Comparative Guide to
American Elementary
&
Secondary Schools

2006
Fourth Edition

Comparative Guide to American Elementary & Secondary Schools

All Public School Districts
Serving 1,500 or More Students

A UNIVERSAL REFERENCE BOOK

Grey House Publishing

PUBLISHER:	Leslie Mackenzie
EDITOR:	David Garoogian
EDITORIAL DIRECTOR:	Laura Mars-Proietti
MARKETING DIRECTOR:	Jessica Moody

A Universal Reference Book
Grey House Publishing, Inc.
185 Millerton Road
Millerton, NY 12546
518.789.8700
FAX 518.789.0545
www.greyhouse.com
e-mail: books @greyhouse.com

First edition 1996
Fourth edition 2006

Printed in the USA

Publisher's Cataloging-In-Publication Data
(Prepared by The Donohue Group, Inc.)

The comparative guide to American elementary & secondary schools : covers all public school districts serving 1,500 or more students. -- 4th ed. --

  1,516 p.; 5.5 cm.
  Includes index.
  ISBN 10: 1-59237-137-X ISBN 13: 978-1-59237-137-2

1. School districts--United States--States--Statistics. 2. School districts--United States--States--Directories. 3. Public schools--United States--States--Statistics. 4. Elementary schools--United States--States--Statistics. 5. High schools--United States--States--Statistics.

LB2817.3 .C66 2005
371.01/0973/021

Table of Contents

Table of Contents

Introduction

Welcome to the fourth edition of *The Comparative Guide to American Elementary & Secondary Schools,* published by Universal Reference Publications, an imprint of Grey House Publishing. This remarkable resource brings together pertinent evaluative and demographic statistics from a wide range of sources for 5,874 public school districts in the United States - all districts with 1,500 or more students. These districts contain and represent nearly 80% of all the public schools in the country.

These demographics and statistics are organized into a highly readable format that saves hours of research time. The logical and consistent format makes important comparative projects possible and easier than ever.

This 2006 edition of *The Comparative Guide to American Elementary & Secondary Schools* is a comprehensive compilation of district details, test scores, and ranking data, convienently arranged in state chapters. Each state chapter has three sections:

Section One — State Educational Profile

This section includes two pages per state, and encompasses all schools in the state regardless of number of students served. The first page includes the following categories: Schools, Students, Diploma Recipients, High School Drop-out Rate, Staff, Student/Staff Ratios, Current Spending and College Entrance Exam Scores.

Page two of the Profile section includes test scores from the *2005 National Assessment of Educational Progress*. Users will find reading and mathematics scores for both 4th grade and 8th grade levels, broken down by gender, race, ethnicity, and class size.

Section Two — School District Profiles

This section is arranged alphabetically by county, then by name of school district. It includes districts with 1,500 or more students. Each district profile includes basic information, including name, address, phone, and web site, and offers data on 9 categories: Grade Span; District Type; Number and Type of Schools; Number of Teachers; Number of Librarians/Media Specialists and Guidance Counselors; Current Spending; Enrollment, Drop-out Rates and Diploma Recipients by Race/ Ethnicity; Male/Female Ratio; and Number of High School Diploma Recipients by Race.

Section Three — School District Rankings

This section ranks 16 pieces of data.

Following the 50 state chapters is a valuable **National Ranking** section where you can compare, state by state, each piece of criteria found in the **School District Profiles**.

To further facilitate research, *The Comparative Guide to American Elementary & Secondary Schools* includes two indexes:

- **School District Index:** an alphabetical listing of all school districts in this edition, including the city they are located in, and the page number of their detailed profile.

- **City Index:** an alphabetical listing of all cities represented by the school districts profiled in this Guide, and the page number of the school district profile it is included in.

Many sources were used to compile the valuable data in this edition. Please refer to the **User's Guide** for a detailed explanation of the sources of the data in this reference work, as well as definitions of terms used.

As always, we welcome comments and suggestions.

USER'S GUIDE

School District Profile

Shown below is a fictitious listing illustrating the kind of information that is or might be included in a School District Profile. Each numbered item of information is described in the paragraphs following the example. Both the State and National Rankings utilize the same criteria and follow the same guidelines.

❶ **Anniston City SD**
1425 Woodstock Ave • Anniston, AL 36207
Mailing Address: PO Box 432 • Anniston, AL 36207-5432
(256) 231-5000 • http://www.anniston.k12.fl.us
❷ **Grade Span:** KG-12; ❸ **Agency Type:** 4
❹ **Schools:** 10
    6 Primary; 1 Middle; 2 High; 1 Other Level
    8 Regular; 0 Special Education; 0 Vocational; 2 Alternative
    1 Magnet; 0 Charter; 7 Title I Eligible; 6 School-wide Title I
❺ **Students:** 2,839   (52.1% male; 47.9% female)
    Individual Education Program: 508 (17.9%)
    English Language Learner: 17 (0.6%); Migrant: 0 (0.0%)
    Eligible for Free Lunch Program: 2,063 (72.7%)
    Eligible for Reduced-Price Lunch Program: 163 (5.7%)
❻ **Teachers:** 194.2 (15.1 to 1)
❼ **Librarians/Media Specialists:** 8.0 (354.9 to 1)
❽ **Guidance Counselors:** 8.1 (350.5 to 1)
❾ **Current Spending:** ($ per student per year)
    Total: $6,136; Instruction: $3,625; Support Services: $2,037
❿ **Enrollment, Drop-out Rates, Diploma Recipients by Race/Eth.**

Category	Total	White	Black	Asian	AIAN	Hisp.
Enrollment (%)	100.0	8.3	90.3	0.1	0.0	1.1
Drop-out Rate (%)	7.4	5.8	8.6	1.3	n/a	2.0
H.S. Diplomas (#)	154	19	129	1	0	5

❶ **Name/Address/Phone/Web Site:** *Source: U.S. Department of Education, National Center for Education Statistics, Common Core of Data, Local Education Agency (School District) Universe Survey: School Year 2003-2004.*
Web site addresses were researched by the editors. Abbreviations used: SD=School District; RD=Regional District; UD=Unified District; ED=Elementary District; ESD=Elementary School District; HSD=High School District; USD=Unified School District; ISD=Independent School District; LSD=Local School District; CSD=Community School District; JSD=Joint School District; MSD=Municipal School District; PSD=Public School District; CCD=Community Consolidated District; CUD=Community Unit District; CISD=Consolidated Independent School District; UFSD=Union Free School District; JUSD=Joint Unified School District; CUSD=Community Unit School District; CHSD=Community High School District; UHSD=Unified High School District; ICSD=Independent Community School District; JUHSD=Joint Union High School District; JUESD=Joint Union Elementary School District

❷ **Grade Span:** The span of grades intended to be served by this school or agency, whether or not there are students currently enrolled in all grades. If a high school also has a prekindergarten program, the grade span of the high school is reported as a high school, not as a PK-12 school. For example, if a school has PK, 9, 10, 11, and 12 grades, the grade span will be reported as Grades 9 through 12 (9-12). Also, the ungraded designation (UG) cannot be used in a grade span unless the whole school is ungraded students, and in this case the grade span is reported as UGUG. *Source: U.S. Department of Education, National Center for Education Statistics, Common Core of Data, Local Education Agency (School District) Universe Survey: School Year 2003-2004.*

❸ **Agency Type:**

1 = Local school district that is not a component of a supervisory union.
2 = Local school district component of a supervisory union sharing a superintendent and administrative services with other local school districts.
3 = Supervisory union administrative center, or a county superintendent serving the same purpose. Type 3 agencies generally do not report student membership, although Massachusetts and Vermont are exceptions.
4 = Regional education services agency, or a county superintendent serving the same purpose.
5 = State-operated institution charged, at least in part, with providing elementary and/or secondary instruction or services to a special need population.
6 = Federally-operated institution charged, at least in part, with providing elementary and/or secondary instruction or services to a special need population.
7 = Other education agencies that do not fit into the first six categories.
Source: U.S. Department of Education, National Center for Education Statistics, Common Core of Data, Local Education Agency (School District) Universe Survey: School Year 2003-2004.

❹ **Schools:** Total number of schools in the district. *Source: U.S. Department of Education, National Center for Education Statistics, Common Core of Data, Public Elementary/Secondary School Universe Survey: School Year 2003-2004.*

Grade Levels:

Primary: Low grade - prekindergarten through 3; high grade - prekindergarten through 8
Middle: Low grade - 4 through 7; high grade - 4 through 9
High: Low grade - 7 through 12; high grade - 12 only
Other Level: Any configuration not falling within the previous three, including ungraded schools

Curriculum:

Regular: A regular school is defined as a public elementary/secondary school that does not focus primarily on vocational, special, or alternative education.

Special Education: A special education school is defined as a public elementary/secondary school that focuses primarily on special education, including instruction for any of the following: autism, deaf-blindness, developmental delay, hearing impairment, mental retardation, multiple disabilities, orthopedic impairment, serious emotional disturbance, specific learning disability, speech or language impairment, traumatic brain injury, visually impaired, and other health impairments. These schools adapt curriculum, materials or instruction for students served.

Vocational: A vocational educational school is defined as a public elementary/secondary school that focuses primarily on providing formal preparation for semi-skilled, skilled, technical, or professional occupations for high school-aged students who have opted to develop or expand their employment opportunities, often in lieu of preparing for college entry.

Alternative: A public elementary/secondary school that addresses needs of students which typically cannot be met in a regular school; provides nontraditional education; serves as an adjunct to a regular school; and falls outside of the categories of regular, special education, or vocational education.

Type:

Magnet: A special school or program designed to attract students of different racial/ethnic backgrounds for the purpose of reducing, preventing or eliminating racial isolation (50 percent or more minority enrollment); and/or to provide an academic or social focus on a particular theme (e.g., science/math, performing arts, gifted/talented, or foreign language).

Charter: A school providing free public elementary and/or secondary education to eligible students under a specific charter granted by the state legislature or other appropriate authority, and designated by such authority to be a charter school.

Title I Eligible: A school designated under appropriate state and federal regulations as being eligible for participation in programs authorized by Title I of Public Law 103-382.

School-wide Title I: A school in which all the pupils in a school are designated under appropriate state and federal regulations as being eligible for participation in programs authorized by Title I of Public Law 103-382.

❺ **Students:** A student is an individual for whom instruction is provided in an elementary or secondary education program that is not an adult education program and is under the jurisdiction of a school, school system, or other education institution. The gender breakdown is shown in parentheses. *Sources: U.S. Department of Education, National Center for Education Statistics, Common Core of Data, Local Education Agency (School District) Universe Survey: School Year 2003-2004 and Public Elementary/Secondary School Universe Survey: School Year 2003-2004*

For the following five categories, the first value shown is the number of students, the second value (in parentheses) is the percent of the entire student population.

Individual Education Program (IEP): A written instructional plan for students with disabilities designated as special education students under IDEA-Part B. The written instructional plan includes a statement of present levels of educational performance of a child; statement of annual goals, including short-term instructional objectives; statement of specific educational services to be provided and the extent to which the child will be able to participate in regular educational programs; the projected date for initiation and anticipated duration of services; the appropriate objectives, criteria and evaluation procedures; and the schedules for determining, on at least an annual basis, whether instructional objectives are being achieved. *Source: U.S. Department of Education, National Center for Education Statistics, Common Core of Data, Local Education Agency (School District) Universe Survey: School Year 2003-2004*

English Language Learner (ELL): Formerly referred to as Limited English Proficient (LEP). Students being served in appropriate programs of language assistance (e.g., English as a Second Language, High Intensity Language Training, bilingual education). Does not include pupils enrolled in a class to learn a language other than English. Also Limited-English-Proficient students are individuals who were not born in the United States or whose native language is a language other than English; or individuals who come from environments where a language other than English is dominant; or individuals who are American Indians and Alaskan Natives and who come from environments where a language other than English has had a significant impact on their level of English language proficiency; and who, by reason thereof, have sufficient difficulty speaking, reading, writing, or understanding the English language, to deny such individuals the opportunity to learn successfully in classrooms where the language of instruction is English or to participate fully in our society. *Source: U.S. Department of Education, National Center for Education Statistics, Common Core of Data, Local Education Agency (School District) Universe Survey: School Year 2003-2004*

Migrant: A migrant student as defined under federal regulation 34 CFR 200.40: 1) (a) Is younger than 22 (and has not graduated from high school or does not hold a high school equivalency certificate), but (b), if the child is too young to attend school-sponsored educational programs, is old enough to benefit from an organized instructional program; and 2) A migrant agricultural worker or a migrant fisher or has a parent, spouse, or guardian who is a migrant agricultural worker or a migrant fisher; and 3) Performs, or has a parent, spouse, or guardian who performs qualifying agricultural or fishing employment as a principal means of livelihood; and 4) Has moved within the preceding 36 months to obtain or to accompany or join a parent, spouse, or guardian to obtain, temporary or seasonal employment in agricultural or fishing work; and 5) Has moved from one school district to another; or in a state that is comprised of a single school district, has moved from one administrative area to another within such district; or resides in a school district of more than 15,000 square miles, and migrates a distance of 20 miles or more to a temporary residence to engage in a fishing activity. Provision 5 currently applies only to Alaska. *Note: Data covers the 2002-2003 school year. Source: U.S. Department of Education, National Center for Education Statistics, Common Core of Data, Public Elementary/Secondary School Universe Survey: School Year 2003-2004*

Eligible for Free Lunch Program: The free lunch program is defined as a program under the National School Lunch Act that provides cash subsidies for free lunches to students based on family size and income criteria. *Source: U.S. Department of Education, National Center for Education Statistics, Common Core of Data, Public Elementary/Secondary School Universe Survey: School Year 2003-2004*

Eligible for Reduced-Price Lunch Program: A student who is eligible to participate in the Reduced-Price Lunch Program under the National School Lunch Act. *Source: U.S. Department of Education, National Center for Education Statistics, Common Core of Data, Public Elementary/Secondary School Universe Survey: School Year 2003-2004*

❻ **Teachers:** Teachers are defined as individuals who provide instruction to pre-kindergarten, kindergarten, grades 1 through 12, or ungraded classes, or individuals who teach in an environment other than a classroom setting, and who maintain daily student attendance records. Numbers reported are full-time equivalents. The students per teacher ratio is shown in parentheses. *Source: U.S. Department of Education, National Center for Education Statistics, Common Core of Data, Local Education Agency (School District) Universe Survey: School Year 2003-2004.*

❼ **Librarians/Media Specialists:** Library and media support staff are defined as staff members who render other professional library and media services; also includes library aides and those involved in library/media support. Their duties include selecting, preparing, caring for, and making available to instructional staff, equipment, films, filmstrips, transparencies, tapes, TV programs, and similar materials maintained separately or as part of an instructional materials center. Also included are activities in the audio-visual center, TV studio, related-work-study areas, and services provided by audio-visual personnel. Numbers reported are full-time equivalents. The students per librarian/media specialist ratio is shown in parentheses. *Source: U.S. Department of Education, National Center for Education Statistics, Common Core of Data, Local Education Agency (School District) Universe Survey: School Year 2003-2004.*

❽ **Guidance Counselors:** Professional staff assigned specific duties and school time for any of the following activities in an elementary or secondary setting: counseling with students and parents; consulting with other staff members on learning problems; evaluating student abilities; assisting students in making educational and career choices; assisting students in personal and social development; providing referral assistance; and/or working with other staff members in planning and conducting guidance programs for students. The state applies its own standards in apportioning the aggregate of guidance counselors/directors into the elementary and secondary level components. Numbers reported are full-time

equivalents. The students per guidance counselor ratio is shown in parentheses. *Source: U.S. Department of Education, National Center for Education Statistics, Common Core of Data, Local Education Agency (School District) Universe Survey: School Year 2003-2004.*

⑨ Current Spending

Total: Expenditure for Instruction, Support Services, and Other Elementary/Secondary Programs. Includes salaries, employee benefits, purchased services, and supplies, as well as payments made by states on behalf of school districts. Also includes transfers made by school districts into their own retirement system. Excludes expenditure for Non-Elementary/Secondary Programs, debt service, capital outlay, and transfers to other governments or school districts. This item is formally called "Current Expenditures for Public Elementary/Secondary Education."

Instruction: Includes payments from all funds for salaries, employee benefits, supplies, materials, and contractual services for elementary/secondary instruction. It excludes capital outlay, debt service, and interfund transfers for elementary/secondary instruction. Instruction covers regular, special, and vocational programs offered in both the regular school year and summer school. It excludes instructional support activities as well as adult education and community services. Instruction salaries includes salaries for teachers and teacher aides and assistants.

Support Services: Relates to support services functions (series 2000) defined in Financial Accounting for Local and State School Systems (National Center for Education Statistics 2000). Includes payments from all funds for salaries, employee benefits, supplies, materials, and contractual services. It excludes capital outlay, debt service, and interfund transfers. It includes expenditure for the following functions:

- Business/Central/Other Support Services
- General Administration
- Instructional Staff Support
- Operation and Maintenance
- Pupil Support Services
- Pupil Transportation Services
- School Administration
- Nonspecified Support Services

Values shown are dollars per pupil per year. They were calculated by dividing the total dollar amounts by the fall membership. Fall membership is comprised of the total student enrollment on October 1 (or the closest school day to October 1) for all grade levels (including prekindergarten and kindergarten) and ungraded pupils. Membership includes students both present and absent on the measurement day. *Source: U.S. Department of Education, National Center for Education Statistics, Common Core of Data, School District Finance Survey (F-33), Fiscal Year 2003.*

⑩ Enrollment, Drop-out Rates, and Diploma Recipients by Race/Ethnicity:

Enrollment: Breakdown of student enrollment by race. *Source: U.S. Department of Education, National Center for Education Statistics, Common Core of Data, Public Elementary/Secondary School Universe Survey: School Year 2003-2004.*

Drop-out: A dropout is a student who was enrolled in school at some time during the previous school year; was not enrolled at the beginning of the current school year; has not graduated from high school or completed a state or district approved educational program; and does not meet any of the following exclusionary conditions: has transferred to another public school district, private school, or state- or district-approved educational program; is temporarily absent due to suspension or school-approved illness; or has died. The values shown are drop-out rates by race and cover grades 9 through 12. *Source: U.S. Department of Education, National Center for Education Statistics, Common Core of Data, Local Education Agency Universe Dropout File: School Year 2001-2002*

H.S. Diplomas: A student who has received a diploma during the previous school year or subsequent summer school. This category includes regular diploma recipients and other diploma recipients. A High School Diploma is a formal document certifying the successful completion of a secondary school program prescribed by the state education agency or other appropriate body. The values shown are the number of high school diploma recipients by race. *Source: U.S. Department of Education, National Center for Education Statistics, Common Core of Data, Local Education Agency (School District) Universe Survey: School Year 2002-2003.*

Race/Ethnicity:

White: A person having origins in any of the original peoples of Europe, North Africa, or the Middle East. Figures include non-Hispanic whites only.

Black: A person having origins in any of the black racial groups of Africa. Figures include non-Hispanic blacks only.

Asian (Asian/Pacific Islander): A person having origins in any of the original peoples of the Far east, Southeast Asia, the Indian subcontinent, or the Pacific Islands. This includes, for example, China, India, Japan, Korea, the Philippine Islands, and Samoa.

AIAN (American Indian/Alaskan Native): A person having origins in any of the original peoples of North America, and who maintains cultural identification through tribal affiliation or community recognition.

Hispanic: A person of Mexican, Puerto Rican, Cuban, Central or South American, or other Spanish culture or origin, regardless of race.

Figures exclude schools that did not report race/ethnicity data.

Note: n/a indicates data not available.

State and National Educational Profiles

Please refer to the District Profile section in the front of this User's Guide for an explanation of data for all items except for the following:

Average Salary: The average teacher salary in 2003-2004. *Source: American Federation of Teachers, Survey & Analysis of Teacher Salary Trends 2004*

College Entrance Exam Scores:

Scholastic Aptitude Test (SAT). *Note: The College Board strongly discourages the comparison or ranking of states on the basis of SAT scores alone. Source: The College Board, Mean SAT Reasoning Test™ Verbal and Math Scores by State, with Changes for Selected Years, 2005*

American College Testing Program (ACT). *ACT, 2005 ACT National and State Scores*

State and National NAEP Test Scores

The National Assessment of Educational Progress (NAEP), also known as "the Nation's Report Card," is the only nationally representative and continuing assessment of what America's students know and can do in various subject areas.

The NAEP 2005 reading and mathematics assessments were administered to representative samples of fourth- and eighth-graders in participating states and other jurisdictions. The national and state results reported in this publication reflect only the performance of students attending public schools.

The results of student performance are presented in two ways: as average scores on the NAEP mathematics/reading scale and as the percentages of students attaining NAEP mathematics/reading achievement levels. The average scale scores represent how students performed on the assessment. The achievement levels (basic, proficient, advanced) represent how that performance measured up against set expectations for achievement. Thus, the average scale scores represent what students know and can do, while the achievement-level results indicate the degree to which student performance meets expectations of what they should know and be able to do.

Mathematics

Average mathematics scale score results are based on the NAEP mathematics scale, which ranges from 0 to 500. The NAEP mathematics assessment is a composite combining separate scales for each of the mathematics content strands: (1) number sense, properties and operations; (2) measurement; (3) geometry and spatial sense; (4) data analysis, statistics and probability; and (5) algebra and functions. Average scale scores are computed for groups, not for individual students. The average scores are based on analyses of the percentages of students who answered each item successfully. While the score ranges at each grade in mathematics are identical, the scale was derived independently at each grade. Therefore, average scale scores across grades cannot be compared. For example, equal scale scores on the grade 4 and grade 8 scales do not imply equal levels of mathematics achievement.

Reading

Average reading scale score results are based on the NAEP reading scale, which ranges from 0 to 500. The NAEP reading assessment scale is a composite combining separate scales for each reading context specified by the reading framework (at grade 4, reading for literary experience and reading for information, and at grade 8, those contexts and reading to perform a task). Average scale scores are computed for groups, not for individual students. The average scores are based on analyses of the percentages of students who answered each item successfully. While the score ranges at each grade in reading are identical, the scale was derived independently at each grade. Therefore, average scale scores across grades cannot be compared. For example, equal scale scores on the grade 4 and grade 8 scales do not imply equal levels of reading achievement.

Standard Error

The average scores and percentages presented in this publication are estimates because they are based on representative samples of students rather than on the entire population of students. Moreover, the collection of subject-area questions used at each grade level is but a sample of the many questions that could have been asked. As such, NAEP results are subject to a measure of uncertainty, reflected in the standard error of the estimates (appears in parentheses).

Rank

The state ranking appears in the column labeled Rank. In most cases, 50 states and the District of Columbia are ranked. However in cases where data was not available, fewer than 51 states may be ranked. For example, a ranking of 32/41 indicates that the state ranked number 32 out of the 41 states with available data. All rankings represent their corresponding values sorted in descending order.

Caution

Readers are cautioned against interpreting NAEP results as implying causal relations. Inferences related to subgroup performance or to the effectiveness of public and nonpublic schools, for example, should take into consideration the many socioeconomic and educational factors that may also impact performance. *Source: U.S. Department of Education, National Center for Education Statistics, The Nation's Report Card, 2005*

Alabama

Alabama Public School Educational Profile

Category	Value	Category	Value
Schools *(2003-2004)*	1,526	**Diploma Recipients** *(2002-2003)*	35,887
Instructional Level		White, Non-Hispanic	23,462
Primary	722	Black, Non-Hispanic	11,374
Middle	249	Asian/Pacific Islander	347
High	365	American Indian/Alaskan Native	459
Other Level	182	Hispanic	245
Curriculum		**High School Drop-out Rate** (%) *(2001-2002)*	3.7
Regular	1,343	White, Non-Hispanic	3.6
Special Education	26	Black, Non-Hispanic	3.9
Vocational	75	Asian/Pacific Islander	1.6
Alternative	74	American Indian/Alaskan Native	2.1
Type		Hispanic	4.5
Magnet	39	**Staff** *(2003-2004)*	
Charter	0	Teachers	48,435.2
Title I Eligible	832	Average Salary ($)	38,282
School-wide Title I	655	Librarians/Media Specialists	1,355.7
Students *(2003-2004)*	731,251	Guidance Counselors	1,593.9
Gender (%)		**Ratios** *(2003-2004)*	
Male	51.7	Student/Teacher Ratio	15.1 to 1
Female	48.3	Student/Librarian Ratio	539.4 to 1
Race/Ethnicity (%)		Student/Counselor Ratio	458.8 to 1
White, Non-Hispanic	59.7	**College Entrance Exam Scores** *(2005)*	
Black, Non-Hispanic	36.3	Scholastic Aptitude Test (SAT)	
Asian/Pacific Islander	0.9	Participation Rate (%)	10
American Indian/Alaskan Native	0.8	Mean SAT Reasoning Test Verbal Score	567
Hispanic	2.1	Mean SAT Reasoning Test Math Score	559
Classification (%)		American College Testing Program (ACT)	
Individual Education Program (IEP)	16.8	Participation Rate (%)	77
Migrant *(2002-2003)*	0.7	Average Composite Score	20.2
English Language Learner (ELL)	1.5	Average English Score	20.3
Eligible for Free Lunch Program	42.3	Average Math Score	19.4
Eligible for Reduced-Price Lunch Program	8.2	Average Reading Score	20.5
Current Spending *($ per student in FY 2003)*	6,395	Average Science Score	20.1
Instruction	3,870		
Support Services	2,089		

Note: *For an explanation of data, please refer to the User's Guide in the front of the book*

Alabama NAEP 2005 Test Scores

Reading			Mathematics		
Grade/Category	Value	Rank	Grade/Category	Value	Rank
4th Grade			**4th Grade**		
Average Proficiency	207.8 (1.20)	45/51	Average Proficiency	225.1 (0.87)	49/51
Proficiency by Gender/Race/Ethnicity			Proficiency by Gender/Race/Ethnicity		
Male	205.2 (1.62)	45/51	Male	225.0 (1.22)	49/51
Female	210.6 (1.56)	47/51	Female	225.2 (0.92)	49/51
White, Non-Hispanic	220.1 (1.33)	47/51	White, Non-Hispanic	234.8 (1.04)	49/51
Black, Non-Hispanic	188.1 (1.75)	41/42	Black, Non-Hispanic	210.7 (1.08)	38/42
Asian, Non-Hispanic	n/a	n/a	Asian, Non-Hispanic	n/a	n/a
American Indian, Non-Hispanic	n/a	n/a	American Indian, Non-Hispanic	n/a	n/a
Hispanic	n/a	n/a	Hispanic	n/a	n/a
Proficiency by Class Size			Proficiency by Class Size		
Less than 16 Students	185.9 (4.98)	33/34	Less than 16 Students	209.1 (4.26)	34/35
16 to 18 Students	206.1 (5.83)	29/33	16 to 18 Students	223.4 (4.35)	29/31
19 to 20 Students	210.5 (3.39)	34/38	19 to 20 Students	226.4 (2.91)	35/38
21 to 25 Students	209.0 (2.07)	46/51	21 to 25 Students	225.8 (1.45)	49/51
Greater than 25 Students	211.4 (2.68)	32/36	Greater than 25 Students	228.2 (3.28)	31/33
Percent Attaining Achievement Levels			Percent Attaining Achievement Levels		
Below Basic	47.3 (1.30)	7/51	Below Basic	33.6 (1.32)	3/51
Basic or Above	52.7 (1.30)	45/51	Basic or Above	66.4 (1.32)	49/51
Proficient or Above	22.3 (1.32)	45/51	Proficient or Above	20.9 (1.11)	48/51
Advanced or Above	4.5 (0.63)	46/51	Advanced or Above	1.7 (0.38)	47/51
8th Grade			**8th Grade**		
Average Proficiency	252.0 (1.44)	46/51	Average Proficiency	262.2 (1.49)	50/51
Proficiency by Gender/Race/Ethnicity			Proficiency by Gender/Race/Ethnicity		
Male	244.5 (1.66)	49/51	Male	260.6 (1.67)	50/51
Female	259.5 (1.75)	44/51	Female	263.8 (1.57)	48/51
White, Non-Hispanic	263.5 (1.73)	48/51	White, Non-Hispanic	275.6 (1.69)	50/51
Black, Non-Hispanic	234.7 (1.91)	40/40	Black, Non-Hispanic	240.0 (1.77)	41/41
Asian, Non-Hispanic	n/a	n/a	Asian, Non-Hispanic	n/a	n/a
American Indian, Non-Hispanic	n/a	n/a	American Indian, Non-Hispanic	n/a	n/a
Hispanic	n/a	n/a	Hispanic	n/a	n/a
Proficiency by Parents Highest Level of Ed.			Proficiency by Parents Highest Level of Ed.		
Did Not Finish High School	237.3 (2.58)	47/49	Did Not Finish High School	244.9 (2.77)	49/50
Graduated High School	244.0 (2.02)	46/50	Graduated High School	253.7 (1.63)	48/50
Some Education After High School	255.1 (2.15)	48/50	Some Education After High School	266.5 (1.81)	49/50
Graduated College	260.8 (1.98)	46/50	Graduated College	272.1 (2.12)	48/50
Percent Attaining Achievement Levels			Percent Attaining Achievement Levels		
Below Basic	47.3 (1.30)	7/51	Below Basic	47.0 (1.91)	4/51
Basic or Above	52.7 (1.30)	45/51	Basic or Above	53.0 (1.91)	48/51
Proficient or Above	22.3 (1.32)	45/51	Proficient or Above	15.2 (1.43)	48/51
Advanced or Above	4.5 (0.63)	46/51	Advanced or Above	2.3 (0.65)	46/51

Note: *For an explanation of data, please refer to the User's Guide in the front of the book; n/a indicates data not available*

Autauga County

Autauga County
153 W 4th St • Prattville, AL 36067-3011
(334) 365-5706 • http://www.autaugacountyschool.org/
Grade Span: KG-12; **Agency Type:** 1
Schools: 13
  5 Primary; 2 Middle; 3 High; 3 Other Level
  11 Regular; 0 Special Education; 1 Vocational; 1 Alternative
  0 Magnet; 0 Charter; 7 Title I Eligible; 3 School-wide Title I
Students: 9,105 (51.4% male; 48.5% female)
  Individual Education Program: 1,515 (16.6%);
  English Language Learner: 98 (1.1%); Migrant: 0 (0.0%)
  Eligible for Free Lunch Program: 2,825 (31.0%)
  Eligible for Reduced-Price Lunch Program: 709 (7.8%)
Teachers: 561.0 (16.2 to 1)
Librarians/Media Specialists: 11.0 (827.7 to 1)
Guidance Counselors: 19.5 (466.9 to 1)
Current Spending: ($ per student per year):
  Total: $5,293; Instruction: $3,396; Support Services: $1,529
Enrollment, Drop-out Rates and Diploma Recipients by Race/Ethnicity

Category	Total	White	Black	Asian	AIAN	Hisp.
Enrollment (%)	100.0	74.3	22.9	0.8	0.1	0.9
Drop-out Rate (%)	5.4	5.4	4.8	7.1	0.0	20.8
H.S. Diplomas (#)	405	317	79	3	1	5

Baldwin County

Baldwin County
2600-A N Hand Ave • Bay Minette, AL 36507-4180
(251) 937-0308 • http://www.bcbe.org/
Grade Span: KG-12; **Agency Type:** 1
Schools: 47
  25 Primary; 10 Middle; 8 High; 2 Other Level
  41 Regular; 0 Special Education; 2 Vocational; 2 Alternative
  0 Magnet; 0 Charter; 18 Title I Eligible; 18 School-wide Title I
Students: 24,037 (51.7% male; 48.2% female)
  Individual Education Program: 6,586 (27.4%);
  English Language Learner: 360 (1.5%); Migrant: 0 (0.0%)
  Eligible for Free Lunch Program: 6,426 (26.7%)
  Eligible for Reduced-Price Lunch Program: 1,966 (8.2%)
Teachers: 1,716.8 (14.0 to 1)
Librarians/Media Specialists: 42.5 (565.6 to 1)
Guidance Counselors: 57.2 (420.2 to 1)
Current Spending: ($ per student per year):
  Total: $6,727; Instruction: $4,203; Support Services: $2,223
Enrollment, Drop-out Rates and Diploma Recipients by Race/Ethnicity

Category	Total	White	Black	Asian	AIAN	Hisp.
Enrollment (%)	100.0	80.4	16.2	0.5	0.5	2.0
Drop-out Rate (%)	3.1	3.0	3.8	3.0	0.0	5.3
H.S. Diplomas (#)	1,093	961	109	8	4	11

Barbour County

Eufaula City
420 Sanford Ave • Eufaula, AL 36027-1450
(334) 687-1100 • http://www.ecs.k12.al.us/
Grade Span: PK-12; **Agency Type:** 1
Schools: 5
  3 Primary; 1 Middle; 1 High; 0 Other Level
  5 Regular; 0 Special Education; 0 Vocational; 0 Alternative
  0 Magnet; 0 Charter; 3 Title I Eligible; 3 School-wide Title I
Students: 2,902 (52.2% male; 47.7% female)
  Individual Education Program: 586 (20.2%);
  English Language Learner: 12 (0.4%); Migrant: 0 (0.0%)
  Eligible for Free Lunch Program: 1,463 (50.4%)
  Eligible for Reduced-Price Lunch Program: 243 (8.4%)
Teachers: 193.7 (15.0 to 1)
Librarians/Media Specialists: 5.0 (580.6 to 1)
Guidance Counselors: 5.0 (580.6 to 1)
Current Spending: ($ per student per year):
  Total: $6,403; Instruction: $3,988; Support Services: $1,944
Enrollment, Drop-out Rates and Diploma Recipients by Race/Ethnicity

Category	Total	White	Black	Asian	AIAN	Hisp.
Enrollment (%)	100.0	46.2	51.9	0.6	0.1	1.2
Drop-out Rate (%)	5.8	5.5	6.0	33.3	0.0	0.0
H.S. Diplomas (#)	154	70	82	0	0	2

Bibb County

Bibb County
157 SW Davidson Dr • Centreville, AL 35042-2277
(205) 926-9881 • http://www.bibbed.org/
Grade Span: KG-12; **Agency Type:** 1
Schools: 10

---

  4 Primary; 3 Middle; 3 High; 0 Other Level
  9 Regular; 0 Special Education; 1 Vocational; 0 Alternative
  0 Magnet; 0 Charter; 9 Title I Eligible; 9 School-wide Title I
Students: 3,529 (52.3% male; 47.6% female)
  Individual Education Program: 645 (18.3%);
  English Language Learner: 11 (0.3%); Migrant: 0 (0.0%)
  Eligible for Free Lunch Program: 1,745 (49.3%)
  Eligible for Reduced-Price Lunch Program: 421 (11.9%)
Teachers: 229.9 (15.4 to 1)
Librarians/Media Specialists: 8.5 (416.0 to 1)
Guidance Counselors: 8.5 (416.0 to 1)
Current Spending: ($ per student per year):
  Total: $6,187; Instruction: $3,841; Support Services: $1,828
Enrollment, Drop-out Rates and Diploma Recipients by Race/Ethnicity

Category	Total	White	Black	Asian	AIAN	Hisp.
Enrollment (%)	100.0	70.0	28.8	0.1	0.1	0.9
Drop-out Rate (%)	2.4	2.2	2.9	0.0	n/a	0.0
H.S. Diplomas (#)	131	103	27	0	0	1

Blount County

Blount County
204 2nd Ave E • Oneonta, AL 35121-0007
Mailing Address: PO Box 578 • Oneonta, AL 35121-0007
(205) 625-4102 • http://blountcountyschools.net/
Grade Span: PK-12; **Agency Type:** 1
Schools: 16
  6 Primary; 1 Middle; 6 High; 3 Other Level
  13 Regular; 1 Special Education; 1 Vocational; 1 Alternative
  0 Magnet; 0 Charter; 9 Title I Eligible; 9 School-wide Title I
Students: 7,740 (51.5% male; 48.4% female)
  Individual Education Program: 1,278 (16.5%);
  English Language Learner: 558 (7.2%); Migrant: 195 (2.5%)
  Eligible for Free Lunch Program: 2,593 (33.5%)
  Eligible for Reduced-Price Lunch Program: 809 (10.5%)
Teachers: 440.5 (17.6 to 1)
Librarians/Media Specialists: 13.0 (595.4 to 1)
Guidance Counselors: 13.0 (595.4 to 1)
Current Spending: ($ per student per year):
  Total: $5,455; Instruction: $3,362; Support Services: $1,701
Enrollment, Drop-out Rates and Diploma Recipients by Race/Ethnicity

Category	Total	White	Black	Asian	AIAN	Hisp.
Enrollment (%)	100.0	91.6	0.4	0.3	0.2	7.6
Drop-out Rate (%)	5.1	5.2	0.0	0.0	0.0	2.9
H.S. Diplomas (#)	313	306	0	0	1	6

Bullock County

Bullock County
108 Hardaway Ave W • Union Springs, AL 36089-0231
Mailing Address: PO Box 231 • Union Springs, AL 36089-0231
(334) 738-2860 • http://bullock.k12.al.us/
Grade Span: KG-12; **Agency Type:** 1
Schools: 5
  2 Primary; 1 Middle; 2 High; 0 Other Level
  4 Regular; 0 Special Education; 1 Vocational; 0 Alternative
  0 Magnet; 0 Charter; 4 Title I Eligible; 4 School-wide Title I
Students: 1,820 (51.2% male; 48.7% female)
  Individual Education Program: 259 (14.2%);
  English Language Learner: 22 (1.2%); Migrant: 0 (0.0%)
  Eligible for Free Lunch Program: 1,545 (84.9%)
  Eligible for Reduced-Price Lunch Program: 127 (7.0%)
Teachers: 121.5 (15.0 to 1)
Librarians/Media Specialists: 4.0 (455.0 to 1)
Guidance Counselors: 5.0 (364.0 to 1)
Current Spending: ($ per student per year):
  Total: $6,583; Instruction: $3,839; Support Services: $2,232
Enrollment, Drop-out Rates and Diploma Recipients by Race/Ethnicity

Category	Total	White	Black	Asian	AIAN	Hisp.
Enrollment (%)	100.0	0.4	98.2	0.0	0.0	1.4
Drop-out Rate (%)	4.3	40.0	3.9	n/a	n/a	0.0
H.S. Diplomas (#)	110	0	110	0	0	0

Butler County

Butler County
215 Administrative Dr • Greenville, AL 36037-1833
(334) 382-2665 • http://www.butlerco.k12.al.us/
Grade Span: KG-12; **Agency Type:** 1
Schools: 8
  3 Primary; 1 Middle; 3 High; 1 Other Level
  7 Regular; 0 Special Education; 1 Vocational; 0 Alternative
  0 Magnet; 0 Charter; 7 Title I Eligible; 7 School-wide Title I
Students: 3,557 (51.1% male; 48.8% female)
  Individual Education Program: 606 (17.0%);

English Language Learner: 8 (0.2%); Migrant: 0 (0.0%)
Eligible for Free Lunch Program: 2,222 (62.5%)
Eligible for Reduced-Price Lunch Program: 400 (11.2%)
Teachers: 215.4 (16.5 to 1)
Librarians/Media Specialists: 6.0 (592.8 to 1)
Guidance Counselors: 9.0 (395.2 to 1)
Current Spending: ($ per student per year):
Total: $6,267; Instruction: $3,875; Support Services: $1,932

Enrollment, Drop-out Rates and Diploma Recipients by Race/Ethnicity

Category	Total	White	Black	Asian	AIAN	Hisp.
Enrollment (%)	100.0	39.1	60.1	0.4	0.1	0.2
Drop-out Rate (%)	5.8	6.3	5.6	0.0	n/a	0.0
H.S. Diplomas (#)	168	85	81	2	0	0

Calhoun County

Anniston City
4804 Mcclellan Blvd • Anniston, AL 36206
Mailing Address: PO Box 1500 • Anniston, AL 36202-1500
(256) 231-5000 • http://www.anniston-k12.org/
Grade Span: PK-12; **Agency Type:** 1
Schools: 9
5 Primary; 0 Middle; 1 High; 3 Other Level
7 Regular; 0 Special Education; 0 Vocational; 2 Alternative
0 Magnet; 0 Charter; 7 Title I Eligible; 4 School-wide Title I
Students: 2,652 (52.4% male; 47.5% female)
Individual Education Program: 408 (15.4%);
English Language Learner: 39 (1.5%); Migrant: 0 (0.0%)
Eligible for Free Lunch Program: 2,009 (75.8%)
Eligible for Reduced-Price Lunch Program: 138 (5.2%)
Teachers: 167.7 (15.8 to 1)
Librarians/Media Specialists: 7.0 (378.9 to 1)
Guidance Counselors: 6.0 (442.0 to 1)
Current Spending: ($ per student per year):
Total: $7,125; Instruction: $3,831; Support Services: $2,630

Enrollment, Drop-out Rates and Diploma Recipients by Race/Ethnicity

Category	Total	White	Black	Asian	AIAN	Hisp.
Enrollment (%)	100.0	5.8	91.9	0.6	0.0	1.7
Drop-out Rate (%)	11.7	10.0	11.9	0.0	n/a	0.0
H.S. Diplomas (#)	77	1	74	1	0	1

Calhoun County
4400 Mcclellan Blvd • Anniston, AL 36206-2809
Mailing Address: PO Box 2084 • Anniston, AL 36202-2084
(256) 741-7404 • http://www.calhoun.k12.al.us/
Grade Span: PK-12; **Agency Type:** 1
Schools: 19
7 Primary; 1 Middle; 4 High; 7 Other Level
16 Regular; 0 Special Education; 1 Vocational; 2 Alternative
0 Magnet; 0 Charter; 9 Title I Eligible; 9 School-wide Title I
Students: 9,018 (51.7% male; 48.2% female)
Individual Education Program: 1,377 (15.3%);
English Language Learner: 64 (0.7%); Migrant: 0 (0.0%)
Eligible for Free Lunch Program: 3,469 (38.5%)
Eligible for Reduced-Price Lunch Program: 945 (10.5%)
Teachers: 588.1 (15.3 to 1)
Librarians/Media Specialists: 17.0 (530.5 to 1)
Guidance Counselors: 18.0 (501.0 to 1)
Current Spending: ($ per student per year):
Total: $6,006; Instruction: $3,407; Support Services: $2,176

Enrollment, Drop-out Rates and Diploma Recipients by Race/Ethnicity

Category	Total	White	Black	Asian	AIAN	Hisp.
Enrollment (%)	100.0	85.0	13.2	0.5	0.2	1.0
Drop-out Rate (%)	3.8	4.0	2.9	0.0	0.0	4.5
H.S. Diplomas (#)	451	399	43	3	0	6

Jacksonville City
123 College St SW • Jacksonville, AL 36265-2154
(256) 782-5682 • http://www.jacksonville.k12.al.us/
Grade Span: KG-12; **Agency Type:** 1
Schools: 2
1 Primary; 0 Middle; 1 High; 0 Other Level
2 Regular; 0 Special Education; 0 Vocational; 0 Alternative
0 Magnet; 0 Charter; 1 Title I Eligible; 0 School-wide Title I
Students: 1,696 (54.0% male; 45.9% female)
Individual Education Program: 318 (18.8%);
English Language Learner: 6 (0.4%); Migrant: 0 (0.0%)
Eligible for Free Lunch Program: 533 (31.4%)
Eligible for Reduced-Price Lunch Program: 135 (8.0%)
Teachers: 100.0 (17.0 to 1)
Librarians/Media Specialists: 1.8 (942.2 to 1)
Guidance Counselors: 4.0 (424.0 to 1)
Current Spending: ($ per student per year):
Total: $5,838; Instruction: $3,770; Support Services: $1,694

Enrollment, Drop-out Rates and Diploma Recipients by Race/Ethnicity

Category	Total	White	Black	Asian	AIAN	Hisp.
Enrollment (%)	100.0	73.9	22.3	1.5	0.2	2.1
Drop-out Rate (%)	1.2	1.6	0.0	0.0	0.0	0.0
H.S. Diplomas (#)	90	72	11	6	0	1

Oxford City
310 E 2nd St • Oxford, AL 36203-1799
(256) 831-0243 • http://www.oxford.k12.al.us/
Grade Span: PK-12; **Agency Type:** 1
Schools: 6
2 Primary; 2 Middle; 2 High; 0 Other Level
5 Regular; 0 Special Education; 1 Vocational; 0 Alternative
0 Magnet; 0 Charter; 2 Title I Eligible; 0 School-wide Title I
Students: 3,721 (50.9% male; 49.0% female)
Individual Education Program: 508 (13.7%);
English Language Learner: 106 (2.8%); Migrant: 0 (0.0%)
Eligible for Free Lunch Program: 1,140 (30.6%)
Eligible for Reduced-Price Lunch Program: 249 (6.7%)
Teachers: 240.2 (15.5 to 1)
Librarians/Media Specialists: 4.0 (930.3 to 1)
Guidance Counselors: 6.3 (590.6 to 1)
Current Spending: ($ per student per year):
Total: $5,851; Instruction: $3,681; Support Services: $1,696

Enrollment, Drop-out Rates and Diploma Recipients by Race/Ethnicity

Category	Total	White	Black	Asian	AIAN	Hisp.
Enrollment (%)	100.0	73.8	19.8	1.3	0.1	4.8
Drop-out Rate (%)	2.7	2.9	2.4	0.0	n/a	0.0
H.S. Diplomas (#)	185	145	35	5	0	0

Chambers County

Chambers County
202 1st Ave SE • Lafayette, AL 36862-2102
Mailing Address: Box 408d • Lafayette, AL 36862-0408
(334) 864-9343 • http://www.chambersk12.org/
Grade Span: KG-12; **Agency Type:** 1
Schools: 11
6 Primary; 2 Middle; 3 High; 0 Other Level
10 Regular; 0 Special Education; 1 Vocational; 0 Alternative
0 Magnet; 0 Charter; 7 Title I Eligible; 7 School-wide Title I
Students: 4,396 (51.1% male; 48.8% female)
Individual Education Program: 615 (14.0%);
English Language Learner: 9 (0.2%); Migrant: 0 (0.0%)
Eligible for Free Lunch Program: 2,495 (56.8%)
Eligible for Reduced-Price Lunch Program: 406 (9.2%)
Teachers: 288.4 (15.2 to 1)
Librarians/Media Specialists: 9.0 (488.4 to 1)
Guidance Counselors: 8.0 (549.5 to 1)
Current Spending: ($ per student per year):
Total: $5,749; Instruction: $3,420; Support Services: $1,869

Enrollment, Drop-out Rates and Diploma Recipients by Race/Ethnicity

Category	Total	White	Black	Asian	AIAN	Hisp.
Enrollment (%)	100.0	47.7	51.6	0.1	0.1	0.3
Drop-out Rate (%)	4.3	5.7	3.2	0.0	0.0	0.0
H.S. Diplomas (#)	199	87	112	0	0	0

Cherokee County

Cherokee County
130 E Main St • Centre, AL 35960-1599
(256) 927-3362 • http://www.tiger.org/
Grade Span: KG-12; **Agency Type:** 1
Schools: 8
1 Primary; 1 Middle; 2 High; 4 Other Level
7 Regular; 0 Special Education; 1 Vocational; 0 Alternative
0 Magnet; 0 Charter; 6 Title I Eligible; 4 School-wide Title I
Students: 4,204 (52.7% male; 47.2% female)
Individual Education Program: 653 (15.5%);
English Language Learner: 5 (0.1%); Migrant: 2 (<0.1%)
Eligible for Free Lunch Program: 1,505 (35.8%)
Eligible for Reduced-Price Lunch Program: 416 (9.9%)
Teachers: 269.6 (15.6 to 1)
Librarians/Media Specialists: 6.8 (618.2 to 1)
Guidance Counselors: 9.3 (452.0 to 1)
Current Spending: ($ per student per year):
Total: $6,112; Instruction: $3,780; Support Services: $1,826

Enrollment, Drop-out Rates and Diploma Recipients by Race/Ethnicity

Category	Total	White	Black	Asian	AIAN	Hisp.
Enrollment (%)	100.0	92.4	6.1	0.2	0.4	0.8
Drop-out Rate (%)	5.0	5.3	1.4	0.0	0.0	0.0
H.S. Diplomas (#)	167	158	8	0	0	1

Chilton County

Chilton County
1705 Lay Dam Rd • Clanton, AL 35045-2032
(205) 280-3000 • http://www.chiltonschools.org/
Grade Span: PK-12; **Agency Type:** 1
Schools: 12
  3 Primary; 2 Middle; 3 High; 4 Other Level
  11 Regular; 0 Special Education; 1 Vocational; 0 Alternative
  0 Magnet; 0 Charter; 9 Title I Eligible; 0 School-wide Title I
Students: 7,102   (52.4% male; 47.5% female)
  Individual Education Program: 1,314 (18.5%);
  English Language Learner: 121 (1.7%); Migrant: 0 (0.0%)
  Eligible for Free Lunch Program: 2,645 (37.2%)
  Eligible for Reduced-Price Lunch Program: 717 (10.1%)
Teachers: 472.8 (15.0 to 1)
Librarians/Media Specialists: 13.5 (526.1 to 1)
Guidance Counselors: 13.9 (510.9 to 1)
Current Spending: ($ per student per year):
  Total: $5,852; Instruction: $3,685; Support Services: $1,746
Enrollment, Drop-out Rates and Diploma Recipients by Race/Ethnicity

Category	Total	White	Black	Asian	AIAN	Hisp.
Enrollment (%)	100.0	80.8	14.5	0.3	0.0	4.4
Drop-out Rate (%)	2.4	2.3	2.5	0.0	n/a	4.8
H.S. Diplomas (#)	329	287	42	0	0	0

Choctaw County

Choctaw County
107 Tom Orr Dr • Butler, AL 36904-3504
(205) 459-3031 • http://choctawboe.k12.al.us/
Grade Span: KG-12; **Agency Type:** 1
Schools: 8
  4 Primary; 0 Middle; 3 High; 1 Other Level
  6 Regular; 0 Special Education; 1 Vocational; 1 Alternative
  0 Magnet; 0 Charter; 6 Title I Eligible; 6 School-wide Title I
Students: 2,147   (52.5% male; 47.4% female)
  Individual Education Program: 348 (16.2%);
  English Language Learner: 0 (0.0%); Migrant: 0 (0.0%)
  Eligible for Free Lunch Program: 1,495 (69.6%)
  Eligible for Reduced-Price Lunch Program: 231 (10.8%)
Teachers: 150.4 (14.3 to 1)
Librarians/Media Specialists: 5.5 (390.4 to 1)
Guidance Counselors: 3.6 (596.4 to 1)
Current Spending: ($ per student per year):
  Total: $6,593; Instruction: $3,799; Support Services: $2,322
Enrollment, Drop-out Rates and Diploma Recipients by Race/Ethnicity

Category	Total	White	Black	Asian	AIAN	Hisp.
Enrollment (%)	100.0	25.4	74.2	0.0	0.1	0.0
Drop-out Rate (%)	4.0	6.6	3.3	0.0	0.0	n/a
H.S. Diplomas (#)	104	21	83	0	0	0

Clarke County

Clarke County
155 W Cobb St • Grove Hill, AL 36451-0936
Mailing Address: Box 936 • Grove Hill, AL 36451-0936
(251) 275-3255
Grade Span: PK-12; **Agency Type:** 1
Schools: 9
  4 Primary; 2 Middle; 3 High; 0 Other Level
  9 Regular; 0 Special Education; 0 Vocational; 0 Alternative
  0 Magnet; 0 Charter; 7 Title I Eligible; 7 School-wide Title I
Students: 3,547   (50.0% male; 49.9% female)
  Individual Education Program: 649 (18.3%);
  English Language Learner: 0 (0.0%); Migrant: 0 (0.0%)
  Eligible for Free Lunch Program: 2,131 (60.1%)
  Eligible for Reduced-Price Lunch Program: 321 (9.0%)
Teachers: 228.5 (15.5 to 1)
Librarians/Media Specialists: 7.7 (460.6 to 1)
Guidance Counselors: 6.9 (514.1 to 1)
Current Spending: ($ per student per year):
  Total: $6,326; Instruction: $3,675; Support Services: $2,091
Enrollment, Drop-out Rates and Diploma Recipients by Race/Ethnicity

Category	Total	White	Black	Asian	AIAN	Hisp.
Enrollment (%)	100.0	34.3	65.2	0.2	0.1	0.3
Drop-out Rate (%)	1.6	2.0	1.4	0.0	0.0	n/a
H.S. Diplomas (#)	176	63	113	0	0	0

Thomasville City
750 Gates Dr • Thomasville, AL 36784-0458
Mailing Address: PO Box 458 • Thomasville, AL 36784-0458
(334) 636-9955 • http://www.thomasvilleschools.org/
Grade Span: KG-12; **Agency Type:** 1
Schools: 3

1 Primary; 1 Middle; 1 High; 0 Other Level
3 Regular; 0 Special Education; 0 Vocational; 0 Alternative
0 Magnet; 0 Charter; 2 Title I Eligible; 1 School-wide Title I
Students: 1,648   (52.2% male; 47.7% female)
  Individual Education Program: 246 (14.9%);
  English Language Learner: 4 (0.2%); Migrant: 0 (0.0%)
  Eligible for Free Lunch Program: 731 (44.4%)
  Eligible for Reduced-Price Lunch Program: 120 (7.3%)
Teachers: 118.9 (13.9 to 1)
Librarians/Media Specialists: 3.0 (549.3 to 1)
Guidance Counselors: 4.5 (366.2 to 1)
Current Spending: ($ per student per year):
  Total: $5,933; Instruction: $3,822; Support Services: $1,759
Enrollment, Drop-out Rates and Diploma Recipients by Race/Ethnicity

Category	Total	White	Black	Asian	AIAN	Hisp.
Enrollment (%)	100.0	55.0	44.5	0.2	0.0	0.1
Drop-out Rate (%)	1.1	1.5	0.5	0.0	n/a	0.0
H.S. Diplomas (#)	87	57	29	0	0	1

Clay County

Clay County
121 2nd Ave N • Ashland, AL 36251-4108
Mailing Address: PO Box 278 • Ashland, AL 36251-0278
(256) 354-5414
Grade Span: KG-12; **Agency Type:** 1
Schools: 4
  2 Primary; 0 Middle; 2 High; 0 Other Level
  4 Regular; 0 Special Education; 0 Vocational; 0 Alternative
  0 Magnet; 0 Charter; 2 Title I Eligible; 2 School-wide Title I
Students: 2,029   (52.3% male; 47.6% female)
  Individual Education Program: 332 (16.4%);
  English Language Learner: 9 (0.4%); Migrant: 0 (0.0%)
  Eligible for Free Lunch Program: 915 (45.1%)
  Eligible for Reduced-Price Lunch Program: 283 (13.9%)
Teachers: 147.2 (13.8 to 1)
Librarians/Media Specialists: 3.0 (676.3 to 1)
Guidance Counselors: 4.0 (507.3 to 1)
Current Spending: ($ per student per year):
  Total: $6,120; Instruction: $3,839; Support Services: $1,859
Enrollment, Drop-out Rates and Diploma Recipients by Race/Ethnicity

Category	Total	White	Black	Asian	AIAN	Hisp.
Enrollment (%)	100.0	73.2	24.3	0.0	0.1	2.4
Drop-out Rate (%)	1.3	1.5	0.7	n/a	0.0	0.0
H.S. Diplomas (#)	149	112	35	0	1	1

Cleburne County

Cleburne County
93 Education St • Heflin, AL 36264-2207
(256) 463-5624 • http://cleburneschools.net/
Grade Span: PK-12; **Agency Type:** 1
Schools: 7
  4 Primary; 0 Middle; 3 High; 0 Other Level
  6 Regular; 0 Special Education; 1 Vocational; 0 Alternative
  0 Magnet; 0 Charter; 4 Title I Eligible; 4 School-wide Title I
Students: 2,611   (51.4% male; 48.5% female)
  Individual Education Program: 477 (18.3%);
  English Language Learner: 16 (0.6%); Migrant: 0 (0.0%)
  Eligible for Free Lunch Program: 1,092 (41.8%)
  Eligible for Reduced-Price Lunch Program: 312 (11.9%)
Teachers: 172.4 (15.1 to 1)
Librarians/Media Specialists: 5.5 (474.7 to 1)
Guidance Counselors: 5.5 (474.7 to 1)
Current Spending: ($ per student per year):
  Total: $5,849; Instruction: $3,639; Support Services: $1,681
Enrollment, Drop-out Rates and Diploma Recipients by Race/Ethnicity

Category	Total	White	Black	Asian	AIAN	Hisp.
Enrollment (%)	100.0	93.9	4.6	0.2	0.1	1.2
Drop-out Rate (%)	4.0	3.9	4.9	n/a	n/a	0.0
H.S. Diplomas (#)	124	121	3	0	0	0

Coffee County

Coffee County
400 Reddoch Hill Rd • Elba, AL 36323-1661
(334) 897-5016 • http://www.coffeecounty.k12.al.us/
Grade Span: KG-12; **Agency Type:** 1
Schools: 4
  1 Primary; 0 Middle; 1 High; 2 Other Level
  4 Regular; 0 Special Education; 0 Vocational; 0 Alternative
  0 Magnet; 0 Charter; 2 Title I Eligible; 2 School-wide Title I
Students: 1,867   (51.2% male; 48.7% female)
  Individual Education Program: 306 (16.4%);
  English Language Learner: 4 (0.2%); Migrant: 193 (10.3%)

Eligible for Free Lunch Program: 637 (34.1%)
Eligible for Reduced-Price Lunch Program: 229 (12.3%)
Teachers: 125.9 (14.8 to 1)
Librarians/Media Specialists: 4.0 (466.8 to 1)
Guidance Counselors: 5.7 (327.5 to 1)
Current Spending: ($ per student per year):
Total: $6,008; Instruction: $3,746; Support Services: $1,875
Enrollment, Drop-out Rates and Diploma Recipients by Race/Ethnicity

Category	Total	White	Black	Asian	AIAN	Hisp.
Enrollment (%)	100.0	89.3	6.4	0.4	3.0	0.2
Drop-out Rate (%)	4.5	4.3	7.0	0.0	0.0	n/a
H.S. Diplomas (#)	105	96	8	0	1	0

Enterprise City
502 E Watts St • Enterprise, AL 36330-1899
Mailing Address: PO Box 311790 • Enterprise, AL 36331-1790
(334) 347-9531 • http://enterpriseschools.net/
Grade Span: KG-12; **Agency Type:** 1
Schools: 10
6 Primary; 1 Middle; 1 High; 2 Other Level
10 Regular; 0 Special Education; 0 Vocational; 0 Alternative
0 Magnet; 0 Charter; 5 Title I Eligible; 0 School-wide Title I
Students: 5,389 (51.5% male; 48.4% female)
Individual Education Program: 868 (16.1%);
English Language Learner: 96 (1.8%); Migrant: 186 (3.5%)
Eligible for Free Lunch Program: 1,552 (28.8%)
Eligible for Reduced-Price Lunch Program: 386 (7.2%)
Teachers: 349.9 (15.4 to 1)
Librarians/Media Specialists: 11.0 (489.9 to 1)
Guidance Counselors: 12.4 (434.6 to 1)
Current Spending: ($ per student per year):
Total: $6,146; Instruction: $3,737; Support Services: $2,031
Enrollment, Drop-out Rates and Diploma Recipients by Race/Ethnicity

Category	Total	White	Black	Asian	AIAN	Hisp.
Enrollment (%)	100.0	64.2	27.0	2.4	0.5	5.7
Drop-out Rate (%)	2.9	2.9	3.4	0.0	0.0	2.9
H.S. Diplomas (#)	318	228	67	11	1	11

Colbert County
1101 Hwy 72 E • Tuscumbia, AL 35674-2412
(256) 386-8565 • http://www.colbertcountyschools.org/
Grade Span: PK-12; **Agency Type:** 1
Schools: 9
5 Primary; 1 Middle; 3 High; 0 Other Level
9 Regular; 0 Special Education; 0 Vocational; 0 Alternative
0 Magnet; 0 Charter; 4 Title I Eligible; 4 School-wide Title I
Students: 3,265 (54.9% male; 45.0% female)
Individual Education Program: 598 (18.3%);
English Language Learner: 21 (0.6%); Migrant: 1 (<0.1%)
Eligible for Free Lunch Program: 1,601 (49.0%)
Eligible for Reduced-Price Lunch Program: 376 (11.5%)
Teachers: 226.8 (14.4 to 1)
Librarians/Media Specialists: 8.0 (408.1 to 1)
Guidance Counselors: 9.0 (362.8 to 1)
Current Spending: ($ per student per year):
Total: $6,627; Instruction: $3,946; Support Services: $2,196
Enrollment, Drop-out Rates and Diploma Recipients by Race/Ethnicity

Category	Total	White	Black	Asian	AIAN	Hisp.
Enrollment (%)	100.0	81.2	16.9	0.1	0.2	1.5
Drop-out Rate (%)	6.2	6.7	4.3	n/a	n/a	11.1
H.S. Diplomas (#)	116	97	19	0	0	0

Muscle Shoals City
3200 S Wilson Dam Rd • Muscle Shoals, AL 35661
Mailing Address: PO Box 2610 • Muscle Shoals, AL 35662-2610
(256) 389-2600 • http://www.mscs.k12.al.us/
Grade Span: KG-12; **Agency Type:** 1
Schools: 7
4 Primary; 1 Middle; 2 High; 0 Other Level
6 Regular; 0 Special Education; 1 Vocational; 0 Alternative
0 Magnet; 0 Charter; 3 Title I Eligible; 0 School-wide Title I
Students: 2,538 (50.1% male; 49.8% female)
Individual Education Program: 252 (9.9%);
English Language Learner: 3 (0.1%); Migrant: 0 (0.0%)
Eligible for Free Lunch Program: 466 (18.4%)
Eligible for Reduced-Price Lunch Program: 201 (7.9%)
Teachers: 168.2 (15.1 to 1)
Librarians/Media Specialists: 4.0 (634.5 to 1)
Guidance Counselors: 5.0 (507.6 to 1)
Current Spending: ($ per student per year):
Total: $6,795; Instruction: $4,095; Support Services: $2,213

Enrollment, Drop-out Rates and Diploma Recipients by Race/Ethnicity

Category	Total	White	Black	Asian	AIAN	Hisp.
Enrollment (%)	100.0	81.0	16.4	0.8	0.3	1.5
Drop-out Rate (%)	1.2	0.9	3.3	0.0	n/a	0.0
H.S. Diplomas (#)	137	116	20	1	0	0

Conecuh County
100 Jackson St • Evergreen, AL 36401-2843
(251) 578-1752
Grade Span: PK-12; **Agency Type:** 1
Schools: 7
5 Primary; 1 Middle; 1 High; 0 Other Level
7 Regular; 0 Special Education; 0 Vocational; 0 Alternative
0 Magnet; 0 Charter; 5 Title I Eligible; 5 School-wide Title I
Students: 1,853 (52.8% male; 47.1% female)
Individual Education Program: 347 (18.7%);
English Language Learner: 0 (0.0%); Migrant: 0 (0.0%)
Eligible for Free Lunch Program: 1,394 (75.2%)
Eligible for Reduced-Price Lunch Program: 178 (9.6%)
Teachers: 124.2 (14.9 to 1)
Librarians/Media Specialists: 8.0 (231.6 to 1)
Guidance Counselors: 4.0 (463.3 to 1)
Current Spending: ($ per student per year):
Total: $6,773; Instruction: $3,967; Support Services: $2,191
Enrollment, Drop-out Rates and Diploma Recipients by Race/Ethnicity

Category	Total	White	Black	Asian	AIAN	Hisp.
Enrollment (%)	100.0	20.5	78.9	0.3	0.1	0.2
Drop-out Rate (%)	6.4	4.3	6.9	n/a	0.0	0.0
H.S. Diplomas (#)	58	16	42	0	0	0

Coosa County
2001 Nixburg Rd • Rockford, AL 35136-0037
Mailing Address: PO Box 37 • Rockford, AL 35136-0037
(256) 377-4913 • http://coosaschools.k12.al.us/
Grade Span: KG-12; **Agency Type:** 1
Schools: 4
1 Primary; 1 Middle; 2 High; 0 Other Level
3 Regular; 0 Special Education; 1 Vocational; 0 Alternative
0 Magnet; 0 Charter; 1 Title I Eligible; 1 School-wide Title I
Students: 1,618 (52.4% male; 47.5% female)
Individual Education Program: 251 (15.5%);
English Language Learner: 4 (0.2%); Migrant: 0 (0.0%)
Eligible for Free Lunch Program: 829 (51.2%)
Eligible for Reduced-Price Lunch Program: 214 (13.2%)
Teachers: 105.2 (15.4 to 1)
Librarians/Media Specialists: 3.0 (539.3 to 1)
Guidance Counselors: 5.4 (299.6 to 1)
Current Spending: ($ per student per year):
Total: $6,308; Instruction: $3,544; Support Services: $2,318
Enrollment, Drop-out Rates and Diploma Recipients by Race/Ethnicity

Category	Total	White	Black	Asian	AIAN	Hisp.
Enrollment (%)	100.0	48.8	50.2	0.1	0.3	0.3
Drop-out Rate (%)	4.3	7.4	1.3	n/a	n/a	0.0
H.S. Diplomas (#)	73	38	35	0	0	0

Andalusia City
122 6th Ave • Andalusia, AL 36420-3152
(334) 222-3186
Grade Span: KG-12; **Agency Type:** 1
Schools: 3
1 Primary; 1 Middle; 1 High; 0 Other Level
3 Regular; 0 Special Education; 0 Vocational; 0 Alternative
0 Magnet; 0 Charter; 2 Title I Eligible; 2 School-wide Title I
Students: 1,695 (51.1% male; 48.8% female)
Individual Education Program: 238 (14.0%);
English Language Learner: 5 (0.3%); Migrant: 0 (0.0%)
Eligible for Free Lunch Program: 686 (40.5%)
Eligible for Reduced-Price Lunch Program: 103 (6.1%)
Teachers: 110.8 (15.3 to 1)
Librarians/Media Specialists: 4.0 (423.8 to 1)
Guidance Counselors: 4.0 (423.8 to 1)
Current Spending: ($ per student per year):
Total: $6,238; Instruction: $4,058; Support Services: $1,790
Enrollment, Drop-out Rates and Diploma Recipients by Race/Ethnicity

Category	Total	White	Black	Asian	AIAN	Hisp.
Enrollment (%)	100.0	66.5	32.1	0.5	0.2	0.6
Drop-out Rate (%)	3.0	3.3	2.3	n/a	0.0	0.0
H.S. Diplomas (#)	113	82	30	0	0	1

Covington County

807 C C Baker Ave • Andalusia, AL 36420-2199
Mailing Address: PO Box 460 • Andalusia, AL 36420-0460
(334) 222-7571 • http://www.covingtoncountyschools.net/
Grade Span: PK-12; **Agency Type:** 1
Schools: 8
   3 Primary; 1 Middle; 2 High; 2 Other Level
   8 Regular; 0 Special Education; 0 Vocational; 0 Alternative
   0 Magnet; 0 Charter; 7 Title I Eligible; 7 School-wide Title I
Students: 3,241 (53.1% male; 46.8% female)
   Individual Education Program: 528 (16.3%);
   English Language Learner: 4 (0.1%); Migrant: 286 (8.8%)
   Eligible for Free Lunch Program: 1,356 (41.8%)
   Eligible for Reduced-Price Lunch Program: 368 (11.4%)
Teachers: 211.9 (15.3 to 1)
Librarians/Media Specialists: 6.0 (540.2 to 1)
Guidance Counselors: 7.1 (456.5 to 1)
Current Spending: ($ per student per year):
   Total: $5,981; Instruction: $3,636; Support Services: $1,936
Enrollment, Drop-out Rates and Diploma Recipients by Race/Ethnicity

Category	Total	White	Black	Asian	AIAN	Hisp.
Enrollment (%)	100.0	89.1	9.5	0.1	0.6	0.5
Drop-out Rate (%)	3.8	4.1	0.9	n/a	10.0	100.0
H.S. Diplomas (#)	132	116	14	0	1	1

Crenshaw County

Crenshaw County

183 Votec Dr • Luverne, AL 36049-0072
(334) 335-6519
Grade Span: PK-12; **Agency Type:** 1
Schools: 4
   0 Primary; 0 Middle; 1 High; 3 Other Level
   3 Regular; 0 Special Education; 1 Vocational; 0 Alternative
   0 Magnet; 0 Charter; 3 Title I Eligible; 3 School-wide Title I
Students: 2,449 (54.5% male; 45.4% female)
   Individual Education Program: 394 (16.1%);
   English Language Learner: 0 (0.0%); Migrant: 0 (0.0%)
   Eligible for Free Lunch Program: 1,251 (51.1%)
   Eligible for Reduced-Price Lunch Program: 311 (12.7%)
Teachers: 152.3 (16.1 to 1)
Librarians/Media Specialists: 4.0 (612.3 to 1)
Guidance Counselors: 5.3 (462.1 to 1)
Current Spending: ($ per student per year):
   Total: $6,317; Instruction: $3,924; Support Services: $1,919
Enrollment, Drop-out Rates and Diploma Recipients by Race/Ethnicity

Category	Total	White	Black	Asian	AIAN	Hisp.
Enrollment (%)	100.0	66.1	32.8	0.3	0.1	0.7
Drop-out Rate (%)	4.0	3.8	4.4	0.0	0.0	0.0
H.S. Diplomas (#)	129	82	44	2	1	0

Cullman County

Cullman City

301 1st St NE Ste 100 • Cullman, AL 35055-3514
(256) 734-2233 • http://www.cullmancats.net/
Grade Span: KG-12; **Agency Type:** 1
Schools: 7
   3 Primary; 1 Middle; 2 High; 1 Other Level
   5 Regular; 0 Special Education; 1 Vocational; 1 Alternative
   0 Magnet; 0 Charter; 2 Title I Eligible; 0 School-wide Title I
Students: 2,657 (52.7% male; 47.2% female)
   Individual Education Program: 308 (11.6%);
   English Language Learner: 109 (4.1%); Migrant: 0 (0.0%)
   Eligible for Free Lunch Program: 546 (20.5%)
   Eligible for Reduced-Price Lunch Program: 147 (5.5%)
Teachers: 177.2 (15.0 to 1)
Librarians/Media Specialists: 4.0 (664.3 to 1)
Guidance Counselors: 6.0 (442.8 to 1)
Current Spending: ($ per student per year):
   Total: $6,195; Instruction: $4,038; Support Services: $1,687
Enrollment, Drop-out Rates and Diploma Recipients by Race/Ethnicity

Category	Total	White	Black	Asian	AIAN	Hisp.
Enrollment (%)	100.0	92.2	0.5	0.8	0.1	6.4
Drop-out Rate (%)	2.4	2.5	n/a	0.0	0.0	0.0
H.S. Diplomas (#)	181	178	0	2	1	0

Cullman County

402 Arnold St NE • Cullman, AL 35055-1964
Mailing Address: PO Box 1590 • Cullman, AL 35056-1590
(256) 734-2933 • http://www.ccboe.org/
Grade Span: PK-12; **Agency Type:** 1
Schools: 27
   13 Primary; 5 Middle; 8 High; 1 Other Level
   25 Regular; 1 Special Education; 1 Vocational; 0 Alternative

---

   0 Magnet; 0 Charter; 14 Title I Eligible; 1 School-wide Title I
Students: 9,759 (51.9% male; 48.0% female)
   Individual Education Program: 1,420 (14.6%);
   English Language Learner: 189 (1.9%); Migrant: 0 (0.0%)
   Eligible for Free Lunch Program: 3,703 (37.9%)
   Eligible for Reduced-Price Lunch Program: 1,257 (12.9%)
Teachers: 632.0 (15.4 to 1)
Librarians/Media Specialists: 16.8 (580.9 to 1)
Guidance Counselors: 16.7 (584.4 to 1)
Current Spending: ($ per student per year):
   Total: $5,885; Instruction: $3,552; Support Services: $1,882
Enrollment, Drop-out Rates and Diploma Recipients by Race/Ethnicity

Category	Total	White	Black	Asian	AIAN	Hisp.
Enrollment (%)	100.0	96.2	1.4	0.1	0.1	2.2
Drop-out Rate (%)	5.2	5.1	7.4	0.0	n/a	9.1
H.S. Diplomas (#)	465	459	4	1	0	1

Dale County

Dale County

111 W Reynolds St • Ozark, AL 36360-1438
Mailing Address: PO Box 948 • Ozark, AL 36361-0948
(334) 774-2355 • http://www.dalecountyboe.org/
Grade Span: KG-12; **Agency Type:** 1
Schools: 7
   3 Primary; 1 Middle; 2 High; 1 Other Level
   7 Regular; 0 Special Education; 0 Vocational; 0 Alternative
   0 Magnet; 0 Charter; 5 Title I Eligible; 5 School-wide Title I
Students: 2,734 (53.2% male; 46.7% female)
   Individual Education Program: 484 (17.7%);
   English Language Learner: 2 (0.1%); Migrant: 1 (<0.1%)
   Eligible for Free Lunch Program: 1,202 (44.0%)
   Eligible for Reduced-Price Lunch Program: 249 (9.1%)
Teachers: 182.7 (15.0 to 1)
Librarians/Media Specialists: 6.2 (441.0 to 1)
Guidance Counselors: 4.0 (683.5 to 1)
Current Spending: ($ per student per year):
   Total: $6,245; Instruction: $3,879; Support Services: $1,982
Enrollment, Drop-out Rates and Diploma Recipients by Race/Ethnicity

Category	Total	White	Black	Asian	AIAN	Hisp.
Enrollment (%)	100.0	79.9	18.6	0.4	0.4	0.5
Drop-out Rate (%)	7.3	8.1	4.4	0.0	n/a	0.0
H.S. Diplomas (#)	140	116	23	0	0	1

Daleville City

626 N Daleville Ave • Daleville, AL 36322-2006
(334) 598-2456 • http://www.daleville.k12.al.us/
Grade Span: KG-12; **Agency Type:** 1
Schools: 4
   1 Primary; 1 Middle; 1 High; 1 Other Level
   3 Regular; 0 Special Education; 0 Vocational; 1 Alternative
   0 Magnet; 0 Charter; 2 Title I Eligible; 2 School-wide Title I
Students: 1,582 (53.6% male; 46.3% female)
   Individual Education Program: 278 (17.6%);
   English Language Learner: 6 (0.4%); Migrant: 0 (0.0%)
   Eligible for Free Lunch Program: 638 (40.3%)
   Eligible for Reduced-Price Lunch Program: 148 (9.4%)
Teachers: 108.0 (14.6 to 1)
Librarians/Media Specialists: 3.0 (527.3 to 1)
Guidance Counselors: 3.0 (527.3 to 1)
Current Spending: ($ per student per year):
   Total: $5,810; Instruction: $3,522; Support Services: $1,932
Enrollment, Drop-out Rates and Diploma Recipients by Race/Ethnicity

Category	Total	White	Black	Asian	AIAN	Hisp.
Enrollment (%)	100.0	54.7	35.7	2.3	0.7	6.6
Drop-out Rate (%)	1.7	2.4	0.6	7.1	0.0	0.0
H.S. Diplomas (#)	90	45	32	4	0	9

Ozark City

1044 Andrews Ave • Ozark, AL 36360-1739
(334) 774-5197 • http://www.ocbe.k12.al.us/
Grade Span: KG-12; **Agency Type:** 1
Schools: 8
   3 Primary; 2 Middle; 3 High; 0 Other Level
   6 Regular; 0 Special Education; 1 Vocational; 1 Alternative
   0 Magnet; 0 Charter; 4 Title I Eligible; 0 School-wide Title I
Students: 2,778 (52.0% male; 48.0% female)
   Individual Education Program: 517 (18.6%);
   English Language Learner: 5 (0.2%); Migrant: 0 (0.0%)
   Eligible for Free Lunch Program: 1,151 (41.4%)
   Eligible for Reduced-Price Lunch Program: 192 (6.9%)
Teachers: 181.9 (15.3 to 1)
Librarians/Media Specialists: 6.0 (463.0 to 1)
Guidance Counselors: 7.0 (396.9 to 1)
Current Spending: ($ per student per year):
   Total: $6,353; Instruction: $3,693; Support Services: $2,188

Enrollment, Drop-out Rates and Diploma Recipients by Race/Ethnicity

Category	Total	White	Black	Asian	AIAN	Hisp.
Enrollment (%)	100.0	54.9	42.9	0.5	0.4	1.2
Drop-out Rate (%)	5.9	6.4	5.3	0.0	0.0	6.7
H.S. Diplomas (#)	161	103	50	0	3	5

Dallas County

Dallas County
429 Lauderdale St • Selma, AL 36701-4581
Mailing Address: PO Box 1056 • Selma, AL 36702-1056
(334) 876-4461 • http://www.dallask12.org/
Grade Span: KG-12; **Agency Type:** 1
Schools: 14
  8 Primary; 2 Middle; 4 High; 0 Other Level
  13 Regular; 0 Special Education; 1 Vocational; 0 Alternative
  0 Magnet; 0 Charter; 9 Title I Eligible; 9 School-wide Title I
Students: 4,482   (50.5% male; 49.4% female)
  Individual Education Program: 688 (15.4%);
  English Language Learner: 5 (0.1%); Migrant: 0 (0.0%)
  Eligible for Free Lunch Program: 3,309 (73.8%)
  Eligible for Reduced-Price Lunch Program: 331 (7.4%)
Teachers: 271.5 (16.5 to 1)
Librarians/Media Specialists: 11.0 (407.5 to 1)
Guidance Counselors: 8.5 (527.3 to 1)
Current Spending: ($ per student per year):
  Total: $6,444; Instruction: $3,757; Support Services: $2,193
Enrollment, Drop-out Rates and Diploma Recipients by Race/Ethnicity

Category	Total	White	Black	Asian	AIAN	Hisp.
Enrollment (%)	100.0	22.1	77.6	0.3	0.0	0.0
Drop-out Rate (%)	7.3	9.3	6.5	14.3	n/a	n/a
H.S. Diplomas (#)	229	51	177	1	0	0

Selma City
300 Washington St • Selma, AL 36701-4454
Mailing Address: PO Box 350 • Selma, AL 36702-0350
(334) 874-1600 •
**http://www.myaasite.com/programs/schools/districtView.asp?District=:;:
%3CCA:**
Grade Span: PK-12; **Agency Type:** 1
Schools: 13
  8 Primary; 2 Middle; 2 High; 1 Other Level
  11 Regular; 0 Special Education; 1 Vocational; 1 Alternative
  0 Magnet; 0 Charter; 6 Title I Eligible; 6 School-wide Title I
Students: 4,287   (49.5% male; 50.4% female)
  Individual Education Program: 453 (10.6%);
  English Language Learner: 6 (0.1%); Migrant: 0 (0.0%)
  Eligible for Free Lunch Program: 3,351 (78.2%)
  Eligible for Reduced-Price Lunch Program: 298 (7.0%)
Teachers: 267.9 (16.0 to 1)
Librarians/Media Specialists: 11.0 (389.7 to 1)
Guidance Counselors: 10.8 (396.9 to 1)
Current Spending: ($ per student per year):
  Total: $6,469; Instruction: $3,962; Support Services: $1,993
Enrollment, Drop-out Rates and Diploma Recipients by Race/Ethnicity

Category	Total	White	Black	Asian	AIAN	Hisp.
Enrollment (%)	100.0	4.8	94.4	0.5	0.0	0.2
Drop-out Rate (%)	1.7	0.0	1.7	0.0	n/a	n/a
H.S. Diplomas (#)	164	0	164	0	0	0

De Kalb County

Dekalb County
306 Main St W • Rainsville, AL 35986-1668
Mailing Address: PO Box 1668 • Rainsville, AL 35986-1668
(256) 638-6921 • http://www.dekalbk12.org/
Grade Span: KG-12; **Agency Type:** 1
Schools: 14
  3 Primary; 0 Middle; 1 High; 10 Other Level
  11 Regular; 1 Special Education; 1 Vocational; 1 Alternative
  0 Magnet; 0 Charter; 8 Title I Eligible; 8 School-wide Title I
Students: 8,123   (52.5% male; 47.4% female)
  Individual Education Program: 1,352 (16.6%);
  English Language Learner: 595 (7.3%); Migrant: 859 (10.6%)
  Eligible for Free Lunch Program: 3,635 (44.7%)
  Eligible for Reduced-Price Lunch Program: 908 (11.2%)
Teachers: 564.4 (14.4 to 1)
Librarians/Media Specialists: 16.5 (492.3 to 1)
Guidance Counselors: 18.5 (439.1 to 1)
Current Spending: ($ per student per year):
  Total: $6,382; Instruction: $3,941; Support Services: $1,974

Enrollment, Drop-out Rates and Diploma Recipients by Race/Ethnicity

Category	Total	White	Black	Asian	AIAN	Hisp.
Enrollment (%)	100.0	75.3	1.0	0.3	12.1	11.3
Drop-out Rate (%)	4.3	5.2	5.9	0.0	0.3	6.8
H.S. Diplomas (#)	372	255	3	0	109	5

Fort Payne City
205 45th St NE • Fort Payne, AL 35967
Mailing Address: PO Box 681029 • Fort Payne, AL 35968-1611
(256) 845-0915 • http://www.ftpayk12.org/
Grade Span: KG-12; **Agency Type:** 1
Schools: 4
  2 Primary; 1 Middle; 1 High; 0 Other Level
  4 Regular; 0 Special Education; 0 Vocational; 0 Alternative
  0 Magnet; 0 Charter; 2 Title I Eligible; 0 School-wide Title I
Students: 2,726   (52.0% male; 47.9% female)
  Individual Education Program: 306 (11.2%);
  English Language Learner: 542 (19.9%); Migrant: 25 (0.9%)
  Eligible for Free Lunch Program: 1,082 (39.7%)
  Eligible for Reduced-Price Lunch Program: 209 (7.7%)
Teachers: 169.9 (16.0 to 1)
Librarians/Media Specialists: 5.0 (545.2 to 1)
Guidance Counselors: 5.0 (545.2 to 1)
Current Spending: ($ per student per year):
  Total: $5,922; Instruction: $3,829; Support Services: $1,578
Enrollment, Drop-out Rates and Diploma Recipients by Race/Ethnicity

Category	Total	White	Black	Asian	AIAN	Hisp.
Enrollment (%)	100.0	73.3	6.0	0.7	0.1	20.0
Drop-out Rate (%)	4.9	3.7	2.9	14.3	0.0	16.4
H.S. Diplomas (#)	136	118	4	1	12	1

Elmore County

Elmore County
203 Hill St • Wetumpka, AL 36092-2722
Mailing Address: PO Box 817 • Wetumpka, AL 36092-0014
(334) 567-1200 • http://www.elmoreco.com/
Grade Span: PK-12; **Agency Type:** 1
Schools: 15
  5 Primary; 5 Middle; 5 High; 0 Other Level
  14 Regular; 0 Special Education; 1 Vocational; 0 Alternative
  0 Magnet; 0 Charter; 10 Title I Eligible; 0 School-wide Title I
Students: 10,213   (52.0% male; 47.9% female)
  Individual Education Program: 1,485 (14.5%);
  English Language Learner: 81 (0.8%); Migrant: 0 (0.0%)
  Eligible for Free Lunch Program: 3,399 (33.3%)
  Eligible for Reduced-Price Lunch Program: 851 (8.3%)
Teachers: 621.0 (16.4 to 1)
Librarians/Media Specialists: 14.0 (729.5 to 1)
Guidance Counselors: 17.0 (600.8 to 1)
Current Spending: ($ per student per year):
  Total: $5,573; Instruction: $3,541; Support Services: $1,680
Enrollment, Drop-out Rates and Diploma Recipients by Race/Ethnicity

Category	Total	White	Black	Asian	AIAN	Hisp.
Enrollment (%)	100.0	70.4	27.2	0.8	0.1	1.3
Drop-out Rate (%)	5.7	5.8	5.3	6.7	20.0	6.3
H.S. Diplomas (#)	430	342	84	3	0	1

Tallassee City
308 King St • Tallassee, AL 36078-1316
(334) 283-6864
Grade Span: KG-12; **Agency Type:** 1
Schools: 3
  1 Primary; 1 Middle; 1 High; 0 Other Level
  3 Regular; 0 Special Education; 0 Vocational; 0 Alternative
  0 Magnet; 0 Charter; 1 Title I Eligible; 0 School-wide Title I
Students: 1,896   (51.4% male; 48.5% female)
  Individual Education Program: 288 (15.2%);
  English Language Learner: 22 (1.2%); Migrant: 0 (0.0%)
  Eligible for Free Lunch Program: 740 (38.8%)
  Eligible for Reduced-Price Lunch Program: 148 (7.8%)
Teachers: 119.5 (15.9 to 1)
Librarians/Media Specialists: 3.0 (635.3 to 1)
Guidance Counselors: 3.0 (635.3 to 1)
Current Spending: ($ per student per year):
  Total: $5,378; Instruction: $3,577; Support Services: $1,345
Enrollment, Drop-out Rates and Diploma Recipients by Race/Ethnicity

Category	Total	White	Black	Asian	AIAN	Hisp.
Enrollment (%)	100.0	71.2	27.0	0.3	0.1	1.4
Drop-out Rate (%)	6.8	5.4	10.7	0.0	n/a	25.0
H.S. Diplomas (#)	94	69	25	0	0	0

Escambia County

Escambia County
301 Belleville Ave • Brewton, AL 36426-2042
Mailing Address: PO Box 307 • Brewton, AL 36427-0307
(251) 867-6251 • http://www.escambiak12.net/
Grade Span: PK-12; **Agency Type:** 1
Schools: 14
   6 Primary; 2 Middle; 5 High; 1 Other Level
   11 Regular; 0 Special Education; 1 Vocational; 2 Alternative
   0 Magnet; 0 Charter; 8 Title I Eligible; 8 School-wide Title I
Students: 4,595   (52.4% male; 47.5% female)
   Individual Education Program: 693 (15.1%);
   English Language Learner: 1 (<0.1%); Migrant: 0 (0.0%)
   Eligible for Free Lunch Program: 2,684 (58.4%)
   Eligible for Reduced-Price Lunch Program: 579 (12.6%)
Teachers: 317.5 (14.5 to 1)
Librarians/Media Specialists: 10.5 (437.6 to 1)
Guidance Counselors: 13.8 (333.0 to 1)
Current Spending: ($ per student per year):
   Total: $6,675; Instruction: $3,898; Support Services: $2,355
Enrollment, Drop-out Rates and Diploma Recipients by Race/Ethnicity

Category	Total	White	Black	Asian	AIAN	Hisp.
Enrollment (%)	100.0	54.5	39.2	0.2	5.3	0.8
Drop-out Rate (%)	3.9	4.3	3.1	0.0	6.5	0.0
H.S. Diplomas (#)	230	138	81	0	11	0

Etowah County

Attalla City
101 Case Ave • Attalla, AL 35954-3404
(256) 538-8051 • http://www.attalla.k12.al.us/
Grade Span: PK-12; **Agency Type:** 1
Schools: 4
   2 Primary; 1 Middle; 1 High; 0 Other Level
   4 Regular; 0 Special Education; 0 Vocational; 0 Alternative
   0 Magnet; 0 Charter; 2 Title I Eligible; 2 School-wide Title I
Students: 1,823   (53.5% male; 46.4% female)
   Individual Education Program: 351 (19.3%);
   English Language Learner: 10 (0.5%); Migrant: 0 (0.0%)
   Eligible for Free Lunch Program: 780 (42.8%)
   Eligible for Reduced-Price Lunch Program: 232 (12.7%)
Teachers: 123.1 (14.8 to 1)
Librarians/Media Specialists: 4.0 (455.8 to 1)
Guidance Counselors: 5.0 (364.6 to 1)
Current Spending: ($ per student per year):
   Total: $6,163; Instruction: $3,860; Support Services: $1,837
Enrollment, Drop-out Rates and Diploma Recipients by Race/Ethnicity

Category	Total	White	Black	Asian	AIAN	Hisp.
Enrollment (%)	100.0	81.3	13.3	0.3	0.2	4.0
Drop-out Rate (%)	5.4	6.1	0.0	n/a	0.0	0.0
H.S. Diplomas (#)	109	98	8	0	1	2

Etowah County
3200 W Meighan Blvd • Gadsden, AL 35904-1732
(256) 549-7578 • http://www.ecboe.org/
Grade Span: PK-12; **Agency Type:** 1
Schools: 23
   10 Primary; 3 Middle; 6 High; 3 Other Level
   19 Regular; 1 Special Education; 1 Vocational; 1 Alternative
   0 Magnet; 0 Charter; 13 Title I Eligible; 9 School-wide Title I
Students: 8,521   (51.8% male; 48.1% female)
   Individual Education Program: 1,407 (16.5%);
   English Language Learner: 60 (0.7%); Migrant: 0 (0.0%)
   Eligible for Free Lunch Program: 2,473 (29.0%)
   Eligible for Reduced-Price Lunch Program: 941 (11.0%)
Teachers: 601.5 (14.2 to 1)
Librarians/Media Specialists: 18.7 (455.7 to 1)
Guidance Counselors: 20.0 (426.1 to 1)
Current Spending: ($ per student per year):
   Total: $5,794; Instruction: $3,694; Support Services: $1,736
Enrollment, Drop-out Rates and Diploma Recipients by Race/Ethnicity

Category	Total	White	Black	Asian	AIAN	Hisp.
Enrollment (%)	100.0	96.5	1.7	0.4	0.2	1.2
Drop-out Rate (%)	2.7	2.8	0.0	0.0	0.0	0.0
H.S. Diplomas (#)	436	424	4	4	0	4

Gadsden City
1026 Chestnut St • Gadsden, AL 35901
Mailing Address: PO Box 184 • Gadsden, AL 35902-0184
(256) 543-3512 • http://www.gcs.k12.al.us/
Grade Span: PK-12; **Agency Type:** 1
Schools: 17
   9 Primary; 3 Middle; 4 High; 1 Other Level
   15 Regular; 0 Special Education; 1 Vocational; 1 Alternative

---

   0 Magnet; 0 Charter; 11 Title I Eligible; 10 School-wide Title I
Students: 5,467   (50.8% male; 49.1% female)
   Individual Education Program: 956 (17.5%);
   English Language Learner: 172 (3.1%); Migrant: 130 (2.4%)
   Eligible for Free Lunch Program: 3,366 (61.6%)
   Eligible for Reduced-Price Lunch Program: 419 (7.7%)
Teachers: 398.2 (13.7 to 1)
Librarians/Media Specialists: 13.7 (399.1 to 1)
Guidance Counselors: 12.6 (433.9 to 1)
Current Spending: ($ per student per year):
   Total: $6,710; Instruction: $4,050; Support Services: $2,195
Enrollment, Drop-out Rates and Diploma Recipients by Race/Ethnicity

Category	Total	White	Black	Asian	AIAN	Hisp.
Enrollment (%)	100.0	40.1	54.6	0.8	0.4	3.8
Drop-out Rate (%)	4.0	5.6	2.8	0.0	0.0	3.6
H.S. Diplomas (#)	257	121	133	1	0	2

Fayette County

Fayette County
103 First Ave NW • Fayette, AL 35555-0599
Mailing Address: PO Box 686 • Fayette, AL 35555-0599
(205) 932-4611 • http://www.fayette.k12.al.us/
Grade Span: KG-12; **Agency Type:** 1
Schools: 6
   2 Primary; 1 Middle; 2 High; 1 Other Level
   6 Regular; 0 Special Education; 0 Vocational; 0 Alternative
   0 Magnet; 0 Charter; 5 Title I Eligible; 3 School-wide Title I
Students: 2,656   (51.5% male; 48.4% female)
   Individual Education Program: 387 (14.6%);
   English Language Learner: 0 (0.0%); Migrant: 0 (0.0%)
   Eligible for Free Lunch Program: 870 (32.8%)
   Eligible for Reduced-Price Lunch Program: 264 (9.9%)
Teachers: 168.9 (15.7 to 1)
Librarians/Media Specialists: 6.0 (442.7 to 1)
Guidance Counselors: 5.0 (531.2 to 1)
Current Spending: ($ per student per year):
   Total: $6,241; Instruction: $3,807; Support Services: $1,984
Enrollment, Drop-out Rates and Diploma Recipients by Race/Ethnicity

Category	Total	White	Black	Asian	AIAN	Hisp.
Enrollment (%)	100.0	82.5	17.1	0.0	0.0	0.4
Drop-out Rate (%)	4.8	5.2	2.8	n/a	n/a	25.0
H.S. Diplomas (#)	145	120	25	0	0	0

Franklin County

Franklin County
500 N Coffee Ave • Russellville, AL 35653-0610
Mailing Address: PO Box 610 • Russellville, AL 35653-0610
(256) 332-1360 • http://www.franklin.k12.al.us/
Grade Span: KG-12; **Agency Type:** 1
Schools: 7
   0 Primary; 0 Middle; 1 High; 6 Other Level
   6 Regular; 0 Special Education; 1 Vocational; 0 Alternative
   0 Magnet; 0 Charter; 6 Title I Eligible; 1 School-wide Title I
Students: 3,040   (51.8% male; 48.1% female)
   Individual Education Program: 544 (17.9%);
   English Language Learner: 113 (3.7%); Migrant: 53 (1.7%)
   Eligible for Free Lunch Program: 1,355 (44.6%)
   Eligible for Reduced-Price Lunch Program: 454 (14.9%)
Teachers: 222.2 (13.7 to 1)
Librarians/Media Specialists: 4.7 (646.8 to 1)
Guidance Counselors: 6.8 (447.1 to 1)
Current Spending: ($ per student per year):
   Total: $6,756; Instruction: $4,187; Support Services: $2,062
Enrollment, Drop-out Rates and Diploma Recipients by Race/Ethnicity

Category	Total	White	Black	Asian	AIAN	Hisp.
Enrollment (%)	100.0	95.0	0.5	0.0	0.1	4.4
Drop-out Rate (%)	6.0	6.1	0.0	0.0	0.0	0.0
H.S. Diplomas (#)	132	128	1	0	1	2

Russellville City
1945 Waterloo Rd • Russellville, AL 35653-0880
Mailing Address: PO Box 880 • Russellville, AL 35653-0880
(256) 331-2000 • http://www.rcs.k12.al.us/
Grade Span: KG-12; **Agency Type:** 1
Schools: 4
   2 Primary; 1 Middle; 1 High; 0 Other Level
   4 Regular; 0 Special Education; 0 Vocational; 0 Alternative
   0 Magnet; 0 Charter; 2 Title I Eligible; 0 School-wide Title I
Students: 2,344   (50.8% male; 49.1% female)
   Individual Education Program: 325 (13.9%);
   English Language Learner: 273 (11.6%); Migrant: 151 (6.4%)
   Eligible for Free Lunch Program: 1,057 (45.1%)
   Eligible for Reduced-Price Lunch Program: 192 (8.2%)

Teachers: 151.0 (15.5 to 1)
Librarians/Media Specialists: 4.0 (586.0 to 1)
Guidance Counselors: 4.0 (586.0 to 1)
Current Spending: ($ per student per year):
  Total: $6,231; Instruction: $3,908; Support Services: $1,738
Enrollment, Drop-out Rates and Diploma Recipients by Race/Ethnicity

Category	Total	White	Black	Asian	AIAN	Hisp.
Enrollment (%)	100.0	70.3	10.9	0.3	0.0	18.5
Drop-out Rate (%)	0.6	0.8	0.0	0.0	n/a	0.0
H.S. Diplomas (#)	110	94	15	0	0	1

Geneva County

Geneva County
Courthouse • Geneva, AL 36340-0250
Mailing Address: PO Box 250 • Geneva, AL 36340-0250
(334) 684-5690
Grade Span: KG-12; **Agency Type:** 1
Schools: 9
  3 Primary; 3 Middle; 3 High; 0 Other Level
  9 Regular; 0 Special Education; 0 Vocational; 0 Alternative
  0 Magnet; 0 Charter; 3 Title I Eligible; 3 School-wide Title I
Students: 2,722 (53.2% male; 46.7% female)
  Individual Education Program: 466 (17.1%);
  English Language Learner: 31 (1.1%); Migrant: 42 (1.5%)
  Eligible for Free Lunch Program: 1,250 (45.9%)
  Eligible for Reduced-Price Lunch Program: 248 (9.1%)
Teachers: 189.0 (14.4 to 1)
Librarians/Media Specialists: 6.0 (453.7 to 1)
Guidance Counselors: 6.0 (453.7 to 1)
Current Spending: ($ per student per year):
  Total: $5,664; Instruction: $3,385; Support Services: $1,782
Enrollment, Drop-out Rates and Diploma Recipients by Race/Ethnicity

Category	Total	White	Black	Asian	AIAN	Hisp.
Enrollment (%)	100.0	80.4	16.2	0.4	0.2	2.6
Drop-out Rate (%)	4.4	4.4	4.8	0.0	0.0	6.3
H.S. Diplomas (#)	143	123	18	0	0	2

Greene County

Greene County
220 Main St • Eutaw, AL 35462-0569
Mailing Address: PO Box 569 • Eutaw, AL 35462-0569
(205) 372-3114
Grade Span: KG-12; **Agency Type:** 1
Schools: 5
  2 Primary; 1 Middle; 2 High; 0 Other Level
  4 Regular; 0 Special Education; 1 Vocational; 0 Alternative
  0 Magnet; 0 Charter; 4 Title I Eligible; 4 School-wide Title I
Students: 1,635 (51.6% male; 48.3% female)
  Individual Education Program: 226 (13.8%)
  English Language Learner: 0 (0.0%); Migrant: 0 (0.0%)
  Eligible for Free Lunch Program: 1,392 (85.1%)
  Eligible for Reduced-Price Lunch Program: 124 (7.6%)
Teachers: 117.6 (13.9 to 1)
Librarians/Media Specialists: 4.0 (408.8 to 1)
Guidance Counselors: 4.0 (408.8 to 1)
Current Spending: ($ per student per year):
  Total: $6,892; Instruction: $3,904; Support Services: $2,442
Enrollment, Drop-out Rates and Diploma Recipients by Race/Ethnicity

Category	Total	White	Black	Asian	AIAN	Hisp.
Enrollment (%)	100.0	0.2	99.8	0.0	0.0	0.0
Drop-out Rate (%)	11.0	n/a	11.0	n/a	n/a	n/a
H.S. Diplomas (#)	68	0	68	0	0	0

Hale County

Hale County
1115 Powers St • Greensboro, AL 36744-0360
Mailing Address: PO Box 360 • Greensboro, AL 36744-0360
(334) 624-8836 • http://www.halek12.org/
Grade Span: PK-12; **Agency Type:** 1
Schools: 10
  4 Primary; 0 Middle; 5 High; 1 Other Level
  9 Regular; 0 Special Education; 1 Vocational; 0 Alternative
  0 Magnet; 0 Charter; 9 Title I Eligible; 9 School-wide Title I
Students: 3,303 (50.8% male; 49.1% female)
  Individual Education Program: 415 (12.6%)
  English Language Learner: 0 (0.0%); Migrant: 0 (0.0%)
  Eligible for Free Lunch Program: 2,247 (68.0%)
  Eligible for Reduced-Price Lunch Program: 257 (7.8%)
Teachers: 230.6 (14.3 to 1)
Librarians/Media Specialists: 8.3 (398.0 to 1)
Guidance Counselors: 7.6 (434.6 to 1)

Current Spending: ($ per student per year):
  Total: $6,271; Instruction: $3,903; Support Services: $1,874
Enrollment, Drop-out Rates and Diploma Recipients by Race/Ethnicity

Category	Total	White	Black	Asian	AIAN	Hisp.
Enrollment (%)	100.0	25.7	73.6	0.0	0.1	0.4
Drop-out Rate (%)	3.2	4.6	2.7	n/a	n/a	0.0
H.S. Diplomas (#)	162	40	120	0	0	2

Henry County

Henry County
101a Doswell St • Abbeville, AL 36310-0635
Mailing Address: PO Box 635 • Abbeville, AL 36310-0635
(334) 585-2206 • http://www.familyeducation.com/al/henry
Grade Span: PK-12; **Agency Type:** 1
Schools: 7
  2 Primary; 2 Middle; 2 High; 1 Other Level
  6 Regular; 0 Special Education; 0 Vocational; 1 Alternative
  0 Magnet; 0 Charter; 2 Title I Eligible; 2 School-wide Title I
Students: 2,667 (50.0% male; 49.9% female)
  Individual Education Program: 433 (16.2%);
  English Language Learner: 0 (0.0%); Migrant: 0 (0.0%)
  Eligible for Free Lunch Program: 1,507 (56.5%)
  Eligible for Reduced-Price Lunch Program: 281 (10.5%)
Teachers: 169.6 (15.7 to 1)
Librarians/Media Specialists: 5.5 (484.9 to 1)
Guidance Counselors: 6.0 (444.5 to 1)
Current Spending: ($ per student per year):
  Total: $6,914; Instruction: $3,889; Support Services: $2,462
Enrollment, Drop-out Rates and Diploma Recipients by Race/Ethnicity

Category	Total	White	Black	Asian	AIAN	Hisp.
Enrollment (%)	100.0	51.4	46.6	0.2	0.1	1.6
Drop-out Rate (%)	6.1	6.5	5.8	0.0	n/a	0.0
H.S. Diplomas (#)	124	78	46	0	0	0

Houston County

Dothan City
500 Dusy St • Dothan, AL 36301-2506
(334) 794-1407 • http://www.dothan.k12.al.us/
Grade Span: PK-12; **Agency Type:** 1
Schools: 19
  11 Primary; 4 Middle; 3 High; 1 Other Level
  17 Regular; 0 Special Education; 1 Vocational; 1 Alternative
  0 Magnet; 0 Charter; 11 Title I Eligible; 9 School-wide Title I
Students: 8,838 (51.4% male; 48.5% female)
  Individual Education Program: 1,545 (17.5%);
  English Language Learner: 73 (0.8%); Migrant: 0 (0.0%)
  Eligible for Free Lunch Program: 4,200 (47.5%)
  Eligible for Reduced-Price Lunch Program: 540 (6.1%)
Teachers: 520.3 (17.0 to 1)
Librarians/Media Specialists: 19.0 (465.2 to 1)
Guidance Counselors: 21.0 (420.9 to 1)
Current Spending: ($ per student per year):
  Total: $6,649; Instruction: $3,939; Support Services: $2,245
Enrollment, Drop-out Rates and Diploma Recipients by Race/Ethnicity

Category	Total	White	Black	Asian	AIAN	Hisp.
Enrollment (%)	100.0	45.2	51.8	1.1	0.2	1.4
Drop-out Rate (%)	5.7	4.1	7.8	2.6	50.0	0.0
H.S. Diplomas (#)	462	304	142	8	1	7

Houston County
404 W Washington St • Dothan, AL 36301-2520
Mailing Address: PO Box 1688 • Dothan, AL 36302-1688
(334) 792-8331 • http://www.hcboe.org/
Grade Span: KG-12; **Agency Type:** 1
Schools: 11
  3 Primary; 1 Middle; 4 High; 3 Other Level
  9 Regular; 0 Special Education; 1 Vocational; 1 Alternative
  0 Magnet; 0 Charter; 3 Title I Eligible; 3 School-wide Title I
Students: 6,161 (51.3% male; 48.6% female)
  Individual Education Program: 985 (16.0%);
  English Language Learner: 0 (0.0%); Migrant: 0 (0.0%)
  Eligible for Free Lunch Program: 2,030 (32.9%)
  Eligible for Reduced-Price Lunch Program: 629 (10.2%)
Teachers: 378.5 (16.3 to 1)
Librarians/Media Specialists: 10.3 (598.2 to 1)
Guidance Counselors: 12.7 (485.1 to 1)
Current Spending: ($ per student per year):
  Total: $5,594; Instruction: $3,481; Support Services: $1,620
Enrollment, Drop-out Rates and Diploma Recipients by Race/Ethnicity

Category	Total	White	Black	Asian	AIAN	Hisp.
Enrollment (%)	100.0	80.1	18.4	0.5	0.1	0.8
Drop-out Rate (%)	2.6	2.3	3.5	0.0	0.0	11.1
H.S. Diplomas (#)	323	271	41	1	2	8

Jackson County

Jackson County

16003 Al Hwy 35 • Scottsboro, AL 35768-0490
Mailing Address: PO Box 490 • Scottsboro, AL 35768-0490
(256) 259-9500 • http://www.jackson.k12.al.us/
Grade Span: PK-12; **Agency Type:** 1
Schools: 19
  8 Primary; 2 Middle; 2 High; 7 Other Level
  17 Regular; 0 Special Education; 1 Vocational; 1 Alternative
  0 Magnet; 0 Charter; 16 Title I Eligible; 16 School-wide Title I
Students: 6,042 (52.1% male; 47.8% female)
  Individual Education Program: 712 (11.8%);
  English Language Learner: 71 (1.2%); Migrant: 0 (0.0%)
  Eligible for Free Lunch Program: 2,720 (45.0%)
  Eligible for Reduced-Price Lunch Program: 796 (13.2%)
Teachers: 430.0 (14.1 to 1)
Librarians/Media Specialists: 14.5 (416.7 to 1)
Guidance Counselors: 11.5 (525.4 to 1)
Current Spending: ($ per student per year):
  Total: $6,376; Instruction: $3,696; Support Services: $2,116
Enrollment, Drop-out Rates and Diploma Recipients by Race/Ethnicity

Category	Total	White	Black	Asian	AIAN	Hisp.
Enrollment (%)	100.0	84.6	4.1	0.2	9.3	1.8
Drop-out Rate (%)	4.5	4.8	3.6	0.0	3.7	0.0
H.S. Diplomas (#)	277	198	9	1	69	0

Scottsboro City

906 S Scott St • Scottsboro, AL 35768-2642
(256) 218-2100 • http://www.scottsboropower.com/~jopat/
Grade Span: PK-12; **Agency Type:** 1
Schools: 6
  3 Primary; 2 Middle; 1 High; 0 Other Level
  6 Regular; 0 Special Education; 0 Vocational; 0 Alternative
  0 Magnet; 0 Charter; 5 Title I Eligible; 0 School-wide Title I
Students: 2,756 (50.4% male; 49.5% female)
  Individual Education Program: 536 (19.4%);
  English Language Learner: 25 (0.9%); Migrant: 0 (0.0%)
  Eligible for Free Lunch Program: 800 (29.0%)
  Eligible for Reduced-Price Lunch Program: 216 (7.8%)
Teachers: 192.3 (14.3 to 1)
Librarians/Media Specialists: 6.0 (459.3 to 1)
Guidance Counselors: 7.7 (357.9 to 1)
Current Spending: ($ per student per year):
  Total: $7,026; Instruction: $4,067; Support Services: $2,399
Enrollment, Drop-out Rates and Diploma Recipients by Race/Ethnicity

Category	Total	White	Black	Asian	AIAN	Hisp.
Enrollment (%)	100.0	89.6	8.1	0.5	0.0	1.7
Drop-out Rate (%)	3.3	3.3	2.6	0.0	n/a	16.7
H.S. Diplomas (#)	149	138	11	0	0	0

Jefferson County

Bessemer City

1621 5th Ave N • Bessemer, AL 35020
Mailing Address: PO Box 1230 • Bessemer, AL 35021-1230
(205) 432-3000 • http://www.bessk12.org/
Grade Span: KG-12; **Agency Type:** 1
Schools: 9
  5 Primary; 1 Middle; 2 High; 1 Other Level
  7 Regular; 0 Special Education; 1 Vocational; 1 Alternative
  0 Magnet; 0 Charter; 7 Title I Eligible; 6 School-wide Title I
Students: 4,116 (51.1% male; 48.8% female)
  Individual Education Program: 575 (14.0%);
  English Language Learner: 41 (1.0%); Migrant: 0 (0.0%)
  Eligible for Free Lunch Program: 3,067 (74.5%)
  Eligible for Reduced-Price Lunch Program: 294 (7.1%)
Teachers: 265.4 (15.5 to 1)
Librarians/Media Specialists: 8.0 (514.5 to 1)
Guidance Counselors: 8.0 (514.5 to 1)
Current Spending: ($ per student per year):
  Total: $6,571; Instruction: $3,783; Support Services: $2,300
Enrollment, Drop-out Rates and Diploma Recipients by Race/Ethnicity

Category	Total	White	Black	Asian	AIAN	Hisp.
Enrollment (%)	100.0	2.6	95.5	0.1	0.0	1.5
Drop-out Rate (%)	1.2	7.4	1.0	0.0	n/a	0.0
H.S. Diplomas (#)	109	3	106	0	0	0

Birmingham City

2015 N Park Pl • Birmingham, AL 35203-2762
Mailing Address: PO Box 10007 • Birmingham, AL 35202-0007
(205) 231-4220 • http://www.bhm.k12.al.us/
Grade Span: PK-12; **Agency Type:** 1
Schools: 80
  45 Primary; 16 Middle; 16 High; 3 Other Level
  64 Regular; 4 Special Education; 1 Vocational; 11 Alternative
  9 Magnet; 0 Charter; 50 Title I Eligible; 49 School-wide Title I
Students: 34,099 (50.8% male; 49.1% female)
  Individual Education Program: 5,154 (15.1%);
  English Language Learner: 342 (1.0%); Migrant: 0 (0.0%)
  Eligible for Free Lunch Program: 22,302 (65.4%)
  Eligible for Reduced-Price Lunch Program: 2,408 (7.1%)
Teachers: 2,210.6 (15.4 to 1)
Librarians/Media Specialists: 70.0 (487.2 to 1)
Guidance Counselors: 71.7 (475.6 to 1)
Current Spending: ($ per student per year):
  Total: $6,890; Instruction: $3,718; Support Services: $2,774
Enrollment, Drop-out Rates and Diploma Recipients by Race/Ethnicity

Category	Total	White	Black	Asian	AIAN	Hisp.
Enrollment (%)	100.0	1.2	97.3	0.2	0.0	1.3
Drop-out Rate (%)	2.1	0.0	2.2	0.0	n/a	0.0
H.S. Diplomas (#)	1,706	13	1,685	5	0	3

Fairfield City

6405 Ave D • Fairfield, AL 35064-0110
(205) 783-6850 • http://www.fairfield.k12.al.us/
Grade Span: KG-12; **Agency Type:** 1
Schools: 7
  3 Primary; 1 Middle; 2 High; 1 Other Level
  5 Regular; 0 Special Education; 1 Vocational; 1 Alternative
  0 Magnet; 0 Charter; 3 Title I Eligible; 3 School-wide Title I
Students: 2,353 (51.1% male; 48.8% female)
  Individual Education Program: 287 (12.2%);
  English Language Learner: 17 (0.7%); Migrant: 0 (0.0%)
  Eligible for Free Lunch Program: 1,463 (62.2%)
  Eligible for Reduced-Price Lunch Program: 199 (8.5%)
Teachers: 168.8 (13.9 to 1)
Librarians/Media Specialists: 5.0 (470.6 to 1)
Guidance Counselors: 4.3 (547.2 to 1)
Current Spending: ($ per student per year):
  Total: $6,497; Instruction: $3,756; Support Services: $2,198
Enrollment, Drop-out Rates and Diploma Recipients by Race/Ethnicity

Category	Total	White	Black	Asian	AIAN	Hisp.
Enrollment (%)	100.0	0.1	99.2	0.0	0.0	0.6
Drop-out Rate (%)	2.0	n/a	1.8	n/a	n/a	0.0
H.S. Diplomas (#)	130	0	129	0	0	1

Homewood City

7 Hollywood Blvd • Homewood, AL 35209
Mailing Address: PO Box 59366 • Homewood, AL 35259-9366
(205) 870-4203 • http://www.homewood.k12.al.us/
Grade Span: PK-12; **Agency Type:** 1
Schools: 5
  3 Primary; 1 Middle; 1 High; 0 Other Level
  5 Regular; 0 Special Education; 0 Vocational; 0 Alternative
  0 Magnet; 0 Charter; 3 Title I Eligible; 1 School-wide Title I
Students: 3,268 (53.2% male; 46.7% female)
  Individual Education Program: 735 (22.5%);
  English Language Learner: 202 (6.2%); Migrant: 0 (0.0%)
  Eligible for Free Lunch Program: 519 (15.9%)
  Eligible for Reduced-Price Lunch Program: 214 (6.5%)
Teachers: 259.0 (12.6 to 1)
Librarians/Media Specialists: 5.0 (653.6 to 1)
Guidance Counselors: 10.0 (326.8 to 1)
Current Spending: ($ per student per year):
  Total: $8,358; Instruction: $5,235; Support Services: $2,674
Enrollment, Drop-out Rates and Diploma Recipients by Race/Ethnicity

Category	Total	White	Black	Asian	AIAN	Hisp.
Enrollment (%)	100.0	63.9	28.5	2.9	0.2	4.2
Drop-out Rate (%)	0.6	0.3	1.4	0.0	n/a	3.8
H.S. Diplomas (#)	231	183	41	5	0	2

Hoover City

2810 Metropolitan Way • Hoover, AL 35243-5500
(205) 439-1015 • http://www.hoover.k12.al.us/
Grade Span: PK-12; **Agency Type:** 1
Schools: 16
  9 Primary; 3 Middle; 2 High; 0 Other Level
  14 Regular; 0 Special Education; 0 Vocational; 0 Alternative
  0 Magnet; 0 Charter; 2 Title I Eligible; 0 School-wide Title I
Students: 11,197 (50.8% male; 49.1% female)
  Individual Education Program: 794 (7.1%);
  English Language Learner: 429 (3.8%); Migrant: 0 (0.0%)
  Eligible for Free Lunch Program: 1,085 (9.7%)
  Eligible for Reduced-Price Lunch Program: 416 (3.7%)
Teachers: 785.4 (14.3 to 1)
Librarians/Media Specialists: 15.0 (746.5 to 1)
Guidance Counselors: 25.5 (439.1 to 1)
Current Spending: ($ per student per year):
  Total: $7,598; Instruction: $4,488; Support Services: $2,638

Enrollment, Drop-out Rates and Diploma Recipients by Race/Ethnicity

Category	Total	White	Black	Asian	AIAN	Hisp.
Enrollment (%)	100.0	75.1	15.6	5.1	0.1	4.1
Drop-out Rate (%)	1.2	1.1	1.9	2.9	0.0	1.7
H.S. Diplomas (#)	660	566	60	23	0	11

Jefferson County
2100 18th St S • Birmingham, AL 35209-1891
(205) 379-2000 • http://www.jefcoed.com/
Grade Span: KG-12; **Agency Type:** 1
Schools: 59
    32 Primary; 7 Middle; 13 High; 6 Other Level
    54 Regular; 2 Special Education; 1 Vocational; 1 Alternative
    0 Magnet; 0 Charter; 17 Title I Eligible; 15 School-wide Title I
Students: 38,659 (51.8% male; 48.1% female)
    Individual Education Program: 6,763 (17.5%);
    English Language Learner: 498 (1.3%); Migrant: 0 (0.0%)
    Eligible for Free Lunch Program: 9,190 (23.8%)
    Eligible for Reduced-Price Lunch Program: 2,951 (7.6%)
Teachers: 2,467.8 (15.7 to 1)
Librarians/Media Specialists: 56.0 (690.3 to 1)
Guidance Counselors: 69.5 (556.2 to 1)
Current Spending: ($ per student per year):
    Total: $5,931; Instruction: $3,718; Support Services: $1,841
Enrollment, Drop-out Rates and Diploma Recipients by Race/Ethnicity

Category	Total	White	Black	Asian	AIAN	Hisp.
Enrollment (%)	100.0	69.2	28.3	0.5	0.1	1.7
Drop-out Rate (%)	4.1	4.0	4.2	1.5	14.3	10.3
H.S. Diplomas (#)	2,278	1,799	459	15	1	4

Mountain Brook City
3 Church St • Mountain Brook, AL 35213-0040
(205) 871-4608
Grade Span: KG-12; **Agency Type:** 1
Schools: 6
    4 Primary; 1 Middle; 1 High; 0 Other Level
    6 Regular; 0 Special Education; 0 Vocational; 0 Alternative
    0 Magnet; 0 Charter; 1 Title I Eligible; 0 School-wide Title I
Students: 4,149 (50.6% male; 49.3% female)
    Individual Education Program: 360 (8.7%);
    English Language Learner: 8 (0.2%); Migrant: 0 (0.0%)
    Eligible for Free Lunch Program: 0 (0.0%)
    Eligible for Reduced-Price Lunch Program: 0 (0.0%)
Teachers: 333.5 (12.4 to 1)
Librarians/Media Specialists: 7.0 (592.7 to 1)
Guidance Counselors: 7.0 (592.7 to 1)
Current Spending: ($ per student per year):
    Total: $8,349; Instruction: $5,300; Support Services: $2,690
Enrollment, Drop-out Rates and Diploma Recipients by Race/Ethnicity

Category	Total	White	Black	Asian	AIAN	Hisp.
Enrollment (%)	100.0	98.4	0.2	0.9	0.0	0.5
Drop-out Rate (%)	0.1	0.1	0.0	0.0	n/a	0.0
H.S. Diplomas (#)	262	260	1	1	0	0

Vestavia Hills City
1204 Montgomery Hwy • Birmingham, AL 35216-2886
Mailing Address: PO Box 660826 • Birmingham, AL 35266-0826
(205) 402-5100 • http://www.vestavia.k12.al.us/
Grade Span: KG-12; **Agency Type:** 1
Schools: 7
    4 Primary; 2 Middle; 1 High; 0 Other Level
    7 Regular; 0 Special Education; 0 Vocational; 0 Alternative
    0 Magnet; 0 Charter; 0 Title I Eligible; 0 School-wide Title I
Students: 5,232 (51.7% male; 48.2% female)
    Individual Education Program: 1,002 (19.2%);
    English Language Learner: 37 (0.7%); Migrant: 0 (0.0%)
    Eligible for Free Lunch Program: 144 (2.8%)
    Eligible for Reduced-Price Lunch Program: 68 (1.3%)
Teachers: 373.0 (14.0 to 1)
Librarians/Media Specialists: 8.0 (654.0 to 1)
Guidance Counselors: 13.0 (402.5 to 1)
Current Spending: ($ per student per year):
    Total: $6,848; Instruction: $4,572; Support Services: $1,966
Enrollment, Drop-out Rates and Diploma Recipients by Race/Ethnicity

Category	Total	White	Black	Asian	AIAN	Hisp.
Enrollment (%)	100.0	88.4	6.5	3.6	0.2	1.0
Drop-out Rate (%)	0.5	0.5	0.0	0.0	0.0	0.0
H.S. Diplomas (#)	343	315	11	12	0	5

Lamar County

Lamar County
150 Butler Cir • Vernon, AL 35592-1379
Mailing Address: PO Box 1379 • Vernon, AL 35592-1379
(205) 695-7615
Grade Span: KG-12; **Agency Type:** 1
Schools: 5
    0 Primary; 0 Middle; 1 High; 4 Other Level
    4 Regular; 0 Special Education; 1 Vocational; 0 Alternative
    0 Magnet; 0 Charter; 4 Title I Eligible; 1 School-wide Title I
Students: 2,472 (50.3% male; 49.6% female)
    Individual Education Program: 295 (11.9%);
    English Language Learner: 0 (0.0%); Migrant: 0 (0.0%)
    Eligible for Free Lunch Program: 963 (39.0%)
    Eligible for Reduced-Price Lunch Program: 209 (8.5%)
Teachers: 169.4 (14.6 to 1)
Librarians/Media Specialists: 5.0 (494.4 to 1)
Guidance Counselors: 6.0 (412.0 to 1)
Current Spending: ($ per student per year):
    Total: $7,049; Instruction: $3,540; Support Services: $2,974
Enrollment, Drop-out Rates and Diploma Recipients by Race/Ethnicity

Category	Total	White	Black	Asian	AIAN	Hisp.
Enrollment (%)	100.0	80.7	18.3	0.2	0.0	0.8
Drop-out Rate (%)	2.5	2.0	4.7	0.0	n/a	0.0
H.S. Diplomas (#)	144	129	15	0	0	0

Lauderdale County

Florence City
541 Riverview Dr • Florence, AL 35630-6024
(256) 768-3015 • http://www.fcs.k12.al.us/
Grade Span: PK-12; **Agency Type:** 1
Schools: 8
    4 Primary; 2 Middle; 2 High; 0 Other Level
    7 Regular; 1 Special Education; 0 Vocational; 0 Alternative
    0 Magnet; 0 Charter; 6 Title I Eligible; 0 School-wide Title I
Students: 4,135 (51.4% male; 48.5% female)
    Individual Education Program: 673 (16.3%);
    English Language Learner: 43 (1.0%); Migrant: 0 (0.0%)
    Eligible for Free Lunch Program: 2,021 (48.9%)
    Eligible for Reduced-Price Lunch Program: 254 (6.1%)
Teachers: 311.8 (13.3 to 1)
Librarians/Media Specialists: 7.0 (590.7 to 1)
Guidance Counselors: 10.0 (413.5 to 1)
Current Spending: ($ per student per year):
    Total: $8,011; Instruction: $5,009; Support Services: $2,576
Enrollment, Drop-out Rates and Diploma Recipients by Race/Ethnicity

Category	Total	White	Black	Asian	AIAN	Hisp.
Enrollment (%)	100.0	58.4	38.0	0.9	0.1	2.5
Drop-out Rate (%)	4.4	5.3	2.6	0.0	n/a	0.0
H.S. Diplomas (#)	277	202	71	2	0	2

Lauderdale County
355 County Rd 61 • Florence, AL 35634
Mailing Address: PO Box 278 • Florence, AL 35631-0278
(256) 760-1300 • http://www.lcschools.org/
Grade Span: KG-12; **Agency Type:** 1
Schools: 13
    3 Primary; 0 Middle; 2 High; 8 Other Level
    12 Regular; 0 Special Education; 1 Vocational; 0 Alternative
    0 Magnet; 0 Charter; 6 Title I Eligible; 3 School-wide Title I
Students: 8,872 (51.8% male; 48.1% female)
    Individual Education Program: 1,180 (13.3%);
    English Language Learner: 26 (0.3%); Migrant: 0 (0.0%)
    Eligible for Free Lunch Program: 2,252 (25.4%)
    Eligible for Reduced-Price Lunch Program: 736 (8.3%)
Teachers: 572.5 (15.5 to 1)
Librarians/Media Specialists: 14.5 (611.9 to 1)
Guidance Counselors: 22.0 (403.3 to 1)
Current Spending: ($ per student per year):
    Total: $6,016; Instruction: $3,807; Support Services: $1,825
Enrollment, Drop-out Rates and Diploma Recipients by Race/Ethnicity

Category	Total	White	Black	Asian	AIAN	Hisp.
Enrollment (%)	100.0	96.2	3.1	0.1	0.0	0.7
Drop-out Rate (%)	0.1	0.1	0.0	0.0	0.0	0.0
H.S. Diplomas (#)	513	493	13	5	1	1

Lawrence County

Lawrence County
14131 Market St • Moulton, AL 35650-1407
(256) 905-2400 • http://www.lawrenceal.org/
Grade Span: KG-12; **Agency Type:** 1
Schools: 16

5 Primary; 2 Middle; 7 High; 2 Other Level
14 Regular; 0 Special Education; 1 Vocational; 1 Alternative
0 Magnet; 0 Charter; 11 Title I Eligible; 11 School-wide Title I
Students: 5,740 (52.8% male; 47.1% female)
Individual Education Program: 814 (14.2%);
English Language Learner: 42 (0.7%); Migrant: 172 (3.0%)
Eligible for Free Lunch Program: 2,346 (40.9%)
Eligible for Reduced-Price Lunch Program: 747 (13.0%)
Teachers: 357.0 (16.1 to 1)
Librarians/Media Specialists: 12.0 (478.3 to 1)
Guidance Counselors: 11.8 (486.4 to 1)
Current Spending: ($ per student per year):
Total: $6,460; Instruction: $3,865; Support Services: $2,121
Enrollment, Drop-out Rates and Diploma Recipients by Race/Ethnicity

Category	Total	White	Black	Asian	AIAN	Hisp.
Enrollment (%)	100.0	62.6	16.5	0.1	19.9	0.9
Drop-out Rate (%)	2.6	3.4	1.9	n/a	1.1	0.0
H.S. Diplomas (#)	343	179	64	0	98	2

Lee County

Auburn City
855 E Samford Ave • Auburn, AL 36830
Mailing Address: PO Box 3270 • Auburn, AL 36831-3270
(334) 887-2100 • http://www.auburnschools.org/
Grade Span: KG-12; **Agency Type:** 1
Schools: 10
6 Primary; 1 Middle; 1 High; 2 Other Level
9 Regular; 0 Special Education; 1 Vocational; 0 Alternative
0 Magnet; 0 Charter; 5 Title I Eligible; 2 School-wide Title I
Students: 4,691 (50.2% male; 49.7% female)
Individual Education Program: 493 (10.5%);
English Language Learner: 70 (1.5%); Migrant: 0 (0.0%)
Eligible for Free Lunch Program: 1,081 (23.0%)
Eligible for Reduced-Price Lunch Program: 274 (5.8%)
Teachers: 321.7 (14.6 to 1)
Librarians/Media Specialists: 9.3 (504.4 to 1)
Guidance Counselors: 13.0 (360.8 to 1)
Current Spending: ($ per student per year):
Total: $7,273; Instruction: $4,345; Support Services: $2,543
Enrollment, Drop-out Rates and Diploma Recipients by Race/Ethnicity

Category	Total	White	Black	Asian	AIAN	Hisp.
Enrollment (%)	100.0	61.9	30.7	5.2	0.3	1.7
Drop-out Rate (%)	0.7	0.4	1.4	0.0	0.0	0.0
H.S. Diplomas (#)	268	184	68	14	0	2

Lee County
100 S 6th St • Opelika, AL 36803-0120
Mailing Address: PO Box 120 • Opelika, AL 36803-0120
(334) 745-9770 • http://www.lee.k12.al.us/indexie.html
Grade Span: PK-12; **Agency Type:** 1
Schools: 12
5 Primary; 3 Middle; 4 High; 0 Other Level
12 Regular; 0 Special Education; 0 Vocational; 0 Alternative
0 Magnet; 0 Charter; 5 Title I Eligible; 4 School-wide Title I
Students: 9,303 (51.4% male; 48.5% female)
Individual Education Program: 1,105 (11.9%);
English Language Learner: 13 (0.1%); Migrant: 0 (0.0%)
Eligible for Free Lunch Program: 3,169 (34.1%)
Eligible for Reduced-Price Lunch Program: 856 (9.2%)
Teachers: 618.0 (15.1 to 1)
Librarians/Media Specialists: 12.0 (775.3 to 1)
Guidance Counselors: 19.0 (489.6 to 1)
Current Spending: ($ per student per year):
Total: $5,991; Instruction: $3,798; Support Services: $1,766
Enrollment, Drop-out Rates and Diploma Recipients by Race/Ethnicity

Category	Total	White	Black	Asian	AIAN	Hisp.
Enrollment (%)	100.0	73.7	23.9	0.4	0.2	1.2
Drop-out Rate (%)	2.1	2.1	2.3	0.0	0.0	2.4
H.S. Diplomas (#)	402	295	96	1	1	9

Opelika City
300 Simmons St • Opelika, AL 36801
Mailing Address: PO Box 2469 • Opelika, AL 36803-2469
(334) 745-9700 • http://www.opelikaschools.org/
Grade Span: PK-12; **Agency Type:** 1
Schools: 9
6 Primary; 1 Middle; 1 High; 1 Other Level
8 Regular; 0 Special Education; 0 Vocational; 1 Alternative
0 Magnet; 0 Charter; 6 Title I Eligible; 6 School-wide Title I
Students: 4,267 (51.7% male; 48.2% female)
Individual Education Program: 415 (9.7%);
English Language Learner: 17 (0.4%); Migrant: 0 (0.0%)
Eligible for Free Lunch Program: 2,218 (52.0%)
Eligible for Reduced-Price Lunch Program: 329 (7.7%)
Teachers: 301.9 (14.1 to 1)

Librarians/Media Specialists: 9.0 (474.1 to 1)
Guidance Counselors: 9.0 (474.1 to 1)
Current Spending: ($ per student per year):
Total: $7,179; Instruction: $4,467; Support Services: $2,228
Enrollment, Drop-out Rates and Diploma Recipients by Race/Ethnicity

Category	Total	White	Black	Asian	AIAN	Hisp.
Enrollment (%)	100.0	34.5	62.8	1.5	0.1	1.1
Drop-out Rate (%)	0.5	0.4	0.5	0.0	0.0	0.0
H.S. Diplomas (#)	218	106	108	1	0	3

Limestone County

Athens City
313 E Washington St • Athens, AL 35611-2653
(256) 233-6600 • http://www.acs-k12.org/
Grade Span: KG-12; **Agency Type:** 1
Schools: 7
4 Primary; 2 Middle; 1 High; 0 Other Level
7 Regular; 0 Special Education; 0 Vocational; 0 Alternative
0 Magnet; 0 Charter; 4 Title I Eligible; 0 School-wide Title I
Students: 2,702 (51.0% male; 48.9% female)
Individual Education Program: 553 (20.5%);
English Language Learner: 201 (7.4%); Migrant: 0 (0.0%)
Eligible for Free Lunch Program: 808 (29.9%)
Eligible for Reduced-Price Lunch Program: 174 (6.4%)
Teachers: 205.5 (13.1 to 1)
Librarians/Media Specialists: 7.0 (386.0 to 1)
Guidance Counselors: 8.0 (337.8 to 1)
Current Spending: ($ per student per year):
Total: $7,386; Instruction: $4,725; Support Services: $2,198
Enrollment, Drop-out Rates and Diploma Recipients by Race/Ethnicity

Category	Total	White	Black	Asian	AIAN	Hisp.
Enrollment (%)	100.0	66.0	25.4	1.1	0.3	7.0
Drop-out Rate (%)	5.0	3.6	7.6	6.7	n/a	13.5
H.S. Diplomas (#)	147	111	31	3	0	2

Limestone County
300 S Jefferson St • Athens, AL 35611-2549
(256) 232-5353 •
http://limestone.schoolinsites.com/websites/LimestoneCountySchools/LimestoneCounty/
Grade Span: KG-12; **Agency Type:** 1
Schools: 13
6 Primary; 0 Middle; 1 High; 6 Other Level
12 Regular; 0 Special Education; 1 Vocational; 0 Alternative
0 Magnet; 0 Charter; 6 Title I Eligible; 1 School-wide Title I
Students: 8,038 (51.9% male; 48.0% female)
Individual Education Program: 1,148 (14.3%);
English Language Learner: 209 (2.6%); Migrant: 0 (0.0%)
Eligible for Free Lunch Program: 2,003 (24.9%)
Eligible for Reduced-Price Lunch Program: 628 (7.8%)
Teachers: 544.3 (14.8 to 1)
Librarians/Media Specialists: 15.0 (535.9 to 1)
Guidance Counselors: 18.0 (446.6 to 1)
Current Spending: ($ per student per year):
Total: $6,221; Instruction: $4,065; Support Services: $1,689
Enrollment, Drop-out Rates and Diploma Recipients by Race/Ethnicity

Category	Total	White	Black	Asian	AIAN	Hisp.
Enrollment (%)	100.0	86.0	10.1	0.3	0.2	3.3
Drop-out Rate (%)	4.0	4.1	3.1	0.0	0.0	11.1
H.S. Diplomas (#)	384	336	44	2	1	1

Lowndes County

Lowndes County
80 Commerce St S • Hayneville, AL 36040-0755
Mailing Address: PO Box 755 • Hayneville, AL 36040-0755
(334) 548-2131 • http://www.lowndesboe.org/
Grade Span: KG-12; **Agency Type:** 1
Schools: 8
3 Primary; 2 Middle; 3 High; 0 Other Level
7 Regular; 0 Special Education; 1 Vocational; 0 Alternative
0 Magnet; 0 Charter; 7 Title I Eligible; 5 School-wide Title I
Students: 2,415 (50.7% male; 49.2% female)
Individual Education Program: 362 (15.0%);
English Language Learner: 0 (0.0%); Migrant: 0 (0.0%)
Eligible for Free Lunch Program: 2,148 (88.9%)
Eligible for Reduced-Price Lunch Program: 128 (5.3%)
Teachers: 155.3 (15.6 to 1)
Librarians/Media Specialists: 6.0 (402.5 to 1)
Guidance Counselors: 5.5 (439.1 to 1)
Current Spending: ($ per student per year):
Total: $7,941; Instruction: $4,440; Support Services: $2,888

Enrollment, Drop-out Rates and Diploma Recipients by Race/Ethnicity

Category	Total	White	Black	Asian	AIAN	Hisp.
Enrollment (%)	100.0	0.4	99.5	0.0	0.0	0.0
Drop-out Rate (%)	1.5	25.0	1.4	0.0	n/a	0.0
H.S. Diplomas (#)	131	0	131	0	0	0

Macon County

Macon County
501 S School St • Tuskegee, AL 36083-0090
Mailing Address: PO Box 830090 • Tuskegee, AL 36083-0090
(334) 727-1600 • http://www.maconk12.org/
Grade Span: PK-12; Agency Type: 1
Schools: 8
  5 Primary; 1 Middle; 1 High; 1 Other Level
  8 Regular; 0 Special Education; 0 Vocational; 0 Alternative
  0 Magnet; 0 Charter; 7 Title I Eligible; 7 School-wide Title I
Students: 3,781   (51.0% male; 48.9% female)
  Individual Education Program: 472 (12.5%);
  English Language Learner: 0 (0.0%); Migrant: 0 (0.0%)
  Eligible for Free Lunch Program: 2,373 (62.8%)
  Eligible for Reduced-Price Lunch Program: 221 (5.8%)
Teachers: 245.9 (15.4 to 1)
Librarians/Media Specialists: 9.0 (420.1 to 1)
Guidance Counselors: 8.0 (472.6 to 1)
Current Spending: ($ per student per year):
  Total: $6,143; Instruction: $3,684; Support Services: $1,938
Enrollment, Drop-out Rates and Diploma Recipients by Race/Ethnicity

Category	Total	White	Black	Asian	AIAN	Hisp.
Enrollment (%)	100.0	2.6	97.4	0.0	0.0	0.0
Drop-out Rate (%)	3.5	2.1	3.6	n/a	n/a	0.0
H.S. Diplomas (#)	153	7	146	0	0	0

Madison County

Huntsville City
200 White St • Huntsville, AL 35801-4152
Mailing Address: PO Box 1256 • Huntsville, AL 35807-4801
(256) 428-6810 • http://www.hsv.k12.al.us/
Grade Span: PK-12; Agency Type: 1
Schools: 49
  28 Primary; 10 Middle; 7 High; 4 Other Level
  44 Regular; 1 Special Education; 1 Vocational; 3 Alternative
  5 Magnet; 0 Charter; 20 Title I Eligible; 20 School-wide Title I
Students: 22,590   (51.3% male; 48.6% female)
  Individual Education Program: 5,114 (22.6%);
  English Language Learner: 279 (1.2%); Migrant: 0 (0.0%)
  Eligible for Free Lunch Program: 8,132 (36.0%)
  Eligible for Reduced-Price Lunch Program: 1,405 (6.2%)
Teachers: 1,600.4 (14.1 to 1)
Librarians/Media Specialists: 45.0 (502.0 to 1)
Guidance Counselors: 65.5 (344.9 to 1)
Current Spending: ($ per student per year):
  Total: $7,164; Instruction: $4,404; Support Services: $2,426
Enrollment, Drop-out Rates and Diploma Recipients by Race/Ethnicity

Category	Total	White	Black	Asian	AIAN	Hisp.
Enrollment (%)	100.0	50.9	43.1	2.5	0.5	2.7
Drop-out Rate (%)	3.1	2.4	4.7	0.0	0.0	0.0
H.S. Diplomas (#)	1,146	737	339	39	13	18

Madison City
4192 Sullivan St • Madison, AL 35758-1615
(256) 464-8370 • http://www.madisoncity.k12.al.us/
Grade Span: KG-12; Agency Type: 1
Schools: 9
  5 Primary; 2 Middle; 1 High; 0 Other Level
  8 Regular; 0 Special Education; 0 Vocational; 0 Alternative
  0 Magnet; 0 Charter; 3 Title I Eligible; 0 School-wide Title I
Students: 6,848   (52.3% male; 47.6% female)
  Individual Education Program: 1,389 (20.3%);
  English Language Learner: 90 (1.3%); Migrant: 0 (0.0%)
  Eligible for Free Lunch Program: 832 (12.1%)
  Eligible for Reduced-Price Lunch Program: 254 (3.7%)
Teachers: 420.4 (16.3 to 1)
Librarians/Media Specialists: 9.0 (760.9 to 1)
Guidance Counselors: 9.5 (720.8 to 1)
Current Spending: ($ per student per year):
  Total: $5,865; Instruction: $3,642; Support Services: $1,877
Enrollment, Drop-out Rates and Diploma Recipients by Race/Ethnicity

Category	Total	White	Black	Asian	AIAN	Hisp.
Enrollment (%)	100.0	71.5	19.2	4.9	1.0	2.4
Drop-out Rate (%)	0.3	0.3	0.3	0.0	0.0	0.0
H.S. Diplomas (#)	409	316	63	17	8	5

Madison County
1275f Jordan Rd Bldg B • Huntsville, AL 35811
Mailing Address: PO Box 226 • Huntsville, AL 35804-0226
(256) 852-2557 • http://www.madison.k12.al.us/
Grade Span: PK-12; Agency Type: 1
Schools: 25
  14 Primary; 4 Middle; 6 High; 1 Other Level
  23 Regular; 0 Special Education; 1 Vocational; 1 Alternative
  0 Magnet; 0 Charter; 7 Title I Eligible; 7 School-wide Title I
Students: 17,023   (51.6% male; 48.3% female)
  Individual Education Program: 2,696 (15.8%);
  English Language Learner: 80 (0.5%); Migrant: 20 (0.1%)
  Eligible for Free Lunch Program: 2,946 (17.3%)
  Eligible for Reduced-Price Lunch Program: 1,064 (6.3%)
Teachers: 1,031.5 (16.5 to 1)
Librarians/Media Specialists: 25.0 (680.9 to 1)
Guidance Counselors: 40.0 (425.6 to 1)
Current Spending: ($ per student per year):
  Total: $5,932; Instruction: $3,590; Support Services: $2,007
Enrollment, Drop-out Rates and Diploma Recipients by Race/Ethnicity

Category	Total	White	Black	Asian	AIAN	Hisp.
Enrollment (%)	100.0	76.9	15.0	0.9	4.9	1.3
Drop-out Rate (%)	4.9	5.2	4.6	0.0	2.1	2.4
H.S. Diplomas (#)	813	637	109	3	62	2

Marengo County

Demopolis City
609 S Cedar St • Demopolis, AL 36732-0759
Mailing Address: PO Drawer 759 • Demopolis, AL 36732-0759
(334) 289-1670 • http://www.westal.net/dcs/index.htm
Grade Span: PK-12; Agency Type: 1
Schools: 4
  2 Primary; 1 Middle; 1 High; 0 Other Level
  4 Regular; 0 Special Education; 0 Vocational; 0 Alternative
  0 Magnet; 0 Charter; 2 Title I Eligible; 2 School-wide Title I
Students: 2,255   (51.4% male; 48.5% female)
  Individual Education Program: 234 (10.4%);
  English Language Learner: 10 (0.4%); Migrant: 0 (0.0%)
  Eligible for Free Lunch Program: 1,115 (49.4%)
  Eligible for Reduced-Price Lunch Program: 219 (9.7%)
Teachers: 151.5 (14.9 to 1)
Librarians/Media Specialists: 4.0 (563.8 to 1)
Guidance Counselors: 4.5 (501.1 to 1)
Current Spending: ($ per student per year):
  Total: $5,733; Instruction: $3,637; Support Services: $1,641
Enrollment, Drop-out Rates and Diploma Recipients by Race/Ethnicity

Category	Total	White	Black	Asian	AIAN	Hisp.
Enrollment (%)	100.0	45.5	52.8	0.2	0.0	1.2
Drop-out Rate (%)	1.2	1.2	1.1	n/a	n/a	0.0
H.S. Diplomas (#)	106	57	49	0	0	0

Marengo County
101 E Coats Ave • Linden, AL 36748-0339
Mailing Address: PO Box 480339 • Linden, AL 36748-0339
(334) 295-4123
Grade Span: KG-12; Agency Type: 1
Schools: 4
  0 Primary; 0 Middle; 0 High; 4 Other Level
  4 Regular; 0 Special Education; 0 Vocational; 0 Alternative
  0 Magnet; 0 Charter; 4 Title I Eligible; 4 School-wide Title I
Students: 1,704   (53.1% male; 46.8% female)
  Individual Education Program: 183 (10.7%);
  English Language Learner: 0 (0.0%); Migrant: 0 (0.0%)
  Eligible for Free Lunch Program: 1,360 (79.8%)
  Eligible for Reduced-Price Lunch Program: 94 (5.5%)
Teachers: 112.8 (15.1 to 1)
Librarians/Media Specialists: 2.9 (587.6 to 1)
Guidance Counselors: 4.4 (387.3 to 1)
Current Spending: ($ per student per year):
  Total: $6,606; Instruction: $3,896; Support Services: $2,064
Enrollment, Drop-out Rates and Diploma Recipients by Race/Ethnicity

Category	Total	White	Black	Asian	AIAN	Hisp.
Enrollment (%)	100.0	14.6	84.5	0.5	0.1	0.3
Drop-out Rate (%)	3.1	4.6	2.9	0.0	0.0	0.0
H.S. Diplomas (#)	88	21	67	0	0	0

Marion County

Marion County
188 Winchester Dr • Hamilton, AL 35570-6626
(205) 921-3191 • http://server.mcbe.net/
Grade Span: PK-12; Agency Type: 1
Schools: 11
  4 Primary; 1 Middle; 3 High; 3 Other Level

10 Regular; 0 Special Education; 0 Vocational; 1 Alternative
0 Magnet; 0 Charter; 5 Title I Eligible; 5 School-wide Title I
Students: 3,663 (52.9% male; 47.0% female)
  Individual Education Program: 595 (16.2%);
  English Language Learner: 28 (0.8%); Migrant: 0 (0.0%)
  Eligible for Free Lunch Program: 1,423 (38.8%)
  Eligible for Reduced-Price Lunch Program: 376 (10.3%)
Teachers: 247.7 (14.8 to 1)
Librarians/Media Specialists: 8.0 (457.9 to 1)
Guidance Counselors: 7.7 (475.7 to 1)
Current Spending: ($ per student per year):
  Total: $6,001; Instruction: $3,825; Support Services: $1,787
Enrollment, Drop-out Rates and Diploma Recipients by Race/Ethnicity

Category	Total	White	Black	Asian	AIAN	Hisp.
Enrollment (%)	100.0	94.0	4.6	0.1	0.2	1.0
Drop-out Rate (%)	4.0	4.2	0.0	n/a	0.0	0.0
H.S. Diplomas (#)	190	186	3	0	0	1

Marshall County

Albertville City
107 W Main St • Albertville, AL 35950-0025
(256) 891-1183 • http://www.albertk12.org/
Grade Span: KG-12; **Agency Type:** 1
Schools: 5
  2 Primary; 2 Middle; 1 High; 0 Other Level
  5 Regular; 0 Special Education; 0 Vocational; 0 Alternative
  0 Magnet; 0 Charter; 4 Title I Eligible; 4 School-wide Title I
Students: 3,621 (51.1% male; 48.8% female)
  Individual Education Program: 471 (13.0%);
  English Language Learner: 457 (12.6%); Migrant: 0 (0.0%)
  Eligible for Free Lunch Program: 1,561 (43.1%)
  Eligible for Reduced-Price Lunch Program: 268 (7.4%)
Teachers: 228.6 (15.8 to 1)
Librarians/Media Specialists: 7.0 (517.3 to 1)
Guidance Counselors: 7.0 (517.3 to 1)
Current Spending: ($ per student per year):
  Total: $5,908; Instruction: $3,792; Support Services: $1,727
Enrollment, Drop-out Rates and Diploma Recipients by Race/Ethnicity

Category	Total	White	Black	Asian	AIAN	Hisp.
Enrollment (%)	100.0	76.1	2.2	0.4	0.1	21.1
Drop-out Rate (%)	3.0	3.4	0.0	0.0	0.0	0.0
H.S. Diplomas (#)	140	132	2	1	0	5

Arab City
750 Arabian Dr NE • Arab, AL 35016-1161
(256) 586-6011 • http://www.arabcityschools.org/
Grade Span: PK-12; **Agency Type:** 1
Schools: 4
  2 Primary; 1 Middle; 1 High; 0 Other Level
  4 Regular; 0 Special Education; 0 Vocational; 0 Alternative
  0 Magnet; 0 Charter; 2 Title I Eligible; 0 School-wide Title I
Students: 2,705 (52.0% male; 47.9% female)
  Individual Education Program: 365 (13.5%);
  English Language Learner: 4 (0.1%); Migrant: 0 (0.0%)
  Eligible for Free Lunch Program: 453 (16.7%)
  Eligible for Reduced-Price Lunch Program: 145 (5.4%)
Teachers: 174.4 (15.5 to 1)
Librarians/Media Specialists: 5.0 (541.0 to 1)
Guidance Counselors: 6.0 (450.8 to 1)
Current Spending: ($ per student per year):
  Total: $5,892; Instruction: $3,647; Support Services: $1,845
Enrollment, Drop-out Rates and Diploma Recipients by Race/Ethnicity

Category	Total	White	Black	Asian	AIAN	Hisp.
Enrollment (%)	100.0	98.3	0.0	0.4	0.1	0.8
Drop-out Rate (%)	3.3	3.3	n/a	0.0	0.0	0.0
H.S. Diplomas (#)	191	191	0	0	0	0

Guntersville City
2208 Ringold St • Guntersville, AL 35976-0129
Mailing Address: PO Box 129 • Guntersville, AL 35976-0129
(256) 582-3159 • http://www.guntersvilleboe.com/
Grade Span: KG-12; **Agency Type:** 1
Schools: 4
  2 Primary; 1 Middle; 1 High; 0 Other Level
  4 Regular; 0 Special Education; 0 Vocational; 0 Alternative
  0 Magnet; 0 Charter; 3 Title I Eligible; 2 School-wide Title I
Students: 1,803 (52.0% male; 47.9% female)
  Individual Education Program: 341 (18.9%);
  English Language Learner: 0 (0.0%); Migrant: 0 (0.0%)
  Eligible for Free Lunch Program: 571 (31.7%)
  Eligible for Reduced-Price Lunch Program: 87 (4.8%)
Teachers: 132.2 (13.6 to 1)
Librarians/Media Specialists: 4.0 (450.8 to 1)
Guidance Counselors: 4.0 (450.8 to 1)

Current Spending: ($ per student per year):
  Total: $6,729; Instruction: $4,108; Support Services: $2,179
Enrollment, Drop-out Rates and Diploma Recipients by Race/Ethnicity

Category	Total	White	Black	Asian	AIAN	Hisp.
Enrollment (%)	100.0	83.6	13.3	1.0	0.0	2.1
Drop-out Rate (%)	3.3	3.3	3.2	0.0	n/a	0.0
H.S. Diplomas (#)	93	81	9	1	0	2

Marshall County
12380 US Hwy 431 S • Guntersville, AL 35976-9351
(256) 582-3171 • http://www.marshallk12.org/
Grade Span: PK-12; **Agency Type:** 1
Schools: 18
  9 Primary; 4 Middle; 4 High; 1 Other Level
  17 Regular; 0 Special Education; 0 Vocational; 1 Alternative
  0 Magnet; 0 Charter; 12 Title I Eligible; 12 School-wide Title I
Students: 7,148 (53.4% male; 46.5% female)
  Individual Education Program: 1,072 (15.0%);
  English Language Learner: 343 (4.8%); Migrant: 170 (2.5%)
  Eligible for Free Lunch Program: 2,977 (44.1%)
  Eligible for Reduced-Price Lunch Program: 722 (10.7%)
Teachers: 449.4 (15.0 to 1)
Librarians/Media Specialists: 17.0 (397.1 to 1)
Guidance Counselors: 18.0 (375.1 to 1)
Current Spending: ($ per student per year):
  Total: $6,369; Instruction: $3,726; Support Services: $2,126
Enrollment, Drop-out Rates and Diploma Recipients by Race/Ethnicity

Category	Total	White	Black	Asian	AIAN	Hisp.
Enrollment (%)	100.0	92.7	0.5	0.3	0.1	6.3
Drop-out Rate (%)	5.6	5.5	0.0	0.0	n/a	12.9
H.S. Diplomas (#)	281	278	1	0	0	2

Mobile County

Mobile County
504 Government St • Mobile, AL 36602-2098
Mailing Address: PO Box 1327 • Mobile, AL 36633-1327
(251) 221-4394 • http://www.mcpss.com/
Grade Span: PK-12; **Agency Type:** 1
Schools: 104
  60 Primary; 21 Middle; 17 High; 6 Other Level
  95 Regular; 2 Special Education; 2 Vocational; 5 Alternative
  8 Magnet; 0 Charter; 71 Title I Eligible; 70 School-wide Title I
Students: 64,774 (51.8% male; 48.1% female)
  Individual Education Program: 11,843 (18.3%);
  English Language Learner: 764 (1.2%); Migrant: 1,749 (2.7%)
  Eligible for Free Lunch Program: 37,809 (58.4%)
  Eligible for Reduced-Price Lunch Program: 6,103 (9.4%)
Teachers: 4,236.5 (15.3 to 1)
Librarians/Media Specialists: 105.0 (616.9 to 1)
Guidance Counselors: 140.0 (462.7 to 1)
Current Spending: ($ per student per year):
  Total: $6,305; Instruction: $3,757; Support Services: $2,122
Enrollment, Drop-out Rates and Diploma Recipients by Race/Ethnicity

Category	Total	White	Black	Asian	AIAN	Hisp.
Enrollment (%)	100.0	46.1	50.1	2.0	0.8	0.7
Drop-out Rate (%)	4.0	3.2	4.8	3.4	7.5	4.8
H.S. Diplomas (#)	2,854	1,415	1,343	65	23	8

Monroe County

Monroe County
#65 Al Ave Monroe Co Courthous • Monroeville, AL 36460
Mailing Address: Box 967 • Monroeville, AL 36461-0967
(251) 575-2168 • http://www.monroe.k12.al.us/
Grade Span: PK-12; **Agency Type:** 1
Schools: 12
  3 Primary; 1 Middle; 3 High; 5 Other Level
  10 Regular; 0 Special Education; 1 Vocational; 1 Alternative
  0 Magnet; 0 Charter; 10 Title I Eligible; 8 School-wide Title I
Students: 4,431 (52.2% male; 47.7% female)
  Individual Education Program: 631 (14.2%);
  English Language Learner: 2 (<0.1%); Migrant: 0 (0.0%)
  Eligible for Free Lunch Program: 2,432 (54.9%)
  Eligible for Reduced-Price Lunch Program: 442 (10.0%)
Teachers: 302.9 (14.6 to 1)
Librarians/Media Specialists: 7.5 (590.8 to 1)
Guidance Counselors: 10.4 (426.1 to 1)
Current Spending: ($ per student per year):
  Total: $6,107; Instruction: $3,832; Support Services: $1,825
Enrollment, Drop-out Rates and Diploma Recipients by Race/Ethnicity

Category	Total	White	Black	Asian	AIAN	Hisp.
Enrollment (%)	100.0	41.9	55.5	1.5	0.8	0.2
Drop-out Rate (%)	3.1	4.1	2.5	0.0	0.0	0.0
H.S. Diplomas (#)	248	111	135	1	1	0

Montgomery County

Montgomery County
307 S Decatur St • Montgomery, AL 36104-4310
Mailing Address: PO Box 1991 • Montgomery, AL 36102-1991
(334) 223-6710 • http://www.mps.k12.al.us/
Grade Span: PK-12; **Agency Type:** 1
Schools: 62
   37 Primary; 12 Middle; 8 High; 5 Other Level
   55 Regular; 3 Special Education; 0 Vocational; 4 Alternative
   10 Magnet; 0 Charter; 29 Title I Eligible; 26 School-wide Title I
Students: 32,553 (51.0% male; 48.9% female)
   Individual Education Program: 4,944 (15.2%);
   English Language Learner: 403 (1.2%); Migrant: 0 (0.0%)
   Eligible for Free Lunch Program: 18,900 (58.1%)
   Eligible for Reduced-Price Lunch Program: 2,136 (6.6%)
Teachers: 2,171.5 (15.0 to 1)
Librarians/Media Specialists: 59.0 (551.7 to 1)
Guidance Counselors: 71.0 (458.5 to 1)
Current Spending: ($ per student per year):
   Total: $6,106; Instruction: $3,672; Support Services: $2,032
Enrollment, Drop-out Rates and Diploma Recipients by Race/Ethnicity

Category	Total	White	Black	Asian	AIAN	Hisp.
Enrollment (%)	100.0	21.4	75.8	1.4	0.2	1.0
Drop-out Rate (%)	4.4	3.9	4.6	2.5	0.0	5.2
H.S. Diplomas (#)	1,607	473	1,101	17	4	12

Morgan County

Decatur City
302 4th Ave NE • Decatur, AL 35601-1972
(256) 552-3000 • http://www.dcs.edu/
Grade Span: PK-12; **Agency Type:** 1
Schools: 18
   12 Primary; 3 Middle; 3 High; 0 Other Level
   17 Regular; 0 Special Education; 0 Vocational; 1 Alternative
   2 Magnet; 0 Charter; 5 Title I Eligible; 5 School-wide Title I
Students: 8,880 (50.5% male; 49.4% female)
   Individual Education Program: 1,598 (18.0%);
   English Language Learner: 513 (5.8%); Migrant: 228 (2.6%)
   Eligible for Free Lunch Program: 3,624 (40.8%)
   Eligible for Reduced-Price Lunch Program: 592 (6.7%)
Teachers: 624.0 (14.2 to 1)
Librarians/Media Specialists: 19.0 (467.4 to 1)
Guidance Counselors: 21.4 (415.0 to 1)
Current Spending: ($ per student per year):
   Total: $7,222; Instruction: $4,440; Support Services: $2,319
Enrollment, Drop-out Rates and Diploma Recipients by Race/Ethnicity

Category	Total	White	Black	Asian	AIAN	Hisp.
Enrollment (%)	100.0	56.4	33.0	0.8	0.3	9.3
Drop-out Rate (%)	2.5	2.0	3.7	0.0	0.0	2.6
H.S. Diplomas (#)	406	307	90	4	0	5

Hartselle City
305 College St NE • Hartselle, AL 35640-2357
(256) 773-5419 • http://www.hcs.k12.al.us/
Grade Span: PK-12; **Agency Type:** 1
Schools: 6
   3 Primary; 1 Middle; 2 High; 0 Other Level
   5 Regular; 0 Special Education; 1 Vocational; 0 Alternative
   0 Magnet; 0 Charter; 2 Title I Eligible; 0 School-wide Title I
Students: 3,070 (51.9% male; 48.0% female)
   Individual Education Program: 481 (15.7%);
   English Language Learner: 0 (0.0%); Migrant: 29 (0.9%)
   Eligible for Free Lunch Program: 519 (16.9%)
   Eligible for Reduced-Price Lunch Program: 167 (5.4%)
Teachers: 200.0 (15.4 to 1)
Librarians/Media Specialists: 5.0 (614.0 to 1)
Guidance Counselors: 5.7 (538.6 to 1)
Current Spending: ($ per student per year):
   Total: $6,273; Instruction: $3,978; Support Services: $1,872
Enrollment, Drop-out Rates and Diploma Recipients by Race/Ethnicity

Category	Total	White	Black	Asian	AIAN	Hisp.
Enrollment (%)	100.0	92.1	5.7	0.2	0.4	1.6
Drop-out Rate (%)	4.8	4.7	9.5	0.0	0.0	0.0
H.S. Diplomas (#)	171	161	7	2	0	1

Morgan County
1325 Point Mallard Pkwy SE • Decatur, AL 35601-6542
(256) 353-6442 • http://www.morgank12.org/
Grade Span: PK-12; **Agency Type:** 1
Schools: 18
   10 Primary; 1 Middle; 4 High; 3 Other Level
   16 Regular; 0 Special Education; 1 Vocational; 1 Alternative
   0 Magnet; 0 Charter; 9 Title I Eligible; 4 School-wide Title I

Students: 7,607 (52.2% male; 47.7% female)
   Individual Education Program: 1,530 (20.1%);
   English Language Learner: 53 (0.7%); Migrant: 245 (3.2%)
   Eligible for Free Lunch Program: 2,330 (30.6%)
   Eligible for Reduced-Price Lunch Program: 728 (9.6%)
Teachers: 552.2 (13.8 to 1)
Librarians/Media Specialists: 14.5 (524.6 to 1)
Guidance Counselors: 13.4 (567.7 to 1)
Current Spending: ($ per student per year):
   Total: $7,090; Instruction: $4,127; Support Services: $2,436
Enrollment, Drop-out Rates and Diploma Recipients by Race/Ethnicity

Category	Total	White	Black	Asian	AIAN	Hisp.
Enrollment (%)	100.0	95.0	2.8	0.2	0.5	1.5
Drop-out Rate (%)	5.3	5.2	9.0	0.0	0.0	10.0
H.S. Diplomas (#)	381	370	7	1	1	2

Perry County

Perry County
200 Monroe St • Marion, AL 36756-2200
Mailing Address: PO Box 900 • Marion, AL 36756-0900
(334) 683-6528
Grade Span: KG-12; **Agency Type:** 1
Schools: 4
   2 Primary; 0 Middle; 2 High; 0 Other Level
   4 Regular; 0 Special Education; 0 Vocational; 0 Alternative
   0 Magnet; 0 Charter; 4 Title I Eligible; 4 School-wide Title I
Students: 2,168 (51.4% male; 48.5% female)
   Individual Education Program: 323 (14.9%);
   English Language Learner: 0 (0.0%); Migrant: 0 (0.0%)
   Eligible for Free Lunch Program: 2,021 (93.2%)
   Eligible for Reduced-Price Lunch Program: 76 (3.5%)
Teachers: 137.2 (15.8 to 1)
Librarians/Media Specialists: 4.0 (542.0 to 1)
Guidance Counselors: 4.0 (542.0 to 1)
Current Spending: ($ per student per year):
   Total: $6,628; Instruction: $4,079; Support Services: $1,998
Enrollment, Drop-out Rates and Diploma Recipients by Race/Ethnicity

Category	Total	White	Black	Asian	AIAN	Hisp.
Enrollment (%)	100.0	0.9	99.1	0.0	0.0	0.0
Drop-out Rate (%)	3.3	0.0	3.3	n/a	n/a	n/a
H.S. Diplomas (#)	120	2	118	0	0	0

Pickens County

Pickens County
377 Ladow Center Circle • Carrollton, AL 35447-0032
Mailing Address: PO Box 32 • Carrollton, AL 35447-0032
(205) 367-2080 • http://www.pickens.k12.al.us/
Grade Span: PK-12; **Agency Type:** 1
Schools: 10
   3 Primary; 1 Middle; 4 High; 2 Other Level
   8 Regular; 0 Special Education; 1 Vocational; 1 Alternative
   0 Magnet; 0 Charter; 8 Title I Eligible; 7 School-wide Title I
Students: 3,317 (50.8% male; 49.1% female)
   Individual Education Program: 402 (12.1%);
   English Language Learner: 1 (<0.1%); Migrant: 0 (0.0%)
   Eligible for Free Lunch Program: 2,011 (60.6%)
   Eligible for Reduced-Price Lunch Program: 318 (9.6%)
Teachers: 222.4 (14.9 to 1)
Librarians/Media Specialists: 8.0 (414.6 to 1)
Guidance Counselors: 8.4 (394.9 to 1)
Current Spending: ($ per student per year):
   Total: $6,588; Instruction: $3,975; Support Services: $2,126
Enrollment, Drop-out Rates and Diploma Recipients by Race/Ethnicity

Category	Total	White	Black	Asian	AIAN	Hisp.
Enrollment (%)	100.0	33.7	65.5	0.5	0.0	0.3
Drop-out Rate (%)	4.5	2.5	5.7	0.0	n/a	n/a
H.S. Diplomas (#)	214	85	129	0	0	0

Pike County

Pike County
101 W Love St • Troy, AL 36081-2613
(334) 566-1850 • http://www.pikecountyschools.com/
Grade Span: KG-12; **Agency Type:** 1
Schools: 6
   3 Primary; 0 Middle; 3 High; 0 Other Level
   5 Regular; 0 Special Education; 1 Vocational; 0 Alternative
   0 Magnet; 0 Charter; 5 Title I Eligible; 5 School-wide Title I
Students: 2,083 (55.2% male; 44.7% female)
   Individual Education Program: 465 (22.3%);
   English Language Learner: 1 (<0.1%); Migrant: 0 (0.0%)
   Eligible for Free Lunch Program: 1,537 (73.8%)
   Eligible for Reduced-Price Lunch Program: 249 (12.0%)

Teachers: 140.7 (14.8 to 1)
Librarians/Media Specialists: 5.0 (416.6 to 1)
Guidance Counselors: 5.0 (416.6 to 1)
Current Spending: ($ per student per year):
    Total: $7,234; Instruction: $4,005; Support Services: $2,746
Enrollment, Drop-out Rates and Diploma Recipients by Race/Ethnicity

Category	Total	White	Black	Asian	AIAN	Hisp.
Enrollment (%)	100.0	46.0	52.6	0.1	0.3	0.7
Drop-out Rate (%)	4.6	6.0	3.8	0.0	0.0	0.0
H.S. Diplomas (#)	80	39	40	0	0	1

Troy City
500 Elm St • Troy, AL 36081-0529
Mailing Address: PO Box 529 • Troy, AL 36081-0529
(334) 566-3741 • http://www.troyschools.net/
Grade Span: KG-12; **Agency Type:** 1
Schools: 5
    1 Primary; 1 Middle; 2 High; 1 Other Level
    3 Regular; 0 Special Education; 1 Vocational; 1 Alternative
    0 Magnet; 0 Charter; 2 Title I Eligible; 2 School-wide Title I
Students: 2,385   (51.9% male; 48.0% female)
    Individual Education Program: 357 (15.0%);
    English Language Learner: 14 (0.6%); Migrant: 0 (0.0%)
    Eligible for Free Lunch Program: 1,203 (50.4%)
    Eligible for Reduced-Price Lunch Program: 112 (4.7%)
Teachers: 148.1 (16.1 to 1)
Librarians/Media Specialists: 3.0 (795.0 to 1)
Guidance Counselors: 5.0 (477.0 to 1)
Current Spending: ($ per student per year):
    Total: $6,011; Instruction: $3,750; Support Services: $1,848
Enrollment, Drop-out Rates and Diploma Recipients by Race/Ethnicity

Category	Total	White	Black	Asian	AIAN	Hisp.
Enrollment (%)	100.0	42.3	56.5	0.8	0.1	0.4
Drop-out Rate (%)	0.3	0.0	0.6	0.0	0.0	n/a
H.S. Diplomas (#)	107	36	69	1	1	0

Randolph County

Randolph County
14 Broad St E • Wedowee, AL 36278-0288
Mailing Address: PO Box 288 • Wedowee, AL 36278-0288
(256) 357-4611 • http://www.randolph.k12.al.us/
Grade Span: KG-12; **Agency Type:** 1
Schools: 6
    1 Primary; 1 Middle; 1 High; 3 Other Level
    5 Regular; 0 Special Education; 1 Vocational; 0 Alternative
    0 Magnet; 0 Charter; 4 Title I Eligible; 4 School-wide Title I
Students: 2,264   (51.8% male; 48.1% female)
    Individual Education Program: 252 (11.1%);
    English Language Learner: 35 (1.5%); Migrant: 0 (0.0%)
    Eligible for Free Lunch Program: 1,000 (44.2%)
    Eligible for Reduced-Price Lunch Program: 215 (9.5%)
Teachers: 145.0 (15.6 to 1)
Librarians/Media Specialists: 3.6 (628.9 to 1)
Guidance Counselors: 5.4 (419.3 to 1)
Current Spending: ($ per student per year):
    Total: $5,953; Instruction: $3,564; Support Services: $1,976
Enrollment, Drop-out Rates and Diploma Recipients by Race/Ethnicity

Category	Total	White	Black	Asian	AIAN	Hisp.
Enrollment (%)	100.0	78.8	18.9	0.4	0.0	1.9
Drop-out Rate (%)	2.6	2.6	2.6	0.0	n/a	0.0
H.S. Diplomas (#)	84	66	18	0	0	0

Russell County

Phenix City
1212 Ninth Ave • Phenix City, AL 36867
Mailing Address: PO Box 460 • Phenix City, AL 36868-0460
(334) 298-0534 • http://www.pcboe.net/
Grade Span: KG-12; **Agency Type:** 1
Schools: 9
    6 Primary; 2 Middle; 1 High; 0 Other Level
    9 Regular; 0 Special Education; 0 Vocational; 0 Alternative
    1 Magnet; 0 Charter; 7 Title I Eligible; 5 School-wide Title I
Students: 5,293   (51.1% male; 48.8% female)
    Individual Education Program: 801 (15.1%);
    English Language Learner: 0 (0.0%); Migrant: 0 (0.0%)
    Eligible for Free Lunch Program: 2,984 (56.4%)
    Eligible for Reduced-Price Lunch Program: 378 (7.1%)
Teachers: 321.9 (16.4 to 1)
Librarians/Media Specialists: 10.0 (529.3 to 1)
Guidance Counselors: 12.0 (441.1 to 1)
Current Spending: ($ per student per year):
    Total: $6,481; Instruction: $3,866; Support Services: $2,073

Enrollment, Drop-out Rates and Diploma Recipients by Race/Ethnicity

Category	Total	White	Black	Asian	AIAN	Hisp.
Enrollment (%)	100.0	35.7	62.3	0.4	0.1	0.9
Drop-out Rate (%)	4.3	4.8	4.0	0.0	n/a	0.0
H.S. Diplomas (#)	146	70	71	1	0	4

Russell County
506 14th St • Phenix City, AL 36867
Mailing Address: PO Box 400 • Phenix City, AL 36868-0400
(334) 298-8791 • http://www.russellcountyschools.org/
Grade Span: PK-12; **Agency Type:** 1
Schools: 11
    6 Primary; 1 Middle; 3 High; 1 Other Level
    8 Regular; 1 Special Education; 1 Vocational; 1 Alternative
    0 Magnet; 0 Charter; 7 Title I Eligible; 7 School-wide Title I
Students: 3,670   (51.5% male; 48.4% female)
    Individual Education Program: 452 (12.3%);
    English Language Learner: 0 (0.0%); Migrant: 0 (0.0%)
    Eligible for Free Lunch Program: 2,202 (60.0%)
    Eligible for Reduced-Price Lunch Program: 401 (10.9%)
Teachers: 230.9 (15.9 to 1)
Librarians/Media Specialists: 8.0 (458.8 to 1)
Guidance Counselors: 8.0 (458.8 to 1)
Current Spending: ($ per student per year):
    Total: $6,224; Instruction: $3,661; Support Services: $2,059
Enrollment, Drop-out Rates and Diploma Recipients by Race/Ethnicity

Category	Total	White	Black	Asian	AIAN	Hisp.
Enrollment (%)	100.0	55.8	41.6	0.7	0.1	1.5
Drop-out Rate (%)	7.5	8.1	6.9	0.0	0.0	7.7
H.S. Diplomas (#)	121	56	62	0	0	3

Shelby County

Shelby County
410 E College St • Columbiana, AL 35051-0410
Mailing Address: PO Box 1910 • Columbiana, AL 35051-1910
(205) 682-7000 • http://www.shelbyed.k12.al.us/
Grade Span: KG-12; **Agency Type:** 1
Schools: 35
    17 Primary; 7 Middle; 8 High; 3 Other Level
    32 Regular; 1 Special Education; 2 Vocational; 0 Alternative
    0 Magnet; 0 Charter; 10 Title I Eligible; 6 School-wide Title I
Students: 22,541   (52.2% male; 47.7% female)
    Individual Education Program: 5,564 (24.7%);
    English Language Learner: 791 (3.5%); Migrant: 0 (0.0%)
    Eligible for Free Lunch Program: 4,059 (18.0%)
    Eligible for Reduced-Price Lunch Program: 1,170 (5.2%)
Teachers: 1,589.8 (14.2 to 1)
Librarians/Media Specialists: 34.0 (663.0 to 1)
Guidance Counselors: 51.5 (437.7 to 1)
Current Spending: ($ per student per year):
    Total: $6,832; Instruction: $4,047; Support Services: $2,315
Enrollment, Drop-out Rates and Diploma Recipients by Race/Ethnicity

Category	Total	White	Black	Asian	AIAN	Hisp.
Enrollment (%)	100.0	83.0	11.5	1.4	0.2	3.7
Drop-out Rate (%)	2.6	2.5	3.1	1.3	0.0	5.8
H.S. Diplomas (#)	1,040	915	103	12	2	8

St. Clair County

Pell City
25 Williamson Dr • Pell City, AL 35125-1227
(205) 884-4440 • http://www.pell.k12.al.us/
Grade Span: PK-12; **Agency Type:** 1
Schools: 7
    4 Primary; 2 Middle; 1 High; 0 Other Level
    7 Regular; 0 Special Education; 0 Vocational; 0 Alternative
    0 Magnet; 0 Charter; 4 Title I Eligible; 4 School-wide Title I
Students: 3,990   (52.8% male; 47.1% female)
    Individual Education Program: 739 (18.5%);
    English Language Learner: 19 (0.5%); Migrant: 0 (0.0%)
    Eligible for Free Lunch Program: 1,513 (37.9%)
    Eligible for Reduced-Price Lunch Program: 282 (7.1%)
Teachers: 240.7 (16.6 to 1)
Librarians/Media Specialists: 8.0 (498.8 to 1)
Guidance Counselors: 8.0 (498.8 to 1)
Current Spending: ($ per student per year):
    Total: $5,776; Instruction: $3,503; Support Services: $1,842
Enrollment, Drop-out Rates and Diploma Recipients by Race/Ethnicity

Category	Total	White	Black	Asian	AIAN	Hisp.
Enrollment (%)	100.0	85.6	12.3	0.5	0.2	1.4
Drop-out Rate (%)	7.7	8.6	3.3	0.0	n/a	0.0
H.S. Diplomas (#)	185	170	14	1	0	0

St Clair County
33205 US Hwy 231 • Ashville, AL 35953-6254
(205) 594-7131 • http://www.stclaircountyschools.net/
Grade Span: PK-12; **Agency Type:** 1
Schools: 17
　5 Primary; 5 Middle; 5 High; 2 Other Level
　15 Regular; 0 Special Education; 1 Vocational; 1 Alternative
　0 Magnet; 0 Charter; 6 Title I Eligible; 5 School-wide Title I
Students: 7,334　(53.4% male; 46.5% female)
　Individual Education Program: 1,141 (15.6%);
　English Language Learner: 106 (1.4%); Migrant: 262 (3.6%)
　Eligible for Free Lunch Program: 2,078 (28.3%)
　Eligible for Reduced-Price Lunch Program: 676 (9.2%)
Teachers: 466.5 (15.7 to 1)
Librarians/Media Specialists: 15.0 (488.9 to 1)
Guidance Counselors: 13.5 (543.3 to 1)
Current Spending: ($ per student per year):
　Total: $5,453; Instruction: $3,467; Support Services: $1,582
Enrollment, Drop-out Rates and Diploma Recipients by Race/Ethnicity

Category	Total	White	Black	Asian	AIAN	Hisp.
Enrollment (%)	100.0	89.7	8.3	0.3	0.3	1.4
Drop-out Rate (%)	3.0	3.1	2.5	0.0	0.0	0.0
H.S. Diplomas (#)	330	302	25	1	1	1

Sumter County

Sumter County
Hwy 28 To Country Club Dr • Livingston, AL 35470-0010
Mailing Address: PO Box 10 • Livingston, AL 35470-0010
(205) 652-9605
Grade Span: PK-12; **Agency Type:** 1
Schools: 7
　4 Primary; 0 Middle; 3 High; 0 Other Level
　6 Regular; 0 Special Education; 1 Vocational; 0 Alternative
　0 Magnet; 0 Charter; 6 Title I Eligible; 6 School-wide Title I
Students: 2,632　(51.8% male; 48.1% female)
　Individual Education Program: 448 (17.0%);
　English Language Learner: 3 (0.1%); Migrant: 0 (0.0%)
　Eligible for Free Lunch Program: 2,136 (81.2%)
　Eligible for Reduced-Price Lunch Program: 126 (4.8%)
Teachers: 182.7 (14.4 to 1)
Librarians/Media Specialists: 6.3 (417.8 to 1)
Guidance Counselors: 6.5 (404.9 to 1)
Current Spending: ($ per student per year):
　Total: $6,996; Instruction: $4,195; Support Services: $2,237
Enrollment, Drop-out Rates and Diploma Recipients by Race/Ethnicity

Category	Total	White	Black	Asian	AIAN	Hisp.
Enrollment (%)	100.0	0.0	99.9	0.0	0.0	0.0
Drop-out Rate (%)	0.9	33.3	0.8	n/a	0.0	n/a
H.S. Diplomas (#)	143	0	143	0	0	0

Talladega County

Sylacauga City
605 W 4th St • Sylacauga, AL 35150-1941
(256) 245-5256 • http://www.sylacauga.k12.al.us/
Grade Span: KG-12; **Agency Type:** 1
Schools: 5
　2 Primary; 1 Middle; 2 High; 0 Other Level
　4 Regular; 0 Special Education; 0 Vocational; 1 Alternative
　0 Magnet; 0 Charter; 3 Title I Eligible; 2 School-wide Title I
Students: 2,338　(50.1% male; 49.8% female)
　Individual Education Program: 383 (16.4%);
　English Language Learner: 20 (0.9%); Migrant: 0 (0.0%)
　Eligible for Free Lunch Program: 953 (40.8%)
　Eligible for Reduced-Price Lunch Program: 148 (6.3%)
Teachers: 159.4 (14.7 to 1)
Librarians/Media Specialists: 4.0 (584.5 to 1)
Guidance Counselors: 5.0 (467.6 to 1)
Current Spending: ($ per student per year):
　Total: $6,676; Instruction: $4,153; Support Services: $2,053
Enrollment, Drop-out Rates and Diploma Recipients by Race/Ethnicity

Category	Total	White	Black	Asian	AIAN	Hisp.
Enrollment (%)	100.0	61.2	37.6	0.5	0.3	0.4
Drop-out Rate (%)	2.6	3.3	1.6	0.0	0.0	0.0
H.S. Diplomas (#)	128	87	40	1	0	0

Talladega City
501 S St E • Talladega, AL 35160-2532
(256) 315-5600
Grade Span: KG-12; **Agency Type:** 1
Schools: 8
　5 Primary; 1 Middle; 2 High; 0 Other Level
　7 Regular; 0 Special Education; 1 Vocational; 0 Alternative
　0 Magnet; 0 Charter; 6 Title I Eligible; 5 School-wide Title I
Students: 2,851　(51.4% male; 48.5% female)
　Individual Education Program: 474 (16.6%);
　English Language Learner: 0 (0.0%); Migrant: 0 (0.0%)
　Eligible for Free Lunch Program: 1,645 (57.7%)
　Eligible for Reduced-Price Lunch Program: 258 (9.0%)
Teachers: 202.1 (14.1 to 1)
Librarians/Media Specialists: 7.0 (407.3 to 1)
Guidance Counselors: 7.0 (407.3 to 1)
Current Spending: ($ per student per year):
　Total: $6,607; Instruction: $4,015; Support Services: $2,054
Enrollment, Drop-out Rates and Diploma Recipients by Race/Ethnicity

Category	Total	White	Black	Asian	AIAN	Hisp.
Enrollment (%)	100.0	44.8	54.5	0.2	0.1	0.4
Drop-out Rate (%)	4.9	7.5	2.9	n/a	0.0	0.0
H.S. Diplomas (#)	150	80	70	0	0	0

Talladega County
106 W S St • Talladega, AL 35160-2455
Mailing Address: PO Box 887 • Talladega, AL 35161-0887
(256) 315-5100 • http://www.tcboe.org/
Grade Span: KG-12; **Agency Type:** 1
Schools: 19
　7 Primary; 2 Middle; 6 High; 3 Other Level
　16 Regular; 0 Special Education; 1 Vocational; 1 Alternative
　0 Magnet; 0 Charter; 12 Title I Eligible; 11 School-wide Title I
Students: 7,712　(52.2% male; 47.7% female)
　Individual Education Program: 1,228 (15.9%);
　English Language Learner: 22 (0.3%); Migrant: 0 (0.0%)
　Eligible for Free Lunch Program: 4,022 (52.2%)
　Eligible for Reduced-Price Lunch Program: 975 (12.6%)
Teachers: 467.9 (16.5 to 1)
Librarians/Media Specialists: 16.0 (482.0 to 1)
Guidance Counselors: 17.0 (453.6 to 1)
Current Spending: ($ per student per year):
　Total: $6,142; Instruction: $3,368; Support Services: $2,287
Enrollment, Drop-out Rates and Diploma Recipients by Race/Ethnicity

Category	Total	White	Black	Asian	AIAN	Hisp.
Enrollment (%)	100.0	58.5	40.7	0.1	0.1	0.6
Drop-out Rate (%)	5.6	7.0	3.9	0.0	n/a	0.0
H.S. Diplomas (#)	341	202	137	1	0	1

Tallapoosa County

Alexander City
375 Lee St • Alexander City, AL 35010-2053
(256) 234-8670 • http://www.alex.k12.al.us/
Grade Span: KG-12; **Agency Type:** 1
Schools: 6
　2 Primary; 2 Middle; 2 High; 0 Other Level
　5 Regular; 0 Special Education; 1 Vocational; 0 Alternative
　0 Magnet; 0 Charter; 3 Title I Eligible; 3 School-wide Title I
Students: 3,549　(52.5% male; 47.4% female)
　Individual Education Program: 545 (15.4%);
　English Language Learner: 42 (1.2%); Migrant: 0 (0.0%)
　Eligible for Free Lunch Program: 1,405 (39.6%)
　Eligible for Reduced-Price Lunch Program: 229 (6.5%)
Teachers: 227.5 (15.6 to 1)
Librarians/Media Specialists: 5.0 (709.8 to 1)
Guidance Counselors: 10.0 (354.9 to 1)
Current Spending: ($ per student per year):
　Total: $6,305; Instruction: $3,978; Support Services: $2,008
Enrollment, Drop-out Rates and Diploma Recipients by Race/Ethnicity

Category	Total	White	Black	Asian	AIAN	Hisp.
Enrollment (%)	100.0	58.4	39.9	0.6	0.1	0.9
Drop-out Rate (%)	9.5	6.9	14.4	0.0	0.0	0.0
H.S. Diplomas (#)	168	114	51	2	0	1

Tallapoosa County
125 N Broadnax St Rm 113 • Dadeville, AL 36853-1371
(256) 825-1020 • http://www2.webshoppe.net./users/tapcobord/index.html
Grade Span: KG-12; **Agency Type:** 1
Schools: 6
　1 Primary; 0 Middle; 2 High; 3 Other Level
　5 Regular; 0 Special Education; 1 Vocational; 0 Alternative
　0 Magnet; 0 Charter; 3 Title I Eligible; 3 School-wide Title I
Students: 3,389　(52.0% male; 47.9% female)
　Individual Education Program: 606 (17.9%);
　English Language Learner: 0 (0.0%); Migrant: 0 (0.0%)
　Eligible for Free Lunch Program: 1,455 (42.9%)
　Eligible for Reduced-Price Lunch Program: 228 (6.7%)
Teachers: 227.5 (14.9 to 1)
Librarians/Media Specialists: 5.5 (616.2 to 1)
Guidance Counselors: 7.5 (451.9 to 1)
Current Spending: ($ per student per year):
　Total: $6,340; Instruction: $4,032; Support Services: $1,776

Enrollment, Drop-out Rates and Diploma Recipients by Race/Ethnicity

Category	Total	White	Black	Asian	AIAN	Hisp.
Enrollment (%)	100.0	60.1	38.9	0.1	0.2	0.5
Drop-out Rate (%)	4.6	4.8	4.5	0.0	0.0	0.0
H.S. Diplomas (#)	177	123	50	0	0	4

Tuscaloosa County

Tuscaloosa City
1210 21st Ave • Tuscaloosa, AL 35401-2934
Mailing Address: PO Box 038991 • Tuscaloosa, AL 35403-8991
(205) 759-3530 • http://www.tusc.k12.al.us/
Grade Span: PK-12; **Agency Type:** 1
Schools: 21
   12 Primary; 3 Middle; 5 High; 1 Other Level
   18 Regular; 1 Special Education; 1 Vocational; 1 Alternative
   3 Magnet; 0 Charter; 11 Title I Eligible; 9 School-wide Title I
Students: 10,244 (50.4% male; 49.5% female)
   Individual Education Program: 2,135 (20.8%);
   English Language Learner: 90 (0.9%); Migrant: 0 (0.0%)
   Eligible for Free Lunch Program: 5,622 (54.9%)
   Eligible for Reduced-Price Lunch Program: 736 (7.2%)
Teachers: 684.9 (15.0 to 1)
Librarians/Media Specialists: 17.0 (602.6 to 1)
Guidance Counselors: 23.0 (445.4 to 1)
Current Spending: ($ per student per year):
   Total: $7,182; Instruction: $4,403; Support Services: $2,317
Enrollment, Drop-out Rates and Diploma Recipients by Race/Ethnicity

Category	Total	White	Black	Asian	AIAN	Hisp.
Enrollment (%)	100.0	25.0	72.5	1.2	0.0	1.2
Drop-out Rate (%)	5.0	1.8	6.5	0.0	0.0	0.0
H.S. Diplomas (#)	383	149	224	9	0	1

Tuscaloosa County
2314 9th St • Tuscaloosa, AL 35401-2319
Mailing Address: PO Drawer 2568 • Tuscaloosa, AL 35403-2568
(205) 758-0411 • http://www.tcss.net/
Grade Span: PK-12; **Agency Type:** 1
Schools: 31
   16 Primary; 7 Middle; 6 High; 2 Other Level
   28 Regular; 1 Special Education; 0 Vocational; 2 Alternative
   0 Magnet; 0 Charter; 9 Title I Eligible; 9 School-wide Title I
Students: 16,073 (51.6% male; 48.3% female)
   Individual Education Program: 2,666 (16.6%);
   English Language Learner: 146 (0.9%); Migrant: 0 (0.0%)
   Eligible for Free Lunch Program: 5,335 (33.2%)
   Eligible for Reduced-Price Lunch Program: 1,480 (9.2%)
Teachers: 1,032.6 (15.6 to 1)
Librarians/Media Specialists: 29.9 (537.6 to 1)
Guidance Counselors: 31.0 (518.5 to 1)
Current Spending: ($ per student per year):
   Total: $5,902; Instruction: $3,719; Support Services: $1,659
Enrollment, Drop-out Rates and Diploma Recipients by Race/Ethnicity

Category	Total	White	Black	Asian	AIAN	Hisp.
Enrollment (%)	100.0	73.9	24.4	0.4	0.1	0.9
Drop-out Rate (%)	3.7	3.2	5.8	0.0	n/a	0.0
H.S. Diplomas (#)	753	607	139	2	1	4

Walker County

Jasper City
110 W 17th St • Jasper, AL 35501
Mailing Address: PO Box 500 • Jasper, AL 35502-0500
(205) 384-6880 • http://www.jasper.k12.al.us/
Grade Span: PK-12; **Agency Type:** 1
Schools: 6
   3 Primary; 1 Middle; 1 High; 1 Other Level
   5 Regular; 1 Special Education; 0 Vocational; 0 Alternative
   0 Magnet; 0 Charter; 3 Title I Eligible; 0 School-wide Title I
Students: 2,732 (51.3% male; 48.6% female)
   Individual Education Program: 355 (13.0%);
   English Language Learner: 15 (0.5%); Migrant: 0 (0.0%)
   Eligible for Free Lunch Program: 785 (28.7%)
   Eligible for Reduced-Price Lunch Program: 149 (5.5%)
Teachers: 182.5 (15.0 to 1)
Librarians/Media Specialists: 5.0 (546.4 to 1)
Guidance Counselors: 8.0 (341.5 to 1)
Current Spending: ($ per student per year):
   Total: $6,626; Instruction: $4,051; Support Services: $2,159
Enrollment, Drop-out Rates and Diploma Recipients by Race/Ethnicity

Category	Total	White	Black	Asian	AIAN	Hisp.
Enrollment (%)	100.0	78.1	19.4	0.8	0.1	1.3
Drop-out Rate (%)	2.7	1.9	5.8	14.3	n/a	0.0
H.S. Diplomas (#)	167	140	26	1	0	0

Walker County
1710 Alabama Av • Jasper, AL 35501-4964
Mailing Address: PO Box 311 • Jasper, AL 35502-0311
(205) 387-0555 • http://www.walkercountyschools.com/
Grade Span: KG-12; **Agency Type:** 1
Schools: 24
   13 Primary; 2 Middle; 7 High; 2 Other Level
   21 Regular; 0 Special Education; 1 Vocational; 2 Alternative
   0 Magnet; 0 Charter; 13 Title I Eligible; 13 School-wide Title I
Students: 8,244 (52.1% male; 47.8% female)
   Individual Education Program: 1,421 (17.2%);
   English Language Learner: 8 (0.1%); Migrant: 0 (0.0%)
   Eligible for Free Lunch Program: 3,532 (42.8%)
   Eligible for Reduced-Price Lunch Program: 961 (11.7%)
Teachers: 549.9 (15.0 to 1)
Librarians/Media Specialists: 17.7 (465.8 to 1)
Guidance Counselors: 19.6 (420.6 to 1)
Current Spending: ($ per student per year):
   Total: $7,007; Instruction: $4,113; Support Services: $2,387
Enrollment, Drop-out Rates and Diploma Recipients by Race/Ethnicity

Category	Total	White	Black	Asian	AIAN	Hisp.
Enrollment (%)	100.0	93.2	6.1	0.1	0.1	0.5
Drop-out Rate (%)	5.1	5.1	5.2	0.0	0.0	0.0
H.S. Diplomas (#)	344	317	26	0	0	1

Washington County

Washington County
Granade St • Chatom, AL 36518-1359
Mailing Address: PO Box 1359 • Chatom, AL 36518-1359
(251) 847-2401
Grade Span: KG-12; **Agency Type:** 1
Schools: 8
   2 Primary; 0 Middle; 1 High; 5 Other Level
   7 Regular; 0 Special Education; 1 Vocational; 0 Alternative
   0 Magnet; 0 Charter; 7 Title I Eligible; 7 School-wide Title I
Students: 3,575 (52.6% male; 47.3% female)
   Individual Education Program: 599 (16.8%);
   English Language Learner: 1 (<0.1%); Migrant: 185 (5.2%)
   Eligible for Free Lunch Program: 1,772 (49.6%)
   Eligible for Reduced-Price Lunch Program: 359 (10.0%)
Teachers: 233.8 (15.3 to 1)
Librarians/Media Specialists: 7.5 (476.7 to 1)
Guidance Counselors: 6.0 (595.8 to 1)
Current Spending: ($ per student per year):
   Total: $6,054; Instruction: $3,800; Support Services: $1,807
Enrollment, Drop-out Rates and Diploma Recipients by Race/Ethnicity

Category	Total	White	Black	Asian	AIAN	Hisp.
Enrollment (%)	100.0	58.4	32.9	0.2	8.3	0.1
Drop-out Rate (%)	1.0	1.2	0.8	0.0	0.9	0.0
H.S. Diplomas (#)	200	107	77	0	16	0

Wilcox County

Wilcox County
2210 Hwy 221 • Camden, AL 36726-0160
Mailing Address: PO Box 160 • Camden, AL 36726-0160
(334) 682-4716
Grade Span: PK-12; **Agency Type:** 1
Schools: 7
   4 Primary; 1 Middle; 1 High; 1 Other Level
   6 Regular; 0 Special Education; 0 Vocational; 1 Alternative
   0 Magnet; 0 Charter; 5 Title I Eligible; 5 School-wide Title I
Students: 2,481 (52.3% male; 47.6% female)
   Individual Education Program: 321 (12.9%);
   English Language Learner: 0 (0.0%); Migrant: 0 (0.0%)
   Eligible for Free Lunch Program: 2,381 (96.0%)
   Eligible for Reduced-Price Lunch Program: 26 (1.0%)
Teachers: 161.3 (15.4 to 1)
Librarians/Media Specialists: 6.0 (413.5 to 1)
Guidance Counselors: 6.0 (413.5 to 1)
Current Spending: ($ per student per year):
   Total: $7,190; Instruction: $4,072; Support Services: $2,495
Enrollment, Drop-out Rates and Diploma Recipients by Race/Ethnicity

Category	Total	White	Black	Asian	AIAN	Hisp.
Enrollment (%)	100.0	0.3	99.6	0.0	0.0	0.1
Drop-out Rate (%)	4.7	0.0	4.7	n/a	n/a	n/a
H.S. Diplomas (#)	126	0	126	0	0	0

Winston County

Haleyville City
2011 20th St • Haleyville, AL 35565-1959
(205) 486-9231 • http://www.havc.k12.al.us/
Grade Span: PK-12; Agency Type: 1
Schools: 3
   1 Primary; 0 Middle; 2 High; 0 Other Level
   2 Regular; 0 Special Education; 1 Vocational; 0 Alternative
   0 Magnet; 0 Charter; 1 Title I Eligible; 1 School-wide Title I
Students: 1,724   (52.0% male; 47.9% female)
   Individual Education Program: 256 (14.8%);
   English Language Learner: 41 (2.4%); Migrant: 0 (0.0%)
   Eligible for Free Lunch Program: 681 (39.5%)
   Eligible for Reduced-Price Lunch Program: 175 (10.2%)
Teachers: 124.2 (13.9 to 1)
Librarians/Media Specialists: 2.0 (862.0 to 1)
Guidance Counselors: 3.0 (574.7 to 1)
Current Spending: ($ per student per year):
   Total: $5,727; Instruction: $3,914; Support Services: $1,391
Enrollment, Drop-out Rates and Diploma Recipients by Race/Ethnicity

Category	Total	White	Black	Asian	AIAN	Hisp.
Enrollment (%)	100.0	94.6	1.2	0.3	0.1	3.8
Drop-out Rate (%)	3.5	3.6	0.0	0.0	0.0	0.0
H.S. Diplomas (#)	104	102	1	1	0	0

Winston County
25125 Hwy 195 • Double Springs, AL 35553-0009
Mailing Address: PO Box 9 • Double Springs, AL 35553-0009
(205) 489-5018 • http://www.winstonk12.org/
Grade Span: KG-12; Agency Type: 1
Schools: 10
   4 Primary; 1 Middle; 5 High; 0 Other Level
   9 Regular; 0 Special Education; 1 Vocational; 0 Alternative
   0 Magnet; 0 Charter; 5 Title I Eligible; 2 School-wide Title I
Students: 2,755   (50.7% male; 49.2% female)
   Individual Education Program: 655 (23.8%);
   English Language Learner: 1 (<0.1%); Migrant: 0 (0.0%)
   Eligible for Free Lunch Program: 1,250 (45.4%)
   Eligible for Reduced-Price Lunch Program: 453 (16.4%)
Teachers: 190.1 (14.5 to 1)
Librarians/Media Specialists: 8.0 (344.4 to 1)
Guidance Counselors: 4.8 (574.0 to 1)
Current Spending: ($ per student per year):
   Total: $6,888; Instruction: $3,802; Support Services: $2,388
Enrollment, Drop-out Rates and Diploma Recipients by Race/Ethnicity

Category	Total	White	Black	Asian	AIAN	Hisp.
Enrollment (%)	100.0	99.7	0.1	0.0	0.0	0.1
Drop-out Rate (%)	2.9	2.9	n/a	0.0	0.0	n/a
H.S. Diplomas (#)	160	159	0	0	1	0

Number of Schools

Rank	Number	District Name	City
1	104	Mobile County	Mobile
2	80	Birmingham City	Birmingham
3	62	Montgomery County	Montgomery
4	59	Jefferson County	Birmingham
5	49	Huntsville City	Huntsville
6	47	Baldwin County	Bay Minette
7	35	Shelby County	Columbiana
8	31	Tuscaloosa County	Tuscaloosa
9	27	Cullman County	Cullman
10	25	Madison County	Huntsville
11	24	Walker County	Jasper
12	23	Etowah County	Gadsden
13	21	Tuscaloosa City	Tuscaloosa
14	19	Calhoun County	Anniston
14	19	Dothan City	Dothan
14	19	Jackson County	Scottsboro
14	19	Talladega County	Talladega
18	18	Decatur City	Decatur
18	18	Marshall County	Guntersville
18	18	Morgan County	Decatur
21	17	Gadsden City	Gadsden
21	17	St Clair County	Ashville
23	16	Blount County	Oneonta
23	16	Hoover City	Hoover
23	16	Lawrence County	Moulton
26	15	Elmore County	Wetumpka
27	14	Dallas County	Selma
27	14	Dekalb County	Rainsville
27	14	Escambia County	Brewton
30	13	Autauga County	Prattville
30	13	Lauderdale County	Florence
30	13	Limestone County	Athens
30	13	Selma City	Selma
34	12	Chilton County	Clanton
34	12	Lee County	Opelika
34	12	Monroe County	Monroeville
37	11	Chambers County	Lafayette
37	11	Houston County	Dothan
37	11	Marion County	Hamilton
37	11	Russell County	Phenix City
41	10	Auburn City	Auburn
41	10	Bibb County	Centreville
41	10	Enterprise City	Enterprise
41	10	Hale County	Greensboro
41	10	Pickens County	Carrollton
41	10	Winston County	Double Springs
47	9	Anniston City	Anniston
47	9	Bessemer City	Bessemer
47	9	Clarke County	Grove Hill
47	9	Colbert County	Tuscumbia
47	9	Geneva County	Geneva
47	9	Madison City	Madison
47	9	Opelika City	Opelika
47	9	Phenix City	Phenix City
55	8	Butler County	Greenville
55	8	Cherokee County	Centre
55	8	Choctaw County	Butler
55	8	Covington County	Andalusia
55	8	Florence City	Florence
55	8	Lowndes County	Hayneville
55	8	Macon County	Tuskegee
55	8	Ozark City	Ozark
55	8	Talladega City	Talladega
55	8	Washington County	Chatom
65	7	Athens City	Athens
65	7	Cleburne County	Heflin
65	7	Conecuh County	Evergreen
65	7	Cullman City	Cullman
65	7	Dale County	Ozark
65	7	Fairfield City	Fairfield
65	7	Franklin County	Russellville
65	7	Henry County	Abbeville
65	7	Muscle Shoals City	Muscle Shoals
65	7	Pell City	Pell City
65	7	Sumter County	Livingston
65	7	Vestavia Hills County	Birmingham
65	7	Wilcox County	Camden
78	6	Alexander City	Alexander City
78	6	Fayette County	Fayette
78	6	Hartselle City	Hartselle
78	6	Jasper City	Jasper
78	6	Mountain Brook City	Mountain Brook
78	6	Oxford City	Oxford
78	6	Pike County	Troy
78	6	Randolph County	Wedowee
78	6	Scottsboro City	Scottsboro
78	6	Tallapoosa County	Dadeville
88	5	Albertville City	Albertville
88	5	Bullock County	Union Springs
88	5	Eufaula City	Eufaula
88	5	Greene County	Eutaw
88	5	Homewood City	Homewood
88	5	Lamar County	Vernon
88	5	Sylacauga City	Sylacauga
88	5	Troy City	Troy
96	4	Arab City	Arab
96	4	Attalla City	Attalla
96	4	Clay County	Ashland
96	4	Coffee County	Elba
96	4	Coosa County	Rockford
96	4	Crenshaw County	Luverne
96	4	Daleville City	Daleville
96	4	Demopolis City	Demopolis
96	4	Fort Payne City	Fort Payne
96	4	Guntersville City	Guntersville
96	4	Marengo County	Linden
96	4	Perry County	Marion
96	4	Russellville City	Russellville
109	3	Andalusia City	Andalusia
109	3	Haleyville City	Haleyville
109	3	Tallassee City	Tallassee
109	3	Thomasville City	Thomasville
113	2	Jacksonville City	Jacksonville

Number of Teachers

Rank	Number	District Name	City
1	4,236	Mobile County	Mobile
2	2,467	Jefferson County	Birmingham
3	2,210	Birmingham City	Birmingham
4	2,171	Montgomery County	Montgomery
5	1,716	Baldwin County	Bay Minette
6	1,600	Huntsville City	Huntsville
7	1,589	Shelby County	Columbiana
8	1,032	Tuscaloosa County	Tuscaloosa
9	1,031	Madison County	Huntsville
10	785	Hoover City	Hoover
11	684	Tuscaloosa City	Tuscaloosa
12	632	Cullman County	Cullman
13	624	Decatur City	Decatur
14	621	Elmore County	Wetumpka
15	618	Lee County	Opelika
16	601	Etowah County	Gadsden
17	588	Calhoun County	Anniston
18	572	Lauderdale County	Florence
19	564	Dekalb County	Rainsville
20	561	Autauga County	Prattville
21	552	Morgan County	Decatur
22	549	Walker County	Jasper
23	544	Limestone County	Athens
24	520	Dothan City	Dothan
25	472	Chilton County	Clanton
26	467	Talladega County	Talladega
27	466	St Clair County	Ashville
28	449	Marshall County	Guntersville
29	440	Blount County	Oneonta
30	430	Jackson County	Scottsboro
31	420	Madison City	Madison
32	398	Gadsden City	Gadsden
33	378	Houston County	Dothan
34	373	Vestavia Hills City	Birmingham
35	357	Lawrence County	Moulton
36	349	Enterprise City	Enterprise
37	333	Mountain Brook City	Mountain Brook
38	321	Phenix City	Phenix City
39	321	Auburn City	Auburn
40	317	Escambia County	Brewton
41	311	Florence City	Florence
42	302	Monroe County	Monroeville
43	301	Opelika City	Opelika
44	288	Chambers County	Lafayette
45	271	Dallas County	Selma
46	269	Cherokee County	Centre
47	267	Selma City	Selma
48	265	Bessemer City	Bessemer
49	259	Homewood City	Homewood
50	247	Marion County	Hamilton
51	245	Macon County	Tuskegee
52	240	Pell City	Pell City
53	240	Oxford City	Oxford
54	233	Washington County	Chatom
55	230	Russell County	Phenix City
56	230	Hale County	Greensboro
57	229	Bibb County	Centreville
58	228	Albertville City	Albertville
59	228	Clarke County	Grove Hill
60	227	Alexander City	Alexander City
60	227	Tallapoosa County	Dadeville
62	226	Colbert County	Tuscumbia
63	222	Pickens County	Carrollton
64	222	Franklin County	Russellville
65	215	Butler County	Greenville
66	211	Covington County	Andalusia
67	205	Athens City	Athens
68	202	Talladega City	Talladega
69	200	Hartselle City	Hartselle
70	193	Eufaula City	Eufaula
71	192	Scottsboro City	Scottsboro
72	190	Winston County	Double Springs
73	189	Geneva County	Geneva
74	182	Dale County	Ozark
74	182	Sumter County	Livingston
76	182	Jasper City	Jasper
77	181	Ozark City	Ozark
78	177	Cullman City	Cullman
79	174	Arab City	Arab
80	172	Cleburne County	Heflin
81	169	Fort Payne City	Fort Payne
82	169	Henry County	Abbeville
83	169	Lamar County	Vernon
84	168	Fayette County	Fayette
85	168	Fairfield City	Fairfield
86	168	Muscle Shoals City	Muscle Shoals
87	167	Anniston City	Anniston
88	161	Wilcox County	Camden
89	159	Sylacauga City	Sylacauga
90	155	Lowndes County	Hayneville
91	152	Crenshaw County	Luverne
92	151	Demopolis City	Demopolis
93	151	Russellville City	Russellville
94	150	Choctaw County	Butler
95	148	Troy City	Troy
96	147	Clay County	Ashland
97	145	Randolph County	Wedowee
98	140	Pike County	Troy
99	137	Perry County	Marion
100	132	Guntersville City	Guntersville
101	125	Coffee County	Elba
102	124	Conecuh County	Evergreen
102	124	Haleyville City	Haleyville
104	123	Attalla City	Attalla
105	121	Bullock County	Union Springs
106	119	Tallassee City	Tallassee
107	118	Thomasville City	Thomasville
108	117	Greene County	Eutaw
109	112	Marengo County	Linden
110	110	Andalusia City	Andalusia
111	108	Daleville City	Daleville
112	105	Coosa County	Rockford
113	100	Jacksonville City	Jacksonville

Number of Students

Rank	Number	District Name	City
1	64,774	Mobile County	Mobile
2	38,659	Jefferson County	Birmingham
3	34,099	Birmingham City	Birmingham
4	32,553	Montgomery County	Montgomery
5	24,037	Baldwin County	Bay Minette
6	22,590	Huntsville City	Huntsville
7	22,541	Shelby County	Columbiana
8	17,023	Madison County	Huntsville
9	16,073	Tuscaloosa County	Tuscaloosa
10	11,197	Hoover City	Hoover
11	10,244	Tuscaloosa City	Tuscaloosa
12	10,213	Elmore County	Wetumpka
13	9,759	Cullman County	Cullman
14	9,303	Lee County	Opelika
15	9,105	Autauga County	Prattville
16	9,018	Calhoun County	Anniston
17	8,880	Decatur City	Decatur
18	8,872	Lauderdale County	Florence
19	8,838	Dothan City	Dothan
20	8,521	Etowah County	Gadsden
21	8,244	Walker County	Jasper
22	8,123	Dekalb County	Rainsville
23	8,038	Limestone County	Athens
24	7,740	Blount County	Oneonta
25	7,712	Talladega County	Talladega
26	7,607	Morgan County	Decatur
27	7,334	St Clair County	Ashville
28	7,148	Marshall County	Guntersville
29	7,102	Chilton County	Clanton
30	6,848	Madison City	Madison
31	6,161	Houston County	Dothan
32	6,042	Jackson County	Scottsboro
33	5,740	Lawrence County	Moulton
34	5,467	Gadsden City	Gadsden
35	5,389	Enterprise City	Enterprise
36	5,293	Phenix City	Phenix City
37	5,232	Vestavia Hills City	Birmingham
38	4,691	Auburn City	Auburn
39	4,595	Escambia County	Brewton
40	4,482	Dallas County	Selma
41	4,431	Monroe County	Monroeville
42	4,396	Chambers County	Lafayette

Rank	Value	District Name	City
43	4,287	Selma City	Selma
44	4,267	Opelika City	Opelika
45	4,204	Cherokee County	Centre
46	4,149	Mountain Brook City	Mountain Brook
47	4,135	Florence City	Florence
48	4,116	Bessemer City	Bessemer
49	3,990	Pell City	Pell City
50	3,781	Macon County	Tuskegee
51	3,721	Oxford City	Oxford
52	3,670	Russell County	Phenix City
53	3,663	Marion County	Hamilton
54	3,621	Albertville City	Albertville
55	3,575	Washington County	Chatom
56	3,557	Butler County	Greenville
57	3,549	Alexander City	Alexander City
58	3,547	Clarke County	Grove Hill
59	3,529	Bibb County	Centreville
60	3,389	Tallapoosa County	Dadeville
61	3,317	Pickens County	Carrollton
62	3,303	Hale County	Greensboro
63	3,268	Homewood City	Homewood
64	3,265	Colbert County	Tuscumbia
65	3,241	Covington County	Andalusia
66	3,070	Hartselle City	Hartselle
67	3,040	Franklin County	Russellville
68	2,902	Eufaula City	Eufaula
69	2,851	Talladega City	Talladega
70	2,778	Ozark City	Ozark
71	2,756	Scottsboro City	Scottsboro
72	2,755	Winston County	Double Springs
73	2,734	Dale County	Ozark
74	2,732	Jasper City	Jasper
75	2,726	Fort Payne City	Fort Payne
76	2,722	Geneva County	Geneva
77	2,705	Arab City	Arab
78	2,702	Athens City	Athens
79	2,667	Henry County	Abbeville
80	2,657	Cullman City	Cullman
81	2,656	Fayette County	Fayette
82	2,652	Anniston City	Anniston
83	2,632	Sumter County	Livingston
84	2,611	Cleburne County	Heflin
85	2,538	Muscle Shoals City	Muscle Shoals
86	2,481	Wilcox County	Camden
87	2,472	Lamar County	Vernon
88	2,449	Crenshaw County	Luverne
89	2,415	Lowndes County	Hayneville
90	2,385	Troy City	Troy
91	2,353	Fairfield City	Fairfield
92	2,344	Russellville City	Russellville
93	2,338	Sylacauga City	Sylacauga
94	2,264	Randolph County	Wedowee
95	2,255	Demopolis City	Demopolis
96	2,168	Perry County	Marion
97	2,147	Choctaw County	Butler
98	2,083	Pike County	Troy
99	2,029	Clay County	Ashland
100	1,896	Tallassee City	Tallassee
101	1,867	Coffee County	Elba
102	1,853	Conecuh County	Evergreen
103	1,823	Attalla City	Attalla
104	1,820	Bullock County	Union Springs
105	1,803	Guntersville City	Guntersville
106	1,724	Haleyville City	Haleyville
107	1,704	Marengo County	Linden
108	1,696	Jacksonville City	Jacksonville
109	1,695	Andalusia City	Andalusia
110	1,648	Thomasville City	Thomasville
111	1,635	Greene County	Eutaw
112	1,618	Coosa County	Rockford
113	1,582	Daleville City	Daleville

Male Students

Rank	Percent	District Name	City
1	55.2	Pike County	Troy
2	54.9	Colbert County	Tuscumbia
3	54.5	Crenshaw County	Luverne
4	54.0	Jacksonville City	Jacksonville
5	53.6	Daleville City	Daleville
6	53.5	Attalla City	Attalla
7	53.4	Marshall County	Guntersville
8	53.4	St Clair County	Ashville
9	53.2	Geneva County	Geneva
9	53.2	Homewood City	Homewood
11	53.2	Dale County	Ozark
12	53.1	Marengo County	Linden
13	53.1	Covington County	Andalusia
14	52.9	Marion County	Hamilton
15	52.8	Conecuh County	Evergreen
16	52.8	Pell City	Pell City
17	52.8	Lawrence County	Moulton
18	52.7	Cullman City	Cullman
19	52.7	Cherokee County	Centre
20	52.6	Washington County	Chatom
21	52.5	Choctaw County	Butler
22	52.5	Dekalb County	Rainsville
23	52.5	Alexander City	Alexander City
24	52.4	Anniston City	Anniston
25	52.4	Chilton County	Clanton
26	52.4	Escambia County	Brewton
27	52.4	Coosa County	Rockford
28	52.3	Bibb County	Centreville
29	52.3	Clay County	Ashland
30	52.3	Madison City	Madison
31	52.3	Wilcox County	Camden
32	52.2	Morgan County	Decatur
33	52.2	Thomasville City	Thomasville
34	52.2	Eufaula City	Eufaula
35	52.2	Monroe County	Monroeville
36	52.2	Talladega County	Talladega
37	52.2	Shelby County	Columbiana
38	52.1	Walker County	Jasper
39	52.1	Jackson County	Scottsboro
40	52.0	Haleyville City	Haleyville
41	52.0	Guntersville City	Guntersville
42	52.0	Elmore County	Wetumpka
43	52.0	Fort Payne City	Fort Payne
44	52.0	Tallapoosa County	Dadeville
45	52.0	Arab City	Arab
46	52.0	Ozark City	Ozark
47	51.9	Troy City	Troy
48	51.9	Cullman County	Cullman
49	51.9	Limestone County	Athens
50	51.9	Hartselle City	Hartselle
51	51.8	Sumter County	Livingston
52	51.8	Mobile County	Mobile
53	51.8	Jefferson County	Birmingham
54	51.8	Franklin County	Russellville
55	51.8	Etowah County	Gadsden
56	51.8	Randolph County	Wedowee
57	51.8	Lauderdale County	Florence
58	51.7	Calhoun County	Anniston
59	51.7	Baldwin County	Bay Minette
60	51.7	Opelika City	Opelika
61	51.7	Vestavia Hills City	Birmingham
62	51.6	Greene County	Eutaw
63	51.6	Tuscaloosa County	Tuscaloosa
64	51.6	Madison County	Huntsville
65	51.5	Russell County	Phenix City
66	51.5	Blount County	Oneonta
67	51.5	Fayette County	Fayette
68	51.5	Enterprise City	Enterprise
69	51.4	Autauga County	Prattville
70	51.4	Tallassee City	Tallassee
71	51.4	Demopolis City	Demopolis
72	51.4	Florence City	Florence
73	51.4	Cleburne County	Heflin
74	51.4	Dothan City	Dothan
75	51.4	Perry County	Marion
76	51.4	Lee County	Opelika
77	51.4	Talladega City	Talladega
78	51.3	Huntsville City	Huntsville
79	51.3	Houston County	Dothan
80	51.3	Jasper City	Jasper
81	51.2	Bullock County	Union Springs
82	51.2	Coffee County	Elba
83	51.1	Bessemer City	Bessemer
84	51.1	Chambers County	Lafayette
85	51.1	Fairfield City	Fairfield
86	51.1	Albertville City	Albertville
87	51.1	Butler County	Greenville
88	51.1	Andalusia City	Andalusia
89	51.1	Phenix City	Phenix City
90	51.0	Montgomery County	Montgomery
91	51.0	Athens City	Athens
92	51.0	Macon County	Tuskegee
93	50.9	Oxford City	Oxford
94	50.8	Hoover City	Hoover
95	50.8	Russellville City	Russellville
96	50.8	Gadsden City	Gadsden
97	50.8	Hale County	Greensboro
98	50.8	Birmingham City	Birmingham
99	50.8	Pickens County	Carrollton
100	50.7	Winston County	Double Springs
101	50.7	Lowndes County	Hayneville
102	50.6	Mountain Brook City	Mountain Brook
103	50.5	Dallas County	Selma
104	50.5	Decatur City	Decatur
105	50.4	Tuscaloosa City	Tuscaloosa
106	50.4	Scottsboro City	Scottsboro
107	50.3	Lamar County	Vernon
108	50.2	Auburn City	Auburn
109	50.1	Muscle Shoals City	Muscle Shoals
110	50.1	Sylacauga City	Sylacauga
111	50.0	Clarke County	Grove Hill
112	50.0	Henry County	Abbeville
113	49.5	Selma City	Selma

Female Students

Rank	Percent	District Name	City
1	50.4	Selma City	Selma
2	49.9	Henry County	Abbeville
3	49.9	Clarke County	Grove Hill
4	49.8	Sylacauga City	Sylacauga
5	49.8	Muscle Shoals City	Muscle Shoals
6	49.7	Auburn City	Auburn
7	49.6	Lamar County	Vernon
8	49.5	Scottsboro City	Scottsboro
9	49.5	Tuscaloosa City	Tuscaloosa
10	49.4	Decatur City	Decatur
11	49.4	Dallas County	Selma
12	49.3	Mountain Brook City	Mountain Brook
13	49.2	Lowndes County	Hayneville
14	49.2	Winston County	Double Springs
15	49.1	Pickens County	Carrollton
16	49.1	Birmingham City	Birmingham
17	49.1	Hale County	Greensboro
18	49.1	Gadsden City	Gadsden
19	49.1	Russellville City	Russellville
20	49.1	Hoover City	Hoover
21	49.0	Oxford City	Oxford
22	48.9	Macon County	Tuskegee
23	48.9	Athens City	Athens
24	48.9	Montgomery County	Montgomery
25	48.8	Phenix City	Phenix City
26	48.8	Andalusia City	Andalusia
27	48.8	Butler County	Greenville
28	48.8	Albertville City	Albertville
29	48.8	Fairfield City	Fairfield
30	48.8	Chambers County	Lafayette
31	48.8	Bessemer City	Bessemer
32	48.7	Coffee County	Elba
33	48.7	Bullock County	Union Springs
34	48.6	Jasper City	Jasper
35	48.6	Houston County	Dothan
36	48.6	Huntsville City	Huntsville
37	48.5	Talladega City	Talladega
38	48.5	Lee County	Opelika
39	48.5	Perry County	Marion
40	48.5	Dothan City	Dothan
41	48.5	Cleburne County	Heflin
42	48.5	Florence City	Florence
43	48.5	Demopolis City	Demopolis
44	48.5	Tallassee City	Tallassee
45	48.5	Autauga County	Prattville
46	48.4	Enterprise City	Enterprise
47	48.4	Fayette County	Fayette
48	48.4	Blount County	Oneonta
49	48.4	Russell County	Phenix City
50	48.3	Madison County	Huntsville
51	48.3	Tuscaloosa County	Tuscaloosa
52	48.3	Greene County	Eutaw
53	48.2	Vestavia Hills City	Birmingham
54	48.2	Opelika City	Opelika
55	48.2	Baldwin County	Bay Minette
56	48.2	Calhoun County	Anniston
57	48.1	Lauderdale County	Florence
58	48.1	Randolph County	Wedowee
59	48.1	Etowah County	Gadsden
60	48.1	Franklin County	Russellville
61	48.1	Jefferson County	Birmingham
62	48.1	Mobile County	Mobile
63	48.1	Sumter County	Livingston
64	48.0	Hartselle City	Hartselle
65	48.0	Limestone County	Athens
66	48.0	Cullman County	Cullman
67	48.0	Troy City	Troy
68	48.0	Ozark City	Ozark
69	47.9	Arab City	Arab
70	47.9	Tallapoosa County	Dadeville
71	47.9	Fort Payne City	Fort Payne
72	47.9	Elmore County	Wetumpka
73	47.9	Guntersville City	Guntersville
74	47.9	Haleyville City	Haleyville
75	47.8	Jackson County	Scottsboro
76	47.8	Walker County	Jasper
77	47.7	Shelby County	Columbiana
78	47.7	Talladega County	Talladega
79	47.7	Monroe County	Monroeville
80	47.7	Eufaula City	Eufaula
81	47.7	Thomasville City	Thomasville
82	47.7	Morgan County	Decatur
83	47.6	Wilcox County	Camden
84	47.6	Madison City	Madison
85	47.6	Clay County	Ashland
86	47.6	Bibb County	Centreville

Rank	Percent	District Name	City
87	47.5	Coosa County	Rockford
88	47.5	Escambia County	Brewton
89	47.5	Chilton County	Clanton
90	47.5	Anniston City	Anniston
91	47.4	Alexander City	Alexander City
92	47.4	Dekalb County	Rainsville
93	47.4	Choctaw County	Butler
94	47.3	Washington County	Chatom
95	47.2	Cherokee County	Centre
96	47.2	Cullman City	Cullman
97	47.1	Lawrence County	Moulton
98	47.1	Pell City	Pell City
99	47.1	Conecuh County	Evergreen
100	47.0	Marion County	Hamilton
101	46.8	Covington County	Andalusia
102	46.8	Marengo County	Linden
103	46.7	Dale County	Ozark
104	46.7	Geneva County	Geneva
104	46.7	Homewood City	Homewood
106	46.5	St Clair County	Ashville
107	46.5	Marshall County	Guntersville
108	46.4	Attalla City	Attalla
109	46.3	Daleville City	Daleville
110	45.9	Jacksonville City	Jacksonville
111	45.4	Crenshaw County	Luverne
112	45.0	Colbert County	Tuscumbia
113	44.7	Pike County	Troy

Individual Education Program Students

Rank	Percent	District Name	City
1	27.4	Baldwin County	Bay Minette
2	24.7	Shelby County	Columbiana
3	23.8	Winston County	Double Springs
4	22.6	Huntsville City	Huntsville
5	22.5	Homewood City	Homewood
6	22.3	Pike County	Troy
7	20.8	Tuscaloosa City	Tuscaloosa
8	20.5	Athens City	Athens
9	20.3	Madison City	Madison
10	20.2	Eufaula City	Eufaula
11	20.1	Morgan County	Decatur
12	19.4	Scottsboro City	Scottsboro
13	19.3	Attalla City	Attalla
14	19.2	Vestavia Hills City	Birmingham
15	18.9	Guntersville City	Guntersville
16	18.8	Jacksonville City	Jacksonville
17	18.7	Conecuh County	Evergreen
18	18.6	Ozark City	Ozark
19	18.5	Chilton County	Clanton
19	18.5	Pell City	Pell City
21	18.3	Bibb County	Centreville
21	18.3	Clarke County	Grove Hill
21	18.3	Cleburne County	Heflin
21	18.3	Colbert County	Tuscumbia
21	18.3	Mobile County	Mobile
26	18.0	Decatur City	Decatur
27	17.9	Franklin County	Russellville
27	17.9	Tallapoosa County	Dadeville
29	17.7	Dale County	Ozark
30	17.6	Daleville City	Daleville
31	17.5	Dothan City	Dothan
31	17.5	Gadsden City	Gadsden
31	17.5	Jefferson County	Birmingham
34	17.2	Walker County	Jasper
35	17.1	Geneva County	Geneva
36	17.0	Butler County	Greenville
36	17.0	Sumter County	Livingston
38	16.8	Washington County	Chatom
39	16.6	Autauga County	Prattville
39	16.6	Dekalb County	Rainsville
39	16.6	Talladega City	Talladega
39	16.6	Tuscaloosa County	Tuscaloosa
43	16.5	Blount County	Oneonta
43	16.5	Etowah County	Gadsden
45	16.4	Clay County	Ashland
45	16.4	Coffee County	Elba
45	16.4	Sylacauga City	Sylacauga
48	16.3	Covington County	Andalusia
48	16.3	Florence City	Florence
50	16.2	Choctaw County	Butler
50	16.2	Henry County	Abbeville
50	16.2	Marion County	Hamilton
53	16.1	Crenshaw County	Luverne
53	16.1	Enterprise City	Enterprise
55	16.0	Houston County	Dothan
56	15.9	Talladega County	Talladega
57	15.8	Madison County	Huntsville
58	15.7	Hartselle City	Hartselle
59	15.6	St Clair County	Ashville
60	15.5	Cherokee County	Centre
60	15.5	Coosa County	Rockford
62	15.4	Alexander City	Alexander City
62	15.4	Anniston City	Anniston
62	15.4	Dallas County	Selma
65	15.3	Calhoun County	Anniston
66	15.2	Montgomery County	Montgomery
66	15.2	Tallassee City	Tallassee
68	15.1	Birmingham City	Birmingham
68	15.1	Escambia County	Brewton
68	15.1	Phenix City	Phenix City
71	15.0	Lowndes County	Hayneville
71	15.0	Marshall County	Guntersville
71	15.0	Troy City	Troy
74	14.9	Perry County	Marion
74	14.9	Thomasville City	Thomasville
76	14.8	Haleyville City	Haleyville
77	14.6	Cullman County	Cullman
77	14.6	Fayette County	Fayette
79	14.5	Elmore County	Wetumpka
80	14.3	Limestone County	Athens
81	14.2	Bullock County	Union Springs
81	14.2	Lawrence County	Moulton
81	14.2	Monroe County	Monroeville
84	14.0	Andalusia City	Andalusia
84	14.0	Bessemer City	Bessemer
84	14.0	Chambers County	Lafayette
87	13.9	Russellville City	Russellville
88	13.8	Greene County	Eutaw
89	13.7	Oxford City	Oxford
90	13.5	Arab City	Arab
91	13.3	Lauderdale County	Florence
92	13.0	Albertville City	Albertville
92	13.0	Jasper City	Jasper
94	12.9	Wilcox County	Camden
95	12.6	Hale County	Greensboro
96	12.5	Macon County	Tuskegee
97	12.3	Russell County	Phenix City
98	12.2	Fairfield City	Fairfield
99	12.1	Pickens County	Carrollton
100	11.9	Lamar County	Vernon
100	11.9	Lee County	Opelika
102	11.8	Jackson County	Scottsboro
103	11.6	Cullman City	Cullman
104	11.2	Fort Payne City	Fort Payne
105	11.1	Randolph County	Wedowee
106	10.7	Marengo County	Linden
107	10.6	Selma City	Selma
108	10.5	Auburn City	Auburn
109	10.4	Demopolis City	Demopolis
110	9.9	Muscle Shoals City	Muscle Shoals
111	9.7	Opelika City	Opelika
112	8.7	Mountain Brook City	Mountain Brook
113	7.1	Hoover City	Hoover

English Language Learner Students

Rank	Percent	District Name	City
1	19.9	Fort Payne City	Fort Payne
2	12.6	Albertville City	Albertville
3	11.6	Russellville City	Russellville
4	7.4	Athens City	Athens
5	7.3	Dekalb County	Rainsville
6	7.2	Blount County	Oneonta
7	6.2	Homewood City	Homewood
8	5.8	Decatur City	Decatur
9	4.8	Marshall County	Guntersville
10	4.1	Cullman City	Cullman
11	3.8	Hoover City	Hoover
12	3.7	Franklin County	Russellville
13	3.5	Shelby County	Columbiana
14	3.1	Gadsden City	Gadsden
15	2.8	Oxford City	Oxford
16	2.6	Limestone County	Athens
17	2.4	Haleyville City	Haleyville
18	1.9	Cullman County	Cullman
19	1.8	Enterprise City	Enterprise
20	1.7	Chilton County	Clanton
21	1.5	Anniston City	Anniston
21	1.5	Auburn City	Auburn
21	1.5	Baldwin County	Bay Minette
21	1.5	Randolph County	Wedowee
25	1.4	St Clair County	Ashville
26	1.3	Jefferson County	Birmingham
26	1.3	Madison County	Madison
28	1.2	Alexander City	Alexander City
28	1.2	Bullock County	Union Springs
28	1.2	Huntsville City	Huntsville
28	1.2	Jackson County	Scottsboro
28	1.2	Mobile County	Mobile
28	1.2	Montgomery County	Montgomery
28	1.2	Tallassee City	Tallassee
35	1.1	Autauga County	Prattville
35	1.1	Geneva County	Geneva
37	1.0	Bessemer City	Bessemer
37	1.0	Birmingham City	Birmingham
37	1.0	Florence City	Florence
40	0.9	Scottsboro City	Scottsboro
40	0.9	Sylacauga City	Sylacauga
40	0.9	Tuscaloosa City	Tuscaloosa
40	0.9	Tuscaloosa County	Tuscaloosa
44	0.8	Dothan City	Dothan
44	0.8	Elmore County	Wetumpka
44	0.8	Marion County	Hamilton
47	0.7	Calhoun County	Anniston
47	0.7	Etowah County	Gadsden
47	0.7	Fairfield City	Fairfield
47	0.7	Lawrence County	Moulton
47	0.7	Morgan County	Decatur
47	0.7	Vestavia Hills City	Birmingham
53	0.6	Cleburne County	Heflin
53	0.6	Colbert County	Tuscumbia
53	0.6	Troy City	Troy
56	0.5	Attalla City	Attalla
56	0.5	Jasper City	Jasper
56	0.5	Madison City	Huntsville
56	0.5	Pell City	Pell City
60	0.4	Clay County	Ashland
60	0.4	Daleville City	Daleville
60	0.4	Demopolis City	Demopolis
60	0.4	Eufaula City	Eufaula
60	0.4	Jacksonville City	Jacksonville
60	0.4	Opelika City	Opelika
66	0.3	Andalusia City	Andalusia
66	0.3	Bibb County	Centreville
66	0.3	Lauderdale County	Florence
66	0.3	Talladega County	Talladega
70	0.2	Butler County	Greenville
70	0.2	Chambers County	Lafayette
70	0.2	Coffee County	Elba
70	0.2	Coosa County	Rockford
70	0.2	Mountain Brook City	Mountain Brook
70	0.2	Ozark City	Ozark
70	0.2	Thomasville City	Thomasville
77	0.1	Arab City	Arab
77	0.1	Cherokee County	Centre
77	0.1	Covington County	Andalusia
77	0.1	Dale County	Ozark
77	0.1	Dallas County	Selma
77	0.1	Lee County	Opelika
77	0.1	Muscle Shoals City	Muscle Shoals
77	0.1	Selma City	Selma
77	0.1	Sumter County	Livingston
77	0.1	Walker County	Jasper
87	0.0	Escambia County	Brewton
87	0.0	Monroe County	Monroeville
87	0.0	Pickens County	Carrollton
87	0.0	Pike County	Troy
87	0.0	Washington County	Chatom
87	0.0	Winston County	Double Springs
93	0.0	Choctaw County	Butler
93	0.0	Clarke County	Grove Hill
93	0.0	Conecuh County	Evergreen
93	0.0	Crenshaw County	Luverne
93	0.0	Fayette County	Fayette
93	0.0	Greene County	Eutaw
93	0.0	Guntersville City	Guntersville
93	0.0	Hale County	Greensboro
93	0.0	Hartselle City	Hartselle
93	0.0	Henry County	Abbeville
93	0.0	Houston County	Dothan
93	0.0	Lamar County	Vernon
93	0.0	Lowndes County	Hayneville
93	0.0	Macon County	Tuskegee
93	0.0	Marengo County	Linden
93	0.0	Perry County	Marion
93	0.0	Phenix City	Phenix City
93	0.0	Russell County	Phenix City
93	0.0	Talladega City	Talladega
93	0.0	Tallapoosa County	Dadeville
93	0.0	Wilcox County	Camden

Migrant Students

Rank	Percent	District Name	City
1	10.6	Dekalb County	Rainsville
2	10.3	Coffee County	Elba
3	8.8	Covington County	Andalusia
4	6.4	Russellville City	Russellville
5	5.2	Washington County	Chatom
6	3.6	St Clair County	Ashville
7	3.5	Enterprise City	Enterprise
8	3.2	Morgan County	Decatur
9	3.0	Lawrence County	Moulton
10	2.7	Mobile County	Mobile
11	2.6	Decatur City	Decatur
12	2.5	Blount County	Oneonta
12	2.5	Marshall County	Guntersville
14	2.4	Gadsden City	Gadsden

Rank	Percent	District Name	City
15	1.7	Franklin County	Russellville
16	1.5	Geneva County	Geneva
17	0.9	Fort Payne City	Fort Payne
17	0.9	Hartselle City	Hartselle
19	0.1	Madison County	Huntsville
20	0.0	Cherokee County	Centre
20	0.0	Colbert County	Tuscumbia
20	0.0	Dale County	Ozark
23	0.0	Albertville City	Albertville
23	0.0	Alexander City	Alexander City
23	0.0	Andalusia City	Andalusia
23	0.0	Anniston City	Anniston
23	0.0	Arab City	Arab
23	0.0	Athens City	Athens
23	0.0	Attalla City	Attalla
23	0.0	Auburn City	Auburn
23	0.0	Autauga County	Prattville
23	0.0	Baldwin County	Bay Minette
23	0.0	Bessemer City	Bessemer
23	0.0	Bibb County	Centreville
23	0.0	Birmingham City	Birmingham
23	0.0	Bullock County	Union Springs
23	0.0	Butler County	Greenville
23	0.0	Calhoun County	Anniston
23	0.0	Chambers County	Lafayette
23	0.0	Chilton County	Clanton
23	0.0	Choctaw County	Butler
23	0.0	Clarke County	Grove Hill
23	0.0	Clay County	Ashland
23	0.0	Cleburne County	Heflin
23	0.0	Conecuh County	Evergreen
23	0.0	Coosa County	Rockford
23	0.0	Crenshaw County	Luverne
23	0.0	Cullman City	Cullman
23	0.0	Cullman County	Cullman
23	0.0	Daleville City	Daleville
23	0.0	Dallas County	Selma
23	0.0	Demopolis City	Demopolis
23	0.0	Dothan City	Dothan
23	0.0	Elmore County	Wetumpka
23	0.0	Escambia County	Brewton
23	0.0	Etowah County	Gadsden
23	0.0	Eufaula City	Eufaula
23	0.0	Fairfield City	Fairfield
23	0.0	Fayette County	Fayette
23	0.0	Florence City	Florence
23	0.0	Greene County	Eutaw
23	0.0	Guntersville City	Guntersville
23	0.0	Hale County	Greensboro
23	0.0	Haleyville City	Haleyville
23	0.0	Henry County	Abbeville
23	0.0	Homewood City	Homewood
23	0.0	Hoover City	Hoover
23	0.0	Houston County	Dothan
23	0.0	Huntsville City	Huntsville
23	0.0	Jackson County	Scottsboro
23	0.0	Jacksonville City	Jacksonville
23	0.0	Jasper City	Jasper
23	0.0	Jefferson County	Birmingham
23	0.0	Lamar County	Vernon
23	0.0	Lauderdale County	Florence
23	0.0	Lee County	Opelika
23	0.0	Limestone County	Athens
23	0.0	Lowndes County	Hayneville
23	0.0	Macon County	Tuskegee
23	0.0	Madison City	Madison
23	0.0	Marengo County	Linden
23	0.0	Marion County	Hamilton
23	0.0	Monroe County	Monroeville
23	0.0	Montgomery County	Montgomery
23	0.0	Mountain Brook City	Mountain Brook
23	0.0	Muscle Shoals City	Muscle Shoals
23	0.0	Opelika City	Opelika
23	0.0	Oxford City	Oxford
23	0.0	Ozark City	Ozark
23	0.0	Pell City	Pell City
23	0.0	Perry County	Marion
23	0.0	Phenix City	Phenix City
23	0.0	Pickens County	Carrollton
23	0.0	Pike County	Troy
23	0.0	Randolph County	Wedowee
23	0.0	Russell County	Phenix City
23	0.0	Scottsboro City	Scottsboro
23	0.0	Selma City	Selma
23	0.0	Shelby County	Columbiana
23	0.0	Sumter County	Livingston
23	0.0	Sylacauga City	Sylacauga
23	0.0	Talladega City	Talladega
23	0.0	Talladega County	Talladega
23	0.0	Tallapoosa County	Dadeville
23	0.0	Tallassee City	Tallassee
23	0.0	Thomasville City	Thomasville
23	0.0	Troy City	Troy
23	0.0	Tuscaloosa City	Tuscaloosa
23	0.0	Tuscaloosa County	Tuscaloosa
23	0.0	Vestavia Hills City	Birmingham
23	0.0	Walker County	Jasper
23	0.0	Wilcox County	Camden
23	0.0	Winston County	Double Springs

Students Eligible for Free Lunch

Rank	Percent	District Name	City
1	96.0	Wilcox County	Camden
2	93.2	Perry County	Marion
3	88.9	Lowndes County	Hayneville
4	85.1	Greene County	Eutaw
5	84.9	Bullock County	Union Springs
6	81.2	Sumter County	Livingston
7	79.8	Marengo County	Linden
8	78.2	Selma City	Selma
9	75.8	Anniston City	Anniston
10	75.2	Conecuh County	Evergreen
11	74.5	Bessemer City	Bessemer
12	73.8	Dallas County	Selma
12	73.8	Pike County	Troy
14	69.6	Choctaw County	Butler
15	68.0	Hale County	Greensboro
16	65.4	Birmingham City	Birmingham
17	62.8	Macon County	Tuskegee
18	62.5	Butler County	Greenville
19	62.2	Fairfield City	Fairfield
20	61.6	Gadsden City	Gadsden
21	60.6	Pickens County	Carrollton
22	60.1	Clarke County	Grove Hill
23	60.0	Russell County	Phenix City
24	58.4	Escambia County	Brewton
24	58.4	Mobile County	Mobile
26	58.1	Montgomery County	Montgomery
27	57.7	Talladega City	Talladega
28	56.8	Chambers County	Lafayette
29	56.5	Henry County	Abbeville
30	56.4	Phenix City	Phenix City
31	54.9	Monroe County	Monroeville
31	54.9	Tuscaloosa City	Tuscaloosa
33	52.2	Talladega County	Talladega
34	52.0	Opelika City	Opelika
35	51.2	Coosa County	Rockford
36	51.1	Crenshaw County	Luverne
37	50.4	Eufaula City	Eufaula
37	50.4	Troy City	Troy
39	49.6	Washington County	Chatom
40	49.4	Demopolis City	Demopolis
41	49.3	Bibb County	Centreville
42	49.0	Colbert County	Tuscumbia
43	48.9	Florence City	Florence
44	47.5	Dothan City	Dothan
45	45.9	Geneva County	Geneva
46	45.4	Winston County	Double Springs
47	45.1	Clay County	Ashland
47	45.1	Russellville City	Russellville
49	45.0	Jackson County	Scottsboro
50	44.7	Dekalb County	Rainsville
51	44.6	Franklin County	Russellville
52	44.4	Thomasville City	Thomasville
53	44.2	Randolph County	Wedowee
54	44.1	Marshall County	Guntersville
55	44.0	Dale County	Ozark
56	43.1	Albertville City	Albertville
57	42.9	Tallapoosa County	Dadeville
58	42.8	Attalla City	Attalla
58	42.8	Walker County	Jasper
60	41.8	Cleburne County	Heflin
60	41.8	Covington County	Andalusia
62	41.4	Ozark City	Ozark
63	40.9	Lawrence County	Moulton
64	40.8	Decatur City	Decatur
64	40.8	Sylacauga City	Sylacauga
66	40.5	Andalusia City	Andalusia
67	40.3	Daleville City	Daleville
68	39.7	Fort Payne City	Fort Payne
69	39.6	Alexander City	Alexander City
70	39.5	Haleyville City	Haleyville
71	39.0	Lamar County	Vernon
72	38.8	Marion County	Hamilton
72	38.8	Tallassee City	Tallassee
74	38.5	Calhoun County	Anniston
75	37.9	Cullman County	Cullman
75	37.9	Pell City	Pell City
77	37.2	Chilton County	Clanton
78	36.0	Huntsville City	Huntsville
79	35.8	Cherokee County	Centre
80	34.1	Coffee County	Elba
80	34.1	Lee County	Opelika
82	33.5	Blount County	Oneonta
83	33.3	Elmore County	Wetumpka
84	33.2	Tuscaloosa County	Tuscaloosa
85	32.9	Houston County	Dothan
86	32.8	Fayette County	Fayette
87	31.7	Guntersville City	Guntersville
88	31.4	Jacksonville City	Jacksonville
89	31.0	Autauga County	Prattville
90	30.6	Morgan County	Decatur
90	30.6	Oxford City	Oxford
92	29.9	Athens City	Athens
93	29.0	Etowah County	Gadsden
93	29.0	Scottsboro City	Scottsboro
95	28.8	Enterprise City	Enterprise
96	28.7	Jasper City	Jasper
97	28.3	St Clair County	Ashville
98	26.7	Baldwin County	Bay Minette
99	25.4	Lauderdale County	Florence
100	24.9	Limestone County	Athens
101	23.8	Jefferson County	Birmingham
102	23.0	Auburn City	Auburn
103	20.5	Cullman City	Cullman
104	18.4	Muscle Shoals City	Muscle Shoals
105	18.0	Shelby County	Columbiana
106	17.3	Madison County	Huntsville
107	16.9	Hartselle City	Hartselle
108	16.7	Arab City	Arab
109	15.9	Homewood City	Homewood
110	12.1	Madison City	Madison
111	9.7	Hoover City	Hoover
112	2.8	Vestavia Hills City	Birmingham
113	0.0	Mountain Brook City	Mountain Brook

Students Eligible for Reduced-Price Lunch

Rank	Percent	District Name	City
1	16.4	Winston County	Double Springs
2	14.9	Franklin County	Russellville
3	13.9	Clay County	Ashland
4	13.2	Coosa County	Rockford
4	13.2	Jackson County	Scottsboro
6	13.0	Lawrence County	Moulton
7	12.9	Cullman County	Cullman
8	12.7	Attalla City	Attalla
8	12.7	Crenshaw County	Luverne
10	12.6	Escambia County	Brewton
10	12.6	Talladega County	Talladega
12	12.3	Coffee County	Elba
13	12.0	Pike County	Troy
14	11.9	Bibb County	Centreville
14	11.9	Cleburne County	Heflin
16	11.7	Walker County	Jasper
17	11.5	Colbert County	Tuscumbia
18	11.4	Covington County	Andalusia
19	11.2	Butler County	Greenville
19	11.2	Dekalb County	Rainsville
21	11.0	Etowah County	Gadsden
22	10.9	Russell County	Phenix City
23	10.8	Choctaw County	Butler
24	10.7	Marshall County	Guntersville
25	10.5	Blount County	Oneonta
25	10.5	Calhoun County	Anniston
25	10.5	Henry County	Abbeville
28	10.3	Marion County	Hamilton
29	10.2	Haleyville City	Haleyville
29	10.2	Houston County	Dothan
31	10.1	Chilton County	Clanton
32	10.0	Monroe County	Monroeville
32	10.0	Washington County	Chatom
34	9.9	Cherokee County	Centre
34	9.9	Fayette County	Fayette
36	9.7	Demopolis City	Demopolis
37	9.6	Conecuh County	Evergreen
37	9.6	Morgan County	Decatur
37	9.6	Pickens County	Carrollton
40	9.5	Randolph County	Wedowee
41	9.4	Daleville City	Daleville
41	9.4	Mobile County	Mobile
43	9.2	Chambers County	Lafayette
43	9.2	Lee County	Opelika
43	9.2	St Clair County	Ashville
43	9.2	Tuscaloosa County	Tuscaloosa
47	9.1	Dale County	Ozark
47	9.1	Geneva County	Geneva
49	9.0	Clarke County	Grove Hill
49	9.0	Talladega City	Talladega
51	8.5	Fairfield City	Fairfield
51	8.5	Lamar County	Vernon
53	8.4	Eufaula City	Eufaula
54	8.3	Elmore County	Wetumpka
54	8.3	Lauderdale County	Florence
56	8.2	Baldwin County	Bay Minette
56	8.2	Russellville City	Russellville

Rank	Ratio	District Name	City
58	8.0	Jacksonville City	Jacksonville
59	7.9	Muscle Shoals City	Muscle Shoals
60	7.8	Autauga County	Prattville
60	7.8	Hale County	Greensboro
60	7.8	Limestone County	Athens
60	7.8	Scottsboro City	Scottsboro
60	7.8	Tallassee City	Tallassee
65	7.7	Fort Payne City	Fort Payne
65	7.7	Gadsden City	Gadsden
65	7.7	Opelika City	Opelika
68	7.6	Greene County	Eutaw
68	7.6	Jefferson County	Birmingham
70	7.4	Albertville City	Albertville
70	7.4	Dallas County	Selma
72	7.3	Thomasville City	Thomasville
73	7.2	Enterprise City	Enterprise
73	7.2	Tuscaloosa City	Tuscaloosa
75	7.1	Bessemer City	Bessemer
75	7.1	Birmingham City	Birmingham
75	7.1	Pell City	Pell City
75	7.1	Phenix City	Phenix City
79	7.0	Bullock County	Union Springs
79	7.0	Selma City	Selma
81	6.9	Ozark City	Ozark
82	6.7	Decatur City	Decatur
82	6.7	Oxford City	Oxford
82	6.7	Tallapoosa County	Dadeville
85	6.6	Montgomery County	Montgomery
86	6.5	Alexander City	Alexander City
86	6.5	Homewood City	Homewood
88	6.4	Athens City	Athens
89	6.3	Madison County	Huntsville
89	6.3	Sylacauga City	Sylacauga
91	6.2	Huntsville City	Huntsville
92	6.1	Andalusia City	Andalusia
92	6.1	Dothan City	Dothan
92	6.1	Florence City	Florence
95	5.8	Auburn City	Auburn
95	5.8	Macon County	Tuskegee
97	5.5	Cullman City	Cullman
97	5.5	Jasper City	Jasper
97	5.5	Marengo County	Linden
100	5.4	Arab City	Arab
100	5.4	Hartselle City	Hartselle
102	5.3	Lowndes County	Hayneville
103	5.2	Anniston City	Anniston
103	5.2	Shelby County	Columbiana
105	4.8	Guntersville City	Guntersville
105	4.8	Sumter County	Livingston
107	4.7	Troy City	Troy
108	3.7	Hoover City	Hoover
108	3.7	Madison City	Madison
110	3.5	Perry County	Marion
111	1.3	Vestavia Hills City	Birmingham
112	1.0	Wilcox County	Camden
113	0.0	Mountain Brook City	Mountain Brook

Student/Teacher Ratio

Rank	Ratio	District Name	City
1	17.6	Blount County	Oneonta
2	17.0	Dothan City	Dothan
2	17.0	Jacksonville City	Jacksonville
4	16.6	Pell City	Pell City
5	16.5	Butler County	Greenville
5	16.5	Dallas County	Selma
5	16.5	Madison County	Huntsville
5	16.5	Talladega County	Talladega
9	16.4	Elmore County	Wetumpka
9	16.4	Phenix City	Phenix City
11	16.3	Houston County	Dothan
11	16.3	Madison City	Madison
13	16.2	Autauga County	Prattville
14	16.1	Crenshaw County	Luverne
14	16.1	Lawrence County	Moulton
14	16.1	Troy City	Troy
17	16.0	Fort Payne City	Fort Payne
17	16.0	Selma City	Selma
19	15.9	Russell County	Phenix City
19	15.9	Tallassee City	Tallassee
21	15.8	Albertville City	Albertville
21	15.8	Anniston City	Anniston
21	15.8	Perry County	Marion
24	15.7	Fayette County	Fayette
24	15.7	Henry County	Abbeville
24	15.7	Jefferson County	Birmingham
24	15.7	St Clair County	Ashville
28	15.6	Alexander City	Alexander City
28	15.6	Cherokee County	Centre
28	15.6	Lowndes County	Hayneville
28	15.6	Randolph County	Wedowee
28	15.6	Tuscaloosa County	Tuscaloosa
33	15.5	Arab City	Arab
33	15.5	Bessemer City	Bessemer
33	15.5	Clarke County	Grove Hill
33	15.5	Lauderdale County	Florence
33	15.5	Oxford City	Oxford
33	15.5	Russellville City	Russellville
39	15.4	Bibb County	Centreville
39	15.4	Birmingham City	Birmingham
39	15.4	Coosa County	Rockford
39	15.4	Cullman County	Cullman
39	15.4	Enterprise City	Enterprise
39	15.4	Hartselle City	Hartselle
39	15.4	Macon County	Tuskegee
39	15.4	Wilcox County	Camden
47	15.3	Andalusia City	Andalusia
47	15.3	Calhoun County	Anniston
47	15.3	Covington County	Andalusia
47	15.3	Mobile County	Mobile
47	15.3	Ozark City	Ozark
47	15.3	Washington County	Chatom
53	15.2	Chambers County	Lafayette
54	15.1	Cleburne County	Heflin
54	15.1	Lee County	Opelika
54	15.1	Marengo County	Linden
54	15.1	Muscle Shoals City	Muscle Shoals
58	15.0	Bullock County	Union Springs
58	15.0	Chilton County	Clanton
58	15.0	Cullman City	Cullman
58	15.0	Dale County	Ozark
58	15.0	Eufaula City	Eufaula
58	15.0	Jasper City	Jasper
58	15.0	Marshall County	Guntersville
58	15.0	Montgomery County	Montgomery
58	15.0	Tuscaloosa City	Tuscaloosa
58	15.0	Walker County	Jasper
68	14.9	Conecuh County	Evergreen
68	14.9	Demopolis City	Demopolis
68	14.9	Pickens County	Carrollton
68	14.9	Tallapoosa County	Dadeville
72	14.8	Attalla City	Attalla
72	14.8	Coffee County	Elba
72	14.8	Limestone County	Athens
72	14.8	Marion County	Hamilton
72	14.8	Pike County	Troy
77	14.7	Sylacauga City	Sylacauga
78	14.6	Auburn City	Auburn
78	14.6	Daleville City	Daleville
78	14.6	Lamar County	Vernon
78	14.6	Monroe County	Monroeville
82	14.5	Escambia County	Brewton
82	14.5	Winston County	Double Springs
84	14.4	Colbert County	Tuscumbia
84	14.4	Dekalb County	Rainsville
84	14.4	Geneva County	Geneva
84	14.4	Sumter County	Livingston
88	14.3	Choctaw County	Butler
88	14.3	Hale County	Greensboro
88	14.3	Hoover City	Hoover
88	14.3	Scottsboro City	Scottsboro
92	14.2	Decatur City	Decatur
92	14.2	Etowah County	Gadsden
92	14.2	Shelby County	Columbiana
95	14.1	Huntsville City	Huntsville
95	14.1	Jackson County	Scottsboro
95	14.1	Opelika City	Opelika
95	14.1	Talladega City	Talladega
99	14.0	Baldwin County	Bay Minette
99	14.0	Vestavia Hills City	Birmingham
101	13.9	Fairfield City	Fairfield
101	13.9	Greene County	Eutaw
101	13.9	Haleyville City	Haleyville
101	13.9	Thomasville City	Thomasville
105	13.8	Clay County	Ashland
105	13.8	Morgan County	Decatur
107	13.7	Franklin County	Russellville
107	13.7	Gadsden City	Gadsden
109	13.6	Guntersville City	Guntersville
110	13.3	Florence City	Florence
111	13.1	Athens City	Athens
112	12.6	Homewood City	Homewood
113	12.4	Mountain Brook City	Mountain Brook

Student/Librarian Ratio

Rank	Ratio	District Name	City
1	942.2	Jacksonville City	Jacksonville
2	930.3	Oxford City	Oxford
3	862.0	Haleyville City	Haleyville
4	827.7	Autauga County	Prattville
5	795.0	Troy City	Troy
6	775.3	Lee County	Opelika
7	760.9	Madison City	Madison
8	746.5	Hoover City	Hoover
9	729.5	Elmore County	Wetumpka
10	709.8	Alexander City	Alexander City
11	690.3	Jefferson County	Birmingham
12	680.9	Madison County	Huntsville
13	676.3	Clay County	Ashland
14	664.3	Cullman City	Cullman
15	663.0	Shelby County	Columbiana
16	654.0	Vestavia Hills City	Birmingham
17	653.6	Homewood City	Homewood
18	646.8	Franklin County	Russellville
19	635.3	Tallassee City	Tallassee
20	634.5	Muscle Shoals City	Muscle Shoals
21	628.9	Randolph County	Wedowee
22	618.2	Cherokee County	Centre
23	616.9	Mobile County	Mobile
24	616.2	Tallapoosa County	Dadeville
25	614.0	Hartselle City	Hartselle
26	612.3	Crenshaw County	Luverne
27	611.9	Lauderdale County	Florence
28	602.6	Tuscaloosa City	Tuscaloosa
29	598.2	Houston County	Dothan
30	595.4	Blount County	Oneonta
31	592.8	Butler County	Greenville
32	592.7	Mountain Brook City	Mountain Brook
33	590.8	Monroe County	Monroeville
34	590.7	Florence City	Florence
35	587.6	Marengo County	Linden
36	586.0	Russellville City	Russellville
37	584.5	Sylacauga City	Sylacauga
38	580.9	Cullman County	Cullman
39	580.6	Eufaula City	Eufaula
40	565.6	Baldwin County	Bay Minette
41	563.8	Demopolis City	Demopolis
42	551.7	Montgomery County	Montgomery
43	549.3	Thomasville City	Thomasville
44	546.4	Jasper City	Jasper
45	545.2	Fort Payne City	Fort Payne
46	542.0	Perry County	Marion
47	541.0	Arab City	Arab
48	540.2	Covington County	Andalusia
49	539.3	Coosa County	Rockford
50	537.6	Tuscaloosa County	Tuscaloosa
51	535.9	Limestone County	Athens
52	530.5	Calhoun County	Anniston
53	529.3	Phenix City	Phenix City
54	527.3	Daleville City	Daleville
55	526.1	Chilton County	Clanton
56	524.6	Morgan County	Decatur
57	517.3	Albertville City	Albertville
58	514.5	Bessemer City	Bessemer
59	504.4	Auburn City	Auburn
60	502.0	Huntsville City	Huntsville
61	498.8	Pell City	Pell City
62	494.4	Lamar County	Vernon
63	492.3	Dekalb County	Rainsville
64	489.9	Enterprise City	Enterprise
65	488.9	St Clair County	Ashville
66	488.4	Chambers County	Lafayette
67	487.2	Birmingham City	Birmingham
68	484.9	Henry County	Abbeville
69	482.0	Talladega County	Talladega
70	478.3	Lawrence County	Moulton
71	476.7	Washington County	Chatom
72	474.7	Cleburne County	Heflin
73	474.1	Opelika City	Opelika
74	470.6	Fairfield City	Fairfield
75	467.4	Decatur City	Decatur
76	466.8	Coffee County	Elba
77	465.8	Walker County	Jasper
78	465.2	Dothan City	Dothan
79	463.0	Ozark City	Ozark
80	460.6	Clarke County	Grove Hill
81	459.3	Scottsboro City	Scottsboro
82	458.8	Russell County	Phenix City
83	457.9	Marion County	Hamilton
84	455.8	Attalla City	Attalla
85	455.7	Etowah County	Gadsden
86	455.0	Bullock County	Union Springs
87	453.7	Geneva County	Geneva
88	450.8	Guntersville City	Guntersville
89	442.7	Fayette County	Fayette
90	441.0	Dale County	Ozark
91	437.6	Escambia County	Brewton
92	423.8	Andalusia City	Andalusia
93	420.1	Macon County	Tuskegee
94	417.8	Sumter County	Livingston
95	416.3	Jackson County	Scottsboro
96	416.0	Pike County	Troy
97	416.0	Bibb County	Centreville
98	414.6	Pickens County	Carrollton
99	413.5	Wilcox County	Camden
100	408.8	Greene County	Eutaw
101	408.1	Colbert County	Tuscumbia
102	407.5	Dallas County	Selma

Rank		District Name	City
103	407.3	Talladega City	Talladega
104	402.5	Lowndes County	Hayneville
105	399.1	Gadsden City	Gadsden
106	398.0	Hale County	Greensboro
107	397.1	Marshall County	Guntersville
108	390.4	Choctaw County	Butler
109	389.7	Selma City	Selma
110	386.0	Athens City	Athens
111	378.9	Anniston City	Anniston
112	344.4	Winston County	Double Springs
113	231.6	Conecuh County	Evergreen

Student/Counselor Ratio

Rank	Ratio	District Name	City
1	720.8	Madison City	Madison
2	683.5	Dale County	Ozark
3	635.3	Tallassee City	Tallassee
4	600.8	Elmore County	Wetumpka
5	596.4	Choctaw County	Butler
6	595.8	Washington County	Chatom
7	595.4	Blount County	Oneonta
8	592.7	Mountain Brook City	Mountain Brook
9	590.6	Oxford City	Oxford
10	586.0	Russellville City	Russellville
11	584.4	Cullman County	Cullman
12	580.6	Eufaula City	Eufaula
13	574.7	Haleyville City	Haleyville
14	574.0	Winston County	Double Springs
15	567.7	Morgan County	Decatur
16	556.2	Jefferson County	Birmingham
17	549.5	Chambers County	Lafayette
18	547.2	Fairfield City	Fairfield
19	545.2	Fort Payne City	Fort Payne
20	543.3	St Clair County	Ashville
21	542.0	Perry County	Marion
22	538.6	Hartselle City	Hartselle
23	531.2	Fayette County	Fayette
24	527.3	Daleville City	Daleville
24	527.3	Dallas County	Selma
26	525.4	Jackson County	Scottsboro
27	518.5	Tuscaloosa County	Tuscaloosa
28	517.3	Albertville City	Albertville
29	514.5	Bessemer City	Bessemer
30	514.1	Clarke County	Grove Hill
31	510.9	Chilton County	Clanton
32	507.6	Muscle Shoals City	Muscle Shoals
33	507.3	Clay County	Ashland
34	501.1	Demopolis City	Demopolis
35	501.0	Calhoun County	Anniston
36	498.8	Pell City	Pell City
37	489.6	Lee County	Opelika
38	486.4	Lawrence County	Moulton
39	485.1	Houston County	Dothan
40	477.0	Troy City	Troy
41	475.7	Marion County	Hamilton
42	475.6	Birmingham City	Birmingham
43	474.7	Cleburne County	Heflin
44	474.1	Opelika City	Opelika
45	472.6	Macon County	Tuskegee
46	467.6	Sylacauga City	Sylacauga
47	466.9	Autauga County	Prattville
48	463.3	Conecuh County	Evergreen
49	462.7	Mobile County	Mobile
50	462.1	Crenshaw County	Luverne
51	458.8	Russell County	Phenix City
52	458.5	Montgomery County	Montgomery
53	456.5	Covington County	Andalusia
54	453.7	Geneva County	Geneva
55	453.6	Talladega County	Talladega
56	452.0	Cherokee County	Centre
57	451.9	Tallapoosa County	Dadeville
58	450.8	Arab City	Arab
58	450.8	Guntersville City	Guntersville
60	447.1	Franklin County	Russellville
61	446.6	Limestone County	Athens
62	445.4	Tuscaloosa City	Tuscaloosa
63	444.5	Henry County	Abbeville
64	442.8	Cullman City	Cullman
65	442.0	Anniston City	Anniston
66	441.1	Phenix City	Phenix City
67	439.1	Dekalb County	Rainsville
67	439.1	Hoover City	Hoover
67	439.1	Lowndes County	Hayneville
70	437.7	Shelby County	Columbiana
71	434.6	Enterprise City	Enterprise
71	434.6	Hale County	Greensboro
73	433.9	Gadsden City	Gadsden
74	426.1	Etowah County	Gadsden
74	426.1	Monroe County	Monroeville
76	425.6	Madison County	Huntsville
77	424.0	Jacksonville City	Jacksonville
78	423.8	Andalusia City	Andalusia
79	420.9	Dothan City	Dothan
80	420.6	Walker County	Jasper
81	420.2	Baldwin County	Bay Minette
82	419.3	Randolph County	Wedowee
83	416.6	Pike County	Troy
84	416.0	Bibb County	Centreville
85	415.0	Decatur City	Decatur
86	413.5	Florence City	Florence
86	413.5	Wilcox County	Camden
88	412.0	Lamar County	Vernon
89	408.8	Greene County	Eutaw
90	407.3	Talladega City	Talladega
91	404.9	Sumter County	Livingston
92	403.3	Lauderdale County	Florence
93	402.5	Vestavia Hills City	Birmingham
94	396.9	Ozark City	Ozark
94	396.9	Selma City	Selma
96	395.2	Butler County	Greenville
97	394.9	Pickens County	Carrollton
98	387.3	Marengo County	Linden
99	375.1	Marshall County	Guntersville
100	366.2	Thomasville City	Thomasville
101	364.6	Attalla City	Attalla
102	364.0	Bullock County	Union Springs
103	362.8	Colbert County	Tuscumbia
104	360.8	Auburn City	Auburn
105	357.9	Scottsboro City	Scottsboro
106	354.9	Alexander City	Alexander City
107	344.9	Huntsville City	Huntsville
108	341.5	Jasper City	Jasper
109	337.8	Athens City	Athens
110	333.0	Escambia County	Brewton
111	327.5	Coffee County	Elba
112	326.8	Homewood City	Homewood
113	299.6	Coosa County	Rockford

Current Spending per Student in FY2003

Rank	Dollars	District Name	City
1	8,358	Homewood City	Homewood
2	8,349	Mountain Brook City	Mountain Brook
3	8,011	Florence City	Florence
4	7,941	Lowndes County	Hayneville
5	7,598	Hoover City	Hoover
6	7,386	Athens City	Athens
7	7,273	Auburn City	Auburn
8	7,234	Pike County	Troy
9	7,222	Decatur City	Decatur
10	7,190	Wilcox County	Camden
11	7,182	Tuscaloosa City	Tuscaloosa
12	7,179	Opelika City	Opelika
13	7,164	Huntsville City	Huntsville
14	7,125	Anniston City	Anniston
15	7,090	Morgan County	Decatur
16	7,049	Lamar County	Vernon
17	7,026	Scottsboro City	Scottsboro
18	7,007	Walker County	Jasper
19	6,996	Sumter County	Livingston
20	6,914	Henry County	Abbeville
21	6,892	Greene County	Eutaw
22	6,890	Birmingham City	Birmingham
23	6,888	Winston County	Double Springs
24	6,848	Vestavia Hills City	Birmingham
25	6,832	Shelby County	Columbiana
26	6,795	Muscle Shoals City	Muscle Shoals
27	6,773	Conecuh County	Evergreen
28	6,756	Franklin County	Russellville
29	6,729	Guntersville City	Guntersville
30	6,727	Baldwin County	Bay Minette
31	6,710	Gadsden City	Gadsden
32	6,676	Sylacauga City	Sylacauga
33	6,675	Escambia County	Brewton
34	6,649	Dothan City	Dothan
35	6,628	Perry County	Marion
36	6,627	Colbert County	Tuscumbia
37	6,626	Jasper City	Jasper
38	6,607	Talladega City	Talladega
39	6,606	Marengo County	Linden
40	6,593	Choctaw County	Butler
41	6,588	Pickens County	Carrollton
42	6,583	Bullock County	Union Springs
43	6,571	Bessemer City	Bessemer
44	6,497	Fairfield City	Fairfield
45	6,481	Phenix City	Phenix City
46	6,469	Selma City	Selma
47	6,460	Lawrence County	Moulton
48	6,444	Dallas County	Selma
49	6,403	Eufaula City	Eufaula
50	6,382	Dekalb County	Rainsville
51	6,376	Jackson County	Scottsboro
52	6,369	Marshall County	Guntersville
53	6,353	Ozark City	Ozark
54	6,340	Tallapoosa County	Dadeville
55	6,326	Clarke County	Grove Hill
56	6,317	Crenshaw County	Luverne
57	6,308	Coosa County	Rockford
58	6,305	Alexander City	Alexander City
58	6,305	Mobile County	Mobile
60	6,273	Hartselle City	Hartselle
61	6,271	Hale County	Greensboro
62	6,267	Butler County	Greenville
63	6,245	Dale County	Ozark
64	6,241	Fayette County	Fayette
65	6,238	Andalusia City	Andalusia
66	6,231	Russellville City	Russellville
67	6,224	Russell County	Phenix City
68	6,221	Limestone County	Athens
69	6,195	Cullman City	Cullman
70	6,187	Bibb County	Centreville
71	6,163	Attalla City	Attalla
72	6,146	Enterprise City	Enterprise
73	6,143	Macon County	Tuskegee
74	6,142	Talladega County	Talladega
75	6,120	Clay County	Ashland
76	6,112	Cherokee County	Centre
77	6,107	Monroe County	Monroeville
78	6,106	Montgomery County	Montgomery
79	6,054	Washington County	Chatom
80	6,016	Lauderdale County	Florence
81	6,011	Troy City	Troy
82	6,008	Coffee County	Elba
83	6,006	Calhoun County	Anniston
84	6,001	Marion County	Hamilton
85	5,991	Lee County	Opelika
86	5,981	Covington County	Andalusia
87	5,953	Randolph County	Wedowee
88	5,933	Thomasville City	Thomasville
89	5,932	Madison City	Huntsville
90	5,931	Jefferson County	Birmingham
91	5,922	Fort Payne City	Fort Payne
92	5,908	Albertville City	Albertville
93	5,902	Tuscaloosa County	Tuscaloosa
94	5,892	Arab City	Arab
95	5,885	Cullman County	Cullman
96	5,865	Madison County	Huntsville
97	5,851	Chilton County	Clanton
98	5,851	Oxford City	Oxford
99	5,849	Cleburne County	Heflin
100	5,838	Jacksonville City	Jacksonville
101	5,810	Daleville City	Daleville
102	5,794	Etowah County	Gadsden
103	5,776	Pell City	Pell City
104	5,749	Chambers County	Lafayette
105	5,733	Demopolis City	Demopolis
106	5,727	Haleyville City	Haleyville
107	5,664	Geneva County	Geneva
108	5,594	Houston County	Dothan
109	5,573	Elmore County	Wetumpka
110	5,455	Blount County	Oneonta
111	5,453	St Clair County	Ashville
112	5,378	Tallassee City	Tallassee
113	5,293	Autauga County	Prattville

Number of Diploma Recipients

Rank	Number	District Name	City
1	2,854	Mobile County	Mobile
2	2,278	Jefferson County	Birmingham
3	1,706	Birmingham City	Birmingham
4	1,607	Montgomery County	Montgomery
5	1,146	Huntsville City	Huntsville
6	1,093	Baldwin County	Bay Minette
7	1,040	Shelby County	Columbiana
8	813	Madison County	Huntsville
9	753	Tuscaloosa County	Tuscaloosa
10	660	Hoover City	Hoover
11	513	Lauderdale County	Florence
12	465	Cullman County	Cullman
13	462	Dothan City	Dothan
14	451	Calhoun County	Anniston
15	436	Etowah County	Gadsden
16	430	Elmore County	Wetumpka
17	409	Madison City	Madison
18	406	Decatur City	Decatur
19	405	Autauga County	Prattville
20	402	Lee County	Opelika
21	384	Limestone County	Athens
22	383	Tuscaloosa City	Tuscaloosa
23	381	Morgan County	Decatur
24	372	Dekalb County	Rainsville
25	344	Walker County	Jasper
26	343	Lawrence County	Moulton
26	343	Vestavia Hills City	Birmingham
28	341	Talladega County	Talladega
29	330	St Clair County	Ashville
30	329	Chilton County	Clanton

Rank		District Name	City
31	323	Houston County	Dothan
32	318	Enterprise City	Enterprise
33	313	Blount County	Oneonta
34	281	Marshall County	Guntersville
35	277	Florence City	Florence
35	277	Jackson County	Scottsboro
37	268	Auburn City	Auburn
38	262	Mountain Brook City	Mountain Brook
39	257	Gadsden City	Gadsden
40	248	Monroe County	Monroeville
41	231	Homewood City	Homewood
42	230	Escambia County	Brewton
43	229	Dallas County	Selma
44	218	Opelika City	Opelika
45	214	Pickens County	Carrollton
46	200	Washington County	Chatom
47	199	Chambers County	Lafayette
48	191	Arab City	Arab
49	190	Marion County	Hamilton
50	185	Oxford City	Oxford
50	185	Pell City	Pell City
52	181	Cullman City	Cullman
53	177	Tallapoosa County	Dadeville
54	176	Clarke County	Grove Hill
55	171	Hartselle City	Hartselle
56	168	Alexander City	Alexander City
56	168	Butler County	Greenville
58	167	Cherokee County	Centre
58	167	Jasper City	Jasper
60	164	Selma City	Selma
61	162	Hale County	Greensboro
62	161	Ozark City	Ozark
63	160	Winston County	Double Springs
64	154	Eufaula City	Eufaula
65	153	Macon County	Tuskegee
66	150	Talladega City	Talladega
67	149	Clay County	Ashland
67	149	Scottsboro City	Scottsboro
69	147	Athens City	Athens
70	146	Phenix City	Phenix City
71	145	Fayette County	Fayette
72	144	Lamar County	Vernon
73	143	Geneva County	Geneva
73	143	Sumter County	Livingston
75	140	Albertville City	Albertville
75	140	Dale County	Ozark
77	137	Muscle Shoals City	Muscle Shoals
78	136	Fort Payne City	Fort Payne
79	132	Covington County	Andalusia
79	132	Franklin County	Russellville
81	131	Bibb County	Centreville
81	131	Lowndes County	Hayneville
83	130	Fairfield City	Fairfield
84	129	Crenshaw County	Luverne
85	128	Sylacauga City	Sylacauga
86	126	Wilcox County	Camden
87	124	Cleburne County	Heflin
87	124	Henry County	Abbeville
89	121	Russell County	Phenix City
90	120	Perry County	Marion
91	116	Colbert County	Tuscumbia
92	113	Andalusia City	Andalusia
93	110	Bullock County	Union Springs
93	110	Russellville City	Russellville
95	109	Attalla City	Attalla
95	109	Bessemer City	Bessemer
97	107	Troy City	Troy
98	106	Demopolis City	Demopolis
99	105	Coffee County	Elba
100	104	Choctaw County	Butler
100	104	Haleyville City	Haleyville
102	94	Tallassee City	Tallassee
103	93	Guntersville City	Guntersville
104	90	Daleville City	Daleville
104	90	Jacksonville City	Jacksonville
106	88	Marengo County	Linden
107	87	Thomasville City	Thomasville
108	84	Randolph County	Wedowee
109	80	Pike County	Troy
110	77	Anniston City	Anniston
111	73	Coosa County	Rockford
112	68	Greene County	Eutaw
113	58	Conecuh County	Evergreen

High School Drop-out Rate

Rank	Percent	District Name	City
1	11.7	Anniston City	Anniston
2	11.0	Greene County	Eutaw
3	9.5	Alexander City	Alexander City
4	7.7	Pell City	Pell City
5	7.5	Russell County	Phenix City
6	7.3	Dale County	Ozark
6	7.3	Dallas County	Selma
8	6.8	Tallassee City	Tallassee
9	6.4	Conecuh County	Evergreen
10	6.2	Colbert County	Tuscumbia
11	6.1	Henry County	Abbeville
12	6.0	Franklin County	Russellville
13	5.9	Ozark City	Ozark
14	5.8	Butler County	Greenville
14	5.8	Eufaula City	Eufaula
16	5.7	Dothan City	Dothan
16	5.7	Elmore County	Wetumpka
18	5.6	Marshall County	Guntersville
18	5.6	Talladega County	Talladega
20	5.4	Attalla City	Attalla
20	5.4	Autauga County	Prattville
22	5.3	Morgan County	Decatur
23	5.2	Cullman County	Cullman
24	5.1	Blount County	Oneonta
24	5.1	Walker County	Jasper
26	5.0	Athens City	Athens
26	5.0	Cherokee County	Centre
26	5.0	Tuscaloosa City	Tuscaloosa
29	4.9	Fort Payne City	Fort Payne
29	4.9	Madison County	Huntsville
29	4.9	Talladega City	Talladega
32	4.8	Fayette County	Fayette
32	4.8	Hartselle City	Hartselle
34	4.7	Wilcox County	Camden
35	4.6	Pike County	Troy
35	4.6	Tallapoosa County	Dadeville
37	4.5	Coffee County	Elba
37	4.5	Jackson County	Scottsboro
37	4.5	Pickens County	Carrollton
40	4.4	Florence City	Florence
40	4.4	Geneva County	Geneva
40	4.4	Montgomery County	Montgomery
43	4.3	Bullock County	Union Springs
43	4.3	Chambers County	Lafayette
43	4.3	Coosa County	Rockford
43	4.3	Dekalb County	Rainsville
43	4.3	Phenix City	Phenix City
48	4.1	Jefferson County	Birmingham
49	4.0	Choctaw County	Butler
49	4.0	Cleburne County	Heflin
49	4.0	Crenshaw County	Luverne
49	4.0	Gadsden City	Gadsden
49	4.0	Limestone County	Athens
49	4.0	Marion County	Hamilton
49	4.0	Mobile County	Mobile
56	3.9	Escambia County	Brewton
57	3.8	Calhoun County	Anniston
57	3.8	Covington County	Andalusia
59	3.7	Tuscaloosa County	Tuscaloosa
60	3.5	Haleyville City	Haleyville
60	3.5	Macon County	Tuskegee
62	3.3	Arab City	Arab
62	3.3	Guntersville City	Guntersville
62	3.3	Perry County	Marion
62	3.3	Scottsboro City	Scottsboro
66	3.2	Hale County	Greensboro
67	3.1	Baldwin County	Bay Minette
67	3.1	Huntsville City	Huntsville
67	3.1	Marengo County	Linden
67	3.1	Monroe County	Monroeville
71	3.0	Albertville City	Albertville
71	3.0	Andalusia City	Andalusia
71	3.0	St Clair County	Ashville
74	2.9	Enterprise City	Enterprise
74	2.9	Winston County	Double Springs
76	2.7	Etowah County	Gadsden
76	2.7	Jasper City	Jasper
76	2.7	Oxford City	Oxford
79	2.6	Houston County	Dothan
79	2.6	Lawrence County	Moulton
79	2.6	Randolph County	Wedowee
79	2.6	Shelby County	Columbiana
79	2.6	Sylacauga City	Sylacauga
84	2.5	Decatur City	Decatur
84	2.5	Lamar County	Vernon
86	2.4	Bibb County	Centreville
86	2.4	Chilton County	Clanton
86	2.4	Cullman City	Cullman
89	2.1	Birmingham City	Birmingham
89	2.1	Lee County	Opelika
91	2.0	Fairfield City	Fairfield
92	1.7	Daleville City	Daleville
92	1.7	Selma City	Selma
94	1.6	Clarke County	Grove Hill
95	1.5	Lowndes County	Hayneville
96	1.3	Clay County	Ashland
97	1.2	Bessemer City	Bessemer
97	1.2	Demopolis City	Demopolis
97	1.2	Hoover City	Hoover
97	1.2	Jacksonville City	Jacksonville
97	1.2	Muscle Shoals City	Muscle Shoals
102	1.1	Thomasville City	Thomasville
103	1.0	Washington County	Chatom
104	0.9	Sumter County	Livingston
105	0.7	Auburn City	Auburn
106	0.6	Homewood City	Homewood
106	0.6	Russellville City	Russellville
108	0.5	Opelika City	Opelika
108	0.5	Vestavia Hills City	Birmingham
110	0.3	Madison City	Madison
110	0.3	Troy City	Troy
112	0.1	Lauderdale County	Florence
112	0.1	Mountain Brook City	Mountain Brook

Alaska

Alaska Public School Educational Profile

Category	Value	Category	Value
Schools *(2003-2004)*	521	**Diploma Recipients** *(2002-2003)*	6,945
Instructional Level		White, Non-Hispanic	4,734
Primary	178	Black, Non-Hispanic	252
Middle	35	Asian/Pacific Islander	422
High	66	American Indian/Alaskan Native	1,340
Other Level	241	Hispanic	197
Curriculum		**High School Drop-out Rate** (%) *(2001-2002)*	8.1
Regular	492	White, Non-Hispanic	6.2
Special Education	3	Black, Non-Hispanic	11.4
Vocational	2	Asian/Pacific Islander	6.7
Alternative	23	American Indian/Alaskan Native	13.4
Type		Hispanic	8.9
Magnet	19	**Staff** *(2003-2004)*	
Charter	19	Teachers	7,807.5
Title I Eligible	345	Average Salary ($)	51,136
School-wide Title I	107	Librarians/Media Specialists	151.5
Students *(2003-2004)*	133,933	Guidance Counselors	273.5
Gender (%)		**Ratios** *(2003-2004)*	
Male	51.5	Student/Teacher Ratio	17.2 to 1
Female	48.5	Student/Librarian Ratio	884.0 to 1
Race/Ethnicity (%)		Student/Counselor Ratio	489.7 to 1
White, Non-Hispanic	58.9	**College Entrance Exam Scores** *(2005)*	
Black, Non-Hispanic	4.7	Scholastic Aptitude Test (SAT)	
Asian/Pacific Islander	6.5	Participation Rate (%)	52
American Indian/Alaskan Native	26.0	Mean SAT Reasoning Test Verbal Score	523
Hispanic	3.9	Mean SAT Reasoning Test Math Score	519
Classification (%)		American College Testing Program (ACT)	
Individual Education Program (IEP)	13.3	Participation Rate (%)	26
Migrant *(2002-2003)*	6.4	Average Composite Score	21.3
English Language Learner (ELL)	14.8	Average English Score	20.5
Eligible for Free Lunch Program	20.1	Average Math Score	21.3
Eligible for Reduced-Price Lunch Program	7.2	Average Reading Score	22.0
Current Spending *($ per student in FY 2003)*	9,919	Average Science Score	21.1
Instruction	5,728		
Support Services	3,856		

Note: *For an explanation of data, please refer to the User's Guide in the front of the book*

Alaska NAEP 2005 Test Scores

Reading			Mathematics		
Grade/Category	Value	Rank	Grade/Category	Value	Rank
4th Grade			**4th Grade**		
Average Proficiency	211.1 (1.35)	42/51	Average Proficiency	235.5 (1.03)	33/51
Proficiency by Gender/Race/Ethnicity			Proficiency by Gender/Race/Ethnicity		
Male	207.4 (1.61)	43/51	Male	235.8 (1.34)	35/51
Female	214.9 (1.74)	42/51	Female	235.2 (1.11)	33/51
White, Non-Hispanic	224.7 (1.27)	36/51	White, Non-Hispanic	243.9 (1.40)	30/51
Black, Non-Hispanic	212.0 (3.88)	1/42	Black, Non-Hispanic	225.7 (2.89)	7/42
Asian, Non-Hispanic	205.8 (3.98)	26/27	Asian, Non-Hispanic	238.1 (2.40)	22/25
American Indian, Non-Hispanic	182.9 (2.98)	7/7	American Indian, Non-Hispanic	219.7 (1.34)	6/7
Hispanic	209.4 (3.58)	12/40	Hispanic	227.3 (3.21)	17/41
Proficiency by Class Size			Proficiency by Class Size		
Less than 16 Students	186.5 (3.58)	32/34	Less than 16 Students	217.2 (2.77)	31/35
16 to 18 Students	187.6 (9.96)	32/33	16 to 18 Students	n/a	n/a
19 to 20 Students	n/a	n/a	19 to 20 Students	n/a	n/a
21 to 25 Students	218.1 (1.82)	35/51	21 to 25 Students	240.4 (1.91)	29/51
Greater than 25 Students	221.9 (1.86)	17/36	Greater than 25 Students	240.4 (1.62)	11/33
Percent Attaining Achievement Levels			Percent Attaining Achievement Levels		
Below Basic	41.9 (1.54)	11/51	Below Basic	23.1 (1.13)	16/51
Basic or Above	58.1 (1.54)	41/51	Basic or Above	76.9 (1.13)	36/51
Proficient or Above	26.7 (1.27)	37/51	Proficient or Above	33.7 (1.73)	34/51
Advanced or Above	5.3 (0.49)	41/51	Advanced or Above	4.5 (0.57)	26/51
8th Grade			**8th Grade**		
Average Proficiency	258.7 (0.87)	35/51	Average Proficiency	279.0 (0.79)	30/51
Proficiency by Gender/Race/Ethnicity			Proficiency by Gender/Race/Ethnicity		
Male	252.7 (1.23)	36/51	Male	280.1 (1.11)	28/51
Female	264.8 (1.01)	35/51	Female	277.7 (1.08)	31/51
White, Non-Hispanic	268.3 (0.90)	27/51	White, Non-Hispanic	288.4 (0.92)	23/51
Black, Non-Hispanic	248.9 (3.76)	7/40	Black, Non-Hispanic	266.2 (3.01)	1/41
Asian, Non-Hispanic	260.0 (2.38)	22/24	Asian, Non-Hispanic	269.8 (2.89)	22/23
American Indian, Non-Hispanic	239.5 (2.08)	8/9	American Indian, Non-Hispanic	264.0 (1.82)	4/10
Hispanic	253.8 (4.13)	6/38	Hispanic	271.8 (3.42)	1/38
Proficiency by Parents Highest Level of Ed.			Proficiency by Parents Highest Level of Ed.		
Did Not Finish High School	n/a	n/a	Did Not Finish High School	n/a	n/a
Graduated High School	n/a	n/a	Graduated High School	n/a	n/a
Some Education After High School	n/a	n/a	Some Education After High School	n/a	n/a
Graduated College	n/a	n/a	Graduated College	n/a	n/a
Percent Attaining Achievement Levels			Percent Attaining Achievement Levels		
Below Basic	41.9 (1.54)	11/51	Below Basic	31.1 (1.54)	22/51
Basic or Above	58.1 (1.54)	41/51	Basic or Above	68.9 (1.54)	30/51
Proficient or Above	26.7 (1.27)	37/51	Proficient or Above	28.7 (1.31)	32/51
Advanced or Above	5.3 (0.49)	41/51	Advanced or Above	5.8 (0.61)	20/51

Note: *For an explanation of data, please refer to the User's Guide in the front of the book; n/a indicates data not available*

Anchorage Borough

Anchorage SD
4600 Debarr Ave • Anchorage, AK 99519-6614
Mailing Address: PO Box 196614 • Anchorage, AK 99519-6614
(907) 742-4312 • http://www.asdk12.org/
Grade Span: PK-12; Agency Type: 1
Schools: 95
  64 Primary; 9 Middle; 13 High; 8 Other Level
  86 Regular; 3 Special Education; 1 Vocational; 4 Alternative
  11 Magnet; 5 Charter; 40 Title I Eligible; 13 School-wide Title I
Students: 49,722   (51.5% male; 48.4% female)
  Individual Education Program: 6,979 (14.0%);
  English Language Learner: 6,017 (12.1%); Migrant: 1,273 (2.6%)
  Eligible for Free Lunch Program: 7,641 (15.4%)
  Eligible for Reduced-Price Lunch Program: 2,865 (5.8%)
Teachers: 2,832.0 (17.6 to 1)
Librarians/Media Specialists: 75.5 (658.6 to 1)
Guidance Counselors: 96.0 (517.9 to 1)
Current Spending: ($ per student per year):
  Total: $7,826; Instruction: $4,638; Support Services: $2,960

Enrollment, Drop-out Rates and Diploma Recipients by Race/Ethnicity

Category	Total	White	Black	Asian	AIAN	Hisp.
Enrollment (%)	100.0	59.2	8.7	11.4	14.2	6.4
Drop-out Rate (%)	8.6	6.6	11.0	8.3	19.3	9.6
H.S. Diplomas (#)	2,505	1,763	174	255	196	117

Bethel Borough

Lower Kuskokwim SD
1004 Ron Edwards Way • Bethel, AK 99559-0305
Mailing Address: PO Box 305 • Bethel, AK 99559-0305
(907) 543-4810 • http://www.lksd.org/
Grade Span: PK-12; Agency Type: 1
Schools: 28
  3 Primary; 0 Middle; 1 High; 24 Other Level
  26 Regular; 0 Special Education; 0 Vocational; 2 Alternative
  1 Magnet; 1 Charter; 27 Title I Eligible; 0 School-wide Title I
Students: 3,816   (51.8% male; 48.1% female)
  Individual Education Program: 515 (13.5%);
  English Language Learner: 2,398 (62.8%); Migrant: 888 (23.3%)
  Eligible for Free Lunch Program: 1,917 (50.2%)
  Eligible for Reduced-Price Lunch Program: 353 (9.3%)
Teachers: 278.3 (13.7 to 1)
Librarians/Media Specialists: 3.0 (1,272.0 to 1)
Guidance Counselors: 2.5 (1,526.4 to 1)
Current Spending: ($ per student per year):
  Total: $17,048; Instruction: $9,234; Support Services: $6,892

Enrollment, Drop-out Rates and Diploma Recipients by Race/Ethnicity

Category	Total	White	Black	Asian	AIAN	Hisp.
Enrollment (%)	100.0	4.8	0.4	0.4	94.1	0.3
Drop-out Rate (%)	16.9	5.2	0.0	33.3	17.8	0.0
H.S. Diplomas (#)	118	11	0	3	104	0

Fairbanks North Star Borough

Fairbanks North Star Boro SD
520 Fifth Ave • Fairbanks, AK 99701-4756
(907) 452-2000 • http://www.northstar.k12.ak.us/
Grade Span: PK-12; Agency Type: 1
Schools: 33
  20 Primary; 4 Middle; 6 High; 3 Other Level
  30 Regular; 0 Special Education; 1 Vocational; 2 Alternative
  1 Magnet; 1 Charter; 11 Title I Eligible; 8 School-wide Title I
Students: 14,810   (51.9% male; 48.0% female)
  Individual Education Program: 2,138 (14.4%);
  English Language Learner: 481 (3.2%); Migrant: 213 (1.4%)
  Eligible for Free Lunch Program: 2,391 (16.1%)
  Eligible for Reduced-Price Lunch Program: 1,510 (10.2%)
Teachers: 842.5 (17.6 to 1)
Librarians/Media Specialists: 8.0 (1,851.3 to 1)
Guidance Counselors: 43.0 (344.4 to 1)
Current Spending: ($ per student per year):
  Total: $9,002; Instruction: $5,231; Support Services: $3,523

Enrollment, Drop-out Rates and Diploma Recipients by Race/Ethnicity

Category	Total	White	Black	Asian	AIAN	Hisp.
Enrollment (%)	100.0	69.9	8.1	3.4	14.2	4.4
Drop-out Rate (%)	11.0	8.7	14.1	5.4	24.1	11.5
H.S. Diplomas (#)	785	637	45	29	60	14

Juneau Borough

Juneau Borough Schools
1208 Glacier Ave • Juneau, AK 99801
Mailing Address: 10014 Crazy Horse Dr • Juneau, AK 99801
(907) 463-1700 • http://www.jsd.k12.ak.us/
Grade Span: PK-12; Agency Type: 1
Schools: 13
  7 Primary; 2 Middle; 1 High; 3 Other Level
  12 Regular; 0 Special Education; 0 Vocational; 1 Alternative
  1 Magnet; 6 Title I Eligible; 0 School-wide Title I
Students: 5,475   (51.5% male; 48.4% female)
  Individual Education Program: 738 (13.5%);
  English Language Learner: 879 (16.1%); Migrant: 0 (0.0%)
  Eligible for Free Lunch Program: 543 (9.9%)
  Eligible for Reduced-Price Lunch Program: 129 (2.4%)
Teachers: 305.0 (18.0 to 1)
Librarians/Media Specialists: 3.0 (1,825.0 to 1)
Guidance Counselors: 11.5 (476.1 to 1)
Current Spending: ($ per student per year):
  Total: $8,670; Instruction: $5,348; Support Services: $3,252

Enrollment, Drop-out Rates and Diploma Recipients by Race/Ethnicity

Category	Total	White	Black	Asian	AIAN	Hisp.
Enrollment (%)	100.0	61.8	1.2	9.8	23.6	3.5
Drop-out Rate (%)	11.1	8.8	36.8	2.6	21.9	7.3
H.S. Diplomas (#)	333	249	1	27	48	8

Kenai Peninsula Borough

Kenai Peninsula Borough Schs
148 N Binkley St • Soldotna, AK 99669
(907) 262-5846 • http://www.kpbsd.k12.ak.us/
Grade Span: PK-12; Agency Type: 1
Schools: 44
  19 Primary; 4 Middle; 9 High; 12 Other Level
  39 Regular; 0 Special Education; 0 Vocational; 5 Alternative
  3 Magnet; 3 Charter; 25 Title I Eligible; 13 School-wide Title I
Students: 9,645   (51.5% male; 48.4% female)
  Individual Education Program: 1,353 (14.0%);
  English Language Learner: 277 (2.9%); Migrant: 463 (4.8%)
  Eligible for Free Lunch Program: 1,881 (19.5%)
  Eligible for Reduced-Price Lunch Program: 943 (9.8%)
Teachers: 550.8 (17.5 to 1)
Librarians/Media Specialists: 12.3 (784.1 to 1)
Guidance Counselors: 14.5 (665.2 to 1)
Current Spending: ($ per student per year):
  Total: $9,261; Instruction: $5,447; Support Services: $3,560

Enrollment, Drop-out Rates and Diploma Recipients by Race/Ethnicity

Category	Total	White	Black	Asian	AIAN	Hisp.
Enrollment (%)	100.0	83.6	0.7	1.8	12.1	1.8
Drop-out Rate (%)	7.2	6.4	11.4	3.8	12.9	9.1
H.S. Diplomas (#)	669	564	15	18	65	7

Ketchikan Gateway Borough

Ketchikan Gateway Borough SD
2610 Fourth Ave • Ketchikan, AK 99901-6278
Mailing Address: 333 Schoenbar Rd • Ketchikan, AK 99901-6278
(907) 225-2118 • http://www.kgbsd.org/
Grade Span: PK-12; Agency Type: 1
Schools: 11
  6 Primary; 1 Middle; 2 High; 2 Other Level
  9 Regular; 0 Special Education; 0 Vocational; 2 Alternative
  0 Magnet; 2 Charter; 6 Title I Eligible; 0 School-wide Title I
Students: 2,387   (51.1% male; 48.8% female)
  Individual Education Program: 337 (14.1%);
  English Language Learner: 58 (2.4%); Migrant: 105 (4.4%)
  Eligible for Free Lunch Program: 459 (19.2%)
  Eligible for Reduced-Price Lunch Program: 126 (5.3%)
Teachers: 138.5 (17.2 to 1)
Librarians/Media Specialists: 2.5 (954.8 to 1)
Guidance Counselors: 2.0 (1,193.5 to 1)
Current Spending: ($ per student per year):
  Total: $8,827; Instruction: $5,180; Support Services: $3,477

Enrollment, Drop-out Rates and Diploma Recipients by Race/Ethnicity

Category	Total	White	Black	Asian	AIAN	Hisp.
Enrollment (%)	100.0	61.0	0.9	6.6	28.9	2.6
Drop-out Rate (%)	8.6	6.2	0.0	9.4	18.1	0.0
H.S. Diplomas (#)	128	104	3	11	9	1

Kodiak Island Borough

Kodiak Island Borough SD
722 Mill Bay Rd • Kodiak, AK 99615
(907) 486-9210 • http://www.kodiak.k12.ak.us/
Grade Span: PK-12; **Agency Type:** 1
Schools: 15
    4 Primary; 1 Middle; 1 High; 9 Other Level
    15 Regular; 0 Special Education; 0 Vocational; 0 Alternative
    0 Magnet; 0 Charter; 9 Title I Eligible; 1 School-wide Title I
Students: 2,697 (52.6% male; 47.3% female)
    Individual Education Program: 411 (15.2%);
    English Language Learner: 440 (16.3%); Migrant: 334 (12.4%)
    Eligible for Free Lunch Program: 630 (23.4%)
    Eligible for Reduced-Price Lunch Program: 278 (10.3%)
Teachers: 172.0 (15.7 to 1)
Librarians/Media Specialists: 1.0 (2,697.0 to 1)
Guidance Counselors: 2.5 (1,078.8 to 1)
Current Spending: ($ per student per year):
    Total: $10,950; Instruction: $6,147; Support Services: $4,504
Enrollment, Drop-out Rates and Diploma Recipients by Race/Ethnicity

Category	Total	White	Black	Asian	AIAN	Hisp.
Enrollment (%)	100.0	45.7	1.2	23.4	23.0	6.7
Drop-out Rate (%)	3.1	2.2	0.0	3.4	5.8	0.0
H.S. Diplomas (#)	184	96	1	38	45	4

Matanuska-Susitna Borough

Matanuska-Susitna Borough Schs
125 W Evergreen • Palmer, AK 99645
(907) 746-9255 • http://www.mat-su.k12.ak.us/schdist
Grade Span: PK-12; **Agency Type:** 1
Schools: 38
    18 Primary; 4 Middle; 7 High; 9 Other Level
    35 Regular; 0 Special Education; 0 Vocational; 3 Alternative
    0 Magnet; 3 Charter; 19 Title I Eligible; 12 School-wide Title I
Students: 14,372 (51.8% male; 48.1% female)
    Individual Education Program: 2,016 (14.0%);
    English Language Learner: 414 (2.9%); Migrant: 351 (2.4%)
    Eligible for Free Lunch Program: 2,928 (20.4%)
    Eligible for Reduced-Price Lunch Program: 1,141 (7.9%)
Teachers: 788.7 (18.2 to 1)
Librarians/Media Specialists: 23.0 (624.9 to 1)
Guidance Counselors: 25.3 (568.1 to 1)
Current Spending: ($ per student per year):
    Total: $9,329; Instruction: $5,006; Support Services: $4,083
Enrollment, Drop-out Rates and Diploma Recipients by Race/Ethnicity

Category	Total	White	Black	Asian	AIAN	Hisp.
Enrollment (%)	100.0	84.1	1.1	1.2	11.5	2.1
Drop-out Rate (%)	6.3	5.7	6.3	0.0	11.6	12.5
H.S. Diplomas (#)	830	739	8	8	54	21

Nome Borough

Bering Strait SD
225 Main St • Unalakleet, AK 99684-0225
Mailing Address: PO Box 225 • Unalakleet, AK 99684-0225
(907) 624-3611 • http://www.bssd.org/
Grade Span: PK-12; **Agency Type:** 1
Schools: 15
    0 Primary; 0 Middle; 0 High; 15 Other Level
    15 Regular; 0 Special Education; 0 Vocational; 0 Alternative
    0 Magnet; 0 Charter; 15 Title I Eligible; 15 School-wide Title I
Students: 1,810 (51.9% male; 48.0% female)
    Individual Education Program: 276 (15.2%);
    English Language Learner: 1,314 (72.6%); Migrant: 615 (34.0%)
    Eligible for Free Lunch Program: 1,037 (57.3%)
    Eligible for Reduced-Price Lunch Program: 208 (11.5%)
Teachers: 159.0 (11.4 to 1)
Librarians/Media Specialists: 1.0 (1,810.0 to 1)
Guidance Counselors: 6.0 (301.7 to 1)
Current Spending: ($ per student per year):
    Total: $20,319; Instruction: $13,645; Support Services: $5,744
Enrollment, Drop-out Rates and Diploma Recipients by Race/Ethnicity

Category	Total	White	Black	Asian	AIAN	Hisp.
Enrollment (%)	100.0	1.9	0.0	0.1	98.0	0.0
Drop-out Rate (%)	14.1	0.0	n/a	0.0	14.2	n/a
H.S. Diplomas (#)	47	2	0	1	44	0

North Slope Borough

North Slope Borough SD
829 Aivak St • Barrow, AK 99723-0169
Mailing Address: PO Box 169 • Barrow, AK 99723-0169
(907) 852-5311 • http://www.nsbsd.k12.ak.us/
Grade Span: PK-12; **Agency Type:** 1
Schools: 10
    1 Primary; 1 Middle; 1 High; 7 Other Level
    10 Regular; 0 Special Education; 0 Vocational; 0 Alternative
    0 Magnet; 0 Charter; 7 Title I Eligible; 0 School-wide Title I
Students: 2,065 (51.9% male; 48.0% female)
    Individual Education Program: 238 (11.5%);
    English Language Learner: 1,284 (62.2%); Migrant: 417 (20.2%)
    Eligible for Free Lunch Program: 302 (14.6%)
    Eligible for Reduced-Price Lunch Program: 251 (12.2%)
Teachers: 192.6 (10.7 to 1)
Librarians/Media Specialists: 3.0 (688.3 to 1)
Guidance Counselors: 8.6 (240.1 to 1)
Current Spending: ($ per student per year):
    Total: $22,637; Instruction: $12,065; Support Services: $8,934
Enrollment, Drop-out Rates and Diploma Recipients by Race/Ethnicity

Category	Total	White	Black	Asian	AIAN	Hisp.
Enrollment (%)	100.0	7.2	0.9	6.7	84.4	0.8
Drop-out Rate (%)	7.1	0.0	33.3	3.0	8.2	0.0
H.S. Diplomas (#)	133	11	0	5	115	2

Northwest Arctic Borough

Northwest Arctic SD
776 Third Ave • Kotzebue, AK 99752
Mailing Address: PO Box 51 • Kotzebue, AK 99752
(907) 442-3472 • http://www.nwabsd.schoolzone.net/
Grade Span: PK-12; **Agency Type:** 1
Schools: 13
    1 Primary; 0 Middle; 0 High; 12 Other Level
    13 Regular; 0 Special Education; 0 Vocational; 0 Alternative
    0 Magnet; 0 Charter; 12 Title I Eligible; 10 School-wide Title I
Students: 2,214 (50.3% male; 49.6% female)
    Individual Education Program: 192 (8.7%);
    English Language Learner: 1,040 (47.0%); Migrant: 693 (31.3%)
    Eligible for Free Lunch Program: 1,046 (47.2%)
    Eligible for Reduced-Price Lunch Program: 218 (9.8%)
Teachers: 169.2 (13.1 to 1)
Librarians/Media Specialists: 2.0 (1,107.0 to 1)
Guidance Counselors: 9.0 (246.0 to 1)
Current Spending: ($ per student per year):
    Total: $18,192; Instruction: $9,750; Support Services: $7,534
Enrollment, Drop-out Rates and Diploma Recipients by Race/Ethnicity

Category	Total	White	Black	Asian	AIAN	Hisp.
Enrollment (%)	100.0	4.1	0.1	0.9	94.9	0.0
Drop-out Rate (%)	10.0	0.0	n/a	0.0	10.5	n/a
H.S. Diplomas (#)	68	5	0	1	62	0

Sitka Borough

Sitka Borough SD
300 Kostrometinoff St • Sitka, AK 99835-0179
(907) 747-8622 • http://www.ssd.k12.ak.us/
Grade Span: PK-12; **Agency Type:** 1
Schools: 6
    2 Primary; 1 Middle; 2 High; 1 Other Level
    6 Regular; 0 Special Education; 0 Vocational; 0 Alternative
    0 Magnet; 0 Charter; 4 Title I Eligible; 0 School-wide Title I
Students: 1,524 (49.8% male; 50.1% female)
    Individual Education Program: 272 (17.8%);
    English Language Learner: 32 (2.1%); Migrant: 79 (5.2%)
    Eligible for Free Lunch Program: 217 (14.2%)
    Eligible for Reduced-Price Lunch Program: 131 (8.6%)
Teachers: 102.5 (14.9 to 1)
Librarians/Media Specialists: 3.0 (508.0 to 1)
Guidance Counselors: 4.5 (338.7 to 1)
Current Spending: ($ per student per year):
    Total: $9,449; Instruction: $6,229; Support Services: $3,020
Enrollment, Drop-out Rates and Diploma Recipients by Race/Ethnicity

Category	Total	White	Black	Asian	AIAN	Hisp.
Enrollment (%)	100.0	58.7	1.0	6.7	30.7	2.8
Drop-out Rate (%)	7.9	4.2	0.0	4.0	18.2	0.0
H.S. Diplomas (#)	89	52	1	5	29	2

Wade Hampton Borough

Lower Yukon SD
1st Bldg Airport Rd • Mountain Village, AK 99632-0089
Mailing Address: PO Box 32089 • Mountain Village, AK 99632-0089
(907) 591-2411 • http://www.lysd.gcisa.net/lysd/default.htm
Grade Span: PK-12; **Agency Type:** 1
Schools: 11
   0 Primary; 0 Middle; 0 High; 11 Other Level
   11 Regular; 0 Special Education; 0 Vocational; 0 Alternative
   0 Magnet; 0 Charter; 11 Title I Eligible; 11 School-wide Title I
Students: 2,023   (52.1% male; 47.8% female)
   Individual Education Program: 235 (11.6%);
   English Language Learner: 1,947 (96.2%); Migrant: 651 (32.2%)
   Eligible for Free Lunch Program: 1,386 (68.5%)
   Eligible for Reduced-Price Lunch Program: 243 (12.0%)
Teachers: 146.1 (13.8 to 1)
Librarians/Media Specialists: 1.0 (2,023.0 to 1)
Guidance Counselors: 8.4 (240.8 to 1)
Current Spending: ($ per student per year):
   Total: $14,503; Instruction: $7,689; Support Services: $5,368

Enrollment, Drop-out Rates and Diploma Recipients by Race/Ethnicity

Category	Total	White	Black	Asian	AIAN	Hisp.
Enrollment (%)	100.0	1.1	0.0	0.0	98.8	0.0
Drop-out Rate (%)	18.8	50.0	n/a	n/a	18.7	n/a
H.S. Diplomas (#)	50	0	0	0	50	0

Yukon-Koyukuk Borough

Galena City SD
299 Antoski Ave • Galena, AK 99741-0299
Mailing Address: PO Box 299 • Galena, AK 99741-0299
(907) 656-1205 • http://www.galenaalaska.org/
Grade Span: PK-12; **Agency Type:** 1
Schools: 4
   1 Primary; 0 Middle; 2 High; 1 Other Level
   4 Regular; 0 Special Education; 0 Vocational; 0 Alternative
   1 Magnet; 0 Charter; 2 Title I Eligible; 0 School-wide Title I
Students: 3,990   (50.1% male; 49.8% female)
   Individual Education Program: 128 (3.2%);
   English Language Learner: 17 (0.4%); Migrant: 27 (0.7%)
   Eligible for Free Lunch Program: 38 (1.0%)
   Eligible for Reduced-Price Lunch Program: 13 (0.3%)
Teachers: 62.7 (63.6 to 1)
Librarians/Media Specialists: 2.5 (1,596.0 to 1)
Guidance Counselors: 3.5 (1,140.0 to 1)
Current Spending: ($ per student per year):
   Total: $5,786; Instruction: $3,344; Support Services: $2,390

Enrollment, Drop-out Rates and Diploma Recipients by Race/Ethnicity

Category	Total	White	Black	Asian	AIAN	Hisp.
Enrollment (%)	100.0	83.0	2.8	1.8	10.8	1.6
Drop-out Rate (%)	1.4	1.7	0.0	12.5	0.0	0.0
H.S. Diplomas (#)	131	97	1	2	28	3

Number of Schools

Rank	Number	District Name	City
1	95	Anchorage SD	Anchorage
2	44	Kenai Peninsula Borough Schs	Soldotna
3	38	Matanuska-Susitna Borough Schs	Palmer
4	33	Fairbanks North Star Boro SD	Fairbanks
5	28	Lower Kuskokwim SD	Bethel
6	15	Bering Strait SD	Unalakleet
6	15	Kodiak Island Borough SD	Kodiak
8	13	Juneau Borough Schools	Juneau
8	13	Northwest Arctic SD	Kotzebue
10	11	Ketchikan Gateway Borough SD	Ketchikan
10	11	Lower Yukon SD	Mountain Vlg
12	10	North Slope Borough SD	Barrow
13	6	Sitka Borough SD	Sitka
14	4	Galena City SD	Galena

Number of Teachers

Rank	Number	District Name	City
1	2,832	Anchorage SD	Anchorage
2	842	Fairbanks North Star Boro SD	Fairbanks
3	788	Matanuska-Susitna Borough Schs	Palmer
4	550	Kenai Peninsula Borough Schs	Soldotna
5	305	Juneau Borough Schools	Juneau
6	278	Lower Kuskokwim SD	Bethel
7	192	North Slope Borough SD	Barrow
8	172	Kodiak Island Borough SD	Kodiak
9	169	Northwest Arctic SD	Kotzebue
10	159	Bering Strait SD	Unalakleet
11	146	Lower Yukon SD	Mountain Vlg
12	138	Ketchikan Gateway Borough SD	Ketchikan
13	102	Sitka Borough SD	Sitka
14	62	Galena City SD	Galena

Number of Students

Rank	Number	District Name	City
1	49,722	Anchorage SD	Anchorage
2	14,810	Fairbanks North Star Boro SD	Fairbanks
3	14,372	Matanuska-Susitna Borough Schs	Palmer
4	9,645	Kenai Peninsula Borough Schs	Soldotna
5	5,475	Juneau Borough Schools	Juneau
6	3,990	Galena City SD	Galena
7	3,816	Lower Kuskokwim SD	Bethel
8	2,697	Kodiak Island Borough SD	Kodiak
9	2,387	Ketchikan Gateway Borough SD	Ketchikan
10	2,214	Northwest Arctic SD	Kotzebue
11	2,065	North Slope Borough SD	Barrow
12	2,023	Lower Yukon SD	Mountain Vlg
13	1,810	Bering Strait SD	Unalakleet
14	1,524	Sitka Borough SD	Sitka

Male Students

Rank	Percent	District Name	City
1	52.6	Kodiak Island Borough SD	Kodiak
2	52.1	Lower Yukon SD	Mountain Vlg
3	51.9	North Slope Borough SD	Barrow
4	51.9	Bering Strait SD	Unalakleet
5	51.9	Fairbanks North Star Boro SD	Fairbanks
6	51.8	Lower Kuskokwim SD	Bethel
7	51.8	Matanuska-Susitna Borough Schs	Palmer
8	51.5	Anchorage SD	Anchorage
9	51.5	Kenai Peninsula Borough Schs	Soldotna
10	51.5	Juneau Borough Schools	Juneau
11	51.1	Ketchikan Gateway Borough SD	Ketchikan
12	50.3	Northwest Arctic SD	Kotzebue
13	50.1	Galena City SD	Galena
14	49.8	Sitka Borough SD	Sitka

Female Students

Rank	Percent	District Name	City
1	50.1	Sitka Borough SD	Sitka
2	49.8	Galena City SD	Galena
3	49.6	Northwest Arctic SD	Kotzebue
4	48.8	Ketchikan Gateway Borough SD	Ketchikan
5	48.4	Juneau Borough Schools	Juneau
6	48.4	Kenai Peninsula Borough Schs	Soldotna
7	48.4	Anchorage SD	Anchorage
8	48.1	Matanuska-Susitna Borough Schs	Palmer
9	48.1	Lower Kuskokwim SD	Bethel
10	48.0	Fairbanks North Star Boro SD	Fairbanks
11	48.0	Bering Strait SD	Unalakleet
12	48.0	North Slope Borough SD	Barrow
13	47.8	Lower Yukon SD	Mountain Vlg
14	47.3	Kodiak Island Borough SD	Kodiak

Individual Education Program Students

Rank	Percent	District Name	City

(continued)

Rank	Percent	District Name	City
1	17.8	Sitka Borough SD	Sitka
2	15.2	Bering Strait SD	Unalakleet
2	15.2	Kodiak Island Borough SD	Kodiak
4	14.4	Fairbanks North Star Boro SD	Fairbanks
5	14.1	Ketchikan Gateway Borough SD	Ketchikan
6	14.0	Anchorage SD	Anchorage
6	14.0	Kenai Peninsula Borough Schs	Soldotna
6	14.0	Matanuska-Susitna Borough Schs	Palmer
9	13.5	Juneau Borough Schools	Juneau
9	13.5	Lower Kuskokwim SD	Bethel
11	11.6	Lower Yukon SD	Mountain Vlg
12	11.5	North Slope Borough SD	Barrow
13	8.7	Northwest Arctic SD	Kotzebue
14	3.2	Galena City SD	Galena

English Language Learner Students

Rank	Percent	District Name	City
1	96.2	Lower Yukon SD	Mountain Vlg
2	72.6	Bering Strait SD	Unalakleet
3	62.8	Lower Kuskokwim SD	Bethel
4	62.2	North Slope Borough SD	Barrow
5	47.0	Northwest Arctic SD	Kotzebue
6	16.3	Kodiak Island Borough SD	Kodiak
7	16.1	Juneau Borough Schools	Juneau
8	12.1	Anchorage SD	Anchorage
9	3.2	Fairbanks North Star Boro SD	Fairbanks
10	2.9	Kenai Peninsula Borough Schs	Soldotna
10	2.9	Matanuska-Susitna Borough Schs	Palmer
12	2.4	Ketchikan Gateway Borough SD	Ketchikan
13	2.1	Sitka Borough SD	Sitka
14	0.4	Galena City SD	Galena

Migrant Students

Rank	Percent	District Name	City
1	34.0	Bering Strait SD	Unalakleet
2	32.2	Lower Yukon SD	Mountain Vlg
3	31.3	Northwest Arctic SD	Kotzebue
4	23.3	Lower Kuskokwim SD	Bethel
5	20.2	North Slope Borough SD	Barrow
6	12.4	Kodiak Island Borough SD	Kodiak
7	5.2	Sitka Borough SD	Sitka
8	4.8	Kenai Peninsula Borough Schs	Soldotna
9	4.4	Ketchikan Gateway Borough SD	Ketchikan
10	2.6	Anchorage SD	Anchorage
11	2.4	Matanuska-Susitna Borough Schs	Palmer
12	1.4	Fairbanks North Star Boro SD	Fairbanks
13	0.7	Galena City SD	Galena
14	0.0	Juneau Borough Schools	Juneau

Students Eligible for Free Lunch

Rank	Percent	District Name	City
1	68.5	Lower Yukon SD	Mountain Vlg
2	57.3	Bering Strait SD	Unalakleet
3	50.2	Lower Kuskokwim SD	Bethel
4	47.2	Northwest Arctic SD	Kotzebue
5	23.4	Kodiak Island Borough SD	Kodiak
6	20.4	Matanuska-Susitna Borough Schs	Palmer
7	19.5	Kenai Peninsula Borough Schs	Soldotna
8	19.2	Ketchikan Gateway Borough SD	Ketchikan
9	16.1	Fairbanks North Star Boro SD	Fairbanks
10	15.4	Anchorage SD	Anchorage
11	14.6	North Slope Borough SD	Barrow
12	14.2	Sitka Borough SD	Sitka
13	9.9	Juneau Borough Schools	Juneau
14	1.0	Galena City SD	Galena

Students Eligible for Reduced-Price Lunch

Rank	Percent	District Name	City
1	12.2	North Slope Borough SD	Barrow
2	12.0	Lower Yukon SD	Mountain Vlg
3	11.5	Bering Strait SD	Unalakleet
4	10.3	Kodiak Island Borough SD	Kodiak
5	10.2	Fairbanks North Star Boro SD	Fairbanks
6	9.8	Kenai Peninsula Borough Schs	Soldotna
7	9.8	Northwest Arctic SD	Kotzebue
8	9.3	Lower Kuskokwim SD	Bethel
9	8.6	Sitka Borough SD	Sitka
10	7.9	Matanuska-Susitna Borough Schs	Palmer
11	5.8	Anchorage SD	Anchorage
12	5.3	Ketchikan Gateway Borough SD	Ketchikan
13	2.4	Juneau Borough Schools	Juneau
14	0.3	Galena City SD	Galena

Student/Teacher Ratio

Rank	Ratio	District Name	City
1	63.6	Galena City SD	Galena
2	18.2	Matanuska-Susitna Borough Schs	Palmer
3	18.0	Juneau Borough Schools	Juneau
4	17.6	Anchorage SD	Anchorage
4	17.6	Fairbanks North Star Boro SD	Fairbanks
6	17.5	Kenai Peninsula Borough Schs	Soldotna
7	17.2	Ketchikan Gateway Borough SD	Ketchikan
8	15.7	Kodiak Island Borough SD	Kodiak
9	14.9	Sitka Borough SD	Sitka
10	13.8	Lower Yukon SD	Mountain Vlg
11	13.7	Lower Kuskokwim SD	Bethel
12	13.1	Northwest Arctic SD	Kotzebue
13	11.4	Bering Strait SD	Unalakleet
14	10.7	North Slope Borough SD	Barrow

Student/Librarian Ratio

Rank	Ratio	District Name	City
1	2,697.0	Kodiak Island Borough SD	Kodiak
2	2,023.0	Lower Yukon SD	Mountain Vlg
3	1,851.3	Fairbanks North Star Boro SD	Fairbanks
4	1,825.0	Juneau Borough Schools	Juneau
5	1,810.0	Bering Strait SD	Unalakleet
6	1,596.0	Galena City SD	Galena
7	1,272.0	Lower Kuskokwim SD	Bethel
8	1,107.0	Northwest Arctic SD	Kotzebue
9	954.8	Ketchikan Gateway Borough SD	Ketchikan
10	784.1	Kenai Peninsula Borough Schs	Soldotna
11	688.3	North Slope Borough SD	Barrow
12	658.6	Anchorage SD	Anchorage
13	624.9	Matanuska-Susitna Borough Schs	Palmer
14	508.0	Sitka Borough SD	Sitka

Student/Counselor Ratio

Rank	Ratio	District Name	City
1	1,526.4	Lower Kuskokwim SD	Bethel
2	1,193.5	Ketchikan Gateway Borough SD	Ketchikan
3	1,140.0	Galena City SD	Galena
4	1,078.8	Kodiak Island Borough SD	Kodiak
5	665.2	Kenai Peninsula Borough Schs	Soldotna
6	568.1	Matanuska-Susitna Borough Schs	Palmer
7	517.9	Anchorage SD	Anchorage
8	476.1	Juneau Borough Schools	Juneau
9	344.4	Fairbanks North Star Boro SD	Fairbanks
10	338.7	Sitka Borough SD	Sitka
11	301.7	Bering Strait SD	Unalakleet
12	246.0	Northwest Arctic SD	Kotzebue
13	240.8	Lower Yukon SD	Mountain Vlg
14	240.1	North Slope Borough SD	Barrow

Current Spending per Student in FY2003

Rank	Dollars	District Name	City
1	22,637	North Slope Borough SD	Barrow
2	20,319	Bering Strait SD	Unalakleet
3	18,192	Northwest Arctic SD	Kotzebue
4	17,048	Lower Kuskokwim SD	Bethel
5	14,503	Lower Yukon SD	Mountain Vlg
6	10,950	Kodiak Island Borough SD	Kodiak
7	9,449	Sitka Borough SD	Sitka
8	9,329	Matanuska-Susitna Borough Schs	Palmer
9	9,261	Kenai Peninsula Borough Schs	Soldotna
10	9,002	Fairbanks North Star Boro SD	Fairbanks
11	8,827	Ketchikan Gateway Borough SD	Ketchikan
12	8,670	Juneau Borough Schools	Juneau
13	7,826	Anchorage SD	Anchorage
14	5,786	Galena City SD	Galena

Number of Diploma Recipients

Rank	Number	District Name	City
1	2,505	Anchorage SD	Anchorage
2	830	Matanuska-Susitna Borough Schs	Palmer
3	785	Fairbanks North Star Boro SD	Fairbanks
4	669	Kenai Peninsula Borough Schs	Soldotna
5	333	Juneau Borough Schools	Juneau
6	184	Kodiak Island Borough SD	Kodiak
7	133	North Slope Borough SD	Barrow
8	131	Galena City SD	Galena
9	128	Ketchikan Gateway Borough SD	Ketchikan
10	118	Lower Kuskokwim SD	Bethel
11	89	Sitka Borough SD	Sitka
12	68	Northwest Arctic SD	Kotzebue
13	50	Lower Yukon SD	Mountain Vlg
14	47	Bering Strait SD	Unalakleet

High School Drop-out Rate

Rank	Percent	District Name	City
1	18.8	Lower Yukon SD	Mountain Vlg
2	16.9	Lower Kuskokwim SD	Bethel
3	14.1	Bering Strait SD	Unalakleet
4	11.1	Juneau Borough Schools	Juneau
5	11.0	Fairbanks North Star Boro SD	Fairbanks

6	10.0	Northwest Arctic SD	Kotzebue
7	8.6	Anchorage SD	Anchorage
7	8.6	Ketchikan Gateway Borough SD	Ketchikan
9	7.9	Sitka Borough SD	Sitka
10	7.2	Kenai Peninsula Borough Schs	Soldotna
11	7.1	North Slope Borough SD	Barrow
12	6.3	Matanuska-Susitna Borough Schs	Palmer
13	3.1	Kodiak Island Borough SD	Kodiak
14	1.4	Galena City SD	Galena

Arizona

Arizona Public School Educational Profile

Category	Value	Category	Value
Schools *(2003-2004)*	2,031	**Diploma Recipients** *(2002-2003)*	46,879
Instructional Level		White, Non-Hispanic	28,481
Primary	1,097	Black, Non-Hispanic	1,989
Middle	255	Asian/Pacific Islander	1,279
High	464	American Indian/Alaskan Native	2,743
Other Level	200	Hispanic	12,387
Curriculum		**High School Drop-out Rate** (%) *(2001-2002)*	10.0
Regular	1,854	White, Non-Hispanic	6.5
Special Education	13	Black, Non-Hispanic	12.8
Vocational	73	Asian/Pacific Islander	3.8
Alternative	76	American Indian/Alaskan Native	17.9
Type		Hispanic	14.8
Magnet	0	**Staff** *(2003-2004)*	
Charter	505	Teachers	47,445.9
Title I Eligible	1,100	Average Salary[1] ($)	42,324
School-wide Title I	653	Librarians/Media Specialists	802.8
Students *(2003-2004)*	1,012,068	Guidance Counselors	1,238.2
Gender (%)		**Ratios** *(2003-2004)*	
Male	51.6	Student/Teacher Ratio	21.3 to 1
Female	48.4	Student/Librarian Ratio	1,260.7 to 1
Race/Ethnicity (%)		Student/Counselor Ratio	817.4 to 1
White, Non-Hispanic	49.2	**College Entrance Exam Scores** *(2005)*	
Black, Non-Hispanic	4.8	Scholastic Aptitude Test (SAT)	
Asian/Pacific Islander	2.2	Participation Rate (%)	33
American Indian/Alaskan Native	6.6	Mean SAT Reasoning Test Verbal Score	526
Hispanic	37.2	Mean SAT Reasoning Test Math Score	530
Classification (%)		American College Testing Program (ACT)	
Individual Education Program (IEP)	10.8	Participation Rate (%)	19
Migrant *(2002-2003)*	0.3	Average Composite Score	21.5
English Language Learner (ELL)	15.4	Average English Score	20.9
Eligible for Free Lunch Program	37.3	Average Math Score	21.7
Eligible for Reduced-Price Lunch Program	7.8	Average Reading Score	21.9
Current Spending *($ per student in FY 2003)*	5,665	Average Science Score	21.2
Instruction	3,127		
Support Services	2,259		

Note: *For an explanation of data, please refer to the User's Guide in the front of the book; (1) AFT estimate*

Arizona NAEP 2005 Test Scores

Reading			Mathematics		
Grade/Category	Value	Rank	Grade/Category	Value	Rank
4th Grade			**4th Grade**		
Average Proficiency	207.1 (1.57)	47/51	Average Proficiency	229.8 (1.12)	47/51
Proficiency by Gender/Race/Ethnicity			Proficiency by Gender/Race/Ethnicity		
Male	203.3 (1.84)	46/51	Male	232.7 (1.29)	41/51
Female	211.2 (1.89)	45/51	Female	226.8 (1.21)	47/51
White, Non-Hispanic	223.6 (1.89)	40/51	White, Non-Hispanic	242.6 (1.32)	35/51
Black, Non-Hispanic	192.6 (3.41)	36/42	Black, Non-Hispanic	217.2 (3.57)	26/42
Asian, Non-Hispanic	224.1 (5.31)	18/27	Asian, Non-Hispanic	240.6 (4.03)	20/25
American Indian, Non-Hispanic	n/a	n/a	American Indian, Non-Hispanic	n/a	n/a
Hispanic	192.2 (1.70)	39/40	Hispanic	218.2 (1.14)	37/41
Proficiency by Class Size			Proficiency by Class Size		
Less than 16 Students	n/a	n/a	Less than 16 Students	n/a	n/a
16 to 18 Students	n/a	n/a	16 to 18 Students	n/a	n/a
19 to 20 Students	n/a	n/a	19 to 20 Students	n/a	n/a
21 to 25 Students	207.7 (2.86)	47/51	21 to 25 Students	230.2 (2.01)	44/51
Greater than 25 Students	207.9 (2.28)	34/36	Greater than 25 Students	230.5 (1.71)	29/33
Percent Attaining Achievement Levels			Percent Attaining Achievement Levels		
Below Basic	47.9 (1.74)	6/51	Below Basic	29.6 (1.33)	5/51
Basic or Above	52.1 (1.74)	46/51	Basic or Above	70.4 (1.33)	47/51
Proficient or Above	23.6 (1.65)	43/51	Proficient or Above	27.9 (1.55)	41/51
Advanced or Above	5.5 (0.64)	40/51	Advanced or Above	3.3 (0.66)	39/51
8th Grade			**8th Grade**		
Average Proficiency	254.8 (1.01)	43/51	Average Proficiency	274.3 (1.07)	35/51
Proficiency by Gender/Race/Ethnicity			Proficiency by Gender/Race/Ethnicity		
Male	249.4 (1.30)	42/51	Male	274.4 (1.39)	37/51
Female	260.3 (1.29)	43/51	Female	274.2 (1.25)	35/51
White, Non-Hispanic	267.0 (1.17)	34/51	White, Non-Hispanic	287.6 (1.32)	25/51
Black, Non-Hispanic	242.3 (4.05)	21/40	Black, Non-Hispanic	260.9 (2.71)	9/41
Asian, Non-Hispanic	n/a	n/a	Asian, Non-Hispanic	n/a	n/a
American Indian, Non-Hispanic	239.5 (5.03)	8/9	American Indian, Non-Hispanic	259.3 (4.76)	8/10
Hispanic	242.1 (1.50)	34/38	Hispanic	260.0 (1.42)	26/38
Proficiency by Parents Highest Level of Ed.			Proficiency by Parents Highest Level of Ed.		
Did Not Finish High School	237.5 (1.94)	46/49	Did Not Finish High School	255.4 (1.72)	36/50
Graduated High School	246.9 (1.46)	43/50	Graduated High School	265.5 (1.59)	31/50
Some Education After High School	263.5 (1.75)	33/50	Some Education After High School	278.0 (1.91)	34/50
Graduated College	266.9 (1.28)	35/50	Graduated College	290.4 (1.48)	23/50
Percent Attaining Achievement Levels			Percent Attaining Achievement Levels		
Below Basic	47.9 (1.74)	6/51	Below Basic	36.1 (1.46)	14/51
Basic or Above	52.1 (1.74)	46/51	Basic or Above	63.9 (1.46)	38/51
Proficient or Above	23.6 (1.65)	43/51	Proficient or Above	25.7 (1.16)	35/51
Advanced or Above	5.5 (0.64)	40/51	Advanced or Above	4.6 (0.43)	32/51

Note: For an explanation of data, please refer to the User's Guide in the front of the book; n/a indicates data not available

Apache County

Chinle Unified District
Navajo Rte 7 & State Hwy 191 • Chinle, AZ 86503-0587
Mailing Address: PO Box 587 • Chinle, AZ 86503-0587
(928) 674-9630 • http://www.chinleusd.k12.az.us/
Grade Span: PK-12; Agency Type: 1
Schools: 8
　　4 Primary; 2 Middle; 2 High; 0 Other Level
　　7 Regular; 0 Special Education; 0 Vocational; 1 Alternative
　　0 Magnet; 0 Charter; 7 Title I Eligible; 7 School-wide Title I
Students: 4,082　(51.4% male; 48.5% female)
　　Individual Education Program: 509 (12.5%);
　　English Language Learner: 2,766 (67.8%); Migrant: 0 (0.0%)
　　Eligible for Free Lunch Program: n/a
　　Eligible for Reduced-Price Lunch Program: n/a
Teachers: 265.7 (15.4 to 1)
Librarians/Media Specialists: 5.0 (816.4 to 1)
Guidance Counselors: 11.0 (371.1 to 1)
Current Spending: ($ per student per year):
　　Total: $8,403; Instruction: $4,122; Support Services: $3,782
Enrollment, Drop-out Rates and Diploma Recipients by Race/Ethnicity

Category	Total	White	Black	Asian	AIAN	Hisp.
Enrollment (%)	100.0	1.2	0.0	0.0	98.6	0.2
Drop-out Rate (%)	17.3	14.3	n/a	n/a	17.3	0.0
H.S. Diplomas (#)	222	2	0	0	219	1

Ganado Unified District
Hwy 264 • Ganado, AZ 86505-1757
Mailing Address: PO Box 1757 • Ganado, AZ 86505-1757
(928) 755-1099 • http://www.ganado.k12.az.us/
Grade Span: PK-12; Agency Type: 1
Schools: 4
　　2 Primary; 1 Middle; 1 High; 0 Other Level
　　4 Regular; 0 Special Education; 0 Vocational; 0 Alternative
　　0 Magnet; 0 Charter; 4 Title I Eligible; 4 School-wide Title I
Students: 2,075　(51.4% male; 48.5% female)
　　Individual Education Program: 161 (7.8%);
　　English Language Learner: 1,466 (70.7%); Migrant: 0 (0.0%)
　　Eligible for Free Lunch Program: 1,717 (82.7%)
　　Eligible for Reduced-Price Lunch Program: 229 (11.0%)
Teachers: 124.3 (16.7 to 1)
Librarians/Media Specialists: 3.0 (691.7 to 1)
Guidance Counselors: 6.9 (300.7 to 1)
Current Spending: ($ per student per year):
　　Total: $9,587; Instruction: $4,328; Support Services: $4,822
Enrollment, Drop-out Rates and Diploma Recipients by Race/Ethnicity

Category	Total	White	Black	Asian	AIAN	Hisp.
Enrollment (%)	100.0	0.9	0.0	0.2	98.9	0.0
Drop-out Rate (%)	9.2	0.0	n/a	n/a	9.3	0.0
H.S. Diplomas (#)	133	1	0	0	132	0

Window Rock Unified District
Navajo Rte 12 • Ft Defiance, AZ 86504-0559
Mailing Address: PO Box 559 • Ft Defiance, AZ 86504-0559
(928) 729-6706 • http://www.wrschool.net/
Grade Span: PK-12; Agency Type: 1
Schools: 6
　　4 Primary; 1 Middle; 1 High; 0 Other Level
　　6 Regular; 0 Special Education; 0 Vocational; 0 Alternative
　　0 Magnet; 0 Charter; 5 Title I Eligible; 5 School-wide Title I
Students: 2,874　(50.9% male; 49.0% female)
　　Individual Education Program: 310 (10.8%);
　　English Language Learner: 1 (<0.1%); Migrant: 0 (0.0%)
　　Eligible for Free Lunch Program: n/a
　　Eligible for Reduced-Price Lunch Program: n/a
Teachers: 196.8 (14.6 to 1)
Librarians/Media Specialists: 4.0 (718.5 to 1)
Guidance Counselors: 7.0 (410.6 to 1)
Current Spending: ($ per student per year):
　　Total: $8,945; Instruction: $5,356; Support Services: $3,278
Enrollment, Drop-out Rates and Diploma Recipients by Race/Ethnicity

Category	Total	White	Black	Asian	AIAN	Hisp.
Enrollment (%)	100.0	0.6	0.1	0.1	99.1	0.0
Drop-out Rate (%)	10.5	0.0	n/a	0.0	10.6	n/a
H.S. Diplomas (#)	128	0	0	1	127	0

Cochise County

Douglas Unified District
1132 12th St • Douglas, AZ 85607
(520) 364-2447 • http://www.dusd.k12.az.us/
Grade Span: PK-12; Agency Type: 1
Schools: 12
　　7 Primary; 2 Middle; 2 High; 1 Other Level

　　12 Regular; 0 Special Education; 0 Vocational; 0 Alternative
　　0 Magnet; 0 Charter; 10 Title I Eligible; 0 School-wide Title I
Students: 4,115　(53.0% male; 46.9% female)
　　Individual Education Program: 386 (9.4%);
　　English Language Learner: 2,296 (55.8%); Migrant: 79 (1.9%)
　　Eligible for Free Lunch Program: 2,733 (66.4%)
　　Eligible for Reduced-Price Lunch Program: 233 (5.7%)
Teachers: 204.0 (20.2 to 1)
Librarians/Media Specialists: 2.0 (2,057.5 to 1)
Guidance Counselors: 5.6 (734.8 to 1)
Current Spending: ($ per student per year):
　　Total: n/a; Instruction: n/a; Support Services: n/a
Enrollment, Drop-out Rates and Diploma Recipients by Race/Ethnicity

Category	Total	White	Black	Asian	AIAN	Hisp.
Enrollment (%)	100.0	3.9	0.3	0.0	0.0	95.7
Drop-out Rate (%)	4.8	3.2	n/a	0.0	n/a	4.8
H.S. Diplomas (#)	226	12	0	1	0	213

Sierra Vista Unified District
3555 Fry Blvd • Sierra Vista, AZ 85635-2972
(520) 515-2700 • http://www.sierravistapublicschools.com/
Grade Span: PK-12; Agency Type: 1
Schools: 9
　　6 Primary; 2 Middle; 1 High; 0 Other Level
　　9 Regular; 0 Special Education; 0 Vocational; 0 Alternative
　　0 Magnet; 0 Charter; 4 Title I Eligible; 2 School-wide Title I
Students: 6,719　(50.3% male; 49.6% female)
　　Individual Education Program: 777 (11.6%);
　　English Language Learner: 213 (3.2%); Migrant: 0 (0.0%)
　　Eligible for Free Lunch Program: 2,318 (34.5%)
　　Eligible for Reduced-Price Lunch Program: 701 (10.4%)
Teachers: 345.6 (19.4 to 1)
Librarians/Media Specialists: 4.0 (1,679.8 to 1)
Guidance Counselors: 10.2 (658.7 to 1)
Current Spending: ($ per student per year):
　　Total: $4,833; Instruction: $2,606; Support Services: $1,943
Enrollment, Drop-out Rates and Diploma Recipients by Race/Ethnicity

Category	Total	White	Black	Asian	AIAN	Hisp.
Enrollment (%)	100.0	56.2	11.1	4.8	1.3	26.7
Drop-out Rate (%)	6.0	6.0	6.9	2.6	0.0	7.1
H.S. Diplomas (#)	572	360	57	45	4	106

Coconino County

Flagstaff Unified District
3285 E Sparrow • Flagstaff, AZ 86004-7795
(928) 527-6000 • http://www.flagstaff.k12.az.us/
Grade Span: PK-12; Agency Type: 1
Schools: 21
　　13 Primary; 3 Middle; 5 High; 0 Other Level
　　20 Regular; 0 Special Education; 0 Vocational; 1 Alternative
　　0 Magnet; 0 Charter; 14 Title I Eligible; 8 School-wide Title I
Students: 11,379　(51.6% male; 48.3% female)
　　Individual Education Program: 1,794 (15.8%);
　　English Language Learner: 1,396 (12.3%); Migrant: 0 (0.0%)
　　Eligible for Free Lunch Program: 3,572 (31.4%)
　　Eligible for Reduced-Price Lunch Program: 1,084 (9.5%)
Teachers: 641.8 (17.7 to 1)
Librarians/Media Specialists: 15.5 (734.1 to 1)
Guidance Counselors: 23.8 (478.1 to 1)
Current Spending: ($ per student per year):
　　Total: $6,109; Instruction: $3,589; Support Services: $2,313
Enrollment, Drop-out Rates and Diploma Recipients by Race/Ethnicity

Category	Total	White	Black	Asian	AIAN	Hisp.
Enrollment (%)	100.0	54.7	2.5	1.2	23.6	18.0
Drop-out Rate (%)	9.8	6.3	9.8	6.0	15.4	17.2
H.S. Diplomas (#)	741	490	6	14	135	96

Page Unified District
500 S Navajo Dr • Page, AZ 86040-1927
Mailing Address: PO Box 1927 • Page, AZ 86040-1927
(928) 608-4100 • http://www.pageud.k12.az.us/
Grade Span: PK-12; Agency Type: 1
Schools: 4
　　2 Primary; 1 Middle; 1 High; 0 Other Level
　　4 Regular; 0 Special Education; 0 Vocational; 0 Alternative
　　0 Magnet; 0 Charter; 4 Title I Eligible; 4 School-wide Title I
Students: 3,017　(53.0% male; 46.9% female)
　　Individual Education Program: 528 (17.5%);
　　English Language Learner: 1,036 (34.3%); Migrant: 0 (0.0%)
　　Eligible for Free Lunch Program: 1,899 (62.9%)
　　Eligible for Reduced-Price Lunch Program: 237 (7.9%)
Teachers: 183.2 (16.5 to 1)
Librarians/Media Specialists: 1.0 (3,017.0 to 1)
Guidance Counselors: 3.0 (1,005.7 to 1)

Current Spending: ($ per student per year):
   Total: $7,278; Instruction: $3,885; Support Services: $3,087
Enrollment, Drop-out Rates and Diploma Recipients by Race/Ethnicity

Category	Total	White	Black	Asian	AIAN	Hisp.
Enrollment (%)	100.0	25.8	0.4	0.3	71.0	2.5
Drop-out Rate (%)	11.7	9.2	0.0	0.0	11.8	60.0
H.S. Diplomas (#)	168	61	0	1	105	1

Tuba City Unified District
E Fir St • Tuba City, AZ 86045-0067
Mailing Address: PO Box 67 • Tuba City, AZ 86045-0067
(928) 283-1001 •
http://www.tcusd.k12.az.us/education/district/district.php?sectionid=1
Grade Span: PK-12; **Agency Type:** 1
Schools: 7
   4 Primary; 1 Middle; 2 High; 0 Other Level
   6 Regular; 0 Special Education; 0 Vocational; 1 Alternative
   0 Magnet; 0 Charter; 7 Title I Eligible; 6 School-wide Title I
Students: 2,565   (51.2% male; 48.7% female)
   Individual Education Program: 391 (15.2%);
   English Language Learner: 1,161 (45.3%); Migrant: 0 (0.0%)
   Eligible for Free Lunch Program: 1,972 (76.9%)
   Eligible for Reduced-Price Lunch Program: 323 (12.6%)
Teachers: 165.6 (15.5 to 1)
Librarians/Media Specialists: 5.0 (513.0 to 1)
Guidance Counselors: 8.6 (298.3 to 1)
Current Spending: ($ per student per year):
   Total: $8,700; Instruction: $3,975; Support Services: $4,386
Enrollment, Drop-out Rates and Diploma Recipients by Race/Ethnicity

Category	Total	White	Black	Asian	AIAN	Hisp.
Enrollment (%)	100.0	2.0	0.1	0.2	97.3	0.3
Drop-out Rate (%)	16.6	17.6	n/a	n/a	16.6	0.0
H.S. Diplomas (#)	149	3	0	0	146	0

Gila County

Globe Unified District
501 E Ash St • Globe, AZ 85501-2295
Mailing Address: 455 N Willow • Globe, AZ 85501-2295
(928) 425-3211 • http://www.globe.k12.az.us/
Grade Span: PK-12; **Agency Type:** 1
Schools: 4
   1 Primary; 2 Middle; 1 High; 0 Other Level
   4 Regular; 0 Special Education; 0 Vocational; 0 Alternative
   0 Magnet; 0 Charter; 3 Title I Eligible; 2 School-wide Title I
Students: 2,133   (51.8% male; 48.1% female)
   Individual Education Program: 229 (10.7%);
   English Language Learner: 41 (1.9%); Migrant: 0 (0.0%)
   Eligible for Free Lunch Program: 1,024 (48.0%)
   Eligible for Reduced-Price Lunch Program: 227 (10.6%)
Teachers: 112.9 (18.9 to 1)
Librarians/Media Specialists: 3.0 (711.0 to 1)
Guidance Counselors: 2.0 (1,066.5 to 1)
Current Spending: ($ per student per year):
   Total: $5,389; Instruction: $2,834; Support Services: $2,229
Enrollment, Drop-out Rates and Diploma Recipients by Race/Ethnicity

Category	Total	White	Black	Asian	AIAN	Hisp.
Enrollment (%)	100.0	45.8	0.8	0.4	22.8	30.3
Drop-out Rate (%)	8.7	7.5	50.0	0.0	13.4	7.4
H.S. Diplomas (#)	105	60	1	1	15	28

Payson Unified District
514 W Wade Ln • Payson, AZ 85541
Mailing Address: PO Box 919 • Payson, AZ 85547-0919
(928) 474-2070 • http://www.pusd.k12.az.us
Grade Span: PK-12; **Agency Type:** 1
Schools: 6
   3 Primary; 1 Middle; 2 High; 0 Other Level
   6 Regular; 0 Special Education; 0 Vocational; 0 Alternative
   0 Magnet; 1 Charter; 6 Title I Eligible; 0 School-wide Title I
Students: 2,816   (51.3% male; 48.6% female)
   Individual Education Program: 355 (12.6%);
   English Language Learner: 111 (3.9%); Migrant: 0 (0.0%)
   Eligible for Free Lunch Program: 913 (32.4%)
   Eligible for Reduced-Price Lunch Program: 270 (9.6%)
Teachers: 154.5 (18.2 to 1)
Librarians/Media Specialists: 5.5 (512.0 to 1)
Guidance Counselors: 5.0 (563.2 to 1)
Current Spending: ($ per student per year):
   Total: $5,129; Instruction: $3,075; Support Services: $1,867
Enrollment, Drop-out Rates and Diploma Recipients by Race/Ethnicity

Category	Total	White	Black	Asian	AIAN	Hisp.
Enrollment (%)	100.0	84.3	0.8	0.7	3.0	11.1
Drop-out Rate (%)	10.3	10.2	0.0	12.5	21.4	7.2
H.S. Diplomas (#)	157	138	0	2	6	11

Graham County

Safford Unified District
734 11th St • Safford, AZ 85546-2967
(928) 348-7000 • http://www.saffordusd.k12.az.us/
Grade Span: PK-12; **Agency Type:** 1
Schools: 6
   2 Primary; 1 Middle; 2 High; 1 Other Level
   6 Regular; 0 Special Education; 0 Vocational; 0 Alternative
   0 Magnet; 0 Charter; 4 Title I Eligible; 1 School-wide Title I
Students: 2,888   (51.2% male; 48.7% female)
   Individual Education Program: 376 (13.0%);
   English Language Learner: 0 (0.0%); Migrant: 0 (0.0%)
   Eligible for Free Lunch Program: 1,148 (39.8%)
   Eligible for Reduced-Price Lunch Program: 230 (8.0%)
Teachers: 149.6 (19.3 to 1)
Librarians/Media Specialists: 5.0 (577.6 to 1)
Guidance Counselors: 6.0 (481.3 to 1)
Current Spending: ($ per student per year):
   Total: $4,975; Instruction: $2,787; Support Services: $1,924
Enrollment, Drop-out Rates and Diploma Recipients by Race/Ethnicity

Category	Total	White	Black	Asian	AIAN	Hisp.
Enrollment (%)	100.0	51.4	2.5	0.5	1.4	44.2
Drop-out Rate (%)	15.9	14.5	37.5	0.0	42.9	16.6
H.S. Diplomas (#)	162	93	3	2	4	60

La Paz County

Parker Unified SD
1608 Laguna Ave • Parker, AZ 85344-1090
Mailing Address: PO Box 1090 • Parker, AZ 85344-1090
(928) 669-9244 • http://www.parkerusd.k12.az.us/
Grade Span: PK-12; **Agency Type:** 1
Schools: 6
   2 Primary; 2 Middle; 1 High; 1 Other Level
   6 Regular; 0 Special Education; 0 Vocational; 0 Alternative
   0 Magnet; 0 Charter; 2 Title I Eligible; 0 School-wide Title I
Students: 1,995   (50.0% male; 49.9% female)
   Individual Education Program: 311 (15.6%);
   English Language Learner: 197 (9.9%); Migrant: 0 (0.0%)
   Eligible for Free Lunch Program: 1,181 (59.2%)
   Eligible for Reduced-Price Lunch Program: 306 (15.3%)
Teachers: 126.9 (15.7 to 1)
Librarians/Media Specialists: 2.0 (997.5 to 1)
Guidance Counselors: 2.0 (997.5 to 1)
Current Spending: ($ per student per year):
   Total: $6,333; Instruction: $3,552; Support Services: $2,541
Enrollment, Drop-out Rates and Diploma Recipients by Race/Ethnicity

Category	Total	White	Black	Asian	AIAN	Hisp.
Enrollment (%)	100.0	28.4	1.3	0.8	36.4	33.1
Drop-out Rate (%)	13.9	9.9	0.0	0.0	20.2	14.4
H.S. Diplomas (#)	116	49	3	1	25	38

Maricopa County

Agua Fria Union High SD
750 E Riley Dr • Avondale, AZ 85323-2154
(623) 932-7000 • http://www.aguafria.org/
Grade Span: 09-12; **Agency Type:** 1
Schools: 3
   0 Primary; 0 Middle; 3 High; 0 Other Level
   3 Regular; 0 Special Education; 0 Vocational; 0 Alternative
   0 Magnet; 0 Charter; 1 Title I Eligible; 0 School-wide Title I
Students: 3,657   (51.3% male; 48.6% female)
   Individual Education Program: 325 (8.9%);
   English Language Learner: 225 (6.2%); Migrant: 12 (0.3%)
   Eligible for Free Lunch Program: 616 (16.8%)
   Eligible for Reduced-Price Lunch Program: 129 (3.5%)
Teachers: 161.2 (22.7 to 1)
Librarians/Media Specialists: 2.2 (1,662.3 to 1)
Guidance Counselors: 9.0 (406.3 to 1)
Current Spending: ($ per student per year):
   Total: $11,195; Instruction: $3,343; Support Services: $7,506
Enrollment, Drop-out Rates and Diploma Recipients by Race/Ethnicity

Category	Total	White	Black	Asian	AIAN	Hisp.
Enrollment (%)	100.0	49.3	8.9	3.3	1.1	37.5
Drop-out Rate (%)	6.9	5.8	5.7	3.7	5.6	9.1
H.S. Diplomas (#)	425	244	28	15	7	131

Alhambra Elementary District
4510 N 37th Ave • Phoenix, AZ 85019
(602) 336-2920 • http://www.alhambra.k12.az.us/
Grade Span: PK-08; **Agency Type:** 1
Schools: 15
   13 Primary; 2 Middle; 0 High; 0 Other Level

15 Regular; 0 Special Education; 0 Vocational; 0 Alternative
0 Magnet; 0 Charter; 14 Title I Eligible; 14 School-wide Title I
Students: 14,742   (51.7% male; 48.2% female)
Individual Education Program: 1,588 (10.8%);
English Language Learner: 7,326 (49.7%); Migrant: 0 (0.0%)
Eligible for Free Lunch Program: 12,471 (84.6%)
Eligible for Reduced-Price Lunch Program: 1,587 (10.8%)
Teachers: 723.9 (20.4 to 1)
Librarians/Media Specialists: 10.5 (1,404.0 to 1)
Guidance Counselors: 12.0 (1,228.5 to 1)
Current Spending: ($ per student per year):
Total: $4,970; Instruction: $3,061; Support Services: $1,517
Enrollment, Drop-out Rates and Diploma Recipients by Race/Ethnicity

Category	Total	White	Black	Asian	AIAN	Hisp.
Enrollment (%)	100.0	14.7	7.9	2.8	3.8	70.7
Drop-out Rate (%)	n/a	n/a	n/a	n/a	n/a	n/a
H.S. Diplomas (#)	n/a	n/a	n/a	n/a	n/a	n/a

Avondale Elementary District
235 W Western Ave • Avondale, AZ 85323-1848
(623) 772-5013 • http://www.avondale.k12.az.us/
Grade Span: PK-08; **Agency Type:** 1
Schools: 7
5 Primary; 2 Middle; 0 High; 0 Other Level
7 Regular; 0 Special Education; 0 Vocational; 0 Alternative
0 Magnet; 0 Charter; 4 Title I Eligible; 4 School-wide Title I
Students: 4,449 (53.0% male; 46.9% female)
Individual Education Program: 529 (11.9%);
English Language Learner: 1,174 (26.4%); Migrant: 11 (0.2%)
Eligible for Free Lunch Program: 2,873 (64.6%)
Eligible for Reduced-Price Lunch Program: 498 (11.2%)
Teachers: 219.5 (20.3 to 1)
Librarians/Media Specialists: 5.0 (889.8 to 1)
Guidance Counselors: 3.0 (1,483.0 to 1)
Current Spending: ($ per student per year):
Total: $4,793; Instruction: $2,968; Support Services: $1,532
Enrollment, Drop-out Rates and Diploma Recipients by Race/Ethnicity

Category	Total	White	Black	Asian	AIAN	Hisp.
Enrollment (%)	100.0	30.0	6.8	0.7	1.1	61.4
Drop-out Rate (%)	n/a	n/a	n/a	n/a	n/a	n/a
H.S. Diplomas (#)	n/a	n/a	n/a	n/a	n/a	n/a

Balsz Elementary District
4825 E Roosevelt • Phoenix, AZ 85008-5917
(602) 629-6400 • http://www.balsz.k12.az.us/
Grade Span: PK-08; **Agency Type:** 1
Schools: 5
5 Primary; 0 Middle; 0 High; 0 Other Level
5 Regular; 0 Special Education; 0 Vocational; 0 Alternative
0 Magnet; 0 Charter; 4 Title I Eligible; 4 School-wide Title I
Students: 3,432 (50.7% male; 49.2% female)
Individual Education Program: 343 (10.0%);
English Language Learner: 1,573 (45.8%); Migrant: 0 (0.0%)
Eligible for Free Lunch Program: 2,940 (85.7%)
Eligible for Reduced-Price Lunch Program: 373 (10.9%)
Teachers: 195.6 (17.5 to 1)
Librarians/Media Specialists: 4.0 (858.0 to 1)
Guidance Counselors: 2.0 (1,716.0 to 1)
Current Spending: ($ per student per year):
Total: $9,160; Instruction: $3,190; Support Services: $5,610
Enrollment, Drop-out Rates and Diploma Recipients by Race/Ethnicity

Category	Total	White	Black	Asian	AIAN	Hisp.
Enrollment (%)	100.0	10.5	10.0	1.3	5.7	72.5
Drop-out Rate (%)	n/a	n/a	n/a	n/a	n/a	n/a
H.S. Diplomas (#)	n/a	n/a	n/a	n/a	n/a	n/a

Cartwright Elementary District
3401 N 67th Ave • Phoenix, AZ 85033-4599
(623) 691-4000 • http://www.cartwright.k12.az.us/
Grade Span: PK-08; **Agency Type:** 1
Schools: 24
20 Primary; 4 Middle; 0 High; 0 Other Level
22 Regular; 2 Special Education; 0 Vocational; 0 Alternative
0 Magnet; 0 Charter; 19 Title I Eligible; 19 School-wide Title I
Students: 19,864 (50.6% male; 49.3% female)
Individual Education Program: 2,295 (11.6%);
English Language Learner: 8,896 (44.8%); Migrant: 0 (0.0%)
Eligible for Free Lunch Program: 14,227 (71.6%)
Eligible for Reduced-Price Lunch Program: 2,296 (11.6%)
Teachers: 961.3 (20.7 to 1)
Librarians/Media Specialists: 5.0 (3,972.8 to 1)
Guidance Counselors: 8.0 (2,483.0 to 1)
Current Spending: ($ per student per year):
Total: $4,947; Instruction: $2,994; Support Services: $1,643

Enrollment, Drop-out Rates and Diploma Recipients by Race/Ethnicity

Category	Total	White	Black	Asian	AIAN	Hisp.
Enrollment (%)	100.0	9.9	5.5	0.6	1.1	83.0
Drop-out Rate (%)	n/a	n/a	n/a	n/a	n/a	n/a
H.S. Diplomas (#)	n/a	n/a	n/a	n/a	n/a	n/a

Cave Creek Unified District
33606 N 60th St • Cave Creek, AZ 85262-5243
Mailing Address: PO Box 426 • Cave Creek, AZ 85327
(480) 575-2016 • http://www.ccusd.k12.az.us/
Grade Span: PK-12; **Agency Type:** 1
Schools: 7
4 Primary; 2 Middle; 1 High; 0 Other Level
7 Regular; 0 Special Education; 0 Vocational; 0 Alternative
0 Magnet; 0 Charter; 2 Title I Eligible; 0 School-wide Title I
Students: 5,388 (51.0% male; 48.9% female)
Individual Education Program: 430 (8.0%);
English Language Learner: 65 (1.2%); Migrant: 0 (0.0%)
Eligible for Free Lunch Program: 244 (4.5%)
Eligible for Reduced-Price Lunch Program: 75 (1.4%)
Teachers: 265.9 (20.3 to 1)
Librarians/Media Specialists: 4.0 (1,347.0 to 1)
Guidance Counselors: 5.0 (1,077.6 to 1)
Current Spending: ($ per student per year):
Total: $5,500; Instruction: $2,915; Support Services: $2,283
Enrollment, Drop-out Rates and Diploma Recipients by Race/Ethnicity

Category	Total	White	Black	Asian	AIAN	Hisp.
Enrollment (%)	100.0	90.6	1.2	1.7	0.3	6.2
Drop-out Rate (%)	2.6	2.4	0.0	0.0	0.0	9.4
H.S. Diplomas (#)	198	187	0	2	1	8

Chandler Unified District
1525 W Frye Rd • Chandler, AZ 85224-6178
(480) 812-7000 • http://www.chandler.k12.az.us/
Grade Span: PK-12; **Agency Type:** 1
Schools: 28
19 Primary; 3 Middle; 2 High; 4 Other Level
26 Regular; 0 Special Education; 0 Vocational; 2 Alternative
0 Magnet; 0 Charter; 5 Title I Eligible; 4 School-wide Title I
Students: 26,915 (51.2% male; 48.7% female)
Individual Education Program: 2,702 (10.0%);
English Language Learner: 3,524 (13.1%); Migrant: 106 (0.4%)
Eligible for Free Lunch Program: 1,218 (4.5%)
Eligible for Reduced-Price Lunch Program: 5,994 (22.3%)
Teachers: 1,221.3 (22.0 to 1)
Librarians/Media Specialists: 23.0 (1,170.2 to 1)
Guidance Counselors: 42.0 (640.8 to 1)
Current Spending: ($ per student per year):
Total: $5,303; Instruction: $3,176; Support Services: $1,838
Enrollment, Drop-out Rates and Diploma Recipients by Race/Ethnicity

Category	Total	White	Black	Asian	AIAN	Hisp.
Enrollment (%)	100.0	57.8	5.9	4.4	1.5	30.4
Drop-out Rate (%)	4.1	2.2	6.1	4.4	4.0	8.1
H.S. Diplomas (#)	1,021	647	70	50	22	232

Creighton Elementary District
2702 E Flower St • Phoenix, AZ 85016-7498
(602) 381-6000 • http://www.creighton.k12.az.us/
Grade Span: PK-12; **Agency Type:** 1
Schools: 10
9 Primary; 0 Middle; 0 High; 1 Other Level
10 Regular; 0 Special Education; 0 Vocational; 0 Alternative
0 Magnet; 0 Charter; 9 Title I Eligible; 9 School-wide Title I
Students: 8,382 (50.1% male; 49.8% female)
Individual Education Program: 785 (9.4%);
English Language Learner: 5,067 (60.5%); Migrant: 0 (0.0%)
Eligible for Free Lunch Program: 7,114 (84.9%)
Eligible for Reduced-Price Lunch Program: 1,196 (14.3%)
Teachers: 482.1 (17.4 to 1)
Librarians/Media Specialists: 5.0 (1,676.4 to 1)
Guidance Counselors: 1.0 (8,382.0 to 1)
Current Spending: ($ per student per year):
Total: $5,755; Instruction: $3,304; Support Services: $2,027
Enrollment, Drop-out Rates and Diploma Recipients by Race/Ethnicity

Category	Total	White	Black	Asian	AIAN	Hisp.
Enrollment (%)	100.0	9.0	3.8	0.5	3.4	83.3
Drop-out Rate (%)	n/a	n/a	n/a	n/a	n/a	n/a
H.S. Diplomas (#)	0	0	0	0	0	0

Deer Valley Unified District
20402 N 15th Ave • Phoenix, AZ 85027-3699
(623) 445-5000 • http://www.dvusd.k12.az.us/
Grade Span: PK-12; **Agency Type:** 1
Schools: 34
25 Primary; 3 Middle; 4 High; 2 Other Level

33 Regular; 0 Special Education; 1 Vocational; 0 Alternative
0 Magnet; 0 Charter; 7 Title I Eligible; 6 School-wide Title I
Students: 31,691 (51.6% male; 48.3% female)
  Individual Education Program: 3,983 (12.6%);
  English Language Learner: 1,566 (4.9%); Migrant: 0 (0.0%)
  Eligible for Free Lunch Program: 5,392 (17.0%)
  Eligible for Reduced-Price Lunch Program: 1,761 (5.6%)
Teachers: 1,585.3 (20.0 to 1)
Librarians/Media Specialists: 31.0 (1,022.3 to 1)
Guidance Counselors: 42.4 (747.4 to 1)
Current Spending: ($ per student per year):
  Total: $5,056; Instruction: $3,070; Support Services: $1,744
Enrollment, Drop-out Rates and Diploma Recipients by Race/Ethnicity

Category	Total	White	Black	Asian	AIAN	Hisp.
Enrollment (%)	100.0	80.4	3.1	3.3	0.9	12.2
Drop-out Rate (%)	6.3	6.0	9.4	3.8	10.0	8.6
H.S. Diplomas (#)	1,320	1,115	27	45	9	124

Dysart Unified District
11405 N Dysart Rd • El Mirage, AZ 85335
(623) 876-7000 • http://dysart.org/
Grade Span: PK-12; **Agency Type:** 1
Schools: 12
  9 Primary; 0 Middle; 2 High; 1 Other Level
  12 Regular; 0 Special Education; 0 Vocational; 0 Alternative
  0 Magnet; 0 Charter; 6 Title I Eligible; 6 School-wide Title I
Students: 11,150 (52.4% male; 47.5% female)
  Individual Education Program: 1,328 (11.9%);
  English Language Learner: 1,631 (14.6%); Migrant: 49 (0.4%)
  Eligible for Free Lunch Program: 5,743 (51.5%)
  Eligible for Reduced-Price Lunch Program: 1,627 (14.6%)
Teachers: 530.9 (21.0 to 1)
Librarians/Media Specialists: 2.0 (5,575.0 to 1)
Guidance Counselors: 11.9 (937.0 to 1)
Current Spending: ($ per student per year):
  Total: $5,175; Instruction: $2,820; Support Services: $2,061
Enrollment, Drop-out Rates and Diploma Recipients by Race/Ethnicity

Category	Total	White	Black	Asian	AIAN	Hisp.
Enrollment (%)	100.0	44.9	8.6	1.9	1.2	43.4
Drop-out Rate (%)	11.0	9.4	8.5	5.6	18.2	12.4
H.S. Diplomas (#)	189	46	17	4	0	122

East Valley Institute of Technology
1601 W Main St • Mesa, AZ 85201-6910
(480) 461-4000 • http://www.evit.com/
Grade Span: 09-12; **Agency Type:** 7
Schools: 12
  0 Primary; 0 Middle; 8 High; 4 Other Level
  0 Regular; 0 Special Education; 12 Vocational; 0 Alternative
  0 Magnet; 0 Charter; 1 Title I Eligible; 0 School-wide Title I
Students: 16,332 (55.8% male; 44.1% female)
  Individual Education Program: 0 (0.0%);
  English Language Learner: 0 (0.0%); Migrant: 0 (0.0%)
  Eligible for Free Lunch Program: n/a
  Eligible for Reduced-Price Lunch Program: n/a
Teachers: n/a
Librarians/Media Specialists: n/a
Guidance Counselors: n/a
Current Spending: ($ per student per year):
  Total: n/a; Instruction: n/a; Support Services: n/a
Enrollment, Drop-out Rates and Diploma Recipients by Race/Ethnicity

Category	Total	White	Black	Asian	AIAN	Hisp.
Enrollment (%)	100.0	66.0	6.2	3.4	2.7	21.7
Drop-out Rate (%)	n/a	n/a	n/a	n/a	n/a	n/a
H.S. Diplomas (#)	0	0	0	0	0	0

Fountain Hills Unified District
16000 E Palisades Blvd • Fountain Hills, AZ 85268-2441
(480) 664-5000 • http://www.fhusd.org/
Grade Span: PK-12; **Agency Type:** 1
Schools: 4
  2 Primary; 1 Middle; 1 High; 0 Other Level
  4 Regular; 0 Special Education; 0 Vocational; 0 Alternative
  0 Magnet; 0 Charter; 2 Title I Eligible; 0 School-wide Title I
Students: 2,542 (53.6% male; 46.3% female)
  Individual Education Program: 248 (9.8%);
  English Language Learner: 19 (0.7%); Migrant: 0 (0.0%)
  Eligible for Free Lunch Program: 195 (7.7%)
  Eligible for Reduced-Price Lunch Program: 61 (2.4%)
Teachers: 136.1 (18.7 to 1)
Librarians/Media Specialists: 3.5 (726.3 to 1)
Guidance Counselors: 4.0 (635.5 to 1)
Current Spending: ($ per student per year):
  Total: $4,999; Instruction: $2,550; Support Services: $2,196

Enrollment, Drop-out Rates and Diploma Recipients by Race/Ethnicity

Category	Total	White	Black	Asian	AIAN	Hisp.
Enrollment (%)	100.0	86.3	0.9	2.0	5.9	4.9
Drop-out Rate (%)	3.6	3.7	0.0	0.0	5.5	0.0
H.S. Diplomas (#)	176	164	1	2	5	4

Fowler Elementary District
1617 S 67th Ave • Phoenix, AZ 85043-7717
(623) 707-4500 • http://www.fesd.org/
Grade Span: PK-08; **Agency Type:** 1
Schools: 6
  4 Primary; 2 Middle; 0 High; 0 Other Level
  6 Regular; 0 Special Education; 0 Vocational; 0 Alternative
  0 Magnet; 0 Charter; 4 Title I Eligible; 3 School-wide Title I
Students: 3,126 (51.2% male; 48.7% female)
  Individual Education Program: 368 (11.8%);
  English Language Learner: 1,149 (36.8%); Migrant: 12 (0.4%)
  Eligible for Free Lunch Program: 2,359 (75.5%)
  Eligible for Reduced-Price Lunch Program: 512 (16.4%)
Teachers: 173.2 (18.0 to 1)
Librarians/Media Specialists: 2.0 (1,563.0 to 1)
Guidance Counselors: 1.0 (3,126.0 to 1)
Current Spending: ($ per student per year):
  Total: $6,215; Instruction: $3,081; Support Services: $2,771
Enrollment, Drop-out Rates and Diploma Recipients by Race/Ethnicity

Category	Total	White	Black	Asian	AIAN	Hisp.
Enrollment (%)	100.0	13.7	9.2	0.7	1.3	75.1
Drop-out Rate (%)	n/a	n/a	n/a	n/a	n/a	n/a
H.S. Diplomas (#)	n/a	n/a	n/a	n/a	n/a	n/a

Gilbert Unified District
140 S Gilbert Rd • Gilbert, AZ 85296-1014
(480) 497-3452 • http://www.gilbert.k12.az.us/index.html
Grade Span: PK-12; **Agency Type:** 1
Schools: 38
  25 Primary; 5 Middle; 6 High; 2 Other Level
  36 Regular; 0 Special Education; 0 Vocational; 2 Alternative
  0 Magnet; 0 Charter; 9 Title I Eligible; 2 School-wide Title I
Students: 35,218 (51.7% male; 48.2% female)
  Individual Education Program: 3,931 (11.2%);
  English Language Learner: 838 (2.4%); Migrant: 0 (0.0%)
  Eligible for Free Lunch Program: 1,763 (5.0%)
  Eligible for Reduced-Price Lunch Program: 1,173 (3.3%)
Teachers: 1,909.0 (18.4 to 1)
Librarians/Media Specialists: 32.5 (1,083.6 to 1)
Guidance Counselors: 35.0 (1,006.2 to 1)
Current Spending: ($ per student per year):
  Total: $4,698; Instruction: $2,869; Support Services: $1,587
Enrollment, Drop-out Rates and Diploma Recipients by Race/Ethnicity

Category	Total	White	Black	Asian	AIAN	Hisp.
Enrollment (%)	100.0	77.1	3.8	3.8	0.9	14.4
Drop-out Rate (%)	2.5	2.2	4.7	1.6	8.9	4.0
H.S. Diplomas (#)	1,817	1,507	40	78	8	184

Glendale Elementary District
7301 N 58th Ave • Glendale, AZ 85301-1893
(623) 842-8100 • http://www.gesd.k12.az.us/
Grade Span: PK-12; **Agency Type:** 1
Schools: 17
  14 Primary; 2 Middle; 0 High; 1 Other Level
  14 Regular; 0 Special Education; 1 Vocational; 2 Alternative
  0 Magnet; 0 Charter; 16 Title I Eligible; 15 School-wide Title I
Students: 13,258 (51.3% male; 48.6% female)
  Individual Education Program: 1,483 (11.2%);
  English Language Learner: 4,445 (33.5%); Migrant: 135 (1.0%)
  Eligible for Free Lunch Program: 8,205 (61.9%)
  Eligible for Reduced-Price Lunch Program: 1,593 (12.0%)
Teachers: 647.2 (20.5 to 1)
Librarians/Media Specialists: 16.0 (828.6 to 1)
Guidance Counselors: 2.0 (6,629.0 to 1)
Current Spending: ($ per student per year):
  Total: $4,886; Instruction: $2,783; Support Services: $1,819
Enrollment, Drop-out Rates and Diploma Recipients by Race/Ethnicity

Category	Total	White	Black	Asian	AIAN	Hisp.
Enrollment (%)	100.0	22.4	9.3	2.3	2.4	63.6
Drop-out Rate (%)	n/a	n/a	n/a	n/a	n/a	n/a
H.S. Diplomas (#)	0	0	0	0	0	0

Glendale Union High SD
7650 N 43rd Ave • Glendale, AZ 85301-1661
(623) 435-6000 • http://guhsdns1.guhsd.k12.az.us/
Grade Span: 09-12; **Agency Type:** 1
Schools: 12
  0 Primary; 0 Middle; 11 High; 1 Other Level
  9 Regular; 0 Special Education; 0 Vocational; 3 Alternative

0 Magnet; 0 Charter; 7 Title I Eligible; 1 School-wide Title I
Students: 14,515 (51.4% male; 48.5% female)
 Individual Education Program: 1,395 (9.6%);
 English Language Learner: 879 (6.1%); Migrant: 48 (0.3%)
 Eligible for Free Lunch Program: 2,331 (16.1%)
 Eligible for Reduced-Price Lunch Program: 423 (2.9%)
Teachers: 681.7 (21.3 to 1)
Librarians/Media Specialists: 8.0 (1,814.4 to 1)
Guidance Counselors: 31.0 (468.2 to 1)
Current Spending: ($ per student per year):
 Total: $6,181; Instruction: $3,441; Support Services: $2,405
Enrollment, Drop-out Rates and Diploma Recipients by Race/Ethnicity

Category	Total	White	Black	Asian	AIAN	Hisp.
Enrollment (%)	100.0	53.4	7.3	3.0	2.7	33.6
Drop-out Rate (%)	4.6	3.8	3.9	2.2	7.7	6.2
H.S. Diplomas (#)	2,609	1,705	152	111	45	596

Higley Unified District
15201 S Higley Rd • Higley, AZ 85236-9715
(480) 279-7000 • http://www.husd.org/
Grade Span: PK-12; **Agency Type:** 1
Schools: 10
 6 Primary; 0 Middle; 2 High; 2 Other Level
 10 Regular; 0 Special Education; 0 Vocational; 0 Alternative
 0 Magnet; 5 Charter; 5 Title I Eligible; 3 School-wide Title I
Students: 5,565 (50.5% male; 49.4% female)
 Individual Education Program: 507 (9.1%);
 English Language Learner: 166 (3.0%); Migrant: 8 (0.1%)
 Eligible for Free Lunch Program: 499 (9.0%)
 Eligible for Reduced-Price Lunch Program: 391 (7.0%)
Teachers: 233.3 (23.9 to 1)
Librarians/Media Specialists: 5.0 (1,113.0 to 1)
Guidance Counselors: 0.0 (n/a to 1)
Current Spending: ($ per student per year):
 Total: $6,091; Instruction: $3,929; Support Services: $1,895
Enrollment, Drop-out Rates and Diploma Recipients by Race/Ethnicity

Category	Total	White	Black	Asian	AIAN	Hisp.
Enrollment (%)	100.0	72.2	3.4	2.7	4.2	17.4
Drop-out Rate (%)	11.0	9.4	3.4	0.0	33.3	12.8
H.S. Diplomas (#)	129	86	8	2	6	27

Isaac Elementary District
3348 W Mcdowell Rd • Phoenix, AZ 85009-2390
(602) 455-6700 • http://isaaceld.org/index.htm
Grade Span: PK-08; **Agency Type:** 1
Schools: 13
 10 Primary; 3 Middle; 0 High; 0 Other Level
 13 Regular; 0 Special Education; 0 Vocational; 0 Alternative
 0 Magnet; 0 Charter; 13 Title I Eligible; 13 School-wide Title I
Students: 8,538 (50.5% male; 49.4% female)
 Individual Education Program: 1,017 (11.9%);
 English Language Learner: 5,207 (61.0%); Migrant: 0 (0.0%)
 Eligible for Free Lunch Program: 8,502 (99.6%)
 Eligible for Reduced-Price Lunch Program: 0 (0.0%)
Teachers: 439.5 (19.4 to 1)
Librarians/Media Specialists: 7.0 (1,219.7 to 1)
Guidance Counselors: 5.0 (1,707.6 to 1)
Current Spending: ($ per student per year):
 Total: $5,987; Instruction: $3,394; Support Services: $2,204
Enrollment, Drop-out Rates and Diploma Recipients by Race/Ethnicity

Category	Total	White	Black	Asian	AIAN	Hisp.
Enrollment (%)	100.0	2.8	1.9	0.4	0.9	94.1
Drop-out Rate (%)	n/a	n/a	n/a	n/a	n/a	n/a
H.S. Diplomas (#)	n/a	n/a	n/a	n/a	n/a	n/a

Kyrene Elementary District
8700 S Kyrene Rd • Tempe, AZ 85284-2197
(480) 783-4000 • http://www.kyrene.k12.az.us/
Grade Span: PK-08; **Agency Type:** 1
Schools: 26
 20 Primary; 6 Middle; 0 High; 0 Other Level
 25 Regular; 0 Special Education; 0 Vocational; 1 Alternative
 0 Magnet; 0 Charter; 4 Title I Eligible; 0 School-wide Title I
Students: 18,579 (51.1% male; 48.8% female)
 Individual Education Program: 1,838 (9.9%);
 English Language Learner: 477 (2.6%); Migrant: 0 (0.0%)
 Eligible for Free Lunch Program: 1,704 (9.2%)
 Eligible for Reduced-Price Lunch Program: 692 (3.7%)
Teachers: 1,016.5 (18.3 to 1)
Librarians/Media Specialists: 28.0 (663.5 to 1)
Guidance Counselors: 12.0 (1,548.3 to 1)
Current Spending: ($ per student per year):
 Total: $4,950; Instruction: $2,969; Support Services: $1,718

Enrollment, Drop-out Rates and Diploma Recipients by Race/Ethnicity

Category	Total	White	Black	Asian	AIAN	Hisp.
Enrollment (%)	100.0	69.7	6.4	7.8	2.4	13.8
Drop-out Rate (%)	n/a	n/a	n/a	n/a	n/a	n/a
H.S. Diplomas (#)	n/a	n/a	n/a	n/a	n/a	n/a

Laveen Elementary District
9401 S 51st Ave • Laveen, AZ 85339-0029
Mailing Address: PO Box 29 • Laveen, AZ 85339-0029
(602) 237-9100 • http://laveeneld.k12.az.us/
Grade Span: PK-08; **Agency Type:** 1
Schools: 3
 2 Primary; 1 Middle; 0 High; 0 Other Level
 3 Regular; 0 Special Education; 0 Vocational; 0 Alternative
 0 Magnet; 0 Charter; 3 Title I Eligible; 3 School-wide Title I
Students: 1,754 (49.6% male; 50.3% female)
 Individual Education Program: 307 (17.5%);
 English Language Learner: 599 (34.2%); Migrant: 0 (0.0%)
 Eligible for Free Lunch Program: 1,338 (76.3%)
 Eligible for Reduced-Price Lunch Program: 202 (11.5%)
Teachers: 94.5 (18.6 to 1)
Librarians/Media Specialists: 3.0 (584.7 to 1)
Guidance Counselors: 2.0 (877.0 to 1)
Current Spending: ($ per student per year):
 Total: $5,315; Instruction: $2,673; Support Services: $2,352
Enrollment, Drop-out Rates and Diploma Recipients by Race/Ethnicity

Category	Total	White	Black	Asian	AIAN	Hisp.
Enrollment (%)	100.0	16.0	6.8	0.6	11.6	65.1
Drop-out Rate (%)	n/a	n/a	n/a	n/a	n/a	n/a
H.S. Diplomas (#)	n/a	n/a	n/a	n/a	n/a	n/a

Liberty Elementary District
19818 W Hwy 85 • Buckeye, AZ 85326-9258
(623) 327-2940
Grade Span: PK-08; **Agency Type:** 1
Schools: 3
 3 Primary; 0 Middle; 0 High; 0 Other Level
 3 Regular; 0 Special Education; 0 Vocational; 0 Alternative
 0 Magnet; 0 Charter; 1 Title I Eligible; 0 School-wide Title I
Students: 2,070 (49.7% male; 50.2% female)
 Individual Education Program: 315 (15.2%);
 English Language Learner: 135 (6.5%); Migrant: 11 (0.5%)
 Eligible for Free Lunch Program: 618 (29.9%)
 Eligible for Reduced-Price Lunch Program: 140 (6.8%)
Teachers: 120.5 (17.2 to 1)
Librarians/Media Specialists: 2.0 (1,035.0 to 1)
Guidance Counselors: 1.5 (1,380.0 to 1)
Current Spending: ($ per student per year):
 Total: $5,232; Instruction: $3,115; Support Services: $1,901
Enrollment, Drop-out Rates and Diploma Recipients by Race/Ethnicity

Category	Total	White	Black	Asian	AIAN	Hisp.
Enrollment (%)	100.0	65.6	2.3	0.8	1.4	29.9
Drop-out Rate (%)	n/a	n/a	n/a	n/a	n/a	n/a
H.S. Diplomas (#)	n/a	n/a	n/a	n/a	n/a	n/a

Litchfield Elementary District
553 Plaza Circle • Litchfield Park, AZ 85340-4996
(623) 535-6000 • http://www.lesd.k12.az.us/
Grade Span: PK-08; **Agency Type:** 1
Schools: 8
 6 Primary; 2 Middle; 0 High; 0 Other Level
 8 Regular; 0 Special Education; 0 Vocational; 0 Alternative
 0 Magnet; 0 Charter; 2 Title I Eligible; 0 School-wide Title I
Students: 6,252 (50.7% male; 49.2% female)
 Individual Education Program: 678 (10.8%);
 English Language Learner: 478 (7.6%); Migrant: 3 (<0.1%)
 Eligible for Free Lunch Program: 1,298 (20.8%)
 Eligible for Reduced-Price Lunch Program: 515 (8.2%)
Teachers: 291.5 (21.4 to 1)
Librarians/Media Specialists: 6.0 (1,042.0 to 1)
Guidance Counselors: 6.0 (1,042.0 to 1)
Current Spending: ($ per student per year):
 Total: $4,871; Instruction: $2,734; Support Services: $1,897
Enrollment, Drop-out Rates and Diploma Recipients by Race/Ethnicity

Category	Total	White	Black	Asian	AIAN	Hisp.
Enrollment (%)	100.0	59.5	7.6	4.1	1.2	27.6
Drop-out Rate (%)	n/a	n/a	n/a	n/a	n/a	n/a
H.S. Diplomas (#)	n/a	n/a	n/a	n/a	n/a	n/a

Littleton Elementary District
1252 S 115th Ave • Cashion, AZ 85329-0280
Mailing Address: PO Box 280 • Cashion, AZ 85329-0280
(623) 478-5610
Grade Span: PK-08; **Agency Type:** 1
Schools: 3

2 Primary; 1 Middle; 0 High; 0 Other Level
3 Regular; 0 Special Education; 0 Vocational; 0 Alternative
0 Magnet; 0 Charter; 3 Title I Eligible; 2 School-wide Title I
Students: 2,415   (51.3% male; 48.6% female)
Individual Education Program: 286 (11.8%);
English Language Learner: 670 (27.7%); Migrant: 5 (0.2%)
Eligible for Free Lunch Program: 1,763 (73.0%)
Eligible for Reduced-Price Lunch Program: 381 (15.8%)
Teachers: 110.5 (21.9 to 1)
Librarians/Media Specialists: 0.0 (n/a to 1)
Guidance Counselors: 0.0 (n/a to 1)
Current Spending: ($ per student per year):
Total: $5,083; Instruction: $2,609; Support Services: $2,111
Enrollment, Drop-out Rates and Diploma Recipients by Race/Ethnicity

Category	Total	White	Black	Asian	AIAN	Hisp.
Enrollment (%)	100.0	23.2	7.2	0.8	1.2	67.6
Drop-out Rate (%)	n/a	n/a	n/a	n/a	n/a	n/a
H.S. Diplomas (#)	n/a	n/a	n/a	n/a	n/a	n/a

Madison Elementary District
5601 N 16th St • Phoenix, AZ 85016-2903
(602) 664-7913 • http://www.msd38.k12.az.us/
Grade Span: PK-12; **Agency Type:** 1
Schools: 9
6 Primary; 1 Middle; 0 High; 1 Other Level
8 Regular; 0 Special Education; 0 Vocational; 0 Alternative
0 Magnet; 0 Charter; 5 Title I Eligible; 2 School-wide Title I
Students: 5,253   (51.6% male; 48.3% female)
Individual Education Program: 573 (10.9%);
English Language Learner: 733 (14.0%); Migrant: 0 (0.0%)
Eligible for Free Lunch Program: 2,447 (46.6%)
Eligible for Reduced-Price Lunch Program: 472 (9.0%)
Teachers: 323.1 (16.3 to 1)
Librarians/Media Specialists: 6.0 (875.5 to 1)
Guidance Counselors: 2.0 (2,626.5 to 1)
Current Spending: ($ per student per year):
Total: $6,642; Instruction: $3,324; Support Services: $2,997
Enrollment, Drop-out Rates and Diploma Recipients by Race/Ethnicity

Category	Total	White	Black	Asian	AIAN	Hisp.
Enrollment (%)	100.0	56.3	5.7	1.8	5.6	30.6
Drop-out Rate (%)	n/a	n/a	n/a	n/a	n/a	n/a
H.S. Diplomas (#)	0	0	0	0	0	0

Maricopa County Regional District
358 N 5th Ave • Phoenix, AZ 85003
(602) 452-4700 • http://www.musd20.org/
Grade Span: PK-12; **Agency Type:** 1
Schools: 14
3 Primary; 1 Middle; 5 High; 4 Other Level
7 Regular; 0 Special Education; 0 Vocational; 6 Alternative
0 Magnet; 0 Charter; 10 Title I Eligible; 9 School-wide Title I
Students: 1,769   (60.3% male; 39.6% female)
Individual Education Program: 163 (9.2%);
English Language Learner: 178 (10.1%); Migrant: 0 (0.0%)
Eligible for Free Lunch Program: 1,109 (62.7%)
Eligible for Reduced-Price Lunch Program: 40 (2.3%)
Teachers: 89.0 (19.9 to 1)
Librarians/Media Specialists: 0.0 (n/a to 1)
Guidance Counselors: 0.6 (2,948.3 to 1)
Current Spending: ($ per student per year):
Total: $5,176; Instruction: $2,063; Support Services: $3,113
Enrollment, Drop-out Rates and Diploma Recipients by Race/Ethnicity

Category	Total	White	Black	Asian	AIAN	Hisp.
Enrollment (%)	100.0	37.6	12.5	0.5	10.7	38.7
Drop-out Rate (%)	n/a	n/a	n/a	n/a	n/a	n/a
H.S. Diplomas (#)	139	71	9	1	3	55

Mesa Unified District
63 E Main St • Mesa, AZ 85201-7422
(480) 472-0200 • http://www.mpsaz.org/
Grade Span: PK-12; **Agency Type:** 1
Schools: 91
59 Primary; 16 Middle; 12 High; 4 Other Level
85 Regular; 1 Special Education; 0 Vocational; 5 Alternative
0 Magnet; 0 Charter; 42 Title I Eligible; 31 School-wide Title I
Students: 75,401   (51.7% male; 48.2% female)
Individual Education Program: 7,237 (9.6%);
English Language Learner: 7,431 (9.9%); Migrant: 147 (0.2%)
Eligible for Free Lunch Program: 29,894 (39.6%)
Eligible for Reduced-Price Lunch Program: 7,882 (10.5%)
Teachers: 3,704.0 (20.4 to 1)
Librarians/Media Specialists: 69.0 (1,092.8 to 1)
Guidance Counselors: 90.1 (836.9 to 1)
Current Spending: ($ per student per year):
Total: $5,289; Instruction: $3,217; Support Services: $1,799

Category	Total	White	Black	Asian	AIAN	Hisp.
Enrollment (%)	100.0	60.7	3.7	2.3	3.8	29.5
Drop-out Rate (%)	3.8	2.8	3.7	1.8	12.5	6.1
H.S. Diplomas (#)	4,014	3,099	103	89	104	619

Murphy Elementary District
2615 W Buckeye Rd • Phoenix, AZ 85009-5783
(602) 353-5000 • http://msd.k12.az.us/
Grade Span: PK-08; **Agency Type:** 1
Schools: 4
4 Primary; 0 Middle; 0 High; 0 Other Level
4 Regular; 0 Special Education; 0 Vocational; 0 Alternative
0 Magnet; 0 Charter; 4 Title I Eligible; 4 School-wide Title I
Students: 2,587   (51.5% male; 48.4% female)
Individual Education Program: 350 (13.5%);
English Language Learner: 1,686 (65.2%); Migrant: 0 (0.0%)
Eligible for Free Lunch Program: 2,354 (91.0%)
Eligible for Reduced-Price Lunch Program: 221 (8.5%)
Teachers: 145.4 (17.8 to 1)
Librarians/Media Specialists: 2.5 (1,034.8 to 1)
Guidance Counselors: 1.0 (2,587.0 to 1)
Current Spending: ($ per student per year):
Total: $6,300; Instruction: $3,232; Support Services: $2,614
Enrollment, Drop-out Rates and Diploma Recipients by Race/Ethnicity

Category	Total	White	Black	Asian	AIAN	Hisp.
Enrollment (%)	100.0	3.8	1.6	0.2	0.5	93.9
Drop-out Rate (%)	n/a	n/a	n/a	n/a	n/a	n/a
H.S. Diplomas (#)	n/a	n/a	n/a	n/a	n/a	n/a

Osborn Elementary District
1226 W Osborn Rd • Phoenix, AZ 85013-3618
(602) 707-2000 • http://www.osbornnet.org/
Grade Span: PK-08; **Agency Type:** 1
Schools: 6
4 Primary; 2 Middle; 0 High; 0 Other Level
2 Regular; 0 Special Education; 0 Vocational; 4 Alternative
0 Magnet; 0 Charter; 6 Title I Eligible; 6 School-wide Title I
Students: 3,715   (51.1% male; 48.8% female)
Individual Education Program: 478 (12.9%);
English Language Learner: 1,181 (31.8%); Migrant: 0 (0.0%)
Eligible for Free Lunch Program: 2,812 (75.7%)
Eligible for Reduced-Price Lunch Program: 368 (9.9%)
Teachers: 219.0 (17.0 to 1)
Librarians/Media Specialists: 5.5 (675.5 to 1)
Guidance Counselors: 2.5 (1,486.0 to 1)
Current Spending: ($ per student per year):
Total: $5,721; Instruction: $2,942; Support Services: $2,441
Enrollment, Drop-out Rates and Diploma Recipients by Race/Ethnicity

Category	Total	White	Black	Asian	AIAN	Hisp.
Enrollment (%)	100.0	18.1	10.0	2.1	10.3	59.5
Drop-out Rate (%)	n/a	n/a	n/a	n/a	n/a	n/a
H.S. Diplomas (#)	n/a	n/a	n/a	n/a	n/a	n/a

Paradise Valley Unified District
15002 N 32nd St • Phoenix, AZ 85032-4441
(602) 867-5135 • http://www.pvusd.k12.az.us/
Grade Span: PK-12; **Agency Type:** 1
Schools: 50
30 Primary; 11 Middle; 9 High; 0 Other Level
48 Regular; 0 Special Education; 1 Vocational; 1 Alternative
0 Magnet; 0 Charter; 8 Title I Eligible; 2 School-wide Title I
Students: 34,884   (51.7% male; 48.2% female)
Individual Education Program: 4,022 (11.5%);
English Language Learner: 3,153 (9.0%); Migrant: 0 (0.0%)
Eligible for Free Lunch Program: 7,249 (20.8%)
Eligible for Reduced-Price Lunch Program: 1,831 (5.2%)
Teachers: 1,788.1 (19.5 to 1)
Librarians/Media Specialists: 34.1 (1,023.0 to 1)
Guidance Counselors: 38.0 (918.0 to 1)
Current Spending: ($ per student per year):
Total: $5,345; Instruction: $3,137; Support Services: $1,993
Enrollment, Drop-out Rates and Diploma Recipients by Race/Ethnicity

Category	Total	White	Black	Asian	AIAN	Hisp.
Enrollment (%)	100.0	75.5	3.1	2.8	1.1	17.5
Drop-out Rate (%)	5.9	4.9	10.2	2.1	13.0	13.6
H.S. Diplomas (#)	2,136	1,843	49	62	9	173

Pendergast Elementary District
3802 N 91st Ave • Phoenix, AZ 85037-2368
(623) 772-2215 • http://pendergast.k12.az.us/
Grade Span: PK-08; **Agency Type:** 1
Schools: 12
12 Primary; 0 Middle; 0 High; 0 Other Level
12 Regular; 0 Special Education; 0 Vocational; 0 Alternative

0 Magnet; 0 Charter; 3 Title I Eligible; 3 School-wide Title I
Students: 10,109 (51.7% male; 48.2% female)
   Individual Education Program: 1,081 (10.7%);
   English Language Learner: 2,241 (22.2%); Migrant: 14 (0.1%)
   Eligible for Free Lunch Program: 4,380 (43.3%)
   Eligible for Reduced-Price Lunch Program: 1,035 (10.2%)
Teachers: 522.8 (19.3 to 1)
Librarians/Media Specialists: 9.0 (1,123.2 to 1)
Guidance Counselors: 11.1 (910.7 to 1)
Current Spending: ($ per student per year):
   Total: $4,788; Instruction: $2,752; Support Services: $1,758
Enrollment, Drop-out Rates and Diploma Recipients by Race/Ethnicity

Category	Total	White	Black	Asian	AIAN	Hisp.
Enrollment (%)	100.0	33.4	9.8	1.9	1.5	53.4
Drop-out Rate (%)	n/a	n/a	n/a	n/a	n/a	n/a
H.S. Diplomas (#)	n/a	n/a	n/a	n/a	n/a	n/a

Peoria Unified SD
6330 W Thunderbird Rd · Glendale, AZ 85306
Mailing Address: PO Box 39 · Peoria, AZ 85380-0039
(623) 486-6032 · http://www.peoriaud.k12.az.us/
Grade Span: PK-12; **Agency Type:** 1
Schools: 37
   29 Primary; 0 Middle; 5 High; 3 Other Level
   36 Regular; 0 Special Education; 0 Vocational; 1 Alternative
   0 Magnet; 0 Charter; 6 Title I Eligible; 0 School-wide Title I
Students: 36,719 (51.8% male; 48.1% female)
   Individual Education Program: 4,478 (12.2%);
   English Language Learner: 1,565 (4.3%); Migrant: 65 (0.2%)
   Eligible for Free Lunch Program: 5,412 (14.7%)
   Eligible for Reduced-Price Lunch Program: 1,711 (4.7%)
Teachers: 1,937.5 (19.0 to 1)
Librarians/Media Specialists: 5.0 (7,343.8 to 1)
Guidance Counselors: 60.5 (606.9 to 1)
Current Spending: ($ per student per year):
   Total: $5,093; Instruction: $3,053; Support Services: $1,808
Enrollment, Drop-out Rates and Diploma Recipients by Race/Ethnicity

Category	Total	White	Black	Asian	AIAN	Hisp.
Enrollment (%)	100.0	70.1	4.9	3.1	1.2	20.8
Drop-out Rate (%)	2.4	2.0	2.4	1.2	0.0	4.8
H.S. Diplomas (#)	1,990	1,559	76	65	5	285

Phoenix Elementary District
1817 N 7th St · Phoenix, AZ 85006
(602) 257-3755 · http://www.phxelem.k12.az.us/
Grade Span: PK-08; **Agency Type:** 1
Schools: 21
   18 Primary; 2 Middle; 0 High; 1 Other Level
   19 Regular; 0 Special Education; 0 Vocational; 2 Alternative
   0 Magnet; 0 Charter; 15 Title I Eligible; 14 School-wide Title I
Students: 8,340 (49.9% male; 50.0% female)
   Individual Education Program: 1,049 (12.6%);
   English Language Learner: 4,142 (49.7%); Migrant: 12 (0.1%)
   Eligible for Free Lunch Program: n/a
   Eligible for Reduced-Price Lunch Program: n/a
Teachers: 471.9 (17.7 to 1)
Librarians/Media Specialists: 4.0 (2,085.0 to 1)
Guidance Counselors: 3.0 (2,780.0 to 1)
Current Spending: ($ per student per year):
   Total: $9,102; Instruction: $3,819; Support Services: $4,804
Enrollment, Drop-out Rates and Diploma Recipients by Race/Ethnicity

Category	Total	White	Black	Asian	AIAN	Hisp.
Enrollment (%)	100.0	5.2	5.8	0.7	2.3	86.0
Drop-out Rate (%)	n/a	n/a	n/a	n/a	n/a	n/a
H.S. Diplomas (#)	n/a	n/a	n/a	n/a	n/a	n/a

Phoenix Union High SD
4502 N Central Ave · Phoenix, AZ 85012
(602) 764-1500 ·
http://www.phxhs.k12.az.us/education/district/district.php?sectionid=1
Grade Span: 09-12; **Agency Type:** 1
Schools: 14
   0 Primary; 0 Middle; 14 High; 0 Other Level
   10 Regular; 1 Special Education; 1 Vocational; 2 Alternative
   0 Magnet; 0 Charter; 11 Title I Eligible; 10 School-wide Title I
Students: 23,989 (50.8% male; 49.1% female)
   Individual Education Program: 2,016 (8.4%);
   English Language Learner: 4,195 (17.5%); Migrant: 58 (0.2%)
   Eligible for Free Lunch Program: 15,610 (65.1%)
   Eligible for Reduced-Price Lunch Program: 2,015 (8.4%)
Teachers: 1,294.8 (18.5 to 1)
Librarians/Media Specialists: 10.0 (2,398.9 to 1)
Guidance Counselors: 83.0 (289.0 to 1)
Current Spending: ($ per student per year):
   Total: $7,556; Instruction: $3,889; Support Services: $3,422

Category	Total	White	Black	Asian	AIAN	Hisp.
Enrollment (%)	100.0	12.3	10.1	1.5	3.3	72.8
Drop-out Rate (%)	11.2	9.6	9.8	4.7	19.0	11.6
H.S. Diplomas (#)	3,534	675	396	91	113	2,259

Queen Creek Unified District
20740 S Ellsworth Rd · Queen Creek, AZ 85242-9314
(480) 987-5935
Grade Span: PK-12; **Agency Type:** 1
Schools: 5
   3 Primary; 1 Middle; 1 High; 0 Other Level
   5 Regular; 0 Special Education; 0 Vocational; 0 Alternative
   0 Magnet; 0 Charter; 5 Title I Eligible; 1 School-wide Title I
Students: 2,516 (52.9% male; 47.0% female)
   Individual Education Program: 245 (9.7%);
   English Language Learner: 227 (9.0%); Migrant: 120 (4.8%)
   Eligible for Free Lunch Program: n/a
   Eligible for Reduced-Price Lunch Program: n/a
Teachers: 146.1 (17.2 to 1)
Librarians/Media Specialists: 1.0 (2,516.0 to 1)
Guidance Counselors: 4.9 (513.5 to 1)
Current Spending: ($ per student per year):
   Total: $5,925; Instruction: $2,685; Support Services: $2,819
Enrollment, Drop-out Rates and Diploma Recipients by Race/Ethnicity

Category	Total	White	Black	Asian	AIAN	Hisp.
Enrollment (%)	100.0	68.4	1.2	0.8	1.0	28.5
Drop-out Rate (%)	5.4	2.2	0.0	0.0	16.7	10.2
H.S. Diplomas (#)	84	52	0	0	0	32

Roosevelt Elementary District
6000 S 7th St · Phoenix, AZ 85042-4294
(602) 243-4800 · http://www.rsd.k12.az.us/
Grade Span: PK-08; **Agency Type:** 1
Schools: 22
   19 Primary; 2 Middle; 0 High; 1 Other Level
   19 Regular; 2 Special Education; 0 Vocational; 1 Alternative
   0 Magnet; 0 Charter; 20 Title I Eligible; 20 School-wide Title I
Students: 11,750 (50.8% male; 49.1% female)
   Individual Education Program: 1,382 (11.8%);
   English Language Learner: 4,862 (41.4%); Migrant: 15 (0.1%)
   Eligible for Free Lunch Program: 7,966 (67.8%)
   Eligible for Reduced-Price Lunch Program: 1,169 (9.9%)
Teachers: 637.0 (18.4 to 1)
Librarians/Media Specialists: 16.0 (734.4 to 1)
Guidance Counselors: 0.0 (n/a to 1)
Current Spending: ($ per student per year):
   Total: $5,966; Instruction: $3,255; Support Services: $2,317
Enrollment, Drop-out Rates and Diploma Recipients by Race/Ethnicity

Category	Total	White	Black	Asian	AIAN	Hisp.
Enrollment (%)	100.0	3.7	15.2	0.2	0.9	80.0
Drop-out Rate (%)	n/a	n/a	n/a	n/a	n/a	n/a
H.S. Diplomas (#)	n/a	n/a	n/a	n/a	n/a	n/a

Scottsdale Unified District
3811 N 44th St · Phoenix, AZ 85018-5489
(480) 484-6100 · http://www.susd.org/
Grade Span: PK-12; **Agency Type:** 1
Schools: 34
   21 Primary; 6 Middle; 5 High; 2 Other Level
   34 Regular; 0 Special Education; 0 Vocational; 0 Alternative
   0 Magnet; 0 Charter; 5 Title I Eligible; 2 School-wide Title I
Students: 26,559 (51.7% male; 48.2% female)
   Individual Education Program: 2,643 (10.0%);
   English Language Learner: 1,880 (7.1%); Migrant: 0 (0.0%)
   Eligible for Free Lunch Program: 3,440 (13.0%)
   Eligible for Reduced-Price Lunch Program: 781 (2.9%)
Teachers: 1,394.5 (19.0 to 1)
Librarians/Media Specialists: 24.5 (1,084.0 to 1)
Guidance Counselors: 30.8 (862.3 to 1)
Current Spending: ($ per student per year):
   Total: $5,607; Instruction: $3,321; Support Services: $2,059
Enrollment, Drop-out Rates and Diploma Recipients by Race/Ethnicity

Category	Total	White	Black	Asian	AIAN	Hisp.
Enrollment (%)	100.0	80.6	2.2	3.4	1.4	12.5
Drop-out Rate (%)	1.4	1.2	0.6	0.7	0.0	4.5
H.S. Diplomas (#)	1,708	1,513	33	67	9	86

Tempe Elementary District
3205 S Rural Rd · Tempe, AZ 85282
Mailing Address: PO Box 27708 · Tempe, AZ 85285-7708
(480) 730-7102 · http://www.tempe3.k12.az.us/
Grade Span: PK-12; **Agency Type:** 1
Schools: 27
   21 Primary; 5 Middle; 0 High; 1 Other Level

26 Regular; 0 Special Education; 0 Vocational; 1 Alternative
0 Magnet; 0 Charter; 17 Title I Eligible; 17 School-wide Title I
Students: 13,717   (50.8% male; 49.1% female)
    Individual Education Program: 1,823 (13.3%);
    English Language Learner: 3,450 (25.2%); Migrant: 0 (0.0%)
    Eligible for Free Lunch Program: 8,131 (59.3%)
    Eligible for Reduced-Price Lunch Program: 1,439 (10.5%)
Teachers: 850.2 (16.1 to 1)
Librarians/Media Specialists: 17.7 (775.0 to 1)
Guidance Counselors: 29.8 (460.3 to 1)
Current Spending: ($ per student per year):
    Total: $6,336; Instruction: $3,418; Support Services: $2,613
Enrollment, Drop-out Rates and Diploma Recipients by Race/Ethnicity

Category	Total	White	Black	Asian	AIAN	Hisp.
Enrollment (%)	100.0	31.8	11.9	3.7	8.2	44.4
Drop-out Rate (%)	n/a	n/a	n/a	n/a	n/a	n/a
H.S. Diplomas (#)	0	0	0	0	0	0

Tempe Union High SD
500 W Guadalupe Rd • Tempe, AZ 85283-3599
(480) 839-0292 • http://www.tuhsd.k12.az.us/
Grade Span: 09-12; **Agency Type:** 1
Schools: 8
    0 Primary; 0 Middle; 7 High; 0 Other Level
    7 Regular; 0 Special Education; 0 Vocational; 0 Alternative
    0 Magnet; 0 Charter; 3 Title I Eligible; 0 School-wide Title I
Students: 13,249   (51.0% male; 48.9% female)
    Individual Education Program: 1,067 (8.1%);
    English Language Learner: 374 (2.8%); Migrant: 0 (0.0%)
    Eligible for Free Lunch Program: 539 (4.1%)
    Eligible for Reduced-Price Lunch Program: 0 (0.0%)
Teachers: 643.9 (20.6 to 1)
Librarians/Media Specialists: 18.8 (704.7 to 1)
Guidance Counselors: 33.6 (394.3 to 1)
Current Spending: ($ per student per year):
    Total: $5,704; Instruction: $3,177; Support Services: $2,284
Enrollment, Drop-out Rates and Diploma Recipients by Race/Ethnicity

Category	Total	White	Black	Asian	AIAN	Hisp.
Enrollment (%)	100.0	62.0	8.2	5.7	3.4	20.7
Drop-out Rate (%)	4.0	2.4	4.8	2.0	11.5	8.4
H.S. Diplomas (#)	2,678	1,850	197	142	61	428

Tolleson Elementary District
9401 W Garfield Rd • Tolleson, AZ 85353-2941
Mailing Address: 9261 W Van Buren • Tolleson, AZ 85353-2941
(623) 936-9740
Grade Span: PK-08; **Agency Type:** 1
Schools: 3
    3 Primary; 0 Middle; 0 High; 0 Other Level
    3 Regular; 0 Special Education; 0 Vocational; 0 Alternative
    0 Magnet; 0 Charter; 3 Title I Eligible; 3 School-wide Title I
Students: 2,035   (52.1% male; 47.8% female)
    Individual Education Program: 136 (6.7%);
    English Language Learner: 596 (29.3%); Migrant: 0 (0.0%)
    Eligible for Free Lunch Program: 1,321 (64.9%)
    Eligible for Reduced-Price Lunch Program: 234 (11.5%)
Teachers: 112.0 (18.2 to 1)
Librarians/Media Specialists: 1.0 (2,035.0 to 1)
Guidance Counselors: 0.0 (n/a to 1)
Current Spending: ($ per student per year):
    Total: $5,256; Instruction: $2,832; Support Services: $2,103
Enrollment, Drop-out Rates and Diploma Recipients by Race/Ethnicity

Category	Total	White	Black	Asian	AIAN	Hisp.
Enrollment (%)	100.0	12.2	6.9	1.2	1.2	78.5
Drop-out Rate (%)	n/a	n/a	n/a	n/a	n/a	n/a
H.S. Diplomas (#)	n/a	n/a	n/a	n/a	n/a	n/a

Tolleson Union High SD
9419 W Van Buren St • Tolleson, AZ 85353-2898
(623) 478-4000 • http://www.tuhsd.org/
Grade Span: 09-12; **Agency Type:** 1
Schools: 3
    0 Primary; 0 Middle; 3 High; 0 Other Level
    3 Regular; 0 Special Education; 0 Vocational; 0 Alternative
    0 Magnet; 0 Charter; 2 Title I Eligible; 2 School-wide Title I
Students: 5,487   (51.2% male; 48.7% female)
    Individual Education Program: 541 (9.9%);
    English Language Learner: 298 (5.4%); Migrant: 124 (2.3%)
    Eligible for Free Lunch Program: 1,894 (34.5%)
    Eligible for Reduced-Price Lunch Program: 399 (7.3%)
Teachers: 267.0 (20.6 to 1)
Librarians/Media Specialists: 3.0 (1,829.0 to 1)
Guidance Counselors: 11.0 (498.8 to 1)
Current Spending: ($ per student per year):
    Total: $6,199; Instruction: $3,117; Support Services: $2,764

Enrollment, Drop-out Rates and Diploma Recipients by Race/Ethnicity

Category	Total	White	Black	Asian	AIAN	Hisp.
Enrollment (%)	100.0	29.7	10.8	2.7	2.1	54.8
Drop-out Rate (%)	6.8	6.4	3.9	1.8	13.4	7.6
H.S. Diplomas (#)	742	352	55	20	13	302

Washington Elementary District
8610 N 19th Ave • Phoenix, AZ 85021-4294
(602) 347-2600 • http://www.wesd.k12.az.us/
Grade Span: PK-08; **Agency Type:** 1
Schools: 32
    27 Primary; 5 Middle; 0 High; 0 Other Level
    32 Regular; 0 Special Education; 0 Vocational; 0 Alternative
    0 Magnet; 0 Charter; 20 Title I Eligible; 11 School-wide Title I
Students: 24,438   (52.4% male; 47.5% female)
    Individual Education Program: 3,618 (14.8%);
    English Language Learner: 4,921 (20.1%); Migrant: 0 (0.0%)
    Eligible for Free Lunch Program: 15,001 (61.4%)
    Eligible for Reduced-Price Lunch Program: 2,548 (10.4%)
Teachers: 1,284.4 (19.0 to 1)
Librarians/Media Specialists: 20.9 (1,169.3 to 1)
Guidance Counselors: 10.5 (2,327.4 to 1)
Current Spending: ($ per student per year):
    Total: $5,732; Instruction: $3,492; Support Services: $1,940
Enrollment, Drop-out Rates and Diploma Recipients by Race/Ethnicity

Category	Total	White	Black	Asian	AIAN	Hisp.
Enrollment (%)	100.0	48.8	6.5	2.9	3.5	38.2
Drop-out Rate (%)	n/a	n/a	n/a	n/a	n/a	n/a
H.S. Diplomas (#)	n/a	n/a	n/a	n/a	n/a	n/a

Western Maricopa Education Center (West-Mec)
4949 W Indian School Rd • Phoenix, AZ 85031
(623) 873-1860
Grade Span: n/a; **Agency Type:** 7
Schools: 6
    0 Primary; 0 Middle; 6 High; 0 Other Level
    0 Regular; 0 Special Education; 6 Vocational; 0 Alternative
    0 Magnet; 0 Charter; 0 Title I Eligible; 0 School-wide Title I
Students: 3,405   (54.0% male; 45.9% female)
    Individual Education Program: 0 (0.0%);
    English Language Learner: 0 (0.0%); Migrant: 0 (0.0%)
    Eligible for Free Lunch Program: n/a
    Eligible for Reduced-Price Lunch Program: n/a
Teachers: n/a
Librarians/Media Specialists: n/a
Guidance Counselors: n/a
Current Spending: ($ per student per year):
    Total: n/a; Instruction: n/a; Support Services: n/a
Enrollment, Drop-out Rates and Diploma Recipients by Race/Ethnicity

Category	Total	White	Black	Asian	AIAN	Hisp.
Enrollment (%)	100.0	55.3	6.2	2.3	1.0	35.2
Drop-out Rate (%)	n/a	n/a	n/a	n/a	n/a	n/a
H.S. Diplomas (#)	n/a	n/a	n/a	n/a	n/a	n/a

Mohave County

Bullhead City Elementary District
1004 Hancock Rd • Bullhead City, AZ 86442-5901
(928) 758-3961 • http://www.bullhead.apscc.k12.az.us/
Grade Span: PK-08; **Agency Type:** 1
Schools: 7
    5 Primary; 2 Middle; 0 High; 0 Other Level
    7 Regular; 0 Special Education; 0 Vocational; 0 Alternative
    0 Magnet; 0 Charter; 4 Title I Eligible; 0 School-wide Title I
Students: 3,888   (52.9% male; 47.0% female)
    Individual Education Program: 367 (9.4%);
    English Language Learner: 557 (14.3%); Migrant: 0 (0.0%)
    Eligible for Free Lunch Program: 2,463 (63.3%)
    Eligible for Reduced-Price Lunch Program: 337 (8.7%)
Teachers: 210.0 (18.5 to 1)
Librarians/Media Specialists: 7.0 (555.4 to 1)
Guidance Counselors: 5.0 (777.6 to 1)
Current Spending: ($ per student per year):
    Total: $4,260; Instruction: $2,582; Support Services: $1,422
Enrollment, Drop-out Rates and Diploma Recipients by Race/Ethnicity

Category	Total	White	Black	Asian	AIAN	Hisp.
Enrollment (%)	100.0	58.2	2.6	1.1	1.1	36.9
Drop-out Rate (%)	n/a	n/a	n/a	n/a	n/a	n/a
H.S. Diplomas (#)	n/a	n/a	n/a	n/a	n/a	n/a

Colorado River Union High SD
5221 Hwy 95 • Fort Mojave, AZ 86426
Mailing Address: PO Box 21479 • Bullhead City, AZ 86439-1479
(928) 768-1665 • http://www.cruhsd.org
Grade Span: 09-12; Agency Type: 1
Schools: 2
   0 Primary; 0 Middle; 2 High; 0 Other Level
   2 Regular; 0 Special Education; 0 Vocational; 0 Alternative
   0 Magnet; 0 Charter; 2 Title I Eligible; 1 School-wide Title I
Students: 2,114   (51.0% male; 48.9% female)
   Individual Education Program: 235 (11.1%);
   English Language Learner: 18 (0.9%); Migrant: 0 (0.0%)
   Eligible for Free Lunch Program: 696 (32.9%)
   Eligible for Reduced-Price Lunch Program: 178 (8.4%)
Teachers: 89.0 (23.8 to 1)
Librarians/Media Specialists: 2.0 (1,057.0 to 1)
Guidance Counselors: 4.0 (528.5 to 1)
Current Spending: ($ per student per year):
   Total: $5,367; Instruction: $2,905; Support Services: $2,083
Enrollment, Drop-out Rates and Diploma Recipients by Race/Ethnicity

Category	Total	White	Black	Asian	AIAN	Hisp.
Enrollment (%)	100.0	70.2	1.1	0.8	2.7	25.2
Drop-out Rate (%)	13.6	12.9	30.4	13.6	14.0	14.9
H.S. Diplomas (#)	320	247	3	7	10	53

Kingman Unified SD
3033 Macdonald Ave • Kingman, AZ 86401
(928) 753-5678 • http://www.kusd.org/
Grade Span: PK-12; Agency Type: 1
Schools: 11
   6 Primary; 1 Middle; 3 High; 1 Other Level
   11 Regular; 0 Special Education; 0 Vocational; 0 Alternative
   0 Magnet; 0 Charter; 8 Title I Eligible; 2 School-wide Title I
Students: 7,298   (51.1% male; 48.8% female)
   Individual Education Program: 1,046 (14.3%);
   English Language Learner: 75 (1.0%); Migrant: 0 (0.0%)
   Eligible for Free Lunch Program: 2,712 (37.2%)
   Eligible for Reduced-Price Lunch Program: 481 (6.6%)
Teachers: 366.6 (19.9 to 1)
Librarians/Media Specialists: 8.0 (912.3 to 1)
Guidance Counselors: 8.0 (912.3 to 1)
Current Spending: ($ per student per year):
   Total: $5,050; Instruction: $2,723; Support Services: $2,159
Enrollment, Drop-out Rates and Diploma Recipients by Race/Ethnicity

Category	Total	White	Black	Asian	AIAN	Hisp.
Enrollment (%)	100.0	82.7	1.2	1.1	2.8	12.1
Drop-out Rate (%)	12.4	12.4	16.7	2.9	17.2	11.5
H.S. Diplomas (#)	442	377	3	11	9	42

Lake Havasu Unified District
2200 Havasupai Blvd • Lake Havasu City, AZ 86403-3798
(928) 855-8466 • http://www.havasu.k12.az.us/
Grade Span: PK-12; Agency Type: 1
Schools: 9
   5 Primary; 2 Middle; 1 High; 1 Other Level
   9 Regular; 0 Special Education; 0 Vocational; 0 Alternative
   0 Magnet; 0 Charter; 5 Title I Eligible; 5 School-wide Title I
Students: 6,495   (51.5% male; 48.4% female)
   Individual Education Program: 725 (11.2%);
   English Language Learner: 263 (4.0%); Migrant: 0 (0.0%)
   Eligible for Free Lunch Program: 2,373 (36.5%)
   Eligible for Reduced-Price Lunch Program: 800 (12.3%)
Teachers: 296.0 (21.9 to 1)
Librarians/Media Specialists: 2.0 (3,247.5 to 1)
Guidance Counselors: 6.4 (1,014.8 to 1)
Current Spending: ($ per student per year):
   Total: $4,475; Instruction: $2,644; Support Services: $1,534
Enrollment, Drop-out Rates and Diploma Recipients by Race/Ethnicity

Category	Total	White	Black	Asian	AIAN	Hisp.
Enrollment (%)	100.0	79.9	0.7	1.1	1.2	17.1
Drop-out Rate (%)	5.3	4.6	0.0	0.0	11.5	11.2
H.S. Diplomas (#)	316	273	2	6	2	33

Mohave Valley Elementary District
8450 S Olive • Mohave Valley, AZ 86440-5070
Mailing Address: PO Box 5070 • Mohave Valley, AZ 86446
(928) 768-2507 • http://www.mvesd16.org/
Grade Span: PK-08; Agency Type: 1
Schools: 4
   3 Primary; 1 Middle; 0 High; 0 Other Level
   4 Regular; 0 Special Education; 0 Vocational; 0 Alternative
   0 Magnet; 0 Charter; 4 Title I Eligible; 1 School-wide Title I
Students: 1,755   (51.9% male; 48.0% female)
   Individual Education Program: 239 (13.6%)
   English Language Learner: 63 (3.6%); Migrant: 0 (0.0%)

   Eligible for Free Lunch Program: 863 (49.2%)
   Eligible for Reduced-Price Lunch Program: 164 (9.3%)
Teachers: 77.5 (22.6 to 1)
Librarians/Media Specialists: 1.0 (1,755.0 to 1)
Guidance Counselors: 0.5 (3,510.0 to 1)
Current Spending: ($ per student per year):
   Total: $4,285; Instruction: $2,443; Support Services: $1,608
Enrollment, Drop-out Rates and Diploma Recipients by Race/Ethnicity

Category	Total	White	Black	Asian	AIAN	Hisp.
Enrollment (%)	100.0	71.7	1.0	0.9	8.3	18.1
Drop-out Rate (%)	n/a	n/a	n/a	n/a	n/a	n/a
H.S. Diplomas (#)	n/a	n/a	n/a	n/a	n/a	n/a

Peach Springs Unified District
16500 E Hwy 66 • Peach Springs, AZ 86403-0360
Mailing Address: PO Box 360 • Peach Springs, AZ 86434-0138
(928) 769-2202
Grade Span: PK-12; Agency Type: 1
Schools: 36
   25 Primary; 2 Middle; 2 High; 6 Other Level
   35 Regular; 0 Special Education; 0 Vocational; 0 Alternative
   0 Magnet; 33 Charter; 18 Title I Eligible; 15 School-wide Title I
Students: 1,719   (50.1% male; 49.8% female)
   Individual Education Program: 30 (1.7%);
   English Language Learner: 0 (0.0%); Migrant: 0 (0.0%)
   Eligible for Free Lunch Program: 274 (15.9%)
   Eligible for Reduced-Price Lunch Program: 127 (7.4%)
Teachers: 20.7 (83.0 to 1)
Librarians/Media Specialists: 0.0 (n/a to 1)
Guidance Counselors: 0.0 (n/a to 1)
Current Spending: ($ per student per year):
   Total: $6,898; Instruction: $5,000; Support Services: $1,748
Enrollment, Drop-out Rates and Diploma Recipients by Race/Ethnicity

Category	Total	White	Black	Asian	AIAN	Hisp.
Enrollment (%)	100.0	55.7	7.3	3.9	21.9	11.2
Drop-out Rate (%)	n/a	n/a	n/a	n/a	n/a	n/a
H.S. Diplomas (#)	47	31	1	0	5	10

Navajo County

Blue Ridge Unified District
1200 W White Mountain Blvd • Lakeside, AZ 85929-0885
(928) 368-6126 • http://www.brusd.k12.az.us/
Grade Span: PK-12; Agency Type: 1
Schools: 4
   1 Primary; 2 Middle; 1 High; 0 Other Level
   4 Regular; 0 Special Education; 0 Vocational; 0 Alternative
   0 Magnet; 0 Charter; 4 Title I Eligible; 0 School-wide Title I
Students: 2,636   (50.3% male; 49.6% female)
   Individual Education Program: 425 (16.1%);
   English Language Learner: 158 (6.0%); Migrant: 0 (0.0%)
   Eligible for Free Lunch Program: 788 (29.9%)
   Eligible for Reduced-Price Lunch Program: 218 (8.3%)
Teachers: 154.4 (17.1 to 1)
Librarians/Media Specialists: 1.0 (2,636.0 to 1)
Guidance Counselors: 4.6 (573.0 to 1)
Current Spending: ($ per student per year):
   Total: $5,187; Instruction: $3,006; Support Services: $1,897
Enrollment, Drop-out Rates and Diploma Recipients by Race/Ethnicity

Category	Total	White	Black	Asian	AIAN	Hisp.
Enrollment (%)	100.0	74.8	0.8	0.8	8.8	14.7
Drop-out Rate (%)	7.0	6.1	0.0	20.0	15.7	7.6
H.S. Diplomas (#)	145	116	0	3	6	20

Holbrook Unified District
1000 N 8th Ave • Holbrook, AZ 86025-0640
Mailing Address: PO Box 640 • Holbrook, AZ 86025-0640
(928) 524-6144 • http://www.holbrook.k12.az.us/
Grade Span: PK-12; Agency Type: 1
Schools: 5
   3 Primary; 1 Middle; 1 High; 0 Other Level
   5 Regular; 0 Special Education; 0 Vocational; 0 Alternative
   0 Magnet; 0 Charter; 5 Title I Eligible; 4 School-wide Title I
Students: 2,073   (50.6% male; 49.3% female)
   Individual Education Program: 243 (11.7%);
   English Language Learner: 474 (22.9%); Migrant: 0 (0.0%)
   Eligible for Free Lunch Program: 744 (35.9%)
   Eligible for Reduced-Price Lunch Program: 152 (7.3%)
Teachers: 137.4 (15.1 to 1)
Librarians/Media Specialists: 1.0 (2,073.0 to 1)
Guidance Counselors: 4.0 (518.3 to 1)
Current Spending: ($ per student per year):
   Total: $7,275; Instruction: $4,090; Support Services: $2,833

Enrollment, Drop-out Rates and Diploma Recipients by Race/Ethnicity

Category	Total	White	Black	Asian	AIAN	Hisp.
Enrollment (%)	100.0	27.7	1.8	0.8	57.4	12.3
Drop-out Rate (%)	10.5	5.6	6.7	0.0	14.4	4.4
H.S. Diplomas (#)	139	42	5	2	77	13

Kayenta Unified District

N Hwy 163 • Kayenta, AZ 86033-0337
Mailing Address: PO Box 337 • Kayenta, AZ 86033-0337
(928) 697-2008 • http://www.kayenta.k12.az.us/
Grade Span: PK-12; Agency Type: 1
Schools: 5
  2 Primary; 1 Middle; 1 High; 0 Other Level
  4 Regular; 0 Special Education; 0 Vocational; 0 Alternative
  0 Magnet; 0 Charter; 4 Title I Eligible; 4 School-wide Title I
Students: 2,570 (51.6% male; 48.3% female)
  Individual Education Program: 243 (9.5%);
  English Language Learner: 1,632 (63.5%); Migrant: 0 (0.0%)
  Eligible for Free Lunch Program: 1,900 (73.9%)
  Eligible for Reduced-Price Lunch Program: 289 (11.2%)
Teachers: 164.5 (15.6 to 1)
Librarians/Media Specialists: 4.0 (642.5 to 1)
Guidance Counselors: 6.5 (395.4 to 1)
Current Spending: ($ per student per year):
  Total: $7,952; Instruction: $3,581; Support Services: $3,986

Enrollment, Drop-out Rates and Diploma Recipients by Race/Ethnicity

Category	Total	White	Black	Asian	AIAN	Hisp.
Enrollment (%)	100.0	1.8	0.0	0.0	98.1	0.2
Drop-out Rate (%)	10.1	0.0	n/a	n/a	10.2	n/a
H.S. Diplomas (#)	188	2	0	0	186	0

Navit

1611 S Main St • Snowflake, AZ 85937
Mailing Address: PO Box 2110 • Snowflake, AZ 85937
(928) 536-6232
Grade Span: 09-12; Agency Type: 1
Schools: 12
  0 Primary; 0 Middle; 10 High; 2 Other Level
  0 Regular; 0 Special Education; 12 Vocational; 0 Alternative
  0 Magnet; 0 Charter; 5 Title I Eligible; 5 School-wide Title I
Students: 4,909 (51.3% male; 48.6% female)
  Individual Education Program: 0 (0.0%);
  English Language Learner: 0 (0.0%); Migrant: 0 (0.0%)
  Eligible for Free Lunch Program: n/a
  Eligible for Reduced-Price Lunch Program: n/a
Teachers: n/a
Librarians/Media Specialists: 0.0 (n/a to 1)
Guidance Counselors: 0.0 (n/a to 1)
Current Spending: ($ per student per year):
  Total: n/a; Instruction: n/a; Support Services: n/a

Enrollment, Drop-out Rates and Diploma Recipients by Race/Ethnicity

Category	Total	White	Black	Asian	AIAN	Hisp.
Enrollment (%)	100.0	60.5	0.9	0.6	28.6	9.4
Drop-out Rate (%)	n/a	n/a	n/a	n/a	n/a	n/a
H.S. Diplomas (#)	0	0	0	0	0	0

Northeast Arizona Technological Institute of Vocational Education

N Hwy 163 - MVHS • Kayenta, AZ 86033
Mailing Address: PO Box 710 • Kayenta, AZ 86033
(928) 697-2500
Grade Span: n/a; Agency Type: 7
Schools: 7
  0 Primary; 0 Middle; 7 High; 0 Other Level
  0 Regular; 0 Special Education; 7 Vocational; 0 Alternative
  0 Magnet; 0 Charter; 0 Title I Eligible; 0 School-wide Title I
Students: 3,264 (53.5% male; 46.4% female)
  Individual Education Program: 0 (0.0%);
  English Language Learner: 0 (0.0%); Migrant: 0 (0.0%)
  Eligible for Free Lunch Program: n/a
  Eligible for Reduced-Price Lunch Program: n/a
Teachers: n/a
Librarians/Media Specialists: n/a
Guidance Counselors: n/a
Current Spending: ($ per student per year):
  Total: n/a; Instruction: n/a; Support Services: n/a

Enrollment, Drop-out Rates and Diploma Recipients by Race/Ethnicity

Category	Total	White	Black	Asian	AIAN	Hisp.
Enrollment (%)	100.0	0.7	0.0	0.0	99.1	0.1
Drop-out Rate (%)	n/a	n/a	n/a	n/a	n/a	n/a
H.S. Diplomas (#)	n/a	n/a	n/a	n/a	n/a	n/a

Pinon Unified District

Navajo Hwy 41 • Pinon, AZ 86510-0839
Mailing Address: PO Box 839 • Pinon, AZ 86510-0839
(928) 725-3450
Grade Span: PK-12; Agency Type: 1
Schools: 4
  1 Primary; 1 Middle; 1 High; 1 Other Level
  4 Regular; 0 Special Education; 0 Vocational; 0 Alternative
  0 Magnet; 0 Charter; 4 Title I Eligible; 4 School-wide Title I
Students: 1,523 (52.9% male; 47.0% female)
  Individual Education Program: 108 (7.1%);
  English Language Learner: 953 (62.6%); Migrant: 0 (0.0%)
  Eligible for Free Lunch Program: n/a
  Eligible for Reduced-Price Lunch Program: n/a
Teachers: 101.0 (15.1 to 1)
Librarians/Media Specialists: 1.0 (1,523.0 to 1)
Guidance Counselors: 2.0 (761.5 to 1)
Current Spending: ($ per student per year):
  Total: $9,470; Instruction: $4,534; Support Services: $4,073

Enrollment, Drop-out Rates and Diploma Recipients by Race/Ethnicity

Category	Total	White	Black	Asian	AIAN	Hisp.
Enrollment (%)	100.0	0.5	0.0	0.0	99.5	0.0
Drop-out Rate (%)	18.7	n/a	n/a	n/a	18.7	0.0
H.S. Diplomas (#)	79	0	0	0	79	0

Show Low Unified District

1350 N Central Ave • Show Low, AZ 85901-4645
Mailing Address: 500 W Old Linden Rd • Show Low, AZ 85901-4645
(928) 537-6001 • http://www.show-low.k12.az.us/
Grade Span: PK-12; Agency Type: 1
Schools: 9
  4 Primary; 3 Middle; 2 High; 0 Other Level
  9 Regular; 0 Special Education; 0 Vocational; 0 Alternative
  0 Magnet; 0 Charter; 8 Title I Eligible; 5 School-wide Title I
Students: 2,625 (53.2% male; 46.7% female)
  Individual Education Program: 343 (13.1%);
  English Language Learner: 45 (1.7%); Migrant: 0 (0.0%)
  Eligible for Free Lunch Program: 1,148 (43.7%)
  Eligible for Reduced-Price Lunch Program: 339 (12.9%)
Teachers: 132.4 (19.8 to 1)
Librarians/Media Specialists: 1.0 (2,625.0 to 1)
Guidance Counselors: 4.0 (656.3 to 1)
Current Spending: ($ per student per year):
  Total: $5,034; Instruction: $2,763; Support Services: $2,081

Enrollment, Drop-out Rates and Diploma Recipients by Race/Ethnicity

Category	Total	White	Black	Asian	AIAN	Hisp.
Enrollment (%)	100.0	83.8	0.8	0.8	4.3	10.2
Drop-out Rate (%)	7.6	6.7	20.0	0.0	5.6	20.0
H.S. Diplomas (#)	198	174	0	1	7	16

Snowflake Unified District

682 School Bus Ln • Snowflake, AZ 85937-1100
(928) 536-4156 • http://www.snowflake.k12.az.us/
Grade Span: PK-12; Agency Type: 1
Schools: 7
  3 Primary; 3 Middle; 1 High; 0 Other Level
  7 Regular; 0 Special Education; 0 Vocational; 0 Alternative
  0 Magnet; 0 Charter; 5 Title I Eligible; 4 School-wide Title I
Students: 2,513 (52.5% male; 47.4% female)
  Individual Education Program: 330 (13.1%);
  English Language Learner: 120 (4.8%); Migrant: 0 (0.0%)
  Eligible for Free Lunch Program: n/a
  Eligible for Reduced-Price Lunch Program: n/a
Teachers: 132.5 (19.0 to 1)
Librarians/Media Specialists: 3.0 (837.7 to 1)
Guidance Counselors: 2.0 (1,256.5 to 1)
Current Spending: ($ per student per year):
  Total: $6,291; Instruction: $4,110; Support Services: $1,967

Enrollment, Drop-out Rates and Diploma Recipients by Race/Ethnicity

Category	Total	White	Black	Asian	AIAN	Hisp.
Enrollment (%)	100.0	81.8	0.4	0.4	7.6	9.9
Drop-out Rate (%)	3.5	2.2	0.0	0.0	3.6	16.7
H.S. Diplomas (#)	139	122	1	0	8	8

Whiteriver Unified District

200 Cemetery Rd • Whiteriver, AZ 85941-0190
Mailing Address: PO Box 190 • Whiteriver, AZ 85941-0190
(928) 338-4842 • http://www.wusd.k12.az.us/
Grade Span: PK-12; Agency Type: 1
Schools: 5
  3 Primary; 1 Middle; 1 High; 0 Other Level
  5 Regular; 0 Special Education; 0 Vocational; 0 Alternative
  0 Magnet; 0 Charter; 5 Title I Eligible; 5 School-wide Title I
Students: 2,467 (50.8% male; 49.1% female)
  Individual Education Program: 363 (14.7%);

English Language Learner: 1,273 (51.6%); Migrant: 0 (0.0%)
Eligible for Free Lunch Program: 1,571 (63.7%)
Eligible for Reduced-Price Lunch Program: 120 (4.9%)
Teachers: 169.8 (14.5 to 1)
Librarians/Media Specialists: 3.0 (822.3 to 1)
Guidance Counselors: 8.0 (308.4 to 1)
Current Spending: ($ per student per year):
Total: $7,270; Instruction: $3,834; Support Services: $3,092
Enrollment, Drop-out Rates and Diploma Recipients by Race/Ethnicity

Category	Total	White	Black	Asian	AIAN	Hisp.
Enrollment (%)	100.0	0.9	0.0	0.0	98.9	0.2
Drop-out Rate (%)	26.8	0.0	n/a	0.0	27.0	0.0
H.S. Diplomas (#)	116	2	0	1	112	1

Winslow Unified District
800 Apache Ave • Winslow, AZ 86047-0580
Mailing Address: PO Box 580 • Winslow, AZ 86047-0580
(928) 289-3375 • http://www.winslowsd.k12.az.us/
Grade Span: PK-12; **Agency Type:** 1
Schools: 5
3 Primary; 1 Middle; 1 High; 0 Other Level
5 Regular; 0 Special Education; 0 Vocational; 0 Alternative
0 Magnet; 0 Charter; 5 Title I Eligible; 5 School-wide Title I
Students: 2,561 (49.3% male; 50.6% female)
Individual Education Program: 346 (13.5%);
English Language Learner: 227 (8.9%); Migrant: 0 (0.0%)
Eligible for Free Lunch Program: 1,167 (45.6%)
Eligible for Reduced-Price Lunch Program: 354 (13.8%)
Teachers: 147.2 (17.4 to 1)
Librarians/Media Specialists: 3.0 (853.7 to 1)
Guidance Counselors: 5.5 (465.6 to 1)
Current Spending: ($ per student per year):
Total: $5,435; Instruction: $3,038; Support Services: $2,174
Enrollment, Drop-out Rates and Diploma Recipients by Race/Ethnicity

Category	Total	White	Black	Asian	AIAN	Hisp.
Enrollment (%)	100.0	26.4	3.7	1.1	45.8	23.0
Drop-out Rate (%)	9.7	4.0	12.5	0.0	12.9	8.7
H.S. Diplomas (#)	148	49	4	1	75	19

Pima County

Amphitheater Unified District
701 W Wetmore • Tucson, AZ 85705-1547
(520) 696-5130 • http://www.amphi.com/
Grade Span: PK-12; **Agency Type:** 1
Schools: 22
13 Primary; 3 Middle; 4 High; 2 Other Level
20 Regular; 1 Special Education; 0 Vocational; 1 Alternative
0 Magnet; 0 Charter; 10 Title I Eligible; 8 School-wide Title I
Students: 16,868 (52.0% male; 47.9% female)
Individual Education Program: 2,414 (14.3%);
English Language Learner: 1,341 (8.0%); Migrant: 0 (0.0%)
Eligible for Free Lunch Program: 5,973 (35.4%)
Eligible for Reduced-Price Lunch Program: 1,286 (7.6%)
Teachers: 925.6 (18.2 to 1)
Librarians/Media Specialists: 10.0 (1,686.8 to 1)
Guidance Counselors: 20.0 (843.4 to 1)
Current Spending: ($ per student per year):
Total: $5,132; Instruction: $2,847; Support Services: $2,099
Enrollment, Drop-out Rates and Diploma Recipients by Race/Ethnicity

Category	Total	White	Black	Asian	AIAN	Hisp.
Enrollment (%)	100.0	59.7	3.7	2.9	2.0	31.7
Drop-out Rate (%)	3.4	2.6	5.3	2.6	5.0	5.1
H.S. Diplomas (#)	947	669	20	37	11	210

Catalina Foothills Unified District
2101 E River Rd • Tucson, AZ 85718-6597
(520) 299-6446 • http://www.cfsd.k12.az.us/
Grade Span: PK-12; **Agency Type:** 1
Schools: 8
5 Primary; 2 Middle; 1 High; 0 Other Level
8 Regular; 0 Special Education; 0 Vocational; 0 Alternative
0 Magnet; 0 Charter; 4 Title I Eligible; 0 School-wide Title I
Students: 5,046 (50.8% male; 49.1% female)
Individual Education Program: 537 (10.6%);
English Language Learner: 115 (2.3%); Migrant: 0 (0.0%)
Eligible for Free Lunch Program: 310 (6.1%)
Eligible for Reduced-Price Lunch Program: 0 (0.0%)
Teachers: 289.2 (17.4 to 1)
Librarians/Media Specialists: 8.0 (630.8 to 1)
Guidance Counselors: 11.2 (450.5 to 1)
Current Spending: ($ per student per year):
Total: $5,920; Instruction: $3,255; Support Services: $2,362

Enrollment, Drop-out Rates and Diploma Recipients by Race/Ethnicity

Category	Total	White	Black	Asian	AIAN	Hisp.
Enrollment (%)	100.0	78.4	1.8	8.4	0.5	10.9
Drop-out Rate (%)	1.1	1.1	0.0	1.6	0.0	0.0
H.S. Diplomas (#)	431	351	4	32	1	43

Flowing Wells Unified District
1556 W Prince Rd • Tucson, AZ 85705-3024
(520) 690-2212 • http://www.flowingwells.k12.az.us/
Grade Span: PK-12; **Agency Type:** 1
Schools: 11
7 Primary; 1 Middle; 3 High; 0 Other Level
10 Regular; 0 Special Education; 0 Vocational; 1 Alternative
0 Magnet; 0 Charter; 5 Title I Eligible; 0 School-wide Title I
Students: 6,041 (50.8% male; 49.1% female)
Individual Education Program: 779 (12.9%)
English Language Learner: 296 (4.9%); Migrant: 0 (0.0%)
Eligible for Free Lunch Program: n/a
Eligible for Reduced-Price Lunch Program: n/a
Teachers: 295.2 (20.5 to 1)
Librarians/Media Specialists: 2.0 (3,020.5 to 1)
Guidance Counselors: 14.0 (431.5 to 1)
Current Spending: ($ per student per year):
Total: $5,395; Instruction: $3,151; Support Services: $1,884
Enrollment, Drop-out Rates and Diploma Recipients by Race/Ethnicity

Category	Total	White	Black	Asian	AIAN	Hisp.
Enrollment (%)	100.0	52.8	2.0	1.5	1.9	41.9
Drop-out Rate (%)	7.3	6.7	2.2	8.6	15.0	8.3
H.S. Diplomas (#)	363	247	12	6	4	94

Marana Unified District
11279 W Grier Rd Ste 115a • Marana, AZ 85653-9776
(520) 682-4749 • http://maranausd.org/
Grade Span: PK-12; **Agency Type:** 1
Schools: 17
10 Primary; 3 Middle; 4 High; 0 Other Level
16 Regular; 0 Special Education; 0 Vocational; 1 Alternative
0 Magnet; 0 Charter; 6 Title I Eligible; 1 School-wide Title I
Students: 12,693 (51.8% male; 48.1% female)
Individual Education Program: 1,614 (12.7%);
English Language Learner: 338 (2.7%); Migrant: 24 (0.2%)
Eligible for Free Lunch Program: 2,868 (22.6%)
Eligible for Reduced-Price Lunch Program: 1,031 (8.1%)
Teachers: 658.9 (19.3 to 1)
Librarians/Media Specialists: 13.0 (976.4 to 1)
Guidance Counselors: 26.6 (477.2 to 1)
Current Spending: ($ per student per year):
Total: $5,034; Instruction: $2,704; Support Services: $2,091
Enrollment, Drop-out Rates and Diploma Recipients by Race/Ethnicity

Category	Total	White	Black	Asian	AIAN	Hisp.
Enrollment (%)	100.0	70.0	3.3	2.0	1.9	22.9
Drop-out Rate (%)	4.8	4.4	3.5	0.0	14.8	6.5
H.S. Diplomas (#)	683	513	22	21	9	118

Sahuarita Unified District
350 W Sahuarita Rd • Sahuarita, AZ 85629-9522
(520) 625-3502 • http://www.sahuarita.k12.az.us/
Grade Span: PK-12; **Agency Type:** 1
Schools: 5
3 Primary; 1 Middle; 1 High; 0 Other Level
5 Regular; 0 Special Education; 0 Vocational; 0 Alternative
0 Magnet; 0 Charter; 5 Title I Eligible; 0 School-wide Title I
Students: 2,607 (51.9% male; 48.0% female)
Individual Education Program: 344 (13.2%);
English Language Learner: 229 (8.8%); Migrant: 0 (0.0%)
Eligible for Free Lunch Program: 1,178 (45.2%)
Eligible for Reduced-Price Lunch Program: 274 (10.5%)
Teachers: 147.9 (17.6 to 1)
Librarians/Media Specialists: 1.0 (2,607.0 to 1)
Guidance Counselors: 4.0 (651.8 to 1)
Current Spending: ($ per student per year):
Total: $5,987; Instruction: $2,883; Support Services: $2,797
Enrollment, Drop-out Rates and Diploma Recipients by Race/Ethnicity

Category	Total	White	Black	Asian	AIAN	Hisp.
Enrollment (%)	100.0	47.6	1.2	1.2	1.2	48.8
Drop-out Rate (%)	5.2	4.1	18.2	0.0	10.0	6.3
H.S. Diplomas (#)	121	72	1	0	1	47

Sunnyside Unified District
2238 E Ginter Rd • Tucson, AZ 85706-5806
(520) 545-2041 • http://www.sunnysideud.k12.az.us/
Grade Span: PK-12; **Agency Type:** 1
Schools: 23
14 Primary; 4 Middle; 2 High; 3 Other Level
23 Regular; 0 Special Education; 0 Vocational; 0 Alternative

0 Magnet; 0 Charter; 17 Title I Eligible; 17 School-wide Title I
Students: 15,861 (52.1% male; 47.8% female)
    Individual Education Program: 2,291 (14.4%);
    English Language Learner: 6,826 (43.0%); Migrant: 0 (0.0%)
    Eligible for Free Lunch Program: 12,887 (81.2%)
    Eligible for Reduced-Price Lunch Program: 1,434 (9.0%)
Teachers: 873.8 (18.2 to 1)
Librarians/Media Specialists: 17.2 (922.2 to 1)
Guidance Counselors: 31.6 (501.9 to 1)
Current Spending: ($ per student per year):
    Total: $5,983; Instruction: $3,421; Support Services: $2,174
Enrollment, Drop-out Rates and Diploma Recipients by Race/Ethnicity

Category	Total	White	Black	Asian	AIAN	Hisp.
Enrollment (%)	100.0	6.5	2.0	0.6	4.2	86.8
Drop-out Rate (%)	12.3	13.6	9.0	0.0	27.1	11.6
H.S. Diplomas (#)	580	73	15	3	16	473

Tucson Unified District
1010 E 10th St • Tucson, AZ 85719
(520) 225-6060 • http://www.tusd.k12.az.us/
Grade Span: PK-12; **Agency Type:** 1
Schools: 126
    79 Primary; 21 Middle; 22 High; 4 Other Level
    118 Regular; 1 Special Education; 0 Vocational; 7 Alternative
    0 Magnet; 0 Charter; 34 Title I Eligible; 26 School-wide Title I
Students: 61,448 (51.3% male; 48.6% female)
    Individual Education Program: 7,935 (12.9%);
    English Language Learner: 8,538 (13.9%); Migrant: 0 (0.0%)
    Eligible for Free Lunch Program: 34,321 (55.9%)
    Eligible for Reduced-Price Lunch Program: 5,138 (8.4%)
Teachers: 3,355.9 (18.3 to 1)
Librarians/Media Specialists: 88.4 (695.1 to 1)
Guidance Counselors: 126.6 (485.4 to 1)
Current Spending: ($ per student per year):
    Total: $5,983; Instruction: $3,119; Support Services: $2,558
Enrollment, Drop-out Rates and Diploma Recipients by Race/Ethnicity

Category	Total	White	Black	Asian	AIAN	Hisp.
Enrollment (%)	100.0	36.1	6.6	2.6	4.1	50.6
Drop-out Rate (%)	4.7	3.0	4.5	1.9	11.0	6.3
H.S. Diplomas (#)	3,309	1,691	201	117	97	1,203

Vail Unified District
13801 E Benson Hwy • Vail, AZ 85641-0800
Mailing Address: PO Box 800 • Vail, AZ 85641-0800
(520) 762-2040 • http://www.vail.k12.az.us/
Grade Span: PK-12; **Agency Type:** 1
Schools: 12
    7 Primary; 1 Middle; 3 High; 1 Other Level
    12 Regular; 0 Special Education; 0 Vocational; 0 Alternative
    0 Magnet; 2 Charter; 3 Title I Eligible; 0 School-wide Title I
Students: 5,648 (52.5% male; 47.4% female)
    Individual Education Program: 613 (10.9%);
    English Language Learner: 115 (2.0%); Migrant: 0 (0.0%)
    Eligible for Free Lunch Program: 632 (11.2%)
    Eligible for Reduced-Price Lunch Program: 438 (7.8%)
Teachers: 323.7 (17.4 to 1)
Librarians/Media Specialists: 8.0 (706.0 to 1)
Guidance Counselors: 3.0 (1,882.7 to 1)
Current Spending: ($ per student per year):
    Total: $5,201; Instruction: $2,952; Support Services: $2,035
Enrollment, Drop-out Rates and Diploma Recipients by Race/Ethnicity

Category	Total	White	Black	Asian	AIAN	Hisp.
Enrollment (%)	100.0	73.8	5.0	2.1	0.7	18.3
Drop-out Rate (%)	2.5	1.9	3.0	0.0	0.0	5.8
H.S. Diplomas (#)	58	42	3	5	0	8

Pinal County

Apache Junction Unified District
1575 W Southern Ave • Apache Junction, AZ 85220
(480) 982-1110 • http://www.ajusd.org/
Grade Span: PK-12; **Agency Type:** 1
Schools: 9
    6 Primary; 2 Middle; 1 High; 0 Other Level
    8 Regular; 0 Special Education; 0 Vocational; 1 Alternative
    0 Magnet; 0 Charter; 6 Title I Eligible; 0 School-wide Title I
Students: 5,758 (51.7% male; 48.2% female)
    Individual Education Program: 777 (13.5%);
    English Language Learner: 72 (1.3%); Migrant: 0 (0.0%)
    Eligible for Free Lunch Program: 1,850 (32.1%)
    Eligible for Reduced-Price Lunch Program: 455 (7.9%)
Teachers: 301.4 (19.1 to 1)
Librarians/Media Specialists: 7.0 (822.6 to 1)
Guidance Counselors: 11.6 (496.4 to 1)
Current Spending: ($ per student per year):
    Total: $5,547; Instruction: $2,732; Support Services: $2,538

Enrollment, Drop-out Rates and Diploma Recipients by Race/Ethnicity

Category	Total	White	Black	Asian	AIAN	Hisp.
Enrollment (%)	100.0	78.5	1.6	1.3	1.4	17.2
Drop-out Rate (%)	4.9	4.9	0.0	0.0	0.0	5.8
H.S. Diplomas (#)	242	208	3	4	2	25

Casa Grande Elementary District
1460 N Pinal Ave • Casa Grande, AZ 85222-3397
(520) 836-2111 • http://www.cgelem.k12.az.us/
Grade Span: PK-08; **Agency Type:** 1
Schools: 10
    8 Primary; 2 Middle; 0 High; 0 Other Level
    10 Regular; 0 Special Education; 0 Vocational; 0 Alternative
    0 Magnet; 0 Charter; 7 Title I Eligible; 2 School-wide Title I
Students: 5,708 (52.4% male; 47.5% female)
    Individual Education Program: 770 (13.5%);
    English Language Learner: 771 (13.5%); Migrant: 48 (0.8%)
    Eligible for Free Lunch Program: 3,029 (53.1%)
    Eligible for Reduced-Price Lunch Program: 559 (9.8%)
Teachers: 296.4 (19.3 to 1)
Librarians/Media Specialists: 9.0 (634.2 to 1)
Guidance Counselors: 2.0 (2,854.0 to 1)
Current Spending: ($ per student per year):
    Total: $5,442; Instruction: $2,987; Support Services: $2,188
Enrollment, Drop-out Rates and Diploma Recipients by Race/Ethnicity

Category	Total	White	Black	Asian	AIAN	Hisp.
Enrollment (%)	100.0	35.5	5.7	0.6	6.7	51.6
Drop-out Rate (%)	n/a	n/a	n/a	n/a	n/a	n/a
H.S. Diplomas (#)	n/a	n/a	n/a	n/a	n/a	n/a

Casa Grande Union High SD
2730 N Trekell Rd • Casa Grande, AZ 85222-4193
Mailing Address: 1362 N Casa Grande Ave • Casa Grande, AZ 85222-4193
(520) 316-3360
Grade Span: 09-12; **Agency Type:** 1
Schools: 3
    0 Primary; 0 Middle; 3 High; 0 Other Level
    3 Regular; 0 Special Education; 0 Vocational; 0 Alternative
    0 Magnet; 1 Charter; 2 Title I Eligible; 0 School-wide Title I
Students: 2,815 (50.0% male; 49.9% female)
    Individual Education Program: 319 (11.3%);
    English Language Learner: 229 (8.1%); Migrant: 24 (0.9%)
    Eligible for Free Lunch Program: 983 (34.9%)
    Eligible for Reduced-Price Lunch Program: 156 (5.5%)
Teachers: 155.1 (18.1 to 1)
Librarians/Media Specialists: 2.0 (1,407.5 to 1)
Guidance Counselors: 8.0 (351.9 to 1)
Current Spending: ($ per student per year):
    Total: $5,847; Instruction: $3,056; Support Services: $2,548
Enrollment, Drop-out Rates and Diploma Recipients by Race/Ethnicity

Category	Total	White	Black	Asian	AIAN	Hisp.
Enrollment (%)	100.0	41.9	4.7	0.6	11.5	41.3
Drop-out Rate (%)	10.9	7.8	8.8	0.0	16.2	12.6
H.S. Diplomas (#)	387	181	8	5	34	159

Central Arizona Valley Institute of Technology
8470 N Overfield Rd • Coolidge, AZ 85228
(520) 423-1944
Grade Span: 09-12; **Agency Type:** 7
Schools: 6
    0 Primary; 0 Middle; 6 High; 0 Other Level
    0 Regular; 0 Special Education; 6 Vocational; 0 Alternative
    0 Magnet; 0 Charter; 0 Title I Eligible; 0 School-wide Title I
Students: 2,998 (50.5% male; 49.4% female)
    Individual Education Program: 0 (0.0%);
    English Language Learner: 0 (0.0%); Migrant: 0 (0.0%)
    Eligible for Free Lunch Program: n/a
    Eligible for Reduced-Price Lunch Program: n/a
Teachers: n/a
Librarians/Media Specialists: n/a
Guidance Counselors: n/a
Current Spending: ($ per student per year):
    Total: n/a; Instruction: n/a; Support Services: n/a
Enrollment, Drop-out Rates and Diploma Recipients by Race/Ethnicity

Category	Total	White	Black	Asian	AIAN	Hisp.
Enrollment (%)	100.0	37.5	5.5	0.4	12.4	44.2
Drop-out Rate (%)	n/a	n/a	n/a	n/a	n/a	n/a
H.S. Diplomas (#)	0	0	0	0	0	0

Coolidge Unified District
221 W Central Ave • Coolidge, AZ 85228-4109
(520) 723-2045 • http://www.cusd.k12.az.us/
Grade Span: PK-12; **Agency Type:** 1
Schools: 8
    4 Primary; 2 Middle; 2 High; 0 Other Level

7 Regular; 0 Special Education; 0 Vocational; 1 Alternative
0 Magnet; 1 Charter; 6 Title I Eligible; 3 School-wide Title I
Students: 3,037   (51.5% male; 48.4% female)
   Individual Education Program: 392 (12.9%);
   English Language Learner: 295 (9.7%); Migrant: 3 (0.1%)
   Eligible for Free Lunch Program: 1,542 (50.8%)
   Eligible for Reduced-Price Lunch Program: 362 (11.9%)
Teachers: 179.1 (17.0 to 1)
Librarians/Media Specialists: 3.0 (1,012.3 to 1)
Guidance Counselors: 4.0 (759.3 to 1)
Current Spending: ($ per student per year):
   Total: $6,110; Instruction: $2,989; Support Services: $2,868
Enrollment, Drop-out Rates and Diploma Recipients by Race/Ethnicity

Category	Total	White	Black	Asian	AIAN	Hisp.
Enrollment (%)	100.0	31.5	9.1	0.3	20.0	39.1
Drop-out Rate (%)	21.0	15.7	24.1	0.0	28.4	20.5
H.S. Diplomas (#)	138	56	15	1	18	48

Florence Unified SD
350 S Main St • Florence, AZ 85232-0829
Mailing Address: PO Box 2850 • Florence, AZ 85232-0829
(520) 866-3500
Grade Span: PK-12; **Agency Type:** 1
Schools: 5
   3 Primary; 1 Middle; 1 High; 0 Other Level
   5 Regular; 0 Special Education; 0 Vocational; 0 Alternative
   0 Magnet; 0 Charter; 5 Title I Eligible; 1 School-wide Title I
Students: 2,417   (51.0% male; 48.9% female)
   Individual Education Program: 282 (11.7%);
   English Language Learner: 12 (0.5%); Migrant: 22 (0.9%)
   Eligible for Free Lunch Program: 999 (41.3%)
   Eligible for Reduced-Price Lunch Program: 350 (14.5%)
Teachers: 142.8 (16.9 to 1)
Librarians/Media Specialists: 0.0 (n/a to 1)
Guidance Counselors: 2.0 (1,208.5 to 1)
Current Spending: ($ per student per year):
   Total: $5,432; Instruction: $3,085; Support Services: $2,077
Enrollment, Drop-out Rates and Diploma Recipients by Race/Ethnicity

Category	Total	White	Black	Asian	AIAN	Hisp.
Enrollment (%)	100.0	61.9	4.3	0.5	2.5	30.8
Drop-out Rate (%)	9.0	11.3	16.0	0.0	6.3	3.6
H.S. Diplomas (#)	78	54	4	0	1	19

Santa Cruz County

Nogales Unified District
310 W Plum St • Nogales, AZ 85621-2611
(520) 375-7800 • http://www.nusd.k12.az.us/
Grade Span: PK-12; **Agency Type:** 1
Schools: 11
   6 Primary; 2 Middle; 2 High; 1 Other Level
   9 Regular; 1 Special Education; 0 Vocational; 1 Alternative
   0 Magnet; 0 Charter; 10 Title I Eligible; 10 School-wide Title I
Students: 6,209   (51.3% male; 48.6% female)
   Individual Education Program: 534 (8.6%);
   English Language Learner: 3,759 (60.5%); Migrant: 0 (0.0%)
   Eligible for Free Lunch Program: 4,118 (66.3%)
   Eligible for Reduced-Price Lunch Program: 630 (10.1%)
Teachers: 321.7 (19.3 to 1)
Librarians/Media Specialists: 4.0 (1,552.3 to 1)
Guidance Counselors: 10.5 (591.3 to 1)
Current Spending: ($ per student per year):
   Total: $5,781; Instruction: $2,748; Support Services: $2,487
Enrollment, Drop-out Rates and Diploma Recipients by Race/Ethnicity

Category	Total	White	Black	Asian	AIAN	Hisp.
Enrollment (%)	100.0	2.0	0.1	0.1	0.0	97.7
Drop-out Rate (%)	9.1	2.2	0.0	0.0	n/a	9.3
H.S. Diplomas (#)	353	9	1	1	0	342

Santa Cruz Valley Unified District
1374 W Frontage Rd • Rio Rico, AZ 85648-2006
(520) 281-8282 • http://www.scvuhs.org/
Grade Span: PK-12; **Agency Type:** 1
Schools: 5
   3 Primary; 1 Middle; 1 High; 0 Other Level
   5 Regular; 0 Special Education; 0 Vocational; 0 Alternative
   0 Magnet; 0 Charter; 4 Title I Eligible; 0 School-wide Title I
Students: 3,087   (52.9% male; 47.0% female)
   Individual Education Program: 237 (7.7%);
   English Language Learner: 1,784 (57.8%); Migrant: 0 (0.0%)
   Eligible for Free Lunch Program: 1,790 (58.0%)
   Eligible for Reduced-Price Lunch Program: 487 (15.8%)
Teachers: 162.5 (19.0 to 1)
Librarians/Media Specialists: 2.0 (1,543.5 to 1)
Guidance Counselors: 5.0 (617.4 to 1)

Current Spending: ($ per student per year):
   Total: $4,853; Instruction: $2,579; Support Services: $1,957
Enrollment, Drop-out Rates and Diploma Recipients by Race/Ethnicity

Category	Total	White	Black	Asian	AIAN	Hisp.
Enrollment (%)	100.0	8.7	0.4	0.6	0.1	90.3
Drop-out Rate (%)	5.4	3.9	50.0	0.0	0.0	5.6
H.S. Diplomas (#)	101	9	0	2	1	89

Yavapai County

Chino Valley Unified District
115 N Hwy 89 • Chino Valley, AZ 86323-0225
Mailing Address: PO Box 225 • Chino Valley, AZ 86323-0225
(928) 636-2458 • http://www.chinleusd.k12.az.us/
Grade Span: PK-12; **Agency Type:** 1
Schools: 4
   2 Primary; 1 Middle; 1 High; 0 Other Level
   4 Regular; 0 Special Education; 0 Vocational; 0 Alternative
   0 Magnet; 0 Charter; 4 Title I Eligible; 0 School-wide Title I
Students: 2,640   (52.7% male; 47.2% female)
   Individual Education Program: 392 (14.8%);
   English Language Learner: 227 (8.6%); Migrant: 0 (0.0%)
   Eligible for Free Lunch Program: 952 (36.1%)
   Eligible for Reduced-Price Lunch Program: 410 (15.5%)
Teachers: 148.5 (17.8 to 1)
Librarians/Media Specialists: 1.0 (2,640.0 to 1)
Guidance Counselors: 3.1 (851.6 to 1)
Current Spending: ($ per student per year):
   Total: $4,776; Instruction: $2,692; Support Services: $1,740
Enrollment, Drop-out Rates and Diploma Recipients by Race/Ethnicity

Category	Total	White	Black	Asian	AIAN	Hisp.
Enrollment (%)	100.0	81.2	0.8	0.4	1.3	16.3
Drop-out Rate (%)	7.8	7.7	0.0	33.3	0.0	9.0
H.S. Diplomas (#)	144	132	1	0	1	10

Cottonwood-Oak Creek Elementary District
1 N Willard St • Cottonwood, AZ 86326-0057
(928) 634-2288 • http://www.cocsd.k12.az.us/
Grade Span: PK-08; **Agency Type:** 1
Schools: 4
   3 Primary; 1 Middle; 0 High; 0 Other Level
   4 Regular; 0 Special Education; 0 Vocational; 0 Alternative
   0 Magnet; 0 Charter; 4 Title I Eligible; 1 School-wide Title I
Students: 2,558   (52.5% male; 47.4% female)
   Individual Education Program: 216 (8.4%);
   English Language Learner: 427 (16.7%); Migrant: 0 (0.0%)
   Eligible for Free Lunch Program: 1,074 (42.0%)
   Eligible for Reduced-Price Lunch Program: 334 (13.1%)
Teachers: 132.9 (19.2 to 1)
Librarians/Media Specialists: 2.0 (1,279.0 to 1)
Guidance Counselors: 0.0 (n/a to 1)
Current Spending: ($ per student per year):
   Total: $5,316; Instruction: $2,729; Support Services: $1,935
Enrollment, Drop-out Rates and Diploma Recipients by Race/Ethnicity

Category	Total	White	Black	Asian	AIAN	Hisp.
Enrollment (%)	100.0	68.1	0.7	0.6	1.7	28.9
Drop-out Rate (%)	n/a	n/a	n/a	n/a	n/a	n/a
H.S. Diplomas (#)	n/a	n/a	n/a	n/a	n/a	n/a

Humboldt Unified District
8766 E Hwy 69 • Prescott Valley, AZ 86314
(928) 759-4000
Grade Span: PK-12; **Agency Type:** 1
Schools: 9
   5 Primary; 2 Middle; 1 High; 0 Other Level
   8 Regular; 0 Special Education; 0 Vocational; 0 Alternative
   0 Magnet; 0 Charter; 4 Title I Eligible; 0 School-wide Title I
Students: 5,236   (51.2% male; 48.7% female)
   Individual Education Program: 786 (15.0%);
   English Language Learner: 359 (6.9%); Migrant: 0 (0.0%)
   Eligible for Free Lunch Program: 1,912 (36.5%)
   Eligible for Reduced-Price Lunch Program: 691 (13.2%)
Teachers: 259.6 (20.2 to 1)
Librarians/Media Specialists: 1.0 (5,236.0 to 1)
Guidance Counselors: 6.8 (770.0 to 1)
Current Spending: ($ per student per year):
   Total: $5,180; Instruction: $2,698; Support Services: $2,213
Enrollment, Drop-out Rates and Diploma Recipients by Race/Ethnicity

Category	Total	White	Black	Asian	AIAN	Hisp.
Enrollment (%)	100.0	76.0	1.0	1.3	1.4	20.4
Drop-out Rate (%)	7.8	7.8	0.0	4.3	7.7	8.9
H.S. Diplomas (#)	281	238	2	2	4	35

Prescott Unified District

146 S Granite St • Prescott, AZ 86303-4786
(928) 445-5400 • http://www.prescott.k12.az.us/
Grade Span: PK-12; **Agency Type:** 1
Schools: 12
  6 Primary; 2 Middle; 1 High; 2 Other Level
  10 Regular; 1 Special Education; 0 Vocational; 0 Alternative
  0 Magnet; 0 Charter; 2 Title I Eligible; 0 School-wide Title I
Students: 5,241 (50.7% male; 49.2% female)
  Individual Education Program: 690 (13.2%);
  English Language Learner: 149 (2.8%); Migrant: 0 (0.0%)
  Eligible for Free Lunch Program: 1,080 (20.6%)
  Eligible for Reduced-Price Lunch Program: 310 (5.9%)
Teachers: 280.0 (18.7 to 1)
Librarians/Media Specialists: 1.0 (5,241.0 to 1)
Guidance Counselors: 7.0 (748.7 to 1)
Current Spending: ($ per student per year):
  Total: $5,013; Instruction: $2,827; Support Services: $1,734
Enrollment, Drop-out Rates and Diploma Recipients by Race/Ethnicity

Category	Total	White	Black	Asian	AIAN	Hisp.
Enrollment (%)	100.0	83.5	1.2	1.5	2.5	11.3
Drop-out Rate (%)	5.6	5.4	0.0	5.0	10.0	7.2
H.S. Diplomas (#)	326	289	2	3	4	28

Yuma County

Crane Elementary District

4250 W 16th St • Yuma, AZ 85364-4099
(928) 373-3400 • http://familyeducation.com/az/crane_elementary
Grade Span: PK-08; **Agency Type:** 1
Schools: 7
  5 Primary; 2 Middle; 0 High; 0 Other Level
  7 Regular; 0 Special Education; 0 Vocational; 0 Alternative
  0 Magnet; 0 Charter; 6 Title I Eligible; 5 School-wide Title I
Students: 5,851 (52.3% male; 47.6% female)
  Individual Education Program: 745 (12.7%);
  English Language Learner: 1,994 (34.1%); Migrant: 130 (2.2%)
  Eligible for Free Lunch Program: 3,390 (57.9%)
  Eligible for Reduced-Price Lunch Program: 883 (15.1%)
Teachers: 323.7 (18.1 to 1)
Librarians/Media Specialists: 0.0 (n/a to 1)
Guidance Counselors: 8.0 (731.4 to 1)
Current Spending: ($ per student per year):
  Total: $4,973; Instruction: $2,849; Support Services: $1,821
Enrollment, Drop-out Rates and Diploma Recipients by Race/Ethnicity

Category	Total	White	Black	Asian	AIAN	Hisp.
Enrollment (%)	100.0	24.5	2.0	1.6	1.1	70.8
Drop-out Rate (%)	n/a	n/a	n/a	n/a	n/a	n/a
H.S. Diplomas (#)	n/a	n/a	n/a	n/a	n/a	n/a

Gadsden Elementary District

1453 N Main St • San Luis, AZ 85349
Mailing Address: PO Box 6870 • San Luis, AZ 85349
(928) 627-6540 • http://www.gesd32.org/district/html/
Grade Span: PK-08; **Agency Type:** 1
Schools: 7
  6 Primary; 1 Middle; 0 High; 0 Other Level
  7 Regular; 0 Special Education; 0 Vocational; 0 Alternative
  0 Magnet; 0 Charter; 4 Title I Eligible; 4 School-wide Title I
Students: 4,432 (50.5% male; 49.4% female)
  Individual Education Program: 369 (8.3%);
  English Language Learner: 4,205 (94.9%); Migrant: 82 (1.9%)
  Eligible for Free Lunch Program: 3,159 (71.3%)
  Eligible for Reduced-Price Lunch Program: 193 (4.4%)
Teachers: 172.3 (25.7 to 1)
Librarians/Media Specialists: 6.0 (738.7 to 1)
Guidance Counselors: 4.0 (1,108.0 to 1)
Current Spending: ($ per student per year):
  Total: $4,832; Instruction: $2,620; Support Services: $1,844
Enrollment, Drop-out Rates and Diploma Recipients by Race/Ethnicity

Category	Total	White	Black	Asian	AIAN	Hisp.
Enrollment (%)	100.0	0.2	0.1	0.0	0.0	99.8
Drop-out Rate (%)	n/a	n/a	n/a	n/a	n/a	n/a
H.S. Diplomas (#)	n/a	n/a	n/a	n/a	n/a	n/a

Somerton Elementary District

215 N Carlisle Ave • Somerton, AZ 85350-3200
Mailing Address: PO Box 3200 • Somerton, AZ 85350-3200
(928) 341-6000 • http://www.somerton.k12.az.us/
Grade Span: PK-08; **Agency Type:** 1
Schools: 4
  3 Primary; 1 Middle; 0 High; 0 Other Level
  4 Regular; 0 Special Education; 0 Vocational; 0 Alternative
  0 Magnet; 0 Charter; 4 Title I Eligible; 4 School-wide Title I
Students: 2,488 (50.8% male; 49.1% female)

  Individual Education Program: 333 (13.4%);
  English Language Learner: 1,800 (72.3%); Migrant: 72 (2.9%)
  Eligible for Free Lunch Program: 2,475 (99.5%)
  Eligible for Reduced-Price Lunch Program: 0 (0.0%)
Teachers: 120.1 (20.7 to 1)
Librarians/Media Specialists: 2.0 (1,244.0 to 1)
Guidance Counselors: 2.0 (1,244.0 to 1)
Current Spending: ($ per student per year):
  Total: $5,580; Instruction: $2,762; Support Services: $2,341
Enrollment, Drop-out Rates and Diploma Recipients by Race/Ethnicity

Category	Total	White	Black	Asian	AIAN	Hisp.
Enrollment (%)	100.0	1.4	0.3	0.0	4.9	93.3
Drop-out Rate (%)	n/a	n/a	n/a	n/a	n/a	n/a
H.S. Diplomas (#)	n/a	n/a	n/a	n/a	n/a	n/a

Yuma Elementary District

4th Ave And 6th St • Yuma, AZ 85364-2973
Mailing Address: 450 W 6th St • Yuma, AZ 85364-2973
(928) 502-4300 • http://www.yuma.org/
Grade Span: PK-08; **Agency Type:** 1
Schools: 17
  12 Primary; 5 Middle; 0 High; 0 Other Level
  17 Regular; 0 Special Education; 0 Vocational; 0 Alternative
  0 Magnet; 0 Charter; 16 Title I Eligible; 16 School-wide Title I
Students: 10,359 (50.7% male; 49.2% female)
  Individual Education Program: 975 (9.4%);
  English Language Learner: 3,465 (33.4%); Migrant: 172 (1.7%)
  Eligible for Free Lunch Program: 5,793 (55.9%)
  Eligible for Reduced-Price Lunch Program: 1,390 (13.4%)
Teachers: 569.1 (18.2 to 1)
Librarians/Media Specialists: 13.5 (767.3 to 1)
Guidance Counselors: 20.0 (518.0 to 1)
Current Spending: ($ per student per year):
  Total: $5,037; Instruction: $2,727; Support Services: $1,957
Enrollment, Drop-out Rates and Diploma Recipients by Race/Ethnicity

Category	Total	White	Black	Asian	AIAN	Hisp.
Enrollment (%)	100.0	29.0	3.1	1.0	1.1	65.7
Drop-out Rate (%)	n/a	n/a	n/a	n/a	n/a	n/a
H.S. Diplomas (#)	n/a	n/a	n/a	n/a	n/a	n/a

Yuma Union High SD

3150 S Ave A • Yuma, AZ 85364-7998
(928) 726-1731 • http://www.yuma.org/
Grade Span: 09-12; **Agency Type:** 1
Schools: 5
  0 Primary; 0 Middle; 5 High; 0 Other Level
  4 Regular; 0 Special Education; 0 Vocational; 1 Alternative
  0 Magnet; 0 Charter; 4 Title I Eligible; 4 School-wide Title I
Students: 9,159 (51.3% male; 48.6% female)
  Individual Education Program: 764 (8.3%);
  English Language Learner: 929 (10.1%); Migrant: 627 (6.8%)
  Eligible for Free Lunch Program: 4,717 (51.5%)
  Eligible for Reduced-Price Lunch Program: 409 (4.5%)
Teachers: 443.9 (20.6 to 1)
Librarians/Media Specialists: 7.2 (1,272.1 to 1)
Guidance Counselors: 26.4 (346.9 to 1)
Current Spending: ($ per student per year):
  Total: $5,187; Instruction: $2,693; Support Services: $2,144
Enrollment, Drop-out Rates and Diploma Recipients by Race/Ethnicity

Category	Total	White	Black	Asian	AIAN	Hisp.
Enrollment (%)	100.0	22.3	1.8	1.0	1.1	73.9
Drop-out Rate (%)	6.9	5.1	7.6	1.1	16.2	7.6
H.S. Diplomas (#)	1,389	415	26	13	5	930

Number of Schools

Rank	Number	District Name	City
1	126	Tucson Unified District	Tucson
2	91	Mesa Unified District	Mesa
3	50	Paradise Valley Unified District	Phoenix
4	38	Gilbert Unified District	Gilbert
5	37	Peoria Unified SD	Glendale
6	36	Peach Springs Unified District	Peach Springs
7	34	Deer Valley Unified District	Phoenix
7	34	Scottsdale Unified District	Phoenix
9	32	Washington Elementary District	Phoenix
10	28	Chandler Unified District	Chandler
11	27	Tempe Elementary District	Tempe
12	26	Kyrene Elementary District	Tempe
13	24	Cartwright Elementary District	Phoenix
14	23	Sunnyside Unified District	Tucson
15	22	Amphitheater Unified District	Tucson
15	22	Roosevelt Elementary District	Phoenix
17	21	Flagstaff Unified District	Flagstaff
17	21	Phoenix Elementary District	Phoenix
19	17	Glendale Elementary District	Glendale
19	17	Marana Unified District	Marana
19	17	Yuma Elementary District	Yuma
22	15	Alhambra Elementary District	Phoenix
23	14	Maricopa County Regional District	Phoenix
23	14	Phoenix Union High SD	Phoenix
25	13	Isaac Elementary District	Phoenix
26	12	Douglas Unified District	Douglas
26	12	Dysart Unified District	El Mirage
26	12	East Valley Institute of Tech	Mesa
26	12	Glendale Union High SD	Glendale
26	12	Navit	Snowflake
26	12	Pendergast Elementary District	Phoenix
26	12	Prescott Unified District	Prescott
26	12	Vail Unified District	Vail
34	11	Flowing Wells Unified District	Tucson
34	11	Kingman Unified SD	Kingman
34	11	Nogales Unified District	Nogales
37	10	Casa Grande Elementary District	Casa Grande
37	10	Creighton Elementary District	Phoenix
37	10	Higley Unified District	Higley
40	9	Apache Junction Unified District	Apache Junction
40	9	Humboldt Unified District	Prescott Valley
40	9	Lake Havasu Unified District	Lk Havasu City
40	9	Madison Elementary District	Phoenix
40	9	Show Low Unified District	Show Low
40	9	Sierra Vista Unified District	Sierra Vista
46	8	Catalina Foothills Unified Dist	Tucson
46	8	Chinle Unified District	Chinle
46	8	Coolidge Unified District	Coolidge
46	8	Litchfield Elementary District	Litchfield Park
46	8	Tempe Union High SD	Tempe
51	7	Avondale Elementary District	Avondale
51	7	Bullhead City Elementary District	Bullhead City
51	7	Cave Creek Unified District	Cave Creek
51	7	Crane Elementary District	Yuma
51	7	Gadsden Elementary District	San Luis
51	7	NE Arizona Tech Inst of Voc Ed	Kayenta
51	7	Snowflake Unified District	Snowflake
51	7	Tuba City Unified District	Tuba City
59	6	Central Ariz Valley Inst of Tech	Coolidge
59	6	Fowler Elementary District	Phoenix
59	6	Osborn Elementary District	Phoenix
59	6	Parker Unified SD	Parker
59	6	Payson Unified District	Payson
59	6	Safford Unified District	Safford
59	6	Western Maricopa Ed Ctr (West-Mec)	Phoenix
59	6	Window Rock Unified District	Ft Defiance
67	5	Balsz Elementary District	Phoenix
67	5	Florence Unified SD	Florence
67	5	Holbrook Unified District	Holbrook
67	5	Kayenta Unified District	Kayenta
67	5	Queen Creek Unified District	Queen Creek
67	5	Sahuarita Unified District	Sahuarita
67	5	Santa Cruz Valley Unified District	Rio Rico
67	5	Whiteriver Unified District	Whiteriver
67	5	Winslow Unified District	Winslow
67	5	Yuma Union High SD	Yuma
77	4	Blue Ridge Unified District	Lakeside
77	4	Chino Valley Unified District	Chino Valley
77	4	Cottonwood-Oak Creek Elem Dist	Cottonwood
77	4	Fountain Hills Unified District	Fountain Hills
77	4	Ganado Unified District	Ganado
77	4	Globe Unified District	Globe
77	4	Mohave Valley Elementary District	Mohave Valley
77	4	Murphy Elementary District	Phoenix
77	4	Page Unified District	Page
77	4	Pinon Unified District	Pinon
77	4	Somerton Elementary District	Somerton
88	3	Agua Fria Union High SD	Avondale
88	3	Casa Grande Union High SD	Casa Grande
88	3	Laveen Elementary District	Laveen
88	3	Liberty Elementary District	Buckeye
88	3	Littleton Elementary District	Cashion
88	3	Tolleson Elementary District	Tolleson
88	3	Tolleson Union High SD	Tolleson
95	2	Colorado River Union High SD	Fort Mojave

Number of Teachers

Rank	Number	District Name	City
1	3,704	Mesa Unified District	Mesa
2	3,355	Tucson Unified District	Tucson
3	1,937	Peoria Unified SD	Glendale
4	1,909	Gilbert Unified District	Gilbert
5	1,788	Paradise Valley Unified District	Phoenix
6	1,585	Deer Valley Unified District	Phoenix
7	1,394	Scottsdale Unified District	Phoenix
8	1,294	Phoenix Union High SD	Phoenix
9	1,284	Washington Elementary District	Phoenix
10	1,221	Chandler Unified District	Chandler
11	1,016	Kyrene Elementary District	Tempe
12	961	Cartwright Elementary District	Phoenix
13	925	Amphitheater Unified District	Tucson
14	873	Sunnyside Unified District	Tucson
15	850	Tempe Elementary District	Tempe
16	723	Alhambra Elementary District	Phoenix
17	681	Glendale Union High SD	Glendale
18	658	Marana Unified District	Marana
19	647	Glendale Elementary District	Glendale
20	643	Tempe Union High SD	Tempe
21	641	Flagstaff Unified District	Flagstaff
22	637	Roosevelt Elementary District	Phoenix
23	569	Yuma Elementary District	Yuma
24	530	Dysart Unified District	El Mirage
25	522	Pendergast Elementary District	Phoenix
26	482	Creighton Elementary District	Phoenix
27	471	Phoenix Elementary District	Phoenix
28	443	Yuma Union High SD	Yuma
29	439	Isaac Elementary District	Phoenix
30	366	Kingman Unified SD	Kingman
31	345	Sierra Vista Unified District	Sierra Vista
32	323	Crane Elementary District	Yuma
32	323	Vail Unified District	Vail
34	323	Madison Elementary District	Phoenix
35	321	Nogales Unified District	Nogales
36	301	Apache Junction Unified District	Apache Junction
37	296	Casa Grande Elementary District	Casa Grande
38	296	Lake Havasu Unified District	Lk Havasu City
39	295	Flowing Wells Unified District	Tucson
40	291	Litchfield Elementary District	Litchfield Park
41	289	Catalina Foothills Unified Dist	Tucson
42	280	Prescott Unified District	Prescott
43	267	Tolleson Union High SD	Tolleson
44	265	Cave Creek Unified District	Cave Creek
45	265	Chinle Unified District	Chinle
46	259	Humboldt Unified District	Prescott Valley
47	233	Higley Unified District	Higley
48	219	Avondale Elementary District	Avondale
49	219	Osborn Elementary District	Phoenix
50	210	Bullhead City Elementary District	Bullhead City
51	204	Douglas Unified District	Douglas
52	196	Window Rock Unified District	Ft Defiance
53	195	Balsz Elementary District	Phoenix
54	183	Page Unified District	Page
55	179	Coolidge Unified District	Coolidge
56	173	Fowler Elementary District	Phoenix
57	172	Gadsden Elementary District	San Luis
58	169	Whiteriver Unified District	Whiteriver
59	165	Tuba City Unified District	Tuba City
60	164	Kayenta Unified District	Kayenta
61	162	Santa Cruz Valley Unified District	Rio Rico
62	161	Agua Fria Union High SD	Avondale
63	155	Casa Grande Union High SD	Casa Grande
64	154	Payson Unified District	Payson
65	154	Blue Ridge Unified District	Lakeside
66	149	Safford Unified District	Safford
67	148	Chino Valley Unified District	Chino Valley
68	147	Sahuarita Unified District	Sahuarita
69	147	Winslow Unified District	Winslow
70	146	Queen Creek Unified District	Queen Creek
71	145	Murphy Elementary District	Phoenix
72	142	Florence Unified SD	Florence
73	137	Holbrook Unified District	Holbrook
74	136	Fountain Hills Unified District	Fountain Hills
75	132	Cottonwood-Oak Creek Elem Dist	Cottonwood
76	132	Snowflake Unified District	Snowflake
77	132	Show Low Unified District	Show Low
78	126	Parker Unified SD	Parker
79	124	Ganado Unified District	Ganado
80	120	Liberty Elementary District	Buckeye
81	120	Somerton Elementary District	Somerton
82	112	Globe Unified District	Globe
83	112	Tolleson Elementary District	Tolleson
84	110	Littleton Elementary District	Cashion
85	101	Pinon Unified District	Pinon
86	94	Laveen Elementary District	Laveen
87	89	Colorado River Union High SD	Fort Mojave
87	89	Maricopa County Regional District	Phoenix
89	77	Mohave Valley Elementary District	Mohave Valley
90	20	Peach Springs Unified District	Peach Springs
91	n/a	Central Ariz Valley Inst of Tech	Coolidge
91	n/a	East Valley Institute of Tech	Mesa
91	n/a	Navit	Snowflake
91	n/a	NE Arizona Tech Inst of Voc Ed	Kayenta
91	n/a	Western Maricopa Ed Ctr (West-Mec)	Phoenix

Number of Students

Rank	Number	District Name	City
1	75,401	Mesa Unified District	Mesa
2	61,448	Tucson Unified District	Tucson
3	36,719	Peoria Unified SD	Glendale
4	35,218	Gilbert Unified District	Gilbert
5	34,884	Paradise Valley Unified District	Phoenix
6	31,691	Deer Valley Unified District	Phoenix
7	26,915	Chandler Unified District	Chandler
8	26,559	Scottsdale Unified District	Phoenix
9	24,438	Washington Elementary District	Phoenix
10	23,989	Phoenix Union High SD	Phoenix
11	19,864	Cartwright Elementary District	Phoenix
12	18,579	Kyrene Elementary District	Tempe
13	16,868	Amphitheater Unified District	Tucson
14	16,332	East Valley Institute of Tech	Mesa
15	15,861	Sunnyside Unified District	Tucson
16	14,742	Alhambra Elementary District	Phoenix
17	14,515	Glendale Union High SD	Glendale
18	13,717	Tempe Elementary District	Tempe
19	13,258	Glendale Elementary District	Glendale
20	13,249	Tempe Union High SD	Tempe
21	12,693	Marana Unified District	Marana
22	11,750	Roosevelt Elementary District	Phoenix
23	11,379	Flagstaff Unified District	Flagstaff
24	11,150	Dysart Unified District	El Mirage
25	10,359	Yuma Elementary District	Yuma
26	10,109	Pendergast Elementary District	Phoenix
27	9,159	Yuma Union High SD	Yuma
28	8,538	Isaac Elementary District	Phoenix
29	8,382	Creighton Elementary District	Phoenix
30	8,340	Phoenix Elementary District	Phoenix
31	7,298	Kingman Unified SD	Kingman
32	6,719	Sierra Vista Unified District	Sierra Vista
33	6,495	Lake Havasu Unified District	Lk Havasu City
34	6,252	Litchfield Elementary District	Litchfield Park
35	6,209	Nogales Unified District	Nogales
36	6,041	Flowing Wells Unified District	Tucson
37	5,851	Crane Elementary District	Yuma
38	5,758	Apache Junction Unified District	Apache Junction
39	5,708	Casa Grande Elementary District	Casa Grande
40	5,648	Vail Unified District	Vail
41	5,565	Higley Unified District	Higley
42	5,487	Tolleson Union High SD	Tolleson
43	5,388	Cave Creek Unified District	Cave Creek
44	5,253	Madison Elementary District	Phoenix
45	5,241	Prescott Unified District	Prescott
46	5,236	Humboldt Unified District	Prescott Valley
47	5,046	Catalina Foothills Unified Dist	Tucson
48	4,909	Navit	Snowflake
49	4,449	Avondale Elementary District	Avondale
50	4,432	Gadsden Elementary District	San Luis
51	4,115	Douglas Unified District	Douglas
52	4,082	Chinle Unified District	Chinle
53	3,888	Bullhead City Elementary District	Bullhead City
54	3,715	Osborn Elementary District	Phoenix
55	3,657	Agua Fria Union High SD	Avondale
56	3,432	Balsz Elementary District	Phoenix
57	3,405	Western Maricopa Ed Ctr (West-Mec)	Phoenix
58	3,264	NE Arizona Tech Inst of Voc Ed	Kayenta
59	3,126	Fowler Elementary District	Phoenix
60	3,087	Santa Cruz Valley Unified District	Rio Rico
61	3,037	Coolidge Unified District	Coolidge
62	3,017	Page Unified District	Page
63	2,998	Central Ariz Valley Inst of Tech	Coolidge
64	2,888	Safford Unified District	Safford
65	2,874	Window Rock Unified District	Ft Defiance
66	2,816	Payson Unified District	Payson
67	2,815	Casa Grande Union High SD	Casa Grande
68	2,640	Chino Valley Unified District	Chino Valley
69	2,636	Blue Ridge Unified District	Lakeside
70	2,625	Show Low Unified District	Show Low
71	2,607	Sahuarita Unified District	Sahuarita
72	2,587	Murphy Elementary District	Phoenix
73	2,570	Kayenta Unified District	Kayenta
74	2,565	Tuba City Unified District	Tuba City
75	2,561	Winslow Unified District	Winslow
76	2,558	Cottonwood-Oak Creek Elem Dist	Cottonwood
77	2,542	Fountain Hills Unified District	Fountain Hills
78	2,516	Queen Creek Unified District	Queen Creek

79	2,513	Snowflake Unified District	Snowflake
80	2,488	Somerton Elementary District	Somerton
81	2,467	Whiteriver Unified District	Whiteriver
82	2,417	Florence Unified SD	Florence
83	2,415	Littleton Elementary District	Cashion
84	2,133	Globe Unified District	Globe
85	2,114	Colorado River Union High SD	Fort Mojave
86	2,075	Ganado Unified District	Ganado
87	2,073	Holbrook Unified District	Holbrook
88	2,070	Liberty Elementary District	Buckeye
89	2,035	Tolleson Elementary District	Tolleson
90	1,995	Parker Unified SD	Parker
91	1,769	Maricopa County Regional District	Phoenix
92	1,755	Mohave Valley Elementary District	Mohave Valley
93	1,754	Laveen Elementary District	Laveen
94	1,719	Peach Springs Unified District	Peach Springs
95	1,523	Pinon Unified District	Pinon

Male Students

Rank	Percent	District Name	City
1	60.3	Maricopa County Regional District	Phoenix
2	55.8	East Valley Institute of Tech	Mesa
3	54.0	Western Maricopa Ed Ctr (West-Mec)	Phoenix
4	53.6	Fountain Hills Unified District	Fountain Hills
5	53.5	NE Arizona Tech Inst of Voc Ed	Kayenta
6	53.2	Show Low Unified District	Show Low
7	53.0	Page Unified District	Page
8	53.0	Douglas Unified District	Douglas
9	53.0	Avondale Elementary District	Avondale
10	52.9	Santa Cruz Valley Unified District	Rio Rico
11	52.9	Bullhead City Elementary District	Bullhead City
12	52.9	Queen Creek Unified District	Queen Creek
13	52.9	Pinon Unified District	Pinon
14	52.7	Chino Valley Unified District	Chino Valley
15	52.5	Snowflake Unified District	Snowflake
16	52.5	Cottonwood-Oak Creek Elem Dist	Cottonwood
17	52.5	Vail Unified District	Vail
18	52.4	Dysart Unified District	El Mirage
19	52.4	Washington Elementary District	Phoenix
20	52.4	Casa Grande Elementary District	Casa Grande
21	52.3	Crane Elementary District	Yuma
22	52.1	Tolleson Elementary District	Tolleson
23	52.1	Sunnyside Unified District	Tucson
24	52.0	Amphitheater Unified District	Tucson
25	51.9	Mohave Valley Elementary District	Mohave Valley
26	51.9	Sahuarita Unified District	Sahuarita
27	51.8	Peoria Unified SD	Glendale
28	51.8	Marana Unified District	Marana
29	51.8	Globe Unified District	Globe
30	51.7	Alhambra Elementary District	Phoenix
31	51.7	Paradise Valley Unified District	Phoenix
32	51.7	Pendergast Elementary District	Phoenix
33	51.7	Gilbert Unified District	Gilbert
34	51.7	Scottsdale Unified District	Phoenix
35	51.7	Apache Junction Unified District	Apache Junction
36	51.7	Mesa Unified District	Mesa
37	51.6	Flagstaff Unified District	Flagstaff
38	51.6	Deer Valley Unified District	Phoenix
39	51.6	Kayenta Unified District	Kayenta
40	51.6	Madison Elementary District	Phoenix
41	51.5	Lake Havasu Unified District	Lk Havasu City
42	51.5	Murphy Elementary District	Phoenix
43	51.5	Coolidge Unified District	Coolidge
44	51.4	Glendale Union High SD	Glendale
45	51.4	Ganado Unified District	Ganado
46	51.4	Chinle Unified District	Chinle
47	51.3	Payson Unified District	Payson
48	51.3	Navit	Snowflake
49	51.3	Agua Fria Union High SD	Avondale
50	51.3	Tucson Unified District	Tucson
51	51.3	Glendale Elementary District	Glendale
52	51.3	Nogales Unified District	Nogales
53	51.3	Yuma Union High SD	Yuma
54	51.3	Littleton Elementary District	Cashion
55	51.2	Tuba City Unified District	Tuba City
56	51.2	Humboldt Unified District	Prescott Valley
57	51.2	Tolleson Union High SD	Tolleson
58	51.2	Chandler Unified District	Chandler
59	51.2	Fowler Elementary District	Phoenix
60	51.2	Safford Unified District	Safford
61	51.1	Kingman Unified SD	Kingman
62	51.1	Osborn Elementary District	Phoenix
63	51.1	Kyrene Elementary District	Tempe
64	51.0	Florence Unified SD	Florence
65	51.0	Tempe Union High SD	Tempe
66	51.0	Colorado River Union High SD	Fort Mojave
67	51.0	Cave Creek Unified District	Cave Creek
68	50.9	Window Rock Unified District	Ft Defiance
69	50.8	Flowing Wells Unified District	Tucson
70	50.8	Catalina Foothills Unified Dist	Tucson
71	50.8	Phoenix Union High SD	Phoenix
72	50.8	Whiteriver Unified District	Whiteriver
73	50.8	Roosevelt Elementary District	Phoenix
74	50.8	Tempe Elementary District	Tempe
75	50.8	Somerton Elementary District	Somerton
76	50.7	Litchfield Elementary District	Litchfield Park
77	50.7	Yuma Elementary District	Yuma
78	50.7	Balsz Elementary District	Phoenix
79	50.7	Prescott Unified District	Prescott
80	50.6	Holbrook Unified District	Holbrook
81	50.6	Cartwright Elementary District	Phoenix
82	50.5	Higley Unified District	Higley
83	50.5	Central Ariz Valley Inst of Tech	Coolidge
84	50.5	Gadsden Elementary District	San Luis
85	50.5	Isaac Elementary District	Phoenix
86	50.3	Sierra Vista Unified District	Sierra Vista
87	50.3	Blue Ridge Unified District	Lakeside
88	50.1	Creighton Elementary District	Phoenix
89	50.1	Peach Springs Unified District	Peach Springs
90	50.0	Parker Unified SD	Parker
91	50.0	Casa Grande Union High SD	Casa Grande
92	49.9	Phoenix Elementary District	Phoenix
93	49.7	Liberty Elementary District	Buckeye
94	49.6	Laveen Elementary District	Laveen
95	49.3	Winslow Unified District	Winslow

Female Students

Rank	Percent	District Name	City
1	50.6	Winslow Unified District	Winslow
2	50.3	Laveen Elementary District	Laveen
3	50.2	Liberty Elementary District	Buckeye
4	50.0	Phoenix Elementary District	Phoenix
5	49.9	Casa Grande Union High SD	Casa Grande
6	49.9	Parker Unified SD	Parker
7	49.8	Peach Springs Unified District	Peach Springs
8	49.8	Creighton Elementary District	Phoenix
9	49.6	Blue Ridge Unified District	Lakeside
10	49.6	Sierra Vista Unified District	Sierra Vista
11	49.4	Isaac Elementary District	Phoenix
12	49.4	Gadsden Elementary District	San Luis
13	49.4	Central Ariz Valley Inst of Tech	Coolidge
14	49.4	Higley Unified District	Higley
15	49.3	Cartwright Elementary District	Phoenix
16	49.3	Holbrook Unified District	Holbrook
17	49.2	Prescott Unified District	Prescott
18	49.2	Balsz Elementary District	Phoenix
19	49.2	Yuma Elementary District	Yuma
20	49.2	Litchfield Elementary District	Litchfield Park
21	49.1	Somerton Elementary District	Somerton
22	49.1	Tempe Elementary District	Tempe
23	49.1	Roosevelt Elementary District	Phoenix
24	49.1	Whiteriver Unified District	Whiteriver
25	49.1	Phoenix Union High SD	Phoenix
26	49.1	Catalina Foothills Unified Dist	Tucson
27	49.1	Flowing Wells Unified District	Tucson
28	49.0	Window Rock Unified District	Ft Defiance
29	48.9	Cave Creek Unified District	Cave Creek
30	48.9	Colorado River Union High SD	Fort Mojave
31	48.9	Tempe Union High SD	Tempe
32	48.9	Florence Unified SD	Florence
33	48.8	Kyrene Elementary District	Tempe
34	48.8	Osborn Elementary District	Phoenix
35	48.8	Kingman Unified SD	Kingman
36	48.7	Safford Unified District	Safford
37	48.7	Fowler Elementary District	Phoenix
38	48.7	Chandler Unified District	Chandler
39	48.7	Tolleson Union High SD	Tolleson
40	48.7	Humboldt Unified District	Prescott Valley
41	48.7	Tuba City Unified District	Tuba City
42	48.6	Littleton Elementary District	Cashion
43	48.6	Yuma Union High SD	Yuma
44	48.6	Nogales Unified District	Nogales
45	48.6	Glendale Elementary District	Glendale
46	48.6	Tucson Unified District	Tucson
47	48.6	Agua Fria Union High SD	Avondale
48	48.6	Navit	Snowflake
49	48.6	Payson Unified District	Payson
50	48.5	Chinle Unified District	Chinle
51	48.5	Ganado Unified District	Ganado
52	48.5	Glendale Union High SD	Glendale
53	48.4	Coolidge Unified District	Coolidge
54	48.4	Murphy Elementary District	Phoenix
55	48.4	Lake Havasu Unified District	Lk Havasu City
56	48.3	Madison Elementary District	Phoenix
57	48.3	Kayenta Unified District	Kayenta
58	48.3	Deer Valley Unified District	Phoenix
59	48.3	Flagstaff Unified District	Flagstaff
60	48.2	Mesa Unified District	Mesa
61	48.2	Apache Junction Unified District	Apache Junction
62	48.2	Scottsdale Unified District	Phoenix
63	48.2	Gilbert Unified District	Gilbert
64	48.2	Pendergast Elementary District	Phoenix
65	48.2	Paradise Valley Unified District	Phoenix
66	48.2	Alhambra Elementary District	Phoenix
67	48.1	Globe Unified District	Globe
68	48.1	Marana Unified District	Marana
69	48.1	Peoria Unified SD	Glendale
70	48.0	Sahuarita Unified District	Sahuarita
71	48.0	Mohave Valley Elementary District	Mohave Valley
72	47.9	Amphitheater Unified District	Tucson
73	47.8	Sunnyside Unified District	Tucson
74	47.8	Tolleson Elementary District	Tolleson
75	47.6	Crane Elementary District	Yuma
76	47.5	Casa Grande Elementary District	Casa Grande
77	47.5	Washington Elementary District	Phoenix
78	47.5	Dysart Unified District	El Mirage
79	47.4	Vail Unified District	Vail
80	47.4	Cottonwood-Oak Creek Elem Dist	Cottonwood
81	47.4	Snowflake Unified District	Snowflake
82	47.2	Chino Valley Unified District	Chino Valley
83	47.0	Pinon Unified District	Pinon
84	47.0	Queen Creek Unified District	Queen Creek
85	47.0	Bullhead City Elementary District	Bullhead City
86	47.0	Santa Cruz Valley Unified District	Rio Rico
87	46.9	Avondale Elementary District	Avondale
88	46.9	Douglas Unified District	Douglas
89	46.9	Page Unified District	Page
90	46.7	Show Low Unified District	Show Low
91	46.4	NE Arizona Tech Inst of Voc Ed	Kayenta
92	46.3	Fountain Hills Unified District	Fountain Hills
93	45.9	Western Maricopa Ed Ctr (West-Mec)	Phoenix
94	44.1	East Valley Institute of Tech	Mesa
95	39.6	Maricopa County Regional District	Phoenix

Individual Education Program Students

Rank	Percent	District Name	City
1	17.5	Laveen Elementary District	Laveen
1	17.5	Page Unified District	Page
3	16.1	Blue Ridge Unified District	Lakeside
4	15.8	Flagstaff Unified District	Flagstaff
5	15.6	Parker Unified SD	Parker
6	15.2	Liberty Elementary District	Buckeye
6	15.2	Tuba City Unified District	Tuba City
8	15.0	Humboldt Unified District	Prescott Valley
9	14.8	Chino Valley Unified District	Chino Valley
9	14.8	Washington Elementary District	Phoenix
11	14.7	Whiteriver Unified District	Whiteriver
12	14.4	Sunnyside Unified District	Tucson
13	14.3	Amphitheater Unified District	Tucson
13	14.3	Kingman Unified SD	Kingman
15	13.6	Mohave Valley Elementary District	Mohave Valley
16	13.5	Apache Junction Unified District	Apache Junction
16	13.5	Casa Grande Elementary District	Casa Grande
16	13.5	Murphy Elementary District	Phoenix
16	13.5	Winslow Unified District	Winslow
20	13.4	Somerton Elementary District	Somerton
21	13.3	Tempe Elementary District	Tempe
22	13.2	Prescott Unified District	Prescott
22	13.2	Sahuarita Unified District	Sahuarita
24	13.1	Show Low Unified District	Show Low
24	13.1	Snowflake Unified District	Snowflake
26	13.0	Safford Unified District	Safford
27	12.9	Coolidge Unified District	Coolidge
27	12.9	Flowing Wells Unified District	Tucson
27	12.9	Osborn Elementary District	Phoenix
27	12.9	Tucson Unified District	Tucson
31	12.7	Crane Elementary District	Yuma
31	12.7	Marana Unified District	Marana
33	12.6	Deer Valley Unified District	Phoenix
33	12.6	Payson Unified District	Payson
33	12.6	Phoenix Elementary District	Phoenix
36	12.5	Chinle Unified District	Chinle
37	12.2	Peoria Unified SD	Glendale
38	11.9	Avondale Elementary District	Avondale
38	11.9	Dysart Unified District	El Mirage
38	11.9	Isaac Elementary District	Phoenix
41	11.8	Fowler Elementary District	Phoenix
41	11.8	Littleton Elementary District	Cashion
41	11.8	Roosevelt Elementary District	Phoenix
44	11.7	Florence Unified SD	Florence
44	11.7	Holbrook Unified District	Holbrook
46	11.6	Cartwright Elementary District	Phoenix
46	11.6	Sierra Vista Unified District	Sierra Vista
48	11.5	Paradise Valley Unified District	Phoenix
49	11.3	Casa Grande Union High SD	Casa Grande
50	11.2	Gilbert Unified District	Gilbert
50	11.2	Glendale Elementary District	Glendale
50	11.2	Lake Havasu Unified District	Lk Havasu City
53	11.1	Colorado River Union High SD	Fort Mojave
54	10.9	Madison Elementary District	Phoenix
54	10.9	Vail Unified District	Vail
56	10.8	Alhambra Elementary District	Phoenix
56	10.8	Litchfield Elementary District	Litchfield Park
56	10.8	Window Rock Unified District	Ft Defiance
59	10.7	Globe Unified District	Globe
59	10.7	Pendergast Elementary District	Phoenix

61	10.6	Catalina Foothills Unified Dist	Tucson
62	10.0	Balsz Elementary District	Phoenix
62	10.0	Chandler Unified District	Chandler
62	10.0	Scottsdale Unified District	Phoenix
65	9.9	Kyrene Elementary District	Tempe
65	9.9	Tolleson Union High SD	Tolleson
67	9.8	Fountain Hills Unified District	Fountain Hills
68	9.7	Queen Creek Unified District	Queen Creek
69	9.6	Glendale Union High SD	Glendale
69	9.6	Mesa Unified District	Mesa
71	9.5	Kayenta Unified District	Kayenta
72	9.4	Bullhead City Elementary District	Bullhead City
72	9.4	Creighton Elementary District	Phoenix
72	9.4	Douglas Unified District	Douglas
72	9.4	Yuma Elementary District	Yuma
76	9.2	Maricopa County Regional District	Phoenix
77	9.1	Higley Unified District	Higley
78	8.9	Agua Fria Union High SD	Avondale
79	8.6	Nogales Unified District	Nogales
80	8.4	Cottonwood-Oak Creek Elem Dist	Cottonwood
80	8.4	Phoenix Union High SD	Phoenix
82	8.3	Gadsden Elementary District	San Luis
82	8.3	Yuma Union High SD	Yuma
84	8.1	Tempe Union High SD	Tempe
85	8.0	Cave Creek Unified District	Cave Creek
86	7.8	Ganado Unified District	Ganado
87	7.7	Santa Cruz Valley Unified District	Rio Rico
88	7.1	Pinon Unified District	Pinon
89	6.7	Tolleson Elementary District	Tolleson
90	1.7	Peach Springs Unified District	Peach Springs
91	0.0	Central Ariz Valley Inst of Tech	Coolidge
91	0.0	East Valley Institute of Tech	Mesa
91	0.0	Navit	Snowflake
91	0.0	NE Arizona Tech Inst of Voc Ed	Kayenta
91	0.0	Western Maricopa Ed Ctr (West-Mec)	Phoenix

English Language Learner Students

Rank	Percent	District Name	City
1	94.9	Gadsden Elementary District	San Luis
2	72.3	Somerton Elementary District	Somerton
3	70.7	Ganado Unified District	Ganado
4	67.8	Chinle Unified District	Chinle
5	65.2	Murphy Elementary District	Phoenix
6	63.5	Kayenta Unified District	Kayenta
7	62.6	Pinon Unified District	Pinon
8	61.0	Isaac Elementary District	Phoenix
9	60.5	Creighton Elementary District	Phoenix
9	60.5	Nogales Unified District	Nogales
11	57.8	Santa Cruz Valley Unified District	Rio Rico
12	55.8	Douglas Unified District	Douglas
13	51.6	Whiteriver Unified District	Whiteriver
14	49.7	Alhambra Elementary District	Phoenix
14	49.7	Phoenix Elementary District	Phoenix
16	45.8	Balsz Elementary District	Phoenix
17	45.3	Tuba City Unified District	Tuba City
18	44.8	Cartwright Elementary District	Phoenix
19	43.0	Sunnyside Unified District	Tucson
20	41.4	Roosevelt Elementary District	Phoenix
21	36.8	Fowler Elementary District	Phoenix
22	34.3	Page Unified District	Page
23	34.2	Laveen Elementary District	Laveen
24	34.1	Crane Elementary District	Yuma
25	33.5	Glendale Elementary District	Glendale
26	33.4	Yuma Elementary District	Yuma
27	31.8	Osborn Elementary District	Phoenix
28	29.3	Tolleson Elementary District	Tolleson
29	27.7	Littleton Elementary District	Cashion
30	26.4	Avondale Elementary District	Avondale
31	25.2	Tempe Elementary District	Tempe
32	22.9	Holbrook Unified District	Holbrook
33	22.2	Pendergast Elementary District	Phoenix
34	20.1	Washington Elementary District	Phoenix
35	17.5	Phoenix Union High SD	Phoenix
36	16.7	Cottonwood-Oak Creek Elem Dist	Cottonwood
37	14.6	Dysart Unified District	El Mirage
38	14.3	Bullhead City Elementary District	Bullhead City
39	14.0	Madison Elementary District	Phoenix
40	13.9	Tucson Unified District	Tucson
41	13.5	Casa Grande Elementary District	Casa Grande
42	13.1	Chandler Unified District	Chandler
43	12.3	Flagstaff Unified District	Flagstaff
44	10.1	Maricopa County Regional District	Phoenix
44	10.1	Yuma Union High SD	Yuma
46	9.9	Mesa Unified District	Mesa
46	9.9	Parker Unified SD	Parker
48	9.7	Coolidge Unified District	Coolidge
49	9.0	Paradise Valley Unified District	Phoenix
49	9.0	Queen Creek Unified District	Queen Creek
51	8.9	Winslow Unified District	Winslow
52	8.8	Sahuarita Unified District	Sahuarita
53	8.6	Chino Valley Unified District	Chino Valley
54	8.1	Casa Grande Union High SD	Casa Grande
55	8.0	Amphitheater Unified District	Tucson
56	7.6	Litchfield Elementary District	Litchfield Park
57	7.1	Scottsdale Unified District	Phoenix
58	6.9	Humboldt Unified District	Prescott Valley
59	6.5	Liberty Elementary District	Buckeye
60	6.2	Agua Fria Union High SD	Avondale
61	6.1	Glendale Union High SD	Glendale
62	6.0	Blue Ridge Unified District	Lakeside
63	5.4	Tolleson Union High SD	Tolleson
64	4.9	Deer Valley Unified District	Phoenix
64	4.9	Flowing Wells Unified District	Tucson
66	4.8	Snowflake Unified District	Snowflake
67	4.3	Peoria Unified SD	Glendale
68	4.0	Lake Havasu Unified District	Lk Havasu City
69	3.9	Payson Unified District	Payson
70	3.6	Mohave Valley Elementary District	Mohave Valley
71	3.2	Sierra Vista Unified District	Sierra Vista
72	3.0	Higley Unified District	Higley
73	2.8	Prescott Unified District	Prescott
73	2.8	Tempe Union High SD	Tempe
75	2.7	Marana Unified District	Marana
76	2.6	Kyrene Elementary District	Tempe
77	2.4	Gilbert Unified District	Gilbert
78	2.3	Catalina Foothills Unified Dist	Tucson
79	2.0	Vail Unified District	Vail
80	1.9	Globe Unified District	Globe
81	1.7	Show Low Unified District	Show Low
82	1.3	Apache Junction Unified District	Apache Junction
83	1.2	Cave Creek Unified District	Cave Creek
84	1.0	Kingman Unified SD	Kingman
85	0.9	Colorado River Union High SD	Fort Mojave
86	0.7	Fountain Hills Unified District	Fountain Hills
87	0.5	Florence Unified SD	Florence
88	0.0	Window Rock Unified District	Ft Defiance
89	0.0	Central Ariz Valley Inst of Tech	Coolidge
89	0.0	East Valley Institute of Tech	Mesa
89	0.0	Navit	Snowflake
89	0.0	NE Arizona Tech Inst of Voc Ed	Kayenta
89	0.0	Peach Springs Unified District	Peach Springs
89	0.0	Safford Unified District	Safford
89	0.0	Western Maricopa Ed Ctr (West-Mec)	Phoenix

Migrant Students

Rank	Percent	District Name	City
1	6.8	Yuma Union High SD	Yuma
2	4.8	Queen Creek Unified District	Queen Creek
3	2.9	Somerton Elementary District	Somerton
4	2.3	Tolleson Union High SD	Tolleson
5	2.2	Crane Elementary District	Yuma
6	1.9	Douglas Unified District	Douglas
6	1.9	Gadsden Elementary District	San Luis
8	1.7	Yuma Elementary District	Yuma
9	1.0	Glendale Elementary District	Glendale
10	0.9	Casa Grande Union High SD	Casa Grande
10	0.9	Florence Unified SD	Florence
12	0.8	Casa Grande Elementary District	Casa Grande
13	0.5	Liberty Elementary District	Buckeye
14	0.4	Chandler Unified District	Chandler
14	0.4	Dysart Unified District	El Mirage
14	0.4	Fowler Elementary District	Phoenix
17	0.3	Agua Fria Union High SD	Avondale
17	0.3	Glendale Union High SD	Glendale
19	0.2	Avondale Elementary District	Avondale
19	0.2	Littleton Elementary District	Cashion
19	0.2	Marana Unified District	Marana
19	0.2	Mesa Unified District	Mesa
19	0.2	Peoria Unified SD	Glendale
19	0.2	Phoenix Union High SD	Phoenix
25	0.1	Coolidge Unified District	Coolidge
25	0.1	Higley Unified District	Higley
25	0.1	Pendergast Elementary District	Phoenix
25	0.1	Phoenix Elementary District	Phoenix
25	0.1	Roosevelt Elementary District	Phoenix
30	0.0	Litchfield Elementary District	Litchfield Park
31	0.0	Alhambra Elementary District	Phoenix
31	0.0	Amphitheater Unified District	Tucson
31	0.0	Apache Junction Unified District	Apache Junction
31	0.0	Balsz Elementary District	Phoenix
31	0.0	Blue Ridge Unified District	Lakeside
31	0.0	Bullhead City Elementary District	Bullhead City
31	0.0	Cartwright Elementary District	Phoenix
31	0.0	Catalina Foothills Unified Dist	Tucson
31	0.0	Cave Creek Unified District	Cave Creek
31	0.0	Central Ariz Valley Inst of Tech	Coolidge
31	0.0	Chinle Unified District	Chinle
31	0.0	Chino Valley Unified District	Chino Valley
31	0.0	Colorado River Union High SD	Fort Mojave
31	0.0	Cottonwood-Oak Creek Elem Dist	Cottonwood
31	0.0	Creighton Elementary District	Phoenix
31	0.0	Deer Valley Unified District	Phoenix
31	0.0	East Valley Institute of Tech	Mesa
31	0.0	Flagstaff Unified District	Flagstaff
31	0.0	Flowing Wells Unified District	Tucson
31	0.0	Fountain Hills Unified District	Fountain Hills
31	0.0	Ganado Unified District	Ganado
31	0.0	Gilbert Unified District	Gilbert
31	0.0	Globe Unified District	Globe
31	0.0	Holbrook Unified District	Holbrook
31	0.0	Humboldt Unified District	Prescott Valley
31	0.0	Isaac Elementary District	Phoenix
31	0.0	Kayenta Unified District	Kayenta
31	0.0	Kingman Unified SD	Kingman
31	0.0	Kyrene Elementary District	Tempe
31	0.0	Lake Havasu Unified District	Lk Havasu City
31	0.0	Laveen Elementary District	Laveen
31	0.0	Madison Elementary District	Phoenix
31	0.0	Maricopa County Regional District	Phoenix
31	0.0	Mohave Valley Elementary District	Mohave Valley
31	0.0	Murphy Elementary District	Phoenix
31	0.0	Navit	Snowflake
31	0.0	Nogales Unified District	Nogales
31	0.0	NE Arizona Tech Inst of Voc Ed	Kayenta
31	0.0	Osborn Elementary District	Phoenix
31	0.0	Page Unified District	Page
31	0.0	Paradise Valley Unified District	Phoenix
31	0.0	Parker Unified SD	Parker
31	0.0	Payson Unified District	Payson
31	0.0	Peach Springs Unified District	Peach Springs
31	0.0	Pinon Unified District	Pinon
31	0.0	Prescott Unified District	Prescott
31	0.0	Safford Unified District	Safford
31	0.0	Sahuarita Unified District	Sahuarita
31	0.0	Santa Cruz Valley Unified District	Rio Rico
31	0.0	Scottsdale Unified District	Phoenix
31	0.0	Show Low Unified District	Show Low
31	0.0	Sierra Vista Unified District	Sierra Vista
31	0.0	Snowflake Unified District	Snowflake
31	0.0	Sunnyside Unified District	Tucson
31	0.0	Tempe Elementary District	Tempe
31	0.0	Tempe Union High SD	Tempe
31	0.0	Tolleson Elementary District	Tolleson
31	0.0	Tuba City Unified District	Tuba City
31	0.0	Tucson Unified District	Tucson
31	0.0	Vail Unified District	Vail
31	0.0	Washington Elementary District	Phoenix
31	0.0	Western Maricopa Ed Ctr (West-Mec)	Phoenix
31	0.0	Whiteriver Unified District	Whiteriver
31	0.0	Window Rock Unified District	Ft Defiance
31	0.0	Winslow Unified District	Winslow

Students Eligible for Free Lunch

Rank	Percent	District Name	City
1	99.6	Isaac Elementary District	Phoenix
2	99.5	Somerton Elementary District	Somerton
3	91.0	Murphy Elementary District	Phoenix
4	85.7	Balsz Elementary District	Phoenix
5	84.9	Creighton Elementary District	Phoenix
6	84.6	Alhambra Elementary District	Phoenix
7	82.7	Ganado Unified District	Ganado
8	81.2	Sunnyside Unified District	Tucson
9	76.9	Tuba City Unified District	Tuba City
10	76.3	Laveen Elementary District	Laveen
11	75.7	Osborn Elementary District	Phoenix
12	75.5	Fowler Elementary District	Phoenix
13	73.9	Kayenta Unified District	Kayenta
14	73.0	Littleton Elementary District	Cashion
15	71.6	Cartwright Elementary District	Phoenix
16	71.3	Gadsden Elementary District	San Luis
17	67.8	Roosevelt Elementary District	Phoenix
18	66.4	Douglas Unified District	Douglas
19	66.3	Nogales Unified District	Nogales
20	65.1	Phoenix Union High SD	Phoenix
21	64.9	Tolleson Elementary District	Tolleson
22	64.6	Avondale Elementary District	Avondale
23	63.7	Whiteriver Unified District	Whiteriver
24	63.3	Bullhead City Elementary District	Bullhead City
25	62.9	Page Unified District	Page
26	62.7	Maricopa County Regional District	Phoenix
27	61.9	Glendale Elementary District	Glendale
28	61.4	Washington Elementary District	Phoenix
29	59.3	Tempe Elementary District	Tempe
30	59.2	Parker Unified SD	Parker
31	58.0	Santa Cruz Valley Unified District	Rio Rico
32	57.9	Crane Elementary District	Yuma
33	55.9	Tucson Unified District	Tucson
33	55.9	Yuma Elementary District	Yuma
35	53.1	Casa Grande Elementary District	Casa Grande
36	51.5	Dysart Unified District	El Mirage
36	51.5	Yuma Union High SD	Yuma
38	50.8	Coolidge Unified District	Coolidge
39	49.2	Mohave Valley Elementary District	Mohave Valley
40	48.0	Globe Unified District	Globe
41	46.6	Madison Elementary District	Phoenix
42	45.6	Winslow Unified District	Winslow

43	45.2	Sahuarita Unified District	Sahuarita
44	43.7	Show Low Unified District	Show Low
45	43.3	Pendergast Elementary District	Phoenix
46	42.0	Cottonwood-Oak Creek Elem Dist	Cottonwood
47	41.3	Florence Unified SD	Florence
48	39.8	Safford Unified District	Safford
49	39.6	Mesa Unified District	Mesa
50	37.2	Kingman Unified SD	Kingman
51	36.5	Humboldt Unified District	Prescott Valley
51	36.5	Lake Havasu Unified District	Lk Havasu City
53	36.1	Chino Valley Unified District	Chino Valley
54	35.9	Holbrook Unified District	Holbrook
55	35.4	Amphitheater Unified District	Tucson
56	34.9	Casa Grande Union High SD	Casa Grande
57	34.5	Sierra Vista Unified District	Sierra Vista
57	34.5	Tolleson Union High SD	Tolleson
59	32.9	Colorado River Union High SD	Fort Mojave
60	32.4	Payson Unified District	Payson
61	32.1	Apache Junction Unified District	Apache Junction
62	31.4	Flagstaff Unified District	Flagstaff
63	29.9	Blue Ridge Unified District	Lakeside
63	29.9	Liberty Elementary District	Buckeye
65	22.6	Marana Unified District	Marana
66	20.8	Litchfield Elementary District	Litchfield Park
66	20.8	Paradise Valley Unified District	Phoenix
68	20.6	Prescott Unified District	Prescott
69	17.0	Deer Valley Unified District	Phoenix
70	16.8	Agua Fria Union High SD	Avondale
71	16.1	Glendale Union High SD	Glendale
72	15.9	Peach Springs Unified District	Peach Springs
73	14.7	Peoria Unified SD	Glendale
74	13.0	Scottsdale Unified District	Phoenix
75	11.2	Vail Unified District	Vail
76	9.2	Kyrene Elementary District	Tempe
77	9.0	Higley Unified District	Higley
78	7.7	Fountain Hills Unified District	Fountain Hills
79	6.1	Catalina Foothills Unified Dist	Tucson
80	5.0	Gilbert Unified District	Gilbert
81	4.5	Cave Creek Unified District	Cave Creek
81	4.5	Chandler Unified District	Chandler
83	4.1	Tempe Union High SD	Tempe
84	n/a	Central Ariz Valley Inst of Tech	Coolidge
84	n/a	Chinle Unified District	Chinle
84	n/a	East Valley Institute of Tech	Mesa
84	n/a	Flowing Wells Unified District	Tucson
84	n/a	Navit	Snowflake
84	n/a	NE Arizona Tech Inst of Voc Ed	Kayenta
84	n/a	Phoenix Elementary District	Phoenix
84	n/a	Pinon Unified District	Pinon
84	n/a	Queen Creek Unified District	Queen Creek
84	n/a	Snowflake Unified District	Snowflake
84	n/a	Western Maricopa Ed Ctr (West-Mec)	Phoenix
84	n/a	Window Rock Unified District	Ft Defiance

Students Eligible for Reduced-Price Lunch

Rank	Percent	District Name	City
1	22.3	Chandler Unified District	Chandler
2	16.4	Fowler Elementary District	Phoenix
3	15.8	Littleton Elementary District	Cashion
3	15.8	Santa Cruz Valley Unified District	Rio Rico
5	15.5	Chino Valley Unified District	Chino Valley
6	15.3	Parker Unified SD	Parker
7	15.1	Crane Elementary District	Yuma
8	14.6	Dysart Unified District	El Mirage
9	14.5	Florence Unified SD	Florence
10	14.3	Creighton Elementary District	Phoenix
11	13.8	Winslow Unified District	Winslow
12	13.4	Yuma Elementary District	Yuma
13	13.2	Humboldt Unified District	Prescott Valley
14	13.1	Cottonwood-Oak Creek Elem Dist	Cottonwood
15	12.9	Show Low Unified District	Show Low
16	12.6	Tuba City Unified District	Tuba City
17	12.3	Lake Havasu Unified District	Lk Havasu City
18	12.0	Glendale Elementary District	Glendale
19	11.9	Coolidge Unified District	Coolidge
20	11.6	Cartwright Elementary District	Phoenix
21	11.5	Laveen Elementary District	Laveen
21	11.5	Tolleson Elementary District	Tolleson
23	11.2	Avondale Elementary District	Avondale
23	11.2	Kayenta Unified District	Kayenta
25	11.0	Ganado Unified District	Ganado
26	10.9	Balsz Elementary District	Phoenix
27	10.8	Alhambra Elementary District	Phoenix
28	10.6	Globe Unified District	Globe
29	10.5	Mesa Unified District	Mesa
29	10.5	Sahuarita Unified District	Sahuarita
29	10.5	Tempe Elementary District	Tempe
32	10.4	Sierra Vista Unified District	Sierra Vista
32	10.4	Washington Elementary District	Phoenix
34	10.2	Pendergast Elementary District	Phoenix
35	10.1	Nogales Unified District	Nogales
36	9.9	Osborn Elementary District	Phoenix
36	9.9	Roosevelt Elementary District	Phoenix
38	9.8	Casa Grande Elementary District	Casa Grande
39	9.6	Payson Unified District	Payson
40	9.5	Flagstaff Unified District	Flagstaff
41	9.3	Mohave Valley Elementary District	Mohave Valley
42	9.0	Madison Elementary District	Phoenix
42	9.0	Sunnyside Unified District	Tucson
44	8.7	Bullhead City Elementary District	Bullhead City
45	8.5	Murphy Elementary District	Phoenix
46	8.4	Colorado River Union High SD	Fort Mojave
46	8.4	Phoenix Union High SD	Phoenix
46	8.4	Tucson Unified District	Tucson
49	8.3	Blue Ridge Unified District	Lakeside
50	8.2	Litchfield Elementary District	Litchfield Park
51	8.1	Marana Unified District	Marana
52	8.0	Safford Unified District	Safford
53	7.9	Apache Junction Unified District	Apache Junction
53	7.9	Page Unified District	Page
55	7.8	Vail Unified District	Vail
56	7.6	Amphitheater Unified District	Tucson
57	7.4	Peach Springs Unified District	Peach Springs
58	7.3	Holbrook Unified District	Holbrook
58	7.3	Tolleson Union High SD	Tolleson
60	7.0	Higley Unified District	Higley
61	6.8	Liberty Elementary District	Buckeye
62	6.6	Kingman Unified SD	Kingman
63	5.9	Prescott Unified District	Prescott
64	5.7	Douglas Unified District	Douglas
65	5.6	Deer Valley Unified District	Phoenix
66	5.5	Casa Grande Union High SD	Casa Grande
67	5.2	Paradise Valley Unified District	Phoenix
68	4.9	Whiteriver Unified District	Whiteriver
69	4.7	Peoria Unified SD	Glendale
70	4.5	Yuma Union High SD	Yuma
71	4.4	Gadsden Elementary District	San Luis
72	3.7	Kyrene Elementary District	Tempe
73	3.5	Agua Fria Union High SD	Avondale
74	3.3	Gilbert Unified District	Gilbert
75	2.9	Glendale Union High SD	Glendale
75	2.9	Scottsdale Unified District	Phoenix
77	2.4	Fountain Hills Unified District	Fountain Hills
78	2.3	Maricopa County Regional District	Phoenix
79	1.4	Cave Creek Unified District	Cave Creek
80	0.0	Catalina Foothills Unified Dist	Tucson
80	0.0	Isaac Elementary District	Phoenix
80	0.0	Somerton Elementary District	Somerton
80	0.0	Tempe Union High SD	Tempe
84	n/a	Central Ariz Valley Inst of Tech	Coolidge
84	n/a	Chinle Unified District	Chinle
84	n/a	East Valley Institute of Tech	Mesa
84	n/a	Flowing Wells Unified District	Tucson
84	n/a	Navit	Snowflake
84	n/a	NE Arizona Tech Inst of Voc Ed	Kayenta
84	n/a	Phoenix Elementary District	Phoenix
84	n/a	Pinon Unified District	Pinon
84	n/a	Queen Creek Unified District	Queen Creek
84	n/a	Snowflake Unified District	Snowflake
84	n/a	Western Maricopa Ed Ctr (West-Mec)	Phoenix
84	n/a	Window Rock Unified District	Ft Defiance

Student/Teacher Ratio

Rank	Ratio	District Name	City
1	83.0	Peach Springs Unified District	Peach Springs
2	25.7	Gadsden Elementary District	San Luis
3	23.9	Higley Unified District	Higley
4	23.8	Colorado River Union High SD	Fort Mojave
5	22.7	Agua Fria Union High SD	Avondale
6	22.6	Mohave Valley Elementary District	Mohave Valley
7	22.0	Chandler Unified District	Chandler
8	21.9	Lake Havasu Unified District	Lk Havasu City
8	21.9	Littleton Elementary District	Cashion
10	21.4	Litchfield Elementary District	Litchfield Park
11	21.3	Glendale Union High SD	Glendale
12	21.0	Dysart Unified District	El Mirage
13	20.7	Cartwright Elementary District	Phoenix
13	20.7	Somerton Elementary District	Somerton
15	20.6	Tempe Union High SD	Tempe
15	20.6	Tolleson Union High SD	Tolleson
15	20.6	Yuma Union High SD	Yuma
18	20.5	Flowing Wells Unified District	Tucson
18	20.5	Glendale Elementary District	Glendale
20	20.4	Alhambra Elementary District	Phoenix
20	20.4	Mesa Unified District	Mesa
22	20.3	Avondale Elementary District	Avondale
22	20.3	Cave Creek Unified District	Cave Creek
24	20.2	Douglas Unified District	Douglas
24	20.2	Humboldt Unified District	Prescott Valley
26	20.0	Deer Valley Unified District	Phoenix
27	19.9	Kingman Unified SD	Kingman
27	19.9	Maricopa County Regional District	Phoenix
29	19.8	Show Low Unified District	Show Low
30	19.5	Paradise Valley Unified District	Phoenix
31	19.4	Isaac Elementary District	Phoenix
31	19.4	Sierra Vista Unified District	Sierra Vista
33	19.3	Casa Grande Elementary District	Casa Grande
33	19.3	Marana Unified District	Marana
33	19.3	Nogales Unified District	Nogales
33	19.3	Pendergast Elementary District	Phoenix
33	19.3	Safford Unified District	Safford
38	19.2	Cottonwood-Oak Creek Elem Dist	Cottonwood
39	19.1	Apache Junction Unified District	Apache Junction
40	19.0	Peoria Unified SD	Glendale
40	19.0	Santa Cruz Valley Unified District	Rio Rico
40	19.0	Scottsdale Unified District	Phoenix
40	19.0	Snowflake Unified District	Snowflake
40	19.0	Washington Elementary District	Phoenix
45	18.9	Globe Unified District	Globe
46	18.7	Fountain Hills Unified District	Fountain Hills
46	18.7	Prescott Unified District	Prescott
48	18.6	Laveen Elementary District	Laveen
49	18.5	Bullhead City Elementary District	Bullhead City
49	18.5	Phoenix Union High SD	Phoenix
51	18.4	Gilbert Unified District	Gilbert
51	18.4	Roosevelt Elementary District	Phoenix
53	18.3	Kyrene Elementary District	Tempe
53	18.3	Tucson Unified District	Tucson
55	18.2	Amphitheater Unified District	Tucson
55	18.2	Payson Unified District	Payson
55	18.2	Sunnyside Unified District	Tucson
55	18.2	Tolleson Elementary District	Tolleson
55	18.2	Yuma Elementary District	Yuma
60	18.1	Casa Grande Union High SD	Casa Grande
60	18.1	Crane Elementary District	Yuma
62	18.0	Fowler Elementary District	Phoenix
63	17.8	Chino Valley Unified District	Chino Valley
63	17.8	Murphy Elementary District	Phoenix
65	17.7	Flagstaff Unified District	Flagstaff
65	17.7	Phoenix Elementary District	Phoenix
67	17.6	Sahuarita Unified District	Sahuarita
68	17.5	Balsz Elementary District	Phoenix
69	17.4	Catalina Foothills Unified Dist	Tucson
69	17.4	Creighton Elementary District	Phoenix
69	17.4	Vail Unified District	Vail
69	17.4	Winslow Unified District	Winslow
73	17.2	Liberty Elementary District	Buckeye
73	17.2	Queen Creek Unified District	Queen Creek
75	17.1	Blue Ridge Unified District	Lakeside
76	17.0	Coolidge Unified District	Coolidge
76	17.0	Osborn Elementary District	Phoenix
78	16.9	Florence Unified SD	Florence
79	16.7	Ganado Unified District	Ganado
80	16.5	Page Unified District	Page
81	16.3	Madison Elementary District	Phoenix
82	16.1	Tempe Elementary District	Tempe
83	15.7	Parker Unified SD	Parker
84	15.6	Kayenta Unified District	Kayenta
85	15.5	Tuba City Unified District	Tuba City
86	15.4	Chinle Unified District	Chinle
87	15.1	Holbrook Unified District	Holbrook
87	15.1	Pinon Unified District	Pinon
89	14.6	Window Rock Unified District	Ft Defiance
90	14.5	Whiteriver Unified District	Whiteriver
91	n/a	Central Ariz Valley Inst of Tech	Coolidge
91	n/a	East Valley Institute of Tech	Mesa
91	n/a	Navit	Snowflake
91	n/a	NE Arizona Tech Inst of Voc Ed	Kayenta
91	n/a	Western Maricopa Ed Ctr (West-Mec)	Phoenix

Student/Librarian Ratio

Rank	Ratio	District Name	City
1	7,343.8	Peoria Unified SD	Glendale
2	5,575.0	Dysart Unified District	El Mirage
3	5,241.0	Prescott Unified District	Prescott
4	5,236.0	Humboldt Unified District	Prescott Valley
5	3,972.8	Cartwright Elementary District	Phoenix
6	3,247.5	Lake Havasu Unified District	Lk Havasu City
7	3,020.5	Flowing Wells Unified District	Tucson
8	3,017.0	Page Unified District	Page
9	2,640.0	Chino Valley Unified District	Chino Valley
10	2,636.0	Blue Ridge Unified District	Lakeside
11	2,625.0	Show Low Unified District	Show Low
12	2,607.0	Sahuarita Unified District	Sahuarita
13	2,516.0	Queen Creek Unified District	Queen Creek
14	2,398.9	Phoenix Union High SD	Phoenix
15	2,085.0	Phoenix Elementary District	Phoenix
16	2,073.0	Holbrook Unified District	Holbrook
17	2,057.5	Douglas Unified District	Douglas
18	2,035.0	Tolleson Elementary District	Tolleson
19	1,829.0	Tolleson Union High SD	Tolleson
20	1,814.4	Glendale Union High SD	Glendale
21	1,755.0	Mohave Valley Elementary District	Mohave Valley
22	1,686.8	Amphitheater Unified District	Tucson

23	1,679.8	Sierra Vista Unified District	Sierra Vista
24	1,676.4	Creighton Elementary District	Phoenix
25	1,662.3	Agua Fria Union High SD	Avondale
26	1,563.0	Fowler Elementary District	Phoenix
27	1,552.3	Nogales Unified District	Nogales
28	1,543.5	Santa Cruz Valley Unified District	Rio Rico
29	1,523.0	Pinon Unified District	Pinon
30	1,407.5	Casa Grande Union High SD	Casa Grande
31	1,404.0	Alhambra Elementary District	Phoenix
32	1,347.0	Cave Creek Unified District	Cave Creek
33	1,279.0	Cottonwood-Oak Creek Elem Dist	Cottonwood
34	1,272.1	Yuma Union High SD	Yuma
35	1,244.0	Somerton Elementary District	Somerton
36	1,219.7	Isaac Elementary District	Phoenix
37	1,170.2	Chandler Unified District	Chandler
38	1,169.3	Washington Elementary District	Phoenix
39	1,123.2	Pendergast Elementary District	Phoenix
40	1,113.0	Higley Unified District	Higley
41	1,092.8	Mesa Unified District	Mesa
42	1,084.0	Scottsdale Unified District	Phoenix
43	1,083.6	Gilbert Unified District	Gilbert
44	1,057.0	Colorado River Union High SD	Fort Mojave
45	1,042.0	Litchfield Elementary District	Litchfield Park
46	1,035.0	Liberty Elementary District	Buckeye
47	1,034.8	Murphy Elementary District	Phoenix
48	1,023.0	Paradise Valley Unified District	Phoenix
49	1,022.3	Deer Valley Unified District	Phoenix
50	1,012.3	Coolidge Unified District	Coolidge
51	997.5	Parker Unified SD	Parker
52	976.4	Marana Unified District	Marana
53	922.2	Sunnyside Unified District	Tucson
54	912.3	Kingman Unified SD	Kingman
55	889.8	Avondale Elementary District	Avondale
56	875.5	Madison Elementary District	Phoenix
57	858.0	Balsz Elementary District	Phoenix
58	853.7	Winslow Unified District	Winslow
59	837.7	Snowflake Unified District	Snowflake
60	828.6	Glendale Elementary District	Glendale
61	822.6	Apache Junction Unified District	Apache Junction
62	822.3	Whiteriver Unified District	Whiteriver
63	816.4	Chinle Unified District	Chinle
64	775.0	Tempe Elementary District	Tempe
65	767.3	Yuma Elementary District	Yuma
66	738.7	Gadsden Elementary District	San Luis
67	734.4	Roosevelt Elementary District	Phoenix
68	734.1	Flagstaff Unified District	Flagstaff
69	726.3	Fountain Hills Unified District	Fountain Hills
70	718.5	Window Rock Unified District	Ft Defiance
71	711.0	Globe Unified District	Globe
72	706.0	Vail Unified District	Vail
73	704.7	Tempe Union High SD	Tempe
74	695.1	Tucson Unified District	Tucson
75	691.7	Ganado Unified District	Ganado
76	675.5	Osborn Elementary District	Phoenix
77	663.5	Kyrene Elementary District	Tempe
78	642.5	Kayenta Unified District	Kayenta
79	634.2	Casa Grande Elementary District	Casa Grande
80	630.8	Catalina Foothills Unified Dist	Tucson
81	584.7	Laveen Elementary District	Laveen
82	577.6	Safford Unified District	Safford
83	555.4	Bullhead City Elementary District	Bullhead City
84	513.0	Tuba City Unified District	Tuba City
85	512.0	Payson Unified District	Payson
86	n/a	Central Ariz Valley Inst of Tech	Coolidge
86	n/a	Crane Elementary District	Yuma
86	n/a	East Valley Institute of Tech	Mesa
86	n/a	Florence Unified SD	Florence
86	n/a	Littleton Elementary District	Cashion
86	n/a	Maricopa County Regional District	Phoenix
86	n/a	Navit	Snowflake
86	n/a	NE Arizona Tech Inst of Voc Ed	Kayenta
86	n/a	Peach Springs Unified District	Peach Springs
86	n/a	Western Maricopa Ed Ctr (West-Mec)	Phoenix

Student/Counselor Ratio

Rank	Ratio	District Name	City
1	8,382.0	Creighton Elementary District	Phoenix
2	6,629.0	Glendale Elementary District	Glendale
3	3,510.0	Mohave Valley Elementary District	Mohave Valley
4	3,126.0	Fowler Elementary District	Phoenix
5	2,948.3	Maricopa County Regional District	Phoenix
6	2,854.0	Casa Grande Elementary District	Casa Grande
7	2,780.0	Phoenix Elementary District	Phoenix
8	2,626.5	Madison Elementary District	Phoenix
9	2,587.0	Murphy Elementary District	Phoenix
10	2,483.0	Cartwright Elementary District	Phoenix
11	2,327.4	Washington Elementary District	Phoenix
12	1,882.7	Vail Unified District	Vail
13	1,716.0	Balsz Elementary District	Phoenix
14	1,707.6	Isaac Elementary District	Phoenix
15	1,548.3	Kyrene Elementary District	Tempe
16	1,486.0	Osborn Elementary District	Phoenix
17	1,483.0	Avondale Elementary District	Avondale
18	1,380.0	Liberty Elementary District	Buckeye
19	1,256.5	Snowflake Unified District	Snowflake
20	1,244.0	Somerton Elementary District	Somerton
21	1,228.5	Alhambra Elementary District	Phoenix
22	1,208.5	Florence Unified SD	Florence
23	1,108.0	Gadsden Elementary District	San Luis
24	1,077.6	Cave Creek Unified District	Cave Creek
25	1,066.5	Globe Unified District	Globe
26	1,042.0	Litchfield Elementary District	Litchfield Park
27	1,014.8	Lake Havasu Unified District	Lk Havasu City
28	1,006.2	Gilbert Unified District	Gilbert
29	1,005.7	Page Unified District	Page
30	997.5	Parker Unified SD	Parker
31	937.0	Dysart Unified District	El Mirage
32	918.0	Paradise Valley Unified District	Phoenix
33	912.3	Kingman Unified SD	Kingman
34	910.7	Pendergast Elementary District	Phoenix
35	877.0	Laveen Elementary District	Laveen
36	862.3	Scottsdale Unified District	Phoenix
37	851.6	Chino Valley Unified District	Chino Valley
38	843.4	Amphitheater Unified District	Tucson
39	836.9	Mesa Unified District	Mesa
40	777.6	Bullhead City Elementary District	Bullhead City
41	770.0	Humboldt Unified District	Prescott Valley
42	761.5	Pinon Unified District	Pinon
43	759.3	Coolidge Unified District	Coolidge
44	748.7	Prescott Unified District	Prescott
45	747.4	Deer Valley Unified District	Phoenix
46	734.8	Douglas Unified District	Douglas
47	731.4	Crane Elementary District	Yuma
48	658.7	Sierra Vista Unified District	Sierra Vista
49	656.3	Show Low Unified District	Show Low
50	651.8	Sahuarita Unified District	Sahuarita
51	640.8	Chandler Unified District	Chandler
52	635.5	Fountain Hills Unified District	Fountain Hills
53	617.4	Santa Cruz Valley Unified District	Rio Rico
54	606.9	Peoria Unified SD	Glendale
55	591.3	Nogales Unified District	Nogales
56	573.0	Blue Ridge Unified District	Lakeside
57	563.2	Payson Unified District	Payson
58	528.5	Colorado River Union High SD	Fort Mojave
59	518.3	Holbrook Unified District	Holbrook
60	518.0	Yuma Elementary District	Yuma
61	513.5	Queen Creek Unified District	Queen Creek
62	501.9	Sunnyside Unified District	Tucson
63	498.8	Tolleson Union High SD	Tolleson
64	496.4	Apache Junction Unified District	Apache Junction
65	485.4	Tucson Unified District	Tucson
66	481.3	Safford Unified District	Safford
67	478.1	Flagstaff Unified District	Flagstaff
68	477.2	Marana Unified District	Marana
69	468.2	Glendale Union High SD	Glendale
70	465.6	Winslow Unified District	Winslow
71	460.3	Tempe Elementary District	Tempe
72	450.5	Catalina Foothills Unified Dist	Tucson
73	431.5	Flowing Wells Unified District	Tucson
74	410.6	Window Rock Unified District	Ft Defiance
75	406.3	Agua Fria Union High SD	Avondale
76	395.4	Kayenta Unified District	Kayenta
77	394.3	Tempe Union High SD	Tempe
78	371.1	Chinle Unified District	Chinle
79	351.9	Casa Grande Union High SD	Casa Grande
80	346.9	Yuma Union High SD	Yuma
81	308.4	Whiteriver Unified District	Whiteriver
82	300.7	Ganado Unified District	Ganado
83	298.3	Tuba City Unified District	Tuba City
84	289.0	Phoenix Union High SD	Phoenix
85	n/a	Central Ariz Valley Inst of Tech	Coolidge
85	n/a	Cottonwood-Oak Creek Elem Dist	Cottonwood
85	n/a	East Valley Institute of Tech	Mesa
85	n/a	Higley Unified District	Higley
85	n/a	Littleton Elementary District	Cashion
85	n/a	Navit	Snowflake
85	n/a	NE Arizona Tech Inst of Voc Ed	Kayenta
85	n/a	Peach Springs Unified District	Peach Springs
85	n/a	Roosevelt Elementary District	Phoenix
85	n/a	Tolleson Elementary District	Tolleson
85	n/a	Western Maricopa Ed Ctr (West-Mec)	Phoenix

Current Spending per Student in FY2003

Rank	Dollars	District Name	City
1	11,195	Agua Fria Union High SD	Avondale
2	9,587	Ganado Unified District	Ganado
3	9,470	Pinon Unified District	Pinon
4	9,160	Balsz Elementary District	Phoenix
5	9,102	Phoenix Elementary District	Phoenix
6	8,945	Window Rock Unified District	Ft Defiance
7	8,700	Tuba City Unified District	Tuba City
8	8,403	Chinle Unified District	Chinle
9	7,952	Kayenta Unified District	Kayenta
10	7,556	Phoenix Union High SD	Phoenix
11	7,278	Page Unified District	Page
12	7,275	Holbrook Unified District	Holbrook
13	7,270	Whiteriver Unified District	Whiteriver
14	6,898	Peach Springs Unified District	Peach Springs
15	6,642	Madison Elementary District	Phoenix
16	6,336	Tempe Elementary District	Tempe
17	6,333	Parker Unified SD	Parker
18	6,300	Murphy Elementary District	Phoenix
19	6,291	Snowflake Unified District	Snowflake
20	6,215	Fowler Elementary District	Phoenix
21	6,199	Tolleson Union High SD	Tolleson
22	6,181	Glendale Union High SD	Glendale
23	6,110	Coolidge Unified District	Coolidge
24	6,109	Flagstaff Unified District	Flagstaff
25	6,091	Higley Unified District	Higley
26	5,987	Isaac Elementary District	Phoenix
26	5,987	Sahuarita Unified District	Sahuarita
28	5,983	Sunnyside Unified District	Tucson
28	5,983	Tucson Unified District	Tucson
30	5,966	Roosevelt Elementary District	Phoenix
31	5,925	Queen Creek Unified District	Queen Creek
32	5,920	Catalina Foothills Unified Dist	Tucson
33	5,847	Casa Grande Union High SD	Casa Grande
34	5,781	Nogales Unified District	Nogales
35	5,755	Creighton Elementary District	Phoenix
36	5,732	Washington Elementary District	Phoenix
37	5,721	Osborn Elementary District	Phoenix
38	5,704	Tempe Union High SD	Tempe
39	5,607	Scottsdale Unified District	Phoenix
40	5,580	Somerton Elementary District	Somerton
41	5,547	Apache Junction Unified District	Apache Junction
42	5,500	Cave Creek Unified District	Cave Creek
43	5,442	Casa Grande Elementary District	Casa Grande
44	5,435	Winslow Unified District	Winslow
45	5,432	Florence Unified SD	Florence
46	5,395	Flowing Wells Unified District	Tucson
47	5,389	Globe Unified District	Globe
48	5,367	Colorado River Union High SD	Fort Mojave
49	5,345	Paradise Valley Unified District	Phoenix
50	5,316	Cottonwood-Oak Creek Elem Dist	Cottonwood
51	5,315	Laveen Elementary District	Laveen
52	5,303	Chandler Unified District	Chandler
53	5,289	Mesa Unified District	Mesa
54	5,256	Tolleson Elementary District	Tolleson
55	5,232	Liberty Elementary District	Buckeye
56	5,201	Vail Unified District	Vail
57	5,187	Blue Ridge Unified District	Lakeside
57	5,187	Yuma Union High SD	Yuma
59	5,180	Humboldt Unified District	Prescott Valley
60	5,176	Maricopa County Regional District	Phoenix
61	5,175	Dysart Unified District	El Mirage
62	5,132	Amphitheater Unified District	Tucson
63	5,129	Payson Unified District	Payson
64	5,093	Peoria Unified SD	Glendale
65	5,083	Littleton Elementary District	Cashion
66	5,056	Deer Valley Unified District	Phoenix
67	5,050	Kingman Unified SD	Kingman
68	5,037	Yuma Elementary District	Yuma
69	5,034	Marana Unified District	Marana
69	5,034	Show Low Unified District	Show Low
71	5,013	Prescott Unified District	Prescott
72	4,999	Fountain Hills Unified District	Fountain Hills
73	4,975	Safford Unified District	Safford
74	4,973	Crane Elementary District	Yuma
75	4,970	Alhambra Elementary District	Phoenix
76	4,950	Kyrene Elementary District	Tempe
77	4,947	Cartwright Elementary District	Phoenix
78	4,886	Glendale Elementary District	Glendale
79	4,871	Litchfield Elementary District	Litchfield Park
80	4,853	Santa Cruz Valley Unified District	Rio Rico
81	4,833	Sierra Vista Unified District	Sierra Vista
82	4,832	Gadsden Elementary District	San Luis
83	4,793	Avondale Elementary District	Avondale
84	4,788	Pendergast Elementary District	Phoenix
85	4,776	Chino Valley Unified District	Chino Valley
86	4,698	Gilbert Unified District	Gilbert
87	4,475	Lake Havasu Unified District	Lk Havasu City
88	4,285	Mohave Valley Elementary District	Mohave Valley
89	4,260	Bullhead City Elementary District	Bullhead City
90	n/a	Central Ariz Valley Inst of Tech	Coolidge
90	n/a	Douglas Unified District	Douglas
90	n/a	East Valley Institute of Tech	Mesa
90	n/a	Navit	Snowflake
90	n/a	NE Arizona Tech Inst of Voc Ed	Kayenta
90	n/a	Western Maricopa Ed Ctr (West-Mec)	Phoenix

Number of Diploma Recipients

Rank	Number	District Name	City
1	4,014	Mesa Unified District	Mesa
2	3,534	Phoenix Union High SD	Phoenix
3	3,309	Tucson Unified District	Tucson
4	2,678	Tempe Union High SD	Tempe

5	2,609	Glendale Union High SD	Glendale
6	2,136	Paradise Valley Unified District	Phoenix
7	1,990	Peoria Unified SD	Glendale
8	1,817	Gilbert Unified District	Gilbert
9	1,708	Scottsdale Unified District	Phoenix
10	1,389	Yuma Union High SD	Yuma
11	1,320	Deer Valley Unified District	Phoenix
12	1,021	Chandler Unified District	Chandler
13	947	Amphitheater Unified District	Tucson
14	742	Tolleson Union High SD	Tolleson
15	741	Flagstaff Unified District	Flagstaff
16	683	Marana Unified District	Marana
17	580	Sunnyside Unified District	Tucson
18	572	Sierra Vista Unified District	Sierra Vista
19	442	Kingman Unified SD	Kingman
20	431	Catalina Foothills Unified Dist	Tucson
21	425	Agua Fria Union High SD	Avondale
22	387	Casa Grande Union High SD	Casa Grande
23	363	Flowing Wells Unified District	Tucson
24	353	Nogales Unified District	Nogales
25	326	Prescott Unified District	Prescott
26	320	Colorado River Union High SD	Fort Mojave
27	316	Lake Havasu Unified District	Lk Havasu City
28	281	Humboldt Unified District	Prescott Valley
29	242	Apache Junction Unified District	Apache Junction
30	226	Douglas Unified District	Douglas
31	222	Chinle Unified District	Chinle
32	198	Cave Creek Unified District	Cave Creek
32	198	Show Low Unified District	Show Low
34	189	Dysart Unified District	El Mirage
35	188	Kayenta Unified District	Kayenta
36	176	Fountain Hills Unified District	Fountain Hills
37	168	Page Unified District	Page
38	162	Safford Unified District	Safford
39	157	Payson Unified District	Payson
40	149	Tuba City Unified District	Tuba City
41	148	Winslow Unified District	Winslow
42	145	Blue Ridge Unified District	Lakeside
43	144	Chino Valley Unified District	Chino Valley
44	139	Holbrook Unified District	Holbrook
44	139	Maricopa County Regional District	Phoenix
44	139	Snowflake Unified District	Snowflake
47	138	Coolidge Unified District	Coolidge
48	133	Ganado Unified District	Ganado
49	129	Higley Unified District	Higley
50	128	Window Rock Unified District	Ft Defiance
51	121	Sahuarita Unified District	Sahuarita
52	116	Parker Unified SD	Parker
52	116	Whiteriver Unified District	Whiteriver
54	105	Globe Unified District	Globe
55	101	Santa Cruz Valley Unified District	Rio Rico
56	84	Queen Creek Unified District	Queen Creek
57	79	Pinon Unified District	Pinon
58	78	Florence Unified SD	Florence
59	58	Vail Unified District	Vail
60	47	Peach Springs Unified District	Peach Springs
61	0	Central Ariz Valley Inst of Tech	Coolidge
61	0	Creighton Elementary District	Phoenix
61	0	East Valley Institute of Tech	Mesa
61	0	Glendale Elementary District	Glendale
61	0	Madison Elementary District	Phoenix
61	0	Navit	Snowflake
61	0	Tempe Elementary District	Tempe
68	n/a	NE Arizona Tech Inst of Voc Ed	Kayenta
68	n/a	Western Maricopa Ed Ctr (West-Mec)	Phoenix
70	n/a	Alhambra Elementary District	Phoenix
70	n/a	Avondale Elementary District	Avondale
70	n/a	Balsz Elementary District	Phoenix
70	n/a	Bullhead City Elementary District	Bullhead City
70	n/a	Cartwright Elementary District	Phoenix
70	n/a	Casa Grande Elementary District	Casa Grande
70	n/a	Cottonwood-Oak Creek Elem Dist	Cottonwood
70	n/a	Crane Elementary District	Yuma
70	n/a	Fowler Elementary District	Phoenix
70	n/a	Gadsden Elementary District	San Luis
70	n/a	Isaac Elementary District	Phoenix
70	n/a	Kyrene Elementary District	Tempe
70	n/a	Laveen Elementary District	Laveen
70	n/a	Liberty Elementary District	Buckeye
70	n/a	Litchfield Elementary District	Litchfield Park
70	n/a	Littleton Elementary District	Cashion
70	n/a	Mohave Valley Elementary District	Mohave Valley
70	n/a	Murphy Elementary District	Phoenix
70	n/a	Osborn Elementary District	Phoenix
70	n/a	Pendergast Elementary District	Phoenix
70	n/a	Phoenix Elementary District	Phoenix
70	n/a	Roosevelt Elementary District	Phoenix
70	n/a	Somerton Elementary District	Somerton
70	n/a	Tolleson Elementary District	Tolleson
70	n/a	Washington Elementary District	Phoenix
70	n/a	Yuma Elementary District	Yuma

High School Drop-out Rate

Rank	Percent	District Name	City
1	51.3	Peach Springs Unified District	Peach Springs
2	44.2	Maricopa County Regional District	Phoenix
3	26.8	Whiteriver Unified District	Whiteriver
4	21.0	Coolidge Unified District	Coolidge
5	18.7	Pinon Unified District	Pinon
6	17.3	Chinle Unified District	Chinle
7	16.6	Tuba City Unified District	Tuba City
8	15.9	Safford Unified District	Safford
9	13.9	Parker Unified SD	Parker
10	13.6	Colorado River Union High SD	Fort Mojave
11	12.4	Kingman Unified SD	Kingman
12	12.3	Sunnyside Unified District	Tucson
13	11.7	Page Unified District	Page
14	11.2	Phoenix Union High SD	Phoenix
15	11.0	Dysart Unified District	El Mirage
15	11.0	Higley Unified District	Higley
17	10.9	Casa Grande Union High SD	Casa Grande
18	10.5	Holbrook Unified District	Holbrook
18	10.5	Window Rock Unified District	Ft Defiance
20	10.3	Payson Unified District	Payson
21	10.1	Kayenta Unified District	Kayenta
22	9.8	Flagstaff Unified District	Flagstaff
23	9.7	Winslow Unified District	Winslow
24	9.2	Ganado Unified District	Ganado
25	9.1	Nogales Unified District	Nogales
26	9.0	Florence Unified SD	Florence
27	8.7	Globe Unified District	Globe
28	7.8	Chino Valley Unified District	Chino Valley
28	7.8	Humboldt Unified District	Prescott Valley
30	7.6	Show Low Unified District	Show Low
31	7.3	Flowing Wells Unified District	Tucson
32	7.0	Blue Ridge Unified District	Lakeside
33	6.9	Agua Fria Union High SD	Avondale
33	6.9	Yuma Union High SD	Yuma
35	6.8	Tolleson Union High SD	Tolleson
36	6.3	Deer Valley Unified District	Phoenix
37	6.0	Sierra Vista Unified District	Sierra Vista
38	5.9	Paradise Valley Unified District	Phoenix
39	5.6	Prescott Unified District	Prescott
40	5.4	Queen Creek Unified District	Queen Creek
40	5.4	Santa Cruz Valley Unified District	Rio Rico
42	5.3	Lake Havasu Unified District	Lk Havasu City
43	5.2	Sahuarita Unified District	Sahuarita
44	4.9	Apache Junction Unified District	Apache Junction
45	4.8	Douglas Unified District	Douglas
45	4.8	Marana Unified District	Marana
47	4.7	Tucson Unified District	Tucson
48	4.6	Glendale Union High SD	Glendale
49	4.1	Chandler Unified District	Chandler
50	4.0	Tempe Union High SD	Tempe
51	3.8	Mesa Unified District	Mesa
52	3.6	Fountain Hills Unified District	Fountain Hills
53	3.5	Snowflake Unified District	Snowflake
54	3.4	Amphitheater Unified District	Tucson
55	2.6	Cave Creek Unified District	Cave Creek
56	2.5	Gilbert Unified District	Gilbert
56	2.5	Vail Unified District	Vail
58	2.4	Peoria Unified SD	Glendale
59	1.4	Scottsdale Unified District	Phoenix
60	1.1	Catalina Foothills Unified Dist	Tucson
61	n/a	NE Arizona Tech Inst of Voc Ed	Kayenta
61	n/a	Western Maricopa Ed Ctr (West-Mec)	Phoenix
63	n/a	Alhambra Elementary District	Phoenix
63	n/a	Avondale Elementary District	Avondale
63	n/a	Balsz Elementary District	Phoenix
63	n/a	Bullhead City Elementary District	Bullhead City
63	n/a	Cartwright Elementary District	Phoenix
63	n/a	Casa Grande Elementary District	Casa Grande
63	n/a	Central Ariz Valley Inst of Tech	Coolidge
63	n/a	Cottonwood-Oak Creek Elem Dist	Cottonwood
63	n/a	Crane Elementary District	Yuma
63	n/a	Creighton Elementary District	Phoenix
63	n/a	East Valley Institute of Tech	Mesa
63	n/a	Fowler Elementary District	Phoenix
63	n/a	Gadsden Elementary District	San Luis
63	n/a	Glendale Elementary District	Glendale
63	n/a	Isaac Elementary District	Phoenix
63	n/a	Kyrene Elementary District	Tempe
63	n/a	Laveen Elementary District	Laveen
63	n/a	Liberty Elementary District	Buckeye
63	n/a	Litchfield Elementary District	Litchfield Park
63	n/a	Littleton Elementary District	Cashion
63	n/a	Madison Elementary District	Phoenix
63	n/a	Mohave Valley Elementary District	Mohave Valley
63	n/a	Murphy Elementary District	Phoenix
63	n/a	Navit	Snowflake
63	n/a	Osborn Elementary District	Phoenix
63	n/a	Pendergast Elementary District	Phoenix
63	n/a	Phoenix Elementary District	Phoenix
63	n/a	Roosevelt Elementary District	Phoenix
63	n/a	Somerton Elementary District	Somerton
63	n/a	Tempe Elementary District	Tempe
63	n/a	Tolleson Elementary District	Tolleson
63	n/a	Washington Elementary District	Phoenix
63	n/a	Yuma Elementary District	Yuma

Arkansas

Arkansas Public School Educational Profile

Category	Value	Category	Value
Schools *(2003-2004)*	1,150	**Diploma Recipients** *(2002-2003)*	26,906
Instructional Level		White, Non-Hispanic	20,100
Primary	569	Black, Non-Hispanic	5,739
Middle	200	Asian/Pacific Islander	323
High	347	American Indian/Alaskan Native	118
Other Level	34	Hispanic	626
Curriculum		**High School Drop-out Rate** (%) *(2001-2002)*	5.3
Regular	1,121	White, Non-Hispanic	4.6
Special Education	4	Black, Non-Hispanic	7.0
Vocational	20	Asian/Pacific Islander	4.3
Alternative	5	American Indian/Alaskan Native	6.9
Type		Hispanic	7.7
Magnet	7	**Staff** *(2003-2004)*	
Charter	13	Teachers	30,876.0
Title I Eligible	824	Average Salary[1] ($)	39,226
School-wide Title I	468	Librarians/Media Specialists	934.0
Students *(2003-2004)*	454,523	Guidance Counselors	1,218.0
Gender (%)		**Ratios** *(2003-2004)*	
Male	51.3	Student/Teacher Ratio	14.7 to 1
Female	48.7	Student/Librarian Ratio	486.6 to 1
Race/Ethnicity (%)		Student/Counselor Ratio	373.2 to 1
White, Non-Hispanic	69.9	**College Entrance Exam Scores** *(2005)*	
Black, Non-Hispanic	23.1	Scholastic Aptitude Test (SAT)	
Asian/Pacific Islander	1.1	Participation Rate (%)	6
American Indian/Alaskan Native	0.6	Mean SAT Reasoning Test Verbal Score	563
Hispanic	5.3	Mean SAT Reasoning Test Math Score	552
Classification (%)		American College Testing Program (ACT)	
Individual Education Program (IEP)	12.7	Participation Rate (%)	76
Migrant *(2002-2003)*	2.4	Average Composite Score	20.3
English Language Learner (ELL)	3.8	Average English Score	20.5
Eligible for Free Lunch Program	41.2	Average Math Score	19.6
Eligible for Reduced-Price Lunch Program	8.6	Average Reading Score	20.6
Current Spending *($ per student in FY 2003)*	6,304	Average Science Score	20.1
Instruction	3,879		
Support Services	2,101		

Note: For an explanation of data, please refer to the User's Guide in the front of the book; (1) Includes extra-duty pay

Arkansas NAEP 2005 Test Scores

Reading			Mathematics		
Grade/Category	Value	Rank	Grade/Category	Value	Rank
4th Grade			**4th Grade**		
Average Proficiency	217.1 (1.05)	32/51	Average Proficiency	235.5 (0.92)	33/51
Proficiency by Gender/Race/Ethnicity			Proficiency by Gender/Race/Ethnicity		
Male	212.8 (1.38)	35/51	Male	236.2 (1.15)	34/51
Female	221.2 (1.19)	31/51	Female	234.8 (1.04)	34/51
White, Non-Hispanic	225.2 (0.99)	33/51	White, Non-Hispanic	242.4 (0.88)	36/51
Black, Non-Hispanic	193.6 (1.93)	34/42	Black, Non-Hispanic	213.9 (1.65)	33/42
Asian, Non-Hispanic	n/a	n/a	Asian, Non-Hispanic	n/a	n/a
American Indian, Non-Hispanic	n/a	n/a	American Indian, Non-Hispanic	n/a	n/a
Hispanic	212.3 (4.17)	6/40	Hispanic	229.2 (2.62)	13/41
Proficiency by Class Size			Proficiency by Class Size		
Less than 16 Students	199.4 (4.30)	21/34	Less than 16 Students	221.5 (4.85)	24/35
16 to 18 Students	212.3 (2.49)	24/33	16 to 18 Students	232.7 (3.42)	23/31
19 to 20 Students	217.6 (3.44)	25/38	19 to 20 Students	239.6 (2.34)	19/38
21 to 25 Students	218.9 (1.89)	33/51	21 to 25 Students	235.1 (1.82)	39/51
Greater than 25 Students	224.1 (2.63)	11/36	Greater than 25 Students	239.0 (1.68)	17/33
Percent Attaining Achievement Levels			Percent Attaining Achievement Levels		
Below Basic	37.4 (1.38)	20/51	Below Basic	22.2 (1.20)	17/51
Basic or Above	62.6 (1.38)	32/51	Basic or Above	77.8 (1.20)	35/51
Proficient or Above	29.7 (1.08)	31/51	Proficient or Above	34.0 (1.42)	33/51
Advanced or Above	6.2 (0.60)	35/51	Advanced or Above	4.2 (0.53)	30/51
8th Grade			**8th Grade**		
Average Proficiency	257.7 (1.10)	38/51	Average Proficiency	271.6 (1.18)	40/51
Proficiency by Gender/Race/Ethnicity			Proficiency by Gender/Race/Ethnicity		
Male	252.2 (1.33)	37/51	Male	270.4 (1.38)	42/51
Female	263.2 (1.26)	37/51	Female	273.0 (1.35)	36/51
White, Non-Hispanic	265.7 (1.12)	37/51	White, Non-Hispanic	280.9 (0.95)	40/51
Black, Non-Hispanic	236.2 (1.95)	37/40	Black, Non-Hispanic	242.8 (1.57)	39/41
Asian, Non-Hispanic	n/a	n/a	Asian, Non-Hispanic	n/a	n/a
American Indian, Non-Hispanic	n/a	n/a	American Indian, Non-Hispanic	n/a	n/a
Hispanic	250.0 (3.70)	12/38	Hispanic	266.3 (4.03)	7/38
Proficiency by Parents Highest Level of Ed.			Proficiency by Parents Highest Level of Ed.		
Did Not Finish High School	248.4 (2.90)	16/49	Did Not Finish High School	262.7 (2.48)	23/50
Graduated High School	249.9 (1.96)	33/50	Graduated High School	263.6 (1.75)	36/50
Some Education After High School	265.0 (1.60)	29/50	Some Education After High School	279.4 (1.53)	31/50
Graduated College	264.1 (1.45)	40/50	Graduated College	279.3 (1.65)	42/50
Percent Attaining Achievement Levels			Percent Attaining Achievement Levels		
Below Basic	37.4 (1.38)	20/51	Below Basic	35.9 (1.61)	15/51
Basic or Above	62.6 (1.38)	32/51	Basic or Above	64.1 (1.61)	37/51
Proficient or Above	29.7 (1.08)	31/51	Proficient or Above	22.0 (1.09)	40/51
Advanced or Above	6.2 (0.60)	35/51	Advanced or Above	3.0 (0.37)	42/51

Note: For an explanation of data, please refer to the User's Guide in the front of the book; n/a indicates data not available

Arkansas County

Stuttgart SD
2501 S Main • Stuttgart, AR 72160-0928
(870) 673-3561 • http://sps.k12.ar.us/
Grade Span: KG-12; **Agency Type:** 1
Schools: 6
   2 Primary; 3 Middle; 1 High; 0 Other Level
   6 Regular; 0 Special Education; 0 Vocational; 0 Alternative
   0 Magnet; 0 Charter; 5 Title I Eligible; 4 School-wide Title I
Students: 1,883   (51.8% male; 48.1% female)
   Individual Education Program: 168 (8.9%);
   English Language Learner: 3 (0.2%); Migrant: 22 (1.2%)
   Eligible for Free Lunch Program: 928 (49.3%)
   Eligible for Reduced-Price Lunch Program: 170 (9.0%)
Teachers: 137.0 (13.7 to 1)
Librarians/Media Specialists: 5.0 (376.6 to 1)
Guidance Counselors: 6.0 (313.8 to 1)
Current Spending: ($ per student per year):
   Total: $6,248; Instruction: $3,839; Support Services: $2,037
Enrollment, Drop-out Rates and Diploma Recipients by Race/Ethnicity

Category	Total	White	Black	Asian	AIAN	Hisp.
Enrollment (%)	100.0	49.3	49.8	0.4	0.1	0.5
Drop-out Rate (%)	5.3	3.1	8.8	0.0	n/a	0.0
H.S. Diplomas (#)	134	86	46	0	0	2

Ashley County

Crossett SD
219 Main • Crossett, AR 71635-3323
(870) 364-3112 • http://csd1.sesc.k12.ar.us/
Grade Span: PK-12; **Agency Type:** 1
Schools: 7
   3 Primary; 2 Middle; 2 High; 0 Other Level
   6 Regular; 0 Special Education; 0 Vocational; 1 Alternative
   0 Magnet; 0 Charter; 4 Title I Eligible; 3 School-wide Title I
Students: 2,461   (49.4% male; 50.5% female)
   Individual Education Program: 261 (10.6%);
   English Language Learner: 13 (0.5%); Migrant: 1 (<0.1%)
   Eligible for Free Lunch Program: 1,033 (42.0%)
   Eligible for Reduced-Price Lunch Program: 156 (6.3%)
Teachers: 157.0 (15.7 to 1)
Librarians/Media Specialists: 6.0 (410.2 to 1)
Guidance Counselors: 6.0 (410.2 to 1)
Current Spending: ($ per student per year):
   Total: $5,819; Instruction: $3,447; Support Services: $2,058
Enrollment, Drop-out Rates and Diploma Recipients by Race/Ethnicity

Category	Total	White	Black	Asian	AIAN	Hisp.
Enrollment (%)	100.0	61.4	37.2	0.2	0.0	1.2
Drop-out Rate (%)	5.5	4.4	7.6	0.0	0.0	0.0
H.S. Diplomas (#)	126	88	37	0	1	0

Hamburg SD
521 E Lincoln • Hamburg, AR 71646-3303
(870) 853-9851 • http://se.sesc.k12.ar.us/hamburg/
Grade Span: PK-12; **Agency Type:** 1
Schools: 6
   3 Primary; 2 Middle; 1 High; 0 Other Level
   6 Regular; 0 Special Education; 0 Vocational; 0 Alternative
   0 Magnet; 0 Charter; 6 Title I Eligible; 5 School-wide Title I
Students: 1,735   (49.5% male; 50.4% female)
   Individual Education Program: 196 (11.3%);
   English Language Learner: 120 (6.9%); Migrant: 48 (2.8%)
   Eligible for Free Lunch Program: 1,113 (64.1%)
   Eligible for Reduced-Price Lunch Program: 65 (3.7%)
Teachers: 115.0 (15.1 to 1)
Librarians/Media Specialists: 4.0 (433.8 to 1)
Guidance Counselors: 4.0 (433.8 to 1)
Current Spending: ($ per student per year):
   Total: $6,871; Instruction: $4,012; Support Services: $2,339
Enrollment, Drop-out Rates and Diploma Recipients by Race/Ethnicity

Category	Total	White	Black	Asian	AIAN	Hisp.
Enrollment (%)	100.0	56.9	35.0	0.0	0.0	8.1
Drop-out Rate (%)	4.8	6.2	2.4	n/a	n/a	9.7
H.S. Diplomas (#)	116	65	47	0	0	4

Baxter County

Mountain Home SD
1230 S Maple • Mountain Home, AR 72653-4840
(870) 425-1201 • http://bombers.k12.ar.us/
Grade Span: KG-12; **Agency Type:** 1
Schools: 6
   2 Primary; 2 Middle; 1 High; 1 Other Level
   6 Regular; 0 Special Education; 0 Vocational; 0 Alternative

   0 Magnet; 1 Charter; 6 Title I Eligible; 6 School-wide Title I
Students: 3,860   (53.1% male; 46.8% female)
   Individual Education Program: 460 (11.9%);
   English Language Learner: 37 (1.0%); Migrant: 0 (0.0%)
   Eligible for Free Lunch Program: 1,284 (33.3%)
   Eligible for Reduced-Price Lunch Program: 324 (8.4%)
Teachers: 223.0 (17.3 to 1)
Librarians/Media Specialists: 6.0 (643.3 to 1)
Guidance Counselors: 9.0 (428.9 to 1)
Current Spending: ($ per student per year):
   Total: $5,852; Instruction: $3,704; Support Services: $1,872
Enrollment, Drop-out Rates and Diploma Recipients by Race/Ethnicity

Category	Total	White	Black	Asian	AIAN	Hisp.
Enrollment (%)	100.0	98.0	0.3	0.6	0.5	0.6
Drop-out Rate (%)	5.4	5.4	n/a	0.0	16.7	0.0
H.S. Diplomas (#)	240	240	0	0	0	0

Benton County

Bentonville SD
400 NW Second St • Bentonville, AR 72712-5238
(479) 254-5000 • http://www.bentonville.k12.ar.us/bps/scripts/home.asp
Grade Span: KG-12; **Agency Type:** 1
Schools: 10
   5 Primary; 4 Middle; 1 High; 0 Other Level
   10 Regular; 0 Special Education; 0 Vocational; 0 Alternative
   0 Magnet; 0 Charter; 5 Title I Eligible; 1 School-wide Title I
Students: 8,346   (50.0% male; 49.9% female)
   Individual Education Program: 943 (11.3%);
   English Language Learner: 279 (3.3%); Migrant: 118 (1.4%)
   Eligible for Free Lunch Program: 1,357 (16.3%)
   Eligible for Reduced-Price Lunch Program: 659 (7.9%)
Teachers: 513.0 (16.3 to 1)
Librarians/Media Specialists: 8.0 (1,043.3 to 1)
Guidance Counselors: 19.0 (439.3 to 1)
Current Spending: ($ per student per year):
   Total: $6,062; Instruction: $3,724; Support Services: $2,018
Enrollment, Drop-out Rates and Diploma Recipients by Race/Ethnicity

Category	Total	White	Black	Asian	AIAN	Hisp.
Enrollment (%)	100.0	88.4	1.4	2.3	1.3	6.6
Drop-out Rate (%)	6.3	6.3	0.0	2.8	5.3	10.0
H.S. Diplomas (#)	392	367	3	6	2	14

Gravette SD
609 Birmingham SE • Gravette, AR 72736-8701
(479) 787-4100
Grade Span: KG-12; **Agency Type:** 1
Schools: 4
   1 Primary; 2 Middle; 1 High; 0 Other Level
   4 Regular; 0 Special Education; 0 Vocational; 0 Alternative
   0 Magnet; 0 Charter; 3 Title I Eligible; 2 School-wide Title I
Students: 1,621   (51.2% male; 48.7% female)
   Individual Education Program: 197 (12.2%);
   English Language Learner: 25 (1.5%); Migrant: 43 (2.7%)
   Eligible for Free Lunch Program: 498 (30.7%)
   Eligible for Reduced-Price Lunch Program: 161 (9.9%)
Teachers: 99.0 (16.4 to 1)
Librarians/Media Specialists: 4.0 (405.3 to 1)
Guidance Counselors: 4.0 (405.3 to 1)
Current Spending: ($ per student per year):
   Total: $5,472; Instruction: $3,444; Support Services: $1,776
Enrollment, Drop-out Rates and Diploma Recipients by Race/Ethnicity

Category	Total	White	Black	Asian	AIAN	Hisp.
Enrollment (%)	100.0	91.9	0.2	1.1	3.2	3.6
Drop-out Rate (%)	4.6	4.1	n/a	0.0	20.0	9.1
H.S. Diplomas (#)	83	76	0	1	1	5

Rogers SD
212 S Third St • Rogers, AR 72756-4547
(479) 636-3910 • http://icu.nwsc.k12.ar.us/
Grade Span: PK-12; **Agency Type:** 1
Schools: 18
   12 Primary; 1 Middle; 1 High; 4 Other Level
   18 Regular; 0 Special Education; 0 Vocational; 0 Alternative
   0 Magnet; 0 Charter; 9 Title I Eligible; 7 School-wide Title I
Students: 12,351   (51.1% male; 48.8% female)
   Individual Education Program: 1,520 (12.3%);
   English Language Learner: 2,771 (22.4%); Migrant: 1,051 (8.5%)
   Eligible for Free Lunch Program: 4,174 (33.8%)
   Eligible for Reduced-Price Lunch Program: 1,130 (9.1%)
Teachers: 708.0 (17.4 to 1)
Librarians/Media Specialists: 17.0 (726.5 to 1)
Guidance Counselors: 28.0 (441.1 to 1)
Current Spending: ($ per student per year):
   Total: $6,042; Instruction: $3,899; Support Services: $1,823

Enrollment, Drop-out Rates and Diploma Recipients by Race/Ethnicity

Category	Total	White	Black	Asian	AIAN	Hisp.
Enrollment (%)	100.0	68.7	0.7	1.6	0.5	28.6
Drop-out Rate (%)	4.7	4.2	12.5	1.7	11.1	6.7
H.S. Diplomas (#)	596	487	3	16	3	87

Siloam Springs SD

847 S Dogwood • Siloam Springs, AR 72761-0798
Mailing Address: PO Box 798 • Siloam Springs, AR 72761-0798
(479) 524-3191 • http://pride.nwsc.k12.ar.us/index.html
Grade Span: KG-12; Agency Type: 1
Schools: 5
 2 Primary; 2 Middle; 1 High; 0 Other Level
 5 Regular; 0 Special Education; 0 Vocational; 0 Alternative
 0 Magnet; 0 Charter; 5 Title I Eligible; 0 School-wide Title I
Students: 3,135 (51.3% male; 48.6% female)
 Individual Education Program: 237 (7.6%);
 English Language Learner: 326 (10.4%); Migrant: 285 (9.1%)
 Eligible for Free Lunch Program: 994 (31.7%)
 Eligible for Reduced-Price Lunch Program: 374 (11.9%)
Teachers: 190.0 (16.5 to 1)
Librarians/Media Specialists: 5.0 (627.0 to 1)
Guidance Counselors: 8.0 (391.9 to 1)
Current Spending: ($ per student per year):
 Total: $5,544; Instruction: $3,567; Support Services: $1,677
Enrollment, Drop-out Rates and Diploma Recipients by Race/Ethnicity

Category	Total	White	Black	Asian	AIAN	Hisp.
Enrollment (%)	100.0	74.1	0.4	2.4	6.8	16.3
Drop-out Rate (%)	1.0	0.8	0.0	0.0	2.6	1.8
H.S. Diplomas (#)	222	191	0	3	6	22

Boone County

Harrison SD

400 S Sycamore • Harrison, AR 72601-5293
Mailing Address: 400 So Sycamore St • Harrison, AR 72601-5293
(870) 741-7600 • http://taurus.oursc.k12.ar.us/
Grade Span: KG-12; Agency Type: 1
Schools: 7
 4 Primary; 1 Middle; 2 High; 0 Other Level
 7 Regular; 0 Special Education; 0 Vocational; 0 Alternative
 0 Magnet; 0 Charter; 4 Title I Eligible; 1 School-wide Title I
Students: 2,792 (51.6% male; 48.3% female)
 Individual Education Program: 299 (10.7%);
 English Language Learner: 4 (0.1%); Migrant: 0 (0.0%)
 Eligible for Free Lunch Program: 830 (29.7%)
 Eligible for Reduced-Price Lunch Program: 240 (8.6%)
Teachers: 178.0 (15.7 to 1)
Librarians/Media Specialists: 7.0 (398.9 to 1)
Guidance Counselors: 9.0 (310.2 to 1)
Current Spending: ($ per student per year):
 Total: $5,537; Instruction: $3,404; Support Services: $1,806
Enrollment, Drop-out Rates and Diploma Recipients by Race/Ethnicity

Category	Total	White	Black	Asian	AIAN	Hisp.
Enrollment (%)	100.0	97.8	0.1	0.3	0.6	1.1
Drop-out Rate (%)	3.9	4.0	0.0	0.0	0.0	0.0
H.S. Diplomas (#)	194	190	2	2	0	0

Bradley County

Warren SD

803 N Walnut • Warren, AR 71671-2008
Mailing Address: PO Box 1210 • Warren, AR 71671-2008
(870) 226-6738 • http://zebra.wsc.k12.ar.us/~wbulldog/
Grade Span: KG-12; Agency Type: 1
Schools: 5
 1 Primary; 2 Middle; 2 High; 0 Other Level
 4 Regular; 0 Special Education; 1 Vocational; 0 Alternative
 0 Magnet; 0 Charter; 3 Title I Eligible; 3 School-wide Title I
Students: 1,573 (50.5% male; 49.4% female)
 Individual Education Program: 155 (9.9%);
 English Language Learner: 77 (4.9%); Migrant: 87 (5.5%)
 Eligible for Free Lunch Program: 851 (54.1%)
 Eligible for Reduced-Price Lunch Program: 130 (8.3%)
Teachers: 116.0 (13.6 to 1)
Librarians/Media Specialists: 4.0 (393.3 to 1)
Guidance Counselors: 5.0 (314.6 to 1)
Current Spending: ($ per student per year):
 Total: $6,855; Instruction: $4,346; Support Services: $2,158
Enrollment, Drop-out Rates and Diploma Recipients by Race/Ethnicity

Category	Total	White	Black	Asian	AIAN	Hisp.
Enrollment (%)	100.0	47.7	40.8	0.1	0.0	11.4
Drop-out Rate (%)	3.1	3.5	2.4	n/a	0.0	4.5
H.S. Diplomas (#)	102	57	39	0	0	6

Carroll County

Berryville SD

215 Ferguson St • Berryville, AR 72616-0408
(870) 423-7065 • http://bobcat.oursc.k12.ar.us/
Grade Span: KG-12; Agency Type: 1
Schools: 3
 1 Primary; 1 Middle; 1 High; 0 Other Level
 3 Regular; 0 Special Education; 0 Vocational; 0 Alternative
 0 Magnet; 0 Charter; 2 Title I Eligible; 0 School-wide Title I
Students: 1,693 (52.3% male; 47.6% female)
 Individual Education Program: 186 (11.0%);
 English Language Learner: 164 (9.7%); Migrant: 210 (12.4%)
 Eligible for Free Lunch Program: 560 (33.1%)
 Eligible for Reduced-Price Lunch Program: 228 (13.5%)
Teachers: 112.0 (15.1 to 1)
Librarians/Media Specialists: 2.0 (846.5 to 1)
Guidance Counselors: 4.0 (423.3 to 1)
Current Spending: ($ per student per year):
 Total: $5,748; Instruction: $3,623; Support Services: $1,825
Enrollment, Drop-out Rates and Diploma Recipients by Race/Ethnicity

Category	Total	White	Black	Asian	AIAN	Hisp.
Enrollment (%)	100.0	80.9	0.1	0.3	0.8	17.9
Drop-out Rate (%)	4.8	4.5	n/a	0.0	0.0	7.0
H.S. Diplomas (#)	100	93	0	0	0	7

Clark County

Arkadelphia SD

234 N 11th • Arkadelphia, AR 71923-4903
Mailing Address: 235 N 11th • Arkadelphia, AR 71923-4903
(870) 246-5564 • http://apsd.k12.ar.us/
Grade Span: PK-12; Agency Type: 1
Schools: 5
 2 Primary; 2 Middle; 1 High; 0 Other Level
 5 Regular; 0 Special Education; 0 Vocational; 0 Alternative
 0 Magnet; 0 Charter; 4 Title I Eligible; 3 School-wide Title I
Students: 2,269 (51.0% male; 48.9% female)
 Individual Education Program: 323 (14.2%);
 English Language Learner: 26 (1.1%); Migrant: 0 (0.0%)
 Eligible for Free Lunch Program: 780 (34.4%)
 Eligible for Reduced-Price Lunch Program: 207 (9.1%)
Teachers: 147.0 (15.4 to 1)
Librarians/Media Specialists: 5.0 (453.8 to 1)
Guidance Counselors: 8.0 (283.6 to 1)
Current Spending: ($ per student per year):
 Total: $5,880; Instruction: $3,463; Support Services: $2,109
Enrollment, Drop-out Rates and Diploma Recipients by Race/Ethnicity

Category	Total	White	Black	Asian	AIAN	Hisp.
Enrollment (%)	100.0	60.2	35.2	1.0	0.0	3.6
Drop-out Rate (%)	3.4	4.2	2.2	0.0	0.0	0.0
H.S. Diplomas (#)	164	99	59	3	0	3

Cleburne County

Heber Springs SD

800 W Moore • Heber Springs, AR 72543-2402
(501) 362-6712 • http://hssdweb.afsc.k12.ar.us/
Grade Span: KG-12; Agency Type: 1
Schools: 3
 1 Primary; 1 Middle; 1 High; 0 Other Level
 3 Regular; 0 Special Education; 0 Vocational; 0 Alternative
 0 Magnet; 0 Charter; 3 Title I Eligible; 3 School-wide Title I
Students: 1,682 (52.4% male; 47.5% female)
 Individual Education Program: 282 (16.8%);
 English Language Learner: 4 (0.2%); Migrant: 0 (0.0%)
 Eligible for Free Lunch Program: 576 (34.2%)
 Eligible for Reduced-Price Lunch Program: 175 (10.4%)
Teachers: 112.0 (15.0 to 1)
Librarians/Media Specialists: 3.0 (560.7 to 1)
Guidance Counselors: 5.0 (336.4 to 1)
Current Spending: ($ per student per year):
 Total: $5,978; Instruction: $3,829; Support Services: $1,790
Enrollment, Drop-out Rates and Diploma Recipients by Race/Ethnicity

Category	Total	White	Black	Asian	AIAN	Hisp.
Enrollment (%)	100.0	98.3	0.1	0.5	0.3	0.7
Drop-out Rate (%)	6.4	6.3	n/a	0.0	n/a	20.0
H.S. Diplomas (#)	95	94	0	1	0	0

Columbia County

Magnolia SD
1400 High School Dr • Magnolia, AR 71754-0649
Mailing Address: PO Box 649 • Magnolia, AR 71754-0649
(870) 234-4933
Grade Span: KG-12; **Agency Type:** 1
Schools: 4
    1 Primary; 2 Middle; 1 High; 0 Other Level
    4 Regular; 0 Special Education; 0 Vocational; 0 Alternative
    0 Magnet; 0 Charter; 4 Title I Eligible; 0 School-wide Title I
Students: 2,786 (50.2% male; 49.7% female)
    Individual Education Program: 244 (8.8%);
    English Language Learner: 21 (0.8%); Migrant: 6 (0.2%)
    Eligible for Free Lunch Program: 1,271 (45.6%)
    Eligible for Reduced-Price Lunch Program: 180 (6.5%)
Teachers: 180.0 (15.5 to 1)
Librarians/Media Specialists: 4.0 (696.5 to 1)
Guidance Counselors: 8.0 (348.3 to 1)
Current Spending: ($ per student per year):
    Total: $5,612; Instruction: $3,566; Support Services: $1,743
Enrollment, Drop-out Rates and Diploma Recipients by Race/Ethnicity

Category	Total	White	Black	Asian	AIAN	Hisp.
Enrollment (%)	100.0	52.2	46.1	0.5	0.1	1.1
Drop-out Rate (%)	3.6	2.4	5.0	0.0	n/a	40.0
H.S. Diplomas (#)	209	143	66	0	0	0

Conway County

So. Conway County SD
704 E Church • Morrilton, AR 72110-3559
Mailing Address: 704 E Church Steet • Morrilton, AR 72110-3559
(501) 354-9400 • http://mdd.k12.ar.us/
Grade Span: KG-12; **Agency Type:** 1
Schools: 6
    3 Primary; 1 Middle; 2 High; 0 Other Level
    5 Regular; 0 Special Education; 1 Vocational; 0 Alternative
    0 Magnet; 0 Charter; 4 Title I Eligible; 3 School-wide Title I
Students: 2,377 (50.2% male; 49.7% female)
    Individual Education Program: 347 (14.6%);
    English Language Learner: 33 (1.4%); Migrant: 0 (0.0%)
    Eligible for Free Lunch Program: 1,096 (46.1%)
    Eligible for Reduced-Price Lunch Program: 279 (11.7%)
Teachers: 179.0 (13.3 to 1)
Librarians/Media Specialists: 4.0 (594.3 to 1)
Guidance Counselors: 6.0 (396.2 to 1)
Current Spending: ($ per student per year):
    Total: $6,245; Instruction: $3,728; Support Services: $2,178
Enrollment, Drop-out Rates and Diploma Recipients by Race/Ethnicity

Category	Total	White	Black	Asian	AIAN	Hisp.
Enrollment (%)	100.0	70.2	25.4	0.8	0.3	3.4
Drop-out Rate (%)	3.3	3.3	3.4	0.0	0.0	6.7
H.S. Diplomas (#)	166	121	44	0	0	1

Craighead County

Jonesboro SD
2506 Southwest Square • Jonesboro, AR 72401-3968
(870) 933-5800 • http://www.jps.k12.ar.us/
Grade Span: KG-12; **Agency Type:** 1
Schools: 10
    5 Primary; 3 Middle; 2 High; 0 Other Level
    9 Regular; 0 Special Education; 1 Vocational; 0 Alternative
    0 Magnet; 0 Charter; 6 Title I Eligible; 2 School-wide Title I
Students: 4,845 (49.7% male; 50.2% female)
    Individual Education Program: 541 (11.2%);
    English Language Learner: 128 (2.6%); Migrant: 136 (2.8%)
    Eligible for Free Lunch Program: 2,187 (45.1%)
    Eligible for Reduced-Price Lunch Program: 346 (7.1%)
Teachers: 290.0 (16.7 to 1)
Librarians/Media Specialists: 9.0 (538.3 to 1)
Guidance Counselors: 14.0 (346.1 to 1)
Current Spending: ($ per student per year):
    Total: $5,988; Instruction: $3,582; Support Services: $2,057
Enrollment, Drop-out Rates and Diploma Recipients by Race/Ethnicity

Category	Total	White	Black	Asian	AIAN	Hisp.
Enrollment (%)	100.0	63.2	31.2	0.7	0.1	4.8
Drop-out Rate (%)	1.8	1.0	3.5	0.0	0.0	4.8
H.S. Diplomas (#)	315	216	84	6	1	8

Nettleton SD
2616 Progress Dr • Jonesboro, AR 72401-7639
(870) 910-7800 • http://nettleton.crsc.k12.ar.us/
Grade Span: KG-12; **Agency Type:** 1
Schools: 7

    3 Primary; 3 Middle; 1 High; 0 Other Level
    7 Regular; 0 Special Education; 0 Vocational; 0 Alternative
    0 Magnet; 1 Charter; 5 Title I Eligible; 0 School-wide Title I
Students: 2,753 (51.2% male; 48.7% female)
    Individual Education Program: 377 (13.7%);
    English Language Learner: 36 (1.3%); Migrant: 11 (0.4%)
    Eligible for Free Lunch Program: 935 (34.0%)
    Eligible for Reduced-Price Lunch Program: 207 (7.5%)
Teachers: 172.0 (16.0 to 1)
Librarians/Media Specialists: 6.0 (458.8 to 1)
Guidance Counselors: 7.0 (393.3 to 1)
Current Spending: ($ per student per year):
    Total: $5,644; Instruction: $3,540; Support Services: $1,776
Enrollment, Drop-out Rates and Diploma Recipients by Race/Ethnicity

Category	Total	White	Black	Asian	AIAN	Hisp.
Enrollment (%)	100.0	76.6	19.1	1.2	0.3	2.8
Drop-out Rate (%)	3.3	2.5	7.8	0.0	0.0	16.7
H.S. Diplomas (#)	152	137	9	5	0	1

Valley View SD
2131 Valley View Dr • Jonesboro, AR 72404-9031
(870) 935-6200
Grade Span: KG-12; **Agency Type:** 1
Schools: 2
    1 Primary; 0 Middle; 1 High; 0 Other Level
    2 Regular; 0 Special Education; 0 Vocational; 0 Alternative
    0 Magnet; 0 Charter; 2 Title I Eligible; 2 School-wide Title I
Students: 1,542 (51.4% male; 48.5% female)
    Individual Education Program: 142 (9.2%);
    English Language Learner: 15 (1.0%); Migrant: 4 (0.3%)
    Eligible for Free Lunch Program: 193 (12.5%)
    Eligible for Reduced-Price Lunch Program: 89 (5.8%)
Teachers: 94.0 (16.4 to 1)
Librarians/Media Specialists: 2.0 (771.0 to 1)
Guidance Counselors: 4.0 (385.5 to 1)
Current Spending: ($ per student per year):
    Total: $5,243; Instruction: $3,454; Support Services: $1,478
Enrollment, Drop-out Rates and Diploma Recipients by Race/Ethnicity

Category	Total	White	Black	Asian	AIAN	Hisp.
Enrollment (%)	100.0	95.3	1.3	0.6	0.9	1.9
Drop-out Rate (%)	5.6	5.5	0.0	0.0	0.0	20.0
H.S. Diplomas (#)	87	86	0	0	0	1

Westside Cons. SD
1630 Hwy 91 W • Jonesboro, AR 72404-9284
(870) 935-7503 • http://crowleys.crsc.k12.ar.us/~westside/
Grade Span: KG-12; **Agency Type:** 1
Schools: 3
    1 Primary; 1 Middle; 1 High; 0 Other Level
    3 Regular; 0 Special Education; 0 Vocational; 0 Alternative
    0 Magnet; 0 Charter; 3 Title I Eligible; 0 School-wide Title I
Students: 1,631 (52.5% male; 47.4% female)
    Individual Education Program: 222 (13.6%);
    English Language Learner: 1 (0.1%); Migrant: 17 (1.0%)
    Eligible for Free Lunch Program: 477 (29.2%)
    Eligible for Reduced-Price Lunch Program: 169 (10.4%)
Teachers: 105.0 (15.5 to 1)
Librarians/Media Specialists: 3.0 (543.7 to 1)
Guidance Counselors: 5.0 (326.2 to 1)
Current Spending: ($ per student per year):
    Total: $6,210; Instruction: $3,580; Support Services: $2,320
Enrollment, Drop-out Rates and Diploma Recipients by Race/Ethnicity

Category	Total	White	Black	Asian	AIAN	Hisp.
Enrollment (%)	100.0	99.1	0.1	0.0	0.0	0.7
Drop-out Rate (%)	1.5	1.5	n/a	n/a	n/a	n/a
H.S. Diplomas (#)	91	91	0	0	0	0

Crawford County

Alma SD
916 Hwy 64 E • Alma, AR 72921-2359
Mailing Address: PO Box 2359 • Alma, AR 72921-2359
(479) 632-4791 • http://alma.wsc.k12.ar.us/
Grade Span: KG-12; **Agency Type:** 1
Schools: 4
    2 Primary; 1 Middle; 1 High; 0 Other Level
    4 Regular; 0 Special Education; 0 Vocational; 0 Alternative
    0 Magnet; 0 Charter; 4 Title I Eligible; 0 School-wide Title I
Students: 3,035 (52.1% male; 47.8% female)
    Individual Education Program: 400 (13.2%);
    English Language Learner: 8 (0.3%); Migrant: 80 (2.6%)
    Eligible for Free Lunch Program: 942 (31.0%)
    Eligible for Reduced-Price Lunch Program: 289 (9.5%)
Teachers: 185.0 (16.4 to 1)
Librarians/Media Specialists: 4.0 (758.8 to 1)
Guidance Counselors: 7.0 (433.6 to 1)

Current Spending: ($ per student per year):
Total: $6,085; Instruction: $3,766; Support Services: $1,976
Enrollment, Drop-out Rates and Diploma Recipients by Race/Ethnicity

Category	Total	White	Black	Asian	AIAN	Hisp.
Enrollment (%)	100.0	96.6	0.8	0.6	0.2	1.8
Drop-out Rate (%)	2.6	2.2	8.3	50.0	0.0	12.5
H.S. Diplomas (#)	188	183	1	2	1	1

Van Buren SD
2221 Pointer Tr • Van Buren, AR 72956-2336
(479) 474-7942 • http://vbschools.k12.ar.us/
Grade Span: PK-12; **Agency Type:** 1
Schools: 11
6 Primary; 4 Middle; 1 High; 0 Other Level
11 Regular; 0 Special Education; 0 Vocational; 0 Alternative
0 Magnet; 0 Charter; 4 Title I Eligible; 3 School-wide Title I
Students: 5,585 (51.7% male; 48.2% female)
Individual Education Program: 723 (12.9%);
English Language Learner: 338 (6.1%); Migrant: 247 (4.4%)
Eligible for Free Lunch Program: 1,992 (35.7%)
Eligible for Reduced-Price Lunch Program: 507 (9.1%)
Teachers: 374.0 (14.9 to 1)
Librarians/Media Specialists: 11.0 (507.7 to 1)
Guidance Counselors: 15.0 (372.3 to 1)
Current Spending: ($ per student per year):
Total: $6,033; Instruction: $3,928; Support Services: $1,787
Enrollment, Drop-out Rates and Diploma Recipients by Race/Ethnicity

Category	Total	White	Black	Asian	AIAN	Hisp.
Enrollment (%)	100.0	84.0	1.8	3.1	1.8	9.3
Drop-out Rate (%)	4.9	5.1	4.3	4.2	9.5	2.8
H.S. Diplomas (#)	300	247	8	19	4	22

Marion SD
200 Manor St • Marion, AR 72364-1909
(870) 739-5100 • http://marion.crsc.k12.ar.us/
Grade Span: KG-12; **Agency Type:** 1
Schools: 6
2 Primary; 2 Middle; 1 High; 1 Other Level
6 Regular; 0 Special Education; 0 Vocational; 0 Alternative
0 Magnet; 0 Charter; 0 Title I Eligible; 0 School-wide Title I
Students: 3,418 (51.2% male; 48.7% female)
Individual Education Program: 390 (11.4%);
English Language Learner: 6 (0.2%); Migrant: 58 (1.7%)
Eligible for Free Lunch Program: 1,177 (34.4%)
Eligible for Reduced-Price Lunch Program: 324 (9.5%)
Teachers: 189.0 (18.1 to 1)
Librarians/Media Specialists: 6.0 (569.7 to 1)
Guidance Counselors: 8.0 (427.3 to 1)
Current Spending: ($ per student per year):
Total: $5,723; Instruction: $3,583; Support Services: $1,816
Enrollment, Drop-out Rates and Diploma Recipients by Race/Ethnicity

Category	Total	White	Black	Asian	AIAN	Hisp.
Enrollment (%)	100.0	70.2	27.3	0.9	0.3	1.4
Drop-out Rate (%)	4.6	4.6	5.1	0.0	0.0	0.0
H.S. Diplomas (#)	158	123	32	3	0	0

West Memphis SD
301 S Avalon • West Memphis, AR 72301
Mailing Address: Pobox 826 • West Memphis, AR 72303-0826
(870) 735-1915 • http://west.grsc.k12.ar.us/
Grade Span: PK-12; **Agency Type:** 1
Schools: 12
8 Primary; 3 Middle; 1 High; 0 Other Level
12 Regular; 0 Special Education; 0 Vocational; 0 Alternative
0 Magnet; 0 Charter; 8 Title I Eligible; 8 School-wide Title I
Students: 6,161 (50.3% male; 49.6% female)
Individual Education Program: 684 (11.1%);
English Language Learner: 0 (0.0%); Migrant: 0 (0.0%)
Eligible for Free Lunch Program: 4,024 (65.3%)
Eligible for Reduced-Price Lunch Program: 317 (5.1%)
Teachers: 394.0 (15.6 to 1)
Librarians/Media Specialists: 12.0 (513.4 to 1)
Guidance Counselors: 14.0 (440.1 to 1)
Current Spending: ($ per student per year):
Total: $5,732; Instruction: $3,728; Support Services: $1,686
Enrollment, Drop-out Rates and Diploma Recipients by Race/Ethnicity

Category	Total	White	Black	Asian	AIAN	Hisp.
Enrollment (%)	100.0	17.7	81.5	0.2	0.0	0.5
Drop-out Rate (%)	6.9	6.0	7.1	0.0	n/a	0.0
H.S. Diplomas (#)	260	53	205	1	0	1

Wynne SD
1300 N Falls Blvd • Wynne, AR 72396-0069
Mailing Address: PO Box 69 • Wynne, AR 72396-0069
(870) 238-5000 • http://wynne.k12.ar.us
Grade Span: KG-12; **Agency Type:** 1
Schools: 4
2 Primary; 1 Middle; 1 High; 0 Other Level
4 Regular; 0 Special Education; 0 Vocational; 0 Alternative
0 Magnet; 0 Charter; 2 Title I Eligible; 0 School-wide Title I
Students: 2,833 (50.9% male; 49.0% female)
Individual Education Program: 345 (12.2%);
English Language Learner: 7 (0.2%); Migrant: 43 (1.5%)
Eligible for Free Lunch Program: 1,269 (44.8%)
Eligible for Reduced-Price Lunch Program: 219 (7.7%)
Teachers: 189.0 (15.0 to 1)
Librarians/Media Specialists: 4.0 (708.3 to 1)
Guidance Counselors: 9.0 (314.8 to 1)
Current Spending: ($ per student per year):
Total: $5,704; Instruction: $3,725; Support Services: $1,648
Enrollment, Drop-out Rates and Diploma Recipients by Race/Ethnicity

Category	Total	White	Black	Asian	AIAN	Hisp.
Enrollment (%)	100.0	69.0	29.8	0.4	0.2	0.6
Drop-out Rate (%)	3.5	2.8	5.2	0.0	n/a	0.0
H.S. Diplomas (#)	196	128	65	1	0	2

Dumas SD
213 Adams St • Dumas, AR 71639
Mailing Address: Caller #8880 • Dumas, AR 71639
(870) 382-4571 • http://wwwdumas.sesc.k12.ar.us/
Grade Span: PK-12; **Agency Type:** 1
Schools: 4
2 Primary; 1 Middle; 1 High; 0 Other Level
4 Regular; 0 Special Education; 0 Vocational; 0 Alternative
0 Magnet; 0 Charter; 3 Title I Eligible; 3 School-wide Title I
Students: 1,614 (49.9% male; 50.0% female)
Individual Education Program: 229 (14.2%);
English Language Learner: 68 (4.2%); Migrant: 32 (2.0%)
Eligible for Free Lunch Program: 1,032 (63.9%)
Eligible for Reduced-Price Lunch Program: 154 (9.5%)
Teachers: 117.0 (13.8 to 1)
Librarians/Media Specialists: 4.0 (403.5 to 1)
Guidance Counselors: 5.0 (322.8 to 1)
Current Spending: ($ per student per year):
Total: $6,482; Instruction: $4,056; Support Services: $2,072
Enrollment, Drop-out Rates and Diploma Recipients by Race/Ethnicity

Category	Total	White	Black	Asian	AIAN	Hisp.
Enrollment (%)	100.0	28.7	64.4	0.2	0.2	6.4
Drop-out Rate (%)	4.0	5.5	3.5	n/a	n/a	3.6
H.S. Diplomas (#)	116	27	83	0	0	6

Monticello SD
935 Scogin Dr • Monticello, AR 71655-5733
(870) 367-4000 • http://msd.sesc.k12.ar.us/
Grade Span: KG-12; **Agency Type:** 1
Schools: 5
2 Primary; 1 Middle; 2 High; 0 Other Level
4 Regular; 0 Special Education; 1 Vocational; 0 Alternative
0 Magnet; 0 Charter; 3 Title I Eligible; 2 School-wide Title I
Students: 2,186 (51.0% male; 48.9% female)
Individual Education Program: 232 (10.6%);
English Language Learner: 0 (0.0%); Migrant: 0 (0.0%)
Eligible for Free Lunch Program: 918 (42.0%)
Eligible for Reduced-Price Lunch Program: 102 (4.7%)
Teachers: 142.0 (15.4 to 1)
Librarians/Media Specialists: 4.0 (546.5 to 1)
Guidance Counselors: 6.0 (364.3 to 1)
Current Spending: ($ per student per year):
Total: $5,933; Instruction: $3,485; Support Services: $2,156
Enrollment, Drop-out Rates and Diploma Recipients by Race/Ethnicity

Category	Total	White	Black	Asian	AIAN	Hisp.
Enrollment (%)	100.0	61.9	36.3	0.3	0.1	1.3
Drop-out Rate (%)	1.3	1.0	1.8	0.0	0.0	0.0
H.S. Diplomas (#)	151	97	51	3	0	0

Faulkner County

Conway SD
2220 Prince St · Conway, AR 72034
(501) 450-4800 · http://www.conwayschools.afsc.k12.ar.us/
Grade Span: KG-12; **Agency Type:** 1
Schools: 13
  8 Primary; 2 Middle; 2 High; 1 Other Level
  12 Regular; 0 Special Education; 1 Vocational; 0 Alternative
  0 Magnet; 0 Charter; 6 Title I Eligible; 1 School-wide Title I
Students: 8,216 (51.0% male; 48.9% female)
  Individual Education Program: 1,171 (14.3%);
  English Language Learner: 119 (1.4%); Migrant: 24 (0.3%)
  Eligible for Free Lunch Program: 2,136 (26.0%)
  Eligible for Reduced-Price Lunch Program: 479 (5.8%)
Teachers: 502.0 (16.4 to 1)
Librarians/Media Specialists: 12.0 (684.7 to 1)
Guidance Counselors: 18.0 (456.4 to 1)
Current Spending: ($ per student per year):
  Total: $5,728; Instruction: $3,550; Support Services: $1,912
Enrollment, Drop-out Rates and Diploma Recipients by Race/Ethnicity

Category	Total	White	Black	Asian	AIAN	Hisp.
Enrollment (%)	100.0	74.4	20.9	1.0	0.2	3.5
Drop-out Rate (%)	5.0	4.6	6.5	0.0	0.0	11.1
H.S. Diplomas (#)	446	371	66	6	0	3

Greenbrier SD
#4 School Dr · Greenbrier, AR 72058-9206
Mailing Address: 4 School Dr · Greenbrier, AR 72058-9206
(501) 679-4808 · http://gps.k12.ar.us/
Grade Span: PK-12; **Agency Type:** 1
Schools: 5
  2 Primary; 1 Middle; 1 High; 1 Other Level
  5 Regular; 0 Special Education; 0 Vocational; 0 Alternative
  0 Magnet; 0 Charter; 5 Title I Eligible; 0 School-wide Title I
Students: 2,427 (51.6% male; 48.3% female)
  Individual Education Program: 347 (14.3%);
  English Language Learner: 1 (<0.1%); Migrant: 2 (0.1%)
  Eligible for Free Lunch Program: 658 (27.1%)
  Eligible for Reduced-Price Lunch Program: 259 (10.7%)
Teachers: 167.0 (14.5 to 1)
Librarians/Media Specialists: 5.0 (485.4 to 1)
Guidance Counselors: 5.0 (485.4 to 1)
Current Spending: ($ per student per year):
  Total: $5,980; Instruction: $3,836; Support Services: $1,856
Enrollment, Drop-out Rates and Diploma Recipients by Race/Ethnicity

Category	Total	White	Black	Asian	AIAN	Hisp.
Enrollment (%)	100.0	97.6	0.6	0.2	0.6	1.1
Drop-out Rate (%)	1.1	1.2	0.0	0.0	0.0	0.0
H.S. Diplomas (#)	143	139	0	1	0	3

Vilonia SD
11 Eagle St · Vilonia, AR 72173-0160
Mailing Address: PO Box 160 · Vilonia, AR 72173-0160
(501) 796-2113 · http://www.byers-soft.com/vilonia/
Grade Span: KG-12; **Agency Type:** 1
Schools: 5
  2 Primary; 1 Middle; 1 High; 1 Other Level
  5 Regular; 0 Special Education; 0 Vocational; 0 Alternative
  0 Magnet; 0 Charter; 3 Title I Eligible; 0 School-wide Title I
Students: 2,646 (51.7% male; 48.2% female)
  Individual Education Program: 379 (14.3%);
  English Language Learner: 2 (0.1%); Migrant: 0 (0.0%)
  Eligible for Free Lunch Program: 510 (19.3%)
  Eligible for Reduced-Price Lunch Program: 227 (8.6%)
Teachers: 151.0 (17.5 to 1)
Librarians/Media Specialists: 4.0 (661.5 to 1)
Guidance Counselors: 6.0 (441.0 to 1)
Current Spending: ($ per student per year):
  Total: $5,561; Instruction: $3,563; Support Services: $1,675
Enrollment, Drop-out Rates and Diploma Recipients by Race/Ethnicity

Category	Total	White	Black	Asian	AIAN	Hisp.
Enrollment (%)	100.0	97.5	0.1	0.5	0.4	1.5
Drop-out Rate (%)	2.4	2.5	0.0	0.0	0.0	0.0
H.S. Diplomas (#)	171	164	2	2	0	3

Franklin County

Ozark SD
1609 Walden Dr · Ozark, AR 72949-0135
Mailing Address: PO Box 135 · Ozark, AR 72949-0135
(479) 667-4118
Grade Span: KG-12; **Agency Type:** 1
Schools: 3
  1 Primary; 1 Middle; 1 High; 0 Other Level

  3 Regular; 0 Special Education; 0 Vocational; 0 Alternative
  0 Magnet; 0 Charter; 2 Title I Eligible; 0 School-wide Title I
Students: 1,576 (51.5% male; 48.4% female)
  Individual Education Program: 166 (10.5%);
  English Language Learner: 8 (0.5%); Migrant: 19 (1.2%)
  Eligible for Free Lunch Program: 502 (31.9%)
  Eligible for Reduced-Price Lunch Program: 138 (8.8%)
Teachers: 108.0 (14.6 to 1)
Librarians/Media Specialists: 3.0 (525.3 to 1)
Guidance Counselors: 4.0 (394.0 to 1)
Current Spending: ($ per student per year):
  Total: $5,573; Instruction: $3,483; Support Services: $1,830
Enrollment, Drop-out Rates and Diploma Recipients by Race/Ethnicity

Category	Total	White	Black	Asian	AIAN	Hisp.
Enrollment (%)	100.0	96.0	0.5	0.9	1.1	1.5
Drop-out Rate (%)	6.2	5.5	14.3	0.0	50.0	33.3
H.S. Diplomas (#)	138	124	10	0	2	2

Garland County

Hot Springs SD
400 Linwood Ave · Hot Springs, AR 71913
(501) 624-3372 · http://hsprings.dsc.k12.ar.us/
Grade Span: PK-12; **Agency Type:** 1
Schools: 6
  4 Primary; 0 Middle; 1 High; 1 Other Level
  6 Regular; 0 Special Education; 0 Vocational; 0 Alternative
  0 Magnet; 0 Charter; 5 Title I Eligible; 5 School-wide Title I
Students: 3,593 (51.2% male; 48.7% female)
  Individual Education Program: 508 (14.1%);
  English Language Learner: 234 (6.5%); Migrant: 3 (0.1%)
  Eligible for Free Lunch Program: 2,239 (62.3%)
  Eligible for Reduced-Price Lunch Program: 304 (8.5%)
Teachers: 258.0 (13.9 to 1)
Librarians/Media Specialists: 6.0 (598.8 to 1)
Guidance Counselors: 9.0 (399.2 to 1)
Current Spending: ($ per student per year):
  Total: $7,803; Instruction: $4,883; Support Services: $2,543
Enrollment, Drop-out Rates and Diploma Recipients by Race/Ethnicity

Category	Total	White	Black	Asian	AIAN	Hisp.
Enrollment (%)	100.0	49.5	41.3	1.4	0.6	7.2
Drop-out Rate (%)	5.3	5.6	5.5	0.0	0.0	2.8
H.S. Diplomas (#)	152	78	66	4	0	4

Lake Hamilton SD
205 Wolf St · Pearcy, AR 71964
(501) 767-2306 · http://wolves.dsc.k12.ar.us/
Grade Span: KG-12; **Agency Type:** 1
Schools: 6
  2 Primary; 2 Middle; 1 High; 1 Other Level
  6 Regular; 0 Special Education; 0 Vocational; 0 Alternative
  0 Magnet; 0 Charter; 3 Title I Eligible; 0 School-wide Title I
Students: 3,803 (53.3% male; 46.7% female)
  Individual Education Program: 479 (12.6%);
  English Language Learner: 41 (1.1%); Migrant: 0 (0.0%)
  Eligible for Free Lunch Program: 915 (24.1%)
  Eligible for Reduced-Price Lunch Program: 378 (9.9%)
Teachers: 208.0 (18.3 to 1)
Librarians/Media Specialists: 6.0 (633.8 to 1)
Guidance Counselors: 13.0 (292.5 to 1)
Current Spending: ($ per student per year):
  Total: $5,862; Instruction: $3,436; Support Services: $1,979
Enrollment, Drop-out Rates and Diploma Recipients by Race/Ethnicity

Category	Total	White	Black	Asian	AIAN	Hisp.
Enrollment (%)	100.0	93.8	2.7	1.0	0.0	2.5
Drop-out Rate (%)	0.4	0.5	0.0	0.0	n/a	0.0
H.S. Diplomas (#)	212	202	5	3	0	2

Lakeside SD
2837 Malvern Ave · Hot Springs, AR 71901-8321
(501) 262-1880 · http://se.sesc.k12.ar.us/lakeside/
Grade Span: KG-12; **Agency Type:** 1
Schools: 5
  2 Primary; 1 Middle; 1 High; 1 Other Level
  5 Regular; 0 Special Education; 0 Vocational; 0 Alternative
  0 Magnet; 0 Charter; 5 Title I Eligible; 0 School-wide Title I
Students: 2,530 (50.4% male; 49.5% female)
  Individual Education Program: 282 (11.1%);
  English Language Learner: 121 (4.8%); Migrant: 1 (<0.1%)
  Eligible for Free Lunch Program: 491 (19.4%)
  Eligible for Reduced-Price Lunch Program: 125 (4.9%)
Teachers: 159.0 (15.9 to 1)
Librarians/Media Specialists: 5.0 (506.0 to 1)
Guidance Counselors: 5.0 (506.0 to 1)
Current Spending: ($ per student per year):
  Total: $5,969; Instruction: $3,675; Support Services: $2,068

Enrollment, Drop-out Rates and Diploma Recipients by Race/Ethnicity

Category	Total	White	Black	Asian	AIAN	Hisp.
Enrollment (%)	100.0	90.7	4.4	1.5	0.5	2.8
Drop-out Rate (%)	2.6	2.8	0.0	0.0	0.0	0.0
H.S. Diplomas (#)	155	140	11	1	1	2

Grant County

Sheridan SD
400 N Rock • Sheridan, AR 72150-2228
(870) 942-3135 • http://jackets.arsc.k12.ar.us/
Grade Span: KG-12; **Agency Type:** 1
Schools: 6
  2 Primary; 3 Middle; 1 High; 0 Other Level
  6 Regular; 0 Special Education; 0 Vocational; 0 Alternative
  0 Magnet; 0 Charter; 6 Title I Eligible; 0 School-wide Title I
Students: 4,164   (51.4% male; 48.5% female)
  Individual Education Program: 514 (12.3%);
  English Language Learner: 48 (1.2%); Migrant: 1 (<0.1%)
  Eligible for Free Lunch Program: 987 (23.7%)
  Eligible for Reduced-Price Lunch Program: 493 (11.8%)
Teachers: 261.0 (16.0 to 1)
Librarians/Media Specialists: 6.0 (694.0 to 1)
Guidance Counselors: 10.0 (416.4 to 1)
Current Spending: ($ per student per year):
  Total: $5,633; Instruction: $3,570; Support Services: $1,750

Enrollment, Drop-out Rates and Diploma Recipients by Race/Ethnicity

Category	Total	White	Black	Asian	AIAN	Hisp.
Enrollment (%)	100.0	96.0	1.8	0.9	0.1	1.2
Drop-out Rate (%)	4.8	4.8	3.3	0.0	0.0	0.0
H.S. Diplomas (#)	246	238	5	2	1	0

Greene County

Greene County Tech SD
5413 W Kingshighway • Paragould, AR 72450-3368
(870) 236-2762 • http://gctsd.nesc.k12.ar.us/
Grade Span: KG-12; **Agency Type:** 1
Schools: 4
  1 Primary; 2 Middle; 1 High; 0 Other Level
  4 Regular; 0 Special Education; 0 Vocational; 0 Alternative
  0 Magnet; 0 Charter; 4 Title I Eligible; 0 School-wide Title I
Students: 2,936   (52.3% male; 47.6% female)
  Individual Education Program: 443 (15.1%);
  English Language Learner: 18 (0.6%); Migrant: 18 (0.6%)
  Eligible for Free Lunch Program: 901 (30.7%)
  Eligible for Reduced-Price Lunch Program: 283 (9.6%)
Teachers: 180.0 (16.3 to 1)
Librarians/Media Specialists: 4.0 (734.0 to 1)
Guidance Counselors: 7.0 (419.4 to 1)
Current Spending: ($ per student per year):
  Total: $5,488; Instruction: $3,374; Support Services: $1,791

Enrollment, Drop-out Rates and Diploma Recipients by Race/Ethnicity

Category	Total	White	Black	Asian	AIAN	Hisp.
Enrollment (%)	100.0	98.9	0.5	0.1	0.0	0.5
Drop-out Rate (%)	3.9	3.8	0.0	0.0	n/a	16.7
H.S. Diplomas (#)	154	151	0	0	0	3

Paragould SD
631 W Court St • Paragould, AR 72450-4248
(870) 239-2105 • http://rams.nesd.k12.ar.us/
Grade Span: KG-12; **Agency Type:** 1
Schools: 6
  3 Primary; 2 Middle; 1 High; 0 Other Level
  6 Regular; 0 Special Education; 0 Vocational; 0 Alternative
  0 Magnet; 0 Charter; 4 Title I Eligible; 4 School-wide Title I
Students: 2,675   (51.5% male; 48.4% female)
  Individual Education Program: 476 (17.8%);
  English Language Learner: 6 (0.2%); Migrant: 19 (0.7%)
  Eligible for Free Lunch Program: 1,090 (40.7%)
  Eligible for Reduced-Price Lunch Program: 272 (10.2%)
Teachers: 173.0 (15.5 to 1)
Librarians/Media Specialists: 6.0 (445.8 to 1)
Guidance Counselors: 7.0 (382.1 to 1)
Current Spending: ($ per student per year):
  Total: $6,281; Instruction: $4,064; Support Services: $1,909

Enrollment, Drop-out Rates and Diploma Recipients by Race/Ethnicity

Category	Total	White	Black	Asian	AIAN	Hisp.
Enrollment (%)	100.0	97.2	1.0	0.2	0.1	1.5
Drop-out Rate (%)	5.9	5.8	0.0	n/a	0.0	11.8
H.S. Diplomas (#)	132	129	0	0	0	3

Hempstead County

Hope SD
117 E Second • Hope, AR 71801-4402
Mailing Address: 117 E Second St • Hope, AR 71801-4402
(870) 722-2700 • http://hhs.swsc.k12.ar.us/
Grade Span: PK-12; **Agency Type:** 1
Schools: 5
  1 Primary; 2 Middle; 2 High; 0 Other Level
  5 Regular; 0 Special Education; 0 Vocational; 0 Alternative
  0 Magnet; 0 Charter; 5 Title I Eligible; 0 School-wide Title I
Students: 2,750   (50.9% male; 49.0% female)
  Individual Education Program: 288 (10.5%);
  English Language Learner: 217 (7.9%); Migrant: 144 (5.2%)
  Eligible for Free Lunch Program: 1,606 (58.4%)
  Eligible for Reduced-Price Lunch Program: 138 (5.0%)
Teachers: 193.0 (14.2 to 1)
Librarians/Media Specialists: 5.0 (550.0 to 1)
Guidance Counselors: 7.0 (392.9 to 1)
Current Spending: ($ per student per year):
  Total: $6,377; Instruction: $4,151; Support Services: $1,887

Enrollment, Drop-out Rates and Diploma Recipients by Race/Ethnicity

Category	Total	White	Black	Asian	AIAN	Hisp.
Enrollment (%)	100.0	34.1	50.7	0.3	0.2	14.7
Drop-out Rate (%)	5.4	2.9	6.5	25.0	0.0	10.3
H.S. Diplomas (#)	178	73	91	1	0	13

Hot Spring County

Malvern SD
1517 S Main St • Malvern, AR 72104-5231
(501) 332-7500 • http://malvern.dsc.k12.ar.us/
Grade Span: KG-12; **Agency Type:** 1
Schools: 4
  1 Primary; 2 Middle; 1 High; 0 Other Level
  4 Regular; 0 Special Education; 0 Vocational; 0 Alternative
  0 Magnet; 0 Charter; 3 Title I Eligible; 0 School-wide Title I
Students: 2,183   (50.4% male; 49.5% female)
  Individual Education Program: 274 (12.6%);
  English Language Learner: 5 (0.2%); Migrant: 1 (<0.1%)
  Eligible for Free Lunch Program: 974 (44.6%)
  Eligible for Reduced-Price Lunch Program: 245 (11.2%)
Teachers: 146.0 (15.0 to 1)
Librarians/Media Specialists: 6.0 (363.8 to 1)
Guidance Counselors: 6.0 (363.8 to 1)
Current Spending: ($ per student per year):
  Total: $6,090; Instruction: $3,831; Support Services: $1,932

Enrollment, Drop-out Rates and Diploma Recipients by Race/Ethnicity

Category	Total	White	Black	Asian	AIAN	Hisp.
Enrollment (%)	100.0	65.3	31.9	0.5	0.2	2.2
Drop-out Rate (%)	5.6	4.3	5.5	0.0	75.0	42.9
H.S. Diplomas (#)	139	93	43	1	0	2

Howard County

Nashville SD
600 N Fourth St • Nashville, AR 71852-3911
Mailing Address: 600 N Fourth • Nashville, AR 71852-3911
(870) 845-3425 • http://nsd.dmsc.k12.ar.us/
Grade Span: KG-12; **Agency Type:** 1
Schools: 4
  1 Primary; 2 Middle; 1 High; 0 Other Level
  4 Regular; 0 Special Education; 0 Vocational; 0 Alternative
  0 Magnet; 0 Charter; 3 Title I Eligible; 2 School-wide Title I
Students: 1,815   (51.1% male; 48.8% female)
  Individual Education Program: 221 (12.2%);
  English Language Learner: 71 (3.9%); Migrant: 81 (4.5%)
  Eligible for Free Lunch Program: 769 (42.4%)
  Eligible for Reduced-Price Lunch Program: 168 (9.3%)
Teachers: 135.0 (13.4 to 1)
Librarians/Media Specialists: 4.0 (453.8 to 1)
Guidance Counselors: 5.0 (363.0 to 1)
Current Spending: ($ per student per year):
  Total: $5,879; Instruction: $3,796; Support Services: $1,736

Enrollment, Drop-out Rates and Diploma Recipients by Race/Ethnicity

Category	Total	White	Black	Asian	AIAN	Hisp.
Enrollment (%)	100.0	63.7	26.0	0.8	0.2	9.3
Drop-out Rate (%)	5.2	4.3	6.3	0.0	0.0	14.3
H.S. Diplomas (#)	105	70	29	0	2	4

Independence County

Batesville SD
330 E College • Batesville, AR 72501-5624
(870) 793-6831 • http://bsd.ncsc.k12.ar.us/
Grade Span: KG-12; **Agency Type:** 1
Schools: 7
　4 Primary; 2 Middle; 1 High; 0 Other Level
　7 Regular; 0 Special Education; 0 Vocational; 0 Alternative
　0 Magnet; 0 Charter; 4 Title I Eligible; 4 School-wide Title I
Students: 2,196　(52.6% male; 47.3% female)
　Individual Education Program: 379 (17.3%);
　English Language Learner: 106 (4.8%); Migrant: 179 (8.2%)
　Eligible for Free Lunch Program: 818 (37.2%)
　Eligible for Reduced-Price Lunch Program: 196 (8.9%)
Teachers: 145.0 (15.1 to 1)
Librarians/Media Specialists: 6.0 (366.0 to 1)
Guidance Counselors: 7.0 (313.7 to 1)
Current Spending: ($ per student per year):
　Total: $6,206; Instruction: $3,806; Support Services: $2,022
Enrollment, Drop-out Rates and Diploma Recipients by Race/Ethnicity

Category	Total	White	Black	Asian	AIAN	Hisp.
Enrollment (%)	100.0	82.3	8.8	1.9	0.3	6.6
Drop-out Rate (%)	4.6	4.6	2.2	0.0	0.0	25.0
H.S. Diplomas (#)	129	121	7	0	1	0

Jackson County

Newport SD
406 Wilkerson Dr • Newport, AR 72112-3949
(870) 523-1312 • http://newport.crsc.k12.ar.us/1024/Index.htm
Grade Span: KG-12; **Agency Type:** 1
Schools: 4
　1 Primary; 2 Middle; 1 High; 0 Other Level
　4 Regular; 0 Special Education; 0 Vocational; 0 Alternative
　0 Magnet; 0 Charter; 3 Title I Eligible; 3 School-wide Title I
Students: 1,609　(52.0% male; 47.9% female)
　Individual Education Program: 231 (14.4%);
　English Language Learner: 16 (1.0%); Migrant: 27 (1.7%)
　Eligible for Free Lunch Program: 859 (53.4%)
　Eligible for Reduced-Price Lunch Program: 182 (11.3%)
Teachers: 132.0 (12.2 to 1)
Librarians/Media Specialists: 3.0 (536.3 to 1)
Guidance Counselors: 4.0 (402.3 to 1)
Current Spending: ($ per student per year):
　Total: $7,101; Instruction: $4,322; Support Services: $2,380
Enrollment, Drop-out Rates and Diploma Recipients by Race/Ethnicity

Category	Total	White	Black	Asian	AIAN	Hisp.
Enrollment (%)	100.0	62.8	34.8	0.7	0.1	1.7
Drop-out Rate (%)	9.3	6.8	12.1	n/a	33.3	100.0
H.S. Diplomas (#)	120	67	52	0	1	0

Jefferson County

Dollarway SD
4900 Dollarway Rd • Pine Bluff, AR 71602-4006
(870) 534-7003 • http://www.dollarway.org/
Grade Span: KG-12; **Agency Type:** 1
Schools: 5
　2 Primary; 2 Middle; 1 High; 0 Other Level
　5 Regular; 0 Special Education; 0 Vocational; 0 Alternative
　0 Magnet; 0 Charter; 4 Title I Eligible; 4 School-wide Title I
Students: 1,543　(51.9% male; 48.0% female)
　Individual Education Program: 202 (13.1%);
　English Language Learner: 0 (0.0%); Migrant: 0 (0.0%)
　Eligible for Free Lunch Program: 1,212 (78.5%)
　Eligible for Reduced-Price Lunch Program: 149 (9.7%)
Teachers: 115.0 (13.4 to 1)
Librarians/Media Specialists: 4.0 (385.8 to 1)
Guidance Counselors: 5.0 (308.6 to 1)
Current Spending: ($ per student per year):
　Total: $6,847; Instruction: $4,014; Support Services: $2,393
Enrollment, Drop-out Rates and Diploma Recipients by Race/Ethnicity

Category	Total	White	Black	Asian	AIAN	Hisp.
Enrollment (%)	100.0	12.4	87.5	0.0	0.0	0.1
Drop-out Rate (%)	5.2	8.1	4.8	n/a	n/a	0.0
H.S. Diplomas (#)	96	14	82	0	0	0

Pine Bluff SD
1215 W Pullen • Pine Bluff, AR 71601
(870) 543-4200 • http://pbweb.arsc.k12.ar.us/
Grade Span: KG-12; **Agency Type:** 1
Schools: 14
　7 Primary; 5 Middle; 1 High; 1 Other Level
　14 Regular; 0 Special Education; 0 Vocational; 0 Alternative

0 Magnet; 0 Charter; 11 Title I Eligible; 11 School-wide Title I
Students: 5,964　(50.3% male; 49.6% female)
　Individual Education Program: 688 (11.5%);
　English Language Learner: 5 (0.1%); Migrant: 1 (<0.1%)
　Eligible for Free Lunch Program: 3,616 (60.6%)
　Eligible for Reduced-Price Lunch Program: 372 (6.2%)
Teachers: 367.0 (16.3 to 1)
Librarians/Media Specialists: 12.0 (497.0 to 1)
Guidance Counselors: 14.0 (426.0 to 1)
Current Spending: ($ per student per year):
　Total: $6,324; Instruction: $3,918; Support Services: $2,119
Enrollment, Drop-out Rates and Diploma Recipients by Race/Ethnicity

Category	Total	White	Black	Asian	AIAN	Hisp.
Enrollment (%)	100.0	5.0	94.4	0.3	0.0	0.3
Drop-out Rate (%)	9.9	7.7	10.1	0.0	n/a	25.0
H.S. Diplomas (#)	319	47	268	2	0	2

Watson Chapel SD
4100 Camden Rd • Pine Bluff, AR 71603-9096
(870) 879-0220 • http://watson2.arsc.k12.ar.us/
Grade Span: KG-12; **Agency Type:** 1
Schools: 5
　2 Primary; 2 Middle; 1 High; 0 Other Level
　5 Regular; 0 Special Education; 0 Vocational; 0 Alternative
　0 Magnet; 0 Charter; 4 Title I Eligible; 3 School-wide Title I
Students: 3,136　(50.9% male; 49.0% female)
　Individual Education Program: 321 (10.2%);
　English Language Learner: 1 (<0.1%); Migrant: 0 (0.0%)
　Eligible for Free Lunch Program: 1,423 (45.4%)
　Eligible for Reduced-Price Lunch Program: 210 (6.7%)
Teachers: 185.0 (17.0 to 1)
Librarians/Media Specialists: 5.0 (627.2 to 1)
Guidance Counselors: 8.0 (392.0 to 1)
Current Spending: ($ per student per year):
　Total: $5,705; Instruction: $3,736; Support Services: $1,710
Enrollment, Drop-out Rates and Diploma Recipients by Race/Ethnicity

Category	Total	White	Black	Asian	AIAN	Hisp.
Enrollment (%)	100.0	40.7	58.6	0.4	0.0	0.4
Drop-out Rate (%)	2.4	1.5	2.9	n/a	n/a	n/a
H.S. Diplomas (#)	225	106	118	0	0	1

White Hall SD
1020 W Holland Ave • White Hall, AR 71602-9572
(870) 247-2002 • http://pinebluff.dina.org/education/whpublic.html
Grade Span: KG-12; **Agency Type:** 1
Schools: 7
　4 Primary; 2 Middle; 1 High; 0 Other Level
　7 Regular; 0 Special Education; 0 Vocational; 0 Alternative
　0 Magnet; 0 Charter; 4 Title I Eligible; 0 School-wide Title I
Students: 3,053　(50.7% male; 49.2% female)
　Individual Education Program: 289 (9.5%);
　English Language Learner: 24 (0.8%); Migrant: 0 (0.0%)
　Eligible for Free Lunch Program: 635 (20.8%)
　Eligible for Reduced-Price Lunch Program: 212 (6.9%)
Teachers: 189.0 (16.2 to 1)
Librarians/Media Specialists: 7.0 (436.1 to 1)
Guidance Counselors: 7.0 (436.1 to 1)
Current Spending: ($ per student per year):
　Total: $5,549; Instruction: $3,468; Support Services: $1,797
Enrollment, Drop-out Rates and Diploma Recipients by Race/Ethnicity

Category	Total	White	Black	Asian	AIAN	Hisp.
Enrollment (%)	100.0	90.1	7.2	1.2	0.3	1.2
Drop-out Rate (%)	1.8	1.7	1.6	7.1	0.0	0.0
H.S. Diplomas (#)	184	162	14	4	1	3

Johnson County

Clarksville SD
1701 Clark Rd • Clarksville, AR 72830-3915
(479) 705-3200 • http://panthernet.wsc.k12.ar.us/
Grade Span: KG-12; **Agency Type:** 1
Schools: 5
　2 Primary; 2 Middle; 1 High; 0 Other Level
　5 Regular; 0 Special Education; 0 Vocational; 0 Alternative
　0 Magnet; 0 Charter; 4 Title I Eligible; 0 School-wide Title I
Students: 2,246　(50.6% male; 49.3% female)
　Individual Education Program: 238 (10.6%);
　English Language Learner: 317 (14.1%); Migrant: 240 (10.7%)
　Eligible for Free Lunch Program: 979 (43.6%)
　Eligible for Reduced-Price Lunch Program: 228 (10.2%)
Teachers: 143.0 (15.7 to 1)
Librarians/Media Specialists: 5.0 (449.2 to 1)
Guidance Counselors: 5.0 (449.2 to 1)
Current Spending: ($ per student per year):
　Total: $5,560; Instruction: $3,595; Support Services: $1,658

Enrollment, Drop-out Rates and Diploma Recipients by Race/Ethnicity

Category	Total	White	Black	Asian	AIAN	Hisp.
Enrollment (%)	100.0	78.0	3.8	0.4	0.2	17.7
Drop-out Rate (%)	7.3	8.0	3.0	0.0	0.0	4.8
H.S. Diplomas (#)	102	85	4	1	0	12

Lee County

Lee County SD
188 W Chestnut St • Marianna, AR 72360-2002
(870) 295-7100 • http://lcsd1.grsc.k12.ar.us/
Grade Span: KG-12; **Agency Type:** 1
Schools: 4
    2 Primary; 1 Middle; 1 High; 0 Other Level
    4 Regular; 0 Special Education; 0 Vocational; 0 Alternative
    0 Magnet; 0 Charter; 0 Title I Eligible; 0 School-wide Title I
Students: 1,569   (49.5% male; 50.4% female)
    Individual Education Program: 215 (13.7%);
    English Language Learner: 0 (0.0%); Migrant: 0 (0.0%)
    Eligible for Free Lunch Program: 1,370 (87.3%)
    Eligible for Reduced-Price Lunch Program: 92 (5.9%)
Teachers: 102.0 (15.4 to 1)
Librarians/Media Specialists: 4.0 (392.3 to 1)
Guidance Counselors: 4.0 (392.3 to 1)
Current Spending: ($ per student per year):
    Total: $7,654; Instruction: $4,070; Support Services: $3,206
Enrollment, Drop-out Rates and Diploma Recipients by Race/Ethnicity

Category	Total	White	Black	Asian	AIAN	Hisp.
Enrollment (%)	100.0	9.8	88.9	0.0	0.1	1.3
Drop-out Rate (%)	9.2	16.2	8.8	n/a	n/a	0.0
H.S. Diplomas (#)	117	2	115	0	0	0

Lincoln County

Star City SD
206 Cleveland St • Star City, AR 71667-5218
(870) 628-4237 • http://se.sesc.k12.ar.us/starcity/
Grade Span: KG-12; **Agency Type:** 1
Schools: 3
    1 Primary; 1 Middle; 1 High; 0 Other Level
    3 Regular; 0 Special Education; 0 Vocational; 0 Alternative
    0 Magnet; 0 Charter; 2 Title I Eligible; 2 School-wide Title I
Students: 1,578   (52.3% male; 47.6% female)
    Individual Education Program: 201 (12.7%);
    English Language Learner: 34 (2.2%); Migrant: 21 (1.3%)
    Eligible for Free Lunch Program: 614 (38.9%)
    Eligible for Reduced-Price Lunch Program: 139 (8.8%)
Teachers: 101.0 (15.6 to 1)
Librarians/Media Specialists: 3.0 (526.0 to 1)
Guidance Counselors: 4.0 (394.5 to 1)
Current Spending: ($ per student per year):
    Total: $5,507; Instruction: $3,531; Support Services: $1,698
Enrollment, Drop-out Rates and Diploma Recipients by Race/Ethnicity

Category	Total	White	Black	Asian	AIAN	Hisp.
Enrollment (%)	100.0	79.4	18.1	0.0	0.1	2.5
Drop-out Rate (%)	8.3	8.6	7.5	n/a	0.0	0.0
H.S. Diplomas (#)	90	69	20	0	0	1

Little River County

Ashdown SD
511 N Second • Ashdown, AR 71822-2706
(870) 898-3208 • http://nexus.dmsc.k12.ar.us/schools/ashdown.htm
Grade Span: KG-12; **Agency Type:** 1
Schools: 5
    2 Primary; 2 Middle; 1 High; 0 Other Level
    5 Regular; 0 Special Education; 0 Vocational; 0 Alternative
    0 Magnet; 0 Charter; 2 Title I Eligible; 1 School-wide Title I
Students: 1,656   (52.0% male; 47.9% female)
    Individual Education Program: 196 (11.8%);
    English Language Learner: 1 (0.1%); Migrant: 0 (0.0%)
    Eligible for Free Lunch Program: 618 (37.3%)
    Eligible for Reduced-Price Lunch Program: 174 (10.5%)
Teachers: 122.0 (13.6 to 1)
Librarians/Media Specialists: 5.0 (331.2 to 1)
Guidance Counselors: 5.0 (331.2 to 1)
Current Spending: ($ per student per year):
    Total: $6,311; Instruction: $3,717; Support Services: $2,290
Enrollment, Drop-out Rates and Diploma Recipients by Race/Ethnicity

Category	Total	White	Black	Asian	AIAN	Hisp.
Enrollment (%)	100.0	65.9	31.4	0.2	1.2	1.2
Drop-out Rate (%)	5.2	5.2	6.1	0.0	0.0	0.0
H.S. Diplomas (#)	100	71	27	0	0	2

Lonoke County

Cabot SD
602 No Lincoln • Cabot, AR 72023-2540
(501) 843-3363 • http://cabot.wmsc.k12.ar.us/
Grade Span: KG-12; **Agency Type:** 1
Schools: 12
    7 Primary; 4 Middle; 1 High; 0 Other Level
    12 Regular; 0 Special Education; 0 Vocational; 0 Alternative
    0 Magnet; 0 Charter; 11 Title I Eligible; 2 School-wide Title I
Students: 7,773   (51.3% male; 48.6% female)
    Individual Education Program: 1,114 (14.3%);
    English Language Learner: 38 (0.5%); Migrant: 31 (0.4%)
    Eligible for Free Lunch Program: 1,778 (22.9%)
    Eligible for Reduced-Price Lunch Program: 534 (6.9%)
Teachers: 480.0 (16.2 to 1)
Librarians/Media Specialists: 12.0 (647.8 to 1)
Guidance Counselors: 19.0 (409.1 to 1)
Current Spending: ($ per student per year):
    Total: $5,742; Instruction: $3,670; Support Services: $1,850
Enrollment, Drop-out Rates and Diploma Recipients by Race/Ethnicity

Category	Total	White	Black	Asian	AIAN	Hisp.
Enrollment (%)	100.0	96.2	0.7	0.9	0.5	1.7
Drop-out Rate (%)	4.7	4.6	28.6	7.1	0.0	5.3
H.S. Diplomas (#)	450	440	0	5	1	4

Lonoke SD
401 W Holly St • Lonoke, AR 72086-0740
Mailing Address: PO Box 740 • Lonoke, AR 72086-0740
(501) 676-2042 • http://170.211.188.150/
Grade Span: KG-12; **Agency Type:** 1
Schools: 4
    2 Primary; 1 Middle; 1 High; 0 Other Level
    4 Regular; 0 Special Education; 0 Vocational; 0 Alternative
    0 Magnet; 0 Charter; 4 Title I Eligible; 0 School-wide Title I
Students: 1,781   (52.1% male; 47.8% female)
    Individual Education Program: 271 (15.2%);
    English Language Learner: 53 (3.0%); Migrant: 31 (1.7%)
    Eligible for Free Lunch Program: 683 (38.3%)
    Eligible for Reduced-Price Lunch Program: 166 (9.3%)
Teachers: 114.0 (15.6 to 1)
Librarians/Media Specialists: 4.0 (445.3 to 1)
Guidance Counselors: 4.0 (445.3 to 1)
Current Spending: ($ per student per year):
    Total: $5,841; Instruction: $3,413; Support Services: $2,054
Enrollment, Drop-out Rates and Diploma Recipients by Race/Ethnicity

Category	Total	White	Black	Asian	AIAN	Hisp.
Enrollment (%)	100.0	74.8	21.3	0.4	0.2	3.4
Drop-out Rate (%)	3.0	2.9	3.8	0.0	0.0	0.0
H.S. Diplomas (#)	104	75	29	0	0	0

Madison County

Huntsville SD
570 W Main • Huntsville, AR 72740-0160
Mailing Address: PO Drawer F • Huntsville, AR 72740-0160
(479) 738-2011 • http://eagle.nwsc.k12.ar.us/
Grade Span: KG-12; **Agency Type:** 1
Schools: 4
    2 Primary; 1 Middle; 1 High; 0 Other Level
    4 Regular; 0 Special Education; 0 Vocational; 0 Alternative
    0 Magnet; 0 Charter; 4 Title I Eligible; 0 School-wide Title I
Students: 2,128   (52.1% male; 47.8% female)
    Individual Education Program: 301 (14.1%);
    English Language Learner: 81 (3.8%); Migrant: 93 (4.4%)
    Eligible for Free Lunch Program: 730 (34.3%)
    Eligible for Reduced-Price Lunch Program: 151 (7.1%)
Teachers: 134.0 (15.9 to 1)
Librarians/Media Specialists: 4.0 (532.0 to 1)
Guidance Counselors: 5.0 (425.6 to 1)
Current Spending: ($ per student per year):
    Total: $5,825; Instruction: $3,563; Support Services: $1,953
Enrollment, Drop-out Rates and Diploma Recipients by Race/Ethnicity

Category	Total	White	Black	Asian	AIAN	Hisp.
Enrollment (%)	100.0	93.0	0.3	0.8	0.6	5.4
Drop-out Rate (%)	5.5	5.7	0.0	n/a	0.0	0.0
H.S. Diplomas (#)	123	118	0	1	1	3

Miller County

Texarkana SD
3512 Grand Ave • Texarkana, AR 71854
(870) 772-3371 • http://darkstar.swsc.k12.ar.us/
Grade Span: KG-12; **Agency Type:** 1
Schools: 9

5 Primary; 2 Middle; 2 High; 0 Other Level
8 Regular; 0 Special Education; 1 Vocational; 0 Alternative
0 Magnet; 0 Charter; 8 Title I Eligible; 8 School-wide Title I
Students: 4,438 (53.3% male; 46.6% female)
Individual Education Program: 733 (16.5%);
English Language Learner: 41 (0.9%); Migrant: 6 (0.1%)
Eligible for Free Lunch Program: 2,329 (52.5%)
Eligible for Reduced-Price Lunch Program: 332 (7.5%)
Teachers: 299.0 (14.8 to 1)
Librarians/Media Specialists: 7.0 (634.0 to 1)
Guidance Counselors: 14.0 (317.0 to 1)
Current Spending: ($ per student per year):
Total: $6,437; Instruction: $4,081; Support Services: $1,996
Enrollment, Drop-out Rates and Diploma Recipients by Race/Ethnicity

Category	Total	White	Black	Asian	AIAN	Hisp.
Enrollment (%)	100.0	49.5	48.1	0.3	0.2	1.9
Drop-out Rate (%)	4.9	4.8	4.8	0.0	0.0	18.2
H.S. Diplomas (#)	217	106	109	1	0	1

Mississippi County

Blytheville SD
405 W Park St • Blytheville, AR 72315
Mailing Address: PO Box 1169 • Blytheville, AR 72316-1169
(870) 762-2053 • http://crowleys.crsc.k12.ar.us/~blythev/
Grade Span: KG-12; **Agency Type:** 1
Schools: 7
3 Primary; 2 Middle; 2 High; 0 Other Level
7 Regular; 0 Special Education; 0 Vocational; 0 Alternative
0 Magnet; 1 Charter; 7 Title I Eligible; 7 School-wide Title I
Students: 3,290 (49.3% male; 50.6% female)
Individual Education Program: 493 (15.0%);
English Language Learner: 11 (0.3%); Migrant: 30 (0.9%)
Eligible for Free Lunch Program: 3,269 (99.4%)
Eligible for Reduced-Price Lunch Program: 0 (0.0%)
Teachers: 229.0 (14.4 to 1)
Librarians/Media Specialists: 6.0 (548.3 to 1)
Guidance Counselors: 9.0 (365.6 to 1)
Current Spending: ($ per student per year):
Total: $6,430; Instruction: $3,795; Support Services: $2,284
Enrollment, Drop-out Rates and Diploma Recipients by Race/Ethnicity

Category	Total	White	Black	Asian	AIAN	Hisp.
Enrollment (%)	100.0	23.3	75.0	0.3	0.1	1.3
Drop-out Rate (%)	8.5	6.9	9.1	0.0	n/a	0.0
H.S. Diplomas (#)	163	48	112	1	0	2

Osceola SD
2750 W Semmes • Osceola, AR 72370-0628
(870) 563-2561 • http://crowleys.crsc.k12.ar.us/~osceola/
Grade Span: PK-12; **Agency Type:** 1
Schools: 6
2 Primary; 3 Middle; 1 High; 0 Other Level
6 Regular; 0 Special Education; 0 Vocational; 0 Alternative
0 Magnet; 1 Charter; 6 Title I Eligible; 5 School-wide Title I
Students: 1,675 (54.6% male; 45.3% female)
Individual Education Program: 279 (16.7%);
English Language Learner: 3 (0.2%); Migrant: 6 (0.4%)
Eligible for Free Lunch Program: 1,626 (97.1%)
Eligible for Reduced-Price Lunch Program: 0 (0.0%)
Teachers: 130.0 (12.9 to 1)
Librarians/Media Specialists: 5.0 (335.0 to 1)
Guidance Counselors: 5.0 (335.0 to 1)
Current Spending: ($ per student per year):
Total: $6,271; Instruction: $4,007; Support Services: $1,836
Enrollment, Drop-out Rates and Diploma Recipients by Race/Ethnicity

Category	Total	White	Black	Asian	AIAN	Hisp.
Enrollment (%)	100.0	25.7	73.6	0.1	0.1	0.5
Drop-out Rate (%)	7.7	7.5	7.6	0.0	n/a	20.0
H.S. Diplomas (#)	124	34	90	0	0	0

Ouachita County

Camden Fairview SD
625 Clifton St • Camden, AR 71701-3327
(870) 836-4193 • http://cfpsd.scsc.k12.ar.us/
Grade Span: KG-12; **Agency Type:** 1
Schools: 7
3 Primary; 2 Middle; 1 High; 1 Other Level
6 Regular; 0 Special Education; 0 Vocational; 1 Alternative
0 Magnet; 0 Charter; 4 Title I Eligible; 1 School-wide Title I
Students: 3,023 (50.4% male; 49.5% female)
Individual Education Program: 332 (11.0%);
English Language Learner: 8 (0.3%); Migrant: 0 (0.0%)
Eligible for Free Lunch Program: 1,638 (54.2%)
Eligible for Reduced-Price Lunch Program: 204 (6.7%)

Teachers: 199.0 (15.2 to 1)
Librarians/Media Specialists: 6.0 (503.8 to 1)
Guidance Counselors: 8.0 (377.9 to 1)
Current Spending: ($ per student per year):
Total: $6,602; Instruction: $3,868; Support Services: $2,346
Enrollment, Drop-out Rates and Diploma Recipients by Race/Ethnicity

Category	Total	White	Black	Asian	AIAN	Hisp.
Enrollment (%)	100.0	37.4	61.6	0.5	0.2	0.4
Drop-out Rate (%)	5.7	4.2	6.8	0.0	0.0	0.0
H.S. Diplomas (#)	230	103	126	0	0	1

Phillips County

Helena/West Helena SD
305 Valley Dr • Helena, AR 72342-0369
Mailing Address: PO Box 369 • Helena, AR 72342-0369
(870) 338-4425 • http://hwh.grsc.k12.ar.us/
Grade Span: KG-12; **Agency Type:** 1
Schools: 6
4 Primary; 0 Middle; 1 High; 1 Other Level
6 Regular; 0 Special Education; 0 Vocational; 0 Alternative
0 Magnet; 0 Charter; 6 Title I Eligible; 6 School-wide Title I
Students: 3,216 (50.4% male; 49.5% female)
Individual Education Program: 417 (13.0%);
English Language Learner: 1 (<0.1%); Migrant: 0 (0.0%)
Eligible for Free Lunch Program: 2,278 (70.8%)
Eligible for Reduced-Price Lunch Program: 213 (6.6%)
Teachers: 243.0 (13.2 to 1)
Librarians/Media Specialists: 7.0 (459.4 to 1)
Guidance Counselors: 8.0 (402.0 to 1)
Current Spending: ($ per student per year):
Total: $7,262; Instruction: $4,315; Support Services: $2,507
Enrollment, Drop-out Rates and Diploma Recipients by Race/Ethnicity

Category	Total	White	Black	Asian	AIAN	Hisp.
Enrollment (%)	100.0	6.6	92.8	0.3	0.0	0.3
Drop-out Rate (%)	10.7	21.0	10.0	0.0	0.0	0.0
H.S. Diplomas (#)	183	9	171	0	1	2

Poinsett County

Trumann SD
221 Pine Ave • Trumann, AR 72472-2700
(870) 483-6444 • http://wildcat.crsc.k12.ar.us/
Grade Span: KG-12; **Agency Type:** 1
Schools: 3
1 Primary; 1 Middle; 1 High; 0 Other Level
3 Regular; 0 Special Education; 0 Vocational; 0 Alternative
0 Magnet; 0 Charter; 2 Title I Eligible; 2 School-wide Title I
Students: 1,735 (50.2% male; 49.7% female)
Individual Education Program: 329 (19.0%);
English Language Learner: 8 (0.5%); Migrant: 96 (5.5%)
Eligible for Free Lunch Program: 933 (53.8%)
Eligible for Reduced-Price Lunch Program: 168 (9.7%)
Teachers: 119.0 (14.6 to 1)
Librarians/Media Specialists: 3.0 (578.3 to 1)
Guidance Counselors: 5.0 (347.0 to 1)
Current Spending: ($ per student per year):
Total: $6,298; Instruction: $3,601; Support Services: $2,369
Enrollment, Drop-out Rates and Diploma Recipients by Race/Ethnicity

Category	Total	White	Black	Asian	AIAN	Hisp.
Enrollment (%)	100.0	89.2	8.2	0.2	0.2	2.2
Drop-out Rate (%)	7.4	7.4	3.8	n/a	n/a	25.0
H.S. Diplomas (#)	81	80	1	0	0	0

Polk County

Mena SD
501 Hickory St • Mena, AR 71953-1945
(479) 394-1710 • http://170.211.34.2/Mena%20Public%202000/index.htm
Grade Span: KG-12; **Agency Type:** 1
Schools: 4
2 Primary; 1 Middle; 1 High; 0 Other Level
4 Regular; 0 Special Education; 0 Vocational; 0 Alternative
0 Magnet; 0 Charter; 2 Title I Eligible; 2 School-wide Title I
Students: 1,878 (51.6% male; 48.3% female)
Individual Education Program: 215 (11.4%);
English Language Learner: 0 (0.0%); Migrant: 0 (0.0%)
Eligible for Free Lunch Program: 772 (41.1%)
Eligible for Reduced-Price Lunch Program: 220 (11.7%)
Teachers: 124.0 (15.1 to 1)
Librarians/Media Specialists: 4.0 (469.5 to 1)
Guidance Counselors: 5.0 (375.6 to 1)
Current Spending: ($ per student per year):
Total: $5,898; Instruction: $3,833; Support Services: $1,741

Enrollment, Drop-out Rates and Diploma Recipients by Race/Ethnicity

Category	Total	White	Black	Asian	AIAN	Hisp.
Enrollment (%)	100.0	97.2	0.1	0.6	0.6	1.5
Drop-out Rate (%)	4.8	4.7	n/a	0.0	20.0	0.0
H.S. Diplomas (#)	117	115	0	1	1	0

Pope County

Russellville SD
220 W 10th St • Russellville, AR 72801-0928
Mailing Address: PO Box 928 • Russellville, AR 72811-0928
(479) 968-1306 • http://rsd.afsc.k12.ar.us/
Grade Span: KG-12; **Agency Type:** 1
Schools: 11
  6 Primary; 2 Middle; 2 High; 1 Other Level
  10 Regular; 0 Special Education; 1 Vocational; 0 Alternative
  0 Magnet; 0 Charter; 5 Title I Eligible; 2 School-wide Title I
Students: 5,116   (52.0% male; 47.9% female)
  Individual Education Program: 546 (10.7%);
  English Language Learner: 186 (3.6%); Migrant: 209 (4.1%)
  Eligible for Free Lunch Program: 1,797 (35.1%)
  Eligible for Reduced-Price Lunch Program: 411 (8.0%)
Teachers: 348.0 (14.7 to 1)
Librarians/Media Specialists: 10.0 (511.6 to 1)
Guidance Counselors: 16.0 (319.8 to 1)
Current Spending: ($ per student per year):
  Total: $6,908; Instruction: $4,441; Support Services: $2,148
Enrollment, Drop-out Rates and Diploma Recipients by Race/Ethnicity

Category	Total	White	Black	Asian	AIAN	Hisp.
Enrollment (%)	100.0	84.1	7.2	1.6	0.7	6.4
Drop-out Rate (%)	5.6	5.5	8.2	0.0	0.0	7.5
H.S. Diplomas (#)	324	288	23	3	2	8

Pulaski County

Little Rock SD
810 W Markham St • Little Rock, AR 72201-1306
(501) 447-1002 • http://www.lrsd.org/
Grade Span: PK-12; **Agency Type:** 1
Schools: 52
  34 Primary; 8 Middle; 8 High; 2 Other Level
  49 Regular; 0 Special Education; 1 Vocational; 2 Alternative
  7 Magnet; 0 Charter; 34 Title I Eligible; 34 School-wide Title I
Students: 25,346   (49.9% male; 50.0% female)
  Individual Education Program: 2,678 (10.6%);
  English Language Learner: 817 (3.2%); Migrant: 0 (0.0%)
  Eligible for Free Lunch Program: 11,808 (46.6%)
  Eligible for Reduced-Price Lunch Program: 1,730 (6.8%)
Teachers: 1,726.0 (14.7 to 1)
Librarians/Media Specialists: 49.0 (517.3 to 1)
Guidance Counselors: 77.0 (329.2 to 1)
Current Spending: ($ per student per year):
  Total: $7,994; Instruction: $4,326; Support Services: $3,387
Enrollment, Drop-out Rates and Diploma Recipients by Race/Ethnicity

Category	Total	White	Black	Asian	AIAN	Hisp.
Enrollment (%)	100.0	25.1	68.6	1.8	0.3	4.2
Drop-out Rate (%)	12.1	10.4	12.9	6.4	25.0	14.2
H.S. Diplomas (#)	1,334	428	865	17	2	22

N. Little Rock SD
2700 Poplar St • North Little Rock, AR 72114
(501) 771-8000 • http://www.nlrsd.k12.ar.us/
Grade Span: PK-12; **Agency Type:** 1
Schools: 20
  14 Primary; 4 Middle; 1 High; 1 Other Level
  20 Regular; 0 Special Education; 0 Vocational; 0 Alternative
  0 Magnet; 1 Charter; 17 Title I Eligible; 8 School-wide Title I
Students: 9,144   (50.8% male; 49.1% female)
  Individual Education Program: 0 (0.0%);
  English Language Learner: 112 (1.2%); Migrant: 0 (0.0%)
  Eligible for Free Lunch Program: 4,766 (52.1%)
  Eligible for Reduced-Price Lunch Program: 381 (4.2%)
Teachers: 634.0 (14.4 to 1)
Librarians/Media Specialists: 16.0 (571.5 to 1)
Guidance Counselors: 23.0 (397.6 to 1)
Current Spending: ($ per student per year):
  Total: $7,304; Instruction: $4,146; Support Services: $2,822
Enrollment, Drop-out Rates and Diploma Recipients by Race/Ethnicity

Category	Total	White	Black	Asian	AIAN	Hisp.
Enrollment (%)	100.0	37.6	58.2	0.5	0.1	3.6
Drop-out Rate (%)	1.1	1.1	1.2	0.0	0.0	1.7
H.S. Diplomas (#)	508	261	222	9	2	14

Pulaski County Spec. SD
925 E Dixon Rd • Little Rock, AR 72216-4199
Mailing Address: PO Box 8601 • Little Rock, AR 72216-8601
(501) 490-2000 • http://pcssdweb.k12.ar.us/
Grade Span: PK-12; **Agency Type:** 1
Schools: 36
  23 Primary; 5 Middle; 6 High; 2 Other Level
  36 Regular; 0 Special Education; 0 Vocational; 0 Alternative
  0 Magnet; 0 Charter; 21 Title I Eligible; 13 School-wide Title I
Students: 18,522   (52.0% male; 47.9% female)
  Individual Education Program: 2,418 (13.1%);
  English Language Learner: 67 (0.4%); Migrant: 0 (0.0%)
  Eligible for Free Lunch Program: 6,331 (34.2%)
  Eligible for Reduced-Price Lunch Program: 1,512 (8.2%)
Teachers: 1,202.0 (15.4 to 1)
Librarians/Media Specialists: 36.0 (514.5 to 1)
Guidance Counselors: 61.0 (303.6 to 1)
Current Spending: ($ per student per year):
  Total: $7,403; Instruction: $4,412; Support Services: $2,661
Enrollment, Drop-out Rates and Diploma Recipients by Race/Ethnicity

Category	Total	White	Black	Asian	AIAN	Hisp.
Enrollment (%)	100.0	57.2	39.6	0.8	0.3	2.1
Drop-out Rate (%)	7.5	7.5	7.4	4.5	0.0	12.7
H.S. Diplomas (#)	816	539	260	8	0	9

Randolph County

Pocahontas SD
2300 N Park • Pocahontas, AR 72455-1306
(870) 892-4573 • http://www.nesc.k12.ar.us/
Grade Span: KG-12; **Agency Type:** 1
Schools: 4
  2 Primary; 1 Middle; 1 High; 0 Other Level
  4 Regular; 0 Special Education; 0 Vocational; 0 Alternative
  0 Magnet; 0 Charter; 4 Title I Eligible; 4 School-wide Title I
Students: 1,821   (53.1% male; 46.8% female)
  Individual Education Program: 241 (13.2%);
  English Language Learner: 3 (0.2%); Migrant: 7 (0.4%)
  Eligible for Free Lunch Program: 761 (41.8%)
  Eligible for Reduced-Price Lunch Program: 282 (15.5%)
Teachers: 109.0 (16.7 to 1)
Librarians/Media Specialists: 4.0 (455.3 to 1)
Guidance Counselors: 6.0 (303.5 to 1)
Current Spending: ($ per student per year):
  Total: $5,785; Instruction: $3,749; Support Services: $1,765
Enrollment, Drop-out Rates and Diploma Recipients by Race/Ethnicity

Category	Total	White	Black	Asian	AIAN	Hisp.
Enrollment (%)	100.0	97.0	1.0	0.3	0.2	1.5
Drop-out Rate (%)	3.8	3.9	0.0	0.0	0.0	0.0
H.S. Diplomas (#)	110	106	0	0	1	3

Saline County

Benton SD
500 River St • Benton, AR 72015
Mailing Address: PO Box 939 • Benton, AR 72015
(501) 778-4861 • http://www.bentonark.com/sindex.html
Grade Span: KG-12; **Agency Type:** 1
Schools: 7
  4 Primary; 1 Middle; 1 High; 1 Other Level
  7 Regular; 0 Special Education; 0 Vocational; 0 Alternative
  0 Magnet; 0 Charter; 0 Title I Eligible; 0 School-wide Title I
Students: 4,258   (51.7% male; 48.2% female)
  Individual Education Program: 435 (10.2%);
  English Language Learner: 76 (1.8%); Migrant: 3 (0.1%)
  Eligible for Free Lunch Program: 879 (20.6%)
  Eligible for Reduced-Price Lunch Program: 225 (5.3%)
Teachers: 260.0 (16.4 to 1)
Librarians/Media Specialists: 7.0 (608.3 to 1)
Guidance Counselors: 11.0 (387.1 to 1)
Current Spending: ($ per student per year):
  Total: $6,004; Instruction: $3,905; Support Services: $1,811
Enrollment, Drop-out Rates and Diploma Recipients by Race/Ethnicity

Category	Total	White	Black	Asian	AIAN	Hisp.
Enrollment (%)	100.0	90.7	5.0	0.7	0.5	3.1
Drop-out Rate (%)	3.2	2.5	15.7	8.3	16.7	0.0
H.S. Diplomas (#)	274	259	9	3	0	3

Bryant SD
200 Northwest Fourth St • Bryant, AR 72022-3424
Mailing Address: 200 NW Fourth St • Bryant, AR 72022-3424
(501) 847-5600 • http://bryant.dsc.k12.ar.us/
Grade Span: KG-12; **Agency Type:** 1
Schools: 7
  5 Primary; 1 Middle; 1 High; 0 Other Level

7 Regular; 0 Special Education; 0 Vocational; 0 Alternative
0 Magnet; 0 Charter; 6 Title I Eligible; 0 School-wide Title I
Students: 6,176   (51.1% male; 48.8% female)
 Individual Education Program: 889 (14.4%);
 English Language Learner: 89 (1.4%); Migrant: 0 (0.0%)
 Eligible for Free Lunch Program: 1,245 (20.2%)
 Eligible for Reduced-Price Lunch Program: 334 (5.4%)
Teachers: 359.0 (17.2 to 1)
Librarians/Media Specialists: 8.0 (772.0 to 1)
Guidance Counselors: 14.0 (441.1 to 1)
Current Spending: ($ per student per year):
 Total: $5,381; Instruction: $3,631; Support Services: $1,526
Enrollment, Drop-out Rates and Diploma Recipients by Race/Ethnicity

Category	Total	White	Black	Asian	AIAN	Hisp.
Enrollment (%)	100.0	94.4	2.4	1.0	0.5	1.7
Drop-out Rate (%)	4.3	4.4	0.0	10.0	0.0	0.0
H.S. Diplomas (#)	388	380	3	2	0	3

Scott County

Waldron SD
1560 W Sixth St • Waldron, AR 72958-1397
(479) 637-3179 • http://zebra.wsc.k12.ar.us/~wbulldog/
Grade Span: KG-12; **Agency Type:** 1
Schools: 3
 1 Primary; 1 Middle; 1 High; 0 Other Level
 3 Regular; 0 Special Education; 0 Vocational; 0 Alternative
 0 Magnet; 0 Charter; 2 Title I Eligible; 2 School-wide Title I
Students: 1,695   (50.8% male; 49.1% female)
 Individual Education Program: 200 (11.8%);
 English Language Learner: 59 (3.5%); Migrant: 194 (11.4%)
 Eligible for Free Lunch Program: 811 (47.8%)
 Eligible for Reduced-Price Lunch Program: 151 (8.9%)
Teachers: 117.0 (14.5 to 1)
Librarians/Media Specialists: 3.0 (565.0 to 1)
Guidance Counselors: 4.0 (423.8 to 1)
Current Spending: ($ per student per year):
 Total: $5,317; Instruction: $3,297; Support Services: $1,729
Enrollment, Drop-out Rates and Diploma Recipients by Race/Ethnicity

Category	Total	White	Black	Asian	AIAN	Hisp.
Enrollment (%)	100.0	89.3	0.3	1.7	1.0	7.7
Drop-out Rate (%)	3.1	2.2	n/a	0.0	12.5	25.0
H.S. Diplomas (#)	110	106	0	1	1	2

Sebastian County

Fort Smith SD
3205 Jenny Lind Rd • Fort Smith, AR 72901-1948
Mailing Address: PO Box 1948 • Fort Smith, AR 72902-1948
(479) 785-2501 • http://clx.fssc.k12.ar.us/
Grade Span: KG-12; **Agency Type:** 1
Schools: 26
 19 Primary; 4 Middle; 3 High; 0 Other Level
 25 Regular; 0 Special Education; 0 Vocational; 1 Alternative
 0 Magnet; 0 Charter; 16 Title I Eligible; 14 School-wide Title I
Students: 12,865   (50.7% male; 49.2% female)
 Individual Education Program: 1,829 (14.2%);
 English Language Learner: 1,825 (14.2%); Migrant: 960 (7.5%)
 Eligible for Free Lunch Program: 5,606 (43.6%)
 Eligible for Reduced-Price Lunch Program: 1,014 (7.9%)
Teachers: 831.0 (15.5 to 1)
Librarians/Media Specialists: 23.0 (559.3 to 1)
Guidance Counselors: 35.0 (367.6 to 1)
Current Spending: ($ per student per year):
 Total: $6,506; Instruction: $3,942; Support Services: $2,227
Enrollment, Drop-out Rates and Diploma Recipients by Race/Ethnicity

Category	Total	White	Black	Asian	AIAN	Hisp.
Enrollment (%)	100.0	59.0	14.6	6.6	3.1	16.6
Drop-out Rate (%)	5.2	5.4	4.9	2.2	3.5	7.8
H.S. Diplomas (#)	822	554	108	86	25	49

Greenwood SD
420 N Main • Greenwood, AR 72936-7016
(479) 996-4142 • http://greenwood.k12.ar.us/
Grade Span: KG-12; **Agency Type:** 1
Schools: 5
 2 Primary; 1 Middle; 1 High; 1 Other Level
 5 Regular; 0 Special Education; 0 Vocational; 0 Alternative
 0 Magnet; 0 Charter; 5 Title I Eligible; 0 School-wide Title I
Students: 3,181   (51.3% male; 48.6% female)
 Individual Education Program: 390 (12.3%);
 English Language Learner: 12 (0.4%); Migrant: 1 (<0.1%)
 Eligible for Free Lunch Program: 475 (14.9%)
 Eligible for Reduced-Price Lunch Program: 218 (6.9%)
Teachers: 189.0 (16.8 to 1)

Librarians/Media Specialists: 5.0 (636.2 to 1)
Guidance Counselors: 8.0 (397.6 to 1)
Current Spending: ($ per student per year):
 Total: $5,779; Instruction: $3,645; Support Services: $1,906
Enrollment, Drop-out Rates and Diploma Recipients by Race/Ethnicity

Category	Total	White	Black	Asian	AIAN	Hisp.
Enrollment (%)	100.0	95.1	0.2	0.9	2.5	1.4
Drop-out Rate (%)	2.9	3.0	n/a	0.0	0.0	0.0
H.S. Diplomas (#)	227	221	0	3	2	1

Sevier County

Dequeen SD
101 N Ninth St • De Queen, AR 71832-0950
Mailing Address: PO Box 950 • De Queen, AR 71832-0950
(870) 584-4312 • http://leopards.k12.ar.us/
Grade Span: KG-12; **Agency Type:** 1
Schools: 4
 2 Primary; 1 Middle; 1 High; 0 Other Level
 4 Regular; 0 Special Education; 0 Vocational; 0 Alternative
 0 Magnet; 0 Charter; 3 Title I Eligible; 3 School-wide Title I
Students: 2,011   (51.2% male; 48.7% female)
 Individual Education Program: 200 (9.9%);
 English Language Learner: 853 (42.4%); Migrant: 575 (28.6%)
 Eligible for Free Lunch Program: 1,158 (57.6%)
 Eligible for Reduced-Price Lunch Program: 159 (7.9%)
Teachers: 125.0 (16.1 to 1)
Librarians/Media Specialists: 4.0 (502.8 to 1)
Guidance Counselors: 5.0 (402.2 to 1)
Current Spending: ($ per student per year):
 Total: $5,744; Instruction: $3,351; Support Services: $1,993
Enrollment, Drop-out Rates and Diploma Recipients by Race/Ethnicity

Category	Total	White	Black	Asian	AIAN	Hisp.
Enrollment (%)	100.0	45.0	6.0	0.1	2.4	46.4
Drop-out Rate (%)	10.2	7.5	15.4	0.0	30.0	13.5
H.S. Diplomas (#)	81	57	1	0	3	20

Sharp County

Highland SD
1 Rebel Circle • Hardy, AR 72542-0419
Mailing Address: PO Box 419 • Hardy, AR 72542-0419
(870) 856-3275
Grade Span: KG-12; **Agency Type:** 1
Schools: 3
 1 Primary; 1 Middle; 1 High; 0 Other Level
 3 Regular; 0 Special Education; 0 Vocational; 0 Alternative
 0 Magnet; 0 Charter; 3 Title I Eligible; 3 School-wide Title I
Students: 1,605   (52.2% male; 47.7% female)
 Individual Education Program: 219 (13.6%);
 English Language Learner: 0 (0.0%); Migrant: 0 (0.0%)
 Eligible for Free Lunch Program: 719 (44.8%)
 Eligible for Reduced-Price Lunch Program: 179 (11.2%)
Teachers: 101.0 (15.9 to 1)
Librarians/Media Specialists: 2.0 (802.5 to 1)
Guidance Counselors: 4.0 (401.3 to 1)
Current Spending: ($ per student per year):
 Total: $5,537; Instruction: $3,503; Support Services: $1,723
Enrollment, Drop-out Rates and Diploma Recipients by Race/Ethnicity

Category	Total	White	Black	Asian	AIAN	Hisp.
Enrollment (%)	100.0	97.3	0.7	0.5	0.4	1.1
Drop-out Rate (%)	4.4	4.5	0.0	0.0	0.0	0.0
H.S. Diplomas (#)	83	82	0	0	0	1

St. Francis County

Forrest City SD
845 N Rosser • Forrest City, AR 72335-2364
(870) 633-1485 • http://mustang.grsc.k12.ar.us/
Grade Span: KG-12; **Agency Type:** 1
Schools: 8
 5 Primary; 1 Middle; 1 High; 1 Other Level
 8 Regular; 0 Special Education; 0 Vocational; 0 Alternative
 0 Magnet; 0 Charter; 8 Title I Eligible; 8 School-wide Title I
Students: 3,998   (50.9% male; 49.0% female)
 Individual Education Program: 533 (13.3%);
 English Language Learner: 6 (0.2%); Migrant: 58 (1.5%)
 Eligible for Free Lunch Program: 3,974 (99.4%)
 Eligible for Reduced-Price Lunch Program: 0 (0.0%)
Teachers: 243.0 (16.5 to 1)
Librarians/Media Specialists: 7.0 (571.1 to 1)
Guidance Counselors: 10.0 (399.8 to 1)
Current Spending: ($ per student per year):
 Total: $6,304; Instruction: $3,694; Support Services: $2,186

Enrollment, Drop-out Rates and Diploma Recipients by Race/Ethnicity

Category	Total	White	Black	Asian	AIAN	Hisp.
Enrollment (%)	100.0	23.9	75.1	0.4	0.0	0.6
Drop-out Rate (%)	7.7	6.2	8.2	0.0	0.0	25.0
H.S. Diplomas (#)	236	51	181	2	2	0

Union County

El Dorado SD
200 W Oak St • El Dorado, AR 71730-5618
(870) 864-5001 • http://www.scsc.k12.ar.us/eldorado/
Grade Span: KG-12; **Agency Type:** 1
Schools: 9
  6 Primary; 2 Middle; 1 High; 0 Other Level
  9 Regular; 0 Special Education; 0 Vocational; 0 Alternative
  0 Magnet; 1 Charter; 9 Title I Eligible; 8 School-wide Title I
Students: 4,276   (51.7% male; 48.2% female)
  Individual Education Program: 407 (9.5%);
  English Language Learner: 46 (1.1%); Migrant: 0 (0.0%)
  Eligible for Free Lunch Program: 2,118 (49.5%)
  Eligible for Reduced-Price Lunch Program: 284 (6.6%)
Teachers: 303.0 (14.1 to 1)
Librarians/Media Specialists: 8.0 (534.5 to 1)
Guidance Counselors: 12.0 (356.3 to 1)
Current Spending: ($ per student per year):
  Total: $5,787; Instruction: $3,678; Support Services: $1,822
Enrollment, Drop-out Rates and Diploma Recipients by Race/Ethnicity

Category	Total	White	Black	Asian	AIAN	Hisp.
Enrollment (%)	100.0	41.1	56.9	0.6	0.0	1.4
Drop-out Rate (%)	0.8	0.8	0.8	0.0	0.0	0.0
H.S. Diplomas (#)	308	135	167	3	0	3

Washington County

Farmington SD
42 S Double Springs Rd • Farmington, AR 72730-2707
Mailing Address: 42 S Dbl Springs Rd • Farmington, AR 72730-2707
(479) 266-1805 • http://farmington.k12.ar.us/
Grade Span: KG-12; **Agency Type:** 1
Schools: 3
  1 Primary; 1 Middle; 1 High; 0 Other Level
  3 Regular; 0 Special Education; 0 Vocational; 0 Alternative
  0 Magnet; 0 Charter; 1 Title I Eligible; 0 School-wide Title I
Students: 1,835   (49.8% male; 50.1% female)
  Individual Education Program: 177 (9.6%);
  English Language Learner: 41 (2.2%); Migrant: 0 (0.0%)
  Eligible for Free Lunch Program: 347 (18.9%)
  Eligible for Reduced-Price Lunch Program: 144 (7.8%)
Teachers: 112.0 (16.4 to 1)
Librarians/Media Specialists: 3.0 (611.7 to 1)
Guidance Counselors: 5.0 (367.0 to 1)
Current Spending: ($ per student per year):
  Total: $5,358; Instruction: $3,296; Support Services: $1,821
Enrollment, Drop-out Rates and Diploma Recipients by Race/Ethnicity

Category	Total	White	Black	Asian	AIAN	Hisp.
Enrollment (%)	100.0	93.4	1.8	0.3	0.8	3.8
Drop-out Rate (%)	2.6	2.8	0.0	0.0	0.0	0.0
H.S. Diplomas (#)	98	95	0	0	2	1

Fayetteville SD
1000 W Stone St • Fayetteville, AR 72701
(479) 444-3000 • http://www.fayar.net/
Grade Span: PK-12; **Agency Type:** 1
Schools: 15
  9 Primary; 2 Middle; 2 High; 2 Other Level
  15 Regular; 0 Special Education; 0 Vocational; 0 Alternative
  0 Magnet; 0 Charter; 0 Title I Eligible; 0 School-wide Title I
Students: 8,061   (50.1% male; 49.8% female)
  Individual Education Program: 1,103 (13.7%);
  English Language Learner: 538 (6.7%); Migrant: 257 (3.2%)
  Eligible for Free Lunch Program: 1,949 (24.2%)
  Eligible for Reduced-Price Lunch Program: 531 (6.6%)
Teachers: 525.0 (15.4 to 1)
Librarians/Media Specialists: 16.0 (503.8 to 1)
Guidance Counselors: 22.0 (366.4 to 1)
Current Spending: ($ per student per year):
  Total: $7,145; Instruction: $4,227; Support Services: $2,625
Enrollment, Drop-out Rates and Diploma Recipients by Race/Ethnicity

Category	Total	White	Black	Asian	AIAN	Hisp.
Enrollment (%)	100.0	79.7	8.5	3.3	1.2	7.4
Drop-out Rate (%)	6.4	5.7	10.5	5.7	15.4	11.3
H.S. Diplomas (#)	539	472	23	16	3	25

Springdale SD
804 W Johnson Ave • Springdale, AR 72765-0008
Mailing Address: PO Box 8 • Springdale, AR 72765-0008
(479) 750-8800 • http://www.sadmin.jonesnet.org/
Grade Span: KG-12; **Agency Type:** 1
Schools: 16
  11 Primary; 2 Middle; 0 High; 3 Other Level
  16 Regular; 0 Special Education; 0 Vocational; 0 Alternative
  0 Magnet; 0 Charter; 6 Title I Eligible; 6 School-wide Title I
Students: 13,678   (52.1% male; 47.8% female)
  Individual Education Program: 1,457 (10.7%);
  English Language Learner: 4,417 (32.3%); Migrant: 1,489 (10.9%)
  Eligible for Free Lunch Program: 5,174 (37.8%)
  Eligible for Reduced-Price Lunch Program: 1,231 (9.0%)
Teachers: 760.0 (18.0 to 1)
Librarians/Media Specialists: 15.0 (911.9 to 1)
Guidance Counselors: 25.0 (547.1 to 1)
Current Spending: ($ per student per year):
  Total: $5,785; Instruction: $3,926; Support Services: $1,582
Enrollment, Drop-out Rates and Diploma Recipients by Race/Ethnicity

Category	Total	White	Black	Asian	AIAN	Hisp.
Enrollment (%)	100.0	63.2	1.2	6.4	0.5	28.7
Drop-out Rate (%)	5.5	4.8	4.0	8.7	0.0	7.7
H.S. Diplomas (#)	554	469	3	25	0	57

White County

Beebe SD
1201 W Center St • Beebe, AR 72012-3103
(501) 882-5463 • http://thor.k12.ar.us/
Grade Span: KG-12; **Agency Type:** 1
Schools: 6
  2 Primary; 2 Middle; 1 High; 1 Other Level
  6 Regular; 0 Special Education; 0 Vocational; 0 Alternative
  0 Magnet; 0 Charter; 3 Title I Eligible; 0 School-wide Title I
Students: 2,453   (52.3% male; 47.6% female)
  Individual Education Program: 349 (14.2%);
  English Language Learner: 1 (<0.1%); Migrant: 4 (0.2%)
  Eligible for Free Lunch Program: 658 (26.8%)
  Eligible for Reduced-Price Lunch Program: 243 (9.9%)
Teachers: 157.0 (15.6 to 1)
Librarians/Media Specialists: 5.0 (490.6 to 1)
Guidance Counselors: 6.0 (408.8 to 1)
Current Spending: ($ per student per year):
  Total: $5,769; Instruction: $3,565; Support Services: $1,818
Enrollment, Drop-out Rates and Diploma Recipients by Race/Ethnicity

Category	Total	White	Black	Asian	AIAN	Hisp.
Enrollment (%)	100.0	95.1	3.1	0.9	0.2	0.7
Drop-out Rate (%)	5.8	6.2	0.0	0.0	0.0	0.0
H.S. Diplomas (#)	118	110	5	1	2	0

Searcy SD
801 N Elm • Searcy, AR 72143-3640
(501) 268-3517 • http://ssweb.wmsc.k12.ar.us/
Grade Span: KG-12; **Agency Type:** 1
Schools: 6
  3 Primary; 2 Middle; 1 High; 0 Other Level
  6 Regular; 0 Special Education; 0 Vocational; 0 Alternative
  0 Magnet; 0 Charter; 3 Title I Eligible; 0 School-wide Title I
Students: 3,663   (50.8% male; 49.1% female)
  Individual Education Program: 378 (10.3%);
  English Language Learner: 18 (0.5%); Migrant: 106 (2.9%)
  Eligible for Free Lunch Program: 941 (25.7%)
  Eligible for Reduced-Price Lunch Program: 309 (8.4%)
Teachers: 219.0 (16.7 to 1)
Librarians/Media Specialists: 6.0 (610.5 to 1)
Guidance Counselors: 9.0 (407.0 to 1)
Current Spending: ($ per student per year):
  Total: $5,393; Instruction: $3,403; Support Services: $1,675
Enrollment, Drop-out Rates and Diploma Recipients by Race/Ethnicity

Category	Total	White	Black	Asian	AIAN	Hisp.
Enrollment (%)	100.0	87.9	9.4	0.4	0.1	2.1
Drop-out Rate (%)	3.0	2.8	2.6	11.1	0.0	13.3
H.S. Diplomas (#)	214	193	17	1	0	3

Yell County

Dardanelle SD
209 Cedar • Dardanelle, AR 72834-3215
Mailing Address: 209 Cedar St • Dardanelle, AR 72834-3215
(479) 229-4111 • http://lizardlink.afsc.k12.ar.us/
Grade Span: KG-12; **Agency Type:** 1
Schools: 4
  2 Primary; 1 Middle; 1 High; 0 Other Level
  4 Regular; 0 Special Education; 0 Vocational; 0 Alternative

0 Magnet; 0 Charter; 4 Title I Eligible; 4 School-wide Title I

Students: 1,777   (52.1% male; 47.8% female)
  Individual Education Program: 235 (13.2%);
  English Language Learner: 246 (13.8%); Migrant: 223 (12.5%)
  Eligible for Free Lunch Program: 766 (43.1%)
  Eligible for Reduced-Price Lunch Program: 206 (11.6%)

Teachers: 120.0 (14.8 to 1)

Librarians/Media Specialists: 4.0 (444.3 to 1)

Guidance Counselors: 4.0 (444.3 to 1)

Current Spending: ($ per student per year):
  Total: $5,512; Instruction: $3,329; Support Services: $1,884

Enrollment, Drop-out Rates and Diploma Recipients by Race/Ethnicity

Category	Total	White	Black	Asian	AIAN	Hisp.
Enrollment (%)	100.0	77.9	3.0	2.3	0.3	16.5
Drop-out Rate (%)	6.2	5.9	0.0	0.0	0.0	12.0
H.S. Diplomas (#)	101	89	4	0	2	6

Number of Schools

Rank	Number	District Name	City
1	52	Little Rock SD	Little Rock
2	36	Pulaski County Spec. SD	Little Rock
3	26	Fort Smith SD	Fort Smith
4	20	N. Little Rock SD	N Little Rock
5	18	Rogers SD	Rogers
6	16	Springdale SD	Springdale
7	15	Fayetteville SD	Fayetteville
8	14	Pine Bluff SD	Pine Bluff
9	13	Conway SD	Conway
10	12	Cabot SD	Cabot
10	12	West Memphis SD	West Memphis
12	11	Russellville SD	Russellville
12	11	Van Buren SD	Van Buren
14	10	Bentonville SD	Bentonville
14	10	Jonesboro SD	Jonesboro
16	9	El Dorado SD	El Dorado
16	9	Texarkana SD	Texarkana
18	8	Forrest City SD	Forrest City
19	7	Batesville SD	Batesville
19	7	Benton SD	Benton
19	7	Blytheville SD	Blytheville
19	7	Bryant SD	Bryant
19	7	Camden Fairview SD	Camden
19	7	Crossett SD	Crossett
19	7	Harrison SD	Harrison
19	7	Nettleton SD	Jonesboro
19	7	White Hall SD	White Hall
28	6	Beebe SD	Beebe
28	6	Hamburg SD	Hamburg
28	6	Helena/West Helena SD	Helena
28	6	Hot Springs SD	Hot Springs
28	6	Lake Hamilton SD	Pearcy
28	6	Marion SD	Marion
28	6	Mountain Home SD	Mountain Home
28	6	Osceola SD	Osceola
28	6	Paragould SD	Paragould
28	6	Searcy SD	Searcy
28	6	Sheridan SD	Sheridan
28	6	So. Conway County SD	Morrilton
28	6	Stuttgart SD	Stuttgart
41	5	Arkadelphia SD	Arkadelphia
41	5	Ashdown SD	Ashdown
41	5	Clarksville SD	Clarksville
41	5	Dollarway SD	Pine Bluff
41	5	Greenbrier SD	Greenbrier
41	5	Greenwood SD	Greenwood
41	5	Hope SD	Hope
41	5	Lakeside SD	Hot Springs
41	5	Monticello SD	Monticello
41	5	Siloam Springs SD	Siloam Springs
41	5	Vilonia SD	Vilonia
41	5	Warren SD	Warren
41	5	Watson Chapel SD	Pine Bluff
54	4	Alma SD	Alma
54	4	Dardanelle SD	Dardanelle
54	4	Dequeen SD	De Queen
54	4	Dumas SD	Dumas
54	4	Gravette SD	Gravette
54	4	Greene County Tech SD	Paragould
54	4	Huntsville SD	Huntsville
54	4	Lee County SD	Marianna
54	4	Lonoke SD	Lonoke
54	4	Magnolia SD	Magnolia
54	4	Malvern SD	Malvern
54	4	Mena SD	Mena
54	4	Nashville SD	Nashville
54	4	Newport SD	Newport
54	4	Pocahontas SD	Pocahontas
54	4	Wynne SD	Wynne
70	3	Berryville SD	Berryville
70	3	Farmington SD	Farmington
70	3	Heber Springs SD	Heber Springs
70	3	Highland SD	Hardy
70	3	Ozark SD	Ozark
70	3	Star City SD	Star City
70	3	Trumann SD	Trumann
70	3	Waldron SD	Waldron
70	3	Westside Cons. SD	Jonesboro
79	2	Valley View SD	Jonesboro

Number of Teachers

Rank	Number	District Name	City
1	1,726	Little Rock SD	Little Rock
2	1,202	Pulaski County Spec. SD	Little Rock
3	831	Fort Smith SD	Fort Smith
4	760	Springdale SD	Springdale
5	708	Rogers SD	Rogers
6	634	N. Little Rock SD	N Little Rock
7	525	Fayetteville SD	Fayetteville
8	513	Bentonville SD	Bentonville
9	502	Conway SD	Conway
10	480	Cabot SD	Cabot
11	394	West Memphis SD	West Memphis
12	374	Van Buren SD	Van Buren
13	367	Pine Bluff SD	Pine Bluff
14	359	Bryant SD	Bryant
15	348	Russellville SD	Russellville
16	303	El Dorado SD	El Dorado
17	299	Texarkana SD	Texarkana
18	290	Jonesboro SD	Jonesboro
19	261	Sheridan SD	Sheridan
20	260	Benton SD	Benton
21	258	Hot Springs SD	Hot Springs
22	243	Forrest City SD	Forrest City
22	243	Helena/West Helena SD	Helena
24	229	Blytheville SD	Blytheville
25	223	Mountain Home SD	Mountain Home
26	219	Searcy SD	Searcy
27	208	Lake Hamilton SD	Pearcy
28	199	Camden Fairview SD	Camden
29	193	Hope SD	Hope
30	190	Siloam Springs SD	Siloam Springs
31	189	Greenwood SD	Greenwood
31	189	Marion SD	Marion
31	189	White Hall SD	White Hall
31	189	Wynne SD	Wynne
35	185	Alma SD	Alma
35	185	Watson Chapel SD	Pine Bluff
37	180	Greene County Tech SD	Paragould
37	180	Magnolia SD	Magnolia
39	179	So. Conway County SD	Morrilton
40	178	Harrison SD	Harrison
41	173	Paragould SD	Paragould
42	172	Nettleton SD	Jonesboro
43	167	Greenbrier SD	Greenbrier
44	159	Lakeside SD	Hot Springs
45	157	Beebe SD	Beebe
45	157	Crossett SD	Crossett
47	151	Vilonia SD	Vilonia
48	147	Arkadelphia SD	Arkadelphia
49	146	Malvern SD	Malvern
50	145	Batesville SD	Batesville
51	143	Clarksville SD	Clarksville
52	142	Monticello SD	Monticello
53	137	Stuttgart SD	Stuttgart
54	135	Nashville SD	Nashville
55	134	Huntsville SD	Huntsville
56	132	Newport SD	Newport
57	130	Osceola SD	Osceola
58	125	Dequeen SD	De Queen
59	124	Mena SD	Mena
60	122	Ashdown SD	Ashdown
61	120	Dardanelle SD	Dardanelle
62	119	Trumann SD	Trumann
63	117	Dumas SD	Dumas
63	117	Waldron SD	Waldron
65	115	Warren SD	Warren
66	115	Dollarway SD	Pine Bluff
66	115	Hamburg SD	Hamburg
68	114	Lonoke SD	Lonoke
69	112	Berryville SD	Berryville
69	112	Farmington SD	Farmington
69	112	Heber Springs SD	Heber Springs
72	109	Pocahontas SD	Pocahontas
73	108	Ozark SD	Ozark
74	105	Westside Cons. SD	Jonesboro
75	102	Lee County SD	Marianna
76	101	Highland SD	Hardy
76	101	Star City SD	Star City
78	99	Gravette SD	Gravette
79	94	Valley View SD	Jonesboro

Number of Students

Rank	Number	District Name	City
1	25,346	Little Rock SD	Little Rock
2	18,522	Pulaski County Spec. SD	Little Rock
3	13,678	Springdale SD	Springdale
4	12,865	Fort Smith SD	Fort Smith
5	12,351	Rogers SD	Rogers
6	9,144	N. Little Rock SD	N Little Rock
7	8,346	Bentonville SD	Bentonville
8	8,216	Conway SD	Conway
9	8,061	Fayetteville SD	Fayetteville
10	7,773	Cabot SD	Cabot
11	6,176	Bryant SD	Bryant
12	6,161	West Memphis SD	West Memphis
13	5,964	Pine Bluff SD	Pine Bluff
14	5,585	Van Buren SD	Van Buren
15	5,116	Russellville SD	Russellville
16	4,845	Jonesboro SD	Jonesboro
17	4,438	Texarkana SD	Texarkana
18	4,276	El Dorado SD	El Dorado
19	4,258	Benton SD	Benton
20	4,164	Sheridan SD	Sheridan
21	3,998	Forrest City SD	Forrest City
22	3,860	Mountain Home SD	Mountain Home
23	3,803	Lake Hamilton SD	Pearcy
24	3,663	Searcy SD	Searcy
25	3,593	Hot Springs SD	Hot Springs
26	3,418	Marion SD	Marion
27	3,290	Blytheville SD	Blytheville
28	3,216	Helena/West Helena SD	Helena
29	3,181	Greenwood SD	Greenwood
30	3,136	Watson Chapel SD	Pine Bluff
31	3,135	Siloam Springs SD	Siloam Springs
32	3,053	White Hall SD	White Hall
33	3,035	Alma SD	Alma
34	3,023	Camden Fairview SD	Camden
35	2,936	Greene County Tech SD	Paragould
36	2,833	Wynne SD	Wynne
37	2,792	Harrison SD	Harrison
38	2,786	Magnolia SD	Magnolia
39	2,753	Nettleton SD	Jonesboro
40	2,750	Hope SD	Hope
41	2,675	Paragould SD	Paragould
42	2,646	Vilonia SD	Vilonia
43	2,530	Lakeside SD	Hot Springs
44	2,461	Crossett SD	Crossett
45	2,453	Beebe SD	Beebe
46	2,427	Greenbrier SD	Greenbrier
47	2,377	So. Conway County SD	Morrilton
48	2,269	Arkadelphia SD	Arkadelphia
49	2,246	Clarksville SD	Clarksville
50	2,196	Batesville SD	Batesville
51	2,186	Monticello SD	Monticello
52	2,183	Malvern SD	Malvern
53	2,128	Huntsville SD	Huntsville
54	2,011	Dequeen SD	De Queen
55	1,883	Stuttgart SD	Stuttgart
56	1,878	Mena SD	Mena
57	1,835	Farmington SD	Farmington
58	1,821	Pocahontas SD	Pocahontas
59	1,815	Nashville SD	Nashville
60	1,781	Lonoke SD	Lonoke
61	1,777	Dardanelle SD	Dardanelle
62	1,735	Hamburg SD	Hamburg
62	1,735	Trumann SD	Trumann
64	1,695	Waldron SD	Waldron
65	1,693	Berryville SD	Berryville
66	1,682	Heber Springs SD	Heber Springs
67	1,675	Osceola SD	Osceola
68	1,656	Ashdown SD	Ashdown
69	1,631	Westside Cons. SD	Jonesboro
70	1,621	Gravette SD	Gravette
71	1,614	Dumas SD	Dumas
72	1,609	Newport SD	Newport
73	1,605	Highland SD	Hardy
74	1,578	Star City SD	Star City
75	1,576	Ozark SD	Ozark
76	1,573	Warren SD	Warren
77	1,569	Lee County SD	Marianna
78	1,543	Dollarway SD	Pine Bluff
79	1,542	Valley View SD	Jonesboro

Male Students

Rank	Percent	District Name	City
1	54.6	Osceola SD	Osceola
2	53.3	Texarkana SD	Texarkana
3	53.3	Lake Hamilton SD	Pearcy
4	53.1	Mountain Home SD	Mountain Home
5	53.1	Pocahontas SD	Pocahontas
6	52.6	Batesville SD	Batesville
7	52.5	Westside Cons. SD	Jonesboro
8	52.4	Heber Springs SD	Heber Springs
9	52.3	Berryville SD	Berryville
10	52.3	Beebe SD	Beebe
11	52.3	Greene County Tech SD	Paragould
12	52.3	Star City SD	Star City
13	52.2	Highland SD	Hardy
14	52.1	Lonoke SD	Lonoke
15	52.1	Alma SD	Alma
16	52.1	Springdale SD	Springdale
17	52.1	Huntsville SD	Huntsville
18	52.1	Dardanelle SD	Dardanelle
19	52.0	Newport SD	Newport
20	52.0	Ashdown SD	Ashdown
21	52.0	Pulaski County Spec. SD	Little Rock
22	52.0	Russellville SD	Russellville
23	51.9	Dollarway SD	Pine Bluff
24	51.8	Stuttgart SD	Stuttgart
25	51.7	Van Buren SD	Van Buren
26	51.7	El Dorado SD	El Dorado
27	51.7	Benton SD	Benton

Rank	Percent	District Name	City
28	51.7	Vilonia SD	Vilonia
29	51.6	Greenbrier SD	Greenbrier
30	51.6	Mena SD	Mena
31	51.6	Harrison SD	Harrison
32	51.5	Ozark SD	Ozark
33	51.5	Paragould SD	Paragould
34	51.4	Sheridan SD	Sheridan
35	51.4	Valley View SD	Jonesboro
36	51.3	Greenwood SD	Greenwood
37	51.3	Cabot SD	Cabot
38	51.3	Siloam Springs SD	Siloam Springs
39	51.2	Nettleton SD	Jonesboro
40	51.2	Marion SD	Marion
41	51.2	Gravette SD	Gravette
42	51.2	Dequeen SD	De Queen
43	51.2	Hot Springs SD	Hot Springs
44	51.1	Nashville SD	Nashville
45	51.1	Rogers SD	Rogers
46	51.1	Bryant SD	Bryant
47	51.0	Conway SD	Conway
48	51.0	Arkadelphia SD	Arkadelphia
49	51.0	Monticello SD	Monticello
50	50.9	Forrest City SD	Forrest City
51	50.9	Hope SD	Hope
52	50.9	Watson Chapel SD	Pine Bluff
53	50.9	Wynne SD	Wynne
54	50.8	Searcy SD	Searcy
55	50.8	N. Little Rock SD	N Little Rock
56	50.8	Waldron SD	Waldron
57	50.7	Fort Smith SD	Fort Smith
58	50.7	White Hall SD	White Hall
59	50.6	Clarksville SD	Clarksville
60	50.5	Warren SD	Warren
61	50.4	Helena/West Helena SD	Helena
62	50.4	Malvern SD	Malvern
63	50.4	Camden Fairview SD	Camden
64	50.4	Lakeside SD	Hot Springs
65	50.3	Pine Bluff SD	Pine Bluff
66	50.3	West Memphis SD	West Memphis
67	50.2	Magnolia SD	Magnolia
68	50.2	So. Conway County SD	Morrilton
69	50.2	Trumann SD	Trumann
70	50.1	Fayetteville SD	Fayetteville
71	50.0	Bentonville SD	Bentonville
72	49.9	Little Rock SD	Little Rock
73	49.9	Dumas SD	Dumas
74	49.8	Farmington SD	Farmington
75	49.7	Jonesboro SD	Jonesboro
76	49.5	Lee County SD	Marianna
77	49.5	Hamburg SD	Hamburg
78	49.4	Crossett SD	Crossett
79	49.3	Blytheville SD	Blytheville

Female Students

Rank	Percent	District Name	City
1	50.6	Blytheville SD	Blytheville
2	50.5	Crossett SD	Crossett
3	50.4	Hamburg SD	Hamburg
4	50.4	Lee County SD	Marianna
5	50.2	Jonesboro SD	Jonesboro
6	50.1	Farmington SD	Farmington
7	50.0	Dumas SD	Dumas
8	50.0	Little Rock SD	Little Rock
9	49.9	Bentonville SD	Bentonville
10	49.8	Fayetteville SD	Fayetteville
11	49.7	Trumann SD	Trumann
12	49.7	So. Conway County SD	Morrilton
13	49.7	Magnolia SD	Magnolia
14	49.6	West Memphis SD	West Memphis
15	49.6	Pine Bluff SD	Pine Bluff
16	49.5	Lakeside SD	Hot Springs
17	49.5	Camden Fairview SD	Camden
18	49.5	Malvern SD	Malvern
19	49.5	Helena/West Helena SD	Helena
20	49.4	Warren SD	Warren
21	49.3	Clarksville SD	Clarksville
22	49.2	White Hall SD	White Hall
23	49.2	Fort Smith SD	Fort Smith
24	49.1	Waldron SD	Waldron
25	49.1	N. Little Rock SD	N Little Rock
26	49.1	Searcy SD	Searcy
27	49.0	Wynne SD	Wynne
28	49.0	Watson Chapel SD	Pine Bluff
29	49.0	Hope SD	Hope
30	49.0	Forrest City SD	Forrest City
31	48.9	Monticello SD	Monticello
32	48.9	Arkadelphia SD	Arkadelphia
33	48.9	Conway SD	Conway
34	48.8	Bryant SD	Bryant
35	48.8	Rogers SD	Rogers
36	48.8	Nashville SD	Nashville
37	48.7	Hot Springs SD	Hot Springs

Rank	Percent	District Name	City
38	48.7	Dequeen SD	De Queen
39	48.7	Gravette SD	Gravette
40	48.7	Marion SD	Marion
41	48.7	Nettleton SD	Jonesboro
42	48.6	Siloam Springs SD	Siloam Springs
43	48.6	Cabot SD	Cabot
44	48.6	Greenwood SD	Greenwood
45	48.5	Valley View SD	Jonesboro
46	48.5	Sheridan SD	Sheridan
47	48.4	Paragould SD	Paragould
48	48.4	Ozark SD	Ozark
49	48.3	Harrison SD	Harrison
50	48.3	Mena SD	Mena
51	48.3	Greenbrier SD	Greenbrier
52	48.2	Vilonia SD	Vilonia
53	48.2	Benton SD	Benton
54	48.2	El Dorado SD	El Dorado
55	48.2	Van Buren SD	Van Buren
56	48.1	Stuttgart SD	Stuttgart
57	48.0	Dollarway SD	Pine Bluff
58	47.9	Russellville SD	Russellville
59	47.9	Pulaski County Spec. SD	Little Rock
60	47.9	Ashdown SD	Ashdown
61	47.9	Newport SD	Newport
62	47.8	Dardanelle SD	Dardanelle
63	47.8	Huntsville SD	Huntsville
64	47.8	Springdale SD	Springdale
65	47.8	Alma SD	Alma
66	47.8	Lonoke SD	Lonoke
67	47.7	Highland SD	Hardy
68	47.6	Star City SD	Star City
69	47.6	Greene County Tech SD	Paragould
70	47.6	Beebe SD	Beebe
71	47.6	Berryville SD	Berryville
72	47.5	Heber Springs SD	Heber Springs
73	47.4	Westside Cons. SD	Jonesboro
74	47.3	Batesville SD	Batesville
75	46.8	Pocahontas SD	Pocahontas
76	46.8	Mountain Home SD	Mountain Home
77	46.7	Lake Hamilton SD	Pearcy
78	46.6	Texarkana SD	Texarkana
79	45.3	Osceola SD	Osceola

Individual Education Program Students

Rank	Percent	District Name	City
1	19.0	Trumann SD	Trumann
2	17.8	Paragould SD	Paragould
3	17.3	Batesville SD	Batesville
4	16.8	Heber Springs SD	Heber Springs
5	16.7	Osceola SD	Osceola
6	16.5	Texarkana SD	Texarkana
7	15.2	Lonoke SD	Lonoke
8	15.1	Greene County Tech SD	Paragould
9	15.0	Blytheville SD	Blytheville
10	14.6	So. Conway County SD	Morrilton
11	14.4	Bryant SD	Bryant
11	14.4	Newport SD	Newport
13	14.3	Cabot SD	Cabot
13	14.3	Conway SD	Conway
13	14.3	Greenbrier SD	Greenbrier
13	14.3	Vilonia SD	Vilonia
17	14.2	Arkadelphia SD	Arkadelphia
17	14.2	Beebe SD	Beebe
17	14.2	Dumas SD	Dumas
17	14.2	Fort Smith SD	Fort Smith
21	14.1	Hot Springs SD	Hot Springs
21	14.1	Huntsville SD	Huntsville
23	13.7	Fayetteville SD	Fayetteville
23	13.7	Lee County SD	Marianna
23	13.7	Nettleton SD	Jonesboro
26	13.6	Highland SD	Hardy
26	13.6	Westside Cons. SD	Jonesboro
28	13.3	Forrest City SD	Forrest City
29	13.2	Alma SD	Alma
29	13.2	Dardanelle SD	Dardanelle
29	13.2	Pocahontas SD	Pocahontas
32	13.1	Dollarway SD	Pine Bluff
32	13.1	Pulaski County Spec. SD	Little Rock
34	13.0	Helena/West Helena SD	Helena
35	12.9	Van Buren SD	Van Buren
36	12.7	Star City SD	Star City
37	12.6	Lake Hamilton SD	Pearcy
37	12.6	Malvern SD	Malvern
39	12.3	Greenwood SD	Greenwood
39	12.3	Rogers SD	Rogers
39	12.3	Sheridan SD	Sheridan
42	12.2	Gravette SD	Gravette
42	12.2	Nashville SD	Nashville
42	12.2	Wynne SD	Wynne
45	11.9	Mountain Home SD	Mountain Home
46	11.8	Ashdown SD	Ashdown
46	11.8	Waldron SD	Waldron

Rank	Percent	District Name	City
48	11.5	Pine Bluff SD	Pine Bluff
49	11.4	Marion SD	Marion
49	11.4	Mena SD	Mena
51	11.3	Bentonville SD	Bentonville
51	11.3	Hamburg SD	Hamburg
53	11.2	Jonesboro SD	Jonesboro
54	11.1	Lakeside SD	Hot Springs
54	11.1	West Memphis SD	West Memphis
56	11.0	Berryville SD	Berryville
56	11.0	Camden Fairview SD	Camden
58	10.7	Harrison SD	Harrison
58	10.7	Russellville SD	Russellville
58	10.7	Springdale SD	Springdale
61	10.6	Clarksville SD	Clarksville
61	10.6	Crossett SD	Crossett
61	10.6	Little Rock SD	Little Rock
61	10.6	Monticello SD	Monticello
65	10.5	Hope SD	Hope
65	10.5	Ozark SD	Ozark
67	10.3	Searcy SD	Searcy
68	10.2	Benton SD	Benton
68	10.2	Watson Chapel SD	Pine Bluff
70	9.9	Dequeen SD	De Queen
70	9.9	Warren SD	Warren
72	9.6	Farmington SD	Farmington
73	9.5	El Dorado SD	El Dorado
73	9.5	White Hall SD	White Hall
75	9.2	Valley View SD	Jonesboro
76	8.9	Stuttgart SD	Stuttgart
77	8.8	Magnolia SD	Magnolia
78	7.6	Siloam Springs SD	Siloam Springs
79	0.0	N. Little Rock SD	N Little Rock

English Language Learner Students

Rank	Percent	District Name	City
1	42.4	Dequeen SD	De Queen
2	32.3	Springdale SD	Springdale
3	22.4	Rogers SD	Rogers
4	14.2	Fort Smith SD	Fort Smith
5	14.1	Clarksville SD	Clarksville
6	13.8	Dardanelle SD	Dardanelle
7	10.4	Siloam Springs SD	Siloam Springs
8	9.7	Berryville SD	Berryville
9	7.9	Hope SD	Hope
10	6.9	Hamburg SD	Hamburg
11	6.7	Fayetteville SD	Fayetteville
12	6.5	Hot Springs SD	Hot Springs
13	6.1	Van Buren SD	Van Buren
14	4.9	Warren SD	Warren
15	4.8	Batesville SD	Batesville
15	4.8	Lakeside SD	Hot Springs
17	4.2	Dumas SD	Dumas
18	3.9	Nashville SD	Nashville
19	3.8	Huntsville SD	Huntsville
20	3.6	Russellville SD	Russellville
21	3.5	Waldron SD	Waldron
22	3.3	Bentonville SD	Bentonville
23	3.2	Little Rock SD	Little Rock
24	3.0	Lonoke SD	Lonoke
25	2.6	Jonesboro SD	Jonesboro
26	2.2	Farmington SD	Farmington
26	2.2	Star City SD	Star City
28	1.8	Benton SD	Benton
29	1.5	Gravette SD	Gravette
30	1.4	Bryant SD	Bryant
30	1.4	Conway SD	Conway
30	1.4	So. Conway County SD	Morrilton
33	1.3	Nettleton SD	Jonesboro
34	1.2	N. Little Rock SD	N Little Rock
34	1.2	Sheridan SD	Sheridan
36	1.1	Arkadelphia SD	Arkadelphia
36	1.1	El Dorado SD	El Dorado
36	1.1	Lake Hamilton SD	Pearcy
39	1.0	Mountain Home SD	Mountain Home
39	1.0	Newport SD	Newport
39	1.0	Valley View SD	Jonesboro
42	0.9	Texarkana SD	Texarkana
43	0.8	Magnolia SD	Magnolia
43	0.8	White Hall SD	White Hall
45	0.6	Greene County Tech SD	Paragould
46	0.5	Cabot SD	Cabot
46	0.5	Crossett SD	Crossett
46	0.5	Ozark SD	Ozark
46	0.5	Searcy SD	Searcy
46	0.5	Trumann SD	Trumann
51	0.4	Greenwood SD	Greenwood
51	0.4	Pulaski County Spec. SD	Little Rock
53	0.3	Alma SD	Alma
53	0.3	Blytheville SD	Blytheville
53	0.3	Camden Fairview SD	Camden
56	0.2	Forrest City SD	Forrest City
56	0.2	Heber Springs SD	Heber Springs

Rank	Percent	District Name	City
56	0.2	Malvern SD	Malvern
56	0.2	Marion SD	Marion
56	0.2	Osceola SD	Osceola
56	0.2	Paragould SD	Paragould
56	0.2	Pocahontas SD	Pocahontas
56	0.2	Stuttgart SD	Stuttgart
56	0.2	Wynne SD	Wynne
65	0.1	Ashdown SD	Ashdown
65	0.1	Harrison SD	Harrison
65	0.1	Pine Bluff SD	Pine Bluff
65	0.1	Vilonia SD	Vilonia
65	0.1	Westside Cons. SD	Jonesboro
70	0.0	Beebe SD	Beebe
70	0.0	Greenbrier SD	Greenbrier
70	0.0	Helena/West Helena SD	Helena
70	0.0	Watson Chapel SD	Pine Bluff
74	0.0	Dollarway SD	Pine Bluff
74	0.0	Highland SD	Hardy
74	0.0	Lee County SD	Marianna
74	0.0	Mena SD	Mena
74	0.0	Monticello SD	Monticello
74	0.0	West Memphis SD	West Memphis

Migrant Students

Rank	Percent	District Name	City
1	28.6	Dequeen SD	De Queen
2	12.5	Dardanelle SD	Dardanelle
3	12.4	Berryville SD	Berryville
4	11.4	Waldron SD	Waldron
5	10.9	Springdale SD	Springdale
6	10.7	Clarksville SD	Clarksville
7	9.1	Siloam Springs SD	Siloam Springs
8	8.5	Rogers SD	Rogers
9	8.2	Batesville SD	Batesville
10	7.5	Fort Smith SD	Fort Smith
11	5.5	Trumann SD	Trumann
11	5.5	Warren SD	Warren
13	5.2	Hope SD	Hope
14	4.5	Nashville SD	Nashville
15	4.4	Huntsville SD	Huntsville
15	4.4	Van Buren SD	Van Buren
17	4.1	Russellville SD	Russellville
18	3.2	Fayetteville SD	Fayetteville
19	2.9	Searcy SD	Searcy
20	2.8	Hamburg SD	Hamburg
20	2.8	Jonesboro SD	Jonesboro
22	2.7	Gravette SD	Gravette
23	2.6	Alma SD	Alma
24	2.0	Dumas SD	Dumas
25	1.7	Lonoke SD	Lonoke
25	1.7	Marion SD	Marion
25	1.7	Newport SD	Newport
28	1.5	Forrest City SD	Forrest City
28	1.5	Wynne SD	Wynne
30	1.4	Bentonville SD	Bentonville
31	1.3	Star City SD	Star City
32	1.2	Ozark SD	Ozark
32	1.2	Stuttgart SD	Stuttgart
34	1.0	Westside Cons. SD	Jonesboro
35	0.9	Blytheville SD	Blytheville
36	0.7	Paragould SD	Paragould
37	0.6	Greene County Tech SD	Paragould
38	0.4	Cabot SD	Cabot
38	0.4	Nettleton SD	Jonesboro
38	0.4	Osceola SD	Osceola
38	0.4	Pocahontas SD	Pocahontas
42	0.3	Conway SD	Conway
42	0.3	Valley View SD	Jonesboro
44	0.2	Beebe SD	Beebe
44	0.2	Magnolia SD	Magnolia
46	0.1	Benton SD	Benton
46	0.1	Greenbrier SD	Greenbrier
46	0.1	Hot Springs SD	Hot Springs
46	0.1	Texarkana SD	Texarkana
50	0.0	Crossett SD	Crossett
50	0.0	Greenwood SD	Greenwood
50	0.0	Lakeside SD	Hot Springs
50	0.0	Malvern SD	Malvern
50	0.0	Pine Bluff SD	Pine Bluff
50	0.0	Sheridan SD	Sheridan
56	0.0	Arkadelphia SD	Arkadelphia
56	0.0	Ashdown SD	Ashdown
56	0.0	Bryant SD	Bryant
56	0.0	Camden Fairview SD	Camden
56	0.0	Dollarway SD	Pine Bluff
56	0.0	El Dorado SD	El Dorado
56	0.0	Farmington SD	Farmington
56	0.0	Harrison SD	Harrison
56	0.0	Heber Springs SD	Heber Springs
56	0.0	Helena/West Helena SD	Helena
56	0.0	Highland SD	Hardy
56	0.0	Lake Hamilton SD	Pearcy
56	0.0	Lee County SD	Marianna
56	0.0	Little Rock SD	Little Rock
56	0.0	Mena SD	Mena
56	0.0	Monticello SD	Monticello
56	0.0	Mountain Home SD	Mountain Home
56	0.0	N. Little Rock SD	N Little Rock
56	0.0	Pulaski County Spec. SD	Little Rock
56	0.0	So. Conway County SD	Morrilton
56	0.0	Vilonia SD	Vilonia
56	0.0	Watson Chapel SD	Pine Bluff
56	0.0	West Memphis SD	West Memphis
56	0.0	White Hall SD	White Hall

Students Eligible for Free Lunch

Rank	Percent	District Name	City
1	99.4	Blytheville SD	Blytheville
1	99.4	Forrest City SD	Forrest City
3	97.1	Osceola SD	Osceola
4	87.3	Lee County SD	Marianna
5	78.5	Dollarway SD	Pine Bluff
6	70.8	Helena/West Helena SD	Helena
7	65.3	West Memphis SD	West Memphis
8	64.1	Hamburg SD	Hamburg
9	63.9	Dumas SD	Dumas
10	62.3	Hot Springs SD	Hot Springs
11	60.6	Pine Bluff SD	Pine Bluff
12	58.4	Hope SD	Hope
13	57.6	Dequeen SD	De Queen
14	54.2	Camden Fairview SD	Camden
15	54.1	Warren SD	Warren
16	53.8	Trumann SD	Trumann
17	53.4	Newport SD	Newport
18	52.5	Texarkana SD	Texarkana
19	52.1	N. Little Rock SD	N Little Rock
20	49.5	El Dorado SD	El Dorado
21	49.3	Stuttgart SD	Stuttgart
22	47.8	Waldron SD	Waldron
23	46.6	Little Rock SD	Little Rock
24	46.1	So. Conway County SD	Morrilton
25	45.6	Magnolia SD	Magnolia
26	45.4	Watson Chapel SD	Pine Bluff
27	45.1	Jonesboro SD	Jonesboro
28	44.8	Highland SD	Hardy
28	44.8	Wynne SD	Wynne
30	44.6	Malvern SD	Malvern
31	43.6	Clarksville SD	Clarksville
31	43.6	Fort Smith SD	Fort Smith
33	43.1	Dardanelle SD	Dardanelle
34	42.4	Nashville SD	Nashville
35	42.0	Crossett SD	Crossett
35	42.0	Monticello SD	Monticello
37	41.8	Pocahontas SD	Pocahontas
38	41.1	Mena SD	Mena
39	40.7	Paragould SD	Paragould
40	38.9	Star City SD	Star City
41	38.3	Lonoke SD	Lonoke
42	37.8	Springdale SD	Springdale
43	37.3	Ashdown SD	Ashdown
44	37.2	Batesville SD	Batesville
45	35.7	Van Buren SD	Van Buren
46	35.1	Russellville SD	Russellville
47	34.4	Arkadelphia SD	Arkadelphia
47	34.4	Marion SD	Marion
49	34.3	Huntsville SD	Huntsville
50	34.2	Heber Springs SD	Heber Springs
50	34.2	Pulaski County Spec. SD	Little Rock
52	34.0	Nettleton SD	Jonesboro
53	33.8	Rogers SD	Rogers
54	33.3	Mountain Home SD	Mountain Home
55	33.1	Berryville SD	Berryville
56	31.9	Ozark SD	Ozark
57	31.7	Siloam Springs SD	Siloam Springs
58	31.0	Alma SD	Alma
59	30.7	Gravette SD	Gravette
59	30.7	Greene County Tech SD	Paragould
61	29.7	Harrison SD	Harrison
62	29.2	Westside Cons. SD	Jonesboro
63	27.1	Greenbrier SD	Greenbrier
64	26.8	Beebe SD	Beebe
65	26.0	Conway SD	Conway
66	25.7	Searcy SD	Searcy
67	24.2	Fayetteville SD	Fayetteville
68	24.1	Lake Hamilton SD	Pearcy
69	23.7	Sheridan SD	Sheridan
70	22.9	Cabot SD	Cabot
71	20.8	White Hall SD	White Hall
72	20.6	Benton SD	Benton
73	20.2	Bryant SD	Bryant
74	19.4	Lakeside SD	Hot Springs
75	19.3	Vilonia SD	Vilonia
76	18.9	Farmington SD	Farmington
77	16.3	Bentonville SD	Bentonville
78	14.9	Greenwood SD	Greenwood
79	12.5	Valley View SD	Jonesboro

Students Eligible for Reduced-Price Lunch

Rank	Percent	District Name	City
1	15.5	Pocahontas SD	Pocahontas
2	13.5	Berryville SD	Berryville
3	11.9	Siloam Springs SD	Siloam Springs
4	11.8	Sheridan SD	Sheridan
5	11.7	Mena SD	Mena
5	11.7	So. Conway County SD	Morrilton
7	11.6	Dardanelle SD	Dardanelle
8	11.3	Newport SD	Newport
9	11.2	Highland SD	Hardy
9	11.2	Malvern SD	Malvern
11	10.7	Greenbrier SD	Greenbrier
12	10.5	Ashdown SD	Ashdown
13	10.4	Heber Springs SD	Heber Springs
13	10.4	Westside Cons. SD	Jonesboro
15	10.2	Clarksville SD	Clarksville
15	10.2	Paragould SD	Paragould
17	9.9	Beebe SD	Beebe
17	9.9	Gravette SD	Gravette
17	9.9	Lake Hamilton SD	Pearcy
20	9.7	Dollarway SD	Pine Bluff
20	9.7	Trumann SD	Trumann
22	9.6	Greene County Tech SD	Paragould
23	9.5	Alma SD	Alma
23	9.5	Dumas SD	Dumas
23	9.5	Marion SD	Marion
26	9.3	Lonoke SD	Lonoke
26	9.3	Nashville SD	Nashville
28	9.1	Arkadelphia SD	Arkadelphia
28	9.1	Rogers SD	Rogers
28	9.1	Van Buren SD	Van Buren
31	9.0	Springdale SD	Springdale
31	9.0	Stuttgart SD	Stuttgart
33	8.9	Batesville SD	Batesville
33	8.9	Waldron SD	Waldron
35	8.8	Ozark SD	Ozark
35	8.8	Star City SD	Star City
37	8.6	Harrison SD	Harrison
37	8.6	Vilonia SD	Vilonia
39	8.5	Hot Springs SD	Hot Springs
40	8.4	Mountain Home SD	Mountain Home
40	8.4	Searcy SD	Searcy
42	8.3	Warren SD	Warren
43	8.2	Pulaski County Spec. SD	Little Rock
44	8.0	Russellville SD	Russellville
45	7.9	Bentonville SD	Bentonville
45	7.9	Dequeen SD	De Queen
45	7.9	Fort Smith SD	Fort Smith
48	7.8	Farmington SD	Farmington
49	7.7	Wynne SD	Wynne
50	7.5	Nettleton SD	Jonesboro
50	7.5	Texarkana SD	Texarkana
52	7.1	Huntsville SD	Huntsville
52	7.1	Jonesboro SD	Jonesboro
54	6.9	Cabot SD	Cabot
54	6.9	Greenwood SD	Greenwood
54	6.9	White Hall SD	White Hall
57	6.8	Little Rock SD	Little Rock
58	6.7	Camden Fairview SD	Camden
58	6.7	Watson Chapel SD	Pine Bluff
60	6.6	El Dorado SD	El Dorado
60	6.6	Fayetteville SD	Fayetteville
60	6.6	Helena/West Helena SD	Helena
63	6.5	Magnolia SD	Magnolia
64	6.3	Crossett SD	Crossett
65	6.2	Pine Bluff SD	Pine Bluff
66	5.9	Lee County SD	Marianna
67	5.8	Conway SD	Conway
67	5.8	Valley View SD	Jonesboro
69	5.4	Bryant SD	Bryant
70	5.3	Benton SD	Benton
71	5.1	West Memphis SD	West Memphis
72	5.0	Hope SD	Hope
73	4.9	Lakeside SD	Hot Springs
74	4.7	Monticello SD	Monticello
75	4.2	N. Little Rock SD	N Little Rock
76	3.7	Hamburg SD	Hamburg
77	0.0	Blytheville SD	Blytheville
77	0.0	Forrest City SD	Forrest City
77	0.0	Osceola SD	Osceola

Student/Teacher Ratio

Rank	Ratio	District Name	City
1	18.3	Lake Hamilton SD	Pearcy
2	18.1	Marion SD	Marion
3	18.0	Springdale SD	Springdale

Rank	Ratio	District Name	City
4	17.5	Vilonia SD	Vilonia
5	17.4	Rogers SD	Rogers
6	17.3	Mountain Home SD	Mountain Home
7	17.2	Bryant SD	Bryant
8	17.0	Watson Chapel SD	Pine Bluff
9	16.8	Greenwood SD	Greenwood
10	16.7	Jonesboro SD	Jonesboro
10	16.7	Pocahontas SD	Pocahontas
10	16.7	Searcy SD	Searcy
13	16.5	Forrest City SD	Forrest City
13	16.5	Siloam Springs SD	Siloam Springs
15	16.4	Alma SD	Alma
15	16.4	Benton SD	Benton
15	16.4	Conway SD	Conway
15	16.4	Farmington SD	Farmington
15	16.4	Gravette SD	Gravette
15	16.4	Valley View SD	Jonesboro
21	16.3	Bentonville SD	Bentonville
21	16.3	Greene County Tech SD	Paragould
21	16.3	Pine Bluff SD	Pine Bluff
24	16.2	Cabot SD	Cabot
24	16.2	White Hall SD	White Hall
26	16.1	Dequeen SD	De Queen
27	16.0	Nettleton SD	Jonesboro
27	16.0	Sheridan SD	Sheridan
29	15.9	Highland SD	Hardy
29	15.9	Huntsville SD	Huntsville
29	15.9	Lakeside SD	Hot Springs
32	15.7	Clarksville SD	Clarksville
32	15.7	Crossett SD	Crossett
32	15.7	Harrison SD	Harrison
35	15.6	Beebe SD	Beebe
35	15.6	Lonoke SD	Lonoke
35	15.6	Star City SD	Star City
35	15.6	West Memphis SD	West Memphis
39	15.5	Fort Smith SD	Fort Smith
39	15.5	Magnolia SD	Magnolia
39	15.5	Paragould SD	Paragould
39	15.5	Westside Cons. SD	Jonesboro
43	15.4	Arkadelphia SD	Arkadelphia
43	15.4	Fayetteville SD	Fayetteville
43	15.4	Lee County SD	Marianna
43	15.4	Monticello SD	Monticello
43	15.4	Pulaski County Spec. SD	Little Rock
48	15.2	Camden Fairview SD	Camden
49	15.1	Batesville SD	Batesville
49	15.1	Berryville SD	Berryville
49	15.1	Hamburg SD	Hamburg
49	15.1	Mena SD	Mena
53	15.0	Heber Springs SD	Heber Springs
53	15.0	Malvern SD	Malvern
53	15.0	Wynne SD	Wynne
56	14.9	Van Buren SD	Van Buren
57	14.8	Dardanelle SD	Dardanelle
57	14.8	Texarkana SD	Texarkana
59	14.7	Little Rock SD	Little Rock
59	14.7	Russellville SD	Russellville
61	14.6	Ozark SD	Ozark
61	14.6	Trumann SD	Trumann
63	14.5	Greenbrier SD	Greenbrier
63	14.5	Waldron SD	Waldron
65	14.4	Blytheville SD	Blytheville
65	14.4	N. Little Rock SD	N Little Rock
67	14.2	Hope SD	Hope
68	14.1	El Dorado SD	El Dorado
69	13.9	Hot Springs SD	Hot Springs
70	13.8	Dumas SD	Dumas
71	13.7	Stuttgart SD	Stuttgart
72	13.6	Ashdown SD	Ashdown
72	13.6	Warren SD	Warren
74	13.4	Dollarway SD	Pine Bluff
74	13.4	Nashville SD	Nashville
76	13.3	So. Conway County SD	Morrilton
77	13.2	Helena/West Helena SD	Helena
78	12.9	Osceola SD	Osceola
79	12.2	Newport SD	Newport

Student/Librarian Ratio

Rank	Ratio	District Name	City
1	1,043.3	Bentonville SD	Bentonville
2	911.9	Springdale SD	Springdale
3	846.5	Berryville SD	Berryville
4	802.5	Highland SD	Hardy
5	772.0	Bryant SD	Bryant
6	771.0	Valley View SD	Jonesboro
7	758.8	Alma SD	Alma
8	734.0	Greene County Tech SD	Paragould
9	726.5	Rogers SD	Rogers
10	708.3	Wynne SD	Wynne
11	696.5	Magnolia SD	Magnolia
12	694.0	Sheridan SD	Sheridan
13	684.7	Conway SD	Conway
14	661.5	Vilonia SD	Vilonia
15	647.8	Cabot SD	Cabot
16	643.3	Mountain Home SD	Mountain Home
17	636.2	Greenwood SD	Greenwood
18	634.0	Texarkana SD	Texarkana
19	633.8	Lake Hamilton SD	Pearcy
20	627.2	Watson Chapel SD	Pine Bluff
21	617.0	Siloam Springs SD	Siloam Springs
22	611.7	Farmington SD	Farmington
23	610.5	Searcy SD	Searcy
24	608.3	Benton SD	Benton
25	598.8	Hot Springs SD	Hot Springs
26	594.3	So. Conway County SD	Morrilton
27	578.3	Trumann SD	Trumann
28	571.5	N. Little Rock SD	N Little Rock
29	571.1	Forrest City SD	Forrest City
30	569.7	Marion SD	Marion
31	565.0	Waldron SD	Waldron
32	560.7	Heber Springs SD	Heber Springs
33	559.3	Fort Smith SD	Fort Smith
34	550.0	Hope SD	Hope
35	548.3	Blytheville SD	Blytheville
36	546.5	Monticello SD	Monticello
37	543.7	Westside Cons. SD	Jonesboro
38	538.3	Jonesboro SD	Jonesboro
39	536.3	Newport SD	Newport
40	534.5	El Dorado SD	El Dorado
41	532.0	Huntsville SD	Huntsville
42	526.0	Star City SD	Star City
43	525.3	Ozark SD	Ozark
44	517.3	Little Rock SD	Little Rock
45	514.5	Pulaski County Spec. SD	Little Rock
46	513.4	West Memphis SD	West Memphis
47	511.6	Russellville SD	Russellville
48	507.7	Van Buren SD	Van Buren
49	506.0	Lakeside SD	Hot Springs
50	503.8	Camden Fairview SD	Camden
50	503.8	Fayetteville SD	Fayetteville
52	502.8	Dequeen SD	De Queen
53	497.0	Pine Bluff SD	Pine Bluff
54	490.6	Beebe SD	Beebe
55	485.4	Greenbrier SD	Greenbrier
56	469.5	Mena SD	Mena
57	459.4	Helena/West Helena SD	Helena
58	458.8	Nettleton SD	Jonesboro
59	455.3	Pocahontas SD	Pocahontas
60	453.8	Arkadelphia SD	Arkadelphia
60	453.8	Nashville SD	Nashville
62	449.2	Clarksville SD	Clarksville
63	445.8	Paragould SD	Paragould
64	445.3	Lonoke SD	Lonoke
65	444.3	Dardanelle SD	Dardanelle
66	436.1	White Hall SD	White Hall
67	433.8	Hamburg SD	Hamburg
68	410.2	Crossett SD	Crossett
69	405.3	Gravette SD	Gravette
70	403.5	Dumas SD	Dumas
71	398.9	Harrison SD	Harrison
72	393.3	Warren SD	Warren
73	392.3	Lee County SD	Marianna
74	385.8	Dollarway SD	Pine Bluff
75	376.6	Stuttgart SD	Stuttgart
76	366.0	Batesville SD	Batesville
77	363.8	Malvern SD	Malvern
78	335.0	Osceola SD	Osceola
79	331.2	Ashdown SD	Ashdown

Student/Counselor Ratio

Rank	Ratio	District Name	City
1	547.1	Springdale SD	Springdale
2	506.0	Lakeside SD	Hot Springs
3	485.4	Greenbrier SD	Greenbrier
4	456.4	Conway SD	Conway
5	449.2	Clarksville SD	Clarksville
6	445.3	Lonoke SD	Lonoke
7	444.3	Dardanelle SD	Dardanelle
8	441.1	Bryant SD	Bryant
8	441.1	Rogers SD	Rogers
10	441.0	Vilonia SD	Vilonia
11	440.1	West Memphis SD	West Memphis
12	439.3	Bentonville SD	Bentonville
13	436.1	White Hall SD	White Hall
14	433.8	Hamburg SD	Hamburg
15	433.6	Alma SD	Alma
16	428.9	Mountain Home SD	Mountain Home
17	427.3	Marion SD	Marion
18	426.0	Pine Bluff SD	Pine Bluff
19	425.6	Huntsville SD	Huntsville
20	423.6	Waldron SD	Waldron
21	423.3	Berryville SD	Berryville
22	419.4	Greene County Tech SD	Paragould
23	416.4	Sheridan SD	Sheridan
24	410.2	Crossett SD	Crossett
25	409.1	Cabot SD	Cabot
26	408.8	Beebe SD	Beebe
27	407.0	Searcy SD	Searcy
28	405.3	Gravette SD	Gravette
29	402.3	Newport SD	Newport
30	402.2	Dequeen SD	De Queen
31	402.0	Helena/West Helena SD	Helena
32	401.3	Highland SD	Hardy
33	399.8	Forrest City SD	Forrest City
34	399.2	Hot Springs SD	Hot Springs
35	397.6	Greenwood SD	Greenwood
35	397.6	N. Little Rock SD	N Little Rock
37	396.2	So. Conway County SD	Morrilton
38	394.5	Star City SD	Star City
39	394.0	Ozark SD	Ozark
40	393.3	Nettleton SD	Jonesboro
41	392.9	Hope SD	Hope
42	392.4	Lee County SD	Marianna
43	392.0	Watson Chapel SD	Pine Bluff
44	391.9	Siloam Springs SD	Siloam Springs
45	387.1	Benton SD	Benton
46	385.5	Valley View SD	Jonesboro
47	382.1	Paragould SD	Paragould
48	377.9	Camden Fairview SD	Camden
49	375.6	Mena SD	Mena
50	372.1	Van Buren SD	Van Buren
51	367.6	Fort Smith SD	Fort Smith
52	367.0	Farmington SD	Farmington
53	366.4	Fayetteville SD	Fayetteville
54	365.6	Blytheville SD	Blytheville
55	364.3	Monticello SD	Monticello
56	363.8	Malvern SD	Malvern
57	363.0	Nashville SD	Nashville
58	356.3	El Dorado SD	El Dorado
59	348.3	Magnolia SD	Magnolia
60	347.0	Trumann SD	Trumann
61	346.1	Jonesboro SD	Jonesboro
62	336.4	Heber Springs SD	Heber Springs
63	335.0	Osceola SD	Osceola
64	331.2	Ashdown SD	Ashdown
65	329.2	Little Rock SD	Little Rock
66	326.2	Westside Cons. SD	Jonesboro
67	322.8	Dumas SD	Dumas
68	319.8	Russellville SD	Russellville
69	317.0	Texarkana SD	Texarkana
70	314.8	Wynne SD	Wynne
71	314.6	Warren SD	Warren
72	313.8	Stuttgart SD	Stuttgart
73	313.7	Batesville SD	Batesville
74	310.2	Harrison SD	Harrison
75	308.6	Dollarway SD	Pine Bluff
76	303.6	Pulaski County Spec. SD	Little Rock
77	303.5	Pocahontas SD	Pocahontas
78	292.5	Lake Hamilton SD	Pearcy
79	283.6	Arkadelphia SD	Arkadelphia

Current Spending per Student in FY2003

Rank	Dollars	District Name	City
1	7,994	Little Rock SD	Little Rock
2	7,803	Hot Springs SD	Hot Springs
3	7,654	Lee County SD	Marianna
4	7,403	Pulaski County Spec. SD	Little Rock
5	7,304	N. Little Rock SD	N Little Rock
6	7,262	Helena/West Helena SD	Helena
7	7,145	Fayetteville SD	Fayetteville
8	7,101	Newport SD	Newport
9	6,908	Russellville SD	Russellville
10	6,871	Hamburg SD	Hamburg
11	6,855	Warren SD	Warren
12	6,847	Dollarway SD	Pine Bluff
13	6,602	Camden Fairview SD	Camden
14	6,506	Fort Smith SD	Fort Smith
15	6,482	Dumas SD	Dumas
16	6,437	Texarkana SD	Texarkana
17	6,430	Blytheville SD	Blytheville
18	6,377	Hope SD	Hope
19	6,324	Pine Bluff SD	Pine Bluff
20	6,311	Ashdown SD	Ashdown
21	6,304	Forrest City SD	Forrest City
22	6,298	Trumann SD	Trumann
23	6,281	Paragould SD	Paragould
24	6,271	Osceola SD	Osceola
25	6,248	Stuttgart SD	Stuttgart
26	6,245	So. Conway County SD	Morrilton
27	6,210	Westside Cons. SD	Jonesboro
28	6,206	Batesville SD	Batesville
29	6,090	Malvern SD	Malvern
30	6,085	Alma SD	Alma
31	6,062	Bentonville SD	Bentonville
32	6,042	Rogers SD	Rogers
33	6,033	Van Buren SD	Van Buren

34	6,004	Benton SD	Benton
35	5,988	Jonesboro SD	Jonesboro
36	5,980	Greenbrier SD	Greenbrier
37	5,978	Heber Springs SD	Heber Springs
38	5,969	Lakeside SD	Hot Springs
39	5,933	Monticello SD	Monticello
40	5,898	Mena SD	Mena
41	5,880	Arkadelphia SD	Arkadelphia
42	5,879	Nashville SD	Nashville
43	5,862	Lake Hamilton SD	Pearcy
44	5,852	Mountain Home SD	Mountain Home
45	5,841	Lonoke SD	Lonoke
46	5,825	Huntsville SD	Huntsville
47	5,819	Crossett SD	Crossett
48	5,787	El Dorado SD	El Dorado
49	5,785	Pocahontas SD	Pocahontas
49	5,785	Springdale SD	Springdale
51	5,779	Greenwood SD	Greenwood
52	5,769	Beebe SD	Beebe
53	5,748	Berryville SD	Berryville
54	5,744	Dequeen SD	De Queen
55	5,742	Cabot SD	Cabot
56	5,732	West Memphis SD	West Memphis
57	5,728	Conway SD	Conway
58	5,723	Marion SD	Marion
59	5,705	Watson Chapel SD	Pine Bluff
60	5,704	Wynne SD	Wynne
61	5,644	Nettleton SD	Jonesboro
62	5,633	Sheridan SD	Sheridan
63	5,612	Magnolia SD	Magnolia
64	5,573	Ozark SD	Ozark
65	5,561	Vilonia SD	Vilonia
66	5,560	Clarksville SD	Clarksville
67	5,549	White Hall SD	White Hall
68	5,544	Siloam Springs SD	Siloam Springs
69	5,537	Harrison SD	Harrison
69	5,537	Highland SD	Hardy
71	5,512	Dardanelle SD	Dardanelle
72	5,507	Star City SD	Star City
73	5,488	Greene County Tech SD	Paragould
74	5,472	Gravette SD	Gravette
75	5,393	Searcy SD	Searcy
76	5,381	Bryant SD	Bryant
77	5,358	Farmington SD	Farmington
78	5,317	Waldron SD	Waldron
79	5,243	Valley View SD	Jonesboro

Number of Diploma Recipients

Rank	Number	District Name	City
1	1,334	Little Rock SD	Little Rock
2	822	Fort Smith SD	Fort Smith
3	816	Pulaski County Spec. SD	Little Rock
4	596	Rogers SD	Rogers
5	554	Springdale SD	Springdale
6	539	Fayetteville SD	Fayetteville
7	508	N. Little Rock SD	N Little Rock
8	450	Cabot SD	Cabot
9	446	Conway SD	Conway
10	392	Bentonville SD	Bentonville
11	388	Bryant SD	Bryant
12	324	Russellville SD	Russellville
13	319	Pine Bluff SD	Pine Bluff
14	315	Jonesboro SD	Jonesboro
15	308	El Dorado SD	El Dorado
16	300	Van Buren SD	Van Buren
17	274	Benton SD	Benton
18	260	West Memphis SD	West Memphis
19	246	Sheridan SD	Sheridan
20	240	Mountain Home SD	Mountain Home
21	236	Forrest City SD	Forrest City
22	230	Camden Fairview SD	Camden
23	227	Greenwood SD	Greenwood
24	225	Watson Chapel SD	Pine Bluff
25	222	Siloam Springs SD	Siloam Springs
26	217	Texarkana SD	Texarkana
27	214	Searcy SD	Searcy
28	212	Lake Hamilton SD	Pearcy
29	209	Magnolia SD	Magnolia
30	196	Wynne SD	Wynne
31	194	Harrison SD	Harrison
32	188	Alma SD	Alma
33	184	White Hall SD	White Hall
34	183	Helena/West Helena SD	Helena
35	178	Hope SD	Hope
36	171	Vilonia SD	Vilonia
37	166	So. Conway County SD	Morrilton
38	164	Arkadelphia SD	Arkadelphia
39	163	Blytheville SD	Blytheville
40	158	Marion SD	Marion
41	155	Lakeside SD	Hot Springs
42	154	Greene County Tech SD	Paragould
43	152	Hot Springs SD	Hot Springs
43	152	Nettleton SD	Jonesboro
45	151	Monticello SD	Monticello
46	143	Greenbrier SD	Greenbrier
47	139	Malvern SD	Malvern
48	138	Ozark SD	Ozark
49	134	Stuttgart SD	Stuttgart
50	132	Paragould SD	Paragould
51	129	Batesville SD	Batesville
52	126	Crossett SD	Crossett
53	124	Osceola SD	Osceola
54	123	Huntsville SD	Huntsville
55	120	Newport SD	Newport
56	118	Beebe SD	Beebe
57	117	Lee County SD	Marianna
57	117	Mena SD	Mena
59	116	Dumas SD	Dumas
59	116	Hamburg SD	Hamburg
61	110	Pocahontas SD	Pocahontas
61	110	Waldron SD	Waldron
63	105	Nashville SD	Nashville
64	104	Lonoke SD	Lonoke
65	102	Clarksville SD	Clarksville
65	102	Warren SD	Warren
67	101	Dardanelle SD	Dardanelle
68	100	Ashdown SD	Ashdown
68	100	Berryville SD	Berryville
70	98	Farmington SD	Farmington
71	96	Dollarway SD	Pine Bluff
72	95	Heber Springs SD	Heber Springs
73	91	Westside Cons. SD	Jonesboro
74	90	Star City SD	Star City
75	87	Valley View SD	Jonesboro
76	83	Gravette SD	Gravette
76	83	Highland SD	Hardy
78	81	Dequeen SD	De Queen
78	81	Trumann SD	Trumann

High School Drop-out Rate

Rank	Percent	District Name	City
1	12.1	Little Rock SD	Little Rock
2	10.7	Helena/West Helena SD	Helena
3	10.2	Dequeen SD	De Queen
4	9.9	Pine Bluff SD	Pine Bluff
5	9.3	Newport SD	Newport
6	9.2	Lee County SD	Marianna
7	8.5	Blytheville SD	Blytheville
8	8.3	Star City SD	Star City
9	7.7	Forrest City SD	Forrest City
9	7.7	Osceola SD	Osceola
11	7.5	Pulaski County Spec. SD	Little Rock
12	7.4	Trumann SD	Trumann
13	7.3	Clarksville SD	Clarksville
14	6.9	West Memphis SD	West Memphis
15	6.4	Fayetteville SD	Fayetteville
15	6.4	Heber Springs SD	Heber Springs
17	6.3	Bentonville SD	Bentonville
18	6.2	Dardanelle SD	Dardanelle
18	6.2	Ozark SD	Ozark
20	5.9	Paragould SD	Paragould
21	5.8	Beebe SD	Beebe
22	5.7	Camden Fairview SD	Camden
23	5.6	Malvern SD	Malvern
23	5.6	Russellville SD	Russellville
23	5.6	Valley View SD	Jonesboro
26	5.5	Crossett SD	Crossett
26	5.5	Huntsville SD	Huntsville
26	5.5	Springdale SD	Springdale
29	5.4	Hope SD	Hope
29	5.4	Mountain Home SD	Mountain Home
31	5.3	Hot Springs SD	Hot Springs
31	5.3	Stuttgart SD	Stuttgart
33	5.2	Ashdown SD	Ashdown
33	5.2	Dollarway SD	Pine Bluff
33	5.2	Fort Smith SD	Fort Smith
33	5.2	Nashville SD	Nashville
37	5.0	Conway SD	Conway
38	4.9	Texarkana SD	Texarkana
38	4.9	Van Buren SD	Van Buren
40	4.8	Berryville SD	Berryville
40	4.8	Hamburg SD	Hamburg
40	4.8	Mena SD	Mena
40	4.8	Sheridan SD	Sheridan
44	4.7	Cabot SD	Cabot
44	4.7	Rogers SD	Rogers
46	4.6	Batesville SD	Batesville
46	4.6	Gravette SD	Gravette
46	4.6	Marion SD	Marion
49	4.4	Highland SD	Hardy
50	4.3	Bryant SD	Bryant
51	4.0	Dumas SD	Dumas
52	3.9	Greene County Tech SD	Paragould
52	3.9	Harrison SD	Harrison
54	3.8	Pocahontas SD	Pocahontas
55	3.6	Magnolia SD	Magnolia
56	3.5	Wynne SD	Wynne
57	3.4	Arkadelphia SD	Arkadelphia
58	3.3	Nettleton SD	Jonesboro
58	3.3	So. Conway County SD	Morrilton
60	3.2	Benton SD	Benton
61	3.1	Waldron SD	Waldron
61	3.1	Warren SD	Warren
63	3.0	Lonoke SD	Lonoke
63	3.0	Searcy SD	Searcy
65	2.9	Greenwood SD	Greenwood
66	2.6	Alma SD	Alma
66	2.6	Farmington SD	Farmington
66	2.6	Lakeside SD	Hot Springs
69	2.4	Vilonia SD	Vilonia
69	2.4	Watson Chapel SD	Pine Bluff
71	1.8	Jonesboro SD	Jonesboro
71	1.8	White Hall SD	White Hall
73	1.5	Westside Cons. SD	Jonesboro
74	1.3	Monticello SD	Monticello
75	1.1	Greenbrier SD	Greenbrier
75	1.1	N. Little Rock SD	N Little Rock
77	1.0	Siloam Springs SD	Siloam Springs
78	0.8	El Dorado SD	El Dorado
79	0.4	Lake Hamilton SD	Pearcy

California

California Public School Educational Profile

Category	Value	Category	Value
Schools *(2003-2004)*	9,237	**Diploma Recipients** *(2002-2003)*	325,895
Instructional Level		White, Non-Hispanic	140,421
Primary	5,580	Black, Non-Hispanic	23,451
Middle	1,341	Asian/Pacific Islander	48,206
High	1,839	American Indian/Alaskan Native	3,036
Other Level	463	Hispanic	109,038
Curriculum		**High School Drop-out Rate** (%) *(2001-2002)*	n/a
Regular	7,908	White, Non-Hispanic	n/a
Special Education	128	Black, Non-Hispanic	n/a
Vocational	0	Asian/Pacific Islander	n/a
Alternative	1,187	American Indian/Alaskan Native	n/a
Type		Hispanic	n/a
Magnet	457	**Staff** *(2003-2004)*	
Charter	444	Teachers	296,727.6
Title I Eligible	5,458	Average Salary[1] ($)	56,444
School-wide Title I	2,924	Librarians/Media Specialists	1,227.9
Students *(2003-2004)*	6,298,928	Guidance Counselors	6,639.6
Gender (%)		**Ratios** *(2003-2004)*	
Male	51.4	Student/Teacher Ratio	21.2 to 1
Female	48.6	Student/Librarian Ratio	5,129.8 to 1
Race/Ethnicity (%)		Student/Counselor Ratio	948.7 to 1
White, Non-Hispanic	32.5	**College Entrance Exam Scores** *(2005)*	
Black, Non-Hispanic	8.1	Scholastic Aptitude Test (SAT)	
Asian/Pacific Islander	11.2	Participation Rate (%)	50
American Indian/Alaskan Native	0.8	Mean SAT Reasoning Test Verbal Score	504
Hispanic	46.0	Mean SAT Reasoning Test Math Score	522
Classification (%)		American College Testing Program (ACT)	
Individual Education Program (IEP)	10.8	Participation Rate (%)	14
Migrant *(2002-2003)*	3.7	Average Composite Score	21.6
English Language Learner (ELL)	25.4	Average English Score	21.1
Eligible for Free Lunch Program	39.6	Average Math Score	22.1
Eligible for Reduced-Price Lunch Program	9.1	Average Reading Score	21.8
Current Spending *($ per student in FY 2003)*	7,695	Average Science Score	20.9
Instruction	4,723		
Support Services	2,702		

Note: *For an explanation of data, please refer to the User's Guide in the front of the book; (1) Includes extra-duty pay*

California NAEP 2005 Test Scores

Reading			Mathematics		
Grade/Category	Value	Rank	Grade/Category	Value	Rank
4th Grade			**4th Grade**		
Average Proficiency	206.5 (0.70)	49/51	Average Proficiency	230.4 (0.58)	43/51
Proficiency by Gender/Race/Ethnicity			Proficiency by Gender/Race/Ethnicity		
Male	203.3 (0.83)	46/51	Male	231.4 (0.69)	44/51
Female	209.7 (0.80)	49/51	Female	229.3 (0.60)	43/51
White, Non-Hispanic	225.4 (1.15)	31/51	White, Non-Hispanic	244.9 (0.81)	23/51
Black, Non-Hispanic	195.1 (1.43)	29/42	Black, Non-Hispanic	215.4 (1.43)	30/42
Asian, Non-Hispanic	222.5 (1.77)	19/27	Asian, Non-Hispanic	248.7 (1.49)	14/25
American Indian, Non-Hispanic	212.9 (3.93)	1/7	American Indian, Non-Hispanic	228.4 (4.18)	2/7
Hispanic	192.8 (0.81)	38/40	Hispanic	219.4 (0.70)	32/41
Proficiency by Class Size			Proficiency by Class Size		
Less than 16 Students	193.3 (5.33)	29/34	Less than 16 Students	219.3 (3.59)	27/35
16 to 18 Students	n/a	n/a	16 to 18 Students	n/a	n/a
19 to 20 Students	n/a	n/a	19 to 20 Students	n/a	n/a
21 to 25 Students	202.4 (3.12)	50/51	21 to 25 Students	222.9 (2.48)	50/51
Greater than 25 Students	207.7 (0.85)	35/36	Greater than 25 Students	231.5 (0.68)	27/33
Percent Attaining Achievement Levels			Percent Attaining Achievement Levels		
Below Basic	50.0 (0.93)	3/51	Below Basic	29.1 (0.74)	6/51
Basic or Above	50.0 (0.93)	49/51	Basic or Above	70.9 (0.74)	46/51
Proficient or Above	21.4 (0.70)	46/51	Proficient or Above	28.0 (0.80)	40/51
Advanced or Above	4.8 (0.35)	44/51	Advanced or Above	3.8 (0.38)	34/51
8th Grade			**8th Grade**		
Average Proficiency	250.4 (0.55)	49/51	Average Proficiency	268.6 (0.65)	45/51
Proficiency by Gender/Race/Ethnicity			Proficiency by Gender/Race/Ethnicity		
Male	245.7 (0.74)	48/51	Male	269.2 (0.86)	44/51
Female	255.2 (0.62)	48/51	Female	267.9 (0.74)	46/51
White, Non-Hispanic	264.1 (0.93)	45/51	White, Non-Hispanic	283.5 (0.88)	37/51
Black, Non-Hispanic	240.1 (1.62)	26/40	Black, Non-Hispanic	248.1 (1.57)	31/41
Asian, Non-Hispanic	264.4 (1.64)	18/24	Asian, Non-Hispanic	292.8 (1.71)	15/23
American Indian, Non-Hispanic	n/a	n/a	American Indian, Non-Hispanic	n/a	n/a
Hispanic	238.6 (0.77)	37/38	Hispanic	254.2 (0.69)	35/38
Proficiency by Parents Highest Level of Ed.			Proficiency by Parents Highest Level of Ed.		
Did Not Finish High School	238.0 (1.21)	44/49	Did Not Finish High School	252.5 (1.19)	42/50
Graduated High School	242.5 (1.14)	48/50	Graduated High School	258.2 (1.26)	45/50
Some Education After High School	258.5 (1.06)	45/50	Some Education After High School	274.4 (1.15)	43/50
Graduated College	263.4 (0.84)	42/50	Graduated College	284.2 (1.00)	36/50
Percent Attaining Achievement Levels			Percent Attaining Achievement Levels		
Below Basic	50.0 (0.93)	3/51	Below Basic	43.0 (0.82)	6/51
Basic or Above	50.0 (0.93)	49/51	Basic or Above	57.0 (0.82)	46/51
Proficient or Above	21.4 (0.70)	46/51	Proficient or Above	21.8 (0.62)	41/51
Advanced or Above	4.8 (0.35)	44/51	Advanced or Above	4.5 (0.36)	34/51

Note: For an explanation of data, please refer to the User's Guide in the front of the book; n/a indicates data not available

Alameda County

Alameda City Unified
2200 Central Ave • Alameda, CA 94501-4450
(510) 337-7060 • http://www.alameda.k12.ca.us/
Grade Span: KG-12; **Agency Type:** 1
Schools: 20
  12 Primary; 3 Middle; 5 High; 0 Other Level
  19 Regular; 0 Special Education; 0 Vocational; 1 Alternative
  0 Magnet; 2 Charter; 6 Title I Eligible; 4 School-wide Title I
Students: 10,621 (50.4% male; 49.5% female)
  Individual Education Program: 1,212 (11.4%);
  English Language Learner: 2,152 (20.3%); Migrant: 2 (<0.1%)
  Eligible for Free Lunch Program: 2,773 (26.1%)
  Eligible for Reduced-Price Lunch Program: 796 (7.5%)
Teachers: 558.8 (19.0 to 1)
Librarians/Media Specialists: 1.0 (10,621.0 to 1)
Guidance Counselors: 12.4 (856.5 to 1)
Current Spending: ($ per student per year):
  Total: $7,166; Instruction: $4,685; Support Services: $2,283
Enrollment, Drop-out Rates and Diploma Recipients by Race/Ethnicity

Category	Total	White	Black	Asian	AIAN	Hisp.
Enrollment (%)	100.0	31.5	15.0	37.9	0.9	11.5
Drop-out Rate (%)	n/a	n/a	n/a	n/a	n/a	n/a
H.S. Diplomas (#)	645	201	84	277	4	66

Albany City Unified
904 Talbot Ave • Albany, CA 94706-2020
(510) 558-3750 • http://www.albany.k12.ca.us/
Grade Span: KG-12; **Agency Type:** 1
Schools: 6
  3 Primary; 1 Middle; 2 High; 0 Other Level
  5 Regular; 0 Special Education; 0 Vocational; 1 Alternative
  0 Magnet; 0 Charter; 3 Title I Eligible; 0 School-wide Title I
Students: 3,314 (51.0% male; 48.9% female)
  Individual Education Program: 325 (9.8%);
  English Language Learner: 368 (11.1%); Migrant: 0 (0.0%)
  Eligible for Free Lunch Program: 280 (8.4%)
  Eligible for Reduced-Price Lunch Program: 156 (4.7%)
Teachers: 160.4 (20.7 to 1)
Librarians/Media Specialists: 1.6 (2,071.3 to 1)
Guidance Counselors: 4.4 (753.2 to 1)
Current Spending: ($ per student per year):
  Total: $7,570; Instruction: $5,155; Support Services: $2,190
Enrollment, Drop-out Rates and Diploma Recipients by Race/Ethnicity

Category	Total	White	Black	Asian	AIAN	Hisp.
Enrollment (%)	100.0	43.2	8.4	32.1	0.5	10.4
Drop-out Rate (%)	n/a	n/a	n/a	n/a	n/a	n/a
H.S. Diplomas (#)	181	85	14	55	0	20

Berkeley Unified
2134 Martin Luther King Jr. W • Berkeley, CA 94704-1109
(510) 644-6147 • http://www.berkeley.k12.ca.us/
Grade Span: KG-12; **Agency Type:** 1
Schools: 16
  11 Primary; 3 Middle; 2 High; 0 Other Level
  15 Regular; 0 Special Education; 0 Vocational; 1 Alternative
  5 Magnet; 0 Charter; 14 Title I Eligible; 6 School-wide Title I
Students: 8,843 (50.8% male; 49.1% female)
  Individual Education Program: 1,082 (12.2%);
  English Language Learner: 1,204 (13.6%); Migrant: 0 (0.0%)
  Eligible for Free Lunch Program: 3,484 (39.4%)
  Eligible for Reduced-Price Lunch Program: 932 (10.5%)
Teachers: 455.4 (19.4 to 1)
Librarians/Media Specialists: 3.6 (2,456.4 to 1)
Guidance Counselors: 9.8 (902.3 to 1)
Current Spending: ($ per student per year):
  Total: $9,766; Instruction: $6,019; Support Services: $3,549
Enrollment, Drop-out Rates and Diploma Recipients by Race/Ethnicity

Category	Total	White	Black	Asian	AIAN	Hisp.
Enrollment (%)	100.0	29.3	31.4	8.2	0.3	15.9
Drop-out Rate (%)	n/a	n/a	n/a	n/a	n/a	n/a
H.S. Diplomas (#)	673	265	217	69	1	65

Castro Valley Unified
4430 Alma Ave • Castro Valley, CA 94546-0146
Mailing Address: PO Box 2146 • Castro Valley, CA 94546-0146
(510) 537-3000 • http://www.cv.k12.ca.us/
Grade Span: KG-12; **Agency Type:** 1
Schools: 15
  9 Primary; 2 Middle; 4 High; 0 Other Level
  13 Regular; 1 Special Education; 0 Vocational; 1 Alternative
  0 Magnet; 0 Charter; 3 Title I Eligible; 0 School-wide Title I
Students: 8,391 (50.6% male; 49.3% female)
  Individual Education Program: 857 (10.2%);

  English Language Learner: 563 (6.7%); Migrant: 0 (0.0%)
  Eligible for Free Lunch Program: 887 (10.6%)
  Eligible for Reduced-Price Lunch Program: 505 (6.0%)
Teachers: 390.3 (21.5 to 1)
Librarians/Media Specialists: 2.0 (4,195.5 to 1)
Guidance Counselors: 12.5 (671.3 to 1)
Current Spending: ($ per student per year):
  Total: $6,719; Instruction: $4,216; Support Services: $2,277
Enrollment, Drop-out Rates and Diploma Recipients by Race/Ethnicity

Category	Total	White	Black	Asian	AIAN	Hisp.
Enrollment (%)	100.0	53.5	5.4	25.9	0.9	14.1
Drop-out Rate (%)	n/a	n/a	n/a	n/a	n/a	n/a
H.S. Diplomas (#)	551	355	17	124	6	48

Dublin Unified
7471 Larkdale Ave • Dublin, CA 94568-1500
(925) 828-2551 • http://www.dublin.k12.ca.us/
Grade Span: KG-12; **Agency Type:** 1
Schools: 8
  5 Primary; 1 Middle; 2 High; 0 Other Level
  7 Regular; 0 Special Education; 0 Vocational; 1 Alternative
  0 Magnet; 0 Charter; 5 Title I Eligible; 0 School-wide Title I
Students: 4,483 (51.2% male; 48.7% female)
  Individual Education Program: 423 (9.4%);
  English Language Learner: 296 (6.6%); Migrant: 0 (0.0%)
  Eligible for Free Lunch Program: 341 (7.6%)
  Eligible for Reduced-Price Lunch Program: 110 (2.5%)
Teachers: 226.8 (19.8 to 1)
Librarians/Media Specialists: 1.0 (4,483.0 to 1)
Guidance Counselors: 3.0 (1,494.3 to 1)
Current Spending: ($ per student per year):
  Total: $7,966; Instruction: $4,962; Support Services: $2,749
Enrollment, Drop-out Rates and Diploma Recipients by Race/Ethnicity

Category	Total	White	Black	Asian	AIAN	Hisp.
Enrollment (%)	100.0	55.8	5.9	19.1	1.0	12.7
Drop-out Rate (%)	n/a	n/a	n/a	n/a	n/a	n/a
H.S. Diplomas (#)	250	161	16	42	3	28

Fremont Unified
4210 Technology Dr • Fremont, CA 94537-5008
Mailing Address: PO Box 5008 • Fremont, CA 94537-5008
(510) 657-2350 • http://www.fremont.k12.ca.us/
Grade Span: KG-12; **Agency Type:** 1
Schools: 41
  28 Primary; 5 Middle; 6 High; 2 Other Level
  39 Regular; 0 Special Education; 0 Vocational; 2 Alternative
  0 Magnet; 1 Charter; 7 Title I Eligible; 2 School-wide Title I
Students: 31,844 (52.3% male; 47.6% female)
  Individual Education Program: 2,806 (8.8%);
  English Language Learner: 4,918 (15.4%); Migrant: 260 (0.8%)
  Eligible for Free Lunch Program: 3,228 (10.1%)
  Eligible for Reduced-Price Lunch Program: 1,432 (4.5%)
Teachers: 1,468.7 (21.7 to 1)
Librarians/Media Specialists: 4.3 (7,405.6 to 1)
Guidance Counselors: 27.0 (1,179.4 to 1)
Current Spending: ($ per student per year):
  Total: $6,892; Instruction: $4,654; Support Services: $2,075
Enrollment, Drop-out Rates and Diploma Recipients by Race/Ethnicity

Category	Total	White	Black	Asian	AIAN	Hisp.
Enrollment (%)	100.0	30.6	5.5	48.2	0.7	14.7
Drop-out Rate (%)	n/a	n/a	n/a	n/a	n/a	n/a
H.S. Diplomas (#)	1,972	865	58	827	8	214

Hayward Unified
24411 Amador St • Hayward, CA 94540-0001
Mailing Address: PO Box 5000 • Hayward, CA 94540-0001
(510) 784-2600 • http://www.husd.k12.ca.us/
Grade Span: KG-12; **Agency Type:** 1
Schools: 33
  23 Primary; 6 Middle; 3 High; 1 Other Level
  32 Regular; 0 Special Education; 0 Vocational; 1 Alternative
  0 Magnet; 0 Charter; 17 Title I Eligible; 14 School-wide Title I
Students: 24,014 (51.5% male; 48.4% female)
  Individual Education Program: 2,469 (10.3%);
  English Language Learner: 8,219 (34.2%); Migrant: 784 (3.3%)
  Eligible for Free Lunch Program: 9,606 (40.0%)
  Eligible for Reduced-Price Lunch Program: 3,433 (14.3%)
Teachers: 1,197.5 (20.1 to 1)
Librarians/Media Specialists: 15.3 (1,569.5 to 1)
Guidance Counselors: 23.8 (1,009.0 to 1)
Current Spending: ($ per student per year):
  Total: $7,381; Instruction: $4,652; Support Services: $2,475

Enrollment, Drop-out Rates and Diploma Recipients by Race/Ethnicity

Category	Total	White	Black	Asian	AIAN	Hisp.
Enrollment (%)	100.0	13.2	15.6	20.5	0.6	47.7
Drop-out Rate (%)	n/a	n/a	n/a	n/a	n/a	n/a
H.S. Diplomas (#)	1,264	253	209	350	11	441

Livermore Valley Joint Unified
685 E Jack London Blvd • Livermore, CA 94550-1800
(925) 606-3200 • http://www.lvjusd.k12.ca.us/
Grade Span: KG-12; **Agency Type:** 1
Schools: 21
     12 Primary; 4 Middle; 4 High; 1 Other Level
     18 Regular; 0 Special Education; 0 Vocational; 3 Alternative
     0 Magnet; 0 Charter; 4 Title I Eligible; 0 School-wide Title I
Students: 14,329   (51.3% male; 48.6% female)
     Individual Education Program: 1,638 (11.4%);
     English Language Learner: 1,569 (10.9%); Migrant: 532 (3.7%)
     Eligible for Free Lunch Program: 1,576 (11.0%)
     Eligible for Reduced-Price Lunch Program: 453 (3.2%)
Teachers: 606.6 (23.6 to 1)
Librarians/Media Specialists: 0.0 (n/a to 1)
Guidance Counselors: 4.5 (3,184.2 to 1)
Current Spending: ($ per student per year):
     Total: $6,690; Instruction: $4,432; Support Services: $2,089

Enrollment, Drop-out Rates and Diploma Recipients by Race/Ethnicity

Category	Total	White	Black	Asian	AIAN	Hisp.
Enrollment (%)	100.0	67.7	3.1	8.8	0.5	18.9
Drop-out Rate (%)	n/a	n/a	n/a	n/a	n/a	n/a
H.S. Diplomas (#)	918	693	22	67	5	125

New Haven Unified
34200 Alvarado-Niles Rd • Union City, CA 94587-4402
(510) 471-1100 • http://www.nhusd.k12.ca.us/
Grade Span: KG-12; **Agency Type:** 1
Schools: 12
     8 Primary; 3 Middle; 1 High; 0 Other Level
     12 Regular; 0 Special Education; 0 Vocational; 0 Alternative
     0 Magnet; 0 Charter; 7 Title I Eligible; 0 School-wide Title I
Students: 13,303   (51.7% male; 48.2% female)
     Individual Education Program: 1,243 (9.3%);
     English Language Learner: 3,163 (23.8%); Migrant: 477 (3.6%)
     Eligible for Free Lunch Program: 2,989 (22.5%)
     Eligible for Reduced-Price Lunch Program: 1,221 (9.2%)
Teachers: 641.6 (20.7 to 1)
Librarians/Media Specialists: 12.7 (1,047.5 to 1)
Guidance Counselors: 17.5 (760.2 to 1)
Current Spending: ($ per student per year):
     Total: $7,133; Instruction: $4,717; Support Services: $2,114

Enrollment, Drop-out Rates and Diploma Recipients by Race/Ethnicity

Category	Total	White	Black	Asian	AIAN	Hisp.
Enrollment (%)	100.0	15.4	11.2	43.1	0.4	29.9
Drop-out Rate (%)	n/a	n/a	n/a	n/a	n/a	n/a
H.S. Diplomas (#)	828	170	83	397	0	178

Newark Unified
5715 Musick Ave • Newark, CA 94560-0385
Mailing Address: PO Box 385 • Newark, CA 94560-0385
(510) 818-4103 • http://www.nusd.k12.ca.us/
Grade Span: KG-12; **Agency Type:** 1
Schools: 14
     8 Primary; 2 Middle; 3 High; 1 Other Level
     10 Regular; 0 Special Education; 0 Vocational; 4 Alternative
     1 Magnet; 0 Charter; 3 Title I Eligible; 0 School-wide Title I
Students: 7,421   (52.0% male; 47.9% female)
     Individual Education Program: 855 (11.5%);
     English Language Learner: 1,492 (20.1%); Migrant: 142 (1.9%)
     Eligible for Free Lunch Program: 472 (6.4%)
     Eligible for Reduced-Price Lunch Program: 2 (<0.1%)
Teachers: 345.5 (21.5 to 1)
Librarians/Media Specialists: 1.0 (7,421.0 to 1)
Guidance Counselors: 4.2 (1,766.9 to 1)
Current Spending: ($ per student per year):
     Total: $7,435; Instruction: $4,389; Support Services: $2,810

Enrollment, Drop-out Rates and Diploma Recipients by Race/Ethnicity

Category	Total	White	Black	Asian	AIAN	Hisp.
Enrollment (%)	100.0	26.6	7.6	24.9	0.5	39.8
Drop-out Rate (%)	n/a	n/a	n/a	n/a	n/a	n/a
H.S. Diplomas (#)	520	180	24	146	6	164

Oakland Unified
1025 Second Ave • Oakland, CA 94606-2212
(510) 879-8100 • http://www.ousd.k12.ca.us/
Grade Span: KG-12; **Agency Type:** 1
Schools: 118
     69 Primary; 22 Middle; 18 High; 9 Other Level

     109 Regular; 2 Special Education; 0 Vocational; 7 Alternative
     0 Magnet; 15 Charter; 87 Title I Eligible; 64 School-wide Title I
Students: 50,437   (50.8% male; 49.1% female)
     Individual Education Program: 5,511 (10.9%);
     English Language Learner: 15,009 (29.8%); Migrant: 612 (1.2%)
     Eligible for Free Lunch Program: 27,987 (55.5%)
     Eligible for Reduced-Price Lunch Program: 4,543 (9.0%)
Teachers: 2,544.1 (19.8 to 1)
Librarians/Media Specialists: 6.0 (8,406.2 to 1)
Guidance Counselors: 41.0 (1,230.2 to 1)
Current Spending: ($ per student per year):
     Total: $8,692; Instruction: $5,152; Support Services: $3,234

Enrollment, Drop-out Rates and Diploma Recipients by Race/Ethnicity

Category	Total	White	Black	Asian	AIAN	Hisp.
Enrollment (%)	100.0	5.8	42.3	17.0	0.5	33.7
Drop-out Rate (%)	n/a	n/a	n/a	n/a	n/a	n/a
H.S. Diplomas (#)	1,617	88	687	519	6	311

Piedmont City Unified
760 Magnolia Ave • Piedmont, CA 94611-4047
(510) 594-2600 • http://www.piedmont.k12.ca.us/
Grade Span: KG-12; **Agency Type:** 1
Schools: 6
     3 Primary; 1 Middle; 2 High; 0 Other Level
     5 Regular; 0 Special Education; 0 Vocational; 1 Alternative
     0 Magnet; 0 Charter; 0 Title I Eligible; 0 School-wide Title I
Students: 2,597   (50.7% male; 49.2% female)
     Individual Education Program: 324 (12.5%);
     English Language Learner: 78 (3.0%); Migrant: 0 (0.0%)
     Eligible for Free Lunch Program: 0 (0.0%)
     Eligible for Reduced-Price Lunch Program: 0 (0.0%)
Teachers: 151.8 (17.1 to 1)
Librarians/Media Specialists: 3.9 (665.9 to 1)
Guidance Counselors: 6.4 (405.8 to 1)
Current Spending: ($ per student per year):
     Total: $8,799; Instruction: $5,717; Support Services: $3,074

Enrollment, Drop-out Rates and Diploma Recipients by Race/Ethnicity

Category	Total	White	Black	Asian	AIAN	Hisp.
Enrollment (%)	100.0	70.4	2.0	20.3	0.2	3.2
Drop-out Rate (%)	n/a	n/a	n/a	n/a	n/a	n/a
H.S. Diplomas (#)	241	166	14	50	2	8

Pleasanton Unified
4665 Bernal Ave • Pleasanton, CA 94566-7449
(925) 462-5500 • http://www.pleasanton.k12.ca.us/
Grade Span: KG-12; **Agency Type:** 1
Schools: 15
     9 Primary; 3 Middle; 3 High; 0 Other Level
     14 Regular; 0 Special Education; 0 Vocational; 1 Alternative
     0 Magnet; 0 Charter; 3 Title I Eligible; 0 School-wide Title I
Students: 14,039   (50.8% male; 49.1% female)
     Individual Education Program: 1,531 (10.9%);
     English Language Learner: 741 (5.3%); Migrant: 1 (<0.1%)
     Eligible for Free Lunch Program: 450 (3.2%)
     Eligible for Reduced-Price Lunch Program: 200 (1.4%)
Teachers: 658.9 (21.3 to 1)
Librarians/Media Specialists: 2.0 (7,019.5 to 1)
Guidance Counselors: 20.7 (678.2 to 1)
Current Spending: ($ per student per year):
     Total: $7,482; Instruction: $4,942; Support Services: $2,247

Enrollment, Drop-out Rates and Diploma Recipients by Race/Ethnicity

Category	Total	White	Black	Asian	AIAN	Hisp.
Enrollment (%)	100.0	68.2	1.9	20.3	0.8	8.2
Drop-out Rate (%)	n/a	n/a	n/a	n/a	n/a	n/a
H.S. Diplomas (#)	910	712	20	109	9	54

San Leandro Unified
14735 Juniper St • San Leandro, CA 94579-1222
(510) 667-3500 • http://www.sanleandro.k12.ca.us/
Grade Span: KG-12; **Agency Type:** 1
Schools: 13
     9 Primary; 2 Middle; 2 High; 0 Other Level
     12 Regular; 0 Special Education; 0 Vocational; 1 Alternative
     0 Magnet; 1 Charter; 5 Title I Eligible; 0 School-wide Title I
Students: 8,653   (51.4% male; 48.5% female)
     Individual Education Program: 884 (10.2%);
     English Language Learner: 2,233 (25.8%); Migrant: 3 (<0.1%)
     Eligible for Free Lunch Program: 2,265 (26.2%)
     Eligible for Reduced-Price Lunch Program: 936 (10.8%)
Teachers: 418.7 (20.7 to 1)
Librarians/Media Specialists: 2.6 (3,328.1 to 1)
Guidance Counselors: 8.2 (1,055.2 to 1)
Current Spending: ($ per student per year):
     Total: $6,779; Instruction: $4,339; Support Services: $2,233

Enrollment, Drop-out Rates and Diploma Recipients by Race/Ethnicity

Category	Total	White	Black	Asian	AIAN	Hisp.
Enrollment (%)	100.0	19.2	16.7	27.2	0.7	34.1
Drop-out Rate (%)	n/a	n/a	n/a	n/a	n/a	n/a
H.S. Diplomas (#)	454	127	79	129	5	113

San Lorenzo Unified
15510 Usher St • San Lorenzo, CA 94580-0037
(510) 317-4600 • http://www.slzusd.k12.ca.us/
Grade Span: KG-12; **Agency Type:** 1
Schools: 15
   9 Primary; 3 Middle; 2 High; 1 Other Level
   14 Regular; 0 Special Education; 0 Vocational; 1 Alternative
   0 Magnet; 0 Charter; 5 Title I Eligible; 0 School-wide Title I
Students: 11,547 (51.6% male; 48.3% female)
   Individual Education Program: 1,204 (10.4%);
   English Language Learner: 2,772 (24.0%); Migrant: 239 (2.1%)
   Eligible for Free Lunch Program: 3,152 (27.3%)
   Eligible for Reduced-Price Lunch Program: 1,110 (9.6%)
Teachers: 566.6 (20.4 to 1)
Librarians/Media Specialists: 5.0 (2,309.4 to 1)
Guidance Counselors: 11.0 (1,049.7 to 1)
Current Spending: ($ per student per year):
   Total: $6,921; Instruction: $4,385; Support Services: $2,228

Enrollment, Drop-out Rates and Diploma Recipients by Race/Ethnicity

Category	Total	White	Black	Asian	AIAN	Hisp.
Enrollment (%)	100.0	22.6	14.9	20.9	1.0	40.6
Drop-out Rate (%)	n/a	n/a	n/a	n/a	n/a	n/a
H.S. Diplomas (#)	660	241	91	137	8	183

Amador County

Amador County Unified
217 Rex Ave No. 7 • Jackson, CA 95642-2020
(209) 223-1750 • http://www.teachnet.k12.ca.us/
Grade Span: KG-12; **Agency Type:** 1
Schools: 12
   6 Primary; 2 Middle; 3 High; 1 Other Level
   10 Regular; 0 Special Education; 0 Vocational; 2 Alternative
   0 Magnet; 0 Charter; 7 Title I Eligible; 1 School-wide Title I
Students: 4,567 (51.7% male; 48.2% female)
   Individual Education Program: 621 (13.6%);
   English Language Learner: 95 (2.1%); Migrant: 0 (0.0%)
   Eligible for Free Lunch Program: 872 (19.1%)
   Eligible for Reduced-Price Lunch Program: 397 (8.7%)
Teachers: 198.8 (23.0 to 1)
Librarians/Media Specialists: 0.0 (n/a to 1)
Guidance Counselors: 5.9 (774.1 to 1)
Current Spending: ($ per student per year):
   Total: $5,795; Instruction: $3,515; Support Services: $2,092

Enrollment, Drop-out Rates and Diploma Recipients by Race/Ethnicity

Category	Total	White	Black	Asian	AIAN	Hisp.
Enrollment (%)	100.0	82.9	1.0	1.7	3.7	9.0
Drop-out Rate (%)	n/a	n/a	n/a	n/a	n/a	n/a
H.S. Diplomas (#)	343	294	2	3	11	26

Butte County

Chico Unified
1163 E Seventh St • Chico, CA 95928-5999
(530) 891-3000 • http://www.cusd.chico.k12.ca.us/
Grade Span: KG-12; **Agency Type:** 1
Schools: 26
   17 Primary; 3 Middle; 3 High; 3 Other Level
   23 Regular; 0 Special Education; 0 Vocational; 3 Alternative
   0 Magnet; 1 Charter; 14 Title I Eligible; 6 School-wide Title I
Students: 13,762 (51.3% male; 48.6% female)
   Individual Education Program: 1,678 (12.2%);
   English Language Learner: 1,748 (12.7%); Migrant: 363 (2.6%)
   Eligible for Free Lunch Program: 3,905 (28.4%)
   Eligible for Reduced-Price Lunch Program: 912 (6.6%)
Teachers: 676.8 (20.3 to 1)
Librarians/Media Specialists: 2.5 (5,504.8 to 1)
Guidance Counselors: 17.9 (768.8 to 1)
Current Spending: ($ per student per year):
   Total: $6,881; Instruction: $4,760; Support Services: $1,894

Enrollment, Drop-out Rates and Diploma Recipients by Race/Ethnicity

Category	Total	White	Black	Asian	AIAN	Hisp.
Enrollment (%)	100.0	70.8	3.5	7.4	1.5	16.1
Drop-out Rate (%)	n/a	n/a	n/a	n/a	n/a	n/a
H.S. Diplomas (#)	967	736	21	72	12	126

Gridley Unified
429 Magnolia St • Gridley, CA 95948-2533
(530) 846-4721 • http://www.bcoe.butte.k12.ca.us/persdir/gridley.htm
Grade Span: KG-12; **Agency Type:** 1
Schools: 7
   3 Primary; 1 Middle; 3 High; 0 Other Level
   4 Regular; 0 Special Education; 0 Vocational; 3 Alternative
   0 Magnet; 0 Charter; 4 Title I Eligible; 4 School-wide Title I
Students: 2,072 (52.9% male; 47.0% female)
   Individual Education Program: 169 (8.2%);
   English Language Learner: 552 (26.6%); Migrant: 373 (18.0%)
   Eligible for Free Lunch Program: 1,074 (51.8%)
   Eligible for Reduced-Price Lunch Program: 156 (7.5%)
Teachers: 108.3 (19.1 to 1)
Librarians/Media Specialists: 0.0 (n/a to 1)
Guidance Counselors: 2.8 (740.0 to 1)
Current Spending: ($ per student per year):
   Total: $7,057; Instruction: $4,534; Support Services: $2,202

Enrollment, Drop-out Rates and Diploma Recipients by Race/Ethnicity

Category	Total	White	Black	Asian	AIAN	Hisp.
Enrollment (%)	100.0	46.7	0.5	5.0	0.4	46.9
Drop-out Rate (%)	n/a	n/a	n/a	n/a	n/a	n/a
H.S. Diplomas (#)	148	92	0	9	0	47

Oroville City Elementary
2795 Yard St • Oroville, CA 95966-5113
(530) 532-3000 • http://www.bcoe.butte.k12.ca.us/persdir/oroelem.htm
Grade Span: KG-08; **Agency Type:** 1
Schools: 7
   6 Primary; 1 Middle; 0 High; 0 Other Level
   7 Regular; 0 Special Education; 0 Vocational; 0 Alternative
   0 Magnet; 0 Charter; 7 Title I Eligible; 6 School-wide Title I
Students: 3,198 (51.8% male; 48.1% female)
   Individual Education Program: 540 (16.9%);
   English Language Learner: 394 (12.3%); Migrant: 96 (3.0%)
   Eligible for Free Lunch Program: 1,855 (58.0%)
   Eligible for Reduced-Price Lunch Program: 337 (10.5%)
Teachers: 162.9 (19.6 to 1)
Librarians/Media Specialists: 1.0 (3,198.0 to 1)
Guidance Counselors: 2.0 (1,599.0 to 1)
Current Spending: ($ per student per year):
   Total: $7,342; Instruction: $4,799; Support Services: $2,201

Enrollment, Drop-out Rates and Diploma Recipients by Race/Ethnicity

Category	Total	White	Black	Asian	AIAN	Hisp.
Enrollment (%)	100.0	61.8	5.4	12.2	5.3	7.6
Drop-out Rate (%)	n/a	n/a	n/a	n/a	n/a	n/a
H.S. Diplomas (#)	n/a	n/a	n/a	n/a	n/a	n/a

Oroville Union High
2211 Washington Ave • Oroville, CA 95966-5440
(530) 538-2300 • http://www.ouhsd.org/
Grade Span: 09-12; **Agency Type:** 1
Schools: 5
   0 Primary; 0 Middle; 5 High; 0 Other Level
   3 Regular; 0 Special Education; 0 Vocational; 2 Alternative
   0 Magnet; 1 Charter; 5 Title I Eligible; 0 School-wide Title I
Students: 2,962 (50.5% male; 49.4% female)
   Individual Education Program: 363 (12.3%);
   English Language Learner: 214 (7.2%); Migrant: 134 (4.5%)
   Eligible for Free Lunch Program: 1,183 (39.9%)
   Eligible for Reduced-Price Lunch Program: 194 (6.5%)
Teachers: 108.9 (27.2 to 1)
Librarians/Media Specialists: 0.0 (n/a to 1)
Guidance Counselors: 4.0 (740.5 to 1)
Current Spending: ($ per student per year):
   Total: $7,121; Instruction: $4,388; Support Services: $2,463

Enrollment, Drop-out Rates and Diploma Recipients by Race/Ethnicity

Category	Total	White	Black	Asian	AIAN	Hisp.
Enrollment (%)	100.0	65.6	3.7	16.3	5.8	8.4
Drop-out Rate (%)	n/a	n/a	n/a	n/a	n/a	n/a
H.S. Diplomas (#)	489	315	17	78	34	45

Paradise Unified
6696 Clark Rd • Paradise, CA 95969-2834
(530) 872-6400 • http://www.paradise.k12.ca.us/
Grade Span: KG-12; **Agency Type:** 1
Schools: 13
   5 Primary; 3 Middle; 3 High; 2 Other Level
   10 Regular; 0 Special Education; 0 Vocational; 3 Alternative
   0 Magnet; 4 Charter; 8 Title I Eligible; 0 School-wide Title I
Students: 5,309 (52.3% male; 47.6% female)
   Individual Education Program: 561 (10.6%);
   English Language Learner: 9 (0.2%); Migrant: 0 (0.0%)
   Eligible for Free Lunch Program: 1,483 (27.9%)
   Eligible for Reduced-Price Lunch Program: 465 (8.8%)

Teachers: 275.9 (19.2 to 1)
Librarians/Media Specialists: 2.0 (2,654.5 to 1)
Guidance Counselors: 6.6 (804.4 to 1)
Current Spending: ($ per student per year):
    Total: $6,746; Instruction: $4,546; Support Services: $1,961

Enrollment, Drop-out Rates and Diploma Recipients by Race/Ethnicity

Category	Total	White	Black	Asian	AIAN	Hisp.
Enrollment (%)	100.0	89.3	0.9	1.5	1.6	6.7
Drop-out Rate (%)	n/a	n/a	n/a	n/a	n/a	n/a
H.S. Diplomas (#)	373	333	2	8	6	24

Calaveras County

Calaveras Unified
501 Gold Strike Rd • San Andreas, CA 95249-0788
Mailing Address: PO Box 788 • San Andreas, CA 95249-0788
(209) 754-3504 • http://www.calaveras.k12.ca.us/
Grade Span: KG-12; **Agency Type:** 1
Schools: 13
    6 Primary; 1 Middle; 4 High; 1 Other Level
    8 Regular; 0 Special Education; 0 Vocational; 4 Alternative
    0 Magnet; 0 Charter; 5 Title I Eligible; 3 School-wide Title I
Students: 3,701   (50.3% male; 49.6% female)
    Individual Education Program: 439 (11.9%);
    English Language Learner: 14 (0.4%); Migrant: 0 (0.0%)
    Eligible for Free Lunch Program: 795 (21.5%)
    Eligible for Reduced-Price Lunch Program: 339 (9.2%)
Teachers: 181.7 (20.4 to 1)
Librarians/Media Specialists: 0.0 (n/a to 1)
Guidance Counselors: 2.0 (1,850.5 to 1)
Current Spending: ($ per student per year):
    Total: $7,744; Instruction: $4,492; Support Services: $3,127

Enrollment, Drop-out Rates and Diploma Recipients by Race/Ethnicity

Category	Total	White	Black	Asian	AIAN	Hisp.
Enrollment (%)	100.0	84.9	1.4	1.3	2.7	8.1
Drop-out Rate (%)	n/a	n/a	n/a	n/a	n/a	n/a
H.S. Diplomas (#)	236	218	2	1	2	13

Contra Costa County

Acalanes Union High
1212 Pleasant Hill Rd • Lafayette, CA 94549-2623
(925) 935-2800 • http://www.acalanes.acalanes.k12.ca.us/
Grade Span: 09-12; **Agency Type:** 1
Schools: 5
    0 Primary; 0 Middle; 5 High; 0 Other Level
    4 Regular; 0 Special Education; 0 Vocational; 1 Alternative
    0 Magnet; 0 Charter; 1 Title I Eligible; 0 School-wide Title I
Students: 5,785   (51.9% male; 48.0% female)
    Individual Education Program: 494 (8.5%);
    English Language Learner: 80 (1.4%); Migrant: 0 (0.0%)
    Eligible for Free Lunch Program: 26 (0.4%)
    Eligible for Reduced-Price Lunch Program: 7 (0.1%)
Teachers: 263.1 (22.0 to 1)
Librarians/Media Specialists: 4.0 (1,446.3 to 1)
Guidance Counselors: 13.0 (445.0 to 1)
Current Spending: ($ per student per year):
    Total: $7,270; Instruction: $4,250; Support Services: $2,866

Enrollment, Drop-out Rates and Diploma Recipients by Race/Ethnicity

Category	Total	White	Black	Asian	AIAN	Hisp.
Enrollment (%)	100.0	73.1	3.3	12.0	0.2	4.6
Drop-out Rate (%)	n/a	n/a	n/a	n/a	n/a	n/a
H.S. Diplomas (#)	1,279	1,047	13	165	7	41

Antioch Unified
510 G St • Antioch, CA 94509-0904
Mailing Address: PO Box 768 • Antioch, CA 94509-0904
(925) 706-4100 • http://www.antioch.k12.ca.us/
Grade Span: KG-12; **Agency Type:** 1
Schools: 23
    13 Primary; 4 Middle; 4 High; 2 Other Level
    20 Regular; 0 Special Education; 0 Vocational; 3 Alternative
    1 Magnet; 1 Charter; 7 Title I Eligible; 6 School-wide Title I
Students: 21,628   (50.8% male; 49.1% female)
    Individual Education Program: 2,264 (10.5%);
    English Language Learner: 2,036 (9.4%); Migrant: 4 (<0.1%)
    Eligible for Free Lunch Program: 6,160 (28.5%)
    Eligible for Reduced-Price Lunch Program: 2,318 (10.7%)
Teachers: 1,002.9 (21.6 to 1)
Librarians/Media Specialists: 0.6 (36,046.7 to 1)
Guidance Counselors: 3.6 (6,007.8 to 1)
Current Spending: ($ per student per year):
    Total: $6,220; Instruction: $4,175; Support Services: $1,833

Enrollment, Drop-out Rates and Diploma Recipients by Race/Ethnicity

Category	Total	White	Black	Asian	AIAN	Hisp.
Enrollment (%)	100.0	37.2	16.8	10.6	1.2	27.0
Drop-out Rate (%)	n/a	n/a	n/a	n/a	n/a	n/a
H.S. Diplomas (#)	1,254	599	152	150	15	285

Brentwood Union Elementary
255 Guthrie Ln • Brentwood, CA 94513-1610
(925) 634-1168 • http://www.brentwood.k12.ca.us/
Grade Span: KG-08; **Agency Type:** 1
Schools: 7
    5 Primary; 2 Middle; 0 High; 0 Other Level
    7 Regular; 0 Special Education; 0 Vocational; 0 Alternative
    0 Magnet; 0 Charter; 4 Title I Eligible; 0 School-wide Title I
Students: 5,927   (50.6% male; 49.3% female)
    Individual Education Program: 703 (11.9%);
    English Language Learner: 867 (14.6%); Migrant: 242 (4.1%)
    Eligible for Free Lunch Program: 936 (15.8%)
    Eligible for Reduced-Price Lunch Program: 310 (5.2%)
Teachers: 291.1 (20.4 to 1)
Librarians/Media Specialists: 0.0 (n/a to 1)
Guidance Counselors: 4.6 (1,288.5 to 1)
Current Spending: ($ per student per year):
    Total: $6,568; Instruction: $4,523; Support Services: $1,818

Enrollment, Drop-out Rates and Diploma Recipients by Race/Ethnicity

Category	Total	White	Black	Asian	AIAN	Hisp.
Enrollment (%)	100.0	60.2	4.6	5.1	0.9	29.2
Drop-out Rate (%)	n/a	n/a	n/a	n/a	n/a	n/a
H.S. Diplomas (#)	n/a	n/a	n/a	n/a	n/a	n/a

John Swett Unified
341 #B (Selby) • Crockett, CA 94525
(510) 787-1141 • http://www.jsusd.k12.ca.us/
Grade Span: KG-12; **Agency Type:** 1
Schools: 4
    1 Primary; 1 Middle; 1 High; 1 Other Level
    3 Regular; 0 Special Education; 0 Vocational; 1 Alternative
    0 Magnet; 0 Charter; 2 Title I Eligible; 0 School-wide Title I
Students: 1,816   (53.1% male; 46.8% female)
    Individual Education Program: 206 (11.3%);
    English Language Learner: 233 (12.8%); Migrant: 0 (0.0%)
    Eligible for Free Lunch Program: 497 (27.4%)
    Eligible for Reduced-Price Lunch Program: 124 (6.8%)
Teachers: 89.1 (20.4 to 1)
Librarians/Media Specialists: 0.0 (n/a to 1)
Guidance Counselors: 1.6 (1,135.0 to 1)
Current Spending: ($ per student per year):
    Total: $7,005; Instruction: $4,623; Support Services: $2,144

Enrollment, Drop-out Rates and Diploma Recipients by Race/Ethnicity

Category	Total	White	Black	Asian	AIAN	Hisp.
Enrollment (%)	100.0	35.2	21.3	16.7	0.7	18.5
Drop-out Rate (%)	n/a	n/a	n/a	n/a	n/a	n/a
H.S. Diplomas (#)	145	59	22	40	2	22

Lafayette Elementary
3477 School St • Lafayette, CA 94549-1029
Mailing Address: PO Box 1029 • Lafayette, CA 94549-1029
(925) 284-7011 • http://www.lafsd.k12.ca.us/
Grade Span: KG-08; **Agency Type:** 1
Schools: 5
    4 Primary; 1 Middle; 0 High; 0 Other Level
    5 Regular; 0 Special Education; 0 Vocational; 0 Alternative
    0 Magnet; 0 Charter; 2 Title I Eligible; 0 School-wide Title I
Students: 3,389   (52.2% male; 47.7% female)
    Individual Education Program: 307 (9.1%);
    English Language Learner: 48 (1.4%); Migrant: 0 (0.0%)
    Eligible for Free Lunch Program: 8 (0.2%)
    Eligible for Reduced-Price Lunch Program: 0 (0.0%)
Teachers: 179.3 (18.9 to 1)
Librarians/Media Specialists: 1.0 (3,389.0 to 1)
Guidance Counselors: 1.6 (2,118.1 to 1)
Current Spending: ($ per student per year):
    Total: $6,572; Instruction: $4,713; Support Services: $1,859

Enrollment, Drop-out Rates and Diploma Recipients by Race/Ethnicity

Category	Total	White	Black	Asian	AIAN	Hisp.
Enrollment (%)	100.0	78.8	0.6	7.8	0.1	2.3
Drop-out Rate (%)	n/a	n/a	n/a	n/a	n/a	n/a
H.S. Diplomas (#)	n/a	n/a	n/a	n/a	n/a	n/a

Liberty Union High
20 Oak St • Brentwood, CA 94513-1379
(925) 634-2166 • http://www.libertyuhsd.k12.ca.us/
Grade Span: 09-12; **Agency Type:** 1
Schools: 4
    0 Primary; 0 Middle; 4 High; 0 Other Level

2 Regular; 0 Special Education; 0 Vocational; 2 Alternative
0 Magnet; 0 Charter; 1 Title I Eligible; 0 School-wide Title I
Students: 4,798 (50.4% male; 49.5% female)
Individual Education Program: 537 (11.2%);
English Language Learner: 385 (8.0%); Migrant: 198 (4.1%)
Eligible for Free Lunch Program: 370 (7.7%)
Eligible for Reduced-Price Lunch Program: 56 (1.2%)
Teachers: 195.7 (24.5 to 1)
Librarians/Media Specialists: 2.0 (2,399.0 to 1)
Guidance Counselors: 8.2 (585.1 to 1)
Current Spending: ($ per student per year):
Total: $7,017; Instruction: $4,013; Support Services: $2,847
Enrollment, Drop-out Rates and Diploma Recipients by Race/Ethnicity

Category	Total	White	Black	Asian	AIAN	Hisp.
Enrollment (%)	100.0	63.0	4.9	4.3	1.0	26.3
Drop-out Rate (%)	n/a	n/a	n/a	n/a	n/a	n/a
H.S. Diplomas (#)	794	555	22	32	4	181

Martinez Unified
921 Susana St • Martinez, CA 94553-1848
(925) 313-0480 • http://www.cccoe.k12.ca.us/cccoe/schools.htm
Grade Span: KG-12; **Agency Type:** 1
Schools: 8
4 Primary; 1 Middle; 2 High; 1 Other Level
6 Regular; 0 Special Education; 0 Vocational; 2 Alternative
0 Magnet; 0 Charter; 4 Title I Eligible; 3 School-wide Title I
Students: 4,320 (51.5% male; 48.4% female)
Individual Education Program: 594 (13.8%);
English Language Learner: 216 (5.0%); Migrant: 0 (0.0%)
Eligible for Free Lunch Program: 487 (11.3%)
Eligible for Reduced-Price Lunch Program: 169 (3.9%)
Teachers: 208.6 (20.7 to 1)
Librarians/Media Specialists: 2.0 (2,160.0 to 1)
Guidance Counselors: 4.5 (960.0 to 1)
Current Spending: ($ per student per year):
Total: $6,492; Instruction: $4,196; Support Services: $2,109
Enrollment, Drop-out Rates and Diploma Recipients by Race/Ethnicity

Category	Total	White	Black	Asian	AIAN	Hisp.
Enrollment (%)	100.0	70.4	3.6	4.9	2.3	16.5
Drop-out Rate (%)	n/a	n/a	n/a	n/a	n/a	n/a
H.S. Diplomas (#)	315	224	12	12	21	46

Moraga Elementary
1540 School St • Moraga, CA 94556-0158
Mailing Address: PO Box 158 • Moraga, CA 94556-0158
(925) 376-5943 • http://www.moraga.k12.ca.us/
Grade Span: KG-08; **Agency Type:** 1
Schools: 4
3 Primary; 1 Middle; 0 High; 0 Other Level
4 Regular; 0 Special Education; 0 Vocational; 0 Alternative
0 Magnet; 0 Charter; 4 Title I Eligible; 0 School-wide Title I
Students: 1,856 (53.9% male; 46.0% female)
Individual Education Program: 168 (9.1%);
English Language Learner: 25 (1.3%); Migrant: 0 (0.0%)
Eligible for Free Lunch Program: 32 (1.7%)
Eligible for Reduced-Price Lunch Program: 0 (0.0%)
Teachers: 90.6 (20.5 to 1)
Librarians/Media Specialists: 0.0 (n/a to 1)
Guidance Counselors: 0.4 (4,640.0 to 1)
Current Spending: ($ per student per year):
Total: $6,949; Instruction: $4,407; Support Services: $2,534
Enrollment, Drop-out Rates and Diploma Recipients by Race/Ethnicity

Category	Total	White	Black	Asian	AIAN	Hisp.
Enrollment (%)	100.0	73.5	0.8	13.7	0.2	2.2
Drop-out Rate (%)	n/a	n/a	n/a	n/a	n/a	n/a
H.S. Diplomas (#)	n/a	n/a	n/a	n/a	n/a	n/a

Mt. Diablo Unified
1936 Carlotta Dr • Concord, CA 94519-1358
(925) 682-8000 • http://www.mdusd.k12.ca.us/
Grade Span: KG-12; **Agency Type:** 1
Schools: 55
30 Primary; 10 Middle; 13 High; 2 Other Level
45 Regular; 1 Special Education; 0 Vocational; 9 Alternative
7 Magnet; 1 Charter; 10 Title I Eligible; 10 School-wide Title I
Students: 36,821 (51.6% male; 48.3% female)
Individual Education Program: 4,781 (13.0%);
English Language Learner: 6,169 (16.8%); Migrant: 3 (<0.1%)
Eligible for Free Lunch Program: 7,859 (21.3%)
Eligible for Reduced-Price Lunch Program: 2,195 (6.0%)
Teachers: 1,845.3 (20.0 to 1)
Librarians/Media Specialists: 35.6 (1,034.3 to 1)
Guidance Counselors: 14.0 (2,630.1 to 1)
Current Spending: ($ per student per year):
Total: $7,062; Instruction: $4,588; Support Services: $2,237

Enrollment, Drop-out Rates and Diploma Recipients by Race/Ethnicity

Category	Total	White	Black	Asian	AIAN	Hisp.
Enrollment (%)	100.0	56.9	5.2	12.4	0.5	25.1
Drop-out Rate (%)	n/a	n/a	n/a	n/a	n/a	n/a
H.S. Diplomas (#)	2,161	1,405	80	321	17	338

Oakley Union Elementary
91 Mercedes Ln • Oakley, CA 94561-0007
(925) 625-0700 • http://www.ouesd.k12.ca.us/
Grade Span: KG-08; **Agency Type:** 1
Schools: 6
4 Primary; 2 Middle; 0 High; 0 Other Level
6 Regular; 0 Special Education; 0 Vocational; 0 Alternative
0 Magnet; 0 Charter; 2 Title I Eligible; 0 School-wide Title I
Students: 4,487 (50.6% male; 49.3% female)
Individual Education Program: 664 (14.8%);
English Language Learner: 447 (10.0%); Migrant: 113 (2.5%)
Eligible for Free Lunch Program: 953 (21.2%)
Eligible for Reduced-Price Lunch Program: 291 (6.5%)
Teachers: 224.3 (20.0 to 1)
Librarians/Media Specialists: 0.0 (n/a to 1)
Guidance Counselors: 1.0 (4,487.0 to 1)
Current Spending: ($ per student per year):
Total: $6,577; Instruction: $4,138; Support Services: $2,214
Enrollment, Drop-out Rates and Diploma Recipients by Race/Ethnicity

Category	Total	White	Black	Asian	AIAN	Hisp.
Enrollment (%)	100.0	55.0	5.7	3.9	0.8	32.0
Drop-out Rate (%)	n/a	n/a	n/a	n/a	n/a	n/a
H.S. Diplomas (#)	n/a	n/a	n/a	n/a	n/a	n/a

Orinda Union Elementary
8 Altarinda Rd • Orinda, CA 94563-2603
(925) 254-4901 • http://www.orinda.k12.ca.us/
Grade Span: KG-08; **Agency Type:** 1
Schools: 5
4 Primary; 1 Middle; 0 High; 0 Other Level
5 Regular; 0 Special Education; 0 Vocational; 0 Alternative
0 Magnet; 0 Charter; 4 Title I Eligible; 0 School-wide Title I
Students: 2,409 (51.3% male; 48.6% female)
Individual Education Program: 197 (8.2%);
English Language Learner: 23 (1.0%); Migrant: 0 (0.0%)
Eligible for Free Lunch Program: 15 (0.6%)
Eligible for Reduced-Price Lunch Program: 0 (0.0%)
Teachers: 128.4 (18.8 to 1)
Librarians/Media Specialists: 4.2 (573.6 to 1)
Guidance Counselors: 2.0 (1,204.5 to 1)
Current Spending: ($ per student per year):
Total: $7,185; Instruction: $4,681; Support Services: $2,443
Enrollment, Drop-out Rates and Diploma Recipients by Race/Ethnicity

Category	Total	White	Black	Asian	AIAN	Hisp.
Enrollment (%)	100.0	78.4	1.3	14.3	0.2	3.4
Drop-out Rate (%)	n/a	n/a	n/a	n/a	n/a	n/a
H.S. Diplomas (#)	n/a	n/a	n/a	n/a	n/a	n/a

Pittsburg Unified
2000 Railroad Ave • Pittsburg, CA 94565-3830
(925) 473-4231 • http://www.pittsburg.k12.ca.us/
Grade Span: KG-12; **Agency Type:** 1
Schools: 11
7 Primary; 2 Middle; 1 High; 1 Other Level
10 Regular; 0 Special Education; 0 Vocational; 1 Alternative
0 Magnet; 0 Charter; 11 Title I Eligible; 10 School-wide Title I
Students: 9,591 (52.4% male; 47.5% female)
Individual Education Program: 999 (10.4%);
English Language Learner: 2,762 (28.8%); Migrant: 0 (0.0%)
Eligible for Free Lunch Program: 4,175 (43.5%)
Eligible for Reduced-Price Lunch Program: 1,715 (17.9%)
Teachers: 462.4 (20.7 to 1)
Librarians/Media Specialists: 1.0 (9,591.0 to 1)
Guidance Counselors: 10.0 (959.1 to 1)
Current Spending: ($ per student per year):
Total: $6,892; Instruction: $4,312; Support Services: $2,242
Enrollment, Drop-out Rates and Diploma Recipients by Race/Ethnicity

Category	Total	White	Black	Asian	AIAN	Hisp.
Enrollment (%)	100.0	11.7	24.6	12.3	0.3	46.8
Drop-out Rate (%)	n/a	n/a	n/a	n/a	n/a	n/a
H.S. Diplomas (#)	428	103	110	78	1	130

San Ramon Valley Unified
699 Old Orchard Dr • Danville, CA 94526-4331
(925) 552-5500 • http://www.srvusd.k12.ca.us/
Grade Span: KG-12; **Agency Type:** 1
Schools: 28
17 Primary; 6 Middle; 4 High; 1 Other Level
26 Regular; 0 Special Education; 0 Vocational; 2 Alternative

3 Magnet; 0 Charter; 9 Title I Eligible; 0 School-wide Title I
Students: 21,988 (50.6% male; 49.3% female)
  Individual Education Program: 2,362 (10.7%);
  English Language Learner: 289 (1.3%); Migrant: 0 (0.0%)
  Eligible for Free Lunch Program: 215 (1.0%)
  Eligible for Reduced-Price Lunch Program: 100 (0.5%)
Teachers: 1,025.8 (21.4 to 1)
Librarians/Media Specialists: 9.0 (2,443.1 to 1)
Guidance Counselors: 23.3 (943.7 to 1)
Current Spending: ($ per student per year):
  Total: $6,634; Instruction: $4,241; Support Services: $2,229
Enrollment, Drop-out Rates and Diploma Recipients by Race/Ethnicity

Category	Total	White	Black	Asian	AIAN	Hisp.
Enrollment (%)	100.0	76.4	1.8	16.3	0.7	4.4
Drop-out Rate (%)	n/a	n/a	n/a	n/a	n/a	n/a
H.S. Diplomas (#)	1,491	1,127	25	245	18	76

Walnut Creek Elementary
960 Ygnacio Valley Rd • Walnut Creek, CA 94597
(925) 944-6850 • http://www.wcsd.k12.ca.us/
Grade Span: KG-08; **Agency Type:** 1
Schools: 6
  5 Primary; 1 Middle; 0 High; 0 Other Level
  6 Regular; 0 Special Education; 0 Vocational; 0 Alternative
  0 Magnet; 0 Charter; 2 Title I Eligible; 0 School-wide Title I
Students: 3,345 (52.0% male; 47.9% female)
  Individual Education Program: 353 (10.6%);
  English Language Learner: 242 (7.2%); Migrant: 0 (0.0%)
  Eligible for Free Lunch Program: 160 (4.8%)
  Eligible for Reduced-Price Lunch Program: 110 (3.3%)
Teachers: 168.0 (19.9 to 1)
Librarians/Media Specialists: 0.0 (n/a to 1)
Guidance Counselors: 1.0 (3,345.0 to 1)
Current Spending: ($ per student per year):
  Total: $6,576; Instruction: $4,333; Support Services: $2,036
Enrollment, Drop-out Rates and Diploma Recipients by Race/Ethnicity

Category	Total	White	Black	Asian	AIAN	Hisp.
Enrollment (%)	100.0	72.4	2.2	12.2	0.6	9.2
Drop-out Rate (%)	n/a	n/a	n/a	n/a	n/a	n/a
H.S. Diplomas (#)	n/a	n/a	n/a	n/a	n/a	n/a

West Contra Costa Unified
1108 Bissell Ave • Richmond, CA 94801-3135
(510) 234-3825 • http://www.wccusd.k12.ca.us/
Grade Span: KG-12; **Agency Type:** 1
Schools: 65
  40 Primary; 8 Middle; 14 High; 2 Other Level
  55 Regular; 1 Special Education; 0 Vocational; 8 Alternative
  1 Magnet; 2 Charter; 29 Title I Eligible; 27 School-wide Title I
Students: 33,672 (51.4% male; 48.5% female)
  Individual Education Program: 4,958 (14.7%);
  English Language Learner: 9,904 (29.4%); Migrant: 0 (0.0%)
  Eligible for Free Lunch Program: 13,168 (39.1%)
  Eligible for Reduced-Price Lunch Program: 4,264 (12.7%)
Teachers: 1,698.2 (19.8 to 1)
Librarians/Media Specialists: 9.8 (3,435.9 to 1)
Guidance Counselors: 32.0 (1,052.3 to 1)
Current Spending: ($ per student per year):
  Total: $7,603; Instruction: $4,637; Support Services: $2,712
Enrollment, Drop-out Rates and Diploma Recipients by Race/Ethnicity

Category	Total	White	Black	Asian	AIAN	Hisp.
Enrollment (%)	100.0	14.2	28.8	16.6	0.2	38.1
Drop-out Rate (%)	n/a	n/a	n/a	n/a	n/a	n/a
H.S. Diplomas (#)	1,770	391	487	442	2	443

Del Norte County

Del Norte County Unified
301 W Washington Blvd • Crescent City, CA 95531-8340
(707) 464-6141 • http://www.delnorte.k12.ca.us/
Grade Span: KG-12; **Agency Type:** 1
Schools: 11
  8 Primary; 1 Middle; 2 High; 0 Other Level
  10 Regular; 0 Special Education; 0 Vocational; 1 Alternative
  1 Magnet; 0 Charter; 11 Title I Eligible; 10 School-wide Title I
Students: 4,292 (51.3% male; 48.6% female)
  Individual Education Program: 588 (13.7%);
  English Language Learner: 332 (7.7%); Migrant: 65 (1.5%)
  Eligible for Free Lunch Program: 2,072 (48.3%)
  Eligible for Reduced-Price Lunch Program: 337 (7.9%)
Teachers: 214.8 (20.0 to 1)
Librarians/Media Specialists: 0.0 (n/a to 1)
Guidance Counselors: 5.0 (858.4 to 1)
Current Spending: ($ per student per year):
  Total: $8,368; Instruction: $5,377; Support Services: $2,643

Category	Total	White	Black	Asian	AIAN	Hisp.
Enrollment (%)	100.0	63.9	0.7	7.7	14.4	13.3
Drop-out Rate (%)	n/a	n/a	n/a	n/a	n/a	n/a
H.S. Diplomas (#)	289	212	4	27	24	22

El Dorado County

Black Oak Mine Unified
6540 Wentworth Springs Rd • Georgetown, CA 95634-9001
Mailing Address: PO Box 4510 • Georgetown, CA 95634-9001
(530) 333-8300 • http://bomusd.k12.ca.us/
Grade Span: KG-12; **Agency Type:** 1
Schools: 7
  4 Primary; 0 Middle; 3 High; 0 Other Level
  5 Regular; 0 Special Education; 0 Vocational; 2 Alternative
  0 Magnet; 0 Charter; 5 Title I Eligible; 0 School-wide Title I
Students: 2,016 (53.5% male; 46.4% female)
  Individual Education Program: 160 (7.9%);
  English Language Learner: 18 (0.9%); Migrant: 1 (<0.1%)
  Eligible for Free Lunch Program: 326 (16.2%)
  Eligible for Reduced-Price Lunch Program: 147 (7.3%)
Teachers: 97.9 (20.6 to 1)
Librarians/Media Specialists: 0.4 (5,040.0 to 1)
Guidance Counselors: 1.2 (1,680.0 to 1)
Current Spending: ($ per student per year):
  Total: $7,056; Instruction: $4,514; Support Services: $2,358
Enrollment, Drop-out Rates and Diploma Recipients by Race/Ethnicity

Category	Total	White	Black	Asian	AIAN	Hisp.
Enrollment (%)	100.0	89.4	0.5	0.7	2.3	4.3
Drop-out Rate (%)	n/a	n/a	n/a	n/a	n/a	n/a
H.S. Diplomas (#)	150	146	0	2	0	2

Buckeye Union Elementary
4560 Buckeye Rd • Shingle Springs, CA 95682-0547
Mailing Address: PO Box 547 • Shingle Springs, CA 95682-0547
(530) 677-2261 • http://buckeye.k12.ca.us/
Grade Span: KG-08; **Agency Type:** 1
Schools: 7
  5 Primary; 2 Middle; 0 High; 0 Other Level
  7 Regular; 0 Special Education; 0 Vocational; 0 Alternative
  0 Magnet; 0 Charter; 1 Title I Eligible; 0 School-wide Title I
Students: 4,279 (50.0% male; 49.9% female)
  Individual Education Program: 221 (5.2%);
  English Language Learner: 28 (0.7%); Migrant: 0 (0.0%)
  Eligible for Free Lunch Program: 172 (4.0%)
  Eligible for Reduced-Price Lunch Program: 75 (1.8%)
Teachers: 197.3 (21.7 to 1)
Librarians/Media Specialists: 1.0 (4,279.0 to 1)
Guidance Counselors: 4.0 (1,069.8 to 1)
Current Spending: ($ per student per year):
  Total: $6,118; Instruction: $4,089; Support Services: $1,931
Enrollment, Drop-out Rates and Diploma Recipients by Race/Ethnicity

Category	Total	White	Black	Asian	AIAN	Hisp.
Enrollment (%)	100.0	86.3	1.1	6.0	0.7	4.8
Drop-out Rate (%)	n/a	n/a	n/a	n/a	n/a	n/a
H.S. Diplomas (#)	n/a	n/a	n/a	n/a	n/a	n/a

El Dorado Union High
4675 Missouri Flat Rd • Placerville, CA 95619-1450
Mailing Address: PO Box 1450 • Diamond Springs, CA 95619-1450
(530) 622-5081 • http://www.eduhsd.k12.ca.us/
Grade Span: 09-12; **Agency Type:** 1
Schools: 10
  0 Primary; 0 Middle; 10 High; 0 Other Level
  5 Regular; 0 Special Education; 0 Vocational; 5 Alternative
  0 Magnet; 1 Charter; 3 Title I Eligible; 0 School-wide Title I
Students: 6,981 (51.0% male; 48.9% female)
  Individual Education Program: 638 (9.1%);
  English Language Learner: 56 (0.8%); Migrant: 15 (0.2%)
  Eligible for Free Lunch Program: 362 (5.2%)
  Eligible for Reduced-Price Lunch Program: 144 (2.1%)
Teachers: 317.7 (22.0 to 1)
Librarians/Media Specialists: 4.2 (1,662.1 to 1)
Guidance Counselors: 13.9 (502.2 to 1)
Current Spending: ($ per student per year):
  Total: $6,828; Instruction: $3,947; Support Services: $2,655
Enrollment, Drop-out Rates and Diploma Recipients by Race/Ethnicity

Category	Total	White	Black	Asian	AIAN	Hisp.
Enrollment (%)	100.0	84.9	0.6	2.6	2.0	6.8
Drop-out Rate (%)	n/a	n/a	n/a	n/a	n/a	n/a
H.S. Diplomas (#)	1,488	1,320	12	37	38	80

Lake Tahoe Unified
1021 Al Tahoe Blvd · South Lake Tahoe, CA 96150-4426
(530) 541-2850 · http://tahoe.ltusd.k12.ca.us/
Grade Span: KG-12; **Agency Type:** 1
Schools: 9
  5 Primary; 1 Middle; 2 High; 1 Other Level
  7 Regular; 0 Special Education; 0 Vocational; 2 Alternative
  0 Magnet; 0 Charter; 5 Title I Eligible; 0 School-wide Title I
Students: 5,083 (52.9% male; 47.0% female)
  Individual Education Program: 713 (14.0%);
  English Language Learner: 1,071 (21.1%); Migrant: 0 (0.0%)
  Eligible for Free Lunch Program: 1,732 (34.1%)
  Eligible for Reduced-Price Lunch Program: 720 (14.2%)
Teachers: 222.4 (22.9 to 1)
Librarians/Media Specialists: 0.0 (n/a to 1)
Guidance Counselors: 7.0 (726.1 to 1)
Current Spending: ($ per student per year):
  Total: $7,366; Instruction: $4,837; Support Services: $2,282
Enrollment, Drop-out Rates and Diploma Recipients by Race/Ethnicity

Category	Total	White	Black	Asian	AIAN	Hisp.
Enrollment (%)	100.0	56.9	0.7	5.7	0.8	32.8
Drop-out Rate (%)	n/a	n/a	n/a	n/a	n/a	n/a
H.S. Diplomas (#)	308	212	2	12	4	78

Mother Lode Union Elementary
3783 Forni Rd · Placerville, CA 95667-6207
(530) 622-6464 · http://www.mlusd.k12.ca.us/
Grade Span: KG-08; **Agency Type:** 1
Schools: 3
  2 Primary; 1 Middle; 0 High; 0 Other Level
  3 Regular; 0 Special Education; 0 Vocational; 0 Alternative
  0 Magnet; 0 Charter; 1 Title I Eligible; 0 School-wide Title I
Students: 1,629 (48.6% male; 51.3% female)
  Individual Education Program: 97 (6.0%);
  English Language Learner: 44 (2.7%); Migrant: 28 (1.7%)
  Eligible for Free Lunch Program: 411 (25.2%)
  Eligible for Reduced-Price Lunch Program: 199 (12.2%)
Teachers: 79.1 (20.6 to 1)
Librarians/Media Specialists: 0.0 (n/a to 1)
Guidance Counselors: 0.0 (n/a to 1)
Current Spending: ($ per student per year):
  Total: $6,637; Instruction: $4,345; Support Services: $2,092
Enrollment, Drop-out Rates and Diploma Recipients by Race/Ethnicity

Category	Total	White	Black	Asian	AIAN	Hisp.
Enrollment (%)	100.0	77.3	0.9	0.9	5.8	14.3
Drop-out Rate (%)	n/a	n/a	n/a	n/a	n/a	n/a
H.S. Diplomas (#)	n/a	n/a	n/a	n/a	n/a	n/a

Rescue Union Elementary
2390 Bass Lake Rd · Rescue, CA 95672-9608
(916) 933-0129 · http://rescue.k12.ca.us/
Grade Span: KG-08; **Agency Type:** 1
Schools: 6
  4 Primary; 2 Middle; 0 High; 0 Other Level
  6 Regular; 0 Special Education; 0 Vocational; 0 Alternative
  0 Magnet; 0 Charter; 2 Title I Eligible; 0 School-wide Title I
Students: 3,624 (52.0% male; 47.9% female)
  Individual Education Program: 186 (5.1%);
  English Language Learner: 64 (1.8%); Migrant: 0 (0.0%)
  Eligible for Free Lunch Program: 229 (6.3%)
  Eligible for Reduced-Price Lunch Program: 106 (2.9%)
Teachers: 174.8 (20.7 to 1)
Librarians/Media Specialists: 0.0 (n/a to 1)
Guidance Counselors: 2.0 (1,812.0 to 1)
Current Spending: ($ per student per year):
  Total: $5,887; Instruction: $3,908; Support Services: $1,871
Enrollment, Drop-out Rates and Diploma Recipients by Race/Ethnicity

Category	Total	White	Black	Asian	AIAN	Hisp.
Enrollment (%)	100.0	86.2	1.3	5.2	1.0	6.0
Drop-out Rate (%)	n/a	n/a	n/a	n/a	n/a	n/a
H.S. Diplomas (#)	n/a	n/a	n/a	n/a	n/a	n/a

Fresno County

Central Unified
4605 N Polk Ave · Fresno, CA 93722-5334
(559) 276-5206 · http://www.centralusd.k12.ca.us/
Grade Span: KG-12; **Agency Type:** 1
Schools: 16
  11 Primary; 2 Middle; 2 High; 1 Other Level
  14 Regular; 0 Special Education; 0 Vocational; 2 Alternative
  0 Magnet; 0 Charter; 12 Title I Eligible; 7 School-wide Title I
Students: 11,851 (51.4% male; 48.5% female)
  Individual Education Program: 1,231 (10.4%);
  English Language Learner: 1,974 (16.7%); Migrant: 388 (3.3%)
  Eligible for Free Lunch Program: 4,265 (36.0%)
  Eligible for Reduced-Price Lunch Program: 1,219 (10.3%)
Teachers: 552.6 (21.4 to 1)
Librarians/Media Specialists: 4.0 (2,962.8 to 1)
Guidance Counselors: 8.9 (1,331.6 to 1)
Current Spending: ($ per student per year):
  Total: $6,770; Instruction: $3,783; Support Services: $2,633
Enrollment, Drop-out Rates and Diploma Recipients by Race/Ethnicity

Category	Total	White	Black	Asian	AIAN	Hisp.
Enrollment (%)	100.0	28.3	8.6	15.6	0.8	44.4
Drop-out Rate (%)	n/a	n/a	n/a	n/a	n/a	n/a
H.S. Diplomas (#)	605	219	38	95	5	247

Clovis Unified
1450 Herndon Ave · Clovis, CA 93611-0567
(559) 397-9000 · http://www.clovisusd.k12.ca.us/
Grade Span: KG-12; **Agency Type:** 1
Schools: 39
  27 Primary; 5 Middle; 6 High; 1 Other Level
  35 Regular; 0 Special Education; 0 Vocational; 4 Alternative
  0 Magnet; 0 Charter; 11 Title I Eligible; 9 School-wide Title I
Students: 34,663 (50.4% male; 49.5% female)
  Individual Education Program: 2,932 (8.5%);
  English Language Learner: 3,041 (8.8%); Migrant: 759 (2.2%)
  Eligible for Free Lunch Program: 6,977 (20.1%)
  Eligible for Reduced-Price Lunch Program: 2,446 (7.1%)
Teachers: 1,604.4 (21.6 to 1)
Librarians/Media Specialists: 9.0 (3,851.4 to 1)
Guidance Counselors: 64.8 (534.9 to 1)
Current Spending: ($ per student per year):
  Total: $7,134; Instruction: $4,195; Support Services: $2,696
Enrollment, Drop-out Rates and Diploma Recipients by Race/Ethnicity

Category	Total	White	Black	Asian	AIAN	Hisp.
Enrollment (%)	100.0	57.9	3.5	13.9	1.3	21.2
Drop-out Rate (%)	n/a	n/a	n/a	n/a	n/a	n/a
H.S. Diplomas (#)	2,052	1,341	58	277	29	345

Coalinga-Huron Joint Unified
657 Sunset St · Coalinga, CA 93210-2927
(559) 935-7500 · http://www.chusd.k12.ca.us/chusd/
Grade Span: KG-12; **Agency Type:** 1
Schools: 11
  5 Primary; 2 Middle; 4 High; 0 Other Level
  8 Regular; 0 Special Education; 0 Vocational; 3 Alternative
  0 Magnet; 0 Charter; 8 Title I Eligible; 7 School-wide Title I
Students: 4,308 (52.8% male; 47.1% female)
  Individual Education Program: 377 (8.8%);
  English Language Learner: 1,560 (36.2%); Migrant: 1,549 (36.0%)
  Eligible for Free Lunch Program: 2,413 (56.0%)
  Eligible for Reduced-Price Lunch Program: 341 (7.9%)
Teachers: 188.1 (22.9 to 1)
Librarians/Media Specialists: 0.0 (n/a to 1)
Guidance Counselors: 6.6 (652.7 to 1)
Current Spending: ($ per student per year):
  Total: $6,818; Instruction: $4,038; Support Services: $2,479
Enrollment, Drop-out Rates and Diploma Recipients by Race/Ethnicity

Category	Total	White	Black	Asian	AIAN	Hisp.
Enrollment (%)	100.0	21.5	0.8	1.3	0.2	75.3
Drop-out Rate (%)	n/a	n/a	n/a	n/a	n/a	n/a
H.S. Diplomas (#)	223	56	2	5	1	157

Firebaugh-Las Deltas Joint Unified
1976 Morris Kyle Dr · Firebaugh, CA 93622-9711
(559) 659-1476
Grade Span: KG-12; **Agency Type:** 1
Schools: 6
  1 Primary; 2 Middle; 3 High; 0 Other Level
  4 Regular; 0 Special Education; 0 Vocational; 2 Alternative
  0 Magnet; 0 Charter; 3 Title I Eligible; 3 School-wide Title I
Students: 2,514 (51.7% male; 48.2% female)
  Individual Education Program: 223 (8.9%);
  English Language Learner: 939 (37.4%); Migrant: 1,265 (50.3%)
  Eligible for Free Lunch Program: 1,798 (71.5%)
  Eligible for Reduced-Price Lunch Program: 247 (9.8%)
Teachers: 122.9 (20.5 to 1)
Librarians/Media Specialists: 1.0 (2,514.0 to 1)
Guidance Counselors: 2.0 (1,257.0 to 1)
Current Spending: ($ per student per year):
  Total: $7,117; Instruction: $4,243; Support Services: $2,487
Enrollment, Drop-out Rates and Diploma Recipients by Race/Ethnicity

Category	Total	White	Black	Asian	AIAN	Hisp.
Enrollment (%)	100.0	6.2	0.8	0.1	0.0	92.7
Drop-out Rate (%)	n/a	n/a	n/a	n/a	n/a	n/a
H.S. Diplomas (#)	103	7	1	0	0	95

Fowler Unified

658 E Adams Ave • Fowler, CA 93625-2111
(559) 834-2591 • http://www.fowler.k12.ca.us/
Grade Span: KG-12; **Agency Type:** 1
Schools: 6
   3 Primary; 1 Middle; 2 High; 0 Other Level
   5 Regular; 0 Special Education; 0 Vocational; 1 Alternative
   0 Magnet; 0 Charter; 4 Title I Eligible; 0 School-wide Title I
Students: 2,235   (52.2% male; 47.7% female)
   Individual Education Program: 249 (11.1%);
   English Language Learner: 491 (22.0%); Migrant: 236 (10.6%)
   Eligible for Free Lunch Program: 986 (44.1%)
   Eligible for Reduced-Price Lunch Program: 200 (8.9%)
Teachers: 109.1 (20.5 to 1)
Librarians/Media Specialists: 1.0 (2,235.0 to 1)
Guidance Counselors: 1.7 (1,314.7 to 1)
Current Spending: ($ per student per year):
   Total: $6,789; Instruction: $4,130; Support Services: $2,318

Enrollment, Drop-out Rates and Diploma Recipients by Race/Ethnicity

Category	Total	White	Black	Asian	AIAN	Hisp.
Enrollment (%)	100.0	18.1	0.9	6.0	0.1	74.1
Drop-out Rate (%)	n/a	n/a	n/a	n/a	n/a	n/a
H.S. Diplomas (#)	143	32	1	12	0	98

Fresno County Office of Education

1111 Van Ness Ave • Fresno, CA 93721-2002
(559) 265-3000 • http://www.fcoe.k12.ca.us/
Grade Span: KG-12; **Agency Type:** 4
Schools: 5
   1 Primary; 0 Middle; 1 High; 3 Other Level
   1 Regular; 1 Special Education; 0 Vocational; 3 Alternative
   0 Magnet; 1 Charter; 0 Title I Eligible; 0 School-wide Title I
Students: 2,178   (67.2% male; 32.7% female)
   Individual Education Program: 1,478 (67.9%);
   English Language Learner: 496 (22.8%); Migrant: 140 (6.4%)
   Eligible for Free Lunch Program: 796 (36.5%)
   Eligible for Reduced-Price Lunch Program: 32 (1.5%)
Teachers: 195.0 (11.2 to 1)
Librarians/Media Specialists: 1.0 (2,178.0 to 1)
Guidance Counselors: 0.0 (n/a to 1)
Current Spending: ($ per student per year):
   Total: $35,115; Instruction: $18,867; Support Services: $16,158

Enrollment, Drop-out Rates and Diploma Recipients by Race/Ethnicity

Category	Total	White	Black	Asian	AIAN	Hisp.
Enrollment (%)	100.0	18.5	23.6	7.1	0.5	49.9
Drop-out Rate (%)	n/a	n/a	n/a	n/a	n/a	n/a
H.S. Diplomas (#)	109	32	10	30	2	35

Fresno Unified

Ed. Cntr. Tulare & M Sts • Fresno, CA 93721-2287
(559) 457-3000 • http://www.fresno.k12.ca.us/
Grade Span: KG-12; **Agency Type:** 1
Schools: 103
   63 Primary; 16 Middle; 18 High; 3 Other Level
   89 Regular; 3 Special Education; 0 Vocational; 8 Alternative
   13 Magnet; 6 Charter; 89 Title I Eligible; 62 School-wide Title I
Students: 81,408   (51.0% male; 48.9% female)
   Individual Education Program: 8,139 (10.0%);
   English Language Learner: 25,319 (31.1%); Migrant: 11,156 (13.7%)
   Eligible for Free Lunch Program: 60,774 (74.7%)
   Eligible for Reduced-Price Lunch Program: 3,620 (4.4%)
Teachers: 3,926.9 (20.7 to 1)
Librarians/Media Specialists: 23.0 (3,539.5 to 1)
Guidance Counselors: 80.9 (1,006.3 to 1)
Current Spending: ($ per student per year):
   Total: $7,799; Instruction: $4,681; Support Services: $2,782

Enrollment, Drop-out Rates and Diploma Recipients by Race/Ethnicity

Category	Total	White	Black	Asian	AIAN	Hisp.
Enrollment (%)	100.0	17.5	11.5	16.6	0.7	53.7
Drop-out Rate (%)	n/a	n/a	n/a	n/a	n/a	n/a
H.S. Diplomas (#)	3,721	974	368	896	27	1,455

Golden Plains Unified

22000 Nevada St • San Joaquin, CA 93660-0520
Mailing Address: PO Box 937 • San Joaquin, CA 93660-0520
(559) 693-1115 • http://www.gpusd.k12.ca.us/
Grade Span: KG-12; **Agency Type:** 1
Schools: 6
   4 Primary; 0 Middle; 2 High; 0 Other Level
   5 Regular; 0 Special Education; 0 Vocational; 1 Alternative
   0 Magnet; 0 Charter; 6 Title I Eligible; 5 School-wide Title I
Students: 1,911   (52.1% male; 47.8% female)
   Individual Education Program: 82 (4.3%);
   English Language Learner: 1,086 (56.8%); Migrant: 1,022 (53.5%)
   Eligible for Free Lunch Program: 1,655 (86.6%)

   Eligible for Reduced-Price Lunch Program: 147 (7.7%)
Teachers: 105.3 (18.1 to 1)
Librarians/Media Specialists: 0.0 (n/a to 1)
Guidance Counselors: 4.0 (477.8 to 1)
Current Spending: ($ per student per year):
   Total: $9,190; Instruction: $4,912; Support Services: $3,892

Enrollment, Drop-out Rates and Diploma Recipients by Race/Ethnicity

Category	Total	White	Black	Asian	AIAN	Hisp.
Enrollment (%)	100.0	3.8	0.2	1.0	0.1	94.7
Drop-out Rate (%)	n/a	n/a	n/a	n/a	n/a	n/a
H.S. Diplomas (#)	104	4	0	2	0	98

Kerman Unified

151 S First St • Kerman, CA 93630-1029
(559) 846-5383 • http://www.kermanusd.k12.ca.us/
Grade Span: KG-12; **Agency Type:** 1
Schools: 7
   2 Primary; 2 Middle; 3 High; 0 Other Level
   5 Regular; 0 Special Education; 0 Vocational; 2 Alternative
   0 Magnet; 0 Charter; 7 Title I Eligible; 6 School-wide Title I
Students: 3,711   (50.6% male; 49.3% female)
   Individual Education Program: 386 (10.4%);
   English Language Learner: 1,231 (33.2%); Migrant: 1,004 (27.1%)
   Eligible for Free Lunch Program: 2,041 (55.0%)
   Eligible for Reduced-Price Lunch Program: 537 (14.5%)
Teachers: 172.1 (21.6 to 1)
Librarians/Media Specialists: 0.9 (4,123.3 to 1)
Guidance Counselors: 1.8 (2,061.7 to 1)
Current Spending: ($ per student per year):
   Total: $6,850; Instruction: $4,098; Support Services: $2,449

Enrollment, Drop-out Rates and Diploma Recipients by Race/Ethnicity

Category	Total	White	Black	Asian	AIAN	Hisp.
Enrollment (%)	100.0	16.7	0.5	6.9	0.2	75.6
Drop-out Rate (%)	n/a	n/a	n/a	n/a	n/a	n/a
H.S. Diplomas (#)	199	51	0	20	0	127

Kings Canyon Joint Unified

675 W Manning Ave • Reedley, CA 93654-2427
(559) 637-1210 • http://www.kc-usd.k12.ca.us/
Grade Span: KG-12; **Agency Type:** 1
Schools: 15
   9 Primary; 3 Middle; 2 High; 1 Other Level
   13 Regular; 0 Special Education; 0 Vocational; 2 Alternative
   0 Magnet; 0 Charter; 12 Title I Eligible; 12 School-wide Title I
Students: 9,067   (50.7% male; 49.2% female)
   Individual Education Program: 924 (10.2%);
   English Language Learner: 3,754 (41.4%); Migrant: 1,259 (13.9%)
   Eligible for Free Lunch Program: 5,675 (62.6%)
   Eligible for Reduced-Price Lunch Program: 912 (10.1%)
Teachers: 441.1 (20.6 to 1)
Librarians/Media Specialists: 2.0 (4,533.5 to 1)
Guidance Counselors: 5.0 (1,813.4 to 1)
Current Spending: ($ per student per year):
   Total: $6,696; Instruction: $4,153; Support Services: $2,218

Enrollment, Drop-out Rates and Diploma Recipients by Race/Ethnicity

Category	Total	White	Black	Asian	AIAN	Hisp.
Enrollment (%)	100.0	17.5	0.5	1.8	0.8	79.5
Drop-out Rate (%)	n/a	n/a	n/a	n/a	n/a	n/a
H.S. Diplomas (#)	510	139	2	21	3	344

Kingsburg Elementary Charter

1310 Stroud Ave • Kingsburg, CA 93631-1000
(559) 897-2331 • http://www.kingsburg-elem.k12.ca.us/
Grade Span: KG-08; **Agency Type:** 1
Schools: 5
   3 Primary; 2 Middle; 0 High; 0 Other Level
   4 Regular; 0 Special Education; 0 Vocational; 1 Alternative
   0 Magnet; 5 Charter; 4 Title I Eligible; 0 School-wide Title I
Students: 2,168   (50.8% male; 49.1% female)
   Individual Education Program: 271 (12.5%);
   English Language Learner: 186 (8.6%); Migrant: 16 (0.7%)
   Eligible for Free Lunch Program: 559 (25.8%)
   Eligible for Reduced-Price Lunch Program: 248 (11.4%)
Teachers: 105.6 (20.5 to 1)
Librarians/Media Specialists: 1.0 (2,168.0 to 1)
Guidance Counselors: 1.0 (2,168.0 to 1)
Current Spending: ($ per student per year):
   Total: $6,394; Instruction: $3,893; Support Services: $2,164

Enrollment, Drop-out Rates and Diploma Recipients by Race/Ethnicity

Category	Total	White	Black	Asian	AIAN	Hisp.
Enrollment (%)	100.0	49.1	0.6	4.3	0.5	43.4
Drop-out Rate (%)	n/a	n/a	n/a	n/a	n/a	n/a
H.S. Diplomas (#)	n/a	n/a	n/a	n/a	n/a	n/a

Mendota Unified
115 Mccabe Ave • Mendota, CA 93640-2000
(559) 655-4942 • http://www.mendotausd.k12.ca.us/
Grade Span: KG-12; **Agency Type:** 1
Schools: 6
  2 Primary; 1 Middle; 3 High; 0 Other Level
  4 Regular; 0 Special Education; 0 Vocational; 2 Alternative
  0 Magnet; 0 Charter; 4 Title I Eligible; 4 School-wide Title I
Students: 2,314   (52.0% male; 47.9% female)
  Individual Education Program: 105 (4.5%);
  English Language Learner: 1,724 (74.5%); Migrant: 1,043 (45.1%)
  Eligible for Free Lunch Program: 2,050 (88.6%)
  Eligible for Reduced-Price Lunch Program: 109 (4.7%)
Teachers: 112.5 (20.6 to 1)
Librarians/Media Specialists: 0.0 (n/a to 1)
Guidance Counselors: 0.0 (n/a to 1)
Current Spending: ($ per student per year):
  Total: $7,845; Instruction: $4,386; Support Services: $2,999

Enrollment, Drop-out Rates and Diploma Recipients by Race/Ethnicity

Category	Total	White	Black	Asian	AIAN	Hisp.
Enrollment (%)	100.0	0.7	0.2	0.4	0.0	98.7
Drop-out Rate (%)	n/a	n/a	n/a	n/a	n/a	n/a
H.S. Diplomas (#)	92	0	0	0	0	92

Parlier Unified
900 Newmark Ave • Parlier, CA 93648-2034
(559) 646-2731 • http://www.parlier.k12.ca.us/
Grade Span: KG-12; **Agency Type:** 1
Schools: 6
  3 Primary; 1 Middle; 2 High; 0 Other Level
  5 Regular; 0 Special Education; 0 Vocational; 1 Alternative
  0 Magnet; 0 Charter; 6 Title I Eligible; 2 School-wide Title I
Students: 3,427   (50.4% male; 49.5% female)
  Individual Education Program: 217 (6.3%);
  English Language Learner: 2,187 (63.8%); Migrant: 1,395 (40.7%)
  Eligible for Free Lunch Program: 2,190 (63.9%)
  Eligible for Reduced-Price Lunch Program: 491 (14.3%)
Teachers: 185.8 (18.4 to 1)
Librarians/Media Specialists: 0.0 (n/a to 1)
Guidance Counselors: 3.0 (1,142.3 to 1)
Current Spending: ($ per student per year):
  Total: $8,070; Instruction: $4,379; Support Services: $3,242

Enrollment, Drop-out Rates and Diploma Recipients by Race/Ethnicity

Category	Total	White	Black	Asian	AIAN	Hisp.
Enrollment (%)	100.0	0.2	0.1	0.3	0.0	98.9
Drop-out Rate (%)	n/a	n/a	n/a	n/a	n/a	n/a
H.S. Diplomas (#)	99	0	0	0	0	99

Riverdale Joint Unified
3086 W Mt. Whitney • Riverdale, CA 93656-1058
Mailing Address: PO Box 1058 • Riverdale, CA 93656-1058
(559) 867-8200 • http://www.riverdale.k12.ca.us/
Grade Span: KG-12; **Agency Type:** 1
Schools: 5
  1 Primary; 1 Middle; 3 High; 0 Other Level
  3 Regular; 0 Special Education; 0 Vocational; 2 Alternative
  0 Magnet; 0 Charter; 4 Title I Eligible; 3 School-wide Title I
Students: 1,575   (50.2% male; 49.7% female)
  Individual Education Program: 93 (5.9%);
  English Language Learner: 444 (28.2%); Migrant: 602 (38.2%)
  Eligible for Free Lunch Program: 1,054 (66.9%)
  Eligible for Reduced-Price Lunch Program: 188 (11.9%)
Teachers: 79.4 (19.8 to 1)
Librarians/Media Specialists: 1.0 (1,575.0 to 1)
Guidance Counselors: 1.7 (926.5 to 1)
Current Spending: ($ per student per year):
  Total: $6,743; Instruction: $4,127; Support Services: $2,218

Enrollment, Drop-out Rates and Diploma Recipients by Race/Ethnicity

Category	Total	White	Black	Asian	AIAN	Hisp.
Enrollment (%)	100.0	23.7	2.2	1.1	0.1	72.9
Drop-out Rate (%)	n/a	n/a	n/a	n/a	n/a	n/a
H.S. Diplomas (#)	100	30	3	2	0	65

Sanger Unified
1905 Seventh St • Sanger, CA 93657-2806
(559) 875-6521 • http://www.sanger.k12.ca.us/
Grade Span: KG-12; **Agency Type:** 1
Schools: 18
  12 Primary; 1 Middle; 3 High; 2 Other Level
  15 Regular; 0 Special Education; 0 Vocational; 3 Alternative
  0 Magnet; 3 Charter; 14 Title I Eligible; 13 School-wide Title I
Students: 8,695   (51.0% male; 48.9% female)
  Individual Education Program: 670 (7.7%);
  English Language Learner: 2,248 (25.9%); Migrant: 343 (3.9%)
  Eligible for Free Lunch Program: 5,438 (62.5%)

Eligible for Reduced-Price Lunch Program: 931 (10.7%)
Teachers: 441.2 (19.7 to 1)
Librarians/Media Specialists: 1.5 (5,796.7 to 1)
Guidance Counselors: 10.0 (869.5 to 1)
Current Spending: ($ per student per year):
  Total: $7,400; Instruction: $4,313; Support Services: $2,690

Enrollment, Drop-out Rates and Diploma Recipients by Race/Ethnicity

Category	Total	White	Black	Asian	AIAN	Hisp.
Enrollment (%)	100.0	19.3	1.2	6.3	0.4	72.8
Drop-out Rate (%)	n/a	n/a	n/a	n/a	n/a	n/a
H.S. Diplomas (#)	497	138	2	33	0	324

Selma Unified
3036 Thompson Ave • Selma, CA 93662-2497
(559) 898-6500 • http://www.selma.k12.ca.us/
Grade Span: KG-12; **Agency Type:** 1
Schools: 12
  8 Primary; 1 Middle; 3 High; 0 Other Level
  10 Regular; 0 Special Education; 0 Vocational; 2 Alternative
  0 Magnet; 0 Charter; 9 Title I Eligible; 9 School-wide Title I
Students: 6,082   (52.0% male; 47.9% female)
  Individual Education Program: 708 (11.6%);
  English Language Learner: 2,054 (33.8%); Migrant: 540 (8.9%)
  Eligible for Free Lunch Program: 4,165 (68.5%)
  Eligible for Reduced-Price Lunch Program: 631 (10.4%)
Teachers: 293.8 (20.7 to 1)
Librarians/Media Specialists: 1.0 (6,082.0 to 1)
Guidance Counselors: 1.4 (4,344.3 to 1)
Current Spending: ($ per student per year):
  Total: $6,324; Instruction: $4,276; Support Services: $1,691

Enrollment, Drop-out Rates and Diploma Recipients by Race/Ethnicity

Category	Total	White	Black	Asian	AIAN	Hisp.
Enrollment (%)	100.0	11.8	0.7	5.3	0.7	80.1
Drop-out Rate (%)	n/a	n/a	n/a	n/a	n/a	n/a
H.S. Diplomas (#)	289	51	2	11	3	216

Sierra Unified
29143 Auberry Rd • Prather, CA 93651
(559) 855-3662 • http://www.sierra.k12.ca.us/
Grade Span: KG-12; **Agency Type:** 1
Schools: 11
  6 Primary; 1 Middle; 4 High; 0 Other Level
  7 Regular; 0 Special Education; 0 Vocational; 4 Alternative
  0 Magnet; 1 Charter; 4 Title I Eligible; 1 School-wide Title I
Students: 2,452   (50.2% male; 49.7% female)
  Individual Education Program: 251 (10.2%);
  English Language Learner: 22 (0.9%); Migrant: 4 (0.2%)
  Eligible for Free Lunch Program: 550 (22.4%)
  Eligible for Reduced-Price Lunch Program: 251 (10.2%)
Teachers: 135.1 (18.1 to 1)
Librarians/Media Specialists: 2.8 (875.7 to 1)
Guidance Counselors: 4.8 (510.8 to 1)
Current Spending: ($ per student per year):
  Total: $9,023; Instruction: $5,315; Support Services: $3,311

Enrollment, Drop-out Rates and Diploma Recipients by Race/Ethnicity

Category	Total	White	Black	Asian	AIAN	Hisp.
Enrollment (%)	100.0	72.3	1.1	3.6	11.5	9.5
Drop-out Rate (%)	n/a	n/a	n/a	n/a	n/a	n/a
H.S. Diplomas (#)	212	173	3	0	21	15

Glenn County

Orland Joint Unified
1320 Sixth St • Orland, CA 95963-1641
(530) 865-1200 • http://www.glenn-co.k12.ca.us/orlandschools.htm
Grade Span: KG-12; **Agency Type:** 1
Schools: 6
  2 Primary; 1 Middle; 3 High; 0 Other Level
  4 Regular; 0 Special Education; 0 Vocational; 2 Alternative
  0 Magnet; 0 Charter; 4 Title I Eligible; 1 School-wide Title I
Students: 2,356   (50.0% male; 49.9% female)
  Individual Education Program: 236 (10.0%);
  English Language Learner: 379 (16.1%); Migrant: 357 (15.2%)
  Eligible for Free Lunch Program: 1,182 (50.2%)
  Eligible for Reduced-Price Lunch Program: 280 (11.9%)
Teachers: 119.0 (19.8 to 1)
Librarians/Media Specialists: 1.0 (2,356.0 to 1)
Guidance Counselors: 3.0 (785.3 to 1)
Current Spending: ($ per student per year):
  Total: $7,022; Instruction: $4,583; Support Services: $2,047

Enrollment, Drop-out Rates and Diploma Recipients by Race/Ethnicity

Category	Total	White	Black	Asian	AIAN	Hisp.
Enrollment (%)	100.0	48.6	1.3	2.0	0.9	45.6
Drop-out Rate (%)	n/a	n/a	n/a	n/a	n/a	n/a
H.S. Diplomas (#)	167	101	2	1	0	63

Willows Unified
334 W Sycamore St • Willows, CA 95988-2830
(530) 934-6600 • http://www.wunif.k12.ca.us/
Grade Span: KG-12; **Agency Type:** 1
Schools: 7
   2 Primary; 2 Middle; 3 High; 0 Other Level
   3 Regular; 0 Special Education; 0 Vocational; 4 Alternative
   0 Magnet; 0 Charter; 4 Title I Eligible; 4 School-wide Title I
Students: 1,846   (52.1% male; 47.8% female)
   Individual Education Program: 0 (0.0%);
   English Language Learner: 300 (16.3%); Migrant: 272 (14.7%)
   Eligible for Free Lunch Program: 835 (45.2%)
   Eligible for Reduced-Price Lunch Program: 142 (7.7%)
Teachers: 87.3 (21.1 to 1)
Librarians/Media Specialists: 0.0 (n/a to 1)
Guidance Counselors: 2.7 (683.7 to 1)
Current Spending: ($ per student per year):
   Total: $6,765; Instruction: $4,054; Support Services: $2,377

Enrollment, Drop-out Rates and Diploma Recipients by Race/Ethnicity

Category	Total	White	Black	Asian	AIAN	Hisp.
Enrollment (%)	100.0	53.6	1.4	8.7	2.9	33.4
Drop-out Rate (%)	n/a	n/a	n/a	n/a	n/a	n/a
H.S. Diplomas (#)	106	70	1	13	3	19

Humboldt County

Eureka City Unified
3200 Walford Ave • Eureka, CA 95503-4887
(707) 441-2400 • http://www.eurekacityschools.org/
Grade Span: KG-12; **Agency Type:** 1
Schools: 13
   6 Primary; 3 Middle; 4 High; 0 Other Level
   9 Regular; 1 Special Education; 0 Vocational; 3 Alternative
   0 Magnet; 0 Charter; 8 Title I Eligible; 6 School-wide Title I
Students: 5,039   (52.2% male; 47.7% female)
   Individual Education Program: 641 (12.7%);
   English Language Learner: 490 (9.7%); Migrant: 0 (0.0%)
   Eligible for Free Lunch Program: 2,047 (40.6%)
   Eligible for Reduced-Price Lunch Program: 516 (10.2%)
Teachers: 264.4 (19.1 to 1)
Librarians/Media Specialists: 2.2 (2,290.5 to 1)
Guidance Counselors: 5.0 (1,007.8 to 1)
Current Spending: ($ per student per year):
   Total: $7,481; Instruction: $4,552; Support Services: $2,637

Enrollment, Drop-out Rates and Diploma Recipients by Race/Ethnicity

Category	Total	White	Black	Asian	AIAN	Hisp.
Enrollment (%)	100.0	66.9	3.4	7.7	12.0	9.7
Drop-out Rate (%)	n/a	n/a	n/a	n/a	n/a	n/a
H.S. Diplomas (#)	419	332	6	30	31	20

Northern Humboldt Union High
2755 Mckinleyville Ave • Mc Kinleyville, CA 95521-3400
(707) 839-6470
Grade Span: 09-12; **Agency Type:** 1
Schools: 5
   0 Primary; 0 Middle; 5 High; 0 Other Level
   2 Regular; 0 Special Education; 0 Vocational; 3 Alternative
   0 Magnet; 0 Charter; 5 Title I Eligible; 0 School-wide Title I
Students: 1,937   (52.2% male; 47.7% female)
   Individual Education Program: 220 (11.4%);
   English Language Learner: 4 (0.2%); Migrant: 0 (0.0%)
   Eligible for Free Lunch Program: 154 (8.0%)
   Eligible for Reduced-Price Lunch Program: 19 (1.0%)
Teachers: 90.8 (21.3 to 1)
Librarians/Media Specialists: 2.0 (968.5 to 1)
Guidance Counselors: 5.0 (387.4 to 1)
Current Spending: ($ per student per year):
   Total: $6,865; Instruction: $4,311; Support Services: $2,542

Enrollment, Drop-out Rates and Diploma Recipients by Race/Ethnicity

Category	Total	White	Black	Asian	AIAN	Hisp.
Enrollment (%)	100.0	80.8	1.3	1.9	8.6	5.1
Drop-out Rate (%)	n/a	n/a	n/a	n/a	n/a	n/a
H.S. Diplomas (#)	402	342	4	7	27	22

Imperial County

Brawley Elementary
261 D St • Brawley, CA 92227-1912
(760) 344-2330 • http://www.icoe.k12.ca.us/besd/besd.htm
Grade Span: KG-08; **Agency Type:** 1
Schools: 5
   4 Primary; 1 Middle; 0 High; 0 Other Level
   5 Regular; 0 Special Education; 0 Vocational; 0 Alternative
   0 Magnet; 0 Charter; 5 Title I Eligible; 5 School-wide Title I
Students: 3,395   (50.8% male; 49.1% female)

   Individual Education Program: 242 (7.1%);
   English Language Learner: 1,147 (33.8%); Migrant: 837 (24.7%)
   Eligible for Free Lunch Program: 2,183 (64.3%)
   Eligible for Reduced-Price Lunch Program: 408 (12.0%)
Teachers: 186.1 (18.2 to 1)
Librarians/Media Specialists: 0.0 (n/a to 1)
Guidance Counselors: 2.0 (1,697.5 to 1)
Current Spending: ($ per student per year):
   Total: $7,103; Instruction: $4,865; Support Services: $1,928

Enrollment, Drop-out Rates and Diploma Recipients by Race/Ethnicity

Category	Total	White	Black	Asian	AIAN	Hisp.
Enrollment (%)	100.0	11.1	2.9	0.7	0.1	85.1
Drop-out Rate (%)	n/a	n/a	n/a	n/a	n/a	n/a
H.S. Diplomas (#)	n/a	n/a	n/a	n/a	n/a	n/a

Brawley Union High
480 N Imperial Ave • Brawley, CA 92227-1625
(760) 312-5819 • http://www.brawleyhigh.org/
Grade Span: 07-12; **Agency Type:** 1
Schools: 3
   0 Primary; 0 Middle; 3 High; 0 Other Level
   1 Regular; 0 Special Education; 0 Vocational; 2 Alternative
   0 Magnet; 0 Charter; 3 Title I Eligible; 1 School-wide Title I
Students: 1,858   (49.7% male; 50.2% female)
   Individual Education Program: 159 (8.6%);
   English Language Learner: 579 (31.2%); Migrant: 481 (25.9%)
   Eligible for Free Lunch Program: 716 (38.5%)
   Eligible for Reduced-Price Lunch Program: 151 (8.1%)
Teachers: 77.3 (24.0 to 1)
Librarians/Media Specialists: 0.0 (n/a to 1)
Guidance Counselors: 7.0 (265.4 to 1)
Current Spending: ($ per student per year):
   Total: $7,551; Instruction: $4,605; Support Services: $2,696

Enrollment, Drop-out Rates and Diploma Recipients by Race/Ethnicity

Category	Total	White	Black	Asian	AIAN	Hisp.
Enrollment (%)	100.0	20.6	1.5	1.1	0.6	75.6
Drop-out Rate (%)	n/a	n/a	n/a	n/a	n/a	n/a
H.S. Diplomas (#)	321	62	4	2	0	253

Calexico Unified
901 Andrade Ave • Calexico, CA 92232-0792
Mailing Address: PO Box 792 • Calexico, CA 92232-0792
(760) 768-3888 • http://bordernet.calexico.k12.ca.us/
Grade Span: KG-12; **Agency Type:** 1
Schools: 10
   6 Primary; 2 Middle; 2 High; 0 Other Level
   9 Regular; 0 Special Education; 0 Vocational; 1 Alternative
   0 Magnet; 0 Charter; 10 Title I Eligible; 7 School-wide Title I
Students: 8,839   (50.7% male; 49.2% female)
   Individual Education Program: 568 (6.4%);
   English Language Learner: 6,463 (73.1%); Migrant: 2,038 (23.1%)
   Eligible for Free Lunch Program: 5,377 (60.8%)
   Eligible for Reduced-Price Lunch Program: 1,500 (17.0%)
Teachers: 399.4 (22.1 to 1)
Librarians/Media Specialists: 0.0 (n/a to 1)
Guidance Counselors: 11.0 (803.5 to 1)
Current Spending: ($ per student per year):
   Total: $7,439; Instruction: $4,586; Support Services: $2,496

Enrollment, Drop-out Rates and Diploma Recipients by Race/Ethnicity

Category	Total	White	Black	Asian	AIAN	Hisp.
Enrollment (%)	100.0	0.7	0.0	0.9	0.0	98.2
Drop-out Rate (%)	n/a	n/a	n/a	n/a	n/a	n/a
H.S. Diplomas (#)	476	7	1	12	0	456

Central Union High
1001 Brighton Ave • El Centro, CA 92243-3110
(760) 336-4500 • http://www.cuhsd.net/
Grade Span: 09-12; **Agency Type:** 1
Schools: 3
   0 Primary; 0 Middle; 3 High; 0 Other Level
   2 Regular; 0 Special Education; 0 Vocational; 1 Alternative
   0 Magnet; 0 Charter; 3 Title I Eligible; 1 School-wide Title I
Students: 3,947   (50.6% male; 49.3% female)
   Individual Education Program: 301 (7.6%);
   English Language Learner: 1,395 (35.3%); Migrant: 765 (19.4%)
   Eligible for Free Lunch Program: 1,652 (41.9%)
   Eligible for Reduced-Price Lunch Program: 361 (9.1%)
Teachers: 164.8 (24.0 to 1)
Librarians/Media Specialists: 1.0 (3,947.0 to 1)
Guidance Counselors: 8.0 (493.4 to 1)
Current Spending: ($ per student per year):
   Total: $7,037; Instruction: $3,994; Support Services: $2,715

Enrollment, Drop-out Rates and Diploma Recipients by Race/Ethnicity

Category	Total	White	Black	Asian	AIAN	Hisp.
Enrollment (%)	100.0	10.1	2.2	1.9	0.1	85.4
Drop-out Rate (%)	n/a	n/a	n/a	n/a	n/a	n/a
H.S. Diplomas (#)	683	104	6	19	0	554

El Centro Elementary
1256 Broadway • El Centro, CA 92243-2317
(760) 352-5712 • http://www.ecsd.k12.ca.us/
Grade Span: KG-08; **Agency Type:** 1
Schools: 11
    9 Primary; 2 Middle; 0 High; 0 Other Level
    11 Regular; 0 Special Education; 0 Vocational; 0 Alternative
    0 Magnet; 0 Charter; 11 Title I Eligible; 11 School-wide Title I
Students: 6,301   (51.7% male; 48.2% female)
    Individual Education Program: 569 (9.0%);
    English Language Learner: 2,806 (44.5%); Migrant: 995 (15.8%)
    Eligible for Free Lunch Program: 3,921 (62.2%)
    Eligible for Reduced-Price Lunch Program: 719 (11.4%)
Teachers: 272.0 (23.2 to 1)
Librarians/Media Specialists: 0.0 (n/a to 1)
Guidance Counselors: 4.0 (1,575.3 to 1)
Current Spending: ($ per student per year):
    Total: $7,364; Instruction: $4,962; Support Services: $2,058

Enrollment, Drop-out Rates and Diploma Recipients by Race/Ethnicity

Category	Total	White	Black	Asian	AIAN	Hisp.
Enrollment (%)	100.0	6.7	2.7	2.5	0.2	88.0
Drop-out Rate (%)	n/a	n/a	n/a	n/a	n/a	n/a
H.S. Diplomas (#)	n/a	n/a	n/a	n/a	n/a	n/a

Holtville Unified
621 E Sixth St • Holtville, CA 92250-1450
(760) 356-2974 • http://www.holtville.k12.ca.us/
Grade Span: KG-12; **Agency Type:** 1
Schools: 5
    2 Primary; 1 Middle; 2 High; 0 Other Level
    4 Regular; 0 Special Education; 0 Vocational; 1 Alternative
    0 Magnet; 0 Charter; 5 Title I Eligible; 0 School-wide Title I
Students: 1,921   (52.1% male; 47.8% female)
    Individual Education Program: 176 (9.2%);
    English Language Learner: 829 (43.2%); Migrant: 582 (30.3%)
    Eligible for Free Lunch Program: 1,213 (63.1%)
    Eligible for Reduced-Price Lunch Program: 161 (8.4%)
Teachers: 94.3 (20.4 to 1)
Librarians/Media Specialists: 0.0 (n/a to 1)
Guidance Counselors: 2.5 (768.4 to 1)
Current Spending: ($ per student per year):
    Total: $7,252; Instruction: $4,557; Support Services: $2,371

Enrollment, Drop-out Rates and Diploma Recipients by Race/Ethnicity

Category	Total	White	Black	Asian	AIAN	Hisp.
Enrollment (%)	100.0	19.9	0.3	1.3	0.2	78.2
Drop-out Rate (%)	n/a	n/a	n/a	n/a	n/a	n/a
H.S. Diplomas (#)	133	36	1	4	1	91

Imperial Unified
219 N E St • Imperial, CA 92251-1176
(760) 355-3200 • http://www.icoe.k12.ca.us/iusd/
Grade Span: KG-12; **Agency Type:** 1
Schools: 6
    3 Primary; 1 Middle; 2 High; 0 Other Level
    5 Regular; 0 Special Education; 0 Vocational; 1 Alternative
    0 Magnet; 0 Charter; 4 Title I Eligible; 0 School-wide Title I
Students: 2,867   (51.0% male; 48.9% female)
    Individual Education Program: 201 (7.0%);
    English Language Learner: 641 (22.4%); Migrant: 130 (4.5%)
    Eligible for Free Lunch Program: 761 (26.5%)
    Eligible for Reduced-Price Lunch Program: 228 (8.0%)
Teachers: 131.5 (21.8 to 1)
Librarians/Media Specialists: 0.0 (n/a to 1)
Guidance Counselors: 3.5 (819.1 to 1)
Current Spending: ($ per student per year):
    Total: $6,779; Instruction: $4,126; Support Services: $2,379

Enrollment, Drop-out Rates and Diploma Recipients by Race/Ethnicity

Category	Total	White	Black	Asian	AIAN	Hisp.
Enrollment (%)	100.0	26.2	2.1	1.8	0.1	69.3
Drop-out Rate (%)	n/a	n/a	n/a	n/a	n/a	n/a
H.S. Diplomas (#)	152	59	5	4	1	82

Kern County

Arvin Union Elementary
737 Bear Mountain Blvd • Arvin, CA 93203-1413
(661) 854-6500 • http://frontpage.lightspeed.net/ausd/
Grade Span: KG-08; **Agency Type:** 1
Schools: 3

    2 Primary; 1 Middle; 0 High; 0 Other Level
    3 Regular; 0 Special Education; 0 Vocational; 0 Alternative
    0 Magnet; 0 Charter; 3 Title I Eligible; 3 School-wide Title I
Students: 2,940   (51.1% male; 48.8% female)
    Individual Education Program: 299 (10.2%);
    English Language Learner: 1,964 (66.8%); Migrant: 1,360 (46.3%)
    Eligible for Free Lunch Program: 1,741 (59.2%)
    Eligible for Reduced-Price Lunch Program: 317 (10.8%)
Teachers: 149.0 (19.7 to 1)
Librarians/Media Specialists: 0.0 (n/a to 1)
Guidance Counselors: 1.0 (2,940.0 to 1)
Current Spending: ($ per student per year):
    Total: $6,973; Instruction: $4,422; Support Services: $2,108

Enrollment, Drop-out Rates and Diploma Recipients by Race/Ethnicity

Category	Total	White	Black	Asian	AIAN	Hisp.
Enrollment (%)	100.0	3.9	1.0	0.5	0.0	94.6
Drop-out Rate (%)	n/a	n/a	n/a	n/a	n/a	n/a
H.S. Diplomas (#)	n/a	n/a	n/a	n/a	n/a	n/a

Bakersfield City Elementary
1300 Baker St • Bakersfield, CA 93305-4326
(661) 631-4600 • http://www.bcsd.k12.ca.us/
Grade Span: KG-08; **Agency Type:** 1
Schools: 43
    32 Primary; 10 Middle; 0 High; 0 Other Level
    40 Regular; 0 Special Education; 0 Vocational; 2 Alternative
    7 Magnet; 0 Charter; 28 Title I Eligible; 28 School-wide Title I
Students: 28,315   (50.9% male; 49.0% female)
    Individual Education Program: 2,816 (9.9%);
    English Language Learner: 6,939 (24.5%); Migrant: 5,375 (19.0%)
    Eligible for Free Lunch Program: 21,626 (76.4%)
    Eligible for Reduced-Price Lunch Program: 2,705 (9.6%)
Teachers: 1,357.3 (20.9 to 1)
Librarians/Media Specialists: 8.0 (3,539.4 to 1)
Guidance Counselors: 27.9 (1,014.9 to 1)
Current Spending: ($ per student per year):
    Total: $7,772; Instruction: $4,938; Support Services: $2,415

Enrollment, Drop-out Rates and Diploma Recipients by Race/Ethnicity

Category	Total	White	Black	Asian	AIAN	Hisp.
Enrollment (%)	100.0	16.1	12.8	1.7	1.2	67.5
Drop-out Rate (%)	n/a	n/a	n/a	n/a	n/a	n/a
H.S. Diplomas (#)	n/a	n/a	n/a	n/a	n/a	n/a

Beardsley Elementary
1001 Roberts Ln • Bakersfield, CA 93308-4503
(661) 393-8550 • http://webup.web.kern.org/districts/beardsley/
Grade Span: KG-08; **Agency Type:** 1
Schools: 3
    1 Primary; 2 Middle; 0 High; 0 Other Level
    3 Regular; 0 Special Education; 0 Vocational; 0 Alternative
    0 Magnet; 0 Charter; 3 Title I Eligible; 2 School-wide Title I
Students: 1,854   (52.5% male; 47.4% female)
    Individual Education Program: 0 (0.0%);
    English Language Learner: 107 (5.8%); Migrant: 6 (0.3%)
    Eligible for Free Lunch Program: 1,313 (70.8%)
    Eligible for Reduced-Price Lunch Program: 214 (11.5%)
Teachers: 91.0 (20.4 to 1)
Librarians/Media Specialists: 0.0 (n/a to 1)
Guidance Counselors: 0.0 (n/a to 1)
Current Spending: ($ per student per year):
    Total: $6,542; Instruction: $4,078; Support Services: $2,131

Enrollment, Drop-out Rates and Diploma Recipients by Race/Ethnicity

Category	Total	White	Black	Asian	AIAN	Hisp.
Enrollment (%)	100.0	72.4	2.3	1.1	1.0	21.8
Drop-out Rate (%)	n/a	n/a	n/a	n/a	n/a	n/a
H.S. Diplomas (#)	n/a	n/a	n/a	n/a	n/a	n/a

Delano Joint Union High
1747 Princeton St • Delano, CA 93215-1501
(661) 725-4000 • http://www.delanohighschool.org/
Grade Span: 09-12; **Agency Type:** 1
Schools: 4
    0 Primary; 0 Middle; 4 High; 0 Other Level
    2 Regular; 0 Special Education; 0 Vocational; 2 Alternative
    0 Magnet; 0 Charter; 2 Title I Eligible; 2 School-wide Title I
Students: 3,936   (50.9% male; 49.0% female)
    Individual Education Program: 318 (8.1%);
    English Language Learner: 1,892 (48.1%); Migrant: 1,433 (36.4%)
    Eligible for Free Lunch Program: 2,314 (58.8%)
    Eligible for Reduced-Price Lunch Program: 529 (13.4%)
Teachers: 166.2 (23.7 to 1)
Librarians/Media Specialists: 0.0 (n/a to 1)
Guidance Counselors: 7.0 (562.3 to 1)
Current Spending: ($ per student per year):
    Total: $7,827; Instruction: $4,535; Support Services: $3,039

Enrollment, Drop-out Rates and Diploma Recipients by Race/Ethnicity

Category	Total	White	Black	Asian	AIAN	Hisp.
Enrollment (%)	100.0	2.9	1.2	15.2	0.0	80.7
Drop-out Rate (%)	n/a	n/a	n/a	n/a	n/a	n/a
H.S. Diplomas (#)	655	22	9	98	1	525

Delano Union Elementary
1405 12th Ave • Delano, CA 93215-2416
(661) 721-5000 • http://www.duesd.org/
Grade Span: KG-08; **Agency Type:** 1
Schools: 10
    7 Primary; 2 Middle; 0 High; 0 Other Level
    9 Regular; 0 Special Education; 0 Vocational; 0 Alternative
    0 Magnet; 0 Charter; 9 Title I Eligible; 1 School-wide Title I
Students: 7,332 (51.3% male; 48.6% female)
    Individual Education Program: 550 (7.5%);
    English Language Learner: 4,090 (55.8%); Migrant: 2,927 (39.9%)
    Eligible for Free Lunch Program: 7,305 (99.6%)
    Eligible for Reduced-Price Lunch Program: 0 (0.0%)
Teachers: 331.0 (22.2 to 1)
Librarians/Media Specialists: 0.0 (n/a to 1)
Guidance Counselors: 0.0 (n/a to 1)
Current Spending: ($ per student per year):
    Total: $6,876; Instruction: $4,299; Support Services: $2,185

Enrollment, Drop-out Rates and Diploma Recipients by Race/Ethnicity

Category	Total	White	Black	Asian	AIAN	Hisp.
Enrollment (%)	100.0	1.6	1.7	14.3	0.1	80.3
Drop-out Rate (%)	n/a	n/a	n/a	n/a	n/a	n/a
H.S. Diplomas (#)	n/a	n/a	n/a	n/a	n/a	n/a

Fairfax Elementary
1500 S Fairfax Rd • Bakersfield, CA 93307-3151
(661) 366-7221
Grade Span: KG-08; **Agency Type:** 1
Schools: 2
    2 Primary; 0 Middle; 0 High; 0 Other Level
    2 Regular; 0 Special Education; 0 Vocational; 0 Alternative
    0 Magnet; 0 Charter; 2 Title I Eligible; 2 School-wide Title I
Students: 1,558 (52.7% male; 47.2% female)
    Individual Education Program: 150 (9.6%);
    English Language Learner: 633 (40.6%); Migrant: 572 (36.7%)
    Eligible for Free Lunch Program: 1,209 (77.6%)
    Eligible for Reduced-Price Lunch Program: 206 (13.2%)
Teachers: 71.9 (21.7 to 1)
Librarians/Media Specialists: 0.0 (n/a to 1)
Guidance Counselors: 0.0 (n/a to 1)
Current Spending: ($ per student per year):
    Total: $6,484; Instruction: $4,045; Support Services: $2,010

Enrollment, Drop-out Rates and Diploma Recipients by Race/Ethnicity

Category	Total	White	Black	Asian	AIAN	Hisp.
Enrollment (%)	100.0	12.6	4.0	1.7	0.7	81.0
Drop-out Rate (%)	n/a	n/a	n/a	n/a	n/a	n/a
H.S. Diplomas (#)	n/a	n/a	n/a	n/a	n/a	n/a

Fruitvale Elementary
7311 Rosedale Hwy • Bakersfield, CA 93308-5738
(661) 589-3830 • http://www.fruitvale.k12.ca.us/
Grade Span: KG-08; **Agency Type:** 1
Schools: 5
    4 Primary; 1 Middle; 0 High; 0 Other Level
    5 Regular; 0 Special Education; 0 Vocational; 0 Alternative
    0 Magnet; 0 Charter; 4 Title I Eligible; 0 School-wide Title I
Students: 3,133 (49.3% male; 50.6% female)
    Individual Education Program: 354 (11.3%);
    English Language Learner: 62 (2.0%); Migrant: 1 (<0.1%)
    Eligible for Free Lunch Program: 376 (12.0%)
    Eligible for Reduced-Price Lunch Program: 332 (10.6%)
Teachers: 146.6 (21.4 to 1)
Librarians/Media Specialists: 0.0 (n/a to 1)
Guidance Counselors: 1.0 (3,133.0 to 1)
Current Spending: ($ per student per year):
    Total: $6,150; Instruction: $4,087; Support Services: $1,869

Enrollment, Drop-out Rates and Diploma Recipients by Race/Ethnicity

Category	Total	White	Black	Asian	AIAN	Hisp.
Enrollment (%)	100.0	63.6	6.6	5.8	1.3	19.8
Drop-out Rate (%)	n/a	n/a	n/a	n/a	n/a	n/a
H.S. Diplomas (#)	n/a	n/a	n/a	n/a	n/a	n/a

Greenfield Union Elementary
1624 Fairview Rd • Bakersfield, CA 93307-5512
(661) 837-6000 • http://www.greenfield.k12.ca.us/
Grade Span: KG-08; **Agency Type:** 1
Schools: 10
    7 Primary; 3 Middle; 0 High; 0 Other Level
    10 Regular; 0 Special Education; 0 Vocational; 0 Alternative

    0 Magnet; 0 Charter; 8 Title I Eligible; 8 School-wide Title I
Students: 7,427 (50.8% male; 49.1% female)
    Individual Education Program: 695 (9.4%);
    English Language Learner: 2,081 (28.0%); Migrant: 1,637 (22.0%)
    Eligible for Free Lunch Program: 4,481 (60.3%)
    Eligible for Reduced-Price Lunch Program: 1,061 (14.3%)
Teachers: 364.0 (20.4 to 1)
Librarians/Media Specialists: 0.0 (n/a to 1)
Guidance Counselors: 4.0 (1,856.8 to 1)
Current Spending: ($ per student per year):
    Total: $6,765; Instruction: $4,194; Support Services: $2,265

Enrollment, Drop-out Rates and Diploma Recipients by Race/Ethnicity

Category	Total	White	Black	Asian	AIAN	Hisp.
Enrollment (%)	100.0	16.5	10.5	3.6	0.6	66.3
Drop-out Rate (%)	n/a	n/a	n/a	n/a	n/a	n/a
H.S. Diplomas (#)	n/a	n/a	n/a	n/a	n/a	n/a

Kern County Office of Education
1300 17th St City Centre • Bakersfield, CA 93301-4504
(661) 636-4000 • http://www.kern.org/
Grade Span: KG-12; **Agency Type:** 4
Schools: 5
    0 Primary; 0 Middle; 0 High; 4 Other Level
    1 Regular; 1 Special Education; 0 Vocational; 2 Alternative
    0 Magnet; 1 Charter; 0 Title I Eligible; 0 School-wide Title I
Students: 2,627 (67.7% male; 32.2% female)
    Individual Education Program: 1,444 (55.0%);
    English Language Learner: 342 (13.0%); Migrant: 5 (0.2%)
    Eligible for Free Lunch Program: 694 (26.4%)
    Eligible for Reduced-Price Lunch Program: 68 (2.6%)
Teachers: 196.5 (13.4 to 1)
Librarians/Media Specialists: 0.0 (n/a to 1)
Guidance Counselors: 2.3 (1,142.2 to 1)
Current Spending: ($ per student per year):
    Total: $38,535; Instruction: $11,975; Support Services: $24,967

Enrollment, Drop-out Rates and Diploma Recipients by Race/Ethnicity

Category	Total	White	Black	Asian	AIAN	Hisp.
Enrollment (%)	100.0	42.8	11.9	0.8	0.4	42.4
Drop-out Rate (%)	n/a	n/a	n/a	n/a	n/a	n/a
H.S. Diplomas (#)	160	84	17	1	0	58

Kern Union High
5801 Sundale Ave • Bakersfield, CA 93309-2924
(661) 827-3100 • http://www.khsd.k12.ca.us/
Grade Span: 09-12; **Agency Type:** 1
Schools: 23
    0 Primary; 0 Middle; 23 High; 0 Other Level
    15 Regular; 2 Special Education; 0 Vocational; 6 Alternative
    0 Magnet; 1 Charter; 0 Title I Eligible; 0 School-wide Title I
Students: 32,357 (50.2% male; 49.7% female)
    Individual Education Program: 2,694 (8.3%);
    English Language Learner: 3,597 (11.1%); Migrant: 3,546 (11.0%)
    Eligible for Free Lunch Program: 11,823 (36.5%)
    Eligible for Reduced-Price Lunch Program: 1,889 (5.8%)
Teachers: 1,410.9 (22.9 to 1)
Librarians/Media Specialists: 15.0 (2,157.1 to 1)
Guidance Counselors: 71.2 (454.5 to 1)
Current Spending: ($ per student per year):
    Total: $7,281; Instruction: $3,887; Support Services: $3,125

Enrollment, Drop-out Rates and Diploma Recipients by Race/Ethnicity

Category	Total	White	Black	Asian	AIAN	Hisp.
Enrollment (%)	100.0	39.6	8.1	4.0	0.8	47.6
Drop-out Rate (%)	n/a	n/a	n/a	n/a	n/a	n/a
H.S. Diplomas (#)	5,741	2,674	372	321	58	2,316

Lamont Elementary
8201 Palm Ave • Lamont, CA 93241-2118
(661) 845-0751 • http://www.lamontschooldistrict.org/
Grade Span: KG-08; **Agency Type:** 1
Schools: 4
    2 Primary; 2 Middle; 0 High; 0 Other Level
    4 Regular; 0 Special Education; 0 Vocational; 0 Alternative
    0 Magnet; 0 Charter; 4 Title I Eligible; 4 School-wide Title I
Students: 2,813 (50.7% male; 49.2% female)
    Individual Education Program: 274 (9.7%);
    English Language Learner: 2,076 (73.8%); Migrant: 1,264 (44.9%)
    Eligible for Free Lunch Program: 2,785 (99.0%)
    Eligible for Reduced-Price Lunch Program: 0 (0.0%)
Teachers: 122.2 (23.0 to 1)
Librarians/Media Specialists: 0.0 (n/a to 1)
Guidance Counselors: 2.0 (1,406.5 to 1)
Current Spending: ($ per student per year):
    Total: $7,715; Instruction: $5,052; Support Services: $2,184

Enrollment, Drop-out Rates and Diploma Recipients by Race/Ethnicity

Category	Total	White	Black	Asian	AIAN	Hisp.
Enrollment (%)	100.0	4.6	0.1	1.0	0.1	93.9
Drop-out Rate (%)	n/a	n/a	n/a	n/a	n/a	n/a
H.S. Diplomas (#)	n/a	n/a	n/a	n/a	n/a	n/a

Mcfarland Unified
601 Second St • Mcfarland, CA 93250-1121
(661) 792-3081
Grade Span: KG-12; **Agency Type:** 1
Schools: 6
    2 Primary; 1 Middle; 3 High; 0 Other Level
    4 Regular; 0 Special Education; 0 Vocational; 2 Alternative
    0 Magnet; 0 Charter; 5 Title I Eligible; 5 School-wide Title I
Students: 2,966   (49.2% male; 50.7% female)
    Individual Education Program: 264 (8.9%);
    English Language Learner: 1,183 (39.9%); Migrant: 1,325 (44.7%)
    Eligible for Free Lunch Program: 2,304 (77.7%)
    Eligible for Reduced-Price Lunch Program: 152 (5.1%)
Teachers: 148.4 (20.0 to 1)
Librarians/Media Specialists: 0.9 (3,295.6 to 1)
Guidance Counselors: 3.0 (988.7 to 1)
Current Spending: ($ per student per year):
    Total: $7,802; Instruction: $4,828; Support Services: $2,533

Enrollment, Drop-out Rates and Diploma Recipients by Race/Ethnicity

Category	Total	White	Black	Asian	AIAN	Hisp.
Enrollment (%)	100.0	4.0	0.5	0.5	0.3	93.4
Drop-out Rate (%)	n/a	n/a	n/a	n/a	n/a	n/a
H.S. Diplomas (#)	194	15	1	1	1	176

Mojave Unified
3500 Douglas Ave • Mojave, CA 93501-1143
(661) 824-4001 • http://www.mojave.k12.ca.us/
Grade Span: KG-12; **Agency Type:** 1
Schools: 9
    3 Primary; 3 Middle; 2 High; 1 Other Level
    6 Regular; 0 Special Education; 0 Vocational; 3 Alternative
    0 Magnet; 0 Charter; 5 Title I Eligible; 3 School-wide Title I
Students: 2,746   (51.5% male; 48.4% female)
    Individual Education Program: 219 (8.0%);
    English Language Learner: 318 (11.6%); Migrant: 42 (1.5%)
    Eligible for Free Lunch Program: 1,244 (45.3%)
    Eligible for Reduced-Price Lunch Program: 169 (6.2%)
Teachers: 125.2 (21.9 to 1)
Librarians/Media Specialists: 0.0 (n/a to 1)
Guidance Counselors: 2.0 (1,373.0 to 1)
Current Spending: ($ per student per year):
    Total: $6,935; Instruction: $4,012; Support Services: $2,637

Enrollment, Drop-out Rates and Diploma Recipients by Race/Ethnicity

Category	Total	White	Black	Asian	AIAN	Hisp.
Enrollment (%)	100.0	44.1	17.3	2.3	1.0	26.6
Drop-out Rate (%)	n/a	n/a	n/a	n/a	n/a	n/a
H.S. Diplomas (#)	169	94	24	7	2	41

Muroc Joint Unified
17100 Foothill Ave • North Edwards, CA 93523-0833
Mailing Address: PO Box 833 • North Edwards, CA 93523-0833
(760) 769-4821 • http://www.muroc.k12.ca.us/
Grade Span: KG-12; **Agency Type:** 1
Schools: 7
    3 Primary; 1 Middle; 2 High; 1 Other Level
    6 Regular; 0 Special Education; 0 Vocational; 1 Alternative
    0 Magnet; 0 Charter; 2 Title I Eligible; 0 School-wide Title I
Students: 2,424   (51.0% male; 48.9% female)
    Individual Education Program: 246 (10.1%);
    English Language Learner: 31 (1.3%); Migrant: 0 (0.0%)
    Eligible for Free Lunch Program: 386 (15.9%)
    Eligible for Reduced-Price Lunch Program: 288 (11.9%)
Teachers: 120.2 (20.2 to 1)
Librarians/Media Specialists: 0.0 (n/a to 1)
Guidance Counselors: 3.0 (808.0 to 1)
Current Spending: ($ per student per year):
    Total: $8,469; Instruction: $5,186; Support Services: $3,032

Enrollment, Drop-out Rates and Diploma Recipients by Race/Ethnicity

Category	Total	White	Black	Asian	AIAN	Hisp.
Enrollment (%)	100.0	63.0	10.6	5.4	0.6	9.1
Drop-out Rate (%)	n/a	n/a	n/a	n/a	n/a	n/a
H.S. Diplomas (#)	135	109	9	12	0	5

Norris Elementary
6940 Calloway Dr • Bakersfield, CA 93312-9005
(661) 387-7000
Grade Span: KG-08; **Agency Type:** 1
Schools: 4
    3 Primary; 1 Middle; 0 High; 0 Other Level

    4 Regular; 0 Special Education; 0 Vocational; 0 Alternative
    0 Magnet; 0 Charter; 0 Title I Eligible; 0 School-wide Title I
Students: 2,073   (51.8% male; 48.1% female)
    Individual Education Program: 117 (5.6%);
    English Language Learner: 25 (1.2%); Migrant: 0 (0.0%)
    Eligible for Free Lunch Program: 133 (6.4%)
    Eligible for Reduced-Price Lunch Program: 137 (6.6%)
Teachers: 100.3 (20.7 to 1)
Librarians/Media Specialists: 1.0 (2,073.0 to 1)
Guidance Counselors: 1.7 (1,219.4 to 1)
Current Spending: ($ per student per year):
    Total: $5,802; Instruction: $3,773; Support Services: $1,827

Enrollment, Drop-out Rates and Diploma Recipients by Race/Ethnicity

Category	Total	White	Black	Asian	AIAN	Hisp.
Enrollment (%)	100.0	74.5	1.5	2.5	0.7	14.3
Drop-out Rate (%)	n/a	n/a	n/a	n/a	n/a	n/a
H.S. Diplomas (#)	n/a	n/a	n/a	n/a	n/a	n/a

Panama Buena Vista Union Elementary
4200 Ashe Rd • Bakersfield, CA 93313-2029
(661) 831-8331 • http://www.pbvusd.k12.ca.us/
Grade Span: KG-08; **Agency Type:** 1
Schools: 20
    16 Primary; 4 Middle; 0 High; 0 Other Level
    20 Regular; 0 Special Education; 0 Vocational; 0 Alternative
    0 Magnet; 0 Charter; 8 Title I Eligible; 0 School-wide Title I
Students: 13,963   (51.0% male; 48.9% female)
    Individual Education Program: 1,168 (8.4%);
    English Language Learner: 920 (6.6%); Migrant: 132 (0.9%)
    Eligible for Free Lunch Program: 4,340 (31.1%)
    Eligible for Reduced-Price Lunch Program: 1,678 (12.0%)
Teachers: 687.3 (20.3 to 1)
Librarians/Media Specialists: 1.0 (13,963.0 to 1)
Guidance Counselors: 4.0 (3,490.8 to 1)
Current Spending: ($ per student per year):
    Total: $7,166; Instruction: $4,538; Support Services: $2,366

Enrollment, Drop-out Rates and Diploma Recipients by Race/Ethnicity

Category	Total	White	Black	Asian	AIAN	Hisp.
Enrollment (%)	100.0	46.9	11.1	7.2	0.7	33.9
Drop-out Rate (%)	n/a	n/a	n/a	n/a	n/a	n/a
H.S. Diplomas (#)	n/a	n/a	n/a	n/a	n/a	n/a

Richland Union Elementary SD
331 Shafter Ave • Shafter, CA 93263-1999
(661) 746-8600
Grade Span: KG-08; **Agency Type:** 1
Schools: 3
    2 Primary; 1 Middle; 0 High; 0 Other Level
    3 Regular; 0 Special Education; 0 Vocational; 0 Alternative
    0 Magnet; 0 Charter; 3 Title I Eligible; 3 School-wide Title I
Students: 2,978   (52.2% male; 47.7% female)
    Individual Education Program: 304 (10.2%);
    English Language Learner: 1,318 (44.3%); Migrant: 1,347 (45.2%)
    Eligible for Free Lunch Program: 2,295 (77.1%)
    Eligible for Reduced-Price Lunch Program: 351 (11.8%)
Teachers: 146.4 (20.3 to 1)
Librarians/Media Specialists: 1.0 (2,978.0 to 1)
Guidance Counselors: 0.5 (5,956.0 to 1)
Current Spending: ($ per student per year):
    Total: $6,963; Instruction: $4,315; Support Services: $2,270

Enrollment, Drop-out Rates and Diploma Recipients by Race/Ethnicity

Category	Total	White	Black	Asian	AIAN	Hisp.
Enrollment (%)	100.0	9.7	0.6	0.7	0.1	88.2
Drop-out Rate (%)	n/a	n/a	n/a	n/a	n/a	n/a
H.S. Diplomas (#)	n/a	n/a	n/a	n/a	n/a	n/a

Rosedale Union Elementary
2553 Old Farm Rd • Bakersfield, CA 93312-3531
(661) 588-6000 • http://www.rosedale.k12.ca.us/schools.htm
Grade Span: KG-08; **Agency Type:** 1
Schools: 8
    6 Primary; 2 Middle; 0 High; 0 Other Level
    8 Regular; 0 Special Education; 0 Vocational; 0 Alternative
    0 Magnet; 0 Charter; 3 Title I Eligible; 0 School-wide Title I
Students: 4,232   (51.2% male; 48.7% female)
    Individual Education Program: 384 (9.1%);
    English Language Learner: 89 (2.1%); Migrant: 15 (0.4%)
    Eligible for Free Lunch Program: 426 (10.1%)
    Eligible for Reduced-Price Lunch Program: 257 (6.1%)
Teachers: 185.5 (22.8 to 1)
Librarians/Media Specialists: 1.0 (4,232.0 to 1)
Guidance Counselors: 2.0 (2,116.0 to 1)
Current Spending: ($ per student per year):
    Total: $5,965; Instruction: $3,916; Support Services: $1,908

Enrollment, Drop-out Rates and Diploma Recipients by Race/Ethnicity

Category	Total	White	Black	Asian	AIAN	Hisp.
Enrollment (%)	100.0	75.7	2.7	3.3	0.2	17.1
Drop-out Rate (%)	n/a	n/a	n/a	n/a	n/a	n/a
H.S. Diplomas (#)	n/a	n/a	n/a	n/a	n/a	n/a

Sierra Sands Unified
113 Felspar • Ridgecrest, CA 93555-3520
(760) 375-3363 • http://www.ssusd.org/
Grade Span: KG-12; **Agency Type:** 1
Schools: 11
  7 Primary; 2 Middle; 2 High; 0 Other Level
  10 Regular; 0 Special Education; 0 Vocational; 1 Alternative
  0 Magnet; 0 Charter; 4 Title I Eligible; 3 School-wide Title I
Students: 5,602 (52.5% male; 47.4% female)
  Individual Education Program: 574 (10.2%);
  English Language Learner: 430 (7.7%); Migrant: 0 (0.0%)
  Eligible for Free Lunch Program: 1,834 (32.7%)
  Eligible for Reduced-Price Lunch Program: 451 (8.1%)
Teachers: 267.2 (21.0 to 1)
Librarians/Media Specialists: 0.8 (7,002.5 to 1)
Guidance Counselors: 7.6 (737.1 to 1)
Current Spending: ($ per student per year):
  Total: $7,230; Instruction: $4,243; Support Services: $2,727

Enrollment, Drop-out Rates and Diploma Recipients by Race/Ethnicity

Category	Total	White	Black	Asian	AIAN	Hisp.
Enrollment (%)	100.0	69.8	5.6	4.5	1.5	14.9
Drop-out Rate (%)	n/a	n/a	n/a	n/a	n/a	n/a
H.S. Diplomas (#)	361	292	14	15	5	33

Southern Kern Unified
3082 Glendower St • Rosamond, CA 93560-0640
Mailing Address: PO Drawer Cc • Rosamond, CA 93560-0640
(661) 256-5000 • http://www.skusd.k12.ca.us/
Grade Span: KG-12; **Agency Type:** 1
Schools: 6
  2 Primary; 1 Middle; 2 High; 1 Other Level
  4 Regular; 0 Special Education; 0 Vocational; 2 Alternative
  0 Magnet; 0 Charter; 2 Title I Eligible; 0 School-wide Title I
Students: 3,267 (50.6% male; 49.3% female)
  Individual Education Program: 295 (9.0%);
  English Language Learner: 258 (7.9%); Migrant: 221 (6.8%)
  Eligible for Free Lunch Program: 1,325 (40.6%)
  Eligible for Reduced-Price Lunch Program: 328 (10.0%)
Teachers: 138.7 (23.6 to 1)
Librarians/Media Specialists: 0.0 (n/a to 1)
Guidance Counselors: 0.0 (n/a to 1)
Current Spending: ($ per student per year):
  Total: $6,152; Instruction: $4,032; Support Services: $1,884

Enrollment, Drop-out Rates and Diploma Recipients by Race/Ethnicity

Category	Total	White	Black	Asian	AIAN	Hisp.
Enrollment (%)	100.0	47.4	9.6	2.5	1.5	38.8
Drop-out Rate (%)	n/a	n/a	n/a	n/a	n/a	n/a
H.S. Diplomas (#)	151	88	5	9	0	49

Standard Elementary
1200 N Chester Ave • Bakersfield, CA 93308-3521
(661) 392-2110
Grade Span: KG-08; **Agency Type:** 1
Schools: 4
  3 Primary; 1 Middle; 0 High; 0 Other Level
  4 Regular; 0 Special Education; 0 Vocational; 0 Alternative
  0 Magnet; 0 Charter; 4 Title I Eligible; 4 School-wide Title I
Students: 2,683 (51.0% male; 48.9% female)
  Individual Education Program: 271 (10.1%);
  English Language Learner: 40 (1.5%); Migrant: 0 (0.0%)
  Eligible for Free Lunch Program: 1,314 (49.0%)
  Eligible for Reduced-Price Lunch Program: 540 (20.1%)
Teachers: 125.7 (21.3 to 1)
Librarians/Media Specialists: 0.0 (n/a to 1)
Guidance Counselors: 2.0 (1,341.5 to 1)
Current Spending: ($ per student per year):
  Total: $7,188; Instruction: $4,502; Support Services: $2,253

Enrollment, Drop-out Rates and Diploma Recipients by Race/Ethnicity

Category	Total	White	Black	Asian	AIAN	Hisp.
Enrollment (%)	100.0	82.6	0.8	0.7	1.3	13.2
Drop-out Rate (%)	n/a	n/a	n/a	n/a	n/a	n/a
H.S. Diplomas (#)	n/a	n/a	n/a	n/a	n/a	n/a

Taft City Elementary
820 N Sixth St • Taft, CA 93268-2306
(661) 763-1521 • http://www.taftcity.k12.ca.us/
Grade Span: KG-08; **Agency Type:** 1
Schools: 7
  4 Primary; 3 Middle; 0 High; 0 Other Level

  6 Regular; 0 Special Education; 0 Vocational; 1 Alternative
  0 Magnet; 0 Charter; 6 Title I Eligible; 5 School-wide Title I
Students: 2,182 (51.2% male; 48.7% female)
  Individual Education Program: 262 (12.0%);
  English Language Learner: 329 (15.1%); Migrant: 449 (20.6%)
  Eligible for Free Lunch Program: 1,253 (57.4%)
  Eligible for Reduced-Price Lunch Program: 223 (10.2%)
Teachers: 109.6 (19.9 to 1)
Librarians/Media Specialists: 0.0 (n/a to 1)
Guidance Counselors: 1.0 (2,182.0 to 1)
Current Spending: ($ per student per year):
  Total: $7,094; Instruction: $4,352; Support Services: $2,354

Enrollment, Drop-out Rates and Diploma Recipients by Race/Ethnicity

Category	Total	White	Black	Asian	AIAN	Hisp.
Enrollment (%)	100.0	68.5	0.6	2.0	0.0	28.9
Drop-out Rate (%)	n/a	n/a	n/a	n/a	n/a	n/a
H.S. Diplomas (#)	n/a	n/a	n/a	n/a	n/a	n/a

Tehachapi Unified
400 S Snyder • Tehachapi, CA 93561-1519
(661) 822-2100 • http://www.teh.k12.ca.us/
Grade Span: KG-12; **Agency Type:** 1
Schools: 6
  3 Primary; 1 Middle; 2 High; 0 Other Level
  5 Regular; 0 Special Education; 0 Vocational; 1 Alternative
  0 Magnet; 0 Charter; 2 Title I Eligible; 0 School-wide Title I
Students: 4,832 (52.0% male; 47.9% female)
  Individual Education Program: 479 (9.9%);
  English Language Learner: 365 (7.6%); Migrant: 190 (3.9%)
  Eligible for Free Lunch Program: 1,228 (25.4%)
  Eligible for Reduced-Price Lunch Program: 374 (7.7%)
Teachers: 194.0 (24.9 to 1)
Librarians/Media Specialists: 1.0 (4,832.0 to 1)
Guidance Counselors: 2.0 (2,416.0 to 1)
Current Spending: ($ per student per year):
  Total: $6,426; Instruction: $4,121; Support Services: $2,108

Enrollment, Drop-out Rates and Diploma Recipients by Race/Ethnicity

Category	Total	White	Black	Asian	AIAN	Hisp.
Enrollment (%)	100.0	72.6	2.6	1.4	1.4	20.9
Drop-out Rate (%)	n/a	n/a	n/a	n/a	n/a	n/a
H.S. Diplomas (#)	304	247	2	3	4	45

Wasco Union Elementary
639 Broadway • Wasco, CA 93280-1899
(661) 758-7100 • http://www.wasco.k12.ca.us/
Grade Span: KG-08; **Agency Type:** 1
Schools: 4
  2 Primary; 2 Middle; 0 High; 0 Other Level
  4 Regular; 0 Special Education; 0 Vocational; 0 Alternative
  0 Magnet; 0 Charter; 4 Title I Eligible; 4 School-wide Title I
Students: 2,990 (52.1% male; 47.8% female)
  Individual Education Program: 204 (6.8%);
  English Language Learner: 1,241 (41.5%); Migrant: 1,657 (55.4%)
  Eligible for Free Lunch Program: 2,410 (80.6%)
  Eligible for Reduced-Price Lunch Program: 293 (9.8%)
Teachers: 144.0 (20.8 to 1)
Librarians/Media Specialists: 0.0 (n/a to 1)
Guidance Counselors: 0.0 (n/a to 1)
Current Spending: ($ per student per year):
  Total: $7,109; Instruction: $4,442; Support Services: $2,198

Enrollment, Drop-out Rates and Diploma Recipients by Race/Ethnicity

Category	Total	White	Black	Asian	AIAN	Hisp.
Enrollment (%)	100.0	8.9	4.7	0.6	0.1	85.1
Drop-out Rate (%)	n/a	n/a	n/a	n/a	n/a	n/a
H.S. Diplomas (#)	n/a	n/a	n/a	n/a	n/a	n/a

Kings County

Central Union Elementary
15783 18th Ave • Lemoore, CA 93245-9742
(559) 924-3405 • http://www.kings.k12.ca.us/central/
Grade Span: KG-08; **Agency Type:** 1
Schools: 4
  4 Primary; 0 Middle; 0 High; 0 Other Level
  4 Regular; 0 Special Education; 0 Vocational; 0 Alternative
  0 Magnet; 0 Charter; 2 Title I Eligible; 2 School-wide Title I
Students: 2,036 (51.5% male; 48.4% female)
  Individual Education Program: 175 (8.6%);
  English Language Learner: 169 (8.3%); Migrant: 184 (9.0%)
  Eligible for Free Lunch Program: 572 (28.1%)
  Eligible for Reduced-Price Lunch Program: 421 (20.7%)
Teachers: 115.0 (17.7 to 1)
Librarians/Media Specialists: 0.0 (n/a to 1)
Guidance Counselors: 1.0 (2,036.0 to 1)
Current Spending: ($ per student per year):
  Total: $8,902; Instruction: $5,816; Support Services: $2,801

Enrollment, Drop-out Rates and Diploma Recipients by Race/Ethnicity

Category	Total	White	Black	Asian	AIAN	Hisp.
Enrollment (%)	100.0	43.2	11.7	8.7	7.3	29.1
Drop-out Rate (%)	n/a	n/a	n/a	n/a	n/a	n/a
H.S. Diplomas (#)	n/a	n/a	n/a	n/a	n/a	n/a

Corcoran Joint Unified
1520 Patterson Ave • Corcoran, CA 93212-1722
(559) 992-3104 • http://www.kings.k12.ca.us/corcoran/
Grade Span: KG-12; **Agency Type:** 1
Schools: 7
  3 Primary; 1 Middle; 3 High; 0 Other Level
  5 Regular; 0 Special Education; 0 Vocational; 2 Alternative
  0 Magnet; 0 Charter; 4 Title I Eligible; 4 School-wide Title I
Students: 3,190   (50.5% male; 49.4% female)
  Individual Education Program: 216 (6.8%);
  English Language Learner: 916 (28.7%); Migrant: 1,188 (37.2%)
  Eligible for Free Lunch Program: 2,057 (64.5%)
  Eligible for Reduced-Price Lunch Program: 403 (12.6%)
Teachers: 155.4 (20.5 to 1)
Librarians/Media Specialists: 0.0 (n/a to 1)
Guidance Counselors: 3.0 (1,063.3 to 1)
Current Spending: ($ per student per year):
  Total: $6,903; Instruction: $4,532; Support Services: $2,047

Enrollment, Drop-out Rates and Diploma Recipients by Race/Ethnicity

Category	Total	White	Black	Asian	AIAN	Hisp.
Enrollment (%)	100.0	13.1	3.9	1.0	0.1	81.9
Drop-out Rate (%)	n/a	n/a	n/a	n/a	n/a	n/a
H.S. Diplomas (#)	121	18	7	0	0	96

Hanford Elementary
714 N White St • Hanford, CA 93232
Mailing Address: PO Box G-1067 • Hanford, CA 93232
(559) 585-2265 • http://www.hesd.k12.ca.us/
Grade Span: KG-08; **Agency Type:** 1
Schools: 11
  9 Primary; 2 Middle; 0 High; 0 Other Level
  10 Regular; 0 Special Education; 0 Vocational; 1 Alternative
  0 Magnet; 0 Charter; 11 Title I Eligible; 7 School-wide Title I
Students: 5,381   (51.3% male; 48.6% female)
  Individual Education Program: 281 (5.2%);
  English Language Learner: 1,145 (21.3%); Migrant: 992 (18.4%)
  Eligible for Free Lunch Program: 3,206 (59.6%)
  Eligible for Reduced-Price Lunch Program: 659 (12.2%)
Teachers: 258.5 (20.8 to 1)
Librarians/Media Specialists: 0.0 (n/a to 1)
Guidance Counselors: 0.0 (n/a to 1)
Current Spending: ($ per student per year):
  Total: $6,979; Instruction: $3,731; Support Services: $2,948

Enrollment, Drop-out Rates and Diploma Recipients by Race/Ethnicity

Category	Total	White	Black	Asian	AIAN	Hisp.
Enrollment (%)	100.0	29.6	7.7	2.5	0.5	59.7
Drop-out Rate (%)	n/a	n/a	n/a	n/a	n/a	n/a
H.S. Diplomas (#)	n/a	n/a	n/a	n/a	n/a	n/a

Hanford Joint Union High
120 E Grangeville Rd • Hanford, CA 93230-3067
(559) 582-4401 • http://www.kings.k12.ca.us/huhsd/
Grade Span: 09-12; **Agency Type:** 1
Schools: 5
  0 Primary; 0 Middle; 5 High; 0 Other Level
  2 Regular; 0 Special Education; 0 Vocational; 3 Alternative
  0 Magnet; 0 Charter; 1 Title I Eligible; 0 School-wide Title I
Students: 3,720   (51.4% male; 48.5% female)
  Individual Education Program: 283 (7.6%);
  English Language Learner: 254 (6.8%); Migrant: 359 (9.7%)
  Eligible for Free Lunch Program: 895 (24.1%)
  Eligible for Reduced-Price Lunch Program: 98 (2.6%)
Teachers: 154.6 (24.1 to 1)
Librarians/Media Specialists: 2.0 (1,860.0 to 1)
Guidance Counselors: 9.0 (413.3 to 1)
Current Spending: ($ per student per year):
  Total: $6,539; Instruction: $3,736; Support Services: $2,638

Enrollment, Drop-out Rates and Diploma Recipients by Race/Ethnicity

Category	Total	White	Black	Asian	AIAN	Hisp.
Enrollment (%)	100.0	41.2	7.4	3.9	0.7	45.4
Drop-out Rate (%)	n/a	n/a	n/a	n/a	n/a	n/a
H.S. Diplomas (#)	533	280	31	23	2	197

Lemoore Union Elementary
100 Vine St • Lemoore, CA 93245-3418
(559) 924-6800 • http://www.luhsd.k12.ca.us/
Grade Span: KG-08; **Agency Type:** 1
Schools: 6
  4 Primary; 2 Middle; 0 High; 0 Other Level

  6 Regular; 0 Special Education; 0 Vocational; 0 Alternative
  0 Magnet; 1 Charter; 5 Title I Eligible; 4 School-wide Title I
Students: 3,253   (52.0% male; 47.9% female)
  Individual Education Program: 266 (8.2%);
  English Language Learner: 633 (19.5%); Migrant: 611 (18.8%)
  Eligible for Free Lunch Program: 1,518 (46.7%)
  Eligible for Reduced-Price Lunch Program: 430 (13.2%)
Teachers: 162.6 (20.0 to 1)
Librarians/Media Specialists: 0.0 (n/a to 1)
Guidance Counselors: 2.0 (1,626.5 to 1)
Current Spending: ($ per student per year):
  Total: $6,113; Instruction: $3,633; Support Services: $2,195

Enrollment, Drop-out Rates and Diploma Recipients by Race/Ethnicity

Category	Total	White	Black	Asian	AIAN	Hisp.
Enrollment (%)	100.0	33.0	8.8	8.9	2.1	47.1
Drop-out Rate (%)	n/a	n/a	n/a	n/a	n/a	n/a
H.S. Diplomas (#)	n/a	n/a	n/a	n/a	n/a	n/a

Lemoore Union High
5 Powell Ave • Lemoore, CA 93245-3601
(559) 924-6610 • http://tigger.luhsd.k12.ca.us/
Grade Span: 09-12; **Agency Type:** 1
Schools: 4
  0 Primary; 0 Middle; 4 High; 0 Other Level
  1 Regular; 0 Special Education; 0 Vocational; 3 Alternative
  0 Magnet; 0 Charter; 3 Title I Eligible; 0 School-wide Title I
Students: 2,098   (50.2% male; 49.7% female)
  Individual Education Program: 197 (9.4%);
  English Language Learner: 95 (4.5%); Migrant: 291 (13.9%)
  Eligible for Free Lunch Program: 420 (20.0%)
  Eligible for Reduced-Price Lunch Program: 82 (3.9%)
Teachers: 98.8 (21.2 to 1)
Librarians/Media Specialists: 0.8 (2,622.5 to 1)
Guidance Counselors: 4.8 (437.1 to 1)
Current Spending: ($ per student per year):
  Total: $7,565; Instruction: $3,762; Support Services: $3,555

Enrollment, Drop-out Rates and Diploma Recipients by Race/Ethnicity

Category	Total	White	Black	Asian	AIAN	Hisp.
Enrollment (%)	100.0	43.0	8.4	9.5	2.6	35.7
Drop-out Rate (%)	n/a	n/a	n/a	n/a	n/a	n/a
H.S. Diplomas (#)	381	204	32	46	4	94

Reef-Sunset Unified
205 N Park Ave • Avenal, CA 93204-1425
(559) 386-9083 • http://www.kings.k12.ca.us/rsusd/
Grade Span: KG-12; **Agency Type:** 1
Schools: 9
  4 Primary; 1 Middle; 4 High; 0 Other Level
  5 Regular; 0 Special Education; 0 Vocational; 4 Alternative
  0 Magnet; 0 Charter; 9 Title I Eligible; 6 School-wide Title I
Students: 2,464   (52.3% male; 47.6% female)
  Individual Education Program: 295 (12.0%);
  English Language Learner: 1,665 (67.6%); Migrant: 1,268 (51.5%)
  Eligible for Free Lunch Program: 2,426 (98.5%)
  Eligible for Reduced-Price Lunch Program: 0 (0.0%)
Teachers: 123.0 (20.0 to 1)
Librarians/Media Specialists: 0.0 (n/a to 1)
Guidance Counselors: 2.0 (1,232.0 to 1)
Current Spending: ($ per student per year):
  Total: $7,577; Instruction: $4,276; Support Services: $2,839

Enrollment, Drop-out Rates and Diploma Recipients by Race/Ethnicity

Category	Total	White	Black	Asian	AIAN	Hisp.
Enrollment (%)	100.0	4.8	1.1	0.2	0.0	93.9
Drop-out Rate (%)	n/a	n/a	n/a	n/a	n/a	n/a
H.S. Diplomas (#)	101	6	2	0	0	93

Lake County

Kelseyville Unified
4325 Main St • Kelseyville, CA 95451-8953
(707) 279-1511 • http://www.kusd.lake.k12.ca.us/
Grade Span: KG-12; **Agency Type:** 1
Schools: 8
  2 Primary; 2 Middle; 4 High; 0 Other Level
  6 Regular; 0 Special Education; 0 Vocational; 2 Alternative
  0 Magnet; 0 Charter; 4 Title I Eligible; 1 School-wide Title I
Students: 1,872   (52.4% male; 47.5% female)
  Individual Education Program: 205 (11.0%);
  English Language Learner: 248 (13.2%); Migrant: 326 (17.4%)
  Eligible for Free Lunch Program: 884 (47.2%)
  Eligible for Reduced-Price Lunch Program: 165 (8.8%)
Teachers: 98.9 (18.9 to 1)
Librarians/Media Specialists: 0.0 (n/a to 1)
Guidance Counselors: 3.0 (624.0 to 1)
Current Spending: ($ per student per year):
  Total: $7,372; Instruction: $4,366; Support Services: $2,687

Enrollment, Drop-out Rates and Diploma Recipients by Race/Ethnicity

Category	Total	White	Black	Asian	AIAN	Hisp.
Enrollment (%)	100.0	67.0	1.5	1.7	2.9	26.4
Drop-out Rate (%)	n/a	n/a	n/a	n/a	n/a	n/a
H.S. Diplomas (#)	157	125	0	1	3	28

Konocti Unified
9430 Lake St • Lower Lake, CA 95457-5000
Mailing Address: PO Box 5000 • Lower Lake, CA 95457-5000
(707) 994-6475 • http://www.konoctiusd.lake.k12.ca.us/kusd/kusd1.html
Grade Span: KG-12; Agency Type: 1
Schools: 9
   5 Primary; 0 Middle; 3 High; 1 Other Level
   6 Regular; 0 Special Education; 0 Vocational; 3 Alternative
   0 Magnet; 0 Charter; 8 Title I Eligible; 8 School-wide Title I
Students: 3,414 (49.8% male; 50.1% female)
   Individual Education Program: 423 (12.4%);
   English Language Learner: 309 (9.1%); Migrant: 200 (5.9%)
   Eligible for Free Lunch Program: 2,434 (71.3%)
   Eligible for Reduced-Price Lunch Program: 357 (10.5%)
Teachers: 155.0 (22.0 to 1)
Librarians/Media Specialists: 0.0 (n/a to 1)
Guidance Counselors: 5.0 (682.8 to 1)
Current Spending: ($ per student per year):
   Total: $7,586; Instruction: $4,504; Support Services: $2,700
Enrollment, Drop-out Rates and Diploma Recipients by Race/Ethnicity

Category	Total	White	Black	Asian	AIAN	Hisp.
Enrollment (%)	100.0	64.8	6.2	1.6	5.4	17.0
Drop-out Rate (%)	n/a	n/a	n/a	n/a	n/a	n/a
H.S. Diplomas (#)	145	113	8	1	6	17

Lakeport Unified
100 Lange St • Lakeport, CA 95453-3297
(707) 262-3000 • http://www.lakeport.k12.ca.us/
Grade Span: KG-12; Agency Type: 1
Schools: 5
   1 Primary; 1 Middle; 2 High; 1 Other Level
   3 Regular; 0 Special Education; 0 Vocational; 2 Alternative
   0 Magnet; 0 Charter; 2 Title I Eligible; 2 School-wide Title I
Students: 1,792 (50.8% male; 49.1% female)
   Individual Education Program: 214 (11.9%);
   English Language Learner: 129 (7.2%); Migrant: 195 (10.9%)
   Eligible for Free Lunch Program: 628 (35.0%)
   Eligible for Reduced-Price Lunch Program: 191 (10.7%)
Teachers: 91.6 (19.6 to 1)
Librarians/Media Specialists: 0.0 (n/a to 1)
Guidance Counselors: 1.7 (1,054.1 to 1)
Current Spending: ($ per student per year):
   Total: $6,756; Instruction: $4,302; Support Services: $2,201
Enrollment, Drop-out Rates and Diploma Recipients by Race/Ethnicity

Category	Total	White	Black	Asian	AIAN	Hisp.
Enrollment (%)	100.0	72.3	2.1	1.4	5.1	18.9
Drop-out Rate (%)	n/a	n/a	n/a	n/a	n/a	n/a
H.S. Diplomas (#)	134	112	4	2	3	13

Middletown Unified
20932 Big Canyon Rd • Middletown, CA 95461-0338
Mailing Address: PO Box 338 • Middletown, CA 95461-0338
(707) 987-4100 • http://www.musd.lake.k12.ca.us/
Grade Span: KG-12; Agency Type: 1
Schools: 8
   4 Primary; 1 Middle; 3 High; 0 Other Level
   5 Regular; 0 Special Education; 0 Vocational; 3 Alternative
   0 Magnet; 0 Charter; 3 Title I Eligible; 0 School-wide Title I
Students: 1,818 (52.1% male; 47.8% female)
   Individual Education Program: 209 (11.5%);
   English Language Learner: 61 (3.4%); Migrant: 57 (3.1%)
   Eligible for Free Lunch Program: 286 (15.7%)
   Eligible for Reduced-Price Lunch Program: 157 (8.6%)
Teachers: 93.3 (19.5 to 1)
Librarians/Media Specialists: 0.0 (n/a to 1)
Guidance Counselors: 1.5 (1,212.0 to 1)
Current Spending: ($ per student per year):
   Total: $6,673; Instruction: $4,138; Support Services: $2,325
Enrollment, Drop-out Rates and Diploma Recipients by Race/Ethnicity

Category	Total	White	Black	Asian	AIAN	Hisp.
Enrollment (%)	100.0	79.8	0.4	1.7	1.5	11.8
Drop-out Rate (%)	n/a	n/a	n/a	n/a	n/a	n/a
H.S. Diplomas (#)	130	107	0	6	5	12

Lassen County

Westwood Unified
Fifth And Delwood Sts. • Westwood, CA 96137-1225
Mailing Address: PO Box 1225 • Westwood, CA 96137-1225
(530) 256-2311
Grade Span: KG-12; Agency Type: 1
Schools: 6
   2 Primary; 0 Middle; 3 High; 1 Other Level
   3 Regular; 0 Special Education; 0 Vocational; 3 Alternative
   0 Magnet; 1 Charter; 2 Title I Eligible; 1 School-wide Title I
Students: 1,547 (53.1% male; 46.8% female)
   Individual Education Program: 0 (0.0%);
   English Language Learner: 20 (1.3%); Migrant: 0 (0.0%)
   Eligible for Free Lunch Program: 429 (27.7%)
   Eligible for Reduced-Price Lunch Program: 93 (6.0%)
Teachers: 67.7 (22.9 to 1)
Librarians/Media Specialists: 0.0 (n/a to 1)
Guidance Counselors: 0.0 (n/a to 1)
Current Spending: ($ per student per year):
   Total: $22,131; Instruction: $19,258; Support Services: $2,654
Enrollment, Drop-out Rates and Diploma Recipients by Race/Ethnicity

Category	Total	White	Black	Asian	AIAN	Hisp.
Enrollment (%)	100.0	38.6	15.6	3.5	2.2	29.1
Drop-out Rate (%)	n/a	n/a	n/a	n/a	n/a	n/a
H.S. Diplomas (#)	45	39	0	0	1	2

Los Angeles County

ABC Unified
16700 Norwalk Blvd • Cerritos, CA 90703-1838
(562) 926-5566 • http://www.abcusd.k12.ca.us/
Grade Span: KG-12; Agency Type: 1
Schools: 30
   19 Primary; 5 Middle; 6 High; 0 Other Level
   28 Regular; 0 Special Education; 0 Vocational; 2 Alternative
   1 Magnet; 0 Charter; 13 Title I Eligible; 9 School-wide Title I
Students: 22,226 (52.1% male; 47.8% female)
   Individual Education Program: 2,194 (9.9%);
   English Language Learner: 4,451 (20.0%); Migrant: 1,526 (6.9%)
   Eligible for Free Lunch Program: 6,213 (28.0%)
   Eligible for Reduced-Price Lunch Program: 1,596 (7.2%)
Teachers: 988.0 (22.5 to 1)
Librarians/Media Specialists: 0.0 (n/a to 1)
Guidance Counselors: 19.9 (1,116.9 to 1)
Current Spending: ($ per student per year):
   Total: $7,035; Instruction: $4,508; Support Services: $2,245
Enrollment, Drop-out Rates and Diploma Recipients by Race/Ethnicity

Category	Total	White	Black	Asian	AIAN	Hisp.
Enrollment (%)	100.0	10.8	9.7	40.1	0.3	38.4
Drop-out Rate (%)	n/a	n/a	n/a	n/a	n/a	n/a
H.S. Diplomas (#)	1,636	250	174	768	4	440

Acton-Agua Dulce Unified
32248 N Crown Valley Rd • Acton, CA 93510-0068
Mailing Address: PO Box 68 • Acton, CA 93510-0068
(661) 269-5999 • http://aadusd.k12.ca.us/
Grade Span: KG-12; Agency Type: 1
Schools: 5
   3 Primary; 1 Middle; 1 High; 0 Other Level
   5 Regular; 0 Special Education; 0 Vocational; 0 Alternative
   0 Magnet; 0 Charter; 2 Title I Eligible; 0 School-wide Title I
Students: 1,994 (49.5% male; 50.4% female)
   Individual Education Program: 296 (14.8%);
   English Language Learner: 123 (6.2%); Migrant: 9 (0.5%)
   Eligible for Free Lunch Program: 0 (0.0%)
   Eligible for Reduced-Price Lunch Program: 0 (0.0%)
Teachers: 88.7 (22.5 to 1)
Librarians/Media Specialists: 0.0 (n/a to 1)
Guidance Counselors: 2.0 (997.0 to 1)
Current Spending: ($ per student per year):
   Total: $6,230; Instruction: $3,779; Support Services: $2,450
Enrollment, Drop-out Rates and Diploma Recipients by Race/Ethnicity

Category	Total	White	Black	Asian	AIAN	Hisp.
Enrollment (%)	100.0	77.7	1.5	1.3	0.8	15.9
Drop-out Rate (%)	n/a	n/a	n/a	n/a	n/a	n/a
H.S. Diplomas (#)	98	82	1	4	0	11

Alhambra City Elementary
15 W Alhambra Rd • Alhambra, CA 91802-2110
Mailing Address: PO Box 110 • Alhambra, CA 91802-2110
(626) 308-2200 • http://www.alhambra.k12.ca.us/
Grade Span: KG-08; Agency Type: 2
Schools: 13
   13 Primary; 0 Middle; 0 High; 0 Other Level

13 Regular; 0 Special Education; 0 Vocational; 0 Alternative
0 Magnet; 0 Charter; 13 Title I Eligible; 13 School-wide Title I
Students: 11,163   (50.5% male; 49.4% female)
  Individual Education Program: 1,044 (9.4%);
  English Language Learner: 4,161 (37.3%); Migrant: 188 (1.7%)
  Eligible for Free Lunch Program: 5,744 (51.5%)
  Eligible for Reduced-Price Lunch Program: 1,664 (14.9%)
Teachers: 503.3 (22.2 to 1)
Librarians/Media Specialists: 0.0 (n/a to 1)
Guidance Counselors: 0.9 (12,403.3 to 1)
Current Spending: ($ per student per year):
  Total: $7,431; Instruction: $4,342; Support Services: $2,801
Enrollment, Drop-out Rates and Diploma Recipients by Race/Ethnicity

Category	Total	White	Black	Asian	AIAN	Hisp.
Enrollment (%)	100.0	7.5	1.1	48.7	0.2	42.5
Drop-out Rate (%)	n/a	n/a	n/a	n/a	n/a	n/a
H.S. Diplomas (#)	n/a	n/a	n/a	n/a	n/a	n/a

Alhambra City High
15 W Alhambra Rd • Alhambra, CA 91802-2110
Mailing Address: PO Box 110 • Alhambra, CA 91802-2110
(626) 308-2200 • http://www.alhambra.k12.ca.us/
Grade Span: 07-12; **Agency Type:** 2
Schools: 6
  0 Primary; 0 Middle; 6 High; 0 Other Level
  3 Regular; 0 Special Education; 0 Vocational; 3 Alternative
  0 Magnet; 0 Charter; 5 Title I Eligible; 4 School-wide Title I
Students: 8,552   (52.1% male; 47.8% female)
  Individual Education Program: 678 (7.9%);
  English Language Learner: 2,746 (32.1%); Migrant: 187 (2.2%)
  Eligible for Free Lunch Program: 4,469 (52.3%)
  Eligible for Reduced-Price Lunch Program: 1,008 (11.8%)
Teachers: 342.1 (25.0 to 1)
Librarians/Media Specialists: 3.0 (2,850.7 to 1)
Guidance Counselors: 16.4 (521.5 to 1)
Current Spending: ($ per student per year):
  Total: n/a; Instruction: n/a; Support Services: n/a
Enrollment, Drop-out Rates and Diploma Recipients by Race/Ethnicity

Category	Total	White	Black	Asian	AIAN	Hisp.
Enrollment (%)	100.0	6.2	0.7	55.1	0.1	38.0
Drop-out Rate (%)	n/a	n/a	n/a	n/a	n/a	n/a
H.S. Diplomas (#)	1,641	93	5	1,059	3	481

Antelope Valley Union High
44811 N Sierra Hwy • Lancaster, CA 93534-3226
(661) 948-7655 • http://www.avdistrict.org/navpage.html
Grade Span: KG-12; **Agency Type:** 1
Schools: 13
  0 Primary; 0 Middle; 12 High; 1 Other Level
  10 Regular; 0 Special Education; 0 Vocational; 3 Alternative
  0 Magnet; 2 Charter; 5 Title I Eligible; 2 School-wide Title I
Students: 22,148   (50.7% male; 49.2% female)
  Individual Education Program: 3,027 (13.7%);
  English Language Learner: 2,571 (11.6%); Migrant: 323 (1.5%)
  Eligible for Free Lunch Program: 6,198 (28.0%)
  Eligible for Reduced-Price Lunch Program: 1,386 (6.3%)
Teachers: 839.0 (26.4 to 1)
Librarians/Media Specialists: 1.5 (14,765.3 to 1)
Guidance Counselors: 41.5 (533.7 to 1)
Current Spending: ($ per student per year):
  Total: $6,408; Instruction: $4,005; Support Services: $2,210
Enrollment, Drop-out Rates and Diploma Recipients by Race/Ethnicity

Category	Total	White	Black	Asian	AIAN	Hisp.
Enrollment (%)	100.0	37.6	21.1	4.0	0.7	36.1
Drop-out Rate (%)	n/a	n/a	n/a	n/a	n/a	n/a
H.S. Diplomas (#)	2,992	1,511	482	154	24	804

Arcadia Unified
234 Campus Dr • Arcadia, CA 91007-6902
(626) 821-8300 • http://www.ausd.k12.ca.us/
Grade Span: KG-12; **Agency Type:** 1
Schools: 11
  6 Primary; 3 Middle; 1 High; 1 Other Level
  10 Regular; 0 Special Education; 0 Vocational; 1 Alternative
  0 Magnet; 0 Charter; 7 Title I Eligible; 0 School-wide Title I
Students: 9,992   (51.5% male; 48.4% female)
  Individual Education Program: 847 (8.5%);
  English Language Learner: 1,159 (11.6%); Migrant: 2 (<0.1%)
  Eligible for Free Lunch Program: 559 (5.6%)
  Eligible for Reduced-Price Lunch Program: 317 (3.2%)
Teachers: 437.4 (22.8 to 1)
Librarians/Media Specialists: 1.0 (9,992.0 to 1)
Guidance Counselors: 12.8 (780.6 to 1)
Current Spending: ($ per student per year):
  Total: $6,314; Instruction: $4,195; Support Services: $1,885

Enrollment, Drop-out Rates and Diploma Recipients by Race/Ethnicity

Category	Total	White	Black	Asian	AIAN	Hisp.
Enrollment (%)	100.0	24.5	1.2	63.4	0.2	10.7
Drop-out Rate (%)	n/a	n/a	n/a	n/a	n/a	n/a
H.S. Diplomas (#)	832	268	7	495	3	59

Azusa Unified
546 S Citrus Ave • Azusa, CA 91702-0500
Mailing Address: PO Box 500 • Azusa, CA 91702-0500
(626) 967-6211 • http://www.azusausd.k12.ca.us/
Grade Span: KG-12; **Agency Type:** 1
Schools: 18
  12 Primary; 3 Middle; 3 High; 0 Other Level
  17 Regular; 0 Special Education; 0 Vocational; 1 Alternative
  0 Magnet; 0 Charter; 12 Title I Eligible; 12 School-wide Title I
Students: 12,134   (51.3% male; 48.6% female)
  Individual Education Program: 1,246 (10.3%);
  English Language Learner: 4,646 (38.3%); Migrant: 105 (0.9%)
  Eligible for Free Lunch Program: 6,043 (49.8%)
  Eligible for Reduced-Price Lunch Program: 2,216 (18.3%)
Teachers: 558.1 (21.7 to 1)
Librarians/Media Specialists: 0.0 (n/a to 1)
Guidance Counselors: 10.5 (1,155.6 to 1)
Current Spending: ($ per student per year):
  Total: $7,366; Instruction: $4,575; Support Services: $2,470
Enrollment, Drop-out Rates and Diploma Recipients by Race/Ethnicity

Category	Total	White	Black	Asian	AIAN	Hisp.
Enrollment (%)	100.0	9.5	2.3	2.9	0.2	85.1
Drop-out Rate (%)	n/a	n/a	n/a	n/a	n/a	n/a
H.S. Diplomas (#)	529	76	16	28	0	409

Baldwin Park Unified
3699 N Holly Ave • Baldwin Park, CA 91706-5397
(626) 962-3311 • http://www.bpusd.net/templates/home.asp?pid=494
Grade Span: KG-12; **Agency Type:** 1
Schools: 22
  13 Primary; 4 Middle; 3 High; 2 Other Level
  20 Regular; 0 Special Education; 0 Vocational; 2 Alternative
  0 Magnet; 1 Charter; 17 Title I Eligible; 17 School-wide Title I
Students: 19,287   (51.1% male; 48.8% female)
  Individual Education Program: 1,562 (8.1%);
  English Language Learner: 6,403 (33.2%); Migrant: 528 (2.7%)
  Eligible for Free Lunch Program: 11,015 (57.1%)
  Eligible for Reduced-Price Lunch Program: 2,808 (14.6%)
Teachers: 779.3 (24.7 to 1)
Librarians/Media Specialists: 1.0 (19,287.0 to 1)
Guidance Counselors: 9.0 (2,143.0 to 1)
Current Spending: ($ per student per year):
  Total: $7,005; Instruction: $4,347; Support Services: $2,388
Enrollment, Drop-out Rates and Diploma Recipients by Race/Ethnicity

Category	Total	White	Black	Asian	AIAN	Hisp.
Enrollment (%)	100.0	6.0	2.0	5.7	0.3	85.2
Drop-out Rate (%)	n/a	n/a	n/a	n/a	n/a	n/a
H.S. Diplomas (#)	713	37	26	61	14	574

Bassett Unified
904 N Willow Ave • La Puente, CA 91746-1615
(626) 931-3000 • http://www.bassett.k12.ca.us/
Grade Span: KG-12; **Agency Type:** 1
Schools: 8
  5 Primary; 1 Middle; 2 High; 0 Other Level
  7 Regular; 0 Special Education; 0 Vocational; 1 Alternative
  0 Magnet; 0 Charter; 8 Title I Eligible; 7 School-wide Title I
Students: 6,039   (50.2% male; 49.7% female)
  Individual Education Program: 642 (10.6%);
  English Language Learner: 1,988 (32.9%); Migrant: 33 (0.5%)
  Eligible for Free Lunch Program: 3,976 (65.8%)
  Eligible for Reduced-Price Lunch Program: 904 (15.0%)
Teachers: 274.9 (22.0 to 1)
Librarians/Media Specialists: 0.0 (n/a to 1)
Guidance Counselors: 7.0 (862.7 to 1)
Current Spending: ($ per student per year):
  Total: $7,267; Instruction: $4,195; Support Services: $2,710
Enrollment, Drop-out Rates and Diploma Recipients by Race/Ethnicity

Category	Total	White	Black	Asian	AIAN	Hisp.
Enrollment (%)	100.0	2.1	1.9	2.9	0.3	92.4
Drop-out Rate (%)	n/a	n/a	n/a	n/a	n/a	n/a
H.S. Diplomas (#)	308	8	1	14	1	276

Bellflower Unified
16703 S Clark Ave • Bellflower, CA 90706-5203
(562) 866-9011 • http://www.citywd.com/bellflower/sch_1.htm
Grade Span: KG-12; **Agency Type:** 1
Schools: 15
  11 Primary; 0 Middle; 3 High; 1 Other Level

13 Regular; 0 Special Education; 0 Vocational; 2 Alternative
1 Magnet; 0 Charter; 9 Title I Eligible; 0 School-wide Title I
Students: 15,522 (51.7% male; 48.2% female)
Individual Education Program: 1,311 (8.4%);
English Language Learner: 2,657 (17.1%); Migrant: 0 (0.0%)
Eligible for Free Lunch Program: 6,075 (39.1%)
Eligible for Reduced-Price Lunch Program: 2,317 (14.9%)
Teachers: 689.7 (22.5 to 1)
Librarians/Media Specialists: 3.2 (4,850.6 to 1)
Guidance Counselors: 9.0 (1,724.7 to 1)
Current Spending: ($ per student per year):
Total: $6,871; Instruction: $4,436; Support Services: $2,129
Enrollment, Drop-out Rates and Diploma Recipients by Race/Ethnicity

Category	Total	White	Black	Asian	AIAN	Hisp.
Enrollment (%)	100.0	22.3	15.9	10.7	0.4	47.2
Drop-out Rate (%)	n/a	n/a	n/a	n/a	n/a	n/a
H.S. Diplomas (#)	780	234	156	109	3	278

Beverly Hills Unified

255 S Lasky Dr • Beverly Hills, CA 90212-3644
(310) 551-5100 • http://www.beverlyhills.k12.ca.us/
Grade Span: KG-12; **Agency Type:** 1
Schools: 6
4 Primary; 0 Middle; 2 High; 0 Other Level
5 Regular; 0 Special Education; 0 Vocational; 1 Alternative
0 Magnet; 0 Charter; 2 Title I Eligible; 0 School-wide Title I
Students: 5,130 (50.6% male; 49.3% female)
Individual Education Program: 610 (11.9%);
English Language Learner: 297 (5.8%); Migrant: 0 (0.0%)
Eligible for Free Lunch Program: 120 (2.3%)
Eligible for Reduced-Price Lunch Program: 90 (1.8%)
Teachers: 280.0 (18.3 to 1)
Librarians/Media Specialists: 3.0 (1,710.0 to 1)
Guidance Counselors: 9.0 (570.0 to 1)
Current Spending: ($ per student per year):
Total: $8,888; Instruction: $5,406; Support Services: $3,340
Enrollment, Drop-out Rates and Diploma Recipients by Race/Ethnicity

Category	Total	White	Black	Asian	AIAN	Hisp.
Enrollment (%)	100.0	76.3	4.3	13.9	0.0	3.8
Drop-out Rate (%)	n/a	n/a	n/a	n/a	n/a	n/a
H.S. Diplomas (#)	472	363	24	65	0	20

Bonita Unified

115 W Allen Ave • San Dimas, CA 91773-1437
(909) 971-8200 • http://www.bonita.k12.ca.us/
Grade Span: KG-12; **Agency Type:** 1
Schools: 14
8 Primary; 2 Middle; 3 High; 1 Other Level
12 Regular; 0 Special Education; 0 Vocational; 2 Alternative
0 Magnet; 0 Charter; 3 Title I Eligible; 0 School-wide Title I
Students: 10,203 (51.1% male; 48.8% female)
Individual Education Program: 1,321 (12.9%);
English Language Learner: 203 (2.0%); Migrant: 3 (<0.1%)
Eligible for Free Lunch Program: 1,687 (16.5%)
Eligible for Reduced-Price Lunch Program: 575 (5.6%)
Teachers: 443.9 (23.0 to 1)
Librarians/Media Specialists: 2.0 (5,101.5 to 1)
Guidance Counselors: 13.0 (784.8 to 1)
Current Spending: ($ per student per year):
Total: $7,083; Instruction: $4,717; Support Services: $2,185
Enrollment, Drop-out Rates and Diploma Recipients by Race/Ethnicity

Category	Total	White	Black	Asian	AIAN	Hisp.
Enrollment (%)	100.0	46.8	3.7	4.1	0.5	27.3
Drop-out Rate (%)	n/a	n/a	n/a	n/a	n/a	n/a
H.S. Diplomas (#)	761	434	50	62	7	202

Burbank Unified

1900 W Olive Ave • Burbank, CA 91506-2460
(818) 729-4400 • http://www.burbank.k12.ca.us/
Grade Span: KG-12; **Agency Type:** 1
Schools: 20
11 Primary; 3 Middle; 4 High; 2 Other Level
16 Regular; 1 Special Education; 0 Vocational; 3 Alternative
0 Magnet; 1 Charter; 5 Title I Eligible; 5 School-wide Title I
Students: 17,066 (51.2% male; 48.7% female)
Individual Education Program: 1,739 (10.2%);
English Language Learner: 2,909 (17.0%); Migrant: 0 (0.0%)
Eligible for Free Lunch Program: 3,822 (22.4%)
Eligible for Reduced-Price Lunch Program: 1,332 (7.8%)
Teachers: 778.5 (21.9 to 1)
Librarians/Media Specialists: 0.0 (n/a to 1)
Guidance Counselors: 14.8 (1,153.1 to 1)
Current Spending: ($ per student per year):
Total: $6,849; Instruction: $4,422; Support Services: $2,225

Enrollment, Drop-out Rates and Diploma Recipients by Race/Ethnicity

Category	Total	White	Black	Asian	AIAN	Hisp.
Enrollment (%)	100.0	49.8	3.0	9.1	0.4	36.8
Drop-out Rate (%)	n/a	n/a	n/a	n/a	n/a	n/a
H.S. Diplomas (#)	1,094	551	23	98	0	383

Castaic Union Elementary

28131 Livingston Ave • Valencia, CA 91355-3359
(661) 257-4500 • http://www.castaic.k12.ca.us/
Grade Span: KG-08; **Agency Type:** 1
Schools: 4
3 Primary; 1 Middle; 0 High; 0 Other Level
4 Regular; 0 Special Education; 0 Vocational; 0 Alternative
0 Magnet; 0 Charter; 1 Title I Eligible; 0 School-wide Title I
Students: 3,589 (52.2% male; 47.7% female)
Individual Education Program: 319 (8.9%);
English Language Learner: 247 (6.9%); Migrant: 0 (0.0%)
Eligible for Free Lunch Program: 339 (9.4%)
Eligible for Reduced-Price Lunch Program: 121 (3.4%)
Teachers: 166.8 (21.5 to 1)
Librarians/Media Specialists: 0.0 (n/a to 1)
Guidance Counselors: 2.9 (1,237.6 to 1)
Current Spending: ($ per student per year):
Total: $6,019; Instruction: $4,037; Support Services: $1,955
Enrollment, Drop-out Rates and Diploma Recipients by Race/Ethnicity

Category	Total	White	Black	Asian	AIAN	Hisp.
Enrollment (%)	100.0	62.9	3.0	8.1	0.1	22.4
Drop-out Rate (%)	n/a	n/a	n/a	n/a	n/a	n/a
H.S. Diplomas (#)	n/a	n/a	n/a	n/a	n/a	n/a

Centinela Valley Union High

14901 S Inglewood Ave • Lawndale, CA 90260-1251
(310) 263-3200 • http://www.centinela.k12.ca.us/
Grade Span: 09-12; **Agency Type:** 1
Schools: 4
0 Primary; 0 Middle; 4 High; 0 Other Level
3 Regular; 0 Special Education; 0 Vocational; 1 Alternative
0 Magnet; 0 Charter; 4 Title I Eligible; 1 School-wide Title I
Students: 7,565 (52.4% male; 47.5% female)
Individual Education Program: 851 (11.2%);
English Language Learner: 2,226 (29.4%); Migrant: 0 (0.0%)
Eligible for Free Lunch Program: 3,972 (52.5%)
Eligible for Reduced-Price Lunch Program: 735 (9.7%)
Teachers: 321.3 (23.5 to 1)
Librarians/Media Specialists: 0.0 (n/a to 1)
Guidance Counselors: 19.0 (398.2 to 1)
Current Spending: ($ per student per year):
Total: $7,274; Instruction: $3,995; Support Services: $2,884
Enrollment, Drop-out Rates and Diploma Recipients by Race/Ethnicity

Category	Total	White	Black	Asian	AIAN	Hisp.
Enrollment (%)	100.0	4.9	22.4	6.8	0.2	65.0
Drop-out Rate (%)	n/a	n/a	n/a	n/a	n/a	n/a
H.S. Diplomas (#)	1,107	53	194	117	3	722

Charter Oak Unified

20240 Cienega Ave • Covina, CA 91723-0009
Mailing Address: PO Box 9 • Covina, CA 91723-0009
(626) 966-8331 • http://www.cousd.k12.ca.us/
Grade Span: KG-12; **Agency Type:** 1
Schools: 10
5 Primary; 1 Middle; 2 High; 2 Other Level
7 Regular; 0 Special Education; 0 Vocational; 3 Alternative
0 Magnet; 0 Charter; 5 Title I Eligible; 0 School-wide Title I
Students: 7,110 (51.1% male; 48.8% female)
Individual Education Program: 686 (9.6%);
English Language Learner: 532 (7.5%); Migrant: 11 (0.2%)
Eligible for Free Lunch Program: 1,354 (19.0%)
Eligible for Reduced-Price Lunch Program: 496 (7.0%)
Teachers: 288.2 (24.7 to 1)
Librarians/Media Specialists: 1.0 (7,110.0 to 1)
Guidance Counselors: 4.9 (1,451.0 to 1)
Current Spending: ($ per student per year):
Total: $6,460; Instruction: $4,185; Support Services: $2,056
Enrollment, Drop-out Rates and Diploma Recipients by Race/Ethnicity

Category	Total	White	Black	Asian	AIAN	Hisp.
Enrollment (%)	100.0	40.0	4.2	8.0	0.2	45.4
Drop-out Rate (%)	n/a	n/a	n/a	n/a	n/a	n/a
H.S. Diplomas (#)	407	188	17	44	3	155

Claremont Unified

2080 N Mountain Ave • Claremont, CA 91711-2643
(909) 398-0600 • http://www.cusd.claremont.edu/
Grade Span: KG-12; **Agency Type:** 1
Schools: 12
8 Primary; 1 Middle; 3 High; 0 Other Level

9 Regular; 1 Special Education; 0 Vocational; 2 Alternative
0 Magnet; 0 Charter; 6 Title I Eligible; 0 School-wide Title I
Students: 6,846   (50.1% male; 49.8% female)
Individual Education Program: 787 (11.5%);
English Language Learner: 615 (9.0%); Migrant: 0 (0.0%)
Eligible for Free Lunch Program: 1,300 (19.0%)
Eligible for Reduced-Price Lunch Program: 531 (7.8%)
Teachers: 309.1 (22.1 to 1)
Librarians/Media Specialists: 1.0 (6,846.0 to 1)
Guidance Counselors: 7.0 (978.0 to 1)
Current Spending: ($ per student per year):
Total: $7,152; Instruction: $4,230; Support Services: $2,662
Enrollment, Drop-out Rates and Diploma Recipients by Race/Ethnicity

Category	Total	White	Black	Asian	AIAN	Hisp.
Enrollment (%)	100.0	48.7	8.4	12.4	0.5	26.5
Drop-out Rate (%)	n/a	n/a	n/a	n/a	n/a	n/a
H.S. Diplomas (#)	585	321	54	99	2	109

Compton Unified
604 S Tamarind Ave • Compton, CA 90220-3826
(310) 639-4321 • http://www.compton.k12.ca.us/
Grade Span: KG-12; **Agency Type:** 1
Schools: 40
24 Primary; 9 Middle; 6 High; 1 Other Level
36 Regular; 0 Special Education; 0 Vocational; 4 Alternative
0 Magnet; 0 Charter; 40 Title I Eligible; 34 School-wide Title I
Students: 32,486   (50.7% male; 49.2% female)
Individual Education Program: 1,686 (5.2%);
English Language Learner: 17,472 (53.8%); Migrant: 13 (<0.1%)
Eligible for Free Lunch Program: 28,403 (87.4%)
Eligible for Reduced-Price Lunch Program: 1,863 (5.7%)
Teachers: 1,373.8 (23.6 to 1)
Librarians/Media Specialists: 2.0 (16,243.0 to 1)
Guidance Counselors: 46.2 (703.2 to 1)
Current Spending: ($ per student per year):
Total: $6,968; Instruction: $4,462; Support Services: $2,134
Enrollment, Drop-out Rates and Diploma Recipients by Race/Ethnicity

Category	Total	White	Black	Asian	AIAN	Hisp.
Enrollment (%)	100.0	0.2	29.2	1.0	0.0	68.8
Drop-out Rate (%)	n/a	n/a	n/a	n/a	n/a	n/a
H.S. Diplomas (#)	902	2	398	8	3	491

Covina-Valley Unified
519 E Badillo St • Covina, CA 91723-0269
Mailing Address: PO Box 269 • Covina, CA 91723-0269
(626) 974-7000 • http://www.cvusd.k12.ca.us/
Grade Span: KG-12; **Agency Type:** 1
Schools: 20
12 Primary; 3 Middle; 4 High; 1 Other Level
18 Regular; 0 Special Education; 0 Vocational; 2 Alternative
0 Magnet; 0 Charter; 10 Title I Eligible; 10 School-wide Title I
Students: 15,035   (51.0% male; 48.9% female)
Individual Education Program: 1,773 (11.8%);
English Language Learner: 1,887 (12.6%); Migrant: 117 (0.8%)
Eligible for Free Lunch Program: 5,384 (35.8%)
Eligible for Reduced-Price Lunch Program: 1,762 (11.7%)
Teachers: 662.3 (22.7 to 1)
Librarians/Media Specialists: 6.0 (2,505.8 to 1)
Guidance Counselors: 16.0 (939.7 to 1)
Current Spending: ($ per student per year):
Total: $6,967; Instruction: $4,241; Support Services: $2,437
Enrollment, Drop-out Rates and Diploma Recipients by Race/Ethnicity

Category	Total	White	Black	Asian	AIAN	Hisp.
Enrollment (%)	100.0	21.9	5.6	9.8	0.3	60.9
Drop-out Rate (%)	n/a	n/a	n/a	n/a	n/a	n/a
H.S. Diplomas (#)	979	318	58	117	5	478

Culver City Unified
4034 Irving Pl • Culver City, CA 90232-2810
(310) 842-4220 • http://www.ccusd.k12.ca.us/
Grade Span: KG-12; **Agency Type:** 1
Schools: 10
5 Primary; 1 Middle; 3 High; 1 Other Level
7 Regular; 0 Special Education; 0 Vocational; 3 Alternative
0 Magnet; 0 Charter; 4 Title I Eligible; 2 School-wide Title I
Students: 6,850   (51.5% male; 48.4% female)
Individual Education Program: 636 (9.3%);
English Language Learner: 1,153 (16.8%); Migrant: 0 (0.0%)
Eligible for Free Lunch Program: 1,479 (21.6%)
Eligible for Reduced-Price Lunch Program: 717 (10.5%)
Teachers: 316.3 (21.7 to 1)
Librarians/Media Specialists: 1.0 (6,850.0 to 1)
Guidance Counselors: 7.5 (913.3 to 1)
Current Spending: ($ per student per year):
Total: $7,046; Instruction: $4,167; Support Services: $2,647

Category	Total	White	Black	Asian	AIAN	Hisp.
Enrollment (%)	100.0	22.6	17.4	10.4	0.1	35.9
Drop-out Rate (%)	n/a	n/a	n/a	n/a	n/a	n/a
H.S. Diplomas (#)	307	88	53	58	0	108

Downey Unified
11627 Brookshire Ave • Downey, CA 90241-7017
Mailing Address: PO Box 7017 • Downey, CA 90241-7017
(562) 904-3500 • http://www.dusd.net/
Grade Span: KG-12; **Agency Type:** 1
Schools: 22
12 Primary; 6 Middle; 3 High; 1 Other Level
20 Regular; 1 Special Education; 0 Vocational; 1 Alternative
0 Magnet; 0 Charter; 14 Title I Eligible; 0 School-wide Title I
Students: 22,523   (51.1% male; 48.8% female)
Individual Education Program: 2,442 (10.8%);
English Language Learner: 5,119 (22.7%); Migrant: 8 (<0.1%)
Eligible for Free Lunch Program: 7,408 (32.9%)
Eligible for Reduced-Price Lunch Program: 4,582 (20.3%)
Teachers: 970.5 (23.2 to 1)
Librarians/Media Specialists: 6.0 (3,753.8 to 1)
Guidance Counselors: 21.3 (1,057.4 to 1)
Current Spending: ($ per student per year):
Total: $6,399; Instruction: $4,240; Support Services: $1,864
Enrollment, Drop-out Rates and Diploma Recipients by Race/Ethnicity

Category	Total	White	Black	Asian	AIAN	Hisp.
Enrollment (%)	100.0	14.1	4.0	5.7	0.4	75.6
Drop-out Rate (%)	n/a	n/a	n/a	n/a	n/a	n/a
H.S. Diplomas (#)	1,292	318	61	114	3	796

Duarte Unified
1620 Huntington Dr • Duarte, CA 91010-2534
(626) 358-1191 • http://www.duarte.k12.ca.us/
Grade Span: KG-12; **Agency Type:** 1
Schools: 8
5 Primary; 1 Middle; 2 High; 0 Other Level
7 Regular; 0 Special Education; 0 Vocational; 1 Alternative
0 Magnet; 0 Charter; 8 Title I Eligible; 5 School-wide Title I
Students: 4,692   (51.3% male; 48.6% female)
Individual Education Program: 383 (8.2%);
English Language Learner: 867 (18.5%); Migrant: 311 (6.6%)
Eligible for Free Lunch Program: 2,290 (48.8%)
Eligible for Reduced-Price Lunch Program: 682 (14.5%)
Teachers: 215.9 (21.7 to 1)
Librarians/Media Specialists: 0.0 (n/a to 1)
Guidance Counselors: 3.0 (1,564.0 to 1)
Current Spending: ($ per student per year):
Total: $6,696; Instruction: $3,842; Support Services: $2,478
Enrollment, Drop-out Rates and Diploma Recipients by Race/Ethnicity

Category	Total	White	Black	Asian	AIAN	Hisp.
Enrollment (%)	100.0	12.5	9.9	6.3	0.2	65.2
Drop-out Rate (%)	n/a	n/a	n/a	n/a	n/a	n/a
H.S. Diplomas (#)	320	51	37	29	0	202

East Whittier City Elementary
14535 E Whittier Blvd • Whittier, CA 90605-2130
(562) 698-0351 • http://www.ewcsd.k12.ca.us/
Grade Span: KG-08; **Agency Type:** 1
Schools: 13
10 Primary; 3 Middle; 0 High; 0 Other Level
13 Regular; 0 Special Education; 0 Vocational; 0 Alternative
0 Magnet; 0 Charter; 7 Title I Eligible; 3 School-wide Title I
Students: 9,332   (51.9% male; 48.0% female)
Individual Education Program: 1,160 (12.4%);
English Language Learner: 1,774 (19.0%); Migrant: 5 (0.1%)
Eligible for Free Lunch Program: 2,348 (25.2%)
Eligible for Reduced-Price Lunch Program: 806 (8.6%)
Teachers: 449.1 (20.8 to 1)
Librarians/Media Specialists: 0.0 (n/a to 1)
Guidance Counselors: 4.6 (2,028.7 to 1)
Current Spending: ($ per student per year):
Total: $6,686; Instruction: $4,513; Support Services: $1,952
Enrollment, Drop-out Rates and Diploma Recipients by Race/Ethnicity

Category	Total	White	Black	Asian	AIAN	Hisp.
Enrollment (%)	100.0	24.2	1.7	2.9	0.5	69.1
Drop-out Rate (%)	n/a	n/a	n/a	n/a	n/a	n/a
H.S. Diplomas (#)	n/a	n/a	n/a	n/a	n/a	n/a

Eastside Union Elementary
45006 30th St E • Lancaster, CA 93535-7849
(661) 952-1200 • http://www.lacoe.edu/sch-dist/eastside/
Grade Span: KG-08; **Agency Type:** 1
Schools: 4
3 Primary; 1 Middle; 0 High; 0 Other Level

4 Regular; 0 Special Education; 0 Vocational; 0 Alternative
0 Magnet; 0 Charter; 4 Title I Eligible; 4 School-wide Title I
Students: 2,720   (50.2% male; 49.7% female)
Individual Education Program: 285 (10.5%);
English Language Learner: 707 (26.0%); Migrant: 160 (5.9%)
Eligible for Free Lunch Program: 1,270 (46.7%)
Eligible for Reduced-Price Lunch Program: 337 (12.4%)
Teachers: 120.3 (22.6 to 1)
Librarians/Media Specialists: 1.0 (2,720.0 to 1)
Guidance Counselors: 0.0 (n/a to 1)
Current Spending: ($ per student per year):
Total: $6,599; Instruction: $4,141; Support Services: $2,190
Enrollment, Drop-out Rates and Diploma Recipients by Race/Ethnicity

Category	Total	White	Black	Asian	AIAN	Hisp.
Enrollment (%)	100.0	29.1	25.3	0.8	0.6	42.8
Drop-out Rate (%)	n/a	n/a	n/a	n/a	n/a	n/a
H.S. Diplomas (#)	n/a	n/a	n/a	n/a	n/a	n/a

El Monte City Elementary
3540 N Lexington Ave • El Monte, CA 91731-2684
(626) 453-3700
Grade Span: KG-08; **Agency Type:** 1
Schools: 19
19 Primary; 0 Middle; 0 High; 0 Other Level
18 Regular; 1 Special Education; 0 Vocational; 0 Alternative
0 Magnet; 0 Charter; 19 Title I Eligible; 16 School-wide Title I
Students: 11,713   (51.1% male; 48.8% female)
Individual Education Program: 1,143 (9.8%);
English Language Learner: 5,296 (45.2%); Migrant: 392 (3.3%)
Eligible for Free Lunch Program: 9,149 (78.1%)
Eligible for Reduced-Price Lunch Program: 1,186 (10.1%)
Teachers: 568.0 (20.6 to 1)
Librarians/Media Specialists: 0.0 (n/a to 1)
Guidance Counselors: 0.0 (n/a to 1)
Current Spending: ($ per student per year):
Total: $7,295; Instruction: $4,721; Support Services: $2,173
Enrollment, Drop-out Rates and Diploma Recipients by Race/Ethnicity

Category	Total	White	Black	Asian	AIAN	Hisp.
Enrollment (%)	100.0	4.2	0.5	14.9	0.2	79.5
Drop-out Rate (%)	n/a	n/a	n/a	n/a	n/a	n/a
H.S. Diplomas (#)	n/a	n/a	n/a	n/a	n/a	n/a

El Monte Union High
3537 Johnson Ave • El Monte, CA 91731-3290
(626) 444-9005 • http://www.emuhsd.k12.ca.us/
Grade Span: 09-12; **Agency Type:** 1
Schools: 7
0 Primary; 0 Middle; 7 High; 0 Other Level
5 Regular; 0 Special Education; 0 Vocational; 2 Alternative
0 Magnet; 0 Charter; 7 Title I Eligible; 2 School-wide Title I
Students: 10,254   (50.9% male; 49.0% female)
Individual Education Program: 913 (8.9%);
English Language Learner: 3,086 (30.1%); Migrant: 356 (3.5%)
Eligible for Free Lunch Program: 5,591 (54.5%)
Eligible for Reduced-Price Lunch Program: 1,196 (11.7%)
Teachers: 401.3 (25.6 to 1)
Librarians/Media Specialists: 5.0 (2,050.8 to 1)
Guidance Counselors: 24.0 (427.3 to 1)
Current Spending: ($ per student per year):
Total: $7,079; Instruction: $4,124; Support Services: $2,673
Enrollment, Drop-out Rates and Diploma Recipients by Race/Ethnicity

Category	Total	White	Black	Asian	AIAN	Hisp.
Enrollment (%)	100.0	4.1	0.6	18.2	0.1	77.0
Drop-out Rate (%)	n/a	n/a	n/a	n/a	n/a	n/a
H.S. Diplomas (#)	1,705	77	9	368	1	1,248

El Rancho Unified
9333 Loch Lomond Dr • Pico Rivera, CA 90660-2913
(562) 942-1500 • http://www.erusd.k12.ca.us/
Grade Span: KG-12; **Agency Type:** 1
Schools: 17
12 Primary; 3 Middle; 2 High; 0 Other Level
16 Regular; 0 Special Education; 0 Vocational; 1 Alternative
0 Magnet; 0 Charter; 17 Title I Eligible; 0 School-wide Title I
Students: 12,166   (51.1% male; 48.8% female)
Individual Education Program: 1,198 (9.8%);
English Language Learner: 3,926 (32.3%); Migrant: 196 (1.6%)
Eligible for Free Lunch Program: 6,184 (50.8%)
Eligible for Reduced-Price Lunch Program: 1,927 (15.8%)
Teachers: 560.0 (21.7 to 1)
Librarians/Media Specialists: 0.0 (n/a to 1)
Guidance Counselors: 10.0 (1,216.6 to 1)
Current Spending: ($ per student per year):
Total: $7,272; Instruction: $4,663; Support Services: $2,338

Enrollment, Drop-out Rates and Diploma Recipients by Race/Ethnicity

Category	Total	White	Black	Asian	AIAN	Hisp.
Enrollment (%)	100.0	2.0	0.4	1.1	0.2	95.9
Drop-out Rate (%)	n/a	n/a	n/a	n/a	n/a	n/a
H.S. Diplomas (#)	596	21	6	18	2	549

El Segundo Unified
641 Sheldon St • El Segundo, CA 90245-3036
(310) 615-2650 • http://www.elsegundousd.com/policies/gate.htm
Grade Span: KG-12; **Agency Type:** 1
Schools: 5
2 Primary; 1 Middle; 2 High; 0 Other Level
4 Regular; 0 Special Education; 0 Vocational; 1 Alternative
0 Magnet; 0 Charter; 1 Title I Eligible; 0 School-wide Title I
Students: 3,196   (49.3% male; 50.6% female)
Individual Education Program: 226 (7.1%);
English Language Learner: 101 (3.2%); Migrant: 0 (0.0%)
Eligible for Free Lunch Program: 207 (6.5%)
Eligible for Reduced-Price Lunch Program: 116 (3.6%)
Teachers: 147.1 (21.7 to 1)
Librarians/Media Specialists: 1.0 (3,196.0 to 1)
Guidance Counselors: 2.6 (1,229.2 to 1)
Current Spending: ($ per student per year):
Total: $6,780; Instruction: $4,339; Support Services: $2,225
Enrollment, Drop-out Rates and Diploma Recipients by Race/Ethnicity

Category	Total	White	Black	Asian	AIAN	Hisp.
Enrollment (%)	100.0	71.4	4.2	9.1	0.2	15.0
Drop-out Rate (%)	n/a	n/a	n/a	n/a	n/a	n/a
H.S. Diplomas (#)	247	159	11	33	2	42

Garvey Elementary
2730 N Del Mar • Rosemead, CA 91770-3026
(626) 307-3400 • http://www.garvey.k12.ca.us/
Grade Span: KG-08; **Agency Type:** 1
Schools: 13
11 Primary; 2 Middle; 0 High; 0 Other Level
13 Regular; 0 Special Education; 0 Vocational; 0 Alternative
0 Magnet; 0 Charter; 13 Title I Eligible; 0 School-wide Title I
Students: 6,584   (50.8% male; 49.1% female)
Individual Education Program: 640 (9.7%);
English Language Learner: 2,867 (43.5%); Migrant: 319 (4.8%)
Eligible for Free Lunch Program: 4,663 (70.8%)
Eligible for Reduced-Price Lunch Program: 472 (7.2%)
Teachers: 315.8 (20.8 to 1)
Librarians/Media Specialists: 2.1 (3,135.2 to 1)
Guidance Counselors: 0.6 (10,973.3 to 1)
Current Spending: ($ per student per year):
Total: $7,681; Instruction: $4,564; Support Services: $2,670
Enrollment, Drop-out Rates and Diploma Recipients by Race/Ethnicity

Category	Total	White	Black	Asian	AIAN	Hisp.
Enrollment (%)	100.0	2.3	0.2	51.0	0.0	46.4
Drop-out Rate (%)	n/a	n/a	n/a	n/a	n/a	n/a
H.S. Diplomas (#)	n/a	n/a	n/a	n/a	n/a	n/a

Glendale Unified
223 N Jackson St • Glendale, CA 91206-4334
(818) 241-3111 • http://www.glendale.k12.ca.us/
Grade Span: KG-12; **Agency Type:** 1
Schools: 32
20 Primary; 4 Middle; 5 High; 3 Other Level
28 Regular; 1 Special Education; 0 Vocational; 3 Alternative
0 Magnet; 0 Charter; 18 Title I Eligible; 17 School-wide Title I
Students: 29,433   (50.9% male; 49.0% female)
Individual Education Program: 2,735 (9.3%);
English Language Learner: 8,822 (30.0%); Migrant: 3 (<0.1%)
Eligible for Free Lunch Program: 10,265 (34.9%)
Eligible for Reduced-Price Lunch Program: 2,707 (9.2%)
Teachers: 1,346.0 (21.9 to 1)
Librarians/Media Specialists: 0.0 (n/a to 1)
Guidance Counselors: 29.0 (1,014.9 to 1)
Current Spending: ($ per student per year):
Total: $7,133; Instruction: $4,809; Support Services: $2,092
Enrollment, Drop-out Rates and Diploma Recipients by Race/Ethnicity

Category	Total	White	Black	Asian	AIAN	Hisp.
Enrollment (%)	100.0	57.0	1.0	18.6	0.2	22.4
Drop-out Rate (%)	n/a	n/a	n/a	n/a	n/a	n/a
H.S. Diplomas (#)	2,002	1,278	14	392	5	313

Glendora Unified
500 N Loraine Ave • Glendora, CA 91741-2964
(626) 963-1611 • http://www.glendora.k12.ca.us/
Grade Span: KG-12; **Agency Type:** 1
Schools: 10
6 Primary; 2 Middle; 2 High; 0 Other Level
9 Regular; 0 Special Education; 0 Vocational; 1 Alternative

0 Magnet; 0 Charter; 5 Title I Eligible; 0 School-wide Title I
Students: 7,924   (50.5% male; 49.4% female)
  Individual Education Program: 774 (9.8%);
  English Language Learner: 271 (3.4%); Migrant: 2 (<0.1%)
  Eligible for Free Lunch Program: 773 (9.8%)
  Eligible for Reduced-Price Lunch Program: 393 (5.0%)
Teachers: 339.4 (23.3 to 1)
Librarians/Media Specialists: 1.0 (7,924.0 to 1)
Guidance Counselors: 7.5 (1,056.5 to 1)
Current Spending: ($ per student per year):
  Total: $5,956; Instruction: $3,918; Support Services: $1,837
Enrollment, Drop-out Rates and Diploma Recipients by Race/Ethnicity

Category	Total	White	Black	Asian	AIAN	Hisp.
Enrollment (%)	100.0	70.0	2.2	6.3	0.4	20.6
Drop-out Rate (%)	n/a	n/a	n/a	n/a	n/a	n/a
H.S. Diplomas (#)	577	405	7	53	4	95

Gorman Elementary
49847 Gorman School Rd • Gorman, CA 93243-0104
Mailing Address: PO Box 104 • Gorman, CA 93243-0104
(661) 248-6816
Grade Span: KG-12; **Agency Type:** 1
Schools: 4
  1 Primary; 1 Middle; 1 High; 1 Other Level
  4 Regular; 0 Special Education; 0 Vocational; 0 Alternative
  0 Magnet; 3 Charter; 4 Title I Eligible; 1 School-wide Title I
Students: 1,995   (47.3% male; 52.6% female)
  Individual Education Program: 143 (7.2%);
  English Language Learner: 37 (1.9%); Migrant: 0 (0.0%)
  Eligible for Free Lunch Program: 26 (1.3%)
  Eligible for Reduced-Price Lunch Program: 6 (0.3%)
Teachers: 67.0 (29.8 to 1)
Librarians/Media Specialists: 0.0 (n/a to 1)
Guidance Counselors: 1.5 (1,330.0 to 1)
Current Spending: ($ per student per year):
  Total: $71,341; Instruction: $55,293; Support Services: $15,000
Enrollment, Drop-out Rates and Diploma Recipients by Race/Ethnicity

Category	Total	White	Black	Asian	AIAN	Hisp.
Enrollment (%)	100.0	55.1	15.4	6.3	1.2	21.9
Drop-out Rate (%)	n/a	n/a	n/a	n/a	n/a	n/a
H.S. Diplomas (#)	28	21	3	1	0	2

Hacienda La Puente Unified
15959 E Gale Ave • City Of Industry, CA 91716-0002
Mailing Address: PO Box 60002 • City Of Industry, CA 91716-0002
(626) 933-1000 • http://www.hlpusd.k12.ca.us/webapps/portal/frameset.jsp
Grade Span: KG-12; **Agency Type:** 1
Schools: 39
  24 Primary; 6 Middle; 6 High; 3 Other Level
  35 Regular; 1 Special Education; 0 Vocational; 3 Alternative
  0 Magnet; 1 Charter; 23 Title I Eligible; 17 School-wide Title I
Students: 25,499   (50.9% male; 49.0% female)
  Individual Education Program: 2,502 (9.8%);
  English Language Learner: 6,586 (25.8%); Migrant: 665 (2.6%)
  Eligible for Free Lunch Program: 10,657 (41.8%)
  Eligible for Reduced-Price Lunch Program: 3,924 (15.4%)
Teachers: 1,171.8 (21.8 to 1)
Librarians/Media Specialists: 2.0 (12,749.5 to 1)
Guidance Counselors: 26.9 (947.9 to 1)
Current Spending: ($ per student per year):
  Total: $7,398; Instruction: $4,532; Support Services: $2,568
Enrollment, Drop-out Rates and Diploma Recipients by Race/Ethnicity

Category	Total	White	Black	Asian	AIAN	Hisp.
Enrollment (%)	100.0	7.4	2.8	16.6	0.4	72.6
Drop-out Rate (%)	n/a	n/a	n/a	n/a	n/a	n/a
H.S. Diplomas (#)	1,345	139	55	359	4	768

Hawthorne Elementary
14120 S Hawthorne Blvd • Hawthorne, CA 90250-5210
(310) 676-2276 • http://www.hawthorne.k12.ca.us/
Grade Span: KG-08; **Agency Type:** 1
Schools: 12
  7 Primary; 4 Middle; 1 High; 0 Other Level
  12 Regular; 0 Special Education; 0 Vocational; 0 Alternative
  0 Magnet; 1 Charter; 11 Title I Eligible; 11 School-wide Title I
Students: 9,875   (50.5% male; 49.4% female)
  Individual Education Program: 917 (9.3%);
  English Language Learner: 4,378 (44.3%); Migrant: 0 (0.0%)
  Eligible for Free Lunch Program: 6,764 (68.5%)
  Eligible for Reduced-Price Lunch Program: 1,549 (15.7%)
Teachers: 452.4 (21.8 to 1)
Librarians/Media Specialists: 0.0 (n/a to 1)
Guidance Counselors: 8.0 (1,234.4 to 1)
Current Spending: ($ per student per year):
  Total: $6,886; Instruction: $3,808; Support Services: $2,652

Enrollment, Drop-out Rates and Diploma Recipients by Race/Ethnicity

Category	Total	White	Black	Asian	AIAN	Hisp.
Enrollment (%)	100.0	2.6	26.2	6.2	0.1	62.8
Drop-out Rate (%)	n/a	n/a	n/a	n/a	n/a	n/a
H.S. Diplomas (#)	n/a	n/a	n/a	n/a	n/a	n/a

Inglewood Unified
401 S Inglewood Ave • Inglewood, CA 90301-2501
(310) 419-2700 • http://inglewood.k12.ca.us/
Grade Span: KG-12; **Agency Type:** 1
Schools: 20
  14 Primary; 2 Middle; 4 High; 0 Other Level
  19 Regular; 0 Special Education; 0 Vocational; 1 Alternative
  6 Magnet; 1 Charter; 17 Title I Eligible; 14 School-wide Title I
Students: 17,969   (50.9% male; 49.0% female)
  Individual Education Program: 1,306 (7.3%);
  English Language Learner: 5,971 (33.2%); Migrant: 0 (0.0%)
  Eligible for Free Lunch Program: 8,020 (44.6%)
  Eligible for Reduced-Price Lunch Program: 1,727 (9.6%)
Teachers: 856.5 (21.0 to 1)
Librarians/Media Specialists: 5.0 (3,593.8 to 1)
Guidance Counselors: 15.0 (1,197.9 to 1)
Current Spending: ($ per student per year):
  Total: $7,429; Instruction: $4,288; Support Services: $2,587
Enrollment, Drop-out Rates and Diploma Recipients by Race/Ethnicity

Category	Total	White	Black	Asian	AIAN	Hisp.
Enrollment (%)	100.0	0.6	41.8	0.8	0.0	56.7
Drop-out Rate (%)	n/a	n/a	n/a	n/a	n/a	n/a
H.S. Diplomas (#)	666	4	284	7	0	371

Keppel Union Elementary
34004 128th St E • Pearblossom, CA 93553-0186
Mailing Address: PO Box 186 • Pearblossom, CA 93553-0186
(661) 944-2155 • http://www.keppel.k12.ca.us/
Grade Span: KG-08; **Agency Type:** 1
Schools: 6
  5 Primary; 1 Middle; 0 High; 0 Other Level
  6 Regular; 0 Special Education; 0 Vocational; 0 Alternative
  0 Magnet; 0 Charter; 6 Title I Eligible; 2 School-wide Title I
Students: 2,976   (51.8% male; 48.1% female)
  Individual Education Program: 340 (11.4%);
  English Language Learner: 691 (23.2%); Migrant: 202 (6.8%)
  Eligible for Free Lunch Program: 1,862 (62.6%)
  Eligible for Reduced-Price Lunch Program: 416 (14.0%)
Teachers: 136.9 (21.7 to 1)
Librarians/Media Specialists: 0.0 (n/a to 1)
Guidance Counselors: 1.0 (2,976.0 to 1)
Current Spending: ($ per student per year):
  Total: $6,362; Instruction: $3,972; Support Services: $2,037
Enrollment, Drop-out Rates and Diploma Recipients by Race/Ethnicity

Category	Total	White	Black	Asian	AIAN	Hisp.
Enrollment (%)	100.0	32.8	10.8	1.3	1.1	52.8
Drop-out Rate (%)	n/a	n/a	n/a	n/a	n/a	n/a
H.S. Diplomas (#)	n/a	n/a	n/a	n/a	n/a	n/a

La Canada Unified
5039 Palm Dr • La Canada, CA 91011-1518
(818) 952-8300 • http://www.lcusd.net/
Grade Span: KG-12; **Agency Type:** 1
Schools: 5
  3 Primary; 0 Middle; 1 High; 1 Other Level
  4 Regular; 1 Special Education; 0 Vocational; 0 Alternative
  0 Magnet; 0 Charter; 0 Title I Eligible; 0 School-wide Title I
Students: 4,343   (51.0% male; 48.9% female)
  Individual Education Program: 423 (9.7%);
  English Language Learner: 102 (2.3%); Migrant: 0 (0.0%)
  Eligible for Free Lunch Program: 20 (0.5%)
  Eligible for Reduced-Price Lunch Program: 11 (0.3%)
Teachers: 187.4 (23.2 to 1)
Librarians/Media Specialists: 1.0 (4,343.0 to 1)
Guidance Counselors: 6.0 (723.8 to 1)
Current Spending: ($ per student per year):
  Total: $7,329; Instruction: $4,712; Support Services: $2,477
Enrollment, Drop-out Rates and Diploma Recipients by Race/Ethnicity

Category	Total	White	Black	Asian	AIAN	Hisp.
Enrollment (%)	100.0	68.8	0.2	24.3	0.0	3.2
Drop-out Rate (%)	n/a	n/a	n/a	n/a	n/a	n/a
H.S. Diplomas (#)	325	212	2	104	0	3

Lancaster Elementary
44711 N Cedar Ave • Lancaster, CA 93534-3210
(661) 948-4661 • http://www.lancaster.k12.ca.us/
Grade Span: KG-08; **Agency Type:** 1
Schools: 18
  14 Primary; 4 Middle; 0 High; 0 Other Level

16 Regular; 0 Special Education; 0 Vocational; 2 Alternative
0 Magnet; 0 Charter; 17 Title I Eligible; 15 School-wide Title I
Students: 15,799   (50.9% male; 49.0% female)
   Individual Education Program: 2,179 (13.8%);
   English Language Learner: 2,333 (14.8%); Migrant: 326 (2.1%)
   Eligible for Free Lunch Program: 8,217 (52.0%)
   Eligible for Reduced-Price Lunch Program: 1,489 (9.4%)
Teachers: 727.5 (21.7 to 1)
Librarians/Media Specialists: 0.0 (n/a to 1)
Guidance Counselors: 0.0 (n/a to 1)
Current Spending: ($ per student per year):
   Total: $6,585; Instruction: $4,453; Support Services: $1,805
Enrollment, Drop-out Rates and Diploma Recipients by Race/Ethnicity

Category	Total	White	Black	Asian	AIAN	Hisp.
Enrollment (%)	100.0	30.2	29.1	3.2	0.7	36.9
Drop-out Rate (%)	n/a	n/a	n/a	n/a	n/a	n/a
H.S. Diplomas (#)	n/a	n/a	n/a	n/a	n/a	n/a

Las Virgenes Unified
4111 N Las Virgenes Rd • Calabasas, CA 91302-1929
(818) 880-4000 • http://www.lvusd.k12.ca.us/
Grade Span: KG-12; **Agency Type:** 1
Schools: 14
   8 Primary; 3 Middle; 3 High; 0 Other Level
   13 Regular; 0 Special Education; 0 Vocational; 1 Alternative
   0 Magnet; 0 Charter; 4 Title I Eligible; 0 School-wide Title I
Students: 12,170   (51.3% male; 48.6% female)
   Individual Education Program: 1,263 (10.4%);
   English Language Learner: 513 (4.2%); Migrant: 0 (0.0%)
   Eligible for Free Lunch Program: 230 (1.9%)
   Eligible for Reduced-Price Lunch Program: 123 (1.0%)
Teachers: 514.6 (23.6 to 1)
Librarians/Media Specialists: 4.8 (2,535.4 to 1)
Guidance Counselors: 9.1 (1,337.4 to 1)
Current Spending: ($ per student per year):
   Total: $6,766; Instruction: $4,471; Support Services: $2,163
Enrollment, Drop-out Rates and Diploma Recipients by Race/Ethnicity

Category	Total	White	Black	Asian	AIAN	Hisp.
Enrollment (%)	100.0	83.5	1.7	7.6	0.2	5.4
Drop-out Rate (%)	n/a	n/a	n/a	n/a	n/a	n/a
H.S. Diplomas (#)	861	754	12	64	1	27

Lawndale Elementary
4161 W 147th St • Lawndale, CA 90260-1709
(310) 973-1300 • http://www.lawndale.k12.ca.us/
Grade Span: KG-12; **Agency Type:** 1
Schools: 8
   6 Primary; 1 Middle; 1 High; 0 Other Level
   8 Regular; 0 Special Education; 0 Vocational; 0 Alternative
   0 Magnet; 1 Charter; 8 Title I Eligible; 7 School-wide Title I
Students: 6,484   (51.4% male; 48.5% female)
   Individual Education Program: 845 (13.0%);
   English Language Learner: 2,768 (42.7%); Migrant: 0 (0.0%)
   Eligible for Free Lunch Program: 4,077 (62.9%)
   Eligible for Reduced-Price Lunch Program: 1,110 (17.1%)
Teachers: 297.4 (21.8 to 1)
Librarians/Media Specialists: 1.6 (4,052.5 to 1)
Guidance Counselors: 3.0 (2,161.3 to 1)
Current Spending: ($ per student per year):
   Total: $7,154; Instruction: $4,801; Support Services: $2,054
Enrollment, Drop-out Rates and Diploma Recipients by Race/Ethnicity

Category	Total	White	Black	Asian	AIAN	Hisp.
Enrollment (%)	100.0	7.5	14.3	9.0	0.5	68.6
Drop-out Rate (%)	n/a	n/a	n/a	n/a	n/a	n/a
H.S. Diplomas (#)	0	0	0	0	0	0

Lennox Elementary
10319 S Firmona Ave • Lennox, CA 90304-1419
(310) 330-4950 • http://www.lennox.k12.ca.us/
Grade Span: KG-12; **Agency Type:** 1
Schools: 8
   5 Primary; 1 Middle; 2 High; 0 Other Level
   8 Regular; 0 Special Education; 0 Vocational; 0 Alternative
   0 Magnet; 2 Charter; 5 Title I Eligible; 5 School-wide Title I
Students: 7,696   (51.3% male; 48.6% female)
   Individual Education Program: 736 (9.6%);
   English Language Learner: 5,313 (69.0%); Migrant: 0 (0.0%)
   Eligible for Free Lunch Program: 5,635 (73.2%)
   Eligible for Reduced-Price Lunch Program: 309 (4.0%)
Teachers: 342.5 (22.5 to 1)
Librarians/Media Specialists: 0.0 (n/a to 1)
Guidance Counselors: 16.0 (481.0 to 1)
Current Spending: ($ per student per year):
   Total: $7,492; Instruction: $5,014; Support Services: $2,081

Enrollment, Drop-out Rates and Diploma Recipients by Race/Ethnicity

Category	Total	White	Black	Asian	AIAN	Hisp.
Enrollment (%)	100.0	0.5	2.2	1.2	0.1	95.6
Drop-out Rate (%)	n/a	n/a	n/a	n/a	n/a	n/a
H.S. Diplomas (#)	0	0	0	0	0	0

Little Lake City Elementary
10515 S Pioneer Blvd • Santa Fe Springs, CA 90670-3703
(562) 868-8241 • http://www.littlelake.k12.ca.us/
Grade Span: KG-08; **Agency Type:** 1
Schools: 9
   7 Primary; 2 Middle; 0 High; 0 Other Level
   9 Regular; 0 Special Education; 0 Vocational; 0 Alternative
   0 Magnet; 0 Charter; 9 Title I Eligible; 0 School-wide Title I
Students: 5,220   (51.6% male; 48.3% female)
   Individual Education Program: 603 (11.6%);
   English Language Learner: 1,400 (26.8%); Migrant: 77 (1.5%)
   Eligible for Free Lunch Program: 2,243 (43.0%)
   Eligible for Reduced-Price Lunch Program: 1,194 (22.9%)
Teachers: 236.0 (22.1 to 1)
Librarians/Media Specialists: 0.0 (n/a to 1)
Guidance Counselors: 2.0 (2,610.0 to 1)
Current Spending: ($ per student per year):
   Total: $6,642; Instruction: $4,467; Support Services: $1,839
Enrollment, Drop-out Rates and Diploma Recipients by Race/Ethnicity

Category	Total	White	Black	Asian	AIAN	Hisp.
Enrollment (%)	100.0	9.5	3.7	4.1	0.1	82.0
Drop-out Rate (%)	n/a	n/a	n/a	n/a	n/a	n/a
H.S. Diplomas (#)	n/a	n/a	n/a	n/a	n/a	n/a

Long Beach Unified
1515 Hughes Way • Long Beach, CA 90810-1839
(562) 997-8000 • http://www.lbusd.k12.ca.us/
Grade Span: KG-12; **Agency Type:** 1
Schools: 91
   60 Primary; 15 Middle; 11 High; 5 Other Level
   86 Regular; 0 Special Education; 0 Vocational; 5 Alternative
   42 Magnet; 3 Charter; 69 Title I Eligible; 61 School-wide Title I
Students: 97,560   (50.9% male; 49.0% female)
   Individual Education Program: 7,808 (8.0%);
   English Language Learner: 28,439 (29.2%); Migrant: 3,715 (3.8%)
   Eligible for Free Lunch Program: 52,820 (54.1%)
   Eligible for Reduced-Price Lunch Program: 11,122 (11.4%)
Teachers: 4,439.2 (22.0 to 1)
Librarians/Media Specialists: 65.9 (1,480.4 to 1)
Guidance Counselors: 166.4 (586.3 to 1)
Current Spending: ($ per student per year):
   Total: $7,365; Instruction: $4,413; Support Services: $2,655
Enrollment, Drop-out Rates and Diploma Recipients by Race/Ethnicity

Category	Total	White	Black	Asian	AIAN	Hisp.
Enrollment (%)	100.0	16.9	18.6	15.1	0.3	49.0
Drop-out Rate (%)	n/a	n/a	n/a	n/a	n/a	n/a
H.S. Diplomas (#)	4,664	1,006	928	1,174	21	1,535

Los Angeles County Office of Education
9300 Imperial Hwy • Downey, CA 90242-2813
(562) 922-6127 • http://www.lacoe.edu/
Grade Span: KG-12; **Agency Type:** 4
Schools: 16
   2 Primary; 0 Middle; 9 High; 5 Other Level
   5 Regular; 1 Special Education; 0 Vocational; 10 Alternative
   0 Magnet; 4 Charter; 1 Title I Eligible; 0 School-wide Title I
Students: 11,829   (69.3% male; 30.6% female)
   Individual Education Program: 6,554 (55.4%);
   English Language Learner: 3,575 (30.2%); Migrant: 100 (0.8%)
   Eligible for Free Lunch Program: 4,940 (41.8%)
   Eligible for Reduced-Price Lunch Program: 428 (3.6%)
Teachers: 1,002.5 (11.8 to 1)
Librarians/Media Specialists: 1.0 (11,829.0 to 1)
Guidance Counselors: 25.0 (473.2 to 1)
Current Spending: ($ per student per year):
   Total: $40,267; Instruction: $26,748; Support Services: $13,517
Enrollment, Drop-out Rates and Diploma Recipients by Race/Ethnicity

Category	Total	White	Black	Asian	AIAN	Hisp.
Enrollment (%)	100.0	15.4	25.7	4.8	0.3	52.5
Drop-out Rate (%)	n/a	n/a	n/a	n/a	n/a	n/a
H.S. Diplomas (#)	851	76	224	96	22	417

Los Angeles Unified
333 S Beaudry Ave • Los Angeles, CA 90017
(213) 241-1000 • http://www.lausd.k12.ca.us/
Grade Span: KG-12; **Agency Type:** 1
Schools: 693
   468 Primary; 81 Middle; 112 High; 32 Other Level
   612 Regular; 18 Special Education; 0 Vocational; 63 Alternative

139 Magnet; 49 Charter; 567 Title I Eligible; 355 School-wide Title I
Students: 747,009 (51.0% male; 48.9% female)
  Individual Education Program: 85,441 (11.4%);
  English Language Learner: 326,893 (43.8%); Migrant: 4,003 (0.5%)
  Eligible for Free Lunch Program: 500,776 (67.0%)
  Eligible for Reduced-Price Lunch Program: 58,197 (7.8%)
Teachers: 35,492.7 (21.0 to 1)
Librarians/Media Specialists: 70.1 (10,656.3 to 1)
Guidance Counselors: 977.4 (764.3 to 1)
Current Spending: ($ per student per year):
  Total: $8,508; Instruction: $4,954; Support Services: $3,265
Enrollment, Drop-out Rates and Diploma Recipients by Race/Ethnicity

Category	Total	White	Black	Asian	AIAN	Hisp.
Enrollment (%)	100.0	9.1	11.8	6.3	0.3	72.5
Drop-out Rate (%)	n/a	n/a	n/a	n/a	n/a	n/a
H.S. Diplomas (#)	27,720	4,285	3,836	3,037	90	16,472

Los Nietos Elementary
8324 S Westman Ave • Whittier, CA 90606-2405
Mailing Address: PO Box 2405 • Whittier, CA 90606-2405
(562) 692-0271 • http://www.losnietos.k12.ca.us/
Grade Span: KG-08; **Agency Type:** 1
Schools: 4
  3 Primary; 1 Middle; 0 High; 0 Other Level
  4 Regular; 0 Special Education; 0 Vocational; 0 Alternative
  0 Magnet; 0 Charter; 4 Title I Eligible; 4 School-wide Title I
Students: 2,385 (52.2% male; 47.7% female)
  Individual Education Program: 257 (10.8%);
  English Language Learner: 782 (32.8%); Migrant: 116 (4.9%)
  Eligible for Free Lunch Program: 2,373 (99.5%)
  Eligible for Reduced-Price Lunch Program: 0 (0.0%)
Teachers: 111.0 (21.5 to 1)
Librarians/Media Specialists: 0.0 (n/a to 1)
Guidance Counselors: 1.0 (2,385.0 to 1)
Current Spending: ($ per student per year):
  Total: $7,219; Instruction: $4,710; Support Services: $2,180
Enrollment, Drop-out Rates and Diploma Recipients by Race/Ethnicity

Category	Total	White	Black	Asian	AIAN	Hisp.
Enrollment (%)	100.0	4.0	1.0	0.8	0.2	94.0
Drop-out Rate (%)	n/a	n/a	n/a	n/a	n/a	n/a
H.S. Diplomas (#)	n/a	n/a	n/a	n/a	n/a	n/a

Lowell Joint
11019 Valley Home Ave • Whittier, CA 90603-3042
(562) 943-0211 • http://www.ljsd.k12.ca.us/
Grade Span: KG-08; **Agency Type:** 1
Schools: 6
  5 Primary; 1 Middle; 0 High; 0 Other Level
  6 Regular; 0 Special Education; 0 Vocational; 0 Alternative
  0 Magnet; 0 Charter; 3 Title I Eligible; 0 School-wide Title I
Students: 3,305 (51.9% male; 48.0% female)
  Individual Education Program: 365 (11.0%);
  English Language Learner: 323 (9.8%); Migrant: 0 (0.0%)
  Eligible for Free Lunch Program: 399 (12.1%)
  Eligible for Reduced-Price Lunch Program: 178 (5.4%)
Teachers: 143.3 (23.1 to 1)
Librarians/Media Specialists: 0.0 (n/a to 1)
Guidance Counselors: 0.0 (n/a to 1)
Current Spending: ($ per student per year):
  Total: $6,559; Instruction: $4,093; Support Services: $2,212
Enrollment, Drop-out Rates and Diploma Recipients by Race/Ethnicity

Category	Total	White	Black	Asian	AIAN	Hisp.
Enrollment (%)	100.0	47.4	1.0	4.3	0.3	40.4
Drop-out Rate (%)	n/a	n/a	n/a	n/a	n/a	n/a
H.S. Diplomas (#)	n/a	n/a	n/a	n/a	n/a	n/a

Lynwood Unified
11321 Bullis Rd • Lynwood, CA 90262-3600
(310) 886-1600 • http://www.lynwood.k12.ca.us
Grade Span: KG-12; **Agency Type:** 1
Schools: 14
  10 Primary; 1 Middle; 3 High; 0 Other Level
  13 Regular; 0 Special Education; 0 Vocational; 1 Alternative
  0 Magnet; 0 Charter; 14 Title I Eligible; 2 School-wide Title I
Students: 19,658 (51.1% male; 48.8% female)
  Individual Education Program: 839 (4.3%);
  English Language Learner: 10,175 (51.8%); Migrant: 622 (3.2%)
  Eligible for Free Lunch Program: 8,971 (45.6%)
  Eligible for Reduced-Price Lunch Program: 829 (4.2%)
Teachers: 732.8 (26.8 to 1)
Librarians/Media Specialists: 2.0 (9,829.0 to 1)
Guidance Counselors: 22.0 (893.5 to 1)
Current Spending: ($ per student per year):
  Total: $6,514; Instruction: $3,938; Support Services: $2,353

Category	Total	White	Black	Asian	AIAN	Hisp.
Enrollment (%)	100.0	0.3	8.8	0.4	0.0	90.1
Drop-out Rate (%)	n/a	n/a	n/a	n/a	n/a	n/a
H.S. Diplomas (#)	824	1	142	21	0	660

Manhattan Beach Unified
325 S Peck Ave • Manhattan Beach, CA 90266-2478
(310) 725-9050 • http://www.manhattan.k12.ca.us/
Grade Span: KG-12; **Agency Type:** 1
Schools: 7
  5 Primary; 1 Middle; 1 High; 0 Other Level
  7 Regular; 0 Special Education; 0 Vocational; 0 Alternative
  0 Magnet; 0 Charter; 1 Title I Eligible; 0 School-wide Title I
Students: 6,441 (51.8% male; 48.1% female)
  Individual Education Program: 713 (11.1%);
  English Language Learner: 119 (1.8%); Migrant: 0 (0.0%)
  Eligible for Free Lunch Program: 207 (3.2%)
  Eligible for Reduced-Price Lunch Program: 100 (1.6%)
Teachers: 315.2 (20.4 to 1)
Librarians/Media Specialists: 1.0 (6,441.0 to 1)
Guidance Counselors: 11.4 (565.0 to 1)
Current Spending: ($ per student per year):
  Total: $8,103; Instruction: $5,288; Support Services: $2,653
Enrollment, Drop-out Rates and Diploma Recipients by Race/Ethnicity

Category	Total	White	Black	Asian	AIAN	Hisp.
Enrollment (%)	100.0	72.7	1.1	7.8	0.1	6.6
Drop-out Rate (%)	n/a	n/a	n/a	n/a	n/a	n/a
H.S. Diplomas (#)	502	390	16	33	0	63

Monrovia Unified
325 E Huntington Dr • Monrovia, CA 91016-3585
(626) 471-2000 • http://www.monroviaschools.net/home.html
Grade Span: KG-12; **Agency Type:** 1
Schools: 11
  6 Primary; 2 Middle; 2 High; 1 Other Level
  10 Regular; 0 Special Education; 0 Vocational; 1 Alternative
  0 Magnet; 0 Charter; 7 Title I Eligible; 7 School-wide Title I
Students: 6,578 (51.2% male; 48.7% female)
  Individual Education Program: 532 (8.1%);
  English Language Learner: 1,269 (19.3%); Migrant: 28 (0.4%)
  Eligible for Free Lunch Program: 2,762 (42.0%)
  Eligible for Reduced-Price Lunch Program: 942 (14.3%)
Teachers: 308.9 (21.3 to 1)
Librarians/Media Specialists: 1.0 (6,578.0 to 1)
Guidance Counselors: 6.1 (1,078.4 to 1)
Current Spending: ($ per student per year):
  Total: $7,344; Instruction: $4,474; Support Services: $2,561
Enrollment, Drop-out Rates and Diploma Recipients by Race/Ethnicity

Category	Total	White	Black	Asian	AIAN	Hisp.
Enrollment (%)	100.0	26.7	12.4	5.5	0.7	52.4
Drop-out Rate (%)	n/a	n/a	n/a	n/a	n/a	n/a
H.S. Diplomas (#)	366	151	50	16	1	148

Montebello Unified
123 S Montebello Blvd • Montebello, CA 90640-4729
(323) 887-7900 • http://www.montebello.k12.ca.us/
Grade Span: KG-12; **Agency Type:** 1
Schools: 29
  18 Primary; 6 Middle; 5 High; 0 Other Level
  27 Regular; 0 Special Education; 0 Vocational; 2 Alternative
  0 Magnet; 0 Charter; 24 Title I Eligible; 24 School-wide Title I
Students: 35,952 (50.5% male; 49.4% female)
  Individual Education Program: 3,037 (8.4%);
  English Language Learner: 15,573 (43.3%); Migrant: 15 (<0.1%)
  Eligible for Free Lunch Program: 24,478 (68.1%)
  Eligible for Reduced-Price Lunch Program: 3,153 (8.8%)
Teachers: 1,507.1 (23.9 to 1)
Librarians/Media Specialists: 8.0 (4,494.0 to 1)
Guidance Counselors: 41.0 (876.9 to 1)
Current Spending: ($ per student per year):
  Total: $7,341; Instruction: $4,620; Support Services: $2,447
Enrollment, Drop-out Rates and Diploma Recipients by Race/Ethnicity

Category	Total	White	Black	Asian	AIAN	Hisp.
Enrollment (%)	100.0	2.6	0.4	4.0	0.1	93.0
Drop-out Rate (%)	n/a	n/a	n/a	n/a	n/a	n/a
H.S. Diplomas (#)	1,543	53	6	148	1	1,335

Mountain View Elementary
3320 Gilman Rd • El Monte, CA 91732-3226
(626) 652-4000 • http://www.mvsd.k12.ca.us/index.htm
Grade Span: KG-08; **Agency Type:** 1
Schools: 12
  10 Primary; 2 Middle; 0 High; 0 Other Level
  12 Regular; 0 Special Education; 0 Vocational; 0 Alternative

0 Magnet; 0 Charter; 12 Title I Eligible; 0 School-wide Title I
Students: 10,192   (51.0% male; 48.9% female)
    Individual Education Program: 919 (9.0%);
    English Language Learner: 5,868 (57.6%); Migrant: 608 (6.0%)
    Eligible for Free Lunch Program: 8,001 (78.5%)
    Eligible for Reduced-Price Lunch Program: 356 (3.5%)
Teachers: 485.8 (21.0 to 1)
Librarians/Media Specialists: 1.0 (10,192.0 to 1)
Guidance Counselors: 2.0 (5,096.0 to 1)
Current Spending: ($ per student per year):
    Total: $7,296; Instruction: $4,837; Support Services: $2,041
Enrollment, Drop-out Rates and Diploma Recipients by Race/Ethnicity

Category	Total	White	Black	Asian	AIAN	Hisp.
Enrollment (%)	100.0	1.0	0.3	6.5	0.0	91.7
Drop-out Rate (%)	n/a	n/a	n/a	n/a	n/a	n/a
H.S. Diplomas (#)	n/a	n/a	n/a	n/a	n/a	n/a

Newhall Elementary
25375 Orchard Village Ste. 20 • Valencia, CA 91355-3055
(661) 286-2200 • http://www.newhall.k12.ca.us/
Grade Span: KG-06; **Agency Type:** 1
Schools: 9
    9 Primary; 0 Middle; 0 High; 0 Other Level
    9 Regular; 0 Special Education; 0 Vocational; 0 Alternative
    0 Magnet; 0 Charter; 4 Title I Eligible; 0 School-wide Title I
Students: 6,672   (52.0% male; 47.9% female)
    Individual Education Program: 622 (9.3%);
    English Language Learner: 1,364 (20.4%); Migrant: 0 (0.0%)
    Eligible for Free Lunch Program: 1,340 (20.1%)
    Eligible for Reduced-Price Lunch Program: 380 (5.7%)
Teachers: 291.5 (22.9 to 1)
Librarians/Media Specialists: 0.0 (n/a to 1)
Guidance Counselors: 2.0 (3,336.0 to 1)
Current Spending: ($ per student per year):
    Total: $5,790; Instruction: $3,954; Support Services: $1,835
Enrollment, Drop-out Rates and Diploma Recipients by Race/Ethnicity

Category	Total	White	Black	Asian	AIAN	Hisp.
Enrollment (%)	100.0	54.1	2.4	8.3	0.2	32.0
Drop-out Rate (%)	n/a	n/a	n/a	n/a	n/a	n/a
H.S. Diplomas (#)	n/a	n/a	n/a	n/a	n/a	n/a

Norwalk-La Mirada Unified
12820 Pioneer Blvd • Norwalk, CA 90650-2894
(562) 868-0431 • http://www.nlmusd.k12.ca.us/
Grade Span: KG-12; **Agency Type:** 1
Schools: 29
    18 Primary; 6 Middle; 4 High; 1 Other Level
    28 Regular; 0 Special Education; 0 Vocational; 1 Alternative
    0 Magnet; 0 Charter; 11 Title I Eligible; 11 School-wide Title I
Students: 24,101   (51.6% male; 48.3% female)
    Individual Education Program: 2,460 (10.2%);
    English Language Learner: 4,603 (19.1%); Migrant: 1,323 (5.5%)
    Eligible for Free Lunch Program: 10,073 (41.8%)
    Eligible for Reduced-Price Lunch Program: 2,342 (9.7%)
Teachers: 1,066.4 (22.6 to 1)
Librarians/Media Specialists: 0.0 (n/a to 1)
Guidance Counselors: 27.0 (892.6 to 1)
Current Spending: ($ per student per year):
    Total: $7,341; Instruction: $4,389; Support Services: $2,624
Enrollment, Drop-out Rates and Diploma Recipients by Race/Ethnicity

Category	Total	White	Black	Asian	AIAN	Hisp.
Enrollment (%)	100.0	16.5	4.3	8.1	0.4	70.7
Drop-out Rate (%)	n/a	n/a	n/a	n/a	n/a	n/a
H.S. Diplomas (#)	1,192	276	67	133	5	711

Palmdale Elementary
39139 10th St East. • Palmdale, CA 93550-3419
(661) 947-7191 • http://www.psd.k12.ca.us/
Grade Span: KG-08; **Agency Type:** 1
Schools: 26
    22 Primary; 4 Middle; 0 High; 0 Other Level
    23 Regular; 1 Special Education; 0 Vocational; 2 Alternative
    1 Magnet; 1 Charter; 24 Title I Eligible; 18 School-wide Title I
Students: 22,736   (51.8% male; 48.1% female)
    Individual Education Program: 2,953 (13.0%);
    English Language Learner: 5,528 (24.3%); Migrant: 610 (2.7%)
    Eligible for Free Lunch Program: 11,381 (50.1%)
    Eligible for Reduced-Price Lunch Program: 3,911 (17.2%)
Teachers: 927.2 (24.5 to 1)
Librarians/Media Specialists: 0.0 (n/a to 1)
Guidance Counselors: 4.0 (5,684.0 to 1)
Current Spending: ($ per student per year):
    Total: $7,009; Instruction: $4,561; Support Services: $2,156

Enrollment, Drop-out Rates and Diploma Recipients by Race/Ethnicity

Category	Total	White	Black	Asian	AIAN	Hisp.
Enrollment (%)	100.0	20.2	20.5	2.8	0.7	54.0
Drop-out Rate (%)	n/a	n/a	n/a	n/a	n/a	n/a
H.S. Diplomas (#)	n/a	n/a	n/a	n/a	n/a	n/a

Palos Verdes Peninsula Unified
3801 Via La Selva • Palos Verdes Estates, CA 90274-1119
(310) 378-9966 • http://www.pvpusd.k12.ca.us/
Grade Span: KG-12; **Agency Type:** 1
Schools: 17
    11 Primary; 3 Middle; 2 High; 1 Other Level
    16 Regular; 0 Special Education; 0 Vocational; 1 Alternative
    0 Magnet; 0 Charter; 7 Title I Eligible; 0 School-wide Title I
Students: 11,605   (51.0% male; 48.9% female)
    Individual Education Program: 1,323 (11.4%);
    English Language Learner: 725 (6.2%); Migrant: 0 (0.0%)
    Eligible for Free Lunch Program: 115 (1.0%)
    Eligible for Reduced-Price Lunch Program: 68 (0.6%)
Teachers: 531.6 (21.8 to 1)
Librarians/Media Specialists: 0.0 (n/a to 1)
Guidance Counselors: 17.4 (667.0 to 1)
Current Spending: ($ per student per year):
    Total: $6,918; Instruction: $4,469; Support Services: $2,050
Enrollment, Drop-out Rates and Diploma Recipients by Race/Ethnicity

Category	Total	White	Black	Asian	AIAN	Hisp.
Enrollment (%)	100.0	66.1	1.6	27.7	0.0	3.9
Drop-out Rate (%)	n/a	n/a	n/a	n/a	n/a	n/a
H.S. Diplomas (#)	736	440	15	250	1	30

Paramount Unified
15110 California Ave • Paramount, CA 90723-4320
(562) 602-6000 • http://www.paramount.k12.ca.us/index.html
Grade Span: KG-12; **Agency Type:** 1
Schools: 18
    14 Primary; 0 Middle; 4 High; 0 Other Level
    16 Regular; 0 Special Education; 0 Vocational; 2 Alternative
    1 Magnet; 0 Charter; 18 Title I Eligible; 16 School-wide Title I
Students: 17,013   (49.7% male; 50.2% female)
    Individual Education Program: 1,390 (8.2%);
    English Language Learner: 7,724 (45.4%); Migrant: 211 (1.2%)
    Eligible for Free Lunch Program: 12,220 (71.8%)
    Eligible for Reduced-Price Lunch Program: 2,474 (14.5%)
Teachers: 786.3 (21.6 to 1)
Librarians/Media Specialists: 0.0 (n/a to 1)
Guidance Counselors: 26.8 (634.8 to 1)
Current Spending: ($ per student per year):
    Total: $6,921; Instruction: $4,173; Support Services: $2,408
Enrollment, Drop-out Rates and Diploma Recipients by Race/Ethnicity

Category	Total	White	Black	Asian	AIAN	Hisp.
Enrollment (%)	100.0	3.1	11.0	3.2	0.2	82.5
Drop-out Rate (%)	n/a	n/a	n/a	n/a	n/a	n/a
H.S. Diplomas (#)	593	22	57	33	1	480

Pasadena Unified
351 S Hudson Ave • Pasadena, CA 91101-3507
(626) 795-6981 • http://www.pasadena.k12.ca.us/
Grade Span: KG-12; **Agency Type:** 1
Schools: 32
    23 Primary; 3 Middle; 4 High; 2 Other Level
    31 Regular; 0 Special Education; 0 Vocational; 1 Alternative
    1 Magnet; 0 Charter; 24 Title I Eligible; 22 School-wide Title I
Students: 22,669   (51.1% male; 48.8% female)
    Individual Education Program: 2,859 (12.6%);
    English Language Learner: 6,109 (26.9%); Migrant: 131 (0.6%)
    Eligible for Free Lunch Program: 12,372 (54.6%)
    Eligible for Reduced-Price Lunch Program: 2,059 (9.1%)
Teachers: 1,076.1 (21.1 to 1)
Librarians/Media Specialists: 5.0 (4,533.8 to 1)
Guidance Counselors: 24.0 (944.5 to 1)
Current Spending: ($ per student per year):
    Total: $8,208; Instruction: $4,995; Support Services: $2,876
Enrollment, Drop-out Rates and Diploma Recipients by Race/Ethnicity

Category	Total	White	Black	Asian	AIAN	Hisp.
Enrollment (%)	100.0	15.7	26.0	3.5	0.1	54.1
Drop-out Rate (%)	n/a	n/a	n/a	n/a	n/a	n/a
H.S. Diplomas (#)	970	165	351	37	4	413

Pomona Unified
800 S Garey Ave • Pomona, CA 91766-3325
Mailing Address: PO Box 2900 • Pomona, CA 91769-2900
(909) 397-4800 • http://www.pomona.k12.ca.us/
Grade Span: KG-12; **Agency Type:** 1
Schools: 40
    27 Primary; 6 Middle; 6 High; 1 Other Level

37 Regular; 0 Special Education; 0 Vocational; 3 Alternative
0 Magnet; 0 Charter; 31 Title I Eligible; 26 School-wide Title I
Students: 35,412   (51.3% male; 48.6% female)
Individual Education Program: 3,714 (10.5%);
English Language Learner: 16,006 (45.2%); Migrant: 443 (1.3%)
Eligible for Free Lunch Program: 18,943 (53.5%)
Eligible for Reduced-Price Lunch Program: 4,342 (12.3%)
Teachers: 1,543.5 (22.9 to 1)
Librarians/Media Specialists: 4.0 (8,853.0 to 1)
Guidance Counselors: 20.0 (1,770.6 to 1)
Current Spending: ($ per student per year):
Total: $7,878; Instruction: $4,690; Support Services: $2,870
Enrollment, Drop-out Rates and Diploma Recipients by Race/Ethnicity

Category	Total	White	Black	Asian	AIAN	Hisp.
Enrollment (%)	100.0	7.3	8.0	6.8	0.1	77.8
Drop-out Rate (%)	n/a	n/a	n/a	n/a	n/a	n/a
H.S. Diplomas (#)	1,410	158	146	159	1	946

Redondo Beach Unified
1401 Inglewood Ave • Redondo Beach, CA 90278-3912
(310) 379-5449 • http://www.beachnet.gen.ca.us/rbsd/
Grade Span: KG-12; **Agency Type:** 1
Schools: 12
8 Primary; 2 Middle; 2 High; 0 Other Level
11 Regular; 0 Special Education; 0 Vocational; 1 Alternative
0 Magnet; 0 Charter; 6 Title I Eligible; 0 School-wide Title I
Students: 8,057   (51.5% male; 48.4% female)
Individual Education Program: 1,060 (13.2%);
English Language Learner: 866 (10.7%); Migrant: 0 (0.0%)
Eligible for Free Lunch Program: 1,101 (13.7%)
Eligible for Reduced-Price Lunch Program: 485 (6.0%)
Teachers: 382.8 (21.0 to 1)
Librarians/Media Specialists: 1.0 (8,057.0 to 1)
Guidance Counselors: 10.8 (746.0 to 1)
Current Spending: ($ per student per year):
Total: $7,498; Instruction: $4,648; Support Services: $2,576
Enrollment, Drop-out Rates and Diploma Recipients by Race/Ethnicity

Category	Total	White	Black	Asian	AIAN	Hisp.
Enrollment (%)	100.0	57.0	6.1	11.5	0.5	24.1
Drop-out Rate (%)	n/a	n/a	n/a	n/a	n/a	n/a
H.S. Diplomas (#)	440	274	11	55	0	100

Rosemead Elementary
3907 Rosemead Blvd • Rosemead, CA 91770-2041
(626) 312-2900 • http://www.rosemead.k12.ca.us/
Grade Span: KG-08; **Agency Type:** 1
Schools: 5
4 Primary; 1 Middle; 0 High; 0 Other Level
5 Regular; 0 Special Education; 0 Vocational; 0 Alternative
0 Magnet; 0 Charter; 5 Title I Eligible; 0 School-wide Title I
Students: 3,355   (52.3% male; 47.6% female)
Individual Education Program: 278 (8.3%);
English Language Learner: 1,072 (32.0%); Migrant: 358 (10.7%)
Eligible for Free Lunch Program: 2,047 (61.0%)
Eligible for Reduced-Price Lunch Program: 704 (21.0%)
Teachers: 156.0 (21.5 to 1)
Librarians/Media Specialists: 0.0 (n/a to 1)
Guidance Counselors: 0.0 (n/a to 1)
Current Spending: ($ per student per year):
Total: $7,034; Instruction: $4,370; Support Services: $2,271
Enrollment, Drop-out Rates and Diploma Recipients by Race/Ethnicity

Category	Total	White	Black	Asian	AIAN	Hisp.
Enrollment (%)	100.0	4.5	1.0	45.1	0.1	48.9
Drop-out Rate (%)	n/a	n/a	n/a	n/a	n/a	n/a
H.S. Diplomas (#)	n/a	n/a	n/a	n/a	n/a	n/a

Rowland Unified
1830 Nogales St • Rowland Heights, CA 91748-0490
(626) 965-2541 • http://www.rowland-unified.org/main.htm
Grade Span: KG-12; **Agency Type:** 1
Schools: 22
15 Primary; 3 Middle; 4 High; 0 Other Level
20 Regular; 0 Special Education; 0 Vocational; 2 Alternative
0 Magnet; 0 Charter; 15 Title I Eligible; 15 School-wide Title I
Students: 18,384   (51.3% male; 48.6% female)
Individual Education Program: 1,796 (9.8%);
English Language Learner: 5,793 (31.5%); Migrant: 43 (0.2%)
Eligible for Free Lunch Program: 7,514 (40.9%)
Eligible for Reduced-Price Lunch Program: 2,573 (14.0%)
Teachers: 827.2 (22.2 to 1)
Librarians/Media Specialists: 1.0 (18,384.0 to 1)
Guidance Counselors: 12.0 (1,532.0 to 1)
Current Spending: ($ per student per year):
Total: $7,216; Instruction: $4,565; Support Services: $2,372

Category	Total	White	Black	Asian	AIAN	Hisp.
Enrollment (%)	100.0	5.9	3.8	28.6	0.1	59.3
Drop-out Rate (%)	n/a	n/a	n/a	n/a	n/a	n/a
H.S. Diplomas (#)	1,072	110	62	435	1	464

San Gabriel Unified
408 Junipero Serra Dr • San Gabriel, CA 91776-4500
(626) 451-5400
Grade Span: KG-12; **Agency Type:** 1
Schools: 9
5 Primary; 1 Middle; 2 High; 1 Other Level
7 Regular; 0 Special Education; 0 Vocational; 2 Alternative
0 Magnet; 1 Charter; 3 Title I Eligible; 3 School-wide Title I
Students: 6,265   (51.6% male; 48.3% female)
Individual Education Program: 517 (8.3%);
English Language Learner: 2,066 (33.0%); Migrant: 18 (0.3%)
Eligible for Free Lunch Program: 2,418 (38.6%)
Eligible for Reduced-Price Lunch Program: 751 (12.0%)
Teachers: 289.1 (21.7 to 1)
Librarians/Media Specialists: 2.0 (3,132.5 to 1)
Guidance Counselors: 8.0 (783.1 to 1)
Current Spending: ($ per student per year):
Total: $6,665; Instruction: $3,918; Support Services: $2,335
Enrollment, Drop-out Rates and Diploma Recipients by Race/Ethnicity

Category	Total	White	Black	Asian	AIAN	Hisp.
Enrollment (%)	100.0	14.4	1.6	42.4	0.3	39.7
Drop-out Rate (%)	n/a	n/a	n/a	n/a	n/a	n/a
H.S. Diplomas (#)	416	73	5	173	3	157

San Marino Unified
1665 W Dr • San Marino, CA 91108-2594
(626) 299-7000 • http://www.san-marino.k12.ca.us/
Grade Span: KG-12; **Agency Type:** 1
Schools: 4
2 Primary; 1 Middle; 1 High; 0 Other Level
4 Regular; 0 Special Education; 0 Vocational; 0 Alternative
0 Magnet; 0 Charter; 0 Title I Eligible; 0 School-wide Title I
Students: 3,266   (51.4% male; 48.5% female)
Individual Education Program: 319 (9.8%);
English Language Learner: 196 (6.0%); Migrant: 0 (0.0%)
Eligible for Free Lunch Program: 25 (0.8%)
Eligible for Reduced-Price Lunch Program: 13 (0.4%)
Teachers: 152.4 (21.4 to 1)
Librarians/Media Specialists: 1.0 (3,266.0 to 1)
Guidance Counselors: 5.0 (653.2 to 1)
Current Spending: ($ per student per year):
Total: $7,116; Instruction: $4,376; Support Services: $2,520
Enrollment, Drop-out Rates and Diploma Recipients by Race/Ethnicity

Category	Total	White	Black	Asian	AIAN	Hisp.
Enrollment (%)	100.0	31.2	0.2	64.5	0.0	3.9
Drop-out Rate (%)	n/a	n/a	n/a	n/a	n/a	n/a
H.S. Diplomas (#)	280	59	2	206	0	11

Santa Monica-Malibu Unified
1651 16th St • Santa Monica, CA 90404-3891
(310) 450-8338 • http://www.smmusd.org/
Grade Span: KG-12; **Agency Type:** 1
Schools: 16
11 Primary; 2 Middle; 2 High; 1 Other Level
14 Regular; 0 Special Education; 0 Vocational; 2 Alternative
0 Magnet; 0 Charter; 4 Title I Eligible; 4 School-wide Title I
Students: 12,842   (51.8% male; 48.1% female)
Individual Education Program: 1,619 (12.6%);
English Language Learner: 1,611 (12.5%); Migrant: 0 (0.0%)
Eligible for Free Lunch Program: 2,372 (18.5%)
Eligible for Reduced-Price Lunch Program: 768 (6.0%)
Teachers: 613.4 (20.9 to 1)
Librarians/Media Specialists: 4.0 (3,210.5 to 1)
Guidance Counselors: 23.6 (544.2 to 1)
Current Spending: ($ per student per year):
Total: $8,097; Instruction: $5,180; Support Services: $2,695
Enrollment, Drop-out Rates and Diploma Recipients by Race/Ethnicity

Category	Total	White	Black	Asian	AIAN	Hisp.
Enrollment (%)	100.0	57.8	8.3	6.3	0.3	27.3
Drop-out Rate (%)	n/a	n/a	n/a	n/a	n/a	n/a
H.S. Diplomas (#)	852	458	78	62	0	254

Saugus Union Elementary
24930 Ave Stanford   • Santa Clarita, CA 91355-1272
(661) 294-7500 • http://www.saugus.k12.ca.us/
Grade Span: KG-06; **Agency Type:** 1
Schools: 14
14 Primary; 0 Middle; 0 High; 0 Other Level
14 Regular; 0 Special Education; 0 Vocational; 0 Alternative

0 Magnet; 0 Charter; 2 Title I Eligible; 0 School-wide Title I
Students: 10,204 (51.4% male; 48.5% female)
    Individual Education Program: 1,157 (11.3%);
    English Language Learner: 428 (4.2%); Migrant: 0 (0.0%)
    Eligible for Free Lunch Program: 863 (8.5%)
    Eligible for Reduced-Price Lunch Program: 415 (4.1%)
Teachers: 479.0 (21.3 to 1)
Librarians/Media Specialists: 0.0 (n/a to 1)
Guidance Counselors: 0.5 (20,408.0 to 1)
Current Spending: ($ per student per year):
    Total: $6,380; Instruction: $4,248; Support Services: $1,777
Enrollment, Drop-out Rates and Diploma Recipients by Race/Ethnicity

Category	Total	White	Black	Asian	AIAN	Hisp.
Enrollment (%)	100.0	67.0	3.4	9.7	0.3	19.3
Drop-out Rate (%)	n/a	n/a	n/a	n/a	n/a	n/a
H.S. Diplomas (#)	n/a	n/a	n/a	n/a	n/a	n/a

South Pasadena Unified
1020 El Centro St • South Pasadena, CA 91030-3118
(626) 441-5810 • http://www.spusd.k12.ca.us/
Grade Span: KG-12; **Agency Type:** 1
Schools: 5
    3 Primary; 1 Middle; 1 High; 0 Other Level
    5 Regular; 0 Special Education; 0 Vocational; 0 Alternative
    0 Magnet; 0 Charter; 3 Title I Eligible; 0 School-wide Title I
Students: 4,199 (50.5% male; 49.4% female)
    Individual Education Program: 351 (8.4%)
    English Language Learner: 257 (6.1%); Migrant: 0 (0.0%)
    Eligible for Free Lunch Program: 209 (5.0%)
    Eligible for Reduced-Price Lunch Program: 114 (2.7%)
Teachers: 175.4 (23.9 to 1)
Librarians/Media Specialists: 2.0 (2,099.5 to 1)
Guidance Counselors: 8.0 (524.9 to 1)
Current Spending: ($ per student per year):
    Total: $6,414; Instruction: $4,129; Support Services: $2,101
Enrollment, Drop-out Rates and Diploma Recipients by Race/Ethnicity

Category	Total	White	Black	Asian	AIAN	Hisp.
Enrollment (%)	100.0	35.2	3.2	36.0	0.3	16.1
Drop-out Rate (%)	n/a	n/a	n/a	n/a	n/a	n/a
H.S. Diplomas (#)	301	97	10	143	1	41

South Whittier Elementary
10120 Painter Ave • Whittier, CA 90605-0037
Mailing Address: PO Box 3037 • Whittier, CA 90605-0037
(562) 944-6231
Grade Span: KG-08; **Agency Type:** 1
Schools: 8
    7 Primary; 1 Middle; 0 High; 0 Other Level
    8 Regular; 0 Special Education; 0 Vocational; 0 Alternative
    0 Magnet; 0 Charter; 8 Title I Eligible; 8 School-wide Title I
Students: 4,556 (50.5% male; 49.4% female)
    Individual Education Program: 417 (9.2%);
    English Language Learner: 1,104 (24.2%); Migrant: 177 (3.9%)
    Eligible for Free Lunch Program: 2,456 (53.9%)
    Eligible for Reduced-Price Lunch Program: 1,187 (26.1%)
Teachers: 205.0 (22.2 to 1)
Librarians/Media Specialists: 0.0 (n/a to 1)
Guidance Counselors: 0.0 (n/a to 1)
Current Spending: ($ per student per year):
    Total: $6,909; Instruction: $4,610; Support Services: $1,946
Enrollment, Drop-out Rates and Diploma Recipients by Race/Ethnicity

Category	Total	White	Black	Asian	AIAN	Hisp.
Enrollment (%)	100.0	5.0	0.9	2.1	0.5	91.5
Drop-out Rate (%)	n/a	n/a	n/a	n/a	n/a	n/a
H.S. Diplomas (#)	n/a	n/a	n/a	n/a	n/a	n/a

Sulphur Springs Union Elementary
17866 Sierra Hwy • Canyon Country, CA 91351-1671
(661) 252-5131 • http://www.sssd.k12.ca.us/
Grade Span: KG-06; **Agency Type:** 1
Schools: 8
    8 Primary; 0 Middle; 0 High; 0 Other Level
    8 Regular; 0 Special Education; 0 Vocational; 0 Alternative
    0 Magnet; 0 Charter; 3 Title I Eligible; 2 School-wide Title I
Students: 5,573 (52.2% male; 47.7% female)
    Individual Education Program: 535 (9.6%);
    English Language Learner: 744 (13.4%); Migrant: 0 (0.0%)
    Eligible for Free Lunch Program: 1,435 (25.7%)
    Eligible for Reduced-Price Lunch Program: 439 (7.9%)
Teachers: 257.3 (21.7 to 1)
Librarians/Media Specialists: 0.0 (n/a to 1)
Guidance Counselors: 0.0 (n/a to 1)
Current Spending: ($ per student per year):
    Total: $6,395; Instruction: $4,293; Support Services: $2,101

Category	Total	White	Black	Asian	AIAN	Hisp.
Enrollment (%)	100.0	56.3	5.3	7.0	0.3	31.1
Drop-out Rate (%)	n/a	n/a	n/a	n/a	n/a	n/a
H.S. Diplomas (#)	n/a	n/a	n/a	n/a	n/a	n/a

Temple City Unified
9700 Las Tunas Dr • Temple City, CA 91780-1610
(626) 548-5000 • http://www.templecity.k12.ca.us/
Grade Span: KG-12; **Agency Type:** 1
Schools: 8
    3 Primary; 2 Middle; 2 High; 1 Other Level
    6 Regular; 0 Special Education; 0 Vocational; 2 Alternative
    0 Magnet; 0 Charter; 4 Title I Eligible; 0 School-wide Title I
Students: 5,702 (51.6% male; 48.3% female)
    Individual Education Program: 463 (8.1%);
    English Language Learner: 851 (14.9%); Migrant: 3 (0.1%)
    Eligible for Free Lunch Program: 1,378 (24.2%)
    Eligible for Reduced-Price Lunch Program: 702 (12.3%)
Teachers: 257.3 (22.2 to 1)
Librarians/Media Specialists: 0.8 (7,127.5 to 1)
Guidance Counselors: 7.1 (803.1 to 1)
Current Spending: ($ per student per year):
    Total: $6,445; Instruction: $4,123; Support Services: $2,138
Enrollment, Drop-out Rates and Diploma Recipients by Race/Ethnicity

Category	Total	White	Black	Asian	AIAN	Hisp.
Enrollment (%)	100.0	24.0	0.8	54.6	0.3	18.2
Drop-out Rate (%)	n/a	n/a	n/a	n/a	n/a	n/a
H.S. Diplomas (#)	395	133	4	201	0	56

Torrance Unified
2335 Plaza Del Amo • Torrance, CA 90501-3420
(310) 972-6500 • http://www.tusd.org/
Grade Span: KG-12; **Agency Type:** 1
Schools: 30
    17 Primary; 8 Middle; 5 High; 0 Other Level
    29 Regular; 0 Special Education; 0 Vocational; 1 Alternative
    0 Magnet; 0 Charter; 7 Title I Eligible; 2 School-wide Title I
Students: 25,229 (51.5% male; 48.4% female)
    Individual Education Program: 2,853 (11.3%);
    English Language Learner: 3,048 (12.1%); Migrant: 0 (0.0%)
    Eligible for Free Lunch Program: 2,911 (11.5%)
    Eligible for Reduced-Price Lunch Program: 1,234 (4.9%)
Teachers: 1,139.2 (22.1 to 1)
Librarians/Media Specialists: 3.0 (8,409.7 to 1)
Guidance Counselors: 35.3 (714.7 to 1)
Current Spending: ($ per student per year):
    Total: $7,001; Instruction: $4,600; Support Services: $2,173
Enrollment, Drop-out Rates and Diploma Recipients by Race/Ethnicity

Category	Total	White	Black	Asian	AIAN	Hisp.
Enrollment (%)	100.0	41.7	3.9	35.5	0.7	18.1
Drop-out Rate (%)	n/a	n/a	n/a	n/a	n/a	n/a
H.S. Diplomas (#)	1,813	783	89	590	96	255

Walnut Valley Unified
880 S Lemon Ave • Walnut, CA 91789-2931
(909) 595-1261 • http://www.walnutvalley.k12.ca.us/
Grade Span: KG-12; **Agency Type:** 1
Schools: 15
    9 Primary; 3 Middle; 3 High; 0 Other Level
    14 Regular; 0 Special Education; 0 Vocational; 1 Alternative
    1 Magnet; 0 Charter; 4 Title I Eligible; 0 School-wide Title I
Students: 15,458 (51.5% male; 48.4% female)
    Individual Education Program: 1,065 (6.9%);
    English Language Learner: 1,082 (7.0%); Migrant: 0 (0.0%)
    Eligible for Free Lunch Program: 911 (5.9%)
    Eligible for Reduced-Price Lunch Program: 675 (4.4%)
Teachers: 685.8 (22.5 to 1)
Librarians/Media Specialists: 0.0 (n/a to 1)
Guidance Counselors: 18.0 (858.8 to 1)
Current Spending: ($ per student per year):
    Total: $6,393; Instruction: $3,946; Support Services: $2,296
Enrollment, Drop-out Rates and Diploma Recipients by Race/Ethnicity

Category	Total	White	Black	Asian	AIAN	Hisp.
Enrollment (%)	100.0	18.7	4.2	58.4	0.1	18.5
Drop-out Rate (%)	n/a	n/a	n/a	n/a	n/a	n/a
H.S. Diplomas (#)	1,288	290	73	733	1	191

West Covina Unified
1717 W Merced Ave • West Covina, CA 91790-3406
(626) 939-4600 • http://www.wcusd.k12.ca.us/
Grade Span: KG-12; **Agency Type:** 1
Schools: 13
    8 Primary; 2 Middle; 2 High; 1 Other Level
    12 Regular; 0 Special Education; 0 Vocational; 1 Alternative

0 Magnet; 1 Charter; 11 Title I Eligible; 9 School-wide Title I
Students: 10,518 (51.3% male; 48.6% female)
  Individual Education Program: 560 (5.3%);
  English Language Learner: 1,175 (11.2%); Migrant: 27 (0.3%)
  Eligible for Free Lunch Program: 2,875 (27.3%)
  Eligible for Reduced-Price Lunch Program: 1,806 (17.2%)
Teachers: 456.6 (23.0 to 1)
Librarians/Media Specialists: 0.0 (n/a to 1)
Guidance Counselors: 10.0 (1,051.8 to 1)
Current Spending: ($ per student per year):
  Total: $6,573; Instruction: $3,970; Support Services: $2,352
Enrollment, Drop-out Rates and Diploma Recipients by Race/Ethnicity

Category	Total	White	Black	Asian	AIAN	Hisp.
Enrollment (%)	100.0	11.3	6.4	14.9	0.4	67.0
Drop-out Rate (%)	n/a	n/a	n/a	n/a	n/a	n/a
H.S. Diplomas (#)	587	97	40	119	1	330

Westside Union Elementary
46809 N 70th St W • Lancaster, CA 93535-7836
(661) 948-2669 • http://www.westside.k12.ca.us/
Grade Span: KG-08; **Agency Type:** 1
Schools: 10
  8 Primary; 2 Middle; 0 High; 0 Other Level
  10 Regular; 0 Special Education; 0 Vocational; 0 Alternative
  0 Magnet; 0 Charter; 4 Title I Eligible; 0 School-wide Title I
Students: 7,433 (50.6% male; 49.3% female)
  Individual Education Program: 828 (11.1%);
  English Language Learner: 208 (2.8%); Migrant: 20 (0.3%)
  Eligible for Free Lunch Program: 1,309 (17.6%)
  Eligible for Reduced-Price Lunch Program: 450 (6.1%)
Teachers: 346.5 (21.5 to 1)
Librarians/Media Specialists: 0.0 (n/a to 1)
Guidance Counselors: 3.0 (2,477.7 to 1)
Current Spending: ($ per student per year):
  Total: $5,912; Instruction: $3,943; Support Services: $1,833
Enrollment, Drop-out Rates and Diploma Recipients by Race/Ethnicity

Category	Total	White	Black	Asian	AIAN	Hisp.
Enrollment (%)	100.0	58.2	9.0	2.9	0.9	16.3
Drop-out Rate (%)	n/a	n/a	n/a	n/a	n/a	n/a
H.S. Diplomas (#)	n/a	n/a	n/a	n/a	n/a	n/a

Whittier City Elementary
7211 S Whittier Ave • Whittier, CA 90602-1123
(562) 789-3000 • http://www.whittiercity.k12.ca.us/
Grade Span: KG-08; **Agency Type:** 1
Schools: 13
  11 Primary; 2 Middle; 0 High; 0 Other Level
  13 Regular; 0 Special Education; 0 Vocational; 0 Alternative
  0 Magnet; 0 Charter; 13 Title I Eligible; 9 School-wide Title I
Students: 7,232 (51.1% male; 48.8% female)
  Individual Education Program: 778 (10.8%);
  English Language Learner: 1,699 (23.5%); Migrant: 6 (0.1%)
  Eligible for Free Lunch Program: 2,961 (40.9%)
  Eligible for Reduced-Price Lunch Program: 1,156 (16.0%)
Teachers: 351.7 (20.6 to 1)
Librarians/Media Specialists: 0.0 (n/a to 1)
Guidance Counselors: 5.2 (1,390.8 to 1)
Current Spending: ($ per student per year):
  Total: $7,171; Instruction: $4,762; Support Services: $2,167
Enrollment, Drop-out Rates and Diploma Recipients by Race/Ethnicity

Category	Total	White	Black	Asian	AIAN	Hisp.
Enrollment (%)	100.0	7.4	1.0	1.4	0.3	87.2
Drop-out Rate (%)	n/a	n/a	n/a	n/a	n/a	n/a
H.S. Diplomas (#)	n/a	n/a	n/a	n/a	n/a	n/a

Whittier Union High
9401 S Painter Ave • Whittier, CA 90605-2798
(562) 698-8121 • http://www.wuhsd.k12.ca.us/
Grade Span: 09-12; **Agency Type:** 1
Schools: 7
  0 Primary; 0 Middle; 7 High; 0 Other Level
  5 Regular; 0 Special Education; 0 Vocational; 2 Alternative
  0 Magnet; 0 Charter; 4 Title I Eligible; 0 School-wide Title I
Students: 12,557 (50.9% male; 49.0% female)
  Individual Education Program: 1,143 (9.1%);
  English Language Learner: 1,935 (15.4%); Migrant: 129 (1.0%)
  Eligible for Free Lunch Program: 3,065 (24.4%)
  Eligible for Reduced-Price Lunch Program: 1,026 (8.2%)
Teachers: 490.2 (25.6 to 1)
Librarians/Media Specialists: 1.0 (12,557.0 to 1)
Guidance Counselors: 33.0 (380.5 to 1)
Current Spending: ($ per student per year):
  Total: $7,419; Instruction: $4,392; Support Services: $2,740

Enrollment, Drop-out Rates and Diploma Recipients by Race/Ethnicity

Category	Total	White	Black	Asian	AIAN	Hisp.
Enrollment (%)	100.0	17.8	1.7	2.7	0.4	77.1
Drop-out Rate (%)	n/a	n/a	n/a	n/a	n/a	n/a
H.S. Diplomas (#)	2,093	495	32	101	8	1,454

William S. Hart Union High
21515 Redview Dr • Santa Clarita, CA 91350-2948
(661) 259-0033 • http://www.hart.k12.ca.us/
Grade Span: 07-12; **Agency Type:** 1
Schools: 13
  0 Primary; 5 Middle; 8 High; 0 Other Level
  11 Regular; 0 Special Education; 0 Vocational; 2 Alternative
  0 Magnet; 1 Charter; 5 Title I Eligible; 0 School-wide Title I
Students: 21,122 (51.5% male; 48.4% female)
  Individual Education Program: 2,335 (11.1%);
  English Language Learner: 1,598 (7.6%); Migrant: 0 (0.0%)
  Eligible for Free Lunch Program: 1,977 (9.4%)
  Eligible for Reduced-Price Lunch Program: 587 (2.8%)
Teachers: 839.2 (25.2 to 1)
Librarians/Media Specialists: 7.0 (3,017.4 to 1)
Guidance Counselors: 44.6 (473.6 to 1)
Current Spending: ($ per student per year):
  Total: $6,551; Instruction: $3,983; Support Services: $2,432
Enrollment, Drop-out Rates and Diploma Recipients by Race/Ethnicity

Category	Total	White	Black	Asian	AIAN	Hisp.
Enrollment (%)	100.0	61.9	4.1	8.3	0.5	24.8
Drop-out Rate (%)	n/a	n/a	n/a	n/a	n/a	n/a
H.S. Diplomas (#)	2,393	1,682	87	165	14	440

Wilsona Elementary
18050 E Ave O • Palmdale, CA 93591-3800
(661) 264-1111 • http://www.theav.com/schools/wilsona.htm
Grade Span: KG-08; **Agency Type:** 1
Schools: 4
  3 Primary; 1 Middle; 0 High; 0 Other Level
  3 Regular; 0 Special Education; 0 Vocational; 1 Alternative
  0 Magnet; 0 Charter; 3 Title I Eligible; 3 School-wide Title I
Students: 2,073 (52.9% male; 47.0% female)
  Individual Education Program: 332 (16.0%);
  English Language Learner: 584 (28.2%); Migrant: 88 (4.2%)
  Eligible for Free Lunch Program: 1,499 (72.3%)
  Eligible for Reduced-Price Lunch Program: 247 (11.9%)
Teachers: 101.4 (20.4 to 1)
Librarians/Media Specialists: 0.0 (n/a to 1)
Guidance Counselors: 1.0 (2,073.0 to 1)
Current Spending: ($ per student per year):
  Total: $7,098; Instruction: $4,471; Support Services: $2,264
Enrollment, Drop-out Rates and Diploma Recipients by Race/Ethnicity

Category	Total	White	Black	Asian	AIAN	Hisp.
Enrollment (%)	100.0	25.6	20.9	0.7	2.1	50.7
Drop-out Rate (%)	n/a	n/a	n/a	n/a	n/a	n/a
H.S. Diplomas (#)	n/a	n/a	n/a	n/a	n/a	n/a

Wiseburn Elementary
13530 Aviation Blvd • Hawthorne, CA 90250-6498
(310) 643-3025 • http://www.wiseburn.k12.ca.us/
Grade Span: KG-08; **Agency Type:** 1
Schools: 4
  3 Primary; 1 Middle; 0 High; 0 Other Level
  4 Regular; 0 Special Education; 0 Vocational; 0 Alternative
  0 Magnet; 0 Charter; 1 Title I Eligible; 0 School-wide Title I
Students: 2,008 (51.5% male; 48.4% female)
  Individual Education Program: 163 (8.1%);
  English Language Learner: 210 (10.5%); Migrant: 0 (0.0%)
  Eligible for Free Lunch Program: 502 (25.0%)
  Eligible for Reduced-Price Lunch Program: 297 (14.8%)
Teachers: 98.4 (20.4 to 1)
Librarians/Media Specialists: 0.0 (n/a to 1)
Guidance Counselors: 0.6 (3,346.7 to 1)
Current Spending: ($ per student per year):
  Total: $6,618; Instruction: $4,234; Support Services: $2,156
Enrollment, Drop-out Rates and Diploma Recipients by Race/Ethnicity

Category	Total	White	Black	Asian	AIAN	Hisp.
Enrollment (%)	100.0	24.2	14.0	8.7	0.0	52.7
Drop-out Rate (%)	n/a	n/a	n/a	n/a	n/a	n/a
H.S. Diplomas (#)	n/a	n/a	n/a	n/a	n/a	n/a

Madera County

Chowchilla Elementary
355 N Fifth St • Chowchilla, CA 93610-0907
Mailing Address: PO Box 910 • Chowchilla, CA 93610-0910
(559) 665-8000 • http://www.chowchillaelem.k12.ca.us/
Grade Span: KG-08; **Agency Type:** 1
Schools: 4
  3 Primary; 1 Middle; 0 High; 0 Other Level
  4 Regular; 0 Special Education; 0 Vocational; 0 Alternative
  0 Magnet; 0 Charter; 4 Title I Eligible; 4 School-wide Title I
Students: 1,779 (53.5% male; 46.4% female)
  Individual Education Program: 60 (3.4%);
  English Language Learner: 565 (31.8%); Migrant: 129 (7.3%)
  Eligible for Free Lunch Program: 957 (53.8%)
  Eligible for Reduced-Price Lunch Program: 107 (6.0%)
Teachers: 84.0 (21.2 to 1)
Librarians/Media Specialists: 0.0 (n/a to 1)
Guidance Counselors: 0.0 (n/a to 1)
Current Spending: ($ per student per year):
  Total: $6,379; Instruction: $3,731; Support Services: $2,323
Enrollment, Drop-out Rates and Diploma Recipients by Race/Ethnicity

Category	Total	White	Black	Asian	AIAN	Hisp.
Enrollment (%)	100.0	43.7	2.2	1.5	1.5	50.8
Drop-out Rate (%)	n/a	n/a	n/a	n/a	n/a	n/a
H.S. Diplomas (#)	n/a	n/a	n/a	n/a	n/a	n/a

Madera Unified
1902 Howard Rd • Madera, CA 93637-5123
(559) 675-4500 • http://www.madera.k12.ca.us/
Grade Span: KG-12; **Agency Type:** 1
Schools: 20
  15 Primary; 2 Middle; 2 High; 1 Other Level
  18 Regular; 0 Special Education; 0 Vocational; 2 Alternative
  0 Magnet; 1 Charter; 19 Title I Eligible; 8 School-wide Title I
Students: 17,247 (50.9% male; 49.0% female)
  Individual Education Program: 1,180 (6.8%);
  English Language Learner: 6,907 (40.0%); Migrant: 2,466 (14.3%)
  Eligible for Free Lunch Program: 11,118 (64.5%)
  Eligible for Reduced-Price Lunch Program: 2,184 (12.7%)
Teachers: 828.4 (20.8 to 1)
Librarians/Media Specialists: 3.0 (5,749.0 to 1)
Guidance Counselors: 14.0 (1,231.9 to 1)
Current Spending: ($ per student per year):
  Total: $6,948; Instruction: $4,236; Support Services: $2,400
Enrollment, Drop-out Rates and Diploma Recipients by Race/Ethnicity

Category	Total	White	Black	Asian	AIAN	Hisp.
Enrollment (%)	100.0	17.3	3.4	1.4	0.2	77.4
Drop-out Rate (%)	n/a	n/a	n/a	n/a	n/a	n/a
H.S. Diplomas (#)	796	236	29	15	0	516

Marin County

Dixie Elementary
380 Nova Albion Way • San Rafael, CA 94903-3523
(415) 492-3700 • http://dixiesd.marin.k12.ca.us/dixieschool/
Grade Span: KG-08; **Agency Type:** 1
Schools: 4
  3 Primary; 1 Middle; 0 High; 0 Other Level
  4 Regular; 0 Special Education; 0 Vocational; 0 Alternative
  0 Magnet; 0 Charter; 4 Title I Eligible; 0 School-wide Title I
Students: 1,817 (49.5% male; 50.4% female)
  Individual Education Program: 202 (11.1%);
  English Language Learner: 48 (2.6%); Migrant: 0 (0.0%)
  Eligible for Free Lunch Program: 76 (4.2%)
  Eligible for Reduced-Price Lunch Program: 14 (0.8%)
Teachers: 95.5 (19.0 to 1)
Librarians/Media Specialists: 1.0 (1,817.0 to 1)
Guidance Counselors: 1.0 (1,817.0 to 1)
Current Spending: ($ per student per year):
  Total: $7,620; Instruction: $4,864; Support Services: $2,706
Enrollment, Drop-out Rates and Diploma Recipients by Race/Ethnicity

Category	Total	White	Black	Asian	AIAN	Hisp.
Enrollment (%)	100.0	78.7	2.7	10.6	0.4	7.2
Drop-out Rate (%)	n/a	n/a	n/a	n/a	n/a	n/a
H.S. Diplomas (#)	n/a	n/a	n/a	n/a	n/a	n/a

Mill Valley Elementary
411 Sycamore Ave • Mill Valley, CA 94941-2231
(415) 389-7700 • http://www.mvschools.org/
Grade Span: KG-08; **Agency Type:** 1
Schools: 6
  5 Primary; 1 Middle; 0 High; 0 Other Level
  6 Regular; 0 Special Education; 0 Vocational; 0 Alternative
  0 Magnet; 0 Charter; 3 Title I Eligible; 0 School-wide Title I
Students: 2,236 (51.6% male; 48.3% female)
  Individual Education Program: 214 (9.6%);
  English Language Learner: 54 (2.4%); Migrant: 0 (0.0%)
  Eligible for Free Lunch Program: 43 (1.9%)
  Eligible for Reduced-Price Lunch Program: 13 (0.6%)
Teachers: 124.9 (17.9 to 1)
Librarians/Media Specialists: 4.5 (496.9 to 1)
Guidance Counselors: 2.9 (771.0 to 1)
Current Spending: ($ per student per year):
  Total: $8,177; Instruction: $5,144; Support Services: $3,021
Enrollment, Drop-out Rates and Diploma Recipients by Race/Ethnicity

Category	Total	White	Black	Asian	AIAN	Hisp.
Enrollment (%)	100.0	78.3	1.6	9.1	0.0	4.6
Drop-out Rate (%)	n/a	n/a	n/a	n/a	n/a	n/a
H.S. Diplomas (#)	n/a	n/a	n/a	n/a	n/a	n/a

Novato Unified
1015 Seventh St • Novato, CA 94945-2205
(415) 897-4201 • http://www.novato.ca.us/nusd/
Grade Span: KG-12; **Agency Type:** 1
Schools: 17
  9 Primary; 3 Middle; 4 High; 1 Other Level
  15 Regular; 0 Special Education; 0 Vocational; 2 Alternative
  0 Magnet; 2 Charter; 8 Title I Eligible; 0 School-wide Title I
Students: 7,813 (51.7% male; 48.2% female)
  Individual Education Program: 916 (11.7%);
  English Language Learner: 854 (10.9%); Migrant: 7 (0.1%)
  Eligible for Free Lunch Program: 898 (11.5%)
  Eligible for Reduced-Price Lunch Program: 392 (5.0%)
Teachers: 382.8 (20.4 to 1)
Librarians/Media Specialists: 6.8 (1,149.0 to 1)
Guidance Counselors: 7.0 (1,116.1 to 1)
Current Spending: ($ per student per year):
  Total: $6,608; Instruction: $4,204; Support Services: $2,251
Enrollment, Drop-out Rates and Diploma Recipients by Race/Ethnicity

Category	Total	White	Black	Asian	AIAN	Hisp.
Enrollment (%)	100.0	69.4	3.0	6.3	0.1	18.4
Drop-out Rate (%)	n/a	n/a	n/a	n/a	n/a	n/a
H.S. Diplomas (#)	481	380	9	39	1	51

Ross Valley Elementary
110 Show Dr • San Anselmo, CA 94960-1112
(415) 454-2162
Grade Span: KG-08; **Agency Type:** 1
Schools: 4
  3 Primary; 1 Middle; 0 High; 0 Other Level
  4 Regular; 0 Special Education; 0 Vocational; 0 Alternative
  1 Magnet; 0 Charter; 2 Title I Eligible; 0 School-wide Title I
Students: 1,816 (49.8% male; 50.1% female)
  Individual Education Program: 225 (12.4%);
  English Language Learner: 60 (3.3%); Migrant: 0 (0.0%)
  Eligible for Free Lunch Program: 109 (6.0%)
  Eligible for Reduced-Price Lunch Program: 38 (2.1%)
Teachers: 95.9 (18.9 to 1)
Librarians/Media Specialists: 0.0 (n/a to 1)
Guidance Counselors: 1.0 (1,816.0 to 1)
Current Spending: ($ per student per year):
  Total: $7,601; Instruction: $4,822; Support Services: $2,663
Enrollment, Drop-out Rates and Diploma Recipients by Race/Ethnicity

Category	Total	White	Black	Asian	AIAN	Hisp.
Enrollment (%)	100.0	85.5	1.8	4.7	0.2	5.8
Drop-out Rate (%)	n/a	n/a	n/a	n/a	n/a	n/a
H.S. Diplomas (#)	n/a	n/a	n/a	n/a	n/a	n/a

San Rafael City Elementary
310 Nova Albion Way • San Rafael, CA 94903-3523
(415) 492-3233 • http://mcoeweb.marin.k12.ca.us/
Grade Span: KG-08; **Agency Type:** 2
Schools: 8
  7 Primary; 1 Middle; 0 High; 0 Other Level
  8 Regular; 0 Special Education; 0 Vocational; 0 Alternative
  0 Magnet; 0 Charter; 6 Title I Eligible; 1 School-wide Title I
Students: 3,500 (52.8% male; 47.1% female)
  Individual Education Program: 501 (14.3%);
  English Language Learner: 1,375 (39.3%); Migrant: 0 (0.0%)
  Eligible for Free Lunch Program: 1,486 (42.5%)
  Eligible for Reduced-Price Lunch Program: 356 (10.2%)
Teachers: 200.4 (17.5 to 1)
Librarians/Media Specialists: 1.0 (3,500.0 to 1)
Guidance Counselors: 2.4 (1,458.3 to 1)
Current Spending: ($ per student per year):
  Total: $7,609; Instruction: $5,134; Support Services: $2,214

Enrollment, Drop-out Rates and Diploma Recipients by Race/Ethnicity

Category	Total	White	Black	Asian	AIAN	Hisp.
Enrollment (%)	100.0	34.3	4.6	5.9	0.2	51.5
Drop-out Rate (%)	n/a	n/a	n/a	n/a	n/a	n/a
H.S. Diplomas (#)	n/a	n/a	n/a	n/a	n/a	n/a

San Rafael City High
310 Nova Albione • San Rafael, CA 94903-3500
(415) 492-3233
Grade Span: 09-12; **Agency Type:** 2
Schools: 3
   0 Primary; 0 Middle; 3 High; 0 Other Level
   2 Regular; 0 Special Education; 0 Vocational; 1 Alternative
   0 Magnet; 0 Charter; 2 Title I Eligible; 0 School-wide Title I
Students: 2,036 (51.4% male; 48.5% female)
   Individual Education Program: 232 (11.4%);
   English Language Learner: 229 (11.2%); Migrant: 0 (0.0%)
   Eligible for Free Lunch Program: 312 (15.3%)
   Eligible for Reduced-Price Lunch Program: 52 (2.6%)
Teachers: 100.2 (20.3 to 1)
Librarians/Media Specialists: 1.0 (2,036.0 to 1)
Guidance Counselors: 4.8 (424.2 to 1)
Current Spending: ($ per student per year):
   Total: $8,946; Instruction: $4,522; Support Services: $3,878
Enrollment, Drop-out Rates and Diploma Recipients by Race/Ethnicity

Category	Total	White	Black	Asian	AIAN	Hisp.
Enrollment (%)	100.0	57.8	3.3	8.0	0.5	29.3
Drop-out Rate (%)	n/a	n/a	n/a	n/a	n/a	n/a
H.S. Diplomas (#)	407	259	12	42	1	91

Tamalpais Union High
395 Doherty Dr • Larkspur, CA 94977-0605
Mailing Address: PO Box 605 • Larkspur, CA 94977-0605
(415) 945-3737 • http://www.tamdistrict.org/
Grade Span: KG-12; **Agency Type:** 1
Schools: 5
   0 Primary; 0 Middle; 5 High; 0 Other Level
   3 Regular; 0 Special Education; 0 Vocational; 2 Alternative
   0 Magnet; 0 Charter; 2 Title I Eligible; 0 School-wide Title I
Students: 3,860 (50.5% male; 49.4% female)
   Individual Education Program: 332 (8.6%);
   English Language Learner: 54 (1.4%); Migrant: 1 (<0.1%)
   Eligible for Free Lunch Program: 78 (2.0%)
   Eligible for Reduced-Price Lunch Program: 14 (0.4%)
Teachers: 210.9 (18.3 to 1)
Librarians/Media Specialists: 3.0 (1,286.7 to 1)
Guidance Counselors: 11.6 (332.8 to 1)
Current Spending: ($ per student per year):
   Total: $10,218; Instruction: $5,878; Support Services: $4,192
Enrollment, Drop-out Rates and Diploma Recipients by Race/Ethnicity

Category	Total	White	Black	Asian	AIAN	Hisp.
Enrollment (%)	100.0	78.1	3.4	6.2	0.7	5.0
Drop-out Rate (%)	n/a	n/a	n/a	n/a	n/a	n/a
H.S. Diplomas (#)	827	693	20	48	5	52

Mariposa County

Mariposa County Unified
5082 Old Hwy N • Mariposa, CA 95338-0008
Mailing Address: PO Box 8 • Mariposa, CA 95338-0008
(209) 742-0250 • http://www.mariposa.k12.ca.us/
Grade Span: KG-12; **Agency Type:** 1
Schools: 14
   7 Primary; 1 Middle; 5 High; 1 Other Level
   11 Regular; 0 Special Education; 0 Vocational; 3 Alternative
   0 Magnet; 0 Charter; 11 Title I Eligible; 1 School-wide Title I
Students: 2,488 (50.6% male; 49.3% female)
   Individual Education Program: 413 (16.6%);
   English Language Learner: 23 (0.9%); Migrant: 0 (0.0%)
   Eligible for Free Lunch Program: 708 (28.5%)
   Eligible for Reduced-Price Lunch Program: 202 (8.1%)
Teachers: 132.6 (18.8 to 1)
Librarians/Media Specialists: 0.0 (n/a to 1)
Guidance Counselors: 5.0 (497.6 to 1)
Current Spending: ($ per student per year):
   Total: $7,853; Instruction: $4,419; Support Services: $3,245
Enrollment, Drop-out Rates and Diploma Recipients by Race/Ethnicity

Category	Total	White	Black	Asian	AIAN	Hisp.
Enrollment (%)	100.0	80.4	0.9	1.2	6.2	6.0
Drop-out Rate (%)	n/a	n/a	n/a	n/a	n/a	n/a
H.S. Diplomas (#)	194	159	2	9	13	10

Mendocino County

Fort Bragg Unified
312 S Lincoln St • Fort Bragg, CA 95437-4416
(707) 961-2850 • http://www.fortbragg.k12.ca.us
Grade Span: KG-12; **Agency Type:** 1
Schools: 8
   3 Primary; 2 Middle; 3 High; 0 Other Level
   5 Regular; 0 Special Education; 0 Vocational; 3 Alternative
   0 Magnet; 0 Charter; 6 Title I Eligible; 0 School-wide Title I
Students: 2,075 (52.5% male; 47.4% female)
   Individual Education Program: 253 (12.2%);
   English Language Learner: 437 (21.1%); Migrant: 334 (16.1%)
   Eligible for Free Lunch Program: 1,040 (50.1%)
   Eligible for Reduced-Price Lunch Program: 263 (12.7%)
Teachers: 121.5 (17.1 to 1)
Librarians/Media Specialists: 0.0 (n/a to 1)
Guidance Counselors: 3.6 (576.4 to 1)
Current Spending: ($ per student per year):
   Total: $7,810; Instruction: $5,002; Support Services: $2,530
Enrollment, Drop-out Rates and Diploma Recipients by Race/Ethnicity

Category	Total	White	Black	Asian	AIAN	Hisp.
Enrollment (%)	100.0	62.7	1.2	1.4	1.0	29.1
Drop-out Rate (%)	n/a	n/a	n/a	n/a	n/a	n/a
H.S. Diplomas (#)	144	110	0	4	2	26

Ukiah Unified
925 N State St • Ukiah, CA 95482-3411
(707) 463-5211 • http://www.uusd.net/
Grade Span: KG-12; **Agency Type:** 1
Schools: 16
   7 Primary; 2 Middle; 3 High; 4 Other Level
   15 Regular; 0 Special Education; 0 Vocational; 1 Alternative
   0 Magnet; 4 Charter; 13 Title I Eligible; 0 School-wide Title I
Students: 6,828 (51.5% male; 48.4% female)
   Individual Education Program: 924 (13.5%);
   English Language Learner: 1,552 (22.7%); Migrant: 1,424 (20.9%)
   Eligible for Free Lunch Program: 3,031 (44.4%)
   Eligible for Reduced-Price Lunch Program: 779 (11.4%)
Teachers: 352.2 (19.4 to 1)
Librarians/Media Specialists: 1.0 (6,828.0 to 1)
Guidance Counselors: 8.0 (853.5 to 1)
Current Spending: ($ per student per year):
   Total: $7,273; Instruction: $4,675; Support Services: $2,280
Enrollment, Drop-out Rates and Diploma Recipients by Race/Ethnicity

Category	Total	White	Black	Asian	AIAN	Hisp.
Enrollment (%)	100.0	57.5	1.1	2.1	6.9	31.9
Drop-out Rate (%)	n/a	n/a	n/a	n/a	n/a	n/a
H.S. Diplomas (#)	509	364	9	18	20	98

Willits Unified
618 S Main St • Willits, CA 95490-3007
(707) 459-5314 • http://ntap.k12.ca.us/wusd/index.shtml
Grade Span: KG-12; **Agency Type:** 1
Schools: 10
   3 Primary; 2 Middle; 3 High; 2 Other Level
   6 Regular; 0 Special Education; 0 Vocational; 4 Alternative
   0 Magnet; 1 Charter; 5 Title I Eligible; 1 School-wide Title I
Students: 2,240 (53.0% male; 46.9% female)
   Individual Education Program: 289 (12.9%);
   English Language Learner: 196 (8.8%); Migrant: 195 (8.7%)
   Eligible for Free Lunch Program: 996 (44.5%)
   Eligible for Reduced-Price Lunch Program: 241 (10.8%)
Teachers: 125.1 (17.9 to 1)
Librarians/Media Specialists: 1.0 (2,240.0 to 1)
Guidance Counselors: 2.7 (829.6 to 1)
Current Spending: ($ per student per year):
   Total: $7,338; Instruction: $4,774; Support Services: $2,292
Enrollment, Drop-out Rates and Diploma Recipients by Race/Ethnicity

Category	Total	White	Black	Asian	AIAN	Hisp.
Enrollment (%)	100.0	70.5	0.5	2.0	6.9	17.9
Drop-out Rate (%)	n/a	n/a	n/a	n/a	n/a	n/a
H.S. Diplomas (#)	165	143	1	5	4	11

Merced County

Atwater Elementary
1401 Broadway Ave • Atwater, CA 95301-3546
(209) 357-6100 • http://www.aesd.k12.ca.us/
Grade Span: KG-08; **Agency Type:** 1
Schools: 9
   7 Primary; 2 Middle; 0 High; 0 Other Level
   9 Regular; 0 Special Education; 0 Vocational; 0 Alternative
   0 Magnet; 0 Charter; 8 Title I Eligible; 8 School-wide Title I
Students: 4,764 (50.8% male; 49.1% female)

Individual Education Program: 436 (9.2%);
English Language Learner: 1,626 (34.1%); Migrant: 374 (7.9%)
Eligible for Free Lunch Program: 2,648 (55.6%)
Eligible for Reduced-Price Lunch Program: 731 (15.3%)
Teachers: 230.1 (20.7 to 1)
Librarians/Media Specialists: 1.0 (4,764.0 to 1)
Guidance Counselors: 2.0 (2,382.0 to 1)
Current Spending: ($ per student per year):
Total: $6,833; Instruction: $4,365; Support Services: $2,054
Enrollment, Drop-out Rates and Diploma Recipients by Race/Ethnicity

Category	Total	White	Black	Asian	AIAN	Hisp.
Enrollment (%)	100.0	29.7	6.2	7.7	0.5	55.5
Drop-out Rate (%)	n/a	n/a	n/a	n/a	n/a	n/a
H.S. Diplomas (#)	n/a	n/a	n/a	n/a	n/a	n/a

Delhi Unified
9716 Hinton Ave • Delhi, CA 95315-0338
Mailing Address: 9715 Hinton Ave • Delhi, CA 95315-0338
(209) 668-6130 • http://www.delhi.k12.ca.us/
Grade Span: KG-12; **Agency Type:** 1
Schools: 5
2 Primary; 1 Middle; 2 High; 0 Other Level
4 Regular; 0 Special Education; 0 Vocational; 1 Alternative
0 Magnet; 0 Charter; 3 Title I Eligible; 2 School-wide Title I
Students: 2,554   (50.0% male; 49.9% female)
Individual Education Program: 269 (10.5%);
English Language Learner: 1,309 (51.3%); Migrant: 239 (9.4%)
Eligible for Free Lunch Program: 1,374 (53.8%)
Eligible for Reduced-Price Lunch Program: 269 (10.5%)
Teachers: 117.0 (21.8 to 1)
Librarians/Media Specialists: 1.0 (2,554.0 to 1)
Guidance Counselors: 0.0 (n/a to 1)
Current Spending: ($ per student per year):
Total: $6,169; Instruction: $3,916; Support Services: $1,980
Enrollment, Drop-out Rates and Diploma Recipients by Race/Ethnicity

Category	Total	White	Black	Asian	AIAN	Hisp.
Enrollment (%)	100.0	19.3	2.3	3.5	0.4	74.5
Drop-out Rate (%)	n/a	n/a	n/a	n/a	n/a	n/a
H.S. Diplomas (#)	80	14	1	1	0	64

Dos Palos Oro Loma Jt. Unified
2041 Almond St • Dos Palos, CA 93620-2303
(209) 392-6101 • http://www.dpol.k12.ca.us/
Grade Span: KG-12; **Agency Type:** 1
Schools: 7
3 Primary; 1 Middle; 2 High; 1 Other Level
6 Regular; 0 Special Education; 0 Vocational; 1 Alternative
1 Magnet; 0 Charter; 6 Title I Eligible; 6 School-wide Title I
Students: 2,685   (52.3% male; 47.6% female)
Individual Education Program: 353 (13.1%);
English Language Learner: 1,035 (38.5%); Migrant: 470 (17.5%)
Eligible for Free Lunch Program: 1,683 (62.7%)
Eligible for Reduced-Price Lunch Program: 316 (11.8%)
Teachers: 137.6 (19.5 to 1)
Librarians/Media Specialists: 2.0 (1,342.5 to 1)
Guidance Counselors: 4.9 (548.0 to 1)
Current Spending: ($ per student per year):
Total: $7,807; Instruction: $4,747; Support Services: $2,722
Enrollment, Drop-out Rates and Diploma Recipients by Race/Ethnicity

Category	Total	White	Black	Asian	AIAN	Hisp.
Enrollment (%)	100.0	25.1	4.1	0.3	0.1	69.2
Drop-out Rate (%)	n/a	n/a	n/a	n/a	n/a	n/a
H.S. Diplomas (#)	171	67	14	1	1	88

Gustine Unified
1500 Meredith Ave • Gustine, CA 95322-1127
(209) 854-3784 • http://www.gustine.k12.ca.us/
Grade Span: KG-12; **Agency Type:** 1
Schools: 5
2 Primary; 1 Middle; 2 High; 0 Other Level
4 Regular; 0 Special Education; 0 Vocational; 1 Alternative
0 Magnet; 0 Charter; 3 Title I Eligible; 3 School-wide Title I
Students: 1,929   (53.4% male; 46.5% female)
Individual Education Program: 157 (8.1%);
English Language Learner: 762 (39.5%); Migrant: 374 (19.4%)
Eligible for Free Lunch Program: 886 (45.9%)
Eligible for Reduced-Price Lunch Program: 235 (12.2%)
Teachers: 99.0 (19.5 to 1)
Librarians/Media Specialists: 0.0 (n/a to 1)
Guidance Counselors: 1.0 (1,929.0 to 1)
Current Spending: ($ per student per year):
Total: $6,760; Instruction: $4,440; Support Services: $2,038

Enrollment, Drop-out Rates and Diploma Recipients by Race/Ethnicity

Category	Total	White	Black	Asian	AIAN	Hisp.
Enrollment (%)	100.0	35.3	0.7	1.0	0.1	62.1
Drop-out Rate (%)	n/a	n/a	n/a	n/a	n/a	n/a
H.S. Diplomas (#)	117	61	0	2	0	54

Hilmar Unified
7807 N Lander Ave • Hilmar, CA 95324-9398
(209) 667-5701 • http://www.hilmar.k12.ca.us/
Grade Span: KG-12; **Agency Type:** 1
Schools: 6
2 Primary; 1 Middle; 3 High; 0 Other Level
4 Regular; 0 Special Education; 0 Vocational; 2 Alternative
0 Magnet; 0 Charter; 3 Title I Eligible; 1 School-wide Title I
Students: 2,330   (50.9% male; 49.0% female)
Individual Education Program: 237 (10.2%);
English Language Learner: 611 (26.2%); Migrant: 82 (3.5%)
Eligible for Free Lunch Program: 698 (30.0%)
Eligible for Reduced-Price Lunch Program: 228 (9.8%)
Teachers: 120.7 (19.3 to 1)
Librarians/Media Specialists: 0.0 (n/a to 1)
Guidance Counselors: 1.0 (2,330.0 to 1)
Current Spending: ($ per student per year):
Total: $6,795; Instruction: $4,368; Support Services: $2,142
Enrollment, Drop-out Rates and Diploma Recipients by Race/Ethnicity

Category	Total	White	Black	Asian	AIAN	Hisp.
Enrollment (%)	100.0	73.9	0.6	2.2	0.2	23.0
Drop-out Rate (%)	n/a	n/a	n/a	n/a	n/a	n/a
H.S. Diplomas (#)	174	142	1	1	1	29

Livingston Union Elementary
922 B St • Livingston, CA 95334-1150
(209) 394-5400 • http://www.lusd.k12.ca.us/
Grade Span: KG-08; **Agency Type:** 1
Schools: 4
3 Primary; 1 Middle; 0 High; 0 Other Level
4 Regular; 0 Special Education; 0 Vocational; 0 Alternative
0 Magnet; 0 Charter; 4 Title I Eligible; 3 School-wide Title I
Students: 2,433   (51.5% male; 48.4% female)
Individual Education Program: 222 (9.1%);
English Language Learner: 1,599 (65.7%); Migrant: 350 (14.4%)
Eligible for Free Lunch Program: 1,745 (71.7%)
Eligible for Reduced-Price Lunch Program: 394 (16.2%)
Teachers: 120.4 (20.2 to 1)
Librarians/Media Specialists: 1.0 (2,433.0 to 1)
Guidance Counselors: 1.5 (1,622.0 to 1)
Current Spending: ($ per student per year):
Total: $7,454; Instruction: $4,838; Support Services: $2,228
Enrollment, Drop-out Rates and Diploma Recipients by Race/Ethnicity

Category	Total	White	Black	Asian	AIAN	Hisp.
Enrollment (%)	100.0	8.9	1.3	12.1	0.0	77.7
Drop-out Rate (%)	n/a	n/a	n/a	n/a	n/a	n/a
H.S. Diplomas (#)	n/a	n/a	n/a	n/a	n/a	n/a

Los Banos Unified
1717 S 11th St • Los Banos, CA 93635-4800
(209) 826-3801 • http://www.losbanosusd.k12.ca.us/
Grade Span: KG-12; **Agency Type:** 1
Schools: 10
5 Primary; 2 Middle; 3 High; 0 Other Level
8 Regular; 0 Special Education; 0 Vocational; 2 Alternative
0 Magnet; 0 Charter; 6 Title I Eligible; 2 School-wide Title I
Students: 8,227   (51.7% male; 48.2% female)
Individual Education Program: 385 (4.7%);
English Language Learner: 2,127 (25.9%); Migrant: 424 (5.2%)
Eligible for Free Lunch Program: 3,444 (41.9%)
Eligible for Reduced-Price Lunch Program: 1,002 (12.2%)
Teachers: 382.1 (21.5 to 1)
Librarians/Media Specialists: 3.2 (2,570.9 to 1)
Guidance Counselors: 0.0 (n/a to 1)
Current Spending: ($ per student per year):
Total: $6,273; Instruction: $3,775; Support Services: $2,244
Enrollment, Drop-out Rates and Diploma Recipients by Race/Ethnicity

Category	Total	White	Black	Asian	AIAN	Hisp.
Enrollment (%)	100.0	25.7	3.9	2.9	0.6	64.4
Drop-out Rate (%)	n/a	n/a	n/a	n/a	n/a	n/a
H.S. Diplomas (#)	424	166	20	21	0	215

Merced City Elementary
444 W 23rd St • Merced, CA 95340-3723
(209) 385-6600 • http://www.mcsd.k12.ca.us/
Grade Span: KG-08; **Agency Type:** 1
Schools: 17
13 Primary; 4 Middle; 0 High; 0 Other Level
16 Regular; 0 Special Education; 0 Vocational; 1 Alternative

0 Magnet; 1 Charter; 16 Title I Eligible; 16 School-wide Title I
Students: 11,414   (50.9% male; 49.0% female)
   Individual Education Program: 1,209 (10.6%);
   English Language Learner: 3,412 (29.9%); Migrant: 535 (4.7%)
   Eligible for Free Lunch Program: 6,966 (61.0%)
   Eligible for Reduced-Price Lunch Program: 1,241 (10.9%)
Teachers: 525.0 (21.7 to 1)
Librarians/Media Specialists: 16.0 (713.4 to 1)
Guidance Counselors: 8.3 (1,375.2 to 1)
Current Spending: ($ per student per year):
   Total: $7,501; Instruction: $5,018; Support Services: $2,115
Enrollment, Drop-out Rates and Diploma Recipients by Race/Ethnicity

Category	Total	White	Black	Asian	AIAN	Hisp.
Enrollment (%)	100.0	24.6	7.4	17.3	0.3	50.3
Drop-out Rate (%)	n/a	n/a	n/a	n/a	n/a	n/a
H.S. Diplomas (#)	n/a	n/a	n/a	n/a	n/a	n/a

Merced Union High
3430 A St · Atwater, CA 95301
Mailing Address: PO Box 2147 · Merced, CA 95344-0147
(209) 385-6412 · http://www.muhsd.k12.ca.us/
Grade Span: 09-12; **Agency Type:** 1
Schools: 7
   0 Primary; 0 Middle; 7 High; 0 Other Level
   5 Regular; 0 Special Education; 0 Vocational; 2 Alternative
   0 Magnet; 0 Charter; 7 Title I Eligible; 5 School-wide Title I
Students: 9,695   (50.2% male; 49.7% female)
   Individual Education Program: 1,147 (11.8%);
   English Language Learner: 1,699 (17.5%); Migrant: 660 (6.8%)
   Eligible for Free Lunch Program: 5,582 (57.6%)
   Eligible for Reduced-Price Lunch Program: 1,097 (11.3%)
Teachers: 411.7 (23.5 to 1)
Librarians/Media Specialists: 5.2 (1,864.4 to 1)
Guidance Counselors: 19.0 (510.3 to 1)
Current Spending: ($ per student per year):
   Total: $6,818; Instruction: $4,037; Support Services: $2,505
Enrollment, Drop-out Rates and Diploma Recipients by Race/Ethnicity

Category	Total	White	Black	Asian	AIAN	Hisp.
Enrollment (%)	100.0	29.3	5.1	17.0	0.4	46.9
Drop-out Rate (%)	n/a	n/a	n/a	n/a	n/a	n/a
H.S. Diplomas (#)	1,951	695	93	367	14	779

Weaver Union Elementary
3076 E Childs Ave · Merced, CA 95340-9583
(209) 723-7606
Grade Span: KG-08; **Agency Type:** 1
Schools: 2
   1 Primary; 1 Middle; 0 High; 0 Other Level
   2 Regular; 0 Special Education; 0 Vocational; 0 Alternative
   0 Magnet; 0 Charter; 2 Title I Eligible; 2 School-wide Title I
Students: 1,683   (51.2% male; 48.7% female)
   Individual Education Program: 151 (9.0%);
   English Language Learner: 787 (46.8%); Migrant: 122 (7.2%)
   Eligible for Free Lunch Program: 1,147 (68.2%)
   Eligible for Reduced-Price Lunch Program: 209 (12.4%)
Teachers: 93.0 (18.1 to 1)
Librarians/Media Specialists: 1.5 (1,122.0 to 1)
Guidance Counselors: 2.0 (841.5 to 1)
Current Spending: ($ per student per year):
   Total: $6,668; Instruction: $4,544; Support Services: $1,786
Enrollment, Drop-out Rates and Diploma Recipients by Race/Ethnicity

Category	Total	White	Black	Asian	AIAN	Hisp.
Enrollment (%)	100.0	23.1	8.5	14.0	0.0	54.4
Drop-out Rate (%)	n/a	n/a	n/a	n/a	n/a	n/a
H.S. Diplomas (#)	n/a	n/a	n/a	n/a	n/a	n/a

Winton Elementary
7000 N Center St · Winton, CA 95388-0008
Mailing Address: PO Box 8 · Winton, CA 95388-0008
(209) 357-6175
Grade Span: KG-08; **Agency Type:** 1
Schools: 3
   2 Primary; 1 Middle; 0 High; 0 Other Level
   3 Regular; 0 Special Education; 0 Vocational; 0 Alternative
   0 Magnet; 0 Charter; 3 Title I Eligible; 3 School-wide Title I
Students: 1,808   (51.3% male; 48.6% female)
   Individual Education Program: 120 (6.6%);
   English Language Learner: 1,012 (56.0%); Migrant: 208 (11.5%)
   Eligible for Free Lunch Program: 1,376 (76.1%)
   Eligible for Reduced-Price Lunch Program: 232 (12.8%)
Teachers: 92.8 (19.5 to 1)
Librarians/Media Specialists: 0.0 (n/a to 1)
Guidance Counselors: 1.0 (1,808.0 to 1)
Current Spending: ($ per student per year):
   Total: $7,070; Instruction: $4,438; Support Services: $2,220

Category	Total	White	Black	Asian	AIAN	Hisp.
Enrollment (%)	100.0	12.4	2.3	7.5	0.2	77.5
Drop-out Rate (%)	n/a	n/a	n/a	n/a	n/a	n/a
H.S. Diplomas (#)	n/a	n/a	n/a	n/a	n/a	n/a

Monterey County

Alisal Union Elementary
1205 E Market St · Salinas, CA 93905-2831
(831) 753-5700 · http://www.monterey.k12.ca.us/~alisaldo/
Grade Span: KG-08; **Agency Type:** 1
Schools: 12
   11 Primary; 1 Middle; 0 High; 0 Other Level
   12 Regular; 0 Special Education; 0 Vocational; 0 Alternative
   0 Magnet; 1 Charter; 11 Title I Eligible; 9 School-wide Title I
Students: 7,951   (51.5% male; 48.4% female)
   Individual Education Program: 518 (6.5%);
   English Language Learner: 5,497 (69.1%); Migrant: 3,933 (49.5%)
   Eligible for Free Lunch Program: 5,430 (68.3%)
   Eligible for Reduced-Price Lunch Program: 1,494 (18.8%)
Teachers: 333.0 (23.9 to 1)
Librarians/Media Specialists: 1.0 (7,951.0 to 1)
Guidance Counselors: 0.0 (n/a to 1)
Current Spending: ($ per student per year):
   Total: $7,658; Instruction: $4,826; Support Services: $2,481
Enrollment, Drop-out Rates and Diploma Recipients by Race/Ethnicity

Category	Total	White	Black	Asian	AIAN	Hisp.
Enrollment (%)	100.0	4.6	1.3	3.7	0.1	89.8
Drop-out Rate (%)	n/a	n/a	n/a	n/a	n/a	n/a
H.S. Diplomas (#)	n/a	n/a	n/a	n/a	n/a	n/a

Carmel Unified
4380 Carmel Valley Rd · Carmel, CA 93922-2700
Mailing Address: PO Box 222700 · Carmel, CA 93922-2700
(831) 624-1546 · http://schools.monterey.k12.ca.us/~carmeldo/
Grade Span: KG-12; **Agency Type:** 1
Schools: 6
   3 Primary; 1 Middle; 2 High; 0 Other Level
   5 Regular; 0 Special Education; 0 Vocational; 1 Alternative
   0 Magnet; 0 Charter; 2 Title I Eligible; 0 School-wide Title I
Students: 2,181   (52.1% male; 47.8% female)
   Individual Education Program: 203 (9.3%);
   English Language Learner: 107 (4.9%); Migrant: 0 (0.0%)
   Eligible for Free Lunch Program: 122 (5.6%)
   Eligible for Reduced-Price Lunch Program: 111 (5.1%)
Teachers: 127.2 (17.1 to 1)
Librarians/Media Specialists: 2.0 (1,090.5 to 1)
Guidance Counselors: 7.0 (311.6 to 1)
Current Spending: ($ per student per year):
   Total: $11,783; Instruction: $6,945; Support Services: $4,639
Enrollment, Drop-out Rates and Diploma Recipients by Race/Ethnicity

Category	Total	White	Black	Asian	AIAN	Hisp.
Enrollment (%)	100.0	77.7	1.1	3.5	0.9	10.5
Drop-out Rate (%)	n/a	n/a	n/a	n/a	n/a	n/a
H.S. Diplomas (#)	177	151	1	9	1	13

Gonzales Unified
600 Elko St · Gonzales, CA 93926-3033
Mailing Address: PO Drawer G · Gonzales, CA 93926-3033
(831) 675-0100 · http://schools.monterey.k12.ca.us/~gonzunif/
Grade Span: KG-12; **Agency Type:** 1
Schools: 4
   1 Primary; 1 Middle; 2 High; 0 Other Level
   3 Regular; 0 Special Education; 0 Vocational; 1 Alternative
   0 Magnet; 0 Charter; 3 Title I Eligible; 3 School-wide Title I
Students: 2,386   (50.2% male; 49.7% female)
   Individual Education Program: 188 (7.9%);
   English Language Learner: 1,410 (59.1%); Migrant: 1,174 (49.2%)
   Eligible for Free Lunch Program: 1,264 (53.0%)
   Eligible for Reduced-Price Lunch Program: 366 (15.3%)
Teachers: 123.8 (19.3 to 1)
Librarians/Media Specialists: 1.0 (2,386.0 to 1)
Guidance Counselors: 4.8 (497.1 to 1)
Current Spending: ($ per student per year):
   Total: $7,400; Instruction: $4,536; Support Services: $2,616
Enrollment, Drop-out Rates and Diploma Recipients by Race/Ethnicity

Category	Total	White	Black	Asian	AIAN	Hisp.
Enrollment (%)	100.0	5.1	0.8	2.7	0.1	91.3
Drop-out Rate (%)	n/a	n/a	n/a	n/a	n/a	n/a
H.S. Diplomas (#)	147	6	6	2	0	133

Greenfield Union Elementary

493 El Camino Real • Greenfield, CA 93927-0097
(831) 674-2840 • http://www.greenfield.k12.ca.us/
Grade Span: KG-08; **Agency Type:** 1
Schools: 4
   3 Primary; 1 Middle; 0 High; 0 Other Level
   4 Regular; 0 Special Education; 0 Vocational; 0 Alternative
   0 Magnet; 0 Charter; 4 Title I Eligible; 4 School-wide Title I
Students: 2,471 (50.3% male; 49.6% female)
   Individual Education Program: 294 (11.9%);
   English Language Learner: 1,409 (57.0%); Migrant: 966 (39.1%)
   Eligible for Free Lunch Program: 1,579 (63.9%)
   Eligible for Reduced-Price Lunch Program: 421 (17.0%)
Teachers: 80.9 (30.5 to 1)
Librarians/Media Specialists: 0.0 (n/a to 1)
Guidance Counselors: 0.0 (n/a to 1)
Current Spending: ($ per student per year):
   Total: $7,706; Instruction: $4,712; Support Services: $2,537
Enrollment, Drop-out Rates and Diploma Recipients by Race/Ethnicity

Category	Total	White	Black	Asian	AIAN	Hisp.
Enrollment (%)	100.0	3.5	0.5	0.6	0.0	95.2
Drop-out Rate (%)	n/a	n/a	n/a	n/a	n/a	n/a
H.S. Diplomas (#)	n/a	n/a	n/a	n/a	n/a	n/a

King City Joint Union High

800 Broadway • King City, CA 93930-3326
(831) 385-0606 • http://www.kingcity.k12.ca.us/
Grade Span: 09-12; **Agency Type:** 1
Schools: 6
   0 Primary; 0 Middle; 6 High; 0 Other Level
   4 Regular; 0 Special Education; 0 Vocational; 2 Alternative
   0 Magnet; 0 Charter; 2 Title I Eligible; 0 School-wide Title I
Students: 2,222 (51.5% male; 48.4% female)
   Individual Education Program: 244 (11.0%);
   English Language Learner: 339 (15.3%); Migrant: 1,292 (58.1%)
   Eligible for Free Lunch Program: 1,196 (53.8%)
   Eligible for Reduced-Price Lunch Program: 325 (14.6%)
Teachers: 91.4 (24.3 to 1)
Librarians/Media Specialists: 0.0 (n/a to 1)
Guidance Counselors: 3.0 (740.7 to 1)
Current Spending: ($ per student per year):
   Total: $6,953; Instruction: $4,523; Support Services: $2,431
Enrollment, Drop-out Rates and Diploma Recipients by Race/Ethnicity

Category	Total	White	Black	Asian	AIAN	Hisp.
Enrollment (%)	100.0	14.4	0.7	1.3	1.6	81.9
Drop-out Rate (%)	n/a	n/a	n/a	n/a	n/a	n/a
H.S. Diplomas (#)	340	64	1	1	2	269

King City Union Elementary

800 Broadway • King City, CA 93930-2984
(831) 385-1144 • http://www.kingcity.k12.ca.us/
Grade Span: KG-08; **Agency Type:** 1
Schools: 3
   2 Primary; 1 Middle; 0 High; 0 Other Level
   3 Regular; 0 Special Education; 0 Vocational; 0 Alternative
   0 Magnet; 0 Charter; 3 Title I Eligible; 0 School-wide Title I
Students: 2,595 (52.4% male; 47.5% female)
   Individual Education Program: 235 (9.1%);
   English Language Learner: 1,357 (52.3%); Migrant: 1,012 (39.0%)
   Eligible for Free Lunch Program: 1,555 (59.9%)
   Eligible for Reduced-Price Lunch Program: 428 (16.5%)
Teachers: 132.5 (19.6 to 1)
Librarians/Media Specialists: 0.0 (n/a to 1)
Guidance Counselors: 1.0 (2,595.0 to 1)
Current Spending: ($ per student per year):
   Total: $6,865; Instruction: $4,403; Support Services: $1,976
Enrollment, Drop-out Rates and Diploma Recipients by Race/Ethnicity

Category	Total	White	Black	Asian	AIAN	Hisp.
Enrollment (%)	100.0	13.2	0.2	1.3	0.3	84.0
Drop-out Rate (%)	n/a	n/a	n/a	n/a	n/a	n/a
H.S. Diplomas (#)	n/a	n/a	n/a	n/a	n/a	n/a

Monterey Peninsula Unified

700 Pacific St • Monterey, CA 93942-1031
(831) 645-1200 • http://www.mpusd.k12.ca.us/
Grade Span: KG-12; **Agency Type:** 1
Schools: 23
   14 Primary; 4 Middle; 4 High; 1 Other Level
   22 Regular; 0 Special Education; 0 Vocational; 1 Alternative
   0 Magnet; 3 Charter; 10 Title I Eligible; 8 School-wide Title I
Students: 12,132 (51.1% male; 48.8% female)
   Individual Education Program: 1,439 (11.9%);
   English Language Learner: 3,071 (25.3%); Migrant: 449 (3.7%)
   Eligible for Free Lunch Program: 4,257 (35.1%)
   Eligible for Reduced-Price Lunch Program: 1,425 (11.7%)

Teachers: 597.8 (20.3 to 1)
Librarians/Media Specialists: 3.5 (3,466.3 to 1)
Guidance Counselors: 13.0 (933.2 to 1)
Current Spending: ($ per student per year):
   Total: $7,317; Instruction: $4,568; Support Services: $2,354
Enrollment, Drop-out Rates and Diploma Recipients by Race/Ethnicity

Category	Total	White	Black	Asian	AIAN	Hisp.
Enrollment (%)	100.0	32.8	11.8	16.4	0.7	36.6
Drop-out Rate (%)	n/a	n/a	n/a	n/a	n/a	n/a
H.S. Diplomas (#)	611	265	84	144	3	115

North Monterey County Unified

8142 Moss Landing Rd • Moss Landing, CA 95039-0049
(831) 633-3343 • http://www.nmcusd.org/
Grade Span: KG-12; **Agency Type:** 1
Schools: 11
   4 Primary; 2 Middle; 3 High; 2 Other Level
   8 Regular; 0 Special Education; 0 Vocational; 3 Alternative
   0 Magnet; 1 Charter; 9 Title I Eligible; 0 School-wide Title I
Students: 6,025 (50.4% male; 49.5% female)
   Individual Education Program: 476 (7.9%);
   English Language Learner: 1,572 (26.1%); Migrant: 1,677 (27.8%)
   Eligible for Free Lunch Program: 2,404 (39.9%)
   Eligible for Reduced-Price Lunch Program: 649 (10.8%)
Teachers: 271.4 (22.2 to 1)
Librarians/Media Specialists: 0.3 (20,083.3 to 1)
Guidance Counselors: 9.0 (669.4 to 1)
Current Spending: ($ per student per year):
   Total: $7,179; Instruction: $4,577; Support Services: $2,368
Enrollment, Drop-out Rates and Diploma Recipients by Race/Ethnicity

Category	Total	White	Black	Asian	AIAN	Hisp.
Enrollment (%)	100.0	37.8	1.4	4.2	0.7	54.6
Drop-out Rate (%)	n/a	n/a	n/a	n/a	n/a	n/a
H.S. Diplomas (#)	415	236	7	21	1	148

Pacific Grove Unified

555 Sinex Ave • Pacific Grove, CA 93950-4320
(831) 646-6520 • http://www.pgusd.org/
Grade Span: KG-12; **Agency Type:** 1
Schools: 5
   2 Primary; 1 Middle; 2 High; 0 Other Level
   4 Regular; 0 Special Education; 0 Vocational; 1 Alternative
   0 Magnet; 0 Charter; 2 Title I Eligible; 0 School-wide Title I
Students: 1,915 (52.7% male; 47.2% female)
   Individual Education Program: 238 (12.4%);
   English Language Learner: 67 (3.5%); Migrant: 0 (0.0%)
   Eligible for Free Lunch Program: 125 (6.5%)
   Eligible for Reduced-Price Lunch Program: 77 (4.0%)
Teachers: 91.3 (21.0 to 1)
Librarians/Media Specialists: 2.0 (957.5 to 1)
Guidance Counselors: 3.0 (638.3 to 1)
Current Spending: ($ per student per year):
   Total: $8,678; Instruction: $5,417; Support Services: $3,064
Enrollment, Drop-out Rates and Diploma Recipients by Race/Ethnicity

Category	Total	White	Black	Asian	AIAN	Hisp.
Enrollment (%)	100.0	76.8	2.3	8.0	0.2	10.4
Drop-out Rate (%)	n/a	n/a	n/a	n/a	n/a	n/a
H.S. Diplomas (#)	174	139	3	17	3	12

Salinas City Elementary

840 S Main St • Salinas, CA 93901-1624
(831) 753-5600 • http://schools.monterey.k12.ca.us/~salcity/
Grade Span: KG-06; **Agency Type:** 1
Schools: 14
   14 Primary; 0 Middle; 0 High; 0 Other Level
   13 Regular; 0 Special Education; 0 Vocational; 1 Alternative
   0 Magnet; 0 Charter; 8 Title I Eligible; 7 School-wide Title I
Students: 8,850 (51.8% male; 48.1% female)
   Individual Education Program: 466 (5.3%);
   English Language Learner: 3,908 (44.2%); Migrant: 3,505 (39.6%)
   Eligible for Free Lunch Program: 4,565 (51.6%)
   Eligible for Reduced-Price Lunch Program: 1,699 (19.2%)
Teachers: 439.5 (20.1 to 1)
Librarians/Media Specialists: 0.0 (n/a to 1)
Guidance Counselors: 0.0 (n/a to 1)
Current Spending: ($ per student per year):
   Total: $7,183; Instruction: $4,733; Support Services: $2,052
Enrollment, Drop-out Rates and Diploma Recipients by Race/Ethnicity

Category	Total	White	Black	Asian	AIAN	Hisp.
Enrollment (%)	100.0	12.6	2.0	6.0	0.3	76.2
Drop-out Rate (%)	n/a	n/a	n/a	n/a	n/a	n/a
H.S. Diplomas (#)	n/a	n/a	n/a	n/a	n/a	n/a

Salinas Union High
431 W Alisal St • Salinas, CA 93901-1624
(831) 796-7000 • http://www.salinas.k12.ca.us/
Grade Span: 07-12; Agency Type: 1
Schools: 10
  0 Primary; 5 Middle; 5 High; 0 Other Level
  8 Regular; 0 Special Education; 0 Vocational; 2 Alternative
  0 Magnet; 0 Charter; 8 Title I Eligible; 0 School-wide Title I
Students: 13,780 (50.9% male; 49.0% female)
  Individual Education Program: 1,131 (8.2%);
  English Language Learner: 5,177 (37.6%); Migrant: 4,303 (31.2%)
  Eligible for Free Lunch Program: 5,256 (38.1%)
  Eligible for Reduced-Price Lunch Program: 2,111 (15.3%)
Teachers: 593.3 (23.2 to 1)
Librarians/Media Specialists: 3.6 (3,827.8 to 1)
Guidance Counselors: 29.1 (473.5 to 1)
Current Spending: ($ per student per year):
  Total: $7,070; Instruction: $3,988; Support Services: $2,860
Enrollment, Drop-out Rates and Diploma Recipients by Race/Ethnicity

Category	Total	White	Black	Asian	AIAN	Hisp.
Enrollment (%)	100.0	15.6	2.3	6.3	0.4	75.2
Drop-out Rate (%)	n/a	n/a	n/a	n/a	n/a	n/a
H.S. Diplomas (#)	1,443	331	43	113	8	948

Santa Rita Union Elementary
57 Russell Rd • Salinas, CA 93906-4325
(831) 443-7200 • http://www.santaritaschools.org/home.html
Grade Span: KG-08; Agency Type: 1
Schools: 4
  3 Primary; 1 Middle; 0 High; 0 Other Level
  4 Regular; 0 Special Education; 0 Vocational; 0 Alternative
  0 Magnet; 0 Charter; 3 Title I Eligible; 1 School-wide Title I
Students: 3,071 (49.9% male; 50.0% female)
  Individual Education Program: 0 (0.0%);
  English Language Learner: 982 (32.0%); Migrant: 364 (11.9%)
  Eligible for Free Lunch Program: 819 (26.7%)
  Eligible for Reduced-Price Lunch Program: 438 (14.3%)
Teachers: 134.3 (22.9 to 1)
Librarians/Media Specialists: 0.0 (n/a to 1)
Guidance Counselors: 1.0 (3,071.0 to 1)
Current Spending: ($ per student per year):
  Total: $6,443; Instruction: $4,315; Support Services: $1,785
Enrollment, Drop-out Rates and Diploma Recipients by Race/Ethnicity

Category	Total	White	Black	Asian	AIAN	Hisp.
Enrollment (%)	100.0	17.6	3.4	10.2	0.6	67.3
Drop-out Rate (%)	n/a	n/a	n/a	n/a	n/a	n/a
H.S. Diplomas (#)	n/a	n/a	n/a	n/a	n/a	n/a

Soledad Unified
1261 Metz Rd • Soledad, CA 93960-0186
Mailing Address: PO Box 186 • Soledad, CA 93960-0186
(831) 678-3987 • http://mainst.monterey.k12.ca.us/
Grade Span: KG-12; Agency Type: 1
Schools: 7
  3 Primary; 1 Middle; 3 High; 0 Other Level
  5 Regular; 0 Special Education; 0 Vocational; 2 Alternative
  0 Magnet; 0 Charter; 7 Title I Eligible; 6 School-wide Title I
Students: 3,839 (51.6% male; 48.3% female)
  Individual Education Program: 268 (7.0%);
  English Language Learner: 2,369 (61.7%); Migrant: 1,222 (31.8%)
  Eligible for Free Lunch Program: 3,167 (82.5%)
  Eligible for Reduced-Price Lunch Program: 254 (6.6%)
Teachers: 175.6 (21.9 to 1)
Librarians/Media Specialists: 1.0 (3,839.0 to 1)
Guidance Counselors: 4.5 (853.1 to 1)
Current Spending: ($ per student per year):
  Total: $7,111; Instruction: $4,341; Support Services: $2,389
Enrollment, Drop-out Rates and Diploma Recipients by Race/Ethnicity

Category	Total	White	Black	Asian	AIAN	Hisp.
Enrollment (%)	100.0	3.9	1.0	2.0	0.1	91.1
Drop-out Rate (%)	n/a	n/a	n/a	n/a	n/a	n/a
H.S. Diplomas (#)	150	4	0	7	0	136

Napa County

Napa Valley Unified
1015 Kaiser Rd • Napa, CA 94558-4931
(707) 253-3715 • http://www.nvusd.k12.ca.us/
Grade Span: KG-12; Agency Type: 1
Schools: 37
  24 Primary; 7 Middle; 4 High; 2 Other Level
  28 Regular; 0 Special Education; 0 Vocational; 9 Alternative
  4 Magnet; 4 Charter; 14 Title I Eligible; 6 School-wide Title I
Students: 17,023 (51.7% male; 48.2% female)
  Individual Education Program: 2,017 (11.8%);
  English Language Learner: 4,289 (25.2%); Migrant: 1,653 (9.7%)
  Eligible for Free Lunch Program: 4,414 (25.9%)
  Eligible for Reduced-Price Lunch Program: 1,918 (11.3%)
Teachers: 833.5 (20.4 to 1)
Librarians/Media Specialists: 3.0 (5,674.3 to 1)
Guidance Counselors: 21.0 (810.6 to 1)
Current Spending: ($ per student per year):
  Total: $7,424; Instruction: $5,000; Support Services: $2,184
Enrollment, Drop-out Rates and Diploma Recipients by Race/Ethnicity

Category	Total	White	Black	Asian	AIAN	Hisp.
Enrollment (%)	100.0	48.5	1.8	4.7	1.5	36.6
Drop-out Rate (%)	n/a	n/a	n/a	n/a	n/a	n/a
H.S. Diplomas (#)	998	681	22	63	12	210

Nevada County

Grass Valley Elementary
10840 Gilmore Way • Grass Valley, CA 95945-5409
(530) 273-4483 • http://www.gvsd.k12.ca.us/
Grade Span: KG-08; Agency Type: 1
Schools: 7
  5 Primary; 2 Middle; 0 High; 0 Other Level
  4 Regular; 0 Special Education; 0 Vocational; 3 Alternative
  0 Magnet; 1 Charter; 3 Title I Eligible; 0 School-wide Title I
Students: 1,848 (52.8% male; 47.1% female)
  Individual Education Program: 197 (10.7%);
  English Language Learner: 50 (2.7%); Migrant: 0 (0.0%)
  Eligible for Free Lunch Program: 578 (31.3%)
  Eligible for Reduced-Price Lunch Program: 196 (10.6%)
Teachers: 98.1 (18.8 to 1)
Librarians/Media Specialists: 0.0 (n/a to 1)
Guidance Counselors: 1.5 (1,232.0 to 1)
Current Spending: ($ per student per year):
  Total: $8,200; Instruction: $5,310; Support Services: $2,198
Enrollment, Drop-out Rates and Diploma Recipients by Race/Ethnicity

Category	Total	White	Black	Asian	AIAN	Hisp.
Enrollment (%)	100.0	83.9	1.5	1.4	3.1	9.4
Drop-out Rate (%)	n/a	n/a	n/a	n/a	n/a	n/a
H.S. Diplomas (#)	n/a	n/a	n/a	n/a	n/a	n/a

Nevada Joint Union High
11645 Ridge Rd • Grass Valley, CA 95945-5024
(530) 273-3351 •
http://www.nuhsd.k12.ca.us/scripts/page.pl?p=dist_scl.htm
Grade Span: 08-12; Agency Type: 1
Schools: 9
  0 Primary; 0 Middle; 9 High; 0 Other Level
  3 Regular; 0 Special Education; 0 Vocational; 6 Alternative
  0 Magnet; 0 Charter; 2 Title I Eligible; 0 School-wide Title I
Students: 4,292 (52.7% male; 47.2% female)
  Individual Education Program: 358 (8.3%);
  English Language Learner: 18 (0.4%); Migrant: 0 (0.0%)
  Eligible for Free Lunch Program: 274 (6.4%)
  Eligible for Reduced-Price Lunch Program: 155 (3.6%)
Teachers: 190.2 (22.6 to 1)
Librarians/Media Specialists: 1.0 (4,292.0 to 1)
Guidance Counselors: 9.4 (456.6 to 1)
Current Spending: ($ per student per year):
  Total: $7,831; Instruction: $4,723; Support Services: $2,934
Enrollment, Drop-out Rates and Diploma Recipients by Race/Ethnicity

Category	Total	White	Black	Asian	AIAN	Hisp.
Enrollment (%)	100.0	91.8	0.8	1.4	1.9	4.1
Drop-out Rate (%)	n/a	n/a	n/a	n/a	n/a	n/a
H.S. Diplomas (#)	907	821	12	21	11	42

Pleasant Ridge Union Elementary
22580 Kingston Ln • Grass Valley, CA 95949-7706
(530) 268-2800 • http://www.pleasantridge.k12.ca.us/
Grade Span: KG-08; Agency Type: 1
Schools: 5
  3 Primary; 2 Middle; 0 High; 0 Other Level
  4 Regular; 0 Special Education; 0 Vocational; 1 Alternative
  0 Magnet; 0 Charter; 4 Title I Eligible; 0 School-wide Title I
Students: 2,073 (52.5% male; 47.4% female)
  Individual Education Program: 162 (7.8%);
  English Language Learner: 7 (0.3%); Migrant: 0 (0.0%)
  Eligible for Free Lunch Program: 235 (11.3%)
  Eligible for Reduced-Price Lunch Program: 107 (5.2%)
Teachers: 100.1 (20.7 to 1)
Librarians/Media Specialists: 0.0 (n/a to 1)
Guidance Counselors: 1.0 (2,073.0 to 1)
Current Spending: ($ per student per year):
  Total: $6,511; Instruction: $4,647; Support Services: $1,759

Enrollment, Drop-out Rates and Diploma Recipients by Race/Ethnicity

Category	Total	White	Black	Asian	AIAN	Hisp.
Enrollment (%)	100.0	83.7	1.1	1.0	0.9	3.8
Drop-out Rate (%)	n/a	n/a	n/a	n/a	n/a	n/a
H.S. Diplomas (#)	n/a	n/a	n/a	n/a	n/a	n/a

Twin Ridges Elementary
18847 Oak Tree Rd Nevada Ci • North San Juan, CA 95960-0529
Mailing Address: PO Box 529 • North San Juan, CA 95960-0529
(530) 292-4221
Grade Span: KG-12; **Agency Type:** 1
Schools: 14
   11 Primary; 1 Middle; 1 High; 1 Other Level
   12 Regular; 0 Special Education; 0 Vocational; 2 Alternative
   0 Magnet; 11 Charter; 4 Title I Eligible; 3 School-wide Title I
Students: 2,191 (50.6% male; 49.3% female)
   Individual Education Program: 168 (7.7%);
   English Language Learner: 21 (1.0%); Migrant: 0 (0.0%)
   Eligible for Free Lunch Program: 48 (2.2%)
   Eligible for Reduced-Price Lunch Program: 496 (22.6%)
Teachers: 115.9 (18.9 to 1)
Librarians/Media Specialists: 0.0 (n/a to 1)
Guidance Counselors: 0.0 (n/a to 1)
Current Spending: ($ per student per year):
   Total: $8,001; Instruction: $4,840; Support Services: $3,120

Enrollment, Drop-out Rates and Diploma Recipients by Race/Ethnicity

Category	Total	White	Black	Asian	AIAN	Hisp.
Enrollment (%)	100.0	84.5	1.9	3.2	2.5	7.4
Drop-out Rate (%)	n/a	n/a	n/a	n/a	n/a	n/a
H.S. Diplomas (#)	33	28	1	1	0	1

Orange County

Anaheim Elementary
1001 S E St • Anaheim, CA 92805-5749
(714) 517-7500 • http://www.acsd.k12.ca.us/
Grade Span: KG-06; **Agency Type:** 1
Schools: 23
   23 Primary; 0 Middle; 0 High; 0 Other Level
   23 Regular; 0 Special Education; 0 Vocational; 0 Alternative
   0 Magnet; 0 Charter; 23 Title I Eligible; 13 School-wide Title I
Students: 21,963 (51.0% male; 48.9% female)
   Individual Education Program: 2,176 (9.9%);
   English Language Learner: 13,722 (62.5%); Migrant: 176 (0.8%)
   Eligible for Free Lunch Program: 12,970 (59.1%)
   Eligible for Reduced-Price Lunch Program: 4,783 (21.8%)
Teachers: 1,027.0 (21.4 to 1)
Librarians/Media Specialists: 0.0 (n/a to 1)
Guidance Counselors: 1.0 (21,963.0 to 1)
Current Spending: ($ per student per year):
   Total: $6,641; Instruction: $4,343; Support Services: $2,298

Enrollment, Drop-out Rates and Diploma Recipients by Race/Ethnicity

Category	Total	White	Black	Asian	AIAN	Hisp.
Enrollment (%)	100.0	7.9	1.8	6.1	0.3	83.4
Drop-out Rate (%)	n/a	n/a	n/a	n/a	n/a	n/a
H.S. Diplomas (#)	n/a	n/a	n/a	n/a	n/a	n/a

Anaheim Union High
501 Crescent Way • Anaheim, CA 92803-3520
Mailing Address: PO Box 3520 • Anaheim, CA 92803-3520
(714) 999-3511 • http://www.auhsd.k12.ca.us/
Grade Span: 07-12; **Agency Type:** 1
Schools: 21
   0 Primary; 8 Middle; 13 High; 0 Other Level
   17 Regular; 1 Special Education; 0 Vocational; 3 Alternative
   0 Magnet; 0 Charter; 9 Title I Eligible; 7 School-wide Title I
Students: 32,468 (51.1% male; 48.8% female)
   Individual Education Program: 3,734 (11.5%);
   English Language Learner: 8,640 (26.6%); Migrant: 248 (0.8%)
   Eligible for Free Lunch Program: 10,334 (31.8%)
   Eligible for Reduced-Price Lunch Program: 4,051 (12.5%)
Teachers: 1,278.1 (25.4 to 1)
Librarians/Media Specialists: 12.0 (2,705.7 to 1)
Guidance Counselors: 57.0 (569.6 to 1)
Current Spending: ($ per student per year):
   Total: $7,617; Instruction: $4,836; Support Services: $2,249

Enrollment, Drop-out Rates and Diploma Recipients by Race/Ethnicity

Category	Total	White	Black	Asian	AIAN	Hisp.
Enrollment (%)	100.0	24.7	3.4	16.2	0.5	55.2
Drop-out Rate (%)	n/a	n/a	n/a	n/a	n/a	n/a
H.S. Diplomas (#)	3,688	1,103	150	735	22	1,678

Brea-Olinda Unified
Number One Civic Cntr. • Brea, CA 92821-9990
Mailing Address: PO Box 300 • Brea, CA 92821-9990
(714) 990-7800 • http://www.bousd.k12.ca.us/
Grade Span: KG-12; **Agency Type:** 1
Schools: 9
   6 Primary; 1 Middle; 2 High; 0 Other Level
   8 Regular; 0 Special Education; 0 Vocational; 1 Alternative
   0 Magnet; 0 Charter; 4 Title I Eligible; 0 School-wide Title I
Students: 6,206 (51.9% male; 48.0% female)
   Individual Education Program: 609 (9.8%);
   English Language Learner: 645 (10.4%); Migrant: 0 (0.0%)
   Eligible for Free Lunch Program: 739 (11.9%)
   Eligible for Reduced-Price Lunch Program: 347 (5.6%)
Teachers: 277.9 (22.3 to 1)
Librarians/Media Specialists: 0.0 (n/a to 1)
Guidance Counselors: 5.2 (1,193.5 to 1)
Current Spending: ($ per student per year):
   Total: $6,878; Instruction: $4,213; Support Services: $2,388

Enrollment, Drop-out Rates and Diploma Recipients by Race/Ethnicity

Category	Total	White	Black	Asian	AIAN	Hisp.
Enrollment (%)	100.0	56.3	1.7	13.8	0.4	24.3
Drop-out Rate (%)	n/a	n/a	n/a	n/a	n/a	n/a
H.S. Diplomas (#)	487	288	7	80	3	84

Buena Park Elementary
6885 Orangethorpe Ave • Buena Park, CA 90620-1348
(714) 522-8412 • http://www.ocde.k12.ca.us/bpsd/
Grade Span: KG-08; **Agency Type:** 1
Schools: 7
   6 Primary; 1 Middle; 0 High; 0 Other Level
   7 Regular; 0 Special Education; 0 Vocational; 0 Alternative
   0 Magnet; 0 Charter; 7 Title I Eligible; 3 School-wide Title I
Students: 6,372 (50.6% male; 49.3% female)
   Individual Education Program: 651 (10.2%);
   English Language Learner: 2,879 (45.2%); Migrant: 6 (0.1%)
   Eligible for Free Lunch Program: 2,951 (46.3%)
   Eligible for Reduced-Price Lunch Program: 956 (15.0%)
Teachers: 279.8 (22.8 to 1)
Librarians/Media Specialists: 0.0 (n/a to 1)
Guidance Counselors: 0.0 (n/a to 1)
Current Spending: ($ per student per year):
   Total: $6,858; Instruction: $4,464; Support Services: $2,037

Enrollment, Drop-out Rates and Diploma Recipients by Race/Ethnicity

Category	Total	White	Black	Asian	AIAN	Hisp.
Enrollment (%)	100.0	17.2	5.6	17.9	0.3	56.8
Drop-out Rate (%)	n/a	n/a	n/a	n/a	n/a	n/a
H.S. Diplomas (#)	n/a	n/a	n/a	n/a	n/a	n/a

Capistrano Unified
32972 Calle Perfecto • San Juan Capistrano, CA 92675-4706
(949) 489-7000 • http://www.capousd.k12.ca.us/
Grade Span: KG-12; **Agency Type:** 1
Schools: 56
   38 Primary; 10 Middle; 7 High; 1 Other Level
   53 Regular; 1 Special Education; 0 Vocational; 2 Alternative
   0 Magnet; 2 Charter; 15 Title I Eligible; 4 School-wide Title I
Students: 49,746 (51.5% male; 48.4% female)
   Individual Education Program: 4,703 (9.5%);
   English Language Learner: 6,465 (13.0%); Migrant: 460 (0.9%)
   Eligible for Free Lunch Program: 5,322 (10.7%)
   Eligible for Reduced-Price Lunch Program: 2,014 (4.0%)
Teachers: 2,158.9 (23.0 to 1)
Librarians/Media Specialists: 1.0 (49,746.0 to 1)
Guidance Counselors: 9.5 (5,236.4 to 1)
Current Spending: ($ per student per year):
   Total: $6,671; Instruction: $4,384; Support Services: $2,116

Enrollment, Drop-out Rates and Diploma Recipients by Race/Ethnicity

Category	Total	White	Black	Asian	AIAN	Hisp.
Enrollment (%)	100.0	69.2	1.3	6.7	0.3	18.2
Drop-out Rate (%)	n/a	n/a	n/a	n/a	n/a	n/a
H.S. Diplomas (#)	2,644	1,951	26	152	8	292

Centralia Elementary
6625 La Palma Ave • Buena Park, CA 90620-2859
(714) 228-3100 • http://www.cesd.k12.ca.us/main.htm
Grade Span: KG-06; **Agency Type:** 1
Schools: 9
   9 Primary; 0 Middle; 0 High; 0 Other Level
   9 Regular; 0 Special Education; 0 Vocational; 0 Alternative
   0 Magnet; 0 Charter; 3 Title I Eligible; 1 School-wide Title I
Students: 5,255 (51.4% male; 48.5% female)
   Individual Education Program: 558 (10.6%);
   English Language Learner: 1,526 (29.0%); Migrant: 9 (0.2%)
   Eligible for Free Lunch Program: 1,790 (34.1%)

Eligible for Reduced-Price Lunch Program: 604 (11.5%)
Teachers: 248.0 (21.2 to 1)
Librarians/Media Specialists: 0.0 (n/a to 1)
Guidance Counselors: 6.0 (875.8 to 1)
Current Spending: ($ per student per year):
    Total: $6,879; Instruction: $4,098; Support Services: $2,509
Enrollment, Drop-out Rates and Diploma Recipients by Race/Ethnicity

Category	Total	White	Black	Asian	AIAN	Hisp.
Enrollment (%)	100.0	25.9	4.6	22.7	0.5	41.7
Drop-out Rate (%)	n/a	n/a	n/a	n/a	n/a	n/a
H.S. Diplomas (#)	n/a	n/a	n/a	n/a	n/a	n/a

Cypress Elementary
9470 Moody St • Cypress, CA 90630-2919
(714) 220-6900 • http://www.cypsd.k12.ca.us/
Grade Span: KG-06; **Agency Type:** 1
Schools: 10
    10 Primary; 0 Middle; 0 High; 0 Other Level
    10 Regular; 0 Special Education; 0 Vocational; 0 Alternative
    0 Magnet; 0 Charter; 2 Title I Eligible; 0 School-wide Title I
Students: 4,727 (52.1% male; 47.8% female)
    Individual Education Program: 513 (10.9%);
    English Language Learner: 580 (12.3%); Migrant: 0 (0.0%)
    Eligible for Free Lunch Program: 746 (15.8%)
    Eligible for Reduced-Price Lunch Program: 380 (8.0%)
Teachers: 225.0 (21.0 to 1)
Librarians/Media Specialists: 0.0 (n/a to 1)
Guidance Counselors: 0.0 (n/a to 1)
Current Spending: ($ per student per year):
    Total: $6,789; Instruction: $4,604; Support Services: $1,905
Enrollment, Drop-out Rates and Diploma Recipients by Race/Ethnicity

Category	Total	White	Black	Asian	AIAN	Hisp.
Enrollment (%)	100.0	43.5	4.8	30.1	0.7	20.3
Drop-out Rate (%)	n/a	n/a	n/a	n/a	n/a	n/a
H.S. Diplomas (#)	n/a	n/a	n/a	n/a	n/a	n/a

Fountain Valley Elementary
17210 Oak St • Fountain Valley, CA 92708-3405
(714) 843-3200 • http://www.fvsd.k12.ca.us/
Grade Span: KG-08; **Agency Type:** 1
Schools: 11
    8 Primary; 3 Middle; 0 High; 0 Other Level
    11 Regular; 0 Special Education; 0 Vocational; 0 Alternative
    0 Magnet; 0 Charter; 5 Title I Eligible; 0 School-wide Title I
Students: 6,250 (51.2% male; 48.7% female)
    Individual Education Program: 650 (10.4%);
    English Language Learner: 496 (7.9%); Migrant: 0 (0.0%)
    Eligible for Free Lunch Program: 479 (7.7%)
    Eligible for Reduced-Price Lunch Program: 306 (4.9%)
Teachers: 262.9 (23.8 to 1)
Librarians/Media Specialists: 0.0 (n/a to 1)
Guidance Counselors: 0.0 (n/a to 1)
Current Spending: ($ per student per year):
    Total: $6,981; Instruction: $4,503; Support Services: $2,336
Enrollment, Drop-out Rates and Diploma Recipients by Race/Ethnicity

Category	Total	White	Black	Asian	AIAN	Hisp.
Enrollment (%)	100.0	59.6	1.1	24.4	0.8	12.6
Drop-out Rate (%)	n/a	n/a	n/a	n/a	n/a	n/a
H.S. Diplomas (#)	n/a	n/a	n/a	n/a	n/a	n/a

Fullerton Elementary
1401 W Valencia Dr • Fullerton, CA 92633-3938
(714) 447-7400 • http://www.fsd.k12.ca.us/
Grade Span: KG-08; **Agency Type:** 1
Schools: 19
    16 Primary; 3 Middle; 0 High; 0 Other Level
    19 Regular; 0 Special Education; 0 Vocational; 0 Alternative
    3 Magnet; 0 Charter; 9 Title I Eligible; 9 School-wide Title I
Students: 13,812 (51.2% male; 48.7% female)
    Individual Education Program: 1,408 (10.2%);
    English Language Learner: 3,914 (28.3%); Migrant: 81 (0.6%)
    Eligible for Free Lunch Program: 4,053 (29.3%)
    Eligible for Reduced-Price Lunch Program: 1,207 (8.7%)
Teachers: 593.2 (23.3 to 1)
Librarians/Media Specialists: 1.1 (12,556.4 to 1)
Guidance Counselors: 3.8 (3,634.7 to 1)
Current Spending: ($ per student per year):
    Total: $6,693; Instruction: $4,298; Support Services: $2,126
Enrollment, Drop-out Rates and Diploma Recipients by Race/Ethnicity

Category	Total	White	Black	Asian	AIAN	Hisp.
Enrollment (%)	100.0	31.5	2.3	19.7	0.3	45.8
Drop-out Rate (%)	n/a	n/a	n/a	n/a	n/a	n/a
H.S. Diplomas (#)	n/a	n/a	n/a	n/a	n/a	n/a

Fullerton Joint Union High
1051 W Bastanchury Rd • Fullerton, CA 92833-2247
(714) 870-2800 • http://www.fjuhsd.k12.ca.us/
Grade Span: 09-12; **Agency Type:** 1
Schools: 8
    0 Primary; 0 Middle; 8 High; 0 Other Level
    6 Regular; 0 Special Education; 0 Vocational; 2 Alternative
    2 Magnet; 0 Charter; 3 Title I Eligible; 0 School-wide Title I
Students: 16,398 (49.1% male; 50.8% female)
    Individual Education Program: 1,166 (7.1%);
    English Language Learner: 4,807 (29.3%); Migrant: 2 (<0.1%)
    Eligible for Free Lunch Program: 1,094 (6.7%)
    Eligible for Reduced-Price Lunch Program: 178 (1.1%)
Teachers: 565.6 (29.0 to 1)
Librarians/Media Specialists: 5.0 (3,279.6 to 1)
Guidance Counselors: 15.7 (1,044.5 to 1)
Current Spending: ($ per student per year):
    Total: $6,096; Instruction: $3,661; Support Services: $2,320
Enrollment, Drop-out Rates and Diploma Recipients by Race/Ethnicity

Category	Total	White	Black	Asian	AIAN	Hisp.
Enrollment (%)	100.0	27.1	2.1	18.5	0.3	47.6
Drop-out Rate (%)	n/a	n/a	n/a	n/a	n/a	n/a
H.S. Diplomas (#)	2,670	1,071	79	618	7	894

Garden Grove Unified
10331 Stanford Ave • Garden Grove, CA 92840-6351
(714) 663-6000 • http://www.ggusd.k12.ca.us/
Grade Span: KG-12; **Agency Type:** 1
Schools: 67
    47 Primary; 10 Middle; 10 High; 0 Other Level
    63 Regular; 2 Special Education; 0 Vocational; 2 Alternative
    0 Magnet; 0 Charter; 55 Title I Eligible; 35 School-wide Title I
Students: 50,172 (50.8% male; 49.1% female)
    Individual Education Program: 5,014 (10.0%);
    English Language Learner: 24,659 (49.1%); Migrant: 10 (<0.1%)
    Eligible for Free Lunch Program: 23,382 (46.6%)
    Eligible for Reduced-Price Lunch Program: 6,929 (13.8%)
Teachers: 2,137.7 (23.5 to 1)
Librarians/Media Specialists: 16.0 (3,135.8 to 1)
Guidance Counselors: 36.0 (1,393.7 to 1)
Current Spending: ($ per student per year):
    Total: $6,935; Instruction: $4,568; Support Services: $2,077
Enrollment, Drop-out Rates and Diploma Recipients by Race/Ethnicity

Category	Total	White	Black	Asian	AIAN	Hisp.
Enrollment (%)	100.0	16.8	1.1	29.9	0.3	51.9
Drop-out Rate (%)	n/a	n/a	n/a	n/a	n/a	n/a
H.S. Diplomas (#)	2,738	643	25	1,095	4	971

Huntington Beach City Elementary
20451 Craimer Ln • Huntington Beach, CA 92646-0071
(714) 964-8888 • http://hbuhsd.k12.ca.us/
Grade Span: KG-08; **Agency Type:** 1
Schools: 10
    8 Primary; 2 Middle; 0 High; 0 Other Level
    10 Regular; 0 Special Education; 0 Vocational; 0 Alternative
    0 Magnet; 0 Charter; 4 Title I Eligible; 0 School-wide Title I
Students: 6,931 (52.4% male; 47.5% female)
    Individual Education Program: 743 (10.7%);
    English Language Learner: 478 (6.9%); Migrant: 0 (0.0%)
    Eligible for Free Lunch Program: 651 (9.4%)
    Eligible for Reduced-Price Lunch Program: 226 (3.3%)
Teachers: 283.0 (24.5 to 1)
Librarians/Media Specialists: 0.0 (n/a to 1)
Guidance Counselors: 0.0 (n/a to 1)
Current Spending: ($ per student per year):
    Total: $6,518; Instruction: $4,386; Support Services: $1,930
Enrollment, Drop-out Rates and Diploma Recipients by Race/Ethnicity

Category	Total	White	Black	Asian	AIAN	Hisp.
Enrollment (%)	100.0	69.1	0.8	9.2	0.8	11.0
Drop-out Rate (%)	n/a	n/a	n/a	n/a	n/a	n/a
H.S. Diplomas (#)	n/a	n/a	n/a	n/a	n/a	n/a

Huntington Beach Union High
10251 Yorktown Ave • Huntington Beach, CA 92646-2999
(714) 964-3339 • http://www2.hbuhsd.org/
Grade Span: 09-12; **Agency Type:** 1
Schools: 9
    0 Primary; 0 Middle; 9 High; 0 Other Level
    6 Regular; 0 Special Education; 0 Vocational; 3 Alternative
    0 Magnet; 0 Charter; 3 Title I Eligible; 1 School-wide Title I
Students: 14,975 (50.9% male; 49.0% female)
    Individual Education Program: 1,505 (10.1%);
    English Language Learner: 1,490 (9.9%); Migrant: 0 (0.0%)
    Eligible for Free Lunch Program: 2,141 (14.3%)
    Eligible for Reduced-Price Lunch Program: 490 (3.3%)

Teachers: 570.0 (26.3 to 1)
Librarians/Media Specialists: 3.0 (4,991.7 to 1)
Guidance Counselors: 1.0 (14,975.0 to 1)
Current Spending: ($ per student per year):
Total: $7,398; Instruction: $4,244; Support Services: $2,946
Enrollment, Drop-out Rates and Diploma Recipients by Race/Ethnicity

Category	Total	White	Black	Asian	AIAN	Hisp.
Enrollment (%)	100.0	50.1	1.3	24.7	5.5	18.4
Drop-out Rate (%)	n/a	n/a	n/a	n/a	n/a	n/a
H.S. Diplomas (#)	2,905	1,449	36	788	212	418

Irvine Unified
5050 Barranca Pkwy • Irvine, CA 92604-4652
(949) 936-5000 • http://www.iusd.k12.ca.us/
Grade Span: KG-12; **Agency Type:** 1
Schools: 33
22 Primary; 5 Middle; 5 High; 1 Other Level
31 Regular; 0 Special Education; 0 Vocational; 2 Alternative
0 Magnet; 0 Charter; 9 Title I Eligible; 0 School-wide Title I
Students: 24,930   (51.7% male; 48.2% female)
Individual Education Program: 2,171 (8.7%);
English Language Learner: 3,064 (12.3%); Migrant: 2 (<0.1%)
Eligible for Free Lunch Program: 1,194 (4.8%)
Eligible for Reduced-Price Lunch Program: 612 (2.5%)
Teachers: 1,075.9 (23.2 to 1)
Librarians/Media Specialists: 5.8 (4,298.3 to 1)
Guidance Counselors: 18.9 (1,319.0 to 1)
Current Spending: ($ per student per year):
Total: $6,675; Instruction: $4,342; Support Services: $2,151
Enrollment, Drop-out Rates and Diploma Recipients by Race/Ethnicity

Category	Total	White	Black	Asian	AIAN	Hisp.
Enrollment (%)	100.0	48.6	2.5	38.0	0.6	7.4
Drop-out Rate (%)	n/a	n/a	n/a	n/a	n/a	n/a
H.S. Diplomas (#)	1,838	1,081	29	628	1	94

La Habra City Elementary
500 N Walnut St • La Habra, CA 90633-0307
Mailing Address: PO Box 307 • La Habra, CA 90633-0307
(562) 690-2300 • http://www.lhcsd.k12.ca.us/
Grade Span: KG-08; **Agency Type:** 1
Schools: 9
7 Primary; 2 Middle; 0 High; 0 Other Level
9 Regular; 0 Special Education; 0 Vocational; 0 Alternative
0 Magnet; 0 Charter; 7 Title I Eligible; 3 School-wide Title I
Students: 6,534   (50.5% male; 49.4% female)
Individual Education Program: 551 (8.4%);
English Language Learner: 2,897 (44.3%); Migrant: 0 (0.0%)
Eligible for Free Lunch Program: 3,557 (54.4%)
Eligible for Reduced-Price Lunch Program: 903 (13.8%)
Teachers: 302.2 (21.6 to 1)
Librarians/Media Specialists: 0.0 (n/a to 1)
Guidance Counselors: 0.0 (n/a to 1)
Current Spending: ($ per student per year):
Total: $7,102; Instruction: $4,581; Support Services: $2,116
Enrollment, Drop-out Rates and Diploma Recipients by Race/Ethnicity

Category	Total	White	Black	Asian	AIAN	Hisp.
Enrollment (%)	100.0	21.3	1.5	2.7	0.0	74.4
Drop-out Rate (%)	n/a	n/a	n/a	n/a	n/a	n/a
H.S. Diplomas (#)	n/a	n/a	n/a	n/a	n/a	n/a

Laguna Beach Unified
550 Blumont St • Laguna Beach, CA 92651-2356
(949) 497-7700 • http://www.lagunabeachschools.org/
Grade Span: KG-12; **Agency Type:** 1
Schools: 4
2 Primary; 1 Middle; 1 High; 0 Other Level
4 Regular; 0 Special Education; 0 Vocational; 0 Alternative
0 Magnet; 0 Charter; 3 Title I Eligible; 0 School-wide Title I
Students: 2,703   (50.9% male; 49.0% female)
Individual Education Program: 225 (8.3%);
English Language Learner: 61 (2.3%); Migrant: 6 (0.2%)
Eligible for Free Lunch Program: 215 (8.0%)
Eligible for Reduced-Price Lunch Program: 66 (2.4%)
Teachers: 124.6 (21.7 to 1)
Librarians/Media Specialists: 0.0 (n/a to 1)
Guidance Counselors: 3.0 (901.0 to 1)
Current Spending: ($ per student per year):
Total: $8,616; Instruction: $5,378; Support Services: $3,027
Enrollment, Drop-out Rates and Diploma Recipients by Race/Ethnicity

Category	Total	White	Black	Asian	AIAN	Hisp.
Enrollment (%)	100.0	84.4	1.1	3.7	0.4	9.7
Drop-out Rate (%)	n/a	n/a	n/a	n/a	n/a	n/a
H.S. Diplomas (#)	195	168	1	7	0	18

Los Alamitos Unified
10293 Bloomfield St • Los Alamitos, CA 90720-2264
(562) 799-4700 • http://www.losalusd.k12.ca.us/
Grade Span: KG-12; **Agency Type:** 1
Schools: 10
6 Primary; 2 Middle; 2 High; 0 Other Level
9 Regular; 0 Special Education; 0 Vocational; 1 Alternative
0 Magnet; 0 Charter; 3 Title I Eligible; 0 School-wide Title I
Students: 9,184   (50.8% male; 49.1% female)
Individual Education Program: 838 (9.1%);
English Language Learner: 196 (2.1%); Migrant: 0 (0.0%)
Eligible for Free Lunch Program: 480 (5.2%)
Eligible for Reduced-Price Lunch Program: 292 (3.2%)
Teachers: 394.1 (23.3 to 1)
Librarians/Media Specialists: 9.8 (937.1 to 1)
Guidance Counselors: 7.0 (1,312.0 to 1)
Current Spending: ($ per student per year):
Total: $7,091; Instruction: $4,711; Support Services: $2,168
Enrollment, Drop-out Rates and Diploma Recipients by Race/Ethnicity

Category	Total	White	Black	Asian	AIAN	Hisp.
Enrollment (%)	100.0	67.6	3.1	12.8	0.5	12.2
Drop-out Rate (%)	n/a	n/a	n/a	n/a	n/a	n/a
H.S. Diplomas (#)	657	469	27	79	2	79

Magnolia Elementary
2705 W Orange Ave • Anaheim, CA 92804-3203
(714) 761-5533 • http://www.msd.k12.ca.us/
Grade Span: KG-06; **Agency Type:** 1
Schools: 9
9 Primary; 0 Middle; 0 High; 0 Other Level
9 Regular; 0 Special Education; 0 Vocational; 0 Alternative
0 Magnet; 0 Charter; 9 Title I Eligible; 8 School-wide Title I
Students: 6,971   (51.0% male; 48.9% female)
Individual Education Program: 726 (10.4%);
English Language Learner: 3,689 (52.9%); Migrant: 29 (0.4%)
Eligible for Free Lunch Program: 4,104 (58.9%)
Eligible for Reduced-Price Lunch Program: 1,014 (14.5%)
Teachers: 346.8 (20.1 to 1)
Librarians/Media Specialists: 0.0 (n/a to 1)
Guidance Counselors: 2.0 (3,485.5 to 1)
Current Spending: ($ per student per year):
Total: $6,937; Instruction: $4,666; Support Services: $1,916
Enrollment, Drop-out Rates and Diploma Recipients by Race/Ethnicity

Category	Total	White	Black	Asian	AIAN	Hisp.
Enrollment (%)	100.0	15.0	3.3	14.0	0.3	66.8
Drop-out Rate (%)	n/a	n/a	n/a	n/a	n/a	n/a
H.S. Diplomas (#)	n/a	n/a	n/a	n/a	n/a	n/a

Newport-Mesa Unified
2985-A Bear St Building A • Costa Mesa, CA 92626
Mailing Address: PO Box 1368 • Newport Beach, CA 92626
(714) 424-5000 • http://www.nmusd.k12.ca.us/
Grade Span: KG-12; **Agency Type:** 1
Schools: 31
20 Primary; 4 Middle; 7 High; 0 Other Level
29 Regular; 0 Special Education; 0 Vocational; 2 Alternative
0 Magnet; 0 Charter; 14 Title I Eligible; 7 School-wide Title I
Students: 22,383   (51.7% male; 48.2% female)
Individual Education Program: 2,552 (11.4%);
English Language Learner: 6,062 (27.1%); Migrant: 199 (0.9%)
Eligible for Free Lunch Program: 7,243 (32.4%)
Eligible for Reduced-Price Lunch Program: 1,529 (6.8%)
Teachers: 1,035.7 (21.6 to 1)
Librarians/Media Specialists: 7.0 (3,197.6 to 1)
Guidance Counselors: 22.4 (999.2 to 1)
Current Spending: ($ per student per year):
Total: $7,614; Instruction: $4,665; Support Services: $2,630
Enrollment, Drop-out Rates and Diploma Recipients by Race/Ethnicity

Category	Total	White	Black	Asian	AIAN	Hisp.
Enrollment (%)	100.0	53.2	1.2	6.1	0.3	39.2
Drop-out Rate (%)	n/a	n/a	n/a	n/a	n/a	n/a
H.S. Diplomas (#)	1,118	740	7	105	4	262

Ocean View Elementary
17200 Pinehurst Ln • Huntington Beach, CA 92647-5569
(714) 847-2551 • http://www.ovsd.org/
Grade Span: KG-08; **Agency Type:** 1
Schools: 15
11 Primary; 4 Middle; 0 High; 0 Other Level
15 Regular; 0 Special Education; 0 Vocational; 0 Alternative
0 Magnet; 0 Charter; 6 Title I Eligible; 0 School-wide Title I
Students: 10,186   (51.9% male; 48.0% female)
Individual Education Program: 1,022 (10.0%);
English Language Learner: 2,133 (20.9%); Migrant: 0 (0.0%)
Eligible for Free Lunch Program: 2,517 (24.7%)

Eligible for Reduced-Price Lunch Program: 786 (7.7%)
Teachers: 480.9 (21.2 to 1)
Librarians/Media Specialists: 0.0 (n/a to 1)
Guidance Counselors: 0.0 (n/a to 1)
Current Spending: ($ per student per year):
  Total: $6,763; Instruction: $4,649; Support Services: $1,902
Enrollment, Drop-out Rates and Diploma Recipients by Race/Ethnicity

Category	Total	White	Black	Asian	AIAN	Hisp.
Enrollment (%)	100.0	50.1	1.1	11.3	0.8	27.8
Drop-out Rate (%)	n/a	n/a	n/a	n/a	n/a	n/a
H.S. Diplomas (#)	n/a	n/a	n/a	n/a	n/a	n/a

Orange County Office of Education
200 Kalmus Dr • Costa Mesa, CA 92628-9050
Mailing Address: PO Box 9050 • Costa Mesa, CA 92628-9050
(714) 966-4000 • http://www.ocde.k12.ca.us/
Grade Span: KG-12; **Agency Type:** 4
Schools: 4
  0 Primary; 0 Middle; 0 High; 4 Other Level
  1 Regular; 1 Special Education; 0 Vocational; 2 Alternative
  0 Magnet; 0 Charter; 0 Title I Eligible; 0 School-wide Title I
Students: 8,617 (60.8% male; 39.1% female)
  Individual Education Program: 1,185 (13.8%);
  English Language Learner: 1,566 (18.2%); Migrant: 3 (<0.1%)
  Eligible for Free Lunch Program: 391 (4.5%)
  Eligible for Reduced-Price Lunch Program: 31 (0.4%)
Teachers: 481.1 (17.9 to 1)
Librarians/Media Specialists: 2.0 (4,308.5 to 1)
Guidance Counselors: 3.0 (2,872.3 to 1)
Current Spending: ($ per student per year):
  Total: $18,489; Instruction: $8,121; Support Services: $10,287
Enrollment, Drop-out Rates and Diploma Recipients by Race/Ethnicity

Category	Total	White	Black	Asian	AIAN	Hisp.
Enrollment (%)	100.0	34.6	3.3	5.5	0.5	50.9
Drop-out Rate (%)	n/a	n/a	n/a	n/a	n/a	n/a
H.S. Diplomas (#)	1,066	419	43	96	5	494

Orange Unified
1401 N Handy St • Orange, CA 92856-8122
Mailing Address: PO Box 11022 • Orange, CA 92856-8122
(714) 997-6100 • http://www.orangeusd.k12.ca.us/
Grade Span: KG-12; **Agency Type:** 1
Schools: 42
  29 Primary; 6 Middle; 4 High; 3 Other Level
  40 Regular; 1 Special Education; 0 Vocational; 1 Alternative
  5 Magnet; 3 Charter; 15 Title I Eligible; 13 School-wide Title I
Students: 32,032 (51.7% male; 48.2% female)
  Individual Education Program: 3,427 (10.7%);
  English Language Learner: 7,201 (22.5%); Migrant: 156 (0.5%)
  Eligible for Free Lunch Program: 8,914 (27.8%)
  Eligible for Reduced-Price Lunch Program: 2,092 (6.5%)
Teachers: 1,520.6 (21.1 to 1)
Librarians/Media Specialists: 9.5 (3,371.8 to 1)
Guidance Counselors: 24.8 (1,291.6 to 1)
Current Spending: ($ per student per year):
  Total: $7,415; Instruction: $4,688; Support Services: $2,511
Enrollment, Drop-out Rates and Diploma Recipients by Race/Ethnicity

Category	Total	White	Black	Asian	AIAN	Hisp.
Enrollment (%)	100.0	41.6	1.7	12.4	0.7	41.7
Drop-out Rate (%)	n/a	n/a	n/a	n/a	n/a	n/a
H.S. Diplomas (#)	2,065	1,015	74	389	15	564

Placentia-Yorba Linda Unified
1301 E Orangethorpe Ave • Placentia, CA 92670-5302
(714) 996-2550 • http://www.pylusd.k12.ca.us/
Grade Span: KG-12; **Agency Type:** 1
Schools: 30
  21 Primary; 4 Middle; 5 High; 0 Other Level
  27 Regular; 1 Special Education; 0 Vocational; 2 Alternative
  2 Magnet; 0 Charter; 6 Title I Eligible; 5 School-wide Title I
Students: 26,774 (51.6% male; 48.3% female)
  Individual Education Program: 2,906 (10.9%);
  English Language Learner: 4,216 (15.7%); Migrant: 377 (1.4%)
  Eligible for Free Lunch Program: 1,762 (6.6%)
  Eligible for Reduced-Price Lunch Program: 449 (1.7%)
Teachers: 1,180.1 (22.7 to 1)
Librarians/Media Specialists: 3.0 (8,924.7 to 1)
Guidance Counselors: 18.0 (1,487.4 to 1)
Current Spending: ($ per student per year):
  Total: $6,929; Instruction: $4,365; Support Services: $2,341
Enrollment, Drop-out Rates and Diploma Recipients by Race/Ethnicity

Category	Total	White	Black	Asian	AIAN	Hisp.
Enrollment (%)	100.0	57.8	1.9	9.5	0.4	30.4
Drop-out Rate (%)	n/a	n/a	n/a	n/a	n/a	n/a
H.S. Diplomas (#)	1,656	1,107	16	197	7	329

Saddleback Valley Unified
25631 Peter A Hartman Way • Mission Viejo, CA 92691-3199
(949) 586-1234 • http://www.svusd.k12.ca.us/
Grade Span: KG-12; **Agency Type:** 1
Schools: 37
  26 Primary; 4 Middle; 7 High; 0 Other Level
  34 Regular; 1 Special Education; 0 Vocational; 2 Alternative
  0 Magnet; 1 Charter; 11 Title I Eligible; 1 School-wide Title I
Students: 35,349 (51.4% male; 48.5% female)
  Individual Education Program: 3,125 (8.8%);
  English Language Learner: 3,020 (8.5%); Migrant: 1 (<0.1%)
  Eligible for Free Lunch Program: 3,575 (10.1%)
  Eligible for Reduced-Price Lunch Program: 1,373 (3.9%)
Teachers: 1,458.8 (24.2 to 1)
Librarians/Media Specialists: 4.0 (8,837.3 to 1)
Guidance Counselors: 15.1 (2,341.0 to 1)
Current Spending: ($ per student per year):
  Total: $6,325; Instruction: $4,356; Support Services: $1,802
Enrollment, Drop-out Rates and Diploma Recipients by Race/Ethnicity

Category	Total	White	Black	Asian	AIAN	Hisp.
Enrollment (%)	100.0	66.6	2.2	10.4	0.4	20.2
Drop-out Rate (%)	n/a	n/a	n/a	n/a	n/a	n/a
H.S. Diplomas (#)	2,157	1,576	37	252	9	283

Santa Ana Unified
1601 E Chestnut Ave • Santa Ana, CA 92701-6322
(714) 558-5501 • http://www.sausd.k12.ca.us/
Grade Span: KG-12; **Agency Type:** 1
Schools: 56
  37 Primary; 9 Middle; 10 High; 0 Other Level
  52 Regular; 0 Special Education; 0 Vocational; 4 Alternative
  2 Magnet; 4 Charter; 47 Title I Eligible; 45 School-wide Title I
Students: 62,874 (50.0% male; 49.9% female)
  Individual Education Program: 5,819 (9.3%);
  English Language Learner: 38,207 (60.8%); Migrant: 1,092 (1.7%)
  Eligible for Free Lunch Program: 37,908 (60.3%)
  Eligible for Reduced-Price Lunch Program: 10,580 (16.8%)
Teachers: 2,833.1 (22.2 to 1)
Librarians/Media Specialists: 5.0 (12,574.8 to 1)
Guidance Counselors: 50.0 (1,257.5 to 1)
Current Spending: ($ per student per year):
  Total: $7,437; Instruction: $4,404; Support Services: $2,687
Enrollment, Drop-out Rates and Diploma Recipients by Race/Ethnicity

Category	Total	White	Black	Asian	AIAN	Hisp.
Enrollment (%)	100.0	3.3	0.7	3.9	0.1	91.3
Drop-out Rate (%)	n/a	n/a	n/a	n/a	n/a	n/a
H.S. Diplomas (#)	2,484	131	30	185	2	2,131

Savanna Elementary
1330 S Knott Ave • Anaheim, CA 92804-4711
(714) 236-3800 • http://www.savsd.k12.ca.us/
Grade Span: KG-06; **Agency Type:** 1
Schools: 4
  4 Primary; 0 Middle; 0 High; 0 Other Level
  4 Regular; 0 Special Education; 0 Vocational; 0 Alternative
  0 Magnet; 0 Charter; 3 Title I Eligible; 1 School-wide Title I
Students: 2,449 (52.5% male; 47.4% female)
  Individual Education Program: 282 (11.5%);
  English Language Learner: 894 (36.5%); Migrant: 3 (0.1%)
  Eligible for Free Lunch Program: 1,001 (40.9%)
  Eligible for Reduced-Price Lunch Program: 364 (14.9%)
Teachers: 113.2 (21.6 to 1)
Librarians/Media Specialists: 0.0 (n/a to 1)
Guidance Counselors: 0.6 (4,081.7 to 1)
Current Spending: ($ per student per year):
  Total: $7,148; Instruction: $5,070; Support Services: $1,812
Enrollment, Drop-out Rates and Diploma Recipients by Race/Ethnicity

Category	Total	White	Black	Asian	AIAN	Hisp.
Enrollment (%)	100.0	24.3	5.2	17.7	0.2	51.1
Drop-out Rate (%)	n/a	n/a	n/a	n/a	n/a	n/a
H.S. Diplomas (#)	n/a	n/a	n/a	n/a	n/a	n/a

Tustin Unified
300 S C St • Tustin, CA 92780-3695
(714) 730-7301 • http://www.tustin.k12.ca.us/
Grade Span: KG-12; **Agency Type:** 1
Schools: 26
  17 Primary; 5 Middle; 4 High; 0 Other Level
  24 Regular; 0 Special Education; 0 Vocational; 2 Alternative
  1 Magnet; 0 Charter; 10 Title I Eligible; 0 School-wide Title I
Students: 18,950 (51.2% male; 48.7% female)
  Individual Education Program: 2,011 (10.6%);
  English Language Learner: 5,145 (27.2%); Migrant: 6 (<0.1%)
  Eligible for Free Lunch Program: 4,831 (25.5%)
  Eligible for Reduced-Price Lunch Program: 1,565 (8.3%)

Teachers: 807.6 (23.5 to 1)
Librarians/Media Specialists: 2.0 (9,475.0 to 1)
Guidance Counselors: 18.5 (1,024.3 to 1)
Current Spending: ($ per student per year):
   Total: $6,408; Instruction: $4,259; Support Services: $1,923
Enrollment, Drop-out Rates and Diploma Recipients by Race/Ethnicity

Category	Total	White	Black	Asian	AIAN	Hisp.
Enrollment (%)	100.0	37.1	2.7	14.3	0.3	43.8
Drop-out Rate (%)	n/a	n/a	n/a	n/a	n/a	n/a
H.S. Diplomas (#)	944	439	36	148	4	315

Westminster Elementary
14121 Cedarwood Ave • Westminster, CA 92683-4482
(714) 894-7311 • http://www.wsd.k12.ca.us/
Grade Span: KG-08; **Agency Type:** 1
Schools: 17
   14 Primary; 3 Middle; 0 High; 0 Other Level
   16 Regular; 0 Special Education; 0 Vocational; 1 Alternative
   0 Magnet; 0 Charter; 12 Title I Eligible; 11 School-wide Title I
Students: 10,253 (51.0% male; 48.9% female)
   Individual Education Program: 1,194 (11.6%);
   English Language Learner: 4,403 (42.9%); Migrant: 1 (<0.1%)
   Eligible for Free Lunch Program: 5,219 (50.9%)
   Eligible for Reduced-Price Lunch Program: 1,259 (12.3%)
Teachers: 484.4 (21.2 to 1)
Librarians/Media Specialists: 0.0 (n/a to 1)
Guidance Counselors: 5.0 (2,050.6 to 1)
Current Spending: ($ per student per year):
   Total: $7,367; Instruction: $5,163; Support Services: $1,913
Enrollment, Drop-out Rates and Diploma Recipients by Race/Ethnicity

Category	Total	White	Black	Asian	AIAN	Hisp.
Enrollment (%)	100.0	20.9	1.2	34.9	0.7	38.3
Drop-out Rate (%)	n/a	n/a	n/a	n/a	n/a	n/a
H.S. Diplomas (#)	n/a	n/a	n/a	n/a	n/a	n/a

Placer County

Auburn Union Elementary
55 College Way • Auburn, CA 95603-5001
(530) 885-7242 • http://www.auesd.k12.ca.us/
Grade Span: KG-08; **Agency Type:** 1
Schools: 5
   4 Primary; 1 Middle; 0 High; 0 Other Level
   5 Regular; 0 Special Education; 0 Vocational; 0 Alternative
   0 Magnet; 0 Charter; 2 Title I Eligible; 0 School-wide Title I
Students: 2,599 (49.8% male; 50.1% female)
   Individual Education Program: 304 (11.7%);
   English Language Learner: 219 (8.4%); Migrant: 15 (0.6%)
   Eligible for Free Lunch Program: 696 (26.8%)
   Eligible for Reduced-Price Lunch Program: 255 (9.8%)
Teachers: 119.7 (21.7 to 1)
Librarians/Media Specialists: 0.0 (n/a to 1)
Guidance Counselors: 3.0 (866.3 to 1)
Current Spending: ($ per student per year):
   Total: $6,716; Instruction: $4,506; Support Services: $1,948
Enrollment, Drop-out Rates and Diploma Recipients by Race/Ethnicity

Category	Total	White	Black	Asian	AIAN	Hisp.
Enrollment (%)	100.0	81.1	1.3	2.4	1.8	12.5
Drop-out Rate (%)	n/a	n/a	n/a	n/a	n/a	n/a
H.S. Diplomas (#)	n/a	n/a	n/a	n/a	n/a	n/a

Dry Creek Joint Elementary
9707 Cook Riolo Rd • Roseville, CA 95747-9793
(916) 771-0646 • http://web.drycreek.k12.ca.us/
Grade Span: KG-08; **Agency Type:** 1
Schools: 8
   6 Primary; 2 Middle; 0 High; 0 Other Level
   8 Regular; 0 Special Education; 0 Vocational; 0 Alternative
   0 Magnet; 0 Charter; 3 Title I Eligible; 0 School-wide Title I
Students: 7,008 (51.0% male; 48.9% female)
   Individual Education Program: 625 (8.9%);
   English Language Learner: 646 (9.2%); Migrant: 0 (0.0%)
   Eligible for Free Lunch Program: 865 (12.3%)
   Eligible for Reduced-Price Lunch Program: 494 (7.0%)
Teachers: 322.0 (21.8 to 1)
Librarians/Media Specialists: 0.0 (n/a to 1)
Guidance Counselors: 4.0 (1,752.0 to 1)
Current Spending: ($ per student per year):
   Total: $5,877; Instruction: $4,026; Support Services: $1,852
Enrollment, Drop-out Rates and Diploma Recipients by Race/Ethnicity

Category	Total	White	Black	Asian	AIAN	Hisp.
Enrollment (%)	100.0	70.9	6.0	10.5	0.6	9.5
Drop-out Rate (%)	n/a	n/a	n/a	n/a	n/a	n/a
H.S. Diplomas (#)	n/a	n/a	n/a	n/a	n/a	n/a

Eureka Union Elementary
5477 Eureka Rd • Granite Bay, CA 95746-8808
(916) 791-4939 • http://www.eurekacityschools.org/
Grade Span: KG-08; **Agency Type:** 1
Schools: 8
   3 Primary; 5 Middle; 0 High; 0 Other Level
   8 Regular; 0 Special Education; 0 Vocational; 0 Alternative
   0 Magnet; 0 Charter; 3 Title I Eligible; 0 School-wide Title I
Students: 4,264 (52.4% male; 47.5% female)
   Individual Education Program: 391 (9.2%);
   English Language Learner: 45 (1.1%); Migrant: 0 (0.0%)
   Eligible for Free Lunch Program: 106 (2.5%)
   Eligible for Reduced-Price Lunch Program: 53 (1.2%)
Teachers: 198.0 (21.5 to 1)
Librarians/Media Specialists: 0.0 (n/a to 1)
Guidance Counselors: 1.0 (4,264.0 to 1)
Current Spending: ($ per student per year):
   Total: $5,958; Instruction: $3,982; Support Services: $1,912
Enrollment, Drop-out Rates and Diploma Recipients by Race/Ethnicity

Category	Total	White	Black	Asian	AIAN	Hisp.
Enrollment (%)	100.0	79.7	1.4	7.9	1.2	5.3
Drop-out Rate (%)	n/a	n/a	n/a	n/a	n/a	n/a
H.S. Diplomas (#)	n/a	n/a	n/a	n/a	n/a	n/a

Loomis Union Elementary
3290 Humphrey Rd • Loomis, CA 95650-9043
(916) 652-1800 • http://www.loomis-usd.k12.ca.us/
Grade Span: KG-08; **Agency Type:** 1
Schools: 4
   4 Primary; 0 Middle; 0 High; 0 Other Level
   4 Regular; 0 Special Education; 0 Vocational; 0 Alternative
   0 Magnet; 0 Charter; 2 Title I Eligible; 0 School-wide Title I
Students: 1,899 (51.7% male; 48.2% female)
   Individual Education Program: 174 (9.2%);
   English Language Learner: 8 (0.4%); Migrant: 0 (0.0%)
   Eligible for Free Lunch Program: 146 (7.7%)
   Eligible for Reduced-Price Lunch Program: 107 (5.6%)
Teachers: 92.0 (20.6 to 1)
Librarians/Media Specialists: 0.0 (n/a to 1)
Guidance Counselors: 0.0 (n/a to 1)
Current Spending: ($ per student per year):
   Total: $6,357; Instruction: $4,126; Support Services: $2,026
Enrollment, Drop-out Rates and Diploma Recipients by Race/Ethnicity

Category	Total	White	Black	Asian	AIAN	Hisp.
Enrollment (%)	100.0	85.8	0.4	2.2	1.5	4.4
Drop-out Rate (%)	n/a	n/a	n/a	n/a	n/a	n/a
H.S. Diplomas (#)	n/a	n/a	n/a	n/a	n/a	n/a

Placer Union High
13000 New Airport Rd • Auburn, CA 95604-5048
Mailing Address: PO Box 5048 • Auburn, CA 95604-5048
(530) 886-4400 • http://www.puhsd.k12.ca.us/
Grade Span: 09-12; **Agency Type:** 1
Schools: 6
   0 Primary; 0 Middle; 6 High; 0 Other Level
   3 Regular; 1 Special Education; 0 Vocational; 2 Alternative
   0 Magnet; 0 Charter; 3 Title I Eligible; 0 School-wide Title I
Students: 4,746 (53.0% male; 46.9% female)
   Individual Education Program: 504 (10.6%);
   English Language Learner: 33 (0.7%); Migrant: 2 (<0.1%)
   Eligible for Free Lunch Program: 357 (7.5%)
   Eligible for Reduced-Price Lunch Program: 190 (4.0%)
Teachers: 202.3 (23.5 to 1)
Librarians/Media Specialists: 0.6 (7,910.0 to 1)
Guidance Counselors: 9.1 (521.5 to 1)
Current Spending: ($ per student per year):
   Total: $7,042; Instruction: $4,090; Support Services: $2,625
Enrollment, Drop-out Rates and Diploma Recipients by Race/Ethnicity

Category	Total	White	Black	Asian	AIAN	Hisp.
Enrollment (%)	100.0	84.8	0.4	1.3	1.1	3.9
Drop-out Rate (%)	n/a	n/a	n/a	n/a	n/a	n/a
H.S. Diplomas (#)	936	839	8	29	9	49

Rocklin Unified
2615 Sierra Meadows Dr • Rocklin, CA 95677-2811
(916) 624-2428 • http://www.rocklin.k12.ca.us/
Grade Span: KG-12; **Agency Type:** 1
Schools: 15
   10 Primary; 2 Middle; 2 High; 1 Other Level
   13 Regular; 0 Special Education; 0 Vocational; 2 Alternative
   0 Magnet; 1 Charter; 4 Title I Eligible; 0 School-wide Title I
Students: 9,171 (51.1% male; 48.8% female)
   Individual Education Program: 957 (10.4%);
   English Language Learner: 251 (2.7%); Migrant: 0 (0.0%)
   Eligible for Free Lunch Program: 595 (6.5%)

Eligible for Reduced-Price Lunch Program: 444 (4.8%)
Teachers: 441.3 (20.8 to 1)
Librarians/Media Specialists: 2.5 (3,668.4 to 1)
Guidance Counselors: 6.8 (1,348.7 to 1)
Current Spending: ($ per student per year):
Total: $6,372; Instruction: $3,962; Support Services: $2,227
Enrollment, Drop-out Rates and Diploma Recipients by Race/Ethnicity

Category	Total	White	Black	Asian	AIAN	Hisp.
Enrollment (%)	100.0	73.6	1.2	6.1	0.4	5.4
Drop-out Rate (%)	n/a	n/a	n/a	n/a	n/a	n/a
H.S. Diplomas (#)	446	368	4	34	3	27

Roseville City Elementary
1000 Darling Way • Roseville, CA 95678-4341
(916) 786-5090 • http://www.rcsdk8.org/
Grade Span: KG-08; **Agency Type:** 1
Schools: 14
11 Primary; 3 Middle; 0 High; 0 Other Level
14 Regular; 0 Special Education; 0 Vocational; 0 Alternative
0 Magnet; 0 Charter; 7 Title I Eligible; 1 School-wide Title I
Students: 7,527   (50.1% male; 49.8% female)
Individual Education Program: 800 (10.6%);
English Language Learner: 560 (7.4%); Migrant: 0 (0.0%)
Eligible for Free Lunch Program: 1,238 (16.4%)
Eligible for Reduced-Price Lunch Program: 609 (8.1%)
Teachers: 365.2 (20.6 to 1)
Librarians/Media Specialists: 0.0 (n/a to 1)
Guidance Counselors: 0.0 (n/a to 1)
Current Spending: ($ per student per year):
Total: $6,411; Instruction: $4,085; Support Services: $1,983
Enrollment, Drop-out Rates and Diploma Recipients by Race/Ethnicity

Category	Total	White	Black	Asian	AIAN	Hisp.
Enrollment (%)	100.0	69.1	2.8	7.6	0.9	17.9
Drop-out Rate (%)	n/a	n/a	n/a	n/a	n/a	n/a
H.S. Diplomas (#)	n/a	n/a	n/a	n/a	n/a	n/a

Roseville Joint Union High
1750 Cirby Way • Roseville, CA 95661-5520
(916) 786-2051 • http://www.rjuhsd.k12.ca.us/
Grade Span: 09-12; **Agency Type:** 1
Schools: 7
0 Primary; 0 Middle; 7 High; 0 Other Level
4 Regular; 0 Special Education; 0 Vocational; 3 Alternative
0 Magnet; 0 Charter; 4 Title I Eligible; 0 School-wide Title I
Students: 8,023   (50.5% male; 49.4% female)
Individual Education Program: 593 (7.4%);
English Language Learner: 102 (1.3%); Migrant: 1 (<0.1%)
Eligible for Free Lunch Program: 370 (4.6%)
Eligible for Reduced-Price Lunch Program: 124 (1.5%)
Teachers: 359.4 (22.3 to 1)
Librarians/Media Specialists: 3.0 (2,674.3 to 1)
Guidance Counselors: 18.8 (426.8 to 1)
Current Spending: ($ per student per year):
Total: $6,844; Instruction: $3,799; Support Services: $2,842
Enrollment, Drop-out Rates and Diploma Recipients by Race/Ethnicity

Category	Total	White	Black	Asian	AIAN	Hisp.
Enrollment (%)	100.0	74.4	3.7	8.5	0.9	11.8
Drop-out Rate (%)	n/a	n/a	n/a	n/a	n/a	n/a
H.S. Diplomas (#)	1,585	1,273	57	102	18	135

Tahoe-Truckee Joint Unified
11839 Donner Pass Rd • Truckee, CA 96161-4951
(530) 582-2500
Grade Span: KG-12; **Agency Type:** 1
Schools: 12
6 Primary; 2 Middle; 3 High; 1 Other Level
10 Regular; 0 Special Education; 0 Vocational; 2 Alternative
2 Magnet; 0 Charter; 5 Title I Eligible; 0 School-wide Title I
Students: 4,589   (50.7% male; 49.2% female)
Individual Education Program: 530 (11.5%);
English Language Learner: 830 (18.1%); Migrant: 0 (0.0%)
Eligible for Free Lunch Program: 655 (14.3%)
Eligible for Reduced-Price Lunch Program: 214 (4.7%)
Teachers: 247.2 (18.6 to 1)
Librarians/Media Specialists: 2.0 (2,294.5 to 1)
Guidance Counselors: 9.6 (478.0 to 1)
Current Spending: ($ per student per year):
Total: $7,146; Instruction: $4,647; Support Services: $2,344
Enrollment, Drop-out Rates and Diploma Recipients by Race/Ethnicity

Category	Total	White	Black	Asian	AIAN	Hisp.
Enrollment (%)	100.0	73.8	0.4	0.9	0.4	24.3
Drop-out Rate (%)	n/a	n/a	n/a	n/a	n/a	n/a
H.S. Diplomas (#)	379	281	4	3	2	64

Western Placer Unified
810 J St • Lincoln, CA 95648-1825
(916) 645-6350 • http://www.wpusd.k12.ca.us/
Grade Span: KG-12; **Agency Type:** 1
Schools: 8
3 Primary; 1 Middle; 2 High; 2 Other Level
7 Regular; 0 Special Education; 0 Vocational; 1 Alternative
0 Magnet; 1 Charter; 7 Title I Eligible; 0 School-wide Title I
Students: 7,309   (49.0% male; 50.9% female)
Individual Education Program: 680 (9.3%);
English Language Learner: 572 (7.8%); Migrant: 0 (0.0%)
Eligible for Free Lunch Program: 868 (11.9%)
Eligible for Reduced-Price Lunch Program: 396 (5.4%)
Teachers: 211.0 (34.6 to 1)
Librarians/Media Specialists: 0.0 (n/a to 1)
Guidance Counselors: 5.0 (1,461.8 to 1)
Current Spending: ($ per student per year):
Total: $4,948; Instruction: $3,643; Support Services: $1,175
Enrollment, Drop-out Rates and Diploma Recipients by Race/Ethnicity

Category	Total	White	Black	Asian	AIAN	Hisp.
Enrollment (%)	100.0	74.0	1.9	2.1	1.1	16.2
Drop-out Rate (%)	n/a	n/a	n/a	n/a	n/a	n/a
H.S. Diplomas (#)	581	435	19	10	8	87

Plumas County

Plumas Unified
50 Church St • Quincy, CA 95971-6009
(530) 283-6500 • http://www.pcoe.k12.ca.us/
Grade Span: KG-12; **Agency Type:** 1
Schools: 16
6 Primary; 1 Middle; 8 High; 1 Other Level
11 Regular; 0 Special Education; 0 Vocational; 5 Alternative
0 Magnet; 1 Charter; 15 Title I Eligible; 0 School-wide Title I
Students: 3,141   (52.3% male; 47.6% female)
Individual Education Program: 386 (12.3%);
English Language Learner: 104 (3.3%); Migrant: 0 (0.0%)
Eligible for Free Lunch Program: 790 (25.2%)
Eligible for Reduced-Price Lunch Program: 272 (8.7%)
Teachers: 165.8 (18.9 to 1)
Librarians/Media Specialists: 0.0 (n/a to 1)
Guidance Counselors: 3.3 (951.8 to 1)
Current Spending: ($ per student per year):
Total: $8,377; Instruction: $5,063; Support Services: $3,032
Enrollment, Drop-out Rates and Diploma Recipients by Race/Ethnicity

Category	Total	White	Black	Asian	AIAN	Hisp.
Enrollment (%)	100.0	78.3	1.9	1.9	7.4	9.7
Drop-out Rate (%)	n/a	n/a	n/a	n/a	n/a	n/a
H.S. Diplomas (#)	264	225	3	8	10	18

Riverside County

Alvord Unified
10365 Keller Ave • Riverside, CA 92505-1349
(909) 509-5000 • http://www.alvord.k12.ca.us/
Grade Span: KG-12; **Agency Type:** 1
Schools: 19
12 Primary; 4 Middle; 3 High; 0 Other Level
18 Regular; 0 Special Education; 0 Vocational; 1 Alternative
0 Magnet; 0 Charter; 10 Title I Eligible; 10 School-wide Title I
Students: 19,441   (51.9% male; 48.0% female)
Individual Education Program: 1,781 (9.2%);
English Language Learner: 7,652 (39.4%); Migrant: 2 (<0.1%)
Eligible for Free Lunch Program: 6,851 (35.2%)
Eligible for Reduced-Price Lunch Program: 2,771 (14.3%)
Teachers: 853.6 (22.8 to 1)
Librarians/Media Specialists: 6.0 (3,240.2 to 1)
Guidance Counselors: 18.0 (1,080.1 to 1)
Current Spending: ($ per student per year):
Total: $6,631; Instruction: $4,274; Support Services: $2,109
Enrollment, Drop-out Rates and Diploma Recipients by Race/Ethnicity

Category	Total	White	Black	Asian	AIAN	Hisp.
Enrollment (%)	100.0	23.1	5.7	5.4	0.4	64.1
Drop-out Rate (%)	n/a	n/a	n/a	n/a	n/a	n/a
H.S. Diplomas (#)	837	305	49	73	2	408

Banning Unified
161 W Williams St • Banning, CA 92220-4746
(909) 922-0201 • http://www.banning.k12.ca.us/
Grade Span: KG-12; **Agency Type:** 1
Schools: 10
4 Primary; 2 Middle; 3 High; 1 Other Level
7 Regular; 0 Special Education; 0 Vocational; 3 Alternative
0 Magnet; 0 Charter; 6 Title I Eligible; 6 School-wide Title I
Students: 4,754   (51.8% male; 48.1% female)

Individual Education Program: 422 (8.9%);
English Language Learner: 1,111 (23.4%); Migrant: 0 (0.0%)
Eligible for Free Lunch Program: 2,887 (60.7%)
Eligible for Reduced-Price Lunch Program: 725 (15.3%)
Teachers: 183.4 (25.9 to 1)
Librarians/Media Specialists: 0.0 (n/a to 1)
Guidance Counselors: 3.0 (1,584.7 to 1)
Current Spending: ($ per student per year):
Total: $6,897; Instruction: $4,342; Support Services: $2,226
Enrollment, Drop-out Rates and Diploma Recipients by Race/Ethnicity

Category	Total	White	Black	Asian	AIAN	Hisp.
Enrollment (%)	100.0	22.5	11.3	9.3	4.9	48.8
Drop-out Rate (%)	n/a	n/a	n/a	n/a	n/a	n/a
H.S. Diplomas (#)	217	57	36	44	10	66

Beaumont Unified

500 Grace Ave • Beaumont, CA 92223-0187
Mailing Address: PO Box 187 • Beaumont, CA 92223-0187
(909) 845-1631 • http://www.beaumontusd.k12.ca.us/
Grade Span: KG-12; **Agency Type:** 1
Schools: 10
5 Primary; 1 Middle; 2 High; 2 Other Level
6 Regular; 0 Special Education; 0 Vocational; 4 Alternative
0 Magnet; 0 Charter; 7 Title I Eligible; 5 School-wide Title I
Students: 4,959   (49.5% male; 50.4% female)
Individual Education Program: 507 (10.2%);
English Language Learner: 694 (14.0%); Migrant: 0 (0.0%)
Eligible for Free Lunch Program: 2,045 (41.2%)
Eligible for Reduced-Price Lunch Program: 889 (17.9%)
Teachers: 221.9 (22.3 to 1)
Librarians/Media Specialists: 0.5 (9,918.0 to 1)
Guidance Counselors: 4.0 (1,239.8 to 1)
Current Spending: ($ per student per year):
Total: $7,343; Instruction: $4,158; Support Services: $2,853
Enrollment, Drop-out Rates and Diploma Recipients by Race/Ethnicity

Category	Total	White	Black	Asian	AIAN	Hisp.
Enrollment (%)	100.0	47.1	3.7	3.9	2.1	42.0
Drop-out Rate (%)	n/a	n/a	n/a	n/a	n/a	n/a
H.S. Diplomas (#)	161	102	3	3	2	51

Coachella Valley Unified

87-225 Church St • Thermal, CA 92274-0847
Mailing Address: PO Box 847 • Thermal, CA 92274-0847
(760) 399-5137 • http://www.coachella.k12.ca.us/
Grade Span: KG-12; **Agency Type:** 1
Schools: 19
13 Primary; 2 Middle; 4 High; 0 Other Level
18 Regular; 0 Special Education; 0 Vocational; 1 Alternative
0 Magnet; 0 Charter; 16 Title I Eligible; 16 School-wide Title I
Students: 14,621   (51.5% male; 48.4% female)
Individual Education Program: 1,150 (7.9%);
English Language Learner: 9,813 (67.1%); Migrant: 3,493 (23.9%)
Eligible for Free Lunch Program: 11,393 (77.9%)
Eligible for Reduced-Price Lunch Program: 1,188 (8.1%)
Teachers: 666.3 (21.9 to 1)
Librarians/Media Specialists: 1.0 (14,621.0 to 1)
Guidance Counselors: 11.0 (1,329.2 to 1)
Current Spending: ($ per student per year):
Total: $7,811; Instruction: $4,862; Support Services: $2,577
Enrollment, Drop-out Rates and Diploma Recipients by Race/Ethnicity

Category	Total	White	Black	Asian	AIAN	Hisp.
Enrollment (%)	100.0	1.4	0.2	0.4	0.4	97.3
Drop-out Rate (%)	n/a	n/a	n/a	n/a	n/a	n/a
H.S. Diplomas (#)	558	17	0	2	0	539

Corona-Norco Unified

2820 Clark Ave • Norco, CA 91760-1903
(909) 736-5000 • http://www.cnusd.k12.ca.us/
Grade Span: KG-12; **Agency Type:** 1
Schools: 42
25 Primary; 6 Middle; 9 High; 2 Other Level
35 Regular; 1 Special Education; 0 Vocational; 6 Alternative
2 Magnet; 0 Charter; 12 Title I Eligible; 7 School-wide Title I
Students: 43,998   (51.3% male; 48.6% female)
Individual Education Program: 4,521 (10.3%);
English Language Learner: 7,370 (16.8%); Migrant: 137 (0.3%)
Eligible for Free Lunch Program: 11,642 (26.5%)
Eligible for Reduced-Price Lunch Program: 5,960 (13.5%)
Teachers: 2,085.9 (21.1 to 1)
Librarians/Media Specialists: 4.0 (10,999.5 to 1)
Guidance Counselors: 44.0 (1,000.0 to 1)
Current Spending: ($ per student per year):
Total: $6,680; Instruction: $4,321; Support Services: $2,090

Enrollment, Drop-out Rates and Diploma Recipients by Race/Ethnicity

Category	Total	White	Black	Asian	AIAN	Hisp.
Enrollment (%)	100.0	41.3	6.2	6.8	0.4	45.3
Drop-out Rate (%)	n/a	n/a	n/a	n/a	n/a	n/a
H.S. Diplomas (#)	2,170	1,050	139	173	4	804

Desert Sands Unified

47-950 Dune Palms Rd • La Quinta, CA 92253-4000
(760) 777-4200 • http://www.dsusd.k12.ca.us/
Grade Span: KG-12; **Agency Type:** 1
Schools: 28
17 Primary; 6 Middle; 4 High; 1 Other Level
27 Regular; 0 Special Education; 0 Vocational; 1 Alternative
3 Magnet; 1 Charter; 16 Title I Eligible; 8 School-wide Title I
Students: 26,122   (50.7% male; 49.2% female)
Individual Education Program: 2,128 (8.1%);
English Language Learner: 7,690 (29.4%); Migrant: 722 (2.8%)
Eligible for Free Lunch Program: 10,235 (39.2%)
Eligible for Reduced-Price Lunch Program: 2,956 (11.3%)
Teachers: 1,190.3 (21.9 to 1)
Librarians/Media Specialists: 4.0 (6,530.5 to 1)
Guidance Counselors: 41.0 (637.1 to 1)
Current Spending: ($ per student per year):
Total: $6,880; Instruction: $4,391; Support Services: $2,202
Enrollment, Drop-out Rates and Diploma Recipients by Race/Ethnicity

Category	Total	White	Black	Asian	AIAN	Hisp.
Enrollment (%)	100.0	29.7	2.0	1.7	0.4	61.8
Drop-out Rate (%)	n/a	n/a	n/a	n/a	n/a	n/a
H.S. Diplomas (#)	1,394	571	25	30	7	756

Hemet Unified

2350 W Latham Ave • Hemet, CA 92545-3632
(909) 765-5100 • http://www.hemetusd.k12.ca.us/
Grade Span: KG-12; **Agency Type:** 1
Schools: 22
13 Primary; 3 Middle; 4 High; 2 Other Level
19 Regular; 0 Special Education; 0 Vocational; 3 Alternative
1 Magnet; 0 Charter; 19 Title I Eligible; 12 School-wide Title I
Students: 19,693   (50.8% male; 49.1% female)
Individual Education Program: 2,256 (11.5%);
English Language Learner: 2,577 (13.1%); Migrant: 5 (<0.1%)
Eligible for Free Lunch Program: 10,241 (52.0%)
Eligible for Reduced-Price Lunch Program: 3,871 (19.7%)
Teachers: 898.5 (21.9 to 1)
Librarians/Media Specialists: 6.0 (3,282.2 to 1)
Guidance Counselors: 21.5 (916.0 to 1)
Current Spending: ($ per student per year):
Total: $6,725; Instruction: $4,278; Support Services: $2,168
Enrollment, Drop-out Rates and Diploma Recipients by Race/Ethnicity

Category	Total	White	Black	Asian	AIAN	Hisp.
Enrollment (%)	100.0	54.0	6.0	3.4	1.1	34.5
Drop-out Rate (%)	n/a	n/a	n/a	n/a	n/a	n/a
H.S. Diplomas (#)	995	699	30	29	5	232

Jurupa Unified

4850 Pedley Rd • Riverside, CA 92509-6611
(909) 360-4100 • http://www.jusd.k12.ca.us/
Grade Span: KG-12; **Agency Type:** 1
Schools: 24
16 Primary; 3 Middle; 5 High; 0 Other Level
21 Regular; 0 Special Education; 0 Vocational; 3 Alternative
0 Magnet; 0 Charter; 17 Title I Eligible; 8 School-wide Title I
Students: 20,924   (50.9% male; 49.0% female)
Individual Education Program: 1,904 (9.1%);
English Language Learner: 5,967 (28.5%); Migrant: 0 (0.0%)
Eligible for Free Lunch Program: 9,882 (47.2%)
Eligible for Reduced-Price Lunch Program: 2,987 (14.3%)
Teachers: 885.4 (23.6 to 1)
Librarians/Media Specialists: 0.3 (69,746.7 to 1)
Guidance Counselors: 17.0 (1,230.8 to 1)
Current Spending: ($ per student per year):
Total: $6,911; Instruction: $4,433; Support Services: $2,176
Enrollment, Drop-out Rates and Diploma Recipients by Race/Ethnicity

Category	Total	White	Black	Asian	AIAN	Hisp.
Enrollment (%)	100.0	26.1	4.4	2.2	0.4	66.9
Drop-out Rate (%)	n/a	n/a	n/a	n/a	n/a	n/a
H.S. Diplomas (#)	797	339	43	19	2	392

Lake Elsinore Unified

545 Chaney St • Lake Elsinore, CA 92530-2723
(909) 674-7731 • http://www.leusd.k12.ca.us/
Grade Span: KG-12; **Agency Type:** 1
Schools: 22
13 Primary; 4 Middle; 4 High; 1 Other Level
19 Regular; 0 Special Education; 0 Vocational; 3 Alternative

1 Magnet; 0 Charter; 12 Title I Eligible; 3 School-wide Title I
Students: 19,711 (51.3% male; 48.6% female)
    Individual Education Program: 2,480 (12.6%);
    English Language Learner: 3,282 (16.7%); Migrant: 0 (0.0%)
    Eligible for Free Lunch Program: 5,922 (30.0%)
    Eligible for Reduced-Price Lunch Program: 2,576 (13.1%)
Teachers: 876.9 (22.5 to 1)
Librarians/Media Specialists: 0.0 (n/a to 1)
Guidance Counselors: 19.0 (1,037.4 to 1)
Current Spending: ($ per student per year):
    Total: $6,655; Instruction: $4,199; Support Services: $2,197
Enrollment, Drop-out Rates and Diploma Recipients by Race/Ethnicity

Category	Total	White	Black	Asian	AIAN	Hisp.
Enrollment (%)	100.0	50.6	4.8	3.6	0.9	39.1
Drop-out Rate (%)	n/a	n/a	n/a	n/a	n/a	n/a
H.S. Diplomas (#)	900	547	37	48	5	256

Menifee Union Elementary
30205 Menifee Rd • Menifee, CA 92584-8109
(909) 672-1851 • http://www.menifeeusd.k12.ca.us/
Grade Span: KG-08; **Agency Type:** 1
Schools: 7
    5 Primary; 2 Middle; 0 High; 0 Other Level
    7 Regular; 0 Special Education; 0 Vocational; 0 Alternative
    0 Magnet; 0 Charter; 1 Title I Eligible; 1 School-wide Title I
Students: 5,920 (50.4% male; 49.5% female)
    Individual Education Program: 472 (8.0%);
    English Language Learner: 907 (15.3%); Migrant: 0 (0.0%)
    Eligible for Free Lunch Program: 1,042 (17.6%)
    Eligible for Reduced-Price Lunch Program: 331 (5.6%)
Teachers: 262.0 (22.6 to 1)
Librarians/Media Specialists: 0.0 (n/a to 1)
Guidance Counselors: 0.0 (n/a to 1)
Current Spending: ($ per student per year):
    Total: $6,048; Instruction: $4,042; Support Services: $1,800
Enrollment, Drop-out Rates and Diploma Recipients by Race/Ethnicity

Category	Total	White	Black	Asian	AIAN	Hisp.
Enrollment (%)	100.0	54.3	3.5	4.5	0.8	33.4
Drop-out Rate (%)	n/a	n/a	n/a	n/a	n/a	n/a
H.S. Diplomas (#)	n/a	n/a	n/a	n/a	n/a	n/a

Moreno Valley Unified
25634 Alessandro Blvd • Moreno Valley, CA 92553-4306
(909) 485-5600 • http://www.mvusd.k12.ca.us/
Grade Span: KG-12; **Agency Type:** 1
Schools: 33
    19 Primary; 6 Middle; 7 High; 1 Other Level
    30 Regular; 0 Special Education; 0 Vocational; 3 Alternative
    7 Magnet; 1 Charter; 21 Title I Eligible; 18 School-wide Title I
Students: 34,792 (51.1% male; 48.8% female)
    Individual Education Program: 3,638 (10.5%);
    English Language Learner: 10,087 (29.0%); Migrant: 0 (0.0%)
    Eligible for Free Lunch Program: 16,013 (46.0%)
    Eligible for Reduced-Price Lunch Program: 5,615 (16.1%)
Teachers: 1,538.5 (22.6 to 1)
Librarians/Media Specialists: 0.0 (n/a to 1)
Guidance Counselors: 60.8 (572.2 to 1)
Current Spending: ($ per student per year):
    Total: $6,582; Instruction: $4,208; Support Services: $2,068
Enrollment, Drop-out Rates and Diploma Recipients by Race/Ethnicity

Category	Total	White	Black	Asian	AIAN	Hisp.
Enrollment (%)	100.0	20.8	22.2	5.5	0.4	50.5
Drop-out Rate (%)	n/a	n/a	n/a	n/a	n/a	n/a
H.S. Diplomas (#)	1,694	635	363	152	3	538

Murrieta Valley Unified
41870 Mcalby Ct • Murrieta, CA 92562-7021
(909) 696-1600 • http://www.murrieta.k12.ca.us/
Grade Span: KG-12; **Agency Type:** 1
Schools: 16
    9 Primary; 3 Middle; 3 High; 1 Other Level
    14 Regular; 0 Special Education; 0 Vocational; 2 Alternative
    0 Magnet; 0 Charter; 5 Title I Eligible; 0 School-wide Title I
Students: 17,480 (50.8% male; 49.1% female)
    Individual Education Program: 1,706 (9.8%);
    English Language Learner: 432 (2.5%); Migrant: 0 (0.0%)
    Eligible for Free Lunch Program: 1,470 (8.4%)
    Eligible for Reduced-Price Lunch Program: 1,063 (6.1%)
Teachers: 773.5 (22.6 to 1)
Librarians/Media Specialists: 3.0 (5,826.7 to 1)
Guidance Counselors: 17.0 (1,028.2 to 1)
Current Spending: ($ per student per year):
    Total: $5,945; Instruction: $3,812; Support Services: $1,950

Enrollment, Drop-out Rates and Diploma Recipients by Race/Ethnicity

Category	Total	White	Black	Asian	AIAN	Hisp.
Enrollment (%)	100.0	61.1	5.9	7.3	0.5	20.0
Drop-out Rate (%)	n/a	n/a	n/a	n/a	n/a	n/a
H.S. Diplomas (#)	690	520	29	26	1	102

Nuview Union Elementary
29780 Lakeview Ave • Nuevo, CA 92567-9261
(909) 928-0066
Grade Span: KG-12; **Agency Type:** 1
Schools: 4
    2 Primary; 1 Middle; 1 High; 0 Other Level
    4 Regular; 0 Special Education; 0 Vocational; 0 Alternative
    0 Magnet; 1 Charter; 2 Title I Eligible; 1 School-wide Title I
Students: 1,523 (52.7% male; 47.2% female)
    Individual Education Program: 107 (7.0%);
    English Language Learner: 408 (26.8%); Migrant: 0 (0.0%)
    Eligible for Free Lunch Program: 604 (39.7%)
    Eligible for Reduced-Price Lunch Program: 188 (12.3%)
Teachers: 68.7 (22.2 to 1)
Librarians/Media Specialists: 0.0 (n/a to 1)
Guidance Counselors: 1.0 (1,523.0 to 1)
Current Spending: ($ per student per year):
    Total: $6,838; Instruction: $4,047; Support Services: $2,388
Enrollment, Drop-out Rates and Diploma Recipients by Race/Ethnicity

Category	Total	White	Black	Asian	AIAN	Hisp.
Enrollment (%)	100.0	47.5	1.4	1.1	0.5	47.9
Drop-out Rate (%)	n/a	n/a	n/a	n/a	n/a	n/a
H.S. Diplomas (#)	0	0	0	0	0	0

Palm Springs Unified
980 E Tahquitz Canyon Way • Palm Springs, CA 92262-1009
(760) 416-6000 • http://www.psusd.k12.ca.us/
Grade Span: KG-12; **Agency Type:** 1
Schools: 23
    14 Primary; 4 Middle; 4 High; 1 Other Level
    22 Regular; 0 Special Education; 0 Vocational; 1 Alternative
    0 Magnet; 0 Charter; 23 Title I Eligible; 6 School-wide Title I
Students: 22,499 (51.2% male; 48.7% female)
    Individual Education Program: 1,945 (8.6%);
    English Language Learner: 7,611 (33.8%); Migrant: 211 (0.9%)
    Eligible for Free Lunch Program: 10,727 (47.7%)
    Eligible for Reduced-Price Lunch Program: 3,065 (13.6%)
Teachers: 1,068.7 (21.1 to 1)
Librarians/Media Specialists: 7.0 (3,214.1 to 1)
Guidance Counselors: 20.5 (1,097.5 to 1)
Current Spending: ($ per student per year):
    Total: $7,006; Instruction: $4,417; Support Services: $2,321
Enrollment, Drop-out Rates and Diploma Recipients by Race/Ethnicity

Category	Total	White	Black	Asian	AIAN	Hisp.
Enrollment (%)	100.0	26.0	5.0	3.7	0.9	64.5
Drop-out Rate (%)	n/a	n/a	n/a	n/a	n/a	n/a
H.S. Diplomas (#)	950	420	41	49	9	431

Palo Verde Unified
295 N First St • Blythe, CA 92225-1703
(760) 922-4164 • http://www.pvusd-bly.k12.ca.us/
Grade Span: KG-12; **Agency Type:** 1
Schools: 6
    3 Primary; 1 Middle; 2 High; 0 Other Level
    5 Regular; 0 Special Education; 0 Vocational; 1 Alternative
    0 Magnet; 0 Charter; 6 Title I Eligible; 3 School-wide Title I
Students: 3,677 (51.7% male; 48.2% female)
    Individual Education Program: 270 (7.3%);
    English Language Learner: 527 (14.3%); Migrant: 372 (10.1%)
    Eligible for Free Lunch Program: 1,629 (44.3%)
    Eligible for Reduced-Price Lunch Program: 313 (8.5%)
Teachers: 162.4 (22.6 to 1)
Librarians/Media Specialists: 0.0 (n/a to 1)
Guidance Counselors: 2.0 (1,838.5 to 1)
Current Spending: ($ per student per year):
    Total: $7,324; Instruction: $4,222; Support Services: $2,804
Enrollment, Drop-out Rates and Diploma Recipients by Race/Ethnicity

Category	Total	White	Black	Asian	AIAN	Hisp.
Enrollment (%)	100.0	33.1	9.9	1.2	0.6	54.2
Drop-out Rate (%)	n/a	n/a	n/a	n/a	n/a	n/a
H.S. Diplomas (#)	185	58	15	3	0	109

Perris Elementary
143 E First St • Perris, CA 92570-2113
(909) 657-3118 • http://www.perris.k12.ca.us/
Grade Span: KG-06; **Agency Type:** 1
Schools: 7
    7 Primary; 0 Middle; 0 High; 0 Other Level
    7 Regular; 0 Special Education; 0 Vocational; 0 Alternative

0 Magnet; 0 Charter; 7 Title I Eligible; 6 School-wide Title I
Students: 5,235   (52.0% male; 47.9% female)
  Individual Education Program: 515 (9.8%);
  English Language Learner: 2,451 (46.8%); Migrant: 171 (3.3%)
  Eligible for Free Lunch Program: 4,017 (76.7%)
  Eligible for Reduced-Price Lunch Program: 660 (12.6%)
Teachers: 254.0 (20.6 to 1)
Librarians/Media Specialists: 0.0 (n/a to 1)
Guidance Counselors: 0.0 (n/a to 1)
Current Spending: ($ per student per year):
  Total: $7,033; Instruction: $3,982; Support Services: $2,368

Enrollment, Drop-out Rates and Diploma Recipients by Race/Ethnicity

Category	Total	White	Black	Asian	AIAN	Hisp.
Enrollment (%)	100.0	8.2	14.2	1.7	0.4	74.8
Drop-out Rate (%)	n/a	n/a	n/a	n/a	n/a	n/a
H.S. Diplomas (#)	n/a	n/a	n/a	n/a	n/a	n/a

Perris Union High

155 E Fourth St • Perris, CA 92570-2124
(909) 943-6369 • http://www.puhsd.org/
Grade Span: 07-12; **Agency Type:** 1
Schools: 7
  0 Primary; 1 Middle; 6 High; 0 Other Level
  4 Regular; 0 Special Education; 0 Vocational; 3 Alternative
  0 Magnet; 2 Charter; 4 Title I Eligible; 1 School-wide Title I
Students: 7,498   (50.8% male; 49.1% female)
  Individual Education Program: 546 (7.3%);
  English Language Learner: 770 (10.3%); Migrant: 89 (1.2%)
  Eligible for Free Lunch Program: 2,657 (35.4%)
  Eligible for Reduced-Price Lunch Program: 548 (7.3%)
Teachers: 297.3 (25.2 to 1)
Librarians/Media Specialists: 3.0 (2,499.3 to 1)
Guidance Counselors: 13.0 (576.8 to 1)
Current Spending: ($ per student per year):
  Total: $6,313; Instruction: $3,785; Support Services: $2,528

Enrollment, Drop-out Rates and Diploma Recipients by Race/Ethnicity

Category	Total	White	Black	Asian	AIAN	Hisp.
Enrollment (%)	100.0	33.2	10.7	2.3	0.6	51.9
Drop-out Rate (%)	n/a	n/a	n/a	n/a	n/a	n/a
H.S. Diplomas (#)	994	423	90	29	12	430

Riverside County Office of Education

3939 13th St • Riverside, CA 92502-0868
Mailing Address: PO Box 868 • Riverside, CA 92502-0868
(909) 826-6530 • http://www.rcoe.k12.ca.us/
Grade Span: KG-12; **Agency Type:** 4
Schools: 5
  0 Primary; 0 Middle; 0 High; 5 Other Level
  1 Regular; 1 Special Education; 0 Vocational; 3 Alternative
  0 Magnet; 0 Charter; 1 Title I Eligible; 0 School-wide Title I
Students: 3,720   (60.4% male; 39.5% female)
  Individual Education Program: 2,854 (76.7%);
  English Language Learner: 687 (18.5%); Migrant: 6 (0.2%)
  Eligible for Free Lunch Program: 889 (23.9%)
  Eligible for Reduced-Price Lunch Program: 20 (0.5%)
Teachers: 289.7 (12.8 to 1)
Librarians/Media Specialists: 1.0 (3,720.0 to 1)
Guidance Counselors: 0.0 (n/a to 1)
Current Spending: ($ per student per year):
  Total: $41,852; Instruction: $18,463; Support Services: $23,261

Enrollment, Drop-out Rates and Diploma Recipients by Race/Ethnicity

Category	Total	White	Black	Asian	AIAN	Hisp.
Enrollment (%)	100.0	30.2	12.8	1.9	0.7	54.1
Drop-out Rate (%)	n/a	n/a	n/a	n/a	n/a	n/a
H.S. Diplomas (#)	285	122	36	10	3	114

Riverside Unified

3380 14th St • Riverside, CA 92516-2800
Mailing Address: PO Box 2800 • Riverside, CA 92516-2800
(909) 788-7134 • http://www.rusd.k12.ca.us/
Grade Span: KG-12; **Agency Type:** 1
Schools: 46
  30 Primary; 6 Middle; 8 High; 2 Other Level
  41 Regular; 1 Special Education; 0 Vocational; 4 Alternative
  0 Magnet; 1 Charter; 22 Title I Eligible; 16 School-wide Title I
Students: 42,012   (51.0% male; 48.9% female)
  Individual Education Program: 4,362 (10.4%);
  English Language Learner: 6,714 (16.0%); Migrant: 0 (0.0%)
  Eligible for Free Lunch Program: 14,164 (33.7%)
  Eligible for Reduced-Price Lunch Program: 5,210 (12.4%)
Teachers: 1,807.7 (23.2 to 1)
Librarians/Media Specialists: 9.0 (4,668.0 to 1)
Guidance Counselors: 43.3 (970.3 to 1)
Current Spending: ($ per student per year):
  Total: $6,567; Instruction: $4,134; Support Services: $2,179

Enrollment, Drop-out Rates and Diploma Recipients by Race/Ethnicity

Category	Total	White	Black	Asian	AIAN	Hisp.
Enrollment (%)	100.0	37.5	10.0	4.8	0.5	47.1
Drop-out Rate (%)	n/a	n/a	n/a	n/a	n/a	n/a
H.S. Diplomas (#)	2,251	1,110	223	156	10	752

Romoland Elementary

25900 Leon Rd • Homeland, CA 92548
(909) 926-9244
Grade Span: KG-08; **Agency Type:** 1
Schools: 2
  2 Primary; 0 Middle; 0 High; 0 Other Level
  2 Regular; 0 Special Education; 0 Vocational; 0 Alternative
  0 Magnet; 0 Charter; 2 Title I Eligible; 2 School-wide Title I
Students: 1,763   (51.6% male; 48.3% female)
  Individual Education Program: 180 (10.2%);
  English Language Learner: 745 (42.3%); Migrant: 3 (0.2%)
  Eligible for Free Lunch Program: 1,053 (59.7%)
  Eligible for Reduced-Price Lunch Program: 286 (16.2%)
Teachers: 75.0 (23.5 to 1)
Librarians/Media Specialists: 0.0 (n/a to 1)
Guidance Counselors: 2.0 (881.5 to 1)
Current Spending: ($ per student per year):
  Total: $6,798; Instruction: $4,151; Support Services: $2,270

Enrollment, Drop-out Rates and Diploma Recipients by Race/Ethnicity

Category	Total	White	Black	Asian	AIAN	Hisp.
Enrollment (%)	100.0	31.7	2.6	0.8	0.4	64.4
Drop-out Rate (%)	n/a	n/a	n/a	n/a	n/a	n/a
H.S. Diplomas (#)	n/a	n/a	n/a	n/a	n/a	n/a

San Jacinto Unified

2045 S San Jacinto Ave • San Jacinto, CA 92583-5626
(909) 929-7700 • http://www.sanjacinto.k12.ca.us/
Grade Span: KG-12; **Agency Type:** 1
Schools: 9
  5 Primary; 2 Middle; 1 High; 1 Other Level
  8 Regular; 0 Special Education; 0 Vocational; 1 Alternative
  0 Magnet; 1 Charter; 8 Title I Eligible; 7 School-wide Title I
Students: 7,093   (51.1% male; 48.8% female)
  Individual Education Program: 877 (12.4%);
  English Language Learner: 2,156 (30.4%); Migrant: 0 (0.0%)
  Eligible for Free Lunch Program: 4,288 (60.5%)
  Eligible for Reduced-Price Lunch Program: 760 (10.7%)
Teachers: 310.7 (22.8 to 1)
Librarians/Media Specialists: 0.0 (n/a to 1)
Guidance Counselors: 4.0 (1,773.3 to 1)
Current Spending: ($ per student per year):
  Total: $6,446; Instruction: $4,092; Support Services: $2,089

Enrollment, Drop-out Rates and Diploma Recipients by Race/Ethnicity

Category	Total	White	Black	Asian	AIAN	Hisp.
Enrollment (%)	100.0	31.6	5.3	2.2	2.7	54.6
Drop-out Rate (%)	n/a	n/a	n/a	n/a	n/a	n/a
H.S. Diplomas (#)	260	109	4	3	9	134

Temecula Valley Unified

31350 Rancho Vista Rd • Temecula, CA 92592-6202
(909) 676-2661 • http://www.tvusd.k12.ca.us/
Grade Span: KG-12; **Agency Type:** 1
Schools: 24
  14 Primary; 5 Middle; 4 High; 1 Other Level
  21 Regular; 0 Special Education; 0 Vocational; 3 Alternative
  0 Magnet; 2 Charter; 4 Title I Eligible; 0 School-wide Title I
Students: 23,496   (50.4% male; 49.5% female)
  Individual Education Program: 2,768 (11.8%);
  English Language Learner: 1,349 (5.7%); Migrant: 0 (0.0%)
  Eligible for Free Lunch Program: 1,774 (7.6%)
  Eligible for Reduced-Price Lunch Program: 1,098 (4.7%)
Teachers: 1,093.7 (21.5 to 1)
Librarians/Media Specialists: 3.0 (7,832.0 to 1)
Guidance Counselors: 23.5 (999.8 to 1)
Current Spending: ($ per student per year):
  Total: $6,349; Instruction: $4,440; Support Services: $1,771

Enrollment, Drop-out Rates and Diploma Recipients by Race/Ethnicity

Category	Total	White	Black	Asian	AIAN	Hisp.
Enrollment (%)	100.0	65.0	5.0	8.5	1.3	19.9
Drop-out Rate (%)	n/a	n/a	n/a	n/a	n/a	n/a
H.S. Diplomas (#)	1,049	771	57	81	4	135

Val Verde Unified

975 E Morgan Rd • Perris, CA 92571-3103
(909) 940-6100 • http://www.valverde.edu/
Grade Span: KG-12; **Agency Type:** 1
Schools: 14
  8 Primary; 3 Middle; 3 High; 0 Other Level
  13 Regular; 0 Special Education; 0 Vocational; 1 Alternative

0 Magnet; 0 Charter; 7 Title I Eligible; 7 School-wide Title I
Students: 13,447 (51.9% male; 48.0% female)
  Individual Education Program: 1,136 (8.4%);
  English Language Learner: 3,771 (28.0%); Migrant: 32 (0.2%)
  Eligible for Free Lunch Program: 6,471 (48.1%)
  Eligible for Reduced-Price Lunch Program: 2,462 (18.3%)
Teachers: 548.6 (24.5 to 1)
Librarians/Media Specialists: 0.0 (n/a to 1)
Guidance Counselors: 13.6 (988.8 to 1)
Current Spending: ($ per student per year):
  Total: $6,545; Instruction: $3,850; Support Services: $2,405
Enrollment, Drop-out Rates and Diploma Recipients by Race/Ethnicity

Category	Total	White	Black	Asian	AIAN	Hisp.
Enrollment (%)	100.0	13.1	19.1	3.5	0.3	63.3
Drop-out Rate (%)	n/a	n/a	n/a	n/a	n/a	n/a
H.S. Diplomas (#)	558	116	127	39	2	274

Sacramento County

Center Joint Unified
8408 Watt Ave · Antelope, CA 95843-9116
(916) 338-6330 · http://www.centerusd.k12.ca.us/
Grade Span: KG-12; **Agency Type:** 1
Schools: 8
  4 Primary; 1 Middle; 2 High; 1 Other Level
  7 Regular; 0 Special Education; 0 Vocational; 1 Alternative
  0 Magnet; 1 Charter; 2 Title I Eligible; 1 School-wide Title I
Students: 6,264 (51.3% male; 48.6% female)
  Individual Education Program: 723 (11.5%);
  English Language Learner: 549 (8.8%); Migrant: 0 (0.0%)
  Eligible for Free Lunch Program: 1,141 (18.2%)
  Eligible for Reduced-Price Lunch Program: 479 (7.6%)
Teachers: 271.8 (23.0 to 1)
Librarians/Media Specialists: 2.0 (3,132.0 to 1)
Guidance Counselors: 6.0 (1,044.0 to 1)
Current Spending: ($ per student per year):
  Total: $6,776; Instruction: $4,377; Support Services: $2,194
Enrollment, Drop-out Rates and Diploma Recipients by Race/Ethnicity

Category	Total	White	Black	Asian	AIAN	Hisp.
Enrollment (%)	100.0	56.6	13.7	11.9	1.1	12.3
Drop-out Rate (%)	n/a	n/a	n/a	n/a	n/a	n/a
H.S. Diplomas (#)	324	191	45	54	4	30

Del Paso Heights Elementary
3780 Rosin Court Ste 270 · Sacramento, CA 95834-1646
(916) 641-5300 ·
http://webpages.grant.k12.ca.us/education/school/school.php?sectionid=1256
Grade Span: KG-06; **Agency Type:** 1
Schools: 5
  5 Primary; 0 Middle; 0 High; 0 Other Level
  5 Regular; 0 Special Education; 0 Vocational; 0 Alternative
  0 Magnet; 0 Charter; 5 Title I Eligible; 0 School-wide Title I
Students: 2,041 (52.3% male; 47.6% female)
  Individual Education Program: 145 (7.1%);
  English Language Learner: 860 (42.1%); Migrant: 8 (0.4%)
  Eligible for Free Lunch Program: 1,852 (90.7%)
  Eligible for Reduced-Price Lunch Program: 131 (6.4%)
Teachers: 99.0 (20.6 to 1)
Librarians/Media Specialists: 0.0 (n/a to 1)
Guidance Counselors: 4.0 (510.3 to 1)
Current Spending: ($ per student per year):
  Total: $8,368; Instruction: $5,391; Support Services: $2,331
Enrollment, Drop-out Rates and Diploma Recipients by Race/Ethnicity

Category	Total	White	Black	Asian	AIAN	Hisp.
Enrollment (%)	100.0	11.0	29.8	34.6	0.4	20.5
Drop-out Rate (%)	n/a	n/a	n/a	n/a	n/a	n/a
H.S. Diplomas (#)	n/a	n/a	n/a	n/a	n/a	n/a

Elk Grove Unified
9510 Elk Grove-Florin Rd · Elk Grove, CA 95624-1801
(916) 686-7700 · http://www.egusd.k12.ca.us/
Grade Span: KG-12; **Agency Type:** 1
Schools: 55
  33 Primary; 6 Middle; 13 High; 3 Other Level
  46 Regular; 1 Special Education; 0 Vocational; 8 Alternative
  0 Magnet; 1 Charter; 12 Title I Eligible; 10 School-wide Title I
Students: 55,613 (51.6% male; 48.3% female)
  Individual Education Program: 4,970 (8.9%);
  English Language Learner: 10,213 (18.4%); Migrant: 112 (0.2%)
  Eligible for Free Lunch Program: 15,748 (28.3%)
  Eligible for Reduced-Price Lunch Program: 5,694 (10.2%)
Teachers: 2,660.3 (20.9 to 1)
Librarians/Media Specialists: 11.5 (4,835.9 to 1)
Guidance Counselors: 60.1 (925.3 to 1)

Current Spending: ($ per student per year):
  Total: $7,359; Instruction: $4,697; Support Services: $2,369
Enrollment, Drop-out Rates and Diploma Recipients by Race/Ethnicity

Category	Total	White	Black	Asian	AIAN	Hisp.
Enrollment (%)	100.0	33.7	18.9	26.3	1.1	19.8
Drop-out Rate (%)	n/a	n/a	n/a	n/a	n/a	n/a
H.S. Diplomas (#)	2,728	1,108	455	773	20	371

Folsom-Cordova Unified
125 E Bidwell St · Folsom, CA 95630-3241
(916) 355-1111 · http://www.fcusd.k12.ca.us/
Grade Span: KG-12; **Agency Type:** 1
Schools: 31
  19 Primary; 4 Middle; 6 High; 2 Other Level
  25 Regular; 1 Special Education; 0 Vocational; 5 Alternative
  0 Magnet; 0 Charter; 8 Title I Eligible; 6 School-wide Title I
Students: 18,041 (50.8% male; 49.1% female)
  Individual Education Program: 2,378 (13.2%);
  English Language Learner: 2,113 (11.7%); Migrant: 23 (0.1%)
  Eligible for Free Lunch Program: 4,718 (26.2%)
  Eligible for Reduced-Price Lunch Program: 1,107 (6.1%)
Teachers: 834.9 (21.6 to 1)
Librarians/Media Specialists: 0.0 (n/a to 1)
Guidance Counselors: 24.7 (730.4 to 1)
Current Spending: ($ per student per year):
  Total: $6,534; Instruction: $4,120; Support Services: $2,168
Enrollment, Drop-out Rates and Diploma Recipients by Race/Ethnicity

Category	Total	White	Black	Asian	AIAN	Hisp.
Enrollment (%)	100.0	65.9	9.1	10.3	0.9	12.9
Drop-out Rate (%)	n/a	n/a	n/a	n/a	n/a	n/a
H.S. Diplomas (#)	898	655	68	85	7	82

Galt Joint Union Elementary
1018 C St Ste 210 · Galt, CA 95632-1733
(209) 744-4545 · http://www.galt.k12.ca.us/
Grade Span: KG-08; **Agency Type:** 1
Schools: 6
  4 Primary; 2 Middle; 0 High; 0 Other Level
  6 Regular; 0 Special Education; 0 Vocational; 0 Alternative
  0 Magnet; 0 Charter; 3 Title I Eligible; 0 School-wide Title I
Students: 4,348 (50.4% male; 49.5% female)
  Individual Education Program: 528 (12.1%);
  English Language Learner: 1,170 (26.9%); Migrant: 600 (13.8%)
  Eligible for Free Lunch Program: 1,541 (35.4%)
  Eligible for Reduced-Price Lunch Program: 564 (13.0%)
Teachers: 245.4 (17.7 to 1)
Librarians/Media Specialists: 0.0 (n/a to 1)
Guidance Counselors: 0.0 (n/a to 1)
Current Spending: ($ per student per year):
  Total: $6,363; Instruction: $4,269; Support Services: $1,848
Enrollment, Drop-out Rates and Diploma Recipients by Race/Ethnicity

Category	Total	White	Black	Asian	AIAN	Hisp.
Enrollment (%)	100.0	47.9	1.7	3.3	1.1	45.9
Drop-out Rate (%)	n/a	n/a	n/a	n/a	n/a	n/a
H.S. Diplomas (#)	n/a	n/a	n/a	n/a	n/a	n/a

Galt Joint Union High
145 N Lincoln Way · Galt, CA 95632-1720
(209) 745-3061 · http://www.ghsd.k12.ca.us/
Grade Span: 09-12; **Agency Type:** 1
Schools: 3
  0 Primary; 0 Middle; 3 High; 0 Other Level
  1 Regular; 0 Special Education; 0 Vocational; 2 Alternative
  0 Magnet; 0 Charter; 2 Title I Eligible; 0 School-wide Title I
Students: 2,131 (51.3% male; 48.6% female)
  Individual Education Program: 199 (9.3%);
  English Language Learner: 367 (17.2%); Migrant: 325 (15.3%)
  Eligible for Free Lunch Program: 628 (29.5%)
  Eligible for Reduced-Price Lunch Program: 131 (6.1%)
Teachers: 100.4 (21.2 to 1)
Librarians/Media Specialists: 0.0 (n/a to 1)
Guidance Counselors: 4.0 (532.8 to 1)
Current Spending: ($ per student per year):
  Total: $7,472; Instruction: $4,421; Support Services: $2,788
Enrollment, Drop-out Rates and Diploma Recipients by Race/Ethnicity

Category	Total	White	Black	Asian	AIAN	Hisp.
Enrollment (%)	100.0	53.8	1.9	4.1	1.8	35.7
Drop-out Rate (%)	n/a	n/a	n/a	n/a	n/a	n/a
H.S. Diplomas (#)	366	231	2	10	9	114

Grant Joint Union High
1333 Grand Ave · Sacramento, CA 95838-3697
(916) 286-4800 · http://www.grant.k12.ca.us/
Grade Span: KG-12; **Agency Type:** 1
Schools: 15

0 Primary; 6 Middle; 8 High; 1 Other Level
11 Regular; 1 Special Education; 0 Vocational; 3 Alternative
0 Magnet; 1 Charter; 10 Title I Eligible; 9 School-wide Title I
Students: 13,015   (52.3% male; 47.6% female)
Individual Education Program: 1,568 (12.0%);
English Language Learner: 3,217 (24.7%); Migrant: 37 (0.3%)
Eligible for Free Lunch Program: 6,690 (51.4%)
Eligible for Reduced-Price Lunch Program: 1,189 (9.1%)
Teachers: 570.3 (22.8 to 1)
Librarians/Media Specialists: 4.0 (3,253.8 to 1)
Guidance Counselors: 26.6 (489.3 to 1)
Current Spending: ($ per student per year):
Total: $8,173; Instruction: $4,249; Support Services: $3,660
Enrollment, Drop-out Rates and Diploma Recipients by Race/Ethnicity

Category	Total	White	Black	Asian	AIAN	Hisp.
Enrollment (%)	100.0	35.7	17.4	15.3	1.4	21.9
Drop-out Rate (%)	n/a	n/a	n/a	n/a	n/a	n/a
H.S. Diplomas (#)	1,345	549	213	292	12	237

Natomas Unified
1901 Arena Blvd • Sacramento, CA 95834-1905
(916) 567-5400 • http://www.natomas.k12.ca.us/
Grade Span: KG-12; **Agency Type:** 1
Schools: 10
5 Primary; 2 Middle; 2 High; 1 Other Level
8 Regular; 0 Special Education; 0 Vocational; 2 Alternative
0 Magnet; 1 Charter; 3 Title I Eligible; 1 School-wide Title I
Students: 8,636   (51.7% male; 48.2% female)
Individual Education Program: 804 (9.3%);
English Language Learner: 1,080 (12.5%); Migrant: 9 (0.1%)
Eligible for Free Lunch Program: 1,952 (22.6%)
Eligible for Reduced-Price Lunch Program: 856 (9.9%)
Teachers: 403.6 (21.4 to 1)
Librarians/Media Specialists: 1.2 (7,196.7 to 1)
Guidance Counselors: 8.2 (1,053.2 to 1)
Current Spending: ($ per student per year):
Total: $6,564; Instruction: $4,230; Support Services: $2,114
Enrollment, Drop-out Rates and Diploma Recipients by Race/Ethnicity

Category	Total	White	Black	Asian	AIAN	Hisp.
Enrollment (%)	100.0	27.1	24.7	18.5	0.8	26.9
Drop-out Rate (%)	n/a	n/a	n/a	n/a	n/a	n/a
H.S. Diplomas (#)	386	125	89	74	2	93

North Sacramento Elementary
670 Dixieanne Ave • Sacramento, CA 95815-3023
(916) 263-8287 • http://www.nssd.k12.ca.us/
Grade Span: KG-06; **Agency Type:** 1
Schools: 11
11 Primary; 0 Middle; 0 High; 0 Other Level
10 Regular; 0 Special Education; 0 Vocational; 1 Alternative
0 Magnet; 0 Charter; 11 Title I Eligible; 10 School-wide Title I
Students: 5,320   (50.8% male; 49.1% female)
Individual Education Program: 616 (11.6%);
English Language Learner: 1,897 (35.7%); Migrant: 72 (1.4%)
Eligible for Free Lunch Program: 3,853 (72.4%)
Eligible for Reduced-Price Lunch Program: 608 (11.4%)
Teachers: 300.7 (17.7 to 1)
Librarians/Media Specialists: 0.0 (n/a to 1)
Guidance Counselors: 11.2 (475.0 to 1)
Current Spending: ($ per student per year):
Total: $8,073; Instruction: $4,885; Support Services: $2,721
Enrollment, Drop-out Rates and Diploma Recipients by Race/Ethnicity

Category	Total	White	Black	Asian	AIAN	Hisp.
Enrollment (%)	100.0	20.2	19.5	13.1	0.9	44.8
Drop-out Rate (%)	n/a	n/a	n/a	n/a	n/a	n/a
H.S. Diplomas (#)	n/a	n/a	n/a	n/a	n/a	n/a

Rio Linda Union Elementary
627 L St • Rio Linda, CA 95673-3430
(916) 991-1704 • http://www.rlusd.com/
Grade Span: KG-08; **Agency Type:** 1
Schools: 23
22 Primary; 1 Middle; 0 High; 0 Other Level
22 Regular; 0 Special Education; 0 Vocational; 1 Alternative
0 Magnet; 1 Charter; 19 Title I Eligible; 18 School-wide Title I
Students: 9,970   (51.8% male; 48.1% female)
Individual Education Program: 1,112 (11.2%);
English Language Learner: 2,119 (21.3%); Migrant: 13 (0.1%)
Eligible for Free Lunch Program: 4,900 (49.1%)
Eligible for Reduced-Price Lunch Program: 1,316 (13.2%)
Teachers: 522.9 (19.1 to 1)
Librarians/Media Specialists: 1.0 (9,970.0 to 1)
Guidance Counselors: 2.6 (3,834.6 to 1)
Current Spending: ($ per student per year):
Total: $7,096; Instruction: $4,724; Support Services: $2,066

Category	Total	White	Black	Asian	AIAN	Hisp.
Enrollment (%)	100.0	54.6	15.9	6.5	1.0	22.0
Drop-out Rate (%)	n/a	n/a	n/a	n/a	n/a	n/a
H.S. Diplomas (#)	n/a	n/a	n/a	n/a	n/a	n/a

River Delta Joint Unified
445 Montezuma • Rio Vista, CA 94571-1651
(707) 374-6381 • http://www.riverdelta.k12.ca.us/
Grade Span: KG-12; **Agency Type:** 1
Schools: 10
5 Primary; 1 Middle; 3 High; 1 Other Level
8 Regular; 0 Special Education; 0 Vocational; 2 Alternative
0 Magnet; 0 Charter; 4 Title I Eligible; 4 School-wide Title I
Students: 2,465   (50.3% male; 49.6% female)
Individual Education Program: 298 (12.1%);
English Language Learner: 689 (28.0%); Migrant: 626 (25.4%)
Eligible for Free Lunch Program: 764 (31.0%)
Eligible for Reduced-Price Lunch Program: 133 (5.4%)
Teachers: 122.6 (20.1 to 1)
Librarians/Media Specialists: 0.0 (n/a to 1)
Guidance Counselors: 5.3 (465.1 to 1)
Current Spending: ($ per student per year):
Total: $7,354; Instruction: $4,333; Support Services: $2,788
Enrollment, Drop-out Rates and Diploma Recipients by Race/Ethnicity

Category	Total	White	Black	Asian	AIAN	Hisp.
Enrollment (%)	100.0	52.3	1.1	2.6	0.5	40.4
Drop-out Rate (%)	n/a	n/a	n/a	n/a	n/a	n/a
H.S. Diplomas (#)	178	113	0	9	0	56

Robla Elementary
5248 Rose St • Sacramento, CA 95838-1633
(916) 991-1728 • http://www.robla.k12.ca.us/
Grade Span: KG-06; **Agency Type:** 1
Schools: 5
5 Primary; 0 Middle; 0 High; 0 Other Level
5 Regular; 0 Special Education; 0 Vocational; 0 Alternative
0 Magnet; 0 Charter; 5 Title I Eligible; 5 School-wide Title I
Students: 2,242   (51.8% male; 48.1% female)
Individual Education Program: 350 (15.6%);
English Language Learner: 891 (39.7%); Migrant: 0 (0.0%)
Eligible for Free Lunch Program: 1,361 (60.7%)
Eligible for Reduced-Price Lunch Program: 366 (16.3%)
Teachers: 121.5 (18.5 to 1)
Librarians/Media Specialists: 0.0 (n/a to 1)
Guidance Counselors: 0.0 (n/a to 1)
Current Spending: ($ per student per year):
Total: $7,619; Instruction: $4,919; Support Services: $2,292
Enrollment, Drop-out Rates and Diploma Recipients by Race/Ethnicity

Category	Total	White	Black	Asian	AIAN	Hisp.
Enrollment (%)	100.0	28.8	15.8	18.9	0.3	29.2
Drop-out Rate (%)	n/a	n/a	n/a	n/a	n/a	n/a
H.S. Diplomas (#)	n/a	n/a	n/a	n/a	n/a	n/a

Sacramento City Unified
5735 47th Ave • Sacramento, CA 95824-6870
Mailing Address: PO Box 246870 • Sacramento, CA 95824-6870
(916) 643-9000 • http://www.scusd.edu/
Grade Span: KG-12; **Agency Type:** 1
Schools: 88
63 Primary; 10 Middle; 14 High; 1 Other Level
84 Regular; 0 Special Education; 0 Vocational; 4 Alternative
26 Magnet; 10 Charter; 65 Title I Eligible; 38 School-wide Title I
Students: 52,103   (51.0% male; 48.9% female)
Individual Education Program: 6,387 (12.3%);
English Language Learner: 15,110 (29.0%); Migrant: 1,217 (2.3%)
Eligible for Free Lunch Program: 31,912 (61.2%)
Eligible for Reduced-Price Lunch Program: 3,029 (5.8%)
Teachers: 2,659.0 (19.6 to 1)
Librarians/Media Specialists: 13.8 (3,775.6 to 1)
Guidance Counselors: 22.9 (2,275.2 to 1)
Current Spending: ($ per student per year):
Total: $8,119; Instruction: $4,829; Support Services: $2,987
Enrollment, Drop-out Rates and Diploma Recipients by Race/Ethnicity

Category	Total	White	Black	Asian	AIAN	Hisp.
Enrollment (%)	100.0	22.4	22.2	23.2	1.5	29.1
Drop-out Rate (%)	n/a	n/a	n/a	n/a	n/a	n/a
H.S. Diplomas (#)	2,237	515	357	886	32	441

San Juan Unified
3738 Walnut Ave • Carmichael, CA 95609-0477
Mailing Address: PO Box 477 • Carmichael, CA 95609-0477
(916) 971-7700 • http://www.sanjuan.edu/
Grade Span: KG-12; **Agency Type:** 1
Schools: 84

52 Primary; 10 Middle; 13 High; 8 Other Level
75 Regular; 3 Special Education; 0 Vocational; 5 Alternative
2 Magnet; 3 Charter; 34 Title I Eligible; 17 School-wide Title I
Students: 50,906   (50.8% male; 49.1% female)
Individual Education Program: 4,924 (9.7%);
English Language Learner: 4,258 (8.4%); Migrant: 20 (<0.1%)
Eligible for Free Lunch Program: 11,506 (22.6%)
Eligible for Reduced-Price Lunch Program: 3,545 (7.0%)
Teachers: 2,418.4 (21.0 to 1)
Librarians/Media Specialists: 3.5 (14,544.6 to 1)
Guidance Counselors: 54.5 (934.1 to 1)
Current Spending: ($ per student per year):
Total: $7,835; Instruction: $4,877; Support Services: $2,735
Enrollment, Drop-out Rates and Diploma Recipients by Race/Ethnicity

Category	Total	White	Black	Asian	AIAN	Hisp.
Enrollment (%)	100.0	70.7	7.5	6.4	2.1	13.1
Drop-out Rate (%)	n/a	n/a	n/a	n/a	n/a	n/a
H.S. Diplomas (#)	3,556	2,804	171	244	54	277

San Benito County

Hollister SD
2690 Cienega Rd • Hollister, CA 95023-4570
(831) 634-2000 • http://www.hollister.goleta.k12.ca.us/
Grade Span: KG-08; **Agency Type:** 1
Schools: 8
6 Primary; 2 Middle; 0 High; 0 Other Level
8 Regular; 0 Special Education; 0 Vocational; 0 Alternative
0 Magnet; 0 Charter; 8 Title I Eligible; 1 School-wide Title I
Students: 6,242   (51.5% male; 48.4% female)
Individual Education Program: 836 (13.4%);
English Language Learner: 1,806 (28.9%); Migrant: 1,825 (29.2%)
Eligible for Free Lunch Program: 1,886 (30.2%)
Eligible for Reduced-Price Lunch Program: 786 (12.6%)
Teachers: 309.2 (20.2 to 1)
Librarians/Media Specialists: 0.0 (n/a to 1)
Guidance Counselors: 1.0 (6,242.0 to 1)
Current Spending: ($ per student per year):
Total: $6,680; Instruction: $4,540; Support Services: $1,930
Enrollment, Drop-out Rates and Diploma Recipients by Race/Ethnicity

Category	Total	White	Black	Asian	AIAN	Hisp.
Enrollment (%)	100.0	31.4	0.9	2.2	0.5	62.7
Drop-out Rate (%)	n/a	n/a	n/a	n/a	n/a	n/a
H.S. Diplomas (#)	n/a	n/a	n/a	n/a	n/a	n/a

San Benito High
1220 Monterey St • Hollister, CA 95023-4708
(831) 637-5831 • http://www.sbhsd.k12.ca.us/
Grade Span: 09-12; **Agency Type:** 1
Schools: 2
0 Primary; 0 Middle; 2 High; 0 Other Level
1 Regular; 0 Special Education; 0 Vocational; 1 Alternative
0 Magnet; 0 Charter; 2 Title I Eligible; 0 School-wide Title I
Students: 3,002   (51.1% male; 48.8% female)
Individual Education Program: 323 (10.8%);
English Language Learner: 159 (5.3%); Migrant: 915 (30.5%)
Eligible for Free Lunch Program: 405 (13.5%)
Eligible for Reduced-Price Lunch Program: 123 (4.1%)
Teachers: 116.4 (25.8 to 1)
Librarians/Media Specialists: 1.0 (3,002.0 to 1)
Guidance Counselors: 5.0 (600.4 to 1)
Current Spending: ($ per student per year):
Total: $7,432; Instruction: $4,415; Support Services: $2,846
Enrollment, Drop-out Rates and Diploma Recipients by Race/Ethnicity

Category	Total	White	Black	Asian	AIAN	Hisp.
Enrollment (%)	100.0	40.9	0.8	2.9	0.4	54.8
Drop-out Rate (%)	n/a	n/a	n/a	n/a	n/a	n/a
H.S. Diplomas (#)	604	270	8	13	1	311

San Bernardino County

Adelanto Elementary
11824 Air Expressway • Adelanto, CA 92301-0070
Mailing Address: PO Box 70 • Adelanto, CA 92301-0070
(760) 246-8691 • http://www.adelanto.k12.ca.us/
Grade Span: KG-08; **Agency Type:** 1
Schools: 9
7 Primary; 2 Middle; 0 High; 0 Other Level
9 Regular; 0 Special Education; 0 Vocational; 0 Alternative
0 Magnet; 0 Charter; 7 Title I Eligible; 7 School-wide Title I
Students: 6,141   (51.0% male; 48.9% female)
Individual Education Program: 637 (10.4%);
English Language Learner: 1,553 (25.3%); Migrant: 0 (0.0%)
Eligible for Free Lunch Program: 3,314 (54.0%)
Eligible for Reduced-Price Lunch Program: 846 (13.8%)

Teachers: 252.5 (24.3 to 1)
Librarians/Media Specialists: 0.0 (n/a to 1)
Guidance Counselors: 3.0 (2,047.0 to 1)
Current Spending: ($ per student per year):
Total: $6,658; Instruction: $4,256; Support Services: $2,057
Enrollment, Drop-out Rates and Diploma Recipients by Race/Ethnicity

Category	Total	White	Black	Asian	AIAN	Hisp.
Enrollment (%)	100.0	26.9	20.0	2.7	0.7	49.7
Drop-out Rate (%)	n/a	n/a	n/a	n/a	n/a	n/a
H.S. Diplomas (#)	n/a	n/a	n/a	n/a	n/a	n/a

Alta Loma Elementary
9340 Baseline Rd • Alta Loma, CA 91701-5821
(909) 484-5151 • http://www.alsd.k12.ca.us/
Grade Span: KG-08; **Agency Type:** 1
Schools: 10
8 Primary; 2 Middle; 0 High; 0 Other Level
10 Regular; 0 Special Education; 0 Vocational; 0 Alternative
0 Magnet; 0 Charter; 4 Title I Eligible; 0 School-wide Title I
Students: 7,503   (51.4% male; 48.5% female)
Individual Education Program: 594 (7.9%);
English Language Learner: 222 (3.0%); Migrant: 0 (0.0%)
Eligible for Free Lunch Program: 836 (11.1%)
Eligible for Reduced-Price Lunch Program: 477 (6.4%)
Teachers: 313.0 (24.0 to 1)
Librarians/Media Specialists: 0.0 (n/a to 1)
Guidance Counselors: 0.0 (n/a to 1)
Current Spending: ($ per student per year):
Total: $6,150; Instruction: $4,258; Support Services: $1,701
Enrollment, Drop-out Rates and Diploma Recipients by Race/Ethnicity

Category	Total	White	Black	Asian	AIAN	Hisp.
Enrollment (%)	100.0	56.7	8.5	6.4	0.3	23.5
Drop-out Rate (%)	n/a	n/a	n/a	n/a	n/a	n/a
H.S. Diplomas (#)	n/a	n/a	n/a	n/a	n/a	n/a

Apple Valley Unified
22974 Bear Valley Rd • Apple Valley, CA 92308-7423
(760) 247-8001 • http://www.avstc.org/stchtml/schools/avusd_m.htm
Grade Span: KG-12; **Agency Type:** 1
Schools: 16
9 Primary; 2 Middle; 3 High; 2 Other Level
14 Regular; 0 Special Education; 0 Vocational; 2 Alternative
0 Magnet; 1 Charter; 13 Title I Eligible; 8 School-wide Title I
Students: 14,475   (51.3% male; 48.6% female)
Individual Education Program: 1,924 (13.3%);
English Language Learner: 556 (3.8%); Migrant: 0 (0.0%)
Eligible for Free Lunch Program: 5,075 (35.1%)
Eligible for Reduced-Price Lunch Program: 1,911 (13.2%)
Teachers: 620.9 (23.3 to 1)
Librarians/Media Specialists: 0.0 (n/a to 1)
Guidance Counselors: 13.9 (1,041.4 to 1)
Current Spending: ($ per student per year):
Total: $6,279; Instruction: $4,056; Support Services: $1,961
Enrollment, Drop-out Rates and Diploma Recipients by Race/Ethnicity

Category	Total	White	Black	Asian	AIAN	Hisp.
Enrollment (%)	100.0	58.8	11.8	2.9	0.6	24.1
Drop-out Rate (%)	n/a	n/a	n/a	n/a	n/a	n/a
H.S. Diplomas (#)	855	574	61	40	6	172

Barstow Unified
551 S Ave H • Barstow, CA 92311-2500
(760) 255-6000 • http://www.barstow.k12.ca.us/
Grade Span: KG-12; **Agency Type:** 1
Schools: 12
8 Primary; 2 Middle; 1 High; 1 Other Level
11 Regular; 0 Special Education; 0 Vocational; 1 Alternative
0 Magnet; 0 Charter; 10 Title I Eligible; 7 School-wide Title I
Students: 7,010   (50.7% male; 49.2% female)
Individual Education Program: 811 (11.6%);
English Language Learner: 676 (9.6%); Migrant: 0 (0.0%)
Eligible for Free Lunch Program: 3,381 (48.2%)
Eligible for Reduced-Price Lunch Program: 661 (9.4%)
Teachers: 326.0 (21.5 to 1)
Librarians/Media Specialists: 1.0 (7,010.0 to 1)
Guidance Counselors: 5.0 (1,402.0 to 1)
Current Spending: ($ per student per year):
Total: $7,029; Instruction: $4,200; Support Services: $2,517
Enrollment, Drop-out Rates and Diploma Recipients by Race/Ethnicity

Category	Total	White	Black	Asian	AIAN	Hisp.
Enrollment (%)	100.0	36.8	15.7	3.1	2.4	41.9
Drop-out Rate (%)	n/a	n/a	n/a	n/a	n/a	n/a
H.S. Diplomas (#)	365	171	43	18	16	117

Bear Valley Unified
42271 Moonridge Rd • Big Bear Lake, CA 92315-1529
Mailing Address: Box 1529 • Big Bear Lake, CA 92315-1529
(909) 866-4631 • http://www.bigbear.k12.ca.us/
Grade Span: KG-12; **Agency Type:** 1
Schools: 8
    4 Primary; 1 Middle; 2 High; 1 Other Level
    7 Regular; 0 Special Education; 0 Vocational; 1 Alternative
    0 Magnet; 1 Charter; 7 Title I Eligible; 0 School-wide Title I
Students: 3,428 (51.8% male; 48.1% female)
    Individual Education Program: 384 (11.2%);
    English Language Learner: 251 (7.3%); Migrant: 0 (0.0%)
    Eligible for Free Lunch Program: 999 (29.1%)
    Eligible for Reduced-Price Lunch Program: 290 (8.5%)
Teachers: 156.8 (21.9 to 1)
Librarians/Media Specialists: 0.4 (8,570.0 to 1)
Guidance Counselors: 3.0 (1,142.7 to 1)
Current Spending: ($ per student per year):
    Total: $6,802; Instruction: $4,418; Support Services: $2,158

Enrollment, Drop-out Rates and Diploma Recipients by Race/Ethnicity

Category	Total	White	Black	Asian	AIAN	Hisp.
Enrollment (%)	100.0	76.8	2.3	1.3	1.1	18.5
Drop-out Rate (%)	n/a	n/a	n/a	n/a	n/a	n/a
H.S. Diplomas (#)	220	191	4	1	0	24

Central Elementary
10601 Church St Ste 112 • Rancho Cucamonga, CA 91730-6863
(909) 989-8541 • http://www.centralusd.k12.ca.us/
Grade Span: KG-08; **Agency Type:** 1
Schools: 7
    5 Primary; 2 Middle; 0 High; 0 Other Level
    7 Regular; 0 Special Education; 0 Vocational; 0 Alternative
    0 Magnet; 0 Charter; 2 Title I Eligible; 0 School-wide Title I
Students: 5,320 (49.5% male; 50.4% female)
    Individual Education Program: 484 (9.1%);
    English Language Learner: 604 (11.4%); Migrant: 0 (0.0%)
    Eligible for Free Lunch Program: 1,360 (25.6%)
    Eligible for Reduced-Price Lunch Program: 604 (11.4%)
Teachers: 225.1 (23.6 to 1)
Librarians/Media Specialists: 0.0 (n/a to 1)
Guidance Counselors: 4.0 (1,330.0 to 1)
Current Spending: ($ per student per year):
    Total: $6,281; Instruction: $4,235; Support Services: $1,808

Enrollment, Drop-out Rates and Diploma Recipients by Race/Ethnicity

Category	Total	White	Black	Asian	AIAN	Hisp.
Enrollment (%)	100.0	34.9	11.2	6.1	1.4	37.0
Drop-out Rate (%)	n/a	n/a	n/a	n/a	n/a	n/a
H.S. Diplomas (#)	n/a	n/a	n/a	n/a	n/a	n/a

Chaffey Joint Union High
211 W Fifth St • Ontario, CA 91762-1698
(909) 988-8511 • http://www.cjuhsd.k12.ca.us/
Grade Span: 09-12; **Agency Type:** 1
Schools: 11
    0 Primary; 0 Middle; 11 High; 0 Other Level
    8 Regular; 0 Special Education; 0 Vocational; 3 Alternative
    0 Magnet; 0 Charter; 5 Title I Eligible; 3 School-wide Title I
Students: 23,341 (50.8% male; 49.1% female)
    Individual Education Program: 2,418 (10.4%);
    English Language Learner: 2,970 (12.7%); Migrant: 0 (0.0%)
    Eligible for Free Lunch Program: 3,394 (14.5%)
    Eligible for Reduced-Price Lunch Program: 884 (3.8%)
Teachers: 939.6 (24.8 to 1)
Librarians/Media Specialists: 8.0 (2,917.6 to 1)
Guidance Counselors: 53.9 (433.0 to 1)
Current Spending: ($ per student per year):
    Total: $6,978; Instruction: $4,447; Support Services: $2,370

Enrollment, Drop-out Rates and Diploma Recipients by Race/Ethnicity

Category	Total	White	Black	Asian	AIAN	Hisp.
Enrollment (%)	100.0	29.4	11.3	5.8	0.4	49.8
Drop-out Rate (%)	n/a	n/a	n/a	n/a	n/a	n/a
H.S. Diplomas (#)	3,873	1,481	435	282	11	1,659

Chino Valley Unified
5130 Riverside Dr • Chino, CA 91710-4130
(909) 628-1201 • http://www.chino.k12.ca.us/
Grade Span: KG-12; **Agency Type:** 1
Schools: 35
    23 Primary; 5 Middle; 7 High; 0 Other Level
    32 Regular; 0 Special Education; 0 Vocational; 3 Alternative
    17 Magnet; 0 Charter; 16 Title I Eligible; 6 School-wide Title I
Students: 33,340 (51.5% male; 48.4% female)
    Individual Education Program: 2,859 (8.6%);
    English Language Learner: 3,163 (9.5%); Migrant: 0 (0.0%)
    Eligible for Free Lunch Program: 6,488 (19.5%)

    Eligible for Reduced-Price Lunch Program: 2,660 (8.0%)
Teachers: 1,382.5 (24.1 to 1)
Librarians/Media Specialists: 3.0 (11,113.3 to 1)
Guidance Counselors: 19.0 (1,754.7 to 1)
Current Spending: ($ per student per year):
    Total: $6,217; Instruction: $4,150; Support Services: $1,879

Enrollment, Drop-out Rates and Diploma Recipients by Race/Ethnicity

Category	Total	White	Black	Asian	AIAN	Hisp.
Enrollment (%)	100.0	33.9	4.4	12.2	0.2	43.5
Drop-out Rate (%)	n/a	n/a	n/a	n/a	n/a	n/a
H.S. Diplomas (#)	1,865	860	120	206	2	677

Colton Joint Unified
1212 Valencia Dr • Colton, CA 92324-1798
(909) 580-5000 • http://www.colton.k12.ca.us/
Grade Span: KG-12; **Agency Type:** 1
Schools: 28
    19 Primary; 4 Middle; 4 High; 1 Other Level
    25 Regular; 0 Special Education; 0 Vocational; 3 Alternative
    4 Magnet; 1 Charter; 11 Title I Eligible; 11 School-wide Title I
Students: 24,936 (51.3% male; 48.6% female)
    Individual Education Program: 2,304 (9.2%);
    English Language Learner: 5,105 (20.5%); Migrant: 0 (0.0%)
    Eligible for Free Lunch Program: 10,704 (42.9%)
    Eligible for Reduced-Price Lunch Program: 2,983 (12.0%)
Teachers: 1,098.8 (22.7 to 1)
Librarians/Media Specialists: 4.5 (5,541.3 to 1)
Guidance Counselors: 37.9 (657.9 to 1)
Current Spending: ($ per student per year):
    Total: $6,412; Instruction: $3,875; Support Services: $2,249

Enrollment, Drop-out Rates and Diploma Recipients by Race/Ethnicity

Category	Total	White	Black	Asian	AIAN	Hisp.
Enrollment (%)	100.0	14.9	9.3	3.8	0.6	70.2
Drop-out Rate (%)	n/a	n/a	n/a	n/a	n/a	n/a
H.S. Diplomas (#)	789	200	51	37	2	497

Cucamonga Elementary
8776 Archibald Ave • Rancho Cucamonga, CA 91730-4698
(909) 987-8942 • http://www.cuca.k12.ca.us/
Grade Span: KG-08; **Agency Type:** 1
Schools: 4
    3 Primary; 1 Middle; 0 High; 0 Other Level
    4 Regular; 0 Special Education; 0 Vocational; 0 Alternative
    0 Magnet; 0 Charter; 4 Title I Eligible; 0 School-wide Title I
Students: 2,898 (51.8% male; 48.1% female)
    Individual Education Program: 270 (9.3%);
    English Language Learner: 707 (24.4%); Migrant: 0 (0.0%)
    Eligible for Free Lunch Program: 1,501 (51.8%)
    Eligible for Reduced-Price Lunch Program: 564 (19.5%)
Teachers: 133.1 (21.8 to 1)
Librarians/Media Specialists: 0.0 (n/a to 1)
Guidance Counselors: 0.0 (n/a to 1)
Current Spending: ($ per student per year):
    Total: $6,300; Instruction: $3,939; Support Services: $2,044

Enrollment, Drop-out Rates and Diploma Recipients by Race/Ethnicity

Category	Total	White	Black	Asian	AIAN	Hisp.
Enrollment (%)	100.0	14.6	15.7	5.2	0.4	62.9
Drop-out Rate (%)	n/a	n/a	n/a	n/a	n/a	n/a
H.S. Diplomas (#)	n/a	n/a	n/a	n/a	n/a	n/a

Etiwanda Elementary
6061 E Ave • Etiwanda, CA 91739-0248
(909) 899-2451 • http://etiwanda.k12.ca.us/eh/ehhome.htm
Grade Span: KG-08; **Agency Type:** 1
Schools: 13
    10 Primary; 3 Middle; 0 High; 0 Other Level
    13 Regular; 0 Special Education; 0 Vocational; 0 Alternative
    0 Magnet; 0 Charter; 4 Title I Eligible; 0 School-wide Title I
Students: 11,294 (51.5% male; 48.4% female)
    Individual Education Program: 985 (8.7%);
    English Language Learner: 300 (2.7%); Migrant: 0 (0.0%)
    Eligible for Free Lunch Program: 1,298 (11.5%)
    Eligible for Reduced-Price Lunch Program: 813 (7.2%)
Teachers: 504.2 (22.4 to 1)
Librarians/Media Specialists: 0.5 (22,588.0 to 1)
Guidance Counselors: 0.0 (n/a to 1)
Current Spending: ($ per student per year):
    Total: $5,687; Instruction: $3,921; Support Services: $1,603

Enrollment, Drop-out Rates and Diploma Recipients by Race/Ethnicity

Category	Total	White	Black	Asian	AIAN	Hisp.
Enrollment (%)	100.0	34.4	15.6	10.9	0.3	30.2
Drop-out Rate (%)	n/a	n/a	n/a	n/a	n/a	n/a
H.S. Diplomas (#)	n/a	n/a	n/a	n/a	n/a	n/a

Fontana Unified
9680 Citrus Ave • Fontana, CA 92335-5571
(909) 357-5000 • http://www.fontana.k12.ca.us/
Grade Span: KG-12; **Agency Type:** 1
Schools: 38
   26 Primary; 7 Middle; 4 High; 1 Other Level
   36 Regular; 0 Special Education; 0 Vocational; 2 Alternative
   0 Magnet; 0 Charter; 26 Title I Eligible; 24 School-wide Title I
Students: 41,343 (50.9% male; 49.0% female)
   Individual Education Program: 4,357 (10.5%);
   English Language Learner: 15,336 (37.1%); Migrant: 0 (0.0%)
   Eligible for Free Lunch Program: 20,250 (49.0%)
   Eligible for Reduced-Price Lunch Program: 5,875 (14.2%)
Teachers: 1,771.0 (23.3 to 1)
Librarians/Media Specialists: 1.0 (41,343.0 to 1)
Guidance Counselors: 51.0 (810.6 to 1)
Current Spending: ($ per student per year):
   Total: $6,795; Instruction: $4,194; Support Services: $2,323
Enrollment, Drop-out Rates and Diploma Recipients by Race/Ethnicity

Category	Total	White	Black	Asian	AIAN	Hisp.
Enrollment (%)	100.0	9.8	8.6	2.1	0.6	78.6
Drop-out Rate (%)	n/a	n/a	n/a	n/a	n/a	n/a
H.S. Diplomas (#)	1,793	353	177	61	5	1,197

Hesperia Unified
9144 Third St • Hesperia, CA 92345-3643
(760) 244-4411 • http://163.150.128.65/
Grade Span: KG-12; **Agency Type:** 1
Schools: 22
   13 Primary; 2 Middle; 6 High; 1 Other Level
   19 Regular; 0 Special Education; 0 Vocational; 3 Alternative
   0 Magnet; 2 Charter; 13 Title I Eligible; 12 School-wide Title I
Students: 17,051 (50.8% male; 49.1% female)
   Individual Education Program: 1,614 (9.5%);
   English Language Learner: 2,612 (15.3%); Migrant: 0 (0.0%)
   Eligible for Free Lunch Program: 7,212 (42.3%)
   Eligible for Reduced-Price Lunch Program: 2,248 (13.2%)
Teachers: 709.7 (24.0 to 1)
Librarians/Media Specialists: 0.0 (n/a to 1)
Guidance Counselors: 13.8 (1,235.6 to 1)
Current Spending: ($ per student per year):
   Total: $6,518; Instruction: $4,214; Support Services: $2,098
Enrollment, Drop-out Rates and Diploma Recipients by Race/Ethnicity

Category	Total	White	Black	Asian	AIAN	Hisp.
Enrollment (%)	100.0	49.0	5.1	2.0	0.5	39.6
Drop-out Rate (%)	n/a	n/a	n/a	n/a	n/a	n/a
H.S. Diplomas (#)	857	511	58	18	7	248

Morongo Unified
5715 Utah Tr • Twentynine Palms, CA 92277-0980
Mailing Address: PO Box 1209 • Twentynine Palms, CA 92277-0980
(760) 367-9191 • http://www.morongo.k12.ca.us/
Grade Span: KG-12; **Agency Type:** 1
Schools: 17
   11 Primary; 2 Middle; 4 High; 0 Other Level
   15 Regular; 0 Special Education; 0 Vocational; 2 Alternative
   0 Magnet; 0 Charter; 15 Title I Eligible; 15 School-wide Title I
Students: 9,473 (51.1% male; 48.8% female)
   Individual Education Program: 1,331 (14.1%);
   English Language Learner: 164 (1.7%); Migrant: 0 (0.0%)
   Eligible for Free Lunch Program: 2,313 (24.4%)
   Eligible for Reduced-Price Lunch Program: 1,144 (12.1%)
Teachers: 448.5 (21.1 to 1)
Librarians/Media Specialists: 0.0 (n/a to 1)
Guidance Counselors: 8.0 (1,184.1 to 1)
Current Spending: ($ per student per year):
   Total: $7,212; Instruction: $4,496; Support Services: $2,443
Enrollment, Drop-out Rates and Diploma Recipients by Race/Ethnicity

Category	Total	White	Black	Asian	AIAN	Hisp.
Enrollment (%)	100.0	64.0	8.1	3.9	1.3	15.9
Drop-out Rate (%)	n/a	n/a	n/a	n/a	n/a	n/a
H.S. Diplomas (#)	456	328	33	39	3	53

Mountain View Elementary
2585 S Archibald Ave • Ontario, CA 91761-8146
(909) 947-2205 • http://www.mvsd.k12.ca.us/index.htm
Grade Span: KG-08; **Agency Type:** 1
Schools: 4
   3 Primary; 1 Middle; 0 High; 0 Other Level
   4 Regular; 0 Special Education; 0 Vocational; 0 Alternative
   0 Magnet; 0 Charter; 2 Title I Eligible; 0 School-wide Title I
Students: 3,482 (51.5% male; 48.4% female)
   Individual Education Program: 316 (9.1%);
   English Language Learner: 507 (14.6%); Migrant: 0 (0.0%)
   Eligible for Free Lunch Program: 813 (23.3%)

Eligible for Reduced-Price Lunch Program: 523 (15.0%)
Teachers: 162.1 (21.5 to 1)
Librarians/Media Specialists: 0.0 (n/a to 1)
Guidance Counselors: 1.0 (3,482.0 to 1)
Current Spending: ($ per student per year):
   Total: $6,183; Instruction: $4,344; Support Services: $1,597
Enrollment, Drop-out Rates and Diploma Recipients by Race/Ethnicity

Category	Total	White	Black	Asian	AIAN	Hisp.
Enrollment (%)	100.0	24.2	14.4	6.3	0.4	53.2
Drop-out Rate (%)	n/a	n/a	n/a	n/a	n/a	n/a
H.S. Diplomas (#)	n/a	n/a	n/a	n/a	n/a	n/a

Ontario-Montclair Elementary
950 W D St • Ontario, CA 91762-3026
(909) 459-2500 • http://www.omsd.k12.ca.us/
Grade Span: KG-08; **Agency Type:** 1
Schools: 34
   28 Primary; 6 Middle; 0 High; 0 Other Level
   33 Regular; 1 Special Education; 0 Vocational; 0 Alternative
   0 Magnet; 0 Charter; 32 Title I Eligible; 23 School-wide Title I
Students: 27,010 (51.0% male; 48.9% female)
   Individual Education Program: 2,485 (9.2%);
   English Language Learner: 13,327 (49.3%); Migrant: 3 (<0.1%)
   Eligible for Free Lunch Program: 17,841 (66.1%)
   Eligible for Reduced-Price Lunch Program: 3,895 (14.4%)
Teachers: 1,194.3 (22.6 to 1)
Librarians/Media Specialists: 0.0 (n/a to 1)
Guidance Counselors: 6.0 (4,501.7 to 1)
Current Spending: ($ per student per year):
   Total: $7,157; Instruction: $4,582; Support Services: $2,287
Enrollment, Drop-out Rates and Diploma Recipients by Race/Ethnicity

Category	Total	White	Black	Asian	AIAN	Hisp.
Enrollment (%)	100.0	9.2	4.5	3.0	0.3	82.9
Drop-out Rate (%)	n/a	n/a	n/a	n/a	n/a	n/a
H.S. Diplomas (#)	n/a	n/a	n/a	n/a	n/a	n/a

Oro Grande Elementary
19175 Third St • Oro Grande, CA 92368-0386
Mailing Address: PO Box 386 • Oro Grande, CA 92368-0386
(760) 245-9260
Grade Span: KG-12; **Agency Type:** 1
Schools: 2
   1 Primary; 0 Middle; 0 High; 1 Other Level
   2 Regular; 0 Special Education; 0 Vocational; 0 Alternative
   0 Magnet; 1 Charter; 2 Title I Eligible; 1 School-wide Title I
Students: 3,237 (51.2% male; 48.7% female)
   Individual Education Program: 14 (0.4%);
   English Language Learner: 424 (13.1%); Migrant: 0 (0.0%)
   Eligible for Free Lunch Program: 807 (24.9%)
   Eligible for Reduced-Price Lunch Program: 0 (0.0%)
Teachers: 138.7 (23.3 to 1)
Librarians/Media Specialists: 0.0 (n/a to 1)
Guidance Counselors: 0.0 (n/a to 1)
Current Spending: ($ per student per year):
   Total: $12,184; Instruction: $6,368; Support Services: $4,919
Enrollment, Drop-out Rates and Diploma Recipients by Race/Ethnicity

Category	Total	White	Black	Asian	AIAN	Hisp.
Enrollment (%)	100.0	44.8	20.6	2.7	0.5	28.8
Drop-out Rate (%)	n/a	n/a	n/a	n/a	n/a	n/a
H.S. Diplomas (#)	100	41	2	1	1	55

Redlands Unified
20 W Lugonia • Redlands, CA 92373-1508
Mailing Address: PO Box 3008 • Redlands, CA 92373-1508
(909) 307-5300 • http://www.redlands.k12.ca.us/
Grade Span: KG-12; **Agency Type:** 1
Schools: 20
   13 Primary; 3 Middle; 4 High; 0 Other Level
   19 Regular; 0 Special Education; 0 Vocational; 1 Alternative
   0 Magnet; 1 Charter; 13 Title I Eligible; 7 School-wide Title I
Students: 20,643 (50.3% male; 49.6% female)
   Individual Education Program: 2,135 (10.3%);
   English Language Learner: 2,135 (10.3%); Migrant: 0 (0.0%)
   Eligible for Free Lunch Program: 5,953 (28.8%)
   Eligible for Reduced-Price Lunch Program: 2,460 (11.9%)
Teachers: 915.9 (22.5 to 1)
Librarians/Media Specialists: 5.0 (4,128.6 to 1)
Guidance Counselors: 33.1 (623.7 to 1)
Current Spending: ($ per student per year):
   Total: $6,586; Instruction: $4,245; Support Services: $2,125
Enrollment, Drop-out Rates and Diploma Recipients by Race/Ethnicity

Category	Total	White	Black	Asian	AIAN	Hisp.
Enrollment (%)	100.0	44.5	8.0	10.4	0.7	33.4
Drop-out Rate (%)	n/a	n/a	n/a	n/a	n/a	n/a
H.S. Diplomas (#)	1,313	682	85	171	13	356

Rialto Unified
182 E Walnut Ave • Rialto, CA 92376-3530
(909) 820-7700 • http://www.rialto.k12.ca.us/
Grade Span: KG-12; **Agency Type:** 1
Schools: 27
   17 Primary; 5 Middle; 5 High; 0 Other Level
   24 Regular; 0 Special Education; 0 Vocational; 3 Alternative
   0 Magnet; 0 Charter; 18 Title I Eligible; 18 School-wide Title I
Students: 30,431 (50.9% male; 49.0% female)
   Individual Education Program: 2,504 (8.2%);
   English Language Learner: 7,452 (24.5%); Migrant: 3 (<0.1%)
   Eligible for Free Lunch Program: 14,883 (48.9%)
   Eligible for Reduced-Price Lunch Program: 2,838 (9.3%)
Teachers: 1,325.0 (23.0 to 1)
Librarians/Media Specialists: 7.0 (4,347.3 to 1)
Guidance Counselors: 32.0 (951.0 to 1)
Current Spending: ($ per student per year):
   Total: $6,731; Instruction: $4,094; Support Services: $2,378
Enrollment, Drop-out Rates and Diploma Recipients by Race/Ethnicity

Category	Total	White	Black	Asian	AIAN	Hisp.
Enrollment (%)	100.0	9.1	23.2	2.5	0.2	64.9
Drop-out Rate (%)	n/a	n/a	n/a	n/a	n/a	n/a
H.S. Diplomas (#)	1,392	207	370	79	0	736

Rim of the World Unified
27614 Hwy 18 • Lake Arrowhead, CA 92352-0430
Mailing Address: PO Box 430 • Lake Arrowhead, CA 92352-0430
(909) 336-2031 • http://www.rimsd.k12.ca.us/
Grade Span: KG-12; **Agency Type:** 1
Schools: 9
   4 Primary; 2 Middle; 2 High; 1 Other Level
   7 Regular; 0 Special Education; 0 Vocational; 2 Alternative
   0 Magnet; 0 Charter; 5 Title I Eligible; 0 School-wide Title I
Students: 5,618 (50.8% male; 49.1% female)
   Individual Education Program: 529 (9.4%);
   English Language Learner: 322 (5.7%); Migrant: 0 (0.0%)
   Eligible for Free Lunch Program: 1,269 (22.6%)
   Eligible for Reduced-Price Lunch Program: 361 (6.4%)
Teachers: 236.3 (23.8 to 1)
Librarians/Media Specialists: 1.0 (5,618.0 to 1)
Guidance Counselors: 6.3 (891.7 to 1)
Current Spending: ($ per student per year):
   Total: $6,777; Instruction: $4,223; Support Services: $2,364
Enrollment, Drop-out Rates and Diploma Recipients by Race/Ethnicity

Category	Total	White	Black	Asian	AIAN	Hisp.
Enrollment (%)	100.0	76.8	1.2	1.3	0.7	16.1
Drop-out Rate (%)	n/a	n/a	n/a	n/a	n/a	n/a
H.S. Diplomas (#)	394	336	2	14	1	38

San Bernardino City Unified
777 N F St • San Bernardino, CA 92410-3017
(909) 381-1100 • http://www.sbcusd.k12.ca.us/
Grade Span: KG-12; **Agency Type:** 1
Schools: 65
   43 Primary; 8 Middle; 11 High; 3 Other Level
   55 Regular; 3 Special Education; 0 Vocational; 7 Alternative
   23 Magnet; 1 Charter; 60 Title I Eligible; 49 School-wide Title I
Students: 57,818 (50.8% male; 49.1% female)
   Individual Education Program: 6,454 (11.2%);
   English Language Learner: 15,501 (26.8%); Migrant: 0 (0.0%)
   Eligible for Free Lunch Program: 38,640 (66.8%)
   Eligible for Reduced-Price Lunch Program: 8,204 (14.2%)
Teachers: 2,691.1 (21.5 to 1)
Librarians/Media Specialists: 3.0 (19,272.7 to 1)
Guidance Counselors: 86.2 (670.7 to 1)
Current Spending: ($ per student per year):
   Total: $7,266; Instruction: $4,165; Support Services: $2,766
Enrollment, Drop-out Rates and Diploma Recipients by Race/Ethnicity

Category	Total	White	Black	Asian	AIAN	Hisp.
Enrollment (%)	100.0	15.9	19.8	2.9	1.0	59.9
Drop-out Rate (%)	n/a	n/a	n/a	n/a	n/a	n/a
H.S. Diplomas (#)	1,933	526	345	132	22	905

San Bernardino County Off. of Education
601 N E St • San Bernardino, CA 92404-2310
(909) 386-2400 • http://www.sbcss.k12.ca.us/sbcss/
Grade Span: KG-12; **Agency Type:** 4
Schools: 6
   0 Primary; 0 Middle; 1 High; 5 Other Level
   0 Regular; 2 Special Education; 0 Vocational; 4 Alternative
   0 Magnet; 0 Charter; 0 Title I Eligible; 0 School-wide Title I
Students: 3,413 (73.5% male; 26.4% female)
   Individual Education Program: n/a;
   English Language Learner: 387 (11.3%); Migrant: 0 (0.0%)
   Eligible for Free Lunch Program: 1,722 (50.5%)
   Eligible for Reduced-Price Lunch Program: 9 (0.3%)
Teachers: 306.1 (11.1 to 1)
Librarians/Media Specialists: 1.3 (2,625.4 to 1)
Guidance Counselors: 3.0 (1,137.7 to 1)
Current Spending: ($ per student per year):
   Total: $45,766; Instruction: $23,433; Support Services: $22,327
Enrollment, Drop-out Rates and Diploma Recipients by Race/Ethnicity

Category	Total	White	Black	Asian	AIAN	Hisp.
Enrollment (%)	100.0	34.2	19.1	3.7	0.4	41.7
Drop-out Rate (%)	n/a	n/a	n/a	n/a	n/a	n/a
H.S. Diplomas (#)	0	0	0	0	0	0

Silver Valley Unified
35320 Daggett Yermo Rd • Yermo, CA 92398-0847
Mailing Address: PO Box 847 • Yermo, CA 92398-0847
(760) 254-2916 • http://www.silvervalley.k12.ca.us/
Grade Span: KG-12; **Agency Type:** 1
Schools: 7
   3 Primary; 1 Middle; 2 High; 1 Other Level
   5 Regular; 0 Special Education; 0 Vocational; 2 Alternative
   0 Magnet; 0 Charter; 3 Title I Eligible; 0 School-wide Title I
Students: 2,630 (50.7% male; 49.2% female)
   Individual Education Program: 259 (9.8%);
   English Language Learner: 56 (2.1%); Migrant: 0 (0.0%)
   Eligible for Free Lunch Program: 748 (28.4%)
   Eligible for Reduced-Price Lunch Program: 504 (19.2%)
Teachers: 136.6 (19.3 to 1)
Librarians/Media Specialists: 0.0 (n/a to 1)
Guidance Counselors: 4.0 (657.5 to 1)
Current Spending: ($ per student per year):
   Total: $9,037; Instruction: $4,742; Support Services: $3,911
Enrollment, Drop-out Rates and Diploma Recipients by Race/Ethnicity

Category	Total	White	Black	Asian	AIAN	Hisp.
Enrollment (%)	100.0	46.6	15.1	4.3	1.1	17.3
Drop-out Rate (%)	n/a	n/a	n/a	n/a	n/a	n/a
H.S. Diplomas (#)	83	49	9	12	2	10

Snowline Joint Unified
4075 Nielson Rd • Phelan, CA 92329-6000
Mailing Address: PO Box 296000 • Phelan, CA 92329-6000
(760) 868-5817 • http://www.snowline.k12.ca.us/
Grade Span: KG-12; **Agency Type:** 1
Schools: 13
   5 Primary; 2 Middle; 3 High; 3 Other Level
   10 Regular; 0 Special Education; 0 Vocational; 3 Alternative
   0 Magnet; 2 Charter; 7 Title I Eligible; 2 School-wide Title I
Students: 9,521 (51.2% male; 48.7% female)
   Individual Education Program: 985 (10.3%);
   English Language Learner: 558 (5.9%); Migrant: 0 (0.0%)
   Eligible for Free Lunch Program: 2,792 (29.3%)
   Eligible for Reduced-Price Lunch Program: 589 (6.2%)
Teachers: 462.7 (20.6 to 1)
Librarians/Media Specialists: 0.0 (n/a to 1)
Guidance Counselors: 9.0 (1,057.9 to 1)
Current Spending: ($ per student per year):
   Total: $5,544; Instruction: $3,466; Support Services: $1,897
Enrollment, Drop-out Rates and Diploma Recipients by Race/Ethnicity

Category	Total	White	Black	Asian	AIAN	Hisp.
Enrollment (%)	100.0	64.8	4.9	1.7	0.9	26.1
Drop-out Rate (%)	n/a	n/a	n/a	n/a	n/a	n/a
H.S. Diplomas (#)	685	358	62	17	3	240

Upland Unified
390 N Euclid Ave • Upland, CA 91785-1239
Mailing Address: PO Box 1239 • Upland, CA 91785-1239
(909) 985-1864 • http://www.upland.k12.ca.us/
Grade Span: KG-12; **Agency Type:** 1
Schools: 15
   9 Primary; 2 Middle; 2 High; 2 Other Level
   13 Regular; 0 Special Education; 0 Vocational; 2 Alternative
   0 Magnet; 1 Charter; 7 Title I Eligible; 5 School-wide Title I
Students: 13,585 (50.1% male; 49.8% female)
   Individual Education Program: 1,019 (7.5%);
   English Language Learner: 1,540 (11.3%); Migrant: 0 (0.0%)
   Eligible for Free Lunch Program: 3,539 (26.1%)
   Eligible for Reduced-Price Lunch Program: 1,035 (7.6%)
Teachers: 593.5 (22.9 to 1)
Librarians/Media Specialists: 1.0 (13,585.0 to 1)
Guidance Counselors: 16.6 (818.4 to 1)
Current Spending: ($ per student per year):
   Total: $5,940; Instruction: $4,052; Support Services: $1,656

Enrollment, Drop-out Rates and Diploma Recipients by Race/Ethnicity

Category	Total	White	Black	Asian	AIAN	Hisp.
Enrollment (%)	100.0	41.1	9.2	6.3	0.6	33.0
Drop-out Rate (%)	n/a	n/a	n/a	n/a	n/a	n/a
H.S. Diplomas (#)	912	481	84	95	1	244

Victor Elementary

15579 Eighth St • Victorville, CA 92392-3348
(760) 245-1691 • http://www.vesd.org/
Grade Span: KG-06; **Agency Type:** 1
Schools: 15
    15 Primary; 0 Middle; 0 High; 0 Other Level
    15 Regular; 0 Special Education; 0 Vocational; 0 Alternative
    0 Magnet; 3 Charter; 10 Title I Eligible; 2 School-wide Title I
Students: 9,805 (49.5% male; 50.4% female)
    Individual Education Program: 760 (7.8%);
    English Language Learner: 1,123 (11.5%); Migrant: 0 (0.0%)
    Eligible for Free Lunch Program: 4,372 (44.6%)
    Eligible for Reduced-Price Lunch Program: 1,151 (11.7%)
Teachers: 406.5 (24.1 to 1)
Librarians/Media Specialists: 0.0 (n/a to 1)
Guidance Counselors: 2.0 (4,902.5 to 1)
Current Spending: ($ per student per year):
    Total: $6,031; Instruction: $4,091; Support Services: $1,715

Enrollment, Drop-out Rates and Diploma Recipients by Race/Ethnicity

Category	Total	White	Black	Asian	AIAN	Hisp.
Enrollment (%)	100.0	36.8	15.5	3.1	0.7	42.1
Drop-out Rate (%)	n/a	n/a	n/a	n/a	n/a	n/a
H.S. Diplomas (#)	n/a	n/a	n/a	n/a	n/a	n/a

Victor Valley Union High

16350 Mojave Dr • Victorville, CA 92392-3655
(760) 955-3200 • http://www.vvuhsd.k12.ca.us/
Grade Span: 07-12; **Agency Type:** 1
Schools: 9
    0 Primary; 3 Middle; 6 High; 0 Other Level
    6 Regular; 0 Special Education; 0 Vocational; 3 Alternative
    0 Magnet; 2 Charter; 6 Title I Eligible; 3 School-wide Title I
Students: 10,852 (50.0% male; 50.0% female)
    Individual Education Program: 1,269 (11.7%);
    English Language Learner: 562 (5.2%); Migrant: 0 (0.0%)
    Eligible for Free Lunch Program: 4,360 (40.2%)
    Eligible for Reduced-Price Lunch Program: 1,100 (10.1%)
Teachers: 424.6 (25.6 to 1)
Librarians/Media Specialists: 1.5 (7,234.7 to 1)
Guidance Counselors: 14.9 (728.3 to 1)
Current Spending: ($ per student per year):
    Total: $5,334; Instruction: $3,043; Support Services: $2,069

Enrollment, Drop-out Rates and Diploma Recipients by Race/Ethnicity

Category	Total	White	Black	Asian	AIAN	Hisp.
Enrollment (%)	100.0	33.0	17.6	3.6	0.7	40.3
Drop-out Rate (%)	n/a	n/a	n/a	n/a	n/a	n/a
H.S. Diplomas (#)	1,145	489	147	63	11	388

Yucaipa-Calimesa Jt. Unified

12797 Third St • Yucaipa, CA 92399-4544
(909) 797-0174 • http://www.ycjusd.k12.ca.us/
Grade Span: KG-12; **Agency Type:** 1
Schools: 14
    7 Primary; 2 Middle; 4 High; 1 Other Level
    11 Regular; 0 Special Education; 0 Vocational; 3 Alternative
    0 Magnet; 0 Charter; 4 Title I Eligible; 0 School-wide Title I
Students: 9,622 (52.2% male; 47.7% female)
    Individual Education Program: 928 (9.6%);
    English Language Learner: 759 (7.9%); Migrant: 0 (0.0%)
    Eligible for Free Lunch Program: 2,348 (24.4%)
    Eligible for Reduced-Price Lunch Program: 670 (7.0%)
Teachers: 406.8 (23.7 to 1)
Librarians/Media Specialists: 0.0 (n/a to 1)
Guidance Counselors: 8.0 (1,202.8 to 1)
Current Spending: ($ per student per year):
    Total: $6,283; Instruction: $4,096; Support Services: $1,959

Enrollment, Drop-out Rates and Diploma Recipients by Race/Ethnicity

Category	Total	White	Black	Asian	AIAN	Hisp.
Enrollment (%)	100.0	67.2	1.4	1.6	0.7	24.6
Drop-out Rate (%)	n/a	n/a	n/a	n/a	n/a	n/a
H.S. Diplomas (#)	635	508	3	12	6	105

San Diego County

Alpine Union Elementary

1323 Administration Way • Alpine, CA 91901-2104
(619) 445-3236 • http://alpineschooldistrict.net/
Grade Span: KG-08; **Agency Type:** 1
Schools: 7

    6 Primary; 1 Middle; 0 High; 0 Other Level
    5 Regular; 0 Special Education; 0 Vocational; 2 Alternative
    0 Magnet; 0 Charter; 5 Title I Eligible; 0 School-wide Title I
Students: 2,329 (52.0% male; 47.9% female)
    Individual Education Program: 260 (11.2%);
    English Language Learner: 92 (4.0%); Migrant: 0 (0.0%)
    Eligible for Free Lunch Program: 273 (11.7%)
    Eligible for Reduced-Price Lunch Program: 86 (3.7%)
Teachers: 112.0 (20.8 to 1)
Librarians/Media Specialists: 0.0 (n/a to 1)
Guidance Counselors: 1.0 (2,329.0 to 1)
Current Spending: ($ per student per year):
    Total: $7,028; Instruction: $4,640; Support Services: $2,151

Enrollment, Drop-out Rates and Diploma Recipients by Race/Ethnicity

Category	Total	White	Black	Asian	AIAN	Hisp.
Enrollment (%)	100.0	76.7	1.0	2.0	4.6	14.4
Drop-out Rate (%)	n/a	n/a	n/a	n/a	n/a	n/a
H.S. Diplomas (#)	n/a	n/a	n/a	n/a	n/a	n/a

Bonsall Union Elementary

31505 Old River Rd • Bonsall, CA 92003-5112
(760) 631-5200 • http://www.nctimes.net/~busd/welcome.html
Grade Span: KG-12; **Agency Type:** 1
Schools: 5
    3 Primary; 1 Middle; 0 High; 1 Other Level
    5 Regular; 0 Special Education; 0 Vocational; 0 Alternative
    0 Magnet; 3 Charter; 3 Title I Eligible; 0 School-wide Title I
Students: 1,865 (50.2% male; 49.7% female)
    Individual Education Program: 173 (9.3%);
    English Language Learner: 446 (23.9%); Migrant: 278 (14.9%)
    Eligible for Free Lunch Program: 437 (23.4%)
    Eligible for Reduced-Price Lunch Program: 130 (7.0%)
Teachers: 92.1 (20.2 to 1)
Librarians/Media Specialists: 0.0 (n/a to 1)
Guidance Counselors: 0.8 (2,331.3 to 1)
Current Spending: ($ per student per year):
    Total: $6,960; Instruction: $4,374; Support Services: $2,290

Enrollment, Drop-out Rates and Diploma Recipients by Race/Ethnicity

Category	Total	White	Black	Asian	AIAN	Hisp.
Enrollment (%)	100.0	54.6	1.3	3.4	7.0	33.5
Drop-out Rate (%)	n/a	n/a	n/a	n/a	n/a	n/a
H.S. Diplomas (#)	0	0	0	0	0	0

Cajon Valley Union Elementary

189 Roanoke Rd • El Cajon, CA 92022-1007
Mailing Address: PO Box 1007 • El Cajon, CA 92022-1007
(619) 588-3000 • http://www.cajon.k12.ca.us/schools/index.htm
Grade Span: KG-08; **Agency Type:** 1
Schools: 28
    22 Primary; 6 Middle; 0 High; 0 Other Level
    26 Regular; 0 Special Education; 0 Vocational; 2 Alternative
    2 Magnet; 0 Charter; 17 Title I Eligible; 13 School-wide Title I
Students: 18,070 (51.3% male; 48.6% female)
    Individual Education Program: 2,562 (14.2%);
    English Language Learner: 3,635 (20.1%); Migrant: 3 (<0.1%)
    Eligible for Free Lunch Program: 6,784 (37.5%)
    Eligible for Reduced-Price Lunch Program: 2,207 (12.2%)
Teachers: 817.5 (22.1 to 1)
Librarians/Media Specialists: 0.0 (n/a to 1)
Guidance Counselors: 5.4 (3,346.3 to 1)
Current Spending: ($ per student per year):
    Total: $7,105; Instruction: $4,669; Support Services: $2,147

Enrollment, Drop-out Rates and Diploma Recipients by Race/Ethnicity

Category	Total	White	Black	Asian	AIAN	Hisp.
Enrollment (%)	100.0	60.4	7.2	3.1	1.0	28.3
Drop-out Rate (%)	n/a	n/a	n/a	n/a	n/a	n/a
H.S. Diplomas (#)	n/a	n/a	n/a	n/a	n/a	n/a

Carlsbad Unified

6225 El Camino Real • Carlsbad, CA 92009
(760) 729-9291 • http://www.carlsbadusd.k12.ca.us/
Grade Span: KG-12; **Agency Type:** 1
Schools: 13
    8 Primary; 2 Middle; 1 High; 2 Other Level
    11 Regular; 0 Special Education; 0 Vocational; 2 Alternative
    0 Magnet; 0 Charter; 5 Title I Eligible; 2 School-wide Title I
Students: 10,098 (52.2% male; 47.7% female)
    Individual Education Program: 959 (9.5%);
    English Language Learner: 885 (8.8%); Migrant: 265 (2.6%)
    Eligible for Free Lunch Program: 1,129 (11.2%)
    Eligible for Reduced-Price Lunch Program: 503 (5.0%)
Teachers: 458.3 (22.0 to 1)
Librarians/Media Specialists: 2.6 (3,883.8 to 1)
Guidance Counselors: 7.0 (1,442.6 to 1)
Current Spending: ($ per student per year):
    Total: $6,470; Instruction: $4,127; Support Services: $2,162

Enrollment, Drop-out Rates and Diploma Recipients by Race/Ethnicity

Category	Total	White	Black	Asian	AIAN	Hisp.
Enrollment (%)	100.0	64.4	2.1	6.0	0.6	23.7
Drop-out Rate (%)	n/a	n/a	n/a	n/a	n/a	n/a
H.S. Diplomas (#)	602	440	17	33	4	108

Chula Vista Elementary
84 E J St • Chula Vista, CA 91910-6115
(619) 425-9600 • http://www.cvesd.k12.ca.us/
Grade Span: KG-06; **Agency Type:** 1
Schools: 40
    40 Primary; 0 Middle; 0 High; 0 Other Level
    40 Regular; 0 Special Education; 0 Vocational; 0 Alternative
    0 Magnet; 6 Charter; 21 Title I Eligible; 17 School-wide Title I
Students: 25,292   (51.6% male; 48.3% female)
    Individual Education Program: 2,799 (11.1%);
    English Language Learner: 8,860 (35.0%); Migrant: 7 (<0.1%)
    Eligible for Free Lunch Program: 7,369 (29.1%)
    Eligible for Reduced-Price Lunch Program: 4,133 (16.3%)
Teachers: 1,291.7 (19.6 to 1)
Librarians/Media Specialists: 7.5 (3,372.3 to 1)
Guidance Counselors: 9.0 (2,810.2 to 1)
Current Spending: ($ per student per year):
    Total: $7,329; Instruction: $4,902; Support Services: $2,150

Enrollment, Drop-out Rates and Diploma Recipients by Race/Ethnicity

Category	Total	White	Black	Asian	AIAN	Hisp.
Enrollment (%)	100.0	17.0	4.9	13.0	0.4	64.3
Drop-out Rate (%)	n/a	n/a	n/a	n/a	n/a	n/a
H.S. Diplomas (#)	n/a	n/a	n/a	n/a	n/a	n/a

Coronado Unified
555 D Ave • Coronado, CA 92118-1714
(619) 522-8900 • http://www.coronado.k12.ca.us/
Grade Span: KG-12; **Agency Type:** 1
Schools: 5
    2 Primary; 1 Middle; 2 High; 0 Other Level
    4 Regular; 0 Special Education; 0 Vocational; 1 Alternative
    0 Magnet; 0 Charter; 1 Title I Eligible; 0 School-wide Title I
Students: 2,915   (50.1% male; 49.8% female)
    Individual Education Program: 348 (11.9%);
    English Language Learner: 39 (1.3%); Migrant: 0 (0.0%)
    Eligible for Free Lunch Program: 99 (3.4%)
    Eligible for Reduced-Price Lunch Program: 126 (4.3%)
Teachers: 136.8 (21.3 to 1)
Librarians/Media Specialists: 0.0 (n/a to 1)
Guidance Counselors: 4.0 (728.8 to 1)
Current Spending: ($ per student per year):
    Total: $7,786; Instruction: $4,895; Support Services: $2,708

Enrollment, Drop-out Rates and Diploma Recipients by Race/Ethnicity

Category	Total	White	Black	Asian	AIAN	Hisp.
Enrollment (%)	100.0	75.1	2.8	6.6	0.9	12.5
Drop-out Rate (%)	n/a	n/a	n/a	n/a	n/a	n/a
H.S. Diplomas (#)	248	204	4	15	0	24

Del Mar Union Elementary
225 Ninth St • Del Mar, CA 92014-2716
(858) 755-9301 • http://delmarschools.com/
Grade Span: KG-06; **Agency Type:** 1
Schools: 6
    6 Primary; 0 Middle; 0 High; 0 Other Level
    6 Regular; 0 Special Education; 0 Vocational; 0 Alternative
    0 Magnet; 0 Charter; 0 Title I Eligible; 0 School-wide Title I
Students: 3,506   (52.4% male; 47.5% female)
    Individual Education Program: 398 (11.4%);
    English Language Learner: 137 (3.9%); Migrant: 3 (0.1%)
    Eligible for Free Lunch Program: 60 (1.7%)
    Eligible for Reduced-Price Lunch Program: 30 (0.9%)
Teachers: 195.4 (17.9 to 1)
Librarians/Media Specialists: 0.0 (n/a to 1)
Guidance Counselors: 0.0 (n/a to 1)
Current Spending: ($ per student per year):
    Total: $7,554; Instruction: $5,229; Support Services: $2,299

Enrollment, Drop-out Rates and Diploma Recipients by Race/Ethnicity

Category	Total	White	Black	Asian	AIAN	Hisp.
Enrollment (%)	100.0	71.8	1.7	22.0	0.1	4.4
Drop-out Rate (%)	n/a	n/a	n/a	n/a	n/a	n/a
H.S. Diplomas (#)	n/a	n/a	n/a	n/a	n/a	n/a

Encinitas Union Elementary
101 S Rancho Santa Fe Rd • Encinitas, CA 92024-4308
(760) 944-4300 • http://www.eusd.k12.ca.us/default.htm
Grade Span: KG-06; **Agency Type:** 1
Schools: 9
    9 Primary; 0 Middle; 0 High; 0 Other Level
    9 Regular; 0 Special Education; 0 Vocational; 0 Alternative

    0 Magnet; 0 Charter; 4 Title I Eligible; 0 School-wide Title I
Students: 5,829   (51.2% male; 48.7% female)
    Individual Education Program: 502 (8.6%);
    English Language Learner: 726 (12.5%); Migrant: 145 (2.5%)
    Eligible for Free Lunch Program: 761 (13.1%)
    Eligible for Reduced-Price Lunch Program: 244 (4.2%)
Teachers: 276.5 (21.1 to 1)
Librarians/Media Specialists: 0.0 (n/a to 1)
Guidance Counselors: 0.6 (9,715.0 to 1)
Current Spending: ($ per student per year):
    Total: $6,716; Instruction: $4,541; Support Services: $2,029

Enrollment, Drop-out Rates and Diploma Recipients by Race/Ethnicity

Category	Total	White	Black	Asian	AIAN	Hisp.
Enrollment (%)	100.0	73.8	0.9	6.2	0.2	18.7
Drop-out Rate (%)	n/a	n/a	n/a	n/a	n/a	n/a
H.S. Diplomas (#)	n/a	n/a	n/a	n/a	n/a	n/a

Escondido Union Elementary
1330 E Grand Ave • Escondido, CA 92027-3099
(760) 432-2400 • http://www.escusd.k12.ca.us/
Grade Span: KG-12; **Agency Type:** 1
Schools: 22
    17 Primary; 4 Middle; 0 High; 1 Other Level
    21 Regular; 1 Special Education; 0 Vocational; 0 Alternative
    0 Magnet; 2 Charter; 14 Title I Eligible; 10 School-wide Title I
Students: 20,164   (51.2% male; 48.7% female)
    Individual Education Program: 2,251 (11.2%);
    English Language Learner: 8,620 (42.7%); Migrant: 780 (3.9%)
    Eligible for Free Lunch Program: 9,270 (46.0%)
    Eligible for Reduced-Price Lunch Program: 2,860 (14.2%)
Teachers: 994.5 (20.3 to 1)
Librarians/Media Specialists: 0.3 (67,213.3 to 1)
Guidance Counselors: 9.0 (2,240.4 to 1)
Current Spending: ($ per student per year):
    Total: $6,582; Instruction: $4,249; Support Services: $2,064

Enrollment, Drop-out Rates and Diploma Recipients by Race/Ethnicity

Category	Total	White	Black	Asian	AIAN	Hisp.
Enrollment (%)	100.0	31.0	3.3	5.3	0.6	59.2
Drop-out Rate (%)	n/a	n/a	n/a	n/a	n/a	n/a
H.S. Diplomas (#)	0	0	0	0	0	0

Escondido Union High
302 N Midway Dr • Escondido, CA 92027-2741
(760) 291-3200 • http://www.escusd.k12.ca.us/
Grade Span: 09-12; **Agency Type:** 1
Schools: 6
    0 Primary; 0 Middle; 6 High; 0 Other Level
    4 Regular; 0 Special Education; 0 Vocational; 2 Alternative
    0 Magnet; 1 Charter; 4 Title I Eligible; 0 School-wide Title I
Students: 8,604   (50.4% male; 49.5% female)
    Individual Education Program: 797 (9.3%);
    English Language Learner: 1,533 (17.8%); Migrant: 271 (3.1%)
    Eligible for Free Lunch Program: 1,061 (12.3%)
    Eligible for Reduced-Price Lunch Program: 286 (3.3%)
Teachers: 347.5 (24.8 to 1)
Librarians/Media Specialists: 0.0 (n/a to 1)
Guidance Counselors: 16.0 (537.8 to 1)
Current Spending: ($ per student per year):
    Total: $6,614; Instruction: $3,985; Support Services: $2,483

Enrollment, Drop-out Rates and Diploma Recipients by Race/Ethnicity

Category	Total	White	Black	Asian	AIAN	Hisp.
Enrollment (%)	100.0	46.3	2.6	5.1	0.7	44.6
Drop-out Rate (%)	n/a	n/a	n/a	n/a	n/a	n/a
H.S. Diplomas (#)	1,556	849	57	93	13	542

Fallbrook Union Elementary
321 N Iowa St • Fallbrook, CA 92088-0698
Mailing Address: PO Box 698 • Fallbrook, CA 92088-0698
(760) 723-7000 • http://www.fuesd.k12.ca.us/
Grade Span: KG-08; **Agency Type:** 1
Schools: 9
    7 Primary; 2 Middle; 0 High; 0 Other Level
    8 Regular; 0 Special Education; 0 Vocational; 1 Alternative
    0 Magnet; 0 Charter; 3 Title I Eligible; 0 School-wide Title I
Students: 6,092   (52.2% male; 47.7% female)
    Individual Education Program: 609 (10.0%);
    English Language Learner: 1,663 (27.3%); Migrant: 557 (9.1%)
    Eligible for Free Lunch Program: 1,964 (32.2%)
    Eligible for Reduced-Price Lunch Program: 730 (12.0%)
Teachers: 281.0 (21.7 to 1)
Librarians/Media Specialists: 0.0 (n/a to 1)
Guidance Counselors: 3.5 (1,740.6 to 1)
Current Spending: ($ per student per year):
    Total: $7,300; Instruction: $4,615; Support Services: $2,434

Enrollment, Drop-out Rates and Diploma Recipients by Race/Ethnicity

Category	Total	White	Black	Asian	AIAN	Hisp.
Enrollment (%)	100.0	44.7	3.7	2.4	0.6	43.1
Drop-out Rate (%)	n/a	n/a	n/a	n/a	n/a	n/a
H.S. Diplomas (#)	n/a	n/a	n/a	n/a	n/a	n/a

Fallbrook Union High
2234 S Stage Coach Ln • Fallbrook, CA 92028
(760) 723-6332
Grade Span: 09-12; **Agency Type:** 1
Schools: 3
    0 Primary; 0 Middle; 3 High; 0 Other Level
    1 Regular; 0 Special Education; 0 Vocational; 2 Alternative
    0 Magnet; 0 Charter; 1 Title I Eligible; 0 School-wide Title I
Students: 3,122   (50.6% male; 49.3% female)
    Individual Education Program: 324 (10.4%);
    English Language Learner: 601 (19.3%); Migrant: 276 (8.8%)
    Eligible for Free Lunch Program: 929 (29.8%)
    Eligible for Reduced-Price Lunch Program: 227 (7.3%)
Teachers: 139.7 (22.3 to 1)
Librarians/Media Specialists: 0.0 (n/a to 1)
Guidance Counselors: 4.4 (709.5 to 1)
Current Spending: ($ per student per year):
    Total: $7,510; Instruction: $4,466; Support Services: $2,799

Enrollment, Drop-out Rates and Diploma Recipients by Race/Ethnicity

Category	Total	White	Black	Asian	AIAN	Hisp.
Enrollment (%)	100.0	51.8	1.7	2.8	2.1	38.1
Drop-out Rate (%)	n/a	n/a	n/a	n/a	n/a	n/a
H.S. Diplomas (#)	595	359	14	23	18	180

Grossmont Union High
1100 Murray Dr • La Mesa, CA 91944-1043
Mailing Address: PO Box 1043 • La Mesa, CA 91944-1043
(619) 644-8000 • http://www.grossmont.k12.ca.us/
Grade Span: 08-12; **Agency Type:** 1
Schools: 19
    0 Primary; 0 Middle; 19 High; 0 Other Level
    12 Regular; 3 Special Education; 0 Vocational; 4 Alternative
    0 Magnet; 1 Charter; 7 Title I Eligible; 2 School-wide Title I
Students: 24,456   (51.1% male; 48.8% female)
    Individual Education Program: 2,931 (12.0%);
    English Language Learner: 1,763 (7.2%); Migrant: 5 (<0.1%)
    Eligible for Free Lunch Program: 4,167 (17.0%)
    Eligible for Reduced-Price Lunch Program: 1,379 (5.6%)
Teachers: 1,186.1 (20.6 to 1)
Librarians/Media Specialists: 3.0 (8,152.0 to 1)
Guidance Counselors: 15.6 (1,567.7 to 1)
Current Spending: ($ per student per year):
    Total: $7,689; Instruction: $4,690; Support Services: $2,780

Enrollment, Drop-out Rates and Diploma Recipients by Race/Ethnicity

Category	Total	White	Black	Asian	AIAN	Hisp.
Enrollment (%)	100.0	61.9	8.2	6.1	2.2	21.3
Drop-out Rate (%)	n/a	n/a	n/a	n/a	n/a	n/a
H.S. Diplomas (#)	4,387	2,996	247	236	99	688

Jamul-Dulzura Union Elementary
14581 Lyons Valley Rd • Jamul, CA 91935-3324
(619) 669-7700
Grade Span: KG-09; **Agency Type:** 1
Schools: 4
    1 Primary; 2 Middle; 0 High; 1 Other Level
    4 Regular; 0 Special Education; 0 Vocational; 0 Alternative
    0 Magnet; 1 Charter; 0 Title I Eligible; 0 School-wide Title I
Students: 1,751   (53.3% male; 46.6% female)
    Individual Education Program: 184 (10.5%);
    English Language Learner: 230 (13.1%); Migrant: 0 (0.0%)
    Eligible for Free Lunch Program: 248 (14.2%)
    Eligible for Reduced-Price Lunch Program: 78 (4.5%)
Teachers: 75.7 (23.1 to 1)
Librarians/Media Specialists: 0.0 (n/a to 1)
Guidance Counselors: 1.0 (1,751.0 to 1)
Current Spending: ($ per student per year):
    Total: $7,461; Instruction: $4,649; Support Services: $2,634

Enrollment, Drop-out Rates and Diploma Recipients by Race/Ethnicity

Category	Total	White	Black	Asian	AIAN	Hisp.
Enrollment (%)	100.0	67.8	2.7	2.0	1.5	22.7
Drop-out Rate (%)	n/a	n/a	n/a	n/a	n/a	n/a
H.S. Diplomas (#)	n/a	n/a	n/a	n/a	n/a	n/a

Julian Union Elementary
1704 Hwy 78 • Julian, CA 92036-0337
Mailing Address: PO Box 337 • Julian, CA 92036-0337
(760) 765-0661
Grade Span: KG-12; **Agency Type:** 1
Schools: 3

    1 Primary; 1 Middle; 0 High; 1 Other Level
    3 Regular; 0 Special Education; 0 Vocational; 0 Alternative
    0 Magnet; 1 Charter; 2 Title I Eligible; 0 School-wide Title I
Students: 1,757   (46.9% male; 53.0% female)
    Individual Education Program: 140 (8.0%);
    English Language Learner: 42 (2.4%); Migrant: 0 (0.0%)
    Eligible for Free Lunch Program: 220 (12.5%)
    Eligible for Reduced-Price Lunch Program: 191 (10.9%)
Teachers: 81.6 (21.5 to 1)
Librarians/Media Specialists: 0.0 (n/a to 1)
Guidance Counselors: 1.0 (1,757.0 to 1)
Current Spending: ($ per student per year):
    Total: $6,460; Instruction: $4,927; Support Services: $1,420

Enrollment, Drop-out Rates and Diploma Recipients by Race/Ethnicity

Category	Total	White	Black	Asian	AIAN	Hisp.
Enrollment (%)	100.0	73.0	4.2	2.7	4.6	13.9
Drop-out Rate (%)	n/a	n/a	n/a	n/a	n/a	n/a
H.S. Diplomas (#)	33	17	0	1	0	6

Julian Union High
1656 Hwy 78 • Julian, CA 92036-0417
Mailing Address: PO Box 417 • Julian, CA 92036-0417
(760) 765-3208
Grade Span: KG-12; **Agency Type:** 1
Schools: 3
    0 Primary; 0 Middle; 2 High; 1 Other Level
    2 Regular; 0 Special Education; 0 Vocational; 1 Alternative
    0 Magnet; 1 Charter; 2 Title I Eligible; 0 School-wide Title I
Students: 1,702   (52.0% male; 47.9% female)
    Individual Education Program: 66 (3.9%);
    English Language Learner: 287 (16.9%); Migrant: 0 (0.0%)
    Eligible for Free Lunch Program: 39 (2.3%)
    Eligible for Reduced-Price Lunch Program: 21 (1.2%)
Teachers: 112.1 (15.2 to 1)
Librarians/Media Specialists: 1.0 (1,702.0 to 1)
Guidance Counselors: 2.2 (773.6 to 1)
Current Spending: ($ per student per year):
    Total: $16,634; Instruction: $12,569; Support Services: $4,028

Enrollment, Drop-out Rates and Diploma Recipients by Race/Ethnicity

Category	Total	White	Black	Asian	AIAN	Hisp.
Enrollment (%)	100.0	57.1	5.6	2.1	2.2	22.0
Drop-out Rate (%)	n/a	n/a	n/a	n/a	n/a	n/a
H.S. Diplomas (#)	109	68	4	6	5	25

La Mesa-Spring Valley
4750 Date Ave • La Mesa, CA 91941-5214
(619) 668-5700 • http://www.lmsvsd.k12.ca.us/
Grade Span: KG-08; **Agency Type:** 1
Schools: 22
    18 Primary; 4 Middle; 0 High; 0 Other Level
    22 Regular; 0 Special Education; 0 Vocational; 0 Alternative
    0 Magnet; 0 Charter; 9 Title I Eligible; 7 School-wide Title I
Students: 14,310   (51.5% male; 48.4% female)
    Individual Education Program: 1,786 (12.5%);
    English Language Learner: 2,499 (17.5%); Migrant: 2 (<0.1%)
    Eligible for Free Lunch Program: 4,243 (29.7%)
    Eligible for Reduced-Price Lunch Program: 1,613 (11.3%)
Teachers: 676.8 (21.1 to 1)
Librarians/Media Specialists: 3.0 (4,770.0 to 1)
Guidance Counselors: 26.8 (534.0 to 1)
Current Spending: ($ per student per year):
    Total: $6,967; Instruction: $4,241; Support Services: $2,434

Enrollment, Drop-out Rates and Diploma Recipients by Race/Ethnicity

Category	Total	White	Black	Asian	AIAN	Hisp.
Enrollment (%)	100.0	41.1	12.3	7.2	0.9	31.2
Drop-out Rate (%)	n/a	n/a	n/a	n/a	n/a	n/a
H.S. Diplomas (#)	n/a	n/a	n/a	n/a	n/a	n/a

Lakeside Union Elementary
12335 Woodside Ave • Lakeside, CA 92040-0578
Mailing Address: PO Box 578 • Lakeside, CA 92040-0578
(619) 390-2600 • http://www.lsschools.k12.ca.us/lakeside/default.htm
Grade Span: KG-12; **Agency Type:** 1
Schools: 11
    7 Primary; 2 Middle; 1 High; 1 Other Level
    10 Regular; 1 Special Education; 0 Vocational; 0 Alternative
    0 Magnet; 2 Charter; 5 Title I Eligible; 0 School-wide Title I
Students: 4,871   (51.0% male; 48.9% female)
    Individual Education Program: 865 (17.8%);
    English Language Learner: 348 (7.1%); Migrant: 0 (0.0%)
    Eligible for Free Lunch Program: 1,029 (21.1%)
    Eligible for Reduced-Price Lunch Program: 549 (11.3%)
Teachers: 224.0 (21.7 to 1)
Librarians/Media Specialists: 0.0 (n/a to 1)
Guidance Counselors: 2.2 (2,214.1 to 1)

Current Spending: ($ per student per year):
Total: $6,985; Instruction: $4,689; Support Services: $2,096
Enrollment, Drop-out Rates and Diploma Recipients by Race/Ethnicity

Category	Total	White	Black	Asian	AIAN	Hisp.
Enrollment (%)	100.0	75.2	3.1	2.0	3.0	16.3
Drop-out Rate (%)	n/a	n/a	n/a	n/a	n/a	n/a
H.S. Diplomas (#)	13	12	1	0	0	0

Lemon Grove Elementary
8025 Lincoln St • Lemon Grove, CA 91945-2515
(619) 825-5600 • http://www.lgsd.k12.ca.us/
Grade Span: KG-08; **Agency Type:** 1
Schools: 8
   6 Primary; 2 Middle; 0 High; 0 Other Level
   8 Regular; 0 Special Education; 0 Vocational; 0 Alternative
   0 Magnet; 0 Charter; 4 Title I Eligible; 4 School-wide Title I
Students: 4,440 (51.6% male; 48.3% female)
   Individual Education Program: 521 (11.7%);
   English Language Learner: 852 (19.2%); Migrant: 5 (0.1%)
   Eligible for Free Lunch Program: 1,960 (44.1%)
   Eligible for Reduced-Price Lunch Program: 807 (18.2%)
Teachers: 212.9 (20.9 to 1)
Librarians/Media Specialists: 0.0 (n/a to 1)
Guidance Counselors: 0.0 (n/a to 1)
Current Spending: ($ per student per year):
Total: $7,214; Instruction: $4,661; Support Services: $2,145
Enrollment, Drop-out Rates and Diploma Recipients by Race/Ethnicity

Category	Total	White	Black	Asian	AIAN	Hisp.
Enrollment (%)	100.0	25.0	25.4	9.9	0.9	37.5
Drop-out Rate (%)	n/a	n/a	n/a	n/a	n/a	n/a
H.S. Diplomas (#)	n/a	n/a	n/a	n/a	n/a	n/a

Mountain Empire Unified
3291 Buckman Springs Rd • Pine Valley, CA 91962-4003
(619) 473-9022 • http://www.meusd.k12.ca.us/
Grade Span: KG-12; **Agency Type:** 1
Schools: 13
   6 Primary; 1 Middle; 6 High; 0 Other Level
   9 Regular; 0 Special Education; 0 Vocational; 4 Alternative
   0 Magnet; 1 Charter; 11 Title I Eligible; 7 School-wide Title I
Students: 1,861 (53.5% male; 46.4% female)
   Individual Education Program: 198 (10.6%);
   English Language Learner: 300 (16.1%); Migrant: 6 (0.3%)
   Eligible for Free Lunch Program: 824 (44.3%)
   Eligible for Reduced-Price Lunch Program: 196 (10.5%)
Teachers: 93.0 (20.0 to 1)
Librarians/Media Specialists: 1.0 (1,861.0 to 1)
Guidance Counselors: 2.6 (715.8 to 1)
Current Spending: ($ per student per year):
Total: $9,260; Instruction: $5,218; Support Services: $3,762
Enrollment, Drop-out Rates and Diploma Recipients by Race/Ethnicity

Category	Total	White	Black	Asian	AIAN	Hisp.
Enrollment (%)	100.0	57.6	1.9	1.3	8.8	30.2
Drop-out Rate (%)	n/a	n/a	n/a	n/a	n/a	n/a
H.S. Diplomas (#)	108	74	1	0	3	30

National Elementary
1500 N Ave • National City, CA 91950-4827
(619) 336-7500 • http://www.sdcoe.k12.ca.us/districts/national/index.html
Grade Span: KG-06; **Agency Type:** 1
Schools: 11
   10 Primary; 1 Middle; 0 High; 0 Other Level
   11 Regular; 0 Special Education; 0 Vocational; 0 Alternative
   0 Magnet; 1 Charter; 10 Title I Eligible; 0 School-wide Title I
Students: 6,535 (52.1% male; 47.8% female)
   Individual Education Program: 676 (10.3%);
   English Language Learner: 3,805 (58.2%); Migrant: 59 (0.9%)
   Eligible for Free Lunch Program: 6,502 (99.5%)
   Eligible for Reduced-Price Lunch Program: 0 (0.0%)
Teachers: 296.4 (22.0 to 1)
Librarians/Media Specialists: 0.0 (n/a to 1)
Guidance Counselors: 2.8 (2,333.9 to 1)
Current Spending: ($ per student per year):
Total: $7,474; Instruction: $4,811; Support Services: $2,245
Enrollment, Drop-out Rates and Diploma Recipients by Race/Ethnicity

Category	Total	White	Black	Asian	AIAN	Hisp.
Enrollment (%)	100.0	3.1	3.4	13.9	0.4	79.3
Drop-out Rate (%)	n/a	n/a	n/a	n/a	n/a	n/a
H.S. Diplomas (#)	n/a	n/a	n/a	n/a	n/a	n/a

Oceanside Unified
2111 Mission Ave • Oceanside, CA 92054-2326
(760) 757-2560 • http://gsh.org/ousdweb/
Grade Span: KG-12; **Agency Type:** 1
Schools: 28

19 Primary; 3 Middle; 5 High; 1 Other Level
25 Regular; 0 Special Education; 0 Vocational; 3 Alternative
1 Magnet; 3 Charter; 20 Title I Eligible; 9 School-wide Title I
Students: 22,484 (50.5% male; 49.4% female)
   Individual Education Program: 2,452 (10.9%);
   English Language Learner: 5,963 (26.5%); Migrant: 1,047 (4.7%)
   Eligible for Free Lunch Program: 8,809 (39.2%)
   Eligible for Reduced-Price Lunch Program: 3,212 (14.3%)
Teachers: 1,068.8 (21.0 to 1)
Librarians/Media Specialists: 4.0 (5,621.0 to 1)
Guidance Counselors: 16.0 (1,405.3 to 1)
Current Spending: ($ per student per year):
Total: $7,541; Instruction: $4,633; Support Services: $2,669
Enrollment, Drop-out Rates and Diploma Recipients by Race/Ethnicity

Category	Total	White	Black	Asian	AIAN	Hisp.
Enrollment (%)	100.0	30.5	10.2	8.2	0.7	50.3
Drop-out Rate (%)	n/a	n/a	n/a	n/a	n/a	n/a
H.S. Diplomas (#)	957	340	144	113	4	356

Poway Unified
13626 Twin Peaks Rd • Poway, CA 92064-3034
(858) 748-0010 • http://powayusd.sdcoe.k12.ca.us/
Grade Span: KG-12; **Agency Type:** 1
Schools: 31
   21 Primary; 5 Middle; 5 High; 0 Other Level
   30 Regular; 0 Special Education; 0 Vocational; 1 Alternative
   0 Magnet; 0 Charter; 5 Title I Eligible; 0 School-wide Title I
Students: 33,051 (51.5% male; 48.4% female)
   Individual Education Program: 3,208 (9.7%);
   English Language Learner: 2,412 (7.3%); Migrant: 3 (<0.1%)
   Eligible for Free Lunch Program: 2,066 (6.3%)
   Eligible for Reduced-Price Lunch Program: 1,084 (3.3%)
Teachers: 1,478.9 (22.3 to 1)
Librarians/Media Specialists: 6.5 (5,084.8 to 1)
Guidance Counselors: 37.3 (886.1 to 1)
Current Spending: ($ per student per year):
Total: $7,154; Instruction: $4,400; Support Services: $2,333
Enrollment, Drop-out Rates and Diploma Recipients by Race/Ethnicity

Category	Total	White	Black	Asian	AIAN	Hisp.
Enrollment (%)	100.0	63.6	3.3	20.2	0.5	9.5
Drop-out Rate (%)	n/a	n/a	n/a	n/a	n/a	n/a
H.S. Diplomas (#)	2,230	1,571	54	412	14	166

Ramona City Unified
720 Ninth St • Ramona, CA 92065-2348
(760) 788-5000 • http://www.ramona.k12.ca.us/
Grade Span: KG-12; **Agency Type:** 1
Schools: 11
   5 Primary; 1 Middle; 4 High; 1 Other Level
   10 Regular; 0 Special Education; 0 Vocational; 1 Alternative
   0 Magnet; 1 Charter; 4 Title I Eligible; 1 School-wide Title I
Students: 7,216 (51.3% male; 48.6% female)
   Individual Education Program: 937 (13.0%);
   English Language Learner: 969 (13.4%); Migrant: 330 (4.6%)
   Eligible for Free Lunch Program: 2,023 (28.0%)
   Eligible for Reduced-Price Lunch Program: 649 (9.0%)
Teachers: 307.2 (23.5 to 1)
Librarians/Media Specialists: 2.0 (3,608.0 to 1)
Guidance Counselors: 6.8 (1,061.2 to 1)
Current Spending: ($ per student per year):
Total: $6,667; Instruction: $4,216; Support Services: $2,219
Enrollment, Drop-out Rates and Diploma Recipients by Race/Ethnicity

Category	Total	White	Black	Asian	AIAN	Hisp.
Enrollment (%)	100.0	70.8	1.0	1.7	1.1	25.2
Drop-out Rate (%)	n/a	n/a	n/a	n/a	n/a	n/a
H.S. Diplomas (#)	483	383	3	2	5	90

San Diego County Office of Education
6401 Linda Vista Rd • San Diego, CA 92111-7319
(858) 292-3500 • http://www.sdcoe.k12.ca.us/
Grade Span: KG-12; **Agency Type:** 4
Schools: 10
   1 Primary; 0 Middle; 2 High; 7 Other Level
   1 Regular; 2 Special Education; 0 Vocational; 7 Alternative
   0 Magnet; 1 Charter; 0 Title I Eligible; 0 School-wide Title I
Students: 3,514 (59.0% male; 40.9% female)
   Individual Education Program: 826 (23.5%);
   English Language Learner: 452 (12.9%); Migrant: 0 (0.0%)
   Eligible for Free Lunch Program: 2,909 (82.8%)
   Eligible for Reduced-Price Lunch Program: 183 (5.2%)
Teachers: 276.5 (12.7 to 1)
Librarians/Media Specialists: 1.0 (3,514.0 to 1)
Guidance Counselors: 1.0 (3,514.0 to 1)
Current Spending: ($ per student per year):
Total: $45,427; Instruction: $17,337; Support Services: $27,826

Enrollment, Drop-out Rates and Diploma Recipients by Race/Ethnicity

Category	Total	White	Black	Asian	AIAN	Hisp.
Enrollment (%)	100.0	33.1	15.8	4.7	1.6	43.7
Drop-out Rate (%)	n/a	n/a	n/a	n/a	n/a	n/a
H.S. Diplomas (#)	214	78	40	15	2	79

San Diego Unified
4100 Normal St • San Diego, CA 92103-2653
(619) 725-8000 • http://www.sdcs.k12.ca.us/
Grade Span: KG-12; **Agency Type:** 1
Schools: 185
　　127 Primary; 27 Middle; 23 High; 8 Other Level
　　176 Regular; 2 Special Education; 0 Vocational; 7 Alternative
　　23 Magnet; 21 Charter; 134 Title I Eligible; 98 School-wide Title I
Students: 137,960   (51.1% male; 48.8% female)
　　Individual Education Program: 17,313 (12.5%);
　　English Language Learner: 38,790 (28.1%); Migrant: 102 (0.1%)
　　Eligible for Free Lunch Program: 56,874 (41.2%)
　　Eligible for Reduced-Price Lunch Program: 13,406 (9.7%)
Teachers: 7,420.7 (18.6 to 1)
Librarians/Media Specialists: 49.0 (2,815.5 to 1)
Guidance Counselors: 315.8 (436.9 to 1)
Current Spending: ($ per student per year):
　　Total: $8,670; Instruction: $5,162; Support Services: $3,200
Enrollment, Drop-out Rates and Diploma Recipients by Race/Ethnicity

Category	Total	White	Black	Asian	AIAN	Hisp.
Enrollment (%)	100.0	25.9	14.5	17.2	0.5	41.9
Drop-out Rate (%)	n/a	n/a	n/a	n/a	n/a	n/a
H.S. Diplomas (#)	6,504	2,230	877	1,632	44	1,721

San Dieguito Union High
710 Encinitas Blvd • Encinitas, CA 92024-3357
(760) 753-6491 • http://www.sduhsd.k12.ca.us/
Grade Span: 07-12; **Agency Type:** 1
Schools: 9
　　0 Primary; 4 Middle; 5 High; 0 Other Level
　　7 Regular; 0 Special Education; 0 Vocational; 2 Alternative
　　0 Magnet; 0 Charter; 3 Title I Eligible; 0 School-wide Title I
Students: 11,690   (53.2% male; 46.7% female)
　　Individual Education Program: 1,191 (10.2%);
　　English Language Learner: 518 (4.4%); Migrant: 184 (1.6%)
　　Eligible for Free Lunch Program: 571 (4.9%)
　　Eligible for Reduced-Price Lunch Program: 204 (1.7%)
Teachers: 475.8 (24.6 to 1)
Librarians/Media Specialists: 5.9 (1,981.4 to 1)
Guidance Counselors: 26.6 (439.5 to 1)
Current Spending: ($ per student per year):
　　Total: $7,672; Instruction: $4,150; Support Services: $3,286
Enrollment, Drop-out Rates and Diploma Recipients by Race/Ethnicity

Category	Total	White	Black	Asian	AIAN	Hisp.
Enrollment (%)	100.0	77.5	0.9	9.5	0.2	11.5
Drop-out Rate (%)	n/a	n/a	n/a	n/a	n/a	n/a
H.S. Diplomas (#)	1,533	1,250	8	120	4	148

San Marcos Unified
1 Civic Center Dr Ste 300 • San Marcos, CA 92069-2952
(760) 744-4776 • http://www.smusd.org/
Grade Span: KG-12; **Agency Type:** 1
Schools: 14
　　9 Primary; 2 Middle; 2 High; 1 Other Level
　　12 Regular; 0 Special Education; 0 Vocational; 2 Alternative
　　0 Magnet; 0 Charter; 9 Title I Eligible; 0 School-wide Title I
Students: 14,589   (51.3% male; 48.6% female)
　　Individual Education Program: 1,631 (11.2%);
　　English Language Learner: 3,998 (27.4%); Migrant: 531 (3.6%)
　　Eligible for Free Lunch Program: 4,295 (29.4%)
　　Eligible for Reduced-Price Lunch Program: 1,335 (9.2%)
Teachers: 618.4 (23.6 to 1)
Librarians/Media Specialists: 2.0 (7,294.5 to 1)
Guidance Counselors: 11.2 (1,302.6 to 1)
Current Spending: ($ per student per year):
　　Total: $6,547; Instruction: $4,286; Support Services: $2,025
Enrollment, Drop-out Rates and Diploma Recipients by Race/Ethnicity

Category	Total	White	Black	Asian	AIAN	Hisp.
Enrollment (%)	100.0	41.2	3.0	6.6	0.8	48.3
Drop-out Rate (%)	n/a	n/a	n/a	n/a	n/a	n/a
H.S. Diplomas (#)	594	313	15	33	2	231

San Ysidro Elementary
4350 Otay Mesa Rd • San Ysidro, CA 92173-1617
(619) 428-4476 • http://www.sysd.k12.ca.us/
Grade Span: KG-08; **Agency Type:** 1
Schools: 7
　　6 Primary; 1 Middle; 0 High; 0 Other Level
　　7 Regular; 0 Special Education; 0 Vocational; 0 Alternative

　　0 Magnet; 0 Charter; 7 Title I Eligible; 0 School-wide Title I
Students: 5,127   (51.9% male; 48.0% female)
　　Individual Education Program: 496 (9.7%);
　　English Language Learner: 3,521 (68.7%); Migrant: 196 (3.8%)
　　Eligible for Free Lunch Program: 3,867 (75.4%)
　　Eligible for Reduced-Price Lunch Program: 682 (13.3%)
Teachers: 239.5 (21.4 to 1)
Librarians/Media Specialists: 0.0 (n/a to 1)
Guidance Counselors: 2.0 (2,563.5 to 1)
Current Spending: ($ per student per year):
　　Total: $8,098; Instruction: $5,175; Support Services: $2,566
Enrollment, Drop-out Rates and Diploma Recipients by Race/Ethnicity

Category	Total	White	Black	Asian	AIAN	Hisp.
Enrollment (%)	100.0	2.5	2.4	3.1	0.1	91.8
Drop-out Rate (%)	n/a	n/a	n/a	n/a	n/a	n/a
H.S. Diplomas (#)	n/a	n/a	n/a	n/a	n/a	n/a

Santee Elementary
9625 Cuyamaca St • Santee, CA 92071-2674
(619) 258-2300 • http://www.santee.k12.ca.us/
Grade Span: KG-08; **Agency Type:** 1
Schools: 11
　　11 Primary; 0 Middle; 0 High; 0 Other Level
　　9 Regular; 0 Special Education; 0 Vocational; 2 Alternative
　　0 Magnet; 0 Charter; 4 Title I Eligible; 0 School-wide Title I
Students: 6,993   (52.1% male; 47.8% female)
　　Individual Education Program: 994 (14.2%);
　　English Language Learner: 473 (6.8%); Migrant: 0 (0.0%)
　　Eligible for Free Lunch Program: 1,051 (15.0%)
　　Eligible for Reduced-Price Lunch Program: 635 (9.1%)
Teachers: 311.3 (22.5 to 1)
Librarians/Media Specialists: 0.0 (n/a to 1)
Guidance Counselors: 0.0 (n/a to 1)
Current Spending: ($ per student per year):
　　Total: $7,011; Instruction: $4,690; Support Services: $2,154
Enrollment, Drop-out Rates and Diploma Recipients by Race/Ethnicity

Category	Total	White	Black	Asian	AIAN	Hisp.
Enrollment (%)	100.0	79.5	2.1	3.3	0.5	14.3
Drop-out Rate (%)	n/a	n/a	n/a	n/a	n/a	n/a
H.S. Diplomas (#)	n/a	n/a	n/a	n/a	n/a	n/a

Solana Beach Elementary
309 N Rios Ave • Solana Beach, CA 92075-1241
(858) 794-3900 • http://www.sbsd.k12.ca.us/
Grade Span: KG-06; **Agency Type:** 1
Schools: 5
　　5 Primary; 0 Middle; 0 High; 0 Other Level
　　5 Regular; 0 Special Education; 0 Vocational; 0 Alternative
　　0 Magnet; 0 Charter; 2 Title I Eligible; 0 School-wide Title I
Students: 2,642   (53.3% male; 46.6% female)
　　Individual Education Program: 361 (13.7%);
　　English Language Learner: 230 (8.7%); Migrant: 89 (3.4%)
　　Eligible for Free Lunch Program: 177 (6.7%)
　　Eligible for Reduced-Price Lunch Program: 67 (2.5%)
Teachers: 147.9 (17.9 to 1)
Librarians/Media Specialists: 0.0 (n/a to 1)
Guidance Counselors: 0.0 (n/a to 1)
Current Spending: ($ per student per year):
　　Total: $9,199; Instruction: $6,168; Support Services: $2,848
Enrollment, Drop-out Rates and Diploma Recipients by Race/Ethnicity

Category	Total	White	Black	Asian	AIAN	Hisp.
Enrollment (%)	100.0	74.5	0.6	13.4	0.2	11.3
Drop-out Rate (%)	n/a	n/a	n/a	n/a	n/a	n/a
H.S. Diplomas (#)	n/a	n/a	n/a	n/a	n/a	n/a

South Bay Union Elementary
601 Elm Ave • Imperial Beach, CA 91932-2029
(619) 628-1600 • http://sbusd.k12.ca.us/sbusd/index.htm
Grade Span: KG-06; **Agency Type:** 1
Schools: 12
　　12 Primary; 0 Middle; 0 High; 0 Other Level
　　12 Regular; 0 Special Education; 0 Vocational; 0 Alternative
　　0 Magnet; 0 Charter; 12 Title I Eligible; 0 School-wide Title I
Students: 9,244   (51.3% male; 48.6% female)
　　Individual Education Program: 989 (10.7%);
　　English Language Learner: 3,902 (42.2%); Migrant: 7 (0.1%)
　　Eligible for Free Lunch Program: 3,576 (38.7%)
　　Eligible for Reduced-Price Lunch Program: 1,489 (16.1%)
Teachers: 442.0 (20.9 to 1)
Librarians/Media Specialists: 0.0 (n/a to 1)
Guidance Counselors: 0.0 (n/a to 1)
Current Spending: ($ per student per year):
　　Total: $7,611; Instruction: $5,044; Support Services: $2,224

Enrollment, Drop-out Rates and Diploma Recipients by Race/Ethnicity

Category	Total	White	Black	Asian	AIAN	Hisp.
Enrollment (%)	100.0	11.3	4.2	7.8	0.3	75.8
Drop-out Rate (%)	n/a	n/a	n/a	n/a	n/a	n/a
H.S. Diplomas (#)	n/a	n/a	n/a	n/a	n/a	n/a

Sweetwater Union High
1130 Fifth Ave • Chula Vista, CA 91911-2812
(619) 691-5500 • http://www.suhsd.k12.ca.us/
Grade Span: 07-12; **Agency Type:** 1
Schools: 28
    0 Primary; 12 Middle; 16 High; 0 Other Level
    23 Regular; 1 Special Education; 0 Vocational; 4 Alternative
    8 Magnet; 1 Charter; 15 Title I Eligible; 10 School-wide Title I
Students: 39,228 (51.5% male; 48.4% female)
    Individual Education Program: 4,407 (11.2%);
    English Language Learner: 10,368 (26.4%); Migrant: 142 (0.4%)
    Eligible for Free Lunch Program: 13,902 (35.4%)
    Eligible for Reduced-Price Lunch Program: 6,277 (16.0%)
Teachers: 1,773.1 (22.1 to 1)
Librarians/Media Specialists: 22.0 (1,783.1 to 1)
Guidance Counselors: 104.2 (376.5 to 1)
Current Spending: ($ per student per year):
    Total: $7,458; Instruction: $4,641; Support Services: $2,634

Enrollment, Drop-out Rates and Diploma Recipients by Race/Ethnicity

Category	Total	White	Black	Asian	AIAN	Hisp.
Enrollment (%)	100.0	13.9	4.8	11.9	0.6	68.9
Drop-out Rate (%)	n/a	n/a	n/a	n/a	n/a	n/a
H.S. Diplomas (#)	4,768	804	195	667	20	3,082

Valley Center-Pauma Unified
28751 Cole Grade Rd • Valley Center, CA 92082-6599
(760) 749-0464
Grade Span: KG-12; **Agency Type:** 1
Schools: 11
    5 Primary; 1 Middle; 2 High; 3 Other Level
    10 Regular; 0 Special Education; 0 Vocational; 1 Alternative
    0 Magnet; 1 Charter; 6 Title I Eligible; 0 School-wide Title I
Students: 4,661 (52.6% male; 47.3% female)
    Individual Education Program: 554 (11.9%);
    English Language Learner: 922 (19.8%); Migrant: 631 (13.5%)
    Eligible for Free Lunch Program: 1,173 (25.2%)
    Eligible for Reduced-Price Lunch Program: 447 (9.6%)
Teachers: 241.9 (19.3 to 1)
Librarians/Media Specialists: 0.0 (n/a to 1)
Guidance Counselors: 5.0 (932.2 to 1)
Current Spending: ($ per student per year):
    Total: $7,940; Instruction: $5,137; Support Services: $2,551

Enrollment, Drop-out Rates and Diploma Recipients by Race/Ethnicity

Category	Total	White	Black	Asian	AIAN	Hisp.
Enrollment (%)	100.0	56.7	0.3	1.3	10.8	30.8
Drop-out Rate (%)	n/a	n/a	n/a	n/a	n/a	n/a
H.S. Diplomas (#)	330	218	1	6	30	75

Vista Unified
1234 Arcadia Ave • Vista, CA 92084-3404
(760) 726-2170 • http://www.vusd.k12.ca.us/
Grade Span: KG-12; **Agency Type:** 1
Schools: 28
    17 Primary; 4 Middle; 4 High; 3 Other Level
    23 Regular; 2 Special Education; 0 Vocational; 3 Alternative
    2 Magnet; 1 Charter; 13 Title I Eligible; 5 School-wide Title I
Students: 26,989 (51.3% male; 48.6% female)
    Individual Education Program: 3,257 (12.1%);
    English Language Learner: 6,585 (24.4%); Migrant: 772 (2.9%)
    Eligible for Free Lunch Program: 8,046 (29.8%)
    Eligible for Reduced-Price Lunch Program: 2,862 (10.6%)
Teachers: 1,192.7 (22.6 to 1)
Librarians/Media Specialists: 5.8 (4,653.3 to 1)
Guidance Counselors: 20.6 (1,310.1 to 1)
Current Spending: ($ per student per year):
    Total: $6,669; Instruction: $4,548; Support Services: $1,884

Enrollment, Drop-out Rates and Diploma Recipients by Race/Ethnicity

Category	Total	White	Black	Asian	AIAN	Hisp.
Enrollment (%)	100.0	40.5	5.3	5.6	0.6	45.3
Drop-out Rate (%)	n/a	n/a	n/a	n/a	n/a	n/a
H.S. Diplomas (#)	1,996	844	182	169	14	739

San Francisco County

San Francisco Unified
555 Franklin St Room 102 • San Francisco, CA 94102-5207
(415) 241-6000 • http://nisus.sfusd.k12.ca.us/
Grade Span: KG-12; **Agency Type:** 1
Schools: 118

    77 Primary; 19 Middle; 21 High; 1 Other Level
    115 Regular; 0 Special Education; 0 Vocational; 3 Alternative
    5 Magnet; 8 Charter; 73 Title I Eligible; 53 School-wide Title I
Students: 57,805 (51.6% male; 48.3% female)
    Individual Education Program: 7,108 (12.3%);
    English Language Learner: 16,391 (28.4%); Migrant: 414 (0.7%)
    Eligible for Free Lunch Program: 26,861 (46.5%)
    Eligible for Reduced-Price Lunch Program: 8,672 (15.0%)
Teachers: 3,139.4 (18.4 to 1)
Librarians/Media Specialists: 20.8 (2,779.1 to 1)
Guidance Counselors: 91.6 (631.1 to 1)
Current Spending: ($ per student per year):
    Total: $8,704; Instruction: $4,937; Support Services: $3,452

Enrollment, Drop-out Rates and Diploma Recipients by Race/Ethnicity

Category	Total	White	Black	Asian	AIAN	Hisp.
Enrollment (%)	100.0	9.6	14.5	51.3	0.6	21.4
Drop-out Rate (%)	n/a	n/a	n/a	n/a	n/a	n/a
H.S. Diplomas (#)	3,399	382	339	2,132	18	520

San Joaquin County

Escalon Unified
1520 Yosemite Ave • Escalon, CA 95320-1753
(209) 838-3591 • http://www.escalonusd.org/
Grade Span: KG-12; **Agency Type:** 1
Schools: 8
    4 Primary; 2 Middle; 2 High; 0 Other Level
    6 Regular; 0 Special Education; 0 Vocational; 2 Alternative
    0 Magnet; 0 Charter; 5 Title I Eligible; 0 School-wide Title I
Students: 3,171 (51.8% male; 48.1% female)
    Individual Education Program: 102 (3.2%);
    English Language Learner: 556 (17.5%); Migrant: 833 (26.3%)
    Eligible for Free Lunch Program: 989 (31.2%)
    Eligible for Reduced-Price Lunch Program: 245 (7.7%)
Teachers: 142.1 (22.3 to 1)
Librarians/Media Specialists: 0.0 (n/a to 1)
Guidance Counselors: 3.6 (880.8 to 1)
Current Spending: ($ per student per year):
    Total: $6,263; Instruction: $4,036; Support Services: $1,960

Enrollment, Drop-out Rates and Diploma Recipients by Race/Ethnicity

Category	Total	White	Black	Asian	AIAN	Hisp.
Enrollment (%)	100.0	62.5	0.5	2.0	0.8	33.2
Drop-out Rate (%)	n/a	n/a	n/a	n/a	n/a	n/a
H.S. Diplomas (#)	216	161	1	6	4	44

Jefferson Elementary
7500 W Linne Rd • Tracy, CA 95376-9278
(209) 836-3388
Grade Span: KG-08; **Agency Type:** 1
Schools: 3
    2 Primary; 1 Middle; 0 High; 0 Other Level
    3 Regular; 0 Special Education; 0 Vocational; 0 Alternative
    0 Magnet; 0 Charter; 3 Title I Eligible; 0 School-wide Title I
Students: 1,850 (50.7% male; 49.2% female)
    Individual Education Program: 128 (6.9%);
    English Language Learner: 255 (13.8%); Migrant: 14 (0.8%)
    Eligible for Free Lunch Program: 131 (7.1%)
    Eligible for Reduced-Price Lunch Program: 58 (3.1%)
Teachers: 92.5 (20.0 to 1)
Librarians/Media Specialists: 0.0 (n/a to 1)
Guidance Counselors: 0.0 (n/a to 1)
Current Spending: ($ per student per year):
    Total: $6,023; Instruction: $3,951; Support Services: $1,765

Enrollment, Drop-out Rates and Diploma Recipients by Race/Ethnicity

Category	Total	White	Black	Asian	AIAN	Hisp.
Enrollment (%)	100.0	48.4	7.7	19.8	1.0	21.9
Drop-out Rate (%)	n/a	n/a	n/a	n/a	n/a	n/a
H.S. Diplomas (#)	n/a	n/a	n/a	n/a	n/a	n/a

Lincoln Unified
2010 W Swain Rd • Stockton, CA 95207-4055
(209) 953-8700 • http://www.lincolnusd.k12.ca.us/
Grade Span: KG-12; **Agency Type:** 1
Schools: 12
    9 Primary; 1 Middle; 2 High; 0 Other Level
    11 Regular; 0 Special Education; 0 Vocational; 1 Alternative
    0 Magnet; 0 Charter; 7 Title I Eligible; 0 School-wide Title I
Students: 9,017 (50.9% male; 49.0% female)
    Individual Education Program: 871 (9.7%);
    English Language Learner: 1,479 (16.4%); Migrant: 46 (0.5%)
    Eligible for Free Lunch Program: 2,343 (26.0%)
    Eligible for Reduced-Price Lunch Program: 868 (9.6%)
Teachers: 441.8 (20.4 to 1)
Librarians/Media Specialists: 1.8 (5,009.4 to 1)
Guidance Counselors: 15.2 (593.2 to 1)

Current Spending: ($ per student per year):
    Total: $6,694; Instruction: $4,428; Support Services: $2,029
Enrollment, Drop-out Rates and Diploma Recipients by Race/Ethnicity

Category	Total	White	Black	Asian	AIAN	Hisp.
Enrollment (%)	100.0	40.5	13.7	19.9	0.7	24.4
Drop-out Rate (%)	n/a	n/a	n/a	n/a	n/a	n/a
H.S. Diplomas (#)	476	225	39	122	2	87

Linden Unified
18527 E Main St • Linden, CA 95236
(209) 887-3894 • http://www.sjcoe.k12.ca.us/LUSD/D.O..html
Grade Span: KG-12; **Agency Type:** 1
Schools: 6
    3 Primary; 1 Middle; 2 High; 0 Other Level
    5 Regular; 0 Special Education; 0 Vocational; 1 Alternative
    0 Magnet; 0 Charter; 3 Title I Eligible; 0 School-wide Title I
Students: 2,465   (49.8% male; 50.1% female)
    Individual Education Program: 257 (10.4%);
    English Language Learner: 526 (21.3%); Migrant: 715 (29.0%)
    Eligible for Free Lunch Program: 845 (34.3%)
    Eligible for Reduced-Price Lunch Program: 212 (8.6%)
Teachers: 125.9 (19.6 to 1)
Librarians/Media Specialists: 0.0 (n/a to 1)
Guidance Counselors: 0.4 (6,162.5 to 1)
Current Spending: ($ per student per year):
    Total: $6,688; Instruction: $4,107; Support Services: $2,325
Enrollment, Drop-out Rates and Diploma Recipients by Race/Ethnicity

Category	Total	White	Black	Asian	AIAN	Hisp.
Enrollment (%)	100.0	55.8	1.1	3.1	0.9	39.0
Drop-out Rate (%)	n/a	n/a	n/a	n/a	n/a	n/a
H.S. Diplomas (#)	150	96	0	7	0	44

Lodi Unified
1305 E Vine St • Lodi, CA 95240-3148
(209) 331-7000 • http://www.lodiusd.net/
Grade Span: KG-12; **Agency Type:** 1
Schools: 47
    33 Primary; 6 Middle; 6 High; 2 Other Level
    41 Regular; 0 Special Education; 0 Vocational; 6 Alternative
    0 Magnet; 4 Charter; 19 Title I Eligible; 13 School-wide Title I
Students: 29,178   (51.1% male; 48.8% female)
    Individual Education Program: 3,407 (11.7%);
    English Language Learner: 8,347 (28.6%); Migrant: 2,552 (8.7%)
    Eligible for Free Lunch Program: 12,228 (41.9%)
    Eligible for Reduced-Price Lunch Program: 3,112 (10.7%)
Teachers: 1,442.6 (20.2 to 1)
Librarians/Media Specialists: 4.4 (6,631.4 to 1)
Guidance Counselors: 38.5 (757.9 to 1)
Current Spending: ($ per student per year):
    Total: $6,927; Instruction: $4,447; Support Services: $2,255
Enrollment, Drop-out Rates and Diploma Recipients by Race/Ethnicity

Category	Total	White	Black	Asian	AIAN	Hisp.
Enrollment (%)	100.0	36.8	7.8	22.2	0.7	32.2
Drop-out Rate (%)	n/a	n/a	n/a	n/a	n/a	n/a
H.S. Diplomas (#)	1,456	703	88	382	2	281

Manteca Unified
2901 E Louise Ave • Manteca, CA 95336-0032
Mailing Address: PO Box 32 • Manteca, CA 95336-0032
(209) 825-3200 • http://www.mantecausd.net/
Grade Span: KG-12; **Agency Type:** 1
Schools: 24
    18 Primary; 0 Middle; 5 High; 1 Other Level
    21 Regular; 0 Special Education; 0 Vocational; 3 Alternative
    0 Magnet; 0 Charter; 10 Title I Eligible; 2 School-wide Title I
Students: 22,627   (50.7% male; 49.2% female)
    Individual Education Program: 1,829 (8.1%);
    English Language Learner: 3,179 (14.0%); Migrant: 1,066 (4.7%)
    Eligible for Free Lunch Program: 5,490 (24.3%)
    Eligible for Reduced-Price Lunch Program: 2,322 (10.3%)
Teachers: 1,016.6 (22.3 to 1)
Librarians/Media Specialists: 4.0 (5,656.8 to 1)
Guidance Counselors: 17.0 (1,331.0 to 1)
Current Spending: ($ per student per year):
    Total: $6,252; Instruction: $3,975; Support Services: $2,065
Enrollment, Drop-out Rates and Diploma Recipients by Race/Ethnicity

Category	Total	White	Black	Asian	AIAN	Hisp.
Enrollment (%)	100.0	39.8	8.6	11.5	1.4	38.7
Drop-out Rate (%)	n/a	n/a	n/a	n/a	n/a	n/a
H.S. Diplomas (#)	1,061	563	67	124	19	288

Ripon Unified
304 N Acacia Ave • Ripon, CA 95366-2404
(209) 599-2131 • http://www.riponusd.net/
Grade Span: KG-12; **Agency Type:** 1
Schools: 6
    4 Primary; 0 Middle; 2 High; 0 Other Level
    5 Regular; 0 Special Education; 0 Vocational; 1 Alternative
    0 Magnet; 0 Charter; 2 Title I Eligible; 0 School-wide Title I
Students: 2,875   (51.9% male; 48.0% female)
    Individual Education Program: 230 (8.0%);
    English Language Learner: 263 (9.1%); Migrant: 353 (12.3%)
    Eligible for Free Lunch Program: 574 (20.0%)
    Eligible for Reduced-Price Lunch Program: 178 (6.2%)
Teachers: 138.6 (20.7 to 1)
Librarians/Media Specialists: 0.0 (n/a to 1)
Guidance Counselors: 1.5 (1,916.7 to 1)
Current Spending: ($ per student per year):
    Total: $6,234; Instruction: $4,273; Support Services: $1,729
Enrollment, Drop-out Rates and Diploma Recipients by Race/Ethnicity

Category	Total	White	Black	Asian	AIAN	Hisp.
Enrollment (%)	100.0	67.0	1.4	2.8	0.7	27.7
Drop-out Rate (%)	n/a	n/a	n/a	n/a	n/a	n/a
H.S. Diplomas (#)	154	124	0	2	1	27

San Joaquin County Off. of Education
2901 Arch-Airport Rd • Stockton, CA 95213-9030
Mailing Address: PO Box 213030 • Stockton, CA 95213-9030
(209) 468-4800 • http://www.sjcoe.k12.ca.us/
Grade Span: KG-12; **Agency Type:** 4
Schools: 4
    0 Primary; 0 Middle; 0 High; 4 Other Level
    1 Regular; 1 Special Education; 0 Vocational; 2 Alternative
    0 Magnet; 1 Charter; 0 Title I Eligible; 0 School-wide Title I
Students: 2,358   (61.2% male; 38.7% female)
    Individual Education Program: 701 (29.7%);
    English Language Learner: 125 (5.3%); Migrant: 53 (2.2%)
    Eligible for Free Lunch Program: 1,041 (44.1%)
    Eligible for Reduced-Price Lunch Program: 198 (8.4%)
Teachers: 152.0 (15.5 to 1)
Librarians/Media Specialists: 0.0 (n/a to 1)
Guidance Counselors: 5.5 (428.7 to 1)
Current Spending: ($ per student per year):
    Total: $31,262; Instruction: $12,739; Support Services: $18,336
Enrollment, Drop-out Rates and Diploma Recipients by Race/Ethnicity

Category	Total	White	Black	Asian	AIAN	Hisp.
Enrollment (%)	100.0	33.0	13.9	11.4	1.7	35.8
Drop-out Rate (%)	n/a	n/a	n/a	n/a	n/a	n/a
H.S. Diplomas (#)	130	45	13	26	0	46

Stockton City Unified
701 N Madison St • Stockton, CA 95202-1634
(209) 953-4050 • http://www.stockton.k12.ca.us/
Grade Span: KG-12; **Agency Type:** 1
Schools: 50
    36 Primary; 4 Middle; 7 High; 3 Other Level
    44 Regular; 2 Special Education; 0 Vocational; 4 Alternative
    9 Magnet; 2 Charter; 42 Title I Eligible; 34 School-wide Title I
Students: 39,483   (50.8% male; 49.1% female)
    Individual Education Program: 3,872 (9.8%);
    English Language Learner: 9,499 (24.1%); Migrant: 6,021 (15.2%)
    Eligible for Free Lunch Program: 23,640 (59.9%)
    Eligible for Reduced-Price Lunch Program: 2,040 (5.2%)
Teachers: 2,004.4 (19.7 to 1)
Librarians/Media Specialists: 8.0 (4,935.4 to 1)
Guidance Counselors: 76.3 (517.5 to 1)
Current Spending: ($ per student per year):
    Total: $7,654; Instruction: $4,724; Support Services: $2,677
Enrollment, Drop-out Rates and Diploma Recipients by Race/Ethnicity

Category	Total	White	Black	Asian	AIAN	Hisp.
Enrollment (%)	100.0	11.6	13.4	19.6	3.4	51.9
Drop-out Rate (%)	n/a	n/a	n/a	n/a	n/a	n/a
H.S. Diplomas (#)	1,309	155	199	408	37	510

Tracy Joint Unified
1875 W Lowell Ave • Tracy, CA 95376-4095
(209) 830-3200 • http://www.tracy.k12.ca.us/
Grade Span: KG-12; **Agency Type:** 1
Schools: 21
    11 Primary; 4 Middle; 6 High; 0 Other Level
    17 Regular; 0 Special Education; 0 Vocational; 4 Alternative
    2 Magnet; 1 Charter; 7 Title I Eligible; 1 School-wide Title I
Students: 16,063   (50.9% male; 49.0% female)
    Individual Education Program: 1,349 (8.4%);
    English Language Learner: 2,427 (15.1%); Migrant: 842 (5.2%)
    Eligible for Free Lunch Program: 3,112 (19.4%)

Eligible for Reduced-Price Lunch Program: 926 (5.8%)
Teachers: 752.3 (21.4 to 1)
Librarians/Media Specialists: 2.2 (7,301.4 to 1)
Guidance Counselors: 16.0 (1,003.9 to 1)
Current Spending: ($ per student per year):
   Total: $6,549; Instruction: $4,040; Support Services: $2,321

Enrollment, Drop-out Rates and Diploma Recipients by Race/Ethnicity

Category	Total	White	Black	Asian	AIAN	Hisp.
Enrollment (%)	100.0	41.1	7.7	15.4	1.2	34.6
Drop-out Rate (%)	n/a	n/a	n/a	n/a	n/a	n/a
H.S. Diplomas (#)	927	505	69	110	10	233

San Luis Obispo County

Atascadero Unified
5601 W Mall • Atascadero, CA 93422-4234
(805) 462-4200 • http://www.atas.k12.ca.us/
Grade Span: KG-12; **Agency Type:** 1
Schools: 12
   7 Primary; 2 Middle; 2 High; 1 Other Level
   10 Regular; 0 Special Education; 0 Vocational; 2 Alternative
   0 Magnet; 0 Charter; 9 Title I Eligible; 0 School-wide Title I
Students: 5,517   (52.1% male; 47.8% female)
   Individual Education Program: 639 (11.6%);
   English Language Learner: 184 (3.3%); Migrant: 32 (0.6%)
   Eligible for Free Lunch Program: 844 (15.3%)
   Eligible for Reduced-Price Lunch Program: 367 (6.7%)
Teachers: 272.9 (20.2 to 1)
Librarians/Media Specialists: 1.0 (5,517.0 to 1)
Guidance Counselors: 7.4 (745.5 to 1)
Current Spending: ($ per student per year):
   Total: $6,630; Instruction: $4,116; Support Services: $2,321

Enrollment, Drop-out Rates and Diploma Recipients by Race/Ethnicity

Category	Total	White	Black	Asian	AIAN	Hisp.
Enrollment (%)	100.0	81.5	2.1	1.6	0.6	14.2
Drop-out Rate (%)	n/a	n/a	n/a	n/a	n/a	n/a
H.S. Diplomas (#)	397	351	4	12	2	28

Lucia Mar Unified
602 Orchard St • Arroyo Grande, CA 93420-4000
(805) 474-3000 • http://www.luciamar.k12.ca.us/
Grade Span: KG-12; **Agency Type:** 1
Schools: 16
   10 Primary; 3 Middle; 3 High; 0 Other Level
   15 Regular; 0 Special Education; 0 Vocational; 1 Alternative
   0 Magnet; 0 Charter; 13 Title I Eligible; 0 School-wide Title I
Students: 10,847   (51.9% male; 48.0% female)
   Individual Education Program: 1,172 (10.8%);
   English Language Learner: 1,399 (12.9%); Migrant: 540 (5.0%)
   Eligible for Free Lunch Program: 2,967 (27.4%)
   Eligible for Reduced-Price Lunch Program: 1,591 (14.7%)
Teachers: 528.3 (20.5 to 1)
Librarians/Media Specialists: 0.2 (54,235.0 to 1)
Guidance Counselors: 10.0 (1,084.7 to 1)
Current Spending: ($ per student per year):
   Total: $6,955; Instruction: $4,546; Support Services: $2,131

Enrollment, Drop-out Rates and Diploma Recipients by Race/Ethnicity

Category	Total	White	Black	Asian	AIAN	Hisp.
Enrollment (%)	100.0	60.2	1.2	3.0	0.4	31.8
Drop-out Rate (%)	n/a	n/a	n/a	n/a	n/a	n/a
H.S. Diplomas (#)	691	472	5	26	4	184

Paso Robles Joint Unified
800 Niblick Rd • Paso Robles, CA 93447-7010
Mailing Address: PO Box 7010 • Paso Robles, CA 93447-7010
(805) 238-2222 • http://king.prps.k12.ca.us/
Grade Span: KG-12; **Agency Type:** 1
Schools: 12
   6 Primary; 2 Middle; 3 High; 1 Other Level
   9 Regular; 0 Special Education; 0 Vocational; 3 Alternative
   0 Magnet; 0 Charter; 9 Title I Eligible; 3 School-wide Title I
Students: 6,771   (51.3% male; 48.6% female)
   Individual Education Program: 730 (10.8%);
   English Language Learner: 1,186 (17.5%); Migrant: 628 (9.3%)
   Eligible for Free Lunch Program: 1,779 (26.3%)
   Eligible for Reduced-Price Lunch Program: 591 (8.7%)
Teachers: 329.7 (20.5 to 1)
Librarians/Media Specialists: 3.0 (2,257.0 to 1)
Guidance Counselors: 9.6 (705.3 to 1)
Current Spending: ($ per student per year):
   Total: $7,182; Instruction: $4,672; Support Services: $2,245

Enrollment, Drop-out Rates and Diploma Recipients by Race/Ethnicity

Category	Total	White	Black	Asian	AIAN	Hisp.
Enrollment (%)	100.0	59.3	3.0	1.6	0.9	33.9
Drop-out Rate (%)	n/a	n/a	n/a	n/a	n/a	n/a
H.S. Diplomas (#)	423	298	17	16	2	87

San Luis Coastal Unified
1500 Lizzie St • San Luis Obispo, CA 93401
(805) 549-1200 • http://www.slcusd.org/
Grade Span: KG-12; **Agency Type:** 1
Schools: 16
   10 Primary; 3 Middle; 3 High; 0 Other Level
   15 Regular; 0 Special Education; 0 Vocational; 1 Alternative
   0 Magnet; 1 Charter; 5 Title I Eligible; 2 School-wide Title I
Students: 7,841   (50.5% male; 49.4% female)
   Individual Education Program: 691 (8.8%);
   English Language Learner: 626 (8.0%); Migrant: 310 (4.0%)
   Eligible for Free Lunch Program: 1,346 (17.2%)
   Eligible for Reduced-Price Lunch Program: 652 (8.3%)
Teachers: 376.3 (20.8 to 1)
Librarians/Media Specialists: 3.3 (2,376.1 to 1)
Guidance Counselors: 17.9 (438.0 to 1)
Current Spending: ($ per student per year):
   Total: $6,985; Instruction: $4,250; Support Services: $2,511

Enrollment, Drop-out Rates and Diploma Recipients by Race/Ethnicity

Category	Total	White	Black	Asian	AIAN	Hisp.
Enrollment (%)	100.0	72.8	1.8	4.6	0.6	18.1
Drop-out Rate (%)	n/a	n/a	n/a	n/a	n/a	n/a
H.S. Diplomas (#)	541	458	7	21	3	50

Templeton Unified
960 Old County Rd • Templeton, CA 93465-9419
(805) 434-5800 • http://www.tusdnet.k12.ca.us/
Grade Span: KG-12; **Agency Type:** 1
Schools: 7
   3 Primary; 1 Middle; 3 High; 0 Other Level
   4 Regular; 0 Special Education; 0 Vocational; 3 Alternative
   0 Magnet; 0 Charter; 4 Title I Eligible; 0 School-wide Title I
Students: 2,721   (49.4% male; 50.5% female)
   Individual Education Program: 185 (6.8%);
   English Language Learner: 64 (2.4%); Migrant: 6 (0.2%)
   Eligible for Free Lunch Program: 185 (6.8%)
   Eligible for Reduced-Price Lunch Program: 134 (4.9%)
Teachers: 123.0 (22.1 to 1)
Librarians/Media Specialists: 0.0 (n/a to 1)
Guidance Counselors: 3.0 (907.0 to 1)
Current Spending: ($ per student per year):
   Total: $6,388; Instruction: $4,115; Support Services: $2,059

Enrollment, Drop-out Rates and Diploma Recipients by Race/Ethnicity

Category	Total	White	Black	Asian	AIAN	Hisp.
Enrollment (%)	100.0	80.0	4.0	1.7	1.4	12.1
Drop-out Rate (%)	n/a	n/a	n/a	n/a	n/a	n/a
H.S. Diplomas (#)	192	167	2	8	3	12

San Mateo County

Belmont-Redwood Shores Elementary
2960 Hallmark Dr • Belmont, CA 94002-2943
(650) 637-4800 • http://www.belmont.gov/educ/district/
Grade Span: KG-08; **Agency Type:** 1
Schools: 6
   5 Primary; 1 Middle; 0 High; 0 Other Level
   6 Regular; 0 Special Education; 0 Vocational; 0 Alternative
   0 Magnet; 0 Charter; 3 Title I Eligible; 0 School-wide Title I
Students: 2,460   (52.6% male; 47.3% female)
   Individual Education Program: 221 (9.0%);
   English Language Learner: 111 (4.5%); Migrant: 0 (0.0%)
   Eligible for Free Lunch Program: 84 (3.4%)
   Eligible for Reduced-Price Lunch Program: 0 (0.0%)
Teachers: 125.4 (19.6 to 1)
Librarians/Media Specialists: 0.0 (n/a to 1)
Guidance Counselors: 0.8 (3,075.0 to 1)
Current Spending: ($ per student per year):
   Total: $8,117; Instruction: $4,768; Support Services: $3,329

Enrollment, Drop-out Rates and Diploma Recipients by Race/Ethnicity

Category	Total	White	Black	Asian	AIAN	Hisp.
Enrollment (%)	100.0	58.6	2.5	22.6	0.4	9.1
Drop-out Rate (%)	n/a	n/a	n/a	n/a	n/a	n/a
H.S. Diplomas (#)	n/a	n/a	n/a	n/a	n/a	n/a

Burlingame Elementary
1825 Trousdale Dr • Burlingame, CA 94010-4509
(650) 259-3800 • http://www.burlingameschools.com/
Grade Span: KG-08; **Agency Type:** 1
Schools: 6

5 Primary; 1 Middle; 0 High; 0 Other Level
6 Regular; 0 Special Education; 0 Vocational; 0 Alternative
0 Magnet; 0 Charter; 3 Title I Eligible; 0 School-wide Title I
Students: 2,369   (51.6% male; 48.3% female)
Individual Education Program: 196 (8.3%);
English Language Learner: 366 (15.4%); Migrant: 0 (0.0%)
Eligible for Free Lunch Program: 76 (3.2%)
Eligible for Reduced-Price Lunch Program: 34 (1.4%)
Teachers: 126.0 (18.8 to 1)
Librarians/Media Specialists: 4.0 (592.3 to 1)
Guidance Counselors: 2.0 (1,184.5 to 1)
Current Spending: ($ per student per year):
Total: $6,617; Instruction: $4,396; Support Services: $2,184
Enrollment, Drop-out Rates and Diploma Recipients by Race/Ethnicity

Category	Total	White	Black	Asian	AIAN	Hisp.
Enrollment (%)	100.0	58.8	1.1	19.6	0.0	11.6
Drop-out Rate (%)	n/a	n/a	n/a	n/a	n/a	n/a
H.S. Diplomas (#)	n/a	n/a	n/a	n/a	n/a	n/a

Cabrillo Unified
498 Kelly Ave • Half Moon Bay, CA 94019-1636
(650) 712-7100 • http://www.coastside.net/cusd/
Grade Span: KG-12; **Agency Type:** 1
Schools: 7
4 Primary; 1 Middle; 2 High; 0 Other Level
6 Regular; 0 Special Education; 0 Vocational; 1 Alternative
0 Magnet; 0 Charter; 3 Title I Eligible; 0 School-wide Title I
Students: 3,633   (49.9% male; 50.0% female)
Individual Education Program: 420 (11.6%);
English Language Learner: 979 (26.9%); Migrant: 465 (12.8%)
Eligible for Free Lunch Program: 651 (17.9%)
Eligible for Reduced-Price Lunch Program: 314 (8.6%)
Teachers: 168.7 (21.5 to 1)
Librarians/Media Specialists: 1.0 (3,633.0 to 1)
Guidance Counselors: 5.0 (726.6 to 1)
Current Spending: ($ per student per year):
Total: $6,958; Instruction: $4,150; Support Services: $2,642
Enrollment, Drop-out Rates and Diploma Recipients by Race/Ethnicity

Category	Total	White	Black	Asian	AIAN	Hisp.
Enrollment (%)	100.0	54.6	0.6	3.9	0.4	37.2
Drop-out Rate (%)	n/a	n/a	n/a	n/a	n/a	n/a
H.S. Diplomas (#)	259	188	2	10	1	58

Jefferson Elementary
101 Lincoln Ave • Daly City, CA 94015-3934
(650) 991-1000 • http://www.smcoe.k12.ca.us/jesd/
Grade Span: KG-08; **Agency Type:** 1
Schools: 16
12 Primary; 4 Middle; 0 High; 0 Other Level
16 Regular; 0 Special Education; 0 Vocational; 0 Alternative
0 Magnet; 0 Charter; 6 Title I Eligible; 0 School-wide Title I
Students: 6,636   (51.2% male; 48.7% female)
Individual Education Program: 437 (6.6%);
English Language Learner: 1,861 (28.0%); Migrant: 0 (0.0%)
Eligible for Free Lunch Program: 2,135 (32.2%)
Eligible for Reduced-Price Lunch Program: 1,278 (19.3%)
Teachers: 301.4 (22.0 to 1)
Librarians/Media Specialists: 3.0 (2,212.0 to 1)
Guidance Counselors: 0.0 (n/a to 1)
Current Spending: ($ per student per year):
Total: $6,890; Instruction: $4,554; Support Services: $2,052
Enrollment, Drop-out Rates and Diploma Recipients by Race/Ethnicity

Category	Total	White	Black	Asian	AIAN	Hisp.
Enrollment (%)	100.0	6.6	5.5	49.2	0.4	31.7
Drop-out Rate (%)	n/a	n/a	n/a	n/a	n/a	n/a
H.S. Diplomas (#)	n/a	n/a	n/a	n/a	n/a	n/a

Jefferson Union High
699 Serramonte Blvd.Ste 100 • Daly City, CA 94015-4132
(650) 550-7900 • http://www.juhsd.k12.ca.us/
Grade Span: 09-12; **Agency Type:** 1
Schools: 5
0 Primary; 0 Middle; 5 High; 0 Other Level
3 Regular; 0 Special Education; 0 Vocational; 2 Alternative
0 Magnet; 0 Charter; 2 Title I Eligible; 0 School-wide Title I
Students: 5,384   (53.2% male; 46.7% female)
Individual Education Program: 390 (7.2%);
English Language Learner: 395 (7.3%); Migrant: 0 (0.0%)
Eligible for Free Lunch Program: 841 (15.6%)
Eligible for Reduced-Price Lunch Program: 463 (8.6%)
Teachers: 238.3 (22.6 to 1)
Librarians/Media Specialists: 4.0 (1,346.0 to 1)
Guidance Counselors: 8.6 (626.0 to 1)
Current Spending: ($ per student per year):
Total: $7,185; Instruction: $4,108; Support Services: $2,902

Category	Total	White	Black	Asian	AIAN	Hisp.
Enrollment (%)	100.0	24.2	5.5	44.4	0.5	25.2
Drop-out Rate (%)	n/a	n/a	n/a	n/a	n/a	n/a
H.S. Diplomas (#)	1,085	317	68	457	6	237

Menlo Park City Elementary
181 Encinal Ave • Atherton, CA 94027-3102
(650) 321-7140 • http://www.mpcsd.k12.ca.us/
Grade Span: KG-08; **Agency Type:** 1
Schools: 4
3 Primary; 1 Middle; 0 High; 0 Other Level
4 Regular; 0 Special Education; 0 Vocational; 0 Alternative
0 Magnet; 0 Charter; 3 Title I Eligible; 0 School-wide Title I
Students: 2,019   (52.3% male; 47.6% female)
Individual Education Program: 229 (11.3%);
English Language Learner: 101 (5.0%); Migrant: 0 (0.0%)
Eligible for Free Lunch Program: 71 (3.5%)
Eligible for Reduced-Price Lunch Program: 8 (0.4%)
Teachers: 121.1 (16.7 to 1)
Librarians/Media Specialists: 3.4 (593.8 to 1)
Guidance Counselors: 2.2 (917.7 to 1)
Current Spending: ($ per student per year):
Total: $9,198; Instruction: $6,483; Support Services: $2,697
Enrollment, Drop-out Rates and Diploma Recipients by Race/Ethnicity

Category	Total	White	Black	Asian	AIAN	Hisp.
Enrollment (%)	100.0	76.2	3.9	10.3	0.0	8.2
Drop-out Rate (%)	n/a	n/a	n/a	n/a	n/a	n/a
H.S. Diplomas (#)	n/a	n/a	n/a	n/a	n/a	n/a

Millbrae Elementary
555 Richmond Dr • Millbrae, CA 94030-1600
(650) 697-5693 • http://www.smcoe.k12.ca.us/msd/do/do.htm
Grade Span: KG-08; **Agency Type:** 1
Schools: 5
4 Primary; 1 Middle; 0 High; 0 Other Level
5 Regular; 0 Special Education; 0 Vocational; 0 Alternative
0 Magnet; 0 Charter; 2 Title I Eligible; 0 School-wide Title I
Students: 2,096   (51.1% male; 48.8% female)
Individual Education Program: 184 (8.8%);
English Language Learner: 528 (25.2%); Migrant: 0 (0.0%)
Eligible for Free Lunch Program: 115 (5.5%)
Eligible for Reduced-Price Lunch Program: 106 (5.1%)
Teachers: 103.2 (20.3 to 1)
Librarians/Media Specialists: 0.0 (n/a to 1)
Guidance Counselors: 1.0 (2,096.0 to 1)
Current Spending: ($ per student per year):
Total: $6,854; Instruction: $4,121; Support Services: $2,503
Enrollment, Drop-out Rates and Diploma Recipients by Race/Ethnicity

Category	Total	White	Black	Asian	AIAN	Hisp.
Enrollment (%)	100.0	31.1	1.5	44.1	0.3	16.5
Drop-out Rate (%)	n/a	n/a	n/a	n/a	n/a	n/a
H.S. Diplomas (#)	n/a	n/a	n/a	n/a	n/a	n/a

Pacifica SD
375 Reina Del Mar • Pacifica, CA 94044-3052
(650) 738-6600 • http://www.lsusd.k12.ca.us/
Grade Span: KG-08; **Agency Type:** 1
Schools: 7
6 Primary; 1 Middle; 0 High; 0 Other Level
7 Regular; 0 Special Education; 0 Vocational; 0 Alternative
3 Magnet; 0 Charter; 3 Title I Eligible; 0 School-wide Title I
Students: 3,169   (51.1% male; 48.8% female)
Individual Education Program: 297 (9.4%);
English Language Learner: 165 (5.2%); Migrant: 0 (0.0%)
Eligible for Free Lunch Program: 361 (11.4%)
Eligible for Reduced-Price Lunch Program: 226 (7.1%)
Teachers: 142.7 (22.2 to 1)
Librarians/Media Specialists: 0.0 (n/a to 1)
Guidance Counselors: 1.0 (3,169.0 to 1)
Current Spending: ($ per student per year):
Total: $7,082; Instruction: $4,130; Support Services: $2,669
Enrollment, Drop-out Rates and Diploma Recipients by Race/Ethnicity

Category	Total	White	Black	Asian	AIAN	Hisp.
Enrollment (%)	100.0	55.3	3.9	17.9	0.7	14.5
Drop-out Rate (%)	n/a	n/a	n/a	n/a	n/a	n/a
H.S. Diplomas (#)	n/a	n/a	n/a	n/a	n/a	n/a

Ravenswood City Elementary
2160 Euclid Ave • East Palo Alto, CA 94303-1703
(650) 329-2800 • http://www.ravenswood.k12.ca.us/
Grade Span: KG-12; **Agency Type:** 1
Schools: 12
8 Primary; 3 Middle; 1 High; 0 Other Level
12 Regular; 0 Special Education; 0 Vocational; 0 Alternative

0 Magnet; 4 Charter; 12 Title I Eligible; 7 School-wide Title I
Students: 5,019 (50.3% male; 49.6% female)
  Individual Education Program: 385 (7.7%);
  English Language Learner: 3,477 (69.3%); Migrant: 595 (11.9%)
  Eligible for Free Lunch Program: 3,407 (67.9%)
  Eligible for Reduced-Price Lunch Program: 826 (16.5%)
Teachers: 254.0 (19.8 to 1)
Librarians/Media Specialists: 0.0 (n/a to 1)
Guidance Counselors: 1.0 (5,019.0 to 1)
Current Spending: ($ per student per year):
  Total: $9,340; Instruction: $5,809; Support Services: $3,150
Enrollment, Drop-out Rates and Diploma Recipients by Race/Ethnicity

Category	Total	White	Black	Asian	AIAN	Hisp.
Enrollment (%)	100.0	0.5	18.1	10.0	0.1	70.5
Drop-out Rate (%)	n/a	n/a	n/a	n/a	n/a	n/a
H.S. Diplomas (#)	0	0	0	0	0	0

Redwood City Elementary
750 Bradford St · Redwood City, CA 94063-1727
(650) 423-2200 · http://www.rcsd.k12.ca.us/
Grade Span: KG-12; **Agency Type:** 1
Schools: 17
  14 Primary; 2 Middle; 1 High; 0 Other Level
  16 Regular; 0 Special Education; 0 Vocational; 1 Alternative
  16 Magnet; 2 Charter; 12 Title I Eligible; 4 School-wide Title I
Students: 8,834 (51.3% male; 48.6% female)
  Individual Education Program: 796 (9.0%);
  English Language Learner: 4,338 (49.1%); Migrant: 554 (6.3%)
  Eligible for Free Lunch Program: 3,700 (41.9%)
  Eligible for Reduced-Price Lunch Program: 1,227 (13.9%)
Teachers: 516.2 (17.1 to 1)
Librarians/Media Specialists: 0.0 (n/a to 1)
Guidance Counselors: 1.0 (8,834.0 to 1)
Current Spending: ($ per student per year):
  Total: $7,851; Instruction: $4,999; Support Services: $2,605
Enrollment, Drop-out Rates and Diploma Recipients by Race/Ethnicity

Category	Total	White	Black	Asian	AIAN	Hisp.
Enrollment (%)	100.0	26.6	2.4	5.9	0.3	64.6
Drop-out Rate (%)	n/a	n/a	n/a	n/a	n/a	n/a
H.S. Diplomas (#)	3	3	0	0	0	0

San Bruno Park Elementary
500 Acacia Ave · San Bruno, CA 94066-4298
(650) 624-3100 · http://sbpsd.k12.ca.us/
Grade Span: KG-08; **Agency Type:** 1
Schools: 8
  7 Primary; 1 Middle; 0 High; 0 Other Level
  8 Regular; 0 Special Education; 0 Vocational; 0 Alternative
  0 Magnet; 0 Charter; 2 Title I Eligible; 0 School-wide Title I
Students: 2,717 (51.6% male; 48.3% female)
  Individual Education Program: 229 (8.4%);
  English Language Learner: 450 (16.6%); Migrant: 0 (0.0%)
  Eligible for Free Lunch Program: 608 (22.4%)
  Eligible for Reduced-Price Lunch Program: 274 (10.1%)
Teachers: 124.3 (21.9 to 1)
Librarians/Media Specialists: 0.0 (n/a to 1)
Guidance Counselors: 2.5 (1,086.8 to 1)
Current Spending: ($ per student per year):
  Total: $6,710; Instruction: $4,223; Support Services: $2,234
Enrollment, Drop-out Rates and Diploma Recipients by Race/Ethnicity

Category	Total	White	Black	Asian	AIAN	Hisp.
Enrollment (%)	100.0	37.4	3.1	24.0	0.5	35.0
Drop-out Rate (%)	n/a	n/a	n/a	n/a	n/a	n/a
H.S. Diplomas (#)	n/a	n/a	n/a	n/a	n/a	n/a

San Carlos Elementary
826 Chestnut St · San Carlos, CA 94070-3802
(650) 508-7333 · http://scsd.sancarlos.k12.ca.us/
Grade Span: KG-08; **Agency Type:** 1
Schools: 8
  5 Primary; 2 Middle; 1 High; 0 Other Level
  8 Regular; 0 Special Education; 0 Vocational; 0 Alternative
  0 Magnet; 7 Charter; 3 Title I Eligible; 0 School-wide Title I
Students: 2,696 (49.5% male; 50.4% female)
  Individual Education Program: 185 (6.9%);
  English Language Learner: 55 (2.0%); Migrant: 0 (0.0%)
  Eligible for Free Lunch Program: 55 (2.0%)
  Eligible for Reduced-Price Lunch Program: 14 (0.5%)
Teachers: 128.9 (20.9 to 1)
Librarians/Media Specialists: 0.0 (n/a to 1)
Guidance Counselors: 2.0 (1,348.0 to 1)
Current Spending: ($ per student per year):
  Total: $9,906; Instruction: $7,748; Support Services: $2,141

Enrollment, Drop-out Rates and Diploma Recipients by Race/Ethnicity

Category	Total	White	Black	Asian	AIAN	Hisp.
Enrollment (%)	100.0	75.9	2.3	9.3	0.4	11.8
Drop-out Rate (%)	n/a	n/a	n/a	n/a	n/a	n/a
H.S. Diplomas (#)	n/a	n/a	n/a	n/a	n/a	n/a

San Mateo Union High
650 N Delaware St · San Mateo, CA 94401-1795
(650) 762-0200 · http://www.smuhsd.k12.ca.us/
Grade Span: 09-12; **Agency Type:** 1
Schools: 8
  0 Primary; 0 Middle; 8 High; 0 Other Level
  6 Regular; 0 Special Education; 0 Vocational; 2 Alternative
  0 Magnet; 0 Charter; 4 Title I Eligible; 0 School-wide Title I
Students: 8,351 (52.0% male; 47.9% female)
  Individual Education Program: 935 (11.2%);
  English Language Learner: 1,065 (12.8%); Migrant: 0 (0.0%)
  Eligible for Free Lunch Program: 326 (3.9%)
  Eligible for Reduced-Price Lunch Program: 183 (2.2%)
Teachers: 398.7 (20.9 to 1)
Librarians/Media Specialists: 6.2 (1,346.9 to 1)
Guidance Counselors: 17.2 (485.5 to 1)
Current Spending: ($ per student per year):
  Total: $9,896; Instruction: $5,431; Support Services: $4,202
Enrollment, Drop-out Rates and Diploma Recipients by Race/Ethnicity

Category	Total	White	Black	Asian	AIAN	Hisp.
Enrollment (%)	100.0	44.6	2.6	30.3	0.3	22.1
Drop-out Rate (%)	n/a	n/a	n/a	n/a	n/a	n/a
H.S. Diplomas (#)	1,763	882	32	549	7	293

San Mateo-Foster City Elementary
300 28th Ave · San Mateo, CA 94402-0058
Mailing Address: PO Box K · San Mateo, CA 94402-0058
(650) 312-7700 · http://www.smfc.k12.ca.us/
Grade Span: KG-08; **Agency Type:** 1
Schools: 20
  16 Primary; 4 Middle; 0 High; 0 Other Level
  20 Regular; 0 Special Education; 0 Vocational; 0 Alternative
  6 Magnet; 0 Charter; 8 Title I Eligible; 0 School-wide Title I
Students: 10,069 (51.0% male; 48.9% female)
  Individual Education Program: 1,314 (13.1%);
  English Language Learner: 2,362 (23.5%); Migrant: 0 (0.0%)
  Eligible for Free Lunch Program: 2,214 (22.0%)
  Eligible for Reduced-Price Lunch Program: 865 (8.6%)
Teachers: 502.0 (20.1 to 1)
Librarians/Media Specialists: 3.5 (2,876.9 to 1)
Guidance Counselors: 9.0 (1,118.8 to 1)
Current Spending: ($ per student per year):
  Total: $7,354; Instruction: $4,736; Support Services: $2,237
Enrollment, Drop-out Rates and Diploma Recipients by Race/Ethnicity

Category	Total	White	Black	Asian	AIAN	Hisp.
Enrollment (%)	100.0	39.7	3.5	25.7	0.2	28.5
Drop-out Rate (%)	n/a	n/a	n/a	n/a	n/a	n/a
H.S. Diplomas (#)	n/a	n/a	n/a	n/a	n/a	n/a

Sequoia Union High
480 James Ave · Redwood City, CA 94062-1041
(650) 369-1411 · http://www.seq.org/
Grade Span: 09-12; **Agency Type:** 1
Schools: 6
  0 Primary; 0 Middle; 6 High; 0 Other Level
  4 Regular; 0 Special Education; 0 Vocational; 2 Alternative
  0 Magnet; 0 Charter; 3 Title I Eligible; 0 School-wide Title I
Students: 7,782 (51.3% male; 48.6% female)
  Individual Education Program: 895 (11.5%);
  English Language Learner: 1,987 (25.5%); Migrant: 435 (5.6%)
  Eligible for Free Lunch Program: 1,289 (16.6%)
  Eligible for Reduced-Price Lunch Program: 379 (4.9%)
Teachers: 372.2 (20.9 to 1)
Librarians/Media Specialists: 4.0 (1,945.5 to 1)
Guidance Counselors: 25.6 (304.0 to 1)
Current Spending: ($ per student per year):
  Total: $9,538; Instruction: $5,012; Support Services: $4,214
Enrollment, Drop-out Rates and Diploma Recipients by Race/Ethnicity

Category	Total	White	Black	Asian	AIAN	Hisp.
Enrollment (%)	100.0	41.3	5.9	9.8	0.4	41.3
Drop-out Rate (%)	n/a	n/a	n/a	n/a	n/a	n/a
H.S. Diplomas (#)	1,197	567	79	120	0	431

South San Francisco Unified
398 B St · S. San Francisco, CA 94080-4423
(650) 877-8700 · http://www.ssfusd.k12.ca.us/
Grade Span: KG-12; **Agency Type:** 1
Schools: 16
  10 Primary; 3 Middle; 3 High; 0 Other Level

15 Regular; 0 Special Education; 0 Vocational; 1 Alternative
0 Magnet; 0 Charter; 6 Title I Eligible; 5 School-wide Title I
Students: 9,362 (52.2% male; 47.7% female)
Individual Education Program: 919 (9.8%);
English Language Learner: 1,898 (20.3%); Migrant: 214 (2.3%)
Eligible for Free Lunch Program: 2,121 (22.7%)
Eligible for Reduced-Price Lunch Program: 821 (8.8%)
Teachers: 429.3 (21.8 to 1)
Librarians/Media Specialists: 2.0 (4,681.0 to 1)
Guidance Counselors: 10.2 (917.8 to 1)
Current Spending: ($ per student per year):
Total: $6,691; Instruction: $3,966; Support Services: $2,460
Enrollment, Drop-out Rates and Diploma Recipients by Race/Ethnicity

Category	Total	White	Black	Asian	AIAN	Hisp.
Enrollment (%)	100.0	17.8	4.5	38.8	0.4	38.6
Drop-out Rate (%)	n/a	n/a	n/a	n/a	n/a	n/a
H.S. Diplomas (#)	633	153	26	279	1	174

Santa Barbara County

Carpinteria Unified
1400 Linden Ave • Carpinteria, CA 93013-1414
(805) 684-4511 • http://www.cusd.net/home/
Grade Span: KG-12; **Agency Type:** 1
Schools: 9
4 Primary; 1 Middle; 3 High; 1 Other Level
6 Regular; 0 Special Education; 0 Vocational; 3 Alternative
0 Magnet; 0 Charter; 4 Title I Eligible; 0 School-wide Title I
Students: 2,919 (51.6% male; 48.3% female)
Individual Education Program: 310 (10.6%);
English Language Learner: 1,126 (38.6%); Migrant: 663 (22.7%)
Eligible for Free Lunch Program: 1,012 (34.7%)
Eligible for Reduced-Price Lunch Program: 457 (15.7%)
Teachers: 142.0 (20.6 to 1)
Librarians/Media Specialists: 0.0 (n/a to 1)
Guidance Counselors: 2.6 (1,122.7 to 1)
Current Spending: ($ per student per year):
Total: $6,750; Instruction: $4,188; Support Services: $2,304
Enrollment, Drop-out Rates and Diploma Recipients by Race/Ethnicity

Category	Total	White	Black	Asian	AIAN	Hisp.
Enrollment (%)	100.0	31.8	1.2	2.7	0.3	62.3
Drop-out Rate (%)	n/a	n/a	n/a	n/a	n/a	n/a
H.S. Diplomas (#)	203	97	2	5	1	98

Goleta Union Elementary
401 N Fairview Ave • Goleta, CA 93117-1732
(805) 681-1200 • http://www.goleta.k12.ca.us/
Grade Span: KG-06; **Agency Type:** 1
Schools: 9
9 Primary; 0 Middle; 0 High; 0 Other Level
9 Regular; 0 Special Education; 0 Vocational; 0 Alternative
0 Magnet; 0 Charter; 5 Title I Eligible; 2 School-wide Title I
Students: 3,964 (50.1% male; 49.8% female)
Individual Education Program: 419 (10.6%);
English Language Learner: 1,052 (26.5%); Migrant: 67 (1.7%)
Eligible for Free Lunch Program: 987 (24.9%)
Eligible for Reduced-Price Lunch Program: 405 (10.2%)
Teachers: 199.4 (19.9 to 1)
Librarians/Media Specialists: 0.0 (n/a to 1)
Guidance Counselors: 0.5 (7,928.0 to 1)
Current Spending: ($ per student per year):
Total: $7,089; Instruction: $4,738; Support Services: $2,130
Enrollment, Drop-out Rates and Diploma Recipients by Race/Ethnicity

Category	Total	White	Black	Asian	AIAN	Hisp.
Enrollment (%)	100.0	46.4	1.7	8.1	0.5	43.2
Drop-out Rate (%)	n/a	n/a	n/a	n/a	n/a	n/a
H.S. Diplomas (#)	n/a	n/a	n/a	n/a	n/a	n/a

Lompoc Unified
1301 N A St • Lompoc, CA 93438-8000
Mailing Address: PO Box 8000 • Lompoc, CA 93438-8000
(805) 736-2371 • http://www1.lusd.org/index.jsp
Grade Span: KG-12; **Agency Type:** 1
Schools: 17
11 Primary; 3 Middle; 3 High; 0 Other Level
15 Regular; 0 Special Education; 0 Vocational; 2 Alternative
0 Magnet; 0 Charter; 11 Title I Eligible; 6 School-wide Title I
Students: 11,559 (51.0% male; 48.9% female)
Individual Education Program: 877 (7.6%);
English Language Learner: 2,231 (19.3%); Migrant: 916 (7.9%)
Eligible for Free Lunch Program: 4,026 (34.8%)
Eligible for Reduced-Price Lunch Program: 1,227 (10.6%)
Teachers: 575.7 (20.1 to 1)
Librarians/Media Specialists: 2.0 (5,779.5 to 1)
Guidance Counselors: 13.3 (869.1 to 1)

Current Spending: ($ per student per year):
Total: $6,629; Instruction: $4,254; Support Services: $2,234
Enrollment, Drop-out Rates and Diploma Recipients by Race/Ethnicity

Category	Total	White	Black	Asian	AIAN	Hisp.
Enrollment (%)	100.0	41.3	6.6	5.1	1.7	45.3
Drop-out Rate (%)	n/a	n/a	n/a	n/a	n/a	n/a
H.S. Diplomas (#)	568	305	47	40	10	166

Orcutt Union Elementary
Soares & Dyer Sts. • Orcutt, CA 93457-2310
Mailing Address: PO Box 2310 • Orcutt, CA 93457-2310
(805) 938-8900 • http://www.orcutt-schools.net/public/
Grade Span: KG-08; **Agency Type:** 1
Schools: 8
6 Primary; 2 Middle; 0 High; 0 Other Level
8 Regular; 0 Special Education; 0 Vocational; 0 Alternative
0 Magnet; 0 Charter; 1 Title I Eligible; 0 School-wide Title I
Students: 4,966 (52.2% male; 47.7% female)
Individual Education Program: 395 (8.0%);
English Language Learner: 274 (5.5%); Migrant: 9 (0.2%)
Eligible for Free Lunch Program: 882 (17.8%)
Eligible for Reduced-Price Lunch Program: 391 (7.9%)
Teachers: 218.5 (22.7 to 1)
Librarians/Media Specialists: 0.0 (n/a to 1)
Guidance Counselors: 0.0 (n/a to 1)
Current Spending: ($ per student per year):
Total: $6,122; Instruction: $3,870; Support Services: $2,066
Enrollment, Drop-out Rates and Diploma Recipients by Race/Ethnicity

Category	Total	White	Black	Asian	AIAN	Hisp.
Enrollment (%)	100.0	63.5	2.2	5.5	1.3	27.5
Drop-out Rate (%)	n/a	n/a	n/a	n/a	n/a	n/a
H.S. Diplomas (#)	n/a	n/a	n/a	n/a	n/a	n/a

Santa Barbara Elementary
720 Santa Barbara St • Santa Barbara, CA 93101-3167
(805) 963-4331 • http://www.sbceo.k12.ca.us/~sbsdweb/
Grade Span: KG-08; **Agency Type:** 2
Schools: 13
13 Primary; 0 Middle; 0 High; 0 Other Level
13 Regular; 0 Special Education; 0 Vocational; 0 Alternative
3 Magnet; 3 Charter; 10 Title I Eligible; 5 School-wide Title I
Students: 6,024 (51.6% male; 48.3% female)
Individual Education Program: 710 (11.8%);
English Language Learner: 2,547 (42.3%); Migrant: 43 (0.7%)
Eligible for Free Lunch Program: 2,570 (42.7%)
Eligible for Reduced-Price Lunch Program: 1,001 (16.6%)
Teachers: 304.2 (19.8 to 1)
Librarians/Media Specialists: 8.4 (717.1 to 1)
Guidance Counselors: 0.0 (n/a to 1)
Current Spending: ($ per student per year):
Total: $6,912; Instruction: $4,925; Support Services: $1,929
Enrollment, Drop-out Rates and Diploma Recipients by Race/Ethnicity

Category	Total	White	Black	Asian	AIAN	Hisp.
Enrollment (%)	100.0	24.4	2.4	2.5	1.0	69.4
Drop-out Rate (%)	n/a	n/a	n/a	n/a	n/a	n/a
H.S. Diplomas (#)	n/a	n/a	n/a	n/a	n/a	n/a

Santa Barbara High
720 Santa Barbara St • Santa Barbara, CA 93101-3167
(805) 963-4331 • http://www.sbceo.k12.ca.us/districts/sbhighsd/
Grade Span: 06-12; **Agency Type:** 2
Schools: 13
0 Primary; 6 Middle; 7 High; 0 Other Level
8 Regular; 0 Special Education; 0 Vocational; 5 Alternative
0 Magnet; 1 Charter; 4 Title I Eligible; 1 School-wide Title I
Students: 10,598 (51.3% male; 48.6% female)
Individual Education Program: 1,117 (10.5%);
English Language Learner: 2,073 (19.6%); Migrant: 107 (1.0%)
Eligible for Free Lunch Program: 1,725 (16.3%)
Eligible for Reduced-Price Lunch Program: 663 (6.3%)
Teachers: 463.8 (22.9 to 1)
Librarians/Media Specialists: 7.0 (1,514.0 to 1)
Guidance Counselors: 24.6 (430.8 to 1)
Current Spending: ($ per student per year):
Total: $6,594; Instruction: $4,229; Support Services: $2,365
Enrollment, Drop-out Rates and Diploma Recipients by Race/Ethnicity

Category	Total	White	Black	Asian	AIAN	Hisp.
Enrollment (%)	100.0	47.8	2.0	4.7	1.2	44.2
Drop-out Rate (%)	n/a	n/a	n/a	n/a	n/a	n/a
H.S. Diplomas (#)	1,358	745	35	60	8	510

Santa Maria Joint Union High

2560 Skyway Dr • Santa Maria, CA 93455-6112
(805) 922-4573 • http://www.smjuhsd.k12.ca.us/
Grade Span: 09-12; **Agency Type:** 1
Schools: 3
   0 Primary; 0 Middle; 3 High; 0 Other Level
   2 Regular; 0 Special Education; 0 Vocational; 1 Alternative
   0 Magnet; 0 Charter; 3 Title I Eligible; 1 School-wide Title I
Students: 6,675 (51.0% male; 48.9% female)
   Individual Education Program: 527 (7.9%);
   English Language Learner: 1,700 (25.5%); Migrant: 1,550 (23.2%)
   Eligible for Free Lunch Program: 1,552 (23.3%)
   Eligible for Reduced-Price Lunch Program: 410 (6.1%)
Teachers: 269.9 (24.7 to 1)
Librarians/Media Specialists: 0.4 (16,687.5 to 1)
Guidance Counselors: 4.0 (1,668.8 to 1)
Current Spending: ($ per student per year):
   Total: $6,641; Instruction: $3,928; Support Services: $2,487
Enrollment, Drop-out Rates and Diploma Recipients by Race/Ethnicity

Category	Total	White	Black	Asian	AIAN	Hisp.
Enrollment (%)	100.0	30.4	1.8	5.5	0.7	59.6
Drop-out Rate (%)	n/a	n/a	n/a	n/a	n/a	n/a
H.S. Diplomas (#)	1,093	451	4	56	10	570

Santa Maria-Bonita Elementary

708 S Miller St • Santa Maria, CA 93454-6230
(805) 928-1783 • http://www.sbceo.k12.ca.us/districts/smbonitasd/
Grade Span: KG-08; **Agency Type:** 1
Schools: 16
   13 Primary; 3 Middle; 0 High; 0 Other Level
   16 Regular; 0 Special Education; 0 Vocational; 0 Alternative
   0 Magnet; 0 Charter; 16 Title I Eligible; 13 School-wide Title I
Students: 12,395 (52.3% male; 47.6% female)
   Individual Education Program: 864 (7.0%);
   English Language Learner: 6,123 (49.4%); Migrant: 2,785 (22.5%)
   Eligible for Free Lunch Program: 8,048 (64.9%)
   Eligible for Reduced-Price Lunch Program: 1,868 (15.1%)
Teachers: 581.3 (21.3 to 1)
Librarians/Media Specialists: 0.0 (n/a to 1)
Guidance Counselors: 6.0 (2,065.8 to 1)
Current Spending: ($ per student per year):
   Total: $7,324; Instruction: $4,716; Support Services: $2,246
Enrollment, Drop-out Rates and Diploma Recipients by Race/Ethnicity

Category	Total	White	Black	Asian	AIAN	Hisp.
Enrollment (%)	100.0	9.6	1.4	3.6	0.6	84.8
Drop-out Rate (%)	n/a	n/a	n/a	n/a	n/a	n/a
H.S. Diplomas (#)	n/a	n/a	n/a	n/a	n/a	n/a

Santa Clara County

Alum Rock Union Elementary

2930 Gay Ave • San Jose, CA 95127-2322
(408) 928-6800 • http://www.alumrock.k12.ca.us/home.htm
Grade Span: KG-08; **Agency Type:** 1
Schools: 25
   19 Primary; 6 Middle; 0 High; 0 Other Level
   25 Regular; 0 Special Education; 0 Vocational; 0 Alternative
   0 Magnet; 0 Charter; 12 Title I Eligible; 10 School-wide Title I
Students: 13,782 (51.2% male; 48.7% female)
   Individual Education Program: 1,484 (10.8%);
   English Language Learner: 8,363 (60.7%); Migrant: 1,010 (7.3%)
   Eligible for Free Lunch Program: 8,556 (62.1%)
   Eligible for Reduced-Price Lunch Program: 2,097 (15.2%)
Teachers: 692.2 (19.9 to 1)
Librarians/Media Specialists: 0.0 (n/a to 1)
Guidance Counselors: 5.0 (2,756.4 to 1)
Current Spending: ($ per student per year):
   Total: $7,694; Instruction: $4,836; Support Services: $2,530
Enrollment, Drop-out Rates and Diploma Recipients by Race/Ethnicity

Category	Total	White	Black	Asian	AIAN	Hisp.
Enrollment (%)	100.0	3.6	3.1	17.7	1.2	74.4
Drop-out Rate (%)	n/a	n/a	n/a	n/a	n/a	n/a
H.S. Diplomas (#)	n/a	n/a	n/a	n/a	n/a	n/a

Berryessa Union Elementary

1376 Piedmont Rd • San Jose, CA 95132-2427
(408) 923-1800 • http://www.berryessa.k12.ca.us/index.html
Grade Span: KG-08; **Agency Type:** 1
Schools: 14
   11 Primary; 3 Middle; 0 High; 0 Other Level
   13 Regular; 0 Special Education; 0 Vocational; 1 Alternative
   0 Magnet; 0 Charter; 9 Title I Eligible; 0 School-wide Title I
Students: 8,479 (51.6% male; 48.3% female)
   Individual Education Program: 721 (8.5%);
   English Language Learner: 2,679 (31.6%); Migrant: 0 (0.0%)

Eligible for Free Lunch Program: 1,467 (17.3%)
   Eligible for Reduced-Price Lunch Program: 661 (7.8%)
Teachers: 398.9 (21.3 to 1)
Librarians/Media Specialists: 0.0 (n/a to 1)
Guidance Counselors: 6.5 (1,304.5 to 1)
Current Spending: ($ per student per year):
   Total: $7,028; Instruction: $4,666; Support Services: $2,143
Enrollment, Drop-out Rates and Diploma Recipients by Race/Ethnicity

Category	Total	White	Black	Asian	AIAN	Hisp.
Enrollment (%)	100.0	11.1	4.0	63.2	0.5	21.3
Drop-out Rate (%)	n/a	n/a	n/a	n/a	n/a	n/a
H.S. Diplomas (#)	n/a	n/a	n/a	n/a	n/a	n/a

Cambrian Elementary

4115 Jacksol Dr • San Jose, CA 95124-3312
(408) 377-2103 • http://www.cambrian.k12.ca.us/
Grade Span: KG-08; **Agency Type:** 1
Schools: 6
   4 Primary; 2 Middle; 0 High; 0 Other Level
   5 Regular; 0 Special Education; 0 Vocational; 1 Alternative
   0 Magnet; 3 Charter; 2 Title I Eligible; 0 School-wide Title I
Students: 2,801 (51.4% male; 48.5% female)
   Individual Education Program: 212 (7.6%);
   English Language Learner: 153 (5.5%); Migrant: 0 (0.0%)
   Eligible for Free Lunch Program: 391 (14.0%)
   Eligible for Reduced-Price Lunch Program: 154 (5.5%)
Teachers: 137.8 (20.3 to 1)
Librarians/Media Specialists: 0.0 (n/a to 1)
Guidance Counselors: 1.0 (2,801.0 to 1)
Current Spending: ($ per student per year):
   Total: $6,585; Instruction: $4,539; Support Services: $2,046
Enrollment, Drop-out Rates and Diploma Recipients by Race/Ethnicity

Category	Total	White	Black	Asian	AIAN	Hisp.
Enrollment (%)	100.0	59.4	3.8	13.8	0.6	22.2
Drop-out Rate (%)	n/a	n/a	n/a	n/a	n/a	n/a
H.S. Diplomas (#)	n/a	n/a	n/a	n/a	n/a	n/a

Campbell Union Elementary

155 N Third St • Campbell, CA 95008-2044
(408) 364-4200 • http://www.campbellusd.k12.ca.us/
Grade Span: KG-08; **Agency Type:** 1
Schools: 12
   9 Primary; 3 Middle; 0 High; 0 Other Level
   12 Regular; 0 Special Education; 0 Vocational; 0 Alternative
   0 Magnet; 1 Charter; 7 Title I Eligible; 0 School-wide Title I
Students: 7,462 (53.1% male; 46.8% female)
   Individual Education Program: 686 (9.2%);
   English Language Learner: 2,367 (31.7%); Migrant: 0 (0.0%)
   Eligible for Free Lunch Program: 2,230 (29.9%)
   Eligible for Reduced-Price Lunch Program: 613 (8.2%)
Teachers: 367.0 (20.3 to 1)
Librarians/Media Specialists: 0.0 (n/a to 1)
Guidance Counselors: 2.0 (3,731.0 to 1)
Current Spending: ($ per student per year):
   Total: $7,156; Instruction: $4,900; Support Services: $2,103
Enrollment, Drop-out Rates and Diploma Recipients by Race/Ethnicity

Category	Total	White	Black	Asian	AIAN	Hisp.
Enrollment (%)	100.0	41.6	5.2	15.1	0.5	36.3
Drop-out Rate (%)	n/a	n/a	n/a	n/a	n/a	n/a
H.S. Diplomas (#)	n/a	n/a	n/a	n/a	n/a	n/a

Campbell Union High

3235 Union Ave • San Jose, CA 95124-2009
(408) 371-0960 • http://www.cuhsd.org/
Grade Span: 09-12; **Agency Type:** 1
Schools: 7
   0 Primary; 0 Middle; 7 High; 0 Other Level
   5 Regular; 0 Special Education; 0 Vocational; 2 Alternative
   0 Magnet; 0 Charter; 2 Title I Eligible; 0 School-wide Title I
Students: 7,500 (51.3% male; 48.6% female)
   Individual Education Program: 778 (10.4%);
   English Language Learner: 339 (4.5%); Migrant: 0 (0.0%)
   Eligible for Free Lunch Program: 575 (7.7%)
   Eligible for Reduced-Price Lunch Program: 186 (2.5%)
Teachers: 300.3 (25.0 to 1)
Librarians/Media Specialists: 1.9 (3,947.4 to 1)
Guidance Counselors: 14.0 (535.7 to 1)
Current Spending: ($ per student per year):
   Total: $6,658; Instruction: $4,150; Support Services: $2,312
Enrollment, Drop-out Rates and Diploma Recipients by Race/Ethnicity

Category	Total	White	Black	Asian	AIAN	Hisp.
Enrollment (%)	100.0	55.9	3.4	10.7	1.0	18.4
Drop-out Rate (%)	n/a	n/a	n/a	n/a	n/a	n/a
H.S. Diplomas (#)	1,414	909	48	217	10	202

Cupertino Union School
10301 Vista Dr • Cupertino, CA 95014-2091
(408) 252-3000 • http://www.cupertino.k12.ca.us/
Grade Span: KG-08; **Agency Type:** 1
Schools: 24
   20 Primary; 4 Middle; 0 High; 0 Other Level
   24 Regular; 0 Special Education; 0 Vocational; 0 Alternative
   0 Magnet; 0 Charter; 5 Title I Eligible; 0 School-wide Title I
Students: 16,048 (51.3% male; 48.6% female)
   Individual Education Program: 997 (6.2%);
   English Language Learner: 2,238 (13.9%); Migrant: 0 (0.0%)
   Eligible for Free Lunch Program: 569 (3.5%)
   Eligible for Reduced-Price Lunch Program: 261 (1.6%)
Teachers: 742.8 (21.6 to 1)
Librarians/Media Specialists: 0.0 (n/a to 1)
Guidance Counselors: 4.4 (3,647.3 to 1)
Current Spending: ($ per student per year):
   Total: $6,408; Instruction: $4,289; Support Services: $1,956
Enrollment, Drop-out Rates and Diploma Recipients by Race/Ethnicity

Category	Total	White	Black	Asian	AIAN	Hisp.
Enrollment (%)	100.0	33.2	1.3	60.8	0.2	4.5
Drop-out Rate (%)	n/a	n/a	n/a	n/a	n/a	n/a
H.S. Diplomas (#)	n/a	n/a	n/a	n/a	n/a	n/a

East Side Union High
830 N Capitol Ave • San Jose, CA 95133-1316
(408) 347-5000 • http://www.esuhsd.k12.ca.us/
Grade Span: KG-12; **Agency Type:** 1
Schools: 21
   0 Primary; 0 Middle; 19 High; 2 Other Level
   15 Regular; 0 Special Education; 0 Vocational; 6 Alternative
   10 Magnet; 4 Charter; 8 Title I Eligible; 0 School-wide Title I
Students: 25,176 (51.7% male; 48.2% female)
   Individual Education Program: 2,588 (10.3%);
   English Language Learner: 6,897 (27.4%); Migrant: 401 (1.6%)
   Eligible for Free Lunch Program: 5,562 (22.1%)
   Eligible for Reduced-Price Lunch Program: 937 (3.7%)
Teachers: 1,146.9 (22.0 to 1)
Librarians/Media Specialists: 12.5 (2,014.1 to 1)
Guidance Counselors: 40.7 (618.6 to 1)
Current Spending: ($ per student per year):
   Total: $8,236; Instruction: $4,657; Support Services: $3,379
Enrollment, Drop-out Rates and Diploma Recipients by Race/Ethnicity

Category	Total	White	Black	Asian	AIAN	Hisp.
Enrollment (%)	100.0	14.0	4.4	36.7	0.4	44.4
Drop-out Rate (%)	n/a	n/a	n/a	n/a	n/a	n/a
H.S. Diplomas (#)	4,467	772	178	2,040	19	1,457

Evergreen Elementary
3188 Quimby Rd • San Jose, CA 95148-3022
(408) 270-6800 • http://www.do.esd.k12.ca.us/
Grade Span: KG-08; **Agency Type:** 1
Schools: 17
   14 Primary; 3 Middle; 0 High; 0 Other Level
   17 Regular; 0 Special Education; 0 Vocational; 0 Alternative
   0 Magnet; 0 Charter; 7 Title I Eligible; 6 School-wide Title I
Students: 13,111 (51.5% male; 48.4% female)
   Individual Education Program: 1,089 (8.3%);
   English Language Learner: 3,792 (28.9%); Migrant: 237 (1.8%)
   Eligible for Free Lunch Program: 3,086 (23.5%)
   Eligible for Reduced-Price Lunch Program: 1,032 (7.9%)
Teachers: 596.4 (22.0 to 1)
Librarians/Media Specialists: 10.6 (1,236.9 to 1)
Guidance Counselors: 0.0 (n/a to 1)
Current Spending: ($ per student per year):
   Total: $6,545; Instruction: $4,488; Support Services: $1,837
Enrollment, Drop-out Rates and Diploma Recipients by Race/Ethnicity

Category	Total	White	Black	Asian	AIAN	Hisp.
Enrollment (%)	100.0	11.7	4.4	50.8	0.5	32.5
Drop-out Rate (%)	n/a	n/a	n/a	n/a	n/a	n/a
H.S. Diplomas (#)	n/a	n/a	n/a	n/a	n/a	n/a

Franklin-Mckinley Elementary
645 Wool Creek Dr • San Jose, CA 95112-2617
(408) 283-6000 • http://www.fmsd.k12.ca.us/
Grade Span: KG-08; **Agency Type:** 1
Schools: 14
   12 Primary; 2 Middle; 0 High; 0 Other Level
   14 Regular; 0 Special Education; 0 Vocational; 0 Alternative
   0 Magnet; 0 Charter; 10 Title I Eligible; 7 School-wide Title I
Students: 9,867 (50.4% male; 49.5% female)
   Individual Education Program: 818 (8.3%);
   English Language Learner: 5,329 (54.0%); Migrant: 1,028 (10.4%)
   Eligible for Free Lunch Program: 5,801 (58.8%)
   Eligible for Reduced-Price Lunch Program: 1,398 (14.2%)

Teachers: 499.4 (19.8 to 1)
Librarians/Media Specialists: 0.0 (n/a to 1)
Guidance Counselors: 5.0 (1,973.4 to 1)
Current Spending: ($ per student per year):
   Total: $7,820; Instruction: $4,955; Support Services: $2,487
Enrollment, Drop-out Rates and Diploma Recipients by Race/Ethnicity

Category	Total	White	Black	Asian	AIAN	Hisp.
Enrollment (%)	100.0	3.2	2.6	33.3	0.4	60.5
Drop-out Rate (%)	n/a	n/a	n/a	n/a	n/a	n/a
H.S. Diplomas (#)	n/a	n/a	n/a	n/a	n/a	n/a

Fremont Union High
589 W Fremont Ave • Sunnyvale, CA 94087
Mailing Address: PO Box F • Sunnyvale, CA 94087
(408) 522-2200 • http://www.fuhsd.org/
Grade Span: 09-12; **Agency Type:** 1
Schools: 6
   0 Primary; 0 Middle; 6 High; 0 Other Level
   5 Regular; 0 Special Education; 0 Vocational; 1 Alternative
   0 Magnet; 0 Charter; 1 Title I Eligible; 0 School-wide Title I
Students: 9,320 (51.0% male; 48.9% female)
   Individual Education Program: 740 (7.9%)
   English Language Learner: 979 (10.5%); Migrant: 29 (0.3%)
   Eligible for Free Lunch Program: 486 (5.2%)
   Eligible for Reduced-Price Lunch Program: 135 (1.4%)
Teachers: 397.4 (23.5 to 1)
Librarians/Media Specialists: 5.0 (1,864.0 to 1)
Guidance Counselors: 10.8 (863.0 to 1)
Current Spending: ($ per student per year):
   Total: $8,142; Instruction: $4,920; Support Services: $3,002
Enrollment, Drop-out Rates and Diploma Recipients by Race/Ethnicity

Category	Total	White	Black	Asian	AIAN	Hisp.
Enrollment (%)	100.0	36.2	2.1	49.5	0.3	11.9
Drop-out Rate (%)	n/a	n/a	n/a	n/a	n/a	n/a
H.S. Diplomas (#)	1,985	741	52	997	6	189

Gilroy Unified
7810 Arroyo Circle • Gilroy, CA 95020-7313
(408) 847-2700 • http://www.gusd.k12.ca.us/
Grade Span: KG-12; **Agency Type:** 1
Schools: 15
   8 Primary; 3 Middle; 4 High; 0 Other Level
   13 Regular; 0 Special Education; 0 Vocational; 2 Alternative
   0 Magnet; 1 Charter; 13 Title I Eligible; 0 School-wide Title I
Students: 9,691 (51.5% male; 48.4% female)
   Individual Education Program: 870 (9.0%);
   English Language Learner: 2,919 (30.1%); Migrant: 1,401 (14.5%)
   Eligible for Free Lunch Program: 3,317 (34.2%)
   Eligible for Reduced-Price Lunch Program: 785 (8.1%)
Teachers: 457.5 (21.2 to 1)
Librarians/Media Specialists: 0.0 (n/a to 1)
Guidance Counselors: 7.5 (1,292.1 to 1)
Current Spending: ($ per student per year):
   Total: $6,988; Instruction: $4,178; Support Services: $2,479
Enrollment, Drop-out Rates and Diploma Recipients by Race/Ethnicity

Category	Total	White	Black	Asian	AIAN	Hisp.
Enrollment (%)	100.0	25.3	1.7	4.4	0.5	66.1
Drop-out Rate (%)	n/a	n/a	n/a	n/a	n/a	n/a
H.S. Diplomas (#)	446	170	13	35	2	226

Los Altos Elementary
201 Covington Rd • Los Altos, CA 94024-4030
(650) 947-1150 • http://www.sccoe.k12.ca.us/district/4320home.html
Grade Span: KG-08; **Agency Type:** 1
Schools: 8
   6 Primary; 2 Middle; 0 High; 0 Other Level
   8 Regular; 0 Special Education; 0 Vocational; 0 Alternative
   0 Magnet; 0 Charter; 0 Title I Eligible; 0 School-wide Title I
Students: 4,050 (50.4% male; 49.5% female)
   Individual Education Program: 364 (9.0%);
   English Language Learner: 210 (5.2%); Migrant: 0 (0.0%)
   Eligible for Free Lunch Program: 76 (1.9%)
   Eligible for Reduced-Price Lunch Program: 9 (0.2%)
Teachers: 204.7 (19.8 to 1)
Librarians/Media Specialists: 0.0 (n/a to 1)
Guidance Counselors: 2.0 (2,025.0 to 1)
Current Spending: ($ per student per year):
   Total: $7,620; Instruction: $5,237; Support Services: $2,376
Enrollment, Drop-out Rates and Diploma Recipients by Race/Ethnicity

Category	Total	White	Black	Asian	AIAN	Hisp.
Enrollment (%)	100.0	68.5	0.7	27.1	0.1	3.5
Drop-out Rate (%)	n/a	n/a	n/a	n/a	n/a	n/a
H.S. Diplomas (#)	n/a	n/a	n/a	n/a	n/a	n/a

Los Gatos Union Elementary
15766 Poppy Ln • Los Gatos, CA 95030-3228
(408) 335-2000 • http://www.lgusd.k12.ca.us/
Grade Span: KG-08; **Agency Type:** 1
Schools: 5
   4 Primary; 1 Middle; 0 High; 0 Other Level
   5 Regular; 0 Special Education; 0 Vocational; 0 Alternative
   0 Magnet; 0 Charter; 4 Title I Eligible; 0 School-wide Title I
Students: 2,581 (51.5% male; 48.4% female)
   Individual Education Program: 297 (11.5%);
   English Language Learner: 43 (1.7%); Migrant: 0 (0.0%)
   Eligible for Free Lunch Program: 50 (1.9%)
   Eligible for Reduced-Price Lunch Program: 8 (0.3%)
Teachers: 135.1 (19.1 to 1)
Librarians/Media Specialists: 1.0 (2,581.0 to 1)
Guidance Counselors: 2.0 (1,290.5 to 1)
Current Spending: ($ per student per year):
   Total: $7,428; Instruction: $4,794; Support Services: $2,452
Enrollment, Drop-out Rates and Diploma Recipients by Race/Ethnicity

Category	Total	White	Black	Asian	AIAN	Hisp.
Enrollment (%)	100.0	78.7	0.7	14.1	0.2	4.8
Drop-out Rate (%)	n/a	n/a	n/a	n/a	n/a	n/a
H.S. Diplomas (#)	n/a	n/a	n/a	n/a	n/a	n/a

Los Gatos-Saratoga Joint Union High
17421 Farley Rd W • Los Gatos, CA 95030-3308
(408) 354-2520 • http://www.eduniverse.com/members/schools
Grade Span: 09-12; **Agency Type:** 1
Schools: 2
   0 Primary; 0 Middle; 2 High; 0 Other Level
   2 Regular; 0 Special Education; 0 Vocational; 0 Alternative
   0 Magnet; 0 Charter; 1 Title I Eligible; 0 School-wide Title I
Students: 2,948 (52.4% male; 47.5% female)
   Individual Education Program: 237 (8.0%);
   English Language Learner: 17 (0.6%); Migrant: 0 (0.0%)
   Eligible for Free Lunch Program: 28 (0.9%)
   Eligible for Reduced-Price Lunch Program: 0 (0.0%)
Teachers: 128.7 (22.9 to 1)
Librarians/Media Specialists: 2.0 (1,474.0 to 1)
Guidance Counselors: 0.0 (n/a to 1)
Current Spending: ($ per student per year):
   Total: $8,876; Instruction: $5,310; Support Services: $3,368
Enrollment, Drop-out Rates and Diploma Recipients by Race/Ethnicity

Category	Total	White	Black	Asian	AIAN	Hisp.
Enrollment (%)	100.0	64.0	0.5	26.9	0.2	4.1
Drop-out Rate (%)	n/a	n/a	n/a	n/a	n/a	n/a
H.S. Diplomas (#)	651	452	3	174	3	17

Milpitas Unified
1331 E Calaveras Blvd • Milpitas, CA 95035-5707
(408) 945-2300 • http://www.milpitas.k12.ca.us/
Grade Span: KG-12; **Agency Type:** 1
Schools: 14
   9 Primary; 2 Middle; 3 High; 0 Other Level
   12 Regular; 0 Special Education; 0 Vocational; 2 Alternative
   0 Magnet; 0 Charter; 6 Title I Eligible; 0 School-wide Title I
Students: 9,528 (51.8% male; 48.1% female)
   Individual Education Program: 862 (9.0%);
   English Language Learner: 2,378 (25.0%); Migrant: 0 (0.0%)
   Eligible for Free Lunch Program: 1,928 (20.2%)
   Eligible for Reduced-Price Lunch Program: 878 (9.2%)
Teachers: 436.5 (21.8 to 1)
Librarians/Media Specialists: 2.0 (4,764.0 to 1)
Guidance Counselors: 7.6 (1,253.7 to 1)
Current Spending: ($ per student per year):
   Total: $7,012; Instruction: $4,444; Support Services: $2,298
Enrollment, Drop-out Rates and Diploma Recipients by Race/Ethnicity

Category	Total	White	Black	Asian	AIAN	Hisp.
Enrollment (%)	100.0	15.1	3.9	54.9	0.4	20.0
Drop-out Rate (%)	n/a	n/a	n/a	n/a	n/a	n/a
H.S. Diplomas (#)	710	165	36	380	2	127

Moreland Elementary
4710 Campbell Ave • San Jose, CA 95130-1709
(408) 874-2900 • http://www.moreland.k12.ca.us/
Grade Span: KG-08; **Agency Type:** 1
Schools: 9
   7 Primary; 2 Middle; 0 High; 0 Other Level
   9 Regular; 0 Special Education; 0 Vocational; 0 Alternative
   0 Magnet; 0 Charter; 3 Title I Eligible; 1 School-wide Title I
Students: 4,438 (51.3% male; 48.6% female)
   Individual Education Program: 421 (9.5%);
   English Language Learner: 898 (20.2%); Migrant: 0 (0.0%)
   Eligible for Free Lunch Program: 775 (17.5%)
   Eligible for Reduced-Price Lunch Program: 301 (6.8%)

Teachers: 216.9 (20.5 to 1)
Librarians/Media Specialists: 0.0 (n/a to 1)
Guidance Counselors: 0.0 (n/a to 1)
Current Spending: ($ per student per year):
   Total: $7,487; Instruction: $4,702; Support Services: $2,522
Enrollment, Drop-out Rates and Diploma Recipients by Race/Ethnicity

Category	Total	White	Black	Asian	AIAN	Hisp.
Enrollment (%)	100.0	44.3	4.4	26.3	0.4	23.9
Drop-out Rate (%)	n/a	n/a	n/a	n/a	n/a	n/a
H.S. Diplomas (#)	n/a	n/a	n/a	n/a	n/a	n/a

Morgan Hill Unified
15600 Concord Circle • Morgan Hill, CA 95037-7110
(408) 201-6023 • http://www.mhu.k12.ca.us/
Grade Span: KG-12; **Agency Type:** 1
Schools: 15
   10 Primary; 2 Middle; 3 High; 0 Other Level
   14 Regular; 0 Special Education; 0 Vocational; 1 Alternative
   0 Magnet; 2 Charter; 6 Title I Eligible; 2 School-wide Title I
Students: 8,880 (50.7% male; 49.2% female)
   Individual Education Program: 988 (11.1%);
   English Language Learner: 1,525 (17.2%); Migrant: 921 (10.4%)
   Eligible for Free Lunch Program: 1,710 (19.3%)
   Eligible for Reduced-Price Lunch Program: 422 (4.8%)
Teachers: 409.3 (21.7 to 1)
Librarians/Media Specialists: 1.0 (8,880.0 to 1)
Guidance Counselors: 5.0 (1,776.0 to 1)
Current Spending: ($ per student per year):
   Total: $6,464; Instruction: $4,115; Support Services: $2,134
Enrollment, Drop-out Rates and Diploma Recipients by Race/Ethnicity

Category	Total	White	Black	Asian	AIAN	Hisp.
Enrollment (%)	100.0	48.2	2.4	8.7	0.6	37.2
Drop-out Rate (%)	n/a	n/a	n/a	n/a	n/a	n/a
H.S. Diplomas (#)	615	365	10	56	1	183

Mountain View-Los Altos Union High
1299 Bryant Ave • Mountain View, CA 94040-4527
(650) 940-4650 • http://www.mvla.k12.ca.us/
Grade Span: 09-12; **Agency Type:** 1
Schools: 4
   0 Primary; 0 Middle; 4 High; 0 Other Level
   2 Regular; 0 Special Education; 0 Vocational; 2 Alternative
   0 Magnet; 0 Charter; 2 Title I Eligible; 0 School-wide Title I
Students: 3,441 (50.2% male; 49.7% female)
   Individual Education Program: 334 (9.7%);
   English Language Learner: 224 (6.5%); Migrant: 1 (<0.1%)
   Eligible for Free Lunch Program: 377 (11.0%)
   Eligible for Reduced-Price Lunch Program: 59 (1.7%)
Teachers: 167.8 (20.5 to 1)
Librarians/Media Specialists: 2.0 (1,720.5 to 1)
Guidance Counselors: 8.4 (409.6 to 1)
Current Spending: ($ per student per year):
   Total: $10,132; Instruction: $5,942; Support Services: $3,983
Enrollment, Drop-out Rates and Diploma Recipients by Race/Ethnicity

Category	Total	White	Black	Asian	AIAN	Hisp.
Enrollment (%)	100.0	53.3	2.9	19.6	0.4	18.1
Drop-out Rate (%)	n/a	n/a	n/a	n/a	n/a	n/a
H.S. Diplomas (#)	639	357	28	141	1	100

Mountain View-Whisman Elementary
750 A San Pierre Way • Mountain View, CA 94043
(650) 526-3500 • http://www.mvsd.k12.ca.us/index.htm
Grade Span: KG-08; **Agency Type:** 1
Schools: 9
   7 Primary; 2 Middle; 0 High; 0 Other Level
   9 Regular; 0 Special Education; 0 Vocational; 0 Alternative
   0 Magnet; 0 Charter; 4 Title I Eligible; 1 School-wide Title I
Students: 4,440 (51.7% male; 48.2% female)
   Individual Education Program: 460 (10.4%);
   English Language Learner: 1,722 (38.8%); Migrant: 1 (<0.1%)
   Eligible for Free Lunch Program: 1,356 (30.5%)
   Eligible for Reduced-Price Lunch Program: 468 (10.5%)
Teachers: 217.8 (20.4 to 1)
Librarians/Media Specialists: 0.0 (n/a to 1)
Guidance Counselors: 0.0 (n/a to 1)
Current Spending: ($ per student per year):
   Total: $7,462; Instruction: $4,669; Support Services: $2,503
Enrollment, Drop-out Rates and Diploma Recipients by Race/Ethnicity

Category	Total	White	Black	Asian	AIAN	Hisp.
Enrollment (%)	100.0	35.3	5.7	17.1	0.3	41.4
Drop-out Rate (%)	n/a	n/a	n/a	n/a	n/a	n/a
H.S. Diplomas (#)	n/a	n/a	n/a	n/a	n/a	n/a

Mt. Pleasant Elementary
3434 Marten Ave • San Jose, CA 95148-1300
(408) 223-3700 • http://www.sccoe.k12.ca.us/district/4328home.html
Grade Span: KG-08; **Agency Type:** 1
Schools: 5
   3 Primary; 2 Middle; 0 High; 0 Other Level
   5 Regular; 0 Special Education; 0 Vocational; 0 Alternative
   1 Magnet; 0 Charter; 2 Title I Eligible; 2 School-wide Title I
Students: 2,906   (51.7% male; 48.2% female)
   Individual Education Program: 306 (10.5%);
   English Language Learner: 1,598 (55.0%); Migrant: 240 (8.3%)
   Eligible for Free Lunch Program: 1,381 (47.5%)
   Eligible for Reduced-Price Lunch Program: 409 (14.1%)
Teachers: 139.8 (20.8 to 1)
Librarians/Media Specialists: 0.0 (n/a to 1)
Guidance Counselors: 1.0 (2,906.0 to 1)
Current Spending: ($ per student per year):
   Total: $7,873; Instruction: $4,427; Support Services: $3,185
Enrollment, Drop-out Rates and Diploma Recipients by Race/Ethnicity

Category	Total	White	Black	Asian	AIAN	Hisp.
Enrollment (%)	100.0	7.3	3.7	19.1	0.0	68.5
Drop-out Rate (%)	n/a	n/a	n/a	n/a	n/a	n/a
H.S. Diplomas (#)	n/a	n/a	n/a	n/a	n/a	n/a

Oak Grove Elementary
6578 Santa Teresa Blvd • San Jose, CA 95119-1204
(408) 227-8300 • http://www.ogsd.k12.ca.us/
Grade Span: KG-08; **Agency Type:** 1
Schools: 20
   16 Primary; 4 Middle; 0 High; 0 Other Level
   19 Regular; 0 Special Education; 0 Vocational; 1 Alternative
   0 Magnet; 0 Charter; 5 Title I Eligible; 5 School-wide Title I
Students: 11,636   (51.9% male; 48.0% female)
   Individual Education Program: 1,174 (10.1%);
   English Language Learner: 3,192 (27.4%); Migrant: 450 (3.9%)
   Eligible for Free Lunch Program: 3,560 (30.6%)
   Eligible for Reduced-Price Lunch Program: 1,232 (10.6%)
Teachers: 559.3 (20.8 to 1)
Librarians/Media Specialists: 0.5 (23,272.0 to 1)
Guidance Counselors: 6.8 (1,711.2 to 1)
Current Spending: ($ per student per year):
   Total: $7,061; Instruction: $4,591; Support Services: $2,202
Enrollment, Drop-out Rates and Diploma Recipients by Race/Ethnicity

Category	Total	White	Black	Asian	AIAN	Hisp.
Enrollment (%)	100.0	28.4	5.8	21.4	0.6	39.1
Drop-out Rate (%)	n/a	n/a	n/a	n/a	n/a	n/a
H.S. Diplomas (#)	n/a	n/a	n/a	n/a	n/a	n/a

Palo Alto Unified
25 Churchill Ave • Palo Alto, CA 94306-1005
(650) 329-3700 • http://www.pausd.palo-alto.ca.us/
Grade Span: KG-12; **Agency Type:** 1
Schools: 19
   13 Primary; 3 Middle; 2 High; 1 Other Level
   18 Regular; 0 Special Education; 0 Vocational; 1 Alternative
   0 Magnet; 0 Charter; 3 Title I Eligible; 0 School-wide Title I
Students: 10,354   (51.7% male; 48.2% female)
   Individual Education Program: 1,136 (11.0%);
   English Language Learner: 790 (7.6%); Migrant: 0 (0.0%)
   Eligible for Free Lunch Program: 376 (3.6%)
   Eligible for Reduced-Price Lunch Program: 178 (1.7%)
Teachers: 612.2 (16.9 to 1)
Librarians/Media Specialists: 14.9 (694.9 to 1)
Guidance Counselors: 12.5 (828.3 to 1)
Current Spending: ($ per student per year):
   Total: $11,045; Instruction: $7,240; Support Services: $3,637
Enrollment, Drop-out Rates and Diploma Recipients by Race/Ethnicity

Category	Total	White	Black	Asian	AIAN	Hisp.
Enrollment (%)	100.0	58.0	4.0	23.4	0.2	7.9
Drop-out Rate (%)	n/a	n/a	n/a	n/a	n/a	n/a
H.S. Diplomas (#)	709	486	19	166	3	35

San Jose Unified
855 Lenzen Ave • San Jose, CA 95126-2736
(408) 535-6000 • http://www.sjusd.k12.ca.us/
Grade Span: KG-12; **Agency Type:** 1
Schools: 57
   32 Primary; 7 Middle; 16 High; 2 Other Level
   46 Regular; 0 Special Education; 0 Vocational; 11 Alternative
   6 Magnet; 1 Charter; 21 Title I Eligible; 17 School-wide Title I
Students: 32,314   (50.3% male; 49.6% female)
   Individual Education Program: 3,768 (11.7%);
   English Language Learner: 8,405 (26.0%); Migrant: 1,578 (4.9%)
   Eligible for Free Lunch Program: 12,287 (38.0%)
   Eligible for Reduced-Price Lunch Program: 3,180 (9.8%)

Teachers: 1,627.0 (19.9 to 1)
Librarians/Media Specialists: 0.0 (n/a to 1)
Guidance Counselors: 34.6 (933.9 to 1)
Current Spending: ($ per student per year):
   Total: $8,624; Instruction: $4,968; Support Services: $3,418
Enrollment, Drop-out Rates and Diploma Recipients by Race/Ethnicity

Category	Total	White	Black	Asian	AIAN	Hisp.
Enrollment (%)	100.0	28.9	3.5	15.2	1.7	50.7
Drop-out Rate (%)	n/a	n/a	n/a	n/a	n/a	n/a
H.S. Diplomas (#)	1,740	632	57	387	20	644

Santa Clara County Off. of Education
1290 Ridder Park Dr • San Jose, CA 95131-2398
(408) 453-6500 • http://www.sccoe.k12.ca.us/
Grade Span: KG-12; **Agency Type:** 4
Schools: 5
   0 Primary; 0 Middle; 2 High; 3 Other Level
   1 Regular; 1 Special Education; 0 Vocational; 3 Alternative
   0 Magnet; 0 Charter; 0 Title I Eligible; 0 School-wide Title I
Students: 2,089   (67.7% male; 32.2% female)
   Individual Education Program: n/a;
   English Language Learner: 296 (14.2%); Migrant: 2 (0.1%)
   Eligible for Free Lunch Program: 416 (19.9%)
   Eligible for Reduced-Price Lunch Program: 4 (0.2%)
Teachers: 237.8 (8.8 to 1)
Librarians/Media Specialists: 1.0 (2,089.0 to 1)
Guidance Counselors: 6.0 (348.2 to 1)
Current Spending: ($ per student per year):
   Total: $63,340; Instruction: $31,845; Support Services: $29,521
Enrollment, Drop-out Rates and Diploma Recipients by Race/Ethnicity

Category	Total	White	Black	Asian	AIAN	Hisp.
Enrollment (%)	100.0	25.8	4.7	20.1	1.0	42.7
Drop-out Rate (%)	n/a	n/a	n/a	n/a	n/a	n/a
H.S. Diplomas (#)	128	29	12	26	5	50

Santa Clara Unified
1889 Lawrence Rd • Santa Clara, CA 95052-0397
Mailing Address: PO Box 397 • Santa Clara, CA 95052-0397
(408) 423-2000 • http://www.scu.k12.ca.us/
Grade Span: KG-12; **Agency Type:** 1
Schools: 23
   16 Primary; 3 Middle; 3 High; 1 Other Level
   21 Regular; 0 Special Education; 0 Vocational; 2 Alternative
   0 Magnet; 0 Charter; 7 Title I Eligible; 7 School-wide Title I
Students: 13,976   (51.1% male; 48.8% female)
   Individual Education Program: 1,644 (11.8%);
   English Language Learner: 3,273 (23.4%); Migrant: 734 (5.3%)
   Eligible for Free Lunch Program: 4,129 (29.5%)
   Eligible for Reduced-Price Lunch Program: 1,801 (12.9%)
Teachers: 652.4 (21.4 to 1)
Librarians/Media Specialists: 5.9 (2,368.8 to 1)
Guidance Counselors: 15.7 (890.2 to 1)
Current Spending: ($ per student per year):
   Total: $9,035; Instruction: $5,346; Support Services: $3,404
Enrollment, Drop-out Rates and Diploma Recipients by Race/Ethnicity

Category	Total	White	Black	Asian	AIAN	Hisp.
Enrollment (%)	100.0	34.3	4.7	29.0	0.7	28.3
Drop-out Rate (%)	n/a	n/a	n/a	n/a	n/a	n/a
H.S. Diplomas (#)	804	339	34	257	5	169

Saratoga Union Elementary
20460 Forrest Hills Dr • Saratoga, CA 95070-6020
(408) 867-3424 • http://www.susd.k12.ca.us/
Grade Span: KG-08; **Agency Type:** 1
Schools: 4
   3 Primary; 1 Middle; 0 High; 0 Other Level
   4 Regular; 0 Special Education; 0 Vocational; 0 Alternative
   0 Magnet; 0 Charter; 0 Title I Eligible; 0 School-wide Title I
Students: 2,413   (52.4% male; 47.5% female)
   Individual Education Program: 212 (8.8%);
   English Language Learner: 43 (1.8%); Migrant: 0 (0.0%)
   Eligible for Free Lunch Program: 15 (0.6%)
   Eligible for Reduced-Price Lunch Program: 4 (0.2%)
Teachers: 117.9 (20.5 to 1)
Librarians/Media Specialists: 1.0 (2,413.0 to 1)
Guidance Counselors: 1.6 (1,508.1 to 1)
Current Spending: ($ per student per year):
   Total: $7,374; Instruction: $4,911; Support Services: $2,321
Enrollment, Drop-out Rates and Diploma Recipients by Race/Ethnicity

Category	Total	White	Black	Asian	AIAN	Hisp.
Enrollment (%)	100.0	49.0	0.1	43.7	0.1	2.7
Drop-out Rate (%)	n/a	n/a	n/a	n/a	n/a	n/a
H.S. Diplomas (#)	n/a	n/a	n/a	n/a	n/a	n/a

Sunnyvale Elementary

819 W Iowa Ave • Sunnyvale, CA 94088-3217
Mailing Address: PO Box 3217 • Sunnyvale, CA 94088-3217
(408) 522-8200 • http://www.sesd.org/index.html
Grade Span: KG-08; **Agency Type:** 1
Schools: 11
     8 Primary; 3 Middle; 0 High; 0 Other Level
     10 Regular; 0 Special Education; 0 Vocational; 1 Alternative
     0 Magnet; 0 Charter; 6 Title I Eligible; 0 School-wide Title I
Students: 5,960   (51.9% male; 48.0% female)
     Individual Education Program: 621 (10.4%);
     English Language Learner: 1,905 (32.0%); Migrant: 59 (1.0%)
     Eligible for Free Lunch Program: 1,705 (28.6%)
     Eligible for Reduced-Price Lunch Program: 638 (10.7%)
Teachers: 300.6 (19.8 to 1)
Librarians/Media Specialists: 0.0 (n/a to 1)
Guidance Counselors: 0.0 (n/a to 1)
Current Spending: ($ per student per year):
     Total: $8,197; Instruction: $4,941; Support Services: $2,953
Enrollment, Drop-out Rates and Diploma Recipients by Race/Ethnicity

Category	Total	White	Black	Asian	AIAN	Hisp.
Enrollment (%)	100.0	23.3	3.5	29.7	0.8	41.3
Drop-out Rate (%)	n/a	n/a	n/a	n/a	n/a	n/a
H.S. Diplomas (#)	n/a	n/a	n/a	n/a	n/a	n/a

Union Elementary

5175 Union Ave • San Jose, CA 95124-5434
(408) 377-8010 • http://www.unionsd.k12.ca.us/
Grade Span: KG-08; **Agency Type:** 1
Schools: 10
     8 Primary; 2 Middle; 0 High; 0 Other Level
     10 Regular; 0 Special Education; 0 Vocational; 0 Alternative
     0 Magnet; 0 Charter; 3 Title I Eligible; 0 School-wide Title I
Students: 4,547   (52.0% male; 47.9% female)
     Individual Education Program: 529 (11.6%);
     English Language Learner: 255 (5.6%); Migrant: 0 (0.0%)
     Eligible for Free Lunch Program: 447 (9.8%)
     Eligible for Reduced-Price Lunch Program: 125 (2.7%)
Teachers: 218.0 (20.9 to 1)
Librarians/Media Specialists: 0.0 (n/a to 1)
Guidance Counselors: 2.0 (2,273.5 to 1)
Current Spending: ($ per student per year):
     Total: $7,267; Instruction: $4,743; Support Services: $2,327
Enrollment, Drop-out Rates and Diploma Recipients by Race/Ethnicity

Category	Total	White	Black	Asian	AIAN	Hisp.
Enrollment (%)	100.0	70.1	2.6	11.5	0.5	13.9
Drop-out Rate (%)	n/a	n/a	n/a	n/a	n/a	n/a
H.S. Diplomas (#)	n/a	n/a	n/a	n/a	n/a	n/a

Santa Cruz County

Live Oak Elementary

984-1 Bostwick Ln • Santa Cruz, CA 95062-1756
(831) 475-6333 • http://www.lodo.santacruz.k12.ca.us/
Grade Span: KG-08; **Agency Type:** 1
Schools: 7
     5 Primary; 1 Middle; 0 High; 1 Other Level
     7 Regular; 0 Special Education; 0 Vocational; 0 Alternative
     0 Magnet; 2 Charter; 4 Title I Eligible; 0 School-wide Title I
Students: 2,114   (52.3% male; 47.6% female)
     Individual Education Program: 316 (14.9%);
     English Language Learner: 559 (26.4%); Migrant: 102 (4.8%)
     Eligible for Free Lunch Program: 686 (32.5%)
     Eligible for Reduced-Price Lunch Program: 235 (11.1%)
Teachers: 103.5 (20.4 to 1)
Librarians/Media Specialists: 0.3 (7,046.7 to 1)
Guidance Counselors: 2.5 (845.6 to 1)
Current Spending: ($ per student per year):
     Total: $8,467; Instruction: $5,042; Support Services: $3,155
Enrollment, Drop-out Rates and Diploma Recipients by Race/Ethnicity

Category	Total	White	Black	Asian	AIAN	Hisp.
Enrollment (%)	100.0	49.4	3.2	3.8	0.9	40.4
Drop-out Rate (%)	n/a	n/a	n/a	n/a	n/a	n/a
H.S. Diplomas (#)	n/a	n/a	n/a	n/a	n/a	n/a

Pajaro Valley Unified School

294 Green Valley Rd • Watsonville, CA 95076
Mailing Address: PO Box 50010 • Watsonville, CA 95077-5010
(831) 786-2100 • http://www.pvusd.santacruz.k12.ca.us/
Grade Span: KG-12; **Agency Type:** 1
Schools: 29
     18 Primary; 5 Middle; 5 High; 1 Other Level
     26 Regular; 0 Special Education; 0 Vocational; 3 Alternative
     0 Magnet; 5 Charter; 18 Title I Eligible; 16 School-wide Title I
Students: 19,522   (50.6% male; 49.3% female)

     Individual Education Program: 2,227 (11.4%);
     English Language Learner: 8,908 (45.6%); Migrant: 8,934 (45.8%)
     Eligible for Free Lunch Program: 9,683 (49.6%)
     Eligible for Reduced-Price Lunch Program: 1,777 (9.1%)
Teachers: 994.8 (19.6 to 1)
Librarians/Media Specialists: 0.0 (n/a to 1)
Guidance Counselors: 17.0 (1,148.4 to 1)
Current Spending: ($ per student per year):
     Total: $8,301; Instruction: $4,793; Support Services: $3,224
Enrollment, Drop-out Rates and Diploma Recipients by Race/Ethnicity

Category	Total	White	Black	Asian	AIAN	Hisp.
Enrollment (%)	100.0	20.7	0.6	2.0	0.2	76.3
Drop-out Rate (%)	n/a	n/a	n/a	n/a	n/a	n/a
H.S. Diplomas (#)	1,009	309	3	32	5	656

San Lorenzo Valley Unified

325 Marion Ave • Ben Lomond, CA 95005-9403
(831) 335-7488 • http://www.slvdo.santacruz.k12.ca.us/index.html
Grade Span: KG-12; **Agency Type:** 1
Schools: 6
     2 Primary; 1 Middle; 2 High; 1 Other Level
     4 Regular; 0 Special Education; 0 Vocational; 2 Alternative
     0 Magnet; 1 Charter; 2 Title I Eligible; 0 School-wide Title I
Students: 3,561   (50.8% male; 49.1% female)
     Individual Education Program: 470 (13.2%);
     English Language Learner: 27 (0.8%); Migrant: 0 (0.0%)
     Eligible for Free Lunch Program: 304 (8.5%)
     Eligible for Reduced-Price Lunch Program: 119 (3.3%)
Teachers: 164.8 (21.6 to 1)
Librarians/Media Specialists: 0.0 (n/a to 1)
Guidance Counselors: 3.0 (1,187.0 to 1)
Current Spending: ($ per student per year):
     Total: $7,313; Instruction: $4,764; Support Services: $2,376
Enrollment, Drop-out Rates and Diploma Recipients by Race/Ethnicity

Category	Total	White	Black	Asian	AIAN	Hisp.
Enrollment (%)	100.0	85.8	1.9	2.4	1.3	5.7
Drop-out Rate (%)	n/a	n/a	n/a	n/a	n/a	n/a
H.S. Diplomas (#)	303	274	3	8	4	14

Santa Cruz City Elementary

405 Old San Jose Rd • Soquel, CA 95073
(831) 429-3800 • http://www.sccs.santacruz.k12.ca.us/
Grade Span: KG-08; **Agency Type:** 2
Schools: 7
     7 Primary; 0 Middle; 0 High; 0 Other Level
     6 Regular; 0 Special Education; 0 Vocational; 1 Alternative
     0 Magnet; 0 Charter; 3 Title I Eligible; 0 School-wide Title I
Students: 2,252   (50.5% male; 49.4% female)
     Individual Education Program: 352 (15.6%);
     English Language Learner: 581 (25.8%); Migrant: 102 (4.5%)
     Eligible for Free Lunch Program: 680 (30.2%)
     Eligible for Reduced-Price Lunch Program: 173 (7.7%)
Teachers: 121.2 (18.6 to 1)
Librarians/Media Specialists: 6.0 (375.3 to 1)
Guidance Counselors: 0.0 (n/a to 1)
Current Spending: ($ per student per year):
     Total: $7,604; Instruction: $4,327; Support Services: $2,891
Enrollment, Drop-out Rates and Diploma Recipients by Race/Ethnicity

Category	Total	White	Black	Asian	AIAN	Hisp.
Enrollment (%)	100.0	48.7	2.7	4.2	0.5	35.0
Drop-out Rate (%)	n/a	n/a	n/a	n/a	n/a	n/a
H.S. Diplomas (#)	n/a	n/a	n/a	n/a	n/a	n/a

Santa Cruz City High

405 Old San Jose Rd • Soquel, CA 95073
(831) 429-3800 • http://www.sccs.santacruz.k12.ca.us/
Grade Span: KG-12; **Agency Type:** 2
Schools: 9
     0 Primary; 2 Middle; 6 High; 1 Other Level
     6 Regular; 0 Special Education; 0 Vocational; 3 Alternative
     0 Magnet; 1 Charter; 6 Title I Eligible; 0 School-wide Title I
Students: 5,432   (53.4% male; 46.5% female)
     Individual Education Program: 690 (12.7%);
     English Language Learner: 462 (8.5%); Migrant: 72 (1.3%)
     Eligible for Free Lunch Program: 727 (13.4%)
     Eligible for Reduced-Price Lunch Program: 195 (3.6%)
Teachers: 217.6 (25.0 to 1)
Librarians/Media Specialists: 5.0 (1,086.4 to 1)
Guidance Counselors: 8.3 (654.5 to 1)
Current Spending: ($ per student per year):
     Total: n/a; Instruction: n/a; Support Services: n/a

Enrollment, Drop-out Rates and Diploma Recipients by Race/Ethnicity

Category	Total	White	Black	Asian	AIAN	Hisp.
Enrollment (%)	100.0	64.0	2.0	4.0	0.5	22.8
Drop-out Rate (%)	n/a	n/a	n/a	n/a	n/a	n/a
H.S. Diplomas (#)	1,051	804	31	54	3	151

Scotts Valley Unified
4444 Scotts Valley Dr Ste 5b • Scotts Valley, CA 95066-4529
(831) 438-1820 • http://www.svusd.santacruz.k12.ca.us/
Grade Span: KG-12; **Agency Type:** 1
Schools: 4
  2 Primary; 1 Middle; 1 High; 0 Other Level
  4 Regular; 0 Special Education; 0 Vocational; 0 Alternative
  0 Magnet; 0 Charter; 2 Title I Eligible; 0 School-wide Title I
Students: 2,763 (50.9% male; 49.0% female)
  Individual Education Program: 226 (8.2%);
  English Language Learner: 40 (1.4%); Migrant: 0 (0.0%)
  Eligible for Free Lunch Program: 101 (3.7%)
  Eligible for Reduced-Price Lunch Program: 38 (1.4%)
Teachers: 130.8 (21.1 to 1)
Librarians/Media Specialists: 0.0 (n/a to 1)
Guidance Counselors: 4.8 (575.6 to 1)
Current Spending: ($ per student per year):
  Total: $6,264; Instruction: $4,388; Support Services: $1,739
Enrollment, Drop-out Rates and Diploma Recipients by Race/Ethnicity

Category	Total	White	Black	Asian	AIAN	Hisp.
Enrollment (%)	100.0	80.6	1.1	6.8	0.5	7.5
Drop-out Rate (%)	n/a	n/a	n/a	n/a	n/a	n/a
H.S. Diplomas (#)	0	0	0	0	0	0

Soquel Union Elementary
620 Monterey Ave • Capitola, CA 95010-3618
(831) 464-5630 • http://www.soqueldo.santacruz.k12.ca.us/
Grade Span: KG-08; **Agency Type:** 1
Schools: 5
  4 Primary; 1 Middle; 0 High; 0 Other Level
  5 Regular; 0 Special Education; 0 Vocational; 0 Alternative
  0 Magnet; 0 Charter; 3 Title I Eligible; 0 School-wide Title I
Students: 2,030 (51.2% male; 48.7% female)
  Individual Education Program: 195 (9.6%);
  English Language Learner: 211 (10.4%); Migrant: 0 (0.0%)
  Eligible for Free Lunch Program: 348 (17.1%)
  Eligible for Reduced-Price Lunch Program: 157 (7.7%)
Teachers: 103.2 (19.7 to 1)
Librarians/Media Specialists: 0.0 (n/a to 1)
Guidance Counselors: 1.0 (2,030.0 to 1)
Current Spending: ($ per student per year):
  Total: $6,953; Instruction: $4,443; Support Services: $2,277
Enrollment, Drop-out Rates and Diploma Recipients by Race/Ethnicity

Category	Total	White	Black	Asian	AIAN	Hisp.
Enrollment (%)	100.0	67.5	2.6	4.3	0.4	25.0
Drop-out Rate (%)	n/a	n/a	n/a	n/a	n/a	n/a
H.S. Diplomas (#)	n/a	n/a	n/a	n/a	n/a	n/a

Shasta County

Anderson Union High
1469 Ferry St • Anderson, CA 96007-3313
(530) 378-0568 • http://forest.anderson.k12.ca.us/
Grade Span: 09-12; **Agency Type:** 1
Schools: 6
  0 Primary; 0 Middle; 6 High; 0 Other Level
  3 Regular; 0 Special Education; 0 Vocational; 3 Alternative
  0 Magnet; 1 Charter; 4 Title I Eligible; 0 School-wide Title I
Students: 2,382 (52.7% male; 47.2% female)
  Individual Education Program: 195 (8.2%);
  English Language Learner: 15 (0.6%); Migrant: 22 (0.9%)
  Eligible for Free Lunch Program: 519 (21.8%)
  Eligible for Reduced-Price Lunch Program: 142 (6.0%)
Teachers: 98.8 (24.1 to 1)
Librarians/Media Specialists: 2.0 (1,191.0 to 1)
Guidance Counselors: 6.6 (360.9 to 1)
Current Spending: ($ per student per year):
  Total: $7,839; Instruction: $4,574; Support Services: $2,991
Enrollment, Drop-out Rates and Diploma Recipients by Race/Ethnicity

Category	Total	White	Black	Asian	AIAN	Hisp.
Enrollment (%)	100.0	83.0	0.6	2.6	6.2	7.0
Drop-out Rate (%)	n/a	n/a	n/a	n/a	n/a	n/a
H.S. Diplomas (#)	475	409	3	16	21	26

Cascade Union Elementary
1645 W Mill St • Anderson, CA 96007-3226
(530) 378-7000 • http://www.shastalink.k12.ca.us/cascade
Grade Span: KG-08; **Agency Type:** 1
Schools: 5

  4 Primary; 1 Middle; 0 High; 0 Other Level
  4 Regular; 0 Special Education; 0 Vocational; 1 Alternative
  0 Magnet; 0 Charter; 5 Title I Eligible; 5 School-wide Title I
Students: 1,554 (54.3% male; 45.6% female)
  Individual Education Program: 227 (14.6%);
  English Language Learner: 80 (5.1%); Migrant: 38 (2.4%)
  Eligible for Free Lunch Program: 849 (54.6%)
  Eligible for Reduced-Price Lunch Program: 286 (18.4%)
Teachers: 79.4 (19.6 to 1)
Librarians/Media Specialists: 0.0 (n/a to 1)
Guidance Counselors: 1.0 (1,554.0 to 1)
Current Spending: ($ per student per year):
  Total: $8,019; Instruction: $4,936; Support Services: $2,617
Enrollment, Drop-out Rates and Diploma Recipients by Race/Ethnicity

Category	Total	White	Black	Asian	AIAN	Hisp.
Enrollment (%)	100.0	71.6	1.3	2.6	12.0	9.1
Drop-out Rate (%)	n/a	n/a	n/a	n/a	n/a	n/a
H.S. Diplomas (#)	n/a	n/a	n/a	n/a	n/a	n/a

Enterprise Elementary
1155 Mistletoe Ln • Redding, CA 96002-0749
(530) 224-4100 • http://www.enterprise.k12.ca.us/
Grade Span: KG-10; **Agency Type:** 1
Schools: 9
  7 Primary; 1 Middle; 0 High; 1 Other Level
  8 Regular; 0 Special Education; 0 Vocational; 1 Alternative
  0 Magnet; 1 Charter; 8 Title I Eligible; 6 School-wide Title I
Students: 3,761 (51.7% male; 48.2% female)
  Individual Education Program: 350 (9.3%);
  English Language Learner: 230 (6.1%); Migrant: 20 (0.5%)
  Eligible for Free Lunch Program: 1,555 (41.3%)
  Eligible for Reduced-Price Lunch Program: 603 (16.0%)
Teachers: 188.5 (20.0 to 1)
Librarians/Media Specialists: 0.0 (n/a to 1)
Guidance Counselors: 1.0 (3,761.0 to 1)
Current Spending: ($ per student per year):
  Total: $7,083; Instruction: $4,801; Support Services: $1,977
Enrollment, Drop-out Rates and Diploma Recipients by Race/Ethnicity

Category	Total	White	Black	Asian	AIAN	Hisp.
Enrollment (%)	100.0	73.8	3.5	8.1	4.3	8.9
Drop-out Rate (%)	n/a	n/a	n/a	n/a	n/a	n/a
H.S. Diplomas (#)	n/a	n/a	n/a	n/a	n/a	n/a

Gateway Unified
4411 Mountain Lakes Blvd • Redding, CA 96003-1446
(530) 245-7900 • http://www.gsd.k12.ca.us/
Grade Span: KG-12; **Agency Type:** 1
Schools: 11
  5 Primary; 2 Middle; 3 High; 1 Other Level
  8 Regular; 0 Special Education; 0 Vocational; 3 Alternative
  0 Magnet; 1 Charter; 6 Title I Eligible; 5 School-wide Title I
Students: 3,612 (52.9% male; 47.0% female)
  Individual Education Program: 428 (11.8%);
  English Language Learner: 149 (4.1%); Migrant: 11 (0.3%)
  Eligible for Free Lunch Program: 1,534 (42.5%)
  Eligible for Reduced-Price Lunch Program: 447 (12.4%)
Teachers: 193.7 (18.6 to 1)
Librarians/Media Specialists: 0.8 (4,515.0 to 1)
Guidance Counselors: 3.1 (1,165.2 to 1)
Current Spending: ($ per student per year):
  Total: $7,722; Instruction: $4,935; Support Services: $2,485
Enrollment, Drop-out Rates and Diploma Recipients by Race/Ethnicity

Category	Total	White	Black	Asian	AIAN	Hisp.
Enrollment (%)	100.0	77.9	1.6	3.9	10.0	6.6
Drop-out Rate (%)	n/a	n/a	n/a	n/a	n/a	n/a
H.S. Diplomas (#)	259	206	1	4	28	20

Redding Elementary
5885 E Bonnyview Rd • Redding, CA 96099-2418
Mailing Address: PO Box 992418 • Redding, CA 96099-2418
(530) 225-0011 • http://redding.echalk.com/
Grade Span: KG-12; **Agency Type:** 1
Schools: 14
  10 Primary; 1 Middle; 1 High; 2 Other Level
  13 Regular; 0 Special Education; 0 Vocational; 1 Alternative
  0 Magnet; 6 Charter; 6 Title I Eligible; 6 School-wide Title I
Students: 4,025 (53.3% male; 46.6% female)
  Individual Education Program: 368 (9.1%);
  English Language Learner: 107 (2.7%); Migrant: 11 (0.3%)
  Eligible for Free Lunch Program: 1,469 (36.5%)
  Eligible for Reduced-Price Lunch Program: 474 (11.8%)
Teachers: 192.2 (20.9 to 1)
Librarians/Media Specialists: 0.0 (n/a to 1)
Guidance Counselors: 3.0 (1,341.7 to 1)
Current Spending: ($ per student per year):
  Total: $6,912; Instruction: $4,585; Support Services: $2,020

Enrollment, Drop-out Rates and Diploma Recipients by Race/Ethnicity

Category	Total	White	Black	Asian	AIAN	Hisp.
Enrollment (%)	100.0	82.5	3.0	4.2	3.8	6.0
Drop-out Rate (%)	n/a	n/a	n/a	n/a	n/a	n/a
H.S. Diplomas (#)	3	3	0	0	0	0

Shasta Union High
2200 Eureka Way Ste B • Redding, CA 96001-1012
(530) 241-3261 • http://www.suhsd.net/
Grade Span: KG-12; **Agency Type:** 1
Schools: 9
　1 Primary; 0 Middle; 7 High; 1 Other Level
　5 Regular; 0 Special Education; 0 Vocational; 4 Alternative
　0 Magnet; 2 Charter; 3 Title I Eligible; 0 School-wide Title I
Students: 5,838　(50.7% male; 49.2% female)
　Individual Education Program: 391 (6.7%);
　English Language Learner: 47 (0.8%); Migrant: 22 (0.4%)
　Eligible for Free Lunch Program: 1,152 (19.7%)
　Eligible for Reduced-Price Lunch Program: 416 (7.1%)
Teachers: 244.6 (23.9 to 1)
Librarians/Media Specialists: 1.0 (5,838.0 to 1)
Guidance Counselors: 14.7 (397.1 to 1)
Current Spending: ($ per student per year):
　Total: $7,487; Instruction: $4,457; Support Services: $2,847

Enrollment, Drop-out Rates and Diploma Recipients by Race/Ethnicity

Category	Total	White	Black	Asian	AIAN	Hisp.
Enrollment (%)	100.0	83.0	1.2	6.5	3.4	4.6
Drop-out Rate (%)	n/a	n/a	n/a	n/a	n/a	n/a
H.S. Diplomas (#)	1,055	893	13	62	39	47

Solano County

Benicia Unified
350 E K St • Benicia, CA 94510-3437
(707) 747-8300 • http://www.benicia.k12.ca.us/
Grade Span: KG-12; **Agency Type:** 1
Schools: 9
　5 Primary; 1 Middle; 2 High; 1 Other Level
　7 Regular; 0 Special Education; 0 Vocational; 2 Alternative
　0 Magnet; 0 Charter; 4 Title I Eligible; 0 School-wide Title I
Students: 5,366　(50.8% male; 49.1% female)
　Individual Education Program: 540 (10.1%);
　English Language Learner: 118 (2.2%); Migrant: 0 (0.0%)
　Eligible for Free Lunch Program: 275 (5.1%)
　Eligible for Reduced-Price Lunch Program: 165 (3.1%)
Teachers: 260.0 (20.6 to 1)
Librarians/Media Specialists: 0.0 (n/a to 1)
Guidance Counselors: 2.8 (1,916.4 to 1)
Current Spending: ($ per student per year):
　Total: $6,591; Instruction: $4,358; Support Services: $2,029

Enrollment, Drop-out Rates and Diploma Recipients by Race/Ethnicity

Category	Total	White	Black	Asian	AIAN	Hisp.
Enrollment (%)	100.0	66.8	8.6	13.1	0.6	10.7
Drop-out Rate (%)	n/a	n/a	n/a	n/a	n/a	n/a
H.S. Diplomas (#)	416	285	24	53	3	50

Dixon Unified
180 S First St #6 • Dixon, CA 95620-2702
(707) 678-5582 • http://www.dixonusd.org/
Grade Span: KG-12; **Agency Type:** 1
Schools: 8
　4 Primary; 1 Middle; 3 High; 0 Other Level
　6 Regular; 0 Special Education; 0 Vocational; 2 Alternative
　0 Magnet; 0 Charter; 7 Title I Eligible; 0 School-wide Title I
Students: 3,929　(52.4% male; 47.5% female)
　Individual Education Program: 421 (10.7%);
　English Language Learner: 633 (16.1%); Migrant: 538 (13.7%)
　Eligible for Free Lunch Program: 1,171 (29.8%)
　Eligible for Reduced-Price Lunch Program: 405 (10.3%)
Teachers: 184.4 (21.3 to 1)
Librarians/Media Specialists: 1.0 (3,929.0 to 1)
Guidance Counselors: 4.5 (873.1 to 1)
Current Spending: ($ per student per year):
　Total: $6,500; Instruction: $4,297; Support Services: $1,946

Enrollment, Drop-out Rates and Diploma Recipients by Race/Ethnicity

Category	Total	White	Black	Asian	AIAN	Hisp.
Enrollment (%)	100.0	46.6	2.4	3.0	0.7	46.3
Drop-out Rate (%)	n/a	n/a	n/a	n/a	n/a	n/a
H.S. Diplomas (#)	200	108	10	7	1	74

Fairfield-Suisun Unified
1975 Pennsylvania Ave • Fairfield, CA 94533-3643
(707) 399-5000 • http://www.fsusd.k12.ca.us/
Grade Span: KG-12; **Agency Type:** 1
Schools: 27

　17 Primary; 5 Middle; 5 High; 0 Other Level
　25 Regular; 0 Special Education; 0 Vocational; 2 Alternative
　0 Magnet; 0 Charter; 9 Title I Eligible; 5 School-wide Title I
Students: 23,241　(50.4% male; 49.5% female)
　Individual Education Program: 2,427 (10.4%);
　English Language Learner: 2,780 (12.0%); Migrant: 330 (1.4%)
　Eligible for Free Lunch Program: 6,728 (28.9%)
　Eligible for Reduced-Price Lunch Program: 2,246 (9.7%)
Teachers: 1,114.1 (20.9 to 1)
Librarians/Media Specialists: 11.0 (2,112.8 to 1)
Guidance Counselors: 14.0 (1,660.1 to 1)
Current Spending: ($ per student per year):
　Total: $6,296; Instruction: $3,931; Support Services: $2,130

Enrollment, Drop-out Rates and Diploma Recipients by Race/Ethnicity

Category	Total	White	Black	Asian	AIAN	Hisp.
Enrollment (%)	100.0	33.7	22.5	16.0	0.9	26.8
Drop-out Rate (%)	n/a	n/a	n/a	n/a	n/a	n/a
H.S. Diplomas (#)	1,106	470	225	232	10	169

Travis Unified
2751 De Ronde Dr • Travis Afb, CA 94533-9710
(707) 437-4604 • http://www.travisusd.k12.ca.us/
Grade Span: KG-12; **Agency Type:** 1
Schools: 10
　5 Primary; 1 Middle; 3 High; 0 Other Level
　7 Regular; 0 Special Education; 0 Vocational; 2 Alternative
　3 Magnet; 0 Charter; 3 Title I Eligible; 0 School-wide Title I
Students: 5,380　(51.3% male; 48.6% female)
　Individual Education Program: 604 (11.2%);
　English Language Learner: 191 (3.6%); Migrant: 0 (0.0%)
　Eligible for Free Lunch Program: 367 (6.8%)
　Eligible for Reduced-Price Lunch Program: 548 (10.2%)
Teachers: 280.6 (19.2 to 1)
Librarians/Media Specialists: 3.0 (1,793.3 to 1)
Guidance Counselors: 6.0 (896.7 to 1)
Current Spending: ($ per student per year):
　Total: $7,393; Instruction: $4,663; Support Services: $2,530

Enrollment, Drop-out Rates and Diploma Recipients by Race/Ethnicity

Category	Total	White	Black	Asian	AIAN	Hisp.
Enrollment (%)	100.0	54.4	15.5	13.8	1.0	12.2
Drop-out Rate (%)	n/a	n/a	n/a	n/a	n/a	n/a
H.S. Diplomas (#)	292	146	64	42	0	40

Vacaville Unified
751 School St • Vacaville, CA 95688-3945
(707) 453-6100 • http://www.vusd.solanocoe.k12.ca.us/
Grade Span: KG-12; **Agency Type:** 1
Schools: 17
　11 Primary; 2 Middle; 3 High; 1 Other Level
　15 Regular; 0 Special Education; 0 Vocational; 2 Alternative
　1 Magnet; 1 Charter; 5 Title I Eligible; 3 School-wide Title I
Students: 13,887　(51.3% male; 48.6% female)
　Individual Education Program: 1,551 (11.2%);
　English Language Learner: 1,455 (10.5%); Migrant: 333 (2.4%)
　Eligible for Free Lunch Program: 2,869 (20.7%)
　Eligible for Reduced-Price Lunch Program: 891 (6.4%)
Teachers: 674.4 (20.6 to 1)
Librarians/Media Specialists: 1.0 (13,887.0 to 1)
Guidance Counselors: 12.0 (1,157.3 to 1)
Current Spending: ($ per student per year):
　Total: $6,413; Instruction: $4,180; Support Services: $2,036

Enrollment, Drop-out Rates and Diploma Recipients by Race/Ethnicity

Category	Total	White	Black	Asian	AIAN	Hisp.
Enrollment (%)	100.0	59.2	8.8	6.1	1.2	22.2
Drop-out Rate (%)	n/a	n/a	n/a	n/a	n/a	n/a
H.S. Diplomas (#)	1,035	688	74	72	15	149

Vallejo City Unified
211 Valle Vista • Vallejo, CA 94590-3256
(707) 556-8921 • http://www.vallejo.k12.ca.us/
Grade Span: KG-12; **Agency Type:** 1
Schools: 29
　17 Primary; 5 Middle; 6 High; 1 Other Level
　26 Regular; 1 Special Education; 0 Vocational; 2 Alternative
　0 Magnet; 2 Charter; 15 Title I Eligible; 10 School-wide Title I
Students: 19,462　(51.4% male; 48.5% female)
　Individual Education Program: 2,295 (11.8%);
　English Language Learner: 3,451 (17.7%); Migrant: 4 (<0.1%)
　Eligible for Free Lunch Program: 6,151 (31.6%)
　Eligible for Reduced-Price Lunch Program: 1,655 (8.5%)
Teachers: 916.1 (21.2 to 1)
Librarians/Media Specialists: 5.0 (3,892.4 to 1)
Guidance Counselors: 26.0 (748.5 to 1)
Current Spending: ($ per student per year):
　Total: $7,703; Instruction: $4,912; Support Services: $2,553

Enrollment, Drop-out Rates and Diploma Recipients by Race/Ethnicity

Category	Total	White	Black	Asian	AIAN	Hisp.
Enrollment (%)	100.0	15.1	34.7	25.1	0.6	23.5
Drop-out Rate (%)	n/a	n/a	n/a	n/a	n/a	n/a
H.S. Diplomas (#)	1,099	180	344	405	14	144

Sonoma County

Bellevue Union Elementary
3223 Primrose Ave • Santa Rosa, CA 95407-7723
(707) 542-5197
Grade Span: KG-06; **Agency Type:** 1
Schools: 3
  3 Primary; 0 Middle; 0 High; 0 Other Level
  3 Regular; 0 Special Education; 0 Vocational; 0 Alternative
  0 Magnet; 0 Charter; 3 Title I Eligible; 0 School-wide Title I
Students: 1,715   (50.2% male; 49.7% female)
  Individual Education Program: 192 (11.2%);
  English Language Learner: 1,133 (66.1%); Migrant: 144 (8.4%)
  Eligible for Free Lunch Program: 1,193 (69.6%)
  Eligible for Reduced-Price Lunch Program: 289 (16.9%)
Teachers: 89.7 (19.1 to 1)
Librarians/Media Specialists: 0.0 (n/a to 1)
Guidance Counselors: 0.2 (8,575.0 to 1)
Current Spending: ($ per student per year):
  Total: $7,522; Instruction: $5,617; Support Services: $1,534

Enrollment, Drop-out Rates and Diploma Recipients by Race/Ethnicity

Category	Total	White	Black	Asian	AIAN	Hisp.
Enrollment (%)	100.0	20.5	3.1	6.1	2.0	67.4
Drop-out Rate (%)	n/a	n/a	n/a	n/a	n/a	n/a
H.S. Diplomas (#)	n/a	n/a	n/a	n/a	n/a	n/a

Cloverdale Unified
97 School St • Cloverdale, CA 95425-3244
(707) 894-1920 • http://www.cusd.org/district/schools.html
Grade Span: KG-12; **Agency Type:** 1
Schools: 4
  1 Primary; 1 Middle; 2 High; 0 Other Level
  3 Regular; 0 Special Education; 0 Vocational; 1 Alternative
  0 Magnet; 0 Charter; 2 Title I Eligible; 1 School-wide Title I
Students: 1,583   (52.4% male; 47.5% female)
  Individual Education Program: 89 (5.6%);
  English Language Learner: 297 (18.8%); Migrant: 290 (18.3%)
  Eligible for Free Lunch Program: 471 (29.8%)
  Eligible for Reduced-Price Lunch Program: 118 (7.5%)
Teachers: 80.5 (19.7 to 1)
Librarians/Media Specialists: 0.0 (n/a to 1)
Guidance Counselors: 1.0 (1,583.0 to 1)
Current Spending: ($ per student per year):
  Total: $7,046; Instruction: $4,907; Support Services: $1,920

Enrollment, Drop-out Rates and Diploma Recipients by Race/Ethnicity

Category	Total	White	Black	Asian	AIAN	Hisp.
Enrollment (%)	100.0	61.5	0.4	0.6	1.5	35.9
Drop-out Rate (%)	n/a	n/a	n/a	n/a	n/a	n/a
H.S. Diplomas (#)	103	78	0	1	2	22

Cotati-Rohnert Park Unified
5860 Labath Ave • Rohnert Park, CA 94928-3606
(707) 792-4722 • http://www.crpusd.sonoma.edu/
Grade Span: KG-12; **Agency Type:** 1
Schools: 15
  8 Primary; 3 Middle; 4 High; 0 Other Level
  11 Regular; 0 Special Education; 0 Vocational; 4 Alternative
  1 Magnet; 0 Charter; 5 Title I Eligible; 1 School-wide Title I
Students: 7,482   (51.8% male; 48.1% female)
  Individual Education Program: 875 (11.7%);
  English Language Learner: 998 (13.3%); Migrant: 110 (1.5%)
  Eligible for Free Lunch Program: 957 (12.8%)
  Eligible for Reduced-Price Lunch Program: 541 (7.2%)
Teachers: 329.7 (22.7 to 1)
Librarians/Media Specialists: 2.0 (3,741.0 to 1)
Guidance Counselors: 9.9 (755.8 to 1)
Current Spending: ($ per student per year):
  Total: $6,875; Instruction: $4,706; Support Services: $1,955

Enrollment, Drop-out Rates and Diploma Recipients by Race/Ethnicity

Category	Total	White	Black	Asian	AIAN	Hisp.
Enrollment (%)	100.0	65.0	3.7	8.6	1.3	20.4
Drop-out Rate (%)	n/a	n/a	n/a	n/a	n/a	n/a
H.S. Diplomas (#)	487	364	13	39	4	66

Healdsburg Unified
1028 Prince St • Healdsburg, CA 95448-3528
(707) 431-3117 • http://www.husd.com/
Grade Span: KG-12; **Agency Type:** 1
Schools: 6

  3 Primary; 1 Middle; 2 High; 0 Other Level
  5 Regular; 0 Special Education; 0 Vocational; 1 Alternative
  0 Magnet; 0 Charter; 3 Title I Eligible; 0 School-wide Title I
Students: 2,734   (52.8% male; 47.1% female)
  Individual Education Program: 263 (9.6%);
  English Language Learner: 636 (23.3%); Migrant: 564 (20.6%)
  Eligible for Free Lunch Program: 712 (26.0%)
  Eligible for Reduced-Price Lunch Program: 331 (12.1%)
Teachers: 125.2 (21.8 to 1)
Librarians/Media Specialists: 0.0 (n/a to 1)
Guidance Counselors: 5.4 (506.3 to 1)
Current Spending: ($ per student per year):
  Total: $7,424; Instruction: $5,025; Support Services: $2,147

Enrollment, Drop-out Rates and Diploma Recipients by Race/Ethnicity

Category	Total	White	Black	Asian	AIAN	Hisp.
Enrollment (%)	100.0	53.6	0.5	0.9	0.6	44.4
Drop-out Rate (%)	n/a	n/a	n/a	n/a	n/a	n/a
H.S. Diplomas (#)	203	148	1	1	2	51

Mark West Union Elementary
305 Mark W Springs Rd • Santa Rosa, CA 95404-1101
(707) 524-2970
Grade Span: KG-06; **Agency Type:** 1
Schools: 3
  3 Primary; 0 Middle; 0 High; 0 Other Level
  3 Regular; 0 Special Education; 0 Vocational; 0 Alternative
  0 Magnet; 0 Charter; 0 Title I Eligible; 0 School-wide Title I
Students: 1,605   (52.4% male; 47.5% female)
  Individual Education Program: 158 (9.8%);
  English Language Learner: 117 (7.3%); Migrant: 10 (0.6%)
  Eligible for Free Lunch Program: 218 (13.6%)
  Eligible for Reduced-Price Lunch Program: 55 (3.4%)
Teachers: 82.0 (19.6 to 1)
Librarians/Media Specialists: 0.0 (n/a to 1)
Guidance Counselors: 1.0 (1,605.0 to 1)
Current Spending: ($ per student per year):
  Total: $6,864; Instruction: $4,899; Support Services: $1,837

Enrollment, Drop-out Rates and Diploma Recipients by Race/Ethnicity

Category	Total	White	Black	Asian	AIAN	Hisp.
Enrollment (%)	100.0	77.3	2.7	4.4	0.9	12.3
Drop-out Rate (%)	n/a	n/a	n/a	n/a	n/a	n/a
H.S. Diplomas (#)	n/a	n/a	n/a	n/a	n/a	n/a

Old Adobe Union Elementary
845 Crinella Dr • Petaluma, CA 94954-4450
(707) 765-4321
Grade Span: KG-06; **Agency Type:** 1
Schools: 5
  5 Primary; 0 Middle; 0 High; 0 Other Level
  5 Regular; 0 Special Education; 0 Vocational; 0 Alternative
  0 Magnet; 0 Charter; 2 Title I Eligible; 0 School-wide Title I
Students: 1,928   (50.6% male; 49.3% female)
  Individual Education Program: 218 (11.3%);
  English Language Learner: 434 (22.5%); Migrant: 53 (2.7%)
  Eligible for Free Lunch Program: 298 (15.5%)
  Eligible for Reduced-Price Lunch Program: 134 (7.0%)
Teachers: 95.9 (20.1 to 1)
Librarians/Media Specialists: 0.0 (n/a to 1)
Guidance Counselors: 0.0 (n/a to 1)
Current Spending: ($ per student per year):
  Total: $6,845; Instruction: $4,760; Support Services: $1,885

Enrollment, Drop-out Rates and Diploma Recipients by Race/Ethnicity

Category	Total	White	Black	Asian	AIAN	Hisp.
Enrollment (%)	100.0	67.0	1.5	7.6	0.9	23.0
Drop-out Rate (%)	n/a	n/a	n/a	n/a	n/a	n/a
H.S. Diplomas (#)	n/a	n/a	n/a	n/a	n/a	n/a

Petaluma City Elementary
200 Douglas St • Petaluma, CA 94952-2575
(707) 778-4604 • http://www.petalumacityschools.org/
Grade Span: KG-08; **Agency Type:** 2
Schools: 9
  9 Primary; 0 Middle; 0 High; 0 Other Level
  8 Regular; 0 Special Education; 0 Vocational; 1 Alternative
  0 Magnet; 2 Charter; 2 Title I Eligible; 2 School-wide Title I
Students: 2,243   (50.8% male; 49.1% female)
  Individual Education Program: 309 (13.8%);
  English Language Learner: 506 (22.6%); Migrant: 50 (2.2%)
  Eligible for Free Lunch Program: 453 (20.2%)
  Eligible for Reduced-Price Lunch Program: 128 (5.7%)
Teachers: 114.6 (19.6 to 1)
Librarians/Media Specialists: 0.0 (n/a to 1)
Guidance Counselors: 0.0 (n/a to 1)
Current Spending: ($ per student per year):
  Total: $7,071; Instruction: $4,609; Support Services: $2,223

Enrollment, Drop-out Rates and Diploma Recipients by Race/Ethnicity

Category	Total	White	Black	Asian	AIAN	Hisp.
Enrollment (%)	100.0	66.2	1.9	3.5	0.7	26.6
Drop-out Rate (%)	n/a	n/a	n/a	n/a	n/a	n/a
H.S. Diplomas (#)	n/a	n/a	n/a	n/a	n/a	n/a

Petaluma Joint Union High
200 Douglas St • Petaluma, CA 94952-2575
(707) 778-4604
Grade Span: KG-12; **Agency Type:** 2
Schools: 10
　1 Primary; 3 Middle; 5 High; 1 Other Level
　5 Regular; 0 Special Education; 0 Vocational; 5 Alternative
　0 Magnet; 1 Charter; 4 Title I Eligible; 0 School-wide Title I
Students: 5,934　(50.2% male; 49.7% female)
　Individual Education Program: 649 (10.9%);
　English Language Learner: 645 (10.9%); Migrant: 98 (1.7%)
　Eligible for Free Lunch Program: 607 (10.2%)
　Eligible for Reduced-Price Lunch Program: 179 (3.0%)
Teachers: 262.5 (22.6 to 1)
Librarians/Media Specialists: 4.0 (1,483.5 to 1)
Guidance Counselors: 13.0 (456.5 to 1)
Current Spending: ($ per student per year):
　Total: n/a; Instruction: n/a; Support Services: n/a
Enrollment, Drop-out Rates and Diploma Recipients by Race/Ethnicity

Category	Total	White	Black	Asian	AIAN	Hisp.
Enrollment (%)	100.0	75.5	1.4	5.0	0.7	17.0
Drop-out Rate (%)	n/a	n/a	n/a	n/a	n/a	n/a
H.S. Diplomas (#)	691	568	5	22	3	93

Piner-Olivet Union Elementary
3450 Coffey Ln • Santa Rosa, CA 95403-1919
(707) 522-3000 • http://www.pousd.k12.ca.us/
Grade Span: KG-08; **Agency Type:** 1
Schools: 5
　4 Primary; 1 Middle; 0 High; 0 Other Level
　5 Regular; 0 Special Education; 0 Vocational; 0 Alternative
　0 Magnet; 1 Charter; 3 Title I Eligible; 0 School-wide Title I
Students: 1,659　(53.5% male; 46.4% female)
　Individual Education Program: 178 (10.7%);
　English Language Learner: 358 (21.6%); Migrant: 18 (1.1%)
　Eligible for Free Lunch Program: 261 (15.7%)
　Eligible for Reduced-Price Lunch Program: 171 (10.3%)
Teachers: 84.0 (19.8 to 1)
Librarians/Media Specialists: 0.0 (n/a to 1)
Guidance Counselors: 0.0 (n/a to 1)
Current Spending: ($ per student per year):
　Total: $6,870; Instruction: $4,849; Support Services: $1,826
Enrollment, Drop-out Rates and Diploma Recipients by Race/Ethnicity

Category	Total	White	Black	Asian	AIAN	Hisp.
Enrollment (%)	100.0	66.4	4.8	8.3	1.3	19.3
Drop-out Rate (%)	n/a	n/a	n/a	n/a	n/a	n/a
H.S. Diplomas (#)	n/a	n/a	n/a	n/a	n/a	n/a

Rincon Valley Union Elementary
1000 Yulupa Ave • Santa Rosa, CA 95405-7020
(707) 542-7375
Grade Span: KG-06; **Agency Type:** 1
Schools: 8
　8 Primary; 0 Middle; 0 High; 0 Other Level
　8 Regular; 0 Special Education; 0 Vocational; 0 Alternative
　0 Magnet; 0 Charter; 5 Title I Eligible; 0 School-wide Title I
Students: 2,770　(50.7% male; 49.2% female)
　Individual Education Program: 330 (11.9%);
　English Language Learner: 152 (5.5%); Migrant: 10 (0.4%)
　Eligible for Free Lunch Program: 435 (15.7%)
　Eligible for Reduced-Price Lunch Program: 198 (7.1%)
Teachers: 142.0 (19.5 to 1)
Librarians/Media Specialists: 0.0 (n/a to 1)
Guidance Counselors: 0.0 (n/a to 1)
Current Spending: ($ per student per year):
　Total: $7,115; Instruction: $4,735; Support Services: $2,127
Enrollment, Drop-out Rates and Diploma Recipients by Race/Ethnicity

Category	Total	White	Black	Asian	AIAN	Hisp.
Enrollment (%)	100.0	73.6	3.9	6.5	1.8	14.1
Drop-out Rate (%)	n/a	n/a	n/a	n/a	n/a	n/a
H.S. Diplomas (#)	n/a	n/a	n/a	n/a	n/a	n/a

Santa Rosa Elementary
211 Ridgway Ave • Santa Rosa, CA 95401-4320
(707) 528-5352 • http://www.srcs.k12.ca.us/
Grade Span: KG-08; **Agency Type:** 2
Schools: 14
　14 Primary; 0 Middle; 0 High; 0 Other Level
　13 Regular; 1 Special Education; 0 Vocational; 0 Alternative

　0 Magnet; 2 Charter; 8 Title I Eligible; 8 School-wide Title I
Students: 4,696　(51.9% male; 48.0% female)
　Individual Education Program: 571 (12.2%);
　English Language Learner: 2,005 (42.7%); Migrant: 473 (10.1%)
　Eligible for Free Lunch Program: 1,784 (38.0%)
　Eligible for Reduced-Price Lunch Program: 672 (14.3%)
Teachers: 273.0 (17.2 to 1)
Librarians/Media Specialists: 0.0 (n/a to 1)
Guidance Counselors: 0.6 (7,826.7 to 1)
Current Spending: ($ per student per year):
　Total: $7,447; Instruction: $4,848; Support Services: $2,288
Enrollment, Drop-out Rates and Diploma Recipients by Race/Ethnicity

Category	Total	White	Black	Asian	AIAN	Hisp.
Enrollment (%)	100.0	37.8	3.3	4.9	1.5	48.0
Drop-out Rate (%)	n/a	n/a	n/a	n/a	n/a	n/a
H.S. Diplomas (#)	n/a	n/a	n/a	n/a	n/a	n/a

Santa Rosa High
211 Ridgway Ave • Santa Rosa, CA 95401-4320
(707) 528-5181 • http://www.srcs.k12.ca.us/
Grade Span: 07-12; **Agency Type:** 2
Schools: 15
　0 Primary; 5 Middle; 10 High; 0 Other Level
　10 Regular; 0 Special Education; 0 Vocational; 5 Alternative
　0 Magnet; 0 Charter; 7 Title I Eligible; 0 School-wide Title I
Students: 12,847　(51.1% male; 48.8% female)
　Individual Education Program: 1,265 (9.8%);
　English Language Learner: 1,988 (15.5%); Migrant: 396 (3.1%)
　Eligible for Free Lunch Program: 1,075 (8.4%)
　Eligible for Reduced-Price Lunch Program: 455 (3.5%)
Teachers: 562.2 (22.9 to 1)
Librarians/Media Specialists: 6.5 (1,976.5 to 1)
Guidance Counselors: 28.0 (458.8 to 1)
Current Spending: ($ per student per year):
　Total: n/a; Instruction: n/a; Support Services: n/a
Enrollment, Drop-out Rates and Diploma Recipients by Race/Ethnicity

Category	Total	White	Black	Asian	AIAN	Hisp.
Enrollment (%)	100.0	59.2	3.0	6.4	1.8	25.2
Drop-out Rate (%)	n/a	n/a	n/a	n/a	n/a	n/a
H.S. Diplomas (#)	1,506	1,045	49	127	16	242

Sonoma Valley Unified
17850 Railroad Ave • Sonoma, CA 95476-6412
(707) 935-6000 • http://www.sonomavly.k12.ca.us/
Grade Span: KG-12; **Agency Type:** 1
Schools: 12
　7 Primary; 1 Middle; 2 High; 1 Other Level
　9 Regular; 0 Special Education; 0 Vocational; 2 Alternative
　0 Magnet; 1 Charter; 6 Title I Eligible; 2 School-wide Title I
Students: 4,921　(52.7% male; 47.2% female)
　Individual Education Program: 572 (11.6%);
　English Language Learner: 1,375 (27.9%); Migrant: 320 (6.5%)
　Eligible for Free Lunch Program: 1,268 (25.8%)
　Eligible for Reduced-Price Lunch Program: 338 (6.9%)
Teachers: 238.3 (20.7 to 1)
Librarians/Media Specialists: 2.0 (2,460.5 to 1)
Guidance Counselors: 9.0 (546.8 to 1)
Current Spending: ($ per student per year):
　Total: $6,997; Instruction: $4,748; Support Services: $2,004
Enrollment, Drop-out Rates and Diploma Recipients by Race/Ethnicity

Category	Total	White	Black	Asian	AIAN	Hisp.
Enrollment (%)	100.0	59.3	0.7	2.1	0.6	36.2
Drop-out Rate (%)	n/a	n/a	n/a	n/a	n/a	n/a
H.S. Diplomas (#)	287	212	4	5	0	65

West Sonoma County Union High
462 Johnson St • Sebastopol, CA 95472-3401
(707) 824-6403 • http://www.wscuhsd.k12.ca.us/
Grade Span: 07-12; **Agency Type:** 1
Schools: 6
　0 Primary; 0 Middle; 6 High; 0 Other Level
　3 Regular; 0 Special Education; 0 Vocational; 3 Alternative
　0 Magnet; 1 Charter; 1 Title I Eligible; 0 School-wide Title I
Students: 2,689　(51.0% male; 48.9% female)
　Individual Education Program: 418 (15.5%);
　English Language Learner: 118 (4.4%); Migrant: 66 (2.5%)
　Eligible for Free Lunch Program: 257 (9.6%)
　Eligible for Reduced-Price Lunch Program: 86 (3.2%)
Teachers: 123.4 (21.8 to 1)
Librarians/Media Specialists: 0.0 (n/a to 1)
Guidance Counselors: 8.9 (302.1 to 1)
Current Spending: ($ per student per year):
　Total: $7,679; Instruction: $5,040; Support Services: $2,431

Enrollment, Drop-out Rates and Diploma Recipients by Race/Ethnicity

Category	Total	White	Black	Asian	AIAN	Hisp.
Enrollment (%)	100.0	77.1	1.2	1.7	1.4	10.7
Drop-out Rate (%)	n/a	n/a	n/a	n/a	n/a	n/a
H.S. Diplomas (#)	590	507	4	19	8	44

Windsor Unified
9291 Old Redwood Hwy Building • Windsor, CA 95492-9217
(707) 837-7700 • http://www.scoe.org/clients/wusd/
Grade Span: KG-12; **Agency Type:** 1
Schools: 7
  3 Primary; 2 Middle; 2 High; 0 Other Level
  6 Regular; 0 Special Education; 0 Vocational; 1 Alternative
  0 Magnet; 1 Charter; 1 Title I Eligible; 0 School-wide Title I
Students: 4,685 (50.2% male; 49.7% female)
  Individual Education Program: 453 (9.7%);
  English Language Learner: 1,067 (22.8%); Migrant: 372 (7.9%)
  Eligible for Free Lunch Program: 992 (21.2%)
  Eligible for Reduced-Price Lunch Program: 373 (8.0%)
Teachers: 228.9 (20.5 to 1)
Librarians/Media Specialists: 0.0 (n/a to 1)
Guidance Counselors: 6.0 (780.8 to 1)
Current Spending: ($ per student per year):
  Total: $7,218; Instruction: $4,973; Support Services: $2,009

Enrollment, Drop-out Rates and Diploma Recipients by Race/Ethnicity

Category	Total	White	Black	Asian	AIAN	Hisp.
Enrollment (%)	100.0	59.8	1.2	3.1	1.6	33.8
Drop-out Rate (%)	n/a	n/a	n/a	n/a	n/a	n/a
H.S. Diplomas (#)	193	135	4	6	1	47

Stanislaus County

Ceres Unified
2503 Lawrence St • Ceres, CA 95307-0307
Mailing Address: PO Box 307 • Ceres, CA 95307-0307
(209) 538-0141 • http://www.ceres.k12.ca.us/default.htm
Grade Span: KG-12; **Agency Type:** 1
Schools: 13
  7 Primary; 2 Middle; 2 High; 2 Other Level
  11 Regular; 0 Special Education; 0 Vocational; 2 Alternative
  0 Magnet; 1 Charter; 11 Title I Eligible; 7 School-wide Title I
Students: 10,211 (50.9% male; 49.0% female)
  Individual Education Program: 1,129 (11.1%);
  English Language Learner: 2,120 (20.8%); Migrant: 1,181 (11.6%)
  Eligible for Free Lunch Program: 4,772 (46.7%)
  Eligible for Reduced-Price Lunch Program: 1,334 (13.1%)
Teachers: 473.0 (21.6 to 1)
Librarians/Media Specialists: 2.0 (5,105.5 to 1)
Guidance Counselors: 6.0 (1,701.8 to 1)
Current Spending: ($ per student per year):
  Total: $7,023; Instruction: $4,608; Support Services: $2,121

Enrollment, Drop-out Rates and Diploma Recipients by Race/Ethnicity

Category	Total	White	Black	Asian	AIAN	Hisp.
Enrollment (%)	100.0	36.3	2.9	6.3	2.0	51.0
Drop-out Rate (%)	n/a	n/a	n/a	n/a	n/a	n/a
H.S. Diplomas (#)	578	250	15	10	4	259

Empire Union Elementary
116 N Mcclure Rd • Modesto, CA 95357-1329
(209) 521-2800 • http://www.empire.k12.ca.us/
Grade Span: KG-08; **Agency Type:** 1
Schools: 7
  5 Primary; 2 Middle; 0 High; 0 Other Level
  7 Regular; 0 Special Education; 0 Vocational; 0 Alternative
  0 Magnet; 0 Charter; 6 Title I Eligible; 4 School-wide Title I
Students: 4,066 (52.8% male; 47.1% female)
  Individual Education Program: 465 (11.4%);
  English Language Learner: 873 (21.5%); Migrant: 318 (7.8%)
  Eligible for Free Lunch Program: 1,724 (42.4%)
  Eligible for Reduced-Price Lunch Program: 629 (15.5%)
Teachers: 200.1 (20.3 to 1)
Librarians/Media Specialists: 1.0 (4,066.0 to 1)
Guidance Counselors: 3.5 (1,161.7 to 1)
Current Spending: ($ per student per year):
  Total: $6,578; Instruction: $4,369; Support Services: $1,860

Enrollment, Drop-out Rates and Diploma Recipients by Race/Ethnicity

Category	Total	White	Black	Asian	AIAN	Hisp.
Enrollment (%)	100.0	40.2	5.9	8.4	0.7	41.8
Drop-out Rate (%)	n/a	n/a	n/a	n/a	n/a	n/a
H.S. Diplomas (#)	n/a	n/a	n/a	n/a	n/a	n/a

Hughson Unified
7448 Fox Rd • Hughson, CA 95326
Mailing Address: PO Box 189 • Hughson, CA 95326
(209) 883-4428 • http://stan-co.k12.ca.us/hughson/do/welcome.html
Grade Span: KG-12; **Agency Type:** 1
Schools: 5
  1 Primary; 2 Middle; 2 High; 0 Other Level
  4 Regular; 0 Special Education; 0 Vocational; 1 Alternative
  0 Magnet; 0 Charter; 3 Title I Eligible; 1 School-wide Title I
Students: 2,048 (50.6% male; 49.3% female)
  Individual Education Program: 158 (7.7%);
  English Language Learner: 440 (21.5%); Migrant: 458 (22.4%)
  Eligible for Free Lunch Program: 751 (36.7%)
  Eligible for Reduced-Price Lunch Program: 157 (7.7%)
Teachers: 97.9 (20.9 to 1)
Librarians/Media Specialists: 0.0 (n/a to 1)
Guidance Counselors: 2.0 (1,024.0 to 1)
Current Spending: ($ per student per year):
  Total: $7,199; Instruction: $4,659; Support Services: $2,161

Enrollment, Drop-out Rates and Diploma Recipients by Race/Ethnicity

Category	Total	White	Black	Asian	AIAN	Hisp.
Enrollment (%)	100.0	58.0	1.5	3.0	0.2	37.0
Drop-out Rate (%)	n/a	n/a	n/a	n/a	n/a	n/a
H.S. Diplomas (#)	191	141	0	3	0	46

Keyes Union Elementary
5465 Seventh St • Keyes, CA 95328-0549
Mailing Address: PO Box 549 • Keyes, CA 95328-0549
(209) 669-2921
Grade Span: KG-12; **Agency Type:** 1
Schools: 6
  3 Primary; 1 Middle; 0 High; 2 Other Level
  6 Regular; 0 Special Education; 0 Vocational; 0 Alternative
  0 Magnet; 4 Charter; 3 Title I Eligible; 1 School-wide Title I
Students: 1,805 (49.6% male; 50.3% female)
  Individual Education Program: 179 (9.9%);
  English Language Learner: 306 (17.0%); Migrant: 147 (8.1%)
  Eligible for Free Lunch Program: 741 (41.1%)
  Eligible for Reduced-Price Lunch Program: 70 (3.9%)
Teachers: 93.9 (19.2 to 1)
Librarians/Media Specialists: 0.0 (n/a to 1)
Guidance Counselors: 0.0 (n/a to 1)
Current Spending: ($ per student per year):
  Total: $6,632; Instruction: $2,794; Support Services: $3,632

Enrollment, Drop-out Rates and Diploma Recipients by Race/Ethnicity

Category	Total	White	Black	Asian	AIAN	Hisp.
Enrollment (%)	100.0	49.5	3.5	3.3	1.1	38.8
Drop-out Rate (%)	n/a	n/a	n/a	n/a	n/a	n/a
H.S. Diplomas (#)	1	1	0	0	0	0

Modesto City Elementary
426 Locust St • Modesto, CA 95351-2631
(209) 576-4011 • http://www.monet.k12.ca.us/
Grade Span: KG-08; **Agency Type:** 2
Schools: 27
  23 Primary; 4 Middle; 0 High; 0 Other Level
  27 Regular; 0 Special Education; 0 Vocational; 0 Alternative
  0 Magnet; 0 Charter; 24 Title I Eligible; 15 School-wide Title I
Students: 18,803 (51.4% male; 48.5% female)
  Individual Education Program: 2,576 (13.7%);
  English Language Learner: 6,113 (32.5%); Migrant: 1,441 (7.7%)
  Eligible for Free Lunch Program: 11,821 (62.9%)
  Eligible for Reduced-Price Lunch Program: 2,005 (10.7%)
Teachers: 925.4 (20.3 to 1)
Librarians/Media Specialists: 19.5 (964.3 to 1)
Guidance Counselors: 0.0 (n/a to 1)
Current Spending: ($ per student per year):
  Total: $6,891; Instruction: $4,363; Support Services: $2,252

Enrollment, Drop-out Rates and Diploma Recipients by Race/Ethnicity

Category	Total	White	Black	Asian	AIAN	Hisp.
Enrollment (%)	100.0	28.6	5.1	7.2	1.0	57.8
Drop-out Rate (%)	n/a	n/a	n/a	n/a	n/a	n/a
H.S. Diplomas (#)	n/a	n/a	n/a	n/a	n/a	n/a

Modesto City High
426 Locust St • Modesto, CA 95351-2631
(209) 576-4011 • http://www.monet.k12.ca.us/
Grade Span: 07-12; **Agency Type:** 2
Schools: 6
  0 Primary; 0 Middle; 5 High; 1 Other Level
  5 Regular; 0 Special Education; 0 Vocational; 1 Alternative
  0 Magnet; 0 Charter; 2 Title I Eligible; 0 School-wide Title I
Students: 15,581 (49.5% male; 50.4% female)
  Individual Education Program: 1,709 (11.0%);
  English Language Learner: 2,291 (14.7%); Migrant: 606 (3.9%)

Eligible for Free Lunch Program: 4,196 (26.9%)
Eligible for Reduced-Price Lunch Program: 719 (4.6%)
Teachers: 631.5 (24.7 to 1)
Librarians/Media Specialists: 4.0 (3,895.3 to 1)
Guidance Counselors: 34.7 (449.0 to 1)
Current Spending: ($ per student per year):
Total: n/a; Instruction: n/a; Support Services: n/a
Enrollment, Drop-out Rates and Diploma Recipients by Race/Ethnicity

Category	Total	White	Black	Asian	AIAN	Hisp.
Enrollment (%)	100.0	45.3	5.1	10.4	1.1	37.2
Drop-out Rate (%)	n/a	n/a	n/a	n/a	n/a	n/a
H.S. Diplomas (#)	2,815	1,476	117	350	28	844

Newman-Crows Landing Unified
890 Main St • Newman, CA 95360-1199
(209) 862-2933 • http://nclusd.k12.ca.us/
Grade Span: KG-12; **Agency Type:** 1
Schools: 9
3 Primary; 2 Middle; 3 High; 1 Other Level
5 Regular; 0 Special Education; 0 Vocational; 4 Alternative
0 Magnet; 0 Charter; 5 Title I Eligible; 4 School-wide Title I
Students: 2,293   (52.3% male; 47.6% female)
Individual Education Program: 231 (10.1%);
English Language Learner: 753 (32.8%); Migrant: 485 (21.2%)
Eligible for Free Lunch Program: 985 (43.0%)
Eligible for Reduced-Price Lunch Program: 280 (12.2%)
Teachers: 120.0 (19.1 to 1)
Librarians/Media Specialists: 0.0 (n/a to 1)
Guidance Counselors: 1.0 (2,293.0 to 1)
Current Spending: ($ per student per year):
Total: $6,829; Instruction: $4,424; Support Services: $2,114
Enrollment, Drop-out Rates and Diploma Recipients by Race/Ethnicity

Category	Total	White	Black	Asian	AIAN	Hisp.
Enrollment (%)	100.0	30.9	1.9	1.8	0.3	62.4
Drop-out Rate (%)	n/a	n/a	n/a	n/a	n/a	n/a
H.S. Diplomas (#)	146	51	2	4	0	89

Oakdale Joint Unified
168 S Third Ave • Oakdale, CA 95361-3935
(209) 848-4884 • http://www.oakdale.k12.ca.us/
Grade Span: KG-12; **Agency Type:** 1
Schools: 8
3 Primary; 1 Middle; 4 High; 0 Other Level
5 Regular; 0 Special Education; 0 Vocational; 3 Alternative
0 Magnet; 1 Charter; 4 Title I Eligible; 2 School-wide Title I
Students: 4,984   (51.0% male; 48.9% female)
Individual Education Program: 524 (10.5%);
English Language Learner: 462 (9.3%); Migrant: 560 (11.2%)
Eligible for Free Lunch Program: 1,460 (29.3%)
Eligible for Reduced-Price Lunch Program: 378 (7.6%)
Teachers: 228.3 (21.8 to 1)
Librarians/Media Specialists: 0.0 (n/a to 1)
Guidance Counselors: 5.0 (996.8 to 1)
Current Spending: ($ per student per year):
Total: $6,849; Instruction: $4,440; Support Services: $2,176
Enrollment, Drop-out Rates and Diploma Recipients by Race/Ethnicity

Category	Total	White	Black	Asian	AIAN	Hisp.
Enrollment (%)	100.0	70.6	0.8	1.6	1.1	23.7
Drop-out Rate (%)	n/a	n/a	n/a	n/a	n/a	n/a
H.S. Diplomas (#)	357	293	0	6	2	52

Patterson Joint Unified
200 N Seventh St • Patterson, CA 95363-0547
Mailing Address: PO Box 547 • Patterson, CA 95363-0547
(209) 892-3700 • http://www.stan-co.k12.ca.us/Patterson/welcome.htm
Grade Span: KG-12; **Agency Type:** 1
Schools: 7
3 Primary; 2 Middle; 2 High; 0 Other Level
6 Regular; 0 Special Education; 0 Vocational; 1 Alternative
0 Magnet; 1 Charter; 6 Title I Eligible; 2 School-wide Title I
Students: 4,407   (50.9% male; 49.0% female)
Individual Education Program: 502 (11.4%);
English Language Learner: 1,841 (41.8%); Migrant: 1,003 (22.8%)
Eligible for Free Lunch Program: 2,004 (45.5%)
Eligible for Reduced-Price Lunch Program: 533 (12.1%)
Teachers: 208.3 (21.2 to 1)
Librarians/Media Specialists: 1.0 (4,407.0 to 1)
Guidance Counselors: 4.0 (1,101.8 to 1)
Current Spending: ($ per student per year):
Total: $6,649; Instruction: $4,170; Support Services: $2,169
Enrollment, Drop-out Rates and Diploma Recipients by Race/Ethnicity

Category	Total	White	Black	Asian	AIAN	Hisp.
Enrollment (%)	100.0	23.8	2.9	3.2	0.9	68.9
Drop-out Rate (%)	n/a	n/a	n/a	n/a	n/a	n/a
H.S. Diplomas (#)	211	76	5	3	0	127

Riverbank Unified
6715 7th St • Riverbank, CA 95367-2345
(209) 869-2538 • http://stan-co.k12.ca.us/riverbank/
Grade Span: KG-12; **Agency Type:** 1
Schools: 5
3 Primary; 1 Middle; 1 High; 0 Other Level
5 Regular; 0 Special Education; 0 Vocational; 0 Alternative
0 Magnet; 0 Charter; 5 Title I Eligible; 4 School-wide Title I
Students: 3,102   (52.1% male; 47.8% female)
Individual Education Program: 285 (9.2%);
English Language Learner: 1,289 (41.6%); Migrant: 793 (25.6%)
Eligible for Free Lunch Program: 1,389 (44.8%)
Eligible for Reduced-Price Lunch Program: 420 (13.5%)
Teachers: 154.3 (20.1 to 1)
Librarians/Media Specialists: 0.0 (n/a to 1)
Guidance Counselors: 4.0 (775.5 to 1)
Current Spending: ($ per student per year):
Total: $7,720; Instruction: $4,696; Support Services: $2,691
Enrollment, Drop-out Rates and Diploma Recipients by Race/Ethnicity

Category	Total	White	Black	Asian	AIAN	Hisp.
Enrollment (%)	100.0	29.1	2.0	0.7	0.8	66.3
Drop-out Rate (%)	n/a	n/a	n/a	n/a	n/a	n/a
H.S. Diplomas (#)	201	78	1	1	1	120

Salida Union Elementary
4801 Sisk Rd • Salida, CA 95368-9226
(209) 545-0339 • http://www.salida.k12.ca.us/
Grade Span: KG-08; **Agency Type:** 1
Schools: 5
4 Primary; 1 Middle; 0 High; 0 Other Level
5 Regular; 0 Special Education; 0 Vocational; 0 Alternative
0 Magnet; 0 Charter; 4 Title I Eligible; 1 School-wide Title I
Students: 3,458   (51.5% male; 48.4% female)
Individual Education Program: 372 (10.8%);
English Language Learner: 546 (15.8%); Migrant: 197 (5.7%)
Eligible for Free Lunch Program: 995 (28.8%)
Eligible for Reduced-Price Lunch Program: 431 (12.5%)
Teachers: 173.8 (19.9 to 1)
Librarians/Media Specialists: 0.0 (n/a to 1)
Guidance Counselors: 2.0 (1,729.0 to 1)
Current Spending: ($ per student per year):
Total: $6,673; Instruction: $4,237; Support Services: $2,092
Enrollment, Drop-out Rates and Diploma Recipients by Race/Ethnicity

Category	Total	White	Black	Asian	AIAN	Hisp.
Enrollment (%)	100.0	44.2	5.1	6.7	0.6	42.6
Drop-out Rate (%)	n/a	n/a	n/a	n/a	n/a	n/a
H.S. Diplomas (#)	n/a	n/a	n/a	n/a	n/a	n/a

Stanislaus Union Elementary
3601 Carver Rd • Modesto, CA 95356-0926
(209) 529-9546 • http://www.stanunion.k12.ca.us/
Grade Span: KG-08; **Agency Type:** 1
Schools: 6
5 Primary; 1 Middle; 0 High; 0 Other Level
6 Regular; 0 Special Education; 0 Vocational; 0 Alternative
0 Magnet; 0 Charter; 5 Title I Eligible; 2 School-wide Title I
Students: 3,267   (51.4% male; 48.5% female)
Individual Education Program: 402 (12.3%);
English Language Learner: 632 (19.3%); Migrant: 101 (3.1%)
Eligible for Free Lunch Program: 1,325 (40.6%)
Eligible for Reduced-Price Lunch Program: 299 (9.2%)
Teachers: 152.7 (21.4 to 1)
Librarians/Media Specialists: 0.0 (n/a to 1)
Guidance Counselors: 0.0 (n/a to 1)
Current Spending: ($ per student per year):
Total: $6,323; Instruction: $4,461; Support Services: $1,672
Enrollment, Drop-out Rates and Diploma Recipients by Race/Ethnicity

Category	Total	White	Black	Asian	AIAN	Hisp.
Enrollment (%)	100.0	39.2	8.6	14.4	0.7	35.7
Drop-out Rate (%)	n/a	n/a	n/a	n/a	n/a	n/a
H.S. Diplomas (#)	n/a	n/a	n/a	n/a	n/a	n/a

Sylvan Union Elementary
605 Sylvan Ave • Modesto, CA 95350-1517
(209) 574-5000 • http://www.sylvan.k12.ca.us/stockard.html
Grade Span: KG-08; **Agency Type:** 1
Schools: 10
8 Primary; 2 Middle; 0 High; 0 Other Level
10 Regular; 0 Special Education; 0 Vocational; 0 Alternative
0 Magnet; 0 Charter; 5 Title I Eligible; 5 School-wide Title I
Students: 7,733   (51.5% male; 48.4% female)
Individual Education Program: 884 (11.4%);
English Language Learner: 723 (9.3%); Migrant: 16 (0.2%)
Eligible for Free Lunch Program: 1,929 (24.9%)
Eligible for Reduced-Price Lunch Program: 687 (8.9%)

Teachers: 381.4 (20.3 to 1)
Librarians/Media Specialists: 2.8 (2,761.8 to 1)
Guidance Counselors: 6.0 (1,288.8 to 1)
Current Spending: ($ per student per year):
  Total: $6,204; Instruction: $4,204; Support Services: $1,718
Enrollment, Drop-out Rates and Diploma Recipients by Race/Ethnicity

Category	Total	White	Black	Asian	AIAN	Hisp.
Enrollment (%)	100.0	55.0	5.2	7.4	0.8	26.9
Drop-out Rate (%)	n/a	n/a	n/a	n/a	n/a	n/a
H.S. Diplomas (#)	n/a	n/a	n/a	n/a	n/a	n/a

Turlock Joint Elementary
1574 E Canal Dr • Turlock, CA 95381-1105
Mailing Address: PO Box 1105 • Turlock, CA 95381-1105
(209) 667-0645 • http://www.turlock.k12.ca.us/
Grade Span: KG-08; **Agency Type:** 2
Schools: 11
  9 Primary; 2 Middle; 0 High; 0 Other Level
  11 Regular; 0 Special Education; 0 Vocational; 0 Alternative
  1 Magnet; 0 Charter; 8 Title I Eligible; 4 School-wide Title I
Students: 8,939   (51.6% male; 48.3% female)
  Individual Education Program: 1,055 (11.8%)
  English Language Learner: 2,489 (27.8%); Migrant: 397 (4.4%)
  Eligible for Free Lunch Program: 4,161 (46.5%)
  Eligible for Reduced-Price Lunch Program: 898 (10.0%)
Teachers: 438.4 (20.4 to 1)
Librarians/Media Specialists: 0.0 (n/a to 1)
Guidance Counselors: 5.4 (1,655.4 to 1)
Current Spending: ($ per student per year):
  Total: $6,756; Instruction: $4,744; Support Services: $1,721
Enrollment, Drop-out Rates and Diploma Recipients by Race/Ethnicity

Category	Total	White	Black	Asian	AIAN	Hisp.
Enrollment (%)	100.0	43.6	1.9	5.2	0.8	47.3
Drop-out Rate (%)	n/a	n/a	n/a	n/a	n/a	n/a
H.S. Diplomas (#)	n/a	n/a	n/a	n/a	n/a	n/a

Turlock Joint Union High
1574 E Canal Dr • Turlock, CA 95381-1105
Mailing Address: PO Box 810913 • Turlock, CA 95381-9013
(209) 667-0645 • http://www.turlock.k12.ca.us/
Grade Span: 09-12; **Agency Type:** 2
Schools: 4
  0 Primary; 0 Middle; 4 High; 0 Other Level
  2 Regular; 0 Special Education; 0 Vocational; 2 Alternative
  0 Magnet; 0 Charter; 3 Title I Eligible; 0 School-wide Title I
Students: 4,597   (50.3% male; 49.6% female)
  Individual Education Program: 493 (10.7%)
  English Language Learner: 711 (15.5%); Migrant: 208 (4.5%)
  Eligible for Free Lunch Program: 991 (21.6%)
  Eligible for Reduced-Price Lunch Program: 212 (4.6%)
Teachers: 202.2 (22.7 to 1)
Librarians/Media Specialists: 0.0 (n/a to 1)
Guidance Counselors: 11.0 (417.9 to 1)
Current Spending: ($ per student per year):
  Total: $7,107; Instruction: $4,385; Support Services: $2,460
Enrollment, Drop-out Rates and Diploma Recipients by Race/Ethnicity

Category	Total	White	Black	Asian	AIAN	Hisp.
Enrollment (%)	100.0	52.9	1.5	6.1	0.9	37.4
Drop-out Rate (%)	n/a	n/a	n/a	n/a	n/a	n/a
H.S. Diplomas (#)	801	478	10	71	10	232

Waterford Unified
12420 Bentley St • Waterford, CA 95386-9158
(209) 874-1809
Grade Span: KG-12; **Agency Type:** 1
Schools: 4
  1 Primary; 1 Middle; 1 High; 1 Other Level
  4 Regular; 0 Special Education; 0 Vocational; 0 Alternative
  0 Magnet; 1 Charter; 3 Title I Eligible; 3 School-wide Title I
Students: 3,135   (49.8% male; 50.1% female)
  Individual Education Program: 298 (9.5%)
  English Language Learner: 560 (17.9%); Migrant: 375 (12.0%)
  Eligible for Free Lunch Program: 1,143 (36.5%)
  Eligible for Reduced-Price Lunch Program: 173 (5.5%)
Teachers: 157.5 (19.9 to 1)
Librarians/Media Specialists: 0.0 (n/a to 1)
Guidance Counselors: 1.0 (3,135.0 to 1)
Current Spending: ($ per student per year):
  Total: $6,812; Instruction: $3,399; Support Services: $3,209
Enrollment, Drop-out Rates and Diploma Recipients by Race/Ethnicity

Category	Total	White	Black	Asian	AIAN	Hisp.
Enrollment (%)	100.0	50.7	2.9	2.9	2.1	34.2
Drop-out Rate (%)	n/a	n/a	n/a	n/a	n/a	n/a
H.S. Diplomas (#)	32	14	0	2	0	16

Sutter County

Live Oak Unified
2201 Pennington Rd • Live Oak, CA 95953-2469
(530) 695-5400 • http://www.hs.lousd.k12.ca.us/lousd/lousd.htm
Grade Span: KG-12; **Agency Type:** 1
Schools: 6
  2 Primary; 1 Middle; 2 High; 1 Other Level
  4 Regular; 0 Special Education; 0 Vocational; 2 Alternative
  0 Magnet; 0 Charter; 5 Title I Eligible; 5 School-wide Title I
Students: 1,877   (51.0% male; 48.9% female)
  Individual Education Program: 91 (4.8%)
  English Language Learner: 497 (26.5%); Migrant: 364 (19.4%)
  Eligible for Free Lunch Program: 1,118 (59.6%)
  Eligible for Reduced-Price Lunch Program: 259 (13.8%)
Teachers: 88.4 (21.2 to 1)
Librarians/Media Specialists: 0.0 (n/a to 1)
Guidance Counselors: 1.0 (1,877.0 to 1)
Current Spending: ($ per student per year):
  Total: $6,296; Instruction: $3,900; Support Services: $2,089
Enrollment, Drop-out Rates and Diploma Recipients by Race/Ethnicity

Category	Total	White	Black	Asian	AIAN	Hisp.
Enrollment (%)	100.0	30.1	0.4	11.2	1.2	54.1
Drop-out Rate (%)	n/a	n/a	n/a	n/a	n/a	n/a
H.S. Diplomas (#)	104	43	0	14	5	42

Yuba City Unified
750 Palora Ave • Yuba City, CA 95991-3627
(530) 822-5200 • http://www.ycusd.k12.ca.us/
Grade Span: KG-12; **Agency Type:** 1
Schools: 18
  12 Primary; 2 Middle; 2 High; 2 Other Level
  16 Regular; 0 Special Education; 0 Vocational; 2 Alternative
  0 Magnet; 1 Charter; 15 Title I Eligible; 9 School-wide Title I
Students: 11,921   (51.8% male; 48.1% female)
  Individual Education Program: 850 (7.1%)
  English Language Learner: 2,410 (20.2%); Migrant: 1,745 (14.6%)
  Eligible for Free Lunch Program: 4,857 (40.7%)
  Eligible for Reduced-Price Lunch Program: 1,235 (10.4%)
Teachers: 570.2 (20.9 to 1)
Librarians/Media Specialists: 4.0 (2,980.3 to 1)
Guidance Counselors: 20.0 (596.1 to 1)
Current Spending: ($ per student per year):
  Total: $6,920; Instruction: $4,445; Support Services: $2,225
Enrollment, Drop-out Rates and Diploma Recipients by Race/Ethnicity

Category	Total	White	Black	Asian	AIAN	Hisp.
Enrollment (%)	100.0	46.5	3.1	16.1	1.7	29.5
Drop-out Rate (%)	n/a	n/a	n/a	n/a	n/a	n/a
H.S. Diplomas (#)	681	357	8	130	12	174

Tehama County

Corning Union Elementary
1590 S St • Corning, CA 96021-2934
(530) 824-7700 • http://www.cuesd.tehama.k12.ca.us/
Grade Span: KG-08; **Agency Type:** 1
Schools: 5
  4 Primary; 1 Middle; 0 High; 0 Other Level
  4 Regular; 0 Special Education; 0 Vocational; 1 Alternative
  0 Magnet; 0 Charter; 4 Title I Eligible; 3 School-wide Title I
Students: 1,989   (51.1% male; 48.8% female)
  Individual Education Program: 117 (5.9%)
  English Language Learner: 525 (26.4%); Migrant: 196 (9.9%)
  Eligible for Free Lunch Program: 1,235 (62.1%)
  Eligible for Reduced-Price Lunch Program: 155 (7.8%)
Teachers: 95.0 (20.9 to 1)
Librarians/Media Specialists: 0.0 (n/a to 1)
Guidance Counselors: 1.0 (1,989.0 to 1)
Current Spending: ($ per student per year):
  Total: $6,982; Instruction: $4,633; Support Services: $1,983
Enrollment, Drop-out Rates and Diploma Recipients by Race/Ethnicity

Category	Total	White	Black	Asian	AIAN	Hisp.
Enrollment (%)	100.0	52.1	0.9	0.9	0.4	45.2
Drop-out Rate (%)	n/a	n/a	n/a	n/a	n/a	n/a
H.S. Diplomas (#)	n/a	n/a	n/a	n/a	n/a	n/a

Red Bluff Joint Union High
1525 Douglass St • Red Bluff, CA 96080-2599
Mailing Address: PO Box 1507 • Red Bluff, CA 96080-2599
(530) 529-8700 • http://www.rbuhsd.k12.ca.us/
Grade Span: 09-12; **Agency Type:** 1
Schools: 4
  0 Primary; 0 Middle; 4 High; 0 Other Level
  1 Regular; 0 Special Education; 0 Vocational; 3 Alternative
  0 Magnet; 0 Charter; 4 Title I Eligible; 4 School-wide Title I

Students: 1,971   (51.1% male; 48.8% female)
   Individual Education Program: 199 (10.1%);
   English Language Learner: 37 (1.9%); Migrant: 25 (1.3%)
   Eligible for Free Lunch Program: 524 (26.6%)
   Eligible for Reduced-Price Lunch Program: 111 (5.6%)
Teachers: 94.2 (20.9 to 1)
Librarians/Media Specialists: 0.0 (n/a to 1)
Guidance Counselors: 4.0 (492.8 to 1)
Current Spending: ($ per student per year):
   Total: $7,643; Instruction: $4,298; Support Services: $3,048
Enrollment, Drop-out Rates and Diploma Recipients by Race/Ethnicity

Category	Total	White	Black	Asian	AIAN	Hisp.
Enrollment (%)	100.0	75.3	1.9	1.0	4.4	15.9
Drop-out Rate (%)	n/a	n/a	n/a	n/a	n/a	n/a
H.S. Diplomas (#)	440	358	4	9	14	55

Red Bluff Union Elementary
1755 Airport Rd • Red Bluff, CA 96080-4514
(530) 527-7200 • http://www.rbuhsd.k12.ca.us/
Grade Span: KG-12; **Agency Type:** 1
Schools: 6
   4 Primary; 1 Middle; 0 High; 1 Other Level
   5 Regular; 0 Special Education; 0 Vocational; 1 Alternative
   0 Magnet; 1 Charter; 4 Title I Eligible; 4 School-wide Title I
Students: 2,307   (52.4% male; 47.5% female)
   Individual Education Program: 159 (6.9%)
   English Language Learner: 230 (10.0%); Migrant: 80 (3.5%)
   Eligible for Free Lunch Program: 1,105 (47.9%)
   Eligible for Reduced-Price Lunch Program: 289 (12.5%)
Teachers: 110.7 (20.8 to 1)
Librarians/Media Specialists: 0.5 (4,614.0 to 1)
Guidance Counselors: 2.0 (1,153.5 to 1)
Current Spending: ($ per student per year):
   Total: $6,831; Instruction: $4,462; Support Services: $2,109
Enrollment, Drop-out Rates and Diploma Recipients by Race/Ethnicity

Category	Total	White	Black	Asian	AIAN	Hisp.
Enrollment (%)	100.0	71.7	1.1	1.4	1.9	22.2
Drop-out Rate (%)	n/a	n/a	n/a	n/a	n/a	n/a
H.S. Diplomas (#)	0	0	0	0	0	0

Tulare County

Burton Elementary
264 N Westwood St • Porterville, CA 93257-2542
(559) 781-8020 • http://burton.davis.k12.ut.us/
Grade Span: KG-08; **Agency Type:** 1
Schools: 5
   3 Primary; 2 Middle; 0 High; 0 Other Level
   5 Regular; 0 Special Education; 0 Vocational; 0 Alternative
   0 Magnet; 0 Charter; 4 Title I Eligible; 4 School-wide Title I
Students: 2,864   (52.4% male; 47.5% female)
   Individual Education Program: 130 (4.5%);
   English Language Learner: 443 (15.5%); Migrant: 72 (2.5%)
   Eligible for Free Lunch Program: 1,176 (41.1%)
   Eligible for Reduced-Price Lunch Program: 461 (16.1%)
Teachers: 138.5 (20.7 to 1)
Librarians/Media Specialists: 0.0 (n/a to 1)
Guidance Counselors: 2.4 (1,193.3 to 1)
Current Spending: ($ per student per year):
   Total: $6,285; Instruction: $4,198; Support Services: $1,712
Enrollment, Drop-out Rates and Diploma Recipients by Race/Ethnicity

Category	Total	White	Black	Asian	AIAN	Hisp.
Enrollment (%)	100.0	44.0	1.0	6.8	0.9	47.3
Drop-out Rate (%)	n/a	n/a	n/a	n/a	n/a	n/a
H.S. Diplomas (#)	n/a	n/a	n/a	n/a	n/a	n/a

Cutler-Orosi Joint Unified
41855 Rd 128 • Orosi, CA 93647-2008
(559) 528-4763 • http://www.cojusd.org/
Grade Span: KG-12; **Agency Type:** 1
Schools: 10
   4 Primary; 1 Middle; 4 High; 1 Other Level
   6 Regular; 0 Special Education; 0 Vocational; 4 Alternative
   0 Magnet; 0 Charter; 10 Title I Eligible; 10 School-wide Title I
Students: 4,017   (51.8% male; 48.1% female)
   Individual Education Program: 137 (3.4%);
   English Language Learner: 2,307 (57.4%); Migrant: 424 (10.6%)
   Eligible for Free Lunch Program: 3,272 (81.5%)
   Eligible for Reduced-Price Lunch Program: 285 (7.1%)
Teachers: 193.8 (20.7 to 1)
Librarians/Media Specialists: 0.0 (n/a to 1)
Guidance Counselors: 2.5 (1,606.8 to 1)
Current Spending: ($ per student per year):
   Total: $7,065; Instruction: $4,297; Support Services: $2,313

Enrollment, Drop-out Rates and Diploma Recipients by Race/Ethnicity

Category	Total	White	Black	Asian	AIAN	Hisp.
Enrollment (%)	100.0	2.5	0.3	4.0	0.0	92.6
Drop-out Rate (%)	n/a	n/a	n/a	n/a	n/a	n/a
H.S. Diplomas (#)	194	7	0	18	0	168

Dinuba Unified
1327 E El Monte Way • Dinuba, CA 93618-1800
(559) 595-7200 • http://www.dinubausd.org/
Grade Span: KG-12; **Agency Type:** 1
Schools: 9
   5 Primary; 1 Middle; 2 High; 1 Other Level
   8 Regular; 0 Special Education; 0 Vocational; 1 Alternative
   0 Magnet; 0 Charter; 8 Title I Eligible; 8 School-wide Title I
Students: 5,542   (52.3% male; 47.6% female)
   Individual Education Program: 369 (6.7%);
   English Language Learner: 1,832 (33.1%); Migrant: 984 (17.8%)
   Eligible for Free Lunch Program: 3,255 (58.7%)
   Eligible for Reduced-Price Lunch Program: 747 (13.5%)
Teachers: 260.2 (21.3 to 1)
Librarians/Media Specialists: 1.0 (5,542.0 to 1)
Guidance Counselors: 7.9 (701.5 to 1)
Current Spending: ($ per student per year):
   Total: $7,068; Instruction: $4,537; Support Services: $2,189
Enrollment, Drop-out Rates and Diploma Recipients by Race/Ethnicity

Category	Total	White	Black	Asian	AIAN	Hisp.
Enrollment (%)	100.0	11.0	0.4	1.7	0.3	86.5
Drop-out Rate (%)	n/a	n/a	n/a	n/a	n/a	n/a
H.S. Diplomas (#)	299	53	0	6	0	240

Earlimart Elementary
785 E Center Ave • Earlimart, CA 93219-1970
Mailing Address: PO Box 11970 • Earlimart, CA 93219-1970
(661) 849-3386 • http://www.earlimart.k12.ca.us/
Grade Span: KG-08; **Agency Type:** 1
Schools: 4
   2 Primary; 2 Middle; 0 High; 0 Other Level
   3 Regular; 0 Special Education; 0 Vocational; 1 Alternative
   0 Magnet; 0 Charter; 3 Title I Eligible; 2 School-wide Title I
Students: 1,903   (49.3% male; 50.6% female)
   Individual Education Program: 81 (4.3%);
   English Language Learner: 1,581 (83.1%); Migrant: 633 (33.3%)
   Eligible for Free Lunch Program: 1,671 (87.8%)
   Eligible for Reduced-Price Lunch Program: 165 (8.7%)
Teachers: 84.6 (22.5 to 1)
Librarians/Media Specialists: 0.0 (n/a to 1)
Guidance Counselors: 0.0 (n/a to 1)
Current Spending: ($ per student per year):
   Total: $6,543; Instruction: $4,118; Support Services: $2,078
Enrollment, Drop-out Rates and Diploma Recipients by Race/Ethnicity

Category	Total	White	Black	Asian	AIAN	Hisp.
Enrollment (%)	100.0	1.9	0.3	3.5	0.1	93.6
Drop-out Rate (%)	n/a	n/a	n/a	n/a	n/a	n/a
H.S. Diplomas (#)	n/a	n/a	n/a	n/a	n/a	n/a

Exeter Union Elementary
134 S E St • Exeter, CA 93221-1731
(559) 592-9421
Grade Span: KG-08; **Agency Type:** 1
Schools: 4
   2 Primary; 2 Middle; 0 High; 0 Other Level
   3 Regular; 0 Special Education; 0 Vocational; 1 Alternative
   0 Magnet; 0 Charter; 3 Title I Eligible; 3 School-wide Title I
Students: 1,980   (51.9% male; 48.0% female)
   Individual Education Program: 108 (5.5%);
   English Language Learner: 395 (19.9%); Migrant: 310 (15.7%)
   Eligible for Free Lunch Program: 1,041 (52.6%)
   Eligible for Reduced-Price Lunch Program: 262 (13.2%)
Teachers: 93.7 (21.1 to 1)
Librarians/Media Specialists: 0.0 (n/a to 1)
Guidance Counselors: 0.0 (n/a to 1)
Current Spending: ($ per student per year):
   Total: $7,080; Instruction: $5,032; Support Services: $1,708
Enrollment, Drop-out Rates and Diploma Recipients by Race/Ethnicity

Category	Total	White	Black	Asian	AIAN	Hisp.
Enrollment (%)	100.0	50.9	0.7	1.0	0.7	45.3
Drop-out Rate (%)	n/a	n/a	n/a	n/a	n/a	n/a
H.S. Diplomas (#)	n/a	n/a	n/a	n/a	n/a	n/a

Farmersville Unified
571 E Citrus • Farmersville, CA 93223-1833
(559) 747-0776 • http://www.farmersville.k12.ca.us/
Grade Span: KG-12; **Agency Type:** 1
Schools: 5
   2 Primary; 1 Middle; 2 High; 0 Other Level

4 Regular; 0 Special Education; 0 Vocational; 1 Alternative
0 Magnet; 0 Charter; 5 Title I Eligible; 3 School-wide Title I
Students: 2,445 (48.7% male; 51.2% female)
  Individual Education Program: 137 (5.6%);
  English Language Learner: 1,134 (46.4%); Migrant: 785 (32.1%)
  Eligible for Free Lunch Program: 1,558 (63.7%)
  Eligible for Reduced-Price Lunch Program: 309 (12.6%)
Teachers: 125.4 (19.5 to 1)
Librarians/Media Specialists: 0.0 (n/a to 1)
Guidance Counselors: 3.5 (698.6 to 1)
Current Spending: ($ per student per year):
  Total: $7,858; Instruction: $4,913; Support Services: $2,577
Enrollment, Drop-out Rates and Diploma Recipients by Race/Ethnicity

Category	Total	White	Black	Asian	AIAN	Hisp.
Enrollment (%)	100.0	10.8	0.2	1.1	0.3	86.9
Drop-out Rate (%)	n/a	n/a	n/a	n/a	n/a	n/a
H.S. Diplomas (#)	118	7	2	0	0	109

Lindsay Unified

519 E Honolulu St • Lindsay, CA 93247-2143
(559) 562-5111 • http://www.lindsay.k12.ca.us/
Grade Span: KG-12; **Agency Type:** 1
Schools: 7
  3 Primary; 1 Middle; 3 High; 0 Other Level
  5 Regular; 0 Special Education; 0 Vocational; 2 Alternative
  0 Magnet; 0 Charter; 7 Title I Eligible; 6 School-wide Title I
Students: 3,586 (50.5% male; 49.4% female)
  Individual Education Program: 107 (3.0%);
  English Language Learner: 2,093 (58.4%); Migrant: 1,310 (36.5%)
  Eligible for Free Lunch Program: 2,422 (67.5%)
  Eligible for Reduced-Price Lunch Program: 397 (11.1%)
Teachers: 179.7 (20.0 to 1)
Librarians/Media Specialists: 1.0 (3,586.0 to 1)
Guidance Counselors: 7.0 (512.3 to 1)
Current Spending: ($ per student per year):
  Total: $8,073; Instruction: $4,845; Support Services: $2,864
Enrollment, Drop-out Rates and Diploma Recipients by Race/Ethnicity

Category	Total	White	Black	Asian	AIAN	Hisp.
Enrollment (%)	100.0	9.4	0.5	0.6	0.1	88.7
Drop-out Rate (%)	n/a	n/a	n/a	n/a	n/a	n/a
H.S. Diplomas (#)	207	27	0	6	0	174

Porterville Unified

600 W Grand Ave • Porterville, CA 93257-2029
(559) 793-2455 • http://porterville.k12.ca.us/dist/Home.html
Grade Span: KG-12; **Agency Type:** 1
Schools: 18
  10 Primary; 2 Middle; 5 High; 1 Other Level
  15 Regular; 0 Special Education; 0 Vocational; 3 Alternative
  1 Magnet; 0 Charter; 16 Title I Eligible; 13 School-wide Title I
Students: 12,580 (51.1% male; 48.8% female)
  Individual Education Program: 709 (5.6%);
  English Language Learner: 2,628 (20.9%); Migrant: 1,435 (11.4%)
  Eligible for Free Lunch Program: 9,352 (74.3%)
  Eligible for Reduced-Price Lunch Program: 957 (7.6%)
Teachers: 588.6 (21.4 to 1)
Librarians/Media Specialists: 2.2 (5,718.2 to 1)
Guidance Counselors: 8.0 (1,572.5 to 1)
Current Spending: ($ per student per year):
  Total: $7,324; Instruction: $4,643; Support Services: $2,323
Enrollment, Drop-out Rates and Diploma Recipients by Race/Ethnicity

Category	Total	White	Black	Asian	AIAN	Hisp.
Enrollment (%)	100.0	24.7	0.6	2.8	2.1	61.2
Drop-out Rate (%)	n/a	n/a	n/a	n/a	n/a	n/a
H.S. Diplomas (#)	972	375	9	73	20	493

Tulare City Elementary

600 N Cherry Ave • Tulare, CA 93274-2920
(559) 685-7200 • http://www.tcsd.k12.ca.us/
Grade Span: KG-08; **Agency Type:** 1
Schools: 14
  9 Primary; 5 Middle; 0 High; 0 Other Level
  13 Regular; 0 Special Education; 0 Vocational; 1 Alternative
  0 Magnet; 0 Charter; 12 Title I Eligible; 12 School-wide Title I
Students: 8,069 (49.7% male; 50.2% female)
  Individual Education Program: 635 (7.9%);
  English Language Learner: 1,707 (21.2%); Migrant: 1,245 (15.4%)
  Eligible for Free Lunch Program: 4,916 (60.9%)
  Eligible for Reduced-Price Lunch Program: 955 (11.8%)
Teachers: 388.9 (20.7 to 1)
Librarians/Media Specialists: 0.0 (n/a to 1)
Guidance Counselors: 3.8 (2,123.4 to 1)
Current Spending: ($ per student per year):
  Total: $6,960; Instruction: $4,861; Support Services: $1,717

Enrollment, Drop-out Rates and Diploma Recipients by Race/Ethnicity

Category	Total	White	Black	Asian	AIAN	Hisp.
Enrollment (%)	100.0	27.3	7.5	0.9	0.5	61.9
Drop-out Rate (%)	n/a	n/a	n/a	n/a	n/a	n/a
H.S. Diplomas (#)	n/a	n/a	n/a	n/a	n/a	n/a

Tulare County Office of Education

2637 W Burrel Ave • Visalia, CA 93278-5091
Mailing Address: PO Box 5091 • Visalia, CA 93278-5091
(559) 733-6300
Grade Span: KG-12; **Agency Type:** 4
Schools: 5
  0 Primary; 0 Middle; 2 High; 3 Other Level
  2 Regular; 1 Special Education; 0 Vocational; 2 Alternative
  0 Magnet; 2 Charter; 0 Title I Eligible; 0 School-wide Title I
Students: 1,656 (66.0% male; 33.9% female)
  Individual Education Program: n/a;
  English Language Learner: 159 (9.6%); Migrant: 0 (0.0%)
  Eligible for Free Lunch Program: 554 (33.5%)
  Eligible for Reduced-Price Lunch Program: 142 (8.6%)
Teachers: 132.5 (12.5 to 1)
Librarians/Media Specialists: 1.0 (1,656.0 to 1)
Guidance Counselors: 2.0 (828.0 to 1)
Current Spending: ($ per student per year):
  Total: $54,368; Instruction: $23,027; Support Services: $29,807
Enrollment, Drop-out Rates and Diploma Recipients by Race/Ethnicity

Category	Total	White	Black	Asian	AIAN	Hisp.
Enrollment (%)	100.0	31.5	3.3	3.0	0.9	57.4
Drop-out Rate (%)	n/a	n/a	n/a	n/a	n/a	n/a
H.S. Diplomas (#)	24	0	0	1	1	19

Tulare Joint Union High

426 N Blackstone • Tulare, CA 93274-4449
(559) 688-2021 • http://www.tulare.k12.ca.us/
Grade Span: 09-12; **Agency Type:** 1
Schools: 5
  0 Primary; 0 Middle; 5 High; 0 Other Level
  2 Regular; 0 Special Education; 0 Vocational; 3 Alternative
  1 Magnet; 0 Charter; 5 Title I Eligible; 5 School-wide Title I
Students: 4,350 (51.7% male; 48.2% female)
  Individual Education Program: 331 (7.6%);
  English Language Learner: 329 (7.6%); Migrant: 546 (12.6%)
  Eligible for Free Lunch Program: 1,654 (38.0%)
  Eligible for Reduced-Price Lunch Program: 187 (4.3%)
Teachers: 177.0 (24.6 to 1)
Librarians/Media Specialists: 2.0 (2,175.0 to 1)
Guidance Counselors: 14.3 (304.2 to 1)
Current Spending: ($ per student per year):
  Total: $7,083; Instruction: $3,919; Support Services: $2,839
Enrollment, Drop-out Rates and Diploma Recipients by Race/Ethnicity

Category	Total	White	Black	Asian	AIAN	Hisp.
Enrollment (%)	100.0	35.1	5.5	2.8	0.6	54.8
Drop-out Rate (%)	n/a	n/a	n/a	n/a	n/a	n/a
H.S. Diplomas (#)	870	376	50	18	5	404

Visalia Unified

5000 W Cypress Ave • Visalia, CA 93277-8300
(559) 730-7300 • http://www2.visalia.k12.ca.us/
Grade Span: KG-12; **Agency Type:** 1
Schools: 32
  21 Primary; 4 Middle; 6 High; 1 Other Level
  30 Regular; 1 Special Education; 0 Vocational; 1 Alternative
  0 Magnet; 2 Charter; 16 Title I Eligible; 16 School-wide Title I
Students: 25,258 (50.5% male; 49.4% female)
  Individual Education Program: 2,282 (9.0%);
  English Language Learner: 5,222 (20.7%); Migrant: 1,405 (5.6%)
  Eligible for Free Lunch Program: 11,060 (43.8%)
  Eligible for Reduced-Price Lunch Program: 1,995 (7.9%)
Teachers: 1,145.0 (22.1 to 1)
Librarians/Media Specialists: 2.0 (12,629.0 to 1)
Guidance Counselors: 13.9 (1,817.1 to 1)
Current Spending: ($ per student per year):
  Total: $7,199; Instruction: $4,657; Support Services: $2,279
Enrollment, Drop-out Rates and Diploma Recipients by Race/Ethnicity

Category	Total	White	Black	Asian	AIAN	Hisp.
Enrollment (%)	100.0	38.2	2.5	6.5	1.1	51.7
Drop-out Rate (%)	n/a	n/a	n/a	n/a	n/a	n/a
H.S. Diplomas (#)	1,310	706	19	112	12	461

Woodlake Union Elementary

300 W Whitney Ave • Woodlake, CA 93286-1238
(559) 564-8081
Grade Span: KG-08; **Agency Type:** 2
Schools: 3
  2 Primary; 1 Middle; 0 High; 0 Other Level

3 Regular; 0 Special Education; 0 Vocational; 0 Alternative
0 Magnet; 0 Charter; 3 Title I Eligible; 3 School-wide Title I
Students: 1,632   (51.5% male; 48.4% female)
  Individual Education Program: 77 (4.7%);
  English Language Learner: 650 (39.8%); Migrant: 543 (33.3%)
  Eligible for Free Lunch Program: 1,286 (78.8%)
  Eligible for Reduced-Price Lunch Program: 107 (6.6%)
Teachers: 82.0 (19.9 to 1)
Librarians/Media Specialists: 0.0 (n/a to 1)
Guidance Counselors: 0.0 (n/a to 1)
Current Spending: ($ per student per year):
  Total: $7,751; Instruction: $4,873; Support Services: $2,352
Enrollment, Drop-out Rates and Diploma Recipients by Race/Ethnicity

Category	Total	White	Black	Asian	AIAN	Hisp.
Enrollment (%)	100.0	11.6	0.1	0.4	0.0	87.9
Drop-out Rate (%)	n/a	n/a	n/a	n/a	n/a	n/a
H.S. Diplomas (#)	n/a	n/a	n/a	n/a	n/a	n/a

Tuolumne County

Sonora Union High
251 S Barretta St • Sonora, CA 95370-5042
(209) 533-8510 • http://www.sonorahs.k12.ca.us/district/
Grade Span: 09-12; **Agency Type:** 1
Schools: 4
  0 Primary; 0 Middle; 4 High; 0 Other Level
  1 Regular; 0 Special Education; 0 Vocational; 3 Alternative
  0 Magnet; 0 Charter; 1 Title I Eligible; 0 School-wide Title I
Students: 1,729   (51.0% male; 48.9% female)
  Individual Education Program: 155 (9.0%);
  English Language Learner: 8 (0.5%); Migrant: 0 (0.0%)
  Eligible for Free Lunch Program: 280 (16.2%)
  Eligible for Reduced-Price Lunch Program: 58 (3.4%)
Teachers: 73.6 (23.5 to 1)
Librarians/Media Specialists: 1.0 (1,729.0 to 1)
Guidance Counselors: 3.0 (576.3 to 1)
Current Spending: ($ per student per year):
  Total: $7,448; Instruction: $4,091; Support Services: $3,100
Enrollment, Drop-out Rates and Diploma Recipients by Race/Ethnicity

Category	Total	White	Black	Asian	AIAN	Hisp.
Enrollment (%)	100.0	79.9	0.6	1.3	3.2	9.3
Drop-out Rate (%)	n/a	n/a	n/a	n/a	n/a	n/a
H.S. Diplomas (#)	359	345	1	1	2	8

Ventura County

Conejo Valley Unified
1400 E Janss Rd • Thousand Oaks, CA 91362-2133
(805) 497-9511 • http://www.conejo.k12.ca.us/
Grade Span: KG-12; **Agency Type:** 1
Schools: 29
  20 Primary; 4 Middle; 5 High; 0 Other Level
  27 Regular; 0 Special Education; 0 Vocational; 2 Alternative
  0 Magnet; 0 Charter; 6 Title I Eligible; 0 School-wide Title I
Students: 22,243   (51.7% male; 48.2% female)
  Individual Education Program: 2,214 (10.0%);
  English Language Learner: 1,808 (8.1%); Migrant: 0 (0.0%)
  Eligible for Free Lunch Program: 1,721 (7.7%)
  Eligible for Reduced-Price Lunch Program: 848 (3.8%)
Teachers: 991.5 (22.4 to 1)
Librarians/Media Specialists: 3.0 (7,414.3 to 1)
Guidance Counselors: 27.0 (823.8 to 1)
Current Spending: ($ per student per year):
  Total: $6,755; Instruction: $4,532; Support Services: $2,033
Enrollment, Drop-out Rates and Diploma Recipients by Race/Ethnicity

Category	Total	White	Black	Asian	AIAN	Hisp.
Enrollment (%)	100.0	71.8	1.6	8.0	0.7	17.2
Drop-out Rate (%)	n/a	n/a	n/a	n/a	n/a	n/a
H.S. Diplomas (#)	1,413	1,137	12	114	3	146

Fillmore Unified
627 Sespe Ave • Fillmore, CA 93016-0697
Mailing Address: PO Box 697 • Fillmore, CA 93016-0697
(805) 524-6000 • http://www.fillmore.k12.ca.us/
Grade Span: KG-12; **Agency Type:** 1
Schools: 6
  3 Primary; 1 Middle; 2 High; 0 Other Level
  5 Regular; 0 Special Education; 0 Vocational; 1 Alternative
  0 Magnet; 0 Charter; 6 Title I Eligible; 5 School-wide Title I
Students: 3,906   (50.0% male; 49.9% female)
  Individual Education Program: 458 (11.7%);
  English Language Learner: 1,533 (39.2%); Migrant: 1,125 (28.8%)
  Eligible for Free Lunch Program: 1,774 (45.4%)
  Eligible for Reduced-Price Lunch Program: 449 (11.5%)
Teachers: 183.1 (21.3 to 1)

Librarians/Media Specialists: 0.0 (n/a to 1)
Guidance Counselors: 3.0 (1,302.0 to 1)
Current Spending: ($ per student per year):
  Total: $6,854; Instruction: $4,224; Support Services: $2,347
Enrollment, Drop-out Rates and Diploma Recipients by Race/Ethnicity

Category	Total	White	Black	Asian	AIAN	Hisp.
Enrollment (%)	100.0	16.2	0.4	0.8	0.6	81.3
Drop-out Rate (%)	n/a	n/a	n/a	n/a	n/a	n/a
H.S. Diplomas (#)	233	58	0	3	2	170

Hueneme Elementary
205 N Ventura Rd • Port Hueneme, CA 93041-3065
(805) 488-3588 • http://www.huensd.k12.ca.us/
Grade Span: KG-08; **Agency Type:** 1
Schools: 11
  9 Primary; 2 Middle; 0 High; 0 Other Level
  11 Regular; 0 Special Education; 0 Vocational; 0 Alternative
  0 Magnet; 0 Charter; 10 Title I Eligible; 3 School-wide Title I
Students: 8,508   (51.2% male; 48.7% female)
  Individual Education Program: 807 (9.5%);
  English Language Learner: 3,776 (44.4%); Migrant: 2,053 (24.1%)
  Eligible for Free Lunch Program: 4,682 (55.0%)
  Eligible for Reduced-Price Lunch Program: 1,429 (16.8%)
Teachers: 399.0 (21.3 to 1)
Librarians/Media Specialists: 0.0 (n/a to 1)
Guidance Counselors: 2.0 (4,254.0 to 1)
Current Spending: ($ per student per year):
  Total: $6,913; Instruction: $4,743; Support Services: $1,870
Enrollment, Drop-out Rates and Diploma Recipients by Race/Ethnicity

Category	Total	White	Black	Asian	AIAN	Hisp.
Enrollment (%)	100.0	12.0	3.9	8.1	0.7	75.3
Drop-out Rate (%)	n/a	n/a	n/a	n/a	n/a	n/a
H.S. Diplomas (#)	n/a	n/a	n/a	n/a	n/a	n/a

Moorpark Unified
30 Flory Ave • Moorpark, CA 93021-1862
(805) 378-6300 • http://www.mrpk.k12.ca.us/
Grade Span: KG-12; **Agency Type:** 1
Schools: 11
  5 Primary; 3 Middle; 3 High; 0 Other Level
  10 Regular; 0 Special Education; 0 Vocational; 1 Alternative
  0 Magnet; 0 Charter; 7 Title I Eligible; 0 School-wide Title I
Students: 7,814   (50.8% male; 49.1% female)
  Individual Education Program: 897 (11.5%);
  English Language Learner: 1,365 (17.5%); Migrant: 370 (4.7%)
  Eligible for Free Lunch Program: 1,772 (22.7%)
  Eligible for Reduced-Price Lunch Program: 483 (6.2%)
Teachers: 364.5 (21.4 to 1)
Librarians/Media Specialists: 0.0 (n/a to 1)
Guidance Counselors: 6.6 (1,183.9 to 1)
Current Spending: ($ per student per year):
  Total: $6,675; Instruction: $4,269; Support Services: $2,184
Enrollment, Drop-out Rates and Diploma Recipients by Race/Ethnicity

Category	Total	White	Black	Asian	AIAN	Hisp.
Enrollment (%)	100.0	53.5	1.8	5.6	1.1	31.5
Drop-out Rate (%)	n/a	n/a	n/a	n/a	n/a	n/a
H.S. Diplomas (#)	569	364	12	45	5	143

Oak Park Unified
5801 E Conifer St • Oak Park, CA 91301-1002
(626) 735-3200 • http://www.opusd.k12.ca.us/
Grade Span: KG-12; **Agency Type:** 1
Schools: 6
  3 Primary; 1 Middle; 2 High; 0 Other Level
  5 Regular; 0 Special Education; 0 Vocational; 1 Alternative
  0 Magnet; 0 Charter; 5 Title I Eligible; 0 School-wide Title I
Students: 3,764   (51.9% male; 48.0% female)
  Individual Education Program: 381 (10.1%);
  English Language Learner: 89 (2.4%); Migrant: 0 (0.0%)
  Eligible for Free Lunch Program: 35 (0.9%)
  Eligible for Reduced-Price Lunch Program: 33 (0.9%)
Teachers: 177.0 (21.3 to 1)
Librarians/Media Specialists: 0.0 (n/a to 1)
Guidance Counselors: 5.0 (752.8 to 1)
Current Spending: ($ per student per year):
  Total: $6,429; Instruction: $4,366; Support Services: $1,911
Enrollment, Drop-out Rates and Diploma Recipients by Race/Ethnicity

Category	Total	White	Black	Asian	AIAN	Hisp.
Enrollment (%)	100.0	84.8	1.3	10.0	0.0	3.6
Drop-out Rate (%)	n/a	n/a	n/a	n/a	n/a	n/a
H.S. Diplomas (#)	232	208	4	13	0	7

Ocean View Elementary
2382 Etting Rd • Oxnard, CA 93033-6864
(805) 488-4441 • http://www.ovsd.k12.ca.us/
Grade Span: KG-08; **Agency Type:** 1
Schools: 4
   3 Primary; 1 Middle; 0 High; 0 Other Level
   4 Regular; 0 Special Education; 0 Vocational; 0 Alternative
   0 Magnet; 0 Charter; 2 Title I Eligible; 0 School-wide Title I
Students: 2,521   (52.2% male; 47.7% female)
   Individual Education Program: 235 (9.3%);
   English Language Learner: 1,284 (50.9%); Migrant: 675 (26.8%)
   Eligible for Free Lunch Program: 1,278 (50.7%)
   Eligible for Reduced-Price Lunch Program: 478 (19.0%)
Teachers: 128.0 (19.7 to 1)
Librarians/Media Specialists: 0.0 (n/a to 1)
Guidance Counselors: 2.0 (1,260.5 to 1)
Current Spending: ($ per student per year):
   Total: $7,560; Instruction: $4,617; Support Services: $2,547
Enrollment, Drop-out Rates and Diploma Recipients by Race/Ethnicity

Category	Total	White	Black	Asian	AIAN	Hisp.
Enrollment (%)	100.0	11.5	5.6	7.0	0.2	74.9
Drop-out Rate (%)	n/a	n/a	n/a	n/a	n/a	n/a
H.S. Diplomas (#)	n/a	n/a	n/a	n/a	n/a	n/a

Ojai Unified
414 E Ojai Ave • Ojai, CA 93024-0878
Mailing Address: PO Box 878 • Ojai, CA 93024-0878
(805) 640-4300 • http://www.ojai.k12.ca.us/
Grade Span: KG-12; **Agency Type:** 1
Schools: 9
   5 Primary; 1 Middle; 2 High; 1 Other Level
   8 Regular; 0 Special Education; 0 Vocational; 1 Alternative
   0 Magnet; 1 Charter; 4 Title I Eligible; 0 School-wide Title I
Students: 3,808   (51.4% male; 48.5% female)
   Individual Education Program: 402 (10.6%);
   English Language Learner: 452 (11.9%); Migrant: 0 (0.0%)
   Eligible for Free Lunch Program: 644 (16.9%)
   Eligible for Reduced-Price Lunch Program: 271 (7.1%)
Teachers: 175.5 (21.7 to 1)
Librarians/Media Specialists: 0.0 (n/a to 1)
Guidance Counselors: 4.4 (865.5 to 1)
Current Spending: ($ per student per year):
   Total: $6,595; Instruction: $4,235; Support Services: $2,112
Enrollment, Drop-out Rates and Diploma Recipients by Race/Ethnicity

Category	Total	White	Black	Asian	AIAN	Hisp.
Enrollment (%)	100.0	69.6	0.9	2.4	1.0	25.0
Drop-out Rate (%)	n/a	n/a	n/a	n/a	n/a	n/a
H.S. Diplomas (#)	274	209	2	6	4	53

Oxnard Elementary
1051 S A St • Oxnard, CA 93030-7442
(805) 487-3918 • http://www.oxnardsd.org/
Grade Span: KG-08; **Agency Type:** 1
Schools: 21
   17 Primary; 4 Middle; 0 High; 0 Other Level
   20 Regular; 1 Special Education; 0 Vocational; 0 Alternative
   0 Magnet; 0 Charter; 18 Title I Eligible; 16 School-wide Title I
Students: 16,851   (50.6% male; 49.3% female)
   Individual Education Program: 1,597 (9.5%);
   English Language Learner: 7,631 (45.3%); Migrant: 1,194 (7.1%)
   Eligible for Free Lunch Program: 9,793 (58.1%)
   Eligible for Reduced-Price Lunch Program: 2,759 (16.4%)
Teachers: 785.1 (21.5 to 1)
Librarians/Media Specialists: 0.0 (n/a to 1)
Guidance Counselors: 0.0 (n/a to 1)
Current Spending: ($ per student per year):
   Total: $7,269; Instruction: $4,756; Support Services: $2,189
Enrollment, Drop-out Rates and Diploma Recipients by Race/Ethnicity

Category	Total	White	Black	Asian	AIAN	Hisp.
Enrollment (%)	100.0	8.8	2.6	3.4	0.5	84.0
Drop-out Rate (%)	n/a	n/a	n/a	n/a	n/a	n/a
H.S. Diplomas (#)	n/a	n/a	n/a	n/a	n/a	n/a

Oxnard Union High
309 S K St • Oxnard, CA 93030-5212
(805) 385-2500 • http://www.ouhsd.k12.ca.us/
Grade Span: KG-12; **Agency Type:** 1
Schools: 9
   0 Primary; 0 Middle; 9 High; 0 Other Level
   6 Regular; 0 Special Education; 0 Vocational; 3 Alternative
   0 Magnet; 0 Charter; 8 Title I Eligible; 0 School-wide Title I
Students: 15,746   (51.3% male; 48.6% female)
   Individual Education Program: 1,585 (10.1%);
   English Language Learner: 3,338 (21.2%); Migrant: 2,907 (18.5%)
   Eligible for Free Lunch Program: 4,138 (26.3%)

   Eligible for Reduced-Price Lunch Program: 2,248 (14.3%)
Teachers: 602.7 (26.1 to 1)
Librarians/Media Specialists: 5.0 (3,149.2 to 1)
Guidance Counselors: 38.0 (414.4 to 1)
Current Spending: ($ per student per year):
   Total: $6,723; Instruction: $4,086; Support Services: $2,382
Enrollment, Drop-out Rates and Diploma Recipients by Race/Ethnicity

Category	Total	White	Black	Asian	AIAN	Hisp.
Enrollment (%)	100.0	23.0	3.5	7.6	1.1	64.2
Drop-out Rate (%)	n/a	n/a	n/a	n/a	n/a	n/a
H.S. Diplomas (#)	2,529	717	98	272	50	1,392

Pleasant Valley School
600 Temple Ave • Camarillo, CA 93010-4835
(805) 482-2763 • http://www.pvsd.k12.ca.us/
Grade Span: KG-08; **Agency Type:** 1
Schools: 13
   11 Primary; 2 Middle; 0 High; 0 Other Level
   13 Regular; 0 Special Education; 0 Vocational; 0 Alternative
   1 Magnet; 1 Charter; 4 Title I Eligible; 0 School-wide Title I
Students: 7,455   (51.7% male; 48.2% female)
   Individual Education Program: 750 (10.1%);
   English Language Learner: 661 (8.9%); Migrant: 173 (2.3%)
   Eligible for Free Lunch Program: 781 (10.5%)
   Eligible for Reduced-Price Lunch Program: 416 (5.6%)
Teachers: 341.2 (21.8 to 1)
Librarians/Media Specialists: 0.0 (n/a to 1)
Guidance Counselors: 4.4 (1,694.3 to 1)
Current Spending: ($ per student per year):
   Total: $6,556; Instruction: $4,285; Support Services: $2,157
Enrollment, Drop-out Rates and Diploma Recipients by Race/Ethnicity

Category	Total	White	Black	Asian	AIAN	Hisp.
Enrollment (%)	100.0	61.0	3.0	10.7	0.7	24.7
Drop-out Rate (%)	n/a	n/a	n/a	n/a	n/a	n/a
H.S. Diplomas (#)	n/a	n/a	n/a	n/a	n/a	n/a

Rio Elementary
3300 Cortez St • Oxnard, CA 93036-1309
(805) 485-3111 • http://www.rio.k12.ca.us/
Grade Span: KG-08; **Agency Type:** 1
Schools: 7
   6 Primary; 1 Middle; 0 High; 0 Other Level
   7 Regular; 0 Special Education; 0 Vocational; 0 Alternative
   0 Magnet; 0 Charter; 7 Title I Eligible; 0 School-wide Title I
Students: 4,146   (51.3% male; 48.6% female)
   Individual Education Program: 423 (10.2%);
   English Language Learner: 1,751 (42.2%); Migrant: 1,316 (31.7%)
   Eligible for Free Lunch Program: 1,801 (43.4%)
   Eligible for Reduced-Price Lunch Program: 663 (16.0%)
Teachers: 185.0 (22.4 to 1)
Librarians/Media Specialists: 0.0 (n/a to 1)
Guidance Counselors: 0.0 (n/a to 1)
Current Spending: ($ per student per year):
   Total: $7,028; Instruction: $4,477; Support Services: $2,226
Enrollment, Drop-out Rates and Diploma Recipients by Race/Ethnicity

Category	Total	White	Black	Asian	AIAN	Hisp.
Enrollment (%)	100.0	9.1	3.2	6.7	0.6	79.7
Drop-out Rate (%)	n/a	n/a	n/a	n/a	n/a	n/a
H.S. Diplomas (#)	n/a	n/a	n/a	n/a	n/a	n/a

Santa Paula Elementary
201 S Steckel Dr • Santa Paula, CA 93060
(805) 933-5342 • http://www.spesd.org/main/
Grade Span: KG-08; **Agency Type:** 1
Schools: 7
   6 Primary; 1 Middle; 0 High; 0 Other Level
   7 Regular; 0 Special Education; 0 Vocational; 0 Alternative
   0 Magnet; 0 Charter; 7 Title I Eligible; 0 School-wide Title I
Students: 4,065   (51.5% male; 48.4% female)
   Individual Education Program: 413 (10.2%);
   English Language Learner: 2,017 (49.6%); Migrant: 992 (24.4%)
   Eligible for Free Lunch Program: 2,055 (50.6%)
   Eligible for Reduced-Price Lunch Program: 882 (21.7%)
Teachers: 168.5 (24.1 to 1)
Librarians/Media Specialists: 0.0 (n/a to 1)
Guidance Counselors: 8.0 (508.1 to 1)
Current Spending: ($ per student per year):
   Total: $7,284; Instruction: $4,449; Support Services: $2,454
Enrollment, Drop-out Rates and Diploma Recipients by Race/Ethnicity

Category	Total	White	Black	Asian	AIAN	Hisp.
Enrollment (%)	100.0	11.3	0.3	0.4	0.2	87.5
Drop-out Rate (%)	n/a	n/a	n/a	n/a	n/a	n/a
H.S. Diplomas (#)	n/a	n/a	n/a	n/a	n/a	n/a

Santa Paula Union High

500 E Santa Barbara St • Santa Paula, CA 93060-2633
(805) 525-0988 • http://www.spuhsd.k12.ca.us/front.html
Grade Span: 09-12; **Agency Type:** 1
Schools: 2
    0 Primary; 0 Middle; 2 High; 0 Other Level
    1 Regular; 0 Special Education; 0 Vocational; 1 Alternative
    0 Magnet; 0 Charter; 2 Title I Eligible; 0 School-wide Title I
Students: 1,715   (51.2% male; 48.7% female)
    Individual Education Program: 173 (10.1%);
    English Language Learner: 233 (13.6%); Migrant: 310 (18.1%)
    Eligible for Free Lunch Program: 725 (42.3%)
    Eligible for Reduced-Price Lunch Program: 191 (11.1%)
Teachers: 64.5 (26.6 to 1)
Librarians/Media Specialists: 0.0 (n/a to 1)
Guidance Counselors: 3.0 (571.7 to 1)
Current Spending: ($ per student per year):
    Total: $6,790; Instruction: $3,836; Support Services: $2,757
Enrollment, Drop-out Rates and Diploma Recipients by Race/Ethnicity

Category	Total	White	Black	Asian	AIAN	Hisp.
Enrollment (%)	100.0	15.8	0.3	0.5	0.1	83.3
Drop-out Rate (%)	n/a	n/a	n/a	n/a	n/a	n/a
H.S. Diplomas (#)	286	41	1	2	0	242

Simi Valley Unified

875 E Cochran • Simi Valley, CA 93065-0999
(805) 520-6500 • http://www.simi.k12.ca.us/
Grade Span: KG-12; **Agency Type:** 1
Schools: 29
    21 Primary; 3 Middle; 4 High; 1 Other Level
    27 Regular; 0 Special Education; 0 Vocational; 2 Alternative
    0 Magnet; 0 Charter; 4 Title I Eligible; 0 School-wide Title I
Students: 21,727   (51.4% male; 48.5% female)
    Individual Education Program: 2,264 (10.4%);
    English Language Learner: 1,784 (8.2%); Migrant: 0 (0.0%)
    Eligible for Free Lunch Program: 2,630 (12.1%)
    Eligible for Reduced-Price Lunch Program: 1,251 (5.8%)
Teachers: 960.5 (22.6 to 1)
Librarians/Media Specialists: 2.0 (10,863.5 to 1)
Guidance Counselors: 18.4 (1,180.8 to 1)
Current Spending: ($ per student per year):
    Total: $6,529; Instruction: $4,309; Support Services: $2,079
Enrollment, Drop-out Rates and Diploma Recipients by Race/Ethnicity

Category	Total	White	Black	Asian	AIAN	Hisp.
Enrollment (%)	100.0	69.7	1.5	7.5	0.9	20.1
Drop-out Rate (%)	n/a	n/a	n/a	n/a	n/a	n/a
H.S. Diplomas (#)	1,148	831	21	111	18	167

Ventura Unified

120 E Santa Clara St • Ventura, CA 93001-2716
(805) 641-5000 • http://www.ventura.k12.ca.us
Grade Span: KG-12; **Agency Type:** 1
Schools: 29
    18 Primary; 4 Middle; 6 High; 1 Other Level
    24 Regular; 0 Special Education; 0 Vocational; 5 Alternative
    2 Magnet; 0 Charter; 12 Title I Eligible; 7 School-wide Title I
Students: 17,794   (51.6% male; 48.3% female)
    Individual Education Program: 1,767 (9.9%);
    English Language Learner: 2,585 (14.5%); Migrant: 722 (4.1%)
    Eligible for Free Lunch Program: 4,353 (24.5%)
    Eligible for Reduced-Price Lunch Program: 2,087 (11.7%)
Teachers: 787.2 (22.6 to 1)
Librarians/Media Specialists: 5.8 (3,067.9 to 1)
Guidance Counselors: 29.2 (609.4 to 1)
Current Spending: ($ per student per year):
    Total: $6,597; Instruction: $4,071; Support Services: $2,227
Enrollment, Drop-out Rates and Diploma Recipients by Race/Ethnicity

Category	Total	White	Black	Asian	AIAN	Hisp.
Enrollment (%)	100.0	52.0	2.3	3.2	1.2	37.8
Drop-out Rate (%)	n/a	n/a	n/a	n/a	n/a	n/a
H.S. Diplomas (#)	1,024	672	24	35	11	275

Yolo County

Davis Joint Unified

526 B St • Davis, CA 95616-3811
(530) 757-5300 • http://www.djusd.k12.ca.us/District/
Grade Span: KG-12; **Agency Type:** 1
Schools: 14
    9 Primary; 2 Middle; 2 High; 1 Other Level
    12 Regular; 0 Special Education; 0 Vocational; 2 Alternative
    3 Magnet; 0 Charter; 6 Title I Eligible; 0 School-wide Title I
Students: 8,711   (49.8% male; 50.1% female)
    Individual Education Program: 718 (8.2%);
    English Language Learner: 813 (9.3%); Migrant: 130 (1.5%)

    Eligible for Free Lunch Program: 830 (9.5%)
    Eligible for Reduced-Price Lunch Program: 233 (2.7%)
Teachers: 427.2 (20.4 to 1)
Librarians/Media Specialists: 6.5 (1,340.2 to 1)
Guidance Counselors: 13.0 (670.1 to 1)
Current Spending: ($ per student per year):
    Total: $6,830; Instruction: $4,395; Support Services: $2,280
Enrollment, Drop-out Rates and Diploma Recipients by Race/Ethnicity

Category	Total	White	Black	Asian	AIAN	Hisp.
Enrollment (%)	100.0	67.4	3.7	15.0	0.9	12.8
Drop-out Rate (%)	n/a	n/a	n/a	n/a	n/a	n/a
H.S. Diplomas (#)	576	420	9	84	5	56

Washington Unified

930 W Acres Rd • West Sacramento, CA 95691-3224
(916) 375-7600 • http://www.wusd.k12.ca.us/
Grade Span: KG-12; **Agency Type:** 1
Schools: 12
    8 Primary; 1 Middle; 2 High; 1 Other Level
    10 Regular; 0 Special Education; 0 Vocational; 2 Alternative
    0 Magnet; 0 Charter; 9 Title I Eligible; 8 School-wide Title I
Students: 6,842   (51.1% male; 48.8% female)
    Individual Education Program: 740 (10.8%);
    English Language Learner: 1,710 (25.0%); Migrant: 13 (0.2%)
    Eligible for Free Lunch Program: 3,311 (48.4%)
    Eligible for Reduced-Price Lunch Program: 1,002 (14.6%)
Teachers: 365.0 (18.7 to 1)
Librarians/Media Specialists: 1.0 (6,842.0 to 1)
Guidance Counselors: 7.0 (977.4 to 1)
Current Spending: ($ per student per year):
    Total: $7,089; Instruction: $4,259; Support Services: $2,494
Enrollment, Drop-out Rates and Diploma Recipients by Race/Ethnicity

Category	Total	White	Black	Asian	AIAN	Hisp.
Enrollment (%)	100.0	40.2	5.6	13.5	2.1	38.2
Drop-out Rate (%)	n/a	n/a	n/a	n/a	n/a	n/a
H.S. Diplomas (#)	327	155	7	48	9	108

Winters Joint Unified

710 Railroad Ave • Winters, CA 95694-1646
(530) 795-6100 • http://winters.k12.ca.us/
Grade Span: KG-12; **Agency Type:** 1
Schools: 6
    2 Primary; 2 Middle; 2 High; 0 Other Level
    5 Regular; 0 Special Education; 0 Vocational; 1 Alternative
    0 Magnet; 0 Charter; 4 Title I Eligible; 0 School-wide Title I
Students: 2,012   (53.9% male; 46.0% female)
    Individual Education Program: 226 (11.2%);
    English Language Learner: 706 (35.1%); Migrant: 371 (18.4%)
    Eligible for Free Lunch Program: 618 (30.7%)
    Eligible for Reduced-Price Lunch Program: 227 (11.3%)
Teachers: 106.6 (18.9 to 1)
Librarians/Media Specialists: 1.0 (2,012.0 to 1)
Guidance Counselors: 4.6 (437.4 to 1)
Current Spending: ($ per student per year):
    Total: $6,918; Instruction: $4,062; Support Services: $2,648
Enrollment, Drop-out Rates and Diploma Recipients by Race/Ethnicity

Category	Total	White	Black	Asian	AIAN	Hisp.
Enrollment (%)	100.0	41.4	0.4	2.7	0.8	52.5
Drop-out Rate (%)	n/a	n/a	n/a	n/a	n/a	n/a
H.S. Diplomas (#)	122	59	0	6	3	54

Woodland Joint Unified

630 Cottonwood St • Woodland, CA 95695-3615
(530) 662-0201 • http://www.wjusd.k12.ca.us/
Grade Span: KG-12; **Agency Type:** 1
Schools: 19
    13 Primary; 3 Middle; 3 High; 0 Other Level
    16 Regular; 0 Special Education; 0 Vocational; 3 Alternative
    0 Magnet; 0 Charter; 10 Title I Eligible; 7 School-wide Title I
Students: 10,515   (51.8% male; 48.1% female)
    Individual Education Program: 1,087 (10.3%);
    English Language Learner: 3,122 (29.7%); Migrant: 1,015 (9.7%)
    Eligible for Free Lunch Program: 3,413 (32.5%)
    Eligible for Reduced-Price Lunch Program: 1,086 (10.3%)
Teachers: 510.2 (20.6 to 1)
Librarians/Media Specialists: 2.0 (5,257.5 to 1)
Guidance Counselors: 10.4 (1,011.1 to 1)
Current Spending: ($ per student per year):
    Total: $6,707; Instruction: $4,005; Support Services: $2,460
Enrollment, Drop-out Rates and Diploma Recipients by Race/Ethnicity

Category	Total	White	Black	Asian	AIAN	Hisp.
Enrollment (%)	100.0	38.9	1.6	5.1	0.6	52.8
Drop-out Rate (%)	n/a	n/a	n/a	n/a	n/a	n/a
H.S. Diplomas (#)	550	273	7	33	3	234

Marysville Joint Unified
1919 B St • Marysville, CA 95901-3731
(530) 741-6000 • http://www.mjusd.k12.ca.us/
Grade Span: KG-12; **Agency Type:** 1
Schools: 24
    14 Primary; 4 Middle; 5 High; 1 Other Level
    21 Regular; 0 Special Education; 0 Vocational; 3 Alternative
    0 Magnet; 2 Charter; 18 Title I Eligible; 15 School-wide Title I
Students: 9,839   (51.3% male; 48.6% female)
    Individual Education Program: 843 (8.6%);
    English Language Learner: 2,311 (23.5%); Migrant: 696 (7.1%)
    Eligible for Free Lunch Program: 6,188 (62.9%)
    Eligible for Reduced-Price Lunch Program: 1,064 (10.8%)
Teachers: 476.3 (20.7 to 1)
Librarians/Media Specialists: 0.0 (n/a to 1)
Guidance Counselors: 3.7 (2,659.2 to 1)
Current Spending: ($ per student per year):
    Total: $7,268; Instruction: $4,518; Support Services: $2,405
Enrollment, Drop-out Rates and Diploma Recipients by Race/Ethnicity

Category	Total	White	Black	Asian	AIAN	Hisp.
Enrollment (%)	100.0	45.8	3.5	15.1	6.6	26.0
Drop-out Rate (%)	n/a	n/a	n/a	n/a	n/a	n/a
H.S. Diplomas (#)	421	201	9	106	36	69

Wheatland Elementary
711 W Olive • Wheatland, CA 95692-0818
Mailing Address: PO Box 818 • Wheatland, CA 95692-0818
(530) 633-3130 • http://www.wheatland.k12.ca.us/
Grade Span: KG-12; **Agency Type:** 1
Schools: 6
    2 Primary; 2 Middle; 0 High; 2 Other Level
    6 Regular; 0 Special Education; 0 Vocational; 0 Alternative
    0 Magnet; 2 Charter; 3 Title I Eligible; 0 School-wide Title I
Students: 2,543   (49.9% male; 50.0% female)
    Individual Education Program: 164 (6.4%);
    English Language Learner: 86 (3.4%); Migrant: 7 (0.3%)
    Eligible for Free Lunch Program: 439 (17.3%)
    Eligible for Reduced-Price Lunch Program: 317 (12.5%)
Teachers: 128.9 (19.7 to 1)
Librarians/Media Specialists: 1.0 (2,543.0 to 1)
Guidance Counselors: 0.0 (n/a to 1)
Current Spending: ($ per student per year):
    Total: $6,152; Instruction: $3,678; Support Services: $2,237
Enrollment, Drop-out Rates and Diploma Recipients by Race/Ethnicity

Category	Total	White	Black	Asian	AIAN	Hisp.
Enrollment (%)	100.0	66.0	8.1	9.6	2.5	13.8
Drop-out Rate (%)	n/a	n/a	n/a	n/a	n/a	n/a
H.S. Diplomas (#)	0	0	0	0	0	0

Number of Schools

Rank	Number	District Name	City
1	693	Los Angeles Unified	Los Angeles
2	185	San Diego Unified	San Diego
3	118	Oakland Unified	Oakland
3	118	San Francisco Unified	San Francisco
5	103	Fresno Unified	Fresno
6	91	Long Beach Unified	Long Beach
7	88	Sacramento City Unified	Sacramento
8	84	San Juan Unified	Carmichael
9	67	Garden Grove Unified	Garden Grove
10	65	San Bernardino City Unified	San Bernardino
10	65	West Contra Costa Unified	Richmond
12	57	San Jose Unified	San Jose
13	56	Capistrano Unified	San Juan Capis
13	56	Santa Ana Unified	Santa Ana
15	55	Elk Grove Unified	Elk Grove
15	55	Mt. Diablo Unified	Concord
17	50	Stockton City Unified	Stockton
18	47	Lodi Unified	Lodi
19	46	Riverside Unified	Riverside
20	43	Bakersfield City Elementary	Bakersfield
21	42	Corona-Norco Unified	Norco
21	42	Orange Unified	Orange
23	41	Fremont Unified	Fremont
24	40	Chula Vista Elementary	Chula Vista
24	40	Compton Unified	Compton
24	40	Pomona Unified	Pomona
27	39	Clovis Unified	Clovis
27	39	Hacienda La Puente Unified	City of Industry
29	38	Fontana Unified	Fontana
30	37	Napa Valley Unified	Napa
30	37	Saddleback Valley Unified	Mission Viejo
32	35	Chino Valley Unified	Chino
33	34	Ontario-Montclair Elementary	Ontario
34	33	Hayward Unified	Hayward
34	33	Irvine Unified	Irvine
34	33	Moreno Valley Unified	Moreno Valley
37	32	Glendale Unified	Glendale
37	32	Pasadena Unified	Pasadena
37	32	Visalia Unified	Visalia
40	31	Folsom-Cordova Unified	Folsom
40	31	Newport-Mesa Unified	Costa Mesa
40	31	Poway Unified	Poway
43	30	ABC Unified	Cerritos
43	30	Placentia-Yorba Linda Unified	Placentia
43	30	Torrance Unified	Torrance
46	29	Conejo Valley Unified	Thousand Oaks
46	29	Montebello Unified	Montebello
46	29	Norwalk-La Mirada Unified	Norwalk
46	29	Pajaro Valley Unified School	Watsonville
46	29	Simi Valley Unified	Simi Valley
46	29	Vallejo City Unified	Vallejo
46	29	Ventura Unified	Ventura
53	28	Cajon Valley Union Elementary	El Cajon
53	28	Colton Joint Unified	Colton
53	28	Desert Sands Unified	La Quinta
53	28	Oceanside Unified	Oceanside
53	28	San Ramon Valley Unified	Danville
53	28	Sweetwater Union High	Chula Vista
53	28	Vista Unified	Vista
60	27	Fairfield-Suisun Unified	Fairfield
60	27	Modesto City Elementary	Modesto
60	27	Rialto Unified	Rialto
63	26	Chico Unified	Chico
63	26	Palmdale Elementary	Palmdale
63	26	Tustin Unified	Tustin
66	25	Alum Rock Union Elementary	San Jose
67	24	Cupertino Union School	Cupertino
67	24	Jurupa Unified	Riverside
67	24	Manteca Unified	Manteca
67	24	Marysville Joint Unified	Marysville
67	24	Temecula Valley Unified	Temecula
72	23	Anaheim Elementary	Anaheim
72	23	Antioch Unified	Antioch
72	23	Kern Union High	Bakersfield
72	23	Monterey Peninsula Unified	Monterey
72	23	Palm Springs Unified	Palm Springs
72	23	Rio Linda Union Elementary	Rio Linda
72	23	Santa Clara Unified	Santa Clara
79	22	Baldwin Park Unified	Baldwin Park
79	22	Downey Unified	Downey
79	22	Escondido Union Elementary	Escondido
79	22	Hemet Unified	Hemet
79	22	Hesperia Unified	Hesperia
79	22	La Mesa-Spring Valley	La Mesa
79	22	Lake Elsinore Unified	Lake Elsinore
79	22	Rowland Unified	Rowland Heights
87	21	Anaheim Union High	Anaheim
87	21	East Side Union High	San Jose
87	21	Livermore Valley Joint Unified	Livermore
87	21	Oxnard Elementary	Oxnard
87	21	Tracy Joint Unified	Tracy
92	20	Alameda City Unified	Alameda
92	20	Burbank Unified	Burbank
92	20	Covina-Valley Unified	Covina
92	20	Inglewood Unified	Inglewood
92	20	Madera Unified	Madera
92	20	Oak Grove Elementary	San Jose
92	20	Panama Buena Vista Union Elem	Bakersfield
92	20	Redlands Unified	Redlands
92	20	San Mateo-Foster City Elementary	San Mateo
101	19	Alvord Unified	Riverside
101	19	Coachella Valley Unified	Thermal
101	19	El Monte City Elementary	El Monte
101	19	Fullerton Elementary	Fullerton
101	19	Grossmont Union High	La Mesa
101	19	Palo Alto Unified	Palo Alto
101	19	Woodland Joint Unified	Woodland
108	18	Azusa Unified	Azusa
108	18	Lancaster Elementary	Lancaster
108	18	Paramount Unified	Paramount
108	18	Porterville Unified	Porterville
108	18	Sanger Unified	Sanger
108	18	Yuba City Unified	Yuba City
114	17	El Rancho Unified	Pico Rivera
114	17	Evergreen Elementary	San Jose
114	17	Lompoc Unified	Lompoc
114	17	Merced City Elementary	Merced
114	17	Morongo Unified	Twentynine Plms
114	17	Novato Unified	Novato
114	17	Palos Verdes Peninsula Unified	Palos Verdes Est
114	17	Redwood City Elementary	Redwood City
114	17	Vacaville Unified	Vacaville
114	17	Westminster Elementary	Westminster
124	16	Apple Valley Unified	Apple Valley
124	16	Berkeley Unified	Berkeley
124	16	Central Unified	Fresno
124	16	Jefferson Elementary	Daly City
124	16	Los Angeles Co Office of Education	Downey
124	16	Lucia Mar Unified	Arroyo Grande
124	16	Murrieta Valley Unified	Murrieta
124	16	Plumas Unified	Quincy
124	16	San Luis Coastal Unified	San Luis Obispo
124	16	Santa Maria-Bonita Elementary	Santa Maria
124	16	Santa Monica-Malibu Unified	Santa Monica
124	16	South San Francisco Unified	S San Francisco
124	16	Ukiah Unified	Ukiah
137	15	Bellflower Unified	Bellflower
137	15	Castro Valley Unified	Castro Valley
137	15	Cotati-Rohnert Park Unified	Rohnert Park
137	15	Gilroy Unified	Gilroy
137	15	Grant Joint Union High	Sacramento
137	15	Kings Canyon Joint Unified	Reedley
137	15	Morgan Hill Unified	Morgan Hill
137	15	Ocean View Elementary	Huntington Bch
137	15	Pleasanton Unified	Pleasanton
137	15	Rocklin Unified	Rocklin
137	15	San Lorenzo Unified	San Lorenzo
137	15	Santa Rosa High	Santa Rosa
137	15	Upland Unified	Upland
137	15	Victor Elementary	Victorville
137	15	Walnut Valley Unified	Walnut
152	14	Berryessa Union Elementary	San Jose
152	14	Bonita Unified	San Dimas
152	14	Davis Joint Unified	Davis
152	14	Franklin-Mckinley Elementary	San Jose
152	14	Las Virgenes Unified	Calabasas
152	14	Lynwood Unified	Lynwood
152	14	Mariposa County Unified	Mariposa
152	14	Milpitas Unified	Milpitas
152	14	Newark Unified	Newark
152	14	Redding Elementary	Redding
152	14	Roseville City Elementary	Roseville
152	14	Salinas City Elementary	Salinas
152	14	San Marcos Unified	San Marcos
152	14	Santa Rosa Elementary	Santa Rosa
152	14	Saugus Union Elementary	Santa Clarita
152	14	Tulare City Elementary	Tulare
152	14	Twin Ridges Elementary	North San Juan
152	14	Val Verde Unified	Perris
152	14	Yucaipa-Calimesa Jt. Unified	Yucaipa
171	13	Alhambra City Elementary	Alhambra
171	13	Antelope Valley Union High	Lancaster
171	13	Calaveras Unified	San Andreas
171	13	Carlsbad Unified	Carlsbad
171	13	Ceres Unified	Ceres
171	13	East Whittier City Elementary	Whittier
171	13	Etiwanda Elementary	Etiwanda
171	13	Eureka City Unified	Eureka
171	13	Garvey Elementary	Rosemead
171	13	Mountain Empire Unified	Pine Valley
171	13	Paradise Unified	Paradise
171	13	Pleasant Valley School	Camarillo
171	13	San Leandro Unified	San Leandro
171	13	Santa Barbara Elementary	Santa Barbara
171	13	Santa Barbara High	Santa Barbara
171	13	Snowline Joint Unified	Phelan
171	13	West Covina Unified	West Covina
171	13	Whittier City Elementary	Whittier
171	13	William S. Hart Union High	Santa Clarita
190	12	Alisal Union Elementary	Salinas
190	12	Amador County Unified	Jackson
190	12	Atascadero Unified	Atascadero
190	12	Barstow Unified	Barstow
190	12	Campbell Union Elementary	Campbell
190	12	Claremont Unified	Claremont
190	12	Hawthorne Elementary	Hawthorne
190	12	Lincoln Unified	Stockton
190	12	Mountain View Elementary	El Monte
190	12	New Haven Unified	Union City
190	12	Paso Robles Joint Unified	Paso Robles
190	12	Ravenswood City Elementary	East Palo Alto
190	12	Redondo Beach Unified	Redondo Beach
190	12	Selma Unified	Selma
190	12	Sonoma Valley Unified	Sonoma
190	12	South Bay Union Elementary	Imperial Beach
190	12	Tahoe-Truckee Joint Unified	Truckee
190	12	Washington Unified	West Sacramento
208	11	Arcadia Unified	Arcadia
208	11	Chaffey Joint Union High	Ontario
208	11	Coalinga-Huron Joint Unified	Coalinga
208	11	Del Norte County Unified	Crescent City
208	11	El Centro Elementary	El Centro
208	11	Fountain Valley Elementary	Fountain Valley
208	11	Gateway Unified	Redding
208	11	Hanford Elementary	Hanford
208	11	Hueneme Elementary	Port Hueneme
208	11	Lakeside Union Elementary	Lakeside
208	11	Monrovia Unified	Monrovia
208	11	Moorpark Unified	Moorpark
208	11	National Elementary	National City
208	11	North Monterey County Unified	Moss Landing
208	11	North Sacramento Elementary	Sacramento
208	11	Pittsburg Unified	Pittsburg
208	11	Ramona City Unified	Ramona
208	11	Santee Elementary	Santee
208	11	Sierra Sands Unified	Ridgecrest
208	11	Sierra Unified	Prather
208	11	Sunnyvale Elementary	Sunnyvale
208	11	Turlock Joint Elementary	Turlock
208	11	Valley Center-Pauma Unified	Valley Center
231	10	Alta Loma Elementary	Alta Loma
231	10	Banning Unified	Banning
231	10	Beaumont Unified	Beaumont
231	10	Calexico Unified	Calexico
231	10	Charter Oak Unified	Covina
231	10	Culver City Unified	Culver City
231	10	Cutler-Orosi Joint Unified	Orosi
231	10	Cypress Elementary	Cypress
231	10	Delano Union Elementary	Delano
231	10	El Dorado Union High	Placerville
231	10	Glendora Unified	Glendora
231	10	Greenfield Union Elementary	Bakersfield
231	10	Huntington Beach City Elementary	Huntington Bch
231	10	Los Alamitos Unified	Los Alamitos
231	10	Los Banos Unified	Los Banos
231	10	Natomas Unified	Sacramento
231	10	Petaluma Joint Union High	Petaluma
231	10	River Delta Joint Unified	Rio Vista
231	10	Salinas Union High	Salinas
231	10	San Diego Co Office of Education	San Diego
231	10	Sylvan Union Elementary	Modesto
231	10	Travis Unified	Travis Afb
231	10	Union Elementary	San Jose
231	10	Westside Union Elementary	Lancaster
231	10	Willits Unified	Willits
256	9	Adelanto Elementary	Adelanto
256	9	Atwater Elementary	Atwater
256	9	Benicia Unified	Benicia
256	9	Brea-Olinda Unified	Brea
256	9	Carpinteria Unified	Carpinteria
256	9	Centralia Elementary	Buena Park
256	9	Dinuba Unified	Dinuba
256	9	Encinitas Union Elementary	Encinitas
256	9	Enterprise Elementary	Redding
256	9	Fallbrook Union Elementary	Fallbrook
256	9	Goleta Union Elementary	Goleta
256	9	Huntington Beach Union High	Huntington Bch
256	9	Konocti Unified	Lower Lake
256	9	La Habra City Elementary	La Habra
256	9	Lake Tahoe Unified	S Lake Tahoe
256	9	Little Lake City Elementary	Santa Fe Spgs
256	9	Magnolia Elementary	Anaheim
256	9	Mojave Unified	Mojave
256	9	Moreland Elementary	San Jose
256	9	Mountain View-Whisman Elementary	Mountain View

256	9	Nevada Joint Union High	Grass Valley
256	9	Newhall Elementary	Valencia
256	9	Newman-Crows Landing Unified	Newman
256	9	Ojai Unified	Ojai
256	9	Oxnard Union High	Oxnard
256	9	Petaluma City Elementary	Petaluma
256	9	Reef-Sunset Unified	Avenal
256	9	Rim of the World Unified	Lake Arrowhead
256	9	San Dieguito Union High	Encinitas
256	9	San Gabriel Unified	San Gabriel
256	9	San Jacinto Unified	San Jacinto
256	9	Santa Cruz City High	Soquel
256	9	Shasta Union High	Redding
256	9	Victor Valley Union High	Victorville
290	8	Bassett Unified	La Puente
290	8	Bear Valley Unified	Big Bear Lake
290	8	Center Joint Unified	Antelope
290	8	Dixon Unified	Dixon
290	8	Dry Creek Joint Elementary	Roseville
290	8	Duarte Unified	Duarte
290	8	Dublin Unified	Dublin
290	8	Escalon Unified	Escalon
290	8	Eureka Union Elementary	Granite Bay
290	8	Fort Bragg Unified	Fort Bragg
290	8	Fullerton Joint Union High	Fullerton
290	8	Hollister SD	Hollister
290	8	Kelseyville Unified	Kelseyville
290	8	Lawndale Elementary	Lawndale
290	8	Lemon Grove Elementary	Lemon Grove
290	8	Lennox Elementary	Lennox
290	8	Los Altos Elementary	Los Altos
290	8	Martinez Unified	Martinez
290	8	Middletown Unified	Middletown
290	8	Oakdale Joint Unified	Oakdale
290	8	Orcutt Union Elementary	Orcutt
290	8	Rincon Valley Union Elementary	Santa Rosa
290	8	Rosedale Union Elementary	Bakersfield
290	8	San Bruno Park Elementary	San Bruno
290	8	San Carlos Elementary	San Carlos
290	8	San Mateo Union High	San Mateo
290	8	San Rafael City Elementary	San Rafael
290	8	South Whittier Elementary	Whittier
290	8	Sulphur Springs Union Elementary	Canyon Country
290	8	Temple City Unified	Temple City
290	8	Western Placer Unified	Lincoln
321	7	Alpine Union Elementary	Alpine
321	7	Black Oak Mine Unified	Georgetown
321	7	Brentwood Union Elementary	Brentwood
321	7	Buckeye Union Elementary	Shingle Springs
321	7	Buena Park Elementary	Buena Park
321	7	Cabrillo Unified	Half Moon Bay
321	7	Campbell Union High	San Jose
321	7	Central Elementary	Rcho Cucamong
321	7	Corcoran Joint Unified	Corcoran
321	7	Dos Palos Oro Loma Jt. Unified	Dos Palos
321	7	El Monte Union High	El Monte
321	7	Empire Union Elementary	Modesto
321	7	Grass Valley Elementary	Grass Valley
321	7	Gridley Unified	Gridley
321	7	Kerman Unified	Kerman
321	7	Lindsay Unified	Lindsay
321	7	Live Oak Elementary	Santa Cruz
321	7	Manhattan Beach Unified	Manhattan Beach
321	7	Menifee Union Elementary	Menifee
321	7	Merced Union High	Atwater
321	7	Muroc Joint Unified	North Edwards
321	7	Oroville City Elementary	Oroville
321	7	Pacifica SD	Pacifica
321	7	Patterson Joint Unified	Patterson
321	7	Perris Elementary	Perris
321	7	Perris Union High	Perris
321	7	Rio Elementary	Oxnard
321	7	Roseville Joint Union High	Roseville
321	7	San Ysidro Elementary	San Ysidro
321	7	Santa Cruz City Elementary	Soquel
321	7	Santa Paula Elementary	Santa Paula
321	7	Silver Valley Unified	Yermo
321	7	Soledad Unified	Soledad
321	7	Taft City Elementary	Taft
321	7	Templeton Unified	Templeton
321	7	Whittier Union High	Whittier
321	7	Willows Unified	Willows
321	7	Windsor Unified	Windsor
359	6	Albany City Unified	Albany
359	6	Alhambra City High	Alhambra
359	6	Anderson Union High	Anderson
359	6	Belmont-Redwood Shores Elementary	Belmont
359	6	Beverly Hills Unified	Beverly Hills
359	6	Burlingame Elementary	Burlingame
359	6	Cambrian Elementary	San Jose
359	6	Carmel Unified	Carmel
359	6	Del Mar Union Elementary	Del Mar
359	6	Escondido Union High	Escondido
359	6	Fillmore Unified	Fillmore
359	6	Firebaugh-Las Deltas Joint Unified	Firebaugh
359	6	Fowler Unified	Fowler
359	6	Fremont Union High	Sunnyvale
359	6	Galt Joint Union Elementary	Galt
359	6	Golden Plains Unified	San Joaquin
359	6	Healdsburg Unified	Healdsburg
359	6	Hilmar Unified	Hilmar
359	6	Imperial Unified	Imperial
359	6	Keppel Union Elementary	Pearblossom
359	6	Keyes Union Elementary	Keyes
359	6	King City Joint Union High	King City
359	6	Lemoore Union Elementary	Lemoore
359	6	Linden Unified	Linden
359	6	Live Oak Unified	Live Oak
359	6	Lowell Joint	Whittier
359	6	Mcfarland Unified	Mcfarland
359	6	Mendota Unified	Mendota
359	6	Mill Valley Elementary	Mill Valley
359	6	Modesto City High	Modesto
359	6	Oak Park Unified	Oak Park
359	6	Oakley Union Elementary	Oakley
359	6	Orland Joint Unified	Orland
359	6	Palo Verde Unified	Blythe
359	6	Parlier Unified	Parlier
359	6	Piedmont City Unified	Piedmont
359	6	Placer Union High	Auburn
359	6	Red Bluff Union Elementary	Red Bluff
359	6	Rescue Union Elementary	Rescue
359	6	Ripon Unified	Ripon
359	6	San Bernardino Co Off of Education	San Bernardino
359	6	San Lorenzo Valley Unified	Ben Lomond
359	6	Sequoia Union High	Redwood City
359	6	Southern Kern Unified	Rosamond
359	6	Stanislaus Union Elementary	Modesto
359	6	Tehachapi Unified	Tehachapi
359	6	Walnut Creek Elementary	Walnut Creek
359	6	West Sonoma County Union High	Sebastopol
359	6	Westwood Unified	Westwood
359	6	Wheatland Elementary	Wheatland
359	6	Winters Joint Unified	Winters
410	5	Acalanes Union High	Lafayette
410	5	Acton-Agua Dulce Unified	Acton
410	5	Auburn Union Elementary	Auburn
410	5	Bonsall Union Elementary	Bonsall
410	5	Brawley Elementary	Brawley
410	5	Burton Elementary	Porterville
410	5	Cascade Union Elementary	Anderson
410	5	Corning Union Elementary	Corning
410	5	Coronado Unified	Coronado
410	5	Del Paso Heights Elementary	Sacramento
410	5	Delhi Unified	Delhi
410	5	El Segundo Unified	El Segundo
410	5	Farmersville Unified	Farmersville
410	5	Fresno County Office of Education	Fresno
410	5	Fruitvale Elementary	Bakersfield
410	5	Gustine Unified	Gustine
410	5	Hanford Joint Union High	Hanford
410	5	Holtville Unified	Holtville
410	5	Hughson Unified	Hughson
410	5	Jefferson Union High	Daly City
410	5	Kern County Office of Education	Bakersfield
410	5	Kingsburg Elementary Charter	Kingsburg
410	5	La Canada Unified	La Canada
410	5	Lafayette Elementary	Lafayette
410	5	Lakeport Unified	Lakeport
410	5	Los Gatos Union Elementary	Los Gatos
410	5	Millbrae Elementary	Millbrae
410	5	Mt. Pleasant Elementary	San Jose
410	5	Northern Humboldt Union High	McKinleyville
410	5	Old Adobe Union Elementary	Petaluma
410	5	Orinda Union Elementary	Orinda
410	5	Oroville Union High	Oroville
410	5	Pacific Grove Unified	Pacific Grove
410	5	Piner-Olivet Union Elementary	Santa Rosa
410	5	Pleasant Ridge Union Elementary	Grass Valley
410	5	Riverbank Unified	Riverbank
410	5	Riverdale Joint Unified	Riverdale
410	5	Riverside Co Office of Education	Riverside
410	5	Robla Elementary	Sacramento
410	5	Rosemead Elementary	Rosemead
410	5	Salida Union Elementary	Salida
410	5	Santa Clara Co Off of Education	San Jose
410	5	Solana Beach Elementary	Solana Beach
410	5	Soquel Union Elementary	Capitola
410	5	South Pasadena Unified	South Pasadena
410	5	Tamalpais Union High	Larkspur
410	5	Tulare County Office of Education	Visalia
410	5	Tulare Joint Union High	Tulare
458	4	Castaic Union Elementary	Valencia
458	4	Centinela Valley Union High	Lawndale
458	4	Central Union Elementary	Lemoore
458	4	Chowchilla Elementary	Chowchilla
458	4	Cloverdale Unified	Cloverdale
458	4	Cucamonga Elementary	Rcho Cucamong
458	4	Delano Joint Union High	Delano
458	4	Dixie Elementary	San Rafael
458	4	Earlimart Elementary	Earlimart
458	4	Eastside Union Elementary	Lancaster
458	4	Exeter Union Elementary	Exeter
458	4	Gonzales Unified	Gonzales
458	4	Gorman Elementary	Gorman
458	4	Greenfield Union Elementary	Greenfield
458	4	Jamul-Dulzura Union Elementary	Jamul
458	4	John Swett Unified	Crockett
458	4	Laguna Beach Unified	Laguna Beach
458	4	Lamont Elementary	Lamont
458	4	Lemoore Union High	Lemoore
458	4	Liberty Union High	Brentwood
458	4	Livingston Union Elementary	Livingston
458	4	Loomis Union Elementary	Loomis
458	4	Los Nietos Elementary	Whittier
458	4	Menlo Park City Elementary	Atherton
458	4	Moraga Elementary	Moraga
458	4	Mountain View Elementary	Ontario
458	4	Mountain View-Los Altos Union High	Mountain View
458	4	Norris Elementary	Bakersfield
458	4	Nuview Union Elementary	Nuevo
458	4	Ocean View Elementary	Oxnard
458	4	Orange County Office of Education	Costa Mesa
458	4	Red Bluff Joint Union High	Red Bluff
458	4	Ross Valley Elementary	San Anselmo
458	4	San Joaquin Co Off of Education	Stockton
458	4	San Marino Unified	San Marino
458	4	Santa Rita Union Elementary	Salinas
458	4	Saratoga Union Elementary	Saratoga
458	4	Savanna Elementary	Anaheim
458	4	Scotts Valley Unified	Scotts Valley
458	4	Sonora Union High	Sonora
458	4	Standard Elementary	Bakersfield
458	4	Turlock Joint Union High	Turlock
458	4	Wasco Union Elementary	Wasco
458	4	Waterford Unified	Waterford
458	4	Wilsona Elementary	Palmdale
458	4	Wiseburn Elementary	Hawthorne
504	3	Arvin Union Elementary	Arvin
504	3	Beardsley Elementary	Bakersfield
504	3	Bellevue Union Elementary	Santa Rosa
504	3	Brawley Union High	Brawley
504	3	Central Union High	El Centro
504	3	Fallbrook Union High	Fallbrook
504	3	Galt Joint Union High	Galt
504	3	Jefferson Elementary	Tracy
504	3	Julian Union Elementary	Julian
504	3	Julian Union High	Julian
504	3	King City Union Elementary	King City
504	3	Mark West Union Elementary	Santa Rosa
504	3	Mother Lode Union Elementary	Placerville
504	3	Richland Union Elementary SD	Shafter
504	3	San Rafael City High	San Rafael
504	3	Santa Maria Joint Union High	Santa Maria
504	3	Winton Elementary	Winton
504	3	Woodlake Union Elementary	Woodlake
522	2	Fairfax Elementary	Bakersfield
522	2	Los Gatos-Saratoga Jt Union High	Los Gatos
522	2	Oro Grande Elementary	Oro Grande
522	2	Romoland Elementary	Homeland
522	2	San Benito High	Hollister
522	2	Santa Paula Union High	Santa Paula
522	2	Weaver Union Elementary	Merced

Number of Teachers

Rank	Number	District Name	City
1	35,492	Los Angeles Unified	Los Angeles
2	7,420	San Diego Unified	San Diego
3	4,439	Long Beach Unified	Long Beach
4	3,926	Fresno Unified	Fresno
5	3,139	San Francisco Unified	San Francisco
6	2,833	Santa Ana Unified	Santa Ana
7	2,691	San Bernardino City Unified	San Bernardino
8	2,660	Elk Grove Unified	Elk Grove
9	2,659	Sacramento City Unified	Sacramento
10	2,544	Oakland Unified	Oakland
11	2,418	San Juan Unified	Carmichael
12	2,158	Capistrano Unified	San Juan Capis
13	2,137	Garden Grove Unified	Garden Grove
14	2,085	Corona-Norco Unified	Norco
15	2,004	Stockton City Unified	Stockton
16	1,845	Mt. Diablo Unified	Concord
17	1,807	Riverside Unified	Riverside
18	1,773	Sweetwater Union High	Chula Vista
19	1,771	Fontana Unified	Fontana
20	1,698	West Contra Costa Unified	Richmond
21	1,627	San Jose Unified	San Jose

22	1,604	Clovis Unified	Clovis
23	1,543	Pomona Unified	Pomona
24	1,538	Moreno Valley Unified	Moreno Valley
25	1,520	Orange Unified	Orange
26	1,507	Montebello Unified	Montebello
27	1,478	Poway Unified	Poway
28	1,468	Fremont Unified	Fremont
29	1,458	Saddleback Valley Unified	Mission Viejo
30	1,442	Lodi Unified	Lodi
31	1,410	Kern Union High	Bakersfield
32	1,382	Chino Valley Unified	Chino
33	1,373	Compton Unified	Compton
34	1,357	Bakersfield City Elementary	Bakersfield
35	1,346	Glendale Unified	Glendale
36	1,325	Rialto Unified	Rialto
37	1,291	Chula Vista Elementary	Chula Vista
38	1,278	Anaheim Union High	Anaheim
39	1,197	Hayward Unified	Hayward
40	1,194	Ontario-Montclair Elementary	Ontario
41	1,192	Vista Unified	Vista
42	1,190	Desert Sands Unified	La Quinta
43	1,186	Grossmont Union High	La Mesa
44	1,180	Placentia-Yorba Linda Unified	Placentia
45	1,171	Hacienda La Puente Unified	City of Industry
46	1,146	East Side Union High	San Jose
47	1,145	Visalia Unified	Visalia
48	1,139	Torrance Unified	Torrance
49	1,114	Fairfield-Suisun Unified	Fairfield
50	1,098	Colton Joint Unified	Colton
51	1,093	Temecula Valley Unified	Temecula
52	1,076	Pasadena Unified	Pasadena
53	1,075	Irvine Unified	Irvine
54	1,068	Oceanside Unified	Oceanside
55	1,068	Palm Springs Unified	Palm Springs
56	1,066	Norwalk-La Mirada Unified	Norwalk
57	1,035	Newport-Mesa Unified	Costa Mesa
58	1,027	Anaheim Elementary	Anaheim
59	1,025	San Ramon Valley Unified	Danville
60	1,016	Manteca Unified	Manteca
61	1,002	Antioch Unified	Antioch
62	1,002	Los Angeles Co Office of Education	Downey
63	994	Pajaro Valley Unified School	Watsonville
64	994	Escondido Union Elementary	Escondido
65	991	Conejo Valley Unified	Thousand Oaks
66	988	ABC Unified	Cerritos
67	970	Downey Unified	Downey
68	960	Simi Valley Unified	Simi Valley
69	939	Chaffey Joint Union High	Ontario
70	927	Palmdale Elementary	Palmdale
71	925	Modesto City Elementary	Modesto
72	916	Vallejo City Unified	Vallejo
73	915	Redlands Unified	Redlands
74	898	Hemet Unified	Hemet
75	885	Jurupa Unified	Riverside
76	876	Lake Elsinore Unified	Lake Elsinore
77	856	Inglewood Unified	Inglewood
78	853	Alvord Unified	Riverside
79	839	William S. Hart Union High	Santa Clarita
80	839	Antelope Valley Union High	Lancaster
81	834	Folsom-Cordova Unified	Folsom
82	833	Napa Valley Unified	Napa
83	828	Madera Unified	Madera
84	827	Rowland Unified	Rowland Heights
85	817	Cajon Valley Union Elementary	El Cajon
86	807	Tustin Unified	Tustin
87	787	Ventura Unified	Ventura
88	786	Paramount Unified	Paramount
89	785	Oxnard Elementary	Oxnard
90	779	Baldwin Park Unified	Baldwin Park
91	778	Burbank Unified	Burbank
92	773	Murrieta Valley Unified	Murrieta
93	752	Tracy Joint Unified	Tracy
94	742	Cupertino Union School	Cupertino
95	732	Lynwood Unified	Lynwood
96	727	Lancaster Elementary	Lancaster
97	709	Hesperia Unified	Hesperia
98	692	Alum Rock Union Elementary	San Jose
99	689	Bellflower Unified	Bellflower
100	687	Panama Buena Vista Union Elem	Bakersfield
101	685	Walnut Valley Unified	Walnut
102	676	Chico Unified	Chico
102	676	La Mesa-Spring Valley	La Mesa
104	674	Vacaville Unified	Vacaville
105	666	Coachella Valley Unified	Thermal
106	662	Covina-Valley Unified	Covina
107	658	Pleasanton Unified	Pleasanton
108	652	Santa Clara Unified	Santa Clara
109	641	New Haven Unified	Union City
110	631	Modesto City High	Modesto
111	620	Apple Valley Unified	Apple Valley
112	618	San Marcos Unified	San Marcos
113	613	Santa Monica-Malibu Unified	Santa Monica
114	612	Palo Alto Unified	Palo Alto
115	606	Livermore Valley Joint Unified	Livermore
116	602	Oxnard Union High	Oxnard
117	597	Monterey Peninsula Unified	Monterey
118	596	Evergreen Elementary	San Jose
119	593	Upland Unified	Upland
120	593	Salinas Union High	Salinas
121	593	Fullerton Elementary	Fullerton
122	588	Porterville Unified	Porterville
123	581	Santa Maria-Bonita Elementary	Santa Maria
124	575	Lompoc Unified	Lompoc
125	570	Grant Joint Union High	Sacramento
126	570	Yuba City Unified	Yuba City
127	570	Huntington Beach Union High	Huntington Bch
128	568	El Monte City Elementary	El Monte
129	566	San Lorenzo Unified	San Lorenzo
130	565	Fullerton Joint Union High	Fullerton
131	562	Santa Rosa High	Santa Rosa
132	560	El Rancho Unified	Pico Rivera
133	559	Oak Grove Elementary	San Jose
134	558	Alameda City Unified	Alameda
135	558	Azusa Unified	Azusa
136	552	Central Unified	Fresno
137	548	Val Verde Unified	Perris
138	531	Palos Verdes Peninsula Unified	Palos Verdes Est
139	528	Lucia Mar Unified	Arroyo Grande
140	525	Merced City Elementary	Merced
141	522	Rio Linda Union Elementary	Rio Linda
142	516	Redwood City Elementary	Redwood City
143	514	Las Virgenes Unified	Calabasas
144	510	Woodland Joint Unified	Woodland
145	504	Etiwanda Elementary	Etiwanda
146	503	Alhambra City Elementary	Alhambra
147	502	San Mateo-Foster City Elementary	San Mateo
148	499	Franklin-Mckinley Elementary	San Jose
149	490	Whittier Union High	Whittier
150	485	Mountain View Elementary	El Monte
151	484	Westminster Elementary	Westminster
152	481	Orange County Office of Education	Costa Mesa
153	480	Ocean View Elementary	Huntington Bch
154	479	Saugus Union Elementary	Santa Clarita
155	476	Marysville Joint Unified	Marysville
156	475	San Dieguito Union High	Encinitas
157	473	Ceres Unified	Ceres
158	463	Santa Barbara High	Santa Barbara
159	462	Snowline Joint Unified	Phelan
160	462	Pittsburg Unified	Pittsburg
161	458	Carlsbad Unified	Carlsbad
162	457	Gilroy Unified	Gilroy
163	456	West Covina Unified	West Covina
164	455	Berkeley Unified	Berkeley
165	452	Hawthorne Elementary	Hawthorne
166	449	East Whittier City Elementary	Whittier
167	448	Morongo Unified	Twentynine Plms
168	443	Bonita Unified	San Dimas
169	442	South Bay Union Elementary	Imperial Beach
170	441	Lincoln Unified	Stockton
171	441	Rocklin Unified	Rocklin
172	441	Sanger Unified	Sanger
173	441	Kings Canyon Joint Unified	Reedley
174	439	Salinas City Elementary	Salinas
175	438	Turlock Joint Elementary	Turlock
176	437	Arcadia Unified	Arcadia
177	436	Milpitas Unified	Milpitas
178	429	South San Francisco Unified	S San Francisco
179	427	Davis Joint Unified	Davis
180	424	Victor Valley Union High	Victorville
181	418	San Leandro Unified	San Leandro
182	411	Merced Union High	Atwater
183	409	Morgan Hill Unified	Morgan Hill
184	406	Yucaipa-Calimesa Jt. Unified	Yucaipa
185	406	Victor Elementary	Victorville
186	403	Natomas Unified	Sacramento
187	401	El Monte Union High	El Monte
188	399	Calexico Unified	Calexico
189	399	Hueneme Elementary	Port Hueneme
190	398	Berryessa Union Elementary	San Jose
191	398	San Mateo Union High	San Mateo
192	397	Fremont Union High	Sunnyvale
193	394	Los Alamitos Unified	Los Alamitos
194	390	Castro Valley Unified	Castro Valley
195	388	Tulare City Elementary	Tulare
196	382	Novato Unified	Novato
196	382	Redondo Beach Unified	Redondo Beach
198	382	Los Banos Unified	Los Banos
199	381	Sylvan Union Elementary	Modesto
200	376	San Luis Coastal Unified	San Luis Obispo
201	372	Sequoia Union High	Redwood City
202	367	Campbell Union Elementary	Campbell
203	365	Roseville City Elementary	Roseville
204	365	Washington Unified	West Sacramento
205	364	Moorpark Unified	Moorpark
206	364	Greenfield Union Elementary	Bakersfield
207	359	Roseville Joint Union High	Roseville
208	352	Ukiah Unified	Ukiah
209	351	Whittier City Elementary	Whittier
210	347	Escondido Union High	Escondido
211	346	Magnolia Elementary	Anaheim
212	346	Westside Union Elementary	Lancaster
213	345	Newark Unified	Newark
214	342	Lennox Elementary	Lennox
215	342	Alhambra City High	Alhambra
216	341	Pleasant Valley School	Camarillo
217	339	Glendora Unified	Glendora
218	333	Alisal Union Elementary	Salinas
219	331	Delano Union Elementary	Delano
220	329	Cotati-Rohnert Park Unified	Rohnert Park
220	329	Paso Robles Joint Unified	Paso Robles
222	326	Barstow Unified	Barstow
223	322	Dry Creek Joint Elementary	Roseville
224	321	Centinela Valley Union High	Lawndale
225	317	El Dorado Union High	Placerville
226	316	Culver City Unified	Culver City
227	315	Garvey Elementary	Rosemead
228	315	Manhattan Beach Unified	Manhattan Beach
229	313	Alta Loma Elementary	Alta Loma
230	311	Santee Elementary	Santee
231	310	San Jacinto Unified	San Jacinto
232	309	Hollister SD	Hollister
233	309	Claremont Unified	Claremont
234	308	Monrovia Unified	Monrovia
235	307	Ramona City Unified	Ramona
236	306	San Bernardino Co Off of Education	San Bernardino
237	304	Santa Barbara Elementary	Santa Barbara
238	302	La Habra City Elementary	La Habra
239	301	Jefferson Elementary	Daly City
240	300	North Sacramento Elementary	Sacramento
241	300	Sunnyvale Elementary	Sunnyvale
242	300	Campbell Union High	San Jose
243	297	Lawndale Elementary	Lawndale
244	297	Perris Union High	Perris
245	296	National Elementary	National City
246	293	Selma Unified	Selma
247	291	Newhall Elementary	Valencia
248	291	Brentwood Union Elementary	Brentwood
249	289	Riverside Co Office of Education	Riverside
250	289	San Gabriel Unified	San Gabriel
251	288	Charter Oak Unified	Covina
252	283	Huntington Beach City Elementary	Huntington Bch
253	281	Fallbrook Union Elementary	Fallbrook
254	280	Travis Unified	Travis Afb
255	280	Beverly Hills Unified	Beverly Hills
256	279	Buena Park Elementary	Buena Park
257	277	Brea-Olinda Unified	Brea
258	276	Encinitas Union Elementary	Encinitas
258	276	San Diego Co Office of Education	San Diego
260	275	Paradise Unified	Paradise
261	274	Bassett Unified	La Puente
262	273	Santa Rosa Elementary	Santa Rosa
263	272	Atascadero Unified	Atascadero
264	272	El Centro Elementary	El Centro
265	271	Center Joint Unified	Antelope
266	271	North Monterey County Unified	Moss Landing
267	269	Santa Maria Joint Union High	Santa Maria
268	267	Sierra Sands Unified	Ridgecrest
269	264	Eureka City Unified	Eureka
270	263	Acalanes Union High	Lafayette
271	262	Fountain Valley Elementary	Fountain Valley
272	262	Petaluma Joint Union High	Petaluma
273	262	Menifee Union Elementary	Menifee
274	260	Dinuba Unified	Dinuba
275	260	Benicia Unified	Benicia
276	258	Hanford Elementary	Hanford
277	257	Sulphur Springs Union Elementary	Canyon Country
277	257	Temple City Unified	Temple City
279	254	Perris Elementary	Perris
279	254	Ravenswood City Elementary	East Palo Alto
281	252	Adelanto Elementary	Adelanto
282	248	Centralia Elementary	Buena Park
283	247	Tahoe-Truckee Joint Unified	Truckee
284	245	Galt Joint Union Elementary	Galt
285	244	Shasta Union High	Redding
286	241	Valley Center-Pauma Unified	Valley Center
287	239	San Ysidro Elementary	San Ysidro
288	238	Jefferson Union High	Daly City
288	238	Sonoma Valley Unified	Sonoma
290	237	Santa Clara Co Off of Education	San Jose
291	236	Rim of the World Unified	Lake Arrowhead
292	236	Little Lake City Elementary	Santa Fe Spgs
293	230	Atwater Elementary	Atwater
294	228	Windsor Unified	Windsor
295	228	Oakdale Joint Unified	Oakdale
296	226	Dublin Unified	Dublin
297	225	Central Elementary	Rcho Cucamong
298	225	Cypress Elementary	Cypress
299	224	Oakley Union Elementary	Oakley

300	224	Lakeside Union Elementary	Lakeside
301	222	Lake Tahoe Unified	S Lake Tahoe
302	221	Beaumont Unified	Beaumont
303	218	Orcutt Union Elementary	Orcutt
304	218	Union Elementary	San Jose
305	217	Mountain View-Whisman Elementary	Mountain View
306	217	Santa Cruz City High	Soquel
307	216	Moreland Elementary	San Jose
308	215	Duarte Unified	Duarte
309	214	Del Norte County Unified	Crescent City
310	212	Lemon Grove Elementary	Lemon Grove
311	211	Western Placer Unified	Lincoln
312	210	Tamalpais Union High	Larkspur
313	208	Martinez Unified	Martinez
314	208	Patterson Joint Unified	Patterson
315	205	South Whittier Elementary	Whittier
316	204	Los Altos Elementary	Los Altos
317	202	Placer Union High	Auburn
318	202	Turlock Joint Union High	Turlock
319	200	San Rafael City Elementary	San Rafael
320	200	Empire Union Elementary	Modesto
321	199	Goleta Union Elementary	Goleta
322	198	Amador County Unified	Jackson
323	198	Eureka Union Elementary	Granite Bay
324	197	Buckeye Union Elementary	Shingle Springs
325	196	Kern County Office of Education	Bakersfield
326	195	Liberty Union High	Brentwood
327	195	Del Mar Union Elementary	Del Mar
328	195	Fresno County Office of Education	Fresno
329	194	Tehachapi Unified	Tehachapi
330	193	Cutler-Orosi Joint Unified	Orosi
331	193	Gateway Unified	Redding
332	192	Redding Elementary	Redding
333	190	Nevada Joint Union High	Grass Valley
334	188	Enterprise Elementary	Redding
335	188	Coalinga-Huron Joint Unified	Coalinga
336	187	La Canada Unified	La Canada
337	186	Brawley Elementary	Brawley
338	185	Parlier Unified	Parlier
339	185	Rosedale Union Elementary	Bakersfield
340	185	Rio Elementary	Oxnard
341	184	Dixon Unified	Dixon
342	183	Banning Unified	Banning
343	183	Fillmore Unified	Fillmore
344	181	Calaveras Unified	San Andreas
345	179	Lindsay Unified	Lindsay
346	179	Lafayette Elementary	Lafayette
347	177	Oak Park Unified	Oak Park
347	177	Tulare Joint Union High	Tulare
349	175	Soledad Unified	Soledad
350	175	Ojai Unified	Ojai
351	175	South Pasadena Unified	South Pasadena
352	174	Rescue Union Elementary	Rescue
353	173	Salida Union Elementary	Salida
354	172	Kerman Unified	Kerman
355	168	Cabrillo Unified	Half Moon Bay
356	168	Santa Paula Elementary	Santa Paula
357	168	Walnut Creek Elementary	Walnut Creek
358	167	Mountain View-Los Altos Union High	Mountain View
359	166	Castaic Union Elementary	Valencia
360	166	Delano Joint Union High	Delano
361	165	Plumas Unified	Quincy
362	164	Central Union High	El Centro
362	164	San Lorenzo Valley Unified	Ben Lomond
364	162	Oroville City Elementary	Oroville
365	162	Lemoore Union Elementary	Lemoore
366	162	Palo Verde Unified	Blythe
367	162	Mountain View Elementary	Ontario
368	160	Albany City Unified	Albany
369	157	Waterford Unified	Waterford
370	156	Bear Valley Unified	Big Bear Lake
371	156	Rosemead Elementary	Rosemead
372	155	Corcoran Joint Unified	Corcoran
373	155	Konocti Unified	Lower Lake
374	154	Hanford Joint Union High	Hanford
375	154	Riverbank Unified	Riverbank
376	152	Stanislaus Union Elementary	Modesto
377	152	San Marino Unified	San Marino
378	152	San Joaquin Co Off of Education	Stockton
379	151	Piedmont City Unified	Piedmont
380	149	Arvin Union Elementary	Arvin
381	148	Mcfarland Unified	Mcfarland
382	147	Solana Beach Elementary	Solana Beach
383	147	El Segundo Unified	El Segundo
384	146	Fruitvale Elementary	Bakersfield
385	146	Richland Union Elementary SD	Shafter
386	144	Wasco Union Elementary	Wasco
387	143	Lowell Joint	Whittier
388	142	Pacifica SD	Pacifica
389	142	Escalon Unified	Escalon
390	142	Carpinteria Unified	Carpinteria
390	142	Rincon Valley Union Elementary	Santa Rosa
392	139	Mt. Pleasant Elementary	San Jose
393	139	Fallbrook Union High	Fallbrook
394	138	Oro Grande Elementary	Oro Grande
394	138	Southern Kern Unified	Rosamond
396	138	Ripon Unified	Ripon
397	138	Burton Elementary	Porterville
398	137	Cambrian Elementary	San Jose
399	137	Dos Palos Oro Loma Jt. Unified	Dos Palos
400	136	Keppel Union Elementary	Pearblossom
401	136	Coronado Unified	Coronado
402	136	Silver Valley Unified	Yermo
403	135	Los Gatos Union Elementary	Los Gatos
403	135	Sierra Unified	Prather
405	134	Santa Rita Union Elementary	Salinas
406	133	Cucamonga Elementary	Rcho Cucamong
407	132	Mariposa County Unified	Mariposa
408	132	King City Union Elementary	King City
408	132	Tulare County Office of Education	Visalia
410	131	Imperial Unified	Imperial
411	130	Scotts Valley Unified	Scotts Valley
412	128	San Carlos Elementary	San Carlos
412	128	Wheatland Elementary	Wheatland
414	128	Los Gatos-Saratoga Jt Union High	Los Gatos
415	128	Orinda Union Elementary	Orinda
416	128	Ocean View Elementary	Oxnard
417	127	Carmel Unified	Carmel
418	126	Burlingame Elementary	Burlingame
419	125	Linden Unified	Linden
420	125	Standard Elementary	Bakersfield
421	125	Belmont-Redwood Shores Elementary	Belmont
421	125	Farmersville Unified	Farmersville
423	125	Healdsburg Unified	Healdsburg
423	125	Mojave Unified	Mojave
425	125	Willits Unified	Willits
426	124	Mill Valley Elementary	Mill Valley
427	124	Laguna Beach Unified	Laguna Beach
428	124	San Bruno Park Elementary	San Bruno
429	123	Gonzales Unified	Gonzales
430	123	West Sonoma County Union High	Sebastopol
431	123	Reef-Sunset Unified	Avenal
431	123	Templeton Unified	Templeton
433	122	Firebaugh-Las Deltas Joint Unified	Firebaugh
434	122	River Delta Joint Unified	Rio Vista
435	122	Lamont Elementary	Lamont
436	121	Fort Bragg Unified	Fort Bragg
436	121	Robla Elementary	Sacramento
438	121	Santa Cruz City Elementary	Soquel
439	121	Menlo Park City Elementary	Atherton
440	120	Hilmar Unified	Hilmar
441	120	Livingston Union Elementary	Livingston
442	120	Eastside Union Elementary	Lancaster
443	120	Muroc Joint Unified	North Edwards
444	120	Newman-Crows Landing Unified	Newman
445	119	Auburn Union Elementary	Auburn
446	119	Orland Joint Unified	Orland
447	117	Saratoga Union Elementary	Saratoga
448	117	Delhi Unified	Delhi
449	116	San Benito High	Hollister
450	115	Twin Ridges Elementary	North San Juan
451	115	Central Union Elementary	Lemoore
452	114	Petaluma City Elementary	Petaluma
453	113	Savanna Elementary	Anaheim
454	112	Mendota Unified	Mendota
455	112	Julian Union High	Julian
456	112	Alpine Union Elementary	Alpine
457	111	Los Nietos Elementary	Whittier
458	110	Red Bluff Union Elementary	Red Bluff
459	109	Taft City Elementary	Taft
460	109	Fowler Unified	Fowler
461	108	Oroville Union High	Oroville
462	108	Gridley Unified	Gridley
463	106	Winters Joint Unified	Winters
464	105	Kingsburg Elementary Charter	Kingsburg
465	105	Golden Plains Unified	San Joaquin
466	103	Live Oak Elementary	Santa Cruz
467	103	Millbrae Elementary	Millbrae
467	103	Soquel Union Elementary	Capitola
469	101	Wilsona Elementary	Palmdale
470	100	Galt Joint Union High	Galt
471	100	Norris Elementary	Bakersfield
472	100	San Rafael City High	San Rafael
473	100	Pleasant Ridge Union Elementary	Grass Valley
474	99	Del Paso Heights Elementary	Sacramento
474	99	Gustine Unified	Gustine
476	98	Kelseyville Unified	Kelseyville
477	98	Anderson Union High	Anderson
477	98	Lemoore Union High	Lemoore
479	98	Wiseburn Elementary	Hawthorne
480	98	Grass Valley Elementary	Grass Valley
481	97	Black Oak Mine Unified	Georgetown
481	97	Hughson Unified	Hughson
483	95	Old Adobe Union Elementary	Petaluma
483	95	Ross Valley Elementary	San Anselmo
485	95	Dixie Elementary	San Rafael
486	95	Corning Union Elementary	Corning
487	94	Holtville Unified	Holtville
488	94	Red Bluff Joint Union High	Red Bluff
489	93	Keyes Union Elementary	Keyes
490	93	Exeter Union Elementary	Exeter
491	93	Middletown Unified	Middletown
492	93	Mountain Empire Unified	Pine Valley
492	93	Weaver Union Elementary	Merced
494	92	Winton Elementary	Winton
495	92	Jefferson Elementary	Tracy
496	92	Bonsall Union Elementary	Bonsall
497	92	Loomis Union Elementary	Loomis
498	91	Lakeport Unified	Lakeport
499	91	King City Joint Union High	King City
500	91	Pacific Grove Unified	Pacific Grove
501	91	Beardsley Elementary	Bakersfield
502	90	Northern Humboldt Union High	McKinleyville
503	90	Moraga Elementary	Moraga
504	89	Bellevue Union Elementary	Santa Rosa
505	89	John Swett Unified	Crockett
506	88	Acton-Agua Dulce Unified	Acton
507	88	Live Oak Unified	Live Oak
508	87	Willows Unified	Willows
509	84	Earlimart Elementary	Earlimart
510	84	Chowchilla Elementary	Chowchilla
510	84	Piner-Olivet Union Elementary	Santa Rosa
512	82	Mark West Union Elementary	Santa Rosa
512	82	Woodlake Union Elementary	Woodlake
514	81	Julian Union Elementary	Julian
515	80	Greenfield Union Elementary	Greenfield
516	80	Cloverdale Unified	Cloverdale
517	79	Cascade Union Elementary	Anderson
517	79	Riverdale Joint Unified	Riverdale
519	79	Mother Lode Union Elementary	Placerville
520	77	Brawley Union High	Brawley
521	75	Jamul-Dulzura Union Elementary	Jamul
522	75	Romoland Elementary	Homeland
523	73	Sonora Union High	Sonora
524	71	Fairfax Elementary	Bakersfield
525	68	Nuview Union Elementary	Nuevo
526	67	Westwood Unified	Westwood
527	67	Gorman Elementary	Gorman
528	64	Santa Paula Union High	Santa Paula

Number of Students

Rank	Number	District Name	City
1	747,009	Los Angeles Unified	Los Angeles
2	137,960	San Diego Unified	San Diego
3	97,560	Long Beach Unified	Long Beach
4	81,408	Fresno Unified	Fresno
5	62,874	Santa Ana Unified	Santa Ana
6	57,818	San Bernardino City Unified	San Bernardino
7	57,805	San Francisco Unified	San Francisco
8	55,613	Elk Grove Unified	Elk Grove
9	52,103	Sacramento City Unified	Sacramento
10	50,906	San Juan Unified	Carmichael
11	50,437	Oakland Unified	Oakland
12	50,172	Garden Grove Unified	Garden Grove
13	49,746	Capistrano Unified	San Juan Capis
14	43,998	Corona-Norco Unified	Norco
15	42,012	Riverside Unified	Riverside
16	41,343	Fontana Unified	Fontana
17	39,483	Stockton City Unified	Stockton
18	39,228	Sweetwater Union High	Chula Vista
19	36,821	Mt. Diablo Unified	Concord
20	35,952	Montebello Unified	Montebello
21	35,412	Pomona Unified	Pomona
22	35,349	Saddleback Valley Unified	Mission Viejo
23	34,792	Moreno Valley Unified	Moreno Valley
24	34,663	Clovis Unified	Clovis
25	33,672	West Contra Costa Unified	Richmond
26	33,340	Chino Valley Unified	Chino
27	33,051	Poway Unified	Poway
28	32,486	Compton Unified	Compton
29	32,468	Anaheim Union High	Anaheim
30	32,357	Kern Union High	Bakersfield
31	32,314	San Jose Unified	San Jose
32	32,032	Orange Unified	Orange
33	31,844	Fremont Unified	Fremont
34	30,431	Rialto Unified	Rialto
35	29,433	Glendale Unified	Glendale
36	29,178	Lodi Unified	Lodi
37	28,315	Bakersfield City Elementary	Bakersfield
38	27,010	Ontario-Montclair Elementary	Ontario
39	26,989	Vista Unified	Vista
40	26,774	Placentia-Yorba Linda Unified	Placentia
41	26,122	Desert Sands Unified	La Quinta
42	25,499	Hacienda La Puente Unified	City of Industry
43	25,292	Chula Vista Elementary	Chula Vista
44	25,258	Visalia Unified	Visalia
45	25,229	Torrance Unified	Torrance

46	25,176	East Side Union High	San Jose
47	24,936	Colton Joint Unified	Colton
48	24,930	Irvine Unified	Irvine
49	24,456	Grossmont Union High	La Mesa
50	24,101	Norwalk-La Mirada Unified	Norwalk
51	24,014	Hayward Unified	Hayward
52	23,496	Temecula Valley Unified	Temecula
53	23,341	Chaffey Joint Union High	Ontario
54	23,241	Fairfield-Suisun Unified	Fairfield
55	22,736	Palmdale Elementary	Palmdale
56	22,669	Pasadena Unified	Pasadena
57	22,627	Manteca Unified	Manteca
58	22,523	Downey Unified	Downey
59	22,499	Palm Springs Unified	Palm Springs
60	22,484	Oceanside Unified	Oceanside
61	22,383	Newport-Mesa Unified	Costa Mesa
62	22,243	Conejo Valley Unified	Thousand Oaks
63	22,226	ABC Unified	Cerritos
64	22,148	Antelope Valley Union High	Lancaster
65	21,988	San Ramon Valley Unified	Danville
66	21,963	Anaheim Elementary	Anaheim
67	21,727	Simi Valley Unified	Simi Valley
68	21,628	Antioch Unified	Antioch
69	21,122	William S. Hart Union High	Santa Clarita
70	20,924	Jurupa Unified	Riverside
71	20,643	Redlands Unified	Redlands
72	20,164	Escondido Union Elementary	Escondido
73	19,711	Lake Elsinore Unified	Lake Elsinore
74	19,693	Hemet Unified	Hemet
75	19,658	Lynwood Unified	Lynwood
76	19,522	Pajaro Valley Unified School	Watsonville
77	19,462	Vallejo City Unified	Vallejo
78	19,441	Alvord Unified	Riverside
79	19,287	Baldwin Park Unified	Baldwin Park
80	18,950	Tustin Unified	Tustin
81	18,803	Modesto City Elementary	Modesto
82	18,384	Rowland Unified	Rowland Heights
83	18,070	Cajon Valley Union Elementary	El Cajon
84	18,041	Folsom-Cordova Unified	Folsom
85	17,969	Inglewood Unified	Inglewood
86	17,794	Ventura Unified	Ventura
87	17,480	Murrieta Valley Unified	Murrieta
88	17,247	Madera Unified	Madera
89	17,066	Burbank Unified	Burbank
90	17,051	Hesperia Unified	Hesperia
91	17,023	Napa Valley Unified	Napa
92	17,013	Paramount Unified	Paramount
93	16,851	Oxnard Elementary	Oxnard
94	16,398	Fullerton Joint Union High	Fullerton
95	16,063	Tracy Joint Unified	Tracy
96	16,048	Cupertino Union School	Cupertino
97	15,799	Lancaster Elementary	Lancaster
98	15,746	Oxnard Union High	Oxnard
99	15,581	Modesto City High	Modesto
100	15,522	Bellflower Unified	Bellflower
101	15,458	Walnut Valley Unified	Walnut
102	15,035	Covina-Valley Unified	Covina
103	14,975	Huntington Beach Union High	Huntington Bch
104	14,621	Coachella Valley Unified	Thermal
105	14,589	San Marcos Unified	San Marcos
106	14,475	Apple Valley Unified	Apple Valley
107	14,329	Livermore Valley Joint Unified	Livermore
108	14,310	La Mesa-Spring Valley	La Mesa
109	14,039	Pleasanton Unified	Pleasanton
110	13,976	Santa Clara Unified	Santa Clara
111	13,963	Panama Buena Vista Union Elem	Bakersfield
112	13,887	Vacaville Unified	Vacaville
113	13,812	Fullerton Elementary	Fullerton
114	13,782	Alum Rock Union Elementary	San Jose
115	13,780	Salinas Union High	Salinas
116	13,762	Chico Unified	Chico
117	13,585	Upland Unified	Upland
118	13,447	Val Verde Unified	Perris
119	13,303	New Haven Unified	Union City
120	13,111	Evergreen Elementary	San Jose
121	13,015	Grant Joint Union High	Sacramento
122	12,847	Santa Rosa High	Santa Rosa
123	12,842	Santa Monica-Malibu Unified	Santa Monica
124	12,580	Porterville Unified	Porterville
125	12,557	Whittier Union High	Whittier
126	12,395	Santa Maria-Bonita Elementary	Santa Maria
127	12,170	Las Virgenes Unified	Calabasas
128	12,166	El Rancho Unified	Pico Rivera
129	12,134	Azusa Unified	Azusa
130	12,132	Monterey Peninsula Unified	Monterey
131	11,921	Yuba City Unified	Yuba City
132	11,851	Central Unified	Fresno
133	11,829	Los Angeles Co Office of Education	Downey
134	11,713	El Monte City Elementary	El Monte
135	11,690	San Dieguito Union High	Encinitas
136	11,636	Oak Grove Elementary	San Jose
137	11,605	Palos Verdes Peninsula Unified	Palos Verdes Est
138	11,559	Lompoc Unified	Lompoc
139	11,547	San Lorenzo Unified	San Lorenzo
140	11,414	Merced City Elementary	Merced
141	11,294	Etiwanda Elementary	Etiwanda
142	11,163	Alhambra City Elementary	Alhambra
143	10,852	Victor Valley Union High	Victorville
144	10,847	Lucia Mar Unified	Arroyo Grande
145	10,621	Alameda City Unified	Alameda
146	10,598	Santa Barbara High	Santa Barbara
147	10,518	West Covina Unified	West Covina
148	10,515	Woodland Joint Unified	Woodland
149	10,354	Palo Alto Unified	Palo Alto
150	10,254	El Monte Union High	El Monte
151	10,253	Westminster Elementary	Westminster
152	10,211	Ceres Unified	Ceres
153	10,204	Saugus Union Elementary	Santa Clarita
154	10,203	Bonita Unified	San Dimas
155	10,192	Mountain View Elementary	El Monte
156	10,186	Ocean View Elementary	Huntington Bch
157	10,098	Carlsbad Unified	Carlsbad
158	10,069	San Mateo-Foster City Elementary	San Mateo
159	9,992	Arcadia Unified	Arcadia
160	9,970	Rio Linda Union Elementary	Rio Linda
161	9,875	Hawthorne Elementary	Hawthorne
162	9,867	Franklin-Mckinley Elementary	San Jose
163	9,839	Marysville Joint Unified	Marysville
164	9,805	Victor Elementary	Victorville
165	9,695	Merced Union High	Atwater
166	9,691	Gilroy Unified	Gilroy
167	9,622	Yucaipa-Calimesa Jt. Unified	Yucaipa
168	9,591	Pittsburg Unified	Pittsburg
169	9,528	Milpitas Unified	Milpitas
170	9,521	Snowline Joint Unified	Phelan
171	9,473	Morongo Unified	Twentynine Plms
172	9,362	South San Francisco Unified	S San Francisco
173	9,332	East Whittier City Elementary	Whittier
174	9,320	Fremont Union High	Sunnyvale
175	9,244	South Bay Union Elementary	Imperial Beach
176	9,184	Los Alamitos Unified	Los Alamitos
177	9,171	Rocklin Unified	Rocklin
178	9,067	Kings Canyon Joint Unified	Reedley
179	9,017	Lincoln Unified	Stockton
180	8,939	Turlock Joint Elementary	Turlock
181	8,880	Morgan Hill Unified	Morgan Hill
182	8,850	Salinas City Elementary	Salinas
183	8,843	Berkeley Unified	Berkeley
184	8,839	Calexico Unified	Calexico
185	8,834	Redwood City Elementary	Redwood City
186	8,711	Davis Joint Unified	Davis
187	8,695	Sanger Unified	Sanger
188	8,653	San Leandro Unified	San Leandro
189	8,636	Natomas Unified	Sacramento
190	8,617	Orange County Office of Education	Costa Mesa
191	8,604	Escondido Union High	Escondido
192	8,552	Alhambra City High	Alhambra
193	8,508	Hueneme Elementary	Port Hueneme
194	8,479	Berryessa Union Elementary	San Jose
195	8,391	Castro Valley Unified	Castro Valley
196	8,351	San Mateo Union High	San Mateo
197	8,227	Los Banos Unified	Los Banos
198	8,069	Tulare City Elementary	Tulare
199	8,057	Redondo Beach Unified	Redondo Beach
200	8,023	Roseville Joint Union High	Roseville
201	7,951	Alisal Union Elementary	Salinas
202	7,924	Glendora Unified	Glendora
203	7,841	San Luis Coastal Unified	San Luis Obispo
204	7,814	Moorpark Unified	Moorpark
205	7,813	Novato Unified	Novato
206	7,782	Sequoia Union High	Redwood City
207	7,733	Sylvan Union Elementary	Modesto
208	7,696	Lennox Elementary	Lennox
209	7,565	Centinela Valley Union High	Lawndale
210	7,527	Roseville City Elementary	Roseville
211	7,503	Alta Loma Elementary	Alta Loma
212	7,500	Campbell Union High	San Jose
213	7,498	Perris Union High	Perris
214	7,482	Cotati-Rohnert Park Unified	Rohnert Park
215	7,462	Campbell Union Elementary	Campbell
216	7,455	Pleasant Valley School	Camarillo
217	7,433	Westside Union Elementary	Lancaster
218	7,427	Greenfield Union Elementary	Bakersfield
219	7,421	Newark Unified	Newark
220	7,332	Delano Union Elementary	Delano
221	7,309	Western Placer Unified	Lincoln
222	7,232	Whittier City Elementary	Whittier
223	7,216	Ramona City Unified	Ramona
224	7,110	Charter Oak Unified	Covina
225	7,093	San Jacinto Unified	San Jacinto
226	7,010	Barstow Unified	Barstow
227	7,008	Dry Creek Joint Elementary	Roseville
228	6,993	Santee Elementary	Santee
229	6,981	El Dorado Union High	Placerville
230	6,971	Magnolia Elementary	Anaheim
231	6,931	Huntington Beach City Elementary	Huntington Bch
232	6,850	Culver City Unified	Culver City
233	6,846	Claremont Unified	Claremont
234	6,842	Washington Unified	West Sacramento
235	6,828	Ukiah Unified	Ukiah
236	6,771	Paso Robles Joint Unified	Paso Robles
237	6,675	Santa Maria Joint Union High	Santa Maria
238	6,672	Newhall Elementary	Valencia
239	6,636	Jefferson Elementary	Daly City
240	6,584	Garvey Elementary	Rosemead
241	6,578	Monrovia Unified	Monrovia
242	6,535	National Elementary	National City
243	6,534	La Habra City Elementary	La Habra
244	6,484	Lawndale Elementary	Lawndale
245	6,441	Manhattan Beach Unified	Manhattan Beach
246	6,372	Buena Park Elementary	Buena Park
247	6,301	El Centro Elementary	El Centro
248	6,265	San Gabriel Unified	San Gabriel
249	6,264	Center Joint Unified	Antelope
250	6,250	Fountain Valley Elementary	Fountain Valley
251	6,242	Hollister SD	Hollister
252	6,206	Brea-Olinda Unified	Brea
253	6,141	Adelanto Elementary	Adelanto
254	6,092	Fallbrook Union Elementary	Fallbrook
255	6,082	Selma Unified	Selma
256	6,039	Bassett Unified	La Puente
257	6,025	North Monterey County Unified	Moss Landing
258	6,024	Santa Barbara Elementary	Santa Barbara
259	5,960	Sunnyvale Elementary	Sunnyvale
260	5,934	Petaluma Joint Union High	Petaluma
261	5,927	Brentwood Union Elementary	Brentwood
262	5,920	Menifee Union Elementary	Menifee
263	5,838	Shasta Union High	Redding
264	5,829	Encinitas Union Elementary	Encinitas
265	5,785	Acalanes Union High	Lafayette
266	5,702	Temple City Unified	Temple City
267	5,618	Rim of the World Unified	Lake Arrowhead
268	5,602	Sierra Sands Unified	Ridgecrest
269	5,573	Sulphur Springs Union Elementary	Canyon Country
270	5,542	Dinuba Unified	Dinuba
271	5,517	Atascadero Unified	Atascadero
272	5,432	Santa Cruz City High	Soquel
273	5,384	Jefferson Union High	Daly City
274	5,381	Hanford Elementary	Hanford
275	5,380	Travis Unified	Travis Afb
276	5,366	Benicia Unified	Benicia
277	5,320	Central Elementary	Rcho Cucamong
277	5,320	North Sacramento Elementary	Sacramento
279	5,309	Paradise Unified	Paradise
280	5,255	Centralia Elementary	Buena Park
281	5,235	Perris Elementary	Perris
282	5,220	Little Lake City Elementary	Santa Fe Spgs
283	5,130	Beverly Hills Unified	Beverly Hills
284	5,127	San Ysidro Elementary	San Ysidro
285	5,083	Lake Tahoe Unified	S Lake Tahoe
286	5,039	Eureka City Unified	Eureka
287	5,019	Ravenswood City Elementary	East Palo Alto
288	4,984	Oakdale Joint Unified	Oakdale
289	4,966	Orcutt Union Elementary	Orcutt
290	4,959	Beaumont Unified	Beaumont
291	4,921	Sonoma Valley Unified	Sonoma
292	4,871	Lakeside Union Elementary	Lakeside
293	4,832	Tehachapi Unified	Tehachapi
294	4,798	Liberty Union High	Brentwood
295	4,764	Atwater Elementary	Atwater
296	4,754	Banning Unified	Banning
297	4,746	Placer Union High	Auburn
298	4,727	Cypress Elementary	Cypress
299	4,696	Santa Rosa Elementary	Santa Rosa
300	4,692	Duarte Unified	Duarte
301	4,685	Windsor Unified	Windsor
302	4,661	Valley Center-Pauma Unified	Valley Center
303	4,597	Turlock Joint Union High	Turlock
304	4,589	Tahoe-Truckee Joint Unified	Truckee
305	4,567	Amador County Unified	Jackson
306	4,556	South Whittier Elementary	Whittier
307	4,547	Union Elementary	San Jose
308	4,487	Oakley Union Elementary	Oakley
309	4,483	Dublin Unified	Dublin
310	4,440	Lemon Grove Elementary	Lemon Grove
310	4,440	Mountain View-Whisman Elementary	Mountain View
312	4,438	Moreland Elementary	San Jose
313	4,407	Patterson Joint Unified	Patterson
314	4,350	Tulare Joint Union High	Tulare
315	4,348	Galt Joint Union Elementary	Galt
316	4,343	La Canada Unified	La Canada
317	4,320	Martinez Unified	Martinez
318	4,308	Coalinga-Huron Joint Unified	Coalinga
319	4,292	Del Norte County Unified	Crescent City
319	4,292	Nevada Joint Union High	Grass Valley
321	4,279	Buckeye Union Elementary	Shingle Springs
322	4,264	Eureka Union Elementary	Granite Bay
323	4,232	Rosedale Union Elementary	Bakersfield

324	4,199	South Pasadena Unified	South Pasadena
325	4,146	Rio Elementary	Oxnard
326	4,066	Empire Union Elementary	Modesto
327	4,065	Santa Paula Elementary	Santa Paula
328	4,050	Los Altos Elementary	Los Altos
329	4,025	Redding Elementary	Redding
330	4,017	Cutler-Orosi Joint Unified	Orosi
331	3,964	Goleta Union Elementary	Goleta
332	3,947	Central Union High	El Centro
333	3,936	Delano Joint Union High	Delano
334	3,929	Dixon Unified	Dixon
335	3,906	Fillmore Unified	Fillmore
336	3,860	Tamalpais Union High	Larkspur
337	3,839	Soledad Unified	Soledad
338	3,808	Ojai Unified	Ojai
339	3,764	Oak Park Unified	Oak Park
340	3,761	Enterprise Elementary	Redding
341	3,720	Hanford Joint Union High	Hanford
341	3,720	Riverside Co Office of Education	Riverside
343	3,711	Kerman Unified	Kerman
344	3,701	Calaveras Unified	San Andreas
345	3,677	Palo Verde Unified	Blythe
346	3,633	Cabrillo Unified	Half Moon Bay
347	3,624	Rescue Union Elementary	Rescue
348	3,612	Gateway Unified	Redding
349	3,589	Castaic Union Elementary	Valencia
350	3,586	Lindsay Unified	Lindsay
351	3,561	San Lorenzo Valley Unified	Ben Lomond
352	3,514	San Diego Co Office of Education	San Diego
353	3,506	Del Mar Union Elementary	Del Mar
354	3,500	San Rafael City Elementary	San Rafael
355	3,482	Mountain View Elementary	Ontario
356	3,458	Salida Union Elementary	Salida
357	3,441	Mountain View-Los Altos Union High	Mountain View
358	3,428	Bear Valley Unified	Big Bear Lake
359	3,427	Parlier Unified	Parlier
360	3,414	Konocti Unified	Lower Lake
361	3,413	San Bernardino Co Off of Education	San Bernardino
362	3,395	Brawley Elementary	Brawley
363	3,389	Lafayette Elementary	Lafayette
364	3,355	Rosemead Elementary	Rosemead
365	3,345	Walnut Creek Elementary	Walnut Creek
366	3,314	Albany City Unified	Albany
367	3,305	Lowell Joint	Whittier
368	3,267	Southern Kern Unified	Rosamond
368	3,267	Stanislaus Union Elementary	Modesto
370	3,266	San Marino Unified	San Marino
371	3,253	Lemoore Union Elementary	Lemoore
372	3,237	Oro Grande Elementary	Oro Grande
373	3,198	Oroville City Elementary	Oroville
374	3,196	El Segundo Unified	El Segundo
375	3,190	Corcoran Joint Unified	Corcoran
376	3,171	Escalon Unified	Escalon
377	3,169	Pacifica SD	Pacifica
378	3,141	Plumas Unified	Quincy
379	3,135	Waterford Unified	Waterford
380	3,133	Fruitvale Elementary	Bakersfield
381	3,122	Fallbrook Union High	Fallbrook
382	3,102	Riverbank Unified	Riverbank
383	3,071	Santa Rita Union Elementary	Salinas
384	3,002	San Benito High	Hollister
385	2,990	Wasco Union Elementary	Wasco
386	2,978	Richland Union Elementary SD	Shafter
387	2,976	Keppel Union Elementary	Pearblossom
388	2,966	Mcfarland Unified	Mcfarland
389	2,962	Oroville Union High	Oroville
390	2,948	Los Gatos-Saratoga Jt Union High	Los Gatos
391	2,940	Arvin Union Elementary	Arvin
392	2,919	Carpinteria Unified	Carpinteria
393	2,915	Coronado Unified	Coronado
394	2,906	Mt. Pleasant Elementary	San Jose
395	2,898	Cucamonga Elementary	Rcho Cucamong
396	2,875	Ripon Unified	Ripon
397	2,867	Imperial Unified	Imperial
398	2,864	Burton Elementary	Porterville
399	2,813	Lamont Elementary	Lamont
400	2,801	Cambrian Elementary	San Jose
401	2,770	Rincon Valley Union Elementary	Santa Rosa
402	2,763	Scotts Valley Unified	Scotts Valley
403	2,746	Mojave Unified	Mojave
404	2,734	Healdsburg Unified	Healdsburg
405	2,721	Templeton Unified	Templeton
406	2,720	Eastside Union Elementary	Lancaster
407	2,717	San Bruno Park Elementary	San Bruno
408	2,703	Laguna Beach Unified	Laguna Beach
409	2,696	San Carlos Elementary	San Carlos
410	2,689	West Sonoma County Union High	Sebastopol
411	2,685	Dos Palos Oro Loma Jt. Unified	Dos Palos
412	2,683	Standard Elementary	Bakersfield
413	2,642	Solana Beach Elementary	Solana Beach
414	2,630	Silver Valley Unified	Yermo
415	2,627	Kern County Office of Education	Bakersfield
416	2,599	Auburn Union Elementary	Auburn
417	2,597	Piedmont City Unified	Piedmont
418	2,595	King City Union Elementary	King City
419	2,581	Los Gatos Union Elementary	Los Gatos
420	2,554	Delhi Unified	Delhi
421	2,543	Wheatland Elementary	Wheatland
422	2,521	Ocean View Elementary	Oxnard
423	2,514	Firebaugh-Las Deltas Joint Unified	Firebaugh
424	2,488	Mariposa County Unified	Mariposa
425	2,471	Greenfield Union Elementary	Greenfield
426	2,465	Linden Unified	Linden
426	2,465	River Delta Joint Unified	Rio Vista
428	2,464	Reef-Sunset Unified	Avenal
429	2,460	Belmont-Redwood Shores Elementary	Belmont
430	2,452	Sierra Unified	Prather
431	2,449	Savanna Elementary	Anaheim
432	2,445	Farmersville Unified	Farmersville
433	2,433	Livingston Union Elementary	Livingston
434	2,424	Muroc Joint Unified	North Edwards
435	2,413	Saratoga Union Elementary	Saratoga
436	2,409	Orinda Union Elementary	Orinda
437	2,386	Gonzales Unified	Gonzales
438	2,385	Los Nietos Elementary	Whittier
439	2,382	Anderson Union High	Anderson
440	2,369	Burlingame Elementary	Burlingame
441	2,358	San Joaquin Co Off of Education	Stockton
442	2,356	Orland Joint Unified	Orland
443	2,330	Hilmar Unified	Hilmar
444	2,329	Alpine Union Elementary	Alpine
445	2,314	Mendota Unified	Mendota
446	2,307	Red Bluff Union Elementary	Red Bluff
447	2,293	Newman-Crows Landing Unified	Newman
448	2,252	Santa Cruz City Elementary	Soquel
449	2,243	Petaluma City Elementary	Petaluma
450	2,242	Robla Elementary	Sacramento
451	2,240	Willits Unified	Willits
452	2,236	Mill Valley Elementary	Mill Valley
453	2,235	Fowler Unified	Fowler
454	2,222	King City Joint Union High	King City
455	2,191	Twin Ridges Elementary	North San Juan
456	2,182	Taft City Elementary	Taft
457	2,181	Carmel Unified	Carmel
458	2,178	Fresno County Office of Education	Fresno
459	2,168	Kingsburg Elementary Charter	Kingsburg
460	2,131	Galt Joint Union High	Galt
461	2,114	Live Oak Elementary	Santa Cruz
462	2,098	Lemoore Union High	Lemoore
463	2,096	Millbrae Elementary	Millbrae
464	2,089	Santa Clara Co Off of Education	San Jose
465	2,075	Fort Bragg Unified	Fort Bragg
466	2,073	Norris Elementary	Bakersfield
466	2,073	Pleasant Ridge Union Elementary	Grass Valley
466	2,073	Wilsona Elementary	Palmdale
469	2,072	Gridley Unified	Gridley
470	2,048	Hughson Unified	Hughson
471	2,041	Del Paso Heights Elementary	Sacramento
472	2,036	Central Union Elementary	Lemoore
472	2,036	San Rafael City High	San Rafael
474	2,030	Soquel Union Elementary	Capitola
475	2,019	Menlo Park City Elementary	Atherton
476	2,016	Black Oak Mine Unified	Georgetown
477	2,012	Winters Joint Unified	Winters
478	2,008	Wiseburn Elementary	Hawthorne
479	1,995	Gorman Elementary	Gorman
480	1,994	Acton-Agua Dulce Unified	Acton
481	1,989	Corning Union Elementary	Corning
482	1,980	Exeter Union Elementary	Exeter
483	1,971	Red Bluff Joint Union High	Red Bluff
484	1,937	Northern Humboldt Union High	McKinleyville
485	1,929	Gustine Unified	Gustine
486	1,928	Old Adobe Union Elementary	Petaluma
487	1,921	Holtville Unified	Holtville
488	1,915	Pacific Grove Unified	Pacific Grove
489	1,911	Golden Plains Unified	San Joaquin
490	1,903	Earlimart Elementary	Earlimart
491	1,899	Loomis Union Elementary	Loomis
492	1,877	Live Oak Unified	Live Oak
493	1,872	Kelseyville Unified	Kelseyville
494	1,865	Bonsall Union Elementary	Bonsall
495	1,861	Mountain Empire Unified	Pine Valley
496	1,858	Brawley Union High	Brawley
497	1,856	Moraga Elementary	Moraga
498	1,854	Beardsley Elementary	Bakersfield
499	1,850	Jefferson Elementary	Tracy
500	1,848	Grass Valley Elementary	Grass Valley
501	1,846	Willows Unified	Willows
502	1,818	Middletown Unified	Middletown
503	1,817	Dixie Elementary	San Rafael
504	1,816	John Swett Unified	Crockett
504	1,816	Ross Valley Elementary	San Anselmo
506	1,808	Winton Elementary	Winton
507	1,805	Keyes Union Elementary	Keyes
508	1,792	Lakeport Unified	Lakeport
509	1,779	Chowchilla Elementary	Chowchilla
510	1,763	Romoland Elementary	Homeland
511	1,757	Julian Union Elementary	Julian
512	1,751	Jamul-Dulzura Union Elementary	Jamul
513	1,729	Sonora Union High	Sonora
514	1,715	Bellevue Union Elementary	Santa Rosa
514	1,715	Santa Paula Union High	Santa Paula
516	1,702	Julian Union High	Julian
517	1,683	Weaver Union Elementary	Merced
518	1,659	Piner-Olivet Union Elementary	Santa Rosa
519	1,656	Tulare County Office of Education	Visalia
520	1,632	Woodlake Union Elementary	Woodlake
521	1,629	Mother Lode Union Elementary	Placerville
522	1,605	Mark West Union Elementary	Santa Rosa
523	1,583	Cloverdale Unified	Cloverdale
524	1,575	Riverdale Joint Unified	Riverdale
525	1,558	Fairfax Elementary	Bakersfield
526	1,554	Cascade Union Elementary	Anderson
527	1,547	Westwood Unified	Westwood
528	1,523	Nuview Union Elementary	Nuevo

Male Students

Rank	Percent	District Name	City
1	73.5	San Bernardino Co Off of Education	San Bernardino
2	69.3	Los Angeles Co Office of Education	Downey
3	67.7	Kern County Office of Education	Bakersfield
4	67.7	Santa Clara Co Off of Education	San Jose
5	67.2	Fresno County Office of Education	Fresno
6	66.0	Tulare County Office of Education	Visalia
7	61.2	San Joaquin Co Off of Education	Stockton
8	60.8	Orange County Office of Education	Costa Mesa
9	60.4	Riverside Co Office of Education	Riverside
10	59.0	San Diego Co Office of Education	San Diego
11	54.3	Cascade Union Elementary	Anderson
12	53.9	Moraga Elementary	Moraga
13	53.9	Winters Joint Unified	Winters
14	53.5	Chowchilla Elementary	Chowchilla
15	53.5	Black Oak Mine Unified	Georgetown
16	53.5	Mountain Empire Unified	Pine Valley
17	53.5	Piner-Olivet Union Elementary	Santa Rosa
18	53.4	Santa Cruz City High	Soquel
19	53.4	Gustine Unified	Gustine
20	53.3	Jamul-Dulzura Union Elementary	Jamul
21	53.3	Solana Beach Elementary	Solana Beach
22	53.3	Redding Elementary	Redding
23	53.2	Jefferson Union High	Daly City
24	53.2	San Dieguito Union High	Encinitas
25	53.1	Campbell Union Elementary	Campbell
26	53.1	John Swett Unified	Crockett
27	53.1	Westwood Unified	Westwood
28	53.0	Placer Union High	Auburn
29	53.0	Willits Unified	Willits
30	52.9	Gateway Unified	Redding
31	52.9	Lake Tahoe Unified	S Lake Tahoe
32	52.9	Wilsona Elementary	Palmdale
33	52.9	Gridley Unified	Gridley
34	52.8	Healdsburg Unified	Healdsburg
35	52.8	San Rafael City Elementary	San Rafael
36	52.8	Grass Valley Elementary	Grass Valley
37	52.8	Coalinga-Huron Joint Unified	Coalinga
38	52.8	Empire Union Elementary	Modesto
39	52.7	Fairfax Elementary	Bakersfield
40	52.7	Pacific Grove Unified	Pacific Grove
41	52.7	Nuview Union Elementary	Nuevo
42	52.7	Sonoma Valley Unified	Sonoma
43	52.7	Anderson Union High	Anderson
44	52.7	Nevada Joint Union High	Grass Valley
45	52.6	Belmont-Redwood Shores Elementary	Belmont
46	52.6	Valley Center-Pauma Unified	Valley Center
47	52.5	Beardsley Elementary	Bakersfield
48	52.5	Fort Bragg Unified	Fort Bragg
49	52.5	Savanna Elementary	Anaheim
50	52.5	Pleasant Ridge Union Elementary	Grass Valley
51	52.5	Sierra Sands Unified	Ridgecrest
52	52.4	Burton Elementary	Porterville
53	52.4	Cloverdale Unified	Cloverdale
54	52.4	Saratoga Union Elementary	Saratoga
55	52.4	Los Gatos-Saratoga Jt Union High	Los Gatos
56	52.4	Huntington Beach City Elementary	Huntington Bch
57	52.4	Kelseyville Unified	Kelseyville
58	52.4	Red Bluff Union Elementary	Red Bluff
59	52.4	Dixon Unified	Dixon
60	52.4	Eureka Union Elementary	Granite Bay
61	52.4	Pittsburg Unified	Pittsburg
62	52.4	Mark West Union Elementary	Santa Rosa
63	52.4	King City Union Elementary	King City
64	52.4	Centinela Valley Union High	Lawndale
65	52.4	Del Mar Union Elementary	Del Mar
66	52.3	Grant Joint Union High	Sacramento
67	52.3	Rosemead Elementary	Rosemead
68	52.3	Fremont Unified	Fremont
69	52.3	Del Paso Heights Elementary	Sacramento

70	52.3	Dinuba Unified	Dinuba
71	52.3	Reef-Sunset Unified	Avenal
72	52.3	Dos Palos Oro Loma Jt. Unified	Dos Palos
73	52.3	Menlo Park City Elementary	Atherton
74	52.3	Paradise Unified	Paradise
75	52.3	Santa Maria-Bonita Elementary	Santa Maria
76	52.3	Plumas Unified	Quincy
77	52.3	Newman-Crows Landing Unified	Newman
78	52.3	Live Oak Elementary	Santa Cruz
79	52.2	Yucaipa-Calimesa Jt. Unified	Yucaipa
80	52.2	Ocean View Elementary	Oxnard
81	52.2	Northern Humboldt Union High	McKinleyville
82	52.2	Fallbrook Union Elementary	Fallbrook
83	52.2	Carlsbad Unified	Carlsbad
84	52.2	Fowler Unified	Fowler
85	52.2	Castaic Union Elementary	Valencia
86	52.2	Lafayette Elementary	Lafayette
87	52.2	Richland Union Elementary SD	Shafter
88	52.2	Orcutt Union Elementary	Orcutt
89	52.2	Eureka City Unified	Eureka
90	52.2	South San Francisco Unified	S San Francisco
91	52.2	Sulphur Springs Union Elementary	Canyon Country
92	52.2	Los Nietos Elementary	Whittier
93	52.1	Santee Elementary	Santee
94	52.1	Alhambra City High	Alhambra
95	52.1	Middletown Unified	Middletown
96	52.1	Riverbank Unified	Riverbank
97	52.1	Golden Plains Unified	San Joaquin
98	52.1	Willows Unified	Willows
99	52.1	Holtville Unified	Holtville
100	52.1	Atascadero Unified	Atascadero
101	52.1	Carmel Unified	Carmel
102	52.1	ABC Unified	Cerritos
103	52.1	Cypress Elementary	Cypress
104	52.1	National Elementary	National City
105	52.1	Wasco Union Elementary	Wasco
106	52.0	Rescue Union Elementary	Rescue
107	52.0	Perris Elementary	Perris
108	52.0	Lemoore Union Elementary	Lemoore
109	52.0	Tehachapi Unified	Tehachapi
110	52.0	Alpine Union Elementary	Alpine
111	52.0	Newark Unified	Newark
112	52.0	Julian Union High	Julian
113	52.0	Union Elementary	San Jose
114	52.0	Newhall Elementary	Valencia
115	52.0	Mendota Unified	Mendota
116	52.0	Selma Unified	Selma
117	52.0	San Mateo Union High	San Mateo
118	52.0	Walnut Creek Elementary	Walnut Creek
119	51.9	Oak Park Unified	Oak Park
120	51.9	Ripon Unified	Ripon
121	51.9	San Ysidro Elementary	San Ysidro
122	51.9	Brea-Olinda Unified	Brea
123	51.9	Exeter Union Elementary	Exeter
124	51.9	Sunnyvale Elementary	Sunnyvale
125	51.9	Oak Grove Elementary	San Jose
126	51.9	Alvord Unified	Riverside
127	51.9	Lowell Joint	Whittier
128	51.9	Lucia Mar Unified	Arroyo Grande
129	51.9	Santa Rosa Elementary	Santa Rosa
130	51.9	Ocean View Elementary	Huntington Bch
131	51.9	East Whittier City Elementary	Whittier
132	51.9	Acalanes Union High	Lafayette
133	51.9	Val Verde Unified	Perris
134	51.8	Robla Elementary	Sacramento
135	51.8	Rio Linda Union Elementary	Rio Linda
136	51.8	Norris Elementary	Bakersfield
137	51.8	Milpitas Unified	Milpitas
138	51.8	Oroville City Elementary	Oroville
139	51.8	Banning Unified	Banning
140	51.8	Palmdale Elementary	Palmdale
141	51.8	Cutler-Orosi Joint Unified	Orosi
142	51.8	Salinas City Elementary	Salinas
143	51.8	Cucamonga Elementary	Rcho Cucamong
144	51.8	Escalon Unified	Escalon
145	51.8	Bear Valley Unified	Big Bear Lake
146	51.8	Manhattan Beach Unified	Manhattan Beach
147	51.8	Woodland Joint Unified	Woodland
148	51.8	Santa Monica-Malibu Unified	Santa Monica
149	51.8	Yuba City Unified	Yuba City
150	51.8	Cotati-Rohnert Park Unified	Rohnert Park
151	51.8	Keppel Union Elementary	Pearblossom
152	51.7	Firebaugh-Las Deltas Joint Unified	Firebaugh
153	51.7	Newport-Mesa Unified	Costa Mesa
154	51.7	Pleasant Valley School	Camarillo
155	51.7	Palo Alto Unified	Palo Alto
156	51.7	Napa Valley Unified	Napa
157	51.7	Los Banos Unified	Los Banos
158	51.7	Enterprise Elementary	Redding
159	51.7	Mt. Pleasant Elementary	San Jose
160	51.7	Amador County Unified	Jackson
161	51.7	Tulare Joint Union High	Tulare
162	51.7	Bellflower Unified	Bellflower
163	51.7	Orange Unified	Orange
164	51.7	New Haven Unified	Union City
165	51.7	Loomis Union Elementary	Loomis
166	51.7	Natomas Unified	Sacramento
167	51.7	Conejo Valley Unified	Thousand Oaks
168	51.7	Palo Verde Unified	Blythe
169	51.7	Mountain View-Whisman Elementary	Mountain View
170	51.7	El Centro Elementary	El Centro
171	51.7	Novato Unified	Novato
172	51.7	East Side Union High	San Jose
173	51.7	Irvine Unified	Irvine
174	51.6	Lemon Grove Elementary	Lemon Grove
175	51.6	Mill Valley Elementary	Mill Valley
176	51.6	San Lorenzo Unified	San Lorenzo
177	51.6	Little Lake City Elementary	Santa Fe Spgs
178	51.6	San Francisco Unified	San Francisco
179	51.6	Norwalk-La Mirada Unified	Norwalk
180	51.6	Berryessa Union Elementary	San Jose
181	51.6	Carpinteria Unified	Carpinteria
182	51.6	Romoland Elementary	Homeland
183	51.6	Temple City Unified	Temple City
184	51.6	Mt. Diablo Unified	Concord
185	51.6	Chula Vista Elementary	Chula Vista
186	51.6	San Gabriel Unified	San Gabriel
187	51.6	Ventura Unified	Ventura
188	51.6	Burlingame Elementary	Burlingame
189	51.6	Soledad Unified	Soledad
190	51.6	Turlock Joint Elementary	Turlock
191	51.6	Elk Grove Unified	Elk Grove
192	51.6	Placentia-Yorba Linda Unified	Placentia
193	51.6	Santa Barbara Elementary	Santa Barbara
194	51.6	San Bruno Park Elementary	San Bruno
195	51.5	Poway Unified	Poway
196	51.5	Hayward Unified	Hayward
197	51.5	William S. Hart Union High	Santa Clarita
198	51.5	Hollister SD	Hollister
199	51.5	Redondo Beach Unified	Redondo Beach
200	51.5	Coachella Valley Unified	Thermal
201	51.5	King City Joint Union High	King City
202	51.5	Ukiah Unified	Ukiah
203	51.5	Wiseburn Elementary	Hawthorne
204	51.5	Salida Union Elementary	Salida
205	51.5	Central Union Elementary	Lemoore
206	51.5	Etiwanda Elementary	Etiwanda
207	51.5	Chino Valley Unified	Chino
208	51.5	Martinez Unified	Martinez
209	51.5	Alisal Union Elementary	Salinas
210	51.5	Sweetwater Union High	Chula Vista
211	51.5	Torrance Unified	Torrance
212	51.5	Gilroy Unified	Gilroy
213	51.5	Sylvan Union Elementary	Modesto
214	51.5	Culver City Unified	Culver City
215	51.5	Mojave Unified	Mojave
216	51.5	Los Gatos Union Elementary	Los Gatos
217	51.5	Woodlake Union Elementary	Woodlake
218	51.5	Walnut Valley Unified	Walnut
219	51.5	Santa Paula Elementary	Santa Paula
220	51.5	Capistrano Unified	San Juan Capis
221	51.5	La Mesa-Spring Valley	La Mesa
222	51.5	Arcadia Unified	Arcadia
223	51.5	Evergreen Elementary	San Jose
224	51.5	Mountain View Elementary	Ontario
225	51.5	Livingston Union Elementary	Livingston
226	51.4	Simi Valley Unified	Simi Valley
227	51.4	West Contra Costa Unified	Richmond
228	51.4	San Leandro Unified	San Leandro
229	51.4	Modesto City Elementary	Modesto
230	51.4	Ojai Unified	Ojai
231	51.4	Central Unified	Fresno
232	51.4	San Rafael City High	San Rafael
233	51.4	Vallejo City Unified	Vallejo
234	51.4	Centralia Elementary	Buena Park
235	51.4	San Marino Unified	San Marino
236	51.4	Saugus Union Elementary	Santa Clarita
237	51.4	Stanislaus Union Elementary	Modesto
238	51.4	Cambrian Elementary	San Jose
239	51.4	Saddleback Valley Unified	Mission Viejo
240	51.4	Hanford Joint Union High	Hanford
241	51.4	Lawndale Elementary	Lawndale
242	51.4	Alta Loma Elementary	Alta Loma
243	51.3	Cajon Valley Union Elementary	El Cajon
244	51.3	Sequoia Union High	Redwood City
245	51.3	Vacaville Unified	Vacaville
246	51.3	Apple Valley Unified	Apple Valley
247	51.3	Hanford Elementary	Hanford
248	51.3	Santa Barbara High	Santa Barbara
249	51.3	Vista Unified	Vista
250	51.3	Corona-Norco Unified	Norco
251	51.3	Ramona City Unified	Ramona
252	51.3	Paso Robles Joint Unified	Paso Robles
253	51.3	Azusa Unified	Azusa
254	51.3	San Marcos Unified	San Marcos
255	51.3	Travis Unified	Travis Afb
256	51.3	Del Norte County Unified	Crescent City
257	51.3	Rio Elementary	Oxnard
258	51.3	Center Joint Unified	Antelope
259	51.3	West Covina Unified	West Covina
260	51.3	Moreland Elementary	San Jose
261	51.3	Redwood City Elementary	Redwood City
262	51.3	Duarte Unified	Duarte
263	51.3	Lake Elsinore Unified	Lake Elsinore
264	51.3	Chico Unified	Chico
265	51.3	Winton Elementary	Winton
266	51.3	Delano Union Elementary	Delano
267	51.3	Marysville Joint Unified	Marysville
268	51.3	Rowland Unified	Rowland Heights
269	51.3	Campbell Union High	San Jose
270	51.3	Orinda Union Elementary	Orinda
271	51.3	Cupertino Union School	Cupertino
272	51.3	Las Virgenes Unified	Calabasas
273	51.3	Lennox Elementary	Lennox
274	51.3	Oxnard Union High	Oxnard
275	51.3	Colton Joint Unified	Colton
276	51.3	Livermore Valley Joint Unified	Livermore
277	51.3	South Bay Union Elementary	Imperial Beach
278	51.3	Galt Joint Union High	Galt
279	51.3	Pomona Unified	Pomona
280	51.2	Burbank Unified	Burbank
281	51.2	Fullerton Elementary	Fullerton
282	51.2	Taft City Elementary	Taft
283	51.2	Encinitas Union Elementary	Encinitas
284	51.2	Weaver Union Elementary	Merced
285	51.2	Jefferson Elementary	Daly City
286	51.2	Santa Paula Union High	Santa Paula
287	51.2	Oro Grande Elementary	Oro Grande
288	51.2	Fountain Valley Elementary	Fountain Valley
289	51.2	Escondido Union Elementary	Escondido
290	51.2	Monrovia Unified	Monrovia
291	51.2	Hueneme Elementary	Port Hueneme
292	51.2	Dublin Unified	Dublin
293	51.2	Alum Rock Union Elementary	San Jose
294	51.2	Soquel Union Elementary	Capitola
295	51.2	Rosedale Union Elementary	Bakersfield
296	51.2	Tustin Unified	Tustin
297	51.2	Palm Springs Unified	Palm Springs
298	51.2	Snowline Joint Unified	Phelan
299	51.1	Lynwood Unified	Lynwood
300	51.1	Washington Unified	West Sacramento
301	51.1	Morongo Unified	Twentynine Plms
302	51.1	Rocklin Unified	Rocklin
303	51.1	Santa Clara Unified	Santa Clara
304	51.1	Red Bluff Joint Union High	Red Bluff
305	51.1	Porterville Unified	Porterville
306	51.1	El Rancho Unified	Pico Rivera
307	51.1	Downey Unified	Downey
308	51.1	El Monte City Elementary	El Monte
309	51.1	Lodi Unified	Lodi
310	51.1	Anaheim Union High	Anaheim
310	51.1	Grossmont Union High	La Mesa
312	51.1	Millbrae Elementary	Millbrae
313	51.1	San Diego Unified	San Diego
314	51.1	San Jacinto Unified	San Jacinto
315	51.1	Santa Rosa High	Santa Rosa
316	51.1	Monterey Peninsula Unified	Monterey
317	51.1	Corning Union Elementary	Corning
318	51.1	San Benito High	Hollister
319	51.1	Bonita Unified	San Dimas
320	51.1	Pacifica SD	Pacifica
321	51.1	Arvin Union Elementary	Arvin
322	51.1	Baldwin Park Unified	Baldwin Park
323	51.1	Charter Oak Unified	Covina
324	51.1	Pasadena Unified	Pasadena
325	51.1	Whittier City Elementary	Whittier
326	51.1	Moreno Valley Unified	Moreno Valley
327	51.0	Covina-Valley Unified	Covina
328	51.0	Anaheim Elementary	Anaheim
329	51.0	San Mateo-Foster City Elementary	San Mateo
330	51.0	Adelanto Elementary	Adelanto
331	51.0	Sanger Unified	Sanger
332	51.0	Santa Maria Joint Union High	Santa Maria
333	51.0	Albany City Unified	Albany
334	51.0	Imperial Unified	Imperial
334	51.0	Mountain View Elementary	El Monte
336	51.0	Magnolia Elementary	Anaheim
337	51.0	Dry Creek Joint Elementary	Roseville
338	51.0	El Dorado Union High	Placerville
339	51.0	Palos Verdes Peninsula Unified	Palos Verdes Est
340	51.0	Live Oak Unified	Live Oak
341	51.0	Fremont Union High	Sunnyvale
342	51.0	Los Angeles Unified	Los Angeles
343	51.0	Ontario-Montclair Elementary	Ontario
344	51.0	West Sonoma County Union High	Sebastopol
345	51.0	Sacramento City Unified	Sacramento
346	51.0	Riverside Unified	Riverside
347	51.0	Standard Elementary	Bakersfield

348	51.0	Lakeside Union Elementary	Lakeside
349	51.0	Lompoc Unified	Lompoc
350	51.0	Oakdale Joint Unified	Oakdale
351	51.0	Sonora Union High	Sonora
352	51.0	Westminster Elementary	Westminster
353	51.0	Panama Buena Vista Union Elem	Bakersfield
354	51.0	Fresno Unified	Fresno
355	51.0	La Canada Unified	La Canada
356	51.0	Muroc Joint Unified	North Edwards
357	50.9	Ceres Unified	Ceres
358	50.9	Lancaster Elementary	Lancaster
359	50.9	Whittier Union High	Whittier
360	50.9	Long Beach Unified	Long Beach
361	50.9	Salinas Union High	Salinas
362	50.9	Huntington Beach Union High	Huntington Bch
363	50.9	Tracy Joint Unified	Tracy
364	50.9	Jurupa Unified	Riverside
365	50.9	Glendale Unified	Glendale
366	50.9	Lincoln Unified	Stockton
367	50.9	Madera Unified	Madera
368	50.9	Hacienda La Puente Unified	City of Industry
369	50.9	Laguna Beach Unified	Laguna Beach
370	50.9	Merced City Elementary	Merced
371	50.9	El Monte Union High	El Monte
372	50.9	Hilmar Unified	Hilmar
373	50.9	Patterson Joint Unified	Patterson
374	50.9	Scotts Valley Unified	Scotts Valley
375	50.9	Bakersfield City Elementary	Bakersfield
376	50.9	Inglewood Unified	Inglewood
377	50.9	Delano Joint Union High	Delano
378	50.9	Rialto Unified	Rialto
379	50.9	Fontana Unified	Fontana
380	50.8	Brawley Elementary	Brawley
381	50.8	North Sacramento Elementary	Sacramento
382	50.8	Kingsburg Elementary Charter	Kingsburg
383	50.8	Greenfield Union Elementary	Bakersfield
384	50.8	Garvey Elementary	Rosemead
385	50.8	Hesperia Unified	Hesperia
386	50.8	Folsom-Cordova Unified	Folsom
387	50.8	Murrieta Valley Unified	Murrieta
388	50.8	Lakeport Unified	Lakeport
389	50.8	Benicia Unified	Benicia
390	50.8	Stockton City Unified	Stockton
391	50.8	Chaffey Joint Union High	Ontario
392	50.8	Garden Grove Unified	Garden Grove
393	50.8	Antioch Unified	Antioch
394	50.8	Hemet Unified	Hemet
395	50.8	Atwater Elementary	Atwater
396	50.8	Perris Union High	Perris
397	50.8	San Juan Unified	Carmichael
398	50.8	San Lorenzo Valley Unified	Ben Lomond
399	50.8	Pleasanton Unified	Pleasanton
400	50.8	Moorpark Unified	Moorpark
401	50.8	Berkeley Unified	Berkeley
402	50.8	Petaluma City Elementary	Petaluma
403	50.8	Rim of the World Unified	Lake Arrowhead
404	50.8	Oakland Unified	Oakland
405	50.8	Los Alamitos Unified	Los Alamitos
406	50.8	San Bernardino City Unified	San Bernardino
407	50.7	Jefferson Elementary	Tracy
408	50.7	Silver Valley Unified	Yermo
409	50.7	Antelope Valley Union High	Lancaster
410	50.7	Kings Canyon Joint Unified	Reedley
411	50.7	Manteca Unified	Manteca
412	50.7	Lamont Elementary	Lamont
413	50.7	Calexico Unified	Calexico
414	50.7	Morgan Hill Unified	Morgan Hill
415	50.7	Compton Unified	Compton
416	50.7	Rincon Valley Union Elementary	Santa Rosa
417	50.7	Desert Sands Unified	La Quinta
418	50.7	Shasta Union High	Redding
419	50.7	Tahoe-Truckee Joint Unified	Truckee
420	50.7	Barstow Unified	Barstow
421	50.7	Piedmont City Unified	Piedmont
422	50.6	Hughson Unified	Hughson
423	50.6	San Ramon Valley Unified	Danville
424	50.6	Fallbrook Union High	Fallbrook
425	50.6	Kerman Unified	Kerman
426	50.6	Central Union High	El Centro
427	50.6	Mariposa County Unified	Mariposa
428	50.6	Brentwood Union Elementary	Brentwood
428	50.6	Buena Park Elementary	Buena Park
430	50.6	Pajaro Valley Unified School	Watsonville
431	50.6	Beverly Hills Unified	Beverly Hills
432	50.6	Old Adobe Union Elementary	Petaluma
433	50.6	Castro Valley Unified	Castro Valley
434	50.6	Oxnard Elementary	Oxnard
435	50.6	Twin Ridges Elementary	North San Juan
436	50.6	Southern Kern Unified	Rosamond
437	50.6	Westside Union Elementary	Lancaster
438	50.6	Oakley Union Elementary	Oakley
439	50.5	Glendora Unified	Glendora
440	50.5	Hawthorne Elementary	Hawthorne
441	50.5	South Whittier Elementary	Whittier
442	50.5	Corcoran Joint Unified	Corcoran
443	50.5	Santa Cruz City Elementary	Soquel
444	50.5	La Habra City Elementary	La Habra
445	50.5	Montebello Unified	Montebello
446	50.5	Alhambra City Elementary	Alhambra
447	50.5	Visalia Unified	Visalia
448	50.5	San Luis Coastal Unified	San Luis Obispo
449	50.5	Roseville Joint Union High	Roseville
450	50.5	Tamalpais Union High	Larkspur
451	50.5	Oroville Union High	Oroville
452	50.5	South Pasadena Unified	South Pasadena
453	50.5	Lindsay Unified	Lindsay
454	50.5	Oceanside Unified	Oceanside
455	50.4	Galt Joint Union Elementary	Galt
456	50.4	Franklin-Mckinley Elementary	San Jose
457	50.4	Clovis Unified	Clovis
458	50.4	Menifee Union Elementary	Menifee
459	50.4	Liberty Union High	Brentwood
460	50.4	Parlier Unified	Parlier
461	50.4	Los Altos Elementary	Los Altos
462	50.4	Escondido Union High	Escondido
463	50.4	Temecula Valley Unified	Temecula
464	50.4	Fairfield-Suisun Unified	Fairfield
465	50.4	North Monterey County Unified	Moss Landing
466	50.4	Alameda City Unified	Alameda
467	50.3	San Jose Unified	San Jose
468	50.3	River Delta Joint Unified	Rio Vista
469	50.3	Calaveras Unified	San Andreas
470	50.3	Redlands Unified	Redlands
471	50.3	Greenfield Union Elementary	Greenfield
472	50.3	Ravenswood City Elementary	East Palo Alto
473	50.3	Turlock Joint Union High	Turlock
474	50.2	Bassett Unified	La Puente
475	50.2	Lemoore Union High	Lemoore
476	50.2	Petaluma Joint Union High	Petaluma
477	50.2	Kern Union High	Bakersfield
478	50.2	Eastside Union Elementary	Lancaster
479	50.2	Sierra Unified	Prather
480	50.2	Mountain View-Los Altos Union High	Mountain View
481	50.2	Bonsall Union Elementary	Bonsall
482	50.2	Windsor Unified	Windsor
483	50.2	Riverdale Joint Unified	Riverdale
484	50.2	Merced Union High	Atwater
485	50.2	Gonzales Unified	Gonzales
486	50.2	Bellevue Union Elementary	Santa Rosa
487	50.1	Roseville City Elementary	Roseville
488	50.1	Coronado Unified	Coronado
489	50.1	Goleta Union Elementary	Goleta
490	50.1	Claremont Unified	Claremont
491	50.1	Upland Unified	Upland
492	50.0	Santa Ana Unified	Santa Ana
493	50.0	Orland Joint Unified	Orland
494	50.0	Buckeye Union Elementary	Shingle Springs
495	50.0	Delhi Unified	Delhi
496	50.0	Fillmore Unified	Fillmore
497	50.0	Victor Valley Union High	Victorville
498	49.9	Wheatland Elementary	Wheatland
499	49.9	Cabrillo Unified	Half Moon Bay
500	49.9	Santa Rita Union Elementary	Salinas
501	49.8	Auburn Union Elementary	Auburn
502	49.8	Linden Unified	Linden
503	49.8	Davis Joint Unified	Davis
504	49.8	Konocti Unified	Lower Lake
505	49.8	Ross Valley Elementary	San Anselmo
506	49.8	Waterford Unified	Waterford
507	49.7	Brawley Union High	Brawley
508	49.7	Tulare City Elementary	Tulare
509	49.7	Paramount Unified	Paramount
510	49.6	Keyes Union Elementary	Keyes
511	49.5	Victor Elementary	Victorville
512	49.5	Acton-Agua Dulce Unified	Acton
513	49.5	Central Elementary	Rcho Cucamong
514	49.5	Beaumont Unified	Beaumont
515	49.5	Modesto City High	Modesto
516	49.5	San Carlos Elementary	San Carlos
517	49.5	Dixie Elementary	San Rafael
518	49.4	Templeton Unified	Templeton
519	49.3	Fruitvale Elementary	Bakersfield
520	49.3	Earlimart Elementary	Earlimart
521	49.3	El Segundo Unified	El Segundo
522	49.2	Mcfarland Unified	Mcfarland
523	49.1	Fullerton Joint Union High	Fullerton
524	49.0	Western Placer Unified	Lincoln
525	48.7	Farmersville Unified	Farmersville
526	48.6	Mother Lode Union Elementary	Placerville
527	47.3	Gorman Elementary	Gorman
528	46.9	Julian Union Elementary	Julian

Female Students

Rank	Percent	District Name	City
1	53.0	Julian Union Elementary	Julian
2	52.6	Gorman Elementary	Gorman
3	51.3	Mother Lode Union Elementary	Placerville
4	51.2	Farmersville Unified	Farmersville
5	50.9	Western Placer Unified	Lincoln
6	50.8	Fullerton Joint Union High	Fullerton
7	50.7	Mcfarland Unified	Mcfarland
8	50.6	El Segundo Unified	El Segundo
9	50.6	Earlimart Elementary	Earlimart
10	50.6	Fruitvale Elementary	Bakersfield
11	50.5	Templeton Unified	Templeton
12	50.4	Dixie Elementary	San Rafael
13	50.4	San Carlos Elementary	San Carlos
14	50.4	Modesto City High	Modesto
15	50.4	Beaumont Unified	Beaumont
16	50.4	Central Elementary	Rcho Cucamong
17	50.4	Acton-Agua Dulce Unified	Acton
18	50.4	Victor Elementary	Victorville
19	50.3	Keyes Union Elementary	Keyes
20	50.2	Paramount Unified	Paramount
21	50.2	Tulare City Elementary	Tulare
22	50.2	Brawley Union High	Brawley
23	50.1	Waterford Unified	Waterford
24	50.1	Ross Valley Elementary	San Anselmo
25	50.1	Konocti Unified	Lower Lake
26	50.1	Davis Joint Unified	Davis
27	50.1	Linden Unified	Linden
28	50.1	Auburn Union Elementary	Auburn
29	50.0	Santa Rita Union Elementary	Salinas
30	50.0	Cabrillo Unified	Half Moon Bay
31	50.0	Wheatland Elementary	Wheatland
32	50.0	Victor Valley Union High	Victorville
33	49.9	Fillmore Unified	Fillmore
34	49.9	Delhi Unified	Delhi
35	49.9	Buckeye Union Elementary	Shingle Springs
36	49.9	Orland Joint Unified	Orland
37	49.9	Santa Ana Unified	Santa Ana
38	49.8	Upland Unified	Upland
39	49.8	Claremont Unified	Claremont
40	49.8	Goleta Union Elementary	Goleta
41	49.8	Coronado Unified	Coronado
42	49.8	Roseville City Elementary	Roseville
43	49.7	Bellevue Union Elementary	Santa Rosa
44	49.7	Gonzales Unified	Gonzales
45	49.7	Merced Union High	Atwater
46	49.7	Riverdale Joint Unified	Riverdale
47	49.7	Windsor Unified	Windsor
48	49.7	Bonsall Union Elementary	Bonsall
49	49.7	Mountain View-Los Altos Union High	Mountain View
50	49.7	Sierra Unified	Prather
51	49.7	Eastside Union Elementary	Lancaster
52	49.7	Kern Union High	Bakersfield
53	49.7	Petaluma Joint Union High	Petaluma
54	49.7	Lemoore Union High	Lemoore
55	49.7	Bassett Unified	La Puente
56	49.6	Turlock Joint Union High	Turlock
57	49.6	Ravenswood City Elementary	East Palo Alto
58	49.6	Greenfield Union Elementary	Greenfield
59	49.6	Redlands Unified	Redlands
60	49.6	Calaveras Unified	San Andreas
61	49.6	River Delta Joint Unified	Rio Vista
62	49.6	San Jose Unified	San Jose
63	49.5	Alameda City Unified	Alameda
64	49.5	North Monterey County Unified	Moss Landing
65	49.5	Fairfield-Suisun Unified	Fairfield
66	49.5	Temecula Valley Unified	Temecula
67	49.5	Escondido Union High	Escondido
68	49.5	Los Altos Elementary	Los Altos
69	49.5	Parlier Unified	Parlier
70	49.5	Liberty Union High	Brentwood
71	49.5	Menifee Union Elementary	Menifee
72	49.5	Clovis Unified	Clovis
73	49.5	Franklin-Mckinley Elementary	San Jose
74	49.5	Galt Joint Union Elementary	Galt
75	49.4	Oceanside Unified	Oceanside
76	49.4	Lindsay Unified	Lindsay
77	49.4	South Pasadena Unified	South Pasadena
78	49.4	Oroville Union High	Oroville
79	49.4	Tamalpais Union High	Larkspur
80	49.4	Roseville Joint Union High	Roseville
81	49.4	San Luis Coastal Unified	San Luis Obispo
82	49.4	Visalia Unified	Visalia
83	49.4	Alhambra City Elementary	Alhambra
84	49.4	Montebello Unified	Montebello
85	49.4	La Habra City Elementary	La Habra
86	49.4	Santa Cruz City Elementary	Soquel
87	49.4	Corcoran Joint Unified	Corcoran
88	49.4	South Whittier Elementary	Whittier
89	49.4	Hawthorne Elementary	Hawthorne
90	49.4	Glendora Unified	Glendora
91	49.3	Oakley Union Elementary	Oakley
92	49.3	Westside Union Elementary	Lancaster

93	49.3	Southern Kern Unified	Rosamond
94	49.3	Twin Ridges Elementary	North San Juan
95	49.3	Oxnard Elementary	Oxnard
96	49.3	Castro Valley Unified	Castro Valley
97	49.3	Old Adobe Union Elementary	Petaluma
98	49.3	Beverly Hills Unified	Beverly Hills
99	49.3	Pajaro Valley Unified School	Watsonville
100	49.3	Brentwood Union Elementary	Brentwood
100	49.3	Buena Park Elementary	Buena Park
102	49.3	Mariposa County Unified	Mariposa
103	49.3	Central Union High	El Centro
104	49.3	Kerman Unified	Kerman
105	49.3	Fallbrook Union High	Fallbrook
106	49.3	San Ramon Valley Unified	Danville
107	49.3	Hughson Unified	Hughson
108	49.2	Piedmont City Unified	Piedmont
109	49.2	Barstow Unified	Barstow
110	49.2	Tahoe-Truckee Joint Unified	Truckee
111	49.2	Shasta Union High	Redding
112	49.2	Desert Sands Unified	La Quinta
113	49.2	Rincon Valley Union Elementary	Santa Rosa
114	49.2	Compton Unified	Compton
115	49.2	Morgan Hill Unified	Morgan Hill
116	49.2	Calexico Unified	Calexico
117	49.2	Lamont Elementary	Lamont
118	49.2	Manteca Unified	Manteca
119	49.2	Kings Canyon Joint Unified	Reedley
120	49.2	Antelope Valley Union High	Lancaster
121	49.2	Silver Valley Unified	Yermo
122	49.2	Jefferson Elementary	Tracy
123	49.1	San Bernardino City Unified	San Bernardino
124	49.1	Los Alamitos Unified	Los Alamitos
125	49.1	Oakland Unified	Oakland
126	49.1	Rim of the World Unified	Lake Arrowhead
127	49.1	Petaluma City Elementary	Petaluma
128	49.1	Berkeley Unified	Berkeley
129	49.1	Moorpark Unified	Moorpark
130	49.1	Pleasanton Unified	Pleasanton
131	49.1	San Lorenzo Valley Unified	Ben Lomond
132	49.1	San Juan Unified	Carmichael
133	49.1	Perris Union High	Perris
134	49.1	Atwater Elementary	Atwater
135	49.1	Hemet Unified	Hemet
136	49.1	Antioch Unified	Antioch
137	49.1	Garden Grove Unified	Garden Grove
138	49.1	Chaffey Joint Union High	Ontario
139	49.1	Stockton City Unified	Stockton
140	49.1	Benicia Unified	Benicia
141	49.1	Lakeport Unified	Lakeport
142	49.1	Murrieta Valley Unified	Murrieta
143	49.1	Folsom-Cordova Unified	Folsom
144	49.1	Hesperia Unified	Hesperia
145	49.1	Garvey Elementary	Rosemead
146	49.1	Greenfield Union Elementary	Bakersfield
147	49.1	Kingsburg Elementary Charter	Kingsburg
148	49.1	North Sacramento Elementary	Sacramento
149	49.1	Brawley Elementary	Brawley
150	49.0	Fontana Unified	Fontana
151	49.0	Rialto Unified	Rialto
152	49.0	Delano Joint Union High	Delano
153	49.0	Inglewood Unified	Inglewood
154	49.0	Bakersfield City Elementary	Bakersfield
155	49.0	Scotts Valley Unified	Scotts Valley
156	49.0	Patterson Joint Unified	Patterson
157	49.0	Hilmar Unified	Hilmar
158	49.0	El Monte Union High	El Monte
159	49.0	Merced City Elementary	Merced
160	49.0	Laguna Beach Unified	Laguna Beach
161	49.0	Hacienda La Puente Unified	City of Industry
162	49.0	Madera Unified	Madera
163	49.0	Lincoln Unified	Stockton
164	49.0	Glendale Unified	Glendale
165	49.0	Jurupa Unified	Riverside
166	49.0	Tracy Joint Unified	Tracy
167	49.0	Huntington Beach Union High	Huntington Bch
168	49.0	Salinas Union High	Salinas
169	49.0	Long Beach Unified	Long Beach
170	49.0	Whittier Union High	Whittier
171	49.0	Lancaster Elementary	Lancaster
172	49.0	Ceres Unified	Ceres
173	48.9	Muroc Joint Unified	North Edwards
174	48.9	La Canada Unified	La Canada
175	48.9	Fresno Unified	Fresno
176	48.9	Panama Buena Vista Union Elem	Bakersfield
177	48.9	Westminster Elementary	Westminster
178	48.9	Sonora Union High	Sonora
179	48.9	Oakdale Joint Unified	Oakdale
180	48.9	Lompoc Unified	Lompoc
181	48.9	Lakeside Union Elementary	Lakeside
182	48.9	Standard Elementary	Bakersfield
183	48.9	Riverside Unified	Riverside
184	48.9	Sacramento City Unified	Sacramento
185	48.9	West Sonoma County Union High	Sebastopol
186	48.9	Ontario-Montclair Elementary	Ontario
187	48.9	Los Angeles Unified	Los Angeles
188	48.9	Fremont Union High	Sunnyvale
189	48.9	Live Oak Unified	Live Oak
190	48.9	Palos Verdes Peninsula Unified	Palos Verdes Est
191	48.9	El Dorado Union High	Placerville
192	48.9	Dry Creek Joint Elementary	Roseville
193	48.9	Magnolia Elementary	Anaheim
194	48.9	Imperial Unified	Imperial
194	48.9	Mountain View Elementary	El Monte
196	48.9	Albany City Unified	Albany
197	48.9	Santa Maria Joint Union High	Santa Maria
198	48.9	Sanger Unified	Sanger
199	48.9	Adelanto Elementary	Adelanto
200	48.9	San Mateo-Foster City Elementary	San Mateo
201	48.9	Anaheim Elementary	Anaheim
202	48.9	Covina-Valley Unified	Covina
203	48.8	Moreno Valley Unified	Moreno Valley
204	48.8	Whittier City Elementary	Whittier
205	48.8	Pasadena Unified	Pasadena
206	48.8	Charter Oak Unified	Covina
207	48.8	Baldwin Park Unified	Baldwin Park
208	48.8	Arvin Union Elementary	Arvin
209	48.8	Pacifica SD	Pacifica
210	48.8	Bonita Unified	San Dimas
211	48.8	San Benito High	Hollister
212	48.8	Corning Union Elementary	Corning
213	48.8	Monterey Peninsula Unified	Monterey
214	48.8	Santa Rosa High	Santa Rosa
215	48.8	San Jacinto Unified	San Jacinto
216	48.8	San Diego Unified	San Diego
217	48.8	Millbrae Elementary	Millbrae
218	48.8	Anaheim Union High	Anaheim
218	48.8	Grossmont Union High	La Mesa
220	48.8	Lodi Unified	Lodi
221	48.8	El Monte City Elementary	El Monte
222	48.8	Downey Unified	Downey
223	48.8	El Rancho Unified	Pico Rivera
224	48.8	Porterville Unified	Porterville
225	48.8	Red Bluff Joint Union High	Red Bluff
226	48.8	Santa Clara Unified	Santa Clara
227	48.8	Rocklin Unified	Rocklin
228	48.8	Morongo Unified	Twentynine Plms
229	48.8	Washington Unified	West Sacramento
230	48.8	Lynwood Unified	Lynwood
231	48.7	Snowline Joint Unified	Phelan
232	48.7	Palm Springs Unified	Palm Springs
233	48.7	Tustin Unified	Tustin
234	48.7	Rosedale Union Elementary	Bakersfield
235	48.7	Soquel Union Elementary	Capitola
236	48.7	Alum Rock Union Elementary	San Jose
237	48.7	Dublin Unified	Dublin
238	48.7	Hueneme Elementary	Port Hueneme
239	48.7	Monrovia Unified	Monrovia
240	48.7	Escondido Union Elementary	Escondido
241	48.7	Fountain Valley Elementary	Fountain Valley
242	48.7	Oro Grande Elementary	Oro Grande
243	48.7	Santa Paula Union High	Santa Paula
244	48.7	Jefferson Elementary	Daly City
245	48.7	Weaver Union Elementary	Merced
246	48.7	Encinitas Union Elementary	Encinitas
247	48.7	Taft City Elementary	Taft
248	48.7	Fullerton Elementary	Fullerton
249	48.7	Burbank Unified	Burbank
250	48.6	Pomona Unified	Pomona
251	48.6	Galt Joint Union High	Galt
252	48.6	South Bay Union Elementary	Imperial Beach
253	48.6	Livermore Valley Joint Unified	Livermore
254	48.6	Colton Joint Unified	Colton
255	48.6	Oxnard Union High	Oxnard
256	48.6	Lennox Elementary	Lennox
257	48.6	Las Virgenes Unified	Calabasas
258	48.6	Cupertino Union School	Cupertino
259	48.6	Orinda Union Elementary	Orinda
260	48.6	Campbell Union High	San Jose
261	48.6	Rowland Unified	Rowland Heights
262	48.6	Marysville Joint Unified	Marysville
263	48.6	Delano Union Elementary	Delano
264	48.6	Winton Elementary	Winton
265	48.6	Chico Unified	Chico
266	48.6	Lake Elsinore Unified	Lake Elsinore
267	48.6	Duarte Unified	Duarte
268	48.6	Redwood City Elementary	Redwood City
269	48.6	Moreland Elementary	San Jose
270	48.6	West Covina Unified	West Covina
271	48.6	Center Joint Unified	Antelope
272	48.6	Rio Elementary	Oxnard
273	48.6	Del Norte County Unified	Crescent City
274	48.6	Travis Unified	Travis Afb
275	48.6	San Marcos Unified	San Marcos
276	48.6	Azusa Unified	Azusa
277	48.6	Paso Robles Joint Unified	Paso Robles
278	48.6	Ramona City Unified	Ramona
279	48.6	Corona-Norco Unified	Norco
280	48.6	Vista Unified	Vista
281	48.6	Santa Barbara High	Santa Barbara
282	48.6	Hanford Elementary	Hanford
283	48.6	Apple Valley Unified	Apple Valley
284	48.6	Vacaville Unified	Vacaville
285	48.6	Sequoia Union High	Redwood City
286	48.6	Cajon Valley Union Elementary	El Cajon
287	48.5	Alta Loma Elementary	Alta Loma
288	48.5	Lawndale Elementary	Lawndale
289	48.5	Hanford Joint Union High	Hanford
290	48.5	Saddleback Valley Unified	Mission Viejo
291	48.5	Cambrian Elementary	San Jose
292	48.5	Stanislaus Union Elementary	Modesto
293	48.5	Saugus Union Elementary	Santa Clarita
294	48.5	San Marino Unified	San Marino
295	48.5	Centralia Elementary	Buena Park
296	48.5	Vallejo City Unified	Vallejo
297	48.5	San Rafael City High	San Rafael
298	48.5	Central Unified	Fresno
299	48.5	Ojai Unified	Ojai
300	48.5	Modesto City Elementary	Modesto
301	48.5	San Leandro Unified	San Leandro
302	48.5	West Contra Costa Unified	Richmond
303	48.5	Simi Valley Unified	Simi Valley
304	48.4	Livingston Union Elementary	Livingston
305	48.4	Mountain View Elementary	Ontario
306	48.4	Evergreen Elementary	San Jose
307	48.4	Arcadia Unified	Arcadia
308	48.4	La Mesa-Spring Valley	La Mesa
309	48.4	Capistrano Unified	San Juan Capis
310	48.4	Santa Paula Elementary	Santa Paula
311	48.4	Walnut Valley Unified	Walnut
312	48.4	Woodlake Union Elementary	Woodlake
313	48.4	Los Gatos Union Elementary	Los Gatos
314	48.4	Mojave Unified	Mojave
315	48.4	Culver City Unified	Culver City
316	48.4	Sylvan Union Elementary	Modesto
317	48.4	Gilroy Unified	Gilroy
318	48.4	Torrance Unified	Torrance
319	48.4	Sweetwater Union High	Chula Vista
320	48.4	Alisal Union Elementary	Salinas
321	48.4	Martinez Unified	Martinez
322	48.4	Chino Valley Unified	Chino
323	48.4	Etiwanda Elementary	Etiwanda
324	48.4	Central Union Elementary	Lemoore
325	48.4	Salida Union Elementary	Salida
326	48.4	Wiseburn Elementary	Hawthorne
327	48.4	Ukiah Unified	Ukiah
328	48.4	King City Joint Union High	King City
329	48.4	Coachella Valley Unified	Thermal
330	48.4	Redondo Beach Unified	Redondo Beach
331	48.4	Hollister SD	Hollister
332	48.4	William S. Hart Union High	Santa Clarita
333	48.4	Hayward Unified	Hayward
334	48.4	Poway Unified	Poway
335	48.3	San Bruno Park Elementary	San Bruno
336	48.3	Santa Barbara Elementary	Santa Barbara
337	48.3	Placentia-Yorba Linda Unified	Placentia
338	48.3	Elk Grove Unified	Elk Grove
339	48.3	Turlock Joint Elementary	Turlock
340	48.3	Soledad Unified	Soledad
341	48.3	Burlingame Elementary	Burlingame
342	48.3	Ventura Unified	Ventura
343	48.3	San Gabriel Unified	San Gabriel
344	48.3	Chula Vista Elementary	Chula Vista
345	48.3	Mt. Diablo Unified	Concord
346	48.3	Temple City Unified	Temple City
347	48.3	Romoland Elementary	Homeland
348	48.3	Carpinteria Unified	Carpinteria
349	48.3	Berryessa Union Elementary	San Jose
350	48.3	Norwalk-La Mirada Unified	Norwalk
351	48.3	San Francisco Unified	San Francisco
352	48.3	Little Lake City Elementary	Santa Fe Spgs
353	48.3	San Lorenzo Unified	San Lorenzo
354	48.3	Mill Valley Elementary	Mill Valley
355	48.3	Lemon Grove Elementary	Lemon Grove
356	48.2	Irvine Unified	Irvine
357	48.2	East Side Union High	San Jose
358	48.2	Novato Unified	Novato
359	48.2	El Centro Elementary	El Centro
360	48.2	Mountain View-Whisman Elementary	Mountain View
361	48.2	Palo Verde Unified	Blythe
362	48.2	Conejo Valley Unified	Thousand Oaks
363	48.2	Natomas Unified	Sacramento
364	48.2	Loomis Union Elementary	Loomis
365	48.2	New Haven Unified	Union City
366	48.2	Orange Unified	Orange
367	48.2	Bellflower Unified	Bellflower
368	48.2	Tulare Joint Union High	Tulare
369	48.2	Amador County Unified	Jackson
370	48.2	Mt. Pleasant Elementary	San Jose

371	48.2	Enterprise Elementary	Redding
372	48.2	Los Banos Unified	Los Banos
373	48.2	Napa Valley Unified	Napa
374	48.2	Palo Alto Unified	Palo Alto
375	48.2	Pleasant Valley School	Camarillo
376	48.2	Newport-Mesa Unified	Costa Mesa
377	48.2	Firebaugh-Las Deltas Joint Unified	Firebaugh
378	48.1	Keppel Union Elementary	Pearblossom
379	48.1	Cotati-Rohnert Park Unified	Rohnert Park
380	48.1	Yuba City Unified	Yuba City
381	48.1	Santa Monica-Malibu Unified	Santa Monica
382	48.1	Woodland Joint Unified	Woodland
383	48.1	Manhattan Beach Unified	Manhattan Beach
384	48.1	Bear Valley Unified	Big Bear Lake
385	48.1	Escalon Unified	Escalon
386	48.1	Cucamonga Elementary	Rcho Cucamong
387	48.1	Salinas City Elementary	Salinas
388	48.1	Cutler-Orosi Joint Unified	Orosi
389	48.1	Palmdale Elementary	Palmdale
390	48.1	Banning Unified	Banning
391	48.1	Oroville City Elementary	Oroville
392	48.1	Milpitas Unified	Milpitas
393	48.1	Norris Elementary	Bakersfield
394	48.1	Rio Linda Union Elementary	Rio Linda
395	48.1	Robla Elementary	Sacramento
396	48.0	Val Verde Unified	Perris
397	48.0	Acalanes Union High	Lafayette
398	48.0	East Whittier City Elementary	Whittier
399	48.0	Ocean View Elementary	Huntington Bch
400	48.0	Santa Rosa Elementary	Santa Rosa
401	48.0	Lucia Mar Unified	Arroyo Grande
402	48.0	Lowell Joint	Whittier
403	48.0	Alvord Unified	Riverside
404	48.0	Oak Grove Elementary	San Jose
405	48.0	Sunnyvale Elementary	Sunnyvale
406	48.0	Exeter Union Elementary	Exeter
407	48.0	Brea-Olinda Unified	Brea
408	48.0	San Ysidro Elementary	San Ysidro
409	48.0	Ripon Unified	Ripon
410	48.0	Oak Park Unified	Oak Park
411	47.9	Walnut Creek Elementary	Walnut Creek
412	47.9	San Mateo Union High	San Mateo
413	47.9	Selma Unified	Selma
414	47.9	Mendota Unified	Mendota
415	47.9	Newhall Elementary	Valencia
416	47.9	Union Elementary	San Jose
417	47.9	Julian Union High	Julian
418	47.9	Newark Unified	Newark
419	47.9	Alpine Union Elementary	Alpine
420	47.9	Tehachapi Unified	Tehachapi
421	47.9	Lemoore Union Elementary	Lemoore
422	47.9	Perris Elementary	Perris
423	47.9	Rescue Union Elementary	Rescue
424	47.8	Wasco Union Elementary	Wasco
425	47.8	National Elementary	National City
426	47.8	Cypress Elementary	Cypress
427	47.8	ABC Unified	Cerritos
428	47.8	Carmel Unified	Carmel
429	47.8	Atascadero Unified	Atascadero
430	47.8	Holtville Unified	Holtville
431	47.8	Willows Unified	Willows
432	47.8	Golden Plains Unified	San Joaquin
433	47.8	Riverbank Unified	Riverbank
434	47.8	Middletown Unified	Middletown
435	47.8	Alhambra City High	Alhambra
436	47.8	Santee Elementary	Santee
437	47.7	Los Nietos Elementary	Whittier
438	47.7	Sulphur Springs Union Elementary	Canyon Country
439	47.7	South San Francisco Unified	S San Francisco
440	47.7	Eureka City Unified	Eureka
441	47.7	Orcutt Union Elementary	Orcutt
442	47.7	Richland Union Elementary SD	Shafter
443	47.7	Lafayette Elementary	Lafayette
444	47.7	Castaic Union Elementary	Valencia
445	47.7	Fowler Unified	Fowler
446	47.7	Carlsbad Unified	Carlsbad
447	47.7	Fallbrook Union Elementary	Fallbrook
448	47.7	Northern Humboldt Union High	McKinleyville
449	47.7	Ocean View Elementary	Oxnard
450	47.7	Yucaipa-Calimesa Jt. Unified	Yucaipa
451	47.6	Live Oak Elementary	Santa Cruz
452	47.6	Newman-Crows Landing Unified	Newman
453	47.6	Plumas Unified	Quincy
454	47.6	Santa Maria-Bonita Elementary	Santa Maria
455	47.6	Paradise Unified	Paradise
456	47.6	Menlo Park City Elementary	Atherton
457	47.6	Dos Palos Oro Loma Jt. Unified	Dos Palos
458	47.6	Reef-Sunset Unified	Avenal
459	47.6	Dinuba Unified	Dinuba
460	47.6	Del Paso Heights Elementary	Sacramento
461	47.6	Fremont Unified	Fremont
462	47.6	Rosemead Elementary	Rosemead
463	47.6	Grant Joint Union High	Sacramento
464	47.5	Del Mar Union Elementary	Del Mar
465	47.5	Centinela Valley Union High	Lawndale
466	47.5	King City Union Elementary	King City
467	47.5	Mark West Union Elementary	Santa Rosa
468	47.5	Pittsburg Unified	Pittsburg
469	47.5	Eureka Union Elementary	Granite Bay
470	47.5	Dixon Unified	Dixon
471	47.5	Red Bluff Union Elementary	Red Bluff
472	47.5	Kelseyville Unified	Kelseyville
473	47.5	Huntington Beach City Elementary	Huntington Bch
474	47.5	Los Gatos-Saratoga Jt Union High	Los Gatos
475	47.5	Saratoga Union Elementary	Saratoga
476	47.5	Cloverdale Unified	Cloverdale
477	47.5	Burton Elementary	Porterville
478	47.4	Sierra Sands Unified	Ridgecrest
479	47.4	Pleasant Ridge Union Elementary	Grass Valley
480	47.4	Savanna Elementary	Anaheim
481	47.4	Fort Bragg Unified	Fort Bragg
482	47.4	Beardsley Elementary	Bakersfield
483	47.3	Valley Center-Pauma Unified	Valley Center
484	47.3	Belmont-Redwood Shores Elementary	Belmont
485	47.2	Nevada Joint Union High	Grass Valley
486	47.2	Anderson Union High	Anderson
487	47.2	Sonoma Valley Unified	Sonoma
488	47.2	Nuview Union Elementary	Nuevo
489	47.2	Pacific Grove Unified	Pacific Grove
490	47.2	Fairfax Elementary	Bakersfield
491	47.1	Empire Union Elementary	Modesto
492	47.1	Coalinga-Huron Joint Unified	Coalinga
493	47.1	Grass Valley Elementary	Grass Valley
494	47.1	San Rafael City Elementary	San Rafael
495	47.1	Healdsburg Unified	Healdsburg
496	47.0	Gridley Unified	Gridley
497	47.0	Wilsona Elementary	Palmdale
498	47.0	Lake Tahoe Unified	S Lake Tahoe
499	47.0	Gateway Unified	Redding
500	46.9	Willits Unified	Willits
501	46.9	Placer Union High	Auburn
502	46.8	Westwood Unified	Westwood
503	46.8	John Swett Unified	Crockett
504	46.8	Campbell Union Elementary	Campbell
505	46.7	San Dieguito Union High	Encinitas
506	46.7	Jefferson Union High	Daly City
507	46.6	Redding Elementary	Redding
508	46.6	Solana Beach Elementary	Solana Beach
509	46.6	Jamul-Dulzura Union Elementary	Jamul
510	46.5	Gustine Unified	Gustine
511	46.5	Santa Cruz City High	Soquel
512	46.4	Piner-Olivet Union Elementary	Santa Rosa
513	46.4	Mountain Empire Unified	Pine Valley
514	46.4	Black Oak Mine Unified	Georgetown
515	46.4	Chowchilla Elementary	Chowchilla
516	46.0	Winters Joint Unified	Winters
517	46.0	Moraga Elementary	Moraga
518	45.6	Cascade Union Elementary	Anderson
519	40.9	San Diego Co Office of Education	San Diego
520	39.5	Riverside Co Office of Education	Riverside
521	39.1	Orange County Office of Education	Costa Mesa
522	38.7	San Joaquin Co Off of Education	Stockton
523	33.9	Tulare County Office of Education	Visalia
524	32.7	Fresno County Office of Education	Fresno
525	32.2	Santa Clara Co Off of Education	San Jose
526	32.2	Kern County Office of Education	Bakersfield
527	30.6	Los Angeles Co Office of Education	Downey
528	26.4	San Bernardino Co Off of Education	San Bernardino

Individual Education Program Students

Rank	Percent	District Name	City
1	76.7	Riverside Co Office of Education	Riverside
2	67.9	Fresno County Office of Education	Fresno
3	55.4	Los Angeles Co Office of Education	Downey
4	55.0	Kern County Office of Education	Bakersfield
5	29.7	San Joaquin Co Off of Education	Stockton
6	23.5	San Diego Co Office of Education	San Diego
7	17.8	Lakeside Union Elementary	Lakeside
8	16.9	Oroville City Elementary	Oroville
9	16.6	Mariposa County Unified	Mariposa
10	16.0	Wilsona Elementary	Palmdale
11	15.6	Robla Elementary	Sacramento
11	15.6	Santa Cruz City Elementary	Soquel
13	15.5	West Sonoma County Union High	Sebastopol
14	14.9	Live Oak Elementary	Santa Cruz
15	14.8	Acton-Agua Dulce Unified	Acton
15	14.8	Oakley Union Elementary	Oakley
17	14.7	West Contra Costa Unified	Richmond
18	14.6	Cascade Union Elementary	Anderson
19	14.3	San Rafael City Elementary	San Rafael
20	14.2	Cajon Valley Union Elementary	El Cajon
20	14.2	Santee Elementary	Santee
22	14.1	Morongo Unified	Twentynine Plms
23	14.0	Lake Tahoe Unified	S Lake Tahoe
24	13.8	Lancaster Elementary	Lancaster
24	13.8	Martinez Unified	Martinez
24	13.8	Orange County Office of Education	Costa Mesa
24	13.8	Petaluma City Elementary	Petaluma
28	13.7	Antelope Valley Union High	Lancaster
28	13.7	Del Norte County Unified	Crescent City
28	13.7	Modesto City Elementary	Modesto
28	13.7	Solana Beach Elementary	Solana Beach
32	13.6	Amador County Unified	Jackson
33	13.5	Ukiah Unified	Ukiah
34	13.4	Hollister SD	Hollister
35	13.3	Apple Valley Unified	Apple Valley
36	13.2	Folsom-Cordova Unified	Folsom
36	13.2	Redondo Beach Unified	Redondo Beach
36	13.2	San Lorenzo Valley Unified	Ben Lomond
39	13.1	Dos Palos Oro Loma Jt. Unified	Dos Palos
39	13.1	San Mateo-Foster City Elementary	San Mateo
41	13.0	Lawndale Elementary	Lawndale
41	13.0	Mt. Diablo Unified	Concord
41	13.0	Palmdale Elementary	Palmdale
41	13.0	Ramona City Unified	Ramona
45	12.9	Bonita Unified	San Dimas
45	12.9	Willits Unified	Willits
47	12.7	Eureka City Unified	Eureka
47	12.7	Santa Cruz City High	Soquel
49	12.6	Lake Elsinore Unified	Lake Elsinore
49	12.6	Pasadena Unified	Pasadena
49	12.6	Santa Monica-Malibu Unified	Santa Monica
52	12.5	Kingsburg Elementary Charter	Kingsburg
52	12.5	La Mesa-Spring Valley	La Mesa
52	12.5	Piedmont City Unified	Piedmont
52	12.5	San Diego Unified	San Diego
56	12.4	East Whittier City Elementary	Whittier
56	12.4	Konocti Unified	Lower Lake
56	12.4	Pacific Grove Unified	Pacific Grove
56	12.4	Ross Valley Elementary	San Anselmo
56	12.4	San Jacinto Unified	San Jacinto
61	12.3	Oroville Union High	Oroville
61	12.3	Plumas Unified	Quincy
61	12.3	Sacramento City Unified	Sacramento
61	12.3	San Francisco Unified	San Francisco
61	12.3	Stanislaus Union Elementary	Modesto
66	12.2	Berkeley Unified	Berkeley
66	12.2	Chico Unified	Chico
66	12.2	Fort Bragg Unified	Fort Bragg
66	12.2	Santa Rosa Elementary	Santa Rosa
70	12.1	Galt Joint Union Elementary	Galt
70	12.1	River Delta Joint Unified	Rio Vista
70	12.1	Vista Unified	Vista
73	12.0	Grant Joint Union High	Sacramento
73	12.0	Grossmont Union High	La Mesa
73	12.0	Reef-Sunset Unified	Avenal
73	12.0	Taft City Elementary	Taft
77	11.9	Beverly Hills Unified	Beverly Hills
77	11.9	Brentwood Union Elementary	Brentwood
77	11.9	Calaveras Unified	San Andreas
77	11.9	Coronado Unified	Coronado
77	11.9	Greenfield Union Elementary	Greenfield
77	11.9	Lakeport Unified	Lakeport
77	11.9	Monterey Peninsula Unified	Monterey
77	11.9	Rincon Valley Union Elementary	Santa Rosa
77	11.9	Valley Center-Pauma Unified	Valley Center
86	11.8	Covina-Valley Unified	Covina
86	11.8	Gateway Unified	Redding
86	11.8	Merced Union High	Atwater
86	11.8	Napa Valley Unified	Napa
86	11.8	Santa Barbara Elementary	Santa Barbara
86	11.8	Santa Clara Unified	Santa Clara
86	11.8	Temecula Valley Unified	Temecula
86	11.8	Turlock Joint Elementary	Turlock
86	11.8	Vallejo City Unified	Vallejo
95	11.7	Auburn Union Elementary	Auburn
95	11.7	Cotati-Rohnert Park Unified	Rohnert Park
95	11.7	Fillmore Unified	Fillmore
95	11.7	Lemon Grove Elementary	Lemon Grove
95	11.7	Lodi Unified	Lodi
95	11.7	Novato Unified	Novato
95	11.7	San Jose Unified	San Jose
95	11.7	Victor Valley Union High	Victorville
103	11.6	Atascadero Unified	Atascadero
103	11.6	Barstow Unified	Barstow
103	11.6	Cabrillo Unified	Half Moon Bay
103	11.6	Little Lake City Elementary	Santa Fe Spgs
103	11.6	North Sacramento Elementary	Sacramento
103	11.6	Selma Unified	Selma
103	11.6	Sonoma Valley Unified	Sonoma
103	11.6	Union Elementary	San Jose
103	11.6	Westminster Elementary	Westminster
112	11.5	Anaheim Union High	Anaheim
112	11.5	Center Joint Unified	Antelope
112	11.5	Claremont Unified	Claremont
112	11.5	Hemet Unified	Hemet

112	11.5	Los Gatos Union Elementary	Los Gatos
112	11.5	Middletown Unified	Middletown
112	11.5	Moorpark Unified	Moorpark
112	11.5	Newark Unified	Newark
112	11.5	Savanna Elementary	Anaheim
112	11.5	Sequoia Union High	Redwood City
112	11.5	Tahoe-Truckee Joint Unified	Truckee
123	11.4	Alameda City Unified	Alameda
123	11.4	Del Mar Union Elementary	Del Mar
123	11.4	Empire Union Elementary	Modesto
123	11.4	Keppel Union Elementary	Pearblossom
123	11.4	Livermore Valley Joint Unified	Livermore
123	11.4	Los Angeles Unified	Los Angeles
123	11.4	Newport-Mesa Unified	Costa Mesa
123	11.4	Northern Humboldt Union High	McKinleyville
123	11.4	Pajaro Valley Unified School	Watsonville
123	11.4	Palos Verdes Peninsula Unified	Palos Verdes Est
123	11.4	Patterson Joint Unified	Patterson
123	11.4	San Rafael City High	San Rafael
123	11.4	Sylvan Union Elementary	Modesto
136	11.3	Fruitvale Elementary	Bakersfield
136	11.3	John Swett Unified	Crockett
136	11.3	Menlo Park City Elementary	Atherton
136	11.3	Old Adobe Union Elementary	Petaluma
136	11.3	Saugus Union Elementary	Santa Clarita
136	11.3	Torrance Unified	Torrance
142	11.2	Alpine Union Elementary	Alpine
142	11.2	Bear Valley Unified	Big Bear Lake
142	11.2	Bellevue Union Elementary	Santa Rosa
142	11.2	Centinela Valley Union High	Lawndale
142	11.2	Escondido Union Elementary	Escondido
142	11.2	Liberty Union High	Brentwood
142	11.2	Rio Linda Union Elementary	Rio Linda
142	11.2	San Bernardino City Unified	San Bernardino
142	11.2	San Marcos Unified	San Marcos
142	11.2	San Mateo Union High	San Mateo
142	11.2	Sweetwater Union High	Chula Vista
142	11.2	Travis Unified	Travis Afb
142	11.2	Vacaville Unified	Vacaville
142	11.2	Winters Joint Unified	Winters
156	11.1	Ceres Unified	Ceres
156	11.1	Chula Vista Elementary	Chula Vista
156	11.1	Dixie Elementary	San Rafael
156	11.1	Fowler Unified	Fowler
156	11.1	Manhattan Beach Unified	Manhattan Beach
156	11.1	Morgan Hill Unified	Morgan Hill
156	11.1	Westside Union Elementary	Lancaster
156	11.1	William S. Hart Union High	Santa Clarita
164	11.0	Kelseyville Unified	Kelseyville
164	11.0	King City Joint Union High	King City
164	11.0	Lowell Joint	Whittier
164	11.0	Modesto City High	Modesto
164	11.0	Palo Alto Unified	Palo Alto
169	10.9	Cypress Elementary	Cypress
169	10.9	Oakland Unified	Oakland
169	10.9	Oceanside Unified	Oceanside
169	10.9	Petaluma Joint Union High	Petaluma
169	10.9	Placentia-Yorba Linda Unified	Placentia
169	10.9	Pleasanton Unified	Pleasanton
175	10.8	Alum Rock Union Elementary	San Jose
175	10.8	Downey Unified	Downey
175	10.8	Los Nietos Elementary	Whittier
175	10.8	Lucia Mar Unified	Arroyo Grande
175	10.8	Paso Robles Joint Unified	Paso Robles
175	10.8	Salida Union Elementary	Salida
175	10.8	San Benito High	Hollister
175	10.8	Washington Unified	West Sacramento
175	10.8	Whittier City Elementary	Whittier
184	10.7	Dixon Unified	Dixon
184	10.7	Grass Valley Elementary	Grass Valley
184	10.7	Huntington Beach City Elementary	Huntington Bch
184	10.7	Orange Unified	Orange
184	10.7	Piner-Olivet Union Elementary	Santa Rosa
184	10.7	San Ramon Valley Unified	Danville
184	10.7	South Bay Union Elementary	Imperial Beach
184	10.7	Turlock Joint Union High	Turlock
192	10.6	Bassett Unified	La Puente
192	10.6	Carpinteria Unified	Carpinteria
192	10.6	Centralia Elementary	Buena Park
192	10.6	Goleta Union Elementary	Goleta
192	10.6	Merced City Elementary	Merced
192	10.6	Mountain Empire Unified	Pine Valley
192	10.6	Ojai Unified	Ojai
192	10.6	Paradise Unified	Paradise
192	10.6	Placer Union High	Auburn
192	10.6	Roseville City Elementary	Roseville
192	10.6	Tustin Unified	Tustin
192	10.6	Walnut Creek Elementary	Walnut Creek
204	10.5	Antioch Unified	Antioch
204	10.5	Delhi Unified	Delhi
204	10.5	Eastside Union Elementary	Lancaster
204	10.5	Fontana Unified	Fontana
204	10.5	Jamul-Dulzura Union Elementary	Jamul
204	10.5	Moreno Valley Unified	Moreno Valley
204	10.5	Mt. Pleasant Elementary	San Jose
204	10.5	Oakdale Joint Unified	Oakdale
204	10.5	Pomona Unified	Pomona
204	10.5	Santa Barbara High	Santa Barbara
214	10.4	Adelanto Elementary	Adelanto
214	10.4	Campbell Union High	San Jose
214	10.4	Central Unified	Fresno
214	10.4	Chaffey Joint Union High	Ontario
214	10.4	Fairfield-Suisun Unified	Fairfield
214	10.4	Fallbrook Union High	Fallbrook
214	10.4	Fountain Valley Elementary	Fountain Valley
214	10.4	Kerman Unified	Kerman
214	10.4	Las Virgenes Unified	Calabasas
214	10.4	Linden Unified	Linden
214	10.4	Magnolia Elementary	Anaheim
214	10.4	Mountain View-Whisman Elementary	Mountain View
214	10.4	Pittsburg Unified	Pittsburg
214	10.4	Riverside Unified	Riverside
214	10.4	Rocklin Unified	Rocklin
214	10.4	San Lorenzo Unified	San Lorenzo
214	10.4	Simi Valley Unified	Simi Valley
214	10.4	Sunnyvale Elementary	Sunnyvale
232	10.3	Azusa Unified	Azusa
232	10.3	Corona-Norco Unified	Norco
232	10.3	East Side Union High	San Jose
232	10.3	Hayward Unified	Hayward
232	10.3	National Elementary	National City
232	10.3	Redlands Unified	Redlands
232	10.3	Snowline Joint Unified	Phelan
232	10.3	Woodland Joint Unified	Woodland
240	10.2	Arvin Union Elementary	Arvin
240	10.2	Beaumont Unified	Beaumont
240	10.2	Buena Park Elementary	Buena Park
240	10.2	Burbank Unified	Burbank
240	10.2	Castro Valley Unified	Castro Valley
240	10.2	Fullerton Elementary	Fullerton
240	10.2	Hilmar Unified	Hilmar
240	10.2	Kings Canyon Joint Unified	Reedley
240	10.2	Norwalk-La Mirada Unified	Norwalk
240	10.2	Richland Union Elementary SD	Shafter
240	10.2	Rio Elementary	Oxnard
240	10.2	Romoland Elementary	Homeland
240	10.2	San Dieguito Union High	Encinitas
240	10.2	San Leandro Unified	San Leandro
240	10.2	Santa Paula Elementary	Santa Paula
240	10.2	Sierra Sands Unified	Ridgecrest
240	10.2	Sierra Unified	Prather
257	10.1	Benicia Unified	Benicia
257	10.1	Huntington Beach Union High	Huntington Bch
257	10.1	Muroc Joint Unified	North Edwards
257	10.1	Newman-Crows Landing Unified	Newman
257	10.1	Oak Grove Elementary	San Jose
257	10.1	Oak Park Unified	Oak Park
257	10.1	Oxnard Union High	Oxnard
257	10.1	Pleasant Valley School	Camarillo
257	10.1	Red Bluff Joint Union High	Red Bluff
257	10.1	Santa Paula Union High	Santa Paula
257	10.1	Standard Elementary	Bakersfield
268	10.0	Conejo Valley Unified	Thousand Oaks
268	10.0	Fallbrook Union Elementary	Fallbrook
268	10.0	Fresno Unified	Fresno
268	10.0	Garden Grove Unified	Garden Grove
268	10.0	Ocean View Elementary	Huntington Bch
268	10.0	Orland Joint Unified	Orland
274	9.9	ABC Unified	Cerritos
274	9.9	Anaheim Elementary	Anaheim
274	9.9	Bakersfield City Elementary	Bakersfield
274	9.9	Keyes Union Elementary	Keyes
274	9.9	Tehachapi Unified	Tehachapi
274	9.9	Ventura Unified	Ventura
280	9.8	Albany City Unified	Albany
280	9.8	Brea-Olinda Unified	Brea
280	9.8	El Monte City Elementary	El Monte
280	9.8	El Rancho Unified	Pico Rivera
280	9.8	Glendora Unified	Glendora
280	9.8	Hacienda La Puente Unified	City of Industry
280	9.8	Mark West Union Elementary	Santa Rosa
280	9.8	Murrieta Valley Unified	Murrieta
280	9.8	Perris Elementary	Perris
280	9.8	Rowland Unified	Rowland Heights
280	9.8	San Marino Unified	San Marino
280	9.8	Santa Rosa High	Santa Rosa
280	9.8	Silver Valley Unified	Yermo
280	9.8	South San Francisco Unified	S San Francisco
280	9.8	Stockton City Unified	Stockton
295	9.7	Garvey Elementary	Rosemead
295	9.7	La Canada Unified	La Canada
295	9.7	Lamont Elementary	Lamont
295	9.7	Lincoln Unified	Stockton
295	9.7	Mountain View-Los Altos Union High	Mountain View
295	9.7	Poway Unified	Poway
295	9.7	San Juan Unified	Carmichael
295	9.7	San Ysidro Elementary	San Ysidro
295	9.7	Windsor Unified	Windsor
304	9.6	Charter Oak Unified	Covina
304	9.6	Fairfax Elementary	Bakersfield
304	9.6	Healdsburg Unified	Healdsburg
304	9.6	Lennox Elementary	Lennox
304	9.6	Mill Valley Elementary	Mill Valley
304	9.6	Soquel Union Elementary	Capitola
304	9.6	Sulphur Springs Union Elementary	Canyon Country
304	9.6	Yucaipa-Calimesa Jt. Unified	Yucaipa
312	9.5	Capistrano Unified	San Juan Capis
312	9.5	Carlsbad Unified	Carlsbad
312	9.5	Hesperia Unified	Hesperia
312	9.5	Hueneme Elementary	Port Hueneme
312	9.5	Moreland Elementary	San Jose
312	9.5	Oxnard Elementary	Oxnard
312	9.5	Waterford Unified	Waterford
319	9.4	Alhambra City Elementary	Alhambra
319	9.4	Dublin Unified	Dublin
319	9.4	Greenfield Union Elementary	Bakersfield
319	9.4	Lemoore Union High	Lemoore
319	9.4	Pacifica SD	Pacifica
319	9.4	Rim of the World Unified	Lake Arrowhead
325	9.3	Bonsall Union Elementary	Bonsall
325	9.3	Carmel Unified	Carmel
325	9.3	Cucamonga Elementary	Rcho Cucamong
325	9.3	Culver City Unified	Culver City
325	9.3	Enterprise Elementary	Redding
325	9.3	Escondido Union High	Escondido
325	9.3	Galt Joint Union High	Galt
325	9.3	Glendale Unified	Glendale
325	9.3	Hawthorne Elementary	Hawthorne
325	9.3	Natomas Unified	Sacramento
325	9.3	New Haven Unified	Union City
325	9.3	Newhall Elementary	Valencia
325	9.3	Ocean View Elementary	Oxnard
325	9.3	Santa Ana Unified	Santa Ana
325	9.3	Western Placer Unified	Lincoln
340	9.2	Alvord Unified	Riverside
340	9.2	Atwater Elementary	Atwater
340	9.2	Campbell Union Elementary	Campbell
340	9.2	Colton Joint Unified	Colton
340	9.2	Eureka Union Elementary	Granite Bay
340	9.2	Holtville Unified	Holtville
340	9.2	Loomis Union Elementary	Loomis
340	9.2	Ontario-Montclair Elementary	Ontario
340	9.2	Riverbank Unified	Riverbank
340	9.2	South Whittier Elementary	Whittier
350	9.1	Central Elementary	Rcho Cucamong
350	9.1	El Dorado Union High	Placerville
350	9.1	Jurupa Unified	Riverside
350	9.1	King City Union Elementary	King City
350	9.1	Lafayette Elementary	Lafayette
350	9.1	Livingston Union Elementary	Livingston
350	9.1	Los Alamitos Unified	Los Alamitos
350	9.1	Moraga Elementary	Moraga
350	9.1	Mountain View Elementary	Ontario
350	9.1	Redding Elementary	Redding
350	9.1	Rosedale Union Elementary	Bakersfield
350	9.1	Whittier Union High	Whittier
362	9.0	Belmont-Redwood Shores Elementary	Belmont
362	9.0	El Centro Elementary	El Centro
362	9.0	Gilroy Unified	Gilroy
362	9.0	Los Altos Elementary	Los Altos
362	9.0	Milpitas Unified	Milpitas
362	9.0	Mountain View Elementary	El Monte
362	9.0	Redwood City Elementary	Redwood City
362	9.0	Sonora Union High	Sonora
362	9.0	Southern Kern Unified	Rosamond
362	9.0	Visalia Unified	Visalia
362	9.0	Weaver Union Elementary	Merced
373	8.9	Banning Unified	Banning
373	8.9	Castaic Union Elementary	Valencia
373	8.9	Dry Creek Joint Elementary	Roseville
373	8.9	El Monte Union High	El Monte
373	8.9	Elk Grove Unified	Elk Grove
373	8.9	Firebaugh-Las Deltas Joint Unified	Firebaugh
373	8.9	Mcfarland Unified	Mcfarland
380	8.8	Coalinga-Huron Joint Unified	Coalinga
380	8.8	Fremont Unified	Fremont
380	8.8	Millbrae Elementary	Millbrae
380	8.8	Saddleback Valley Unified	Mission Viejo
380	8.8	San Luis Coastal Unified	San Luis Obispo
380	8.8	Saratoga Union Elementary	Saratoga
386	8.7	Etiwanda Elementary	Etiwanda
386	8.7	Irvine Unified	Irvine
388	8.6	Brawley Union High	Brawley
388	8.6	Central Union Elementary	Lemoore
388	8.6	Chino Valley Unified	Chino
388	8.6	Encinitas Union Elementary	Encinitas
388	8.6	Marysville Joint Unified	Marysville

388	8.6	Palm Springs Unified	Palm Springs
388	8.6	Tamalpais Union High	Larkspur
395	8.5	Acalanes Union High	Lafayette
395	8.5	Arcadia Unified	Arcadia
395	8.5	Berryessa Union Elementary	San Jose
395	8.5	Clovis Unified	Clovis
399	8.4	Bellflower Unified	Bellflower
399	8.4	La Habra City Elementary	La Habra
399	8.4	Montebello Unified	Montebello
399	8.4	Panama Buena Vista Union Elem	Bakersfield
399	8.4	San Bruno Park Elementary	San Bruno
399	8.4	South Pasadena Unified	South Pasadena
399	8.4	Tracy Joint Unified	Tracy
399	8.4	Val Verde Unified	Perris
407	8.3	Burlingame Elementary	Burlingame
407	8.3	Evergreen Elementary	San Jose
407	8.3	Franklin-Mckinley Elementary	San Jose
407	8.3	Kern Union High	Bakersfield
407	8.3	Laguna Beach Unified	Laguna Beach
407	8.3	Nevada Joint Union High	Grass Valley
407	8.3	Rosemead Elementary	Rosemead
407	8.3	San Gabriel Unified	San Gabriel
415	8.2	Anderson Union High	Anderson
415	8.2	Davis Joint Unified	Davis
415	8.2	Duarte Unified	Duarte
415	8.2	Gridley Unified	Gridley
415	8.2	Lemoore Union Elementary	Lemoore
415	8.2	Orinda Union Elementary	Orinda
415	8.2	Paramount Unified	Paramount
415	8.2	Rialto Unified	Rialto
415	8.2	Salinas Union High	Salinas
415	8.2	Scotts Valley Unified	Scotts Valley
425	8.1	Baldwin Park Unified	Baldwin Park
425	8.1	Delano Joint Union High	Delano
425	8.1	Desert Sands Unified	La Quinta
425	8.1	Gustine Unified	Gustine
425	8.1	Manteca Unified	Manteca
425	8.1	Monrovia Unified	Monrovia
425	8.1	Temple City Unified	Temple City
425	8.1	Wiseburn Elementary	Hawthorne
433	8.0	Julian Union Elementary	Julian
433	8.0	Long Beach Unified	Long Beach
433	8.0	Los Gatos-Saratoga Jt Union High	Los Gatos
433	8.0	Menifee Union Elementary	Menifee
433	8.0	Mojave Unified	Mojave
433	8.0	Orcutt Union Elementary	Orcutt
433	8.0	Ripon Unified	Ripon
440	7.9	Alhambra City High	Alhambra
440	7.9	Alta Loma Elementary	Alta Loma
440	7.9	Black Oak Mine Unified	Georgetown
440	7.9	Coachella Valley Unified	Thermal
440	7.9	Fremont Union High	Sunnyvale
440	7.9	Gonzales Unified	Gonzales
440	7.9	North Monterey County Unified	Moss Landing
440	7.9	Santa Maria Joint Union High	Santa Maria
440	7.9	Tulare City Elementary	Tulare
449	7.8	Pleasant Ridge Union Elementary	Grass Valley
449	7.8	Victor Elementary	Victorville
451	7.7	Hughson Unified	Hughson
451	7.7	Ravenswood City Elementary	East Palo Alto
451	7.7	Sanger Unified	Sanger
451	7.7	Twin Ridges Elementary	North San Juan
455	7.6	Cambrian Elementary	San Jose
455	7.6	Central Union High	El Centro
455	7.6	Hanford Joint Union High	Hanford
455	7.6	Lompoc Unified	Lompoc
455	7.6	Tulare Joint Union High	Tulare
460	7.5	Delano Union Elementary	Delano
460	7.5	Upland Unified	Upland
462	7.4	Roseville Joint Union High	Roseville
463	7.3	Inglewood Unified	Inglewood
463	7.3	Palo Verde Unified	Blythe
463	7.3	Perris Union High	Perris
466	7.2	Gorman Elementary	Gorman
466	7.2	Jefferson Union High	Daly City
468	7.1	Brawley Elementary	Brawley
468	7.1	Del Paso Heights Elementary	Sacramento
468	7.1	El Segundo Unified	El Segundo
468	7.1	Fullerton Joint Union High	Fullerton
468	7.1	Yuba City Unified	Yuba City
473	7.0	Imperial Unified	Imperial
473	7.0	Nuview Union Elementary	Nuevo
473	7.0	Santa Maria-Bonita Elementary	Santa Maria
473	7.0	Soledad Unified	Soledad
477	6.9	Jefferson Elementary	Tracy
477	6.9	Red Bluff Union Elementary	Red Bluff
477	6.9	San Carlos Elementary	San Carlos
477	6.9	Walnut Valley Unified	Walnut
481	6.8	Corcoran Joint Unified	Corcoran
481	6.8	Madera Unified	Madera
481	6.8	Templeton Unified	Templeton
481	6.8	Wasco Union Elementary	Wasco
485	6.7	Dinuba Unified	Dinuba
485	6.7	Shasta Union High	Redding
487	6.6	Jefferson Elementary	Daly City
487	6.6	Winton Elementary	Winton
489	6.5	Alisal Union Elementary	Salinas
490	6.4	Calexico Unified	Calexico
490	6.4	Wheatland Elementary	Wheatland
492	6.3	Parlier Unified	Parlier
493	6.2	Cupertino Union School	Cupertino
494	6.0	Mother Lode Union Elementary	Placerville
495	5.9	Corning Union Elementary	Corning
495	5.9	Riverdale Joint Unified	Riverdale
497	5.6	Cloverdale Unified	Cloverdale
497	5.6	Farmersville Unified	Farmersville
497	5.6	Norris Elementary	Bakersfield
497	5.6	Porterville Unified	Porterville
501	5.5	Exeter Union Elementary	Exeter
502	5.3	Salinas City Elementary	Salinas
502	5.3	West Covina Unified	West Covina
504	5.2	Buckeye Union Elementary	Shingle Springs
504	5.2	Compton Unified	Compton
504	5.2	Hanford Elementary	Hanford
507	5.1	Rescue Union Elementary	Rescue
508	4.8	Live Oak Unified	Live Oak
509	4.7	Los Banos Unified	Los Banos
509	4.7	Woodlake Union Elementary	Woodlake
511	4.5	Burton Elementary	Porterville
511	4.5	Mendota Unified	Mendota
513	4.3	Earlimart Elementary	Earlimart
513	4.3	Golden Plains Unified	San Joaquin
513	4.3	Lynwood Unified	Lynwood
516	3.9	Julian Union High	Julian
517	3.4	Chowchilla Elementary	Chowchilla
517	3.4	Cutler-Orosi Joint Unified	Orosi
519	3.2	Escalon Unified	Escalon
520	3.0	Lindsay Unified	Lindsay
521	0.4	Oro Grande Elementary	Oro Grande
522	0.0	Beardsley Elementary	Bakersfield
522	0.0	Santa Rita Union Elementary	Salinas
522	0.0	Westwood Unified	Westwood
522	0.0	Willows Unified	Willows
526	n/a	San Bernardino Co Off of Education	San Bernardino
526	n/a	Santa Clara Co Off of Education	San Jose
526	n/a	Tulare County Office of Education	Visalia

English Language Learner Students

Rank	Percent	District Name	City
1	83.1	Earlimart Elementary	Earlimart
2	74.5	Mendota Unified	Mendota
3	73.8	Lamont Elementary	Lamont
4	73.1	Calexico Unified	Calexico
5	69.3	Ravenswood City Elementary	East Palo Alto
6	69.1	Alisal Union Elementary	Salinas
7	69.0	Lennox Elementary	Lennox
8	68.7	San Ysidro Elementary	San Ysidro
9	67.6	Reef-Sunset Unified	Avenal
10	67.1	Coachella Valley Unified	Thermal
11	66.8	Arvin Union Elementary	Arvin
12	66.1	Bellevue Union Elementary	Santa Rosa
13	65.7	Livingston Union Elementary	Livingston
14	63.8	Parlier Unified	Parlier
15	62.5	Anaheim Elementary	Anaheim
16	61.7	Soledad Unified	Soledad
17	60.8	Santa Ana Unified	Santa Ana
18	60.7	Alum Rock Union Elementary	San Jose
19	59.1	Gonzales Unified	Gonzales
20	58.4	Lindsay Unified	Lindsay
21	58.2	National Elementary	National City
22	57.6	Mountain View Elementary	El Monte
23	57.4	Cutler-Orosi Joint Unified	Orosi
24	57.0	Greenfield Union Elementary	Greenfield
25	56.8	Golden Plains Unified	San Joaquin
26	56.0	Winton Elementary	Winton
27	55.8	Delano Union Elementary	Delano
28	55.0	Mt. Pleasant Elementary	San Jose
29	54.0	Franklin-Mckinley Elementary	San Jose
30	53.8	Compton Unified	Compton
31	52.9	Magnolia Elementary	Anaheim
32	52.3	King City Union Elementary	King City
33	51.8	Lynwood Unified	Lynwood
34	51.3	Delhi Unified	Delhi
35	50.9	Ocean View Elementary	Oxnard
36	49.6	Santa Paula Elementary	Santa Paula
37	49.4	Santa Maria-Bonita Elementary	Santa Maria
38	49.3	Ontario-Montclair Elementary	Ontario
39	49.1	Garden Grove Unified	Garden Grove
39	49.1	Redwood City Elementary	Redwood City
41	48.1	Delano Joint Union High	Delano
42	46.8	Perris Elementary	Perris
42	46.8	Weaver Union Elementary	Merced
44	46.4	Farmersville Unified	Farmersville
45	45.6	Pajaro Valley Unified School	Watsonville
46	45.4	Paramount Unified	Paramount
47	45.3	Oxnard Elementary	Oxnard
48	45.2	Buena Park Elementary	Buena Park
48	45.2	El Monte City Elementary	El Monte
48	45.2	Pomona Unified	Pomona
51	44.5	El Centro Elementary	El Centro
52	44.4	Hueneme Elementary	Port Hueneme
53	44.3	Hawthorne Elementary	Hawthorne
53	44.3	La Habra City Elementary	La Habra
53	44.3	Richland Union Elementary SD	Shafter
56	44.2	Salinas City Elementary	Salinas
57	43.8	Los Angeles Unified	Los Angeles
58	43.5	Garvey Elementary	Rosemead
59	43.3	Montebello Unified	Montebello
60	43.2	Holtville Unified	Holtville
61	42.9	Westminster Elementary	Westminster
62	42.7	Escondido Union Elementary	Escondido
62	42.7	Lawndale Elementary	Lawndale
62	42.7	Santa Rosa Elementary	Santa Rosa
65	42.3	Romoland Elementary	Homeland
65	42.3	Santa Barbara Elementary	Santa Barbara
67	42.2	Rio Elementary	Oxnard
67	42.2	South Bay Union Elementary	Imperial Beach
69	42.1	Del Paso Heights Elementary	Sacramento
70	41.8	Patterson Joint Unified	Patterson
71	41.6	Riverbank Unified	Riverbank
72	41.5	Wasco Union Elementary	Wasco
73	41.4	Kings Canyon Joint Unified	Reedley
74	40.6	Fairfax Elementary	Bakersfield
75	40.0	Madera Unified	Madera
76	39.9	Mcfarland Unified	Mcfarland
77	39.8	Woodlake Union Elementary	Woodlake
78	39.7	Robla Elementary	Sacramento
79	39.5	Gustine Unified	Gustine
80	39.4	Alvord Unified	Riverside
81	39.3	San Rafael City Elementary	San Rafael
82	39.2	Fillmore Unified	Fillmore
83	38.8	Mountain View-Whisman Elementary	Mountain View
84	38.6	Carpinteria Unified	Carpinteria
85	38.5	Dos Palos Oro Loma Jt. Unified	Dos Palos
86	38.3	Azusa Unified	Azusa
87	37.6	Salinas Union High	Salinas
88	37.4	Firebaugh-Las Deltas Joint Unified	Firebaugh
89	37.3	Alhambra City Elementary	Alhambra
90	37.1	Fontana Unified	Fontana
91	36.5	Savanna Elementary	Anaheim
92	36.2	Coalinga-Huron Joint Unified	Coalinga
93	35.7	North Sacramento Elementary	Sacramento
94	35.3	Central Union High	El Centro
95	35.1	Winters Joint Unified	Winters
96	35.0	Chula Vista Elementary	Chula Vista
97	34.2	Hayward Unified	Hayward
98	34.1	Atwater Elementary	Atwater
99	33.8	Brawley Elementary	Brawley
99	33.8	Palm Springs Unified	Palm Springs
99	33.8	Selma Unified	Selma
102	33.2	Baldwin Park Unified	Baldwin Park
102	33.2	Inglewood Unified	Inglewood
102	33.2	Kerman Unified	Kerman
105	33.1	Dinuba Unified	Dinuba
106	33.0	San Gabriel Unified	San Gabriel
107	32.9	Bassett Unified	La Puente
108	32.8	Los Nietos Elementary	Whittier
108	32.8	Newman-Crows Landing Unified	Newman
110	32.5	Modesto City Elementary	Modesto
111	32.3	El Rancho Unified	Pico Rivera
112	32.1	Alhambra City High	Alhambra
113	32.0	Rosemead Elementary	Rosemead
113	32.0	Santa Rita Union Elementary	Salinas
113	32.0	Sunnyvale Elementary	Sunnyvale
116	31.8	Chowchilla Elementary	Chowchilla
117	31.7	Campbell Union Elementary	Campbell
118	31.6	Berryessa Union Elementary	San Jose
119	31.5	Rowland Unified	Rowland Heights
120	31.2	Brawley Union High	Brawley
121	31.1	Fresno Unified	Fresno
122	30.4	San Jacinto Unified	San Jacinto
123	30.2	Los Angeles Co Office of Education	Downey
124	30.1	El Monte Union High	El Monte
124	30.1	Gilroy Unified	Gilroy
126	30.0	Glendale Unified	Glendale
127	29.9	Merced City Elementary	Merced
128	29.8	Oakland Unified	Oakland
129	29.7	Woodland Joint Unified	Woodland
130	29.4	Centinela Valley Union High	Lawndale
130	29.4	Desert Sands Unified	La Quinta
130	29.4	West Contra Costa Unified	Richmond
133	29.3	Fullerton Joint Union High	Fullerton
134	29.2	Long Beach Unified	Long Beach
135	29.0	Centralia Elementary	Buena Park
135	29.0	Moreno Valley Unified	Moreno Valley
135	29.0	Sacramento City Unified	Sacramento
138	28.9	Evergreen Elementary	San Jose

138	28.9	Hollister SD	Hollister
140	28.8	Pittsburg Unified	Pittsburg
141	28.7	Corcoran Joint Unified	Corcoran
142	28.6	Lodi Unified	Lodi
143	28.5	Jurupa Unified	Riverside
144	28.4	San Francisco Unified	San Francisco
145	28.3	Fullerton Elementary	Fullerton
146	28.2	Riverdale Joint Unified	Riverdale
146	28.2	Wilsona Elementary	Palmdale
148	28.1	San Diego Unified	San Diego
149	28.0	Greenfield Union Elementary	Bakersfield
149	28.0	Jefferson Elementary	Daly City
149	28.0	River Delta Joint Unified	Rio Vista
149	28.0	Val Verde Unified	Perris
153	27.9	Sonoma Valley Unified	Sonoma
154	27.8	Turlock Joint Elementary	Turlock
155	27.4	East Side Union High	San Jose
155	27.4	Oak Grove Elementary	San Jose
155	27.4	San Marcos Unified	San Marcos
158	27.3	Fallbrook Union Elementary	Fallbrook
159	27.2	Tustin Unified	Tustin
160	27.1	Newport-Mesa Unified	Costa Mesa
161	26.9	Cabrillo Unified	Half Moon Bay
161	26.9	Galt Joint Union Elementary	Galt
161	26.9	Pasadena Unified	Pasadena
164	26.8	Little Lake City Elementary	Santa Fe Spgs
164	26.8	Nuview Union Elementary	Nuevo
164	26.8	San Bernardino City Unified	San Bernardino
167	26.6	Anaheim Union High	Anaheim
167	26.6	Gridley Unified	Gridley
169	26.5	Goleta Union Elementary	Goleta
169	26.5	Live Oak Unified	Live Oak
169	26.5	Oceanside Unified	Oceanside
172	26.4	Corning Union Elementary	Corning
172	26.4	Live Oak Elementary	Santa Cruz
172	26.4	Sweetwater Union High	Chula Vista
175	26.2	Hilmar Unified	Hilmar
176	26.1	North Monterey County Unified	Moss Landing
177	26.0	Eastside Union Elementary	Lancaster
177	26.0	San Jose Unified	San Jose
179	25.9	Los Banos Unified	Los Banos
179	25.9	Sanger Unified	Sanger
181	25.8	Hacienda La Puente Unified	City of Industry
181	25.8	San Leandro Unified	San Leandro
181	25.8	Santa Cruz City Elementary	Soquel
184	25.5	Santa Maria Joint Union High	Santa Maria
184	25.5	Sequoia Union High	Redwood City
186	25.3	Adelanto Elementary	Adelanto
186	25.3	Monterey Peninsula Unified	Monterey
188	25.2	Millbrae Elementary	Millbrae
188	25.2	Napa Valley Unified	Napa
190	25.0	Milpitas Unified	Milpitas
190	25.0	Washington Unified	West Sacramento
192	24.7	Grant Joint Union High	Sacramento
193	24.5	Bakersfield City Elementary	Bakersfield
193	24.5	Rialto Unified	Rialto
195	24.4	Cucamonga Elementary	Rcho Cucamong
195	24.4	Vista Unified	Vista
197	24.3	Palmdale Elementary	Palmdale
198	24.2	South Whittier Elementary	Whittier
199	24.1	Stockton City Unified	Stockton
200	24.0	San Lorenzo Unified	San Lorenzo
201	23.9	Bonsall Union Elementary	Bonsall
202	23.8	New Haven Unified	Union City
203	23.5	Marysville Joint Unified	Marysville
203	23.5	San Mateo-Foster City Elementary	San Mateo
203	23.5	Whittier City Elementary	Whittier
206	23.4	Banning Unified	Banning
206	23.4	Santa Clara Unified	Santa Clara
208	23.3	Healdsburg Unified	Healdsburg
209	23.2	Keppel Union Elementary	Pearblossom
210	22.8	Fresno County Office of Education	Fresno
210	22.8	Windsor Unified	Windsor
212	22.7	Downey Unified	Downey
212	22.7	Ukiah Unified	Ukiah
214	22.6	Petaluma City Elementary	Petaluma
215	22.5	Old Adobe Union Elementary	Petaluma
215	22.5	Orange Unified	Orange
217	22.4	Imperial Unified	Imperial
218	22.0	Fowler Unified	Fowler
219	21.6	Piner-Olivet Union Elementary	Santa Rosa
220	21.5	Empire Union Elementary	Modesto
220	21.5	Hughson Unified	Hughson
222	21.3	Hanford Elementary	Hanford
222	21.3	Linden Unified	Linden
222	21.3	Rio Linda Union Elementary	Rio Linda
225	21.2	Oxnard Union High	Oxnard
225	21.2	Tulare City Elementary	Tulare
227	21.1	Fort Bragg Unified	Fort Bragg
227	21.1	Lake Tahoe Unified	S Lake Tahoe
229	20.9	Ocean View Elementary	Huntington Bch
229	20.9	Porterville Unified	Porterville
231	20.8	Ceres Unified	Ceres
232	20.7	Visalia Unified	Visalia
233	20.5	Colton Joint Unified	Colton
234	20.4	Newhall Elementary	Valencia
235	20.3	Alameda City Unified	Alameda
235	20.3	South San Francisco Unified	S San Francisco
237	20.2	Moreland Elementary	San Jose
237	20.2	Yuba City Unified	Yuba City
239	20.1	Cajon Valley Union Elementary	El Cajon
239	20.1	Newark Unified	Newark
241	20.0	ABC Unified	Cerritos
242	19.9	Exeter Union Elementary	Exeter
243	19.8	Valley Center-Pauma Unified	Valley Center
244	19.6	Santa Barbara High	Santa Barbara
245	19.5	Lemoore Union Elementary	Lemoore
246	19.3	Fallbrook Union High	Fallbrook
246	19.3	Lompoc Unified	Lompoc
246	19.3	Monrovia Unified	Monrovia
246	19.3	Stanislaus Union Elementary	Modesto
250	19.2	Lemon Grove Elementary	Lemon Grove
251	19.1	Norwalk-La Mirada Unified	Norwalk
252	19.0	East Whittier City Elementary	Whittier
253	18.8	Cloverdale Unified	Cloverdale
254	18.5	Duarte Unified	Duarte
254	18.5	Riverside Co Office of Education	Riverside
256	18.4	Elk Grove Unified	Elk Grove
257	18.2	Orange County Office of Education	Costa Mesa
258	18.1	Tahoe-Truckee Joint Unified	Truckee
259	17.9	Waterford Unified	Waterford
260	17.8	Escondido Union High	Escondido
261	17.7	Vallejo City Unified	Vallejo
262	17.5	Escalon Unified	Escalon
262	17.5	La Mesa-Spring Valley	La Mesa
262	17.5	Merced Union High	Atwater
262	17.5	Moorpark Unified	Moorpark
262	17.5	Paso Robles Joint Unified	Paso Robles
267	17.2	Galt Joint Union High	Galt
267	17.2	Morgan Hill Unified	Morgan Hill
269	17.1	Bellflower Unified	Bellflower
270	17.0	Burbank Unified	Burbank
270	17.0	Keyes Union Elementary	Keyes
272	16.9	Julian Union High	Julian
273	16.8	Corona-Norco Unified	Norco
273	16.8	Culver City Unified	Culver City
273	16.8	Mt. Diablo Unified	Concord
276	16.7	Central Unified	Fresno
276	16.7	Lake Elsinore Unified	Lake Elsinore
278	16.6	San Bruno Park Elementary	San Bruno
279	16.4	Lincoln Unified	Stockton
280	16.3	Willows Unified	Willows
281	16.1	Dixon Unified	Dixon
281	16.1	Mountain Empire Unified	Pine Valley
281	16.1	Orland Joint Unified	Orland
284	16.0	Riverside Unified	Riverside
285	15.8	Salida Union Elementary	Salida
286	15.7	Placentia-Yorba Linda Unified	Placentia
287	15.5	Burton Elementary	Porterville
287	15.5	Santa Rosa High	Santa Rosa
287	15.5	Turlock Joint Union High	Turlock
290	15.4	Burlingame Elementary	Burlingame
290	15.4	Fremont Unified	Fremont
290	15.4	Whittier Union High	Whittier
293	15.3	Hesperia Unified	Hesperia
293	15.3	King City Joint Union High	King City
293	15.3	Menifee Union Elementary	Menifee
296	15.1	Taft City Elementary	Taft
296	15.1	Tracy Joint Unified	Tracy
298	14.9	Temple City Unified	Temple City
299	14.8	Lancaster Elementary	Lancaster
300	14.7	Modesto City High	Modesto
301	14.6	Brentwood Union Elementary	Brentwood
301	14.6	Mountain View Elementary	Ontario
303	14.5	Ventura Unified	Ventura
304	14.3	Palo Verde Unified	Blythe
305	14.2	Santa Clara Co Off of Education	San Jose
306	14.0	Beaumont Unified	Beaumont
306	14.0	Manteca Unified	Manteca
308	13.9	Cupertino Union School	Cupertino
309	13.8	Jefferson Elementary	Tracy
310	13.6	Berkeley Unified	Berkeley
310	13.6	Santa Paula Union High	Santa Paula
312	13.4	Ramona City Unified	Ramona
312	13.4	Sulphur Springs Union Elementary	Canyon Country
314	13.3	Cotati-Rohnert Park Unified	Rohnert Park
315	13.2	Kelseyville Unified	Kelseyville
316	13.1	Hemet Unified	Hemet
316	13.1	Jamul-Dulzura Union Elementary	Jamul
316	13.1	Oro Grande Elementary	Oro Grande
319	13.0	Capistrano Unified	San Juan Capis
319	13.0	Kern County Office of Education	Bakersfield
321	12.9	Lucia Mar Unified	Arroyo Grande
321	12.9	San Diego Co Office of Education	San Diego
323	12.8	John Swett Unified	Crockett
323	12.8	San Mateo Union High	San Mateo
325	12.7	Chaffey Joint Union High	Ontario
325	12.7	Chico Unified	Chico
327	12.6	Covina-Valley Unified	Covina
328	12.5	Encinitas Union Elementary	Encinitas
328	12.5	Natomas Unified	Sacramento
328	12.5	Santa Monica-Malibu Unified	Santa Monica
331	12.3	Cypress Elementary	Cypress
331	12.3	Irvine Unified	Irvine
331	12.3	Oroville City Elementary	Oroville
334	12.1	Torrance Unified	Torrance
335	12.0	Fairfield-Suisun Unified	Fairfield
336	11.9	Ojai Unified	Ojai
337	11.7	Folsom-Cordova Unified	Folsom
338	11.6	Antelope Valley Union High	Lancaster
338	11.6	Arcadia Unified	Arcadia
338	11.6	Mojave Unified	Mojave
341	11.5	Victor Elementary	Victorville
342	11.4	Central Elementary	Rcho Cucamong
343	11.3	San Bernardino Co Off of Education	San Bernardino
343	11.3	Upland Unified	Upland
345	11.2	San Rafael City High	San Rafael
345	11.2	West Covina Unified	West Covina
347	11.1	Albany City Unified	Albany
347	11.1	Kern Union High	Bakersfield
349	10.9	Livermore Valley Joint Unified	Livermore
349	10.9	Novato Unified	Novato
349	10.9	Petaluma Joint Union High	Petaluma
352	10.7	Redondo Beach Unified	Redondo Beach
353	10.5	Fremont Union High	Sunnyvale
353	10.5	Vacaville Unified	Vacaville
353	10.5	Wiseburn Elementary	Hawthorne
356	10.4	Brea-Olinda Unified	Brea
356	10.4	Soquel Union Elementary	Capitola
358	10.3	Perris Union High	Perris
358	10.3	Redlands Unified	Redlands
360	10.0	Oakley Union Elementary	Oakley
360	10.0	Red Bluff Union Elementary	Red Bluff
362	9.9	Huntington Beach Union High	Huntington Bch
363	9.8	Lowell Joint	Whittier
364	9.7	Eureka City Unified	Eureka
365	9.6	Barstow Unified	Barstow
365	9.6	Tulare County Office of Education	Visalia
367	9.5	Chino Valley Unified	Chino
368	9.4	Antioch Unified	Antioch
369	9.3	Davis Joint Unified	Davis
369	9.3	Oakdale Joint Unified	Oakdale
369	9.3	Sylvan Union Elementary	Modesto
372	9.2	Dry Creek Joint Elementary	Roseville
373	9.1	Konocti Unified	Lower Lake
373	9.1	Ripon Unified	Ripon
375	9.0	Claremont Unified	Claremont
376	8.9	Pleasant Valley School	Camarillo
377	8.8	Carlsbad Unified	Carlsbad
377	8.8	Center Joint Unified	Antelope
377	8.8	Clovis Unified	Clovis
377	8.8	Willits Unified	Willits
381	8.7	Solana Beach Elementary	Solana Beach
382	8.6	Kingsburg Elementary Charter	Kingsburg
383	8.5	Saddleback Valley Unified	Mission Viejo
383	8.5	Santa Cruz City High	Soquel
385	8.4	Auburn Union Elementary	Auburn
385	8.4	San Juan Unified	Carmichael
387	8.3	Central Union Elementary	Lemoore
388	8.2	Simi Valley Unified	Simi Valley
389	8.1	Conejo Valley Unified	Thousand Oaks
390	8.0	Liberty Union High	Brentwood
390	8.0	San Luis Coastal Unified	San Luis Obispo
392	7.9	Fountain Valley Elementary	Fountain Valley
392	7.9	Southern Kern Unified	Rosamond
392	7.9	Yucaipa-Calimesa Jt. Unified	Yucaipa
395	7.8	Western Placer Unified	Lincoln
396	7.7	Del Norte County Unified	Crescent City
396	7.7	Sierra Sands Unified	Ridgecrest
398	7.6	Palo Alto Unified	Palo Alto
398	7.6	Tehachapi Unified	Tehachapi
398	7.6	Tulare Joint Union High	Tulare
398	7.6	William S. Hart Union High	Santa Clarita
402	7.5	Charter Oak Unified	Covina
403	7.4	Roseville City Elementary	Roseville
404	7.3	Bear Valley Unified	Big Bear Lake
404	7.3	Jefferson Union High	Daly City
404	7.3	Mark West Union Elementary	Santa Rosa
404	7.3	Poway Unified	Poway
408	7.2	Grossmont Union High	La Mesa
408	7.2	Lakeport Unified	Lakeport
408	7.2	Oroville Union High	Oroville
408	7.2	Walnut Creek Elementary	Walnut Creek
412	7.1	Lakeside Union Elementary	Lakeside
413	7.0	Walnut Valley Unified	Walnut
414	6.9	Castaic Union Elementary	Valencia
414	6.9	Huntington Beach City Elementary	Huntington Bch

416	6.8	Hanford Joint Union High	Hanford
416	6.8	Santee Elementary	Santee
418	6.7	Castro Valley Unified	Castro Valley
419	6.6	Dublin Unified	Dublin
419	6.6	Panama Buena Vista Union Elem	Bakersfield
421	6.5	Mountain View-Los Altos Union High	Mountain View
422	6.2	Acton-Agua Dulce Unified	Acton
422	6.2	Palos Verdes Peninsula Unified	Palos Verdes Est
424	6.1	Enterprise Elementary	Redding
424	6.1	South Pasadena Unified	South Pasadena
426	6.0	San Marino Unified	San Marino
427	5.9	Snowline Joint Unified	Phelan
428	5.8	Beardsley Elementary	Bakersfield
428	5.8	Beverly Hills Unified	Beverly Hills
430	5.7	Rim of the World Unified	Lake Arrowhead
430	5.7	Temecula Valley Unified	Temecula
432	5.6	Union Elementary	San Jose
433	5.5	Cambrian Elementary	San Jose
433	5.5	Orcutt Union Elementary	Orcutt
433	5.5	Rincon Valley Union Elementary	Santa Rosa
436	5.3	Pleasanton Unified	Pleasanton
436	5.3	San Benito High	Hollister
436	5.3	San Joaquin Co Off of Education	Stockton
439	5.2	Los Altos Elementary	Los Altos
439	5.2	Pacifica SD	Pacifica
439	5.2	Victor Valley Union High	Victorville
442	5.1	Cascade Union Elementary	Anderson
443	5.0	Martinez Unified	Martinez
443	5.0	Menlo Park City Elementary	Atherton
445	4.9	Carmel Unified	Carmel
446	4.5	Belmont-Redwood Shores Elementary	Belmont
446	4.5	Campbell Union High	San Jose
446	4.5	Lemoore Union High	Lemoore
449	4.4	San Dieguito Union High	Encinitas
449	4.4	West Sonoma County Union High	Sebastopol
451	4.2	Las Virgenes Unified	Calabasas
451	4.2	Saugus Union Elementary	Santa Clarita
453	4.1	Gateway Unified	Redding
454	4.0	Alpine Union Elementary	Alpine
455	3.9	Del Mar Union Elementary	Del Mar
456	3.8	Apple Valley Unified	Apple Valley
457	3.6	Travis Unified	Travis Afb
458	3.5	Pacific Grove Unified	Pacific Grove
459	3.4	Glendora Unified	Glendora
459	3.4	Middletown Unified	Middletown
459	3.4	Wheatland Elementary	Wheatland
462	3.3	Atascadero Unified	Atascadero
462	3.3	Plumas Unified	Quincy
462	3.3	Ross Valley Elementary	San Anselmo
465	3.2	El Segundo Unified	El Segundo
466	3.0	Alta Loma Elementary	Alta Loma
466	3.0	Piedmont City Unified	Piedmont
468	2.8	Westside Union Elementary	Lancaster
469	2.7	Etiwanda Elementary	Etiwanda
469	2.7	Grass Valley Elementary	Grass Valley
469	2.7	Mother Lode Union Elementary	Placerville
469	2.7	Redding Elementary	Redding
469	2.7	Rocklin Unified	Rocklin
474	2.6	Dixie Elementary	San Rafael
475	2.5	Murrieta Valley Unified	Murrieta
476	2.4	Julian Union Elementary	Julian
476	2.4	Mill Valley Elementary	Mill Valley
476	2.4	Oak Park Unified	Oak Park
476	2.4	Templeton Unified	Templeton
480	2.3	La Canada Unified	La Canada
480	2.3	Laguna Beach Unified	Laguna Beach
482	2.2	Benicia Unified	Benicia
483	2.1	Amador County Unified	Jackson
483	2.1	Los Alamitos Unified	Los Alamitos
483	2.1	Rosedale Union Elementary	Bakersfield
483	2.1	Silver Valley Unified	Yermo
487	2.0	Bonita Unified	San Dimas
487	2.0	Fruitvale Elementary	Bakersfield
487	2.0	San Carlos Elementary	San Carlos
490	1.9	Gorman Elementary	Gorman
490	1.9	Red Bluff Joint Union High	Red Bluff
492	1.8	Manhattan Beach Unified	Manhattan Beach
492	1.8	Rescue Union Elementary	Rescue
492	1.8	Saratoga Union Elementary	Saratoga
495	1.7	Los Gatos Union Elementary	Los Gatos
495	1.7	Morongo Unified	Twentynine Plms
497	1.5	Standard Elementary	Bakersfield
498	1.4	Acalanes Union High	Lafayette
498	1.4	Lafayette Elementary	Lafayette
498	1.4	Scotts Valley Unified	Scotts Valley
498	1.4	Tamalpais Union High	Larkspur
502	1.3	Coronado Unified	Coronado
502	1.3	Moraga Elementary	Moraga
502	1.3	Muroc Joint Unified	North Edwards
502	1.3	Roseville Joint Union High	Roseville
502	1.3	San Ramon Valley Unified	Danville
502	1.3	Westwood Unified	Westwood
508	1.2	Norris Elementary	Bakersfield
509	1.1	Eureka Union Elementary	Granite Bay
510	1.0	Orinda Union Elementary	Orinda
510	1.0	Twin Ridges Elementary	North San Juan
512	0.9	Black Oak Mine Unified	Georgetown
512	0.9	Mariposa County Unified	Mariposa
512	0.9	Sierra Unified	Prather
515	0.8	El Dorado Union High	Placerville
515	0.8	San Lorenzo Valley Unified	Ben Lomond
515	0.8	Shasta Union High	Redding
518	0.7	Buckeye Union Elementary	Shingle Springs
518	0.7	Placer Union High	Auburn
520	0.6	Anderson Union High	Anderson
520	0.6	Los Gatos-Saratoga Jt Union High	Los Gatos
522	0.5	Sonora Union High	Sonora
523	0.4	Calaveras Unified	San Andreas
523	0.4	Loomis Union Elementary	Loomis
523	0.4	Nevada Joint Union High	Grass Valley
526	0.3	Pleasant Ridge Union Elementary	Grass Valley
527	0.2	Northern Humboldt Union High	McKinleyville
527	0.2	Paradise Unified	Paradise

Migrant Students

Rank	Percent	District Name	City
1	58.1	King City Joint Union High	King City
2	55.4	Wasco Union Elementary	Wasco
3	53.5	Golden Plains Unified	San Joaquin
4	51.5	Reef-Sunset Unified	Avenal
5	50.3	Firebaugh-Las Deltas Joint Unified	Firebaugh
6	49.5	Alisal Union Elementary	Salinas
7	49.2	Gonzales Unified	Gonzales
8	46.3	Arvin Union Elementary	Arvin
9	45.8	Pajaro Valley Unified School	Watsonville
10	45.2	Richland Union Elementary SD	Shafter
11	45.1	Mendota Unified	Mendota
12	44.9	Lamont Elementary	Lamont
13	44.7	Mcfarland Unified	Mcfarland
14	40.7	Parlier Unified	Parlier
15	39.9	Delano Union Elementary	Delano
16	39.6	Salinas City Elementary	Salinas
17	39.1	Greenfield Union Elementary	Greenfield
18	39.0	King City Union Elementary	King City
19	38.2	Riverdale Joint Unified	Riverdale
20	37.2	Corcoran Joint Unified	Corcoran
21	36.7	Fairfax Elementary	Bakersfield
22	36.5	Lindsay Unified	Lindsay
23	36.4	Delano Joint Union High	Delano
24	36.0	Coalinga-Huron Joint Unified	Coalinga
25	33.3	Earlimart Elementary	Earlimart
25	33.3	Woodlake Union Elementary	Woodlake
27	32.1	Farmersville Unified	Farmersville
28	31.8	Soledad Unified	Soledad
29	31.7	Rio Elementary	Oxnard
30	31.2	Salinas Union High	Salinas
31	30.5	San Benito High	Hollister
32	30.3	Holtville Unified	Holtville
33	29.2	Hollister SD	Hollister
34	29.0	Linden Unified	Linden
35	28.8	Fillmore Unified	Fillmore
36	27.8	North Monterey County Unified	Moss Landing
37	27.1	Kerman Unified	Kerman
38	26.8	Ocean View Elementary	Oxnard
39	26.3	Escalon Unified	Escalon
40	25.9	Brawley Union High	Brawley
41	25.6	Riverbank Unified	Riverbank
42	25.4	River Delta Joint Unified	Rio Vista
43	24.7	Brawley Elementary	Brawley
44	24.4	Santa Paula Elementary	Santa Paula
45	24.1	Hueneme Elementary	Port Hueneme
46	23.9	Coachella Valley Unified	Thermal
47	23.2	Santa Maria Joint Union High	Santa Maria
48	23.1	Calexico Unified	Calexico
49	22.8	Patterson Joint Unified	Patterson
50	22.7	Carpinteria Unified	Carpinteria
51	22.5	Santa Maria-Bonita Elementary	Santa Maria
52	22.4	Hughson Unified	Hughson
53	22.0	Greenfield Union Elementary	Bakersfield
54	21.2	Newman-Crows Landing Unified	Newman
55	20.9	Ukiah Unified	Ukiah
56	20.6	Healdsburg Unified	Healdsburg
56	20.6	Taft City Elementary	Taft
58	19.4	Central Union High	El Centro
58	19.4	Gustine Unified	Gustine
58	19.4	Live Oak Unified	Live Oak
61	19.0	Bakersfield City Elementary	Bakersfield
62	18.8	Lemoore Union Elementary	Lemoore
63	18.5	Oxnard Union High	Oxnard
64	18.4	Hanford Elementary	Hanford
64	18.4	Winters Joint Unified	Winters
66	18.3	Cloverdale Unified	Cloverdale
67	18.1	Santa Paula Union High	Santa Paula
68	18.0	Gridley Unified	Gridley
69	17.8	Dinuba Unified	Dinuba
70	17.5	Dos Palos Oro Loma Jt. Unified	Dos Palos
71	17.4	Kelseyville Unified	Kelseyville
72	16.1	Fort Bragg Unified	Fort Bragg
73	15.8	El Centro Elementary	El Centro
74	15.7	Exeter Union Elementary	Exeter
75	15.4	Tulare City Elementary	Tulare
76	15.3	Galt Joint Union High	Galt
77	15.2	Orland Joint Unified	Orland
77	15.2	Stockton City Unified	Stockton
79	14.9	Bonsall Union Elementary	Bonsall
80	14.7	Willows Unified	Willows
81	14.6	Yuba City Unified	Yuba City
82	14.5	Gilroy Unified	Gilroy
83	14.4	Livingston Union Elementary	Livingston
84	14.3	Madera Unified	Madera
85	13.9	Kings Canyon Joint Unified	Reedley
85	13.9	Lemoore Union High	Lemoore
87	13.8	Galt Joint Union Elementary	Galt
88	13.7	Dixon Unified	Dixon
88	13.7	Fresno Unified	Fresno
90	13.5	Valley Center-Pauma Unified	Valley Center
91	12.8	Cabrillo Unified	Half Moon Bay
92	12.6	Tulare Joint Union High	Tulare
93	12.3	Ripon Unified	Ripon
94	12.0	Waterford Unified	Waterford
95	11.9	Ravenswood City Elementary	East Palo Alto
95	11.9	Santa Rita Union Elementary	Salinas
97	11.6	Ceres Unified	Ceres
98	11.5	Winton Elementary	Winton
99	11.4	Porterville Unified	Porterville
100	11.2	Oakdale Joint Unified	Oakdale
101	11.0	Kern Union High	Bakersfield
102	10.9	Lakeport Unified	Lakeport
103	10.7	Rosemead Elementary	Rosemead
104	10.6	Cutler-Orosi Joint Unified	Orosi
104	10.6	Fowler Unified	Fowler
106	10.4	Franklin-Mckinley Elementary	San Jose
106	10.4	Morgan Hill Unified	Morgan Hill
108	10.1	Palo Verde Unified	Blythe
108	10.1	Santa Rosa Elementary	Santa Rosa
110	9.9	Corning Union Elementary	Corning
111	9.7	Hanford Joint Union High	Hanford
111	9.7	Napa Valley Unified	Napa
111	9.7	Woodland Joint Unified	Woodland
114	9.4	Delhi Unified	Delhi
115	9.3	Paso Robles Joint Unified	Paso Robles
116	9.1	Fallbrook Union Elementary	Fallbrook
117	9.0	Central Union Elementary	Lemoore
118	8.9	Selma Unified	Selma
119	8.8	Fallbrook Union High	Fallbrook
120	8.7	Lodi Unified	Lodi
120	8.7	Willits Unified	Willits
122	8.4	Bellevue Union Elementary	Santa Rosa
123	8.3	Mt. Pleasant Elementary	San Jose
124	8.1	Keyes Union Elementary	Keyes
125	7.9	Atwater Elementary	Atwater
125	7.9	Lompoc Unified	Lompoc
125	7.9	Windsor Unified	Windsor
128	7.8	Empire Union Elementary	Modesto
129	7.7	Modesto City Elementary	Modesto
130	7.3	Alum Rock Union Elementary	San Jose
130	7.3	Chowchilla Elementary	Chowchilla
132	7.2	Weaver Union Elementary	Merced
133	7.1	Marysville Joint Unified	Marysville
133	7.1	Oxnard Elementary	Oxnard
135	6.9	ABC Unified	Cerritos
136	6.8	Keppel Union Elementary	Pearblossom
136	6.8	Merced Union High	Atwater
136	6.8	Southern Kern Unified	Rosamond
139	6.6	Duarte Unified	Duarte
140	6.5	Sonoma Valley Unified	Sonoma
141	6.4	Fresno County Office of Education	Fresno
142	6.3	Redwood City Elementary	Redwood City
143	6.0	Mountain View Elementary	El Monte
144	5.9	Eastside Union Elementary	Lancaster
144	5.9	Konocti Unified	Lower Lake
146	5.7	Salida Union Elementary	Salida
147	5.6	Sequoia Union High	Redwood City
147	5.6	Visalia Unified	Visalia
149	5.5	Norwalk-La Mirada Unified	Norwalk
150	5.3	Santa Clara Unified	Santa Clara
151	5.2	Los Banos Unified	Los Banos
151	5.2	Tracy Joint Unified	Tracy
153	5.0	Lucia Mar Unified	Arroyo Grande
154	4.9	Los Nietos Elementary	Whittier
154	4.9	San Jose Unified	San Jose
156	4.8	Garvey Elementary	Rosemead
156	4.8	Live Oak Elementary	Santa Cruz
158	4.7	Manteca Unified	Manteca
158	4.7	Merced City Elementary	Merced
158	4.7	Moorpark Unified	Moorpark
158	4.7	Oceanside Unified	Oceanside
162	4.6	Ramona City Unified	Ramona

163	4.5	Imperial Unified	Imperial
163	4.5	Oroville Union High	Oroville
163	4.5	Santa Cruz City Elementary	Soquel
163	4.5	Turlock Joint Union High	Turlock
167	4.4	Turlock Joint Elementary	Turlock
168	4.2	Wilsona Elementary	Palmdale
169	4.1	Brentwood Union Elementary	Brentwood
169	4.1	Liberty Union High	Brentwood
169	4.1	Ventura Unified	Ventura
172	4.0	San Luis Coastal Unified	San Luis Obispo
173	3.9	Escondido Union Elementary	Escondido
173	3.9	Modesto City High	Modesto
173	3.9	Oak Grove Elementary	San Jose
173	3.9	Sanger Unified	Sanger
173	3.9	South Whittier Elementary	Whittier
173	3.9	Tehachapi Unified	Tehachapi
179	3.8	Long Beach Unified	Long Beach
179	3.8	San Ysidro Elementary	San Ysidro
181	3.7	Livermore Valley Joint Unified	Livermore
181	3.7	Monterey Peninsula Unified	Monterey
183	3.6	New Haven Unified	Union City
183	3.6	San Marcos Unified	San Marcos
185	3.5	El Monte Union High	El Monte
185	3.5	Hilmar Unified	Hilmar
185	3.5	Red Bluff Union Elementary	Red Bluff
188	3.4	Solana Beach Elementary	Solana Beach
189	3.3	Central Unified	Fresno
189	3.3	El Monte City Elementary	El Monte
189	3.3	Hayward Unified	Hayward
189	3.3	Perris Elementary	Perris
193	3.2	Lynwood Unified	Lynwood
194	3.1	Escondido Union High	Escondido
194	3.1	Middletown Unified	Middletown
194	3.1	Santa Rosa High	Santa Rosa
194	3.1	Stanislaus Union Elementary	Modesto
198	3.0	Oroville City Elementary	Oroville
199	2.9	Vista Unified	Vista
200	2.8	Desert Sands Unified	La Quinta
201	2.7	Baldwin Park Unified	Baldwin Park
201	2.7	Old Adobe Union Elementary	Petaluma
201	2.7	Palmdale Elementary	Palmdale
204	2.6	Carlsbad Unified	Carlsbad
204	2.6	Chico Unified	Chico
204	2.6	Hacienda La Puente Unified	City of Industry
207	2.5	Burton Elementary	Porterville
207	2.5	Encinitas Union Elementary	Encinitas
207	2.5	Oakley Union Elementary	Oakley
207	2.5	West Sonoma County Union High	Sebastopol
211	2.4	Cascade Union Elementary	Anderson
211	2.4	Vacaville Unified	Vacaville
213	2.3	Pleasant Valley School	Camarillo
213	2.3	Sacramento City Unified	Sacramento
213	2.3	South San Francisco Unified	S San Francisco
216	2.2	Alhambra City High	Alhambra
216	2.2	Clovis Unified	Clovis
216	2.2	Petaluma City Elementary	Petaluma
216	2.2	San Joaquin Co Off of Education	Stockton
220	2.1	Lancaster Elementary	Lancaster
220	2.1	San Lorenzo Unified	San Lorenzo
222	1.9	Newark Unified	Newark
223	1.8	Evergreen Elementary	San Jose
224	1.7	Alhambra City Elementary	Alhambra
224	1.7	Goleta Union Elementary	Goleta
224	1.7	Mother Lode Union Elementary	Placerville
224	1.7	Petaluma Joint Union High	Petaluma
224	1.7	Santa Ana Unified	Santa Ana
229	1.6	East Side Union High	San Jose
229	1.6	El Rancho Unified	Pico Rivera
229	1.6	San Dieguito Union High	Encinitas
232	1.5	Antelope Valley Union High	Lancaster
232	1.5	Cotati-Rohnert Park Unified	Rohnert Park
232	1.5	Davis Joint Unified	Davis
232	1.5	Del Norte County Unified	Crescent City
232	1.5	Little Lake City Elementary	Santa Fe Spgs
232	1.5	Mojave Unified	Mojave
238	1.4	Fairfield-Suisun Unified	Fairfield
238	1.4	North Sacramento Elementary	Sacramento
238	1.4	Placentia-Yorba Linda Unified	Placentia
241	1.3	Pomona Unified	Pomona
241	1.3	Red Bluff Joint Union High	Red Bluff
241	1.3	Santa Cruz City High	Soquel
244	1.2	Oakland Unified	Oakland
244	1.2	Paramount Unified	Paramount
244	1.2	Perris Union High	Perris
247	1.1	Piner-Olivet Union Elementary	Santa Rosa
248	1.0	Santa Barbara High	Santa Barbara
248	1.0	Sunnyvale Elementary	Sunnyvale
248	1.0	Whittier Union High	Whittier
251	0.9	Anderson Union High	Anderson
251	0.9	Azusa Unified	Azusa
251	0.9	Capistrano Unified	San Juan Capis
251	0.9	National Elementary	National City
251	0.9	Newport-Mesa Unified	Costa Mesa
251	0.9	Palm Springs Unified	Palm Springs
251	0.9	Panama Buena Vista Union Elem	Bakersfield
258	0.8	Anaheim Elementary	Anaheim
258	0.8	Anaheim Union High	Anaheim
258	0.8	Covina-Valley Unified	Covina
258	0.8	Fremont Unified	Fremont
258	0.8	Jefferson Elementary	Tracy
258	0.8	Los Angeles Co Office of Education	Downey
264	0.7	Kingsburg Elementary Charter	Kingsburg
264	0.7	San Francisco Unified	San Francisco
264	0.7	Santa Barbara Elementary	Santa Barbara
267	0.6	Atascadero Unified	Atascadero
267	0.6	Auburn Union Elementary	Auburn
267	0.6	Fullerton Elementary	Fullerton
267	0.6	Mark West Union Elementary	Santa Rosa
267	0.6	Pasadena Unified	Pasadena
272	0.5	Acton-Agua Dulce Unified	Acton
272	0.5	Bassett Unified	La Puente
272	0.5	Enterprise Elementary	Redding
272	0.5	Lincoln Unified	Stockton
272	0.5	Los Angeles Unified	Los Angeles
272	0.5	Orange Unified	Orange
278	0.4	Del Paso Heights Elementary	Sacramento
278	0.4	Magnolia Elementary	Anaheim
278	0.4	Monrovia Unified	Monrovia
278	0.4	Rincon Valley Union Elementary	Santa Rosa
278	0.4	Rosedale Union Elementary	Bakersfield
278	0.4	Shasta Union High	Redding
278	0.4	Sweetwater Union High	Chula Vista
285	0.3	Beardsley Elementary	Bakersfield
285	0.3	Corona-Norco Unified	Norco
285	0.3	Fremont Union High	Sunnyvale
285	0.3	Gateway Unified	Redding
285	0.3	Grant Joint Union High	Sacramento
285	0.3	Mountain Empire Unified	Pine Valley
285	0.3	Redding Elementary	Redding
285	0.3	San Gabriel Unified	San Gabriel
285	0.3	West Covina Unified	West Covina
285	0.3	Westside Union Elementary	Lancaster
285	0.3	Wheatland Elementary	Wheatland
296	0.2	Centralia Elementary	Buena Park
296	0.2	Charter Oak Unified	Covina
296	0.2	El Dorado Union High	Placerville
296	0.2	Elk Grove Unified	Elk Grove
296	0.2	Kern County Office of Education	Bakersfield
296	0.2	Laguna Beach Unified	Laguna Beach
296	0.2	Orcutt Union Elementary	Orcutt
296	0.2	Riverside Co Office of Education	Riverside
296	0.2	Romoland Elementary	Homeland
296	0.2	Rowland Unified	Rowland Heights
296	0.2	Sierra Unified	Prather
296	0.2	Sylvan Union Elementary	Modesto
296	0.2	Templeton Unified	Templeton
296	0.2	Val Verde Unified	Perris
296	0.2	Washington Unified	West Sacramento
311	0.1	Buena Park Elementary	Buena Park
311	0.1	Del Mar Union Elementary	Del Mar
311	0.1	East Whittier City Elementary	Whittier
311	0.1	Folsom-Cordova Unified	Folsom
311	0.1	Lemon Grove Elementary	Lemon Grove
311	0.1	Natomas Unified	Sacramento
311	0.1	Novato Unified	Novato
311	0.1	Rio Linda Union Elementary	Rio Linda
311	0.1	San Diego Unified	San Diego
311	0.1	Santa Clara Co Off of Education	San Jose
311	0.1	Savanna Elementary	Anaheim
311	0.1	South Bay Union Elementary	Imperial Beach
311	0.1	Temple City Unified	Temple City
311	0.1	Whittier City Elementary	Whittier
325	0.0	Alameda City Unified	Alameda
325	0.0	Alvord Unified	Riverside
325	0.0	Antioch Unified	Antioch
325	0.0	Arcadia Unified	Arcadia
325	0.0	Black Oak Mine Unified	Georgetown
325	0.0	Bonita Unified	San Dimas
325	0.0	Cajon Valley Union Elementary	El Cajon
325	0.0	Chula Vista Elementary	Chula Vista
325	0.0	Compton Unified	Compton
325	0.0	Downey Unified	Downey
325	0.0	Fruitvale Elementary	Bakersfield
325	0.0	Fullerton Joint Union High	Fullerton
325	0.0	Garden Grove Unified	Garden Grove
325	0.0	Glendale Unified	Glendale
325	0.0	Glendora Unified	Glendora
325	0.0	Grossmont Union High	La Mesa
325	0.0	Hemet Unified	Hemet
325	0.0	Irvine Unified	Irvine
325	0.0	La Mesa-Spring Valley	La Mesa
325	0.0	Montebello Unified	Montebello
325	0.0	Mountain View-Los Altos Union High	Mountain View
325	0.0	Mountain View-Whisman Elementary	Mountain View
325	0.0	Mt. Diablo Unified	Concord
325	0.0	Ontario-Montclair Elementary	Ontario
325	0.0	Orange County Office of Education	Costa Mesa
325	0.0	Placer Union High	Auburn
325	0.0	Pleasanton Unified	Pleasanton
325	0.0	Poway Unified	Poway
325	0.0	Rialto Unified	Rialto
325	0.0	Roseville Joint Union High	Roseville
325	0.0	Saddleback Valley Unified	Mission Viejo
325	0.0	San Juan Unified	Carmichael
325	0.0	San Leandro Unified	San Leandro
325	0.0	Tamalpais Union High	Larkspur
325	0.0	Tustin Unified	Tustin
325	0.0	Vallejo City Unified	Vallejo
325	0.0	Westminster Elementary	Westminster
362	0.0	Acalanes Union High	Lafayette
362	0.0	Adelanto Elementary	Adelanto
362	0.0	Albany City Unified	Albany
362	0.0	Alpine Union Elementary	Alpine
362	0.0	Alta Loma Elementary	Alta Loma
362	0.0	Amador County Unified	Jackson
362	0.0	Apple Valley Unified	Apple Valley
362	0.0	Banning Unified	Banning
362	0.0	Barstow Unified	Barstow
362	0.0	Bear Valley Unified	Big Bear Lake
362	0.0	Beaumont Unified	Beaumont
362	0.0	Bellflower Unified	Bellflower
362	0.0	Belmont-Redwood Shores Elementary	Belmont
362	0.0	Benicia Unified	Benicia
362	0.0	Berkeley Unified	Berkeley
362	0.0	Berryessa Union Elementary	San Jose
362	0.0	Beverly Hills Unified	Beverly Hills
362	0.0	Brea-Olinda Unified	Brea
362	0.0	Buckeye Union Elementary	Shingle Springs
362	0.0	Burbank Unified	Burbank
362	0.0	Burlingame Elementary	Burlingame
362	0.0	Calaveras Unified	San Andreas
362	0.0	Cambrian Elementary	San Jose
362	0.0	Campbell Union Elementary	Campbell
362	0.0	Campbell Union High	San Jose
362	0.0	Carmel Unified	Carmel
362	0.0	Castaic Union Elementary	Valencia
362	0.0	Castro Valley Unified	Castro Valley
362	0.0	Center Joint Unified	Antelope
362	0.0	Centinela Valley Union High	Lawndale
362	0.0	Central Elementary	Rcho Cucamong
362	0.0	Chaffey Joint Union High	Ontario
362	0.0	Chino Valley Unified	Chino
362	0.0	Claremont Unified	Claremont
362	0.0	Colton Joint Unified	Colton
362	0.0	Conejo Valley Unified	Thousand Oaks
362	0.0	Coronado Unified	Coronado
362	0.0	Cucamonga Elementary	Rcho Cucamong
362	0.0	Culver City Unified	Culver City
362	0.0	Cupertino Union School	Cupertino
362	0.0	Cypress Elementary	Cypress
362	0.0	Dixie Elementary	San Rafael
362	0.0	Dry Creek Joint Elementary	Roseville
362	0.0	Dublin Unified	Dublin
362	0.0	El Segundo Unified	El Segundo
362	0.0	Etiwanda Elementary	Etiwanda
362	0.0	Eureka City Unified	Eureka
362	0.0	Eureka Union Elementary	Granite Bay
362	0.0	Fontana Unified	Fontana
362	0.0	Fountain Valley Elementary	Fountain Valley
362	0.0	Gorman Elementary	Gorman
362	0.0	Grass Valley Elementary	Grass Valley
362	0.0	Hawthorne Elementary	Hawthorne
362	0.0	Hesperia Unified	Hesperia
362	0.0	Huntington Beach City Elementary	Huntington Bch
362	0.0	Huntington Beach Union High	Huntington Bch
362	0.0	Inglewood Unified	Inglewood
362	0.0	Jamul-Dulzura Union Elementary	Jamul
362	0.0	Jefferson Elementary	Daly City
362	0.0	Jefferson Union High	Daly City
362	0.0	John Swett Unified	Crockett
362	0.0	Julian Union Elementary	Julian
362	0.0	Julian Union High	Julian
362	0.0	Jurupa Unified	Riverside
362	0.0	La Canada Unified	La Canada
362	0.0	La Habra City Elementary	La Habra
362	0.0	Lafayette Elementary	Lafayette
362	0.0	Lake Elsinore Unified	Lake Elsinore
362	0.0	Lake Tahoe Unified	S Lake Tahoe
362	0.0	Lakeside Union Elementary	Lakeside
362	0.0	Las Virgenes Unified	Calabasas
362	0.0	Lawndale Elementary	Lawndale
362	0.0	Lennox Elementary	Lennox
362	0.0	Loomis Union Elementary	Loomis
362	0.0	Los Alamitos Unified	Los Alamitos
362	0.0	Los Altos Elementary	Los Altos
362	0.0	Los Gatos Union Elementary	Los Gatos
362	0.0	Los Gatos-Saratoga Jt Union High	Los Gatos

362	0.0	Lowell Joint	Whittier
362	0.0	Manhattan Beach Unified	Manhattan Beach
362	0.0	Mariposa County Unified	Mariposa
362	0.0	Martinez Unified	Martinez
362	0.0	Menifee Union Elementary	Menifee
362	0.0	Menlo Park City Elementary	Atherton
362	0.0	Mill Valley Elementary	Mill Valley
362	0.0	Millbrae Elementary	Millbrae
362	0.0	Milpitas Unified	Milpitas
362	0.0	Moraga Elementary	Moraga
362	0.0	Moreland Elementary	San Jose
362	0.0	Moreno Valley Unified	Moreno Valley
362	0.0	Morongo Unified	Twentynine Plms
362	0.0	Mountain View Elementary	Ontario
362	0.0	Muroc Joint Unified	North Edwards
362	0.0	Murrieta Valley Unified	Murrieta
362	0.0	Nevada Joint Union High	Grass Valley
362	0.0	Newhall Elementary	Valencia
362	0.0	Norris Elementary	Bakersfield
362	0.0	Northern Humboldt Union High	McKinleyville
362	0.0	Nuview Union Elementary	Nuevo
362	0.0	Oak Park Unified	Oak Park
362	0.0	Ocean View Elementary	Huntington Bch
362	0.0	Ojai Unified	Ojai
362	0.0	Orinda Union Elementary	Orinda
362	0.0	Oro Grande Elementary	Oro Grande
362	0.0	Pacific Grove Unified	Pacific Grove
362	0.0	Pacifica SD	Pacifica
362	0.0	Palo Alto Unified	Palo Alto
362	0.0	Palos Verdes Peninsula Unified	Palos Verdes Est
362	0.0	Paradise Unified	Paradise
362	0.0	Piedmont City Unified	Piedmont
362	0.0	Pittsburg Unified	Pittsburg
362	0.0	Pleasant Ridge Union Elementary	Grass Valley
362	0.0	Plumas Unified	Quincy
362	0.0	Redlands Unified	Redlands
362	0.0	Redondo Beach Unified	Redondo Beach
362	0.0	Rescue Union Elementary	Rescue
362	0.0	Rim of the World Unified	Lake Arrowhead
362	0.0	Riverside Unified	Riverside
362	0.0	Robla Elementary	Sacramento
362	0.0	Rocklin Unified	Rocklin
362	0.0	Roseville City Elementary	Roseville
362	0.0	Ross Valley Elementary	San Anselmo
362	0.0	San Bernardino City Unified	San Bernardino
362	0.0	San Bernardino Co Off of Education	San Bernardino
362	0.0	San Bruno Park Elementary	San Bruno
362	0.0	San Carlos Elementary	San Carlos
362	0.0	San Diego Co Office of Education	San Diego
362	0.0	San Jacinto Unified	San Jacinto
362	0.0	San Lorenzo Valley Unified	Ben Lomond
362	0.0	San Marino Unified	San Marino
362	0.0	San Mateo Union High	San Mateo
362	0.0	San Mateo-Foster City Elementary	San Mateo
362	0.0	San Rafael City Elementary	San Rafael
362	0.0	San Rafael City High	San Rafael
362	0.0	San Ramon Valley Unified	Danville
362	0.0	Santa Monica-Malibu Unified	Santa Monica
362	0.0	Santee Elementary	Santee
362	0.0	Saratoga Union Elementary	Saratoga
362	0.0	Saugus Union Elementary	Santa Clarita
362	0.0	Scotts Valley Unified	Scotts Valley
362	0.0	Sierra Sands Unified	Ridgecrest
362	0.0	Silver Valley Unified	Yermo
362	0.0	Simi Valley Unified	Simi Valley
362	0.0	Snowline Joint Unified	Phelan
362	0.0	Sonora Union High	Sonora
362	0.0	Soquel Union Elementary	Capitola
362	0.0	South Pasadena Unified	South Pasadena
362	0.0	Standard Elementary	Bakersfield
362	0.0	Sulphur Springs Union Elementary	Canyon Country
362	0.0	Tahoe-Truckee Joint Unified	Truckee
362	0.0	Temecula Valley Unified	Temecula
362	0.0	Torrance Unified	Torrance
362	0.0	Travis Unified	Travis Afb
362	0.0	Tulare County Office of Education	Visalia
362	0.0	Twin Ridges Elementary	North San Juan
362	0.0	Union Elementary	San Jose
362	0.0	Upland Unified	Upland
362	0.0	Victor Elementary	Victorville
362	0.0	Victor Valley Union High	Victorville
362	0.0	Walnut Creek Elementary	Walnut Creek
362	0.0	Walnut Valley Unified	Walnut
362	0.0	West Contra Costa Unified	Richmond
362	0.0	Western Placer Unified	Lincoln
362	0.0	Westwood Unified	Westwood
362	0.0	William S. Hart Union High	Santa Clarita
362	0.0	Wiseburn Elementary	Hawthorne
362	0.0	Yucaipa-Calimesa Jt. Unified	Yucaipa

Students Eligible for Free Lunch

Rank	Percent	District Name	City
1	99.6	Delano Union Elementary	Delano
2	99.5	Los Nietos Elementary	Whittier
2	99.5	National Elementary	National City
4	99.0	Lamont Elementary	Lamont
5	98.5	Reef-Sunset Unified	Avenal
6	90.7	Del Paso Heights Elementary	Sacramento
7	88.6	Mendota Unified	Mendota
8	87.8	Earlimart Elementary	Earlimart
9	87.4	Compton Unified	Compton
10	86.6	Golden Plains Unified	San Joaquin
11	82.8	San Diego Co Office of Education	San Diego
12	82.5	Soledad Unified	Soledad
13	81.5	Cutler-Orosi Joint Unified	Orosi
14	80.6	Wasco Union Elementary	Wasco
15	78.8	Woodlake Union Elementary	Woodlake
16	78.5	Mountain View Elementary	El Monte
17	78.1	El Monte City Elementary	El Monte
18	77.9	Coachella Valley Unified	Thermal
19	77.7	Mcfarland Unified	Mcfarland
20	77.6	Fairfax Elementary	Bakersfield
21	77.1	Richland Union Elementary SD	Shafter
22	76.7	Perris Elementary	Perris
23	76.4	Bakersfield City Elementary	Bakersfield
24	76.1	Winton Elementary	Winton
25	75.4	San Ysidro Elementary	San Ysidro
26	74.7	Fresno Unified	Fresno
27	74.3	Porterville Unified	Porterville
28	73.2	Lennox Elementary	Lennox
29	72.4	North Sacramento Elementary	Sacramento
30	72.3	Wilsona Elementary	Palmdale
31	71.8	Paramount Unified	Paramount
32	71.7	Livingston Union Elementary	Livingston
33	71.5	Firebaugh-Las Deltas Joint Unified	Firebaugh
34	71.3	Konocti Unified	Lower Lake
35	70.8	Beardsley Elementary	Bakersfield
35	70.8	Garvey Elementary	Rosemead
37	69.6	Bellevue Union Elementary	Santa Rosa
38	68.5	Hawthorne Elementary	Hawthorne
38	68.5	Selma Unified	Selma
40	68.3	Alisal Union Elementary	Salinas
41	68.2	Weaver Union Elementary	Merced
42	68.1	Montebello Unified	Montebello
43	67.9	Ravenswood City Elementary	East Palo Alto
44	67.5	Lindsay Unified	Lindsay
45	67.0	Los Angeles Unified	Los Angeles
46	66.9	Riverdale Joint Unified	Riverdale
47	66.8	San Bernardino City Unified	San Bernardino
48	66.1	Ontario-Montclair Elementary	Ontario
49	65.8	Bassett Unified	La Puente
50	64.9	Santa Maria-Bonita Elementary	Santa Maria
51	64.5	Corcoran Joint Unified	Corcoran
51	64.5	Madera Unified	Madera
53	64.3	Brawley Elementary	Brawley
54	63.9	Greenfield Union Elementary	Greenfield
54	63.9	Parlier Unified	Parlier
56	63.7	Farmersville Unified	Farmersville
57	63.1	Holtville Unified	Holtville
58	62.9	Lawndale Elementary	Lawndale
58	62.9	Marysville Joint Unified	Marysville
58	62.9	Modesto City Elementary	Modesto
61	62.7	Dos Palos Oro Loma Jt. Unified	Dos Palos
62	62.6	Keppel Union Elementary	Pearblossom
62	62.6	Kings Canyon Joint Unified	Reedley
64	62.5	Sanger Unified	Sanger
65	62.2	El Centro Elementary	El Centro
66	62.1	Alum Rock Union Elementary	San Jose
66	62.1	Corning Union Elementary	Corning
68	61.2	Sacramento City Unified	Sacramento
69	61.0	Merced City Elementary	Merced
69	61.0	Rosemead Elementary	Rosemead
71	60.9	Tulare City Elementary	Tulare
72	60.8	Calexico Unified	Calexico
73	60.7	Banning Unified	Banning
73	60.7	Robla Elementary	Sacramento
75	60.5	San Jacinto Unified	San Jacinto
76	60.3	Greenfield Union Elementary	Bakersfield
76	60.3	Santa Ana Unified	Santa Ana
78	59.9	King City Union Elementary	King City
78	59.9	Stockton City Unified	Stockton
80	59.7	Romoland Elementary	Homeland
81	59.6	Hanford Elementary	Hanford
81	59.6	Live Oak Unified	Live Oak
83	59.2	Arvin Union Elementary	Arvin
84	59.1	Anaheim Elementary	Anaheim
85	58.9	Magnolia Elementary	Anaheim
86	58.8	Delano Joint Union High	Delano
86	58.8	Franklin-Mckinley Elementary	San Jose
88	58.7	Dinuba Unified	Dinuba
89	58.1	Oxnard Elementary	Oxnard
90	58.0	Oroville City Elementary	Oroville
91	57.6	Merced Union High	Atwater
92	57.4	Taft City Elementary	Taft
93	57.1	Baldwin Park Unified	Baldwin Park
94	56.0	Coalinga-Huron Joint Unified	Coalinga
95	55.6	Atwater Elementary	Atwater
96	55.5	Oakland Unified	Oakland
97	55.0	Hueneme Elementary	Port Hueneme
97	55.0	Kerman Unified	Kerman
99	54.6	Cascade Union Elementary	Anderson
99	54.6	Pasadena Unified	Pasadena
101	54.5	El Monte Union High	El Monte
102	54.4	La Habra City Elementary	La Habra
103	54.1	Long Beach Unified	Long Beach
104	54.0	Adelanto Elementary	Adelanto
105	53.9	South Whittier Elementary	Whittier
106	53.8	Chowchilla Elementary	Chowchilla
106	53.8	Delhi Unified	Delhi
106	53.8	King City Joint Union High	King City
109	53.5	Pomona Unified	Pomona
110	53.0	Gonzales Unified	Gonzales
111	52.6	Exeter Union Elementary	Exeter
112	52.5	Centinela Valley Union High	Lawndale
113	52.3	Alhambra City High	Alhambra
114	52.0	Hemet Unified	Hemet
114	52.0	Lancaster Elementary	Lancaster
116	51.8	Cucamonga Elementary	Rcho Cucamong
116	51.8	Gridley Unified	Gridley
118	51.6	Salinas City Elementary	Salinas
119	51.5	Alhambra City Elementary	Alhambra
120	51.4	Grant Joint Union High	Sacramento
121	50.9	Westminster Elementary	Westminster
122	50.8	El Rancho Unified	Pico Rivera
123	50.7	Ocean View Elementary	Oxnard
124	50.6	Santa Paula Elementary	Santa Paula
125	50.5	San Bernardino Co Off of Education	San Bernardino
126	50.2	Orland Joint Unified	Orland
127	50.1	Fort Bragg Unified	Fort Bragg
127	50.1	Palmdale Elementary	Palmdale
129	49.8	Azusa Unified	Azusa
130	49.6	Pajaro Valley Unified School	Watsonville
131	49.1	Rio Linda Union Elementary	Rio Linda
132	49.0	Fontana Unified	Fontana
132	49.0	Standard Elementary	Bakersfield
134	48.9	Rialto Unified	Rialto
135	48.8	Duarte Unified	Duarte
136	48.4	Washington Unified	West Sacramento
137	48.3	Del Norte County Unified	Crescent City
138	48.2	Barstow Unified	Barstow
139	48.1	Val Verde Unified	Perris
140	47.9	Red Bluff Union Elementary	Red Bluff
141	47.7	Palm Springs Unified	Palm Springs
142	47.5	Mt. Pleasant Elementary	San Jose
143	47.2	Jurupa Unified	Riverside
143	47.2	Kelseyville Unified	Kelseyville
145	46.7	Ceres Unified	Ceres
145	46.7	Eastside Union Elementary	Lancaster
145	46.7	Lemoore Union Elementary	Lemoore
148	46.6	Garden Grove Unified	Garden Grove
149	46.5	San Francisco Unified	San Francisco
149	46.5	Turlock Joint Elementary	Turlock
151	46.3	Buena Park Elementary	Buena Park
152	46.0	Escondido Union Elementary	Escondido
152	46.0	Moreno Valley Unified	Moreno Valley
154	45.9	Gustine Unified	Gustine
155	45.6	Lynwood Unified	Lynwood
156	45.5	Patterson Joint Unified	Patterson
157	45.4	Fillmore Unified	Fillmore
158	45.3	Mojave Unified	Mojave
159	45.2	Willows Unified	Willows
160	44.8	Riverbank Unified	Riverbank
161	44.6	Inglewood Unified	Inglewood
161	44.6	Victor Elementary	Victorville
163	44.5	Willits Unified	Willits
164	44.4	Ukiah Unified	Ukiah
165	44.3	Mountain Empire Unified	Pine Valley
165	44.3	Palo Verde Unified	Blythe
167	44.1	Fowler Unified	Fowler
167	44.1	Lemon Grove Elementary	Lemon Grove
167	44.1	San Joaquin Co Off of Education	Stockton
170	43.8	Visalia Unified	Visalia
171	43.5	Pittsburg Unified	Pittsburg
172	43.4	Rio Elementary	Oxnard
173	43.0	Little Lake City Elementary	Santa Fe Spgs
173	43.0	Newman-Crows Landing Unified	Newman
175	42.9	Colton Joint Unified	Colton
176	42.7	Santa Barbara Elementary	Santa Barbara
177	42.5	Gateway Unified	Redding
177	42.5	San Rafael City Elementary	San Rafael
179	42.4	Empire Union Elementary	Modesto
180	42.3	Hesperia Unified	Hesperia
180	42.3	Santa Paula Union High	Santa Paula
182	42.0	Monrovia Unified	Monrovia
183	41.9	Central Union High	El Centro
183	41.9	Lodi Unified	Lodi
183	41.9	Los Banos Unified	Los Banos

183	41.9	Redwood City Elementary	Redwood City
187	41.8	Hacienda La Puente Unified	City of Industry
187	41.8	Los Angeles Co Office of Education	Downey
187	41.8	Norwalk-La Mirada Unified	Norwalk
190	41.3	Enterprise Elementary	Redding
191	41.2	Beaumont Unified	Beaumont
191	41.2	San Diego Unified	San Diego
193	41.1	Burton Elementary	Porterville
193	41.1	Keyes Union Elementary	Keyes
195	40.9	Rowland Unified	Rowland Heights
195	40.9	Savanna Elementary	Anaheim
195	40.9	Whittier City Elementary	Whittier
198	40.7	Yuba City Unified	Yuba City
199	40.6	Eureka City Unified	Eureka
199	40.6	Southern Kern Unified	Rosamond
199	40.6	Stanislaus Union Elementary	Modesto
202	40.2	Victor Valley Union High	Victorville
203	40.0	Hayward Unified	Hayward
204	39.9	North Monterey County Unified	Moss Landing
204	39.9	Oroville Union High	Oroville
206	39.7	Nuview Union Elementary	Nuevo
207	39.4	Berkeley Unified	Berkeley
208	39.2	Desert Sands Unified	La Quinta
208	39.2	Oceanside Unified	Oceanside
210	39.1	Bellflower Unified	Bellflower
210	39.1	West Contra Costa Unified	Richmond
212	38.7	South Bay Union Elementary	Imperial Beach
213	38.6	San Gabriel Unified	San Gabriel
214	38.5	Brawley Union High	Brawley
215	38.1	Salinas Union High	Salinas
216	38.0	San Jose Unified	San Jose
216	38.0	Santa Rosa Elementary	Santa Rosa
216	38.0	Tulare Joint Union High	Tulare
219	37.5	Cajon Valley Union Elementary	El Cajon
220	36.7	Hughson Unified	Hughson
221	36.5	Fresno County Office of Education	Fresno
221	36.5	Kern Union High	Bakersfield
221	36.5	Redding Elementary	Redding
221	36.5	Waterford Unified	Waterford
225	36.0	Central Unified	Fresno
226	35.8	Covina-Valley Unified	Covina
227	35.4	Galt Joint Union Elementary	Galt
227	35.4	Perris Union High	Perris
227	35.4	Sweetwater Union High	Chula Vista
230	35.2	Alvord Unified	Riverside
231	35.1	Apple Valley Unified	Apple Valley
231	35.1	Monterey Peninsula Unified	Monterey
233	35.0	Lakeport Unified	Lakeport
234	34.9	Glendale Unified	Glendale
235	34.8	Lompoc Unified	Lompoc
236	34.7	Carpinteria Unified	Carpinteria
237	34.3	Linden Unified	Linden
238	34.2	Gilroy Unified	Gilroy
239	34.1	Centralia Elementary	Buena Park
239	34.1	Lake Tahoe Unified	S Lake Tahoe
241	33.7	Riverside Unified	Riverside
242	33.5	Tulare County Office of Education	Visalia
243	32.9	Downey Unified	Downey
244	32.7	Sierra Sands Unified	Ridgecrest
245	32.5	Live Oak Elementary	Santa Cruz
245	32.5	Woodland Joint Unified	Woodland
247	32.4	Newport-Mesa Unified	Costa Mesa
248	32.2	Fallbrook Union Elementary	Fallbrook
248	32.2	Jefferson Elementary	Daly City
250	31.8	Anaheim Union High	Anaheim
251	31.6	Vallejo City Unified	Vallejo
252	31.3	Grass Valley Elementary	Grass Valley
253	31.2	Escalon Unified	Escalon
254	31.1	Panama Buena Vista Union Elem	Bakersfield
255	31.0	River Delta Joint Unified	Rio Vista
256	30.7	Winters Joint Unified	Winters
257	30.6	Oak Grove Elementary	San Jose
258	30.5	Mountain View-Whisman Elementary	Mountain View
259	30.2	Hollister SD	Hollister
259	30.2	Santa Cruz City Elementary	Soquel
261	30.0	Hilmar Unified	Hilmar
261	30.0	Lake Elsinore Unified	Lake Elsinore
263	29.9	Campbell Union Elementary	Campbell
264	29.8	Cloverdale Unified	Cloverdale
264	29.8	Dixon Unified	Dixon
264	29.8	Fallbrook Union High	Fallbrook
264	29.8	Vista Unified	Vista
268	29.7	La Mesa-Spring Valley	La Mesa
269	29.5	Galt Joint Union High	Galt
269	29.5	Santa Clara Unified	Santa Clara
271	29.4	San Marcos Unified	San Marcos
272	29.3	Fullerton Elementary	Fullerton
272	29.3	Oakdale Joint Unified	Oakdale
272	29.3	Snowline Joint Unified	Phelan
275	29.1	Bear Valley Unified	Big Bear Lake
275	29.1	Chula Vista Elementary	Chula Vista
277	28.9	Fairfield-Suisun Unified	Fairfield
278	28.8	Redlands Unified	Redlands
278	28.8	Salida Union Elementary	Salida
280	28.6	Sunnyvale Elementary	Sunnyvale
281	28.5	Antioch Unified	Antioch
281	28.5	Mariposa County Unified	Mariposa
283	28.4	Chico Unified	Chico
283	28.4	Silver Valley Unified	Yermo
285	28.3	Elk Grove Unified	Elk Grove
286	28.1	Central Union Elementary	Lemoore
287	28.0	ABC Unified	Cerritos
287	28.0	Antelope Valley Union High	Lancaster
287	28.0	Ramona City Unified	Ramona
290	27.9	Paradise Unified	Paradise
291	27.8	Orange Unified	Orange
292	27.7	Westwood Unified	Westwood
293	27.4	John Swett Unified	Crockett
293	27.4	Lucia Mar Unified	Arroyo Grande
295	27.3	San Lorenzo Unified	San Lorenzo
295	27.3	West Covina Unified	West Covina
297	26.9	Modesto City High	Modesto
298	26.8	Auburn Union Elementary	Auburn
299	26.7	Santa Rita Union Elementary	Salinas
300	26.6	Red Bluff Joint Union High	Red Bluff
301	26.5	Corona-Norco Unified	Norco
301	26.5	Imperial Unified	Imperial
303	26.4	Kern County Office of Education	Bakersfield
304	26.3	Oxnard Union High	Oxnard
304	26.3	Paso Robles Joint Unified	Paso Robles
306	26.2	Folsom-Cordova Unified	Folsom
306	26.2	San Leandro Unified	San Leandro
308	26.1	Alameda City Unified	Alameda
308	26.1	Upland Unified	Upland
310	26.0	Healdsburg Unified	Healdsburg
310	26.0	Lincoln Unified	Stockton
312	25.9	Napa Valley Unified	Napa
313	25.8	Kingsburg Elementary Charter	Kingsburg
313	25.8	Sonoma Valley Unified	Sonoma
315	25.7	Sulphur Springs Union Elementary	Canyon Country
316	25.6	Central Elementary	Rcho Cucamong
317	25.5	Tustin Unified	Tustin
318	25.4	Tehachapi Unified	Tehachapi
319	25.2	East Whittier City Elementary	Whittier
319	25.2	Mother Lode Union Elementary	Placerville
319	25.2	Plumas Unified	Quincy
319	25.2	Valley Center-Pauma Unified	Valley Center
323	25.0	Wiseburn Elementary	Hawthorne
324	24.9	Goleta Union Elementary	Goleta
324	24.9	Oro Grande Elementary	Oro Grande
324	24.9	Sylvan Union Elementary	Modesto
327	24.7	Ocean View Elementary	Huntington Bch
328	24.5	Ventura Unified	Ventura
329	24.4	Morongo Unified	Twentynine Plms
329	24.4	Whittier Union High	Whittier
329	24.4	Yucaipa-Calimesa Jt. Unified	Yucaipa
332	24.3	Manteca Unified	Manteca
333	24.2	Temple City Unified	Temple City
334	24.1	Hanford Joint Union High	Hanford
335	23.9	Riverside Co Office of Education	Riverside
336	23.5	Evergreen Elementary	San Jose
337	23.4	Bonsall Union Elementary	Bonsall
338	23.3	Mountain View Elementary	Ontario
338	23.3	Santa Maria Joint Union High	Santa Maria
340	22.7	Moorpark Unified	Moorpark
340	22.7	South San Francisco Unified	S San Francisco
342	22.6	Natomas Unified	Sacramento
342	22.6	Rim of the World Unified	Lake Arrowhead
342	22.6	San Juan Unified	Carmichael
345	22.5	New Haven Unified	Union City
346	22.4	Burbank Unified	Burbank
346	22.4	San Bruno Park Elementary	San Bruno
346	22.4	Sierra Unified	Prather
349	22.1	East Side Union High	San Jose
350	22.0	San Mateo-Foster City Elementary	San Mateo
351	21.8	Anderson Union High	Anderson
352	21.6	Culver City Unified	Culver City
352	21.6	Turlock Joint Union High	Turlock
354	21.5	Calaveras Unified	San Andreas
355	21.3	Mt. Diablo Unified	Concord
356	21.2	Oakley Union Elementary	Oakley
356	21.2	Windsor Unified	Windsor
358	21.1	Lakeside Union Elementary	Lakeside
359	20.7	Vacaville Unified	Vacaville
360	20.2	Milpitas Unified	Milpitas
360	20.2	Petaluma City Elementary	Petaluma
362	20.1	Clovis Unified	Clovis
362	20.1	Newhall Elementary	Valencia
364	20.0	Lemoore Union High	Lemoore
364	20.0	Ripon Unified	Ripon
366	19.9	Santa Clara Co Off of Education	San Jose
367	19.7	Shasta Union High	Redding
368	19.5	Chino Valley Unified	Chino
369	19.4	Tracy Joint Unified	Tracy
370	19.3	Morgan Hill Unified	Morgan Hill
371	19.1	Amador County Unified	Jackson
372	19.0	Charter Oak Unified	Covina
372	19.0	Claremont Unified	Claremont
374	18.5	Santa Monica-Malibu Unified	Santa Monica
375	18.2	Center Joint Unified	Antelope
376	17.9	Cabrillo Unified	Half Moon Bay
377	17.8	Orcutt Union Elementary	Orcutt
378	17.6	Menifee Union Elementary	Menifee
378	17.6	Westside Union Elementary	Lancaster
380	17.5	Moreland Elementary	San Jose
381	17.3	Berryessa Union Elementary	San Jose
381	17.3	Wheatland Elementary	Wheatland
383	17.2	San Luis Coastal Unified	San Luis Obispo
384	17.1	Soquel Union Elementary	Capitola
385	17.0	Grossmont Union High	La Mesa
386	16.9	Ojai Unified	Ojai
387	16.6	Sequoia Union High	Redwood City
388	16.5	Bonita Unified	San Dimas
389	16.4	Roseville City Elementary	Roseville
390	16.3	Santa Barbara High	Santa Barbara
391	16.2	Black Oak Mine Unified	Georgetown
391	16.2	Sonora Union High	Sonora
393	15.9	Muroc Joint Unified	North Edwards
394	15.8	Brentwood Union Elementary	Brentwood
394	15.8	Cypress Elementary	Cypress
396	15.7	Middletown Unified	Middletown
396	15.7	Piner-Olivet Union Elementary	Santa Rosa
396	15.7	Rincon Valley Union Elementary	Santa Rosa
399	15.6	Jefferson Union High	Daly City
400	15.5	Old Adobe Union Elementary	Petaluma
401	15.3	Atascadero Unified	Atascadero
401	15.3	San Rafael City High	San Rafael
403	15.0	Santee Elementary	Santee
404	14.5	Chaffey Joint Union High	Ontario
405	14.3	Huntington Beach Union High	Huntington Bch
405	14.3	Tahoe-Truckee Joint Unified	Truckee
407	14.2	Jamul-Dulzura Union Elementary	Jamul
408	14.0	Cambrian Elementary	San Jose
409	13.7	Redondo Beach Unified	Redondo Beach
410	13.6	Mark West Union Elementary	Santa Rosa
411	13.5	San Benito High	Hollister
412	13.4	Santa Cruz City High	Soquel
413	13.1	Encinitas Union Elementary	Encinitas
414	12.8	Cotati-Rohnert Park Unified	Rohnert Park
415	12.5	Julian Union Elementary	Julian
416	12.3	Dry Creek Joint Elementary	Roseville
416	12.3	Escondido Union High	Escondido
418	12.1	Lowell Joint	Whittier
418	12.1	Simi Valley Unified	Simi Valley
420	12.0	Fruitvale Elementary	Bakersfield
421	11.9	Brea-Olinda Unified	Brea
421	11.9	Western Placer Unified	Lincoln
423	11.7	Alpine Union Elementary	Alpine
424	11.5	Etiwanda Elementary	Etiwanda
424	11.5	Novato Unified	Novato
424	11.5	Torrance Unified	Torrance
427	11.4	Pacifica SD	Pacifica
428	11.3	Martinez Unified	Martinez
428	11.3	Pleasant Ridge Union Elementary	Grass Valley
430	11.2	Carlsbad Unified	Carlsbad
431	11.1	Alta Loma Elementary	Alta Loma
432	11.0	Livermore Valley Joint Unified	Livermore
432	11.0	Mountain View-Los Altos Union High	Mountain View
434	10.7	Capistrano Unified	San Juan Capis
435	10.6	Castro Valley Unified	Castro Valley
436	10.5	Pleasant Valley School	Camarillo
437	10.2	Petaluma Joint Union High	Petaluma
438	10.1	Fremont Unified	Fremont
438	10.1	Rosedale Union Elementary	Bakersfield
438	10.1	Saddleback Valley Unified	Mission Viejo
441	9.8	Glendora Unified	Glendora
441	9.8	Union Elementary	San Jose
443	9.6	West Sonoma County Union High	Sebastopol
444	9.5	Davis Joint Unified	Davis
445	9.4	Castaic Union Elementary	Valencia
445	9.4	Huntington Beach City Elementary	Huntington Bch
445	9.4	William S. Hart Union High	Santa Clarita
448	8.5	San Lorenzo Valley Unified	Ben Lomond
448	8.5	Saugus Union Elementary	Santa Clarita
450	8.4	Albany City Unified	Albany
450	8.4	Murrieta Valley Unified	Murrieta
450	8.4	Santa Rosa High	Santa Rosa
453	8.0	Laguna Beach Unified	Laguna Beach
453	8.0	Northern Humboldt Union High	McKinleyville
455	7.7	Campbell Union High	San Jose
455	7.7	Conejo Valley Unified	Thousand Oaks
455	7.7	Fountain Valley Elementary	Fountain Valley
455	7.7	Liberty Union High	Brentwood
455	7.7	Loomis Union Elementary	Loomis
460	7.6	Dublin Unified	Dublin
460	7.6	Temecula Valley Unified	Temecula
462	7.5	Placer Union High	Auburn

463	7.1	Jefferson Elementary	Tracy
464	6.8	Templeton Unified	Templeton
464	6.8	Travis Unified	Travis Afb
466	6.7	Fullerton Joint Union High	Fullerton
466	6.7	Solana Beach Elementary	Solana Beach
468	6.6	Placentia-Yorba Linda Unified	Placentia
469	6.5	El Segundo Unified	El Segundo
469	6.5	Pacific Grove Unified	Pacific Grove
469	6.5	Rocklin Unified	Rocklin
472	6.4	Nevada Joint Union High	Grass Valley
472	6.4	Newark Unified	Newark
472	6.4	Norris Elementary	Bakersfield
475	6.3	Poway Unified	Poway
475	6.3	Rescue Union Elementary	Rescue
477	6.0	Ross Valley Elementary	San Anselmo
478	5.9	Walnut Valley Unified	Walnut
479	5.6	Arcadia Unified	Arcadia
479	5.6	Carmel Unified	Carmel
481	5.5	Millbrae Elementary	Millbrae
482	5.2	El Dorado Union High	Placerville
482	5.2	Fremont Union High	Sunnyvale
482	5.2	Los Alamitos Unified	Los Alamitos
485	5.1	Benicia Unified	Benicia
486	5.0	South Pasadena Unified	South Pasadena
487	4.9	San Dieguito Union High	Encinitas
488	4.8	Irvine Unified	Irvine
488	4.8	Walnut Creek Elementary	Walnut Creek
490	4.6	Roseville Joint Union High	Roseville
491	4.5	Orange County Office of Education	Costa Mesa
492	4.2	Dixie Elementary	San Rafael
493	4.0	Buckeye Union Elementary	Shingle Springs
494	3.9	San Mateo Union High	San Mateo
495	3.7	Scotts Valley Unified	Scotts Valley
496	3.6	Palo Alto Unified	Palo Alto
497	3.5	Cupertino Union School	Cupertino
497	3.5	Menlo Park City Elementary	Atherton
499	3.4	Belmont-Redwood Shores Elementary	Belmont
499	3.4	Coronado Unified	Coronado
501	3.2	Burlingame Elementary	Burlingame
501	3.2	Manhattan Beach Unified	Manhattan Beach
501	3.2	Pleasanton Unified	Pleasanton
504	2.5	Eureka Union Elementary	Granite Bay
505	2.3	Beverly Hills Unified	Beverly Hills
505	2.3	Julian Union High	Julian
507	2.2	Twin Ridges Elementary	North San Juan
508	2.0	San Carlos Elementary	San Carlos
508	2.0	Tamalpais Union High	Larkspur
510	1.9	Las Virgenes Unified	Calabasas
510	1.9	Los Altos Elementary	Los Altos
510	1.9	Los Gatos Union Elementary	Los Gatos
510	1.9	Mill Valley Elementary	Mill Valley
514	1.7	Del Mar Union Elementary	Del Mar
514	1.7	Moraga Elementary	Moraga
516	1.3	Gorman Elementary	Gorman
517	1.0	Palos Verdes Peninsula Unified	Palos Verdes Est
517	1.0	San Ramon Valley Unified	Danville
519	0.9	Los Gatos-Saratoga Jt Union High	Los Gatos
519	0.9	Oak Park Unified	Oak Park
521	0.8	San Marino Unified	San Marino
522	0.6	Orinda Union Elementary	Orinda
522	0.6	Saratoga Union Elementary	Saratoga
524	0.5	La Canada Unified	La Canada
525	0.4	Acalanes Union High	Lafayette
526	0.2	Lafayette Elementary	Lafayette
527	0.0	Acton-Agua Dulce Unified	Acton
527	0.0	Piedmont City Unified	Piedmont

Students Eligible for Reduced-Price Lunch

Rank	Percent	District Name	City
1	26.1	South Whittier Elementary	Whittier
2	22.9	Little Lake City Elementary	Santa Fe Spgs
3	22.6	Twin Ridges Elementary	North San Juan
4	21.8	Anaheim Elementary	Anaheim
5	21.7	Santa Paula Elementary	Santa Paula
6	21.0	Rosemead Elementary	Rosemead
7	20.7	Central Union Elementary	Lemoore
8	20.3	Downey Unified	Downey
9	20.1	Standard Elementary	Bakersfield
10	19.7	Hemet Unified	Hemet
11	19.5	Cucamonga Elementary	Rcho Cucamong
12	19.3	Jefferson Elementary	Daly City
13	19.2	Salinas City Elementary	Salinas
13	19.2	Silver Valley Unified	Yermo
15	19.0	Ocean View Elementary	Oxnard
16	18.8	Alisal Union Elementary	Salinas
17	18.4	Cascade Union Elementary	Anderson
18	18.3	Azusa Unified	Azusa
18	18.3	Val Verde Unified	Perris
20	18.2	Lemon Grove Elementary	Lemon Grove
21	17.9	Beaumont Unified	Beaumont
21	17.9	Pittsburg Unified	Pittsburg
23	17.2	Palmdale Elementary	Palmdale
23	17.2	West Covina Unified	West Covina
25	17.1	Lawndale Elementary	Lawndale
26	17.0	Calexico Unified	Calexico
26	17.0	Greenfield Union Elementary	Greenfield
28	16.9	Bellevue Union Elementary	Santa Rosa
29	16.8	Hueneme Elementary	Port Hueneme
29	16.8	Santa Ana Unified	Santa Ana
31	16.6	Santa Barbara Elementary	Santa Barbara
32	16.5	King City Union Elementary	King City
32	16.5	Ravenswood City Elementary	East Palo Alto
34	16.4	Oxnard Elementary	Oxnard
35	16.3	Chula Vista Elementary	Chula Vista
35	16.3	Robla Elementary	Sacramento
37	16.2	Livingston Union Elementary	Livingston
37	16.2	Romoland Elementary	Homeland
39	16.1	Burton Elementary	Porterville
39	16.1	Moreno Valley Unified	Moreno Valley
39	16.1	South Bay Union Elementary	Imperial Beach
42	16.0	Enterprise Elementary	Redding
42	16.0	Rio Elementary	Oxnard
42	16.0	Sweetwater Union High	Chula Vista
42	16.0	Whittier City Elementary	Whittier
46	15.8	El Rancho Unified	Pico Rivera
47	15.7	Carpinteria Unified	Carpinteria
47	15.7	Hawthorne Elementary	Hawthorne
49	15.5	Empire Union Elementary	Modesto
50	15.4	Hacienda La Puente Unified	City of Industry
51	15.3	Atwater Elementary	Atwater
51	15.3	Banning Unified	Banning
51	15.3	Gonzales Unified	Gonzales
51	15.3	Salinas Union High	Salinas
55	15.2	Alum Rock Union Elementary	San Jose
56	15.1	Santa Maria-Bonita Elementary	Santa Maria
57	15.0	Bassett Unified	La Puente
57	15.0	Buena Park Elementary	Buena Park
57	15.0	Mountain View Elementary	Ontario
57	15.0	San Francisco Unified	San Francisco
61	14.9	Alhambra City Elementary	Alhambra
61	14.9	Bellflower Unified	Bellflower
61	14.9	Savanna Elementary	Anaheim
64	14.8	Wiseburn Elementary	Hawthorne
65	14.7	Lucia Mar Unified	Arroyo Grande
66	14.6	Baldwin Park Unified	Baldwin Park
66	14.6	King City Joint Union High	King City
66	14.6	Washington Unified	West Sacramento
69	14.5	Duarte Unified	Duarte
69	14.5	Kerman Unified	Kerman
69	14.5	Magnolia Elementary	Anaheim
69	14.5	Paramount Unified	Paramount
73	14.4	Ontario-Montclair Elementary	Ontario
74	14.3	Alvord Unified	Riverside
74	14.3	Greenfield Union Elementary	Bakersfield
74	14.3	Hayward Unified	Hayward
74	14.3	Jurupa Unified	Riverside
74	14.3	Monrovia Unified	Monrovia
74	14.3	Oceanside Unified	Oceanside
74	14.3	Oxnard Union High	Oxnard
74	14.3	Parlier Unified	Parlier
74	14.3	Santa Rita Union Elementary	Salinas
74	14.3	Santa Rosa Elementary	Santa Rosa
84	14.2	Escondido Union Elementary	Escondido
84	14.2	Fontana Unified	Fontana
84	14.2	Franklin-Mckinley Elementary	San Jose
84	14.2	Lake Tahoe Unified	S Lake Tahoe
84	14.2	San Bernardino City Unified	San Bernardino
89	14.1	Mt. Pleasant Elementary	San Jose
90	14.0	Keppel Union Elementary	Pearblossom
90	14.0	Rowland Unified	Rowland Heights
92	13.9	Redwood City Elementary	Redwood City
93	13.8	Adelanto Elementary	Adelanto
93	13.8	Garden Grove Unified	Garden Grove
93	13.8	La Habra City Elementary	La Habra
93	13.8	Live Oak Unified	Live Oak
97	13.6	Palm Springs Unified	Palm Springs
98	13.5	Corona-Norco Unified	Norco
98	13.5	Dinuba Unified	Dinuba
98	13.5	Riverbank Unified	Riverbank
101	13.4	Delano Joint Union High	Delano
102	13.3	San Ysidro Elementary	San Ysidro
103	13.2	Apple Valley Unified	Apple Valley
103	13.2	Exeter Union Elementary	Exeter
103	13.2	Fairfax Elementary	Bakersfield
103	13.2	Hesperia Unified	Hesperia
103	13.2	Lemoore Union Elementary	Lemoore
103	13.2	Rio Linda Union Elementary	Rio Linda
109	13.1	Ceres Unified	Ceres
109	13.1	Lake Elsinore Unified	Lake Elsinore
111	13.0	Galt Joint Union Elementary	Galt
112	12.9	Santa Clara Unified	Santa Clara
113	12.8	Winton Elementary	Winton
114	12.7	Fort Bragg Unified	Fort Bragg
114	12.7	Madera Unified	Madera
114	12.7	West Contra Costa Unified	Richmond
117	12.6	Corcoran Joint Unified	Corcoran
117	12.6	Farmersville Unified	Farmersville
117	12.6	Hollister SD	Hollister
117	12.6	Perris Elementary	Perris
121	12.5	Anaheim Union High	Anaheim
121	12.5	Red Bluff Union Elementary	Red Bluff
121	12.5	Salida Union Elementary	Salida
121	12.5	Wheatland Elementary	Wheatland
125	12.4	Eastside Union Elementary	Lancaster
125	12.4	Gateway Unified	Redding
125	12.4	Riverside Unified	Riverside
125	12.4	Weaver Union Elementary	Merced
129	12.3	Nuview Union Elementary	Nuevo
129	12.3	Pomona Unified	Pomona
129	12.3	Temple City Unified	Temple City
129	12.3	Westminster Elementary	Westminster
133	12.2	Cajon Valley Union Elementary	El Cajon
133	12.2	Gustine Unified	Gustine
133	12.2	Hanford Elementary	Hanford
133	12.2	Los Banos Unified	Los Banos
133	12.2	Mother Lode Union Elementary	Placerville
133	12.2	Newman-Crows Landing Unified	Newman
139	12.1	Healdsburg Unified	Healdsburg
139	12.1	Morongo Unified	Twentynine Plms
139	12.1	Patterson Joint Unified	Patterson
142	12.0	Brawley Elementary	Brawley
142	12.0	Colton Joint Unified	Colton
142	12.0	Fallbrook Union Elementary	Fallbrook
142	12.0	Panama Buena Vista Union Elem	Bakersfield
142	12.0	San Gabriel Unified	San Gabriel
147	11.9	Muroc Joint Unified	North Edwards
147	11.9	Orland Joint Unified	Orland
147	11.9	Redlands Unified	Redlands
147	11.9	Riverdale Joint Unified	Riverdale
147	11.9	Wilsona Elementary	Palmdale
152	11.8	Alhambra City High	Alhambra
152	11.8	Dos Palos Oro Loma Jt. Unified	Dos Palos
152	11.8	Redding Elementary	Redding
152	11.8	Richland Union Elementary SD	Shafter
152	11.8	Tulare City Elementary	Tulare
157	11.7	Covina-Valley Unified	Covina
157	11.7	El Monte Union High	El Monte
157	11.7	Monterey Peninsula Unified	Monterey
157	11.7	Ventura Unified	Ventura
157	11.7	Victor Elementary	Victorville
162	11.5	Beardsley Elementary	Bakersfield
162	11.5	Centralia Elementary	Buena Park
162	11.5	Fillmore Unified	Fillmore
165	11.4	Central Elementary	Rcho Cucamong
165	11.4	El Centro Elementary	El Centro
165	11.4	Kingsburg Elementary Charter	Kingsburg
165	11.4	Long Beach Unified	Long Beach
165	11.4	North Sacramento Elementary	Sacramento
165	11.4	Ukiah Unified	Ukiah
171	11.3	Desert Sands Unified	La Quinta
171	11.3	La Mesa-Spring Valley	La Mesa
171	11.3	Lakeside Union Elementary	Lakeside
171	11.3	Merced Union High	Atwater
171	11.3	Napa Valley Unified	Napa
171	11.3	Winters Joint Unified	Winters
177	11.1	Lindsay Unified	Lindsay
177	11.1	Live Oak Elementary	Santa Cruz
177	11.1	Santa Paula Union High	Santa Paula
180	10.9	Julian Union Elementary	Julian
180	10.9	Merced City Elementary	Merced
182	10.8	Arvin Union Elementary	Arvin
182	10.8	Marysville Joint Unified	Marysville
182	10.8	North Monterey County Unified	Moss Landing
182	10.8	San Leandro Unified	San Leandro
182	10.8	Willits Unified	Willits
187	10.7	Antioch Unified	Antioch
187	10.7	Lakeport Unified	Lakeport
187	10.7	Lodi Unified	Lodi
187	10.7	Modesto City Elementary	Modesto
187	10.7	San Jacinto Unified	San Jacinto
187	10.7	Sanger Unified	Sanger
187	10.7	Sunnyvale Elementary	Sunnyvale
194	10.6	Fruitvale Elementary	Bakersfield
194	10.6	Grass Valley Elementary	Grass Valley
194	10.6	Lompoc Unified	Lompoc
194	10.6	Oak Grove Elementary	San Jose
194	10.6	Vista Unified	Vista
199	10.5	Berkeley Unified	Berkeley
199	10.5	Culver City Unified	Culver City
199	10.5	Delhi Unified	Delhi
199	10.5	Konocti Unified	Lower Lake
199	10.5	Mountain Empire Unified	Pine Valley
199	10.5	Mountain View-Whisman Elementary	Mountain View
199	10.5	Oroville City Elementary	Oroville
206	10.4	Selma Unified	Selma

206	10.4	Yuba City Unified	Yuba City
208	10.3	Central Unified	Fresno
208	10.3	Dixon Unified	Dixon
208	10.3	Manteca Unified	Manteca
208	10.3	Piner-Olivet Union Elementary	Santa Rosa
208	10.3	Woodland Joint Unified	Woodland
213	10.2	Elk Grove Unified	Elk Grove
213	10.2	Eureka City Unified	Eureka
213	10.2	Goleta Union Elementary	Goleta
213	10.2	San Rafael City Elementary	San Rafael
213	10.2	Sierra Unified	Prather
213	10.2	Taft City Elementary	Taft
213	10.2	Travis Unified	Travis Afb
220	10.1	El Monte City Elementary	El Monte
220	10.1	Kings Canyon Joint Unified	Reedley
220	10.1	San Bruno Park Elementary	San Bruno
220	10.1	Victor Valley Union High	Victorville
224	10.0	Southern Kern Unified	Rosamond
224	10.0	Turlock Joint Elementary	Turlock
226	9.9	Natomas Unified	Sacramento
227	9.8	Auburn Union Elementary	Auburn
227	9.8	Firebaugh-Las Deltas Joint Unified	Firebaugh
227	9.8	Hilmar Unified	Hilmar
227	9.8	San Jose Unified	San Jose
227	9.8	Wasco Union Elementary	Wasco
232	9.7	Centinela Valley Union High	Lawndale
232	9.7	Fairfield-Suisun Unified	Fairfield
232	9.7	Norwalk-La Mirada Unified	Norwalk
232	9.7	San Diego Unified	San Diego
236	9.6	Bakersfield City Elementary	Bakersfield
236	9.6	Inglewood Unified	Inglewood
236	9.6	Lincoln Unified	Stockton
236	9.6	San Lorenzo Unified	San Lorenzo
236	9.6	Valley Center-Pauma Unified	Valley Center
241	9.4	Barstow Unified	Barstow
241	9.4	Lancaster Elementary	Lancaster
243	9.3	Rialto Unified	Rialto
244	9.2	Calaveras Unified	San Andreas
244	9.2	Glendale Unified	Glendale
244	9.2	Milpitas Unified	Milpitas
244	9.2	New Haven Unified	Union City
244	9.2	San Marcos Unified	San Marcos
244	9.2	Stanislaus Union Elementary	Modesto
250	9.1	Central Union High	El Centro
250	9.1	Grant Joint Union High	Sacramento
250	9.1	Pajaro Valley Unified School	Watsonville
250	9.1	Pasadena Unified	Pasadena
250	9.1	Santee Elementary	Santee
255	9.0	Oakland Unified	Oakland
255	9.0	Ramona City Unified	Ramona
257	8.9	Fowler Unified	Fowler
257	8.9	Sylvan Union Elementary	Modesto
259	8.8	Kelseyville Unified	Kelseyville
259	8.8	Montebello Unified	Montebello
259	8.8	Paradise Unified	Paradise
259	8.8	South San Francisco Unified	S San Francisco
263	8.7	Amador County Unified	Jackson
263	8.7	Earlimart Elementary	Earlimart
263	8.7	Fullerton Elementary	Fullerton
263	8.7	Paso Robles Joint Unified	Paso Robles
263	8.7	Plumas Unified	Quincy
268	8.6	Cabrillo Unified	Half Moon Bay
268	8.6	East Whittier City Elementary	Whittier
268	8.6	Jefferson Union High	Daly City
268	8.6	Linden Unified	Linden
268	8.6	Middletown Unified	Middletown
268	8.6	San Mateo-Foster City Elementary	San Mateo
268	8.6	Tulare County Office of Education	Visalia
275	8.5	Bear Valley Unified	Big Bear Lake
275	8.5	Palo Verde Unified	Blythe
275	8.5	Vallejo City Unified	Vallejo
278	8.4	Holtville Unified	Holtville
278	8.4	San Joaquin Co Off of Education	Stockton
280	8.3	San Luis Coastal Unified	San Luis Obispo
280	8.3	Tustin Unified	Tustin
282	8.2	Campbell Union Elementary	Campbell
282	8.2	Whittier Union High	Whittier
284	8.1	Brawley Union High	Brawley
284	8.1	Coachella Valley Unified	Thermal
284	8.1	Gilroy Unified	Gilroy
284	8.1	Mariposa County Unified	Mariposa
284	8.1	Roseville City Elementary	Roseville
284	8.1	Sierra Sands Unified	Ridgecrest
290	8.0	Chino Valley Unified	Chino
290	8.0	Cypress Elementary	Cypress
290	8.0	Imperial Unified	Imperial
290	8.0	Windsor Unified	Windsor
294	7.9	Coalinga-Huron Joint Unified	Coalinga
294	7.9	Del Norte County Unified	Crescent City
294	7.9	Evergreen Elementary	San Jose
294	7.9	Orcutt Union Elementary	Orcutt
294	7.9	Sulphur Springs Union Elementary	Canyon Country
294	7.9	Visalia Unified	Visalia
300	7.8	Berryessa Union Elementary	San Jose
300	7.8	Burbank Unified	Burbank
300	7.8	Claremont Unified	Claremont
300	7.8	Corning Union Elementary	Corning
300	7.8	Los Angeles Unified	Los Angeles
305	7.7	Escalon Unified	Escalon
305	7.7	Golden Plains Unified	San Joaquin
305	7.7	Hughson Unified	Hughson
305	7.7	Ocean View Elementary	Huntington Bch
305	7.7	Santa Cruz City Elementary	Soquel
305	7.7	Soquel Union Elementary	Capitola
305	7.7	Tehachapi Unified	Tehachapi
305	7.7	Willows Unified	Willows
313	7.6	Center Joint Unified	Antelope
313	7.6	Oakdale Joint Unified	Oakdale
313	7.6	Porterville Unified	Porterville
313	7.6	Upland Unified	Upland
317	7.5	Alameda City Unified	Alameda
317	7.5	Cloverdale Unified	Cloverdale
317	7.5	Gridley Unified	Gridley
320	7.3	Black Oak Mine Unified	Georgetown
320	7.3	Fallbrook Union High	Fallbrook
320	7.3	Perris Union High	Perris
323	7.2	ABC Unified	Cerritos
323	7.2	Cotati-Rohnert Park Unified	Rohnert Park
323	7.2	Etiwanda Elementary	Etiwanda
323	7.2	Garvey Elementary	Rosemead
327	7.1	Clovis Unified	Clovis
327	7.1	Cutler-Orosi Joint Unified	Orosi
327	7.1	Ojai Unified	Ojai
327	7.1	Pacifica SD	Pacifica
327	7.1	Rincon Valley Union Elementary	Santa Rosa
327	7.1	Shasta Union High	Redding
333	7.0	Bonsall Union Elementary	Bonsall
333	7.0	Charter Oak Unified	Covina
333	7.0	Dry Creek Joint Elementary	Roseville
333	7.0	Old Adobe Union Elementary	Petaluma
333	7.0	San Juan Unified	Carmichael
333	7.0	Yucaipa-Calimesa Jt. Unified	Yucaipa
339	6.9	Sonoma Valley Unified	Sonoma
340	6.8	John Swett Unified	Crockett
340	6.8	Moreland Elementary	San Jose
340	6.8	Newport-Mesa Unified	Costa Mesa
343	6.7	Atascadero Unified	Atascadero
344	6.6	Chico Unified	Chico
344	6.6	Norris Elementary	Bakersfield
344	6.6	Soledad Unified	Soledad
344	6.6	Woodlake Union Elementary	Woodlake
348	6.5	Oakley Union Elementary	Oakley
348	6.5	Orange Unified	Orange
348	6.5	Oroville Union High	Oroville
351	6.4	Alta Loma Elementary	Alta Loma
351	6.4	Del Paso Heights Elementary	Sacramento
351	6.4	Rim of the World Unified	Lake Arrowhead
351	6.4	Vacaville Unified	Vacaville
355	6.3	Antelope Valley Union High	Lancaster
355	6.3	Santa Barbara High	Santa Barbara
357	6.2	Mojave Unified	Mojave
357	6.2	Moorpark Unified	Moorpark
357	6.2	Ripon Unified	Ripon
357	6.2	Snowline Joint Unified	Phelan
361	6.1	Folsom-Cordova Unified	Folsom
361	6.1	Galt Joint Union High	Galt
361	6.1	Murrieta Valley Unified	Murrieta
361	6.1	Rosedale Union Elementary	Bakersfield
361	6.1	Santa Maria Joint Union High	Santa Maria
361	6.1	Westside Union Elementary	Lancaster
367	6.0	Anderson Union High	Anderson
367	6.0	Castro Valley Unified	Castro Valley
367	6.0	Chowchilla Elementary	Chowchilla
367	6.0	Mt. Diablo Unified	Concord
367	6.0	Redondo Beach Unified	Redondo Beach
367	6.0	Santa Monica-Malibu Unified	Santa Monica
367	6.0	Westwood Unified	Westwood
374	5.8	Kern Union High	Bakersfield
374	5.8	Sacramento City Unified	Sacramento
374	5.8	Simi Valley Unified	Simi Valley
374	5.8	Tracy Joint Unified	Tracy
378	5.7	Compton Unified	Compton
378	5.7	Newhall Elementary	Valencia
378	5.7	Petaluma City Elementary	Petaluma
381	5.6	Bonita Unified	San Dimas
381	5.6	Brea-Olinda Unified	Brea
381	5.6	Grossmont Union High	La Mesa
381	5.6	Loomis Union Elementary	Loomis
381	5.6	Menifee Union Elementary	Menifee
381	5.6	Pleasant Valley School	Camarillo
381	5.6	Red Bluff Joint Union High	Red Bluff
388	5.5	Cambrian Elementary	San Jose
388	5.5	Waterford Unified	Waterford
390	5.4	Lowell Joint	Whittier
390	5.4	River Delta Joint Unified	Rio Vista
390	5.4	Western Placer Unified	Lincoln
393	5.2	Brentwood Union Elementary	Brentwood
393	5.2	Pleasant Ridge Union Elementary	Grass Valley
393	5.2	San Diego Co Office of Education	San Diego
393	5.2	Stockton City Unified	Stockton
397	5.1	Carmel Unified	Carmel
397	5.1	Mcfarland Unified	Mcfarland
397	5.1	Millbrae Elementary	Millbrae
400	5.0	Carlsbad Unified	Carlsbad
400	5.0	Glendora Unified	Glendora
400	5.0	Novato Unified	Novato
403	4.9	Fountain Valley Elementary	Fountain Valley
403	4.9	Sequoia Union High	Redwood City
403	4.9	Templeton Unified	Templeton
403	4.9	Torrance Unified	Torrance
407	4.8	Morgan Hill Unified	Morgan Hill
407	4.8	Rocklin Unified	Rocklin
409	4.7	Albany City Unified	Albany
409	4.7	Mendota Unified	Mendota
409	4.7	Tahoe-Truckee Joint Unified	Truckee
409	4.7	Temecula Valley Unified	Temecula
413	4.6	Modesto City High	Modesto
413	4.6	Turlock Joint Union High	Turlock
415	4.5	Fremont Unified	Fremont
415	4.5	Jamul-Dulzura Union Elementary	Jamul
417	4.4	Fresno Unified	Fresno
417	4.4	Walnut Valley Unified	Walnut
419	4.3	Coronado Unified	Coronado
419	4.3	Tulare Joint Union High	Tulare
421	4.2	Encinitas Union Elementary	Encinitas
421	4.2	Lynwood Unified	Lynwood
423	4.1	San Benito High	Hollister
423	4.1	Saugus Union Elementary	Santa Clarita
425	4.0	Capistrano Unified	San Juan Capis
425	4.0	Lennox Elementary	Lennox
425	4.0	Pacific Grove Unified	Pacific Grove
425	4.0	Placer Union High	Auburn
429	3.9	Keyes Union Elementary	Keyes
429	3.9	Lemoore Union High	Lemoore
429	3.9	Martinez Unified	Martinez
429	3.9	Saddleback Valley Unified	Mission Viejo
433	3.8	Chaffey Joint Union High	Ontario
433	3.8	Conejo Valley Unified	Thousand Oaks
435	3.7	Alpine Union Elementary	Alpine
435	3.7	East Side Union High	San Jose
437	3.6	El Segundo Unified	El Segundo
437	3.6	Los Angeles Co Office of Education	Downey
437	3.6	Nevada Joint Union High	Grass Valley
437	3.6	Santa Cruz City High	Soquel
441	3.5	Mountain View Elementary	El Monte
441	3.5	Santa Rosa High	Santa Rosa
443	3.4	Castaic Union Elementary	Valencia
443	3.4	Mark West Union Elementary	Santa Rosa
443	3.4	Sonora Union High	Sonora
446	3.3	Escondido Union High	Escondido
446	3.3	Huntington Beach City Elementary	Huntington Bch
446	3.3	Huntington Beach Union High	Huntington Bch
446	3.3	Poway Unified	Poway
446	3.3	San Lorenzo Valley Unified	Ben Lomond
446	3.3	Walnut Creek Elementary	Walnut Creek
452	3.2	Arcadia Unified	Arcadia
452	3.2	Livermore Valley Joint Unified	Livermore
452	3.2	Los Alamitos Unified	Los Alamitos
452	3.2	West Sonoma County Union High	Sebastopol
456	3.1	Benicia Unified	Benicia
456	3.1	Jefferson Elementary	Tracy
458	3.0	Petaluma Joint Union High	Petaluma
459	2.9	Rescue Union Elementary	Rescue
460	2.8	William S. Hart Union High	Santa Clarita
461	2.7	Davis Joint Unified	Davis
461	2.7	South Pasadena Unified	South Pasadena
461	2.7	Union Elementary	San Jose
464	2.6	Hanford Joint Union High	Hanford
464	2.6	Kern County Office of Education	Bakersfield
464	2.6	San Rafael City High	San Rafael
467	2.5	Campbell Union High	San Jose
467	2.5	Dublin Unified	Dublin
467	2.5	Irvine Unified	Irvine
467	2.5	Solana Beach Elementary	Solana Beach
471	2.4	Laguna Beach Unified	Laguna Beach
472	2.2	San Mateo Union High	San Mateo
473	2.1	El Dorado Union High	Placerville
473	2.1	Ross Valley Elementary	San Anselmo
475	1.8	Beverly Hills Unified	Beverly Hills
475	1.8	Buckeye Union Elementary	Shingle Springs
477	1.7	Mountain View-Los Altos Union High	Mountain View
477	1.7	Palo Alto Unified	Palo Alto
477	1.7	Placentia-Yorba Linda Unified	Placentia
477	1.7	San Dieguito Union High	Encinitas
481	1.6	Cupertino Union School	Cupertino
481	1.6	Manhattan Beach Unified	Manhattan Beach
483	1.5	Fresno County Office of Education	Fresno
483	1.5	Roseville Joint Union High	Roseville

485	1.4	Burlingame Elementary	Burlingame
485	1.4	Fremont Union High	Sunnyvale
485	1.4	Pleasanton Unified	Pleasanton
485	1.4	Scotts Valley Unified	Scotts Valley
489	1.2	Eureka Union Elementary	Granite Bay
489	1.2	Julian Union High	Julian
489	1.2	Liberty Union High	Brentwood
492	1.1	Fullerton Joint Union High	Fullerton
493	1.0	Las Virgenes Unified	Calabasas
493	1.0	Northern Humboldt Union High	McKinleyville
495	0.9	Del Mar Union Elementary	Del Mar
495	0.9	Oak Park Unified	Oak Park
497	0.8	Dixie Elementary	San Rafael
498	0.6	Mill Valley Elementary	Mill Valley
498	0.6	Palos Verdes Peninsula Unified	Palos Verdes Est
500	0.5	Riverside Co Office of Education	Riverside
500	0.5	San Carlos Elementary	San Carlos
500	0.5	San Ramon Valley Unified	Danville
503	0.4	Menlo Park City Elementary	Atherton
503	0.4	Orange County Office of Education	Costa Mesa
503	0.4	San Marino Unified	San Marino
503	0.4	Tamalpais Union High	Larkspur
507	0.3	Gorman Elementary	Gorman
507	0.3	La Canada Unified	La Canada
507	0.3	Los Gatos Union Elementary	Los Gatos
507	0.3	San Bernardino Co Off of Education	San Bernardino
511	0.2	Los Altos Elementary	Los Altos
511	0.2	Santa Clara Co Off of Education	San Jose
511	0.2	Saratoga Union Elementary	Saratoga
514	0.1	Acalanes Union High	Lafayette
515	0.0	Newark Unified	Newark
516	0.0	Acton-Agua Dulce Unified	Acton
516	0.0	Belmont-Redwood Shores Elementary	Belmont
516	0.0	Delano Union Elementary	Delano
516	0.0	Lafayette Elementary	Lafayette
516	0.0	Lamont Elementary	Lamont
516	0.0	Los Gatos-Saratoga Jt Union High	Los Gatos
516	0.0	Los Nietos Elementary	Whittier
516	0.0	Moraga Elementary	Moraga
516	0.0	National Elementary	National City
516	0.0	Orinda Union Elementary	Orinda
516	0.0	Oro Grande Elementary	Oro Grande
516	0.0	Piedmont City Unified	Piedmont
516	0.0	Reef-Sunset Unified	Avenal

Student/Teacher Ratio

Rank	Ratio	District Name	City
1	34.6	Western Placer Unified	Lincoln
2	30.5	Greenfield Union Elementary	Greenfield
3	29.8	Gorman Elementary	Gorman
4	29.0	Fullerton Joint Union High	Fullerton
5	27.2	Oroville Union High	Oroville
6	26.8	Lynwood Unified	Lynwood
7	26.6	Santa Paula Union High	Santa Paula
8	26.4	Antelope Valley Union High	Lancaster
9	26.3	Huntington Beach Union High	Huntington Bch
10	26.1	Oxnard Union High	Oxnard
11	25.9	Banning Unified	Banning
12	25.8	San Benito High	Hollister
13	25.6	El Monte Union High	El Monte
13	25.6	Victor Valley Union High	Victorville
13	25.6	Whittier Union High	Whittier
16	25.4	Anaheim Union High	Anaheim
17	25.2	Perris Union High	Perris
17	25.2	William S. Hart Union High	Santa Clarita
19	25.0	Alhambra City High	Alhambra
19	25.0	Campbell Union High	San Jose
19	25.0	Santa Cruz City High	Soquel
22	24.9	Tehachapi Unified	Tehachapi
23	24.8	Chaffey Joint Union High	Ontario
23	24.8	Escondido Union High	Escondido
25	24.7	Baldwin Park Unified	Baldwin Park
25	24.7	Charter Oak Unified	Covina
25	24.7	Modesto City High	Modesto
25	24.7	Santa Maria Joint Union High	Santa Maria
29	24.6	San Dieguito Union High	Encinitas
29	24.6	Tulare Joint Union High	Tulare
31	24.5	Huntington Beach City Elementary	Huntington Bch
31	24.5	Liberty Union High	Brentwood
31	24.5	Palmdale Elementary	Palmdale
31	24.5	Val Verde Unified	Perris
35	24.3	Adelanto Elementary	Adelanto
35	24.3	King City Joint Union High	King City
37	24.2	Saddleback Valley Unified	Mission Viejo
38	24.1	Anderson Union High	Anderson
38	24.1	Chino Valley Unified	Chino
38	24.1	Hanford Joint Union High	Hanford
38	24.1	Santa Paula Elementary	Santa Paula
38	24.1	Victor Elementary	Victorville
43	24.0	Alta Loma Elementary	Alta Loma
43	24.0	Brawley Union High	Brawley
43	24.0	Central Union High	El Centro
43	24.0	Hesperia Unified	Hesperia
47	23.9	Alisal Union Elementary	Salinas
47	23.9	Montebello Unified	Montebello
47	23.9	Shasta Union High	Redding
47	23.9	South Pasadena Unified	South Pasadena
51	23.8	Fountain Valley Elementary	Fountain Valley
51	23.8	Rim of the World Unified	Lake Arrowhead
53	23.7	Delano Joint Union High	Delano
53	23.7	Yucaipa-Calimesa Jt. Unified	Yucaipa
55	23.6	Central Elementary	Rcho Cucamong
55	23.6	Compton Unified	Compton
55	23.6	Jurupa Unified	Riverside
55	23.6	Las Virgenes Unified	Calabasas
55	23.6	Livermore Valley Joint Unified	Livermore
55	23.6	San Marcos Unified	San Marcos
55	23.6	Southern Kern Unified	Rosamond
62	23.5	Centinela Valley Union High	Lawndale
62	23.5	Fremont Union High	Sunnyvale
62	23.5	Garden Grove Unified	Garden Grove
62	23.5	Merced Union High	Atwater
62	23.5	Placer Union High	Auburn
62	23.5	Ramona City Unified	Ramona
62	23.5	Romoland Elementary	Homeland
62	23.5	Sonora Union High	Sonora
62	23.5	Tustin Unified	Tustin
71	23.3	Apple Valley Unified	Apple Valley
71	23.3	Fontana Unified	Fontana
71	23.3	Fullerton Elementary	Fullerton
71	23.3	Glendora Unified	Glendora
71	23.3	Los Alamitos Unified	Los Alamitos
71	23.3	Oro Grande Elementary	Oro Grande
77	23.2	Downey Unified	Downey
77	23.2	El Centro Elementary	El Centro
77	23.2	Irvine Unified	Irvine
77	23.2	La Canada Unified	La Canada
77	23.2	Riverside Unified	Riverside
77	23.2	Salinas Union High	Salinas
83	23.1	Jamul-Dulzura Union Elementary	Jamul
83	23.1	Lowell Joint	Whittier
85	23.0	Amador County Unified	Jackson
85	23.0	Bonita Unified	San Dimas
85	23.0	Capistrano Unified	San Juan Capis
85	23.0	Center Joint Unified	Antelope
85	23.0	Lamont Elementary	Lamont
85	23.0	Rialto Unified	Rialto
85	23.0	West Covina Unified	West Covina
92	22.9	Coalinga-Huron Joint Unified	Coalinga
92	22.9	Kern Union High	Bakersfield
92	22.9	Lake Tahoe Unified	S Lake Tahoe
92	22.9	Los Gatos-Saratoga Jt Union High	Los Gatos
92	22.9	Newhall Elementary	Valencia
92	22.9	Pomona Unified	Pomona
92	22.9	Santa Barbara High	Santa Barbara
92	22.9	Santa Rita Union Elementary	Salinas
92	22.9	Santa Rosa High	Santa Rosa
92	22.9	Upland Unified	Upland
92	22.9	Westwood Unified	Westwood
103	22.8	Alvord Unified	Riverside
103	22.8	Arcadia Unified	Arcadia
103	22.8	Buena Park Elementary	Buena Park
103	22.8	Grant Joint Union High	Sacramento
103	22.8	Rosedale Union Elementary	Bakersfield
103	22.8	San Jacinto Unified	San Jacinto
109	22.7	Colton Joint Unified	Colton
109	22.7	Cotati-Rohnert Park Unified	Rohnert Park
109	22.7	Covina-Valley Unified	Covina
109	22.7	Orcutt Union Elementary	Orcutt
109	22.7	Placentia-Yorba Linda Unified	Placentia
109	22.7	Turlock Joint Union High	Turlock
115	22.6	Eastside Union Elementary	Lancaster
115	22.6	Jefferson Union High	Daly City
115	22.6	Menifee Union Elementary	Menifee
115	22.6	Moreno Valley Unified	Moreno Valley
115	22.6	Murrieta Valley Unified	Murrieta
115	22.6	Nevada Joint Union High	Grass Valley
115	22.6	Norwalk-La Mirada Unified	Norwalk
115	22.6	Ontario-Montclair Elementary	Ontario
115	22.6	Palo Verde Unified	Blythe
115	22.6	Petaluma Joint Union High	Petaluma
115	22.6	Simi Valley Unified	Simi Valley
115	22.6	Ventura Unified	Ventura
115	22.6	Vista Unified	Vista
128	22.5	ABC Unified	Cerritos
128	22.5	Acton-Agua Dulce Unified	Acton
128	22.5	Bellflower Unified	Bellflower
128	22.5	Earlimart Elementary	Earlimart
128	22.5	Lake Elsinore Unified	Lake Elsinore
128	22.5	Lennox Elementary	Lennox
128	22.5	Redlands Unified	Redlands
128	22.5	Santee Elementary	Santee
128	22.5	Walnut Valley Unified	Walnut
137	22.4	Conejo Valley Unified	Thousand Oaks
137	22.4	Etiwanda Elementary	Etiwanda
137	22.4	Rio Elementary	Oxnard
140	22.3	Beaumont Unified	Beaumont
140	22.3	Brea-Olinda Unified	Brea
140	22.3	Escalon Unified	Escalon
140	22.3	Fallbrook Union High	Fallbrook
140	22.3	Manteca Unified	Manteca
140	22.3	Poway Unified	Poway
140	22.3	Roseville Joint Union High	Roseville
147	22.2	Alhambra City Elementary	Alhambra
147	22.2	Delano Union Elementary	Delano
147	22.2	North Monterey County Unified	Moss Landing
147	22.2	Nuview Union Elementary	Nuevo
147	22.2	Pacifica SD	Pacifica
147	22.2	Rowland Unified	Rowland Heights
147	22.2	Santa Ana Unified	Santa Ana
147	22.2	South Whittier Elementary	Whittier
147	22.2	Temple City Unified	Temple City
156	22.1	Cajon Valley Union Elementary	El Cajon
156	22.1	Calexico Unified	Calexico
156	22.1	Claremont Unified	Claremont
156	22.1	Little Lake City Elementary	Santa Fe Spgs
156	22.1	Sweetwater Union High	Chula Vista
156	22.1	Templeton Unified	Templeton
156	22.1	Torrance Unified	Torrance
156	22.1	Visalia Unified	Visalia
164	22.0	Acalanes Union High	Lafayette
164	22.0	Bassett Unified	La Puente
164	22.0	Carlsbad Unified	Carlsbad
164	22.0	East Side Union High	San Jose
164	22.0	El Dorado Union High	Placerville
164	22.0	Evergreen Elementary	San Jose
164	22.0	Jefferson Elementary	Daly City
164	22.0	Konocti Unified	Lower Lake
164	22.0	Long Beach Unified	Long Beach
164	22.0	National Elementary	National City
174	21.9	Bear Valley Unified	Big Bear Lake
174	21.9	Burbank Unified	Burbank
174	21.9	Coachella Valley Unified	Thermal
174	21.9	Desert Sands Unified	La Quinta
174	21.9	Glendale Unified	Glendale
174	21.9	Hemet Unified	Hemet
174	21.9	Mojave Unified	Mojave
174	21.9	San Bruno Park Elementary	San Bruno
174	21.9	Soledad Unified	Soledad
183	21.8	Cucamonga Elementary	Rcho Cucamong
183	21.8	Delhi Unified	Delhi
183	21.8	Dry Creek Joint Elementary	Roseville
183	21.8	Hacienda La Puente Unified	City of Industry
183	21.8	Hawthorne Elementary	Hawthorne
183	21.8	Healdsburg Unified	Healdsburg
183	21.8	Imperial Unified	Imperial
183	21.8	Lawndale Elementary	Lawndale
183	21.8	Milpitas Unified	Milpitas
183	21.8	Oakdale Joint Unified	Oakdale
183	21.8	Palos Verdes Peninsula Unified	Palos Verdes Est
183	21.8	Pleasant Valley School	Camarillo
183	21.8	South San Francisco Unified	S San Francisco
183	21.8	West Sonoma County Union High	Sebastopol
197	21.7	Auburn Union Elementary	Auburn
197	21.7	Azusa Unified	Azusa
197	21.7	Buckeye Union Elementary	Shingle Springs
197	21.7	Culver City Unified	Culver City
197	21.7	Duarte Unified	Duarte
197	21.7	El Rancho Unified	Pico Rivera
197	21.7	El Segundo Unified	El Segundo
197	21.7	Fairfax Elementary	Bakersfield
197	21.7	Fallbrook Union Elementary	Fallbrook
197	21.7	Fremont Unified	Fremont
197	21.7	Keppel Union Elementary	Pearblossom
197	21.7	Laguna Beach Unified	Laguna Beach
197	21.7	Lakeside Union Elementary	Lakeside
197	21.7	Lancaster Elementary	Lancaster
197	21.7	Merced City Elementary	Merced
197	21.7	Morgan Hill Unified	Morgan Hill
197	21.7	Ojai Unified	Ojai
197	21.7	San Gabriel Unified	San Gabriel
197	21.7	Sulphur Springs Union Elementary	Canyon Country
216	21.6	Antioch Unified	Antioch
216	21.6	Ceres Unified	Ceres
216	21.6	Clovis Unified	Clovis
216	21.6	Cupertino Union School	Cupertino
216	21.6	Folsom-Cordova Unified	Folsom
216	21.6	Kerman Unified	Kerman
216	21.6	La Habra City Elementary	La Habra
216	21.6	Newport-Mesa Unified	Costa Mesa
216	21.6	Paramount Unified	Paramount
216	21.6	San Lorenzo Valley Unified	Ben Lomond
216	21.6	Savanna Elementary	Anaheim
227	21.5	Barstow Unified	Barstow
227	21.5	Cabrillo Unified	Half Moon Bay
227	21.5	Castaic Union Elementary	Valencia
227	21.5	Castro Valley Unified	Castro Valley

227	21.5	Eureka Union Elementary	Granite Bay
227	21.5	Julian Union Elementary	Julian
227	21.5	Los Banos Unified	Los Banos
227	21.5	Los Nietos Elementary	Whittier
227	21.5	Mountain View Elementary	Ontario
227	21.5	Newark Unified	Newark
227	21.5	Oxnard Elementary	Oxnard
227	21.5	Rosemead Elementary	Rosemead
227	21.5	San Bernardino City Unified	San Bernardino
227	21.5	Temecula Valley Unified	Temecula
227	21.5	Westside Union Elementary	Lancaster
242	21.4	Anaheim Elementary	Anaheim
242	21.4	Central Unified	Fresno
242	21.4	Fruitvale Elementary	Bakersfield
242	21.4	Moorpark Unified	Moorpark
242	21.4	Natomas Unified	Sacramento
242	21.4	Porterville Unified	Porterville
242	21.4	San Marino Unified	San Marino
242	21.4	San Ramon Valley Unified	Danville
242	21.4	San Ysidro Elementary	San Ysidro
242	21.4	Santa Clara Unified	Santa Clara
242	21.4	Stanislaus Union Elementary	Modesto
242	21.4	Tracy Joint Unified	Tracy
254	21.3	Berryessa Union Elementary	San Jose
254	21.3	Coronado Unified	Coronado
254	21.3	Dinuba Unified	Dinuba
254	21.3	Dixon Unified	Dixon
254	21.3	Fillmore Unified	Fillmore
254	21.3	Hueneme Elementary	Port Hueneme
254	21.3	Monrovia Unified	Monrovia
254	21.3	Northern Humboldt Union High	McKinleyville
254	21.3	Oak Park Unified	Oak Park
254	21.3	Pleasanton Unified	Pleasanton
254	21.3	Santa Maria-Bonita Elementary	Santa Maria
254	21.3	Saugus Union Elementary	Santa Clarita
254	21.3	Standard Elementary	Bakersfield
267	21.2	Centralia Elementary	Buena Park
267	21.2	Chowchilla Elementary	Chowchilla
267	21.2	Galt Joint Union High	Galt
267	21.2	Gilroy Unified	Gilroy
267	21.2	Lemoore Union High	Lemoore
267	21.2	Live Oak Unified	Live Oak
267	21.2	Ocean View Elementary	Huntington Bch
267	21.2	Patterson Joint Unified	Patterson
267	21.2	Vallejo City Unified	Vallejo
267	21.2	Westminster Elementary	Westminster
277	21.1	Corona-Norco Unified	Norco
277	21.1	Encinitas Union Elementary	Encinitas
277	21.1	Exeter Union Elementary	Exeter
277	21.1	La Mesa-Spring Valley	La Mesa
277	21.1	Morongo Unified	Twentynine Plms
277	21.1	Orange Unified	Orange
277	21.1	Palm Springs Unified	Palm Springs
277	21.1	Pasadena Unified	Pasadena
277	21.1	Scotts Valley Unified	Scotts Valley
277	21.1	Willows Unified	Willows
287	21.0	Cypress Elementary	Cypress
287	21.0	Inglewood Unified	Inglewood
287	21.0	Los Angeles Unified	Los Angeles
287	21.0	Mountain View Elementary	El Monte
287	21.0	Oceanside Unified	Oceanside
287	21.0	Pacific Grove Unified	Pacific Grove
287	21.0	Redondo Beach Unified	Redondo Beach
287	21.0	San Juan Unified	Carmichael
287	21.0	Sierra Sands Unified	Ridgecrest
296	20.9	Bakersfield City Elementary	Bakersfield
296	20.9	Corning Union Elementary	Corning
296	20.9	Elk Grove Unified	Elk Grove
296	20.9	Fairfield-Suisun Unified	Fairfield
296	20.9	Hughson Unified	Hughson
296	20.9	Lemon Grove Elementary	Lemon Grove
296	20.9	Red Bluff Joint Union High	Red Bluff
296	20.9	Redding Elementary	Redding
296	20.9	San Carlos Elementary	San Carlos
296	20.9	San Mateo Union High	San Mateo
296	20.9	Santa Monica-Malibu Unified	Santa Monica
296	20.9	Sequoia Union High	Redwood City
296	20.9	South Bay Union Elementary	Imperial Beach
296	20.9	Union Elementary	San Jose
296	20.9	Yuba City Unified	Yuba City
311	20.8	Alpine Union Elementary	Alpine
311	20.8	East Whittier City Elementary	Whittier
311	20.8	Garvey Elementary	Rosemead
311	20.8	Hanford Elementary	Hanford
311	20.8	Madera Unified	Madera
311	20.8	Mt. Pleasant Elementary	San Jose
311	20.8	Oak Grove Elementary	San Jose
311	20.8	Red Bluff Union Elementary	Red Bluff
311	20.8	Rocklin Unified	Rocklin
311	20.8	San Luis Coastal Unified	San Luis Obispo
311	20.8	Wasco Union Elementary	Wasco
322	20.7	Albany City Unified	Albany
322	20.7	Atwater Elementary	Atwater
322	20.7	Burton Elementary	Porterville
322	20.7	Cutler-Orosi Joint Unified	Orosi
322	20.7	Fresno Unified	Fresno
322	20.7	Martinez Unified	Martinez
322	20.7	Marysville Joint Unified	Marysville
322	20.7	New Haven Unified	Union City
322	20.7	Norris Elementary	Bakersfield
322	20.7	Pittsburg Unified	Pittsburg
322	20.7	Pleasant Ridge Union Elementary	Grass Valley
322	20.7	Rescue Union Elementary	Rescue
322	20.7	Ripon Unified	Ripon
322	20.7	San Leandro Unified	San Leandro
322	20.7	Selma Unified	Selma
322	20.7	Sonoma Valley Unified	Sonoma
322	20.7	Tulare City Elementary	Tulare
339	20.6	Benicia Unified	Benicia
339	20.6	Black Oak Mine Unified	Georgetown
339	20.6	Carpinteria Unified	Carpinteria
339	20.6	Del Paso Heights Elementary	Sacramento
339	20.6	El Monte City Elementary	El Monte
339	20.6	Grossmont Union High	La Mesa
339	20.6	Kings Canyon Joint Unified	Reedley
339	20.6	Loomis Union Elementary	Loomis
339	20.6	Mendota Unified	Mendota
339	20.6	Mother Lode Union Elementary	Placerville
339	20.6	Perris Elementary	Perris
339	20.6	Roseville City Elementary	Roseville
339	20.6	Snowline Joint Unified	Phelan
339	20.6	Vacaville Unified	Vacaville
339	20.6	Whittier City Elementary	Whittier
339	20.6	Woodland Joint Unified	Woodland
355	20.5	Corcoran Joint Unified	Corcoran
355	20.5	Firebaugh-Las Deltas Joint Unified	Firebaugh
355	20.5	Fowler Unified	Fowler
355	20.5	Kingsburg Elementary Charter	Kingsburg
355	20.5	Lucia Mar Unified	Arroyo Grande
355	20.5	Moraga Elementary	Moraga
355	20.5	Moreland Elementary	San Jose
355	20.5	Mountain View-Los Altos Union High	Mountain View
355	20.5	Paso Robles Joint Unified	Paso Robles
355	20.5	Saratoga Union Elementary	Saratoga
355	20.5	Windsor Unified	Windsor
366	20.4	Beardsley Elementary	Bakersfield
366	20.4	Brentwood Union Elementary	Brentwood
366	20.4	Calaveras Unified	San Andreas
366	20.4	Davis Joint Unified	Davis
366	20.4	Greenfield Union Elementary	Bakersfield
366	20.4	Holtville Unified	Holtville
366	20.4	John Swett Unified	Crockett
366	20.4	Lincoln Unified	Stockton
366	20.4	Live Oak Elementary	Santa Cruz
366	20.4	Manhattan Beach Unified	Manhattan Beach
366	20.4	Mountain View-Whisman Elementary	Mountain View
366	20.4	Napa Valley Unified	Napa
366	20.4	Novato Unified	Novato
366	20.4	San Lorenzo Unified	San Lorenzo
366	20.4	Turlock Joint Elementary	Turlock
366	20.4	Wilsona Elementary	Palmdale
366	20.4	Wiseburn Elementary	Hawthorne
383	20.3	Cambrian Elementary	San Jose
383	20.3	Campbell Union Elementary	Campbell
383	20.3	Chico Unified	Chico
383	20.3	Empire Union Elementary	Modesto
383	20.3	Escondido Union Elementary	Escondido
383	20.3	Millbrae Elementary	Millbrae
383	20.3	Modesto City Elementary	Modesto
383	20.3	Monterey Peninsula Unified	Monterey
383	20.3	Panama Buena Vista Union Elem	Bakersfield
383	20.3	Richland Union Elementary SD	Shafter
383	20.3	San Rafael City High	San Rafael
383	20.3	Sylvan Union Elementary	Modesto
395	20.2	Atascadero Unified	Atascadero
395	20.2	Bonsall Union Elementary	Bonsall
395	20.2	Hollister SD	Hollister
395	20.2	Livingston Union Elementary	Livingston
395	20.2	Lodi Unified	Lodi
395	20.2	Muroc Joint Unified	North Edwards
401	20.1	Hayward Unified	Hayward
401	20.1	Lompoc Unified	Lompoc
401	20.1	Magnolia Elementary	Anaheim
401	20.1	Old Adobe Union Elementary	Petaluma
401	20.1	River Delta Joint Unified	Rio Vista
401	20.1	Riverbank Unified	Riverbank
401	20.1	Salinas City Elementary	Salinas
401	20.1	San Mateo-Foster City Elementary	San Mateo
409	20.0	Del Norte County Unified	Crescent City
409	20.0	Enterprise Elementary	Redding
409	20.0	Jefferson Elementary	Tracy
409	20.0	Lemoore Union Elementary	Lemoore
409	20.0	Lindsay Unified	Lindsay
409	20.0	Mcfarland Unified	Mcfarland
409	20.0	Mountain Empire Unified	Pine Valley
409	20.0	Mt. Diablo Unified	Concord
409	20.0	Oakley Union Elementary	Oakley
409	20.0	Reef-Sunset Unified	Avenal
419	19.9	Alum Rock Union Elementary	San Jose
419	19.9	Goleta Union Elementary	Goleta
419	19.9	Salida Union Elementary	Salida
419	19.9	San Jose Unified	San Jose
419	19.9	Taft City Elementary	Taft
419	19.9	Walnut Creek Elementary	Walnut Creek
419	19.9	Waterford Unified	Waterford
419	19.9	Woodlake Union Elementary	Woodlake
427	19.8	Dublin Unified	Dublin
427	19.8	Franklin-Mckinley Elementary	San Jose
427	19.8	Los Altos Elementary	Los Altos
427	19.8	Oakland Unified	Oakland
427	19.8	Orland Joint Unified	Orland
427	19.8	Piner-Olivet Union Elementary	Santa Rosa
427	19.8	Ravenswood City Elementary	East Palo Alto
427	19.8	Riverdale Joint Unified	Riverdale
427	19.8	Santa Barbara Elementary	Santa Barbara
427	19.8	Sunnyvale Elementary	Sunnyvale
427	19.8	West Contra Costa Unified	Richmond
438	19.7	Arvin Union Elementary	Arvin
438	19.7	Cloverdale Unified	Cloverdale
438	19.7	Ocean View Elementary	Oxnard
438	19.7	Sanger Unified	Sanger
438	19.7	Soquel Union Elementary	Capitola
438	19.7	Stockton City Unified	Stockton
438	19.7	Wheatland Elementary	Wheatland
445	19.6	Belmont-Redwood Shores Elementary	Belmont
445	19.6	Cascade Union Elementary	Anderson
445	19.6	Chula Vista Elementary	Chula Vista
445	19.6	King City Union Elementary	King City
445	19.6	Lakeport Unified	Lakeport
445	19.6	Linden Unified	Linden
445	19.6	Mark West Union Elementary	Santa Rosa
445	19.6	Oroville City Elementary	Oroville
445	19.6	Pajaro Valley Unified School	Watsonville
445	19.6	Petaluma City Elementary	Petaluma
445	19.6	Sacramento City Unified	Sacramento
456	19.5	Dos Palos Oro Loma Jt. Unified	Dos Palos
456	19.5	Farmersville Unified	Farmersville
456	19.5	Gustine Unified	Gustine
456	19.5	Middletown Unified	Middletown
456	19.5	Rincon Valley Union Elementary	Santa Rosa
456	19.5	Winton Elementary	Winton
462	19.4	Berkeley Unified	Berkeley
462	19.4	Ukiah Unified	Ukiah
464	19.3	Gonzales Unified	Gonzales
464	19.3	Hilmar Unified	Hilmar
464	19.3	Silver Valley Unified	Yermo
464	19.3	Valley Center-Pauma Unified	Valley Center
468	19.2	Keyes Union Elementary	Keyes
468	19.2	Paradise Unified	Paradise
468	19.2	Travis Unified	Travis Afb
471	19.1	Bellevue Union Elementary	Santa Rosa
471	19.1	Eureka City Unified	Eureka
471	19.1	Gridley Unified	Gridley
471	19.1	Los Gatos Union Elementary	Los Gatos
471	19.1	Newman-Crows Landing Unified	Newman
471	19.1	Rio Linda Union Elementary	Rio Linda
477	19.0	Alameda City Unified	Alameda
477	19.0	Dixie Elementary	San Rafael
479	18.9	Kelseyville Unified	Kelseyville
479	18.9	Lafayette Elementary	Lafayette
479	18.9	Plumas Unified	Quincy
479	18.9	Ross Valley Elementary	San Anselmo
479	18.9	Twin Ridges Elementary	North San Juan
479	18.9	Winters Joint Unified	Winters
485	18.8	Burlingame Elementary	Burlingame
485	18.8	Grass Valley Elementary	Grass Valley
485	18.8	Mariposa County Unified	Mariposa
485	18.8	Orinda Union Elementary	Orinda
489	18.7	Washington Unified	West Sacramento
490	18.6	Gateway Unified	Redding
490	18.6	San Diego Unified	San Diego
490	18.6	Santa Cruz City Elementary	Soquel
490	18.6	Tahoe-Truckee Joint Unified	Truckee
494	18.5	Robla Elementary	Sacramento
495	18.4	Parlier Unified	Parlier
495	18.4	San Francisco Unified	San Francisco
497	18.3	Beverly Hills Unified	Beverly Hills
497	18.3	Tamalpais Union High	Larkspur
499	18.2	Brawley Elementary	Brawley
500	18.1	Golden Plains Unified	San Joaquin
500	18.1	Sierra Unified	Prather
500	18.1	Weaver Union Elementary	Merced
503	17.9	Del Mar Union Elementary	Del Mar
503	17.9	Mill Valley Elementary	Mill Valley
503	17.9	Orange County Office of Education	Costa Mesa
503	17.9	Solana Beach Elementary	Solana Beach
503	17.9	Willits Unified	Willits
508	17.7	Central Union Elementary	Lemoore

508	17.7	Galt Joint Union Elementary	Galt
508	17.7	North Sacramento Elementary	Sacramento
511	17.5	San Rafael City Elementary	San Rafael
512	17.2	Santa Rosa Elementary	Santa Rosa
513	17.1	Carmel Unified	Carmel
513	17.1	Fort Bragg Unified	Fort Bragg
513	17.1	Piedmont City Unified	Piedmont
513	17.1	Redwood City Elementary	Redwood City
517	16.9	Palo Alto Unified	Palo Alto
518	16.7	Menlo Park City Elementary	Atherton
519	15.5	San Joaquin Co Off of Education	Stockton
520	15.2	Julian Union High	Julian
521	13.4	Kern County Office of Education	Bakersfield
522	12.8	Riverside Co Office of Education	Riverside
523	12.7	San Diego Co Office of Education	San Diego
524	12.5	Tulare County Office of Education	Visalia
525	11.8	Los Angeles Co Office of Education	Downey
526	11.2	Fresno County Office of Education	Fresno
527	11.1	San Bernardino Co Off of Education	San Bernardino
528	8.8	Santa Clara Co Off of Education	San Jose

Student/Librarian Ratio

Rank	Ratio	District Name	City
1	69,746.7	Jurupa Unified	Riverside
2	67,213.3	Escondido Union Elementary	Escondido
3	54,235.0	Lucia Mar Unified	Arroyo Grande
4	49,746.0	Capistrano Unified	San Juan Capis
5	41,343.0	Fontana Unified	Fontana
6	36,046.7	Antioch Unified	Antioch
7	23,272.0	Oak Grove Elementary	San Jose
8	22,588.0	Etiwanda Elementary	Etiwanda
9	20,083.3	North Monterey County Unified	Moss Landing
10	19,287.0	Baldwin Park Unified	Baldwin Park
11	19,272.7	San Bernardino City Unified	San Bernardino
12	18,384.0	Rowland Unified	Rowland Heights
13	16,687.5	Santa Maria Joint Union High	Santa Maria
14	16,243.0	Compton Unified	Compton
15	14,765.3	Antelope Valley Union High	Lancaster
16	14,621.0	Coachella Valley Unified	Thermal
17	14,544.6	San Juan Unified	Carmichael
18	13,963.0	Panama Buena Vista Union Elem	Bakersfield
19	13,887.0	Vacaville Unified	Vacaville
20	13,585.0	Upland Unified	Upland
21	12,749.5	Hacienda La Puente Unified	City of Industry
22	12,629.0	Visalia Unified	Visalia
23	12,574.8	Santa Ana Unified	Santa Ana
24	12,557.0	Whittier Union High	Whittier
25	12,556.4	Fullerton Elementary	Fullerton
26	11,829.0	Los Angeles Co Office of Education	Downey
27	11,113.3	Chino Valley Unified	Chino
28	10,999.5	Corona-Norco Unified	Norco
29	10,863.5	Simi Valley Unified	Simi Valley
30	10,656.3	Los Angeles Unified	Los Angeles
31	10,621.0	Alameda City Unified	Alameda
32	10,192.0	Mountain View Elementary	El Monte
33	9,992.0	Arcadia Unified	Arcadia
34	9,970.0	Rio Linda Union Elementary	Rio Linda
35	9,918.0	Beaumont Unified	Beaumont
36	9,829.0	Lynwood Unified	Lynwood
37	9,591.0	Pittsburg Unified	Pittsburg
38	9,475.0	Tustin Unified	Tustin
39	8,924.7	Placentia-Yorba Linda Unified	Placentia
40	8,880.0	Morgan Hill Unified	Morgan Hill
41	8,853.0	Pomona Unified	Pomona
42	8,837.3	Saddleback Valley Unified	Mission Viejo
43	8,570.0	Bear Valley Unified	Big Bear Lake
44	8,409.7	Torrance Unified	Torrance
45	8,406.2	Oakland Unified	Oakland
46	8,152.0	Grossmont Union High	La Mesa
47	8,057.0	Redondo Beach Unified	Redondo Beach
48	7,951.0	Alisal Union Elementary	Salinas
49	7,924.0	Glendora Unified	Glendora
50	7,910.0	Placer Union High	Auburn
51	7,832.0	Temecula Valley Unified	Temecula
52	7,421.0	Newark Unified	Newark
53	7,414.3	Conejo Valley Unified	Thousand Oaks
54	7,405.6	Fremont Unified	Fremont
55	7,301.4	Tracy Joint Unified	Tracy
56	7,294.5	San Marcos Unified	San Marcos
57	7,234.7	Victor Valley Union High	Victorville
58	7,196.7	Natomas Unified	Sacramento
59	7,127.5	Temple City Unified	Temple City
60	7,110.0	Charter Oak Unified	Covina
61	7,046.7	Live Oak Elementary	Santa Cruz
62	7,019.5	Pleasanton Unified	Pleasanton
63	7,010.0	Barstow Unified	Barstow
64	7,002.5	Sierra Sands Unified	Ridgecrest
65	6,850.0	Culver City Unified	Culver City
66	6,846.0	Claremont Unified	Claremont
67	6,842.0	Washington Unified	West Sacramento
68	6,828.0	Ukiah Unified	Ukiah
69	6,631.4	Lodi Unified	Lodi
70	6,578.0	Monrovia Unified	Monrovia
71	6,530.5	Desert Sands Unified	La Quinta
72	6,441.0	Manhattan Beach Unified	Manhattan Beach
73	6,082.0	Selma Unified	Selma
74	5,838.0	Shasta Union High	Redding
75	5,826.7	Murrieta Valley Unified	Murrieta
76	5,796.7	Sanger Unified	Sanger
77	5,779.5	Lompoc Unified	Lompoc
78	5,749.0	Madera Unified	Madera
79	5,718.2	Porterville Unified	Porterville
80	5,674.3	Napa Valley Unified	Napa
81	5,656.8	Manteca Unified	Manteca
82	5,621.0	Oceanside Unified	Oceanside
83	5,618.0	Rim of the World Unified	Lake Arrowhead
84	5,542.0	Dinuba Unified	Dinuba
85	5,541.3	Colton Joint Unified	Colton
86	5,517.0	Atascadero Unified	Atascadero
87	5,504.8	Chico Unified	Chico
88	5,257.5	Woodland Joint Unified	Woodland
89	5,105.5	Ceres Unified	Ceres
90	5,101.5	Bonita Unified	San Dimas
91	5,084.8	Poway Unified	Poway
92	5,040.0	Black Oak Mine Unified	Georgetown
93	5,009.4	Lincoln Unified	Stockton
94	4,991.7	Huntington Beach Union High	Huntington Bch
95	4,935.4	Stockton City Unified	Stockton
96	4,850.6	Bellflower Unified	Bellflower
97	4,835.9	Elk Grove Unified	Elk Grove
98	4,832.0	Tehachapi Unified	Tehachapi
99	4,770.0	La Mesa-Spring Valley	La Mesa
100	4,764.0	Atwater Elementary	Atwater
100	4,764.0	Milpitas Unified	Milpitas
102	4,681.0	South San Francisco Unified	S San Francisco
103	4,668.0	Riverside Unified	Riverside
104	4,653.3	Vista Unified	Vista
105	4,614.0	Red Bluff Union Elementary	Red Bluff
106	4,533.8	Pasadena Unified	Pasadena
107	4,533.5	Kings Canyon Joint Unified	Reedley
108	4,515.0	Gateway Unified	Redding
109	4,494.0	Montebello Unified	Montebello
110	4,483.0	Dublin Unified	Dublin
111	4,407.0	Patterson Joint Unified	Patterson
112	4,347.3	Rialto Unified	Rialto
113	4,343.0	La Canada Unified	La Canada
114	4,308.5	Orange County Office of Education	Costa Mesa
115	4,298.3	Irvine Unified	Irvine
116	4,292.0	Nevada Joint Union High	Grass Valley
117	4,279.0	Buckeye Union Elementary	Shingle Springs
118	4,232.0	Rosedale Union Elementary	Bakersfield
119	4,195.5	Castro Valley Unified	Castro Valley
120	4,128.6	Redlands Unified	Redlands
121	4,123.3	Kerman Unified	Kerman
122	4,066.0	Empire Union Elementary	Modesto
123	4,052.5	Lawndale Elementary	Lawndale
124	3,947.4	Campbell Union High	San Jose
125	3,947.0	Central Union High	El Centro
126	3,929.0	Dixon Unified	Dixon
127	3,895.3	Modesto City High	Modesto
128	3,892.4	Vallejo City Unified	Vallejo
129	3,883.8	Carlsbad Unified	Carlsbad
130	3,851.4	Clovis Unified	Clovis
131	3,839.0	Soledad Unified	Soledad
132	3,827.8	Salinas Union High	Salinas
133	3,775.6	Sacramento City Unified	Sacramento
134	3,753.8	Downey Unified	Downey
135	3,741.0	Cotati-Rohnert Park Unified	Rohnert Park
136	3,720.0	Riverside Co Office of Education	Riverside
137	3,668.4	Rocklin Unified	Rocklin
138	3,633.0	Cabrillo Unified	Half Moon Bay
139	3,608.0	Ramona City Unified	Ramona
140	3,593.8	Inglewood Unified	Inglewood
141	3,586.0	Lindsay Unified	Lindsay
142	3,539.5	Fresno Unified	Fresno
143	3,539.4	Bakersfield City Elementary	Bakersfield
144	3,514.0	San Diego Co Office of Education	San Diego
145	3,500.0	San Rafael City Elementary	San Rafael
146	3,466.3	Monterey Peninsula Unified	Monterey
147	3,435.9	West Contra Costa Unified	Richmond
148	3,389.0	Lafayette Elementary	Lafayette
149	3,372.3	Chula Vista Elementary	Chula Vista
150	3,371.8	Orange Unified	Orange
151	3,328.1	San Leandro Unified	San Leandro
152	3,295.6	Mcfarland Unified	Mcfarland
153	3,282.2	Hemet Unified	Hemet
154	3,279.6	Fullerton Joint Union High	Fullerton
155	3,266.0	San Marino Unified	San Marino
156	3,253.8	Grant Joint Union High	Sacramento
157	3,240.2	Alvord Unified	Riverside
158	3,214.1	Palm Springs Unified	Palm Springs
159	3,210.5	Santa Monica-Malibu Unified	Santa Monica
160	3,198.0	Oroville City Elementary	Oroville
161	3,197.6	Newport-Mesa Unified	Costa Mesa
162	3,196.0	El Segundo Unified	El Segundo
163	3,149.2	Oxnard Union High	Oxnard
164	3,135.8	Garden Grove Unified	Garden Grove
165	3,135.2	Garvey Elementary	Rosemead
166	3,132.5	San Gabriel Unified	San Gabriel
167	3,132.0	Center Joint Unified	Antelope
168	3,067.9	Ventura Unified	Ventura
169	3,017.4	William S. Hart Union High	Santa Clarita
170	3,002.0	San Benito High	Hollister
171	2,980.3	Yuba City Unified	Yuba City
172	2,978.0	Richland Union Elementary SD	Shafter
173	2,962.8	Central Unified	Fresno
174	2,917.6	Chaffey Joint Union High	Ontario
175	2,876.9	San Mateo-Foster City Elementary	San Mateo
176	2,850.7	Alhambra City High	Alhambra
177	2,815.5	San Diego Unified	San Diego
178	2,779.1	San Francisco Unified	San Francisco
179	2,761.8	Sylvan Union Elementary	Modesto
180	2,720.0	Eastside Union Elementary	Lancaster
181	2,705.7	Anaheim Union High	Anaheim
182	2,674.3	Roseville Joint Union High	Roseville
183	2,654.5	Paradise Unified	Paradise
184	2,625.4	San Bernardino Co Off of Education	San Bernardino
185	2,622.5	Lemoore Union High	Lemoore
186	2,581.0	Los Gatos Union Elementary	Los Gatos
187	2,570.9	Los Banos Unified	Los Banos
188	2,554.0	Delhi Unified	Delhi
189	2,543.0	Wheatland Elementary	Wheatland
190	2,535.4	Las Virgenes Unified	Calabasas
191	2,514.0	Firebaugh-Las Deltas Joint Unified	Firebaugh
192	2,505.8	Covina-Valley Unified	Covina
193	2,499.3	Perris Union High	Perris
194	2,460.5	Sonoma Valley Unified	Sonoma
195	2,456.4	Berkeley Unified	Berkeley
196	2,443.1	San Ramon Valley Unified	Danville
197	2,433.0	Livingston Union Elementary	Livingston
198	2,413.0	Saratoga Union Elementary	Saratoga
199	2,399.0	Liberty Union High	Brentwood
200	2,386.0	Gonzales Unified	Gonzales
201	2,376.1	San Luis Coastal Unified	San Luis Obispo
202	2,368.8	Santa Clara Unified	Santa Clara
203	2,356.0	Orland Joint Unified	Orland
204	2,309.4	San Lorenzo Unified	San Lorenzo
205	2,294.5	Tahoe-Truckee Joint Unified	Truckee
206	2,290.5	Eureka City Unified	Eureka
207	2,257.0	Paso Robles Joint Unified	Paso Robles
208	2,240.0	Willits Unified	Willits
209	2,235.0	Fowler Unified	Fowler
210	2,212.0	Jefferson Elementary	Daly City
211	2,178.0	Fresno County Office of Education	Fresno
212	2,175.0	Tulare Joint Union High	Tulare
213	2,168.0	Kingsburg Elementary Charter	Kingsburg
214	2,160.0	Martinez Unified	Martinez
215	2,157.1	Kern Union High	Bakersfield
216	2,112.8	Fairfield-Suisun Unified	Fairfield
217	2,099.5	South Pasadena Unified	South Pasadena
218	2,089.0	Santa Clara Co Off of Education	San Jose
219	2,073.0	Norris Elementary	Bakersfield
220	2,071.3	Albany City Unified	Albany
221	2,050.8	El Monte Union High	El Monte
222	2,036.0	San Rafael City High	San Rafael
223	2,014.1	East Side Union High	San Jose
224	2,012.0	Winters Joint Unified	Winters
225	1,981.4	San Dieguito Union High	Encinitas
226	1,976.5	Santa Rosa High	Santa Rosa
227	1,945.5	Sequoia Union High	Redwood City
228	1,864.4	Merced Union High	Atwater
229	1,864.0	Fremont Union High	Sunnyvale
230	1,861.0	Mountain Empire Unified	Pine Valley
231	1,860.0	Hanford Joint Union High	Hanford
232	1,817.0	Dixie Elementary	San Rafael
233	1,793.3	Travis Unified	Travis Afb
234	1,783.1	Sweetwater Union High	Chula Vista
235	1,729.0	Sonora Union High	Sonora
236	1,720.5	Mountain View-Los Altos Union High	Mountain View
237	1,710.0	Beverly Hills Unified	Beverly Hills
238	1,702.0	Julian Union High	Julian
239	1,662.1	El Dorado Union High	Placerville
240	1,656.0	Tulare County Office of Education	Visalia
241	1,575.0	Riverdale Joint Unified	Riverdale
242	1,569.5	Hayward Unified	Hayward
243	1,514.0	Santa Barbara High	Santa Barbara
244	1,483.5	Petaluma Joint Union High	Petaluma
245	1,480.4	Long Beach Unified	Long Beach
246	1,474.0	Los Gatos-Saratoga Jt Union High	Los Gatos
247	1,446.3	Acalanes Union High	Lafayette
248	1,346.9	San Mateo Union High	San Mateo
249	1,346.0	Jefferson Union High	Daly City
250	1,342.5	Dos Palos Oro Loma Jt. Unified	Dos Palos
251	1,340.2	Davis Joint Unified	Davis
252	1,286.7	Tamalpais Union High	Larkspur
253	1,236.9	Evergreen Elementary	San Jose
254	1,191.0	Anderson Union High	Anderson

255	1,149.0	Novato Unified	Novato
256	1,122.0	Weaver Union Elementary	Merced
257	1,090.5	Carmel Unified	Carmel
258	1,086.4	Santa Cruz City High	Soquel
259	1,047.5	New Haven Unified	Union City
260	1,034.3	Mt. Diablo Unified	Concord
261	968.5	Northern Humboldt Union High	McKinleyville
262	964.3	Modesto City Elementary	Modesto
263	957.5	Pacific Grove Unified	Pacific Grove
264	937.1	Los Alamitos Unified	Los Alamitos
265	875.7	Sierra Unified	Prather
266	717.1	Santa Barbara Elementary	Santa Barbara
267	713.4	Merced City Elementary	Merced
268	694.9	Palo Alto Unified	Palo Alto
269	665.9	Piedmont City Unified	Piedmont
270	593.8	Menlo Park City Elementary	Atherton
271	592.3	Burlingame Elementary	Burlingame
272	573.6	Orinda Union Elementary	Orinda
273	496.9	Mill Valley Elementary	Mill Valley
274	375.3	Santa Cruz City Elementary	Soquel
275	n/a	ABC Unified	Cerritos
275	n/a	Acton-Agua Dulce Unified	Acton
275	n/a	Adelanto Elementary	Adelanto
275	n/a	Alhambra City Elementary	Alhambra
275	n/a	Alpine Union Elementary	Alpine
275	n/a	Alta Loma Elementary	Alta Loma
275	n/a	Alum Rock Union Elementary	San Jose
275	n/a	Amador County Unified	Jackson
275	n/a	Anaheim Elementary	Anaheim
275	n/a	Apple Valley Unified	Apple Valley
275	n/a	Arvin Union Elementary	Arvin
275	n/a	Auburn Union Elementary	Auburn
275	n/a	Azusa Unified	Azusa
275	n/a	Banning Unified	Banning
275	n/a	Bassett Unified	La Puente
275	n/a	Beardsley Elementary	Bakersfield
275	n/a	Bellevue Union Elementary	Santa Rosa
275	n/a	Belmont-Redwood Shores Elementary	Belmont
275	n/a	Benicia Unified	Benicia
275	n/a	Berryessa Union Elementary	San Jose
275	n/a	Bonsall Union Elementary	Bonsall
275	n/a	Brawley Elementary	Brawley
275	n/a	Brawley Union High	Brawley
275	n/a	Brea-Olinda Unified	Brea
275	n/a	Brentwood Union Elementary	Brentwood
275	n/a	Buena Park Elementary	Buena Park
275	n/a	Burbank Unified	Burbank
275	n/a	Burton Elementary	Porterville
275	n/a	Cajon Valley Union Elementary	El Cajon
275	n/a	Calaveras Unified	San Andreas
275	n/a	Calexico Unified	Calexico
275	n/a	Cambrian Elementary	San Jose
275	n/a	Campbell Union Elementary	Campbell
275	n/a	Carpinteria Unified	Carpinteria
275	n/a	Cascade Union Elementary	Anderson
275	n/a	Castaic Union Elementary	Valencia
275	n/a	Centinela Valley Union High	Lawndale
275	n/a	Central Elementary	Rcho Cucamong
275	n/a	Central Union Elementary	Lemoore
275	n/a	Centralia Elementary	Buena Park
275	n/a	Chowchilla Elementary	Chowchilla
275	n/a	Cloverdale Unified	Cloverdale
275	n/a	Coalinga-Huron Joint Unified	Coalinga
275	n/a	Corcoran Joint Unified	Corcoran
275	n/a	Corning Union Elementary	Corning
275	n/a	Coronado Unified	Coronado
275	n/a	Cucamonga Elementary	Rcho Cucamong
275	n/a	Cupertino Union School	Cupertino
275	n/a	Cutler-Orosi Joint Unified	Orosi
275	n/a	Cypress Elementary	Cypress
275	n/a	Del Mar Union Elementary	Del Mar
275	n/a	Del Norte County Unified	Crescent City
275	n/a	Del Paso Heights Elementary	Sacramento
275	n/a	Delano Joint Union High	Delano
275	n/a	Delano Union Elementary	Delano
275	n/a	Dry Creek Joint Elementary	Roseville
275	n/a	Duarte Unified	Duarte
275	n/a	Earlimart Elementary	Earlimart
275	n/a	East Whittier City Elementary	Whittier
275	n/a	El Centro Elementary	El Centro
275	n/a	El Monte City Elementary	El Monte
275	n/a	El Rancho Unified	Pico Rivera
275	n/a	Encinitas Union Elementary	Encinitas
275	n/a	Enterprise Elementary	Redding
275	n/a	Escalon Unified	Escalon
275	n/a	Escondido Union High	Escondido
275	n/a	Eureka Union Elementary	Granite Bay
275	n/a	Exeter Union Elementary	Exeter
275	n/a	Fairfax Elementary	Bakersfield
275	n/a	Fallbrook Union Elementary	Fallbrook
275	n/a	Fallbrook Union High	Fallbrook
275	n/a	Farmersville Unified	Farmersville
275	n/a	Fillmore Unified	Fillmore
275	n/a	Folsom-Cordova Unified	Folsom
275	n/a	Fort Bragg Unified	Fort Bragg
275	n/a	Fountain Valley Elementary	Fountain Valley
275	n/a	Franklin-Mckinley Elementary	San Jose
275	n/a	Fruitvale Elementary	Bakersfield
275	n/a	Galt Joint Union Elementary	Galt
275	n/a	Galt Joint Union High	Galt
275	n/a	Gilroy Unified	Gilroy
275	n/a	Glendale Unified	Glendale
275	n/a	Golden Plains Unified	San Joaquin
275	n/a	Goleta Union Elementary	Goleta
275	n/a	Gorman Elementary	Gorman
275	n/a	Grass Valley Elementary	Grass Valley
275	n/a	Greenfield Union Elementary	Greenfield
275	n/a	Greenfield Union Elementary	Bakersfield
275	n/a	Gridley Unified	Gridley
275	n/a	Gustine Unified	Gustine
275	n/a	Hanford Elementary	Hanford
275	n/a	Hawthorne Elementary	Hawthorne
275	n/a	Healdsburg Unified	Healdsburg
275	n/a	Hesperia Unified	Hesperia
275	n/a	Hilmar Unified	Hilmar
275	n/a	Hollister SD	Hollister
275	n/a	Holtville Unified	Holtville
275	n/a	Hueneme Elementary	Port Hueneme
275	n/a	Hughson Unified	Hughson
275	n/a	Huntington Beach City Elementary	Huntington Bch
275	n/a	Imperial Unified	Imperial
275	n/a	Jamul-Dulzura Union Elementary	Jamul
275	n/a	Jefferson Elementary	Tracy
275	n/a	John Swett Unified	Crockett
275	n/a	Julian Union Elementary	Julian
275	n/a	Kelseyville Unified	Kelseyville
275	n/a	Keppel Union Elementary	Pearblossom
275	n/a	Kern County Office of Education	Bakersfield
275	n/a	Keyes Union Elementary	Keyes
275	n/a	King City Joint Union High	King City
275	n/a	King City Union Elementary	King City
275	n/a	Konocti Unified	Lower Lake
275	n/a	La Habra City Elementary	La Habra
275	n/a	Laguna Beach Unified	Laguna Beach
275	n/a	Lake Elsinore Unified	Lake Elsinore
275	n/a	Lake Tahoe Unified	S Lake Tahoe
275	n/a	Lakeport Unified	Lakeport
275	n/a	Lakeside Union Elementary	Lakeside
275	n/a	Lamont Elementary	Lamont
275	n/a	Lancaster Elementary	Lancaster
275	n/a	Lemon Grove Elementary	Lemon Grove
275	n/a	Lemoore Union Elementary	Lemoore
275	n/a	Lennox Elementary	Lennox
275	n/a	Linden Unified	Linden
275	n/a	Little Lake City Elementary	Santa Fe Spgs
275	n/a	Live Oak Unified	Live Oak
275	n/a	Livermore Valley Joint Unified	Livermore
275	n/a	Loomis Union Elementary	Loomis
275	n/a	Los Altos Elementary	Los Altos
275	n/a	Los Nietos Elementary	Whittier
275	n/a	Lowell Joint	Whittier
275	n/a	Magnolia Elementary	Anaheim
275	n/a	Mariposa County Unified	Mariposa
275	n/a	Mark West Union Elementary	Santa Rosa
275	n/a	Marysville Joint Unified	Marysville
275	n/a	Mendota Unified	Mendota
275	n/a	Menifee Union Elementary	Menifee
275	n/a	Middletown Unified	Middletown
275	n/a	Millbrae Elementary	Millbrae
275	n/a	Mojave Unified	Mojave
275	n/a	Moorpark Unified	Moorpark
275	n/a	Moraga Elementary	Moraga
275	n/a	Moreland Elementary	San Jose
275	n/a	Moreno Valley Unified	Moreno Valley
275	n/a	Morongo Unified	Twentynine Plms
275	n/a	Mother Lode Union Elementary	Placerville
275	n/a	Mountain View Elementary	Ontario
275	n/a	Mountain View-Whisman Elementary	Mountain View
275	n/a	Mt. Pleasant Elementary	San Jose
275	n/a	Muroc Joint Unified	North Edwards
275	n/a	National Elementary	National City
275	n/a	Newhall Elementary	Valencia
275	n/a	Newman-Crows Landing Unified	Newman
275	n/a	North Sacramento Elementary	Sacramento
275	n/a	Norwalk-La Mirada Unified	Norwalk
275	n/a	Nuview Union Elementary	Nuevo
275	n/a	Oak Park Unified	Oak Park
275	n/a	Oakdale Joint Unified	Oakdale
275	n/a	Oakley Union Elementary	Oakley
275	n/a	Ocean View Elementary	Huntington Bch
275	n/a	Ocean View Elementary	Oxnard
275	n/a	Ojai Unified	Ojai
275	n/a	Old Adobe Union Elementary	Petaluma
275	n/a	Ontario-Montclair Elementary	Ontario
275	n/a	Orcutt Union Elementary	Orcutt
275	n/a	Oro Grande Elementary	Oro Grande
275	n/a	Oroville Union High	Oroville
275	n/a	Oxnard Elementary	Oxnard
275	n/a	Pacifica SD	Pacifica
275	n/a	Pajaro Valley Unified School	Watsonville
275	n/a	Palmdale Elementary	Palmdale
275	n/a	Palo Verde Unified	Blythe
275	n/a	Palos Verdes Peninsula Unified	Palos Verdes Est
275	n/a	Paramount Unified	Paramount
275	n/a	Parlier Unified	Parlier
275	n/a	Perris Elementary	Perris
275	n/a	Petaluma City Elementary	Petaluma
275	n/a	Piner-Olivet Union Elementary	Santa Rosa
275	n/a	Pleasant Ridge Union Elementary	Grass Valley
275	n/a	Pleasant Valley School	Camarillo
275	n/a	Plumas Unified	Quincy
275	n/a	Ravenswood City Elementary	East Palo Alto
275	n/a	Red Bluff Joint Union High	Red Bluff
275	n/a	Redding Elementary	Redding
275	n/a	Redwood City Elementary	Redwood City
275	n/a	Reef-Sunset Unified	Avenal
275	n/a	Rescue Union Elementary	Rescue
275	n/a	Rincon Valley Union Elementary	Santa Rosa
275	n/a	Rio Elementary	Oxnard
275	n/a	Ripon Unified	Ripon
275	n/a	River Delta Joint Unified	Rio Vista
275	n/a	Riverbank Unified	Riverbank
275	n/a	Robla Elementary	Sacramento
275	n/a	Romoland Elementary	Homeland
275	n/a	Rosemead Elementary	Rosemead
275	n/a	Roseville City Elementary	Roseville
275	n/a	Ross Valley Elementary	San Anselmo
275	n/a	Salida Union Elementary	Salida
275	n/a	Salinas City Elementary	Salinas
275	n/a	San Bruno Park Elementary	San Bruno
275	n/a	San Carlos Elementary	San Carlos
275	n/a	San Jacinto Unified	San Jacinto
275	n/a	San Joaquin Co Off of Education	Stockton
275	n/a	San Jose Unified	San Jose
275	n/a	San Lorenzo Valley Unified	Ben Lomond
275	n/a	San Ysidro Elementary	San Ysidro
275	n/a	Santa Maria-Bonita Elementary	Santa Maria
275	n/a	Santa Paula Elementary	Santa Paula
275	n/a	Santa Paula Union High	Santa Paula
275	n/a	Santa Rita Union Elementary	Salinas
275	n/a	Santa Rosa Elementary	Santa Rosa
275	n/a	Santee Elementary	Santee
275	n/a	Saugus Union Elementary	Santa Clarita
275	n/a	Savanna Elementary	Anaheim
275	n/a	Scotts Valley Unified	Scotts Valley
275	n/a	Silver Valley Unified	Yermo
275	n/a	Snowline Joint Unified	Phelan
275	n/a	Solana Beach Elementary	Solana Beach
275	n/a	Soquel Union Elementary	Capitola
275	n/a	South Bay Union Elementary	Imperial Beach
275	n/a	South Whittier Elementary	Whittier
275	n/a	Southern Kern Unified	Rosamond
275	n/a	Standard Elementary	Bakersfield
275	n/a	Stanislaus Union Elementary	Modesto
275	n/a	Sulphur Springs Union Elementary	Canyon Country
275	n/a	Sunnyvale Elementary	Sunnyvale
275	n/a	Taft City Elementary	Taft
275	n/a	Templeton Unified	Templeton
275	n/a	Tulare City Elementary	Tulare
275	n/a	Turlock Joint Elementary	Turlock
275	n/a	Turlock Joint Union High	Turlock
275	n/a	Twin Ridges Elementary	North San Juan
275	n/a	Union Elementary	San Jose
275	n/a	Val Verde Unified	Perris
275	n/a	Valley Center-Pauma Unified	Valley Center
275	n/a	Victor Elementary	Victorville
275	n/a	Walnut Creek Elementary	Walnut Creek
275	n/a	Walnut Valley Unified	Walnut
275	n/a	Wasco Union Elementary	Wasco
275	n/a	Waterford Unified	Waterford
275	n/a	West Covina Unified	West Covina
275	n/a	West Sonoma County Union High	Sebastopol
275	n/a	Western Placer Unified	Lincoln
275	n/a	Westminster Elementary	Westminster
275	n/a	Westside Union Elementary	Lancaster
275	n/a	Westwood Unified	Westwood
275	n/a	Whittier City Elementary	Whittier
275	n/a	Willows Unified	Willows
275	n/a	Wilsona Elementary	Palmdale
275	n/a	Windsor Unified	Windsor
275	n/a	Winton Elementary	Winton
275	n/a	Wiseburn Elementary	Hawthorne
275	n/a	Woodlake Union Elementary	Woodlake
275	n/a	Yucaipa-Calimesa Jt. Unified	Yucaipa

Student/Counselor Ratio

Rank	Ratio	District Name	City

1	21,963.0	Anaheim Elementary	Anaheim
2	20,408.0	Saugus Union Elementary	Santa Clarita
3	14,975.0	Huntington Beach Union High	Huntington Bch
4	12,403.3	Alhambra City Elementary	Alhambra
5	10,973.3	Garvey Elementary	Rosemead
6	9,715.0	Encinitas Union Elementary	Encinitas
7	8,834.0	Redwood City Elementary	Redwood City
8	8,575.0	Bellevue Union Elementary	Santa Rosa
9	7,928.0	Goleta Union Elementary	Goleta
10	7,826.7	Santa Rosa Elementary	Santa Rosa
11	6,242.0	Hollister SD	Hollister
12	6,162.5	Linden Unified	Linden
13	6,007.8	Antioch Unified	Antioch
14	5,956.0	Richland Union Elementary SD	Shafter
15	5,684.0	Palmdale Elementary	Palmdale
16	5,236.4	Capistrano Unified	San Juan Capis
17	5,096.0	Mountain View Elementary	El Monte
18	5,019.0	Ravenswood City Elementary	East Palo Alto
19	4,902.5	Victor Elementary	Victorville
20	4,640.0	Moraga Elementary	Moraga
21	4,501.7	Ontario-Montclair Elementary	Ontario
22	4,487.0	Oakley Union Elementary	Oakley
23	4,344.3	Selma Unified	Selma
24	4,264.0	Eureka Union Elementary	Granite Bay
25	4,254.0	Hueneme Elementary	Port Hueneme
26	4,081.7	Savanna Elementary	Anaheim
27	3,834.6	Rio Linda Union Elementary	Rio Linda
28	3,761.0	Enterprise Elementary	Redding
29	3,731.0	Campbell Union Elementary	Campbell
30	3,647.3	Cupertino Union School	Cupertino
31	3,634.7	Fullerton Elementary	Fullerton
32	3,514.0	San Diego Co Office of Education	San Diego
33	3,490.8	Panama Buena Vista Union Elem	Bakersfield
34	3,485.5	Magnolia Elementary	Anaheim
35	3,482.0	Mountain View Elementary	Ontario
36	3,346.7	Wiseburn Elementary	Hawthorne
37	3,346.3	Cajon Valley Union Elementary	El Cajon
38	3,345.0	Walnut Creek Elementary	Walnut Creek
39	3,336.0	Newhall Elementary	Valencia
40	3,184.2	Livermore Valley Joint Unified	Livermore
41	3,169.0	Pacifica SD	Pacifica
42	3,135.0	Waterford Unified	Waterford
43	3,133.0	Fruitvale Elementary	Bakersfield
44	3,075.0	Belmont-Redwood Shores Elementary	Belmont
45	3,071.0	Santa Rita Union Elementary	Salinas
46	2,976.0	Keppel Union Elementary	Pearblossom
47	2,940.0	Arvin Union Elementary	Arvin
48	2,906.0	Mt. Pleasant Elementary	San Jose
49	2,872.3	Orange County Office of Education	Costa Mesa
50	2,810.2	Chula Vista Elementary	Chula Vista
51	2,801.0	Cambrian Elementary	San Jose
52	2,756.4	Alum Rock Union Elementary	San Jose
53	2,659.2	Marysville Joint Unified	Marysville
54	2,630.1	Mt. Diablo Unified	Concord
55	2,610.0	Little Lake City Elementary	Santa Fe Spgs
56	2,595.0	King City Union Elementary	King City
57	2,563.5	San Ysidro Elementary	San Ysidro
58	2,477.7	Westside Union Elementary	Lancaster
59	2,416.0	Tehachapi Unified	Tehachapi
60	2,385.0	Los Nietos Elementary	Whittier
61	2,382.0	Atwater Elementary	Atwater
62	2,341.0	Saddleback Valley Unified	Mission Viejo
63	2,333.9	National Elementary	National City
64	2,331.3	Bonsall Union Elementary	Bonsall
65	2,330.0	Hilmar Unified	Hilmar
66	2,329.0	Alpine Union Elementary	Alpine
67	2,293.0	Newman-Crows Landing Unified	Newman
68	2,275.2	Sacramento City Unified	Sacramento
69	2,273.5	Union Elementary	San Jose
70	2,240.4	Escondido Union Elementary	Escondido
71	2,214.1	Lakeside Union Elementary	Lakeside
72	2,182.0	Taft City Elementary	Taft
73	2,168.0	Kingsburg Elementary Charter	Kingsburg
74	2,161.3	Lawndale Elementary	Lawndale
75	2,143.0	Baldwin Park Unified	Baldwin Park
76	2,123.4	Tulare City Elementary	Tulare
77	2,118.1	Lafayette Elementary	Lafayette
78	2,116.0	Rosedale Union Elementary	Bakersfield
79	2,096.0	Millbrae Elementary	Millbrae
80	2,073.0	Pleasant Ridge Union Elementary	Grass Valley
80	2,073.0	Wilsona Elementary	Palmdale
82	2,065.8	Santa Maria-Bonita Elementary	Santa Maria
83	2,061.7	Kerman Unified	Kerman
84	2,050.6	Westminster Elementary	Westminster
85	2,047.0	Adelanto Elementary	Adelanto
86	2,036.0	Central Union Elementary	Lemoore
87	2,030.0	Soquel Union Elementary	Capitola
88	2,028.7	East Whittier City Elementary	Whittier
89	2,025.0	Los Altos Elementary	Los Altos
90	1,989.0	Corning Union Elementary	Corning
91	1,973.4	Franklin-Mckinley Elementary	San Jose
92	1,929.0	Gustine Unified	Gustine
93	1,916.7	Ripon Unified	Ripon
94	1,916.4	Benicia Unified	Benicia
95	1,877.0	Live Oak Unified	Live Oak
96	1,856.8	Greenfield Union Elementary	Bakersfield
97	1,850.5	Calaveras Unified	San Andreas
98	1,838.5	Palo Verde Unified	Blythe
99	1,817.1	Visalia Unified	Visalia
100	1,817.0	Dixie Elementary	San Rafael
101	1,816.0	Ross Valley Elementary	San Anselmo
102	1,813.4	Kings Canyon Joint Unified	Reedley
103	1,812.0	Rescue Union Elementary	Rescue
104	1,808.0	Winton Elementary	Winton
105	1,776.0	Morgan Hill Unified	Morgan Hill
106	1,773.3	San Jacinto Unified	San Jacinto
107	1,770.6	Pomona Unified	Pomona
108	1,766.9	Newark Unified	Newark
109	1,757.0	Julian Union Elementary	Julian
110	1,754.7	Chino Valley Unified	Chino
111	1,752.0	Dry Creek Joint Elementary	Roseville
112	1,751.0	Jamul-Dulzura Union Elementary	Jamul
113	1,740.6	Fallbrook Union Elementary	Fallbrook
114	1,729.0	Salida Union Elementary	Salida
115	1,724.7	Bellflower Unified	Bellflower
116	1,711.2	Oak Grove Elementary	San Jose
117	1,701.8	Ceres Unified	Ceres
118	1,697.5	Brawley Elementary	Brawley
119	1,694.3	Pleasant Valley School	Camarillo
120	1,680.0	Black Oak Mine Unified	Georgetown
121	1,668.8	Santa Maria Joint Union High	Santa Maria
122	1,660.1	Fairfield-Suisun Unified	Fairfield
123	1,655.4	Turlock Joint Elementary	Turlock
124	1,626.5	Lemoore Union Elementary	Lemoore
125	1,622.0	Livingston Union Elementary	Livingston
126	1,606.8	Cutler-Orosi Joint Unified	Orosi
127	1,605.0	Mark West Union Elementary	Santa Rosa
128	1,599.0	Oroville City Elementary	Oroville
129	1,584.7	Banning Unified	Banning
130	1,583.0	Cloverdale Unified	Cloverdale
131	1,575.3	El Centro Elementary	El Centro
132	1,572.5	Porterville Unified	Porterville
133	1,567.7	Grossmont Union High	La Mesa
134	1,564.0	Duarte Unified	Duarte
135	1,554.0	Cascade Union Elementary	Anderson
136	1,532.0	Rowland Unified	Rowland Heights
137	1,523.0	Nuview Union Elementary	Nuevo
138	1,508.1	Saratoga Union Elementary	Saratoga
139	1,494.3	Dublin Unified	Dublin
140	1,487.4	Placentia-Yorba Linda Unified	Placentia
141	1,461.8	Western Placer Unified	Lincoln
142	1,458.3	San Rafael City Elementary	San Rafael
143	1,451.0	Charter Oak Unified	Covina
144	1,442.6	Carlsbad Unified	Carlsbad
145	1,406.5	Lamont Elementary	Lamont
146	1,405.3	Oceanside Unified	Oceanside
147	1,402.0	Barstow Unified	Barstow
148	1,393.7	Garden Grove Unified	Garden Grove
149	1,390.8	Whittier City Elementary	Whittier
150	1,375.2	Merced City Elementary	Merced
151	1,373.0	Mojave Unified	Mojave
152	1,348.7	Rocklin Unified	Rocklin
153	1,348.0	San Carlos Elementary	San Carlos
154	1,341.7	Redding Elementary	Redding
155	1,341.5	Standard Elementary	Bakersfield
156	1,337.4	Las Virgenes Unified	Calabasas
157	1,331.6	Central Unified	Fresno
158	1,331.0	Manteca Unified	Manteca
159	1,330.0	Central Elementary	Rcho Cucamong
159	1,330.0	Gorman Elementary	Gorman
161	1,329.2	Coachella Valley Unified	Thermal
162	1,319.0	Irvine Unified	Irvine
163	1,314.7	Fowler Unified	Fowler
164	1,312.0	Los Alamitos Unified	Los Alamitos
165	1,310.1	Vista Unified	Vista
166	1,304.5	Berryessa Union Elementary	San Jose
167	1,302.6	San Marcos Unified	San Marcos
168	1,302.0	Fillmore Unified	Fillmore
169	1,292.1	Gilroy Unified	Gilroy
170	1,291.6	Orange Unified	Orange
171	1,290.5	Los Gatos Union Elementary	Los Gatos
172	1,288.8	Sylvan Union Elementary	Modesto
173	1,288.5	Brentwood Union Elementary	Brentwood
174	1,260.5	Ocean View Elementary	Oxnard
175	1,257.5	Santa Ana Unified	Santa Ana
176	1,257.0	Firebaugh-Las Deltas Joint Unified	Firebaugh
177	1,253.7	Milpitas Unified	Milpitas
178	1,239.8	Beaumont Unified	Beaumont
179	1,237.6	Castaic Union Elementary	Valencia
180	1,235.6	Hesperia Unified	Hesperia
181	1,234.4	Hawthorne Elementary	Hawthorne
182	1,232.0	Grass Valley Elementary	Grass Valley
182	1,232.0	Reef-Sunset Unified	Avenal
184	1,231.9	Madera Unified	Madera
185	1,230.8	Jurupa Unified	Riverside
186	1,230.2	Oakland Unified	Oakland
187	1,229.2	El Segundo Unified	El Segundo
188	1,219.4	Norris Elementary	Bakersfield
189	1,216.6	El Rancho Unified	Pico Rivera
190	1,212.0	Middletown Unified	Middletown
191	1,204.5	Orinda Union Elementary	Orinda
192	1,202.8	Yucaipa-Calimesa Jt. Unified	Yucaipa
193	1,197.9	Inglewood Unified	Inglewood
194	1,193.5	Brea-Olinda Unified	Brea
195	1,193.3	Burton Elementary	Porterville
196	1,187.0	San Lorenzo Valley Unified	Ben Lomond
197	1,184.5	Burlingame Elementary	Burlingame
198	1,184.1	Morongo Unified	Twentynine Plms
199	1,183.9	Moorpark Unified	Moorpark
200	1,180.8	Simi Valley Unified	Simi Valley
201	1,179.4	Fremont Unified	Fremont
202	1,165.2	Gateway Unified	Redding
203	1,161.7	Empire Union Elementary	Modesto
204	1,157.3	Vacaville Unified	Vacaville
205	1,155.6	Azusa Unified	Azusa
206	1,153.5	Red Bluff Union Elementary	Red Bluff
207	1,153.1	Burbank Unified	Burbank
208	1,148.4	Pajaro Valley Unified School	Watsonville
209	1,142.7	Bear Valley Unified	Big Bear Lake
210	1,142.3	Parlier Unified	Parlier
211	1,142.2	Kern County Office of Education	Bakersfield
212	1,137.7	San Bernardino Co Off of Education	San Bernardino
213	1,135.0	John Swett Unified	Crockett
214	1,122.7	Carpinteria Unified	Carpinteria
215	1,118.8	San Mateo-Foster City Elementary	San Mateo
216	1,116.9	ABC Unified	Cerritos
217	1,116.1	Novato Unified	Novato
218	1,101.8	Patterson Joint Unified	Patterson
219	1,097.5	Palm Springs Unified	Palm Springs
220	1,086.8	San Bruno Park Elementary	San Bruno
221	1,084.7	Lucia Mar Unified	Arroyo Grande
222	1,080.1	Alvord Unified	Riverside
223	1,078.4	Monrovia Unified	Monrovia
224	1,069.8	Buckeye Union Elementary	Shingle Springs
225	1,063.3	Corcoran Joint Unified	Corcoran
226	1,061.2	Ramona City Unified	Ramona
227	1,057.9	Snowline Joint Unified	Phelan
228	1,057.4	Downey Unified	Downey
229	1,056.5	Glendora Unified	Glendora
230	1,055.2	San Leandro Unified	San Leandro
231	1,054.1	Lakeport Unified	Lakeport
232	1,053.2	Natomas Unified	Sacramento
233	1,052.3	West Contra Costa Unified	Richmond
234	1,051.8	West Covina Unified	West Covina
235	1,049.7	San Lorenzo Unified	San Lorenzo
236	1,044.5	Fullerton Joint Union High	Fullerton
237	1,044.0	Center Joint Unified	Antelope
238	1,041.4	Apple Valley Unified	Apple Valley
239	1,037.4	Lake Elsinore Unified	Lake Elsinore
240	1,028.2	Murrieta Valley Unified	Murrieta
241	1,024.3	Tustin Unified	Tustin
242	1,024.0	Hughson Unified	Hughson
243	1,014.9	Bakersfield City Elementary	Bakersfield
243	1,014.9	Glendale Unified	Glendale
245	1,011.1	Woodland Joint Unified	Woodland
246	1,009.0	Hayward Unified	Hayward
247	1,007.8	Eureka City Unified	Eureka
248	1,006.3	Fresno Unified	Fresno
249	1,003.9	Tracy Joint Unified	Tracy
250	1,000.0	Corona-Norco Unified	Norco
251	999.8	Temecula Valley Unified	Temecula
252	999.2	Newport-Mesa Unified	Costa Mesa
253	997.0	Acton-Agua Dulce Unified	Acton
254	996.8	Oakdale Joint Unified	Oakdale
255	988.8	Val Verde Unified	Perris
256	988.7	Mcfarland Unified	Mcfarland
257	978.0	Claremont Unified	Claremont
258	977.4	Washington Unified	West Sacramento
259	970.3	Riverside Unified	Riverside
260	960.0	Martinez Unified	Martinez
261	959.1	Pittsburg Unified	Pittsburg
262	951.8	Plumas Unified	Quincy
263	951.0	Rialto Unified	Rialto
264	947.9	Hacienda La Puente Unified	City of Industry
265	944.5	Pasadena Unified	Pasadena
266	943.7	San Ramon Valley Unified	Danville
267	939.7	Covina-Valley Unified	Covina
268	934.1	San Juan Unified	Carmichael
269	933.9	San Jose Unified	San Jose
270	933.2	Monterey Peninsula Unified	Monterey
271	932.2	Valley Center-Pauma Unified	Valley Center
272	926.5	Riverdale Joint Unified	Riverdale
273	925.3	Elk Grove Unified	Elk Grove
274	917.8	South San Francisco Unified	S San Francisco
275	917.7	Menlo Park City Elementary	Atherton
276	916.0	Hemet Unified	Hemet
277	913.3	Culver City Unified	Culver City

278	907.0	Templeton Unified	Templeton
279	902.3	Berkeley Unified	Berkeley
280	901.0	Laguna Beach Unified	Laguna Beach
281	896.7	Travis Unified	Travis Afb
282	893.5	Lynwood Unified	Lynwood
283	892.6	Norwalk-La Mirada Unified	Norwalk
284	891.7	Rim of the World Unified	Lake Arrowhead
285	890.2	Santa Clara Unified	Santa Clara
286	886.1	Poway Unified	Poway
287	881.5	Romoland Elementary	Homeland
288	880.8	Escalon Unified	Escalon
289	876.9	Montebello Unified	Montebello
290	875.8	Centralia Elementary	Buena Park
291	873.1	Dixon Unified	Dixon
292	869.5	Sanger Unified	Sanger
293	869.1	Lompoc Unified	Lompoc
294	866.3	Auburn Union Elementary	Auburn
295	865.5	Ojai Unified	Ojai
296	863.0	Fremont Union High	Sunnyvale
297	862.7	Bassett Unified	La Puente
298	858.8	Walnut Valley Unified	Walnut
299	858.4	Del Norte County Unified	Crescent City
300	856.5	Alameda City Unified	Alameda
301	853.5	Ukiah Unified	Ukiah
302	853.1	Soledad Unified	Soledad
303	845.6	Live Oak Elementary	Santa Cruz
304	841.5	Weaver Union Elementary	Merced
305	829.6	Willits Unified	Willits
306	828.3	Palo Alto Unified	Palo Alto
307	828.0	Tulare County Office of Education	Visalia
308	823.8	Conejo Valley Unified	Thousand Oaks
309	819.1	Imperial Unified	Imperial
310	818.4	Upland Unified	Upland
311	810.6	Fontana Unified	Fontana
311	810.6	Napa Valley Unified	Napa
313	808.0	Muroc Joint Unified	North Edwards
314	804.4	Paradise Unified	Paradise
315	803.5	Calexico Unified	Calexico
316	803.1	Temple City Unified	Temple City
317	785.3	Orland Joint Unified	Orland
318	784.8	Bonita Unified	San Dimas
319	783.1	San Gabriel Unified	San Gabriel
320	780.8	Windsor Unified	Windsor
321	780.6	Arcadia Unified	Arcadia
322	775.5	Riverbank Unified	Riverbank
323	774.1	Amador County Unified	Jackson
324	773.6	Julian Union High	Julian
325	771.0	Mill Valley Elementary	Mill Valley
326	768.8	Chico Unified	Chico
327	768.4	Holtville Unified	Holtville
328	764.3	Los Angeles Unified	Los Angeles
329	760.2	New Haven Unified	Union City
330	757.9	Lodi Unified	Lodi
331	755.8	Cotati-Rohnert Park Unified	Rohnert Park
332	753.2	Albany City Unified	Albany
333	752.8	Oak Park Unified	Oak Park
334	748.5	Vallejo City Unified	Vallejo
335	746.0	Redondo Beach Unified	Redondo Beach
336	745.5	Atascadero Unified	Atascadero
337	740.7	King City Joint Union High	King City
338	740.5	Oroville Union High	Oroville
339	740.0	Gridley Unified	Gridley
340	737.1	Sierra Sands Unified	Ridgecrest
341	730.4	Folsom-Cordova Unified	Folsom
342	728.8	Coronado Unified	Coronado
343	728.3	Victor Valley Union High	Victorville
344	726.6	Cabrillo Unified	Half Moon Bay
345	726.1	Lake Tahoe Unified	S Lake Tahoe
346	723.8	La Canada Unified	La Canada
347	715.8	Mountain Empire Unified	Pine Valley
348	714.7	Torrance Unified	Torrance
349	709.5	Fallbrook Union High	Fallbrook
350	705.3	Paso Robles Joint Unified	Paso Robles
351	703.2	Compton Unified	Compton
352	701.5	Dinuba Unified	Dinuba
353	698.6	Farmersville Unified	Farmersville
354	683.7	Willows Unified	Willows
355	682.8	Konocti Unified	Lower Lake
356	678.2	Pleasanton Unified	Pleasanton
357	671.3	Castro Valley Unified	Castro Valley
358	670.7	San Bernardino City Unified	San Bernardino
359	670.1	Davis Joint Unified	Davis
360	669.4	North Monterey County Unified	Moss Landing
361	667.0	Palos Verdes Peninsula Unified	Palos Verdes Est
362	657.9	Colton Joint Unified	Colton
363	657.5	Silver Valley Unified	Yermo
364	654.5	Santa Cruz City High	Soquel
365	653.2	San Marino Unified	San Marino
366	652.7	Coalinga-Huron Joint Unified	Coalinga
367	638.3	Pacific Grove Unified	Pacific Grove
368	637.1	Desert Sands Unified	La Quinta
369	634.8	Paramount Unified	Paramount
370	631.1	San Francisco Unified	San Francisco
371	626.0	Jefferson Union High	Daly City
372	624.0	Kelseyville Unified	Kelseyville
373	623.7	Redlands Unified	Redlands
374	618.6	East Side Union High	San Jose
375	609.4	Ventura Unified	Ventura
376	600.4	San Benito High	Hollister
377	596.1	Yuba City Unified	Yuba City
378	593.2	Lincoln Unified	Stockton
379	586.3	Long Beach Unified	Long Beach
380	585.1	Liberty Union High	Brentwood
381	576.8	Perris Union High	Perris
382	576.4	Fort Bragg Unified	Fort Bragg
383	576.3	Sonora Union High	Sonora
384	575.6	Scotts Valley Unified	Scotts Valley
385	572.2	Moreno Valley Unified	Moreno Valley
386	571.7	Santa Paula Union High	Santa Paula
387	570.0	Beverly Hills Unified	Beverly Hills
388	569.6	Anaheim Union High	Anaheim
389	565.0	Manhattan Beach Unified	Manhattan Beach
390	562.3	Delano Joint Union High	Delano
391	548.0	Dos Palos Oro Loma Jt. Unified	Dos Palos
392	546.8	Sonoma Valley Unified	Sonoma
393	544.2	Santa Monica-Malibu Unified	Santa Monica
394	537.8	Escondido Union High	Escondido
395	535.7	Campbell Union High	San Jose
396	534.9	Clovis Unified	Clovis
397	534.0	La Mesa-Spring Valley	La Mesa
398	533.7	Antelope Valley Union High	Lancaster
399	532.8	Galt Joint Union High	Galt
400	524.9	South Pasadena Unified	South Pasadena
401	521.5	Alhambra City High	Alhambra
401	521.5	Placer Union High	Auburn
403	517.5	Stockton City Unified	Stockton
404	512.3	Lindsay Unified	Lindsay
405	510.8	Sierra Unified	Prather
406	510.3	Del Paso Heights Elementary	Sacramento
406	510.3	Merced Union High	Atwater
408	508.1	Santa Paula Elementary	Santa Paula
409	506.3	Healdsburg Unified	Healdsburg
410	502.2	El Dorado Union High	Placerville
411	497.6	Mariposa County Unified	Mariposa
412	497.1	Gonzales Unified	Gonzales
413	493.4	Central Union High	El Centro
414	492.8	Red Bluff Joint Union High	Red Bluff
415	489.3	Grant Joint Union High	Sacramento
416	485.5	San Mateo Union High	San Mateo
417	481.0	Lennox Elementary	Lennox
418	478.0	Tahoe-Truckee Joint Unified	Truckee
419	477.8	Golden Plains Unified	San Joaquin
420	475.0	North Sacramento Elementary	Sacramento
421	473.6	William S. Hart Union High	Santa Clarita
422	473.5	Salinas Union High	Salinas
423	473.2	Los Angeles Co Office of Education	Downey
424	465.1	River Delta Joint Unified	Rio Vista
425	458.8	Santa Rosa High	Santa Rosa
426	456.6	Nevada Joint Union High	Grass Valley
427	456.5	Petaluma Joint Union High	Petaluma
428	454.5	Kern Union High	Bakersfield
429	449.0	Modesto City High	Modesto
430	445.0	Acalanes Union High	Lafayette
431	439.5	San Dieguito Union High	Encinitas
432	438.0	San Luis Coastal Unified	San Luis Obispo
433	437.4	Winters Joint Unified	Winters
434	437.1	Lemoore Union High	Lemoore
435	436.9	San Diego Unified	San Diego
436	433.0	Chaffey Joint Union High	Ontario
437	430.8	Santa Barbara High	Santa Barbara
438	428.7	San Joaquin Co Off of Education	Stockton
439	427.3	El Monte Union High	El Monte
440	426.8	Roseville Joint Union High	Roseville
441	424.2	San Rafael City High	San Rafael
442	417.9	Turlock Joint Union High	Turlock
443	414.4	Oxnard Union High	Oxnard
444	413.3	Hanford Joint Union High	Hanford
445	409.6	Mountain View-Los Altos Union High	Mountain View
446	405.8	Piedmont City Unified	Piedmont
447	398.2	Centinela Valley Union High	Lawndale
448	397.1	Shasta Union High	Redding
449	387.4	Northern Humboldt Union High	McKinleyville
450	380.5	Whittier Union High	Whittier
451	376.5	Sweetwater Union High	Chula Vista
452	360.9	Anderson Union High	Anderson
453	348.2	Santa Clara Co Off of Education	San Jose
454	332.8	Tamalpais Union High	Larkspur
455	311.6	Carmel Unified	Carmel
456	304.2	Tulare Joint Union High	Tulare
457	304.0	Sequoia Union High	Redwood City
458	302.1	West Sonoma County Union High	Sebastopol
459	265.4	Brawley Union High	Brawley
460	n/a	Alisal Union Elementary	Salinas
460	n/a	Alta Loma Elementary	Alta Loma
460	n/a	Beardsley Elementary	Bakersfield
460	n/a	Buena Park Elementary	Buena Park
460	n/a	Chowchilla Elementary	Chowchilla
460	n/a	Cucamonga Elementary	Rcho Cucamong
460	n/a	Cypress Elementary	Cypress
460	n/a	Del Mar Union Elementary	Del Mar
460	n/a	Delano Union Elementary	Delano
460	n/a	Delhi Unified	Delhi
460	n/a	Earlimart Elementary	Earlimart
460	n/a	Eastside Union Elementary	Lancaster
460	n/a	El Monte City Elementary	El Monte
460	n/a	Etiwanda Elementary	Etiwanda
460	n/a	Evergreen Elementary	San Jose
460	n/a	Exeter Union Elementary	Exeter
460	n/a	Fairfax Elementary	Bakersfield
460	n/a	Fountain Valley Elementary	Fountain Valley
460	n/a	Fresno County Office of Education	Fresno
460	n/a	Galt Joint Union Elementary	Galt
460	n/a	Greenfield Union Elementary	Greenfield
460	n/a	Hanford Elementary	Hanford
460	n/a	Huntington Beach City Elementary	Huntington Bch
460	n/a	Jefferson Elementary	Daly City
460	n/a	Jefferson Elementary	Tracy
460	n/a	Keyes Union Elementary	Keyes
460	n/a	La Habra City Elementary	La Habra
460	n/a	Lancaster Elementary	Lancaster
460	n/a	Lemon Grove Elementary	Lemon Grove
460	n/a	Loomis Union Elementary	Loomis
460	n/a	Los Banos Unified	Los Banos
460	n/a	Los Gatos-Saratoga Jt Union High	Los Gatos
460	n/a	Lowell Joint	Whittier
460	n/a	Mendota Unified	Mendota
460	n/a	Menifee Union Elementary	Menifee
460	n/a	Modesto City Elementary	Modesto
460	n/a	Moreland Elementary	San Jose
460	n/a	Mother Lode Union Elementary	Placerville
460	n/a	Mountain View-Whisman Elementary	Mountain View
460	n/a	Ocean View Elementary	Huntington Bch
460	n/a	Old Adobe Union Elementary	Petaluma
460	n/a	Orcutt Union Elementary	Orcutt
460	n/a	Oro Grande Elementary	Oro Grande
460	n/a	Oxnard Elementary	Oxnard
460	n/a	Perris Elementary	Perris
460	n/a	Petaluma City Elementary	Petaluma
460	n/a	Piner-Olivet Union Elementary	Santa Rosa
460	n/a	Rincon Valley Union Elementary	Santa Rosa
460	n/a	Rio Elementary	Oxnard
460	n/a	Riverside Co Office of Education	Riverside
460	n/a	Robla Elementary	Sacramento
460	n/a	Rosemead Elementary	Rosemead
460	n/a	Roseville City Elementary	Roseville
460	n/a	Salinas City Elementary	Salinas
460	n/a	Santa Barbara Elementary	Santa Barbara
460	n/a	Santa Cruz City Elementary	Soquel
460	n/a	Santee Elementary	Santee
460	n/a	Solana Beach Elementary	Solana Beach
460	n/a	South Bay Union Elementary	Imperial Beach
460	n/a	South Whittier Elementary	Whittier
460	n/a	Southern Kern Unified	Rosamond
460	n/a	Stanislaus Union Elementary	Modesto
460	n/a	Sulphur Springs Union Elementary	Canyon Country
460	n/a	Sunnyvale Elementary	Sunnyvale
460	n/a	Twin Ridges Elementary	North San Juan
460	n/a	Wasco Union Elementary	Wasco
460	n/a	Westwood Unified	Westwood
460	n/a	Wheatland Elementary	Wheatland
460	n/a	Woodlake Union Elementary	Woodlake

Current Spending per Student in FY2003

Rank	Dollars	District Name	City
1	71,341	Gorman Elementary	Gorman
2	63,340	Santa Clara Co Off of Education	San Jose
3	54,368	Tulare County Office of Education	Visalia
4	45,766	San Bernardino Co Off of Education	San Bernardino
5	45,427	San Diego Co Office of Education	San Diego
6	41,852	Riverside Co Office of Education	Riverside
7	40,267	Los Angeles Co Office of Education	Downey
8	38,535	Kern County Office of Education	Bakersfield
9	35,115	Fresno County Office of Education	Fresno
10	31,262	San Joaquin Co Off of Education	Stockton
11	22,131	Westwood Unified	Westwood
12	18,489	Orange County Office of Education	Costa Mesa
13	16,634	Julian Union High	Julian
14	12,184	Oro Grande Elementary	Oro Grande
15	11,783	Carmel Unified	Carmel
16	11,045	Palo Alto Unified	Palo Alto
17	10,218	Tamalpais Union High	Larkspur
18	10,132	Mountain View-Los Altos Union High	Mountain View
19	9,906	San Carlos Elementary	San Carlos
20	9,896	San Mateo Union High	San Mateo
21	9,766	Berkeley Unified	Berkeley
22	9,538	Sequoia Union High	Redwood City
23	9,340	Ravenswood City Elementary	East Palo Alto

24	9,260	Mountain Empire Unified	Pine Valley
25	9,199	Solana Beach Elementary	Solana Beach
26	9,198	Menlo Park City Elementary	Atherton
27	9,190	Golden Plains Unified	San Joaquin
28	9,037	Silver Valley Unified	Yermo
29	9,035	Santa Clara Unified	Santa Clara
30	9,023	Sierra Unified	Prather
31	8,946	San Rafael City High	San Rafael
32	8,902	Central Union Elementary	Lemoore
33	8,888	Beverly Hills Unified	Beverly Hills
34	8,876	Los Gatos-Saratoga Jt Union High	Los Gatos
35	8,799	Piedmont City Unified	Piedmont
36	8,704	San Francisco Unified	San Francisco
37	8,692	Oakland Unified	Oakland
38	8,678	Pacific Grove Unified	Pacific Grove
39	8,670	San Diego Unified	San Diego
40	8,624	San Jose Unified	San Jose
41	8,616	Laguna Beach Unified	Laguna Beach
42	8,508	Los Angeles Unified	Los Angeles
43	8,469	Muroc Joint Unified	North Edwards
44	8,467	Live Oak Elementary	Santa Cruz
45	8,377	Plumas Unified	Quincy
46	8,368	Del Norte County Unified	Crescent City
46	8,368	Del Paso Heights Elementary	Sacramento
48	8,301	Pajaro Valley Unified School	Watsonville
49	8,236	East Side Union High	San Jose
50	8,208	Pasadena Unified	Pasadena
51	8,200	Grass Valley Elementary	Grass Valley
52	8,197	Sunnyvale Elementary	Sunnyvale
53	8,177	Mill Valley Elementary	Mill Valley
54	8,173	Grant Joint Union High	Sacramento
55	8,142	Fremont Union High	Sunnyvale
56	8,119	Sacramento City Unified	Sacramento
57	8,117	Belmont-Redwood Shores Elementary	Belmont
58	8,103	Manhattan Beach Unified	Manhattan Beach
59	8,098	San Ysidro Elementary	San Ysidro
60	8,097	Santa Monica-Malibu Unified	Santa Monica
61	8,073	Lindsay Unified	Lindsay
61	8,073	North Sacramento Elementary	Sacramento
63	8,070	Parlier Unified	Parlier
64	8,019	Cascade Union Elementary	Anderson
65	8,001	Twin Ridges Elementary	North San Juan
66	7,966	Dublin Unified	Dublin
67	7,940	Valley Center-Pauma Unified	Valley Center
68	7,878	Pomona Unified	Pomona
69	7,873	Mt. Pleasant Elementary	San Jose
70	7,858	Farmersville Unified	Farmersville
71	7,853	Mariposa County Unified	Mariposa
72	7,851	Redwood City Elementary	Redwood City
73	7,845	Mendota Unified	Mendota
74	7,839	Anderson Union High	Anderson
75	7,835	San Juan Unified	Carmichael
76	7,831	Nevada Joint Union High	Grass Valley
77	7,827	Delano Joint Union High	Delano
78	7,820	Franklin-Mckinley Elementary	San Jose
79	7,811	Coachella Valley Unified	Thermal
80	7,810	Fort Bragg Unified	Fort Bragg
81	7,807	Dos Palos Oro Loma Jt. Unified	Dos Palos
82	7,802	Mcfarland Unified	Mcfarland
83	7,799	Fresno Unified	Fresno
84	7,786	Coronado Unified	Coronado
85	7,772	Bakersfield City Elementary	Bakersfield
86	7,751	Woodlake Union Elementary	Woodlake
87	7,744	Calaveras Unified	San Andreas
88	7,722	Gateway Unified	Redding
89	7,720	Riverbank Unified	Riverbank
90	7,715	Lamont Elementary	Lamont
91	7,706	Greenfield Union Elementary	Greenfield
92	7,703	Vallejo City Unified	Vallejo
93	7,694	Alum Rock Union Elementary	San Jose
94	7,689	Grossmont Union High	La Mesa
95	7,681	Garvey Elementary	Rosemead
96	7,679	West Sonoma County Union High	Sebastopol
97	7,672	San Dieguito Union High	Encinitas
98	7,658	Alisal Union Elementary	Salinas
99	7,654	Stockton City Unified	Stockton
100	7,643	Red Bluff Joint Union High	Red Bluff
101	7,620	Dixie Elementary	San Rafael
101	7,620	Los Altos Elementary	Los Altos
103	7,619	Robla Elementary	Sacramento
104	7,617	Anaheim Union High	Anaheim
105	7,614	Newport-Mesa Unified	Costa Mesa
106	7,611	South Bay Union Elementary	Imperial Beach
107	7,609	San Rafael City Elementary	San Rafael
108	7,604	Santa Cruz City Elementary	Soquel
109	7,603	West Contra Costa Unified	Richmond
110	7,601	Ross Valley Elementary	San Anselmo
111	7,586	Konocti Unified	Lower Lake
112	7,577	Reef-Sunset Unified	Avenal
113	7,570	Albany City Unified	Albany
114	7,565	Lemoore Union High	Lemoore
115	7,560	Ocean View Elementary	Oxnard
116	7,554	Del Mar Union Elementary	Del Mar
117	7,551	Brawley Union High	Brawley
118	7,541	Oceanside Unified	Oceanside
119	7,522	Bellevue Union Elementary	Santa Rosa
120	7,510	Fallbrook Union High	Fallbrook
121	7,501	Merced City Elementary	Merced
122	7,498	Redondo Beach Unified	Redondo Beach
123	7,492	Lennox Elementary	Lennox
124	7,487	Moreland Elementary	San Jose
124	7,487	Shasta Union High	Redding
126	7,482	Pleasanton Unified	Pleasanton
127	7,481	Eureka City Unified	Eureka
128	7,474	National Elementary	National City
129	7,472	Galt Joint Union High	Galt
130	7,462	Mountain View-Whisman Elementary	Mountain View
131	7,461	Jamul-Dulzura Union Elementary	Jamul
132	7,458	Sweetwater Union High	Chula Vista
133	7,454	Livingston Union Elementary	Livingston
134	7,448	Sonora Union High	Sonora
135	7,447	Santa Rosa Elementary	Santa Rosa
136	7,439	Calexico Unified	Calexico
137	7,437	Santa Ana Unified	Santa Ana
138	7,435	Newark Unified	Newark
139	7,432	San Benito High	Hollister
140	7,431	Alhambra City Elementary	Alhambra
141	7,429	Inglewood Unified	Inglewood
142	7,428	Los Gatos Union Elementary	Los Gatos
143	7,424	Healdsburg Unified	Healdsburg
143	7,424	Napa Valley Unified	Napa
145	7,419	Whittier Union High	Whittier
146	7,415	Orange Unified	Orange
147	7,400	Gonzales Unified	Gonzales
147	7,400	Sanger Unified	Sanger
149	7,398	Hacienda La Puente Unified	City of Industry
149	7,398	Huntington Beach Union High	Huntington Bch
151	7,393	Travis Unified	Travis Afb
152	7,381	Hayward Unified	Hayward
153	7,374	Saratoga Union Elementary	Saratoga
154	7,372	Kelseyville Unified	Kelseyville
155	7,367	Westminster Elementary	Westminster
156	7,366	Azusa Unified	Azusa
156	7,366	Lake Tahoe Unified	S Lake Tahoe
158	7,365	Long Beach Unified	Long Beach
159	7,364	El Centro Elementary	El Centro
160	7,359	Elk Grove Unified	Elk Grove
161	7,354	River Delta Joint Unified	Rio Vista
161	7,354	San Mateo-Foster City Elementary	San Mateo
163	7,344	Monrovia Unified	Monrovia
164	7,343	Beaumont Unified	Beaumont
165	7,342	Oroville City Elementary	Oroville
166	7,341	Montebello Unified	Montebello
166	7,341	Norwalk-La Mirada Unified	Norwalk
168	7,338	Willits Unified	Willits
169	7,329	Chula Vista Elementary	Chula Vista
169	7,329	La Canada Unified	La Canada
171	7,324	Palo Verde Unified	Blythe
171	7,324	Porterville Unified	Porterville
171	7,324	Santa Maria-Bonita Elementary	Santa Maria
174	7,317	Monterey Peninsula Unified	Monterey
175	7,313	San Lorenzo Valley Unified	Ben Lomond
176	7,300	Fallbrook Union Elementary	Fallbrook
177	7,296	Mountain View Elementary	El Monte
178	7,295	El Monte City Elementary	El Monte
179	7,284	Santa Paula Elementary	Santa Paula
180	7,281	Kern Union High	Bakersfield
181	7,274	Centinela Valley Union High	Lawndale
182	7,273	Ukiah Unified	Ukiah
183	7,272	El Rancho Unified	Pico Rivera
184	7,270	Acalanes Union High	Lafayette
185	7,269	Oxnard Elementary	Oxnard
186	7,268	Marysville Joint Unified	Marysville
187	7,267	Bassett Unified	La Puente
187	7,267	Union Elementary	San Jose
189	7,266	San Bernardino City Unified	San Bernardino
190	7,252	Holtville Unified	Holtville
191	7,230	Sierra Sands Unified	Ridgecrest
192	7,219	Los Nietos Elementary	Whittier
193	7,218	Windsor Unified	Windsor
194	7,216	Rowland Unified	Rowland Heights
195	7,214	Lemon Grove Elementary	Lemon Grove
196	7,212	Morongo Unified	Twentynine Plms
197	7,199	Hughson Unified	Hughson
197	7,199	Visalia Unified	Visalia
199	7,188	Standard Elementary	Bakersfield
200	7,185	Jefferson Union High	Daly City
200	7,185	Orinda Union Elementary	Orinda
202	7,183	Salinas City Elementary	Salinas
203	7,182	Paso Robles Joint Unified	Paso Robles
204	7,179	North Monterey County Unified	Moss Landing
205	7,171	Whittier City Elementary	Whittier
206	7,166	Alameda City Unified	Alameda
206	7,166	Panama Buena Vista Union Elem	Bakersfield
208	7,157	Ontario-Montclair Elementary	Ontario
209	7,156	Campbell Union Elementary	Campbell
210	7,154	Lawndale Elementary	Lawndale
210	7,154	Poway Unified	Poway
212	7,152	Claremont Unified	Claremont
213	7,148	Savanna Elementary	Anaheim
214	7,146	Tahoe-Truckee Joint Unified	Truckee
215	7,134	Clovis Unified	Clovis
216	7,133	Glendale Unified	Glendale
216	7,133	New Haven Unified	Union City
218	7,121	Oroville Union High	Oroville
219	7,117	Firebaugh-Las Deltas Joint Unified	Firebaugh
220	7,116	San Marino Unified	San Marino
221	7,115	Rincon Valley Union Elementary	Santa Rosa
222	7,111	Soledad Unified	Soledad
223	7,109	Wasco Union Elementary	Wasco
224	7,107	Turlock Joint Union High	Turlock
225	7,105	Cajon Valley Union Elementary	El Cajon
226	7,103	Brawley Elementary	Brawley
227	7,102	La Habra City Elementary	La Habra
228	7,098	Wilsona Elementary	Palmdale
229	7,096	Rio Linda Union Elementary	Rio Linda
230	7,094	Taft City Elementary	Taft
231	7,091	Los Alamitos Unified	Los Alamitos
232	7,089	Goleta Union Elementary	Goleta
232	7,089	Washington Unified	West Sacramento
234	7,083	Bonita Unified	San Dimas
234	7,083	Enterprise Elementary	Redding
234	7,083	Tulare Joint Union High	Tulare
237	7,082	Pacifica SD	Pacifica
238	7,080	Exeter Union Elementary	Exeter
239	7,079	El Monte Union High	El Monte
240	7,071	Petaluma City Elementary	Petaluma
241	7,070	Salinas Union High	Salinas
241	7,070	Winton Elementary	Winton
243	7,068	Dinuba Unified	Dinuba
244	7,065	Cutler-Orosi Joint Unified	Orosi
245	7,062	Mt. Diablo Unified	Concord
246	7,061	Oak Grove Elementary	San Jose
247	7,057	Gridley Unified	Gridley
248	7,056	Black Oak Mine Unified	Georgetown
249	7,046	Cloverdale Unified	Cloverdale
249	7,046	Culver City Unified	Culver City
251	7,042	Placer Union High	Auburn
252	7,037	Central Union High	El Centro
253	7,035	ABC Unified	Cerritos
254	7,034	Rosemead Elementary	Rosemead
255	7,033	Perris Elementary	Perris
256	7,029	Barstow Unified	Barstow
257	7,028	Alpine Union Elementary	Alpine
257	7,028	Berryessa Union Elementary	San Jose
257	7,028	Rio Elementary	Oxnard
260	7,023	Ceres Unified	Ceres
261	7,022	Orland Joint Unified	Orland
262	7,017	Liberty Union High	Brentwood
263	7,012	Milpitas Unified	Milpitas
264	7,011	Santee Elementary	Santee
265	7,009	Palmdale Elementary	Palmdale
266	7,006	Palm Springs Unified	Palm Springs
267	7,005	Baldwin Park Unified	Baldwin Park
267	7,005	John Swett Unified	Crockett
269	7,001	Torrance Unified	Torrance
270	6,997	Sonoma Valley Unified	Sonoma
271	6,988	Gilroy Unified	Gilroy
272	6,985	Lakeside Union Elementary	Lakeside
272	6,985	San Luis Coastal Unified	San Luis Obispo
274	6,982	Corning Union Elementary	Corning
275	6,981	Fountain Valley Elementary	Fountain Valley
276	6,979	Hanford Elementary	Hanford
277	6,978	Chaffey Joint Union High	Ontario
278	6,973	Arvin Union Elementary	Arvin
279	6,968	Compton Unified	Compton
280	6,967	Covina-Valley Unified	Covina
280	6,967	La Mesa-Spring Valley	La Mesa
282	6,963	Richland Union Elementary SD	Shafter
283	6,960	Bonsall Union Elementary	Bonsall
283	6,960	Tulare City Elementary	Tulare
285	6,958	Cabrillo Unified	Half Moon Bay
286	6,955	Lucia Mar Unified	Arroyo Grande
287	6,953	King City Joint Union High	King City
287	6,953	Soquel Union Elementary	Capitola
289	6,949	Moraga Elementary	Moraga
290	6,948	Madera Unified	Madera
291	6,937	Magnolia Elementary	Anaheim
292	6,935	Garden Grove Unified	Garden Grove
292	6,935	Mojave Unified	Mojave
294	6,929	Placentia-Yorba Linda Unified	Placentia
295	6,927	Lodi Unified	Lodi
296	6,921	Paramount Unified	Paramount
296	6,921	San Lorenzo Unified	San Lorenzo
298	6,920	Yuba City Unified	Yuba City
299	6,918	Palos Verdes Peninsula Unified	Palos Verdes Est
299	6,918	Winters Joint Unified	Winters

301	6,913	Hueneme Elementary	Port Hueneme
302	6,912	Redding Elementary	Redding
302	6,912	Santa Barbara Elementary	Santa Barbara
304	6,911	Jurupa Unified	Riverside
305	6,909	South Whittier Elementary	Whittier
306	6,903	Corcoran Joint Unified	Corcoran
307	6,897	Banning Unified	Banning
308	6,892	Fremont Unified	Fremont
308	6,892	Pittsburg Unified	Pittsburg
310	6,891	Modesto City Elementary	Modesto
311	6,890	Jefferson Elementary	Daly City
312	6,886	Hawthorne Elementary	Hawthorne
313	6,881	Chico Unified	Chico
314	6,880	Desert Sands Unified	La Quinta
315	6,879	Centralia Elementary	Buena Park
316	6,878	Brea-Olinda Unified	Brea
317	6,876	Delano Union Elementary	Delano
318	6,875	Cotati-Rohnert Park Unified	Rohnert Park
319	6,871	Bellflower Unified	Bellflower
320	6,870	Piner-Olivet Union Elementary	Santa Rosa
321	6,865	King City Union Elementary	King City
321	6,865	Northern Humboldt Union High	McKinleyville
323	6,864	Mark West Union Elementary	Santa Rosa
324	6,858	Buena Park Elementary	Buena Park
325	6,854	Fillmore Unified	Fillmore
325	6,854	Millbrae Elementary	Millbrae
327	6,850	Kerman Unified	Kerman
328	6,849	Burbank Unified	Burbank
328	6,849	Oakdale Joint Unified	Oakdale
330	6,845	Old Adobe Union Elementary	Petaluma
331	6,844	Roseville Joint Union High	Roseville
332	6,838	Nuview Union Elementary	Nuevo
333	6,833	Atwater Elementary	Atwater
334	6,831	Red Bluff Union Elementary	Red Bluff
335	6,830	Davis Joint Unified	Davis
336	6,829	Newman-Crows Landing Unified	Newman
337	6,828	El Dorado Union High	Placerville
338	6,818	Coalinga-Huron Joint Unified	Coalinga
338	6,818	Merced Union High	Atwater
340	6,812	Waterford Unified	Waterford
341	6,802	Bear Valley Unified	Big Bear Lake
342	6,798	Romoland Elementary	Homeland
343	6,795	Fontana Unified	Fontana
343	6,795	Hilmar Unified	Hilmar
345	6,790	Santa Paula Union High	Santa Paula
346	6,789	Cypress Elementary	Cypress
346	6,789	Fowler Unified	Fowler
348	6,780	El Segundo Unified	El Segundo
349	6,779	Imperial Unified	Imperial
349	6,779	San Leandro Unified	San Leandro
351	6,777	Rim of the World Unified	Lake Arrowhead
352	6,776	Center Joint Unified	Antelope
353	6,770	Central Unified	Fresno
354	6,766	Las Virgenes Unified	Calabasas
355	6,765	Greenfield Union Elementary	Bakersfield
355	6,765	Willows Unified	Willows
357	6,763	Ocean View Elementary	Huntington Bch
358	6,760	Gustine Unified	Gustine
359	6,756	Lakeport Unified	Lakeport
359	6,756	Turlock Joint Elementary	Turlock
361	6,755	Conejo Valley Unified	Thousand Oaks
362	6,750	Carpinteria Unified	Carpinteria
363	6,746	Paradise Unified	Paradise
364	6,743	Riverdale Joint Unified	Riverdale
365	6,731	Rialto Unified	Rialto
366	6,725	Hemet Unified	Hemet
367	6,723	Oxnard Union High	Oxnard
368	6,719	Castro Valley Unified	Castro Valley
369	6,716	Auburn Union Elementary	Auburn
369	6,716	Encinitas Union Elementary	Encinitas
371	6,710	San Bruno Park Elementary	San Bruno
372	6,707	Woodland Joint Unified	Woodland
373	6,696	Duarte Unified	Duarte
373	6,696	Kings Canyon Joint Unified	Reedley
375	6,694	Lincoln Unified	Stockton
376	6,693	Fullerton Elementary	Fullerton
377	6,691	South San Francisco Unified	S San Francisco
378	6,690	Livermore Valley Joint Unified	Livermore
379	6,688	Linden Unified	Linden
380	6,686	East Whittier City Elementary	Whittier
381	6,680	Corona-Norco Unified	Norco
381	6,680	Hollister SD	Hollister
383	6,675	Irvine Unified	Irvine
383	6,675	Moorpark Unified	Moorpark
385	6,673	Middletown Unified	Middletown
385	6,673	Salida Union Elementary	Salida
387	6,671	Capistrano Unified	San Juan Capis
388	6,669	Vista Unified	Vista
389	6,668	Weaver Union Elementary	Merced
390	6,667	Ramona City Unified	Ramona
391	6,665	San Gabriel Unified	San Gabriel
392	6,658	Adelanto Elementary	Adelanto
392	6,658	Campbell Union High	San Jose
394	6,655	Lake Elsinore Unified	Lake Elsinore
395	6,649	Patterson Joint Unified	Patterson
396	6,642	Little Lake City Elementary	Santa Fe Spgs
397	6,641	Anaheim Elementary	Anaheim
397	6,641	Santa Maria Joint Union High	Santa Maria
399	6,637	Mother Lode Union Elementary	Placerville
400	6,634	San Ramon Valley Unified	Danville
401	6,632	Keyes Union Elementary	Keyes
402	6,631	Alvord Unified	Riverside
403	6,630	Atascadero Unified	Atascadero
404	6,629	Lompoc Unified	Lompoc
405	6,618	Wiseburn Elementary	Hawthorne
406	6,617	Burlingame Elementary	Burlingame
407	6,614	Escondido Union High	Escondido
408	6,608	Novato Unified	Novato
409	6,599	Eastside Union Elementary	Lancaster
410	6,597	Ventura Unified	Ventura
411	6,595	Ojai Unified	Ojai
412	6,594	Santa Barbara High	Santa Barbara
413	6,591	Benicia Unified	Benicia
414	6,586	Redlands Unified	Redlands
415	6,585	Cambrian Elementary	San Jose
415	6,585	Lancaster Elementary	Lancaster
417	6,582	Escondido Union Elementary	Escondido
417	6,582	Moreno Valley Unified	Moreno Valley
419	6,578	Empire Union Elementary	Modesto
420	6,577	Oakley Union Elementary	Oakley
421	6,576	Walnut Creek Elementary	Walnut Creek
422	6,573	West Covina Unified	West Covina
423	6,572	Lafayette Elementary	Lafayette
424	6,568	Brentwood Union Elementary	Brentwood
425	6,567	Riverside Unified	Riverside
426	6,564	Natomas Unified	Sacramento
427	6,559	Lowell Joint	Whittier
428	6,556	Pleasant Valley School	Camarillo
429	6,551	William S. Hart Union High	Santa Clarita
430	6,549	Tracy Joint Unified	Tracy
431	6,547	San Marcos Unified	San Marcos
432	6,545	Evergreen Elementary	San Jose
432	6,545	Val Verde Unified	Perris
434	6,543	Earlimart Elementary	Earlimart
435	6,542	Beardsley Elementary	Bakersfield
436	6,539	Hanford Joint Union High	Hanford
437	6,534	Folsom-Cordova Unified	Folsom
438	6,529	Simi Valley Unified	Simi Valley
439	6,518	Hesperia Unified	Hesperia
439	6,518	Huntington Beach City Elementary	Huntington Bch
441	6,514	Lynwood Unified	Lynwood
442	6,511	Pleasant Ridge Union Elementary	Grass Valley
443	6,500	Dixon Unified	Dixon
444	6,492	Martinez Unified	Martinez
445	6,484	Fairfax Elementary	Bakersfield
446	6,470	Carlsbad Unified	Carlsbad
447	6,464	Morgan Hill Unified	Morgan Hill
448	6,460	Charter Oak Unified	Covina
448	6,460	Julian Union Elementary	Julian
450	6,446	San Jacinto Unified	San Jacinto
451	6,445	Temple City Unified	Temple City
452	6,443	Santa Rita Union Elementary	Salinas
453	6,429	Oak Park Unified	Oak Park
454	6,426	Tehachapi Unified	Tehachapi
455	6,414	South Pasadena Unified	South Pasadena
456	6,413	Vacaville Unified	Vacaville
457	6,412	Colton Joint Unified	Colton
458	6,411	Roseville City Elementary	Roseville
459	6,408	Antelope Valley Union High	Lancaster
459	6,408	Cupertino Union School	Cupertino
459	6,408	Tustin Unified	Tustin
462	6,399	Downey Unified	Downey
463	6,395	Sulphur Springs Union Elementary	Canyon Country
464	6,394	Kingsburg Elementary Charter	Kingsburg
465	6,393	Walnut Valley Unified	Walnut
466	6,388	Templeton Unified	Templeton
467	6,380	Saugus Union Elementary	Santa Clarita
468	6,379	Chowchilla Elementary	Chowchilla
469	6,372	Rocklin Unified	Rocklin
470	6,363	Galt Joint Union Elementary	Galt
471	6,362	Keppel Union Elementary	Pearblossom
472	6,357	Loomis Union Elementary	Loomis
473	6,349	Temecula Valley Unified	Temecula
474	6,325	Saddleback Valley Unified	Mission Viejo
475	6,324	Selma Unified	Selma
476	6,323	Stanislaus Union Elementary	Modesto
477	6,314	Arcadia Unified	Arcadia
478	6,313	Perris Union High	Perris
479	6,300	Cucamonga Elementary	Rcho Cucamong
480	6,296	Fairfield-Suisun Unified	Fairfield
480	6,296	Live Oak Unified	Live Oak
482	6,285	Burton Elementary	Porterville
483	6,283	Yucaipa-Calimesa Jt. Unified	Yucaipa
484	6,281	Central Elementary	Rcho Cucamong
485	6,279	Apple Valley Unified	Apple Valley
486	6,273	Los Banos Unified	Los Banos
487	6,264	Scotts Valley Unified	Scotts Valley
488	6,263	Escalon Unified	Escalon
489	6,252	Manteca Unified	Manteca
490	6,234	Ripon Unified	Ripon
491	6,230	Acton-Agua Dulce Unified	Acton
492	6,220	Antioch Unified	Antioch
493	6,217	Chino Valley Unified	Chino
494	6,204	Sylvan Union Elementary	Modesto
495	6,183	Mountain View Elementary	Ontario
496	6,169	Delhi Unified	Delhi
497	6,152	Southern Kern Unified	Rosamond
497	6,152	Wheatland Elementary	Wheatland
499	6,150	Alta Loma Elementary	Alta Loma
499	6,150	Fruitvale Elementary	Bakersfield
501	6,122	Orcutt Union Elementary	Orcutt
502	6,118	Buckeye Union Elementary	Shingle Springs
503	6,113	Lemoore Union Elementary	Lemoore
504	6,096	Fullerton Joint Union High	Fullerton
505	6,048	Menifee Union Elementary	Menifee
506	6,031	Victor Elementary	Victorville
507	6,023	Jefferson Elementary	Tracy
508	6,019	Castaic Union Elementary	Valencia
509	5,965	Rosedale Union Elementary	Bakersfield
510	5,958	Eureka Union Elementary	Granite Bay
511	5,956	Glendora Unified	Glendora
512	5,945	Murrieta Valley Unified	Murrieta
513	5,940	Upland Unified	Upland
514	5,912	Westside Union Elementary	Lancaster
515	5,887	Rescue Union Elementary	Rescue
516	5,877	Dry Creek Joint Elementary	Roseville
517	5,802	Norris Elementary	Bakersfield
518	5,795	Amador County Unified	Jackson
519	5,790	Newhall Elementary	Valencia
520	5,687	Etiwanda Elementary	Etiwanda
521	5,544	Snowline Joint Unified	Phelan
522	5,334	Victor Valley Union High	Victorville
523	4,948	Western Placer Unified	Lincoln
524	n/a	Alhambra City High	Alhambra
524	n/a	Modesto City High	Modesto
524	n/a	Petaluma Joint Union High	Petaluma
524	n/a	Santa Cruz City High	Soquel
524	n/a	Santa Rosa High	Santa Rosa

Number of Diploma Recipients

Rank	Number	District Name	City
1	27,720	Los Angeles Unified	Los Angeles
2	6,504	San Diego Unified	San Diego
3	5,741	Kern Union High	Bakersfield
4	4,768	Sweetwater Union High	Chula Vista
5	4,664	Long Beach Unified	Long Beach
6	4,467	East Side Union High	San Jose
7	4,387	Grossmont Union High	La Mesa
8	3,873	Chaffey Joint Union High	Ontario
9	3,721	Fresno Unified	Fresno
10	3,688	Anaheim Union High	Anaheim
11	3,556	San Juan Unified	Carmichael
12	3,399	San Francisco Unified	San Francisco
13	2,992	Antelope Valley Union High	Lancaster
14	2,905	Huntington Beach Union High	Huntington Bch
15	2,815	Modesto City High	Modesto
16	2,738	Garden Grove Unified	Garden Grove
17	2,728	Elk Grove Unified	Elk Grove
18	2,670	Fullerton Joint Union High	Fullerton
19	2,644	Capistrano Unified	San Juan Capis
20	2,529	Oxnard Union High	Oxnard
21	2,484	Santa Ana Unified	Santa Ana
22	2,393	William S. Hart Union High	Santa Clarita
23	2,251	Riverside Unified	Riverside
24	2,237	Sacramento City Unified	Sacramento
25	2,230	Poway Unified	Poway
26	2,170	Corona-Norco Unified	Norco
27	2,161	Mt. Diablo Unified	Concord
28	2,157	Saddleback Valley Unified	Mission Viejo
29	2,093	Whittier Union High	Whittier
30	2,065	Orange Unified	Orange
31	2,052	Clovis Unified	Clovis
32	2,002	Glendale Unified	Glendale
33	1,996	Vista Unified	Vista
34	1,985	Fremont Union High	Sunnyvale
35	1,972	Fremont Unified	Fremont
36	1,951	Merced Union High	Atwater
37	1,933	San Bernardino City Unified	San Bernardino
38	1,865	Chino Valley Unified	Chino
39	1,838	Irvine Unified	Irvine
40	1,813	Torrance Unified	Torrance
41	1,793	Fontana Unified	Fontana
42	1,770	West Contra Costa Unified	Richmond
43	1,763	San Mateo Union High	San Mateo
44	1,740	San Jose Unified	San Jose
45	1,705	El Monte Union High	El Monte
46	1,694	Moreno Valley Unified	Moreno Valley

47	1,656	Placentia-Yorba Linda Unified	Placentia
48	1,641	Alhambra City High	Alhambra
49	1,636	ABC Unified	Cerritos
50	1,617	Oakland Unified	Oakland
51	1,585	Roseville Joint Union High	Roseville
52	1,556	Escondido Union High	Escondido
53	1,543	Montebello Unified	Montebello
54	1,533	San Dieguito Union High	Encinitas
55	1,506	Santa Rosa High	Santa Rosa
56	1,491	San Ramon Valley Unified	Danville
57	1,488	El Dorado Union High	Placerville
58	1,456	Lodi Unified	Lodi
59	1,443	Salinas Union High	Salinas
60	1,414	Campbell Union High	San Jose
61	1,413	Conejo Valley Unified	Thousand Oaks
62	1,410	Pomona Unified	Pomona
63	1,394	Desert Sands Unified	La Quinta
64	1,392	Rialto Unified	Rialto
65	1,358	Santa Barbara High	Santa Barbara
66	1,345	Grant Joint Union High	Sacramento
66	1,345	Hacienda La Puente Unified	City of Industry
68	1,313	Redlands Unified	Redlands
69	1,310	Visalia Unified	Visalia
70	1,309	Stockton City Unified	Stockton
71	1,292	Downey Unified	Downey
72	1,288	Walnut Valley Unified	Walnut
73	1,279	Acalanes Union High	Lafayette
74	1,264	Hayward Unified	Hayward
75	1,254	Antioch Unified	Antioch
76	1,197	Sequoia Union High	Redwood City
77	1,192	Norwalk-La Mirada Unified	Norwalk
78	1,148	Simi Valley Unified	Simi Valley
79	1,145	Victor Valley Union High	Victorville
80	1,118	Newport-Mesa Unified	Costa Mesa
81	1,107	Centinela Valley Union High	Lawndale
82	1,106	Fairfield-Suisun Unified	Fairfield
83	1,099	Vallejo City Unified	Vallejo
84	1,094	Burbank Unified	Burbank
85	1,093	Santa Maria Joint Union High	Santa Maria
86	1,085	Jefferson Union High	Daly City
87	1,072	Rowland Unified	Rowland Heights
88	1,066	Orange County Office of Education	Costa Mesa
89	1,061	Manteca Unified	Manteca
90	1,055	Shasta Union High	Redding
91	1,051	Santa Cruz City High	Soquel
92	1,049	Temecula Valley Unified	Temecula
93	1,035	Vacaville Unified	Vacaville
94	1,024	Ventura Unified	Ventura
95	1,009	Pajaro Valley Unified School	Watsonville
96	998	Napa Valley Unified	Napa
97	995	Hemet Unified	Hemet
98	994	Perris Union High	Perris
99	979	Covina-Valley Unified	Covina
100	972	Porterville Unified	Porterville
101	970	Pasadena Unified	Pasadena
102	967	Chico Unified	Chico
103	957	Oceanside Unified	Oceanside
104	950	Palm Springs Unified	Palm Springs
105	944	Tustin Unified	Tustin
106	936	Placer Union High	Auburn
107	927	Tracy Joint Unified	Tracy
108	918	Livermore Valley Joint Unified	Livermore
109	912	Upland Unified	Upland
110	910	Pleasanton Unified	Pleasanton
111	907	Nevada Joint Union High	Grass Valley
112	902	Compton Unified	Compton
113	900	Lake Elsinore Unified	Lake Elsinore
114	898	Folsom-Cordova Unified	Folsom
115	870	Tulare Joint Union High	Tulare
116	861	Las Virgenes Unified	Calabasas
117	857	Hesperia Unified	Hesperia
118	855	Apple Valley Unified	Apple Valley
119	852	Santa Monica-Malibu Unified	Santa Monica
120	851	Los Angeles Co Office of Education	Downey
121	837	Alvord Unified	Riverside
122	832	Arcadia Unified	Arcadia
123	828	New Haven Unified	Union City
124	827	Tamalpais Union High	Larkspur
125	824	Lynwood Unified	Lynwood
126	804	Santa Clara Unified	Santa Clara
127	801	Turlock Joint Union High	Turlock
128	797	Jurupa Unified	Riverside
129	796	Madera Unified	Madera
130	794	Liberty Union High	Brentwood
131	789	Colton Joint Unified	Colton
132	780	Bellflower Unified	Bellflower
133	761	Bonita Unified	San Dimas
134	736	Palos Verdes Peninsula Unified	Palos Verdes Est
135	713	Baldwin Park Unified	Baldwin Park
136	710	Milpitas Unified	Milpitas
137	709	Palo Alto Unified	Palo Alto
138	691	Lucia Mar Unified	Arroyo Grande
138	691	Petaluma Joint Union High	Petaluma
140	690	Murrieta Valley Unified	Murrieta
141	685	Snowline Joint Unified	Phelan
142	683	Central Union High	El Centro
143	681	Yuba City Unified	Yuba City
144	673	Berkeley Unified	Berkeley
145	666	Inglewood Unified	Inglewood
146	660	San Lorenzo Unified	San Lorenzo
147	657	Los Alamitos Unified	Los Alamitos
148	655	Delano Joint Union High	Delano
149	651	Los Gatos-Saratoga Jt Union High	Los Gatos
150	645	Alameda City Unified	Alameda
151	639	Mountain View-Los Altos Union High	Mountain View
152	635	Yucaipa-Calimesa Jt. Unified	Yucaipa
153	633	South San Francisco Unified	S San Francisco
154	615	Morgan Hill Unified	Morgan Hill
155	611	Monterey Peninsula Unified	Monterey
156	605	Central Unified	Fresno
157	604	San Benito High	Hollister
158	602	Carlsbad Unified	Carlsbad
159	596	El Rancho Unified	Pico Rivera
160	595	Fallbrook Union High	Fallbrook
161	594	San Marcos Unified	San Marcos
162	593	Paramount Unified	Paramount
163	590	West Sonoma County Union High	Sebastopol
164	587	West Covina Unified	West Covina
165	585	Claremont Unified	Claremont
166	581	Western Placer Unified	Lincoln
167	578	Ceres Unified	Ceres
168	577	Glendora Unified	Glendora
169	576	Davis Joint Unified	Davis
170	569	Moorpark Unified	Moorpark
171	568	Lompoc Unified	Lompoc
172	558	Coachella Valley Unified	Thermal
172	558	Val Verde Unified	Perris
174	551	Castro Valley Unified	Castro Valley
175	550	Woodland Joint Unified	Woodland
176	541	San Luis Coastal Unified	San Luis Obispo
177	533	Hanford Joint Union High	Hanford
178	529	Azusa Unified	Azusa
179	520	Newark Unified	Newark
180	510	Kings Canyon Joint Unified	Reedley
181	509	Ukiah Unified	Ukiah
182	502	Manhattan Beach Unified	Manhattan Beach
183	497	Sanger Unified	Sanger
184	489	Oroville Union High	Oroville
185	487	Brea-Olinda Unified	Brea
185	487	Cotati-Rohnert Park Unified	Rohnert Park
187	483	Ramona City Unified	Ramona
188	481	Novato Unified	Novato
189	476	Calexico Unified	Calexico
189	476	Lincoln Unified	Stockton
191	475	Anderson Union High	Anderson
192	472	Beverly Hills Unified	Beverly Hills
193	456	Morongo Unified	Twentynine Plms
194	454	San Leandro Unified	San Leandro
195	446	Gilroy Unified	Gilroy
195	446	Rocklin Unified	Rocklin
197	440	Red Bluff Joint Union High	Red Bluff
197	440	Redondo Beach Unified	Redondo Beach
199	428	Pittsburg Unified	Pittsburg
200	424	Los Banos Unified	Los Banos
201	423	Paso Robles Joint Unified	Paso Robles
202	421	Marysville Joint Unified	Marysville
203	419	Eureka City Unified	Eureka
204	416	Benicia Unified	Benicia
204	416	San Gabriel Unified	San Gabriel
206	415	North Monterey County Unified	Moss Landing
207	407	Charter Oak Unified	Covina
207	407	San Rafael City High	San Rafael
209	402	Northern Humboldt Union High	McKinleyville
210	397	Atascadero Unified	Atascadero
211	395	Temple City Unified	Temple City
212	394	Rim of the World Unified	Lake Arrowhead
213	386	Natomas Unified	Sacramento
214	381	Lemoore Union High	Lemoore
215	379	Tahoe-Truckee Joint Unified	Truckee
216	373	Paradise Unified	Paradise
217	366	Galt Joint Union High	Galt
217	366	Monrovia Unified	Monrovia
219	365	Barstow Unified	Barstow
220	361	Sierra Sands Unified	Ridgecrest
221	359	Sonora Union High	Sonora
222	357	Oakdale Joint Unified	Oakdale
223	343	Amador County Unified	Jackson
224	340	King City Joint Union High	King City
225	330	Valley Center-Pauma Unified	Valley Center
226	327	Washington Unified	West Sacramento
227	325	La Canada Unified	La Canada
228	324	Center Joint Unified	Antelope
229	321	Brawley Union High	Brawley
230	320	Duarte Unified	Duarte
231	315	Martinez Unified	Martinez
232	308	Bassett Unified	La Puente
232	308	Lake Tahoe Unified	S Lake Tahoe
234	307	Culver City Unified	Culver City
235	304	Tehachapi Unified	Tehachapi
236	303	San Lorenzo Valley Unified	Ben Lomond
237	301	South Pasadena Unified	South Pasadena
238	299	Dinuba Unified	Dinuba
239	292	Travis Unified	Travis Afb
240	289	Del Norte County Unified	Crescent City
240	289	Selma Unified	Selma
242	287	Sonoma Valley Unified	Sonoma
243	286	Santa Paula Union High	Santa Paula
244	285	Riverside Co Office of Education	Riverside
245	280	San Marino Unified	San Marino
246	274	Ojai Unified	Ojai
247	264	Plumas Unified	Quincy
248	260	San Jacinto Unified	San Jacinto
249	259	Cabrillo Unified	Half Moon Bay
249	259	Gateway Unified	Redding
251	250	Dublin Unified	Dublin
252	248	Coronado Unified	Coronado
253	247	El Segundo Unified	El Segundo
254	241	Piedmont City Unified	Piedmont
255	236	Calaveras Unified	San Andreas
256	233	Fillmore Unified	Fillmore
257	232	Oak Park Unified	Oak Park
258	223	Coalinga-Huron Joint Unified	Coalinga
259	220	Bear Valley Unified	Big Bear Lake
260	217	Banning Unified	Banning
261	216	Escalon Unified	Escalon
262	214	San Diego Co Office of Education	San Diego
263	212	Sierra Unified	Prather
264	211	Patterson Joint Unified	Patterson
265	207	Lindsay Unified	Lindsay
266	203	Carpinteria Unified	Carpinteria
266	203	Healdsburg Unified	Healdsburg
268	201	Riverbank Unified	Riverbank
269	200	Dixon Unified	Dixon
270	199	Kerman Unified	Kerman
271	195	Laguna Beach Unified	Laguna Beach
272	194	Cutler-Orosi Joint Unified	Orosi
272	194	Mariposa County Unified	Mariposa
272	194	Mcfarland Unified	Mcfarland
275	193	Windsor Unified	Windsor
276	192	Templeton Unified	Templeton
277	191	Hughson Unified	Hughson
278	185	Palo Verde Unified	Blythe
279	181	Albany City Unified	Albany
280	178	River Delta Joint Unified	Rio Vista
281	177	Carmel Unified	Carmel
282	174	Hilmar Unified	Hilmar
282	174	Pacific Grove Unified	Pacific Grove
284	171	Dos Palos Oro Loma Jt. Unified	Dos Palos
285	169	Mojave Unified	Mojave
286	167	Orland Joint Unified	Orland
287	165	Willits Unified	Willits
288	161	Beaumont Unified	Beaumont
289	160	Kern County Office of Education	Bakersfield
290	157	Kelseyville Unified	Kelseyville
291	154	Ripon Unified	Ripon
292	152	Imperial Unified	Imperial
293	151	Southern Kern Unified	Rosamond
294	150	Black Oak Mine Unified	Georgetown
294	150	Linden Unified	Linden
294	150	Soledad Unified	Soledad
297	148	Gridley Unified	Gridley
298	147	Gonzales Unified	Gonzales
299	146	Newman-Crows Landing Unified	Newman
300	145	John Swett Unified	Crockett
300	145	Konocti Unified	Lower Lake
302	144	Fort Bragg Unified	Fort Bragg
303	143	Fowler Unified	Fowler
304	135	Muroc Joint Unified	North Edwards
305	134	Lakeport Unified	Lakeport
306	133	Holtville Unified	Holtville
307	130	Middletown Unified	Middletown
307	130	San Joaquin Co Off of Education	Stockton
309	128	Santa Clara Co Off of Education	San Jose
310	122	Winters Joint Unified	Winters
311	121	Corcoran Joint Unified	Corcoran
312	118	Farmersville Unified	Farmersville
313	117	Gustine Unified	Gustine
314	109	Fresno County Office of Education	Fresno
314	109	Julian Union High	Julian
316	108	Mountain Empire Unified	Pine Valley
317	106	Willows Unified	Willows
318	104	Golden Plains Unified	San Joaquin
318	104	Live Oak Unified	Live Oak
320	103	Cloverdale Unified	Cloverdale
320	103	Firebaugh-Las Deltas Joint Unified	Firebaugh
322	101	Reef-Sunset Unified	Avenal
323	100	Oro Grande Elementary	Oro Grande

323	100	Riverdale Joint Unified	Riverdale
325	99	Parlier Unified	Parlier
326	98	Acton-Agua Dulce Unified	Acton
327	92	Mendota Unified	Mendota
328	83	Silver Valley Unified	Yermo
329	80	Delhi Unified	Delhi
330	45	Westwood Unified	Westwood
331	33	Julian Union Elementary	Julian
331	33	Twin Ridges Elementary	North San Juan
333	32	Waterford Unified	Waterford
334	28	Gorman Elementary	Gorman
335	24	Tulare County Office of Education	Visalia
336	13	Lakeside Union Elementary	Lakeside
337	3	Redding Elementary	Redding
337	3	Redwood City Elementary	Redwood City
339	1	Keyes Union Elementary	Keyes
340	0	Bonsall Union Elementary	Bonsall
340	0	Escondido Union Elementary	Escondido
340	0	Lawndale Elementary	Lawndale
340	0	Lennox Elementary	Lennox
340	0	Nuview Union Elementary	Nuevo
340	0	Ravenswood City Elementary	East Palo Alto
340	0	Red Bluff Union Elementary	Red Bluff
340	0	San Bernardino Co Off of Education	San Bernardino
340	0	Scotts Valley Unified	Scotts Valley
340	0	Wheatland Elementary	Wheatland
350	n/a	Adelanto Elementary	Adelanto
350	n/a	Alhambra City Elementary	Alhambra
350	n/a	Alisal Union Elementary	Salinas
350	n/a	Alpine Union Elementary	Alpine
350	n/a	Alta Loma Elementary	Alta Loma
350	n/a	Alum Rock Union Elementary	San Jose
350	n/a	Anaheim Elementary	Anaheim
350	n/a	Arvin Union Elementary	Arvin
350	n/a	Atwater Elementary	Atwater
350	n/a	Auburn Union Elementary	Auburn
350	n/a	Bakersfield City Elementary	Bakersfield
350	n/a	Beardsley Elementary	Bakersfield
350	n/a	Bellevue Union Elementary	Santa Rosa
350	n/a	Belmont-Redwood Shores Elementary	Belmont
350	n/a	Berryessa Union Elementary	San Jose
350	n/a	Brawley Elementary	Brawley
350	n/a	Brentwood Union Elementary	Brentwood
350	n/a	Buckeye Union Elementary	Shingle Springs
350	n/a	Buena Park Elementary	Buena Park
350	n/a	Burlingame Elementary	Burlingame
350	n/a	Burton Elementary	Porterville
350	n/a	Cajon Valley Union Elementary	El Cajon
350	n/a	Cambrian Elementary	San Jose
350	n/a	Campbell Union Elementary	Campbell
350	n/a	Cascade Union Elementary	Anderson
350	n/a	Castaic Union Elementary	Valencia
350	n/a	Central Elementary	Rcho Cucamong
350	n/a	Central Union Elementary	Lemoore
350	n/a	Centralia Elementary	Buena Park
350	n/a	Chowchilla Elementary	Chowchilla
350	n/a	Chula Vista Elementary	Chula Vista
350	n/a	Corning Union Elementary	Corning
350	n/a	Cucamonga Elementary	Rcho Cucamong
350	n/a	Cupertino Union School	Cupertino
350	n/a	Cypress Elementary	Cypress
350	n/a	Del Mar Union Elementary	Del Mar
350	n/a	Del Paso Heights Elementary	Sacramento
350	n/a	Delano Union Elementary	Delano
350	n/a	Dixie Elementary	San Rafael
350	n/a	Dry Creek Joint Elementary	Roseville
350	n/a	Earlimart Elementary	Earlimart
350	n/a	East Whittier City Elementary	Whittier
350	n/a	Eastside Union Elementary	Lancaster
350	n/a	El Centro Elementary	El Centro
350	n/a	El Monte City Elementary	El Monte
350	n/a	Empire Union Elementary	Modesto
350	n/a	Encinitas Union Elementary	Encinitas
350	n/a	Enterprise Elementary	Redding
350	n/a	Etiwanda Elementary	Etiwanda
350	n/a	Eureka Union Elementary	Granite Bay
350	n/a	Evergreen Elementary	San Jose
350	n/a	Exeter Union Elementary	Exeter
350	n/a	Fairfax Elementary	Bakersfield
350	n/a	Fallbrook Union Elementary	Fallbrook
350	n/a	Fountain Valley Elementary	Fountain Valley
350	n/a	Franklin-Mckinley Elementary	San Jose
350	n/a	Fruitvale Elementary	Bakersfield
350	n/a	Fullerton Elementary	Fullerton
350	n/a	Galt Joint Union Elementary	Galt
350	n/a	Garvey Elementary	Rosemead
350	n/a	Goleta Union Elementary	Goleta
350	n/a	Grass Valley Elementary	Grass Valley
350	n/a	Greenfield Union Elementary	Bakersfield
350	n/a	Greenfield Union Elementary	Greenfield
350	n/a	Hanford Elementary	Hanford
350	n/a	Hawthorne Elementary	Hawthorne
350	n/a	Hollister SD	Hollister
350	n/a	Hueneme Elementary	Port Hueneme
350	n/a	Huntington Beach City Elementary	Huntington Bch
350	n/a	Jamul-Dulzura Union Elementary	Jamul
350	n/a	Jefferson Elementary	Tracy
350	n/a	Jefferson Elementary	Daly City
350	n/a	Keppel Union Elementary	Pearblossom
350	n/a	King City Union Elementary	King City
350	n/a	Kingsburg Elementary Charter	Kingsburg
350	n/a	La Habra City Elementary	La Habra
350	n/a	La Mesa-Spring Valley	La Mesa
350	n/a	Lafayette Elementary	Lafayette
350	n/a	Lamont Elementary	Lamont
350	n/a	Lancaster Elementary	Lancaster
350	n/a	Lemon Grove Elementary	Lemon Grove
350	n/a	Lemoore Union Elementary	Lemoore
350	n/a	Little Lake City Elementary	Santa Fe Spgs
350	n/a	Live Oak Elementary	Santa Cruz
350	n/a	Livingston Union Elementary	Livingston
350	n/a	Loomis Union Elementary	Loomis
350	n/a	Los Altos Elementary	Los Altos
350	n/a	Los Gatos Union Elementary	Los Gatos
350	n/a	Los Nietos Elementary	Whittier
350	n/a	Lowell Joint	Whittier
350	n/a	Magnolia Elementary	Anaheim
350	n/a	Mark West Union Elementary	Santa Rosa
350	n/a	Menifee Union Elementary	Menifee
350	n/a	Menlo Park City Elementary	Atherton
350	n/a	Merced City Elementary	Merced
350	n/a	Mill Valley Elementary	Mill Valley
350	n/a	Millbrae Elementary	Millbrae
350	n/a	Modesto City Elementary	Modesto
350	n/a	Moraga Elementary	Moraga
350	n/a	Moreland Elementary	San Jose
350	n/a	Mother Lode Union Elementary	Placerville
350	n/a	Mountain View Elementary	Ontario
350	n/a	Mountain View Elementary	El Monte
350	n/a	Mountain View-Whisman Elementary	Mountain View
350	n/a	Mt. Pleasant Elementary	San Jose
350	n/a	National Elementary	National City
350	n/a	Newhall Elementary	Valencia
350	n/a	Norris Elementary	Bakersfield
350	n/a	North Sacramento Elementary	Sacramento
350	n/a	Oak Grove Elementary	San Jose
350	n/a	Oakley Union Elementary	Oakley
350	n/a	Ocean View Elementary	Huntington Bch
350	n/a	Ocean View Elementary	Oxnard
350	n/a	Old Adobe Union Elementary	Petaluma
350	n/a	Ontario-Montclair Elementary	Ontario
350	n/a	Orcutt Union Elementary	Orcutt
350	n/a	Orinda Union Elementary	Orinda
350	n/a	Oroville City Elementary	Oroville
350	n/a	Oxnard Elementary	Oxnard
350	n/a	Pacifica SD	Pacifica
350	n/a	Palmdale Elementary	Palmdale
350	n/a	Panama Buena Vista Union Elem	Bakersfield
350	n/a	Perris Elementary	Perris
350	n/a	Petaluma City Elementary	Petaluma
350	n/a	Piner-Olivet Union Elementary	Santa Rosa
350	n/a	Pleasant Ridge Union Elementary	Grass Valley
350	n/a	Pleasant Valley School	Camarillo
350	n/a	Rescue Union Elementary	Rescue
350	n/a	Richland Union Elementary SD	Shafter
350	n/a	Rincon Valley Union Elementary	Santa Rosa
350	n/a	Rio Elementary	Oxnard
350	n/a	Rio Linda Union Elementary	Rio Linda
350	n/a	Robla Elementary	Sacramento
350	n/a	Romoland Elementary	Homeland
350	n/a	Rosedale Union Elementary	Bakersfield
350	n/a	Rosemead Elementary	Rosemead
350	n/a	Roseville City Elementary	Roseville
350	n/a	Ross Valley Elementary	San Anselmo
350	n/a	Salida Union Elementary	Salida
350	n/a	Salinas City Elementary	Salinas
350	n/a	San Bruno Park Elementary	San Bruno
350	n/a	San Carlos Elementary	San Carlos
350	n/a	San Mateo-Foster City Elementary	San Mateo
350	n/a	San Rafael City Elementary	San Rafael
350	n/a	San Ysidro Elementary	San Ysidro
350	n/a	Santa Barbara Elementary	Santa Barbara
350	n/a	Santa Cruz City Elementary	Soquel
350	n/a	Santa Maria-Bonita Elementary	Santa Maria
350	n/a	Santa Paula Elementary	Santa Paula
350	n/a	Santa Rita Union Elementary	Salinas
350	n/a	Santa Rosa Elementary	Santa Rosa
350	n/a	Santee Elementary	Santee
350	n/a	Saratoga Union Elementary	Saratoga
350	n/a	Saugus Union Elementary	Santa Clarita
350	n/a	Savanna Elementary	Anaheim
350	n/a	Solana Beach Elementary	Solana Beach
350	n/a	Soquel Union Elementary	Capitola
350	n/a	South Bay Union Elementary	Imperial Beach
350	n/a	South Whittier Elementary	Whittier
350	n/a	Standard Elementary	Bakersfield
350	n/a	Stanislaus Union Elementary	Modesto
350	n/a	Sulphur Springs Union Elementary	Canyon Country
350	n/a	Sunnyvale Elementary	Sunnyvale
350	n/a	Sylvan Union Elementary	Modesto
350	n/a	Taft City Elementary	Taft
350	n/a	Tulare City Elementary	Tulare
350	n/a	Turlock Joint Elementary	Turlock
350	n/a	Union Elementary	San Jose
350	n/a	Victor Elementary	Victorville
350	n/a	Walnut Creek Elementary	Walnut Creek
350	n/a	Wasco Union Elementary	Wasco
350	n/a	Weaver Union Elementary	Merced
350	n/a	Westminster Elementary	Westminster
350	n/a	Westside Union Elementary	Lancaster
350	n/a	Whittier City Elementary	Whittier
350	n/a	Wilsona Elementary	Palmdale
350	n/a	Winton Elementary	Winton
350	n/a	Wiseburn Elementary	Hawthorne
350	n/a	Woodlake Union Elementary	Woodlake

High School Drop-out Rate

Rank	Percent	District Name	City
1	n/a	ABC Unified	Cerritos
1	n/a	Acalanes Union High	Lafayette
1	n/a	Acton-Agua Dulce Unified	Acton
1	n/a	Adelanto Elementary	Adelanto
1	n/a	Alameda City Unified	Alameda
1	n/a	Albany City Unified	Albany
1	n/a	Alhambra City Elementary	Alhambra
1	n/a	Alhambra City High	Alhambra
1	n/a	Alisal Union Elementary	Salinas
1	n/a	Alpine Union Elementary	Alpine
1	n/a	Alta Loma Elementary	Alta Loma
1	n/a	Alum Rock Union Elementary	San Jose
1	n/a	Alvord Unified	Riverside
1	n/a	Amador County Unified	Jackson
1	n/a	Anaheim Elementary	Anaheim
1	n/a	Anaheim Union High	Anaheim
1	n/a	Anderson Union High	Anderson
1	n/a	Antelope Valley Union High	Lancaster
1	n/a	Antioch Unified	Antioch
1	n/a	Apple Valley Unified	Apple Valley
1	n/a	Arcadia Unified	Arcadia
1	n/a	Arvin Union Elementary	Arvin
1	n/a	Atascadero Unified	Atascadero
1	n/a	Atwater Elementary	Atwater
1	n/a	Auburn Union Elementary	Auburn
1	n/a	Azusa Unified	Azusa
1	n/a	Bakersfield City Elementary	Bakersfield
1	n/a	Baldwin Park Unified	Baldwin Park
1	n/a	Banning Unified	Banning
1	n/a	Barstow Unified	Barstow
1	n/a	Bassett Unified	La Puente
1	n/a	Bear Valley Unified	Big Bear Lake
1	n/a	Beardsley Elementary	Bakersfield
1	n/a	Beaumont Unified	Beaumont
1	n/a	Bellevue Union Elementary	Santa Rosa
1	n/a	Bellflower Unified	Bellflower
1	n/a	Belmont-Redwood Shores Elementary	Belmont
1	n/a	Benicia Unified	Benicia
1	n/a	Berkeley Unified	Berkeley
1	n/a	Berryessa Union Elementary	San Jose
1	n/a	Beverly Hills Unified	Beverly Hills
1	n/a	Black Oak Mine Unified	Georgetown
1	n/a	Bonita Unified	San Dimas
1	n/a	Bonsall Union Elementary	Bonsall
1	n/a	Brawley Elementary	Brawley
1	n/a	Brawley Union High	Brawley
1	n/a	Brea-Olinda Unified	Brea
1	n/a	Brentwood Union Elementary	Brentwood
1	n/a	Buckeye Union Elementary	Shingle Springs
1	n/a	Buena Park Elementary	Buena Park
1	n/a	Burbank Unified	Burbank
1	n/a	Burlingame Elementary	Burlingame
1	n/a	Burton Elementary	Porterville
1	n/a	Cabrillo Unified	Half Moon Bay
1	n/a	Cajon Valley Union Elementary	El Cajon
1	n/a	Calaveras Unified	San Andreas
1	n/a	Calexico Unified	Calexico
1	n/a	Cambrian Elementary	San Jose
1	n/a	Campbell Union Elementary	Campbell
1	n/a	Campbell Union High	San Jose
1	n/a	Capistrano Unified	San Juan Capis
1	n/a	Carlsbad Unified	Carlsbad
1	n/a	Carmel Unified	Carmel
1	n/a	Carpinteria Unified	Carpinteria
1	n/a	Cascade Union Elementary	Anderson
1	n/a	Castaic Union Elementary	Valencia
1	n/a	Castro Valley Unified	Castro Valley
1	n/a	Center Joint Unified	Antelope
1	n/a	Centinela Valley Union High	Lawndale

1	n/a	Central Elementary	Rcho Cucamong
1	n/a	Central Unified	Fresno
1	n/a	Central Union Elementary	Lemoore
1	n/a	Central Union High	El Centro
1	n/a	Centralia Elementary	Buena Park
1	n/a	Ceres Unified	Ceres
1	n/a	Chaffey Joint Union High	Ontario
1	n/a	Charter Oak Unified	Covina
1	n/a	Chico Unified	Chico
1	n/a	Chino Valley Unified	Chino
1	n/a	Chowchilla Elementary	Chowchilla
1	n/a	Chula Vista Elementary	Chula Vista
1	n/a	Claremont Unified	Claremont
1	n/a	Cloverdale Unified	Cloverdale
1	n/a	Clovis Unified	Clovis
1	n/a	Coachella Valley Unified	Thermal
1	n/a	Coalinga-Huron Joint Unified	Coalinga
1	n/a	Colton Joint Unified	Colton
1	n/a	Compton Unified	Compton
1	n/a	Conejo Valley Unified	Thousand Oaks
1	n/a	Corcoran Joint Unified	Corcoran
1	n/a	Corning Union Elementary	Corning
1	n/a	Corona-Norco Unified	Norco
1	n/a	Coronado Unified	Coronado
1	n/a	Cotati-Rohnert Park Unified	Rohnert Park
1	n/a	Covina-Valley Unified	Covina
1	n/a	Cucamonga Elementary	Rcho Cucamong
1	n/a	Culver City Unified	Culver City
1	n/a	Cupertino Union School	Cupertino
1	n/a	Cutler-Orosi Joint Unified	Orosi
1	n/a	Cypress Elementary	Cypress
1	n/a	Davis Joint Unified	Davis
1	n/a	Del Mar Union Elementary	Del Mar
1	n/a	Del Norte County Unified	Crescent City
1	n/a	Del Paso Heights Elementary	Sacramento
1	n/a	Delano Joint Union High	Delano
1	n/a	Delano Union Elementary	Delano
1	n/a	Delhi Unified	Delhi
1	n/a	Desert Sands Unified	La Quinta
1	n/a	Dinuba Unified	Dinuba
1	n/a	Dixie Elementary	San Rafael
1	n/a	Dixon Unified	Dixon
1	n/a	Dos Palos Oro Loma Jt. Unified	Dos Palos
1	n/a	Downey Unified	Downey
1	n/a	Dry Creek Joint Elementary	Roseville
1	n/a	Duarte Unified	Duarte
1	n/a	Dublin Unified	Dublin
1	n/a	Earlimart Elementary	Earlimart
1	n/a	East Side Union High	San Jose
1	n/a	East Whittier City Elementary	Whittier
1	n/a	Eastside Union Elementary	Lancaster
1	n/a	El Centro Elementary	El Centro
1	n/a	El Dorado Union High	Placerville
1	n/a	El Monte City Elementary	El Monte
1	n/a	El Monte Union High	El Monte
1	n/a	El Rancho Unified	Pico Rivera
1	n/a	El Segundo Unified	El Segundo
1	n/a	Elk Grove Unified	Elk Grove
1	n/a	Empire Union Elementary	Modesto
1	n/a	Encinitas Union Elementary	Encinitas
1	n/a	Enterprise Elementary	Redding
1	n/a	Escalon Unified	Escalon
1	n/a	Escondido Union Elementary	Escondido
1	n/a	Escondido Union High	Escondido
1	n/a	Etiwanda Elementary	Etiwanda
1	n/a	Eureka City Unified	Eureka
1	n/a	Eureka Union Elementary	Granite Bay
1	n/a	Evergreen Elementary	San Jose
1	n/a	Exeter Union Elementary	Exeter
1	n/a	Fairfax Elementary	Bakersfield
1	n/a	Fairfield-Suisun Unified	Fairfield
1	n/a	Fallbrook Union Elementary	Fallbrook
1	n/a	Fallbrook Union High	Fallbrook
1	n/a	Farmersville Unified	Farmersville
1	n/a	Fillmore Unified	Fillmore
1	n/a	Firebaugh-Las Deltas Joint Unified	Firebaugh
1	n/a	Folsom-Cordova Unified	Folsom
1	n/a	Fontana Unified	Fontana
1	n/a	Fort Bragg Unified	Fort Bragg
1	n/a	Fountain Valley Elementary	Fountain Valley
1	n/a	Fowler Unified	Fowler
1	n/a	Franklin-Mckinley Elementary	San Jose
1	n/a	Fremont Unified	Fremont
1	n/a	Fremont Union High	Sunnyvale
1	n/a	Fresno County Office of Education	Fresno
1	n/a	Fresno Unified	Fresno
1	n/a	Fruitvale Elementary	Bakersfield
1	n/a	Fullerton Elementary	Fullerton
1	n/a	Fullerton Joint Union High	Fullerton
1	n/a	Galt Joint Union Elementary	Galt
1	n/a	Galt Joint Union High	Galt
1	n/a	Garden Grove Unified	Garden Grove
1	n/a	Garvey Elementary	Rosemead
1	n/a	Gateway Unified	Redding
1	n/a	Gilroy Unified	Gilroy
1	n/a	Glendale Unified	Glendale
1	n/a	Glendora Unified	Glendora
1	n/a	Golden Plains Unified	San Joaquin
1	n/a	Goleta Union Elementary	Goleta
1	n/a	Gonzales Unified	Gonzales
1	n/a	Gorman Elementary	Gorman
1	n/a	Grant Joint Union High	Sacramento
1	n/a	Grass Valley Elementary	Grass Valley
1	n/a	Greenfield Union Elementary	Greenfield
1	n/a	Greenfield Union Elementary	Bakersfield
1	n/a	Gridley Unified	Gridley
1	n/a	Grossmont Union High	La Mesa
1	n/a	Gustine Unified	Gustine
1	n/a	Hacienda La Puente Unified	City of Industry
1	n/a	Hanford Elementary	Hanford
1	n/a	Hanford Joint Union High	Hanford
1	n/a	Hawthorne Elementary	Hawthorne
1	n/a	Hayward Unified	Hayward
1	n/a	Healdsburg Unified	Healdsburg
1	n/a	Hemet Unified	Hemet
1	n/a	Hesperia Unified	Hesperia
1	n/a	Hilmar Unified	Hilmar
1	n/a	Hollister SD	Hollister
1	n/a	Holtville Unified	Holtville
1	n/a	Hueneme Elementary	Port Hueneme
1	n/a	Hughson Unified	Hughson
1	n/a	Huntington Beach City Elementary	Huntington Bch
1	n/a	Huntington Beach Union High	Huntington Bch
1	n/a	Imperial Unified	Imperial
1	n/a	Inglewood Unified	Inglewood
1	n/a	Irvine Unified	Irvine
1	n/a	Jamul-Dulzura Union Elementary	Jamul
1	n/a	Jefferson Elementary	Daly City
1	n/a	Jefferson Elementary	Tracy
1	n/a	Jefferson Union High	Daly City
1	n/a	John Swett Unified	Crockett
1	n/a	Julian Union Elementary	Julian
1	n/a	Julian Union High	Julian
1	n/a	Jurupa Unified	Riverside
1	n/a	Kelseyville Unified	Kelseyville
1	n/a	Keppel Union Elementary	Pearblossom
1	n/a	Kerman Unified	Kerman
1	n/a	Kern County Office of Education	Bakersfield
1	n/a	Kern Union High	Bakersfield
1	n/a	Keyes Union Elementary	Keyes
1	n/a	King City Joint Union High	King City
1	n/a	King City Union Elementary	King City
1	n/a	Kings Canyon Joint Unified	Reedley
1	n/a	Kingsburg Elementary Charter	Kingsburg
1	n/a	Konocti Unified	Lower Lake
1	n/a	La Canada Unified	La Canada
1	n/a	La Habra City Elementary	La Habra
1	n/a	La Mesa-Spring Valley	La Mesa
1	n/a	Lafayette Elementary	Lafayette
1	n/a	Laguna Beach Unified	Laguna Beach
1	n/a	Lake Elsinore Unified	Lake Elsinore
1	n/a	Lake Tahoe Unified	S Lake Tahoe
1	n/a	Lakeport Unified	Lakeport
1	n/a	Lakeside Union Elementary	Lakeside
1	n/a	Lamont Elementary	Lamont
1	n/a	Lancaster Elementary	Lancaster
1	n/a	Las Virgenes Unified	Calabasas
1	n/a	Lawndale Elementary	Lawndale
1	n/a	Lemon Grove Elementary	Lemon Grove
1	n/a	Lemoore Union Elementary	Lemoore
1	n/a	Lemoore Union High	Lemoore
1	n/a	Lennox Elementary	Lennox
1	n/a	Liberty Union High	Brentwood
1	n/a	Lincoln Unified	Stockton
1	n/a	Linden Unified	Linden
1	n/a	Lindsay Unified	Lindsay
1	n/a	Little Lake City Elementary	Santa Fe Spgs
1	n/a	Live Oak Elementary	Santa Cruz
1	n/a	Live Oak Unified	Live Oak
1	n/a	Livermore Valley Joint Unified	Livermore
1	n/a	Livingston Union Elementary	Livingston
1	n/a	Lodi Unified	Lodi
1	n/a	Lompoc Unified	Lompoc
1	n/a	Long Beach Unified	Long Beach
1	n/a	Loomis Union Elementary	Loomis
1	n/a	Los Alamitos Unified	Los Alamitos
1	n/a	Los Altos Elementary	Los Altos
1	n/a	Los Angeles Co Office of Education	Downey
1	n/a	Los Angeles Unified	Los Angeles
1	n/a	Los Banos Unified	Los Banos
1	n/a	Los Gatos Union Elementary	Los Gatos
1	n/a	Los Gatos-Saratoga Jt Union High	Los Gatos
1	n/a	Los Nietos Elementary	Whittier
1	n/a	Lowell Joint	Whittier
1	n/a	Lucia Mar Unified	Arroyo Grande
1	n/a	Lynwood Unified	Lynwood
1	n/a	Madera Unified	Madera
1	n/a	Magnolia Elementary	Anaheim
1	n/a	Manhattan Beach Unified	Manhattan Beach
1	n/a	Manteca Unified	Manteca
1	n/a	Mariposa County Unified	Mariposa
1	n/a	Mark West Union Elementary	Santa Rosa
1	n/a	Martinez Unified	Martinez
1	n/a	Marysville Joint Unified	Marysville
1	n/a	Mcfarland Unified	Mcfarland
1	n/a	Mendota Unified	Mendota
1	n/a	Menifee Union Elementary	Menifee
1	n/a	Menlo Park City Elementary	Atherton
1	n/a	Merced City Elementary	Merced
1	n/a	Merced Union High	Atwater
1	n/a	Middletown Unified	Middletown
1	n/a	Mill Valley Elementary	Mill Valley
1	n/a	Millbrae Elementary	Millbrae
1	n/a	Milpitas Unified	Milpitas
1	n/a	Modesto City Elementary	Modesto
1	n/a	Modesto City High	Modesto
1	n/a	Mojave Unified	Mojave
1	n/a	Monrovia Unified	Monrovia
1	n/a	Montebello Unified	Montebello
1	n/a	Monterey Peninsula Unified	Monterey
1	n/a	Moorpark Unified	Moorpark
1	n/a	Moraga Elementary	Moraga
1	n/a	Moreland Elementary	San Jose
1	n/a	Moreno Valley Unified	Moreno Valley
1	n/a	Morgan Hill Unified	Morgan Hill
1	n/a	Morongo Unified	Twentynine Plms
1	n/a	Mother Lode Union Elementary	Placerville
1	n/a	Mountain Empire Unified	Pine Valley
1	n/a	Mountain View Elementary	El Monte
1	n/a	Mountain View Elementary	Ontario
1	n/a	Mountain View-Los Altos Union High	Mountain View
1	n/a	Mountain View-Whisman Elementary	Mountain View
1	n/a	Mt. Diablo Unified	Concord
1	n/a	Mt. Pleasant Elementary	San Jose
1	n/a	Muroc Joint Unified	North Edwards
1	n/a	Murrieta Valley Unified	Murrieta
1	n/a	Napa Valley Unified	Napa
1	n/a	National Elementary	National City
1	n/a	Natomas Unified	Sacramento
1	n/a	Nevada Joint Union High	Grass Valley
1	n/a	New Haven Unified	Union City
1	n/a	Newark Unified	Newark
1	n/a	Newhall Elementary	Valencia
1	n/a	Newman-Crows Landing Unified	Newman
1	n/a	Newport-Mesa Unified	Costa Mesa
1	n/a	Norris Elementary	Bakersfield
1	n/a	North Monterey County Unified	Moss Landing
1	n/a	North Sacramento Elementary	Sacramento
1	n/a	Northern Humboldt Union High	McKinleyville
1	n/a	Norwalk-La Mirada Unified	Norwalk
1	n/a	Novato Unified	Novato
1	n/a	Nuview Union Elementary	Nuevo
1	n/a	Oak Grove Elementary	San Jose
1	n/a	Oak Park Unified	Oak Park
1	n/a	Oakdale Joint Unified	Oakdale
1	n/a	Oakland Unified	Oakland
1	n/a	Oakley Union Elementary	Oakley
1	n/a	Ocean View Elementary	Oxnard
1	n/a	Ocean View Elementary	Huntington Bch
1	n/a	Oceanside Unified	Oceanside
1	n/a	Ojai Unified	Ojai
1	n/a	Old Adobe Union Elementary	Petaluma
1	n/a	Ontario-Montclair Elementary	Ontario
1	n/a	Orange County Office of Education	Costa Mesa
1	n/a	Orange Unified	Orange
1	n/a	Orcutt Union Elementary	Orcutt
1	n/a	Orinda Union Elementary	Orinda
1	n/a	Orland Joint Unified	Orland
1	n/a	Oro Grande Elementary	Oro Grande
1	n/a	Oroville City Elementary	Oroville
1	n/a	Oroville Union High	Oroville
1	n/a	Oxnard Elementary	Oxnard
1	n/a	Oxnard Union High	Oxnard
1	n/a	Pacific Grove Unified	Pacific Grove
1	n/a	Pacifica SD	Pacifica
1	n/a	Pajaro Valley Unified School	Watsonville
1	n/a	Palm Springs Unified	Palm Springs
1	n/a	Palmdale Elementary	Palmdale
1	n/a	Palo Alto Unified	Palo Alto
1	n/a	Palo Verde Unified	Blythe
1	n/a	Palos Verdes Peninsula Unified	Palos Verdes Est
1	n/a	Panama Buena Vista Union Elem	Bakersfield
1	n/a	Paradise Unified	Paradise
1	n/a	Paramount Unified	Paramount
1	n/a	Parlier Unified	Parlier
1	n/a	Pasadena Unified	Pasadena
1	n/a	Paso Robles Joint Unified	Paso Robles
1	n/a	Patterson Joint Unified	Patterson

1	n/a	Perris Elementary	Perris
1	n/a	Perris Union High	Perris
1	n/a	Petaluma City Elementary	Petaluma
1	n/a	Petaluma Joint Union High	Petaluma
1	n/a	Piedmont City Unified	Piedmont
1	n/a	Piner-Olivet Union Elementary	Santa Rosa
1	n/a	Pittsburg Unified	Pittsburg
1	n/a	Placentia-Yorba Linda Unified	Placentia
1	n/a	Placer Union High	Auburn
1	n/a	Pleasant Ridge Union Elementary	Grass Valley
1	n/a	Pleasant Valley School	Camarillo
1	n/a	Pleasanton Unified	Pleasanton
1	n/a	Plumas Unified	Quincy
1	n/a	Pomona Unified	Pomona
1	n/a	Porterville Unified	Porterville
1	n/a	Poway Unified	Poway
1	n/a	Ramona City Unified	Ramona
1	n/a	Ravenswood City Elementary	East Palo Alto
1	n/a	Red Bluff Joint Union High	Red Bluff
1	n/a	Red Bluff Union Elementary	Red Bluff
1	n/a	Redding Elementary	Redding
1	n/a	Redlands Unified	Redlands
1	n/a	Redondo Beach Unified	Redondo Beach
1	n/a	Redwood City Elementary	Redwood City
1	n/a	Reef-Sunset Unified	Avenal
1	n/a	Rescue Union Elementary	Rescue
1	n/a	Rialto Unified	Rialto
1	n/a	Richland Union Elementary SD	Shafter
1	n/a	Rim of the World Unified	Lake Arrowhead
1	n/a	Rincon Valley Union Elementary	Santa Rosa
1	n/a	Rio Elementary	Oxnard
1	n/a	Rio Linda Union Elementary	Rio Linda
1	n/a	Ripon Unified	Ripon
1	n/a	River Delta Joint Unified	Rio Vista
1	n/a	Riverbank Unified	Riverbank
1	n/a	Riverdale Joint Unified	Riverdale
1	n/a	Riverside Co Office of Education	Riverside
1	n/a	Riverside Unified	Riverside
1	n/a	Robla Elementary	Sacramento
1	n/a	Rocklin Unified	Rocklin
1	n/a	Romoland Elementary	Homeland
1	n/a	Rosedale Union Elementary	Bakersfield
1	n/a	Rosemead Elementary	Rosemead
1	n/a	Roseville City Elementary	Roseville
1	n/a	Roseville Joint Union High	Roseville
1	n/a	Ross Valley Elementary	San Anselmo
1	n/a	Rowland Unified	Rowland Heights
1	n/a	Sacramento City Unified	Sacramento
1	n/a	Saddleback Valley Unified	Mission Viejo
1	n/a	Salida Union Elementary	Salida
1	n/a	Salinas City Elementary	Salinas
1	n/a	Salinas Union High	Salinas
1	n/a	San Benito High	Hollister
1	n/a	San Bernardino City Unified	San Bernardino
1	n/a	San Bernardino Co Off of Education	San Bernardino
1	n/a	San Bruno Park Elementary	San Bruno
1	n/a	San Carlos Elementary	San Carlos
1	n/a	San Diego Co Office of Education	San Diego
1	n/a	San Diego Unified	San Diego
1	n/a	San Dieguito Union High	Encinitas
1	n/a	San Francisco Unified	San Francisco
1	n/a	San Gabriel Unified	San Gabriel
1	n/a	San Jacinto Unified	San Jacinto
1	n/a	San Joaquin Co Off of Education	Stockton
1	n/a	San Jose Unified	San Jose
1	n/a	San Juan Unified	Carmichael
1	n/a	San Leandro Unified	San Leandro
1	n/a	San Lorenzo Unified	San Lorenzo
1	n/a	San Lorenzo Valley Unified	Ben Lomond
1	n/a	San Luis Coastal Unified	San Luis Obispo
1	n/a	San Marcos Unified	San Marcos
1	n/a	San Marino Unified	San Marino
1	n/a	San Mateo Union High	San Mateo
1	n/a	San Mateo-Foster City Elementary	San Mateo
1	n/a	San Rafael City Elementary	San Rafael
1	n/a	San Rafael City High	San Rafael
1	n/a	San Ramon Valley Unified	Danville
1	n/a	San Ysidro Elementary	San Ysidro
1	n/a	Sanger Unified	Sanger
1	n/a	Santa Ana Unified	Santa Ana
1	n/a	Santa Barbara Elementary	Santa Barbara
1	n/a	Santa Barbara High	Santa Barbara
1	n/a	Santa Clara Co Off of Education	San Jose
1	n/a	Santa Clara Unified	Santa Clara
1	n/a	Santa Cruz City Elementary	Soquel
1	n/a	Santa Cruz City High	Soquel
1	n/a	Santa Maria Joint Union High	Santa Maria
1	n/a	Santa Maria-Bonita Elementary	Santa Maria
1	n/a	Santa Monica-Malibu Unified	Santa Monica
1	n/a	Santa Paula Elementary	Santa Paula
1	n/a	Santa Paula Union High	Santa Paula
1	n/a	Santa Rita Union Elementary	Salinas
1	n/a	Santa Rosa Elementary	Santa Rosa
1	n/a	Santa Rosa High	Santa Rosa
1	n/a	Santee Elementary	Santee
1	n/a	Saratoga Union Elementary	Saratoga
1	n/a	Saugus Union Elementary	Santa Clarita
1	n/a	Savanna Elementary	Anaheim
1	n/a	Scotts Valley Unified	Scotts Valley
1	n/a	Selma Unified	Selma
1	n/a	Sequoia Union High	Redwood City
1	n/a	Shasta Union High	Redding
1	n/a	Sierra Sands Unified	Ridgecrest
1	n/a	Sierra Unified	Prather
1	n/a	Silver Valley Unified	Yermo
1	n/a	Simi Valley Unified	Simi Valley
1	n/a	Snowline Joint Unified	Phelan
1	n/a	Solana Beach Elementary	Solana Beach
1	n/a	Soledad Unified	Soledad
1	n/a	Sonoma Valley Unified	Sonoma
1	n/a	Sonora Union High	Sonora
1	n/a	Soquel Union Elementary	Capitola
1	n/a	South Bay Union Elementary	Imperial Beach
1	n/a	South Pasadena Unified	South Pasadena
1	n/a	South San Francisco Unified	S San Francisco
1	n/a	South Whittier Elementary	Whittier
1	n/a	Southern Kern Unified	Rosamond
1	n/a	Standard Elementary	Bakersfield
1	n/a	Stanislaus Union Elementary	Modesto
1	n/a	Stockton City Unified	Stockton
1	n/a	Sulphur Springs Union Elementary	Canyon Country
1	n/a	Sunnyvale Elementary	Sunnyvale
1	n/a	Sweetwater Union High	Chula Vista
1	n/a	Sylvan Union Elementary	Modesto
1	n/a	Taft City Elementary	Taft
1	n/a	Tahoe-Truckee Joint Unified	Truckee
1	n/a	Tamalpais Union High	Larkspur
1	n/a	Tehachapi Unified	Tehachapi
1	n/a	Temecula Valley Unified	Temecula
1	n/a	Temple City Unified	Temple City
1	n/a	Templeton Unified	Templeton
1	n/a	Torrance Unified	Torrance
1	n/a	Tracy Joint Unified	Tracy
1	n/a	Travis Unified	Travis Afb
1	n/a	Tulare City Elementary	Tulare
1	n/a	Tulare County Office of Education	Visalia
1	n/a	Tulare Joint Union High	Tulare
1	n/a	Turlock Joint Elementary	Turlock
1	n/a	Turlock Joint Union High	Turlock
1	n/a	Tustin Unified	Tustin
1	n/a	Twin Ridges Elementary	North San Juan
1	n/a	Ukiah Unified	Ukiah
1	n/a	Union Elementary	San Jose
1	n/a	Upland Unified	Upland
1	n/a	Vacaville Unified	Vacaville
1	n/a	Val Verde Unified	Perris
1	n/a	Vallejo City Unified	Vallejo
1	n/a	Valley Center-Pauma Unified	Valley Center
1	n/a	Ventura Unified	Ventura
1	n/a	Victor Elementary	Victorville
1	n/a	Victor Valley Union High	Victorville
1	n/a	Visalia Unified	Visalia
1	n/a	Vista Unified	Vista
1	n/a	Walnut Creek Elementary	Walnut Creek
1	n/a	Walnut Valley Unified	Walnut
1	n/a	Wasco Union Elementary	Wasco
1	n/a	Washington Unified	West Sacramento
1	n/a	Waterford Unified	Waterford
1	n/a	Weaver Union Elementary	Merced
1	n/a	West Contra Costa Unified	Richmond
1	n/a	West Covina Unified	West Covina
1	n/a	West Sonoma County Union High	Sebastopol
1	n/a	Western Placer Unified	Lincoln
1	n/a	Westminster Elementary	Westminster
1	n/a	Westside Union Elementary	Lancaster
1	n/a	Westwood Unified	Westwood
1	n/a	Wheatland Elementary	Wheatland
1	n/a	Whittier City Elementary	Whittier
1	n/a	Whittier Union High	Whittier
1	n/a	William S. Hart Union High	Santa Clarita
1	n/a	Willits Unified	Willits
1	n/a	Willows Unified	Willows
1	n/a	Wilsona Elementary	Palmdale
1	n/a	Windsor Unified	Windsor
1	n/a	Winters Joint Unified	Winters
1	n/a	Winton Elementary	Winton
1	n/a	Wiseburn Elementary	Hawthorne
1	n/a	Woodlake Union Elementary	Woodlake
1	n/a	Woodland Joint Unified	Woodland
1	n/a	Yuba City Unified	Yuba City
1	n/a	Yucaipa-Calimesa Jt. Unified	Yucaipa

Colorado

Colorado Public School Educational Profile

Category	Value	Category	Value
Schools *(2003-2004)*	1,672	**Diploma Recipients** *(2002-2003)*	40,760
Instructional Level		White, Non-Hispanic	31,506
Primary	968	Black, Non-Hispanic	1,798
Middle	289	Asian/Pacific Islander	1,442
High	337	American Indian/Alaskan Native	314
Other Level	78	Hispanic	5,700
Curriculum		**High School Drop-out Rate** (%) *(2001-2002)*	n/a
Regular	1,579	White, Non-Hispanic	n/a
Special Education	17	Black, Non-Hispanic	n/a
Vocational	2	Asian/Pacific Islander	n/a
Alternative	74	American Indian/Alaskan Native	n/a
Type		Hispanic	n/a
Magnet	4	**Staff** *(2003-2004)*	
Charter	96	Teachers	44,904.3
Title I Eligible	868	Average Salary ($)	43,318
School-wide Title I	327	Librarians/Media Specialists	844.9
Students *(2003-2004)*	756,912	Guidance Counselors	1,371.0
Gender (%)		**Ratios** *(2003-2004)*	
Male	51.4	Student/Teacher Ratio	16.9 to 1
Female	48.6	Student/Librarian Ratio	895.9 to 1
Race/Ethnicity (%)		Student/Counselor Ratio	552.1 to 1
White, Non-Hispanic	64.5	**College Entrance Exam Scores** *(2005)*	
Black, Non-Hispanic	5.8	Scholastic Aptitude Test (SAT)	
Asian/Pacific Islander	3.1	Participation Rate (%)	26
American Indian/Alaskan Native	1.2	Mean SAT Reasoning Test Verbal Score	560
Hispanic	25.3	Mean SAT Reasoning Test Math Score	560
Classification (%)		American College Testing Program (ACT)	
Individual Education Program (IEP)	10.0	Participation Rate (%)	100
Migrant *(2002-2003)*	2.5	Average Composite Score	20.2
English Language Learner (ELL)	12.8	Average English Score	19.3
Eligible for Free Lunch Program	23.9	Average Math Score	20.0
Eligible for Reduced-Price Lunch Program	6.3	Average Reading Score	20.6
Current Spending *($ per student in FY 2003)*	7,250	Average Science Score	20.2
Instruction	4,189		
Support Services	2,818		

Note: For an explanation of data, please refer to the User's Guide in the front of the book

Colorado NAEP 2005 Test Scores

Reading			Mathematics		
Grade/Category	Value	Rank	Grade/Category	Value	Rank
4th Grade			**4th Grade**		
Average Proficiency	223.7 (1.14)	11/51	Average Proficiency	239.2 (1.08)	24/51
Proficiency by Gender/Race/Ethnicity			Proficiency by Gender/Race/Ethnicity		
Male	220.8 (1.36)	12/51	Male	240.7 (1.29)	23/51
Female	226.7 (1.46)	14/51	Female	237.6 (1.17)	27/51
White, Non-Hispanic	232.2 (1.15)	8/51	White, Non-Hispanic	247.5 (0.98)	13/51
Black, Non-Hispanic	207.2 (3.01)	6/42	Black, Non-Hispanic	222.4 (2.65)	14/42
Asian, Non-Hispanic	231.1 (3.89)	12/27	Asian, Non-Hispanic	241.7 (3.70)	19/25
American Indian, Non-Hispanic	n/a	n/a	American Indian, Non-Hispanic	n/a	n/a
Hispanic	205.8 (1.57)	17/40	Hispanic	222.7 (1.74)	27/41
Proficiency by Class Size			Proficiency by Class Size		
Less than 16 Students	219.0 (4.07)	5/34	Less than 16 Students	233.3 (5.78)	9/35
16 to 18 Students	n/a	n/a	16 to 18 Students	n/a	n/a
19 to 20 Students	225.7 (3.01)	9/38	19 to 20 Students	238.4 (3.07)	24/38
21 to 25 Students	225.3 (1.59)	15/51	21 to 25 Students	240.8 (1.49)	25/51
Greater than 25 Students	220.4 (3.27)	20/36	Greater than 25 Students	238.4 (2.99)	20/33
Percent Attaining Achievement Levels			Percent Attaining Achievement Levels		
Below Basic	30.5 (1.26)	38/51	Below Basic	19.5 (1.36)	24/51
Basic or Above	69.5 (1.26)	14/51	Basic or Above	80.5 (1.36)	28/51
Proficient or Above	36.6 (1.56)	8/51	Proficient or Above	38.8 (1.56)	19/51
Advanced or Above	8.3 (0.89)	9/51	Advanced or Above	6.2 (0.76)	9/51
8th Grade			**8th Grade**		
Average Proficiency	264.8 (1.07)	20/51	Average Proficiency	280.8 (1.18)	26/51
Proficiency by Gender/Race/Ethnicity			Proficiency by Gender/Race/Ethnicity		
Male	261.5 (1.28)	14/51	Male	280.8 (1.65)	26/51
Female	268.3 (1.27)	27/51	Female	280.8 (1.30)	20/51
White, Non-Hispanic	272.9 (0.98)	9/51	White, Non-Hispanic	291.5 (1.08)	11/51
Black, Non-Hispanic	254.2 (3.87)	2/40	Black, Non-Hispanic	255.8 (3.08)	18/41
Asian, Non-Hispanic	269.2 (5.54)	15/24	Asian, Non-Hispanic	n/a	n/a
American Indian, Non-Hispanic	n/a	n/a	American Indian, Non-Hispanic	n/a	n/a
Hispanic	246.5 (1.88)	22/38	Hispanic	260.2 (1.91)	25/38
Proficiency by Parents Highest Level of Ed.			Proficiency by Parents Highest Level of Ed.		
Did Not Finish High School	242.4 (2.86)	34/49	Did Not Finish High School	256.8 (1.91)	34/50
Graduated High School	252.2 (1.82)	28/50	Graduated High School	266.3 (1.99)	30/50
Some Education After High School	268.3 (1.78)	19/50	Some Education After High School	282.4 (1.90)	25/50
Graduated College	275.2 (1.40)	12/50	Graduated College	294.0 (1.05)	9/50
Percent Attaining Achievement Levels			Percent Attaining Achievement Levels		
Below Basic	30.5 (1.26)	38/51	Below Basic	29.5 (1.57)	25/51
Basic or Above	69.5 (1.26)	14/51	Basic or Above	70.5 (1.57)	27/51
Proficient or Above	36.6 (1.56)	8/51	Proficient or Above	32.0 (1.36)	18/51
Advanced or Above	8.3 (0.89)	9/51	Advanced or Above	6.3 (0.76)	16/51

Note: For an explanation of data, please refer to the User's Guide in the front of the book; n/a indicates data not available

Adams County

Adams 12 Five Star Schools
1500 E 128th Ave • Thornton, CO 80241
(720) 972-4000 • http://www.adams12.org/
Grade Span: PK-12; **Agency Type:** 1
Schools: 47
  30 Primary; 8 Middle; 6 High; 3 Other Level
  45 Regular; 0 Special Education; 0 Vocational; 2 Alternative
  0 Magnet; 4 Charter; 19 Title I Eligible; 5 School-wide Title I
Students: 34,869 (50.4% male; 49.5% female)
  Individual Education Program: 3,292 (9.4%);
  English Language Learner: 3,333 (9.6%); Migrant: 754 (2.2%)
  Eligible for Free Lunch Program: 6,675 (19.1%)
  Eligible for Reduced-Price Lunch Program: 2,067 (5.9%)
Teachers: 1,767.2 (19.7 to 1)
Librarians/Media Specialists: 45.1 (773.1 to 1)
Guidance Counselors: 42.5 (820.4 to 1)
Current Spending: ($ per student per year):
  Total: $6,355; Instruction: $3,834; Support Services: $2,349
Enrollment, Drop-out Rates and Diploma Recipients by Race/Ethnicity

Category	Total	White	Black	Asian	AIAN	Hisp.
Enrollment (%)	100.0	64.9	2.5	5.0	1.1	26.6
Drop-out Rate (%)	n/a	n/a	n/a	n/a	n/a	n/a
H.S. Diplomas (#)	1,566	1,156	36	81	8	285

Adams County 14
4720 E 69th Ave • Commerce City, CO 80022-2358
(303) 289-3950 • http://www.acsd14.k12.co.us/
Grade Span: PK-12; **Agency Type:** 1
Schools: 13
  9 Primary; 2 Middle; 2 High; 0 Other Level
  12 Regular; 0 Special Education; 0 Vocational; 1 Alternative
  0 Magnet; 0 Charter; 9 Title I Eligible; 7 School-wide Title I
Students: 6,528 (51.5% male; 48.4% female)
  Individual Education Program: 612 (9.4%);
  English Language Learner: 2,640 (40.4%); Migrant: 1,056 (16.2%)
  Eligible for Free Lunch Program: 3,973 (60.9%)
  Eligible for Reduced-Price Lunch Program: 541 (8.3%)
Teachers: 366.7 (17.8 to 1)
Librarians/Media Specialists: 5.0 (1,305.6 to 1)
Guidance Counselors: 8.8 (741.8 to 1)
Current Spending: ($ per student per year):
  Total: $7,758; Instruction: $4,738; Support Services: $2,759
Enrollment, Drop-out Rates and Diploma Recipients by Race/Ethnicity

Category	Total	White	Black	Asian	AIAN	Hisp.
Enrollment (%)	100.0	23.3	3.5	0.7	1.7	70.8
Drop-out Rate (%)	n/a	n/a	n/a	n/a	n/a	n/a
H.S. Diplomas (#)	236	105	3	0	3	125

Brighton 27J
630 S Eighth St • Brighton, CO 80601-3295
(303) 655-2900 • http://www.brightonps27j.k12.co.us/
Grade Span: PK-12; **Agency Type:** 1
Schools: 15
  10 Primary; 2 Middle; 1 High; 2 Other Level
  14 Regular; 0 Special Education; 0 Vocational; 1 Alternative
  0 Magnet; 3 Charter; 5 Title I Eligible; 1 School-wide Title I
Students: 8,261 (51.3% male; 48.6% female)
  Individual Education Program: 786 (9.5%);
  English Language Learner: 1,568 (19.0%); Migrant: 470 (5.7%)
  Eligible for Free Lunch Program: 1,927 (23.3%)
  Eligible for Reduced-Price Lunch Program: 572 (6.9%)
Teachers: 481.4 (17.2 to 1)
Librarians/Media Specialists: 1.5 (5,507.3 to 1)
Guidance Counselors: 12.2 (677.1 to 1)
Current Spending: ($ per student per year):
  Total: $6,460; Instruction: $3,738; Support Services: $2,414
Enrollment, Drop-out Rates and Diploma Recipients by Race/Ethnicity

Category	Total	White	Black	Asian	AIAN	Hisp.
Enrollment (%)	100.0	54.5	1.5	1.8	0.8	41.4
Drop-out Rate (%)	n/a	n/a	n/a	n/a	n/a	n/a
H.S. Diplomas (#)	271	180	1	8	1	81

Mapleton 1
591 E 80th Ave • Denver, CO 80229-5806
(303) 853-1000 • http://www.acsd1.k12.co.us/
Grade Span: PK-12; **Agency Type:** 1
Schools: 9
  6 Primary; 2 Middle; 1 High; 0 Other Level
  9 Regular; 0 Special Education; 0 Vocational; 0 Alternative
  0 Magnet; 0 Charter; 5 Title I Eligible; 3 School-wide Title I
Students: 5,716 (51.8% male; 48.1% female)
  Individual Education Program: 498 (8.7%);
  English Language Learner: 1,694 (29.6%); Migrant: 292 (5.1%)

  Eligible for Free Lunch Program: 1,872 (32.8%)
  Eligible for Reduced-Price Lunch Program: 619 (10.8%)
Teachers: 286.5 (20.0 to 1)
Librarians/Media Specialists: 3.0 (1,905.3 to 1)
Guidance Counselors: 9.5 (601.7 to 1)
Current Spending: ($ per student per year):
  Total: $6,838; Instruction: $3,849; Support Services: $2,779
Enrollment, Drop-out Rates and Diploma Recipients by Race/Ethnicity

Category	Total	White	Black	Asian	AIAN	Hisp.
Enrollment (%)	100.0	37.4	2.6	3.4	1.9	54.8
Drop-out Rate (%)	n/a	n/a	n/a	n/a	n/a	n/a
H.S. Diplomas (#)	210	124	4	7	2	73

Westminster 50
4476 W 68th Ave • Westminster, CO 80030-5898
(303) 428-3511 • http://www.adams50.k12.co.us/
Grade Span: PK-12; **Agency Type:** 1
Schools: 23
  17 Primary; 4 Middle; 2 High; 0 Other Level
  23 Regular; 0 Special Education; 0 Vocational; 0 Alternative
  0 Magnet; 1 Charter; 16 Title I Eligible; 9 School-wide Title I
Students: 10,467 (51.4% male; 48.5% female)
  Individual Education Program: 980 (9.4%);
  English Language Learner: 3,509 (33.5%); Migrant: 489 (4.7%)
  Eligible for Free Lunch Program: 4,895 (46.8%)
  Eligible for Reduced-Price Lunch Program: 1,079 (10.3%)
Teachers: 671.0 (15.6 to 1)
Librarians/Media Specialists: 5.7 (1,836.3 to 1)
Guidance Counselors: 17.8 (588.0 to 1)
Current Spending: ($ per student per year):
  Total: $6,961; Instruction: $4,396; Support Services: $2,351
Enrollment, Drop-out Rates and Diploma Recipients by Race/Ethnicity

Category	Total	White	Black	Asian	AIAN	Hisp.
Enrollment (%)	100.0	34.1	2.2	8.2	1.1	54.4
Drop-out Rate (%)	n/a	n/a	n/a	n/a	n/a	n/a
H.S. Diplomas (#)	498	272	8	57	10	151

Alamosa County

Alamosa RE-11J
209 Victoria Ave • Alamosa, CO 81101-4204
(719) 587-1600 • http://www.alamosa.k12.co.us/
Grade Span: PK-12; **Agency Type:** 1
Schools: 6
  2 Primary; 2 Middle; 1 High; 1 Other Level
  5 Regular; 0 Special Education; 0 Vocational; 1 Alternative
  0 Magnet; 0 Charter; 4 Title I Eligible; 3 School-wide Title I
Students: 2,454 (52.6% male; 47.3% female)
  Individual Education Program: 297 (12.1%);
  English Language Learner: 238 (9.7%); Migrant: 707 (28.8%)
  Eligible for Free Lunch Program: 1,218 (49.6%)
  Eligible for Reduced-Price Lunch Program: 233 (9.5%)
Teachers: 142.5 (17.2 to 1)
Librarians/Media Specialists: 3.0 (818.0 to 1)
Guidance Counselors: 9.3 (263.9 to 1)
Current Spending: ($ per student per year):
  Total: $6,793; Instruction: $3,962; Support Services: $2,644
Enrollment, Drop-out Rates and Diploma Recipients by Race/Ethnicity

Category	Total	White	Black	Asian	AIAN	Hisp.
Enrollment (%)	100.0	39.6	0.7	1.1	1.0	57.7
Drop-out Rate (%)	n/a	n/a	n/a	n/a	n/a	n/a
H.S. Diplomas (#)	132	72	0	4	0	56

Arapahoe County

Adams-Arapahoe 28J
1085 Peoria St • Aurora, CO 80011-6297
(303) 344-8060 • http://www.aps.k12.co.us/
Grade Span: PK-12; **Agency Type:** 1
Schools: 47
  33 Primary; 7 Middle; 6 High; 1 Other Level
  44 Regular; 0 Special Education; 0 Vocational; 3 Alternative
  0 Magnet; 1 Charter; 24 Title I Eligible; 18 School-wide Title I
Students: 32,530 (51.6% male; 48.3% female)
  Individual Education Program: 3,378 (10.4%);
  English Language Learner: 12,534 (38.5%); Migrant: 1,612 (5.0%)
  Eligible for Free Lunch Program: 11,690 (35.9%)
  Eligible for Reduced-Price Lunch Program: 2,025 (6.2%)
Teachers: 1,739.0 (18.7 to 1)
Librarians/Media Specialists: 19.9 (1,634.7 to 1)
Guidance Counselors: 46.0 (707.2 to 1)
Current Spending: ($ per student per year):
  Total: $6,887; Instruction: $4,192; Support Services: $2,490

Enrollment, Drop-out Rates and Diploma Recipients by Race/Ethnicity

Category	Total	White	Black	Asian	AIAN	Hisp.
Enrollment (%)	100.0	31.8	22.0	4.0	0.8	41.4
Drop-out Rate (%)	n/a	n/a	n/a	n/a	n/a	n/a
H.S. Diplomas (#)	1,120	569	233	95	11	212

Cherry Creek 5
4700 S Yosemite St • Greenwood Village, CO 80111-1394
(303) 773-1184 • http://www.ccsd.k12.co.us/index.htm
Grade Span: PK-12; **Agency Type:** 1
Schools: 50
  36 Primary; 8 Middle; 6 High; 0 Other Level
  50 Regular; 0 Special Education; 0 Vocational; 0 Alternative
  1 Magnet; 1 Charter; 17 Title I Eligible; 0 School-wide Title I
Students: 46,594 (51.1% male; 48.8% female)
  Individual Education Program: 5,109 (11.0%);
  English Language Learner: 6,044 (13.0%); Migrant: 9 (<0.1%)
  Eligible for Free Lunch Program: 4,235 (9.1%)
  Eligible for Reduced-Price Lunch Program: 2,176 (4.7%)
Teachers: 2,737.8 (17.0 to 1)
Librarians/Media Specialists: 59.7 (780.5 to 1)
Guidance Counselors: 71.3 (653.5 to 1)
Current Spending: ($ per student per year):
  Total: $7,427; Instruction: $4,719; Support Services: $2,284

Enrollment, Drop-out Rates and Diploma Recipients by Race/Ethnicity

Category	Total	White	Black	Asian	AIAN	Hisp.
Enrollment (%)	100.0	70.8	11.9	6.9	0.5	9.9
Drop-out Rate (%)	n/a	n/a	n/a	n/a	n/a	n/a
H.S. Diplomas (#)	2,922	2,368	221	193	5	135

Englewood 1
4101 S Bannock St • Englewood, CO 80110-4600
(303) 761-7050 • http://www.englewoodschools.org/
Grade Span: PK-12; **Agency Type:** 1
Schools: 11
  6 Primary; 3 Middle; 2 High; 0 Other Level
  10 Regular; 0 Special Education; 0 Vocational; 1 Alternative
  0 Magnet; 0 Charter; 6 Title I Eligible; 0 School-wide Title I
Students: 4,084 (52.5% male; 47.4% female)
  Individual Education Program: 530 (13.0%);
  English Language Learner: 229 (5.6%); Migrant: 2 (<0.1%)
  Eligible for Free Lunch Program: 1,100 (26.9%)
  Eligible for Reduced-Price Lunch Program: 266 (6.5%)
Teachers: 225.0 (18.2 to 1)
Librarians/Media Specialists: 3.0 (1,361.3 to 1)
Guidance Counselors: 9.6 (425.4 to 1)
Current Spending: ($ per student per year):
  Total: $7,344; Instruction: $4,629; Support Services: $2,523

Enrollment, Drop-out Rates and Diploma Recipients by Race/Ethnicity

Category	Total	White	Black	Asian	AIAN	Hisp.
Enrollment (%)	100.0	65.8	4.4	1.8	2.6	25.3
Drop-out Rate (%)	n/a	n/a	n/a	n/a	n/a	n/a
H.S. Diplomas (#)	290	223	11	5	2	49

Littleton 6
5776 S Crocker St • Littleton, CO 80120-2012
(303) 347-3300 • http://www.lps.k12.co.us/
Grade Span: PK-12; **Agency Type:** 1
Schools: 25
  18 Primary; 4 Middle; 3 High; 0 Other Level
  25 Regular; 0 Special Education; 0 Vocational; 0 Alternative
  0 Magnet; 2 Charter; 11 Title I Eligible; 0 School-wide Title I
Students: 16,458 (50.8% male; 49.1% female)
  Individual Education Program: 1,713 (10.4%);
  English Language Learner: 830 (5.0%); Migrant: 21 (0.1%)
  Eligible for Free Lunch Program: 1,380 (8.4%)
  Eligible for Reduced-Price Lunch Program: 464 (2.8%)
Teachers: 945.2 (17.4 to 1)
Librarians/Media Specialists: 11.6 (1,418.8 to 1)
Guidance Counselors: 32.0 (514.3 to 1)
Current Spending: ($ per student per year):
  Total: $6,947; Instruction: $4,341; Support Services: $2,266

Enrollment, Drop-out Rates and Diploma Recipients by Race/Ethnicity

Category	Total	White	Black	Asian	AIAN	Hisp.
Enrollment (%)	100.0	85.3	2.1	3.0	0.7	9.0
Drop-out Rate (%)	n/a	n/a	n/a	n/a	n/a	n/a
H.S. Diplomas (#)	1,223	1,127	14	37	2	43

Sheridan 2
4000 S Lowell Blvd • Sheridan, CO 80236
Mailing Address: PO Box 1198 • Englewood, CO 80150-1198
(720) 833-6991
Grade Span: PK-12; **Agency Type:** 1
Schools: 5
  3 Primary; 1 Middle; 1 High; 0 Other Level

  5 Regular; 0 Special Education; 0 Vocational; 0 Alternative
  0 Magnet; 0 Charter; 4 Title I Eligible; 3 School-wide Title I
Students: 1,861 (52.3% male; 47.6% female)
  Individual Education Program: 229 (12.3%);
  English Language Learner: 577 (31.0%); Migrant: 46 (2.5%)
  Eligible for Free Lunch Program: 958 (51.5%)
  Eligible for Reduced-Price Lunch Program: 192 (10.3%)
Teachers: 122.4 (15.2 to 1)
Librarians/Media Specialists: 3.6 (516.9 to 1)
Guidance Counselors: 5.0 (372.2 to 1)
Current Spending: ($ per student per year):
  Total: $8,583; Instruction: $4,841; Support Services: $3,418

Enrollment, Drop-out Rates and Diploma Recipients by Race/Ethnicity

Category	Total	White	Black	Asian	AIAN	Hisp.
Enrollment (%)	100.0	32.0	3.2	3.9	1.9	59.1
Drop-out Rate (%)	n/a	n/a	n/a	n/a	n/a	n/a
H.S. Diplomas (#)	76	46	2	3	1	24

Archuleta County

Archuleta County 50 Jt
309 Lewis St • Pagosa Springs, CO 81147-1498
Mailing Address: PO Box 1498 • Pagosa Springs, CO 81147-1498
(970) 264-2228 • http://www.pagosa.k12.co.us/
Grade Span: KG-12; **Agency Type:** 1
Schools: 4
  1 Primary; 2 Middle; 1 High; 0 Other Level
  4 Regular; 0 Special Education; 0 Vocational; 0 Alternative
  0 Magnet; 0 Charter; 2 Title I Eligible; 0 School-wide Title I
Students: 1,553 (53.3% male; 46.6% female)
  Individual Education Program: 99 (6.4%);
  English Language Learner: 27 (1.7%); Migrant: 0 (0.0%)
  Eligible for Free Lunch Program: 425 (27.4%)
  Eligible for Reduced-Price Lunch Program: 181 (11.7%)
Teachers: 92.1 (16.9 to 1)
Librarians/Media Specialists: 3.1 (501.0 to 1)
Guidance Counselors: 4.0 (388.3 to 1)
Current Spending: ($ per student per year):
  Total: $6,829; Instruction: $3,729; Support Services: $2,319

Enrollment, Drop-out Rates and Diploma Recipients by Race/Ethnicity

Category	Total	White	Black	Asian	AIAN	Hisp.
Enrollment (%)	100.0	77.6	1.1	0.5	1.3	19.5
Drop-out Rate (%)	n/a	n/a	n/a	n/a	n/a	n/a
H.S. Diplomas (#)	100	80	0	0	0	20

Boulder County

Boulder Valley Re 2
6500 Arapahoe Ave • Boulder, CO 80303
Mailing Address: PO Box 9011 6500 Arapahoe Av • Boulder, CO 80301-9011
(303) 447-1010 • http://www.bvsd.k12.co.us/
Grade Span: PK-12; **Agency Type:** 1
Schools: 53
  33 Primary; 9 Middle; 7 High; 4 Other Level
  52 Regular; 1 Special Education; 0 Vocational; 0 Alternative
  0 Magnet; 4 Charter; 21 Title I Eligible; 6 School-wide Title I
Students: 27,804 (50.8% male; 49.1% female)
  Individual Education Program: 3,033 (10.9%);
  English Language Learner: 4,021 (14.5%); Migrant: 529 (1.9%)
  Eligible for Free Lunch Program: 2,983 (10.7%)
  Eligible for Reduced-Price Lunch Program: 655 (2.4%)
Teachers: 1,629.3 (17.1 to 1)
Librarians/Media Specialists: 39.3 (707.5 to 1)
Guidance Counselors: 54.8 (507.4 to 1)
Current Spending: ($ per student per year):
  Total: $7,639; Instruction: $4,904; Support Services: $2,563

Enrollment, Drop-out Rates and Diploma Recipients by Race/Ethnicity

Category	Total	White	Black	Asian	AIAN	Hisp.
Enrollment (%)	100.0	78.9	1.6	5.8	0.7	13.0
Drop-out Rate (%)	n/a	n/a	n/a	n/a	n/a	n/a
H.S. Diplomas (#)	1,810	1,536	29	95	9	141

St Vrain Valley RE-1J
395 S Pratt Pkwy • Longmont, CO 80501-6436
(303) 776-6200 • http://www.stvrain.k12.co.us/
Grade Span: PK-12; **Agency Type:** 1
Schools: 37
  21 Primary; 6 Middle; 7 High; 3 Other Level
  35 Regular; 0 Special Education; 0 Vocational; 2 Alternative
  0 Magnet; 2 Charter; 13 Title I Eligible; 0 School-wide Title I
Students: 21,596 (51.6% male; 48.3% female)
  Individual Education Program: 1,616 (7.5%);
  English Language Learner: 3,457 (16.0%); Migrant: 552 (2.6%)
  Eligible for Free Lunch Program: 3,672 (17.0%)

Eligible for Reduced-Price Lunch Program: 804 (3.7%)
Teachers: 1,217.6 (17.7 to 1)
Librarians/Media Specialists: 17.5 (1,234.1 to 1)
Guidance Counselors: 46.9 (460.5 to 1)
Current Spending: ($ per student per year):
   Total: $6,605; Instruction: $3,983; Support Services: $2,415
Enrollment, Drop-out Rates and Diploma Recipients by Race/Ethnicity

Category	Total	White	Black	Asian	AIAN	Hisp.
Enrollment (%)	100.0	69.9	1.1	3.1	0.9	25.1
Drop-out Rate (%)	n/a	n/a	n/a	n/a	n/a	n/a
H.S. Diplomas (#)	1,134	970	6	29	13	116

Delta County

Delta County 50(J)
765 2075 Rd • Delta, CO 81416-8390
Mailing Address: 7655 2075 Rd • Delta, CO 81416-8390
(970) 874-4438 • http://www.delta.k12.co.us/
Grade Span: PK-12; **Agency Type:** 1
Schools: 14
   6 Primary; 2 Middle; 5 High; 1 Other Level
   14 Regular; 0 Special Education; 0 Vocational; 0 Alternative
   0 Magnet; 0 Charter; 7 Title I Eligible; 5 School-wide Title I
Students: 5,087   (51.9% male; 48.0% female)
   Individual Education Program: 571 (11.2%);
   English Language Learner: 400 (7.9%); Migrant: 255 (5.0%)
   Eligible for Free Lunch Program: 1,581 (31.1%)
   Eligible for Reduced-Price Lunch Program: 568 (11.2%)
Teachers: 279.4 (18.2 to 1)
Librarians/Media Specialists: 0.0 (n/a to 1)
Guidance Counselors: 9.9 (513.8 to 1)
Current Spending: ($ per student per year):
   Total: $6,594; Instruction: $4,037; Support Services: $2,287
Enrollment, Drop-out Rates and Diploma Recipients by Race/Ethnicity

Category	Total	White	Black	Asian	AIAN	Hisp.
Enrollment (%)	100.0	80.9	0.6	0.7	1.2	16.6
Drop-out Rate (%)	n/a	n/a	n/a	n/a	n/a	n/a
H.S. Diplomas (#)	306	274	1	4	2	25

Denver County

Denver County 1
900 Grant St • Denver, CO 80203-2996
(303) 764-3200 • http://dpsnet.denver.k12.co.us/
Grade Span: PK-12; **Agency Type:** 1
Schools: 145
   95 Primary; 21 Middle; 21 High; 8 Other Level
   137 Regular; 0 Special Education; 1 Vocational; 7 Alternative
   0 Magnet; 12 Charter; 95 Title I Eligible; 89 School-wide Title I
Students: 72,100   (50.9% male; 49.0% female)
   Individual Education Program: 8,287 (11.5%);
   English Language Learner: 21,523 (29.9%); Migrant: 1,377 (1.9%)
   Eligible for Free Lunch Program: 39,788 (55.2%)
   Eligible for Reduced-Price Lunch Program: 5,196 (7.2%)
Teachers: 4,217.8 (17.1 to 1)
Librarians/Media Specialists: 109.0 (661.5 to 1)
Guidance Counselors: 69.3 (1,040.4 to 1)
Current Spending: ($ per student per year):
   Total: $7,888; Instruction: $4,290; Support Services: $3,329
Enrollment, Drop-out Rates and Diploma Recipients by Race/Ethnicity

Category	Total	White	Black	Asian	AIAN	Hisp.
Enrollment (%)	100.0	19.7	18.8	3.1	1.2	57.1
Drop-out Rate (%)	n/a	n/a	n/a	n/a	n/a	n/a
H.S. Diplomas (#)	2,612	882	566	155	13	996

Douglas County

Douglas County Re 1
620 Wilcox St • Castle Rock, CO 80104-1739
(303) 387-0100 • http://www.dcsd.k12.co.us/
Grade Span: PK-12; **Agency Type:** 1
Schools: 63
   43 Primary; 9 Middle; 9 High; 2 Other Level
   59 Regular; 1 Special Education; 0 Vocational; 3 Alternative
   1 Magnet; 5 Charter; 26 Title I Eligible; 0 School-wide Title I
Students: 41,924   (51.1% male; 48.8% female)
   Individual Education Program: 3,574 (8.5%);
   English Language Learner: 1,030 (2.5%); Migrant: 15 (<0.1%)
   Eligible for Free Lunch Program: 713 (1.7%)
   Eligible for Reduced-Price Lunch Program: 485 (1.2%)
Teachers: 2,351.4 (17.8 to 1)
Librarians/Media Specialists: 14.5 (2,891.3 to 1)
Guidance Counselors: 49.0 (855.6 to 1)
Current Spending: ($ per student per year):
   Total: $7,049; Instruction: $4,089; Support Services: $2,683

Enrollment, Drop-out Rates and Diploma Recipients by Race/Ethnicity

Category	Total	White	Black	Asian	AIAN	Hisp.
Enrollment (%)	100.0	87.7	1.8	3.6	0.6	6.3
Drop-out Rate (%)	n/a	n/a	n/a	n/a	n/a	n/a
H.S. Diplomas (#)	1,898	1,689	29	68	12	100

Eagle County

Eagle County Re 50
757 E 3rd St • Eagle, CO 81631-0740
Mailing Address: PO Box 740 • Eagle, CO 81631-0740
(970) 328-6321 • http://ecsd2.re50j.k12.co.us/ECSD/
Grade Span: PK-12; **Agency Type:** 1
Schools: 16
   9 Primary; 4 Middle; 3 High; 0 Other Level
   15 Regular; 0 Special Education; 0 Vocational; 1 Alternative
   0 Magnet; 1 Charter; 9 Title I Eligible; 0 School-wide Title I
Students: 5,067   (51.4% male; 48.5% female)
   Individual Education Program: 447 (8.8%);
   English Language Learner: 1,509 (29.8%); Migrant: 145 (2.9%)
   Eligible for Free Lunch Program: 922 (18.2%)
   Eligible for Reduced-Price Lunch Program: 361 (7.1%)
Teachers: 341.3 (14.8 to 1)
Librarians/Media Specialists: 11.2 (452.4 to 1)
Guidance Counselors: 13.4 (378.1 to 1)
Current Spending: ($ per student per year):
   Total: $8,732; Instruction: $4,654; Support Services: $3,807
Enrollment, Drop-out Rates and Diploma Recipients by Race/Ethnicity

Category	Total	White	Black	Asian	AIAN	Hisp.
Enrollment (%)	100.0	56.1	0.4	0.8	0.4	42.2
Drop-out Rate (%)	n/a	n/a	n/a	n/a	n/a	n/a
H.S. Diplomas (#)	237	185	1	4	0	47

El Paso County

Academy 20
7610 N Union Blvd • Colorado Springs, CO 80920-3899
(719) 234-1200 • http://www.d20.co.edu/
Grade Span: PK-12; **Agency Type:** 1
Schools: 26
   16 Primary; 4 Middle; 5 High; 1 Other Level
   25 Regular; 0 Special Education; 0 Vocational; 1 Alternative
   0 Magnet; 2 Charter; 14 Title I Eligible; 2 School-wide Title I
Students: 19,083   (51.3% male; 48.6% female)
   Individual Education Program: 1,393 (7.3%);
   English Language Learner: 396 (2.1%); Migrant: 0 (0.0%)
   Eligible for Free Lunch Program: 627 (3.3%)
   Eligible for Reduced-Price Lunch Program: 435 (2.3%)
Teachers: 1,165.4 (16.4 to 1)
Librarians/Media Specialists: 11.4 (1,673.9 to 1)
Guidance Counselors: 46.0 (414.8 to 1)
Current Spending: ($ per student per year):
   Total: $6,921; Instruction: $4,223; Support Services: $2,549
Enrollment, Drop-out Rates and Diploma Recipients by Race/Ethnicity

Category	Total	White	Black	Asian	AIAN	Hisp.
Enrollment (%)	100.0	84.7	3.7	4.4	0.9	6.3
Drop-out Rate (%)	n/a	n/a	n/a	n/a	n/a	n/a
H.S. Diplomas (#)	1,205	1,069	42	30	15	49

Cheyenne Mountain 12
1118 W Cheyenne Rd • Colorado Springs, CO 80906-2497
(719) 475-6100 • http://www.cmsd.k12.co.us/
Grade Span: PK-12; **Agency Type:** 1
Schools: 9
   7 Primary; 1 Middle; 1 High; 0 Other Level
   9 Regular; 0 Special Education; 0 Vocational; 0 Alternative
   0 Magnet; 1 Charter; 4 Title I Eligible; 1 School-wide Title I
Students: 4,506   (50.6% male; 49.3% female)
   Individual Education Program: 228 (5.1%);
   English Language Learner: 393 (8.7%); Migrant: 0 (0.0%)
   Eligible for Free Lunch Program: 202 (4.5%)
   Eligible for Reduced-Price Lunch Program: 92 (2.0%)
Teachers: 267.3 (16.9 to 1)
Librarians/Media Specialists: 7.9 (570.4 to 1)
Guidance Counselors: 12.6 (357.6 to 1)
Current Spending: ($ per student per year):
   Total: $6,029; Instruction: $3,655; Support Services: $2,225
Enrollment, Drop-out Rates and Diploma Recipients by Race/Ethnicity

Category	Total	White	Black	Asian	AIAN	Hisp.
Enrollment (%)	100.0	83.2	2.7	4.8	0.7	8.6
Drop-out Rate (%)	n/a	n/a	n/a	n/a	n/a	n/a
H.S. Diplomas (#)	316	282	7	13	2	12

Colorado Springs 11

1115 N El Paso St • Colorado Springs, CO 80903-2599
(719) 520-2000 • http://www.cssd11.k12.co.us/
Grade Span: PK-12; **Agency Type:** 1
Schools: 65
    40 Primary; 10 Middle; 11 High; 4 Other Level
    57 Regular; 2 Special Education; 0 Vocational; 6 Alternative
    0 Magnet; 5 Charter; 35 Title I Eligible; 17 School-wide Title I
Students: 31,840   (51.5% male; 48.4% female)
    Individual Education Program: 2,311 (7.3%);
    English Language Learner: 2,002 (6.3%); Migrant: 453 (1.4%)
    Eligible for Free Lunch Program: 8,217 (25.8%)
    Eligible for Reduced-Price Lunch Program: 2,860 (9.0%)
Teachers: 1,917.9 (16.6 to 1)
Librarians/Media Specialists: 57.6 (552.8 to 1)
Guidance Counselors: 40.3 (790.1 to 1)
Current Spending: ($ per student per year):
    Total: $7,918; Instruction: $4,009; Support Services: $3,714
Enrollment, Drop-out Rates and Diploma Recipients by Race/Ethnicity

Category	Total	White	Black	Asian	AIAN	Hisp.
Enrollment (%)	100.0	66.6	10.2	2.7	1.5	19.0
Drop-out Rate (%)	n/a	n/a	n/a	n/a	n/a	n/a
H.S. Diplomas (#)	1,816	1,350	154	63	25	224

Falcon 49

10850 E Woodmen Rd • Falcon, CO 80831-8127
(719) 495-3601 • http://d49.org/
Grade Span: PK-12; **Agency Type:** 1
Schools: 12
    7 Primary; 3 Middle; 2 High; 0 Other Level
    12 Regular; 0 Special Education; 0 Vocational; 0 Alternative
    0 Magnet; 0 Charter; 5 Title I Eligible; 2 School-wide Title I
Students: 8,660   (51.2% male; 48.7% female)
    Individual Education Program: 902 (10.4%);
    English Language Learner: 53 (0.6%); Migrant: 2 (<0.1%)
    Eligible for Free Lunch Program: 790 (9.1%)
    Eligible for Reduced-Price Lunch Program: 477 (5.5%)
Teachers: 497.6 (17.4 to 1)
Librarians/Media Specialists: 12.0 (721.7 to 1)
Guidance Counselors: 20.4 (424.5 to 1)
Current Spending: ($ per student per year):
    Total: $5,800; Instruction: $3,354; Support Services: $2,253
Enrollment, Drop-out Rates and Diploma Recipients by Race/Ethnicity

Category	Total	White	Black	Asian	AIAN	Hisp.
Enrollment (%)	100.0	73.2	8.0	4.6	1.7	12.5
Drop-out Rate (%)	n/a	n/a	n/a	n/a	n/a	n/a
H.S. Diplomas (#)	327	242	37	20	3	25

Fountain 8

425 W Alabama Ave • Fountain, CO 80817-1703
(719) 382-1300 • http://www.ffc8.org/
Grade Span: PK-12; **Agency Type:** 1
Schools: 10
    6 Primary; 2 Middle; 2 High; 0 Other Level
    9 Regular; 0 Special Education; 0 Vocational; 1 Alternative
    0 Magnet; 0 Charter; 5 Title I Eligible; 3 School-wide Title I
Students: 5,879   (51.9% male; 48.0% female)
    Individual Education Program: 663 (11.3%);
    English Language Learner: 95 (1.6%); Migrant: 36 (0.6%)
    Eligible for Free Lunch Program: 1,121 (19.1%)
    Eligible for Reduced-Price Lunch Program: 779 (13.3%)
Teachers: 245.5 (23.9 to 1)
Librarians/Media Specialists: 4.1 (1,433.9 to 1)
Guidance Counselors: 10.6 (554.6 to 1)
Current Spending: ($ per student per year):
    Total: $6,190; Instruction: $3,548; Support Services: $2,391
Enrollment, Drop-out Rates and Diploma Recipients by Race/Ethnicity

Category	Total	White	Black	Asian	AIAN	Hisp.
Enrollment (%)	100.0	59.4	18.3	4.1	2.4	15.8
Drop-out Rate (%)	n/a	n/a	n/a	n/a	n/a	n/a
H.S. Diplomas (#)	184	114	39	7	1	23

Harrison 2

1060 Harrison Rd • Colorado Springs, CO 80906-3586
(719) 579-2000 • http://www.harrison.k12.co.us/
Grade Span: PK-12; **Agency Type:** 1
Schools: 25
    14 Primary; 4 Middle; 7 High; 0 Other Level
    22 Regular; 0 Special Education; 0 Vocational; 3 Alternative
    0 Magnet; 3 Charter; 17 Title I Eligible; 13 School-wide Title I
Students: 10,943   (51.1% male; 48.8% female)
    Individual Education Program: 1,062 (9.7%);
    English Language Learner: 1,050 (9.6%); Migrant: 319 (2.9%)
    Eligible for Free Lunch Program: 4,977 (45.5%)
    Eligible for Reduced-Price Lunch Program: 1,300 (11.9%)

Teachers: 750.2 (14.6 to 1)
Librarians/Media Specialists: 8.8 (1,243.5 to 1)
Guidance Counselors: 33.5 (326.7 to 1)
Current Spending: ($ per student per year):
    Total: $7,592; Instruction: $4,304; Support Services: $3,006
Enrollment, Drop-out Rates and Diploma Recipients by Race/Ethnicity

Category	Total	White	Black	Asian	AIAN	Hisp.
Enrollment (%)	100.0	36.0	24.8	5.1	1.7	32.4
Drop-out Rate (%)	n/a	n/a	n/a	n/a	n/a	n/a
H.S. Diplomas (#)	400	162	123	34	2	79

Lewis-Palmer 38

146 Jefferson St • Monument, CO 80132-0040
Mailing Address: PO Box 40 • Monument, CO 80132-0040
(719) 488-4700 • http://www.lpsd.k12.co.us/
Grade Span: PK-12; **Agency Type:** 1
Schools: 9
    5 Primary; 2 Middle; 1 High; 1 Other Level
    9 Regular; 0 Special Education; 0 Vocational; 0 Alternative
    0 Magnet; 1 Charter; 3 Title I Eligible; 0 School-wide Title I
Students: 5,370   (51.8% male; 48.1% female)
    Individual Education Program: 419 (7.8%);
    English Language Learner: 62 (1.2%); Migrant: 0 (0.0%)
    Eligible for Free Lunch Program: 169 (3.1%)
    Eligible for Reduced-Price Lunch Program: 77 (1.4%)
Teachers: 327.6 (16.4 to 1)
Librarians/Media Specialists: 2.1 (2,557.1 to 1)
Guidance Counselors: 14.0 (383.6 to 1)
Current Spending: ($ per student per year):
    Total: $5,794; Instruction: $3,403; Support Services: $2,244
Enrollment, Drop-out Rates and Diploma Recipients by Race/Ethnicity

Category	Total	White	Black	Asian	AIAN	Hisp.
Enrollment (%)	100.0	91.2	1.4	2.2	0.6	4.5
Drop-out Rate (%)	n/a	n/a	n/a	n/a	n/a	n/a
H.S. Diplomas (#)	295	286	1	2	0	6

Widefield 3

1820 Main St • Colorado Springs, CO 80911-1152
(719) 391-3000 • http://www.wsd3.k12.co.us/
Grade Span: PK-12; **Agency Type:** 1
Schools: 17
    11 Primary; 3 Middle; 3 High; 0 Other Level
    16 Regular; 0 Special Education; 0 Vocational; 1 Alternative
    0 Magnet; 1 Charter; 12 Title I Eligible; 2 School-wide Title I
Students: 8,475   (51.4% male; 48.5% female)
    Individual Education Program: 1,056 (12.5%);
    English Language Learner: 190 (2.2%); Migrant: 2 (<0.1%)
    Eligible for Free Lunch Program: 1,166 (13.8%)
    Eligible for Reduced-Price Lunch Program: 481 (5.7%)
Teachers: 480.4 (17.6 to 1)
Librarians/Media Specialists: 6.2 (1,366.9 to 1)
Guidance Counselors: 26.8 (316.2 to 1)
Current Spending: ($ per student per year):
    Total: $5,803; Instruction: $3,431; Support Services: $2,156
Enrollment, Drop-out Rates and Diploma Recipients by Race/Ethnicity

Category	Total	White	Black	Asian	AIAN	Hisp.
Enrollment (%)	100.0	62.9	15.6	4.0	1.4	16.1
Drop-out Rate (%)	n/a	n/a	n/a	n/a	n/a	n/a
H.S. Diplomas (#)	532	354	66	39	5	68

Elbert County

Elizabeth C-1

634 S Elbert St • Elizabeth, CO 80107-0610
Mailing Address: PO Box 610 • Elizabeth, CO 80107-0610
(303) 646-4441 • http://www.elizabeth.k12.co.us/
Grade Span: PK-12; **Agency Type:** 1
Schools: 8
    5 Primary; 1 Middle; 2 High; 0 Other Level
    8 Regular; 0 Special Education; 0 Vocational; 0 Alternative
    0 Magnet; 1 Charter; 3 Title I Eligible; 0 School-wide Title I
Students: 2,867   (51.4% male; 48.5% female)
    Individual Education Program: 273 (9.5%);
    English Language Learner: 12 (0.4%); Migrant: 0 (0.0%)
    Eligible for Free Lunch Program: 108 (3.8%)
    Eligible for Reduced-Price Lunch Program: 53 (1.8%)
Teachers: 163.9 (17.5 to 1)
Librarians/Media Specialists: 0.9 (3,185.6 to 1)
Guidance Counselors: 5.9 (485.9 to 1)
Current Spending: ($ per student per year):
    Total: $6,455; Instruction: $3,488; Support Services: $2,688

Enrollment, Drop-out Rates and Diploma Recipients by Race/Ethnicity

Category	Total	White	Black	Asian	AIAN	Hisp.
Enrollment (%)	100.0	90.3	1.3	1.3	0.9	6.1
Drop-out Rate (%)	n/a	n/a	n/a	n/a	n/a	n/a
H.S. Diplomas (#)	215	194	3	2	4	12

Fremont County

Canon City Re-1
101 N 14th St • Canon City, CO 81212-3564
(719) 276-5700 • http://www.canoncityschools.org/profile.htm
Grade Span: KG-12; **Agency Type:** 1
Schools: 10
  7 Primary; 1 Middle; 2 High; 0 Other Level
  9 Regular; 0 Special Education; 0 Vocational; 1 Alternative
  0 Magnet; 1 Charter; 6 Title I Eligible; 5 School-wide Title I
Students: 4,114   (51.0% male; 48.9% female)
  Individual Education Program: 488 (11.9%);
  English Language Learner: 17 (0.4%); Migrant: 4 (0.1%)
  Eligible for Free Lunch Program: 1,198 (29.1%)
  Eligible for Reduced-Price Lunch Program: 378 (9.2%)
Teachers: 248.8 (16.5 to 1)
Librarians/Media Specialists: 2.0 (2,057.0 to 1)
Guidance Counselors: 7.3 (563.6 to 1)
Current Spending: ($ per student per year):
  Total: $6,384; Instruction: $3,891; Support Services: $2,271

Enrollment, Drop-out Rates and Diploma Recipients by Race/Ethnicity

Category	Total	White	Black	Asian	AIAN	Hisp.
Enrollment (%)	100.0	90.0	0.8	1.2	0.9	7.1
Drop-out Rate (%)	n/a	n/a	n/a	n/a	n/a	n/a
H.S. Diplomas (#)	279	255	3	2	8	11

Florence Re-2
403 W 5th St • Florence, CO 81226-1103
(719) 784-6312
Grade Span: KG-12; **Agency Type:** 1
Schools: 5
  2 Primary; 2 Middle; 1 High; 0 Other Level
  5 Regular; 0 Special Education; 0 Vocational; 0 Alternative
  0 Magnet; 0 Charter; 3 Title I Eligible; 3 School-wide Title I
Students: 1,844   (52.8% male; 47.1% female)
  Individual Education Program: 285 (15.5%);
  English Language Learner: 16 (0.9%); Migrant: 3 (0.2%)
  Eligible for Free Lunch Program: 523 (28.4%)
  Eligible for Reduced-Price Lunch Program: 168 (9.1%)
Teachers: 114.9 (16.0 to 1)
Librarians/Media Specialists: 1.0 (1,844.0 to 1)
Guidance Counselors: 5.3 (347.9 to 1)
Current Spending: ($ per student per year):
  Total: $6,237; Instruction: $3,979; Support Services: $2,021

Enrollment, Drop-out Rates and Diploma Recipients by Race/Ethnicity

Category	Total	White	Black	Asian	AIAN	Hisp.
Enrollment (%)	100.0	85.8	1.2	0.8	0.8	11.4
Drop-out Rate (%)	n/a	n/a	n/a	n/a	n/a	n/a
H.S. Diplomas (#)	87	76	0	1	0	10

Garfield County

Garfield Re-2
839 Whiteriver • Rifle, CO 81650-3500
(970) 625-7600 • http://www.garfieldre2.k12.co.us/
Grade Span: PK-12; **Agency Type:** 1
Schools: 7
  4 Primary; 2 Middle; 1 High; 0 Other Level
  7 Regular; 0 Special Education; 0 Vocational; 0 Alternative
  0 Magnet; 0 Charter; 6 Title I Eligible; 4 School-wide Title I
Students: 3,810   (51.4% male; 48.5% female)
  Individual Education Program: 315 (8.3%);
  English Language Learner: 741 (19.4%); Migrant: 58 (1.5%)
  Eligible for Free Lunch Program: 905 (23.8%)
  Eligible for Reduced-Price Lunch Program: 308 (8.1%)
Teachers: 212.2 (18.0 to 1)
Librarians/Media Specialists: 2.0 (1,905.0 to 1)
Guidance Counselors: 8.7 (437.9 to 1)
Current Spending: ($ per student per year):
  Total: $5,819; Instruction: $3,297; Support Services: $2,300

Enrollment, Drop-out Rates and Diploma Recipients by Race/Ethnicity

Category	Total	White	Black	Asian	AIAN	Hisp.
Enrollment (%)	100.0	70.0	0.5	0.4	0.7	28.4
Drop-out Rate (%)	n/a	n/a	n/a	n/a	n/a	n/a
H.S. Diplomas (#)	156	146	0	2	4	4

Roaring Fork Re-1
1405 Grand Ave • Glenwood Springs, CO 81601-3807
(970) 384-6000 • http://www.rfsd.k12.co.us/
Grade Span: PK-12; **Agency Type:** 1
Schools: 13
  6 Primary; 3 Middle; 4 High; 0 Other Level
  12 Regular; 0 Special Education; 0 Vocational; 1 Alternative
  0 Magnet; 1 Charter; 8 Title I Eligible; 5 School-wide Title I
Students: 4,882   (52.5% male; 47.4% female)
  Individual Education Program: 334 (6.8%);
  English Language Learner: 1,349 (27.6%); Migrant: 13 (0.3%)
  Eligible for Free Lunch Program: 740 (15.2%)
  Eligible for Reduced-Price Lunch Program: 310 (6.3%)
Teachers: 333.1 (14.7 to 1)
Librarians/Media Specialists: 8.3 (588.2 to 1)
Guidance Counselors: 10.8 (452.0 to 1)
Current Spending: ($ per student per year):
  Total: $7,118; Instruction: $4,505; Support Services: $2,427

Enrollment, Drop-out Rates and Diploma Recipients by Race/Ethnicity

Category	Total	White	Black	Asian	AIAN	Hisp.
Enrollment (%)	100.0	62.2	0.3	0.9	0.3	36.3
Drop-out Rate (%)	n/a	n/a	n/a	n/a	n/a	n/a
H.S. Diplomas (#)	311	276	0	5	0	30

Gunnison County

Gunnison Watershed RE-1J
800 N Blvd • Gunnison, CO 81230-2604
(970) 641-7760 • http://tomichi.ghs.gunnison.k12.co.us/
Grade Span: PK-12; **Agency Type:** 1
Schools: 7
  3 Primary; 0 Middle; 2 High; 2 Other Level
  6 Regular; 0 Special Education; 0 Vocational; 1 Alternative
  0 Magnet; 1 Charter; 3 Title I Eligible; 0 School-wide Title I
Students: 1,641   (52.1% male; 47.8% female)
  Individual Education Program: 133 (8.1%);
  English Language Learner: 66 (4.0%); Migrant: 34 (2.1%)
  Eligible for Free Lunch Program: 238 (14.5%)
  Eligible for Reduced-Price Lunch Program: 82 (5.0%)
Teachers: 120.2 (13.7 to 1)
Librarians/Media Specialists: 1.8 (911.7 to 1)
Guidance Counselors: 4.6 (356.7 to 1)
Current Spending: ($ per student per year):
  Total: $7,044; Instruction: $4,169; Support Services: $2,363

Enrollment, Drop-out Rates and Diploma Recipients by Race/Ethnicity

Category	Total	White	Black	Asian	AIAN	Hisp.
Enrollment (%)	100.0	86.0	0.4	1.1	2.5	10.0
Drop-out Rate (%)	n/a	n/a	n/a	n/a	n/a	n/a
H.S. Diplomas (#)	109	103	1	1	0	4

Jefferson County

Jefferson County R-1
1829 Denver W Dr Bldg #27 • Golden, CO 80401-0001
Mailing Address: PO Box 4001 • Golden, CO 80401-0001
(303) 982-6500 • http://jeffco.k12.co.us/
Grade Span: PK-12; **Agency Type:** 1
Schools: 167
  107 Primary; 24 Middle; 27 High; 9 Other Level
  154 Regular; 7 Special Education; 1 Vocational; 5 Alternative
  0 Magnet; 14 Charter; 61 Title I Eligible; 13 School-wide Title I
Students: 87,172   (51.4% male; 48.5% female)
  Individual Education Program: 7,911 (9.1%);
  English Language Learner: 4,858 (5.6%); Migrant: 1,051 (1.2%)
  Eligible for Free Lunch Program: 11,309 (13.0%)
  Eligible for Reduced-Price Lunch Program: 4,018 (4.6%)
Teachers: 4,764.6 (18.3 to 1)
Librarians/Media Specialists: 131.2 (664.4 to 1)
Guidance Counselors: 127.4 (684.2 to 1)
Current Spending: ($ per student per year):
  Total: $8,230; Instruction: $4,276; Support Services: $3,750

Enrollment, Drop-out Rates and Diploma Recipients by Race/Ethnicity

Category	Total	White	Black	Asian	AIAN	Hisp.
Enrollment (%)	100.0	78.3	1.8	3.5	1.1	15.2
Drop-out Rate (%)	n/a	n/a	n/a	n/a	n/a	n/a
H.S. Diplomas (#)	5,334	4,614	66	197	29	428

La Plata County

Durango 9-R
201 E 12th St • Durango, CO 81301
(970) 247-5411 • http://www.durango.k12.co.us/
Grade Span: PK-12; **Agency Type:** 1
Schools: 12
  7 Primary; 2 Middle; 1 High; 2 Other Level

11 Regular; 0 Special Education; 0 Vocational; 1 Alternative
0 Magnet; 1 Charter; 8 Title I Eligible; 0 School-wide Title I
Students: 4,618 (51.6% male; 48.3% female)
Individual Education Program: 497 (10.8%);
English Language Learner: 106 (2.3%); Migrant: 1 (<0.1%)
Eligible for Free Lunch Program: 665 (14.4%)
Eligible for Reduced-Price Lunch Program: 245 (5.3%)
Teachers: 322.1 (14.3 to 1)
Librarians/Media Specialists: 9.3 (496.6 to 1)
Guidance Counselors: 17.3 (266.9 to 1)
Current Spending: ($ per student per year):
Total: $7,014; Instruction: $4,481; Support Services: $2,323
Enrollment, Drop-out Rates and Diploma Recipients by Race/Ethnicity

Category	Total	White	Black	Asian	AIAN	Hisp.
Enrollment (%)	100.0	81.3	0.8	1.1	5.0	11.9
Drop-out Rate (%)	n/a	n/a	n/a	n/a	n/a	n/a
H.S. Diplomas (#)	319	300	2	2	3	12

Larimer County

Poudre R-1
2407 La Porte Ave • Fort Collins, CO 80521-2297
(970) 482-7420 • http://www.psd.k12.co.us/
Grade Span: PK-12; **Agency Type:** 1
Schools: 50
31 Primary; 9 Middle; 7 High; 3 Other Level
46 Regular; 0 Special Education; 0 Vocational; 4 Alternative
0 Magnet; 3 Charter; 22 Title I Eligible; 2 School-wide Title I
Students: 24,891 (51.5% male; 48.4% female)
Individual Education Program: 2,346 (9.4%);
English Language Learner: 2,532 (10.2%); Migrant: 304 (1.2%)
Eligible for Free Lunch Program: 3,811 (15.3%)
Eligible for Reduced-Price Lunch Program: 985 (4.0%)
Teachers: 1,434.3 (17.4 to 1)
Librarians/Media Specialists: 33.7 (738.6 to 1)
Guidance Counselors: 55.2 (450.9 to 1)
Current Spending: ($ per student per year):
Total: $7,857; Instruction: $4,039; Support Services: $3,619
Enrollment, Drop-out Rates and Diploma Recipients by Race/Ethnicity

Category	Total	White	Black	Asian	AIAN	Hisp.
Enrollment (%)	100.0	79.8	1.9	3.3	1.1	13.9
Drop-out Rate (%)	n/a	n/a	n/a	n/a	n/a	n/a
H.S. Diplomas (#)	1,503	1,310	13	50	12	118

Thompson R-2J
535 N Douglas Ave • Loveland, CO 80537-5396
(970) 613-5000 • http://www.thompson.k12.co.us/
Grade Span: PK-12; **Agency Type:** 1
Schools: 29
19 Primary; 5 Middle; 5 High; 0 Other Level
28 Regular; 0 Special Education; 0 Vocational; 1 Alternative
0 Magnet; 0 Charter; 14 Title I Eligible; 4 School-wide Title I
Students: 14,966 (51.4% male; 48.5% female)
Individual Education Program: 1,681 (11.2%);
English Language Learner: 489 (3.3%); Migrant: 227 (1.5%)
Eligible for Free Lunch Program: 2,715 (18.1%)
Eligible for Reduced-Price Lunch Program: 1,149 (7.7%)
Teachers: 863.6 (17.3 to 1)
Librarians/Media Specialists: 9.0 (1,662.9 to 1)
Guidance Counselors: 35.6 (420.4 to 1)
Current Spending: ($ per student per year):
Total: $6,608; Instruction: $3,918; Support Services: $2,467
Enrollment, Drop-out Rates and Diploma Recipients by Race/Ethnicity

Category	Total	White	Black	Asian	AIAN	Hisp.
Enrollment (%)	100.0	85.3	1.0	1.3	0.8	11.6
Drop-out Rate (%)	n/a	n/a	n/a	n/a	n/a	n/a
H.S. Diplomas (#)	924	842	5	20	6	51

Las Animas County

Trinidad 1
215 S Maple St • Trinidad, CO 81082-3300
(719) 846-3324
Grade Span: PK-12; **Agency Type:** 1
Schools: 4
2 Primary; 1 Middle; 1 High; 0 Other Level
4 Regular; 0 Special Education; 0 Vocational; 0 Alternative
0 Magnet; 0 Charter; 3 Title I Eligible; 1 School-wide Title I
Students: 1,519 (51.5% male; 48.4% female)
Individual Education Program: 146 (9.6%);
English Language Learner: 23 (1.5%); Migrant: 0 (0.0%)
Eligible for Free Lunch Program: 780 (51.3%)
Eligible for Reduced-Price Lunch Program: 203 (13.4%)
Teachers: 95.8 (15.9 to 1)
Librarians/Media Specialists: 0.9 (1,687.8 to 1)

Guidance Counselors: 5.0 (303.8 to 1)
Current Spending: ($ per student per year):
Total: $7,192; Instruction: $4,194; Support Services: $2,550
Enrollment, Drop-out Rates and Diploma Recipients by Race/Ethnicity

Category	Total	White	Black	Asian	AIAN	Hisp.
Enrollment (%)	100.0	34.4	0.1	0.7	1.8	63.0
Drop-out Rate (%)	n/a	n/a	n/a	n/a	n/a	n/a
H.S. Diplomas (#)	65	32	0	0	0	33

Logan County

Valley Re-1
415 Beattie St • Sterling, CO 80751-0910
(970) 522-0792 • http://www.re1valleyschools.com/
Grade Span: PK-12; **Agency Type:** 1
Schools: 9
5 Primary; 1 Middle; 3 High; 0 Other Level
8 Regular; 0 Special Education; 0 Vocational; 1 Alternative
0 Magnet; 0 Charter; 7 Title I Eligible; 2 School-wide Title I
Students: 2,751 (51.4% male; 48.5% female)
Individual Education Program: 369 (13.4%);
English Language Learner: 144 (5.2%); Migrant: 20 (0.7%)
Eligible for Free Lunch Program: 785 (28.5%)
Eligible for Reduced-Price Lunch Program: 255 (9.3%)
Teachers: 171.0 (16.1 to 1)
Librarians/Media Specialists: 2.0 (1,375.5 to 1)
Guidance Counselors: 3.7 (743.5 to 1)
Current Spending: ($ per student per year):
Total: $6,093; Instruction: $3,736; Support Services: $2,120
Enrollment, Drop-out Rates and Diploma Recipients by Race/Ethnicity

Category	Total	White	Black	Asian	AIAN	Hisp.
Enrollment (%)	100.0	79.6	1.1	0.6	0.9	17.8
Drop-out Rate (%)	n/a	n/a	n/a	n/a	n/a	n/a
H.S. Diplomas (#)	168	146	0	0	1	21

Mesa County

Mesa County Valley 51
2115 Grand Ave • Grand Junction, CO 81501-8063
(970) 254-5100 • http://www.mesa.k12.co.us/
Grade Span: PK-12; **Agency Type:** 1
Schools: 38
23 Primary; 8 Middle; 4 High; 3 Other Level
36 Regular; 0 Special Education; 0 Vocational; 2 Alternative
0 Magnet; 0 Charter; 20 Title I Eligible; 7 School-wide Title I
Students: 20,167 (50.9% male; 49.0% female)
Individual Education Program: 2,340 (11.6%);
English Language Learner: 951 (4.7%); Migrant: 663 (3.3%)
Eligible for Free Lunch Program: 6,171 (30.6%)
Eligible for Reduced-Price Lunch Program: 1,865 (9.2%)
Teachers: 1,154.8 (17.5 to 1)
Librarians/Media Specialists: 14.0 (1,440.5 to 1)
Guidance Counselors: 39.8 (506.7 to 1)
Current Spending: ($ per student per year):
Total: $6,390; Instruction: $3,972; Support Services: $2,214
Enrollment, Drop-out Rates and Diploma Recipients by Race/Ethnicity

Category	Total	White	Black	Asian	AIAN	Hisp.
Enrollment (%)	100.0	80.8	1.1	0.9	1.3	15.9
Drop-out Rate (%)	n/a	n/a	n/a	n/a	n/a	n/a
H.S. Diplomas (#)	1,179	1,042	4	21	11	101

Moffat County

Moffat County Re:No 1
775 Yampa Ave • Craig, CO 81625-2532
(970) 824-3268 • http://www.moffat.k12.co.us/
Grade Span: PK-12; **Agency Type:** 1
Schools: 8
5 Primary; 2 Middle; 1 High; 0 Other Level
8 Regular; 0 Special Education; 0 Vocational; 0 Alternative
0 Magnet; 0 Charter; 5 Title I Eligible; 0 School-wide Title I
Students: 2,507 (51.6% male; 48.3% female)
Individual Education Program: 297 (11.8%);
English Language Learner: 159 (6.3%); Migrant: 14 (0.6%)
Eligible for Free Lunch Program: 464 (18.5%)
Eligible for Reduced-Price Lunch Program: 144 (5.7%)
Teachers: 146.8 (17.1 to 1)
Librarians/Media Specialists: 2.1 (1,193.8 to 1)
Guidance Counselors: 6.7 (374.2 to 1)
Current Spending: ($ per student per year):
Total: $7,176; Instruction: $4,416; Support Services: $2,556

Enrollment, Drop-out Rates and Diploma Recipients by Race/Ethnicity

Category	Total	White	Black	Asian	AIAN	Hisp.
Enrollment (%)	100.0	84.3	0.2	0.8	1.8	12.8
Drop-out Rate (%)	n/a	n/a	n/a	n/a	n/a	n/a
H.S. Diplomas (#)	165	151	0	2	0	12

Montezuma County

Montezuma-Cortez Re-1
121 E First St • Cortez, CO 81321-0708
Mailing Address: Drawer R • Cortez, CO 81321-0708
(970) 565-7282 • http://www.cortez.k12.co.us/
Grade Span: PK-12; Agency Type: 1
Schools: 13
   10 Primary; 1 Middle; 2 High; 0 Other Level
   12 Regular; 0 Special Education; 0 Vocational; 1 Alternative
   0 Magnet; 2 Charter; 9 Title I Eligible; 4 School-wide Title I
Students: 3,346 (51.5% male; 48.4% female)
   Individual Education Program: 412 (12.3%);
   English Language Learner: 1,148 (34.3%); Migrant: 0 (0.0%)
   Eligible for Free Lunch Program: 1,304 (39.0%)
   Eligible for Reduced-Price Lunch Program: 343 (10.3%)
Teachers: 211.0 (15.9 to 1)
Librarians/Media Specialists: 2.0 (1,673.0 to 1)
Guidance Counselors: 9.5 (352.2 to 1)
Current Spending: ($ per student per year):
   Total: $6,201; Instruction: $3,868; Support Services: $2,104

Enrollment, Drop-out Rates and Diploma Recipients by Race/Ethnicity

Category	Total	White	Black	Asian	AIAN	Hisp.
Enrollment (%)	100.0	60.8	0.6	0.6	25.0	13.1
Drop-out Rate (%)	n/a	n/a	n/a	n/a	n/a	n/a
H.S. Diplomas (#)	164	116	1	2	22	23

Montrose County

Montrose County RE-1J
126 S 5th St • Montrose, CO 81401
Mailing Address: PO Box 10000 • Montrose, CO 81402-9701
(970) 249-7726 • http://www.mcsd.org/
Grade Span: PK-12; Agency Type: 1
Schools: 14
   7 Primary; 3 Middle; 4 High; 0 Other Level
   12 Regular; 0 Special Education; 0 Vocational; 2 Alternative
   0 Magnet; 1 Charter; 8 Title I Eligible; 3 School-wide Title I
Students: 5,610 (51.0% male; 48.9% female)
   Individual Education Program: 682 (12.2%);
   English Language Learner: 638 (11.4%); Migrant: 475 (8.5%)
   Eligible for Free Lunch Program: 1,708 (30.4%)
   Eligible for Reduced-Price Lunch Program: 501 (8.9%)
Teachers: 335.4 (16.7 to 1)
Librarians/Media Specialists: 4.1 (1,368.3 to 1)
Guidance Counselors: 10.6 (529.2 to 1)
Current Spending: ($ per student per year):
   Total: $6,779; Instruction: $3,815; Support Services: $2,738

Enrollment, Drop-out Rates and Diploma Recipients by Race/Ethnicity

Category	Total	White	Black	Asian	AIAN	Hisp.
Enrollment (%)	100.0	71.6	0.6	0.8	0.7	26.3
Drop-out Rate (%)	n/a	n/a	n/a	n/a	n/a	n/a
H.S. Diplomas (#)	348	300	0	2	2	44

Morgan County

Brush Re-2(J)
527 Industrial Park Rd • Brush, CO 80723-0585
Mailing Address: PO Box 585 • Brush, CO 80723-0585
(970) 842-5176 • http://brushschools.org/
Grade Span: PK-12; Agency Type: 1
Schools: 4
   2 Primary; 1 Middle; 1 High; 0 Other Level
   4 Regular; 0 Special Education; 0 Vocational; 0 Alternative
   0 Magnet; 0 Charter; 2 Title I Eligible; 0 School-wide Title I
Students: 1,588 (49.4% male; 50.5% female)
   Individual Education Program: 174 (11.0%);
   English Language Learner: 390 (24.6%); Migrant: 159 (10.0%)
   Eligible for Free Lunch Program: 503 (31.7%)
   Eligible for Reduced-Price Lunch Program: 227 (14.3%)
Teachers: 110.0 (14.4 to 1)
Librarians/Media Specialists: 0.8 (1,985.0 to 1)
Guidance Counselors: 3.8 (417.9 to 1)
Current Spending: ($ per student per year):
   Total: $6,666; Instruction: $3,860; Support Services: $2,481

Enrollment, Drop-out Rates and Diploma Recipients by Race/Ethnicity

Category	Total	White	Black	Asian	AIAN	Hisp.
Enrollment (%)	100.0	57.3	0.8	0.5	0.4	41.1
Drop-out Rate (%)	n/a	n/a	n/a	n/a	n/a	n/a
H.S. Diplomas (#)	94	76	0	0	0	18

Fort Morgan Re-3
230 Walnut St • Fort Morgan, CO 80701-2640
(970) 867-5633 • http://www.morgan.k12.co.us/
Grade Span: PK-12; Agency Type: 1
Schools: 8
   4 Primary; 2 Middle; 2 High; 0 Other Level
   7 Regular; 0 Special Education; 0 Vocational; 1 Alternative
   0 Magnet; 0 Charter; 7 Title I Eligible; 4 School-wide Title I
Students: 3,294 (50.5% male; 49.4% female)
   Individual Education Program: 370 (11.2%);
   English Language Learner: 585 (17.8%); Migrant: 696 (21.1%)
   Eligible for Free Lunch Program: 1,511 (45.9%)
   Eligible for Reduced-Price Lunch Program: 383 (11.6%)
Teachers: 204.2 (16.1 to 1)
Librarians/Media Specialists: 2.5 (1,317.6 to 1)
Guidance Counselors: 5.3 (621.5 to 1)
Current Spending: ($ per student per year):
   Total: $6,468; Instruction: $3,903; Support Services: $2,278

Enrollment, Drop-out Rates and Diploma Recipients by Race/Ethnicity

Category	Total	White	Black	Asian	AIAN	Hisp.
Enrollment (%)	100.0	47.2	0.4	0.4	0.3	51.8
Drop-out Rate (%)	n/a	n/a	n/a	n/a	n/a	n/a
H.S. Diplomas (#)	157	119	1	2	0	35

Otero County

East Otero R-1
1802 Colorado Ave Ste 200 • La Junta, CO 81050-3381
(719) 384-6900 • http://lajunta.k12.co.us/
Grade Span: PK-12; Agency Type: 1
Schools: 5
   2 Primary; 1 Middle; 2 High; 0 Other Level
   4 Regular; 0 Special Education; 0 Vocational; 1 Alternative
   0 Magnet; 0 Charter; 2 Title I Eligible; 2 School-wide Title I
Students: 1,604 (50.3% male; 49.6% female)
   Individual Education Program: 220 (13.7%);
   English Language Learner: 9 (0.6%); Migrant: 25 (1.6%)
   Eligible for Free Lunch Program: 752 (46.9%)
   Eligible for Reduced-Price Lunch Program: 202 (12.6%)
Teachers: 113.9 (14.1 to 1)
Librarians/Media Specialists: 1.0 (1,604.0 to 1)
Guidance Counselors: 5.1 (314.5 to 1)
Current Spending: ($ per student per year):
   Total: $6,317; Instruction: $3,686; Support Services: $2,370

Enrollment, Drop-out Rates and Diploma Recipients by Race/Ethnicity

Category	Total	White	Black	Asian	AIAN	Hisp.
Enrollment (%)	100.0	43.8	1.2	0.6	1.9	52.4
Drop-out Rate (%)	n/a	n/a	n/a	n/a	n/a	n/a
H.S. Diplomas (#)	128	59	3	1	0	65

Pitkin County

Aspen 1
0235 High School Rd • Aspen, CO 81611-3357
(970) 925-3760
Grade Span: PK-12; Agency Type: 1
Schools: 5
   3 Primary; 1 Middle; 1 High; 0 Other Level
   5 Regular; 0 Special Education; 0 Vocational; 0 Alternative
   0 Magnet; 1 Charter; 2 Title I Eligible; 0 School-wide Title I
Students: 1,554 (54.0% male; 45.9% female)
   Individual Education Program: 73 (4.7%);
   English Language Learner: 195 (12.5%); Migrant: 0 (0.0%)
   Eligible for Free Lunch Program: 0 (0.0%)
   Eligible for Reduced-Price Lunch Program: 28 (1.8%)
Teachers: 130.0 (12.0 to 1)
Librarians/Media Specialists: 0.0 (n/a to 1)
Guidance Counselors: 4.2 (370.0 to 1)
Current Spending: ($ per student per year):
   Total: $10,195; Instruction: $7,106; Support Services: $3,089

Enrollment, Drop-out Rates and Diploma Recipients by Race/Ethnicity

Category	Total	White	Black	Asian	AIAN	Hisp.
Enrollment (%)	100.0	83.9	0.5	2.6	0.3	12.7
Drop-out Rate (%)	n/a	n/a	n/a	n/a	n/a	n/a
H.S. Diplomas (#)	95	90	1	0	0	4

Prowers County

Lamar Re-2
210 W Pearl • Lamar, CO 81052-3173
(719) 336-3251 • http://www.lamar.k12.co.us/
Grade Span: PK-12; **Agency Type:** 1
Schools: 8
  5 Primary; 1 Middle; 2 High; 0 Other Level
  7 Regular; 0 Special Education; 0 Vocational; 1 Alternative
  0 Magnet; 1 Charter; 4 Title I Eligible; 2 School-wide Title I
Students: 1,846   (53.1% male; 46.8% female)
  Individual Education Program: 234 (12.7%);
  English Language Learner: 328 (17.8%); Migrant: 176 (9.5%)
  Eligible for Free Lunch Program: 793 (43.0%)
  Eligible for Reduced-Price Lunch Program: 227 (12.3%)
Teachers: 121.0 (15.3 to 1)
Librarians/Media Specialists: 2.6 (710.0 to 1)
Guidance Counselors: 3.0 (615.3 to 1)
Current Spending: ($ per student per year):
  Total: $5,894; Instruction: $3,755; Support Services: $1,906
Enrollment, Drop-out Rates and Diploma Recipients by Race/Ethnicity

Category	Total	White	Black	Asian	AIAN	Hisp.
Enrollment (%)	100.0	53.5	0.9	0.4	0.8	44.5
Drop-out Rate (%)	n/a	n/a	n/a	n/a	n/a	n/a
H.S. Diplomas (#)	90	71	0	2	0	17

Pueblo County

Pueblo City 60
315 W 11th St • Pueblo, CO 81003-2804
(719) 549-7100 • http://www.pueblo60.k12.co.us/
Grade Span: PK-12; **Agency Type:** 1
Schools: 38
  24 Primary; 6 Middle; 6 High; 2 Other Level
  36 Regular; 1 Special Education; 0 Vocational; 1 Alternative
  0 Magnet; 3 Charter; 24 Title I Eligible; 18 School-wide Title I
Students: 17,693   (51.6% male; 48.3% female)
  Individual Education Program: 2,037 (11.5%);
  English Language Learner: 2,314 (13.1%); Migrant: 345 (1.9%)
  Eligible for Free Lunch Program: 8,733 (49.4%)
  Eligible for Reduced-Price Lunch Program: 1,873 (10.6%)
Teachers: 1,104.2 (16.0 to 1)
Librarians/Media Specialists: 31.0 (570.7 to 1)
Guidance Counselors: 49.4 (358.2 to 1)
Current Spending: ($ per student per year):
  Total: $6,852; Instruction: $3,843; Support Services: $2,741
Enrollment, Drop-out Rates and Diploma Recipients by Race/Ethnicity

Category	Total	White	Black	Asian	AIAN	Hisp.
Enrollment (%)	100.0	38.3	2.4	0.6	1.7	57.0
Drop-out Rate (%)	n/a	n/a	n/a	n/a	n/a	n/a
H.S. Diplomas (#)	907	475	24	8	12	388

Pueblo County Rural 70
24951 E Hwy 50 • Pueblo, CO 81006
(719) 542-0220 • http://www.dist70.k12.co.us/
Grade Span: PK-12; **Agency Type:** 1
Schools: 22
  10 Primary; 7 Middle; 4 High; 1 Other Level
  21 Regular; 0 Special Education; 0 Vocational; 1 Alternative
  0 Magnet; 2 Charter; 11 Title I Eligible; 1 School-wide Title I
Students: 8,045   (51.2% male; 48.7% female)
  Individual Education Program: 868 (10.8%);
  English Language Learner: 149 (1.9%); Migrant: 117 (1.5%)
  Eligible for Free Lunch Program: 1,781 (22.1%)
  Eligible for Reduced-Price Lunch Program: 806 (10.0%)
Teachers: 429.1 (18.7 to 1)
Librarians/Media Specialists: 2.8 (2,873.2 to 1)
Guidance Counselors: 19.9 (404.3 to 1)
Current Spending: ($ per student per year):
  Total: $5,988; Instruction: $3,350; Support Services: $2,399
Enrollment, Drop-out Rates and Diploma Recipients by Race/Ethnicity

Category	Total	White	Black	Asian	AIAN	Hisp.
Enrollment (%)	100.0	71.3	1.3	0.6	0.8	26.0
Drop-out Rate (%)	n/a	n/a	n/a	n/a	n/a	n/a
H.S. Diplomas (#)	349	271	3	2	4	69

Routt County

Steamboat Springs Re-2
325 7th St • Steamboat Springs, CO 80487
Mailing Address: PO Box 774368 • Steamboat Springs, CO 80477-4368
(970) 879-1530 • http://sailors.steamboat.k12.co.us/
Grade Span: KG-12; **Agency Type:** 1
Schools: 5
  3 Primary; 1 Middle; 1 High; 0 Other Level

  5 Regular; 0 Special Education; 0 Vocational; 0 Alternative
  0 Magnet; 1 Charter; 3 Title I Eligible; 0 School-wide Title I
Students: 1,912   (53.3% male; 46.6% female)
  Individual Education Program: 217 (11.3%);
  English Language Learner: 38 (2.0%); Migrant: 4 (0.2%)
  Eligible for Free Lunch Program: 52 (2.7%)
  Eligible for Reduced-Price Lunch Program: 40 (2.1%)
Teachers: 134.7 (14.2 to 1)
Librarians/Media Specialists: 4.0 (478.0 to 1)
Guidance Counselors: 5.9 (324.1 to 1)
Current Spending: ($ per student per year):
  Total: $8,691; Instruction: $4,885; Support Services: $3,488
Enrollment, Drop-out Rates and Diploma Recipients by Race/Ethnicity

Category	Total	White	Black	Asian	AIAN	Hisp.
Enrollment (%)	100.0	95.0	0.6	1.0	0.4	3.0
Drop-out Rate (%)	n/a	n/a	n/a	n/a	n/a	n/a
H.S. Diplomas (#)	132	127	0	1	0	4

Summit County

Summit Re-1
0150 School Rd • Frisco, CO 80443-0007
Mailing Address: PO Box 7 • Frisco, CO 80443-0007
(970) 668-3011 • http://summit.k12.co.us/
Grade Span: PK-12; **Agency Type:** 1
Schools: 8
  6 Primary; 1 Middle; 1 High; 0 Other Level
  8 Regular; 0 Special Education; 0 Vocational; 0 Alternative
  0 Magnet; 0 Charter; 4 Title I Eligible; 0 School-wide Title I
Students: 2,829   (52.6% male; 47.3% female)
  Individual Education Program: 269 (9.5%);
  English Language Learner: 515 (18.2%); Migrant: 8 (0.3%)
  Eligible for Free Lunch Program: 312 (11.0%)
  Eligible for Reduced-Price Lunch Program: 130 (4.6%)
Teachers: 215.0 (13.2 to 1)
Librarians/Media Specialists: 8.0 (353.6 to 1)
Guidance Counselors: 9.8 (288.7 to 1)
Current Spending: ($ per student per year):
  Total: $9,144; Instruction: $4,986; Support Services: $3,946
Enrollment, Drop-out Rates and Diploma Recipients by Race/Ethnicity

Category	Total	White	Black	Asian	AIAN	Hisp.
Enrollment (%)	100.0	79.5	0.3	1.8	0.2	18.2
Drop-out Rate (%)	n/a	n/a	n/a	n/a	n/a	n/a
H.S. Diplomas (#)	165	150	0	5	0	10

Teller County

Woodland Park Re-2
211 N Baldwin St • Woodland Park, CO 80866-0099
Mailing Address: PO Box 99 • Woodland Park, CO 80866-0099
(719) 687-6048 • http://www.wpsdk12.org/
Grade Span: PK-12; **Agency Type:** 1
Schools: 5
  3 Primary; 1 Middle; 1 High; 0 Other Level
  5 Regular; 0 Special Education; 0 Vocational; 0 Alternative
  0 Magnet; 0 Charter; 4 Title I Eligible; 0 School-wide Title I
Students: 3,116   (51.9% male; 48.0% female)
  Individual Education Program: 298 (9.6%);
  English Language Learner: 12 (0.4%); Migrant: 0 (0.0%)
  Eligible for Free Lunch Program: 323 (10.4%)
  Eligible for Reduced-Price Lunch Program: 129 (4.1%)
Teachers: 188.9 (16.5 to 1)
Librarians/Media Specialists: 5.0 (623.2 to 1)
Guidance Counselors: 8.0 (389.5 to 1)
Current Spending: ($ per student per year):
  Total: $5,993; Instruction: $3,538; Support Services: $2,294
Enrollment, Drop-out Rates and Diploma Recipients by Race/Ethnicity

Category	Total	White	Black	Asian	AIAN	Hisp.
Enrollment (%)	100.0	91.8	1.0	1.2	1.3	4.7
Drop-out Rate (%)	n/a	n/a	n/a	n/a	n/a	n/a
H.S. Diplomas (#)	210	194	3	0	4	9

Weld County

Eaton Re-2
200 Park Ave • Eaton, CO 80615-3528
(970) 454-3402
Grade Span: KG-12; **Agency Type:** 1
Schools: 5
  3 Primary; 1 Middle; 1 High; 0 Other Level
  5 Regular; 0 Special Education; 0 Vocational; 0 Alternative
  0 Magnet; 0 Charter; 4 Title I Eligible; 0 School-wide Title I
Students: 1,563   (52.5% male; 47.4% female)
  Individual Education Program: 132 (8.4%);
  English Language Learner: 134 (8.6%); Migrant: 137 (8.8%)

Eligible for Free Lunch Program: 257 (16.4%)
Eligible for Reduced-Price Lunch Program: 88 (5.6%)
Teachers: 96.0 (16.3 to 1)
Librarians/Media Specialists: 1.9 (822.6 to 1)
Guidance Counselors: 3.8 (411.3 to 1)
Current Spending: ($ per student per year):
Total: $5,828; Instruction: $3,487; Support Services: $2,119
Enrollment, Drop-out Rates and Diploma Recipients by Race/Ethnicity

Category	Total	White	Black	Asian	AIAN	Hisp.
Enrollment (%)	100.0	79.8	0.5	0.4	0.1	19.1
Drop-out Rate (%)	n/a	n/a	n/a	n/a	n/a	n/a
H.S. Diplomas (#)	79	62	1	1	0	15

Greeley 6
1025 9th Ave • Greeley, CO 80631-4686
(970) 348-6000 • http://www.greeleyschools.org/
Grade Span: PK-12; **Agency Type:** 1
Schools: 31
17 Primary; 5 Middle; 6 High; 3 Other Level
28 Regular; 1 Special Education; 0 Vocational; 2 Alternative
1 Magnet; 3 Charter; 16 Title I Eligible; 8 School-wide Title I
Students: 17,598   (51.6% male; 48.3% female)
Individual Education Program: 1,791 (10.2%);
English Language Learner: 3,895 (22.1%); Migrant: 1,688 (9.6%)
Eligible for Free Lunch Program: 6,921 (39.3%)
Eligible for Reduced-Price Lunch Program: 1,504 (8.5%)
Teachers: 1,055.0 (16.7 to 1)
Librarians/Media Specialists: 0.0 (n/a to 1)
Guidance Counselors: 26.5 (664.1 to 1)
Current Spending: ($ per student per year):
Total: $6,326; Instruction: $4,146; Support Services: $1,933
Enrollment, Drop-out Rates and Diploma Recipients by Race/Ethnicity

Category	Total	White	Black	Asian	AIAN	Hisp.
Enrollment (%)	100.0	48.9	1.2	0.9	0.7	48.3
Drop-out Rate (%)	n/a	n/a	n/a	n/a	n/a	n/a
H.S. Diplomas (#)	870	603	6	11	3	247

Johnstown-Milliken RE-5J
110 So Centennial Dr Ste 1 • Milliken, CO 80543
Mailing Address: 110 So Centennial Dr Ste A • Milliken, CO 80543
(970) 587-2336
Grade Span: PK-12; **Agency Type:** 1
Schools: 5
3 Primary; 1 Middle; 1 High; 0 Other Level
5 Regular; 0 Special Education; 0 Vocational; 0 Alternative
0 Magnet; 1 Charter; 2 Title I Eligible; 0 School-wide Title I
Students: 2,126   (52.6% male; 47.3% female)
Individual Education Program: 220 (10.3%);
English Language Learner: 437 (20.6%); Migrant: 125 (5.9%)
Eligible for Free Lunch Program: 370 (17.4%)
Eligible for Reduced-Price Lunch Program: 155 (7.3%)
Teachers: 127.2 (16.7 to 1)
Librarians/Media Specialists: 3.0 (708.7 to 1)
Guidance Counselors: 4.2 (506.2 to 1)
Current Spending: ($ per student per year):
Total: $5,908; Instruction: $3,734; Support Services: $1,911
Enrollment, Drop-out Rates and Diploma Recipients by Race/Ethnicity

Category	Total	White	Black	Asian	AIAN	Hisp.
Enrollment (%)	100.0	63.0	0.5	0.5	0.2	35.7
Drop-out Rate (%)	n/a	n/a	n/a	n/a	n/a	n/a
H.S. Diplomas (#)	89	59	0	0	0	30

Keenesburg Re-3(J)
95 W Broadway • Keenesburg, CO 80643-0269
Mailing Address: PO Box 269 • Keenesburg, CO 80643-0269
(303) 536-2000 • http://www.rebel-net.tec.co.us/admin/index.asp
Grade Span: PK-12; **Agency Type:** 1
Schools: 6
4 Primary; 1 Middle; 1 High; 0 Other Level
6 Regular; 0 Special Education; 0 Vocational; 0 Alternative
0 Magnet; 1 Charter; 2 Title I Eligible; 0 School-wide Title I
Students: 1,916   (53.0% male; 46.9% female)
Individual Education Program: 251 (13.1%);
English Language Learner: 301 (15.7%); Migrant: 186 (9.7%)
Eligible for Free Lunch Program: 523 (27.3%)
Eligible for Reduced-Price Lunch Program: 223 (11.6%)
Teachers: 128.4 (14.9 to 1)
Librarians/Media Specialists: 0.9 (2,128.9 to 1)
Guidance Counselors: 2.0 (958.0 to 1)
Current Spending: ($ per student per year):
Total: $6,161; Instruction: $3,522; Support Services: $2,349

Category	Total	White	Black	Asian	AIAN	Hisp.
Enrollment (%)	100.0	70.1	0.4	0.7	0.2	28.5
Drop-out Rate (%)	n/a	n/a	n/a	n/a	n/a	n/a
H.S. Diplomas (#)	85	74	0	1	0	10

Weld County Re-1
14827 W.C.R. 42 • Gilcrest, CO 80623-0157
Mailing Address: PO Box 157 • Gilcrest, CO 80623-0157
(970) 737-2403 • http://www.weld-re1.k12.co.us/
Grade Span: PK-12; **Agency Type:** 1
Schools: 6
3 Primary; 2 Middle; 1 High; 0 Other Level
6 Regular; 0 Special Education; 0 Vocational; 0 Alternative
0 Magnet; 0 Charter; 4 Title I Eligible; 0 School-wide Title I
Students: 2,001   (51.1% male; 48.8% female)
Individual Education Program: 278 (13.9%);
English Language Learner: 461 (23.0%); Migrant: 344 (17.2%)
Eligible for Free Lunch Program: 688 (34.4%)
Eligible for Reduced-Price Lunch Program: 177 (8.8%)
Teachers: 149.3 (13.4 to 1)
Librarians/Media Specialists: 0.6 (3,335.0 to 1)
Guidance Counselors: 5.0 (400.2 to 1)
Current Spending: ($ per student per year):
Total: $7,457; Instruction: $4,815; Support Services: $2,335
Enrollment, Drop-out Rates and Diploma Recipients by Race/Ethnicity

Category	Total	White	Black	Asian	AIAN	Hisp.
Enrollment (%)	100.0	51.2	0.7	0.5	0.4	47.1
Drop-out Rate (%)	n/a	n/a	n/a	n/a	n/a	n/a
H.S. Diplomas (#)	105	68	2	0	0	35

Weld County SD Re-8
301 Reynolds St • Fort Lupton, CO 80621-1329
(303) 857-3200 • http://www.weld-re1.k12.co.us/
Grade Span: PK-12; **Agency Type:** 1
Schools: 4
2 Primary; 1 Middle; 1 High; 0 Other Level
4 Regular; 0 Special Education; 0 Vocational; 0 Alternative
0 Magnet; 0 Charter; 3 Title I Eligible; 2 School-wide Title I
Students: 2,586   (53.0% male; 46.9% female)
Individual Education Program: 325 (12.6%);
English Language Learner: 1,123 (43.4%); Migrant: 644 (24.9%)
Eligible for Free Lunch Program: 1,158 (44.8%)
Eligible for Reduced-Price Lunch Program: 246 (9.5%)
Teachers: 156.1 (16.6 to 1)
Librarians/Media Specialists: 1.7 (1,521.2 to 1)
Guidance Counselors: 7.4 (349.5 to 1)
Current Spending: ($ per student per year):
Total: $7,249; Instruction: $4,177; Support Services: $2,815
Enrollment, Drop-out Rates and Diploma Recipients by Race/Ethnicity

Category	Total	White	Black	Asian	AIAN	Hisp.
Enrollment (%)	100.0	38.1	0.5	0.7	0.4	60.4
Drop-out Rate (%)	n/a	n/a	n/a	n/a	n/a	n/a
H.S. Diplomas (#)	143	72	0	3	1	67

Windsor Re-4
1020 Main St • Windsor, CO 80550-4776
Mailing Address: PO Box 609 • Windsor, CO 80550-4776
(970) 686-8000 • http://www.windsor.k12.co.us/
Grade Span: PK-12; **Agency Type:** 1
Schools: 7
5 Primary; 1 Middle; 1 High; 0 Other Level
7 Regular; 0 Special Education; 0 Vocational; 0 Alternative
0 Magnet; 1 Charter; 3 Title I Eligible; 0 School-wide Title I
Students: 2,989   (51.6% male; 48.3% female)
Individual Education Program: 282 (9.4%);
English Language Learner: 79 (2.6%); Migrant: 27 (0.9%)
Eligible for Free Lunch Program: 195 (6.5%)
Eligible for Reduced-Price Lunch Program: 105 (3.5%)
Teachers: 191.2 (15.6 to 1)
Librarians/Media Specialists: 6.0 (498.2 to 1)
Guidance Counselors: 7.0 (427.0 to 1)
Current Spending: ($ per student per year):
Total: $6,032; Instruction: $3,581; Support Services: $2,256
Enrollment, Drop-out Rates and Diploma Recipients by Race/Ethnicity

Category	Total	White	Black	Asian	AIAN	Hisp.
Enrollment (%)	100.0	85.7	1.0	1.2	1.2	10.9
Drop-out Rate (%)	n/a	n/a	n/a	n/a	n/a	n/a
H.S. Diplomas (#)	158	125	0	1	2	30

Number of Schools

Rank	Number	District Name	City
1	167	Jefferson County R-1	Golden
2	145	Denver County 1	Denver
3	65	Colorado Springs 11	Colorado Spgs
4	63	Douglas County Re 1	Castle Rock
5	53	Boulder Valley Re 2	Boulder
6	50	Cherry Creek 5	Greenwood Vlg
6	50	Poudre R-1	Fort Collins
8	47	Adams 12 Five Star Schools	Thornton
8	47	Adams-Arapahoe 28J	Aurora
10	38	Mesa County Valley 51	Grand Junction
10	38	Pueblo City 60	Pueblo
12	37	St Vrain Valley RE-1J	Longmont
13	31	Greeley 6	Greeley
14	29	Thompson R-2J	Loveland
15	26	Academy 20	Colorado Spgs
16	25	Harrison 2	Colorado Spgs
16	25	Littleton 6	Littleton
18	23	Westminster 50	Westminster
19	22	Pueblo County Rural 70	Pueblo
20	17	Widefield 3	Colorado Spgs
21	16	Eagle County Re 50	Eagle
22	15	Brighton 27J	Brighton
23	14	Delta County 50(J)	Delta
23	14	Montrose County RE-1J	Montrose
25	13	Adams County 14	Commerce City
25	13	Montezuma-Cortez Re-1	Cortez
25	13	Roaring Fork Re-1	Glenwood Spgs
28	12	Durango 9-R	Durango
28	12	Falcon 49	Falcon
30	11	Englewood 1	Englewood
31	10	Canon City Re-1	Canon City
31	10	Fountain 8	Fountain
33	9	Cheyenne Mountain 12	Colorado Spgs
33	9	Lewis-Palmer 38	Monument
33	9	Mapleton 1	Denver
33	9	Valley Re-1	Sterling
37	8	Elizabeth C-1	Elizabeth
37	8	Fort Morgan Re-3	Fort Morgan
37	8	Lamar Re-2	Lamar
37	8	Moffat County Re:No 1	Craig
37	8	Summit Re-1	Frisco
42	7	Garfield Re-2	Rifle
42	7	Gunnison Watershed RE-1J	Gunnison
42	7	Windsor Re-4	Windsor
45	6	Alamosa RE-11J	Alamosa
45	6	Keenesburg Re-3(J)	Keenesburg
45	6	Weld County Re-1	Gilcrest
48	5	Aspen 1	Aspen
48	5	East Otero R-1	La Junta
48	5	Eaton Re-2	Eaton
48	5	Florence Re-2	Florence
48	5	Johnstown-Milliken RE-5J	Milliken
48	5	Sheridan 2	Sheridan
48	5	Steamboat Springs Re-2	Steamboat Spgs
48	5	Woodland Park Re-2	Woodland Park
56	4	Archuleta County 50 Jt	Pagosa Springs
56	4	Brush Re-2(J)	Brush
56	4	Trinidad 1	Trinidad
56	4	Weld County SD Re-8	Fort Lupton

Number of Teachers

Rank	Number	District Name	City
1	4,764	Jefferson County R-1	Golden
2	4,217	Denver County 1	Denver
3	2,737	Cherry Creek 5	Greenwood Vlg
4	2,351	Douglas County Re 1	Castle Rock
5	1,917	Colorado Springs 11	Colorado Spgs
6	1,767	Adams 12 Five Star Schools	Thornton
7	1,739	Adams-Arapahoe 28J	Aurora
8	1,629	Boulder Valley Re 2	Boulder
9	1,434	Poudre R-1	Fort Collins
10	1,217	St Vrain Valley RE-1J	Longmont
11	1,165	Academy 20	Colorado Spgs
12	1,154	Mesa County Valley 51	Grand Junction
13	1,104	Pueblo City 60	Pueblo
14	1,055	Greeley 6	Greeley
15	945	Littleton 6	Littleton
16	863	Thompson R-2J	Loveland
17	750	Harrison 2	Colorado Spgs
18	671	Westminster 50	Westminster
19	497	Falcon 49	Falcon
20	481	Brighton 27J	Brighton
21	480	Widefield 3	Colorado Spgs
22	429	Pueblo County Rural 70	Pueblo
23	366	Adams County 14	Commerce City
24	341	Eagle County Re 50	Eagle
25	335	Montrose County RE-1J	Montrose
26	333	Roaring Fork Re-1	Glenwood Spgs
27	327	Lewis-Palmer 38	Monument
28	322	Durango 9-R	Durango
29	286	Mapleton 1	Denver
30	279	Delta County 50(J)	Delta
31	267	Cheyenne Mountain 12	Colorado Spgs
32	248	Canon City Re-1	Canon City
33	245	Fountain 8	Fountain
34	225	Englewood 1	Englewood
35	215	Summit Re-1	Frisco
36	212	Garfield Re-2	Rifle
37	211	Montezuma-Cortez Re-1	Cortez
38	204	Fort Morgan Re-3	Fort Morgan
39	191	Windsor Re-4	Windsor
40	188	Woodland Park Re-2	Woodland Park
41	171	Valley Re-1	Sterling
42	163	Elizabeth C-1	Elizabeth
43	156	Weld County SD Re-8	Fort Lupton
44	149	Weld County Re-1	Gilcrest
45	146	Moffat County Re:No 1	Craig
46	142	Alamosa RE-11J	Alamosa
47	134	Steamboat Springs Re-2	Steamboat Spgs
48	130	Aspen 1	Aspen
49	128	Keenesburg Re-3(J)	Keenesburg
50	127	Johnstown-Milliken RE-5J	Milliken
51	122	Sheridan 2	Sheridan
52	121	Lamar Re-2	Lamar
53	120	Gunnison Watershed RE-1J	Gunnison
54	114	Florence Re-2	Florence
55	113	East Otero R-1	La Junta
56	110	Brush Re-2(J)	Brush
57	96	Eaton Re-2	Eaton
58	95	Trinidad 1	Trinidad
59	92	Archuleta County 50 Jt	Pagosa Springs

Number of Students

Rank	Number	District Name	City
1	87,172	Jefferson County R-1	Golden
2	72,100	Denver County 1	Denver
3	46,594	Cherry Creek 5	Greenwood Vlg
4	41,924	Douglas County Re 1	Castle Rock
5	34,869	Adams 12 Five Star Schools	Thornton
6	32,530	Adams-Arapahoe 28J	Aurora
7	31,840	Colorado Springs 11	Colorado Spgs
8	27,804	Boulder Valley Re 2	Boulder
9	24,891	Poudre R-1	Fort Collins
10	21,596	St Vrain Valley RE-1J	Longmont
11	20,167	Mesa County Valley 51	Grand Junction
12	19,083	Academy 20	Colorado Spgs
13	17,693	Pueblo City 60	Pueblo
14	17,598	Greeley 6	Greeley
15	16,458	Littleton 6	Littleton
16	14,966	Thompson R-2J	Loveland
17	10,943	Harrison 2	Colorado Spgs
18	10,467	Westminster 50	Westminster
19	8,660	Falcon 49	Falcon
20	8,475	Widefield 3	Colorado Spgs
21	8,261	Brighton 27J	Brighton
22	8,045	Pueblo County Rural 70	Pueblo
23	6,528	Adams County 14	Commerce City
24	5,879	Fountain 8	Fountain
25	5,716	Mapleton 1	Denver
26	5,610	Montrose County RE-1J	Montrose
27	5,370	Lewis-Palmer 38	Monument
28	5,087	Delta County 50(J)	Delta
29	5,067	Eagle County Re 50	Eagle
30	4,882	Roaring Fork Re-1	Glenwood Spgs
31	4,618	Durango 9-R	Durango
32	4,506	Cheyenne Mountain 12	Colorado Spgs
33	4,114	Canon City Re-1	Canon City
34	4,084	Englewood 1	Englewood
35	3,810	Garfield Re-2	Rifle
36	3,346	Montezuma-Cortez Re-1	Cortez
37	3,294	Fort Morgan Re-3	Fort Morgan
38	3,116	Woodland Park Re-2	Woodland Park
39	2,989	Windsor Re-4	Windsor
40	2,867	Elizabeth C-1	Elizabeth
41	2,829	Summit Re-1	Frisco
42	2,751	Valley Re-1	Sterling
43	2,586	Weld County SD Re-8	Fort Lupton
44	2,507	Moffat County Re:No 1	Craig
45	2,454	Alamosa RE-11J	Alamosa
46	2,126	Johnstown-Milliken RE-5J	Milliken
47	2,001	Weld County Re-1	Gilcrest
48	1,916	Keenesburg Re-3(J)	Keenesburg
49	1,912	Steamboat Springs Re-2	Steamboat Spgs
50	1,861	Sheridan 2	Sheridan
51	1,844	Lamar Re-2	Lamar
52	1,844	Florence Re-2	Florence
53	1,641	Gunnison Watershed RE-1J	Gunnison
54	1,604	East Otero R-1	La Junta
55	1,588	Brush Re-2(J)	Brush
56	1,563	Eaton Re-2	Eaton
57	1,554	Aspen 1	Aspen
58	1,553	Archuleta County 50 Jt	Pagosa Springs
59	1,519	Trinidad 1	Trinidad

Male Students

Rank	Percent	District Name	City
1	54.0	Aspen 1	Aspen
2	53.3	Archuleta County 50 Jt	Pagosa Springs
3	53.3	Steamboat Springs Re-2	Steamboat Spgs
4	53.1	Lamar Re-2	Lamar
5	53.0	Weld County SD Re-8	Fort Lupton
6	53.0	Keenesburg Re-3(J)	Keenesburg
7	52.8	Florence Re-2	Florence
8	52.6	Alamosa RE-11J	Alamosa
9	52.6	Johnstown-Milliken RE-5J	Milliken
10	52.6	Summit Re-1	Frisco
11	52.5	Eaton Re-2	Eaton
12	52.5	Roaring Fork Re-1	Glenwood Spgs
13	52.5	Englewood 1	Englewood
14	52.3	Sheridan 2	Sheridan
15	52.1	Gunnison Watershed RE-1J	Gunnison
16	51.9	Woodland Park Re-2	Woodland Park
17	51.9	Delta County 50(J)	Delta
18	51.9	Fountain 8	Fountain
19	51.8	Lewis-Palmer 38	Monument
20	51.8	Mapleton 1	Denver
21	51.6	Moffat County Re:No 1	Craig
22	51.6	Windsor Re-4	Windsor
23	51.6	Durango 9-R	Durango
24	51.6	St Vrain Valley RE-1J	Longmont
25	51.6	Greeley 6	Greeley
26	51.6	Adams-Arapahoe 28J	Aurora
27	51.6	Pueblo City 60	Pueblo
28	51.5	Poudre R-1	Fort Collins
29	51.5	Adams County 14	Commerce City
30	51.5	Trinidad 1	Trinidad
31	51.5	Colorado Springs 11	Colorado Spgs
32	51.5	Montezuma-Cortez Re-1	Cortez
33	51.4	Elizabeth C-1	Elizabeth
34	51.4	Jefferson County R-1	Golden
35	51.4	Garfield Re-2	Rifle
36	51.4	Valley Re-1	Sterling
37	51.4	Eagle County Re 50	Eagle
38	51.4	Thompson R-2J	Loveland
39	51.4	Westminster 50	Westminster
40	51.4	Widefield 3	Colorado Spgs
41	51.3	Brighton 27J	Brighton
42	51.3	Academy 20	Colorado Spgs
43	51.2	Pueblo County Rural 70	Pueblo
44	51.2	Falcon 49	Falcon
45	51.1	Douglas County Re 1	Castle Rock
46	51.1	Weld County Re-1	Gilcrest
47	51.1	Harrison 2	Colorado Spgs
48	51.1	Cherry Creek 5	Greenwood Vlg
49	51.0	Canon City Re-1	Canon City
50	51.0	Montrose County RE-1J	Montrose
51	50.9	Denver County 1	Denver
52	50.9	Mesa County Valley 51	Grand Junction
53	50.8	Boulder Valley Re 2	Boulder
54	50.8	Littleton 6	Littleton
55	50.6	Cheyenne Mountain 12	Colorado Spgs
56	50.5	Fort Morgan Re-3	Fort Morgan
57	50.4	Adams 12 Five Star Schools	Thornton
58	50.3	East Otero R-1	La Junta
59	49.4	Brush Re-2(J)	Brush

Female Students

Rank	Percent	District Name	City
1	50.5	Brush Re-2(J)	Brush
2	49.6	East Otero R-1	La Junta
3	49.5	Adams 12 Five Star Schools	Thornton
4	49.5	Fort Morgan Re-3	Fort Morgan
5	49.3	Cheyenne Mountain 12	Colorado Spgs
6	49.1	Littleton 6	Littleton
7	49.1	Boulder Valley Re 2	Boulder
8	49.0	Mesa County Valley 51	Grand Junction
9	49.0	Denver County 1	Denver
10	48.9	Montrose County RE-1J	Montrose
11	48.9	Canon City Re-1	Canon City
12	48.8	Cherry Creek 5	Greenwood Vlg
13	48.8	Harrison 2	Colorado Spgs
14	48.8	Weld County Re-1	Gilcrest
15	48.8	Douglas County Re 1	Castle Rock
16	48.7	Falcon 49	Falcon
17	48.7	Pueblo County Rural 70	Pueblo
18	48.6	Academy 20	Colorado Spgs
19	48.6	Brighton 27J	Brighton
20	48.5	Widefield 3	Colorado Spgs
21	48.5	Westminster 50	Westminster
22	48.5	Thompson R-2J	Loveland
23	48.5	Eagle County Re 50	Eagle
24	48.5	Valley Re-1	Sterling

Rank	Percent	District Name	City
25	48.5	Garfield Re-2	Rifle
26	48.5	Jefferson County R-1	Golden
27	48.5	Elizabeth C-1	Elizabeth
28	48.4	Montezuma-Cortez Re-1	Cortez
29	48.4	Colorado Springs 11	Colorado Spgs
30	48.4	Trinidad 1	Trinidad
31	48.4	Adams County 14	Commerce City
32	48.4	Poudre R-1	Fort Collins
33	48.3	Pueblo City 60	Pueblo
34	48.3	Adams-Arapahoe 28J	Aurora
35	48.3	Greeley 6	Greeley
36	48.3	St Vrain Valley RE-1J	Longmont
37	48.3	Durango 9-R	Durango
38	48.3	Windsor Re-4	Windsor
39	48.3	Moffat County Re:No 1	Craig
40	48.1	Mapleton 1	Denver
41	48.1	Lewis-Palmer 38	Monument
42	48.0	Fountain 8	Fountain
43	48.0	Delta County 50(J)	Delta
44	48.0	Woodland Park Re-2	Woodland Park
45	47.8	Gunnison Watershed RE-1J	Gunnison
46	47.6	Sheridan 2	Sheridan
47	47.4	Englewood 1	Englewood
48	47.4	Roaring Fork Re-1	Glenwood Spgs
49	47.4	Eaton Re-2	Eaton
50	47.3	Summit Re-1	Frisco
51	47.3	Johnstown-Milliken RE-5J	Milliken
52	47.3	Alamosa RE-11J	Alamosa
53	47.1	Florence Re-2	Florence
54	46.9	Keenesburg Re-3(J)	Keenesburg
55	46.9	Weld County SD Re-8	Fort Lupton
56	46.8	Lamar Re-2	Lamar
57	46.6	Steamboat Springs Re-2	Steamboat Spgs
58	46.6	Archuleta County 50 Jt	Pagosa Springs
59	45.9	Aspen 1	Aspen

Individual Education Program Students

Rank	Percent	District Name	City
1	15.5	Florence Re-2	Florence
2	13.9	Weld County Re-1	Gilcrest
3	13.7	East Otero R-1	La Junta
4	13.4	Valley Re-1	Sterling
5	13.1	Keenesburg Re-3(J)	Keenesburg
6	13.0	Englewood 1	Englewood
7	12.7	Lamar Re-2	Lamar
8	12.6	Weld County SD Re-8	Fort Lupton
9	12.5	Widefield 3	Colorado Spgs
10	12.3	Montezuma-Cortez Re-1	Cortez
10	12.3	Sheridan 2	Sheridan
12	12.2	Montrose County RE-1J	Montrose
13	12.1	Alamosa RE-11J	Alamosa
14	11.9	Canon City Re-1	Canon City
15	11.8	Moffat County Re:No 1	Craig
16	11.6	Mesa County Valley 51	Grand Junction
17	11.5	Denver County 1	Denver
17	11.5	Pueblo City 60	Pueblo
19	11.3	Fountain 8	Fountain
19	11.3	Steamboat Springs Re-2	Steamboat Spgs
21	11.2	Delta County 50(J)	Delta
21	11.2	Fort Morgan Re-3	Fort Morgan
21	11.2	Thompson R-2J	Loveland
24	11.0	Brush Re-2(J)	Brush
24	11.0	Cherry Creek 5	Greenwood Vlg
26	10.9	Boulder Valley Re 2	Boulder
27	10.8	Durango 9-R	Durango
27	10.8	Pueblo County Rural 70	Pueblo
29	10.4	Adams-Arapahoe 28J	Aurora
29	10.4	Falcon 49	Falcon
29	10.4	Littleton 6	Littleton
32	10.3	Johnstown-Milliken RE-5J	Milliken
33	10.2	Greeley 6	Greeley
34	9.7	Harrison 2	Colorado Spgs
35	9.6	Trinidad 1	Trinidad
35	9.6	Woodland Park Re-2	Woodland Park
37	9.5	Brighton 27J	Brighton
37	9.5	Elizabeth C-1	Elizabeth
37	9.5	Summit Re-1	Frisco
40	9.4	Adams 12 Five Star Schools	Thornton
40	9.4	Adams County 14	Commerce City
40	9.4	Poudre R-1	Fort Collins
40	9.4	Westminster 50	Westminster
40	9.4	Windsor Re-4	Windsor
45	9.1	Jefferson County R-1	Golden
46	8.8	Eagle County Re 50	Eagle
47	8.7	Mapleton 1	Denver
48	8.5	Douglas County Re 1	Castle Rock
49	8.4	Eaton Re-2	Eaton
50	8.3	Garfield Re-2	Rifle
51	8.1	Gunnison Watershed RE-1J	Gunnison
52	7.8	Lewis-Palmer 38	Monument
53	7.5	St Vrain Valley RE-1J	Longmont
54	7.3	Academy 20	Colorado Spgs
54	7.3	Colorado Springs 11	Colorado Spgs
56	6.8	Roaring Fork Re-1	Glenwood Spgs
57	6.4	Archuleta County 50 Jt	Pagosa Springs
58	5.1	Cheyenne Mountain 12	Colorado Spgs
59	4.7	Aspen 1	Aspen

English Language Learner Students

Rank	Percent	District Name	City
1	43.4	Weld County SD Re-8	Fort Lupton
2	40.4	Adams County 14	Commerce City
3	38.5	Adams-Arapahoe 28J	Aurora
4	34.3	Montezuma-Cortez Re-1	Cortez
5	33.5	Westminster 50	Westminster
6	31.0	Sheridan 2	Sheridan
7	29.9	Denver County 1	Denver
8	29.8	Eagle County Re 50	Eagle
9	29.6	Mapleton 1	Denver
10	27.6	Roaring Fork Re-1	Glenwood Spgs
11	24.6	Brush Re-2(J)	Brush
12	23.0	Weld County Re-1	Gilcrest
13	22.1	Greeley 6	Greeley
14	20.6	Johnstown-Milliken RE-5J	Milliken
15	19.4	Garfield Re-2	Rifle
16	19.0	Brighton 27J	Brighton
17	18.2	Summit Re-1	Frisco
18	17.8	Fort Morgan Re-3	Fort Morgan
18	17.8	Lamar Re-2	Lamar
20	16.0	St Vrain Valley RE-1J	Longmont
21	15.7	Keenesburg Re-3(J)	Keenesburg
22	14.5	Boulder Valley Re 2	Boulder
23	13.1	Pueblo City 60	Pueblo
24	13.0	Cherry Creek 5	Greenwood Vlg
25	12.5	Aspen 1	Aspen
26	11.4	Montrose County RE-1J	Montrose
27	10.2	Poudre R-1	Fort Collins
28	9.7	Alamosa RE-11J	Alamosa
29	9.6	Adams 12 Five Star Schools	Thornton
29	9.6	Harrison 2	Colorado Spgs
31	8.7	Cheyenne Mountain 12	Colorado Spgs
32	8.6	Eaton Re-2	Eaton
33	7.9	Delta County 50(J)	Delta
34	6.3	Colorado Springs 11	Colorado Spgs
34	6.3	Moffat County Re:No 1	Craig
36	5.6	Englewood 1	Englewood
36	5.6	Jefferson County R-1	Golden
38	5.2	Valley Re-1	Sterling
39	5.0	Littleton 6	Littleton
40	4.7	Mesa County Valley 51	Grand Junction
41	4.0	Gunnison Watershed RE-1J	Gunnison
42	3.3	Thompson R-2J	Loveland
43	2.6	Windsor Re-4	Windsor
44	2.5	Douglas County Re 1	Castle Rock
45	2.3	Durango 9-R	Durango
46	2.2	Widefield 3	Colorado Spgs
47	2.1	Academy 20	Colorado Spgs
48	2.0	Steamboat Springs Re-2	Steamboat Spgs
49	1.9	Pueblo County Rural 70	Pueblo
50	1.7	Archuleta County 50 Jt	Pagosa Springs
51	1.6	Fountain 8	Fountain
52	1.5	Trinidad 1	Trinidad
53	1.2	Lewis-Palmer 38	Monument
54	0.9	Florence Re-2	Florence
55	0.6	East Otero R-1	La Junta
55	0.6	Falcon 49	Falcon
57	0.4	Canon City Re-1	Canon City
57	0.4	Elizabeth C-1	Elizabeth
57	0.4	Woodland Park Re-2	Woodland Park

Migrant Students

Rank	Percent	District Name	City
1	28.8	Alamosa RE-11J	Alamosa
2	24.9	Weld County SD Re-8	Fort Lupton
3	21.1	Fort Morgan Re-3	Fort Morgan
4	17.2	Weld County Re-1	Gilcrest
5	16.2	Adams County 14	Commerce City
6	10.0	Brush Re-2(J)	Brush
7	9.7	Keenesburg Re-3(J)	Keenesburg
8	9.6	Greeley 6	Greeley
9	9.5	Lamar Re-2	Lamar
10	8.8	Eaton Re-2	Eaton
11	8.5	Montrose County RE-1J	Montrose
12	5.9	Johnstown-Milliken RE-5J	Milliken
13	5.7	Brighton 27J	Brighton
14	5.1	Mapleton 1	Denver
15	5.0	Adams-Arapahoe 28J	Aurora
15	5.0	Delta County 50(J)	Delta
17	4.7	Westminster 50	Westminster
18	3.3	Mesa County Valley 51	Grand Junction
19	2.9	Eagle County Re 50	Eagle
19	2.9	Harrison 2	Colorado Spgs
21	2.6	St Vrain Valley RE-1J	Longmont

Rank	Percent	District Name	City
22	2.5	Sheridan 2	Sheridan
23	2.2	Adams 12 Five Star Schools	Thornton
24	2.1	Gunnison Watershed RE-1J	Gunnison
25	1.9	Boulder Valley Re 2	Boulder
25	1.9	Denver County 1	Denver
25	1.9	Pueblo City 60	Pueblo
28	1.6	East Otero R-1	La Junta
29	1.5	Garfield Re-2	Rifle
29	1.5	Pueblo County Rural 70	Pueblo
29	1.5	Thompson R-2J	Loveland
32	1.4	Colorado Springs 11	Colorado Spgs
33	1.2	Jefferson County R-1	Golden
33	1.2	Poudre R-1	Fort Collins
35	0.9	Windsor Re-4	Windsor
36	0.7	Valley Re-1	Sterling
37	0.6	Fountain 8	Fountain
37	0.6	Moffat County Re:No 1	Craig
39	0.3	Roaring Fork Re-1	Glenwood Spgs
39	0.3	Summit Re-1	Frisco
41	0.2	Florence Re-2	Florence
41	0.2	Steamboat Springs Re-2	Steamboat Spgs
43	0.1	Canon City Re-1	Canon City
43	0.1	Littleton 6	Littleton
45	0.0	Cherry Creek 5	Greenwood Vlg
45	0.0	Douglas County Re 1	Castle Rock
45	0.0	Durango 9-R	Durango
45	0.0	Englewood 1	Englewood
45	0.0	Falcon 49	Falcon
45	0.0	Widefield 3	Colorado Spgs
51	0.0	Academy 20	Colorado Spgs
51	0.0	Archuleta County 50 Jt	Pagosa Springs
51	0.0	Aspen 1	Aspen
51	0.0	Cheyenne Mountain 12	Colorado Spgs
51	0.0	Elizabeth C-1	Elizabeth
51	0.0	Lewis-Palmer 38	Monument
51	0.0	Montezuma-Cortez Re-1	Cortez
51	0.0	Trinidad 1	Trinidad
51	0.0	Woodland Park Re-2	Woodland Park

Students Eligible for Free Lunch

Rank	Percent	District Name	City
1	60.9	Adams County 14	Commerce City
2	55.2	Denver County 1	Denver
3	51.5	Sheridan 2	Sheridan
4	51.3	Trinidad 1	Trinidad
5	49.6	Alamosa RE-11J	Alamosa
6	49.4	Pueblo City 60	Pueblo
7	46.9	East Otero R-1	La Junta
8	46.8	Westminster 50	Westminster
9	45.9	Fort Morgan Re-3	Fort Morgan
10	45.5	Harrison 2	Colorado Spgs
11	44.8	Weld County SD Re-8	Fort Lupton
12	43.0	Lamar Re-2	Lamar
13	39.3	Greeley 6	Greeley
14	39.0	Montezuma-Cortez Re-1	Cortez
15	35.9	Adams-Arapahoe 28J	Aurora
16	34.4	Weld County Re-1	Gilcrest
17	32.8	Mapleton 1	Denver
18	31.7	Brush Re-2(J)	Brush
19	31.1	Delta County 50(J)	Delta
20	30.6	Mesa County Valley 51	Grand Junction
21	30.4	Montrose County RE-1J	Montrose
22	29.1	Canon City Re-1	Canon City
23	28.5	Valley Re-1	Sterling
24	28.4	Florence Re-2	Florence
25	27.4	Archuleta County 50 Jt	Pagosa Springs
26	27.3	Keenesburg Re-3(J)	Keenesburg
27	26.9	Englewood 1	Englewood
28	25.8	Colorado Springs 11	Colorado Spgs
29	23.8	Garfield Re-2	Rifle
30	23.3	Brighton 27J	Brighton
31	22.1	Pueblo County Rural 70	Pueblo
32	19.1	Adams 12 Five Star Schools	Thornton
32	19.1	Fountain 8	Fountain
34	18.5	Moffat County Re:No 1	Craig
35	18.2	Eagle County Re 50	Eagle
36	18.1	Thompson R-2J	Loveland
37	17.4	Johnstown-Milliken RE-5J	Milliken
38	17.0	St Vrain Valley RE-1J	Longmont
39	16.4	Eaton Re-2	Eaton
40	15.3	Poudre R-1	Fort Collins
41	15.2	Roaring Fork Re-1	Glenwood Spgs
42	14.5	Gunnison Watershed RE-1J	Gunnison
43	14.4	Durango 9-R	Durango
44	13.8	Widefield 3	Colorado Spgs
45	13.0	Jefferson County R-1	Golden
46	11.0	Summit Re-1	Frisco
47	10.7	Boulder Valley Re 2	Boulder
48	10.4	Woodland Park Re-2	Woodland Park
49	9.1	Cherry Creek 5	Greenwood Vlg
49	9.1	Falcon 49	Falcon
51	8.4	Littleton 6	Littleton

52	6.5	Windsor Re-4	Windsor
53	4.5	Cheyenne Mountain 12	Colorado Spgs
54	3.8	Elizabeth C-1	Elizabeth
55	3.3	Academy 20	Colorado Spgs
56	3.1	Lewis-Palmer 38	Monument
57	2.7	Steamboat Springs Re-2	Steamboat Spgs
58	1.7	Douglas County Re 1	Castle Rock
59	0.0	Aspen 1	Aspen

Students Eligible for Reduced-Price Lunch

Rank	Percent	District Name	City
1	14.3	Brush Re-2(J)	Brush
2	13.4	Trinidad 1	Trinidad
3	13.3	Fountain 8	Fountain
4	12.6	East Otero R-1	La Junta
5	12.3	Lamar Re-2	Lamar
6	11.9	Harrison 2	Colorado Spgs
7	11.7	Archuleta County 50 Jt	Pagosa Springs
8	11.6	Fort Morgan Re-3	Fort Morgan
8	11.6	Keensburg Re-3(J)	Keenesburg
10	11.2	Delta County 50(J)	Delta
11	10.8	Mapleton 1	Denver
12	10.6	Pueblo City 60	Pueblo
13	10.3	Montezuma-Cortez Re-1	Cortez
13	10.3	Sheridan 2	Sheridan
13	10.3	Westminster 50	Westminster
16	10.0	Pueblo County Rural 70	Pueblo
17	9.5	Alamosa RE-11J	Alamosa
17	9.5	Weld County SD Re-8	Fort Lupton
19	9.3	Valley Re-1	Sterling
20	9.2	Canon City Re-1	Canon City
20	9.2	Mesa County Valley 51	Grand Junction
22	9.1	Florence Re-2	Florence
23	9.0	Colorado Springs 11	Colorado Spgs
24	8.9	Montrose County RE-1J	Montrose
25	8.8	Weld County Re-1	Gilcrest
26	8.5	Greeley 6	Greeley
27	8.3	Adams County 14	Commerce City
28	8.1	Garfield Re-2	Rifle
29	7.7	Thompson R-2J	Loveland
30	7.3	Johnstown-Milliken RE-5J	Milliken
31	7.2	Denver County 1	Denver
32	7.1	Eagle County Re 50	Eagle
33	6.9	Brighton 27J	Brighton
34	6.5	Englewood 1	Englewood
35	6.3	Roaring Fork Re-1	Glenwood Spgs
36	6.2	Adams-Arapahoe 28J	Aurora
37	5.9	Adams 12 Five Star Schools	Thornton
38	5.7	Moffat County Re:No 1	Craig
38	5.7	Widefield 3	Colorado Spgs
40	5.6	Eaton Re-2	Eaton
41	5.5	Falcon 49	Falcon
42	5.3	Durango 9-R	Durango
43	5.0	Gunnison Watershed RE-1J	Gunnison
44	4.7	Cherry Creek 5	Greenwood Vlg
45	4.6	Jefferson County R-1	Golden
45	4.6	Summit Re-1	Frisco
47	4.1	Woodland Park Re-2	Woodland Park
48	4.0	Poudre R-1	Fort Collins
49	3.7	St Vrain Valley RE-1J	Longmont
50	3.5	Windsor Re-4	Windsor
51	2.8	Littleton 6	Littleton
52	2.4	Boulder Valley Re 2	Boulder
53	2.3	Academy 20	Colorado Spgs
54	2.1	Steamboat Springs Re-2	Steamboat Spgs
55	2.0	Cheyenne Mountain 12	Colorado Spgs
56	1.8	Aspen 1	Aspen
56	1.8	Elizabeth C-1	Elizabeth
58	1.4	Lewis-Palmer 38	Monument
59	1.2	Douglas County Re 1	Castle Rock

Student/Teacher Ratio

Rank	Ratio	District Name	City
1	23.9	Fountain 8	Fountain
2	20.0	Mapleton 1	Denver
3	19.7	Adams 12 Five Star Schools	Thornton
4	18.7	Adams-Arapahoe 28J	Aurora
4	18.7	Pueblo County Rural 70	Pueblo
6	18.3	Jefferson County R-1	Golden
7	18.2	Delta County 50(J)	Delta
7	18.2	Englewood 1	Englewood
9	18.0	Garfield Re-2	Rifle
10	17.8	Adams County 14	Commerce City
10	17.8	Douglas County Re 1	Castle Rock
12	17.7	St Vrain Valley RE-1J	Longmont
13	17.6	Widefield 3	Colorado Spgs
14	17.5	Elizabeth C-1	Elizabeth
14	17.5	Mesa County Valley 51	Grand Junction
16	17.4	Falcon 49	Falcon
16	17.4	Littleton 6	Littleton
16	17.4	Poudre R-1	Fort Collins
19	17.3	Thompson R-2J	Loveland
20	17.2	Alamosa RE-11J	Alamosa
20	17.2	Brighton 27J	Brighton
22	17.1	Boulder Valley Re 2	Boulder
22	17.1	Denver County 1	Denver
22	17.1	Moffat County Re:No 1	Craig
25	17.0	Cherry Creek 5	Greenwood Vlg
26	16.9	Archuleta County 50 Jt	Pagosa Springs
26	16.9	Cheyenne Mountain 12	Colorado Spgs
28	16.7	Greeley 6	Greeley
28	16.7	Johnstown-Milliken RE-5J	Milliken
28	16.7	Montrose County RE-1J	Montrose
31	16.6	Colorado Springs 11	Colorado Spgs
31	16.6	Weld County SD Re-8	Fort Lupton
33	16.5	Canon City Re-1	Canon City
33	16.5	Woodland Park Re-2	Woodland Park
35	16.4	Academy 20	Colorado Spgs
35	16.4	Lewis-Palmer 38	Monument
37	16.3	Eaton Re-2	Eaton
38	16.1	Fort Morgan Re-3	Fort Morgan
38	16.1	Valley Re-1	Sterling
40	16.0	Florence Re-2	Florence
40	16.0	Pueblo City 60	Pueblo
42	15.9	Montezuma-Cortez Re-1	Cortez
42	15.9	Trinidad 1	Trinidad
44	15.6	Westminster 50	Westminster
44	15.6	Windsor Re-4	Windsor
46	15.3	Lamar Re-2	Lamar
47	15.2	Sheridan 2	Sheridan
48	14.9	Keensburg Re-3(J)	Keenesburg
49	14.8	Eagle County Re 50	Eagle
50	14.7	Roaring Fork Re-1	Glenwood Spgs
51	14.6	Harrison 2	Colorado Spgs
52	14.4	Brush Re-2(J)	Brush
53	14.3	Durango 9-R	Durango
54	14.2	Steamboat Springs Re-2	Steamboat Spgs
55	14.1	East Otero R-1	La Junta
56	13.7	Gunnison Watershed RE-1J	Gunnison
57	13.4	Weld County Re-1	Gilcrest
58	13.2	Summit Re-1	Frisco
59	12.0	Aspen 1	Aspen

Student/Librarian Ratio

Rank	Ratio	District Name	City
1	5,507.3	Brighton 27J	Brighton
2	3,335.0	Weld County Re-1	Gilcrest
3	3,185.6	Elizabeth C-1	Elizabeth
4	2,891.3	Douglas County Re 1	Castle Rock
5	2,873.2	Pueblo County Rural 70	Pueblo
6	2,557.1	Lewis-Palmer 38	Monument
7	2,128.9	Keensburg Re-3(J)	Keenesburg
8	2,057.0	Canon City Re-1	Canon City
9	1,985.0	Brush Re-2(J)	Brush
10	1,905.3	Mapleton 1	Denver
11	1,905.0	Garfield Re-2	Rifle
12	1,844.0	Florence Re-2	Florence
13	1,836.3	Westminster 50	Westminster
14	1,687.8	Trinidad 1	Trinidad
15	1,673.9	Academy 20	Colorado Spgs
16	1,673.0	Montezuma-Cortez Re-1	Cortez
17	1,662.9	Thompson R-2J	Loveland
18	1,634.7	Adams-Arapahoe 28J	Aurora
19	1,604.0	East Otero R-1	La Junta
20	1,521.2	Weld County SD Re-8	Fort Lupton
21	1,440.5	Mesa County Valley 51	Grand Junction
22	1,433.9	Fountain 8	Fountain
23	1,418.8	Littleton 6	Littleton
24	1,375.5	Valley Re-1	Sterling
25	1,368.3	Montrose County RE-1J	Montrose
26	1,366.9	Widefield 3	Colorado Spgs
27	1,361.3	Englewood 1	Englewood
28	1,317.6	Fort Morgan Re-3	Fort Morgan
29	1,305.6	Adams County 14	Commerce City
30	1,243.5	Harrison 2	Colorado Spgs
31	1,234.1	St Vrain Valley RE-1J	Longmont
32	1,193.8	Moffat County Re:No 1	Craig
33	911.7	Gunnison Watershed RE-1J	Gunnison
34	822.6	Eaton Re-2	Eaton
35	818.0	Alamosa RE-11J	Alamosa
36	780.5	Cherry Creek 5	Greenwood Vlg
37	773.1	Adams 12 Five Star Schools	Thornton
38	738.6	Poudre R-1	Fort Collins
39	721.7	Falcon 49	Falcon
40	710.0	Lamar Re-2	Lamar
41	708.7	Johnstown-Milliken RE-5J	Milliken
42	707.5	Boulder Valley Re 2	Boulder
43	664.4	Jefferson County R-1	Golden
44	661.5	Denver County 1	Denver
45	623.2	Woodland Park Re-2	Woodland Park
46	588.2	Roaring Fork Re-1	Glenwood Spgs
47	570.7	Pueblo City 60	Pueblo
48	570.4	Cheyenne Mountain 12	Colorado Spgs
49	552.8	Colorado Springs 11	Colorado Spgs
50	516.9	Sheridan 2	Sheridan
51	501.0	Archuleta County 50 Jt	Pagosa Springs
52	498.2	Windsor Re-4	Windsor
53	496.6	Durango 9-R	Durango
54	478.0	Steamboat Springs Re-2	Steamboat Spgs
55	452.4	Eagle County Re 50	Eagle
56	353.6	Summit Re-1	Frisco
57	n/a	Aspen 1	Aspen
57	n/a	Delta County 50(J)	Delta
57	n/a	Greeley 6	Greeley

Student/Counselor Ratio

Rank	Ratio	District Name	City
1	1,040.4	Denver County 1	Denver
2	958.0	Keensburg Re-3(J)	Keenesburg
3	855.6	Douglas County Re 1	Castle Rock
4	820.4	Adams 12 Five Star Schools	Thornton
5	790.1	Colorado Springs 11	Colorado Spgs
6	743.5	Valley Re-1	Sterling
7	741.8	Adams County 14	Commerce City
8	707.2	Adams-Arapahoe 28J	Aurora
9	684.2	Jefferson County R-1	Golden
10	677.1	Brighton 27J	Brighton
11	664.1	Greeley 6	Greeley
12	653.5	Cherry Creek 5	Greenwood Vlg
13	621.5	Fort Morgan Re-3	Fort Morgan
14	615.3	Lamar Re-2	Lamar
15	601.7	Mapleton 1	Denver
16	588.0	Westminster 50	Westminster
17	563.6	Canon City Re-1	Canon City
18	554.6	Fountain 8	Fountain
19	529.2	Montrose County RE-1J	Montrose
20	514.3	Littleton 6	Littleton
21	513.8	Delta County 50(J)	Delta
22	507.4	Boulder Valley Re 2	Boulder
23	506.7	Mesa County Valley 51	Grand Junction
24	506.2	Johnstown-Milliken RE-5J	Milliken
25	485.9	Elizabeth C-1	Elizabeth
26	460.5	St Vrain Valley RE-1J	Longmont
27	452.0	Roaring Fork Re-1	Glenwood Spgs
28	450.9	Poudre R-1	Fort Collins
29	437.9	Garfield Re-2	Rifle
30	427.0	Windsor Re-4	Windsor
31	425.4	Englewood 1	Englewood
32	424.5	Falcon 49	Falcon
33	420.4	Thompson R-2J	Loveland
34	417.9	Brush Re-2(J)	Brush
35	414.8	Academy 20	Colorado Spgs
36	411.3	Eaton Re-2	Eaton
37	404.3	Pueblo County Rural 70	Pueblo
38	400.2	Weld County Re-1	Gilcrest
39	389.5	Woodland Park Re-2	Woodland Park
40	388.3	Archuleta County 50 Jt	Pagosa Springs
41	383.6	Lewis-Palmer 38	Monument
42	378.1	Eagle County Re 50	Eagle
43	374.2	Moffat County Re:No 1	Craig
44	372.2	Sheridan 2	Sheridan
45	370.0	Aspen 1	Aspen
46	358.2	Pueblo City 60	Pueblo
47	357.6	Cheyenne Mountain 12	Colorado Spgs
48	356.7	Gunnison Watershed RE-1J	Gunnison
49	352.2	Montezuma-Cortez Re-1	Cortez
50	349.5	Weld County SD Re-8	Fort Lupton
51	347.9	Florence Re-2	Florence
52	326.7	Harrison 2	Colorado Spgs
53	324.1	Steamboat Springs Re-2	Steamboat Spgs
54	316.2	Widefield 3	Colorado Spgs
55	314.5	East Otero R-1	La Junta
56	303.8	Trinidad 1	Trinidad
57	288.7	Summit Re-1	Frisco
58	266.9	Durango 9-R	Durango
59	263.9	Alamosa RE-11J	Alamosa

Current Spending per Student in FY2003

Rank	Dollars	District Name	City
1	10,195	Aspen 1	Aspen
2	9,144	Summit Re-1	Frisco
3	8,732	Eagle County Re 50	Eagle
4	8,691	Steamboat Springs Re-2	Steamboat Spgs
5	8,583	Sheridan 2	Sheridan
6	8,230	Jefferson County R-1	Golden
7	7,918	Colorado Springs 11	Colorado Spgs
8	7,888	Denver County 1	Denver
9	7,857	Poudre R-1	Fort Collins
10	7,758	Adams County 14	Commerce City
11	7,639	Boulder Valley Re 2	Boulder
12	7,592	Harrison 2	Colorado Spgs
13	7,457	Weld County Re-1	Gilcrest
14	7,427	Cherry Creek 5	Greenwood Vlg

15	7,344	Englewood 1	Englewood
16	7,249	Weld County SD Re-8	Fort Lupton
17	7,192	Trinidad 1	Trinidad
18	7,176	Moffat County Re:No 1	Craig
19	7,118	Roaring Fork Re-1	Glenwood Spgs
20	7,049	Douglas County Re 1	Castle Rock
21	7,044	Gunnison Watershed RE-1J	Gunnison
22	7,014	Durango 9-R	Durango
23	6,961	Westminster 50	Westminster
24	6,947	Littleton 6	Littleton
25	6,921	Academy 20	Colorado Spgs
26	6,887	Adams-Arapahoe 28J	Aurora
27	6,852	Pueblo City 60	Pueblo
28	6,838	Mapleton 1	Denver
29	6,829	Archuleta County 50 Jt	Pagosa Springs
30	6,793	Alamosa RE-11J	Alamosa
31	6,779	Montrose County RE-1J	Montrose
32	6,666	Brush Re-2(J)	Brush
33	6,608	Thompson R-2J	Loveland
34	6,605	St Vrain Valley RE-1J	Longmont
35	6,594	Delta County 50(J)	Delta
36	6,468	Fort Morgan Re-3	Fort Morgan
37	6,460	Brighton 27J	Brighton
38	6,455	Elizabeth C-1	Elizabeth
39	6,390	Mesa County Valley 51	Grand Junction
40	6,384	Canon City Re-1	Canon City
41	6,355	Adams 12 Five Star Schools	Thornton
42	6,326	Greeley 6	Greeley
43	6,317	East Otero R-1	La Junta
44	6,237	Florence Re-2	Florence
45	6,201	Montezuma-Cortez Re-1	Cortez
46	6,190	Fountain 8	Fountain
47	6,161	Keenesburg Re-3(J)	Keenesburg
48	6,093	Valley Re-1	Sterling
49	6,032	Windsor Re-4	Windsor
50	6,029	Cheyenne Mountain 12	Colorado Spgs
51	5,993	Woodland Park Re-2	Woodland Park
52	5,988	Pueblo County Rural 70	Pueblo
53	5,908	Johnstown-Milliken RE-5J	Milliken
54	5,894	Lamar Re-2	Lamar
55	5,828	Eaton Re-2	Eaton
56	5,819	Garfield Re-2	Rifle
57	5,803	Widefield 3	Colorado Spgs
58	5,800	Falcon 49	Falcon
59	5,794	Lewis-Palmer 38	Monument

Number of Diploma Recipients

Rank	Number	District Name	City
1	5,334	Jefferson County R-1	Golden
2	2,922	Cherry Creek 5	Greenwood Vlg
3	2,612	Denver County 1	Denver
4	1,898	Douglas County Re 1	Castle Rock
5	1,816	Colorado Springs 11	Colorado Spgs
6	1,810	Boulder Valley Re 2	Boulder
7	1,566	Adams 12 Five Star Schools	Thornton
8	1,503	Poudre R-1	Fort Collins
9	1,223	Littleton 6	Littleton
10	1,205	Academy 20	Colorado Spgs
11	1,179	Mesa County Valley 51	Grand Junction
12	1,134	St Vrain Valley RE-1J	Longmont
13	1,120	Adams-Arapahoe 28J	Aurora
14	924	Thompson R-2J	Loveland
15	907	Pueblo City 60	Pueblo
16	870	Greeley 6	Greeley
17	532	Widefield 3	Colorado Spgs
18	498	Westminster 50	Westminster
19	400	Harrison 2	Colorado Spgs
20	349	Pueblo County Rural 70	Pueblo
21	348	Montrose County RE-1J	Montrose
22	327	Falcon 49	Falcon
23	319	Durango 9-R	Durango
24	316	Cheyenne Mountain 12	Colorado Spgs
25	311	Roaring Fork Re-1	Glenwood Spgs
26	306	Delta County 50(J)	Delta
27	295	Lewis-Palmer 38	Monument
28	290	Englewood 1	Englewood
29	279	Canon City Re-1	Canon City
30	271	Brighton 27J	Brighton
31	237	Eagle County Re 50	Eagle
32	236	Adams County 14	Commerce City
33	215	Elizabeth C-1	Elizabeth
34	210	Mapleton 1	Denver
34	210	Woodland Park Re-2	Woodland Park
36	184	Fountain 8	Fountain
37	168	Valley Re-1	Sterling
38	165	Moffat County Re:No 1	Craig
38	165	Summit Re-1	Frisco
40	164	Montezuma-Cortez Re-1	Cortez
41	158	Windsor Re-4	Windsor
42	157	Fort Morgan Re-3	Fort Morgan
43	156	Garfield Re-2	Rifle
44	143	Weld County SD Re-8	Fort Lupton

45	132	Alamosa RE-11J	Alamosa
45	132	Steamboat Springs Re-2	Steamboat Spgs
47	128	East Otero R-1	La Junta
48	109	Gunnison Watershed RE-1J	Gunnison
49	105	Weld County Re-1	Gilcrest
50	100	Archuleta County 50 Jt	Pagosa Springs
51	95	Aspen 1	Aspen
52	94	Brush Re-2(J)	Brush
53	90	Lamar Re-2	Lamar
54	89	Johnstown-Milliken RE-5J	Milliken
55	87	Florence Re-2	Florence
56	85	Keenesburg Re-3(J)	Keenesburg
57	79	Eaton Re-2	Eaton
58	76	Sheridan 2	Sheridan
59	65	Trinidad 1	Trinidad

High School Drop-out Rate

Rank	Percent	District Name	City
1	n/a	Academy 20	Colorado Spgs
1	n/a	Adams 12 Five Star Schools	Thornton
1	n/a	Adams County 14	Commerce City
1	n/a	Adams-Arapahoe 28J	Aurora
1	n/a	Alamosa RE-11J	Alamosa
1	n/a	Archuleta County 50 Jt	Pagosa Springs
1	n/a	Aspen 1	Aspen
1	n/a	Boulder Valley Re 2	Boulder
1	n/a	Brighton 27J	Brighton
1	n/a	Brush Re-2(J)	Brush
1	n/a	Canon City Re-1	Canon City
1	n/a	Cherry Creek 5	Greenwood Vlg
1	n/a	Cheyenne Mountain 12	Colorado Spgs
1	n/a	Colorado Springs 11	Colorado Spgs
1	n/a	Delta County 50(J)	Delta
1	n/a	Denver County 1	Denver
1	n/a	Douglas County Re 1	Castle Rock
1	n/a	Durango 9-R	Durango
1	n/a	Eagle County Re 50	Eagle
1	n/a	East Otero R-1	La Junta
1	n/a	Eaton Re-2	Eaton
1	n/a	Elizabeth C-1	Elizabeth
1	n/a	Englewood 1	Englewood
1	n/a	Falcon 49	Falcon
1	n/a	Florence Re-2	Florence
1	n/a	Fort Morgan Re-3	Fort Morgan
1	n/a	Fountain 8	Fountain
1	n/a	Garfield Re-2	Rifle
1	n/a	Greeley 6	Greeley
1	n/a	Gunnison Watershed RE-1J	Gunnison
1	n/a	Harrison 2	Colorado Spgs
1	n/a	Jefferson County R-1	Golden
1	n/a	Johnstown-Milliken RE-5J	Milliken
1	n/a	Keenesburg Re-3(J)	Keenesburg
1	n/a	Lamar Re-2	Lamar
1	n/a	Lewis-Palmer 38	Monument
1	n/a	Littleton 6	Littleton
1	n/a	Mapleton 1	Denver
1	n/a	Mesa County Valley 51	Grand Junction
1	n/a	Moffat County Re:No 1	Craig
1	n/a	Montezuma-Cortez Re-1	Cortez
1	n/a	Montrose County RE-1J	Montrose
1	n/a	Poudre R-1	Fort Collins
1	n/a	Pueblo City 60	Pueblo
1	n/a	Pueblo County Rural 70	Pueblo
1	n/a	Roaring Fork Re-1	Glenwood Spgs
1	n/a	Sheridan 2	Sheridan
1	n/a	St Vrain Valley RE-1J	Longmont
1	n/a	Steamboat Springs Re-2	Steamboat Spgs
1	n/a	Summit Re-1	Frisco
1	n/a	Thompson R-2J	Loveland
1	n/a	Trinidad 1	Trinidad
1	n/a	Valley Re-1	Sterling
1	n/a	Weld County Re-1	Gilcrest
1	n/a	Weld County SD Re-8	Fort Lupton
1	n/a	Westminster 50	Westminster
1	n/a	Widefield 3	Colorado Spgs
1	n/a	Windsor Re-4	Windsor
1	n/a	Woodland Park Re-2	Woodland Park

Connecticut

Connecticut Public School Educational Profile

Category	Value	Category	Value
Schools *(2003-2004)*	1,250	**Diploma Recipients** *(2002-2003)*	32,193
Instructional Level		White, Non-Hispanic	24,595
Primary	663	Black, Non-Hispanic	3,617
Middle	192	Asian/Pacific Islander	1,024
High	202	American Indian/Alaskan Native	74
Other Level	190	Hispanic	2,883
Curriculum		**High School Drop-out Rate** (%) *(2001-2002)*	2.6
Regular	1,003	White, Non-Hispanic	1.9
Special Education	27	Black, Non-Hispanic	4.0
Vocational	17	Asian/Pacific Islander	2.4
Alternative	200	American Indian/Alaskan Native	4.9
Type		Hispanic	5.3
Magnet	38	**Staff** *(2003-2004)*	
Charter	12	Teachers	42,033.5
Title I Eligible	487	Average Salary ($)	56,516
School-wide Title I	134	Librarians/Media Specialists	781.0
Students *(2003-2004)*	577,203	Guidance Counselors	1,297.1
Gender (%)		**Ratios** *(2003-2004)*	
Male	51.5	Student/Teacher Ratio	13.7 to 1
Female	48.5	Student/Librarian Ratio	739.1 to 1
Race/Ethnicity (%)		Student/Counselor Ratio	445.0 to 1
White, Non-Hispanic	68.3	**College Entrance Exam Scores** *(2005)*	
Black, Non-Hispanic	13.6	Scholastic Aptitude Test (SAT)	
Asian/Pacific Islander	3.2	Participation Rate (%)	86
American Indian/Alaskan Native	0.3	Mean SAT Reasoning Test Verbal Score	517
Hispanic	14.6	Mean SAT Reasoning Test Math Score	517
Classification (%)		American College Testing Program (ACT)	
Individual Education Program (IEP)	12.1	Participation Rate (%)	10
Migrant *(2002-2003)*	1.8	Average Composite Score	22.8
English Language Learner (ELL)	4.5	Average English Score	22.5
Eligible for Free Lunch Program	0.0	Average Math Score	22.7
Eligible for Reduced-Price Lunch Program	0.0	Average Reading Score	23.4
Current Spending *($ per student in FY 2003)*	10,653	Average Science Score	22.0
Instruction	6,728		
Support Services	3,533		

Note: *For an explanation of data, please refer to the User's Guide in the front of the book*

Connecticut NAEP 2005 Test Scores

Reading			Mathematics		
Grade/Category	Value	Rank	Grade/Category	Value	Rank
4th Grade			**4th Grade**		
Average Proficiency	225.8 (1.02)	4/51	Average Proficiency	242.1 (0.78)	9/51
Proficiency by Gender/Race/Ethnicity			Proficiency by Gender/Race/Ethnicity		
Male	221.6 (1.21)	8/51	Male	243.6 (1.02)	10/51
Female	230.2 (1.21)	4/51	Female	240.6 (0.93)	12/51
White, Non-Hispanic	234.4 (1.12)	4/51	White, Non-Hispanic	250.1 (0.82)	6/51
Black, Non-Hispanic	201.1 (1.85)	14/42	Black, Non-Hispanic	218.5 (1.64)	25/42
Asian, Non-Hispanic	236.2 (4.16)	8/27	Asian, Non-Hispanic	252.6 (2.48)	13/25
American Indian, Non-Hispanic	n/a	n/a	American Indian, Non-Hispanic	n/a	n/a
Hispanic	203.1 (2.24)	23/40	Hispanic	223.3 (1.63)	25/41
Proficiency by Class Size			Proficiency by Class Size		
Less than 16 Students	n/a	n/a	Less than 16 Students	n/a	n/a
16 to 18 Students	218.4 (2.70)	14/33	16 to 18 Students	239.6 (1.96)	12/31
19 to 20 Students	225.6 (2.81)	11/38	19 to 20 Students	242.3 (2.32)	10/38
21 to 25 Students	231.7 (1.51)	2/51	21 to 25 Students	245.6 (1.27)	4/51
Greater than 25 Students	n/a	n/a	Greater than 25 Students	n/a	n/a
Percent Attaining Achievement Levels			Percent Attaining Achievement Levels		
Below Basic	29.4 (1.20)	41/51	Below Basic	15.7 (1.00)	37/51
Basic or Above	70.6 (1.20)	11/51	Basic or Above	84.3 (1.00)	14/51
Proficient or Above	38.3 (1.22)	4/51	Proficient or Above	42.5 (1.37)	8/51
Advanced or Above	11.7 (1.00)	1/51	Advanced or Above	6.5 (0.60)	8/51
8th Grade			**8th Grade**		
Average Proficiency	264.0 (1.30)	24/51	Average Proficiency	281.1 (1.43)	21/51
Proficiency by Gender/Race/Ethnicity			Proficiency by Gender/Race/Ethnicity		
Male	258.5 (1.44)	23/51	Male	281.0 (1.61)	25/51
Female	269.9 (1.48)	21/51	Female	281.1 (1.74)	19/51
White, Non-Hispanic	272.4 (1.39)	10/51	White, Non-Hispanic	293.4 (1.09)	7/51
Black, Non-Hispanic	240.2 (3.31)	25/40	Black, Non-Hispanic	249.5 (2.67)	27/41
Asian, Non-Hispanic	278.9 (4.46)	7/24	Asian, Non-Hispanic	291.8 (5.27)	16/23
American Indian, Non-Hispanic	n/a	n/a	American Indian, Non-Hispanic	n/a	n/a
Hispanic	244.6 (3.86)	31/38	Hispanic	254.1 (2.78)	36/38
Proficiency by Parents Highest Level of Ed.			Proficiency by Parents Highest Level of Ed.		
Did Not Finish High School	245.4 (4.45)	22/49	Did Not Finish High School	251.9 (3.58)	45/50
Graduated High School	253.9 (2.28)	25/50	Graduated High School	264.1 (1.79)	35/50
Some Education After High School	265.4 (1.79)	28/50	Some Education After High School	280.3 (1.71)	28/50
Graduated College	273.4 (1.35)	21/50	Graduated College	294.3 (1.53)	8/50
Percent Attaining Achievement Levels			Percent Attaining Achievement Levels		
Below Basic	29.4 (1.20)	41/51	Below Basic	30.1 (1.73)	23/51
Basic or Above	70.6 (1.20)	11/51	Basic or Above	69.9 (1.73)	29/51
Proficient or Above	38.3 (1.22)	4/51	Proficient or Above	34.6 (1.41)	10/51
Advanced or Above	11.7 (1.00)	1/51	Advanced or Above	7.8 (0.73)	7/51

Note: *For an explanation of data, please refer to the User's Guide in the front of the book; n/a indicates data not available*

Fairfield County

Bethel SD
1 School St • Bethel, CT 06801-0253
Mailing Address: PO Box 253 • Bethel, CT 06801-0253
(203) 794-8601 • http://www.bethel.k12.ct.us/
Grade Span: PK-12; Agency Type: 1
Schools: 6
  2 Primary; 2 Middle; 1 High; 1 Other Level
  5 Regular; 0 Special Education; 0 Vocational; 1 Alternative
  0 Magnet; 0 Charter; 0 Title I Eligible; 0 School-wide Title I
Students: 3,254 (51.8% male; 48.1% female)
  Individual Education Program: 298 (9.2%);
  English Language Learner: 106 (3.3%); Migrant: 14 (0.4%)
  Eligible for Free Lunch Program: n/a
  Eligible for Reduced-Price Lunch Program: n/a
Teachers: 242.3 (13.4 to 1)
Librarians/Media Specialists: 6.0 (540.2 to 1)
Guidance Counselors: 9.0 (360.1 to 1)
Current Spending: ($ per student per year):
  Total: $10,432; Instruction: $6,360; Support Services: $3,691
Enrollment, Drop-out Rates and Diploma Recipients by Race/Ethnicity

Category	Total	White	Black	Asian	AIAN	Hisp.
Enrollment (%)	100.0	84.3	1.9	6.3	0.2	7.3
Drop-out Rate (%)	0.5	0.6	0.0	0.0	0.0	0.0
H.S. Diplomas (#)	186	161	2	12	0	11

Bridgeport SD
45 Lyon Terrace • Bridgeport, CT 06604-4023
(203) 576-7302 • http://www.bridgeportedu.com
Grade Span: PK-12; Agency Type: 1
Schools: 38
  30 Primary; 0 Middle; 2 High; 3 Other Level
  35 Regular; 0 Special Education; 0 Vocational; 0 Alternative
  2 Magnet; 0 Charter; 27 Title I Eligible; 27 School-wide Title I
Students: 22,828 (51.0% male; 48.9% female)
  Individual Education Program: 2,532 (11.1%);
  English Language Learner: 2,796 (12.2%); Migrant: 2,482 (11.1%)
  Eligible for Free Lunch Program: n/a
  Eligible for Reduced-Price Lunch Program: n/a
Teachers: 1,485.5 (15.1 to 1)
Librarians/Media Specialists: 19.0 (1,179.1 to 1)
Guidance Counselors: 46.0 (487.0 to 1)
Current Spending: ($ per student per year):
  Total: $10,815; Instruction: $7,168; Support Services: $3,067
Enrollment, Drop-out Rates and Diploma Recipients by Race/Ethnicity

Category	Total	White	Black	Asian	AIAN	Hisp.
Enrollment (%)	100.0	10.3	43.3	3.1	0.1	43.2
Drop-out Rate (%)	10.0	11.4	6.8	12.3	0.0	13.0
H.S. Diplomas (#)	834	91	391	35	0	317

Brookfield SD
100 Pocono Rd • Brookfield, CT 06804-3331
(203) 775-7620 • http://www.brookfield.k12.ct.us/
Grade Span: PK-12; Agency Type: 1
Schools: 5
  2 Primary; 1 Middle; 1 High; 1 Other Level
  4 Regular; 0 Special Education; 0 Vocational; 1 Alternative
  0 Magnet; 0 Charter; 2 Title I Eligible; 0 School-wide Title I
Students: 3,060 (50.6% male; 49.3% female)
  Individual Education Program: 143 (4.7%);
  English Language Learner: 7 (0.2%); Migrant: 3 (0.1%)
  Eligible for Free Lunch Program: n/a
  Eligible for Reduced-Price Lunch Program: n/a
Teachers: 218.4 (14.0 to 1)
Librarians/Media Specialists: 3.0 (1,018.0 to 1)
Guidance Counselors: 7.0 (436.3 to 1)
Current Spending: ($ per student per year):
  Total: $9,897; Instruction: $5,936; Support Services: $3,583
Enrollment, Drop-out Rates and Diploma Recipients by Race/Ethnicity

Category	Total	White	Black	Asian	AIAN	Hisp.
Enrollment (%)	100.0	94.1	0.9	2.7	0.1	2.2
Drop-out Rate (%)	0.6	0.6	0.0	0.0	n/a	0.0
H.S. Diplomas (#)	182	165	1	12	0	4

Danbury SD
63 Beaver Brook Rd • Danbury, CT 06810-6211
(203) 797-4701 • http://www.danbury.k12.ct.us/
Grade Span: PK-12; Agency Type: 1
Schools: 18
  13 Primary; 2 Middle; 2 High; 1 Other Level
  16 Regular; 0 Special Education; 0 Vocational; 2 Alternative
  0 Magnet; 0 Charter; 8 Title I Eligible; 7 School-wide Title I
Students: 9,527 (50.8% male; 49.1% female)
  Individual Education Program: 1,164 (12.2%);

English Language Learner: 1,067 (11.2%); Migrant: 573 (6.0%)
  Eligible for Free Lunch Program: n/a
  Eligible for Reduced-Price Lunch Program: n/a
Teachers: 657.3 (14.5 to 1)
Librarians/Media Specialists: 21.0 (453.7 to 1)
Guidance Counselors: 19.0 (501.4 to 1)
Current Spending: ($ per student per year):
  Total: $9,712; Instruction: $6,452; Support Services: $2,842
Enrollment, Drop-out Rates and Diploma Recipients by Race/Ethnicity

Category	Total	White	Black	Asian	AIAN	Hisp.
Enrollment (%)	100.0	56.3	10.8	8.9	0.1	23.9
Drop-out Rate (%)	3.8	2.9	4.0	5.1	0.0	6.1
H.S. Diplomas (#)	506	351	44	47	0	64

Darien SD
2 Renshaw Rd • Darien, CT 06820-1167
Mailing Address: PO Box 1167 • Darien, CT 06820-1167
(203) 656-7400 • http://www.darien.k12.ct.us/boe/default.php
Grade Span: PK-12; Agency Type: 1
Schools: 8
  5 Primary; 1 Middle; 1 High; 1 Other Level
  7 Regular; 0 Special Education; 0 Vocational; 1 Alternative
  0 Magnet; 0 Charter; 0 Title I Eligible; 0 School-wide Title I
Students: 4,277 (52.2% male; 47.7% female)
  Individual Education Program: 510 (11.9%);
  English Language Learner: 37 (0.9%); Migrant: 0 (0.0%)
  Eligible for Free Lunch Program: n/a
  Eligible for Reduced-Price Lunch Program: n/a
Teachers: 351.1 (12.1 to 1)
Librarians/Media Specialists: 10.0 (426.3 to 1)
Guidance Counselors: 10.0 (426.3 to 1)
Current Spending: ($ per student per year):
  Total: $12,116; Instruction: $8,022; Support Services: $3,480
Enrollment, Drop-out Rates and Diploma Recipients by Race/Ethnicity

Category	Total	White	Black	Asian	AIAN	Hisp.
Enrollment (%)	100.0	95.0	0.5	2.6	0.4	1.4
Drop-out Rate (%)	0.2	0.2	0.0	0.0	n/a	0.0
H.S. Diplomas (#)	190	179	2	7	0	2

Fairfield SD
785 Unquowa Rd • Fairfield, CT 06825
Mailing Address: PO Box 222 • Fairfield, CT 06430-0222
(203) 255-8371 • http://www.fairfield.k12.ct.us/
Grade Span: PK-12; Agency Type: 1
Schools: 16
  11 Primary; 3 Middle; 1 High; 1 Other Level
  15 Regular; 1 Special Education; 0 Vocational; 0 Alternative
  0 Magnet; 0 Charter; 3 Title I Eligible; 0 School-wide Title I
Students: 8,803 (50.3% male; 49.6% female)
  Individual Education Program: 1,058 (12.0%);
  English Language Learner: 117 (1.3%); Migrant: 16 (0.2%)
  Eligible for Free Lunch Program: n/a
  Eligible for Reduced-Price Lunch Program: n/a
Teachers: 703.6 (12.5 to 1)
Librarians/Media Specialists: 18.0 (489.1 to 1)
Guidance Counselors: 20.0 (440.2 to 1)
Current Spending: ($ per student per year):
  Total: $12,109; Instruction: $7,062; Support Services: $4,703
Enrollment, Drop-out Rates and Diploma Recipients by Race/Ethnicity

Category	Total	White	Black	Asian	AIAN	Hisp.
Enrollment (%)	100.0	89.8	2.2	4.0	0.2	3.9
Drop-out Rate (%)	0.6	0.4	2.6	1.1	0.0	3.0
H.S. Diplomas (#)	459	422	4	21	0	12

Greenwich SD
Havemeyer Building • Greenwich, CT 06830-6521
(203) 625-7400 • http://www.greenwichschools.org/
Grade Span: PK-12; Agency Type: 1
Schools: 16
  11 Primary; 3 Middle; 1 High; 1 Other Level
  15 Regular; 0 Special Education; 0 Vocational; 1 Alternative
  0 Magnet; 0 Charter; 3 Title I Eligible; 0 School-wide Title I
Students: 9,081 (52.3% male; 47.6% female)
  Individual Education Program: 1,084 (11.9%);
  English Language Learner: 618 (6.8%); Migrant: 0 (0.0%)
  Eligible for Free Lunch Program: n/a
  Eligible for Reduced-Price Lunch Program: n/a
Teachers: 749.9 (12.1 to 1)
Librarians/Media Specialists: 22.0 (412.6 to 1)
Guidance Counselors: 25.0 (363.1 to 1)
Current Spending: ($ per student per year):
  Total: $14,356; Instruction: $9,275; Support Services: $4,649

Enrollment, Drop-out Rates and Diploma Recipients by Race/Ethnicity

Category	Total	White	Black	Asian	AIAN	Hisp.
Enrollment (%)	100.0	78.2	2.4	8.0	0.1	11.4
Drop-out Rate (%)	1.7	1.2	8.5	1.4	n/a	3.6
H.S. Diplomas (#)	474	390	7	28	0	49

Monroe SD
375 Monroe Turnpike • Monroe, CT 06468-2362
(203) 452-6501 • http://www.monroe.k12.ct.us/
Grade Span: PK-12; **Agency Type:** 1
Schools: 7
   3 Primary; 2 Middle; 1 High; 1 Other Level
   6 Regular; 0 Special Education; 0 Vocational; 1 Alternative
   0 Magnet; 0 Charter; 1 Title I Eligible; 0 School-wide Title I
Students: 4,310 (51.7% male; 48.2% female)
   Individual Education Program: 417 (9.7%);
   English Language Learner: 25 (0.6%); Migrant: 0 (0.0%)
   Eligible for Free Lunch Program: n/a
   Eligible for Reduced-Price Lunch Program: n/a
Teachers: 289.3 (14.9 to 1)
Librarians/Media Specialists: 3.0 (1,436.3 to 1)
Guidance Counselors: 12.0 (359.1 to 1)
Current Spending: ($ per student per year):
   Total: $9,474; Instruction: $6,060; Support Services: $3,059

Enrollment, Drop-out Rates and Diploma Recipients by Race/Ethnicity

Category	Total	White	Black	Asian	AIAN	Hisp.
Enrollment (%)	100.0	91.9	1.3	2.8	0.3	3.6
Drop-out Rate (%)	0.1	0.1	0.0	0.0	0.0	0.0
H.S. Diplomas (#)	286	270	5	6	0	5

New Canaan SD
39 Locust Ave • New Canaan, CT 06840-4723
(203) 594-4000 • http://www.newcanaan.k12.ct.us/
Grade Span: PK-12; **Agency Type:** 1
Schools: 7
   3 Primary; 1 Middle; 1 High; 2 Other Level
   6 Regular; 0 Special Education; 0 Vocational; 1 Alternative
   0 Magnet; 0 Charter; 1 Title I Eligible; 0 School-wide Title I
Students: 3,988 (52.0% male; 47.9% female)
   Individual Education Program: 365 (9.2%);
   English Language Learner: 22 (0.6%); Migrant: 0 (0.0%)
   Eligible for Free Lunch Program: n/a
   Eligible for Reduced-Price Lunch Program: n/a
Teachers: 297.4 (13.4 to 1)
Librarians/Media Specialists: 7.0 (569.4 to 1)
Guidance Counselors: 11.0 (362.4 to 1)
Current Spending: ($ per student per year):
   Total: $12,756; Instruction: $7,944; Support Services: $4,380

Enrollment, Drop-out Rates and Diploma Recipients by Race/Ethnicity

Category	Total	White	Black	Asian	AIAN	Hisp.
Enrollment (%)	100.0	95.1	0.7	2.8	0.0	1.5
Drop-out Rate (%)	0.6	0.7	0.0	0.0	n/a	0.0
H.S. Diplomas (#)	233	219	1	9	0	4

New Fairfield SD
3 Brush Hill Rd • New Fairfield, CT 06812-2618
(203) 312-5770
Grade Span: PK-12; **Agency Type:** 1
Schools: 5
   2 Primary; 1 Middle; 1 High; 1 Other Level
   4 Regular; 0 Special Education; 0 Vocational; 1 Alternative
   0 Magnet; 0 Charter; 0 Title I Eligible; 0 School-wide Title I
Students: 3,131 (51.5% male; 48.4% female)
   Individual Education Program: 313 (10.0%);
   English Language Learner: 0 (0.0%); Migrant: 0 (0.0%)
   Eligible for Free Lunch Program: n/a
   Eligible for Reduced-Price Lunch Program: n/a
Teachers: 217.0 (14.3 to 1)
Librarians/Media Specialists: 4.0 (774.3 to 1)
Guidance Counselors: 7.0 (442.4 to 1)
Current Spending: ($ per student per year):
   Total: $8,865; Instruction: $5,806; Support Services: $2,727

Enrollment, Drop-out Rates and Diploma Recipients by Race/Ethnicity

Category	Total	White	Black	Asian	AIAN	Hisp.
Enrollment (%)	100.0	95.8	0.4	1.4	0.0	2.4
Drop-out Rate (%)	0.7	0.7	0.0	0.0	0.0	0.0
H.S. Diplomas (#)	197	184	1	7	0	5

Newtown SD
4 Fairfield Circle S • Newtown, CT 06470-2151
(203) 426-7620 • http://www.newtown.k12.ct.us/
Grade Span: PK-12; **Agency Type:** 1
Schools: 8
   4 Primary; 2 Middle; 1 High; 1 Other Level
   7 Regular; 0 Special Education; 0 Vocational; 1 Alternative

   0 Magnet; 0 Charter; 2 Title I Eligible; 0 School-wide Title I
Students: 5,399 (51.6% male; 48.3% female)
   Individual Education Program: 487 (9.0%);
   English Language Learner: 0 (0.0%); Migrant: 7 (0.1%)
   Eligible for Free Lunch Program: n/a
   Eligible for Reduced-Price Lunch Program: n/a
Teachers: 344.1 (15.6 to 1)
Librarians/Media Specialists: 8.0 (672.5 to 1)
Guidance Counselors: 9.0 (597.8 to 1)
Current Spending: ($ per student per year):
   Total: $9,616; Instruction: $5,726; Support Services: $3,494

Enrollment, Drop-out Rates and Diploma Recipients by Race/Ethnicity

Category	Total	White	Black	Asian	AIAN	Hisp.
Enrollment (%)	100.0	94.4	0.8	2.3	0.0	2.4
Drop-out Rate (%)	0.8	0.8	0.0	0.0	n/a	0.0
H.S. Diplomas (#)	286	278	1	5	0	2

Norwalk SD
125 E Ave • Norwalk, CT 06852-6001
(203) 854-4001 • http://www.norwalkpublicschools.org/
Grade Span: PK-12; **Agency Type:** 1
Schools: 20
   12 Primary; 4 Middle; 3 High; 1 Other Level
   18 Regular; 0 Special Education; 0 Vocational; 2 Alternative
   0 Magnet; 0 Charter; 5 Title I Eligible; 0 School-wide Title I
Students: 11,109 (52.0% male; 47.9% female)
   Individual Education Program: 1,305 (11.7%);
   English Language Learner: 1,124 (10.1%); Migrant: 0 (0.0%)
   Eligible for Free Lunch Program: n/a
   Eligible for Reduced-Price Lunch Program: n/a
Teachers: 787.0 (14.1 to 1)
Librarians/Media Specialists: 3.0 (3,702.7 to 1)
Guidance Counselors: 26.0 (427.2 to 1)
Current Spending: ($ per student per year):
   Total: $12,232; Instruction: $8,159; Support Services: $3,730

Enrollment, Drop-out Rates and Diploma Recipients by Race/Ethnicity

Category	Total	White	Black	Asian	AIAN	Hisp.
Enrollment (%)	100.0	45.5	25.4	3.8	0.1	25.2
Drop-out Rate (%)	2.7	1.8	3.5	0.0	0.0	4.1
H.S. Diplomas (#)	613	328	149	22	3	111

Ridgefield SD
70 Prospect St • Ridgefield, CT 06877-0629
(203) 431-2800 • http://www.ridgefield.org/
Grade Span: PK-12; **Agency Type:** 1
Schools: 10
   6 Primary; 2 Middle; 1 High; 1 Other Level
   9 Regular; 0 Special Education; 0 Vocational; 1 Alternative
   0 Magnet; 0 Charter; 0 Title I Eligible; 0 School-wide Title I
Students: 5,485 (49.9% male; 50.0% female)
   Individual Education Program: 598 (10.9%);
   English Language Learner: 35 (0.6%); Migrant: 11 (0.2%)
   Eligible for Free Lunch Program: n/a
   Eligible for Reduced-Price Lunch Program: n/a
Teachers: 362.4 (15.1 to 1)
Librarians/Media Specialists: 11.0 (498.6 to 1)
Guidance Counselors: 12.0 (457.1 to 1)
Current Spending: ($ per student per year):
   Total: $10,428; Instruction: $6,706; Support Services: $3,300

Enrollment, Drop-out Rates and Diploma Recipients by Race/Ethnicity

Category	Total	White	Black	Asian	AIAN	Hisp.
Enrollment (%)	100.0	93.2	0.6	3.3	0.1	2.8
Drop-out Rate (%)	0.5	0.6	0.0	0.0	0.0	0.0
H.S. Diplomas (#)	280	261	2	9	1	7

Shelton SD
124 Meadow St • Shelton, CT 06484-2265
Mailing Address: PO Box 846 • Shelton, CT 06484-2265
(203) 924-1023 • http://www.sheltonpublicschools.org/
Grade Span: PK-12; **Agency Type:** 1
Schools: 10
   6 Primary; 1 Middle; 1 High; 2 Other Level
   8 Regular; 1 Special Education; 0 Vocational; 1 Alternative
   0 Magnet; 0 Charter; 2 Title I Eligible; 0 School-wide Title I
Students: 5,739 (51.9% male; 48.0% female)
   Individual Education Program: 427 (7.4%);
   English Language Learner: 104 (1.8%); Migrant: 0 (0.0%)
   Eligible for Free Lunch Program: n/a
   Eligible for Reduced-Price Lunch Program: n/a
Teachers: 373.2 (15.4 to 1)
Librarians/Media Specialists: 5.0 (1,147.8 to 1)
Guidance Counselors: 15.0 (382.6 to 1)
Current Spending: ($ per student per year):
   Total: $9,766; Instruction: $6,047; Support Services: $3,353

Enrollment, Drop-out Rates and Diploma Recipients by Race/Ethnicity

Category	Total	White	Black	Asian	AIAN	Hisp.
Enrollment (%)	100.0	89.6	2.3	3.2	0.2	4.7
Drop-out Rate (%)	1.7	1.7	0.0	2.5	0.0	3.0
H.S. Diplomas (#)	344	304	8	14	0	18

Stamford SD
888 Washington Blvd • Stamford, CT 06901-9310
Mailing Address: PO Box 9310 • Stamford, CT 06901-9310
(203) 977-4543 • http://stamford.k12.ct.us/
Grade Span: PK-12; Agency Type: 1
Schools: 22
13 Primary; 5 Middle; 3 High; 1 Other Level
20 Regular; 1 Special Education; 0 Vocational; 1 Alternative
2 Magnet; 0 Charter; 10 Title I Eligible; 0 School-wide Title I
Students: 15,307 (51.7% male; 48.2% female)
Individual Education Program: 1,720 (11.2%);
English Language Learner: 2,155 (14.1%); Migrant: 0 (0.0%)
Eligible for Free Lunch Program: n/a
Eligible for Reduced-Price Lunch Program: n/a
Teachers: 1,209.6 (12.7 to 1)
Librarians/Media Specialists: 19.0 (805.6 to 1)
Guidance Counselors: 33.0 (463.8 to 1)
Current Spending: ($ per student per year):
Total: $12,313; Instruction: $7,894; Support Services: $4,175
Enrollment, Drop-out Rates and Diploma Recipients by Race/Ethnicity

Category	Total	White	Black	Asian	AIAN	Hisp.
Enrollment (%)	100.0	43.7	24.5	5.5	0.0	26.3
Drop-out Rate (%)	2.7	1.3	3.0	3.9	n/a	5.4
H.S. Diplomas (#)	795	370	259	38	0	128

Stratford SD
1000 E Broadway • Stratford, CT 06615-2739
(203) 385-4210 • http://www.stratford.k12.ct.us/
Grade Span: PK-12; Agency Type: 1
Schools: 14
9 Primary; 2 Middle; 2 High; 1 Other Level
13 Regular; 0 Special Education; 0 Vocational; 1 Alternative
0 Magnet; 0 Charter; 4 Title I Eligible; 0 School-wide Title I
Students: 7,666 (50.5% male; 49.4% female)
Individual Education Program: 785 (10.2%);
English Language Learner: 125 (1.6%); Migrant: 16 (0.2%)
Eligible for Free Lunch Program: n/a
Eligible for Reduced-Price Lunch Program: n/a
Teachers: 517.0 (14.8 to 1)
Librarians/Media Specialists: 14.0 (545.3 to 1)
Guidance Counselors: 15.0 (508.9 to 1)
Current Spending: ($ per student per year):
Total: $9,452; Instruction: $5,768; Support Services: $3,295
Enrollment, Drop-out Rates and Diploma Recipients by Race/Ethnicity

Category	Total	White	Black	Asian	AIAN	Hisp.
Enrollment (%)	100.0	63.6	20.5	2.6	0.4	13.0
Drop-out Rate (%)	2.5	2.8	1.5	3.6	22.2	1.1
H.S. Diplomas (#)	470	320	83	11	4	52

Trumbull SD
6254 Main St • Trumbull, CT 06611-2052
(203) 452-4301 • http://www.trumbullps.org/index.asp
Grade Span: PK-12; Agency Type: 1
Schools: 11
7 Primary; 2 Middle; 1 High; 1 Other Level
10 Regular; 0 Special Education; 0 Vocational; 1 Alternative
0 Magnet; 0 Charter; 0 Title I Eligible; 0 School-wide Title I
Students: 6,612 (50.5% male; 49.4% female)
Individual Education Program: 548 (8.3%);
English Language Learner: 41 (0.6%); Migrant: 0 (0.0%)
Eligible for Free Lunch Program: n/a
Eligible for Reduced-Price Lunch Program: n/a
Teachers: 429.0 (15.4 to 1)
Librarians/Media Specialists: 10.0 (661.2 to 1)
Guidance Counselors: 16.0 (413.3 to 1)
Current Spending: ($ per student per year):
Total: $9,966; Instruction: $5,815; Support Services: $3,766
Enrollment, Drop-out Rates and Diploma Recipients by Race/Ethnicity

Category	Total	White	Black	Asian	AIAN	Hisp.
Enrollment (%)	100.0	88.7	3.4	4.3	0.1	3.4
Drop-out Rate (%)	2.6	2.4	5.6	1.6	28.6	1.4
H.S. Diplomas (#)	416	377	15	6	1	17

Weston SD
24 School Rd • Weston, CT 06883-1698
(203) 291-1401
Grade Span: PK-12; Agency Type: 1
Schools: 4
1 Primary; 1 Middle; 1 High; 1 Other Level

3 Regular; 0 Special Education; 0 Vocational; 1 Alternative
0 Magnet; 0 Charter; 0 Title I Eligible; 0 School-wide Title I
Students: 2,474 (48.7% male; 51.2% female)
Individual Education Program: 213 (8.6%);
English Language Learner: 10 (0.4%); Migrant: 0 (0.0%)
Eligible for Free Lunch Program: n/a
Eligible for Reduced-Price Lunch Program: n/a
Teachers: 198.1 (12.4 to 1)
Librarians/Media Specialists: 5.0 (490.2 to 1)
Guidance Counselors: 8.0 (306.4 to 1)
Current Spending: ($ per student per year):
Total: $13,906; Instruction: $8,421; Support Services: $4,766
Enrollment, Drop-out Rates and Diploma Recipients by Race/Ethnicity

Category	Total	White	Black	Asian	AIAN	Hisp.
Enrollment (%)	100.0	94.2	1.8	2.5	0.0	1.5
Drop-out Rate (%)	0.0	0.0	0.0	0.0	n/a	0.0
H.S. Diplomas (#)	135	125	2	3	0	5

Westport SD
110 Myrtle Ave • Westport, CT 06880-3513
(203) 341-1025 • http://teachers.westport.k12.ct.us/westportk12ctu/
Grade Span: PK-12; Agency Type: 1
Schools: 9
5 Primary; 2 Middle; 1 High; 1 Other Level
7 Regular; 1 Special Education; 0 Vocational; 1 Alternative
0 Magnet; 0 Charter; 1 Title I Eligible; 0 School-wide Title I
Students: 5,223 (50.6% male; 49.3% female)
Individual Education Program: 569 (10.9%);
English Language Learner: 87 (1.7%); Migrant: 0 (0.0%)
Eligible for Free Lunch Program: n/a
Eligible for Reduced-Price Lunch Program: n/a
Teachers: 445.6 (11.7 to 1)
Librarians/Media Specialists: 8.0 (652.9 to 1)
Guidance Counselors: 12.1 (431.7 to 1)
Current Spending: ($ per student per year):
Total: $13,900; Instruction: $8,024; Support Services: $5,346
Enrollment, Drop-out Rates and Diploma Recipients by Race/Ethnicity

Category	Total	White	Black	Asian	AIAN	Hisp.
Enrollment (%)	100.0	92.9	1.4	3.4	0.0	2.4
Drop-out Rate (%)	1.0	0.9	0.0	2.0	0.0	2.4
H.S. Diplomas (#)	255	231	9	8	0	7

Wilton SD
395 Danbury Rd • Wilton, CT 06897-0277
(203) 762-3381 • http://www.wilton.k12.ct.us/
Grade Span: PK-12; Agency Type: 1
Schools: 6
3 Primary; 1 Middle; 1 High; 1 Other Level
5 Regular; 0 Special Education; 0 Vocational; 1 Alternative
0 Magnet; 0 Charter; 2 Title I Eligible; 0 School-wide Title I
Students: 4,229 (53.9% male; 46.0% female)
Individual Education Program: 483 (11.4%);
English Language Learner: 17 (0.4%); Migrant: 0 (0.0%)
Eligible for Free Lunch Program: n/a
Eligible for Reduced-Price Lunch Program: n/a
Teachers: 305.7 (13.8 to 1)
Librarians/Media Specialists: 9.0 (469.7 to 1)
Guidance Counselors: 11.2 (377.4 to 1)
Current Spending: ($ per student per year):
Total: $11,585; Instruction: $6,994; Support Services: $4,448
Enrollment, Drop-out Rates and Diploma Recipients by Race/Ethnicity

Category	Total	White	Black	Asian	AIAN	Hisp.
Enrollment (%)	100.0	94.7	0.6	3.2	0.3	1.2
Drop-out Rate (%)	0.4	0.4	0.0	0.0	n/a	0.0
H.S. Diplomas (#)	230	210	2	13	0	5

Hartford County

Avon SD
34 Simsbury Rd • Avon, CT 06001-3730
(860) 404-4700 • http://www.avon.k12.ct.us/
Grade Span: PK-12; Agency Type: 1
Schools: 6
2 Primary; 2 Middle; 1 High; 1 Other Level
5 Regular; 0 Special Education; 0 Vocational; 1 Alternative
0 Magnet; 0 Charter; 0 Title I Eligible; 0 School-wide Title I
Students: 3,239 (49.4% male; 50.5% female)
Individual Education Program: 322 (9.9%);
English Language Learner: 37 (1.1%); Migrant: 0 (0.0%)
Eligible for Free Lunch Program: n/a
Eligible for Reduced-Price Lunch Program: n/a
Teachers: 215.6 (15.0 to 1)
Librarians/Media Specialists: 5.0 (646.6 to 1)
Guidance Counselors: 9.0 (359.2 to 1)
Current Spending: ($ per student per year):
Total: $10,224; Instruction: $6,394; Support Services: $3,451

Enrollment, Drop-out Rates and Diploma Recipients by Race/Ethnicity

Category	Total	White	Black	Asian	AIAN	Hisp.
Enrollment (%)	100.0	89.8	2.2	5.4	0.1	2.5
Drop-out Rate (%)	0.0	0.0	0.0	0.0	n/a	0.0
H.S. Diplomas (#)	181	160	5	13	0	3

Berlin SD

238 Kensington Rd • Berlin, CT 06037-2648
(860) 828-6581 • http://www.berlinschools.org/
Grade Span: PK-12; **Agency Type:** 1
Schools: 6
    3 Primary; 1 Middle; 1 High; 1 Other Level
    5 Regular; 0 Special Education; 0 Vocational; 1 Alternative
    0 Magnet; 0 Charter; 0 Title I Eligible; 0 School-wide Title I
Students: 3,345   (51.1% male; 48.8% female)
    Individual Education Program: 366 (10.9%);
    English Language Learner: 109 (3.3%); Migrant: 0 (0.0%)
    Eligible for Free Lunch Program: n/a
    Eligible for Reduced-Price Lunch Program: n/a
Teachers: 227.5 (14.7 to 1)
Librarians/Media Specialists: 5.0 (667.4 to 1)
Guidance Counselors: 8.0 (417.1 to 1)
Current Spending: ($ per student per year):
    Total: $9,667; Instruction: $5,581; Support Services: $3,670

Enrollment, Drop-out Rates and Diploma Recipients by Race/Ethnicity

Category	Total	White	Black	Asian	AIAN	Hisp.
Enrollment (%)	100.0	95.0	0.7	2.9	0.2	1.2
Drop-out Rate (%)	1.7	1.7	0.0	0.0	0.0	0.0
H.S. Diplomas (#)	247	236	1	8	0	2

Bloomfield SD

11 Turkey Hill Rd • Bloomfield, CT 06002-3099
(860) 769-4211 • http://www.blmfld.org/
Grade Span: PK-12; **Agency Type:** 1
Schools: 6
    3 Primary; 0 Middle; 1 High; 2 Other Level
    5 Regular; 0 Special Education; 0 Vocational; 1 Alternative
    0 Magnet; 0 Charter; 3 Title I Eligible; 0 School-wide Title I
Students: 2,455   (54.0% male; 45.9% female)
    Individual Education Program: 282 (11.5%);
    English Language Learner: 2 (0.1%); Migrant: 0 (0.0%)
    Eligible for Free Lunch Program: n/a
    Eligible for Reduced-Price Lunch Program: n/a
Teachers: 205.8 (11.9 to 1)
Librarians/Media Specialists: 2.0 (1,227.5 to 1)
Guidance Counselors: 7.0 (350.7 to 1)
Current Spending: ($ per student per year):
    Total: $12,795; Instruction: $7,199; Support Services: $5,033

Enrollment, Drop-out Rates and Diploma Recipients by Race/Ethnicity

Category	Total	White	Black	Asian	AIAN	Hisp.
Enrollment (%)	100.0	4.9	88.6	1.2	0.1	5.3
Drop-out Rate (%)	3.4	4.5	3.5	0.0	n/a	0.0
H.S. Diplomas (#)	173	10	157	1	0	5

Bristol SD

129 Church St • Bristol, CT 06011-0450
Mailing Address: PO Box 450 • Bristol, CT 06011-0450
(860) 584-7002 •
**http://www.bristol.k12.ct.us/directory_of_services/technology_in_schools
/**
Grade Span: PK-12; **Agency Type:** 1
Schools: 16
    10 Primary; 3 Middle; 3 High; 0 Other Level
    15 Regular; 0 Special Education; 0 Vocational; 1 Alternative
    0 Magnet; 0 Charter; 9 Title I Eligible; 1 School-wide Title I
Students: 9,004   (51.2% male; 48.7% female)
    Individual Education Program: 1,138 (12.6%);
    English Language Learner: 225 (2.5%); Migrant: 0 (0.0%)
    Eligible for Free Lunch Program: n/a
    Eligible for Reduced-Price Lunch Program: n/a
Teachers: 603.6 (14.8 to 1)
Librarians/Media Specialists: 5.0 (1,790.8 to 1)
Guidance Counselors: 19.0 (471.3 to 1)
Current Spending: ($ per student per year):
    Total: $9,273; Instruction: $6,154; Support Services: $2,698

Enrollment, Drop-out Rates and Diploma Recipients by Race/Ethnicity

Category	Total	White	Black	Asian	AIAN	Hisp.
Enrollment (%)	100.0	79.7	6.9	2.2	0.2	11.0
Drop-out Rate (%)	1.3	1.1	1.5	3.1	0.0	2.9
H.S. Diplomas (#)	558	485	34	10	0	29

Canton SD

39 Dyer Ave • Canton, CT 06019-1008
(860) 693-7704 • http://www.pccs.k12.mi.us/
Grade Span: PK-12; **Agency Type:** 1
Schools: 4
    1 Primary; 1 Middle; 1 High; 1 Other Level
    3 Regular; 0 Special Education; 0 Vocational; 1 Alternative
    0 Magnet; 0 Charter; 3 Title I Eligible; 0 School-wide Title I
Students: 1,638   (52.8% male; 47.1% female)
    Individual Education Program: 161 (9.8%);
    English Language Learner: 8 (0.5%); Migrant: 0 (0.0%)
    Eligible for Free Lunch Program: n/a
    Eligible for Reduced-Price Lunch Program: n/a
Teachers: 112.1 (14.6 to 1)
Librarians/Media Specialists: 3.0 (544.0 to 1)
Guidance Counselors: 4.0 (408.0 to 1)
Current Spending: ($ per student per year):
    Total: $9,860; Instruction: $6,421; Support Services: $3,231

Enrollment, Drop-out Rates and Diploma Recipients by Race/Ethnicity

Category	Total	White	Black	Asian	AIAN	Hisp.
Enrollment (%)	100.0	94.7	2.3	1.5	0.1	1.4
Drop-out Rate (%)	0.0	0.0	0.0	0.0	n/a	0.0
H.S. Diplomas (#)	100	90	4	3	0	3

Capitol Region Education Council

111 Charter Oak Ave • Hartford, CT 06106-3567
(860) 524-4063
Grade Span: PK-12; **Agency Type:** 4
Schools: 6
    3 Primary; 1 Middle; 0 High; 2 Other Level
    5 Regular; 1 Special Education; 0 Vocational; 0 Alternative
    5 Magnet; 0 Charter; 2 Title I Eligible; 0 School-wide Title I
Students: 2,445   (53.2% male; 46.7% female)
    Individual Education Program: 458 (18.7%);
    English Language Learner: 37 (1.5%); Migrant: 0 (0.0%)
    Eligible for Free Lunch Program: n/a
    Eligible for Reduced-Price Lunch Program: n/a
Teachers: 236.8 (10.3 to 1)
Librarians/Media Specialists: 2.0 (1,214.0 to 1)
Guidance Counselors: 7.0 (346.9 to 1)
Current Spending: ($ per student per year):
    Total: n/a; Instruction: n/a; Support Services: n/a

Enrollment, Drop-out Rates and Diploma Recipients by Race/Ethnicity

Category	Total	White	Black	Asian	AIAN	Hisp.
Enrollment (%)	100.0	41.8	38.9	3.0	0.4	16.0
Drop-out Rate (%)	6.8	9.4	4.1	0.0	0.0	4.7
H.S. Diplomas (#)	18	14	2	0	0	2

East Hartford SD

31 School St • East Hartford, CT 06108-2681
(860) 622-5107 • http://www.easthartford.org/
Grade Span: PK-12; **Agency Type:** 1
Schools: 16
    9 Primary; 2 Middle; 2 High; 3 Other Level
    14 Regular; 1 Special Education; 0 Vocational; 1 Alternative
    1 Magnet; 0 Charter; 8 Title I Eligible; 8 School-wide Title I
Students: 7,926   (51.7% male; 48.2% female)
    Individual Education Program: 1,032 (13.0%);
    English Language Learner: 325 (4.1%); Migrant: 0 (0.0%)
    Eligible for Free Lunch Program: n/a
    Eligible for Reduced-Price Lunch Program: n/a
Teachers: 542.4 (14.4 to 1)
Librarians/Media Specialists: 4.0 (1,954.0 to 1)
Guidance Counselors: 13.0 (601.2 to 1)
Current Spending: ($ per student per year):
    Total: $10,443; Instruction: $7,116; Support Services: $2,880

Enrollment, Drop-out Rates and Diploma Recipients by Race/Ethnicity

Category	Total	White	Black	Asian	AIAN	Hisp.
Enrollment (%)	100.0	31.4	34.7	4.4	0.4	29.0
Drop-out Rate (%)	2.8	2.3	3.4	1.4	0.0	3.1
H.S. Diplomas (#)	475	210	137	28	0	100

East Windsor SD

47 Rye St • East Windsor, CT 06016-9552
Mailing Address: 14 Rye St • East Windsor, CT 06016-9552
(860) 623-3346 • http://www.eastwindsorschools.org/
Grade Span: PK-12; **Agency Type:** 1
Schools: 4
    1 Primary; 1 Middle; 1 High; 1 Other Level
    3 Regular; 0 Special Education; 0 Vocational; 1 Alternative
    0 Magnet; 0 Charter; 2 Title I Eligible; 0 School-wide Title I
Students: 1,590   (52.6% male; 47.3% female)
    Individual Education Program: 211 (13.3%);
    English Language Learner: 42 (2.6%); Migrant: 0 (0.0%)
    Eligible for Free Lunch Program: n/a

Eligible for Reduced-Price Lunch Program: n/a
Teachers: 107.2 (14.8 to 1)
Librarians/Media Specialists: 1.0 (1,587.0 to 1)
Guidance Counselors: 3.0 (529.0 to 1)
Current Spending: ($ per student per year):
    Total: $9,451; Instruction: $5,856; Support Services: $3,301
Enrollment, Drop-out Rates and Diploma Recipients by Race/Ethnicity

Category	Total	White	Black	Asian	AIAN	Hisp.
Enrollment (%)	100.0	79.4	10.8	3.5	0.4	6.0
Drop-out Rate (%)	4.6	4.8	0.0	0.0	0.0	10.5
H.S. Diplomas (#)	78	72	2	2	0	2

Enfield SD
27 Shaker Rd • Enfield, CT 06082-3199
(860) 253-6500 • http://www.enfieldschools.org/
Grade Span: PK-12; **Agency Type:** 1
Schools: 14
    10 Primary; 1 Middle; 2 High; 1 Other Level
    13 Regular; 0 Special Education; 0 Vocational; 1 Alternative
    0 Magnet; 0 Charter; 2 Title I Eligible; 0 School-wide Title I
Students: 6,744 (50.8% male; 49.1% female)
    Individual Education Program: 800 (11.9%);
    English Language Learner: 64 (0.9%); Migrant: 0 (0.0%)
    Eligible for Free Lunch Program: n/a
    Eligible for Reduced-Price Lunch Program: n/a
Teachers: 493.4 (13.6 to 1)
Librarians/Media Specialists: 4.0 (1,677.8 to 1)
Guidance Counselors: 21.4 (313.6 to 1)
Current Spending: ($ per student per year):
    Total: $9,875; Instruction: $6,446; Support Services: $3,045
Enrollment, Drop-out Rates and Diploma Recipients by Race/Ethnicity

Category	Total	White	Black	Asian	AIAN	Hisp.
Enrollment (%)	100.0	88.0	5.9	2.3	0.3	3.5
Drop-out Rate (%)	3.1	2.9	3.8	4.1	14.3	4.2
H.S. Diplomas (#)	448	413	13	12	1	9

Farmington SD
1 Monteith Dr • Farmington, CT 06032-1041
Mailing Address: One Monteith Dr • Farmington, CT 06032-1041
(860) 673-8270 • http://www.fpsct.org/
Grade Span: PK-12; **Agency Type:** 1
Schools: 8
    4 Primary; 2 Middle; 1 High; 1 Other Level
    7 Regular; 0 Special Education; 0 Vocational; 1 Alternative
    0 Magnet; 0 Charter; 3 Title I Eligible; 0 School-wide Title I
Students: 4,316 (51.9% male; 48.0% female)
    Individual Education Program: 362 (8.4%);
    English Language Learner: 45 (1.0%); Migrant: 0 (0.0%)
    Eligible for Free Lunch Program: n/a
    Eligible for Reduced-Price Lunch Program: n/a
Teachers: 309.5 (13.9 to 1)
Librarians/Media Specialists: 6.0 (717.3 to 1)
Guidance Counselors: 10.0 (430.4 to 1)
Current Spending: ($ per student per year):
    Total: $10,090; Instruction: $5,973; Support Services: $3,626
Enrollment, Drop-out Rates and Diploma Recipients by Race/Ethnicity

Category	Total	White	Black	Asian	AIAN	Hisp.
Enrollment (%)	100.0	86.0	4.8	6.2	0.2	2.8
Drop-out Rate (%)	0.8	0.8	0.0	1.7	0.0	0.0
H.S. Diplomas (#)	280	249	8	18	0	5

Glastonbury SD
232 Williams St • Glastonbury, CT 06033-2354
(860) 652-7961 • http://www.glastonburyus.org/
Grade Span: PK-12; **Agency Type:** 1
Schools: 9
    5 Primary; 2 Middle; 1 High; 1 Other Level
    8 Regular; 0 Special Education; 0 Vocational; 1 Alternative
    0 Magnet; 0 Charter; 0 Title I Eligible; 0 School-wide Title I
Students: 6,537 (50.1% male; 49.8% female)
    Individual Education Program: 782 (12.0%);
    English Language Learner: 158 (2.4%); Migrant: 0 (0.0%)
    Eligible for Free Lunch Program: n/a
    Eligible for Reduced-Price Lunch Program: n/a
Teachers: 447.8 (14.6 to 1)
Librarians/Media Specialists: 9.0 (726.3 to 1)
Guidance Counselors: 15.0 (435.8 to 1)
Current Spending: ($ per student per year):
    Total: $9,455; Instruction: $5,874; Support Services: $3,209
Enrollment, Drop-out Rates and Diploma Recipients by Race/Ethnicity

Category	Total	White	Black	Asian	AIAN	Hisp.
Enrollment (%)	100.0	88.7	2.5	5.4	0.1	3.3
Drop-out Rate (%)	0.5	0.6	0.0	0.0	0.0	0.0
H.S. Diplomas (#)	414	366	12	24	1	11

Granby SD
15b N Granby Rd • Granby, CT 06035-9449
Mailing Address: 15_B N Granby Rd • Granby, CT 06035-9449
(860) 844-5250 • http://www.granby.k12.ct.us/
Grade Span: KG-12; **Agency Type:** 1
Schools: 6
    3 Primary; 1 Middle; 1 High; 1 Other Level
    5 Regular; 0 Special Education; 0 Vocational; 1 Alternative
    0 Magnet; 0 Charter; 1 Title I Eligible; 0 School-wide Title I
Students: 2,198 (51.8% male; 48.1% female)
    Individual Education Program: 220 (10.0%);
    English Language Learner: 5 (0.2%); Migrant: 0 (0.0%)
    Eligible for Free Lunch Program: n/a
    Eligible for Reduced-Price Lunch Program: n/a
Teachers: 133.1 (16.4 to 1)
Librarians/Media Specialists: 2.0 (1,091.5 to 1)
Guidance Counselors: 6.0 (363.8 to 1)
Current Spending: ($ per student per year):
    Total: $9,351; Instruction: $5,930; Support Services: $3,158
Enrollment, Drop-out Rates and Diploma Recipients by Race/Ethnicity

Category	Total	White	Black	Asian	AIAN	Hisp.
Enrollment (%)	100.0	95.9	1.7	0.8	0.2	1.4
Drop-out Rate (%)	0.9	0.9	0.0	0.0	n/a	0.0
H.S. Diplomas (#)	125	121	2	1	0	1

Hartford SD
153 Market St • Hartford, CT 06103-1009
(860) 695-8000 • http://www.hartfordschools.org/
Grade Span: PK-12; **Agency Type:** 1
Schools: 40
    28 Primary; 4 Middle; 5 High; 3 Other Level
    38 Regular; 2 Special Education; 0 Vocational; 0 Alternative
    5 Magnet; 0 Charter; 37 Title I Eligible; 35 School-wide Title I
Students: 22,578 (51.2% male; 48.7% female)
    Individual Education Program: 3,530 (15.6%);
    English Language Learner: 3,708 (16.4%); Migrant: 0 (0.0%)
    Eligible for Free Lunch Program: n/a
    Eligible for Reduced-Price Lunch Program: n/a
Teachers: 1,717.4 (13.0 to 1)
Librarians/Media Specialists: 37.0 (601.1 to 1)
Guidance Counselors: 42.0 (529.5 to 1)
Current Spending: ($ per student per year):
    Total: $13,763; Instruction: $8,604; Support Services: $4,703
Enrollment, Drop-out Rates and Diploma Recipients by Race/Ethnicity

Category	Total	White	Black	Asian	AIAN	Hisp.
Enrollment (%)	100.0	4.6	40.3	0.8	0.1	54.3
Drop-out Rate (%)	6.3	5.9	7.0	3.8	0.0	5.8
H.S. Diplomas (#)	785	56	367	59	0	303

Manchester SD
45 N School St • Manchester, CT 06040-2022
(860) 647-3441
Grade Span: PK-12; **Agency Type:** 1
Schools: 17
    11 Primary; 2 Middle; 3 High; 1 Other Level
    15 Regular; 1 Special Education; 0 Vocational; 1 Alternative
    1 Magnet; 0 Charter; 6 Title I Eligible; 5 School-wide Title I
Students: 7,655 (50.9% male; 49.0% female)
    Individual Education Program: 983 (12.8%);
    English Language Learner: 193 (2.5%); Migrant: 0 (0.0%)
    Eligible for Free Lunch Program: n/a
    Eligible for Reduced-Price Lunch Program: n/a
Teachers: 541.0 (14.1 to 1)
Librarians/Media Specialists: 9.0 (848.2 to 1)
Guidance Counselors: 17.0 (449.1 to 1)
Current Spending: ($ per student per year):
    Total: $10,721; Instruction: $7,004; Support Services: $3,300
Enrollment, Drop-out Rates and Diploma Recipients by Race/Ethnicity

Category	Total	White	Black	Asian	AIAN	Hisp.
Enrollment (%)	100.0	59.9	19.2	4.8	0.4	15.7
Drop-out Rate (%)	1.3	1.0	1.0	2.6	0.0	3.2
H.S. Diplomas (#)	408	295	55	18	0	40

New Britain SD
272 Main St • New Britain, CT 06050-1960
Mailing Address: PO Box 1960 • New Britain, CT 06050-1960
(860) 827-2200 • http://www.new-britain.k12.ct.us/
Grade Span: PK-12; **Agency Type:** 1
Schools: 16
    11 Primary; 3 Middle; 1 High; 1 Other Level
    15 Regular; 0 Special Education; 0 Vocational; 1 Alternative
    1 Magnet; 0 Charter; 14 Title I Eligible; 0 School-wide Title I
Students: 10,789 (51.0% male; 48.9% female)
    Individual Education Program: 1,926 (17.9%);
    English Language Learner: 1,365 (12.7%); Migrant: 535 (5.0%)

Eligible for Free Lunch Program: n/a
Eligible for Reduced-Price Lunch Program: n/a
Teachers: 729.8 (14.8 to 1)
Librarians/Media Specialists: 12.0 (899.1 to 1)
Guidance Counselors: 20.0 (539.5 to 1)
Current Spending: ($ per student per year):
    Total: $11,116; Instruction: $7,767; Support Services: $3,044
Enrollment, Drop-out Rates and Diploma Recipients by Race/Ethnicity

Category	Total	White	Black	Asian	AIAN	Hisp.
Enrollment (%)	100.0	28.4	17.5	2.3	0.2	51.6
Drop-out Rate (%)	6.9	4.2	4.7	6.3	0.0	11.0
H.S. Diplomas (#)	445	232	83	13	0	117

Newington SD

131 Cedar St • Newington, CT 06111-2698
(860) 665-8610 • http://www.newington-schools.org/
Grade Span: PK-12; **Agency Type:** 1
Schools: 8
    4 Primary; 2 Middle; 1 High; 1 Other Level
    7 Regular; 0 Special Education; 0 Vocational; 1 Alternative
    0 Magnet; 0 Charter; 0 Title I Eligible; 0 School-wide Title I
Students: 4,610 (52.5% male; 47.4% female)
    Individual Education Program: 435 (9.4%);
    English Language Learner: 121 (2.6%); Migrant: 0 (0.0%)
    Eligible for Free Lunch Program: n/a
    Eligible for Reduced-Price Lunch Program: n/a
Teachers: 295.1 (15.6 to 1)
Librarians/Media Specialists: 8.0 (574.1 to 1)
Guidance Counselors: 11.0 (417.5 to 1)
Current Spending: ($ per student per year):
    Total: $9,637; Instruction: $5,930; Support Services: $3,366
Enrollment, Drop-out Rates and Diploma Recipients by Race/Ethnicity

Category	Total	White	Black	Asian	AIAN	Hisp.
Enrollment (%)	100.0	83.1	4.5	5.6	0.2	6.6
Drop-out Rate (%)	0.5	0.3	6.0	0.0	0.0	1.3
H.S. Diplomas (#)	268	239	11	13	0	5

Plainville SD

47 Robert Holcomb Way • Plainville, CT 06062-2398
(860) 793-3200 • http://www.plainvilleschools.org/
Grade Span: PK-12; **Agency Type:** 1
Schools: 7
    4 Primary; 2 Middle; 1 High; 0 Other Level
    6 Regular; 0 Special Education; 0 Vocational; 1 Alternative
    0 Magnet; 0 Charter; 3 Title I Eligible; 0 School-wide Title I
Students: 2,650 (50.4% male; 49.5% female)
    Individual Education Program: 298 (11.2%);
    English Language Learner: 78 (2.9%); Migrant: 0 (0.0%)
    Eligible for Free Lunch Program: n/a
    Eligible for Reduced-Price Lunch Program: n/a
Teachers: 187.3 (14.1 to 1)
Librarians/Media Specialists: 5.0 (530.0 to 1)
Guidance Counselors: 8.0 (331.3 to 1)
Current Spending: ($ per student per year):
    Total: $10,690; Instruction: $6,846; Support Services: $3,465
Enrollment, Drop-out Rates and Diploma Recipients by Race/Ethnicity

Category	Total	White	Black	Asian	AIAN	Hisp.
Enrollment (%)	100.0	86.6	6.0	2.2	0.2	4.9
Drop-out Rate (%)	0.5	0.4	0.0	6.7	0.0	0.0
H.S. Diplomas (#)	188	171	7	4	0	6

Regional SD 10

24 Lyon Rd • Burlington, CT 06013-1313
(860) 673-2538 • http://users.ntplx.net/~region10/
Grade Span: PK-12; **Agency Type:** 1
Schools: 5
    2 Primary; 1 Middle; 1 High; 1 Other Level
    4 Regular; 0 Special Education; 0 Vocational; 1 Alternative
    0 Magnet; 0 Charter; 0 Title I Eligible; 0 School-wide Title I
Students: 2,687 (51.2% male; 48.7% female)
    Individual Education Program: 244 (9.1%);
    English Language Learner: 0 (0.0%); Migrant: 0 (0.0%)
    Eligible for Free Lunch Program: n/a
    Eligible for Reduced-Price Lunch Program: n/a
Teachers: 198.8 (13.4 to 1)
Librarians/Media Specialists: 3.0 (885.3 to 1)
Guidance Counselors: 6.0 (442.7 to 1)
Current Spending: ($ per student per year):
    Total: $9,435; Instruction: $5,598; Support Services: $3,635
Enrollment, Drop-out Rates and Diploma Recipients by Race/Ethnicity

Category	Total	White	Black	Asian	AIAN	Hisp.
Enrollment (%)	100.0	96.6	0.3	1.6	0.2	1.3
Drop-out Rate (%)	0.3	0.3	n/a	0.0	0.0	0.0
H.S. Diplomas (#)	162	157	0	2	0	3

Rocky Hill SD

761 Old Main St • Rocky Hill, CT 06067-0627
(860) 258-7701 • http://www.rockyhillps.us/
Grade Span: PK-12; **Agency Type:** 1
Schools: 6
    4 Primary; 1 Middle; 1 High; 0 Other Level
    5 Regular; 0 Special Education; 0 Vocational; 1 Alternative
    0 Magnet; 0 Charter; 0 Title I Eligible; 0 School-wide Title I
Students: 2,485 (50.1% male; 49.8% female)
    Individual Education Program: 234 (9.4%);
    English Language Learner: 50 (2.0%); Migrant: 0 (0.0%)
    Eligible for Free Lunch Program: n/a
    Eligible for Reduced-Price Lunch Program: n/a
Teachers: 186.3 (13.3 to 1)
Librarians/Media Specialists: 4.0 (619.3 to 1)
Guidance Counselors: 5.0 (495.4 to 1)
Current Spending: ($ per student per year):
    Total: $9,907; Instruction: $6,655; Support Services: $3,001
Enrollment, Drop-out Rates and Diploma Recipients by Race/Ethnicity

Category	Total	White	Black	Asian	AIAN	Hisp.
Enrollment (%)	100.0	85.5	4.2	5.8	0.1	4.3
Drop-out Rate (%)	0.0	0.0	0.0	0.0	n/a	0.0
H.S. Diplomas (#)	143	128	6	6	0	3

Simsbury SD

933 Hopmeadow St • Simsbury, CT 06070-1897
(860) 651-3361 • http://www.simsbury.k12.ct.us/
Grade Span: PK-12; **Agency Type:** 1
Schools: 8
    5 Primary; 1 Middle; 1 High; 1 Other Level
    7 Regular; 0 Special Education; 0 Vocational; 1 Alternative
    0 Magnet; 0 Charter; 0 Title I Eligible; 0 School-wide Title I
Students: 5,037 (53.3% male; 46.6% female)
    Individual Education Program: 666 (13.2%);
    English Language Learner: 45 (0.9%); Migrant: 0 (0.0%)
    Eligible for Free Lunch Program: n/a
    Eligible for Reduced-Price Lunch Program: n/a
Teachers: 334.5 (15.0 to 1)
Librarians/Media Specialists: 6.0 (833.8 to 1)
Guidance Counselors: 10.0 (500.3 to 1)
Current Spending: ($ per student per year):
    Total: $9,737; Instruction: $6,244; Support Services: $3,185
Enrollment, Drop-out Rates and Diploma Recipients by Race/Ethnicity

Category	Total	White	Black	Asian	AIAN	Hisp.
Enrollment (%)	100.0	92.7	2.7	3.0	0.1	1.5
Drop-out Rate (%)	0.8	0.6	4.9	2.2	0.0	0.0
H.S. Diplomas (#)	346	330	5	8	0	3

South Windsor SD

1737 Main St • South Windsor, CT 06074-1093
(860) 291-1205 • http://www.swindsor.k12.ct.us/
Grade Span: PK-12; **Agency Type:** 1
Schools: 8
    5 Primary; 1 Middle; 1 High; 1 Other Level
    7 Regular; 0 Special Education; 0 Vocational; 1 Alternative
    0 Magnet; 0 Charter; 0 Title I Eligible; 0 School-wide Title I
Students: 5,100 (50.7% male; 49.2% female)
    Individual Education Program: 624 (12.2%);
    English Language Learner: 67 (1.3%); Migrant: 0 (0.0%)
    Eligible for Free Lunch Program: n/a
    Eligible for Reduced-Price Lunch Program: n/a
Teachers: 329.4 (15.4 to 1)
Librarians/Media Specialists: 2.0 (2,538.0 to 1)
Guidance Counselors: 10.0 (507.6 to 1)
Current Spending: ($ per student per year):
    Total: $9,380; Instruction: $5,838; Support Services: $3,108
Enrollment, Drop-out Rates and Diploma Recipients by Race/Ethnicity

Category	Total	White	Black	Asian	AIAN	Hisp.
Enrollment (%)	100.0	85.2	5.2	5.8	0.4	3.3
Drop-out Rate (%)	1.3	1.2	1.6	3.1	0.0	0.0
H.S. Diplomas (#)	317	285	14	11	0	7

Southington SD

49 Beecher St • Southington, CT 06489-3097
(860) 628-3202 • http://www.southingtonschools.org/
Grade Span: PK-12; **Agency Type:** 1
Schools: 13
    9 Primary; 2 Middle; 2 High; 0 Other Level
    12 Regular; 0 Special Education; 0 Vocational; 1 Alternative
    0 Magnet; 0 Charter; 3 Title I Eligible; 0 School-wide Title I
Students: 6,769 (51.5% male; 48.4% female)
    Individual Education Program: 793 (11.7%);
    English Language Learner: 48 (0.7%); Migrant: 0 (0.0%)
    Eligible for Free Lunch Program: n/a
    Eligible for Reduced-Price Lunch Program: n/a

Teachers: 496.7 (13.4 to 1)
Librarians/Media Specialists: 10.0 (667.6 to 1)
Guidance Counselors: 20.1 (332.1 to 1)
Current Spending: ($ per student per year):
    Total: $9,591; Instruction: $6,498; Support Services: $2,831
Enrollment, Drop-out Rates and Diploma Recipients by Race/Ethnicity

Category	Total	White	Black	Asian	AIAN	Hisp.
Enrollment (%)	100.0	93.2	1.4	1.9	0.3	3.2
Drop-out Rate (%)	1.7	1.7	0.0	0.0	0.0	1.5
H.S. Diplomas (#)	479	445	8	10	2	14

Suffield SD
350 Mountain Rd • Suffield, CT 06078-2078
(860) 668-3800 • http://www.suffield.org/
Grade Span: PK-12; **Agency Type:** 1
Schools: 6
    3 Primary; 1 Middle; 1 High; 1 Other Level
    5 Regular; 0 Special Education; 0 Vocational; 1 Alternative
    0 Magnet; 0 Charter; 2 Title I Eligible; 0 School-wide Title I
Students: 2,471   (49.3% male; 50.6% female)
    Individual Education Program: 267 (10.8%);
    English Language Learner: 2 (0.1%); Migrant: 0 (0.0%)
    Eligible for Free Lunch Program: n/a
    Eligible for Reduced-Price Lunch Program: n/a
Teachers: 168.8 (14.6 to 1)
Librarians/Media Specialists: 3.0 (820.0 to 1)
Guidance Counselors: 5.0 (492.0 to 1)
Current Spending: ($ per student per year):
    Total: $8,985; Instruction: $6,002; Support Services: $2,665
Enrollment, Drop-out Rates and Diploma Recipients by Race/Ethnicity

Category	Total	White	Black	Asian	AIAN	Hisp.
Enrollment (%)	100.0	95.9	1.8	0.9	0.2	1.3
Drop-out Rate (%)	1.8	1.9	0.0	0.0	n/a	0.0
H.S. Diplomas (#)	144	139	4	1	0	0

West Hartford SD
28 S Main St • West Hartford, CT 06107-2447
(860) 523-3500 • http://www.whps.org/
Grade Span: PK-12; **Agency Type:** 1
Schools: 16
    11 Primary; 2 Middle; 2 High; 1 Other Level
    15 Regular; 0 Special Education; 0 Vocational; 1 Alternative
    0 Magnet; 0 Charter; 4 Title I Eligible; 0 School-wide Title I
Students: 9,816   (50.1% male; 49.8% female)
    Individual Education Program: 1,282 (13.1%);
    English Language Learner: 556 (5.7%); Migrant: 0 (0.0%)
    Eligible for Free Lunch Program: n/a
    Eligible for Reduced-Price Lunch Program: n/a
Teachers: 751.6 (13.0 to 1)
Librarians/Media Specialists: 17.0 (575.4 to 1)
Guidance Counselors: 24.0 (407.5 to 1)
Current Spending: ($ per student per year):
    Total: $10,306; Instruction: $6,203; Support Services: $3,648
Enrollment, Drop-out Rates and Diploma Recipients by Race/Ethnicity

Category	Total	White	Black	Asian	AIAN	Hisp.
Enrollment (%)	100.0	69.8	9.4	8.6	0.2	11.8
Drop-out Rate (%)	2.1	1.7	1.5	2.0	9.1	5.0
H.S. Diplomas (#)	668	484	61	57	1	65

Wethersfield SD
51 Willow St • Wethersfield, CT 06109-2798
(860) 571-8110 • http://www.wethersfield.k12.ct.us/
Grade Span: PK-12; **Agency Type:** 1
Schools: 8
    5 Primary; 1 Middle; 1 High; 1 Other Level
    7 Regular; 0 Special Education; 0 Vocational; 1 Alternative
    0 Magnet; 0 Charter; 3 Title I Eligible; 0 School-wide Title I
Students: 3,689   (51.2% male; 48.7% female)
    Individual Education Program: 438 (11.9%);
    English Language Learner: 193 (5.2%); Migrant: 0 (0.0%)
    Eligible for Free Lunch Program: n/a
    Eligible for Reduced-Price Lunch Program: n/a
Teachers: 244.2 (15.0 to 1)
Librarians/Media Specialists: 2.0 (1,836.5 to 1)
Guidance Counselors: 7.0 (524.7 to 1)
Current Spending: ($ per student per year):
    Total: $10,055; Instruction: $6,444; Support Services: $3,132
Enrollment, Drop-out Rates and Diploma Recipients by Race/Ethnicity

Category	Total	White	Black	Asian	AIAN	Hisp.
Enrollment (%)	100.0	83.6	4.1	2.9	0.1	9.3
Drop-out Rate (%)	1.4	1.4	2.9	0.0	n/a	1.4
H.S. Diplomas (#)	241	205	13	9	0	14

Windsor Locks SD
58 S Elm St • Windsor Locks, CT 06096-2399
(860) 292-5000
Grade Span: PK-12; **Agency Type:** 1
Schools: 5
    2 Primary; 1 Middle; 1 High; 1 Other Level
    4 Regular; 0 Special Education; 0 Vocational; 1 Alternative
    0 Magnet; 0 Charter; 1 Title I Eligible; 0 School-wide Title I
Students: 1,917   (49.9% male; 50.0% female)
    Individual Education Program: 314 (16.4%);
    English Language Learner: 43 (2.2%); Migrant: 0 (0.0%)
    Eligible for Free Lunch Program: n/a
    Eligible for Reduced-Price Lunch Program: n/a
Teachers: 157.4 (12.2 to 1)
Librarians/Media Specialists: 4.0 (479.3 to 1)
Guidance Counselors: 7.0 (273.9 to 1)
Current Spending: ($ per student per year):
    Total: $10,820; Instruction: $7,045; Support Services: $3,319
Enrollment, Drop-out Rates and Diploma Recipients by Race/Ethnicity

Category	Total	White	Black	Asian	AIAN	Hisp.
Enrollment (%)	100.0	86.2	5.5	5.1	0.1	3.1
Drop-out Rate (%)	5.1	4.2	25.0	0.0	25.0	8.7
H.S. Diplomas (#)	128	109	6	4	1	8

Windsor SD
601 Matianuck Ave • Windsor, CT 06095-0010
(860) 687-2000 • http://www.windsorct.org/
Grade Span: PK-12; **Agency Type:** 1
Schools: 8
    5 Primary; 1 Middle; 1 High; 1 Other Level
    7 Regular; 0 Special Education; 0 Vocational; 1 Alternative
    0 Magnet; 0 Charter; 3 Title I Eligible; 0 School-wide Title I
Students: 4,410   (51.9% male; 48.0% female)
    Individual Education Program: 563 (12.8%);
    English Language Learner: 65 (1.5%); Migrant: 0 (0.0%)
    Eligible for Free Lunch Program: n/a
    Eligible for Reduced-Price Lunch Program: n/a
Teachers: 344.1 (12.8 to 1)
Librarians/Media Specialists: 7.0 (630.0 to 1)
Guidance Counselors: 9.0 (490.0 to 1)
Current Spending: ($ per student per year):
    Total: $11,268; Instruction: $6,578; Support Services: $4,183
Enrollment, Drop-out Rates and Diploma Recipients by Race/Ethnicity

Category	Total	White	Black	Asian	AIAN	Hisp.
Enrollment (%)	100.0	40.7	46.6	3.9	0.4	8.4
Drop-out Rate (%)	3.3	2.3	3.9	3.4	0.0	6.1
H.S. Diplomas (#)	315	167	111	13	2	22

Litchfield County

New Milford SD
50 E St • New Milford, CT 06776-3099
(860) 355-8406 • http://www.new-milford.k12.ct.us/
Grade Span: PK-12; **Agency Type:** 1
Schools: 7
    3 Primary; 2 Middle; 1 High; 1 Other Level
    6 Regular; 0 Special Education; 0 Vocational; 1 Alternative
    0 Magnet; 0 Charter; 4 Title I Eligible; 0 School-wide Title I
Students: 5,267   (50.9% male; 49.0% female)
    Individual Education Program: 651 (12.4%);
    English Language Learner: 119 (2.3%); Migrant: 6 (0.1%)
    Eligible for Free Lunch Program: n/a
    Eligible for Reduced-Price Lunch Program: n/a
Teachers: 349.6 (15.0 to 1)
Librarians/Media Specialists: 6.0 (873.3 to 1)
Guidance Counselors: 12.0 (436.7 to 1)
Current Spending: ($ per student per year):
    Total: $8,986; Instruction: $5,673; Support Services: $2,939
Enrollment, Drop-out Rates and Diploma Recipients by Race/Ethnicity

Category	Total	White	Black	Asian	AIAN	Hisp.
Enrollment (%)	100.0	90.8	1.9	2.8	0.1	4.4
Drop-out Rate (%)	0.2	0.2	0.0	0.0	n/a	0.0
H.S. Diplomas (#)	241	233	1	3	0	4

Plymouth SD
77 Main St • Terryville, CT 06786-5104
Mailing Address: 77 E Main St • Terryville, CT 06786-5104
(860) 314-8005 • http://www.pccs.k12.mi.us/
Grade Span: PK-12; **Agency Type:** 1
Schools: 6
    3 Primary; 1 Middle; 1 High; 1 Other Level
    5 Regular; 0 Special Education; 0 Vocational; 1 Alternative
    0 Magnet; 0 Charter; 3 Title I Eligible; 0 School-wide Title I
Students: 1,914   (51.3% male; 48.6% female)
    Individual Education Program: 210 (11.0%);

English Language Learner: 26 (1.4%); Migrant: 0 (0.0%)
Eligible for Free Lunch Program: n/a
Eligible for Reduced-Price Lunch Program: n/a
Teachers: 141.0 (13.0 to 1)
Librarians/Media Specialists: 0.0 (n/a to 1)
Guidance Counselors: 4.0 (457.0 to 1)
Current Spending: ($ per student per year):
Total: $10,071; Instruction: $6,277; Support Services: $3,504

Enrollment, Drop-out Rates and Diploma Recipients by Race/Ethnicity

Category	Total	White	Black	Asian	AIAN	Hisp.
Enrollment (%)	100.0	95.7	0.8	0.9	0.5	2.1
Drop-out Rate (%)	2.6	2.4	33.3	0.0	n/a	0.0
H.S. Diplomas (#)	120	119	1	0	0	0

Regional SD 14
5 Minortown Ln • Woodbury, CT 06798-0469
Mailing Address: PO Box 469 • Woodbury, CT 06798-0469
(203) 263-4339 • http://www.ctreg14.com/
Grade Span: PK-12; **Agency Type:** 1
Schools: 6
3 Primary; 1 Middle; 1 High; 1 Other Level
4 Regular; 1 Special Education; 0 Vocational; 1 Alternative
0 Magnet; 0 Charter; 2 Title I Eligible; 0 School-wide Title I
Students: 2,318 (49.1% male; 50.8% female)
Individual Education Program: 259 (11.2%);
English Language Learner: 0 (0.0%); Migrant: 4 (0.2%)
Eligible for Free Lunch Program: n/a
Eligible for Reduced-Price Lunch Program: n/a
Teachers: 175.3 (13.2 to 1)
Librarians/Media Specialists: 4.0 (579.5 to 1)
Guidance Counselors: 6.0 (386.3 to 1)
Current Spending: ($ per student per year):
Total: $9,327; Instruction: $5,654; Support Services: $3,249

Enrollment, Drop-out Rates and Diploma Recipients by Race/Ethnicity

Category	Total	White	Black	Asian	AIAN	Hisp.
Enrollment (%)	100.0	95.2	0.6	1.4	0.3	2.4
Drop-out Rate (%)	0.9	0.7	0.0	7.1	0.0	6.7
H.S. Diplomas (#)	180	176	2	1	0	1

Torrington SD
355 Migeon Ave • Torrington, CT 06790-4822
(860) 489-2327 • http://www.torrington.org/
Grade Span: PK-12; **Agency Type:** 1
Schools: 9
5 Primary; 1 Middle; 2 High; 1 Other Level
7 Regular; 1 Special Education; 0 Vocational; 1 Alternative
0 Magnet; 0 Charter; 3 Title I Eligible; 0 School-wide Title I
Students: 5,027 (52.0% male; 47.9% female)
Individual Education Program: 628 (12.5%);
English Language Learner: 201 (4.0%); Migrant: 0 (0.0%)
Eligible for Free Lunch Program: n/a
Eligible for Reduced-Price Lunch Program: n/a
Teachers: 311.9 (16.0 to 1)
Librarians/Media Specialists: 6.0 (829.8 to 1)
Guidance Counselors: 9.0 (553.2 to 1)
Current Spending: ($ per student per year):
Total: $9,831; Instruction: $6,424; Support Services: $3,063

Enrollment, Drop-out Rates and Diploma Recipients by Race/Ethnicity

Category	Total	White	Black	Asian	AIAN	Hisp.
Enrollment (%)	100.0	85.1	5.3	2.7	0.3	6.6
Drop-out Rate (%)	6.0	6.1	8.0	5.8	0.0	1.7
H.S. Diplomas (#)	267	248	7	5	1	6

Watertown SD
10 Deforest St • Watertown, CT 06795-2190
(860) 945-4801 • http://watertownctschools.org/
Grade Span: PK-12; **Agency Type:** 1
Schools: 7
3 Primary; 2 Middle; 1 High; 1 Other Level
6 Regular; 0 Special Education; 0 Vocational; 1 Alternative
0 Magnet; 0 Charter; 0 Title I Eligible; 0 School-wide Title I
Students: 3,536 (50.0% male; 49.9% female)
Individual Education Program: 403 (11.4%);
English Language Learner: 48 (1.4%); Migrant: 0 (0.0%)
Eligible for Free Lunch Program: n/a
Eligible for Reduced-Price Lunch Program: n/a
Teachers: 233.3 (15.1 to 1)
Librarians/Media Specialists: 3.0 (1,175.3 to 1)
Guidance Counselors: 6.0 (587.7 to 1)
Current Spending: ($ per student per year):
Total: $8,676; Instruction: $5,440; Support Services: $2,965

Enrollment, Drop-out Rates and Diploma Recipients by Race/Ethnicity

Category	Total	White	Black	Asian	AIAN	Hisp.
Enrollment (%)	100.0	94.2	1.1	2.1	0.6	2.0
Drop-out Rate (%)	2.4	2.6	0.0	0.0	0.0	0.0
H.S. Diplomas (#)	203	194	1	4	0	4

Middlesex County

Clinton SD
137-B Glenwood Circle • Clinton, CT 06413-1493
Mailing Address: 137 B Glenwood Circle • Clinton, CT 06413-1493
(860) 664-6500 • http://www.clintonpublic.org/
Grade Span: PK-12; **Agency Type:** 1
Schools: 5
1 Primary; 2 Middle; 1 High; 1 Other Level
4 Regular; 0 Special Education; 0 Vocational; 1 Alternative
0 Magnet; 0 Charter; 1 Title I Eligible; 0 School-wide Title I
Students: 2,178 (50.6% male; 49.3% female)
Individual Education Program: 278 (12.8%);
English Language Learner: 22 (1.0%); Migrant: 6 (0.3%)
Eligible for Free Lunch Program: n/a
Eligible for Reduced-Price Lunch Program: n/a
Teachers: 170.6 (12.6 to 1)
Librarians/Media Specialists: 4.0 (536.5 to 1)
Guidance Counselors: 6.0 (357.7 to 1)
Current Spending: ($ per student per year):
Total: $10,710; Instruction: $7,383; Support Services: $2,987

Enrollment, Drop-out Rates and Diploma Recipients by Race/Ethnicity

Category	Total	White	Black	Asian	AIAN	Hisp.
Enrollment (%)	100.0	91.8	0.5	2.7	0.1	4.8
Drop-out Rate (%)	4.3	4.3	0.0	0.0	0.0	6.1
H.S. Diplomas (#)	157	147	0	3	0	7

Cromwell SD
9 Mann Memorial Dr • Cromwell, CT 06416-1398
(860) 632-4830
Grade Span: PK-12; **Agency Type:** 1
Schools: 4
1 Primary; 1 Middle; 1 High; 1 Other Level
3 Regular; 0 Special Education; 0 Vocational; 1 Alternative
0 Magnet; 0 Charter; 2 Title I Eligible; 0 School-wide Title I
Students: 1,881 (48.9% male; 51.0% female)
Individual Education Program: 244 (13.0%);
English Language Learner: 70 (3.7%); Migrant: 0 (0.0%)
Eligible for Free Lunch Program: n/a
Eligible for Reduced-Price Lunch Program: n/a
Teachers: 149.1 (12.6 to 1)
Librarians/Media Specialists: 2.0 (939.0 to 1)
Guidance Counselors: 4.0 (469.5 to 1)
Current Spending: ($ per student per year):
Total: $10,520; Instruction: $6,871; Support Services: $3,295

Enrollment, Drop-out Rates and Diploma Recipients by Race/Ethnicity

Category	Total	White	Black	Asian	AIAN	Hisp.
Enrollment (%)	100.0	87.1	5.5	2.7	0.2	4.6
Drop-out Rate (%)	0.2	0.0	4.2	0.0	0.0	0.0
H.S. Diplomas (#)	101	90	4	2	1	4

East Hampton SD
94 Main St • East Hampton, CT 06424-1119
(860) 365-4000
Grade Span: PK-12; **Agency Type:** 1
Schools: 5
1 Primary; 2 Middle; 1 High; 1 Other Level
4 Regular; 0 Special Education; 0 Vocational; 1 Alternative
0 Magnet; 0 Charter; 2 Title I Eligible; 0 School-wide Title I
Students: 2,085 (49.6% male; 50.3% female)
Individual Education Program: 230 (11.0%);
English Language Learner: 4 (0.2%); Migrant: 0 (0.0%)
Eligible for Free Lunch Program: n/a
Eligible for Reduced-Price Lunch Program: n/a
Teachers: 139.9 (14.9 to 1)
Librarians/Media Specialists: 1.0 (2,085.0 to 1)
Guidance Counselors: 3.0 (695.0 to 1)
Current Spending: ($ per student per year):
Total: $9,786; Instruction: $6,257; Support Services: $3,296

Enrollment, Drop-out Rates and Diploma Recipients by Race/Ethnicity

Category	Total	White	Black	Asian	AIAN	Hisp.
Enrollment (%)	100.0	96.7	0.7	1.4	0.1	1.0
Drop-out Rate (%)	0.8	0.8	0.0	0.0	n/a	0.0
H.S. Diplomas (#)	125	120	0	3	0	1

Middletown SD
311 Hunting Hill Ave • Middletown, CT 06457-4356
(860) 638-1401 • http://www.middletownschools.org/
Grade Span: PK-12; **Agency Type:** 1
Schools: 12
  8 Primary; 2 Middle; 1 High; 1 Other Level
  12 Regular; 0 Special Education; 0 Vocational; 0 Alternative
  0 Magnet; 0 Charter; 7 Title I Eligible; 4 School-wide Title I
Students: 5,186   (50.0% male; 49.9% female)
  Individual Education Program: 628 (12.1%);
  English Language Learner: 105 (2.0%); Migrant: 0 (0.0%)
  Eligible for Free Lunch Program: n/a
  Eligible for Reduced-Price Lunch Program: n/a
Teachers: 394.3 (13.1 to 1)
Librarians/Media Specialists: 4.0 (1,290.8 to 1)
Guidance Counselors: 9.0 (573.7 to 1)
Current Spending: ($ per student per year):
  Total: $11,088; Instruction: $7,387; Support Services: $3,321
Enrollment, Drop-out Rates and Diploma Recipients by Race/Ethnicity

Category	Total	White	Black	Asian	AIAN	Hisp.
Enrollment (%)	100.0	59.0	26.9	4.0	0.1	10.0
Drop-out Rate (%)	0.8	0.7	1.0	0.0	0.0	1.2
H.S. Diplomas (#)	246	168	59	9	0	10

Old Saybrook SD
50 Sheffield St • Old Saybrook, CT 06475-2399
(860) 395-3157
Grade Span: PK-12; **Agency Type:** 1
Schools: 4
  1 Primary; 1 Middle; 1 High; 1 Other Level
  3 Regular; 0 Special Education; 0 Vocational; 1 Alternative
  0 Magnet; 0 Charter; 2 Title I Eligible; 0 School-wide Title I
Students: 1,588   (50.4% male; 49.5% female)
  Individual Education Program: 210 (13.2%);
  English Language Learner: 55 (3.5%); Migrant: 0 (0.0%)
  Eligible for Free Lunch Program: n/a
  Eligible for Reduced-Price Lunch Program: n/a
Teachers: 136.6 (11.6 to 1)
Librarians/Media Specialists: 3.0 (528.3 to 1)
Guidance Counselors: 4.0 (396.3 to 1)
Current Spending: ($ per student per year):
  Total: $9,964; Instruction: $5,817; Support Services: $3,618
Enrollment, Drop-out Rates and Diploma Recipients by Race/Ethnicity

Category	Total	White	Black	Asian	AIAN	Hisp.
Enrollment (%)	100.0	89.0	2.5	4.7	0.2	3.7
Drop-out Rate (%)	0.0	0.0	0.0	0.0	n/a	0.0
H.S. Diplomas (#)	95	85	3	3	0	4

Regional SD 13
135-A Pickett Ln • Durham, CT 06422-2001
(860) 349-7200 • http://www.reg13.k12.ct.us
Grade Span: PK-12; **Agency Type:** 1
Schools: 7
  3 Primary; 2 Middle; 1 High; 1 Other Level
  6 Regular; 0 Special Education; 0 Vocational; 1 Alternative
  0 Magnet; 0 Charter; 4 Title I Eligible; 0 School-wide Title I
Students: 2,147   (51.0% male; 48.9% female)
  Individual Education Program: 236 (11.0%);
  English Language Learner: 0 (0.0%); Migrant: 0 (0.0%)
  Eligible for Free Lunch Program: n/a
  Eligible for Reduced-Price Lunch Program: n/a
Teachers: 171.8 (12.5 to 1)
Librarians/Media Specialists: 2.0 (1,073.0 to 1)
Guidance Counselors: 3.0 (715.3 to 1)
Current Spending: ($ per student per year):
  Total: $10,680; Instruction: $6,301; Support Services: $4,057
Enrollment, Drop-out Rates and Diploma Recipients by Race/Ethnicity

Category	Total	White	Black	Asian	AIAN	Hisp.
Enrollment (%)	100.0	96.7	0.7	1.1	0.2	1.4
Drop-out Rate (%)	0.7	0.7	0.0	0.0	n/a	0.0
H.S. Diplomas (#)	110	105	1	3	0	1

Regional SD 17
95 Little City Rd • Higganum, CT 06441-4323
(860) 345-4534 • http://www.rsd17.k12.ct.us/
Grade Span: PK-12; **Agency Type:** 1
Schools: 6
  3 Primary; 0 Middle; 2 High; 1 Other Level
  5 Regular; 0 Special Education; 0 Vocational; 1 Alternative
  0 Magnet; 0 Charter; 1 Title I Eligible; 0 School-wide Title I
Students: 2,387   (52.8% male; 47.1% female)
  Individual Education Program: 297 (12.4%);
  English Language Learner: 0 (0.0%); Migrant: 0 (0.0%)
  Eligible for Free Lunch Program: n/a
  Eligible for Reduced-Price Lunch Program: n/a

Teachers: 199.4 (12.0 to 1)
Librarians/Media Specialists: 1.0 (2,386.0 to 1)
Guidance Counselors: 6.0 (397.7 to 1)
Current Spending: ($ per student per year):
  Total: $6,408; Instruction: $6,408; Support Services: $3,707
Enrollment, Drop-out Rates and Diploma Recipients by Race/Ethnicity

Category	Total	White	Black	Asian	AIAN	Hisp.
Enrollment (%)	100.0	96.2	1.0	1.6	0.2	1.0
Drop-out Rate (%)	0.2	0.2	0.0	0.0	0.0	0.0
H.S. Diplomas (#)	146	138	3	3	0	2

State Vocational-Technical Schools
25 Industrial Park Rd • Middletown, CT 06457-1543
(860) 807-2200
Grade Span: 09-12; **Agency Type:** 5
Schools: 17
  0 Primary; 0 Middle; 17 High; 0 Other Level
  0 Regular; 0 Special Education; 17 Vocational; 0 Alternative
  0 Magnet; 0 Charter; 5 Title I Eligible; 5 School-wide Title I
Students: 11,253   (64.1% male; 35.8% female)
  Individual Education Program: 1,668 (14.8%);
  English Language Learner: 828 (7.4%); Migrant: 115 (1.0%)
  Eligible for Free Lunch Program: n/a
  Eligible for Reduced-Price Lunch Program: n/a
Teachers: 1,086.5 (10.4 to 1)
Librarians/Media Specialists: 17.0 (661.9 to 1)
Guidance Counselors: 66.0 (170.5 to 1)
Current Spending: ($ per student per year):
  Total: n/a; Instruction: n/a; Support Services: n/a
Enrollment, Drop-out Rates and Diploma Recipients by Race/Ethnicity

Category	Total	White	Black	Asian	AIAN	Hisp.
Enrollment (%)	100.0	58.4	15.9	0.6	0.9	24.2
Drop-out Rate (%)	0.9	1.1	0.5	1.7	0.0	0.9
H.S. Diplomas (#)	2,013	1,270	317	13	4	409

New Haven County

Ansonia SD
42 Grove St • Ansonia, CT 06401-1798
(203) 736-5095 • http://electronicvalley.org/ansonia/k12/
Grade Span: PK-12; **Agency Type:** 1
Schools: 5
  2 Primary; 1 Middle; 1 High; 1 Other Level
  4 Regular; 0 Special Education; 0 Vocational; 1 Alternative
  0 Magnet; 0 Charter; 3 Title I Eligible; 0 School-wide Title I
Students: 2,691   (52.2% male; 47.7% female)
  Individual Education Program: 343 (12.7%);
  English Language Learner: 97 (3.6%); Migrant: 0 (0.0%)
  Eligible for Free Lunch Program: n/a
  Eligible for Reduced-Price Lunch Program: n/a
Teachers: 164.5 (16.1 to 1)
Librarians/Media Specialists: 1.0 (2,652.0 to 1)
Guidance Counselors: 5.0 (530.4 to 1)
Current Spending: ($ per student per year):
  Total: $8,575; Instruction: $5,540; Support Services: $2,603
Enrollment, Drop-out Rates and Diploma Recipients by Race/Ethnicity

Category	Total	White	Black	Asian	AIAN	Hisp.
Enrollment (%)	100.0	64.4	17.5	1.2	0.5	16.4
Drop-out Rate (%)	5.7	5.1	4.0	0.0	n/a	12.1
H.S. Diplomas (#)	118	86	15	2	0	15

Area Cooperative Educational Services
350 State St • North Haven, CT 06473-3108
(203) 498-6817
Grade Span: PK-12; **Agency Type:** 4
Schools: 4
  1 Primary; 1 Middle; 1 High; 1 Other Level
  2 Regular; 2 Special Education; 0 Vocational; 0 Alternative
  3 Magnet; 0 Charter; 2 Title I Eligible; 0 School-wide Title I
Students: 2,030   (59.3% male; 40.6% female)
  Individual Education Program: 701 (34.5%);
  English Language Learner: 28 (1.4%); Migrant: 4 (0.2%)
  Eligible for Free Lunch Program: n/a
  Eligible for Reduced-Price Lunch Program: n/a
Teachers: 219.4 (9.2 to 1)
Librarians/Media Specialists: 2.0 (1,010.0 to 1)
Guidance Counselors: 5.0 (404.0 to 1)
Current Spending: ($ per student per year):
  Total: n/a; Instruction: n/a; Support Services: n/a
Enrollment, Drop-out Rates and Diploma Recipients by Race/Ethnicity

Category	Total	White	Black	Asian	AIAN	Hisp.
Enrollment (%)	100.0	54.2	26.0	2.6	0.0	17.2
Drop-out Rate (%)	0.7	0.9	0.8	0.0	n/a	0.0
H.S. Diplomas (#)	24	16	6	0	0	2

Branford SD

1111 Main St • **Branford, CT 06405-3717**
(203) 315-7800 • http://www.branford.k12.ct.us/prod/index.jsp
Grade Span: PK-12; **Agency Type:** 1
Schools: 7
  4 Primary; 1 Middle; 1 High; 1 Other Level
  6 Regular; 0 Special Education; 0 Vocational; 1 Alternative
  0 Magnet; 0 Charter; 3 Title I Eligible; 0 School-wide Title I
Students: 3,674 (50.3% male; 49.6% female)
  Individual Education Program: 225 (6.1%);
  English Language Learner: 76 (2.1%); Migrant: 0 (0.0%)
  Eligible for Free Lunch Program: n/a
  Eligible for Reduced-Price Lunch Program: n/a
Teachers: 274.9 (13.4 to 1)
Librarians/Media Specialists: 7.0 (524.6 to 1)
Guidance Counselors: 10.0 (367.2 to 1)
Current Spending: ($ per student per year):
  Total: $10,126; Instruction: $6,298; Support Services: $3,399
Enrollment, Drop-out Rates and Diploma Recipients by Race/Ethnicity

Category	Total	White	Black	Asian	AIAN	Hisp.
Enrollment (%)	100.0	89.2	2.5	5.5	0.1	2.7
Drop-out Rate (%)	1.8	1.7	0.0	4.4	0.0	0.0
H.S. Diplomas (#)	238	219	4	13	0	2

Cheshire SD

29 Main St • **Cheshire, CT 06410-2495**
(203) 250-2400 • http://www.cheshirect.org/
Grade Span: PK-12; **Agency Type:** 1
Schools: 9
  5 Primary; 1 Middle; 1 High; 2 Other Level
  7 Regular; 1 Special Education; 0 Vocational; 1 Alternative
  0 Magnet; 0 Charter; 0 Title I Eligible; 0 School-wide Title I
Students: 5,184 (51.4% male; 48.5% female)
  Individual Education Program: 507 (9.8%);
  English Language Learner: 30 (0.6%); Migrant: 0 (0.0%)
  Eligible for Free Lunch Program: n/a
  Eligible for Reduced-Price Lunch Program: n/a
Teachers: 316.1 (16.4 to 1)
Librarians/Media Specialists: 8.0 (647.5 to 1)
Guidance Counselors: 12.0 (431.7 to 1)
Current Spending: ($ per student per year):
  Total: $9,851; Instruction: $6,095; Support Services: $3,420
Enrollment, Drop-out Rates and Diploma Recipients by Race/Ethnicity

Category	Total	White	Black	Asian	AIAN	Hisp.
Enrollment (%)	100.0	91.0	1.7	5.4	0.1	1.8
Drop-out Rate (%)	1.0	1.1	0.0	0.0	0.0	0.0
H.S. Diplomas (#)	348	333	2	9	1	3

Derby SD

1 Elizabeth St • **Derby, CT 06418-0373**
Mailing Address: PO Box 373 • **Derby, CT 06418-0373**
(203) 736-5027 • http://www.derbyps.org/
Grade Span: PK-12; **Agency Type:** 1
Schools: 4
  2 Primary; 0 Middle; 1 High; 1 Other Level
  3 Regular; 0 Special Education; 0 Vocational; 1 Alternative
  0 Magnet; 0 Charter; 1 Title I Eligible; 0 School-wide Title I
Students: 1,571 (52.2% male; 47.7% female)
  Individual Education Program: 155 (9.9%);
  English Language Learner: 115 (7.3%); Migrant: 1 (0.1%)
  Eligible for Free Lunch Program: n/a
  Eligible for Reduced-Price Lunch Program: n/a
Teachers: 100.2 (15.4 to 1)
Librarians/Media Specialists: 3.0 (515.7 to 1)
Guidance Counselors: 3.0 (515.7 to 1)
Current Spending: ($ per student per year):
  Total: $9,506; Instruction: $5,770; Support Services: $3,057
Enrollment, Drop-out Rates and Diploma Recipients by Race/Ethnicity

Category	Total	White	Black	Asian	AIAN	Hisp.
Enrollment (%)	100.0	71.8	9.5	1.5	0.2	17.0
Drop-out Rate (%)	2.9	1.9	9.1	0.0	0.0	7.3
H.S. Diplomas (#)	80	59	4	4	1	12

East Haven SD

35 Wheelbarrow Ln • **East Haven, CT 06513-1597**
(203) 468-3261 • http://www.east-haven.k12.ct.us/
Grade Span: PK-12; **Agency Type:** 1
Schools: 13
  9 Primary; 1 Middle; 2 High; 1 Other Level
  11 Regular; 1 Special Education; 0 Vocational; 1 Alternative
  0 Magnet; 0 Charter; 0 Title I Eligible; 0 School-wide Title I
Students: 3,964 (51.5% male; 48.4% female)
  Individual Education Program: 469 (11.8%);
  English Language Learner: 96 (2.4%); Migrant: 4 (0.1%)
  Eligible for Free Lunch Program: n/a

  Eligible for Reduced-Price Lunch Program: n/a
Teachers: 252.9 (15.6 to 1)
Librarians/Media Specialists: 6.0 (657.8 to 1)
Guidance Counselors: 8.0 (493.4 to 1)
Current Spending: ($ per student per year):
  Total: $9,374; Instruction: $5,543; Support Services: $3,373
Enrollment, Drop-out Rates and Diploma Recipients by Race/Ethnicity

Category	Total	White	Black	Asian	AIAN	Hisp.
Enrollment (%)	100.0	87.7	1.8	3.1	0.1	7.3
Drop-out Rate (%)	0.7	0.6	0.0	4.3	0.0	0.0
H.S. Diplomas (#)	215	197	1	3	0	14

Guilford SD

701 New England Rd • **Guilford, CT 06437-1838**
Mailing Address: PO Box 367 • **Guilford, CT 06437-1838**
(203) 453-8200 • http://www.guilford.k12.ct.us/
Grade Span: PK-12; **Agency Type:** 1
Schools: 8
  4 Primary; 2 Middle; 1 High; 1 Other Level
  7 Regular; 0 Special Education; 0 Vocational; 1 Alternative
  0 Magnet; 0 Charter; 3 Title I Eligible; 0 School-wide Title I
Students: 3,891 (50.8% male; 49.1% female)
  Individual Education Program: 398 (10.2%);
  English Language Learner: 31 (0.8%); Migrant: 0 (0.0%)
  Eligible for Free Lunch Program: n/a
  Eligible for Reduced-Price Lunch Program: n/a
Teachers: 250.2 (15.6 to 1)
Librarians/Media Specialists: 8.0 (486.4 to 1)
Guidance Counselors: 10.0 (389.1 to 1)
Current Spending: ($ per student per year):
  Total: $9,970; Instruction: $6,379; Support Services: $3,282
Enrollment, Drop-out Rates and Diploma Recipients by Race/Ethnicity

Category	Total	White	Black	Asian	AIAN	Hisp.
Enrollment (%)	100.0	93.0	0.9	2.8	0.2	3.1
Drop-out Rate (%)	0.3	0.3	0.0	0.0	0.0	0.0
H.S. Diplomas (#)	287	274	1	4	0	8

Hamden SD

60 Putnam Ave • **Hamden, CT 06517-2825**
(203) 407-2000 • http://www.hamden.k12.ct.us/
Grade Span: PK-12; **Agency Type:** 1
Schools: 12
  9 Primary; 1 Middle; 1 High; 1 Other Level
  11 Regular; 0 Special Education; 0 Vocational; 1 Alternative
  0 Magnet; 0 Charter; 6 Title I Eligible; 0 School-wide Title I
Students: 6,340 (52.5% male; 47.4% female)
  Individual Education Program: 792 (12.5%);
  English Language Learner: 30 (0.5%); Migrant: 9 (0.1%)
  Eligible for Free Lunch Program: n/a
  Eligible for Reduced-Price Lunch Program: n/a
Teachers: 404.4 (15.6 to 1)
Librarians/Media Specialists: 13.0 (486.3 to 1)
Guidance Counselors: 10.0 (632.2 to 1)
Current Spending: ($ per student per year):
  Total: $11,956; Instruction: $7,935; Support Services: $3,700
Enrollment, Drop-out Rates and Diploma Recipients by Race/Ethnicity

Category	Total	White	Black	Asian	AIAN	Hisp.
Enrollment (%)	100.0	56.6	29.3	5.4	0.1	8.7
Drop-out Rate (%)	3.8	2.9	6.8	4.9	n/a	1.9
H.S. Diplomas (#)	401	286	88	11	0	16

Madison SD

10 Campus Dr • **Madison, CT 06443-2562**
Mailing Address: PO Box 71 • **Madison, CT 06443-2562**
(203) 245-6300 • http://www.madisonps.org/
Grade Span: PK-12; **Agency Type:** 1
Schools: 8
  4 Primary; 2 Middle; 1 High; 1 Other Level
  7 Regular; 0 Special Education; 0 Vocational; 1 Alternative
  0 Magnet; 0 Charter; 0 Title I Eligible; 0 School-wide Title I
Students: 3,715 (49.9% male; 50.0% female)
  Individual Education Program: 482 (13.0%);
  English Language Learner: 9 (0.2%); Migrant: 0 (0.0%)
  Eligible for Free Lunch Program: n/a
  Eligible for Reduced-Price Lunch Program: n/a
Teachers: 261.4 (14.2 to 1)
Librarians/Media Specialists: 4.0 (928.8 to 1)
Guidance Counselors: 7.0 (530.7 to 1)
Current Spending: ($ per student per year):
  Total: $9,199; Instruction: $5,541; Support Services: $3,239
Enrollment, Drop-out Rates and Diploma Recipients by Race/Ethnicity

Category	Total	White	Black	Asian	AIAN	Hisp.
Enrollment (%)	100.0	95.2	0.8	3.0	0.1	1.0
Drop-out Rate (%)	1.2	1.0	0.0	0.0	33.3	5.0
H.S. Diplomas (#)	210	196	1	5	0	8

Meriden SD
22 Liberty St • Meriden, CT 06450-0848
Mailing Address: PO Box 848 • Meriden, CT 06450-0848
(203) 630-4171 • http://www.meriden.k12.ct.us/
Grade Span: PK-12; Agency Type: 1
Schools: 13
   8 Primary; 2 Middle; 2 High; 1 Other Level
   12 Regular; 0 Special Education; 0 Vocational; 1 Alternative
   0 Magnet; 0 Charter; 8 Title I Eligible; 0 School-wide Title I
Students: 8,894 (51.1% male; 48.8% female)
   Individual Education Program: 1,241 (14.0%);
   English Language Learner: 609 (6.8%); Migrant: 581 (6.5%)
   Eligible for Free Lunch Program: n/a
   Eligible for Reduced-Price Lunch Program: n/a
Teachers: 612.6 (14.5 to 1)
Librarians/Media Specialists: 10.0 (888.6 to 1)
Guidance Counselors: 21.3 (417.2 to 1)
Current Spending: ($ per student per year):
   Total: $10,488; Instruction: $6,709; Support Services: $3,386
Enrollment, Drop-out Rates and Diploma Recipients by Race/Ethnicity

Category	Total	White	Black	Asian	AIAN	Hisp.
Enrollment (%)	100.0	47.4	12.6	1.7	0.2	38.0
Drop-out Rate (%)	2.7	2.2	2.2	1.9	0.0	4.0
H.S. Diplomas (#)	433	301	32	9	0	91

Milford SD
70 W River St • Milford, CT 06460-3364
(203) 783-3402 • http://www.milforded.org/
Grade Span: PK-12; Agency Type: 1
Schools: 16
   9 Primary; 3 Middle; 3 High; 1 Other Level
   14 Regular; 0 Special Education; 0 Vocational; 2 Alternative
   0 Magnet; 0 Charter; 8 Title I Eligible; 0 School-wide Title I
Students: 7,559 (50.9% male; 49.0% female)
   Individual Education Program: 965 (12.8%);
   English Language Learner: 139 (1.8%); Migrant: 0 (0.0%)
   Eligible for Free Lunch Program: n/a
   Eligible for Reduced-Price Lunch Program: n/a
Teachers: 576.6 (13.1 to 1)
Librarians/Media Specialists: 14.0 (537.5 to 1)
Guidance Counselors: 12.0 (627.1 to 1)
Current Spending: ($ per student per year):
   Total: $10,638; Instruction: $7,377; Support Services: $2,930
Enrollment, Drop-out Rates and Diploma Recipients by Race/Ethnicity

Category	Total	White	Black	Asian	AIAN	Hisp.
Enrollment (%)	100.0	87.9	3.3	4.4	0.2	4.2
Drop-out Rate (%)	1.7	1.5	4.5	5.6	0.0	2.5
H.S. Diplomas (#)	464	424	9	15	0	16

Naugatuck SD
380 Church St • Naugatuck, CT 06770-2887
(203) 720-5265
Grade Span: PK-12; Agency Type: 1
Schools: 12
   7 Primary; 3 Middle; 1 High; 1 Other Level
   11 Regular; 0 Special Education; 0 Vocational; 1 Alternative
   0 Magnet; 0 Charter; 8 Title I Eligible; 0 School-wide Title I
Students: 5,429 (51.1% male; 48.8% female)
   Individual Education Program: 642 (11.8%);
   English Language Learner: 183 (3.4%); Migrant: 8 (0.1%)
   Eligible for Free Lunch Program: n/a
   Eligible for Reduced-Price Lunch Program: n/a
Teachers: 345.3 (15.7 to 1)
Librarians/Media Specialists: 4.0 (1,354.3 to 1)
Guidance Counselors: 13.0 (416.7 to 1)
Current Spending: ($ per student per year):
   Total: $8,954; Instruction: $5,925; Support Services: $2,723
Enrollment, Drop-out Rates and Diploma Recipients by Race/Ethnicity

Category	Total	White	Black	Asian	AIAN	Hisp.
Enrollment (%)	100.0	83.3	6.1	2.4	0.3	7.9
Drop-out Rate (%)	3.0	3.0	0.0	4.3	0.0	4.5
H.S. Diplomas (#)	326	287	16	3	1	19

New Haven SD
140 Dewitt St • New Haven, CT 06519-1743
(203) 946-8888 • http://www.nhps.net/
Grade Span: PK-12; Agency Type: 1
Schools: 50
   33 Primary; 5 Middle; 8 High; 4 Other Level
   41 Regular; 1 Special Education; 0 Vocational; 8 Alternative
   14 Magnet; 0 Charter; 25 Title I Eligible; 25 School-wide Title I
Students: 20,457 (50.9% male; 49.0% female)
   Individual Education Program: 1,852 (9.1%);
   English Language Learner: 1,998 (9.8%); Migrant: 2,093 (10.4%)
   Eligible for Free Lunch Program: n/a

Eligible for Reduced-Price Lunch Program: n/a
Teachers: 1,410.9 (14.2 to 1)
Librarians/Media Specialists: 39.0 (514.1 to 1)
Guidance Counselors: 42.0 (477.4 to 1)
Current Spending: ($ per student per year):
   Total: $12,966; Instruction: $8,143; Support Services: $4,267
Enrollment, Drop-out Rates and Diploma Recipients by Race/Ethnicity

Category	Total	White	Black	Asian	AIAN	Hisp.
Enrollment (%)	100.0	11.1	55.5	1.2	0.0	32.2
Drop-out Rate (%)	5.2	3.3	5.2	2.7	0.0	7.0
H.S. Diplomas (#)	788	149	451	18	2	168

North Branford SD
1388 Middletown Ave • Northford, CT 06472-1380
(203) 484-1440 • http://www.northbranfordschools.org/
Grade Span: PK-12; Agency Type: 1
Schools: 6
   3 Primary; 1 Middle; 1 High; 1 Other Level
   5 Regular; 0 Special Education; 0 Vocational; 1 Alternative
   0 Magnet; 0 Charter; 0 Title I Eligible; 0 School-wide Title I
Students: 2,506 (51.7% male; 48.2% female)
   Individual Education Program: 273 (10.9%);
   English Language Learner: 16 (0.6%); Migrant: 0 (0.0%)
   Eligible for Free Lunch Program: n/a
   Eligible for Reduced-Price Lunch Program: n/a
Teachers: 147.5 (16.9 to 1)
Librarians/Media Specialists: 3.0 (833.3 to 1)
Guidance Counselors: 5.0 (500.0 to 1)
Current Spending: ($ per student per year):
   Total: $9,207; Instruction: $5,348; Support Services: $3,474
Enrollment, Drop-out Rates and Diploma Recipients by Race/Ethnicity

Category	Total	White	Black	Asian	AIAN	Hisp.
Enrollment (%)	100.0	95.5	1.4	0.7	0.3	2.0
Drop-out Rate (%)	1.4	1.5	0.0	0.0	0.0	0.0
H.S. Diplomas (#)	148	137	3	1	2	5

North Haven SD
5 Linsley St • North Haven, CT 06473-2586
(203) 239-2581 • http://www.north-haven.k12.ct.us/
Grade Span: PK-12; Agency Type: 1
Schools: 7
   4 Primary; 1 Middle; 1 High; 1 Other Level
   6 Regular; 0 Special Education; 0 Vocational; 1 Alternative
   0 Magnet; 0 Charter; 0 Title I Eligible; 0 School-wide Title I
Students: 3,777 (51.1% male; 48.8% female)
   Individual Education Program: 345 (9.1%);
   English Language Learner: 65 (1.7%); Migrant: 0 (0.0%)
   Eligible for Free Lunch Program: n/a
   Eligible for Reduced-Price Lunch Program: n/a
Teachers: 243.0 (15.5 to 1)
Librarians/Media Specialists: 7.0 (539.0 to 1)
Guidance Counselors: 7.0 (539.0 to 1)
Current Spending: ($ per student per year):
   Total: $9,562; Instruction: $5,891; Support Services: $3,329
Enrollment, Drop-out Rates and Diploma Recipients by Race/Ethnicity

Category	Total	White	Black	Asian	AIAN	Hisp.
Enrollment (%)	100.0	89.1	2.7	5.6	0.1	2.7
Drop-out Rate (%)	2.2	2.0	13.3	2.5	0.0	0.0
H.S. Diplomas (#)	214	197	4	9	0	4

Regional SD 05
25 Newton Rd • Woodbridge, CT 06525-1598
(203) 397-4811 • http://www.amityregion5.org/District_Page/
Grade Span: 07-12; Agency Type: 1
Schools: 4
   0 Primary; 2 Middle; 1 High; 1 Other Level
   3 Regular; 0 Special Education; 0 Vocational; 1 Alternative
   0 Magnet; 0 Charter; 2 Title I Eligible; 0 School-wide Title I
Students: 2,468 (49.3% male; 50.6% female)
   Individual Education Program: 294 (11.9%);
   English Language Learner: 6 (0.2%); Migrant: 0 (0.0%)
   Eligible for Free Lunch Program: n/a
   Eligible for Reduced-Price Lunch Program: n/a
Teachers: 182.8 (13.5 to 1)
Librarians/Media Specialists: 4.0 (615.3 to 1)
Guidance Counselors: 14.0 (175.8 to 1)
Current Spending: ($ per student per year):
   Total: $11,986; Instruction: $5,899; Support Services: $5,594
Enrollment, Drop-out Rates and Diploma Recipients by Race/Ethnicity

Category	Total	White	Black	Asian	AIAN	Hisp.
Enrollment (%)	100.0	90.1	1.8	6.3	0.1	1.7
Drop-out Rate (%)	1.0	1.1	0.0	0.0	0.0	0.0
H.S. Diplomas (#)	323	294	6	21	0	2

Regional SD 15
286 Whittemore Rd • Middlebury, CT 06762-0395
Mailing Address: PO Box 395 • Middlebury, CT 06762-0395
(203) 758-8258 • http://www.region15.org/default.shtml
Grade Span: PK-12; **Agency Type:** 1
Schools: 8
  4 Primary; 2 Middle; 1 High; 1 Other Level
  7 Regular; 0 Special Education; 0 Vocational; 1 Alternative
  0 Magnet; 0 Charter; 4 Title I Eligible; 0 School-wide Title I
Students: 4,484 (51.0% male; 48.9% female)
  Individual Education Program: 550 (12.3%);
  English Language Learner: 36 (0.8%); Migrant: 2 (<0.1%)
  Eligible for Free Lunch Program: n/a
  Eligible for Reduced-Price Lunch Program: n/a
Teachers: 290.3 (15.4 to 1)
Librarians/Media Specialists: 7.0 (637.9 to 1)
Guidance Counselors: 13.0 (343.5 to 1)
Current Spending: ($ per student per year):
  Total: $10,000; Instruction: $5,915; Support Services: $3,675
Enrollment, Drop-out Rates and Diploma Recipients by Race/Ethnicity

Category	Total	White	Black	Asian	AIAN	Hisp.
Enrollment (%)	100.0	94.9	0.5	2.6	0.1	1.9
Drop-out Rate (%)	2.3	2.4	0.0	0.0	0.0	0.0
H.S. Diplomas (#)	243	231	2	3	2	5

Regional SD 16
207 New Haven Rd • Prospect, CT 06712-1629
(203) 758-6671
Grade Span: PK-11; **Agency Type:** 1
Schools: 6
  2 Primary; 2 Middle; 1 High; 1 Other Level
  5 Regular; 0 Special Education; 0 Vocational; 1 Alternative
  0 Magnet; 0 Charter; 5 Title I Eligible; 0 School-wide Title I
Students: 2,603 (51.4% male; 48.5% female)
  Individual Education Program: 260 (10.0%);
  English Language Learner: 3 (0.1%); Migrant: 0 (0.0%)
  Eligible for Free Lunch Program: n/a
  Eligible for Reduced-Price Lunch Program: n/a
Teachers: 189.9 (13.6 to 1)
Librarians/Media Specialists: 1.0 (2,590.0 to 1)
Guidance Counselors: 8.0 (323.8 to 1)
Current Spending: ($ per student per year):
  Total: $9,391; Instruction: $5,452; Support Services: $3,494
Enrollment, Drop-out Rates and Diploma Recipients by Race/Ethnicity

Category	Total	White	Black	Asian	AIAN	Hisp.
Enrollment (%)	100.0	95.3	1.7	0.7	0.0	2.2
Drop-out Rate (%)	0.0	0.0	0.0	0.0	0.0	0.0
H.S. Diplomas (#)	n/a	n/a	n/a	n/a	n/a	n/a

Seymour SD
98 Bank St • Seymour, CT 06483-2892
(203) 888-4564 • http://www.seymourschools.org/
Grade Span: PK-12; **Agency Type:** 1
Schools: 6
  3 Primary; 1 Middle; 1 High; 1 Other Level
  5 Regular; 0 Special Education; 0 Vocational; 1 Alternative
  0 Magnet; 0 Charter; 4 Title I Eligible; 0 School-wide Title I
Students: 2,733 (49.7% male; 50.2% female)
  Individual Education Program: 163 (6.0%);
  English Language Learner: 47 (1.7%); Migrant: 0 (0.0%)
  Eligible for Free Lunch Program: n/a
  Eligible for Reduced-Price Lunch Program: n/a
Teachers: 190.4 (14.3 to 1)
Librarians/Media Specialists: 3.0 (908.7 to 1)
Guidance Counselors: 9.0 (302.9 to 1)
Current Spending: ($ per student per year):
  Total: $8,473; Instruction: $5,167; Support Services: $2,878
Enrollment, Drop-out Rates and Diploma Recipients by Race/Ethnicity

Category	Total	White	Black	Asian	AIAN	Hisp.
Enrollment (%)	100.0	90.1	1.7	3.1	0.2	5.0
Drop-out Rate (%)	2.3	2.4	7.1	0.0	n/a	0.0
H.S. Diplomas (#)	240	220	3	6	0	11

Wallingford SD
142 Hope Hill Rd • Wallingford, CT 06492-2254
(203) 949-6500 • http://www.wallingford.k12.ct.us/index2.html
Grade Span: PK-12; **Agency Type:** 1
Schools: 14
  8 Primary; 2 Middle; 3 High; 1 Other Level
  12 Regular; 0 Special Education; 0 Vocational; 2 Alternative
  0 Magnet; 0 Charter; 5 Title I Eligible; 0 School-wide Title I
Students: 7,154 (50.1% male; 49.8% female)
  Individual Education Program: 705 (9.9%);
  English Language Learner: 203 (2.8%); Migrant: 8 (0.1%)
  Eligible for Free Lunch Program: n/a

Eligible for Reduced-Price Lunch Program: n/a
Teachers: 521.6 (13.7 to 1)
Librarians/Media Specialists: 13.0 (550.3 to 1)
Guidance Counselors: 16.0 (447.1 to 1)
Current Spending: ($ per student per year):
  Total: $9,232; Instruction: $5,490; Support Services: $3,370
Enrollment, Drop-out Rates and Diploma Recipients by Race/Ethnicity

Category	Total	White	Black	Asian	AIAN	Hisp.
Enrollment (%)	100.0	86.3	2.5	3.3	0.3	7.6
Drop-out Rate (%)	1.1	0.9	2.1	1.7	0.0	4.2
H.S. Diplomas (#)	462	410	10	17	0	25

Waterbury SD
236 Grand St • Waterbury, CT 06702-1972
(203) 574-8004 • http://www.waterbury.k12.ct.us/
Grade Span: PK-12; **Agency Type:** 1
Schools: 29
  21 Primary; 3 Middle; 3 High; 2 Other Level
  26 Regular; 2 Special Education; 0 Vocational; 1 Alternative
  2 Magnet; 0 Charter; 26 Title I Eligible; 0 School-wide Title I
Students: 17,714 (51.0% male; 48.9% female)
  Individual Education Program: 2,829 (16.0%);
  English Language Learner: 1,944 (11.0%); Migrant: 2,273 (12.8%)
  Eligible for Free Lunch Program: n/a
  Eligible for Reduced-Price Lunch Program: n/a
Teachers: 1,308.2 (13.5 to 1)
Librarians/Media Specialists: 18.0 (984.1 to 1)
Guidance Counselors: 18.0 (984.1 to 1)
Current Spending: ($ per student per year):
  Total: $11,001; Instruction: $6,391; Support Services: $4,011
Enrollment, Drop-out Rates and Diploma Recipients by Race/Ethnicity

Category	Total	White	Black	Asian	AIAN	Hisp.
Enrollment (%)	100.0	31.0	26.7	2.1	0.4	39.8
Drop-out Rate (%)	3.0	2.4	2.4	0.0	7.1	4.0
H.S. Diplomas (#)	578	236	158	11	3	170

West Haven SD
25 Ogden St • West Haven, CT 06516-1800
(203) 937-4300 • http://www.whschools.org/
Grade Span: PK-12; **Agency Type:** 1
Schools: 13
  9 Primary; 2 Middle; 1 High; 1 Other Level
  11 Regular; 0 Special Education; 0 Vocational; 2 Alternative
  0 Magnet; 0 Charter; 6 Title I Eligible; 0 School-wide Title I
Students: 7,177 (50.3% male; 49.6% female)
  Individual Education Program: 626 (8.7%);
  English Language Learner: 351 (4.9%); Migrant: 41 (0.6%)
  Eligible for Free Lunch Program: n/a
  Eligible for Reduced-Price Lunch Program: n/a
Teachers: 479.6 (14.9 to 1)
Librarians/Media Specialists: 9.0 (792.7 to 1)
Guidance Counselors: 10.0 (713.4 to 1)
Current Spending: ($ per student per year):
  Total: $10,112; Instruction: $6,106; Support Services: $3,586
Enrollment, Drop-out Rates and Diploma Recipients by Race/Ethnicity

Category	Total	White	Black	Asian	AIAN	Hisp.
Enrollment (%)	100.0	53.7	26.0	3.4	0.6	16.4
Drop-out Rate (%)	1.6	1.3	1.4	3.5	0.0	3.0
H.S. Diplomas (#)	340	213	70	15	2	40

Wolcott SD
154 Center St • Wolcott, CT 06716-2035
(203) 879-8183
Grade Span: PK-12; **Agency Type:** 1
Schools: 6
  3 Primary; 1 Middle; 1 High; 1 Other Level
  5 Regular; 0 Special Education; 0 Vocational; 1 Alternative
  0 Magnet; 0 Charter; 2 Title I Eligible; 0 School-wide Title I
Students: 2,939 (50.1% male; 49.8% female)
  Individual Education Program: 491 (16.7%);
  English Language Learner: 6 (0.2%); Migrant: 0 (0.0%)
  Eligible for Free Lunch Program: n/a
  Eligible for Reduced-Price Lunch Program: n/a
Teachers: 210.9 (13.9 to 1)
Librarians/Media Specialists: 2.0 (1,460.5 to 1)
Guidance Counselors: 6.0 (486.8 to 1)
Current Spending: ($ per student per year):
  Total: $9,065; Instruction: $6,151; Support Services: $2,439
Enrollment, Drop-out Rates and Diploma Recipients by Race/Ethnicity

Category	Total	White	Black	Asian	AIAN	Hisp.
Enrollment (%)	100.0	95.2	1.2	1.1	0.1	2.4
Drop-out Rate (%)	1.3	1.3	0.0	0.0	0.0	0.0
H.S. Diplomas (#)	202	198	1	1	1	1

New London County

Colchester SD
127 Norwich Ave • Colchester, CT 06415-1260
(860) 537-7267 • http://www.colchesterct.org/
Grade Span: PK-12; **Agency Type:** 1
Schools: 6
  2 Primary; 2 Middle; 1 High; 1 Other Level
  5 Regular; 0 Special Education; 0 Vocational; 1 Alternative
  0 Magnet; 0 Charter; 3 Title I Eligible; 0 School-wide Title I
Students: 3,158 (50.4% male; 49.5% female)
  Individual Education Program: 367 (11.6%);
  English Language Learner: 16 (0.5%); Migrant: 0 (0.0%)
  Eligible for Free Lunch Program: n/a
  Eligible for Reduced-Price Lunch Program: n/a
Teachers: 231.3 (13.6 to 1)
Librarians/Media Specialists: 4.0 (788.5 to 1)
Guidance Counselors: 6.0 (525.7 to 1)
Current Spending: ($ per student per year):
  Total: $8,824; Instruction: $5,574; Support Services: $2,943
Enrollment, Drop-out Rates and Diploma Recipients by Race/Ethnicity

Category	Total	White	Black	Asian	AIAN	Hisp.
Enrollment (%)	100.0	93.3	2.8	1.1	0.5	2.3
Drop-out Rate (%)	1.2	1.2	0.0	0.0	0.0	0.0
H.S. Diplomas (#)	135	128	1	1	2	3

East Lyme SD
Boston Post Rd • East Lyme, CT 06333-0176
Mailing Address: PO Box 176 • Est Lyme, CT 06333-0176
(860) 739-3966 • http://www.eastlymeschools.org/
Grade Span: PK-12; **Agency Type:** 1
Schools: 6
  3 Primary; 1 Middle; 1 High; 1 Other Level
  5 Regular; 0 Special Education; 0 Vocational; 1 Alternative
  0 Magnet; 0 Charter; 4 Title I Eligible; 0 School-wide Title I
Students: 3,262 (50.5% male; 49.4% female)
  Individual Education Program: 368 (11.3%);
  English Language Learner: 23 (0.7%); Migrant: 0 (0.0%)
  Eligible for Free Lunch Program: n/a
  Eligible for Reduced-Price Lunch Program: n/a
Teachers: 234.3 (13.8 to 1)
Librarians/Media Specialists: 4.0 (807.0 to 1)
Guidance Counselors: 7.0 (461.1 to 1)
Current Spending: ($ per student per year):
  Total: $9,450; Instruction: $5,993; Support Services: $3,073
Enrollment, Drop-out Rates and Diploma Recipients by Race/Ethnicity

Category	Total	White	Black	Asian	AIAN	Hisp.
Enrollment (%)	100.0	88.8	1.5	5.9	1.0	2.7
Drop-out Rate (%)	1.2	1.3	0.0	0.0	0.0	0.0
H.S. Diplomas (#)	235	213	5	14	1	2

Griswold SD
267 Slater Ave • Griswold, CT 06351-2540
(860) 376-7600 • http://www.griswold.k12.ct.us/
Grade Span: PK-12; **Agency Type:** 1
Schools: 4
  1 Primary; 1 Middle; 1 High; 1 Other Level
  3 Regular; 0 Special Education; 0 Vocational; 1 Alternative
  0 Magnet; 0 Charter; 2 Title I Eligible; 0 School-wide Title I
Students: 2,224 (51.3% male; 48.6% female)
  Individual Education Program: 264 (11.9%);
  English Language Learner: 12 (0.5%); Migrant: 0 (0.0%)
  Eligible for Free Lunch Program: n/a
  Eligible for Reduced-Price Lunch Program: n/a
Teachers: 158.9 (14.0 to 1)
Librarians/Media Specialists: 3.0 (740.7 to 1)
Guidance Counselors: 7.0 (317.4 to 1)
Current Spending: ($ per student per year):
  Total: $9,694; Instruction: $6,247; Support Services: $3,012
Enrollment, Drop-out Rates and Diploma Recipients by Race/Ethnicity

Category	Total	White	Black	Asian	AIAN	Hisp.
Enrollment (%)	100.0	92.7	1.9	1.7	1.6	2.1
Drop-out Rate (%)	2.8	3.0	0.0	0.0	0.0	0.0
H.S. Diplomas (#)	126	119	3	1	1	2

Groton SD
1300 Flanders Rd • Mystic, CT 06355-1042
(860) 572-2120 • http://www.groton.k12.ct.us/
Grade Span: PK-12; **Agency Type:** 1
Schools: 14
  9 Primary; 2 Middle; 1 High; 2 Other Level
  13 Regular; 0 Special Education; 0 Vocational; 1 Alternative
  0 Magnet; 0 Charter; 6 Title I Eligible; 0 School-wide Title I
Students: 5,753 (50.8% male; 49.1% female)
  Individual Education Program: 838 (14.6%);

English Language Learner: 109 (1.9%); Migrant: 0 (0.0%)
  Eligible for Free Lunch Program: n/a
  Eligible for Reduced-Price Lunch Program: n/a
Teachers: 436.8 (13.0 to 1)
Librarians/Media Specialists: 14.0 (406.9 to 1)
Guidance Counselors: 12.0 (474.8 to 1)
Current Spending: ($ per student per year):
  Total: $11,470; Instruction: $7,173; Support Services: $4,038
Enrollment, Drop-out Rates and Diploma Recipients by Race/Ethnicity

Category	Total	White	Black	Asian	AIAN	Hisp.
Enrollment (%)	100.0	72.0	12.8	5.4	1.5	8.3
Drop-out Rate (%)	0.7	0.7	1.2	0.0	0.0	0.0
H.S. Diplomas (#)	239	195	23	11	2	8

Lebanon SD
891 Exeter Rd • Lebanon, CT 06249-1742
Mailing Address: PO Box 166 • Lebanon, CT 06249-1742
(860) 642-7795
Grade Span: PK-12; **Agency Type:** 1
Schools: 4
  1 Primary; 1 Middle; 1 High; 1 Other Level
  3 Regular; 0 Special Education; 0 Vocational; 1 Alternative
  0 Magnet; 0 Charter; 1 Title I Eligible; 0 School-wide Title I
Students: 1,543 (47.8% male; 52.1% female)
  Individual Education Program: 182 (11.8%);
  English Language Learner: 4 (0.3%); Migrant: 3 (0.2%)
  Eligible for Free Lunch Program: n/a
  Eligible for Reduced-Price Lunch Program: n/a
Teachers: 109.7 (14.0 to 1)
Librarians/Media Specialists: 3.0 (511.7 to 1)
Guidance Counselors: 5.0 (307.0 to 1)
Current Spending: ($ per student per year):
  Total: $8,930; Instruction: $5,276; Support Services: $3,351
Enrollment, Drop-out Rates and Diploma Recipients by Race/Ethnicity

Category	Total	White	Black	Asian	AIAN	Hisp.
Enrollment (%)	100.0	96.7	0.6	0.4	0.6	1.8
Drop-out Rate (%)	1.2	1.3	0.0	0.0	0.0	0.0
H.S. Diplomas (#)	128	125	1	2	0	0

Ledyard SD
4 Blonder Blvd • Ledyard, CT 06339-1504
(860) 464-9255 • http://www.ledyardschools.org/
Grade Span: PK-12; **Agency Type:** 1
Schools: 7
  4 Primary; 1 Middle; 1 High; 1 Other Level
  6 Regular; 0 Special Education; 0 Vocational; 1 Alternative
  0 Magnet; 0 Charter; 2 Title I Eligible; 0 School-wide Title I
Students: 2,989 (50.0% male; 49.9% female)
  Individual Education Program: 353 (11.8%);
  English Language Learner: 21 (0.7%); Migrant: 0 (0.0%)
  Eligible for Free Lunch Program: n/a
  Eligible for Reduced-Price Lunch Program: n/a
Teachers: 208.6 (14.2 to 1)
Librarians/Media Specialists: 4.0 (739.8 to 1)
Guidance Counselors: 7.0 (422.7 to 1)
Current Spending: ($ per student per year):
  Total: $8,934; Instruction: $5,808; Support Services: $3,017
Enrollment, Drop-out Rates and Diploma Recipients by Race/Ethnicity

Category	Total	White	Black	Asian	AIAN	Hisp.
Enrollment (%)	100.0	84.1	4.4	3.0	4.4	4.0
Drop-out Rate (%)	16.9	16.4	27.3	20.0	29.7	7.8
H.S. Diplomas (#)	230	205	6	5	2	12

Montville SD
Old Colchester Rd • Oakdale, CT 06370-0078
(860) 848-1228 • http://www.montvilleschools.org/
Grade Span: PK-12; **Agency Type:** 1
Schools: 7
  3 Primary; 1 Middle; 2 High; 1 Other Level
  5 Regular; 0 Special Education; 0 Vocational; 2 Alternative
  0 Magnet; 0 Charter; 3 Title I Eligible; 0 School-wide Title I
Students: 2,933 (52.9% male; 47.0% female)
  Individual Education Program: 428 (14.6%);
  English Language Learner: 63 (2.1%); Migrant: 0 (0.0%)
  Eligible for Free Lunch Program: n/a
  Eligible for Reduced-Price Lunch Program: n/a
Teachers: 227.8 (12.8 to 1)
Librarians/Media Specialists: 5.0 (585.2 to 1)
Guidance Counselors: 6.0 (487.7 to 1)
Current Spending: ($ per student per year):
  Total: $10,254; Instruction: $6,640; Support Services: $3,211

Enrollment, Drop-out Rates and Diploma Recipients by Race/Ethnicity

Category	Total	White	Black	Asian	AIAN	Hisp.
Enrollment (%)	100.0	84.4	4.7	3.8	2.1	5.0
Drop-out Rate (%)	2.0	1.5	6.5	0.0	9.5	3.4
H.S. Diplomas (#)	159	141	5	4	6	3

New London SD

134 Williams St • New London, CT 06320-5296
(860) 447-6000 • http://www.newlondon.org/
Grade Span: PK-12; **Agency Type:** 1
Schools: 9
    5 Primary; 1 Middle; 1 High; 2 Other Level
    8 Regular; 0 Special Education; 0 Vocational; 1 Alternative
    0 Magnet; 0 Charter; 5 Title I Eligible; 5 School-wide Title I
Students: 3,205   (52.4% male; 47.5% female)
    Individual Education Program: 464 (14.5%);
    English Language Learner: 639 (19.9%); Migrant: 207 (6.9%)
    Eligible for Free Lunch Program: n/a
    Eligible for Reduced-Price Lunch Program: n/a
Teachers: 240.2 (12.4 to 1)
Librarians/Media Specialists: 3.0 (994.3 to 1)
Guidance Counselors: 8.0 (372.9 to 1)
Current Spending: ($ per student per year):
    Total: $13,618; Instruction: $8,709; Support Services: $4,409

Enrollment, Drop-out Rates and Diploma Recipients by Race/Ethnicity

Category	Total	White	Black	Asian	AIAN	Hisp.
Enrollment (%)	100.0	18.8	32.7	2.0	1.5	45.0
Drop-out Rate (%)	13.4	17.7	11.2	25.0	66.7	12.2
H.S. Diplomas (#)	121	34	47	3	3	34

Norwich Free Academy

305 Broadway • Norwich, CT 06360-3563
(860) 887-2004 • http://WWW.norwichfreeacademy.com/
Grade Span: 09-12; **Agency Type:** 7
Schools: 1
    0 Primary; 0 Middle; 1 High; 0 Other Level
    1 Regular; 0 Special Education; 0 Vocational; 0 Alternative
    0 Magnet; 0 Charter; 0 Title I Eligible; 0 School-wide Title I
Students: 2,348   (46.8% male; 53.1% female)
    Individual Education Program: 245 (10.4%);
    English Language Learner: 64 (2.7%); Migrant: 3 (0.1%)
    Eligible for Free Lunch Program: n/a
    Eligible for Reduced-Price Lunch Program: n/a
Teachers: 148.4 (15.8 to 1)
Librarians/Media Specialists: 2.0 (1,170.5 to 1)
Guidance Counselors: 11.0 (212.8 to 1)
Current Spending: ($ per student per year):
    Total: $0; Instruction: $0; Support Services: $0

Enrollment, Drop-out Rates and Diploma Recipients by Race/Ethnicity

Category	Total	White	Black	Asian	AIAN	Hisp.
Enrollment (%)	100.0	76.4	10.3	4.1	1.9	7.4
Drop-out Rate (%)	4.0	3.6	5.2	1.5	2.5	9.5
H.S. Diplomas (#)	497	414	44	18	6	15

Norwich SD

90 Town St • Norwich, CT 06360-2324
(860) 823-4200 • http://www.norwichschools.org
Grade Span: PK-12; **Agency Type:** 1
Schools: 15
    9 Primary; 3 Middle; 3 High; 0 Other Level
    12 Regular; 1 Special Education; 0 Vocational; 2 Alternative
    0 Magnet; 0 Charter; 12 Title I Eligible; 8 School-wide Title I
Students: 4,002   (50.2% male; 49.7% female)
    Individual Education Program: 606 (15.1%);
    English Language Learner: 256 (6.4%); Migrant: 21 (0.5%)
    Eligible for Free Lunch Program: n/a
    Eligible for Reduced-Price Lunch Program: n/a
Teachers: 254.0 (15.8 to 1)
Librarians/Media Specialists: 4.0 (1,000.5 to 1)
Guidance Counselors: 9.0 (444.7 to 1)
Current Spending: ($ per student per year):
    Total: $10,682; Instruction: $6,872; Support Services: $3,440

Enrollment, Drop-out Rates and Diploma Recipients by Race/Ethnicity

Category	Total	White	Black	Asian	AIAN	Hisp.
Enrollment (%)	100.0	58.4	20.0	4.7	2.0	14.8
Drop-out Rate (%)	30.6	28.1	52.9	0.0	0.0	27.3
H.S. Diplomas (#)	11	8	2	0	0	1

Regional SD 18

4 Davis Rd W • Old Lyme, CT 06371-2334
(860) 434-7238
Grade Span: PK-12; **Agency Type:** 1
Schools: 6
    3 Primary; 1 Middle; 1 High; 1 Other Level
    5 Regular; 0 Special Education; 0 Vocational; 1 Alternative

    0 Magnet; 0 Charter; 1 Title I Eligible; 0 School-wide Title I
Students: 1,567   (50.0% male; 49.9% female)
    Individual Education Program: 179 (11.4%);
    English Language Learner: 5 (0.3%); Migrant: 0 (0.0%)
    Eligible for Free Lunch Program: n/a
    Eligible for Reduced-Price Lunch Program: n/a
Teachers: 125.0 (12.5 to 1)
Librarians/Media Specialists: 5.0 (313.4 to 1)
Guidance Counselors: 3.0 (522.3 to 1)
Current Spending: ($ per student per year):
    Total: $12,982; Instruction: $7,045; Support Services: $5,489

Enrollment, Drop-out Rates and Diploma Recipients by Race/Ethnicity

Category	Total	White	Black	Asian	AIAN	Hisp.
Enrollment (%)	100.0	94.8	0.8	3.0	0.1	1.3
Drop-out Rate (%)	1.1	0.9	50.0	0.0	n/a	0.0
H.S. Diplomas (#)	94	92	0	0	0	2

Stonington SD

49 N Stonington Rd • Old Mystic, CT 06372-0479
(860) 572-0506 • http://stamford.k12.ct.us/
Grade Span: PK-12; **Agency Type:** 1
Schools: 8
    4 Primary; 2 Middle; 1 High; 1 Other Level
    6 Regular; 1 Special Education; 0 Vocational; 1 Alternative
    0 Magnet; 0 Charter; 3 Title I Eligible; 0 School-wide Title I
Students: 2,479   (52.1% male; 47.8% female)
    Individual Education Program: 285 (11.5%);
    English Language Learner: 10 (0.4%); Migrant: 0 (0.0%)
    Eligible for Free Lunch Program: n/a
    Eligible for Reduced-Price Lunch Program: n/a
Teachers: 179.7 (13.6 to 1)
Librarians/Media Specialists: 4.0 (611.3 to 1)
Guidance Counselors: 4.0 (611.3 to 1)
Current Spending: ($ per student per year):
    Total: $10,315; Instruction: $6,291; Support Services: $3,616

Enrollment, Drop-out Rates and Diploma Recipients by Race/Ethnicity

Category	Total	White	Black	Asian	AIAN	Hisp.
Enrollment (%)	100.0	92.1	1.7	2.4	1.5	2.3
Drop-out Rate (%)	1.9	1.8	0.0	0.0	0.0	14.3
H.S. Diplomas (#)	141	136	2	1	0	2

Waterford SD

15 Rope Ferry Rd • Waterford, CT 06385-2886
(860) 444-5870 • http://www.waterfordschools.org/
Grade Span: PK-12; **Agency Type:** 1
Schools: 9
    6 Primary; 1 Middle; 0 High; 2 Other Level
    8 Regular; 0 Special Education; 0 Vocational; 1 Alternative
    0 Magnet; 0 Charter; 4 Title I Eligible; 0 School-wide Title I
Students: 3,109   (50.4% male; 49.5% female)
    Individual Education Program: 368 (11.8%);
    English Language Learner: 16 (0.5%); Migrant: 0 (0.0%)
    Eligible for Free Lunch Program: n/a
    Eligible for Reduced-Price Lunch Program: n/a
Teachers: 234.1 (13.2 to 1)
Librarians/Media Specialists: 2.0 (1,547.5 to 1)
Guidance Counselors: 8.0 (386.9 to 1)
Current Spending: ($ per student per year):
    Total: $11,101; Instruction: $7,013; Support Services: $3,659

Enrollment, Drop-out Rates and Diploma Recipients by Race/Ethnicity

Category	Total	White	Black	Asian	AIAN	Hisp.
Enrollment (%)	100.0	87.6	4.2	4.3	0.5	3.5
Drop-out Rate (%)	0.9	1.0	0.0	0.0	0.0	0.0
H.S. Diplomas (#)	191	171	9	7	2	2

Tolland County

Coventry SD

1700 Main St • Coventry, CT 06238-1654
(860) 742-7317 • http://www.CoventryPS.org/
Grade Span: PK-12; **Agency Type:** 1
Schools: 5
    3 Primary; 1 Middle; 1 High; 0 Other Level
    4 Regular; 0 Special Education; 0 Vocational; 1 Alternative
    0 Magnet; 0 Charter; 2 Title I Eligible; 0 School-wide Title I
Students: 2,101   (51.3% male; 48.6% female)
    Individual Education Program: 267 (12.7%);
    English Language Learner: 0 (0.0%); Migrant: 0 (0.0%)
    Eligible for Free Lunch Program: n/a
    Eligible for Reduced-Price Lunch Program: n/a
Teachers: 153.9 (13.6 to 1)
Librarians/Media Specialists: 1.0 (2,095.0 to 1)
Guidance Counselors: 4.0 (523.8 to 1)
Current Spending: ($ per student per year):
    Total: $8,929; Instruction: $5,459; Support Services: $3,028

Enrollment, Drop-out Rates and Diploma Recipients by Race/Ethnicity

Category	Total	White	Black	Asian	AIAN	Hisp.
Enrollment (%)	100.0	96.1	1.0	0.6	0.5	1.9
Drop-out Rate (%)	4.3	4.3	0.0	0.0	0.0	20.0
H.S. Diplomas (#)	101	98	1	1	0	1

Ellington SD

47 Main St • Ellington, CT 06029-3341
Mailing Address: PO Box 157 • Ellington, CT 06029-3341
(860) 896-2300 • http://www.ellingtonschools.org/
Grade Span: PK-12; Agency Type: 1
Schools: 6
   3 Primary; 1 Middle; 1 High; 1 Other Level
   5 Regular; 0 Special Education; 0 Vocational; 1 Alternative
   0 Magnet; 0 Charter; 2 Title I Eligible; 0 School-wide Title I
Students: 2,371 (50.0% male; 49.9% female)
   Individual Education Program: 220 (9.3%);
   English Language Learner: 23 (1.0%); Migrant: 0 (0.0%)
   Eligible for Free Lunch Program: n/a
   Eligible for Reduced-Price Lunch Program: n/a
Teachers: 163.3 (14.5 to 1)
Librarians/Media Specialists: 3.0 (790.3 to 1)
Guidance Counselors: 5.0 (474.2 to 1)
Current Spending: ($ per student per year):
   Total: $9,530; Instruction: $6,173; Support Services: $2,961
Enrollment, Drop-out Rates and Diploma Recipients by Race/Ethnicity

Category	Total	White	Black	Asian	AIAN	Hisp.
Enrollment (%)	100.0	94.8	1.4	2.1	0.0	1.6
Drop-out Rate (%)	0.5	0.5	0.0	0.0	0.0	0.0
H.S. Diplomas (#)	113	110	0	1	2	0

Regional SD 08

33 Pendleton Dr • Hebron, CT 06248-1525
(860) 228-9417
Grade Span: 07-12; Agency Type: 1
Schools: 3
   0 Primary; 1 Middle; 1 High; 1 Other Level
   2 Regular; 0 Special Education; 0 Vocational; 1 Alternative
   0 Magnet; 0 Charter; 1 Title I Eligible; 0 School-wide Title I
Students: 1,574 (51.5% male; 48.4% female)
   Individual Education Program: 148 (9.4%);
   English Language Learner: 0 (0.0%); Migrant: 0 (0.0%)
   Eligible for Free Lunch Program: n/a
   Eligible for Reduced-Price Lunch Program: n/a
Teachers: 127.4 (12.3 to 1)
Librarians/Media Specialists: 2.0 (786.0 to 1)
Guidance Counselors: 6.0 (262.0 to 1)
Current Spending: ($ per student per year):
   Total: $10,544; Instruction: $6,693; Support Services: $3,343
Enrollment, Drop-out Rates and Diploma Recipients by Race/Ethnicity

Category	Total	White	Black	Asian	AIAN	Hisp.
Enrollment (%)	100.0	96.7	0.8	1.0	0.3	1.3
Drop-out Rate (%)	1.4	1.5	0.0	0.0	0.0	0.0
H.S. Diplomas (#)	205	201	2	1	0	1

Somers SD

Ninth District Rd • Somers, CT 06071-9609
(860) 749-2270 • http://www.somers.k12.ct.us/
Grade Span: PK-12; Agency Type: 1
Schools: 4
   2 Primary; 1 Middle; 1 High; 0 Other Level
   3 Regular; 0 Special Education; 0 Vocational; 1 Alternative
   0 Magnet; 0 Charter; 0 Title I Eligible; 0 School-wide Title I
Students: 1,735 (51.2% male; 48.7% female)
   Individual Education Program: 148 (8.5%);
   English Language Learner: 1 (0.1%); Migrant: 0 (0.0%)
   Eligible for Free Lunch Program: n/a
   Eligible for Reduced-Price Lunch Program: n/a
Teachers: 125.3 (13.8 to 1)
Librarians/Media Specialists: 4.0 (432.5 to 1)
Guidance Counselors: 3.0 (576.7 to 1)
Current Spending: ($ per student per year):
   Total: $9,012; Instruction: $5,994; Support Services: $2,914
Enrollment, Drop-out Rates and Diploma Recipients by Race/Ethnicity

Category	Total	White	Black	Asian	AIAN	Hisp.
Enrollment (%)	100.0	96.9	1.0	0.9	0.1	1.0
Drop-out Rate (%)	4.2	3.7	0.0	0.0	n/a	42.9
H.S. Diplomas (#)	95	93	0	2	0	0

Stafford SD

263 E St Route 19 • Stafford Springs, CT 06076-0147
Mailing Address: PO Box 147 • Stafford Springs, CT 06076-0147
(860) 684-4211 • http://www.stafford.ctschool.net/
Grade Span: PK-12; Agency Type: 1
Schools: 7

   3 Primary; 2 Middle; 1 High; 1 Other Level
   6 Regular; 0 Special Education; 0 Vocational; 1 Alternative
   0 Magnet; 0 Charter; 2 Title I Eligible; 0 School-wide Title I
Students: 1,994 (48.7% male; 51.2% female)
   Individual Education Program: 195 (9.8%);
   English Language Learner: 16 (0.8%); Migrant: 0 (0.0%)
   Eligible for Free Lunch Program: n/a
   Eligible for Reduced-Price Lunch Program: n/a
Teachers: 162.7 (12.2 to 1)
Librarians/Media Specialists: 2.0 (994.0 to 1)
Guidance Counselors: 3.0 (662.7 to 1)
Current Spending: ($ per student per year):
   Total: $10,064; Instruction: $6,310; Support Services: $3,410
Enrollment, Drop-out Rates and Diploma Recipients by Race/Ethnicity

Category	Total	White	Black	Asian	AIAN	Hisp.
Enrollment (%)	100.0	94.8	1.5	1.4	0.2	2.2
Drop-out Rate (%)	2.5	2.5	25.0	0.0	0.0	0.0
H.S. Diplomas (#)	92	85	1	3	0	3

Tolland SD

51 Tolland Green • Tolland, CT 06084-3099
(860) 870-7737 • http://www.tolland.k12.ct.us/
Grade Span: PK-12; Agency Type: 1
Schools: 5
   2 Primary; 1 Middle; 1 High; 1 Other Level
   4 Regular; 0 Special Education; 0 Vocational; 1 Alternative
   0 Magnet; 0 Charter; 2 Title I Eligible; 0 School-wide Title I
Students: 3,053 (51.8% male; 48.1% female)
   Individual Education Program: 338 (11.1%);
   English Language Learner: 13 (0.4%); Migrant: 0 (0.0%)
   Eligible for Free Lunch Program: n/a
   Eligible for Reduced-Price Lunch Program: n/a
Teachers: 232.6 (13.0 to 1)
Librarians/Media Specialists: 4.0 (754.5 to 1)
Guidance Counselors: 8.0 (377.3 to 1)
Current Spending: ($ per student per year):
   Total: $8,920; Instruction: $5,710; Support Services: $2,874
Enrollment, Drop-out Rates and Diploma Recipients by Race/Ethnicity

Category	Total	White	Black	Asian	AIAN	Hisp.
Enrollment (%)	100.0	95.7	1.0	2.0	0.3	1.0
Drop-out Rate (%)	1.9	1.9	0.0	0.0	n/a	0.0
H.S. Diplomas (#)	169	163	0	4	1	1

Vernon SD

30 Park St • Vernon, CT 06066-3244
Mailing Address: PO Box 600 • Vernon, CT 06066-3244
(860) 870-6000 • http://www.vernonct.com/
Grade Span: PK-12; Agency Type: 1
Schools: 8
   5 Primary; 1 Middle; 1 High; 1 Other Level
   7 Regular; 0 Special Education; 0 Vocational; 1 Alternative
   0 Magnet; 0 Charter; 4 Title I Eligible; 0 School-wide Title I
Students: 4,021 (50.1% male; 49.8% female)
   Individual Education Program: 340 (8.5%);
   English Language Learner: 87 (2.2%); Migrant: 0 (0.0%)
   Eligible for Free Lunch Program: n/a
   Eligible for Reduced-Price Lunch Program: n/a
Teachers: 300.3 (13.4 to 1)
Librarians/Media Specialists: 0.0 (n/a to 1)
Guidance Counselors: 9.0 (446.4 to 1)
Current Spending: ($ per student per year):
   Total: $10,388; Instruction: $6,804; Support Services: $3,318
Enrollment, Drop-out Rates and Diploma Recipients by Race/Ethnicity

Category	Total	White	Black	Asian	AIAN	Hisp.
Enrollment (%)	100.0	78.2	9.4	5.4	0.6	6.3
Drop-out Rate (%)	2.8	2.6	2.6	0.0	n/a	11.1
H.S. Diplomas (#)	235	225	3	6	0	1

Windham County

Killingly SD

369 Main St • Danielson, CT 06239-0210
Mailing Address: PO Box 210 • Danielson, CT 06239-0210
(860) 779-6600 • http://killingly.k12.ct.us/
Grade Span: PK-12; Agency Type: 1
Schools: 6
   3 Primary; 1 Middle; 1 High; 1 Other Level
   5 Regular; 0 Special Education; 0 Vocational; 1 Alternative
   0 Magnet; 0 Charter; 2 Title I Eligible; 0 School-wide Title I
Students: 2,924 (51.7% male; 48.2% female)
   Individual Education Program: 411 (14.1%);
   English Language Learner: 90 (3.1%); Migrant: 46 (1.6%)
   Eligible for Free Lunch Program: n/a
   Eligible for Reduced-Price Lunch Program: n/a
Teachers: 209.3 (14.0 to 1)
Librarians/Media Specialists: 4.0 (731.0 to 1)

Guidance Counselors: 6.0 (487.3 to 1)
Current Spending: ($ per student per year):
   Total: $9,934; Instruction: $6,265; Support Services: $3,345
Enrollment, Drop-out Rates and Diploma Recipients by Race/Ethnicity

Category	Total	White	Black	Asian	AIAN	Hisp.
Enrollment (%)	100.0	89.3	3.9	2.3	1.0	3.5
Drop-out Rate (%)	5.7	5.8	7.4	4.3	n/a	0.0
H.S. Diplomas (#)	203	187	5	9	0	2

Plainfield SD

651 Norwich Rd • Plainfield, CT 06374
Mailing Address: 99 Putnam Rd • Plainfield, CT 06374
(860) 564-6403 • http://www.plainfieldschools.org/
Grade Span: PK-12; Agency Type: 1
Schools: 7
   3 Primary; 2 Middle; 1 High; 1 Other Level
   5 Regular; 0 Special Education; 0 Vocational; 2 Alternative
   0 Magnet; 0 Charter; 5 Title I Eligible; 0 School-wide Title I
Students: 2,633   (52.7% male; 47.2% female)
   Individual Education Program: 301 (11.4%);
   English Language Learner: 3 (0.1%); Migrant: 0 (0.0%)
   Eligible for Free Lunch Program: n/a
   Eligible for Reduced-Price Lunch Program: n/a
Teachers: 174.0 (15.1 to 1)
Librarians/Media Specialists: 1.0 (2,630.0 to 1)
Guidance Counselors: 8.0 (328.8 to 1)
Current Spending: ($ per student per year):
   Total: $9,966; Instruction: $6,300; Support Services: $3,348
Enrollment, Drop-out Rates and Diploma Recipients by Race/Ethnicity

Category	Total	White	Black	Asian	AIAN	Hisp.
Enrollment (%)	100.0	92.4	1.8	0.9	1.5	3.5
Drop-out Rate (%)	6.0	6.0	0.0	0.0	0.0	9.1
H.S. Diplomas (#)	164	153	1	2	2	6

Windham SD

322 Prospect St • Willimantic, CT 06226-2202
(860) 465-2310 • http://www.windham.k12.ct.us/
Grade Span: PK-12; Agency Type: 1
Schools: 10
   6 Primary; 1 Middle; 1 High; 2 Other Level
   8 Regular; 1 Special Education; 0 Vocational; 1 Alternative
   0 Magnet; 0 Charter; 4 Title I Eligible; 4 School-wide Title I
Students: 3,597   (51.8% male; 48.1% female)
   Individual Education Program: 501 (13.9%);
   English Language Learner: 480 (13.3%); Migrant: 985 (27.6%)
   Eligible for Free Lunch Program: n/a
   Eligible for Reduced-Price Lunch Program: n/a
Teachers: 278.8 (12.8 to 1)
Librarians/Media Specialists: 4.0 (891.8 to 1)
Guidance Counselors: 8.0 (445.9 to 1)
Current Spending: ($ per student per year):
   Total: $12,360; Instruction: $7,685; Support Services: $4,185
Enrollment, Drop-out Rates and Diploma Recipients by Race/Ethnicity

Category	Total	White	Black	Asian	AIAN	Hisp.
Enrollment (%)	100.0	39.4	5.1	1.1	0.5	53.9
Drop-out Rate (%)	5.0	3.6	6.8	0.0	0.0	6.9
H.S. Diplomas (#)	196	135	9	7	0	45

Number of Schools

Rank	Number	District Name	City
1	50	New Haven SD	New Haven
2	40	Hartford SD	Hartford
3	38	Bridgeport SD	Bridgeport
4	29	Waterbury SD	Waterbury
5	22	Stamford SD	Stamford
6	20	Norwalk SD	Norwalk
7	18	Danbury SD	Danbury
8	17	Manchester SD	Manchester
8	17	State Vocational-Technical Schools	Middletown
10	16	Bristol SD	Bristol
10	16	East Hartford SD	East Hartford
10	16	Fairfield SD	Fairfield
10	16	Greenwich SD	Greenwich
10	16	Milford SD	Milford
10	16	New Britain SD	New Britain
10	16	West Hartford SD	West Hartford
17	15	Norwich SD	Norwich
18	14	Enfield SD	Enfield
18	14	Groton SD	Mystic
18	14	Stratford SD	Stratford
18	14	Wallingford SD	Wallingford
22	13	East Haven SD	East Haven
22	13	Meriden SD	Meriden
22	13	Southington SD	Southington
22	13	West Haven SD	West Haven
26	12	Hamden SD	Hamden
26	12	Middletown SD	Middletown
26	12	Naugatuck SD	Naugatuck
29	11	Trumbull SD	Trumbull
30	10	Ridgefield SD	Ridgefield
30	10	Shelton SD	Shelton
30	10	Windham SD	Willimantic
33	9	Cheshire SD	Cheshire
33	9	Glastonbury SD	Glastonbury
33	9	New London SD	New London
33	9	Torrington SD	Torrington
33	9	Waterford SD	Waterford
33	9	Westport SD	Westport
39	8	Darien SD	Darien
39	8	Farmington SD	Farmington
39	8	Guilford SD	Guilford
39	8	Madison SD	Madison
39	8	Newington SD	Newington
39	8	Newtown SD	Newtown
39	8	Regional SD 15	Middlebury
39	8	Simsbury SD	Simsbury
39	8	South Windsor SD	South Windsor
39	8	Stonington SD	Old Mystic
39	8	Vernon SD	Vernon
39	8	Wethersfield SD	Wethersfield
39	8	Windsor SD	Windsor
52	7	Branford SD	Branford
52	7	Ledyard SD	Ledyard
52	7	Monroe SD	Monroe
52	7	Montville SD	Oakdale
52	7	New Canaan SD	New Canaan
52	7	New Milford SD	New Milford
52	7	North Haven SD	North Haven
52	7	Plainfield SD	Plainfield
52	7	Plainville SD	Plainville
52	7	Regional SD 13	Durham
52	7	Stafford SD	Stafford Spgs
52	7	Watertown SD	Watertown
64	6	Avon SD	Avon
64	6	Berlin SD	Berlin
64	6	Bethel SD	Bethel
64	6	Bloomfield SD	Bloomfield
64	6	Capitol Region Education Council	Hartford
64	6	Colchester SD	Colchester
64	6	East Lyme SD	East Lyme
64	6	Ellington SD	Ellington
64	6	Granby SD	Granby
64	6	Killingly SD	Danielson
64	6	North Branford SD	Northford
64	6	Plymouth SD	Terryville
64	6	Regional SD 14	Woodbury
64	6	Regional SD 16	Prospect
64	6	Regional SD 17	Higganum
64	6	Regional SD 18	Old Lyme
64	6	Rocky Hill SD	Rocky Hill
64	6	Seymour SD	Seymour
64	6	Suffield SD	Suffield
64	6	Wilton SD	Wilton
64	6	Wolcott SD	Wolcott
85	5	Ansonia SD	Ansonia
85	5	Brookfield SD	Brookfield
85	5	Clinton SD	Clinton
85	5	Coventry SD	Coventry
85	5	East Hampton SD	East Hampton
85	5	New Fairfield SD	New Fairfield
85	5	Regional SD 10	Burlington
85	5	Tolland SD	Tolland
85	5	Windsor Locks SD	Windsor Locks
94	4	Area Coop Educational Services	North Haven
94	4	Canton SD	Canton
94	4	Cromwell SD	Cromwell
94	4	Derby SD	Derby
94	4	East Windsor SD	East Windsor
94	4	Griswold SD	Griswold
94	4	Lebanon SD	Lebanon
94	4	Old Saybrook SD	Old Saybrook
94	4	Regional SD 05	Woodbridge
94	4	Somers SD	Somers
94	4	Weston SD	Weston
105	3	Regional SD 08	Hebron
106	1	Norwich Free Academy	Norwich

Number of Teachers

Rank	Number	District Name	City
1	1,717	Hartford SD	Hartford
2	1,485	Bridgeport SD	Bridgeport
3	1,410	New Haven SD	New Haven
4	1,308	Waterbury SD	Waterbury
5	1,209	Stamford SD	Stamford
6	1,086	State Vocational-Technical Schools	Middletown
7	787	Norwalk SD	Norwalk
8	751	West Hartford SD	West Hartford
9	749	Greenwich SD	Greenwich
10	729	New Britain SD	New Britain
11	703	Fairfield SD	Fairfield
12	657	Danbury SD	Danbury
13	612	Meriden SD	Meriden
14	603	Bristol SD	Bristol
15	576	Milford SD	Milford
16	542	East Hartford SD	East Hartford
17	541	Manchester SD	Manchester
18	521	Wallingford SD	Wallingford
19	517	Stratford SD	Stratford
20	496	Southington SD	Southington
21	493	Enfield SD	Enfield
22	479	West Haven SD	West Haven
23	447	Glastonbury SD	Glastonbury
24	445	Westport SD	Westport
25	436	Groton SD	Mystic
26	429	Trumbull SD	Trumbull
27	404	Hamden SD	Hamden
28	394	Middletown SD	Middletown
29	373	Shelton SD	Shelton
30	362	Ridgefield SD	Ridgefield
31	351	Darien SD	Darien
32	349	New Milford SD	New Milford
33	345	Naugatuck SD	Naugatuck
34	344	Newtown SD	Newtown
34	344	Windsor SD	Windsor
36	334	Simsbury SD	Simsbury
37	329	South Windsor SD	South Windsor
38	316	Cheshire SD	Cheshire
39	311	Torrington SD	Torrington
40	309	Farmington SD	Farmington
41	305	Wilton SD	Wilton
42	300	Vernon SD	Vernon
43	297	New Canaan SD	New Canaan
44	295	Newington SD	Newington
45	290	Regional SD 15	Middlebury
46	289	Monroe SD	Monroe
47	278	Windham SD	Willimantic
48	274	Branford SD	Branford
49	261	Madison SD	Madison
50	254	Norwich SD	Norwich
51	252	East Haven SD	East Haven
52	250	Guilford SD	Guilford
53	244	Wethersfield SD	Wethersfield
54	243	North Haven SD	North Haven
55	242	Bethel SD	Bethel
56	240	New London SD	New London
57	236	Capitol Region Education Council	Hartford
58	234	East Lyme SD	East Lyme
59	234	Waterford SD	Waterford
60	233	Watertown SD	Watertown
61	232	Tolland SD	Tolland
62	231	Colchester SD	Colchester
63	227	Montville SD	Oakdale
64	227	Berlin SD	Berlin
65	219	Area Coop Educational Services	North Haven
66	218	Brookfield SD	Brookfield
67	217	New Fairfield SD	New Fairfield
68	215	Avon SD	Avon
69	210	Wolcott SD	Wolcott
70	209	Killingly SD	Danielson
71	208	Ledyard SD	Ledyard
72	205	Bloomfield SD	Bloomfield
73	199	Regional SD 17	Higganum
74	198	Regional SD 10	Burlington
75	198	Weston SD	Weston
76	190	Seymour SD	Seymour
77	189	Regional SD 16	Prospect
78	187	Plainville SD	Plainville
79	186	Rocky Hill SD	Rocky Hill
80	182	Regional SD 05	Woodbridge
81	179	Stonington SD	Old Mystic
82	175	Regional SD 14	Woodbury
83	174	Plainfield SD	Plainfield
84	171	Regional SD 13	Durham
85	170	Clinton SD	Clinton
86	168	Suffield SD	Suffield
87	164	Ansonia SD	Ansonia
88	163	Ellington SD	Ellington
89	162	Stafford SD	Stafford Spgs
90	158	Griswold SD	Griswold
91	157	Windsor Locks SD	Windsor Locks
92	153	Coventry SD	Coventry
93	149	Cromwell SD	Cromwell
94	148	Norwich Free Academy	Norwich
95	147	North Branford SD	Northford
96	141	Plymouth SD	Terryville
97	139	East Hampton SD	East Hampton
98	136	Old Saybrook SD	Old Saybrook
99	133	Granby SD	Granby
100	127	Regional SD 08	Hebron
101	125	Somers SD	Somers
102	125	Regional SD 18	Old Lyme
103	112	Canton SD	Canton
104	109	Lebanon SD	Lebanon
105	107	East Windsor SD	East Windsor
106	100	Derby SD	Derby

Number of Students

Rank	Number	District Name	City
1	22,828	Bridgeport SD	Bridgeport
2	22,578	Hartford SD	Hartford
3	20,457	New Haven SD	New Haven
4	17,714	Waterbury SD	Waterbury
5	15,307	Stamford SD	Stamford
6	11,253	State Vocational-Technical Schools	Middletown
7	11,109	Norwalk SD	Norwalk
8	10,789	New Britain SD	New Britain
9	9,816	West Hartford SD	West Hartford
10	9,527	Danbury SD	Danbury
11	9,081	Greenwich SD	Greenwich
12	9,004	Bristol SD	Bristol
13	8,894	Meriden SD	Meriden
14	8,803	Fairfield SD	Fairfield
15	7,926	East Hartford SD	East Hartford
16	7,666	Stratford SD	Stratford
17	7,655	Manchester SD	Manchester
18	7,559	Milford SD	Milford
19	7,177	West Haven SD	West Haven
20	7,154	Wallingford SD	Wallingford
21	6,769	Southington SD	Southington
22	6,744	Enfield SD	Enfield
23	6,612	Trumbull SD	Trumbull
24	6,537	Glastonbury SD	Glastonbury
25	6,340	Hamden SD	Hamden
26	5,753	Groton SD	Mystic
27	5,739	Shelton SD	Shelton
28	5,485	Ridgefield SD	Ridgefield
29	5,429	Naugatuck SD	Naugatuck
30	5,399	Newtown SD	Newtown
31	5,267	New Milford SD	New Milford
32	5,223	Westport SD	Westport
33	5,186	Middletown SD	Middletown
34	5,184	Cheshire SD	Cheshire
35	5,100	South Windsor SD	South Windsor
36	5,037	Simsbury SD	Simsbury
37	5,027	Torrington SD	Torrington
38	4,610	Newington SD	Newington
39	4,484	Regional SD 15	Middlebury
40	4,410	Windsor SD	Windsor
41	4,316	Farmington SD	Farmington
42	4,310	Monroe SD	Monroe
43	4,277	Darien SD	Darien
44	4,229	Wilton SD	Wilton
45	4,021	Vernon SD	Vernon
46	4,002	Norwich SD	Norwich
47	3,988	New Canaan SD	New Canaan
48	3,964	East Haven SD	East Haven
49	3,891	Guilford SD	Guilford
50	3,777	North Haven SD	North Haven
51	3,715	Madison SD	Madison
52	3,689	Wethersfield SD	Wethersfield
53	3,674	Branford SD	Branford
54	3,597	Windham SD	Willimantic
55	3,536	Watertown SD	Watertown
56	3,345	Berlin SD	Berlin

Rank		District Name	City
57	3,262	East Lyme SD	East Lyme
58	3,254	Bethel SD	Bethel
59	3,239	Avon SD	Avon
60	3,205	New London SD	New London
61	3,158	Colchester SD	Colchester
62	3,131	New Fairfield SD	New Fairfield
63	3,109	Waterford SD	Waterford
64	3,060	Brookfield SD	Brookfield
65	3,053	Tolland SD	Tolland
66	2,989	Ledyard SD	Ledyard
67	2,939	Wolcott SD	Wolcott
68	2,933	Montville SD	Oakdale
69	2,924	Killingly SD	Danielson
70	2,733	Seymour SD	Seymour
71	2,691	Ansonia SD	Ansonia
72	2,687	Regional SD 10	Burlington
73	2,650	Plainville SD	Plainville
74	2,633	Plainfield SD	Plainfield
75	2,603	Regional SD 16	Prospect
76	2,506	North Branford SD	Northford
77	2,485	Rocky Hill SD	Rocky Hill
78	2,479	Stonington SD	Old Mystic
79	2,474	Weston SD	Weston
80	2,471	Suffield SD	Suffield
81	2,468	Regional SD 05	Woodbridge
82	2,455	Bloomfield SD	Bloomfield
83	2,445	Capitol Region Education Council	Hartford
84	2,387	Regional SD 17	Higganum
85	2,371	Ellington SD	Ellington
86	2,348	Norwich Free Academy	Norwich
87	2,318	Regional SD 14	Woodbury
88	2,224	Griswold SD	Griswold
89	2,198	Granby SD	Granby
90	2,178	Clinton SD	Clinton
91	2,147	Regional SD 13	Durham
92	2,101	Coventry SD	Coventry
93	2,085	East Hampton SD	East Hampton
94	2,030	Area Coop Educational Services	North Haven
95	1,994	Stafford SD	Stafford Spgs
96	1,917	Windsor Locks SD	Windsor Locks
97	1,914	Plymouth SD	Terryville
98	1,881	Cromwell SD	Cromwell
99	1,735	Somers SD	Somers
100	1,638	Canton SD	Canton
101	1,590	East Windsor SD	East Windsor
102	1,588	Old Saybrook SD	Old Saybrook
103	1,574	Regional SD 08	Hebron
104	1,571	Derby SD	Derby
105	1,567	Regional SD 18	Old Lyme
106	1,543	Lebanon SD	Lebanon

Male Students

Rank	Percent	District Name	City
1	64.1	State Vocational-Technical Schools	Middletown
2	59.3	Area Coop Educational Services	North Haven
3	54.0	Bloomfield SD	Bloomfield
4	53.9	Wilton SD	Wilton
5	53.3	Simsbury SD	Simsbury
6	53.2	Capitol Region Education Council	Hartford
7	52.9	Montville SD	Oakdale
8	52.8	Regional SD 17	Higganum
9	52.8	Canton SD	Canton
10	52.7	Plainfield SD	Plainfield
11	52.6	East Windsor SD	East Windsor
12	52.5	Hamden SD	Hamden
13	52.5	Newington SD	Newington
14	52.4	New London SD	New London
15	52.3	Greenwich SD	Greenwich
16	52.2	Ansonia SD	Ansonia
17	52.2	Derby SD	Derby
18	52.2	Darien SD	Darien
19	52.1	Stonington SD	Old Mystic
20	52.0	Norwalk SD	Norwalk
21	52.0	New Canaan SD	New Canaan
22	52.0	Torrington SD	Torrington
23	51.9	Farmington SD	Farmington
24	51.9	Windsor SD	Windsor
25	51.9	Shelton SD	Shelton
26	51.8	Tolland SD	Tolland
27	51.8	Granby SD	Granby
28	51.8	Windham SD	Willimantic
29	51.8	Bethel SD	Bethel
30	51.7	Stamford SD	Stamford
31	51.7	Monroe SD	Monroe
32	51.7	Killingly SD	Danielson
33	51.7	East Hartford SD	East Hartford
34	51.7	North Branford SD	Northford
35	51.6	Newtown SD	Newtown
36	51.5	Southington SD	Southington
37	51.5	East Haven SD	East Haven
38	51.5	Regional SD 08	Hebron
39	51.5	New Fairfield SD	New Fairfield
40	51.4	Cheshire SD	Cheshire
41	51.4	Regional SD 16	Prospect
42	51.3	Plymouth SD	Terryville
43	51.3	Griswold SD	Griswold
44	51.3	Coventry SD	Coventry
45	51.2	Bristol SD	Bristol
46	51.2	Wethersfield SD	Wethersfield
47	51.2	Somers SD	Somers
48	51.2	Hartford SD	Hartford
49	51.2	Regional SD 10	Burlington
50	51.1	Meriden SD	Meriden
51	51.1	North Haven SD	North Haven
52	51.1	Berlin SD	Berlin
53	51.1	Naugatuck SD	Naugatuck
54	51.0	Waterbury SD	Waterbury
55	51.0	Regional SD 13	Durham
56	51.0	Bridgeport SD	Bridgeport
57	51.0	New Britain SD	New Britain
58	51.0	Regional SD 15	Middlebury
59	50.9	New Milford SD	New Milford
60	50.9	New Haven SD	New Haven
61	50.9	Milford SD	Milford
62	50.9	Manchester SD	Manchester
63	50.8	Guilford SD	Guilford
64	50.8	Danbury SD	Danbury
65	50.8	Groton SD	Mystic
66	50.8	Enfield SD	Enfield
67	50.7	South Windsor SD	South Windsor
68	50.6	Clinton SD	Clinton
69	50.6	Brookfield SD	Brookfield
70	50.6	Westport SD	Westport
71	50.6	Trumbull SD	Trumbull
72	50.5	East Lyme SD	East Lyme
73	50.5	Stratford SD	Stratford
74	50.4	Colchester SD	Colchester
75	50.4	Plainville SD	Plainville
76	50.4	Old Saybrook SD	Old Saybrook
77	50.4	Waterford SD	Waterford
78	50.3	Fairfield SD	Fairfield
79	50.3	West Haven SD	West Haven
80	50.3	Branford SD	Branford
81	50.2	Norwich SD	Norwich
82	50.1	Wallingford SD	Wallingford
83	50.1	West Hartford SD	West Hartford
84	50.1	Glastonbury SD	Glastonbury
85	50.1	Vernon SD	Vernon
86	50.1	Wolcott SD	Wolcott
87	50.1	Rocky Hill SD	Rocky Hill
88	50.0	Watertown SD	Watertown
89	50.0	Ledyard SD	Ledyard
90	50.0	Middletown SD	Middletown
91	50.0	Regional SD 18	Old Lyme
92	50.0	Ellington SD	Ellington
93	49.9	Ridgefield SD	Ridgefield
94	49.9	Madison SD	Madison
95	49.9	Windsor Locks SD	Windsor Locks
96	49.7	Seymour SD	Seymour
97	49.6	East Hampton SD	East Hampton
98	49.4	Avon SD	Avon
99	49.3	Regional SD 05	Woodbridge
100	49.3	Suffield SD	Suffield
101	49.1	Regional SD 14	Woodbury
102	48.9	Cromwell SD	Cromwell
103	48.7	Stafford SD	Stafford Spgs
104	48.7	Weston SD	Weston
105	47.8	Lebanon SD	Lebanon
106	46.8	Norwich Free Academy	Norwich

Female Students

Rank	Percent	District Name	City
1	53.1	Norwich Free Academy	Norwich
2	52.1	Lebanon SD	Lebanon
3	51.2	Weston SD	Weston
4	51.2	Stafford SD	Stafford Spgs
5	51.0	Cromwell SD	Cromwell
6	50.8	Regional SD 14	Woodbury
7	50.6	Suffield SD	Suffield
8	50.6	Regional SD 05	Woodbridge
9	50.5	Avon SD	Avon
10	50.3	East Hampton SD	East Hampton
11	50.2	Seymour SD	Seymour
12	50.0	Windsor Locks SD	Windsor Locks
13	50.0	Madison SD	Madison
14	50.0	Ridgefield SD	Ridgefield
15	49.9	Ellington SD	Ellington
16	49.9	Regional SD 18	Old Lyme
17	49.9	Middletown SD	Middletown
18	49.9	Ledyard SD	Ledyard
19	49.9	Watertown SD	Watertown
20	49.8	Rocky Hill SD	Rocky Hill
21	49.8	Wolcott SD	Wolcott
22	49.8	Vernon SD	Vernon
23	49.8	Glastonbury SD	Glastonbury
24	49.8	West Hartford SD	West Hartford
25	49.8	Wallingford SD	Wallingford
26	49.7	Norwich SD	Norwich
27	49.6	Branford SD	Branford
28	49.6	West Haven SD	West Haven
29	49.6	Fairfield SD	Fairfield
30	49.5	Waterford SD	Waterford
31	49.5	Old Saybrook SD	Old Saybrook
32	49.5	Plainville SD	Plainville
33	49.5	Colchester SD	Colchester
34	49.4	Stratford SD	Stratford
35	49.4	East Lyme SD	East Lyme
36	49.4	Trumbull SD	Trumbull
37	49.3	Westport SD	Westport
38	49.3	Brookfield SD	Brookfield
39	49.3	Clinton SD	Clinton
40	49.2	South Windsor SD	South Windsor
41	49.1	Enfield SD	Enfield
42	49.1	Groton SD	Mystic
43	49.1	Danbury SD	Danbury
44	49.1	Guilford SD	Guilford
45	49.0	Manchester SD	Manchester
46	49.0	Milford SD	Milford
47	49.0	New Haven SD	New Haven
48	49.0	New Milford SD	New Milford
49	48.9	Regional SD 15	Middlebury
50	48.9	New Britain SD	New Britain
51	48.9	Bridgeport SD	Bridgeport
52	48.9	Regional SD 13	Durham
53	48.9	Waterbury SD	Waterbury
54	48.8	Naugatuck SD	Naugatuck
55	48.8	Berlin SD	Berlin
56	48.8	North Haven SD	North Haven
57	48.8	Meriden SD	Meriden
58	48.7	Regional SD 10	Burlington
59	48.7	Hartford SD	Hartford
60	48.7	Somers SD	Somers
61	48.7	Wethersfield SD	Wethersfield
62	48.7	Bristol SD	Bristol
63	48.6	Coventry SD	Coventry
64	48.6	Griswold SD	Griswold
65	48.6	Plymouth SD	Terryville
66	48.5	Regional SD 16	Prospect
67	48.5	Cheshire SD	Cheshire
68	48.4	New Fairfield SD	New Fairfield
69	48.4	Regional SD 08	Hebron
70	48.4	East Haven SD	East Haven
71	48.4	Southington SD	Southington
72	48.3	Newtown SD	Newtown
73	48.2	North Branford SD	Northford
74	48.2	East Hartford SD	East Hartford
75	48.2	Killingly SD	Danielson
76	48.2	Monroe SD	Monroe
77	48.2	Stamford SD	Stamford
78	48.1	Bethel SD	Bethel
79	48.1	Windham SD	Willimantic
80	48.1	Granby SD	Granby
81	48.1	Tolland SD	Tolland
82	48.0	Shelton SD	Shelton
83	48.0	Windsor SD	Windsor
84	48.0	Farmington SD	Farmington
85	47.9	Torrington SD	Torrington
86	47.9	New Canaan SD	New Canaan
87	47.9	Norwalk SD	Norwalk
88	47.8	Stonington SD	Old Mystic
89	47.7	Darien SD	Darien
90	47.7	Derby SD	Derby
91	47.7	Ansonia SD	Ansonia
92	47.6	Greenwich SD	Greenwich
93	47.5	New London SD	New London
94	47.4	Newington SD	Newington
95	47.4	Hamden SD	Hamden
96	47.3	East Windsor SD	East Windsor
97	47.1	Plainfield SD	Plainfield
98	47.1	Canton SD	Canton
99	47.1	Regional SD 17	Higganum
100	47.0	Montville SD	Oakdale
101	46.7	Capitol Region Education Council	Hartford
102	46.6	Simsbury SD	Simsbury
103	46.0	Wilton SD	Wilton
104	45.9	Bloomfield SD	Bloomfield
105	40.6	Area Coop Educational Services	North Haven
106	35.8	State Vocational-Technical Schools	Middletown

Individual Education Program Students

Rank	Percent	District Name	City
1	34.5	Area Coop Educational Services	North Haven
2	18.7	Capitol Region Education Council	Hartford
3	17.9	New Britain SD	New Britain
4	16.7	Wolcott SD	Wolcott
5	16.4	Windsor Locks SD	Windsor Locks

Rank		District Name	City
6	16.0	Waterbury SD	Waterbury
7	15.6	Hartford SD	Hartford
8	15.1	Norwich SD	Norwich
9	14.8	State Vocational-Technical Schools	Middletown
10	14.6	Groton SD	Mystic
10	14.6	Montville SD	Oakdale
12	14.5	New London SD	New London
13	14.1	Killingly SD	Danielson
14	14.0	Meriden SD	Meriden
15	13.9	Windham SD	Willimantic
16	13.3	East Windsor SD	East Windsor
17	13.2	Old Saybrook SD	Old Saybrook
17	13.2	Simsbury SD	Simsbury
19	13.1	West Hartford SD	West Hartford
20	13.0	Cromwell SD	Cromwell
20	13.0	East Hartford SD	East Hartford
20	13.0	Madison SD	Madison
23	12.8	Clinton SD	Clinton
23	12.8	Manchester SD	Manchester
23	12.8	Milford SD	Milford
23	12.8	Windsor SD	Windsor
27	12.7	Ansonia SD	Ansonia
27	12.7	Coventry SD	Coventry
29	12.6	Bristol SD	Bristol
30	12.5	Hamden SD	Hamden
30	12.5	Torrington SD	Torrington
32	12.4	New Milford SD	New Milford
32	12.4	Regional SD 17	Higganum
34	12.3	Regional SD 15	Middlebury
35	12.2	Danbury SD	Danbury
35	12.2	South Windsor SD	South Windsor
37	12.1	Middletown SD	Middletown
38	12.0	Fairfield SD	Fairfield
38	12.0	Glastonbury SD	Glastonbury
40	11.9	Darien SD	Darien
40	11.9	Enfield SD	Enfield
40	11.9	Greenwich SD	Greenwich
40	11.9	Griswold SD	Griswold
40	11.9	Regional SD 05	Woodbridge
40	11.9	Wethersfield SD	Wethersfield
46	11.8	East Haven SD	East Haven
46	11.8	Lebanon SD	Lebanon
46	11.8	Ledyard SD	Ledyard
46	11.8	Naugatuck SD	Naugatuck
46	11.8	Waterford SD	Waterford
51	11.7	Norwalk SD	Norwalk
51	11.7	Southington SD	Southington
53	11.6	Colchester SD	Colchester
54	11.5	Bloomfield SD	Bloomfield
54	11.5	Stonington SD	Old Mystic
56	11.4	Plainfield SD	Plainfield
56	11.4	Regional SD 18	Old Lyme
56	11.4	Watertown SD	Watertown
56	11.4	Wilton SD	Wilton
60	11.3	East Lyme SD	East Lyme
61	11.2	Plainville SD	Plainville
61	11.2	Regional SD 14	Woodbury
61	11.2	Stamford SD	Stamford
64	11.1	Bridgeport SD	Bridgeport
64	11.1	Tolland SD	Tolland
66	11.0	East Hampton SD	East Hampton
66	11.0	Plymouth SD	Terryville
66	11.0	Regional SD 13	Durham
69	10.9	Berlin SD	Berlin
69	10.9	North Branford SD	Northford
69	10.9	Ridgefield SD	Ridgefield
69	10.9	Westport SD	Westport
73	10.8	Suffield SD	Suffield
74	10.4	Norwich Free Academy	Norwich
75	10.2	Guilford SD	Guilford
75	10.2	Stratford SD	Stratford
77	10.0	Granby SD	Granby
77	10.0	New Fairfield SD	New Fairfield
77	10.0	Regional SD 16	Prospect
80	9.9	Avon SD	Avon
80	9.9	Derby SD	Derby
80	9.9	Wallingford SD	Wallingford
83	9.8	Canton SD	Canton
83	9.8	Cheshire SD	Cheshire
83	9.8	Stafford SD	Stafford Spgs
86	9.7	Monroe SD	Monroe
87	9.4	Newington SD	Newington
87	9.4	Regional SD 08	Hebron
87	9.4	Rocky Hill SD	Rocky Hill
90	9.3	Ellington SD	Ellington
91	9.2	Bethel SD	Bethel
91	9.2	New Canaan SD	New Canaan
93	9.1	New Haven SD	New Haven
93	9.1	North Haven SD	North Haven
93	9.1	Regional SD 10	Burlington
96	9.0	Newtown SD	Newtown
97	8.7	West Haven SD	West Haven
98	8.6	Weston SD	Weston
99	8.5	Somers SD	Somers
99	8.5	Vernon SD	Vernon
101	8.4	Farmington SD	Farmington
102	8.3	Trumbull SD	Trumbull
103	7.4	Shelton SD	Shelton
104	6.1	Branford SD	Branford
105	6.0	Seymour SD	Seymour
106	4.7	Brookfield SD	Brookfield

English Language Learner Students

Rank	Percent	District Name	City
1	19.9	New London SD	New London
2	16.4	Hartford SD	Hartford
3	14.1	Stamford SD	Stamford
4	13.3	Windham SD	Willimantic
5	12.7	New Britain SD	New Britain
6	12.2	Bridgeport SD	Bridgeport
7	11.2	Danbury SD	Danbury
8	11.0	Waterbury SD	Waterbury
9	10.1	Norwalk SD	Norwalk
10	9.8	New Haven SD	New Haven
11	7.4	State Vocational-Technical Schools	Middletown
12	7.3	Derby SD	Derby
13	6.8	Greenwich SD	Greenwich
13	6.8	Meriden SD	Meriden
15	6.4	Norwich SD	Norwich
16	5.7	West Hartford SD	West Hartford
17	5.2	Wethersfield SD	Wethersfield
18	4.9	West Haven SD	West Haven
19	4.1	East Hartford SD	East Hartford
20	4.0	Torrington SD	Torrington
21	3.7	Cromwell SD	Cromwell
22	3.6	Ansonia SD	Ansonia
23	3.5	Old Saybrook SD	Old Saybrook
24	3.4	Naugatuck SD	Naugatuck
25	3.3	Berlin SD	Berlin
25	3.3	Bethel SD	Bethel
27	3.1	Killingly SD	Danielson
28	2.9	Plainville SD	Plainville
29	2.8	Wallingford SD	Wallingford
30	2.7	Norwich Free Academy	Norwich
31	2.6	East Windsor SD	East Windsor
31	2.6	Newington SD	Newington
33	2.5	Bristol SD	Bristol
33	2.5	Manchester SD	Manchester
35	2.4	East Haven SD	East Haven
35	2.4	Glastonbury SD	Glastonbury
37	2.3	New Milford SD	New Milford
38	2.2	Vernon SD	Vernon
38	2.2	Windsor Locks SD	Windsor Locks
40	2.1	Branford SD	Branford
40	2.1	Montville SD	Oakdale
42	2.0	Middletown SD	Middletown
42	2.0	Rocky Hill SD	Rocky Hill
44	1.9	Groton SD	Mystic
45	1.8	Milford SD	Milford
45	1.8	Shelton SD	Shelton
47	1.7	North Haven SD	North Haven
47	1.7	Seymour SD	Seymour
47	1.7	Westport SD	Westport
50	1.6	Stratford SD	Stratford
51	1.5	Capitol Region Education Council	Hartford
51	1.5	Windsor SD	Windsor
53	1.4	Area Coop Educational Services	North Haven
53	1.4	Plymouth SD	Terryville
53	1.4	Watertown SD	Watertown
56	1.3	Fairfield SD	Fairfield
56	1.3	South Windsor SD	South Windsor
58	1.1	Avon SD	Avon
59	1.0	Clinton SD	Clinton
59	1.0	Ellington SD	Ellington
59	1.0	Farmington SD	Farmington
62	0.9	Darien SD	Darien
62	0.9	Enfield SD	Enfield
62	0.9	Simsbury SD	Simsbury
65	0.8	Guilford SD	Guilford
65	0.8	Regional SD 15	Middlebury
65	0.8	Stafford SD	Stafford Spgs
68	0.7	East Lyme SD	East Lyme
68	0.7	Ledyard SD	Ledyard
68	0.7	Southington SD	Southington
71	0.6	Cheshire SD	Cheshire
71	0.6	Monroe SD	Monroe
71	0.6	New Canaan SD	New Canaan
71	0.6	North Branford SD	Northford
71	0.6	Ridgefield SD	Ridgefield
71	0.6	Trumbull SD	Trumbull
77	0.5	Canton SD	Canton
77	0.5	Colchester SD	Colchester
77	0.5	Griswold SD	Griswold
77	0.5	Hamden SD	Hamden
77	0.5	Waterford SD	Waterford
82	0.4	Stonington SD	Old Mystic
82	0.4	Tolland SD	Tolland
82	0.4	Weston SD	Weston
82	0.4	Wilton SD	Wilton
86	0.3	Lebanon SD	Lebanon
86	0.3	Regional SD 18	Old Lyme
88	0.2	Brookfield SD	Brookfield
88	0.2	East Hampton SD	East Hampton
88	0.2	Granby SD	Granby
88	0.2	Madison SD	Madison
88	0.2	Regional SD 05	Woodbridge
88	0.2	Wolcott SD	Wolcott
94	0.1	Bloomfield SD	Bloomfield
94	0.1	Plainfield SD	Plainfield
94	0.1	Regional SD 16	Prospect
94	0.1	Somers SD	Somers
94	0.1	Suffield SD	Suffield
99	0.0	Coventry SD	Coventry
99	0.0	New Fairfield SD	New Fairfield
99	0.0	Newtown SD	Newtown
99	0.0	Regional SD 08	Hebron
99	0.0	Regional SD 10	Burlington
99	0.0	Regional SD 13	Durham
99	0.0	Regional SD 14	Woodbury
99	0.0	Regional SD 17	Higganum

Migrant Students

Rank	Percent	District Name	City
1	27.6	Windham SD	Willimantic
2	12.8	Waterbury SD	Waterbury
3	11.1	Bridgeport SD	Bridgeport
4	10.4	New Haven SD	New Haven
5	6.9	New London SD	New London
6	6.5	Meriden SD	Meriden
7	6.0	Danbury SD	Danbury
8	5.0	New Britain SD	New Britain
9	1.6	Killingly SD	Danielson
10	1.0	State Vocational-Technical Schools	Middletown
11	0.6	West Haven SD	West Haven
12	0.5	Norwich SD	Norwich
13	0.4	Bethel SD	Bethel
14	0.3	Clinton SD	Clinton
15	0.2	Area Coop Educational Services	North Haven
15	0.2	Fairfield SD	Fairfield
15	0.2	Lebanon SD	Lebanon
15	0.2	Regional SD 14	Woodbury
15	0.2	Ridgefield SD	Ridgefield
15	0.2	Stratford SD	Stratford
21	0.1	Brookfield SD	Brookfield
21	0.1	Derby SD	Derby
21	0.1	East Haven SD	East Haven
21	0.1	Hamden SD	Hamden
21	0.1	Naugatuck SD	Naugatuck
21	0.1	New Milford SD	New Milford
21	0.1	Newtown SD	Newtown
21	0.1	Norwich Free Academy	Norwich
21	0.1	Wallingford SD	Wallingford
30	0.0	Regional SD 15	Middlebury
31	0.0	Ansonia SD	Ansonia
31	0.0	Avon SD	Avon
31	0.0	Berlin SD	Berlin
31	0.0	Bloomfield SD	Bloomfield
31	0.0	Branford SD	Branford
31	0.0	Bristol SD	Bristol
31	0.0	Canton SD	Canton
31	0.0	Capitol Region Education Council	Hartford
31	0.0	Cheshire SD	Cheshire
31	0.0	Colchester SD	Colchester
31	0.0	Coventry SD	Coventry
31	0.0	Cromwell SD	Cromwell
31	0.0	Darien SD	Darien
31	0.0	East Hampton SD	East Hampton
31	0.0	East Hartford SD	East Hartford
31	0.0	East Lyme SD	East Lyme
31	0.0	East Windsor SD	East Windsor
31	0.0	Ellington SD	Ellington
31	0.0	Enfield SD	Enfield
31	0.0	Farmington SD	Farmington
31	0.0	Glastonbury SD	Glastonbury
31	0.0	Granby SD	Granby
31	0.0	Greenwich SD	Greenwich
31	0.0	Griswold SD	Griswold
31	0.0	Groton SD	Mystic
31	0.0	Guilford SD	Guilford
31	0.0	Hartford SD	Hartford
31	0.0	Ledyard SD	Ledyard
31	0.0	Madison SD	Madison
31	0.0	Manchester SD	Manchester
31	0.0	Middletown SD	Middletown
31	0.0	Milford SD	Milford
31	0.0	Monroe SD	Monroe

Rank	Percent	District Name	City
31	0.0	Montville SD	Oakdale
31	0.0	New Canaan SD	New Canaan
31	0.0	New Fairfield SD	New Fairfield
31	0.0	Newington SD	Newington
31	0.0	North Branford SD	Northford
31	0.0	North Haven SD	North Haven
31	0.0	Norwalk SD	Norwalk
31	0.0	Old Saybrook SD	Old Saybrook
31	0.0	Plainfield SD	Plainfield
31	0.0	Plainville SD	Plainville
31	0.0	Plymouth SD	Terryville
31	0.0	Regional SD 05	Woodbridge
31	0.0	Regional SD 08	Hebron
31	0.0	Regional SD 10	Burlington
31	0.0	Regional SD 13	Durham
31	0.0	Regional SD 16	Prospect
31	0.0	Regional SD 17	Higganum
31	0.0	Regional SD 18	Old Lyme
31	0.0	Rocky Hill SD	Rocky Hill
31	0.0	Seymour SD	Seymour
31	0.0	Shelton SD	Shelton
31	0.0	Simsbury SD	Simsbury
31	0.0	Somers SD	Somers
31	0.0	South Windsor SD	South Windsor
31	0.0	Southington SD	Southington
31	0.0	Stafford SD	Stafford Spgs
31	0.0	Stamford SD	Stamford
31	0.0	Stonington SD	Old Mystic
31	0.0	Suffield SD	Suffield
31	0.0	Tolland SD	Tolland
31	0.0	Torrington SD	Torrington
31	0.0	Trumbull SD	Trumbull
31	0.0	Vernon SD	Vernon
31	0.0	Waterford SD	Waterford
31	0.0	Watertown SD	Watertown
31	0.0	West Hartford SD	West Hartford
31	0.0	Weston SD	Weston
31	0.0	Westport SD	Westport
31	0.0	Wethersfield SD	Wethersfield
31	0.0	Wilton SD	Wilton
31	0.0	Windsor Locks SD	Windsor Locks
31	0.0	Windsor SD	Windsor
31	0.0	Wolcott SD	Wolcott

Students Eligible for Free Lunch

Rank	Percent	District Name	City
1	n/a	Ansonia SD	Ansonia
1	n/a	Area Coop Educational Services	North Haven
1	n/a	Avon SD	Avon
1	n/a	Berlin SD	Berlin
1	n/a	Bethel SD	Bethel
1	n/a	Bloomfield SD	Bloomfield
1	n/a	Branford SD	Branford
1	n/a	Bridgeport SD	Bridgeport
1	n/a	Bristol SD	Bristol
1	n/a	Brookfield SD	Brookfield
1	n/a	Canton SD	Canton
1	n/a	Capitol Region Education Council	Hartford
1	n/a	Cheshire SD	Cheshire
1	n/a	Clinton SD	Clinton
1	n/a	Colchester SD	Colchester
1	n/a	Coventry SD	Coventry
1	n/a	Cromwell SD	Cromwell
1	n/a	Danbury SD	Danbury
1	n/a	Darien SD	Darien
1	n/a	Derby SD	Derby
1	n/a	East Hampton SD	East Hampton
1	n/a	East Hartford SD	East Hartford
1	n/a	East Haven SD	East Haven
1	n/a	East Lyme SD	East Lyme
1	n/a	East Windsor SD	East Windsor
1	n/a	Ellington SD	Ellington
1	n/a	Enfield SD	Enfield
1	n/a	Fairfield SD	Fairfield
1	n/a	Farmington SD	Farmington
1	n/a	Glastonbury SD	Glastonbury
1	n/a	Granby SD	Granby
1	n/a	Greenwich SD	Greenwich
1	n/a	Griswold SD	Griswold
1	n/a	Groton SD	Mystic
1	n/a	Guilford SD	Guilford
1	n/a	Hamden SD	Hamden
1	n/a	Hartford SD	Hartford
1	n/a	Killingly SD	Danielson
1	n/a	Lebanon SD	Lebanon
1	n/a	Ledyard SD	Ledyard
1	n/a	Madison SD	Madison
1	n/a	Manchester SD	Manchester
1	n/a	Meriden SD	Meriden
1	n/a	Middletown SD	Middletown
1	n/a	Milford SD	Milford
1	n/a	Monroe SD	Monroe
1	n/a	Montville SD	Oakdale
1	n/a	Naugatuck SD	Naugatuck
1	n/a	New Britain SD	New Britain
1	n/a	New Canaan SD	New Canaan
1	n/a	New Fairfield SD	New Fairfield
1	n/a	New Haven SD	New Haven
1	n/a	New London SD	New London
1	n/a	New Milford SD	New Milford
1	n/a	Newington SD	Newington
1	n/a	Newtown SD	Newtown
1	n/a	North Branford SD	Northford
1	n/a	North Haven SD	North Haven
1	n/a	Norwalk SD	Norwalk
1	n/a	Norwich Free Academy	Norwich
1	n/a	Norwich SD	Norwich
1	n/a	Old Saybrook SD	Old Saybrook
1	n/a	Plainfield SD	Plainfield
1	n/a	Plainville SD	Plainville
1	n/a	Plymouth SD	Terryville
1	n/a	Regional SD 05	Woodbridge
1	n/a	Regional SD 08	Hebron
1	n/a	Regional SD 10	Burlington
1	n/a	Regional SD 13	Durham
1	n/a	Regional SD 14	Woodbury
1	n/a	Regional SD 15	Middlebury
1	n/a	Regional SD 16	Prospect
1	n/a	Regional SD 17	Higganum
1	n/a	Regional SD 18	Old Lyme
1	n/a	Ridgefield SD	Ridgefield
1	n/a	Rocky Hill SD	Rocky Hill
1	n/a	Seymour SD	Seymour
1	n/a	Shelton SD	Shelton
1	n/a	Simsbury SD	Simsbury
1	n/a	Somers SD	Somers
1	n/a	South Windsor SD	South Windsor
1	n/a	Southington SD	Southington
1	n/a	Stafford SD	Stafford Spgs
1	n/a	Stamford SD	Stamford
1	n/a	State Vocational-Technical Schools	Middletown
1	n/a	Stonington SD	Old Mystic
1	n/a	Stratford SD	Stratford
1	n/a	Suffield SD	Suffield
1	n/a	Tolland SD	Tolland
1	n/a	Torrington SD	Torrington
1	n/a	Trumbull SD	Trumbull
1	n/a	Vernon SD	Vernon
1	n/a	Wallingford SD	Wallingford
1	n/a	Waterbury SD	Waterbury
1	n/a	Waterford SD	Waterford
1	n/a	Watertown SD	Watertown
1	n/a	West Hartford SD	West Hartford
1	n/a	West Haven SD	West Haven
1	n/a	Weston SD	Weston
1	n/a	Westport SD	Westport
1	n/a	Wethersfield SD	Wethersfield
1	n/a	Wilton SD	Wilton
1	n/a	Windham SD	Willimantic
1	n/a	Windsor Locks SD	Windsor Locks
1	n/a	Windsor SD	Windsor
1	n/a	Wolcott SD	Wolcott

Students Eligible for Reduced-Price Lunch

Rank	Percent	District Name	City
1	n/a	Ansonia SD	Ansonia
1	n/a	Area Coop Educational Services	North Haven
1	n/a	Avon SD	Avon
1	n/a	Berlin SD	Berlin
1	n/a	Bethel SD	Bethel
1	n/a	Bloomfield SD	Bloomfield
1	n/a	Branford SD	Branford
1	n/a	Bridgeport SD	Bridgeport
1	n/a	Bristol SD	Bristol
1	n/a	Brookfield SD	Brookfield
1	n/a	Canton SD	Canton
1	n/a	Capitol Region Education Council	Hartford
1	n/a	Cheshire SD	Cheshire
1	n/a	Clinton SD	Clinton
1	n/a	Colchester SD	Colchester
1	n/a	Coventry SD	Coventry
1	n/a	Cromwell SD	Cromwell
1	n/a	Danbury SD	Danbury
1	n/a	Darien SD	Darien
1	n/a	Derby SD	Derby
1	n/a	East Hampton SD	East Hampton
1	n/a	East Hartford SD	East Hartford
1	n/a	East Haven SD	East Haven
1	n/a	East Lyme SD	East Lyme
1	n/a	East Windsor SD	East Windsor
1	n/a	Ellington SD	Ellington
1	n/a	Enfield SD	Enfield
1	n/a	Fairfield SD	Fairfield
1	n/a	Farmington SD	Farmington
1	n/a	Glastonbury SD	Glastonbury
1	n/a	Granby SD	Granby
1	n/a	Greenwich SD	Greenwich
1	n/a	Griswold SD	Griswold
1	n/a	Groton SD	Mystic
1	n/a	Guilford SD	Guilford
1	n/a	Hamden SD	Hamden
1	n/a	Hartford SD	Hartford
1	n/a	Killingly SD	Danielson
1	n/a	Lebanon SD	Lebanon
1	n/a	Ledyard SD	Ledyard
1	n/a	Madison SD	Madison
1	n/a	Manchester SD	Manchester
1	n/a	Meriden SD	Meriden
1	n/a	Middletown SD	Middletown
1	n/a	Milford SD	Milford
1	n/a	Monroe SD	Monroe
1	n/a	Montville SD	Oakdale
1	n/a	Naugatuck SD	Naugatuck
1	n/a	New Britain SD	New Britain
1	n/a	New Canaan SD	New Canaan
1	n/a	New Fairfield SD	New Fairfield
1	n/a	New Haven SD	New Haven
1	n/a	New London SD	New London
1	n/a	New Milford SD	New Milford
1	n/a	Newington SD	Newington
1	n/a	Newtown SD	Newtown
1	n/a	North Branford SD	Northford
1	n/a	North Haven SD	North Haven
1	n/a	Norwalk SD	Norwalk
1	n/a	Norwich Free Academy	Norwich
1	n/a	Norwich SD	Norwich
1	n/a	Old Saybrook SD	Old Saybrook
1	n/a	Plainfield SD	Plainfield
1	n/a	Plainville SD	Plainville
1	n/a	Plymouth SD	Terryville
1	n/a	Regional SD 05	Woodbridge
1	n/a	Regional SD 08	Hebron
1	n/a	Regional SD 10	Burlington
1	n/a	Regional SD 13	Durham
1	n/a	Regional SD 14	Woodbury
1	n/a	Regional SD 15	Middlebury
1	n/a	Regional SD 16	Prospect
1	n/a	Regional SD 17	Higganum
1	n/a	Regional SD 18	Old Lyme
1	n/a	Ridgefield SD	Ridgefield
1	n/a	Rocky Hill SD	Rocky Hill
1	n/a	Seymour SD	Seymour
1	n/a	Shelton SD	Shelton
1	n/a	Simsbury SD	Simsbury
1	n/a	Somers SD	Somers
1	n/a	South Windsor SD	South Windsor
1	n/a	Southington SD	Southington
1	n/a	Stafford SD	Stafford Spgs
1	n/a	Stamford SD	Stamford
1	n/a	State Vocational-Technical Schools	Middletown
1	n/a	Stonington SD	Old Mystic
1	n/a	Stratford SD	Stratford
1	n/a	Suffield SD	Suffield
1	n/a	Tolland SD	Tolland
1	n/a	Torrington SD	Torrington
1	n/a	Trumbull SD	Trumbull
1	n/a	Vernon SD	Vernon
1	n/a	Wallingford SD	Wallingford
1	n/a	Waterbury SD	Waterbury
1	n/a	Waterford SD	Waterford
1	n/a	Watertown SD	Watertown
1	n/a	West Hartford SD	West Hartford
1	n/a	West Haven SD	West Haven
1	n/a	Weston SD	Weston
1	n/a	Westport SD	Westport
1	n/a	Wethersfield SD	Wethersfield
1	n/a	Wilton SD	Wilton
1	n/a	Windham SD	Willimantic
1	n/a	Windsor Locks SD	Windsor Locks
1	n/a	Windsor SD	Windsor
1	n/a	Wolcott SD	Wolcott

Student/Teacher Ratio

Rank	Ratio	District Name	City
1	16.9	North Branford SD	Northford
2	16.4	Cheshire SD	Cheshire
2	16.4	Granby SD	Granby
4	16.1	Ansonia SD	Ansonia
5	16.0	Torrington SD	Torrington
6	15.8	Norwich Free Academy	Norwich
6	15.8	Norwich SD	Norwich
8	15.7	Naugatuck SD	Naugatuck
9	15.6	East Haven SD	East Haven
9	15.6	Guilford SD	Guilford

Rank	Ratio	District Name	City
9	15.6	Hamden SD	Hamden
9	15.6	Newington SD	Newington
9	15.6	Newtown SD	Newtown
14	15.5	North Haven SD	North Haven
15	15.4	Derby SD	Derby
15	15.4	Regional SD 15	Middlebury
15	15.4	Shelton SD	Shelton
15	15.4	South Windsor SD	South Windsor
15	15.4	Trumbull SD	Trumbull
20	15.1	Bridgeport SD	Bridgeport
20	15.1	Plainfield SD	Plainfield
20	15.1	Ridgefield SD	Ridgefield
20	15.1	Watertown SD	Watertown
24	15.0	Avon SD	Avon
24	15.0	New Milford SD	New Milford
24	15.0	Simsbury SD	Simsbury
24	15.0	Wethersfield SD	Wethersfield
28	14.9	East Hampton SD	East Hampton
28	14.9	Monroe SD	Monroe
28	14.9	West Haven SD	West Haven
31	14.8	Bristol SD	Bristol
31	14.8	East Windsor SD	East Windsor
31	14.8	New Britain SD	New Britain
31	14.8	Stratford SD	Stratford
35	14.7	Berlin SD	Berlin
36	14.6	Canton SD	Canton
36	14.6	Glastonbury SD	Glastonbury
36	14.6	Suffield SD	Suffield
39	14.5	Danbury SD	Danbury
39	14.5	Ellington SD	Ellington
39	14.5	Meriden SD	Meriden
42	14.4	East Hartford SD	East Hartford
43	14.3	New Fairfield SD	New Fairfield
43	14.3	Seymour SD	Seymour
45	14.2	Ledyard SD	Ledyard
45	14.2	Madison SD	Madison
45	14.2	New Haven SD	New Haven
48	14.1	Manchester SD	Manchester
48	14.1	Norwalk SD	Norwalk
48	14.1	Plainville SD	Plainville
51	14.0	Brookfield SD	Brookfield
51	14.0	Griswold SD	Griswold
51	14.0	Killingly SD	Danielson
51	14.0	Lebanon SD	Lebanon
55	13.9	Farmington SD	Farmington
55	13.9	Wolcott SD	Wolcott
57	13.8	East Lyme SD	East Lyme
57	13.8	Somers SD	Somers
57	13.8	Wilton SD	Wilton
60	13.7	Wallingford SD	Wallingford
61	13.6	Colchester SD	Colchester
61	13.6	Coventry SD	Coventry
61	13.6	Enfield SD	Enfield
61	13.6	Regional SD 16	Prospect
61	13.6	Stonington SD	Old Mystic
66	13.5	Regional SD 05	Woodbridge
66	13.5	Waterbury SD	Waterbury
68	13.4	Bethel SD	Bethel
68	13.4	Branford SD	Branford
68	13.4	New Canaan SD	New Canaan
68	13.4	Regional SD 10	Burlington
68	13.4	Southington SD	Southington
68	13.4	Vernon SD	Vernon
74	13.3	Rocky Hill SD	Rocky Hill
75	13.2	Regional SD 14	Woodbury
75	13.2	Waterford SD	Waterford
77	13.1	Middletown SD	Middletown
77	13.1	Milford SD	Milford
79	13.0	Groton SD	Mystic
79	13.0	Hartford SD	Hartford
79	13.0	Plymouth SD	Terryville
79	13.0	Tolland SD	Tolland
79	13.0	West Hartford SD	West Hartford
84	12.8	Montville SD	Oakdale
84	12.8	Windham SD	Willimantic
84	12.8	Windsor SD	Windsor
87	12.7	Stamford SD	Stamford
88	12.6	Clinton SD	Clinton
88	12.6	Cromwell SD	Cromwell
90	12.5	Fairfield SD	Fairfield
90	12.5	Regional SD 13	Durham
90	12.5	Regional SD 18	Old Lyme
93	12.4	New London SD	New London
93	12.4	Weston SD	Weston
95	12.3	Regional SD 08	Hebron
96	12.2	Stafford SD	Stafford Spgs
96	12.2	Windsor Locks SD	Windsor Locks
98	12.1	Darien SD	Darien
98	12.1	Greenwich SD	Greenwich
100	12.0	Regional SD 17	Higganum
101	11.9	Bloomfield SD	Bloomfield
102	11.7	Westport SD	Westport
103	11.6	Old Saybrook SD	Old Saybrook
104	10.4	State Vocational-Technical Schools	Middletown
105	10.3	Capitol Region Education Council	Hartford
106	9.2	Area Coop Educational Services	North Haven

Student/Librarian Ratio

Rank	Ratio	District Name	City
1	3,702.7	Norwalk SD	Norwalk
2	2,652.0	Ansonia SD	Ansonia
3	2,630.0	Plainfield SD	Plainfield
4	2,590.0	Regional SD 16	Prospect
5	2,538.0	South Windsor SD	South Windsor
6	2,386.0	Regional SD 17	Higganum
7	2,095.0	Coventry SD	Coventry
8	2,085.0	East Hampton SD	East Hampton
9	1,954.0	East Hartford SD	East Hartford
10	1,836.5	Wethersfield SD	Wethersfield
11	1,790.8	Bristol SD	Bristol
12	1,677.8	Enfield SD	Enfield
13	1,587.0	East Windsor SD	East Windsor
14	1,547.5	Waterford SD	Waterford
15	1,460.5	Wolcott SD	Wolcott
16	1,436.3	Monroe SD	Monroe
17	1,354.3	Naugatuck SD	Naugatuck
18	1,290.8	Middletown SD	Middletown
19	1,227.5	Bloomfield SD	Bloomfield
20	1,214.0	Capitol Region Education Council	Hartford
21	1,179.1	Bridgeport SD	Bridgeport
22	1,175.3	Watertown SD	Watertown
23	1,170.5	Norwich Free Academy	Norwich
24	1,147.8	Shelton SD	Shelton
25	1,091.5	Granby SD	Granby
26	1,073.0	Regional SD 13	Durham
27	1,018.0	Brookfield SD	Brookfield
28	1,010.0	Area Coop Educational Services	North Haven
29	1,000.5	Norwich SD	Norwich
30	994.3	New London SD	New London
31	994.0	Stafford SD	Stafford Spgs
32	984.1	Waterbury SD	Waterbury
33	939.0	Cromwell SD	Cromwell
34	928.8	Madison SD	Madison
35	908.7	Seymour SD	Seymour
36	899.1	New Britain SD	New Britain
37	891.8	Windham SD	Willimantic
38	888.6	Meriden SD	Meriden
39	885.3	Regional SD 10	Burlington
40	873.3	New Milford SD	New Milford
41	848.2	Manchester SD	Manchester
42	833.8	Simsbury SD	Simsbury
43	833.3	North Branford SD	Northford
44	829.8	Torrington SD	Torrington
45	820.0	Suffield SD	Suffield
46	807.0	East Lyme SD	East Lyme
47	805.6	Stamford SD	Stamford
48	792.7	West Haven SD	West Haven
49	790.3	Ellington SD	Ellington
50	788.5	Colchester SD	Colchester
51	786.0	Regional SD 08	Hebron
52	774.3	New Fairfield SD	New Fairfield
53	754.5	Tolland SD	Tolland
54	740.7	Griswold SD	Griswold
55	739.8	Ledyard SD	Ledyard
56	731.0	Killingly SD	Danielson
57	726.3	Glastonbury SD	Glastonbury
58	717.3	Farmington SD	Farmington
59	672.5	Newtown SD	Newtown
60	667.6	Southington SD	Southington
61	667.4	Berlin SD	Berlin
62	661.9	State Vocational-Technical Schools	Middletown
63	661.2	Trumbull SD	Trumbull
64	657.8	East Haven SD	East Haven
65	652.9	Westport SD	Westport
66	647.5	Cheshire SD	Cheshire
67	646.6	Avon SD	Avon
68	637.9	Regional SD 15	Middlebury
69	630.0	Windsor SD	Windsor
70	619.3	Rocky Hill SD	Rocky Hill
71	615.3	Regional SD 05	Woodbridge
72	611.3	Stonington SD	Old Mystic
73	601.1	Hartford SD	Hartford
74	585.2	Montville SD	Oakdale
75	579.5	Regional SD 14	Woodbury
76	575.4	West Hartford SD	West Hartford
77	574.1	Newington SD	Newington
78	569.4	New Canaan SD	New Canaan
79	550.3	Wallingford SD	Wallingford
80	545.3	Stratford SD	Stratford
81	544.0	Canton SD	Canton
82	540.2	Bethel SD	Bethel
83	539.0	North Haven SD	North Haven
84	537.5	Milford SD	Milford
85	536.5	Clinton SD	Clinton
86	530.0	Plainville SD	Plainville
87	528.3	Old Saybrook SD	Old Saybrook
88	524.6	Branford SD	Branford
89	515.7	Derby SD	Derby
90	514.1	New Haven SD	New Haven
91	511.7	Lebanon SD	Lebanon
92	498.6	Ridgefield SD	Ridgefield
93	490.2	Weston SD	Weston
94	489.1	Fairfield SD	Fairfield
95	486.4	Guilford SD	Guilford
96	486.3	Hamden SD	Hamden
97	479.3	Windsor Locks SD	Windsor Locks
98	469.7	Wilton SD	Wilton
99	453.7	Danbury SD	Danbury
100	432.5	Somers SD	Somers
101	426.3	Darien SD	Darien
102	412.6	Greenwich SD	Greenwich
103	406.9	Groton SD	Mystic
104	313.4	Regional SD 18	Old Lyme
105	n/a	Plymouth SD	Terryville
105	n/a	Vernon SD	Vernon

Student/Counselor Ratio

Rank	Ratio	District Name	City
1	984.1	Waterbury SD	Waterbury
2	715.3	Regional SD 13	Durham
3	713.4	West Haven SD	West Haven
4	695.0	East Hampton SD	East Hampton
5	662.7	Stafford SD	Stafford Spgs
6	632.2	Hamden SD	Hamden
7	627.1	Milford SD	Milford
8	611.3	Stonington SD	Old Mystic
9	601.2	East Hartford SD	East Hartford
10	597.8	Newtown SD	Newtown
11	587.7	Watertown SD	Watertown
12	576.7	Somers SD	Somers
13	573.7	Middletown SD	Middletown
14	553.2	Torrington SD	Torrington
15	539.5	New Britain SD	New Britain
16	539.0	North Haven SD	North Haven
17	530.7	Madison SD	Madison
18	530.4	Ansonia SD	Ansonia
19	529.5	Hartford SD	Hartford
20	529.0	East Windsor SD	East Windsor
21	525.7	Colchester SD	Colchester
22	524.7	Wethersfield SD	Wethersfield
23	523.8	Coventry SD	Coventry
24	522.3	Regional SD 18	Old Lyme
25	515.7	Derby SD	Derby
26	508.9	Stratford SD	Stratford
27	507.6	South Windsor SD	South Windsor
28	501.4	Danbury SD	Danbury
29	500.3	Simsbury SD	Simsbury
30	500.0	North Branford SD	Northford
31	495.4	Rocky Hill SD	Rocky Hill
32	493.4	East Haven SD	East Haven
33	492.0	Suffield SD	Suffield
34	490.0	Windsor SD	Windsor
35	487.7	Montville SD	Oakdale
36	487.3	Killingly SD	Danielson
37	487.0	Bridgeport SD	Bridgeport
38	486.8	Wolcott SD	Wolcott
39	477.4	New Haven SD	New Haven
40	474.8	Groton SD	Mystic
41	474.2	Ellington SD	Ellington
42	471.3	Bristol SD	Bristol
43	469.5	Cromwell SD	Cromwell
44	463.8	Stamford SD	Stamford
45	461.1	East Lyme SD	East Lyme
46	457.1	Ridgefield SD	Ridgefield
47	457.0	Plymouth SD	Terryville
48	449.1	Manchester SD	Manchester
49	447.1	Wallingford SD	Wallingford
50	446.4	Vernon SD	Vernon
51	445.9	Windham SD	Willimantic
52	444.7	Norwich SD	Norwich
53	442.7	Regional SD 10	Burlington
54	442.4	New Fairfield SD	New Fairfield
55	440.2	Fairfield SD	Fairfield
56	436.7	New Milford SD	New Milford
57	436.3	Brookfield SD	Brookfield
58	435.8	Glastonbury SD	Glastonbury
59	431.7	Cheshire SD	Cheshire
59	431.7	Westport SD	Westport
61	430.4	Farmington SD	Farmington
62	427.2	Norwalk SD	Norwalk
63	426.3	Darien SD	Darien
64	422.7	Ledyard SD	Ledyard
65	417.5	Newington SD	Newington
66	417.2	Meriden SD	Meriden
67	417.1	Berlin SD	Berlin
68	416.7	Naugatuck SD	Naugatuck

69	413.3	Trumbull SD	Trumbull
70	408.0	Canton SD	Canton
71	407.5	West Hartford SD	West Hartford
72	404.0	Area Coop Educational Services	North Haven
73	397.7	Regional SD 17	Higganum
74	396.3	Old Saybrook SD	Old Saybrook
75	389.1	Guilford SD	Guilford
76	386.9	Waterford SD	Waterford
77	386.3	Regional SD 14	Woodbury
78	382.6	Shelton SD	Shelton
79	377.4	Wilton SD	Wilton
80	377.3	Tolland SD	Tolland
81	372.9	New London SD	New London
82	367.2	Branford SD	Branford
83	363.8	Granby SD	Granby
84	363.1	Greenwich SD	Greenwich
85	362.4	New Canaan SD	New Canaan
86	360.1	Bethel SD	Bethel
87	359.2	Avon SD	Avon
88	359.1	Monroe SD	Monroe
89	357.7	Clinton SD	Clinton
90	350.7	Bloomfield SD	Bloomfield
91	346.9	Capitol Region Education Council	Hartford
92	343.5	Regional SD 15	Middlebury
93	332.1	Southington SD	Southington
94	331.3	Plainville SD	Plainville
95	328.8	Plainfield SD	Plainfield
96	323.8	Regional SD 16	Prospect
97	317.4	Griswold SD	Griswold
98	313.6	Enfield SD	Enfield
99	307.0	Lebanon SD	Lebanon
100	306.4	Weston SD	Weston
101	302.9	Seymour SD	Seymour
102	273.9	Windsor Locks SD	Windsor Locks
103	262.0	Regional SD 08	Hebron
104	212.8	Norwich Free Academy	Norwich
105	175.8	Regional SD 05	Woodbridge
106	170.5	State Vocational-Technical Schools	Middletown

Current Spending per Student in FY2003

Rank	Dollars	District Name	City
1	14,356	Greenwich SD	Greenwich
2	13,906	Weston SD	Weston
3	13,900	Westport SD	Westport
4	13,763	Hartford SD	Hartford
5	13,618	New London SD	New London
6	12,982	Regional SD 18	Old Lyme
7	12,966	New Haven SD	New Haven
8	12,795	Bloomfield SD	Bloomfield
9	12,756	New Canaan SD	New Canaan
10	12,360	Windham SD	Willimantic
11	12,313	Stamford SD	Stamford
12	12,232	Norwalk SD	Norwalk
13	12,116	Darien SD	Darien
14	12,109	Fairfield SD	Fairfield
15	11,986	Regional SD 05	Woodbridge
16	11,956	Hamden SD	Hamden
17	11,585	Wilton SD	Wilton
18	11,470	Groton SD	Mystic
19	11,268	Windsor SD	Windsor
20	11,116	New Britain SD	New Britain
21	11,101	Waterford SD	Waterford
22	11,088	Middletown SD	Middletown
23	11,001	Waterbury SD	Waterbury
24	10,820	Windsor Locks SD	Windsor Locks
25	10,815	Bridgeport SD	Bridgeport
26	10,721	Manchester SD	Manchester
27	10,710	Clinton SD	Clinton
28	10,690	Plainville SD	Plainville
29	10,682	Norwich SD	Norwich
30	10,680	Regional SD 13	Durham
31	10,638	Milford SD	Milford
32	10,544	Regional SD 08	Hebron
33	10,520	Cromwell SD	Cromwell
34	10,488	Meriden SD	Meriden
35	10,468	Regional SD 17	Higganum
36	10,443	East Hartford SD	East Hartford
37	10,432	Bethel SD	Bethel
38	10,428	Ridgefield SD	Ridgefield
39	10,388	Vernon SD	Vernon
40	10,315	Stonington SD	Old Mystic
41	10,306	West Hartford SD	West Hartford
42	10,254	Montville SD	Oakdale
43	10,224	Avon SD	Avon
44	10,126	Branford SD	Branford
45	10,112	West Haven SD	West Haven
46	10,090	Farmington SD	Farmington
47	10,071	Plymouth SD	Terryville
48	10,064	Stafford SD	Stafford Spgs
49	10,055	Wethersfield SD	Wethersfield
50	10,000	Regional SD 15	Middlebury
51	9,970	Guilford SD	Guilford
52	9,966	Plainfield SD	Plainfield
52	9,966	Trumbull SD	Trumbull
54	9,964	Old Saybrook SD	Old Saybrook
55	9,934	Killingly SD	Danielson
56	9,907	Rocky Hill SD	Rocky Hill
57	9,897	Brookfield SD	Brookfield
58	9,875	Enfield SD	Enfield
59	9,860	Canton SD	Canton
60	9,851	Cheshire SD	Cheshire
61	9,831	Torrington SD	Torrington
62	9,786	East Hampton SD	East Hampton
63	9,766	Shelton SD	Shelton
64	9,737	Simsbury SD	Simsbury
65	9,712	Danbury SD	Danbury
66	9,694	Griswold SD	Griswold
67	9,667	Berlin SD	Berlin
68	9,637	Newington SD	Newington
69	9,616	Newtown SD	Newtown
70	9,591	Southington SD	Southington
71	9,562	North Haven SD	North Haven
72	9,530	Ellington SD	Ellington
73	9,506	Derby SD	Derby
74	9,474	Monroe SD	Monroe
75	9,455	Glastonbury SD	Glastonbury
76	9,452	Stratford SD	Stratford
77	9,451	East Windsor SD	East Windsor
78	9,450	East Lyme SD	East Lyme
79	9,435	Regional SD 10	Burlington
80	9,391	Regional SD 16	Prospect
81	9,380	South Windsor SD	South Windsor
82	9,374	East Haven SD	East Haven
83	9,351	Granby SD	Granby
84	9,327	Regional SD 14	Woodbury
85	9,273	Bristol SD	Bristol
86	9,232	Wallingford SD	Wallingford
87	9,207	North Branford SD	Northford
88	9,199	Madison SD	Madison
89	9,065	Wolcott SD	Wolcott
90	9,012	Somers SD	Somers
91	8,986	New Milford SD	New Milford
92	8,985	Suffield SD	Suffield
93	8,954	Naugatuck SD	Naugatuck
94	8,934	Ledyard SD	Ledyard
95	8,930	Lebanon SD	Lebanon
96	8,929	Coventry SD	Coventry
97	8,920	Tolland SD	Tolland
98	8,865	New Fairfield SD	New Fairfield
99	8,824	Colchester SD	Colchester
100	8,676	Watertown SD	Watertown
101	8,575	Ansonia SD	Ansonia
102	8,473	Seymour SD	Seymour
103	n/a	Norwich Free Academy	Norwich
104	n/a	Area Coop Educational Services	North Haven
104	n/a	Capitol Region Education Council	Hartford
104	n/a	State Vocational-Technical Schools	Middletown

Number of Diploma Recipients

Rank	Number	District Name	City
1	2,013	State Vocational-Technical Schools	Middletown
2	834	Bridgeport SD	Bridgeport
3	795	Stamford SD	Stamford
4	788	New Haven SD	New Haven
5	785	Hartford SD	Hartford
6	668	West Hartford SD	West Hartford
7	613	Norwalk SD	Norwalk
8	578	Waterbury SD	Waterbury
9	558	Bristol SD	Bristol
10	506	Danbury SD	Danbury
11	497	Norwich Free Academy	Norwich
12	479	Southington SD	Southington
13	475	East Hartford SD	East Hartford
14	474	Greenwich SD	Greenwich
15	470	Stratford SD	Stratford
16	464	Milford SD	Milford
17	462	Wallingford SD	Wallingford
18	459	Fairfield SD	Fairfield
19	448	Enfield SD	Enfield
20	445	New Britain SD	New Britain
21	433	Meriden SD	Meriden
22	416	Trumbull SD	Trumbull
23	414	Glastonbury SD	Glastonbury
24	408	Manchester SD	Manchester
25	401	Hamden SD	Hamden
26	348	Cheshire SD	Cheshire
27	346	Simsbury SD	Simsbury
28	344	Shelton SD	Shelton
29	340	West Haven SD	West Haven
30	326	Naugatuck SD	Naugatuck
31	323	Regional SD 05	Woodbridge
32	317	South Windsor SD	South Windsor
33	315	Windsor SD	Windsor
34	287	Guilford SD	Guilford
35	286	Monroe SD	Monroe
35	286	Newtown SD	Newtown
37	280	Farmington SD	Farmington
37	280	Ridgefield SD	Ridgefield
39	268	Newington SD	Newington
40	267	Torrington SD	Torrington
41	255	Westport SD	Westport
42	247	Berlin SD	Berlin
43	246	Middletown SD	Middletown
44	243	Regional SD 15	Middlebury
45	241	New Milford SD	New Milford
45	241	Wethersfield SD	Wethersfield
47	240	Seymour SD	Seymour
48	239	Groton SD	Mystic
49	238	Branford SD	Branford
50	235	East Lyme SD	East Lyme
50	235	Vernon SD	Vernon
52	233	New Canaan SD	New Canaan
53	230	Ledyard SD	Ledyard
53	230	Wilton SD	Wilton
55	215	East Haven SD	East Haven
56	214	North Haven SD	North Haven
57	210	Madison SD	Madison
58	205	Regional SD 08	Hebron
59	203	Killingly SD	Danielson
59	203	Watertown SD	Watertown
61	202	Wolcott SD	Wolcott
62	197	New Fairfield SD	New Fairfield
63	196	Windham SD	Willimantic
64	191	Waterford SD	Waterford
65	190	Darien SD	Darien
66	188	Plainville SD	Plainville
67	186	Bethel SD	Bethel
68	182	Brookfield SD	Brookfield
69	181	Avon SD	Avon
70	180	Regional SD 14	Woodbury
71	173	Bloomfield SD	Bloomfield
72	169	Tolland SD	Tolland
73	164	Plainfield SD	Plainfield
74	162	Regional SD 10	Burlington
75	159	Montville SD	Oakdale
76	157	Clinton SD	Clinton
77	148	North Branford SD	Northford
78	146	Regional SD 17	Higganum
79	144	Suffield SD	Suffield
80	143	Rocky Hill SD	Rocky Hill
81	141	Stonington SD	Old Mystic
82	135	Colchester SD	Colchester
82	135	Weston SD	Weston
84	128	Lebanon SD	Lebanon
84	128	Windsor Locks SD	Windsor Locks
86	126	Griswold SD	Griswold
87	125	East Hampton SD	East Hampton
87	125	Granby SD	Granby
89	121	New London SD	New London
90	120	Plymouth SD	Terryville
91	118	Ansonia SD	Ansonia
92	113	Ellington SD	Ellington
93	110	Regional SD 13	Durham
94	101	Coventry SD	Coventry
94	101	Cromwell SD	Cromwell
96	100	Canton SD	Canton
97	95	Old Saybrook SD	Old Saybrook
97	95	Somers SD	Somers
99	94	Regional SD 18	Old Lyme
100	92	Stafford SD	Stafford Spgs
101	80	Derby SD	Derby
102	78	East Windsor SD	East Windsor
103	24	Area Coop Educational Services	North Haven
104	18	Capitol Region Education Council	Hartford
105	11	Norwich SD	Norwich
106	n/a	Regional SD 16	Prospect

High School Drop-out Rate

Rank	Percent	District Name	City
1	30.6	Norwich SD	Norwich
2	16.9	Ledyard SD	Ledyard
3	13.4	New London SD	New London
4	10.0	Bridgeport SD	Bridgeport
5	6.9	New Britain SD	New Britain
6	6.8	Capitol Region Education Council	Hartford
7	6.3	Hartford SD	Hartford
8	6.0	Plainfield SD	Plainfield
8	6.0	Torrington SD	Torrington
10	5.7	Ansonia SD	Ansonia
10	5.7	Killingly SD	Danielson
12	5.2	New Haven SD	New Haven
13	5.1	Windsor Locks SD	Windsor Locks
14	5.0	Windham SD	Willimantic
15	4.6	East Windsor SD	East Windsor
16	4.3	Clinton SD	Clinton
16	4.3	Coventry SD	Coventry

18	4.2	Somers SD	Somers
19	4.0	Norwich Free Academy	Norwich
20	3.8	Danbury SD	Danbury
20	3.8	Hamden SD	Hamden
22	3.4	Bloomfield SD	Bloomfield
23	3.3	Windsor SD	Windsor
24	3.1	Enfield SD	Enfield
25	3.0	Naugatuck SD	Naugatuck
25	3.0	Waterbury SD	Waterbury
27	2.9	Derby SD	Derby
28	2.8	East Hartford SD	East Hartford
28	2.8	Griswold SD	Griswold
28	2.8	Vernon SD	Vernon
31	2.7	Meriden SD	Meriden
31	2.7	Norwalk SD	Norwalk
31	2.7	Stamford SD	Stamford
34	2.6	Plymouth SD	Terryville
34	2.6	Trumbull SD	Trumbull
36	2.5	Stafford SD	Stafford Spgs
36	2.5	Stratford SD	Stratford
38	2.4	Watertown SD	Watertown
39	2.3	Regional SD 15	Middlebury
39	2.3	Seymour SD	Seymour
41	2.2	North Haven SD	North Haven
42	2.1	West Hartford SD	West Hartford
43	2.0	Montville SD	Oakdale
44	1.9	Stonington SD	Old Mystic
44	1.9	Tolland SD	Tolland
46	1.8	Branford SD	Branford
46	1.8	Suffield SD	Suffield
48	1.7	Berlin SD	Berlin
48	1.7	Greenwich SD	Greenwich
48	1.7	Milford SD	Milford
48	1.7	Shelton SD	Shelton
48	1.7	Southington SD	Southington
53	1.6	West Haven SD	West Haven
54	1.4	North Branford SD	Northford
54	1.4	Regional SD 08	Hebron
54	1.4	Wethersfield SD	Wethersfield
57	1.3	Bristol SD	Bristol
57	1.3	Manchester SD	Manchester
57	1.3	South Windsor SD	South Windsor
57	1.3	Wolcott SD	Wolcott
61	1.2	Colchester SD	Colchester
61	1.2	East Lyme SD	East Lyme
61	1.2	Lebanon SD	Lebanon
61	1.2	Madison SD	Madison
65	1.1	Regional SD 18	Old Lyme
65	1.1	Wallingford SD	Wallingford
67	1.0	Cheshire SD	Cheshire
67	1.0	Regional SD 05	Woodbridge
67	1.0	Westport SD	Westport
70	0.9	Granby SD	Granby
70	0.9	Regional SD 14	Woodbury
70	0.9	State Vocational-Technical Schools	Middletown
70	0.9	Waterford SD	Waterford
74	0.8	East Hampton SD	East Hampton
74	0.8	Farmington SD	Farmington
74	0.8	Middletown SD	Middletown
74	0.8	Newtown SD	Newtown
74	0.8	Simsbury SD	Simsbury
79	0.7	Area Coop Educational Services	North Haven
79	0.7	East Haven SD	East Haven
79	0.7	Groton SD	Mystic
79	0.7	New Fairfield SD	New Fairfield
79	0.7	Regional SD 13	Durham
84	0.6	Brookfield SD	Brookfield
84	0.6	Fairfield SD	Fairfield
84	0.6	New Canaan SD	New Canaan
87	0.5	Bethel SD	Bethel
87	0.5	Ellington SD	Ellington
87	0.5	Glastonbury SD	Glastonbury
87	0.5	Newington SD	Newington
87	0.5	Plainville SD	Plainville
87	0.5	Ridgefield SD	Ridgefield
93	0.4	Wilton SD	Wilton
94	0.3	Guilford SD	Guilford
94	0.3	Regional SD 10	Burlington
96	0.2	Cromwell SD	Cromwell
96	0.2	Darien SD	Darien
96	0.2	New Milford SD	New Milford
96	0.2	Regional SD 17	Higganum
100	0.1	Monroe SD	Monroe
101	0.0	Avon SD	Avon
101	0.0	Canton SD	Canton
101	0.0	Old Saybrook SD	Old Saybrook
101	0.0	Regional SD 16	Prospect
101	0.0	Rocky Hill SD	Rocky Hill
101	0.0	Weston SD	Weston

Delaware

Delaware Public School Educational Profile

Category	Value	Category	Value
Schools (2003-2004)	205	**Diploma Recipients** (2002-2003)	6,481
Instructional Level		White, Non-Hispanic	4,357
Primary	105	Black, Non-Hispanic	1,683
Middle	43	Asian/Pacific Islander	185
High	32	American Indian/Alaskan Native	15
Other Level	24	Hispanic	241
Curriculum		**High School Drop-out Rate** (%) (2001-2002)	6.2
Regular	173	White, Non-Hispanic	4.6
Special Education	16	Black, Non-Hispanic	9.0
Vocational	5	Asian/Pacific Islander	3.5
Alternative	10	American Indian/Alaskan Native	5.1
Type		Hispanic	11.6
Magnet	2	**Staff** (2003-2004)	
Charter	13	Teachers	7,748.8
Title I Eligible	103	Average Salary ($)	51,122
School-wide Title I	58	Librarians/Media Specialists	129.0
Students (2003-2004)	117,777	Guidance Counselors	262.6
Gender (%)		**Ratios** (2003-2004)	
Male	51.7	Student/Teacher Ratio	15.2 to 1
Female	48.3	Student/Librarian Ratio	913.0 to 1
Race/Ethnicity (%)		Student/Counselor Ratio	448.5 to 1
White, Non-Hispanic	57.3	**College Entrance Exam Scores** (2005)	
Black, Non-Hispanic	31.9	Scholastic Aptitude Test (SAT)	
Asian/Pacific Islander	2.6	Participation Rate (%)	74
American Indian/Alaskan Native	0.3	Mean SAT Reasoning Test Verbal Score	503
Hispanic	7.9	Mean SAT Reasoning Test Math Score	502
Classification (%)		American College Testing Program (ACT)	
Individual Education Program (IEP)	14.6	Participation Rate (%)	4
Migrant (2002-2003)	0.2	Average Composite Score	20.8
English Language Learner (ELL)	3.4	Average English Score	20.2
Eligible for Free Lunch Program	27.7	Average Math Score	20.5
Eligible for Reduced-Price Lunch Program	6.1	Average Reading Score	21.4
Current Spending ($ per student in FY 2003)	9,588	Average Science Score	20.6
Instruction	5,960		
Support Services	3,275		

Note: For an explanation of data, please refer to the User's Guide in the front of the book

Delaware NAEP 2005 Test Scores

Reading			Mathematics		
Grade/Category	Value	Rank	Grade/Category	Value	Rank
4th Grade			**4th Grade**		
Average Proficiency	225.8 (0.78)	4/51	Average Proficiency	239.7 (0.46)	23/51
Proficiency by Gender/Race/Ethnicity			Proficiency by Gender/Race/Ethnicity		
Male	222.9 (0.96)	5/51	Male	240.9 (0.69)	22/51
Female	228.7 (0.99)	6/51	Female	238.5 (0.75)	21/51
White, Non-Hispanic	234.7 (0.91)	3/51	White, Non-Hispanic	248.8 (0.73)	11/51
Black, Non-Hispanic	211.7 (1.12)	2/42	Black, Non-Hispanic	225.9 (1.03)	5/42
Asian, Non-Hispanic	238.8 (4.53)	4/27	Asian, Non-Hispanic	260.2 (3.71)	4/25
American Indian, Non-Hispanic	n/a	n/a	American Indian, Non-Hispanic	n/a	n/a
Hispanic	216.4 (2.17)	3/40	Hispanic	228.5 (1.86)	16/41
Proficiency by Class Size			Proficiency by Class Size		
Less than 16 Students	n/a	n/a	Less than 16 Students	221.8 (3.16)	23/35
16 to 18 Students	219.1 (3.04)	13/33	16 to 18 Students	235.7 (2.40)	18/31
19 to 20 Students	222.3 (2.20)	20/38	19 to 20 Students	238.9 (1.23)	22/38
21 to 25 Students	226.9 (0.79)	10/51	21 to 25 Students	240.8 (0.68)	25/51
Greater than 25 Students	226.8 (1.73)	2/36	Greater than 25 Students	240.3 (0.98)	13/33
Percent Attaining Achievement Levels			Percent Attaining Achievement Levels		
Below Basic	26.7 (1.43)	49/51	Below Basic	15.8 (0.84)	36/51
Basic or Above	73.3 (1.43)	3/51	Basic or Above	84.2 (0.84)	16/51
Proficient or Above	34.2 (1.16)	16/51	Proficient or Above	36.1 (1.19)	29/51
Advanced or Above	6.6 (0.80)	32/51	Advanced or Above	4.4 (0.46)	29/51
8th Grade			**8th Grade**		
Average Proficiency	266.0 (0.62)	18/51	Average Proficiency	281.0 (0.61)	24/51
Proficiency by Gender/Race/Ethnicity			Proficiency by Gender/Race/Ethnicity		
Male	261.2 (0.86)	17/51	Male	282.6 (0.98)	21/51
Female	270.5 (0.94)	19/51	Female	279.3 (0.97)	27/51
White, Non-Hispanic	274.4 (0.79)	6/51	White, Non-Hispanic	291.3 (0.76)	12/51
Black, Non-Hispanic	252.4 (1.16)	4/40	Black, Non-Hispanic	264.4 (0.97)	3/41
Asian, Non-Hispanic	275.8 (4.32)	8/24	Asian, Non-Hispanic	305.6 (3.91)	4/23
American Indian, Non-Hispanic	n/a	n/a	American Indian, Non-Hispanic	n/a	n/a
Hispanic	253.4 (2.70)	7/38	Hispanic	268.0 (2.19)	5/38
Proficiency by Parents Highest Level of Ed.			Proficiency by Parents Highest Level of Ed.		
Did Not Finish High School	261.1 (2.82)	1/49	Did Not Finish High School	266.8 (2.66)	7/50
Graduated High School	261.1 (1.18)	6/50	Graduated High School	270.8 (1.68)	19/50
Some Education After High School	268.4 (1.29)	17/50	Some Education After High School	284.1 (1.23)	15/50
Graduated College	271.0 (0.97)	29/50	Graduated College	288.7 (0.99)	31/50
Percent Attaining Achievement Levels			Percent Attaining Achievement Levels		
Below Basic	26.7 (1.43)	49/51	Below Basic	27.7 (1.03)	31/51
Basic or Above	73.3 (1.43)	3/51	Basic or Above	72.3 (1.03)	20/51
Proficient or Above	34.2 (1.16)	16/51	Proficient or Above	29.7 (0.99)	27/51
Advanced or Above	6.6 (0.80)	32/51	Advanced or Above	5.0 (0.51)	28/51

Note: For an explanation of data, please refer to the User's Guide in the front of the book; n/a indicates data not available

Kent County

Caesar Rodney SD
219 Old N Rd • Wyoming, DE 19934-1252
Mailing Address: PO Box 188 • Wyoming, DE 19934-1252
(302) 697-2173 • http://www.k12.de.us/caesarrodney/index.htm
Grade Span: PK-12; Agency Type: 1
Schools: 14
  8 Primary; 3 Middle; 1 High; 2 Other Level
  12 Regular; 2 Special Education; 0 Vocational; 0 Alternative
  0 Magnet; 0 Charter; 6 Title I Eligible; 0 School-wide Title I
Students: 6,608 (51.9% male; 48.0% female)
  Individual Education Program: 1,102 (16.7%);
  English Language Learner: 74 (1.1%); Migrant: 37 (0.6%)
  Eligible for Free Lunch Program: 1,433 (21.7%)
  Eligible for Reduced-Price Lunch Program: 586 (8.9%)
Teachers: 447.0 (14.8 to 1)
Librarians/Media Specialists: 10.0 (660.8 to 1)
Guidance Counselors: 17.0 (388.7 to 1)
Current Spending: ($ per student per year):
  Total: $9,451; Instruction: $5,904; Support Services: $3,129
Enrollment, Drop-out Rates and Diploma Recipients by Race/Ethnicity

Category	Total	White	Black	Asian	AIAN	Hisp.
Enrollment (%)	100.0	66.6	25.6	2.7	0.4	4.7
Drop-out Rate (%)	2.5	2.0	3.5	5.4	0.0	5.2
H.S. Diplomas (#)	310	221	67	8	1	13

Capital SD
945 Forest St • Dover, DE 19904-3498
(302) 672-1556 • http://www.k12.de.us/capital
Grade Span: PK-12; Agency Type: 1
Schools: 12
  7 Primary; 2 Middle; 2 High; 1 Other Level
  10 Regular; 2 Special Education; 0 Vocational; 0 Alternative
  0 Magnet; 0 Charter; 6 Title I Eligible; 6 School-wide Title I
Students: 5,909 (51.8% male; 48.1% female)
  Individual Education Program: 997 (16.9%)
  English Language Learner: 164 (2.8%); Migrant: 2 (<0.1%)
  Eligible for Free Lunch Program: 2,201 (37.2%)
  Eligible for Reduced-Price Lunch Program: 361 (6.1%)
Teachers: 416.4 (14.2 to 1)
Librarians/Media Specialists: 6.0 (984.8 to 1)
Guidance Counselors: 15.0 (393.9 to 1)
Current Spending: ($ per student per year):
  Total: $9,052; Instruction: $5,930; Support Services: $2,784
Enrollment, Drop-out Rates and Diploma Recipients by Race/Ethnicity

Category	Total	White	Black	Asian	AIAN	Hisp.
Enrollment (%)	100.0	44.6	46.7	2.4	0.7	5.6
Drop-out Rate (%)	5.8	5.3	6.4	0.0	0.0	8.5
H.S. Diplomas (#)	267	144	105	10	1	7

Lake Forest SD
5423 Killens Pond Rd • Felton, DE 19943-9801
(302) 284-3020 • http://www.k12.de.us/lakeforest
Grade Span: PK-12; Agency Type: 1
Schools: 6
  3 Primary; 2 Middle; 1 High; 0 Other Level
  6 Regular; 0 Special Education; 0 Vocational; 0 Alternative
  0 Magnet; 0 Charter; 3 Title I Eligible; 3 School-wide Title I
Students: 3,397 (50.5% male; 49.4% female)
  Individual Education Program: 514 (15.1%);
  English Language Learner: 53 (1.6%); Migrant: 2 (0.1%)
  Eligible for Free Lunch Program: 1,032 (30.4%)
  Eligible for Reduced-Price Lunch Program: 303 (8.9%)
Teachers: 244.2 (13.9 to 1)
Librarians/Media Specialists: 2.0 (1,698.5 to 1)
Guidance Counselors: 9.0 (377.4 to 1)
Current Spending: ($ per student per year):
  Total: $9,176; Instruction: $5,411; Support Services: $3,325
Enrollment, Drop-out Rates and Diploma Recipients by Race/Ethnicity

Category	Total	White	Black	Asian	AIAN	Hisp.
Enrollment (%)	100.0	75.5	20.1	1.1	0.4	2.9
Drop-out Rate (%)	5.4	4.4	8.2	9.1	0.0	10.0
H.S. Diplomas (#)	154	117	31	2	0	4

Milford SD
906 Lakeview Ave • Milford, DE 19963-1799
(302) 422-1600 • http://www.milford.k12.de.us
Grade Span: PK-12; Agency Type: 1
Schools: 6
  3 Primary; 1 Middle; 1 High; 1 Other Level
  5 Regular; 1 Special Education; 0 Vocational; 0 Alternative
  0 Magnet; 0 Charter; 4 Title I Eligible; 4 School-wide Title I
Students: 3,795 (51.1% male; 48.8% female)
  Individual Education Program: 607 (16.0%);

English Language Learner: 234 (6.2%); Migrant: 37 (1.0%)
  Eligible for Free Lunch Program: 1,284 (33.8%)
  Eligible for Reduced-Price Lunch Program: 211 (5.6%)
Teachers: 250.7 (15.1 to 1)
Librarians/Media Specialists: 4.0 (948.8 to 1)
Guidance Counselors: 7.7 (492.9 to 1)
Current Spending: ($ per student per year):
  Total: $8,540; Instruction: $5,557; Support Services: $2,544
Enrollment, Drop-out Rates and Diploma Recipients by Race/Ethnicity

Category	Total	White	Black	Asian	AIAN	Hisp.
Enrollment (%)	100.0	62.4	27.8	1.0	0.2	8.5
Drop-out Rate (%)	5.9	4.9	8.1	0.0	0.0	10.8
H.S. Diplomas (#)	198	142	51	0	0	5

Smyrna SD
22 S Main St • Smyrna, DE 19977-1493
(302) 653-8585 • http://www.smyrna.k12.de.us
Grade Span: PK-12; Agency Type: 1
Schools: 7
  3 Primary; 2 Middle; 1 High; 0 Other Level
  6 Regular; 0 Special Education; 0 Vocational; 0 Alternative
  0 Magnet; 0 Charter; 3 Title I Eligible; 0 School-wide Title I
Students: 3,311 (50.6% male; 49.3% female)
  Individual Education Program: 586 (17.7%);
  English Language Learner: 52 (1.6%); Migrant: 9 (0.3%)
  Eligible for Free Lunch Program: 560 (16.9%)
  Eligible for Reduced-Price Lunch Program: 135 (4.1%)
Teachers: 200.0 (16.6 to 1)
Librarians/Media Specialists: 3.0 (1,103.7 to 1)
Guidance Counselors: 8.0 (413.9 to 1)
Current Spending: ($ per student per year):
  Total: $8,433; Instruction: $5,124; Support Services: $2,897
Enrollment, Drop-out Rates and Diploma Recipients by Race/Ethnicity

Category	Total	White	Black	Asian	AIAN	Hisp.
Enrollment (%)	100.0	79.0	16.7	1.3	0.2	2.8
Drop-out Rate (%)	3.9	4.4	1.5	0.0	0.0	4.5
H.S. Diplomas (#)	202	172	25	1	0	4

New Castle County

Appoquinimink SD
118 S Sixth St • Odessa, DE 19730-4010
Mailing Address: PO Box 4010 • Odessa, DE 19730-4010
(302) 378-5010 • http://www.k12.de.us/appoquinimink
Grade Span: PK-12; Agency Type: 1
Schools: 9
  6 Primary; 2 Middle; 1 High; 0 Other Level
  9 Regular; 0 Special Education; 0 Vocational; 0 Alternative
  0 Magnet; 0 Charter; 5 Title I Eligible; 0 School-wide Title I
Students: 6,393 (51.2% male; 48.7% female)
  Individual Education Program: 825 (12.9%);
  English Language Learner: 43 (0.7%); Migrant: 2 (<0.1%)
  Eligible for Free Lunch Program: 424 (6.6%)
  Eligible for Reduced-Price Lunch Program: 151 (2.4%)
Teachers: 357.9 (17.9 to 1)
Librarians/Media Specialists: 8.0 (799.1 to 1)
Guidance Counselors: 13.0 (491.8 to 1)
Current Spending: ($ per student per year):
  Total: $8,228; Instruction: $4,730; Support Services: $3,222
Enrollment, Drop-out Rates and Diploma Recipients by Race/Ethnicity

Category	Total	White	Black	Asian	AIAN	Hisp.
Enrollment (%)	100.0	77.0	17.1	2.3	0.3	3.3
Drop-out Rate (%)	6.0	5.4	10.3	0.0	n/a	0.0
H.S. Diplomas (#)	284	241	38	3	0	2

Brandywine SD
1000 Pennsylvania Ave • Claymont, DE 19703-1237
(302) 792-3800 • http://www.bsd.k12.de.us
Grade Span: PK-12; Agency Type: 1
Schools: 20
  10 Primary; 5 Middle; 3 High; 2 Other Level
  17 Regular; 3 Special Education; 0 Vocational; 0 Alternative
  0 Magnet; 0 Charter; 8 Title I Eligible; 8 School-wide Title I
Students: 10,601 (51.7% male; 48.2% female)
  Individual Education Program: 1,347 (12.7%);
  English Language Learner: 340 (3.2%); Migrant: 4 (<0.1%)
  Eligible for Free Lunch Program: 2,692 (25.4%)
  Eligible for Reduced-Price Lunch Program: 510 (4.8%)
Teachers: 679.9 (15.6 to 1)
Librarians/Media Specialists: 13.0 (814.3 to 1)
Guidance Counselors: 32.5 (325.7 to 1)
Current Spending: ($ per student per year):
  Total: $9,702; Instruction: $5,865; Support Services: $3,492

Enrollment, Drop-out Rates and Diploma Recipients by Race/Ethnicity

Category	Total	White	Black	Asian	AIAN	Hisp.
Enrollment (%)	100.0	55.5	37.6	3.6	0.2	3.1
Drop-out Rate (%)	5.8	3.5	10.0	3.2	0.0	10.8
H.S. Diplomas (#)	694	494	164	23	1	12

Christina SD
83 E Main St • Newark, DE 19711-4671
(302) 454-2000 • http://www.christina.k12.de.us
Grade Span: PK-12; **Agency Type:** 1
Schools: 28
  15 Primary; 7 Middle; 3 High; 3 Other Level
  26 Regular; 2 Special Education; 0 Vocational; 0 Alternative
  0 Magnet; 0 Charter; 15 Title I Eligible; 10 School-wide Title I
Students: 19,407 (53.4% male; 46.5% female)
  Individual Education Program: 3,048 (15.7%);
  English Language Learner: 559 (2.9%); Migrant: 5 (<0.1%)
  Eligible for Free Lunch Program: 5,745 (29.7%)
  Eligible for Reduced-Price Lunch Program: 1,151 (5.9%)
Teachers: 1,315.8 (14.7 to 1)
Librarians/Media Specialists: 25.0 (774.6 to 1)
Guidance Counselors: 17.0 (1,139.1 to 1)
Current Spending: ($ per student per year):
  Total: $10,604; Instruction: $6,698; Support Services: $3,636

Enrollment, Drop-out Rates and Diploma Recipients by Race/Ethnicity

Category	Total	White	Black	Asian	AIAN	Hisp.
Enrollment (%)	100.0	47.0	38.9	4.0	0.1	9.9
Drop-out Rate (%)	10.5	7.2	14.2	9.0	15.4	18.5
H.S. Diplomas (#)	857	492	272	50	3	40

Colonial SD
318 E Basin Rd • New Castle, DE 19720-4214
(302) 323-2700 • http://www.dataservice.org/colonial
Grade Span: PK-12; **Agency Type:** 1
Schools: 15
  9 Primary; 3 Middle; 1 High; 2 Other Level
  13 Regular; 1 Special Education; 0 Vocational; 1 Alternative
  0 Magnet; 0 Charter; 8 Title I Eligible; 0 School-wide Title I
Students: 10,339 (51.9% male; 48.0% female)
  Individual Education Program: 1,562 (15.1%);
  English Language Learner: 444 (4.3%); Migrant: 0 (0.0%)
  Eligible for Free Lunch Program: 3,359 (32.5%)
  Eligible for Reduced-Price Lunch Program: 714 (6.9%)
Teachers: 644.8 (16.0 to 1)
Librarians/Media Specialists: 11.0 (938.4 to 1)
Guidance Counselors: 28.0 (368.6 to 1)
Current Spending: ($ per student per year):
  Total: $9,085; Instruction: $5,775; Support Services: $2,898

Enrollment, Drop-out Rates and Diploma Recipients by Race/Ethnicity

Category	Total	White	Black	Asian	AIAN	Hisp.
Enrollment (%)	100.0	44.4	41.9	2.4	0.3	11.0
Drop-out Rate (%)	13.7	14.6	13.5	5.0	0.0	13.8
H.S. Diplomas (#)	406	201	176	10	0	19

New Castle County Votech SD
1417 Newport Rd • Wilmington, DE 19804-3499
(302) 995-8000 • http://www.nccvotech.org
Grade Span: 08-12; **Agency Type:** 1
Schools: 3
  0 Primary; 0 Middle; 3 High; 0 Other Level
  0 Regular; 0 Special Education; 3 Vocational; 0 Alternative
  0 Magnet; 0 Charter; 2 Title I Eligible; 0 School-wide Title I
Students: 3,392 (50.3% male; 49.6% female)
  Individual Education Program: 465 (13.7%);
  English Language Learner: 22 (0.6%); Migrant: 0 (0.0%)
  Eligible for Free Lunch Program: 576 (17.0%)
  Eligible for Reduced-Price Lunch Program: 215 (6.3%)
Teachers: 282.3 (12.0 to 1)
Librarians/Media Specialists: 3.0 (1,130.7 to 1)
Guidance Counselors: 11.7 (289.9 to 1)
Current Spending: ($ per student per year):
  Total: $14,373; Instruction: $8,592; Support Services: $5,388

Enrollment, Drop-out Rates and Diploma Recipients by Race/Ethnicity

Category	Total	White	Black	Asian	AIAN	Hisp.
Enrollment (%)	100.0	59.9	34.3	0.5	0.2	5.2
Drop-out Rate (%)	2.3	2.0	2.6	0.0	0.0	3.6
H.S. Diplomas (#)	691	440	211	4	0	36

Red Clay Consolidated SD
2916 Duncan Rd • Wilmington, DE 19808
(302) 651-2600 • http://www.redclay.k12.de.us
Grade Span: PK-12; **Agency Type:** 1
Schools: 28
  14 Primary; 5 Middle; 3 High; 6 Other Level
  22 Regular; 2 Special Education; 0 Vocational; 4 Alternative

  1 Magnet; 0 Charter; 9 Title I Eligible; 2 School-wide Title I
Students: 15,556 (50.8% male; 49.1% female)
  Individual Education Program: 2,123 (13.6%);
  English Language Learner: 1,052 (6.8%); Migrant: 9 (0.1%)
  Eligible for Free Lunch Program: 4,770 (30.7%)
  Eligible for Reduced-Price Lunch Program: 765 (4.9%)
Teachers: 964.5 (16.1 to 1)
Librarians/Media Specialists: 18.0 (863.3 to 1)
Guidance Counselors: 31.0 (501.3 to 1)
Current Spending: ($ per student per year):
  Total: $9,910; Instruction: $6,225; Support Services: $3,356

Enrollment, Drop-out Rates and Diploma Recipients by Race/Ethnicity

Category	Total	White	Black	Asian	AIAN	Hisp.
Enrollment (%)	100.0	50.7	28.8	3.8	0.1	16.6
Drop-out Rate (%)	7.9	4.7	11.9	1.4	0.0	16.1
H.S. Diplomas (#)	758	484	177	38	1	58

Sussex County

Cape Henlopen SD
1270 Kings Hwy • Lewes, DE 19958-1798
(302) 645-6686 • http://www.k12.de.us/capehenlopen/
Grade Span: PK-12; **Agency Type:** 1
Schools: 8
  4 Primary; 2 Middle; 1 High; 1 Other Level
  7 Regular; 1 Special Education; 0 Vocational; 0 Alternative
  0 Magnet; 0 Charter; 4 Title I Eligible; 4 School-wide Title I
Students: 4,262 (51.5% male; 48.4% female)
  Individual Education Program: 722 (16.9%);
  English Language Learner: 90 (2.1%); Migrant: 21 (0.5%)
  Eligible for Free Lunch Program: 1,160 (27.2%)
  Eligible for Reduced-Price Lunch Program: 249 (5.8%)
Teachers: 290.5 (14.7 to 1)
Librarians/Media Specialists: 4.0 (1,065.5 to 1)
Guidance Counselors: 6.7 (636.1 to 1)
Current Spending: ($ per student per year):
  Total: $10,153; Instruction: $6,424; Support Services: $3,316

Enrollment, Drop-out Rates and Diploma Recipients by Race/Ethnicity

Category	Total	White	Black	Asian	AIAN	Hisp.
Enrollment (%)	100.0	72.7	20.4	1.3	0.8	4.8
Drop-out Rate (%)	5.7	4.9	8.5	7.1	0.0	6.5
H.S. Diplomas (#)	237	188	39	4	0	6

Indian River SD
31 Hoosier St • Selbyville, DE 19975
Mailing Address: Route 2 Box 156 • Selbyville, DE 19975
(302) 436-1000 • http://www.k12.de.us/indianriver
Grade Span: PK-12; **Agency Type:** 1
Schools: 14
  8 Primary; 2 Middle; 2 High; 2 Other Level
  11 Regular; 1 Special Education; 0 Vocational; 2 Alternative
  1 Magnet; 0 Charter; 8 Title I Eligible; 7 School-wide Title I
Students: 7,757 (50.2% male; 49.7% female)
  Individual Education Program: 1,422 (18.3%);
  English Language Learner: 486 (6.3%); Migrant: 117 (1.5%)
  Eligible for Free Lunch Program: 2,543 (32.8%)
  Eligible for Reduced-Price Lunch Program: 627 (8.1%)
Teachers: 572.0 (13.6 to 1)
Librarians/Media Specialists: 8.0 (969.4 to 1)
Guidance Counselors: 20.0 (387.8 to 1)
Current Spending: ($ per student per year):
  Total: $9,312; Instruction: $5,927; Support Services: $2,982

Enrollment, Drop-out Rates and Diploma Recipients by Race/Ethnicity

Category	Total	White	Black	Asian	AIAN	Hisp.
Enrollment (%)	100.0	65.4	20.5	1.0	0.5	12.6
Drop-out Rate (%)	5.8	5.0	7.9	0.0	20.0	5.8
H.S. Diplomas (#)	379	279	76	4	3	17

Laurel SD
1160 S Central Ave • Laurel, DE 19956-1413
(302) 875-6100 • http://www.k12.de.us/laurel
Grade Span: PK-12; **Agency Type:** 1
Schools: 6
  2 Primary; 2 Middle; 2 High; 0 Other Level
  5 Regular; 0 Special Education; 0 Vocational; 1 Alternative
  0 Magnet; 0 Charter; 2 Title I Eligible; 2 School-wide Title I
Students: 2,008 (50.7% male; 49.2% female)
  Individual Education Program: 270 (13.4%);
  English Language Learner: 63 (3.1%); Migrant: 7 (0.3%)
  Eligible for Free Lunch Program: 804 (40.0%)
  Eligible for Reduced-Price Lunch Program: 162 (8.1%)
Teachers: 130.0 (15.4 to 1)
Librarians/Media Specialists: 3.0 (669.3 to 1)
Guidance Counselors: 5.0 (401.6 to 1)
Current Spending: ($ per student per year):
  Total: $9,095; Instruction: $5,532; Support Services: $3,088

Enrollment, Drop-out Rates and Diploma Recipients by Race/Ethnicity

Category	Total	White	Black	Asian	AIAN	Hisp.
Enrollment (%)	100.0	65.0	30.2	1.6	0.1	3.1
Drop-out Rate (%)	3.5	1.2	8.0	0.0	n/a	9.1
H.S. Diplomas (#)	102	71	30	1	0	0

Seaford SD
390 N Market St Extend • Seaford, DE 19973-1433
(302) 629-4587 • http://www.seaford.k12.de.us
Grade Span: PK-12; **Agency Type:** 1
Schools: 7
    4 Primary; 1 Middle; 1 High; 1 Other Level
    6 Regular; 1 Special Education; 0 Vocational; 0 Alternative
    0 Magnet; 0 Charter; 5 Title I Eligible; 5 School-wide Title I
Students: 3,447   (51.8% male; 48.1% female)
    Individual Education Program: 535 (15.5%);
    English Language Learner: 192 (5.6%); Migrant: 10 (0.3%)
    Eligible for Free Lunch Program: 1,442 (41.8%)
    Eligible for Reduced-Price Lunch Program: 306 (8.9%)
Teachers: 222.2 (15.5 to 1)
Librarians/Media Specialists: 4.0 (861.8 to 1)
Guidance Counselors: 9.0 (383.0 to 1)
Current Spending: ($ per student per year):
    Total: $8,960; Instruction: $5,844; Support Services: $2,704

Enrollment, Drop-out Rates and Diploma Recipients by Race/Ethnicity

Category	Total	White	Black	Asian	AIAN	Hisp.
Enrollment (%)	100.0	54.0	39.7	1.2	0.1	5.0
Drop-out Rate (%)	4.6	3.5	6.4	8.3	0.0	0.0
H.S. Diplomas (#)	186	111	69	4	0	2

Woodbridge SD
Governors Ave • Greenwood, DE 19950
Mailing Address: PO Box 869 • Greenwood, DE 19950
(302) 337-8296
Grade Span: PK-12; **Agency Type:** 1
Schools: 4
    2 Primary; 1 Middle; 1 High; 0 Other Level
    4 Regular; 0 Special Education; 0 Vocational; 0 Alternative
    0 Magnet; 0 Charter; 3 Title I Eligible; 3 School-wide Title I
Students: 1,915   (49.8% male; 50.1% female)
    Individual Education Program: 226 (11.8%);
    English Language Learner: 70 (3.7%); Migrant: 19 (1.0%)
    Eligible for Free Lunch Program: 852 (44.5%)
    Eligible for Reduced-Price Lunch Program: 184 (9.6%)
Teachers: 138.0 (13.9 to 1)
Librarians/Media Specialists: 2.0 (957.5 to 1)
Guidance Counselors: 8.0 (239.4 to 1)
Current Spending: ($ per student per year):
    Total: $9,280; Instruction: $5,407; Support Services: $3,364

Enrollment, Drop-out Rates and Diploma Recipients by Race/Ethnicity

Category	Total	White	Black	Asian	AIAN	Hisp.
Enrollment (%)	100.0	57.2	34.0	0.5	0.4	7.8
Drop-out Rate (%)	13.7	12.6	15.9	n/a	n/a	11.8
H.S. Diplomas (#)	65	51	13	0	0	1

Number of Schools

Rank	Number	District Name	City
1	28	Christina SD	Newark
1	28	Red Clay Consolidated SD	Wilmington
3	20	Brandywine SD	Claymont
4	15	Colonial SD	New Castle
5	14	Caesar Rodney SD	Wyoming
5	14	Indian River SD	Selbyville
7	12	Capital SD	Dover
8	9	Appoquinimink SD	Odessa
9	8	Cape Henlopen SD	Lewes
10	7	Seaford SD	Seaford
10	7	Smyrna SD	Smyrna
12	6	Lake Forest SD	Felton
12	6	Laurel SD	Laurel
12	6	Milford SD	Milford
15	4	Woodbridge SD	Greenwood
16	3	New Castle County Votech SD	Wilmington

Number of Teachers

Rank	Number	District Name	City
1	1,315	Christina SD	Newark
2	964	Red Clay Consolidated SD	Wilmington
3	679	Brandywine SD	Claymont
4	644	Colonial SD	New Castle
5	572	Indian River SD	Selbyville
6	447	Caesar Rodney SD	Wyoming
7	416	Capital SD	Dover
8	357	Appoquinimink SD	Odessa
9	290	Cape Henlopen SD	Lewes
10	282	New Castle County Votech SD	Wilmington
11	250	Milford SD	Milford
12	244	Lake Forest SD	Felton
13	222	Seaford SD	Seaford
14	200	Smyrna SD	Smyrna
15	138	Woodbridge SD	Greenwood
16	130	Laurel SD	Laurel

Number of Students

Rank	Number	District Name	City
1	19,407	Christina SD	Newark
2	15,556	Red Clay Consolidated SD	Wilmington
3	10,601	Brandywine SD	Claymont
4	10,339	Colonial SD	New Castle
5	7,757	Indian River SD	Selbyville
6	6,608	Caesar Rodney SD	Wyoming
7	6,393	Appoquinimink SD	Odessa
8	5,909	Capital SD	Dover
9	4,262	Cape Henlopen SD	Lewes
10	3,795	Milford SD	Milford
11	3,447	Seaford SD	Seaford
12	3,397	Lake Forest SD	Felton
13	3,392	New Castle County Votech SD	Wilmington
14	3,311	Smyrna SD	Smyrna
15	2,008	Laurel SD	Laurel
16	1,915	Woodbridge SD	Greenwood

Male Students

Rank	Percent	District Name	City
1	53.4	Christina SD	Newark
2	51.9	Colonial SD	New Castle
3	51.9	Caesar Rodney SD	Wyoming
4	51.8	Seaford SD	Seaford
5	51.8	Capital SD	Dover
6	51.7	Brandywine SD	Claymont
7	51.5	Cape Henlopen SD	Lewes
8	51.2	Appoquinimink SD	Odessa
9	51.1	Milford SD	Milford
10	50.8	Red Clay Consolidated SD	Wilmington
11	50.7	Laurel SD	Laurel
12	50.6	Smyrna SD	Smyrna
13	50.5	Lake Forest SD	Felton
14	50.3	New Castle County Votech SD	Wilmington
15	50.2	Indian River SD	Selbyville
16	49.8	Woodbridge SD	Greenwood

Female Students

Rank	Percent	District Name	City
1	50.1	Woodbridge SD	Greenwood
2	49.7	Indian River SD	Selbyville
3	49.6	New Castle County Votech SD	Wilmington
4	49.4	Lake Forest SD	Felton
5	49.3	Smyrna SD	Smyrna
6	49.2	Laurel SD	Laurel
7	49.1	Red Clay Consolidated SD	Wilmington
8	48.8	Milford SD	Milford
9	48.7	Appoquinimink SD	Odessa
10	48.4	Cape Henlopen SD	Lewes
11	48.2	Brandywine SD	Claymont
12	48.1	Capital SD	Dover
13	48.1	Seaford SD	Seaford
14	48.0	Caesar Rodney SD	Wyoming
15	48.0	Colonial SD	New Castle
16	46.5	Christina SD	Newark

Individual Education Program Students

Rank	Percent	District Name	City
1	18.3	Indian River SD	Selbyville
2	17.7	Smyrna SD	Smyrna
3	16.9	Cape Henlopen SD	Lewes
3	16.9	Capital SD	Dover
5	16.7	Caesar Rodney SD	Wyoming
6	16.0	Milford SD	Milford
7	15.7	Christina SD	Newark
8	15.5	Seaford SD	Seaford
9	15.1	Colonial SD	New Castle
9	15.1	Lake Forest SD	Felton
11	13.7	New Castle County Votech SD	Wilmington
12	13.6	Red Clay Consolidated SD	Wilmington
13	13.4	Laurel SD	Laurel
14	12.9	Appoquinimink SD	Odessa
15	12.7	Brandywine SD	Claymont
16	11.8	Woodbridge SD	Greenwood

English Language Learner Students

Rank	Percent	District Name	City
1	6.8	Red Clay Consolidated SD	Wilmington
2	6.3	Indian River SD	Selbyville
3	6.2	Milford SD	Milford
4	5.6	Seaford SD	Seaford
5	4.3	Colonial SD	New Castle
6	3.7	Woodbridge SD	Greenwood
7	3.2	Brandywine SD	Claymont
8	3.1	Laurel SD	Laurel
9	2.9	Christina SD	Newark
10	2.8	Capital SD	Dover
11	2.1	Cape Henlopen SD	Lewes
12	1.6	Lake Forest SD	Felton
12	1.6	Smyrna SD	Smyrna
14	1.1	Caesar Rodney SD	Wyoming
15	0.7	Appoquinimink SD	Odessa
16	0.6	New Castle County Votech SD	Wilmington

Migrant Students

Rank	Percent	District Name	City
1	1.5	Indian River SD	Selbyville
2	1.0	Milford SD	Milford
2	1.0	Woodbridge SD	Greenwood
4	0.6	Caesar Rodney SD	Wyoming
5	0.5	Cape Henlopen SD	Lewes
6	0.3	Laurel SD	Laurel
6	0.3	Seaford SD	Seaford
6	0.3	Smyrna SD	Smyrna
9	0.1	Lake Forest SD	Felton
9	0.1	Red Clay Consolidated SD	Wilmington
11	0.0	Appoquinimink SD	Odessa
11	0.0	Brandywine SD	Claymont
11	0.0	Capital SD	Dover
11	0.0	Christina SD	Newark
15	0.0	Colonial SD	New Castle
15	0.0	New Castle County Votech SD	Wilmington

Students Eligible for Free Lunch

Rank	Percent	District Name	City
1	44.5	Woodbridge SD	Greenwood
2	41.8	Seaford SD	Seaford
3	40.0	Laurel SD	Laurel
4	37.2	Capital SD	Dover
5	33.8	Milford SD	Milford
6	32.8	Indian River SD	Selbyville
7	32.5	Colonial SD	New Castle
8	30.7	Red Clay Consolidated SD	Wilmington
9	30.4	Lake Forest SD	Felton
10	29.7	Christina SD	Newark
11	27.2	Cape Henlopen SD	Lewes
12	25.4	Brandywine SD	Claymont
13	21.7	Caesar Rodney SD	Wyoming
14	17.0	New Castle County Votech SD	Wilmington
15	16.9	Smyrna SD	Smyrna
16	6.6	Appoquinimink SD	Odessa

Students Eligible for Reduced-Price Lunch

Rank	Percent	District Name	City
1	9.6	Woodbridge SD	Greenwood
2	8.9	Caesar Rodney SD	Wyoming
2	8.9	Lake Forest SD	Felton
2	8.9	Seaford SD	Seaford
5	8.1	Indian River SD	Selbyville
5	8.1	Laurel SD	Laurel
7	6.9	Colonial SD	New Castle
8	6.3	New Castle County Votech SD	Wilmington
9	6.1	Capital SD	Dover
10	5.9	Christina SD	Newark
11	5.8	Cape Henlopen SD	Lewes
12	5.6	Milford SD	Milford
13	4.9	Red Clay Consolidated SD	Wilmington
14	4.8	Brandywine SD	Claymont
15	4.1	Smyrna SD	Smyrna
16	2.4	Appoquinimink SD	Odessa

Student/Teacher Ratio

Rank	Ratio	District Name	City
1	17.9	Appoquinimink SD	Odessa
2	16.6	Smyrna SD	Smyrna
3	16.1	Red Clay Consolidated SD	Wilmington
4	16.0	Colonial SD	New Castle
5	15.6	Brandywine SD	Claymont
6	15.5	Seaford SD	Seaford
7	15.4	Laurel SD	Laurel
8	15.1	Milford SD	Milford
9	14.8	Caesar Rodney SD	Wyoming
10	14.7	Cape Henlopen SD	Lewes
10	14.7	Christina SD	Newark
12	14.2	Capital SD	Dover
13	13.9	Lake Forest SD	Felton
13	13.9	Woodbridge SD	Greenwood
15	13.6	Indian River SD	Selbyville
16	12.0	New Castle County Votech SD	Wilmington

Student/Librarian Ratio

Rank	Ratio	District Name	City
1	1,698.5	Lake Forest SD	Felton
2	1,130.7	New Castle County Votech SD	Wilmington
3	1,103.7	Smyrna SD	Smyrna
4	1,065.5	Cape Henlopen SD	Lewes
5	984.8	Capital SD	Dover
6	969.4	Indian River SD	Selbyville
7	957.5	Woodbridge SD	Greenwood
8	948.8	Milford SD	Milford
9	938.4	Colonial SD	New Castle
10	863.3	Red Clay Consolidated SD	Wilmington
11	861.8	Seaford SD	Seaford
12	814.3	Brandywine SD	Claymont
13	799.1	Appoquinimink SD	Odessa
14	774.6	Christina SD	Newark
15	669.3	Laurel SD	Laurel
16	660.8	Caesar Rodney SD	Wyoming

Student/Counselor Ratio

Rank	Ratio	District Name	City
1	1,139.1	Christina SD	Newark
2	636.1	Cape Henlopen SD	Lewes
3	501.3	Red Clay Consolidated SD	Wilmington
4	492.9	Milford SD	Milford
5	491.8	Appoquinimink SD	Odessa
6	413.9	Smyrna SD	Smyrna
7	401.6	Laurel SD	Laurel
8	393.9	Capital SD	Dover
9	388.7	Caesar Rodney SD	Wyoming
10	387.8	Indian River SD	Selbyville
11	383.0	Seaford SD	Seaford
12	377.4	Lake Forest SD	Felton
13	368.6	Colonial SD	New Castle
14	325.7	Brandywine SD	Claymont
15	289.9	New Castle County Votech SD	Wilmington
16	239.4	Woodbridge SD	Greenwood

Current Spending per Student in FY2003

Rank	Dollars	District Name	City
1	14,373	New Castle County Votech SD	Wilmington
2	10,604	Christina SD	Newark
3	10,153	Cape Henlopen SD	Lewes
4	9,910	Red Clay Consolidated SD	Wilmington
5	9,702	Brandywine SD	Claymont
6	9,451	Caesar Rodney SD	Wyoming
7	9,312	Indian River SD	Selbyville
8	9,280	Woodbridge SD	Greenwood
9	9,176	Lake Forest SD	Felton
10	9,095	Laurel SD	Laurel
11	9,085	Colonial SD	New Castle
12	9,052	Capital SD	Dover
13	8,960	Seaford SD	Seaford
14	8,540	Milford SD	Milford
15	8,433	Smyrna SD	Smyrna

| 16 | 8,228 | Appoquinimink SD | Odessa |

Number of Diploma Recipients

Rank	Number	District Name	City
1	857	Christina SD	Newark
2	758	Red Clay Consolidated SD	Wilmington
3	694	Brandywine SD	Claymont
4	691	New Castle County Votech SD	Wilmington
5	406	Colonial SD	New Castle
6	379	Indian River SD	Selbyville
7	310	Caesar Rodney SD	Wyoming
8	284	Appoquinimink SD	Odessa
9	267	Capital SD	Dover
10	237	Cape Henlopen SD	Lewes
11	202	Smyrna SD	Smyrna
12	198	Milford SD	Milford
13	186	Seaford SD	Seaford
14	154	Lake Forest SD	Felton
15	102	Laurel SD	Laurel
16	65	Woodbridge SD	Greenwood

High School Drop-out Rate

Rank	Percent	District Name	City
1	13.7	Colonial SD	New Castle
1	13.7	Woodbridge SD	Greenwood
3	10.5	Christina SD	Newark
4	7.9	Red Clay Consolidated SD	Wilmington
5	6.0	Appoquinimink SD	Odessa
6	5.9	Milford SD	Milford
7	5.8	Brandywine SD	Claymont
7	5.8	Capital SD	Dover
7	5.8	Indian River SD	Selbyville
10	5.7	Cape Henlopen SD	Lewes
11	5.4	Lake Forest SD	Felton
12	4.6	Seaford SD	Seaford
13	3.9	Smyrna SD	Smyrna
14	3.5	Laurel SD	Laurel
15	2.5	Caesar Rodney SD	Wyoming
16	2.3	New Castle County Votech SD	Wilmington

District of Columbia

District of Columbia Public School Educational Profile

Category	Value	Category	Value
Schools *(2003-2004)*	207	**Diploma Recipients** *(2002-2003)*	3,085
Instructional Level		White, Non-Hispanic	128
Primary	122	Black, Non-Hispanic	2,679
Middle	29	Asian/Pacific Islander	66
High	32	American Indian/Alaskan Native	3
Other Level	23	Hispanic	209
Curriculum		**High School Drop-out Rate** (%) *(2001-2002)*	n/a
Regular	184	White, Non-Hispanic	n/a
Special Education	13	Black, Non-Hispanic	n/a
Vocational	2	Asian/Pacific Islander	n/a
Alternative	7	American Indian/Alaskan Native	n/a
Type		Hispanic	n/a
Magnet	3	**Staff** *(2003-2004)*	
Charter	37	Teachers	5,676.0
Title I Eligible	169	Average Salary ($)	62,909
School-wide Title I	159	Librarians/Media Specialists	40.0
Students *(2003-2004)*	78,057	Guidance Counselors	60.0
Gender (%)		**Ratios** *(2003-2004)*	
Male	50.4	Student/Teacher Ratio	13.8 to 1
Female	49.6	Student/Librarian Ratio	1,951.4 to 1
Race/Ethnicity (%)		Student/Counselor Ratio	1,301.0 to 1
White, Non-Hispanic	4.3	**College Entrance Exam Scores** *(2005)*	
Black, Non-Hispanic	84.7	Scholastic Aptitude Test (SAT)	
Asian/Pacific Islander	1.5	Participation Rate (%)	79
American Indian/Alaskan Native	0.1	Mean SAT Reasoning Test Verbal Score	490
Hispanic	9.5	Mean SAT Reasoning Test Math Score	478
Classification (%)		American College Testing Program (ACT)	
Individual Education Program (IEP)	17.0	Participation Rate (%)	29
Migrant *(2002-2003)*	1.2	Average Composite Score	18.0
English Language Learner (ELL)	7.3	Average English Score	17.2
Eligible for Free Lunch Program	47.3	Average Math Score	18.0
Eligible for Reduced-Price Lunch Program	4.2	Average Reading Score	18.5
Current Spending *($ per student in FY 2003)*	13,363	Average Science Score	17.8
Instruction	7,011		
Support Services	6,014		

Note: *For an explanation of data, please refer to the User's Guide in the front of the book*

District of Columbia NAEP 2005 Test Scores

Reading			Mathematics		
Grade/Category	Value	Rank	Grade/Category	Value	Rank
4th Grade			**4th Grade**		
Average Proficiency	190.8 (0.98)	51/51	Average Proficiency	211.1 (0.76)	51/51
Proficiency by Gender/Race/Ethnicity			Proficiency by Gender/Race/Ethnicity		
Male	185.8 (1.32)	51/51	Male	211.5 (1.00)	51/51
Female	195.1 (1.29)	51/51	Female	210.7 (1.00)	51/51
White, Non-Hispanic	252.3 (3.87)	1/51	White, Non-Hispanic	265.6 (2.60)	1/51
Black, Non-Hispanic	186.7 (1.03)	42/42	Black, Non-Hispanic	207.4 (0.71)	42/42
Asian, Non-Hispanic	n/a	n/a	Asian, Non-Hispanic	n/a	n/a
American Indian, Non-Hispanic	n/a	n/a	American Indian, Non-Hispanic	n/a	n/a
Hispanic	193.4 (3.44)	37/40	Hispanic	214.9 (2.41)	40/41
Proficiency by Class Size			Proficiency by Class Size		
Less than 16 Students	184.4 (3.84)	34/34	Less than 16 Students	207.0 (2.31)	35/35
16 to 18 Students	182.7 (1.88)	33/33	16 to 18 Students	209.1 (1.41)	31/31
19 to 20 Students	192.5 (2.46)	38/38	19 to 20 Students	210.0 (1.26)	38/38
21 to 25 Students	196.6 (1.28)	51/51	21 to 25 Students	214.6 (1.06)	51/51
Greater than 25 Students	188.1 (2.98)	36/36	Greater than 25 Students	207.7 (2.17)	33/33
Percent Attaining Achievement Levels			Percent Attaining Achievement Levels		
Below Basic	67.0 (1.00)	1/51	Below Basic	55.4 (1.16)	1/51
Basic or Above	33.0 (1.00)	51/51	Basic or Above	44.6 (1.16)	51/51
Proficient or Above	11.2 (0.84)	51/51	Proficient or Above	9.6 (0.78)	51/51
Advanced or Above	2.2 (0.35)	51/51	Advanced or Above	1.3 (0.33)	50/51
8th Grade			**8th Grade**		
Average Proficiency	238.2 (0.87)	51/51	Average Proficiency	245.2 (0.86)	51/51
Proficiency by Gender/Race/Ethnicity			Proficiency by Gender/Race/Ethnicity		
Male	230.0 (1.25)	51/51	Male	245.6 (1.19)	51/51
Female	245.5 (1.38)	51/51	Female	244.9 (1.22)	51/51
White, Non-Hispanic	300.6 (5.18)	1/51	White, Non-Hispanic	317.3 (4.24)	1/51
Black, Non-Hispanic	234.9 (0.90)	39/40	Black, Non-Hispanic	241.2 (0.95)	40/41
Asian, Non-Hispanic	n/a	n/a	Asian, Non-Hispanic	n/a	n/a
American Indian, Non-Hispanic	n/a	n/a	American Indian, Non-Hispanic	n/a	n/a
Hispanic	247.5 (3.21)	16/38	Hispanic	252.1 (2.98)	37/38
Proficiency by Parents Highest Level of Ed.			Proficiency by Parents Highest Level of Ed.		
Did Not Finish High School	233.1 (3.00)	49/49	Did Not Finish High School	242.7 (3.57)	50/50
Graduated High School	232.3 (1.87)	50/50	Graduated High School	237.8 (1.29)	50/50
Some Education After High School	247.2 (1.97)	50/50	Some Education After High School	252.4 (1.84)	50/50
Graduated College	244.0 (1.52)	50/50	Graduated College	252.8 (1.32)	50/50
Percent Attaining Achievement Levels			Percent Attaining Achievement Levels		
Below Basic	67.0 (1.00)	1/51	Below Basic	69.3 (1.34)	1/51
Basic or Above	33.0 (1.00)	51/51	Basic or Above	30.7 (1.34)	51/51
Proficient or Above	11.2 (0.84)	51/51	Proficient or Above	6.9 (0.64)	51/51
Advanced or Above	2.2 (0.35)	51/51	Advanced or Above	1.8 (0.31)	47/51

Note: *For an explanation of data, please refer to the User's Guide in the front of the book; n/a indicates data not available*

District Of Columbia County

District of Columbia Pub Schls
825 Northcapitol St NE • Washington, DC 20002-4232
Mailing Address: 825 N Capitol St NE • Washington, DC 20003
(202) 442-5885 • http://www.k12.dc.us/dcps/home.html
Grade Span: PK-12; **Agency Type:** 1
Schools: 170
   107 Primary; 23 Middle; 20 High; 19 Other Level
   147 Regular; 13 Special Education; 2 Vocational; 7 Alternative
   3 Magnet; 0 Charter; 132 Title I Eligible; 126 School-wide Title I
Students: 65,099 (50.4% male; 49.5% female)
   Individual Education Program: 11,977 (18.4%);
   English Language Learner: 5,201 (8.0%); Migrant: 881 (1.4%)
   Eligible for Free Lunch Program: 36,889 (56.7%)
   Eligible for Reduced-Price Lunch Program: 3,250 (5.0%)
Teachers: 4,898.0 (13.3 to 1)
Librarians/Media Specialists: 40.0 (1,627.5 to 1)
Guidance Counselors: 60.0 (1,085.0 to 1)
Current Spending: ($ per student per year):
   Total: $13,363; Instruction: $7,011; Support Services: $6,014

Enrollment, Drop-out Rates and Diploma Recipients by Race/Ethnicity

Category	Total	White	Black	Asian	AIAN	Hisp.
Enrollment (%)	100.0	4.9	83.6	1.7	0.1	9.7
Drop-out Rate (%)	n/a	n/a	n/a	n/a	n/a	n/a
H.S. Diplomas (#)	2,894	128	2,507	63	1	195

Edison-Friendship Public Charter School Agency
1345 Potomac Ave SE • Washington, DC 20002
(202) 547-5800
Grade Span: PK-12; **Agency Type:** 7
Schools: 1
   0 Primary; 0 Middle; 0 High; 1 Other Level
   1 Regular; 0 Special Education; 0 Vocational; 0 Alternative
   0 Magnet; 1 Charter; 1 Title I Eligible; 1 School-wide Title I
Students: 3,017 (n/a% male; n/a% female)
   Individual Education Program: 297 (9.8%);
   English Language Learner: 2 (0.1%); Migrant: 0 (0.0%)
   Eligible for Free Lunch Program: n/a
   Eligible for Reduced-Price Lunch Program: n/a
Teachers: 71.0 (42.5 to 1)
Librarians/Media Specialists: n/a
Guidance Counselors: n/a
Current Spending: ($ per student per year):
   Total: n/a; Instruction: n/a; Support Services: n/a

Enrollment, Drop-out Rates and Diploma Recipients by Race/Ethnicity

Category	Total	White	Black	Asian	AIAN	Hisp.
Enrollment (%)	100.0	0.0	100.0	0.0	0.0	0.0
Drop-out Rate (%)	n/a	n/a	n/a	n/a	n/a	n/a
H.S. Diplomas (#)	n/a	n/a	n/a	n/a	n/a	n/a

Number of Schools

Rank	Number	District Name	City
1	170	District of Columbia Pub Schls	Washington
2	1	Edison-Friendship Public Charter	Washington

Number of Teachers

Rank	Number	District Name	City
1	4,898	District of Columbia Pub Schls	Washington
2	71	Edison-Friendship Public Charter	Washington

Number of Students

Rank	Number	District Name	City
1	65,099	District of Columbia Pub Schls	Washington
2	3,017	Edison-Friendship Public Charter	Washington

Male Students

Rank	Percent	District Name	City
1	50.4	District of Columbia Pub Schls	Washington
2	n/a	Edison-Friendship Public Charter	Washington

Female Students

Rank	Percent	District Name	City
1	49.5	District of Columbia Pub Schls	Washington
2	n/a	Edison-Friendship Public Charter	Washington

Individual Education Program Students

Rank	Percent	District Name	City
1	18.4	District of Columbia Pub Schls	Washington
2	9.8	Edison-Friendship Public Charter	Washington

English Language Learner Students

Rank	Percent	District Name	City
1	8.0	District of Columbia Pub Schls	Washington
2	0.1	Edison-Friendship Public Charter	Washington

Migrant Students

Rank	Percent	District Name	City
1	1.4	District of Columbia Pub Schls	Washington
2	0.0	Edison-Friendship Public Charter	Washington

Students Eligible for Free Lunch

Rank	Percent	District Name	City
1	56.7	District of Columbia Pub Schls	Washington
2	n/a	Edison-Friendship Public Charter	Washington

Students Eligible for Reduced-Price Lunch

Rank	Percent	District Name	City
1	5.0	District of Columbia Pub Schls	Washington
2	n/a	Edison-Friendship Public Charter	Washington

Student/Teacher Ratio

Rank	Ratio	District Name	City
1	42.5	Edison-Friendship Public Charter	Washington
2	13.3	District of Columbia Pub Schls	Washington

Student/Librarian Ratio

Rank	Ratio	District Name	City
1	1,627.5	District of Columbia Pub Schls	Washington
2	n/a	Edison-Friendship Public Charter	Washington

Student/Counselor Ratio

Rank	Ratio	District Name	City
1	1,085.0	District of Columbia Pub Schls	Washington
2	n/a	Edison-Friendship Public Charter	Washington

Current Spending per Student in FY2003

Rank	Dollars	District Name	City
1	13,363	District of Columbia Pub Schls	Washington
2	n/a	Edison-Friendship Public Charter	Washington

Number of Diploma Recipients

Rank	Number	District Name	City
1	2,894	District of Columbia Pub Schls	Washington
2	n/a	Edison-Friendship Public Charter	Washington

High School Drop-out Rate

Rank	Percent	District Name	City
1	n/a	District of Columbia Pub Schls	Washington
1	n/a	Edison-Friendship Public Charter	Washington

Florida

Florida Public School Educational Profile

Category	Value	Category	Value
Schools *(2003-2004)*	3,529	**Diploma Recipients** *(2002-2003)*	119,490
Instructional Level		White, Non-Hispanic	70,825
Primary	1,862	Black, Non-Hispanic	24,905
Middle	517	Asian/Pacific Islander	3,331
High	448	American Indian/Alaskan Native	304
Other Level	600	Hispanic	20,125
Curriculum		**High School Drop-out Rate** (%) *(2001-2002)*	3.7
Regular	3,099	White, Non-Hispanic	3.0
Special Education	117	Black, Non-Hispanic	4.9
Vocational	26	Asian/Pacific Islander	1.9
Alternative	185	American Indian/Alaskan Native	3.6
Type		Hispanic	4.5
Magnet	0	**Staff** *(2003-2004)*	
Charter	257	Teachers	144,955.0
Title I Eligible	1,428	Average Salary ($)	40,598
School-wide Title I	1,352	Librarians/Media Specialists	2,710.0
Students *(2003-2004)*	2,600,203	Guidance Counselors	5,772.0
Gender (%)		**Ratios** *(2003-2004)*	
Male	51.5	Student/Teacher Ratio	17.9 to 1
Female	48.5	Student/Librarian Ratio	959.5 to 1
Race/Ethnicity (%)		Student/Counselor Ratio	450.5 to 1
White, Non-Hispanic	51.3	**College Entrance Exam Scores** *(2005)*	
Black, Non-Hispanic	24.3	Scholastic Aptitude Test (SAT)	
Asian/Pacific Islander	2.0	Participation Rate (%)	65
American Indian/Alaskan Native	0.3	Mean SAT Reasoning Test Verbal Score	498
Hispanic	22.1	Mean SAT Reasoning Test Math Score	498
Classification (%)		American College Testing Program (ACT)	
Individual Education Program (IEP)	15.4	Participation Rate (%)	41
Migrant *(2002-2003)*	1.7	Average Composite Score	20.4
English Language Learner (ELL)	7.5	Average English Score	19.8
Eligible for Free Lunch Program	37.0	Average Math Score	20.4
Eligible for Reduced-Price Lunch Program	9.0	Average Reading Score	20.9
Current Spending *($ per student in FY 2003)*	6,450	Average Science Score	20.1
Instruction	3,793		
Support Services	2,341		

Note: For an explanation of data, please refer to the User's Guide in the front of the book

Florida NAEP 2005 Test Scores

Reading			Mathematics		
Grade/Category	Value	Rank	Grade/Category	Value	Rank
4th Grade			**4th Grade**		
Average Proficiency	219.5 (0.93)	28/51	Average Proficiency	238.9 (0.66)	25/51
Proficiency by Gender/Race/Ethnicity			Proficiency by Gender/Race/Ethnicity		
Male	217.1 (1.08)	26/51	Male	240.0 (0.86)	25/51
Female	221.9 (1.19)	28/51	Female	237.9 (0.72)	25/51
White, Non-Hispanic	228.2 (1.40)	15/51	White, Non-Hispanic	247.4 (0.96)	14/51
Black, Non-Hispanic	202.7 (1.62)	12/42	Black, Non-Hispanic	224.4 (0.84)	9/42
Asian, Non-Hispanic	229.9 (4.04)	14/27	Asian, Non-Hispanic	259.3 (3.16)	5/25
American Indian, Non-Hispanic	n/a	n/a	American Indian, Non-Hispanic	n/a	n/a
Hispanic	215.3 (1.61)	4/40	Hispanic	233.3 (0.92)	7/41
Proficiency by Class Size			Proficiency by Class Size		
Less than 16 Students	196.8 (3.23)	23/34	Less than 16 Students	222.2 (2.38)	22/35
16 to 18 Students	208.6 (4.36)	28/33	16 to 18 Students	233.8 (3.61)	19/31
19 to 20 Students	216.4 (2.79)	28/38	19 to 20 Students	234.9 (2.38)	29/38
21 to 25 Students	222.0 (1.38)	24/51	21 to 25 Students	241.4 (1.05)	21/51
Greater than 25 Students	224.6 (1.55)	8/36	Greater than 25 Students	238.7 (1.72)	18/33
Percent Attaining Achievement Levels			Percent Attaining Achievement Levels		
Below Basic	35.2 (1.03)	25/51	Below Basic	17.8 (0.64)	27/51
Basic or Above	64.8 (1.03)	27/51	Basic or Above	82.2 (0.64)	24/51
Proficient or Above	30.1 (1.21)	30/51	Proficient or Above	36.6 (1.11)	28/51
Advanced or Above	7.0 (0.67)	27/51	Advanced or Above	5.4 (0.68)	16/51
8th Grade			**8th Grade**		
Average Proficiency	255.8 (1.19)	41/51	Average Proficiency	274.0 (1.13)	36/51
Proficiency by Gender/Race/Ethnicity			Proficiency by Gender/Race/Ethnicity		
Male	249.2 (1.53)	43/51	Male	276.0 (1.33)	35/51
Female	262.1 (1.23)	41/51	Female	272.0 (1.38)	39/51
White, Non-Hispanic	264.6 (1.24)	42/51	White, Non-Hispanic	286.3 (1.03)	29/51
Black, Non-Hispanic	238.2 (1.74)	34/40	Black, Non-Hispanic	251.0 (1.79)	24/41
Asian, Non-Hispanic	273.3 (4.99)	13/24	Asian, Non-Hispanic	299.1 (5.18)	10/23
American Indian, Non-Hispanic	n/a	n/a	American Indian, Non-Hispanic	n/a	n/a
Hispanic	251.7 (1.91)	9/38	Hispanic	264.9 (1.90)	13/38
Proficiency by Parents Highest Level of Ed.			Proficiency by Parents Highest Level of Ed.		
Did Not Finish High School	246.8 (2.70)	20/49	Did Not Finish High School	260.1 (2.05)	30/50
Graduated High School	248.2 (1.97)	39/50	Graduated High School	267.3 (1.81)	29/50
Some Education After High School	264.2 (1.67)	32/50	Some Education After High School	278.6 (1.59)	33/50
Graduated College	262.6 (1.49)	43/50	Graduated College	282.4 (1.47)	39/50
Percent Attaining Achievement Levels			Percent Attaining Achievement Levels		
Below Basic	35.2 (1.03)	25/51	Below Basic	35.0 (1.27)	17/51
Basic or Above	64.8 (1.03)	27/51	Basic or Above	65.0 (1.27)	35/51
Proficient or Above	30.1 (1.21)	30/51	Proficient or Above	25.6 (1.18)	36/51
Advanced or Above	7.0 (0.67)	27/51	Advanced or Above	4.6 (0.68)	32/51

Note: For an explanation of data, please refer to the User's Guide in the front of the book; n/a indicates data not available

Alachua County

Alachua County SD
620 E University Ave • Gainesville, FL 32601-5498
(352) 955-7880 • http://www.sbac.edu/
Grade Span: PK-12; **Agency Type:** 1
Schools: 66
    37 Primary; 11 Middle; 7 High; 9 Other Level
    59 Regular; 3 Special Education; 0 Vocational; 2 Alternative
    0 Magnet; 14 Charter; 32 Title I Eligible; 28 School-wide Title I
Students: 29,448   (50.3% male; 49.6% female)
    Individual Education Program: 5,729 (19.5%);
    English Language Learner: 450 (1.5%); Migrant: 95 (0.3%)
    Eligible for Free Lunch Program: 11,808 (40.2%)
    Eligible for Reduced-Price Lunch Program: 2,555 (8.7%)
Teachers: 1,667.0 (17.6 to 1)
Librarians/Media Specialists: 51.0 (575.4 to 1)
Guidance Counselors: 74.0 (396.6 to 1)
Current Spending: ($ per student per year):
    Total: $6,486; Instruction: $3,529; Support Services: $2,620
Enrollment, Drop-out Rates and Diploma Recipients by Race/Ethnicity

Category	Total	White	Black	Asian	AIAN	Hisp.
Enrollment (%)	100.0	53.2	38.6	3.3	0.2	4.7
Drop-out Rate (%)	6.1	4.3	10.0	1.5	10.5	6.0
H.S. Diplomas (#)	1,651	1,126	404	49	4	68

Baker County

Baker County SD
392 S Blvd E • Macclenny, FL 32063-2540
(904) 259-0401 • http://prod.schoolcruiser.com/bcsd/
Grade Span: PK-12; **Agency Type:** 1
Schools: 7
    3 Primary; 1 Middle; 0 High; 2 Other Level
    5 Regular; 0 Special Education; 0 Vocational; 1 Alternative
    0 Magnet; 0 Charter; 4 Title I Eligible; 4 School-wide Title I
Students: 4,606   (52.4% male; 47.5% female)
    Individual Education Program: 555 (12.0%);
    English Language Learner: 3 (0.1%); Migrant: 9 (0.2%)
    Eligible for Free Lunch Program: 1,447 (31.4%)
    Eligible for Reduced-Price Lunch Program: 403 (8.8%)
Teachers: 254.0 (18.1 to 1)
Librarians/Media Specialists: 6.0 (767.3 to 1)
Guidance Counselors: 9.0 (511.6 to 1)
Current Spending: ($ per student per year):
    Total: $5,967; Instruction: $3,162; Support Services: $2,464
Enrollment, Drop-out Rates and Diploma Recipients by Race/Ethnicity

Category	Total	White	Black	Asian	AIAN	Hisp.
Enrollment (%)	100.0	84.4	14.6	0.3	0.0	0.6
Drop-out Rate (%)	4.7	4.7	4.0	0.0	0.0	20.0
H.S. Diplomas (#)	223	194	26	2	1	0

Bay County

Bay County SD
1311 Balboa Ave • Panama City, FL 32401-2080
(850) 872-7700 • http://www.bay.k12.fl.us/district_schools.asp
Grade Span: PK-12; **Agency Type:** 1
Schools: 44
    20 Primary; 6 Middle; 6 High; 9 Other Level
    38 Regular; 3 Special Education; 0 Vocational; 0 Alternative
    0 Magnet; 1 Charter; 20 Title I Eligible; 20 School-wide Title I
Students: 26,708   (51.6% male; 48.3% female)
    Individual Education Program: 5,253 (19.7%);
    English Language Learner: 228 (0.9%); Migrant: 149 (0.6%)
    Eligible for Free Lunch Program: 9,379 (35.2%)
    Eligible for Reduced-Price Lunch Program: 3,256 (12.2%)
Teachers: 1,564.0 (17.0 to 1)
Librarians/Media Specialists: 40.0 (665.5 to 1)
Guidance Counselors: 70.0 (380.3 to 1)
Current Spending: ($ per student per year):
    Total: $6,140; Instruction: $3,687; Support Services: $2,105
Enrollment, Drop-out Rates and Diploma Recipients by Race/Ethnicity

Category	Total	White	Black	Asian	AIAN	Hisp.
Enrollment (%)	100.0	79.5	16.2	1.9	0.4	2.0
Drop-out Rate (%)	1.8	1.8	1.7	2.4	0.0	0.0
H.S. Diplomas (#)	1,230	1,043	141	29	4	13

Bradford County

Bradford County SD
501 W Washington St • Starke, FL 32091-2525
(904) 966-6018 • http://www.bradford.k12.fl.us/
Grade Span: PK-12; **Agency Type:** 1
Schools: 12

6 Primary; 1 Middle; 2 High; 2 Other Level
    10 Regular; 0 Special Education; 1 Vocational; 0 Alternative
    0 Magnet; 0 Charter; 5 Title I Eligible; 5 School-wide Title I
Students: 3,909   (52.5% male; 47.4% female)
    Individual Education Program: 948 (24.3%);
    English Language Learner: 16 (0.4%); Migrant: 9 (0.2%)
    Eligible for Free Lunch Program: 1,917 (49.2%)
    Eligible for Reduced-Price Lunch Program: 486 (12.5%)
Teachers: 246.0 (15.8 to 1)
Librarians/Media Specialists: 6.0 (649.5 to 1)
Guidance Counselors: 9.0 (433.0 to 1)
Current Spending: ($ per student per year):
    Total: $6,728; Instruction: $3,920; Support Services: $2,482
Enrollment, Drop-out Rates and Diploma Recipients by Race/Ethnicity

Category	Total	White	Black	Asian	AIAN	Hisp.
Enrollment (%)	100.0	73.0	24.8	0.6	0.1	1.4
Drop-out Rate (%)	4.3	4.2	4.3	0.0	0.0	18.2
H.S. Diplomas (#)	214	167	45	1	0	1

Brevard County

Brevard County SD
2700 Judge Fran • Viera, FL 32940-6699
(321) 631-1911 • http://plx.brevard.k12.fl.us/bre/schools.pl
Grade Span: PK-12; **Agency Type:** 1
Schools: 108
    64 Primary; 14 Middle; 12 High; 17 Other Level
    98 Regular; 4 Special Education; 0 Vocational; 5 Alternative
    0 Magnet; 10 Charter; 36 Title I Eligible; 36 School-wide Title I
Students: 73,901   (51.3% male; 48.6% female)
    Individual Education Program: 12,911 (17.5%);
    English Language Learner: 1,133 (1.5%); Migrant: 54 (0.1%)
    Eligible for Free Lunch Program: 16,007 (21.8%)
    Eligible for Reduced-Price Lunch Program: 4,666 (6.3%)
Teachers: 4,303.0 (17.1 to 1)
Librarians/Media Specialists: 113.0 (650.8 to 1)
Guidance Counselors: 155.0 (474.5 to 1)
Current Spending: ($ per student per year):
    Total: $6,023; Instruction: $3,718; Support Services: $2,030
Enrollment, Drop-out Rates and Diploma Recipients by Race/Ethnicity

Category	Total	White	Black	Asian	AIAN	Hisp.
Enrollment (%)	100.0	78.3	14.0	1.7	0.3	5.7
Drop-out Rate (%)	0.9	0.8	1.6	0.5	2.0	0.9
H.S. Diplomas (#)	3,578	2,927	385	87	8	171

Broward County

Broward County SD
600 SE 3rd Ave • Fort Lauderdale, FL 33301-3125
Mailing Address: 600 SE 3rd Ave • Fort Lauderdale, FL 33301-3125
(754) 321-2600 • http://www.browardschools.com/
Grade Span: PK-12; **Agency Type:** 1
Schools: 264
    152 Primary; 44 Middle; 33 High; 30 Other Level
    241 Regular; 9 Special Education; 2 Vocational; 7 Alternative
    0 Magnet; 21 Charter; 90 Title I Eligible; 90 School-wide Title I
Students: 272,835   (51.7% male; 48.2% female)
    Individual Education Program: 31,128 (11.4%);
    English Language Learner: 29,612 (10.9%); Migrant: 879 (0.3%)
    Eligible for Free Lunch Program: 86,228 (31.7%)
    Eligible for Reduced-Price Lunch Program: 23,446 (8.6%)
Teachers: 14,264.0 (19.1 to 1)
Librarians/Media Specialists: 227.0 (1,197.8 to 1)
Guidance Counselors: 541.0 (502.6 to 1)
Current Spending: ($ per student per year):
    Total: $6,239; Instruction: $3,559; Support Services: $2,442
Enrollment, Drop-out Rates and Diploma Recipients by Race/Ethnicity

Category	Total	White	Black	Asian	AIAN	Hisp.
Enrollment (%)	100.0	36.3	36.8	3.0	0.3	23.5
Drop-out Rate (%)	1.6	1.3	1.9	0.9	2.5	1.8
H.S. Diplomas (#)	11,654	5,119	3,864	464	38	2,169

Calhoun County

Calhoun County SD
20859 E Central Ave G-20 • Blountstown, FL 32424-2264
Mailing Address: 20859 E Central Ave G • Blountstown, FL 32424-2264
(850) 674-5927 • http://www.paec.org/calhoun/district/
Grade Span: PK-12; **Agency Type:** 1
Schools: 7
    2 Primary; 1 Middle; 0 High; 2 Other Level
    5 Regular; 0 Special Education; 0 Vocational; 0 Alternative
    0 Magnet; 0 Charter; 4 Title I Eligible; 4 School-wide Title I
Students: 2,225   (50.5% male; 49.4% female)
    Individual Education Program: 502 (22.6%);

English Language Learner: 2 (0.1%); Migrant: 19 (0.9%)
Eligible for Free Lunch Program: 901 (40.6%)
Eligible for Reduced-Price Lunch Program: 230 (10.4%)
Teachers: 156.0 (14.2 to 1)
Librarians/Media Specialists: 5.0 (444.0 to 1)
Guidance Counselors: 6.0 (370.0 to 1)
Current Spending: ($ per student per year):
Total: $6,228; Instruction: $3,638; Support Services: $2,269
Enrollment, Drop-out Rates and Diploma Recipients by Race/Ethnicity

Category	Total	White	Black	Asian	AIAN	Hisp.
Enrollment (%)	100.0	83.8	13.7	0.8	0.2	1.5
Drop-out Rate (%)	3.2	2.5	8.7	0.0	0.0	0.0
H.S. Diplomas (#)	106	83	17	0	1	5

Charlotte County

Charlotte County SD
1445 Education Way • Port Charlotte, FL 33948-1053
(941) 255-0808 • http://www.ccps.k12.fl.us/
Grade Span: PK-12; **Agency Type:** 1
Schools: 23
11 Primary; 4 Middle; 5 High; 2 Other Level
20 Regular; 1 Special Education; 1 Vocational; 0 Alternative
0 Magnet; 0 Charter; 8 Title I Eligible; 8 School-wide Title I
Students: 18,298   (50.8% male; 49.1% female)
Individual Education Program: 3,561 (19.5%);
English Language Learner: 164 (0.9%); Migrant: 0 (0.0%)
Eligible for Free Lunch Program: 4,365 (24.0%)
Eligible for Reduced-Price Lunch Program: 1,844 (10.1%)
Teachers: 970.0 (18.8 to 1)
Librarians/Media Specialists: 21.0 (866.2 to 1)
Guidance Counselors: 38.0 (478.7 to 1)
Current Spending: ($ per student per year):
Total: $6,352; Instruction: $3,583; Support Services: $2,417
Enrollment, Drop-out Rates and Diploma Recipients by Race/Ethnicity

Category	Total	White	Black	Asian	AIAN	Hisp.
Enrollment (%)	100.0	84.5	8.4	1.4	0.3	5.4
Drop-out Rate (%)	4.2	4.3	3.0	4.2	0.0	5.6
H.S. Diplomas (#)	1,076	915	101	14	4	42

Citrus County

Citrus County SD
1007 W Main St • Inverness, FL 34450-4625
(352) 726-1931 • http://www.citrus.k12.fl.us/
Grade Span: PK-12; **Agency Type:** 1
Schools: 25
10 Primary; 4 Middle; 6 High; 3 Other Level
19 Regular; 1 Special Education; 2 Vocational; 1 Alternative
0 Magnet; 1 Charter; 11 Title I Eligible; 11 School-wide Title I
Students: 15,517   (52.1% male; 47.8% female)
Individual Education Program: 2,848 (18.4%);
English Language Learner: 97 (0.6%); Migrant: 59 (0.4%)
Eligible for Free Lunch Program: 5,225 (33.8%)
Eligible for Reduced-Price Lunch Program: 1,686 (10.9%)
Teachers: 949.0 (16.3 to 1)
Librarians/Media Specialists: 22.0 (702.9 to 1)
Guidance Counselors: 37.0 (417.9 to 1)
Current Spending: ($ per student per year):
Total: $6,454; Instruction: $3,666; Support Services: $2,530
Enrollment, Drop-out Rates and Diploma Recipients by Race/Ethnicity

Category	Total	White	Black	Asian	AIAN	Hisp.
Enrollment (%)	100.0	90.6	4.3	1.3	0.4	3.5
Drop-out Rate (%)	4.8	4.8	6.6	0.0	5.3	3.1
H.S. Diplomas (#)	830	750	41	15	1	23

Clay County

Clay County SD
900 Walnut St • Green Cove Springs, FL 32043-3129
(904) 284-6510 • http://www.clay.k12.fl.us/school_sites.htm
Grade Span: PK-12; **Agency Type:** 1
Schools: 33
20 Primary; 4 Middle; 6 High; 3 Other Level
32 Regular; 0 Special Education; 0 Vocational; 1 Alternative
0 Magnet; 0 Charter; 8 Title I Eligible; 7 School-wide Title I
Students: 31,370   (51.2% male; 48.7% female)
Individual Education Program: 6,208 (19.8%);
English Language Learner: 203 (0.6%); Migrant: 124 (0.4%)
Eligible for Free Lunch Program: 5,685 (18.2%)
Eligible for Reduced-Price Lunch Program: 2,496 (8.0%)
Teachers: 1,797.0 (17.4 to 1)
Librarians/Media Specialists: 38.0 (821.1 to 1)
Guidance Counselors: 77.0 (405.2 to 1)

Current Spending: ($ per student per year):
Total: $5,628; Instruction: $3,437; Support Services: $1,964
Enrollment, Drop-out Rates and Diploma Recipients by Race/Ethnicity

Category	Total	White	Black	Asian	AIAN	Hisp.
Enrollment (%)	100.0	82.3	10.6	2.2	0.2	4.7
Drop-out Rate (%)	2.8	2.6	4.6	0.9	4.3	3.4
H.S. Diplomas (#)	1,627	1,385	140	42	5	55

Collier County

Collier County SD
5775 Osceola Tr • Naples, FL 34109-0919
(239) 254-4100 • http://www.collier.k12.fl.us/
Grade Span: PK-12; **Agency Type:** 1
Schools: 57
29 Primary; 9 Middle; 7 High; 11 Other Level
49 Regular; 2 Special Education; 0 Vocational; 5 Alternative
0 Magnet; 2 Charter; 16 Title I Eligible; 16 School-wide Title I
Students: 40,157   (51.4% male; 48.5% female)
Individual Education Program: 6,221 (15.5%);
English Language Learner: 5,757 (14.3%); Migrant: 4,992 (12.5%)
Eligible for Free Lunch Program: 6,233 (15.6%)
Eligible for Reduced-Price Lunch Program: 2,355 (5.9%)
Teachers: 2,332.0 (17.2 to 1)
Librarians/Media Specialists: 43.0 (931.1 to 1)
Guidance Counselors: 126.0 (317.7 to 1)
Current Spending: ($ per student per year):
Total: $7,435; Instruction: $4,495; Support Services: $2,581
Enrollment, Drop-out Rates and Diploma Recipients by Race/Ethnicity

Category	Total	White	Black	Asian	AIAN	Hisp.
Enrollment (%)	100.0	50.7	11.2	0.9	0.4	36.9
Drop-out Rate (%)	4.4	2.7	5.9	3.0	10.8	7.3
H.S. Diplomas (#)	1,711	1,097	198	17	5	394

Columbia County

Columbia County SD
372 W Duval St • Lake City, FL 32055-3990
(386) 755-8000 • http://www.columbia.k12.fl.us/schools.html
Grade Span: PK-12; **Agency Type:** 1
Schools: 15
8 Primary; 1 Middle; 1 High; 5 Other Level
15 Regular; 0 Special Education; 0 Vocational; 0 Alternative
0 Magnet; 0 Charter; 8 Title I Eligible; 8 School-wide Title I
Students: 9,790   (51.6% male; 48.3% female)
Individual Education Program: 1,800 (18.4%);
English Language Learner: 31 (0.3%); Migrant: 40 (0.4%)
Eligible for Free Lunch Program: 4,361 (44.8%)
Eligible for Reduced-Price Lunch Program: 1,133 (11.6%)
Teachers: 590.0 (16.5 to 1)
Librarians/Media Specialists: 11.0 (884.9 to 1)
Guidance Counselors: 23.0 (423.2 to 1)
Current Spending: ($ per student per year):
Total: $6,103; Instruction: $3,486; Support Services: $2,291
Enrollment, Drop-out Rates and Diploma Recipients by Race/Ethnicity

Category	Total	White	Black	Asian	AIAN	Hisp.
Enrollment (%)	100.0	73.2	22.9	0.8	0.3	2.8
Drop-out Rate (%)	1.7	1.1	3.3	0.0	0.0	2.9
H.S. Diplomas (#)	441	327	97	6	1	10

De Soto County

Desoto County SD
530 Lasolona Ave • Arcadia, FL 34265-2000
Mailing Address: PO Drawer 2000 • Arcadia, FL 34265-2000
(863) 494-4222 • http://www.desotoschools.com/web_site_links.htm
Grade Span: PK-12; **Agency Type:** 1
Schools: 13
4 Primary; 1 Middle; 1 High; 6 Other Level
10 Regular; 1 Special Education; 0 Vocational; 1 Alternative
0 Magnet; 0 Charter; 3 Title I Eligible; 3 School-wide Title I
Students: 4,975   (53.0% male; 46.9% female)
Individual Education Program: 995 (20.0%);
English Language Learner: 426 (8.6%); Migrant: 587 (11.8%)
Eligible for Free Lunch Program: 2,656 (53.5%)
Eligible for Reduced-Price Lunch Program: 478 (9.6%)
Teachers: 287.0 (17.3 to 1)
Librarians/Media Specialists: 6.0 (828.0 to 1)
Guidance Counselors: 9.0 (552.0 to 1)
Current Spending: ($ per student per year):
Total: $6,940; Instruction: $4,108; Support Services: $2,418

Enrollment, Drop-out Rates and Diploma Recipients by Race/Ethnicity

Category	Total	White	Black	Asian	AIAN	Hisp.
Enrollment (%)	100.0	53.4	19.4	0.5	0.1	26.5
Drop-out Rate (%)	3.7	2.7	3.9	0.0	0.0	6.3
H.S. Diplomas (#)	204	130	35	4	1	34

Dixie County

Dixie County SD
16077 SE 19 Hwy • Cross City, FL 32628-0890
Mailing Address: PO Box 890 • Cross City, FL 32628-0890
(352) 498-6131 • http://dixieschools.dixie.k12.fl.us/
Grade Span: PK-12; Agency Type: 1
Schools: 5
    1 Primary; 0 Middle; 1 High; 2 Other Level
    4 Regular; 0 Special Education; 0 Vocational; 0 Alternative
    0 Magnet; 0 Charter; 3 Title I Eligible; 3 School-wide Title I
Students: 2,169   (51.6% male; 48.3% female)
    Individual Education Program: 509 (23.5%);
    English Language Learner: 0 (0.0%); Migrant: 58 (2.7%)
    Eligible for Free Lunch Program: 1,155 (53.3%)
    Eligible for Reduced-Price Lunch Program: 263 (12.1%)
Teachers: 123.0 (17.6 to 1)
Librarians/Media Specialists: 1.0 (2,167.0 to 1)
Guidance Counselors: 5.0 (433.4 to 1)
Current Spending: ($ per student per year):
    Total: $6,771; Instruction: $3,744; Support Services: $2,613

Enrollment, Drop-out Rates and Diploma Recipients by Race/Ethnicity

Category	Total	White	Black	Asian	AIAN	Hisp.
Enrollment (%)	100.0	88.9	9.5	0.1	0.0	1.5
Drop-out Rate (%)	3.6	3.3	6.9	0.0	n/a	0.0
H.S. Diplomas (#)	150	138	11	0	0	1

Duval County

Duval County SD
1701 Prudential Dr • Jacksonville, FL 32207-8182
(904) 390-2115 • http://www.educationcentral.org/
Grade Span: PK-12; Agency Type: 1
Schools: 179
    110 Primary; 28 Middle; 19 High; 20 Other Level
    170 Regular; 3 Special Education; 0 Vocational; 4 Alternative
    0 Magnet; 7 Charter; 71 Title I Eligible; 71 School-wide Title I
Students: 129,557   (50.8% male; 49.1% female)
    Individual Education Program: 20,355 (15.7%);
    English Language Learner: 2,936 (2.3%); Migrant: 0 (0.0%)
    Eligible for Free Lunch Program: 44,337 (34.6%)
    Eligible for Reduced-Price Lunch Program: 11,822 (9.2%)
Teachers: 6,976.0 (18.4 to 1)
Librarians/Media Specialists: 145.0 (883.0 to 1)
Guidance Counselors: 238.0 (537.9 to 1)
Current Spending: ($ per student per year):
    Total: $6,350; Instruction: $3,706; Support Services: $2,332

Enrollment, Drop-out Rates and Diploma Recipients by Race/Ethnicity

Category	Total	White	Black	Asian	AIAN	Hisp.
Enrollment (%)	100.0	47.8	44.1	3.1	0.2	4.8
Drop-out Rate (%)	6.7	6.2	7.6	3.6	3.6	6.6
H.S. Diplomas (#)	5,260	2,922	1,871	237	10	220

Escambia County

Escambia County SD
215 W Garden St • Pensacola, FL 32501
(850) 469-6130 • http://www.escambia.k12.fl.us/schools.htm
Grade Span: PK-12; Agency Type: 1
Schools: 77
    39 Primary; 12 Middle; 10 High; 15 Other Level
    65 Regular; 5 Special Education; 0 Vocational; 6 Alternative
    0 Magnet; 6 Charter; 52 Title I Eligible; 52 School-wide Title I
Students: 43,998   (51.1% male; 48.8% female)
    Individual Education Program: 7,486 (17.0%);
    English Language Learner: 315 (0.7%); Migrant: 395 (0.9%)
    Eligible for Free Lunch Program: 20,251 (46.3%)
    Eligible for Reduced-Price Lunch Program: 5,255 (12.0%)
Teachers: 2,511.0 (17.4 to 1)
Librarians/Media Specialists: 60.0 (729.4 to 1)
Guidance Counselors: 98.0 (446.6 to 1)
Current Spending: ($ per student per year):
    Total: $6,056; Instruction: $3,456; Support Services: $2,248

Enrollment, Drop-out Rates and Diploma Recipients by Race/Ethnicity

Category	Total	White	Black	Asian	AIAN	Hisp.
Enrollment (%)	100.0	57.6	37.0	2.7	0.7	1.9
Drop-out Rate (%)	2.8	2.0	4.5	2.4	1.3	1.0
H.S. Diplomas (#)	2,320	1,473	699	101	15	32

Flagler County

Flagler County SD
Hwy 100 E • Bunnell, FL 32110-0755
Mailing Address: PO Box 755 • Bunnell, FL 32110-0755
(386) 437-7526 • http://www.flagler.k12.fl.us/
Grade Span: PK-12; Agency Type: 1
Schools: 8
    4 Primary; 1 Middle; 2 High; 1 Other Level
    8 Regular; 0 Special Education; 0 Vocational; 0 Alternative
    0 Magnet; 0 Charter; 4 Title I Eligible; 1 School-wide Title I
Students: 8,564   (51.7% male; 48.2% female)
    Individual Education Program: 1,455 (17.0%);
    English Language Learner: 236 (2.8%); Migrant: 20 (0.2%)
    Eligible for Free Lunch Program: 2,250 (26.3%)
    Eligible for Reduced-Price Lunch Program: 820 (9.6%)
Teachers: 497.0 (17.2 to 1)
Librarians/Media Specialists: 6.0 (1,425.7 to 1)
Guidance Counselors: 17.0 (503.2 to 1)
Current Spending: ($ per student per year):
    Total: $6,319; Instruction: $3,489; Support Services: $2,545

Enrollment, Drop-out Rates and Diploma Recipients by Race/Ethnicity

Category	Total	White	Black	Asian	AIAN	Hisp.
Enrollment (%)	100.0	78.4	12.5	1.9	0.3	6.9
Drop-out Rate (%)	2.3	1.9	4.2	3.1	0.0	3.4
H.S. Diplomas (#)	385	301	59	2	0	23

Gadsden County

Gadsden County SD
35 Martin Luther King Blv • Quincy, FL 32351-4400
Mailing Address: 35 Martin Luther King Bou • Quincy, FL 32351-4400
(850) 627-9651 • http://www.gcps.k12.fl.us/schs.html
Grade Span: PK-12; Agency Type: 1
Schools: 22
    11 Primary; 2 Middle; 1 High; 6 Other Level
    17 Regular; 2 Special Education; 0 Vocational; 1 Alternative
    0 Magnet; 1 Charter; 14 Title I Eligible; 14 School-wide Title I
Students: 6,948   (50.7% male; 49.2% female)
    Individual Education Program: 1,238 (17.8%);
    English Language Learner: 398 (5.7%); Migrant: 607 (8.8%)
    Eligible for Free Lunch Program: 4,614 (66.8%)
    Eligible for Reduced-Price Lunch Program: 663 (9.6%)
Teachers: 440.0 (15.7 to 1)
Librarians/Media Specialists: 12.0 (575.9 to 1)
Guidance Counselors: 18.0 (383.9 to 1)
Current Spending: ($ per student per year):
    Total: $6,913; Instruction: $3,533; Support Services: $2,896

Enrollment, Drop-out Rates and Diploma Recipients by Race/Ethnicity

Category	Total	White	Black	Asian	AIAN	Hisp.
Enrollment (%)	100.0	5.0	83.1	0.2	0.0	11.7
Drop-out Rate (%)	5.4	5.2	5.1	0.0	n/a	8.5
H.S. Diplomas (#)	346	21	312	0	0	13

Gilchrist County

Gilchrist County SD
310 NW 11th Ave • Trenton, FL 32693-3804
(352) 463-3200 • http://www.gilchristschools.org/
Grade Span: PK-12; Agency Type: 1
Schools: 4
    1 Primary; 0 Middle; 0 High; 3 Other Level
    4 Regular; 0 Special Education; 0 Vocational; 0 Alternative
    0 Magnet; 0 Charter; 2 Title I Eligible; 2 School-wide Title I
Students: 2,832   (51.2% male; 48.7% female)
    Individual Education Program: 721 (25.5%);
    English Language Learner: 10 (0.4%); Migrant: 96 (3.4%)
    Eligible for Free Lunch Program: 1,156 (40.9%)
    Eligible for Reduced-Price Lunch Program: 375 (13.3%)
Teachers: 169.0 (16.7 to 1)
Librarians/Media Specialists: 4.0 (706.3 to 1)
Guidance Counselors: 8.0 (353.1 to 1)
Current Spending: ($ per student per year):
    Total: $6,601; Instruction: $3,673; Support Services: $2,474

Enrollment, Drop-out Rates and Diploma Recipients by Race/Ethnicity

Category	Total	White	Black	Asian	AIAN	Hisp.
Enrollment (%)	100.0	93.2	4.4	0.0	0.2	2.2
Drop-out Rate (%)	2.9	2.9	5.4	0.0	0.0	0.0
H.S. Diplomas (#)	141	133	8	0	0	0

Gulf County

Gulf County SD
150 Middle School Rd • Port St. Joe, FL 32456-2261
(850) 229-8256
Grade Span: PK-12; **Agency Type:** 1
Schools: 8
   3 Primary; 2 Middle; 2 High; 0 Other Level
   7 Regular; 0 Special Education; 0 Vocational; 0 Alternative
   0 Magnet; 0 Charter; 2 Title I Eligible; 2 School-wide Title I
Students: 2,150   (52.0% male; 47.9% female)
   Individual Education Program: 411 (19.1%);
   English Language Learner: 1 (<0.1%); Migrant: 0 (0.0%)
   Eligible for Free Lunch Program: 798 (37.1%)
   Eligible for Reduced-Price Lunch Program: 223 (10.4%)
Teachers: 131.0 (16.4 to 1)
Librarians/Media Specialists: 4.0 (537.5 to 1)
Guidance Counselors: 8.0 (268.8 to 1)
Current Spending: ($ per student per year):
   Total: $6,982; Instruction: $3,945; Support Services: $2,722
Enrollment, Drop-out Rates and Diploma Recipients by Race/Ethnicity

Category	Total	White	Black	Asian	AIAN	Hisp.
Enrollment (%)	100.0	82.3	16.6	0.4	0.2	0.4
Drop-out Rate (%)	0.5	0.0	2.8	0.0	n/a	0.0
H.S. Diplomas (#)	117	91	23	1	0	2

Hamilton County

Hamilton County SD
4280 SW County Rd #152 • Jasper, FL 32052-3774
(386) 792-6501 •
http://www.firn.edu/schools/hamilton/hamilton/schools.htm
Grade Span: PK-12; **Agency Type:** 1
Schools: 7
   3 Primary; 0 Middle; 1 High; 2 Other Level
   5 Regular; 1 Special Education; 0 Vocational; 0 Alternative
   0 Magnet; 0 Charter; 4 Title I Eligible; 4 School-wide Title I
Students: 2,057   (51.3% male; 48.6% female)
   Individual Education Program: 357 (17.4%);
   English Language Learner: 66 (3.2%); Migrant: 69 (3.4%)
   Eligible for Free Lunch Program: 1,302 (63.7%)
   Eligible for Reduced-Price Lunch Program: 184 (9.0%)
Teachers: 126.0 (16.2 to 1)
Librarians/Media Specialists: 3.0 (681.0 to 1)
Guidance Counselors: 4.0 (510.8 to 1)
Current Spending: ($ per student per year):
   Total: $7,362; Instruction: $3,912; Support Services: $2,997
Enrollment, Drop-out Rates and Diploma Recipients by Race/Ethnicity

Category	Total	White	Black	Asian	AIAN	Hisp.
Enrollment (%)	100.0	43.8	47.3	0.4	0.2	8.4
Drop-out Rate (%)	2.8	0.0	5.3	0.0	0.0	4.8
H.S. Diplomas (#)	119	61	56	1	0	1

Hardee County

Hardee County SD
1001-1009 N Sixth Ave • Wauchula, FL 33873-1678
Mailing Address: PO Drawer 1678 • Wauchula, FL 33873-1678
(863) 773-9058 • http://www.hardee.k12.fl.us/schools.htm
Grade Span: PK-12; **Agency Type:** 1
Schools: 9
   4 Primary; 0 Middle; 1 High; 3 Other Level
   7 Regular; 0 Special Education; 0 Vocational; 1 Alternative
   0 Magnet; 0 Charter; 4 Title I Eligible; 4 School-wide Title I
Students: 5,221   (52.6% male; 47.3% female)
   Individual Education Program: 1,080 (20.7%);
   English Language Learner: 439 (8.4%); Migrant: 1,622 (31.1%)
   Eligible for Free Lunch Program: 3,243 (62.1%)
   Eligible for Reduced-Price Lunch Program: 451 (8.6%)
Teachers: 305.0 (17.1 to 1)
Librarians/Media Specialists: 7.0 (745.7 to 1)
Guidance Counselors: 9.0 (580.0 to 1)
Current Spending: ($ per student per year):
   Total: $6,356; Instruction: $3,693; Support Services: $2,278
Enrollment, Drop-out Rates and Diploma Recipients by Race/Ethnicity

Category	Total	White	Black	Asian	AIAN	Hisp.
Enrollment (%)	100.0	41.1	8.0	0.9	0.1	50.0
Drop-out Rate (%)	7.5	5.2	7.1	0.0	0.0	11.1
H.S. Diplomas (#)	213	125	19	2	1	66

Hendry County

Hendry County SD
25 E Hickpochee Ave • La Belle, FL 33975-1980
Mailing Address: PO Box 1980 • La Belle, FL 33975-1980
(863) 674-4642 • http://www.hendry-schools.org/
Grade Span: PK-12; **Agency Type:** 1
Schools: 14
   6 Primary; 0 Middle; 2 High; 5 Other Level
   12 Regular; 1 Special Education; 0 Vocational; 0 Alternative
   0 Magnet; 0 Charter; 8 Title I Eligible; 6 School-wide Title I
Students: 7,664   (51.7% male; 48.2% female)
   Individual Education Program: 1,300 (17.0%);
   English Language Learner: 642 (8.4%); Migrant: 2,300 (30.0%)
   Eligible for Free Lunch Program: 4,590 (59.9%)
   Eligible for Reduced-Price Lunch Program: 750 (9.8%)
Teachers: 392.0 (19.5 to 1)
Librarians/Media Specialists: 10.0 (766.1 to 1)
Guidance Counselors: 16.0 (478.8 to 1)
Current Spending: ($ per student per year):
   Total: $6,379; Instruction: $3,576; Support Services: $2,380
Enrollment, Drop-out Rates and Diploma Recipients by Race/Ethnicity

Category	Total	White	Black	Asian	AIAN	Hisp.
Enrollment (%)	100.0	35.4	16.2	0.5	0.4	47.6
Drop-out Rate (%)	6.1	4.5	5.5	16.7	0.0	8.5
H.S. Diplomas (#)	290	155	39	5	0	91

Hernando County

Hernando County SD
919 N Broad St • Brooksville, FL 34601-2397
(352) 797-7001 • http://www.hcsb.k12.fl.us/
Grade Span: PK-12; **Agency Type:** 1
Schools: 23
   10 Primary; 4 Middle; 4 High; 2 Other Level
   19 Regular; 0 Special Education; 0 Vocational; 1 Alternative
   0 Magnet; 1 Charter; 9 Title I Eligible; 9 School-wide Title I
Students: 19,596   (51.1% male; 48.8% female)
   Individual Education Program: 3,441 (17.6%);
   English Language Learner: 292 (1.5%); Migrant: 0 (0.0%)
   Eligible for Free Lunch Program: 6,698 (34.3%)
   Eligible for Reduced-Price Lunch Program: 2,268 (11.6%)
Teachers: 1,090.0 (17.9 to 1)
Librarians/Media Specialists: 22.0 (887.8 to 1)
Guidance Counselors: 54.0 (361.7 to 1)
Current Spending: ($ per student per year):
   Total: $5,830; Instruction: $3,285; Support Services: $2,269
Enrollment, Drop-out Rates and Diploma Recipients by Race/Ethnicity

Category	Total	White	Black	Asian	AIAN	Hisp.
Enrollment (%)	100.0	83.4	6.9	0.9	0.3	8.5
Drop-out Rate (%)	2.3	2.1	4.6	3.5	11.1	2.3
H.S. Diplomas (#)	923	799	54	17	2	51

Highlands County

Highlands County SD
426 School St • Sebring, FL 33870-4048
(863) 471-5564 • http://www.highlands.k12.fl.us/
Grade Span: PK-12; **Agency Type:** 1
Schools: 18
   8 Primary; 4 Middle; 3 High; 3 Other Level
   18 Regular; 0 Special Education; 0 Vocational; 0 Alternative
   0 Magnet; 1 Charter; 8 Title I Eligible; 8 School-wide Title I
Students: 11,666   (51.6% male; 48.3% female)
   Individual Education Program: 2,068 (17.7%);
   English Language Learner: 486 (4.2%); Migrant: 1,266 (10.9%)
   Eligible for Free Lunch Program: 5,856 (50.3%)
   Eligible for Reduced-Price Lunch Program: 1,103 (9.5%)
Teachers: 697.0 (16.7 to 1)
Librarians/Media Specialists: 15.0 (776.2 to 1)
Guidance Counselors: 27.0 (431.2 to 1)
Current Spending: ($ per student per year):
   Total: $6,585; Instruction: $3,660; Support Services: $2,512
Enrollment, Drop-out Rates and Diploma Recipients by Race/Ethnicity

Category	Total	White	Black	Asian	AIAN	Hisp.
Enrollment (%)	100.0	58.5	19.8	1.1	0.6	19.9
Drop-out Rate (%)	5.3	4.3	7.4	0.0	0.0	7.0
H.S. Diplomas (#)	561	360	111	8	1	81

Hillsborough County

Hillsborough County SD
901 E Kennedy Blvd • Tampa, FL 33601-3408
Mailing Address: PO Box 3408 • Tampa, FL 33601-3408
(813) 272-4050 • http://apps.sdhc.k12.fl.us/sdhc2/schoolsite
Grade Span: PK-12; **Agency Type:** 1
Schools: 237
  135 Primary; 41 Middle; 27 High; 29 Other Level
  216 Regular; 8 Special Education; 0 Vocational; 8 Alternative
  0 Magnet; 20 Charter; 106 Title I Eligible; 106 School-wide Title I
Students: 181,900 (51.3% male; 48.6% female)
  Individual Education Program: 28,458 (15.6%);
  English Language Learner: 18,928 (10.4%); Migrant: 3,996 (2.2%)
  Eligible for Free Lunch Program: 72,830 (40.2%)
  Eligible for Reduced-Price Lunch Program: 17,756 (9.8%)
Teachers: 11,020.0 (16.5 to 1)
Librarians/Media Specialists: 208.0 (871.6 to 1)
Guidance Counselors: 419.0 (432.7 to 1)
Current Spending: ($ per student per year):
  Total: $6,411; Instruction: $3,800; Support Services: $2,223
Enrollment, Drop-out Rates and Diploma Recipients by Race/Ethnicity

Category	Total	White	Black	Asian	AIAN	Hisp.
Enrollment (%)	100.0	48.7	23.6	2.4	0.3	25.0
Drop-out Rate (%)	2.8	2.0	4.1	1.6	4.1	3.6
H.S. Diplomas (#)	7,968	4,567	1,539	280	32	1,550

Holmes County

Holmes County SD
701 E Pennsylvania Ave • Bonifay, FL 32425-2349
(850) 547-9341 • http://www.firn.edu/schools/holmes/holmessb/
Grade Span: PK-12; **Agency Type:** 1
Schools: 9
  2 Primary; 1 Middle; 2 High; 4 Other Level
  9 Regular; 0 Special Education; 0 Vocational; 0 Alternative
  0 Magnet; 0 Charter; 5 Title I Eligible; 5 School-wide Title I
Students: 3,383 (52.8% male; 47.1% female)
  Individual Education Program: 509 (15.0%);
  English Language Learner: 10 (0.3%); Migrant: 33 (1.0%)
  Eligible for Free Lunch Program: 1,459 (43.1%)
  Eligible for Reduced-Price Lunch Program: 471 (13.9%)
Teachers: 216.0 (15.7 to 1)
Librarians/Media Specialists: 8.0 (422.9 to 1)
Guidance Counselors: 9.0 (375.9 to 1)
Current Spending: ($ per student per year):
  Total: $6,673; Instruction: $3,858; Support Services: $2,438
Enrollment, Drop-out Rates and Diploma Recipients by Race/Ethnicity

Category	Total	White	Black	Asian	AIAN	Hisp.
Enrollment (%)	100.0	94.4	3.5	0.8	0.1	1.2
Drop-out Rate (%)	3.1	3.1	0.0	0.0	0.0	14.3
H.S. Diplomas (#)	203	196	5	1	0	1

Indian River County

Indian River County SD
1990 25th St • Vero Beach, FL 32960-3395
(772) 564-3150 • http://www.indian-river.k12.fl.us/
Grade Span: PK-12; **Agency Type:** 1
Schools: 28
  16 Primary; 4 Middle; 3 High; 3 Other Level
  24 Regular; 2 Special Education; 0 Vocational; 0 Alternative
  0 Magnet; 5 Charter; 12 Title I Eligible; 12 School-wide Title I
Students: 16,637 (51.8% male; 48.1% female)
  Individual Education Program: 2,490 (15.0%);
  English Language Learner: 647 (3.9%); Migrant: 791 (4.8%)
  Eligible for Free Lunch Program: 4,890 (29.4%)
  Eligible for Reduced-Price Lunch Program: 1,431 (8.6%)
Teachers: 932.0 (17.8 to 1)
Librarians/Media Specialists: 20.0 (830.6 to 1)
Guidance Counselors: 25.0 (664.4 to 1)
Current Spending: ($ per student per year):
  Total: $6,260; Instruction: $3,487; Support Services: $2,379
Enrollment, Drop-out Rates and Diploma Recipients by Race/Ethnicity

Category	Total	White	Black	Asian	AIAN	Hisp.
Enrollment (%)	100.0	70.1	15.8	1.2	0.3	12.6
Drop-out Rate (%)	1.8	1.4	3.2	0.0	0.0	2.0
H.S. Diplomas (#)	821	620	129	8	2	62

Jackson County

Jackson County SD
2003 Jefferson St • Marianna, FL 32447-5958
Mailing Address: PO Box 5958 • Marianna, FL 32447-5958
(850) 482-1200 • http://www.firn.edu/schools/jackson/jacksonsb/schools/
Grade Span: PK-12; **Agency Type:** 1
Schools: 21
  7 Primary; 1 Middle; 3 High; 8 Other Level
  17 Regular; 2 Special Education; 0 Vocational; 0 Alternative
  0 Magnet; 1 Charter; 12 Title I Eligible; 12 School-wide Title I
Students: 7,192 (51.4% male; 48.5% female)
  Individual Education Program: 1,434 (19.9%);
  English Language Learner: 33 (0.5%); Migrant: 37 (0.5%)
  Eligible for Free Lunch Program: 3,058 (42.6%)
  Eligible for Reduced-Price Lunch Program: 786 (11.0%)
Teachers: 425.0 (16.9 to 1)
Librarians/Media Specialists: 12.0 (598.0 to 1)
Guidance Counselors: 21.0 (341.7 to 1)
Current Spending: ($ per student per year):
  Total: $6,761; Instruction: $3,769; Support Services: $2,592
Enrollment, Drop-out Rates and Diploma Recipients by Race/Ethnicity

Category	Total	White	Black	Asian	AIAN	Hisp.
Enrollment (%)	100.0	64.8	32.2	0.5	0.6	1.8
Drop-out Rate (%)	2.7	2.1	3.6	0.0	12.5	6.7
H.S. Diplomas (#)	409	261	140	0	2	6

Lake County

Lake County SD
201 W Burleigh Blvd • Tavares, FL 32778-2496
(352) 253-6510 • http://www.lake.k12.fl.us/
Grade Span: PK-12; **Agency Type:** 1
Schools: 52
  25 Primary; 10 Middle; 9 High; 7 Other Level
  45 Regular; 2 Special Education; 1 Vocational; 3 Alternative
  0 Magnet; 8 Charter; 26 Title I Eligible; 24 School-wide Title I
Students: 33,992 (51.0% male; 48.9% female)
  Individual Education Program: 5,680 (16.7%);
  English Language Learner: 1,348 (4.0%); Migrant: 295 (0.9%)
  Eligible for Free Lunch Program: 10,271 (30.4%)
  Eligible for Reduced-Price Lunch Program: 3,079 (9.1%)
Teachers: 1,758.0 (19.2 to 1)
Librarians/Media Specialists: 43.0 (786.6 to 1)
Guidance Counselors: 83.0 (407.5 to 1)
Current Spending: ($ per student per year):
  Total: $5,956; Instruction: $3,449; Support Services: $2,182
Enrollment, Drop-out Rates and Diploma Recipients by Race/Ethnicity

Category	Total	White	Black	Asian	AIAN	Hisp.
Enrollment (%)	100.0	71.2	15.6	1.3	0.4	11.5
Drop-out Rate (%)	5.5	5.1	6.9	0.9	8.0	7.2
H.S. Diplomas (#)	1,531	1,210	182	25	1	113

Lee County

Lee County SD
2055 Central Ave • Fort Myers, FL 33901-3916
(239) 337-8301 • http://www.lee.k12.fl.us/
Grade Span: PK-12; **Agency Type:** 1
Schools: 83
  42 Primary; 12 Middle; 12 High; 15 Other Level
  71 Regular; 4 Special Education; 3 Vocational; 3 Alternative
  0 Magnet; 4 Charter; 31 Title I Eligible; 25 School-wide Title I
Students: 66,466 (51.3% male; 48.6% female)
  Individual Education Program: 10,066 (15.1%);
  English Language Learner: 6,579 (9.9%); Migrant: 1,574 (2.4%)
  Eligible for Free Lunch Program: 24,253 (36.6%)
  Eligible for Reduced-Price Lunch Program: 6,763 (10.2%)
Teachers: 3,624.0 (18.3 to 1)
Librarians/Media Specialists: 47.0 (1,408.6 to 1)
Guidance Counselors: 125.0 (529.6 to 1)
Current Spending: ($ per student per year):
  Total: $6,206; Instruction: $3,414; Support Services: $2,491
Enrollment, Drop-out Rates and Diploma Recipients by Race/Ethnicity

Category	Total	White	Black	Asian	AIAN	Hisp.
Enrollment (%)	100.0	62.2	15.0	1.3	0.4	21.1
Drop-out Rate (%)	9.0	7.2	15.3	2.7	2.1	11.9
H.S. Diplomas (#)	2,846	2,105	352	56	10	323

Leon County

Florida State University Laboratory School
3000 School House Rd • Tallahassee, FL 32311
(850) 245-3700
Grade Span: PK-12; **Agency Type:** 7
Schools: 2
  1 Primary; 0 Middle; 0 High; 1 Other Level
  2 Regular; 0 Special Education; 0 Vocational; 0 Alternative
  0 Magnet; 2 Charter; 1 Title I Eligible; 0 School-wide Title I
Students: 2,217   (49.4% male; 50.5% female)
  Individual Education Program: 190 (8.6%);
  English Language Learner: 57 (2.6%); Migrant: 1 (<0.1%)
  Eligible for Free Lunch Program: 240 (10.8%)
  Eligible for Reduced-Price Lunch Program: 175 (7.9%)
Teachers: 141.0 (15.7 to 1)
Librarians/Media Specialists: 2.0 (1,106.0 to 1)
Guidance Counselors: 5.0 (442.4 to 1)
Current Spending: ($ per student per year):
  Total: n/a; Instruction: n/a; Support Services: n/a
Enrollment, Drop-out Rates and Diploma Recipients by Race/Ethnicity

Category	Total	White	Black	Asian	AIAN	Hisp.
Enrollment (%)	100.0	54.2	23.3	2.9	0.5	19.2
Drop-out Rate (%)	1.9	2.8	0.7	0.0	0.0	0.0
H.S. Diplomas (#)	93	53	26	2	1	11

Leon County SD
2757 W Pensacola St • Tallahassee, FL 32304-2907
(850) 487-7147 •
http://www.leon.k12.fl.us/districtserver/Schools/Index.html
Grade Span: PK-12; **Agency Type:** 1
Schools: 56
  27 Primary; 9 Middle; 6 High; 11 Other Level
  47 Regular; 4 Special Education; 1 Vocational; 1 Alternative
  0 Magnet; 2 Charter; 18 Title I Eligible; 18 School-wide Title I
Students: 32,194   (51.0% male; 48.9% female)
  Individual Education Program: 6,322 (19.6%);
  English Language Learner: 320 (1.0%); Migrant: 0 (0.0%)
  Eligible for Free Lunch Program: 9,545 (29.9%)
  Eligible for Reduced-Price Lunch Program: 2,075 (6.5%)
Teachers: 1,817.0 (17.6 to 1)
Librarians/Media Specialists: 41.0 (779.9 to 1)
Guidance Counselors: 72.0 (444.1 to 1)
Current Spending: ($ per student per year):
  Total: $6,179; Instruction: $3,398; Support Services: $2,508
Enrollment, Drop-out Rates and Diploma Recipients by Race/Ethnicity

Category	Total	White	Black	Asian	AIAN	Hisp.
Enrollment (%)	100.0	54.1	41.1	2.2	0.1	2.5
Drop-out Rate (%)	3.7	2.9	5.4	2.4	8.3	4.1
H.S. Diplomas (#)	1,788	1,173	543	32	3	37

Levy County

Levy County SD
480 Marshburn Dr • Bronson, FL 32621-0129
Mailing Address: PO Drawer 129 • Bronson, FL 32621-0129
(352) 486-5231 • http://www.levy.k12.fl.us/
Grade Span: PK-12; **Agency Type:** 1
Schools: 16
  5 Primary; 2 Middle; 2 High; 6 Other Level
  13 Regular; 0 Special Education; 0 Vocational; 2 Alternative
  0 Magnet; 2 Charter; 11 Title I Eligible; 11 School-wide Title I
Students: 6,208   (51.7% male; 48.2% female)
  Individual Education Program: 1,491 (24.0%);
  English Language Learner: 157 (2.5%); Migrant: 276 (4.5%)
  Eligible for Free Lunch Program: 2,791 (45.3%)
  Eligible for Reduced-Price Lunch Program: 655 (10.6%)
Teachers: 387.0 (15.9 to 1)
Librarians/Media Specialists: 11.0 (560.5 to 1)
Guidance Counselors: 12.0 (513.8 to 1)
Current Spending: ($ per student per year):
  Total: $6,564; Instruction: $3,825; Support Services: $2,386
Enrollment, Drop-out Rates and Diploma Recipients by Race/Ethnicity

Category	Total	White	Black	Asian	AIAN	Hisp.
Enrollment (%)	100.0	78.9	15.9	0.6	0.1	4.6
Drop-out Rate (%)	3.6	3.7	4.3	0.0	0.0	0.0
H.S. Diplomas (#)	301	237	53	3	0	8

Madison County

Madison County SD
312 N E Duval St • Madison, FL 32340-2552
Mailing Address: 312 NE Duval St • Madison, FL 32340-2552
(850) 973-5022 • http://janusgroup.com/madison/
Grade Span: PK-12; **Agency Type:** 1
Schools: 9
  4 Primary; 0 Middle; 1 High; 4 Other Level
  8 Regular; 0 Special Education; 0 Vocational; 1 Alternative
  0 Magnet; 0 Charter; 4 Title I Eligible; 4 School-wide Title I
Students: 3,245   (54.8% male; 45.1% female)
  Individual Education Program: 811 (25.0%);
  English Language Learner: 5 (0.2%); Migrant: 25 (0.8%)
  Eligible for Free Lunch Program: 1,731 (53.5%)
  Eligible for Reduced-Price Lunch Program: 253 (7.8%)
Teachers: 175.0 (18.5 to 1)
Librarians/Media Specialists: 3.0 (1,077.7 to 1)
Guidance Counselors: 5.0 (646.6 to 1)
Current Spending: ($ per student per year):
  Total: $6,602; Instruction: $3,597; Support Services: $2,614
Enrollment, Drop-out Rates and Diploma Recipients by Race/Ethnicity

Category	Total	White	Black	Asian	AIAN	Hisp.
Enrollment (%)	100.0	39.9	57.5	0.2	0.2	2.2
Drop-out Rate (%)	6.8	6.8	6.9	0.0	0.0	8.3
H.S. Diplomas (#)	180	100	75	3	0	2

Manatee County

Manatee County SD
215 Manatee Ave W • Bradenton, FL 34206-9069
Mailing Address: PO Box 9069 • Bradenton, FL 34206-9069
(941) 708-8770 • http://www.manatee.k12.fl.us/school_sites.htm
Grade Span: PK-12; **Agency Type:** 1
Schools: 73
  35 Primary; 9 Middle; 9 High; 17 Other Level
  54 Regular; 8 Special Education; 0 Vocational; 8 Alternative
  0 Magnet; 7 Charter; 16 Title I Eligible; 9 School-wide Title I
Students: 40,269   (51.6% male; 48.3% female)
  Individual Education Program: 7,899 (19.6%);
  English Language Learner: 2,548 (6.3%); Migrant: 1,734 (4.3%)
  Eligible for Free Lunch Program: 13,418 (33.5%)
  Eligible for Reduced-Price Lunch Program: 3,231 (8.1%)
Teachers: 2,279.0 (17.6 to 1)
Librarians/Media Specialists: 48.0 (833.5 to 1)
Guidance Counselors: 90.0 (444.5 to 1)
Current Spending: ($ per student per year):
  Total: $6,510; Instruction: $3,878; Support Services: $2,323
Enrollment, Drop-out Rates and Diploma Recipients by Race/Ethnicity

Category	Total	White	Black	Asian	AIAN	Hisp.
Enrollment (%)	100.0	64.2	16.4	1.0	0.1	18.2
Drop-out Rate (%)	3.7	2.6	6.9	4.5	0.0	6.1
H.S. Diplomas (#)	1,709	1,309	258	23	2	117

Marion County

Marion County SD
512 SE 3rd St • Ocala, FL 34478-0670
Mailing Address: PO Box 670 • Ocala, FL 34478-0670
(352) 671-7702 • http://www.marionschoolsk12.org/schooldir.htm
Grade Span: PK-12; **Agency Type:** 1
Schools: 65
  34 Primary; 8 Middle; 9 High; 11 Other Level
  53 Regular; 5 Special Education; 0 Vocational; 4 Alternative
  0 Magnet; 2 Charter; 32 Title I Eligible; 32 School-wide Title I
Students: 40,382   (51.5% male; 48.4% female)
  Individual Education Program: 7,137 (17.7%);
  English Language Learner: 1,115 (2.8%); Migrant: 69 (0.2%)
  Eligible for Free Lunch Program: 16,682 (41.4%)
  Eligible for Reduced-Price Lunch Program: 4,516 (11.2%)
Teachers: 2,299.0 (17.5 to 1)
Librarians/Media Specialists: 44.0 (916.1 to 1)
Guidance Counselors: 91.0 (442.9 to 1)
Current Spending: ($ per student per year):
  Total: $6,233; Instruction: $3,658; Support Services: $2,229
Enrollment, Drop-out Rates and Diploma Recipients by Race/Ethnicity

Category	Total	White	Black	Asian	AIAN	Hisp.
Enrollment (%)	100.0	67.7	20.8	1.0	0.4	10.2
Drop-out Rate (%)	3.5	2.8	5.6	0.0	6.7	4.5
H.S. Diplomas (#)	1,960	1,457	338	25	3	137

Martin County

Martin County SD
500 E Ocean Blvd • Stuart, FL 34994-2578
(772) 219-1200 • http://www.sbmc.org/
Grade Span: PK-12; **Agency Type:** 1
Schools: 29
    14 Primary; 4 Middle; 2 High; 7 Other Level
    20 Regular; 4 Special Education; 0 Vocational; 3 Alternative
    0 Magnet; 0 Charter; 5 Title I Eligible; 4 School-wide Title I
Students: 17,783   (51.3% male; 48.6% female)
    Individual Education Program: 2,999 (16.9%);
    English Language Learner: 1,666 (9.4%); Migrant: 383 (2.2%)
    Eligible for Free Lunch Program: 4,811 (27.1%)
    Eligible for Reduced-Price Lunch Program: 1,080 (6.1%)
Teachers: 974.0 (18.2 to 1)
Librarians/Media Specialists: 17.0 (1,043.4 to 1)
Guidance Counselors: 39.0 (454.8 to 1)
Current Spending: ($ per student per year):
    Total: $6,720; Instruction: $4,011; Support Services: $2,430
Enrollment, Drop-out Rates and Diploma Recipients by Race/Ethnicity

Category	Total	White	Black	Asian	AIAN	Hisp.
Enrollment (%)	100.0	72.7	10.0	1.0	0.2	16.0
Drop-out Rate (%)	0.6	0.3	1.0	0.0	0.0	2.6
H.S. Diplomas (#)	842	711	63	15	2	51

Miami-Dade County

Dade County SD
1450 NE 2nd Ave #912 • Miami, FL 33132-1394
Mailing Address: 1450 NE 2nd Ave #912 • Miami, FL 33132-1394
(305) 995-1428 • http://www.dade.k12.fl.us/schools/
Grade Span: PK-12; **Agency Type:** 1
Schools: 375
    228 Primary; 58 Middle; 46 High; 30 Other Level
    345 Regular; 5 Special Education; 1 Vocational; 11 Alternative
    0 Magnet; 31 Charter; 188 Title I Eligible; 186 School-wide Title I
Students: 371,785   (51.2% male; 48.7% female)
    Individual Education Program: 44,355 (11.9%);
    English Language Learner: 62,180 (16.7%); Migrant: 2,950 (0.8%)
    Eligible for Free Lunch Program: 201,868 (54.7%)
    Eligible for Reduced-Price Lunch Program: 33,145 (9.0%)
Teachers: 18,887.0 (19.5 to 1)
Librarians/Media Specialists: 362.0 (1,020.0 to 1)
Guidance Counselors: 1,004.0 (367.8 to 1)
Current Spending: ($ per student per year):
    Total: $6,956; Instruction: $4,246; Support Services: $2,379
Enrollment, Drop-out Rates and Diploma Recipients by Race/Ethnicity

Category	Total	White	Black	Asian	AIAN	Hisp.
Enrollment (%)	100.0	10.4	28.9	1.1	0.1	59.4
Drop-out Rate (%)	4.8	3.7	5.4	2.3	2.3	4.7
H.S. Diplomas (#)	16,638	2,424	4,864	321	13	9,016

Monroe County

Monroe County SD
241 Trumbo Rd • Key West, FL 33041-1788
Mailing Address: PO Box 1788 • Key West, FL 33041-1788
(305) 293-1400 • http://www.monroe.k12.fl.us/district/schools.htm
Grade Span: PK-12; **Agency Type:** 1
Schools: 19
    11 Primary; 1 Middle; 3 High; 3 Other Level
    17 Regular; 0 Special Education; 0 Vocational; 1 Alternative
    0 Magnet; 3 Charter; 8 Title I Eligible; 0 School-wide Title I
Students: 9,140   (52.7% male; 47.2% female)
    Individual Education Program: 1,653 (18.1%);
    English Language Learner: 570 (6.2%); Migrant: 35 (0.4%)
    Eligible for Free Lunch Program: 2,575 (28.3%)
    Eligible for Reduced-Price Lunch Program: 861 (9.5%)
Teachers: 538.0 (16.9 to 1)
Librarians/Media Specialist: 5.0 (1,820.0 to 1)
Guidance Counselors: 14.0 (650.0 to 1)
Current Spending: ($ per student per year):
    Total: $7,097; Instruction: $3,919; Support Services: $2,915
Enrollment, Drop-out Rates and Diploma Recipients by Race/Ethnicity

Category	Total	White	Black	Asian	AIAN	Hisp.
Enrollment (%)	100.0	66.4	9.4	1.1	0.4	22.7
Drop-out Rate (%)	4.2	3.7	3.5	0.0	11.1	6.3
H.S. Diplomas (#)	486	346	46	6	0	88

Nassau County

Nassau County SD
1201 Atlantic Ave • Fernandina Beach, FL 32034-3499
(904) 491-9901 • http://www.nassau.k12.fl.us/
Grade Span: PK-12; **Agency Type:** 1
Schools: 19
    8 Primary; 2 Middle; 2 High; 6 Other Level
    17 Regular; 0 Special Education; 0 Vocational; 1 Alternative
    0 Magnet; 0 Charter; 10 Title I Eligible; 0 School-wide Title I
Students: 10,563   (51.7% male; 48.2% female)
    Individual Education Program: 1,613 (15.3%);
    English Language Learner: 26 (0.2%); Migrant: 22 (0.2%)
    Eligible for Free Lunch Program: 2,467 (23.4%)
    Eligible for Reduced-Price Lunch Program: 971 (9.2%)
Teachers: 594.0 (17.7 to 1)
Librarians/Media Specialists: 16.0 (657.7 to 1)
Guidance Counselors: 22.0 (478.3 to 1)
Current Spending: ($ per student per year):
    Total: $5,490; Instruction: $3,088; Support Services: $2,102
Enrollment, Drop-out Rates and Diploma Recipients by Race/Ethnicity

Category	Total	White	Black	Asian	AIAN	Hisp.
Enrollment (%)	100.0	88.9	8.9	0.6	0.3	1.3
Drop-out Rate (%)	4.0	3.8	5.9	0.0	0.0	3.1
H.S. Diplomas (#)	577	513	53	5	0	6

Okaloosa County

Okaloosa County SD
120 Lowery Place SE • Fort Walton Beach, FL 32548-5595
(850) 833-3109 • http://www.okaloosa.k12.fl.us/schools/
Grade Span: PK-12; **Agency Type:** 1
Schools: 55
    24 Primary; 8 Middle; 9 High; 13 Other Level
    49 Regular; 1 Special Education; 2 Vocational; 2 Alternative
    0 Magnet; 3 Charter; 14 Title I Eligible; 9 School-wide Title I
Students: 31,489   (51.6% male; 48.3% female)
    Individual Education Program: 5,124 (16.3%);
    English Language Learner: 169 (0.5%); Migrant: 13 (<0.1%)
    Eligible for Free Lunch Program: 6,607 (21.4%)
    Eligible for Reduced-Price Lunch Program: 2,784 (9.0%)
Teachers: 1,695.0 (18.2 to 1)
Librarians/Media Specialists: 32.0 (964.8 to 1)
Guidance Counselors: 60.0 (514.6 to 1)
Current Spending: ($ per student per year):
    Total: $5,782; Instruction: $3,541; Support Services: $1,992
Enrollment, Drop-out Rates and Diploma Recipients by Race/Ethnicity

Category	Total	White	Black	Asian	AIAN	Hisp.
Enrollment (%)	100.0	80.4	12.5	2.8	0.5	3.8
Drop-out Rate (%)	3.6	3.4	5.3	2.6	0.0	3.5
H.S. Diplomas (#)	1,978	1,615	218	72	7	66

Okeechobee County

Okeechobee County SD
700 SW 2nd Ave • Okeechobee, FL 34974-5117
Mailing Address: 700 SW 2nd Ave • Okeechobee, FL 34974-5117
(863) 462-5000 • http://www.okee.k12.fl.us/web.nsf
Grade Span: PK-12; **Agency Type:** 1
Schools: 18
    7 Primary; 2 Middle; 1 High; 7 Other Level
    10 Regular; 2 Special Education; 0 Vocational; 5 Alternative
    0 Magnet; 0 Charter; 5 Title I Eligible; 5 School-wide Title I
Students: 7,279   (52.4% male; 47.5% female)
    Individual Education Program: 1,559 (21.4%);
    English Language Learner: 432 (5.9%); Migrant: 1,207 (16.6%)
    Eligible for Free Lunch Program: 3,249 (44.7%)
    Eligible for Reduced-Price Lunch Program: 759 (10.4%)
Teachers: 382.0 (19.0 to 1)
Librarians/Media Specialists: 7.0 (1,039.3 to 1)
Guidance Counselors: 14.0 (519.6 to 1)
Current Spending: ($ per student per year):
    Total: $6,378; Instruction: $3,645; Support Services: $2,373
Enrollment, Drop-out Rates and Diploma Recipients by Race/Ethnicity

Category	Total	White	Black	Asian	AIAN	Hisp.
Enrollment (%)	100.0	64.0	8.9	0.5	2.4	24.2
Drop-out Rate (%)	5.6	5.5	3.7	0.0	19.0	6.7
H.S. Diplomas (#)	339	248	28	2	3	58

FLORIDA: District Profiles / Orange County   259

Orange County

Florida Virtual School
445 W Amelia St • Orlando, FL 32801-1153
Mailing Address: 445 W Amelia St Ste 301 • Orlando, FL 32801-1153
(407) 317-3326
Grade Span: n/a; Agency Type: 5
Schools: 2
  0 Primary; 1 Middle; 1 High; 0 Other Level
  2 Regular; 0 Special Education; 0 Vocational; 0 Alternative
  0 Magnet; 0 Charter; 0 Title I Eligible; 0 School-wide Title I
Students: 1,710 (36.3% male; 63.6% female)
  Individual Education Program: 0 (0.0%);
  English Language Learner: 0 (0.0%); Migrant: 0 (0.0%)
  Eligible for Free Lunch Program: 0 (0.0%)
  Eligible for Reduced-Price Lunch Program: 0 (0.0%)
Teachers: 77.0 (22.2 to 1)
Librarians/Media Specialists: 0.0 (n/a to 1)
Guidance Counselors: 4.0 (427.5 to 1)
Current Spending: ($ per student per year):
  Total: n/a; Instruction: n/a; Support Services: n/a

Enrollment, Drop-out Rates and Diploma Recipients by Race/Ethnicity

Category	Total	White	Black	Asian	AIAN	Hisp.
Enrollment (%)	100.0	77.1	5.0	6.4	0.6	10.8
Drop-out Rate (%)	n/a	n/a	n/a	n/a	n/a	n/a
H.S. Diplomas (#)	n/a	n/a	n/a	n/a	n/a	n/a

Orange County SD
445 W Amelia St • Orlando, FL 32802-0271
Mailing Address: PO Box 271 • Orlando, FL 32802-0271
(407) 317-3202 • http://www.ocps.k12.fl.us/schools/
Grade Span: PK-12; Agency Type: 1
Schools: 190
  118 Primary; 28 Middle; 21 High; 20 Other Level
  172 Regular; 5 Special Education; 3 Vocational; 7 Alternative
  0 Magnet; 16 Charter; 50 Title I Eligible; 50 School-wide Title I
Students: 165,992 (51.4% male; 48.5% female)
  Individual Education Program: 26,581 (16.0%);
  English Language Learner: 11,305 (6.8%); Migrant: 1,566 (0.9%)
  Eligible for Free Lunch Program: 55,270 (33.4%)
  Eligible for Reduced-Price Lunch Program: 13,543 (8.2%)
Teachers: 9,495.0 (17.4 to 1)
Librarians/Media Specialists: 101.0 (1,637.7 to 1)
Guidance Counselors: 294.0 (562.6 to 1)
Current Spending: ($ per student per year):
  Total: $6,358; Instruction: $3,601; Support Services: $2,449

Enrollment, Drop-out Rates and Diploma Recipients by Race/Ethnicity

Category	Total	White	Black	Asian	AIAN	Hisp.
Enrollment (%)	100.0	40.3	28.5	3.8	0.4	26.9
Drop-out Rate (%)	3.4	2.4	4.6	1.5	1.9	4.2
H.S. Diplomas (#)	7,361	3,737	1,713	401	34	1,476

Osceola County

Osceola County SD
817 Bill Beck Blvd • Kissimmee, FL 34744-4495
(407) 870-4008 • http://www.osceola.k12.fl.us/
Grade Span: PK-12; Agency Type: 1
Schools: 58
  25 Primary; 9 Middle; 7 High; 16 Other Level
  48 Regular; 1 Special Education; 0 Vocational; 8 Alternative
  0 Magnet; 10 Charter; 24 Title I Eligible; 20 School-wide Title I
Students: 43,911 (51.4% male; 48.5% female)
  Individual Education Program: 6,723 (15.3%);
  English Language Learner: 6,901 (15.7%); Migrant: 159 (0.4%)
  Eligible for Free Lunch Program: 17,873 (40.8%)
  Eligible for Reduced-Price Lunch Program: 5,979 (13.6%)
Teachers: 2,219.0 (19.8 to 1)
Librarians/Media Specialists: 35.0 (1,252.7 to 1)
Guidance Counselors: 91.0 (481.8 to 1)
Current Spending: ($ per student per year):
  Total: $5,859; Instruction: $3,318; Support Services: $2,247

Enrollment, Drop-out Rates and Diploma Recipients by Race/Ethnicity

Category	Total	White	Black	Asian	AIAN	Hisp.
Enrollment (%)	100.0	42.4	9.7	2.3	0.2	45.5
Drop-out Rate (%)	5.6	5.6	6.4	3.5	0.0	5.6
H.S. Diplomas (#)	1,853	979	172	71	1	630

Palm Beach County

Palm Beach County SD
3330 Forest Hill Blvd • West Palm Beach, FL 33406-5869
Mailing Address: 3330 Forest Hill Boulevar • West Palm Beach, FL 33406-5869
(561) 434-8200 • http://www.palmbeach.k12.fl.us/schools/
Grade Span: PK-12; Agency Type: 1
Schools: 213
  122 Primary; 29 Middle; 31 High; 26 Other Level
  190 Regular; 3 Special Education; 0 Vocational; 15 Alternative
  0 Magnet; 28 Charter; 95 Title I Eligible; 95 School-wide Title I
Students: 170,260 (51.4% male; 48.5% female)
  Individual Education Program: 25,250 (14.8%);
  English Language Learner: 19,599 (11.5%); Migrant: 5,551 (3.3%)
  Eligible for Free Lunch Program: 61,691 (36.4%)
  Eligible for Reduced-Price Lunch Program: 11,775 (7.0%)
Teachers: 9,359.0 (18.1 to 1)
Librarians/Media Specialists: 159.0 (1,065.3 to 1)
Guidance Counselors: 365.0 (464.1 to 1)
Current Spending: ($ per student per year):
  Total: $6,983; Instruction: $4,284; Support Services: $2,402

Enrollment, Drop-out Rates and Diploma Recipients by Race/Ethnicity

Category	Total	White	Black	Asian	AIAN	Hisp.
Enrollment (%)	100.0	46.3	29.7	2.3	0.6	21.1
Drop-out Rate (%)	3.1	1.9	4.3	1.4	4.8	4.5
H.S. Diplomas (#)	7,687	4,387	1,904	243	21	1,132

Pasco County

Pasco County SD
7227 Land O'lakes Blvd • Land O' Lakes, FL 34639-2899
Mailing Address: 7227 Land O'lakes Bouleva • Land O' Lakes, FL 34639-2899
(813) 794-2651 • http://www.pasco.k12.fl.us/schoollist.html
Grade Span: PK-12; Agency Type: 1
Schools: 73
  36 Primary; 9 Middle; 8 High; 18 Other Level
  69 Regular; 0 Special Education; 1 Vocational; 1 Alternative
  0 Magnet; 5 Charter; 20 Title I Eligible; 20 School-wide Title I
Students: 57,510 (51.4% male; 48.5% female)
  Individual Education Program: 11,082 (19.3%);
  English Language Learner: 1,650 (2.9%); Migrant: 487 (0.8%)
  Eligible for Free Lunch Program: 20,955 (36.5%)
  Eligible for Reduced-Price Lunch Program: 6,447 (11.2%)
Teachers: 3,196.0 (17.9 to 1)
Librarians/Media Specialists: 71.0 (807.6 to 1)
Guidance Counselors: 138.0 (415.5 to 1)
Current Spending: ($ per student per year):
  Total: $6,011; Instruction: $3,336; Support Services: $2,317

Enrollment, Drop-out Rates and Diploma Recipients by Race/Ethnicity

Category	Total	White	Black	Asian	AIAN	Hisp.
Enrollment (%)	100.0	84.6	4.1	1.4	0.3	9.7
Drop-out Rate (%)	4.2	4.0	6.2	2.6	6.7	5.7
H.S. Diplomas (#)	2,453	2,159	81	46	7	160

Pinellas County

Pinellas County SD
301 4th St SW • Largo, FL 33770-3536
(727) 588-6011 • http://www.pinellas.k12.fl.us/
Grade Span: PK-12; Agency Type: 1
Schools: 169
  85 Primary; 26 Middle; 18 High; 34 Other Level
  144 Regular; 8 Special Education; 2 Vocational; 9 Alternative
  0 Magnet; 3 Charter; 54 Title I Eligible; 54 School-wide Title I
Students: 114,510 (51.5% male; 48.4% female)
  Individual Education Program: 20,092 (17.5%);
  English Language Learner: 3,094 (2.7%); Migrant: 0 (0.0%)
  Eligible for Free Lunch Program: 35,407 (31.1%)
  Eligible for Reduced-Price Lunch Program: 10,006 (8.8%)
Teachers: 6,632.0 (17.2 to 1)
Librarians/Media Specialists: 124.0 (918.2 to 1)
Guidance Counselors: 240.0 (474.4 to 1)
Current Spending: ($ per student per year):
  Total: $6,407; Instruction: $3,735; Support Services: $2,376

Enrollment, Drop-out Rates and Diploma Recipients by Race/Ethnicity

Category	Total	White	Black	Asian	AIAN	Hisp.
Enrollment (%)	100.0	70.2	19.5	3.3	0.3	6.7
Drop-out Rate (%)	6.3	5.5	9.7	3.6	2.8	8.1
H.S. Diplomas (#)	5,413	4,332	672	207	12	190

Polk County

Polk County SD
1915 S Floral Ave • Bartow, FL 33831-0391
Mailing Address: PO Box 391 • Bartow, FL 33831-0391
(863) 534-0521 • http://www.pinellas.k12.fl.us/
Grade Span: PK-12; Agency Type: 1
Schools: 147
76 Primary; 21 Middle; 17 High; 33 Other Level
124 Regular; 3 Special Education; 2 Vocational; 18 Alternative
0 Magnet; 15 Charter; 61 Title I Eligible; 61 School-wide Title I
Students: 84,135 (51.8% male; 48.1% female)
Individual Education Program: 12,752 (15.2%);
English Language Learner: 4,057 (4.8%); Migrant: 1,856 (2.2%)
Eligible for Free Lunch Program: 38,026 (45.3%)
Eligible for Reduced-Price Lunch Program: 8,999 (10.7%)
Teachers: 5,284.0 (15.9 to 1)
Librarians/Media Specialists: 116.0 (722.9 to 1)
Guidance Counselors: 185.0 (453.3 to 1)
Current Spending: ($ per student per year):
Total: $6,654; Instruction: $4,101; Support Services: $2,154
Enrollment, Drop-out Rates and Diploma Recipients by Race/Ethnicity

Category	Total	White	Black	Asian	AIAN	Hisp.
Enrollment (%)	100.0	60.7	22.4	1.1	0.2	15.6
Drop-out Rate (%)	3.6	3.4	3.4	1.7	2.9	5.5
H.S. Diplomas (#)	3,815	2,594	832	67	5	317

Putnam County

Putnam County SD
200 S 7th St • Palatka, FL 32177-4615
(386) 329-0510 • http://www.putnamschools.org/
Grade Span: PK-12; Agency Type: 1
Schools: 23
11 Primary; 5 Middle; 3 High; 3 Other Level
19 Regular; 2 Special Education; 0 Vocational; 1 Alternative
0 Magnet; 1 Charter; 16 Title I Eligible; 13 School-wide Title I
Students: 12,241 (53.1% male; 46.8% female)
Individual Education Program: 2,295 (18.7%);
English Language Learner: 454 (3.7%); Migrant: 421 (3.4%)
Eligible for Free Lunch Program: 6,371 (52.1%)
Eligible for Reduced-Price Lunch Program: 1,088 (8.9%)
Teachers: 736.0 (16.6 to 1)
Librarians/Media Specialists: 16.0 (764.3 to 1)
Guidance Counselors: 32.0 (382.2 to 1)
Current Spending: ($ per student per year):
Total: $6,261; Instruction: $3,336; Support Services: $2,541
Enrollment, Drop-out Rates and Diploma Recipients by Race/Ethnicity

Category	Total	White	Black	Asian	AIAN	Hisp.
Enrollment (%)	100.0	62.4	27.1	0.5	0.1	9.8
Drop-out Rate (%)	2.5	1.8	3.6	0.0	0.0	5.4
H.S. Diplomas (#)	447	318	107	2	1	19

Santa Rosa County

Santa Rosa County SD
5086 Canal St • Milton, FL 32570-6726
(850) 983-5010 • http://www.santarosa.k12.fl.us/
Grade Span: PK-12; Agency Type: 1
Schools: 37
14 Primary; 5 Middle; 9 High; 8 Other Level
34 Regular; 1 Special Education; 1 Vocational; 0 Alternative
0 Magnet; 4 Charter; 14 Title I Eligible; 10 School-wide Title I
Students: 24,429 (52.0% male; 47.9% female)
Individual Education Program: 3,957 (16.2%);
English Language Learner: 69 (0.3%); Migrant: 5 (<0.1%)
Eligible for Free Lunch Program: 5,221 (21.4%)
Eligible for Reduced-Price Lunch Program: 2,258 (9.2%)
Teachers: 1,329.0 (18.4 to 1)
Librarians/Media Specialists: 30.0 (814.0 to 1)
Guidance Counselors: 48.0 (508.8 to 1)
Current Spending: ($ per student per year):
Total: $5,627; Instruction: $3,128; Support Services: $2,191
Enrollment, Drop-out Rates and Diploma Recipients by Race/Ethnicity

Category	Total	White	Black	Asian	AIAN	Hisp.
Enrollment (%)	100.0	90.5	5.3	1.6	0.6	2.1
Drop-out Rate (%)	2.1	2.1	3.4	1.9	2.2	0.8
H.S. Diplomas (#)	1,333	1,221	45	22	12	33

Sarasota County

Sarasota County SD
1960 Landings Blvd • Sarasota, FL 34231-3331
(941) 927-9000 • http://www.sarasota.k12.fl.us/
Grade Span: PK-12; Agency Type: 1
Schools: 49
23 Primary; 8 Middle; 8 High; 9 Other Level
41 Regular; 3 Special Education; 1 Vocational; 3 Alternative
0 Magnet; 6 Charter; 12 Title I Eligible; 12 School-wide Title I
Students: 39,534 (51.2% male; 48.7% female)
Individual Education Program: 6,627 (16.8%)
English Language Learner: 1,706 (4.3%); Migrant: 147 (0.4%)
Eligible for Free Lunch Program: 9,595 (24.4%)
Eligible for Reduced-Price Lunch Program: 3,932 (10.0%)
Teachers: 2,389.0 (16.4 to 1)
Librarians/Media Specialists: 18.0 (2,182.2 to 1)
Guidance Counselors: 70.0 (561.1 to 1)
Current Spending: ($ per student per year):
Total: $7,019; Instruction: $4,159; Support Services: $2,545
Enrollment, Drop-out Rates and Diploma Recipients by Race/Ethnicity

Category	Total	White	Black	Asian	AIAN	Hisp.
Enrollment (%)	100.0	79.4	9.5	1.6	0.2	9.3
Drop-out Rate (%)	3.6	2.9	9.3	0.0	20.0	5.3
H.S. Diplomas (#)	1,895	1,634	118	47	1	95

Seminole County

Seminole County SD
400 E Lake Mary Blvd • Sanford, FL 32773-7127
Mailing Address: 400 E Lake Mary Boulev • Sanford, FL 32773-7127
(407) 320-0006 • http://www.scps.k12.fl.us/
Grade Span: PK-12; Agency Type: 1
Schools: 72
38 Primary; 12 Middle; 8 High; 14 Other Level
59 Regular; 3 Special Education; 0 Vocational; 10 Alternative
0 Magnet; 3 Charter; 21 Title I Eligible; 21 School-wide Title I
Students: 64,904 (51.3% male; 48.6% female)
Individual Education Program: 8,753 (13.5%);
English Language Learner: 1,933 (3.0%); Migrant: 0 (0.0%)
Eligible for Free Lunch Program: 14,777 (22.9%)
Eligible for Reduced-Price Lunch Program: 4,968 (7.7%)
Teachers: 3,788.0 (17.1 to 1)
Librarians/Media Specialists: 39.0 (1,657.2 to 1)
Guidance Counselors: 111.0 (582.3 to 1)
Current Spending: ($ per student per year):
Total: $5,849; Instruction: $3,667; Support Services: $1,902
Enrollment, Drop-out Rates and Diploma Recipients by Race/Ethnicity

Category	Total	White	Black	Asian	AIAN	Hisp.
Enrollment (%)	100.0	67.2	13.8	3.1	0.2	15.6
Drop-out Rate (%)	1.5	1.2	3.4	0.8	3.8	1.6
H.S. Diplomas (#)	3,420	2,516	355	138	9	402

St. Johns County

St. Johns County SD
40 Orange St • St. Augustine, FL 32084-3693
(904) 819-7502 • http://macserver.stjohns.k12.fl.us/
Grade Span: PK-12; Agency Type: 1
Schools: 36
16 Primary; 5 Middle; 6 High; 6 Other Level
32 Regular; 0 Special Education; 0 Vocational; 1 Alternative
0 Magnet; 4 Charter; 11 Title I Eligible; 8 School-wide Title I
Students: 23,191 (51.9% male; 48.0% female)
Individual Education Program: 3,565 (15.4%);
English Language Learner: 117 (0.5%); Migrant: 39 (0.2%)
Eligible for Free Lunch Program: 3,275 (14.2%)
Eligible for Reduced-Price Lunch Program: 1,073 (4.6%)
Teachers: 1,319.0 (17.5 to 1)
Librarians/Media Specialists: 28.0 (824.6 to 1)
Guidance Counselors: 53.0 (435.7 to 1)
Current Spending: ($ per student per year):
Total: $6,569; Instruction: $4,043; Support Services: $2,233
Enrollment, Drop-out Rates and Diploma Recipients by Race/Ethnicity

Category	Total	White	Black	Asian	AIAN	Hisp.
Enrollment (%)	100.0	86.8	9.1	1.4	0.1	2.6
Drop-out Rate (%)	2.5	2.4	3.8	0.0	0.0	3.6
H.S. Diplomas (#)	1,097	965	82	11	1	38

St. Lucie County

St. Lucie County SD
2909 Delaware Ave • Fort Pierce, FL 34947-7299
Mailing Address: 4204 Okeechobee Rd • Fort Pierce, FL 34947-7299
(772) 429-3925 • http://plato.stlucie.k12.fl.us/
Grade Span: PK-12; **Agency Type:** 1
Schools: 43
   21 Primary; 6 Middle; 4 High; 11 Other Level
   34 Regular; 2 Special Education; 0 Vocational; 6 Alternative
   0 Magnet; 0 Charter; 28 Title I Eligible; 28 School-wide Title I
Students: 32,799 (50.8% male; 49.1% female)
   Individual Education Program: 4,594 (14.0%);
   English Language Learner: 1,730 (5.3%); Migrant: 4,144 (12.7%)
   Eligible for Free Lunch Program: 14,382 (44.0%)
   Eligible for Reduced-Price Lunch Program: 3,239 (9.9%)
Teachers: 1,645.0 (19.9 to 1)
Librarians/Media Specialists: 37.0 (883.6 to 1)
Guidance Counselors: 83.0 (393.9 to 1)
Current Spending: ($ per student per year):
   Total: $6,192; Instruction: $3,521; Support Services: $2,317
Enrollment, Drop-out Rates and Diploma Recipients by Race/Ethnicity

Category	Total	White	Black	Asian	AIAN	Hisp.
Enrollment (%)	100.0	55.1	29.1	1.4	0.3	14.2
Drop-out Rate (%)	1.6	1.1	3.0	0.0	5.3	1.0
H.S. Diplomas (#)	1,258	758	368	24	3	105

Sumter County

Sumter County SD
2680 Wc 476 • Bushnell, FL 33513-3574
(352) 793-2315 • http://www.sumter.k12.fl.us/
Grade Span: PK-12; **Agency Type:** 1
Schools: 14
   6 Primary; 3 Middle; 1 High; 4 Other Level
   12 Regular; 1 Special Education; 0 Vocational; 1 Alternative
   0 Magnet; 3 Charter; 5 Title I Eligible; 5 School-wide Title I
Students: 6,857 (51.5% male; 48.4% female)
   Individual Education Program: 1,114 (16.2%);
   English Language Learner: 272 (4.0%); Migrant: 345 (5.0%)
   Eligible for Free Lunch Program: 2,972 (43.4%)
   Eligible for Reduced-Price Lunch Program: 834 (12.2%)
Teachers: 389.0 (17.6 to 1)
Librarians/Media Specialists: 12.0 (570.9 to 1)
Guidance Counselors: 14.0 (489.4 to 1)
Current Spending: ($ per student per year):
   Total: $6,527; Instruction: $3,816; Support Services: $2,296
Enrollment, Drop-out Rates and Diploma Recipients by Race/Ethnicity

Category	Total	White	Black	Asian	AIAN	Hisp.
Enrollment (%)	100.0	71.6	19.8	0.7	0.2	7.6
Drop-out Rate (%)	2.8	2.2	4.6	0.0	20.0	3.2
H.S. Diplomas (#)	261	187	54	1	3	16

Suwannee County

Suwannee County SD
702 Second St NW • Live Oak, FL 32064-1608
(386) 364-2604 • http://www.suwannee.k12.fl.us/
Grade Span: PK-12; **Agency Type:** 1
Schools: 10
   3 Primary; 1 Middle; 1 High; 4 Other Level
   9 Regular; 0 Special Education; 0 Vocational; 0 Alternative
   0 Magnet; 0 Charter; 4 Title I Eligible; 4 School-wide Title I
Students: 5,857 (52.6% male; 47.3% female)
   Individual Education Program: 823 (14.1%);
   English Language Learner: 127 (2.2%); Migrant: 158 (2.7%)
   Eligible for Free Lunch Program: 2,478 (42.6%)
   Eligible for Reduced-Price Lunch Program: 530 (9.1%)
Teachers: 338.0 (17.2 to 1)
Librarians/Media Specialists: 7.0 (831.4 to 1)
Guidance Counselors: 14.0 (415.7 to 1)
Current Spending: ($ per student per year):
   Total: $6,387; Instruction: $3,756; Support Services: $2,278
Enrollment, Drop-out Rates and Diploma Recipients by Race/Ethnicity

Category	Total	White	Black	Asian	AIAN	Hisp.
Enrollment (%)	100.0	76.4	17.0	0.8	0.3	5.5
Drop-out Rate (%)	3.5	3.4	4.0	0.0	0.0	4.3
H.S. Diplomas (#)	284	228	46	2	1	7

Taylor County

Taylor County SD
318 N Clark St • Perry, FL 32347-2930
(850) 838-2500 • http://www.taylor.k12.fl.us/
Grade Span: PK-12; **Agency Type:** 1
Schools: 9
   4 Primary; 1 Middle; 2 High; 2 Other Level
   7 Regular; 0 Special Education; 1 Vocational; 1 Alternative
   0 Magnet; 0 Charter; 4 Title I Eligible; 3 School-wide Title I
Students: 3,563 (51.4% male; 48.5% female)
   Individual Education Program: 685 (19.2%);
   English Language Learner: 1 (<0.1%); Migrant: 1 (<0.1%)
   Eligible for Free Lunch Program: 1,708 (48.0%)
   Eligible for Reduced-Price Lunch Program: 276 (7.8%)
Teachers: 206.0 (17.3 to 1)
Librarians/Media Specialists: 4.0 (890.0 to 1)
Guidance Counselors: 5.0 (712.0 to 1)
Current Spending: ($ per student per year):
   Total: $7,096; Instruction: $4,166; Support Services: $2,583
Enrollment, Drop-out Rates and Diploma Recipients by Race/Ethnicity

Category	Total	White	Black	Asian	AIAN	Hisp.
Enrollment (%)	100.0	73.9	23.9	0.6	0.6	1.1
Drop-out Rate (%)	3.0	2.7	4.3	0.0	0.0	0.0
H.S. Diplomas (#)	203	160	39	2	1	1

Union County

Union County SD
55 SW 6th St • Lake Butler, FL 32054-2599
Mailing Address: 55 SW 6th St • Lake Butler, FL 32054-2599
(386) 496-2045 • http://www.union.k12.fl.us/
Grade Span: PK-12; **Agency Type:** 1
Schools: 6
   1 Primary; 1 Middle; 1 High; 2 Other Level
   4 Regular; 0 Special Education; 0 Vocational; 1 Alternative
   0 Magnet; 0 Charter; 2 Title I Eligible; 0 School-wide Title I
Students: 2,171 (52.5% male; 47.4% female)
   Individual Education Program: 384 (17.7%);
   English Language Learner: 3 (0.1%); Migrant: 17 (0.8%)
   Eligible for Free Lunch Program: 835 (38.5%)
   Eligible for Reduced-Price Lunch Program: 193 (8.9%)
Teachers: 162.0 (13.4 to 1)
Librarians/Media Specialists: 3.0 (723.7 to 1)
Guidance Counselors: 3.0 (723.7 to 1)
Current Spending: ($ per student per year):
   Total: $6,014; Instruction: $3,400; Support Services: $2,285
Enrollment, Drop-out Rates and Diploma Recipients by Race/Ethnicity

Category	Total	White	Black	Asian	AIAN	Hisp.
Enrollment (%)	100.0	79.1	18.3	0.3	0.0	2.3
Drop-out Rate (%)	1.9	1.8	1.9	0.0	0.0	14.3
H.S. Diplomas (#)	129	105	22	0	1	1

Volusia County

Volusia County SD
200 N Clara Ave • Deland, FL 32721-2118
Mailing Address: PO Box 2118 • Deland, FL 32721-2118
(386) 734-7190 • http://www.volusia.k12.fl.us/
Grade Span: PK-12; **Agency Type:** 1
Schools: 87
   46 Primary; 11 Middle; 10 High; 20 Other Level
   80 Regular; 1 Special Education; 0 Vocational; 6 Alternative
   0 Magnet; 3 Charter; 48 Title I Eligible; 46 School-wide Title I
Students: 64,089 (51.6% male; 48.3% female)
   Individual Education Program: 11,569 (18.1%);
   English Language Learner: 2,081 (3.2%); Migrant: 1,165 (1.8%)
   Eligible for Free Lunch Program: 20,459 (32.0%)
   Eligible for Reduced-Price Lunch Program: 5,693 (8.9%)
Teachers: 3,807.0 (16.8 to 1)
Librarians/Media Specialists: 70.0 (912.8 to 1)
Guidance Counselors: 184.0 (347.3 to 1)
Current Spending: ($ per student per year):
   Total: $6,360; Instruction: $3,805; Support Services: $2,273
Enrollment, Drop-out Rates and Diploma Recipients by Race/Ethnicity

Category	Total	White	Black	Asian	AIAN	Hisp.
Enrollment (%)	100.0	71.7	15.2	1.2	0.2	11.6
Drop-out Rate (%)	1.9	1.5	2.8	2.0	0.0	4.0
H.S. Diplomas (#)	3,386	2,675	396	59	3	253

Wakulla County

Wakulla County SD
126 High Dr • Crawfordville, FL 32326-0100
Mailing Address: PO Box 100 • Crawfordville, FL 32326-0100
(850) 926-7131 • http://www.firn.edu/schools/wakulla/wakulla/
Grade Span: PK-12; Agency Type: 1
Schools: 11
    5 Primary; 2 Middle; 1 High; 2 Other Level
    8 Regular; 0 Special Education; 0 Vocational; 2 Alternative
    0 Magnet; 1 Charter; 5 Title I Eligible; 2 School-wide Title I
Students: 4,733   (52.1% male; 47.8% female)
    Individual Education Program: 922 (19.5%);
    English Language Learner: 5 (0.1%); Migrant: 0 (0.0%)
    Eligible for Free Lunch Program: 1,247 (26.5%)
    Eligible for Reduced-Price Lunch Program: 419 (8.9%)
Teachers: 263.0 (17.9 to 1)
Librarians/Media Specialists: 6.0 (785.7 to 1)
Guidance Counselors: 8.0 (589.3 to 1)
Current Spending: ($ per student per year):
    Total: $6,226; Instruction: $3,517; Support Services: $2,409
Enrollment, Drop-out Rates and Diploma Recipients by Race/Ethnicity

Category	Total	White	Black	Asian	AIAN	Hisp.
Enrollment (%)	100.0	87.2	11.5	0.3	0.2	0.8
Drop-out Rate (%)	5.7	5.6	5.9	33.3	0.0	11.1
H.S. Diplomas (#)	233	198	30	1	2	2

Walton County

Walton County SD
145 Park St Ste #3 • Defuniak Springs, FL 32433-3344
(850) 892-8331 • http://www.walton.k12.fl.us/
Grade Span: PK-12; Agency Type: 1
Schools: 17
    5 Primary; 2 Middle; 3 High; 7 Other Level
    16 Regular; 0 Special Education; 1 Vocational; 0 Alternative
    0 Magnet; 2 Charter; 7 Title I Eligible; 7 School-wide Title I
Students: 6,530   (52.2% male; 47.7% female)
    Individual Education Program: 1,041 (15.9%);
    English Language Learner: 82 (1.3%); Migrant: 56 (0.9%)
    Eligible for Free Lunch Program: 2,545 (39.1%)
    Eligible for Reduced-Price Lunch Program: 855 (13.1%)
Teachers: 371.0 (17.5 to 1)
Librarians/Media Specialists: 10.0 (651.1 to 1)
Guidance Counselors: 13.0 (500.8 to 1)
Current Spending: ($ per student per year):
    Total: $6,700; Instruction: $3,871; Support Services: $2,480
Enrollment, Drop-out Rates and Diploma Recipients by Race/Ethnicity

Category	Total	White	Black	Asian	AIAN	Hisp.
Enrollment (%)	100.0	87.5	8.7	0.7	0.6	2.5
Drop-out Rate (%)	6.1	5.8	10.0	9.1	0.0	2.9
H.S. Diplomas (#)	246	221	20	0	1	4

Washington County

Washington County SD
652 Third St • Chipley, FL 32428-1442
(850) 638-6222 • http://www.firn.edu/schools/washington/wash/index.htm
Grade Span: PK-12; Agency Type: 1
Schools: 8
    2 Primary; 2 Middle; 2 High; 2 Other Level
    7 Regular; 0 Special Education; 0 Vocational; 1 Alternative
    0 Magnet; 0 Charter; 6 Title I Eligible; 6 School-wide Title I
Students: 3,425   (51.4% male; 48.5% female)
    Individual Education Program: 526 (15.4%);
    English Language Learner: 0 (0.0%); Migrant: 7 (0.2%)
    Eligible for Free Lunch Program: 1,637 (47.8%)
    Eligible for Reduced-Price Lunch Program: 361 (10.5%)
Teachers: 238.0 (14.4 to 1)
Librarians/Media Specialists: 5.0 (684.8 to 1)
Guidance Counselors: 9.0 (380.4 to 1)
Current Spending: ($ per student per year):
    Total: $8,396; Instruction: $4,791; Support Services: $3,216
Enrollment, Drop-out Rates and Diploma Recipients by Race/Ethnicity

Category	Total	White	Black	Asian	AIAN	Hisp.
Enrollment (%)	100.0	78.5	19.0	0.6	0.9	1.0
Drop-out Rate (%)	3.2	3.4	2.2	0.0	0.0	0.0
H.S. Diplomas (#)	191	153	36	1	0	1

Number of Schools

Rank	Number	District Name	City
1	375	Dade County SD	Miami
2	264	Broward County SD	Fort Lauderdale
3	237	Hillsborough County SD	Tampa
4	213	Palm Beach County SD	West Palm Beach
5	190	Orange County SD	Orlando
6	179	Duval County SD	Jacksonville
7	169	Pinellas County SD	Largo
8	147	Polk County SD	Bartow
9	108	Brevard County SD	Viera
10	87	Volusia County SD	Deland
11	83	Lee County SD	Fort Myers
12	77	Escambia County SD	Pensacola
13	73	Manatee County SD	Bradenton
13	73	Pasco County SD	Land O' Lakes
15	72	Seminole County SD	Sanford
16	66	Alachua County SD	Gainesville
17	65	Marion County SD	Ocala
18	58	Osceola County SD	Kissimmee
19	57	Collier County SD	Naples
20	56	Leon County SD	Tallahassee
21	55	Okaloosa County SD	Ft Walton Beach
22	52	Lake County SD	Tavares
23	49	Sarasota County SD	Sarasota
24	44	Bay County SD	Panama City
25	43	St. Lucie County SD	Fort Pierce
26	37	Santa Rosa County SD	Milton
27	36	St. Johns County SD	St. Augustine
28	33	Clay County SD	Green Cove Spgs
29	29	Martin County SD	Stuart
30	28	Indian River County SD	Vero Beach
31	25	Citrus County SD	Inverness
32	23	Charlotte County SD	Port Charlotte
32	23	Hernando County SD	Brooksville
32	23	Putnam County SD	Palatka
35	22	Gadsden County SD	Quincy
36	21	Jackson County SD	Marianna
37	19	Monroe County SD	Key West
37	19	Nassau County SD	Fernandina Bch
39	18	Highlands County SD	Sebring
39	18	Okeechobee County SD	Okeechobee
41	17	Walton County SD	Defuniak Spgs
42	16	Levy County SD	Bronson
43	15	Columbia County SD	Lake City
44	14	Hendry County SD	La Belle
44	14	Sumter County SD	Bushnell
46	13	Desoto County SD	Arcadia
47	12	Bradford County SD	Starke
48	11	Wakulla County SD	Crawfordville
49	10	Suwannee County SD	Live Oak
50	9	Hardee County SD	Wauchula
50	9	Holmes County SD	Bonifay
50	9	Madison County SD	Madison
50	9	Taylor County SD	Perry
54	8	Flagler County SD	Bunnell
54	8	Gulf County SD	Port St. Joe
54	8	Washington County SD	Chipley
57	7	Baker County SD	Macclenny
57	7	Calhoun County SD	Blountstown
57	7	Hamilton County SD	Jasper
60	6	Union County SD	Lake Butler
61	5	Dixie County SD	Cross City
62	4	Gilchrist County SD	Trenton
63	2	Florida State Univ Lab School	Tallahassee
63	2	Florida Virtual School	Orlando

Number of Teachers

Rank	Number	District Name	City
1	18,887	Dade County SD	Miami
2	14,264	Broward County SD	Fort Lauderdale
3	11,020	Hillsborough County SD	Tampa
4	9,495	Orange County SD	Orlando
5	9,359	Palm Beach County SD	West Palm Beach
6	6,976	Duval County SD	Jacksonville
7	6,632	Pinellas County SD	Largo
8	5,284	Polk County SD	Bartow
9	4,303	Brevard County SD	Viera
10	3,807	Volusia County SD	Deland
11	3,788	Seminole County SD	Sanford
12	3,624	Lee County SD	Fort Myers
13	3,196	Pasco County SD	Land O' Lakes
14	2,511	Escambia County SD	Pensacola
15	2,389	Sarasota County SD	Sarasota
16	2,332	Collier County SD	Naples
17	2,299	Marion County SD	Ocala
18	2,279	Manatee County SD	Bradenton
19	2,219	Osceola County SD	Kissimmee
20	1,817	Leon County SD	Tallahassee
21	1,797	Clay County SD	Green Cove Spgs
22	1,758	Lake County SD	Tavares

Number of Students

Rank	Number	District Name	City
1	371,785	Dade County SD	Miami
2	272,835	Broward County SD	Fort Lauderdale
3	181,900	Hillsborough County SD	Tampa
4	170,260	Palm Beach County SD	West Palm Beach
5	165,992	Orange County SD	Orlando
6	129,557	Duval County SD	Jacksonville
7	114,510	Pinellas County SD	Largo
8	84,135	Polk County SD	Bartow
9	73,901	Brevard County SD	Viera
10	66,466	Lee County SD	Fort Myers
11	64,904	Seminole County SD	Sanford
12	64,089	Volusia County SD	Deland
13	57,510	Pasco County SD	Land O' Lakes
14	43,998	Escambia County SD	Pensacola
15	43,911	Osceola County SD	Kissimmee
16	40,382	Marion County SD	Ocala
17	40,269	Manatee County SD	Bradenton
18	40,157	Collier County SD	Naples
19	39,534	Sarasota County SD	Sarasota
20	33,992	Lake County SD	Tavares
21	32,799	St. Lucie County SD	Fort Pierce
22	32,194	Leon County SD	Tallahassee
23	31,489	Okaloosa County SD	Ft Walton Beach
24	31,370	Clay County SD	Green Cove Spgs
25	29,448	Alachua County SD	Gainesville
26	26,708	Bay County SD	Panama City
27	24,429	Santa Rosa County SD	Milton
28	23,191	St. Johns County SD	St. Augustine
29	19,596	Hernando County SD	Brooksville
30	18,298	Charlotte County SD	Port Charlotte
31	17,783	Martin County SD	Stuart
32	16,637	Indian River County SD	Vero Beach
33	15,517	Citrus County SD	Inverness
34	12,241	Putnam County SD	Palatka
35	11,666	Highlands County SD	Sebring
36	10,563	Nassau County SD	Fernandina Bch
37	9,790	Columbia County SD	Lake City
38	9,140	Monroe County SD	Key West
39	8,564	Flagler County SD	Bunnell
40	7,664	Hendry County SD	La Belle
41	7,279	Okeechobee County SD	Okeechobee
42	7,192	Jackson County SD	Marianna
43	6,948	Gadsden County SD	Quincy
44	6,857	Sumter County SD	Bushnell
45	6,530	Walton County SD	Defuniak Spgs
46	6,208	Levy County SD	Bronson
47	5,857	Suwannee County SD	Live Oak
48	5,221	Hardee County SD	Wauchula
49	4,975	Desoto County SD	Arcadia
50	4,733	Wakulla County SD	Crawfordville
51	4,606	Baker County SD	Macclenny
52	3,909	Bradford County SD	Starke
53	3,563	Taylor County SD	Perry
54	3,425	Washington County SD	Chipley
55	3,383	Holmes County SD	Bonifay
56	3,245	Madison County SD	Madison
57	2,832	Gilchrist County SD	Trenton
58	2,225	Calhoun County SD	Blountstown
59	2,217	Florida State Univ Lab School	Tallahassee
60	2,171	Union County SD	Lake Butler
61	2,169	Dixie County SD	Cross City
62	2,150	Gulf County SD	Port St. Joe
63	2,057	Hamilton County SD	Jasper
64	1,710	Florida Virtual School	Orlando

Male Students

Rank	Percent	District Name	City
1	54.8	Madison County SD	Madison
2	53.1	Putnam County SD	Palatka
3	53.0	Desoto County SD	Arcadia
4	52.8	Holmes County SD	Bonifay
5	52.7	Monroe County SD	Key West
6	52.6	Suwannee County SD	Live Oak
7	52.6	Hardee County SD	Wauchula
8	52.5	Bradford County SD	Starke
9	52.5	Union County SD	Lake Butler
10	52.4	Okeechobee County SD	Okeechobee
11	52.4	Baker County SD	Macclenny
12	52.2	Walton County SD	Defuniak Spgs
13	52.1	Citrus County SD	Inverness
14	52.1	Wakulla County SD	Crawfordville
15	52.0	Gulf County SD	Port St. Joe
16	52.0	Santa Rosa County SD	Milton
17	51.9	St. Johns County SD	St. Augustine
18	51.8	Polk County SD	Bartow
19	51.8	Indian River County SD	Vero Beach
20	51.7	Levy County SD	Bronson
21	51.7	Flagler County SD	Bunnell
22	51.7	Hendry County SD	La Belle
23	51.7	Broward County SD	Fort Lauderdale
24	51.7	Nassau County SD	Fernandina Bch
25	51.6	Dixie County SD	Cross City
26	51.6	Manatee County SD	Bradenton
27	51.6	Columbia County SD	Lake City
28	51.6	Highlands County SD	Sebring
29	51.6	Okaloosa County SD	Ft Walton Beach
30	51.6	Bay County SD	Panama City
31	51.6	Volusia County SD	Deland
32	51.5	Marion County SD	Ocala
33	51.5	Sumter County SD	Bushnell
34	51.5	Pinellas County SD	Largo
35	51.4	Palm Beach County SD	West Palm Beach
36	51.4	Orange County SD	Orlando
37	51.4	Taylor County SD	Perry
38	51.4	Collier County SD	Naples
39	51.4	Osceola County SD	Kissimmee
40	51.4	Washington County SD	Chipley
41	51.4	Pasco County SD	Land O' Lakes
42	51.4	Jackson County SD	Marianna
43	51.3	Hamilton County SD	Jasper
44	51.3	Seminole County SD	Sanford
45	51.3	Brevard County SD	Viera
46	51.3	Martin County SD	Stuart
47	51.3	Lee County SD	Fort Myers
48	51.3	Hillsborough County SD	Tampa
49	51.2	Gilchrist County SD	Trenton
50	51.2	Sarasota County SD	Sarasota
51	51.2	Dade County SD	Miami
52	51.2	Clay County SD	Green Cove Spgs
53	51.1	Escambia County SD	Pensacola
54	51.1	Hernando County SD	Brooksville
55	51.0	Leon County SD	Tallahassee
56	51.0	Lake County SD	Tavares
57	50.8	St. Lucie County SD	Fort Pierce
58	50.8	Duval County SD	Jacksonville
59	50.8	Charlotte County SD	Port Charlotte
60	50.7	Gadsden County SD	Quincy
61	50.5	Calhoun County SD	Blountstown
62	50.3	Alachua County SD	Gainesville
63	49.4	Florida State Univ Lab School	Tallahassee
64	36.3	Florida Virtual School	Orlando

Female Students

Rank	Percent	District Name	City
1	63.6	Florida Virtual School	Orlando
2	50.5	Florida State Univ Lab School	Tallahassee
3	49.6	Alachua County SD	Gainesville
4	49.4	Calhoun County SD	Blountstown

5	49.2	Gadsden County SD	Quincy
6	49.1	Charlotte County SD	Port Charlotte
7	49.1	Duval County SD	Jacksonville
8	49.1	St. Lucie County SD	Fort Pierce
9	48.9	Lake County SD	Tavares
10	48.9	Leon County SD	Tallahassee
11	48.8	Hernando County SD	Brooksville
12	48.8	Escambia County SD	Pensacola
13	48.7	Clay County SD	Green Cove Spgs
14	48.7	Dade County SD	Miami
15	48.7	Sarasota County SD	Sarasota
16	48.7	Gilchrist County SD	Trenton
17	48.6	Hillsborough County SD	Tampa
18	48.6	Lee County SD	Fort Myers
19	48.6	Martin County SD	Stuart
20	48.6	Brevard County SD	Viera
21	48.6	Seminole County SD	Sanford
22	48.6	Hamilton County SD	Jasper
23	48.5	Jackson County SD	Marianna
24	48.5	Pasco County SD	Land O' Lakes
25	48.5	Washington County SD	Chipley
26	48.5	Osceola County SD	Kissimmee
27	48.5	Collier County SD	Naples
28	48.5	Taylor County SD	Perry
29	48.5	Orange County SD	Orlando
30	48.5	Palm Beach County SD	West Palm Beach
31	48.4	Pinellas County SD	Largo
32	48.4	Sumter County SD	Bushnell
33	48.4	Marion County SD	Ocala
34	48.3	Volusia County SD	Deland
35	48.3	Bay County SD	Panama City
36	48.3	Okaloosa County SD	Ft Walton Beach
37	48.3	Highlands County SD	Sebring
38	48.3	Columbia County SD	Lake City
39	48.3	Manatee County SD	Bradenton
40	48.3	Dixie County SD	Cross City
41	48.2	Nassau County SD	Fernandina Bch
42	48.2	Broward County SD	Fort Lauderdale
43	48.2	Hendry County SD	La Belle
44	48.2	Flagler County SD	Bunnell
45	48.2	Levy County SD	Bronson
46	48.1	Indian River County SD	Vero Beach
47	48.1	Polk County SD	Bartow
48	48.0	St. Johns County SD	St. Augustine
49	47.9	Santa Rosa County SD	Milton
50	47.9	Gulf County SD	Port St. Joe
51	47.8	Wakulla County SD	Crawfordville
52	47.8	Citrus County SD	Inverness
53	47.7	Walton County SD	Defuniak Spgs
54	47.5	Baker County SD	Macclenny
55	47.5	Okeechobee County SD	Okeechobee
56	47.4	Union County SD	Lake Butler
57	47.4	Bradford County SD	Starke
58	47.3	Hardee County SD	Wauchula
59	47.3	Suwannee County SD	Live Oak
60	47.2	Monroe County SD	Key West
61	47.1	Holmes County SD	Bonifay
62	46.9	Desoto County SD	Arcadia
63	46.8	Putnam County SD	Palatka
64	45.1	Madison County SD	Madison

Individual Education Program Students

Rank	Percent	District Name	City
1	25.5	Gilchrist County SD	Trenton
2	25.0	Madison County SD	Madison
3	24.3	Bradford County SD	Starke
4	24.0	Levy County SD	Bronson
5	23.5	Dixie County SD	Cross City
6	22.6	Calhoun County SD	Blountstown
7	21.4	Okeechobee County SD	Okeechobee
8	20.7	Hardee County SD	Wauchula
9	20.0	Desoto County SD	Arcadia
10	19.9	Jackson County SD	Marianna
11	19.8	Clay County SD	Green Cove Spgs
12	19.7	Bay County SD	Panama City
13	19.6	Leon County SD	Tallahassee
13	19.6	Manatee County SD	Bradenton
15	19.5	Alachua County SD	Gainesville
15	19.5	Charlotte County SD	Port Charlotte
15	19.5	Wakulla County SD	Crawfordville
18	19.3	Pasco County SD	Land O' Lakes
19	19.2	Taylor County SD	Perry
20	19.1	Gulf County SD	Port St. Joe
21	18.7	Putnam County SD	Palatka
22	18.4	Citrus County SD	Inverness
22	18.4	Columbia County SD	Lake City
24	18.1	Monroe County SD	Key West
24	18.1	Volusia County SD	Deland
26	17.8	Gadsden County SD	Quincy
27	17.7	Highlands County SD	Sebring
27	17.7	Marion County SD	Ocala
27	17.7	Union County SD	Lake Butler
30	17.6	Hernando County SD	Brooksville
31	17.5	Brevard County SD	Viera
31	17.5	Pinellas County SD	Largo
33	17.4	Hamilton County SD	Jasper
34	17.0	Escambia County SD	Pensacola
34	17.0	Flagler County SD	Bunnell
34	17.0	Hendry County SD	La Belle
37	16.9	Martin County SD	Stuart
38	16.8	Sarasota County SD	Sarasota
39	16.7	Lake County SD	Tavares
40	16.3	Okaloosa County SD	Ft Walton Beach
41	16.2	Santa Rosa County SD	Milton
41	16.2	Sumter County SD	Bushnell
43	16.0	Orange County SD	Orlando
44	15.9	Walton County SD	Defuniak Spgs
45	15.7	Duval County SD	Jacksonville
46	15.6	Hillsborough County SD	Tampa
47	15.5	Collier County SD	Naples
48	15.4	St. Johns County SD	St. Augustine
48	15.4	Washington County SD	Chipley
50	15.3	Nassau County SD	Fernandina Bch
50	15.3	Osceola County SD	Kissimmee
52	15.2	Polk County SD	Bartow
53	15.1	Lee County SD	Fort Myers
54	15.0	Holmes County SD	Bonifay
54	15.0	Indian River County SD	Vero Beach
56	14.8	Palm Beach County SD	West Palm Beach
57	14.1	Suwannee County SD	Live Oak
58	14.0	St. Lucie County SD	Fort Pierce
59	13.5	Seminole County SD	Sanford
60	12.0	Baker County SD	Macclenny
61	11.9	Dade County SD	Miami
62	11.4	Broward County SD	Fort Lauderdale
63	8.6	Florida State Univ Lab School	Tallahassee
64	0.0	Florida Virtual School	Orlando

English Language Learner Students

Rank	Percent	District Name	City
1	16.7	Dade County SD	Miami
2	15.7	Osceola County SD	Kissimmee
3	14.3	Collier County SD	Naples
4	11.5	Palm Beach County SD	West Palm Beach
5	10.9	Broward County SD	Fort Lauderdale
6	10.4	Hillsborough County SD	Tampa
7	9.9	Lee County SD	Fort Myers
8	9.4	Martin County SD	Stuart
9	8.6	Desoto County SD	Arcadia
10	8.4	Hardee County SD	Wauchula
10	8.4	Hendry County SD	La Belle
12	6.8	Orange County SD	Orlando
13	6.3	Manatee County SD	Bradenton
14	6.2	Monroe County SD	Key West
15	5.9	Okeechobee County SD	Okeechobee
16	5.7	Gadsden County SD	Quincy
17	5.3	St. Lucie County SD	Fort Pierce
18	4.8	Polk County SD	Bartow
19	4.3	Sarasota County SD	Sarasota
20	4.2	Highlands County SD	Sebring
21	4.0	Lake County SD	Tavares
21	4.0	Sumter County SD	Bushnell
23	3.9	Indian River County SD	Vero Beach
24	3.7	Putnam County SD	Palatka
25	3.2	Hamilton County SD	Jasper
25	3.2	Volusia County SD	Deland
27	3.0	Seminole County SD	Sanford
28	2.9	Pasco County SD	Land O' Lakes
29	2.8	Flagler County SD	Bunnell
29	2.8	Marion County SD	Ocala
31	2.7	Pinellas County SD	Largo
32	2.6	Florida State Univ Lab School	Tallahassee
33	2.5	Levy County SD	Bronson
34	2.3	Duval County SD	Jacksonville
35	2.2	Suwannee County SD	Live Oak
36	1.5	Alachua County SD	Gainesville
36	1.5	Brevard County SD	Viera
36	1.5	Hernando County SD	Brooksville
39	1.3	Walton County SD	Defuniak Spgs
40	1.0	Leon County SD	Tallahassee
41	0.9	Bay County SD	Panama City
41	0.9	Charlotte County SD	Port Charlotte
43	0.7	Escambia County SD	Pensacola
44	0.6	Citrus County SD	Inverness
44	0.6	Clay County SD	Green Cove Spgs
46	0.5	Jackson County SD	Marianna
46	0.5	Okaloosa County SD	Ft Walton Beach
46	0.5	St. Johns County SD	St. Augustine
49	0.4	Bradford County SD	Starke
49	0.4	Gilchrist County SD	Trenton
51	0.3	Columbia County SD	Lake City
51	0.3	Holmes County SD	Bonifay
51	0.3	Santa Rosa County SD	Milton
54	0.2	Madison County SD	Madison
54	0.2	Nassau County SD	Fernandina Bch
56	0.1	Baker County SD	Macclenny
56	0.1	Calhoun County SD	Blountstown
56	0.1	Union County SD	Lake Butler
56	0.1	Wakulla County SD	Crawfordville
60	0.0	Gulf County SD	Port St. Joe
60	0.0	Taylor County SD	Perry
62	0.0	Dixie County SD	Cross City
62	0.0	Florida Virtual School	Orlando
62	0.0	Washington County SD	Chipley

Migrant Students

Rank	Percent	District Name	City
1	31.1	Hardee County SD	Wauchula
2	30.0	Hendry County SD	La Belle
3	16.6	Okeechobee County SD	Okeechobee
4	12.7	St. Lucie County SD	Fort Pierce
5	12.5	Collier County SD	Naples
6	11.8	Desoto County SD	Arcadia
7	10.9	Highlands County SD	Sebring
8	8.8	Gadsden County SD	Quincy
9	5.0	Sumter County SD	Bushnell
10	4.8	Indian River County SD	Vero Beach
11	4.5	Levy County SD	Bronson
12	4.3	Manatee County SD	Bradenton
13	3.4	Gilchrist County SD	Trenton
13	3.4	Hamilton County SD	Jasper
13	3.4	Putnam County SD	Palatka
16	3.3	Palm Beach County SD	West Palm Beach
17	2.7	Dixie County SD	Cross City
17	2.7	Suwannee County SD	Live Oak
19	2.4	Lee County SD	Fort Myers
20	2.2	Hillsborough County SD	Tampa
20	2.2	Martin County SD	Stuart
20	2.2	Polk County SD	Bartow
23	1.8	Volusia County SD	Deland
24	1.0	Holmes County SD	Bonifay
25	0.9	Calhoun County SD	Blountstown
25	0.9	Escambia County SD	Pensacola
25	0.9	Lake County SD	Tavares
25	0.9	Orange County SD	Orlando
25	0.9	Walton County SD	Defuniak Spgs
30	0.8	Dade County SD	Miami
30	0.8	Madison County SD	Madison
30	0.8	Pasco County SD	Land O' Lakes
30	0.8	Union County SD	Lake Butler
34	0.6	Bay County SD	Panama City
35	0.5	Jackson County SD	Marianna
36	0.4	Citrus County SD	Inverness
36	0.4	Clay County SD	Green Cove Spgs
36	0.4	Columbia County SD	Lake City
36	0.4	Monroe County SD	Key West
36	0.4	Osceola County SD	Kissimmee
36	0.4	Sarasota County SD	Sarasota
42	0.3	Alachua County SD	Gainesville
42	0.3	Broward County SD	Fort Lauderdale
44	0.2	Baker County SD	Macclenny
44	0.2	Bradford County SD	Starke
44	0.2	Flagler County SD	Bunnell
44	0.2	Marion County SD	Ocala
44	0.2	Nassau County SD	Fernandina Bch
44	0.2	St. Johns County SD	St. Augustine
44	0.2	Washington County SD	Chipley
51	0.1	Brevard County SD	Viera
52	0.0	Florida State Univ Lab School	Tallahassee
52	0.0	Okaloosa County SD	Ft Walton Beach
52	0.0	Santa Rosa County SD	Milton
52	0.0	Taylor County SD	Perry
56	0.0	Charlotte County SD	Port Charlotte
56	0.0	Duval County SD	Jacksonville
56	0.0	Florida Virtual School	Orlando
56	0.0	Gulf County SD	Port St. Joe
56	0.0	Hernando County SD	Brooksville
56	0.0	Leon County SD	Tallahassee
56	0.0	Pinellas County SD	Largo
56	0.0	Seminole County SD	Sanford
56	0.0	Wakulla County SD	Crawfordville

Students Eligible for Free Lunch

Rank	Percent	District Name	City
1	66.8	Gadsden County SD	Quincy
2	63.7	Hamilton County SD	Jasper
3	62.1	Hardee County SD	Wauchula
4	59.9	Hendry County SD	La Belle
5	54.7	Dade County SD	Miami
6	53.5	Desoto County SD	Arcadia
6	53.5	Madison County SD	Madison
8	53.3	Dixie County SD	Cross City
9	52.1	Putnam County SD	Palatka
10	50.3	Highlands County SD	Sebring
11	49.2	Bradford County SD	Starke

12	48.0	Taylor County SD	Perry
13	47.8	Washington County SD	Chipley
14	46.3	Escambia County SD	Pensacola
15	45.3	Levy County SD	Bronson
15	45.3	Polk County SD	Bartow
17	44.8	Columbia County SD	Lake City
18	44.7	Okeechobee County SD	Okeechobee
19	44.0	St. Lucie County SD	Fort Pierce
20	43.4	Sumter County SD	Bushnell
21	43.1	Holmes County SD	Bonifay
22	42.6	Jackson County SD	Marianna
22	42.6	Suwannee County SD	Live Oak
24	41.4	Marion County SD	Ocala
25	40.9	Gilchrist County SD	Trenton
26	40.8	Osceola County SD	Kissimmee
27	40.6	Calhoun County SD	Blountstown
28	40.2	Alachua County SD	Gainesville
28	40.2	Hillsborough County SD	Tampa
30	39.1	Walton County SD	Defuniak Spgs
31	38.5	Union County SD	Lake Butler
32	37.1	Gulf County SD	Port St. Joe
33	36.6	Lee County SD	Fort Myers
34	36.5	Pasco County SD	Land O' Lakes
35	36.4	Palm Beach County SD	West Palm Beach
36	35.2	Bay County SD	Panama City
37	34.6	Duval County SD	Jacksonville
38	34.3	Hernando County SD	Brooksville
39	33.8	Citrus County SD	Inverness
40	33.5	Manatee County SD	Bradenton
41	33.4	Orange County SD	Orlando
42	32.0	Volusia County SD	Deland
43	31.7	Broward County SD	Fort Lauderdale
44	31.4	Baker County SD	Macclenny
45	31.1	Pinellas County SD	Largo
46	30.4	Lake County SD	Tavares
47	29.9	Leon County SD	Tallahassee
48	29.4	Indian River County SD	Vero Beach
49	28.3	Monroe County SD	Key West
50	27.1	Martin County SD	Stuart
51	26.5	Wakulla County SD	Crawfordville
52	26.3	Flagler County SD	Bunnell
53	24.4	Sarasota County SD	Sarasota
54	24.0	Charlotte County SD	Port Charlotte
55	23.4	Nassau County SD	Fernandina Bch
56	22.9	Seminole County SD	Sanford
57	21.8	Brevard County SD	Viera
58	21.4	Okaloosa County SD	Ft Walton Beach
58	21.4	Santa Rosa County SD	Milton
60	18.2	Clay County SD	Green Cove Spgs
61	15.6	Collier County SD	Naples
62	14.2	St. Johns County SD	St. Augustine
63	10.8	Florida State Univ Lab School	Tallahassee
64	0.0	Florida Virtual School	Orlando

Students Eligible for Reduced-Price Lunch

Rank	Percent	District Name	City
1	13.9	Holmes County SD	Bonifay
2	13.6	Osceola County SD	Kissimmee
3	13.3	Gilchrist County SD	Trenton
4	13.1	Walton County SD	Defuniak Spgs
5	12.5	Bradford County SD	Starke
6	12.2	Bay County SD	Panama City
6	12.2	Sumter County SD	Bushnell
8	12.1	Dixie County SD	Cross City
9	12.0	Escambia County SD	Pensacola
10	11.6	Columbia County SD	Lake City
10	11.6	Hernando County SD	Brooksville
12	11.2	Marion County SD	Ocala
12	11.2	Pasco County SD	Land O' Lakes
14	11.0	Jackson County SD	Marianna
15	10.9	Citrus County SD	Inverness
16	10.7	Polk County SD	Bartow
17	10.6	Levy County SD	Bronson
18	10.5	Washington County SD	Chipley
19	10.4	Calhoun County SD	Blountstown
19	10.4	Gulf County SD	Port St. Joe
19	10.4	Okeechobee County SD	Okeechobee
22	10.2	Lee County SD	Fort Myers
23	10.1	Charlotte County SD	Port Charlotte
24	10.0	Sarasota County SD	Sarasota
25	9.9	St. Lucie County SD	Fort Pierce
26	9.8	Hendry County SD	La Belle
26	9.8	Hillsborough County SD	Tampa
28	9.6	Desoto County SD	Arcadia
28	9.6	Flagler County SD	Bunnell
28	9.6	Gadsden County SD	Quincy
31	9.5	Highlands County SD	Sebring
31	9.5	Monroe County SD	Key West
33	9.2	Duval County SD	Jacksonville
33	9.2	Nassau County SD	Fernandina Bch
33	9.2	Santa Rosa County SD	Milton
36	9.1	Lake County SD	Tavares
36	9.1	Suwannee County SD	Live Oak
38	9.0	Dade County SD	Miami
38	9.0	Hamilton County SD	Jasper
38	9.0	Okaloosa County SD	Ft Walton Beach
41	8.9	Putnam County SD	Palatka
41	8.9	Union County SD	Lake Butler
41	8.9	Volusia County SD	Deland
41	8.9	Wakulla County SD	Crawfordville
45	8.8	Baker County SD	Macclenny
45	8.8	Pinellas County SD	Largo
47	8.7	Alachua County SD	Gainesville
48	8.6	Broward County SD	Fort Lauderdale
48	8.6	Hardee County SD	Wauchula
48	8.6	Indian River County SD	Vero Beach
51	8.2	Orange County SD	Orlando
52	8.1	Manatee County SD	Bradenton
53	8.0	Clay County SD	Green Cove Spgs
54	7.9	Florida State Univ Lab School	Tallahassee
55	7.8	Madison County SD	Madison
55	7.8	Taylor County SD	Perry
57	7.7	Seminole County SD	Sanford
58	7.0	Palm Beach County SD	West Palm Beach
59	6.5	Leon County SD	Tallahassee
60	6.3	Brevard County SD	Viera
61	6.1	Martin County SD	Stuart
62	5.9	Collier County SD	Naples
63	4.6	St. Johns County SD	St. Augustine
64	0.0	Florida Virtual School	Orlando

Student/Teacher Ratio

Rank	Ratio	District Name	City
1	22.2	Florida Virtual School	Orlando
2	19.9	St. Lucie County SD	Fort Pierce
3	19.8	Osceola County SD	Kissimmee
4	19.5	Dade County SD	Miami
4	19.5	Hendry County SD	La Belle
6	19.2	Lake County SD	Tavares
7	19.1	Broward County SD	Fort Lauderdale
8	19.0	Okeechobee County SD	Okeechobee
9	18.8	Charlotte County SD	Port Charlotte
10	18.5	Madison County SD	Madison
11	18.4	Duval County SD	Jacksonville
11	18.4	Santa Rosa County SD	Milton
13	18.3	Lee County SD	Fort Myers
14	18.2	Martin County SD	Stuart
14	18.2	Okaloosa County SD	Ft Walton Beach
16	18.1	Baker County SD	Macclenny
16	18.1	Palm Beach County SD	West Palm Beach
18	17.9	Hernando County SD	Brooksville
18	17.9	Pasco County SD	Land O' Lakes
18	17.9	Wakulla County SD	Crawfordville
21	17.8	Indian River County SD	Vero Beach
22	17.7	Nassau County SD	Fernandina Bch
23	17.6	Alachua County SD	Gainesville
23	17.6	Dixie County SD	Cross City
23	17.6	Leon County SD	Tallahassee
23	17.6	Manatee County SD	Bradenton
23	17.6	Sumter County SD	Bushnell
28	17.5	Marion County SD	Ocala
28	17.5	St. Johns County SD	St. Augustine
28	17.5	Walton County SD	Defuniak Spgs
31	17.4	Clay County SD	Green Cove Spgs
31	17.4	Escambia County SD	Pensacola
31	17.4	Orange County SD	Orlando
34	17.3	Desoto County SD	Arcadia
34	17.3	Taylor County SD	Perry
36	17.2	Collier County SD	Naples
36	17.2	Flagler County SD	Bunnell
36	17.2	Pinellas County SD	Largo
36	17.2	Suwannee County SD	Live Oak
40	17.1	Brevard County SD	Viera
40	17.1	Hardee County SD	Wauchula
40	17.1	Seminole County SD	Sanford
43	17.0	Bay County SD	Panama City
44	16.9	Jackson County SD	Marianna
44	16.9	Monroe County SD	Key West
46	16.8	Volusia County SD	Deland
47	16.7	Gilchrist County SD	Trenton
47	16.7	Highlands County SD	Sebring
49	16.6	Putnam County SD	Palatka
50	16.5	Columbia County SD	Lake City
50	16.5	Hillsborough County SD	Tampa
52	16.4	Gulf County SD	Port St. Joe
52	16.4	Sarasota County SD	Sarasota
54	16.3	Citrus County SD	Inverness
55	16.2	Hamilton County SD	Jasper
56	15.9	Levy County SD	Bronson
56	15.9	Polk County SD	Bartow
58	15.8	Bradford County SD	Starke
59	15.7	Florida State Univ Lab School	Tallahassee
59	15.7	Gadsden County SD	Quincy
59	15.7	Holmes County SD	Bonifay
62	14.4	Washington County SD	Chipley
63	14.2	Calhoun County SD	Blountstown
64	13.4	Union County SD	Lake Butler

Student/Librarian Ratio

Rank	Ratio	District Name	City
1	2,182.2	Sarasota County SD	Sarasota
2	2,167.0	Dixie County SD	Cross City
3	1,820.0	Monroe County SD	Key West
4	1,657.2	Seminole County SD	Sanford
5	1,637.7	Orange County SD	Orlando
6	1,425.7	Flagler County SD	Bunnell
7	1,408.6	Lee County SD	Fort Myers
8	1,252.7	Osceola County SD	Kissimmee
9	1,197.8	Broward County SD	Fort Lauderdale
10	1,106.0	Florida State Univ Lab School	Tallahassee
11	1,077.7	Madison County SD	Madison
12	1,065.3	Palm Beach County SD	West Palm Beach
13	1,043.4	Martin County SD	Stuart
14	1,039.3	Okeechobee County SD	Okeechobee
15	1,020.0	Dade County SD	Miami
16	964.8	Okaloosa County SD	Ft Walton Beach
17	931.1	Collier County SD	Naples
18	918.2	Pinellas County SD	Largo
19	916.1	Marion County SD	Ocala
20	912.8	Volusia County SD	Deland
21	890.0	Taylor County SD	Perry
22	887.8	Hernando County SD	Brooksville
23	884.9	Columbia County SD	Lake City
24	883.6	St. Lucie County SD	Fort Pierce
25	883.0	Duval County SD	Jacksonville
26	871.6	Hillsborough County SD	Tampa
27	866.2	Charlotte County SD	Port Charlotte
28	833.5	Manatee County SD	Bradenton
29	831.4	Suwannee County SD	Live Oak
30	830.6	Indian River County SD	Vero Beach
31	828.0	Desoto County SD	Arcadia
32	824.6	St. Johns County SD	St. Augustine
33	821.1	Clay County SD	Green Cove Spgs
34	814.0	Santa Rosa County SD	Milton
35	807.6	Pasco County SD	Land O' Lakes
36	786.6	Lake County SD	Tavares
37	785.7	Wakulla County SD	Crawfordville
38	779.9	Leon County SD	Tallahassee
39	776.2	Highlands County SD	Sebring
40	767.3	Baker County SD	Macclenny
41	766.1	Hendry County SD	La Belle
42	764.3	Putnam County SD	Palatka
43	745.7	Hardee County SD	Wauchula
44	729.4	Escambia County SD	Pensacola
45	723.7	Union County SD	Lake Butler
46	722.9	Polk County SD	Bartow
47	706.3	Gilchrist County SD	Trenton
48	702.9	Citrus County SD	Inverness
49	684.8	Washington County SD	Chipley
50	681.0	Hamilton County SD	Jasper
51	665.5	Bay County SD	Panama City
52	657.7	Nassau County SD	Fernandina Bch
53	651.1	Walton County SD	Defuniak Spgs
54	650.8	Brevard County SD	Viera
55	649.5	Bradford County SD	Starke
56	598.0	Jackson County SD	Marianna
57	575.9	Gadsden County SD	Quincy
58	575.4	Alachua County SD	Gainesville
59	570.9	Sumter County SD	Bushnell
60	560.5	Levy County SD	Bronson
61	537.5	Gulf County SD	Port St. Joe
62	444.0	Calhoun County SD	Blountstown
63	422.9	Holmes County SD	Bonifay
64	n/a	Florida Virtual School	Orlando

Student/Counselor Ratio

Rank	Ratio	District Name	City
1	723.7	Union County SD	Lake Butler
2	712.0	Taylor County SD	Perry
3	664.4	Indian River County SD	Vero Beach
4	650.0	Monroe County SD	Key West
5	646.6	Madison County SD	Madison
6	589.3	Wakulla County SD	Crawfordville
7	582.3	Seminole County SD	Sanford
8	580.0	Hardee County SD	Wauchula
9	562.6	Orange County SD	Orlando
10	561.1	Sarasota County SD	Sarasota
11	552.0	Desoto County SD	Arcadia
12	537.9	Duval County SD	Jacksonville
13	529.6	Lee County SD	Fort Myers
14	519.6	Okeechobee County SD	Okeechobee
15	514.6	Okaloosa County SD	Ft Walton Beach
16	513.8	Levy County SD	Bronson

Rank		District Name	City
17	511.6	Baker County SD	Macclenny
18	510.8	Hamilton County SD	Jasper
19	508.8	Santa Rosa County SD	Milton
20	503.2	Flagler County SD	Bunnell
21	502.6	Broward County SD	Fort Lauderdale
22	500.8	Walton County SD	Defuniak Spgs
23	489.4	Sumter County SD	Bushnell
24	481.8	Osceola County SD	Kissimmee
25	478.8	Hendry County SD	La Belle
26	478.7	Charlotte County SD	Port Charlotte
27	478.3	Nassau County SD	Fernandina Bch
28	474.5	Brevard County SD	Viera
29	474.4	Pinellas County SD	Largo
30	464.1	Palm Beach County SD	West Palm Beach
31	454.8	Martin County SD	Stuart
32	453.3	Polk County SD	Bartow
33	446.6	Escambia County SD	Pensacola
34	444.5	Manatee County SD	Bradenton
35	444.1	Leon County SD	Tallahassee
36	442.9	Marion County SD	Ocala
37	442.4	Florida State Univ Lab School	Tallahassee
38	435.7	St. Johns County SD	St. Augustine
39	433.4	Dixie County SD	Cross City
40	433.0	Bradford County SD	Starke
41	432.7	Hillsborough County SD	Tampa
42	431.2	Highlands County SD	Sebring
43	427.5	Florida Virtual School	Orlando
44	423.2	Columbia County SD	Lake City
45	417.9	Citrus County SD	Inverness
46	415.7	Suwannee County SD	Live Oak
47	415.5	Pasco County SD	Land O' Lakes
48	407.5	Lake County SD	Tavares
49	405.2	Clay County SD	Green Cove Spgs
50	396.6	Alachua County SD	Gainesville
51	393.9	St. Lucie County SD	Fort Pierce
52	383.9	Gadsden County SD	Quincy
53	382.2	Putnam County SD	Palatka
54	380.4	Washington County SD	Chipley
55	380.3	Bay County SD	Panama City
56	375.9	Holmes County SD	Bonifay
57	370.0	Calhoun County SD	Blountstown
58	367.8	Dade County SD	Miami
59	361.7	Hernando County SD	Brooksville
60	353.1	Gilchrist County SD	Trenton
61	347.3	Volusia County SD	Deland
62	341.7	Jackson County SD	Marianna
63	317.7	Collier County SD	Naples
64	268.8	Gulf County SD	Port St. Joe

Current Spending per Student in FY2003

Rank	Dollars	District Name	City
1	8,396	Washington County SD	Chipley
2	7,435	Collier County SD	Naples
3	7,362	Hamilton County SD	Jasper
4	7,097	Monroe County SD	Key West
5	7,096	Taylor County SD	Perry
6	7,019	Sarasota County SD	Sarasota
7	6,983	Palm Beach County SD	West Palm Beach
8	6,982	Gulf County SD	Port St. Joe
9	6,956	Dade County SD	Miami
10	6,940	Desoto County SD	Arcadia
11	6,913	Gadsden County SD	Quincy
12	6,771	Dixie County SD	Cross City
13	6,761	Jackson County SD	Marianna
14	6,728	Bradford County SD	Starke
15	6,720	Martin County SD	Stuart
16	6,700	Walton County SD	Defuniak Spgs
17	6,673	Holmes County SD	Bonifay
18	6,654	Polk County SD	Bartow
19	6,602	Madison County SD	Madison
20	6,601	Gilchrist County SD	Trenton
21	6,585	Highlands County SD	Sebring
22	6,569	St. Johns County SD	St. Augustine
23	6,564	Levy County SD	Bronson
24	6,527	Sumter County SD	Bushnell
25	6,510	Manatee County SD	Bradenton
26	6,486	Alachua County SD	Gainesville
27	6,454	Citrus County SD	Inverness
28	6,411	Hillsborough County SD	Tampa
29	6,407	Pinellas County SD	Largo
30	6,387	Suwannee County SD	Live Oak
31	6,379	Hendry County SD	La Belle
32	6,378	Okeechobee County SD	Okeechobee
33	6,360	Volusia County SD	Deland
34	6,358	Orange County SD	Orlando
35	6,356	Hardee County SD	Wauchula
36	6,352	Charlotte County SD	Port Charlotte
37	6,350	Duval County SD	Jacksonville
38	6,319	Flagler County SD	Bunnell
39	6,261	Putnam County SD	Palatka
40	6,260	Indian River County SD	Vero Beach
41	6,239	Broward County SD	Fort Lauderdale
42	6,233	Marion County SD	Ocala
43	6,228	Calhoun County SD	Blountstown
44	6,226	Wakulla County SD	Crawfordville
45	6,206	Lee County SD	Fort Myers
46	6,192	St. Lucie County SD	Fort Pierce
47	6,179	Leon County SD	Tallahassee
48	6,140	Bay County SD	Panama City
49	6,103	Columbia County SD	Lake City
50	6,056	Escambia County SD	Pensacola
51	6,023	Brevard County SD	Viera
52	6,014	Union County SD	Lake Butler
53	6,011	Pasco County SD	Land O' Lakes
54	5,967	Baker County SD	Macclenny
55	5,956	Lake County SD	Tavares
56	5,859	Osceola County SD	Kissimmee
57	5,849	Seminole County SD	Sanford
58	5,830	Hernando County SD	Brooksville
59	5,782	Okaloosa County SD	Ft Walton Beach
60	5,628	Clay County SD	Green Cove Spgs
61	5,627	Santa Rosa County SD	Milton
62	5,490	Nassau County SD	Fernandina Bch
63	n/a	Florida State Univ Lab School	Tallahassee
63	n/a	Florida Virtual School	Orlando

Number of Diploma Recipients

Rank	Number	District Name	City
1	16,638	Dade County SD	Miami
2	11,654	Broward County SD	Fort Lauderdale
3	7,968	Hillsborough County SD	Tampa
4	7,687	Palm Beach County SD	West Palm Beach
5	7,361	Orange County SD	Orlando
6	5,413	Pinellas County SD	Largo
7	5,260	Duval County SD	Jacksonville
8	3,815	Polk County SD	Bartow
9	3,578	Brevard County SD	Viera
10	3,420	Seminole County SD	Sanford
11	3,386	Volusia County SD	Deland
12	2,846	Lee County SD	Fort Myers
13	2,453	Pasco County SD	Land O' Lakes
14	2,320	Escambia County SD	Pensacola
15	1,978	Okaloosa County SD	Ft Walton Beach
16	1,960	Marion County SD	Ocala
17	1,895	Sarasota County SD	Sarasota
18	1,853	Osceola County SD	Kissimmee
19	1,788	Leon County SD	Tallahassee
20	1,711	Collier County SD	Naples
21	1,709	Manatee County SD	Bradenton
22	1,651	Alachua County SD	Gainesville
23	1,627	Clay County SD	Green Cove Spgs
24	1,531	Lake County SD	Tavares
25	1,333	Santa Rosa County SD	Milton
26	1,258	St. Lucie County SD	Fort Pierce
27	1,230	Bay County SD	Panama City
28	1,097	St. Johns County SD	St. Augustine
29	1,076	Charlotte County SD	Port Charlotte
30	923	Hernando County SD	Brooksville
31	842	Martin County SD	Stuart
32	830	Citrus County SD	Inverness
33	821	Indian River County SD	Vero Beach
34	577	Nassau County SD	Fernandina Bch
35	561	Highlands County SD	Sebring
36	486	Monroe County SD	Key West
37	447	Putnam County SD	Palatka
38	441	Columbia County SD	Lake City
39	409	Jackson County SD	Marianna
40	385	Flagler County SD	Bunnell
41	346	Gadsden County SD	Quincy
42	339	Okeechobee County SD	Okeechobee
43	301	Levy County SD	Bronson
44	290	Hendry County SD	La Belle
45	284	Suwannee County SD	Live Oak
46	261	Sumter County SD	Bushnell
47	246	Walton County SD	Defuniak Spgs
48	233	Wakulla County SD	Crawfordville
49	223	Baker County SD	Macclenny
50	214	Bradford County SD	Starke
51	213	Hardee County SD	Wauchula
52	204	Desoto County SD	Arcadia
53	203	Holmes County SD	Bonifay
53	203	Taylor County SD	Perry
55	191	Washington County SD	Chipley
56	180	Madison County SD	Madison
57	150	Dixie County SD	Cross City
58	141	Gilchrist County SD	Trenton
59	129	Union County SD	Lake Butler
60	119	Hamilton County SD	Jasper
61	117	Gulf County SD	Port St. Joe
62	106	Calhoun County SD	Blountstown
63	93	Florida State Univ Lab School	Tallahassee
64	n/a	Florida Virtual School	Orlando

High School Drop-out Rate

Rank	Percent	District Name	City
1	9.0	Lee County SD	Fort Myers
2	7.5	Hardee County SD	Wauchula
3	6.8	Madison County SD	Madison
4	6.7	Duval County SD	Jacksonville
5	6.3	Pinellas County SD	Largo
6	6.1	Alachua County SD	Gainesville
6	6.1	Hendry County SD	La Belle
6	6.1	Walton County SD	Defuniak Spgs
9	5.7	Wakulla County SD	Crawfordville
10	5.6	Okeechobee County SD	Okeechobee
10	5.6	Osceola County SD	Kissimmee
12	5.5	Lake County SD	Tavares
13	5.4	Gadsden County SD	Quincy
14	5.3	Highlands County SD	Sebring
15	4.8	Citrus County SD	Inverness
15	4.8	Dade County SD	Miami
17	4.7	Baker County SD	Macclenny
18	4.4	Collier County SD	Naples
19	4.3	Bradford County SD	Starke
20	4.2	Charlotte County SD	Port Charlotte
20	4.2	Monroe County SD	Key West
20	4.2	Pasco County SD	Land O' Lakes
23	4.0	Nassau County SD	Fernandina Bch
24	3.7	Desoto County SD	Arcadia
24	3.7	Leon County SD	Tallahassee
24	3.7	Manatee County SD	Bradenton
27	3.6	Dixie County SD	Cross City
27	3.6	Levy County SD	Bronson
27	3.6	Okaloosa County SD	Ft Walton Beach
27	3.6	Polk County SD	Bartow
27	3.6	Sarasota County SD	Sarasota
32	3.5	Marion County SD	Ocala
32	3.5	Suwannee County SD	Live Oak
34	3.4	Orange County SD	Orlando
35	3.2	Calhoun County SD	Blountstown
35	3.2	Washington County SD	Chipley
37	3.1	Holmes County SD	Bonifay
37	3.1	Palm Beach County SD	West Palm Beach
39	3.0	Taylor County SD	Perry
40	2.9	Gilchrist County SD	Trenton
41	2.8	Clay County SD	Green Cove Spgs
41	2.8	Escambia County SD	Pensacola
41	2.8	Hamilton County SD	Jasper
41	2.8	Hillsborough County SD	Tampa
41	2.8	Sumter County SD	Bushnell
46	2.7	Jackson County SD	Marianna
47	2.5	Putnam County SD	Palatka
47	2.5	St. Johns County SD	St. Augustine
49	2.3	Flagler County SD	Bunnell
49	2.3	Hernando County SD	Brooksville
51	2.1	Santa Rosa County SD	Milton
52	1.9	Florida State Univ Lab School	Tallahassee
52	1.9	Union County SD	Lake Butler
52	1.9	Volusia County SD	Deland
55	1.8	Bay County SD	Panama City
55	1.8	Indian River County SD	Vero Beach
57	1.7	Columbia County SD	Lake City
58	1.6	Broward County SD	Fort Lauderdale
58	1.6	St. Lucie County SD	Fort Pierce
60	1.5	Seminole County SD	Sanford
61	0.9	Brevard County SD	Viera
62	0.6	Martin County SD	Stuart
63	0.5	Gulf County SD	Port St. Joe
64	n/a	Florida Virtual School	Orlando

Georgia

Georgia Public School Educational Profile

Category	Value	Category	Value
Schools (2003-2004)	2,458	**Diploma Recipients** (2002-2003)	65,983
Instructional Level		White, Non-Hispanic	40,801
Primary	1,224	Black, Non-Hispanic	21,357
Middle	429	Asian/Pacific Islander	2,151
High	336	American Indian/Alaskan Native	81
Other Level	469	Hispanic	1,593
Curriculum		**High School Drop-out Rate** (%) (2001-2002)	6.5
Regular	2,013	White, Non-Hispanic	5.8
Special Education	271	Black, Non-Hispanic	7.6
Vocational	0	Asian/Pacific Islander	3.6
Alternative	174	American Indian/Alaskan Native	7.5
Type		Hispanic	9.8
Magnet	59	**Staff** (2003-2004)	
Charter	51	Teachers	97,152.7
Title I Eligible	1,079	Average Salary ($)	45,848
School-wide Title I	862	Librarians/Media Specialists	2,170.0
Students (2003-2004)	1,522,611	Guidance Counselors	3,339.1
Gender (%)		**Ratios** (2003-2004)	
Male	51.2	Student/Teacher Ratio	15.7 to 1
Female	48.8	Student/Librarian Ratio	701.7 to 1
Race/Ethnicity (%)		Student/Counselor Ratio	456.0 to 1
White, Non-Hispanic	52.1	**College Entrance Exam Scores** (2005)	
Black, Non-Hispanic	38.3	Scholastic Aptitude Test (SAT)	
Asian/Pacific Islander	2.5	Participation Rate (%)	75
American Indian/Alaskan Native	0.2	Mean SAT Reasoning Test Verbal Score	497
Hispanic	6.9	Mean SAT Reasoning Test Math Score	496
Classification (%)		American College Testing Program (ACT)	
Individual Education Program (IEP)	12.2	Participation Rate (%)	29
Migrant (2002-2003)	0.7	Average Composite Score	20.0
English Language Learner (ELL)	4.3	Average English Score	19.4
Eligible for Free Lunch Program	38.2	Average Math Score	19.8
Eligible for Reduced-Price Lunch Program	8.2	Average Reading Score	20.3
Current Spending ($ per student in FY 2003)	7,653	Average Science Score	19.8
Instruction	4,900		
Support Services	2,364		

Note: For an explanation of data, please refer to the User's Guide in the front of the book

Georgia NAEP 2005 Test Scores

Reading			Mathematics		
Grade/Category	Value	Rank	Grade/Category	Value	Rank
4th Grade			**4th Grade**		
Average Proficiency	214.4 (1.21)	38/51	Average Proficiency	233.6 (0.97)	37/51
Proficiency by Gender/Race/Ethnicity			Proficiency by Gender/Race/Ethnicity		
Male	209.6 (1.52)	41/51	Male	234.2 (1.26)	38/51
Female	219.2 (1.38)	36/51	Female	233.1 (0.99)	36/51
White, Non-Hispanic	226.3 (1.18)	26/51	White, Non-Hispanic	243.3 (1.17)	32/51
Black, Non-Hispanic	199.2 (1.52)	22/42	Black, Non-Hispanic	220.8 (1.25)	18/42
Asian, Non-Hispanic	242.6 (5.11)	1/27	Asian, Non-Hispanic	255.1 (3.57)	11/25
American Indian, Non-Hispanic	n/a	n/a	American Indian, Non-Hispanic	n/a	n/a
Hispanic	203.1 (4.15)	23/40	Hispanic	229.2 (2.29)	13/41
Proficiency by Class Size			Proficiency by Class Size		
Less than 16 Students	196.6 (3.09)	24/34	Less than 16 Students	218.0 (2.43)	29/35
16 to 18 Students	209.1 (3.74)	27/33	16 to 18 Students	229.0 (2.42)	26/31
19 to 20 Students	n/a	n/a	19 to 20 Students	n/a	n/a
21 to 25 Students	217.9 (1.68)	37/51	21 to 25 Students	238.7 (1.36)	32/51
Greater than 25 Students	219.9 (3.64)	21/36	Greater than 25 Students	236.2 (2.91)	23/33
Percent Attaining Achievement Levels			Percent Attaining Achievement Levels		
Below Basic	41.7 (1.46)	12/51	Below Basic	24.0 (1.27)	14/51
Basic or Above	58.3 (1.46)	40/51	Basic or Above	76.0 (1.27)	38/51
Proficient or Above	26.3 (1.48)	39/51	Proficient or Above	29.5 (1.45)	38/51
Advanced or Above	6.2 (0.70)	35/51	Advanced or Above	3.7 (0.54)	36/51
8th Grade			**8th Grade**		
Average Proficiency	256.9 (1.31)	40/51	Average Proficiency	272.2 (1.11)	39/51
Proficiency by Gender/Race/Ethnicity			Proficiency by Gender/Race/Ethnicity		
Male	250.9 (1.55)	40/51	Male	272.6 (1.36)	38/51
Female	262.6 (1.31)	39/51	Female	271.8 (1.28)	40/51
White, Non-Hispanic	267.9 (1.54)	28/51	White, Non-Hispanic	284.4 (1.34)	34/51
Black, Non-Hispanic	240.7 (1.30)	23/40	Black, Non-Hispanic	255.3 (1.40)	19/41
Asian, Non-Hispanic	274.9 (7.48)	11/24	Asian, Non-Hispanic	301.1 (3.96)	7/23
American Indian, Non-Hispanic	n/a	n/a	American Indian, Non-Hispanic	n/a	n/a
Hispanic	247.5 (3.42)	16/38	Hispanic	257.5 (3.02)	28/38
Proficiency by Parents Highest Level of Ed.			Proficiency by Parents Highest Level of Ed.		
Did Not Finish High School	243.9 (2.52)	31/49	Did Not Finish High School	252.1 (2.63)	43/50
Graduated High School	245.7 (1.88)	44/50	Graduated High School	261.4 (1.99)	42/50
Some Education After High School	260.6 (2.14)	43/50	Some Education After High School	274.9 (1.88)	41/50
Graduated College	264.6 (1.67)	39/50	Graduated College	283.6 (1.48)	38/50
Percent Attaining Achievement Levels			Percent Attaining Achievement Levels		
Below Basic	41.7 (1.46)	12/51	Below Basic	38.2 (1.25)	11/51
Basic or Above	58.3 (1.46)	40/51	Basic or Above	61.8 (1.25)	41/51
Proficient or Above	26.3 (1.48)	39/51	Proficient or Above	23.2 (1.16)	38/51
Advanced or Above	6.2 (0.70)	35/51	Advanced or Above	4.3 (0.51)	36/51

Note: *For an explanation of data, please refer to the User's Guide in the front of the book; n/a indicates data not available*

Appling County

Appling County
249 Blackshear Hwy • Baxley, GA 31513-1513
(912) 367-8600 • http://www.appling.k12.ga.us
Grade Span: PK-12; **Agency Type:** 1
Schools: 9
    4 Primary; 1 Middle; 1 High; 3 Other Level
    6 Regular; 2 Special Education; 0 Vocational; 1 Alternative
    0 Magnet; 0 Charter; 4 Title I Eligible; 4 School-wide Title I
Students: 3,362 (52.2% male; 47.7% female)
    Individual Education Program: 551 (16.4%)
    English Language Learner: 90 (2.7%); Migrant: 266 (7.9%)
    Eligible for Free Lunch Program: 1,760 (52.3%)
    Eligible for Reduced-Price Lunch Program: 285 (8.5%)
Teachers: 211.3 (15.9 to 1)
Librarians/Media Specialists: 6.0 (560.3 to 1)
Guidance Counselors: 7.8 (431.0 to 1)
Current Spending: ($ per student per year):
    Total: $7,966; Instruction: $5,183; Support Services: $2,429
Enrollment, Drop-out Rates and Diploma Recipients by Race/Ethnicity

Category	Total	White	Black	Asian	AIAN	Hisp.
Enrollment (%)	100.0	67.9	25.6	0.4	0.0	6.1
Drop-out Rate (%)	7.4	8.7	4.2	0.0	n/a	10.3
H.S. Diplomas (#)	178	128	47	1	0	2

Atkinson County

Atkinson County
506 Roberts Ave • Pearson, GA 31642-1642
(912) 422-7373 • http://www.atkinson.k12.ga.us/
Grade Span: PK-12; **Agency Type:** 1
Schools: 4
    2 Primary; 0 Middle; 1 High; 1 Other Level
    3 Regular; 1 Special Education; 0 Vocational; 0 Alternative
    0 Magnet; 0 Charter; 2 Title I Eligible; 2 School-wide Title I
Students: 1,695 (51.6% male; 48.3% female)
    Individual Education Program: 225 (13.3%);
    English Language Learner: 75 (4.4%); Migrant: 313 (18.5%)
    Eligible for Free Lunch Program: 1,139 (67.2%)
    Eligible for Reduced-Price Lunch Program: 231 (13.6%)
Teachers: 100.5 (16.9 to 1)
Librarians/Media Specialists: 3.0 (565.0 to 1)
Guidance Counselors: 4.1 (413.4 to 1)
Current Spending: ($ per student per year):
    Total: $6,785; Instruction: $4,269; Support Services: $2,059
Enrollment, Drop-out Rates and Diploma Recipients by Race/Ethnicity

Category	Total	White	Black	Asian	AIAN	Hisp.
Enrollment (%)	100.0	53.2	20.1	0.2	0.1	26.4
Drop-out Rate (%)	10.8	10.9	7.4	n/a	n/a	18.4
H.S. Diplomas (#)	53	42	6	0	0	5

Bacon County

Bacon County
601 N Pierce St • Alma, GA 31510-1510
(912) 632-7363 • http://www.bcraiders.com/
Grade Span: PK-12; **Agency Type:** 1
Schools: 5
    2 Primary; 1 Middle; 1 High; 1 Other Level
    4 Regular; 1 Special Education; 0 Vocational; 0 Alternative
    0 Magnet; 0 Charter; 3 Title I Eligible; 3 School-wide Title I
Students: 1,884 (52.0% male; 47.9% female)
    Individual Education Program: 271 (14.4%);
    English Language Learner: 20 (1.1%); Migrant: 115 (6.1%)
    Eligible for Free Lunch Program: 814 (43.2%)
    Eligible for Reduced-Price Lunch Program: 183 (9.7%)
Teachers: 120.3 (15.7 to 1)
Librarians/Media Specialists: 3.0 (628.0 to 1)
Guidance Counselors: 3.0 (628.0 to 1)
Current Spending: ($ per student per year):
    Total: $7,137; Instruction: $4,637; Support Services: $2,093
Enrollment, Drop-out Rates and Diploma Recipients by Race/Ethnicity

Category	Total	White	Black	Asian	AIAN	Hisp.
Enrollment (%)	100.0	74.1	22.2	0.4	0.0	3.3
Drop-out Rate (%)	8.0	7.5	8.9	n/a	n/a	25.0
H.S. Diplomas (#)	76	58	18	0	0	0

Baldwin County

Baldwin County
110 N Abc St • Milledgeville, GA 31061-1061
(478) 453-4176 • http://www.baldwin-county-schools.com
Grade Span: PK-12; **Agency Type:** 1
Schools: 12

---

    5 Primary; 1 Middle; 1 High; 5 Other Level
    7 Regular; 3 Special Education; 0 Vocational; 2 Alternative
    0 Magnet; 0 Charter; 6 Title I Eligible; 6 School-wide Title I
Students: 5,947 (50.3% male; 49.6% female)
    Individual Education Program: 1,054 (17.7%);
    English Language Learner: 43 (0.7%); Migrant: 0 (0.0%)
    Eligible for Free Lunch Program: 2,841 (47.8%)
    Eligible for Reduced-Price Lunch Program: 585 (9.8%)
Teachers: 439.0 (13.5 to 1)
Librarians/Media Specialists: 7.0 (849.6 to 1)
Guidance Counselors: 10.0 (594.7 to 1)
Current Spending: ($ per student per year):
    Total: $7,467; Instruction: $4,841; Support Services: $2,209
Enrollment, Drop-out Rates and Diploma Recipients by Race/Ethnicity

Category	Total	White	Black	Asian	AIAN	Hisp.
Enrollment (%)	100.0	35.4	62.3	1.2	0.1	1.0
Drop-out Rate (%)	3.7	5.4	2.7	3.3	n/a	0.0
H.S. Diplomas (#)	238	98	132	8	0	0

Banks County

Banks County
102 Hwy 51 S • Homer, GA 30547-0547
(706) 677-2224 • http://www.banks.k12.ga.us
Grade Span: PK-12; **Agency Type:** 1
Schools: 6
    2 Primary; 2 Middle; 1 High; 1 Other Level
    5 Regular; 1 Special Education; 0 Vocational; 0 Alternative
    0 Magnet; 0 Charter; 4 Title I Eligible; 4 School-wide Title I
Students: 2,457 (51.9% male; 48.0% female)
    Individual Education Program: 322 (13.1%);
    English Language Learner: 92 (3.7%); Migrant: 22 (0.9%)
    Eligible for Free Lunch Program: 1,014 (41.3%)
    Eligible for Reduced-Price Lunch Program: 345 (14.0%)
Teachers: 149.9 (16.4 to 1)
Librarians/Media Specialists: 4.0 (614.3 to 1)
Guidance Counselors: 6.0 (409.5 to 1)
Current Spending: ($ per student per year):
    Total: $6,582; Instruction: $4,234; Support Services: $1,923
Enrollment, Drop-out Rates and Diploma Recipients by Race/Ethnicity

Category	Total	White	Black	Asian	AIAN	Hisp.
Enrollment (%)	100.0	90.3	3.1	1.1	0.1	5.4
Drop-out Rate (%)	8.6	8.9	7.7	0.0	n/a	0.0
H.S. Diplomas (#)	94	90	1	1	0	2

Barrow County

Barrow County
179 W Athens St • Winder, GA 30680-0680
(770) 867-4527 • http://www.barrow.k12.ga.us
Grade Span: PK-12; **Agency Type:** 1
Schools: 16
    8 Primary; 3 Middle; 2 High; 3 Other Level
    13 Regular; 3 Special Education; 0 Vocational; 0 Alternative
    0 Magnet; 0 Charter; 5 Title I Eligible; 4 School-wide Title I
Students: 9,767 (51.7% male; 48.2% female)
    Individual Education Program: 1,579 (16.2%);
    English Language Learner: 446 (4.6%); Migrant: 20 (0.2%)
    Eligible for Free Lunch Program: 2,699 (27.6%)
    Eligible for Reduced-Price Lunch Program: 951 (9.7%)
Teachers: 626.9 (15.6 to 1)
Librarians/Media Specialists: 15.0 (651.1 to 1)
Guidance Counselors: 19.0 (514.1 to 1)
Current Spending: ($ per student per year):
    Total: $7,597; Instruction: $4,960; Support Services: $2,265
Enrollment, Drop-out Rates and Diploma Recipients by Race/Ethnicity

Category	Total	White	Black	Asian	AIAN	Hisp.
Enrollment (%)	100.0	76.2	12.5	5.7	0.1	5.4
Drop-out Rate (%)	6.6	6.5	7.3	5.5	50.0	5.5
H.S. Diplomas (#)	350	288	45	14	0	3

Bartow County

Bartow County
65 Gilreath Rd NW • Cartersville, GA 30120-0120
(770) 606-5800 • http://www.bartow.k12.ga.us
Grade Span: PK-12; **Agency Type:** 1
Schools: 21
    11 Primary; 4 Middle; 3 High; 3 Other Level
    18 Regular; 2 Special Education; 0 Vocational; 1 Alternative
    2 Magnet; 6 Charter; 6 Title I Eligible; 2 School-wide Title I
Students: 13,696 (51.3% male; 48.6% female)
    Individual Education Program: 1,981 (14.5%);
    English Language Learner: 220 (1.6%); Migrant: 0 (0.0%)
    Eligible for Free Lunch Program: 4,259 (31.1%)

Eligible for Reduced-Price Lunch Program: 1,143 (8.3%)
Teachers: 850.4 (16.1 to 1)
Librarians/Media Specialists: 20.0 (684.8 to 1)
Guidance Counselors: 30.0 (456.5 to 1)
Current Spending: ($ per student per year):
    Total: $7,449; Instruction: $4,876; Support Services: $2,179
Enrollment, Drop-out Rates and Diploma Recipients by Race/Ethnicity

Category	Total	White	Black	Asian	AIAN	Hisp.
Enrollment (%)	100.0	86.7	7.8	0.3	0.6	4.6
Drop-out Rate (%)	7.9	8.1	5.8	6.3	0.0	9.7
H.S. Diplomas (#)	485	422	48	3	5	7

Cartersville City
15 Nelson St • Cartersville, GA 30120-0120
(770) 382-5880 • http://www.cartersville.k12.ga.us
Grade Span: PK-12; **Agency Type:** 1
Schools: 5
    2 Primary; 1 Middle; 1 High; 1 Other Level
    4 Regular; 1 Special Education; 0 Vocational; 0 Alternative
    0 Magnet; 4 Charter; 3 Title I Eligible; 0 School-wide Title I
Students: 3,907 (51.7% male; 48.2% female)
    Individual Education Program: 346 (8.9%);
    English Language Specialist: 191 (4.9%); Migrant: 0 (0.0%)
    Eligible for Free Lunch Program: 1,247 (31.9%)
    Eligible for Reduced-Price Lunch Program: 304 (7.8%)
Teachers: 241.4 (16.2 to 1)
Librarians/Media Specialists: 5.0 (781.4 to 1)
Guidance Counselors: 8.5 (459.6 to 1)
Current Spending: ($ per student per year):
    Total: $7,212; Instruction: $4,561; Support Services: $2,245
Enrollment, Drop-out Rates and Diploma Recipients by Race/Ethnicity

Category	Total	White	Black	Asian	AIAN	Hisp.
Enrollment (%)	100.0	63.6	24.2	0.7	0.3	11.2
Drop-out Rate (%)	4.1	3.1	7.3	0.0	25.0	3.5
H.S. Diplomas (#)	180	142	33	0	0	5

Ben Hill County

Ben Hill County
509 W Palm St • Fitzgerald, GA 31750-1750
(229) 426-5500 • http://www.ben-hill.k12.ga.us
Grade Span: PK-12; **Agency Type:** 1
Schools: 7
    2 Primary; 1 Middle; 1 High; 3 Other Level
    4 Regular; 2 Special Education; 0 Vocational; 1 Alternative
    0 Magnet; 0 Charter; 3 Title I Eligible; 3 School-wide Title I
Students: 3,309 (50.4% male; 49.5% female)
    Individual Education Program: 486 (14.7%)
    English Language Learner: 125 (3.8%); Migrant: 23 (0.7%)
    Eligible for Free Lunch Program: 1,898 (57.4%)
    Eligible for Reduced-Price Lunch Program: 266 (8.0%)
Teachers: 211.5 (15.6 to 1)
Librarians/Media Specialists: 4.0 (827.3 to 1)
Guidance Counselors: 8.0 (413.6 to 1)
Current Spending: ($ per student per year):
    Total: $7,373; Instruction: $4,903; Support Services: $2,056
Enrollment, Drop-out Rates and Diploma Recipients by Race/Ethnicity

Category	Total	White	Black	Asian	AIAN	Hisp.
Enrollment (%)	100.0	49.0	45.6	0.5	0.0	4.9
Drop-out Rate (%)	10.0	7.9	12.2	0.0	33.3	19.0
H.S. Diplomas (#)	157	106	49	0	1	1

Berrien County

Berrien County
100 E Smith Ave • Nashville, GA 31639-1639
(229) 686-2081 • http://www.berrien.k12.ga.us
Grade Span: PK-12; **Agency Type:** 1
Schools: 6
    2 Primary; 1 Middle; 1 High; 2 Other Level
    4 Regular; 1 Special Education; 0 Vocational; 1 Alternative
    0 Magnet; 0 Charter; 3 Title I Eligible; 3 School-wide Title I
Students: 3,044 (50.8% male; 49.1% female)
    Individual Education Program: 406 (13.3%);
    English Language Learner: 0 (0.0%); Migrant: 69 (2.3%)
    Eligible for Free Lunch Program: 1,343 (44.1%)
    Eligible for Reduced-Price Lunch Program: 273 (9.0%)
Teachers: 150.8 (20.2 to 1)
Librarians/Media Specialists: 3.4 (895.3 to 1)
Guidance Counselors: 6.0 (507.3 to 1)
Current Spending: ($ per student per year):
    Total: $6,853; Instruction: $4,389; Support Services: $1,986

Enrollment, Drop-out Rates and Diploma Recipients by Race/Ethnicity

Category	Total	White	Black	Asian	AIAN	Hisp.
Enrollment (%)	100.0	80.8	15.5	0.2	0.1	3.4
Drop-out Rate (%)	8.4	7.9	10.1	0.0	n/a	20.0
H.S. Diplomas (#)	127	109	16	0	0	2

Bibb County

Bibb County
484 Mulberry St • Macon, GA 31201
(478) 765-8711 • http://www.bibb.k12.ga.us
Grade Span: PK-12; **Agency Type:** 1
Schools: 45
    29 Primary; 5 Middle; 6 High; 5 Other Level
    41 Regular; 1 Special Education; 0 Vocational; 3 Alternative
    4 Magnet; 0 Charter; 24 Title I Eligible; 20 School-wide Title I
Students: 25,276 (50.2% male; 49.7% female)
    Individual Education Program: 2,916 (11.5%);
    English Language Learner: 261 (1.0%); Migrant: 16 (0.1%)
    Eligible for Free Lunch Program: 15,423 (61.0%)
    Eligible for Reduced-Price Lunch Program: 1,693 (6.7%)
Teachers: 1,487.1 (17.0 to 1)
Librarians/Media Specialists: 43.0 (587.8 to 1)
Guidance Counselors: 56.5 (447.4 to 1)
Current Spending: ($ per student per year):
    Total: $7,256; Instruction: $4,353; Support Services: $2,442
Enrollment, Drop-out Rates and Diploma Recipients by Race/Ethnicity

Category	Total	White	Black	Asian	AIAN	Hisp.
Enrollment (%)	100.0	25.9	71.4	1.3	0.3	1.2
Drop-out Rate (%)	10.3	8.0	11.2	3.8	6.7	12.8
H.S. Diplomas (#)	831	276	541	11	0	3

Bleckley County

Bleckley County
909 Northeast Dykes St • Cochran, GA 31014-1014
(478) 934-2821 • http://www.bleckley.k12.ga.us
Grade Span: PK-12; **Agency Type:** 1
Schools: 5
    2 Primary; 1 Middle; 1 High; 1 Other Level
    4 Regular; 1 Special Education; 0 Vocational; 0 Alternative
    0 Magnet; 0 Charter; 2 Title I Eligible; 2 School-wide Title I
Students: 2,432 (49.8% male; 50.1% female)
    Individual Education Program: 339 (13.9%);
    English Language Learner: 13 (0.5%); Migrant: 7 (0.3%)
    Eligible for Free Lunch Program: 996 (41.0%)
    Eligible for Reduced-Price Lunch Program: 224 (9.2%)
Teachers: 145.2 (16.7 to 1)
Librarians/Media Specialists: 4.0 (608.0 to 1)
Guidance Counselors: 5.0 (486.4 to 1)
Current Spending: ($ per student per year):
    Total: $6,945; Instruction: $4,557; Support Services: $1,930
Enrollment, Drop-out Rates and Diploma Recipients by Race/Ethnicity

Category	Total	White	Black	Asian	AIAN	Hisp.
Enrollment (%)	100.0	68.7	29.1	0.9	0.0	1.3
Drop-out Rate (%)	7.8	8.4	6.8	0.0	n/a	0.0
H.S. Diplomas (#)	101	81	18	2	0	0

Brantley County

Brantley County
122 School Circle • Nahunta, GA 31553-1553
Mailing Address: Route 2 Box 22-T • Nahunta, GA 31553-1553
(912) 462-6176
Grade Span: PK-12; **Agency Type:** 1
Schools: 7
    3 Primary; 2 Middle; 1 High; 1 Other Level
    6 Regular; 1 Special Education; 0 Vocational; 0 Alternative
    0 Magnet; 0 Charter; 5 Title I Eligible; 5 School-wide Title I
Students: 3,330 (51.1% male; 48.8% female)
    Individual Education Program: 476 (14.3%);
    English Language Learner: 3 (0.1%); Migrant: 11 (0.3%)
    Eligible for Free Lunch Program: 1,435 (43.1%)
    Eligible for Reduced-Price Lunch Program: 409 (12.3%)
Teachers: 207.8 (16.0 to 1)
Librarians/Media Specialists: 6.0 (555.0 to 1)
Guidance Counselors: 7.0 (475.7 to 1)
Current Spending: ($ per student per year):
    Total: $6,382; Instruction: $4,043; Support Services: $1,960
Enrollment, Drop-out Rates and Diploma Recipients by Race/Ethnicity

Category	Total	White	Black	Asian	AIAN	Hisp.
Enrollment (%)	100.0	94.8	4.2	0.1	0.2	0.8
Drop-out Rate (%)	10.4	10.2	15.4	n/a	n/a	0.0
H.S. Diplomas (#)	121	118	3	0	0	0

Brooks County

Brooks County
489 Barwick Rd • Quitman, GA 31643-1643
(229) 263-7531 • http://www.brooks.k12.ga.us
Grade Span: PK-12; **Agency Type:** 1
Schools: 5
  2 Primary; 1 Middle; 1 High; 1 Other Level
  4 Regular; 1 Special Education; 0 Vocational; 0 Alternative
  0 Magnet; 0 Charter; 4 Title I Eligible; 4 School-wide Title I
Students: 2,524   (52.0% male; 47.9% female)
  Individual Education Program: 333 (13.2%);
  English Language Learner: 22 (0.9%); Migrant: 59 (2.3%)
  Eligible for Free Lunch Program: 1,647 (65.3%)
  Eligible for Reduced-Price Lunch Program: 253 (10.0%)
Teachers: 156.5 (16.1 to 1)
Librarians/Media Specialists: 4.0 (631.0 to 1)
Guidance Counselors: 5.0 (504.8 to 1)
Current Spending: ($ per student per year):
  Total: $7,540; Instruction: $4,520; Support Services: $2,540
Enrollment, Drop-out Rates and Diploma Recipients by Race/Ethnicity

Category	Total	White	Black	Asian	AIAN	Hisp.
Enrollment (%)	100.0	34.7	61.2	0.2	0.3	3.6
Drop-out Rate (%)	9.3	9.6	9.3	0.0	n/a	7.1
H.S. Diplomas (#)	95	37	55	1	0	2

Bryan County

Bryan County
66 S Industrial Blvd • Pembroke, GA 31321-1321
(912) 626-5000 • http://www.bryan.k12.ga.us
Grade Span: PK-12; **Agency Type:** 1
Schools: 13
  4 Primary; 3 Middle; 2 High; 4 Other Level
  9 Regular; 3 Special Education; 0 Vocational; 1 Alternative
  0 Magnet; 0 Charter; 4 Title I Eligible; 0 School-wide Title I
Students: 5,768   (52.0% male; 47.9% female)
  Individual Education Program: 551 (9.6%);
  English Language Learner: 12 (0.2%); Migrant: 2 (<0.1%)
  Eligible for Free Lunch Program: 1,450 (25.1%)
  Eligible for Reduced-Price Lunch Program: 502 (8.7%)
Teachers: 341.5 (16.9 to 1)
Librarians/Media Specialists: 9.0 (640.9 to 1)
Guidance Counselors: 10.0 (576.8 to 1)
Current Spending: ($ per student per year):
  Total: $6,060; Instruction: $3,935; Support Services: $1,784
Enrollment, Drop-out Rates and Diploma Recipients by Race/Ethnicity

Category	Total	White	Black	Asian	AIAN	Hisp.
Enrollment (%)	100.0	80.3	16.5	1.0	0.1	2.0
Drop-out Rate (%)	5.7	5.2	8.2	0.0	n/a	6.9
H.S. Diplomas (#)	289	244	36	3	0	6

Bulloch County

Bulloch County
150 Williams Rd Ste A • Statesboro, GA 30458-0458
(912) 764-6201 • http://www.bulloch.k12.ga.us
Grade Span: PK-12; **Agency Type:** 1
Schools: 17
  9 Primary; 3 Middle; 2 High; 3 Other Level
  15 Regular; 1 Special Education; 0 Vocational; 1 Alternative
  0 Magnet; 0 Charter; 13 Title I Eligible; 13 School-wide Title I
Students: 8,498   (51.4% male; 48.5% female)
  Individual Education Program: 1,255 (14.8%);
  English Language Learner: 102 (1.2%); Migrant: 117 (1.4%)
  Eligible for Free Lunch Program: 3,914 (46.1%)
  Eligible for Reduced-Price Lunch Program: 868 (10.2%)
Teachers: 581.9 (14.6 to 1)
Librarians/Media Specialists: 16.0 (531.1 to 1)
Guidance Counselors: 19.0 (447.3 to 1)
Current Spending: ($ per student per year):
  Total: $8,204; Instruction: $5,286; Support Services: $2,476
Enrollment, Drop-out Rates and Diploma Recipients by Race/Ethnicity

Category	Total	White	Black	Asian	AIAN	Hisp.
Enrollment (%)	100.0	57.9	39.3	0.8	0.1	1.9
Drop-out Rate (%)	7.0	6.4	8.3	4.0	0.0	5.9
H.S. Diplomas (#)	408	284	119	4	0	1

Burke County

Burke County
789 Perimeter Rd • Waynesboro, GA 30830-0830
(706) 554-5101 • http://www.burke.k12.ga.us
Grade Span: PK-12; **Agency Type:** 1
Schools: 7

  3 Primary; 1 Middle; 1 High; 2 Other Level
  5 Regular; 1 Special Education; 0 Vocational; 1 Alternative
  0 Magnet; 0 Charter; 3 Title I Eligible; 2 School-wide Title I
Students: 4,657   (51.1% male; 48.8% female)
  Individual Education Program: 492 (10.6%);
  English Language Learner: 0 (0.0%); Migrant: 5 (0.1%)
  Eligible for Free Lunch Program: 3,069 (65.9%)
  Eligible for Reduced-Price Lunch Program: 640 (13.7%)
Teachers: 253.0 (18.4 to 1)
Librarians/Media Specialists: 6.0 (776.2 to 1)
Guidance Counselors: 12.0 (388.1 to 1)
Current Spending: ($ per student per year):
  Total: $7,632; Instruction: $4,508; Support Services: $2,665
Enrollment, Drop-out Rates and Diploma Recipients by Race/Ethnicity

Category	Total	White	Black	Asian	AIAN	Hisp.
Enrollment (%)	100.0	31.2	67.7	0.1	0.0	0.9
Drop-out Rate (%)	9.3	6.8	10.4	11.1	0.0	33.3
H.S. Diplomas (#)	213	90	120	2	0	1

Butts County

Butts County
181 N Mulberry St • Jackson, GA 30233-0233
(770) 504-2300 • http://www.butts.k12.ga.us
Grade Span: PK-12; **Agency Type:** 1
Schools: 6
  3 Primary; 1 Middle; 1 High; 1 Other Level
  5 Regular; 1 Special Education; 0 Vocational; 0 Alternative
  0 Magnet; 0 Charter; 3 Title I Eligible; 3 School-wide Title I
Students: 3,412   (51.9% male; 48.0% female)
  Individual Education Program: 407 (11.9%);
  English Language Learner: 0 (0.0%); Migrant: 0 (0.0%)
  Eligible for Free Lunch Program: 1,312 (38.5%)
  Eligible for Reduced-Price Lunch Program: 354 (10.4%)
Teachers: 178.7 (19.1 to 1)
Librarians/Media Specialists: 5.0 (682.4 to 1)
Guidance Counselors: 7.0 (487.4 to 1)
Current Spending: ($ per student per year):
  Total: $6,955; Instruction: $4,167; Support Services: $2,423
Enrollment, Drop-out Rates and Diploma Recipients by Race/Ethnicity

Category	Total	White	Black	Asian	AIAN	Hisp.
Enrollment (%)	100.0	63.7	34.1	0.6	0.1	1.6
Drop-out Rate (%)	3.5	3.8	2.7	0.0	n/a	20.0
H.S. Diplomas (#)	130	82	47	1	0	0

Camden County

Camden County
311 S E St • Kingsland, GA 31548-1548
(912) 729-5687 • http://www.camden.k12.ga.us/
Grade Span: PK-12; **Agency Type:** 1
Schools: 14
  9 Primary; 2 Middle; 1 High; 2 Other Level
  12 Regular; 1 Special Education; 0 Vocational; 1 Alternative
  0 Magnet; 0 Charter; 9 Title I Eligible; 9 School-wide Title I
Students: 9,669   (51.4% male; 48.5% female)
  Individual Education Program: 1,166 (12.1%);
  English Language Learner: 37 (0.4%); Migrant: 0 (0.0%)
  Eligible for Free Lunch Program: 2,647 (27.4%)
  Eligible for Reduced-Price Lunch Program: 1,087 (11.2%)
Teachers: 588.7 (16.4 to 1)
Librarians/Media Specialists: 14.0 (690.6 to 1)
Guidance Counselors: 24.0 (402.9 to 1)
Current Spending: ($ per student per year):
  Total: $6,766; Instruction: $4,112; Support Services: $2,175
Enrollment, Drop-out Rates and Diploma Recipients by Race/Ethnicity

Category	Total	White	Black	Asian	AIAN	Hisp.
Enrollment (%)	100.0	68.9	26.2	1.0	0.3	3.7
Drop-out Rate (%)	6.8	6.5	7.5	0.0	20.0	10.0
H.S. Diplomas (#)	445	322	115	0	1	7

Candler County

Candler County
210 S College St • Metter, GA 30439-0439
(912) 685-5713 • http://www.metter.org/
Grade Span: PK-12; **Agency Type:** 1
Schools: 6
  1 Primary; 2 Middle; 1 High; 2 Other Level
  4 Regular; 2 Special Education; 0 Vocational; 0 Alternative
  0 Magnet; 0 Charter; 4 Title I Eligible; 4 School-wide Title I
Students: 1,931   (52.3% male; 47.6% female)
  Individual Education Program: 253 (13.1%);
  English Language Learner: 117 (6.1%); Migrant: 223 (11.5%)
  Eligible for Free Lunch Program: 1,098 (56.9%)

Eligible for Reduced-Price Lunch Program: 216 (11.2%)
Teachers: 108.6 (17.8 to 1)
Librarians/Media Specialists: 3.0 (643.7 to 1)
Guidance Counselors: 3.8 (508.2 to 1)
Current Spending: ($ per student per year):
    Total: $7,051; Instruction: $4,473; Support Services: $2,072
Enrollment, Drop-out Rates and Diploma Recipients by Race/Ethnicity

Category	Total	White	Black	Asian	AIAN	Hisp.
Enrollment (%)	100.0	54.6	32.9	0.3	0.1	12.1
Drop-out Rate (%)	10.1	9.6	8.9	0.0	n/a	22.6
H.S. Diplomas (#)	72	42	28	1	0	1

Carroll County

Carroll County
164 Independence Dr • Carrollton, GA 30116-0116
(770) 832-3568 • http://www.carrollcountyschools.com
Grade Span: PK-12; **Agency Type:** 1
Schools: 23
    10 Primary; 4 Middle; 5 High; 4 Other Level
    20 Regular; 1 Special Education; 0 Vocational; 2 Alternative
    0 Magnet; 0 Charter; 9 Title I Eligible; 9 School-wide Title I
Students: 13,769   (51.5% male; 48.4% female)
    Individual Education Program: 2,055 (14.9%);
    English Language Learner: 186 (1.4%); Migrant: 0 (0.0%)
    Eligible for Free Lunch Program: 5,059 (36.7%)
    Eligible for Reduced-Price Lunch Program: 1,506 (10.9%)
Teachers: 830.2 (16.6 to 1)
Librarians/Media Specialists: 23.4 (588.4 to 1)
Guidance Counselors: 25.5 (540.0 to 1)
Current Spending: ($ per student per year):
    Total: $7,131; Instruction: $4,647; Support Services: $2,080
Enrollment, Drop-out Rates and Diploma Recipients by Race/Ethnicity

Category	Total	White	Black	Asian	AIAN	Hisp.
Enrollment (%)	100.0	79.6	17.2	0.5	0.2	2.4
Drop-out Rate (%)	7.6	7.9	5.8	4.8	25.0	11.1
H.S. Diplomas (#)	536	453	77	4	0	2

Carrollton City
106 Trojan Dr • Carrollton, GA 30117-0117
(770) 832-9633 • http://www.carrolltoncityschools.net
Grade Span: PK-12; **Agency Type:** 1
Schools: 4
    1 Primary; 1 Middle; 1 High; 1 Other Level
    3 Regular; 1 Special Education; 0 Vocational; 0 Alternative
    0 Magnet; 0 Charter; 1 Title I Eligible; 0 School-wide Title I
Students: 3,629   (51.5% male; 48.4% female)
    Individual Education Program: 525 (14.5%);
    English Language Learner: 125 (3.4%); Migrant: 0 (0.0%)
    Eligible for Free Lunch Program: 1,398 (38.5%)
    Eligible for Reduced-Price Lunch Program: 233 (6.4%)
Teachers: 207.3 (17.5 to 1)
Librarians/Media Specialists: 3.0 (1,209.7 to 1)
Guidance Counselors: 7.8 (465.3 to 1)
Current Spending: ($ per student per year):
    Total: $7,816; Instruction: $4,783; Support Services: $2,610
Enrollment, Drop-out Rates and Diploma Recipients by Race/Ethnicity

Category	Total	White	Black	Asian	AIAN	Hisp.
Enrollment (%)	100.0	53.1	38.7	1.8	0.0	6.4
Drop-out Rate (%)	3.8	2.1	5.7	12.5	0.0	12.1
H.S. Diplomas (#)	186	125	58	1	0	2

Catoosa County

Catoosa County
307 Cleveland St • Ringgold, GA 30736-0736
(706) 965-2297 • http://www.catoosa.k12.ga.us
Grade Span: PK-12; **Agency Type:** 1
Schools: 16
    9 Primary; 2 Middle; 2 High; 3 Other Level
    13 Regular; 2 Special Education; 0 Vocational; 1 Alternative
    0 Magnet; 0 Charter; 6 Title I Eligible; 5 School-wide Title I
Students: 10,120   (50.7% male; 49.2% female)
    Individual Education Program: 1,369 (13.5%);
    English Language Learner: 49 (0.5%); Migrant: 0 (0.0%)
    Eligible for Free Lunch Program: 2,658 (26.3%)
    Eligible for Reduced-Price Lunch Program: 1,028 (10.2%)
Teachers: 614.6 (16.5 to 1)
Librarians/Media Specialists: 16.0 (632.5 to 1)
Guidance Counselors: 21.0 (481.9 to 1)
Current Spending: ($ per student per year):
    Total: $6,916; Instruction: $4,539; Support Services: $1,991

Enrollment, Drop-out Rates and Diploma Recipients by Race/Ethnicity

Category	Total	White	Black	Asian	AIAN	Hisp.
Enrollment (%)	100.0	95.6	1.6	1.4	0.1	1.3
Drop-out Rate (%)	7.0	7.1	3.7	2.7	0.0	5.9
H.S. Diplomas (#)	446	429	3	8	4	2

Charlton County

Charlton County
500 S Third St • Folkston, GA 31537-1537
(912) 496-2596 • http://boe.charlton.k12.ga.us/
Grade Span: PK-12; **Agency Type:** 1
Schools: 6
    3 Primary; 0 Middle; 1 High; 2 Other Level
    4 Regular; 1 Special Education; 0 Vocational; 1 Alternative
    0 Magnet; 0 Charter; 3 Title I Eligible; 1 School-wide Title I
Students: 2,044   (51.7% male; 48.2% female)
    Individual Education Program: 271 (13.3%);
    English Language Learner: 0 (0.0%); Migrant: 0 (0.0%)
    Eligible for Free Lunch Program: 995 (48.7%)
    Eligible for Reduced-Price Lunch Program: 262 (12.8%)
Teachers: 115.6 (17.7 to 1)
Librarians/Media Specialists: 4.0 (511.0 to 1)
Guidance Counselors: 3.5 (584.0 to 1)
Current Spending: ($ per student per year):
    Total: $7,050; Instruction: $4,397; Support Services: $2,268
Enrollment, Drop-out Rates and Diploma Recipients by Race/Ethnicity

Category	Total	White	Black	Asian	AIAN	Hisp.
Enrollment (%)	100.0	65.2	33.6	0.8	0.1	0.3
Drop-out Rate (%)	6.5	7.1	5.6	0.0	n/a	0.0
H.S. Diplomas (#)	92	71	19	2	0	0

Chatham County

Chatham County
208 Bull St • Savannah, GA 31401-1401
(912) 201-5600 • http://www.savannah.chatham.k12.ga.us/
Grade Span: PK-12; **Agency Type:** 1
Schools: 55
    29 Primary; 11 Middle; 4 High; 11 Other Level
    48 Regular; 1 Special Education; 0 Vocational; 6 Alternative
    13 Magnet; 4 Charter; 29 Title I Eligible; 22 School-wide Title I
Students: 34,514   (50.9% male; 49.0% female)
    Individual Education Program: 4,079 (11.8%);
    English Language Learner: 161 (0.5%); Migrant: 0 (0.0%)
    Eligible for Free Lunch Program: 16,073 (46.6%)
    Eligible for Reduced-Price Lunch Program: 2,981 (8.6%)
Teachers: 2,336.5 (14.8 to 1)
Librarians/Media Specialists: 52.0 (663.7 to 1)
Guidance Counselors: 80.5 (428.7 to 1)
Current Spending: ($ per student per year):
    Total: $7,576; Instruction: $4,907; Support Services: $2,307
Enrollment, Drop-out Rates and Diploma Recipients by Race/Ethnicity

Category	Total	White	Black	Asian	AIAN	Hisp.
Enrollment (%)	100.0	29.5	66.1	1.7	0.2	2.5
Drop-out Rate (%)	16.8	18.5	15.9	12.4	38.5	24.8
H.S. Diplomas (#)	1,197	430	695	43	3	26

Chattooga County

Chattooga County
33 Middle School Rd • Summerville, GA 30747-0747
(706) 857-3447 • http://www.chattooga.k12.ga.us/
Grade Span: PK-12; **Agency Type:** 1
Schools: 11
    4 Primary; 2 Middle; 1 High; 4 Other Level
    7 Regular; 3 Special Education; 0 Vocational; 1 Alternative
    0 Magnet; 0 Charter; 5 Title I Eligible; 5 School-wide Title I
Students: 2,988   (53.1% male; 46.8% female)
    Individual Education Program: 648 (21.7%);
    English Language Learner: 32 (1.1%); Migrant: 0 (0.0%)
    Eligible for Free Lunch Program: 1,420 (47.5%)
    Eligible for Reduced-Price Lunch Program: 382 (12.8%)
Teachers: 191.8 (15.6 to 1)
Librarians/Media Specialists: 7.0 (426.9 to 1)
Guidance Counselors: 6.0 (498.0 to 1)
Current Spending: ($ per student per year):
    Total: $8,328; Instruction: $5,441; Support Services: $2,449
Enrollment, Drop-out Rates and Diploma Recipients by Race/Ethnicity

Category	Total	White	Black	Asian	AIAN	Hisp.
Enrollment (%)	100.0	85.3	12.0	0.1	0.1	2.5
Drop-out Rate (%)	8.8	9.3	7.2	n/a	n/a	0.0
H.S. Diplomas (#)	92	85	7	0	0	0

Cherokee County

Cherokee County
221 W Main St • Canton, GA 30169
Mailing Address: 221 W Main St / P.O. Bo • Canton, GA 30169
(770) 479-1871 • http://www.cherokee.k12.ga.us
Grade Span: PK-12; **Agency Type:** 1
Schools: 34
  22 Primary; 5 Middle; 5 High; 2 Other Level
  31 Regular; 1 Special Education; 0 Vocational; 2 Alternative
  0 Magnet; 0 Charter; 9 Title I Eligible; 3 School-wide Title I
Students: 29,711 (51.4% male; 48.5% female)
  Individual Education Program: 3,656 (12.3%);
  English Language Learner: 807 (2.7%); Migrant: 92 (0.3%)
  Eligible for Free Lunch Program: 4,034 (13.6%)
  Eligible for Reduced-Price Lunch Program: 1,415 (4.8%)
Teachers: 1,897.8 (15.7 to 1)
Librarians/Media Specialists: 35.7 (832.2 to 1)
Guidance Counselors: 55.5 (535.3 to 1)
Current Spending: ($ per student per year):
  Total: $7,226; Instruction: $4,706; Support Services: $2,199
Enrollment, Drop-out Rates and Diploma Recipients by Race/Ethnicity

Category	Total	White	Black	Asian	AIAN	Hisp.
Enrollment (%)	100.0	86.2	4.6	1.2	0.3	7.8
Drop-out Rate (%)	4.5	4.2	6.7	4.0	6.7	7.8
H.S. Diplomas (#)	1,271	1,176	40	28	1	26

Clarke County

Clarke County
240 Mitchell Bridge Rd • Athens, GA 30606
(706) 546-7721 • http://www.clarke.k12.ga.us
Grade Span: PK-12; **Agency Type:** 1
Schools: 23
  13 Primary; 4 Middle; 3 High; 3 Other Level
  20 Regular; 1 Special Education; 0 Vocational; 2 Alternative
  0 Magnet; 0 Charter; 12 Title I Eligible; 12 School-wide Title I
Students: 11,502 (50.1% male; 49.8% female)
  Individual Education Program: 1,734 (15.1%);
  English Language Learner: 723 (6.3%); Migrant: 465 (4.0%)
  Eligible for Free Lunch Program: 6,662 (57.9%)
  Eligible for Reduced-Price Lunch Program: 925 (8.0%)
Teachers: 842.3 (13.7 to 1)
Librarians/Media Specialists: 20.0 (575.1 to 1)
Guidance Counselors: 25.0 (460.1 to 1)
Current Spending: ($ per student per year):
  Total: $9,013; Instruction: $5,321; Support Services: $3,235
Enrollment, Drop-out Rates and Diploma Recipients by Race/Ethnicity

Category	Total	White	Black	Asian	AIAN	Hisp.
Enrollment (%)	100.0	26.3	56.7	2.9	0.1	14.0
Drop-out Rate (%)	10.7	8.8	11.3	8.4	0.0	16.5
H.S. Diplomas (#)	390	211	155	12	0	12

Clayton County

Clayton County
1058 Fifth Ave • Jonesboro, GA 30236-0236
(770) 473-2700 • http://www.ccps.ga.net
Grade Span: PK-12; **Agency Type:** 1
Schools: 57
  33 Primary; 12 Middle; 7 High; 5 Other Level
  53 Regular; 3 Special Education; 0 Vocational; 1 Alternative
  0 Magnet; 0 Charter; 29 Title I Eligible; 29 School-wide Title I
Students: 50,555 (51.1% male; 48.8% female)
  Individual Education Program: 4,863 (9.6%);
  English Language Learner: 2,510 (5.0%); Migrant: 3 (<0.1%)
  Eligible for Free Lunch Program: 25,656 (50.7%)
  Eligible for Reduced-Price Lunch Program: 7,064 (14.0%)
Teachers: 2,954.0 (17.1 to 1)
Librarians/Media Specialists: 61.5 (822.0 to 1)
Guidance Counselors: 108.5 (465.9 to 1)
Current Spending: ($ per student per year):
  Total: $7,151; Instruction: $4,572; Support Services: $2,112
Enrollment, Drop-out Rates and Diploma Recipients by Race/Ethnicity

Category	Total	White	Black	Asian	AIAN	Hisp.
Enrollment (%)	100.0	13.1	72.8	4.4	0.1	9.6
Drop-out Rate (%)	8.2	8.7	7.6	8.3	0.0	13.3
H.S. Diplomas (#)	1,791	473	1,112	140	3	63

Cobb County

Cobb County
514 Glover St • Marietta, GA 30061-0061
(770) 426-3300 • http://www.cobb.k12.ga.us
Grade Span: PK-12; **Agency Type:** 1
Schools: 106
  65 Primary; 21 Middle; 15 High; 5 Other Level
  101 Regular; 1 Special Education; 0 Vocational; 4 Alternative
  4 Magnet; 8 Charter; 26 Title I Eligible; 19 School-wide Title I
Students: 102,034 (51.4% male; 48.5% female)
  Individual Education Program: 13,022 (12.8%);
  English Language Learner: 5,134 (5.0%); Migrant: 23 (<0.1%)
  Eligible for Free Lunch Program: 22,458 (22.0%)
  Eligible for Reduced-Price Lunch Program: 6,091 (6.0%)
Teachers: 6,867.3 (14.9 to 1)
Librarians/Media Specialists: 115.0 (887.3 to 1)
Guidance Counselors: 244.6 (417.1 to 1)
Current Spending: ($ per student per year):
  Total: $7,529; Instruction: $5,173; Support Services: $2,055
Enrollment, Drop-out Rates and Diploma Recipients by Race/Ethnicity

Category	Total	White	Black	Asian	AIAN	Hisp.
Enrollment (%)	100.0	57.9	27.7	3.8	0.2	10.3
Drop-out Rate (%)	3.6	2.9	4.6	2.5	2.1	8.5
H.S. Diplomas (#)	5,231	3,924	927	215	7	158

Marietta City
250 Howard St • Marietta, GA 30060
(770) 422-3500 • http://www.marietta-city.k12.ga.us
Grade Span: PK-12; **Agency Type:** 1
Schools: 12
  7 Primary; 2 Middle; 1 High; 2 Other Level
  10 Regular; 1 Special Education; 0 Vocational; 1 Alternative
  0 Magnet; 0 Charter; 9 Title I Eligible; 5 School-wide Title I
Students: 7,599 (51.0% male; 48.9% female)
  Individual Education Program: 1,087 (14.3%);
  English Language Learner: 1,421 (18.7%); Migrant: 4 (0.1%)
  Eligible for Free Lunch Program: 3,911 (51.5%)
  Eligible for Reduced-Price Lunch Program: 687 (9.0%)
Teachers: 511.3 (14.9 to 1)
Librarians/Media Specialists: 11.0 (690.8 to 1)
Guidance Counselors: 18.0 (422.2 to 1)
Current Spending: ($ per student per year):
  Total: $9,236; Instruction: $6,003; Support Services: $2,834
Enrollment, Drop-out Rates and Diploma Recipients by Race/Ethnicity

Category	Total	White	Black	Asian	AIAN	Hisp.
Enrollment (%)	100.0	25.9	48.3	2.5	0.1	23.3
Drop-out Rate (%)	6.8	4.3	8.2	2.2	0.0	10.6
H.S. Diplomas (#)	268	138	104	12	1	13

Coffee County

Coffee County
1311 S Peterson Ave • Douglas, GA 31533
(912) 384-2086 • http://coffee.k12.ga.us/
Grade Span: PK-12; **Agency Type:** 1
Schools: 13
  9 Primary; 1 Middle; 1 High; 2 Other Level
  11 Regular; 1 Special Education; 0 Vocational; 1 Alternative
  0 Magnet; 0 Charter; 8 Title I Eligible; 8 School-wide Title I
Students: 7,808 (50.6% male; 49.3% female)
  Individual Education Program: 912 (11.7%);
  English Language Learner: 377 (4.8%); Migrant: 683 (8.7%)
  Eligible for Free Lunch Program: 4,447 (57.0%)
  Eligible for Reduced-Price Lunch Program: 842 (10.8%)
Teachers: 440.0 (17.7 to 1)
Librarians/Media Specialists: 12.0 (650.7 to 1)
Guidance Counselors: 14.0 (557.7 to 1)
Current Spending: ($ per student per year):
  Total: $7,411; Instruction: $4,694; Support Services: $2,226
Enrollment, Drop-out Rates and Diploma Recipients by Race/Ethnicity

Category	Total	White	Black	Asian	AIAN	Hisp.
Enrollment (%)	100.0	56.4	34.4	0.1	0.0	9.1
Drop-out Rate (%)	9.3	9.0	9.2	5.3	n/a	13.4
H.S. Diplomas (#)	260	174	76	3	0	7

Colquitt County

Colquitt County
710 28th Ave SE • Moultrie, GA 31768
(229) 890-6200 • http://www.colquitt.k12.ga.us
Grade Span: PK-12; **Agency Type:** 1
Schools: 17
  10 Primary; 2 Middle; 1 High; 4 Other Level
  13 Regular; 3 Special Education; 0 Vocational; 1 Alternative

0 Magnet; 0 Charter; 12 Title I Eligible; 11 School-wide Title I
Students: 8,419 (51.1% male; 48.8% female)
  Individual Education Program: 1,159 (13.8%);
  English Language Learner: 340 (4.0%); Migrant: 782 (9.3%)
  Eligible for Free Lunch Program: 4,515 (53.6%)
  Eligible for Reduced-Price Lunch Program: 753 (8.9%)
Teachers: 480.7 (17.5 to 1)
Librarians/Media Specialists: 15.0 (561.3 to 1)
Guidance Counselors: 17.0 (495.2 to 1)
Current Spending: ($ per student per year):
  Total: $7,270; Instruction: $4,582; Support Services: $2,213
Enrollment, Drop-out Rates and Diploma Recipients by Race/Ethnicity

Category	Total	White	Black	Asian	AIAN	Hisp.
Enrollment (%)	100.0	56.7	31.1	0.2	0.0	12.0
Drop-out Rate (%)	7.6	5.3	9.6	0.0	33.3	19.7
H.S. Diplomas (#)	308	223	75	1	1	8

Columbia County

Columbia County
6430 Pollards Pond Rd • Appling, GA 30802-0802
(706) 541-0650 • http://www.ccboe.net
Grade Span: PK-12; **Agency Type:** 1
Schools: 28
  15 Primary; 7 Middle; 4 High; 2 Other Level
  26 Regular; 1 Special Education; 0 Vocational; 1 Alternative
  0 Magnet; 0 Charter; 12 Title I Eligible; 5 School-wide Title I
Students: 20,063 (51.3% male; 48.6% female)
  Individual Education Program: 2,003 (10.0%);
  English Language Learner: 109 (0.5%); Migrant: 0 (0.0%)
  Eligible for Free Lunch Program: 2,956 (14.7%)
  Eligible for Reduced-Price Lunch Program: 1,144 (5.7%)
Teachers: 1,185.1 (16.9 to 1)
Librarians/Media Specialists: 29.0 (691.8 to 1)
Guidance Counselors: 47.0 (426.9 to 1)
Current Spending: ($ per student per year):
  Total: $6,541; Instruction: $4,395; Support Services: $1,818
Enrollment, Drop-out Rates and Diploma Recipients by Race/Ethnicity

Category	Total	White	Black	Asian	AIAN	Hisp.
Enrollment (%)	100.0	79.9	14.3	3.3	0.1	2.4
Drop-out Rate (%)	4.8	4.9	4.6	2.4	0.0	6.0
H.S. Diplomas (#)	1,051	831	136	56	2	26

Cook County

Cook County
1109 N Parrish Ave • Adel, GA 31620-1620
(229) 896-2294 • http://www.cook.k12.ga.us
Grade Span: PK-12; **Agency Type:** 1
Schools: 5
  1 Primary; 1 Middle; 1 High; 2 Other Level
  3 Regular; 2 Special Education; 0 Vocational; 0 Alternative
  0 Magnet; 0 Charter; 2 Title I Eligible; 2 School-wide Title I
Students: 3,158 (50.9% male; 49.0% female)
  Individual Education Program: 391 (12.4%);
  English Language Learner: 33 (1.0%); Migrant: 59 (1.9%)
  Eligible for Free Lunch Program: 1,569 (49.7%)
  Eligible for Reduced-Price Lunch Program: 288 (9.1%)
Teachers: 191.3 (16.5 to 1)
Librarians/Media Specialists: 3.5 (902.3 to 1)
Guidance Counselors: 5.5 (574.2 to 1)
Current Spending: ($ per student per year):
  Total: $6,872; Instruction: $4,174; Support Services: $2,306
Enrollment, Drop-out Rates and Diploma Recipients by Race/Ethnicity

Category	Total	White	Black	Asian	AIAN	Hisp.
Enrollment (%)	100.0	57.7	37.9	0.8	0.1	3.5
Drop-out Rate (%)	7.7	6.7	8.5	0.0	n/a	21.4
H.S. Diplomas (#)	131	76	55	0	0	0

Coweta County

Coweta County
237 Jackson St • Newnan, GA 30263
(770) 254-2801 • http://www.coweta.k12.ga.us
Grade Span: PK-12; **Agency Type:** 1
Schools: 28
  16 Primary; 5 Middle; 3 High; 4 Other Level
  25 Regular; 2 Special Education; 0 Vocational; 1 Alternative
  0 Magnet; 1 Charter; 8 Title I Eligible; 7 School-wide Title I
Students: 19,035 (51.4% male; 48.5% female)
  Individual Education Program: 2,847 (15.0%);
  English Language Learner: 243 (1.3%); Migrant: 0 (0.0%)
  Eligible for Free Lunch Program: 4,272 (22.4%)
  Eligible for Reduced-Price Lunch Program: 1,042 (5.5%)
Teachers: 1,171.7 (16.2 to 1)

Librarians/Media Specialists: 28.0 (679.8 to 1)
Guidance Counselors: 41.0 (464.3 to 1)
Current Spending: ($ per student per year):
  Total: $7,020; Instruction: $4,576; Support Services: $2,136
Enrollment, Drop-out Rates and Diploma Recipients by Race/Ethnicity

Category	Total	White	Black	Asian	AIAN	Hisp.
Enrollment (%)	100.0	73.4	22.2	0.7	0.1	3.6
Drop-out Rate (%)	5.5	4.6	8.4	4.3	0.0	1.3
H.S. Diplomas (#)	788	627	147	8	1	5

Crawford County

Crawford County
190 Crusselle St • Roberta, GA 31078-1078
(478) 836-3131 • http://www.crawford.k12.ga.us
Grade Span: PK-12; **Agency Type:** 1
Schools: 6
  1 Primary; 1 Middle; 1 High; 3 Other Level
  3 Regular; 2 Special Education; 0 Vocational; 1 Alternative
  0 Magnet; 0 Charter; 3 Title I Eligible; 3 School-wide Title I
Students: 2,078 (52.9% male; 47.0% female)
  Individual Education Program: 361 (17.4%);
  English Language Learner: 1 (<0.1%); Migrant: 10 (0.5%)
  Eligible for Free Lunch Program: 1,003 (48.3%)
  Eligible for Reduced-Price Lunch Program: 267 (12.8%)
Teachers: 121.5 (17.1 to 1)
Librarians/Media Specialists: 3.0 (692.7 to 1)
Guidance Counselors: 4.0 (519.5 to 1)
Current Spending: ($ per student per year):
  Total: $7,350; Instruction: $4,757; Support Services: $2,098
Enrollment, Drop-out Rates and Diploma Recipients by Race/Ethnicity

Category	Total	White	Black	Asian	AIAN	Hisp.
Enrollment (%)	100.0	70.5	28.1	0.2	0.1	1.1
Drop-out Rate (%)	5.6	5.3	6.4	0.0	0.0	0.0
H.S. Diplomas (#)	89	57	32	0	0	0

Crisp County

Crisp County
201 Seventh St S • Cordele, GA 31015
(229) 276-3400 • http://www.crisp.k12.ga.us
Grade Span: PK-12; **Agency Type:** 1
Schools: 8
  4 Primary; 1 Middle; 1 High; 2 Other Level
  6 Regular; 1 Special Education; 0 Vocational; 1 Alternative
  0 Magnet; 0 Charter; 5 Title I Eligible; 5 School-wide Title I
Students: 4,388 (50.6% male; 49.3% female)
  Individual Education Program: 481 (11.0%);
  English Language Learner: 32 (0.7%); Migrant: 24 (0.5%)
  Eligible for Free Lunch Program: 2,678 (61.0%)
  Eligible for Reduced-Price Lunch Program: 320 (7.3%)
Teachers: 283.0 (15.5 to 1)
Librarians/Media Specialists: 6.0 (731.3 to 1)
Guidance Counselors: 7.5 (585.1 to 1)
Current Spending: ($ per student per year):
  Total: $7,933; Instruction: $4,932; Support Services: $2,507
Enrollment, Drop-out Rates and Diploma Recipients by Race/Ethnicity

Category	Total	White	Black	Asian	AIAN	Hisp.
Enrollment (%)	100.0	39.1	58.7	0.6	0.0	1.5
Drop-out Rate (%)	9.8	8.4	11.1	0.0	0.0	0.0
H.S. Diplomas (#)	165	89	74	1	1	0

Dade County

Dade County
52 Tradition Ln • Trenton, GA 30752-0752
(706) 657-4361 • http://www.dade.k12.ga.us
Grade Span: PK-12; **Agency Type:** 1
Schools: 6
  2 Primary; 1 Middle; 1 High; 2 Other Level
  4 Regular; 1 Special Education; 0 Vocational; 1 Alternative
  0 Magnet; 0 Charter; 2 Title I Eligible; 2 School-wide Title I
Students: 2,638 (53.8% male; 46.1% female)
  Individual Education Program: 332 (12.6%);
  English Language Learner: 0 (0.0%); Migrant: 0 (0.0%)
  Eligible for Free Lunch Program: 748 (28.4%)
  Eligible for Reduced-Price Lunch Program: 316 (12.0%)
Teachers: 162.3 (16.3 to 1)
Librarians/Media Specialists: 5.0 (527.6 to 1)
Guidance Counselors: 6.4 (412.2 to 1)
Current Spending: ($ per student per year):
  Total: $7,117; Instruction: $4,656; Support Services: $2,019

Enrollment, Drop-out Rates and Diploma Recipients by Race/Ethnicity

Category	Total	White	Black	Asian	AIAN	Hisp.
Enrollment (%)	100.0	98.5	0.0	0.3	0.1	1.0
Drop-out Rate (%)	4.0	4.1	0.0	0.0	0.0	n/a
H.S. Diplomas (#)	134	132	0	0	2	0

Dawson County

Dawson County
517 Allen St • Dawsonville, GA 30534-0534
(706) 265-3246 • http://www.dawson.k12.ga.us
Grade Span: PK-12; **Agency Type:** 1
Schools: 7
   3 Primary; 1 Middle; 1 High; 2 Other Level
   5 Regular; 1 Special Education; 0 Vocational; 1 Alternative
   0 Magnet; 0 Charter; 3 Title I Eligible; 1 School-wide Title I
Students: 3,023 (51.6% male; 48.3% female)
   Individual Education Program: 396 (13.1%);
   English Language Learner: 27 (0.9%); Migrant: 2 (0.1%)
   Eligible for Free Lunch Program: 679 (22.5%)
   Eligible for Reduced-Price Lunch Program: 217 (7.2%)
Teachers: 229.8 (13.2 to 1)
Librarians/Media Specialists: 5.0 (604.6 to 1)
Guidance Counselors: 6.0 (503.8 to 1)
Current Spending: ($ per student per year):
   Total: $7,728; Instruction: $4,786; Support Services: $2,522
Enrollment, Drop-out Rates and Diploma Recipients by Race/Ethnicity

Category	Total	White	Black	Asian	AIAN	Hisp.
Enrollment (%)	100.0	97.1	0.1	0.6	0.1	2.2
Drop-out Rate (%)	7.5	7.7	n/a	0.0	n/a	0.0
H.S. Diplomas (#)	113	109	0	2	0	2

De Kalb County

Decatur City
320 N Mcdonough St • Decatur, GA 30030-0030
(404) 370-4400 • http://www.decatur-city.k12.ga.us
Grade Span: PK-12; **Agency Type:** 1
Schools: 8
   6 Primary; 1 Middle; 1 High; 0 Other Level
   8 Regular; 0 Special Education; 0 Vocational; 0 Alternative
   0 Magnet; 0 Charter; 4 Title I Eligible; 2 School-wide Title I
Students: 2,517 (52.0% male; 47.9% female)
   Individual Education Program: 333 (13.2%);
   English Language Learner: 35 (1.4%); Migrant: 0 (0.0%)
   Eligible for Free Lunch Program: 876 (34.8%)
   Eligible for Reduced-Price Lunch Program: 110 (4.4%)
Teachers: 206.9 (12.2 to 1)
Librarians/Media Specialists: 7.0 (359.6 to 1)
Guidance Counselors: 7.0 (359.6 to 1)
Current Spending: ($ per student per year):
   Total: $12,179; Instruction: $7,430; Support Services: $4,271
Enrollment, Drop-out Rates and Diploma Recipients by Race/Ethnicity

Category	Total	White	Black	Asian	AIAN	Hisp.
Enrollment (%)	100.0	49.2	48.7	1.4	0.0	0.7
Drop-out Rate (%)	1.0	0.3	1.7	0.0	n/a	0.0
H.S. Diplomas (#)	125	76	43	4	0	2

Dekalb County
3770 N Decatur Rd • Decatur, GA 30032-0032
(678) 676-1200 • http://www.dekalb.k12.ga.us
Grade Span: PK-12; **Agency Type:** 1
Schools: 141
   86 Primary; 21 Middle; 22 High; 12 Other Level
   130 Regular; 6 Special Education; 0 Vocational; 5 Alternative
   14 Magnet; 7 Charter; 66 Title I Eligible; 37 School-wide Title I
Students: 99,550 (51.1% male; 48.8% female)
   Individual Education Program: 9,366 (9.4%);
   English Language Learner: 13,585 (13.6%); Migrant: 6 (<0.1%)
   Eligible for Free Lunch Program: 49,672 (49.9%)
   Eligible for Reduced-Price Lunch Program: 9,023 (9.1%)
Teachers: 6,408.7 (15.5 to 1)
Librarians/Media Specialists: 156.5 (636.1 to 1)
Guidance Counselors: 269.1 (369.9 to 1)
Current Spending: ($ per student per year):
   Total: $8,476; Instruction: $5,349; Support Services: $2,705
Enrollment, Drop-out Rates and Diploma Recipients by Race/Ethnicity

Category	Total	White	Black	Asian	AIAN	Hisp.
Enrollment (%)	100.0	11.7	77.8	3.4	0.1	7.0
Drop-out Rate (%)	6.8	5.4	6.8	5.7	12.5	11.7
H.S. Diplomas (#)	4,191	638	3,251	217	4	81

Decatur County

Decatur County
100 W Street; PO Drawer 129 • Bainbridge, GA 39818
(229) 248-2200 • http://www.decatur.k12.ga.us
Grade Span: PK-12; **Agency Type:** 1
Schools: 11
   6 Primary; 2 Middle; 1 High; 2 Other Level
   9 Regular; 1 Special Education; 0 Vocational; 1 Alternative
   0 Magnet; 0 Charter; 9 Title I Eligible; 8 School-wide Title I
Students: 5,714 (51.4% male; 48.5% female)
   Individual Education Program: 640 (11.2%);
   English Language Learner: 67 (1.2%); Migrant: 205 (3.6%)
   Eligible for Free Lunch Program: 3,303 (57.8%)
   Eligible for Reduced-Price Lunch Program: 509 (8.9%)
Teachers: 377.8 (15.1 to 1)
Librarians/Media Specialists: 10.1 (565.7 to 1)
Guidance Counselors: 15.2 (375.9 to 1)
Current Spending: ($ per student per year):
   Total: $6,992; Instruction: $4,560; Support Services: $2,015
Enrollment, Drop-out Rates and Diploma Recipients by Race/Ethnicity

Category	Total	White	Black	Asian	AIAN	Hisp.
Enrollment (%)	100.0	42.2	52.8	0.3	0.0	4.6
Drop-out Rate (%)	7.8	5.7	10.0	0.0	n/a	9.7
H.S. Diplomas (#)	270	154	112	3	0	1

Dodge County

Dodge County
720 College St • Eastman, GA 31023-1023
(478) 374-3783 • http://www.dodge.k12.ga.us
Grade Span: PK-12; **Agency Type:** 1
Schools: 6
   2 Primary; 1 Middle; 1 High; 2 Other Level
   4 Regular; 2 Special Education; 0 Vocational; 0 Alternative
   0 Magnet; 0 Charter; 4 Title I Eligible; 4 School-wide Title I
Students: 3,542 (52.1% male; 47.8% female)
   Individual Education Program: 425 (12.0%);
   English Language Learner: 3 (0.1%); Migrant: 11 (0.3%)
   Eligible for Free Lunch Program: 1,781 (50.3%)
   Eligible for Reduced-Price Lunch Program: 415 (11.7%)
Teachers: 211.6 (16.7 to 1)
Librarians/Media Specialists: 4.0 (885.5 to 1)
Guidance Counselors: 6.5 (544.9 to 1)
Current Spending: ($ per student per year):
   Total: $6,897; Instruction: $4,684; Support Services: $1,753
Enrollment, Drop-out Rates and Diploma Recipients by Race/Ethnicity

Category	Total	White	Black	Asian	AIAN	Hisp.
Enrollment (%)	100.0	61.6	36.6	0.4	0.1	1.4
Drop-out Rate (%)	5.9	6.1	5.2	n/a	n/a	0.0
H.S. Diplomas (#)	161	118	43	0	0	0

Dooly County

Dooly County
202 Cotton St • Vienna, GA 31092-1092
(229) 268-4761 • http://www.dooly.k12.ga.us/
Grade Span: PK-12; **Agency Type:** 1
Schools: 4
   1 Primary; 1 Middle; 1 High; 1 Other Level
   3 Regular; 1 Special Education; 0 Vocational; 0 Alternative
   0 Magnet; 0 Charter; 0 Title I Eligible; 0 School-wide Title I
Students: 1,570 (51.9% male; 48.0% female)
   Individual Education Program: 137 (8.7%);
   English Language Learner: 38 (2.4%); Migrant: 29 (1.8%)
   Eligible for Free Lunch Program: 1,195 (76.1%)
   Eligible for Reduced-Price Lunch Program: 138 (8.8%)
Teachers: 78.0 (20.1 to 1)
Librarians/Media Specialists: 3.0 (523.3 to 1)
Guidance Counselors: 3.0 (523.3 to 1)
Current Spending: ($ per student per year):
   Total: $8,981; Instruction: $5,185; Support Services: $3,254
Enrollment, Drop-out Rates and Diploma Recipients by Race/Ethnicity

Category	Total	White	Black	Asian	AIAN	Hisp.
Enrollment (%)	100.0	12.9	77.1	0.6	0.0	9.4
Drop-out Rate (%)	12.1	22.9	10.2	0.0	n/a	13.3
H.S. Diplomas (#)	57	11	43	3	0	0

Dougherty County

Dougherty County
200 Pine Ave • Albany, GA 31701
(229) 431-1285 • http://www.dougherty.k12.ga.us
Grade Span: PK-12; **Agency Type:** 1
Schools: 29

16 Primary; 6 Middle; 4 High; 3 Other Level
26 Regular; 2 Special Education; 0 Vocational; 1 Alternative
2 Magnet; 0 Charter; 21 Title I Eligible; 21 School-wide Title I
Students: 16,844   (50.4% male; 49.5% female)
  Individual Education Program: 2,083 (12.4%);
  English Language Learner: 38 (0.2%); Migrant: 16 (0.1%)
  Eligible for Free Lunch Program: 10,149 (60.3%)
  Eligible for Reduced-Price Lunch Program: 1,542 (9.2%)
Teachers: 1,028.5 (16.4 to 1)
Librarians/Media Specialists: 30.0 (561.5 to 1)
Guidance Counselors: 39.5 (426.4 to 1)
Current Spending: ($ per student per year):
  Total: $8,056; Instruction: $4,778; Support Services: $2,719
Enrollment, Drop-out Rates and Diploma Recipients by Race/Ethnicity

Category	Total	White	Black	Asian	AIAN	Hisp.
Enrollment (%)	100.0	15.0	83.8	0.4	0.1	0.7
Drop-out Rate (%)	8.0	8.5	8.0	4.2	0.0	5.9
H.S. Diplomas (#)	711	122	580	6	0	3

Douglas County

Douglas County
9030 Hwy 5 • Douglasville, GA 30133-0134
(770) 651-2000 • http://www.douglas.k12.ga.us
Grade Span: PK-12; **Agency Type:** 1
Schools: 31
18 Primary; 6 Middle; 4 High; 3 Other Level
28 Regular; 1 Special Education; 0 Vocational; 2 Alternative
0 Magnet; 0 Charter; 3 Title I Eligible; 3 School-wide Title I
Students: 19,697   (51.5% male; 48.4% female)
  Individual Education Program: 2,364 (12.0%);
  English Language Learner: 368 (1.9%); Migrant: 0 (0.0%)
  Eligible for Free Lunch Program: 5,614 (28.5%)
  Eligible for Reduced-Price Lunch Program: 1,817 (9.2%)
Teachers: 1,122.1 (17.6 to 1)
Librarians/Media Specialists: 33.0 (596.9 to 1)
Guidance Counselors: 38.0 (518.3 to 1)
Current Spending: ($ per student per year):
  Total: $7,120; Instruction: $4,493; Support Services: $2,216
Enrollment, Drop-out Rates and Diploma Recipients by Race/Ethnicity

Category	Total	White	Black	Asian	AIAN	Hisp.
Enrollment (%)	100.0	60.3	33.4	1.4	0.1	4.8
Drop-out Rate (%)	5.7	6.1	4.3	4.9	0.0	10.0
H.S. Diplomas (#)	899	689	171	16	3	20

Early County

Early County
11927 Columbia St • Blakely, GA 39823
(229) 723-4337 • http://www.early.k12.ga.us
Grade Span: PK-12; **Agency Type:** 1
Schools: 5
1 Primary; 1 Middle; 1 High; 2 Other Level
3 Regular; 1 Special Education; 0 Vocational; 1 Alternative
0 Magnet; 0 Charter; 2 Title I Eligible; 2 School-wide Title I
Students: 2,711   (50.8% male; 49.1% female)
  Individual Education Program: 417 (15.4%);
  English Language Learner: 13 (0.5%); Migrant: 38 (1.4%)
  Eligible for Free Lunch Program: 1,750 (64.6%)
  Eligible for Reduced-Price Lunch Program: 249 (9.2%)
Teachers: 158.1 (17.1 to 1)
Librarians/Media Specialists: 3.0 (903.7 to 1)
Guidance Counselors: 6.5 (417.1 to 1)
Current Spending: ($ per student per year):
  Total: $7,166; Instruction: $4,465; Support Services: $2,301
Enrollment, Drop-out Rates and Diploma Recipients by Race/Ethnicity

Category	Total	White	Black	Asian	AIAN	Hisp.
Enrollment (%)	100.0	36.1	62.2	0.4	0.0	1.3
Drop-out Rate (%)	4.7	4.8	4.7	0.0	0.0	0.0
H.S. Diplomas (#)	131	61	70	0	0	0

Effingham County

Effingham County
405 N Ash St • Springfield, GA 31329-1329
(912) 754-6491 • http://www.effingham.k12.ga.us
Grade Span: PK-12; **Agency Type:** 1
Schools: 14
7 Primary; 3 Middle; 2 High; 2 Other Level
12 Regular; 1 Special Education; 0 Vocational; 1 Alternative
0 Magnet; 0 Charter; 3 Title I Eligible; 2 School-wide Title I
Students: 9,350   (51.0% male; 48.9% female)
  Individual Education Program: 1,358 (14.5%);
  English Language Learner: 41 (0.4%); Migrant: 1 (<0.1%)
  Eligible for Free Lunch Program: 1,975 (21.1%)

  Eligible for Reduced-Price Lunch Program: 824 (8.8%)
Teachers: 524.6 (17.8 to 1)
Librarians/Media Specialists: 14.0 (667.9 to 1)
Guidance Counselors: 18.0 (519.4 to 1)
Current Spending: ($ per student per year):
  Total: $6,528; Instruction: $4,158; Support Services: $2,018
Enrollment, Drop-out Rates and Diploma Recipients by Race/Ethnicity

Category	Total	White	Black	Asian	AIAN	Hisp.
Enrollment (%)	100.0	82.2	15.6	0.7	0.1	1.5
Drop-out Rate (%)	5.8	5.8	6.1	0.0	0.0	4.3
H.S. Diplomas (#)	426	374	45	1	0	6

Elbert County

Elbert County
50 Laurel Dr • Elberton, GA 30635-0635
(706) 213-4000 • http://www.elbert.k12.ga.us
Grade Span: PK-12; **Agency Type:** 1
Schools: 10
5 Primary; 1 Middle; 1 High; 3 Other Level
8 Regular; 1 Special Education; 0 Vocational; 1 Alternative
0 Magnet; 0 Charter; 6 Title I Eligible; 6 School-wide Title I
Students: 3,740   (51.0% male; 48.9% female)
  Individual Education Program: 463 (12.4%);
  English Language Learner: 93 (2.5%); Migrant: 23 (0.6%)
  Eligible for Free Lunch Program: 1,793 (47.9%)
  Eligible for Reduced-Price Lunch Program: 345 (9.2%)
Teachers: 237.9 (15.7 to 1)
Librarians/Media Specialists: 8.0 (467.5 to 1)
Guidance Counselors: 5.0 (748.0 to 1)
Current Spending: ($ per student per year):
  Total: $7,658; Instruction: $4,862; Support Services: $2,322
Enrollment, Drop-out Rates and Diploma Recipients by Race/Ethnicity

Category	Total	White	Black	Asian	AIAN	Hisp.
Enrollment (%)	100.0	56.2	39.8	0.4	0.0	3.6
Drop-out Rate (%)	7.1	7.6	6.5	0.0	n/a	6.3
H.S. Diplomas (#)	176	122	54	0	0	0

Emanuel County

Emanuel County
201 N Main St • Swainsboro, GA 30401-0401
(478) 237-6674 • http://www.emanuel.k12.ga.us/
Grade Span: PK-12; **Agency Type:** 1
Schools: 12
4 Primary; 1 Middle; 1 High; 6 Other Level
7 Regular; 4 Special Education; 0 Vocational; 1 Alternative
0 Magnet; 0 Charter; 6 Title I Eligible; 6 School-wide Title I
Students: 4,581   (51.5% male; 48.4% female)
  Individual Education Program: 755 (16.5%);
  English Language Learner: 37 (0.8%); Migrant: 72 (1.6%)
  Eligible for Free Lunch Program: 2,725 (59.5%)
  Eligible for Reduced-Price Lunch Program: 481 (10.5%)
Teachers: 288.9 (15.9 to 1)
Librarians/Media Specialists: 6.8 (673.7 to 1)
Guidance Counselors: 7.8 (587.3 to 1)
Current Spending: ($ per student per year):
  Total: $7,038; Instruction: $4,619; Support Services: $1,922
Enrollment, Drop-out Rates and Diploma Recipients by Race/Ethnicity

Category	Total	White	Black	Asian	AIAN	Hisp.
Enrollment (%)	100.0	52.2	45.4	0.3	0.0	2.2
Drop-out Rate (%)	7.0	6.5	7.8	0.0	0.0	0.0
H.S. Diplomas (#)	214	137	77	0	0	0

Evans County

Evans County
613 W Main St • Claxton, GA 30417-0417
(912) 739-3544 • http://www.evans.k12.ga.us/
Grade Span: PK-12; **Agency Type:** 1
Schools: 5
1 Primary; 1 Middle; 1 High; 2 Other Level
3 Regular; 1 Special Education; 0 Vocational; 1 Alternative
0 Magnet; 0 Charter; 2 Title I Eligible; 2 School-wide Title I
Students: 1,888   (54.1% male; 45.8% female)
  Individual Education Program: 345 (18.3%);
  English Language Learner: 94 (5.0%); Migrant: 146 (7.7%)
  Eligible for Free Lunch Program: 1,134 (60.1%)
  Eligible for Reduced-Price Lunch Program: 262 (13.9%)
Teachers: 123.3 (15.3 to 1)
Librarians/Media Specialists: 3.0 (629.3 to 1)
Guidance Counselors: 4.0 (472.0 to 1)
Current Spending: ($ per student per year):
  Total: $7,471; Instruction: $4,670; Support Services: $2,347

Enrollment, Drop-out Rates and Diploma Recipients by Race/Ethnicity

Category	Total	White	Black	Asian	AIAN	Hisp.
Enrollment (%)	100.0	44.8	45.7	0.4	0.0	9.2
Drop-out Rate (%)	6.0	5.5	5.3	0.0	n/a	28.6
H.S. Diplomas (#)	84	51	31	1	0	1

Fannin County

Fannin County
2290 E First St · Blue Ridge, GA 30513-0513
(706) 632-3771 · http://www.fannin.k12.ga.us
Grade Span: PK-12; **Agency Type:** 1
Schools: 6
  3 Primary; 1 Middle; 1 High; 1 Other Level
  5 Regular; 1 Special Education; 0 Vocational; 0 Alternative
  0 Magnet; 0 Charter; 4 Title I Eligible; 0 School-wide Title I
Students: 3,123   (51.7% male; 48.2% female)
  Individual Education Program: 422 (13.5%);
  English Language Learner: 0 (0.0%); Migrant: 0 (0.0%)
  Eligible for Free Lunch Program: 984 (31.5%)
  Eligible for Reduced-Price Lunch Program: 419 (13.4%)
Teachers: 180.3 (17.3 to 1)
Librarians/Media Specialists: 5.0 (624.6 to 1)
Guidance Counselors: 6.0 (520.5 to 1)
Current Spending: ($ per student per year):
  Total: $7,605; Instruction: $4,860; Support Services: $2,294
Enrollment, Drop-out Rates and Diploma Recipients by Race/Ethnicity

Category	Total	White	Black	Asian	AIAN	Hisp.
Enrollment (%)	100.0	98.3	0.2	0.5	0.1	0.8
Drop-out Rate (%)	4.9	4.9	0.0	0.0	0.0	10.0
H.S. Diplomas (#)	147	145	0	1	0	1

Fayette County

Fayette County
210 Stonewall Ave · Fayetteville, GA 30214-0214
(770) 460-3535 · http://www.fcboe.org
Grade Span: PK-12; **Agency Type:** 1
Schools: 30
  17 Primary; 5 Middle; 5 High; 3 Other Level
  27 Regular; 1 Special Education; 0 Vocational; 2 Alternative
  0 Magnet; 0 Charter; 7 Title I Eligible; 0 School-wide Title I
Students: 21,224   (51.1% male; 48.8% female)
  Individual Education Program: 2,433 (11.5%);
  English Language Learner: 489 (2.3%); Migrant: 0 (0.0%)
  Eligible for Free Lunch Program: 1,610 (7.6%)
  Eligible for Reduced-Price Lunch Program: 582 (2.7%)
Teachers: 1,394.1 (15.2 to 1)
Librarians/Media Specialists: 33.0 (643.2 to 1)
Guidance Counselors: 52.0 (408.2 to 1)
Current Spending: ($ per student per year):
  Total: $7,331; Instruction: $4,878; Support Services: $2,184
Enrollment, Drop-out Rates and Diploma Recipients by Race/Ethnicity

Category	Total	White	Black	Asian	AIAN	Hisp.
Enrollment (%)	100.0	75.6	17.9	3.2	0.1	3.2
Drop-out Rate (%)	2.0	2.0	1.4	2.3	0.0	4.7
H.S. Diplomas (#)	1,380	1,130	190	37	1	22

Floyd County

Floyd County
600 Riverside Pkwy NE · Rome, GA 30161-0161
(706) 234-1031 · http://www.floydboe.net
Grade Span: PK-12; **Agency Type:** 1
Schools: 23
  10 Primary; 5 Middle; 5 High; 3 Other Level
  20 Regular; 1 Special Education; 0 Vocational; 2 Alternative
  0 Magnet; 0 Charter; 7 Title I Eligible; 7 School-wide Title I
Students: 10,382   (50.9% male; 49.0% female)
  Individual Education Program: 2,533 (24.4%);
  English Language Learner: 264 (2.5%); Migrant: 7 (0.1%)
  Eligible for Free Lunch Program: 3,309 (31.9%)
  Eligible for Reduced-Price Lunch Program: 991 (9.5%)
Teachers: 656.6 (15.8 to 1)
Librarians/Media Specialists: 19.0 (546.4 to 1)
Guidance Counselors: 25.0 (415.3 to 1)
Current Spending: ($ per student per year):
  Total: $7,508; Instruction: $4,789; Support Services: $2,342
Enrollment, Drop-out Rates and Diploma Recipients by Race/Ethnicity

Category	Total	White	Black	Asian	AIAN	Hisp.
Enrollment (%)	100.0	90.5	4.3	0.7	0.2	4.2
Drop-out Rate (%)	6.8	6.7	6.4	0.0	22.2	10.2
H.S. Diplomas (#)	454	422	21	4	0	7

Rome City
508 E Second St · Rome, GA 30161-0161
(706) 236-5050 · http://www.rcs.rome.ga.us
Grade Span: PK-12; **Agency Type:** 1
Schools: 12
  8 Primary; 1 Middle; 1 High; 2 Other Level
  10 Regular; 1 Special Education; 0 Vocational; 1 Alternative
  0 Magnet; 0 Charter; 8 Title I Eligible; 8 School-wide Title I
Students: 5,306   (49.6% male; 50.3% female)
  Individual Education Program: 645 (12.2%);
  English Language Learner: 628 (11.8%); Migrant: 101 (1.9%)
  Eligible for Free Lunch Program: 2,939 (55.4%)
  Eligible for Reduced-Price Lunch Program: 346 (6.5%)
Teachers: 332.5 (16.0 to 1)
Librarians/Media Specialists: 11.0 (482.4 to 1)
Guidance Counselors: 12.0 (442.2 to 1)
Current Spending: ($ per student per year):
  Total: $7,600; Instruction: $5,178; Support Services: $1,959
Enrollment, Drop-out Rates and Diploma Recipients by Race/Ethnicity

Category	Total	White	Black	Asian	AIAN	Hisp.
Enrollment (%)	100.0	37.6	43.1	2.9	0.6	15.7
Drop-out Rate (%)	8.3	5.4	11.4	5.8	n/a	9.3
H.S. Diplomas (#)	238	135	83	9	0	11

Forsyth County

Forsyth County
1120 Dahlonega Hwy · Cumming, GA 30040-0040
(770) 887-2461 · http://www.forsyth.k12.ga.us
Grade Span: PK-12; **Agency Type:** 1
Schools: 24
  14 Primary; 5 Middle; 3 High; 2 Other Level
  22 Regular; 1 Special Education; 0 Vocational; 1 Alternative
  0 Magnet; 0 Charter; 2 Title I Eligible; 0 School-wide Title I
Students: 22,067   (51.6% male; 48.3% female)
  Individual Education Program: 2,868 (13.0%);
  English Language Learner: 1,026 (4.6%); Migrant: 65 (0.3%)
  Eligible for Free Lunch Program: 2,104 (9.5%)
  Eligible for Reduced-Price Lunch Program: 774 (3.5%)
Teachers: 1,361.0 (16.2 to 1)
Librarians/Media Specialists: 22.0 (1,003.0 to 1)
Guidance Counselors: 47.5 (464.6 to 1)
Current Spending: ($ per student per year):
  Total: $7,435; Instruction: $4,801; Support Services: $2,320
Enrollment, Drop-out Rates and Diploma Recipients by Race/Ethnicity

Category	Total	White	Black	Asian	AIAN	Hisp.
Enrollment (%)	100.0	90.9	0.8	1.3	0.1	7.0
Drop-out Rate (%)	2.7	2.4	0.0	11.5	10.0	8.4
H.S. Diplomas (#)	765	739	4	4	1	17

Franklin County

Franklin County
919 Hull Ave · Carnesville, GA 30521-0521
(706) 384-4554 · http://www.franklin.k12.ga.us
Grade Span: PK-12; **Agency Type:** 1
Schools: 6
  3 Primary; 1 Middle; 1 High; 1 Other Level
  5 Regular; 1 Special Education; 0 Vocational; 0 Alternative
  0 Magnet; 0 Charter; 4 Title I Eligible; 4 School-wide Title I
Students: 3,657   (51.6% male; 48.3% female)
  Individual Education Program: 638 (17.4%);
  English Language Learner: 19 (0.5%); Migrant: 0 (0.0%)
  Eligible for Free Lunch Program: 1,211 (33.1%)
  Eligible for Reduced-Price Lunch Program: 319 (8.7%)
Teachers: 238.9 (15.3 to 1)
Librarians/Media Specialists: 5.0 (731.4 to 1)
Guidance Counselors: 7.0 (522.4 to 1)
Current Spending: ($ per student per year):
  Total: $6,967; Instruction: $4,754; Support Services: $1,878
Enrollment, Drop-out Rates and Diploma Recipients by Race/Ethnicity

Category	Total	White	Black	Asian	AIAN	Hisp.
Enrollment (%)	100.0	85.7	12.2	0.6	0.0	1.5
Drop-out Rate (%)	6.9	6.8	8.1	0.0	n/a	0.0
H.S. Diplomas (#)	145	134	11	0	0	0

Fulton County

Atlanta City
210 Pryor St SW · Atlanta, GA 30335
(404) 827-8075 · http://www.atlanta.k12.ga.us
Grade Span: PK-12; **Agency Type:** 1
Schools: 105
  67 Primary; 18 Middle; 13 High; 7 Other Level
  96 Regular; 2 Special Education; 0 Vocational; 7 Alternative

6 Magnet; 7 Charter; 84 Title I Eligible; 84 School-wide Title I
Students: 52,103 (49.8% male; 50.1% female)
  Individual Education Program: 4,481 (8.6%);
  English Language Learner: 2,195 (4.2%); Migrant: 0 (0.0%)
  Eligible for Free Lunch Program: 34,333 (65.9%)
  Eligible for Reduced-Price Lunch Program: 2,163 (4.2%)
Teachers: 3,692.0 (14.1 to 1)
Librarians/Media Specialists: 92.0 (566.3 to 1)
Guidance Counselors: 133.0 (391.8 to 1)
Current Spending: ($ per student per year):
  Total: $11,435; Instruction: $6,442; Support Services: $4,424
Enrollment, Drop-out Rates and Diploma Recipients by Race/Ethnicity

Category	Total	White	Black	Asian	AIAN	Hisp.
Enrollment (%)	100.0	7.6	88.2	0.6	0.0	3.6
Drop-out Rate (%)	8.9	1.3	9.4	4.9	0.0	6.7
H.S. Diplomas (#)	2,270	112	2,100	38	0	20

Fulton County

786 Cleveland Ave SW • Atlanta, GA 30315-0315
(404) 768-3600 • http://www.fulton.k12.ga.us
Grade Span: PK-12; **Agency Type:** 1
Schools: 87
  51 Primary; 18 Middle; 11 High; 7 Other Level
  81 Regular; 2 Special Education; 0 Vocational; 4 Alternative
  1 Magnet; 6 Charter; 31 Title I Eligible; 25 School-wide Title I
Students: 73,319 (51.1% male; 48.8% female)
  Individual Education Program: 7,800 (10.6%);
  English Language Learner: 4,286 (5.8%); Migrant: 0 (0.0%)
  Eligible for Free Lunch Program: 20,220 (27.6%)
  Eligible for Reduced-Price Lunch Program: 3,251 (4.4%)
Teachers: 4,891.4 (15.0 to 1)
Librarians/Media Specialists: 87.0 (842.7 to 1)
Guidance Counselors: 175.2 (418.5 to 1)
Current Spending: ($ per student per year):
  Total: $8,599; Instruction: $5,596; Support Services: $2,698
Enrollment, Drop-out Rates and Diploma Recipients by Race/Ethnicity

Category	Total	White	Black	Asian	AIAN	Hisp.
Enrollment (%)	100.0	45.2	39.3	6.6	0.1	8.8
Drop-out Rate (%)	2.5	1.7	3.8	0.9	11.1	3.5
H.S. Diplomas (#)	3,360	1,980	1,044	236	1	99

Gilmer County

497 Bobcat Tr • Ellijay, GA 30540-5212
(706) 276-5000 •
http://www.gilmerschools.com/education/district/district.php?sectionid=1
Grade Span: PK-12; **Agency Type:** 1
Schools: 7
  4 Primary; 1 Middle; 1 High; 1 Other Level
  6 Regular; 1 Special Education; 0 Vocational; 0 Alternative
  0 Magnet; 0 Charter; 6 Title I Eligible; 6 School-wide Title I
Students: 4,036 (52.0% male; 47.9% female)
  Individual Education Program: 474 (11.7%);
  English Language Learner: 245 (6.1%); Migrant: 237 (5.9%)
  Eligible for Free Lunch Program: 1,630 (40.4%)
  Eligible for Reduced-Price Lunch Program: 468 (11.6%)
Teachers: 259.5 (15.6 to 1)
Librarians/Media Specialists: 6.0 (672.7 to 1)
Guidance Counselors: 7.0 (576.6 to 1)
Current Spending: ($ per student per year):
  Total: $7,374; Instruction: $4,939; Support Services: $2,031
Enrollment, Drop-out Rates and Diploma Recipients by Race/Ethnicity

Category	Total	White	Black	Asian	AIAN	Hisp.
Enrollment (%)	100.0	88.6	0.1	0.2	0.0	11.1
Drop-out Rate (%)	5.8	5.5	100.0	0.0	0.0	9.6
H.S. Diplomas (#)	139	134	0	0	0	5

Glynn County

1313 Egmont St • Brunswick, GA 31520
(912) 267-4100 • http://www.glynn.k12.ga.us
Grade Span: PK-12; **Agency Type:** 1
Schools: 19
  9 Primary; 4 Middle; 2 High; 4 Other Level
  15 Regular; 3 Special Education; 0 Vocational; 1 Alternative
  0 Magnet; 0 Charter; 7 Title I Eligible; 6 School-wide Title I
Students: 12,017 (50.6% male; 49.3% female)
  Individual Education Program: 1,610 (13.4%);
  English Language Learner: 131 (1.1%); Migrant: 168 (1.4%)
  Eligible for Free Lunch Program: 4,651 (38.7%)
  Eligible for Reduced-Price Lunch Program: 830 (6.9%)
Teachers: 781.6 (15.4 to 1)
Librarians/Media Specialists: 17.0 (706.9 to 1)

Guidance Counselors: 27.4 (438.6 to 1)
Current Spending: ($ per student per year):
  Total: $7,567; Instruction: $5,158; Support Services: $2,043
Enrollment, Drop-out Rates and Diploma Recipients by Race/Ethnicity

Category	Total	White	Black	Asian	AIAN	Hisp.
Enrollment (%)	100.0	56.5	38.6	0.7	0.1	4.0
Drop-out Rate (%)	10.0	9.5	10.6	0.0	50.0	17.5
H.S. Diplomas (#)	516	350	152	8	0	6

Calhoun City

700 W Line St • Calhoun, GA 30701-0701
(706) 629-2900 • http://www.calhoun-city.k12.ga.us
Grade Span: PK-12; **Agency Type:** 1
Schools: 7
  2 Primary; 1 Middle; 1 High; 3 Other Level
  4 Regular; 2 Special Education; 0 Vocational; 1 Alternative
  0 Magnet; 0 Charter; 2 Title I Eligible; 2 School-wide Title I
Students: 2,777 (51.0% male; 48.9% female)
  Individual Education Program: 301 (10.8%);
  English Language Learner: 248 (8.9%); Migrant: 1 (<0.1%)
  Eligible for Free Lunch Program: 924 (33.3%)
  Eligible for Reduced-Price Lunch Program: 213 (7.7%)
Teachers: 168.0 (16.5 to 1)
Librarians/Media Specialists: 3.0 (925.7 to 1)
Guidance Counselors: 5.0 (555.4 to 1)
Current Spending: ($ per student per year):
  Total: $7,153; Instruction: $4,622; Support Services: $2,031
Enrollment, Drop-out Rates and Diploma Recipients by Race/Ethnicity

Category	Total	White	Black	Asian	AIAN	Hisp.
Enrollment (%)	100.0	70.6	8.5	1.5	0.0	19.3
Drop-out Rate (%)	4.0	2.1	10.8	5.6	n/a	9.1
H.S. Diplomas (#)	124	103	10	4	0	7

Gordon County

205 Warrior Path • Calhoun, GA 30703-0127
(706) 629-7366 • http://www.gcbe.org
Grade Span: PK-12; **Agency Type:** 1
Schools: 10
  5 Primary; 2 Middle; 1 High; 2 Other Level
  8 Regular; 2 Special Education; 0 Vocational; 0 Alternative
  0 Magnet; 0 Charter; 6 Title I Eligible; 6 School-wide Title I
Students: 6,399 (50.3% male; 49.6% female)
  Individual Education Program: 980 (15.3%);
  English Language Learner: 235 (3.7%); Migrant: 0 (0.0%)
  Eligible for Free Lunch Program: 2,181 (34.1%)
  Eligible for Reduced-Price Lunch Program: 683 (10.7%)
Teachers: 369.9 (17.3 to 1)
Librarians/Media Specialists: 9.0 (711.0 to 1)
Guidance Counselors: 10.0 (639.9 to 1)
Current Spending: ($ per student per year):
  Total: $7,234; Instruction: $4,629; Support Services: $2,180
Enrollment, Drop-out Rates and Diploma Recipients by Race/Ethnicity

Category	Total	White	Black	Asian	AIAN	Hisp.
Enrollment (%)	100.0	89.3	2.0	0.5	0.2	8.0
Drop-out Rate (%)	9.4	9.2	5.3	8.3	14.3	15.0
H.S. Diplomas (#)	217	209	3	2	1	2

Grady County

122 N Broad • Cairo, GA 31728-1728
(229) 377-3701 • http://www.grady.k12.ga.us
Grade Span: PK-12; **Agency Type:** 1
Schools: 9
  5 Primary; 1 Middle; 1 High; 2 Other Level
  7 Regular; 1 Special Education; 0 Vocational; 1 Alternative
  0 Magnet; 0 Charter; 4 Title I Eligible; 4 School-wide Title I
Students: 4,481 (48.5% male; 51.4% female)
  Individual Education Program: 519 (11.6%);
  English Language Learner: 139 (3.1%); Migrant: 218 (4.9%)
  Eligible for Free Lunch Program: 2,200 (49.1%)
  Eligible for Reduced-Price Lunch Program: 345 (7.7%)
Teachers: 274.2 (16.3 to 1)
Librarians/Media Specialists: 8.0 (560.1 to 1)
Guidance Counselors: 10.0 (448.1 to 1)
Current Spending: ($ per student per year):
  Total: $6,996; Instruction: $4,477; Support Services: $2,143
Enrollment, Drop-out Rates and Diploma Recipients by Race/Ethnicity

Category	Total	White	Black	Asian	AIAN	Hisp.
Enrollment (%)	100.0	54.0	40.0	0.5	0.1	5.3
Drop-out Rate (%)	6.7	6.0	7.0	0.0	0.0	25.0
H.S. Diplomas (#)	173	105	67	0	0	1

Greene County

Greene County
201 N Main St P. O. B • Greensboro, GA 31728
(706) 453-7688 • http://www.greene.k12.ga.us
Grade Span: PK-12; **Agency Type:** 1
Schools: 7
  2 Primary; 1 Middle; 1 High; 3 Other Level
  4 Regular; 2 Special Education; 0 Vocational; 1 Alternative
  0 Magnet; 0 Charter; 3 Title I Eligible; 3 School-wide Title I
Students: 2,263 (51.8% male; 48.1% female)
  Individual Education Program: 344 (15.2%);
  English Language Learner: 31 (1.4%); Migrant: 7 (0.3%)
  Eligible for Free Lunch Program: 1,680 (74.2%)
  Eligible for Reduced-Price Lunch Program: 142 (6.3%)
Teachers: 158.2 (14.3 to 1)
Librarians/Media Specialists: 4.0 (565.8 to 1)
Guidance Counselors: 6.0 (377.2 to 1)
Current Spending: ($ per student per year):
  Total: $9,563; Instruction: $5,731; Support Services: $3,304
Enrollment, Drop-out Rates and Diploma Recipients by Race/Ethnicity

Category	Total	White	Black	Asian	AIAN	Hisp.
Enrollment (%)	100.0	27.3	69.7	0.2	0.0	2.7
Drop-out Rate (%)	2.0	2.8	1.6	0.0	n/a	20.0
H.S. Diplomas (#)	82	21	59	1	0	1

Gwinnett County

Buford City
70 Wiley Dr Ste 200 • Buford, GA 30518-0518
(770) 945-5035 • http://www.bufordcityschools.org
Grade Span: PK-12; **Agency Type:** 1
Schools: 5
  2 Primary; 1 Middle; 1 High; 1 Other Level
  4 Regular; 1 Special Education; 0 Vocational; 0 Alternative
  0 Magnet; 0 Charter; 3 Title I Eligible; 2 School-wide Title I
Students: 2,288 (51.3% male; 48.6% female)
  Individual Education Program: 290 (12.7%);
  English Language Learner: 243 (10.6%); Migrant: 21 (0.9%)
  Eligible for Free Lunch Program: 849 (37.1%)
  Eligible for Reduced-Price Lunch Program: 112 (4.9%)
Teachers: 148.8 (15.4 to 1)
Librarians/Media Specialists: 4.0 (572.0 to 1)
Guidance Counselors: 5.0 (457.6 to 1)
Current Spending: ($ per student per year):
  Total: $9,455; Instruction: $5,841; Support Services: $3,130
Enrollment, Drop-out Rates and Diploma Recipients by Race/Ethnicity

Category	Total	White	Black	Asian	AIAN	Hisp.
Enrollment (%)	100.0	60.6	15.3	1.4	0.2	22.6
Drop-out Rate (%)	4.6	3.7	6.4	0.0	n/a	8.1
H.S. Diplomas (#)	100	80	14	0	0	6

Gwinnett County
52 Gwinnett Dr • Lawrenceville, GA 30046
(770) 963-8651 • http://www.gwinnett.k12.ga.us
Grade Span: PK-12; **Agency Type:** 1
Schools: 98
  61 Primary; 16 Middle; 15 High; 6 Other Level
  91 Regular; 4 Special Education; 0 Vocational; 3 Alternative
  0 Magnet; 0 Charter; 23 Title I Eligible; 8 School-wide Title I
Students: 129,014 (51.4% male; 48.5% female)
  Individual Education Program: 14,826 (11.5%);
  English Language Learner: 13,661 (10.6%); Migrant: 22 (<0.1%)
  Eligible for Free Lunch Program: 30,561 (23.7%)
  Eligible for Reduced-Price Lunch Program: 9,115 (7.1%)
Teachers: 8,220.8 (15.7 to 1)
Librarians/Media Specialists: 108.4 (1,190.2 to 1)
Guidance Counselors: 266.5 (484.1 to 1)
Current Spending: ($ per student per year):
  Total: $7,545; Instruction: $4,909; Support Services: $2,347
Enrollment, Drop-out Rates and Diploma Recipients by Race/Ethnicity

Category	Total	White	Black	Asian	AIAN	Hisp.
Enrollment (%)	100.0	52.7	21.4	9.7	0.1	16.0
Drop-out Rate (%)	3.2	2.4	4.4	2.3	9.8	7.9
H.S. Diplomas (#)	6,116	4,370	760	645	10	331

Habersham County

Habersham County
132 W Stanford Mill Rd • Clarkesville, GA 30523-0523
(706) 754-2118 • http://www.habersham.k12.ga.us
Grade Span: KG-12; **Agency Type:** 1
Schools: 12
  7 Primary; 2 Middle; 1 High; 2 Other Level
  10 Regular; 1 Special Education; 0 Vocational; 1 Alternative

  0 Magnet; 0 Charter; 4 Title I Eligible; 2 School-wide Title I
Students: 6,043 (52.1% male; 47.8% female)
  Individual Education Program: 818 (13.5%);
  English Language Learner: 325 (5.4%); Migrant: 479 (7.9%)
  Eligible for Free Lunch Program: 1,866 (30.9%)
  Eligible for Reduced-Price Lunch Program: 485 (8.0%)
Teachers: 380.7 (15.9 to 1)
Librarians/Media Specialists: 9.5 (636.1 to 1)
Guidance Counselors: 12.0 (503.6 to 1)
Current Spending: ($ per student per year):
  Total: $7,302; Instruction: $4,707; Support Services: $2,252
Enrollment, Drop-out Rates and Diploma Recipients by Race/Ethnicity

Category	Total	White	Black	Asian	AIAN	Hisp.
Enrollment (%)	100.0	79.2	2.3	2.5	0.2	15.8
Drop-out Rate (%)	7.5	6.3	6.5	7.3	100.0	22.0
H.S. Diplomas (#)	270	254	2	6	0	8

Hall County

Gainesville City
508 Oak St NW • Gainesville, GA 30501-3506
(770) 536-5275 • http://www.gainesville-city.k12.ga.us
Grade Span: PK-12; **Agency Type:** 1
Schools: 8
  4 Primary; 1 Middle; 1 High; 2 Other Level
  7 Regular; 1 Special Education; 0 Vocational; 0 Alternative
  0 Magnet; 0 Charter; 5 Title I Eligible; 4 School-wide Title I
Students: 4,724 (50.1% male; 49.8% female)
  Individual Education Program: 291 (6.2%);
  English Language Learner: 1,328 (28.1%); Migrant: 532 (11.3%)
  Eligible for Free Lunch Program: 2,872 (60.8%)
  Eligible for Reduced-Price Lunch Program: 404 (8.6%)
Teachers: 284.3 (16.6 to 1)
Librarians/Media Specialists: 6.0 (787.3 to 1)
Guidance Counselors: 8.0 (590.5 to 1)
Current Spending: ($ per student per year):
  Total: $8,381; Instruction: $5,372; Support Services: $2,637
Enrollment, Drop-out Rates and Diploma Recipients by Race/Ethnicity

Category	Total	White	Black	Asian	AIAN	Hisp.
Enrollment (%)	100.0	26.1	22.7	2.6	0.1	48.5
Drop-out Rate (%)	15.5	7.1	11.7	28.8	n/a	28.3
H.S. Diplomas (#)	186	114	32	10	0	30

Hall County
711 Green St Ste 100 • Gainesville, GA 30505
(770) 534-1080 • http://www.hallco.org
Grade Span: PK-12; **Agency Type:** 1
Schools: 33
  19 Primary; 6 Middle; 7 High; 1 Other Level
  31 Regular; 1 Special Education; 0 Vocational; 1 Alternative
  0 Magnet; 0 Charter; 8 Title I Eligible; 8 School-wide Title I
Students: 22,535 (52.1% male; 47.8% female)
  Individual Education Program: 2,335 (10.4%);
  English Language Learner: 3,772 (16.7%); Migrant: 999 (4.4%)
  Eligible for Free Lunch Program: 7,908 (35.1%)
  Eligible for Reduced-Price Lunch Program: 1,896 (8.4%)
Teachers: 1,394.6 (16.2 to 1)
Librarians/Media Specialists: 33.0 (682.9 to 1)
Guidance Counselors: 47.4 (475.4 to 1)
Current Spending: ($ per student per year):
  Total: $7,027; Instruction: $4,624; Support Services: $2,008
Enrollment, Drop-out Rates and Diploma Recipients by Race/Ethnicity

Category	Total	White	Black	Asian	AIAN	Hisp.
Enrollment (%)	100.0	66.9	5.5	1.0	0.4	26.2
Drop-out Rate (%)	6.2	5.7	8.8	1.5	4.0	8.3
H.S. Diplomas (#)	869	745	37	17	4	66

Hancock County

Hancock County
Augusta Hwy • Sparta, GA 31087-1087
(706) 444-5775 • http://www.hancock.k12.ga.us/
Grade Span: PK-12; **Agency Type:** 1
Schools: 5
  2 Primary; 0 Middle; 0 High; 3 Other Level
  3 Regular; 1 Special Education; 0 Vocational; 1 Alternative
  0 Magnet; 0 Charter; 3 Title I Eligible; 0 School-wide Title I
Students: 1,590 (50.5% male; 49.4% female)
  Individual Education Program: 219 (13.8%);
  English Language Learner: 4 (0.3%); Migrant: 0 (0.0%)
  Eligible for Free Lunch Program: 1,187 (74.7%)
  Eligible for Reduced-Price Lunch Program: 140 (8.8%)
Teachers: 94.8 (16.8 to 1)
Librarians/Media Specialists: 2.0 (795.0 to 1)
Guidance Counselors: 3.5 (454.3 to 1)

Current Spending: ($ per student per year):
Total: $8,600; Instruction: $4,700; Support Services: $3,295
Enrollment, Drop-out Rates and Diploma Recipients by Race/Ethnicity

Category	Total	White	Black	Asian	AIAN	Hisp.
Enrollment (%)	100.0	1.6	98.3	0.0	0.1	0.1
Drop-out Rate (%)	12.0	33.3	11.7	n/a	n/a	n/a
H.S. Diplomas (#)	82	0	82	0	0	0

Haralson County

Bremen City
504 Laurel St · Bremen, GA 30110-0110
(770) 537-5508
Grade Span: PK-12; **Agency Type:** 1
Schools: 4
  1 Primary; 1 Middle; 1 High; 1 Other Level
  3 Regular; 1 Special Education; 0 Vocational; 0 Alternative
  0 Magnet; 0 Charter; 1 Title I Eligible; 0 School-wide Title I
Students: 1,618 (49.5% male; 50.4% female)
  Individual Education Program: 215 (13.3%);
  English Language Learner: 0 (0.0%); Migrant: 0 (0.0%)
  Eligible for Free Lunch Program: 211 (13.0%)
  Eligible for Reduced-Price Lunch Program: 63 (3.9%)
Teachers: 94.3 (17.2 to 1)
Librarians/Media Specialists: 2.0 (809.0 to 1)
Guidance Counselors: 2.5 (647.2 to 1)
Current Spending: ($ per student per year):
Total: $7,021; Instruction: $4,674; Support Services: $1,961
Enrollment, Drop-out Rates and Diploma Recipients by Race/Ethnicity

Category	Total	White	Black	Asian	AIAN	Hisp.
Enrollment (%)	100.0	91.8	7.2	0.6	0.2	0.2
Drop-out Rate (%)	1.8	1.9	0.0	0.0	n/a	n/a
H.S. Diplomas (#)	89	85	4	0	0	0

Haralson County
10 Van Wert St · Buchanan, GA 30113-0113
(770) 646-3882 · http://www.haralson.k12.ga.us
Grade Span: PK-12; **Agency Type:** 1
Schools: 9
  4 Primary; 1 Middle; 1 High; 3 Other Level
  6 Regular; 2 Special Education; 0 Vocational; 1 Alternative
  0 Magnet; 0 Charter; 4 Title I Eligible; 4 School-wide Title I
Students: 3,811 (52.7% male; 47.2% female)
  Individual Education Program: 742 (19.5%);
  English Language Learner: 0 (0.0%); Migrant: 112 (2.9%)
  Eligible for Free Lunch Program: 1,362 (35.7%)
  Eligible for Reduced-Price Lunch Program: 389 (10.2%)
Teachers: 234.2 (16.3 to 1)
Librarians/Media Specialists: 6.0 (635.2 to 1)
Guidance Counselors: 8.0 (476.4 to 1)
Current Spending: ($ per student per year):
Total: $6,980; Instruction: $4,659; Support Services: $1,971
Enrollment, Drop-out Rates and Diploma Recipients by Race/Ethnicity

Category	Total	White	Black	Asian	AIAN	Hisp.
Enrollment (%)	100.0	94.9	4.4	0.2	0.1	0.4
Drop-out Rate (%)	10.3	10.6	7.4	0.0	0.0	0.0
H.S. Diplomas (#)	142	131	9	1	1	0

Harris County

Harris County
132 Barnes Mill Rd · Hamilton, GA 31811-1811
(706) 628-4206 · http://www.harris.k12.ga.us/
Grade Span: PK-12; **Agency Type:** 1
Schools: 8
  4 Primary; 1 Middle; 1 High; 2 Other Level
  6 Regular; 1 Special Education; 0 Vocational; 1 Alternative
  0 Magnet; 0 Charter; 3 Title I Eligible; 2 School-wide Title I
Students: 4,410 (52.2% male; 47.7% female)
  Individual Education Program: 393 (8.9%);
  English Language Learner: 1 (<0.1%); Migrant: 0 (0.0%)
  Eligible for Free Lunch Program: 1,101 (25.0%)
  Eligible for Reduced-Price Lunch Program: 412 (9.3%)
Teachers: 275.9 (16.0 to 1)
Librarians/Media Specialists: 7.0 (630.0 to 1)
Guidance Counselors: 11.0 (400.9 to 1)
Current Spending: ($ per student per year):
Total: $7,049; Instruction: $4,425; Support Services: $2,203
Enrollment, Drop-out Rates and Diploma Recipients by Race/Ethnicity

Category	Total	White	Black	Asian	AIAN	Hisp.
Enrollment (%)	100.0	76.3	22.4	0.4	0.0	0.8
Drop-out Rate (%)	6.0	6.2	5.3	0.0	0.0	16.7
H.S. Diplomas (#)	221	174	44	2	0	1

Hart County

Hart County
284 Campbell Dr · Hartwell, GA 30643-0643
(706) 376-5141 · http://www.pioneer.resa.k12.ga.us
Grade Span: PK-12; **Agency Type:** 1
Schools: 7
  3 Primary; 1 Middle; 1 High; 2 Other Level
  5 Regular; 1 Special Education; 0 Vocational; 1 Alternative
  0 Magnet; 0 Charter; 3 Title I Eligible; 0 School-wide Title I
Students: 3,562 (53.6% male; 46.3% female)
  Individual Education Program: 415 (11.7%);
  English Language Learner: 49 (1.4%); Migrant: 11 (0.3%)
  Eligible for Free Lunch Program: 1,311 (36.8%)
  Eligible for Reduced-Price Lunch Program: 348 (9.8%)
Teachers: 216.6 (16.4 to 1)
Librarians/Media Specialists: 5.0 (712.4 to 1)
Guidance Counselors: 7.0 (508.9 to 1)
Current Spending: ($ per student per year):
Total: $7,616; Instruction: $4,992; Support Services: $2,227
Enrollment, Drop-out Rates and Diploma Recipients by Race/Ethnicity

Category	Total	White	Black	Asian	AIAN	Hisp.
Enrollment (%)	100.0	69.8	27.4	0.7	0.0	2.0
Drop-out Rate (%)	5.8	5.5	6.4	0.0	n/a	14.3
H.S. Diplomas (#)	211	155	54	2	0	0

Heard County

Heard County
131 E Court Square · Franklin, GA 30217-0217
Mailing Address: 131 E Court Square P.O. Bo · Franklin, GA 30217-0217
(706) 675-3320 · http://www.heard.k12.ga.us
Grade Span: PK-12; **Agency Type:** 1
Schools: 6
  3 Primary; 1 Middle; 1 High; 1 Other Level
  5 Regular; 1 Special Education; 0 Vocational; 0 Alternative
  0 Magnet; 0 Charter; 3 Title I Eligible; 3 School-wide Title I
Students: 2,147 (51.2% male; 48.7% female)
  Individual Education Program: 256 (11.9%);
  English Language Learner: 0 (0.0%); Migrant: 0 (0.0%)
  Eligible for Free Lunch Program: 891 (41.5%)
  Eligible for Reduced-Price Lunch Program: 231 (10.8%)
Teachers: 140.2 (15.3 to 1)
Librarians/Media Specialists: 4.0 (536.8 to 1)
Guidance Counselors: 4.0 (536.8 to 1)
Current Spending: ($ per student per year):
Total: $6,713; Instruction: $4,388; Support Services: $1,945
Enrollment, Drop-out Rates and Diploma Recipients by Race/Ethnicity

Category	Total	White	Black	Asian	AIAN	Hisp.
Enrollment (%)	100.0	87.3	11.6	0.1	0.0	0.9
Drop-out Rate (%)	4.5	4.5	5.1	0.0	n/a	0.0
H.S. Diplomas (#)	69	67	1	1	0	0

Henry County

Henry County
396 Tomlinson St · Mcdonough, GA 30253-0253
(770) 957-6601 · http://www.henry.k12.ga.us/
Grade Span: PK-12; **Agency Type:** 1
Schools: 32
  17 Primary; 7 Middle; 4 High; 4 Other Level
  29 Regular; 1 Special Education; 0 Vocational; 2 Alternative
  0 Magnet; 0 Charter; 7 Title I Eligible; 0 School-wide Title I
Students: 29,843 (51.2% male; 48.7% female)
  Individual Education Program: 3,421 (11.5%);
  English Language Learner: 373 (1.2%); Migrant: 0 (0.0%)
  Eligible for Free Lunch Program: 5,202 (17.4%)
  Eligible for Reduced-Price Lunch Program: 1,716 (5.8%)
Teachers: 1,843.9 (16.2 to 1)
Librarians/Media Specialists: 33.0 (904.3 to 1)
Guidance Counselors: 63.0 (473.7 to 1)
Current Spending: ($ per student per year):
Total: $6,571; Instruction: $4,419; Support Services: $1,864
Enrollment, Drop-out Rates and Diploma Recipients by Race/Ethnicity

Category	Total	White	Black	Asian	AIAN	Hisp.
Enrollment (%)	100.0	66.1	28.0	2.1	0.2	3.6
Drop-out Rate (%)	4.0	3.9	4.6	0.6	0.0	6.5
H.S. Diplomas (#)	1,157	878	222	38	0	19

Houston County

Houston County
1100 Main St • Perry, GA 31069-1069
(478) 988-6200 • http://www.houston.k12.ga.us
Grade Span: PK-12; **Agency Type:** 1
Schools: 37
  22 Primary; 8 Middle; 6 High; 1 Other Level
  34 Regular; 1 Special Education; 0 Vocational; 2 Alternative
  0 Magnet; 0 Charter; 15 Title I Eligible; 10 School-wide Title I
Students: 23,395 (51.9% male; 48.0% female)
  Individual Education Program: 3,141 (13.4%);
  English Language Learner: 215 (0.9%); Migrant: 61 (0.3%)
  Eligible for Free Lunch Program: 7,015 (30.0%)
  Eligible for Reduced-Price Lunch Program: 2,241 (9.6%)
Teachers: 1,527.7 (15.3 to 1)
Librarians/Media Specialists: 35.0 (668.4 to 1)
Guidance Counselors: 46.0 (508.6 to 1)
Current Spending: ($ per student per year):
  Total: $7,469; Instruction: $5,002; Support Services: $2,091
Enrollment, Drop-out Rates and Diploma Recipients by Race/Ethnicity

Category	Total	White	Black	Asian	AIAN	Hisp.
Enrollment (%)	100.0	61.8	33.1	1.8	0.2	3.0
Drop-out Rate (%)	5.8	5.8	5.7	2.7	7.1	10.9
H.S. Diplomas (#)	1,208	760	390	34	2	22

Irwin County

Irwin County
210 Apple St • Ocilla, GA 31774-1774
(229) 468-7485 • http://www.irwin.k12.ga.us
Grade Span: PK-12; **Agency Type:** 1
Schools: 5
  1 Primary; 1 Middle; 1 High; 2 Other Level
  3 Regular; 1 Special Education; 0 Vocational; 1 Alternative
  0 Magnet; 0 Charter; 2 Title I Eligible; 2 School-wide Title I
Students: 1,822 (50.4% male; 49.5% female)
  Individual Education Program: 348 (19.1%);
  English Language Learner: 0 (0.0%); Migrant: 16 (0.9%)
  Eligible for Free Lunch Program: 947 (52.0%)
  Eligible for Reduced-Price Lunch Program: 223 (12.2%)
Teachers: 117.5 (15.5 to 1)
Librarians/Media Specialists: 2.0 (911.0 to 1)
Guidance Counselors: 5.0 (364.4 to 1)
Current Spending: ($ per student per year):
  Total: $8,432; Instruction: $5,310; Support Services: $2,660
Enrollment, Drop-out Rates and Diploma Recipients by Race/Ethnicity

Category	Total	White	Black	Asian	AIAN	Hisp.
Enrollment (%)	100.0	62.2	36.2	0.2	0.0	1.4
Drop-out Rate (%)	8.0	6.4	10.3	0.0	n/a	0.0
H.S. Diplomas (#)	77	42	35	0	0	0

Jackson County

Jackson County
1660 Winder Hwy • Jefferson, GA 30549-0549
(706) 367-5151 • http://www.jackson.k12.ga.us/
Grade Span: PK-12; **Agency Type:** 1
Schools: 13
  7 Primary; 2 Middle; 2 High; 2 Other Level
  10 Regular; 1 Special Education; 0 Vocational; 2 Alternative
  0 Magnet; 0 Charter; 0 Title I Eligible; 0 School-wide Title I
Students: 5,679 (52.1% male; 47.8% female)
  Individual Education Program: 878 (15.5%);
  English Language Learner: 88 (1.5%); Migrant: 30 (0.5%)
  Eligible for Free Lunch Program: 1,932 (34.0%)
  Eligible for Reduced-Price Lunch Program: 604 (10.6%)
Teachers: 354.7 (16.0 to 1)
Librarians/Media Specialists: 11.0 (516.3 to 1)
Guidance Counselors: 11.0 (516.3 to 1)
Current Spending: ($ per student per year):
  Total: $7,886; Instruction: $4,767; Support Services: $2,623
Enrollment, Drop-out Rates and Diploma Recipients by Race/Ethnicity

Category	Total	White	Black	Asian	AIAN	Hisp.
Enrollment (%)	100.0	87.9	4.7	2.0	0.6	4.8
Drop-out Rate (%)	9.8	9.8	12.2	6.3	0.0	6.7
H.S. Diplomas (#)	236	205	22	8	0	1

Jefferson City
575 Washington St • Jefferson, GA 30549-0549
(706) 367-2880
Grade Span: KG-12; **Agency Type:** 1
Schools: 4
  1 Primary; 1 Middle; 1 High; 1 Other Level
  3 Regular; 1 Special Education; 0 Vocational; 0 Alternative

  0 Magnet; 0 Charter; 1 Title I Eligible; 0 School-wide Title I
Students: 1,704 (51.4% male; 48.5% female)
  Individual Education Program: 179 (10.5%);
  English Language Learner: 38 (2.2%); Migrant: 3 (0.2%)
  Eligible for Free Lunch Program: 382 (22.4%)
  Eligible for Reduced-Price Lunch Program: 84 (4.9%)
Teachers: 111.3 (15.3 to 1)
Librarians/Media Specialists: 3.0 (568.0 to 1)
Guidance Counselors: 3.5 (486.9 to 1)
Current Spending: ($ per student per year):
  Total: $7,468; Instruction: $4,955; Support Services: $2,145
Enrollment, Drop-out Rates and Diploma Recipients by Race/Ethnicity

Category	Total	White	Black	Asian	AIAN	Hisp.
Enrollment (%)	100.0	82.3	12.4	1.4	0.1	3.8
Drop-out Rate (%)	2.2	2.1	2.9	0.0	0.0	0.0
H.S. Diplomas (#)	65	57	6	1	0	1

Jasper County

Jasper County
1125-A Fred Smith St • Monticello, GA 31064-1064
(706) 468-6350 • http://www.jasper.k12.ga.us
Grade Span: PK-12; **Agency Type:** 1
Schools: 6
  2 Primary; 1 Middle; 1 High; 2 Other Level
  4 Regular; 1 Special Education; 0 Vocational; 1 Alternative
  0 Magnet; 0 Charter; 2 Title I Eligible; 2 School-wide Title I
Students: 2,094 (50.6% male; 49.3% female)
  Individual Education Program: 323 (15.4%);
  English Language Learner: 35 (1.7%); Migrant: 0 (0.0%)
  Eligible for Free Lunch Program: 1,020 (48.7%)
  Eligible for Reduced-Price Lunch Program: 200 (9.6%)
Teachers: 136.7 (15.3 to 1)
Librarians/Media Specialists: 3.0 (698.0 to 1)
Guidance Counselors: 4.0 (523.5 to 1)
Current Spending: ($ per student per year):
  Total: $6,675; Instruction: $4,022; Support Services: $2,195
Enrollment, Drop-out Rates and Diploma Recipients by Race/Ethnicity

Category	Total	White	Black	Asian	AIAN	Hisp.
Enrollment (%)	100.0	64.2	32.4	0.2	0.0	3.1
Drop-out Rate (%)	10.3	12.2	7.6	n/a	n/a	0.0
H.S. Diplomas (#)	74	48	25	0	0	1

Jeff Davis County

Jeff Davis County
44 Charles Rogers Blvd • Hazlehurst, GA 31539-1539
(912) 375-6700 • http://www.jeff-davis.k12.ga.us
Grade Span: PK-12; **Agency Type:** 1
Schools: 6
  2 Primary; 1 Middle; 1 High; 2 Other Level
  4 Regular; 1 Special Education; 0 Vocational; 1 Alternative
  0 Magnet; 0 Charter; 4 Title I Eligible; 4 School-wide Title I
Students: 2,593 (50.3% male; 49.6% female)
  Individual Education Program: 336 (13.0%);
  English Language Learner: 76 (2.9%); Migrant: 174 (6.7%)
  Eligible for Free Lunch Program: 1,248 (48.1%)
  Eligible for Reduced-Price Lunch Program: 266 (10.3%)
Teachers: 152.3 (17.0 to 1)
Librarians/Media Specialists: 4.1 (632.4 to 1)
Guidance Counselors: 5.0 (518.6 to 1)
Current Spending: ($ per student per year):
  Total: $8,111; Instruction: $5,465; Support Services: $2,221
Enrollment, Drop-out Rates and Diploma Recipients by Race/Ethnicity

Category	Total	White	Black	Asian	AIAN	Hisp.
Enrollment (%)	100.0	76.1	15.7	0.3	0.1	7.8
Drop-out Rate (%)	7.9	7.9	7.2	0.0	n/a	17.6
H.S. Diplomas (#)	157	118	36	0	0	3

Jefferson County

Jefferson County
1001 Peachtree St • Louisville, GA 30434-0434
(478) 625-7626 • http://www.jefferson.k12.ga.us
Grade Span: PK-12; **Agency Type:** 1
Schools: 8
  3 Primary; 2 Middle; 1 High; 2 Other Level
  6 Regular; 1 Special Education; 0 Vocational; 1 Alternative
  0 Magnet; 0 Charter; 6 Title I Eligible; 6 School-wide Title I
Students: 3,402 (51.2% male; 48.7% female)
  Individual Education Program: 471 (13.8%);
  English Language Learner: 19 (0.6%); Migrant: 12 (0.4%)
  Eligible for Free Lunch Program: 2,675 (78.6%)
  Eligible for Reduced-Price Lunch Program: 239 (7.0%)
Teachers: 185.7 (18.3 to 1)

Librarians/Media Specialists: 6.0 (567.0 to 1)
Guidance Counselors: 7.0 (486.0 to 1)
Current Spending: ($ per student per year):
  Total: $7,211; Instruction: $4,440; Support Services: $2,319
Enrollment, Drop-out Rates and Diploma Recipients by Race/Ethnicity

Category	Total	White	Black	Asian	AIAN	Hisp.
Enrollment (%)	100.0	24.1	74.8	0.1	0.0	1.0
Drop-out Rate (%)	5.2	4.7	5.2	0.0	n/a	25.0
H.S. Diplomas (#)	146	41	105	0	0	0

Jenkins County

Jenkins County
527 Barney Ave • Millen, GA 30442-0442
(478) 982-6000 • http://www.jenkins.k12.ga.us
Grade Span: PK-12; **Agency Type:** 1
Schools: 5
  1 Primary; 1 Middle; 1 High; 2 Other Level
  3 Regular; 1 Special Education; 0 Vocational; 1 Alternative
  0 Magnet; 0 Charter; 1 Title I Eligible; 1 School-wide Title I
Students: 1,721 (52.5% male; 47.4% female)
  Individual Education Program: 247 (14.4%);
  English Language Learner: 0 (0.0%); Migrant: 41 (2.4%)
  Eligible for Free Lunch Program: 1,118 (65.0%)
  Eligible for Reduced-Price Lunch Program: 212 (12.3%)
Teachers: 115.1 (15.0 to 1)
Librarians/Media Specialists: 2.0 (860.5 to 1)
Guidance Counselors: 4.0 (430.3 to 1)
Current Spending: ($ per student per year):
  Total: $7,227; Instruction: $4,649; Support Services: $2,071
Enrollment, Drop-out Rates and Diploma Recipients by Race/Ethnicity

Category	Total	White	Black	Asian	AIAN	Hisp.
Enrollment (%)	100.0	44.5	53.1	0.0	0.0	2.4
Drop-out Rate (%)	12.1	9.4	13.7	n/a	n/a	40.0
H.S. Diplomas (#)	79	35	44	0	0	0

Jones County

Jones County
125 Stewart Ave • Gray, GA 31032-1032
(478) 986-6580 • http://www.jones.k12.ga.us/
Grade Span: PK-12; **Agency Type:** 1
Schools: 10
  4 Primary; 2 Middle; 1 High; 3 Other Level
  7 Regular; 2 Special Education; 0 Vocational; 1 Alternative
  0 Magnet; 0 Charter; 2 Title I Eligible; 0 School-wide Title I
Students: 5,187 (51.8% male; 48.1% female)
  Individual Education Program: 612 (11.8%);
  English Language Learner: 1 (<0.1%); Migrant: 0 (0.0%)
  Eligible for Free Lunch Program: 1,338 (25.8%)
  Eligible for Reduced-Price Lunch Program: 377 (7.3%)
Teachers: 296.0 (17.5 to 1)
Librarians/Media Specialists: 8.0 (648.4 to 1)
Guidance Counselors: 9.5 (546.0 to 1)
Current Spending: ($ per student per year):
  Total: $6,070; Instruction: $3,972; Support Services: $1,771
Enrollment, Drop-out Rates and Diploma Recipients by Race/Ethnicity

Category	Total	White	Black	Asian	AIAN	Hisp.
Enrollment (%)	100.0	73.9	24.8	0.6	0.1	0.6
Drop-out Rate (%)	8.2	8.2	8.3	0.0	n/a	0.0
H.S. Diplomas (#)	240	191	49	0	0	0

Lamar County

Lamar County
Three Trojan Way • Barnesville, GA 30204
(706) 358-1159 • http://www.lamar.k12.ga.us
Grade Span: PK-12; **Agency Type:** 1
Schools: 4
  1 Primary; 1 Middle; 1 High; 1 Other Level
  3 Regular; 1 Special Education; 0 Vocational; 0 Alternative
  0 Magnet; 0 Charter; 2 Title I Eligible; 2 School-wide Title I
Students: 2,592 (50.3% male; 49.6% female)
  Individual Education Program: 267 (10.3%);
  English Language Learner: 0 (0.0%); Migrant: 0 (0.0%)
  Eligible for Free Lunch Program: 1,202 (46.4%)
  Eligible for Reduced-Price Lunch Program: 297 (11.5%)
Teachers: 141.7 (18.3 to 1)
Librarians/Media Specialists: 3.0 (864.0 to 1)
Guidance Counselors: 5.0 (518.4 to 1)
Current Spending: ($ per student per year):
  Total: $6,791; Instruction: $4,142; Support Services: $2,214

Enrollment, Drop-out Rates and Diploma Recipients by Race/Ethnicity

Category	Total	White	Black	Asian	AIAN	Hisp.
Enrollment (%)	100.0	58.9	39.6	0.6	0.1	0.8
Drop-out Rate (%)	5.9	5.9	6.0	0.0	n/a	0.0
H.S. Diplomas (#)	106	69	37	0	0	0

Laurens County

Dublin City
207 Shamrock Dr • Dublin, GA 31021-1021
(478) 272-3440 • http://www.dublinirish.org/
Grade Span: PK-12; **Agency Type:** 1
Schools: 8
  2 Primary; 2 Middle; 1 High; 3 Other Level
  5 Regular; 2 Special Education; 0 Vocational; 1 Alternative
  0 Magnet; 0 Charter; 2 Title I Eligible; 2 School-wide Title I
Students: 3,174 (51.8% male; 48.1% female)
  Individual Education Program: 521 (16.4%);
  English Language Learner: 15 (0.5%); Migrant: 10 (0.3%)
  Eligible for Free Lunch Program: 1,894 (59.7%)
  Eligible for Reduced-Price Lunch Program: 248 (7.8%)
Teachers: 230.7 (13.8 to 1)
Librarians/Media Specialists: 5.0 (634.8 to 1)
Guidance Counselors: 6.9 (460.0 to 1)
Current Spending: ($ per student per year):
  Total: $7,746; Instruction: $4,888; Support Services: $2,405
Enrollment, Drop-out Rates and Diploma Recipients by Race/Ethnicity

Category	Total	White	Black	Asian	AIAN	Hisp.
Enrollment (%)	100.0	24.7	72.7	1.4	0.2	1.0
Drop-out Rate (%)	8.6	2.5	12.4	0.0	n/a	16.7
H.S. Diplomas (#)	148	89	57	2	0	0

Laurens County
467 Firetower Rd • Dublin, GA 31021
(478) 272-4767 • http://www.lcboe.net/
Grade Span: PK-12; **Agency Type:** 1
Schools: 10
  4 Primary; 2 Middle; 2 High; 2 Other Level
  8 Regular; 1 Special Education; 0 Vocational; 1 Alternative
  0 Magnet; 0 Charter; 3 Title I Eligible; 3 School-wide Title I
Students: 6,121 (51.8% male; 48.1% female)
  Individual Education Program: 653 (10.7%);
  English Language Learner: 41 (0.7%); Migrant: 87 (1.4%)
  Eligible for Free Lunch Program: 2,954 (48.3%)
  Eligible for Reduced-Price Lunch Program: 590 (9.6%)
Teachers: 381.0 (16.1 to 1)
Librarians/Media Specialists: 9.5 (644.3 to 1)
Guidance Counselors: 13.0 (470.8 to 1)
Current Spending: ($ per student per year):
  Total: $6,576; Instruction: $4,461; Support Services: $1,690
Enrollment, Drop-out Rates and Diploma Recipients by Race/Ethnicity

Category	Total	White	Black	Asian	AIAN	Hisp.
Enrollment (%)	100.0	66.5	31.4	0.3	0.1	1.8
Drop-out Rate (%)	4.6	5.4	2.7	0.0	n/a	36.4
H.S. Diplomas (#)	307	203	103	0	0	1

Lee County

Lee County
126 Starksville Ave N • Leesburg, GA 31763-1763
Mailing Address: PO Box 399 (126 Starksvill • Leesburg, GA 31763-1763
(229) 903-2100 • http://www.lee.k12.ga.us
Grade Span: PK-12; **Agency Type:** 1
Schools: 8
  4 Primary; 1 Middle; 1 High; 2 Other Level
  6 Regular; 1 Special Education; 0 Vocational; 1 Alternative
  0 Magnet; 0 Charter; 2 Title I Eligible; 0 School-wide Title I
Students: 5,449 (50.8% male; 49.1% female)
  Individual Education Program: 481 (8.8%);
  English Language Learner: 0 (0.0%); Migrant: 0 (0.0%)
  Eligible for Free Lunch Program: 1,319 (24.2%)
  Eligible for Reduced-Price Lunch Program: 349 (6.4%)
Teachers: 320.3 (17.0 to 1)
Librarians/Media Specialists: 8.0 (681.1 to 1)
Guidance Counselors: 11.0 (495.4 to 1)
Current Spending: ($ per student per year):
  Total: $6,459; Instruction: $4,257; Support Services: $1,878
Enrollment, Drop-out Rates and Diploma Recipients by Race/Ethnicity

Category	Total	White	Black	Asian	AIAN	Hisp.
Enrollment (%)	100.0	83.4	14.4	1.1	0.2	0.8
Drop-out Rate (%)	2.8	2.3	5.6	0.0	0.0	0.0
H.S. Diplomas (#)	291	254	31	4	0	2

Liberty County

Liberty County
110 S Gause St · Hinesville, GA 31313-1313
(912) 876-2161 · http://www.liberty.k12.ga.us
Grade Span: PK-12; **Agency Type:** 1
Schools: 17
   8 Primary; 3 Middle; 1 High; 5 Other Level
   13 Regular; 3 Special Education; 0 Vocational; 1 Alternative
   0 Magnet; 0 Charter; 10 Title I Eligible; 10 School-wide Title I
Students: 11,615 (50.3% male; 49.6% female)
   Individual Education Program: 1,351 (11.6%);
   English Language Learner: 87 (0.7%); Migrant: 3 (<0.1%)
   Eligible for Free Lunch Program: 4,254 (36.6%)
   Eligible for Reduced-Price Lunch Program: 1,767 (15.2%)
Teachers: 615.1 (18.9 to 1)
Librarians/Media Specialists: 16.0 (725.9 to 1)
Guidance Counselors: 22.0 (528.0 to 1)
Current Spending: ($ per student per year):
   Total: $6,925; Instruction: $4,469; Support Services: $2,066
Enrollment, Drop-out Rates and Diploma Recipients by Race/Ethnicity

Category	Total	White	Black	Asian	AIAN	Hisp.
Enrollment (%)	100.0	34.9	56.5	1.8	0.3	6.5
Drop-out Rate (%)	4.3	4.4	4.5	3.5	0.0	3.0
H.S. Diplomas (#)	505	172	275	11	0	47

Long County

Long County
Mcdonald St · Ludowici, GA 31316-1316
(912) 545-2367 · http://www.long.k12.ga.us
Grade Span: PK-12; **Agency Type:** 1
Schools: 3
   1 Primary; 0 Middle; 0 High; 2 Other Level
   2 Regular; 1 Special Education; 0 Vocational; 0 Alternative
   0 Magnet; 0 Charter; 2 Title I Eligible; 2 School-wide Title I
Students: 2,069 (51.2% male; 48.7% female)
   Individual Education Program: 204 (9.9%);
   English Language Learner: 129 (6.2%); Migrant: 221 (10.7%)
   Eligible for Free Lunch Program: 1,099 (53.1%)
   Eligible for Reduced-Price Lunch Program: 280 (13.5%)
Teachers: 105.7 (19.6 to 1)
Librarians/Media Specialists: 2.0 (1,034.5 to 1)
Guidance Counselors: 3.0 (689.7 to 1)
Current Spending: ($ per student per year):
   Total: $5,986; Instruction: $3,755; Support Services: $1,793
Enrollment, Drop-out Rates and Diploma Recipients by Race/Ethnicity

Category	Total	White	Black	Asian	AIAN	Hisp.
Enrollment (%)	100.0	62.4	25.3	1.0	0.4	10.9
Drop-out Rate (%)	10.8	10.3	10.3	0.0	0.0	24.0
H.S. Diplomas (#)	75	46	27	1	0	1

Lowndes County

Lowndes County
1592 Norman Dr · Valdosta, GA 31603-1227
(229) 245-2250 · http://www.lowndes.k12.ga.us
Grade Span: PK-12; **Agency Type:** 1
Schools: 12
   7 Primary; 2 Middle; 1 High; 2 Other Level
   10 Regular; 1 Special Education; 0 Vocational; 1 Alternative
   0 Magnet; 0 Charter; 7 Title I Eligible; 3 School-wide Title I
Students: 9,298 (51.3% male; 48.6% female)
   Individual Education Program: 1,429 (15.4%);
   English Language Learner: 59 (0.6%); Migrant: 79 (0.8%)
   Eligible for Free Lunch Program: 2,683 (28.9%)
   Eligible for Reduced-Price Lunch Program: 844 (9.1%)
Teachers: 598.6 (15.5 to 1)
Librarians/Media Specialists: 13.0 (715.2 to 1)
Guidance Counselors: 18.0 (516.6 to 1)
Current Spending: ($ per student per year):
   Total: $7,346; Instruction: $4,783; Support Services: $2,180
Enrollment, Drop-out Rates and Diploma Recipients by Race/Ethnicity

Category	Total	White	Black	Asian	AIAN	Hisp.
Enrollment (%)	100.0	72.6	23.3	1.0	0.2	3.1
Drop-out Rate (%)	6.5	6.8	5.2	11.1	25.0	7.9
H.S. Diplomas (#)	468	341	114	5	2	6

Valdosta City
1204 Williams St · Valdosta, GA 31603-5407
Mailing Address: PO Box 5407 1204 Williams S · Valdosta, GA 31603-5407
(229) 333-8500 · http://wildcat.gocats.org/
Grade Span: PK-12; **Agency Type:** 1
Schools: 11
   4 Primary; 4 Middle; 1 High; 2 Other Level

   9 Regular; 1 Special Education; 0 Vocational; 1 Alternative
   0 Magnet; 0 Charter; 7 Title I Eligible; 6 School-wide Title I
Students: 7,062 (50.3% male; 49.6% female)
   Individual Education Program: 1,064 (15.1%);
   English Language Learner: 52 (0.7%); Migrant: 21 (0.3%)
   Eligible for Free Lunch Program: 4,253 (60.2%)
   Eligible for Reduced-Price Lunch Program: 606 (8.6%)
Teachers: 461.3 (15.3 to 1)
Librarians/Media Specialists: 12.0 (588.5 to 1)
Guidance Counselors: 15.0 (470.8 to 1)
Current Spending: ($ per student per year):
   Total: $6,889; Instruction: $4,540; Support Services: $1,904
Enrollment, Drop-out Rates and Diploma Recipients by Race/Ethnicity

Category	Total	White	Black	Asian	AIAN	Hisp.
Enrollment (%)	100.0	22.4	74.4	1.5	0.2	1.5
Drop-out Rate (%)	10.4	6.6	12.2	3.0	0.0	11.5
H.S. Diplomas (#)	305	120	174	10	0	0

Lumpkin County

Lumpkin County
51 Mountain View Dr · Dahlonega, GA 30533-0533
(706) 864-3611 · http://www.lumpkin.k12.ga.us
Grade Span: PK-12; **Agency Type:** 1
Schools: 7
   3 Primary; 1 Middle; 1 High; 2 Other Level
   5 Regular; 1 Special Education; 0 Vocational; 1 Alternative
   0 Magnet; 0 Charter; 4 Title I Eligible; 4 School-wide Title I
Students: 3,549 (52.2% male; 47.7% female)
   Individual Education Program: 466 (13.1%);
   English Language Learner: 37 (1.0%); Migrant: 22 (0.6%)
   Eligible for Free Lunch Program: 1,037 (29.2%)
   Eligible for Reduced-Price Lunch Program: 292 (8.2%)
Teachers: 226.5 (15.7 to 1)
Librarians/Media Specialists: 5.0 (709.8 to 1)
Guidance Counselors: 8.0 (443.6 to 1)
Current Spending: ($ per student per year):
   Total: $7,421; Instruction: $4,635; Support Services: $2,480
Enrollment, Drop-out Rates and Diploma Recipients by Race/Ethnicity

Category	Total	White	Black	Asian	AIAN	Hisp.
Enrollment (%)	100.0	92.0	1.6	0.7	0.5	5.2
Drop-out Rate (%)	4.7	4.7	0.0	0.0	0.0	8.6
H.S. Diplomas (#)	141	130	3	1	1	6

Macon County

Macon County
Hwy 49 · Oglethorpe, GA 31068-1068
(478) 472-8188 · http://www.macon.k12.ga.us./
Grade Span: PK-12; **Agency Type:** 1
Schools: 4
   1 Primary; 1 Middle; 1 High; 1 Other Level
   3 Regular; 0 Special Education; 0 Vocational; 1 Alternative
   0 Magnet; 0 Charter; 1 Title I Eligible; 1 School-wide Title I
Students: 2,160 (50.7% male; 49.2% female)
   Individual Education Program: 204 (9.4%);
   English Language Learner: 48 (2.2%); Migrant: 69 (3.2%)
   Eligible for Free Lunch Program: 1,508 (69.8%)
   Eligible for Reduced-Price Lunch Program: 268 (12.4%)
Teachers: 133.2 (16.2 to 1)
Librarians/Media Specialists: 4.0 (540.0 to 1)
Guidance Counselors: 5.0 (432.0 to 1)
Current Spending: ($ per student per year):
   Total: $7,954; Instruction: $4,720; Support Services: $2,698
Enrollment, Drop-out Rates and Diploma Recipients by Race/Ethnicity

Category	Total	White	Black	Asian	AIAN	Hisp.
Enrollment (%)	100.0	11.4	84.0	1.5	0.0	3.1
Drop-out Rate (%)	8.7	9.1	8.6	0.0	n/a	50.0
H.S. Diplomas (#)	76	15	60	1	0	0

Madison County

Madison County
55 Mary Ellen Court · Danielsville, GA 30633-0633
(706) 795-2191 · http://www.madison.k12.ga.us
Grade Span: PK-12; **Agency Type:** 1
Schools: 9
   5 Primary; 1 Middle; 1 High; 2 Other Level
   7 Regular; 1 Special Education; 0 Vocational; 1 Alternative
   0 Magnet; 0 Charter; 6 Title I Eligible; 5 School-wide Title I
Students: 4,636 (51.1% male; 48.8% female)
   Individual Education Program: 778 (16.8%);
   English Language Learner: 57 (1.2%); Migrant: 2 (<0.1%)
   Eligible for Free Lunch Program: 1,506 (32.5%)
   Eligible for Reduced-Price Lunch Program: 479 (10.3%)

Teachers: 291.4 (15.9 to 1)
Librarians/Media Specialists: 9.0 (515.1 to 1)
Guidance Counselors: 10.0 (463.6 to 1)
Current Spending: ($ per student per year):
  Total: $7,104; Instruction: $4,644; Support Services: $2,106
Enrollment, Drop-out Rates and Diploma Recipients by Race/Ethnicity

Category	Total	White	Black	Asian	AIAN	Hisp.
Enrollment (%)	100.0	88.4	9.2	0.2	0.0	2.2
Drop-out Rate (%)	6.4	6.5	5.2	n/a	n/a	8.7
H.S. Diplomas (#)	191	168	22	0	0	1

Marion County

Marion County
1697 Pineville Rd • Buena Vista, GA 31803-1803
(229) 649-2234 • http://www.marion.k12.ga.us
Grade Span: PK-12; **Agency Type:** 1
Schools: 4
  1 Primary; 1 Middle; 1 High; 1 Other Level
  3 Regular; 1 Special Education; 0 Vocational; 0 Alternative
  0 Magnet; 0 Charter; 3 Title I Eligible; 0 School-wide Title I
Students: 1,715 (50.6% male; 49.3% female)
  Individual Education Program: 166 (9.7%);
  English Language Learner: 62 (3.6%); Migrant: 47 (2.7%)
  Eligible for Free Lunch Program: 957 (55.8%)
  Eligible for Reduced-Price Lunch Program: 186 (10.8%)
Teachers: 106.4 (16.1 to 1)
Librarians/Media Specialists: 3.0 (571.7 to 1)
Guidance Counselors: 3.0 (571.7 to 1)
Current Spending: ($ per student per year):
  Total: $7,686; Instruction: $4,313; Support Services: $2,876
Enrollment, Drop-out Rates and Diploma Recipients by Race/Ethnicity

Category	Total	White	Black	Asian	AIAN	Hisp.
Enrollment (%)	100.0	54.8	40.0	0.9	0.1	4.1
Drop-out Rate (%)	12.9	10.7	11.5	n/a	100.0	87.5
H.S. Diplomas (#)	108	53	55	0	0	0

Mcduffie County

Mcduffie County
716 N Lee St • Thomson, GA 30824-0824
(706) 595-1918 • http://www.mcduffie.k12.ga.us
Grade Span: PK-12; **Agency Type:** 1
Schools: 8
  3 Primary; 2 Middle; 1 High; 2 Other Level
  6 Regular; 1 Special Education; 0 Vocational; 1 Alternative
  0 Magnet; 0 Charter; 4 Title I Eligible; 4 School-wide Title I
Students: 4,310 (51.5% male; 48.4% female)
  Individual Education Program: 541 (12.6%);
  English Language Learner: 21 (0.5%); Migrant: 7 (0.2%)
  Eligible for Free Lunch Program: 2,325 (53.9%)
  Eligible for Reduced-Price Lunch Program: 361 (8.4%)
Teachers: 264.4 (16.3 to 1)
Librarians/Media Specialists: 7.0 (615.7 to 1)
Guidance Counselors: 10.4 (414.4 to 1)
Current Spending: ($ per student per year):
  Total: $6,751; Instruction: $4,361; Support Services: $2,015
Enrollment, Drop-out Rates and Diploma Recipients by Race/Ethnicity

Category	Total	White	Black	Asian	AIAN	Hisp.
Enrollment (%)	100.0	48.7	49.4	0.3	0.0	1.5
Drop-out Rate (%)	6.6	7.0	6.5	0.0	n/a	0.0
H.S. Diplomas (#)	231	122	103	3	0	3

Mcintosh County

Mcintosh County
200 Pine St • Darien, GA 31305-1305
(912) 437-6645 • http://www.mcintosh.k12.ga.us/
Grade Span: PK-12; **Agency Type:** 1
Schools: 4
  1 Primary; 1 Middle; 1 High; 1 Other Level
  3 Regular; 1 Special Education; 0 Vocational; 0 Alternative
  0 Magnet; 0 Charter; 2 Title I Eligible; 1 School-wide Title I
Students: 1,933 (50.2% male; 49.7% female)
  Individual Education Program: 153 (7.9%)
  English Language Learner: 4 (0.2%); Migrant: 0 (0.0%)
  Eligible for Free Lunch Program: 1,228 (63.5%)
  Eligible for Reduced-Price Lunch Program: 152 (7.9%)
Teachers: 113.7 (17.0 to 1)
Librarians/Media Specialists: 2.3 (840.4 to 1)
Guidance Counselors: 4.0 (483.3 to 1)
Current Spending: ($ per student per year):
  Total: $7,339; Instruction: $4,448; Support Services: $2,369

Enrollment, Drop-out Rates and Diploma Recipients by Race/Ethnicity

Category	Total	White	Black	Asian	AIAN	Hisp.
Enrollment (%)	100.0	46.9	51.8	0.7	0.1	0.6
Drop-out Rate (%)	13.4	15.3	11.8	0.0	n/a	0.0
H.S. Diplomas (#)	69	40	28	0	0	1

Meriwether County

Meriwether County
2100 Gaston St • Greenville, GA 30222-0070
(706) 672-4297 • http://www.meriwether.k12.ga.us
Grade Span: PK-12; **Agency Type:** 1
Schools: 11
  3 Primary; 2 Middle; 2 High; 4 Other Level
  7 Regular; 3 Special Education; 0 Vocational; 1 Alternative
  0 Magnet; 0 Charter; 5 Title I Eligible; 5 School-wide Title I
Students: 3,866 (52.7% male; 47.2% female)
  Individual Education Program: 967 (25.0%);
  English Language Learner: 6 (0.2%); Migrant: 0 (0.0%)
  Eligible for Free Lunch Program: 2,639 (68.3%)
  Eligible for Reduced-Price Lunch Program: 488 (12.6%)
Teachers: 297.6 (13.0 to 1)
Librarians/Media Specialists: 7.0 (552.3 to 1)
Guidance Counselors: 8.5 (454.8 to 1)
Current Spending: ($ per student per year):
  Total: $8,809; Instruction: $5,403; Support Services: $2,941
Enrollment, Drop-out Rates and Diploma Recipients by Race/Ethnicity

Category	Total	White	Black	Asian	AIAN	Hisp.
Enrollment (%)	100.0	39.4	59.7	0.3	0.0	0.5
Drop-out Rate (%)	9.4	12.7	7.7	0.0	n/a	0.0
H.S. Diplomas (#)	138	59	79	0	0	0

Mitchell County

Mitchell County
108 S Harney St • Camilla, GA 31730-1730
(229) 336-2100 • http://www.mitchell.k12.ga.us
Grade Span: PK-12; **Agency Type:** 1
Schools: 8
  2 Primary; 1 Middle; 1 High; 4 Other Level
  5 Regular; 2 Special Education; 0 Vocational; 1 Alternative
  0 Magnet; 1 Charter; 3 Title I Eligible; 3 School-wide Title I
Students: 2,867 (51.4% male; 48.5% female)
  Individual Education Program: 371 (12.9%);
  English Language Learner: 13 (0.5%); Migrant: 53 (1.8%)
  Eligible for Free Lunch Program: 1,591 (55.5%)
  Eligible for Reduced-Price Lunch Program: 285 (9.9%)
Teachers: 202.7 (14.1 to 1)
Librarians/Media Specialists: 4.0 (716.8 to 1)
Guidance Counselors: 5.1 (562.2 to 1)
Current Spending: ($ per student per year):
  Total: $7,290; Instruction: $4,592; Support Services: $2,248
Enrollment, Drop-out Rates and Diploma Recipients by Race/Ethnicity

Category	Total	White	Black	Asian	AIAN	Hisp.
Enrollment (%)	100.0	27.8	68.8	0.4	0.1	2.9
Drop-out Rate (%)	11.0	12.8	10.6	0.0	0.0	8.3
H.S. Diplomas (#)	132	30	98	2	0	2

Pelham City
188 W Railroad St S • Pelham, GA 31779-1779
(912) 229-8715 • http://www.pelham-city.k12.ga.us/
Grade Span: PK-12; **Agency Type:** 1
Schools: 4
  1 Primary; 1 Middle; 1 High; 1 Other Level
  3 Regular; 1 Special Education; 0 Vocational; 0 Alternative
  0 Magnet; 0 Charter; 2 Title I Eligible; 2 School-wide Title I
Students: 1,583 (49.8% male; 50.1% female)
  Individual Education Program: 253 (16.0%);
  English Language Learner: 15 (0.9%); Migrant: 18 (1.1%)
  Eligible for Free Lunch Program: 954 (60.3%)
  Eligible for Reduced-Price Lunch Program: 180 (11.4%)
Teachers: 100.2 (15.8 to 1)
Librarians/Media Specialists: 2.2 (719.5 to 1)
Guidance Counselors: 3.1 (510.6 to 1)
Current Spending: ($ per student per year):
  Total: $6,823; Instruction: $4,577; Support Services: $1,819
Enrollment, Drop-out Rates and Diploma Recipients by Race/Ethnicity

Category	Total	White	Black	Asian	AIAN	Hisp.
Enrollment (%)	100.0	41.7	54.6	0.5	0.3	3.0
Drop-out Rate (%)	9.6	9.6	8.3	0.0	0.0	40.0
H.S. Diplomas (#)	73	39	31	0	0	3

Monroe County

Monroe County
25 Brooklyn Ave • Forsyth, GA 31029-1029
(478) 994-2031 • http://www.monroe.k12.ga.us/
Grade Span: PK-12; **Agency Type:** 1
Schools: 6
   2 Primary; 1 Middle; 1 High; 2 Other Level
   4 Regular; 1 Special Education; 0 Vocational; 1 Alternative
   0 Magnet; 0 Charter; 4 Title I Eligible; 4 School-wide Title I
Students: 3,820 (51.7% male; 48.2% female)
   Individual Education Program: 590 (15.4%);
   English Language Learner: 24 (0.6%); Migrant: 13 (0.3%)
   Eligible for Free Lunch Program: 1,512 (39.6%)
   Eligible for Reduced-Price Lunch Program: 293 (7.7%)
Teachers: 222.7 (17.2 to 1)
Librarians/Media Specialists: 4.0 (955.0 to 1)
Guidance Counselors: 7.3 (523.3 to 1)
Current Spending: ($ per student per year):
   Total: $7,024; Instruction: $4,394; Support Services: $2,256

Enrollment, Drop-out Rates and Diploma Recipients by Race/Ethnicity

Category	Total	White	Black	Asian	AIAN	Hisp.
Enrollment (%)	100.0	63.8	34.4	0.7	0.0	1.1
Drop-out Rate (%)	5.4	6.3	3.9	0.0	0.0	0.0
H.S. Diplomas (#)	195	133	58	0	3	1

Morgan County

Morgan County
1065 E Ave • Madison, GA 30650-0650
(706) 342-0752 • http://www.morgan.k12.ga.us
Grade Span: PK-12; **Agency Type:** 1
Schools: 6
   2 Primary; 1 Middle; 1 High; 2 Other Level
   4 Regular; 1 Special Education; 0 Vocational; 1 Alternative
   0 Magnet; 0 Charter; 2 Title I Eligible; 2 School-wide Title I
Students: 3,204 (50.3% male; 49.6% female)
   Individual Education Program: 434 (13.5%);
   English Language Learner: 20 (0.6%); Migrant: 0 (0.0%)
   Eligible for Free Lunch Program: 1,033 (32.2%)
   Eligible for Reduced-Price Lunch Program: 197 (6.1%)
Teachers: 209.2 (15.3 to 1)
Librarians/Media Specialists: 4.0 (801.0 to 1)
Guidance Counselors: 7.5 (427.2 to 1)
Current Spending: ($ per student per year):
   Total: $7,259; Instruction: $4,986; Support Services: $1,910

Enrollment, Drop-out Rates and Diploma Recipients by Race/Ethnicity

Category	Total	White	Black	Asian	AIAN	Hisp.
Enrollment (%)	100.0	64.8	32.5	0.7	0.0	2.1
Drop-out Rate (%)	3.3	3.3	3.5	0.0	0.0	0.0
H.S. Diplomas (#)	147	114	33	0	0	0

Murray County

Murray County
715 Chestnut St • Chatsworth, GA 30705-0705
(706) 695-4531 • http://www.murray.k12.ga.us
Grade Span: PK-12; **Agency Type:** 1
Schools: 10
   5 Primary; 2 Middle; 1 High; 2 Other Level
   8 Regular; 1 Special Education; 0 Vocational; 1 Alternative
   0 Magnet; 0 Charter; 8 Title I Eligible; 8 School-wide Title I
Students: 7,474 (51.6% male; 48.3% female)
   Individual Education Program: 861 (11.5%);
   English Language Learner: 188 (2.5%); Migrant: 3 (<0.1%)
   Eligible for Free Lunch Program: 2,892 (38.7%)
   Eligible for Reduced-Price Lunch Program: 1,077 (14.4%)
Teachers: 453.6 (16.5 to 1)
Librarians/Media Specialists: 9.0 (830.4 to 1)
Guidance Counselors: 14.0 (533.9 to 1)
Current Spending: ($ per student per year):
   Total: $6,725; Instruction: $4,636; Support Services: $1,667

Enrollment, Drop-out Rates and Diploma Recipients by Race/Ethnicity

Category	Total	White	Black	Asian	AIAN	Hisp.
Enrollment (%)	100.0	86.6	0.2	0.4	0.1	12.6
Drop-out Rate (%)	11.7	11.9	0.0	0.0	n/a	9.8
H.S. Diplomas (#)	218	210	1	0	0	7

Muscogee County

Muscogee County
1200 Bradley Dr • Columbus, GA 31906
Mailing Address: PO Box 2427 1200 Bradley Dr • Columbus, GA 31906
(706) 649-0500 • http://www.mindspring.com/~muscogee
Grade Span: PK-12; **Agency Type:** 1
Schools: 62
   33 Primary; 11 Middle; 8 High; 10 Other Level
   52 Regular; 4 Special Education; 0 Vocational; 6 Alternative
   7 Magnet; 0 Charter; 0 Title I Eligible; 0 School-wide Title I
Students: 33,055 (50.4% male; 49.5% female)
   Individual Education Program: 4,233 (12.8%);
   English Language Learner: 319 (1.0%); Migrant: 21 (0.1%)
   Eligible for Free Lunch Program: 15,631 (47.3%)
   Eligible for Reduced-Price Lunch Program: 2,888 (8.7%)
Teachers: 2,187.2 (15.1 to 1)
Librarians/Media Specialists: 58.1 (568.9 to 1)
Guidance Counselors: 91.3 (362.0 to 1)
Current Spending: ($ per student per year):
   Total: $7,599; Instruction: $4,788; Support Services: $2,354

Enrollment, Drop-out Rates and Diploma Recipients by Race/Ethnicity

Category	Total	White	Black	Asian	AIAN	Hisp.
Enrollment (%)	100.0	34.8	60.5	1.4	0.2	3.2
Drop-out Rate (%)	6.8	5.8	7.7	2.6	16.7	4.0
H.S. Diplomas (#)	1,502	683	731	28	3	57

Newton County

Newton County
2109 Newton Dr NE • Covington, GA 30014
(770) 787-1330 • http://www.newton.k12.ga.us
Grade Span: PK-12; **Agency Type:** 1
Schools: 20
   11 Primary; 4 Middle; 2 High; 3 Other Level
   17 Regular; 2 Special Education; 0 Vocational; 1 Alternative
   0 Magnet; 0 Charter; 12 Title I Eligible; 3 School-wide Title I
Students: 14,713 (51.4% male; 48.5% female)
   Individual Education Program: 2,021 (13.7%);
   English Language Learner: 191 (1.3%); Migrant: 0 (0.0%)
   Eligible for Free Lunch Program: 5,356 (36.4%)
   Eligible for Reduced-Price Lunch Program: 1,582 (10.8%)
Teachers: 908.9 (16.2 to 1)
Librarians/Media Specialists: 19.0 (774.4 to 1)
Guidance Counselors: 26.0 (565.9 to 1)
Current Spending: ($ per student per year):
   Total: $6,915; Instruction: $4,590; Support Services: $1,957

Enrollment, Drop-out Rates and Diploma Recipients by Race/Ethnicity

Category	Total	White	Black	Asian	AIAN	Hisp.
Enrollment (%)	100.0	57.8	37.8	0.8	0.7	2.9
Drop-out Rate (%)	5.0	4.9	5.0	7.1	3.8	8.2
H.S. Diplomas (#)	370	253	104	2	2	9

Oconee County

Oconee County
34 School St • Watkinsville, GA 30677-0677
(706) 769-5130 • http://www.oconee.k12.ga.us
Grade Span: PK-12; **Agency Type:** 1
Schools: 10
   5 Primary; 2 Middle; 1 High; 2 Other Level
   8 Regular; 2 Special Education; 0 Vocational; 0 Alternative
   0 Magnet; 0 Charter; 5 Title I Eligible; 0 School-wide Title I
Students: 5,767 (52.3% male; 47.6% female)
   Individual Education Program: 635 (11.0%);
   English Language Learner: 82 (1.4%); Migrant: 13 (0.2%)
   Eligible for Free Lunch Program: 762 (13.2%)
   Eligible for Reduced-Price Lunch Program: 249 (4.3%)
Teachers: 367.4 (15.7 to 1)
Librarians/Media Specialists: 8.0 (720.9 to 1)
Guidance Counselors: 12.0 (480.6 to 1)
Current Spending: ($ per student per year):
   Total: $6,837; Instruction: $4,558; Support Services: $1,959

Enrollment, Drop-out Rates and Diploma Recipients by Race/Ethnicity

Category	Total	White	Black	Asian	AIAN	Hisp.
Enrollment (%)	100.0	87.3	6.1	2.5	0.2	3.9
Drop-out Rate (%)	2.6	2.3	5.1	7.7	0.0	7.4
H.S. Diplomas (#)	359	328	22	6	0	3

Oglethorpe County

Oglethorpe County
735 Athens Rd • Lexington, GA 30648-0648
(706) 743-8128 • http://www.oglethorpe.k12.ga.us
Grade Span: PK-12; **Agency Type:** 1
Schools: 6
  2 Primary; 1 Middle; 1 High; 2 Other Level
  4 Regular; 1 Special Education; 0 Vocational; 1 Alternative
  0 Magnet; 0 Charter; 4 Title I Eligible; 4 School-wide Title I
Students: 2,252   (51.5% male; 48.4% female)
  Individual Education Program: 343 (15.2%);
  English Language Learner: 1 (<0.1%); Migrant: 1 (<0.1%)
  Eligible for Free Lunch Program: 783 (34.8%)
  Eligible for Reduced-Price Lunch Program: 228 (10.1%)
Teachers: 146.0 (15.4 to 1)
Librarians/Media Specialists: 4.0 (563.0 to 1)
Guidance Counselors: 5.0 (450.4 to 1)
Current Spending: ($ per student per year):
  Total: $7,455; Instruction: $4,724; Support Services: $2,415
Enrollment, Drop-out Rates and Diploma Recipients by Race/Ethnicity

Category	Total	White	Black	Asian	AIAN	Hisp.
Enrollment (%)	100.0	76.1	21.6	0.2	0.0	2.0
Drop-out Rate (%)	5.2	5.2	5.5	0.0	n/a	0.0
H.S. Diplomas (#)	86	61	23	1	0	1

Paulding County

Paulding County
522 Hardee St • Dallas, GA 30132-0132
(770) 443-8000 • http://www.paulding.k12.ga.us
Grade Span: PK-12; **Agency Type:** 1
Schools: 26
  16 Primary; 5 Middle; 3 High; 2 Other Level
  24 Regular; 1 Special Education; 0 Vocational; 1 Alternative
  0 Magnet; 0 Charter; 9 Title I Eligible; 1 School-wide Title I
Students: 20,459   (51.3% male; 48.6% female)
  Individual Education Program: 2,585 (12.6%);
  English Language Learner: 93 (0.5%); Migrant: 1 (<0.1%)
  Eligible for Free Lunch Program: 3,257 (15.9%)
  Eligible for Reduced-Price Lunch Program: 1,597 (7.8%)
Teachers: 1,257.3 (16.3 to 1)
Librarians/Media Specialists: 27.0 (757.7 to 1)
Guidance Counselors: 43.0 (475.8 to 1)
Current Spending: ($ per student per year):
  Total: $6,279; Instruction: $4,254; Support Services: $1,715
Enrollment, Drop-out Rates and Diploma Recipients by Race/Ethnicity

Category	Total	White	Black	Asian	AIAN	Hisp.
Enrollment (%)	100.0	83.0	13.9	0.3	0.4	2.4
Drop-out Rate (%)	7.7	8.2	4.3	0.0	6.3	7.8
H.S. Diplomas (#)	652	582	54	3	2	11

Peach County

Peach County
523 Vineville St • Fort Valley, GA 31030-1030
(478) 825-5933 • http://www.peach.k12.ga.us/
Grade Span: PK-12; **Agency Type:** 1
Schools: 8
  3 Primary; 2 Middle; 1 High; 2 Other Level
  6 Regular; 1 Special Education; 0 Vocational; 1 Alternative
  0 Magnet; 0 Charter; 3 Title I Eligible; 3 School-wide Title I
Students: 4,005   (50.7% male; 49.2% female)
  Individual Education Program: 490 (12.2%);
  English Language Learner: 90 (2.2%); Migrant: 225 (5.6%)
  Eligible for Free Lunch Program: 2,272 (56.7%)
  Eligible for Reduced-Price Lunch Program: 346 (8.6%)
Teachers: 256.9 (15.6 to 1)
Librarians/Media Specialists: 6.0 (667.5 to 1)
Guidance Counselors: 9.0 (445.0 to 1)
Current Spending: ($ per student per year):
  Total: $7,615; Instruction: $4,767; Support Services: $2,339
Enrollment, Drop-out Rates and Diploma Recipients by Race/Ethnicity

Category	Total	White	Black	Asian	AIAN	Hisp.
Enrollment (%)	100.0	38.7	53.4	0.6	0.1	7.2
Drop-out Rate (%)	15.4	14.3	15.4	33.3	0.0	22.6
H.S. Diplomas (#)	159	72	83	0	0	4

Pickens County

Pickens County
159 Stegall Dr • Jasper, GA 30143-0143
(706) 253-1700 • http://www.pickens.k12.ga.us/
Grade Span: PK-12; **Agency Type:** 1
Schools: 7

3 Primary; 2 Middle; 1 High; 1 Other Level
  6 Regular; 1 Special Education; 0 Vocational; 0 Alternative
  0 Magnet; 0 Charter; 5 Title I Eligible; 4 School-wide Title I
Students: 4,126   (51.3% male; 48.6% female)
  Individual Education Program: 523 (12.7%);
  English Language Learner: 27 (0.7%); Migrant: 4 (0.1%)
  Eligible for Free Lunch Program: 1,309 (31.7%)
  Eligible for Reduced-Price Lunch Program: 409 (9.9%)
Teachers: 247.7 (16.7 to 1)
Librarians/Media Specialists: 7.0 (589.4 to 1)
Guidance Counselors: 8.0 (515.8 to 1)
Current Spending: ($ per student per year):
  Total: $7,467; Instruction: $4,541; Support Services: $2,534
Enrollment, Drop-out Rates and Diploma Recipients by Race/Ethnicity

Category	Total	White	Black	Asian	AIAN	Hisp.
Enrollment (%)	100.0	96.1	1.3	0.3	0.1	2.2
Drop-out Rate (%)	6.0	6.0	0.0	0.0	n/a	16.7
H.S. Diplomas (#)	123	122	0	0	0	1

Pierce County

Pierce County
114 Strickland Ave • Blackshear, GA 31516-1516
(912) 449-2044 • http://www.pierce.k12.ga.us
Grade Span: PK-12; **Agency Type:** 1
Schools: 5
  2 Primary; 1 Middle; 1 High; 1 Other Level
  4 Regular; 1 Special Education; 0 Vocational; 0 Alternative
  0 Magnet; 0 Charter; 4 Title I Eligible; 4 School-wide Title I
Students: 3,283   (52.0% male; 47.9% female)
  Individual Education Program: 520 (15.8%);
  English Language Learner: 111 (3.4%); Migrant: 121 (3.7%)
  Eligible for Free Lunch Program: 1,398 (42.6%)
  Eligible for Reduced-Price Lunch Program: 449 (13.7%)
Teachers: 162.1 (20.3 to 1)
Librarians/Media Specialists: 4.0 (820.8 to 1)
Guidance Counselors: 7.0 (469.0 to 1)
Current Spending: ($ per student per year):
  Total: $6,951; Instruction: $4,606; Support Services: $1,929
Enrollment, Drop-out Rates and Diploma Recipients by Race/Ethnicity

Category	Total	White	Black	Asian	AIAN	Hisp.
Enrollment (%)	100.0	83.7	12.3	0.2	0.1	3.8
Drop-out Rate (%)	6.4	6.4	4.9	0.0	0.0	21.4
H.S. Diplomas (#)	115	95	19	0	0	1

Pike County

Pike County
115 W Jackson St • Zebulon, GA 30295-0295
(770) 567-8489 • http://www.pike.k12.ga.us/
Grade Span: PK-12; **Agency Type:** 1
Schools: 5
  2 Primary; 1 Middle; 1 High; 1 Other Level
  4 Regular; 1 Special Education; 0 Vocational; 0 Alternative
  0 Magnet; 0 Charter; 2 Title I Eligible; 0 School-wide Title I
Students: 3,005   (52.8% male; 47.1% female)
  Individual Education Program: 305 (10.1%);
  English Language Learner: 1 (<0.1%); Migrant: 0 (0.0%)
  Eligible for Free Lunch Program: 657 (21.9%)
  Eligible for Reduced-Price Lunch Program: 168 (5.6%)
Teachers: 158.7 (18.9 to 1)
Librarians/Media Specialists: 3.0 (1,001.7 to 1)
Guidance Counselors: 5.0 (601.0 to 1)
Current Spending: ($ per student per year):
  Total: $5,929; Instruction: $3,937; Support Services: $1,701
Enrollment, Drop-out Rates and Diploma Recipients by Race/Ethnicity

Category	Total	White	Black	Asian	AIAN	Hisp.
Enrollment (%)	100.0	84.0	14.4	0.4	0.2	1.0
Drop-out Rate (%)	7.2	7.5	6.0	0.0	n/a	0.0
H.S. Diplomas (#)	143	126	16	1	0	0

Polk County

Polk County
612 S College St • Cedartown, GA 30125-0128
(770) 748-3821 • http://polk.ga.net
Grade Span: PK-12; **Agency Type:** 1
Schools: 12
  6 Primary; 2 Middle; 2 High; 2 Other Level
  10 Regular; 1 Special Education; 0 Vocational; 1 Alternative
  0 Magnet; 0 Charter; 5 Title I Eligible; 5 School-wide Title I
Students: 7,065   (52.2% male; 47.7% female)
  Individual Education Program: 1,164 (16.5%);
  English Language Learner: 357 (5.1%); Migrant: 249 (3.5%)
  Eligible for Free Lunch Program: 2,625 (37.2%)

Eligible for Reduced-Price Lunch Program: 498 (7.0%)
Teachers: 451.3 (15.7 to 1)
Librarians/Media Specialists: 11.8 (598.7 to 1)
Guidance Counselors: 14.0 (504.6 to 1)
Current Spending: ($ per student per year):
    Total: $7,146; Instruction: $4,727; Support Services: $2,050
Enrollment, Drop-out Rates and Diploma Recipients by Race/Ethnicity

Category	Total	White	Black	Asian	AIAN	Hisp.
Enrollment (%)	100.0	72.4	16.9	0.4	0.1	10.3
Drop-out Rate (%)	10.0	9.7	10.4	0.0	50.0	13.9
H.S. Diplomas (#)	276	223	38	2	1	12

Pulaski County

Pulaski County
206 Mccormick Ave • Hawkinsville, GA 31036-1036
(478) 783-7200 • http://www.pulaski.k12.ga.us/
Grade Span: PK-12; **Agency Type:** 1
Schools: 6
    1 Primary; 1 Middle; 1 High; 3 Other Level
    3 Regular; 2 Special Education; 0 Vocational; 1 Alternative
    0 Magnet; 0 Charter; 1 Title I Eligible; 1 School-wide Title I
Students: 1,674   (51.6% male; 48.3% female)
    Individual Education Program: 243 (14.5%);
    English Language Learner: 9 (0.5%); Migrant: 14 (0.8%)
    Eligible for Free Lunch Program: 788 (47.1%)
    Eligible for Reduced-Price Lunch Program: 164 (9.8%)
Teachers: 123.0 (13.6 to 1)
Librarians/Media Specialists: 2.0 (837.0 to 1)
Guidance Counselors: 4.0 (418.5 to 1)
Current Spending: ($ per student per year):
    Total: $7,472; Instruction: $4,768; Support Services: $2,309
Enrollment, Drop-out Rates and Diploma Recipients by Race/Ethnicity

Category	Total	White	Black	Asian	AIAN	Hisp.
Enrollment (%)	100.0	55.4	41.5	0.8	0.0	2.2
Drop-out Rate (%)	9.2	10.3	7.5	0.0	n/a	33.3
H.S. Diplomas (#)	87	58	27	1	0	1

Putnam County

Putnam County
158 Old Glenwood Springs Road • Eatonton, GA 31024-1024
(706) 485-5381 • http://www.putnam.k12.ga.us
Grade Span: PK-12; **Agency Type:** 1
Schools: 5
    1 Primary; 1 Middle; 1 High; 2 Other Level
    3 Regular; 1 Special Education; 0 Vocational; 1 Alternative
    0 Magnet; 0 Charter; 2 Title I Eligible; 2 School-wide Title I
Students: 2,622   (52.2% male; 47.7% female)
    Individual Education Program: 394 (15.0%);
    English Language Learner: 57 (2.2%); Migrant: 26 (1.0%)
    Eligible for Free Lunch Program: 1,391 (53.1%)
    Eligible for Reduced-Price Lunch Program: 304 (11.6%)
Teachers: 190.4 (13.8 to 1)
Librarians/Media Specialists: 3.9 (672.3 to 1)
Guidance Counselors: 5.0 (524.4 to 1)
Current Spending: ($ per student per year):
    Total: $8,520; Instruction: $5,153; Support Services: $2,852
Enrollment, Drop-out Rates and Diploma Recipients by Race/Ethnicity

Category	Total	White	Black	Asian	AIAN	Hisp.
Enrollment (%)	100.0	45.5	48.1	1.1	0.0	5.3
Drop-out Rate (%)	10.5	15.9	6.5	20.0	n/a	0.0
H.S. Diplomas (#)	101	37	61	3	0	0

Rabun County

Rabun County
41 Education St • Clayton, GA 30525
(706) 746-5376
Grade Span: PK-12; **Agency Type:** 1
Schools: 7
    2 Primary; 2 Middle; 1 High; 2 Other Level
    5 Regular; 1 Special Education; 0 Vocational; 1 Alternative
    0 Magnet; 0 Charter; 4 Title I Eligible; 0 School-wide Title I
Students: 2,192   (51.5% male; 48.4% female)
    Individual Education Program: 341 (15.6%);
    English Language Learner: 102 (4.7%); Migrant: 18 (0.8%)
    Eligible for Free Lunch Program: 742 (33.9%)
    Eligible for Reduced-Price Lunch Program: 370 (16.9%)
Teachers: 150.4 (14.6 to 1)
Librarians/Media Specialists: 5.0 (438.4 to 1)
Guidance Counselors: 5.0 (438.4 to 1)
Current Spending: ($ per student per year):
    Total: $7,971; Instruction: $5,296; Support Services: $2,258

Enrollment, Drop-out Rates and Diploma Recipients by Race/Ethnicity

Category	Total	White	Black	Asian	AIAN	Hisp.
Enrollment (%)	100.0	91.6	0.4	0.3	0.5	7.2
Drop-out Rate (%)	9.6	9.7	0.0	n/a	0.0	7.7
H.S. Diplomas (#)	115	109	0	0	0	6

Randolph County

Randolph County
1208 Andrew St • Cuthbert, GA 39840
(229) 732-2641
Grade Span: PK-12; **Agency Type:** 1
Schools: 5
    1 Primary; 1 Middle; 1 High; 2 Other Level
    3 Regular; 1 Special Education; 0 Vocational; 1 Alternative
    0 Magnet; 0 Charter; 3 Title I Eligible; 1 School-wide Title I
Students: 1,610   (51.6% male; 48.3% female)
    Individual Education Program: 182 (11.3%);
    English Language Learner: 0 (0.0%); Migrant: 0 (0.0%)
    Eligible for Free Lunch Program: 1,299 (80.7%)
    Eligible for Reduced-Price Lunch Program: 134 (8.3%)
Teachers: 111.3 (14.5 to 1)
Librarians/Media Specialists: 3.0 (536.7 to 1)
Guidance Counselors: 3.0 (536.7 to 1)
Current Spending: ($ per student per year):
    Total: $9,335; Instruction: $4,965; Support Services: $3,656
Enrollment, Drop-out Rates and Diploma Recipients by Race/Ethnicity

Category	Total	White	Black	Asian	AIAN	Hisp.
Enrollment (%)	100.0	11.1	87.3	0.2	0.4	0.9
Drop-out Rate (%)	7.9	10.4	7.6	0.0	n/a	n/a
H.S. Diplomas (#)	83	12	71	0	0	0

Richmond County

Richmond County
2083 Heckle St • Augusta, GA 30904-0904
(706) 737-7200 • http://www.richmond.k12.ga.us
Grade Span: PK-12; **Agency Type:** 1
Schools: 58
    35 Primary; 10 Middle; 9 High; 4 Other Level
    55 Regular; 1 Special Education; 0 Vocational; 2 Alternative
    3 Magnet; 0 Charter; 50 Title I Eligible; 50 School-wide Title I
Students: 34,400   (50.4% male; 49.5% female)
    Individual Education Program: 3,568 (10.4%);
    English Language Learner: 128 (0.4%); Migrant: 0 (0.0%)
    Eligible for Free Lunch Program: 18,982 (55.2%)
    Eligible for Reduced-Price Lunch Program: 3,297 (9.6%)
Teachers: 2,209.2 (15.6 to 1)
Librarians/Media Specialists: 56.9 (604.6 to 1)
Guidance Counselors: 72.5 (474.5 to 1)
Current Spending: ($ per student per year):
    Total: $7,450; Instruction: $4,580; Support Services: $2,450
Enrollment, Drop-out Rates and Diploma Recipients by Race/Ethnicity

Category	Total	White	Black	Asian	AIAN	Hisp.
Enrollment (%)	100.0	25.6	71.2	1.0	0.1	2.0
Drop-out Rate (%)	5.0	6.1	4.6	3.0	8.3	6.2
H.S. Diplomas (#)	1,576	499	1,014	29	2	32

Rockdale County

Rockdale County
954 N Main St • Conyers, GA 30012-0012
(770) 483-4713 • http://www.rockdale.k12.ga.us
Grade Span: PK-12; **Agency Type:** 1
Schools: 19
    11 Primary; 3 Middle; 3 High; 2 Other Level
    17 Regular; 1 Special Education; 0 Vocational; 1 Alternative
    0 Magnet; 0 Charter; 8 Title I Eligible; 5 School-wide Title I
Students: 14,266   (51.2% male; 48.7% female)
    Individual Education Program: 1,493 (10.5%);
    English Language Learner: 699 (4.9%); Migrant: 0 (0.0%)
    Eligible for Free Lunch Program: 4,234 (29.7%)
    Eligible for Reduced-Price Lunch Program: 1,146 (8.0%)
Teachers: 883.6 (16.1 to 1)
Librarians/Media Specialists: 19.8 (720.5 to 1)
Guidance Counselors: 30.0 (475.5 to 1)
Current Spending: ($ per student per year):
    Total: $7,251; Instruction: $4,628; Support Services: $2,233
Enrollment, Drop-out Rates and Diploma Recipients by Race/Ethnicity

Category	Total	White	Black	Asian	AIAN	Hisp.
Enrollment (%)	100.0	54.2	36.6	2.0	0.2	7.0
Drop-out Rate (%)	4.2	3.4	6.1	2.4	0.0	7.3
H.S. Diplomas (#)	722	550	133	29	2	8

Screven County

Screven County
216 Mims Rd • Sylvania, GA 30467-0467
(912) 564-7114 • http://www.screven.k12.ga.us
Grade Span: PK-12; **Agency Type:** 1
Schools: 5
  1 Primary; 1 Middle; 1 High; 2 Other Level
  3 Regular; 1 Special Education; 0 Vocational; 1 Alternative
  0 Magnet; 0 Charter; 3 Title I Eligible; 3 School-wide Title I
Students: 3,049   (49.2% male; 50.7% female)
  Individual Education Program: 516 (16.9%);
  English Language Learner: 1 (<0.1%); Migrant: 60 (2.0%)
  Eligible for Free Lunch Program: 1,926 (63.2%)
  Eligible for Reduced-Price Lunch Program: 481 (15.8%)
Teachers: 187.2 (16.3 to 1)
Librarians/Media Specialists: 3.0 (1,016.3 to 1)
Guidance Counselors: 6.0 (508.2 to 1)
Current Spending: ($ per student per year):
  Total: $7,164; Instruction: $4,406; Support Services: $2,297
Enrollment, Drop-out Rates and Diploma Recipients by Race/Ethnicity

Category	Total	White	Black	Asian	AIAN	Hisp.
Enrollment (%)	100.0	43.8	55.3	0.3	0.0	0.6
Drop-out Rate (%)	7.3	5.4	8.7	n/a	n/a	0.0
H.S. Diplomas (#)	161	78	83	0	0	0

Seminole County

Seminole County
800 S Woolfork Ave • Donalsonville, GA 39845
(229) 524-2433 • http://www.seminole.k12.ga.us
Grade Span: PK-12; **Agency Type:** 1
Schools: 4
  1 Primary; 0 Middle; 0 High; 3 Other Level
  2 Regular; 1 Special Education; 0 Vocational; 1 Alternative
  0 Magnet; 0 Charter; 2 Title I Eligible; 2 School-wide Title I
Students: 1,758   (51.5% male; 48.4% female)
  Individual Education Program: 253 (14.4%);
  English Language Learner: 0 (0.0%); Migrant: 47 (2.7%)
  Eligible for Free Lunch Program: 1,076 (61.2%)
  Eligible for Reduced-Price Lunch Program: 129 (7.3%)
Teachers: 118.0 (14.9 to 1)
Librarians/Media Specialists: 2.0 (879.0 to 1)
Guidance Counselors: 4.0 (439.5 to 1)
Current Spending: ($ per student per year):
  Total: $7,902; Instruction: $4,933; Support Services: $2,467
Enrollment, Drop-out Rates and Diploma Recipients by Race/Ethnicity

Category	Total	White	Black	Asian	AIAN	Hisp.
Enrollment (%)	100.0	45.7	51.9	0.3	0.0	2.0
Drop-out Rate (%)	29.1	36.4	23.0	n/a	n/a	0.0
H.S. Diplomas (#)	87	30	57	0	0	0

Spalding County

Spalding County
216 S Sixth St • Griffin, GA 30224-0224
(770) 229-3700 • http://web.spalding.k12.ga.us/
Grade Span: PK-12; **Agency Type:** 1
Schools: 20
  10 Primary; 4 Middle; 2 High; 4 Other Level
  16 Regular; 2 Special Education; 0 Vocational; 2 Alternative
  0 Magnet; 2 Charter; 11 Title I Eligible; 11 School-wide Title I
Students: 10,693   (50.9% male; 49.0% female)
  Individual Education Program: 1,547 (14.5%);
  English Language Learner: 119 (1.1%); Migrant: 0 (0.0%)
  Eligible for Free Lunch Program: 5,182 (48.5%)
  Eligible for Reduced-Price Lunch Program: 952 (8.9%)
Teachers: 681.9 (15.7 to 1)
Librarians/Media Specialists: 20.0 (534.7 to 1)
Guidance Counselors: 23.5 (455.0 to 1)
Current Spending: ($ per student per year):
  Total: $7,593; Instruction: $4,698; Support Services: $2,464
Enrollment, Drop-out Rates and Diploma Recipients by Race/Ethnicity

Category	Total	White	Black	Asian	AIAN	Hisp.
Enrollment (%)	100.0	51.9	44.9	0.8	0.1	2.2
Drop-out Rate (%)	13.2	10.7	16.9	0.0	25.0	8.3
H.S. Diplomas (#)	401	239	153	7	0	2

Stephens County

Stephens County
Rt. 1 Box 1050 • Toccoa, GA 30577-0577
(706) 886-9415 • http://www.stephenscountyschools.com/
Grade Span: PK-12; **Agency Type:** 1
Schools: 8

---

  4 Primary; 1 Middle; 1 High; 2 Other Level
  6 Regular; 1 Special Education; 0 Vocational; 1 Alternative
  0 Magnet; 0 Charter; 3 Title I Eligible; 3 School-wide Title I
Students: 4,313   (51.6% male; 48.3% female)
  Individual Education Program: 604 (14.0%);
  English Language Learner: 26 (0.6%); Migrant: 0 (0.0%)
  Eligible for Free Lunch Program: 1,632 (37.8%)
  Eligible for Reduced-Price Lunch Program: 369 (8.6%)
Teachers: 297.0 (14.5 to 1)
Librarians/Media Specialists: 7.0 (616.1 to 1)
Guidance Counselors: 9.9 (435.7 to 1)
Current Spending: ($ per student per year):
  Total: $7,817; Instruction: $5,107; Support Services: $2,328
Enrollment, Drop-out Rates and Diploma Recipients by Race/Ethnicity

Category	Total	White	Black	Asian	AIAN	Hisp.
Enrollment (%)	100.0	82.0	16.0	0.5	0.2	1.3
Drop-out Rate (%)	9.2	9.2	7.9	0.0	0.0	37.5
H.S. Diplomas (#)	177	157	19	1	0	0

Sumter County

Sumter County
100 Learning Ln • Americus, GA 31719
(229) 931-8500 • http://www.sumter.k12.ga.us
Grade Span: PK-12; **Agency Type:** 1
Schools: 10
  4 Primary; 2 Middle; 2 High; 2 Other Level
  8 Regular; 1 Special Education; 0 Vocational; 1 Alternative
  0 Magnet; 0 Charter; 6 Title I Eligible; 6 School-wide Title I
Students: 5,704   (50.8% male; 49.1% female)
  Individual Education Program: 559 (9.8%);
  English Language Learner: 2 (<0.1%); Migrant: 140 (2.5%)
  Eligible for Free Lunch Program: 3,726 (65.3%)
  Eligible for Reduced-Price Lunch Program: 541 (9.5%)
Teachers: 363.4 (15.7 to 1)
Librarians/Media Specialists: 8.0 (713.0 to 1)
Guidance Counselors: 11.7 (487.5 to 1)
Current Spending: ($ per student per year):
  Total: $7,028; Instruction: $4,500; Support Services: $2,038
Enrollment, Drop-out Rates and Diploma Recipients by Race/Ethnicity

Category	Total	White	Black	Asian	AIAN	Hisp.
Enrollment (%)	100.0	22.2	74.1	0.6	0.1	3.0
Drop-out Rate (%)	14.0	15.2	13.2	0.0	0.0	25.7
H.S. Diplomas (#)	185	58	122	1	0	4

Tattnall County

Tattnall County
147 Brazell St • Reidsville, GA 30453-0157
(912) 557-4726 • http://www.tattnallcountyschools.org/
Grade Span: PK-12; **Agency Type:** 1
Schools: 9
  3 Primary; 3 Middle; 1 High; 2 Other Level
  7 Regular; 1 Special Education; 0 Vocational; 1 Alternative
  0 Magnet; 0 Charter; 6 Title I Eligible; 6 School-wide Title I
Students: 3,310   (52.0% male; 47.9% female)
  Individual Education Program: 421 (12.7%);
  English Language Learner: 183 (5.5%); Migrant: 541 (16.3%)
  Eligible for Free Lunch Program: 1,945 (58.8%)
  Eligible for Reduced-Price Lunch Program: 335 (10.1%)
Teachers: 205.7 (16.1 to 1)
Librarians/Media Specialists: 6.0 (551.7 to 1)
Guidance Counselors: 7.0 (472.9 to 1)
Current Spending: ($ per student per year):
  Total: $7,057; Instruction: $4,407; Support Services: $2,179
Enrollment, Drop-out Rates and Diploma Recipients by Race/Ethnicity

Category	Total	White	Black	Asian	AIAN	Hisp.
Enrollment (%)	100.0	55.1	30.6	0.6	0.0	13.7
Drop-out Rate (%)	8.1	7.3	7.5	0.0	0.0	17.7
H.S. Diplomas (#)	112	80	27	0	0	5

Taylor County

Taylor County
229 Mulberry St • Butler, GA 31006-3106
(478) 862-5224 • http://www.taylor.k12.ga.us
Grade Span: PK-12; **Agency Type:** 1
Schools: 4
  1 Primary; 1 Middle; 1 High; 1 Other Level
  3 Regular; 1 Special Education; 0 Vocational; 0 Alternative
  0 Magnet; 0 Charter; 2 Title I Eligible; 0 School-wide Title I
Students: 1,696   (51.0% male; 48.9% female)
  Individual Education Program: 161 (9.5%);
  English Language Learner: 0 (0.0%); Migrant: 11 (0.6%)
  Eligible for Free Lunch Program: 978 (57.7%)

Eligible for Reduced-Price Lunch Program: 170 (10.0%)
Teachers: 97.5 (17.4 to 1)
Librarians/Media Specialists: 2.0 (848.0 to 1)
Guidance Counselors: 4.0 (424.0 to 1)
Current Spending: ($ per student per year):
Total: $7,081; Instruction: $4,451; Support Services: $2,110
Enrollment, Drop-out Rates and Diploma Recipients by Race/Ethnicity

Category	Total	White	Black	Asian	AIAN	Hisp.
Enrollment (%)	100.0	46.9	51.9	0.4	0.0	0.8
Drop-out Rate (%)	12.5	7.9	15.9	n/a	n/a	50.0
H.S. Diplomas (#)	79	47	32	0	0	0

Telfair County

Telfair County
210-B Parsonage St • Mcrae, GA 31055-1055
(229) 868-5661
Grade Span: PK-12; **Agency Type:** 1
Schools: 5
1 Primary; 1 Middle; 1 High; 2 Other Level
3 Regular; 1 Special Education; 0 Vocational; 1 Alternative
0 Magnet; 0 Charter; 2 Title I Eligible; 2 School-wide Title I
Students: 1,702   (52.0% male; 47.9% female)
Individual Education Program: 248 (14.6%);
English Language Learner: 34 (2.0%); Migrant: 4 (0.2%)
Eligible for Free Lunch Program: 1,038 (61.0%)
Eligible for Reduced-Price Lunch Program: 168 (9.9%)
Teachers: 116.5 (14.6 to 1)
Librarians/Media Specialists: 2.0 (851.0 to 1)
Guidance Counselors: 3.0 (567.3 to 1)
Current Spending: ($ per student per year):
Total: $8,492; Instruction: $5,708; Support Services: $2,297
Enrollment, Drop-out Rates and Diploma Recipients by Race/Ethnicity

Category	Total	White	Black	Asian	AIAN	Hisp.
Enrollment (%)	100.0	48.8	48.5	0.5	0.2	2.1
Drop-out Rate (%)	8.2	7.6	8.6	0.0	n/a	100.0
H.S. Diplomas (#)	80	38	42	0	0	0

Terrell County

Terrell County
955 Forrester Dr SE • Dawson, GA 31742-1742
(229) 995-4425
Grade Span: PK-12; **Agency Type:** 1
Schools: 4
2 Primary; 0 Middle; 0 High; 2 Other Level
3 Regular; 1 Special Education; 0 Vocational; 0 Alternative
0 Magnet; 0 Charter; 3 Title I Eligible; 3 School-wide Title I
Students: 1,676   (51.0% male; 48.9% female)
Individual Education Program: 229 (13.7%);
English Language Learner: 0 (0.0%); Migrant: 2 (0.1%)
Eligible for Free Lunch Program: 1,006 (60.0%)
Eligible for Reduced-Price Lunch Program: 166 (9.9%)
Teachers: 99.1 (16.9 to 1)
Librarians/Media Specialists: 3.0 (558.7 to 1)
Guidance Counselors: 2.9 (577.9 to 1)
Current Spending: ($ per student per year):
Total: $8,259; Instruction: $5,084; Support Services: $2,677
Enrollment, Drop-out Rates and Diploma Recipients by Race/Ethnicity

Category	Total	White	Black	Asian	AIAN	Hisp.
Enrollment (%)	100.0	3.3	96.2	0.1	0.1	0.4
Drop-out Rate (%)	6.4	0.0	6.7	n/a	n/a	0.0
H.S. Diplomas (#)	54	3	50	0	0	1

Thomas County

Thomas County
11343 U.S Hwy 319 N • Thomasville, GA 31757
(229) 225-4380 • http://www.thomas.k12.ga.us/
Grade Span: PK-12; **Agency Type:** 1
Schools: 8
2 Primary; 1 Middle; 2 High; 3 Other Level
5 Regular; 2 Special Education; 0 Vocational; 1 Alternative
0 Magnet; 1 Charter; 3 Title I Eligible; 3 School-wide Title I
Students: 5,523   (50.8% male; 49.1% female)
Individual Education Program: 957 (17.3%);
English Language Learner: 9 (0.2%); Migrant: 123 (2.2%)
Eligible for Free Lunch Program: 2,657 (48.1%)
Eligible for Reduced-Price Lunch Program: 509 (9.2%)
Teachers: 343.8 (16.1 to 1)
Librarians/Media Specialists: 5.0 (1,104.6 to 1)
Guidance Counselors: 9.7 (569.4 to 1)
Current Spending: ($ per student per year):
Total: $7,997; Instruction: $5,422; Support Services: $2,164

Thomasville City
915 E Jackson St • Thomasville, GA 31792-4776
(229) 225-2600 • http://www.tcitys.org/
Grade Span: PK-12; **Agency Type:** 1
Schools: 9
4 Primary; 1 Middle; 1 High; 3 Other Level
6 Regular; 1 Special Education; 0 Vocational; 2 Alternative
0 Magnet; 0 Charter; 3 Title I Eligible; 3 School-wide Title I
Students: 3,062   (49.8% male; 50.1% female)
Individual Education Program: 396 (12.9%);
English Language Learner: 0 (0.0%); Migrant: 0 (0.0%)
Eligible for Free Lunch Program: 1,701 (55.6%)
Eligible for Reduced-Price Lunch Program: 244 (8.0%)
Teachers: 202.3 (15.1 to 1)
Librarians/Media Specialists: 5.0 (612.4 to 1)
Guidance Counselors: 5.7 (537.2 to 1)
Current Spending: ($ per student per year):
Total: $8,210; Instruction: $5,041; Support Services: $2,624
Enrollment, Drop-out Rates and Diploma Recipients by Race/Ethnicity

Category	Total	White	Black	Asian	AIAN	Hisp.
Enrollment (%)	100.0	24.2	75.0	0.3	0.0	0.5
Drop-out Rate (%)	7.7	4.7	8.7	0.0	n/a	n/a
H.S. Diplomas (#)	159	46	111	2	0	0

Tift County

Tift County
207 N Ridge Ave • Tifton, GA 31793-0389
Mailing Address: PO Box 389 207 N Ridge • Tifton, GA 31793-0389
(229) 386-6500 • http://www.tift.k12.ga.us
Grade Span: PK-12; **Agency Type:** 1
Schools: 14
5 Primary; 4 Middle; 1 High; 4 Other Level
11 Regular; 2 Special Education; 0 Vocational; 1 Alternative
0 Magnet; 0 Charter; 4 Title I Eligible; 4 School-wide Title I
Students: 7,661   (50.4% male; 49.5% female)
Individual Education Program: 957 (12.5%);
English Language Learner: 426 (5.6%); Migrant: 432 (5.6%)
Eligible for Free Lunch Program: 3,735 (48.8%)
Eligible for Reduced-Price Lunch Program: 620 (8.1%)
Teachers: 471.2 (16.3 to 1)
Librarians/Media Specialists: 12.0 (638.4 to 1)
Guidance Counselors: 14.5 (528.3 to 1)
Current Spending: ($ per student per year):
Total: $6,576; Instruction: $4,475; Support Services: $1,758
Enrollment, Drop-out Rates and Diploma Recipients by Race/Ethnicity

Category	Total	White	Black	Asian	AIAN	Hisp.
Enrollment (%)	100.0	50.8	38.2	1.0	0.0	10.0
Drop-out Rate (%)	9.4	6.9	11.8	5.6	0.0	20.9
H.S. Diplomas (#)	342	239	91	6	0	6

Toombs County

Toombs County
117 E Wesley Ave • Lyons, GA 30436-0436
(912) 526-3141 • http://www.toombs.k12.ga.us
Grade Span: PK-12; **Agency Type:** 1
Schools: 6
3 Primary; 1 Middle; 1 High; 1 Other Level
5 Regular; 1 Special Education; 0 Vocational; 0 Alternative
0 Magnet; 0 Charter; 1 Title I Eligible; 1 School-wide Title I
Students: 2,758   (50.8% male; 49.1% female)
Individual Education Program: 415 (15.0%);
English Language Learner: 241 (8.7%); Migrant: 217 (7.9%)
Eligible for Free Lunch Program: 1,668 (60.5%)
Eligible for Reduced-Price Lunch Program: 328 (11.9%)
Teachers: 172.1 (16.0 to 1)
Librarians/Media Specialists: 4.0 (689.5 to 1)
Guidance Counselors: 4.9 (562.9 to 1)
Current Spending: ($ per student per year):
Total: $6,766; Instruction: $4,461; Support Services: $1,839
Enrollment, Drop-out Rates and Diploma Recipients by Race/Ethnicity

Category	Total	White	Black	Asian	AIAN	Hisp.
Enrollment (%)	100.0	62.1	19.7	0.2	0.0	18.0
Drop-out Rate (%)	8.7	7.8	7.1	0.0	n/a	21.2
H.S. Diplomas (#)	94	67	17	1	0	9

Vidalia City

301 Adams St • Vidalia, GA 30474-0474
(912) 537-3088 • http://www.vidalia-city.k12.ga.us/
Grade Span: PK-12; **Agency Type:** 1
Schools: 6
  2 Primary; 1 Middle; 1 High; 2 Other Level
  4 Regular; 1 Special Education; 0 Vocational; 1 Alternative
  0 Magnet; 0 Charter; 3 Title I Eligible; 3 School-wide Title I
Students: 2,491 (49.7% male; 50.2% female)
  Individual Education Program: 181 (7.3%);
  English Language Learner: 7 (0.3%); Migrant: 14 (0.6%)
  Eligible for Free Lunch Program: 1,193 (47.9%)
  Eligible for Reduced-Price Lunch Program: 180 (7.2%)
Teachers: 147.6 (16.9 to 1)
Librarians/Media Specialists: 4.0 (622.8 to 1)
Guidance Counselors: 5.0 (498.2 to 1)
Current Spending: ($ per student per year):
  Total: $7,212; Instruction: $4,893; Support Services: $1,938
Enrollment, Drop-out Rates and Diploma Recipients by Race/Ethnicity

Category	Total	White	Black	Asian	AIAN	Hisp.
Enrollment (%)	100.0	47.3	49.3	1.2	0.1	2.1
Drop-out Rate (%)	3.8	3.3	4.7	0.0	n/a	0.0
H.S. Diplomas (#)	137	77	56	2	0	2

Towns County

Towns County

67 Lakeview Circle Ste C • Hiawassee, GA 30546-0546
(706) 896-2279
Grade Span: PK-12; **Agency Type:** 1
Schools: 5
  1 Primary; 1 Middle; 2 High; 1 Other Level
  3 Regular; 1 Special Education; 0 Vocational; 1 Alternative
  0 Magnet; 0 Charter; 0 Title I Eligible; 0 School-wide Title I
Students: 1,597 (50.2% male; 49.7% female)
  Individual Education Program: 124 (7.8%);
  English Language Learner: 11 (0.7%); Migrant: 0 (0.0%)
  Eligible for Free Lunch Program: 335 (21.0%)
  Eligible for Reduced-Price Lunch Program: 130 (8.1%)
Teachers: 142.3 (11.2 to 1)
Librarians/Media Specialists: 2.0 (798.5 to 1)
Guidance Counselors: 3.0 (532.3 to 1)
Current Spending: ($ per student per year):
  Total: $6,958; Instruction: $4,495; Support Services: $2,200
Enrollment, Drop-out Rates and Diploma Recipients by Race/Ethnicity

Category	Total	White	Black	Asian	AIAN	Hisp.
Enrollment (%)	100.0	98.4	0.1	0.7	0.1	0.8
Drop-out Rate (%)	n/a	n/a	n/a	n/a	n/a	n/a
H.S. Diplomas (#)	99	98	1	0	0	0

Troup County

Troup County

200 Mooty Bridge Rd • Lagrange, GA 30240
(706) 812-7900 • http://www.troup.k12.ga.us
Grade Span: PK-12; **Agency Type:** 1
Schools: 22
  13 Primary; 3 Middle; 3 High; 3 Other Level
  19 Regular; 1 Special Education; 0 Vocational; 2 Alternative
  2 Magnet; 0 Charter; 19 Title I Eligible; 19 School-wide Title I
Students: 11,993 (51.2% male; 48.7% female)
  Individual Education Program: 1,488 (12.4%);
  English Language Learner: 79 (0.7%); Migrant: 0 (0.0%)
  Eligible for Free Lunch Program: 5,536 (46.2%)
  Eligible for Reduced-Price Lunch Program: 985 (8.2%)
Teachers: 793.0 (15.1 to 1)
Librarians/Media Specialists: 21.0 (571.1 to 1)
Guidance Counselors: 27.5 (436.1 to 1)
Current Spending: ($ per student per year):
  Total: $7,388; Instruction: $4,670; Support Services: $2,535
Enrollment, Drop-out Rates and Diploma Recipients by Race/Ethnicity

Category	Total	White	Black	Asian	AIAN	Hisp.
Enrollment (%)	100.0	56.1	41.9	0.3	0.4	1.4
Drop-out Rate (%)	6.9	7.2	6.7	0.0	0.0	3.3
H.S. Diplomas (#)	484	323	153	4	0	4

Turner County

Turner County

423 Noth Cleveland St • Ashburn, GA 31714-1714
Mailing Address: PO Box 609 423 N Clevel • Ashburn, GA 31714-1714
(229) 567-3338 • http://www.turner.k12.ga.us
Grade Span: PK-12; **Agency Type:** 1
Schools: 7
  1 Primary; 1 Middle; 1 High; 4 Other Level

---

  3 Regular; 2 Special Education; 0 Vocational; 2 Alternative
  0 Magnet; 0 Charter; 2 Title I Eligible; 2 School-wide Title I
Students: 1,898 (51.3% male; 48.6% female)
  Individual Education Program: 221 (11.6%);
  English Language Learner: 0 (0.0%); Migrant: 8 (0.4%)
  Eligible for Free Lunch Program: 1,141 (60.1%)
  Eligible for Reduced-Price Lunch Program: 139 (7.3%)
Teachers: 135.8 (14.0 to 1)
Librarians/Media Specialists: 2.0 (949.0 to 1)
Guidance Counselors: 4.5 (421.8 to 1)
Current Spending: ($ per student per year):
  Total: $8,253; Instruction: $5,397; Support Services: $2,449
Enrollment, Drop-out Rates and Diploma Recipients by Race/Ethnicity

Category	Total	White	Black	Asian	AIAN	Hisp.
Enrollment (%)	100.0	42.2	56.0	0.4	0.1	1.3
Drop-out Rate (%)	6.7	4.1	9.0	n/a	0.0	0.0
H.S. Diplomas (#)	82	42	40	0	0	0

Union County

Union County

10 Hughes St • Blairsville, GA 30512-0512
(706) 745-2322 • http://www.union.k12.ga.us
Grade Span: KG-12; **Agency Type:** 1
Schools: 8
  2 Primary; 1 Middle; 1 High; 4 Other Level
  5 Regular; 1 Special Education; 0 Vocational; 2 Alternative
  0 Magnet; 0 Charter; 2 Title I Eligible; 2 School-wide Title I
Students: 2,626 (50.4% male; 49.5% female)
  Individual Education Program: 483 (18.4%);
  English Language Learner: 19 (0.7%); Migrant: 0 (0.0%)
  Eligible for Free Lunch Program: 906 (34.5%)
  Eligible for Reduced-Price Lunch Program: 364 (13.9%)
Teachers: 182.3 (14.4 to 1)
Librarians/Media Specialists: 3.9 (673.3 to 1)
Guidance Counselors: 4.9 (535.9 to 1)
Current Spending: ($ per student per year):
  Total: $8,098; Instruction: $5,070; Support Services: $2,538
Enrollment, Drop-out Rates and Diploma Recipients by Race/Ethnicity

Category	Total	White	Black	Asian	AIAN	Hisp.
Enrollment (%)	100.0	98.2	0.1	0.1	0.5	1.1
Drop-out Rate (%)	2.6	2.6	0.0	0.0	n/a	0.0
H.S. Diplomas (#)	145	145	0	0	0	0

Upson County

Thomaston-Upson County

205 Civic Center Dr • Thomaston, GA 30286-4233
(706) 647-9621 • http://www.upson.k12.ga.us/
Grade Span: PK-12; **Agency Type:** 1
Schools: 8
  3 Primary; 1 Middle; 1 High; 3 Other Level
  5 Regular; 2 Special Education; 0 Vocational; 1 Alternative
  0 Magnet; 0 Charter; 4 Title I Eligible; 4 School-wide Title I
Students: 4,992 (51.9% male; 48.0% female)
  Individual Education Program: 735 (14.7%);
  English Language Learner: 3 (0.1%); Migrant: 1 (<0.1%)
  Eligible for Free Lunch Program: 2,250 (45.1%)
  Eligible for Reduced-Price Lunch Program: 478 (9.6%)
Teachers: 299.1 (16.7 to 1)
Librarians/Media Specialists: 7.0 (713.1 to 1)
Guidance Counselors: 8.8 (567.3 to 1)
Current Spending: ($ per student per year):
  Total: $6,673; Instruction: $4,407; Support Services: $1,850
Enrollment, Drop-out Rates and Diploma Recipients by Race/Ethnicity

Category	Total	White	Black	Asian	AIAN	Hisp.
Enrollment (%)	100.0	61.6	37.0	0.3	0.1	0.9
Drop-out Rate (%)	8.3	8.5	8.2	0.0	0.0	8.3
H.S. Diplomas (#)	228	160	62	4	0	2

Walker County

Walker County

201 S Duke St • Lafayette, GA 30728-0728
(706) 638-1240 • http://www.walkerschools.org/
Grade Span: PK-12; **Agency Type:** 1
Schools: 16
  9 Primary; 3 Middle; 2 High; 2 Other Level
  14 Regular; 1 Special Education; 0 Vocational; 1 Alternative
  0 Magnet; 0 Charter; 9 Title I Eligible; 9 School-wide Title I
Students: 8,820 (52.3% male; 47.6% female)
  Individual Education Program: 1,328 (15.1%);
  English Language Learner: 31 (0.4%); Migrant: 35 (0.4%)
  Eligible for Free Lunch Program: 3,537 (40.1%)
  Eligible for Reduced-Price Lunch Program: 1,159 (13.1%)

Teachers: 566.7 (15.6 to 1)
Librarians/Media Specialists: 15.0 (588.0 to 1)
Guidance Counselors: 19.5 (452.3 to 1)
Current Spending: ($ per student per year):
  Total: $7,465; Instruction: $4,821; Support Services: $2,225
Enrollment, Drop-out Rates and Diploma Recipients by Race/Ethnicity

Category	Total	White	Black	Asian	AIAN	Hisp.
Enrollment (%)	100.0	93.1	5.5	0.2	0.1	1.0
Drop-out Rate (%)	10.9	11.2	8.0	0.0	0.0	5.6
H.S. Diplomas (#)	317	301	8	2	0	6

Walton County

Walton County
200 Double Springs Church Road • Monroe, GA 30656
(770) 266-4520 • http://www.walton.k12.ga.us
Grade Span: PK-12; **Agency Type:** 1
Schools: 15
  8 Primary; 2 Middle; 2 High; 3 Other Level
  12 Regular; 2 Special Education; 0 Vocational; 1 Alternative
  0 Magnet; 0 Charter; 4 Title I Eligible; 3 School-wide Title I
Students: 10,722 (49.9% male; 50.0% female)
  Individual Education Program: 1,445 (13.5%);
  English Language Learner: 165 (1.5%); Migrant: 3 (<0.1%)
  Eligible for Free Lunch Program: 3,100 (28.9%)
  Eligible for Reduced-Price Lunch Program: 827 (7.7%)
Teachers: 698.6 (15.3 to 1)
Librarians/Media Specialists: 15.0 (714.8 to 1)
Guidance Counselors: 24.0 (446.8 to 1)
Current Spending: ($ per student per year):
  Total: $7,748; Instruction: $4,954; Support Services: $2,268
Enrollment, Drop-out Rates and Diploma Recipients by Race/Ethnicity

Category	Total	White	Black	Asian	AIAN	Hisp.
Enrollment (%)	100.0	76.9	19.1	1.5	0.3	2.1
Drop-out Rate (%)	3.5	3.1	6.2	0.0	0.0	0.0
H.S. Diplomas (#)	344	295	42	4	0	3

Ware County

Ware County
1301 Bailey St • Waycross, GA 31503
(912) 283-8656 • http://www.warecoschools.com
Grade Span: PK-12; **Agency Type:** 1
Schools: 13
  6 Primary; 2 Middle; 1 High; 4 Other Level
  10 Regular; 2 Special Education; 0 Vocational; 1 Alternative
  1 Magnet; 0 Charter; 9 Title I Eligible; 7 School-wide Title I
Students: 6,343 (51.2% male; 48.7% female)
  Individual Education Program: 912 (14.4%);
  English Language Learner: 66 (1.0%); Migrant: 119 (1.9%)
  Eligible for Free Lunch Program: 3,222 (50.8%)
  Eligible for Reduced-Price Lunch Program: 578 (9.1%)
Teachers: 418.4 (15.2 to 1)
Librarians/Media Specialists: 11.0 (576.6 to 1)
Guidance Counselors: 12.1 (524.2 to 1)
Current Spending: ($ per student per year):
  Total: $7,598; Instruction: $4,903; Support Services: $2,262
Enrollment, Drop-out Rates and Diploma Recipients by Race/Ethnicity

Category	Total	White	Black	Asian	AIAN	Hisp.
Enrollment (%)	100.0	60.0	37.1	0.7	0.2	1.9
Drop-out Rate (%)	9.5	9.8	8.5	12.5	0.0	23.1
H.S. Diplomas (#)	270	191	76	2	0	1

Washington County

Washington County
501 Industrial Dr • Sandersville, GA 31082-1082
(478) 552-3981 • http://www.washington.k12.ga.us
Grade Span: PK-12; **Agency Type:** 1
Schools: 8
  4 Primary; 1 Middle; 1 High; 2 Other Level
  6 Regular; 1 Special Education; 0 Vocational; 1 Alternative
  0 Magnet; 0 Charter; 5 Title I Eligible; 5 School-wide Title I
Students: 3,711 (50.4% male; 49.5% female)
  Individual Education Program: 433 (11.7%);
  English Language Learner: 0 (0.0%); Migrant: 1 (<0.1%)
  Eligible for Free Lunch Program: 2,043 (55.1%)
  Eligible for Reduced-Price Lunch Program: 507 (13.7%)
Teachers: 220.9 (16.8 to 1)
Librarians/Media Specialists: 6.8 (545.7 to 1)
Guidance Counselors: 6.0 (618.5 to 1)
Current Spending: ($ per student per year):
  Total: $7,479; Instruction: $4,404; Support Services: $2,649

Category	Total	White	Black	Asian	AIAN	Hisp.
Enrollment (%)	100.0	30.2	69.2	0.2	0.1	0.4
Drop-out Rate (%)	5.6	3.1	6.9	n/a	n/a	0.0
H.S. Diplomas (#)	207	78	128	0	0	1

Wayne County

Wayne County
555 S Sunset Boulvard • Jesup, GA 31545-1545
(912) 427-1003 • http://www.wayne.k12.ga.us/
Grade Span: PK-12; **Agency Type:** 1
Schools: 11
  4 Primary; 3 Middle; 2 High; 2 Other Level
  8 Regular; 2 Special Education; 0 Vocational; 1 Alternative
  0 Magnet; 0 Charter; 5 Title I Eligible; 4 School-wide Title I
Students: 5,312 (51.9% male; 48.0% female)
  Individual Education Program: 739 (13.9%);
  English Language Learner: 84 (1.6%); Migrant: 22 (0.4%)
  Eligible for Free Lunch Program: 2,361 (44.4%)
  Eligible for Reduced-Price Lunch Program: 470 (8.8%)
Teachers: 318.1 (16.7 to 1)
Librarians/Media Specialists: 9.0 (590.2 to 1)
Guidance Counselors: 10.5 (505.9 to 1)
Current Spending: ($ per student per year):
  Total: $6,983; Instruction: $4,490; Support Services: $2,118
Enrollment, Drop-out Rates and Diploma Recipients by Race/Ethnicity

Category	Total	White	Black	Asian	AIAN	Hisp.
Enrollment (%)	100.0	72.6	23.5	0.7	0.2	3.1
Drop-out Rate (%)	10.9	10.9	10.4	0.0	0.0	24.2
H.S. Diplomas (#)	214	162	48	2	0	2

White County

White County
113 N Brooks St • Cleveland, GA 30528-0528
(706) 865-2315 • http://www.white.k12.ga.us
Grade Span: PK-12; **Agency Type:** 1
Schools: 8
  3 Primary; 1 Middle; 1 High; 3 Other Level
  6 Regular; 2 Special Education; 0 Vocational; 0 Alternative
  0 Magnet; 0 Charter; 3 Title I Eligible; 0 School-wide Title I
Students: 3,863 (52.1% male; 47.8% female)
  Individual Education Program: 515 (13.3%);
  English Language Learner: 26 (0.7%); Migrant: 6 (0.2%)
  Eligible for Free Lunch Program: 1,107 (28.7%)
  Eligible for Reduced-Price Lunch Program: 392 (10.1%)
Teachers: 247.5 (15.6 to 1)
Librarians/Media Specialists: 6.0 (643.8 to 1)
Guidance Counselors: 7.5 (515.1 to 1)
Current Spending: ($ per student per year):
  Total: $7,056; Instruction: $4,590; Support Services: $2,068
Enrollment, Drop-out Rates and Diploma Recipients by Race/Ethnicity

Category	Total	White	Black	Asian	AIAN	Hisp.
Enrollment (%)	100.0	95.1	2.1	0.6	0.5	1.7
Drop-out Rate (%)	5.2	5.4	0.0	0.0	0.0	0.0
H.S. Diplomas (#)	152	147	2	2	1	0

Whitfield County

Dalton City
100 S Hamilton St • Dalton, GA 30720
(706) 278-8766 • http://www.dalton.k12.ga.us
Grade Span: PK-12; **Agency Type:** 1
Schools: 10
  4 Primary; 2 Middle; 1 High; 3 Other Level
  7 Regular; 1 Special Education; 0 Vocational; 2 Alternative
  0 Magnet; 0 Charter; 7 Title I Eligible; 6 School-wide Title I
Students: 5,934 (51.2% male; 48.7% female)
  Individual Education Program: 695 (11.7%);
  English Language Learner: 1,259 (21.2%); Migrant: 432 (7.3%)
  Eligible for Free Lunch Program: 2,852 (48.1%)
  Eligible for Reduced-Price Lunch Program: 667 (11.2%)
Teachers: 388.6 (15.3 to 1)
Librarians/Media Specialists: 9.0 (659.3 to 1)
Guidance Counselors: 14.0 (423.9 to 1)
Current Spending: ($ per student per year):
  Total: $8,993; Instruction: $5,639; Support Services: $2,993
Enrollment, Drop-out Rates and Diploma Recipients by Race/Ethnicity

Category	Total	White	Black	Asian	AIAN	Hisp.
Enrollment (%)	100.0	28.3	7.3	2.6	0.2	61.6
Drop-out Rate (%)	3.1	1.3	0.7	n/a	0.0	5.4
H.S. Diplomas (#)	235	138	24	9	0	64

Whitfield County

1306 S Thornton Ave • Dalton, GA 30720
(706) 278-8070 • http://www.whitfield.k12.ga.us
Grade Span: PK-12; **Agency Type:** 1
Schools: 22
   11 Primary; 4 Middle; 3 High; 4 Other Level
   17 Regular; 2 Special Education; 0 Vocational; 3 Alternative
   0 Magnet; 0 Charter; 6 Title I Eligible; 5 School-wide Title I
Students: 12,237 (51.7% male; 48.2% female)
   Individual Education Program: 1,449 (11.8%);
   English Language Learner: 971 (7.9%); Migrant: 217 (1.8%)
   Eligible for Free Lunch Program: 4,549 (37.2%)
   Eligible for Reduced-Price Lunch Program: 1,368 (11.2%)
Teachers: 777.3 (15.7 to 1)
Librarians/Media Specialists: 21.4 (571.8 to 1)
Guidance Counselors: 26.3 (465.3 to 1)
Current Spending: ($ per student per year):
   Total: $7,515; Instruction: $4,915; Support Services: $2,210
Enrollment, Drop-out Rates and Diploma Recipients by Race/Ethnicity

Category	Total	White	Black	Asian	AIAN	Hisp.
Enrollment (%)	100.0	74.1	2.2	0.7	0.1	23.0
Drop-out Rate (%)	11.0	9.6	21.2	7.1	0.0	17.6
H.S. Diplomas (#)	553	499	14	1	0	39

Wilkes County

Wilkes County

313-A N Alexander Ave • Washington, GA 30673-0673
(706) 678-2718 • http://www.wilkes.k12.ga.us/
Grade Span: PK-12; **Agency Type:** 1
Schools: 6
   2 Primary; 1 Middle; 1 High; 2 Other Level
   4 Regular; 1 Special Education; 0 Vocational; 1 Alternative
   0 Magnet; 0 Charter; 3 Title I Eligible; 3 School-wide Title I
Students: 1,853 (51.1% male; 48.8% female)
   Individual Education Program: 265 (14.3%);
   English Language Learner: 11 (0.6%); Migrant: 4 (0.2%)
   Eligible for Free Lunch Program: 919 (49.6%)
   Eligible for Reduced-Price Lunch Program: 223 (12.0%)
Teachers: 119.6 (15.5 to 1)
Librarians/Media Specialists: 3.0 (617.7 to 1)
Guidance Counselors: 4.0 (463.3 to 1)
Current Spending: ($ per student per year):
   Total: $7,459; Instruction: $4,519; Support Services: $2,393
Enrollment, Drop-out Rates and Diploma Recipients by Race/Ethnicity

Category	Total	White	Black	Asian	AIAN	Hisp.
Enrollment (%)	100.0	46.9	51.3	0.2	0.1	1.6
Drop-out Rate (%)	9.3	8.7	9.6	50.0	0.0	0.0
H.S. Diplomas (#)	99	58	40	1	0	0

Wilkinson County

Wilkinson County

100 Bacon St • Irwinton, GA 31042-1042
Mailing Address: PO Box 206 • Irwinton, GA 31042-1042
(478) 946-5521
Grade Span: PK-12; **Agency Type:** 1
Schools: 5
   2 Primary; 1 Middle; 1 High; 1 Other Level
   4 Regular; 1 Special Education; 0 Vocational; 0 Alternative
   0 Magnet; 0 Charter; 2 Title I Eligible; 2 School-wide Title I
Students: 1,713 (51.3% male; 48.6% female)
   Individual Education Program: 269 (15.7%);
   English Language Learner: 5 (0.3%); Migrant: 7 (0.4%)
   Eligible for Free Lunch Program: 1,003 (58.6%)
   Eligible for Reduced-Price Lunch Program: 251 (14.7%)
Teachers: 119.6 (14.3 to 1)
Librarians/Media Specialists: 2.0 (856.5 to 1)
Guidance Counselors: 3.0 (571.0 to 1)
Current Spending: ($ per student per year):
   Total: $8,139; Instruction: $4,968; Support Services: $2,710
Enrollment, Drop-out Rates and Diploma Recipients by Race/Ethnicity

Category	Total	White	Black	Asian	AIAN	Hisp.
Enrollment (%)	100.0	40.5	58.8	0.1	0.0	0.6
Drop-out Rate (%)	8.0	9.4	7.0	n/a	n/a	100.0
H.S. Diplomas (#)	100	22	78	0	0	0

Worth County

Worth County

504 E Price St • Sylvester, GA 31791-1791
(912) 229-8600 • http://www.peanut.org/wcbe
Grade Span: PK-12; **Agency Type:** 1
Schools: 7
   3 Primary; 1 Middle; 1 High; 2 Other Level

---

   5 Regular; 1 Special Education; 0 Vocational; 1 Alternative
   0 Magnet; 0 Charter; 4 Title I Eligible; 4 School-wide Title I
Students: 4,106 (51.7% male; 48.2% female)
   Individual Education Program: 318 (7.7%);
   English Language Learner: 4 (0.1%); Migrant: 6 (0.1%)
   Eligible for Free Lunch Program: 2,214 (53.9%)
   Eligible for Reduced-Price Lunch Program: 347 (8.5%)
Teachers: 266.5 (15.4 to 1)
Librarians/Media Specialists: 7.0 (586.6 to 1)
Guidance Counselors: 10.0 (410.6 to 1)
Current Spending: ($ per student per year):
   Total: $6,952; Instruction: $4,309; Support Services: $2,205
Enrollment, Drop-out Rates and Diploma Recipients by Race/Ethnicity

Category	Total	White	Black	Asian	AIAN	Hisp.
Enrollment (%)	100.0	57.4	41.1	0.3	0.2	1.1
Drop-out Rate (%)	9.5	8.6	11.0	0.0	33.3	9.1
H.S. Diplomas (#)	188	124	64	0	0	0

Number of Schools

Rank	Number	District Name	City
1	141	Dekalb County	Decatur
2	106	Cobb County	Marietta
3	105	Atlanta City	Atlanta
4	98	Gwinnett County	Lawrenceville
5	87	Fulton County	Atlanta
6	62	Muscogee County	Columbus
7	58	Richmond County	Augusta
8	57	Clayton County	Jonesboro
9	55	Chatham County	Savannah
10	45	Bibb County	Macon
11	37	Houston County	Perry
12	34	Cherokee County	Canton
13	33	Hall County	Gainesville
14	32	Henry County	Mcdonough
15	31	Douglas County	Douglasville
16	30	Fayette County	Fayetteville
17	29	Dougherty County	Albany
18	28	Columbia County	Appling
18	28	Coweta County	Newnan
20	26	Paulding County	Dallas
21	24	Forsyth County	Cumming
22	23	Carroll County	Carrollton
22	23	Clarke County	Athens
22	23	Floyd County	Rome
25	22	Troup County	Lagrange
25	22	Whitfield County	Dalton
27	21	Bartow County	Cartersville
28	20	Newton County	Covington
28	20	Spalding County	Griffin
30	19	Glynn County	Brunswick
30	19	Rockdale County	Conyers
32	17	Bulloch County	Statesboro
32	17	Colquitt County	Moultrie
32	17	Liberty County	Hinesville
35	16	Barrow County	Winder
35	16	Catoosa County	Ringgold
35	16	Walker County	Lafayette
38	15	Walton County	Monroe
39	14	Camden County	Kingsland
39	14	Effingham County	Springfield
39	14	Tift County	Tifton
42	13	Bryan County	Pembroke
42	13	Coffee County	Douglas
42	13	Jackson County	Jefferson
42	13	Ware County	Waycross
46	12	Baldwin County	Milledgeville
46	12	Emanuel County	Swainsboro
46	12	Habersham County	Clarkesville
46	12	Lowndes County	Valdosta
46	12	Marietta City	Marietta
46	12	Polk County	Cedartown
46	12	Rome City	Rome
53	11	Chattooga County	Summerville
53	11	Decatur County	Bainbridge
53	11	Meriwether County	Greenville
53	11	Valdosta City	Valdosta
53	11	Wayne County	Jesup
58	10	Dalton City	Dalton
58	10	Elbert County	Elberton
58	10	Gordon County	Calhoun
58	10	Jones County	Gray
58	10	Laurens County	Dublin
58	10	Murray County	Chatsworth
58	10	Oconee County	Watkinsville
58	10	Sumter County	Americus
66	9	Appling County	Baxley
66	9	Grady County	Cairo
66	9	Haralson County	Buchanan
66	9	Madison County	Danielsville
66	9	Tattnall County	Reidsville
66	9	Thomasville City	Thomasville
72	8	Crisp County	Cordele
72	8	Decatur City	Decatur
72	8	Dublin City	Dublin
72	8	Gainesville City	Gainesville
72	8	Harris County	Hamilton
72	8	Jefferson County	Louisville
72	8	Lee County	Leesburg
72	8	Mcduffie County	Thomson
72	8	Mitchell County	Camilla
72	8	Peach County	Fort Valley
72	8	Stephens County	Toccoa
72	8	Thomas County	Thomasville
72	8	Thomaston-Upson County	Thomaston
72	8	Union County	Blairsville
72	8	Washington County	Sandersville
72	8	White County	Cleveland
88	7	Ben Hill County	Fitzgerald
88	7	Brantley County	Nahunta
88	7	Burke County	Waynesboro
88	7	Calhoun City	Calhoun
88	7	Dawson County	Dawsonville
88	7	Gilmer County	Ellijay
88	7	Greene County	Greensboro
88	7	Hart County	Hartwell
88	7	Lumpkin County	Dahlonega
88	7	Pickens County	Jasper
88	7	Rabun County	Clayton
88	7	Turner County	Ashburn
88	7	Worth County	Sylvester
101	6	Banks County	Homer
101	6	Berrien County	Nashville
101	6	Butts County	Jackson
101	6	Candler County	Metter
101	6	Charlton County	Folkston
101	6	Crawford County	Roberta
101	6	Dade County	Trenton
101	6	Dodge County	Eastman
101	6	Fannin County	Blue Ridge
101	6	Franklin County	Carnesville
101	6	Heard County	Franklin
101	6	Jasper County	Monticello
101	6	Jeff Davis County	Hazlehurst
101	6	Monroe County	Forsyth
101	6	Morgan County	Madison
101	6	Oglethorpe County	Lexington
101	6	Pulaski County	Hawkinsville
101	6	Toombs County	Lyons
101	6	Vidalia City	Vidalia
101	6	Wilkes County	Washington
121	5	Bacon County	Alma
121	5	Bleckley County	Cochran
121	5	Brooks County	Quitman
121	5	Buford City	Buford
121	5	Cartersville City	Cartersville
121	5	Cook County	Adel
121	5	Early County	Blakely
121	5	Evans County	Claxton
121	5	Hancock County	Sparta
121	5	Irwin County	Ocilla
121	5	Jenkins County	Millen
121	5	Pierce County	Blackshear
121	5	Pike County	Zebulon
121	5	Putnam County	Eatonton
121	5	Randolph County	Cuthbert
121	5	Screven County	Sylvania
121	5	Telfair County	Mcrae
121	5	Towns County	Hiawassee
121	5	Wilkinson County	Irwinton
140	4	Atkinson County	Pearson
140	4	Bremen City	Bremen
140	4	Carrollton City	Carrollton
140	4	Dooly County	Vienna
140	4	Jefferson City	Jefferson
140	4	Lamar County	Barnesville
140	4	Macon County	Oglethorpe
140	4	Marion County	Buena Vista
140	4	Mcintosh County	Darien
140	4	Pelham City	Pelham
140	4	Seminole County	Donalsonville
140	4	Taylor County	Butler
140	4	Terrell County	Dawson
153	3	Long County	Ludowici

Number of Teachers

Rank	Number	District Name	City
1	8,220	Gwinnett County	Lawrenceville
2	6,867	Cobb County	Marietta
3	6,408	Dekalb County	Decatur
4	4,891	Fulton County	Atlanta
5	3,692	Atlanta City	Atlanta
6	2,954	Clayton County	Jonesboro
7	2,336	Chatham County	Savannah
8	2,209	Richmond County	Augusta
9	2,187	Muscogee County	Columbus
10	1,897	Cherokee County	Canton
11	1,843	Henry County	Mcdonough
12	1,527	Houston County	Perry
13	1,487	Bibb County	Macon
14	1,394	Hall County	Gainesville
15	1,394	Fayette County	Fayetteville
16	1,361	Forsyth County	Cumming
17	1,257	Paulding County	Dallas
18	1,185	Columbia County	Appling
19	1,171	Coweta County	Newnan
20	1,122	Douglas County	Douglasville
21	1,028	Dougherty County	Albany
22	908	Newton County	Covington
23	883	Rockdale County	Conyers
24	850	Bartow County	Cartersville
25	842	Clarke County	Athens
26	830	Carroll County	Carrollton
27	793	Troup County	Lagrange
28	781	Glynn County	Brunswick
29	777	Whitfield County	Dalton
30	698	Walton County	Monroe
31	681	Spalding County	Griffin
32	656	Floyd County	Rome
33	626	Barrow County	Winder
34	615	Liberty County	Hinesville
35	614	Catoosa County	Ringgold
36	598	Lowndes County	Valdosta
37	588	Camden County	Kingsland
38	581	Bulloch County	Statesboro
39	566	Walker County	Lafayette
40	524	Effingham County	Springfield
41	511	Marietta City	Marietta
42	480	Colquitt County	Moultrie
43	471	Tift County	Tifton
44	461	Valdosta City	Valdosta
45	453	Murray County	Chatsworth
46	451	Polk County	Cedartown
47	440	Coffee County	Douglas
48	439	Baldwin County	Milledgeville
49	418	Ware County	Waycross
50	388	Dalton City	Dalton
51	381	Laurens County	Dublin
52	380	Habersham County	Clarkesville
53	377	Decatur County	Bainbridge
54	369	Gordon County	Calhoun
55	367	Oconee County	Watkinsville
56	363	Sumter County	Americus
57	354	Jackson County	Jefferson
58	343	Thomas County	Thomasville
59	341	Bryan County	Pembroke
60	332	Rome City	Rome
61	320	Lee County	Leesburg
62	318	Wayne County	Jesup
63	299	Thomaston-Upson County	Thomaston
64	297	Meriwether County	Greenville
65	297	Stephens County	Toccoa
66	296	Jones County	Gray
67	291	Madison County	Danielsville
68	288	Emanuel County	Swainsboro
69	284	Gainesville City	Gainesville
70	283	Crisp County	Cordele
71	275	Harris County	Hamilton
72	274	Grady County	Cairo
73	266	Worth County	Sylvester
74	264	Mcduffie County	Thomson
75	259	Gilmer County	Ellijay
76	256	Peach County	Fort Valley
77	253	Burke County	Waynesboro
78	247	Pickens County	Jasper
79	247	White County	Cleveland
80	241	Cartersville City	Cartersville
81	238	Franklin County	Carnesville
82	237	Elbert County	Elberton
83	234	Haralson County	Buchanan
84	230	Dublin City	Dublin
85	229	Dawson County	Dawsonville
86	226	Lumpkin County	Dahlonega
87	222	Monroe County	Forsyth
88	220	Washington County	Sandersville
89	216	Hart County	Hartwell
90	211	Dodge County	Eastman
91	211	Ben Hill County	Fitzgerald
92	211	Appling County	Baxley
93	209	Morgan County	Madison
94	207	Brantley County	Nahunta
95	207	Carrollton City	Carrollton
96	206	Decatur City	Decatur
97	205	Tattnall County	Reidsville
98	202	Mitchell County	Camilla
99	202	Thomasville City	Thomasville
100	191	Chattooga County	Summerville
101	191	Cook County	Adel
102	190	Putnam County	Eatonton
103	187	Screven County	Sylvania
104	185	Jefferson County	Louisville
105	182	Union County	Blairsville
106	180	Fannin County	Blue Ridge
107	178	Butts County	Jackson
108	172	Toombs County	Lyons
109	168	Calhoun City	Calhoun
110	162	Dade County	Trenton
111	162	Pierce County	Blackshear
112	158	Pike County	Zebulon
113	158	Greene County	Greensboro
114	158	Early County	Blakely
115	156	Brooks County	Quitman
116	152	Jeff Davis County	Hazlehurst
117	150	Berrien County	Nashville
118	150	Rabun County	Clayton
119	149	Banks County	Homer

120	148	Buford City	Buford
121	147	Vidalia City	Vidalia
122	146	Oglethorpe County	Lexington
123	145	Bleckley County	Cochran
124	142	Towns County	Hiawassee
125	141	Lamar County	Barnesville
126	140	Heard County	Franklin
127	136	Jasper County	Monticello
128	135	Turner County	Ashburn
129	133	Macon County	Oglethorpe
130	123	Evans County	Claxton
131	123	Pulaski County	Hawkinsville
132	121	Crawford County	Roberta
133	120	Bacon County	Alma
134	119	Wilkes County	Washington
134	119	Wilkinson County	Irwinton
136	118	Seminole County	Donalsonville
137	117	Irwin County	Ocilla
138	116	Telfair County	Mcrae
139	115	Charlton County	Folkston
140	115	Jenkins County	Millen
141	113	Mcintosh County	Darien
142	111	Jefferson City	Jefferson
142	111	Randolph County	Cuthbert
144	108	Candler County	Metter
145	106	Marion County	Buena Vista
146	105	Long County	Ludowici
147	100	Atkinson County	Pearson
148	100	Pelham City	Pelham
149	99	Terrell County	Dawson
150	97	Taylor County	Butler
151	94	Hancock County	Sparta
152	94	Bremen City	Bremen
153	78	Dooly County	Vienna

Number of Students

Rank	Number	District Name	City
1	129,014	Gwinnett County	Lawrenceville
2	102,034	Cobb County	Marietta
3	99,550	Dekalb County	Decatur
4	73,319	Fulton County	Atlanta
5	52,103	Atlanta City	Atlanta
6	50,555	Clayton County	Jonesboro
7	34,514	Chatham County	Savannah
8	34,400	Richmond County	Augusta
9	33,055	Muscogee County	Columbus
10	29,843	Henry County	Mcdonough
11	29,711	Cherokee County	Canton
12	25,276	Bibb County	Macon
13	23,395	Houston County	Perry
14	22,535	Hall County	Gainesville
15	22,067	Forsyth County	Cumming
16	21,224	Fayette County	Fayetteville
17	20,459	Paulding County	Dallas
18	20,063	Columbia County	Appling
19	19,697	Douglas County	Douglasville
20	19,035	Coweta County	Newnan
21	16,844	Dougherty County	Albany
22	14,713	Newton County	Covington
23	14,266	Rockdale County	Conyers
24	13,769	Carroll County	Carrollton
25	13,696	Bartow County	Cartersville
26	12,237	Whitfield County	Dalton
27	12,017	Glynn County	Brunswick
28	11,993	Troup County	Lagrange
29	11,615	Liberty County	Hinesville
30	11,502	Clarke County	Athens
31	10,722	Walton County	Monroe
32	10,693	Spalding County	Griffin
33	10,382	Floyd County	Rome
34	10,120	Catoosa County	Ringgold
35	9,767	Barrow County	Winder
36	9,669	Camden County	Kingsland
37	9,350	Effingham County	Springfield
38	9,298	Lowndes County	Valdosta
39	8,820	Walker County	Lafayette
40	8,498	Bulloch County	Statesboro
41	8,419	Colquitt County	Moultrie
42	7,808	Coffee County	Douglas
43	7,661	Tift County	Tifton
44	7,599	Marietta City	Marietta
45	7,474	Murray County	Chatsworth
46	7,065	Polk County	Cedartown
47	7,062	Valdosta City	Valdosta
48	6,399	Gordon County	Calhoun
49	6,343	Ware County	Waycross
50	6,121	Laurens County	Dublin
51	6,043	Habersham County	Clarkesville
52	5,947	Baldwin County	Milledgeville
53	5,934	Dalton City	Dalton
54	5,768	Bryan County	Pembroke
55	5,767	Oconee County	Watkinsville
56	5,714	Decatur County	Bainbridge
57	5,704	Sumter County	Americus
58	5,679	Jackson County	Jefferson
59	5,523	Thomas County	Thomasville
60	5,449	Lee County	Leesburg
61	5,312	Wayne County	Jesup
62	5,306	Rome City	Rome
63	5,187	Jones County	Gray
64	4,992	Thomaston-Upson County	Thomaston
65	4,724	Gainesville City	Gainesville
66	4,657	Burke County	Waynesboro
67	4,636	Madison County	Danielsville
68	4,581	Emanuel County	Swainsboro
69	4,481	Grady County	Cairo
70	4,410	Harris County	Hamilton
71	4,388	Crisp County	Cordele
72	4,313	Stephens County	Toccoa
73	4,310	Mcduffie County	Thomson
74	4,126	Pickens County	Jasper
75	4,106	Worth County	Sylvester
76	4,036	Gilmer County	Ellijay
77	4,005	Peach County	Fort Valley
78	3,907	Cartersville City	Cartersville
79	3,866	Meriwether County	Greenville
80	3,863	White County	Cleveland
81	3,820	Monroe County	Forsyth
82	3,811	Haralson County	Buchanan
83	3,740	Elbert County	Elberton
84	3,711	Washington County	Sandersville
85	3,657	Franklin County	Carnesville
86	3,629	Carrollton City	Carrollton
87	3,562	Hart County	Hartwell
88	3,549	Lumpkin County	Dahlonega
89	3,542	Dodge County	Eastman
90	3,412	Butts County	Jackson
91	3,402	Jefferson County	Louisville
92	3,362	Appling County	Baxley
93	3,330	Brantley County	Nahunta
94	3,310	Tattnall County	Reidsville
95	3,309	Ben Hill County	Fitzgerald
96	3,283	Pierce County	Blackshear
97	3,204	Morgan County	Madison
98	3,174	Dublin City	Dublin
99	3,158	Cook County	Adel
100	3,123	Fannin County	Blue Ridge
101	3,062	Thomasville City	Thomasville
102	3,049	Screven County	Sylvania
103	3,044	Berrien County	Nashville
104	3,023	Dawson County	Dawsonville
105	3,005	Pike County	Zebulon
106	2,988	Chattooga County	Summerville
107	2,867	Mitchell County	Camilla
108	2,777	Calhoun City	Calhoun
109	2,758	Toombs County	Lyons
110	2,711	Early County	Blakely
111	2,638	Dade County	Trenton
112	2,626	Union County	Blairsville
113	2,622	Putnam County	Eatonton
114	2,593	Jeff Davis County	Hazlehurst
115	2,592	Lamar County	Barnesville
116	2,524	Brooks County	Quitman
117	2,517	Decatur City	Decatur
118	2,491	Vidalia City	Vidalia
119	2,457	Banks County	Homer
120	2,432	Bleckley County	Cochran
121	2,288	Buford City	Buford
122	2,263	Greene County	Greensboro
123	2,252	Oglethorpe County	Lexington
124	2,192	Rabun County	Clayton
125	2,160	Macon County	Oglethorpe
126	2,147	Heard County	Franklin
127	2,094	Jasper County	Monticello
128	2,078	Crawford County	Roberta
129	2,069	Long County	Ludowici
130	2,044	Charlton County	Folkston
131	1,933	Mcintosh County	Darien
132	1,931	Candler County	Metter
133	1,898	Turner County	Ashburn
134	1,888	Evans County	Claxton
135	1,884	Bacon County	Alma
136	1,853	Wilkes County	Washington
137	1,822	Irwin County	Ocilla
138	1,758	Seminole County	Donalsonville
139	1,721	Jenkins County	Millen
140	1,715	Marion County	Buena Vista
141	1,713	Wilkinson County	Irwinton
142	1,704	Jefferson City	Jefferson
143	1,702	Telfair County	Mcrae
144	1,696	Taylor County	Butler
145	1,695	Atkinson County	Pearson
146	1,676	Terrell County	Dawson
147	1,674	Pulaski County	Hawkinsville
148	1,618	Bremen City	Bremen
149	1,610	Randolph County	Cuthbert
150	1,597	Towns County	Hiawassee
151	1,590	Hancock County	Sparta
152	1,583	Pelham City	Pelham
153	1,570	Dooly County	Vienna

Male Students

Rank	Percent	District Name	City
1	54.1	Evans County	Claxton
2	53.8	Dade County	Trenton
3	53.6	Hart County	Hartwell
4	53.1	Chattooga County	Summerville
5	52.9	Crawford County	Roberta
6	52.8	Pike County	Zebulon
7	52.7	Haralson County	Buchanan
8	52.7	Meriwether County	Greenville
9	52.5	Jenkins County	Millen
10	52.3	Oconee County	Watkinsville
11	52.3	Walker County	Lafayette
12	52.3	Candler County	Metter
13	52.2	Lumpkin County	Dahlonega
14	52.2	Appling County	Baxley
15	52.2	Putnam County	Eatonton
16	52.2	Harris County	Hamilton
17	52.2	Polk County	Cedartown
18	52.1	White County	Cleveland
19	52.1	Jackson County	Jefferson
20	52.1	Hall County	Gainesville
21	52.1	Habersham County	Clarkesville
22	52.1	Dodge County	Eastman
23	52.0	Pierce County	Blackshear
24	52.0	Decatur City	Decatur
25	52.0	Bryan County	Pembroke
26	52.0	Bacon County	Alma
27	52.0	Brooks County	Quitman
28	52.0	Telfair County	Mcrae
29	52.0	Gilmer County	Ellijay
30	52.0	Tattnall County	Reidsville
31	51.9	Wayne County	Jesup
32	51.9	Banks County	Homer
33	51.9	Butts County	Jackson
34	51.9	Houston County	Perry
35	51.9	Dooly County	Vienna
36	51.9	Thomaston-Upson County	Thomaston
37	51.8	Jones County	Gray
38	51.8	Dublin City	Dublin
39	51.8	Greene County	Greensboro
40	51.8	Laurens County	Dublin
41	51.7	Worth County	Sylvester
42	51.7	Charlton County	Folkston
43	51.7	Monroe County	Forsyth
44	51.7	Fannin County	Blue Ridge
45	51.7	Whitfield County	Dalton
46	51.7	Barrow County	Winder
47	51.7	Cartersville City	Cartersville
48	51.6	Franklin County	Carnesville
49	51.6	Atkinson County	Pearson
50	51.6	Forsyth County	Cumming
51	51.6	Randolph County	Cuthbert
52	51.6	Murray County	Chatsworth
53	51.6	Stephens County	Toccoa
54	51.6	Pulaski County	Hawkinsville
55	51.6	Dawson County	Dawsonville
56	51.5	Emanuel County	Swainsboro
57	51.5	Douglas County	Douglasville
58	51.5	Oglethorpe County	Lexington
59	51.5	Seminole County	Donalsonville
60	51.5	Mcduffie County	Thomson
61	51.5	Carrollton City	Carrollton
62	51.5	Carroll County	Carrollton
63	51.5	Rabun County	Clayton
64	51.4	Cherokee County	Canton
65	51.4	Gwinnett County	Lawrenceville
66	51.4	Mitchell County	Camilla
67	51.4	Newton County	Covington
68	51.4	Coweta County	Newnan
69	51.4	Camden County	Kingsland
70	51.4	Bulloch County	Statesboro
71	51.4	Decatur County	Bainbridge
72	51.4	Cobb County	Marietta
73	51.4	Jefferson City	Jefferson
74	51.3	Lowndes County	Valdosta
75	51.3	Pickens County	Jasper
76	51.3	Bartow County	Cartersville
77	51.3	Turner County	Ashburn
78	51.3	Wilkinson County	Irwinton
79	51.3	Columbia County	Appling
80	51.3	Buford City	Buford
81	51.3	Paulding County	Dallas
82	51.2	Henry County	Mcdonough
83	51.2	Jefferson County	Louisville
84	51.2	Troup County	Lagrange

Rank	Percent	District Name	City
85	51.2	Rockdale County	Conyers
86	51.2	Ware County	Waycross
87	51.2	Heard County	Franklin
88	51.2	Long County	Ludowici
89	51.2	Dalton City	Dalton
90	51.1	Dekalb County	Decatur
91	51.1	Colquitt County	Moultrie
92	51.1	Burke County	Waynesboro
93	51.1	Madison County	Danielsville
94	51.1	Brantley County	Nahunta
95	51.1	Fulton County	Atlanta
96	51.1	Clayton County	Jonesboro
97	51.1	Wilkes County	Washington
98	51.1	Fayette County	Fayetteville
99	51.0	Calhoun City	Calhoun
100	51.0	Marietta City	Marietta
101	51.0	Terrell County	Dawson
102	51.0	Effingham County	Springfield
103	51.0	Elbert County	Elberton
104	51.0	Taylor County	Butler
105	50.9	Floyd County	Rome
106	50.9	Chatham County	Savannah
107	50.9	Cook County	Adel
108	50.9	Spalding County	Griffin
109	50.8	Sumter County	Americus
110	50.8	Early County	Blakely
111	50.8	Thomas County	Thomasville
112	50.8	Lee County	Leesburg
113	50.8	Toombs County	Lyons
114	50.8	Berrien County	Nashville
115	50.7	Catoosa County	Ringgold
116	50.7	Macon County	Oglethorpe
117	50.7	Peach County	Fort Valley
118	50.6	Jasper County	Monticello
119	50.6	Crisp County	Cordele
120	50.6	Glynn County	Brunswick
121	50.6	Coffee County	Douglas
122	50.6	Marion County	Buena Vista
123	50.5	Hancock County	Sparta
124	50.4	Ben Hill County	Fitzgerald
125	50.4	Union County	Blairsville
126	50.4	Irwin County	Ocilla
127	50.4	Dougherty County	Albany
128	50.4	Muscogee County	Columbus
129	50.4	Washington County	Sandersville
130	50.4	Richmond County	Augusta
131	50.4	Tift County	Tifton
132	50.3	Lamar County	Barnesville
133	50.3	Baldwin County	Milledgeville
134	50.3	Jeff Davis County	Hazlehurst
135	50.3	Gordon County	Calhoun
136	50.3	Morgan County	Madison
137	50.3	Liberty County	Hinesville
138	50.3	Valdosta City	Valdosta
139	50.2	Mcintosh County	Darien
140	50.2	Bibb County	Macon
141	50.2	Towns County	Hiawassee
142	50.1	Gainesville City	Gainesville
143	50.1	Clarke County	Athens
144	49.9	Walton County	Monroe
145	49.8	Atlanta City	Atlanta
146	49.8	Bleckley County	Cochran
147	49.8	Pelham City	Pelham
148	49.8	Thomasville City	Thomasville
149	49.7	Vidalia City	Vidalia
150	49.6	Rome City	Rome
151	49.5	Bremen City	Bremen
152	49.2	Screven County	Sylvania
153	48.5	Grady County	Cairo

Female Students

Rank	Percent	District Name	City
1	51.4	Grady County	Cairo
2	50.7	Screven County	Sylvania
3	50.4	Bremen City	Bremen
4	50.3	Rome City	Rome
5	50.2	Vidalia City	Vidalia
6	50.1	Thomasville City	Thomasville
7	50.1	Pelham City	Pelham
8	50.1	Bleckley County	Cochran
9	50.1	Atlanta City	Atlanta
10	50.0	Walton County	Monroe
11	49.8	Clarke County	Athens
12	49.8	Gainesville City	Gainesville
13	49.7	Towns County	Hiawassee
14	49.7	Bibb County	Macon
15	49.7	Mcintosh County	Darien
16	49.6	Valdosta City	Valdosta
17	49.6	Liberty County	Hinesville
18	49.6	Morgan County	Madison
19	49.6	Gordon County	Calhoun
20	49.6	Jeff Davis County	Hazlehurst
21	49.6	Baldwin County	Milledgeville
22	49.6	Lamar County	Barnesville
23	49.5	Tift County	Tifton
24	49.5	Richmond County	Augusta
25	49.5	Washington County	Sandersville
26	49.5	Muscogee County	Columbus
27	49.5	Dougherty County	Albany
28	49.5	Irwin County	Ocilla
29	49.5	Union County	Blairsville
30	49.5	Ben Hill County	Fitzgerald
31	49.4	Hancock County	Sparta
32	49.3	Marion County	Buena Vista
33	49.3	Coffee County	Douglas
34	49.3	Glynn County	Brunswick
35	49.3	Crisp County	Cordele
36	49.3	Jasper County	Monticello
37	49.2	Peach County	Fort Valley
38	49.2	Macon County	Oglethorpe
39	49.2	Catoosa County	Ringgold
40	49.1	Berrien County	Nashville
41	49.1	Toombs County	Lyons
42	49.1	Lee County	Leesburg
43	49.1	Thomas County	Thomasville
44	49.1	Early County	Blakely
45	49.1	Sumter County	Americus
46	49.0	Spalding County	Griffin
47	49.0	Cook County	Adel
48	49.0	Chatham County	Savannah
49	49.0	Floyd County	Rome
50	48.9	Taylor County	Butler
51	48.9	Elbert County	Elberton
52	48.9	Effingham County	Springfield
53	48.9	Terrell County	Dawson
54	48.9	Marietta City	Marietta
55	48.9	Calhoun City	Calhoun
56	48.8	Fayette County	Fayetteville
57	48.8	Wilkes County	Washington
58	48.8	Clayton County	Jonesboro
59	48.8	Fulton County	Atlanta
60	48.8	Brantley County	Nahunta
61	48.8	Madison County	Danielsville
62	48.8	Burke County	Waynesboro
63	48.8	Colquitt County	Moultrie
64	48.8	Dekalb County	Decatur
65	48.7	Dalton City	Dalton
66	48.7	Long County	Ludowici
67	48.7	Heard County	Franklin
68	48.7	Ware County	Waycross
69	48.7	Rockdale County	Conyers
70	48.7	Troup County	Lagrange
71	48.7	Jefferson County	Louisville
72	48.7	Henry County	Mcdonough
73	48.6	Paulding County	Dallas
74	48.6	Buford City	Buford
75	48.6	Columbia County	Appling
76	48.6	Wilkinson County	Irwinton
77	48.6	Turner County	Ashburn
78	48.6	Bartow County	Cartersville
79	48.6	Pickens County	Jasper
80	48.6	Lowndes County	Valdosta
81	48.5	Jefferson City	Jefferson
82	48.5	Cobb County	Marietta
83	48.5	Decatur County	Bainbridge
84	48.5	Bulloch County	Statesboro
85	48.5	Camden County	Kingsland
86	48.5	Coweta County	Newnan
87	48.5	Newton County	Covington
88	48.5	Mitchell County	Camilla
89	48.5	Gwinnett County	Lawrenceville
90	48.5	Cherokee County	Canton
91	48.4	Rabun County	Clayton
92	48.4	Carroll County	Carrollton
93	48.4	Carrollton City	Carrollton
94	48.4	Mcduffie County	Thomson
95	48.4	Seminole County	Donalsonville
96	48.4	Oglethorpe County	Lexington
97	48.4	Douglas County	Douglasville
98	48.4	Emanuel County	Swainsboro
99	48.3	Dawson County	Dawsonville
100	48.3	Pulaski County	Hawkinsville
101	48.3	Stephens County	Toccoa
102	48.3	Murray County	Chatsworth
103	48.3	Randolph County	Cuthbert
104	48.3	Forsyth County	Cumming
105	48.3	Atkinson County	Pearson
106	48.3	Franklin County	Carnesville
107	48.2	Cartersville City	Cartersville
108	48.2	Barrow County	Winder
109	48.2	Whitfield County	Dalton
110	48.2	Fannin County	Blue Ridge
111	48.2	Monroe County	Forsyth
112	48.2	Charlton County	Folkston
113	48.2	Worth County	Sylvester
114	48.1	Laurens County	Dublin
115	48.1	Greene County	Greensboro
116	48.1	Dublin City	Dublin
117	48.1	Jones County	Gray
118	48.0	Thomaston-Upson County	Thomaston
119	48.0	Dooly County	Vienna
120	48.0	Houston County	Perry
121	48.0	Butts County	Jackson
122	48.0	Banks County	Homer
123	48.0	Wayne County	Jesup
124	47.9	Tattnall County	Reidsville
125	47.9	Gilmer County	Ellijay
126	47.9	Telfair County	Mcrae
127	47.9	Brooks County	Quitman
128	47.9	Bacon County	Alma
129	47.9	Bryan County	Pembroke
130	47.9	Decatur City	Decatur
131	47.9	Pierce County	Blackshear
132	47.8	Dodge County	Eastman
133	47.8	Habersham County	Clarkesville
134	47.8	Hall County	Gainesville
135	47.8	Jackson County	Jefferson
136	47.8	White County	Cleveland
137	47.7	Polk County	Cedartown
138	47.7	Harris County	Hamilton
139	47.7	Putnam County	Eatonton
140	47.7	Appling County	Baxley
141	47.7	Lumpkin County	Dahlonega
142	47.6	Candler County	Metter
143	47.6	Walker County	Lafayette
144	47.6	Oconee County	Watkinsville
145	47.4	Jenkins County	Millen
146	47.2	Meriwether County	Greenville
147	47.2	Haralson County	Buchanan
148	47.1	Pike County	Zebulon
149	47.0	Crawford County	Roberta
150	46.8	Chattooga County	Summerville
151	46.3	Hart County	Hartwell
152	46.1	Dade County	Trenton
153	45.8	Evans County	Claxton

Individual Education Program Students

Rank	Percent	District Name	City
1	25.0	Meriwether County	Greenville
2	24.4	Floyd County	Rome
3	21.7	Chattooga County	Summerville
4	19.5	Haralson County	Buchanan
5	19.1	Irwin County	Ocilla
6	18.4	Union County	Blairsville
7	18.3	Evans County	Claxton
8	17.7	Baldwin County	Milledgeville
9	17.4	Crawford County	Roberta
9	17.4	Franklin County	Carnesville
11	17.3	Thomas County	Thomasville
12	16.9	Screven County	Sylvania
13	16.8	Madison County	Danielsville
14	16.5	Emanuel County	Swainsboro
14	16.5	Polk County	Cedartown
16	16.4	Appling County	Baxley
16	16.4	Dublin City	Dublin
18	16.2	Barrow County	Winder
19	16.0	Pelham City	Pelham
20	15.8	Pierce County	Blackshear
21	15.7	Wilkinson County	Irwinton
22	15.6	Rabun County	Clayton
23	15.5	Jackson County	Jefferson
24	15.4	Early County	Blakely
24	15.4	Jasper County	Monticello
24	15.4	Lowndes County	Valdosta
24	15.4	Monroe County	Forsyth
28	15.3	Gordon County	Calhoun
29	15.2	Greene County	Greensboro
29	15.2	Oglethorpe County	Lexington
31	15.1	Clarke County	Athens
31	15.1	Valdosta City	Valdosta
31	15.1	Walker County	Lafayette
34	15.0	Coweta County	Newnan
34	15.0	Putnam County	Eatonton
34	15.0	Toombs County	Lyons
37	14.9	Carroll County	Carrollton
38	14.8	Bulloch County	Statesboro
39	14.7	Ben Hill County	Fitzgerald
39	14.7	Thomaston-Upson County	Thomaston
41	14.6	Telfair County	Mcrae
42	14.5	Bartow County	Cartersville
42	14.5	Carrollton City	Carrollton
42	14.5	Effingham County	Springfield
42	14.5	Pulaski County	Hawkinsville
42	14.5	Spalding County	Griffin
47	14.4	Bacon County	Alma
47	14.4	Jenkins County	Millen
47	14.4	Seminole County	Donalsonville

		District	City
47	14.4	Ware County	Waycross
51	14.3	Brantley County	Nahunta
51	14.3	Marietta City	Marietta
51	14.3	Wilkes County	Washington
54	14.0	Stephens County	Toccoa
55	13.9	Bleckley County	Cochran
55	13.9	Wayne County	Jesup
57	13.8	Colquitt County	Moultrie
57	13.8	Hancock County	Sparta
57	13.8	Jefferson County	Louisville
60	13.7	Newton County	Covington
60	13.7	Terrell County	Dawson
62	13.5	Catoosa County	Ringgold
62	13.5	Fannin County	Blue Ridge
62	13.5	Habersham County	Clarkesville
62	13.5	Morgan County	Madison
62	13.5	Walton County	Monroe
67	13.4	Glynn County	Brunswick
67	13.4	Houston County	Perry
69	13.3	Atkinson County	Pearson
69	13.3	Berrien County	Nashville
69	13.3	Bremen City	Bremen
69	13.3	Charlton County	Folkston
69	13.3	White County	Cleveland
74	13.2	Brooks County	Quitman
74	13.2	Decatur City	Decatur
76	13.1	Banks County	Homer
76	13.1	Candler County	Metter
76	13.1	Dawson County	Dawsonville
76	13.1	Lumpkin County	Dahlonega
80	13.0	Forsyth County	Cumming
80	13.0	Jeff Davis County	Hazlehurst
82	12.9	Mitchell County	Camilla
82	12.9	Thomasville City	Thomasville
84	12.8	Cobb County	Marietta
84	12.8	Muscogee County	Columbus
86	12.7	Buford City	Buford
86	12.7	Pickens County	Jasper
86	12.7	Tattnall County	Reidsville
89	12.6	Dade County	Trenton
89	12.6	Mcduffie County	Thomson
89	12.6	Paulding County	Dallas
92	12.5	Tift County	Tifton
93	12.4	Cook County	Adel
93	12.4	Dougherty County	Albany
93	12.4	Elbert County	Elberton
93	12.4	Troup County	Lagrange
97	12.3	Cherokee County	Canton
98	12.2	Peach County	Fort Valley
98	12.2	Rome City	Rome
100	12.1	Camden County	Kingsland
101	12.0	Dodge County	Eastman
101	12.0	Douglas County	Douglasville
103	11.9	Butts County	Jackson
103	11.9	Heard County	Franklin
105	11.8	Chatham County	Savannah
105	11.8	Jones County	Gray
105	11.8	Whitfield County	Dalton
108	11.7	Coffee County	Douglas
108	11.7	Dalton City	Dalton
108	11.7	Gilmer County	Ellijay
108	11.7	Hart County	Hartwell
108	11.7	Washington County	Sandersville
113	11.6	Grady County	Cairo
113	11.6	Liberty County	Hinesville
113	11.6	Turner County	Ashburn
116	11.5	Bibb County	Macon
116	11.5	Fayette County	Fayetteville
116	11.5	Gwinnett County	Lawrenceville
116	11.5	Henry County	Mcdonough
116	11.5	Murray County	Chatsworth
121	11.3	Randolph County	Cuthbert
122	11.2	Decatur County	Bainbridge
123	11.0	Crisp County	Cordele
123	11.0	Oconee County	Watkinsville
125	10.8	Calhoun City	Calhoun
126	10.7	Laurens County	Dublin
127	10.6	Burke County	Waynesboro
127	10.6	Fulton County	Atlanta
129	10.5	Jefferson City	Jefferson
129	10.5	Rockdale County	Conyers
131	10.4	Hall County	Gainesville
131	10.4	Richmond County	Augusta
133	10.3	Lamar County	Barnesville
134	10.1	Pike County	Zebulon
135	10.0	Columbia County	Appling
136	9.9	Long County	Ludowici
137	9.8	Sumter County	Americus
138	9.7	Marion County	Buena Vista
139	9.6	Bryan County	Pembroke
139	9.6	Clayton County	Jonesboro
141	9.5	Taylor County	Butler
142	9.4	Dekalb County	Decatur
142	9.4	Macon County	Oglethorpe
144	8.9	Cartersville City	Cartersville
144	8.9	Harris County	Hamilton
146	8.8	Lee County	Leesburg
147	8.7	Dooly County	Vienna
148	8.6	Atlanta City	Atlanta
149	7.9	Mcintosh County	Darien
150	7.8	Towns County	Hiawassee
151	7.7	Worth County	Sylvester
152	7.3	Vidalia City	Vidalia
153	6.2	Gainesville City	Gainesville

English Language Learner Students

Rank	Percent	District Name	City
1	28.1	Gainesville City	Gainesville
2	21.2	Dalton City	Dalton
3	18.7	Marietta City	Marietta
4	16.7	Hall County	Gainesville
5	13.6	Dekalb County	Decatur
6	11.8	Rome City	Rome
7	10.6	Buford City	Buford
7	10.6	Gwinnett County	Lawrenceville
9	8.9	Calhoun City	Calhoun
10	8.7	Toombs County	Lyons
11	7.9	Whitfield County	Dalton
12	6.3	Clarke County	Athens
13	6.2	Long County	Ludowici
14	6.1	Candler County	Metter
14	6.1	Gilmer County	Ellijay
16	5.8	Fulton County	Atlanta
17	5.6	Tift County	Tifton
18	5.5	Tattnall County	Reidsville
19	5.4	Habersham County	Clarkesville
20	5.1	Polk County	Cedartown
21	5.0	Clayton County	Jonesboro
21	5.0	Cobb County	Marietta
21	5.0	Evans County	Claxton
24	4.9	Cartersville City	Cartersville
24	4.9	Rockdale County	Conyers
26	4.8	Coffee County	Douglas
27	4.7	Rabun County	Clayton
28	4.6	Barrow County	Winder
28	4.6	Forsyth County	Cumming
30	4.4	Atkinson County	Pearson
31	4.2	Atlanta City	Atlanta
32	4.0	Colquitt County	Moultrie
33	3.8	Ben Hill County	Fitzgerald
34	3.7	Banks County	Homer
34	3.7	Gordon County	Calhoun
36	3.6	Marion County	Buena Vista
37	3.4	Carrollton City	Carrollton
37	3.4	Pierce County	Blackshear
39	3.1	Grady County	Cairo
40	2.9	Jeff Davis County	Hazlehurst
41	2.7	Appling County	Baxley
41	2.7	Cherokee County	Canton
43	2.5	Elbert County	Elberton
43	2.5	Floyd County	Rome
43	2.5	Murray County	Chatsworth
46	2.4	Dooly County	Vienna
47	2.3	Fayette County	Fayetteville
48	2.2	Jefferson City	Jefferson
48	2.2	Macon County	Oglethorpe
48	2.2	Peach County	Fort Valley
48	2.2	Putnam County	Eatonton
52	2.0	Telfair County	Mcrae
53	1.9	Douglas County	Douglasville
54	1.7	Jasper County	Monticello
55	1.6	Bartow County	Cartersville
55	1.6	Wayne County	Jesup
57	1.5	Jackson County	Jefferson
57	1.5	Walton County	Monroe
59	1.4	Carroll County	Carrollton
59	1.4	Decatur City	Decatur
59	1.4	Greene County	Greensboro
59	1.4	Hart County	Hartwell
59	1.4	Oconee County	Watkinsville
64	1.3	Coweta County	Newnan
64	1.3	Newton County	Covington
66	1.2	Bulloch County	Statesboro
66	1.2	Decatur County	Bainbridge
66	1.2	Henry County	Mcdonough
66	1.2	Madison County	Danielsville
70	1.1	Bacon County	Alma
70	1.1	Chattooga County	Summerville
70	1.1	Glynn County	Brunswick
70	1.1	Spalding County	Griffin
74	1.0	Bibb County	Macon
74	1.0	Cook County	Adel
74	1.0	Lumpkin County	Dahlonega
74	1.0	Muscogee County	Columbus
74	1.0	Ware County	Waycross
79	0.9	Brooks County	Quitman
79	0.9	Dawson County	Dawsonville
79	0.9	Houston County	Perry
79	0.9	Pelham City	Pelham
83	0.8	Emanuel County	Swainsboro
84	0.7	Baldwin County	Milledgeville
84	0.7	Crisp County	Cordele
84	0.7	Laurens County	Dublin
84	0.7	Liberty County	Hinesville
84	0.7	Pickens County	Jasper
84	0.7	Towns County	Hiawassee
84	0.7	Troup County	Lagrange
84	0.7	Union County	Blairsville
84	0.7	Valdosta City	Valdosta
84	0.7	White County	Cleveland
94	0.6	Jefferson County	Louisville
94	0.6	Lowndes County	Valdosta
94	0.6	Monroe County	Forsyth
94	0.6	Morgan County	Madison
94	0.6	Stephens County	Toccoa
94	0.6	Wilkes County	Washington
100	0.5	Bleckley County	Cochran
100	0.5	Catoosa County	Ringgold
100	0.5	Chatham County	Savannah
100	0.5	Columbia County	Appling
100	0.5	Dublin City	Dublin
100	0.5	Early County	Blakely
100	0.5	Franklin County	Carnesville
100	0.5	Mcduffie County	Thomson
100	0.5	Mitchell County	Camilla
100	0.5	Paulding County	Dallas
100	0.5	Pulaski County	Hawkinsville
111	0.4	Camden County	Kingsland
111	0.4	Effingham County	Springfield
111	0.4	Richmond County	Augusta
111	0.4	Walker County	Lafayette
115	0.3	Hancock County	Sparta
115	0.3	Vidalia City	Vidalia
115	0.3	Wilkinson County	Irwinton
118	0.2	Bryan County	Pembroke
118	0.2	Dougherty County	Albany
118	0.2	Mcintosh County	Darien
118	0.2	Meriwether County	Greenville
118	0.2	Thomas County	Thomasville
123	0.1	Brantley County	Nahunta
123	0.1	Dodge County	Eastman
123	0.1	Thomaston-Upson County	Thomaston
123	0.1	Worth County	Sylvester
127	0.0	Crawford County	Roberta
127	0.0	Harris County	Hamilton
127	0.0	Jones County	Gray
127	0.0	Oglethorpe County	Lexington
127	0.0	Pike County	Zebulon
127	0.0	Screven County	Sylvania
127	0.0	Sumter County	Americus
134	0.0	Berrien County	Nashville
134	0.0	Bremen City	Bremen
134	0.0	Burke County	Waynesboro
134	0.0	Butts County	Jackson
134	0.0	Charlton County	Folkston
134	0.0	Dade County	Trenton
134	0.0	Fannin County	Blue Ridge
134	0.0	Haralson County	Buchanan
134	0.0	Heard County	Franklin
134	0.0	Irwin County	Ocilla
134	0.0	Jenkins County	Millen
134	0.0	Lamar County	Barnesville
134	0.0	Lee County	Leesburg
134	0.0	Randolph County	Cuthbert
134	0.0	Seminole County	Donalsonville
134	0.0	Taylor County	Butler
134	0.0	Terrell County	Dawson
134	0.0	Thomasville City	Thomasville
134	0.0	Turner County	Ashburn
134	0.0	Washington County	Sandersville

Migrant Students

Rank	Percent	District Name	City
1	18.5	Atkinson County	Pearson
2	16.3	Tattnall County	Reidsville
3	11.5	Candler County	Metter
4	11.3	Gainesville City	Gainesville
5	10.7	Long County	Ludowici
6	9.3	Colquitt County	Moultrie
7	8.7	Coffee County	Douglas
8	7.9	Appling County	Baxley
8	7.9	Habersham County	Clarkesville
8	7.9	Toombs County	Lyons
11	7.7	Evans County	Claxton
12	7.3	Dalton City	Dalton
13	6.7	Jeff Davis County	Hazlehurst
14	6.1	Bacon County	Alma

Rank		District	City
15	5.9	Gilmer County	Ellijay
16	5.6	Peach County	Fort Valley
16	5.6	Tift County	Tifton
18	4.9	Grady County	Cairo
19	4.4	Hall County	Gainesville
20	4.0	Clarke County	Athens
21	3.7	Pierce County	Blackshear
22	3.6	Decatur County	Bainbridge
23	3.5	Polk County	Cedartown
24	3.2	Macon County	Oglethorpe
25	2.9	Haralson County	Buchanan
26	2.7	Marion County	Buena Vista
26	2.7	Seminole County	Donalsonville
28	2.5	Sumter County	Americus
29	2.4	Jenkins County	Millen
30	2.3	Berrien County	Nashville
30	2.3	Brooks County	Quitman
32	2.2	Thomas County	Thomasville
33	2.0	Screven County	Sylvania
34	1.9	Cook County	Adel
34	1.9	Rome City	Rome
34	1.9	Ware County	Waycross
37	1.8	Dooly County	Vienna
37	1.8	Mitchell County	Camilla
37	1.8	Whitfield County	Dalton
40	1.6	Emanuel County	Swainsboro
41	1.4	Bulloch County	Statesboro
41	1.4	Early County	Blakely
41	1.4	Glynn County	Brunswick
41	1.4	Laurens County	Dublin
45	1.1	Pelham City	Pelham
46	1.0	Putnam County	Eatonton
47	0.9	Banks County	Homer
47	0.9	Buford City	Buford
47	0.9	Irwin County	Ocilla
50	0.8	Lowndes County	Valdosta
50	0.8	Pulaski County	Hawkinsville
50	0.8	Rabun County	Clayton
53	0.7	Ben Hill County	Fitzgerald
54	0.6	Elbert County	Elberton
54	0.6	Lumpkin County	Dahlonega
54	0.6	Taylor County	Butler
54	0.6	Vidalia City	Vidalia
58	0.5	Crawford County	Roberta
58	0.5	Crisp County	Cordele
58	0.5	Jackson County	Jefferson
61	0.4	Jefferson County	Louisville
61	0.4	Turner County	Ashburn
61	0.4	Walker County	Lafayette
61	0.4	Wayne County	Jesup
61	0.4	Wilkinson County	Irwinton
66	0.3	Bleckley County	Cochran
66	0.3	Brantley County	Nahunta
66	0.3	Cherokee County	Canton
66	0.3	Dodge County	Eastman
66	0.3	Dublin City	Dublin
66	0.3	Forsyth County	Cumming
66	0.3	Greene County	Greensboro
66	0.3	Hart County	Hartwell
66	0.3	Houston County	Perry
66	0.3	Monroe County	Forsyth
66	0.3	Valdosta City	Valdosta
77	0.2	Barrow County	Winder
77	0.2	Jefferson City	Jefferson
77	0.2	Mcduffie County	Thomson
77	0.2	Oconee County	Watkinsville
77	0.2	Telfair County	Mcrae
77	0.2	White County	Cleveland
77	0.2	Wilkes County	Washington
84	0.1	Bibb County	Macon
84	0.1	Burke County	Waynesboro
84	0.1	Dawson County	Dawsonville
84	0.1	Dougherty County	Albany
84	0.1	Floyd County	Rome
84	0.1	Marietta City	Marietta
84	0.1	Muscogee County	Columbus
84	0.1	Pickens County	Jasper
84	0.1	Terrell County	Dawson
84	0.1	Worth County	Sylvester
94	0.0	Bryan County	Pembroke
94	0.0	Calhoun City	Calhoun
94	0.0	Clayton County	Jonesboro
94	0.0	Cobb County	Marietta
94	0.0	Dekalb County	Decatur
94	0.0	Effingham County	Springfield
94	0.0	Gwinnett County	Lawrenceville
94	0.0	Liberty County	Hinesville
94	0.0	Madison County	Danielsville
94	0.0	Murray County	Chatsworth
94	0.0	Oglethorpe County	Lexington
94	0.0	Paulding County	Dallas
94	0.0	Thomaston-Upson County	Thomaston
94	0.0	Walton County	Monroe
94	0.0	Washington County	Sandersville
109	0.0	Atlanta City	Atlanta
109	0.0	Baldwin County	Milledgeville
109	0.0	Bartow County	Cartersville
109	0.0	Bremen City	Bremen
109	0.0	Butts County	Jackson
109	0.0	Camden County	Kingsland
109	0.0	Carroll County	Carrollton
109	0.0	Carrollton City	Carrollton
109	0.0	Cartersville City	Cartersville
109	0.0	Catoosa County	Ringgold
109	0.0	Charlton County	Folkston
109	0.0	Chatham County	Savannah
109	0.0	Chattooga County	Summerville
109	0.0	Columbia County	Appling
109	0.0	Coweta County	Newnan
109	0.0	Dade County	Trenton
109	0.0	Decatur City	Decatur
109	0.0	Douglas County	Douglasville
109	0.0	Fannin County	Blue Ridge
109	0.0	Fayette County	Fayetteville
109	0.0	Franklin County	Carnesville
109	0.0	Fulton County	Atlanta
109	0.0	Gordon County	Calhoun
109	0.0	Hancock County	Sparta
109	0.0	Harris County	Hamilton
109	0.0	Heard County	Franklin
109	0.0	Henry County	Mcdonough
109	0.0	Jasper County	Monticello
109	0.0	Jones County	Gray
109	0.0	Lamar County	Barnesville
109	0.0	Lee County	Leesburg
109	0.0	Mcintosh County	Darien
109	0.0	Meriwether County	Greenville
109	0.0	Morgan County	Madison
109	0.0	Newton County	Covington
109	0.0	Pike County	Zebulon
109	0.0	Randolph County	Cuthbert
109	0.0	Richmond County	Augusta
109	0.0	Rockdale County	Conyers
109	0.0	Spalding County	Griffin
109	0.0	Stephens County	Toccoa
109	0.0	Thomasville City	Thomasville
109	0.0	Towns County	Hiawassee
109	0.0	Troup County	Lagrange
109	0.0	Union County	Blairsville

Students Eligible for Free Lunch

Rank	Percent	District Name	City
1	80.7	Randolph County	Cuthbert
2	78.6	Jefferson County	Louisville
3	76.1	Dooly County	Vienna
4	74.7	Hancock County	Sparta
5	74.2	Greene County	Greensboro
6	69.8	Macon County	Oglethorpe
7	68.3	Meriwether County	Greenville
8	67.2	Atkinson County	Pearson
9	65.9	Atlanta City	Atlanta
9	65.9	Burke County	Waynesboro
11	65.3	Brooks County	Quitman
11	65.3	Sumter County	Americus
13	65.0	Jenkins County	Millen
14	64.6	Early County	Blakely
15	63.5	Mcintosh County	Darien
16	63.2	Screven County	Sylvania
17	61.2	Seminole County	Donalsonville
18	61.0	Bibb County	Macon
18	61.0	Crisp County	Cordele
18	61.0	Telfair County	Mcrae
21	60.8	Gainesville City	Gainesville
22	60.5	Toombs County	Lyons
23	60.3	Dougherty County	Albany
23	60.3	Pelham City	Pelham
25	60.2	Valdosta City	Valdosta
26	60.1	Evans County	Claxton
26	60.1	Turner County	Ashburn
28	60.0	Terrell County	Dawson
29	59.7	Dublin City	Dublin
30	59.5	Emanuel County	Swainsboro
31	58.8	Tattnall County	Reidsville
32	58.6	Wilkinson County	Irwinton
33	57.9	Clarke County	Athens
34	57.8	Decatur County	Bainbridge
35	57.7	Taylor County	Butler
36	57.4	Ben Hill County	Fitzgerald
37	57.0	Coffee County	Douglas
38	56.9	Candler County	Metter
39	56.7	Peach County	Fort Valley
40	55.8	Marion County	Buena Vista
41	55.6	Thomasville City	Thomasville
42	55.5	Mitchell County	Camilla
43	55.4	Rome City	Rome
44	55.2	Richmond County	Augusta
45	55.1	Washington County	Sandersville
46	53.9	Mcduffie County	Thomson
46	53.9	Worth County	Sylvester
48	53.6	Colquitt County	Moultrie
49	53.1	Long County	Ludowici
49	53.1	Putnam County	Eatonton
51	52.3	Appling County	Baxley
52	52.0	Irwin County	Ocilla
53	51.5	Marietta City	Marietta
54	50.8	Ware County	Waycross
55	50.7	Clayton County	Jonesboro
56	50.3	Dodge County	Eastman
57	49.9	Dekalb County	Decatur
58	49.7	Cook County	Adel
59	49.6	Wilkes County	Washington
60	49.1	Grady County	Cairo
61	48.8	Tift County	Tifton
62	48.7	Charlton County	Folkston
62	48.7	Jasper County	Monticello
64	48.5	Spalding County	Griffin
65	48.3	Crawford County	Roberta
65	48.3	Laurens County	Dublin
67	48.1	Dalton City	Dalton
67	48.1	Jeff Davis County	Hazlehurst
67	48.1	Thomas County	Thomasville
70	47.9	Elbert County	Elberton
70	47.9	Vidalia City	Vidalia
72	47.8	Baldwin County	Milledgeville
73	47.5	Chattooga County	Summerville
74	47.3	Muscogee County	Columbus
75	47.1	Pulaski County	Hawkinsville
76	46.6	Chatham County	Savannah
77	46.4	Lamar County	Barnesville
78	46.2	Troup County	Lagrange
79	46.1	Bulloch County	Statesboro
80	45.1	Thomaston-Upson County	Thomaston
81	44.4	Wayne County	Jesup
82	44.1	Berrien County	Nashville
83	43.2	Bacon County	Alma
84	43.1	Brantley County	Nahunta
85	42.6	Pierce County	Blackshear
86	41.5	Heard County	Franklin
87	41.3	Banks County	Homer
88	41.0	Bleckley County	Cochran
89	40.4	Gilmer County	Ellijay
90	40.1	Walker County	Lafayette
91	39.6	Monroe County	Forsyth
92	38.7	Glynn County	Brunswick
92	38.7	Murray County	Chatsworth
94	38.5	Butts County	Jackson
94	38.5	Carrollton City	Carrollton
96	37.8	Stephens County	Toccoa
97	37.2	Polk County	Cedartown
97	37.2	Whitfield County	Dalton
99	37.1	Buford City	Buford
100	36.8	Hart County	Hartwell
101	36.7	Carroll County	Carrollton
102	36.6	Liberty County	Hinesville
103	36.4	Newton County	Covington
104	35.7	Haralson County	Buchanan
105	35.1	Hall County	Gainesville
106	34.8	Decatur City	Decatur
106	34.8	Oglethorpe County	Lexington
108	34.5	Union County	Blairsville
109	34.1	Gordon County	Calhoun
110	34.0	Jackson County	Jefferson
111	33.9	Rabun County	Clayton
112	33.3	Calhoun City	Calhoun
113	33.1	Franklin County	Carnesville
114	32.5	Madison County	Danielsville
115	32.2	Morgan County	Madison
116	31.9	Cartersville City	Cartersville
116	31.9	Floyd County	Rome
118	31.7	Pickens County	Jasper
119	31.5	Fannin County	Blue Ridge
120	31.1	Bartow County	Cartersville
121	30.9	Habersham County	Clarkesville
122	30.0	Houston County	Perry
123	29.7	Rockdale County	Conyers
124	29.2	Lumpkin County	Dahlonega
125	28.9	Lowndes County	Valdosta
125	28.9	Walton County	Monroe
127	28.7	White County	Cleveland
128	28.5	Douglas County	Douglasville
129	28.4	Dade County	Trenton
130	27.6	Barrow County	Winder
130	27.6	Fulton County	Atlanta
132	27.4	Camden County	Kingsland
133	26.3	Catoosa County	Ringgold
134	25.8	Jones County	Gray
135	25.1	Bryan County	Pembroke
136	25.0	Harris County	Hamilton

137	24.2	Lee County	Leesburg
138	23.7	Gwinnett County	Lawrenceville
139	22.5	Dawson County	Dawsonville
140	22.4	Coweta County	Newnan
140	22.4	Jefferson City	Jefferson
142	22.0	Cobb County	Marietta
143	21.9	Pike County	Zebulon
144	21.1	Effingham County	Springfield
145	21.0	Towns County	Hiawassee
146	17.4	Henry County	Mcdonough
147	15.9	Paulding County	Dallas
148	14.7	Columbia County	Appling
149	13.6	Cherokee County	Canton
150	13.2	Oconee County	Watkinsville
151	13.0	Bremen City	Bremen
152	9.5	Forsyth County	Cumming
153	7.6	Fayette County	Fayetteville

Students Eligible for Reduced-Price Lunch

Rank	Percent	District Name	City
1	16.9	Rabun County	Clayton
2	15.8	Screven County	Sylvania
3	15.2	Liberty County	Hinesville
4	14.7	Wilkinson County	Irwinton
5	14.4	Murray County	Chatsworth
6	14.0	Banks County	Homer
6	14.0	Clayton County	Jonesboro
8	13.9	Evans County	Claxton
8	13.9	Union County	Blairsville
10	13.7	Burke County	Waynesboro
10	13.7	Pierce County	Blackshear
10	13.7	Washington County	Sandersville
13	13.6	Atkinson County	Pearson
14	13.5	Long County	Ludowici
15	13.4	Fannin County	Blue Ridge
16	13.1	Walker County	Lafayette
17	12.8	Charlton County	Folkston
17	12.8	Chattooga County	Summerville
17	12.8	Crawford County	Roberta
20	12.6	Meriwether County	Greenville
21	12.4	Macon County	Oglethorpe
22	12.3	Brantley County	Nahunta
22	12.3	Jenkins County	Millen
24	12.2	Irwin County	Ocilla
25	12.0	Dade County	Trenton
25	12.0	Wilkes County	Washington
27	11.9	Toombs County	Lyons
28	11.7	Dodge County	Eastman
29	11.6	Gilmer County	Ellijay
29	11.6	Putnam County	Eatonton
31	11.5	Lamar County	Barnesville
32	11.4	Pelham City	Pelham
33	11.2	Camden County	Kingsland
33	11.2	Candler County	Metter
33	11.2	Dalton City	Dalton
33	11.2	Whitfield County	Dalton
37	10.9	Carroll County	Carrollton
38	10.8	Coffee County	Douglas
38	10.8	Heard County	Franklin
38	10.8	Marion County	Buena Vista
38	10.8	Newton County	Covington
42	10.7	Gordon County	Calhoun
43	10.6	Jackson County	Jefferson
44	10.5	Emanuel County	Swainsboro
45	10.4	Butts County	Jackson
46	10.3	Jeff Davis County	Hazlehurst
46	10.3	Madison County	Danielsville
48	10.2	Bulloch County	Statesboro
48	10.2	Catoosa County	Ringgold
48	10.2	Haralson County	Buchanan
51	10.1	Oglethorpe County	Lexington
51	10.1	Tattnall County	Reidsville
51	10.1	White County	Cleveland
54	10.0	Brooks County	Quitman
54	10.0	Taylor County	Butler
56	9.9	Mitchell County	Camilla
56	9.9	Pickens County	Jasper
56	9.9	Telfair County	Mcrae
56	9.9	Terrell County	Dawson
60	9.8	Baldwin County	Milledgeville
60	9.8	Hart County	Hartwell
60	9.8	Pulaski County	Hawkinsville
63	9.7	Bacon County	Alma
63	9.7	Barrow County	Winder
65	9.6	Houston County	Perry
65	9.6	Jasper County	Monticello
65	9.6	Laurens County	Dublin
65	9.6	Richmond County	Augusta
65	9.6	Thomaston-Upson County	Thomaston
70	9.5	Floyd County	Rome
70	9.5	Sumter County	Americus
72	9.3	Harris County	Hamilton
73	9.2	Bleckley County	Cochran
73	9.2	Dougherty County	Albany
73	9.2	Douglas County	Douglasville
73	9.2	Early County	Blakely
73	9.2	Elbert County	Elberton
73	9.2	Thomas County	Thomasville
79	9.1	Cook County	Adel
79	9.1	Dekalb County	Decatur
79	9.1	Lowndes County	Valdosta
79	9.1	Ware County	Waycross
83	9.0	Berrien County	Nashville
83	9.0	Marietta City	Marietta
85	8.9	Colquitt County	Moultrie
85	8.9	Decatur County	Bainbridge
85	8.9	Spalding County	Griffin
88	8.8	Dooly County	Vienna
88	8.8	Effingham County	Springfield
88	8.8	Hancock County	Sparta
88	8.8	Wayne County	Jesup
92	8.7	Bryan County	Pembroke
92	8.7	Franklin County	Carnesville
92	8.7	Muscogee County	Columbus
95	8.6	Chatham County	Savannah
95	8.6	Gainesville City	Gainesville
95	8.6	Peach County	Fort Valley
95	8.6	Stephens County	Toccoa
95	8.6	Valdosta City	Valdosta
100	8.5	Appling County	Baxley
100	8.5	Worth County	Sylvester
102	8.4	Hall County	Gainesville
102	8.4	Mcduffie County	Thomson
104	8.3	Bartow County	Cartersville
104	8.3	Randolph County	Cuthbert
106	8.2	Lumpkin County	Dahlonega
106	8.2	Troup County	Lagrange
108	8.1	Tift County	Tifton
108	8.1	Towns County	Hiawassee
110	8.0	Ben Hill County	Fitzgerald
110	8.0	Clarke County	Athens
110	8.0	Habersham County	Clarkesville
110	8.0	Rockdale County	Conyers
110	8.0	Thomasville City	Thomasville
115	7.9	Mcintosh County	Darien
116	7.8	Cartersville City	Cartersville
116	7.8	Dublin City	Dublin
116	7.8	Paulding County	Dallas
119	7.7	Calhoun City	Calhoun
119	7.7	Grady County	Cairo
119	7.7	Monroe County	Forsyth
119	7.7	Walton County	Monroe
123	7.3	Crisp County	Cordele
123	7.3	Jones County	Gray
123	7.3	Seminole County	Donalsonville
123	7.3	Turner County	Ashburn
127	7.2	Dawson County	Dawsonville
127	7.2	Vidalia City	Vidalia
129	7.1	Gwinnett County	Lawrenceville
130	7.0	Jefferson County	Louisville
130	7.0	Polk County	Cedartown
132	6.9	Glynn County	Brunswick
133	6.7	Bibb County	Macon
134	6.5	Rome City	Rome
135	6.4	Carrollton City	Carrollton
135	6.4	Lee County	Leesburg
137	6.3	Greene County	Greensboro
138	6.1	Morgan County	Madison
139	6.0	Cobb County	Marietta
140	5.8	Henry County	Mcdonough
141	5.7	Columbia County	Appling
142	5.6	Pike County	Zebulon
143	5.5	Coweta County	Newnan
144	4.9	Buford City	Buford
144	4.9	Jefferson City	Jefferson
146	4.8	Cherokee County	Canton
147	4.4	Decatur City	Decatur
147	4.4	Fulton County	Atlanta
149	4.3	Oconee County	Watkinsville
150	4.2	Atlanta City	Atlanta
151	3.9	Bremen City	Bremen
152	3.5	Forsyth County	Cumming
153	2.7	Fayette County	Fayetteville

Student/Teacher Ratio

Rank	Ratio	District Name	City
1	20.3	Pierce County	Blackshear
2	20.2	Berrien County	Nashville
3	20.1	Dooly County	Vienna
4	19.6	Long County	Ludowici
5	19.1	Butts County	Jackson
6	18.9	Liberty County	Hinesville
6	18.9	Pike County	Zebulon
8	18.4	Burke County	Waynesboro
9	18.3	Jefferson County	Louisville
9	18.3	Lamar County	Barnesville
11	17.8	Candler County	Metter
11	17.8	Effingham County	Springfield
13	17.7	Charlton County	Folkston
13	17.7	Coffee County	Douglas
15	17.6	Douglas County	Douglasville
16	17.5	Carrollton City	Carrollton
16	17.5	Colquitt County	Moultrie
16	17.5	Jones County	Gray
19	17.4	Taylor County	Butler
20	17.3	Fannin County	Blue Ridge
20	17.3	Gordon County	Calhoun
22	17.2	Bremen City	Bremen
22	17.2	Monroe County	Forsyth
24	17.1	Clayton County	Jonesboro
24	17.1	Crawford County	Roberta
24	17.1	Early County	Blakely
27	17.0	Bibb County	Macon
27	17.0	Jeff Davis County	Hazlehurst
27	17.0	Lee County	Leesburg
27	17.0	Mcintosh County	Darien
31	16.9	Atkinson County	Pearson
31	16.9	Bryan County	Pembroke
31	16.9	Columbia County	Appling
31	16.9	Terrell County	Dawson
31	16.9	Vidalia City	Vidalia
36	16.8	Hancock County	Sparta
36	16.8	Washington County	Sandersville
38	16.7	Bleckley County	Cochran
38	16.7	Dodge County	Eastman
38	16.7	Pickens County	Jasper
38	16.7	Thomaston-Upson County	Thomaston
38	16.7	Wayne County	Jesup
43	16.6	Carroll County	Carrollton
43	16.6	Gainesville City	Gainesville
45	16.5	Calhoun City	Calhoun
45	16.5	Catoosa County	Ringgold
45	16.5	Cook County	Adel
45	16.5	Murray County	Chatsworth
49	16.4	Banks County	Homer
49	16.4	Camden County	Kingsland
49	16.4	Dougherty County	Albany
49	16.4	Hart County	Hartwell
53	16.3	Dade County	Trenton
53	16.3	Grady County	Cairo
53	16.3	Haralson County	Buchanan
53	16.3	Mcduffie County	Thomson
53	16.3	Paulding County	Dallas
53	16.3	Screven County	Sylvania
53	16.3	Tift County	Tifton
60	16.2	Cartersville City	Cartersville
60	16.2	Coweta County	Newnan
60	16.2	Forsyth County	Cumming
60	16.2	Hall County	Gainesville
60	16.2	Henry County	Mcdonough
60	16.2	Macon County	Oglethorpe
60	16.2	Newton County	Covington
67	16.1	Bartow County	Cartersville
67	16.1	Brooks County	Quitman
67	16.1	Laurens County	Dublin
67	16.1	Marion County	Buena Vista
67	16.1	Rockdale County	Conyers
67	16.1	Tattnall County	Reidsville
67	16.1	Thomas County	Thomasville
74	16.0	Brantley County	Nahunta
74	16.0	Harris County	Hamilton
74	16.0	Jackson County	Jefferson
74	16.0	Rome City	Rome
74	16.0	Toombs County	Lyons
79	15.9	Appling County	Baxley
79	15.9	Emanuel County	Swainsboro
79	15.9	Habersham County	Clarkesville
79	15.9	Madison County	Danielsville
83	15.8	Floyd County	Rome
83	15.8	Pelham City	Pelham
85	15.7	Bacon County	Alma
85	15.7	Cherokee County	Canton
85	15.7	Elbert County	Elberton
85	15.7	Gwinnett County	Lawrenceville
85	15.7	Lumpkin County	Dahlonega
85	15.7	Oconee County	Watkinsville
85	15.7	Polk County	Cedartown
85	15.7	Spalding County	Griffin
85	15.7	Sumter County	Americus
85	15.7	Whitfield County	Dalton
95	15.6	Barrow County	Winder
95	15.6	Ben Hill County	Fitzgerald
95	15.6	Chattooga County	Summerville
95	15.6	Gilmer County	Ellijay

Rank	Ratio	District	City
95	15.6	Peach County	Fort Valley
95	15.6	Richmond County	Augusta
95	15.6	Walker County	Lafayette
95	15.6	White County	Cleveland
103	15.5	Crisp County	Cordele
103	15.5	Dekalb County	Decatur
103	15.5	Irwin County	Ocilla
103	15.5	Lowndes County	Valdosta
103	15.5	Wilkes County	Washington
108	15.4	Buford City	Buford
108	15.4	Glynn County	Brunswick
108	15.4	Oglethorpe County	Lexington
108	15.4	Worth County	Sylvester
112	15.3	Dalton City	Dalton
112	15.3	Evans County	Claxton
112	15.3	Franklin County	Carnesville
112	15.3	Heard County	Franklin
112	15.3	Houston County	Perry
112	15.3	Jasper County	Monticello
112	15.3	Jefferson City	Jefferson
112	15.3	Morgan County	Madison
112	15.3	Valdosta City	Valdosta
112	15.3	Walton County	Monroe
122	15.2	Fayette County	Fayetteville
122	15.2	Ware County	Waycross
124	15.1	Decatur County	Bainbridge
124	15.1	Muscogee County	Columbus
124	15.1	Thomasville City	Thomasville
124	15.1	Troup County	Lagrange
128	15.0	Fulton County	Atlanta
128	15.0	Jenkins County	Millen
130	14.9	Cobb County	Marietta
130	14.9	Marietta City	Marietta
130	14.9	Seminole County	Donalsonville
133	14.8	Chatham County	Savannah
134	14.6	Bulloch County	Statesboro
134	14.6	Rabun County	Clayton
134	14.6	Telfair County	Mcrae
137	14.5	Randolph County	Cuthbert
137	14.5	Stephens County	Toccoa
139	14.4	Union County	Blairsville
140	14.3	Greene County	Greensboro
140	14.3	Wilkinson County	Irwinton
142	14.1	Atlanta City	Atlanta
142	14.1	Mitchell County	Camilla
144	14.0	Turner County	Ashburn
145	13.8	Dublin City	Dublin
145	13.8	Putnam County	Eatonton
147	13.7	Clarke County	Athens
148	13.6	Pulaski County	Hawkinsville
149	13.5	Baldwin County	Milledgeville
150	13.2	Dawson County	Dawsonville
151	13.0	Meriwether County	Greenville
152	12.2	Decatur City	Decatur
153	11.2	Towns County	Hiawassee

Student/Librarian Ratio

Rank	Ratio	District Name	City
1	1,209.7	Carrollton City	Carrollton
2	1,190.2	Gwinnett County	Lawrenceville
3	1,104.6	Thomas County	Thomasville
4	1,034.5	Long County	Ludowici
5	1,016.3	Screven County	Sylvania
6	1,003.0	Forsyth County	Cumming
7	1,001.7	Pike County	Zebulon
8	955.0	Monroe County	Forsyth
9	949.0	Turner County	Ashburn
10	925.7	Calhoun City	Calhoun
11	911.0	Irwin County	Ocilla
12	904.3	Henry County	Mcdonough
13	903.7	Early County	Blakely
14	902.3	Cook County	Adel
15	895.3	Berrien County	Nashville
16	887.3	Cobb County	Marietta
17	885.5	Dodge County	Eastman
18	879.0	Seminole County	Donalsonville
19	864.0	Lamar County	Barnesville
20	860.5	Jenkins County	Millen
21	856.5	Wilkinson County	Irwinton
22	851.0	Telfair County	Mcrae
23	849.6	Baldwin County	Milledgeville
24	848.0	Taylor County	Butler
25	842.7	Fulton County	Atlanta
26	840.4	Mcintosh County	Darien
27	837.0	Pulaski County	Hawkinsville
28	832.2	Cherokee County	Canton
29	830.4	Murray County	Chatsworth
30	827.3	Ben Hill County	Fitzgerald
31	822.0	Clayton County	Jonesboro
32	820.8	Pierce County	Blackshear
33	809.0	Bremen City	Bremen
34	801.0	Morgan County	Madison
35	798.5	Towns County	Hiawassee
36	795.0	Hancock County	Sparta
37	787.3	Gainesville City	Gainesville
38	781.4	Cartersville City	Cartersville
39	776.2	Burke County	Waynesboro
40	774.4	Newton County	Covington
41	757.7	Paulding County	Dallas
42	731.4	Franklin County	Carnesville
43	731.3	Crisp County	Cordele
44	725.9	Liberty County	Hinesville
45	720.9	Oconee County	Watkinsville
46	720.5	Rockdale County	Conyers
47	719.5	Pelham City	Pelham
48	716.8	Mitchell County	Camilla
49	715.2	Lowndes County	Valdosta
50	714.8	Walton County	Monroe
51	713.1	Thomaston-Upson County	Thomaston
52	713.0	Sumter County	Americus
53	712.4	Hart County	Hartwell
54	711.0	Gordon County	Calhoun
55	709.8	Lumpkin County	Dahlonega
56	706.9	Glynn County	Brunswick
57	698.0	Jasper County	Monticello
58	692.7	Crawford County	Roberta
59	691.8	Columbia County	Appling
60	690.8	Marietta City	Marietta
61	690.6	Camden County	Kingsland
62	689.5	Toombs County	Lyons
63	684.8	Bartow County	Cartersville
64	682.9	Hall County	Gainesville
65	682.4	Butts County	Jackson
66	681.1	Lee County	Leesburg
67	679.8	Coweta County	Newnan
68	673.7	Emanuel County	Swainsboro
69	673.3	Union County	Blairsville
70	672.7	Gilmer County	Ellijay
71	672.3	Putnam County	Eatonton
72	668.4	Houston County	Perry
73	667.9	Effingham County	Springfield
74	667.5	Peach County	Fort Valley
75	663.7	Chatham County	Savannah
76	659.3	Dalton City	Dalton
77	651.1	Barrow County	Winder
78	650.7	Coffee County	Douglas
79	648.4	Jones County	Gray
80	644.3	Laurens County	Dublin
81	643.8	White County	Cleveland
82	643.7	Candler County	Metter
83	643.2	Fayette County	Fayetteville
84	640.9	Bryan County	Pembroke
85	638.4	Tift County	Tifton
86	636.1	Dekalb County	Decatur
86	636.1	Habersham County	Clarkesville
88	635.2	Haralson County	Buchanan
89	634.8	Dublin City	Dublin
90	632.5	Catoosa County	Ringgold
91	632.4	Jeff Davis County	Hazlehurst
92	631.0	Brooks County	Quitman
93	630.0	Harris County	Hamilton
94	629.3	Evans County	Claxton
95	628.0	Bacon County	Alma
96	624.6	Fannin County	Blue Ridge
97	622.8	Vidalia City	Vidalia
98	617.7	Wilkes County	Washington
99	616.1	Stephens County	Toccoa
100	615.7	Mcduffie County	Thomson
101	614.3	Banks County	Homer
102	612.4	Thomasville City	Thomasville
103	608.0	Bleckley County	Cochran
104	604.6	Dawson County	Dawsonville
104	604.6	Richmond County	Augusta
106	598.7	Polk County	Cedartown
107	596.9	Douglas County	Douglasville
108	590.2	Wayne County	Jesup
109	589.4	Pickens County	Jasper
110	588.5	Valdosta City	Valdosta
111	588.4	Carroll County	Carrollton
112	588.0	Walker County	Lafayette
113	587.8	Bibb County	Macon
114	586.6	Worth County	Sylvester
115	576.6	Ware County	Waycross
116	575.1	Clarke County	Athens
117	572.0	Buford City	Buford
118	571.8	Whitfield County	Dalton
119	571.7	Marion County	Buena Vista
120	571.1	Troup County	Lagrange
121	568.9	Muscogee County	Columbus
122	568.0	Jefferson City	Jefferson
123	567.0	Jefferson County	Louisville
124	566.3	Atlanta City	Atlanta
125	565.8	Greene County	Greensboro
126	565.7	Decatur County	Bainbridge
127	565.0	Atkinson County	Pearson
128	563.0	Oglethorpe County	Lexington
129	561.5	Dougherty County	Albany
130	561.3	Colquitt County	Moultrie
131	560.3	Appling County	Baxley
132	560.1	Grady County	Cairo
133	558.7	Terrell County	Dawson
134	555.0	Brantley County	Nahunta
135	552.3	Meriwether County	Greenville
136	551.7	Tattnall County	Reidsville
137	546.4	Floyd County	Rome
138	545.7	Washington County	Sandersville
139	540.0	Macon County	Oglethorpe
140	536.8	Heard County	Franklin
141	536.7	Randolph County	Cuthbert
142	534.7	Spalding County	Griffin
143	531.1	Bulloch County	Statesboro
144	527.6	Dade County	Trenton
145	523.3	Dooly County	Vienna
146	516.3	Jackson County	Jefferson
147	515.1	Madison County	Danielsville
148	511.0	Charlton County	Folkston
149	482.4	Rome City	Rome
150	467.5	Elbert County	Elberton
151	438.4	Rabun County	Clayton
152	426.9	Chattooga County	Summerville
153	359.6	Decatur City	Decatur

Student/Counselor Ratio

Rank	Ratio	District Name	City
1	748.0	Elbert County	Elberton
2	689.7	Long County	Ludowici
3	647.2	Bremen City	Bremen
4	639.9	Gordon County	Calhoun
5	628.0	Bacon County	Alma
6	618.5	Washington County	Sandersville
7	601.0	Pike County	Zebulon
8	594.7	Baldwin County	Milledgeville
9	590.5	Gainesville City	Gainesville
10	587.3	Emanuel County	Swainsboro
11	585.1	Crisp County	Cordele
12	584.0	Charlton County	Folkston
13	577.9	Terrell County	Dawson
14	576.8	Bryan County	Pembroke
15	576.6	Gilmer County	Ellijay
16	574.2	Cook County	Adel
17	571.7	Marion County	Buena Vista
18	571.0	Wilkinson County	Irwinton
19	569.4	Thomas County	Thomasville
20	567.3	Telfair County	Mcrae
20	567.3	Thomaston-Upson County	Thomaston
22	565.9	Newton County	Covington
23	562.9	Toombs County	Lyons
24	562.2	Mitchell County	Camilla
25	557.7	Coffee County	Douglas
26	554.4	Calhoun City	Calhoun
27	546.0	Jones County	Gray
28	544.9	Dodge County	Eastman
29	540.0	Carroll County	Carrollton
30	537.2	Thomasville City	Thomasville
31	536.8	Heard County	Franklin
32	536.7	Randolph County	Cuthbert
33	535.9	Union County	Blairsville
34	535.3	Cherokee County	Canton
35	533.9	Murray County	Chatsworth
36	532.3	Towns County	Hiawassee
37	528.3	Tift County	Tifton
38	528.0	Liberty County	Hinesville
39	524.4	Putnam County	Eatonton
40	524.2	Ware County	Waycross
41	523.5	Jasper County	Monticello
42	523.3	Dooly County	Vienna
42	523.3	Monroe County	Forsyth
44	522.4	Franklin County	Carnesville
45	520.5	Fannin County	Blue Ridge
46	519.5	Crawford County	Roberta
47	519.4	Effingham County	Springfield
48	518.6	Jeff Davis County	Hazlehurst
49	518.4	Lamar County	Barnesville
50	518.3	Douglas County	Douglasville
51	516.6	Lowndes County	Valdosta
52	516.3	Jackson County	Jefferson
53	515.8	Pickens County	Jasper
54	515.1	White County	Cleveland
55	510.6	Barrow County	Winder
56	510.6	Pelham City	Pelham
57	508.9	Hart County	Hartwell
58	508.6	Houston County	Perry
59	508.2	Candler County	Metter
59	508.2	Screven County	Sylvania
61	507.3	Berrien County	Nashville
62	505.9	Wayne County	Jesup

63	504.8	Brooks County	Quitman
64	504.6	Polk County	Cedartown
65	503.8	Dawson County	Dawsonville
66	503.6	Habersham County	Clarkesville
67	498.2	Vidalia City	Vidalia
68	498.0	Chattooga County	Summerville
69	495.4	Lee County	Leesburg
70	495.2	Colquitt County	Moultrie
71	487.5	Sumter County	Americus
72	487.4	Butts County	Jackson
73	486.9	Jefferson City	Jefferson
74	486.4	Bleckley County	Cochran
75	486.0	Jefferson County	Louisville
76	484.1	Gwinnett County	Lawrenceville
77	483.3	Mcintosh County	Darien
78	481.9	Catoosa County	Ringgold
79	480.6	Oconee County	Watkinsville
80	476.4	Haralson County	Buchanan
81	475.8	Paulding County	Dallas
82	475.7	Brantley County	Nahunta
83	475.5	Rockdale County	Conyers
84	475.4	Hall County	Gainesville
85	474.5	Richmond County	Augusta
86	473.7	Henry County	Mcdonough
87	472.9	Tattnall County	Reidsville
88	472.0	Evans County	Claxton
89	470.8	Laurens County	Dublin
89	470.8	Valdosta City	Valdosta
91	469.0	Pierce County	Blackshear
92	465.9	Clayton County	Jonesboro
93	465.3	Carrollton City	Carrollton
93	465.3	Whitfield County	Dalton
95	464.6	Forsyth County	Cumming
96	464.3	Coweta County	Newnan
97	463.6	Madison County	Danielsville
98	463.3	Wilkes County	Washington
99	460.1	Clarke County	Athens
100	460.0	Dublin City	Dublin
101	459.6	Cartersville City	Cartersville
102	457.6	Buford City	Buford
103	456.5	Bartow County	Cartersville
104	455.0	Spalding County	Griffin
105	454.8	Meriwether County	Greenville
106	454.3	Hancock County	Sparta
107	452.3	Walker County	Lafayette
108	450.4	Oglethorpe County	Lexington
109	448.1	Grady County	Cairo
110	447.4	Bibb County	Macon
111	447.3	Bulloch County	Statesboro
112	446.8	Walton County	Monroe
113	445.0	Peach County	Fort Valley
114	443.6	Lumpkin County	Dahlonega
115	442.2	Rome City	Rome
116	439.5	Seminole County	Donalsonville
117	438.6	Glynn County	Brunswick
118	438.4	Rabun County	Clayton
119	436.1	Troup County	Lagrange
120	435.7	Stephens County	Toccoa
121	432.0	Macon County	Oglethorpe
122	431.0	Appling County	Baxley
123	430.3	Jenkins County	Millen
124	428.7	Chatham County	Savannah
125	427.2	Morgan County	Madison
126	426.9	Columbia County	Appling
127	426.4	Dougherty County	Albany
128	424.0	Taylor County	Butler
129	423.9	Dalton City	Dalton
130	422.2	Marietta City	Marietta
131	421.8	Turner County	Ashburn
132	418.5	Fulton County	Atlanta
132	418.5	Pulaski County	Hawkinsville
134	417.1	Cobb County	Marietta
134	417.1	Early County	Blakely
136	415.3	Floyd County	Rome
137	414.4	Mcduffie County	Thomson
138	413.6	Ben Hill County	Fitzgerald
139	413.4	Atkinson County	Pearson
140	412.2	Dade County	Trenton
141	410.6	Worth County	Sylvester
142	409.5	Banks County	Homer
143	408.2	Fayette County	Fayetteville
144	402.9	Camden County	Kingsland
145	400.9	Harris County	Hamilton
146	391.8	Atlanta City	Atlanta
147	388.1	Burke County	Waynesboro
148	377.2	Greene County	Greensboro
149	375.9	Decatur County	Bainbridge
150	369.9	Dekalb County	Decatur
151	364.4	Irwin County	Ocilla
152	362.0	Muscogee County	Columbus
153	359.6	Decatur City	Decatur

Current Spending per Student in FY2003

Rank	Dollars	District Name	City
1	12,179	Decatur City	Decatur
2	11,435	Atlanta City	Atlanta
3	9,563	Greene County	Greensboro
4	9,455	Buford City	Buford
5	9,335	Randolph County	Cuthbert
6	9,236	Marietta City	Marietta
7	9,013	Clarke County	Athens
8	8,993	Dalton City	Dalton
9	8,981	Dooly County	Vienna
10	8,809	Meriwether County	Greenville
11	8,600	Hancock County	Sparta
12	8,599	Fulton County	Atlanta
13	8,520	Putnam County	Eatonton
14	8,492	Telfair County	Mcrae
15	8,476	Dekalb County	Decatur
16	8,432	Irwin County	Ocilla
17	8,381	Gainesville City	Gainesville
18	8,328	Chattooga County	Summerville
19	8,259	Terrell County	Dawson
20	8,253	Turner County	Ashburn
21	8,210	Thomasville City	Thomasville
22	8,204	Bulloch County	Statesboro
23	8,139	Wilkinson County	Irwinton
24	8,111	Jeff Davis County	Hazlehurst
25	8,098	Union County	Blairsville
26	8,056	Dougherty County	Albany
27	7,997	Thomas County	Thomasville
28	7,971	Rabun County	Clayton
29	7,966	Appling County	Baxley
30	7,954	Macon County	Oglethorpe
31	7,933	Crisp County	Cordele
32	7,902	Seminole County	Donalsonville
33	7,886	Jackson County	Jefferson
34	7,817	Stephens County	Toccoa
35	7,816	Carrollton City	Carrollton
36	7,748	Walton County	Monroe
37	7,746	Dublin City	Dublin
38	7,728	Dawson County	Dawsonville
39	7,686	Marion County	Buena Vista
40	7,658	Elbert County	Elberton
41	7,632	Burke County	Waynesboro
42	7,616	Hart County	Hartwell
43	7,615	Peach County	Fort Valley
44	7,605	Fannin County	Blue Ridge
45	7,600	Rome City	Rome
46	7,599	Muscogee County	Columbus
47	7,598	Ware County	Waycross
48	7,597	Barrow County	Winder
49	7,593	Spalding County	Griffin
50	7,576	Chatham County	Savannah
51	7,567	Glynn County	Brunswick
52	7,545	Gwinnett County	Lawrenceville
53	7,540	Brooks County	Quitman
54	7,529	Cobb County	Marietta
55	7,515	Whitfield County	Dalton
56	7,508	Floyd County	Rome
57	7,479	Washington County	Sandersville
58	7,472	Pulaski County	Hawkinsville
59	7,471	Evans County	Claxton
60	7,469	Houston County	Perry
61	7,468	Jefferson City	Jefferson
62	7,467	Baldwin County	Milledgeville
62	7,467	Pickens County	Jasper
64	7,465	Walker County	Lafayette
65	7,459	Wilkes County	Washington
66	7,455	Oglethorpe County	Lexington
67	7,450	Richmond County	Augusta
68	7,449	Bartow County	Cartersville
69	7,435	Forsyth County	Cumming
70	7,421	Lumpkin County	Dahlonega
71	7,411	Coffee County	Douglas
72	7,388	Troup County	Lagrange
73	7,374	Gilmer County	Ellijay
74	7,373	Ben Hill County	Fitzgerald
75	7,350	Crawford County	Roberta
76	7,346	Lowndes County	Valdosta
77	7,339	Mcintosh County	Darien
78	7,331	Fayette County	Fayetteville
79	7,302	Habersham County	Clarkesville
80	7,290	Mitchell County	Camilla
81	7,270	Colquitt County	Moultrie
82	7,259	Morgan County	Madison
83	7,256	Bibb County	Macon
84	7,251	Rockdale County	Conyers
85	7,234	Gordon County	Calhoun
86	7,227	Jenkins County	Millen
87	7,226	Cherokee County	Canton
88	7,212	Cartersville City	Cartersville
88	7,212	Vidalia City	Vidalia
90	7,211	Jefferson County	Louisville

91	7,166	Early County	Blakely
92	7,164	Screven County	Sylvania
93	7,153	Calhoun City	Calhoun
94	7,151	Clayton County	Jonesboro
95	7,146	Polk County	Cedartown
96	7,137	Bacon County	Alma
97	7,131	Carroll County	Carrollton
98	7,120	Douglas County	Douglasville
99	7,117	Dade County	Trenton
100	7,104	Madison County	Danielsville
101	7,081	Taylor County	Butler
102	7,057	Tattnall County	Reidsville
103	7,056	White County	Cleveland
104	7,051	Candler County	Metter
105	7,050	Charlton County	Folkston
106	7,049	Harris County	Hamilton
107	7,038	Emanuel County	Swainsboro
108	7,028	Sumter County	Americus
109	7,027	Hall County	Gainesville
110	7,024	Monroe County	Forsyth
111	7,021	Bremen City	Bremen
112	7,020	Coweta County	Newnan
113	6,996	Grady County	Cairo
114	6,992	Decatur County	Bainbridge
115	6,983	Wayne County	Jesup
116	6,980	Haralson County	Buchanan
117	6,967	Franklin County	Carnesville
118	6,958	Towns County	Hiawassee
119	6,955	Butts County	Jackson
120	6,952	Worth County	Sylvester
121	6,951	Pierce County	Blackshear
122	6,945	Bleckley County	Cochran
123	6,925	Liberty County	Hinesville
124	6,916	Catoosa County	Ringgold
125	6,915	Newton County	Covington
126	6,897	Dodge County	Eastman
127	6,889	Valdosta City	Valdosta
128	6,872	Cook County	Adel
129	6,853	Berrien County	Nashville
130	6,837	Oconee County	Watkinsville
131	6,823	Pelham City	Pelham
132	6,791	Lamar County	Barnesville
133	6,785	Atkinson County	Pearson
134	6,766	Camden County	Kingsland
134	6,766	Toombs County	Lyons
136	6,751	Mcduffie County	Thomson
137	6,725	Murray County	Chatsworth
138	6,713	Heard County	Franklin
139	6,675	Jasper County	Monticello
140	6,673	Thomaston-Upson County	Thomaston
141	6,582	Banks County	Homer
142	6,576	Laurens County	Dublin
142	6,576	Tift County	Tifton
144	6,571	Henry County	Mcdonough
145	6,541	Columbia County	Appling
146	6,528	Effingham County	Springfield
147	6,459	Lee County	Leesburg
148	6,382	Brantley County	Nahunta
149	6,279	Paulding County	Dallas
150	6,070	Jones County	Gray
151	6,060	Bryan County	Pembroke
152	5,986	Long County	Ludowici
153	5,929	Pike County	Zebulon

Number of Diploma Recipients

Rank	Number	District Name	City
1	6,116	Gwinnett County	Lawrenceville
2	5,231	Cobb County	Marietta
3	4,191	Dekalb County	Decatur
4	3,360	Fulton County	Atlanta
5	2,270	Atlanta City	Atlanta
6	1,791	Clayton County	Jonesboro
7	1,576	Richmond County	Augusta
8	1,502	Muscogee County	Columbus
9	1,380	Fayette County	Fayetteville
10	1,271	Cherokee County	Canton
11	1,208	Houston County	Perry
12	1,197	Chatham County	Savannah
13	1,157	Henry County	Mcdonough
14	1,051	Columbia County	Appling
15	899	Douglas County	Douglasville
16	869	Hall County	Gainesville
17	831	Bibb County	Macon
18	788	Coweta County	Newnan
19	765	Forsyth County	Cumming
20	722	Rockdale County	Conyers
21	711	Dougherty County	Albany
22	652	Paulding County	Dallas
23	553	Whitfield County	Dalton
24	536	Carroll County	Carrollton
25	516	Glynn County	Brunswick
26	505	Liberty County	Hinesville

Rank		District Name	City
27	485	Bartow County	Cartersville
28	484	Troup County	Lagrange
29	468	Lowndes County	Valdosta
30	454	Floyd County	Rome
31	446	Catoosa County	Ringgold
32	445	Camden County	Kingsland
33	426	Effingham County	Springfield
34	408	Bulloch County	Statesboro
35	401	Spalding County	Griffin
36	390	Clarke County	Athens
37	370	Newton County	Covington
38	359	Oconee County	Watkinsville
39	350	Barrow County	Winder
40	344	Walton County	Monroe
41	342	Tift County	Tifton
42	317	Walker County	Lafayette
43	308	Colquitt County	Moultrie
44	307	Laurens County	Dublin
45	305	Valdosta City	Valdosta
46	291	Lee County	Leesburg
47	289	Bryan County	Pembroke
48	276	Polk County	Cedartown
49	270	Decatur County	Bainbridge
49	270	Habersham County	Clarkesville
49	270	Ware County	Waycross
52	268	Marietta City	Marietta
53	266	Thomas County	Thomasville
54	260	Coffee County	Douglas
55	240	Jones County	Gray
56	238	Baldwin County	Milledgeville
56	238	Rome City	Rome
58	236	Jackson County	Jefferson
59	235	Dalton City	Dalton
60	231	Mcduffie County	Thomson
61	228	Thomaston-Upson County	Thomaston
62	221	Harris County	Hamilton
63	218	Murray County	Chatsworth
64	217	Gordon County	Calhoun
65	214	Emanuel County	Swainsboro
65	214	Wayne County	Jesup
67	213	Burke County	Waynesboro
68	211	Hart County	Hartwell
69	207	Washington County	Sandersville
70	195	Monroe County	Forsyth
71	191	Madison County	Danielsville
72	188	Worth County	Sylvester
73	186	Carrollton City	Carrollton
73	186	Gainesville City	Gainesville
75	185	Sumter County	Americus
76	180	Cartersville City	Cartersville
77	178	Appling County	Baxley
78	177	Stephens County	Toccoa
79	176	Elbert County	Elberton
80	173	Grady County	Cairo
81	165	Crisp County	Cordele
82	161	Dodge County	Eastman
82	161	Screven County	Sylvania
84	159	Peach County	Fort Valley
84	159	Thomasville City	Thomasville
86	157	Ben Hill County	Fitzgerald
86	157	Jeff Davis County	Hazlehurst
88	152	White County	Cleveland
89	148	Dublin City	Dublin
90	147	Fannin County	Blue Ridge
90	147	Morgan County	Madison
92	146	Jefferson County	Louisville
93	145	Franklin County	Carnesville
93	145	Union County	Blairsville
95	143	Pike County	Zebulon
96	142	Haralson County	Buchanan
97	141	Lumpkin County	Dahlonega
98	139	Gilmer County	Ellijay
99	138	Meriwether County	Greenville
100	137	Vidalia City	Vidalia
101	134	Dade County	Trenton
102	132	Mitchell County	Camilla
103	131	Cook County	Adel
103	131	Early County	Blakely
105	130	Butts County	Jackson
106	127	Berrien County	Nashville
107	125	Decatur City	Decatur
108	124	Calhoun City	Calhoun
109	123	Pickens County	Jasper
110	121	Brantley County	Nahunta
111	115	Pierce County	Blackshear
111	115	Rabun County	Clayton
113	113	Dawson County	Dawsonville
114	112	Tattnall County	Reidsville
115	108	Marion County	Buena Vista
116	106	Lamar County	Barnesville
117	101	Bleckley County	Cochran
117	101	Putnam County	Eatonton
119	100	Buford City	Buford
119	100	Wilkinson County	Irwinton
121	99	Towns County	Hiawassee
121	99	Wilkes County	Washington
123	95	Brooks County	Quitman
124	94	Banks County	Homer
124	94	Toombs County	Lyons
126	92	Charlton County	Folkston
126	92	Chattooga County	Summerville
128	89	Bremen City	Bremen
128	89	Crawford County	Roberta
130	87	Pulaski County	Hawkinsville
130	87	Seminole County	Donalsonville
132	86	Oglethorpe County	Lexington
133	84	Evans County	Claxton
134	83	Randolph County	Cuthbert
135	82	Greene County	Greensboro
135	82	Hancock County	Sparta
135	82	Turner County	Ashburn
138	80	Telfair County	Mcrae
139	79	Jenkins County	Millen
139	79	Taylor County	Butler
141	77	Irwin County	Ocilla
142	76	Bacon County	Alma
142	76	Macon County	Oglethorpe
144	75	Long County	Ludowici
145	74	Jasper County	Monticello
146	73	Pelham City	Pelham
147	72	Candler County	Metter
148	69	Heard County	Franklin
148	69	Mcintosh County	Darien
150	65	Jefferson City	Jefferson
151	57	Dooly County	Vienna
152	54	Terrell County	Dawson
153	53	Atkinson County	Pearson

High School Drop-out Rate

Rank	Percent	District Name	City
1	29.1	Seminole County	Donalsonville
2	16.8	Chatham County	Savannah
3	15.5	Gainesville City	Gainesville
4	15.4	Peach County	Fort Valley
5	14.0	Sumter County	Americus
6	13.4	Mcintosh County	Darien
7	13.2	Spalding County	Griffin
8	12.9	Marion County	Buena Vista
9	12.5	Taylor County	Butler
10	12.1	Dooly County	Vienna
10	12.1	Jenkins County	Millen
12	12.0	Hancock County	Sparta
13	11.7	Murray County	Chatsworth
14	11.0	Mitchell County	Camilla
14	11.0	Whitfield County	Dalton
16	10.9	Walker County	Lafayette
16	10.9	Wayne County	Jesup
18	10.8	Atkinson County	Pearson
18	10.8	Long County	Ludowici
20	10.7	Clarke County	Athens
21	10.5	Putnam County	Eatonton
22	10.4	Brantley County	Nahunta
22	10.4	Valdosta City	Valdosta
24	10.3	Bibb County	Macon
24	10.3	Haralson County	Buchanan
24	10.3	Jasper County	Monticello
27	10.1	Candler County	Metter
28	10.0	Ben Hill County	Fitzgerald
28	10.0	Glynn County	Brunswick
28	10.0	Polk County	Cedartown
31	9.8	Crisp County	Cordele
31	9.8	Jackson County	Jefferson
33	9.6	Pelham City	Pelham
33	9.6	Rabun County	Clayton
35	9.5	Ware County	Waycross
35	9.5	Worth County	Sylvester
37	9.4	Gordon County	Calhoun
37	9.4	Meriwether County	Greenville
37	9.4	Tift County	Tifton
40	9.3	Brooks County	Quitman
40	9.3	Burke County	Waynesboro
40	9.3	Coffee County	Douglas
40	9.3	Wilkes County	Washington
44	9.2	Pulaski County	Hawkinsville
44	9.2	Stephens County	Toccoa
46	8.9	Atlanta City	Atlanta
47	8.8	Chattooga County	Summerville
48	8.7	Macon County	Oglethorpe
48	8.7	Toombs County	Lyons
50	8.6	Banks County	Homer
50	8.6	Dublin City	Dublin
52	8.4	Berrien County	Nashville
53	8.3	Rome City	Rome
53	8.3	Thomaston-Upson County	Thomaston
55	8.2	Clayton County	Jonesboro
55	8.2	Jones County	Gray
55	8.2	Telfair County	Mcrae
58	8.1	Tattnall County	Reidsville
59	8.0	Bacon County	Alma
59	8.0	Dougherty County	Albany
59	8.0	Irwin County	Ocilla
59	8.0	Wilkinson County	Irwinton
63	7.9	Bartow County	Cartersville
63	7.9	Jeff Davis County	Hazlehurst
63	7.9	Randolph County	Cuthbert
66	7.8	Bleckley County	Cochran
66	7.8	Decatur County	Bainbridge
68	7.7	Cook County	Adel
68	7.7	Paulding County	Dallas
68	7.7	Thomasville City	Thomasville
71	7.6	Carroll County	Carrollton
71	7.6	Colquitt County	Moultrie
73	7.5	Dawson County	Dawsonville
73	7.5	Habersham County	Clarkesville
75	7.4	Appling County	Baxley
76	7.3	Screven County	Sylvania
77	7.2	Pike County	Zebulon
78	7.1	Elbert County	Elberton
79	7.0	Bulloch County	Statesboro
79	7.0	Catoosa County	Ringgold
79	7.0	Emanuel County	Swainsboro
82	6.9	Franklin County	Carnesville
82	6.9	Troup County	Lagrange
84	6.8	Camden County	Kingsland
84	6.8	Dekalb County	Decatur
84	6.8	Floyd County	Rome
84	6.8	Marietta City	Marietta
84	6.8	Muscogee County	Columbus
89	6.7	Grady County	Cairo
89	6.7	Turner County	Ashburn
91	6.6	Barrow County	Winder
91	6.6	Mcduffie County	Thomson
93	6.5	Charlton County	Folkston
93	6.5	Lowndes County	Valdosta
95	6.4	Madison County	Danielsville
95	6.4	Pierce County	Blackshear
95	6.4	Terrell County	Dawson
98	6.2	Hall County	Gainesville
99	6.0	Evans County	Claxton
99	6.0	Harris County	Hamilton
99	6.0	Pickens County	Jasper
102	5.9	Dodge County	Eastman
102	5.9	Lamar County	Barnesville
104	5.8	Effingham County	Springfield
104	5.8	Gilmer County	Ellijay
104	5.8	Hart County	Hartwell
104	5.8	Houston County	Perry
108	5.7	Bryan County	Pembroke
108	5.7	Douglas County	Douglasville
110	5.6	Crawford County	Roberta
110	5.6	Washington County	Sandersville
112	5.5	Coweta County	Newnan
113	5.4	Monroe County	Forsyth
114	5.2	Jefferson County	Louisville
114	5.2	Oglethorpe County	Lexington
114	5.2	White County	Cleveland
117	5.0	Newton County	Covington
117	5.0	Richmond County	Augusta
119	4.9	Fannin County	Blue Ridge
120	4.8	Columbia County	Appling
121	4.7	Early County	Blakely
121	4.7	Lumpkin County	Dahlonega
123	4.6	Buford City	Buford
123	4.6	Laurens County	Dublin
125	4.5	Cherokee County	Canton
125	4.5	Heard County	Franklin
127	4.3	Liberty County	Hinesville
128	4.2	Rockdale County	Conyers
129	4.1	Cartersville City	Cartersville
130	4.0	Calhoun City	Calhoun
130	4.0	Dade County	Trenton
130	4.0	Henry County	Mcdonough
133	3.8	Carrollton City	Carrollton
133	3.8	Vidalia City	Vidalia
135	3.7	Baldwin County	Milledgeville
136	3.6	Cobb County	Marietta
137	3.5	Butts County	Jackson
137	3.5	Walton County	Monroe
139	3.3	Morgan County	Madison
140	3.2	Gwinnett County	Lawrenceville
141	3.1	Dalton City	Dalton
142	2.8	Lee County	Leesburg
143	2.7	Forsyth County	Cumming
144	2.6	Oconee County	Watkinsville
144	2.6	Union County	Blairsville
146	2.5	Fulton County	Atlanta
147	2.4	Thomas County	Thomasville
148	2.2	Jefferson City	Jefferson

149	2.0	Fayette County	Fayetteville
149	2.0	Greene County	Greensboro
151	1.8	Bremen City	Bremen
152	1.0	Decatur City	Decatur
153	n/a	Towns County	Hiawassee

Hawaii

Hawaii Public School Educational Profile

Category	Value	Category	Value
Schools *(2003-2004)*	284	**Diploma Recipients** *(2002-2003)*	10,452
Instructional Level		White, Non-Hispanic	2,013
Primary	183	Black, Non-Hispanic	167
Middle	36	Asian/Pacific Islander	7,771
High	42	American Indian/Alaskan Native	34
Other Level	23	Hispanic	467
Curriculum		**High School Drop-out Rate** (%) *(2001-2002)*	5.1
Regular	280	White, Non-Hispanic	5.5
Special Education	3	Black, Non-Hispanic	5.5
Vocational	0	Asian/Pacific Islander	4.9
Alternative	1	American Indian/Alaskan Native	6.6
Type		Hispanic	6.4
Magnet	0	**Staff** *(2003-2004)*	
Charter	26	Teachers	11,128.5
Title I Eligible	205	Average Salary[1] ($)	45,456
School-wide Title I	181	Librarians/Media Specialists	290.0
Students *(2003-2004)*	183,609	Guidance Counselors	647.5
Gender (%)		**Ratios** *(2003-2004)*	
Male	52.0	Student/Teacher Ratio	16.5 to 1
Female	48.0	Student/Librarian Ratio	633.1 to 1
Race/Ethnicity (%)		Student/Counselor Ratio	283.6 to 1
White, Non-Hispanic	20.2	**College Entrance Exam Scores** *(2005)*	
Black, Non-Hispanic	2.4	Scholastic Aptitude Test (SAT)	
Asian/Pacific Islander	72.4	Participation Rate (%)	61
American Indian/Alaskan Native	0.5	Mean SAT Reasoning Test Verbal Score	490
Hispanic	4.5	Mean SAT Reasoning Test Math Score	516
Classification (%)		American College Testing Program (ACT)	
Individual Education Program (IEP)	12.3	Participation Rate (%)	16
Migrant *(2002-2003)*	0.8	Average Composite Score	21.9
English Language Learner (ELL)	7.0	Average English Score	21.0
Eligible for Free Lunch Program	31.5	Average Math Score	22.7
Eligible for Reduced-Price Lunch Program	11.0	Average Reading Score	21.9
Current Spending *($ per student in FY 2003)*	8,100	Average Science Score	21.6
Instruction	4,833		
Support Services	2,839		

Note: For an explanation of data, please refer to the User's Guide in the front of the book; (1) Includes extra-duty pay and fringe benefits such as healthcare where applicable

Hawaii NAEP 2005 Test Scores

Reading			Mathematics		
Grade/Category	Value	Rank	Grade/Category	Value	Rank
4th Grade			**4th Grade**		
Average Proficiency	209.6 (1.01)	43/51	Average Proficiency	230.1 (0.84)	45/51
Proficiency by Gender/Race/Ethnicity			Proficiency by Gender/Race/Ethnicity		
Male	205.4 (1.32)	44/51	Male	229.1 (1.04)	47/51
Female	213.8 (1.13)	43/51	Female	231.2 (1.05)	40/51
White, Non-Hispanic	224.1 (1.70)	39/51	White, Non-Hispanic	241.4 (1.37)	39/51
Black, Non-Hispanic	205.5 (4.84)	10/42	Black, Non-Hispanic	220.5 (3.10)	20/42
Asian, Non-Hispanic	205.5 (1.11)	27/27	Asian, Non-Hispanic	228.7 (1.07)	25/25
American Indian, Non-Hispanic	n/a	n/a	American Indian, Non-Hispanic	n/a	n/a
Hispanic	210.7 (4.77)	7/40	Hispanic	218.8 (4.50)	34/41
Proficiency by Class Size			Proficiency by Class Size		
Less than 16 Students	190.7 (4.75)	30/34	Less than 16 Students	214.7 (4.08)	33/35
16 to 18 Students	n/a	n/a	16 to 18 Students	n/a	n/a
19 to 20 Students	n/a	n/a	19 to 20 Students	n/a	n/a
21 to 25 Students	210.1 (2.18)	44/51	21 to 25 Students	230.2 (1.67)	44/51
Greater than 25 Students	215.0 (1.80)	29/36	Greater than 25 Students	233.2 (1.54)	26/33
Percent Attaining Achievement Levels			Percent Attaining Achievement Levels		
Below Basic	47.2 (1.24)	8/51	Below Basic	27.4 (1.14)	8/51
Basic or Above	52.8 (1.24)	44/51	Basic or Above	72.6 (1.14)	44/51
Proficient or Above	23.4 (1.39)	44/51	Proficient or Above	26.7 (1.33)	43/51
Advanced or Above	5.3 (0.59)	41/51	Advanced or Above	2.6 (0.39)	43/51
8th Grade			**8th Grade**		
Average Proficiency	248.5 (0.86)	50/51	Average Proficiency	265.6 (0.66)	47/51
Proficiency by Gender/Race/Ethnicity			Proficiency by Gender/Race/Ethnicity		
Male	241.8 (1.44)	50/51	Male	265.1 (1.01)	47/51
Female	256.1 (1.10)	47/51	Female	266.3 (1.13)	47/51
White, Non-Hispanic	261.3 (1.93)	49/51	White, Non-Hispanic	276.9 (1.84)	48/51
Black, Non-Hispanic	n/a	n/a	Black, Non-Hispanic	n/a	n/a
Asian, Non-Hispanic	246.3 (1.14)	24/24	Asian, Non-Hispanic	264.0 (0.80)	23/23
American Indian, Non-Hispanic	n/a	n/a	American Indian, Non-Hispanic	n/a	n/a
Hispanic	241.8 (4.36)	35/38	Hispanic	257.1 (5.08)	29/38
Proficiency by Parents Highest Level of Ed.			Proficiency by Parents Highest Level of Ed.		
Did Not Finish High School	237.9 (3.26)	45/49	Did Not Finish High School	249.9 (4.44)	47/50
Graduated High School	240.4 (1.34)	49/50	Graduated High School	254.9 (1.66)	46/50
Some Education After High School	256.3 (2.03)	46/50	Some Education After High School	271.2 (1.43)	46/50
Graduated College	255.9 (1.21)	48/50	Graduated College	273.9 (1.27)	47/50
Percent Attaining Achievement Levels			Percent Attaining Achievement Levels		
Below Basic	47.2 (1.24)	8/51	Below Basic	44.3 (0.99)	5/51
Basic or Above	52.8 (1.24)	44/51	Basic or Above	55.7 (0.99)	47/51
Proficient or Above	23.4 (1.39)	44/51	Proficient or Above	18.2 (0.79)	45/51
Advanced or Above	5.3 (0.59)	41/51	Advanced or Above	2.5 (0.37)	44/51

Note: *For an explanation of data, please refer to the User's Guide in the front of the book; n/a indicates data not available*

Hawaii Department of Education
1390 Miller St • Honolulu, HI 96813
Mailing Address: PO Box 2360 • Honolulu, HI 96804-2360
(808) 837-8012 • http://www.k12.hi.us/
Grade Span: PK-12; Agency Type: 1
Schools: 284
   183 Primary; 36 Middle; 42 High; 23 Other Level
   280 Regular; 3 Special Education; 0 Vocational; 1 Alternative
   0 Magnet; 26 Charter; 205 Title I Eligible; 181 School-wide Title I
Students: 183,609   (52.0% male; 47.9% female)
   Individual Education Program: 22,533 (12.3%);
   English Language Learner: 12,850 (7.0%); Migrant: 1,395 (0.8%)
   Eligible for Free Lunch Program: 57,897 (31.5%)
   Eligible for Reduced-Price Lunch Program: 20,204 (11.0%)
Teachers: 11,128.5 (16.5 to 1)
Librarians/Media Specialists: 290.0 (633.1 to 1)
Guidance Counselors: 647.5 (283.6 to 1)
Current Spending: ($ per student per year):
   Total: $8,100; Instruction: $4,833; Support Services: $2,839
Enrollment, Drop-out Rates and Diploma Recipients by Race/Ethnicity

Category	Total	White	Black	Asian	AIAN	Hisp.
Enrollment (%)	100.0	20.2	2.4	72.4	0.5	4.5
Drop-out Rate (%)	5.1	5.5	5.5	4.9	6.6	6.4
H.S. Diplomas (#)	10,452	2,013	167	7,771	34	467

Number of Schools

Rank	Number	District Name	City
1	284	Hawaii Department of Education	Honolulu

Number of Teachers

Rank	Number	District Name	City
1	11,128	Hawaii Department of Education	Honolulu

Number of Students

Rank	Number	District Name	City
1	183,609	Hawaii Department of Education	Honolulu

Male Students

Rank	Percent	District Name	City
1	52.0	Hawaii Department of Education	Honolulu

Female Students

Rank	Percent	District Name	City
1	47.9	Hawaii Department of Education	Honolulu

Individual Education Program Students

Rank	Percent	District Name	City
1	12.3	Hawaii Department of Education	Honolulu

English Language Learner Students

Rank	Percent	District Name	City
1	7.0	Hawaii Department of Education	Honolulu

Migrant Students

Rank	Percent	District Name	City
1	0.8	Hawaii Department of Education	Honolulu

Students Eligible for Free Lunch

Rank	Percent	District Name	City
1	31.5	Hawaii Department of Education	Honolulu

Students Eligible for Reduced-Price Lunch

Rank	Percent	District Name	City
1	11.0	Hawaii Department of Education	Honolulu

Student/Teacher Ratio

Rank	Ratio	District Name	City
1	16.5	Hawaii Department of Education	Honolulu

Student/Librarian Ratio

Rank	Ratio	District Name	City
1	633.1	Hawaii Department of Education	Honolulu

Student/Counselor Ratio

Rank	Ratio	District Name	City
1	283.6	Hawaii Department of Education	Honolulu

Current Spending per Student in FY2003

Rank	Dollars	District Name	City
1	8,100	Hawaii Department of Education	Honolulu

Number of Diploma Recipients

Rank	Number	District Name	City
1	10,452	Hawaii Department of Education	Honolulu

High School Drop-out Rate

Rank	Percent	District Name	City
1	5.1	Hawaii Department of Education	Honolulu

Idaho

Idaho Public School Educational Profile

Category	Value	Category	Value
Schools (2003-2004)	691	**Diploma Recipients** (2002-2003)	15,874
Instructional Level		White, Non-Hispanic	14,296
Primary	347	Black, Non-Hispanic	76
Middle	111	Asian/Pacific Islander	248
High	180	American Indian/Alaskan Native	191
Other Level	47	Hispanic	1,063
Curriculum		**High School Drop-out Rate** (%) (2001-2002)	3.9
Regular	599	White, Non-Hispanic	n/a
Special Education	10	Black, Non-Hispanic	n/a
Vocational	9	Asian/Pacific Islander	n/a
Alternative	67	American Indian/Alaskan Native	n/a
Type		Hispanic	n/a
Magnet	0	**Staff** (2003-2004)	
Charter	17	Teachers	14,049.6
Title I Eligible	480	Average Salary ($)	40,111
School-wide Title I	80	Librarians/Media Specialists	170.1
Students (2003-2004)	252,120	Guidance Counselors	575.4
Gender (%)		**Ratios** (2003-2004)	
Male	51.6	Student/Teacher Ratio	17.9 to 1
Female	48.4	Student/Librarian Ratio	1,482.2 to 1
Race/Ethnicity (%)		Student/Counselor Ratio	438.2 to 1
White, Non-Hispanic	84.1	**College Entrance Exam Scores** (2005)	
Black, Non-Hispanic	0.9	Scholastic Aptitude Test (SAT)	
Asian/Pacific Islander	1.5	Participation Rate (%)	21
American Indian/Alaskan Native	1.6	Mean SAT Reasoning Test Verbal Score	544
Hispanic	12.0	Mean SAT Reasoning Test Math Score	542
Classification (%)		American College Testing Program (ACT)	
Individual Education Program (IEP)	11.4	Participation Rate (%)	58
Migrant (2002-2003)	3.3	Average Composite Score	21.3
English Language Learner (ELL)	7.8	Average English Score	20.5
Eligible for Free Lunch Program	27.5	Average Math Score	20.9
Eligible for Reduced-Price Lunch Program	9.5	Average Reading Score	21.9
Current Spending ($ per student in FY 2003)	6,034	Average Science Score	21.2
Instruction	3,720		
Support Services	2,053		

Note: For an explanation of data, please refer to the User's Guide in the front of the book

Idaho NAEP 2005 Test Scores

Reading			Mathematics		
Grade/Category	Value	Rank	Grade/Category	Value	Rank
4th Grade			**4th Grade**		
Average Proficiency	221.9 (0.87)	19/51	Average Proficiency	241.7 (0.74)	12/51
Proficiency by Gender/Race/Ethnicity			Proficiency by Gender/Race/Ethnicity		
Male	218.3 (1.21)	21/51	Male	242.5 (0.99)	15/51
Female	225.3 (1.07)	19/51	Female	240.8 (0.75)	10/51
White, Non-Hispanic	226.1 (0.82)	29/51	White, Non-Hispanic	244.5 (0.77)	28/51
Black, Non-Hispanic	n/a	n/a	Black, Non-Hispanic	n/a	n/a
Asian, Non-Hispanic	n/a	n/a	Asian, Non-Hispanic	n/a	n/a
American Indian, Non-Hispanic	n/a	n/a	American Indian, Non-Hispanic	n/a	n/a
Hispanic	199.3 (2.79)	32/40	Hispanic	225.5 (1.87)	21/41
Proficiency by Class Size			Proficiency by Class Size		
Less than 16 Students	n/a	n/a	Less than 16 Students	n/a	n/a
16 to 18 Students	n/a	n/a	16 to 18 Students	n/a	n/a
19 to 20 Students	n/a	n/a	19 to 20 Students	n/a	n/a
21 to 25 Students	221.1 (1.24)	29/51	21 to 25 Students	241.1 (1.06)	23/51
Greater than 25 Students	226.1 (1.76)	4/36	Greater than 25 Students	243.6 (1.29)	3/33
Percent Attaining Achievement Levels			Percent Attaining Achievement Levels		
Below Basic	31.0 (1.13)	37/51	Below Basic	13.6 (0.81)	42/51
Basic or Above	69.0 (1.13)	15/51	Basic or Above	86.4 (0.81)	9/51
Proficient or Above	32.9 (1.36)	22/51	Proficient or Above	40.4 (1.63)	13/51
Advanced or Above	6.6 (0.61)	32/51	Advanced or Above	4.8 (0.64)	23/51
8th Grade			**8th Grade**		
Average Proficiency	264.3 (1.05)	23/51	Average Proficiency	281.0 (0.89)	24/51
Proficiency by Gender/Race/Ethnicity			Proficiency by Gender/Race/Ethnicity		
Male	258.1 (1.41)	26/51	Male	280.3 (1.41)	27/51
Female	270.8 (1.22)	18/51	Female	281.6 (1.08)	17/51
White, Non-Hispanic	266.5 (1.05)	36/51	White, Non-Hispanic	284.0 (0.89)	35/51
Black, Non-Hispanic	n/a	n/a	Black, Non-Hispanic	n/a	n/a
Asian, Non-Hispanic	n/a	n/a	Asian, Non-Hispanic	n/a	n/a
American Indian, Non-Hispanic	n/a	n/a	American Indian, Non-Hispanic	n/a	n/a
Hispanic	246.5 (2.06)	22/38	Hispanic	260.8 (2.07)	24/38
Proficiency by Parents Highest Level of Ed.			Proficiency by Parents Highest Level of Ed.		
Did Not Finish High School	248.9 (2.96)	14/49	Did Not Finish High School	264.5 (2.31)	13/50
Graduated High School	255.6 (1.64)	24/50	Graduated High School	269.5 (1.86)	25/50
Some Education After High School	269.1 (1.77)	12/50	Some Education After High School	283.4 (2.16)	17/50
Graduated College	271.9 (1.20)	27/50	Graduated College	290.4 (1.01)	23/50
Percent Attaining Achievement Levels			Percent Attaining Achievement Levels		
Below Basic	31.0 (1.13)	37/51	Below Basic	26.7 (1.10)	33/51
Basic or Above	69.0 (1.13)	15/51	Basic or Above	73.3 (1.10)	19/51
Proficient or Above	32.9 (1.36)	22/51	Proficient or Above	30.0 (1.16)	24/51
Advanced or Above	6.6 (0.61)	32/51	Advanced or Above	4.5 (0.56)	34/51

Note: For an explanation of data, please refer to the User's Guide in the front of the book; n/a indicates data not available

Ada County

Boise Independent District
1207 W Fort St • Boise, ID 83702-5399
Mailing Address: 8169 W Victory Rd • Boise, ID 83709
(208) 338-3400 • http://www.sd01.k12.id.us/
Grade Span: PK-12; **Agency Type:** 1
Schools: 54
  35 Primary; 7 Middle; 8 High; 4 Other Level
  49 Regular; 0 Special Education; 0 Vocational; 5 Alternative
  0 Magnet; 3 Charter; 27 Title I Eligible; 17 School-wide Title I
Students: 26,211 (51.7% male; 48.2% female)
  Individual Education Program: 3,003 (11.5%);
  English Language Learner: 1,323 (5.0%); Migrant: 0 (0.0%)
  Eligible for Free Lunch Program: 6,322 (24.1%)
  Eligible for Reduced-Price Lunch Program: 1,939 (7.4%)
Teachers: 1,466.2 (17.9 to 1)
Librarians/Media Specialists: 11.2 (2,340.3 to 1)
Guidance Counselors: 77.5 (338.2 to 1)
Current Spending: ($ per student per year):
  Total: $7,314; Instruction: $4,527; Support Services: $2,523
Enrollment, Drop-out Rates and Diploma Recipients by Race/Ethnicity

Category	Total	White	Black	Asian	AIAN	Hisp.
Enrollment (%)	100.0	87.4	1.9	3.1	0.6	7.0
Drop-out Rate (%)	4.0	n/a	n/a	n/a	n/a	n/a
H.S. Diplomas (#)	1,737	1,600	17	36	28	56

Kuna Joint District
610 N School Ave • Kuna, ID 83634-1807
Mailing Address: 1450 Boise St • Kuna, ID 83634-1807
(208) 922-1000 • http://www.kunaschools.org/
Grade Span: PK-12; **Agency Type:** 1
Schools: 7
  3 Primary; 2 Middle; 2 High; 0 Other Level
  6 Regular; 0 Special Education; 0 Vocational; 1 Alternative
  0 Magnet; 0 Charter; 5 Title I Eligible; 0 School-wide Title I
Students: 3,612 (51.2% male; 48.7% female)
  Individual Education Program: 335 (9.3%);
  English Language Learner: 68 (1.9%); Migrant: 0 (0.0%)
  Eligible for Free Lunch Program: 563 (15.6%)
  Eligible for Reduced-Price Lunch Program: 375 (10.4%)
Teachers: 179.3 (20.1 to 1)
Librarians/Media Specialists: 2.0 (1,803.5 to 1)
Guidance Counselors: 5.3 (680.6 to 1)
Current Spending: ($ per student per year):
  Total: $4,987; Instruction: $3,079; Support Services: $1,681
Enrollment, Drop-out Rates and Diploma Recipients by Race/Ethnicity

Category	Total	White	Black	Asian	AIAN	Hisp.
Enrollment (%)	100.0	93.7	0.8	0.8	0.2	4.5
Drop-out Rate (%)	6.1	n/a	n/a	n/a	n/a	n/a
H.S. Diplomas (#)	186	172	0	2	4	8

Meridian Joint District
911 Meridian St • Meridian, ID 83642-2241
Mailing Address: 911 Meridian Rd • Meridian, ID 83642-2241
(208) 888-6701 • http://www.meridianschools.org/
Grade Span: PK-12; **Agency Type:** 1
Schools: 42
  25 Primary; 6 Middle; 9 High; 0 Other Level
  36 Regular; 0 Special Education; 1 Vocational; 3 Alternative
  0 Magnet; 3 Charter; 12 Title I Eligible; 1 School-wide Title I
Students: 26,987 (51.8% male; 48.1% female)
  Individual Education Program: 2,750 (10.2%);
  English Language Learner: 641 (2.4%); Migrant: 0 (0.0%)
  Eligible for Free Lunch Program: 3,214 (12.0%)
  Eligible for Reduced-Price Lunch Program: 1,530 (5.7%)
Teachers: 1,360.7 (19.7 to 1)
Librarians/Media Specialists: 9.0 (2,985.9 to 1)
Guidance Counselors: 63.8 (421.2 to 1)
Current Spending: ($ per student per year):
  Total: $5,066; Instruction: $3,129; Support Services: $1,733
Enrollment, Drop-out Rates and Diploma Recipients by Race/Ethnicity

Category	Total	White	Black	Asian	AIAN	Hisp.
Enrollment (%)	100.0	92.0	1.4	2.5	0.8	3.4
Drop-out Rate (%)	3.5	n/a	n/a	n/a	n/a	n/a
H.S. Diplomas (#)	1,498	1,395	10	40	10	43

Bannock County

Pocatello District
3115 Pole Line Rd • Pocatello, ID 83204-6119
(208) 232-3563 • http://www.d25.k12.id.us/
Grade Span: PK-12; **Agency Type:** 1
Schools: 30
  18 Primary; 4 Middle; 6 High; 2 Other Level
  23 Regular; 1 Special Education; 1 Vocational; 5 Alternative
  0 Magnet; 1 Charter; 16 Title I Eligible; 2 School-wide Title I
Students: 12,111 (51.9% male; 48.0% female)
  Individual Education Program: 1,555 (12.8%);
  English Language Learner: 75 (0.6%); Migrant: 0 (0.0%)
  Eligible for Free Lunch Program: 3,318 (27.4%)
  Eligible for Reduced-Price Lunch Program: 957 (7.9%)
Teachers: 617.1 (19.6 to 1)
Librarians/Media Specialists: 12.6 (961.2 to 1)
Guidance Counselors: 28.5 (424.9 to 1)
Current Spending: ($ per student per year):
  Total: $6,001; Instruction: $3,573; Support Services: $2,154
Enrollment, Drop-out Rates and Diploma Recipients by Race/Ethnicity

Category	Total	White	Black	Asian	AIAN	Hisp.
Enrollment (%)	100.0	85.1	1.3	1.7	5.4	6.5
Drop-out Rate (%)	4.5	n/a	n/a	n/a	n/a	n/a
H.S. Diplomas (#)	843	771	6	15	17	34

Bingham County

Blackfoot District
270 E Bridge St • Blackfoot, ID 83221-2865
(208) 785-8800 • http://www.d55.k12.id.us/
Grade Span: PK-12; **Agency Type:** 1
Schools: 15
  9 Primary; 3 Middle; 2 High; 1 Other Level
  11 Regular; 2 Special Education; 0 Vocational; 2 Alternative
  0 Magnet; 1 Charter; 12 Title I Eligible; 6 School-wide Title I
Students: 4,163 (51.0% male; 48.9% female)
  Individual Education Program: 517 (12.4%);
  English Language Learner: 868 (20.9%); Migrant: 367 (8.8%)
  Eligible for Free Lunch Program: 1,538 (36.9%)
  Eligible for Reduced-Price Lunch Program: 426 (10.2%)
Teachers: 225.6 (18.5 to 1)
Librarians/Media Specialists: 1.8 (2,312.8 to 1)
Guidance Counselors: 7.6 (547.8 to 1)
Current Spending: ($ per student per year):
  Total: $5,973; Instruction: $3,539; Support Services: $2,161
Enrollment, Drop-out Rates and Diploma Recipients by Race/Ethnicity

Category	Total	White	Black	Asian	AIAN	Hisp.
Enrollment (%)	100.0	66.3	0.4	1.5	13.6	18.2
Drop-out Rate (%)	5.5	n/a	n/a	n/a	n/a	n/a
H.S. Diplomas (#)	266	218	0	4	15	29

Shelley Joint District
545 Seminary Ave • Shelley, ID 83274-1461
(208) 357-3411 • http://sd60.k12.id.us/
Grade Span: PK-12; **Agency Type:** 1
Schools: 5
  2 Primary; 1 Middle; 1 High; 0 Other Level
  4 Regular; 0 Special Education; 0 Vocational; 0 Alternative
  0 Magnet; 0 Charter; 3 Title I Eligible; 0 School-wide Title I
Students: 2,048 (52.0% male; 47.9% female)
  Individual Education Program: 257 (12.5%);
  English Language Learner: 124 (6.1%); Migrant: 52 (2.5%)
  Eligible for Free Lunch Program: 482 (23.5%)
  Eligible for Reduced-Price Lunch Program: 222 (10.8%)
Teachers: 97.5 (21.0 to 1)
Librarians/Media Specialists: 1.0 (2,048.0 to 1)
Guidance Counselors: 4.4 (465.5 to 1)
Current Spending: ($ per student per year):
  Total: $5,074; Instruction: $3,385; Support Services: $1,455
Enrollment, Drop-out Rates and Diploma Recipients by Race/Ethnicity

Category	Total	White	Black	Asian	AIAN	Hisp.
Enrollment (%)	100.0	88.4	0.5	0.3	0.6	10.2
Drop-out Rate (%)	1.1	n/a	n/a	n/a	n/a	n/a
H.S. Diplomas (#)	160	142	2	1	1	14

Snake River District
103 S 900 W • Blackfoot, ID 83221-6065
(208) 684-3001 • http://srnt.sd52.k12.id.us/
Grade Span: PK-12; **Agency Type:** 1
Schools: 7
  3 Primary; 2 Middle; 2 High; 0 Other Level
  7 Regular; 0 Special Education; 0 Vocational; 0 Alternative
  0 Magnet; 1 Charter; 5 Title I Eligible; 0 School-wide Title I
Students: 2,042 (49.9% male; 50.0% female)
  Individual Education Program: 190 (9.3%);
  English Language Learner: 327 (16.0%); Migrant: 111 (5.4%)
  Eligible for Free Lunch Program: 527 (25.8%)
  Eligible for Reduced-Price Lunch Program: 279 (13.7%)
Teachers: 103.4 (19.7 to 1)
Librarians/Media Specialists: 1.0 (2,042.0 to 1)
Guidance Counselors: 4.6 (443.9 to 1)
Current Spending: ($ per student per year):
  Total: $5,636; Instruction: $3,534; Support Services: $1,871

Enrollment, Drop-out Rates and Diploma Recipients by Race/Ethnicity

Category	Total	White	Black	Asian	AIAN	Hisp.
Enrollment (%)	100.0	80.3	0.3	0.4	1.3	17.6
Drop-out Rate (%)	0.7	n/a	n/a	n/a	n/a	n/a
H.S. Diplomas (#)	173	153	1	3	1	15

Blaine County

Blaine County District
118 W Bullion St • Hailey, ID 83333
(208) 788-2296 • http://www.bcsd.k12.id.us/
Grade Span: PK-12; **Agency Type:** 1
Schools: 8
  4 Primary; 1 Middle; 2 High; 1 Other Level
  6 Regular; 1 Special Education; 0 Vocational; 1 Alternative
  0 Magnet; 0 Charter; 3 Title I Eligible; 0 School-wide Title I
Students: 3,155 (51.8% male; 48.1% female)
  Individual Education Program: 366 (11.6%);
  English Language Learner: 470 (14.9%); Migrant: 8 (0.3%)
  Eligible for Free Lunch Program: 573 (18.2%)
  Eligible for Reduced-Price Lunch Program: 207 (6.6%)
Teachers: 224.0 (14.1 to 1)
Librarians/Media Specialists: 2.0 (1,577.5 to 1)
Guidance Counselors: 6.5 (485.4 to 1)
Current Spending: ($ per student per year):
  Total: $9,915; Instruction: $6,722; Support Services: $2,981
Enrollment, Drop-out Rates and Diploma Recipients by Race/Ethnicity

Category	Total	White	Black	Asian	AIAN	Hisp.
Enrollment (%)	100.0	78.6	0.3	1.2	0.3	19.6
Drop-out Rate (%)	5.0	n/a	n/a	n/a	n/a	n/a
H.S. Diplomas (#)	171	146	1	3	0	21

Bonner County

Lake Pend Oreille District
901 Triangle Dr • Sandpoint, ID 83864
Mailing Address: 901 N Triangle Dr • Ponderay, ID 83852
(208) 263-2184 • http://www.sd84.k12.id.us/production/
Grade Span: PK-12; **Agency Type:** 1
Schools: 13
  7 Primary; 2 Middle; 3 High; 1 Other Level
  11 Regular; 0 Special Education; 0 Vocational; 2 Alternative
  0 Magnet; 1 Charter; 10 Title I Eligible; 3 School-wide Title I
Students: 4,076 (51.0% male; 48.9% female)
  Individual Education Program: 505 (12.4%);
  English Language Learner: 1 (<0.1%); Migrant: 0 (0.0%)
  Eligible for Free Lunch Program: 1,221 (30.0%)
  Eligible for Reduced-Price Lunch Program: 483 (11.8%)
Teachers: 244.8 (16.7 to 1)
Librarians/Media Specialists: 3.0 (1,358.7 to 1)
Guidance Counselors: 11.1 (367.2 to 1)
Current Spending: ($ per student per year):
  Total: $6,172; Instruction: $3,726; Support Services: $2,173
Enrollment, Drop-out Rates and Diploma Recipients by Race/Ethnicity

Category	Total	White	Black	Asian	AIAN	Hisp.
Enrollment (%)	100.0	96.2	0.5	1.1	0.7	1.4
Drop-out Rate (%)	5.7	n/a	n/a	n/a	n/a	n/a
H.S. Diplomas (#)	277	268	0	3	3	3

West Bonner County District
119 S Main St • Sandpoint, ID 83856
Mailing Address: PO Box 2531 • Priest River, ID 83856
(208) 448-4629 • http://www.sd83.k12.id.us/
Grade Span: PK-12; **Agency Type:** 1
Schools: 6
  3 Primary; 1 Middle; 2 High; 0 Other Level
  5 Regular; 0 Special Education; 0 Vocational; 1 Alternative
  0 Magnet; 0 Charter; 6 Title I Eligible; 0 School-wide Title I
Students: 1,580 (52.0% male; 47.9% female)
  Individual Education Program: 201 (12.7%);
  English Language Learner: 0 (0.0%); Migrant: 0 (0.0%)
  Eligible for Free Lunch Program: 587 (37.2%)
  Eligible for Reduced-Price Lunch Program: 252 (15.9%)
Teachers: 85.8 (18.4 to 1)
Librarians/Media Specialists: 1.0 (1,580.0 to 1)
Guidance Counselors: 3.3 (478.8 to 1)
Current Spending: ($ per student per year):
  Total: $6,334; Instruction: $3,539; Support Services: $2,487
Enrollment, Drop-out Rates and Diploma Recipients by Race/Ethnicity

Category	Total	White	Black	Asian	AIAN	Hisp.
Enrollment (%)	100.0	96.4	0.7	0.3	1.1	1.5
Drop-out Rate (%)	3.6	n/a	n/a	n/a	n/a	n/a
H.S. Diplomas (#)	87	82	0	1	1	3

Bonneville County

Bonneville Joint District
3497 N Ammon Rd • Idaho Falls, ID 83401
(208) 525-4400 • http://d93.k12.id.us/
Grade Span: PK-12; **Agency Type:** 1
Schools: 16
  9 Primary; 2 Middle; 3 High; 2 Other Level
  14 Regular; 0 Special Education; 0 Vocational; 2 Alternative
  0 Magnet; 1 Charter; 10 Title I Eligible; 0 School-wide Title I
Students: 7,997 (51.2% male; 48.7% female)
  Individual Education Program: 832 (10.4%);
  English Language Learner: 357 (4.5%); Migrant: 143 (1.8%)
  Eligible for Free Lunch Program: 1,732 (21.7%)
  Eligible for Reduced-Price Lunch Program: 708 (8.9%)
Teachers: 399.5 (20.0 to 1)
Librarians/Media Specialists: 2.7 (2,952.6 to 1)
Guidance Counselors: 17.5 (455.5 to 1)
Current Spending: ($ per student per year):
  Total: $5,063; Instruction: $3,265; Support Services: $1,548
Enrollment, Drop-out Rates and Diploma Recipients by Race/Ethnicity

Category	Total	White	Black	Asian	AIAN	Hisp.
Enrollment (%)	100.0	90.2	0.6	1.0	0.5	7.8
Drop-out Rate (%)	1.1	n/a	n/a	n/a	n/a	n/a
H.S. Diplomas (#)	579	543	0	5	4	27

Idaho Falls District
690 John Adams Pkwy • Idaho Falls, ID 83401-4073
(208) 525-7500 • http://www.d91.k12.id.us/
Grade Span: PK-12; **Agency Type:** 1
Schools: 22
  14 Primary; 3 Middle; 5 High; 0 Other Level
  19 Regular; 0 Special Education; 1 Vocational; 2 Alternative
  0 Magnet; 0 Charter; 12 Title I Eligible; 0 School-wide Title I
Students: 10,385 (51.3% male; 48.6% female)
  Individual Education Program: 1,241 (11.9%);
  English Language Learner: 761 (7.3%); Migrant: 423 (4.1%)
  Eligible for Free Lunch Program: 2,388 (23.0%)
  Eligible for Reduced-Price Lunch Program: 653 (6.3%)
Teachers: 538.4 (19.3 to 1)
Librarians/Media Specialists: 5.0 (2,077.0 to 1)
Guidance Counselors: 18.5 (561.4 to 1)
Current Spending: ($ per student per year):
  Total: $5,657; Instruction: $3,497; Support Services: $1,928
Enrollment, Drop-out Rates and Diploma Recipients by Race/Ethnicity

Category	Total	White	Black	Asian	AIAN	Hisp.
Enrollment (%)	100.0	84.5	1.0	1.5	0.9	12.1
Drop-out Rate (%)	5.9	n/a	n/a	n/a	n/a	n/a
H.S. Diplomas (#)	737	670	1	17	3	46

Boundary County

Boundary County District
7188 Oak St • Bonners Ferry, ID 83805-8580
Mailing Address: PO Box 899 • Bonners Ferry, ID 83805-8580
(208) 267-3146 • http://www.bcsd101.com/
Grade Span: PK-12; **Agency Type:** 1
Schools: 7
  4 Primary; 1 Middle; 2 High; 0 Other Level
  6 Regular; 0 Special Education; 0 Vocational; 1 Alternative
  0 Magnet; 0 Charter; 6 Title I Eligible; 1 School-wide Title I
Students: 1,569 (51.7% male; 48.2% female)
  Individual Education Program: 172 (11.0%);
  English Language Learner: 109 (6.9%); Migrant: 60 (3.8%)
  Eligible for Free Lunch Program: 539 (34.4%)
  Eligible for Reduced-Price Lunch Program: 230 (14.7%)
Teachers: 95.6 (16.4 to 1)
Librarians/Media Specialists: 1.2 (1,307.5 to 1)
Guidance Counselors: 4.6 (341.1 to 1)
Current Spending: ($ per student per year):
  Total: $6,348; Instruction: $4,063; Support Services: $2,021
Enrollment, Drop-out Rates and Diploma Recipients by Race/Ethnicity

Category	Total	White	Black	Asian	AIAN	Hisp.
Enrollment (%)	100.0	92.1	1.2	1.3	1.6	3.8
Drop-out Rate (%)	9.0	n/a	n/a	n/a	n/a	n/a
H.S. Diplomas (#)	110	106	0	0	2	2

Butte County

Butte County Joint District
250 S Water • Arco, ID 83213
Mailing Address: PO Box 89 • Arco, ID 83213
(208) 527-8235
Grade Span: PK-12; **Agency Type:** 1
Schools: 5

3 Primary; 1 Middle; 1 High; 0 Other Level
5 Regular; 0 Special Education; 0 Vocational; 0 Alternative
0 Magnet; 1 Charter; 4 Title I Eligible; 1 School-wide Title I
Students: 2,409   (50.8% male; 49.1% female)
  Individual Education Program: 79 (3.3%);
  English Language Learner: 0 (0.0%); Migrant: 0 (0.0%)
  Eligible for Free Lunch Program: 178 (7.4%)
  Eligible for Reduced-Price Lunch Program: 87 (3.6%)
Teachers: 76.8 (31.4 to 1)
Librarians/Media Specialists: 1.0 (2,409.0 to 1)
Guidance Counselors: 1.8 (1,338.3 to 1)
Current Spending: ($ per student per year):
  Total: $5,566; Instruction: $3,909; Support Services: $1,545
Enrollment, Drop-out Rates and Diploma Recipients by Race/Ethnicity

Category	Total	White	Black	Asian	AIAN	Hisp.
Enrollment (%)	100.0	93.6	0.5	0.5	1.2	4.2
Drop-out Rate (%)	3.0	n/a	n/a	n/a	n/a	n/a
H.S. Diplomas (#)	36	35	0	0	0	1

Canyon County

Caldwell District
1101 Cleveland Blvd • Caldwell, ID 83605-3855
(208) 455-3300 • http://www.sd132.k12.id.us/
Grade Span: PK-12; **Agency Type:** 1
Schools: 10
  5 Primary; 1 Middle; 2 High; 2 Other Level
  8 Regular; 0 Special Education; 0 Vocational; 2 Alternative
  0 Magnet; 0 Charter; 10 Title I Eligible; 0 School-wide Title I
Students: 5,926   (51.9% male; 48.0% female)
  Individual Education Program: 681 (11.5%);
  English Language Learner: 1,088 (18.4%); Migrant: 471 (8.0%)
  Eligible for Free Lunch Program: 3,157 (53.3%)
  Eligible for Reduced-Price Lunch Program: 581 (9.8%)
Teachers: 336.9 (17.6 to 1)
Librarians/Media Specialists: 2.7 (2,193.0 to 1)
Guidance Counselors: 12.5 (473.7 to 1)
Current Spending: ($ per student per year):
  Total: $5,440; Instruction: $3,283; Support Services: $1,832
Enrollment, Drop-out Rates and Diploma Recipients by Race/Ethnicity

Category	Total	White	Black	Asian	AIAN	Hisp.
Enrollment (%)	100.0	51.2	0.5	0.7	0.5	47.2
Drop-out Rate (%)	5.1	n/a	n/a	n/a	n/a	n/a
H.S. Diplomas (#)	233	157	5	4	1	66

Middleton District
5 S 3rd Ave W • Middleton, ID 83644-5563
(208) 585-3027 • http://www.sd134.k12.id.us/
Grade Span: PK-12; **Agency Type:** 1
Schools: 6
  3 Primary; 1 Middle; 2 High; 0 Other Level
  5 Regular; 0 Special Education; 0 Vocational; 1 Alternative
  0 Magnet; 0 Charter; 3 Title I Eligible; 0 School-wide Title I
Students: 2,451   (50.5% male; 49.4% female)
  Individual Education Program: 248 (10.1%);
  English Language Learner: 72 (2.9%); Migrant: 9 (0.4%)
  Eligible for Free Lunch Program: 667 (27.2%)
  Eligible for Reduced-Price Lunch Program: 290 (11.8%)
Teachers: 127.9 (19.2 to 1)
Librarians/Media Specialists: 4.0 (612.8 to 1)
Guidance Counselors: 6.4 (383.0 to 1)
Current Spending: ($ per student per year):
  Total: $5,405; Instruction: $3,268; Support Services: $1,888
Enrollment, Drop-out Rates and Diploma Recipients by Race/Ethnicity

Category	Total	White	Black	Asian	AIAN	Hisp.
Enrollment (%)	100.0	91.1	0.4	0.4	0.1	7.9
Drop-out Rate (%)	7.4	n/a	n/a	n/a	n/a	n/a
H.S. Diplomas (#)	143	134	1	0	0	8

Nampa SD
619 S Canyon St • Nampa, ID 83686-6634
(208) 465-2700 • http://www.sd131.k12.id.us/
Grade Span: PK-12; **Agency Type:** 1
Schools: 24
  12 Primary; 3 Middle; 7 High; 2 Other Level
  19 Regular; 0 Special Education; 1 Vocational; 4 Alternative
  0 Magnet; 1 Charter; 14 Title I Eligible; 0 School-wide Title I
Students: 13,437   (51.4% male; 48.5% female)
  Individual Education Program: 1,507 (11.2%);
  English Language Learner: 2,310 (17.2%); Migrant: 744 (5.5%)
  Eligible for Free Lunch Program: 4,536 (33.8%)
  Eligible for Reduced-Price Lunch Program: 1,252 (9.3%)
Teachers: 706.4 (19.0 to 1)
Librarians/Media Specialists: 3.0 (4,479.0 to 1)
Guidance Counselors: 20.6 (652.3 to 1)

Current Spending: ($ per student per year):
  Total: $5,228; Instruction: $3,377; Support Services: $1,587
Enrollment, Drop-out Rates and Diploma Recipients by Race/Ethnicity

Category	Total	White	Black	Asian	AIAN	Hisp.
Enrollment (%)	100.0	72.7	0.7	1.3	0.5	24.8
Drop-out Rate (%)	3.6	n/a	n/a	n/a	n/a	n/a
H.S. Diplomas (#)	514	400	5	12	2	95

Vallivue SD
5207 S Montana Ave • Caldwell, ID 83605-4477
(208) 454-0445 • http://sd139.k12.id.us/default.htm
Grade Span: PK-12; **Agency Type:** 1
Schools: 6
  4 Primary; 1 Middle; 1 High; 0 Other Level
  6 Regular; 0 Special Education; 0 Vocational; 0 Alternative
  0 Magnet; 0 Charter; 6 Title I Eligible; 3 School-wide Title I
Students: 4,691   (51.3% male; 48.6% female)
  Individual Education Program: 504 (10.7%);
  English Language Learner: 607 (12.9%); Migrant: 366 (7.8%)
  Eligible for Free Lunch Program: 1,683 (35.9%)
  Eligible for Reduced-Price Lunch Program: 527 (11.2%)
Teachers: 237.2 (19.8 to 1)
Librarians/Media Specialists: 2.0 (2,344.0 to 1)
Guidance Counselors: 10.5 (446.5 to 1)
Current Spending: ($ per student per year):
  Total: $5,835; Instruction: $3,504; Support Services: $2,026
Enrollment, Drop-out Rates and Diploma Recipients by Race/Ethnicity

Category	Total	White	Black	Asian	AIAN	Hisp.
Enrollment (%)	100.0	74.0	0.7	1.2	0.7	23.4
Drop-out Rate (%)	7.6	n/a	n/a	n/a	n/a	n/a
H.S. Diplomas (#)	224	193	0	2	2	27

Cassia County

Cassia County Joint District
237 E 19th St • Burley, ID 83318-2444
(208) 878-6600 • http://www.sd151.k12.id.us/
Grade Span: PK-12; **Agency Type:** 1
Schools: 17
  8 Primary; 3 Middle; 6 High; 0 Other Level
  15 Regular; 0 Special Education; 1 Vocational; 1 Alternative
  0 Magnet; 0 Charter; 14 Title I Eligible; 0 School-wide Title I
Students: 5,002   (51.6% male; 48.3% female)
  Individual Education Program: 578 (11.6%);
  English Language Learner: 1,008 (20.2%); Migrant: 650 (13.0%)
  Eligible for Free Lunch Program: 1,833 (36.6%)
  Eligible for Reduced-Price Lunch Program: 616 (12.3%)
Teachers: 283.2 (17.7 to 1)
Librarians/Media Specialists: 4.2 (1,191.0 to 1)
Guidance Counselors: 13.0 (384.8 to 1)
Current Spending: ($ per student per year):
  Total: $5,508; Instruction: $3,369; Support Services: $1,887
Enrollment, Drop-out Rates and Diploma Recipients by Race/Ethnicity

Category	Total	White	Black	Asian	AIAN	Hisp.
Enrollment (%)	100.0	73.8	0.3	0.6	0.3	25.0
Drop-out Rate (%)	3.0	n/a	n/a	n/a	n/a	n/a
H.S. Diplomas (#)	350	305	0	3	0	42

Elmore County

Mountain Home District
140 N 3rd E • Mountain Home, ID 83647-2731
Mailing Address: PO Box 1390 • Mountain Home, ID 83647-2731
(208) 587-2580 • http://www.mtnhomesd.org/
Grade Span: PK-12; **Agency Type:** 1
Schools: 12
  5 Primary; 2 Middle; 3 High; 1 Other Level
  10 Regular; 0 Special Education; 0 Vocational; 1 Alternative
  0 Magnet; 1 Charter; 8 Title I Eligible; 1 School-wide Title I
Students: 4,454   (51.4% male; 48.5% female)
  Individual Education Program: 683 (15.3%);
  English Language Learner: 419 (9.4%); Migrant: 166 (3.7%)
  Eligible for Free Lunch Program: 955 (21.4%)
  Eligible for Reduced-Price Lunch Program: 518 (11.6%)
Teachers: 240.3 (18.5 to 1)
Librarians/Media Specialists: 2.0 (2,227.0 to 1)
Guidance Counselors: 6.0 (742.3 to 1)
Current Spending: ($ per student per year):
  Total: $5,908; Instruction: $3,516; Support Services: $2,162
Enrollment, Drop-out Rates and Diploma Recipients by Race/Ethnicity

Category	Total	White	Black	Asian	AIAN	Hisp.
Enrollment (%)	100.0	78.6	3.7	3.4	0.8	13.5
Drop-out Rate (%)	4.4	n/a	n/a	n/a	n/a	n/a
H.S. Diplomas (#)	249	207	7	9	1	25

Franklin County

Preston Joint District
120 E 2nd S St • Preston, ID 83263-1527
(208) 852-0283 • http://www.preston.k12.id.us/district/index.htm
Grade Span: PK-12; **Agency Type:** 1
Schools: 5
　　2 Primary; 1 Middle; 2 High; 0 Other Level
　　5 Regular; 0 Special Education; 0 Vocational; 0 Alternative
　　0 Magnet; 0 Charter; 5 Title I Eligible; 1 School-wide Title I
Students: 2,445   (50.8% male; 49.1% female)
　　Individual Education Program: 247 (10.1%);
　　English Language Learner: 93 (3.8%); Migrant: 0 (0.0%)
　　Eligible for Free Lunch Program: 671 (27.4%)
　　Eligible for Reduced-Price Lunch Program: 360 (14.7%)
Teachers: 121.9 (20.1 to 1)
Librarians/Media Specialists: 1.0 (2,445.0 to 1)
Guidance Counselors: 3.0 (815.0 to 1)
Current Spending: ($ per student per year):
　　Total: $4,746; Instruction: $2,966; Support Services: $1,481
Enrollment, Drop-out Rates and Diploma Recipients by Race/Ethnicity

Category	Total	White	Black	Asian	AIAN	Hisp.
Enrollment (%)	100.0	91.5	0.2	0.3	0.5	7.4
Drop-out Rate (%)	0.4	n/a	n/a	n/a	n/a	n/a
H.S. Diplomas (#)	167	161	0	0	0	6

Fremont County

Fremont County Joint District
147 N 2nd W St • St. Anthony, ID 83445-1422
(208) 624-7542 • http://www.sd215.net/
Grade Span: PK-12; **Agency Type:** 1
Schools: 10
　　4 Primary; 3 Middle; 3 High; 0 Other Level
　　8 Regular; 0 Special Education; 0 Vocational; 2 Alternative
　　0 Magnet; 0 Charter; 7 Title I Eligible; 0 School-wide Title I
Students: 2,390   (58.0% male; 41.9% female)
　　Individual Education Program: 333 (13.9%);
　　English Language Learner: 266 (11.1%); Migrant: 302 (12.3%)
　　Eligible for Free Lunch Program: 707 (28.9%)
　　Eligible for Reduced-Price Lunch Program: 336 (13.7%)
Teachers: 135.5 (18.1 to 1)
Librarians/Media Specialists: 2.4 (1,019.6 to 1)
Guidance Counselors: 3.8 (643.9 to 1)
Current Spending: ($ per student per year):
　　Total: $6,061; Instruction: $3,995; Support Services: $1,809
Enrollment, Drop-out Rates and Diploma Recipients by Race/Ethnicity

Category	Total	White	Black	Asian	AIAN	Hisp.
Enrollment (%)	100.0	82.3	0.5	0.7	0.6	15.9
Drop-out Rate (%)	1.9	n/a	n/a	n/a	n/a	n/a
H.S. Diplomas (#)	165	151	0	1	1	12

Gem County

Emmett Independent Dist
601 E Third St • Emmett, ID 83617-3111
(208) 365-6301 • http://www.sd221.k12.id.us/
Grade Span: PK-12; **Agency Type:** 1
Schools: 8
　　4 Primary; 2 Middle; 2 High; 0 Other Level
　　7 Regular; 0 Special Education; 0 Vocational; 1 Alternative
　　0 Magnet; 0 Charter; 6 Title I Eligible; 0 School-wide Title I
Students: 2,996   (51.1% male; 48.8% female)
　　Individual Education Program: 337 (11.2%);
　　English Language Learner: 162 (5.4%); Migrant: 87 (2.9%)
　　Eligible for Free Lunch Program: 1,002 (33.5%)
　　Eligible for Reduced-Price Lunch Program: 331 (11.1%)
Teachers: 157.8 (18.9 to 1)
Librarians/Media Specialists: 2.9 (1,031.0 to 1)
Guidance Counselors: 6.0 (498.3 to 1)
Current Spending: ($ per student per year):
　　Total: $5,302; Instruction: $3,467; Support Services: $1,641
Enrollment, Drop-out Rates and Diploma Recipients by Race/Ethnicity

Category	Total	White	Black	Asian	AIAN	Hisp.
Enrollment (%)	100.0	85.9	0.9	2.3	1.0	9.9
Drop-out Rate (%)	7.3	n/a	n/a	n/a	n/a	n/a
H.S. Diplomas (#)	178	169	0	0	0	9

Jefferson County

Jefferson County Jt District
201 Idaho Ave • Rigby, ID 83442-1413
(208) 745-6693 • http://www.d251.k12.id.us/
Grade Span: PK-12; **Agency Type:** 1
Schools: 9

　　4 Primary; 2 Middle; 2 High; 1 Other Level
　　7 Regular; 0 Special Education; 0 Vocational; 2 Alternative
　　0 Magnet; 0 Charter; 7 Title I Eligible; 3 School-wide Title I
Students: 3,956   (50.7% male; 49.2% female)
　　Individual Education Program: 381 (9.6%);
　　English Language Learner: 330 (8.3%); Migrant: 200 (5.1%)
　　Eligible for Free Lunch Program: 983 (24.8%)
　　Eligible for Reduced-Price Lunch Program: 475 (12.0%)
Teachers: 205.5 (19.3 to 1)
Librarians/Media Specialists: 2.0 (1,978.0 to 1)
Guidance Counselors: 10.0 (395.6 to 1)
Current Spending: ($ per student per year):
　　Total: $5,264; Instruction: $3,312; Support Services: $1,709
Enrollment, Drop-out Rates and Diploma Recipients by Race/Ethnicity

Category	Total	White	Black	Asian	AIAN	Hisp.
Enrollment (%)	100.0	86.6	0.5	0.8	0.6	11.5
Drop-out Rate (%)	1.6	n/a	n/a	n/a	n/a	n/a
H.S. Diplomas (#)	263	238	1	0	0	24

Jerome County

Jerome Joint District
107 W 3rd St • Jerome, ID 83338
(208) 324-2392 • http://www.d261.k12.id.us/
Grade Span: PK-12; **Agency Type:** 1
Schools: 7
　　2 Primary; 2 Middle; 2 High; 1 Other Level
　　6 Regular; 0 Special Education; 0 Vocational; 1 Alternative
　　0 Magnet; 0 Charter; 5 Title I Eligible; 3 School-wide Title I
Students: 3,069   (51.6% male; 48.3% female)
　　Individual Education Program: 326 (10.6%);
　　English Language Learner: 578 (18.8%); Migrant: 167 (5.4%)
　　Eligible for Free Lunch Program: 1,240 (40.4%)
　　Eligible for Reduced-Price Lunch Program: 340 (11.1%)
Teachers: 175.3 (17.5 to 1)
Librarians/Media Specialists: 2.7 (1,136.7 to 1)
Guidance Counselors: 5.0 (613.8 to 1)
Current Spending: ($ per student per year):
　　Total: $5,707; Instruction: $3,410; Support Services: $2,029
Enrollment, Drop-out Rates and Diploma Recipients by Race/Ethnicity

Category	Total	White	Black	Asian	AIAN	Hisp.
Enrollment (%)	100.0	68.8	0.4	0.5	0.5	29.8
Drop-out Rate (%)	7.2	n/a	n/a	n/a	n/a	n/a
H.S. Diplomas (#)	223	181	1	11	0	30

Kootenai County

Coeur D Alene District
311 N 10th St • Coeur D Alene, ID 83814-4280
(208) 664-8241 • http://www.sd271.k12.id.us/
Grade Span: PK-12; **Agency Type:** 1
Schools: 19
　　10 Primary; 3 Middle; 4 High; 2 Other Level
　　16 Regular; 0 Special Education; 1 Vocational; 2 Alternative
　　0 Magnet; 1 Charter; 11 Title I Eligible; 0 School-wide Title I
Students: 9,781   (51.6% male; 48.3% female)
　　Individual Education Program: 976 (10.0%);
　　English Language Learner: 32 (0.3%); Migrant: 0 (0.0%)
　　Eligible for Free Lunch Program: 2,323 (23.9%)
　　Eligible for Reduced-Price Lunch Program: 905 (9.3%)
Teachers: 515.5 (18.8 to 1)
Librarians/Media Specialists: 4.5 (2,157.6 to 1)
Guidance Counselors: 23.1 (420.3 to 1)
Current Spending: ($ per student per year):
　　Total: $5,554; Instruction: $3,444; Support Services: $1,830
Enrollment, Drop-out Rates and Diploma Recipients by Race/Ethnicity

Category	Total	White	Black	Asian	AIAN	Hisp.
Enrollment (%)	100.0	95.3	0.6	1.1	0.6	2.3
Drop-out Rate (%)	4.2	n/a	n/a	n/a	n/a	n/a
H.S. Diplomas (#)	552	527	1	12	2	10

Lakeland District
1564 Washington St • Rathdrum, ID 83858-9043
Mailing Address: PO Box 39 • Rathdrum, ID 83858-9043
(208) 687-0431 • http://www.sd272.k12.id.us/DistIntranet/index.htm
Grade Span: PK-12; **Agency Type:** 1
Schools: 9
　　5 Primary; 1 Middle; 3 High; 0 Other Level
　　8 Regular; 0 Special Education; 0 Vocational; 1 Alternative
　　0 Magnet; 0 Charter; 7 Title I Eligible; 0 School-wide Title I
Students: 4,189   (51.9% male; 48.0% female)
　　Individual Education Program: 417 (10.0%);
　　English Language Learner: 0 (0.0%); Migrant: 0 (0.0%)
　　Eligible for Free Lunch Program: 1,046 (25.0%)
　　Eligible for Reduced-Price Lunch Program: 495 (11.8%)

Teachers: 224.9 (18.6 to 1)
Librarians/Media Specialists: 4.0 (1,047.3 to 1)
Guidance Counselors: 12.0 (349.1 to 1)
Current Spending: ($ per student per year):
  Total: $5,032; Instruction: $3,280; Support Services: $1,532
Enrollment, Drop-out Rates and Diploma Recipients by Race/Ethnicity

Category	Total	White	Black	Asian	AIAN	Hisp.
Enrollment (%)	100.0	96.3	0.5	0.5	0.6	2.1
Drop-out Rate (%)	2.1	n/a	n/a	n/a	n/a	n/a
H.S. Diplomas (#)	250	238	0	5	2	5

Post Falls District
206 W Mullan Ave • Post Falls, ID 83877-7255
Mailing Address: PO Box 40 • Post Falls, ID 83877-7255
(208) 773-1658 • http://www.pfsd.com/index.html
Grade Span: PK-12; **Agency Type:** 1
Schools: 8
  5 Primary; 1 Middle; 2 High; 0 Other Level
  7 Regular; 0 Special Education; 0 Vocational; 1 Alternative
  0 Magnet; 0 Charter; 7 Title I Eligible; 0 School-wide Title I
Students: 4,944   (51.2% male; 48.7% female)
  Individual Education Program: 526 (10.6%);
  English Language Learner: 10 (0.2%); Migrant: 0 (0.0%)
  Eligible for Free Lunch Program: 1,308 (26.5%)
  Eligible for Reduced-Price Lunch Program: 734 (14.8%)
Teachers: 244.8 (20.2 to 1)
Librarians/Media Specialists: 3.0 (1,648.0 to 1)
Guidance Counselors: 10.6 (466.4 to 1)
Current Spending: ($ per student per year):
  Total: $4,992; Instruction: $3,420; Support Services: $1,313
Enrollment, Drop-out Rates and Diploma Recipients by Race/Ethnicity

Category	Total	White	Black	Asian	AIAN	Hisp.
Enrollment (%)	100.0	94.5	0.8	0.8	1.3	2.5
Drop-out Rate (%)	2.9	n/a	n/a	n/a	n/a	n/a
H.S. Diplomas (#)	232	219	0	3	4	6

Latah County

Moscow District
650 N Cleveland • Moscow, ID 83843-2923
(208) 882-1120 • http://www.sd281.k12.id.us/index.html
Grade Span: PK-12; **Agency Type:** 1
Schools: 9
  4 Primary; 2 Middle; 2 High; 1 Other Level
  8 Regular; 0 Special Education; 0 Vocational; 1 Alternative
  0 Magnet; 2 Charter; 5 Title I Eligible; 0 School-wide Title I
Students: 2,551   (51.9% male; 48.0% female)
  Individual Education Program: 290 (11.4%);
  English Language Learner: 34 (1.3%); Migrant: 0 (0.0%)
  Eligible for Free Lunch Program: 334 (13.1%)
  Eligible for Reduced-Price Lunch Program: 150 (5.9%)
Teachers: 163.7 (15.6 to 1)
Librarians/Media Specialists: 3.0 (850.3 to 1)
Guidance Counselors: 7.4 (344.7 to 1)
Current Spending: ($ per student per year):
  Total: $7,278; Instruction: $4,426; Support Services: $2,602
Enrollment, Drop-out Rates and Diploma Recipients by Race/Ethnicity

Category	Total	White	Black	Asian	AIAN	Hisp.
Enrollment (%)	100.0	90.7	2.0	3.9	1.1	2.4
Drop-out Rate (%)	2.9	n/a	n/a	n/a	n/a	n/a
H.S. Diplomas (#)	192	180	1	10	1	0

Madison County

Madison District
290 N 1st E • Rexburg, ID 83440-1520
Mailing Address: PO Box 830 • Rexburg, ID 83440-1520
(208) 359-3300 • http://d321.k12.id.us/
Grade Span: PK-12; **Agency Type:** 1
Schools: 11
  7 Primary; 1 Middle; 2 High; 1 Other Level
  10 Regular; 0 Special Education; 0 Vocational; 1 Alternative
  0 Magnet; 0 Charter; 9 Title I Eligible; 3 School-wide Title I
Students: 4,131   (52.4% male; 47.5% female)
  Individual Education Program: 403 (9.8%);
  English Language Learner: 307 (7.4%); Migrant: 329 (8.0%)
  Eligible for Free Lunch Program: 1,058 (25.7%)
  Eligible for Reduced-Price Lunch Program: 558 (13.6%)
Teachers: 216.4 (19.0 to 1)
Librarians/Media Specialists: 1.0 (4,109.0 to 1)
Guidance Counselors: 7.0 (587.0 to 1)
Current Spending: ($ per student per year):
  Total: $5,331; Instruction: $3,268; Support Services: $1,824

Enrollment, Drop-out Rates and Diploma Recipients by Race/Ethnicity

Category	Total	White	Black	Asian	AIAN	Hisp.
Enrollment (%)	100.0	91.9	0.5	1.0	0.3	6.3
Drop-out Rate (%)	3.0	n/a	n/a	n/a	n/a	n/a
H.S. Diplomas (#)	348	319	1	4	4	20

Minidoka County

Minidoka County Joint District
633 Fremont Ave • Rupert, ID 83350-1610
(208) 436-4727 • http://www.sd331.k12.id.us/
Grade Span: PK-12; **Agency Type:** 1
Schools: 12
  5 Primary; 2 Middle; 4 High; 1 Other Level
  9 Regular; 0 Special Education; 1 Vocational; 2 Alternative
  0 Magnet; 0 Charter; 10 Title I Eligible; 5 School-wide Title I
Students: 4,247   (51.1% male; 48.8% female)
  Individual Education Program: 460 (10.8%);
  English Language Learner: 767 (18.1%); Migrant: 475 (11.2%)
  Eligible for Free Lunch Program: 2,003 (47.2%)
  Eligible for Reduced-Price Lunch Program: 452 (10.6%)
Teachers: 238.4 (17.8 to 1)
Librarians/Media Specialists: 1.7 (2,498.2 to 1)
Guidance Counselors: 6.2 (685.0 to 1)
Current Spending: ($ per student per year):
  Total: $5,657; Instruction: $3,556; Support Services: $1,807
Enrollment, Drop-out Rates and Diploma Recipients by Race/Ethnicity

Category	Total	White	Black	Asian	AIAN	Hisp.
Enrollment (%)	100.0	59.5	0.4	0.7	0.5	38.9
Drop-out Rate (%)	5.3	n/a	n/a	n/a	n/a	n/a
H.S. Diplomas (#)	264	201	0	1	2	60

Nez Perce County

Lewiston Independent District
3317 12th St • Lewiston, ID 83501-5308
(208) 746-2337 • http://www.lewiston.k12.id.us/
Grade Span: PK-12; **Agency Type:** 1
Schools: 13
  7 Primary; 2 Middle; 3 High; 1 Other Level
  10 Regular; 0 Special Education; 1 Vocational; 2 Alternative
  0 Magnet; 0 Charter; 7 Title I Eligible; 0 School-wide Title I
Students: 5,010   (51.4% male; 48.5% female)
  Individual Education Program: 573 (11.4%);
  English Language Learner: 11 (0.2%); Migrant: 0 (0.0%)
  Eligible for Free Lunch Program: 1,024 (20.7%)
  Eligible for Reduced-Price Lunch Program: 374 (7.6%)
Teachers: 284.4 (17.4 to 1)
Librarians/Media Specialists: 4.0 (1,236.8 to 1)
Guidance Counselors: 13.0 (380.5 to 1)
Current Spending: ($ per student per year):
  Total: $6,848; Instruction: $4,330; Support Services: $2,254
Enrollment, Drop-out Rates and Diploma Recipients by Race/Ethnicity

Category	Total	White	Black	Asian	AIAN	Hisp.
Enrollment (%)	100.0	93.5	0.4	1.0	3.1	2.0
Drop-out Rate (%)	6.2	n/a	n/a	n/a	n/a	n/a
H.S. Diplomas (#)	332	315	0	4	10	3

Payette County

Fruitland District
303 Southwest 3rd St • Fruitland, ID 83619
Mailing Address: PO Box A • Fruitland, ID 83619
(208) 452-3595
Grade Span: PK-12; **Agency Type:** 1
Schools: 3
  1 Primary; 1 Middle; 1 High; 0 Other Level
  3 Regular; 0 Special Education; 0 Vocational; 0 Alternative
  0 Magnet; 0 Charter; 2 Title I Eligible; 0 School-wide Title I
Students: 1,558   (52.1% male; 47.8% female)
  Individual Education Program: 171 (11.0%);
  English Language Learner: 213 (13.7%); Migrant: 163 (10.5%)
  Eligible for Free Lunch Program: 499 (32.1%)
  Eligible for Reduced-Price Lunch Program: 146 (9.4%)
Teachers: 84.2 (18.5 to 1)
Librarians/Media Specialists: 1.7 (914.7 to 1)
Guidance Counselors: 3.0 (518.3 to 1)
Current Spending: ($ per student per year):
  Total: $5,602; Instruction: $3,735; Support Services: $1,640
Enrollment, Drop-out Rates and Diploma Recipients by Race/Ethnicity

Category	Total	White	Black	Asian	AIAN	Hisp.
Enrollment (%)	100.0	78.1	0.6	1.5	0.2	19.5
Drop-out Rate (%)	1.6	n/a	n/a	n/a	n/a	n/a
H.S. Diplomas (#)	106	99	0	2	0	5

Payette Joint District

20 N 12th St • Payette, ID 83661-2603
(208) 642-9366 • http://www.payettesd.k12.id.us/
Grade Span: PK-12; **Agency Type:** 1
Schools: 5
    1 Primary; 2 Middle; 2 High; 0 Other Level
    4 Regular; 0 Special Education; 0 Vocational; 1 Alternative
    0 Magnet; 0 Charter; 4 Title I Eligible; 0 School-wide Title I
Students: 1,851 (50.2% male; 49.7% female)
    Individual Education Program: 208 (11.2%);
    English Language Learner: 199 (10.8%); Migrant: 55 (3.0%)
    Eligible for Free Lunch Program: 690 (37.4%)
    Eligible for Reduced-Price Lunch Program: 127 (6.9%)
Teachers: 99.7 (18.5 to 1)
Librarians/Media Specialists: 2.0 (923.5 to 1)
Guidance Counselors: 5.0 (369.4 to 1)
Current Spending: ($ per student per year):
    Total: $5,446; Instruction: $3,396; Support Services: $1,725

Enrollment, Drop-out Rates and Diploma Recipients by Race/Ethnicity

Category	Total	White	Black	Asian	AIAN	Hisp.
Enrollment (%)	100.0	76.8	0.2	1.0	1.1	20.8
Drop-out Rate (%)	6.1	n/a	n/a	n/a	n/a	n/a
H.S. Diplomas (#)	115	95	0	0	0	20

Power County

American Falls Joint District

827 Fort Hall Ave • American Falls, ID 83211-1463
(208) 226-5173 • http://wtms@sd381.k12.id.us/
Grade Span: PK-12; **Agency Type:** 1
Schools: 5
    1 Primary; 2 Middle; 2 High; 0 Other Level
    3 Regular; 0 Special Education; 0 Vocational; 2 Alternative
    0 Magnet; 0 Charter; 5 Title I Eligible; 3 School-wide Title I
Students: 1,619 (50.8% male; 49.1% female)
    Individual Education Program: 202 (12.5%);
    English Language Learner: 577 (35.6%); Migrant: 266 (16.4%)
    Eligible for Free Lunch Program: 759 (46.9%)
    Eligible for Reduced-Price Lunch Program: 156 (9.6%)
Teachers: 92.2 (17.6 to 1)
Librarians/Media Specialists: 3.0 (539.7 to 1)
Guidance Counselors: 5.0 (323.8 to 1)
Current Spending: ($ per student per year):
    Total: $7,179; Instruction: $4,042; Support Services: $2,814

Enrollment, Drop-out Rates and Diploma Recipients by Race/Ethnicity

Category	Total	White	Black	Asian	AIAN	Hisp.
Enrollment (%)	100.0	60.8	0.2	0.9	2.8	35.3
Drop-out Rate (%)	3.7	n/a	n/a	n/a	n/a	n/a
H.S. Diplomas (#)	108	85	0	0	3	20

Twin Falls County

Twin Falls District

201 Main Ave W • Twin Falls, ID 83301-6103
(208) 733-6900 • http://www.tfsd.k12.id.us/tfsd/
Grade Span: PK-12; **Agency Type:** 1
Schools: 13
    7 Primary; 3 Middle; 2 High; 1 Other Level
    10 Regular; 0 Special Education; 0 Vocational; 3 Alternative
    0 Magnet; 0 Charter; 9 Title I Eligible; 3 School-wide Title I
Students: 7,052 (50.5% male; 49.4% female)
    Individual Education Program: 709 (10.1%);
    English Language Learner: 592 (8.4%); Migrant: 221 (3.1%)
    Eligible for Free Lunch Program: 2,117 (30.0%)
    Eligible for Reduced-Price Lunch Program: 747 (10.6%)
Teachers: 390.3 (18.1 to 1)
Librarians/Media Specialists: 3.0 (2,350.7 to 1)
Guidance Counselors: 15.5 (455.0 to 1)
Current Spending: ($ per student per year):
    Total: $5,297; Instruction: $3,098; Support Services: $1,927

Enrollment, Drop-out Rates and Diploma Recipients by Race/Ethnicity

Category	Total	White	Black	Asian	AIAN	Hisp.
Enrollment (%)	100.0	84.2	0.7	2.0	0.6	12.5
Drop-out Rate (%)	4.4	n/a	n/a	n/a	n/a	n/a
H.S. Diplomas (#)	395	372	1	0	3	19

Washington County

Weiser District

925 Pioneer Rd • Weiser, ID 83672-1146
(208) 414-0616 • http://www.sd431.k12.id.us/index.html.htm
Grade Span: PK-12; **Agency Type:** 1
Schools: 4
    1 Primary; 2 Middle; 1 High; 0 Other Level
    4 Regular; 0 Special Education; 0 Vocational; 0 Alternative

---

    0 Magnet; 0 Charter; 4 Title I Eligible; 1 School-wide Title I
Students: 1,620 (49.0% male; 50.9% female)
    Individual Education Program: 161 (9.9%);
    English Language Learner: 310 (19.1%); Migrant: 149 (9.2%)
    Eligible for Free Lunch Program: 598 (37.0%)
    Eligible for Reduced-Price Lunch Program: 213 (13.2%)
Teachers: 90.0 (18.0 to 1)
Librarians/Media Specialists: 2.0 (809.0 to 1)
Guidance Counselors: 4.0 (404.5 to 1)
Current Spending: ($ per student per year):
    Total: $5,732; Instruction: $3,652; Support Services: $1,774

Enrollment, Drop-out Rates and Diploma Recipients by Race/Ethnicity

Category	Total	White	Black	Asian	AIAN	Hisp.
Enrollment (%)	100.0	73.9	0.1	0.7	0.3	24.9
Drop-out Rate (%)	5.1	n/a	n/a	n/a	n/a	n/a
H.S. Diplomas (#)	106	80	0	5	0	21

Number of Schools

Rank	Number	District Name	City
1	54	Boise Independent District	Boise
2	42	Meridian Joint District	Meridian
3	30	Pocatello District	Pocatello
4	24	Nampa SD	Nampa
5	22	Idaho Falls District	Idaho Falls
6	19	Coeur D Alene District	Coeur D Alene
7	17	Cassia County Joint District	Burley
8	16	Bonneville Joint District	Idaho Falls
9	15	Blackfoot District	Blackfoot
10	13	Lake Pend Oreille District	Sandpoint
10	13	Lewiston Independent District	Lewiston
10	13	Twin Falls District	Twin Falls
13	12	Minidoka County Joint District	Rupert
13	12	Mountain Home District	Mountain Home
15	11	Madison District	Rexburg
16	10	Caldwell District	Caldwell
16	10	Fremont County Joint District	St. Anthony
18	9	Jefferson County Jt District	Rigby
18	9	Lakeland District	Rathdrum
18	9	Moscow District	Moscow
21	8	Blaine County District	Hailey
21	8	Emmett Independent Dist	Emmett
21	8	Post Falls District	Post Falls
24	7	Boundary County District	Bonners Ferry
24	7	Jerome Joint District	Jerome
24	7	Kuna Joint District	Kuna
24	7	Snake River District	Blackfoot
28	6	Middleton District	Middleton
28	6	Vallivue SD	Caldwell
28	6	West Bonner County District	Sandpoint
31	5	American Falls Joint District	American Falls
31	5	Butte County Joint District	Arco
31	5	Payette Joint District	Payette
31	5	Preston Joint District	Preston
31	5	Shelley Joint District	Shelley
36	4	Weiser District	Weiser
37	3	Fruitland District	Fruitland

Number of Teachers

Rank	Number	District Name	City
1	1,466	Boise Independent District	Boise
2	1,360	Meridian Joint District	Meridian
3	706	Nampa SD	Nampa
4	617	Pocatello District	Pocatello
5	538	Idaho Falls District	Idaho Falls
6	515	Coeur D Alene District	Coeur D Alene
7	399	Bonneville Joint District	Idaho Falls
8	390	Twin Falls District	Twin Falls
9	336	Caldwell District	Caldwell
10	284	Lewiston Independent District	Lewiston
11	283	Cassia County Joint District	Burley
12	244	Lake Pend Oreille District	Sandpoint
12	244	Post Falls District	Post Falls
14	240	Mountain Home District	Mountain Home
15	238	Minidoka County Joint District	Rupert
16	237	Vallivue SD	Caldwell
17	225	Blackfoot District	Blackfoot
18	224	Lakeland District	Rathdrum
19	224	Blaine County District	Hailey
20	216	Madison District	Rexburg
21	205	Jefferson County Jt District	Rigby
22	179	Kuna Joint District	Kuna
23	175	Jerome Joint District	Jerome
24	163	Moscow District	Moscow
25	157	Emmett Independent Dist	Emmett
26	135	Fremont County Joint District	St. Anthony
27	127	Middleton District	Middleton
28	121	Preston Joint District	Preston
29	103	Snake River District	Blackfoot
30	99	Payette Joint District	Payette
31	97	Shelley Joint District	Shelley
32	95	Boundary County District	Bonners Ferry
33	92	American Falls Joint District	American Falls
34	90	Weiser District	Weiser
35	85	West Bonner County District	Sandpoint
36	84	Fruitland District	Fruitland
37	76	Butte County Joint District	Arco

Number of Students

Rank	Number	District Name	City
1	26,987	Meridian Joint District	Meridian
2	26,211	Boise Independent District	Boise
3	13,437	Nampa SD	Nampa
4	12,111	Pocatello District	Pocatello
5	10,385	Idaho Falls District	Idaho Falls
6	9,781	Coeur D Alene District	Coeur D Alene
7	7,997	Bonneville Joint District	Idaho Falls
8	7,052	Twin Falls District	Twin Falls
9	5,926	Caldwell District	Caldwell
10	5,010	Lewiston Independent District	Lewiston
11	5,002	Cassia County Joint District	Burley
12	4,944	Post Falls District	Post Falls
13	4,691	Vallivue SD	Caldwell
14	4,454	Mountain Home District	Mountain Home
15	4,247	Minidoka County Joint District	Rupert
16	4,189	Lakeland District	Rathdrum
17	4,163	Blackfoot District	Blackfoot
18	4,131	Madison District	Rexburg
19	4,076	Lake Pend Oreille District	Sandpoint
20	3,956	Jefferson County Jt District	Rigby
21	3,612	Kuna Joint District	Kuna
22	3,155	Blaine County District	Hailey
23	3,069	Jerome Joint District	Jerome
24	2,996	Emmett Independent Dist	Emmett
25	2,551	Moscow District	Moscow
26	2,451	Middleton District	Middleton
27	2,445	Preston Joint District	Preston
28	2,409	Butte County Joint District	Arco
29	2,390	Fremont County Joint District	St. Anthony
30	2,048	Shelley Joint District	Shelley
31	2,042	Snake River District	Blackfoot
32	1,851	Payette Joint District	Payette
33	1,620	Weiser District	Weiser
34	1,619	American Falls Joint District	American Falls
35	1,580	West Bonner County District	Sandpoint
36	1,569	Boundary County District	Bonners Ferry
37	1,558	Fruitland District	Fruitland

Male Students

Rank	Percent	District Name	City
1	58.0	Fremont County Joint District	St. Anthony
2	52.4	Madison District	Rexburg
3	52.1	Fruitland District	Fruitland
4	52.0	Shelley Joint District	Shelley
5	52.0	West Bonner County District	Sandpoint
6	51.9	Caldwell District	Caldwell
7	51.9	Lakeland District	Rathdrum
8	51.9	Moscow District	Moscow
9	51.9	Pocatello District	Pocatello
10	51.8	Meridian Joint District	Meridian
11	51.8	Blaine County District	Hailey
12	51.7	Boundary County District	Bonners Ferry
13	51.7	Boise Independent District	Boise
14	51.6	Cassia County Joint District	Burley
15	51.6	Coeur D Alene District	Coeur D Alene
16	51.6	Jerome Joint District	Jerome
17	51.4	Nampa SD	Nampa
18	51.4	Lewiston Independent District	Lewiston
19	51.4	Mountain Home District	Mountain Home
20	51.3	Vallivue SD	Caldwell
21	51.3	Idaho Falls District	Idaho Falls
22	51.2	Kuna Joint District	Kuna
23	51.2	Post Falls District	Post Falls
24	51.2	Bonneville Joint District	Idaho Falls
25	51.1	Minidoka County Joint District	Rupert
26	51.1	Emmett Independent Dist	Emmett
27	51.0	Blackfoot District	Blackfoot
28	51.0	Lake Pend Oreille District	Sandpoint
29	50.8	Butte County Joint District	Arco
30	50.8	Preston Joint District	Preston
31	50.8	American Falls Joint District	American Falls
32	50.7	Jefferson County Jt District	Rigby
33	50.5	Twin Falls District	Twin Falls
34	50.5	Middleton District	Middleton
35	50.2	Payette Joint District	Payette
36	49.9	Snake River District	Blackfoot
37	49.0	Weiser District	Weiser

Female Students

Rank	Percent	District Name	City
1	50.9	Weiser District	Weiser
2	50.0	Snake River District	Blackfoot
3	49.7	Payette Joint District	Payette
4	49.4	Middleton District	Middleton
5	49.4	Twin Falls District	Twin Falls
6	49.2	Jefferson County Jt District	Rigby
7	49.1	American Falls Joint District	American Falls
8	49.1	Preston Joint District	Preston
9	49.1	Butte County Joint District	Arco
10	48.9	Lake Pend Oreille District	Sandpoint
11	48.9	Blackfoot District	Blackfoot
12	48.8	Emmett Independent Dist	Emmett
13	48.8	Minidoka County Joint District	Rupert
14	48.7	Bonneville Joint District	Idaho Falls
15	48.7	Post Falls District	Post Falls
16	48.7	Kuna Joint District	Kuna
17	48.6	Idaho Falls District	Idaho Falls
18	48.6	Vallivue SD	Caldwell
19	48.5	Mountain Home District	Mountain Home
20	48.5	Lewiston Independent District	Lewiston
21	48.5	Nampa SD	Nampa
22	48.3	Jerome Joint District	Jerome
23	48.3	Coeur D Alene District	Coeur D Alene
24	48.3	Cassia County Joint District	Burley
25	48.2	Boise Independent District	Boise
26	48.2	Boundary County District	Bonners Ferry
27	48.1	Blaine County District	Hailey
28	48.1	Meridian Joint District	Meridian
29	48.0	Pocatello District	Pocatello
30	48.0	Moscow District	Moscow
31	48.0	Lakeland District	Rathdrum
32	48.0	Caldwell District	Caldwell
33	47.9	West Bonner County District	Sandpoint
34	47.9	Shelley Joint District	Shelley
35	47.8	Fruitland District	Fruitland
36	47.5	Madison District	Rexburg
37	41.9	Fremont County Joint District	St. Anthony

Individual Education Program Students

Rank	Percent	District Name	City
1	15.3	Mountain Home District	Mountain Home
2	13.9	Fremont County Joint District	St. Anthony
3	12.8	Pocatello District	Pocatello
4	12.7	West Bonner County District	Sandpoint
5	12.5	American Falls Joint District	American Falls
5	12.5	Shelley Joint District	Shelley
7	12.4	Blackfoot District	Blackfoot
7	12.4	Lake Pend Oreille District	Sandpoint
9	11.9	Idaho Falls District	Idaho Falls
10	11.6	Blaine County District	Hailey
10	11.6	Cassia County Joint District	Burley
12	11.5	Boise Independent District	Boise
12	11.5	Caldwell District	Caldwell
14	11.4	Lewiston Independent District	Lewiston
14	11.4	Moscow District	Moscow
16	11.2	Emmett Independent Dist	Emmett
16	11.2	Nampa SD	Nampa
16	11.2	Payette Joint District	Payette
19	11.0	Boundary County District	Bonners Ferry
19	11.0	Fruitland District	Fruitland
21	10.8	Minidoka County Joint District	Rupert
22	10.7	Vallivue SD	Caldwell
23	10.6	Jerome Joint District	Jerome
23	10.6	Post Falls District	Post Falls
25	10.4	Bonneville Joint District	Idaho Falls
26	10.2	Meridian Joint District	Meridian
27	10.1	Middleton District	Middleton
27	10.1	Preston Joint District	Preston
27	10.1	Twin Falls District	Twin Falls
30	10.0	Coeur D Alene District	Coeur D Alene
30	10.0	Lakeland District	Rathdrum
32	9.9	Weiser District	Weiser
33	9.8	Madison District	Rexburg
34	9.6	Jefferson County Jt District	Rigby
35	9.3	Kuna Joint District	Kuna
35	9.3	Snake River District	Blackfoot
37	3.3	Butte County Joint District	Arco

English Language Learner Students

Rank	Percent	District Name	City
1	35.6	American Falls Joint District	American Falls
2	20.9	Blackfoot District	Blackfoot
3	20.2	Cassia County Joint District	Burley
4	19.1	Weiser District	Weiser
5	18.8	Jerome Joint District	Jerome
6	18.4	Caldwell District	Caldwell
7	18.1	Minidoka County Joint District	Rupert
8	17.2	Nampa SD	Nampa
9	16.0	Snake River District	Blackfoot
10	14.9	Blaine County District	Hailey
11	13.7	Fruitland District	Fruitland
12	12.9	Vallivue SD	Caldwell
13	11.1	Fremont County Joint District	St. Anthony
14	10.8	Payette Joint District	Payette
15	9.4	Mountain Home District	Mountain Home
16	8.4	Twin Falls District	Twin Falls
17	8.3	Jefferson County Jt District	Rigby
18	7.4	Madison District	Rexburg
19	7.3	Idaho Falls District	Idaho Falls
20	6.9	Boundary County District	Bonners Ferry
21	6.1	Shelley Joint District	Shelley
22	5.4	Emmett Independent Dist	Emmett
23	5.0	Boise Independent District	Boise
24	4.5	Bonneville Joint District	Idaho Falls
25	3.8	Preston Joint District	Preston
26	2.9	Middleton District	Middleton
27	2.4	Meridian Joint District	Meridian
28	1.9	Kuna Joint District	Kuna
29	1.3	Moscow District	Moscow
30	0.6	Pocatello District	Pocatello

31	0.3	Coeur D Alene District	Coeur D Alene
32	0.2	Lewiston Independent District	Lewiston
32	0.2	Post Falls District	Post Falls
34	0.0	Lake Pend Oreille District	Sandpoint
35	0.0	Butte County Joint District	Arco
35	0.0	Lakeland District	Rathdrum
35	0.0	West Bonner County District	Sandpoint

Migrant Students

Rank	Percent	District Name	City
1	16.4	American Falls Joint District	American Falls
2	13.0	Cassia County Joint District	Burley
3	12.3	Fremont County Joint District	St. Anthony
4	11.2	Minidoka County Joint District	Rupert
5	10.5	Fruitland District	Fruitland
6	9.2	Weiser District	Weiser
7	8.8	Blackfoot District	Blackfoot
8	8.0	Caldwell District	Caldwell
8	8.0	Madison District	Rexburg
10	7.8	Vallivue SD	Caldwell
11	5.5	Nampa SD	Nampa
12	5.4	Jerome Joint District	Jerome
12	5.4	Snake River District	Blackfoot
14	5.1	Jefferson County Jt District	Rigby
15	4.1	Idaho Falls District	Idaho Falls
16	3.8	Boundary County District	Bonners Ferry
17	3.7	Mountain Home District	Mountain Home
18	3.1	Twin Falls District	Twin Falls
19	3.0	Payette Joint District	Payette
20	2.9	Emmett Independent Dist	Emmett
21	2.5	Shelley Joint District	Shelley
22	1.8	Bonneville Joint District	Idaho Falls
23	0.4	Middleton District	Middleton
24	0.3	Blaine County District	Hailey
25	0.0	Boise Independent District	Boise
25	0.0	Butte County Joint District	Arco
25	0.0	Coeur D Alene District	Coeur D Alene
25	0.0	Kuna Joint District	Kuna
25	0.0	Lake Pend Oreille District	Sandpoint
25	0.0	Lakeland District	Rathdrum
25	0.0	Lewiston Independent District	Lewiston
25	0.0	Meridian Joint District	Meridian
25	0.0	Moscow District	Moscow
25	0.0	Pocatello District	Pocatello
25	0.0	Post Falls District	Post Falls
25	0.0	Preston Joint District	Preston
25	0.0	West Bonner County District	Sandpoint

Students Eligible for Free Lunch

Rank	Percent	District Name	City
1	53.3	Caldwell District	Caldwell
2	47.2	Minidoka County Joint District	Rupert
3	46.9	American Falls Joint District	American Falls
4	40.4	Jerome Joint District	Jerome
5	37.4	Payette Joint District	Payette
6	37.2	West Bonner County District	Sandpoint
7	37.0	Weiser District	Weiser
8	36.9	Blackfoot District	Blackfoot
9	36.6	Cassia County Joint District	Burley
10	35.9	Vallivue SD	Caldwell
11	34.4	Boundary County District	Bonners Ferry
12	33.8	Nampa SD	Nampa
13	33.5	Emmett Independent Dist	Emmett
14	32.1	Fruitland District	Fruitland
15	30.0	Lake Pend Oreille District	Sandpoint
15	30.0	Twin Falls District	Twin Falls
17	28.9	Fremont County Joint District	St. Anthony
18	27.4	Pocatello District	Pocatello
18	27.4	Preston Joint District	Preston
20	27.2	Middleton District	Middleton
21	26.5	Post Falls District	Post Falls
22	25.8	Snake River District	Blackfoot
23	25.7	Madison District	Rexburg
24	25.0	Lakeland District	Rathdrum
25	24.8	Jefferson County Jt District	Rigby
26	24.1	Boise Independent District	Boise
27	23.9	Coeur D Alene District	Coeur D Alene
28	23.5	Shelley Joint District	Shelley
29	23.0	Idaho Falls District	Idaho Falls
30	21.7	Bonneville Joint District	Idaho Falls
31	21.4	Mountain Home District	Mountain Home
32	20.7	Lewiston Independent District	Lewiston
33	18.2	Blaine County District	Hailey
34	15.6	Kuna Joint District	Kuna
35	13.1	Moscow District	Moscow
36	12.0	Meridian Joint District	Meridian
37	7.4	Butte County Joint District	Arco

Students Eligible for Reduced-Price Lunch

Rank	Percent	District Name	City
1	15.9	West Bonner County District	Sandpoint
2	14.8	Post Falls District	Post Falls
3	14.7	Boundary County District	Bonners Ferry
3	14.7	Preston Joint District	Preston
5	13.7	Fremont County Joint District	St. Anthony
5	13.7	Snake River District	Blackfoot
7	13.6	Madison District	Rexburg
8	13.2	Weiser District	Weiser
9	12.3	Cassia County Joint District	Burley
10	12.0	Jefferson County Jt District	Rigby
11	11.8	Lake Pend Oreille District	Sandpoint
11	11.8	Lakeland District	Rathdrum
11	11.8	Middleton District	Middleton
14	11.6	Mountain Home District	Mountain Home
15	11.2	Vallivue SD	Caldwell
16	11.1	Emmett Independent Dist	Emmett
16	11.1	Jerome Joint District	Jerome
18	10.8	Shelley Joint District	Shelley
19	10.6	Minidoka County Joint District	Rupert
19	10.6	Twin Falls District	Twin Falls
21	10.4	Kuna Joint District	Kuna
22	10.2	Blackfoot District	Blackfoot
23	9.8	Caldwell District	Caldwell
24	9.6	American Falls Joint District	American Falls
25	9.4	Fruitland District	Fruitland
26	9.3	Coeur D Alene District	Coeur D Alene
26	9.3	Nampa SD	Nampa
28	8.9	Bonneville Joint District	Idaho Falls
29	7.9	Pocatello District	Pocatello
30	7.6	Lewiston Independent District	Lewiston
31	7.4	Boise Independent District	Boise
32	6.9	Payette Joint District	Payette
33	6.6	Blaine County District	Hailey
34	6.3	Idaho Falls District	Idaho Falls
35	5.9	Moscow District	Moscow
36	5.7	Meridian Joint District	Meridian
37	3.6	Butte County Joint District	Arco

Student/Teacher Ratio

Rank	Ratio	District Name	City
1	31.4	Butte County Joint District	Arco
2	21.0	Shelley Joint District	Shelley
3	20.2	Post Falls District	Post Falls
4	20.1	Kuna Joint District	Kuna
4	20.1	Preston Joint District	Preston
6	20.0	Bonneville Joint District	Idaho Falls
7	19.8	Vallivue SD	Caldwell
8	19.7	Meridian Joint District	Meridian
8	19.7	Snake River District	Blackfoot
10	19.6	Pocatello District	Pocatello
11	19.3	Idaho Falls District	Idaho Falls
11	19.3	Jefferson County Jt District	Rigby
13	19.2	Middleton District	Middleton
14	19.0	Madison District	Rexburg
14	19.0	Nampa SD	Nampa
16	18.9	Emmett Independent Dist	Emmett
17	18.8	Coeur D Alene District	Coeur D Alene
18	18.6	Lakeland District	Rathdrum
19	18.5	Blackfoot District	Blackfoot
19	18.5	Fruitland District	Fruitland
19	18.5	Mountain Home District	Mountain Home
19	18.5	Payette Joint District	Payette
23	18.4	West Bonner County District	Sandpoint
24	18.1	Fremont County Joint District	St. Anthony
24	18.1	Twin Falls District	Twin Falls
26	18.0	Weiser District	Weiser
27	17.9	Boise Independent District	Boise
28	17.8	Minidoka County Joint District	Rupert
29	17.7	Cassia County Joint District	Burley
30	17.6	American Falls Joint District	American Falls
30	17.6	Caldwell District	Caldwell
32	17.5	Jerome Joint District	Jerome
33	17.4	Lewiston Independent District	Lewiston
34	16.7	Lake Pend Oreille District	Sandpoint
35	16.4	Boundary County District	Bonners Ferry
36	15.6	Moscow District	Moscow
37	14.1	Blaine County District	Hailey

Student/Librarian Ratio

Rank	Ratio	District Name	City
1	4,479.0	Nampa SD	Nampa
2	4,109.0	Madison District	Rexburg
3	2,985.9	Meridian Joint District	Meridian
4	2,952.6	Bonneville Joint District	Idaho Falls
5	2,498.2	Minidoka County Joint District	Rupert
6	2,445.0	Preston Joint District	Preston
7	2,409.0	Butte County Joint District	Arco
8	2,350.7	Twin Falls District	Twin Falls
9	2,344.0	Vallivue SD	Caldwell
10	2,340.3	Boise Independent District	Boise
11	2,312.8	Blackfoot District	Blackfoot
12	2,227.0	Mountain Home District	Mountain Home
13	2,193.0	Caldwell District	Caldwell
14	2,157.6	Coeur D Alene District	Coeur D Alene
15	2,077.0	Idaho Falls District	Idaho Falls
16	2,048.0	Shelley Joint District	Shelley
17	2,042.0	Snake River District	Blackfoot
18	1,978.0	Jefferson County Jt District	Rigby
19	1,803.5	Kuna Joint District	Kuna
20	1,648.0	Post Falls District	Post Falls
21	1,580.0	West Bonner County District	Sandpoint
22	1,577.5	Blaine County District	Hailey
23	1,358.7	Lake Pend Oreille District	Sandpoint
24	1,307.5	Boundary County District	Bonners Ferry
25	1,236.8	Lewiston Independent District	Lewiston
26	1,191.0	Cassia County Joint District	Burley
27	1,136.7	Jerome Joint District	Jerome
28	1,047.3	Lakeland District	Rathdrum
29	1,031.0	Emmett Independent Dist	Emmett
30	1,019.6	Fremont County Joint District	St. Anthony
31	961.2	Pocatello District	Pocatello
32	923.5	Payette Joint District	Payette
33	914.7	Fruitland District	Fruitland
34	850.3	Moscow District	Moscow
35	809.0	Weiser District	Weiser
36	612.8	Middleton District	Middleton
37	539.7	American Falls Joint District	American Falls

Student/Counselor Ratio

Rank	Ratio	District Name	City
1	1,338.3	Butte County Joint District	Arco
2	815.0	Preston Joint District	Preston
3	742.3	Mountain Home District	Mountain Home
4	685.0	Minidoka County Joint District	Rupert
5	680.6	Kuna Joint District	Kuna
6	652.3	Nampa SD	Nampa
7	643.9	Fremont County Joint District	St. Anthony
8	613.8	Jerome Joint District	Jerome
9	587.0	Madison District	Rexburg
10	561.4	Idaho Falls District	Idaho Falls
11	547.8	Blackfoot District	Blackfoot
12	518.3	Fruitland District	Fruitland
13	498.3	Emmett Independent Dist	Emmett
14	485.4	Blaine County District	Hailey
15	478.8	West Bonner County District	Sandpoint
16	473.7	Caldwell District	Caldwell
17	466.4	Post Falls District	Post Falls
18	465.5	Shelley Joint District	Shelley
19	455.5	Bonneville Joint District	Idaho Falls
20	455.0	Twin Falls District	Twin Falls
21	446.5	Vallivue SD	Caldwell
22	443.9	Snake River District	Blackfoot
23	424.9	Pocatello District	Pocatello
24	421.2	Meridian Joint District	Meridian
25	420.3	Coeur D Alene District	Coeur D Alene
26	404.5	Weiser District	Weiser
27	395.6	Jefferson County Jt District	Rigby
28	384.8	Cassia County Joint District	Burley
29	383.0	Middleton District	Middleton
30	380.5	Lewiston Independent District	Lewiston
31	369.4	Payette Joint District	Payette
32	367.2	Lake Pend Oreille District	Sandpoint
33	349.1	Lakeland District	Rathdrum
34	344.7	Moscow District	Moscow
35	341.1	Boundary County District	Bonners Ferry
36	338.2	Boise Independent District	Boise
37	323.8	American Falls Joint District	American Falls

Current Spending per Student in FY2003

Rank	Dollars	District Name	City
1	9,915	Blaine County District	Hailey
2	7,314	Boise Independent District	Boise
3	7,278	Moscow District	Moscow
4	7,179	American Falls Joint District	American Falls
5	6,848	Lewiston Independent District	Lewiston
6	6,348	Boundary County District	Bonners Ferry
7	6,334	West Bonner County District	Sandpoint
8	6,172	Lake Pend Oreille District	Sandpoint
9	6,061	Fremont County Joint District	St. Anthony
10	6,001	Pocatello District	Pocatello
11	5,973	Blackfoot District	Blackfoot
12	5,908	Mountain Home District	Mountain Home
13	5,835	Vallivue SD	Caldwell
14	5,732	Weiser District	Weiser
15	5,707	Jerome Joint District	Jerome
16	5,657	Idaho Falls District	Idaho Falls
16	5,657	Minidoka County Joint District	Rupert
18	5,636	Snake River District	Blackfoot

19	5,602	Fruitland District	Fruitland
20	5,566	Butte County Joint District	Arco
21	5,554	Coeur D Alene District	Coeur D Alene
22	5,508	Cassia County Joint District	Burley
23	5,446	Payette Joint District	Payette
24	5,440	Caldwell District	Caldwell
25	5,405	Middleton District	Middleton
26	5,331	Madison District	Rexburg
27	5,302	Emmett Independent Dist	Emmett
28	5,297	Twin Falls District	Twin Falls
29	5,264	Jefferson County Jt District	Rigby
30	5,228	Nampa SD	Nampa
31	5,074	Shelley Joint District	Shelley
32	5,066	Meridian Joint District	Meridian
33	5,063	Bonneville Joint District	Idaho Falls
34	5,032	Lakeland District	Rathdrum
35	4,992	Post Falls District	Post Falls
36	4,987	Kuna Joint District	Kuna
37	4,746	Preston Joint District	Preston

30	2.1	Lakeland District	Rathdrum
31	1.9	Fremont County Joint District	St. Anthony
32	1.6	Fruitland District	Fruitland
32	1.6	Jefferson County Jt District	Rigby
34	1.1	Bonneville Joint District	Idaho Falls
34	1.1	Shelley Joint District	Shelley
36	0.7	Snake River District	Blackfoot
37	0.4	Preston Joint District	Preston

Number of Diploma Recipients

Rank	Number	District Name	City
1	1,737	Boise Independent District	Boise
2	1,498	Meridian Joint District	Meridian
3	843	Pocatello District	Pocatello
4	737	Idaho Falls District	Idaho Falls
5	579	Bonneville Joint District	Idaho Falls
6	552	Coeur D Alene District	Coeur D Alene
7	514	Nampa SD	Nampa
8	395	Twin Falls District	Twin Falls
9	350	Cassia County Joint District	Burley
10	348	Madison District	Rexburg
11	332	Lewiston Independent District	Lewiston
12	277	Lake Pend Oreille District	Sandpoint
13	266	Blackfoot District	Blackfoot
14	264	Minidoka County Joint District	Rupert
15	263	Jefferson County Jt District	Rigby
16	250	Lakeland District	Rathdrum
17	249	Mountain Home District	Mountain Home
18	233	Caldwell District	Caldwell
19	232	Post Falls District	Post Falls
20	224	Vallivue SD	Caldwell
21	223	Jerome Joint District	Jerome
22	192	Moscow District	Moscow
23	186	Kuna Joint District	Kuna
24	178	Emmett Independent Dist	Emmett
25	173	Snake River District	Blackfoot
26	171	Blaine County District	Hailey
27	167	Preston Joint District	Preston
28	165	Fremont County Joint District	St. Anthony
29	160	Shelley Joint District	Shelley
30	143	Middleton District	Middleton
31	115	Payette Joint District	Payette
32	110	Boundary County District	Bonners Ferry
33	108	American Falls Joint District	American Falls
34	106	Fruitland District	Fruitland
34	106	Weiser District	Weiser
36	87	West Bonner County District	Sandpoint
37	36	Butte County Joint District	Arco

High School Drop-out Rate

Rank	Percent	District Name	City
1	9.0	Boundary County District	Bonners Ferry
2	7.6	Vallivue SD	Caldwell
3	7.4	Middleton District	Middleton
4	7.3	Emmett Independent Dist	Emmett
5	7.2	Jerome Joint District	Jerome
6	6.2	Lewiston Independent District	Lewiston
7	6.1	Kuna Joint District	Kuna
7	6.1	Payette Joint District	Payette
9	5.9	Idaho Falls District	Idaho Falls
10	5.7	Lake Pend Oreille District	Sandpoint
11	5.5	Blackfoot District	Blackfoot
12	5.3	Minidoka County Joint District	Rupert
13	5.1	Caldwell District	Caldwell
13	5.1	Weiser District	Weiser
15	5.0	Blaine County District	Hailey
16	4.5	Pocatello District	Pocatello
17	4.4	Mountain Home District	Mountain Home
17	4.4	Twin Falls District	Twin Falls
19	4.2	Coeur D Alene District	Coeur D Alene
20	4.0	Boise Independent District	Boise
21	3.7	American Falls Joint District	American Falls
22	3.6	Nampa SD	Nampa
22	3.6	West Bonner County District	Sandpoint
24	3.5	Meridian Joint District	Meridian
25	3.0	Butte County Joint District	Arco
25	3.0	Cassia County Joint District	Burley
25	3.0	Madison District	Rexburg
28	2.9	Moscow District	Moscow
28	2.9	Post Falls District	Post Falls

Illinois

Illinois Public School Educational Profile

Category	Value	Category	Value
Schools (2003-2004)	4,416	**Diploma Recipients** (2002-2003)	116,569
Instructional Level		White, Non-Hispanic	82,366
Primary	2,605	Black, Non-Hispanic	16,294
Middle	744	Asian/Pacific Islander	5,234
High	759	American Indian/Alaskan Native	433
Other Level	308	Hispanic	12,242
Curriculum		**High School Drop-out Rate** (%) (2001-2002)	6.4
Regular	3,937	White, Non-Hispanic	3.7
Special Education	256	Black, Non-Hispanic	13.6
Vocational	54	Asian/Pacific Islander	2.6
Alternative	169	American Indian/Alaskan Native	5.7
Type		Hispanic	10.4
Magnet	376	**Staff** (2003-2004)	
Charter	28	Teachers	127,669.7
Title I Eligible	2,344	Average Salary[1] ($)	53,820
School-wide Title I	1,014	Librarians/Media Specialists	2,200.1
Students (2003-2004)	2,100,403	Guidance Counselors	3,048.9
Gender (%)		**Ratios** (2003-2004)	
Male	51.5	Student/Teacher Ratio	16.5 to 1
Female	48.5	Student/Librarian Ratio	954.7 to 1
Race/Ethnicity (%)		Student/Counselor Ratio	688.9 to 1
White, Non-Hispanic	57.4	**College Entrance Exam Scores** (2005)	
Black, Non-Hispanic	21.2	Scholastic Aptitude Test (SAT)	
Asian/Pacific Islander	3.6	Participation Rate (%)	10
American Indian/Alaskan Native	0.2	Mean SAT Reasoning Test Verbal Score	594
Hispanic	17.7	Mean SAT Reasoning Test Math Score	606
Classification (%)		American College Testing Program (ACT)	
Individual Education Program (IEP)	15.1	Participation Rate (%)	100
Migrant (2002-2003)	0.0	Average Composite Score	20.3
English Language Learner (ELL)	0.0	Average English Score	19.9
Eligible for Free Lunch Program	31.5	Average Math Score	20.2
Eligible for Reduced-Price Lunch Program	5.4	Average Reading Score	20.3
Current Spending ($ per student in FY 2003)	8,096	Average Science Score	20.4
Instruction	4,890		
Support Services	2,925		

Note: For an explanation of data, please refer to the User's Guide in the front of the book; (1) Includes extra-duty pay and employer pick-up of employee pension contributions where applicable

Illinois NAEP 2005 Test Scores

Reading			Mathematics		
Grade/Category	**Value**	**Rank**	**Grade/Category**	**Value**	**Rank**
4th Grade			**4th Grade**		
Average Proficiency	216.5 (1.17)	35/51	Average Proficiency	233.1 (0.98)	39/51
Proficiency by Gender/Race/Ethnicity			Proficiency by Gender/Race/Ethnicity		
Male	215.2 (1.33)	31/51	Male	234.4 (1.15)	37/51
Female	217.9 (1.43)	38/51	Female	231.7 (1.07)	39/51
White, Non-Hispanic	230.3 (1.14)	12/51	White, Non-Hispanic	244.6 (0.94)	27/51
Black, Non-Hispanic	194.0 (2.12)	32/42	Black, Non-Hispanic	212.0 (1.34)	36/42
Asian, Non-Hispanic	230.2 (4.76)	13/27	Asian, Non-Hispanic	258.5 (3.40)	6/25
American Indian, Non-Hispanic	n/a	n/a	American Indian, Non-Hispanic	n/a	n/a
Hispanic	199.4 (2.52)	30/40	Hispanic	218.8 (2.07)	34/41
Proficiency by Class Size			Proficiency by Class Size		
Less than 16 Students	n/a	n/a	Less than 16 Students	217.0 (4.42)	32/35
16 to 18 Students	n/a	n/a	16 to 18 Students	n/a	n/a
19 to 20 Students	215.7 (4.27)	29/38	19 to 20 Students	236.1 (2.85)	27/38
21 to 25 Students	222.3 (1.79)	23/51	21 to 25 Students	238.9 (1.22)	31/51
Greater than 25 Students	212.5 (2.42)	30/36	Greater than 25 Students	228.2 (2.11)	31/33
Percent Attaining Achievement Levels			Percent Attaining Achievement Levels		
Below Basic	37.8 (1.32)	18/51	Below Basic	26.1 (1.18)	10/51
Basic or Above	62.2 (1.32)	34/51	Basic or Above	73.9 (1.18)	42/51
Proficient or Above	29.4 (1.33)	33/51	Proficient or Above	31.6 (1.46)	35/51
Advanced or Above	6.8 (0.70)	28/51	Advanced or Above	4.6 (0.75)	25/51
8th Grade			**8th Grade**		
Average Proficiency	263.5 (1.01)	26/51	Average Proficiency	277.7 (1.06)	32/51
Proficiency by Gender/Race/Ethnicity			Proficiency by Gender/Race/Ethnicity		
Male	258.2 (1.36)	24/51	Male	278.9 (1.17)	32/51
Female	268.9 (1.08)	25/51	Female	276.4 (1.36)	32/51
White, Non-Hispanic	271.9 (1.18)	14/51	White, Non-Hispanic	289.1 (1.01)	20/51
Black, Non-Hispanic	243.9 (2.01)	13/40	Black, Non-Hispanic	248.8 (1.69)	28/41
Asian, Non-Hispanic	281.2 (4.42)	5/24	Asian, Non-Hispanic	299.9 (3.46)	9/23
American Indian, Non-Hispanic	n/a	n/a	American Indian, Non-Hispanic	n/a	n/a
Hispanic	253.3 (1.61)	8/38	Hispanic	265.2 (1.46)	11/38
Proficiency by Parents Highest Level of Ed.			Proficiency by Parents Highest Level of Ed.		
Did Not Finish High School	245.1 (2.80)	25/49	Did Not Finish High School	255.0 (1.98)	38/50
Graduated High School	253.5 (1.69)	26/50	Graduated High School	265.5 (1.35)	31/50
Some Education After High School	265.8 (1.35)	26/50	Some Education After High School	279.3 (1.41)	32/50
Graduated College	272.5 (1.47)	26/50	Graduated College	289.2 (1.36)	29/50
Percent Attaining Achievement Levels			Percent Attaining Achievement Levels		
Below Basic	37.8 (1.32)	18/51	Below Basic	31.7 (1.15)	21/51
Basic or Above	62.2 (1.32)	34/51	Basic or Above	68.3 (1.15)	31/51
Proficient or Above	29.4 (1.33)	33/51	Proficient or Above	28.6 (1.27)	33/51
Advanced or Above	6.8 (0.70)	28/51	Advanced or Above	5.4 (0.62)	25/51

Note: For an explanation of data, please refer to the User's Guide in the front of the book; n/a indicates data not available

Adams County

Quincy SD 172
1444 Maine St · Quincy, IL 62301-4261
(217) 223-8700 · http://www.qps.org/
Grade Span: PK-12; **Agency Type:** 1
Schools: 16
  10 Primary; 2 Middle; 2 High; 2 Other Level
  11 Regular; 5 Special Education; 0 Vocational; 0 Alternative
  0 Magnet; 0 Charter; 5 Title I Eligible; 5 School-wide Title I
Students: 7,182   (50.9% male; 49.0% female)
  Individual Education Program: 1,321 (18.4%);
  English Language Learner: n/a; Migrant: 0 (0.0%)
  Eligible for Free Lunch Program: 2,554 (35.6%)
  Eligible for Reduced-Price Lunch Program: 731 (10.2%)
Teachers: 368.2 (19.5 to 1)
Librarians/Media Specialists: 0.0 (n/a to 1)
Guidance Counselors: 12.0 (598.5 to 1)
Current Spending: ($ per student per year):
  Total: $6,595; Instruction: $3,720; Support Services: $2,524
Enrollment, Drop-out Rates and Diploma Recipients by Race/Ethnicity

Category	Total	White	Black	Asian	AIAN	Hisp.
Enrollment (%)	100.0	87.5	10.6	0.8	0.1	1.1
Drop-out Rate (%)	5.1	4.9	8.5	0.0	0.0	0.0
H.S. Diplomas (#)	490	462	23	2	0	3

Bond County

Bond County CUSD 2
1008 N Hena St · Greenville, IL 62246-1378
(618) 664-0170 · http://www.bccu2.k12.il.us
Grade Span: PK-12; **Agency Type:** 1
Schools: 5
  3 Primary; 1 Middle; 1 High; 0 Other Level
  5 Regular; 0 Special Education; 0 Vocational; 0 Alternative
  0 Magnet; 0 Charter; 0 Title I Eligible; 0 School-wide Title I
Students: 1,975   (52.5% male; 47.4% female)
  Individual Education Program: 328 (16.6%);
  English Language Learner: n/a; Migrant: 0 (0.0%)
  Eligible for Free Lunch Program: 393 (19.9%)
  Eligible for Reduced-Price Lunch Program: 124 (6.3%)
Teachers: 114.1 (17.3 to 1)
Librarians/Media Specialists: 2.0 (987.5 to 1)
Guidance Counselors: 3.0 (658.3 to 1)
Current Spending: ($ per student per year):
  Total: $6,093; Instruction: $3,695; Support Services: $2,149
Enrollment, Drop-out Rates and Diploma Recipients by Race/Ethnicity

Category	Total	White	Black	Asian	AIAN	Hisp.
Enrollment (%)	100.0	93.8	4.7	0.3	0.1	1.1
Drop-out Rate (%)	1.2	1.3	0.0	0.0	n/a	0.0
H.S. Diplomas (#)	132	127	4	0	0	1

Boone County

Belvidere CUSD 100
1201 5th Ave · Belvidere, IL 61008-5125
(815) 544-0301 · http://www.district100.net/
Grade Span: PK-12; **Agency Type:** 1
Schools: 9
  6 Primary; 2 Middle; 1 High; 0 Other Level
  9 Regular; 0 Special Education; 0 Vocational; 0 Alternative
  0 Magnet; 0 Charter; 4 Title I Eligible; 0 School-wide Title I
Students: 7,574   (51.1% male; 48.8% female)
  Individual Education Program: 944 (12.5%);
  English Language Learner: n/a; Migrant: 0 (0.0%)
  Eligible for Free Lunch Program: 1,705 (22.5%)
  Eligible for Reduced-Price Lunch Program: 352 (4.6%)
Teachers: 388.8 (19.5 to 1)
Librarians/Media Specialists: 6.0 (1,262.3 to 1)
Guidance Counselors: 7.0 (1,082.0 to 1)
Current Spending: ($ per student per year):
  Total: $5,370; Instruction: $3,245; Support Services: $1,863
Enrollment, Drop-out Rates and Diploma Recipients by Race/Ethnicity

Category	Total	White	Black	Asian	AIAN	Hisp.
Enrollment (%)	100.0	73.4	2.4	1.1	0.2	23.0
Drop-out Rate (%)	1.2	1.1	5.6	0.0	n/a	1.7
H.S. Diplomas (#)	353	305	2	0	0	46

Champaign County

Champaign Community Unit SD 4
703 S New St · Champaign, IL 61820-5818
(217) 351-3800 · http://www.cmi.k12.il.us/Champaign/
Grade Span: PK-12; **Agency Type:** 1
Schools: 18

---

  12 Primary; 3 Middle; 3 High; 0 Other Level
  16 Regular; 2 Special Education; 0 Vocational; 0 Alternative
  1 Magnet; 0 Charter; 9 Title I Eligible; 3 School-wide Title I
Students: 9,371   (51.1% male; 48.8% female)
  Individual Education Program: 1,683 (18.0%);
  English Language Learner: n/a; Migrant: 0 (0.0%)
  Eligible for Free Lunch Program: 2,940 (31.4%)
  Eligible for Reduced-Price Lunch Program: 430 (4.6%)
Teachers: 643.2 (14.6 to 1)
Librarians/Media Specialists: 12.5 (749.7 to 1)
Guidance Counselors: 15.0 (624.7 to 1)
Current Spending: ($ per student per year):
  Total: $8,060; Instruction: $5,208; Support Services: $2,648
Enrollment, Drop-out Rates and Diploma Recipients by Race/Ethnicity

Category	Total	White	Black	Asian	AIAN	Hisp.
Enrollment (%)	100.0	52.5	35.6	7.2	0.3	4.4
Drop-out Rate (%)	5.0	3.9	9.7	0.0	0.0	4.0
H.S. Diplomas (#)	640	471	112	42	0	15

Mahomet-Seymour CUSD 3
PO Box 229 · Mahomet, IL 61853-0229
(217) 586-4995 · http://www.ms.k12.il.us/
Grade Span: PK-12; **Agency Type:** 1
Schools: 5
  3 Primary; 1 Middle; 1 High; 0 Other Level
  5 Regular; 0 Special Education; 0 Vocational; 0 Alternative
  0 Magnet; 0 Charter; 2 Title I Eligible; 0 School-wide Title I
Students: 2,673   (50.9% male; 49.0% female)
  Individual Education Program: 358 (13.4%);
  English Language Learner: n/a; Migrant: 0 (0.0%)
  Eligible for Free Lunch Program: 214 (8.0%)
  Eligible for Reduced-Price Lunch Program: 21 (0.8%)
Teachers: 154.4 (17.3 to 1)
Librarians/Media Specialists: 4.0 (668.3 to 1)
Guidance Counselors: 4.0 (668.3 to 1)
Current Spending: ($ per student per year):
  Total: $6,742; Instruction: $4,425; Support Services: $2,106
Enrollment, Drop-out Rates and Diploma Recipients by Race/Ethnicity

Category	Total	White	Black	Asian	AIAN	Hisp.
Enrollment (%)	100.0	97.0	0.6	1.0	0.2	1.2
Drop-out Rate (%)	1.4	1.2	0.0	25.0	0.0	0.0
H.S. Diplomas (#)	188	187	0	0	0	1

Rantoul City SD 137
400 E Wabash Ave · Rantoul, IL 61866-3013
(217) 893-4171 · http://www.rcs.k12.il.us/
Grade Span: KG-08; **Agency Type:** 1
Schools: 5
  4 Primary; 1 Middle; 0 High; 0 Other Level
  5 Regular; 0 Special Education; 0 Vocational; 0 Alternative
  0 Magnet; 0 Charter; 4 Title I Eligible; 1 School-wide Title I
Students: 1,690   (51.9% male; 48.0% female)
  Individual Education Program: 366 (21.7%);
  English Language Learner: n/a; Migrant: 0 (0.0%)
  Eligible for Free Lunch Program: 841 (49.8%)
  Eligible for Reduced-Price Lunch Program: 134 (7.9%)
Teachers: 101.5 (16.7 to 1)
Librarians/Media Specialists: 0.0 (n/a to 1)
Guidance Counselors: 0.0 (n/a to 1)
Current Spending: ($ per student per year):
  Total: $6,687; Instruction: $4,356; Support Services: $2,022
Enrollment, Drop-out Rates and Diploma Recipients by Race/Ethnicity

Category	Total	White	Black	Asian	AIAN	Hisp.
Enrollment (%)	100.0	55.6	35.4	2.0	0.2	6.9
Drop-out Rate (%)	n/a	n/a	n/a	n/a	n/a	n/a
H.S. Diplomas (#)	n/a	n/a	n/a	n/a	n/a	n/a

Urbana SD 116
PO Box 3039 · Urbana, IL 61803-3039
(217) 384-3636 · http://www.cmi.k12.il.us/Urbana/
Grade Span: PK-12; **Agency Type:** 1
Schools: 9
  7 Primary; 1 Middle; 1 High; 0 Other Level
  8 Regular; 1 Special Education; 0 Vocational; 0 Alternative
  0 Magnet; 0 Charter; 7 Title I Eligible; 2 School-wide Title I
Students: 4,570   (51.4% male; 48.5% female)
  Individual Education Program: 982 (21.5%);
  English Language Learner: n/a; Migrant: 0 (0.0%)
  Eligible for Free Lunch Program: 1,851 (40.5%)
  Eligible for Reduced-Price Lunch Program: 214 (4.7%)
Teachers: 318.8 (14.3 to 1)
Librarians/Media Specialists: 8.0 (571.3 to 1)
Guidance Counselors: 7.0 (652.9 to 1)
Current Spending: ($ per student per year):
  Total: $9,191; Instruction: $5,549; Support Services: $3,378

Enrollment, Drop-out Rates and Diploma Recipients by Race/Ethnicity

Category	Total	White	Black	Asian	AIAN	Hisp.
Enrollment (%)	100.0	51.8	37.2	6.5	0.2	4.3
Drop-out Rate (%)	6.1	4.4	9.3	7.2	0.0	14.3
H.S. Diplomas (#)	354	227	107	15	0	5

Christian County

Pana Community Unit SD 8
PO Box 377 • Pana, IL 62557-0377
(217) 562-3976
Grade Span: PK-12; **Agency Type:** 1
Schools: 5
  3 Primary; 1 Middle; 1 High; 0 Other Level
  5 Regular; 0 Special Education; 0 Vocational; 0 Alternative
  0 Magnet; 0 Charter; 4 Title I Eligible; 0 School-wide Title I
Students: 1,518　(50.0% male; 49.9% female)
  Individual Education Program: 252 (16.6%);
  English Language Learner: n/a; Migrant: 0 (0.0%)
  Eligible for Free Lunch Program: 547 (36.0%)
  Eligible for Reduced-Price Lunch Program: 137 (9.0%)
Teachers: 98.4 (15.4 to 1)
Librarians/Media Specialists: 2.0 (759.0 to 1)
Guidance Counselors: 1.0 (1,518.0 to 1)
Current Spending: ($ per student per year):
  Total: $6,356; Instruction: $3,592; Support Services: $2,475
Enrollment, Drop-out Rates and Diploma Recipients by Race/Ethnicity

Category	Total	White	Black	Asian	AIAN	Hisp.
Enrollment (%)	100.0	99.0	0.7	0.3	0.1	0.0
Drop-out Rate (%)	6.7	6.7	n/a	0.0	n/a	n/a
H.S. Diplomas (#)	78	78	0	0	0	0

Taylorville CUSD 3
101 E Adams St • Taylorville, IL 62568-2288
(217) 824-4951 • http://www.taylorvilleschools.com/
Grade Span: PK-12; **Agency Type:** 1
Schools: 8
  6 Primary; 1 Middle; 1 High; 0 Other Level
  8 Regular; 0 Special Education; 0 Vocational; 0 Alternative
  0 Magnet; 0 Charter; 5 Title I Eligible; 0 School-wide Title I
Students: 3,120　(50.8% male; 49.1% female)
  Individual Education Program: 526 (16.9%);
  English Language Learner: n/a; Migrant: 0 (0.0%)
  Eligible for Free Lunch Program: 775 (24.8%)
  Eligible for Reduced-Price Lunch Program: 214 (6.9%)
Teachers: 165.9 (18.8 to 1)
Librarians/Media Specialists: 3.0 (1,040.0 to 1)
Guidance Counselors: 3.0 (1,040.0 to 1)
Current Spending: ($ per student per year):
  Total: $5,532; Instruction: $3,533; Support Services: $1,657
Enrollment, Drop-out Rates and Diploma Recipients by Race/Ethnicity

Category	Total	White	Black	Asian	AIAN	Hisp.
Enrollment (%)	100.0	97.1	1.3	0.8	0.1	0.8
Drop-out Rate (%)	5.2	5.3	0.0	0.0	0.0	0.0
H.S. Diplomas (#)	212	210	1	1	0	0

Clay County

Flora Community Unit SD 35
444 S Locust St • Flora, IL 62839-2119
(618) 662-2412
Grade Span: PK-12; **Agency Type:** 1
Schools: 6
  3 Primary; 2 Middle; 1 High; 0 Other Level
  6 Regular; 0 Special Education; 0 Vocational; 0 Alternative
  0 Magnet; 0 Charter; 6 Title I Eligible; 0 School-wide Title I
Students: 1,508　(49.8% male; 50.1% female)
  Individual Education Program: 297 (19.7%);
  English Language Learner: n/a; Migrant: 0 (0.0%)
  Eligible for Free Lunch Program: 440 (29.2%)
  Eligible for Reduced-Price Lunch Program: 135 (9.0%)
Teachers: 99.3 (15.2 to 1)
Librarians/Media Specialists: 1.0 (1,508.0 to 1)
Guidance Counselors: 3.0 (502.7 to 1)
Current Spending: ($ per student per year):
  Total: $6,857; Instruction: $4,353; Support Services: $2,221
Enrollment, Drop-out Rates and Diploma Recipients by Race/Ethnicity

Category	Total	White	Black	Asian	AIAN	Hisp.
Enrollment (%)	100.0	95.6	1.1	1.7	0.1	1.5
Drop-out Rate (%)	7.4	7.5	n/a	0.0	n/a	0.0
H.S. Diplomas (#)	103	100	0	0	0	3

Coles County

Charleston CUSD 1
410 W Polk Ave • Charleston, IL 61920-2557
(217) 345-2106 • http://www.charleston.k12.il.us/index.html
Grade Span: PK-12; **Agency Type:** 1
Schools: 7
  5 Primary; 1 Middle; 1 High; 0 Other Level
  7 Regular; 0 Special Education; 0 Vocational; 0 Alternative
  0 Magnet; 0 Charter; 5 Title I Eligible; 0 School-wide Title I
Students: 2,952　(51.8% male; 48.1% female)
  Individual Education Program: 724 (24.5%);
  English Language Learner: n/a; Migrant: 0 (0.0%)
  Eligible for Free Lunch Program: 704 (23.8%)
  Eligible for Reduced-Price Lunch Program: 162 (5.5%)
Teachers: 177.3 (16.6 to 1)
Librarians/Media Specialists: 5.0 (590.4 to 1)
Guidance Counselors: 5.5 (536.7 to 1)
Current Spending: ($ per student per year):
  Total: $7,010; Instruction: $4,139; Support Services: $2,648
Enrollment, Drop-out Rates and Diploma Recipients by Race/Ethnicity

Category	Total	White	Black	Asian	AIAN	Hisp.
Enrollment (%)	100.0	94.3	3.2	1.2	0.1	1.2
Drop-out Rate (%)	4.2	4.1	10.0	0.0	0.0	0.0
H.S. Diplomas (#)	224	211	9	1	0	3

Mattoon CUSD 2
1701 Charleston Ave • Mattoon, IL 61938-3970
(217) 238-8850 • http://www.mattoon.k12.il.us/
Grade Span: PK-12; **Agency Type:** 1
Schools: 5
  2 Primary; 1 Middle; 1 High; 1 Other Level
  5 Regular; 0 Special Education; 0 Vocational; 0 Alternative
  0 Magnet; 0 Charter; 2 Title I Eligible; 0 School-wide Title I
Students: 3,323　(51.4% male; 48.5% female)
  Individual Education Program: 702 (21.1%);
  English Language Learner: n/a; Migrant: 0 (0.0%)
  Eligible for Free Lunch Program: 893 (26.9%)
  Eligible for Reduced-Price Lunch Program: 150 (4.5%)
Teachers: 237.8 (14.0 to 1)
Librarians/Media Specialists: 4.0 (830.8 to 1)
Guidance Counselors: 4.0 (830.8 to 1)
Current Spending: ($ per student per year):
  Total: $7,606; Instruction: $4,632; Support Services: $2,623
Enrollment, Drop-out Rates and Diploma Recipients by Race/Ethnicity

Category	Total	White	Black	Asian	AIAN	Hisp.
Enrollment (%)	100.0	94.6	2.9	0.8	0.0	1.8
Drop-out Rate (%)	6.2	6.1	7.7	0.0	33.3	11.8
H.S. Diplomas (#)	204	194	4	2	1	3

Cook County

Alsip-Hazlgrn-Oaklwn SD 126
11900 S Kostner Ave • Alsip, IL 60803-2307
(708) 389-1900
Grade Span: PK-08; **Agency Type:** 1
Schools: 4
  3 Primary; 1 Middle; 0 High; 0 Other Level
  4 Regular; 0 Special Education; 0 Vocational; 0 Alternative
  0 Magnet; 0 Charter; 1 Title I Eligible; 0 School-wide Title I
Students: 1,695　(51.3% male; 48.6% female)
  Individual Education Program: 300 (17.7%);
  English Language Learner: n/a; Migrant: 0 (0.0%)
  Eligible for Free Lunch Program: 181 (10.7%)
  Eligible for Reduced-Price Lunch Program: 49 (2.9%)
Teachers: 103.5 (16.4 to 1)
Librarians/Media Specialists: 4.0 (423.8 to 1)
Guidance Counselors: 0.0 (n/a to 1)
Current Spending: ($ per student per year):
  Total: $7,589; Instruction: $4,408; Support Services: $3,083
Enrollment, Drop-out Rates and Diploma Recipients by Race/Ethnicity

Category	Total	White	Black	Asian	AIAN	Hisp.
Enrollment (%)	100.0	79.4	4.3	2.5	0.1	13.7
Drop-out Rate (%)	n/a	n/a	n/a	n/a	n/a	n/a
H.S. Diplomas (#)	n/a	n/a	n/a	n/a	n/a	n/a

Argo Community HSD 217
7329 W 63rd St • Summit, IL 60501-1829
(708) 728-3200 • http://www.argo217.k12.il.us/
Grade Span: 09-12; **Agency Type:** 1
Schools: 1
  0 Primary; 0 Middle; 1 High; 0 Other Level
  1 Regular; 0 Special Education; 0 Vocational; 0 Alternative
  0 Magnet; 0 Charter; 1 Title I Eligible; 1 School-wide Title I
Students: 1,687　(50.8% male; 49.1% female)

Individual Education Program: 222 (13.2%);
  English Language Learner: n/a; Migrant: 0 (0.0%)
  Eligible for Free Lunch Program: 525 (31.1%)
  Eligible for Reduced-Price Lunch Program: 134 (7.9%)
Teachers: 98.8 (17.1 to 1)
Librarians/Media Specialists: 1.0 (1,687.0 to 1)
Guidance Counselors: 6.0 (281.2 to 1)
Current Spending: ($ per student per year):
  Total: $11,072; Instruction: $6,003; Support Services: $4,696
Enrollment, Drop-out Rates and Diploma Recipients by Race/Ethnicity

Category	Total	White	Black	Asian	AIAN	Hisp.
Enrollment (%)	100.0	56.3	13.0	0.5	0.1	30.1
Drop-out Rate (%)	3.5	2.8	6.3	0.0	n/a	3.6
H.S. Diplomas (#)	359	222	37	3	0	97

Arlington Heights SD 25
1200 S Dunton Ave • Arlington Heights, IL 60005-3122
(847) 758-4900 • http://www.ahsd25.n-cook.k12.il.us/
Grade Span: PK-08; **Agency Type:** 1
Schools: 9
  7 Primary; 2 Middle; 0 High; 0 Other Level
  9 Regular; 0 Special Education; 0 Vocational; 0 Alternative
  0 Magnet; 0 Charter; 2 Title I Eligible; 0 School-wide Title I
Students: 4,913 (50.7% male; 49.2% female)
  Individual Education Program: 952 (19.4%);
  English Language Learner: n/a; Migrant: 0 (0.0%)
  Eligible for Free Lunch Program: 223 (4.5%)
  Eligible for Reduced-Price Lunch Program: 94 (1.9%)
Teachers: 316.6 (15.5 to 1)
Librarians/Media Specialists: 2.0 (2,456.5 to 1)
Guidance Counselors: 0.0 (n/a to 1)
Current Spending: ($ per student per year):
  Total: $9,027; Instruction: $5,401; Support Services: $3,415
Enrollment, Drop-out Rates and Diploma Recipients by Race/Ethnicity

Category	Total	White	Black	Asian	AIAN	Hisp.
Enrollment (%)	100.0	88.9	1.2	5.1	0.3	4.6
Drop-out Rate (%)	n/a	n/a	n/a	n/a	n/a	n/a
H.S. Diplomas (#)	n/a	n/a	n/a	n/a	n/a	n/a

Bellwood SD 88
640 Eastern Ave • Bellwood, IL 60104-1878
(708) 344-9344 • http://bwshome.northstarnet.org/educatio.htm
Grade Span: PK-08; **Agency Type:** 1
Schools: 7
  6 Primary; 1 Middle; 0 High; 0 Other Level
  6 Regular; 1 Special Education; 0 Vocational; 0 Alternative
  0 Magnet; 0 Charter; 5 Title I Eligible; 0 School-wide Title I
Students: 3,347 (52.4% male; 47.5% female)
  Individual Education Program: 483 (14.4%);
  English Language Learner: n/a; Migrant: 0 (0.0%)
  Eligible for Free Lunch Program: 1,380 (41.2%)
  Eligible for Reduced-Price Lunch Program: 347 (10.4%)
Teachers: 164.0 (20.4 to 1)
Librarians/Media Specialists: 1.0 (3,347.0 to 1)
Guidance Counselors: 0.0 (n/a to 1)
Current Spending: ($ per student per year):
  Total: $6,303; Instruction: $3,561; Support Services: $2,464
Enrollment, Drop-out Rates and Diploma Recipients by Race/Ethnicity

Category	Total	White	Black	Asian	AIAN	Hisp.
Enrollment (%)	100.0	1.3	64.6	0.2	0.5	33.4
Drop-out Rate (%)	n/a	n/a	n/a	n/a	n/a	n/a
H.S. Diplomas (#)	n/a	n/a	n/a	n/a	n/a	n/a

Berkeley SD 87
1200 N Wolf Rd • Berkeley, IL 60163-1219
(708) 449-3350 • http://bwshome.northstarnet.org/educatio.htm
Grade Span: PK-08; **Agency Type:** 1
Schools: 6
  4 Primary; 2 Middle; 0 High; 0 Other Level
  6 Regular; 0 Special Education; 0 Vocational; 0 Alternative
  1 Magnet; 0 Charter; 6 Title I Eligible; 0 School-wide Title I
Students: 2,949 (50.8% male; 49.1% female)
  Individual Education Program: 528 (17.9%);
  English Language Learner: n/a; Migrant: 0 (0.0%)
  Eligible for Free Lunch Program: 1,318 (44.7%)
  Eligible for Reduced-Price Lunch Program: 360 (12.2%)
Teachers: 171.1 (17.2 to 1)
Librarians/Media Specialists: 1.0 (2,949.0 to 1)
Guidance Counselors: 4.0 (737.3 to 1)
Current Spending: ($ per student per year):
  Total: $6,825; Instruction: $3,589; Support Services: $2,924

Enrollment, Drop-out Rates and Diploma Recipients by Race/Ethnicity

Category	Total	White	Black	Asian	AIAN	Hisp.
Enrollment (%)	100.0	12.4	33.2	2.4	0.1	51.9
Drop-out Rate (%)	n/a	n/a	n/a	n/a	n/a	n/a
H.S. Diplomas (#)	n/a	n/a	n/a	n/a	n/a	n/a

Berwyn North SD 98
6633 W 16th St • Berwyn, IL 60402-1320
(708) 484-6200 • http://www.d98.cook.k12.il.us/web/index.htm
Grade Span: PK-08; **Agency Type:** 1
Schools: 4
  3 Primary; 1 Middle; 0 High; 0 Other Level
  4 Regular; 0 Special Education; 0 Vocational; 0 Alternative
  0 Magnet; 0 Charter; 0 Title I Eligible; 0 School-wide Title I
Students: 3,139 (51.3% male; 48.6% female)
  Individual Education Program: 383 (12.2%);
  English Language Learner: n/a; Migrant: 0 (0.0%)
  Eligible for Free Lunch Program: 1,845 (58.8%)
  Eligible for Reduced-Price Lunch Program: 412 (13.1%)
Teachers: 149.3 (21.0 to 1)
Librarians/Media Specialists: 4.0 (784.8 to 1)
Guidance Counselors: 0.0 (n/a to 1)
Current Spending: ($ per student per year):
  Total: $5,687; Instruction: $3,389; Support Services: $2,053
Enrollment, Drop-out Rates and Diploma Recipients by Race/Ethnicity

Category	Total	White	Black	Asian	AIAN	Hisp.
Enrollment (%)	100.0	24.2	4.0	2.3	0.0	69.5
Drop-out Rate (%)	n/a	n/a	n/a	n/a	n/a	n/a
H.S. Diplomas (#)	n/a	n/a	n/a	n/a	n/a	n/a

Berwyn South SD 100
3401 S Gunderson Ave • Berwyn, IL 60402-3773
(708) 795-2300 • http://www.schooldistrict100.org/
Grade Span: PK-08; **Agency Type:** 1
Schools: 7
  6 Primary; 1 Middle; 0 High; 0 Other Level
  7 Regular; 0 Special Education; 0 Vocational; 0 Alternative
  0 Magnet; 0 Charter; 7 Title I Eligible; 1 School-wide Title I
Students: 3,421 (50.9% male; 49.0% female)
  Individual Education Program: 581 (17.0%);
  English Language Learner: n/a; Migrant: 0 (0.0%)
  Eligible for Free Lunch Program: 1,327 (38.8%)
  Eligible for Reduced-Price Lunch Program: 528 (15.4%)
Teachers: 219.5 (15.6 to 1)
Librarians/Media Specialists: 1.0 (3,421.0 to 1)
Guidance Counselors: 0.0 (n/a to 1)
Current Spending: ($ per student per year):
  Total: $7,224; Instruction: $4,404; Support Services: $2,548
Enrollment, Drop-out Rates and Diploma Recipients by Race/Ethnicity

Category	Total	White	Black	Asian	AIAN	Hisp.
Enrollment (%)	100.0	33.1	1.1	1.2	0.1	64.5
Drop-out Rate (%)	n/a	n/a	n/a	n/a	n/a	n/a
H.S. Diplomas (#)	n/a	n/a	n/a	n/a	n/a	n/a

Bloom Twp High SD 206
100 W 10th St • Chicago Heights, IL 60411-2002
(708) 755-7010 • http://www.bloomdistrict206.org/
Grade Span: 09-12; **Agency Type:** 1
Schools: 3
  0 Primary; 0 Middle; 3 High; 0 Other Level
  2 Regular; 1 Special Education; 0 Vocational; 0 Alternative
  0 Magnet; 0 Charter; 2 Title I Eligible; 0 School-wide Title I
Students: 3,038 (52.9% male; 47.0% female)
  Individual Education Program: 511 (16.8%);
  English Language Learner: n/a; Migrant: 0 (0.0%)
  Eligible for Free Lunch Program: 1,312 (43.2%)
  Eligible for Reduced-Price Lunch Program: 206 (6.8%)
Teachers: 199.0 (15.3 to 1)
Librarians/Media Specialists: 2.0 (1,519.0 to 1)
Guidance Counselors: 11.0 (276.2 to 1)
Current Spending: ($ per student per year):
  Total: $13,103; Instruction: $7,696; Support Services: $5,003
Enrollment, Drop-out Rates and Diploma Recipients by Race/Ethnicity

Category	Total	White	Black	Asian	AIAN	Hisp.
Enrollment (%)	100.0	26.8	50.0	0.2	0.8	22.2
Drop-out Rate (%)	8.6	7.4	10.4	0.0	2.8	7.0
H.S. Diplomas (#)	491	193	202	0	7	89

Bremen Community HS District 228
15233 Pulaski Rd • Midlothian, IL 60445-3799
(708) 389-1175 • http://www.bhsd228.s-cook.k12.il.us/
Grade Span: 09-12; **Agency Type:** 1
Schools: 4
  0 Primary; 0 Middle; 4 High; 0 Other Level
  4 Regular; 0 Special Education; 0 Vocational;

0 Magnet; 0 Charter; 2 Title I Eligible; 0 School-wide Title I
Students: 4,857 (51.1% male; 48.8% female)
  Individual Education Program: 768 (15.8%);
  English Language Learner: n/a; Migrant: 0 (0.0%)
  Eligible for Free Lunch Program: 0 (0.0%)
  Eligible for Reduced-Price Lunch Program: 0 (0.0%)
Teachers: 314.6 (15.4 to 1)
Librarians/Media Specialists: 6.0 (809.5 to 1)
Guidance Counselors: 13.6 (357.1 to 1)
Current Spending: ($ per student per year):
  Total: $11,996; Instruction: $7,264; Support Services: $4,732
Enrollment, Drop-out Rates and Diploma Recipients by Race/Ethnicity

Category	Total	White	Black	Asian	AIAN	Hisp.
Enrollment (%)	100.0	53.7	35.5	2.5	0.4	7.9
Drop-out Rate (%)	3.2	2.6	3.4	5.4	0.0	7.6
H.S. Diplomas (#)	953	600	290	23	1	39

Burbank SD 111
7600 S Central Ave • Burbank, IL 60459-1397
(708) 496-0500 • http://www.burbank.k12.il.us/
Grade Span: PK-08; **Agency Type:** 1
Schools: 7
  7 Primary; 0 Middle; 0 High; 0 Other Level
  7 Regular; 0 Special Education; 0 Vocational; 0 Alternative
  0 Magnet; 0 Charter; 6 Title I Eligible; 0 School-wide Title I
Students: 3,377 (51.0% male; 48.9% female)
  Individual Education Program: 481 (14.2%);
  English Language Learner: n/a; Migrant: 0 (0.0%)
  Eligible for Free Lunch Program: 0 (0.0%)
  Eligible for Reduced-Price Lunch Program: 0 (0.0%)
Teachers: 179.6 (18.8 to 1)
Librarians/Media Specialists: 4.0 (844.3 to 1)
Guidance Counselors: 0.0 (n/a to 1)
Current Spending: ($ per student per year):
  Total: $6,597; Instruction: $4,047; Support Services: $2,470
Enrollment, Drop-out Rates and Diploma Recipients by Race/Ethnicity

Category	Total	White	Black	Asian	AIAN	Hisp.
Enrollment (%)	100.0	74.3	0.4	1.8	0.3	23.2
Drop-out Rate (%)	n/a	n/a	n/a	n/a	n/a	n/a
H.S. Diplomas (#)	n/a	n/a	n/a	n/a	n/a	n/a

Chicago Heights SD 170
30 W 16th St • Chicago Heights, IL 60411-3412
(708) 756-4165 •
http://66.99.25.40/education/district/district.php?sectionid=1
Grade Span: PK-08; **Agency Type:** 1
Schools: 12
  11 Primary; 1 Middle; 0 High; 0 Other Level
  11 Regular; 1 Special Education; 0 Vocational; 0 Alternative
  0 Magnet; 0 Charter; 10 Title I Eligible; 10 School-wide Title I
Students: 3,471 (51.3% male; 48.6% female)
  Individual Education Program: 539 (15.5%);
  English Language Learner: n/a; Migrant: 0 (0.0%)
  Eligible for Free Lunch Program: 2,709 (78.0%)
  Eligible for Reduced-Price Lunch Program: 172 (5.0%)
Teachers: 214.0 (16.2 to 1)
Librarians/Media Specialists: 0.0 (n/a to 1)
Guidance Counselors: 1.0 (3,471.0 to 1)
Current Spending: ($ per student per year):
  Total: $8,118; Instruction: $4,807; Support Services: $2,944
Enrollment, Drop-out Rates and Diploma Recipients by Race/Ethnicity

Category	Total	White	Black	Asian	AIAN	Hisp.
Enrollment (%)	100.0	8.0	48.1	0.2	0.1	43.6
Drop-out Rate (%)	n/a	n/a	n/a	n/a	n/a	n/a
H.S. Diplomas (#)	n/a	n/a	n/a	n/a	n/a	n/a

Cicero SD 99
5110 W 24th St • Cicero, IL 60804-2931
(708) 863-4856 • http://bdcweb.cicd99.edu/
Grade Span: PK-08; **Agency Type:** 1
Schools: 16
  12 Primary; 4 Middle; 0 High; 0 Other Level
  16 Regular; 0 Special Education; 0 Vocational; 0 Alternative
  0 Magnet; 0 Charter; 14 Title I Eligible; 14 School-wide Title I
Students: 13,479 (52.2% male; 47.7% female)
  Individual Education Program: 1,859 (13.8%);
  English Language Learner: n/a; Migrant: 0 (0.0%)
  Eligible for Free Lunch Program: 8,499 (63.1%)
  Eligible for Reduced-Price Lunch Program: 1,731 (12.8%)
Teachers: 746.0 (18.1 to 1)
Librarians/Media Specialists: 11.0 (1,225.4 to 1)
Guidance Counselors: 0.0 (n/a to 1)
Current Spending: ($ per student per year):
  Total: $5,974; Instruction: $3,595; Support Services: $2,122

Category	Total	White	Black	Asian	AIAN	Hisp.
Enrollment (%)	100.0	4.6	1.1	0.3	0.0	94.0
Drop-out Rate (%)	n/a	n/a	n/a	n/a	n/a	n/a
H.S. Diplomas (#)	n/a	n/a	n/a	n/a	n/a	n/a

City of Chicago SD 299
125 S Clark • Chicago, IL 60603-4016
(773) 553-1000 • http://www.cps.k12.il.us/
Grade Span: PK-12; **Agency Type:** 1
Schools: 633
  480 Primary; 23 Middle; 83 High; 47 Other Level
  610 Regular; 23 Special Education; 0 Vocational; 0 Alternative
  312 Magnet; 22 Charter; 469 Title I Eligible; 459 School-wide Title I
Students: 434,419 (50.4% male; 49.5% female)
  Individual Education Program: 55,033 (12.7%);
  English Language Learner: n/a; Migrant: 2 (<0.1%)
  Eligible for Free Lunch Program: 305,872 (70.4%)
  Eligible for Reduced-Price Lunch Program: 36,776 (8.5%)
Teachers: 22,950.8 (18.9 to 1)
Librarians/Media Specialists: 512.3 (848.0 to 1)
Guidance Counselors: 867.2 (500.9 to 1)
Current Spending: ($ per student per year):
  Total: $7,967; Instruction: $4,937; Support Services: $2,616
Enrollment, Drop-out Rates and Diploma Recipients by Race/Ethnicity

Category	Total	White	Black	Asian	AIAN	Hisp.
Enrollment (%)	100.0	9.1	50.3	3.2	0.2	37.3
Drop-out Rate (%)	17.6	15.5	20.3	8.1	8.8	15.2
H.S. Diplomas (#)	15,653	2,018	7,623	931	26	5,055

Community CSD 168
21899 S Torrence Ave • Sauk Village, IL 60411-4405
(708) 758-1610
Grade Span: PK-08; **Agency Type:** 1
Schools: 3
  2 Primary; 1 Middle; 0 High; 0 Other Level
  3 Regular; 0 Special Education; 0 Vocational; 0 Alternative
  0 Magnet; 0 Charter; 1 Title I Eligible; 1 School-wide Title I
Students: 1,772 (51.1% male; 48.8% female)
  Individual Education Program: 280 (15.8%);
  English Language Learner: n/a; Migrant: 0 (0.0%)
  Eligible for Free Lunch Program: 742 (41.9%)
  Eligible for Reduced-Price Lunch Program: 141 (8.0%)
Teachers: 94.0 (18.9 to 1)
Librarians/Media Specialists: 0.0 (n/a to 1)
Guidance Counselors: 1.0 (1,772.0 to 1)
Current Spending: ($ per student per year):
  Total: $5,403; Instruction: $3,083; Support Services: $2,084
Enrollment, Drop-out Rates and Diploma Recipients by Race/Ethnicity

Category	Total	White	Black	Asian	AIAN	Hisp.
Enrollment (%)	100.0	26.0	62.5	0.3	0.2	11.0
Drop-out Rate (%)	n/a	n/a	n/a	n/a	n/a	n/a
H.S. Diplomas (#)	n/a	n/a	n/a	n/a	n/a	n/a

Community CSD 59
2123 S Arlington Hts • Arlington Heights, IL 60005-4596
(847) 593-4300 • http://www.elk-grove.k12.il.us/
Grade Span: PK-08; **Agency Type:** 1
Schools: 14
  11 Primary; 3 Middle; 0 High; 0 Other Level
  14 Regular; 0 Special Education; 0 Vocational; 0 Alternative
  0 Magnet; 0 Charter; 2 Title I Eligible; 0 School-wide Title I
Students: 6,389 (52.4% male; 47.5% female)
  Individual Education Program: 754 (11.8%);
  English Language Learner: n/a; Migrant: 0 (0.0%)
  Eligible for Free Lunch Program: 1,307 (20.5%)
  Eligible for Reduced-Price Lunch Program: 396 (6.2%)
Teachers: 398.1 (16.0 to 1)
Librarians/Media Specialists: 14.0 (456.4 to 1)
Guidance Counselors: 0.0 (n/a to 1)
Current Spending: ($ per student per year):
  Total: $9,548; Instruction: $5,346; Support Services: $3,961
Enrollment, Drop-out Rates and Diploma Recipients by Race/Ethnicity

Category	Total	White	Black	Asian	AIAN	Hisp.
Enrollment (%)	100.0	57.0	3.4	12.7	0.3	26.6
Drop-out Rate (%)	n/a	n/a	n/a	n/a	n/a	n/a
H.S. Diplomas (#)	n/a	n/a	n/a	n/a	n/a	n/a

Community Consolidated SD 62
777 E Algonquin Rd • Des Plaines, IL 60016-6296
(847) 824-1136 • http://www.d62.org/
Grade Span: PK-08; **Agency Type:** 1
Schools: 11
  9 Primary; 2 Middle; 0 High; 0 Other Level
  11 Regular; 0 Special Education; 0 Vocational; 0 Alternative

0 Magnet; 0 Charter; 3 Title I Eligible; 0 School-wide Title I
Students: 5,085   (51.3% male; 48.6% female)
    Individual Education Program: 1,088 (21.4%);
    English Language Learner: n/a; Migrant: 0 (0.0%)
    Eligible for Free Lunch Program: 1,089 (21.4%)
    Eligible for Reduced-Price Lunch Program: 436 (8.6%)
Teachers: 335.9 (15.1 to 1)
Librarians/Media Specialists: 10.0 (508.5 to 1)
Guidance Counselors: 0.0 (n/a to 1)
Current Spending: ($ per student per year):
    Total: $9,699; Instruction: $6,393; Support Services: $3,137

Enrollment, Drop-out Rates and Diploma Recipients by Race/Ethnicity

Category	Total	White	Black	Asian	AIAN	Hisp.
Enrollment (%)	100.0	54.3	3.6	9.2	0.0	32.9
Drop-out Rate (%)	n/a	n/a	n/a	n/a	n/a	n/a
H.S. Diplomas (#)	n/a	n/a	n/a	n/a	n/a	n/a

Community High SD 218
10701 Kilpatrick Ave · Oak Lawn, IL 60453-5464
(708) 424-2000 · http://www.chsd218.org/
Grade Span: 09-12; **Agency Type:** 1
Schools: 4
    0 Primary; 0 Middle; 4 High; 0 Other Level
    3 Regular; 1 Special Education; 0 Vocational; 0 Alternative
    0 Magnet; 0 Charter; 2 Title I Eligible; 0 School-wide Title I
Students: 5,153   (50.3% male; 49.6% female)
    Individual Education Program: 778 (15.1%);
    English Language Learner: n/a; Migrant: 0 (0.0%)
    Eligible for Free Lunch Program: 1,477 (28.7%)
    Eligible for Reduced-Price Lunch Program: 355 (6.9%)
Teachers: 280.9 (18.3 to 1)
Librarians/Media Specialists: 4.5 (1,145.1 to 1)
Guidance Counselors: 14.3 (360.3 to 1)
Current Spending: ($ per student per year):
    Total: $12,378; Instruction: $7,146; Support Services: $4,968

Enrollment, Drop-out Rates and Diploma Recipients by Race/Ethnicity

Category	Total	White	Black	Asian	AIAN	Hisp.
Enrollment (%)	100.0	55.1	26.2	1.4	0.2	17.1
Drop-out Rate (%)	5.4	4.5	7.3	1.5	17.6	5.3
H.S. Diplomas (#)	894	544	190	6	2	152

Cons High SD 230
15100 S 94th Ave · Orland Park, IL 60462-3820
(708) 745-5210 · http://www.d230.org/
Grade Span: 09-12; **Agency Type:** 1
Schools: 4
    0 Primary; 0 Middle; 3 High; 1 Other Level
    3 Regular; 1 Special Education; 0 Vocational; 0 Alternative
    0 Magnet; 0 Charter; 3 Title I Eligible; 0 School-wide Title I
Students: 8,197   (50.1% male; 49.8% female)
    Individual Education Program: 870 (10.6%);
    English Language Learner: n/a; Migrant: 0 (0.0%)
    Eligible for Free Lunch Program: 0 (0.0%)
    Eligible for Reduced-Price Lunch Program: 0 (0.0%)
Teachers: 478.3 (17.1 to 1)
Librarians/Media Specialists: 8.0 (1,024.6 to 1)
Guidance Counselors: 27.0 (303.6 to 1)
Current Spending: ($ per student per year):
    Total: $11,443; Instruction: $5,993; Support Services: $5,206

Enrollment, Drop-out Rates and Diploma Recipients by Race/Ethnicity

Category	Total	White	Black	Asian	AIAN	Hisp.
Enrollment (%)	100.0	90.9	1.6	2.5	0.1	4.9
Drop-out Rate (%)	1.2	1.1	4.5	0.0	9.1	3.1
H.S. Diplomas (#)	1,796	1,663	19	45	22	47

Cook County SD 130
12300 S Greenwood Av · Blue Island, IL 60406-1558
(708) 385-6800 · http://www.lincolnnet.net/users/lsd130/
Grade Span: PK-08; **Agency Type:** 1
Schools: 11
    6 Primary; 5 Middle; 0 High; 0 Other Level
    10 Regular; 1 Special Education; 0 Vocational; 0 Alternative
    0 Magnet; 0 Charter; 10 Title I Eligible; 10 School-wide Title I
Students: 3,841   (53.1% male; 46.8% female)
    Individual Education Program: 781 (20.3%);
    English Language Learner: n/a; Migrant: 0 (0.0%)
    Eligible for Free Lunch Program: 2,437 (63.4%)
    Eligible for Reduced-Price Lunch Program: 242 (6.3%)
Teachers: 245.6 (15.6 to 1)
Librarians/Media Specialists: 6.0 (640.2 to 1)
Guidance Counselors: 0.0 (n/a to 1)
Current Spending: ($ per student per year):
    Total: $7,892; Instruction: $4,422; Support Services: $3,293

Enrollment, Drop-out Rates and Diploma Recipients by Race/Ethnicity

Category	Total	White	Black	Asian	AIAN	Hisp.
Enrollment (%)	100.0	25.7	24.6	0.4	0.0	49.3
Drop-out Rate (%)	n/a	n/a	n/a	n/a	n/a	n/a
H.S. Diplomas (#)	n/a	n/a	n/a	n/a	n/a	n/a

Country Club Hills SD 160
4411 W 185th St · Country Club Hill, IL 60478-5219
(708) 957-6200 · http://www.d160.s-cook.k12.il.us/
Grade Span: PK-08; **Agency Type:** 1
Schools: 3
    2 Primary; 1 Middle; 0 High; 0 Other Level
    3 Regular; 0 Special Education; 0 Vocational; 0 Alternative
    0 Magnet; 0 Charter; 3 Title I Eligible; 3 School-wide Title I
Students: 1,620   (51.1% male; 48.8% female)
    Individual Education Program: 247 (15.2%);
    English Language Learner: n/a; Migrant: 0 (0.0%)
    Eligible for Free Lunch Program: 592 (36.5%)
    Eligible for Reduced-Price Lunch Program: 72 (4.4%)
Teachers: 106.6 (15.2 to 1)
Librarians/Media Specialists: 1.0 (1,620.0 to 1)
Guidance Counselors: 2.0 (810.0 to 1)
Current Spending: ($ per student per year):
    Total: $8,391; Instruction: $4,968; Support Services: $3,145

Enrollment, Drop-out Rates and Diploma Recipients by Race/Ethnicity

Category	Total	White	Black	Asian	AIAN	Hisp.
Enrollment (%)	100.0	1.0	96.2	1.2	0.1	1.5
Drop-out Rate (%)	n/a	n/a	n/a	n/a	n/a	n/a
H.S. Diplomas (#)	n/a	n/a	n/a	n/a	n/a	n/a

Dolton SD 148
114 W 144thst · Riverdale, IL 60827-2703
(708) 841-2290
Grade Span: PK-08; **Agency Type:** 1
Schools: 10
    8 Primary; 2 Middle; 0 High; 0 Other Level
    9 Regular; 1 Special Education; 0 Vocational; 0 Alternative
    0 Magnet; 0 Charter; 8 Title I Eligible; 8 School-wide Title I
Students: 3,299   (52.1% male; 47.8% female)
    Individual Education Program: 427 (12.9%);
    English Language Learner: n/a; Migrant: 0 (0.0%)
    Eligible for Free Lunch Program: 2,044 (62.0%)
    Eligible for Reduced-Price Lunch Program: 302 (9.2%)
Teachers: 182.0 (18.1 to 1)
Librarians/Media Specialists: 8.0 (412.4 to 1)
Guidance Counselors: 0.0 (n/a to 1)
Current Spending: ($ per student per year):
    Total: $6,737; Instruction: $3,853; Support Services: $2,612

Enrollment, Drop-out Rates and Diploma Recipients by Race/Ethnicity

Category	Total	White	Black	Asian	AIAN	Hisp.
Enrollment (%)	100.0	0.9	97.3	0.1	0.0	1.7
Drop-out Rate (%)	n/a	n/a	n/a	n/a	n/a	n/a
H.S. Diplomas (#)	n/a	n/a	n/a	n/a	n/a	n/a

Dolton SD 149
292 Torrence Ave · Calumet City, IL 60409-1941
(708) 868-7861
Grade Span: PK-08; **Agency Type:** 1
Schools: 6
    5 Primary; 1 Middle; 0 High; 0 Other Level
    6 Regular; 0 Special Education; 0 Vocational; 0 Alternative
    0 Magnet; 0 Charter; 6 Title I Eligible; 0 School-wide Title I
Students: 3,980   (52.3% male; 47.6% female)
    Individual Education Program: 515 (12.9%);
    English Language Learner: n/a; Migrant: 0 (0.0%)
    Eligible for Free Lunch Program: 2,259 (56.8%)
    Eligible for Reduced-Price Lunch Program: 356 (8.9%)
Teachers: 201.4 (19.8 to 1)
Librarians/Media Specialists: 1.0 (3,980.0 to 1)
Guidance Counselors: 2.0 (1,990.0 to 1)
Current Spending: ($ per student per year):
    Total: $7,636; Instruction: $4,670; Support Services: $2,731

Enrollment, Drop-out Rates and Diploma Recipients by Race/Ethnicity

Category	Total	White	Black	Asian	AIAN	Hisp.
Enrollment (%)	100.0	0.4	97.6	0.0	0.0	2.1
Drop-out Rate (%)	n/a	n/a	n/a	n/a	n/a	n/a
H.S. Diplomas (#)	n/a	n/a	n/a	n/a	n/a	n/a

East Maine SD 63
10150 Dee Rd · Des Plaines, IL 60016-1597
(847) 299-1900 · http://www.emsd63.n-cook.k12.il.us/
Grade Span: PK-08; **Agency Type:** 1
Schools: 7
    6 Primary; 1 Middle; 0 High; 0 Other Level
    7 Regular; 0 Special Education; 0 Vocational; 0 Alternative

0 Magnet; 0 Charter; 3 Title I Eligible; 0 School-wide Title I
Students: 3,558 (50.8% male; 49.1% female)
  Individual Education Program: 541 (15.2%);
  English Language Learner: n/a; Migrant: 0 (0.0%)
  Eligible for Free Lunch Program: 778 (21.9%)
  Eligible for Reduced-Price Lunch Program: 145 (4.1%)
Teachers: 222.8 (16.0 to 1)
Librarians/Media Specialists: 6.7 (531.0 to 1)
Guidance Counselors: 0.9 (3,953.3 to 1)
Current Spending: ($ per student per year):
  Total: $8,884; Instruction: $5,109; Support Services: $3,469
Enrollment, Drop-out Rates and Diploma Recipients by Race/Ethnicity

Category	Total	White	Black	Asian	AIAN	Hisp.
Enrollment (%)	100.0	42.3	4.5	36.1	0.0	17.1
Drop-out Rate (%)	n/a	n/a	n/a	n/a	n/a	n/a
H.S. Diplomas (#)	n/a	n/a	n/a	n/a	n/a	n/a

Elem SD 159

6202 Vollmer Rd • Matteson, IL 60443-1058
(708) 720-1300 • http://www.dist159.com/
Grade Span: PK-08; **Agency Type:** 1
Schools: 4
  4 Primary; 0 Middle; 0 High; 0 Other Level
  4 Regular; 0 Special Education; 0 Vocational; 0 Alternative
  0 Magnet; 0 Charter; 2 Title I Eligible; 0 School-wide Title I
Students: 1,833 (51.5% male; 48.4% female)
  Individual Education Program: 293 (16.0%);
  English Language Learner: n/a; Migrant: 0 (0.0%)
  Eligible for Free Lunch Program: 543 (29.6%)
  Eligible for Reduced-Price Lunch Program: 165 (9.0%)
Teachers: 120.5 (15.2 to 1)
Librarians/Media Specialists: 3.5 (523.7 to 1)
Guidance Counselors: 0.0 (n/a to 1)
Current Spending: ($ per student per year):
  Total: $9,812; Instruction: $6,700; Support Services: $2,711
Enrollment, Drop-out Rates and Diploma Recipients by Race/Ethnicity

Category	Total	White	Black	Asian	AIAN	Hisp.
Enrollment (%)	100.0	7.2	88.3	1.2	0.2	3.2
Drop-out Rate (%)	n/a	n/a	n/a	n/a	n/a	n/a
H.S. Diplomas (#)	n/a	n/a	n/a	n/a	n/a	n/a

Elmwood Park CUSD 401

8201 W Fullerton Ave • Elmwood Park, IL 60707-2499
(708) 583-5830 • http://www.epcusd.w-cook.k12.il.us/
Grade Span: PK-12; **Agency Type:** 1
Schools: 5
  3 Primary; 1 Middle; 1 High; 0 Other Level
  5 Regular; 0 Special Education; 0 Vocational; 0 Alternative
  0 Magnet; 0 Charter; 3 Title I Eligible; 0 School-wide Title I
Students: 2,951 (50.6% male; 49.3% female)
  Individual Education Program: 525 (17.8%);
  English Language Learner: n/a; Migrant: 0 (0.0%)
  Eligible for Free Lunch Program: 265 (9.0%)
  Eligible for Reduced-Price Lunch Program: 147 (5.0%)
Teachers: 162.3 (18.2 to 1)
Librarians/Media Specialists: 1.0 (2,951.0 to 1)
Guidance Counselors: 2.0 (1,475.5 to 1)
Current Spending: ($ per student per year):
  Total: $7,780; Instruction: $4,592; Support Services: $2,966
Enrollment, Drop-out Rates and Diploma Recipients by Race/Ethnicity

Category	Total	White	Black	Asian	AIAN	Hisp.
Enrollment (%)	100.0	75.1	0.7	2.0	0.1	22.2
Drop-out Rate (%)	5.6	5.5	n/a	0.0	n/a	6.7
H.S. Diplomas (#)	187	164	0	4	0	19

Evanston CCSD 65

1500 Mcdaniel • Evanston, IL 60201-3976
(847) 859-8010 • http://www.d65.k12.il.us/
Grade Span: PK-08; **Agency Type:** 1
Schools: 17
  14 Primary; 3 Middle; 0 High; 0 Other Level
  15 Regular; 2 Special Education; 0 Vocational; 0 Alternative
  2 Magnet; 0 Charter; 8 Title I Eligible; 0 School-wide Title I
Students: 6,957 (50.8% male; 49.1% female)
  Individual Education Program: 1,307 (18.8%);
  English Language Learner: n/a; Migrant: 0 (0.0%)
  Eligible for Free Lunch Program: 1,913 (27.5%)
  Eligible for Reduced-Price Lunch Program: 487 (7.0%)
Teachers: 528.7 (13.2 to 1)
Librarians/Media Specialists: 15.0 (463.8 to 1)
Guidance Counselors: 0.0 (n/a to 1)
Current Spending: ($ per student per year):
  Total: $10,747; Instruction: $6,222; Support Services: $4,200

Evanston Twp HSD 202

1600 Dodge Ave • Evanston, IL 60204-3450
(847) 424-7220 • http://www.eths.k12.il.us/
Grade Span: 09-12; **Agency Type:** 1
Schools: 1
  0 Primary; 0 Middle; 1 High; 0 Other Level
  1 Regular; 0 Special Education; 0 Vocational; 0 Alternative
  0 Magnet; 0 Charter; 1 Title I Eligible; 0 School-wide Title I
Students: 3,118 (50.6% male; 49.3% female)
  Individual Education Program: 444 (14.2%);
  English Language Learner: n/a; Migrant: 0 (0.0%)
  Eligible for Free Lunch Program: 808 (25.9%)
  Eligible for Reduced-Price Lunch Program: 184 (5.9%)
Teachers: 251.2 (12.4 to 1)
Librarians/Media Specialists: 5.0 (623.6 to 1)
Guidance Counselors: 16.0 (194.9 to 1)
Current Spending: ($ per student per year):
  Total: $17,632; Instruction: $9,810; Support Services: $7,270
Enrollment, Drop-out Rates and Diploma Recipients by Race/Ethnicity

Category	Total	White	Black	Asian	AIAN	Hisp.
Enrollment (%)	100.0	48.0	41.3	2.1	0.1	8.5
Drop-out Rate (%)	1.9	0.5	3.2	0.0	0.0	5.9
H.S. Diplomas (#)	667	352	237	22	1	55

Evergreen Pk Elem SD 124

9400 S Sawyer Ave • Evergreen Park, IL 60805-2384
(708) 423-0950 • http://www.d124.s-cook.k12.il.us/
Grade Span: PK-08; **Agency Type:** 1
Schools: 5
  4 Primary; 1 Middle; 0 High; 0 Other Level
  5 Regular; 0 Special Education; 0 Vocational; 0 Alternative
  0 Magnet; 0 Charter; 2 Title I Eligible; 0 School-wide Title I
Students: 2,022 (51.7% male; 48.2% female)
  Individual Education Program: 399 (19.7%);
  English Language Learner: n/a; Migrant: 0 (0.0%)
  Eligible for Free Lunch Program: 303 (15.0%)
  Eligible for Reduced-Price Lunch Program: 91 (4.5%)
Teachers: 129.3 (15.6 to 1)
Librarians/Media Specialists: 1.0 (2,022.0 to 1)
Guidance Counselors: 0.0 (n/a to 1)
Current Spending: ($ per student per year):
  Total: $7,031; Instruction: $4,024; Support Services: $2,848
Enrollment, Drop-out Rates and Diploma Recipients by Race/Ethnicity

Category	Total	White	Black	Asian	AIAN	Hisp.
Enrollment (%)	100.0	70.3	17.5	1.7	0.1	10.3
Drop-out Rate (%)	n/a	n/a	n/a	n/a	n/a	n/a
H.S. Diplomas (#)	n/a	n/a	n/a	n/a	n/a	n/a

Flossmoor SD 161

41 E Elmwood • Chicago Heights, IL 60411-1104
(708) 647-7000 • http://www.sd161.org/
Grade Span: PK-08; **Agency Type:** 1
Schools: 5
  4 Primary; 1 Middle; 0 High; 0 Other Level
  5 Regular; 0 Special Education; 0 Vocational; 0 Alternative
  0 Magnet; 0 Charter; 2 Title I Eligible; 0 School-wide Title I
Students: 2,597 (51.6% male; 48.3% female)
  Individual Education Program: 280 (10.8%);
  English Language Learner: n/a; Migrant: 0 (0.0%)
  Eligible for Free Lunch Program: 0 (0.0%)
  Eligible for Reduced-Price Lunch Program: 0 (0.0%)
Teachers: 162.5 (16.0 to 1)
Librarians/Media Specialists: 1.0 (2,597.0 to 1)
Guidance Counselors: 2.0 (1,298.5 to 1)
Current Spending: ($ per student per year):
  Total: $8,262; Instruction: $4,670; Support Services: $3,581
Enrollment, Drop-out Rates and Diploma Recipients by Race/Ethnicity

Category	Total	White	Black	Asian	AIAN	Hisp.
Enrollment (%)	100.0	38.0	54.9	1.6	0.0	5.4
Drop-out Rate (%)	n/a	n/a	n/a	n/a	n/a	n/a
H.S. Diplomas (#)	n/a	n/a	n/a	n/a	n/a	n/a

Forest Ridge SD 142

15000 S Laramie Ave • Oak Forest, IL 60452-2325
(708) 687-3334 • http://www.d142.s-cook.k12.il.us/frsd142index.htm
Grade Span: PK-08; **Agency Type:** 1
Schools: 4
  3 Primary; 1 Middle; 0 High; 0 Other Level
  4 Regular; 0 Special Education; 0 Vocational; 0 Alternative

0 Magnet; 0 Charter; 2 Title I Eligible; 0 School-wide Title I
Students: 1,762   (52.7% male; 47.2% female)
   Individual Education Program: 293 (16.6%);
   English Language Learner: n/a; Migrant: 0 (0.0%)
   Eligible for Free Lunch Program: n/a
   Eligible for Reduced-Price Lunch Program: n/a
Teachers: 113.8 (15.5 to 1)
Librarians/Media Specialists: 0.0 (n/a to 1)
Guidance Counselors: 1.0 (1,762.0 to 1)
Current Spending: ($ per student per year):
   Total: $6,753; Instruction: $3,899; Support Services: $2,724
Enrollment, Drop-out Rates and Diploma Recipients by Race/Ethnicity

Category	Total	White	Black	Asian	AIAN	Hisp.
Enrollment (%)	100.0	87.5	3.2	1.3	0.2	7.8
Drop-out Rate (%)	n/a	n/a	n/a	n/a	n/a	n/a
H.S. Diplomas (#)	n/a	n/a	n/a	n/a	n/a	n/a

Glenview CCSD 34
1401 Greenwood Rd • Glenview, IL 60025-1599
(847) 998-5000 • http://www.ncook.k12.il.us/
Grade Span: PK-08; **Agency Type:** 1
Schools: 8
   6 Primary; 2 Middle; 0 High; 0 Other Level
   8 Regular; 0 Special Education; 0 Vocational; 0 Alternative
   0 Magnet; 0 Charter; 3 Title I Eligible; 0 School-wide Title I
Students: 3,975   (51.2% male; 48.7% female)
   Individual Education Program: 641 (16.1%);
   English Language Learner: n/a; Migrant: 0 (0.0%)
   Eligible for Free Lunch Program: 524 (13.2%)
   Eligible for Reduced-Price Lunch Program: 309 (7.8%)
Teachers: 278.8 (14.3 to 1)
Librarians/Media Specialists: 8.0 (496.9 to 1)
Guidance Counselors: 0.0 (n/a to 1)
Current Spending: ($ per student per year):
   Total: $9,658; Instruction: $5,737; Support Services: $3,657
Enrollment, Drop-out Rates and Diploma Recipients by Race/Ethnicity

Category	Total	White	Black	Asian	AIAN	Hisp.
Enrollment (%)	100.0	74.8	2.9	11.6	0.1	10.6
Drop-out Rate (%)	n/a	n/a	n/a	n/a	n/a	n/a
H.S. Diplomas (#)	n/a	n/a	n/a	n/a	n/a	n/a

Harvey SD 152
16001 Lincoln Ave • Harvey, IL 60426-4916
(708) 333-0300 • http://www.harvey152.org/
Grade Span: PK-08; **Agency Type:** 1
Schools: 8
   7 Primary; 1 Middle; 0 High; 0 Other Level
   7 Regular; 1 Special Education; 0 Vocational; 0 Alternative
   0 Magnet; 0 Charter; 8 Title I Eligible; 8 School-wide Title I
Students: 3,122   (51.3% male; 48.6% female)
   Individual Education Program: 444 (14.2%);
   English Language Learner: n/a; Migrant: 0 (0.0%)
   Eligible for Free Lunch Program: 2,531 (81.1%)
   Eligible for Reduced-Price Lunch Program: 138 (4.4%)
Teachers: 148.0 (21.1 to 1)
Librarians/Media Specialists: 1.0 (3,122.0 to 1)
Guidance Counselors: 1.0 (3,122.0 to 1)
Current Spending: ($ per student per year):
   Total: $7,220; Instruction: $3,922; Support Services: $2,911
Enrollment, Drop-out Rates and Diploma Recipients by Race/Ethnicity

Category	Total	White	Black	Asian	AIAN	Hisp.
Enrollment (%)	100.0	0.5	84.0	0.9	0.1	14.5
Drop-out Rate (%)	n/a	n/a	n/a	n/a	n/a	n/a
H.S. Diplomas (#)	n/a	n/a	n/a	n/a	n/a	n/a

Homewood Flossmoor CHSD 233
999 Kedzie Ave • Flossmoor, IL 60422-2299
(708) 799-3000 • http://www.hfhighschool.org/
Grade Span: 09-12; **Agency Type:** 1
Schools: 1
   0 Primary; 0 Middle; 1 High; 0 Other Level
   1 Regular; 0 Special Education; 0 Vocational; 0 Alternative
   0 Magnet; 0 Charter; 0 Title I Eligible; 0 School-wide Title I
Students: 2,767   (50.2% male; 49.7% female)
   Individual Education Program: 290 (10.5%);
   English Language Learner: n/a; Migrant: 0 (0.0%)
   Eligible for Free Lunch Program: 211 (7.6%)
   Eligible for Reduced-Price Lunch Program: 44 (1.6%)
Teachers: 156.6 (17.7 to 1)
Librarians/Media Specialists: 3.0 (922.3 to 1)
Guidance Counselors: 6.0 (461.2 to 1)
Current Spending: ($ per student per year):
   Total: $11,695; Instruction: $6,069; Support Services: $5,423

Enrollment, Drop-out Rates and Diploma Recipients by Race/Ethnicity

Category	Total	White	Black	Asian	AIAN	Hisp.
Enrollment (%)	100.0	52.4	42.4	1.8	0.1	3.3
Drop-out Rate (%)	1.0	0.8	1.7	0.0	0.0	0.0
H.S. Diplomas (#)	563	372	163	17	0	11

Homewood SD 153
18205 Aberdeen St • Homewood, IL 60430-2400
(708) 799-5661 • http://www.homewoodsd153.org/
Grade Span: PK-08; **Agency Type:** 1
Schools: 4
   2 Primary; 2 Middle; 0 High; 0 Other Level
   4 Regular; 0 Special Education; 0 Vocational; 0 Alternative
   0 Magnet; 0 Charter; 3 Title I Eligible; 0 School-wide Title I
Students: 2,133   (50.3% male; 49.6% female)
   Individual Education Program: 344 (16.1%);
   English Language Learner: n/a; Migrant: 0 (0.0%)
   Eligible for Free Lunch Program: 173 (8.1%)
   Eligible for Reduced-Price Lunch Program: 48 (2.3%)
Teachers: 150.2 (14.2 to 1)
Librarians/Media Specialists: 0.0 (n/a to 1)
Guidance Counselors: 0.0 (n/a to 1)
Current Spending: ($ per student per year):
   Total: $7,668; Instruction: $4,272; Support Services: $3,195
Enrollment, Drop-out Rates and Diploma Recipients by Race/Ethnicity

Category	Total	White	Black	Asian	AIAN	Hisp.
Enrollment (%)	100.0	58.7	33.7	2.1	0.0	5.4
Drop-out Rate (%)	n/a	n/a	n/a	n/a	n/a	n/a
H.S. Diplomas (#)	n/a	n/a	n/a	n/a	n/a	n/a

Indian Springs SD 109
7540 S 86th Ave • Justice, IL 60458-1168
(708) 496-8700 • http://www.indianspringsschools.org/
Grade Span: PK-08; **Agency Type:** 1
Schools: 6
   5 Primary; 1 Middle; 0 High; 0 Other Level
   6 Regular; 0 Special Education; 0 Vocational; 0 Alternative
   0 Magnet; 0 Charter; 3 Title I Eligible; 0 School-wide Title I
Students: 3,016   (51.3% male; 48.6% female)
   Individual Education Program: 334 (11.1%);
   English Language Learner: n/a; Migrant: 0 (0.0%)
   Eligible for Free Lunch Program: 928 (30.8%)
   Eligible for Reduced-Price Lunch Program: 168 (5.6%)
Teachers: 171.4 (17.6 to 1)
Librarians/Media Specialists: 0.0 (n/a to 1)
Guidance Counselors: 0.0 (n/a to 1)
Current Spending: ($ per student per year):
   Total: $6,397; Instruction: $3,328; Support Services: $2,772
Enrollment, Drop-out Rates and Diploma Recipients by Race/Ethnicity

Category	Total	White	Black	Asian	AIAN	Hisp.
Enrollment (%)	100.0	68.6	17.0	1.7	0.3	12.4
Drop-out Rate (%)	n/a	n/a	n/a	n/a	n/a	n/a
H.S. Diplomas (#)	n/a	n/a	n/a	n/a	n/a	n/a

J S Morton HS District 201
2423 S Austin Blvd • Cicero, IL 60804-2695
(708) 222-5702 • http://www.jsmortonhs.com/
Grade Span: 09-12; **Agency Type:** 1
Schools: 3
   0 Primary; 0 Middle; 3 High; 0 Other Level
   2 Regular; 1 Special Education; 0 Vocational; 0 Alternative
   0 Magnet; 0 Charter; 1 Title I Eligible; 0 School-wide Title I
Students: 7,529   (51.5% male; 48.4% female)
   Individual Education Program: 841 (11.2%);
   English Language Learner: n/a; Migrant: 0 (0.0%)
   Eligible for Free Lunch Program: 3,378 (44.9%)
   Eligible for Reduced-Price Lunch Program: 998 (13.3%)
Teachers: 412.1 (18.3 to 1)
Librarians/Media Specialists: 4.4 (1,711.1 to 1)
Guidance Counselors: 25.0 (301.2 to 1)
Current Spending: ($ per student per year):
   Total: $9,062; Instruction: $5,441; Support Services: $3,218
Enrollment, Drop-out Rates and Diploma Recipients by Race/Ethnicity

Category	Total	White	Black	Asian	AIAN	Hisp.
Enrollment (%)	100.0	21.0	1.2	1.0	0.1	76.8
Drop-out Rate (%)	6.3	7.0	8.2	3.8	0.0	6.1
H.S. Diplomas (#)	1,222	359	7	12	4	840

Kirby SD 140
16931 S Grissom Dr • Tinley Park, IL 60477-0098
(708) 532-6462 • http://www.ksd140.org/
Grade Span: PK-08; **Agency Type:** 1
Schools: 8
   6 Primary; 2 Middle; 0 High; 0 Other Level
   8 Regular; 0 Special Education; 0 Vocational; 0 Alternative

0 Magnet; 0 Charter; 0 Title I Eligible; 0 School-wide Title I
Students: 4,592   (51.7% male; 48.2% female)
  Individual Education Program: 653 (14.2%);
  English Language Learner: n/a; Migrant: 0 (0.0%)
  Eligible for Free Lunch Program: 0 (0.0%)
  Eligible for Reduced-Price Lunch Program: 0 (0.0%)
Teachers: 286.9 (16.0 to 1)
Librarians/Media Specialists: 8.0 (574.0 to 1)
Guidance Counselors: 5.0 (918.4 to 1)
Current Spending: ($ per student per year):
  Total: $7,267; Instruction: $4,537; Support Services: $2,720
Enrollment, Drop-out Rates and Diploma Recipients by Race/Ethnicity

Category	Total	White	Black	Asian	AIAN	Hisp.
Enrollment (%)	100.0	90.4	1.4	3.3	0.3	4.6
Drop-out Rate (%)	n/a	n/a	n/a	n/a	n/a	n/a
H.S. Diplomas (#)	n/a	n/a	n/a	n/a	n/a	n/a

La Grange SD 102
333 N Park Rd • La Grange Park, IL 60526-1898
(708) 482-2400 • http://www.dist102.k12.il.us/
Grade Span: PK-08; **Agency Type:** 1
Schools: 5
  4 Primary; 1 Middle; 0 High; 0 Other Level
  5 Regular; 0 Special Education; 0 Vocational; 0 Alternative
  0 Magnet; 0 Charter; 3 Title I Eligible; 0 School-wide Title I
Students: 2,666   (52.8% male; 47.1% female)
  Individual Education Program: 445 (16.7%);
  English Language Learner: n/a; Migrant: 0 (0.0%)
  Eligible for Free Lunch Program: 211 (7.9%)
  Eligible for Reduced-Price Lunch Program: 31 (1.2%)
Teachers: 185.0 (14.4 to 1)
Librarians/Media Specialists: 4.0 (666.5 to 1)
Guidance Counselors: 0.0 (n/a to 1)
Current Spending: ($ per student per year):
  Total: $8,258; Instruction: $4,982; Support Services: $3,101
Enrollment, Drop-out Rates and Diploma Recipients by Race/Ethnicity

Category	Total	White	Black	Asian	AIAN	Hisp.
Enrollment (%)	100.0	81.5	7.8	1.9	0.1	8.7
Drop-out Rate (%)	n/a	n/a	n/a	n/a	n/a	n/a
H.S. Diplomas (#)	n/a	n/a	n/a	n/a	n/a	n/a

Lansing SD 158
18300 Greenbay Ave • Lansing, IL 60438-3009
(708) 474-6700 • http://www.d158.s-cook.k12.il.us/
Grade Span: PK-08; **Agency Type:** 1
Schools: 5
  4 Primary; 1 Middle; 0 High; 0 Other Level
  4 Regular; 1 Special Education; 0 Vocational; 0 Alternative
  0 Magnet; 0 Charter; 1 Title I Eligible; 0 School-wide Title I
Students: 2,119   (51.1% male; 48.8% female)
  Individual Education Program: 439 (20.7%);
  English Language Learner: n/a; Migrant: 0 (0.0%)
  Eligible for Free Lunch Program: 0 (0.0%)
  Eligible for Reduced-Price Lunch Program: 0 (0.0%)
Teachers: 118.5 (17.9 to 1)
Librarians/Media Specialists: 5.0 (423.8 to 1)
Guidance Counselors: 0.0 (n/a to 1)
Current Spending: ($ per student per year):
  Total: $6,663; Instruction: $4,243; Support Services: $2,391
Enrollment, Drop-out Rates and Diploma Recipients by Race/Ethnicity

Category	Total	White	Black	Asian	AIAN	Hisp.
Enrollment (%)	100.0	56.6	31.8	0.6	0.0	11.0
Drop-out Rate (%)	n/a	n/a	n/a	n/a	n/a	n/a
H.S. Diplomas (#)	n/a	n/a	n/a	n/a	n/a	n/a

Lemont-Bromberek CSD 113a
16100 127th St • Lemont, IL 60439-7462
(630) 257-2286 • http://www.sd113a.org/
Grade Span: PK-08; **Agency Type:** 1
Schools: 4
  3 Primary; 1 Middle; 0 High; 0 Other Level
  4 Regular; 0 Special Education; 0 Vocational; 0 Alternative
  0 Magnet; 0 Charter; 0 Title I Eligible; 0 School-wide Title I
Students: 2,532   (51.3% male; 48.6% female)
  Individual Education Program: 259 (10.2%);
  English Language Learner: n/a; Migrant: 0 (0.0%)
  Eligible for Free Lunch Program: 82 (3.2%)
  Eligible for Reduced-Price Lunch Program: 23 (0.9%)
Teachers: 139.7 (18.1 to 1)
Librarians/Media Specialists: 1.0 (2,532.0 to 1)
Guidance Counselors: 3.0 (844.0 to 1)
Current Spending: ($ per student per year):
  Total: $6,113; Instruction: $3,696; Support Services: $2,271

Enrollment, Drop-out Rates and Diploma Recipients by Race/Ethnicity

Category	Total	White	Black	Asian	AIAN	Hisp.
Enrollment (%)	100.0	94.8	0.6	1.2	0.1	3.4
Drop-out Rate (%)	n/a	n/a	n/a	n/a	n/a	n/a
H.S. Diplomas (#)	n/a	n/a	n/a	n/a	n/a	n/a

Leyden Community HSD 212
3400 Rose St • Franklin Park, IL 60131-2155
(847) 451-3000 • http://www.leyhs.w-cook.k12.il.us/Home/leyden.htm
Grade Span: 09-12; **Agency Type:** 1
Schools: 2
  0 Primary; 0 Middle; 2 High; 0 Other Level
  2 Regular; 0 Special Education; 0 Vocational; 0 Alternative
  0 Magnet; 0 Charter; 2 Title I Eligible; 0 School-wide Title I
Students: 3,491   (51.0% male; 48.9% female)
  Individual Education Program: 505 (14.5%);
  English Language Learner: n/a; Migrant: 0 (0.0%)
  Eligible for Free Lunch Program: 385 (11.0%)
  Eligible for Reduced-Price Lunch Program: 147 (4.2%)
Teachers: 211.0 (16.5 to 1)
Librarians/Media Specialists: 5.4 (646.5 to 1)
Guidance Counselors: 12.8 (272.7 to 1)
Current Spending: ($ per student per year):
  Total: $12,018; Instruction: $6,286; Support Services: $5,437
Enrollment, Drop-out Rates and Diploma Recipients by Race/Ethnicity

Category	Total	White	Black	Asian	AIAN	Hisp.
Enrollment (%)	100.0	54.5	1.2	3.7	0.3	40.3
Drop-out Rate (%)	5.2	5.1	13.6	5.3	13.3	5.0
H.S. Diplomas (#)	732	471	14	31	2	214

Lyons SD 103
4100 S Joliet Ave • Lyons, IL 60534-1595
(708) 783-4100 • http://www.district103.w-cook.k12.il.us/
Grade Span: PK-08; **Agency Type:** 1
Schools: 6
  5 Primary; 1 Middle; 0 High; 0 Other Level
  6 Regular; 0 Special Education; 0 Vocational; 0 Alternative
  0 Magnet; 0 Charter; 4 Title I Eligible; 0 School-wide Title I
Students: 2,274   (50.3% male; 49.6% female)
  Individual Education Program: 330 (14.5%);
  English Language Learner: n/a; Migrant: 6 (0.3%)
  Eligible for Free Lunch Program: 485 (21.3%)
  Eligible for Reduced-Price Lunch Program: 136 (6.0%)
Teachers: 129.9 (17.5 to 1)
Librarians/Media Specialists: 1.0 (2,274.0 to 1)
Guidance Counselors: 1.0 (2,274.0 to 1)
Current Spending: ($ per student per year):
  Total: $6,942; Instruction: $4,290; Support Services: $2,424
Enrollment, Drop-out Rates and Diploma Recipients by Race/Ethnicity

Category	Total	White	Black	Asian	AIAN	Hisp.
Enrollment (%)	100.0	56.7	2.6	1.0	0.3	39.4
Drop-out Rate (%)	n/a	n/a	n/a	n/a	n/a	n/a
H.S. Diplomas (#)	n/a	n/a	n/a	n/a	n/a	n/a

Lyons Twp HSD 204
100 S Brainard • La Grange, IL 60525-2100
(708) 579-6451 • http://www.lths.net/
Grade Span: 08-12; **Agency Type:** 1
Schools: 1
  0 Primary; 0 Middle; 1 High; 0 Other Level
  1 Regular; 0 Special Education; 0 Vocational; 0 Alternative
  0 Magnet; 0 Charter; 1 Title I Eligible; 0 School-wide Title I
Students: 3,564   (49.7% male; 50.2% female)
  Individual Education Program: 386 (10.8%);
  English Language Learner: n/a; Migrant: 0 (0.0%)
  Eligible for Free Lunch Program: 0 (0.0%)
  Eligible for Reduced-Price Lunch Program: 0 (0.0%)
Teachers: 206.3 (17.3 to 1)
Librarians/Media Specialists: 4.0 (891.0 to 1)
Guidance Counselors: 13.9 (256.4 to 1)
Current Spending: ($ per student per year):
  Total: $12,994; Instruction: $7,022; Support Services: $5,723
Enrollment, Drop-out Rates and Diploma Recipients by Race/Ethnicity

Category	Total	White	Black	Asian	AIAN	Hisp.
Enrollment (%)	100.0	86.8	3.1	1.8	0.2	8.2
Drop-out Rate (%)	1.0	1.1	0.9	0.0	0.0	0.0
H.S. Diplomas (#)	734	656	29	8	0	41

Maine Township HSD 207
1131 S Dee Rd • Park Ridge, IL 60068-4398
(847) 696-3600 • http://www.maine207.k12.il.us/
Grade Span: 07-12; **Agency Type:** 1
Schools: 5
  0 Primary; 0 Middle; 5 High; 0 Other Level
  3 Regular; 2 Special Education; 0 Vocational; 0 Alternative

0 Magnet; 0 Charter; 2 Title I Eligible; 0 School-wide Title I
Students: 6,882   (52.0% male; 47.9% female)
   Individual Education Program: 1,061 (15.4%);
   English Language Learner: n/a; Migrant: 0 (0.0%)
   Eligible for Free Lunch Program: n/a
   Eligible for Reduced-Price Lunch Program: n/a
Teachers: 488.5 (14.1 to 1)
Librarians/Media Specialists: 8.0 (860.3 to 1)
Guidance Counselors: 26.0 (264.7 to 1)
Current Spending: ($ per student per year):
   Total: $13,583; Instruction: $8,139; Support Services: $5,192
Enrollment, Drop-out Rates and Diploma Recipients by Race/Ethnicity

Category	Total	White	Black	Asian	AIAN	Hisp.
Enrollment (%)	100.0	69.6	2.8	14.0	0.4	13.2
Drop-out Rate (%)	1.3	1.0	3.9	0.5	4.5	3.6
H.S. Diplomas (#)	1,523	1,106	21	238	4	154

Mannheim SD 83
10401 W Grand Ave • Franklin Park, IL 60131-2208
(847) 455-4413 • http://www.d83.org/
Grade Span: PK-12; **Agency Type:** 1
Schools: 5
   3 Primary; 1 Middle; 0 High; 1 Other Level
   4 Regular; 1 Special Education; 0 Vocational; 0 Alternative
   0 Magnet; 0 Charter; 3 Title I Eligible; 0 School-wide Title I
Students: 2,835   (54.0% male; 45.9% female)
   Individual Education Program: 449 (15.8%);
   English Language Learner: n/a; Migrant: 0 (0.0%)
   Eligible for Free Lunch Program: 835 (29.5%)
   Eligible for Reduced-Price Lunch Program: 263 (9.3%)
Teachers: 181.0 (15.7 to 1)
Librarians/Media Specialists: 4.0 (708.8 to 1)
Guidance Counselors: 0.0 (n/a to 1)
Current Spending: ($ per student per year):
   Total: $8,660; Instruction: $5,878; Support Services: $2,497
Enrollment, Drop-out Rates and Diploma Recipients by Race/Ethnicity

Category	Total	White	Black	Asian	AIAN	Hisp.
Enrollment (%)	100.0	33.0	2.6	3.5	0.1	60.8
Drop-out Rate (%)	0.0	0.0	n/a	n/a	n/a	0.0
H.S. Diplomas (#)	1	0	0	0	0	1

Matteson Elem SD 162
3625 W 215th St • Matteson, IL 60443-2707
(708) 748-0100 • http://www.lincolnnet.net/users/lsd162/home.htm
Grade Span: PK-08; **Agency Type:** 1
Schools: 6
   5 Primary; 1 Middle; 0 High; 0 Other Level
   6 Regular; 0 Special Education; 0 Vocational; 0 Alternative
   1 Magnet; 0 Charter; 4 Title I Eligible; 0 School-wide Title I
Students: 3,024   (51.5% male; 48.4% female)
   Individual Education Program: 513 (17.0%);
   English Language Learner: n/a; Migrant: 0 (0.0%)
   Eligible for Free Lunch Program: 878 (29.0%)
   Eligible for Reduced-Price Lunch Program: 131 (4.3%)
Teachers: 182.0 (16.6 to 1)
Librarians/Media Specialists: 6.0 (504.0 to 1)
Guidance Counselors: 3.0 (1,008.0 to 1)
Current Spending: ($ per student per year):
   Total: $7,324; Instruction: $3,945; Support Services: $3,195
Enrollment, Drop-out Rates and Diploma Recipients by Race/Ethnicity

Category	Total	White	Black	Asian	AIAN	Hisp.
Enrollment (%)	100.0	15.3	80.9	1.1	0.0	2.7
Drop-out Rate (%)	n/a	n/a	n/a	n/a	n/a	n/a
H.S. Diplomas (#)	n/a	n/a	n/a	n/a	n/a	n/a

Maywood-Melrose Park-Broadview-89
906 Walton St • Melrose Park, IL 60160
(708) 450-2000
Grade Span: PK-08; **Agency Type:** 1
Schools: 11
   11 Primary; 0 Middle; 0 High; 0 Other Level
   10 Regular; 1 Special Education; 0 Vocational; 0 Alternative
   0 Magnet; 0 Charter; 10 Title I Eligible; 10 School-wide Title I
Students: 5,917   (50.4% male; 49.5% female)
   Individual Education Program: 703 (11.9%);
   English Language Learner: n/a; Migrant: 0 (0.0%)
   Eligible for Free Lunch Program: 4,255 (71.9%)
   Eligible for Reduced-Price Lunch Program: 575 (9.7%)
Teachers: 332.0 (17.8 to 1)
Librarians/Media Specialists: 1.0 (5,917.0 to 1)
Guidance Counselors: 0.0 (n/a to 1)
Current Spending: ($ per student per year):
   Total: $6,806; Instruction: $3,784; Support Services: $2,717

Category	Total	White	Black	Asian	AIAN	Hisp.
Enrollment (%)	100.0	3.4	56.0	0.4	0.0	40.1
Drop-out Rate (%)	n/a	n/a	n/a	n/a	n/a	n/a
H.S. Diplomas (#)	53	0	52	0	0	1

Midlothian SD 143
14959 S Pulaski Rd • Midlothian, IL 60445-2833
(708) 388-6450
Grade Span: PK-08; **Agency Type:** 1
Schools: 4
   4 Primary; 0 Middle; 0 High; 0 Other Level
   4 Regular; 0 Special Education; 0 Vocational; 0 Alternative
   0 Magnet; 0 Charter; 3 Title I Eligible; 0 School-wide Title I
Students: 1,822   (52.6% male; 47.3% female)
   Individual Education Program: 376 (20.6%);
   English Language Learner: n/a; Migrant: 0 (0.0%)
   Eligible for Free Lunch Program: 274 (15.0%)
   Eligible for Reduced-Price Lunch Program: 9 (0.5%)
Teachers: 104.5 (17.4 to 1)
Librarians/Media Specialists: 0.0 (n/a to 1)
Guidance Counselors: 0.0 (n/a to 1)
Current Spending: ($ per student per year):
   Total: $6,653; Instruction: $3,891; Support Services: $2,650
Enrollment, Drop-out Rates and Diploma Recipients by Race/Ethnicity

Category	Total	White	Black	Asian	AIAN	Hisp.
Enrollment (%)	100.0	55.8	28.7	2.1	0.1	13.3
Drop-out Rate (%)	n/a	n/a	n/a	n/a	n/a	n/a
H.S. Diplomas (#)	n/a	n/a	n/a	n/a	n/a	n/a

Mount Prospect SD 57
701 W Gregory St • Mount Prospect, IL 60056-2296
(847) 394-7300 • http://www.dist57.org/
Grade Span: PK-08; **Agency Type:** 1
Schools: 3
   3 Primary; 0 Middle; 0 High; 0 Other Level
   3 Regular; 0 Special Education; 0 Vocational; 0 Alternative
   0 Magnet; 0 Charter; 1 Title I Eligible; 0 School-wide Title I
Students: 2,023   (51.9% male; 48.0% female)
   Individual Education Program: 324 (16.0%);
   English Language Learner: n/a; Migrant: 0 (0.0%)
   Eligible for Free Lunch Program: 23 (1.1%)
   Eligible for Reduced-Price Lunch Program: 13 (0.6%)
Teachers: 118.1 (17.1 to 1)
Librarians/Media Specialists: 3.0 (674.3 to 1)
Guidance Counselors: 0.0 (n/a to 1)
Current Spending: ($ per student per year):
   Total: $8,094; Instruction: $4,220; Support Services: $3,789
Enrollment, Drop-out Rates and Diploma Recipients by Race/Ethnicity

Category	Total	White	Black	Asian	AIAN	Hisp.
Enrollment (%)	100.0	86.9	1.7	6.2	0.0	5.2
Drop-out Rate (%)	n/a	n/a	n/a	n/a	n/a	n/a
H.S. Diplomas (#)	n/a	n/a	n/a	n/a	n/a	n/a

New Trier Twp HSD 203
7 Happ Rd • Northfield, IL 60093-4295
(847) 446-7000 • http://www.nths.newtrier.k12.il.us/
Grade Span: 09-12; **Agency Type:** 1
Schools: 2
   0 Primary; 0 Middle; 1 High; 1 Other Level
   2 Regular; 0 Special Education; 0 Vocational; 0 Alternative
   0 Magnet; 0 Charter; 0 Title I Eligible; 0 School-wide Title I
Students: 3,958   (51.7% male; 48.2% female)
   Individual Education Program: 629 (15.9%);
   English Language Learner: n/a; Migrant: 0 (0.0%)
   Eligible for Free Lunch Program: n/a
   Eligible for Reduced-Price Lunch Program: n/a
Teachers: 320.9 (12.3 to 1)
Librarians/Media Specialists: 9.6 (412.3 to 1)
Guidance Counselors: 9.0 (439.8 to 1)
Current Spending: ($ per student per year):
   Total: $15,746; Instruction: $8,866; Support Services: $6,556
Enrollment, Drop-out Rates and Diploma Recipients by Race/Ethnicity

Category	Total	White	Black	Asian	AIAN	Hisp.
Enrollment (%)	100.0	88.8	0.6	8.3	0.4	1.9
Drop-out Rate (%)	0.2	0.2	0.0	0.3	0.0	1.8
H.S. Diplomas (#)	948	813	9	106	0	20

Niles Twp Community High SD 219
7700 Gross Point Rd • Skokie, IL 60077-2600
(847) 626-3000 • http://www.niles-hs.k12.il.us/
Grade Span: 09-12; **Agency Type:** 1
Schools: 2
   0 Primary; 0 Middle; 2 High; 0 Other Level
   2 Regular; 0 Special Education; 0 Vocational; 0 Alternative

0 Magnet; 0 Charter; 1 Title I Eligible; 0 School-wide Title I
Students: 4,808   (52.1% male; 47.8% female)
  Individual Education Program: 707 (14.7%);
  English Language Learner: n/a; Migrant: 0 (0.0%)
  Eligible for Free Lunch Program: 0 (0.0%)
  Eligible for Reduced-Price Lunch Program: 0 (0.0%)
Teachers: 319.6 (15.0 to 1)
Librarians/Media Specialists: 7.0 (686.9 to 1)
Guidance Counselors: 20.0 (240.4 to 1)
Current Spending: ($ per student per year):
  Total: $14,694; Instruction: $8,481; Support Services: $6,203
Enrollment, Drop-out Rates and Diploma Recipients by Race/Ethnicity

Category	Total	White	Black	Asian	AIAN	Hisp.
Enrollment (%)	100.0	57.5	3.6	31.4	0.1	7.4
Drop-out Rate (%)	1.0	1.0	1.5	0.8	0.0	2.3
H.S. Diplomas (#)	1,051	598	29	356	1	67

North Palos SD 117
7825 W 103rd St • Palos Hills, IL 60465-1252
(708) 598-5500
Grade Span: PK-08; **Agency Type:** 1
Schools: 5
  4 Primary; 1 Middle; 0 High; 0 Other Level
  4 Regular; 1 Special Education; 0 Vocational; 0 Alternative
  0 Magnet; 0 Charter; 3 Title I Eligible; 0 School-wide Title I
Students: 2,706   (53.2% male; 46.7% female)
  Individual Education Program: 406 (15.0%);
  English Language Learner: n/a; Migrant: 0 (0.0%)
  Eligible for Free Lunch Program: 411 (15.2%)
  Eligible for Reduced-Price Lunch Program: 37 (1.4%)
Teachers: 149.0 (18.2 to 1)
Librarians/Media Specialists: 5.0 (541.2 to 1)
Guidance Counselors: 0.0 (n/a to 1)
Current Spending: ($ per student per year):
  Total: $7,833; Instruction: $4,771; Support Services: $2,840
Enrollment, Drop-out Rates and Diploma Recipients by Race/Ethnicity

Category	Total	White	Black	Asian	AIAN	Hisp.
Enrollment (%)	100.0	84.2	6.4	0.5	0.0	9.0
Drop-out Rate (%)	n/a	n/a	n/a	n/a	n/a	n/a
H.S. Diplomas (#)	n/a	n/a	n/a	n/a	n/a	n/a

Northbrook SD 28
1475 Maple Ave • Northbrook, IL 60062-5418
(847) 498-7900 • http://www.district28.k12.il.us/
Grade Span: PK-08; **Agency Type:** 1
Schools: 4
  3 Primary; 1 Middle; 0 High; 0 Other Level
  4 Regular; 0 Special Education; 0 Vocational; 0 Alternative
  0 Magnet; 0 Charter; 0 Title I Eligible; 0 School-wide Title I
Students: 1,793   (52.9% male; 47.0% female)
  Individual Education Program: 359 (20.0%);
  English Language Learner: n/a; Migrant: 0 (0.0%)
  Eligible for Free Lunch Program: 0 (0.0%)
  Eligible for Reduced-Price Lunch Program: 0 (0.0%)
Teachers: 153.0 (11.7 to 1)
Librarians/Media Specialists: 4.0 (448.3 to 1)
Guidance Counselors: 4.0 (448.3 to 1)
Current Spending: ($ per student per year):
  Total: $13,391; Instruction: $9,015; Support Services: $4,284
Enrollment, Drop-out Rates and Diploma Recipients by Race/Ethnicity

Category	Total	White	Black	Asian	AIAN	Hisp.
Enrollment (%)	100.0	90.5	0.6	6.9	1.1	1.0
Drop-out Rate (%)	n/a	n/a	n/a	n/a	n/a	n/a
H.S. Diplomas (#)	n/a	n/a	n/a	n/a	n/a	n/a

Northfield Twp High SD 225
1835 Landwehr Rd • Glenview, IL 60025-1289
(847) 998-6100 • http://www.glenbrook.k12.il.us/
Grade Span: 09-12; **Agency Type:** 1
Schools: 3
  0 Primary; 0 Middle; 3 High; 0 Other Level
  2 Regular; 1 Special Education; 0 Vocational; 0 Alternative
  0 Magnet; 0 Charter; 1 Title I Eligible; 0 School-wide Title I
Students: 4,776   (52.0% male; 47.9% female)
  Individual Education Program: 534 (11.2%);
  English Language Learner: n/a; Migrant: 0 (0.0%)
  Eligible for Free Lunch Program: n/a
  Eligible for Reduced-Price Lunch Program: n/a
Teachers: 329.2 (14.5 to 1)
Librarians/Media Specialists: 7.0 (682.3 to 1)
Guidance Counselors: 21.0 (227.4 to 1)
Current Spending: ($ per student per year):
  Total: $15,738; Instruction: $8,197; Support Services: $7,211

Enrollment, Drop-out Rates and Diploma Recipients by Race/Ethnicity

Category	Total	White	Black	Asian	AIAN	Hisp.
Enrollment (%)	100.0	79.0	1.3	15.3	0.1	4.2
Drop-out Rate (%)	0.7	0.7	0.0	0.4	0.0	2.7
H.S. Diplomas (#)	1,127	883	10	196	2	36

Oak Lawn Community HSD 229
9400 SW Hwy • Oak Lawn, IL 60453-2396
(708) 424-5200
Grade Span: 09-12; **Agency Type:** 1
Schools: 1
  0 Primary; 0 Middle; 1 High; 0 Other Level
  1 Regular; 0 Special Education; 0 Vocational; 0 Alternative
  0 Magnet; 0 Charter; 0 Title I Eligible; 0 School-wide Title I
Students: 1,697   (50.2% male; 49.7% female)
  Individual Education Program: 241 (14.2%);
  English Language Learner: n/a; Migrant: 0 (0.0%)
  Eligible for Free Lunch Program: n/a
  Eligible for Reduced-Price Lunch Program: n/a
Teachers: 89.0 (19.1 to 1)
Librarians/Media Specialists: 2.0 (848.5 to 1)
Guidance Counselors: 5.0 (339.4 to 1)
Current Spending: ($ per student per year):
  Total: $10,261; Instruction: $5,112; Support Services: $4,772
Enrollment, Drop-out Rates and Diploma Recipients by Race/Ethnicity

Category	Total	White	Black	Asian	AIAN	Hisp.
Enrollment (%)	100.0	85.4	1.0	1.5	0.7	11.3
Drop-out Rate (%)	2.5	2.8	0.0	0.0	0.0	0.8
H.S. Diplomas (#)	352	311	1	12	1	27

Oak Lawn-Hometown SD 123
4201 W 93rd St • Oak Lawn, IL 60453-1907
(708) 423-0150 • http://www.d123.s-cook.k12.il.us/
Grade Span: PK-08; **Agency Type:** 1
Schools: 6
  5 Primary; 1 Middle; 0 High; 0 Other Level
  6 Regular; 0 Special Education; 0 Vocational; 0 Alternative
  0 Magnet; 0 Charter; 3 Title I Eligible; 0 School-wide Title I
Students: 2,851   (53.3% male; 46.6% female)
  Individual Education Program: 457 (16.0%);
  English Language Learner: n/a; Migrant: 0 (0.0%)
  Eligible for Free Lunch Program: 0 (0.0%)
  Eligible for Reduced-Price Lunch Program: 0 (0.0%)
Teachers: 197.1 (14.5 to 1)
Librarians/Media Specialists: 7.0 (407.3 to 1)
Guidance Counselors: 0.0 (n/a to 1)
Current Spending: ($ per student per year):
  Total: $7,843; Instruction: $4,873; Support Services: $2,898
Enrollment, Drop-out Rates and Diploma Recipients by Race/Ethnicity

Category	Total	White	Black	Asian	AIAN	Hisp.
Enrollment (%)	100.0	81.3	1.9	2.0	0.4	14.5
Drop-out Rate (%)	n/a	n/a	n/a	n/a	n/a	n/a
H.S. Diplomas (#)	n/a	n/a	n/a	n/a	n/a	n/a

Oak Park & River Forest Dist 200
201 N Scoville Ave • Oak Park, IL 60302-2296
(708) 383-0700 • http://www.oprfhs.org/
Grade Span: 09-12; **Agency Type:** 1
Schools: 1
  0 Primary; 0 Middle; 1 High; 0 Other Level
  1 Regular; 0 Special Education; 0 Vocational; 0 Alternative
  0 Magnet; 0 Charter; 1 Title I Eligible; 0 School-wide Title I
Students: 3,023   (50.5% male; 49.4% female)
  Individual Education Program: 456 (15.1%);
  English Language Learner: n/a; Migrant: 0 (0.0%)
  Eligible for Free Lunch Program: 230 (7.6%)
  Eligible for Reduced-Price Lunch Program: 67 (2.2%)
Teachers: 188.6 (16.0 to 1)
Librarians/Media Specialists: 3.0 (1,007.7 to 1)
Guidance Counselors: 11.0 (274.8 to 1)
Current Spending: ($ per student per year):
  Total: $15,081; Instruction: $8,698; Support Services: $5,897
Enrollment, Drop-out Rates and Diploma Recipients by Race/Ethnicity

Category	Total	White	Black	Asian	AIAN	Hisp.
Enrollment (%)	100.0	66.0	26.0	2.9	0.4	4.7
Drop-out Rate (%)	n/a	n/a	n/a	n/a	n/a	n/a
H.S. Diplomas (#)	0	0	0	0	0	0

Oak Park Elem SD 97
970 Madison St • Oak Park, IL 60302-4480
(708) 524-3000 • http://www.op97.k12.il.us/
Grade Span: PK-08; **Agency Type:** 1
Schools: 10
  8 Primary; 2 Middle; 0 High; 0 Other Level
  10 Regular; 0 Special Education; 0 Vocational; 0 Alternative

0 Magnet; 0 Charter; 6 Title I Eligible; 0 School-wide Title I
Students: 4,938   (51.8% male; 48.1% female)
  Individual Education Program: 949 (19.2%);
  English Language Learner: n/a; Migrant: 0 (0.0%)
  Eligible for Free Lunch Program: 673 (13.6%)
  Eligible for Reduced-Price Lunch Program: 221 (4.5%)
Teachers: 357.2 (13.8 to 1)
Librarians/Media Specialists: 9.0 (548.7 to 1)
Guidance Counselors: 0.0 (n/a to 1)
Current Spending: ($ per student per year):
  Total: $10,901; Instruction: $6,427; Support Services: $4,264
Enrollment, Drop-out Rates and Diploma Recipients by Race/Ethnicity

Category	Total	White	Black	Asian	AIAN	Hisp.
Enrollment (%)	100.0	60.5	31.8	3.5	0.1	4.1
Drop-out Rate (%)	n/a	n/a	n/a	n/a	n/a	n/a
H.S. Diplomas (#)	n/a	n/a	n/a	n/a	n/a	n/a

Orland SD 135

15100 S 94th Ave • Orland Park, IL 60462-3820
(708) 364-3306 • http://www.orland135.org/
Grade Span: PK-08; **Agency Type:** 1
Schools: 10
  7 Primary; 3 Middle; 0 High; 0 Other Level
  10 Regular; 0 Special Education; 0 Vocational; 0 Alternative
  0 Magnet; 0 Charter; 7 Title I Eligible; 0 School-wide Title I
Students: 5,937   (51.8% male; 48.1% female)
  Individual Education Program: 908 (15.3%);
  English Language Learner: n/a; Migrant: 0 (0.0%)
  Eligible for Free Lunch Program: 0 (0.0%)
  Eligible for Reduced-Price Lunch Program: 0 (0.0%)
Teachers: 354.6 (16.7 to 1)
Librarians/Media Specialists: 10.0 (593.7 to 1)
Guidance Counselors: 4.0 (1,484.3 to 1)
Current Spending: ($ per student per year):
  Total: $8,313; Instruction: $4,693; Support Services: $3,497
Enrollment, Drop-out Rates and Diploma Recipients by Race/Ethnicity

Category	Total	White	Black	Asian	AIAN	Hisp.
Enrollment (%)	100.0	88.7	2.3	4.2	0.0	4.8
Drop-out Rate (%)	n/a	n/a	n/a	n/a	n/a	n/a
H.S. Diplomas (#)	n/a	n/a	n/a	n/a	n/a	n/a

Palatine CCSD 15

580 N First Bank Dr • Palatine, IL 60067-8108
(847) 963-3000 • http://www.ccsd15.net/Home/
Grade Span: PK-08; **Agency Type:** 1
Schools: 20
  16 Primary; 3 Middle; 0 High; 1 Other Level
  18 Regular; 2 Special Education; 0 Vocational; 0 Alternative
  1 Magnet; 0 Charter; 10 Title I Eligible; 0 School-wide Title I
Students: 12,882   (51.5% male; 48.4% female)
  Individual Education Program: 1,658 (12.9%);
  English Language Learner: n/a; Migrant: 0 (0.0%)
  Eligible for Free Lunch Program: 2,254 (17.5%)
  Eligible for Reduced-Price Lunch Program: 498 (3.9%)
Teachers: 748.9 (17.2 to 1)
Librarians/Media Specialists: 21.3 (604.8 to 1)
Guidance Counselors: 5.1 (2,525.9 to 1)
Current Spending: ($ per student per year):
  Total: $9,357; Instruction: $5,622; Support Services: $3,555
Enrollment, Drop-out Rates and Diploma Recipients by Race/Ethnicity

Category	Total	White	Black	Asian	AIAN	Hisp.
Enrollment (%)	100.0	64.5	4.0	10.0	0.1	21.4
Drop-out Rate (%)	n/a	n/a	n/a	n/a	n/a	n/a
H.S. Diplomas (#)	n/a	n/a	n/a	n/a	n/a	n/a

Palos Community CSD 118

8800 W 119th St • Palos Park, IL 60464-1099
(708) 448-4800 • http://www.palos118.org/
Grade Span: PK-08; **Agency Type:** 1
Schools: 3
  2 Primary; 1 Middle; 0 High; 0 Other Level
  3 Regular; 0 Special Education; 0 Vocational; 0 Alternative
  0 Magnet; 0 Charter; 2 Title I Eligible; 0 School-wide Title I
Students: 2,009   (49.7% male; 50.2% female)
  Individual Education Program: 348 (17.3%);
  English Language Learner: n/a; Migrant: 0 (0.0%)
  Eligible for Free Lunch Program: 110 (5.5%)
  Eligible for Reduced-Price Lunch Program: 16 (0.8%)
Teachers: 125.0 (16.1 to 1)
Librarians/Media Specialists: 2.0 (1,004.5 to 1)
Guidance Counselors: 1.0 (2,009.0 to 1)
Current Spending: ($ per student per year):
  Total: $8,212; Instruction: $4,825; Support Services: $3,236

Enrollment, Drop-out Rates and Diploma Recipients by Race/Ethnicity

Category	Total	White	Black	Asian	AIAN	Hisp.
Enrollment (%)	100.0	94.5	0.4	1.7	0.3	3.0
Drop-out Rate (%)	n/a	n/a	n/a	n/a	n/a	n/a
H.S. Diplomas (#)	n/a	n/a	n/a	n/a	n/a	n/a

Park Forest SD 163

242 S Orchard Dr • Park Forest, IL 60466-2045
(708) 748-7050 • http://www.sd163.com/
Grade Span: PK-08; **Agency Type:** 1
Schools: 6
  5 Primary; 1 Middle; 0 High; 0 Other Level
  6 Regular; 0 Special Education; 0 Vocational; 0 Alternative
  0 Magnet; 0 Charter; 6 Title I Eligible; 6 School-wide Title I
Students: 2,219   (51.0% male; 48.9% female)
  Individual Education Program: 373 (16.8%);
  English Language Learner: n/a; Migrant: 0 (0.0%)
  Eligible for Free Lunch Program: 1,520 (68.5%)
  Eligible for Reduced-Price Lunch Program: 165 (7.4%)
Teachers: 130.7 (17.0 to 1)
Librarians/Media Specialists: 1.0 (2,219.0 to 1)
Guidance Counselors: 0.0 (n/a to 1)
Current Spending: ($ per student per year):
  Total: $9,199; Instruction: $5,559; Support Services: $3,288
Enrollment, Drop-out Rates and Diploma Recipients by Race/Ethnicity

Category	Total	White	Black	Asian	AIAN	Hisp.
Enrollment (%)	100.0	12.6	77.6	0.3	0.2	9.3
Drop-out Rate (%)	n/a	n/a	n/a	n/a	n/a	n/a
H.S. Diplomas (#)	n/a	n/a	n/a	n/a	n/a	n/a

Park Ridge CCSD 64

164 S Prospect Ave • Park Ridge, IL 60068-4079
(847) 318-4300 • http://www.d64.k12.il.us/
Grade Span: PK-08; **Agency Type:** 1
Schools: 8
  6 Primary; 2 Middle; 0 High; 0 Other Level
  7 Regular; 1 Special Education; 0 Vocational; 0 Alternative
  0 Magnet; 0 Charter; 0 Title I Eligible; 0 School-wide Title I
Students: 4,404   (51.9% male; 48.0% female)
  Individual Education Program: 771 (17.5%);
  English Language Learner: n/a; Migrant: 0 (0.0%)
  Eligible for Free Lunch Program: 0 (0.0%)
  Eligible for Reduced-Price Lunch Program: 0 (0.0%)
Teachers: 314.8 (14.0 to 1)
Librarians/Media Specialists: 1.0 (4,404.0 to 1)
Guidance Counselors: 2.0 (2,202.0 to 1)
Current Spending: ($ per student per year):
  Total: $9,787; Instruction: $6,721; Support Services: $2,970
Enrollment, Drop-out Rates and Diploma Recipients by Race/Ethnicity

Category	Total	White	Black	Asian	AIAN	Hisp.
Enrollment (%)	100.0	93.6	0.4	2.8	0.2	3.0
Drop-out Rate (%)	n/a	n/a	n/a	n/a	n/a	n/a
H.S. Diplomas (#)	n/a	n/a	n/a	n/a	n/a	n/a

Posen-Robbins El SD 143-5

14025 Harrison Ave • Posen, IL 60469-1055
(708) 388-7200
Grade Span: PK-08; **Agency Type:** 1
Schools: 6
  4 Primary; 2 Middle; 0 High; 0 Other Level
  6 Regular; 0 Special Education; 0 Vocational; 0 Alternative
  0 Magnet; 0 Charter; 6 Title I Eligible; 6 School-wide Title I
Students: 1,542   (52.4% male; 47.5% female)
  Individual Education Program: 185 (12.0%);
  English Language Learner: n/a; Migrant: 0 (0.0%)
  Eligible for Free Lunch Program: 1,148 (74.4%)
  Eligible for Reduced-Price Lunch Program: 97 (6.3%)
Teachers: 81.2 (19.0 to 1)
Librarians/Media Specialists: 1.0 (1,542.0 to 1)
Guidance Counselors: 0.0 (n/a to 1)
Current Spending: ($ per student per year):
  Total: $7,212; Instruction: $4,116; Support Services: $2,802
Enrollment, Drop-out Rates and Diploma Recipients by Race/Ethnicity

Category	Total	White	Black	Asian	AIAN	Hisp.
Enrollment (%)	100.0	6.8	53.8	0.0	0.0	39.4
Drop-out Rate (%)	n/a	n/a	n/a	n/a	n/a	n/a
H.S. Diplomas (#)	n/a	n/a	n/a	n/a	n/a	n/a

Prairie-Hills Elem SD 144

3015 W 163rd St • Markham, IL 60426-5685
(708) 210-2888
Grade Span: PK-08; **Agency Type:** 1
Schools: 8
  7 Primary; 1 Middle; 0 High; 0 Other Level
  8 Regular; 0 Special Education; 0 Vocational; 0 Alternative

0 Magnet; 0 Charter; 8 Title I Eligible; 8 School-wide Title I
Students: 2,914   (50.8% male; 49.1% female)
Individual Education Program: 548 (18.8%);
English Language Learner: n/a; Migrant: 0 (0.0%)
Eligible for Free Lunch Program: 2,193 (75.3%)
Eligible for Reduced-Price Lunch Program: 252 (8.6%)
Teachers: 173.0 (16.8 to 1)
Librarians/Media Specialists: 0.0 (n/a to 1)
Guidance Counselors: 0.0 (n/a to 1)
Current Spending: ($ per student per year):
Total: $7,173; Instruction: $3,792; Support Services: $3,114
Enrollment, Drop-out Rates and Diploma Recipients by Race/Ethnicity

Category	Total	White	Black	Asian	AIAN	Hisp.
Enrollment (%)	100.0	5.5	88.8	0.5	0.0	5.2
Drop-out Rate (%)	n/a	n/a	n/a	n/a	n/a	n/a
H.S. Diplomas (#)	n/a	n/a	n/a	n/a	n/a	n/a

Prospect Heights SD 23
700 N Schoenbeck Rd • Prospect Heights, IL 60070-1299
(847) 870-3850 • http://www.d23.org/
Grade Span: PK-08; **Agency Type:** 1
Schools: 4
3 Primary; 1 Middle; 0 High; 0 Other Level
4 Regular; 0 Special Education; 0 Vocational; 0 Alternative
0 Magnet; 0 Charter; 0 Title I Eligible; 0 School-wide Title I
Students: 1,529   (51.4% male; 48.5% female)
Individual Education Program: 293 (19.2%);
English Language Learner: n/a; Migrant: 0 (0.0%)
Eligible for Free Lunch Program: 0 (0.0%)
Eligible for Reduced-Price Lunch Program: 0 (0.0%)
Teachers: 111.9 (13.7 to 1)
Librarians/Media Specialists: 3.0 (509.7 to 1)
Guidance Counselors: 0.0 (n/a to 1)
Current Spending: ($ per student per year):
Total: $9,423; Instruction: $5,987; Support Services: $3,257
Enrollment, Drop-out Rates and Diploma Recipients by Race/Ethnicity

Category	Total	White	Black	Asian	AIAN	Hisp.
Enrollment (%)	100.0	81.9	1.2	9.2	0.3	7.4
Drop-out Rate (%)	n/a	n/a	n/a	n/a	n/a	n/a
H.S. Diplomas (#)	n/a	n/a	n/a	n/a	n/a	n/a

Proviso Twp HSD 209
807 S 1st Ave • Maywood, IL 60153-2307
(708) 344-7000 • http://www.proviso.w-cook.k12.il.us/
Grade Span: 09-12; **Agency Type:** 1
Schools: 2
0 Primary; 0 Middle; 2 High; 0 Other Level
2 Regular; 0 Special Education; 0 Vocational; 0 Alternative
0 Magnet; 0 Charter; 1 Title I Eligible; 0 School-wide Title I
Students: 4,852   (49.4% male; 50.5% female)
Individual Education Program: 930 (19.2%);
English Language Learner: n/a; Migrant: 0 (0.0%)
Eligible for Free Lunch Program: 1,107 (22.8%)
Eligible for Reduced-Price Lunch Program: 136 (2.8%)
Teachers: 265.0 (18.3 to 1)
Librarians/Media Specialists: 2.0 (2,426.0 to 1)
Guidance Counselors: 11.0 (441.1 to 1)
Current Spending: ($ per student per year):
Total: $11,237; Instruction: $5,989; Support Services: $5,092
Enrollment, Drop-out Rates and Diploma Recipients by Race/Ethnicity

Category	Total	White	Black	Asian	AIAN	Hisp.
Enrollment (%)	100.0	4.3	68.7	1.1	0.4	25.6
Drop-out Rate (%)	8.3	12.1	7.4	7.3	4.3	10.0
H.S. Diplomas (#)	772	37	542	13	0	180

Reavis Twp HSD 220
6034 W 77th St • Burbank, IL 60459-3199
(708) 599-7200 • http://www.rhsd.s-cook.k12.il.us/
Grade Span: 09-12; **Agency Type:** 1
Schools: 1
0 Primary; 0 Middle; 1 High; 0 Other Level
1 Regular; 0 Special Education; 0 Vocational; 0 Alternative
0 Magnet; 0 Charter; 1 Title I Eligible; 0 School-wide Title I
Students: 1,631   (49.5% male; 50.4% female)
Individual Education Program: 141 (8.6%);
English Language Learner: n/a; Migrant: 0 (0.0%)
Eligible for Free Lunch Program: n/a
Eligible for Reduced-Price Lunch Program: n/a
Teachers: 90.8 (18.0 to 1)
Librarians/Media Specialists: 1.0 (1,631.0 to 1)
Guidance Counselors: 5.0 (326.2 to 1)
Current Spending: ($ per student per year):
Total: $11,070; Instruction: $5,951; Support Services: $5,088

Enrollment, Drop-out Rates and Diploma Recipients by Race/Ethnicity

Category	Total	White	Black	Asian	AIAN	Hisp.
Enrollment (%)	100.0	80.4	0.2	1.7	0.2	17.4
Drop-out Rate (%)	4.0	3.3	n/a	0.0	0.0	8.8
H.S. Diplomas (#)	310	265	0	9	1	35

Rich Twp HS District 227
20290 Governors Hiwy • Olympia Fields, IL 60461-1053
(708) 679-5800 • http://www.rich227.org/
Grade Span: 09-12; **Agency Type:** 1
Schools: 4
0 Primary; 0 Middle; 4 High; 0 Other Level
3 Regular; 1 Special Education; 0 Vocational; 0 Alternative
0 Magnet; 0 Charter; 2 Title I Eligible; 0 School-wide Title I
Students: 3,534   (50.5% male; 49.4% female)
Individual Education Program: 551 (15.6%);
English Language Learner: n/a; Migrant: 0 (0.0%)
Eligible for Free Lunch Program: 1,375 (38.9%)
Eligible for Reduced-Price Lunch Program: 281 (8.0%)
Teachers: 209.9 (16.8 to 1)
Librarians/Media Specialists: 3.0 (1,178.0 to 1)
Guidance Counselors: 15.0 (235.6 to 1)
Current Spending: ($ per student per year):
Total: $12,910; Instruction: $7,318; Support Services: $5,160
Enrollment, Drop-out Rates and Diploma Recipients by Race/Ethnicity

Category	Total	White	Black	Asian	AIAN	Hisp.
Enrollment (%)	100.0	14.7	80.7	0.9	0.2	3.5
Drop-out Rate (%)	1.1	1.1	1.2	0.0	0.0	0.0
H.S. Diplomas (#)	734	184	521	12	0	17

Ridgeland SD 122
6500 W 95th St • Oak Lawn, IL 60453-2195
(708) 599-5550 • http://www.ridgeland122.com/
Grade Span: PK-08; **Agency Type:** 1
Schools: 5
4 Primary; 1 Middle; 0 High; 0 Other Level
5 Regular; 0 Special Education; 0 Vocational; 0 Alternative
1 Magnet; 0 Charter; 2 Title I Eligible; 0 School-wide Title I
Students: 2,283   (51.9% male; 48.0% female)
Individual Education Program: 373 (16.3%);
English Language Learner: n/a; Migrant: 0 (0.0%)
Eligible for Free Lunch Program: 296 (13.0%)
Eligible for Reduced-Price Lunch Program: 75 (3.3%)
Teachers: 122.5 (18.6 to 1)
Librarians/Media Specialists: 5.0 (456.6 to 1)
Guidance Counselors: 1.0 (2,283.0 to 1)
Current Spending: ($ per student per year):
Total: $6,811; Instruction: $3,688; Support Services: $3,085
Enrollment, Drop-out Rates and Diploma Recipients by Race/Ethnicity

Category	Total	White	Black	Asian	AIAN	Hisp.
Enrollment (%)	100.0	82.0	1.6	1.9	0.2	14.4
Drop-out Rate (%)	n/a	n/a	n/a	n/a	n/a	n/a
H.S. Diplomas (#)	n/a	n/a	n/a	n/a	n/a	n/a

River Trails SD 26
1900 E Kensington Rd • Mount Prospect, IL 60056-1999
(847) 297-4120 • http://www.rtsd26.org/
Grade Span: PK-08; **Agency Type:** 1
Schools: 3
2 Primary; 1 Middle; 0 High; 0 Other Level
3 Regular; 0 Special Education; 0 Vocational; 0 Alternative
0 Magnet; 0 Charter; 0 Title I Eligible; 0 School-wide Title I
Students: 1,650   (52.2% male; 47.7% female)
Individual Education Program: 283 (17.2%);
English Language Learner: n/a; Migrant: 0 (0.0%)
Eligible for Free Lunch Program: 359 (21.8%)
Eligible for Reduced-Price Lunch Program: 73 (4.4%)
Teachers: 117.3 (14.1 to 1)
Librarians/Media Specialists: 3.0 (550.0 to 1)
Guidance Counselors: 0.0 (n/a to 1)
Current Spending: ($ per student per year):
Total: $10,836; Instruction: $6,367; Support Services: $4,225
Enrollment, Drop-out Rates and Diploma Recipients by Race/Ethnicity

Category	Total	White	Black	Asian	AIAN	Hisp.
Enrollment (%)	100.0	63.4	2.4	12.2	0.1	21.9
Drop-out Rate (%)	n/a	n/a	n/a	n/a	n/a	n/a
H.S. Diplomas (#)	n/a	n/a	n/a	n/a	n/a	n/a

Schaumburg CCSD 54
524 E Schaumburg Rd • Schaumburg, IL 60194-3510
(847) 885-6700 • http://web54.sd54.k12.il.us/
Grade Span: PK-08; **Agency Type:** 1
Schools: 27
22 Primary; 5 Middle; 0 High; 0 Other Level
27 Regular; 0 Special Education; 0 Vocational;

0 Magnet; 0 Charter; 5 Title I Eligible; 0 School-wide Title I
Students: 14,948 (52.0% male; 47.9% female)
  Individual Education Program: 2,257 (15.1%);
  English Language Learner: n/a; Migrant: 0 (0.0%)
  Eligible for Free Lunch Program: 0 (0.0%)
  Eligible for Reduced-Price Lunch Program: 0 (0.0%)
Teachers: 916.1 (16.3 to 1)
Librarians/Media Specialists: 0.0 (n/a to 1)
Guidance Counselors: 5.0 (2,989.6 to 1)
Current Spending: ($ per student per year):
  Total: $9,465; Instruction: $5,929; Support Services: $3,404
Enrollment, Drop-out Rates and Diploma Recipients by Race/Ethnicity

Category	Total	White	Black	Asian	AIAN	Hisp.
Enrollment (%)	100.0	60.4	7.8	17.5	0.2	14.1
Drop-out Rate (%)	n/a	n/a	n/a	n/a	n/a	n/a
H.S. Diplomas (#)	n/a	n/a	n/a	n/a	n/a	n/a

Skokie SD 68
9440 N Kenton Ave • Skokie, IL 60076-1337
(847) 676-9000 • http://www.sd68.k12.il.us/
Grade Span: KG-08; **Agency Type:** 1
Schools: 4
  3 Primary; 1 Middle; 0 High; 0 Other Level
  4 Regular; 0 Special Education; 0 Vocational; 0 Alternative
  0 Magnet; 0 Charter; 3 Title I Eligible; 0 School-wide Title I
Students: 1,636 (51.2% male; 48.7% female)
  Individual Education Program: 328 (20.0%);
  English Language Learner: n/a; Migrant: 0 (0.0%)
  Eligible for Free Lunch Program: 205 (12.5%)
  Eligible for Reduced-Price Lunch Program: 111 (6.8%)
Teachers: 122.5 (13.4 to 1)
Librarians/Media Specialists: 4.0 (409.0 to 1)
Guidance Counselors: 0.0 (n/a to 1)
Current Spending: ($ per student per year):
  Total: $11,162; Instruction: $6,479; Support Services: $4,414
Enrollment, Drop-out Rates and Diploma Recipients by Race/Ethnicity

Category	Total	White	Black	Asian	AIAN	Hisp.
Enrollment (%)	100.0	52.1	6.5	33.0	0.1	8.3
Drop-out Rate (%)	n/a	n/a	n/a	n/a	n/a	n/a
H.S. Diplomas (#)	n/a	n/a	n/a	n/a	n/a	n/a

Steger SD 194
3753 Park Ave • Steger, IL 60475-1864
(708) 755-0022 • http://www.sd194.org/
Grade Span: PK-08; **Agency Type:** 1
Schools: 4
  3 Primary; 1 Middle; 0 High; 0 Other Level
  4 Regular; 0 Special Education; 0 Vocational; 0 Alternative
  0 Magnet; 0 Charter; 3 Title I Eligible; 0 School-wide Title I
Students: 1,638 (51.7% male; 48.2% female)
  Individual Education Program: 285 (17.4%);
  English Language Learner: n/a; Migrant: 0 (0.0%)
  Eligible for Free Lunch Program: 562 (34.3%)
  Eligible for Reduced-Price Lunch Program: 181 (11.1%)
Teachers: 108.4 (15.1 to 1)
Librarians/Media Specialists: 0.0 (n/a to 1)
Guidance Counselors: 0.0 (n/a to 1)
Current Spending: ($ per student per year):
  Total: $5,925; Instruction: $3,724; Support Services: $1,982
Enrollment, Drop-out Rates and Diploma Recipients by Race/Ethnicity

Category	Total	White	Black	Asian	AIAN	Hisp.
Enrollment (%)	100.0	69.8	14.8	1.3	0.2	13.7
Drop-out Rate (%)	n/a	n/a	n/a	n/a	n/a	n/a
H.S. Diplomas (#)	n/a	n/a	n/a	n/a	n/a	n/a

Summit SD 104
6021 S 74th Ave • Summit, IL 60501-1554
(708) 458-0505 • http://www.sd104.s-cook.k12.il.us/
Grade Span: PK-08; **Agency Type:** 1
Schools: 5
  4 Primary; 1 Middle; 0 High; 0 Other Level
  5 Regular; 0 Special Education; 0 Vocational; 0 Alternative
  0 Magnet; 0 Charter; 5 Title I Eligible; 5 School-wide Title I
Students: 1,692 (52.0% male; 47.9% female)
  Individual Education Program: 284 (16.8%);
  English Language Learner: n/a; Migrant: 0 (0.0%)
  Eligible for Free Lunch Program: 878 (51.9%)
  Eligible for Reduced-Price Lunch Program: 219 (12.9%)
Teachers: 118.0 (14.3 to 1)
Librarians/Media Specialists: 0.0 (n/a to 1)
Guidance Counselors: 0.0 (n/a to 1)
Current Spending: ($ per student per year):
  Total: $8,786; Instruction: $4,947; Support Services: $2,362

Enrollment, Drop-out Rates and Diploma Recipients by Race/Ethnicity

Category	Total	White	Black	Asian	AIAN	Hisp.
Enrollment (%)	100.0	22.5	10.9	0.3	0.0	66.3
Drop-out Rate (%)	n/a	n/a	n/a	n/a	n/a	n/a
H.S. Diplomas (#)	n/a	n/a	n/a	n/a	n/a	n/a

Thornton Fractional T HS D 215
1601 Wentworth Ave • Calumet City, IL 60409-6399
(708) 585-2309 • http://www.tfd215.s-cook.k12.il.us/
Grade Span: 09-12; **Agency Type:** 1
Schools: 3
  0 Primary; 0 Middle; 2 High; 1 Other Level
  2 Regular; 1 Special Education; 0 Vocational; 0 Alternative
  0 Magnet; 0 Charter; 0 Title I Eligible; 0 School-wide Title I
Students: 3,074 (51.5% male; 48.4% female)
  Individual Education Program: 394 (12.8%);
  English Language Learner: n/a; Migrant: 0 (0.0%)
  Eligible for Free Lunch Program: 928 (30.2%)
  Eligible for Reduced-Price Lunch Program: 274 (8.9%)
Teachers: 195.6 (15.7 to 1)
Librarians/Media Specialists: 2.0 (1,537.0 to 1)
Guidance Counselors: 9.0 (341.6 to 1)
Current Spending: ($ per student per year):
  Total: $11,531; Instruction: $6,484; Support Services: $4,793
Enrollment, Drop-out Rates and Diploma Recipients by Race/Ethnicity

Category	Total	White	Black	Asian	AIAN	Hisp.
Enrollment (%)	100.0	38.9	45.0	1.0	0.7	14.4
Drop-out Rate (%)	3.6	2.1	5.2	0.0	4.8	4.2
H.S. Diplomas (#)	576	305	203	1	4	63

Thornton Twp HSD 205
465 E 170th St • South Holland, IL 60473-3481
(708) 225-4000 • http://www.district205.net/
Grade Span: 09-12; **Agency Type:** 1
Schools: 3
  0 Primary; 0 Middle; 3 High; 0 Other Level
  3 Regular; 0 Special Education; 0 Vocational; 0 Alternative
  0 Magnet; 0 Charter; 3 Title I Eligible; 0 School-wide Title I
Students: 6,635 (50.5% male; 49.4% female)
  Individual Education Program: 1,087 (16.4%);
  English Language Learner: n/a; Migrant: 0 (0.0%)
  Eligible for Free Lunch Program: 2,555 (38.5%)
  Eligible for Reduced-Price Lunch Program: 409 (6.2%)
Teachers: 424.8 (15.6 to 1)
Librarians/Media Specialists: 2.0 (3,317.5 to 1)
Guidance Counselors: 16.0 (414.7 to 1)
Current Spending: ($ per student per year):
  Total: $10,905; Instruction: $7,508; Support Services: $3,175
Enrollment, Drop-out Rates and Diploma Recipients by Race/Ethnicity

Category	Total	White	Black	Asian	AIAN	Hisp.
Enrollment (%)	100.0	2.5	93.0	0.2	0.0	4.4
Drop-out Rate (%)	6.6	6.7	6.5	5.9	0.0	8.1
H.S. Diplomas (#)	1,136	51	827	5	207	46

Tinley Park Community Cons Sch Dst 146
6611 W 171st St • Tinley Park, IL 60477-3514
(708) 614-4500 • http://www.ccsd146.k12.il.us/
Grade Span: PK-08; **Agency Type:** 1
Schools: 6
  5 Primary; 1 Middle; 0 High; 0 Other Level
  6 Regular; 0 Special Education; 0 Vocational; 0 Alternative
  0 Magnet; 0 Charter; 4 Title I Eligible; 0 School-wide Title I
Students: 2,420 (52.0% male; 47.9% female)
  Individual Education Program: 383 (15.8%);
  English Language Learner: n/a; Migrant: 0 (0.0%)
  Eligible for Free Lunch Program: 280 (11.6%)
  Eligible for Reduced-Price Lunch Program: 85 (3.5%)
Teachers: 171.8 (14.1 to 1)
Librarians/Media Specialists: 6.0 (403.3 to 1)
Guidance Counselors: 0.0 (n/a to 1)
Current Spending: ($ per student per year):
  Total: $9,153; Instruction: $5,381; Support Services: $3,640
Enrollment, Drop-out Rates and Diploma Recipients by Race/Ethnicity

Category	Total	White	Black	Asian	AIAN	Hisp.
Enrollment (%)	100.0	87.5	2.9	3.0	0.3	6.3
Drop-out Rate (%)	n/a	n/a	n/a	n/a	n/a	n/a
H.S. Diplomas (#)	n/a	n/a	n/a	n/a	n/a	n/a

Township HSD 211
1750 S Roselle Rd • Palatine, IL 60067-7336
(847) 755-6600 • http://www.d211.org/
Grade Span: 09-12; **Agency Type:** 1
Schools: 6
  0 Primary; 0 Middle; 6 High; 0 Other Level
  5 Regular; 1 Special Education; 0 Vocational; 0 Alternative

0 Magnet; 0 Charter; 0 Title I Eligible; 0 School-wide Title I
Students: 12,935   (51.3% male; 48.6% female)
  Individual Education Program: 1,480 (11.4%);
  English Language Learner: n/a; Migrant: 0 (0.0%)
  Eligible for Free Lunch Program: 960 (7.4%)
  Eligible for Reduced-Price Lunch Program: 357 (2.8%)
Teachers: 796.0 (16.3 to 1)
Librarians/Media Specialists: 15.0 (862.3 to 1)
Guidance Counselors: 42.4 (305.1 to 1)
Current Spending: ($ per student per year):
  Total: $13,073; Instruction: $7,492; Support Services: $5,239
Enrollment, Drop-out Rates and Diploma Recipients by Race/Ethnicity

Category	Total	White	Black	Asian	AIAN	Hisp.
Enrollment (%)	100.0	70.1	5.2	13.9	0.2	10.6
Drop-out Rate (%)	1.1	0.8	1.8	0.5	3.8	3.3
H.S. Diplomas (#)	2,725	2,040	93	401	5	186

Township High SD 214
2121 S Goebbert Rd • Arlington Heights, IL 60005-4297
(847) 718-7600 • http://www.dist214.k12.il.us/
Grade Span: 09-12; **Agency Type:** 1
Schools: 12
  0 Primary; 0 Middle; 11 High; 1 Other Level
  6 Regular; 6 Special Education; 0 Vocational; 0 Alternative
  0 Magnet; 0 Charter; 4 Title I Eligible; 0 School-wide Title I
Students: 12,209   (52.1% male; 47.8% female)
  Individual Education Program: 1,555 (12.7%);
  English Language Learner: n/a; Migrant: 0 (0.0%)
  Eligible for Free Lunch Program: 1,159 (9.5%)
  Eligible for Reduced-Price Lunch Program: 330 (2.7%)
Teachers: 765.9 (15.9 to 1)
Librarians/Media Specialists: 7.0 (1,744.1 to 1)
Guidance Counselors: 59.6 (204.8 to 1)
Current Spending: ($ per student per year):
  Total: $13,643; Instruction: $7,068; Support Services: $6,255
Enrollment, Drop-out Rates and Diploma Recipients by Race/Ethnicity

Category	Total	White	Black	Asian	AIAN	Hisp.
Enrollment (%)	100.0	74.5	2.8	7.7	0.4	14.6
Drop-out Rate (%)	3.4	2.2	9.4	2.1	9.1	9.5
H.S. Diplomas (#)	2,815	2,152	80	252	5	326

W Harvey-Dixmoor Public Schools Dist147
191 W 155th Place • Harvey, IL 60426-3413
(708) 339-9500 • http://www.whd147.org/
Grade Span: PK-08; **Agency Type:** 1
Schools: 6
  5 Primary; 1 Middle; 0 High; 0 Other Level
  6 Regular; 0 Special Education; 0 Vocational; 0 Alternative
  0 Magnet; 0 Charter; 6 Title I Eligible; 6 School-wide Title I
Students: 1,838   (51.2% male; 48.7% female)
  Individual Education Program: 302 (16.4%);
  English Language Learner: n/a; Migrant: 0 (0.0%)
  Eligible for Free Lunch Program: 1,678 (91.3%)
  Eligible for Reduced-Price Lunch Program: 66 (3.6%)
Teachers: 102.0 (18.0 to 1)
Librarians/Media Specialists: 5.0 (367.6 to 1)
Guidance Counselors: 4.0 (459.5 to 1)
Current Spending: ($ per student per year):
  Total: $9,698; Instruction: $4,453; Support Services: $4,769
Enrollment, Drop-out Rates and Diploma Recipients by Race/Ethnicity

Category	Total	White	Black	Asian	AIAN	Hisp.
Enrollment (%)	100.0	1.6	85.5	0.0	0.0	12.9
Drop-out Rate (%)	n/a	n/a	n/a	n/a	n/a	n/a
H.S. Diplomas (#)	n/a	n/a	n/a	n/a	n/a	n/a

Wheeling CCSD 21
999 W Dundee Rd • Wheeling, IL 60090-3777
(847) 537-8270 • http://www.d21.k12.il.us/
Grade Span: PK-08; **Agency Type:** 1
Schools: 12
  9 Primary; 3 Middle; 0 High; 0 Other Level
  12 Regular; 0 Special Education; 0 Vocational; 0 Alternative
  0 Magnet; 0 Charter; 4 Title I Eligible; 0 School-wide Title I
Students: 7,024   (50.8% male; 49.1% female)
  Individual Education Program: 1,168 (16.6%);
  English Language Learner: n/a; Migrant: 0 (0.0%)
  Eligible for Free Lunch Program: 1,712 (24.4%)
  Eligible for Reduced-Price Lunch Program: 505 (7.2%)
Teachers: 468.7 (15.0 to 1)
Librarians/Media Specialists: 13.0 (540.3 to 1)
Guidance Counselors: 1.0 (7,024.0 to 1)
Current Spending: ($ per student per year):
  Total: $8,727; Instruction: $5,212; Support Services: $3,305

Category	Total	White	Black	Asian	AIAN	Hisp.
Enrollment (%)	100.0	53.4	2.6	6.5	0.0	37.4
Drop-out Rate (%)	n/a	n/a	n/a	n/a	n/a	n/a
H.S. Diplomas (#)	n/a	n/a	n/a	n/a	n/a	n/a

Wilmette SD 39
615 Locust Rd • Wilmette, IL 60091-2299
(847) 256-2450 • http://wilmette.nttc.org/
Grade Span: PK-08; **Agency Type:** 1
Schools: 6
  4 Primary; 2 Middle; 0 High; 0 Other Level
  6 Regular; 0 Special Education; 0 Vocational; 0 Alternative
  0 Magnet; 0 Charter; 0 Title I Eligible; 0 School-wide Title I
Students: 3,595   (51.5% male; 48.4% female)
  Individual Education Program: 535 (14.9%);
  English Language Learner: n/a; Migrant: 0 (0.0%)
  Eligible for Free Lunch Program: 0 (0.0%)
  Eligible for Reduced-Price Lunch Program: 0 (0.0%)
Teachers: 269.2 (13.4 to 1)
Librarians/Media Specialists: 6.0 (599.2 to 1)
Guidance Counselors: 0.0 (n/a to 1)
Current Spending: ($ per student per year):
  Total: $8,755; Instruction: $5,123; Support Services: $3,324
Enrollment, Drop-out Rates and Diploma Recipients by Race/Ethnicity

Category	Total	White	Black	Asian	AIAN	Hisp.
Enrollment (%)	100.0	88.6	0.4	9.7	0.0	1.2
Drop-out Rate (%)	n/a	n/a	n/a	n/a	n/a	n/a
H.S. Diplomas (#)	n/a	n/a	n/a	n/a	n/a	n/a

Winnetka SD 36
1235 Oak St • Winnetka, IL 60093-2168
(847) 446-9400 • http://www.winnetka.k12.il.us/
Grade Span: PK-08; **Agency Type:** 1
Schools: 5
  3 Primary; 2 Middle; 0 High; 0 Other Level
  5 Regular; 0 Special Education; 0 Vocational; 0 Alternative
  0 Magnet; 0 Charter; 0 Title I Eligible; 0 School-wide Title I
Students: 2,079   (52.9% male; 47.0% female)
  Individual Education Program: 358 (17.2%);
  English Language Learner: n/a; Migrant: 0 (0.0%)
  Eligible for Free Lunch Program: 0 (0.0%)
  Eligible for Reduced-Price Lunch Program: 0 (0.0%)
Teachers: 146.9 (14.2 to 1)
Librarians/Media Specialists: 6.2 (335.3 to 1)
Guidance Counselors: 2.0 (1,039.5 to 1)
Current Spending: ($ per student per year):
  Total: $11,260; Instruction: $6,906; Support Services: $4,217
Enrollment, Drop-out Rates and Diploma Recipients by Race/Ethnicity

Category	Total	White	Black	Asian	AIAN	Hisp.
Enrollment (%)	100.0	95.1	0.2	3.6	0.0	1.0
Drop-out Rate (%)	n/a	n/a	n/a	n/a	n/a	n/a
H.S. Diplomas (#)	n/a	n/a	n/a	n/a	n/a	n/a

Crawford County

Robinson CUSD 2
PO Box 190 • Robinson, IL 62454-0190
(618) 544-7511 •
http://nuttall.rob.crwfrd.k12.il.us/education/district/district.php
Grade Span: PK-12; **Agency Type:** 1
Schools: 4
  2 Primary; 1 Middle; 1 High; 0 Other Level
  4 Regular; 0 Special Education; 0 Vocational; 0 Alternative
  0 Magnet; 0 Charter; 3 Title I Eligible; 0 School-wide Title I
Students: 1,777   (52.3% male; 47.6% female)
  Individual Education Program: 377 (21.2%);
  English Language Learner: n/a; Migrant: 0 (0.0%)
  Eligible for Free Lunch Program: 528 (29.7%)
  Eligible for Reduced-Price Lunch Program: 139 (7.8%)
Teachers: 107.3 (16.6 to 1)
Librarians/Media Specialists: 3.0 (592.3 to 1)
Guidance Counselors: 4.0 (444.3 to 1)
Current Spending: ($ per student per year):
  Total: $8,179; Instruction: $4,236; Support Services: $3,632
Enrollment, Drop-out Rates and Diploma Recipients by Race/Ethnicity

Category	Total	White	Black	Asian	AIAN	Hisp.
Enrollment (%)	100.0	94.0	2.3	0.9	0.2	2.6
Drop-out Rate (%)	2.4	2.5	0.0	0.0	n/a	0.0
H.S. Diplomas (#)	123	116	2	1	0	4

De Kalb County

Dekalb Community Unit SD 428
901 S Fourth St • De Kalb, IL 60115-4411
(815) 754-2350 • http://www.dist428.dekalb.k12.il.us/
Grade Span: PK-12; **Agency Type:** 1
Schools: 11
  8 Primary; 2 Middle; 1 High; 0 Other Level
  11 Regular; 0 Special Education; 0 Vocational; 0 Alternative
  0 Charter; 0 Magnet; 6 Title I Eligible; 0 School-wide Title I
Students: 5,473   (50.4% male; 49.5% female)
  Individual Education Program: 611 (11.2%);
  English Language Learner: n/a; Migrant: 0 (0.0%)
  Eligible for Free Lunch Program: 1,239 (22.6%)
  Eligible for Reduced-Price Lunch Program: 227 (4.1%)
Teachers: 336.8 (16.3 to 1)
Librarians/Media Specialists: 1.0 (5,473.0 to 1)
Guidance Counselors: 7.0 (781.9 to 1)
Current Spending: ($ per student per year):
  Total: $7,735; Instruction: $4,785; Support Services: $2,762
Enrollment, Drop-out Rates and Diploma Recipients by Race/Ethnicity

Category	Total	White	Black	Asian	AIAN	Hisp.
Enrollment (%)	100.0	72.7	10.5	2.3	0.3	14.1
Drop-out Rate (%)	3.0	2.1	0.9	0.0	0.0	11.5
H.S. Diplomas (#)	308	257	17	8	0	26

Genoa Kingston CUSD 424
980 Park Ave • Genoa, IL 60135-1423
(815) 784-6222
Grade Span: PK-12; **Agency Type:** 1
Schools: 5
  2 Primary; 2 Middle; 1 High; 0 Other Level
  5 Regular; 0 Special Education; 0 Vocational; 0 Alternative
  0 Magnet; 0 Charter; 2 Title I Eligible; 0 School-wide Title I
Students: 1,776   (50.6% male; 49.3% female)
  Individual Education Program: 235 (13.2%);
  English Language Learner: n/a; Migrant: 0 (0.0%)
  Eligible for Free Lunch Program: 210 (11.8%)
  Eligible for Reduced-Price Lunch Program: 101 (5.7%)
Teachers: 108.5 (16.4 to 1)
Librarians/Media Specialists: 1.0 (1,776.0 to 1)
Guidance Counselors: 3.0 (592.0 to 1)
Current Spending: ($ per student per year):
  Total: $5,120; Instruction: $3,108; Support Services: $1,830
Enrollment, Drop-out Rates and Diploma Recipients by Race/Ethnicity

Category	Total	White	Black	Asian	AIAN	Hisp.
Enrollment (%)	100.0	88.7	0.8	0.3	0.1	10.0
Drop-out Rate (%)	3.0	3.0	n/a	n/a	n/a	3.0
H.S. Diplomas (#)	91	83	0	0	0	8

Sandwich CUSD 430
720 S Wells St • Sandwich, IL 60548-2493
(815) 786-2187 • http://www.sandwich430.org
Grade Span: PK-12; **Agency Type:** 1
Schools: 6
  3 Primary; 2 Middle; 1 High; 0 Other Level
  6 Regular; 0 Special Education; 0 Vocational; 0 Alternative
  0 Magnet; 0 Charter; 2 Title I Eligible; 0 School-wide Title I
Students: 2,454   (51.7% male; 48.2% female)
  Individual Education Program: 410 (16.7%);
  English Language Learner: n/a; Migrant: 0 (0.0%)
  Eligible for Free Lunch Program: 200 (8.2%)
  Eligible for Reduced-Price Lunch Program: 99 (4.0%)
Teachers: 142.6 (17.2 to 1)
Librarians/Media Specialists: 1.0 (2,454.0 to 1)
Guidance Counselors: 3.0 (818.0 to 1)
Current Spending: ($ per student per year):
  Total: $5,420; Instruction: $3,358; Support Services: $1,824
Enrollment, Drop-out Rates and Diploma Recipients by Race/Ethnicity

Category	Total	White	Black	Asian	AIAN	Hisp.
Enrollment (%)	100.0	90.0	0.4	0.8	0.0	8.8
Drop-out Rate (%)	3.6	2.8	n/a	0.0	0.0	19.4
H.S. Diplomas (#)	151	141	0	2	3	5

Sycamore CUSD 427
245 W Exchange St • Sycamore, IL 60178-1406
(815) 899-8103 • http://www.syc.dekalb.k12.il.us/
Grade Span: KG-12; **Agency Type:** 1
Schools: 6
  4 Primary; 1 Middle; 1 High; 0 Other Level
  6 Regular; 0 Special Education; 0 Vocational; 0 Alternative
  0 Magnet; 0 Charter; 0 Title I Eligible; 0 School-wide Title I
Students: 3,138   (51.8% male; 48.1% female)
  Individual Education Program: 362 (11.5%);
  English Language Learner: n/a; Migrant: 0 (0.0%)

  Eligible for Free Lunch Program: 230 (7.3%)
  Eligible for Reduced-Price Lunch Program: 62 (2.0%)
Teachers: 192.8 (16.3 to 1)
Librarians/Media Specialists: 2.0 (1,569.0 to 1)
Guidance Counselors: 5.0 (627.6 to 1)
Current Spending: ($ per student per year):
  Total: $7,639; Instruction: $4,524; Support Services: $2,871
Enrollment, Drop-out Rates and Diploma Recipients by Race/Ethnicity

Category	Total	White	Black	Asian	AIAN	Hisp.
Enrollment (%)	100.0	90.4	3.5	1.1	0.4	4.5
Drop-out Rate (%)	1.7	1.5	3.8	7.7	0.0	4.5
H.S. Diplomas (#)	216	197	8	5	0	6

De Witt County

Clinton CUSD 15
220 N Monroe • Clinton, IL 61727-1713
(217) 935-8321 • http://www.cusd15.k12.il.us/
Grade Span: PK-12; **Agency Type:** 1
Schools: 6
  4 Primary; 1 Middle; 0 High; 1 Other Level
  6 Regular; 0 Special Education; 0 Vocational; 0 Alternative
  0 Magnet; 0 Charter; 2 Title I Eligible; 0 School-wide Title I
Students: 2,137   (50.8% male; 49.1% female)
  Individual Education Program: 365 (17.1%);
  English Language Learner: n/a; Migrant: 0 (0.0%)
  Eligible for Free Lunch Program: 501 (23.4%)
  Eligible for Reduced-Price Lunch Program: 103 (4.8%)
Teachers: 151.3 (14.1 to 1)
Librarians/Media Specialists: 4.0 (534.3 to 1)
Guidance Counselors: 4.0 (534.3 to 1)
Current Spending: ($ per student per year):
  Total: $9,007; Instruction: $5,923; Support Services: $2,798
Enrollment, Drop-out Rates and Diploma Recipients by Race/Ethnicity

Category	Total	White	Black	Asian	AIAN	Hisp.
Enrollment (%)	100.0	94.6	1.1	1.1	0.3	2.9
Drop-out Rate (%)	6.5	6.8	0.0	0.0	0.0	0.0
H.S. Diplomas (#)	144	140	0	0	0	4

Du Page County

Addison SD 4
222 N Kennedy Dr • Addison, IL 60101-2497
(630) 458-2425 • http://www.asd4.org/
Grade Span: PK-08; **Agency Type:** 1
Schools: 8
  7 Primary; 1 Middle; 0 High; 0 Other Level
  8 Regular; 0 Special Education; 0 Vocational; 0 Alternative
  0 Magnet; 0 Charter; 3 Title I Eligible; 0 School-wide Title I
Students: 3,918   (50.1% male; 49.8% female)
  Individual Education Program: 594 (15.2%);
  English Language Learner: n/a; Migrant: 0 (0.0%)
  Eligible for Free Lunch Program: 908 (23.2%)
  Eligible for Reduced-Price Lunch Program: 193 (4.9%)
Teachers: 219.4 (17.9 to 1)
Librarians/Media Specialists: 1.0 (3,918.0 to 1)
Guidance Counselors: 1.0 (3,918.0 to 1)
Current Spending: ($ per student per year):
  Total: $6,787; Instruction: $4,136; Support Services: $2,445
Enrollment, Drop-out Rates and Diploma Recipients by Race/Ethnicity

Category	Total	White	Black	Asian	AIAN	Hisp.
Enrollment (%)	100.0	42.0	2.2	5.2	0.0	50.7
Drop-out Rate (%)	n/a	n/a	n/a	n/a	n/a	n/a
H.S. Diplomas (#)	n/a	n/a	n/a	n/a	n/a	n/a

Bensenville SD 2
210 S Church Rd • Bensenville, IL 60106-2303
(630) 766-5940 • http://www.bensenville2.k12.il.us/
Grade Span: PK-08; **Agency Type:** 1
Schools: 5
  4 Primary; 1 Middle; 0 High; 0 Other Level
  5 Regular; 0 Special Education; 0 Vocational; 0 Alternative
  0 Magnet; 0 Charter; 3 Title I Eligible; 0 School-wide Title I
Students: 2,325   (52.8% male; 47.1% female)
  Individual Education Program: 350 (15.1%);
  English Language Learner: n/a; Migrant: 0 (0.0%)
  Eligible for Free Lunch Program: 98 (4.2%)
  Eligible for Reduced-Price Lunch Program: 26 (1.1%)
Teachers: 140.1 (16.6 to 1)
Librarians/Media Specialists: 5.0 (465.0 to 1)
Guidance Counselors: 2.0 (1,162.5 to 1)
Current Spending: ($ per student per year):
  Total: $7,141; Instruction: $4,433; Support Services: $2,593

Enrollment, Drop-out Rates and Diploma Recipients by Race/Ethnicity

Category	Total	White	Black	Asian	AIAN	Hisp.
Enrollment (%)	100.0	30.8	2.8	6.9	0.0	59.4
Drop-out Rate (%)	n/a	n/a	n/a	n/a	n/a	n/a
H.S. Diplomas (#)	n/a	n/a	n/a	n/a	n/a	n/a

CCSD 181
5905 S County Rd • Hinsdale, IL 60521-4870
(630) 887-1070 • http://www.schooldistrict181.org/
Grade Span: PK-08; **Agency Type:** 1
Schools: 9
   7 Primary; 2 Middle; 0 High; 0 Other Level
   9 Regular; 0 Special Education; 0 Vocational; 0 Alternative
   0 Magnet; 0 Charter; 3 Title I Eligible; 0 School-wide Title I
Students: 4,028 (50.7% male; 49.2% female)
   Individual Education Program: 576 (14.3%);
   English Language Learner: n/a; Migrant: 0 (0.0%)
   Eligible for Free Lunch Program: n/a
   Eligible for Reduced-Price Lunch Program: n/a
Teachers: 243.1 (16.6 to 1)
Librarians/Media Specialists: 8.0 (503.5 to 1)
Guidance Counselors: 1.0 (4,028.0 to 1)
Current Spending: ($ per student per year):
   Total: $9,186; Instruction: $5,771; Support Services: $3,245

Enrollment, Drop-out Rates and Diploma Recipients by Race/Ethnicity

Category	Total	White	Black	Asian	AIAN	Hisp.
Enrollment (%)	100.0	93.8	0.8	3.6	0.0	1.8
Drop-out Rate (%)	n/a	n/a	n/a	n/a	n/a	n/a
H.S. Diplomas (#)	n/a	n/a	n/a	n/a	n/a	n/a

Community Consolidated S D 93
PO Box 88093 • Carol Stream, IL 60188-0093
(630) 893-9393 • http://www.d93.dupage.k12.il.us/
Grade Span: PK-08; **Agency Type:** 1
Schools: 8
   6 Primary; 2 Middle; 0 High; 0 Other Level
   8 Regular; 0 Special Education; 0 Vocational; 0 Alternative
   0 Magnet; 0 Charter; 3 Title I Eligible; 0 School-wide Title I
Students: 4,900 (52.0% male; 47.9% female)
   Individual Education Program: 615 (12.6%);
   English Language Learner: n/a; Migrant: 11 (0.2%)
   Eligible for Free Lunch Program: 0 (0.0%)
   Eligible for Reduced-Price Lunch Program: 0 (0.0%)
Teachers: 296.8 (16.5 to 1)
Librarians/Media Specialists: 8.0 (612.5 to 1)
Guidance Counselors: 0.0 (n/a to 1)
Current Spending: ($ per student per year):
   Total: $7,675; Instruction: $4,515; Support Services: $2,967

Enrollment, Drop-out Rates and Diploma Recipients by Race/Ethnicity

Category	Total	White	Black	Asian	AIAN	Hisp.
Enrollment (%)	100.0	66.5	5.2	15.8	0.2	12.3
Drop-out Rate (%)	n/a	n/a	n/a	n/a	n/a	n/a
H.S. Diplomas (#)	n/a	n/a	n/a	n/a	n/a	n/a

Community High SD 94
326 Joliet St • West Chicago, IL 60185-3142
(630) 876-6200 • http://www.district94.dupage.k12.il.us/
Grade Span: 09-12; **Agency Type:** 1
Schools: 1
   0 Primary; 0 Middle; 1 High; 0 Other Level
   1 Regular; 0 Special Education; 0 Vocational; 0 Alternative
   0 Magnet; 0 Charter; 1 Title I Eligible; 0 School-wide Title I
Students: 2,146 (50.5% male; 49.4% female)
   Individual Education Program: 213 (9.9%);
   English Language Learner: n/a; Migrant: 0 (0.0%)
   Eligible for Free Lunch Program: 0 (0.0%)
   Eligible for Reduced-Price Lunch Program: 0 (0.0%)
Teachers: 125.4 (17.1 to 1)
Librarians/Media Specialists: 1.0 (2,146.0 to 1)
Guidance Counselors: 7.8 (275.1 to 1)
Current Spending: ($ per student per year):
   Total: $9,902; Instruction: $6,068; Support Services: $3,594

Enrollment, Drop-out Rates and Diploma Recipients by Race/Ethnicity

Category	Total	White	Black	Asian	AIAN	Hisp.
Enrollment (%)	100.0	60.1	1.0	1.8	0.5	36.6
Drop-out Rate (%)	3.3	2.1	11.1	0.0	0.0	5.6
H.S. Diplomas (#)	438	305	6	13	1	113

Community High SD 99
6301 Springside • Downers Grove, IL 60516-2489
(630) 795-7100 • http://www.csd99.k12.il.us/
Grade Span: 08-12; **Agency Type:** 1
Schools: 2
   0 Primary; 0 Middle; 2 High; 0 Other Level
   2 Regular; 0 Special Education; 0 Vocational; 0 Alternative

   0 Magnet; 0 Charter; 1 Title I Eligible; 0 School-wide Title I
Students: 5,490 (51.9% male; 48.0% female)
   Individual Education Program: 725 (13.2%);
   English Language Learner: n/a; Migrant: 0 (0.0%)
   Eligible for Free Lunch Program: 254 (4.6%)
   Eligible for Reduced-Price Lunch Program: 77 (1.4%)
Teachers: 311.8 (17.6 to 1)
Librarians/Media Specialists: 6.0 (915.0 to 1)
Guidance Counselors: 21.0 (261.4 to 1)
Current Spending: ($ per student per year):
   Total: $11,954; Instruction: $7,690; Support Services: $3,981

Enrollment, Drop-out Rates and Diploma Recipients by Race/Ethnicity

Category	Total	White	Black	Asian	AIAN	Hisp.
Enrollment (%)	100.0	78.3	6.5	9.0	0.3	5.9
Drop-out Rate (%)	1.2	1.2	0.7	0.4	0.0	3.2
H.S. Diplomas (#)	1,207	964	62	123	3	55

Community Unit SD 200
130 W Park Ave • Wheaton, IL 60187-6460
(630) 682-2002 • http://www.cusd200.org/
Grade Span: PK-12; **Agency Type:** 1
Schools: 20
   14 Primary; 4 Middle; 2 High; 0 Other Level
   19 Regular; 1 Special Education; 0 Vocational; 0 Alternative
   0 Magnet; 0 Charter; 9 Title I Eligible; 0 School-wide Title I
Students: 14,191 (52.3% male; 47.6% female)
   Individual Education Program: 2,143 (15.1%);
   English Language Learner: n/a; Migrant: 0 (0.0%)
   Eligible for Free Lunch Program: 1,429 (10.1%)
   Eligible for Reduced-Price Lunch Program: 365 (2.6%)
Teachers: 860.5 (16.5 to 1)
Librarians/Media Specialists: 19.7 (720.4 to 1)
Guidance Counselors: 27.0 (525.6 to 1)
Current Spending: ($ per student per year):
   Total: $8,709; Instruction: $5,419; Support Services: $3,109

Enrollment, Drop-out Rates and Diploma Recipients by Race/Ethnicity

Category	Total	White	Black	Asian	AIAN	Hisp.
Enrollment (%)	100.0	81.4	6.2	4.3	0.1	8.0
Drop-out Rate (%)	2.7	2.3	3.2	2.7	0.0	10.2
H.S. Diplomas (#)	1,018	879	36	60	0	43

Darien SD 61
7414 S Cass Ave • Darien, IL 60561-3697
(630) 968-7505 • http://www.darien61.com/
Grade Span: PK-08; **Agency Type:** 1
Schools: 4
   3 Primary; 1 Middle; 0 High; 0 Other Level
   4 Regular; 0 Special Education; 0 Vocational; 0 Alternative
   0 Magnet; 0 Charter; 2 Title I Eligible; 0 School-wide Title I
Students: 1,766 (53.3% male; 46.6% female)
   Individual Education Program: 207 (11.7%);
   English Language Learner: n/a; Migrant: 0 (0.0%)
   Eligible for Free Lunch Program: 152 (8.6%)
   Eligible for Reduced-Price Lunch Program: 41 (2.3%)
Teachers: 125.5 (14.1 to 1)
Librarians/Media Specialists: 1.0 (1,766.0 to 1)
Guidance Counselors: 1.0 (1,766.0 to 1)
Current Spending: ($ per student per year):
   Total: $7,845; Instruction: $4,858; Support Services: $2,755

Enrollment, Drop-out Rates and Diploma Recipients by Race/Ethnicity

Category	Total	White	Black	Asian	AIAN	Hisp.
Enrollment (%)	100.0	67.7	10.6	12.4	0.0	9.3
Drop-out Rate (%)	n/a	n/a	n/a	n/a	n/a	n/a
H.S. Diplomas (#)	n/a	n/a	n/a	n/a	n/a	n/a

Downers Grove Grade SD 58
1860 63rd St • Downers Grove, IL 60516-1995
(630) 719-5800 • http://www.dg58.dupage.k12.il.us/
Grade Span: PK-08; **Agency Type:** 1
Schools: 12
   10 Primary; 2 Middle; 0 High; 0 Other Level
   12 Regular; 0 Special Education; 0 Vocational; 0 Alternative
   0 Magnet; 0 Charter; 0 Title I Eligible; 0 School-wide Title I
Students: 4,771 (50.9% male; 49.0% female)
   Individual Education Program: 738 (15.5%);
   English Language Learner: n/a; Migrant: 0 (0.0%)
   Eligible for Free Lunch Program: 40 (0.8%)
   Eligible for Reduced-Price Lunch Program: 5 (0.1%)
Teachers: 264.2 (18.1 to 1)
Librarians/Media Specialists: 12.0 (397.6 to 1)
Guidance Counselors: 4.0 (1,192.8 to 1)
Current Spending: ($ per student per year):
   Total: $8,472; Instruction: $4,856; Support Services: $3,527

Enrollment, Drop-out Rates and Diploma Recipients by Race/Ethnicity

Category	Total	White	Black	Asian	AIAN	Hisp.
Enrollment (%)	100.0	84.7	3.9	6.3	0.3	4.8
Drop-out Rate (%)	n/a	n/a	n/a	n/a	n/a	n/a
H.S. Diplomas (#)	n/a	n/a	n/a	n/a	n/a	n/a

Du Page High SD 88
101 W High Ridge Rd • Villa Park, IL 60181-3205
(630) 530-3980 • http://www.hsdist88.dupage.k12.il.us/
Grade Span: 09-12; **Agency Type:** 1
Schools: 2
  0 Primary; 0 Middle; 2 High; 0 Other Level
  2 Regular; 0 Special Education; 0 Vocational; 0 Alternative
  0 Magnet; 0 Charter; 2 Title I Eligible; 0 School-wide Title I
Students: 4,017 (52.5% male; 47.4% female)
  Individual Education Program: 562 (14.0%);
  English Language Learner: n/a; Migrant: 6 (0.1%)
  Eligible for Free Lunch Program: 630 (15.7%)
  Eligible for Reduced-Price Lunch Program: 131 (3.3%)
Teachers: 239.3 (16.8 to 1)
Librarians/Media Specialists: 2.0 (2,008.5 to 1)
Guidance Counselors: 14.0 (286.9 to 1)
Current Spending: ($ per student per year):
  Total: $11,383; Instruction: $5,943; Support Services: $5,214

Enrollment, Drop-out Rates and Diploma Recipients by Race/Ethnicity

Category	Total	White	Black	Asian	AIAN	Hisp.
Enrollment (%)	100.0	72.0	3.0	6.1	0.0	18.9
Drop-out Rate (%)	3.8	2.9	3.7	3.9	0.0	7.2
H.S. Diplomas (#)	780	588	24	47	1	120

Elmhurst SD 205
130 W Madison St • Elmhurst, IL 60126-3320
(630) 834-4530 • http://www.elmhurst.k12.il.us/
Grade Span: PK-12; **Agency Type:** 1
Schools: 13
  9 Primary; 3 Middle; 1 High; 0 Other Level
  12 Regular; 1 Special Education; 0 Vocational; 0 Alternative
  0 Magnet; 0 Charter; 1 Title I Eligible; 0 School-wide Title I
Students: 7,416 (52.3% male; 47.6% female)
  Individual Education Program: 1,015 (13.7%);
  English Language Learner: n/a; Migrant: 0 (0.0%)
  Eligible for Free Lunch Program: 73 (1.0%)
  Eligible for Reduced-Price Lunch Program: 15 (0.2%)
Teachers: 449.8 (16.5 to 1)
Librarians/Media Specialists: 13.0 (570.5 to 1)
Guidance Counselors: 19.0 (390.3 to 1)
Current Spending: ($ per student per year):
  Total: $9,540; Instruction: $6,024; Support Services: $3,351

Enrollment, Drop-out Rates and Diploma Recipients by Race/Ethnicity

Category	Total	White	Black	Asian	AIAN	Hisp.
Enrollment (%)	100.0	86.1	1.6	5.5	0.1	6.8
Drop-out Rate (%)	1.0	1.1	0.0	0.0	0.0	0.0
H.S. Diplomas (#)	504	432	3	41	3	25

Fenton Community HSD 100
1000 W Green St • Bensenville, IL 60106-2099
(630) 860-6257
Grade Span: 09-12; **Agency Type:** 1
Schools: 1
  0 Primary; 0 Middle; 1 High; 0 Other Level
  1 Regular; 0 Special Education; 0 Vocational; 0 Alternative
  0 Magnet; 0 Charter; 1 Title I Eligible; 0 School-wide Title I
Students: 1,501 (53.8% male; 46.1% female)
  Individual Education Program: 252 (16.8%);
  English Language Learner: n/a; Migrant: 0 (0.0%)
  Eligible for Free Lunch Program: 0 (0.0%)
  Eligible for Reduced-Price Lunch Program: 0 (0.0%)
Teachers: 96.4 (15.6 to 1)
Librarians/Media Specialists: 1.0 (1,501.0 to 1)
Guidance Counselors: 6.0 (250.2 to 1)
Current Spending: ($ per student per year):
  Total: $13,617; Instruction: $7,609; Support Services: $5,617

Enrollment, Drop-out Rates and Diploma Recipients by Race/Ethnicity

Category	Total	White	Black	Asian	AIAN	Hisp.
Enrollment (%)	100.0	56.8	1.6	6.3	0.1	35.2
Drop-out Rate (%)	3.6	1.8	6.7	1.0	n/a	7.1
H.S. Diplomas (#)	329	195	1	28	0	105

Glen Ellyn CCSD 89
22w600 Butterfield • Glen Ellyn, IL 60137-2848
(630) 469-8900 • http://www.d89.dupage.k12.il.us/
Grade Span: PK-08; **Agency Type:** 1
Schools: 5
  4 Primary; 1 Middle; 0 High; 0 Other Level
  5 Regular; 0 Special Education; 0 Vocational; 0 Alternative

  0 Magnet; 0 Charter; 3 Title I Eligible; 0 School-wide Title I
Students: 2,379 (50.9% male; 49.0% female)
  Individual Education Program: 322 (13.5%);
  English Language Learner: n/a; Migrant: 0 (0.0%)
  Eligible for Free Lunch Program: 0 (0.0%)
  Eligible for Reduced-Price Lunch Program: 0 (0.0%)
Teachers: 153.2 (15.5 to 1)
Librarians/Media Specialists: 5.0 (475.8 to 1)
Guidance Counselors: 2.0 (1,189.5 to 1)
Current Spending: ($ per student per year):
  Total: $8,271; Instruction: $5,295; Support Services: $2,914

Enrollment, Drop-out Rates and Diploma Recipients by Race/Ethnicity

Category	Total	White	Black	Asian	AIAN	Hisp.
Enrollment (%)	100.0	77.2	7.7	9.7	0.0	5.3
Drop-out Rate (%)	n/a	n/a	n/a	n/a	n/a	n/a
H.S. Diplomas (#)	n/a	n/a	n/a	n/a	n/a	n/a

Glen Ellyn SD 41
793 N Main St • Glen Ellyn, IL 60137-3999
(630) 790-6400 • http://www.d41.dupage.k12.il.us/
Grade Span: PK-08; **Agency Type:** 1
Schools: 5
  4 Primary; 1 Middle; 0 High; 0 Other Level
  5 Regular; 0 Special Education; 0 Vocational; 0 Alternative
  0 Magnet; 0 Charter; 3 Title I Eligible; 0 School-wide Title I
Students: 3,482 (51.8% male; 48.1% female)
  Individual Education Program: 458 (13.2%);
  English Language Learner: n/a; Migrant: 0 (0.0%)
  Eligible for Free Lunch Program: 0 (0.0%)
  Eligible for Reduced-Price Lunch Program: 0 (0.0%)
Teachers: 222.0 (15.7 to 1)
Librarians/Media Specialists: 5.0 (696.4 to 1)
Guidance Counselors: 3.0 (1,160.7 to 1)
Current Spending: ($ per student per year):
  Total: $7,530; Instruction: $4,691; Support Services: $2,739

Enrollment, Drop-out Rates and Diploma Recipients by Race/Ethnicity

Category	Total	White	Black	Asian	AIAN	Hisp.
Enrollment (%)	100.0	81.0	4.5	7.4	0.2	6.9
Drop-out Rate (%)	n/a	n/a	n/a	n/a	n/a	n/a
H.S. Diplomas (#)	n/a	n/a	n/a	n/a	n/a	n/a

Glenbard Twp HSD 87
596 Crescent Blvd • Glen Ellyn, IL 60137-4297
(630) 469-9100 • http://www.glenbard.org/
Grade Span: 09-12; **Agency Type:** 1
Schools: 4
  0 Primary; 0 Middle; 4 High; 0 Other Level
  4 Regular; 0 Special Education; 0 Vocational; 0 Alternative
  0 Magnet; 0 Charter; 1 Title I Eligible; 0 School-wide Title I
Students: 8,944 (52.0% male; 47.9% female)
  Individual Education Program: 1,034 (11.6%);
  English Language Learner: n/a; Migrant: 0 (0.0%)
  Eligible for Free Lunch Program: 572 (6.4%)
  Eligible for Reduced-Price Lunch Program: 137 (1.5%)
Teachers: 464.3 (19.3 to 1)
Librarians/Media Specialists: 9.0 (993.8 to 1)
Guidance Counselors: 35.3 (253.4 to 1)
Current Spending: ($ per student per year):
  Total: $11,048; Instruction: $6,715; Support Services: $4,162

Enrollment, Drop-out Rates and Diploma Recipients by Race/Ethnicity

Category	Total	White	Black	Asian	AIAN	Hisp.
Enrollment (%)	100.0	70.5	5.4	13.9	0.3	9.8
Drop-out Rate (%)	1.8	1.6	3.1	1.2	7.4	3.1
H.S. Diplomas (#)	1,946	1,457	64	264	6	155

Hinsdale Twp HSD 86
55th And Grant St • Hinsdale, IL 60521-4578
(630) 655-6100 • http://www.district86.k12.il.us/
Grade Span: 09-12; **Agency Type:** 1
Schools: 2
  0 Primary; 0 Middle; 2 High; 0 Other Level
  2 Regular; 0 Special Education; 0 Vocational; 0 Alternative
  0 Magnet; 0 Charter; 1 Title I Eligible; 0 School-wide Title I
Students: 4,239 (51.2% male; 48.7% female)
  Individual Education Program: 430 (10.1%);
  English Language Learner: n/a; Migrant: 0 (0.0%)
  Eligible for Free Lunch Program: 0 (0.0%)
  Eligible for Reduced-Price Lunch Program: 0 (0.0%)
Teachers: 275.4 (15.4 to 1)
Librarians/Media Specialists: 6.0 (706.5 to 1)
Guidance Counselors: 18.0 (235.5 to 1)
Current Spending: ($ per student per year):
  Total: $12,587; Instruction: $7,820; Support Services: $4,728

Enrollment, Drop-out Rates and Diploma Recipients by Race/Ethnicity

Category	Total	White	Black	Asian	AIAN	Hisp.
Enrollment (%)	100.0	77.8	4.3	13.1	0.3	4.5
Drop-out Rate (%)	2.2	1.8	10.3	2.0	0.0	5.1
H.S. Diplomas (#)	993	785	36	136	1	35

Indian Prairie CUSD 204
780 Shoreline Dr • Aurora, IL 60504-6192
(630) 375-3000 • http://www.ipsd.org/index.asp
Grade Span: PK-12; **Agency Type:** 1
Schools: 31
    22 Primary; 6 Middle; 3 High; 0 Other Level
    29 Regular; 2 Special Education; 0 Vocational; 0 Alternative
    0 Magnet; 0 Charter; 6 Title I Eligible; 0 School-wide Title I
Students: 26,779 (50.9% male; 49.0% female)
    Individual Education Program: 3,208 (12.0%);
    English Language Learner: n/a; Migrant: 0 (0.0%)
    Eligible for Free Lunch Program: 0 (0.0%)
    Eligible for Reduced-Price Lunch Program: 0 (0.0%)
Teachers: 1,638.8 (16.3 to 1)
Librarians/Media Specialists: 28.0 (956.4 to 1)
Guidance Counselors: 41.0 (653.1 to 1)
Current Spending: ($ per student per year):
    Total: $7,449; Instruction: $5,040; Support Services: $2,366

Enrollment, Drop-out Rates and Diploma Recipients by Race/Ethnicity

Category	Total	White	Black	Asian	AIAN	Hisp.
Enrollment (%)	100.0	73.6	8.5	11.8	0.2	5.9
Drop-out Rate (%)	0.9	0.9	1.9	0.6	0.0	0.7
H.S. Diplomas (#)	1,282	1,000	105	124	0	53

Keeneyville SD 20
5540 Arlington Dr E • Hanover Park, IL 60133-5569
(630) 894-2250 • http://www.esd20.dupage.k12.il.us/
Grade Span: PK-08; **Agency Type:** 1
Schools: 3
    2 Primary; 1 Middle; 0 High; 0 Other Level
    3 Regular; 0 Special Education; 0 Vocational; 0 Alternative
    0 Magnet; 0 Charter; 2 Title I Eligible; 0 School-wide Title I
Students: 1,727 (53.4% male; 46.5% female)
    Individual Education Program: 283 (16.4%);
    English Language Learner: n/a; Migrant: 0 (0.0%)
    Eligible for Free Lunch Program: 0 (0.0%)
    Eligible for Reduced-Price Lunch Program: 0 (0.0%)
Teachers: 107.0 (16.1 to 1)
Librarians/Media Specialists: 3.0 (575.7 to 1)
Guidance Counselors: 0.0 (n/a to 1)
Current Spending: ($ per student per year):
    Total: $9,125; Instruction: $5,031; Support Services: $4,026

Enrollment, Drop-out Rates and Diploma Recipients by Race/Ethnicity

Category	Total	White	Black	Asian	AIAN	Hisp.
Enrollment (%)	100.0	53.8	11.3	13.4	0.3	21.2
Drop-out Rate (%)	n/a	n/a	n/a	n/a	n/a	n/a
H.S. Diplomas (#)	n/a	n/a	n/a	n/a	n/a	n/a

Lake Park Community HSD 108
450 Spring Court • Roselle, IL 60172-1978
(630) 529-4500 • http://www.lphs.dupage.k12.il.us/
Grade Span: 09-12; **Agency Type:** 1
Schools: 1
    0 Primary; 0 Middle; 1 High; 0 Other Level
    1 Regular; 0 Special Education; 0 Vocational; 0 Alternative
    0 Magnet; 0 Charter; 1 Title I Eligible; 0 School-wide Title I
Students: 2,921 (51.7% male; 48.2% female)
    Individual Education Program: 369 (12.6%);
    English Language Learner: n/a; Migrant: 0 (0.0%)
    Eligible for Free Lunch Program: 0 (0.0%)
    Eligible for Reduced-Price Lunch Program: 0 (0.0%)
Teachers: 154.3 (18.9 to 1)
Librarians/Media Specialists: 2.0 (1,460.5 to 1)
Guidance Counselors: 10.0 (292.1 to 1)
Current Spending: ($ per student per year):
    Total: $11,246; Instruction: $6,210; Support Services: $4,746

Enrollment, Drop-out Rates and Diploma Recipients by Race/Ethnicity

Category	Total	White	Black	Asian	AIAN	Hisp.
Enrollment (%)	100.0	78.7	3.4	7.5	0.7	9.7
Drop-out Rate (%)	1.3	1.3	0.0	0.0	0.0	2.5
H.S. Diplomas (#)	636	529	15	51	1	40

Lisle CUSD 202
5211 Center Ave • Lisle, IL 60532-2399
(630) 493-8000 • http://www.lisle.dupage.k12.il.us/
Grade Span: PK-12; **Agency Type:** 1
Schools: 4
    2 Primary; 1 Middle; 1 High; 0 Other Level
    4 Regular; 0 Special Education; 0 Vocational; 0 Alternative

0 Magnet; 0 Charter; 3 Title I Eligible; 0 School-wide Title I
Students: 1,808 (51.6% male; 48.3% female)
    Individual Education Program: 258 (14.3%);
    English Language Learner: n/a; Migrant: 0 (0.0%)
    Eligible for Free Lunch Program: 135 (7.5%)
    Eligible for Reduced-Price Lunch Program: 54 (3.0%)
Teachers: 113.9 (15.9 to 1)
Librarians/Media Specialists: 4.0 (452.0 to 1)
Guidance Counselors: 3.0 (602.7 to 1)
Current Spending: ($ per student per year):
    Total: $10,991; Instruction: $6,160; Support Services: $4,609

Enrollment, Drop-out Rates and Diploma Recipients by Race/Ethnicity

Category	Total	White	Black	Asian	AIAN	Hisp.
Enrollment (%)	100.0	81.0	7.9	5.3	0.0	5.9
Drop-out Rate (%)	1.3	1.6	0.0	0.0	0.0	0.0
H.S. Diplomas (#)	153	127	10	11	0	5

Lombard SD 44
150 W Madison St • Lombard, IL 60148-5199
(630) 827-4400 • http://www.district44.dupage.k12.il.us/
Grade Span: PK-08; **Agency Type:** 1
Schools: 7
    6 Primary; 1 Middle; 0 High; 0 Other Level
    7 Regular; 0 Special Education; 0 Vocational; 0 Alternative
    0 Magnet; 0 Charter; 3 Title I Eligible; 0 School-wide Title I
Students: 3,307 (51.8% male; 48.1% female)
    Individual Education Program: 573 (17.3%);
    English Language Learner: n/a; Migrant: 0 (0.0%)
    Eligible for Free Lunch Program: 342 (10.3%)
    Eligible for Reduced-Price Lunch Program: 130 (3.9%)
Teachers: 199.8 (16.6 to 1)
Librarians/Media Specialists: 4.5 (734.9 to 1)
Guidance Counselors: 3.0 (1,102.3 to 1)
Current Spending: ($ per student per year):
    Total: $8,849; Instruction: $5,335; Support Services: $3,270

Enrollment, Drop-out Rates and Diploma Recipients by Race/Ethnicity

Category	Total	White	Black	Asian	AIAN	Hisp.
Enrollment (%)	100.0	75.0	5.9	9.0	0.4	9.8
Drop-out Rate (%)	n/a	n/a	n/a	n/a	n/a	n/a
H.S. Diplomas (#)	n/a	n/a	n/a	n/a	n/a	n/a

Marquardt SD 15
2174 Gladstone Ste C • Glendale Heights, IL 60139-1653
(630) 295-5450 • http://www.d15.dupage.k12.il.us/
Grade Span: PK-08; **Agency Type:** 1
Schools: 5
    4 Primary; 1 Middle; 0 High; 0 Other Level
    5 Regular; 0 Special Education; 0 Vocational; 0 Alternative
    0 Magnet; 0 Charter; 3 Title I Eligible; 0 School-wide Title I
Students: 2,672 (51.1% male; 48.8% female)
    Individual Education Program: 303 (11.3%);
    English Language Learner: n/a; Migrant: 0 (0.0%)
    Eligible for Free Lunch Program: 599 (22.4%)
    Eligible for Reduced-Price Lunch Program: 145 (5.4%)
Teachers: 154.3 (17.3 to 1)
Librarians/Media Specialists: 2.0 (1,336.0 to 1)
Guidance Counselors: 0.0 (n/a to 1)
Current Spending: ($ per student per year):
    Total: $7,264; Instruction: $4,635; Support Services: $2,441

Enrollment, Drop-out Rates and Diploma Recipients by Race/Ethnicity

Category	Total	White	Black	Asian	AIAN	Hisp.
Enrollment (%)	100.0	38.4	12.3	16.2	0.1	33.0
Drop-out Rate (%)	n/a	n/a	n/a	n/a	n/a	n/a
H.S. Diplomas (#)	n/a	n/a	n/a	n/a	n/a	n/a

Naperville C U Dist 203
203 W Hillside • Naperville, IL 60540-6589
(630) 420-6300 • http://www.ncusd203.org/
Grade Span: PK-12; **Agency Type:** 1
Schools: 21
    14 Primary; 5 Middle; 2 High; 0 Other Level
    21 Regular; 0 Special Education; 0 Vocational; 0 Alternative
    0 Magnet; 0 Charter; 5 Title I Eligible; 0 School-wide Title I
Students: 18,933 (52.4% male; 47.5% female)
    Individual Education Program: 2,316 (12.2%);
    English Language Learner: n/a; Migrant: 0 (0.0%)
    Eligible for Free Lunch Program: 161 (0.9%)
    Eligible for Reduced-Price Lunch Program: 20 (0.1%)
Teachers: 1,049.7 (18.0 to 1)
Librarians/Media Specialists: 23.0 (823.2 to 1)
Guidance Counselors: 34.0 (556.9 to 1)
Current Spending: ($ per student per year):
    Total: $8,577; Instruction: $5,436; Support Services: $2,995

Enrollment, Drop-out Rates and Diploma Recipients by Race/Ethnicity

Category	Total	White	Black	Asian	AIAN	Hisp.
Enrollment (%)	100.0	79.8	3.3	13.4	0.1	3.4
Drop-out Rate (%)	0.5	0.4	1.3	0.4	0.0	2.2
H.S. Diplomas (#)	1,348	1,117	35	167	7	22

Queen Bee SD 16
1560 Bloomingdale Rd • Glendale Heights, IL 60139-2796
(630) 260-6100 • http://www.d16.dupage.k12.il.us/
Grade Span: PK-08; **Agency Type:** 1
Schools: 3
  1 Primary; 2 Middle; 0 High; 0 Other Level
  3 Regular; 0 Special Education; 0 Vocational; 0 Alternative
  0 Magnet; 0 Charter; 2 Title I Eligible; 0 School-wide Title I
Students: 2,112   (50.3% male; 49.6% female)
  Individual Education Program: 303 (14.3%);
  English Language Learner: n/a; Migrant: 0 (0.0%)
  Eligible for Free Lunch Program: 0 (0.0%)
  Eligible for Reduced-Price Lunch Program: 0 (0.0%)
Teachers: 139.2 (15.2 to 1)
Librarians/Media Specialists: 4.0 (528.0 to 1)
Guidance Counselors: 1.0 (2,112.0 to 1)
Current Spending: ($ per student per year):
  Total: $6,874; Instruction: $4,294; Support Services: $2,491
Enrollment, Drop-out Rates and Diploma Recipients by Race/Ethnicity

Category	Total	White	Black	Asian	AIAN	Hisp.
Enrollment (%)	100.0	40.6	5.7	21.9	0.1	31.7
Drop-out Rate (%)	n/a	n/a	n/a	n/a	n/a	n/a
H.S. Diplomas (#)	n/a	n/a	n/a	n/a	n/a	n/a

SD 45 Dupage County
255 W Vermont St • Villa Park, IL 60181-1943
(630) 530-6200 • http://www.d45.dupage.k12.il.us/
Grade Span: PK-08; **Agency Type:** 1
Schools: 8
  6 Primary; 2 Middle; 0 High; 0 Other Level
  8 Regular; 0 Special Education; 0 Vocational; 0 Alternative
  0 Magnet; 0 Charter; 4 Title I Eligible; 1 School-wide Title I
Students: 3,820   (51.6% male; 48.3% female)
  Individual Education Program: 554 (14.5%);
  English Language Learner: n/a; Migrant: 0 (0.0%)
  Eligible for Free Lunch Program: 858 (22.5%)
  Eligible for Reduced-Price Lunch Program: 177 (4.6%)
Teachers: 233.7 (16.3 to 1)
Librarians/Media Specialists: 2.0 (1,910.0 to 1)
Guidance Counselors: 1.0 (3,820.0 to 1)
Current Spending: ($ per student per year):
  Total: $8,034; Instruction: $5,245; Support Services: $2,586
Enrollment, Drop-out Rates and Diploma Recipients by Race/Ethnicity

Category	Total	White	Black	Asian	AIAN	Hisp.
Enrollment (%)	100.0	62.7	6.8	6.2	0.3	24.0
Drop-out Rate (%)	n/a	n/a	n/a	n/a	n/a	n/a
H.S. Diplomas (#)	n/a	n/a	n/a	n/a	n/a	n/a

West Chicago Elem SD 33
312 E Forest Ave • West Chicago, IL 60185-3599
(630) 293-6000 • http://www.wegoed33.k12.il.us/
Grade Span: PK-08; **Agency Type:** 1
Schools: 7
  6 Primary; 1 Middle; 0 High; 0 Other Level
  7 Regular; 0 Special Education; 0 Vocational; 0 Alternative
  1 Magnet; 0 Charter; 4 Title I Eligible; 4 School-wide Title I
Students: 3,841   (51.6% male; 48.3% female)
  Individual Education Program: 639 (16.6%);
  English Language Learner: n/a; Migrant: 0 (0.0%)
  Eligible for Free Lunch Program: 1,276 (33.2%)
  Eligible for Reduced-Price Lunch Program: 357 (9.3%)
Teachers: 232.3 (16.5 to 1)
Librarians/Media Specialists: 7.0 (548.7 to 1)
Guidance Counselors: 2.0 (1,920.5 to 1)
Current Spending: ($ per student per year):
  Total: $8,850; Instruction: $5,997; Support Services: $2,645
Enrollment, Drop-out Rates and Diploma Recipients by Race/Ethnicity

Category	Total	White	Black	Asian	AIAN	Hisp.
Enrollment (%)	100.0	33.1	2.1	1.4	0.0	63.3
Drop-out Rate (%)	n/a	n/a	n/a	n/a	n/a	n/a
H.S. Diplomas (#)	n/a	n/a	n/a	n/a	n/a	n/a

Westmont CUSD 201
200 N Linden Ave • Westmont, IL 60559-1776
(630) 969-7741 • http://www.westmont.dupage.k12.il.us/
Grade Span: PK-12; **Agency Type:** 1
Schools: 5
  3 Primary; 1 Middle; 1 High; 0 Other Level
  5 Regular; 0 Special Education; 0 Vocational; 0 Alternative

---

  0 Magnet; 0 Charter; 1 Title I Eligible; 0 School-wide Title I
Students: 1,696   (52.0% male; 47.9% female)
  Individual Education Program: 256 (15.1%);
  English Language Learner: n/a; Migrant: 0 (0.0%)
  Eligible for Free Lunch Program: 354 (20.9%)
  Eligible for Reduced-Price Lunch Program: 61 (3.6%)
Teachers: 113.8 (14.9 to 1)
Librarians/Media Specialists: 2.0 (848.0 to 1)
Guidance Counselors: 1.0 (1,696.0 to 1)
Current Spending: ($ per student per year):
  Total: $10,227; Instruction: $6,594; Support Services: $3,283
Enrollment, Drop-out Rates and Diploma Recipients by Race/Ethnicity

Category	Total	White	Black	Asian	AIAN	Hisp.
Enrollment (%)	100.0	75.9	8.6	6.4	0.0	9.0
Drop-out Rate (%)	1.3	1.3	0.0	2.9	n/a	0.0
H.S. Diplomas (#)	91	74	6	6	0	5

Woodridge SD 68
7925 Janes Ave • Woodridge, IL 60517-3821
(630) 985-7925 • http://wdgdst68.dupage.k12.il.us/
Grade Span: PK-08; **Agency Type:** 1
Schools: 7
  6 Primary; 1 Middle; 0 High; 0 Other Level
  7 Regular; 0 Special Education; 0 Vocational; 0 Alternative
  0 Magnet; 0 Charter; 2 Title I Eligible; 0 School-wide Title I
Students: 3,103   (52.0% male; 47.9% female)
  Individual Education Program: 497 (16.0%);
  English Language Learner: n/a; Migrant: 0 (0.0%)
  Eligible for Free Lunch Program: 617 (19.9%)
  Eligible for Reduced-Price Lunch Program: 197 (6.3%)
Teachers: 188.2 (16.5 to 1)
Librarians/Media Specialists: 6.0 (517.2 to 1)
Guidance Counselors: 2.0 (1,551.5 to 1)
Current Spending: ($ per student per year):
  Total: $8,058; Instruction: $4,975; Support Services: $2,915
Enrollment, Drop-out Rates and Diploma Recipients by Race/Ethnicity

Category	Total	White	Black	Asian	AIAN	Hisp.
Enrollment (%)	100.0	58.8	15.7	9.5	0.0	16.0
Drop-out Rate (%)	n/a	n/a	n/a	n/a	n/a	n/a
H.S. Diplomas (#)	n/a	n/a	n/a	n/a	n/a	n/a

Edgar County

Paris-Union SD 95
414 S Main St • Paris, IL 61944-2399
(217) 465-8448 • http://www.paris95.k12.il.us/
Grade Span: PK-12; **Agency Type:** 1
Schools: 6
  3 Primary; 2 Middle; 1 High; 0 Other Level
  4 Regular; 2 Special Education; 0 Vocational; 0 Alternative
  0 Magnet; 0 Charter; 4 Title I Eligible; 0 School-wide Title I
Students: 1,695   (47.9% male; 52.0% female)
  Individual Education Program: 340 (20.1%);
  English Language Learner: n/a; Migrant: 0 (0.0%)
  Eligible for Free Lunch Program: 510 (30.1%)
  Eligible for Reduced-Price Lunch Program: 101 (6.0%)
Teachers: 110.0 (15.4 to 1)
Librarians/Media Specialists: 1.0 (1,695.0 to 1)
Guidance Counselors: 2.0 (847.5 to 1)
Current Spending: ($ per student per year):
  Total: $6,445; Instruction: $4,100; Support Services: $2,146
Enrollment, Drop-out Rates and Diploma Recipients by Race/Ethnicity

Category	Total	White	Black	Asian	AIAN	Hisp.
Enrollment (%)	100.0	97.3	0.6	0.3	0.9	0.8
Drop-out Rate (%)	4.5	4.5	0.0	0.0	0.0	0.0
H.S. Diplomas (#)	99	98	0	0	0	1

Effingham County

Effingham Community Unit SD 40
PO Box 130 • Effingham, IL 62401-0130
(217) 540-1501 • http://www.effingham.k12.il.us/
Grade Span: PK-12; **Agency Type:** 1
Schools: 8
  6 Primary; 1 Middle; 1 High; 0 Other Level
  7 Regular; 1 Special Education; 0 Vocational; 0 Alternative
  0 Magnet; 0 Charter; 5 Title I Eligible; 0 School-wide Title I
Students: 3,005   (52.5% male; 47.4% female)
  Individual Education Program: 505 (16.8%);
  English Language Learner: n/a; Migrant: 0 (0.0%)
  Eligible for Free Lunch Program: 641 (21.3%)
  Eligible for Reduced-Price Lunch Program: 129 (4.3%)
Teachers: 178.9 (16.8 to 1)
Librarians/Media Specialists: 2.0 (1,502.5 to 1)
Guidance Counselors: 7.0 (429.3 to 1)

Current Spending: ($ per student per year):
Total: $6,434; Instruction: $3,769; Support Services: $2,323

Enrollment, Drop-out Rates and Diploma Recipients by Race/Ethnicity

Category	Total	White	Black	Asian	AIAN	Hisp.
Enrollment (%)	100.0	97.0	0.7	0.8	0.1	1.5
Drop-out Rate (%)	2.0	2.0	0.0	0.0	n/a	0.0
H.S. Diplomas (#)	189	187	0	1	0	1

Fayette County

Vandalia CUSD 203
1109 N 8th St • Vandalia, IL 62471-1240
(618) 283-4525 • http://www.fayette.k12.il.us/washington/district.htm
Grade Span: PK-12; **Agency Type:** 1
Schools: 4
  2 Primary; 1 Middle; 1 High; 0 Other Level
  4 Regular; 0 Special Education; 0 Vocational; 0 Alternative
  0 Magnet; 0 Charter; 3 Title I Eligible; 0 School-wide Title I
Students: 1,782   (51.7% male; 48.2% female)
  Individual Education Program: 260 (14.6%);
  English Language Learner: n/a; Migrant: 0 (0.0%)
  Eligible for Free Lunch Program: 513 (28.8%)
  Eligible for Reduced-Price Lunch Program: 100 (5.6%)
Teachers: 99.9 (17.8 to 1)
Librarians/Media Specialists: 2.0 (891.0 to 1)
Guidance Counselors: 4.5 (396.0 to 1)
Current Spending: ($ per student per year):
Total: $6,280; Instruction: $3,578; Support Services: $2,356

Enrollment, Drop-out Rates and Diploma Recipients by Race/Ethnicity

Category	Total	White	Black	Asian	AIAN	Hisp.
Enrollment (%)	100.0	98.0	1.0	0.2	0.2	0.6
Drop-out Rate (%)	6.6	6.6	0.0	n/a	n/a	n/a
H.S. Diplomas (#)	108	108	0	0	0	0

Franklin County

Frankfort Community Unit SD 168
PO Box 425 • West Frankfort, IL 62896-2326
(618) 937-2421 • http://www.wf168.frnkln.k12.il.us/Index.htm
Grade Span: PK-12; **Agency Type:** 1
Schools: 4
  2 Primary; 1 Middle; 1 High; 0 Other Level
  4 Regular; 0 Special Education; 0 Vocational; 0 Alternative
  0 Magnet; 0 Charter; 3 Title I Eligible; 2 School-wide Title I
Students: 1,852   (50.8% male; 49.1% female)
  Individual Education Program: 426 (23.0%);
  English Language Learner: n/a; Migrant: 0 (0.0%)
  Eligible for Free Lunch Program: 608 (32.8%)
  Eligible for Reduced-Price Lunch Program: 167 (9.0%)
Teachers: 109.7 (16.9 to 1)
Librarians/Media Specialists: 1.0 (1,852.0 to 1)
Guidance Counselors: 1.0 (1,852.0 to 1)
Current Spending: ($ per student per year):
Total: $7,111; Instruction: $4,829; Support Services: $2,073

Enrollment, Drop-out Rates and Diploma Recipients by Race/Ethnicity

Category	Total	White	Black	Asian	AIAN	Hisp.
Enrollment (%)	100.0	98.4	0.5	0.3	0.3	0.5
Drop-out Rate (%)	3.3	3.4	n/a	0.0	0.0	0.0
H.S. Diplomas (#)	120	120	0	0	0	0

Fulton County

Canton Union SD 66
20 W Walnut St • Canton, IL 61520-2591
(309) 647-9411 • http://www.cantonusd.org/
Grade Span: PK-12; **Agency Type:** 1
Schools: 5
  3 Primary; 1 Middle; 1 High; 0 Other Level
  5 Regular; 0 Special Education; 0 Vocational; 0 Alternative
  0 Magnet; 0 Charter; 0 Title I Eligible; 0 School-wide Title I
Students: 2,769   (52.5% male; 47.4% female)
  Individual Education Program: 452 (16.3%);
  English Language Learner: n/a; Migrant: 0 (0.0%)
  Eligible for Free Lunch Program: 920 (33.2%)
  Eligible for Reduced-Price Lunch Program: 230 (8.3%)
Teachers: 171.5 (16.1 to 1)
Librarians/Media Specialists: 2.0 (1,384.5 to 1)
Guidance Counselors: 3.0 (923.0 to 1)
Current Spending: ($ per student per year):
Total: $7,009; Instruction: $4,594; Support Services: $2,148

Enrollment, Drop-out Rates and Diploma Recipients by Race/Ethnicity

Category	Total	White	Black	Asian	AIAN	Hisp.
Enrollment (%)	100.0	96.6	1.5	0.7	0.4	0.8
Drop-out Rate (%)	4.0	3.9	33.3	0.0	0.0	0.0
H.S. Diplomas (#)	179	171	1	3	1	3

Grundy County

Coal City CUSD 1
100 S Baima St • Coal City, IL 60416-1663
(815) 634-2287 • http://www.coalcity.k12.il.us/
Grade Span: PK-12; **Agency Type:** 1
Schools: 4
  2 Primary; 1 Middle; 1 High; 0 Other Level
  4 Regular; 0 Special Education; 0 Vocational; 0 Alternative
  0 Magnet; 0 Charter; 1 Title I Eligible; 0 School-wide Title I
Students: 1,920   (49.7% male; 50.2% female)
  Individual Education Program: 273 (14.2%);
  English Language Learner: n/a; Migrant: 0 (0.0%)
  Eligible for Free Lunch Program: 330 (17.2%)
  Eligible for Reduced-Price Lunch Program: 115 (6.0%)
Teachers: 110.9 (17.3 to 1)
Librarians/Media Specialists: 1.0 (1,920.0 to 1)
Guidance Counselors: 3.0 (640.0 to 1)
Current Spending: ($ per student per year):
Total: $7,788; Instruction: $4,372; Support Services: $3,113

Enrollment, Drop-out Rates and Diploma Recipients by Race/Ethnicity

Category	Total	White	Black	Asian	AIAN	Hisp.
Enrollment (%)	100.0	93.9	0.7	0.6	0.4	4.4
Drop-out Rate (%)	1.6	1.7	0.0	n/a	n/a	0.0
H.S. Diplomas (#)	120	115	0	0	0	5

Minooka Community CSD 201
333 W Mcevilly Rd • Minooka, IL 60447-9118
(815) 467-6121
Grade Span: PK-08; **Agency Type:** 1
Schools: 3
  2 Primary; 1 Middle; 0 High; 0 Other Level
  3 Regular; 0 Special Education; 0 Vocational; 0 Alternative
  0 Magnet; 0 Charter; 2 Title I Eligible; 0 School-wide Title I
Students: 1,778   (52.1% male; 47.8% female)
  Individual Education Program: 289 (16.3%);
  English Language Learner: n/a; Migrant: 0 (0.0%)
  Eligible for Free Lunch Program: 105 (5.9%)
  Eligible for Reduced-Price Lunch Program: 27 (1.5%)
Teachers: 91.7 (19.4 to 1)
Librarians/Media Specialists: 4.0 (444.5 to 1)
Guidance Counselors: 0.0 (n/a to 1)
Current Spending: ($ per student per year):
Total: $6,939; Instruction: $4,028; Support Services: $2,731

Enrollment, Drop-out Rates and Diploma Recipients by Race/Ethnicity

Category	Total	White	Black	Asian	AIAN	Hisp.
Enrollment (%)	100.0	92.0	2.1	0.6	0.1	5.3
Drop-out Rate (%)	n/a	n/a	n/a	n/a	n/a	n/a
H.S. Diplomas (#)	n/a	n/a	n/a	n/a	n/a	n/a

Minooka Community HS District 111
PO Box 827 • Minooka, IL 60447-0827
(815) 467-2557
Grade Span: 09-12; **Agency Type:** 1
Schools: 1
  0 Primary; 0 Middle; 1 High; 0 Other Level
  1 Regular; 0 Special Education; 0 Vocational; 0 Alternative
  0 Magnet; 0 Charter; 0 Title I Eligible; 0 School-wide Title I
Students: 1,534   (51.6% male; 48.3% female)
  Individual Education Program: 165 (10.8%);
  English Language Learner: n/a; Migrant: 0 (0.0%)
  Eligible for Free Lunch Program: 0 (0.0%)
  Eligible for Reduced-Price Lunch Program: 0 (0.0%)
Teachers: 83.6 (18.3 to 1)
Librarians/Media Specialists: 1.0 (1,534.0 to 1)
Guidance Counselors: 4.0 (383.5 to 1)
Current Spending: ($ per student per year):
Total: $8,382; Instruction: $4,363; Support Services: $3,763

Enrollment, Drop-out Rates and Diploma Recipients by Race/Ethnicity

Category	Total	White	Black	Asian	AIAN	Hisp.
Enrollment (%)	100.0	95.7	0.6	0.2	0.3	3.3
Drop-out Rate (%)	n/a	n/a	n/a	n/a	n/a	n/a
H.S. Diplomas (#)	0	0	0	0	0	0

Henry County

Geneseo Community Unit SD 228

209 S College Ave • Geneseo, IL 61254-1405
(309) 945-0450
Grade Span: PK-12; **Agency Type:** 1
Schools: 7
    4 Primary; 1 Middle; 2 High; 0 Other Level
    6 Regular; 1 Special Education; 0 Vocational; 0 Alternative
    0 Magnet; 0 Charter; 4 Title I Eligible; 0 School-wide Title I
Students: 2,877   (53.1% male; 46.8% female)
    Individual Education Program: 360 (12.5%);
    English Language Learner: n/a; Migrant: 0 (0.0%)
    Eligible for Free Lunch Program: 331 (11.5%)
    Eligible for Reduced-Price Lunch Program: 115 (4.0%)
Teachers: 165.7 (17.4 to 1)
Librarians/Media Specialists: 3.0 (959.0 to 1)
Guidance Counselors: 5.0 (575.4 to 1)
Current Spending: ($ per student per year):
    Total: $6,850; Instruction: $4,183; Support Services: $2,378
Enrollment, Drop-out Rates and Diploma Recipients by Race/Ethnicity

Category	Total	White	Black	Asian	AIAN	Hisp.
Enrollment (%)	100.0	96.8	0.7	0.6	0.1	1.9
Drop-out Rate (%)	3.5	3.0	18.2	16.7	n/a	15.8
H.S. Diplomas (#)	213	210	0	1	0	2

Kewanee Community Unit SD 229

210 Lyle St • Kewanee, IL 61443-2999
(309) 853-3341 • http://www.kewaneecommunityschools.org/
Grade Span: PK-12; **Agency Type:** 1
Schools: 6
    4 Primary; 1 Middle; 1 High; 0 Other Level
    5 Regular; 1 Special Education; 0 Vocational; 0 Alternative
    0 Magnet; 0 Charter; 4 Title I Eligible; 0 School-wide Title I
Students: 1,856   (51.2% male; 48.7% female)
    Individual Education Program: 342 (18.4%);
    English Language Learner: n/a; Migrant: 7 (0.4%)
    Eligible for Free Lunch Program: 905 (48.8%)
    Eligible for Reduced-Price Lunch Program: 131 (7.1%)
Teachers: 96.0 (19.3 to 1)
Librarians/Media Specialists: 1.0 (1,856.0 to 1)
Guidance Counselors: 1.0 (1,856.0 to 1)
Current Spending: ($ per student per year):
    Total: $6,030; Instruction: $3,593; Support Services: $2,103
Enrollment, Drop-out Rates and Diploma Recipients by Race/Ethnicity

Category	Total	White	Black	Asian	AIAN	Hisp.
Enrollment (%)	100.0	76.5	8.2	0.1	0.0	15.2
Drop-out Rate (%)	8.0	7.2	26.3	n/a	n/a	7.8
H.S. Diplomas (#)	100	87	5	0	0	8

Jackson County

Murphysboro CUSD 186

819 Walnut St • Murphysboro, IL 62966-2196
(618) 684-3781 • http://www.mboro.jacksn.k12.il.us/
Grade Span: PK-12; **Agency Type:** 1
Schools: 5
    3 Primary; 1 Middle; 1 High; 0 Other Level
    5 Regular; 0 Special Education; 0 Vocational; 0 Alternative
    0 Magnet; 0 Charter; 5 Title I Eligible; 4 School-wide Title I
Students: 2,205   (51.4% male; 48.5% female)
    Individual Education Program: 476 (21.6%);
    English Language Learner: n/a; Migrant: 0 (0.0%)
    Eligible for Free Lunch Program: 936 (42.4%)
    Eligible for Reduced-Price Lunch Program: 116 (5.3%)
Teachers: 135.1 (16.3 to 1)
Librarians/Media Specialists: 2.0 (1,102.5 to 1)
Guidance Counselors: 4.0 (551.3 to 1)
Current Spending: ($ per student per year):
    Total: $8,319; Instruction: $5,034; Support Services: $2,897
Enrollment, Drop-out Rates and Diploma Recipients by Race/Ethnicity

Category	Total	White	Black	Asian	AIAN	Hisp.
Enrollment (%)	100.0	82.6	15.0	0.2	0.1	2.1
Drop-out Rate (%)	4.6	4.5	4.9	0.0	0.0	9.1
H.S. Diplomas (#)	172	156	15	0	0	1

Jasper County

Jasper County Community Unit Dist 1

609 S Lafayette • Newton, IL 62448-1317
(618) 783-8459 • http://www.cusd1.jasper.k12.il.us/
Grade Span: PK-12; **Agency Type:** 1
Schools: 8
    5 Primary; 1 Middle; 0 High; 2 Other Level
    8 Regular; 0 Special Education; 0 Vocational; 0 Alternative

0 Magnet; 0 Charter; 4 Title I Eligible; 4 School-wide Title I
Students: 1,609   (50.9% male; 49.0% female)
    Individual Education Program: 291 (18.1%);
    English Language Learner: n/a; Migrant: 0 (0.0%)
    Eligible for Free Lunch Program: 391 (24.3%)
    Eligible for Reduced-Price Lunch Program: 120 (7.5%)
Teachers: 109.0 (14.8 to 1)
Librarians/Media Specialists: 2.0 (804.5 to 1)
Guidance Counselors: 4.0 (402.3 to 1)
Current Spending: ($ per student per year):
    Total: $7,784; Instruction: $4,633; Support Services: $2,878
Enrollment, Drop-out Rates and Diploma Recipients by Race/Ethnicity

Category	Total	White	Black	Asian	AIAN	Hisp.
Enrollment (%)	100.0	98.3	0.9	0.2	0.1	0.6
Drop-out Rate (%)	2.8	2.8	0.0	0.0	n/a	0.0
H.S. Diplomas (#)	124	124	0	0	0	0

Jefferson County

Mount Vernon SD 80

1722 Oakland • Mount Vernon, IL 62864-6304
(618) 244-8080 • http://www.district.mtv80.org/education/district/
Grade Span: PK-08; **Agency Type:** 1
Schools: 4
    2 Primary; 2 Middle; 0 High; 0 Other Level
    3 Regular; 1 Special Education; 0 Vocational; 0 Alternative
    0 Magnet; 0 Charter; 3 Title I Eligible; 3 School-wide Title I
Students: 1,897   (49.1% male; 50.8% female)
    Individual Education Program: 520 (27.4%);
    English Language Learner: n/a; Migrant: 0 (0.0%)
    Eligible for Free Lunch Program: 1,211 (63.8%)
    Eligible for Reduced-Price Lunch Program: 123 (6.5%)
Teachers: 117.0 (16.2 to 1)
Librarians/Media Specialists: 1.0 (1,897.0 to 1)
Guidance Counselors: 2.0 (948.5 to 1)
Current Spending: ($ per student per year):
    Total: $8,069; Instruction: $4,900; Support Services: $2,725
Enrollment, Drop-out Rates and Diploma Recipients by Race/Ethnicity

Category	Total	White	Black	Asian	AIAN	Hisp.
Enrollment (%)	100.0	63.8	32.7	1.3	0.0	2.1
Drop-out Rate (%)	n/a	n/a	n/a	n/a	n/a	n/a
H.S. Diplomas (#)	n/a	n/a	n/a	n/a	n/a	n/a

Jersey County

Jersey CUSD 100

100 Lincoln St • Jerseyville, IL 62052-1425
(618) 498-5561 • http://www.jersey100.k12.il.us/
Grade Span: PK-12; **Agency Type:** 1
Schools: 8
    6 Primary; 1 Middle; 1 High; 0 Other Level
    8 Regular; 0 Special Education; 0 Vocational; 0 Alternative
    0 Magnet; 0 Charter; 5 Title I Eligible; 0 School-wide Title I
Students: 3,026   (50.9% male; 49.0% female)
    Individual Education Program: 383 (12.7%);
    English Language Learner: n/a; Migrant: 0 (0.0%)
    Eligible for Free Lunch Program: 737 (24.4%)
    Eligible for Reduced-Price Lunch Program: 254 (8.4%)
Teachers: 183.0 (16.5 to 1)
Librarians/Media Specialists: 2.0 (1,513.0 to 1)
Guidance Counselors: 4.0 (756.5 to 1)
Current Spending: ($ per student per year):
    Total: $6,967; Instruction: $4,244; Support Services: $2,469
Enrollment, Drop-out Rates and Diploma Recipients by Race/Ethnicity

Category	Total	White	Black	Asian	AIAN	Hisp.
Enrollment (%)	100.0	98.5	0.8	0.3	0.0	0.4
Drop-out Rate (%)	2.3	2.3	0.0	0.0	n/a	0.0
H.S. Diplomas (#)	238	237	0	1	0	0

Kane County

Aurora East Unit SD 131

417 Fifth St • Aurora, IL 60505-4744
(630) 299-5554 • http://www.d131.kane.k12.il.us/home.htm
Grade Span: KG-12; **Agency Type:** 1
Schools: 16
    12 Primary; 3 Middle; 1 High; 0 Other Level
    16 Regular; 0 Special Education; 0 Vocational; 0 Alternative
    0 Magnet; 0 Charter; 16 Title I Eligible; 16 School-wide Title I
Students: 11,420   (50.8% male; 49.1% female)
    Individual Education Program: 1,493 (13.1%);
    English Language Learner: n/a; Migrant: 51 (0.4%)
    Eligible for Free Lunch Program: 6,430 (56.3%)
    Eligible for Reduced-Price Lunch Program: 1,119 (9.8%)
Teachers: 603.1 (18.9 to 1)

Librarians/Media Specialists: 5.0 (2,284.0 to 1)
Guidance Counselors: 10.0 (1,142.0 to 1)
Current Spending: ($ per student per year):
　　Total: $7,742; Instruction: $4,618; Support Services: $2,871
Enrollment, Drop-out Rates and Diploma Recipients by Race/Ethnicity

Category	Total	White	Black	Asian	AIAN	Hisp.
Enrollment (%)	100.0	9.2	12.0	0.7	0.2	77.9
Drop-out Rate (%)	7.1	7.4	7.5	13.3	0.0	6.9
H.S. Diplomas (#)	424	95	64	3	0	262

Aurora West Unit SD 129
80 So River St • Aurora, IL 60506-4108
(630) 844-4400 • http://www.sd129.org/
Grade Span: PK-12; **Agency Type:** 1
Schools: 17
　　12 Primary; 3 Middle; 1 High; 1 Other Level
　　16 Regular; 1 Special Education; 0 Vocational; 0 Alternative
　　1 Magnet; 0 Charter; 7 Title I Eligible; 6 School-wide Title I
Students: 11,717　(51.1% male; 48.8% female)
　　Individual Education Program: 1,797 (15.3%);
　　English Language Learner: n/a; Migrant: 0 (0.0%)
　　Eligible for Free Lunch Program: 3,237 (27.6%)
　　Eligible for Reduced-Price Lunch Program: 596 (5.1%)
Teachers: 646.9 (18.1 to 1)
Librarians/Media Specialists: 15.0 (781.1 to 1)
Guidance Counselors: 9.0 (1,301.9 to 1)
Current Spending: ($ per student per year):
　　Total: $6,732; Instruction: $4,309; Support Services: $2,188
Enrollment, Drop-out Rates and Diploma Recipients by Race/Ethnicity

Category	Total	White	Black	Asian	AIAN	Hisp.
Enrollment (%)	100.0	42.7	18.2	2.1	0.1	36.9
Drop-out Rate (%)	6.1	3.3	10.2	2.0	0.0	9.5
H.S. Diplomas (#)	573	338	83	9	0	143

Batavia Unit SD 101
335 W Wilson • Batavia, IL 60510-1998
(630) 879-4600 • http://dist.bps101.net/
Grade Span: PK-12; **Agency Type:** 1
Schools: 8
　　6 Primary; 1 Middle; 1 High; 0 Other Level
　　8 Regular; 0 Special Education; 0 Vocational; 0 Alternative
　　1 Magnet; 0 Charter; 5 Title I Eligible; 0 School-wide Title I
Students: 5,956　(51.2% male; 48.7% female)
　　Individual Education Program: 668 (11.2%);
　　English Language Learner: n/a; Migrant: 0 (0.0%)
　　Eligible for Free Lunch Program: 109 (1.8%)
　　Eligible for Reduced-Price Lunch Program: 40 (0.7%)
Teachers: 346.2 (17.2 to 1)
Librarians/Media Specialists: 8.0 (744.5 to 1)
Guidance Counselors: 7.0 (850.9 to 1)
Current Spending: ($ per student per year):
　　Total: $7,291; Instruction: $5,284; Support Services: $1,844
Enrollment, Drop-out Rates and Diploma Recipients by Race/Ethnicity

Category	Total	White	Black	Asian	AIAN	Hisp.
Enrollment (%)	100.0	87.8	3.3	2.6	0.2	6.1
Drop-out Rate (%)	1.2	1.2	2.4	0.0	0.0	0.0
H.S. Diplomas (#)	370	342	9	4	0	15

Central Community Unit SD 301
PO Box 396 • Burlington, IL 60109-0396
(847) 464-6005 • http://www.burlington.k12.il.us/
Grade Span: PK-12; **Agency Type:** 1
Schools: 5
　　3 Primary; 1 Middle; 1 High; 0 Other Level
　　5 Regular; 0 Special Education; 0 Vocational; 0 Alternative
　　0 Magnet; 0 Charter; 0 Title I Eligible; 0 School-wide Title I
Students: 2,413　(50.1% male; 49.8% female)
　　Individual Education Program: 289 (12.0%);
　　English Language Learner: n/a; Migrant: 0 (0.0%)
　　Eligible for Free Lunch Program: 26 (1.1%)
　　Eligible for Reduced-Price Lunch Program: 3 (0.1%)
Teachers: 146.5 (16.5 to 1)
Librarians/Media Specialists: 2.0 (1,206.5 to 1)
Guidance Counselors: 3.0 (804.3 to 1)
Current Spending: ($ per student per year):
　　Total: $8,443; Instruction: $4,983; Support Services: $3,257
Enrollment, Drop-out Rates and Diploma Recipients by Race/Ethnicity

Category	Total	White	Black	Asian	AIAN	Hisp.
Enrollment (%)	100.0	91.5	1.9	2.2	0.2	4.3
Drop-out Rate (%)	1.5	1.2	0.0	0.0	0.0	10.0
H.S. Diplomas (#)	153	145	2	3	0	3

Community Unit SD 300
300 Cleveland Ave • Carpentersville, IL 60110-1943
(847) 426-1300 • http://www.d300.kane.k12.il.us/
Grade Span: PK-12; **Agency Type:** 1
Schools: 24
　　15 Primary; 5 Middle; 3 High; 1 Other Level
　　22 Regular; 2 Special Education; 0 Vocational; 0 Alternative
　　0 Magnet; 0 Charter; 6 Title I Eligible; 5 School-wide Title I
Students: 18,175　(51.1% male; 48.8% female)
　　Individual Education Program: 2,981 (16.4%);
　　English Language Learner: n/a; Migrant: 0 (0.0%)
　　Eligible for Free Lunch Program: 3,745 (20.6%)
　　Eligible for Reduced-Price Lunch Program: 845 (4.6%)
Teachers: 864.2 (21.0 to 1)
Librarians/Media Specialists: 14.0 (1,298.2 to 1)
Guidance Counselors: 16.7 (1,088.3 to 1)
Current Spending: ($ per student per year):
　　Total: $7,348; Instruction: $4,523; Support Services: $2,600
Enrollment, Drop-out Rates and Diploma Recipients by Race/Ethnicity

Category	Total	White	Black	Asian	AIAN	Hisp.
Enrollment (%)	100.0	67.2	4.5	3.5	0.5	24.3
Drop-out Rate (%)	3.0	1.8	10.4	0.9	0.0	7.8
H.S. Diplomas (#)	1,037	844	23	21	4	145

Geneva Community Unit SD 304
227 N Fourth St • Geneva, IL 60134-1307
(630) 463-3000 • http://www.geneva304.org/
Grade Span: PK-12; **Agency Type:** 1
Schools: 8
　　6 Primary; 1 Middle; 1 High; 0 Other Level
　　7 Regular; 1 Special Education; 0 Vocational; 0 Alternative
　　0 Magnet; 0 Charter; 0 Title I Eligible; 0 School-wide Title I
Students: 5,549　(51.1% male; 48.8% female)
　　Individual Education Program: 692 (12.5%);
　　English Language Learner: n/a; Migrant: 0 (0.0%)
　　Eligible for Free Lunch Program: 0 (0.0%)
　　Eligible for Reduced-Price Lunch Program: 0 (0.0%)
Teachers: 321.9 (17.2 to 1)
Librarians/Media Specialists: 6.5 (853.7 to 1)
Guidance Counselors: 8.0 (693.6 to 1)
Current Spending: ($ per student per year):
　　Total: $7,854; Instruction: $4,911; Support Services: $2,733
Enrollment, Drop-out Rates and Diploma Recipients by Race/Ethnicity

Category	Total	White	Black	Asian	AIAN	Hisp.
Enrollment (%)	100.0	93.4	0.5	2.3	0.2	3.6
Drop-out Rate (%)	1.5	1.6	0.0	0.0	n/a	0.0
H.S. Diplomas (#)	321	311	0	8	0	2

Kaneland CUSD 302
47w326 Keslinger Rd • Maple Park, IL 60151-9720
(630) 365-5100 • http://www.kaneland.org/
Grade Span: PK-12; **Agency Type:** 1
Schools: 4
　　2 Primary; 1 Middle; 1 High; 0 Other Level
　　4 Regular; 0 Special Education; 0 Vocational; 0 Alternative
　　0 Magnet; 0 Charter; 1 Title I Eligible; 0 School-wide Title I
Students: 3,325　(51.6% male; 48.3% female)
　　Individual Education Program: 455 (13.7%);
　　English Language Learner: n/a; Migrant: 0 (0.0%)
　　Eligible for Free Lunch Program: 55 (1.7%)
　　Eligible for Reduced-Price Lunch Program: 22 (0.7%)
Teachers: 196.6 (16.9 to 1)
Librarians/Media Specialists: 3.0 (1,108.3 to 1)
Guidance Counselors: 4.0 (831.3 to 1)
Current Spending: ($ per student per year):
　　Total: $7,582; Instruction: $4,546; Support Services: $2,742
Enrollment, Drop-out Rates and Diploma Recipients by Race/Ethnicity

Category	Total	White	Black	Asian	AIAN	Hisp.
Enrollment (%)	100.0	92.8	1.1	1.1	0.1	5.0
Drop-out Rate (%)	2.0	2.0	0.0	0.0	0.0	0.0
H.S. Diplomas (#)	190	180	2	1	1	6

SD 46
355 E Chicago St • Elgin, IL 60120-6543
(847) 888-5000 • http://www.u46.k12.il.us/
Grade Span: PK-12; **Agency Type:** 1
Schools: 53
　　40 Primary; 7 Middle; 6 High; 0 Other Level
　　50 Regular; 3 Special Education; 0 Vocational; 0 Alternative
　　13 Magnet; 0 Charter; 15 Title I Eligible; 2 School-wide Title I
Students: 38,821　(51.2% male; 48.7% female)
　　Individual Education Program: 4,635 (11.9%);
　　English Language Learner: n/a; Migrant: 0 (0.0%)
　　Eligible for Free Lunch Program: 10,953 (28.2%)
　　Eligible for Reduced-Price Lunch Program: 2,448 (6.3%)

Teachers: 1,878.0 (20.7 to 1)
Librarians/Media Specialists: 15.0 (2,588.1 to 1)
Guidance Counselors: 26.9 (1,443.2 to 1)
Current Spending: ($ per student per year):
    Total: $8,441; Instruction: $5,206; Support Services: $3,020
Enrollment, Drop-out Rates and Diploma Recipients by Race/Ethnicity

Category	Total	White	Black	Asian	AIAN	Hisp.
Enrollment (%)	100.0	49.2	7.4	7.1	0.2	36.2
Drop-out Rate (%)	4.7	3.4	8.5	2.9	0.0	7.0
H.S. Diplomas (#)	1,914	1,178	113	166	1	456

St Charles CUSD 303

201 S 7th St • Saint Charles, IL 60174-1489
(630) 513-3030 • http://www.st-charles.k12.il.us/
Grade Span: PK-12; **Agency Type:** 1
Schools: 17
    12 Primary; 3 Middle; 2 High; 0 Other Level
    17 Regular; 0 Special Education; 0 Vocational; 0 Alternative
    0 Magnet; 0 Charter; 7 Title I Eligible; 0 School-wide Title I
Students: 12,939   (51.4% male; 48.5% female)
    Individual Education Program: 1,566 (12.1%);
    English Language Learner: n/a; Migrant: 0 (0.0%)
    Eligible for Free Lunch Program: 298 (2.3%)
    Eligible for Reduced-Price Lunch Program: 95 (0.7%)
Teachers: 728.3 (17.8 to 1)
Librarians/Media Specialists: 18.0 (718.8 to 1)
Guidance Counselors: 18.0 (718.8 to 1)
Current Spending: ($ per student per year):
    Total: $7,326; Instruction: $4,163; Support Services: $2,954
Enrollment, Drop-out Rates and Diploma Recipients by Race/Ethnicity

Category	Total	White	Black	Asian	AIAN	Hisp.
Enrollment (%)	100.0	89.3	1.3	3.7	0.3	5.5
Drop-out Rate (%)	1.2	1.2	3.0	1.0	0.0	0.7
H.S. Diplomas (#)	763	697	5	17	3	41

Kankakee County

Bourbonnais SD 53

281 W John Casey Rd • Bourbonnais, IL 60914-1368
(815) 939-2574 • http://www.besd53.k12.il.us/
Grade Span: PK-08; **Agency Type:** 1
Schools: 5
    4 Primary; 1 Middle; 0 High; 0 Other Level
    5 Regular; 0 Special Education; 0 Vocational; 0 Alternative
    0 Magnet; 0 Charter; 3 Title I Eligible; 0 School-wide Title I
Students: 2,426   (53.4% male; 46.5% female)
    Individual Education Program: 358 (14.8%);
    English Language Learner: n/a; Migrant: 0 (0.0%)
    Eligible for Free Lunch Program: 352 (14.5%)
    Eligible for Reduced-Price Lunch Program: 73 (3.0%)
Teachers: 133.8 (18.1 to 1)
Librarians/Media Specialists: 4.0 (606.5 to 1)
Guidance Counselors: 0.0 (n/a to 1)
Current Spending: ($ per student per year):
    Total: $5,778; Instruction: $3,442; Support Services: $2,119
Enrollment, Drop-out Rates and Diploma Recipients by Race/Ethnicity

Category	Total	White	Black	Asian	AIAN	Hisp.
Enrollment (%)	100.0	83.7	8.2	2.6	0.5	5.1
Drop-out Rate (%)	n/a	n/a	n/a	n/a	n/a	n/a
H.S. Diplomas (#)	n/a	n/a	n/a	n/a	n/a	n/a

Bradley Bourbonnais CHSD 307

700 W N St • Bradley, IL 60915-1099
(815) 937-3707 • http://www.bbchs.k12.il.us/
Grade Span: 09-12; **Agency Type:** 1
Schools: 1
    0 Primary; 0 Middle; 1 High; 0 Other Level
    1 Regular; 0 Special Education; 0 Vocational; 0 Alternative
    0 Magnet; 0 Charter; 1 Title I Eligible; 0 School-wide Title I
Students: 1,783   (51.6% male; 48.3% female)
    Individual Education Program: 262 (14.7%);
    English Language Learner: n/a; Migrant: 0 (0.0%)
    Eligible for Free Lunch Program: 171 (9.6%)
    Eligible for Reduced-Price Lunch Program: 69 (3.9%)
Teachers: 89.0 (20.0 to 1)
Librarians/Media Specialists: 1.0 (1,783.0 to 1)
Guidance Counselors: 6.7 (266.1 to 1)
Current Spending: ($ per student per year):
    Total: $7,428; Instruction: $4,225; Support Services: $3,023
Enrollment, Drop-out Rates and Diploma Recipients by Race/Ethnicity

Category	Total	White	Black	Asian	AIAN	Hisp.
Enrollment (%)	100.0	87.9	4.6	2.2	0.3	4.9
Drop-out Rate (%)	2.9	3.0	1.7	0.0	0.0	5.1
H.S. Diplomas (#)	376	349	12	5	2	8

Bradley SD 61

200 W State St • Bradley, IL 60915-2064
(815) 933-3371
Grade Span: PK-08; **Agency Type:** 1
Schools: 3
    2 Primary; 1 Middle; 0 High; 0 Other Level
    3 Regular; 0 Special Education; 0 Vocational; 0 Alternative
    0 Magnet; 0 Charter; 2 Title I Eligible; 0 School-wide Title I
Students: 1,553   (52.1% male; 47.8% female)
    Individual Education Program: 316 (20.3%);
    English Language Learner: n/a; Migrant: 0 (0.0%)
    Eligible for Free Lunch Program: 310 (20.0%)
    Eligible for Reduced-Price Lunch Program: 100 (6.4%)
Teachers: 85.0 (18.3 to 1)
Librarians/Media Specialists: 1.0 (1,553.0 to 1)
Guidance Counselors: 0.0 (n/a to 1)
Current Spending: ($ per student per year):
    Total: $6,089; Instruction: $4,097; Support Services: $1,808
Enrollment, Drop-out Rates and Diploma Recipients by Race/Ethnicity

Category	Total	White	Black	Asian	AIAN	Hisp.
Enrollment (%)	100.0	87.2	4.9	1.2	0.1	6.6
Drop-out Rate (%)	n/a	n/a	n/a	n/a	n/a	n/a
H.S. Diplomas (#)	n/a	n/a	n/a	n/a	n/a	n/a

Herscher Community Unit SD 2

PO Box 504 • Herscher, IL 60941-0504
(815) 426-2162 • http://www.hsd2.k12.il.us/
Grade Span: PK-12; **Agency Type:** 1
Schools: 5
    4 Primary; 0 Middle; 1 High; 0 Other Level
    5 Regular; 0 Special Education; 0 Vocational; 0 Alternative
    0 Magnet; 0 Charter; 3 Title I Eligible; 0 School-wide Title I
Students: 2,175   (52.7% male; 47.2% female)
    Individual Education Program: 277 (12.7%);
    English Language Learner: n/a; Migrant: 0 (0.0%)
    Eligible for Free Lunch Program: 243 (11.2%)
    Eligible for Reduced-Price Lunch Program: 115 (5.3%)
Teachers: 143.0 (15.2 to 1)
Librarians/Media Specialists: 3.0 (725.0 to 1)
Guidance Counselors: 3.0 (725.0 to 1)
Current Spending: ($ per student per year):
    Total: $7,094; Instruction: $4,424; Support Services: $2,412
Enrollment, Drop-out Rates and Diploma Recipients by Race/Ethnicity

Category	Total	White	Black	Asian	AIAN	Hisp.
Enrollment (%)	100.0	97.9	1.0	0.2	0.1	0.8
Drop-out Rate (%)	2.8	2.7	n/a	0.0	0.0	12.5
H.S. Diplomas (#)	150	147	0	1	1	1

Kankakee SD 111

240 Warren Ave • Kankakee, IL 60901-4319
(815) 933-0700 • http://www.k111.k12.il.us/
Grade Span: PK-12; **Agency Type:** 1
Schools: 14
    9 Primary; 2 Middle; 2 High; 1 Other Level
    11 Regular; 3 Special Education; 0 Vocational; 0 Alternative
    6 Magnet; 0 Charter; 10 Title I Eligible; 10 School-wide Title I
Students: 5,804   (50.9% male; 49.0% female)
    Individual Education Program: 1,120 (19.3%);
    English Language Learner: n/a; Migrant: 0 (0.0%)
    Eligible for Free Lunch Program: 4,085 (70.4%)
    Eligible for Reduced-Price Lunch Program: 395 (6.8%)
Teachers: 324.3 (17.9 to 1)
Librarians/Media Specialists: 2.0 (2,902.0 to 1)
Guidance Counselors: 6.0 (967.3 to 1)
Current Spending: ($ per student per year):
    Total: $8,201; Instruction: $4,830; Support Services: $2,992
Enrollment, Drop-out Rates and Diploma Recipients by Race/Ethnicity

Category	Total	White	Black	Asian	AIAN	Hisp.
Enrollment (%)	100.0	22.9	61.6	0.3	0.1	15.1
Drop-out Rate (%)	8.3	6.1	9.1	0.0	n/a	9.5
H.S. Diplomas (#)	246	88	137	1	0	20

Manteno Community Unit SD 5

250 N Poplar St • Manteno, IL 60950-1098
(815) 928-7000 • http://www.manteno.k12.il.us/
Grade Span: KG-12; **Agency Type:** 1
Schools: 5
    2 Primary; 1 Middle; 2 High; 0 Other Level
    4 Regular; 1 Special Education; 0 Vocational; 0 Alternative
    0 Magnet; 0 Charter; 3 Title I Eligible; 0 School-wide Title I
Students: 1,948   (51.1% male; 48.8% female)
    Individual Education Program: 293 (15.0%);
    English Language Learner: n/a; Migrant: 0 (0.0%)
    Eligible for Free Lunch Program: 95 (4.9%)
    Eligible for Reduced-Price Lunch Program: 14 (0.7%)

Teachers: 120.9 (16.1 to 1)
Librarians/Media Specialists: 1.0 (1,948.0 to 1)
Guidance Counselors: 1.5 (1,298.7 to 1)
Current Spending: ($ per student per year):
    Total: $6,603; Instruction: $4,204; Support Services: $2,245
Enrollment, Drop-out Rates and Diploma Recipients by Race/Ethnicity

Category	Total	White	Black	Asian	AIAN	Hisp.
Enrollment (%)	100.0	93.0	3.7	0.5	0.0	2.8
Drop-out Rate (%)	1.7	1.4	5.4	0.0	n/a	0.0
H.S. Diplomas (#)	117	109	4	0	0	4

Kendall County

Oswego Community Unit SD 308
4175 Rte 71 • Oswego, IL 60543-9781
(630) 554-3447 •
http://www.oswego.kendall.k12.il.us/oswego308/default.htm
Grade Span: PK-12; **Agency Type:** 1
Schools: 12
    8 Primary; 3 Middle; 1 High; 0 Other Level
    12 Regular; 0 Special Education; 0 Vocational; 0 Alternative
    0 Magnet; 0 Charter; 11 Title I Eligible; 0 School-wide Title I
Students: 9,771 (52.4% male; 47.6% female)
    Individual Education Program: 1,294 (13.2%);
    English Language Learner: n/a; Migrant: 0 (0.0%)
    Eligible for Free Lunch Program: 535 (5.5%)
    Eligible for Reduced-Price Lunch Program: 328 (3.4%)
Teachers: 483.6 (20.2 to 1)
Librarians/Media Specialists: 8.5 (1,149.5 to 1)
Guidance Counselors: 10.2 (957.9 to 1)
Current Spending: ($ per student per year):
    Total: $6,238; Instruction: $3,652; Support Services: $2,265
Enrollment, Drop-out Rates and Diploma Recipients by Race/Ethnicity

Category	Total	White	Black	Asian	AIAN	Hisp.
Enrollment (%)	100.0	74.6	6.6	3.9	0.5	14.5
Drop-out Rate (%)	3.0	2.7	5.6	2.7	0.0	5.2
H.S. Diplomas (#)	421	361	10	14	3	33

Yorkville Community Unit SD 115
PO Box 579 • Yorkville, IL 60560-0579
(630) 553-4382 • http://www.yorkville.k12.il.us/
Grade Span: PK-12; **Agency Type:** 1
Schools: 5
    3 Primary; 1 Middle; 1 High; 0 Other Level
    5 Regular; 0 Special Education; 0 Vocational; 0 Alternative
    0 Magnet; 0 Charter; 0 Title I Eligible; 0 School-wide Title I
Students: 2,832 (52.0% male; 47.9% female)
    Individual Education Program: 376 (13.3%);
    English Language Learner: n/a; Migrant: 0 (0.0%)
    Eligible for Free Lunch Program: 0 (0.0%)
    Eligible for Reduced-Price Lunch Program: 0 (0.0%)
Teachers: 145.3 (19.5 to 1)
Librarians/Media Specialists: 2.6 (1,089.2 to 1)
Guidance Counselors: 4.0 (708.0 to 1)
Current Spending: ($ per student per year):
    Total: $6,249; Instruction: $3,542; Support Services: $2,676
Enrollment, Drop-out Rates and Diploma Recipients by Race/Ethnicity

Category	Total	White	Black	Asian	AIAN	Hisp.
Enrollment (%)	100.0	93.3	1.6	0.7	0.0	4.3
Drop-out Rate (%)	1.2	1.1	0.0	0.0	0.0	3.7
H.S. Diplomas (#)	175	169	0	1	1	4

Knox County

Galesburg CUSD 205
P O B0x 1206 • Galesburg, IL 61402-1206
(309) 343-1151 • http://www.galesburg205.org/
Grade Span: PK-12; **Agency Type:** 1
Schools: 12
    8 Primary; 2 Middle; 1 High; 1 Other Level
    10 Regular; 2 Special Education; 0 Vocational; 0 Alternative
    1 Magnet; 0 Charter; 7 Title I Eligible; 7 School-wide Title I
Students: 4,940 (53.1% male; 46.8% female)
    Individual Education Program: 757 (15.3%);
    English Language Learner: n/a; Migrant: 0 (0.0%)
    Eligible for Free Lunch Program: 2,001 (40.5%)
    Eligible for Reduced-Price Lunch Program: 405 (8.2%)
Teachers: 300.2 (16.5 to 1)
Librarians/Media Specialists: 7.0 (705.7 to 1)
Guidance Counselors: 4.3 (1,148.8 to 1)
Current Spending: ($ per student per year):
    Total: $6,269; Instruction: $3,940; Support Services: $2,040

Enrollment, Drop-out Rates and Diploma Recipients by Race/Ethnicity

Category	Total	White	Black	Asian	AIAN	Hisp.
Enrollment (%)	100.0	74.3	18.4	0.6	0.2	6.5
Drop-out Rate (%)	6.5	6.1	8.3	0.0	0.0	10.7
H.S. Diplomas (#)	275	229	32	5	0	9

La Salle County

Ottawa Elem SD 141
320 W Main • Ottawa, IL 61350-2848
(815) 433-1133 • http://www.ottawaelem.lasall.k12.il.us/
Grade Span: PK-08; **Agency Type:** 1
Schools: 5
    3 Primary; 2 Middle; 0 High; 0 Other Level
    5 Regular; 0 Special Education; 0 Vocational; 0 Alternative
    0 Magnet; 0 Charter; 2 Title I Eligible; 0 School-wide Title I
Students: 2,055 (50.4% male; 49.5% female)
    Individual Education Program: 413 (20.1%);
    English Language Learner: n/a; Migrant: 0 (0.0%)
    Eligible for Free Lunch Program: 542 (26.4%)
    Eligible for Reduced-Price Lunch Program: 128 (6.2%)
Teachers: 129.6 (15.9 to 1)
Librarians/Media Specialists: 2.0 (1,027.5 to 1)
Guidance Counselors: 4.0 (513.8 to 1)
Current Spending: ($ per student per year):
    Total: $8,398; Instruction: $5,423; Support Services: $2,693
Enrollment, Drop-out Rates and Diploma Recipients by Race/Ethnicity

Category	Total	White	Black	Asian	AIAN	Hisp.
Enrollment (%)	100.0	89.5	3.5	0.9	0.4	5.7
Drop-out Rate (%)	n/a	n/a	n/a	n/a	n/a	n/a
H.S. Diplomas (#)	n/a	n/a	n/a	n/a	n/a	n/a

Ottawa Twp HSD 140
211 E Main St • Ottawa, IL 61350-3199
(815) 433-1323 • http://www.ottawahigh.com/
Grade Span: 09-12; **Agency Type:** 1
Schools: 1
    0 Primary; 0 Middle; 1 High; 0 Other Level
    1 Regular; 0 Special Education; 0 Vocational; 0 Alternative
    0 Magnet; 0 Charter; 1 Title I Eligible; 0 School-wide Title I
Students: 1,576 (51.4% male; 48.5% female)
    Individual Education Program: 293 (18.6%);
    English Language Learner: n/a; Migrant: 0 (0.0%)
    Eligible for Free Lunch Program: 0 (0.0%)
    Eligible for Reduced-Price Lunch Program: 0 (0.0%)
Teachers: 97.0 (16.2 to 1)
Librarians/Media Specialists: 1.0 (1,576.0 to 1)
Guidance Counselors: 4.5 (350.2 to 1)
Current Spending: ($ per student per year):
    Total: $8,582; Instruction: $5,226; Support Services: $2,991
Enrollment, Drop-out Rates and Diploma Recipients by Race/Ethnicity

Category	Total	White	Black	Asian	AIAN	Hisp.
Enrollment (%)	100.0	94.4	1.1	0.6	0.1	3.8
Drop-out Rate (%)	4.9	4.8	9.5	0.0	0.0	6.4
H.S. Diplomas (#)	330	313	4	2	0	11

Streator Elem SD 44
1520 N Bloomington • Streator, IL 61364-1312
(815) 672-2926 • http://www.streatoril.com/education/
Grade Span: PK-08; **Agency Type:** 1
Schools: 5
    5 Primary; 0 Middle; 0 High; 0 Other Level
    5 Regular; 0 Special Education; 0 Vocational; 0 Alternative
    0 Magnet; 0 Charter; 4 Title I Eligible; 0 School-wide Title I
Students: 1,886 (51.3% male; 48.6% female)
    Individual Education Program: 432 (22.9%);
    English Language Learner: n/a; Migrant: 0 (0.0%)
    Eligible for Free Lunch Program: 814 (43.2%)
    Eligible for Reduced-Price Lunch Program: 181 (9.6%)
Teachers: 122.6 (15.4 to 1)
Librarians/Media Specialists: 1.0 (1,886.0 to 1)
Guidance Counselors: 0.0 (n/a to 1)
Current Spending: ($ per student per year):
    Total: $7,685; Instruction: $4,682; Support Services: $2,738
Enrollment, Drop-out Rates and Diploma Recipients by Race/Ethnicity

Category	Total	White	Black	Asian	AIAN	Hisp.
Enrollment (%)	100.0	79.5	8.2	0.7	0.0	11.6
Drop-out Rate (%)	n/a	n/a	n/a	n/a	n/a	n/a
H.S. Diplomas (#)	n/a	n/a	n/a	n/a	n/a	n/a

Lake County

Adlai E Stevenson Dist 125
Two Stevenson Dr • Lincolnshire, IL 60069-2815
(847) 634-4000 • http://www.district125.k12.il.us/
Grade Span: 09-12; **Agency Type:** 1
Schools: 1
  0 Primary; 0 Middle; 1 High; 0 Other Level
  1 Regular; 0 Special Education; 0 Vocational; 0 Alternative
  0 Magnet; 0 Charter; 1 Title I Eligible; 1 School-wide Title I
Students: 4,351 (52.0% male; 47.9% female)
  Individual Education Program: 450 (10.3%);
  English Language Learner: n/a; Migrant: 0 (0.0%)
  Eligible for Free Lunch Program: n/a
  Eligible for Reduced-Price Lunch Program: n/a
Teachers: 269.2 (16.2 to 1)
Librarians/Media Specialists: 2.0 (2,175.5 to 1)
Guidance Counselors: 19.0 (229.0 to 1)
Current Spending: ($ per student per year):
  Total: $11,821; Instruction: $7,336; Support Services: $4,183
Enrollment, Drop-out Rates and Diploma Recipients by Race/Ethnicity

Category	Total	White	Black	Asian	AIAN	Hisp.
Enrollment (%)	100.0	83.2	1.1	12.6	0.0	3.0
Drop-out Rate (%)	0.4	0.4	0.0	0.4	0.0	1.0
H.S. Diplomas (#)	931	799	5	104	4	19

Antioch CCSD 34
800 N Main St • Antioch, IL 60002-1542
(847) 838-8400 • http://www.dist34.lake.k12.il.us/
Grade Span: PK-08; **Agency Type:** 1
Schools: 5
  4 Primary; 1 Middle; 0 High; 0 Other Level
  5 Regular; 0 Special Education; 0 Vocational; 0 Alternative
  0 Magnet; 0 Charter; 3 Title I Eligible; 0 School-wide Title I
Students: 2,541 (52.1% male; 47.8% female)
  Individual Education Program: 567 (22.3%);
  English Language Learner: n/a; Migrant: 0 (0.0%)
  Eligible for Free Lunch Program: 243 (9.6%)
  Eligible for Reduced-Price Lunch Program: 70 (2.8%)
Teachers: 151.1 (16.8 to 1)
Librarians/Media Specialists: 1.0 (2,541.0 to 1)
Guidance Counselors: 0.0 (n/a to 1)
Current Spending: ($ per student per year):
  Total: $6,867; Instruction: $3,904; Support Services: $2,774
Enrollment, Drop-out Rates and Diploma Recipients by Race/Ethnicity

Category	Total	White	Black	Asian	AIAN	Hisp.
Enrollment (%)	100.0	90.3	2.6	2.0	0.5	4.6
Drop-out Rate (%)	n/a	n/a	n/a	n/a	n/a	n/a
H.S. Diplomas (#)	n/a	n/a	n/a	n/a	n/a	n/a

Aptakisic-Tripp CCSD 102
1231 Weiland Rd • Buffalo Grove, IL 60089-7040
(847) 353-5660
Grade Span: PK-08; **Agency Type:** 1
Schools: 4
  2 Primary; 2 Middle; 0 High; 0 Other Level
  4 Regular; 0 Special Education; 0 Vocational; 0 Alternative
  0 Magnet; 0 Charter; 0 Title I Eligible; 0 School-wide Title I
Students: 2,314 (50.4% male; 49.5% female)
  Individual Education Program: 388 (16.8%);
  English Language Learner: n/a; Migrant: 0 (0.0%)
  Eligible for Free Lunch Program: 71 (3.1%)
  Eligible for Reduced-Price Lunch Program: 31 (1.3%)
Teachers: 159.0 (14.6 to 1)
Librarians/Media Specialists: 3.0 (771.3 to 1)
Guidance Counselors: 0.0 (n/a to 1)
Current Spending: ($ per student per year):
  Total: $8,884; Instruction: $5,081; Support Services: $3,533
Enrollment, Drop-out Rates and Diploma Recipients by Race/Ethnicity

Category	Total	White	Black	Asian	AIAN	Hisp.
Enrollment (%)	100.0	81.3	0.7	14.6	0.3	3.1
Drop-out Rate (%)	n/a	n/a	n/a	n/a	n/a	n/a
H.S. Diplomas (#)	n/a	n/a	n/a	n/a	n/a	n/a

Barrington CUSD 220
310 James St • Barrington, IL 60010-1799
(847) 381-6300 • http://www.cusd220.lake.k12.il.us/
Grade Span: PK-12; **Agency Type:** 1
Schools: 12
  9 Primary; 2 Middle; 1 High; 0 Other Level
  11 Regular; 1 Special Education; 0 Vocational; 0 Alternative
  0 Magnet; 0 Charter; 2 Title I Eligible; 0 School-wide Title I
Students: 8,721 (50.9% male; 49.0% female)
  Individual Education Program: 1,344 (15.4%);
  English Language Learner: n/a; Migrant: 0 (0.0%)
  Eligible for Free Lunch Program: 602 (6.9%)
  Eligible for Reduced-Price Lunch Program: 200 (2.3%)
Teachers: 518.5 (16.8 to 1)
Librarians/Media Specialists: 12.0 (726.8 to 1)
Guidance Counselors: 15.0 (581.4 to 1)
Current Spending: ($ per student per year):
  Total: $9,569; Instruction: $5,884; Support Services: $3,442
Enrollment, Drop-out Rates and Diploma Recipients by Race/Ethnicity

Category	Total	White	Black	Asian	AIAN	Hisp.
Enrollment (%)	100.0	80.7	1.7	7.0	0.0	10.5
Drop-out Rate (%)	0.3	0.2	0.0	0.6	0.0	1.1
H.S. Diplomas (#)	577	501	3	46	1	26

Beach Park CCSD 3
11315 W Wadsworth • Beach Park, IL 60099-3399
(847) 599-5070
Grade Span: PK-08; **Agency Type:** 1
Schools: 5
  4 Primary; 1 Middle; 0 High; 0 Other Level
  5 Regular; 0 Special Education; 0 Vocational; 0 Alternative
  0 Magnet; 0 Charter; 3 Title I Eligible; 0 School-wide Title I
Students: 2,238 (51.4% male; 48.5% female)
  Individual Education Program: 311 (13.9%);
  English Language Learner: n/a; Migrant: 0 (0.0%)
  Eligible for Free Lunch Program: 585 (26.1%)
  Eligible for Reduced-Price Lunch Program: 130 (5.8%)
Teachers: 124.1 (18.0 to 1)
Librarians/Media Specialists: 2.0 (1,119.0 to 1)
Guidance Counselors: 0.0 (n/a to 1)
Current Spending: ($ per student per year):
  Total: $6,813; Instruction: $4,139; Support Services: $2,487
Enrollment, Drop-out Rates and Diploma Recipients by Race/Ethnicity

Category	Total	White	Black	Asian	AIAN	Hisp.
Enrollment (%)	100.0	55.5	20.0	3.3	0.6	20.6
Drop-out Rate (%)	n/a	n/a	n/a	n/a	n/a	n/a
H.S. Diplomas (#)	n/a	n/a	n/a	n/a	n/a	n/a

Community Consolidated SD 46
565 Frederick Rd • Grayslake, IL 60030-3909
(847) 543-5319 • http://www.d46.k12.il.us/
Grade Span: PK-08; **Agency Type:** 1
Schools: 6
  4 Primary; 2 Middle; 0 High; 0 Other Level
  6 Regular; 0 Special Education; 0 Vocational; 0 Alternative
  0 Magnet; 0 Charter; 1 Title I Eligible; 0 School-wide Title I
Students: 4,013 (52.3% male; 47.6% female)
  Individual Education Program: 604 (15.1%);
  English Language Learner: n/a; Migrant: 0 (0.0%)
  Eligible for Free Lunch Program: 280 (7.0%)
  Eligible for Reduced-Price Lunch Program: 141 (3.5%)
Teachers: 210.8 (19.0 to 1)
Librarians/Media Specialists: 6.0 (668.8 to 1)
Guidance Counselors: 0.0 (n/a to 1)
Current Spending: ($ per student per year):
  Total: $7,643; Instruction: $4,144; Support Services: $3,343
Enrollment, Drop-out Rates and Diploma Recipients by Race/Ethnicity

Category	Total	White	Black	Asian	AIAN	Hisp.
Enrollment (%)	100.0	80.4	3.1	5.1	0.2	11.1
Drop-out Rate (%)	n/a	n/a	n/a	n/a	n/a	n/a
H.S. Diplomas (#)	n/a	n/a	n/a	n/a	n/a	n/a

Community High SD 117
1625 Deep Lake Rd • Lake Villa, IL 60046
(847) 395-1421
Grade Span: 02-12; **Agency Type:** 1
Schools: 3
  0 Primary; 0 Middle; 2 High; 1 Other Level
  1 Regular; 2 Special Education; 0 Vocational; 0 Alternative
  0 Magnet; 0 Charter; 1 Title I Eligible; 0 School-wide Title I
Students: 2,329 (53.4% male; 46.5% female)
  Individual Education Program: 363 (15.6%);
  English Language Learner: n/a; Migrant: 0 (0.0%)
  Eligible for Free Lunch Program: 0 (0.0%)
  Eligible for Reduced-Price Lunch Program: 0 (0.0%)
Teachers: 133.4 (17.5 to 1)
Librarians/Media Specialists: 2.0 (1,164.5 to 1)
Guidance Counselors: 6.0 (388.2 to 1)
Current Spending: ($ per student per year):
  Total: $9,143; Instruction: $5,208; Support Services: $3,734
Enrollment, Drop-out Rates and Diploma Recipients by Race/Ethnicity

Category	Total	White	Black	Asian	AIAN	Hisp.
Enrollment (%)	100.0	90.8	4.0	1.3	0.6	3.4
Drop-out Rate (%)	3.9	2.5	42.3	0.0	0.0	14.3
H.S. Diplomas (#)	466	430	8	7	6	15

Community High SD 128
940 W Park Ave • Libertyville, IL 60048-2699
(847) 367-3159 • http://www.lchs.lake.k12.il.us/
Grade Span: 09-12; **Agency Type:** 1
Schools: 2
   0 Primary; 0 Middle; 2 High; 0 Other Level
   2 Regular; 0 Special Education; 0 Vocational; 0 Alternative
   0 Magnet; 0 Charter; 0 Title I Eligible; 0 School-wide Title I
Students: 3,007 (53.2% male; 46.7% female)
   Individual Education Program: 417 (13.9%);
   English Language Learner: n/a; Migrant: 0 (0.0%)
   Eligible for Free Lunch Program: n/a
   Eligible for Reduced-Price Lunch Program: n/a
Teachers: 190.4 (15.8 to 1)
Librarians/Media Specialists: 3.0 (1,002.3 to 1)
Guidance Counselors: 18.0 (167.1 to 1)
Current Spending: ($ per student per year):
   Total: $14,077; Instruction: $7,628; Support Services: $6,175
Enrollment, Drop-out Rates and Diploma Recipients by Race/Ethnicity

Category	Total	White	Black	Asian	AIAN	Hisp.
Enrollment (%)	100.0	84.2	1.6	9.1	0.1	5.1
Drop-out Rate (%)	0.9	0.7	0.0	0.8	0.0	5.2
H.S. Diplomas (#)	631	529	18	60	0	24

Deerfield SD 109
517 Deerfield Rd • Deerfield, IL 60015-4419
(847) 945-1844 • http://www.dps109.lake.k12.il.us/
Grade Span: PK-08; **Agency Type:** 1
Schools: 6
   4 Primary; 2 Middle; 0 High; 0 Other Level
   6 Regular; 0 Special Education; 0 Vocational; 0 Alternative
   0 Magnet; 0 Charter; 6 Title I Eligible; 0 School-wide Title I
Students: 3,157 (51.7% male; 48.2% female)
   Individual Education Program: 623 (19.7%);
   English Language Learner: n/a; Migrant: 0 (0.0%)
   Eligible for Free Lunch Program: 0 (0.0%)
   Eligible for Reduced-Price Lunch Program: 0 (0.0%)
Teachers: 226.6 (13.9 to 1)
Librarians/Media Specialists: 6.0 (526.2 to 1)
Guidance Counselors: 1.0 (3,157.0 to 1)
Current Spending: ($ per student per year):
   Total: $8,744; Instruction: $5,337; Support Services: $3,328
Enrollment, Drop-out Rates and Diploma Recipients by Race/Ethnicity

Category	Total	White	Black	Asian	AIAN	Hisp.
Enrollment (%)	100.0	95.6	0.7	2.3	0.0	1.4
Drop-out Rate (%)	n/a	n/a	n/a	n/a	n/a	n/a
H.S. Diplomas (#)	n/a	n/a	n/a	n/a	n/a	n/a

Fremont SD 79
28855 N Fremont Ctr • Mundelein, IL 60060-9470
(847) 566-0169
Grade Span: PK-08; **Agency Type:** 1
Schools: 2
   2 Primary; 0 Middle; 0 High; 0 Other Level
   2 Regular; 0 Special Education; 0 Vocational; 0 Alternative
   0 Magnet; 0 Charter; 2 Title I Eligible; 0 School-wide Title I
Students: 1,561 (49.9% male; 50.0% female)
   Individual Education Program: 272 (17.4%);
   English Language Learner: n/a; Migrant: 0 (0.0%)
   Eligible for Free Lunch Program: 0 (0.0%)
   Eligible for Reduced-Price Lunch Program: 0 (0.0%)
Teachers: 88.2 (17.7 to 1)
Librarians/Media Specialists: 2.0 (780.5 to 1)
Guidance Counselors: 0.0 (n/a to 1)
Current Spending: ($ per student per year):
   Total: $7,724; Instruction: $4,007; Support Services: $3,476
Enrollment, Drop-out Rates and Diploma Recipients by Race/Ethnicity

Category	Total	White	Black	Asian	AIAN	Hisp.
Enrollment (%)	100.0	85.5	0.9	7.4	0.9	5.3
Drop-out Rate (%)	n/a	n/a	n/a	n/a	n/a	n/a
H.S. Diplomas (#)	n/a	n/a	n/a	n/a	n/a	n/a

Grayslake Community High SD 127
400 N Lake St • Grayslake, IL 60030-1499
(847) 223-8621 • http://www.gchs.lake.k12.il.us/
Grade Span: 09-12; **Agency Type:** 1
Schools: 1
   0 Primary; 0 Middle; 1 High; 0 Other Level
   1 Regular; 0 Special Education; 0 Vocational; 0 Alternative
   0 Magnet; 0 Charter; 1 Title I Eligible; 0 School-wide Title I
Students: 2,057 (51.1% male; 48.8% female)
   Individual Education Program: 265 (12.9%);
   English Language Learner: n/a; Migrant: 0 (0.0%)
   Eligible for Free Lunch Program: 0 (0.0%)
   Eligible for Reduced-Price Lunch Program: 0 (0.0%)

Teachers: 124.4 (16.5 to 1)
Librarians/Media Specialists: 1.0 (2,057.0 to 1)
Guidance Counselors: 7.0 (293.9 to 1)
Current Spending: ($ per student per year):
   Total: $8,092; Instruction: $4,311; Support Services: $3,771
Enrollment, Drop-out Rates and Diploma Recipients by Race/Ethnicity

Category	Total	White	Black	Asian	AIAN	Hisp.
Enrollment (%)	100.0	82.2	2.6	4.6	0.4	10.3
Drop-out Rate (%)	1.4	1.4	0.0	0.0	0.0	2.4
H.S. Diplomas (#)	342	299	8	13	1	21

Gurnee SD 56
900 Kilbourne Rd • Gurnee, IL 60031-1998
(847) 336-0800 • http://www.d56.lake.k12.il.us/district/
Grade Span: PK-08; **Agency Type:** 1
Schools: 4
   3 Primary; 1 Middle; 0 High; 0 Other Level
   4 Regular; 0 Special Education; 0 Vocational; 0 Alternative
   0 Magnet; 0 Charter; 1 Title I Eligible; 0 School-wide Title I
Students: 2,240 (52.2% male; 47.7% female)
   Individual Education Program: 303 (13.5%);
   English Language Learner: n/a; Migrant: 0 (0.0%)
   Eligible for Free Lunch Program: 0 (0.0%)
   Eligible for Reduced-Price Lunch Program: 0 (0.0%)
Teachers: 129.2 (17.3 to 1)
Librarians/Media Specialists: 3.0 (746.7 to 1)
Guidance Counselors: 0.0 (n/a to 1)
Current Spending: ($ per student per year):
   Total: $8,293; Instruction: $4,781; Support Services: $3,471
Enrollment, Drop-out Rates and Diploma Recipients by Race/Ethnicity

Category	Total	White	Black	Asian	AIAN	Hisp.
Enrollment (%)	100.0	59.4	14.2	6.7	0.6	19.2
Drop-out Rate (%)	n/a	n/a	n/a	n/a	n/a	n/a
H.S. Diplomas (#)	n/a	n/a	n/a	n/a	n/a	n/a

Hawthorn CCSD 73
201 Hawthorn Pkwy • Vernon Hills, IL 60061-1498
(847) 990-4210 • http://www.hawthorn.k12.il.us/
Grade Span: PK-08; **Agency Type:** 1
Schools: 6
   5 Primary; 1 Middle; 0 High; 0 Other Level
   6 Regular; 0 Special Education; 0 Vocational; 0 Alternative
   1 Magnet; 0 Charter; 3 Title I Eligible; 0 School-wide Title I
Students: 3,718 (51.1% male; 48.8% female)
   Individual Education Program: 483 (13.0%);
   English Language Learner: n/a; Migrant: 0 (0.0%)
   Eligible for Free Lunch Program: 469 (12.6%)
   Eligible for Reduced-Price Lunch Program: 105 (2.8%)
Teachers: 227.3 (16.4 to 1)
Librarians/Media Specialists: 4.6 (808.3 to 1)
Guidance Counselors: 0.0 (n/a to 1)
Current Spending: ($ per student per year):
   Total: $8,141; Instruction: $4,826; Support Services: $3,044
Enrollment, Drop-out Rates and Diploma Recipients by Race/Ethnicity

Category	Total	White	Black	Asian	AIAN	Hisp.
Enrollment (%)	100.0	62.9	2.8	12.6	0.2	21.4
Drop-out Rate (%)	n/a	n/a	n/a	n/a	n/a	n/a
H.S. Diplomas (#)	n/a	n/a	n/a	n/a	n/a	n/a

Kildeer Countryside CCSD 96
1050 Ivy Hall Ln • Buffalo Grove, IL 60089-1700
(847) 459-4260 • http://www.district96.k12.il.us/
Grade Span: PK-08; **Agency Type:** 1
Schools: 7
   5 Primary; 2 Middle; 0 High; 0 Other Level
   7 Regular; 0 Special Education; 0 Vocational; 0 Alternative
   0 Magnet; 0 Charter; 2 Title I Eligible; 0 School-wide Title I
Students: 3,487 (50.3% male; 49.6% female)
   Individual Education Program: 546 (15.7%);
   English Language Learner: n/a; Migrant: 0 (0.0%)
   Eligible for Free Lunch Program: 59 (1.7%)
   Eligible for Reduced-Price Lunch Program: 25 (0.7%)
Teachers: 220.0 (15.9 to 1)
Librarians/Media Specialists: 7.0 (498.1 to 1)
Guidance Counselors: 1.0 (3,487.0 to 1)
Current Spending: ($ per student per year):
   Total: $8,614; Instruction: $5,290; Support Services: $3,144
Enrollment, Drop-out Rates and Diploma Recipients by Race/Ethnicity

Category	Total	White	Black	Asian	AIAN	Hisp.
Enrollment (%)	100.0	85.1	1.2	11.1	0.1	2.5
Drop-out Rate (%)	n/a	n/a	n/a	n/a	n/a	n/a
H.S. Diplomas (#)	n/a	n/a	n/a	n/a	n/a	n/a

Lake Forest Community HS District 115
1285 N Mckinley Rd • Lake Forest, IL 60045-1371
(847) 234-3600 • http://www.lfhs.org/
Grade Span: 09-12; **Agency Type:** 1
Schools: 1
   0 Primary; 0 Middle; 1 High; 0 Other Level
   1 Regular; 0 Special Education; 0 Vocational; 0 Alternative
   0 Magnet; 0 Charter; 1 Title I Eligible; 0 School-wide Title I
Students: 1,735   (50.4% male; 49.5% female)
   Individual Education Program: 291 (16.8%);
   English Language Learner: n/a; Migrant: 0 (0.0%)
   Eligible for Free Lunch Program: 0 (0.0%)
   Eligible for Reduced-Price Lunch Program: 0 (0.0%)
Teachers: 121.3 (14.3 to 1)
Librarians/Media Specialists: 1.0 (1,735.0 to 1)
Guidance Counselors: 8.0 (216.9 to 1)
Current Spending: ($ per student per year):
   Total: $14,253; Instruction: $7,995; Support Services: $5,943
Enrollment, Drop-out Rates and Diploma Recipients by Race/Ethnicity

Category	Total	White	Black	Asian	AIAN	Hisp.
Enrollment (%)	100.0	94.3	0.6	3.9	0.0	1.2
Drop-out Rate (%)	0.2	0.2	0.0	0.0	n/a	0.0
H.S. Diplomas (#)	397	362	5	23	0	7

Lake Forest SD 67
67 W Deerpath • Lake Forest, IL 60045-2198
(847) 234-6010 • http://www.lfelem.lfc.edu/
Grade Span: PK-08; **Agency Type:** 1
Schools: 4
   3 Primary; 1 Middle; 0 High; 0 Other Level
   4 Regular; 0 Special Education; 0 Vocational; 0 Alternative
   0 Magnet; 0 Charter; 4 Title I Eligible; 0 School-wide Title I
Students: 2,194   (52.1% male; 47.8% female)
   Individual Education Program: 341 (15.5%);
   English Language Learner: n/a; Migrant: 0 (0.0%)
   Eligible for Free Lunch Program: 0 (0.0%)
   Eligible for Reduced-Price Lunch Program: 0 (0.0%)
Teachers: 177.0 (12.4 to 1)
Librarians/Media Specialists: 1.0 (2,194.0 to 1)
Guidance Counselors: 1.7 (1,290.6 to 1)
Current Spending: ($ per student per year):
   Total: $10,484; Instruction: $6,079; Support Services: $4,199
Enrollment, Drop-out Rates and Diploma Recipients by Race/Ethnicity

Category	Total	White	Black	Asian	AIAN	Hisp.
Enrollment (%)	100.0	94.1	0.6	3.4	0.0	1.8
Drop-out Rate (%)	n/a	n/a	n/a	n/a	n/a	n/a
H.S. Diplomas (#)	n/a	n/a	n/a	n/a	n/a	n/a

Lake Villa CCSD 41
131 Mckinley Ave • Lake Villa, IL 60046-8986
(847) 356-2385 • http://www.district41.org/
Grade Span: PK-08; **Agency Type:** 1
Schools: 5
   4 Primary; 1 Middle; 0 High; 0 Other Level
   5 Regular; 0 Special Education; 0 Vocational; 0 Alternative
   0 Magnet; 0 Charter; 0 Title I Eligible; 0 School-wide Title I
Students: 3,288   (53.4% male; 46.5% female)
   Individual Education Program: 757 (23.0%);
   English Language Learner: n/a; Migrant: 0 (0.0%)
   Eligible for Free Lunch Program: 212 (6.4%)
   Eligible for Reduced-Price Lunch Program: 104 (3.2%)
Teachers: 214.3 (15.3 to 1)
Librarians/Media Specialists: 3.5 (939.4 to 1)
Guidance Counselors: 0.0 (n/a to 1)
Current Spending: ($ per student per year):
   Total: $6,392; Instruction: $3,939; Support Services: $2,281
Enrollment, Drop-out Rates and Diploma Recipients by Race/Ethnicity

Category	Total	White	Black	Asian	AIAN	Hisp.
Enrollment (%)	100.0	79.7	4.6	3.9	0.3	11.5
Drop-out Rate (%)	n/a	n/a	n/a	n/a	n/a	n/a
H.S. Diplomas (#)	n/a	n/a	n/a	n/a	n/a	n/a

Lake Zurich CUSD 95
400 S Old Rand Rd • Lake Zurich, IL 60047-2459
(847) 438-2831 • http://www.lz95.lake.k12.il.us/
Grade Span: KG-12; **Agency Type:** 1
Schools: 9
   6 Primary; 2 Middle; 1 High; 0 Other Level
   9 Regular; 0 Special Education; 0 Vocational; 0 Alternative
   0 Magnet; 0 Charter; 8 Title I Eligible; 0 School-wide Title I
Students: 6,489   (51.1% male; 48.8% female)
   Individual Education Program: 855 (13.2%);
   English Language Learner: n/a; Migrant: 0 (0.0%)
   Eligible for Free Lunch Program: 169 (2.6%)
   Eligible for Reduced-Price Lunch Program: 50 (0.8%)

Teachers: 427.1 (15.2 to 1)
Librarians/Media Specialists: 8.0 (811.1 to 1)
Guidance Counselors: 8.0 (811.1 to 1)
Current Spending: ($ per student per year):
   Total: $7,694; Instruction: $4,747; Support Services: $2,761
Enrollment, Drop-out Rates and Diploma Recipients by Race/Ethnicity

Category	Total	White	Black	Asian	AIAN	Hisp.
Enrollment (%)	100.0	90.4	1.0	4.1	0.1	4.4
Drop-out Rate (%)	1.2	1.0	0.0	4.1	0.0	2.9
H.S. Diplomas (#)	427	395	3	13	0	16

Libertyville SD 70
1381 Lake St • Libertyville, IL 60048-1731
(847) 362-9695 • http://www.d70.k12.il.us/
Grade Span: KG-08; **Agency Type:** 1
Schools: 5
   4 Primary; 1 Middle; 0 High; 0 Other Level
   5 Regular; 0 Special Education; 0 Vocational; 0 Alternative
   0 Magnet; 0 Charter; 2 Title I Eligible; 0 School-wide Title I
Students: 2,653   (52.3% male; 47.6% female)
   Individual Education Program: 417 (15.7%);
   English Language Learner: n/a; Migrant: 0 (0.0%)
   Eligible for Free Lunch Program: 0 (0.0%)
   Eligible for Reduced-Price Lunch Program: 0 (0.0%)
Teachers: 161.9 (16.4 to 1)
Librarians/Media Specialists: 5.0 (530.6 to 1)
Guidance Counselors: 2.0 (1,326.5 to 1)
Current Spending: ($ per student per year):
   Total: $8,434; Instruction: $5,077; Support Services: $3,296
Enrollment, Drop-out Rates and Diploma Recipients by Race/Ethnicity

Category	Total	White	Black	Asian	AIAN	Hisp.
Enrollment (%)	100.0	90.2	2.1	4.7	0.1	2.9
Drop-out Rate (%)	n/a	n/a	n/a	n/a	n/a	n/a
H.S. Diplomas (#)	n/a	n/a	n/a	n/a	n/a	n/a

Lincolnshire-Prairieview S D 103
1370 Riverwoods Rd • Lincolnshire, IL 60069-2402
(847) 295-4030 • http://www.district103.k12.il.us/
Grade Span: KG-08; **Agency Type:** 1
Schools: 3
   2 Primary; 1 Middle; 0 High; 0 Other Level
   3 Regular; 0 Special Education; 0 Vocational; 0 Alternative
   0 Magnet; 0 Charter; 3 Title I Eligible; 0 School-wide Title I
Students: 1,724   (49.4% male; 50.5% female)
   Individual Education Program: 337 (19.5%);
   English Language Learner: n/a; Migrant: 0 (0.0%)
   Eligible for Free Lunch Program: 0 (0.0%)
   Eligible for Reduced-Price Lunch Program: 0 (0.0%)
Teachers: 121.4 (14.2 to 1)
Librarians/Media Specialists: 3.0 (574.7 to 1)
Guidance Counselors: 0.0 (n/a to 1)
Current Spending: ($ per student per year):
   Total: $10,583; Instruction: $6,258; Support Services: $4,275
Enrollment, Drop-out Rates and Diploma Recipients by Race/Ethnicity

Category	Total	White	Black	Asian	AIAN	Hisp.
Enrollment (%)	100.0	85.2	0.6	12.2	0.0	2.0
Drop-out Rate (%)	n/a	n/a	n/a	n/a	n/a	n/a
H.S. Diplomas (#)	n/a	n/a	n/a	n/a	n/a	n/a

Mundelein Cons High SD 120
1350 W Hawley St • Mundelein, IL 60060-1519
(847) 949-2200 • http://www.mundelein.lake.k12.il.us/
Grade Span: 09-12; **Agency Type:** 1
Schools: 1
   0 Primary; 0 Middle; 1 High; 0 Other Level
   1 Regular; 0 Special Education; 0 Vocational; 0 Alternative
   0 Magnet; 0 Charter; 1 Title I Eligible; 0 School-wide Title I
Students: 2,078   (52.0% male; 47.9% female)
   Individual Education Program: 311 (15.0%);
   English Language Learner: n/a; Migrant: 0 (0.0%)
   Eligible for Free Lunch Program: 314 (15.1%)
   Eligible for Reduced-Price Lunch Program: 111 (5.3%)
Teachers: 117.4 (17.7 to 1)
Librarians/Media Specialists: 2.0 (1,039.0 to 1)
Guidance Counselors: 10.6 (196.0 to 1)
Current Spending: ($ per student per year):
   Total: $10,943; Instruction: $6,645; Support Services: $4,037
Enrollment, Drop-out Rates and Diploma Recipients by Race/Ethnicity

Category	Total	White	Black	Asian	AIAN	Hisp.
Enrollment (%)	100.0	67.5	1.3	5.1	0.1	26.1
Drop-out Rate (%)	5.1	3.5	4.2	2.0	0.0	10.5
H.S. Diplomas (#)	468	325	16	96	0	31

Mundelein Elem SD 75
470 N Lake St • Mundelein, IL 60060-1884
(847) 949-2700 • http://www.d75.lake.k12.il.us/
Grade Span: PK-08; **Agency Type:** 1
Schools: 5
    4 Primary; 1 Middle; 0 High; 0 Other Level
    4 Regular; 1 Special Education; 0 Vocational; 0 Alternative
    0 Magnet; 0 Charter; 2 Title I Eligible; 0 School-wide Title I
Students: 2,219 (50.8% male; 49.1% female)
    Individual Education Program: 386 (17.4%);
    English Language Learner: n/a; Migrant: 0 (0.0%)
    Eligible for Free Lunch Program: 343 (15.5%)
    Eligible for Reduced-Price Lunch Program: 140 (6.3%)
Teachers: 141.1 (15.7 to 1)
Librarians/Media Specialists: 4.0 (554.8 to 1)
Guidance Counselors: 1.0 (2,219.0 to 1)
Current Spending: ($ per student per year):
    Total: $6,153; Instruction: $3,488; Support Services: $2,483
Enrollment, Drop-out Rates and Diploma Recipients by Race/Ethnicity

Category	Total	White	Black	Asian	AIAN	Hisp.
Enrollment (%)	100.0	60.0	2.3	5.9	0.2	31.5
Drop-out Rate (%)	n/a	n/a	n/a	n/a	n/a	n/a
H.S. Diplomas (#)	n/a	n/a	n/a	n/a	n/a	n/a

North Chicago SD 187
2000 Lewis Ave • North Chicago, IL 60064-2532
(847) 689-8150 • http://www.nchi.lfc.edu/
Grade Span: PK-12; **Agency Type:** 1
Schools: 10
    7 Primary; 2 Middle; 1 High; 0 Other Level
    10 Regular; 0 Special Education; 0 Vocational; 0 Alternative
    0 Magnet; 0 Charter; 10 Title I Eligible; 10 School-wide Title I
Students: 4,552 (50.9% male; 49.0% female)
    Individual Education Program: 737 (16.2%);
    English Language Learner: n/a; Migrant: 0 (0.0%)
    Eligible for Free Lunch Program: 2,355 (51.7%)
    Eligible for Reduced-Price Lunch Program: 371 (8.2%)
Teachers: 274.4 (16.6 to 1)
Librarians/Media Specialists: 1.0 (4,552.0 to 1)
Guidance Counselors: 7.0 (650.3 to 1)
Current Spending: ($ per student per year):
    Total: $8,970; Instruction: $5,130; Support Services: $3,602
Enrollment, Drop-out Rates and Diploma Recipients by Race/Ethnicity

Category	Total	White	Black	Asian	AIAN	Hisp.
Enrollment (%)	100.0	12.4	54.5	2.5	0.3	30.2
Drop-out Rate (%)	2.7	0.0	2.7	0.0	n/a	4.1
H.S. Diplomas (#)	138	13	94	0	1	30

North Shore SD 112
1936 Green Bay Rd • Highland Park, IL 60035-3112
(847) 681-6700 • http://www.nsn.org/hpkhome/dist112/
Grade Span: PK-08; **Agency Type:** 1
Schools: 11
    8 Primary; 3 Middle; 0 High; 0 Other Level
    11 Regular; 0 Special Education; 0 Vocational; 0 Alternative
    0 Magnet; 0 Charter; 2 Title I Eligible; 0 School-wide Title I
Students: 4,421 (50.9% male; 49.0% female)
    Individual Education Program: 684 (15.5%);
    English Language Learner: n/a; Migrant: 0 (0.0%)
    Eligible for Free Lunch Program: 350 (7.9%)
    Eligible for Reduced-Price Lunch Program: 0 (0.0%)
Teachers: 331.4 (13.3 to 1)
Librarians/Media Specialists: 10.0 (442.1 to 1)
Guidance Counselors: 2.0 (2,210.5 to 1)
Current Spending: ($ per student per year):
    Total: $10,438; Instruction: $6,463; Support Services: $3,846
Enrollment, Drop-out Rates and Diploma Recipients by Race/Ethnicity

Category	Total	White	Black	Asian	AIAN	Hisp.
Enrollment (%)	100.0	81.1	2.0	1.7	0.0	15.2
Drop-out Rate (%)	n/a	n/a	n/a	n/a	n/a	n/a
H.S. Diplomas (#)	n/a	n/a	n/a	n/a	n/a	n/a

Round Lake Area Schs - Dist 116
316 S Rosedale Ct • Round Lake, IL 60073-2999
(847) 270-9000 • http://www.rlas-116.org/
Grade Span: PK-12; **Agency Type:** 1
Schools: 8
    6 Primary; 1 Middle; 1 High; 0 Other Level
    8 Regular; 0 Special Education; 0 Vocational; 0 Alternative
    0 Magnet; 0 Charter; 7 Title I Eligible; 0 School-wide Title I
Students: 6,333 (51.3% male; 48.6% female)
    Individual Education Program: 1,022 (16.1%);
    English Language Learner: n/a; Migrant: 0 (0.0%)
    Eligible for Free Lunch Program: 2,377 (37.5%)
    Eligible for Reduced-Price Lunch Program: 540 (8.5%)

Teachers: 301.5 (21.0 to 1)
Librarians/Media Specialists: 1.0 (6,333.0 to 1)
Guidance Counselors: 3.0 (2,111.0 to 1)
Current Spending: ($ per student per year):
    Total: $5,898; Instruction: $3,658; Support Services: $2,015
Enrollment, Drop-out Rates and Diploma Recipients by Race/Ethnicity

Category	Total	White	Black	Asian	AIAN	Hisp.
Enrollment (%)	100.0	34.6	6.4	2.0	0.2	56.8
Drop-out Rate (%)	6.2	4.7	7.6	6.3	25.0	7.7
H.S. Diplomas (#)	254	155	8	3	0	88

Township High SD 113
1040 Park Ave W • Highland Park, IL 60035-2283
(847) 926-9301 • http://www.d113.lake.k12.il.us/
Grade Span: 09-12; **Agency Type:** 1
Schools: 2
    0 Primary; 0 Middle; 2 High; 0 Other Level
    2 Regular; 0 Special Education; 0 Vocational; 0 Alternative
    0 Magnet; 0 Charter; 1 Title I Eligible; 0 School-wide Title I
Students: 3,512 (51.3% male; 48.6% female)
    Individual Education Program: 557 (15.9%);
    English Language Learner: n/a; Migrant: 0 (0.0%)
    Eligible for Free Lunch Program: n/a
    Eligible for Reduced-Price Lunch Program: n/a
Teachers: 235.1 (14.9 to 1)
Librarians/Media Specialists: 7.0 (501.7 to 1)
Guidance Counselors: 18.0 (195.1 to 1)
Current Spending: ($ per student per year):
    Total: $17,826; Instruction: $9,454; Support Services: $8,341
Enrollment, Drop-out Rates and Diploma Recipients by Race/Ethnicity

Category	Total	White	Black	Asian	AIAN	Hisp.
Enrollment (%)	100.0	86.8	1.4	2.6	0.0	9.1
Drop-out Rate (%)	1.5	0.8	0.0	0.0	0.0	9.6
H.S. Diplomas (#)	750	656	16	19	1	58

Warren Twp High SD 121
17962 W Gages Lake • Gages Lake, IL 60030
(847) 662-1400 • http://www.wths.net/
Grade Span: 09-12; **Agency Type:** 1
Schools: 1
    0 Primary; 0 Middle; 1 High; 0 Other Level
    1 Regular; 0 Special Education; 0 Vocational; 0 Alternative
    0 Magnet; 0 Charter; 1 Title I Eligible; 0 School-wide Title I
Students: 3,627 (50.5% male; 49.4% female)
    Individual Education Program: 489 (13.5%);
    English Language Learner: n/a; Migrant: 0 (0.0%)
    Eligible for Free Lunch Program: 0 (0.0%)
    Eligible for Reduced-Price Lunch Program: 0 (0.0%)
Teachers: 194.0 (18.7 to 1)
Librarians/Media Specialists: 3.0 (1,209.0 to 1)
Guidance Counselors: 9.0 (403.0 to 1)
Current Spending: ($ per student per year):
    Total: $8,701; Instruction: $5,043; Support Services: $3,330
Enrollment, Drop-out Rates and Diploma Recipients by Race/Ethnicity

Category	Total	White	Black	Asian	AIAN	Hisp.
Enrollment (%)	100.0	68.4	8.4	8.9	0.8	13.5
Drop-out Rate (%)	2.8	2.5	3.4	2.1	0.0	4.8
H.S. Diplomas (#)	674	506	44	57	2	65

Wauconda Community Unit SD 118
555 N Main St • Wauconda, IL 60084-1299
(847) 526-7690 • http://www.wauconda118.org/
Grade Span: PK-12; **Agency Type:** 1
Schools: 5
    2 Primary; 2 Middle; 1 High; 0 Other Level
    5 Regular; 0 Special Education; 0 Vocational; 0 Alternative
    0 Magnet; 0 Charter; 2 Title I Eligible; 0 School-wide Title I
Students: 3,970 (51.8% male; 48.1% female)
    Individual Education Program: 644 (16.2%);
    English Language Learner: n/a; Migrant: 0 (0.0%)
    Eligible for Free Lunch Program: 414 (10.4%)
    Eligible for Reduced-Price Lunch Program: 71 (1.8%)
Teachers: 233.6 (17.0 to 1)
Librarians/Media Specialists: 5.0 (794.0 to 1)
Guidance Counselors: 5.0 (794.0 to 1)
Current Spending: ($ per student per year):
    Total: $7,249; Instruction: $3,942; Support Services: $3,074
Enrollment, Drop-out Rates and Diploma Recipients by Race/Ethnicity

Category	Total	White	Black	Asian	AIAN	Hisp.
Enrollment (%)	100.0	82.6	0.7	2.0	0.3	14.5
Drop-out Rate (%)	2.2	1.5	37.5	15.4	0.0	3.8
H.S. Diplomas (#)	218	201	1	1	1	14

Waukegan CUSD 60
1201 N Sheridan Rd • Waukegan, IL 60085-2099
(847) 336-3100 • http://www.waukeganschools.org/
Grade Span: PK-12; **Agency Type:** 1
Schools: 24
  15 Primary; 5 Middle; 3 High; 1 Other Level
  21 Regular; 3 Special Education; 0 Vocational; 0 Alternative
  2 Magnet; 0 Charter; 20 Title I Eligible; 19 School-wide Title I
Students: 16,260 (51.1% male; 48.8% female)
  Individual Education Program: 2,626 (16.2%);
  English Language Learner: n/a; Migrant: 0 (0.0%)
  Eligible for Free Lunch Program: 7,142 (43.9%)
  Eligible for Reduced-Price Lunch Program: 1,699 (10.4%)
Teachers: 859.9 (18.9 to 1)
Librarians/Media Specialists: 9.0 (1,806.7 to 1)
Guidance Counselors: 22.0 (739.1 to 1)
Current Spending: ($ per student per year):
  Total: $7,274; Instruction: $4,136; Support Services: $2,896
Enrollment, Drop-out Rates and Diploma Recipients by Race/Ethnicity

Category	Total	White	Black	Asian	AIAN	Hisp.
Enrollment (%)	100.0	9.7	20.7	2.2	0.1	67.4
Drop-out Rate (%)	11.2	6.4	12.1	5.6	16.7	12.3
H.S. Diplomas (#)	648	137	163	27	2	319

Woodland CCSD 50
1105 N Hunt Club Rd • Gurnee, IL 60031
(847) 856-3590
Grade Span: PK-08; **Agency Type:** 1
Schools: 4
  3 Primary; 1 Middle; 0 High; 0 Other Level
  4 Regular; 0 Special Education; 0 Vocational; 0 Alternative
  0 Magnet; 0 Charter; 4 Title I Eligible; 0 School-wide Title I
Students: 7,055 (51.7% male; 48.2% female)
  Individual Education Program: 1,181 (16.7%);
  English Language Learner: n/a; Migrant: 0 (0.0%)
  Eligible for Free Lunch Program: 510 (7.2%)
  Eligible for Reduced-Price Lunch Program: 198 (2.8%)
Teachers: 467.5 (15.1 to 1)
Librarians/Media Specialists: 5.0 (1,411.0 to 1)
Guidance Counselors: 0.0 (n/a to 1)
Current Spending: ($ per student per year):
  Total: $7,480; Instruction: $3,961; Support Services: $3,348
Enrollment, Drop-out Rates and Diploma Recipients by Race/Ethnicity

Category	Total	White	Black	Asian	AIAN	Hisp.
Enrollment (%)	100.0	69.1	7.2	10.1	0.2	13.5
Drop-out Rate (%)	n/a	n/a	n/a	n/a	n/a	n/a
H.S. Diplomas (#)	n/a	n/a	n/a	n/a	n/a	n/a

Zion Elementary SD 6
2200 Bethesda Blvd • Zion, IL 60099-2589
(847) 872-5455 • http://www.zion.k12.il.us/
Grade Span: PK-08; **Agency Type:** 1
Schools: 7
  6 Primary; 1 Middle; 0 High; 0 Other Level
  6 Regular; 1 Special Education; 0 Vocational; 0 Alternative
  0 Magnet; 0 Charter; 6 Title I Eligible; 6 School-wide Title I
Students: 2,934 (49.5% male; 50.4% female)
  Individual Education Program: 640 (21.8%);
  English Language Learner: n/a; Migrant: 0 (0.0%)
  Eligible for Free Lunch Program: 1,692 (57.7%)
  Eligible for Reduced-Price Lunch Program: 257 (8.8%)
Teachers: 151.6 (19.4 to 1)
Librarians/Media Specialists: 0.0 (n/a to 1)
Guidance Counselors: 0.0 (n/a to 1)
Current Spending: ($ per student per year):
  Total: $7,219; Instruction: $4,654; Support Services: $2,298
Enrollment, Drop-out Rates and Diploma Recipients by Race/Ethnicity

Category	Total	White	Black	Asian	AIAN	Hisp.
Enrollment (%)	100.0	22.7	47.5	1.1	0.2	28.5
Drop-out Rate (%)	n/a	n/a	n/a	n/a	n/a	n/a
H.S. Diplomas (#)	n/a	n/a	n/a	n/a	n/a	n/a

Zion-Benton Twp HSD 126
One Z-B Way • Zion, IL 60099-2387
(847) 746-1202 • http://www.zbths.k12.il.us/
Grade Span: 09-12; **Agency Type:** 1
Schools: 1
  0 Primary; 0 Middle; 1 High; 0 Other Level
  1 Regular; 0 Special Education; 0 Vocational; 0 Alternative
  0 Magnet; 0 Charter; 1 Title I Eligible; 0 School-wide Title I
Students: 2,396 (51.8% male; 48.1% female)
  Individual Education Program: 389 (16.2%);
  English Language Learner: n/a; Migrant: 0 (0.0%)
  Eligible for Free Lunch Program: 484 (20.2%)
  Eligible for Reduced-Price Lunch Program: 103 (4.3%)

Teachers: 125.8 (19.0 to 1)
Librarians/Media Specialists: 1.0 (2,396.0 to 1)
Guidance Counselors: 6.0 (399.3 to 1)
Current Spending: ($ per student per year):
  Total: $9,434; Instruction: $5,033; Support Services: $4,138
Enrollment, Drop-out Rates and Diploma Recipients by Race/Ethnicity

Category	Total	White	Black	Asian	AIAN	Hisp.
Enrollment (%)	100.0	56.9	25.4	2.3	0.6	14.8
Drop-out Rate (%)	6.9	5.9	8.1	2.0	16.7	9.1
H.S. Diplomas (#)	378	247	77	12	8	34

Lee County

Dixon Unit SD 170
1335 Franklin Gr Rd • Dixon, IL 61021-9149
(815) 284-7722 • http://www.leeogle.lth2.k12.il.us/directory/dixon.html
Grade Span: PK-12; **Agency Type:** 1
Schools: 5
  3 Primary; 1 Middle; 1 High; 0 Other Level
  5 Regular; 0 Special Education; 0 Vocational; 0 Alternative
  0 Magnet; 0 Charter; 3 Title I Eligible; 0 School-wide Title I
Students: 2,992 (50.7% male; 49.2% female)
  Individual Education Program: 415 (13.9%);
  English Language Learner: n/a; Migrant: 0 (0.0%)
  Eligible for Free Lunch Program: 738 (24.7%)
  Eligible for Reduced-Price Lunch Program: 192 (6.4%)
Teachers: 170.5 (17.5 to 1)
Librarians/Media Specialists: 1.0 (2,992.0 to 1)
Guidance Counselors: 5.0 (598.4 to 1)
Current Spending: ($ per student per year):
  Total: $7,307; Instruction: $4,565; Support Services: $2,567
Enrollment, Drop-out Rates and Diploma Recipients by Race/Ethnicity

Category	Total	White	Black	Asian	AIAN	Hisp.
Enrollment (%)	100.0	88.7	4.5	2.4	0.1	4.3
Drop-out Rate (%)	5.8	5.4	16.0	0.0	n/a	12.5
H.S. Diplomas (#)	221	205	3	6	0	7

Livingston County

Prairie Central CUSD 8
PO Box 496 • Forrest, IL 61741-0496
(815) 657-8237
Grade Span: PK-12; **Agency Type:** 1
Schools: 6
  3 Primary; 2 Middle; 1 High; 0 Other Level
  6 Regular; 0 Special Education; 0 Vocational; 0 Alternative
  0 Magnet; 0 Charter; 5 Title I Eligible; 0 School-wide Title I
Students: 1,889 (51.4% male; 48.5% female)
  Individual Education Program: 372 (19.7%);
  English Language Learner: n/a; Migrant: 0 (0.0%)
  Eligible for Free Lunch Program: 407 (21.5%)
  Eligible for Reduced-Price Lunch Program: 102 (5.4%)
Teachers: 131.8 (14.3 to 1)
Librarians/Media Specialists: 3.5 (539.7 to 1)
Guidance Counselors: 2.8 (674.6 to 1)
Current Spending: ($ per student per year):
  Total: $7,121; Instruction: $4,638; Support Services: $2,174
Enrollment, Drop-out Rates and Diploma Recipients by Race/Ethnicity

Category	Total	White	Black	Asian	AIAN	Hisp.
Enrollment (%)	100.0	93.8	1.4	0.6	0.4	3.9
Drop-out Rate (%)	2.2	2.2	0.0	0.0	0.0	6.7
H.S. Diplomas (#)	154	149	1	1	0	3

Macon County

Decatur SD 61
101 W Cerro Gordo St • Decatur, IL 62523-1001
(217) 424-3011 • http://www.dps61.org/
Grade Span: PK-12; **Agency Type:** 1
Schools: 26
  20 Primary; 3 Middle; 2 High; 1 Other Level
  24 Regular; 2 Special Education; 0 Vocational; 0 Alternative
  4 Magnet; 1 Charter; 21 Title I Eligible; 21 School-wide Title I
Students: 10,111 (50.8% male; 49.1% female)
  Individual Education Program: 1,693 (16.7%);
  English Language Learner: n/a; Migrant: 0 (0.0%)
  Eligible for Free Lunch Program: 5,163 (51.1%)
  Eligible for Reduced-Price Lunch Program: 662 (6.5%)
Teachers: 453.7 (22.3 to 1)
Librarians/Media Specialists: 3.0 (3,370.3 to 1)
Guidance Counselors: 13.5 (749.0 to 1)
Current Spending: ($ per student per year):
  Total: $6,140; Instruction: $3,123; Support Services: $2,760

Enrollment, Drop-out Rates and Diploma Recipients by Race/Ethnicity

Category	Total	White	Black	Asian	AIAN	Hisp.
Enrollment (%)	100.0	51.4	46.5	0.9	0.0	1.2
Drop-out Rate (%)	10.7	9.6	13.1	4.0	0.0	0.0
H.S. Diplomas (#)	521	352	161	3	1	4

Mt Zion Community Unit SD 3
455 Elm St • Mt Zion, IL 62549-1314
(217) 864-2366 • http://www.mtzion.k12.il.us/
Grade Span: PK-12; **Agency Type:** 1
Schools: 6
  3 Primary; 2 Middle; 1 High; 0 Other Level
  6 Regular; 0 Special Education; 0 Vocational; 0 Alternative
  0 Magnet; 0 Charter; 3 Title I Eligible; 0 School-wide Title I
Students: 2,458   (50.0% male; 50.0% female)
  Individual Education Program: 216 (8.8%);
  English Language Learner: n/a; Migrant: 0 (0.0%)
  Eligible for Free Lunch Program: 174 (7.1%)
  Eligible for Reduced-Price Lunch Program: 69 (2.8%)
Teachers: 123.2 (20.0 to 1)
Librarians/Media Specialists: 3.0 (819.3 to 1)
Guidance Counselors: 4.0 (614.5 to 1)
Current Spending: ($ per student per year):
  Total: $5,884; Instruction: $3,230; Support Services: $2,334
Enrollment, Drop-out Rates and Diploma Recipients by Race/Ethnicity

Category	Total	White	Black	Asian	AIAN	Hisp.
Enrollment (%)	100.0	97.3	1.3	1.0	0.0	0.3
Drop-out Rate (%)	1.5	1.5	0.0	0.0	n/a	0.0
H.S. Diplomas (#)	195	192	0	3	0	0

Macoupin County

Carlinville CUSD 1
18456 Shipman Rd • Carlinville, IL 62626-1731
(217) 854-9823 • http://www.carlinville.macoupin.k12.il.us/
Grade Span: PK-12; **Agency Type:** 1
Schools: 5
  2 Primary; 2 Middle; 1 High; 0 Other Level
  5 Regular; 0 Special Education; 0 Vocational; 0 Alternative
  0 Magnet; 0 Charter; 3 Title I Eligible; 0 School-wide Title I
Students: 1,600   (51.8% male; 48.1% female)
  Individual Education Program: 222 (13.9%);
  English Language Learner: n/a; Migrant: 0 (0.0%)
  Eligible for Free Lunch Program: 369 (23.1%)
  Eligible for Reduced-Price Lunch Program: 103 (6.4%)
Teachers: 85.5 (18.7 to 1)
Librarians/Media Specialists: 2.0 (800.0 to 1)
Guidance Counselors: 2.0 (800.0 to 1)
Current Spending: ($ per student per year):
  Total: $6,124; Instruction: $3,659; Support Services: $2,171
Enrollment, Drop-out Rates and Diploma Recipients by Race/Ethnicity

Category	Total	White	Black	Asian	AIAN	Hisp.
Enrollment (%)	100.0	96.4	2.4	0.4	0.0	0.8
Drop-out Rate (%)	2.4	2.3	14.3	0.0	n/a	0.0
H.S. Diplomas (#)	134	133	1	0	0	0

Southwestern CUSD 9
PO Box 99 • Piasa, IL 62079-0099
(618) 729-3221 • http://www.sw.macoupin.k12.il.us/
Grade Span: PK-12; **Agency Type:** 1
Schools: 6
  4 Primary; 1 Middle; 1 High; 0 Other Level
  6 Regular; 0 Special Education; 0 Vocational; 0 Alternative
  0 Magnet; 0 Charter; 3 Title I Eligible; 0 School-wide Title I
Students: 1,798   (51.7% male; 48.2% female)
  Individual Education Program: 285 (15.9%);
  English Language Learner: n/a; Migrant: 0 (0.0%)
  Eligible for Free Lunch Program: 261 (14.5%)
  Eligible for Reduced-Price Lunch Program: 102 (5.7%)
Teachers: 99.6 (18.1 to 1)
Librarians/Media Specialists: 2.0 (899.0 to 1)
Guidance Counselors: 2.0 (899.0 to 1)
Current Spending: ($ per student per year):
  Total: $7,276; Instruction: $4,581; Support Services: $2,348
Enrollment, Drop-out Rates and Diploma Recipients by Race/Ethnicity

Category	Total	White	Black	Asian	AIAN	Hisp.
Enrollment (%)	100.0	98.2	1.3	0.4	0.0	0.1
Drop-out Rate (%)	2.9	2.9	0.0	0.0	n/a	n/a
H.S. Diplomas (#)	150	148	2	0	0	0

Madison County

Alton Community Unit SD 11
PO Box 9028 • Alton, IL 62002-9028
(618) 474-2600 • http://www.alton.madison.k12.il.us/
Grade Span: PK-12; **Agency Type:** 1
Schools: 13
  10 Primary; 2 Middle; 1 High; 0 Other Level
  11 Regular; 2 Special Education; 0 Vocational; 0 Alternative
  0 Magnet; 0 Charter; 11 Title I Eligible; 11 School-wide Title I
Students: 6,906   (51.1% male; 48.8% female)
  Individual Education Program: 1,507 (21.8%);
  English Language Learner: n/a; Migrant: 0 (0.0%)
  Eligible for Free Lunch Program: 2,635 (38.2%)
  Eligible for Reduced-Price Lunch Program: 408 (5.9%)
Teachers: 420.6 (16.4 to 1)
Librarians/Media Specialists: 5.0 (1,381.2 to 1)
Guidance Counselors: 6.0 (1,151.0 to 1)
Current Spending: ($ per student per year):
  Total: $7,621; Instruction: $4,416; Support Services: $2,940
Enrollment, Drop-out Rates and Diploma Recipients by Race/Ethnicity

Category	Total	White	Black	Asian	AIAN	Hisp.
Enrollment (%)	100.0	61.9	36.5	0.6	0.1	0.8
Drop-out Rate (%)	6.7	4.2	12.6	0.0	33.3	0.0
H.S. Diplomas (#)	432	323	102	2	1	4

Bethalto CUSD 8
322 E Central St • Bethalto, IL 62010-1399
(618) 377-7200 • http://www.bethalto.org/education/district/
Grade Span: PK-12; **Agency Type:** 1
Schools: 6
  2 Primary; 3 Middle; 1 High; 0 Other Level
  6 Regular; 0 Special Education; 0 Vocational; 0 Alternative
  0 Magnet; 0 Charter; 2 Title I Eligible; 0 School-wide Title I
Students: 2,796   (51.5% male; 48.4% female)
  Individual Education Program: 551 (19.7%);
  English Language Learner: n/a; Migrant: 0 (0.0%)
  Eligible for Free Lunch Program: 556 (19.9%)
  Eligible for Reduced-Price Lunch Program: 128 (4.6%)
Teachers: 171.9 (16.3 to 1)
Librarians/Media Specialists: 2.0 (1,398.0 to 1)
Guidance Counselors: 1.0 (2,796.0 to 1)
Current Spending: ($ per student per year):
  Total: $7,002; Instruction: $4,132; Support Services: $2,520
Enrollment, Drop-out Rates and Diploma Recipients by Race/Ethnicity

Category	Total	White	Black	Asian	AIAN	Hisp.
Enrollment (%)	100.0	95.7	3.0	0.7	0.0	0.6
Drop-out Rate (%)	4.3	4.2	7.7	0.0	n/a	0.0
H.S. Diplomas (#)	217	214	3	0	0	0

Collinsville CUSD 10
201 W Clay St • Collinsville, IL 62234-3219
(618) 346-6350 • http://isd.cusd10.madison.k12.il.us/CUSD/
Grade Span: PK-12; **Agency Type:** 1
Schools: 11
  9 Primary; 1 Middle; 1 High; 0 Other Level
  11 Regular; 0 Special Education; 0 Vocational; 0 Alternative
  0 Magnet; 0 Charter; 6 Title I Eligible; 5 School-wide Title I
Students: 6,078   (52.5% male; 47.4% female)
  Individual Education Program: 1,055 (17.4%);
  English Language Learner: n/a; Migrant: 0 (0.0%)
  Eligible for Free Lunch Program: 1,848 (30.4%)
  Eligible for Reduced-Price Lunch Program: 471 (7.7%)
Teachers: 342.7 (17.7 to 1)
Librarians/Media Specialists: 2.0 (3,039.0 to 1)
Guidance Counselors: 4.0 (1,519.5 to 1)
Current Spending: ($ per student per year):
  Total: $6,923; Instruction: $3,991; Support Services: $2,652
Enrollment, Drop-out Rates and Diploma Recipients by Race/Ethnicity

Category	Total	White	Black	Asian	AIAN	Hisp.
Enrollment (%)	100.0	81.5	9.3	0.9	0.2	8.1
Drop-out Rate (%)	4.4	3.7	12.0	0.0	0.0	11.1
H.S. Diplomas (#)	360	319	20	5	0	16

Edwardsville CUSD 7
708 St Louis St • Edwardsville, IL 62025-1427
(618) 656-1182 • http://www.ecusd7.org/
Grade Span: PK-12; **Agency Type:** 1
Schools: 12
  7 Primary; 3 Middle; 2 High; 0 Other Level
  11 Regular; 1 Special Education; 0 Vocational; 0 Alternative
  0 Magnet; 0 Charter; 4 Title I Eligible; 0 School-wide Title I
Students: 6,992   (50.9% male; 49.0% female)
  Individual Education Program: 1,069 (15.3%);
  English Language Learner: n/a; Migrant: 0 (0.0%)

Eligible for Free Lunch Program: 742 (10.6%)
Eligible for Reduced-Price Lunch Program: 276 (3.9%)
Teachers: 400.8 (17.4 to 1)
Librarians/Media Specialists: 4.0 (1,748.0 to 1)
Guidance Counselors: 5.2 (1,344.6 to 1)
Current Spending: ($ per student per year):
Total: $6,711; Instruction: $3,929; Support Services: $2,555
Enrollment, Drop-out Rates and Diploma Recipients by Race/Ethnicity

Category	Total	White	Black	Asian	AIAN	Hisp.
Enrollment (%)	100.0	87.8	9.3	2.0	0.1	0.9
Drop-out Rate (%)	3.1	3.5	0.6	0.0	n/a	0.0
H.S. Diplomas (#)	491	439	39	8	0	5

Granite City CUSD 9
1947 Adams St • Granite City, IL 62040-3397
(618) 451-5800 • http://www.granitecityschools.org/
Grade Span: PK-12; **Agency Type:** 1
Schools: 10
7 Primary; 2 Middle; 1 High; 0 Other Level
10 Regular; 0 Special Education; 0 Vocational; 0 Alternative
0 Magnet; 0 Charter; 7 Title I Eligible; 5 School-wide Title I
Students: 7,583 (51.5% male; 48.4% female)
Individual Education Program: 1,324 (17.5%);
English Language Learner: n/a; Migrant: 4 (0.1%)
Eligible for Free Lunch Program: 2,486 (32.8%)
Eligible for Reduced-Price Lunch Program: 553 (7.3%)
Teachers: 361.0 (21.0 to 1)
Librarians/Media Specialists: 2.0 (3,791.5 to 1)
Guidance Counselors: 7.0 (1,083.3 to 1)
Current Spending: ($ per student per year):
Total: $6,830; Instruction: $4,046; Support Services: $2,437
Enrollment, Drop-out Rates and Diploma Recipients by Race/Ethnicity

Category	Total	White	Black	Asian	AIAN	Hisp.
Enrollment (%)	100.0	89.7	6.4	0.8	0.2	2.9
Drop-out Rate (%)	8.4	8.1	16.3	0.0	0.0	15.4
H.S. Diplomas (#)	462	448	10	2	0	2

Highland Community Unit SD 5
PO Box 149 • Highland, IL 62249-0149
(618) 654-2106 • http://www.highland.madison.k12.il.us/
Grade Span: PK-12; **Agency Type:** 1
Schools: 8
5 Primary; 2 Middle; 1 High; 0 Other Level
8 Regular; 0 Special Education; 0 Vocational; 0 Alternative
0 Magnet; 0 Charter; 3 Title I Eligible; 0 School-wide Title I
Students: 3,008 (50.6% male; 49.3% female)
Individual Education Program: 457 (15.2%);
English Language Learner: n/a; Migrant: 0 (0.0%)
Eligible for Free Lunch Program: 319 (10.6%)
Eligible for Reduced-Price Lunch Program: 155 (5.2%)
Teachers: 189.6 (15.9 to 1)
Librarians/Media Specialists: 3.0 (1,002.7 to 1)
Guidance Counselors: 4.0 (752.0 to 1)
Current Spending: ($ per student per year):
Total: $6,957; Instruction: $4,252; Support Services: $2,393
Enrollment, Drop-out Rates and Diploma Recipients by Race/Ethnicity

Category	Total	White	Black	Asian	AIAN	Hisp.
Enrollment (%)	100.0	98.1	0.4	0.7	0.0	0.7
Drop-out Rate (%)	3.1	3.2	0.0	0.0	n/a	0.0
H.S. Diplomas (#)	234	230	2	1	0	1

Roxana Community Unit SD 1
401 Chaffer Ave • Roxana, IL 62084-1199
(618) 254-7544
Grade Span: PK-12; **Agency Type:** 1
Schools: 4
2 Primary; 1 Middle; 1 High; 0 Other Level
4 Regular; 0 Special Education; 0 Vocational; 0 Alternative
0 Magnet; 0 Charter; 2 Title I Eligible; 0 School-wide Title I
Students: 1,877 (49.4% male; 50.5% female)
Individual Education Program: 403 (21.5%);
English Language Learner: n/a; Migrant: 0 (0.0%)
Eligible for Free Lunch Program: 500 (26.6%)
Eligible for Reduced-Price Lunch Program: 156 (8.3%)
Teachers: 114.0 (16.5 to 1)
Librarians/Media Specialists: 2.0 (938.5 to 1)
Guidance Counselors: 3.0 (625.7 to 1)
Current Spending: ($ per student per year):
Total: $7,540; Instruction: $4,554; Support Services: $2,653
Enrollment, Drop-out Rates and Diploma Recipients by Race/Ethnicity

Category	Total	White	Black	Asian	AIAN	Hisp.
Enrollment (%)	100.0	97.7	1.0	0.2	0.2	0.9
Drop-out Rate (%)	7.8	7.9	0.0	0.0	n/a	0.0
H.S. Diplomas (#)	129	129	0	0	0	0

Triad Community Unit SD 2
PO Box 360 • Troy, IL 62294-0360
(618) 667-8851 • http://www.triad.madison.k12.il.us/
Grade Span: PK-12; **Agency Type:** 1
Schools: 7
5 Primary; 1 Middle; 1 High; 0 Other Level
7 Regular; 0 Special Education; 0 Vocational; 0 Alternative
0 Magnet; 0 Charter; 4 Title I Eligible; 0 School-wide Title I
Students: 3,768 (51.1% male; 48.8% female)
Individual Education Program: 579 (15.4%);
English Language Learner: n/a; Migrant: 0 (0.0%)
Eligible for Free Lunch Program: 367 (9.7%)
Eligible for Reduced-Price Lunch Program: 182 (4.8%)
Teachers: 214.5 (17.6 to 1)
Librarians/Media Specialists: 1.0 (3,768.0 to 1)
Guidance Counselors: 4.0 (942.0 to 1)
Current Spending: ($ per student per year):
Total: $6,480; Instruction: $4,137; Support Services: $2,048
Enrollment, Drop-out Rates and Diploma Recipients by Race/Ethnicity

Category	Total	White	Black	Asian	AIAN	Hisp.
Enrollment (%)	100.0	95.7	2.1	1.2	0.1	0.9
Drop-out Rate (%)	1.0	1.1	0.0	0.0	0.0	0.0
H.S. Diplomas (#)	273	266	3	2	0	2

Massac County

Massac Unit District #1
PO Box 530 • Metropolis, IL 62960-0530
(618) 524-9376 • http://www.unit1.massac.k12.il.us/
Grade Span: PK-12; **Agency Type:** 1
Schools: 9
7 Primary; 1 Middle; 1 High; 0 Other Level
7 Regular; 2 Special Education; 0 Vocational; 0 Alternative
1 Magnet; 0 Charter; 1 Title I Eligible; 1 School-wide Title I
Students: 2,369 (51.0% male; 48.9% female)
Individual Education Program: 402 (17.0%);
English Language Learner: n/a; Migrant: 0 (0.0%)
Eligible for Free Lunch Program: 544 (23.0%)
Eligible for Reduced-Price Lunch Program: 92 (3.9%)
Teachers: 134.5 (17.6 to 1)
Librarians/Media Specialists: 1.0 (2,369.0 to 1)
Guidance Counselors: 3.0 (789.7 to 1)
Current Spending: ($ per student per year):
Total: $6,267; Instruction: $3,583; Support Services: $2,380
Enrollment, Drop-out Rates and Diploma Recipients by Race/Ethnicity

Category	Total	White	Black	Asian	AIAN	Hisp.
Enrollment (%)	100.0	88.8	9.6	0.3	0.0	1.2
Drop-out Rate (%)	1.2	1.1	2.1	0.0	0.0	0.0
H.S. Diplomas (#)	139	130	8	0	0	1

Mcdonough County

Macomb Community Unit SD 185
323 W Washington • Macomb, IL 61455-2197
(309) 833-4161 • http://www.macomb.com/~dist185/
Grade Span: PK-12; **Agency Type:** 1
Schools: 5
3 Primary; 1 Middle; 1 High; 0 Other Level
4 Regular; 1 Special Education; 0 Vocational; 0 Alternative
0 Magnet; 0 Charter; 2 Title I Eligible; 1 School-wide Title I
Students: 1,965 (50.1% male; 49.8% female)
Individual Education Program: 383 (19.5%);
English Language Learner: n/a; Migrant: 0 (0.0%)
Eligible for Free Lunch Program: 582 (29.6%)
Eligible for Reduced-Price Lunch Program: 141 (7.2%)
Teachers: 131.4 (15.0 to 1)
Librarians/Media Specialists: 2.0 (982.5 to 1)
Guidance Counselors: 5.0 (393.0 to 1)
Current Spending: ($ per student per year):
Total: $8,244; Instruction: $4,812; Support Services: $3,147
Enrollment, Drop-out Rates and Diploma Recipients by Race/Ethnicity

Category	Total	White	Black	Asian	AIAN	Hisp.
Enrollment (%)	100.0	85.5	10.1	3.1	0.2	1.1
Drop-out Rate (%)	2.5	2.6	0.0	0.0	100.0	0.0
H.S. Diplomas (#)	128	115	8	3	0	2

Mchenry County

Cary CCSD 26
400 Haber Dr • Cary, IL 60013-2445
(847) 639-7788 •
http://www.northstarnet.org/cpqhome/schools/distwelcome.html
Grade Span: PK-08; **Agency Type:** 1
Schools: 7
5 Primary; 2 Middle; 0 High; 0 Other Level

7 Regular; 0 Special Education; 0 Vocational; 0 Alternative
0 Magnet; 0 Charter; 0 Title I Eligible; 0 School-wide Title I
Students: 3,663 (52.9% male; 47.0% female)
   Individual Education Program: 715 (19.5%);
   English Language Learner: n/a; Migrant: 0 (0.0%)
   Eligible for Free Lunch Program: 174 (4.8%)
   Eligible for Reduced-Price Lunch Program: 73 (2.0%)
Teachers: 218.5 (16.8 to 1)
Librarians/Media Specialists: 7.0 (523.3 to 1)
Guidance Counselors: 0.0 (n/a to 1)
Current Spending: ($ per student per year):
   Total: $7,216; Instruction: $4,289; Support Services: $2,747
Enrollment, Drop-out Rates and Diploma Recipients by Race/Ethnicity

Category	Total	White	Black	Asian	AIAN	Hisp.
Enrollment (%)	100.0	90.9	0.8	1.6	0.0	6.7
Drop-out Rate (%)	n/a	n/a	n/a	n/a	n/a	n/a
H.S. Diplomas (#)	n/a	n/a	n/a	n/a	n/a	n/a

Community High SD 155
1 S Virginia Rd • Crystal Lake, IL 60014-6195
(815) 455-8500 • http://www.d155.org/
Grade Span: 09-12; **Agency Type:** 1
Schools: 4
   0 Primary; 0 Middle; 4 High; 0 Other Level
   4 Regular; 0 Special Education; 0 Vocational; 0 Alternative
   0 Magnet; 0 Charter; 0 Title I Eligible; 0 School-wide Title I
Students: 6,343 (51.3% male; 48.6% female)
   Individual Education Program: 844 (13.3%);
   English Language Learner: n/a; Migrant: 0 (0.0%)
   Eligible for Free Lunch Program: 195 (3.1%)
   Eligible for Reduced-Price Lunch Program: 36 (0.6%)
Teachers: 360.3 (17.6 to 1)
Librarians/Media Specialists: 4.0 (1,585.8 to 1)
Guidance Counselors: 19.0 (333.8 to 1)
Current Spending: ($ per student per year):
   Total: $9,148; Instruction: $6,394; Support Services: $2,501
Enrollment, Drop-out Rates and Diploma Recipients by Race/Ethnicity

Category	Total	White	Black	Asian	AIAN	Hisp.
Enrollment (%)	100.0	92.9	0.5	1.7	0.1	4.7
Drop-out Rate (%)	2.1	1.9	4.5	1.2	0.0	8.1
H.S. Diplomas (#)	1,226	1,158	7	14	0	47

Consolidated SD 158
11302 Lincoln St • Huntley, IL 60142-9792
(847) 659-6158 • http://www.d158.k12.il.us/
Grade Span: PK-12; **Agency Type:** 1
Schools: 6
   4 Primary; 1 Middle; 1 High; 0 Other Level
   5 Regular; 1 Special Education; 0 Vocational; 0 Alternative
   0 Magnet; 0 Charter; 1 Title I Eligible; 0 School-wide Title I
Students: 5,416 (51.3% male; 48.6% female)
   Individual Education Program: 630 (11.6%);
   English Language Learner: n/a; Migrant: 0 (0.0%)
   Eligible for Free Lunch Program: 123 (2.3%)
   Eligible for Reduced-Price Lunch Program: 80 (1.5%)
Teachers: 331.8 (16.3 to 1)
Librarians/Media Specialists: 5.5 (984.7 to 1)
Guidance Counselors: 7.0 (773.7 to 1)
Current Spending: ($ per student per year):
   Total: $7,972; Instruction: $4,400; Support Services: $3,360
Enrollment, Drop-out Rates and Diploma Recipients by Race/Ethnicity

Category	Total	White	Black	Asian	AIAN	Hisp.
Enrollment (%)	100.0	83.8	1.8	4.8	0.4	9.1
Drop-out Rate (%)	1.7	1.8	7.1	3.1	0.0	0.0
H.S. Diplomas (#)	130	106	2	4	0	18

Crystal Lake CCSD 47
300 Commerce Dr • Crystal Lake, IL 60014-8041
(815) 459-6070 • http://www.d47schools.org/
Grade Span: PK-08; **Agency Type:** 1
Schools: 12
   9 Primary; 3 Middle; 0 High; 0 Other Level
   12 Regular; 0 Special Education; 0 Vocational; 0 Alternative
   0 Magnet; 0 Charter; 5 Title I Eligible; 0 School-wide Title I
Students: 9,115 (51.6% male; 48.3% female)
   Individual Education Program: 1,275 (14.0%);
   English Language Learner: n/a; Migrant: 0 (0.0%)
   Eligible for Free Lunch Program: 546 (6.0%)
   Eligible for Reduced-Price Lunch Program: 217 (2.4%)
Teachers: 524.9 (17.4 to 1)
Librarians/Media Specialists: 12.0 (759.6 to 1)
Guidance Counselors: 0.0 (n/a to 1)
Current Spending: ($ per student per year):
   Total: $6,525; Instruction: $4,100; Support Services: $2,241

Enrollment, Drop-out Rates and Diploma Recipients by Race/Ethnicity

Category	Total	White	Black	Asian	AIAN	Hisp.
Enrollment (%)	100.0	89.1	1.3	2.7	0.0	6.9
Drop-out Rate (%)	n/a	n/a	n/a	n/a	n/a	n/a
H.S. Diplomas (#)	n/a	n/a	n/a	n/a	n/a	n/a

Harvard CUSD 50
1101 N Jefferson St • Harvard, IL 60033-1798
(815) 943-4022 • http://www.d50.mchenry.k12.il.us/
Grade Span: PK-12; **Agency Type:** 1
Schools: 5
   3 Primary; 1 Middle; 1 High; 0 Other Level
   5 Regular; 0 Special Education; 0 Vocational; 0 Alternative
   0 Magnet; 0 Charter; 2 Title I Eligible; 0 School-wide Title I
Students: 2,284 (53.0% male; 46.9% female)
   Individual Education Program: 369 (16.2%);
   English Language Learner: n/a; Migrant: 70 (3.1%)
   Eligible for Free Lunch Program: 776 (34.0%)
   Eligible for Reduced-Price Lunch Program: 159 (7.0%)
Teachers: 132.8 (17.2 to 1)
Librarians/Media Specialists: 3.0 (761.3 to 1)
Guidance Counselors: 3.0 (761.3 to 1)
Current Spending: ($ per student per year):
   Total: $6,694; Instruction: $4,305; Support Services: $2,115
Enrollment, Drop-out Rates and Diploma Recipients by Race/Ethnicity

Category	Total	White	Black	Asian	AIAN	Hisp.
Enrollment (%)	100.0	54.1	0.8	0.7	0.0	44.4
Drop-out Rate (%)	4.7	3.1	0.0	0.0	n/a	9.9
H.S. Diplomas (#)	121	109	2	0	0	10

Johnsburg CUSD 12
2222 W Church St • Johnsburg, IL 60050-1910
(815) 385-6916 • http://www.jburgd12.k12.il.us/
Grade Span: PK-12; **Agency Type:** 1
Schools: 4
   2 Primary; 1 Middle; 1 High; 0 Other Level
   4 Regular; 0 Special Education; 0 Vocational; 0 Alternative
   0 Magnet; 0 Charter; 2 Title I Eligible; 0 School-wide Title I
Students: 2,695 (51.6% male; 48.3% female)
   Individual Education Program: 368 (13.7%);
   English Language Learner: n/a; Migrant: 0 (0.0%)
   Eligible for Free Lunch Program: 139 (5.2%)
   Eligible for Reduced-Price Lunch Program: 52 (1.9%)
Teachers: 145.7 (18.5 to 1)
Librarians/Media Specialists: 3.0 (898.3 to 1)
Guidance Counselors: 3.0 (898.3 to 1)
Current Spending: ($ per student per year):
   Total: $7,284; Instruction: $4,823; Support Services: $2,224
Enrollment, Drop-out Rates and Diploma Recipients by Race/Ethnicity

Category	Total	White	Black	Asian	AIAN	Hisp.
Enrollment (%)	100.0	96.5	0.3	0.3	0.1	2.7
Drop-out Rate (%)	1.8	1.7	0.0	0.0	n/a	5.3
H.S. Diplomas (#)	181	175	1	2	0	3

Mchenry CCSD 15
1011 N Green St • Mc Henry, IL 60050-5434
(815) 385-7210
Grade Span: PK-08; **Agency Type:** 1
Schools: 8
   5 Primary; 3 Middle; 0 High; 0 Other Level
   8 Regular; 0 Special Education; 0 Vocational; 0 Alternative
   0 Magnet; 0 Charter; 6 Title I Eligible; 0 School-wide Title I
Students: 4,723 (52.4% male; 47.5% female)
   Individual Education Program: 930 (19.7%);
   English Language Learner: n/a; Migrant: 0 (0.0%)
   Eligible for Free Lunch Program: 523 (11.1%)
   Eligible for Reduced-Price Lunch Program: 97 (2.1%)
Teachers: 259.6 (18.2 to 1)
Librarians/Media Specialists: 6.0 (787.2 to 1)
Guidance Counselors: 0.0 (n/a to 1)
Current Spending: ($ per student per year):
   Total: $6,292; Instruction: $4,041; Support Services: $2,046
Enrollment, Drop-out Rates and Diploma Recipients by Race/Ethnicity

Category	Total	White	Black	Asian	AIAN	Hisp.
Enrollment (%)	100.0	87.7	1.2	1.2	0.4	9.6
Drop-out Rate (%)	n/a	n/a	n/a	n/a	n/a	n/a
H.S. Diplomas (#)	n/a	n/a	n/a	n/a	n/a	n/a

Mchenry Community HSD 156
4716 Crystal Lake Rd • Mc Henry, IL 60050-5427
(815) 385-7900
Grade Span: 09-12; **Agency Type:** 1
Schools: 2
   0 Primary; 0 Middle; 2 High; 0 Other Level
   2 Regular; 0 Special Education; 0 Vocational; 0 Alternative

0 Magnet; 0 Charter; 1 Title I Eligible; 0 School-wide Title I
Students: 2,325   (52.8% male; 47.1% female)
   Individual Education Program: 409 (17.6%);
   English Language Learner: n/a; Migrant: 0 (0.0%)
   Eligible for Free Lunch Program: n/a
   Eligible for Reduced-Price Lunch Program: n/a
Teachers: 133.4 (17.4 to 1)
Librarians/Media Specialists: 2.0 (1,162.5 to 1)
Guidance Counselors: 6.0 (387.5 to 1)
Current Spending: ($ per student per year):
   Total: $8,497; Instruction: $5,258; Support Services: $3,018

Enrollment, Drop-out Rates and Diploma Recipients by Race/Ethnicity

Category	Total	White	Black	Asian	AIAN	Hisp.
Enrollment (%)	100.0	92.4	0.3	1.0	0.3	6.0
Drop-out Rate (%)	3.0	2.6	0.0	0.0	33.3	11.1
H.S. Diplomas (#)	453	433	0	3	1	16

Nippersink SD 2
10006 Main St • Richmond, IL 60071-9503
(815) 678-4242
Grade Span: KG-08; **Agency Type:** 1
Schools: 3
   2 Primary; 1 Middle; 0 High; 0 Other Level
   3 Regular; 0 Special Education; 0 Vocational; 0 Alternative
   0 Magnet; 0 Charter; 1 Title I Eligible; 0 School-wide Title I
Students: 1,585   (52.2% male; 47.7% female)
   Individual Education Program: 221 (13.9%);
   English Language Learner: n/a; Migrant: 0 (0.0%)
   Eligible for Free Lunch Program: 52 (3.3%)
   Eligible for Reduced-Price Lunch Program: 17 (1.1%)
Teachers: 102.5 (15.5 to 1)
Librarians/Media Specialists: 1.0 (1,585.0 to 1)
Guidance Counselors: 1.0 (1,585.0 to 1)
Current Spending: ($ per student per year):
   Total: $6,796; Instruction: $3,995; Support Services: $2,617

Enrollment, Drop-out Rates and Diploma Recipients by Race/Ethnicity

Category	Total	White	Black	Asian	AIAN	Hisp.
Enrollment (%)	100.0	96.2	0.6	0.8	0.0	2.5
Drop-out Rate (%)	n/a	n/a	n/a	n/a	n/a	n/a
H.S. Diplomas (#)	n/a	n/a	n/a	n/a	n/a	n/a

Woodstock CUSD 200
227 W Judd St • Woodstock, IL 60098-3799
(815) 337-5406 • http://www.d200.mchenry.k12.il.us/
Grade Span: PK-12; **Agency Type:** 1
Schools: 9
   6 Primary; 2 Middle; 1 High; 0 Other Level
   9 Regular; 0 Special Education; 0 Vocational; 0 Alternative
   0 Magnet; 0 Charter; 4 Title I Eligible; 0 School-wide Title I
Students: 5,831   (52.3% male; 47.6% female)
   Individual Education Program: 913 (15.7%);
   English Language Learner: n/a; Migrant: 5 (0.1%)
   Eligible for Free Lunch Program: 1,133 (19.4%)
   Eligible for Reduced-Price Lunch Program: 408 (7.0%)
Teachers: 321.4 (18.1 to 1)
Librarians/Media Specialists: 7.5 (777.5 to 1)
Guidance Counselors: 8.0 (728.9 to 1)
Current Spending: ($ per student per year):
   Total: $7,744; Instruction: $4,610; Support Services: $2,857

Enrollment, Drop-out Rates and Diploma Recipients by Race/Ethnicity

Category	Total	White	Black	Asian	AIAN	Hisp.
Enrollment (%)	100.0	75.0	1.5	1.4	0.3	21.8
Drop-out Rate (%)	5.6	5.0	21.4	6.9	33.3	7.2
H.S. Diplomas (#)	303	259	2	4	0	38

Mclean County

Bloomington SD 87
300 E Monroe St • Bloomington, IL 61701-4083
(309) 827-6031 • http://www.district87.org/
Grade Span: PK-12; **Agency Type:** 1
Schools: 9
   7 Primary; 1 Middle; 1 High; 0 Other Level
   8 Regular; 1 Special Education; 0 Vocational; 0 Alternative
   0 Magnet; 0 Charter; 3 Title I Eligible; 2 School-wide Title I
Students: 5,674   (51.6% male; 48.3% female)
   Individual Education Program: 1,003 (17.7%);
   English Language Learner: n/a; Migrant: 0 (0.0%)
   Eligible for Free Lunch Program: 1,809 (31.9%)
   Eligible for Reduced-Price Lunch Program: 420 (7.4%)
Teachers: 355.5 (16.0 to 1)
Librarians/Media Specialists: 7.0 (810.6 to 1)
Guidance Counselors: 11.6 (489.1 to 1)
Current Spending: ($ per student per year):
   Total: $8,104; Instruction: $4,899; Support Services: $2,804

Enrollment, Drop-out Rates and Diploma Recipients by Race/Ethnicity

Category	Total	White	Black	Asian	AIAN	Hisp.
Enrollment (%)	100.0	64.6	24.1	4.3	0.0	6.9
Drop-out Rate (%)	5.0	4.1	9.6	0.0	0.0	1.4
H.S. Diplomas (#)	264	215	37	4	0	8

Mclean County Unit Dist No 5
1809 W Hovey Ave • Normal, IL 61761-4339
(309) 452-4476 • http://www.unit5.org/
Grade Span: PK-12; **Agency Type:** 1
Schools: 21
   16 Primary; 3 Middle; 2 High; 0 Other Level
   21 Regular; 0 Special Education; 0 Vocational; 0 Alternative
   0 Magnet; 0 Charter; 6 Title I Eligible; 2 School-wide Title I
Students: 10,932   (51.9% male; 48.0% female)
   Individual Education Program: 1,683 (15.4%);
   English Language Learner: n/a; Migrant: 0 (0.0%)
   Eligible for Free Lunch Program: 1,517 (13.9%)
   Eligible for Reduced-Price Lunch Program: 340 (3.1%)
Teachers: 726.1 (15.1 to 1)
Librarians/Media Specialists: 18.0 (607.3 to 1)
Guidance Counselors: 15.0 (728.8 to 1)
Current Spending: ($ per student per year):
   Total: $7,720; Instruction: $4,755; Support Services: $2,715

Enrollment, Drop-out Rates and Diploma Recipients by Race/Ethnicity

Category	Total	White	Black	Asian	AIAN	Hisp.
Enrollment (%)	100.0	78.2	13.8	3.8	0.2	4.1
Drop-out Rate (%)	5.4	4.5	12.3	9.5	0.0	9.1
H.S. Diplomas (#)	615	552	37	15	0	11

Olympia CUSD 16
903 E 800 N Rd • Stanford, IL 61774-9612
(309) 379-6011 • http://www.olympia.org/
Grade Span: PK-12; **Agency Type:** 1
Schools: 8
   6 Primary; 1 Middle; 1 High; 0 Other Level
   8 Regular; 0 Special Education; 0 Vocational; 0 Alternative
   0 Magnet; 0 Charter; 5 Title I Eligible; 0 School-wide Title I
Students: 2,231   (51.2% male; 48.7% female)
   Individual Education Program: 452 (20.3%);
   English Language Learner: n/a; Migrant: 0 (0.0%)
   Eligible for Free Lunch Program: 336 (15.1%)
   Eligible for Reduced-Price Lunch Program: 134 (6.0%)
Teachers: 151.0 (14.8 to 1)
Librarians/Media Specialists: 2.0 (1,115.5 to 1)
Guidance Counselors: 3.0 (743.7 to 1)
Current Spending: ($ per student per year):
   Total: $7,754; Instruction: $4,561; Support Services: $2,897

Enrollment, Drop-out Rates and Diploma Recipients by Race/Ethnicity

Category	Total	White	Black	Asian	AIAN	Hisp.
Enrollment (%)	100.0	98.1	0.4	0.4	0.0	1.0
Drop-out Rate (%)	4.5	4.5	0.0	0.0	0.0	0.0
H.S. Diplomas (#)	143	142	1	0	0	0

Monroe County

Columbia Community Unit SD 4
100 Parkview Dr • Columbia, IL 62236-1130
(618) 281-4772 • http://admin.chseagles.com/
Grade Span: PK-12; **Agency Type:** 1
Schools: 3
   1 Primary; 1 Middle; 1 High; 0 Other Level
   3 Regular; 0 Special Education; 0 Vocational; 0 Alternative
   0 Magnet; 0 Charter; 1 Title I Eligible; 0 School-wide Title I
Students: 1,717   (52.3% male; 47.6% female)
   Individual Education Program: 197 (11.5%);
   English Language Learner: n/a; Migrant: 0 (0.0%)
   Eligible for Free Lunch Program: 69 (4.0%)
   Eligible for Reduced-Price Lunch Program: 23 (1.3%)
Teachers: 104.6 (16.4 to 1)
Librarians/Media Specialists: 1.0 (1,717.0 to 1)
Guidance Counselors: 3.0 (572.3 to 1)
Current Spending: ($ per student per year):
   Total: $6,481; Instruction: $3,901; Support Services: $2,368

Enrollment, Drop-out Rates and Diploma Recipients by Race/Ethnicity

Category	Total	White	Black	Asian	AIAN	Hisp.
Enrollment (%)	100.0	97.7	0.4	0.8	0.3	0.8
Drop-out Rate (%)	1.4	1.5	0.0	0.0	n/a	0.0
H.S. Diplomas (#)	121	119	0	1	0	1

Waterloo Community Unit SD 5
200 N Rogers St • Waterloo, IL 62298-1575
(618) 939-3453 • http://www.wcusd5.net/
Grade Span: PK-12; **Agency Type:** 1
Schools: 4

2 Primary; 1 Middle; 1 High; 0 Other Level
4 Regular; 0 Special Education; 0 Vocational; 0 Alternative
0 Magnet; 0 Charter; 1 Title I Eligible; 0 School-wide Title I
Students: 2,601   (51.1% male; 48.8% female)
Individual Education Program: 376 (14.5%);
English Language Learner: n/a; Migrant: 0 (0.0%)
Eligible for Free Lunch Program: 184 (7.1%)
Eligible for Reduced-Price Lunch Program: 85 (3.3%)
Teachers: 151.6 (17.2 to 1)
Librarians/Media Specialists: 1.0 (2,601.0 to 1)
Guidance Counselors: 2.0 (1,300.5 to 1)
Current Spending: ($ per student per year):
Total: $6,301; Instruction: $3,727; Support Services: $2,288
Enrollment, Drop-out Rates and Diploma Recipients by Race/Ethnicity

Category	Total	White	Black	Asian	AIAN	Hisp.
Enrollment (%)	100.0	98.9	0.2	0.5	0.1	0.4
Drop-out Rate (%)	1.9	1.9	0.0	0.0	0.0	0.0
H.S. Diplomas (#)	179	179	0	0	0	0

Montgomery County

Hillsboro Community Unit SD 3
1311 Vandalia Rd • Hillsboro, IL 62049-2034
(217) 532-2942 • http://www.montgomery.k12.il.us/hillsboro/
Grade Span: PK-12; **Agency Type:** 1
Schools: 5
3 Primary; 1 Middle; 1 High; 0 Other Level
5 Regular; 0 Special Education; 0 Vocational; 0 Alternative
0 Magnet; 0 Charter; 3 Title I Eligible; 0 School-wide Title I
Students: 2,046   (51.4% male; 48.5% female)
Individual Education Program: 348 (17.0%);
English Language Learner: n/a; Migrant: 0 (0.0%)
Eligible for Free Lunch Program: 574 (28.1%)
Eligible for Reduced-Price Lunch Program: 119 (5.8%)
Teachers: 119.4 (17.1 to 1)
Librarians/Media Specialists: 2.0 (1,023.0 to 1)
Guidance Counselors: 3.0 (682.0 to 1)
Current Spending: ($ per student per year):
Total: $7,032; Instruction: $4,376; Support Services: $2,320
Enrollment, Drop-out Rates and Diploma Recipients by Race/Ethnicity

Category	Total	White	Black	Asian	AIAN	Hisp.
Enrollment (%)	100.0	97.3	1.5	0.1	0.2	0.8
Drop-out Rate (%)	3.6	3.7	0.0	0.0	n/a	0.0
H.S. Diplomas (#)	129	127	1	0	0	1

Litchfield CUSD 12
1702 N State St • Litchfield, IL 62056-1196
(217) 324-2157 • http://www.litchfield.k12.il.us/
Grade Span: PK-12; **Agency Type:** 1
Schools: 7
3 Primary; 3 Middle; 1 High; 0 Other Level
6 Regular; 1 Special Education; 0 Vocational; 0 Alternative
0 Magnet; 0 Charter; 2 Title I Eligible; 0 School-wide Title I
Students: 1,654   (51.6% male; 48.3% female)
Individual Education Program: 281 (17.0%);
English Language Learner: n/a; Migrant: 0 (0.0%)
Eligible for Free Lunch Program: 422 (25.5%)
Eligible for Reduced-Price Lunch Program: 92 (5.6%)
Teachers: 90.4 (18.3 to 1)
Librarians/Media Specialists: 1.0 (1,654.0 to 1)
Guidance Counselors: 2.0 (827.0 to 1)
Current Spending: ($ per student per year):
Total: $6,266; Instruction: $3,746; Support Services: $2,233
Enrollment, Drop-out Rates and Diploma Recipients by Race/Ethnicity

Category	Total	White	Black	Asian	AIAN	Hisp.
Enrollment (%)	100.0	96.9	1.3	1.2	0.0	0.5
Drop-out Rate (%)	1.5	1.4	20.0	0.0	n/a	0.0
H.S. Diplomas (#)	113	110	2	0	0	1

Morgan County

Jacksonville SD 117
516 Jordan St • Jacksonville, IL 62650-1941
(217) 243-9411 • http://www.morgan.k12.il.us/jvsd117/
Grade Span: PK-12; **Agency Type:** 1
Schools: 12
10 Primary; 1 Middle; 1 High; 0 Other Level
10 Regular; 2 Special Education; 0 Vocational; 0 Alternative
0 Magnet; 0 Charter; 5 Title I Eligible; 3 School-wide Title I
Students: 3,788   (50.7% male; 49.2% female)
Individual Education Program: 775 (20.5%);
English Language Learner: n/a; Migrant: 0 (0.0%)
Eligible for Free Lunch Program: 1,331 (35.1%)
Eligible for Reduced-Price Lunch Program: 303 (8.0%)
Teachers: 253.5 (14.9 to 1)

Librarians/Media Specialists: 2.0 (1,894.0 to 1)
Guidance Counselors: 5.0 (757.6 to 1)
Current Spending: ($ per student per year):
Total: $7,199; Instruction: $4,405; Support Services: $2,499
Enrollment, Drop-out Rates and Diploma Recipients by Race/Ethnicity

Category	Total	White	Black	Asian	AIAN	Hisp.
Enrollment (%)	100.0	85.5	11.9	0.8	0.2	1.7
Drop-out Rate (%)	3.9	4.1	1.5	0.0	n/a	0.0
H.S. Diplomas (#)	249	237	8	2	0	2

Ogle County

Byron Community Unit SD 226
PO Box 911 • Byron, IL 61010-0911
(815) 234-5491
Grade Span: PK-12; **Agency Type:** 1
Schools: 4
2 Primary; 1 Middle; 1 High; 0 Other Level
4 Regular; 0 Special Education; 0 Vocational; 0 Alternative
0 Magnet; 0 Charter; 2 Title I Eligible; 0 School-wide Title I
Students: 1,786   (50.2% male; 49.7% female)
Individual Education Program: 292 (16.3%);
English Language Learner: n/a; Migrant: 0 (0.0%)
Eligible for Free Lunch Program: 105 (5.9%)
Eligible for Reduced-Price Lunch Program: 40 (2.2%)
Teachers: 124.2 (14.4 to 1)
Librarians/Media Specialists: 1.0 (1,786.0 to 1)
Guidance Counselors: 3.6 (496.1 to 1)
Current Spending: ($ per student per year):
Total: $11,029; Instruction: $6,954; Support Services: $3,803
Enrollment, Drop-out Rates and Diploma Recipients by Race/Ethnicity

Category	Total	White	Black	Asian	AIAN	Hisp.
Enrollment (%)	100.0	95.0	1.5	1.8	0.2	1.6
Drop-out Rate (%)	1.0	1.1	0.0	0.0	n/a	0.0
H.S. Diplomas (#)	146	146	0	0	0	0

Meridian CUSD 223
207 W Main St • Stillman Valley, IL 61084-8943
(815) 645-2606 • http://www.roe47.k12.il.us/cusd223/
Grade Span: PK-12; **Agency Type:** 1
Schools: 4
2 Primary; 1 Middle; 1 High; 0 Other Level
4 Regular; 0 Special Education; 0 Vocational; 0 Alternative
0 Magnet; 0 Charter; 4 Title I Eligible; 0 School-wide Title I
Students: 1,758   (50.0% male; 50.0% female)
Individual Education Program: 204 (11.6%);
English Language Learner: n/a; Migrant: 0 (0.0%)
Eligible for Free Lunch Program: 131 (7.5%)
Eligible for Reduced-Price Lunch Program: 20 (1.1%)
Teachers: 90.7 (19.4 to 1)
Librarians/Media Specialists: 2.0 (879.0 to 1)
Guidance Counselors: 2.0 (879.0 to 1)
Current Spending: ($ per student per year):
Total: $5,902; Instruction: $3,377; Support Services: $2,308
Enrollment, Drop-out Rates and Diploma Recipients by Race/Ethnicity

Category	Total	White	Black	Asian	AIAN	Hisp.
Enrollment (%)	100.0	95.3	1.0	0.7	0.1	2.8
Drop-out Rate (%)	2.0	2.0	0.0	0.0	n/a	0.0
H.S. Diplomas (#)	94	89	1	1	0	3

Oregon C U School Dist-220
206 S 10th St • Oregon, IL 61061-1711
(815) 732-2186 • http://www.ohs.ogle.k12.il.us/
Grade Span: PK-12; **Agency Type:** 1
Schools: 5
2 Primary; 2 Middle; 1 High; 0 Other Level
5 Regular; 0 Special Education; 0 Vocational; 0 Alternative
1 Magnet; 0 Charter; 4 Title I Eligible; 0 School-wide Title I
Students: 1,803   (52.9% male; 47.0% female)
Individual Education Program: 307 (17.0%);
English Language Learner: n/a; Migrant: 0 (0.0%)
Eligible for Free Lunch Program: 310 (17.2%)
Eligible for Reduced-Price Lunch Program: 82 (4.5%)
Teachers: 100.5 (17.9 to 1)
Librarians/Media Specialists: 2.0 (901.5 to 1)
Guidance Counselors: 3.0 (601.0 to 1)
Current Spending: ($ per student per year):
Total: $7,342; Instruction: $4,925; Support Services: $2,244
Enrollment, Drop-out Rates and Diploma Recipients by Race/Ethnicity

Category	Total	White	Black	Asian	AIAN	Hisp.
Enrollment (%)	100.0	95.1	0.6	1.1	0.3	2.9
Drop-out Rate (%)	2.3	2.4	n/a	0.0	0.0	0.0
H.S. Diplomas (#)	146	143	0	1	0	2

Rochelle Community CD 231
444 N Eighth St • Rochelle, IL 61068-1460
(815) 562-6363 • http://www.leeogle.lth2.k12.il.us/directory/rochelem.html
Grade Span: PK-08; **Agency Type:** 1
Schools: 5
    4 Primary; 1 Middle; 0 High; 0 Other Level
    5 Regular; 0 Special Education; 0 Vocational; 0 Alternative
    0 Magnet; 0 Charter; 2 Title I Eligible; 0 School-wide Title I
Students: 1,845   (51.7% male; 48.2% female)
    Individual Education Program: 341 (18.5%);
    English Language Learner: n/a; Migrant: 11 (0.6%)
    Eligible for Free Lunch Program: 554 (30.0%)
    Eligible for Reduced-Price Lunch Program: 82 (4.4%)
Teachers: 118.5 (15.6 to 1)
Librarians/Media Specialists: 1.0 (1,845.0 to 1)
Guidance Counselors: 4.0 (461.3 to 1)
Current Spending: ($ per student per year):
    Total: $6,169; Instruction: $4,270; Support Services: $1,691
Enrollment, Drop-out Rates and Diploma Recipients by Race/Ethnicity

Category	Total	White	Black	Asian	AIAN	Hisp.
Enrollment (%)	100.0	66.3	3.3	0.1	0.0	30.4
Drop-out Rate (%)	n/a	n/a	n/a	n/a	n/a	n/a
H.S. Diplomas (#)	n/a	n/a	n/a	n/a	n/a	n/a

Peoria County

Dunlap CUSD 323
PO Box 395 • Dunlap, IL 61525-0395
(309) 243-7716 • http://www.dunlapcusd.net/
Grade Span: PK-12; **Agency Type:** 1
Schools: 6
    4 Primary; 1 Middle; 1 High; 0 Other Level
    6 Regular; 0 Special Education; 0 Vocational; 0 Alternative
    0 Magnet; 0 Charter; 3 Title I Eligible; 0 School-wide Title I
Students: 2,519   (50.8% male; 49.1% female)
    Individual Education Program: 309 (12.3%);
    English Language Learner: n/a; Migrant: 0 (0.0%)
    Eligible for Free Lunch Program: 127 (5.0%)
    Eligible for Reduced-Price Lunch Program: 32 (1.3%)
Teachers: 134.3 (18.8 to 1)
Librarians/Media Specialists: 2.0 (1,259.5 to 1)
Guidance Counselors: 5.0 (503.8 to 1)
Current Spending: ($ per student per year):
    Total: $5,872; Instruction: $3,505; Support Services: $2,114
Enrollment, Drop-out Rates and Diploma Recipients by Race/Ethnicity

Category	Total	White	Black	Asian	AIAN	Hisp.
Enrollment (%)	100.0	85.4	5.1	6.4	0.2	3.0
Drop-out Rate (%)	1.1	1.2	0.0	0.0	n/a	0.0
H.S. Diplomas (#)	180	162	5	9	0	4

Il Valley Central Unit Dist 321
1300 W Sycamore • Chillicothe, IL 61523-1373
(309) 274-5418 • http://www.ivc.k12.il.us/
Grade Span: PK-12; **Agency Type:** 1
Schools: 4
    3 Primary; 0 Middle; 1 High; 0 Other Level
    4 Regular; 0 Special Education; 0 Vocational; 0 Alternative
    0 Magnet; 0 Charter; 3 Title I Eligible; 0 School-wide Title I
Students: 2,104   (51.8% male; 48.1% female)
    Individual Education Program: 349 (16.6%);
    English Language Learner: n/a; Migrant: 0 (0.0%)
    Eligible for Free Lunch Program: 324 (15.4%)
    Eligible for Reduced-Price Lunch Program: 103 (4.9%)
Teachers: 134.6 (15.6 to 1)
Librarians/Media Specialists: 1.0 (2,104.0 to 1)
Guidance Counselors: 4.0 (526.0 to 1)
Current Spending: ($ per student per year):
    Total: $6,641; Instruction: $4,469; Support Services: $1,961
Enrollment, Drop-out Rates and Diploma Recipients by Race/Ethnicity

Category	Total	White	Black	Asian	AIAN	Hisp.
Enrollment (%)	100.0	94.2	1.6	1.2	0.4	2.5
Drop-out Rate (%)	4.8	4.9	0.0	0.0	n/a	8.0
H.S. Diplomas (#)	146	137	1	1	3	4

Peoria SD 150
3202 N Wisconsin Ave • Peoria, IL 61603-1260
(309) 672-6768 • http://www.peoria.psd150.org/
Grade Span: PK-12; **Agency Type:** 1
Schools: 45
    19 Primary; 12 Middle; 5 High; 9 Other Level
    32 Regular; 13 Special Education; 0 Vocational; 0 Alternative
    5 Magnet; 0 Charter; 16 Title I Eligible; 16 School-wide Title I
Students: 15,863   (51.3% male; 48.6% female)
    Individual Education Program: 3,816 (24.1%);
    English Language Learner: n/a; Migrant: 1 (<0.1%)
    Eligible for Free Lunch Program: 8,816 (55.6%)
    Eligible for Reduced-Price Lunch Program: 952 (6.0%)
Teachers: 1,066.1 (14.9 to 1)
Librarians/Media Specialists: 7.0 (2,266.1 to 1)
Guidance Counselors: 11.6 (1,367.5 to 1)
Current Spending: ($ per student per year):
    Total: $9,003; Instruction: $5,276; Support Services: $3,438
Enrollment, Drop-out Rates and Diploma Recipients by Race/Ethnicity

Category	Total	White	Black	Asian	AIAN	Hisp.
Enrollment (%)	100.0	34.9	59.0	2.2	0.1	3.8
Drop-out Rate (%)	12.1	9.6	15.2	1.3	0.0	6.9
H.S. Diplomas (#)	775	431	312	13	0	19

Piatt County

Monticello CUSD 25
2 Sage Dr • Monticello, IL 61856-1996
(217) 762-8511 • http://www.monticello.k12.il.us/
Grade Span: PK-12; **Agency Type:** 1
Schools: 5
    3 Primary; 1 Middle; 1 High; 0 Other Level
    5 Regular; 0 Special Education; 0 Vocational; 0 Alternative
    0 Magnet; 0 Charter; 2 Title I Eligible; 0 School-wide Title I
Students: 1,615   (52.5% male; 47.4% female)
    Individual Education Program: 190 (11.8%);
    English Language Learner: n/a; Migrant: 0 (0.0%)
    Eligible for Free Lunch Program: 111 (6.9%)
    Eligible for Reduced-Price Lunch Program: 53 (3.3%)
Teachers: 103.9 (15.5 to 1)
Librarians/Media Specialists: 3.0 (538.3 to 1)
Guidance Counselors: 3.0 (538.3 to 1)
Current Spending: ($ per student per year):
    Total: $6,382; Instruction: $3,800; Support Services: $2,275
Enrollment, Drop-out Rates and Diploma Recipients by Race/Ethnicity

Category	Total	White	Black	Asian	AIAN	Hisp.
Enrollment (%)	100.0	98.1	0.7	0.6	0.0	0.6
Drop-out Rate (%)	1.6	1.6	n/a	0.0	n/a	0.0
H.S. Diplomas (#)	114	113	0	1	0	0

Randolph County

Sparta CUSD 140
203b Dean Ave • Sparta, IL 62286-2099
(618) 443-5331 • http://www.sparta.k12.il.us/
Grade Span: PK-12; **Agency Type:** 1
Schools: 5
    3 Primary; 1 Middle; 1 High; 0 Other Level
    5 Regular; 0 Special Education; 0 Vocational; 0 Alternative
    0 Magnet; 0 Charter; 4 Title I Eligible; 4 School-wide Title I
Students: 1,589   (49.9% male; 50.0% female)
    Individual Education Program: 299 (18.8%);
    English Language Learner: n/a; Migrant: 0 (0.0%)
    Eligible for Free Lunch Program: 677 (42.6%)
    Eligible for Reduced-Price Lunch Program: 119 (7.5%)
Teachers: 97.7 (16.3 to 1)
Librarians/Media Specialists: 1.0 (1,589.0 to 1)
Guidance Counselors: 2.0 (794.5 to 1)
Current Spending: ($ per student per year):
    Total: $7,063; Instruction: $4,553; Support Services: $2,204
Enrollment, Drop-out Rates and Diploma Recipients by Race/Ethnicity

Category	Total	White	Black	Asian	AIAN	Hisp.
Enrollment (%)	100.0	79.1	19.4	0.4	0.3	0.8
Drop-out Rate (%)	0.0	0.0	0.0	0.0	0.0	0.0
H.S. Diplomas (#)	115	103	11	0	0	1

Richland County

East Richland CUSD 1
1100 E Laurel • Olney, IL 62450-2599
(618) 395-2324 • http://www.east.rchlnd.k12.il.us/
Grade Span: PK-12; **Agency Type:** 1
Schools: 3
    1 Primary; 1 Middle; 0 High; 1 Other Level
    3 Regular; 0 Special Education; 0 Vocational; 0 Alternative
    0 Magnet; 0 Charter; 1 Title I Eligible; 1 School-wide Title I
Students: 2,085   (52.2% male; 47.7% female)
    Individual Education Program: 356 (17.1%);
    English Language Learner: n/a; Migrant: 0 (0.0%)
    Eligible for Free Lunch Program: 738 (35.4%)
    Eligible for Reduced-Price Lunch Program: 105 (5.0%)
Teachers: 134.4 (15.5 to 1)
Librarians/Media Specialists: 3.0 (695.0 to 1)
Guidance Counselors: 4.0 (521.3 to 1)
Current Spending: ($ per student per year):
    Total: $6,631; Instruction: $4,043; Support Services: $2,255

Enrollment, Drop-out Rates and Diploma Recipients by Race/Ethnicity

Category	Total	White	Black	Asian	AIAN	Hisp.
Enrollment (%)	100.0	97.0	1.4	0.7	0.2	0.6
Drop-out Rate (%)	3.6	3.6	0.0	0.0	0.0	20.0
H.S. Diplomas (#)	146	145	0	1	0	0

Rock Island County

East Moline SD 37
836 17th Ave • East Moline, IL 61244-2199
(309) 755-4533 • http://www.emsd37.org/
Grade Span: PK-08; **Agency Type:** 1
Schools: 5
 4 Primary; 1 Middle; 0 High; 0 Other Level
 5 Regular; 0 Special Education; 0 Vocational; 0 Alternative
 0 Magnet; 0 Charter; 5 Title I Eligible; 2 School-wide Title I
Students: 2,473 (51.9% male; 48.0% female)
 Individual Education Program: 458 (18.5%);
 English Language Learner: n/a; Migrant: 0 (0.0%)
 Eligible for Free Lunch Program: 1,086 (43.9%)
 Eligible for Reduced-Price Lunch Program: 151 (6.1%)
Teachers: 159.7 (15.5 to 1)
Librarians/Media Specialists: 5.0 (494.6 to 1)
Guidance Counselors: 5.0 (494.6 to 1)
Current Spending: ($ per student per year):
 Total: $8,122; Instruction: $5,177; Support Services: $2,694
Enrollment, Drop-out Rates and Diploma Recipients by Race/Ethnicity

Category	Total	White	Black	Asian	AIAN	Hisp.
Enrollment (%)	100.0	57.1	15.1	1.5	0.6	25.6
Drop-out Rate (%)	n/a	n/a	n/a	n/a	n/a	n/a
H.S. Diplomas (#)	n/a	n/a	n/a	n/a	n/a	n/a

Moline Unit SD 40
1619 11th Ave • Moline, IL 61265-3198
(309) 743-1600 • http://www.moline.lth2.k12.il.us/
Grade Span: PK-12; **Agency Type:** 1
Schools: 20
 14 Primary; 2 Middle; 2 High; 2 Other Level
 16 Regular; 4 Special Education; 0 Vocational; 0 Alternative
 0 Magnet; 0 Charter; 8 Title I Eligible; 4 School-wide Title I
Students: 7,767 (51.8% male; 48.1% female)
 Individual Education Program: 1,221 (15.7%);
 English Language Learner: n/a; Migrant: 9 (0.1%)
 Eligible for Free Lunch Program: 2,389 (30.8%)
 Eligible for Reduced-Price Lunch Program: 413 (5.3%)
Teachers: 451.6 (17.2 to 1)
Librarians/Media Specialists: 12.0 (647.3 to 1)
Guidance Counselors: 11.0 (706.1 to 1)
Current Spending: ($ per student per year):
 Total: $7,652; Instruction: $5,092; Support Services: $2,334
Enrollment, Drop-out Rates and Diploma Recipients by Race/Ethnicity

Category	Total	White	Black	Asian	AIAN	Hisp.
Enrollment (%)	100.0	74.6	6.2	1.9	0.2	17.1
Drop-out Rate (%)	3.8	3.1	6.3	0.0	8.3	7.7
H.S. Diplomas (#)	541	452	23	11	0	55

Rock Island SD 41
2101 6th Ave • Rock Island, IL 61201-8116
(309) 793-5900 • http://www.rockis.k12.il.us/
Grade Span: PK-12; **Agency Type:** 1
Schools: 18
 13 Primary; 3 Middle; 1 High; 1 Other Level
 15 Regular; 3 Special Education; 0 Vocational; 0 Alternative
 0 Magnet; 0 Charter; 12 Title I Eligible; 12 School-wide Title I
Students: 6,677 (50.8% male; 49.1% female)
 Individual Education Program: 1,226 (18.4%);
 English Language Learner: n/a; Migrant: 0 (0.0%)
 Eligible for Free Lunch Program: 3,365 (50.4%)
 Eligible for Reduced-Price Lunch Program: 425 (6.4%)
Teachers: 402.2 (16.6 to 1)
Librarians/Media Specialists: 2.0 (3,338.5 to 1)
Guidance Counselors: 7.0 (953.9 to 1)
Current Spending: ($ per student per year):
 Total: $7,726; Instruction: $5,072; Support Services: $2,357
Enrollment, Drop-out Rates and Diploma Recipients by Race/Ethnicity

Category	Total	White	Black	Asian	AIAN	Hisp.
Enrollment (%)	100.0	53.4	36.6	0.6	0.2	9.3
Drop-out Rate (%)	4.6	3.7	6.4	0.0	0.0	6.5
H.S. Diplomas (#)	300	227	63	0	0	10

Sherrard Community Unit SD 200
PO Box 369 • Sherrard, IL 61281-0369
(309) 593-4075
Grade Span: PK-12; **Agency Type:** 1
Schools: 6

 3 Primary; 2 Middle; 1 High; 0 Other Level
 6 Regular; 0 Special Education; 0 Vocational; 0 Alternative
 0 Magnet; 0 Charter; 3 Title I Eligible; 0 School-wide Title I
Students: 1,765 (50.3% male; 49.6% female)
 Individual Education Program: 221 (12.5%);
 English Language Learner: n/a; Migrant: 0 (0.0%)
 Eligible for Free Lunch Program: 283 (16.0%)
 Eligible for Reduced-Price Lunch Program: 82 (4.6%)
Teachers: 125.3 (14.1 to 1)
Librarians/Media Specialists: 1.0 (1,765.0 to 1)
Guidance Counselors: 2.6 (678.8 to 1)
Current Spending: ($ per student per year):
 Total: $6,549; Instruction: $3,979; Support Services: $2,255
Enrollment, Drop-out Rates and Diploma Recipients by Race/Ethnicity

Category	Total	White	Black	Asian	AIAN	Hisp.
Enrollment (%)	100.0	97.1	0.9	0.7	0.1	1.2
Drop-out Rate (%)	2.7	2.7	0.0	0.0	n/a	0.0
H.S. Diplomas (#)	106	103	0	0	0	3

United Twp HS District 30
1275 Ave The Cities • East Moline, IL 61244-4100
(309) 752-1633 • http://uths.revealed.net/
Grade Span: 09-12; **Agency Type:** 1
Schools: 1
 0 Primary; 0 Middle; 1 High; 0 Other Level
 1 Regular; 0 Special Education; 0 Vocational; 0 Alternative
 0 Magnet; 0 Charter; 1 Title I Eligible; 0 School-wide Title I
Students: 1,816 (52.5% male; 47.4% female)
 Individual Education Program: 389 (21.4%);
 English Language Learner: n/a; Migrant: 0 (0.0%)
 Eligible for Free Lunch Program: 530 (29.2%)
 Eligible for Reduced-Price Lunch Program: 159 (8.8%)
Teachers: 93.0 (19.5 to 1)
Librarians/Media Specialists: 1.0 (1,816.0 to 1)
Guidance Counselors: 5.0 (363.2 to 1)
Current Spending: ($ per student per year):
 Total: $7,315; Instruction: $4,202; Support Services: $2,815
Enrollment, Drop-out Rates and Diploma Recipients by Race/Ethnicity

Category	Total	White	Black	Asian	AIAN	Hisp.
Enrollment (%)	100.0	73.0	8.8	1.5	0.7	16.0
Drop-out Rate (%)	6.1	5.4	13.3	3.2	6.3	6.0
H.S. Diplomas (#)	347	280	22	8	2	35

Saline County

Harrisburg CUSD 3
40 S Main St • Harrisburg, IL 62946-1638
(618) 253-7637 • http://www.hbg.saline.k12.il.us/
Grade Span: PK-12; **Agency Type:** 1
Schools: 4
 2 Primary; 1 Middle; 1 High; 0 Other Level
 4 Regular; 0 Special Education; 0 Vocational; 0 Alternative
 0 Magnet; 0 Charter; 2 Title I Eligible; 2 School-wide Title I
Students: 2,208 (51.2% male; 48.7% female)
 Individual Education Program: 362 (16.4%);
 English Language Learner: n/a; Migrant: 0 (0.0%)
 Eligible for Free Lunch Program: 601 (27.2%)
 Eligible for Reduced-Price Lunch Program: 96 (4.3%)
Teachers: 130.8 (16.9 to 1)
Librarians/Media Specialists: 4.0 (552.0 to 1)
Guidance Counselors: 2.0 (1,104.0 to 1)
Current Spending: ($ per student per year):
 Total: $7,009; Instruction: $4,578; Support Services: $2,187
Enrollment, Drop-out Rates and Diploma Recipients by Race/Ethnicity

Category	Total	White	Black	Asian	AIAN	Hisp.
Enrollment (%)	100.0	92.2	6.0	1.0	0.1	0.7
Drop-out Rate (%)	5.5	5.6	0.0	0.0	0.0	14.3
H.S. Diplomas (#)	119	113	6	0	0	0

Sangamon County

Ball Chatham CUSD 5
201 W Mulberry • Chatham, IL 62629-1615
(217) 483-2416 • http://dist5.bcsd.k12.il.us/default.htm
Grade Span: PK-12; **Agency Type:** 1
Schools: 5
 2 Primary; 2 Middle; 1 High; 0 Other Level
 5 Regular; 0 Special Education; 0 Vocational; 0 Alternative
 0 Magnet; 0 Charter; 4 Title I Eligible; 0 School-wide Title I
Students: 4,060 (51.8% male; 48.1% female)
 Individual Education Program: 531 (13.1%);
 English Language Learner: n/a; Migrant: 0 (0.0%)
 Eligible for Free Lunch Program: 224 (5.5%)
 Eligible for Reduced-Price Lunch Program: 45 (1.1%)
Teachers: 217.0 (18.7 to 1)

Librarians/Media Specialists: 5.0 (812.0 to 1)
Guidance Counselors: 7.0 (580.0 to 1)
Current Spending: ($ per student per year):
 Total: $5,883; Instruction: $3,172; Support Services: $2,376
Enrollment, Drop-out Rates and Diploma Recipients by Race/Ethnicity

Category	Total	White	Black	Asian	AIAN	Hisp.
Enrollment (%)	100.0	93.5	2.7	2.4	0.4	0.9
Drop-out Rate (%)	1.0	0.9	0.0	0.0	n/a	7.7
H.S. Diplomas (#)	305	291	5	5	0	4

Corrections SD 428 Dept of
1301 Concordia Court • Springfield, IL 62702-2737
(217) 522-2666 • http://www.idoc.state.il.us/
Grade Span: 06-12; **Agency Type:** 5
Schools: 38
 0 Primary; 0 Middle; 37 High; 1 Other Level
 0 Regular; 0 Special Education; 0 Vocational; 38 Alternative
 0 Magnet; 0 Charter; 0 Title I Eligible; 0 School-wide Title I
Students: 10,118 (91.4% male; 8.5% female)
 Individual Education Program: 727 (7.2%);
 English Language Learner: n/a; Migrant: 0 (0.0%)
 Eligible for Free Lunch Program: 2,163 (21.4%)
 Eligible for Reduced-Price Lunch Program: 0 (0.0%)
Teachers: 276.4 (36.6 to 1)
Librarians/Media Specialists: 0.0 (n/a to 1)
Guidance Counselors: 0.0 (n/a to 1)
Current Spending: ($ per student per year):
 Total: n/a; Instruction: n/a; Support Services: n/a
Enrollment, Drop-out Rates and Diploma Recipients by Race/Ethnicity

Category	Total	White	Black	Asian	AIAN	Hisp.
Enrollment (%)	100.0	26.5	57.9	0.3	0.1	15.1
Drop-out Rate (%)	n/a	n/a	n/a	n/a	n/a	n/a
H.S. Diplomas (#)	0	0	0	0	0	0

Rochester Community Unit SD 3a
4 Rocket Dr • Rochester, IL 62563-9282
(217) 498-6210 • http://209.7.254.7/rocket1/pform.htm
Grade Span: PK-12; **Agency Type:** 1
Schools: 4
 1 Primary; 2 Middle; 1 High; 0 Other Level
 4 Regular; 0 Special Education; 0 Vocational; 0 Alternative
 0 Magnet; 0 Charter; 0 Title I Eligible; 0 School-wide Title I
Students: 1,912 (53.0% male; 46.9% female)
 Individual Education Program: 281 (14.7%);
 English Language Learner: n/a; Migrant: 0 (0.0%)
 Eligible for Free Lunch Program: 32 (1.7%)
 Eligible for Reduced-Price Lunch Program: 16 (0.8%)
Teachers: 108.8 (17.6 to 1)
Librarians/Media Specialists: 2.0 (956.0 to 1)
Guidance Counselors: 2.0 (956.0 to 1)
Current Spending: ($ per student per year):
 Total: $5,569; Instruction: $3,091; Support Services: $2,230
Enrollment, Drop-out Rates and Diploma Recipients by Race/Ethnicity

Category	Total	White	Black	Asian	AIAN	Hisp.
Enrollment (%)	100.0	96.9	0.9	0.8	0.3	1.0
Drop-out Rate (%)	0.3	0.3	n/a	0.0	n/a	0.0
H.S. Diplomas (#)	154	150	2	1	0	1

Springfield SD 186
1900 W Monroe St • Springfield, IL 62704-1599
(217) 525-3002 • http://www.springfield.k12.il.us/
Grade Span: PK-12; **Agency Type:** 1
Schools: 36
 25 Primary; 5 Middle; 3 High; 3 Other Level
 32 Regular; 4 Special Education; 0 Vocational; 0 Alternative
 4 Magnet; 1 Charter; 20 Title I Eligible; 15 School-wide Title I
Students: 15,212 (51.3% male; 48.6% female)
 Individual Education Program: 2,838 (18.7%);
 English Language Learner: n/a; Migrant: 0 (0.0%)
 Eligible for Free Lunch Program: 7,340 (48.3%)
 Eligible for Reduced-Price Lunch Program: 1,018 (6.7%)
Teachers: 944.7 (16.1 to 1)
Librarians/Media Specialists: 7.0 (2,173.1 to 1)
Guidance Counselors: 0.0 (n/a to 1)
Current Spending: ($ per student per year):
 Total: $7,659; Instruction: $4,317; Support Services: $2,991
Enrollment, Drop-out Rates and Diploma Recipients by Race/Ethnicity

Category	Total	White	Black	Asian	AIAN	Hisp.
Enrollment (%)	100.0	58.8	37.8	2.0	0.2	1.2
Drop-out Rate (%)	3.6	3.5	3.7	2.5	0.0	4.9
H.S. Diplomas (#)	803	593	181	21	0	8

Belleville SD 118
105 W A St • Belleville, IL 62220-1326
(618) 233-2830 • http://www.belleville118.stclair.k12.il.us/
Grade Span: PK-08; **Agency Type:** 1
Schools: 11
 9 Primary; 2 Middle; 0 High; 0 Other Level
 11 Regular; 0 Special Education; 0 Vocational; 0 Alternative
 0 Magnet; 0 Charter; 6 Title I Eligible; 1 School-wide Title I
Students: 3,740 (52.4% male; 47.5% female)
 Individual Education Program: 869 (23.2%);
 English Language Learner: n/a; Migrant: 0 (0.0%)
 Eligible for Free Lunch Program: 1,365 (36.5%)
 Eligible for Reduced-Price Lunch Program: 390 (10.4%)
Teachers: 199.5 (18.7 to 1)
Librarians/Media Specialists: 0.0 (n/a to 1)
Guidance Counselors: 0.0 (n/a to 1)
Current Spending: ($ per student per year):
 Total: $8,000; Instruction: $4,577; Support Services: $2,959
Enrollment, Drop-out Rates and Diploma Recipients by Race/Ethnicity

Category	Total	White	Black	Asian	AIAN	Hisp.
Enrollment (%)	100.0	62.2	33.3	1.8	0.7	2.1
Drop-out Rate (%)	n/a	n/a	n/a	n/a	n/a	n/a
H.S. Diplomas (#)	n/a	n/a	n/a	n/a	n/a	n/a

Belleville Twp HSD 201
2600 W Main St • Belleville, IL 62226-6651
(618) 222-8200 • http://www.bths201.stclair.k12.il.us/
Grade Span: 09-12; **Agency Type:** 1
Schools: 3
 0 Primary; 0 Middle; 3 High; 0 Other Level
 2 Regular; 1 Special Education; 0 Vocational; 0 Alternative
 0 Magnet; 0 Charter; 2 Title I Eligible; 0 School-wide Title I
Students: 4,939 (50.8% male; 49.1% female)
 Individual Education Program: 828 (16.8%);
 English Language Learner: n/a; Migrant: 0 (0.0%)
 Eligible for Free Lunch Program: 839 (17.0%)
 Eligible for Reduced-Price Lunch Program: 259 (5.2%)
Teachers: 240.9 (20.5 to 1)
Librarians/Media Specialists: 4.0 (1,234.8 to 1)
Guidance Counselors: 10.0 (493.9 to 1)
Current Spending: ($ per student per year):
 Total: $7,141; Instruction: $4,539; Support Services: $2,363
Enrollment, Drop-out Rates and Diploma Recipients by Race/Ethnicity

Category	Total	White	Black	Asian	AIAN	Hisp.
Enrollment (%)	100.0	72.8	23.3	1.7	0.3	1.9
Drop-out Rate (%)	3.8	3.6	4.5	0.0	13.3	9.4
H.S. Diplomas (#)	1,009	800	176	18	5	10

Cahokia Community Unit SD 187
1700 Jerome Ln • Cahokia, IL 62206-2329
(618) 332-3700 • http://www.cahokia.stclair.k12.il.us/
Grade Span: PK-12; **Agency Type:** 1
Schools: 10
 7 Primary; 1 Middle; 1 High; 1 Other Level
 9 Regular; 1 Special Education; 0 Vocational; 0 Alternative
 0 Magnet; 1 Charter; 9 Title I Eligible; 8 School-wide Title I
Students: 5,098 (50.0% male; 49.9% female)
 Individual Education Program: 1,006 (19.7%);
 English Language Learner: n/a; Migrant: 0 (0.0%)
 Eligible for Free Lunch Program: 3,285 (64.4%)
 Eligible for Reduced-Price Lunch Program: 358 (7.0%)
Teachers: 248.9 (20.5 to 1)
Librarians/Media Specialists: 1.0 (5,098.0 to 1)
Guidance Counselors: 4.0 (1,274.5 to 1)
Current Spending: ($ per student per year):
 Total: $7,727; Instruction: $4,464; Support Services: $2,979
Enrollment, Drop-out Rates and Diploma Recipients by Race/Ethnicity

Category	Total	White	Black	Asian	AIAN	Hisp.
Enrollment (%)	100.0	18.9	79.5	0.1	0.0	1.5
Drop-out Rate (%)	6.6	10.7	5.4	0.0	n/a	0.0
H.S. Diplomas (#)	189	57	129	0	0	3

East St Louis SD 189
1005 State St • East Saint Louis, IL 62201-1907
(618) 646-3009 • http://www.estlouis.stclair.k12.il.us/
Grade Span: PK-12; **Agency Type:** 1
Schools: 28
 19 Primary; 3 Middle; 3 High; 3 Other Level
 24 Regular; 4 Special Education; 0 Vocational; 0 Alternative
 0 Magnet; 2 Charter; 24 Title I Eligible; 24 School-wide Title I
Students: 10,349 (49.3% male; 50.6% female)
 Individual Education Program: 1,670 (16.1%);
 English Language Learner: n/a; Migrant: 0 (0.0%)

Eligible for Free Lunch Program: 7,174 (69.3%)
Eligible for Reduced-Price Lunch Program: 573 (5.5%)
Teachers: 600.3 (17.2 to 1)
Librarians/Media Specialists: 6.0 (1,724.8 to 1)
Guidance Counselors: 16.0 (646.8 to 1)
Current Spending: ($ per student per year):
    Total: $8,291; Instruction: $4,939; Support Services: $2,973
Enrollment, Drop-out Rates and Diploma Recipients by Race/Ethnicity

Category	Total	White	Black	Asian	AIAN	Hisp.
Enrollment (%)	100.0	0.2	98.9	0.0	0.0	0.9
Drop-out Rate (%)	10.2	8.3	10.3	n/a	n/a	0.0
H.S. Diplomas (#)	328	1	327	0	0	0

Mascoutah C U District 19
720 W Harnett St • Mascoutah, IL 62258-1121
(618) 566-7414 • http://www.mascoutah19.k12.il.us/
Grade Span: PK-12; **Agency Type:** 1
Schools: 4
    2 Primary; 1 Middle; 1 High; 0 Other Level
    4 Regular; 0 Special Education; 0 Vocational; 0 Alternative
    0 Magnet; 0 Charter; 1 Title I Eligible; 1 School-wide Title I
Students: 2,873 (50.2% male; 49.7% female)
    Individual Education Program: 452 (15.7%);
    English Language Learner: n/a; Migrant: 0 (0.0%)
    Eligible for Free Lunch Program: 288 (10.0%)
    Eligible for Reduced-Price Lunch Program: 313 (10.9%)
Teachers: 184.5 (15.6 to 1)
Librarians/Media Specialists: 3.0 (957.7 to 1)
Guidance Counselors: 4.0 (718.3 to 1)
Current Spending: ($ per student per year):
    Total: $8,080; Instruction: $4,688; Support Services: $3,079
Enrollment, Drop-out Rates and Diploma Recipients by Race/Ethnicity

Category	Total	White	Black	Asian	AIAN	Hisp.
Enrollment (%)	100.0	79.1	14.0	3.1	0.7	3.2
Drop-out Rate (%)	0.7	0.8	0.0	0.0	0.0	0.0
H.S. Diplomas (#)	172	143	21	5	0	3

O Fallon CCSD 90
707 N Smiley St • Ofallon, IL 62269-1353
(618) 632-3666 • http://www.ofallon90.stclair.k12.il.us/
Grade Span: PK-08; **Agency Type:** 1
Schools: 6
    5 Primary; 1 Middle; 0 High; 0 Other Level
    6 Regular; 0 Special Education; 0 Vocational; 0 Alternative
    0 Magnet; 0 Charter; 2 Title I Eligible; 0 School-wide Title I
Students: 3,143 (51.7% male; 48.2% female)
    Individual Education Program: 545 (17.3%);
    English Language Learner: n/a; Migrant: 0 (0.0%)
    Eligible for Free Lunch Program: 442 (14.1%)
    Eligible for Reduced-Price Lunch Program: 104 (3.3%)
Teachers: 166.1 (18.9 to 1)
Librarians/Media Specialists: 1.0 (3,143.0 to 1)
Guidance Counselors: 0.0 (n/a to 1)
Current Spending: ($ per student per year):
    Total: $5,898; Instruction: $3,903; Support Services: $1,789
Enrollment, Drop-out Rates and Diploma Recipients by Race/Ethnicity

Category	Total	White	Black	Asian	AIAN	Hisp.
Enrollment (%)	100.0	77.9	16.7	2.8	0.3	2.3
Drop-out Rate (%)	n/a	n/a	n/a	n/a	n/a	n/a
H.S. Diplomas (#)	n/a	n/a	n/a	n/a	n/a	n/a

O Fallon Twp High SD 203
600 S Smiley St • Ofallon, IL 62269-2399
(618) 632-3507 • http://www.oths.k12.il.us/
Grade Span: 09-12; **Agency Type:** 1
Schools: 1
    0 Primary; 0 Middle; 1 High; 0 Other Level
    1 Regular; 0 Special Education; 0 Vocational; 0 Alternative
    0 Magnet; 0 Charter; 1 Title I Eligible; 0 School-wide Title I
Students: 2,150 (50.8% male; 49.1% female)
    Individual Education Program: 219 (10.2%);
    English Language Learner: n/a; Migrant: 0 (0.0%)
    Eligible for Free Lunch Program: 132 (6.1%)
    Eligible for Reduced-Price Lunch Program: 46 (2.1%)
Teachers: 106.9 (20.1 to 1)
Librarians/Media Specialists: 1.0 (2,150.0 to 1)
Guidance Counselors: 5.0 (430.0 to 1)
Current Spending: ($ per student per year):
    Total: $7,059; Instruction: $4,018; Support Services: $2,438
Enrollment, Drop-out Rates and Diploma Recipients by Race/Ethnicity

Category	Total	White	Black	Asian	AIAN	Hisp.
Enrollment (%)	100.0	77.0	16.4	4.0	0.0	2.7
Drop-out Rate (%)	2.0	1.8	3.4	0.0	n/a	3.1
H.S. Diplomas (#)	471	390	60	15	0	6

Stephenson County

Freeport SD 145
501 E S St • Freeport, IL 61032-9676
(815) 232-0300 • http://www.freeportschooldistrict.com/index.cfm
Grade Span: PK-12; **Agency Type:** 1
Schools: 10
    6 Primary; 2 Middle; 1 High; 1 Other Level
    9 Regular; 1 Special Education; 0 Vocational; 0 Alternative
    0 Magnet; 0 Charter; 7 Title I Eligible; 2 School-wide Title I
Students: 4,467 (50.7% male; 49.2% female)
    Individual Education Program: 620 (13.9%);
    English Language Learner: n/a; Migrant: 0 (0.0%)
    Eligible for Free Lunch Program: 1,801 (40.3%)
    Eligible for Reduced-Price Lunch Program: 362 (8.1%)
Teachers: 285.8 (15.6 to 1)
Librarians/Media Specialists: 3.0 (1,489.0 to 1)
Guidance Counselors: 5.0 (893.4 to 1)
Current Spending: ($ per student per year):
    Total: $7,464; Instruction: $4,356; Support Services: $2,782
Enrollment, Drop-out Rates and Diploma Recipients by Race/Ethnicity

Category	Total	White	Black	Asian	AIAN	Hisp.
Enrollment (%)	100.0	68.1	26.1	1.7	0.1	4.0
Drop-out Rate (%)	7.5	5.1	15.3	12.0	0.0	16.7
H.S. Diplomas (#)	307	255	42	5	0	5

Tazewell County

East Peoria SD 86
601 Taylor St • East Peoria, IL 61611-2643
(309) 427-5100 • http://www.epd86.org/
Grade Span: PK-08; **Agency Type:** 1
Schools: 7
    6 Primary; 1 Middle; 0 High; 0 Other Level
    7 Regular; 0 Special Education; 0 Vocational; 0 Alternative
    0 Magnet; 0 Charter; 5 Title I Eligible; 0 School-wide Title I
Students: 1,883 (52.3% male; 47.6% female)
    Individual Education Program: 344 (18.3%);
    English Language Learner: n/a; Migrant: 0 (0.0%)
    Eligible for Free Lunch Program: 516 (27.4%)
    Eligible for Reduced-Price Lunch Program: 63 (3.3%)
Teachers: 122.7 (15.3 to 1)
Librarians/Media Specialists: 2.0 (941.5 to 1)
Guidance Counselors: 1.0 (1,883.0 to 1)
Current Spending: ($ per student per year):
    Total: $7,295; Instruction: $4,575; Support Services: $2,432
Enrollment, Drop-out Rates and Diploma Recipients by Race/Ethnicity

Category	Total	White	Black	Asian	AIAN	Hisp.
Enrollment (%)	100.0	94.5	1.8	0.9	0.1	2.7
Drop-out Rate (%)	n/a	n/a	n/a	n/a	n/a	n/a
H.S. Diplomas (#)	n/a	n/a	n/a	n/a	n/a	n/a

Morton CUSD 709
235 E Jackson St • Morton, IL 61550-1600
(309) 263-2581 • http://www.morton709.org/
Grade Span: PK-12; **Agency Type:** 1
Schools: 6
    4 Primary; 1 Middle; 1 High; 0 Other Level
    6 Regular; 0 Special Education; 0 Vocational; 0 Alternative
    0 Magnet; 0 Charter; 2 Title I Eligible; 0 School-wide Title I
Students: 2,659 (51.7% male; 48.2% female)
    Individual Education Program: 385 (14.5%);
    English Language Learner: n/a; Migrant: 0 (0.0%)
    Eligible for Free Lunch Program: 129 (4.9%)
    Eligible for Reduced-Price Lunch Program: 21 (0.8%)
Teachers: 169.3 (15.7 to 1)
Librarians/Media Specialists: 4.7 (565.7 to 1)
Guidance Counselors: 4.0 (664.8 to 1)
Current Spending: ($ per student per year):
    Total: $7,891; Instruction: $5,013; Support Services: $2,676
Enrollment, Drop-out Rates and Diploma Recipients by Race/Ethnicity

Category	Total	White	Black	Asian	AIAN	Hisp.
Enrollment (%)	100.0	96.4	0.6	1.7	0.2	1.1
Drop-out Rate (%)	1.4	1.2	n/a	7.1	0.0	11.1
H.S. Diplomas (#)	230	224	0	2	1	3

Pekin Community HSD 303
320 Stadium Dr • Pekin, IL 61554-5295
(309) 477-4222 • http://www.pekinhigh.net/
Grade Span: 09-12; **Agency Type:** 1
Schools: 1
    0 Primary; 0 Middle; 1 High; 0 Other Level
    1 Regular; 0 Special Education; 0 Vocational; 0 Alternative
    0 Magnet; 0 Charter; 1 Title I Eligible; 0 School-wide Title I
Students: 2,078 (50.2% male; 49.7% female)

Individual Education Program: 279 (13.4%);
English Language Learner: n/a; Migrant: 0 (0.0%)
Eligible for Free Lunch Program: 418 (20.1%)
Eligible for Reduced-Price Lunch Program: 137 (6.6%)
Teachers: 116.0 (17.9 to 1)
Librarians/Media Specialists: 1.0 (2,078.0 to 1)
Guidance Counselors: 7.0 (296.9 to 1)
Current Spending: ($ per student per year):
Total: $7,249; Instruction: $4,131; Support Services: $2,894

Enrollment, Drop-out Rates and Diploma Recipients by Race/Ethnicity

Category	Total	White	Black	Asian	AIAN	Hisp.
Enrollment (%)	100.0	97.9	0.3	1.1	0.2	0.5
Drop-out Rate (%)	3.5	3.5	0.0	0.0	n/a	0.0
H.S. Diplomas (#)	413	411	1	1	0	0

Pekin Public SD 108

501 Washington St • Pekin, IL 61554-4239
(309) 477-4740 • http://www.pekin.net/pekin108/
Grade Span: PK-12; **Agency Type:** 1
Schools: 11
6 Primary; 4 Middle; 0 High; 1 Other Level
10 Regular; 1 Special Education; 0 Vocational; 0 Alternative
0 Magnet; 0 Charter; 8 Title I Eligible; 0 School-wide Title I
Students: 3,835 (50.8% male; 49.1% female)
Individual Education Program: 835 (21.8%);
English Language Learner: n/a; Migrant: 0 (0.0%)
Eligible for Free Lunch Program: 1,310 (34.2%)
Eligible for Reduced-Price Lunch Program: 354 (9.2%)
Teachers: 240.8 (15.9 to 1)
Librarians/Media Specialists: 9.0 (426.1 to 1)
Guidance Counselors: 4.0 (958.8 to 1)
Current Spending: ($ per student per year):
Total: $6,756; Instruction: $3,986; Support Services: $2,551

Enrollment, Drop-out Rates and Diploma Recipients by Race/Ethnicity

Category	Total	White	Black	Asian	AIAN	Hisp.
Enrollment (%)	100.0	97.0	0.8	0.7	0.4	1.1
Drop-out Rate (%)	0.0	0.0	n/a	n/a	n/a	n/a
H.S. Diplomas (#)	0	0	0	0	0	0

Vermilion County

Danville CCSD 118

516 N Jackson St • Danville, IL 61832-4684
(217) 444-1004 • http://www.danville.k12.il.us/Home.asp
Grade Span: PK-12; **Agency Type:** 1
Schools: 11
8 Primary; 2 Middle; 1 High; 0 Other Level
11 Regular; 0 Special Education; 0 Vocational; 0 Alternative
1 Magnet; 0 Charter; 10 Title I Eligible; 10 School-wide Title I
Students: 6,379 (50.5% male; 49.4% female)
Individual Education Program: 1,259 (19.7%);
English Language Learner: n/a; Migrant: 0 (0.0%)
Eligible for Free Lunch Program: 3,627 (56.9%)
Eligible for Reduced-Price Lunch Program: 427 (6.7%)
Teachers: 361.0 (17.7 to 1)
Librarians/Media Specialists: 1.0 (6,379.0 to 1)
Guidance Counselors: 5.0 (1,275.8 to 1)
Current Spending: ($ per student per year):
Total: $8,416; Instruction: $5,261; Support Services: $2,841

Enrollment, Drop-out Rates and Diploma Recipients by Race/Ethnicity

Category	Total	White	Black	Asian	AIAN	Hisp.
Enrollment (%)	100.0	55.2	37.6	1.1	0.3	5.8
Drop-out Rate (%)	11.3	10.2	13.2	9.7	50.0	15.5
H.S. Diplomas (#)	272	205	52	6	0	9

Wabash County

Wabash CUSD 348

218 W 13th St • Mount Carmel, IL 62863-1297
(618) 262-4181 • http://www.d348.wabash.k12.il.us/
Grade Span: PK-12; **Agency Type:** 1
Schools: 4
2 Primary; 1 Middle; 1 High; 0 Other Level
4 Regular; 0 Special Education; 0 Vocational; 0 Alternative
0 Magnet; 0 Charter; 2 Title I Eligible; 2 School-wide Title I
Students: 1,884 (51.1% male; 48.8% female)
Individual Education Program: 317 (16.8%);
English Language Learner: n/a; Migrant: 0 (0.0%)
Eligible for Free Lunch Program: 465 (24.7%)
Eligible for Reduced-Price Lunch Program: 141 (7.5%)
Teachers: 116.7 (16.1 to 1)
Librarians/Media Specialists: 1.0 (1,884.0 to 1)
Guidance Counselors: 3.0 (628.0 to 1)
Current Spending: ($ per student per year):
Total: $6,657; Instruction: $4,296; Support Services: $2,157

Enrollment, Drop-out Rates and Diploma Recipients by Race/Ethnicity

Category	Total	White	Black	Asian	AIAN	Hisp.
Enrollment (%)	100.0	97.8	1.0	0.5	0.2	0.5
Drop-out Rate (%)	6.1	6.1	n/a	n/a	n/a	n/a
H.S. Diplomas (#)	158	158	0	0	0	0

Warren County

Monmouth Unit SD 38

321 E Euclid Ave • Monmouth, IL 61462-2473
(309) 734-4712 • http://zippers.warren.k12.il.us/district/welcome.htm
Grade Span: PK-12; **Agency Type:** 1
Schools: 6
3 Primary; 2 Middle; 1 High; 0 Other Level
5 Regular; 1 Special Education; 0 Vocational; 0 Alternative
0 Magnet; 0 Charter; 4 Title I Eligible; 2 School-wide Title I
Students: 1,531 (50.2% male; 49.7% female)
Individual Education Program: 257 (16.8%);
English Language Learner: n/a; Migrant: 0 (0.0%)
Eligible for Free Lunch Program: 592 (38.7%)
Eligible for Reduced-Price Lunch Program: 96 (6.3%)
Teachers: 100.5 (15.2 to 1)
Librarians/Media Specialists: 5.0 (306.2 to 1)
Guidance Counselors: 5.0 (306.2 to 1)
Current Spending: ($ per student per year):
Total: $5,915; Instruction: $3,834; Support Services: $1,837

Enrollment, Drop-out Rates and Diploma Recipients by Race/Ethnicity

Category	Total	White	Black	Asian	AIAN	Hisp.
Enrollment (%)	100.0	80.5	6.4	0.8	1.2	11.0
Drop-out Rate (%)	4.2	4.7	0.0	0.0	0.0	0.0
H.S. Diplomas (#)	93	83	4	0	0	6

Whiteside County

Sterling C U Dist 5

410 E Le Fevre Rd • Sterling, IL 61081-1399
(815) 626-5050 • http://www.sterlingschools.org/
Grade Span: PK-12; **Agency Type:** 1
Schools: 6
4 Primary; 1 Middle; 1 High; 0 Other Level
6 Regular; 0 Special Education; 0 Vocational; 0 Alternative
0 Magnet; 0 Charter; 5 Title I Eligible; 2 School-wide Title I
Students: 3,556 (50.7% male; 49.2% female)
Individual Education Program: 618 (17.4%);
English Language Learner: n/a; Migrant: 0 (0.0%)
Eligible for Free Lunch Program: 985 (27.7%)
Eligible for Reduced-Price Lunch Program: 290 (8.2%)
Teachers: 198.0 (18.0 to 1)
Librarians/Media Specialists: 1.0 (3,556.0 to 1)
Guidance Counselors: 5.6 (635.0 to 1)
Current Spending: ($ per student per year):
Total: $7,146; Instruction: $4,706; Support Services: $2,198

Enrollment, Drop-out Rates and Diploma Recipients by Race/Ethnicity

Category	Total	White	Black	Asian	AIAN	Hisp.
Enrollment (%)	100.0	71.2	4.3	0.8	0.3	23.5
Drop-out Rate (%)	5.4	5.0	0.0	0.0	0.0	9.0
H.S. Diplomas (#)	231	186	9	7	0	29

Will County

Crete Monee CUSD 201u

1500 Sangamon St • Crete, IL 60417-2899
(708) 672-2680 • http://www.cm201u.org/
Grade Span: PK-12; **Agency Type:** 1
Schools: 8
5 Primary; 2 Middle; 1 High; 0 Other Level
8 Regular; 0 Special Education; 0 Vocational; 0 Alternative
0 Magnet; 0 Charter; 2 Title I Eligible; 2 School-wide Title I
Students: 4,837 (51.3% male; 48.6% female)
Individual Education Program: 902 (18.6%);
English Language Learner: n/a; Migrant: 0 (0.0%)
Eligible for Free Lunch Program: 1,773 (36.7%)
Eligible for Reduced-Price Lunch Program: 401 (8.3%)
Teachers: 252.5 (19.2 to 1)
Librarians/Media Specialists: 1.0 (4,837.0 to 1)
Guidance Counselors: 5.5 (879.5 to 1)
Current Spending: ($ per student per year):
Total: $7,515; Instruction: $4,044; Support Services: $3,165

Enrollment, Drop-out Rates and Diploma Recipients by Race/Ethnicity

Category	Total	White	Black	Asian	AIAN	Hisp.
Enrollment (%)	100.0	40.4	54.0	0.9	0.1	4.7
Drop-out Rate (%)	1.4	1.1	1.7	0.0	n/a	3.0
H.S. Diplomas (#)	266	133	118	3	0	12

Frankfort CCSD 157c
10482 W Nebraska St • Frankfort, IL 60423-2235
(815) 469-5922 • http://www.fsd157c.org/
Grade Span: PK-08; **Agency Type:** 1
Schools: 3
   1 Primary; 2 Middle; 0 High; 0 Other Level
   3 Regular; 0 Special Education; 0 Vocational; 0 Alternative
   0 Magnet; 0 Charter; 0 Title I Eligible; 0 School-wide Title I
Students: 1,921 (51.8% male; 48.1% female)
   Individual Education Program: 261 (13.6%);
   English Language Learner: n/a; Migrant: 0 (0.0%)
   Eligible for Free Lunch Program: 0 (0.0%)
   Eligible for Reduced-Price Lunch Program: 0 (0.0%)
Teachers: 111.1 (17.3 to 1)
Librarians/Media Specialists: 0.0 (n/a to 1)
Guidance Counselors: 0.0 (n/a to 1)
Current Spending: ($ per student per year):
   Total: $6,327; Instruction: $3,713; Support Services: $2,598
Enrollment, Drop-out Rates and Diploma Recipients by Race/Ethnicity

Category	Total	White	Black	Asian	AIAN	Hisp.
Enrollment (%)	100.0	92.8	2.2	2.2	0.0	2.8
Drop-out Rate (%)	n/a	n/a	n/a	n/a	n/a	n/a
H.S. Diplomas (#)	n/a	n/a	n/a	n/a	n/a	n/a

Homer Community CSD 33c
15733 Bell Rd • Homer Glen, IL 60491
(708) 301-3034 • http://www.homerschools.org/
Grade Span: KG-08; **Agency Type:** 1
Schools: 6
   4 Primary; 2 Middle; 0 High; 0 Other Level
   6 Regular; 0 Special Education; 0 Vocational; 0 Alternative
   0 Magnet; 0 Charter; 2 Title I Eligible; 0 School-wide Title I
Students: 3,129 (52.0% male; 47.9% female)
   Individual Education Program: 519 (16.6%);
   English Language Learner: n/a; Migrant: 0 (0.0%)
   Eligible for Free Lunch Program: 0 (0.0%)
   Eligible for Reduced-Price Lunch Program: 0 (0.0%)
Teachers: 162.1 (19.3 to 1)
Librarians/Media Specialists: 1.0 (3,129.0 to 1)
Guidance Counselors: 5.0 (625.8 to 1)
Current Spending: ($ per student per year):
   Total: $7,174; Instruction: $4,376; Support Services: $2,768
Enrollment, Drop-out Rates and Diploma Recipients by Race/Ethnicity

Category	Total	White	Black	Asian	AIAN	Hisp.
Enrollment (%)	100.0	91.8	1.7	1.3	0.1	5.1
Drop-out Rate (%)	n/a	n/a	n/a	n/a	n/a	n/a
H.S. Diplomas (#)	n/a	n/a	n/a	n/a	n/a	n/a

Joliet Public SD 86
420 N Raynor Ave • Joliet, IL 60435-6097
(815) 740-3196 • http://www.joliet86.will.k12.il.us/
Grade Span: PK-08; **Agency Type:** 1
Schools: 24
   18 Primary; 4 Middle; 0 High; 2 Other Level
   21 Regular; 3 Special Education; 0 Vocational; 0 Alternative
   4 Magnet; 0 Charter; 16 Title I Eligible; 15 School-wide Title I
Students: 10,016 (50.7% male; 49.2% female)
   Individual Education Program: 1,587 (15.8%);
   English Language Learner: n/a; Migrant: 10 (0.1%)
   Eligible for Free Lunch Program: 5,856 (58.5%)
   Eligible for Reduced-Price Lunch Program: 1,039 (10.4%)
Teachers: 562.7 (17.8 to 1)
Librarians/Media Specialists: 2.0 (5,008.0 to 1)
Guidance Counselors: 0.0 (n/a to 1)
Current Spending: ($ per student per year):
   Total: $7,448; Instruction: $4,333; Support Services: $2,818
Enrollment, Drop-out Rates and Diploma Recipients by Race/Ethnicity

Category	Total	White	Black	Asian	AIAN	Hisp.
Enrollment (%)	100.0	22.6	37.0	0.8	1.5	38.1
Drop-out Rate (%)	n/a	n/a	n/a	n/a	n/a	n/a
H.S. Diplomas (#)	n/a	n/a	n/a	n/a	n/a	n/a

Joliet Twp HSD 204
201 E Jefferson St • Joliet, IL 60432-2848
(815) 727-6970 • http://www.jths.org/
Grade Span: 09-12; **Agency Type:** 1
Schools: 3
   0 Primary; 0 Middle; 3 High; 0 Other Level
   2 Regular; 1 Special Education; 0 Vocational; 0 Alternative
   0 Magnet; 0 Charter; 2 Title I Eligible; 2 School-wide Title I
Students: 5,069 (50.2% male; 49.7% female)
   Individual Education Program: 957 (18.9%);
   English Language Learner: n/a; Migrant: 0 (0.0%)
   Eligible for Free Lunch Program: 2,230 (44.0%)
   Eligible for Reduced-Price Lunch Program: 591 (11.7%)

Teachers: 303.0 (16.7 to 1)
Librarians/Media Specialists: 6.0 (844.8 to 1)
Guidance Counselors: 14.5 (349.6 to 1)
Current Spending: ($ per student per year):
   Total: $10,889; Instruction: $6,320; Support Services: $4,311
Enrollment, Drop-out Rates and Diploma Recipients by Race/Ethnicity

Category	Total	White	Black	Asian	AIAN	Hisp.
Enrollment (%)	100.0	40.2	31.3	1.3	0.2	27.1
Drop-out Rate (%)	3.3	2.8	3.9	1.3	0.0	3.7
H.S. Diplomas (#)	811	378	243	17	3	170

Lincoln Way Community HSD 210
1801 E Lincoln Hwy • New Lenox, IL 60451-2098
(815) 462-2100 • http://lwhs.will.k12.il.us/
Grade Span: 09-12; **Agency Type:** 1
Schools: 2
   0 Primary; 0 Middle; 2 High; 0 Other Level
   2 Regular; 0 Special Education; 0 Vocational; 0 Alternative
   0 Magnet; 0 Charter; 2 Title I Eligible; 0 School-wide Title I
Students: 5,854 (50.9% male; 49.0% female)
   Individual Education Program: 562 (9.6%);
   English Language Learner: n/a; Migrant: 0 (0.0%)
   Eligible for Free Lunch Program: 92 (1.6%)
   Eligible for Reduced-Price Lunch Program: 68 (1.2%)
Teachers: 291.5 (20.1 to 1)
Librarians/Media Specialists: 2.0 (2,927.0 to 1)
Guidance Counselors: 17.5 (334.5 to 1)
Current Spending: ($ per student per year):
   Total: $7,870; Instruction: $4,502; Support Services: $3,092
Enrollment, Drop-out Rates and Diploma Recipients by Race/Ethnicity

Category	Total	White	Black	Asian	AIAN	Hisp.
Enrollment (%)	100.0	92.6	1.3	1.8	0.2	4.1
Drop-out Rate (%)	0.6	0.6	0.0	0.0	0.0	0.6
H.S. Diplomas (#)	1,070	1,011	11	14	7	27

Lockport Twp HSD 205
1323 E 7th St • Lockport, IL 60441-3899
(815) 588-8100 • http://www.lths.org/
Grade Span: 09-12; **Agency Type:** 1
Schools: 1
   0 Primary; 0 Middle; 1 High; 0 Other Level
   1 Regular; 0 Special Education; 0 Vocational; 0 Alternative
   0 Magnet; 0 Charter; 1 Title I Eligible; 0 School-wide Title I
Students: 3,297 (51.7% male; 48.2% female)
   Individual Education Program: 407 (12.3%);
   English Language Learner: n/a; Migrant: 0 (0.0%)
   Eligible for Free Lunch Program: n/a
   Eligible for Reduced-Price Lunch Program: n/a
Teachers: 174.4 (18.9 to 1)
Librarians/Media Specialists: 2.0 (1,648.5 to 1)
Guidance Counselors: 9.0 (366.3 to 1)
Current Spending: ($ per student per year):
   Total: $9,615; Instruction: $5,736; Support Services: $3,833
Enrollment, Drop-out Rates and Diploma Recipients by Race/Ethnicity

Category	Total	White	Black	Asian	AIAN	Hisp.
Enrollment (%)	100.0	85.9	5.1	1.2	0.6	7.2
Drop-out Rate (%)	3.0	2.7	4.5	2.3	10.0	6.1
H.S. Diplomas (#)	643	564	28	14	1	36

Mokena SD 159
11244 W Willowcrest • Mokena, IL 60448-1398
(708) 342-4900 • http://207.63.182.252/
Grade Span: PK-08; **Agency Type:** 1
Schools: 3
   1 Primary; 2 Middle; 0 High; 0 Other Level
   3 Regular; 0 Special Education; 0 Vocational; 0 Alternative
   0 Magnet; 0 Charter; 1 Title I Eligible; 0 School-wide Title I
Students: 2,355 (51.4% male; 48.5% female)
   Individual Education Program: 340 (14.4%);
   English Language Learner: n/a; Migrant: 0 (0.0%)
   Eligible for Free Lunch Program: 87 (3.7%)
   Eligible for Reduced-Price Lunch Program: 25 (1.1%)
Teachers: 119.5 (19.7 to 1)
Librarians/Media Specialists: 0.0 (n/a to 1)
Guidance Counselors: 0.0 (n/a to 1)
Current Spending: ($ per student per year):
   Total: $5,167; Instruction: $2,815; Support Services: $2,200
Enrollment, Drop-out Rates and Diploma Recipients by Race/Ethnicity

Category	Total	White	Black	Asian	AIAN	Hisp.
Enrollment (%)	100.0	93.4	1.3	1.7	0.5	3.1
Drop-out Rate (%)	n/a	n/a	n/a	n/a	n/a	n/a
H.S. Diplomas (#)	n/a	n/a	n/a	n/a	n/a	n/a

New Lenox SD 122
102 S Cedar Rd • New Lenox, IL 60451-1499
(815) 485-2169 • http://www.myschoolonline.com/
Grade Span: PK-08; **Agency Type:** 1
Schools: 9
 4 Primary; 5 Middle; 0 High; 0 Other Level
 9 Regular; 0 Special Education; 0 Vocational; 0 Alternative
 0 Magnet; 0 Charter; 4 Title I Eligible; 0 School-wide Title I
Students: 5,180 (51.4% male; 48.5% female)
 Individual Education Program: 788 (15.2%)
 English Language Learner: n/a; Migrant: 0 (0.0%)
 Eligible for Free Lunch Program: 130 (2.5%)
 Eligible for Reduced-Price Lunch Program: 92 (1.8%)
Teachers: 256.0 (20.2 to 1)
Librarians/Media Specialists: 8.0 (647.5 to 1)
Guidance Counselors: 7.0 (740.0 to 1)
Current Spending: ($ per student per year):
 Total: $5,380; Instruction: $2,674; Support Services: $2,561
Enrollment, Drop-out Rates and Diploma Recipients by Race/Ethnicity

Category	Total	White	Black	Asian	AIAN	Hisp.
Enrollment (%)	100.0	95.6	0.6	0.7	0.1	2.9
Drop-out Rate (%)	n/a	n/a	n/a	n/a	n/a	n/a
H.S. Diplomas (#)	n/a	n/a	n/a	n/a	n/a	n/a

Peotone CUSD 207u
212 W Wilson St • Peotone, IL 60468-9205
(708) 258-0991 • http://www.peotone.will.k12.il.us/
Grade Span: PK-12; **Agency Type:** 1
Schools: 6
 3 Primary; 2 Middle; 1 High; 0 Other Level
 6 Regular; 0 Special Education; 0 Vocational; 0 Alternative
 0 Magnet; 0 Charter; 1 Title I Eligible; 0 School-wide Title I
Students: 1,839 (52.3% male; 47.6% female)
 Individual Education Program: 254 (13.8%);
 English Language Learner: n/a; Migrant: 0 (0.0%)
 Eligible for Free Lunch Program: 86 (4.7%)
 Eligible for Reduced-Price Lunch Program: 31 (1.7%)
Teachers: 104.6 (17.6 to 1)
Librarians/Media Specialists: 1.0 (1,839.0 to 1)
Guidance Counselors: 1.0 (1,839.0 to 1)
Current Spending: ($ per student per year):
 Total: $6,416; Instruction: $4,278; Support Services: $1,982
Enrollment, Drop-out Rates and Diploma Recipients by Race/Ethnicity

Category	Total	White	Black	Asian	AIAN	Hisp.
Enrollment (%)	100.0	95.9	0.5	0.9	0.1	2.6
Drop-out Rate (%)	0.7	0.6	0.0	0.0	0.0	11.1
H.S. Diplomas (#)	122	117	0	2	0	3

Plainfield SD 202
15732 Howard St • Plainfield, IL 60544-2399
(815) 577-4000 • http://www.plainfield.will.k12.il.us/
Grade Span: PK-12; **Agency Type:** 1
Schools: 20
 13 Primary; 4 Middle; 3 High; 0 Other Level
 18 Regular; 2 Special Education; 0 Vocational; 0 Alternative
 0 Magnet; 0 Charter; 8 Title I Eligible; 0 School-wide Title I
Students: 18,964 (51.2% male; 48.7% female)
 Individual Education Program: 2,510 (13.2%);
 English Language Learner: n/a; Migrant: 0 (0.0%)
 Eligible for Free Lunch Program: 413 (2.2%)
 Eligible for Reduced-Price Lunch Program: 201 (1.1%)
Teachers: 1,061.4 (17.9 to 1)
Librarians/Media Specialists: 14.0 (1,354.6 to 1)
Guidance Counselors: 12.1 (1,567.3 to 1)
Current Spending: ($ per student per year):
 Total: $6,569; Instruction: $4,292; Support Services: $2,073
Enrollment, Drop-out Rates and Diploma Recipients by Race/Ethnicity

Category	Total	White	Black	Asian	AIAN	Hisp.
Enrollment (%)	100.0	75.8	7.5	3.3	0.2	13.3
Drop-out Rate (%)	3.0	2.6	7.6	1.1	11.1	5.1
H.S. Diplomas (#)	748	661	26	12	2	47

Reed Custer CUSD 255u
255 Comet Dr • Braidwood, IL 60408-2098
(815) 458-2307 • http://rc255.will.k12.il.us/255/rc255.html
Grade Span: PK-12; **Agency Type:** 1
Schools: 4
 2 Primary; 1 Middle; 1 High; 0 Other Level
 4 Regular; 0 Special Education; 0 Vocational; 0 Alternative
 0 Magnet; 0 Charter; 2 Title I Eligible; 0 School-wide Title I
Students: 1,806 (49.3% male; 50.6% female)
 Individual Education Program: 353 (19.5%);
 English Language Learner: n/a; Migrant: 0 (0.0%)
 Eligible for Free Lunch Program: 296 (16.4%)
 Eligible for Reduced-Price Lunch Program: 97 (5.4%)

Teachers: 115.5 (15.6 to 1)
Librarians/Media Specialists: 4.0 (451.5 to 1)
Guidance Counselors: 3.0 (602.0 to 1)
Current Spending: ($ per student per year):
 Total: $9,982; Instruction: $6,200; Support Services: $3,488
Enrollment, Drop-out Rates and Diploma Recipients by Race/Ethnicity

Category	Total	White	Black	Asian	AIAN	Hisp.
Enrollment (%)	100.0	95.1	0.7	0.2	0.1	3.9
Drop-out Rate (%)	2.9	3.0	n/a	n/a	0.0	0.0
H.S. Diplomas (#)	113	108	0	0	2	3

Summit Hill SD 161
21133 S 80th Ave • Frankfort, IL 60423-9326
(815) 469-9103 •
http://www.myschoolonline.com/site/0,1876,17809-27273-21-23795,00.html
Grade Span: PK-08; **Agency Type:** 1
Schools: 6
 4 Primary; 2 Middle; 0 High; 0 Other Level
 6 Regular; 0 Special Education; 0 Vocational; 0 Alternative
 0 Magnet; 0 Charter; 4 Title I Eligible; 0 School-wide Title I
Students: 3,470 (49.6% male; 50.3% female)
 Individual Education Program: 480 (13.8%);
 English Language Learner: n/a; Migrant: 0 (0.0%)
 Eligible for Free Lunch Program: 54 (1.6%)
 Eligible for Reduced-Price Lunch Program: 11 (0.3%)
Teachers: 182.0 (19.1 to 1)
Librarians/Media Specialists: 1.0 (3,470.0 to 1)
Guidance Counselors: 0.0 (n/a to 1)
Current Spending: ($ per student per year):
 Total: $4,858; Instruction: $3,125; Support Services: $1,716
Enrollment, Drop-out Rates and Diploma Recipients by Race/Ethnicity

Category	Total	White	Black	Asian	AIAN	Hisp.
Enrollment (%)	100.0	90.2	2.1	2.5	0.1	5.2
Drop-out Rate (%)	n/a	n/a	n/a	n/a	n/a	n/a
H.S. Diplomas (#)	n/a	n/a	n/a	n/a	n/a	n/a

Troy Community CSD 30c
5800 W Theodore St • Plainfield, IL 60544-5269
(815) 577-6760
Grade Span: PK-08; **Agency Type:** 1
Schools: 5
 4 Primary; 1 Middle; 0 High; 0 Other Level
 5 Regular; 0 Special Education; 0 Vocational; 0 Alternative
 0 Magnet; 0 Charter; 4 Title I Eligible; 0 School-wide Title I
Students: 3,533 (51.2% male; 48.7% female)
 Individual Education Program: 517 (14.6%);
 English Language Learner: n/a; Migrant: 0 (0.0%)
 Eligible for Free Lunch Program: 302 (8.5%)
 Eligible for Reduced-Price Lunch Program: 142 (4.0%)
Teachers: 199.0 (17.8 to 1)
Librarians/Media Specialists: 1.0 (3,533.0 to 1)
Guidance Counselors: 7.0 (504.7 to 1)
Current Spending: ($ per student per year):
 Total: $7,308; Instruction: $4,485; Support Services: $2,611
Enrollment, Drop-out Rates and Diploma Recipients by Race/Ethnicity

Category	Total	White	Black	Asian	AIAN	Hisp.
Enrollment (%)	100.0	72.5	10.1	2.2	0.2	15.0
Drop-out Rate (%)	n/a	n/a	n/a	n/a	n/a	n/a
H.S. Diplomas (#)	n/a	n/a	n/a	n/a	n/a	n/a

Valley View Cusd #365u
755 Luther Dr • Romeoville, IL 60446-1157
(815) 886-2700 • http://www.vvsd.org/
Grade Span: PK-12; **Agency Type:** 1
Schools: 17
 11 Primary; 4 Middle; 2 High; 0 Other Level
 17 Regular; 0 Special Education; 0 Vocational; 0 Alternative
 0 Magnet; 0 Charter; 5 Title I Eligible; 1 School-wide Title I
Students: 15,949 (51.7% male; 48.2% female)
 Individual Education Program: 1,891 (11.9%);
 English Language Learner: n/a; Migrant: 0 (0.0%)
 Eligible for Free Lunch Program: 3,475 (21.8%)
 Eligible for Reduced-Price Lunch Program: 1,174 (7.4%)
Teachers: 785.7 (20.3 to 1)
Librarians/Media Specialists: 13.5 (1,181.4 to 1)
Guidance Counselors: 15.0 (1,063.3 to 1)
Current Spending: ($ per student per year):
 Total: $7,246; Instruction: $4,521; Support Services: $2,418
Enrollment, Drop-out Rates and Diploma Recipients by Race/Ethnicity

Category	Total	White	Black	Asian	AIAN	Hisp.
Enrollment (%)	100.0	45.9	25.8	5.3	0.0	23.0
Drop-out Rate (%)	3.8	3.7	3.9	2.9	n/a	4.6
H.S. Diplomas (#)	753	438	183	46	0	86

Will County SD 92

708 N State St • Lockport, IL 60441-2291
(815) 838-8031 • http://www.d92.will.k12.il.us/
Grade Span: PK-08; Agency Type: 1
Schools: 4
    2 Primary; 2 Middle; 0 High; 0 Other Level
    4 Regular; 0 Special Education; 0 Vocational; 0 Alternative
    0 Magnet; 0 Charter; 4 Title I Eligible; 0 School-wide Title I
Students: 2,055 (53.2% male; 46.7% female)
    Individual Education Program: 287 (14.0%);
    English Language Learner: n/a; Migrant: 0 (0.0%)
    Eligible for Free Lunch Program: 70 (3.4%)
    Eligible for Reduced-Price Lunch Program: 23 (1.1%)
Teachers: 102.5 (20.0 to 1)
Librarians/Media Specialists: 0.0 (n/a to 1)
Guidance Counselors: 0.0 (n/a to 1)
Current Spending: ($ per student per year):
    Total: $5,729; Instruction: $3,470; Support Services: $2,147

Enrollment, Drop-out Rates and Diploma Recipients by Race/Ethnicity

Category	Total	White	Black	Asian	AIAN	Hisp.
Enrollment (%)	100.0	93.7	0.6	0.7	0.5	4.5
Drop-out Rate (%)	n/a	n/a	n/a	n/a	n/a	n/a
H.S. Diplomas (#)	n/a	n/a	n/a	n/a	n/a	n/a

Wilmington CUSD 209u

715 S Joliet St • Wilmington, IL 60481-1494
(815) 476-2594 • http://www.wilmington.will.k12.il.us/
Grade Span: PK-12; Agency Type: 1
Schools: 4
    2 Primary; 1 Middle; 1 High; 0 Other Level
    4 Regular; 0 Special Education; 0 Vocational; 0 Alternative
    0 Magnet; 0 Charter; 4 Title I Eligible; 0 School-wide Title I
Students: 1,518 (51.3% male; 48.6% female)
    Individual Education Program: 300 (19.8%);
    English Language Learner: n/a; Migrant: 0 (0.0%)
    Eligible for Free Lunch Program: 222 (14.6%)
    Eligible for Reduced-Price Lunch Program: 90 (5.9%)
Teachers: 89.4 (17.0 to 1)
Librarians/Media Specialists: 2.0 (759.0 to 1)
Guidance Counselors: 2.0 (759.0 to 1)
Current Spending: ($ per student per year):
    Total: $6,218; Instruction: $3,354; Support Services: $2,618

Enrollment, Drop-out Rates and Diploma Recipients by Race/Ethnicity

Category	Total	White	Black	Asian	AIAN	Hisp.
Enrollment (%)	100.0	95.0	0.6	0.4	0.1	4.0
Drop-out Rate (%)	3.4	3.5	n/a	n/a	0.0	0.0
H.S. Diplomas (#)	122	117	0	0	1	4

Carterville CUSD 5

306 Virginia Ave • Carterville, IL 62918-1239
(618) 985-4826
Grade Span: PK-12; Agency Type: 1
Schools: 3
    1 Primary; 1 Middle; 1 High; 0 Other Level
    3 Regular; 0 Special Education; 0 Vocational; 0 Alternative
    0 Magnet; 0 Charter; 2 Title I Eligible; 0 School-wide Title I
Students: 1,632 (50.1% male; 49.8% female)
    Individual Education Program: 344 (21.1%);
    English Language Learner: n/a; Migrant: 0 (0.0%)
    Eligible for Free Lunch Program: 200 (12.3%)
    Eligible for Reduced-Price Lunch Program: 33 (2.0%)
Teachers: 83.0 (19.7 to 1)
Librarians/Media Specialists: 1.0 (1,632.0 to 1)
Guidance Counselors: 2.0 (816.0 to 1)
Current Spending: ($ per student per year):
    Total: $5,062; Instruction: $3,007; Support Services: $1,762

Enrollment, Drop-out Rates and Diploma Recipients by Race/Ethnicity

Category	Total	White	Black	Asian	AIAN	Hisp.
Enrollment (%)	100.0	93.7	3.0	1.3	0.4	1.6
Drop-out Rate (%)	1.9	2.0	0.0	0.0	0.0	0.0
H.S. Diplomas (#)	104	97	4	0	1	2

Herrin CUSD 4

500 N 10th St • Herrin, IL 62948-3399
(618) 988-8024 • http://www.neola.com/herrin-IL/
Grade Span: PK-12; Agency Type: 1
Schools: 4
    2 Primary; 1 Middle; 1 High; 0 Other Level
    4 Regular; 0 Special Education; 0 Vocational; 0 Alternative
    0 Magnet; 0 Charter; 3 Title I Eligible; 3 School-wide Title I
Students: 2,248 (49.8% male; 50.1% female)
    Individual Education Program: 511 (22.7%);
    English Language Learner: n/a; Migrant: 0 (0.0%)
    Eligible for Free Lunch Program: 976 (43.4%)
    Eligible for Reduced-Price Lunch Program: 129 (5.7%)

Teachers: 120.2 (18.7 to 1)
Librarians/Media Specialists: 2.0 (1,124.0 to 1)
Guidance Counselors: 4.0 (562.0 to 1)
Current Spending: ($ per student per year):
    Total: $6,390; Instruction: $3,770; Support Services: $2,322

Enrollment, Drop-out Rates and Diploma Recipients by Race/Ethnicity

Category	Total	White	Black	Asian	AIAN	Hisp.
Enrollment (%)	100.0	91.5	5.8	0.8	0.4	1.6
Drop-out Rate (%)	0.7	0.8	0.0	0.0	0.0	0.0
H.S. Diplomas (#)	129	124	3	2	0	0

Marion Community Unit SD 2

1700 W Cherry St • Marion, IL 62959-1212
(618) 993-2321 • http://www.marion.wilmsn.k12.il.us/
Grade Span: PK-12; Agency Type: 1
Schools: 7
    5 Primary; 1 Middle; 1 High; 0 Other Level
    7 Regular; 0 Special Education; 0 Vocational; 0 Alternative
    0 Magnet; 0 Charter; 7 Title I Eligible; 7 School-wide Title I
Students: 3,953 (52.1% male; 47.8% female)
    Individual Education Program: 836 (21.1%);
    English Language Learner: n/a; Migrant: 0 (0.0%)
    Eligible for Free Lunch Program: 1,116 (28.2%)
    Eligible for Reduced-Price Lunch Program: 210 (5.3%)
Teachers: 202.5 (19.5 to 1)
Librarians/Media Specialists: 3.0 (1,317.7 to 1)
Guidance Counselors: 9.0 (439.2 to 1)
Current Spending: ($ per student per year):
    Total: $5,654; Instruction: $3,511; Support Services: $1,798

Enrollment, Drop-out Rates and Diploma Recipients by Race/Ethnicity

Category	Total	White	Black	Asian	AIAN	Hisp.
Enrollment (%)	100.0	88.2	9.1	1.0	0.3	1.4
Drop-out Rate (%)	4.8	5.1	3.2	0.0	0.0	0.0
H.S. Diplomas (#)	232	211	9	3	3	6

Winnebago County

Harlem Unit Dist 122

PO Box 2021 • Loves Park, IL 61130-2021
(815) 654-4500 • http://www.harlem.winbgo.k12.il.us/
Grade Span: PK-12; Agency Type: 1
Schools: 11
    8 Primary; 2 Middle; 1 High; 0 Other Level
    11 Regular; 0 Special Education; 0 Vocational; 0 Alternative
    2 Magnet; 0 Charter; 5 Title I Eligible; 0 School-wide Title I
Students: 7,886 (51.9% male; 48.0% female)
    Individual Education Program: 1,166 (14.8%);
    English Language Learner: n/a; Migrant: 8 (0.1%)
    Eligible for Free Lunch Program: 1,311 (16.6%)
    Eligible for Reduced-Price Lunch Program: 506 (6.4%)
Teachers: 470.6 (16.8 to 1)
Librarians/Media Specialists: 11.0 (716.9 to 1)
Guidance Counselors: 8.0 (985.8 to 1)
Current Spending: ($ per student per year):
    Total: $7,421; Instruction: $4,684; Support Services: $2,496

Enrollment, Drop-out Rates and Diploma Recipients by Race/Ethnicity

Category	Total	White	Black	Asian	AIAN	Hisp.
Enrollment (%)	100.0	89.0	3.8	1.8	0.4	5.1
Drop-out Rate (%)	3.5	3.5	5.0	0.0	0.0	3.9
H.S. Diplomas (#)	372	346	8	5	0	13

Hononegah Community HSD 207

307 Salem St • Rockton, IL 61072-2630
(815) 624-5010 • http://www.hononegah.org/
Grade Span: 08-12; Agency Type: 1
Schools: 1
    0 Primary; 0 Middle; 1 High; 0 Other Level
    1 Regular; 0 Special Education; 0 Vocational; 0 Alternative
    0 Magnet; 0 Charter; 0 Title I Eligible; 0 School-wide Title I
Students: 1,855 (52.1% male; 47.8% female)
    Individual Education Program: 188 (10.1%);
    English Language Learner: n/a; Migrant: 0 (0.0%)
    Eligible for Free Lunch Program: 119 (6.4%)
    Eligible for Reduced-Price Lunch Program: 18 (1.0%)
Teachers: 106.0 (17.5 to 1)
Librarians/Media Specialists: 1.0 (1,855.0 to 1)
Guidance Counselors: 5.0 (371.0 to 1)
Current Spending: ($ per student per year):
    Total: $9,186; Instruction: $5,656; Support Services: $3,169

Enrollment, Drop-out Rates and Diploma Recipients by Race/Ethnicity

Category	Total	White	Black	Asian	AIAN	Hisp.
Enrollment (%)	100.0	96.5	1.2	0.8	0.3	1.2
Drop-out Rate (%)	1.4	1.4	0.0	0.0	0.0	4.2
H.S. Diplomas (#)	378	354	4	7	2	11

Kinnikinnick CCSD 131

5410 Pine Ln • Roscoe, IL 61073-9220
(815) 623-2837 • http://www.stateline-il.com/kms/
Grade Span: PK-08; Agency Type: 1
Schools: 4
   2 Primary; 2 Middle; 0 High; 0 Other Level
   4 Regular; 0 Special Education; 0 Vocational; 0 Alternative
   0 Magnet; 0 Charter; 0 Title I Eligible; 0 School-wide Title I
Students: 1,871   (51.5% male; 48.4% female)
   Individual Education Program: 260 (13.9%);
   English Language Learner: n/a; Migrant: 0 (0.0%)
   Eligible for Free Lunch Program: 103 (5.5%)
   Eligible for Reduced-Price Lunch Program: 54 (2.9%)
Teachers: 99.9 (18.7 to 1)
Librarians/Media Specialists: 0.0 (n/a to 1)
Guidance Counselors: 1.0 (1,871.0 to 1)
Current Spending: ($ per student per year):
   Total: $5,665; Instruction: $3,665; Support Services: $1,806
Enrollment, Drop-out Rates and Diploma Recipients by Race/Ethnicity

Category	Total	White	Black	Asian	AIAN	Hisp.
Enrollment (%)	100.0	94.4	1.7	1.3	0.1	2.5
Drop-out Rate (%)	n/a	n/a	n/a	n/a	n/a	n/a
H.S. Diplomas (#)	n/a	n/a	n/a	n/a	n/a	n/a

Rockford SD 205

201 S Madison St • Rockford, IL 61104-2092
(815) 966-3101 • http://www.rps205.com/
Grade Span: PK-12; Agency Type: 1
Schools: 53
   40 Primary; 6 Middle; 4 High; 3 Other Level
   49 Regular; 4 Special Education; 0 Vocational; 0 Alternative
   9 Magnet; 0 Charter; 22 Title I Eligible; 22 School-wide Title I
Students: 28,612   (51.1% male; 48.8% female)
   Individual Education Program: 4,138 (14.5%);
   English Language Learner: n/a; Migrant: 0 (0.0%)
   Eligible for Free Lunch Program: 14,539 (50.8%)
   Eligible for Reduced-Price Lunch Program: 2,562 (9.0%)
Teachers: 1,681.2 (17.0 to 1)
Librarians/Media Specialists: 15.5 (1,845.9 to 1)
Guidance Counselors: 54.3 (526.9 to 1)
Current Spending: ($ per student per year):
   Total: $8,606; Instruction: $5,189; Support Services: $3,131
Enrollment, Drop-out Rates and Diploma Recipients by Race/Ethnicity

Category	Total	White	Black	Asian	AIAN	Hisp.
Enrollment (%)	100.0	46.1	32.2	3.2	0.2	18.3
Drop-out Rate (%)	6.4	4.2	10.5	1.7	0.0	8.1
H.S. Diplomas (#)	1,187	775	249	47	4	112

Winnebago CUSD 323

304 E Mcnair Rd • Winnebago, IL 61088-9074
(815) 335-2456 • http://www.winnebagoschools.org/
Grade Span: PK-12; Agency Type: 1
Schools: 5
   2 Primary; 2 Middle; 1 High; 0 Other Level
   5 Regular; 0 Special Education; 0 Vocational; 0 Alternative
   0 Magnet; 0 Charter; 0 Title I Eligible; 0 School-wide Title I
Students: 1,680   (53.0% male; 46.9% female)
   Individual Education Program: 277 (16.5%);
   English Language Learner: n/a; Migrant: 0 (0.0%)
   Eligible for Free Lunch Program: 123 (7.3%)
   Eligible for Reduced-Price Lunch Program: 39 (2.3%)
Teachers: 94.3 (17.8 to 1)
Librarians/Media Specialists: 1.0 (1,680.0 to 1)
Guidance Counselors: 2.5 (672.0 to 1)
Current Spending: ($ per student per year):
   Total: $6,914; Instruction: $4,229; Support Services: $2,456
Enrollment, Drop-out Rates and Diploma Recipients by Race/Ethnicity

Category	Total	White	Black	Asian	AIAN	Hisp.
Enrollment (%)	100.0	95.5	2.5	0.7	0.3	1.0
Drop-out Rate (%)	5.6	5.6	14.3	0.0	n/a	0.0
H.S. Diplomas (#)	107	103	1	2	0	1

Woodford County

Eureka C U Dist 140

109 W Cruger Ave • Eureka, IL 61530-1345
(309) 467-3737 • http://www.eureka.wodfrd.k12.il.us/
Grade Span: PK-12; Agency Type: 1
Schools: 5
   3 Primary; 1 Middle; 1 High; 0 Other Level
   5 Regular; 0 Special Education; 0 Vocational; 0 Alternative
   0 Magnet; 0 Charter; 2 Title I Eligible; 0 School-wide Title I
Students: 1,629   (51.6% male; 48.3% female)
   Individual Education Program: 217 (13.3%);
   English Language Learner: n/a; Migrant: 0 (0.0%)

   Eligible for Free Lunch Program: 186 (11.4%)
   Eligible for Reduced-Price Lunch Program: 44 (2.7%)
Teachers: 98.1 (16.6 to 1)
Librarians/Media Specialists: 2.0 (814.5 to 1)
Guidance Counselors: 3.0 (543.0 to 1)
Current Spending: ($ per student per year):
   Total: $6,940; Instruction: $4,197; Support Services: $2,492
Enrollment, Drop-out Rates and Diploma Recipients by Race/Ethnicity

Category	Total	White	Black	Asian	AIAN	Hisp.
Enrollment (%)	100.0	97.1	1.4	0.6	0.2	0.9
Drop-out Rate (%)	1.2	1.2	0.0	0.0	0.0	0.0
H.S. Diplomas (#)	107	103	0	1	0	3

Number of Schools

Rank	Number	District Name	City
1	633	City of Chicago SD 299	Chicago
2	53	Rockford SD 205	Rockford
2	53	SD 46	Elgin
4	45	Peoria SD 150	Peoria
5	38	Corrections SD 428 Dept of	Springfield
6	36	Springfield SD 186	Springfield
7	31	Indian Prairie CUSD 204	Aurora
8	28	East St Louis SD 189	E Saint Louis
9	27	Schaumburg CCSD 54	Schaumburg
10	26	Decatur SD 61	Decatur
11	24	Community Unit SD 300	Carpentersville
11	24	Joliet Public SD 86	Joliet
11	24	Waukegan CUSD 60	Waukegan
14	21	Mclean County Unit Dist No 5	Normal
14	21	Naperville C U Dist 203	Naperville
16	20	Community Unit SD 200	Wheaton
16	20	Moline Unit SD 40	Moline
16	20	Palatine CCSD 15	Palatine
16	20	Plainfield SD 202	Plainfield
20	18	Champaign Community Unit SD 4	Champaign
20	18	Rock Island SD 41	Rock Island
22	17	Aurora West Unit SD 129	Aurora
22	17	Evanston CCSD 65	Evanston
22	17	St Charles CUSD 303	Saint Charles
22	17	Valley View Cusd #365u	Romeoville
26	16	Aurora East Unit SD 131	Aurora
26	16	Cicero SD 99	Cicero
26	16	Quincy SD 172	Quincy
29	14	Community CSD 59	Arlington Hgts
29	14	Kankakee SD 111	Kankakee
31	13	Alton Community Unit SD 11	Alton
31	13	Elmhurst SD 205	Elmhurst
33	12	Barrington CUSD 220	Barrington
33	12	Chicago Heights SD 170	Chicago Heights
33	12	Crystal Lake CCSD 47	Crystal Lake
33	12	Downers Grove Grade SD 58	Downers Grove
33	12	Edwardsville CUSD 7	Edwardsville
33	12	Galesburg CUSD 205	Galesburg
33	12	Jacksonville SD 117	Jacksonville
33	12	Oswego Community Unit SD 308	Oswego
33	12	Township High SD 214	Arlington Hgts
33	12	Wheeling CCSD 21	Wheeling
43	11	Belleville SD 118	Belleville
43	11	Collinsville CUSD 10	Collinsville
43	11	Community Consolidated SD 62	Des Plaines
43	11	Cook County SD 130	Blue Island
43	11	Danville CCSD 118	Danville
43	11	Dekalb Community Unit SD 428	De Kalb
43	11	Harlem Unit Dist 122	Loves Park
43	11	Maywood-Melrose Park-Broadview-89	Melrose Park
43	11	North Shore SD 112	Highland Park
43	11	Pekin Public SD 108	Pekin
53	10	Cahokia Community Unit SD 187	Cahokia
53	10	Dolton SD 148	Riverdale
53	10	Freeport SD 145	Freeport
53	10	Granite City CUSD 9	Granite City
53	10	North Chicago SD 187	North Chicago
53	10	Oak Park Elem SD 97	Oak Park
53	10	Orland SD 135	Orland Park
60	9	Arlington Heights SD 25	Arlington Hgts
60	9	Belvidere CUSD 100	Belvidere
60	9	Bloomington SD 87	Bloomington
60	9	CCSD 181	Hinsdale
60	9	Lake Zurich CUSD 95	Lake Zurich
60	9	Massac Unit District #1	Metropolis
60	9	New Lenox SD 122	New Lenox
60	9	Urbana SD 116	Urbana
60	9	Woodstock CUSD 200	Woodstock
69	8	Addison SD 4	Addison
69	8	Batavia Unit SD 101	Batavia
69	8	Community Consolidated S D 93	Carol Stream
69	8	Crete Monee CUSD 201u	Crete
69	8	Effingham Community Unit SD 40	Effingham
69	8	Geneva Community Unit SD 304	Geneva
69	8	Glenview CCSD 34	Glenview
69	8	Harvey SD 152	Harvey
69	8	Highland Community Unit SD 5	Highland
69	8	Jasper County Comm Unit Dist 1	Newton
69	8	Jersey CUSD 100	Jerseyville
69	8	Kirby SD 140	Tinley Park
69	8	Mchenry CCSD 15	Mc Henry
69	8	Olympia CUSD 16	Stanford
69	8	Park Ridge CCSD 64	Park Ridge
69	8	Prairie-Hills Elem SD 144	Markham
69	8	Round Lake Area Schs - Dist 116	Round Lake
69	8	SD 45 Dupage County	Villa Park
69	8	Taylorville CUSD 3	Taylorville
88	7	Bellwood SD 88	Bellwood
88	7	Berwyn South SD 100	Berwyn
88	7	Burbank SD 111	Burbank
88	7	Cary CCSD 26	Cary
88	7	Charleston CUSD 1	Charleston
88	7	East Maine SD 63	Des Plaines
88	7	East Peoria SD 86	East Peoria
88	7	Geneseo Community Unit SD 228	Geneseo
88	7	Kildeer Countryside CCSD 96	Buffalo Grove
88	7	Litchfield CUSD 12	Litchfield
88	7	Lombard SD 44	Lombard
88	7	Marion Community Unit SD 2	Marion
88	7	Triad Community Unit SD 2	Troy
88	7	West Chicago Elem SD 33	West Chicago
88	7	Woodridge SD 68	Woodridge
88	7	Zion Elementary SD 6	Zion
104	6	Berkeley SD 87	Berkeley
104	6	Bethalto CUSD 8	Bethalto
104	6	Clinton CUSD 15	Clinton
104	6	Community Consolidated SD 46	Grayslake
104	6	Consolidated SD 158	Huntley
104	6	Deerfield SD 109	Deerfield
104	6	Dolton SD 149	Calumet City
104	6	Dunlap CUSD 323	Dunlap
104	6	Flora Community Unit SD 35	Flora
104	6	Hawthorn CCSD 73	Vernon Hills
104	6	Homer Community CSD 33c	Homer Glen
104	6	Indian Springs SD 109	Justice
104	6	Kewanee Community Unit SD 229	Kewanee
104	6	Lyons SD 103	Lyons
104	6	Matteson Elem SD 162	Matteson
104	6	Monmouth Unit SD 38	Monmouth
104	6	Morton CUSD 709	Morton
104	6	Mt Zion Community Unit SD 3	Mt Zion
104	6	O Fallon CCSD 90	Ofallon
104	6	Oak Lawn-Hometown SD 123	Oak Lawn
104	6	Paris-Union SD 95	Paris
104	6	Park Forest SD 163	Park Forest
104	6	Peotone CUSD 207u	Peotone
104	6	Posen-Robbins El SD 143-5	Posen
104	6	Prairie Central CUSD 8	Forrest
104	6	Sandwich CUSD 430	Sandwich
104	6	Sherrard Community Unit SD 200	Sherrard
104	6	Southwestern CUSD 9	Piasa
104	6	Sterling C U Dist 5	Sterling
104	6	Summit Hill SD 161	Frankfort
104	6	Sycamore CUSD 427	Sycamore
104	6	Tinley Park Comm Cons Sch Dst 146	Tinley Park
104	6	Township HSD 211	Palatine
104	6	W Harvey-Dixmoor PS Dist 147	Harvey
104	6	Wilmette SD 39	Wilmette
139	5	Antioch CCSD 34	Antioch
139	5	Ball Chatham CUSD 5	Chatham
139	5	Beach Park CCSD 3	Beach Park
139	5	Bensenville SD 2	Bensenville
139	5	Bond County CUSD 2	Greenville
139	5	Bourbonnais SD 53	Bourbonnais
139	5	Canton Union SD 66	Canton
139	5	Carlinville CUSD 1	Carlinville
139	5	Central Community Unit SD 301	Burlington
139	5	Dixon Unit SD 170	Dixon
139	5	East Moline SD 37	East Moline
139	5	Elmwood Park CUSD 401	Elmwood Park
139	5	Eureka C U Dist 140	Eureka
139	5	Evergreen Pk Elem SD 124	Evergreen Park
139	5	Flossmoor SD 161	Chicago Heights
139	5	Genoa Kingston CUSD 424	Genoa
139	5	Glen Ellyn CCSD 89	Glen Ellyn
139	5	Glen Ellyn SD 41	Glen Ellyn
139	5	Harvard CUSD 50	Harvard
139	5	Herscher Community Unit SD 2	Herscher
139	5	Hillsboro Community Unit SD 3	Hillsboro
139	5	La Grange SD 102	La Grange Park
139	5	Lake Villa CCSD 41	Lake Villa
139	5	Lansing SD 158	Lansing
139	5	Libertyville SD 70	Libertyville
139	5	Macomb Community Unit SD 185	Macomb
139	5	Mahomet-Seymour CUSD 3	Mahomet
139	5	Maine Township HSD 207	Park Ridge
139	5	Mannheim SD 83	Franklin Park
139	5	Manteno Community Unit SD 5	Manteno
139	5	Marquardt SD 15	Glendale Hgts
139	5	Mattoon CUSD 2	Mattoon
139	5	Monticello CUSD 25	Monticello
139	5	Mundelein Elem SD 75	Mundelein
139	5	Murphysboro CUSD 186	Murphysboro
139	5	North Palos SD 117	Palos Hills
139	5	Oregon C U School Dist-220	Oregon
139	5	Ottawa Elem SD 141	Ottawa
139	5	Pana Community Unit SD 8	Pana
139	5	Rantoul City SD 137	Rantoul
139	5	Ridgeland SD 122	Oak Lawn
139	5	Rochelle Community CD 231	Rochelle
139	5	Sparta CUSD 140	Sparta
139	5	Streator Elem SD 44	Streator
139	5	Summit SD 104	Summit
139	5	Troy Community CSD 30c	Plainfield
139	5	Wauconda Community Unit SD 118	Wauconda
139	5	Westmont CUSD 201	Westmont
139	5	Winnebago CUSD 323	Winnebago
139	5	Winnetka SD 36	Winnetka
139	5	Yorkville Community Unit SD 115	Yorkville
190	4	Alsip-Hazlgrn-Oaklwn SD 126	Alsip
190	4	Aptakisic-Tripp CCSD 102	Buffalo Grove
190	4	Berwyn North SD 98	Berwyn
190	4	Bremen Community HS District 228	Midlothian
190	4	Byron Community Unit SD 226	Byron
190	4	Coal City CUSD 1	Coal City
190	4	Community High SD 155	Crystal Lake
190	4	Community High SD 218	Oak Lawn
190	4	Cons High SD 230	Orland Park
190	4	Darien SD 61	Darien
190	4	Elem SD 159	Matteson
190	4	Forest Ridge SD 142	Oak Forest
190	4	Frankfort Community Unit SD 168	West Frankfort
190	4	Glenbard Twp HSD 87	Glen Ellyn
190	4	Gurnee SD 56	Gurnee
190	4	Harrisburg CUSD 3	Harrisburg
190	4	Herrin CUSD 4	Herrin
190	4	Homewood SD 153	Homewood
190	4	Il Valley Central Unit Dist 321	Chillicothe
190	4	Johnsburg CUSD 12	Johnsburg
190	4	Kaneland CUSD 302	Maple Park
190	4	Kinnikinnick CCSD 131	Roscoe
190	4	Lake Forest SD 67	Lake Forest
190	4	Lemont-Bromberek CSD 113a	Lemont
190	4	Lisle CUSD 202	Lisle
190	4	Mascoutah C U District 19	Mascoutah
190	4	Meridian CUSD 223	Stillman Valley
190	4	Midlothian SD 143	Midlothian
190	4	Mount Vernon SD 80	Mount Vernon
190	4	Northbrook SD 28	Northbrook
190	4	Prospect Heights SD 23	Prospect Hgts
190	4	Reed Custer CUSD 255u	Braidwood
190	4	Rich Twp HS District 227	Olympia Fields
190	4	Robinson CUSD 2	Robinson
190	4	Rochester Community Unit SD 3a	Rochester
190	4	Roxana Community Unit SD 1	Roxana
190	4	Skokie SD 68	Skokie
190	4	Steger SD 194	Steger
190	4	Vandalia CUSD 203	Vandalia
190	4	Wabash CUSD 348	Mount Carmel
190	4	Waterloo Community Unit SD 5	Waterloo
190	4	Will County SD 92	Lockport
190	4	Wilmington CUSD 209u	Wilmington
190	4	Woodland CCSD 50	Gurnee
234	3	Belleville Twp HSD 201	Belleville
234	3	Bloom Twp High SD 206	Chicago Heights
234	3	Bradley SD 61	Bradley
234	3	Carterville CUSD 5	Carterville
234	3	Columbia Community Unit SD 4	Columbia
234	3	Community CSD 168	Sauk Village
234	3	Community High SD 117	Lake Villa
234	3	Country Club Hills SD 160	Ctry Club Hill
234	3	East Richland CUSD 1	Olney
234	3	Frankfort CCSD 157c	Frankfort
234	3	J S Morton HS District 201	Cicero
234	3	Joliet Twp HSD 204	Joliet
234	3	Keeneyville SD 20	Hanover Park
234	3	Lincolnshire-Prairieview S D 103	Lincolnshire
234	3	Minooka Community CSD 201	Minooka
234	3	Mokena SD 159	Mokena
234	3	Mount Prospect SD 57	Mount Prospect
234	3	Nippersink SD 2	Richmond
234	3	Northfield Twp High SD 225	Glenview
234	3	Palos Community CSD 118	Palos Park
234	3	Queen Bee SD 16	Glendale Hgts
234	3	River Trails SD 26	Mount Prospect
234	3	Thornton Fractional T HS D 215	Calumet City
234	3	Thornton Twp HSD 205	South Holland
258	2	Community High SD 128	Libertyville
258	2	Community High SD 99	Downers Grove
258	2	Du Page High SD 88	Villa Park
258	2	Fremont SD 79	Mundelein
258	2	Hinsdale Twp HSD 86	Hinsdale
258	2	Leyden Community HSD 212	Franklin Park
258	2	Lincoln Way Community HSD 210	New Lenox
258	2	Mchenry Community HSD 156	Mc Henry
258	2	New Trier Twp HSD 203	Northfield
258	2	Niles Twp Community High SD 219	Skokie
258	2	Proviso Twp HSD 209	Maywood
258	2	Township High SD 113	Highland Park
270	1	Adlai E Stevenson Dist 125	Lincolnshire
270	1	Argo Community HSD 217	Summit
270	1	Bradley Bourbonnais CHSD 307	Bradley
270	1	Community High SD 94	West Chicago
270	1	Evanston Twp HSD 202	Evanston
270	1	Fenton Community HSD 100	Bensenville

270	1	Grayslake Community High SD 127	Grayslake
270	1	Homewood Flossmoor CHSD 233	Flossmoor
270	1	Hononegah Community HSD 207	Rockton
270	1	Lake Forest Community HS Dist 115	Lake Forest
270	1	Lake Park Community HSD 108	Roselle
270	1	Lockport Twp HSD 205	Lockport
270	1	Lyons Twp HSD 204	La Grange
270	1	Minooka Community HS District 111	Minooka
270	1	Mundelein Cons High SD 120	Mundelein
270	1	O Fallon Twp High SD 203	Ofallon
270	1	Oak Lawn Community HSD 229	Oak Lawn
270	1	Oak Park & River Forest Dist 200	Oak Park
270	1	Ottawa Twp HSD 140	Ottawa
270	1	Pekin Community HSD 303	Pekin
270	1	Reavis Twp HSD 220	Burbank
270	1	United Twp HS District 30	East Moline
270	1	Warren Twp High SD 121	Gages Lake
270	1	Zion-Benton Twp HSD 126	Zion

Number of Teachers

Rank	Number	District Name	City
1	22,950	City of Chicago SD 299	Chicago
2	1,878	SD 46	Elgin
3	1,681	Rockford SD 205	Rockford
4	1,638	Indian Prairie CUSD 204	Aurora
5	1,066	Peoria SD 150	Peoria
6	1,061	Plainfield SD 202	Plainfield
7	1,049	Naperville C U Dist 203	Naperville
8	944	Springfield SD 186	Springfield
9	916	Schaumburg CCSD 54	Schaumburg
10	864	Community Unit SD 300	Carpentersville
11	860	Community Unit SD 200	Wheaton
12	859	Waukegan CUSD 60	Waukegan
13	796	Township HSD 211	Palatine
14	785	Valley View Cusd #365u	Romeoville
15	765	Township High SD 214	Arlington Hgts
16	748	Palatine CCSD 15	Palatine
17	746	Cicero SD 99	Cicero
18	728	St Charles CUSD 303	Saint Charles
19	726	Mclean County Unit Dist No 5	Normal
20	646	Aurora West Unit SD 129	Aurora
21	643	Champaign Community Unit SD 4	Champaign
22	603	Aurora East Unit SD 131	Aurora
23	600	East St Louis SD 189	E Saint Louis
24	562	Joliet Public SD 86	Joliet
25	528	Evanston CCSD 65	Evanston
26	524	Crystal Lake CCSD 47	Crystal Lake
27	518	Barrington CUSD 220	Barrington
28	488	Maine Township HSD 207	Park Ridge
29	483	Oswego Community Unit SD 308	Oswego
30	478	Cons High SD 230	Orland Park
31	470	Harlem Unit Dist 122	Loves Park
32	468	Wheeling CCSD 21	Wheeling
33	467	Woodland CCSD 50	Gurnee
34	464	Glenbard Twp HSD 87	Glen Ellyn
35	453	Decatur SD 61	Decatur
36	451	Moline Unit SD 40	Moline
37	449	Elmhurst SD 205	Elmhurst
38	427	Lake Zurich CUSD 95	Lake Zurich
39	424	Thornton Twp HSD 205	South Holland
40	420	Alton Community Unit SD 11	Alton
41	412	J S Morton HS District 201	Cicero
42	402	Rock Island SD 41	Rock Island
43	400	Edwardsville CUSD 7	Edwardsville
44	398	Community CSD 59	Arlington Hgts
45	388	Belvidere CUSD 100	Belvidere
46	368	Quincy SD 172	Quincy
47	361	Danville CCSD 118	Danville
47	361	Granite City CUSD 9	Granite City
49	360	Community High SD 155	Crystal Lake
50	357	Oak Park Elem SD 97	Oak Park
51	355	Bloomington SD 87	Bloomington
52	354	Orland SD 135	Orland Park
53	346	Batavia Unit SD 101	Batavia
54	342	Collinsville CUSD 10	Collinsville
55	336	Dekalb Community Unit SD 428	De Kalb
56	335	Community Consolidated SD 62	Des Plaines
57	332	Maywood-Melrose Park-Broadview-89	Melrose Park
58	331	Consolidated SD 158	Huntley
59	331	North Shore SD 112	Highland Park
60	329	Northfield Twp High SD 225	Glenview
61	324	Kankakee SD 111	Kankakee
62	321	Geneva Community Unit SD 304	Geneva
63	321	Woodstock CUSD 200	Woodstock
64	320	New Trier Twp HSD 203	Northfield
65	319	Niles Twp Community High SD 219	Skokie
66	318	Urbana SD 116	Urbana
67	316	Arlington Heights SD 25	Arlington Hgts
68	314	Park Ridge CCSD 64	Park Ridge
69	314	Bremen Community HS District 228	Midlothian
70	311	Community High SD 99	Downers Grove
71	303	Joliet Twp HSD 204	Joliet
72	301	Round Lake Area Schs - Dist 116	Round Lake
73	300	Galesburg CUSD 205	Galesburg
74	296	Community Consolidated S D 93	Carol Stream
75	291	Lincoln Way Community HSD 210	New Lenox
76	286	Kirby SD 140	Tinley Park
77	285	Freeport SD 145	Freeport
78	280	Community High SD 218	Oak Lawn
79	278	Glenview CCSD 34	Glenview
80	276	Corrections SD 428 Dept of	Springfield
81	275	Hinsdale Twp HSD 86	Hinsdale
82	274	North Chicago SD 187	North Chicago
83	269	Adlai E Stevenson Dist 125	Lincolnshire
83	269	Wilmette SD 39	Wilmette
85	265	Proviso Twp HSD 209	Maywood
86	264	Downers Grove Grade SD 58	Downers Grove
87	259	Mchenry CCSD 15	Mc Henry
88	256	New Lenox SD 122	New Lenox
89	253	Jacksonville SD 117	Jacksonville
90	252	Crete Monee CUSD 201u	Crete
91	251	Evanston Twp HSD 202	Evanston
92	248	Cahokia Community Unit SD 187	Cahokia
93	245	Cook County SD 130	Blue Island
94	243	CCSD 181	Hinsdale
95	240	Belleville Twp HSD 201	Belleville
96	240	Pekin Public SD 108	Pekin
97	239	Du Page High SD 88	Villa Park
98	237	Mattoon CUSD 2	Mattoon
99	235	Township High SD 113	Highland Park
100	233	SD 45 Dupage County	Villa Park
101	233	Wauconda Community Unit SD 118	Wauconda
102	232	West Chicago Elem SD 33	West Chicago
103	227	Hawthorn CCSD 73	Vernon Hills
104	226	Deerfield SD 109	Deerfield
105	222	East Maine SD 63	Des Plaines
106	222	Glen Ellyn SD 41	Glen Ellyn
107	220	Kildeer Countryside CCSD 96	Buffalo Grove
108	219	Berwyn South SD 100	Berwyn
109	219	Addison SD 4	Addison
110	218	Cary CCSD 26	Cary
111	217	Ball Chatham CUSD 5	Chatham
112	214	Triad Community Unit SD 2	Troy
113	214	Lake Villa CCSD 41	Lake Villa
114	214	Chicago Heights SD 170	Chicago Heights
115	211	Leyden Community HSD 212	Franklin Park
116	210	Community Consolidated SD 46	Grayslake
117	209	Rich Twp HS District 227	Olympia Fields
118	206	Lyons Twp HSD 204	La Grange
119	202	Marion Community Unit SD 2	Marion
120	201	Dolton SD 149	Calumet City
121	199	Lombard SD 44	Lombard
122	199	Belleville SD 118	Belleville
123	199	Bloom Twp High SD 206	Chicago Heights
123	199	Troy Community CSD 30c	Plainfield
125	198	Sterling C U Dist 5	Sterling
126	197	Oak Lawn-Hometown SD 123	Oak Lawn
127	196	Kaneland CUSD 302	Maple Park
128	195	Thornton Fractional T H S D 215	Calumet City
129	194	Warren Twp High SD 121	Gages Lake
130	192	Sycamore CUSD 427	Sycamore
131	190	Community High SD 128	Libertyville
132	189	Highland Community Unit SD 5	Highland
133	188	Oak Park & River Forest Dist 200	Oak Park
134	188	Woodridge SD 68	Woodridge
135	185	La Grange SD 102	La Grange Park
136	184	Mascoutah C U District 19	Mascoutah
137	183	Jersey CUSD 100	Jerseyville
138	182	Dolton SD 148	Riverdale
138	182	Matteson Elem SD 162	Matteson
138	182	Summit Hill SD 161	Frankfort
141	181	Mannheim SD 83	Franklin Park
142	179	Burbank SD 111	Burbank
143	178	Effingham Community Unit SD 40	Effingham
144	177	Charleston CUSD 1	Charleston
145	177	Lake Forest SD 67	Lake Forest
146	174	Lockport Twp HSD 205	Lockport
147	173	Prairie-Hills Elem SD 144	Markham
148	171	Bethalto CUSD 8	Bethalto
149	171	Tinley Park Comm Cons Sch Dst 146	Tinley Park
150	171	Canton Union SD 66	Canton
151	171	Indian Springs SD 109	Justice
152	171	Berkeley SD 87	Berkeley
153	170	Dixon Unit SD 170	Dixon
154	169	Morton CUSD 709	Morton
155	166	O Fallon CCSD 90	Ofallon
156	165	Taylorville CUSD 3	Taylorville
157	165	Geneseo Community Unit SD 228	Geneseo
158	164	Bellwood SD 88	Bellwood
159	162	Flossmoor SD 161	Chicago Heights
160	162	Elmwood Park CUSD 401	Elmwood Park
161	162	Homer Community CSD 33c	Homer Glen
162	161	Libertyville SD 70	Libertyville
163	159	East Moline SD 37	East Moline
164	159	Aptakisic-Tripp CCSD 102	Buffalo Grove
165	156	Homewood Flossmoor CHSD 233	Flossmoor
166	154	Mahomet-Seymour CUSD 3	Mahomet
167	154	Lake Park Community HSD 108	Roselle
167	154	Marquardt SD 15	Glendale Hgts
169	153	Glen Ellyn CCSD 89	Glen Ellyn
170	153	Northbrook SD 28	Northbrook
171	151	Waterloo Community Unit SD 5	Waterloo
171	151	Zion Elementary SD 6	Zion
173	151	Clinton CUSD 15	Clinton
174	151	Antioch CCSD 34	Antioch
175	151	Olympia CUSD 16	Stanford
176	150	Homewood SD 153	Homewood
177	149	Berwyn North SD 98	Berwyn
178	149	North Palos SD 117	Palos Hills
179	148	Harvey SD 152	Harvey
180	146	Winnetka SD 36	Winnetka
181	146	Central Community Unit SD 301	Burlington
182	145	Johnsburg CUSD 12	Johnsburg
183	145	Yorkville Community Unit SD 115	Yorkville
184	143	Herscher Community Unit SD 2	Herscher
185	142	Sandwich CUSD 430	Sandwich
186	141	Mundelein Elem SD 75	Mundelein
187	140	Bensenville SD 2	Bensenville
188	139	Lemont-Bromberek CSD 113a	Lemont
189	139	Queen Bee SD 16	Glendale Hgts
190	135	Murphysboro CUSD 186	Murphysboro
191	134	Il Valley Central Unit Dist 321	Chillicothe
192	134	Massac Unit District #1	Metropolis
193	134	East Richland CUSD 1	Olney
194	134	Dunlap CUSD 323	Dunlap
195	133	Bourbonnais SD 53	Bourbonnais
196	133	Community High SD 117	Lake Villa
196	133	Mchenry Community HSD 156	Mc Henry
198	132	Harvard CUSD 50	Harvard
199	131	Prairie Central CUSD 8	Forrest
200	131	Macomb Community Unit SD 185	Macomb
201	130	Harrisburg CUSD 3	Harrisburg
202	130	Park Forest SD 163	Park Forest
203	129	Lyons SD 103	Lyons
204	129	Ottawa Elem SD 141	Ottawa
205	129	Evergreen Pk Elem SD 124	Evergreen Park
206	129	Gurnee SD 56	Gurnee
207	125	Zion-Benton Twp HSD 126	Zion
208	125	Darien SD 61	Darien
209	125	Community High SD 94	West Chicago
210	125	Sherrard Community Unit SD 200	Sherrard
211	125	Palos Community CSD 118	Palos Park
212	124	Grayslake Community High SD 127	Grayslake
213	124	Byron Community Unit SD 226	Byron
214	124	Beach Park CCSD 3	Beach Park
215	123	Mt Zion Community Unit SD 3	Mt Zion
216	122	East Peoria SD 86	East Peoria
217	122	Streator Elem SD 44	Streator
218	122	Ridgeland SD 122	Oak Lawn
218	122	Skokie SD 68	Skokie
220	121	Lincolnshire-Prairieview S D 103	Lincolnshire
221	121	Lake Forest Community HS Dist 115	Lake Forest
222	120	Manteno Community Unit SD 5	Manteno
223	120	Elem SD 159	Matteson
224	120	Herrin CUSD 4	Herrin
225	119	Mokena SD 159	Mokena
226	119	Hillsboro Community Unit SD 3	Hillsboro
227	118	Lansing SD 158	Lansing
227	118	Rochelle Community CD 231	Rochelle
229	118	Mount Prospect SD 57	Mount Prospect
230	118	Summit SD 104	Summit
231	117	Mundelein Cons High SD 120	Mundelein
232	117	River Trails SD 26	Mount Prospect
233	117	Mount Vernon SD 80	Mount Vernon
234	116	Wabash CUSD 348	Mount Carmel
235	116	Pekin Community HSD 303	Pekin
236	115	Reed Custer CUSD 255u	Braidwood
237	114	Bond County CUSD 2	Greenville
238	114	Roxana Community Unit SD 1	Roxana
239	113	Lisle CUSD 202	Lisle
240	113	Forest Ridge SD 142	Oak Forest
240	113	Westmont CUSD 201	Westmont
242	111	Prospect Heights SD 23	Prospect Hgts
243	111	Frankfort CCSD 157c	Frankfort
244	110	Coal City CUSD 1	Coal City
245	110	Paris-Union SD 95	Paris
246	109	Frankfort Community Unit SD 168	West Frankfort
247	109	Jasper County Comm Unit Dist 1	Newton
248	108	Rochester Community Unit SD 3a	Rochester
249	108	Genoa Kingston CUSD 424	Genoa
250	108	Steger SD 194	Steger
251	107	Robinson CUSD 2	Robinson
252	107	Keeneyville SD 20	Hanover Park
253	106	O Fallon Twp High SD 203	Ofallon
254	106	Country Club Hills SD 160	Ctry Club Hill
255	106	Hononegah Community HSD 207	Rockton
256	104	Columbia Community Unit SD 4	Columbia

256	104	Peotone CUSD 207u	Peotone
258	104	Midlothian SD 143	Midlothian
259	103	Monticello CUSD 25	Monticello
260	103	Alsip-Hazlgrn-Oaklwn SD 126	Alsip
261	102	Nippersink SD 2	Richmond
261	102	Will County SD 92	Lockport
263	102	W Harvey-Dixmoor PS Dist 147	Harvey
264	101	Rantoul City SD 137	Rantoul
265	100	Monmouth Unit SD 38	Monmouth
265	100	Oregon C U School Dist-220	Oregon
267	99	Kinnikinnick CCSD 131	Roscoe
267	99	Vandalia CUSD 203	Vandalia
269	99	Southwestern CUSD 9	Piasa
270	99	Flora Community Unit SD 35	Flora
271	98	Argo Community HSD 217	Summit
272	98	Pana Community Unit SD 8	Pana
273	98	Eureka C U Dist 140	Eureka
274	97	Sparta CUSD 140	Sparta
275	97	Ottawa Twp HSD 140	Ottawa
276	96	Fenton Community HSD 100	Bensenville
277	96	Kewanee Community Unit SD 229	Kewanee
278	94	Winnebago CUSD 323	Winnebago
279	94	Community CSD 168	Sauk Village
280	93	United Twp HS District 30	East Moline
281	91	Minooka Community CSD 201	Minooka
282	90	Reavis Twp HSD 220	Burbank
283	90	Meridian CUSD 223	Stillman Valley
284	90	Litchfield CUSD 12	Litchfield
285	89	Wilmington CUSD 209u	Wilmington
286	89	Bradley Bourbonnais CHSD 307	Bradley
286	89	Oak Lawn Community HSD 229	Oak Lawn
288	88	Fremont SD 79	Mundelein
289	85	Carlinville CUSD 1	Carlinville
290	85	Bradley SD 61	Bradley
291	83	Minooka Community HS District 111	Minooka
292	83	Carterville CUSD 5	Carterville
293	81	Posen-Robbins El SD 143-5	Posen

Number of Students

Rank	Number	District Name	City
1	434,419	City of Chicago SD 299	Chicago
2	38,821	SD 46	Elgin
3	28,612	Rockford SD 205	Rockford
4	26,779	Indian Prairie CUSD 204	Aurora
5	18,964	Plainfield SD 202	Plainfield
6	18,933	Naperville C U Dist 203	Naperville
7	18,175	Community Unit SD 300	Carpentersville
8	16,260	Waukegan CUSD 60	Waukegan
9	15,949	Valley View Cusd #365u	Romeoville
10	15,863	Peoria SD 150	Peoria
11	15,212	Springfield SD 186	Springfield
12	14,948	Schaumburg CCSD 54	Schaumburg
13	14,191	Community Unit SD 200	Wheaton
14	13,479	Cicero SD 99	Cicero
15	12,939	St Charles CUSD 303	Saint Charles
16	12,935	Township HSD 211	Palatine
17	12,882	Palatine CCSD 15	Palatine
18	12,209	Township High SD 214	Arlington Hgts
19	11,717	Aurora West Unit SD 129	Aurora
20	11,420	Aurora East Unit SD 131	Aurora
21	10,932	Mclean County Unit Dist No 5	Normal
22	10,349	East St Louis SD 189	E Saint Louis
23	10,118	Corrections SD 428 Dept of	Springfield
24	10,111	Decatur SD 61	Decatur
25	10,016	Joliet Public SD 86	Joliet
26	9,771	Oswego Community Unit SD 308	Oswego
27	9,371	Champaign Community Unit SD 4	Champaign
28	9,115	Crystal Lake CCSD 47	Crystal Lake
29	8,944	Glenbard Twp HSD 87	Glen Ellyn
30	8,721	Barrington CUSD 220	Barrington
31	8,197	Cons High SD 230	Orland Park
32	7,886	Harlem Unit Dist 122	Loves Park
33	7,767	Moline Unit SD 40	Moline
34	7,583	Granite City CUSD 9	Granite City
35	7,574	Belvidere CUSD 100	Belvidere
36	7,529	J S Morton HS District 201	Cicero
37	7,416	Elmhurst SD 205	Elmhurst
38	7,182	Quincy SD 172	Quincy
39	7,055	Woodland CCSD 50	Gurnee
40	7,024	Wheeling CCSD 21	Wheeling
41	6,992	Edwardsville CUSD 7	Edwardsville
42	6,957	Evanston CCSD 65	Evanston
43	6,906	Alton Community Unit SD 11	Alton
44	6,882	Maine Township HSD 207	Park Ridge
45	6,677	Rock Island SD 41	Rock Island
46	6,635	Thornton Twp HSD 205	South Holland
47	6,489	Lake Zurich CUSD 95	Lake Zurich
48	6,389	Community CSD 59	Arlington Hgts
49	6,379	Danville CCSD 118	Danville
50	6,343	Community High SD 155	Crystal Lake
51	6,333	Round Lake Area Schs - Dist 116	Round Lake
52	6,078	Collinsville CUSD 10	Collinsville
53	5,956	Batavia Unit SD 101	Batavia
54	5,937	Orland SD 135	Orland Park
55	5,917	Maywood-Melrose Park-Broadview-89	Melrose Park
56	5,854	Lincoln Way Community HSD 210	New Lenox
57	5,831	Woodstock CUSD 200	Woodstock
58	5,804	Kankakee SD 111	Kankakee
59	5,674	Bloomington SD 87	Bloomington
60	5,549	Geneva Community Unit SD 304	Geneva
61	5,490	Community High SD 99	Downers Grove
62	5,473	Dekalb Community Unit SD 428	De Kalb
63	5,416	Consolidated SD 158	Huntley
64	5,180	New Lenox SD 122	New Lenox
65	5,153	Community High SD 218	Oak Lawn
66	5,098	Cahokia Community Unit SD 187	Cahokia
67	5,085	Community Consolidated SD 62	Des Plaines
68	5,069	Joliet Twp HSD 204	Joliet
69	4,940	Galesburg CUSD 205	Galesburg
70	4,939	Belleville Twp HSD 201	Belleville
71	4,938	Oak Park Elem SD 97	Oak Park
72	4,913	Arlington Heights SD 25	Arlington Hgts
73	4,900	Community Consolidated S D 93	Carol Stream
74	4,857	Bremen Community HS District 228	Midlothian
75	4,852	Proviso Twp HSD 209	Maywood
76	4,837	Crete Monee CUSD 201u	Crete
77	4,808	Niles Twp Community High SD 219	Skokie
78	4,776	Northfield Twp High SD 225	Glenview
79	4,771	Downers Grove Grade SD 58	Downers Grove
80	4,723	Mchenry CCSD 15	Mc Henry
81	4,592	Kirby SD 140	Tinley Park
82	4,570	Urbana SD 116	Urbana
83	4,552	North Chicago SD 187	North Chicago
84	4,467	Freeport SD 145	Freeport
85	4,421	North Shore SD 112	Highland Park
86	4,404	Park Ridge CCSD 64	Park Ridge
87	4,351	Adlai E Stevenson Dist 125	Lincolnshire
88	4,239	Hinsdale Twp HSD 86	Hinsdale
89	4,060	Ball Chatham CUSD 5	Chatham
90	4,028	CCSD 181	Hinsdale
91	4,017	Du Page High SD 88	Villa Park
92	4,013	Community Consolidated SD 46	Grayslake
93	3,980	Dolton SD 149	Calumet City
94	3,975	Glenview CCSD 34	Glenview
95	3,970	Wauconda Community Unit SD 118	Wauconda
96	3,958	New Trier Twp HSD 203	Northfield
97	3,953	Marion Community Unit SD 2	Marion
98	3,918	Addison SD 4	Addison
99	3,841	Cook County SD 130	Blue Island
99	3,841	West Chicago Elem SD 33	West Chicago
101	3,835	Pekin Public SD 108	Pekin
102	3,820	SD 45 Dupage County	Villa Park
103	3,788	Jacksonville SD 117	Jacksonville
104	3,768	Triad Community Unit SD 2	Troy
105	3,740	Belleville SD 118	Belleville
106	3,718	Hawthorn CCSD 73	Vernon Hills
107	3,663	Cary CCSD 26	Cary
108	3,627	Warren Twp High SD 121	Gages Lake
109	3,595	Wilmette SD 39	Wilmette
110	3,564	Lyons Twp HSD 204	La Grange
111	3,558	East Maine SD 63	Des Plaines
112	3,556	Sterling C U Dist 5	Sterling
113	3,534	Rich Twp HS District 227	Olympia Fields
114	3,533	Troy Community CSD 30c	Plainfield
115	3,512	Township High SD 113	Highland Park
116	3,491	Leyden Community HSD 212	Franklin Park
117	3,487	Kildeer Countryside CCSD 96	Buffalo Grove
118	3,482	Glen Ellyn SD 41	Glen Ellyn
119	3,471	Chicago Heights SD 170	Chicago Heights
120	3,470	Summit Hill SD 161	Frankfort
121	3,421	Berwyn South SD 100	Berwyn
122	3,377	Burbank SD 111	Burbank
123	3,347	Bellwood SD 88	Bellwood
124	3,325	Kaneland CUSD 302	Maple Park
125	3,323	Mattoon CUSD 2	Mattoon
126	3,307	Lombard SD 44	Lombard
127	3,299	Dolton SD 148	Riverdale
128	3,297	Lockport Twp HSD 205	Lockport
129	3,288	Lake Villa CCSD 41	Lake Villa
130	3,157	Deerfield SD 109	Deerfield
131	3,143	O Fallon CCSD 90	Ofallon
132	3,139	Berwyn North SD 98	Berwyn
133	3,138	Sycamore CUSD 427	Sycamore
134	3,129	Homer Community CSD 33c	Homer Glen
135	3,122	Harvey SD 152	Harvey
136	3,120	Taylorville CUSD 3	Taylorville
137	3,118	Evanston Twp HSD 202	Evanston
138	3,103	Woodridge SD 68	Woodridge
139	3,074	Thornton Fractional T HS D 215	Calumet City
140	3,038	Bloom Twp High SD 206	Chicago Heights
141	3,026	Jersey CUSD 100	Jerseyville
142	3,024	Matteson Elem SD 162	Matteson
143	3,023	Oak Park & River Forest Dist 200	Oak Park
144	3,016	Indian Springs SD 109	Justice
145	3,008	Highland Community Unit SD 5	Highland
146	3,007	Community High SD 128	Libertyville
147	3,005	Effingham Community Unit SD 40	Effingham
148	2,992	Dixon Unit SD 170	Dixon
149	2,952	Charleston CUSD 1	Charleston
150	2,951	Elmwood Park CUSD 401	Elmwood Park
151	2,949	Berkeley SD 87	Berkeley
152	2,934	Zion Elementary SD 6	Zion
153	2,921	Lake Park Community HSD 108	Roselle
154	2,914	Prairie-Hills Elem SD 144	Markham
155	2,877	Geneseo Community Unit SD 228	Geneseo
156	2,873	Mascoutah C U District 19	Mascoutah
157	2,851	Oak Lawn-Hometown SD 123	Oak Lawn
158	2,835	Mannheim SD 83	Franklin Park
159	2,832	Yorkville Community Unit SD 115	Yorkville
160	2,796	Bethalto CUSD 8	Bethalto
161	2,769	Canton Union SD 66	Canton
162	2,767	Homewood Flossmoor CHSD 233	Flossmoor
163	2,706	North Palos SD 117	Palos Hills
164	2,695	Johnsburg CUSD 12	Johnsburg
165	2,673	Mahomet-Seymour CUSD 3	Mahomet
166	2,672	Marquardt SD 15	Glendale Hgts
167	2,666	La Grange SD 102	La Grange Park
168	2,659	Morton CUSD 709	Morton
169	2,653	Libertyville SD 70	Libertyville
170	2,601	Waterloo Community Unit SD 5	Waterloo
171	2,597	Flossmoor SD 161	Chicago Heights
172	2,541	Antioch CCSD 34	Antioch
173	2,532	Lemont-Bromberek CSD 113a	Lemont
174	2,519	Dunlap CUSD 323	Dunlap
175	2,473	East Moline SD 37	East Moline
176	2,458	Mt Zion Community Unit SD 3	Mt Zion
177	2,454	Sandwich CUSD 430	Sandwich
178	2,426	Bourbonnais SD 53	Bourbonnais
179	2,420	Tinley Park Comm Cons Sch Dst 146	Tinley Park
180	2,413	Central Community Unit SD 301	Burlington
181	2,396	Zion-Benton Twp HSD 126	Zion
182	2,379	Glen Ellyn CCSD 89	Glen Ellyn
183	2,369	Massac Unit District #1	Metropolis
184	2,355	Mokena SD 159	Mokena
185	2,329	Community High SD 117	Lake Villa
186	2,325	Bensenville SD 2	Bensenville
186	2,325	Mchenry Community HSD 156	Mc Henry
188	2,314	Aptakisic-Tripp CCSD 102	Buffalo Grove
189	2,284	Harvard CUSD 50	Harvard
190	2,283	Ridgeland SD 122	Oak Lawn
191	2,274	Lyons SD 103	Lyons
192	2,248	Herrin CUSD 4	Herrin
193	2,240	Gurnee SD 56	Gurnee
194	2,238	Beach Park CCSD 3	Beach Park
195	2,231	Olympia CUSD 16	Stanford
196	2,219	Mundelein Elem SD 75	Mundelein
196	2,219	Park Forest SD 163	Park Forest
198	2,208	Harrisburg CUSD 3	Harrisburg
199	2,205	Murphysboro CUSD 186	Murphysboro
200	2,194	Lake Forest SD 67	Lake Forest
201	2,175	Herscher Community Unit SD 2	Herscher
202	2,150	O Fallon Twp High SD 203	Ofallon
203	2,146	Community High SD 94	West Chicago
204	2,137	Clinton CUSD 15	Clinton
205	2,133	Homewood SD 153	Homewood
206	2,119	Lansing SD 158	Lansing
207	2,112	Queen Bee SD 16	Glendale Hgts
208	2,104	Il Valley Central Unit Dist 321	Chillicothe
209	2,085	East Richland CUSD 1	Olney
210	2,079	Winnetka SD 36	Winnetka
211	2,078	Mundelein Cons High SD 120	Mundelein
211	2,078	Pekin Community HSD 303	Pekin
213	2,057	Grayslake Community High SD 127	Grayslake
214	2,055	Ottawa Elem SD 141	Ottawa
214	2,055	Will County SD 92	Lockport
216	2,046	Hillsboro Community Unit SD 3	Hillsboro
217	2,023	Mount Prospect SD 57	Mount Prospect
218	2,022	Evergreen Pk Elem SD 124	Evergreen Park
219	2,009	Palos Community CSD 118	Palos Park
220	1,975	Bond County CUSD 2	Greenville
221	1,965	Macomb Community Unit SD 185	Macomb
222	1,948	Manteno Community Unit SD 5	Manteno
223	1,921	Frankfort CCSD 157c	Frankfort
224	1,920	Coal City CUSD 1	Coal City
225	1,912	Rochester Community Unit SD 3a	Rochester
226	1,897	Mount Vernon SD 80	Mount Vernon
227	1,889	Prairie Central CUSD 8	Forrest
228	1,886	Streator Elem SD 44	Streator
229	1,884	Wabash CUSD 348	Mount Carmel
230	1,883	East Peoria SD 86	East Peoria
231	1,877	Roxana Community Unit SD 1	Roxana
232	1,871	Kinnikinnick CCSD 131	Roscoe
233	1,856	Kewanee Community Unit SD 229	Kewanee
234	1,855	Hononegah Community HSD 207	Rockton
235	1,852	Frankfort Community Unit SD 168	West Frankfort
236	1,845	Rochelle Community CD 231	Rochelle

237	1,839	Peotone CUSD 207u	Peotone
238	1,838	W Harvey-Dixmoor PS Dist 147	Harvey
239	1,833	Elem SD 159	Matteson
240	1,822	Midlothian SD 143	Midlothian
241	1,816	United Twp HS District 30	East Moline
242	1,808	Lisle CUSD 202	Lisle
243	1,806	Reed Custer CUSD 255u	Braidwood
244	1,803	Oregon C U School Dist-220	Oregon
245	1,798	Southwestern CUSD 9	Piasa
246	1,793	Northbrook SD 28	Northbrook
247	1,786	Byron Community Unit SD 226	Byron
248	1,783	Bradley Bourbonnais CHSD 307	Bradley
249	1,782	Vandalia CUSD 203	Vandalia
250	1,778	Minooka Community CSD 201	Minooka
251	1,777	Robinson CUSD 2	Robinson
252	1,776	Genoa Kingston CUSD 424	Genoa
253	1,772	Community CSD 168	Sauk Village
254	1,766	Darien SD 61	Darien
255	1,765	Sherrard Community Unit SD 200	Sherrard
256	1,762	Forest Ridge SD 142	Oak Forest
257	1,758	Meridian CUSD 223	Stillman Valley
258	1,735	Lake Forest Community HS Dist 115	Lake Forest
259	1,727	Keeneyville SD 20	Hanover Park
260	1,724	Lincolnshire-Prairieview S D 103	Lincolnshire
261	1,717	Columbia Community Unit SD 4	Columbia
262	1,697	Oak Lawn Community HSD 229	Oak Lawn
263	1,696	Westmont CUSD 201	Westmont
264	1,695	Alsip-Hazlgrn-Oaklwn SD 126	Alsip
264	1,695	Paris-Union SD 95	Paris
266	1,692	Summit SD 104	Summit
267	1,690	Rantoul City SD 137	Rantoul
268	1,687	Argo Community HSD 217	Summit
269	1,680	Winnebago CUSD 323	Winnebago
270	1,654	Litchfield CUSD 12	Litchfield
271	1,650	River Trails SD 26	Mount Prospect
272	1,638	Steger SD 194	Steger
273	1,636	Skokie SD 68	Skokie
274	1,632	Carterville CUSD 5	Carterville
275	1,631	Reavis Twp HSD 220	Burbank
276	1,629	Eureka C U Dist 140	Eureka
277	1,620	Country Club Hills SD 160	Ctry Club Hill
278	1,615	Monticello CUSD 25	Monticello
279	1,609	Jasper County Comm Unit Dist 1	Newton
280	1,600	Carlinville CUSD 1	Carlinville
281	1,589	Sparta CUSD 140	Sparta
282	1,585	Nippersink SD 2	Richmond
283	1,576	Ottawa Twp HSD 140	Ottawa
284	1,561	Fremont SD 79	Mundelein
285	1,553	Bradley SD 61	Bradley
286	1,542	Posen-Robbins El SD 143-5	Posen
287	1,534	Minooka Community HS District 111	Minooka
288	1,531	Monmouth Unit SD 38	Monmouth
289	1,529	Prospect Heights SD 23	Prospect Hgts
290	1,518	Pana Community Unit SD 8	Pana
290	1,518	Wilmington CUSD 209u	Wilmington
292	1,508	Flora Community Unit SD 35	Flora
293	1,501	Fenton Community HSD 100	Bensenville

Male Students

Rank	Percent	District Name	City
1	91.4	Corrections SD 428 Dept of	Springfield
2	54.0	Mannheim SD 83	Franklin Park
3	53.8	Fenton Community HSD 100	Bensenville
4	53.4	Bourbonnais SD 53	Bourbonnais
5	53.4	Community High SD 117	Lake Villa
6	53.4	Keeneyville SD 20	Hanover Park
7	53.4	Lake Villa CCSD 41	Lake Villa
8	53.3	Darien SD 61	Darien
9	53.3	Oak Lawn-Hometown SD 123	Oak Lawn
10	53.2	Will County SD 92	Lockport
11	53.2	Community High SD 128	Libertyville
12	53.2	North Palos SD 117	Palos Hills
13	53.1	Geneseo Community Unit SD 228	Geneseo
14	53.1	Galesburg CUSD 205	Galesburg
15	53.1	Cook County SD 130	Blue Island
16	53.0	Winnebago CUSD 323	Winnebago
17	53.0	Rochester Community Unit SD 3a	Rochester
18	53.0	Harvard CUSD 50	Harvard
19	52.9	Cary CCSD 26	Cary
20	52.9	Bloom Twp High SD 206	Chicago Heights
21	52.9	Northbrook SD 28	Northbrook
22	52.9	Oregon C U School Dist-220	Oregon
23	52.9	Winnetka SD 36	Winnetka
24	52.8	La Grange SD 102	La Grange Park
25	52.8	Bensenville SD 2	Bensenville
26	52.8	Mchenry Community HSD 156	Mc Henry
27	52.7	Forest Ridge SD 142	Oak Forest
28	52.7	Herscher Community Unit SD 2	Herscher
29	52.6	Midlothian SD 143	Midlothian
30	52.5	United Twp HS District 30	East Moline
31	52.5	Canton Union SD 66	Canton
32	52.5	Collinsville CUSD 10	Collinsville
33	52.5	Bond County CUSD 2	Greenville
34	52.5	Du Page High SD 88	Villa Park
35	52.5	Effingham Community Unit SD 40	Effingham
36	52.5	Monticello CUSD 25	Monticello
37	52.4	Posen-Robbins El SD 143-5	Posen
38	52.4	Naperville C U Dist 203	Naperville
39	52.4	Community CSD 59	Arlington Hgts
40	52.4	Belleville SD 118	Belleville
41	52.4	Bellwood SD 88	Bellwood
42	52.4	Mchenry CCSD 15	Mc Henry
43	52.4	Oswego Community Unit SD 308	Oswego
44	52.3	Columbia Community Unit SD 4	Columbia
45	52.3	Libertyville SD 70	Libertyville
46	52.3	Community Consolidated SD 46	Grayslake
47	52.3	Community Unit SD 200	Wheaton
48	52.3	Dolton SD 149	Calumet City
49	52.3	Robinson CUSD 2	Robinson
50	52.3	Elmhurst SD 205	Elmhurst
51	52.3	Peotone CUSD 207u	Peotone
52	52.3	East Peoria SD 86	East Peoria
53	52.3	Woodstock CUSD 200	Woodstock
54	52.2	Cicero SD 99	Cicero
55	52.2	East Richland CUSD 1	Olney
56	52.2	River Trails SD 26	Mount Prospect
57	52.2	Nippersink SD 2	Richmond
58	52.2	Gurnee SD 56	Gurnee
59	52.1	Hononegah Community HSD 207	Rockton
60	52.1	Township High SD 214	Arlington Hgts
61	52.1	Bradley SD 61	Bradley
62	52.1	Antioch CCSD 34	Antioch
63	52.1	Niles Twp Community High SD 219	Skokie
64	52.1	Lake Forest SD 67	Lake Forest
65	52.1	Marion Community Unit SD 2	Marion
66	52.1	Minooka Community CSD 201	Minooka
67	52.1	Dolton SD 148	Riverdale
68	52.0	Northfield Twp High SD 225	Glenview
69	52.0	Summit SD 104	Summit
70	52.0	Tinley Park Comm Cons Sch Dst 146	Tinley Park
71	52.0	Westmont CUSD 201	Westmont
72	52.0	Homer Community CSD 33c	Homer Glen
73	52.0	Schaumburg CCSD 54	Schaumburg
74	52.0	Adlai E Stevenson Dist 125	Lincolnshire
75	52.0	Maine Township HSD 207	Park Ridge
76	52.0	Glenbard Twp HSD 87	Glen Ellyn
77	52.0	Mundelein Cons High SD 120	Mundelein
78	52.0	Community Consolidated S D 93	Carol Stream
79	52.0	Woodridge SD 68	Woodridge
80	52.0	Yorkville Community Unit SD 115	Yorkville
81	51.9	Mclean County Unit Dist No 5	Normal
82	51.9	Community High SD 99	Downers Grove
83	51.9	Harlem Unit Dist 122	Loves Park
84	51.9	Rantoul City SD 137	Rantoul
85	51.9	East Moline SD 37	East Moline
86	51.9	Park Ridge CCSD 64	Park Ridge
87	51.9	Ridgeland SD 122	Oak Lawn
88	51.9	Mount Prospect SD 57	Mount Prospect
89	51.8	Ball Chatham CUSD 5	Chatham
90	51.8	Orland SD 135	Orland Park
91	51.8	Carlinville CUSD 1	Carlinville
92	51.8	Moline Unit SD 40	Moline
93	51.8	Glen Ellyn SD 41	Glen Ellyn
94	51.8	Wauconda Community Unit SD 118	Wauconda
95	51.8	Charleston CUSD 1	Charleston
96	51.8	Il Valley Central Unit Dist 321	Chillicothe
97	51.8	Frankfort CCSD 157c	Frankfort
98	51.8	Zion-Benton Twp HSD 126	Zion
99	51.8	Lombard SD 44	Lombard
100	51.8	Sycamore CUSD 427	Sycamore
101	51.8	Oak Park Elem SD 97	Oak Park
102	51.7	Lake Park Community HSD 108	Roselle
103	51.7	Vandalia CUSD 203	Vandalia
104	51.7	New Trier Twp HSD 203	Northfield
105	51.7	Evergreen Pk Elem SD 124	Evergreen Park
106	51.7	Valley View Cusd #365u	Romeoville
107	51.7	Woodland CCSD 50	Gurnee
108	51.7	Kirby SD 140	Tinley Park
109	51.7	Rochelle Community CD 231	Rochelle
110	51.7	Morton CUSD 709	Morton
111	51.7	Deerfield SD 109	Deerfield
112	51.7	Southwestern CUSD 9	Piasa
113	51.7	Lockport Twp HSD 205	Lockport
114	51.7	Sandwich CUSD 430	Sandwich
115	51.7	Steger SD 194	Steger
116	51.7	O Fallon CCSD 90	Ofallon
117	51.6	Minooka Community HS District 111	Minooka
118	51.6	Bloomington SD 87	Bloomington
119	51.6	Johnsburg CUSD 12	Johnsburg
120	51.6	Eureka C U Dist 140	Eureka
121	51.6	Flossmoor SD 161	Chicago Heights
122	51.6	Kaneland CUSD 302	Maple Park
123	51.6	Lisle CUSD 202	Lisle
124	51.6	Bradley Bourbonnais CHSD 307	Bradley
125	51.6	SD 45 Dupage County	Villa Park
126	51.6	Litchfield CUSD 12	Litchfield
127	51.6	Crystal Lake CCSD 47	Crystal Lake
128	51.6	West Chicago Elem SD 33	West Chicago
129	51.5	Wilmette SD 39	Wilmette
130	51.5	Thornton Fractional T HS D 215	Calumet City
131	51.5	Palatine CCSD 15	Palatine
132	51.5	Granite City CUSD 9	Granite City
133	51.5	Kinnikinnick CCSD 131	Roscoe
134	51.5	Matteson Elem SD 162	Matteson
135	51.5	J S Morton HS District 201	Cicero
136	51.5	Bethalto CUSD 8	Bethalto
137	51.5	Elem SD 159	Matteson
138	51.4	Mattoon CUSD 2	Mattoon
139	51.4	Urbana SD 116	Urbana
140	51.4	Beach Park CCSD 3	Beach Park
141	51.4	Murphysboro CUSD 186	Murphysboro
142	51.4	Prospect Heights SD 23	Prospect Hgts
143	51.4	Mokena SD 159	Mokena
144	51.4	Ottawa Twp HSD 140	Ottawa
145	51.4	New Lenox SD 122	New Lenox
146	51.4	St Charles CUSD 303	Saint Charles
147	51.4	Hillsboro Community Unit SD 3	Hillsboro
148	51.4	Prairie Central CUSD 8	Forrest
149	51.3	Township High SD 113	Highland Park
150	51.3	Wilmington CUSD 209u	Wilmington
151	51.3	Community High SD 155	Crystal Lake
152	51.3	Harvey SD 152	Harvey
153	51.3	Chicago Heights SD 170	Chicago Heights
154	51.3	Round Lake Area Schs - Dist 116	Round Lake
155	51.3	Indian Springs SD 109	Justice
156	51.3	Springfield SD 186	Springfield
157	51.3	Peoria SD 150	Peoria
158	51.3	Crete Monee CUSD 201u	Crete
159	51.3	Alsip-Hazlgrn-Oaklwn SD 126	Alsip
159	51.3	Community Consolidated SD 62	Des Plaines
161	51.3	Township HSD 211	Palatine
162	51.3	Streator Elem SD 44	Streator
163	51.3	Berwyn North SD 98	Berwyn
164	51.3	Consolidated SD 158	Huntley
165	51.3	Lemont-Bromberek CSD 113a	Lemont
166	51.2	Skokie SD 68	Skokie
167	51.2	Batavia Unit SD 101	Batavia
168	51.2	Harrisburg CUSD 3	Harrisburg
169	51.2	W Harvey-Dixmoor PS Dist 147	Harvey
170	51.2	SD 46	Elgin
171	51.2	Kewanee Community Unit SD 229	Kewanee
172	51.2	Hinsdale Twp HSD 86	Hinsdale
173	51.2	Olympia CUSD 16	Stanford
174	51.2	Troy Community CSD 30c	Plainfield
175	51.2	Glenview CCSD 34	Glenview
176	51.2	Plainfield SD 202	Plainfield
177	51.1	Marquardt SD 15	Glendale Hgts
178	51.1	Hawthorn CCSD 73	Vernon Hills
179	51.1	Manteno Community Unit SD 5	Manteno
180	51.1	Waterloo Community Unit SD 5	Waterloo
181	51.1	Rockford SD 205	Rockford
182	51.1	Geneva Community Unit SD 304	Geneva
183	51.1	Belvidere CUSD 100	Belvidere
184	51.1	Waukegan CUSD 60	Waukegan
185	51.1	Grayslake Community High SD 127	Grayslake
186	51.1	Lake Zurich CUSD 95	Lake Zurich
187	51.1	Community CSD 168	Sauk Village
188	51.1	Community Unit SD 300	Carpentersville
189	51.1	Champaign Community Unit SD 4	Champaign
190	51.1	Alton Community Unit SD 11	Alton
191	51.1	Triad Community Unit SD 2	Troy
191	51.1	Wabash CUSD 348	Mount Carmel
193	51.1	Aurora West Unit SD 129	Aurora
194	51.1	Country Club Hills SD 160	Ctry Club Hill
195	51.1	Lansing SD 158	Lansing
196	51.1	Bremen Community HS District 228	Midlothian
197	51.0	Leyden Community HSD 212	Franklin Park
198	51.0	Park Forest SD 163	Park Forest
199	51.0	Massac Unit District #1	Metropolis
200	51.0	Burbank SD 111	Burbank
201	50.9	Downers Grove Grade SD 58	Downers Grove
202	50.9	Barrington CUSD 220	Barrington
203	50.9	Jersey CUSD 100	Jerseyville
203	50.9	Mahomet-Seymour CUSD 3	Mahomet
205	50.9	Glen Ellyn CCSD 89	Glen Ellyn
206	50.9	Kankakee SD 111	Kankakee
207	50.9	Berwyn South SD 100	Berwyn
208	50.9	Indian Prairie CUSD 204	Aurora
209	50.9	Jasper County Comm Unit Dist 1	Newton
210	50.9	North Shore SD 112	Highland Park
211	50.9	Edwardsville CUSD 7	Edwardsville
212	50.9	Quincy SD 172	Quincy
213	50.9	Lincoln Way Community HSD 210	New Lenox
214	50.9	North Chicago SD 187	North Chicago
215	50.8	Berkeley SD 87	Berkeley
216	50.8	Wheeling CCSD 21	Wheeling
217	50.8	Dunlap CUSD 323	Dunlap

218	50.8	Prairie-Hills Elem SD 144	Markham
219	50.8	Belleville Twp HSD 201	Belleville
220	50.8	Pekin Public SD 108	Pekin
221	50.8	East Maine SD 63	Des Plaines
222	50.8	Decatur SD 61	Decatur
223	50.8	Frankfort Community Unit SD 168	West Frankfort
224	50.8	O Fallon Twp High SD 203	Ofallon
225	50.8	Mundelein Elem SD 75	Mundelein
226	50.8	Taylorville CUSD 3	Taylorville
227	50.8	Evanston CCSD 65	Evanston
228	50.8	Clinton CUSD 15	Clinton
229	50.8	Rock Island SD 41	Rock Island
230	50.8	Aurora East Unit SD 131	Aurora
231	50.8	Argo Community HSD 217	Summit
232	50.7	Freeport SD 145	Freeport
233	50.7	Arlington Heights SD 25	Arlington Hgts
234	50.7	CCSD 181	Hinsdale
235	50.7	Jacksonville SD 117	Jacksonville
236	50.7	Sterling C U Dist 5	Sterling
237	50.7	Joliet Public SD 86	Joliet
238	50.7	Dixon Unit SD 170	Dixon
239	50.6	Highland Community Unit SD 5	Highland
240	50.6	Elmwood Park CUSD 401	Elmwood Park
241	50.6	Evanston Twp HSD 202	Evanston
242	50.6	Genoa Kingston CUSD 424	Genoa
243	50.5	Oak Park & River Forest Dist 200	Oak Park
244	50.5	Rich Twp HS District 227	Olympia Fields
245	50.5	Thornton Twp HSD 205	South Holland
246	50.5	Community High SD 94	West Chicago
247	50.5	Warren Twp High SD 121	Gages Lake
248	50.5	Danville CCSD 118	Danville
249	50.4	Lake Forest Community HS Dist 115	Lake Forest
250	50.4	Aptakisic-Tripp CCSD 102	Buffalo Grove
251	50.4	Dekalb Community Unit SD 428	De Kalb
252	50.4	Maywood-Melrose Park-Broadview-89	Melrose Park
253	50.4	City of Chicago SD 299	Chicago
254	50.4	Ottawa Elem SD 141	Ottawa
255	50.3	Homewood SD 153	Homewood
256	50.3	Sherrard Community Unit SD 200	Sherrard
257	50.3	Community High SD 218	Oak Lawn
258	50.3	Lyons SD 103	Lyons
259	50.3	Queen Bee SD 16	Glendale Hgts
260	50.3	Kildeer Countryside CCSD 96	Buffalo Grove
261	50.2	Mascoutah C U District 19	Mascoutah
262	50.2	Byron Community Unit SD 226	Byron
263	50.2	Homewood Flossmoor CHSD 233	Flossmoor
264	50.2	Joliet Twp HSD 204	Joliet
265	50.2	Oak Lawn Community HSD 229	Oak Lawn
266	50.2	Pekin Community HSD 303	Pekin
267	50.2	Monmouth Unit SD 38	Monmouth
268	50.1	Carterville CUSD 5	Carterville
269	50.1	Central Community Unit SD 301	Burlington
270	50.1	Addison SD 4	Addison
271	50.1	Macomb Community Unit SD 185	Macomb
272	50.1	Cons High SD 230	Orland Park
273	50.0	Pana Community Unit SD 8	Pana
274	50.0	Cahokia Community Unit SD 187	Cahokia
275	50.0	Meridian CUSD 223	Stillman Valley
275	50.0	Mt Zion Community Unit SD 3	Mt Zion
277	49.9	Sparta CUSD 140	Sparta
278	49.9	Fremont SD 79	Mundelein
279	49.8	Herrin CUSD 4	Herrin
280	49.8	Flora Community Unit SD 35	Flora
281	49.7	Palos Community CSD 118	Palos Park
282	49.7	Lyons Twp HSD 204	La Grange
283	49.7	Coal City CUSD 1	Coal City
284	49.6	Summit Hill SD 161	Frankfort
285	49.5	Reavis Twp HSD 220	Burbank
286	49.5	Zion Elementary SD 6	Zion
287	49.4	Roxana Community Unit SD 1	Roxana
288	49.4	Proviso Twp HSD 209	Maywood
289	49.4	Lincolnshire-Prairieview S D 103	Lincolnshire
290	49.3	Reed Custer CUSD 255u	Braidwood
291	49.3	East St Louis SD 189	E Saint Louis
292	49.1	Mount Vernon SD 80	Mount Vernon
293	47.9	Paris-Union SD 95	Paris

Female Students

Rank	Percent	District Name	City
1	52.0	Paris-Union SD 95	Paris
2	50.8	Mount Vernon SD 80	Mount Vernon
3	50.6	East St Louis SD 189	E Saint Louis
4	50.6	Reed Custer CUSD 255u	Braidwood
5	50.5	Lincolnshire-Prairieview S D 103	Lincolnshire
6	50.5	Proviso Twp HSD 209	Maywood
7	50.5	Roxana Community Unit SD 1	Roxana
8	50.4	Zion Elementary SD 6	Zion
9	50.4	Reavis Twp HSD 220	Burbank
10	50.3	Summit Hill SD 161	Frankfort
11	50.2	Coal City CUSD 1	Coal City
12	50.2	Lyons Twp HSD 204	La Grange
13	50.2	Palos Community CSD 118	Palos Park
14	50.1	Flora Community Unit SD 35	Flora
15	50.1	Herrin CUSD 4	Herrin
16	50.0	Fremont SD 79	Mundelein
17	50.0	Sparta CUSD 140	Sparta
18	50.0	Meridian CUSD 223	Stillman Valley
18	50.0	Mt Zion Community Unit SD 3	Mt Zion
20	49.9	Cahokia Community Unit SD 187	Cahokia
21	49.9	Pana Community Unit SD 8	Pana
22	49.8	Cons High SD 230	Orland Park
23	49.8	Macomb Community Unit SD 185	Macomb
24	49.8	Addison SD 4	Addison
25	49.8	Central Community Unit SD 301	Burlington
26	49.8	Carterville CUSD 5	Carterville
27	49.7	Monmouth Unit SD 38	Monmouth
28	49.7	Pekin Community HSD 303	Pekin
29	49.7	Oak Lawn Community HSD 229	Oak Lawn
30	49.7	Joliet Twp HSD 204	Joliet
31	49.7	Homewood Flossmoor CHSD 233	Flossmoor
32	49.7	Byron Community Unit SD 226	Byron
33	49.7	Mascoutah C U District 19	Mascoutah
34	49.6	Kildeer Countryside CCSD 96	Buffalo Grove
35	49.6	Queen Bee SD 16	Glendale Hgts
36	49.6	Lyons SD 103	Lyons
37	49.6	Community High SD 218	Oak Lawn
38	49.6	Sherrard Community Unit SD 200	Sherrard
39	49.6	Homewood SD 153	Homewood
40	49.5	Ottawa Elem SD 141	Ottawa
41	49.5	City of Chicago SD 299	Chicago
42	49.5	Maywood-Melrose Park-Broadview-89	Melrose Park
43	49.5	Dekalb Community Unit SD 428	De Kalb
44	49.5	Aptakisic-Tripp CCSD 102	Buffalo Grove
45	49.5	Lake Forest Community HS Dist 115	Lake Forest
46	49.4	Danville CCSD 118	Danville
47	49.4	Warren Twp High SD 121	Gages Lake
48	49.4	Community High SD 94	West Chicago
49	49.4	Thornton Twp HSD 205	South Holland
50	49.4	Rich Twp HS District 227	Olympia Fields
51	49.4	Oak Park & River Forest Dist 200	Oak Park
52	49.3	Genoa Kingston CUSD 424	Genoa
53	49.3	Evanston Twp HSD 202	Evanston
54	49.3	Elmwood Park CUSD 401	Elmwood Park
55	49.3	Highland Community Unit SD 5	Highland
56	49.2	Dixon Unit SD 170	Dixon
57	49.2	Joliet Public SD 86	Joliet
58	49.2	Sterling C U Dist 5	Sterling
59	49.2	Jacksonville SD 117	Jacksonville
60	49.2	CCSD 181	Hinsdale
61	49.2	Arlington Heights SD 25	Arlington Hgts
62	49.2	Freeport SD 145	Freeport
63	49.1	Argo Community HSD 217	Summit
64	49.1	Aurora East Unit SD 131	Aurora
65	49.1	Rock Island SD 41	Rock Island
66	49.1	Clinton CUSD 15	Clinton
67	49.1	Evanston CCSD 65	Evanston
68	49.1	Taylorville CUSD 3	Taylorville
69	49.1	Mundelein Elem SD 75	Mundelein
70	49.1	O Fallon Twp High SD 203	Ofallon
71	49.1	Frankfort Community Unit SD 168	West Frankfort
72	49.1	Decatur SD 61	Decatur
73	49.1	East Maine SD 63	Des Plaines
74	49.1	Pekin Public SD 108	Pekin
75	49.1	Belleville Twp HSD 201	Belleville
76	49.1	Prairie-Hills Elem SD 144	Markham
77	49.1	Dunlap CUSD 323	Dunlap
78	49.1	Wheeling CCSD 21	Wheeling
79	49.1	Berkeley SD 87	Berkeley
80	49.1	North Chicago SD 187	North Chicago
81	49.0	Lincoln Way Community HSD 210	New Lenox
82	49.0	Quincy SD 172	Quincy
83	49.0	Edwardsville CUSD 7	Edwardsville
84	49.0	North Shore SD 112	Highland Park
85	49.0	Jasper County Comm Unit Dist 1	Newton
86	49.0	Indian Prairie CUSD 204	Aurora
87	49.0	Berwyn South SD 100	Berwyn
88	49.0	Kankakee SD 111	Kankakee
89	49.0	Glen Ellyn CCSD 89	Glen Ellyn
90	49.0	Jersey CUSD 100	Jerseyville
90	49.0	Mahomet-Seymour CUSD 3	Mahomet
92	49.0	Barrington CUSD 220	Barrington
93	49.0	Downers Grove Grade SD 58	Downers Grove
94	48.9	Burbank SD 111	Burbank
95	48.9	Massac Unit District #1	Metropolis
96	48.9	Park Forest SD 163	Park Forest
97	48.9	Leyden Community HSD 212	Franklin Park
98	48.8	Bremen Community HS District 228	Midlothian
99	48.8	Lansing SD 158	Lansing
100	48.8	Country Club Hills SD 160	Ctry Club Hill
101	48.8	Aurora West Unit SD 129	Aurora
102	48.8	Triad Community Unit SD 2	Troy
102	48.8	Wabash CUSD 348	Mount Carmel
104	48.8	Alton Community Unit SD 11	Alton
105	48.8	Champaign Community Unit SD 4	Champaign
106	48.8	Community Unit SD 300	Carpentersville
107	48.8	Community CSD 168	Sauk Village
108	48.8	Lake Zurich CUSD 95	Lake Zurich
109	48.8	Grayslake Community High SD 127	Grayslake
110	48.8	Waukegan CUSD 60	Waukegan
111	48.8	Belvidere CUSD 100	Belvidere
112	48.8	Geneva Community Unit SD 304	Geneva
113	48.8	Rockford SD 205	Rockford
114	48.8	Waterloo Community Unit SD 5	Waterloo
115	48.8	Manteno Community Unit SD 5	Manteno
116	48.8	Hawthorn CCSD 73	Vernon Hills
117	48.8	Marquardt SD 15	Glendale Hgts
118	48.7	Plainfield SD 202	Plainfield
119	48.7	Glenview CCSD 34	Glenview
120	48.7	Troy Community CSD 30c	Plainfield
121	48.7	Olympia CUSD 16	Stanford
122	48.7	Hinsdale Twp HSD 86	Hinsdale
123	48.7	Kewanee Community Unit SD 229	Kewanee
124	48.7	SD 46	Elgin
125	48.7	W Harvey-Dixmoor PS Dist 147	Harvey
126	48.7	Harrisburg CUSD 3	Harrisburg
127	48.7	Batavia Unit SD 101	Batavia
128	48.7	Skokie SD 68	Skokie
129	48.6	Lemont-Bromberek CSD 113a	Lemont
130	48.6	Consolidated SD 158	Huntley
131	48.6	Berwyn North SD 98	Berwyn
132	48.6	Streator Elem SD 44	Streator
133	48.6	Township HSD 211	Palatine
134	48.6	Alsip-Hazlgrn-Oaklwn SD 126	Alsip
134	48.6	Community Consolidated SD 62	Des Plaines
136	48.6	Crete Monee CUSD 201u	Crete
137	48.6	Peoria SD 150	Peoria
138	48.6	Springfield SD 186	Springfield
139	48.6	Indian Springs SD 109	Justice
140	48.6	Round Lake Area Schs - Dist 116	Round Lake
141	48.6	Chicago Heights SD 170	Chicago Heights
142	48.6	Harvey SD 152	Harvey
143	48.6	Community High SD 155	Crystal Lake
144	48.6	Wilmington CUSD 209u	Wilmington
145	48.6	Township High SD 113	Highland Park
146	48.5	Prairie Central CUSD 8	Forrest
147	48.5	Hillsboro Community Unit SD 3	Hillsboro
148	48.5	St Charles CUSD 303	Saint Charles
149	48.5	New Lenox SD 122	New Lenox
150	48.5	Ottawa Twp HSD 140	Ottawa
151	48.5	Mokena SD 159	Mokena
152	48.5	Prospect Heights SD 23	Prospect Hgts
153	48.5	Murphysboro CUSD 186	Murphysboro
154	48.5	Beach Park CCSD 3	Beach Park
155	48.5	Urbana SD 116	Urbana
156	48.5	Mattoon CUSD 2	Mattoon
157	48.4	Elem SD 159	Matteson
158	48.4	Bethalto CUSD 8	Bethalto
159	48.4	J S Morton HS District 201	Cicero
160	48.4	Matteson Elem SD 162	Matteson
161	48.4	Kinnikinnick CCSD 131	Roscoe
162	48.4	Granite City CUSD 9	Granite City
163	48.4	Palatine CCSD 15	Palatine
164	48.4	Thornton Fractional T HS D 215	Calumet City
165	48.4	Wilmette SD 39	Wilmette
166	48.3	West Chicago Elem SD 33	West Chicago
167	48.3	Crystal Lake CCSD 47	Crystal Lake
168	48.3	Litchfield CUSD 12	Litchfield
169	48.3	SD 45 Dupage County	Villa Park
170	48.3	Bradley Bourbonnais CHSD 307	Bradley
171	48.3	Lisle CUSD 202	Lisle
172	48.3	Kaneland CUSD 302	Maple Park
173	48.3	Flossmoor SD 161	Chicago Heights
174	48.3	Eureka C U Dist 140	Eureka
175	48.3	Johnsburg CUSD 12	Johnsburg
176	48.3	Bloomington SD 87	Bloomington
177	48.3	Minooka Community HS District 111	Minooka
178	48.2	O Fallon CCSD 90	Ofallon
179	48.2	Steger SD 194	Steger
180	48.2	Sandwich CUSD 430	Sandwich
181	48.2	Lockport Twp HSD 205	Lockport
182	48.2	Southwestern CUSD 9	Piasa
183	48.2	Deerfield SD 109	Deerfield
184	48.2	Morton CUSD 709	Morton
185	48.2	Rochelle Community CD 231	Rochelle
186	48.2	Kirby SD 140	Tinley Park
187	48.2	Woodland CCSD 50	Gurnee
188	48.2	Valley View Cusd #365u	Romeoville
189	48.2	Evergreen Pk Elem SD 124	Evergreen Park
190	48.2	New Trier Twp HSD 203	Northfield
191	48.2	Vandalia CUSD 203	Vandalia
192	48.2	Lake Park Community HSD 108	Roselle
193	48.1	Oak Park Elem SD 97	Oak Park
194	48.1	Sycamore CUSD 427	Sycamore
195	48.1	Lombard SD 44	Lombard
196	48.1	Zion-Benton Twp HSD 126	Zion
197	48.1	Frankfort CCSD 157c	Frankfort
198	48.1	Il Valley Central Unit Dist 321	Chillicothe

199	48.1	Charleston CUSD 1	Charleston
200	48.1	Wauconda Community Unit SD 118	Wauconda
201	48.1	Glen Ellyn SD 41	Glen Ellyn
202	48.1	Moline Unit SD 40	Moline
203	48.1	Carlinville CUSD 1	Carlinville
204	48.1	Orland SD 135	Orland Park
205	48.1	Ball Chatham CUSD 5	Chatham
206	48.0	Mount Prospect SD 57	Mount Prospect
207	48.0	Ridgeland SD 122	Oak Lawn
208	48.0	Park Ridge CCSD 64	Park Ridge
209	48.0	East Moline SD 37	East Moline
210	48.0	Rantoul City SD 137	Rantoul
211	48.0	Harlem Unit Dist 122	Loves Park
212	48.0	Community High SD 99	Downers Grove
213	48.0	Mclean County Unit Dist No 5	Normal
214	47.9	Yorkville Community Unit SD 115	Yorkville
215	47.9	Woodridge SD 68	Woodridge
216	47.9	Community Consolidated S D 93	Carol Stream
217	47.9	Mundelein Cons High SD 120	Mundelein
218	47.9	Glenbard Twp HSD 87	Glen Ellyn
219	47.9	Maine Township HSD 207	Park Ridge
220	47.9	Adlai E Stevenson Dist 125	Lincolnshire
221	47.9	Schaumburg CCSD 54	Schaumburg
222	47.9	Homer Community CSD 33c	Homer Glen
223	47.9	Westmont CUSD 201	Westmont
224	47.9	Tinley Park Comm Cons Sch Dst 146	Tinley Park
225	47.9	Summit SD 104	Summit
226	47.9	Northfield Twp High SD 225	Glenview
227	47.8	Dolton SD 148	Riverdale
228	47.8	Minooka Community CSD 201	Minooka
229	47.8	Marion Community Unit SD 2	Marion
230	47.8	Lake Forest SD 67	Lake Forest
231	47.8	Niles Twp Community High SD 219	Skokie
232	47.8	Antioch CCSD 34	Antioch
233	47.8	Bradley SD 61	Bradley
234	47.8	Township High SD 214	Arlington Hgts
235	47.8	Hononegah Community HSD 207	Rockton
236	47.7	Gurnee SD 56	Gurnee
237	47.7	Nippersink SD 2	Richmond
238	47.7	River Trails SD 26	Mount Prospect
239	47.7	East Richland CUSD 1	Olney
240	47.7	Cicero SD 99	Cicero
241	47.6	Woodstock CUSD 200	Woodstock
242	47.6	East Peoria SD 86	East Peoria
243	47.6	Peotone CUSD 207u	Peotone
244	47.6	Elmhurst SD 205	Elmhurst
245	47.6	Robinson CUSD 2	Robinson
246	47.6	Dolton SD 149	Calumet City
247	47.6	Community Unit SD 200	Wheaton
248	47.6	Community Consolidated SD 46	Grayslake
249	47.6	Libertyville SD 70	Libertyville
250	47.6	Columbia Community Unit SD 4	Columbia
251	47.6	Oswego Community Unit SD 308	Oswego
252	47.5	Mchenry CCSD 15	Mc Henry
253	47.5	Bellwood SD 88	Bellwood
254	47.5	Belleville SD 118	Belleville
255	47.5	Community CSD 59	Arlington Hgts
256	47.5	Naperville C U Dist 203	Naperville
257	47.5	Posen-Robbins El SD 143-5	Posen
258	47.4	Monticello CUSD 25	Monticello
259	47.4	Effingham Community Unit SD 40	Effingham
260	47.4	Du Page High SD 88	Villa Park
261	47.4	Bond County CUSD 2	Greenville
262	47.4	Collinsville CUSD 10	Collinsville
263	47.4	Canton Union SD 66	Canton
264	47.4	United Twp HS District 30	East Moline
265	47.3	Midlothian SD 143	Midlothian
266	47.2	Herscher Community Unit SD 2	Herscher
267	47.2	Forest Ridge SD 142	Oak Forest
268	47.1	Bensenville SD 2	Bensenville
268	47.1	Mchenry Community HSD 156	Mc Henry
270	47.1	La Grange SD 102	La Grange Park
271	47.0	Winnetka SD 36	Winnetka
272	47.0	Oregon C U School Dist-220	Oregon
273	47.0	Northbrook SD 28	Northbrook
274	47.0	Bloom Twp High SD 206	Chicago Heights
275	47.0	Cary CCSD 26	Cary
276	46.9	Harvard CUSD 50	Harvard
277	46.9	Rochester Community Unit SD 3a	Rochester
278	46.9	Winnebago CUSD 323	Winnebago
279	46.8	Cook County SD 130	Blue Island
280	46.8	Galesburg CUSD 205	Galesburg
281	46.8	Geneseo Community Unit SD 228	Geneseo
282	46.7	North Palos SD 117	Palos Hills
283	46.7	Community High SD 128	Libertyville
284	46.7	Will County SD 92	Lockport
285	46.6	Oak Lawn-Hometown SD 123	Oak Lawn
286	46.6	Darien SD 61	Darien
287	46.5	Lake Villa CCSD 41	Lake Villa
288	46.5	Keeneyville SD 20	Hanover Park
289	46.5	Community High SD 117	Lake Villa
290	46.5	Bourbonnais SD 53	Bourbonnais
291	46.1	Fenton Community HSD 100	Bensenville
292	45.9	Mannheim SD 83	Franklin Park
293	8.5	Corrections SD 428 Dept of	Springfield

Individual Education Program Students

Rank	Percent	District Name	City
1	27.4	Mount Vernon SD 80	Mount Vernon
2	24.5	Charleston CUSD 1	Charleston
3	24.1	Peoria SD 150	Peoria
4	23.2	Belleville SD 118	Belleville
5	23.0	Frankfort Community Unit SD 168	West Frankfort
5	23.0	Lake Villa CCSD 41	Lake Villa
7	22.9	Streator Elem SD 44	Streator
8	22.7	Herrin CUSD 4	Herrin
9	22.3	Antioch CCSD 34	Antioch
10	21.8	Alton Community Unit SD 11	Alton
10	21.8	Pekin Public SD 108	Pekin
10	21.8	Zion Elementary SD 6	Zion
13	21.7	Rantoul City SD 137	Rantoul
14	21.6	Murphysboro CUSD 186	Murphysboro
15	21.5	Roxana Community Unit SD 1	Roxana
15	21.5	Urbana SD 116	Urbana
17	21.4	Community Consolidated SD 62	Des Plaines
17	21.4	United Twp HS District 30	East Moline
19	21.2	Robinson CUSD 2	Robinson
20	21.1	Carterville CUSD 5	Carterville
20	21.1	Marion Community Unit SD 2	Marion
20	21.1	Mattoon CUSD 2	Mattoon
23	20.7	Lansing SD 158	Lansing
24	20.6	Midlothian SD 143	Midlothian
25	20.5	Jacksonville SD 117	Jacksonville
26	20.3	Bradley SD 61	Bradley
26	20.3	Cook County SD 130	Blue Island
26	20.3	Olympia CUSD 16	Stanford
29	20.1	Ottawa Elem SD 141	Ottawa
29	20.1	Paris-Union SD 95	Paris
31	20.0	Northbrook SD 28	Northbrook
31	20.0	Skokie SD 68	Skokie
33	19.8	Wilmington CUSD 209u	Wilmington
34	19.7	Bethalto CUSD 8	Bethalto
34	19.7	Cahokia Community Unit SD 187	Cahokia
34	19.7	Danville CCSD 118	Danville
34	19.7	Deerfield SD 109	Deerfield
34	19.7	Evergreen Pk Elem SD 124	Evergreen Park
34	19.7	Flora Community Unit SD 35	Flora
34	19.7	Mchenry CCSD 15	Mc Henry
34	19.7	Prairie Central CUSD 8	Forrest
42	19.5	Cary CCSD 26	Cary
42	19.5	Lincolnshire-Prairieview S D 103	Lincolnshire
42	19.5	Macomb Community Unit SD 185	Macomb
42	19.5	Reed Custer CUSD 255u	Braidwood
46	19.4	Arlington Heights SD 25	Arlington Hgts
47	19.3	Kankakee SD 111	Kankakee
48	19.2	Oak Park Elem SD 97	Oak Park
48	19.2	Prospect Heights SD 23	Prospect Hgts
48	19.2	Proviso Twp HSD 209	Maywood
51	18.9	Joliet Twp HSD 204	Joliet
52	18.8	Evanston CCSD 65	Evanston
52	18.8	Prairie-Hills Elem SD 144	Markham
52	18.8	Sparta CUSD 140	Sparta
55	18.7	Springfield SD 186	Springfield
56	18.6	Crete Monee CUSD 201u	Crete
56	18.6	Ottawa Twp HSD 140	Ottawa
58	18.5	East Moline SD 37	East Moline
58	18.5	Rochelle Community CD 231	Rochelle
60	18.4	Kewanee Community Unit SD 229	Kewanee
60	18.4	Quincy SD 172	Quincy
60	18.4	Rock Island SD 41	Rock Island
63	18.3	East Peoria SD 86	East Peoria
64	18.1	Jasper County Comm Unit Dist 1	Newton
65	18.0	Champaign Community Unit SD 4	Champaign
66	17.9	Berkeley SD 87	Berkeley
67	17.8	Elmwood Park CUSD 401	Elmwood Park
68	17.7	Alsip-Hazlgrn-Oaklwn SD 126	Alsip
68	17.7	Bloomington SD 87	Bloomington
70	17.6	Mchenry Community HSD 156	Mc Henry
71	17.5	Granite City CUSD 9	Granite City
71	17.5	Park Ridge CCSD 64	Park Ridge
73	17.4	Collinsville CUSD 10	Collinsville
73	17.4	Fremont SD 79	Mundelein
73	17.4	Mundelein Elem SD 75	Mundelein
73	17.4	Steger SD 194	Steger
73	17.4	Sterling C U Dist 5	Sterling
78	17.3	Lombard SD 44	Lombard
78	17.3	O Fallon CCSD 90	Ofallon
78	17.3	Palos Community CSD 118	Palos Park
81	17.2	River Trails SD 26	Mount Prospect
81	17.2	Winnetka SD 36	Winnetka
83	17.1	Clinton CUSD 15	Clinton
83	17.1	East Richland CUSD 1	Olney
85	17.0	Berwyn South SD 100	Berwyn
85	17.0	Hillsboro Community Unit SD 3	Hillsboro
85	17.0	Litchfield CUSD 12	Litchfield
85	17.0	Massac Unit District #1	Metropolis
85	17.0	Matteson Elem SD 162	Matteson
85	17.0	Oregon C U School Dist-220	Oregon
91	16.9	Taylorville CUSD 3	Taylorville
92	16.8	Aptakisic-Tripp CCSD 102	Buffalo Grove
92	16.8	Belleville Twp HSD 201	Belleville
92	16.8	Bloom Twp High SD 206	Chicago Heights
92	16.8	Effingham Community Unit SD 40	Effingham
92	16.8	Fenton Community HSD 100	Bensenville
92	16.8	Lake Forest Community HS Dist 115	Lake Forest
92	16.8	Monmouth Unit SD 38	Monmouth
92	16.8	Park Forest SD 163	Park Forest
92	16.8	Summit SD 104	Summit
92	16.8	Wabash CUSD 348	Mount Carmel
102	16.7	Decatur SD 61	Decatur
102	16.7	La Grange SD 102	La Grange Park
102	16.7	Sandwich CUSD 430	Sandwich
102	16.7	Woodland CCSD 50	Gurnee
106	16.6	Bond County CUSD 2	Greenville
106	16.6	Forest Ridge SD 142	Oak Forest
106	16.6	Homer Community CSD 33c	Homer Glen
106	16.6	Il Valley Central Unit Dist 321	Chillicothe
106	16.6	Pana Community Unit SD 8	Pana
106	16.6	West Chicago Elem SD 33	West Chicago
106	16.6	Wheeling CCSD 21	Wheeling
113	16.5	Winnebago CUSD 323	Winnebago
114	16.4	Community Unit SD 300	Carpentersville
114	16.4	Harrisburg CUSD 3	Harrisburg
114	16.4	Keeneyville SD 20	Hanover Park
114	16.4	Thornton Twp HSD 205	South Holland
114	16.4	W Harvey-Dixmoor PS Dist 147	Harvey
119	16.3	Byron Community Unit SD 226	Byron
119	16.3	Canton Union SD 66	Canton
119	16.3	Minooka Community CSD 201	Minooka
119	16.3	Ridgeland SD 122	Oak Lawn
123	16.2	Harvard CUSD 50	Harvard
123	16.2	North Chicago SD 187	North Chicago
123	16.2	Wauconda Community Unit SD 118	Wauconda
123	16.2	Waukegan CUSD 60	Waukegan
123	16.2	Zion-Benton Twp HSD 126	Zion
128	16.1	East St Louis SD 189	E Saint Louis
128	16.1	Glenview CCSD 34	Glenview
128	16.1	Homewood SD 153	Homewood
128	16.1	Round Lake Area Schs - Dist 116	Round Lake
132	16.0	Elem SD 159	Matteson
132	16.0	Mount Prospect SD 57	Mount Prospect
132	16.0	Oak Lawn-Hometown SD 123	Oak Lawn
132	16.0	Woodridge SD 68	Woodridge
136	15.9	New Trier Twp HSD 203	Northfield
136	15.9	Southwestern CUSD 9	Piasa
136	15.9	Township High SD 113	Highland Park
139	15.8	Bremen Community HS District 228	Midlothian
139	15.8	Community CSD 168	Sauk Village
139	15.8	Joliet Public SD 86	Joliet
139	15.8	Mannheim SD 83	Franklin Park
139	15.8	Tinley Park Comm Cons Sch Dst 146	Tinley Park
144	15.7	Kildeer Countryside CCSD 96	Buffalo Grove
144	15.7	Libertyville SD 70	Libertyville
144	15.7	Mascoutah C U District 19	Mascoutah
144	15.7	Moline Unit SD 40	Moline
144	15.7	Woodstock CUSD 200	Woodstock
149	15.6	Community High SD 117	Lake Villa
149	15.6	Rich Twp HS District 227	Olympia Fields
151	15.5	Chicago Heights SD 170	Chicago Heights
151	15.5	Downers Grove Grade SD 58	Downers Grove
151	15.5	Lake Forest SD 67	Lake Forest
151	15.5	North Shore SD 112	Highland Park
155	15.4	Barrington CUSD 220	Barrington
155	15.4	Maine Township HSD 207	Park Ridge
155	15.4	Mclean County Unit Dist No 5	Normal
155	15.4	Triad Community Unit SD 2	Troy
159	15.3	Aurora West Unit SD 129	Aurora
159	15.3	Edwardsville CUSD 7	Edwardsville
159	15.3	Galesburg CUSD 205	Galesburg
159	15.3	Orland SD 135	Orland Park
163	15.2	Addison SD 4	Addison
163	15.2	Country Club Hills SD 160	Ctry Club Hill
163	15.2	East Maine SD 63	Des Plaines
163	15.2	Highland Community Unit SD 5	Highland
163	15.2	New Lenox SD 122	New Lenox
168	15.1	Bensenville SD 2	Bensenville
168	15.1	Community Consolidated SD 46	Grayslake
168	15.1	Community High SD 218	Oak Lawn
168	15.1	Community Unit SD 200	Wheaton
168	15.1	Oak Park & River Forest Dist 200	Oak Park
168	15.1	Schaumburg CCSD 54	Schaumburg
168	15.1	Westmont CUSD 201	Westmont
175	15.0	Manteno Community Unit SD 5	Manteno
175	15.0	Mundelein Cons High SD 120	Mundelein
175	15.0	North Palos SD 117	Palos Hills
178	14.9	Wilmette SD 39	Wilmette
179	14.8	Bourbonnais SD 53	Bourbonnais

179	14.8	Harlem Unit Dist 122	Loves Park
181	14.7	Bradley Bourbonnais CHSD 307	Bradley
181	14.7	Niles Twp Community High SD 219	Skokie
181	14.7	Rochester Community Unit SD 3a	Rochester
184	14.6	Troy Community CSD 30c	Plainfield
184	14.6	Vandalia CUSD 203	Vandalia
186	14.5	Leyden Community HSD 212	Franklin Park
186	14.5	Lyons SD 103	Lyons
186	14.5	Morton CUSD 709	Morton
186	14.5	Rockford SD 205	Rockford
186	14.5	SD 45 Dupage County	Villa Park
186	14.5	Waterloo Community Unit SD 5	Waterloo
192	14.4	Bellwood SD 88	Bellwood
192	14.4	Mokena SD 159	Mokena
194	14.3	CCSD 181	Hinsdale
194	14.3	Lisle CUSD 202	Lisle
194	14.3	Queen Bee SD 16	Glendale Hgts
197	14.2	Burbank SD 111	Burbank
197	14.2	Coal City CUSD 1	Coal City
197	14.2	Evanston Twp HSD 202	Evanston
197	14.2	Harvey SD 152	Harvey
197	14.2	Kirby SD 140	Tinley Park
197	14.2	Oak Lawn Community HSD 229	Oak Lawn
203	14.0	Crystal Lake CCSD 47	Crystal Lake
203	14.0	Du Page High SD 88	Villa Park
203	14.0	Will County SD 92	Lockport
206	13.9	Beach Park CCSD 3	Beach Park
206	13.9	Carlinville CUSD 1	Carlinville
206	13.9	Community High SD 128	Libertyville
206	13.9	Dixon Unit SD 170	Dixon
206	13.9	Freeport SD 145	Freeport
206	13.9	Kinnikinnick CCSD 131	Roscoe
206	13.9	Nippersink SD 2	Richmond
213	13.8	Cicero SD 99	Cicero
213	13.8	Peotone CUSD 207u	Peotone
213	13.8	Summit Hill SD 161	Frankfort
216	13.7	Elmhurst SD 205	Elmhurst
216	13.7	Johnsburg CUSD 12	Johnsburg
216	13.7	Kaneland CUSD 302	Maple Park
219	13.6	Frankfort CCSD 157c	Frankfort
220	13.5	Glen Ellyn CCSD 89	Glen Ellyn
220	13.5	Gurnee SD 56	Gurnee
220	13.5	Warren Twp High SD 121	Gages Lake
223	13.4	Mahomet-Seymour CUSD 3	Mahomet
223	13.4	Pekin Community HSD 303	Pekin
225	13.3	Community High SD 155	Crystal Lake
225	13.3	Eureka C U Dist 140	Eureka
225	13.3	Yorkville Community Unit SD 115	Yorkville
228	13.2	Argo Community HSD 217	Summit
228	13.2	Community High SD 99	Downers Grove
228	13.2	Genoa Kingston CUSD 424	Genoa
228	13.2	Glen Ellyn SD 41	Glen Ellyn
228	13.2	Lake Zurich CUSD 95	Lake Zurich
228	13.2	Oswego Community Unit SD 308	Oswego
228	13.2	Plainfield SD 202	Plainfield
235	13.1	Aurora East Unit SD 131	Aurora
235	13.1	Ball Chatham CUSD 5	Chatham
237	13.0	Hawthorn CCSD 73	Vernon Hills
238	12.9	Dolton SD 148	Riverdale
238	12.9	Dolton SD 149	Calumet City
238	12.9	Grayslake Community High SD 127	Grayslake
238	12.9	Palatine CCSD 15	Palatine
242	12.8	Thornton Fractional T HS D 215	Calumet City
243	12.7	City of Chicago SD 299	Chicago
243	12.7	Herscher Community Unit SD 2	Herscher
243	12.7	Jersey CUSD 100	Jerseyville
243	12.7	Township High SD 214	Arlington Hgts
247	12.6	Community Consolidated S D 93	Carol Stream
247	12.6	Lake Park Community HSD 108	Roselle
249	12.5	Belvidere CUSD 100	Belvidere
249	12.5	Geneseo Community Unit SD 228	Geneseo
249	12.5	Geneva Community Unit SD 304	Geneva
249	12.5	Sherrard Community Unit SD 200	Sherrard
253	12.3	Dunlap CUSD 323	Dunlap
253	12.3	Lockport Twp HSD 205	Lockport
255	12.2	Berwyn North SD 98	Berwyn
255	12.2	Naperville C U Dist 203	Naperville
257	12.1	St Charles CUSD 303	Saint Charles
258	12.0	Central Community Unit SD 301	Burlington
258	12.0	Indian Prairie CUSD 204	Aurora
258	12.0	Posen-Robbins El SD 143-5	Posen
261	11.9	Maywood-Melrose Park-Broadview-89	Melrose Park
261	11.9	SD 46	Elgin
261	11.9	Valley View Cusd #365u	Romeoville
264	11.8	Community CSD 59	Arlington Hgts
264	11.8	Monticello CUSD 25	Monticello
266	11.7	Darien SD 61	Darien
267	11.6	Consolidated SD 158	Huntley
267	11.6	Glenbard Twp HSD 87	Glen Ellyn
267	11.6	Meridian CUSD 223	Stillman Valley
270	11.5	Columbia Community Unit SD 4	Columbia
270	11.5	Sycamore CUSD 427	Sycamore
272	11.4	Township HSD 211	Palatine
273	11.3	Marquardt SD 15	Glendale Hgts
274	11.2	Batavia Unit SD 101	Batavia
274	11.2	Dekalb Community Unit SD 428	De Kalb
274	11.2	J S Morton HS District 201	Cicero
274	11.2	Northfield Twp High SD 225	Glenview
278	11.1	Indian Springs SD 109	Justice
279	10.8	Flossmoor SD 161	Chicago Heights
279	10.8	Lyons Twp HSD 204	La Grange
279	10.8	Minooka Community HS District 111	Minooka
282	10.6	Cons High SD 230	Orland Park
283	10.5	Homewood Flossmoor CHSD 233	Flossmoor
284	10.3	Adlai E Stevenson Dist 125	Lincolnshire
285	10.2	Lemont-Bromberek CSD 113a	Lemont
285	10.2	O Fallon Twp High SD 203	Ofallon
287	10.1	Hinsdale Twp HSD 86	Hinsdale
287	10.1	Hononegah Community HSD 207	Rockton
289	9.9	Community High SD 94	West Chicago
290	9.6	Lincoln Way Community HSD 210	New Lenox
291	8.8	Mt Zion Community Unit SD 3	Mt Zion
292	8.6	Reavis Twp HSD 220	Burbank
293	7.2	Corrections SD 428 Dept of	Springfield

English Language Learner Students

Rank	Percent	District Name	City
1	n/a	Addison SD 4	Addison
1	n/a	Adlai E Stevenson Dist 125	Lincolnshire
1	n/a	Alsip-Hazlgrn-Oaklwn SD 126	Alsip
1	n/a	Alton Community Unit SD 11	Alton
1	n/a	Antioch CCSD 34	Antioch
1	n/a	Aptakisic-Tripp CCSD 102	Buffalo Grove
1	n/a	Argo Community HSD 217	Summit
1	n/a	Arlington Heights SD 25	Arlington Hgts
1	n/a	Aurora East Unit SD 131	Aurora
1	n/a	Aurora West Unit SD 129	Aurora
1	n/a	Ball Chatham CUSD 5	Chatham
1	n/a	Barrington CUSD 220	Barrington
1	n/a	Batavia Unit SD 101	Batavia
1	n/a	Beach Park CCSD 3	Beach Park
1	n/a	Belleville SD 118	Belleville
1	n/a	Belleville Twp HSD 201	Belleville
1	n/a	Bellwood SD 88	Bellwood
1	n/a	Belvidere CUSD 100	Belvidere
1	n/a	Bensenville SD 2	Bensenville
1	n/a	Berkeley SD 87	Berkeley
1	n/a	Berwyn North SD 98	Berwyn
1	n/a	Berwyn South SD 100	Berwyn
1	n/a	Bethalto CUSD 8	Bethalto
1	n/a	Bloom Twp High SD 206	Chicago Heights
1	n/a	Bloomington SD 87	Bloomington
1	n/a	Bond County CUSD 2	Greenville
1	n/a	Bourbonnais SD 53	Bourbonnais
1	n/a	Bradley Bourbonnais CHSD 307	Bradley
1	n/a	Bradley SD 61	Bradley
1	n/a	Bremen Community HS District 228	Midlothian
1	n/a	Burbank SD 111	Burbank
1	n/a	Byron Community Unit SD 226	Byron
1	n/a	CCSD 181	Hinsdale
1	n/a	Cahokia Community Unit SD 187	Cahokia
1	n/a	Canton Union SD 66	Canton
1	n/a	Carlinville CUSD 1	Carlinville
1	n/a	Carterville CUSD 5	Carterville
1	n/a	Cary CCSD 26	Cary
1	n/a	Central Community Unit SD 301	Burlington
1	n/a	Champaign Community Unit SD 4	Champaign
1	n/a	Charleston CUSD 1	Charleston
1	n/a	Chicago Heights SD 170	Chicago Heights
1	n/a	Cicero SD 99	Cicero
1	n/a	City of Chicago SD 299	Chicago
1	n/a	Clinton CUSD 15	Clinton
1	n/a	Coal City CUSD 1	Coal City
1	n/a	Collinsville CUSD 10	Collinsville
1	n/a	Columbia Community Unit SD 4	Columbia
1	n/a	Community CSD 168	Sauk Village
1	n/a	Community CSD 59	Arlington Hgts
1	n/a	Community Consolidated S D 93	Carol Stream
1	n/a	Community Consolidated SD 46	Grayslake
1	n/a	Community Consolidated SD 62	Des Plaines
1	n/a	Community High SD 117	Lake Villa
1	n/a	Community High SD 128	Libertyville
1	n/a	Community High SD 155	Crystal Lake
1	n/a	Community High SD 218	Oak Lawn
1	n/a	Community High SD 94	West Chicago
1	n/a	Community High SD 99	Downers Grove
1	n/a	Community Unit SD 200	Wheaton
1	n/a	Community Unit SD 300	Carpentersville
1	n/a	Cons High SD 230	Orland Park
1	n/a	Consolidated SD 158	Huntley
1	n/a	Cook County SD 130	Blue Island
1	n/a	Corrections SD 428 Dept of	Springfield
1	n/a	Country Club Hills SD 160	Ctry Club Hill
1	n/a	Crete Monee CUSD 201u	Crete
1	n/a	Crystal Lake CCSD 47	Crystal Lake
1	n/a	Danville CCSD 118	Danville
1	n/a	Darien SD 61	Darien
1	n/a	Decatur SD 61	Decatur
1	n/a	Deerfield SD 109	Deerfield
1	n/a	Dekalb Community Unit SD 428	De Kalb
1	n/a	Dixon Unit SD 170	Dixon
1	n/a	Dolton SD 148	Riverdale
1	n/a	Dolton SD 149	Calumet City
1	n/a	Downers Grove Grade SD 58	Downers Grove
1	n/a	Du Page High SD 88	Villa Park
1	n/a	Dunlap CUSD 323	Dunlap
1	n/a	East Maine SD 63	Des Plaines
1	n/a	East Moline SD 37	East Moline
1	n/a	East Peoria SD 86	East Peoria
1	n/a	East Richland CUSD 1	Olney
1	n/a	East St Louis SD 189	E Saint Louis
1	n/a	Edwardsville CUSD 7	Edwardsville
1	n/a	Effingham Community Unit SD 40	Effingham
1	n/a	Elem SD 159	Matteson
1	n/a	Elmhurst SD 205	Elmhurst
1	n/a	Elmwood Park CUSD 401	Elmwood Park
1	n/a	Eureka C U Dist 140	Eureka
1	n/a	Evanston CCSD 65	Evanston
1	n/a	Evanston Twp HSD 202	Evanston
1	n/a	Evergreen Pk Elem SD 124	Evergreen Park
1	n/a	Fenton Community HSD 100	Bensenville
1	n/a	Flora Community Unit SD 35	Flora
1	n/a	Flossmoor SD 161	Chicago Heights
1	n/a	Forest Ridge SD 142	Oak Forest
1	n/a	Frankfort CCSD 157c	Frankfort
1	n/a	Frankfort Community Unit SD 168	West Frankfort
1	n/a	Freeport SD 145	Freeport
1	n/a	Fremont SD 79	Mundelein
1	n/a	Galesburg CUSD 205	Galesburg
1	n/a	Geneseo Community Unit SD 228	Geneseo
1	n/a	Geneva Community Unit SD 304	Geneva
1	n/a	Genoa Kingston CUSD 424	Genoa
1	n/a	Glen Ellyn CCSD 89	Glen Ellyn
1	n/a	Glen Ellyn SD 41	Glen Ellyn
1	n/a	Glenbard Twp HSD 87	Glen Ellyn
1	n/a	Glenview CCSD 34	Glenview
1	n/a	Granite City CUSD 9	Granite City
1	n/a	Grayslake Community High SD 127	Grayslake
1	n/a	Gurnee SD 56	Gurnee
1	n/a	Harlem Unit Dist 122	Loves Park
1	n/a	Harrisburg CUSD 3	Harrisburg
1	n/a	Harvard CUSD 50	Harvard
1	n/a	Harvey SD 152	Harvey
1	n/a	Hawthorn CCSD 73	Vernon Hills
1	n/a	Herrin CUSD 4	Herrin
1	n/a	Herscher Community Unit SD 2	Herscher
1	n/a	Highland Community Unit SD 5	Highland
1	n/a	Hillsboro Community Unit SD 3	Hillsboro
1	n/a	Hinsdale Twp HSD 86	Hinsdale
1	n/a	Homer Community CSD 33c	Homer Glen
1	n/a	Homewood Flossmoor CHSD 233	Flossmoor
1	n/a	Homewood SD 153	Homewood
1	n/a	Hononegah Community HSD 207	Rockton
1	n/a	Il Valley Central Unit Dist 321	Chillicothe
1	n/a	Indian Prairie CUSD 204	Aurora
1	n/a	Indian Springs SD 109	Justice
1	n/a	J S Morton HS District 201	Cicero
1	n/a	Jacksonville SD 117	Jacksonville
1	n/a	Jasper County Comm Unit Dist 1	Newton
1	n/a	Jersey CUSD 100	Jerseyville
1	n/a	Johnsburg CUSD 12	Johnsburg
1	n/a	Joliet Public SD 86	Joliet
1	n/a	Joliet Twp HSD 204	Joliet
1	n/a	Kaneland CUSD 302	Maple Park
1	n/a	Kankakee SD 111	Kankakee
1	n/a	Keeneyville SD 20	Hanover Park
1	n/a	Kewanee Community Unit SD 229	Kewanee
1	n/a	Kildeer Countryside CCSD 96	Buffalo Grove
1	n/a	Kinnikinnick CCSD 131	Roscoe
1	n/a	Kirby SD 140	Tinley Park
1	n/a	La Grange SD 102	La Grange Park
1	n/a	Lake Forest Community HS Dist 115	Lake Forest
1	n/a	Lake Forest SD 67	Lake Forest
1	n/a	Lake Park Community HSD 108	Roselle
1	n/a	Lake Villa CCSD 41	Lake Villa
1	n/a	Lake Zurich CUSD 95	Lake Zurich
1	n/a	Lansing SD 158	Lansing
1	n/a	Lemont-Bromberek CSD 113a	Lemont
1	n/a	Leyden Community HSD 212	Franklin Park
1	n/a	Libertyville SD 70	Libertyville
1	n/a	Lincoln Way Community HSD 210	New Lenox
1	n/a	Lincolnshire-Prairieview S D 103	Lincolnshire
1	n/a	Lisle CUSD 202	Lisle
1	n/a	Litchfield CUSD 12	Litchfield
1	n/a	Lockport Twp HSD 205	Lockport
1	n/a	Lombard SD 44	Lombard
1	n/a	Lyons SD 103	Lyons

1	n/a	Lyons Twp HSD 204	La Grange
1	n/a	Macomb Community Unit SD 185	Macomb
1	n/a	Mahomet-Seymour CUSD 3	Mahomet
1	n/a	Maine Township HSD 207	Park Ridge
1	n/a	Mannheim SD 83	Franklin Park
1	n/a	Manteno Community Unit SD 5	Manteno
1	n/a	Marion Community Unit SD 2	Marion
1	n/a	Marquardt SD 15	Glendale Hgts
1	n/a	Mascoutah C U District 19	Mascoutah
1	n/a	Massac Unit District #1	Metropolis
1	n/a	Matteson Elem SD 162	Matteson
1	n/a	Mattoon CUSD 2	Mattoon
1	n/a	Maywood-Melrose Park-Broadview-89	Melrose Park
1	n/a	Mchenry CCSD 15	Mc Henry
1	n/a	Mchenry Community HSD 156	Mc Henry
1	n/a	Mclean County Unit Dist No 5	Normal
1	n/a	Meridian CUSD 223	Stillman Valley
1	n/a	Midlothian SD 143	Midlothian
1	n/a	Minooka Community CSD 201	Minooka
1	n/a	Minooka Community HS District 111	Minooka
1	n/a	Mokena SD 159	Mokena
1	n/a	Moline Unit SD 40	Moline
1	n/a	Monmouth Unit SD 38	Monmouth
1	n/a	Monticello CUSD 25	Monticello
1	n/a	Morton CUSD 709	Morton
1	n/a	Mount Prospect SD 57	Mount Prospect
1	n/a	Mount Vernon SD 80	Mount Vernon
1	n/a	Mt Zion Community Unit SD 3	Mt Zion
1	n/a	Mundelein Cons High SD 120	Mundelein
1	n/a	Mundelein Elem SD 75	Mundelein
1	n/a	Murphysboro CUSD 186	Murphysboro
1	n/a	Naperville C U Dist 203	Naperville
1	n/a	New Lenox SD 122	New Lenox
1	n/a	New Trier Twp HSD 203	Northfield
1	n/a	Niles Twp Community High SD 219	Skokie
1	n/a	Nippersink SD 2	Richmond
1	n/a	North Chicago SD 187	North Chicago
1	n/a	North Palos SD 117	Palos Hills
1	n/a	North Shore SD 112	Highland Park
1	n/a	Northbrook SD 28	Northbrook
1	n/a	Northfield Twp High SD 225	Glenview
1	n/a	O Fallon CCSD 90	Ofallon
1	n/a	O Fallon Twp High SD 203	Ofallon
1	n/a	Oak Lawn Community HSD 229	Oak Lawn
1	n/a	Oak Lawn-Hometown SD 123	Oak Lawn
1	n/a	Oak Park & River Forest Dist 200	Oak Park
1	n/a	Oak Park Elem SD 97	Oak Park
1	n/a	Olympia CUSD 16	Stanford
1	n/a	Oregon C U School Dist-220	Oregon
1	n/a	Orland SD 135	Orland Park
1	n/a	Oswego Community Unit SD 308	Oswego
1	n/a	Ottawa Elem SD 141	Ottawa
1	n/a	Ottawa Twp HSD 140	Ottawa
1	n/a	Palatine CCSD 15	Palatine
1	n/a	Palos Community CSD 118	Palos Park
1	n/a	Pana Community Unit SD 8	Pana
1	n/a	Paris-Union SD 95	Paris
1	n/a	Park Forest SD 163	Park Forest
1	n/a	Park Ridge CCSD 64	Park Ridge
1	n/a	Pekin Community HSD 303	Pekin
1	n/a	Pekin Public SD 108	Pekin
1	n/a	Peoria SD 150	Peoria
1	n/a	Peotone CUSD 207u	Peotone
1	n/a	Plainfield SD 202	Plainfield
1	n/a	Posen-Robbins El SD 143-5	Posen
1	n/a	Prairie Central CUSD 8	Forrest
1	n/a	Prairie-Hills Elem SD 144	Markham
1	n/a	Prospect Heights SD 23	Prospect Hgts
1	n/a	Proviso Twp HSD 209	Maywood
1	n/a	Queen Bee SD 16	Glendale Hgts
1	n/a	Quincy SD 172	Quincy
1	n/a	Rantoul City SD 137	Rantoul
1	n/a	Reavis Twp HSD 220	Burbank
1	n/a	Reed Custer CUSD 255u	Braidwood
1	n/a	Rich Twp HS District 227	Olympia Fields
1	n/a	Ridgeland SD 122	Oak Lawn
1	n/a	River Trails SD 26	Mount Prospect
1	n/a	Robinson CUSD 2	Robinson
1	n/a	Rochelle Community CD 231	Rochelle
1	n/a	Rochester Community Unit SD 3a	Rochester
1	n/a	Rock Island SD 41	Rock Island
1	n/a	Rockford SD 205	Rockford
1	n/a	Round Lake Area Schs - Dist 116	Round Lake
1	n/a	Roxana Community Unit SD 1	Roxana
1	n/a	SD 45 Dupage County	Villa Park
1	n/a	SD 46	Elgin
1	n/a	Sandwich CUSD 430	Sandwich
1	n/a	Schaumburg CCSD 54	Schaumburg
1	n/a	Sherrard Community Unit SD 200	Sherrard
1	n/a	Skokie SD 68	Skokie
1	n/a	Southwestern CUSD 9	Piasa
1	n/a	Sparta CUSD 140	Sparta
1	n/a	Springfield SD 186	Springfield
1	n/a	St Charles CUSD 303	Saint Charles
1	n/a	Steger SD 194	Steger
1	n/a	Sterling C U Dist 5	Sterling
1	n/a	Streator Elem SD 44	Streator
1	n/a	Summit Hill SD 161	Frankfort
1	n/a	Summit SD 104	Summit
1	n/a	Sycamore CUSD 427	Sycamore
1	n/a	Taylorville CUSD 3	Taylorville
1	n/a	Thornton Fractional T HS D 215	Calumet City
1	n/a	Thornton Twp HSD 205	South Holland
1	n/a	Tinley Park Comm Cons Sch Dst 146	Tinley Park
1	n/a	Township HSD 211	Palatine
1	n/a	Township High SD 113	Highland Park
1	n/a	Township High SD 214	Arlington Hgts
1	n/a	Triad Community Unit SD 2	Troy
1	n/a	Troy Community CSD 30c	Plainfield
1	n/a	United Twp HS District 30	East Moline
1	n/a	Urbana SD 116	Urbana
1	n/a	Valley View Cusd #365u	Romeoville
1	n/a	Vandalia CUSD 203	Vandalia
1	n/a	W Harvey-Dixmoor PS Dist 147	Harvey
1	n/a	Wabash CUSD 348	Mount Carmel
1	n/a	Warren Twp High SD 121	Gages Lake
1	n/a	Waterloo Community Unit SD 5	Waterloo
1	n/a	Wauconda Community Unit SD 118	Wauconda
1	n/a	Waukegan CUSD 60	Waukegan
1	n/a	West Chicago Elem SD 33	West Chicago
1	n/a	Westmont CUSD 201	Westmont
1	n/a	Wheeling CCSD 21	Wheeling
1	n/a	Will County SD 92	Lockport
1	n/a	Wilmette SD 39	Wilmette
1	n/a	Wilmington CUSD 209u	Wilmington
1	n/a	Winnebago CUSD 323	Winnebago
1	n/a	Winnetka SD 36	Winnetka
1	n/a	Woodland CCSD 50	Gurnee
1	n/a	Woodridge SD 68	Woodridge
1	n/a	Woodstock CUSD 200	Woodstock
1	n/a	Yorkville Community Unit SD 115	Yorkville
1	n/a	Zion Elementary SD 6	Zion
1	n/a	Zion-Benton Twp HSD 126	Zion

Migrant Students

Rank	Percent	District Name	City
1	3.1	Harvard CUSD 50	Harvard
2	0.6	Rochelle Community CD 231	Rochelle
3	0.4	Aurora East Unit SD 131	Aurora
3	0.4	Kewanee Community Unit SD 229	Kewanee
5	0.3	Lyons SD 103	Lyons
6	0.2	Community Consolidated S D 93	Carol Stream
7	0.1	Du Page High SD 88	Villa Park
7	0.1	Granite City CUSD 9	Granite City
7	0.1	Harlem Unit Dist 122	Loves Park
7	0.1	Joliet Public SD 86	Joliet
7	0.1	Moline Unit SD 40	Moline
7	0.1	Woodstock CUSD 200	Woodstock
13	0.0	City of Chicago SD 299	Chicago
13	0.0	Peoria SD 150	Peoria
15	0.0	Addison SD 4	Addison
15	0.0	Adlai E Stevenson Dist 125	Lincolnshire
15	0.0	Alsip-Hazlgrn-Oaklwn SD 126	Alsip
15	0.0	Alton Community Unit SD 11	Alton
15	0.0	Antioch CCSD 34	Antioch
15	0.0	Aptakisic-Tripp CCSD 102	Buffalo Grove
15	0.0	Argo Community HSD 217	Summit
15	0.0	Arlington Heights SD 25	Arlington Hgts
15	0.0	Aurora West Unit SD 129	Aurora
15	0.0	Ball Chatham CUSD 5	Chatham
15	0.0	Barrington CUSD 220	Barrington
15	0.0	Batavia Unit SD 101	Batavia
15	0.0	Beach Park CCSD 3	Beach Park
15	0.0	Belleville SD 118	Belleville
15	0.0	Belleville Twp HSD 201	Belleville
15	0.0	Bellwood SD 88	Bellwood
15	0.0	Belvidere CUSD 100	Belvidere
15	0.0	Bensenville SD 2	Bensenville
15	0.0	Berkeley SD 87	Berkeley
15	0.0	Berwyn North SD 98	Berwyn
15	0.0	Berwyn South SD 100	Berwyn
15	0.0	Bethalto CUSD 8	Bethalto
15	0.0	Bloom Twp High SD 206	Chicago Heights
15	0.0	Bloomington SD 87	Bloomington
15	0.0	Bond County CUSD 2	Greenville
15	0.0	Bourbonnais SD 53	Bourbonnais
15	0.0	Bradley Bourbonnais CHSD 307	Bradley
15	0.0	Bradley SD 61	Bradley
15	0.0	Bremen Community HS District 228	Midlothian
15	0.0	Burbank SD 111	Burbank
15	0.0	Byron Community Unit SD 226	Byron
15	0.0	CCSD 181	Hinsdale
15	0.0	Cahokia Community Unit SD 187	Cahokia
15	0.0	Canton Union SD 66	Canton
15	0.0	Carlinville CUSD 1	Carlinville
15	0.0	Carterville CUSD 5	Carterville
15	0.0	Cary CCSD 26	Cary
15	0.0	Central Community Unit SD 301	Burlington
15	0.0	Champaign Community Unit SD 4	Champaign
15	0.0	Charleston CUSD 1	Charleston
15	0.0	Chicago Heights SD 170	Chicago Heights
15	0.0	Cicero SD 99	Cicero
15	0.0	Clinton CUSD 15	Clinton
15	0.0	Coal City CUSD 1	Coal City
15	0.0	Collinsville CUSD 10	Collinsville
15	0.0	Columbia Community Unit SD 4	Columbia
15	0.0	Community CSD 168	Sauk Village
15	0.0	Community CSD 59	Arlington Hgts
15	0.0	Community Consolidated SD 46	Grayslake
15	0.0	Community Consolidated SD 62	Des Plaines
15	0.0	Community High SD 117	Lake Villa
15	0.0	Community High SD 128	Libertyville
15	0.0	Community High SD 155	Crystal Lake
15	0.0	Community High SD 218	Oak Lawn
15	0.0	Community High SD 94	West Chicago
15	0.0	Community High SD 99	Downers Grove
15	0.0	Community Unit SD 200	Wheaton
15	0.0	Community Unit SD 300	Carpentersville
15	0.0	Cons High SD 230	Orland Park
15	0.0	Consolidated SD 158	Huntley
15	0.0	Cook County SD 130	Blue Island
15	0.0	Corrections SD 428 Dept of	Springfield
15	0.0	Country Club Hills SD 160	Ctry Club Hill
15	0.0	Crete Monee CUSD 201u	Crete
15	0.0	Crystal Lake CCSD 47	Crystal Lake
15	0.0	Danville CCSD 118	Danville
15	0.0	Darien SD 61	Darien
15	0.0	Decatur SD 61	Decatur
15	0.0	Deerfield SD 109	Deerfield
15	0.0	Dekalb Community Unit SD 428	De Kalb
15	0.0	Dixon Unit SD 170	Dixon
15	0.0	Dolton SD 148	Riverdale
15	0.0	Dolton SD 149	Calumet City
15	0.0	Downers Grove Grade SD 58	Downers Grove
15	0.0	Dunlap CUSD 323	Dunlap
15	0.0	East Maine SD 63	Des Plaines
15	0.0	East Moline SD 37	East Moline
15	0.0	East Peoria SD 86	East Peoria
15	0.0	East Richland CUSD 1	Olney
15	0.0	East St Louis SD 189	E Saint Louis
15	0.0	Edwardsville CUSD 7	Edwardsville
15	0.0	Effingham Community Unit SD 40	Effingham
15	0.0	Elem SD 159	Matteson
15	0.0	Elmhurst SD 205	Elmhurst
15	0.0	Elmwood Park CUSD 401	Elmwood Park
15	0.0	Eureka C U Dist 140	Eureka
15	0.0	Evanston CCSD 65	Evanston
15	0.0	Evanston Twp HSD 202	Evanston
15	0.0	Evergreen Pk Elem SD 124	Evergreen Park
15	0.0	Fenton Community HSD 100	Bensenville
15	0.0	Flora Community Unit SD 35	Flora
15	0.0	Flossmoor SD 161	Chicago Heights
15	0.0	Forest Ridge SD 142	Oak Forest
15	0.0	Frankfort CCSD 157c	Frankfort
15	0.0	Frankfort Community Unit SD 168	West Frankfort
15	0.0	Freeport SD 145	Freeport
15	0.0	Fremont SD 79	Mundelein
15	0.0	Galesburg CUSD 205	Galesburg
15	0.0	Geneseo Community Unit SD 228	Geneseo
15	0.0	Geneva Community Unit SD 304	Geneva
15	0.0	Genoa Kingston CUSD 424	Genoa
15	0.0	Glen Ellyn CCSD 89	Glen Ellyn
15	0.0	Glen Ellyn SD 41	Glen Ellyn
15	0.0	Glenbard Twp HSD 87	Glen Ellyn
15	0.0	Glenview CCSD 34	Glenview
15	0.0	Grayslake Community High SD 127	Grayslake
15	0.0	Gurnee SD 56	Gurnee
15	0.0	Harrisburg CUSD 3	Harrisburg
15	0.0	Harvey SD 152	Harvey
15	0.0	Hawthorn CCSD 73	Vernon Hills
15	0.0	Herrin CUSD 4	Herrin
15	0.0	Herscher Community Unit SD 2	Herscher
15	0.0	Highland Community Unit SD 5	Highland
15	0.0	Hillsboro Community Unit SD 3	Hillsboro
15	0.0	Hinsdale Twp HSD 86	Hinsdale
15	0.0	Homer Community CSD 33c	Homer Glen
15	0.0	Homewood Flossmoor CHSD 233	Flossmoor
15	0.0	Homewood SD 153	Homewood
15	0.0	Hononegah Community HSD 207	Rockton
15	0.0	Il Valley Central Unit Dist 321	Chillicothe
15	0.0	Indian Prairie CUSD 204	Aurora
15	0.0	Indian Springs SD 109	Justice
15	0.0	J S Morton HS District 201	Cicero
15	0.0	Jacksonville SD 117	Jacksonville
15	0.0	Jasper County Comm Unit Dist 1	Newton
15	0.0	Jersey CUSD 100	Jerseyville

15	0.0	Johnsburg CUSD 12	Johnsburg
15	0.0	Joliet Twp HSD 204	Joliet
15	0.0	Kaneland CUSD 302	Maple Park
15	0.0	Kankakee SD 111	Kankakee
15	0.0	Keeneyville SD 20	Hanover Park
15	0.0	Kildeer Countryside CCSD 96	Buffalo Grove
15	0.0	Kinnikinnick CCSD 131	Roscoe
15	0.0	Kirby SD 140	Tinley Park
15	0.0	La Grange SD 102	La Grange Park
15	0.0	Lake Forest Community HS Dist 115	Lake Forest
15	0.0	Lake Forest SD 67	Lake Forest
15	0.0	Lake Park Community HSD 108	Roselle
15	0.0	Lake Villa CCSD 41	Lake Villa
15	0.0	Lake Zurich CUSD 95	Lake Zurich
15	0.0	Lansing SD 158	Lansing
15	0.0	Lemont-Bromberek CSD 113a	Lemont
15	0.0	Leyden Community HSD 212	Franklin Park
15	0.0	Libertyville SD 70	Libertyville
15	0.0	Lincoln Way Community HSD 210	New Lenox
15	0.0	Lincolnshire-Prairieview S D 103	Lincolnshire
15	0.0	Lisle CUSD 202	Lisle
15	0.0	Litchfield CUSD 12	Litchfield
15	0.0	Lockport Twp HSD 205	Lockport
15	0.0	Lombard SD 44	Lombard
15	0.0	Lyons Twp HSD 204	La Grange
15	0.0	Macomb Community Unit SD 185	Macomb
15	0.0	Mahomet-Seymour CUSD 3	Mahomet
15	0.0	Maine Township HSD 207	Park Ridge
15	0.0	Mannheim SD 83	Franklin Park
15	0.0	Manteno Community Unit SD 5	Manteno
15	0.0	Marion Community Unit SD 2	Marion
15	0.0	Marquardt SD 15	Glendale Hgts
15	0.0	Mascoutah C U District 19	Mascoutah
15	0.0	Massac Unit District #1	Metropolis
15	0.0	Matteson Elem SD 162	Matteson
15	0.0	Mattoon CUSD 2	Mattoon
15	0.0	Maywood-Melrose Park-Broadview-89	Melrose Park
15	0.0	Mchenry CCSD 15	Mc Henry
15	0.0	Mchenry Community HSD 156	Mc Henry
15	0.0	Mclean County Unit Dist No 5	Normal
15	0.0	Meridian CUSD 223	Stillman Valley
15	0.0	Midlothian SD 143	Midlothian
15	0.0	Minooka Community CSD 201	Minooka
15	0.0	Minooka Community HS District 111	Minooka
15	0.0	Mokena SD 159	Mokena
15	0.0	Monmouth Unit SD 38	Monmouth
15	0.0	Monticello CUSD 25	Monticello
15	0.0	Morton CUSD 709	Morton
15	0.0	Mount Prospect SD 57	Mount Prospect
15	0.0	Mount Vernon SD 80	Mount Vernon
15	0.0	Mt Zion Community Unit SD 3	Mt Zion
15	0.0	Mundelein Cons High SD 120	Mundelein
15	0.0	Mundelein Elem SD 75	Mundelein
15	0.0	Murphysboro CUSD 186	Murphysboro
15	0.0	Naperville C U Dist 203	Naperville
15	0.0	New Lenox SD 122	New Lenox
15	0.0	New Trier Twp HSD 203	Northfield
15	0.0	Niles Twp Community High SD 219	Skokie
15	0.0	Nippersink SD 2	Richmond
15	0.0	North Chicago SD 187	North Chicago
15	0.0	North Palos SD 117	Palos Hills
15	0.0	North Shore SD 112	Highland Park
15	0.0	Northbrook SD 28	Northbrook
15	0.0	Northfield Twp High SD 225	Glenview
15	0.0	O Fallon CCSD 90	Ofallon
15	0.0	O Fallon Twp High SD 203	Ofallon
15	0.0	Oak Lawn Community HSD 229	Oak Lawn
15	0.0	Oak Lawn-Hometown SD 123	Oak Lawn
15	0.0	Oak Park & River Forest Dist 200	Oak Park
15	0.0	Oak Park Elem SD 97	Oak Park
15	0.0	Olympia CUSD 16	Stanford
15	0.0	Oregon C U School Dist-220	Oregon
15	0.0	Orland SD 135	Orland Park
15	0.0	Oswego Community Unit SD 308	Oswego
15	0.0	Ottawa Elem SD 141	Ottawa
15	0.0	Ottawa Twp HSD 140	Ottawa
15	0.0	Palatine CCSD 15	Palatine
15	0.0	Palos Community CSD 118	Palos Park
15	0.0	Pana Community Unit SD 8	Pana
15	0.0	Paris-Union SD 95	Paris
15	0.0	Park Forest SD 163	Park Forest
15	0.0	Park Ridge CCSD 64	Park Ridge
15	0.0	Pekin Community HSD 303	Pekin
15	0.0	Pekin Public SD 108	Pekin
15	0.0	Peotone CUSD 207u	Peotone
15	0.0	Plainfield SD 202	Plainfield
15	0.0	Posen-Robbins El SD 143-5	Posen
15	0.0	Prairie Central CUSD 8	Forrest
15	0.0	Prairie-Hills Elem SD 144	Markham
15	0.0	Prospect Heights SD 23	Prospect Hgts
15	0.0	Proviso Twp HSD 209	Maywood
15	0.0	Queen Bee SD 16	Glendale Hgts
15	0.0	Quincy SD 172	Quincy
15	0.0	Rantoul City SD 137	Rantoul
15	0.0	Reavis Twp HSD 220	Burbank
15	0.0	Reed Custer CUSD 255u	Braidwood
15	0.0	Rich Twp HS District 227	Olympia Fields
15	0.0	Ridgeland SD 122	Oak Lawn
15	0.0	River Trails SD 26	Mount Prospect
15	0.0	Robinson CUSD 2	Robinson
15	0.0	Rochester Community Unit SD 3a	Rochester
15	0.0	Rock Island SD 41	Rock Island
15	0.0	Rockford SD 205	Rockford
15	0.0	Round Lake Area Schs - Dist 116	Round Lake
15	0.0	Roxana Community Unit SD 1	Roxana
15	0.0	SD 45 Dupage County	Villa Park
15	0.0	SD 46	Elgin
15	0.0	Sandwich CUSD 430	Sandwich
15	0.0	Schaumburg CCSD 54	Schaumburg
15	0.0	Sherrard Community Unit SD 200	Sherrard
15	0.0	Skokie SD 68	Skokie
15	0.0	Southwestern CUSD 9	Piasa
15	0.0	Sparta CUSD 140	Sparta
15	0.0	Springfield SD 186	Springfield
15	0.0	St Charles CUSD 303	Saint Charles
15	0.0	Steger SD 194	Steger
15	0.0	Sterling C U Dist 5	Sterling
15	0.0	Streator Elem SD 44	Streator
15	0.0	Summit Hill SD 161	Frankfort
15	0.0	Summit SD 104	Summit
15	0.0	Sycamore CUSD 427	Sycamore
15	0.0	Taylorville CUSD 3	Taylorville
15	0.0	Thornton Fractional T H S D 215	Calumet City
15	0.0	Thornton Twp HSD 205	South Holland
15	0.0	Tinley Park Comm Cons Sch Dst 146	Tinley Park
15	0.0	Township HSD 211	Palatine
15	0.0	Township High SD 113	Highland Park
15	0.0	Township High SD 214	Arlington Hgts
15	0.0	Triad Community Unit SD 2	Troy
15	0.0	Troy Community CSD 30c	Plainfield
15	0.0	United Twp HS District 30	East Moline
15	0.0	Urbana SD 116	Urbana
15	0.0	Valley View Cusd #365u	Romeoville
15	0.0	Vandalia CUSD 203	Vandalia
15	0.0	W Harvey-Dixmoor PS Dist 147	Harvey
15	0.0	Wabash CUSD 348	Mount Carmel
15	0.0	Warren Twp High SD 121	Gages Lake
15	0.0	Waterloo Community Unit SD 5	Waterloo
15	0.0	Wauconda Community Unit SD 118	Wauconda
15	0.0	Waukegan CUSD 60	Waukegan
15	0.0	West Chicago Elem SD 33	West Chicago
15	0.0	Westmont CUSD 201	Westmont
15	0.0	Wheeling CCSD 21	Wheeling
15	0.0	Will County SD 92	Lockport
15	0.0	Wilmette SD 39	Wilmette
15	0.0	Wilmington CUSD 209u	Wilmington
15	0.0	Winnebago CUSD 323	Winnebago
15	0.0	Winnetka SD 36	Winnetka
15	0.0	Woodland CCSD 50	Gurnee
15	0.0	Woodridge SD 68	Woodridge
15	0.0	Yorkville Community Unit SD 115	Yorkville
15	0.0	Zion Elementary SD 6	Zion
15	0.0	Zion-Benton Twp HSD 126	Zion

Students Eligible for Free Lunch

Rank	Percent	District Name	City
1	91.3	W Harvey-Dixmoor PS Dist 147	Harvey
2	81.1	Harvey SD 152	Harvey
3	78.0	Chicago Heights SD 170	Chicago Heights
4	75.3	Prairie-Hills Elem SD 144	Markham
5	74.4	Posen-Robbins El SD 143-5	Posen
6	71.9	Maywood-Melrose Park-Broadview-89	Melrose Park
7	70.4	City of Chicago SD 299	Chicago
7	70.4	Kankakee SD 111	Kankakee
9	69.3	East St Louis SD 189	E Saint Louis
10	68.5	Park Forest SD 163	Park Forest
11	64.4	Cahokia Community Unit SD 187	Cahokia
12	63.8	Mount Vernon SD 80	Mount Vernon
13	63.4	Cook County SD 130	Blue Island
14	63.1	Cicero SD 99	Cicero
15	62.0	Dolton SD 148	Riverdale
16	58.8	Berwyn North SD 98	Berwyn
17	58.5	Joliet Public SD 86	Joliet
18	57.7	Zion Elementary SD 6	Zion
19	56.9	Danville CCSD 118	Danville
20	56.8	Dolton SD 149	Calumet City
21	56.3	Aurora East Unit SD 131	Aurora
22	55.6	Peoria SD 150	Peoria
23	51.9	Summit SD 104	Summit
24	51.7	North Chicago SD 187	North Chicago
25	51.1	Decatur SD 61	Decatur
26	50.8	Rockford SD 205	Rockford
27	50.4	Rock Island SD 41	Rock Island
28	49.8	Rantoul City SD 137	Rantoul
29	48.8	Kewanee Community Unit SD 229	Kewanee
30	48.3	Springfield SD 186	Springfield
31	44.9	J S Morton HS District 201	Cicero
32	44.7	Berkeley SD 87	Berkeley
33	44.0	Joliet Twp HSD 204	Joliet
34	43.9	East Moline SD 37	East Moline
34	43.9	Waukegan CUSD 60	Waukegan
36	43.4	Herrin CUSD 4	Herrin
37	43.2	Bloom Twp High SD 206	Chicago Heights
37	43.2	Streator Elem SD 44	Streator
39	42.6	Sparta CUSD 140	Sparta
40	42.4	Murphysboro CUSD 186	Murphysboro
41	41.9	Community CSD 168	Sauk Village
42	41.2	Bellwood SD 88	Bellwood
43	40.5	Galesburg CUSD 205	Galesburg
43	40.5	Urbana SD 116	Urbana
45	40.3	Freeport SD 145	Freeport
46	38.9	Rich Twp HS District 227	Olympia Fields
47	38.8	Berwyn South SD 100	Berwyn
48	38.7	Monmouth Unit SD 38	Monmouth
49	38.5	Thornton Twp HSD 205	South Holland
50	38.2	Alton Community Unit SD 11	Alton
51	37.5	Round Lake Area Schs - Dist 116	Round Lake
52	36.7	Crete Monee CUSD 201u	Crete
53	36.5	Belleville SD 118	Belleville
53	36.5	Country Club Hills SD 160	Ctry Club Hill
55	36.0	Pana Community Unit SD 8	Pana
56	35.6	Quincy SD 172	Quincy
57	35.4	East Richland CUSD 1	Olney
58	35.1	Jacksonville SD 117	Jacksonville
59	34.3	Steger SD 194	Steger
60	34.2	Pekin Public SD 108	Pekin
61	34.0	Harvard CUSD 50	Harvard
62	33.2	Canton Union SD 66	Canton
62	33.2	West Chicago Elem SD 33	West Chicago
64	32.8	Frankfort Community Unit SD 168	West Frankfort
64	32.8	Granite City CUSD 9	Granite City
66	31.9	Bloomington SD 87	Bloomington
67	31.4	Champaign Community Unit SD 4	Champaign
68	31.1	Argo Community HSD 217	Summit
69	30.8	Indian Springs SD 109	Justice
69	30.8	Moline Unit SD 40	Moline
71	30.4	Collinsville CUSD 10	Collinsville
72	30.2	Thornton Fractional T H S D 215	Calumet City
73	30.1	Paris-Union SD 95	Paris
74	30.0	Rochelle Community CD 231	Rochelle
75	29.7	Robinson CUSD 2	Robinson
76	29.6	Elem SD 159	Matteson
76	29.6	Macomb Community Unit SD 185	Macomb
78	29.5	Mannheim SD 83	Franklin Park
79	29.2	Flora Community Unit SD 35	Flora
79	29.2	United Twp HS District 30	East Moline
81	29.0	Matteson Elem SD 162	Matteson
82	28.8	Vandalia CUSD 203	Vandalia
83	28.7	Community High SD 218	Oak Lawn
84	28.2	Marion Community Unit SD 2	Marion
84	28.2	SD 46	Elgin
86	28.1	Hillsboro Community Unit SD 3	Hillsboro
87	27.7	Sterling C U Dist 5	Sterling
88	27.6	Aurora West Unit SD 129	Aurora
89	27.5	Evanston CCSD 65	Evanston
90	27.4	East Peoria SD 86	East Peoria
91	27.2	Harrisburg CUSD 3	Harrisburg
92	26.9	Mattoon CUSD 2	Mattoon
93	26.6	Roxana Community Unit SD 1	Roxana
94	26.4	Ottawa Elem SD 141	Ottawa
95	26.1	Beach Park CCSD 3	Beach Park
96	25.9	Evanston Twp HSD 202	Evanston
97	25.5	Litchfield CUSD 12	Litchfield
98	24.8	Taylorville CUSD 3	Taylorville
99	24.7	Dixon Unit SD 170	Dixon
99	24.7	Wabash CUSD 348	Mount Carmel
101	24.4	Jersey CUSD 100	Jerseyville
101	24.4	Wheeling CCSD 21	Wheeling
103	24.3	Jasper County Comm Unit Dist 1	Newton
104	23.8	Charleston CUSD 1	Charleston
105	23.4	Clinton CUSD 15	Clinton
106	23.2	Addison SD 4	Addison
107	23.1	Carlinville CUSD 1	Carlinville
108	23.0	Massac Unit District #1	Metropolis
109	22.8	Proviso Twp HSD 209	Maywood
110	22.6	Dekalb Community Unit SD 428	De Kalb
111	22.5	Belvidere CUSD 100	Belvidere
111	22.5	SD 45 Dupage County	Villa Park
113	22.4	Marquardt SD 15	Glendale Hgts
114	21.9	East Maine SD 63	Des Plaines
115	21.8	River Trails SD 26	Mount Prospect
115	21.8	Valley View Cusd #365u	Romeoville
117	21.5	Prairie Central CUSD 8	Forrest
118	21.4	Community Consolidated SD 62	Des Plaines
118	21.4	Corrections SD 428 Dept of	Springfield
120	21.3	Effingham Community Unit SD 40	Effingham
120	21.3	Lyons SD 103	Lyons

122	20.9	Westmont CUSD 201	Westmont
123	20.6	Community Unit SD 300	Carpentersville
124	20.5	Community CSD 59	Arlington Hgts
125	20.2	Zion-Benton Twp HSD 126	Zion
126	20.1	Pekin Community HSD 303	Pekin
127	20.0	Bradley SD 61	Bradley
128	19.9	Bethalto CUSD 8	Bethalto
128	19.9	Bond County CUSD 2	Greenville
128	19.9	Woodridge SD 68	Woodridge
131	19.4	Woodstock CUSD 200	Woodstock
132	17.5	Palatine CCSD 15	Palatine
133	17.2	Coal City CUSD 1	Coal City
133	17.2	Oregon C U School Dist-220	Oregon
135	17.0	Belleville Twp HSD 201	Belleville
136	16.6	Harlem Unit Dist 122	Loves Park
137	16.4	Reed Custer CUSD 255u	Braidwood
138	16.0	Sherrard Community Unit SD 200	Sherrard
139	15.7	Du Page High SD 88	Villa Park
140	15.5	Mundelein Elem SD 75	Mundelein
141	15.4	Il Valley Central Unit Dist 321	Chillicothe
142	15.2	North Palos SD 117	Palos Hills
143	15.1	Mundelein Cons High SD 120	Mundelein
143	15.1	Olympia CUSD 16	Stanford
145	15.0	Evergreen Pk Elem SD 124	Evergreen Park
145	15.0	Midlothian SD 143	Midlothian
147	14.6	Wilmington CUSD 209u	Wilmington
148	14.5	Bourbonnais SD 53	Bourbonnais
148	14.5	Southwestern CUSD 9	Piasa
150	14.1	O Fallon CCSD 90	Ofallon
151	13.9	Mclean County Unit Dist No 5	Normal
152	13.6	Oak Park Elem SD 97	Oak Park
153	13.2	Glenview CCSD 34	Glenview
154	13.0	Ridgeland SD 122	Oak Lawn
155	12.6	Hawthorn CCSD 73	Vernon Hills
156	12.5	Skokie SD 68	Skokie
157	12.3	Carterville CUSD 5	Carterville
158	11.8	Genoa Kingston CUSD 424	Genoa
159	11.6	Tinley Park Comm Cons Sch Dst 146	Tinley Park
160	11.5	Geneseo Community Unit SD 228	Geneseo
161	11.4	Eureka C U Dist 140	Eureka
162	11.2	Herscher Community Unit SD 2	Herscher
163	11.1	Mchenry CCSD 15	Mc Henry
164	11.0	Leyden Community HSD 212	Franklin Park
165	10.7	Alsip-Hazlgrn-Oaklwn SD 126	Alsip
166	10.6	Edwardsville CUSD 7	Edwardsville
166	10.6	Highland Community Unit SD 5	Highland
168	10.4	Wauconda Community Unit SD 118	Wauconda
169	10.3	Lombard SD 44	Lombard
170	10.1	Community Unit SD 200	Wheaton
171	10.0	Mascoutah C U District 19	Mascoutah
172	9.7	Triad Community Unit SD 2	Troy
173	9.6	Antioch CCSD 34	Antioch
173	9.6	Bradley Bourbonnais CHSD 307	Bradley
175	9.5	Township High SD 214	Arlington Hgts
176	9.0	Elmwood Park CUSD 401	Elmwood Park
177	8.6	Darien SD 61	Darien
178	8.5	Troy Community CSD 30c	Plainfield
179	8.2	Sandwich CUSD 430	Sandwich
180	8.1	Homewood SD 153	Homewood
181	8.0	Mahomet-Seymour CUSD 3	Mahomet
182	7.9	La Grange SD 102	La Grange Park
182	7.9	North Shore SD 112	Highland Park
184	7.6	Homewood Flossmoor CHSD 233	Flossmoor
184	7.6	Oak Park & River Forest Dist 200	Oak Park
186	7.5	Lisle CUSD 202	Lisle
186	7.5	Meridian CUSD 223	Stillman Valley
188	7.4	Township HSD 211	Palatine
189	7.3	Sycamore CUSD 427	Sycamore
189	7.3	Winnebago CUSD 323	Winnebago
191	7.2	Woodland CCSD 50	Gurnee
192	7.1	Mt Zion Community Unit SD 3	Mt Zion
192	7.1	Waterloo Community Unit SD 5	Waterloo
194	7.0	Community Consolidated SD 46	Grayslake
195	6.9	Barrington CUSD 220	Barrington
195	6.9	Monticello CUSD 25	Monticello
197	6.4	Glenbard Twp HSD 87	Glen Ellyn
197	6.4	Hononegah Community HSD 207	Rockton
197	6.4	Lake Villa CCSD 41	Lake Villa
200	6.1	O Fallon Twp High SD 203	Ofallon
201	6.0	Crystal Lake CCSD 47	Crystal Lake
202	5.9	Byron Community Unit SD 226	Byron
202	5.9	Minooka Community CSD 201	Minooka
204	5.5	Ball Chatham CUSD 5	Chatham
204	5.5	Kinnikinnick CCSD 131	Roscoe
204	5.5	Oswego Community Unit SD 308	Oswego
204	5.5	Palos Community CSD 118	Palos Park
208	5.2	Johnsburg CUSD 12	Johnsburg
209	5.0	Dunlap CUSD 323	Dunlap
210	4.9	Manteno Community Unit SD 5	Manteno
210	4.9	Morton CUSD 709	Morton
212	4.8	Cary CCSD 26	Cary
213	4.7	Peotone CUSD 207u	Peotone
214	4.6	Community High SD 99	Downers Grove
215	4.5	Arlington Heights SD 25	Arlington Hgts
216	4.2	Bensenville SD 2	Bensenville
217	4.0	Columbia Community Unit SD 4	Columbia
218	3.7	Mokena SD 159	Mokena
219	3.4	Will County SD 92	Lockport
220	3.3	Nippersink SD 2	Richmond
221	3.2	Lemont-Bromberek CSD 113a	Lemont
222	3.1	Aptakisic-Tripp CCSD 102	Buffalo Grove
222	3.1	Community High SD 155	Crystal Lake
224	2.6	Lake Zurich CUSD 95	Lake Zurich
225	2.5	New Lenox SD 122	New Lenox
226	2.3	Consolidated SD 158	Huntley
226	2.3	St Charles CUSD 303	Saint Charles
228	2.2	Plainfield SD 202	Plainfield
229	1.8	Batavia Unit SD 101	Batavia
230	1.7	Kaneland CUSD 302	Maple Park
230	1.7	Kildeer Countryside CCSD 96	Buffalo Grove
230	1.7	Rochester Community Unit SD 3a	Rochester
233	1.6	Lincoln Way Community HSD 210	New Lenox
233	1.6	Summit Hill SD 161	Frankfort
235	1.1	Central Community Unit SD 301	Burlington
235	1.1	Mount Prospect SD 57	Mount Prospect
237	1.0	Elmhurst SD 205	Elmhurst
238	0.9	Naperville C U Dist 203	Naperville
239	0.8	Downers Grove Grade SD 58	Downers Grove
240	0.0	Bremen Community HS District 228	Midlothian
240	0.0	Burbank SD 111	Burbank
240	0.0	Community Consolidated S D 93	Carol Stream
240	0.0	Community High SD 117	Lake Villa
240	0.0	Community High SD 94	West Chicago
240	0.0	Cons High SD 230	Orland Park
240	0.0	Deerfield SD 109	Deerfield
240	0.0	Fenton Community HSD 100	Bensenville
240	0.0	Flossmoor SD 161	Chicago Heights
240	0.0	Frankfort CCSD 157c	Frankfort
240	0.0	Fremont SD 79	Mundelein
240	0.0	Geneva Community Unit SD 304	Geneva
240	0.0	Glen Ellyn CCSD 89	Glen Ellyn
240	0.0	Glen Ellyn SD 41	Glen Ellyn
240	0.0	Grayslake Community High SD 127	Grayslake
240	0.0	Gurnee SD 56	Gurnee
240	0.0	Hinsdale Twp HSD 86	Hinsdale
240	0.0	Homer Community CSD 33c	Homer Glen
240	0.0	Indian Prairie CUSD 204	Aurora
240	0.0	Keeneyville SD 20	Hanover Park
240	0.0	Kirby SD 140	Tinley Park
240	0.0	Lake Forest Community HS Dist 115	Lake Forest
240	0.0	Lake Forest SD 67	Lake Forest
240	0.0	Lake Park Community HSD 108	Roselle
240	0.0	Lansing SD 158	Lansing
240	0.0	Libertyville SD 70	Libertyville
240	0.0	Lincolnshire-Prairieview S D 103	Lincolnshire
240	0.0	Lyons Twp HSD 204	La Grange
240	0.0	Minooka Community HS District 111	Minooka
240	0.0	Niles Twp Community High SD 219	Skokie
240	0.0	Northbrook SD 28	Northbrook
240	0.0	Oak Lawn-Hometown SD 123	Oak Lawn
240	0.0	Orland SD 135	Orland Park
240	0.0	Ottawa Twp HSD 140	Ottawa
240	0.0	Park Ridge CCSD 64	Park Ridge
240	0.0	Prospect Heights SD 23	Prospect Hgts
240	0.0	Queen Bee SD 16	Glendale Hgts
240	0.0	Schaumburg CCSD 54	Schaumburg
240	0.0	Warren Twp High SD 121	Gages Lake
240	0.0	Wilmette SD 39	Wilmette
240	0.0	Winnetka SD 36	Winnetka
240	0.0	Yorkville Community Unit SD 115	Yorkville
282	n/a	Adlai E Stevenson Dist 125	Lincolnshire
282	n/a	CCSD 181	Hinsdale
282	n/a	Community High SD 128	Libertyville
282	n/a	Forest Ridge SD 142	Oak Forest
282	n/a	Lockport Twp HSD 205	Lockport
282	n/a	Maine Township HSD 207	Park Ridge
282	n/a	Mchenry Community HSD 156	Mc Henry
282	n/a	New Trier Twp HSD 203	Northfield
282	n/a	Northfield Twp High SD 225	Glenview
282	n/a	Oak Lawn Community HSD 229	Oak Lawn
282	n/a	Reavis Twp HSD 220	Burbank
282	n/a	Township High SD 113	Highland Park

Students Eligible for Reduced-Price Lunch

Rank	Percent	District Name	City
1	15.4	Berwyn South SD 100	Berwyn
2	13.3	J S Morton HS District 201	Cicero
3	13.1	Berwyn North SD 98	Berwyn
4	12.9	Summit SD 104	Summit
5	12.8	Cicero SD 99	Cicero
6	12.2	Berkeley SD 87	Berkeley
7	11.7	Joliet Twp HSD 204	Joliet
8	11.1	Steger SD 194	Steger
9	10.9	Mascoutah C U District 19	Mascoutah
10	10.4	Belleville SD 118	Belleville
10	10.4	Bellwood SD 88	Bellwood
10	10.4	Joliet Public SD 86	Joliet
10	10.4	Waukegan CUSD 60	Waukegan
14	10.2	Quincy SD 172	Quincy
15	9.8	Aurora East Unit SD 131	Aurora
16	9.7	Maywood-Melrose Park-Broadview-89	Melrose Park
17	9.6	Streator Elem SD 44	Streator
18	9.3	Mannheim SD 83	Franklin Park
18	9.3	West Chicago Elem SD 33	West Chicago
20	9.2	Dolton SD 148	Riverdale
20	9.2	Pekin Public SD 108	Pekin
22	9.0	Elem SD 159	Matteson
22	9.0	Flora Community Unit SD 35	Flora
22	9.0	Frankfort Community Unit SD 168	West Frankfort
22	9.0	Pana Community Unit SD 8	Pana
22	9.0	Rockford SD 205	Rockford
27	8.9	Dolton SD 149	Calumet City
27	8.9	Thornton Fractional T HS D 215	Calumet City
29	8.8	United Twp HS District 30	East Moline
29	8.8	Zion Elementary SD 6	Zion
31	8.6	Community Consolidated SD 62	Des Plaines
31	8.6	Prairie-Hills Elem SD 144	Markham
33	8.5	City of Chicago SD 299	Chicago
33	8.5	Round Lake Area Schs - Dist 116	Round Lake
35	8.4	Jersey CUSD 100	Jerseyville
36	8.3	Canton Union SD 66	Canton
36	8.3	Crete Monee CUSD 201u	Crete
36	8.3	Roxana Community Unit SD 1	Roxana
39	8.2	Galesburg CUSD 205	Galesburg
39	8.2	North Chicago SD 187	North Chicago
39	8.2	Sterling C U Dist 5	Sterling
42	8.1	Freeport SD 145	Freeport
43	8.0	Community CSD 168	Sauk Village
43	8.0	Jacksonville SD 117	Jacksonville
43	8.0	Rich Twp HS District 227	Olympia Fields
46	7.9	Argo Community HSD 217	Summit
46	7.9	Rantoul City SD 137	Rantoul
48	7.8	Glenview CCSD 34	Glenview
48	7.8	Robinson CUSD 2	Robinson
50	7.7	Collinsville CUSD 10	Collinsville
51	7.5	Jasper County Comm Unit Dist 1	Newton
51	7.5	Sparta CUSD 140	Sparta
51	7.5	Wabash CUSD 348	Mount Carmel
54	7.4	Bloomington SD 87	Bloomington
54	7.4	Park Forest SD 163	Park Forest
54	7.4	Valley View Cusd #365u	Romeoville
57	7.3	Granite City CUSD 9	Granite City
58	7.2	Macomb Community Unit SD 185	Macomb
58	7.2	Wheeling CCSD 21	Wheeling
60	7.1	Kewanee Community Unit SD 229	Kewanee
61	7.0	Cahokia Community Unit SD 187	Cahokia
61	7.0	Evanston CCSD 65	Evanston
61	7.0	Harvard CUSD 50	Harvard
61	7.0	Woodstock CUSD 200	Woodstock
65	6.9	Community High SD 218	Oak Lawn
65	6.9	Taylorville CUSD 3	Taylorville
67	6.8	Bloom Twp High SD 206	Chicago Heights
67	6.8	Kankakee SD 111	Kankakee
67	6.8	Skokie SD 68	Skokie
70	6.7	Danville CCSD 118	Danville
70	6.7	Springfield SD 186	Springfield
72	6.6	Pekin Community HSD 303	Pekin
73	6.5	Decatur SD 61	Decatur
73	6.5	Mount Vernon SD 80	Mount Vernon
75	6.4	Bradley SD 61	Bradley
75	6.4	Carlinville CUSD 1	Carlinville
75	6.4	Dixon Unit SD 170	Dixon
75	6.4	Harlem Unit Dist 122	Loves Park
75	6.4	Rock Island SD 41	Rock Island
80	6.3	Bond County CUSD 2	Greenville
80	6.3	Cook County SD 130	Blue Island
80	6.3	Monmouth Unit SD 38	Monmouth
80	6.3	Mundelein Elem SD 75	Mundelein
80	6.3	Posen-Robbins El SD 143-5	Posen
80	6.3	SD 46	Elgin
80	6.3	Woodridge SD 68	Woodridge
87	6.2	Community CSD 59	Arlington Hgts
87	6.2	Ottawa Elem SD 141	Ottawa
87	6.2	Thornton Twp HSD 205	South Holland
90	6.1	East Moline SD 37	East Moline
91	6.0	Coal City CUSD 1	Coal City
91	6.0	Lyons SD 103	Lyons
91	6.0	Olympia CUSD 16	Stanford
91	6.0	Paris-Union SD 95	Paris
91	6.0	Peoria SD 150	Peoria
96	5.9	Alton Community Unit SD 11	Alton
96	5.9	Evanston Twp HSD 202	Evanston
96	5.9	Wilmington CUSD 209u	Wilmington
99	5.8	Beach Park CCSD 3	Beach Park
99	5.8	Hillsboro Community Unit SD 3	Hillsboro
101	5.7	Genoa Kingston CUSD 424	Genoa

101	5.7	Herrin CUSD 4	Herrin
101	5.7	Southwestern CUSD 9	Piasa
104	5.6	Indian Springs SD 109	Justice
104	5.6	Litchfield CUSD 12	Litchfield
104	5.6	Vandalia CUSD 203	Vandalia
107	5.5	Charleston CUSD 1	Charleston
107	5.5	East St Louis SD 189	E Saint Louis
109	5.4	Marquardt SD 15	Glendale Hgts
109	5.4	Prairie Central CUSD 8	Forrest
109	5.4	Reed Custer CUSD 255u	Braidwood
112	5.3	Herscher Community Unit SD 2	Herscher
112	5.3	Marion Community Unit SD 2	Marion
112	5.3	Moline Unit SD 40	Moline
112	5.3	Mundelein Cons High SD 120	Mundelein
112	5.3	Murphysboro CUSD 186	Murphysboro
117	5.2	Belleville Twp HSD 201	Belleville
117	5.2	Highland Community Unit SD 5	Highland
119	5.1	Aurora West Unit SD 129	Aurora
120	5.0	Chicago Heights SD 170	Chicago Heights
120	5.0	East Richland CUSD 1	Olney
120	5.0	Elmwood Park CUSD 401	Elmwood Park
123	4.9	Addison SD 4	Addison
123	4.9	Il Valley Central Unit Dist 321	Chillicothe
125	4.8	Clinton CUSD 15	Clinton
125	4.8	Triad Community Unit SD 2	Troy
127	4.7	Urbana SD 116	Urbana
128	4.6	Belvidere CUSD 100	Belvidere
128	4.6	Bethalto CUSD 8	Bethalto
128	4.6	Champaign Community Unit SD 4	Champaign
128	4.6	Community Unit SD 300	Carpentersville
128	4.6	SD 45 Dupage County	Villa Park
128	4.6	Sherrard Community Unit SD 200	Sherrard
134	4.5	Evergreen Pk Elem SD 124	Evergreen Park
134	4.5	Mattoon CUSD 2	Mattoon
134	4.5	Oak Park Elem SD 97	Oak Park
134	4.5	Oregon C U School Dist-220	Oregon
138	4.4	Country Club Hills SD 160	Ctry Club Hill
138	4.4	Harvey SD 152	Harvey
138	4.4	River Trails SD 26	Mount Prospect
138	4.4	Rochelle Community CD 231	Rochelle
142	4.3	Effingham Community Unit SD 40	Effingham
142	4.3	Harrisburg CUSD 3	Harrisburg
142	4.3	Matteson Elem SD 162	Matteson
142	4.3	Zion-Benton Twp HSD 126	Zion
146	4.2	Leyden Community HSD 212	Franklin Park
147	4.1	Dekalb Community Unit SD 428	De Kalb
147	4.1	East Maine SD 63	Des Plaines
149	4.0	Geneseo Community Unit SD 228	Geneseo
149	4.0	Sandwich CUSD 430	Sandwich
149	4.0	Troy Community CSD 30c	Plainfield
152	3.9	Bradley Bourbonnais CHSD 307	Bradley
152	3.9	Edwardsville CUSD 7	Edwardsville
152	3.9	Lombard SD 44	Lombard
152	3.9	Massac Unit District #1	Metropolis
152	3.9	Palatine CCSD 15	Palatine
157	3.6	W Harvey-Dixmoor PS Dist 147	Harvey
157	3.6	Westmont CUSD 201	Westmont
159	3.5	Community Consolidated SD 46	Grayslake
159	3.5	Tinley Park Comm Cons Sch Dst 146	Tinley Park
161	3.4	Oswego Community Unit SD 308	Oswego
162	3.3	Du Page High SD 88	Villa Park
162	3.3	East Peoria SD 86	East Peoria
162	3.3	Monticello CUSD 25	Monticello
162	3.3	O Fallon CCSD 90	Ofallon
162	3.3	Ridgeland SD 122	Oak Lawn
162	3.3	Waterloo Community Unit SD 5	Waterloo
168	3.2	Lake Villa CCSD 41	Lake Villa
169	3.1	Mclean County Unit Dist No 5	Normal
170	3.0	Bourbonnais SD 53	Bourbonnais
170	3.0	Lisle CUSD 202	Lisle
172	2.9	Alsip-Hazlgrn-Oaklwn SD 126	Alsip
172	2.9	Kinnikinnick CCSD 131	Roscoe
174	2.8	Antioch CCSD 34	Antioch
174	2.8	Hawthorn CCSD 73	Vernon Hills
174	2.8	Mt Zion Community Unit SD 3	Mt Zion
174	2.8	Proviso Twp HSD 209	Maywood
174	2.8	Township HSD 211	Palatine
174	2.8	Woodland CCSD 50	Gurnee
180	2.7	Eureka C U Dist 140	Eureka
180	2.7	Township High SD 214	Arlington Hgts
182	2.6	Community Unit SD 200	Wheaton
183	2.4	Crystal Lake CCSD 47	Crystal Lake
184	2.3	Barrington CUSD 220	Barrington
184	2.3	Darien SD 61	Darien
184	2.3	Homewood SD 153	Homewood
184	2.3	Winnebago CUSD 323	Winnebago
188	2.2	Byron Community Unit SD 226	Byron
188	2.2	Oak Park & River Forest Dist 200	Oak Park
190	2.1	Mchenry CCSD 15	Mc Henry
190	2.1	O Fallon Twp High SD 203	Ofallon
192	2.0	Carterville CUSD 5	Carterville
192	2.0	Cary CCSD 26	Cary
192	2.0	Sycamore CUSD 427	Sycamore
195	1.9	Arlington Heights SD 25	Arlington Hgts
195	1.9	Johnsburg CUSD 12	Johnsburg
197	1.8	New Lenox SD 122	New Lenox
197	1.8	Wauconda Community Unit SD 118	Wauconda
199	1.7	Peotone CUSD 207u	Peotone
200	1.6	Homewood Flossmoor CHSD 233	Flossmoor
201	1.5	Consolidated SD 158	Huntley
201	1.5	Glenbard Twp HSD 87	Glen Ellyn
201	1.5	Minooka Community CSD 201	Minooka
204	1.4	Community High SD 99	Downers Grove
204	1.4	North Palos SD 117	Palos Hills
206	1.3	Aptakisic-Tripp CCSD 102	Buffalo Grove
206	1.3	Columbia Community Unit SD 4	Columbia
206	1.3	Dunlap CUSD 323	Dunlap
209	1.2	La Grange SD 102	La Grange Park
209	1.2	Lincoln Way Community HSD 210	New Lenox
211	1.1	Ball Chatham CUSD 5	Chatham
211	1.1	Bensenville SD 2	Bensenville
211	1.1	Meridian CUSD 223	Stillman Valley
211	1.1	Mokena SD 159	Mokena
211	1.1	Nippersink SD 2	Richmond
211	1.1	Plainfield SD 202	Plainfield
211	1.1	Will County SD 92	Lockport
218	1.0	Hononegah Community HSD 207	Rockton
219	0.9	Lemont-Bromberek CSD 113a	Lemont
220	0.8	Lake Zurich CUSD 95	Lake Zurich
220	0.8	Mahomet-Seymour CUSD 3	Mahomet
220	0.8	Morton CUSD 709	Morton
220	0.8	Palos Community CSD 118	Palos Park
220	0.8	Rochester Community Unit SD 3a	Rochester
225	0.7	Batavia Unit SD 101	Batavia
225	0.7	Kaneland CUSD 302	Maple Park
225	0.7	Kildeer Countryside CCSD 96	Buffalo Grove
225	0.7	Manteno Community Unit SD 5	Manteno
225	0.7	St Charles CUSD 303	Saint Charles
230	0.6	Community High SD 155	Crystal Lake
230	0.6	Mount Prospect SD 57	Mount Prospect
232	0.5	Midlothian SD 143	Midlothian
233	0.3	Summit Hill SD 161	Frankfort
234	0.2	Elmhurst SD 205	Elmhurst
235	0.1	Central Community Unit SD 301	Burlington
235	0.1	Downers Grove Grade SD 58	Downers Grove
235	0.1	Naperville C U Dist 203	Naperville
238	0.0	Bremen Community HS District 228	Midlothian
238	0.0	Burbank SD 111	Burbank
238	0.0	Community Consolidated S D 93	Carol Stream
238	0.0	Community High SD 117	Lake Villa
238	0.0	Community High SD 94	West Chicago
238	0.0	Cons High SD 230	Orland Park
238	0.0	Corrections SD 428 Dept of	Springfield
238	0.0	Deerfield SD 109	Deerfield
238	0.0	Fenton Community HSD 100	Bensenville
238	0.0	Flossmoor SD 161	Chicago Heights
238	0.0	Frankfort CCSD 157c	Frankfort
238	0.0	Fremont SD 79	Mundelein
238	0.0	Geneva Community Unit SD 304	Geneva
238	0.0	Glen Ellyn CCSD 89	Glen Ellyn
238	0.0	Glen Ellyn SD 41	Glen Ellyn
238	0.0	Grayslake Community High SD 127	Grayslake
238	0.0	Gurnee SD 56	Gurnee
238	0.0	Hinsdale Twp HSD 86	Hinsdale
238	0.0	Homer Community CSD 33c	Homer Glen
238	0.0	Indian Prairie CUSD 204	Aurora
238	0.0	Keeneyville SD 20	Hanover Park
238	0.0	Kirby SD 140	Tinley Park
238	0.0	Lake Forest Community HS Dist 115	Lake Forest
238	0.0	Lake Forest SD 67	Lake Forest
238	0.0	Lake Park Community HSD 108	Roselle
238	0.0	Lansing SD 158	Lansing
238	0.0	Libertyville SD 70	Libertyville
238	0.0	Lincolnshire-Prairieview S D 103	Lincolnshire
238	0.0	Lyons Twp HSD 204	La Grange
238	0.0	Minooka Community HS District 111	Minooka
238	0.0	Niles Twp Community High SD 219	Skokie
238	0.0	North Shore SD 112	Highland Park
238	0.0	Northbrook SD 28	Northbrook
238	0.0	Oak Lawn-Hometown SD 123	Oak Lawn
238	0.0	Orland SD 135	Orland Park
238	0.0	Ottawa Twp HSD 140	Ottawa
238	0.0	Park Ridge CCSD 64	Park Ridge
238	0.0	Prospect Heights SD 23	Prospect Hgts
238	0.0	Queen Bee SD 16	Glendale Hgts
238	0.0	Schaumburg CCSD 54	Schaumburg
238	0.0	Warren Twp High SD 121	Gages Lake
238	0.0	Wilmette SD 39	Wilmette
238	0.0	Winnetka SD 36	Winnetka
238	0.0	Yorkville Community Unit SD 115	Yorkville
282	n/a	Adlai E Stevenson Dist 125	Lincolnshire
282	n/a	CCSD 181	Hinsdale
282	n/a	Community High SD 128	Libertyville
282	n/a	Forest Ridge SD 142	Oak Forest
282	n/a	Lockport Twp HSD 205	Lockport
282	n/a	Maine Township HSD 207	Park Ridge
282	n/a	Mchenry Community HSD 156	Mc Henry
282	n/a	New Trier Twp HSD 203	Northfield
282	n/a	Northfield Twp High SD 225	Glenview
282	n/a	Oak Lawn Community HSD 229	Oak Lawn
282	n/a	Reavis Twp HSD 220	Burbank
282	n/a	Township High SD 113	Highland Park

Student/Teacher Ratio

Rank	Ratio	District Name	City
1	36.6	Corrections SD 428 Dept of	Springfield
2	22.3	Decatur SD 61	Decatur
3	21.1	Harvey SD 152	Harvey
4	21.0	Berwyn North SD 98	Berwyn
4	21.0	Community Unit SD 300	Carpentersville
4	21.0	Granite City CUSD 9	Granite City
4	21.0	Round Lake Area Schs - Dist 116	Round Lake
8	20.7	SD 46	Elgin
9	20.5	Belleville Twp HSD 201	Belleville
9	20.5	Cahokia Community Unit SD 187	Cahokia
11	20.4	Bellwood SD 88	Bellwood
12	20.3	Valley View Cusd #365u	Romeoville
13	20.2	New Lenox SD 122	New Lenox
13	20.2	Oswego Community Unit SD 308	Oswego
15	20.1	Lincoln Way Community HSD 210	New Lenox
15	20.1	O Fallon Twp High SD 203	Ofallon
17	20.0	Bradley Bourbonnais CHSD 307	Bradley
17	20.0	Mt Zion Community Unit SD 3	Mt Zion
17	20.0	Will County SD 92	Lockport
20	19.8	Dolton SD 149	Calumet City
21	19.7	Carterville CUSD 5	Carterville
21	19.7	Mokena SD 159	Mokena
23	19.5	Belvidere CUSD 100	Belvidere
23	19.5	Marion Community Unit SD 2	Marion
23	19.5	Quincy SD 172	Quincy
23	19.5	United Twp HS District 30	East Moline
23	19.5	Yorkville Community Unit SD 115	Yorkville
28	19.4	Meridian CUSD 223	Stillman Valley
28	19.4	Minooka Community CSD 201	Minooka
28	19.4	Zion Elementary SD 6	Zion
31	19.3	Glenbard Twp HSD 87	Glen Ellyn
31	19.3	Homer Community CSD 33c	Homer Glen
31	19.3	Kewanee Community Unit SD 229	Kewanee
34	19.2	Crete Monee CUSD 201u	Crete
35	19.1	Oak Lawn Community HSD 229	Oak Lawn
35	19.1	Summit Hill SD 161	Frankfort
37	19.0	Community Consolidated SD 46	Grayslake
37	19.0	Posen-Robbins El SD 143-5	Posen
37	19.0	Zion-Benton Twp HSD 126	Zion
40	18.9	Aurora East Unit SD 131	Aurora
40	18.9	City of Chicago SD 299	Chicago
40	18.9	Community CSD 168	Sauk Village
40	18.9	Lake Park Community HSD 108	Roselle
40	18.9	Lockport Twp HSD 205	Lockport
40	18.9	O Fallon CCSD 90	Ofallon
40	18.9	Waukegan CUSD 60	Waukegan
47	18.8	Burbank SD 111	Burbank
47	18.8	Dunlap CUSD 323	Dunlap
47	18.8	Taylorville CUSD 3	Taylorville
50	18.7	Ball Chatham CUSD 5	Chatham
50	18.7	Belleville SD 118	Belleville
50	18.7	Carlinville CUSD 1	Carlinville
50	18.7	Herrin CUSD 4	Herrin
50	18.7	Kinnikinnick CCSD 131	Roscoe
50	18.7	Warren Twp High SD 121	Gages Lake
56	18.6	Ridgeland SD 122	Oak Lawn
57	18.5	Johnsburg CUSD 12	Johnsburg
58	18.3	Bradley SD 61	Bradley
58	18.3	Community High SD 218	Oak Lawn
58	18.3	J S Morton HS District 201	Cicero
58	18.3	Litchfield CUSD 12	Litchfield
58	18.3	Minooka Community HS District 111	Minooka
58	18.3	Proviso Twp HSD 209	Maywood
64	18.2	Elmwood Park CUSD 401	Elmwood Park
64	18.2	Mchenry CCSD 15	Mc Henry
64	18.2	North Palos SD 117	Palos Hills
67	18.1	Aurora West Unit SD 129	Aurora
67	18.1	Bourbonnais SD 53	Bourbonnais
67	18.1	Cicero SD 99	Cicero
67	18.1	Dolton SD 148	Riverdale
67	18.1	Downers Grove Grade SD 58	Downers Grove
67	18.1	Lemont-Bromberek CSD 113a	Lemont
67	18.1	Southwestern CUSD 9	Piasa
67	18.1	Woodstock CUSD 200	Woodstock
75	18.0	Beach Park CCSD 3	Beach Park
75	18.0	Naperville C U Dist 203	Naperville
75	18.0	Reavis Twp HSD 220	Burbank
75	18.0	Sterling C U Dist 5	Sterling
75	18.0	W Harvey-Dixmoor PS Dist 147	Harvey
80	17.9	Addison SD 4	Addison
80	17.9	Kankakee SD 111	Kankakee
80	17.9	Lansing SD 158	Lansing

80	17.9	Oregon C U School Dist-220	Oregon
80	17.9	Pekin Community HSD 303	Pekin
80	17.9	Plainfield SD 202	Plainfield
86	17.8	Joliet Public SD 86	Joliet
86	17.8	Maywood-Melrose Park-Broadview-89	Melrose Park
86	17.8	St Charles CUSD 303	Saint Charles
86	17.8	Troy Community CSD 30c	Plainfield
86	17.8	Vandalia CUSD 203	Vandalia
86	17.8	Winnebago CUSD 323	Winnebago
92	17.7	Collinsville CUSD 10	Collinsville
92	17.7	Danville CCSD 118	Danville
92	17.7	Fremont SD 79	Mundelein
92	17.7	Homewood Flossmoor CHSD 233	Flossmoor
92	17.7	Mundelein Cons High SD 120	Mundelein
97	17.6	Community High SD 155	Crystal Lake
97	17.6	Community High SD 99	Downers Grove
97	17.6	Indian Springs SD 109	Justice
97	17.6	Massac Unit District #1	Metropolis
97	17.6	Peotone CUSD 207u	Peotone
97	17.6	Rochester Community Unit SD 3a	Rochester
97	17.6	Triad Community Unit SD 2	Troy
104	17.5	Community High SD 117	Lake Villa
104	17.5	Dixon Unit SD 170	Dixon
104	17.5	Hononegah Community HSD 207	Rockton
104	17.5	Lyons SD 103	Lyons
108	17.4	Crystal Lake CCSD 47	Crystal Lake
108	17.4	Edwardsville CUSD 7	Edwardsville
108	17.4	Geneseo Community Unit SD 228	Geneseo
108	17.4	Mchenry Community HSD 156	Mc Henry
108	17.4	Midlothian SD 143	Midlothian
113	17.3	Bond County CUSD 2	Greenville
113	17.3	Coal City CUSD 1	Coal City
113	17.3	Frankfort CCSD 157c	Frankfort
113	17.3	Gurnee SD 56	Gurnee
113	17.3	Lyons Twp HSD 204	La Grange
113	17.3	Mahomet-Seymour CUSD 3	Mahomet
113	17.3	Marquardt SD 15	Glendale Hgts
120	17.2	Batavia Unit SD 101	Batavia
120	17.2	Berkeley SD 87	Berkeley
120	17.2	East St Louis SD 189	E Saint Louis
120	17.2	Geneva Community Unit SD 304	Geneva
120	17.2	Harvard CUSD 50	Harvard
120	17.2	Moline Unit SD 40	Moline
120	17.2	Palatine CCSD 15	Palatine
120	17.2	Sandwich CUSD 430	Sandwich
120	17.2	Waterloo Community Unit SD 5	Waterloo
129	17.1	Argo Community HSD 217	Summit
129	17.1	Community High SD 94	West Chicago
129	17.1	Cons High SD 230	Orland Park
129	17.1	Hillsboro Community Unit SD 3	Hillsboro
129	17.1	Mount Prospect SD 57	Mount Prospect
134	17.0	Park Forest SD 163	Park Forest
134	17.0	Rockford SD 205	Rockford
134	17.0	Wauconda Community Unit SD 118	Wauconda
134	17.0	Wilmington CUSD 209u	Wilmington
138	16.9	Frankfort Community Unit SD 168	West Frankfort
138	16.9	Harrisburg CUSD 3	Harrisburg
138	16.9	Kaneland CUSD 302	Maple Park
141	16.8	Antioch CCSD 34	Antioch
141	16.8	Barrington CUSD 220	Barrington
141	16.8	Cary CCSD 26	Cary
141	16.8	Du Page High SD 88	Villa Park
141	16.8	Effingham Community Unit SD 40	Effingham
141	16.8	Harlem Unit Dist 122	Loves Park
141	16.8	Prairie-Hills Elem SD 144	Markham
141	16.8	Rich Twp HS District 227	Olympia Fields
149	16.7	Joliet Twp HSD 204	Joliet
149	16.7	Orland SD 135	Orland Park
149	16.7	Rantoul City SD 137	Rantoul
152	16.6	Bensenville SD 2	Bensenville
152	16.6	CCSD 181	Hinsdale
152	16.6	Charleston CUSD 1	Charleston
152	16.6	Eureka C U Dist 140	Eureka
152	16.6	Lombard SD 44	Lombard
152	16.6	Matteson Elem SD 162	Matteson
152	16.6	North Chicago SD 187	North Chicago
152	16.6	Robinson CUSD 2	Robinson
152	16.6	Rock Island SD 41	Rock Island
161	16.5	Central Community Unit SD 301	Burlington
161	16.5	Community Consolidated S D 93	Carol Stream
161	16.5	Community Unit SD 200	Wheaton
161	16.5	Elmhurst SD 205	Elmhurst
161	16.5	Galesburg CUSD 205	Galesburg
161	16.5	Grayslake Community High SD 127	Grayslake
161	16.5	Jersey CUSD 100	Jerseyville
161	16.5	Leyden Community HSD 212	Franklin Park
161	16.5	Roxana Community Unit SD 1	Roxana
161	16.5	West Chicago Elem SD 33	West Chicago
161	16.5	Woodridge SD 68	Woodridge
172	16.4	Alsip-Hazlgrn-Oaklwn SD 126	Alsip
172	16.4	Alton Community Unit SD 11	Alton
172	16.4	Columbia Community Unit SD 4	Columbia
172	16.4	Genoa Kingston CUSD 424	Genoa
172	16.4	Hawthorn CCSD 73	Vernon Hills
172	16.4	Libertyville SD 70	Libertyville
178	16.3	Bethalto CUSD 8	Bethalto
178	16.3	Consolidated SD 158	Huntley
178	16.3	Dekalb Community Unit SD 428	De Kalb
178	16.3	Indian Prairie CUSD 204	Aurora
178	16.3	Murphysboro CUSD 186	Murphysboro
178	16.3	SD 45 Dupage County	Villa Park
178	16.3	Schaumburg CCSD 54	Schaumburg
178	16.3	Sparta CUSD 140	Sparta
178	16.3	Sycamore CUSD 427	Sycamore
178	16.3	Township HSD 211	Palatine
188	16.2	Adlai E Stevenson Dist 125	Lincolnshire
188	16.2	Chicago Heights SD 170	Chicago Heights
188	16.2	Mount Vernon SD 80	Mount Vernon
188	16.2	Ottawa Twp HSD 140	Ottawa
192	16.1	Canton Union SD 66	Canton
192	16.1	Keeneyville SD 20	Hanover Park
192	16.1	Manteno Community Unit SD 5	Manteno
192	16.1	Palos Community CSD 118	Palos Park
192	16.1	Springfield SD 186	Springfield
192	16.1	Wabash CUSD 348	Mount Carmel
198	16.0	Bloomington SD 87	Bloomington
198	16.0	Community CSD 59	Arlington Hgts
198	16.0	East Maine SD 63	Des Plaines
198	16.0	Flossmoor SD 161	Chicago Heights
198	16.0	Kirby SD 140	Tinley Park
198	16.0	Oak Park & River Forest Dist 200	Oak Park
204	15.9	Highland Community Unit SD 5	Highland
204	15.9	Kildeer Countryside CCSD 96	Buffalo Grove
204	15.9	Lisle CUSD 202	Lisle
204	15.9	Ottawa Elem SD 141	Ottawa
204	15.9	Pekin Public SD 108	Pekin
204	15.9	Township High SD 214	Arlington Hgts
210	15.8	Community High SD 128	Libertyville
211	15.7	Glen Ellyn SD 41	Glen Ellyn
211	15.7	Mannheim SD 83	Franklin Park
211	15.7	Morton CUSD 709	Morton
211	15.7	Mundelein Elem SD 75	Mundelein
211	15.7	Thornton Fractional T HS D 215	Calumet City
216	15.6	Berwyn South SD 100	Berwyn
216	15.6	Cook County SD 130	Blue Island
216	15.6	Evergreen Pk Elem SD 124	Evergreen Park
216	15.6	Fenton Community HSD 100	Bensenville
216	15.6	Freeport SD 145	Freeport
216	15.6	Il Valley Central Unit Dist 321	Chillicothe
216	15.6	Mascoutah C U District 19	Mascoutah
216	15.6	Reed Custer CUSD 255u	Braidwood
216	15.6	Rochelle Community CD 231	Rochelle
216	15.6	Thornton Twp HSD 205	South Holland
226	15.5	Arlington Heights SD 25	Arlington Hgts
226	15.5	East Moline SD 37	East Moline
226	15.5	East Richland CUSD 1	Olney
226	15.5	Forest Ridge SD 142	Oak Forest
226	15.5	Glen Ellyn CCSD 89	Glen Ellyn
226	15.5	Monticello CUSD 25	Monticello
226	15.5	Nippersink SD 2	Richmond
233	15.4	Bremen Community HS District 228	Midlothian
233	15.4	Hinsdale Twp HSD 86	Hinsdale
233	15.4	Pana Community Unit SD 8	Pana
233	15.4	Paris-Union SD 95	Paris
233	15.4	Streator Elem SD 44	Streator
238	15.3	Bloom Twp High SD 206	Chicago Heights
238	15.3	East Peoria SD 86	East Peoria
238	15.3	Lake Villa CCSD 41	Lake Villa
241	15.2	Country Club Hills SD 160	Ctry Club Hill
241	15.2	Elem SD 159	Matteson
241	15.2	Flora Community Unit SD 35	Flora
241	15.2	Herscher Community Unit SD 2	Herscher
241	15.2	Lake Zurich CUSD 95	Lake Zurich
241	15.2	Monmouth Unit SD 38	Monmouth
241	15.2	Queen Bee SD 16	Glendale Hgts
248	15.1	Community Consolidated SD 62	Des Plaines
248	15.1	Mclean County Unit Dist No 5	Normal
248	15.1	Steger SD 194	Steger
248	15.1	Woodland CCSD 50	Gurnee
252	15.0	Macomb Community Unit SD 185	Macomb
252	15.0	Niles Twp Community High SD 219	Skokie
252	15.0	Wheeling CCSD 21	Wheeling
255	14.9	Jacksonville SD 117	Jacksonville
255	14.9	Peoria SD 150	Peoria
255	14.9	Township High SD 113	Highland Park
255	14.9	Westmont CUSD 201	Westmont
259	14.8	Jasper County Comm Unit Dist 1	Newton
259	14.8	Olympia CUSD 16	Stanford
261	14.6	Aptakisic-Tripp CCSD 102	Buffalo Grove
261	14.6	Champaign Community Unit SD 4	Champaign
263	14.5	Northfield Twp High SD 225	Glenview
263	14.5	Oak Lawn-Hometown SD 123	Oak Lawn
265	14.4	Byron Community Unit SD 226	Byron
265	14.4	La Grange SD 102	La Grange Park
267	14.3	Glenview CCSD 34	Glenview
267	14.3	Lake Forest Community HS Dist 115	Lake Forest
267	14.3	Prairie Central CUSD 8	Forrest
267	14.3	Summit SD 104	Summit
267	14.3	Urbana SD 116	Urbana
272	14.2	Homewood SD 153	Homewood
272	14.2	Lincolnshire-Prairieview S D 103	Lincolnshire
272	14.2	Winnetka SD 36	Winnetka
275	14.1	Clinton CUSD 15	Clinton
275	14.1	Darien SD 61	Darien
275	14.1	Maine Township HSD 207	Park Ridge
275	14.1	River Trails SD 26	Mount Prospect
275	14.1	Sherrard Community Unit SD 200	Sherrard
275	14.1	Tinley Park Comm Cons Sch Dst 146	Tinley Park
281	14.0	Mattoon CUSD 2	Mattoon
281	14.0	Park Ridge CCSD 64	Park Ridge
283	13.9	Deerfield SD 109	Deerfield
284	13.8	Oak Park Elem SD 97	Oak Park
285	13.7	Prospect Heights SD 23	Prospect Hgts
286	13.4	Skokie SD 68	Skokie
286	13.4	Wilmette SD 39	Wilmette
288	13.3	North Shore SD 112	Highland Park
289	13.2	Evanston CCSD 65	Evanston
290	12.4	Evanston Twp HSD 202	Evanston
290	12.4	Lake Forest SD 67	Lake Forest
292	12.3	New Trier Twp HSD 203	Northfield
293	11.7	Northbrook SD 28	Northbrook

Student/Librarian Ratio

Rank	Ratio	District Name	City
1	6,379.0	Danville CCSD 118	Danville
2	6,333.0	Round Lake Area Schs - Dist 116	Round Lake
3	5,917.0	Maywood-Melrose Park-Broadview-89	Melrose Park
4	5,473.0	Dekalb Community Unit SD 428	De Kalb
5	5,098.0	Cahokia Community Unit SD 187	Cahokia
6	5,008.0	Joliet Public SD 86	Joliet
7	4,837.0	Crete Monee CUSD 201u	Crete
8	4,552.0	North Chicago SD 187	North Chicago
9	4,404.0	Park Ridge CCSD 64	Park Ridge
10	3,980.0	Dolton SD 149	Calumet City
11	3,918.0	Addison SD 4	Addison
12	3,791.5	Granite City CUSD 9	Granite City
13	3,768.0	Triad Community Unit SD 2	Troy
14	3,556.0	Sterling C U Dist 5	Sterling
15	3,533.0	Troy Community CSD 30c	Plainfield
16	3,470.0	Summit Hill SD 161	Frankfort
17	3,421.0	Berwyn South SD 100	Berwyn
18	3,370.3	Decatur SD 61	Decatur
19	3,347.0	Bellwood SD 88	Bellwood
20	3,338.5	Rock Island SD 41	Rock Island
21	3,317.5	Thornton Twp HSD 205	South Holland
22	3,143.0	O Fallon CCSD 90	Ofallon
23	3,129.0	Homer Community CSD 33c	Homer Glen
24	3,122.0	Harvey SD 152	Harvey
25	3,039.0	Collinsville CUSD 10	Collinsville
26	2,992.0	Dixon Unit SD 170	Dixon
27	2,951.0	Elmwood Park CUSD 401	Elmwood Park
28	2,949.0	Berkeley SD 87	Berkeley
29	2,927.0	Lincoln Way Community HSD 210	New Lenox
30	2,902.0	Kankakee SD 111	Kankakee
31	2,601.0	Waterloo Community Unit SD 5	Waterloo
32	2,597.0	Flossmoor SD 161	Chicago Heights
33	2,588.1	SD 46	Elgin
34	2,541.0	Antioch CCSD 34	Antioch
35	2,532.0	Lemont-Bromberek CSD 113a	Lemont
36	2,456.5	Arlington Heights SD 25	Arlington Hgts
37	2,454.0	Sandwich CUSD 430	Sandwich
38	2,426.0	Proviso Twp HSD 209	Maywood
39	2,396.0	Zion-Benton Twp HSD 126	Zion
40	2,369.0	Massac Unit District #1	Metropolis
41	2,284.0	Aurora East Unit SD 131	Aurora
42	2,274.0	Lyons SD 103	Lyons
43	2,266.1	Peoria SD 150	Peoria
44	2,219.0	Park Forest SD 163	Park Forest
45	2,194.0	Lake Forest SD 67	Lake Forest
46	2,175.5	Adlai E Stevenson Dist 125	Lincolnshire
47	2,173.1	Springfield SD 186	Springfield
48	2,150.0	O Fallon Twp High SD 203	Ofallon
49	2,146.0	Community High SD 94	West Chicago
50	2,104.0	Il Valley Central Unit Dist 321	Chillicothe
51	2,078.0	Pekin Community HSD 303	Pekin
52	2,057.0	Grayslake Community High SD 127	Grayslake
53	2,022.0	Evergreen Pk Elem SD 124	Evergreen Park
54	2,008.5	Du Page High SD 88	Villa Park
55	1,948.0	Manteno Community Unit SD 5	Manteno
56	1,920.0	Coal City CUSD 1	Coal City
57	1,910.0	SD 45 Dupage County	Villa Park
58	1,897.0	Mount Vernon SD 80	Mount Vernon
59	1,894.0	Jacksonville SD 117	Jacksonville
60	1,886.0	Streator Elem SD 44	Streator
61	1,884.0	Wabash CUSD 348	Mount Carmel
62	1,856.0	Kewanee Community Unit SD 229	Kewanee

63	1,855.0	Hononegah Community HSD 207	Rockton
64	1,852.0	Frankfort Community Unit SD 168	West Frankfort
65	1,845.9	Rockford SD 205	Rockford
66	1,845.0	Rochelle Community CD 231	Rochelle
67	1,839.0	Peotone CUSD 207u	Peotone
68	1,816.0	United Twp HS District 30	East Moline
69	1,806.7	Waukegan CUSD 60	Waukegan
70	1,786.0	Byron Community Unit SD 226	Byron
71	1,783.0	Bradley Bourbonnais CHSD 307	Bradley
72	1,776.0	Genoa Kingston CUSD 424	Genoa
73	1,766.0	Darien SD 61	Darien
74	1,765.0	Sherrard Community Unit SD 200	Sherrard
75	1,748.0	Edwardsville CUSD 7	Edwardsville
76	1,744.1	Township High SD 214	Arlington Hgts
77	1,735.0	Lake Forest Community HS Dist 115	Lake Forest
78	1,724.8	East St Louis SD 189	E Saint Louis
79	1,717.0	Columbia Community Unit SD 4	Columbia
80	1,711.1	J S Morton HS District 201	Cicero
81	1,695.0	Paris-Union SD 95	Paris
82	1,687.0	Argo Community HSD 217	Summit
83	1,680.0	Winnebago CUSD 323	Winnebago
84	1,654.0	Litchfield CUSD 12	Litchfield
85	1,648.5	Lockport Twp HSD 205	Lockport
86	1,632.0	Carterville CUSD 5	Carterville
87	1,631.0	Reavis Twp HSD 220	Burbank
88	1,620.0	Country Club Hills SD 160	Ctry Club Hill
89	1,589.0	Sparta CUSD 140	Sparta
90	1,585.8	Community High SD 155	Crystal Lake
91	1,585.0	Nippersink SD 2	Richmond
92	1,576.0	Ottawa Twp HSD 140	Ottawa
93	1,569.0	Sycamore CUSD 427	Sycamore
94	1,553.0	Bradley SD 61	Bradley
95	1,542.0	Posen-Robbins El SD 143-5	Posen
96	1,537.0	Thornton Fractional T HS D 215	Calumet City
97	1,534.0	Minooka Community HS District 111	Minooka
98	1,519.0	Bloom Twp High SD 206	Chicago Heights
99	1,513.0	Jersey CUSD 100	Jerseyville
100	1,508.0	Flora Community Unit SD 35	Flora
101	1,502.5	Effingham Community Unit SD 40	Effingham
102	1,501.0	Fenton Community HSD 100	Bensenville
103	1,489.0	Freeport SD 145	Freeport
104	1,460.5	Lake Park Community HSD 108	Roselle
105	1,411.0	Woodland CCSD 50	Gurnee
106	1,398.0	Bethalto CUSD 8	Bethalto
107	1,384.5	Canton Union SD 66	Canton
108	1,381.2	Alton Community Unit SD 11	Alton
109	1,354.6	Plainfield SD 202	Plainfield
110	1,336.0	Marquardt SD 15	Glendale Hgts
111	1,317.7	Marion Community Unit SD 2	Marion
112	1,298.2	Community Unit SD 300	Carpentersville
113	1,262.3	Belvidere CUSD 100	Belvidere
114	1,259.5	Dunlap CUSD 323	Dunlap
115	1,234.8	Belleville Twp HSD 201	Belleville
116	1,225.4	Cicero SD 99	Cicero
117	1,209.0	Warren Twp High SD 121	Gages Lake
118	1,206.5	Central Community Unit SD 301	Burlington
119	1,181.4	Valley View Cusd #365u	Romeoville
120	1,178.0	Rich Twp HS District 227	Olympia Fields
121	1,164.5	Community High SD 117	Lake Villa
122	1,162.5	Mchenry Community HSD 156	Mc Henry
123	1,149.5	Oswego Community Unit SD 308	Oswego
124	1,145.1	Community High SD 218	Oak Lawn
125	1,124.0	Herrin CUSD 4	Herrin
126	1,119.0	Beach Park CCSD 3	Beach Park
127	1,115.5	Olympia CUSD 16	Stanford
128	1,108.3	Kaneland CUSD 302	Maple Park
129	1,102.5	Murphysboro CUSD 186	Murphysboro
130	1,089.2	Yorkville Community Unit SD 115	Yorkville
131	1,040.0	Taylorville CUSD 3	Taylorville
132	1,039.0	Mundelein Cons High SD 120	Mundelein
133	1,027.5	Ottawa Elem SD 141	Ottawa
134	1,024.6	Cons High SD 230	Orland Park
135	1,023.0	Hillsboro Community Unit SD 3	Hillsboro
136	1,007.7	Oak Park & River Forest Dist 200	Oak Park
137	1,004.5	Palos Community CSD 118	Palos Park
138	1,002.7	Highland Community Unit SD 5	Highland
139	1,002.3	Community High SD 128	Libertyville
140	993.8	Glenbard Twp HSD 87	Glen Ellyn
141	987.5	Bond County CUSD 2	Greenville
142	984.7	Consolidated SD 158	Huntley
143	982.5	Macomb Community Unit SD 185	Macomb
144	959.0	Geneseo Community Unit SD 228	Geneseo
145	957.7	Mascoutah C U District 19	Mascoutah
146	956.4	Indian Prairie CUSD 204	Aurora
147	956.0	Rochester Community Unit SD 3a	Rochester
148	941.5	East Peoria SD 86	East Peoria
149	939.4	Lake Villa CCSD 41	Lake Villa
150	938.5	Roxana Community Unit SD 1	Roxana
151	922.3	Homewood Flossmoor CHSD 233	Flossmoor
152	915.0	Community High SD 99	Downers Grove
153	901.5	Oregon C U School Dist-220	Oregon
154	899.0	Southwestern CUSD 9	Piasa
155	898.3	Johnsburg CUSD 12	Johnsburg
156	891.0	Lyons Twp HSD 204	La Grange
156	891.0	Vandalia CUSD 203	Vandalia
158	879.0	Meridian CUSD 223	Stillman Valley
159	862.3	Township HSD 211	Palatine
160	860.3	Maine Township HSD 207	Park Ridge
161	853.7	Geneva Community Unit SD 304	Geneva
162	848.5	Oak Lawn Community HSD 229	Oak Lawn
163	848.0	City of Chicago SD 299	Chicago
163	848.0	Westmont CUSD 201	Westmont
165	844.8	Joliet Twp HSD 204	Joliet
166	844.3	Burbank SD 111	Burbank
167	830.8	Mattoon CUSD 2	Mattoon
168	823.2	Naperville C U Dist 203	Naperville
169	819.3	Mt Zion Community Unit SD 3	Mt Zion
170	814.5	Eureka C U Dist 140	Eureka
171	812.0	Ball Chatham CUSD 5	Chatham
172	811.1	Lake Zurich CUSD 95	Lake Zurich
173	810.6	Bloomington SD 87	Bloomington
174	809.5	Bremen Community HS District 228	Midlothian
175	808.3	Hawthorn CCSD 73	Vernon Hills
176	804.5	Jasper County Comm Unit Dist 1	Newton
177	800.0	Carlinville CUSD 1	Carlinville
178	794.0	Wauconda Community Unit SD 118	Wauconda
179	787.2	Mchenry CCSD 15	Mc Henry
180	784.8	Berwyn North SD 98	Berwyn
181	781.1	Aurora West Unit SD 129	Aurora
182	780.5	Fremont SD 79	Mundelein
183	777.5	Woodstock CUSD 200	Woodstock
184	771.3	Aptakisic-Tripp CCSD 102	Buffalo Grove
185	761.3	Harvard CUSD 50	Harvard
186	759.6	Crystal Lake CCSD 47	Crystal Lake
187	759.0	Pana Community Unit SD 8	Pana
187	759.0	Wilmington CUSD 209u	Wilmington
189	749.7	Champaign Community Unit SD 4	Champaign
190	746.7	Gurnee SD 56	Gurnee
191	744.5	Batavia Unit SD 101	Batavia
192	734.9	Lombard SD 44	Lombard
193	726.8	Barrington CUSD 220	Barrington
194	725.0	Herscher Community Unit SD 2	Herscher
195	720.4	Community Unit SD 200	Wheaton
196	718.8	St Charles CUSD 303	Saint Charles
197	716.9	Harlem Unit Dist 122	Loves Park
198	708.8	Mannheim SD 83	Franklin Park
199	706.5	Hinsdale Twp HSD 86	Hinsdale
200	705.7	Galesburg CUSD 205	Galesburg
201	696.4	Glen Ellyn SD 41	Glen Ellyn
202	695.0	East Richland CUSD 1	Olney
203	686.9	Niles Twp Community High SD 219	Skokie
204	682.3	Northfield Twp High SD 225	Glenview
205	674.3	Mount Prospect SD 57	Mount Prospect
206	668.8	Community Consolidated SD 46	Grayslake
207	668.3	Mahomet-Seymour CUSD 3	Mahomet
208	666.5	La Grange SD 102	La Grange Park
209	647.5	New Lenox SD 122	New Lenox
210	647.3	Moline Unit SD 40	Moline
211	646.5	Leyden Community HSD 212	Franklin Park
212	640.2	Cook County SD 130	Blue Island
213	623.6	Evanston Twp HSD 202	Evanston
214	612.5	Community Consolidated S D 93	Carol Stream
215	607.3	Mclean County Unit Dist No 5	Normal
216	606.5	Bourbonnais SD 53	Bourbonnais
217	604.8	Palatine CCSD 15	Palatine
218	599.2	Wilmette SD 39	Wilmette
219	593.7	Orland SD 135	Orland Park
220	592.3	Robinson CUSD 2	Robinson
221	590.4	Charleston CUSD 1	Charleston
222	575.7	Keeneyville SD 20	Hanover Park
223	574.7	Lincolnshire-Prairieview S D 103	Lincolnshire
224	574.0	Kirby SD 140	Tinley Park
225	571.3	Urbana SD 116	Urbana
226	570.5	Elmhurst SD 205	Elmhurst
227	565.7	Morton CUSD 709	Morton
228	554.8	Mundelein Elem SD 75	Mundelein
229	552.0	Harrisburg CUSD 3	Harrisburg
230	550.0	River Trails SD 26	Mount Prospect
231	548.7	Oak Park Elem SD 97	Oak Park
231	548.7	West Chicago Elem SD 33	West Chicago
233	541.2	North Palos SD 117	Palos Hills
234	540.3	Wheeling CCSD 21	Wheeling
235	539.7	Prairie Central CUSD 8	Forrest
236	538.3	Monticello CUSD 25	Monticello
237	534.3	Clinton CUSD 15	Clinton
238	531.0	East Maine SD 63	Des Plaines
239	530.6	Libertyville SD 70	Libertyville
240	528.0	Queen Bee SD 16	Glendale Hgts
241	526.2	Deerfield SD 109	Deerfield
242	523.7	Elem SD 159	Matteson
243	523.3	Cary CCSD 26	Cary
244	517.2	Woodridge SD 68	Woodridge
245	509.7	Prospect Heights SD 23	Prospect Hgts
246	508.5	Community Consolidated SD 62	Des Plaines
247	504.0	Matteson Elem SD 162	Matteson
248	503.5	CCSD 181	Hinsdale
249	501.7	Township High SD 113	Highland Park
250	498.1	Kildeer Countryside CCSD 96	Buffalo Grove
251	496.9	Glenview CCSD 34	Glenview
252	494.6	East Moline SD 37	East Moline
253	475.8	Glen Ellyn CCSD 89	Glen Ellyn
254	465.0	Bensenville SD 2	Bensenville
255	463.8	Evanston CCSD 65	Evanston
256	456.6	Ridgeland SD 122	Oak Lawn
257	456.4	Community CSD 59	Arlington Hgts
258	452.0	Lisle CUSD 202	Lisle
259	451.5	Reed Custer CUSD 255u	Braidwood
260	448.3	Northbrook SD 28	Northbrook
261	444.5	Minooka Community CSD 201	Minooka
262	442.1	North Shore SD 112	Highland Park
263	426.1	Pekin Public SD 108	Pekin
264	423.8	Alsip-Hazlgrn-Oaklwn SD 126	Alsip
264	423.8	Lansing SD 158	Lansing
266	412.4	Dolton SD 148	Riverdale
267	412.3	New Trier Twp HSD 203	Northfield
268	409.0	Skokie SD 68	Skokie
269	407.3	Oak Lawn-Hometown SD 123	Oak Lawn
270	403.3	Tinley Park Comm Cons Sch Dst 146	Tinley Park
271	397.6	Downers Grove Grade SD 58	Downers Grove
272	367.6	W Harvey-Dixmoor PS Dist 147	Harvey
273	335.3	Winnetka SD 36	Winnetka
274	306.2	Monmouth Unit SD 38	Monmouth
275	n/a	Belleville SD 118	Belleville
275	n/a	Chicago Heights SD 170	Chicago Heights
275	n/a	Community CSD 168	Sauk Village
275	n/a	Corrections SD 428 Dept of	Springfield
275	n/a	Forest Ridge SD 142	Oak Forest
275	n/a	Frankfort CCSD 157c	Frankfort
275	n/a	Homewood SD 153	Homewood
275	n/a	Indian Springs SD 109	Justice
275	n/a	Kinnikinnick CCSD 131	Roscoe
275	n/a	Midlothian SD 143	Midlothian
275	n/a	Mokena SD 159	Mokena
275	n/a	Prairie-Hills Elem SD 144	Markham
275	n/a	Quincy SD 172	Quincy
275	n/a	Rantoul City SD 137	Rantoul
275	n/a	Schaumburg CCSD 54	Schaumburg
275	n/a	Steger SD 194	Steger
275	n/a	Summit SD 104	Summit
275	n/a	Will County SD 92	Lockport
275	n/a	Zion Elementary SD 6	Zion

Student/Counselor Ratio

Rank	Ratio	District Name	City
1	7,024.0	Wheeling CCSD 21	Wheeling
2	4,028.0	CCSD 181	Hinsdale
3	3,953.3	East Maine SD 63	Des Plaines
4	3,918.0	Addison SD 4	Addison
5	3,820.0	SD 45 Dupage County	Villa Park
6	3,487.0	Kildeer Countryside CCSD 96	Buffalo Grove
7	3,471.0	Chicago Heights SD 170	Chicago Heights
8	3,157.0	Deerfield SD 109	Deerfield
9	3,122.0	Harvey SD 152	Harvey
10	2,989.6	Schaumburg CCSD 54	Schaumburg
11	2,796.0	Bethalto CUSD 8	Bethalto
12	2,525.9	Palatine CCSD 15	Palatine
13	2,283.0	Ridgeland SD 122	Oak Lawn
14	2,274.0	Lyons SD 103	Lyons
15	2,219.0	Mundelein Elem SD 75	Mundelein
16	2,210.5	North Shore SD 112	Highland Park
17	2,202.0	Park Ridge CCSD 64	Park Ridge
18	2,112.0	Queen Bee SD 16	Glendale Hgts
19	2,111.0	Round Lake Area Schs - Dist 116	Round Lake
20	2,009.0	Palos Community CSD 118	Palos Park
21	1,990.0	Dolton SD 149	Calumet City
22	1,920.5	West Chicago Elem SD 33	West Chicago
23	1,883.0	East Peoria SD 86	East Peoria
24	1,871.0	Kinnikinnick CCSD 131	Roscoe
25	1,856.0	Kewanee Community Unit SD 229	Kewanee
26	1,852.0	Frankfort Community Unit SD 168	West Frankfort
27	1,839.0	Peotone CUSD 207u	Peotone
28	1,772.0	Community CSD 168	Sauk Village
29	1,766.0	Darien SD 61	Darien
30	1,762.0	Forest Ridge SD 142	Oak Forest
31	1,696.0	Westmont CUSD 201	Westmont
32	1,585.0	Nippersink SD 2	Richmond
33	1,567.3	Plainfield SD 202	Plainfield
34	1,551.5	Woodridge SD 68	Woodridge
35	1,519.5	Collinsville CUSD 10	Collinsville
36	1,518.0	Pana Community Unit SD 8	Pana
37	1,484.3	Orland SD 135	Orland Park
38	1,475.5	Elmwood Park CUSD 401	Elmwood Park
39	1,443.2	SD 46	Elgin
40	1,367.5	Peoria SD 150	Peoria
41	1,344.6	Edwardsville CUSD 7	Edwardsville
42	1,326.5	Libertyville SD 70	Libertyville
43	1,301.9	Aurora West Unit SD 129	Aurora

44	1,300.5	Waterloo Community Unit SD 5	Waterloo
45	1,298.7	Manteno Community Unit SD 5	Manteno
46	1,298.5	Flossmoor SD 161	Chicago Heights
47	1,290.6	Lake Forest SD 67	Lake Forest
48	1,275.8	Danville CCSD 118	Danville
49	1,274.5	Cahokia Community Unit SD 187	Cahokia
50	1,192.8	Downers Grove Grade SD 58	Downers Grove
51	1,189.5	Glen Ellyn CCSD 89	Glen Ellyn
52	1,162.5	Bensenville SD 2	Bensenville
53	1,160.7	Glen Ellyn SD 41	Glen Ellyn
54	1,151.0	Alton Community Unit SD 11	Alton
55	1,148.8	Galesburg CUSD 205	Galesburg
56	1,142.0	Aurora East Unit SD 131	Aurora
57	1,104.0	Harrisburg CUSD 3	Harrisburg
58	1,102.3	Lombard SD 44	Lombard
59	1,088.3	Community Unit SD 300	Carpentersville
60	1,083.3	Granite City CUSD 9	Granite City
61	1,082.0	Belvidere CUSD 100	Belvidere
62	1,063.3	Valley View Cusd #365u	Romeoville
63	1,040.0	Taylorville CUSD 3	Taylorville
64	1,039.5	Winnetka SD 36	Winnetka
65	1,008.0	Matteson Elem SD 162	Matteson
66	985.8	Harlem Unit Dist 122	Loves Park
67	967.3	Kankakee SD 111	Kankakee
68	958.8	Pekin Public SD 108	Pekin
69	957.9	Oswego Community Unit SD 308	Oswego
70	956.0	Rochester Community Unit SD 3a	Rochester
71	953.9	Rock Island SD 41	Rock Island
72	948.5	Mount Vernon SD 80	Mount Vernon
73	942.0	Triad Community Unit SD 2	Troy
74	923.0	Canton Union SD 66	Canton
75	918.4	Kirby SD 140	Tinley Park
76	899.0	Southwestern CUSD 9	Piasa
77	898.3	Johnsburg CUSD 12	Johnsburg
78	893.4	Freeport SD 145	Freeport
79	879.5	Crete Monee CUSD 201u	Crete
80	879.0	Meridian CUSD 223	Stillman Valley
81	850.9	Batavia Unit SD 101	Batavia
82	847.5	Paris-Union SD 95	Paris
83	844.0	Lemont-Bromberek CSD 113a	Lemont
84	831.3	Kaneland CUSD 302	Maple Park
85	830.8	Mattoon CUSD 2	Mattoon
86	827.0	Litchfield CUSD 12	Litchfield
87	818.0	Sandwich CUSD 430	Sandwich
88	816.0	Carterville CUSD 5	Carterville
89	811.1	Lake Zurich CUSD 95	Lake Zurich
90	810.0	Country Club Hills SD 160	Ctry Club Hill
91	804.3	Central Community Unit SD 301	Burlington
92	800.0	Carlinville CUSD 1	Carlinville
93	794.5	Sparta CUSD 140	Sparta
94	794.0	Wauconda Community Unit SD 118	Wauconda
95	789.7	Massac Unit District #1	Metropolis
96	781.9	Dekalb Community Unit SD 428	De Kalb
97	773.7	Consolidated SD 158	Huntley
98	761.3	Harvard CUSD 50	Harvard
99	759.0	Wilmington CUSD 209u	Wilmington
100	757.6	Jacksonville SD 117	Jacksonville
101	756.5	Jersey CUSD 100	Jerseyville
102	752.0	Highland Community Unit SD 5	Highland
103	749.0	Decatur SD 61	Decatur
104	743.7	Olympia CUSD 16	Stanford
105	740.0	New Lenox SD 122	New Lenox
106	739.1	Waukegan CUSD 60	Waukegan
107	737.3	Berkeley SD 87	Berkeley
108	728.9	Woodstock CUSD 200	Woodstock
109	728.8	Mclean County Unit Dist No 5	Normal
110	725.0	Herscher Community Unit SD 2	Herscher
111	718.8	St Charles CUSD 303	Saint Charles
112	718.3	Mascoutah C U District 19	Mascoutah
113	708.0	Yorkville Community Unit SD 115	Yorkville
114	706.1	Moline Unit SD 40	Moline
115	693.6	Geneva Community Unit SD 304	Geneva
116	682.0	Hillsboro Community Unit SD 3	Hillsboro
117	678.8	Sherrard Community Unit SD 200	Sherrard
118	674.6	Prairie Central CUSD 8	Forrest
119	672.0	Winnebago CUSD 323	Winnebago
120	668.3	Mahomet-Seymour CUSD 3	Mahomet
121	664.8	Morton CUSD 709	Morton
122	658.3	Bond County CUSD 2	Greenville
123	653.1	Indian Prairie CUSD 204	Aurora
124	652.9	Urbana SD 116	Urbana
125	650.3	North Chicago SD 187	North Chicago
126	646.8	East St Louis SD 189	E Saint Louis
127	640.0	Coal City CUSD 1	Coal City
128	635.0	Sterling C U Dist 5	Sterling
129	628.0	Wabash CUSD 348	Mount Carmel
130	627.6	Sycamore CUSD 427	Sycamore
131	625.8	Homer Community CSD 33c	Homer Glen
132	625.7	Roxana Community Unit SD 1	Roxana
133	624.7	Champaign Community Unit SD 4	Champaign
134	614.5	Mt Zion Community Unit SD 3	Mt Zion
135	602.7	Lisle CUSD 202	Lisle
136	602.0	Reed Custer CUSD 255u	Braidwood
137	601.0	Oregon C U School Dist-220	Oregon
138	598.5	Quincy SD 172	Quincy
139	598.4	Dixon Unit SD 170	Dixon
140	592.0	Genoa Kingston CUSD 424	Genoa
141	581.4	Barrington CUSD 220	Barrington
142	580.0	Ball Chatham CUSD 5	Chatham
143	575.4	Geneseo Community Unit SD 228	Geneseo
144	572.3	Columbia Community Unit SD 4	Columbia
145	562.0	Herrin CUSD 4	Herrin
146	556.9	Naperville C U Dist 203	Naperville
147	551.3	Murphysboro CUSD 186	Murphysboro
148	543.0	Eureka C U Dist 140	Eureka
149	538.3	Monticello CUSD 25	Monticello
150	536.7	Charleston CUSD 1	Charleston
151	534.3	Clinton CUSD 15	Clinton
152	526.9	Rockford SD 205	Rockford
153	526.0	Il Valley Central Unit Dist 321	Chillicothe
154	525.6	Community Unit SD 200	Wheaton
155	521.3	East Richland CUSD 1	Olney
156	513.8	Ottawa Elem SD 141	Ottawa
157	504.7	Troy Community CSD 30c	Plainfield
158	503.8	Dunlap CUSD 323	Dunlap
159	502.7	Flora Community Unit SD 35	Flora
160	500.9	City of Chicago SD 299	Chicago
161	496.1	Byron Community Unit SD 226	Byron
162	494.6	East Moline SD 37	East Moline
163	493.9	Belleville Twp HSD 201	Belleville
164	489.1	Bloomington SD 87	Bloomington
165	461.3	Rochelle Community CD 231	Rochelle
166	461.2	Homewood Flossmoor CHSD 233	Flossmoor
167	459.5	W Harvey-Dixmoor PS Dist 147	Harvey
168	448.3	Northbrook SD 28	Northbrook
169	444.3	Robinson CUSD 2	Robinson
170	441.1	Proviso Twp HSD 209	Maywood
171	439.8	New Trier Twp HSD 203	Northfield
172	439.2	Marion Community Unit SD 2	Marion
173	430.0	O Fallon Twp High SD 203	Ofallon
174	429.3	Effingham Community Unit SD 40	Effingham
175	414.7	Thornton Twp HSD 205	South Holland
176	403.0	Warren Twp High SD 121	Gages Lake
177	402.3	Jasper County Comm Unit Dist 1	Newton
178	399.3	Zion-Benton Twp HSD 126	Zion
179	396.0	Vandalia CUSD 203	Vandalia
180	393.0	Macomb Community Unit SD 185	Macomb
181	390.3	Elmhurst SD 205	Elmhurst
182	388.2	Community High SD 117	Lake Villa
183	387.5	Mchenry Community HSD 156	Mc Henry
184	383.5	Minooka Community HS District 111	Minooka
185	371.0	Hononegah Community HSD 207	Rockton
186	366.3	Lockport Twp HSD 205	Lockport
187	363.2	United Twp HS District 30	East Moline
188	360.3	Community High SD 218	Oak Lawn
189	357.1	Bremen Community HS District 228	Midlothian
190	350.2	Ottawa Twp HSD 140	Ottawa
191	349.6	Joliet Twp HSD 204	Joliet
192	341.6	Thornton Fractional T HS D 215	Calumet City
193	339.4	Oak Lawn Community HSD 229	Oak Lawn
194	334.5	Lincoln Way Community HSD 210	New Lenox
195	333.8	Community High SD 155	Crystal Lake
196	326.2	Reavis Twp HSD 220	Burbank
197	306.2	Monmouth Unit SD 38	Monmouth
198	305.1	Township HSD 211	Palatine
199	303.6	Cons High SD 230	Orland Park
200	301.2	J S Morton HS District 201	Cicero
201	296.9	Pekin Community HSD 303	Pekin
202	293.9	Grayslake Community High SD 127	Grayslake
203	292.1	Lake Park Community HSD 108	Roselle
204	286.9	Du Page High SD 88	Villa Park
205	281.2	Argo Community HSD 217	Summit
206	276.2	Bloom Twp High SD 206	Chicago Heights
207	275.1	Community High SD 94	West Chicago
208	274.8	Oak Park & River Forest Dist 200	Oak Park
209	272.7	Leyden Community HSD 212	Franklin Park
210	266.1	Bradley Bourbonnais CHSD 307	Bradley
211	264.7	Maine Township HSD 207	Park Ridge
212	261.4	Community High SD 99	Downers Grove
213	256.4	Lyons Twp HSD 204	La Grange
214	253.4	Glenbard Twp HSD 87	Glen Ellyn
215	250.2	Fenton Community HSD 100	Bensenville
216	240.4	Niles Twp Community High SD 219	Skokie
217	235.6	Rich Twp HS District 227	Olympia Fields
218	235.5	Hinsdale Twp HSD 86	Hinsdale
219	229.0	Adlai E Stevenson Dist 125	Lincolnshire
220	227.4	Northfield Twp High SD 225	Glenview
221	216.9	Lake Forest Community HS Dist 115	Lake Forest
222	204.8	Township High SD 214	Arlington Hgts
223	196.0	Mundelein Cons High SD 120	Mundelein
224	195.1	Township High SD 113	Highland Park
225	194.9	Evanston Twp HSD 202	Evanston
226	167.1	Community High SD 128	Libertyville
227	n/a	Alsip-Hazlgrn-Oaklwn SD 126	Alsip
227	n/a	Antioch CCSD 34	Antioch
227	n/a	Aptakisic-Tripp CCSD 102	Buffalo Grove
227	n/a	Arlington Heights SD 25	Arlington Hgts
227	n/a	Beach Park CCSD 3	Beach Park
227	n/a	Belleville SD 118	Belleville
227	n/a	Bellwood SD 88	Bellwood
227	n/a	Berwyn North SD 98	Berwyn
227	n/a	Berwyn South SD 100	Berwyn
227	n/a	Bourbonnais SD 53	Bourbonnais
227	n/a	Bradley SD 61	Bradley
227	n/a	Burbank SD 111	Burbank
227	n/a	Cary CCSD 26	Cary
227	n/a	Cicero SD 99	Cicero
227	n/a	Community CSD 59	Arlington Hgts
227	n/a	Community Consolidated S D 93	Carol Stream
227	n/a	Community Consolidated SD 46	Grayslake
227	n/a	Community Consolidated SD 62	Des Plaines
227	n/a	Cook County SD 130	Blue Island
227	n/a	Corrections SD 428 Dept of	Springfield
227	n/a	Crystal Lake CCSD 47	Crystal Lake
227	n/a	Dolton SD 148	Riverdale
227	n/a	Elem SD 159	Matteson
227	n/a	Evanston CCSD 65	Evanston
227	n/a	Evergreen Pk Elem SD 124	Evergreen Park
227	n/a	Frankfort CCSD 157c	Frankfort
227	n/a	Fremont SD 79	Mundelein
227	n/a	Glenview CCSD 34	Glenview
227	n/a	Gurnee SD 56	Gurnee
227	n/a	Hawthorn CCSD 73	Vernon Hills
227	n/a	Homewood SD 153	Homewood
227	n/a	Indian Springs SD 109	Justice
227	n/a	Joliet Public SD 86	Joliet
227	n/a	Keeneyville SD 20	Hanover Park
227	n/a	La Grange SD 102	La Grange Park
227	n/a	Lake Villa CCSD 41	Lake Villa
227	n/a	Lansing SD 158	Lansing
227	n/a	Lincolnshire-Prairieview S D 103	Lincolnshire
227	n/a	Mannheim SD 83	Franklin Park
227	n/a	Marquardt SD 15	Glendale Hgts
227	n/a	Maywood-Melrose Park-Broadview-89	Melrose Park
227	n/a	Mchenry CCSD 15	Mc Henry
227	n/a	Midlothian SD 143	Midlothian
227	n/a	Minooka Community CSD 201	Minooka
227	n/a	Mokena SD 159	Mokena
227	n/a	Mount Prospect SD 57	Mount Prospect
227	n/a	North Palos SD 117	Palos Hills
227	n/a	O Fallon CCSD 90	Ofallon
227	n/a	Oak Lawn-Hometown SD 123	Oak Lawn
227	n/a	Oak Park Elem SD 97	Oak Park
227	n/a	Park Forest SD 163	Park Forest
227	n/a	Posen-Robbins El SD 143-5	Posen
227	n/a	Prairie-Hills Elem SD 144	Markham
227	n/a	Prospect Heights SD 23	Prospect Hgts
227	n/a	Rantoul City SD 137	Rantoul
227	n/a	River Trails SD 26	Mount Prospect
227	n/a	Skokie SD 68	Skokie
227	n/a	Springfield SD 186	Springfield
227	n/a	Steger SD 194	Steger
227	n/a	Streator Elem SD 44	Streator
227	n/a	Summit Hill SD 161	Frankfort
227	n/a	Summit SD 104	Summit
227	n/a	Tinley Park Comm Cons Sch Dst 146	Tinley Park
227	n/a	Will County SD 92	Lockport
227	n/a	Wilmette SD 39	Wilmette
227	n/a	Woodland CCSD 50	Gurnee
227	n/a	Zion Elementary SD 6	Zion

Current Spending per Student in FY2003

Rank	Dollars	District Name	City
1	17,826	Township High SD 113	Highland Park
2	17,632	Evanston Twp HSD 202	Evanston
3	15,746	New Trier Twp HSD 203	Northfield
4	15,738	Northfield Twp High SD 225	Glenview
5	15,081	Oak Park & River Forest Dist 200	Oak Park
6	14,694	Niles Twp Community High SD 219	Skokie
7	14,253	Lake Forest Community HS Dist 115	Lake Forest
8	14,077	Community High SD 128	Libertyville
9	13,643	Township High SD 214	Arlington Hgts
10	13,617	Fenton Community HSD 100	Bensenville
11	13,583	Maine Township HSD 207	Park Ridge
12	13,391	Northbrook SD 28	Northbrook
13	13,103	Bloom Twp High SD 206	Chicago Heights
14	13,073	Township HSD 211	Palatine
15	12,994	Lyons Twp HSD 204	La Grange
16	12,910	Rich Twp HS District 227	Olympia Fields
17	12,587	Hinsdale Twp HSD 86	Hinsdale
18	12,378	Community High SD 218	Oak Lawn
19	12,018	Leyden Community HSD 212	Franklin Park
20	11,996	Bremen Community HS District 228	Midlothian
21	11,954	Community High SD 99	Downers Grove
22	11,821	Adlai E Stevenson Dist 125	Lincolnshire
23	11,695	Homewood Flossmoor CHSD 233	Flossmoor
24	11,531	Thornton Fractional T HS D 215	Calumet City

25	11,443	Cons High SD 230	Orland Park
26	11,383	Du Page High SD 88	Villa Park
27	11,260	Winnetka SD 36	Winnetka
28	11,246	Lake Park Community HSD 108	Roselle
29	11,237	Proviso Twp HSD 209	Maywood
30	11,162	Skokie SD 68	Skokie
31	11,072	Argo Community HSD 217	Summit
32	11,070	Reavis Twp HSD 220	Burbank
33	11,048	Glenbard Twp HSD 87	Glen Ellyn
34	11,029	Byron Community Unit SD 226	Byron
35	10,991	Lisle CUSD 202	Lisle
36	10,943	Mundelein Cons High SD 120	Mundelein
37	10,905	Thornton Twp HSD 205	South Holland
38	10,901	Oak Park Elem SD 97	Oak Park
39	10,889	Joliet Twp HSD 204	Joliet
40	10,836	River Trails SD 26	Mount Prospect
41	10,747	Evanston CCSD 65	Evanston
42	10,583	Lincolnshire-Prairieview S D 103	Lincolnshire
43	10,484	Lake Forest SD 67	Lake Forest
44	10,438	North Shore SD 112	Highland Park
45	10,261	Oak Lawn Community HSD 229	Oak Lawn
46	10,227	Westmont CUSD 201	Westmont
47	9,982	Reed Custer CUSD 255u	Braidwood
48	9,902	Community High SD 94	West Chicago
49	9,812	Elem SD 159	Matteson
50	9,787	Park Ridge CCSD 64	Park Ridge
51	9,699	Community Consolidated SD 62	Des Plaines
52	9,698	W Harvey-Dixmoor PS Dist 147	Harvey
53	9,658	Glenview CCSD 34	Glenview
54	9,615	Lockport Twp HSD 205	Lockport
55	9,569	Barrington CUSD 220	Barrington
56	9,548	Community CSD 59	Arlington Hgts
57	9,540	Elmhurst SD 205	Elmhurst
58	9,465	Schaumburg CCSD 54	Schaumburg
59	9,434	Zion-Benton Twp HSD 126	Zion
60	9,423	Prospect Heights SD 23	Prospect Hgts
61	9,357	Palatine CCSD 15	Palatine
62	9,199	Park Forest SD 163	Park Forest
63	9,191	Urbana SD 116	Urbana
64	9,186	CCSD 181	Hinsdale
64	9,186	Hononegah Community HSD 207	Rockton
66	9,153	Tinley Park Comm Cons Sch Dst 146	Tinley Park
67	9,148	Community High SD 155	Crystal Lake
68	9,143	Community High SD 117	Lake Villa
69	9,125	Keeneyville SD 20	Hanover Park
70	9,062	J S Morton HS District 201	Cicero
71	9,027	Arlington Heights SD 25	Arlington Hgts
72	9,007	Clinton CUSD 15	Clinton
73	9,003	Peoria SD 150	Peoria
74	8,970	North Chicago SD 187	North Chicago
75	8,884	Aptakisic-Tripp CCSD 102	Buffalo Grove
75	8,884	East Maine SD 63	Des Plaines
77	8,850	West Chicago Elem SD 33	West Chicago
78	8,849	Lombard SD 44	Lombard
79	8,786	Summit SD 104	Summit
80	8,755	Wilmette SD 39	Wilmette
81	8,744	Deerfield SD 109	Deerfield
82	8,727	Wheeling CCSD 21	Wheeling
83	8,709	Community Unit SD 200	Wheaton
84	8,701	Warren Twp High SD 121	Gages Lake
85	8,660	Mannheim SD 83	Franklin Park
86	8,614	Kildeer Countryside CCSD 96	Buffalo Grove
87	8,606	Rockford SD 205	Rockford
88	8,582	Ottawa Twp HSD 140	Ottawa
89	8,577	Naperville C U Dist 203	Naperville
90	8,497	Mchenry Community HSD 156	Mc Henry
91	8,472	Downers Grove Grade SD 58	Downers Grove
92	8,443	Central Community Unit SD 301	Burlington
93	8,441	SD 46	Elgin
94	8,434	Libertyville SD 70	Libertyville
95	8,416	Danville CCSD 118	Danville
96	8,398	Ottawa Elem SD 141	Ottawa
97	8,391	Country Club Hills SD 160	Ctry Club Hill
98	8,382	Minooka Community HS District 111	Minooka
99	8,319	Murphysboro CUSD 186	Murphysboro
100	8,313	Orland SD 135	Orland Park
101	8,293	Gurnee SD 56	Gurnee
102	8,291	East St Louis SD 189	E Saint Louis
103	8,271	Glen Ellyn CCSD 89	Glen Ellyn
104	8,262	Flossmoor SD 161	Chicago Heights
105	8,258	La Grange SD 102	La Grange Park
106	8,244	Macomb Community Unit SD 185	Macomb
107	8,212	Palos Community CSD 118	Palos Park
108	8,201	Kankakee SD 111	Kankakee
109	8,179	Robinson CUSD 2	Robinson
110	8,141	Hawthorn CCSD 73	Vernon Hills
111	8,122	East Moline SD 37	East Moline
112	8,118	Chicago Heights SD 170	Chicago Heights
113	8,104	Bloomington SD 87	Bloomington
114	8,094	Mount Prospect SD 57	Mount Prospect
115	8,092	Grayslake Community High SD 127	Grayslake
116	8,080	Mascoutah C U District 19	Mascoutah
117	8,069	Mount Vernon SD 80	Mount Vernon
118	8,060	Champaign Community Unit SD 4	Champaign
119	8,058	Woodridge SD 68	Woodridge
120	8,034	SD 45 Dupage County	Villa Park
121	8,000	Belleville SD 118	Belleville
122	7,972	Consolidated SD 158	Huntley
123	7,967	City of Chicago SD 299	Chicago
124	7,892	Cook County SD 130	Blue Island
125	7,891	Morton CUSD 709	Morton
126	7,870	Lincoln Way Community HSD 210	New Lenox
127	7,854	Geneva Community Unit SD 304	Geneva
128	7,845	Darien SD 61	Darien
129	7,843	Oak Lawn-Hometown SD 123	Oak Lawn
130	7,833	North Palos SD 117	Palos Hills
131	7,788	Coal City CUSD 1	Coal City
132	7,784	Jasper County Comm Unit Dist 1	Newton
133	7,780	Elmwood Park CUSD 401	Elmwood Park
134	7,754	Olympia CUSD 16	Stanford
135	7,744	Woodstock CUSD 200	Woodstock
136	7,742	Aurora East Unit SD 131	Aurora
137	7,735	Dekalb Community Unit SD 428	De Kalb
138	7,727	Cahokia Community Unit SD 187	Cahokia
139	7,726	Rock Island SD 41	Rock Island
140	7,724	Fremont SD 79	Mundelein
141	7,720	Mclean County Unit Dist No 5	Normal
142	7,694	Lake Zurich CUSD 95	Lake Zurich
143	7,685	Streator Elem SD 44	Streator
144	7,675	Community Consolidated S D 93	Carol Stream
145	7,668	Homewood SD 153	Homewood
146	7,659	Springfield SD 186	Springfield
147	7,652	Moline Unit SD 40	Moline
148	7,643	Community Consolidated SD 46	Grayslake
149	7,639	Sycamore CUSD 427	Sycamore
150	7,636	Dolton SD 149	Calumet City
151	7,621	Alton Community Unit SD 11	Alton
152	7,606	Mattoon CUSD 2	Mattoon
153	7,589	Alsip-Hazlgrn-Oaklwn SD 126	Alsip
154	7,582	Kaneland CUSD 302	Maple Park
155	7,540	Roxana Community Unit SD 1	Roxana
156	7,530	Glen Ellyn SD 41	Glen Ellyn
157	7,515	Crete Monee CUSD 201u	Crete
158	7,480	Woodland CCSD 50	Gurnee
159	7,464	Freeport SD 145	Freeport
160	7,449	Indian Prairie CUSD 204	Aurora
161	7,448	Joliet Public SD 86	Joliet
162	7,428	Bradley Bourbonnais CHSD 307	Bradley
163	7,421	Harlem Unit Dist 122	Loves Park
164	7,348	Community Unit SD 300	Carpentersville
165	7,342	Oregon C U School Dist-220	Oregon
166	7,326	St Charles CUSD 303	Saint Charles
167	7,324	Matteson Elem SD 162	Matteson
168	7,315	United Twp HS District 30	East Moline
169	7,308	Troy Community CSD 30c	Plainfield
170	7,307	Dixon Unit SD 170	Dixon
171	7,295	East Peoria SD 86	East Peoria
172	7,291	Batavia Unit SD 101	Batavia
173	7,284	Johnsburg CUSD 12	Johnsburg
174	7,276	Southwestern CUSD 9	Piasa
175	7,274	Waukegan CUSD 60	Waukegan
176	7,267	Kirby SD 140	Tinley Park
177	7,264	Marquardt SD 15	Glendale Hgts
178	7,249	Pekin Community HSD 303	Pekin
178	7,249	Wauconda Community Unit SD 118	Wauconda
180	7,246	Valley View Cusd #365u	Romeoville
181	7,224	Berwyn South SD 100	Berwyn
182	7,220	Harvey SD 152	Harvey
183	7,219	Zion Elementary SD 6	Zion
184	7,216	Cary CCSD 26	Cary
185	7,212	Posen-Robbins El SD 143-5	Posen
186	7,199	Jacksonville SD 117	Jacksonville
187	7,174	Homer Community CSD 33c	Homer Glen
188	7,173	Prairie-Hills Elem SD 144	Markham
189	7,146	Sterling C U Dist 5	Sterling
190	7,141	Belleville Twp HSD 201	Belleville
190	7,141	Bensenville SD 2	Bensenville
192	7,121	Prairie Central CUSD 8	Forrest
193	7,111	Frankfort Community Unit SD 168	West Frankfort
194	7,094	Herscher Community Unit SD 2	Herscher
195	7,063	Sparta CUSD 140	Sparta
196	7,059	O Fallon Twp High SD 203	Ofallon
197	7,032	Hillsboro Community Unit SD 3	Hillsboro
198	7,031	Evergreen Pk Elem SD 124	Evergreen Park
199	7,010	Charleston CUSD 1	Charleston
200	7,009	Canton Union SD 66	Canton
200	7,009	Harrisburg CUSD 3	Harrisburg
202	7,002	Bethalto CUSD 8	Bethalto
203	6,967	Jersey CUSD 100	Jerseyville
204	6,957	Highland Community Unit SD 5	Highland
205	6,942	Lyons SD 103	Lyons
206	6,940	Eureka C U Dist 140	Eureka
207	6,939	Minooka Community CSD 201	Minooka
208	6,923	Collinsville CUSD 10	Collinsville
209	6,914	Winnebago CUSD 323	Winnebago
210	6,874	Queen Bee SD 16	Glendale Hgts
211	6,867	Antioch CCSD 34	Antioch
212	6,857	Flora Community Unit SD 35	Flora
213	6,850	Geneseo Community Unit SD 228	Geneseo
214	6,830	Granite City CUSD 9	Granite City
215	6,825	Berkeley SD 87	Berkeley
216	6,813	Beach Park CCSD 3	Beach Park
217	6,811	Ridgeland SD 122	Oak Lawn
218	6,806	Maywood-Melrose Park-Broadview-89	Melrose Park
219	6,796	Nippersink SD 2	Richmond
220	6,787	Addison SD 4	Addison
221	6,756	Pekin Public SD 108	Pekin
222	6,753	Forest Ridge SD 142	Oak Forest
223	6,742	Mahomet-Seymour CUSD 3	Mahomet
224	6,737	Dolton SD 148	Riverdale
225	6,732	Aurora West Unit SD 129	Aurora
226	6,711	Edwardsville CUSD 7	Edwardsville
227	6,694	Harvard CUSD 50	Harvard
228	6,687	Rantoul City SD 137	Rantoul
229	6,663	Lansing SD 158	Lansing
230	6,657	Wabash CUSD 348	Mount Carmel
231	6,653	Midlothian SD 143	Midlothian
232	6,641	Il Valley Central Unit Dist 321	Chillicothe
233	6,631	East Richland CUSD 1	Olney
234	6,603	Manteno Community Unit SD 5	Manteno
235	6,597	Burbank SD 111	Burbank
236	6,595	Quincy SD 172	Quincy
237	6,569	Plainfield SD 202	Plainfield
238	6,549	Sherrard Community Unit SD 200	Sherrard
239	6,525	Crystal Lake CCSD 47	Crystal Lake
240	6,481	Columbia Community Unit SD 4	Columbia
241	6,480	Triad Community Unit SD 2	Troy
242	6,445	Paris-Union SD 95	Paris
243	6,434	Effingham Community Unit SD 40	Effingham
244	6,416	Peotone CUSD 207u	Peotone
245	6,397	Indian Springs SD 109	Justice
246	6,392	Lake Villa CCSD 41	Lake Villa
247	6,390	Herrin CUSD 4	Herrin
248	6,382	Monticello CUSD 25	Monticello
249	6,356	Pana Community Unit SD 8	Pana
250	6,327	Frankfort CCSD 157c	Frankfort
251	6,303	Bellwood SD 88	Bellwood
252	6,301	Waterloo Community Unit SD 5	Waterloo
253	6,292	Mchenry CCSD 15	Mc Henry
254	6,280	Vandalia CUSD 203	Vandalia
255	6,269	Galesburg CUSD 205	Galesburg
256	6,267	Massac Unit District #1	Metropolis
257	6,266	Litchfield CUSD 12	Litchfield
258	6,249	Yorkville Community Unit SD 115	Yorkville
259	6,238	Oswego Community Unit SD 308	Oswego
260	6,218	Wilmington CUSD 209u	Wilmington
261	6,169	Rochelle Community CD 231	Rochelle
262	6,153	Mundelein Elem SD 75	Mundelein
263	6,140	Decatur SD 61	Decatur
264	6,124	Carlinville CUSD 1	Carlinville
265	6,113	Lemont-Bromberek CSD 113a	Lemont
266	6,093	Bond County CUSD 2	Greenville
267	6,089	Bradley SD 61	Bradley
268	6,030	Kewanee Community Unit SD 229	Kewanee
269	5,974	Cicero SD 99	Cicero
270	5,925	Steger SD 194	Steger
271	5,915	Monmouth Unit SD 38	Monmouth
272	5,902	Meridian CUSD 223	Stillman Valley
273	5,898	O Fallon CCSD 90	Ofallon
273	5,898	Round Lake Area Schs - Dist 116	Round Lake
275	5,884	Mt Zion Community Unit SD 3	Mt Zion
276	5,883	Ball Chatham CUSD 5	Chatham
277	5,872	Dunlap CUSD 323	Dunlap
278	5,778	Bourbonnais SD 53	Bourbonnais
279	5,729	Will County SD 92	Lockport
280	5,687	Berwyn North SD 98	Berwyn
281	5,665	Kinnikinnick CCSD 131	Roscoe
282	5,654	Marion Community Unit SD 2	Marion
283	5,569	Rochester Community Unit SD 3a	Rochester
284	5,532	Taylorville CUSD 3	Taylorville
285	5,420	Sandwich CUSD 430	Sandwich
286	5,403	Community CSD 168	Sauk Village
287	5,380	New Lenox SD 122	New Lenox
288	5,370	Belvidere CUSD 100	Belvidere
289	5,167	Mokena SD 159	Mokena
290	5,120	Genoa Kingston CUSD 424	Genoa
291	5,062	Carterville CUSD 5	Carterville
292	4,858	Summit Hill SD 161	Frankfort
293	n/a	Corrections SD 428 Dept of	Springfield

Number of Diploma Recipients

Rank	Number	District Name	City
1	15,653	City of Chicago SD 299	Chicago
2	2,815	Township High SD 214	Arlington Hgts
3	2,725	Township HSD 211	Palatine
4	1,946	Glenbard Twp HSD 87	Glen Ellyn
5	1,914	SD 46	Elgin

6	1,796	Cons High SD 230	Orland Park
7	1,523	Maine Township HSD 207	Park Ridge
8	1,348	Naperville C U Dist 203	Naperville
9	1,282	Indian Prairie CUSD 204	Aurora
10	1,226	Community High SD 155	Crystal Lake
11	1,222	J S Morton HS District 201	Cicero
12	1,207	Community High SD 99	Downers Grove
13	1,187	Rockford SD 205	Rockford
14	1,136	Thornton Twp HSD 205	South Holland
15	1,127	Northfield Twp High SD 225	Glenview
16	1,070	Lincoln Way Community HSD 210	New Lenox
17	1,051	Niles Twp Community High SD 219	Skokie
18	1,037	Community Unit SD 300	Carpentersville
19	1,018	Community Unit SD 200	Wheaton
20	1,009	Belleville Twp HSD 201	Belleville
21	993	Hinsdale Twp HSD 86	Hinsdale
22	953	Bremen Community HS District 228	Midlothian
23	948	New Trier Twp HSD 203	Northfield
24	931	Adlai E Stevenson Dist 125	Lincolnshire
25	894	Community High SD 218	Oak Lawn
26	811	Joliet Twp HSD 204	Joliet
27	803	Springfield SD 186	Springfield
28	780	Du Page High SD 88	Villa Park
29	775	Peoria SD 150	Peoria
30	772	Proviso Twp HSD 209	Maywood
31	763	St Charles CUSD 303	Saint Charles
32	753	Valley View Cusd #365u	Romeoville
33	750	Township High SD 113	Highland Park
34	748	Plainfield SD 202	Plainfield
35	734	Lyons Twp HSD 204	La Grange
35	734	Rich Twp HS District 227	Olympia Fields
37	732	Leyden Community HSD 212	Franklin Park
38	674	Warren Twp High SD 121	Gages Lake
39	667	Evanston Twp HSD 202	Evanston
40	648	Waukegan CUSD 60	Waukegan
41	643	Lockport Twp HSD 205	Lockport
42	640	Champaign Community Unit SD 4	Champaign
43	636	Lake Park Community HSD 108	Roselle
44	631	Community High SD 128	Libertyville
45	615	Mclean County Unit Dist No 5	Normal
46	577	Barrington CUSD 220	Barrington
47	576	Thornton Fractional T HS D 215	Calumet City
48	573	Aurora West Unit SD 129	Aurora
49	563	Homewood Flossmoor CHSD 233	Flossmoor
50	541	Moline Unit SD 40	Moline
51	521	Decatur SD 61	Decatur
52	504	Elmhurst SD 205	Elmhurst
53	491	Bloom Twp High SD 206	Chicago Heights
53	491	Edwardsville CUSD 7	Edwardsville
55	490	Quincy SD 172	Quincy
56	471	O Fallon Twp High SD 203	Ofallon
57	468	Mundelein Cons High SD 120	Mundelein
58	466	Community High SD 117	Lake Villa
59	462	Granite City CUSD 9	Granite City
60	453	Mchenry Community HSD 156	Mc Henry
61	438	Community High SD 94	West Chicago
62	432	Alton Community Unit SD 11	Alton
63	427	Lake Zurich CUSD 95	Lake Zurich
64	424	Aurora East Unit SD 131	Aurora
65	421	Oswego Community Unit SD 308	Oswego
66	413	Pekin Community HSD 303	Pekin
67	397	Lake Forest Community HS Dist 115	Lake Forest
68	378	Hononegah Community HSD 207	Rockton
68	378	Zion-Benton Twp HSD 126	Zion
70	376	Bradley Bourbonnais CHSD 307	Bradley
71	372	Harlem Unit Dist 122	Loves Park
72	370	Batavia Unit SD 101	Batavia
73	360	Collinsville CUSD 10	Collinsville
74	359	Argo Community HSD 217	Summit
75	354	Urbana SD 116	Urbana
76	353	Belvidere CUSD 100	Belvidere
77	352	Oak Lawn Community HSD 229	Oak Lawn
78	347	United Twp HS District 30	East Moline
79	342	Grayslake Community High SD 127	Grayslake
80	330	Ottawa Twp HSD 140	Ottawa
81	329	Fenton Community HSD 100	Bensenville
82	328	East St Louis SD 189	E Saint Louis
83	321	Geneva Community Unit SD 304	Geneva
84	310	Reavis Twp HSD 220	Burbank
85	308	Dekalb Community Unit SD 428	De Kalb
86	307	Freeport SD 145	Freeport
87	305	Ball Chatham CUSD 5	Chatham
88	303	Woodstock CUSD 200	Woodstock
89	300	Rock Island SD 41	Rock Island
90	275	Galesburg CUSD 205	Galesburg
91	273	Triad Community Unit SD 2	Troy
92	272	Danville CCSD 118	Danville
93	266	Crete Monee CUSD 201u	Crete
94	264	Bloomington SD 87	Bloomington
95	254	Round Lake Area Schs - Dist 116	Round Lake
96	249	Jacksonville SD 117	Jacksonville
97	246	Kankakee SD 111	Kankakee
98	238	Jersey CUSD 100	Jerseyville
99	234	Highland Community Unit SD 5	Highland
100	232	Marion Community Unit SD 2	Marion
101	231	Sterling C U Dist 5	Sterling
102	230	Morton CUSD 709	Morton
103	224	Charleston CUSD 1	Charleston
104	221	Dixon Unit SD 170	Dixon
105	218	Wauconda Community Unit SD 118	Wauconda
106	217	Bethalto CUSD 8	Bethalto
107	216	Sycamore CUSD 427	Sycamore
108	213	Geneseo Community Unit SD 228	Geneseo
109	212	Taylorville CUSD 3	Taylorville
110	204	Mattoon CUSD 2	Mattoon
111	195	Mt Zion Community Unit SD 3	Mt Zion
112	190	Kaneland CUSD 302	Maple Park
113	189	Cahokia Community Unit SD 187	Cahokia
113	189	Effingham Community Unit SD 40	Effingham
115	188	Mahomet-Seymour CUSD 3	Mahomet
116	187	Elmwood Park CUSD 401	Elmwood Park
117	181	Johnsburg CUSD 12	Johnsburg
118	180	Dunlap CUSD 323	Dunlap
119	179	Canton Union SD 66	Canton
119	179	Waterloo Community Unit SD 5	Waterloo
121	175	Yorkville Community Unit SD 115	Yorkville
122	172	Mascoutah C U District 19	Mascoutah
122	172	Murphysboro CUSD 186	Murphysboro
124	158	Wabash CUSD 348	Mount Carmel
125	154	Prairie Central CUSD 8	Forrest
125	154	Rochester Community Unit SD 3a	Rochester
127	153	Central Community Unit SD 301	Burlington
127	153	Lisle CUSD 202	Lisle
129	151	Sandwich CUSD 430	Sandwich
130	150	Herscher Community Unit SD 2	Herscher
130	150	Southwestern CUSD 9	Piasa
132	146	Byron Community Unit SD 226	Byron
132	146	East Richland CUSD 1	Olney
132	146	Il Valley Central Unit Dist 321	Chillicothe
132	146	Oregon C U School Dist-220	Oregon
136	144	Clinton CUSD 15	Clinton
137	143	Olympia CUSD 16	Stanford
138	139	Massac Unit District #1	Metropolis
139	138	North Chicago SD 187	North Chicago
140	134	Carlinville CUSD 1	Carlinville
141	132	Bond County CUSD 2	Greenville
142	130	Consolidated SD 158	Huntley
143	129	Herrin CUSD 4	Herrin
143	129	Hillsboro Community Unit SD 3	Hillsboro
143	129	Roxana Community Unit SD 1	Roxana
146	128	Macomb Community Unit SD 185	Macomb
147	124	Jasper County Comm Unit Dist 1	Newton
148	123	Robinson CUSD 2	Robinson
149	122	Peotone CUSD 207u	Peotone
149	122	Wilmington CUSD 209u	Wilmington
151	121	Columbia Community Unit SD 4	Columbia
151	121	Harvard CUSD 50	Harvard
153	120	Coal City CUSD 1	Coal City
153	120	Frankfort Community Unit SD 168	West Frankfort
155	119	Harrisburg CUSD 3	Harrisburg
156	117	Manteno Community Unit SD 5	Manteno
157	115	Sparta CUSD 140	Sparta
158	114	Monticello CUSD 25	Monticello
159	113	Litchfield CUSD 12	Litchfield
159	113	Reed Custer CUSD 255u	Braidwood
161	108	Vandalia CUSD 203	Vandalia
162	107	Eureka C U Dist 140	Eureka
162	107	Winnebago CUSD 323	Winnebago
164	106	Sherrard Community Unit SD 200	Sherrard
165	104	Carterville CUSD 5	Carterville
166	103	Flora Community Unit SD 35	Flora
167	100	Kewanee Community Unit SD 229	Kewanee
168	99	Paris-Union SD 95	Paris
169	94	Meridian CUSD 223	Stillman Valley
170	93	Monmouth Unit SD 38	Monmouth
171	91	Genoa Kingston CUSD 424	Genoa
171	91	Westmont CUSD 201	Westmont
173	78	Pana Community Unit SD 8	Pana
174	53	Maywood-Melrose Park-Broadview-89	Melrose Park
175	1	Mannheim SD 83	Franklin Park
176	0	Corrections SD 428 Dept of	Springfield
176	0	Minooka Community HS District 111	Minooka
176	0	Oak Park & River Forest Dist 200	Oak Park
176	0	Pekin Public SD 108	Pekin
180	n/a	Addison SD 4	Addison
180	n/a	Alsip-Hazlgrn-Oaklwn SD 126	Alsip
180	n/a	Antioch CCSD 34	Antioch
180	n/a	Aptakisic-Tripp CCSD 102	Buffalo Grove
180	n/a	Arlington Heights SD 25	Arlington Hgts
180	n/a	Beach Park CCSD 3	Beach Park
180	n/a	Belleville SD 118	Belleville
180	n/a	Bellwood SD 88	Bellwood
180	n/a	Bensenville SD 2	Bensenville
180	n/a	Berkeley SD 87	Berkeley
180	n/a	Berwyn North SD 98	Berwyn
180	n/a	Berwyn South SD 100	Berwyn
180	n/a	Bourbonnais SD 53	Bourbonnais
180	n/a	Bradley SD 61	Bradley
180	n/a	Burbank SD 111	Burbank
180	n/a	CCSD 181	Hinsdale
180	n/a	Cary CCSD 26	Cary
180	n/a	Chicago Heights SD 170	Chicago Heights
180	n/a	Cicero SD 99	Cicero
180	n/a	Community CSD 168	Sauk Village
180	n/a	Community CSD 59	Arlington Hgts
180	n/a	Community Consolidated S D 93	Carol Stream
180	n/a	Community Consolidated SD 46	Grayslake
180	n/a	Community Consolidated SD 62	Des Plaines
180	n/a	Cook County SD 130	Blue Island
180	n/a	Country Club Hills SD 160	Ctry Club Hill
180	n/a	Crystal Lake CCSD 47	Crystal Lake
180	n/a	Darien SD 61	Darien
180	n/a	Deerfield SD 109	Deerfield
180	n/a	Dolton SD 148	Riverdale
180	n/a	Dolton SD 149	Calumet City
180	n/a	Downers Grove Grade SD 58	Downers Grove
180	n/a	East Maine SD 63	Des Plaines
180	n/a	East Moline SD 37	East Moline
180	n/a	East Peoria SD 86	East Peoria
180	n/a	Elem SD 159	Matteson
180	n/a	Evanston CCSD 65	Evanston
180	n/a	Evergreen Pk Elem SD 124	Evergreen Park
180	n/a	Flossmoor SD 161	Chicago Heights
180	n/a	Forest Ridge SD 142	Oak Forest
180	n/a	Frankfort CCSD 157c	Frankfort
180	n/a	Fremont SD 79	Mundelein
180	n/a	Glen Ellyn CCSD 89	Glen Ellyn
180	n/a	Glen Ellyn SD 41	Glen Ellyn
180	n/a	Glenview CCSD 34	Glenview
180	n/a	Gurnee SD 56	Gurnee
180	n/a	Harvey SD 152	Harvey
180	n/a	Hawthorn CCSD 73	Vernon Hills
180	n/a	Homer Community CSD 33c	Homer Glen
180	n/a	Homewood SD 153	Homewood
180	n/a	Indian Springs SD 109	Justice
180	n/a	Joliet Public SD 86	Joliet
180	n/a	Keeneyville SD 20	Hanover Park
180	n/a	Kildeer Countryside CCSD 96	Buffalo Grove
180	n/a	Kinnikinnick CCSD 131	Roscoe
180	n/a	Kirby SD 140	Tinley Park
180	n/a	La Grange SD 102	La Grange Park
180	n/a	Lake Forest SD 67	Lake Forest
180	n/a	Lake Villa CCSD 41	Lake Villa
180	n/a	Lansing SD 158	Lansing
180	n/a	Lemont-Bromberek CSD 113a	Lemont
180	n/a	Libertyville SD 70	Libertyville
180	n/a	Lincolnshire-Prairieview S D 103	Lincolnshire
180	n/a	Lombard SD 44	Lombard
180	n/a	Lyons SD 103	Lyons
180	n/a	Marquardt SD 15	Glendale Hgts
180	n/a	Matteson Elem SD 162	Matteson
180	n/a	Mchenry CCSD 15	Mc Henry
180	n/a	Midlothian SD 143	Midlothian
180	n/a	Minooka Community CSD 201	Minooka
180	n/a	Mokena SD 159	Mokena
180	n/a	Mount Prospect SD 57	Mount Prospect
180	n/a	Mount Vernon SD 80	Mount Vernon
180	n/a	Mundelein Elem SD 75	Mundelein
180	n/a	New Lenox SD 122	New Lenox
180	n/a	Nippersink SD 2	Richmond
180	n/a	North Palos SD 117	Palos Hills
180	n/a	North Shore SD 112	Highland Park
180	n/a	Northbrook SD 28	Northbrook
180	n/a	O Fallon CCSD 90	Ofallon
180	n/a	Oak Lawn-Hometown SD 123	Oak Lawn
180	n/a	Oak Park Elem SD 97	Oak Park
180	n/a	Orland SD 135	Orland Park
180	n/a	Ottawa Elem SD 141	Ottawa
180	n/a	Palatine CCSD 15	Palatine
180	n/a	Palos Community CSD 118	Palos Park
180	n/a	Park Forest SD 163	Park Forest
180	n/a	Park Ridge CCSD 64	Park Ridge
180	n/a	Posen-Robbins El SD 143-5	Posen
180	n/a	Prairie-Hills Elem SD 144	Markham
180	n/a	Prospect Heights SD 23	Prospect Hgts
180	n/a	Queen Bee SD 16	Glendale Hgts
180	n/a	Rantoul City SD 137	Rantoul
180	n/a	Ridgeland SD 122	Oak Lawn
180	n/a	River Trails SD 26	Mount Prospect
180	n/a	Rochelle Community CD 231	Rochelle
180	n/a	SD 45 Dupage County	Villa Park
180	n/a	Schaumburg CCSD 54	Schaumburg
180	n/a	Skokie SD 68	Skokie
180	n/a	Steger SD 194	Steger
180	n/a	Streator Elem SD 44	Streator
180	n/a	Summit Hill SD 161	Frankfort
180	n/a	Summit SD 104	Summit

180	n/a	Tinley Park Comm Cons Sch Dst 146	Tinley Park
180	n/a	Troy Community CSD 30c	Plainfield
180	n/a	W Harvey-Dixmoor PS Dist 147	Harvey
180	n/a	West Chicago Elem SD 33	West Chicago
180	n/a	Wheeling CCSD 21	Wheeling
180	n/a	Will County SD 92	Lockport
180	n/a	Wilmette SD 39	Wilmette
180	n/a	Winnetka SD 36	Winnetka
180	n/a	Woodland CCSD 50	Gurnee
180	n/a	Woodridge SD 68	Woodridge
180	n/a	Zion Elementary SD 6	Zion

High School Drop-out Rate

Rank	Percent	District Name	City
1	17.6	City of Chicago SD 299	Chicago
2	12.1	Peoria SD 150	Peoria
3	11.3	Danville CCSD 118	Danville
4	11.2	Waukegan CUSD 60	Waukegan
5	10.7	Decatur SD 61	Decatur
6	10.2	East St Louis SD 189	E Saint Louis
7	8.6	Bloom Twp High SD 206	Chicago Heights
8	8.4	Granite City CUSD 9	Granite City
9	8.3	Kankakee SD 111	Kankakee
9	8.3	Proviso Twp HSD 209	Maywood
11	8.0	Kewanee Community Unit SD 229	Kewanee
12	7.8	Roxana Community Unit SD 1	Roxana
13	7.5	Freeport SD 145	Freeport
14	7.4	Flora Community Unit SD 35	Flora
15	7.1	Aurora East Unit SD 131	Aurora
16	6.9	Zion-Benton Twp HSD 126	Zion
17	6.7	Alton Community Unit SD 11	Alton
17	6.7	Pana Community Unit SD 8	Pana
19	6.6	Cahokia Community Unit SD 187	Cahokia
19	6.6	Thornton Twp HSD 205	South Holland
19	6.6	Vandalia CUSD 203	Vandalia
22	6.5	Clinton CUSD 15	Clinton
22	6.5	Galesburg CUSD 205	Galesburg
24	6.4	Rockford SD 205	Rockford
25	6.3	J S Morton HS District 201	Cicero
26	6.2	Mattoon CUSD 2	Mattoon
26	6.2	Round Lake Area Schs - Dist 116	Round Lake
28	6.1	Aurora West Unit SD 129	Aurora
28	6.1	United Twp HS District 30	East Moline
28	6.1	Urbana SD 116	Urbana
28	6.1	Wabash CUSD 348	Mount Carmel
32	5.8	Dixon Unit SD 170	Dixon
33	5.6	Elmwood Park CUSD 401	Elmwood Park
33	5.6	Winnebago CUSD 323	Winnebago
33	5.6	Woodstock CUSD 200	Woodstock
36	5.5	Harrisburg CUSD 3	Harrisburg
37	5.4	Community High SD 218	Oak Lawn
37	5.4	Mclean County Unit Dist No 5	Normal
37	5.4	Sterling C U Dist 5	Sterling
40	5.2	Leyden Community HSD 212	Franklin Park
40	5.2	Taylorville CUSD 3	Taylorville
42	5.1	Mundelein Cons High SD 120	Mundelein
42	5.1	Quincy SD 172	Quincy
44	5.0	Bloomington SD 87	Bloomington
44	5.0	Champaign Community Unit SD 4	Champaign
46	4.9	Ottawa Twp HSD 140	Ottawa
47	4.8	Il Valley Central Unit Dist 321	Chillicothe
47	4.8	Marion Community Unit SD 2	Marion
49	4.7	Harvard CUSD 50	Harvard
49	4.7	SD 46	Elgin
51	4.6	Murphysboro CUSD 186	Murphysboro
51	4.6	Rock Island SD 41	Rock Island
53	4.5	Olympia CUSD 16	Stanford
53	4.5	Paris-Union SD 95	Paris
55	4.4	Collinsville CUSD 10	Collinsville
56	4.3	Bethalto CUSD 8	Bethalto
57	4.2	Charleston CUSD 1	Charleston
57	4.2	Monmouth Unit SD 38	Monmouth
59	4.0	Canton Union SD 66	Canton
59	4.0	Reavis Twp HSD 220	Burbank
61	3.9	Community High SD 117	Lake Villa
61	3.9	Jacksonville SD 117	Jacksonville
63	3.8	Belleville Twp HSD 201	Belleville
63	3.8	Du Page High SD 88	Villa Park
63	3.8	Moline Unit SD 40	Moline
63	3.8	Valley View Cusd #365u	Romeoville
67	3.6	East Richland CUSD 1	Olney
67	3.6	Fenton Community HSD 100	Bensenville
67	3.6	Hillsboro Community Unit SD 3	Hillsboro
67	3.6	Sandwich CUSD 430	Sandwich
67	3.6	Springfield SD 186	Springfield
67	3.6	Thornton Fractional T H S D 215	Calumet City
73	3.5	Argo Community HSD 217	Summit
73	3.5	Geneseo Community Unit SD 228	Geneseo
73	3.5	Harlem Unit Dist 122	Loves Park
73	3.5	Pekin Community HSD 303	Pekin
77	3.4	Township High SD 214	Arlington Hgts
77	3.4	Wilmington CUSD 209u	Wilmington
79	3.3	Community High SD 94	West Chicago
79	3.3	Frankfort Community Unit SD 168	West Frankfort
79	3.3	Joliet Twp HSD 204	Joliet
82	3.2	Bremen Community HS District 228	Midlothian
83	3.1	Edwardsville CUSD 7	Edwardsville
83	3.1	Highland Community Unit SD 5	Highland
85	3.0	Community Unit SD 300	Carpentersville
85	3.0	Dekalb Community Unit SD 428	De Kalb
85	3.0	Genoa Kingston CUSD 424	Genoa
85	3.0	Lockport Twp HSD 205	Lockport
85	3.0	Mchenry Community HSD 156	Mc Henry
85	3.0	Oswego Community Unit SD 308	Oswego
85	3.0	Plainfield SD 202	Plainfield
92	2.9	Bradley Bourbonnais CHSD 307	Bradley
92	2.9	Reed Custer CUSD 255u	Braidwood
92	2.9	Southwestern CUSD 9	Piasa
95	2.8	Herscher Community Unit SD 2	Herscher
95	2.8	Jasper County Comm Unit Dist 1	Newton
95	2.8	Warren Twp High SD 121	Gages Lake
98	2.7	Community Unit SD 200	Wheaton
98	2.7	North Chicago SD 187	North Chicago
98	2.7	Sherrard Community Unit SD 200	Sherrard
101	2.5	Macomb Community Unit SD 185	Macomb
101	2.5	Oak Lawn Community HSD 229	Oak Lawn
103	2.4	Carlinville CUSD 1	Carlinville
103	2.4	Robinson CUSD 2	Robinson
105	2.3	Jersey CUSD 100	Jerseyville
105	2.3	Oregon C U School Dist-220	Oregon
107	2.2	Hinsdale Twp HSD 86	Hinsdale
107	2.2	Prairie Central CUSD 8	Forrest
107	2.2	Wauconda Community Unit SD 118	Wauconda
110	2.1	Community High SD 155	Crystal Lake
111	2.0	Effingham Community Unit SD 40	Effingham
111	2.0	Kaneland CUSD 302	Maple Park
111	2.0	Meridian CUSD 223	Stillman Valley
111	2.0	O Fallon Twp High SD 203	Ofallon
115	1.9	Carterville CUSD 5	Carterville
115	1.9	Evanston Twp HSD 202	Evanston
115	1.9	Waterloo Community Unit SD 5	Waterloo
118	1.8	Glenbard Twp HSD 87	Glen Ellyn
118	1.8	Johnsburg CUSD 12	Johnsburg
120	1.7	Consolidated SD 158	Huntley
120	1.7	Manteno Community Unit SD 5	Manteno
120	1.7	Sycamore CUSD 427	Sycamore
123	1.6	Coal City CUSD 1	Coal City
123	1.6	Monticello CUSD 25	Monticello
125	1.5	Central Community Unit SD 301	Burlington
125	1.5	Geneva Community Unit SD 304	Geneva
125	1.5	Litchfield CUSD 12	Litchfield
125	1.5	Mt Zion Community Unit SD 3	Mt Zion
125	1.5	Township High SD 113	Highland Park
130	1.4	Columbia Community Unit SD 4	Columbia
130	1.4	Crete Monee CUSD 201u	Crete
130	1.4	Grayslake Community High SD 127	Grayslake
130	1.4	Hononegah Community HSD 207	Rockton
130	1.4	Mahomet-Seymour CUSD 3	Mahomet
130	1.4	Morton CUSD 709	Morton
136	1.3	Lake Park Community HSD 108	Roselle
136	1.3	Lisle CUSD 202	Lisle
136	1.3	Maine Township HSD 207	Park Ridge
136	1.3	Westmont CUSD 201	Westmont
140	1.2	Batavia Unit SD 101	Batavia
140	1.2	Belvidere CUSD 100	Belvidere
140	1.2	Bond County CUSD 2	Greenville
140	1.2	Community High SD 99	Downers Grove
140	1.2	Cons High SD 230	Orland Park
140	1.2	Eureka C U Dist 140	Eureka
140	1.2	Lake Zurich CUSD 95	Lake Zurich
140	1.2	Massac Unit District #1	Metropolis
140	1.2	St Charles CUSD 303	Saint Charles
140	1.2	Yorkville Community Unit SD 115	Yorkville
150	1.1	Dunlap CUSD 323	Dunlap
150	1.1	Rich Twp HS District 227	Olympia Fields
150	1.1	Township HSD 211	Palatine
153	1.0	Ball Chatham CUSD 5	Chatham
153	1.0	Byron Community Unit SD 226	Byron
153	1.0	Elmhurst SD 205	Elmhurst
153	1.0	Homewood Flossmoor CHSD 233	Flossmoor
153	1.0	Lyons Twp HSD 204	La Grange
153	1.0	Niles Twp Community High SD 219	Skokie
153	1.0	Triad Community Unit SD 2	Troy
160	0.9	Community High SD 128	Libertyville
160	0.9	Indian Prairie CUSD 204	Aurora
162	0.7	Herrin CUSD 4	Herrin
162	0.7	Mascoutah C U District 19	Mascoutah
162	0.7	Northfield Twp High SD 225	Glenview
162	0.7	Peotone CUSD 207u	Peotone
166	0.6	Lincoln Way Community HSD 210	New Lenox
167	0.5	Naperville C U Dist 203	Naperville
168	0.4	Adlai E Stevenson Dist 125	Lincolnshire
169	0.3	Barrington CUSD 220	Barrington
169	0.3	Rochester Community Unit SD 3a	Rochester
171	0.2	Lake Forest Community HS Dist 115	Lake Forest
171	0.2	New Trier Twp HSD 203	Northfield
173	0.0	Mannheim SD 83	Franklin Park
173	0.0	Pekin Public SD 108	Pekin
173	0.0	Sparta CUSD 140	Sparta
176	n/a	Addison SD 4	Addison
176	n/a	Alsip-Hazlgrn-Oaklwn SD 126	Alsip
176	n/a	Antioch CCSD 34	Antioch
176	n/a	Aptakisic-Tripp CCSD 102	Buffalo Grove
176	n/a	Arlington Heights SD 25	Arlington Hgts
176	n/a	Beach Park CCSD 3	Beach Park
176	n/a	Belleville SD 118	Belleville
176	n/a	Bellwood SD 88	Bellwood
176	n/a	Bensenville SD 2	Bensenville
176	n/a	Berkeley SD 87	Berkeley
176	n/a	Berwyn North SD 98	Berwyn
176	n/a	Berwyn South SD 100	Berwyn
176	n/a	Bourbonnais SD 53	Bourbonnais
176	n/a	Bradley SD 61	Bradley
176	n/a	Burbank SD 111	Burbank
176	n/a	CCSD 181	Hinsdale
176	n/a	Cary CCSD 26	Cary
176	n/a	Chicago Heights SD 170	Chicago Heights
176	n/a	Cicero SD 99	Cicero
176	n/a	Community CSD 168	Sauk Village
176	n/a	Community CSD 59	Arlington Hgts
176	n/a	Community Consolidated S D 93	Carol Stream
176	n/a	Community Consolidated SD 46	Grayslake
176	n/a	Community Consolidated SD 62	Des Plaines
176	n/a	Cook County SD 130	Blue Island
176	n/a	Corrections SD 428 Dept of	Springfield
176	n/a	Country Club Hills SD 160	Ctry Club Hill
176	n/a	Crystal Lake CCSD 47	Crystal Lake
176	n/a	Darien SD 61	Darien
176	n/a	Deerfield SD 109	Deerfield
176	n/a	Dolton SD 148	Riverdale
176	n/a	Dolton SD 149	Calumet City
176	n/a	Downers Grove Grade SD 58	Downers Grove
176	n/a	East Maine SD 63	Des Plaines
176	n/a	East Moline SD 37	East Moline
176	n/a	East Peoria SD 86	East Peoria
176	n/a	Elem SD 159	Matteson
176	n/a	Evanston CCSD 65	Evanston
176	n/a	Evergreen Pk Elem SD 124	Evergreen Park
176	n/a	Flossmoor SD 161	Chicago Heights
176	n/a	Forest Ridge SD 142	Oak Forest
176	n/a	Frankfort CCSD 157c	Frankfort
176	n/a	Fremont SD 79	Mundelein
176	n/a	Glen Ellyn CCSD 89	Glen Ellyn
176	n/a	Glen Ellyn SD 41	Glen Ellyn
176	n/a	Glenview CCSD 34	Glenview
176	n/a	Gurnee SD 56	Gurnee
176	n/a	Harvey SD 152	Harvey
176	n/a	Hawthorn CCSD 73	Vernon Hills
176	n/a	Homer Community CSD 33c	Homer Glen
176	n/a	Homewood SD 153	Homewood
176	n/a	Indian Springs SD 109	Justice
176	n/a	Joliet Public SD 86	Joliet
176	n/a	Keeneyville SD 20	Hanover Park
176	n/a	Kildeer Countryside CCSD 96	Buffalo Grove
176	n/a	Kinnikinnick CCSD 131	Roscoe
176	n/a	Kirby SD 140	Tinley Park
176	n/a	La Grange SD 102	La Grange Park
176	n/a	Lake Forest SD 67	Lake Forest
176	n/a	Lake Villa CCSD 41	Lake Villa
176	n/a	Lansing SD 158	Lansing
176	n/a	Lemont-Bromberek CSD 113a	Lemont
176	n/a	Libertyville SD 70	Libertyville
176	n/a	Lincolnshire-Prairieview S D 103	Lincolnshire
176	n/a	Lombard SD 44	Lombard
176	n/a	Lyons SD 103	Lyons
176	n/a	Marquardt SD 15	Glendale Hgts
176	n/a	Matteson Elem SD 162	Matteson
176	n/a	Maywood-Melrose Park-Broadview-89	Melrose Park
176	n/a	Mchenry CCSD 15	Mc Henry
176	n/a	Midlothian SD 143	Midlothian
176	n/a	Minooka Community CSD 201	Minooka
176	n/a	Minooka Community HS District 111	Minooka
176	n/a	Mokena SD 159	Mokena
176	n/a	Mount Prospect SD 57	Mount Prospect
176	n/a	Mount Vernon SD 80	Mount Vernon
176	n/a	Mundelein Elem SD 75	Mundelein
176	n/a	New Lenox SD 122	New Lenox
176	n/a	Nippersink SD 2	Richmond
176	n/a	North Palos SD 117	Palos Hills
176	n/a	North Shore SD 112	Highland Park
176	n/a	Northbrook SD 28	Northbrook
176	n/a	O Fallon CCSD 90	Ofallon
176	n/a	Oak Lawn-Hometown SD 123	Oak Lawn
176	n/a	Oak Park & River Forest Dist 200	Oak Park
176	n/a	Oak Park Elem SD 97	Oak Park
176	n/a	Orland SD 135	Orland Park
176	n/a	Ottawa Elem SD 141	Ottawa

176	n/a	Palatine CCSD 15	Palatine
176	n/a	Palos Community CSD 118	Palos Park
176	n/a	Park Forest SD 163	Park Forest
176	n/a	Park Ridge CCSD 64	Park Ridge
176	n/a	Posen-Robbins El SD 143-5	Posen
176	n/a	Prairie-Hills Elem SD 144	Markham
176	n/a	Prospect Heights SD 23	Prospect Hgts
176	n/a	Queen Bee SD 16	Glendale Hgts
176	n/a	Rantoul City SD 137	Rantoul
176	n/a	Ridgeland SD 122	Oak Lawn
176	n/a	River Trails SD 26	Mount Prospect
176	n/a	Rochelle Community CD 231	Rochelle
176	n/a	SD 45 Dupage County	Villa Park
176	n/a	Schaumburg CCSD 54	Schaumburg
176	n/a	Skokie SD 68	Skokie
176	n/a	Steger SD 194	Steger
176	n/a	Streator Elem SD 44	Streator
176	n/a	Summit Hill SD 161	Frankfort
176	n/a	Summit SD 104	Summit
176	n/a	Tinley Park Comm Cons Sch Dst 146	Tinley Park
176	n/a	Troy Community CSD 30c	Plainfield
176	n/a	W Harvey-Dixmoor PS Dist 147	Harvey
176	n/a	West Chicago Elem SD 33	West Chicago
176	n/a	Wheeling CCSD 21	Wheeling
176	n/a	Will County SD 92	Lockport
176	n/a	Wilmette SD 39	Wilmette
176	n/a	Winnetka SD 36	Winnetka
176	n/a	Woodland CCSD 50	Gurnee
176	n/a	Woodridge SD 68	Woodridge
176	n/a	Zion Elementary SD 6	Zion

Indiana

Indiana Public School Educational Profile

Category	Value	Category	Value
Schools *(2003-2004)*	1,986	**Diploma Recipients** *(2002-2003)*	56,569
Instructional Level		White, Non-Hispanic	49,721
Primary	1,158	Black, Non-Hispanic	4,644
Middle	336	Asian/Pacific Islander	637
High	348	American Indian/Alaskan Native	140
Other Level	144	Hispanic	1,427
Curriculum		**High School Drop-out Rate** *(%) (2001-2002)*	2.3
Regular	1,859	White, Non-Hispanic	2.1
Special Education	51	Black, Non-Hispanic	3.1
Vocational	29	Asian/Pacific Islander	1.1
Alternative	47	American Indian/Alaskan Native	2.8
Type		Hispanic	4.0
Magnet	26	**Staff** *(2003-2004)*	
Charter	17	Teachers	59,923.3
Title I Eligible	1,065	Average Salary ($)	45,791
School-wide Title I	181	Librarians/Media Specialists	1,004.6
Students *(2003-2004)*	1,011,130	Guidance Counselors	1,804.2
Gender (%)		**Ratios** *(2003-2004)*	
Male	51.4	Student/Teacher Ratio	16.9 to 1
Female	48.6	Student/Librarian Ratio	1,006.5 to 1
Race/Ethnicity (%)		Student/Counselor Ratio	560.4 to 1
White, Non-Hispanic	81.5	**College Entrance Exam Scores** *(2005)*	
Black, Non-Hispanic	12.4	Scholastic Aptitude Test (SAT)	
Asian/Pacific Islander	1.1	Participation Rate (%)	66
American Indian/Alaskan Native	0.2	Mean SAT Reasoning Test Verbal Score	504
Hispanic	4.8	Mean SAT Reasoning Test Math Score	508
Classification (%)		American College Testing Program (ACT)	
Individual Education Program (IEP)	16.9	Participation Rate (%)	21
Migrant *(2002-2003)*	0.0	Average Composite Score	21.7
English Language Learner (ELL)	4.2	Average English Score	21.2
Eligible for Free Lunch Program	26.8	Average Math Score	21.5
Eligible for Reduced-Price Lunch Program	7.7	Average Reading Score	22.2
Current Spending *($ per student in FY 2003)*	7,836	Average Science Score	21.4
Instruction	4,712		
Support Services	2,809		

Note: *For an explanation of data, please refer to the User's Guide in the front of the book*

Indiana NAEP 2005 Test Scores

Reading			Mathematics		
Grade/Category	**Value**	**Rank**	**Grade/Category**	**Value**	**Rank**
4th Grade			**4th Grade**		
Average Proficiency	218.1 (1.07)	31/51	Average Proficiency	240.1 (0.85)	21/51
Proficiency by Gender/Race/Ethnicity			Proficiency by Gender/Race/Ethnicity		
Male	214.4 (1.32)	32/51	Male	239.9 (1.14)	26/51
Female	221.7 (1.39)	30/51	Female	240.2 (0.93)	14/51
White, Non-Hispanic	223.2 (1.16)	42/51	White, Non-Hispanic	244.8 (0.91)	25/51
Black, Non-Hispanic	196.9 (2.35)	24/42	Black, Non-Hispanic	221.3 (1.45)	17/42
Asian, Non-Hispanic	n/a	n/a	Asian, Non-Hispanic	n/a	n/a
American Indian, Non-Hispanic	n/a	n/a	American Indian, Non-Hispanic	n/a	n/a
Hispanic	207.5 (2.94)	15/40	Hispanic	230.1 (2.63)	11/41
Proficiency by Class Size			Proficiency by Class Size		
Less than 16 Students	210.6 (7.92)	15/34	Less than 16 Students	223.9 (6.57)	20/35
16 to 18 Students	n/a	n/a	16 to 18 Students	n/a	n/a
19 to 20 Students	216.8 (3.66)	27/38	19 to 20 Students	240.0 (2.61)	18/38
21 to 25 Students	218.1 (1.74)	35/51	21 to 25 Students	241.0 (1.04)	24/51
Greater than 25 Students	219.8 (3.15)	22/36	Greater than 25 Students	241.5 (1.95)	9/33
Percent Attaining Achievement Levels			Percent Attaining Achievement Levels		
Below Basic	36.0 (1.31)	23/51	Below Basic	16.2 (0.92)	32/51
Basic or Above	64.0 (1.31)	29/51	Basic or Above	83.8 (0.92)	19/51
Proficient or Above	30.3 (1.37)	29/51	Proficient or Above	38.2 (1.69)	22/51
Advanced or Above	6.8 (0.67)	28/51	Advanced or Above	5.0 (0.56)	21/51
8th Grade			**8th Grade**		
Average Proficiency	261.0 (1.12)	30/51	Average Proficiency	281.7 (1.00)	19/51
Proficiency by Gender/Race/Ethnicity			Proficiency by Gender/Race/Ethnicity		
Male	255.7 (1.37)	31/51	Male	283.2 (1.23)	16/51
Female	266.6 (1.25)	29/51	Female	280.2 (1.09)	24/51
White, Non-Hispanic	264.8 (1.09)	40/51	White, Non-Hispanic	286.3 (1.00)	29/51
Black, Non-Hispanic	240.5 (2.81)	24/40	Black, Non-Hispanic	257.0 (2.63)	14/41
Asian, Non-Hispanic	n/a	n/a	Asian, Non-Hispanic	n/a	n/a
American Indian, Non-Hispanic	n/a	n/a	American Indian, Non-Hispanic	n/a	n/a
Hispanic	246.7 (4.94)	21/38	Hispanic	260.9 (3.96)	23/38
Proficiency by Parents Highest Level of Ed.			Proficiency by Parents Highest Level of Ed.		
Did Not Finish High School	244.4 (2.65)	28/49	Did Not Finish High School	264.4 (2.47)	14/50
Graduated High School	251.5 (1.78)	30/50	Graduated High School	274.1 (1.46)	9/50
Some Education After High School	266.2 (1.79)	25/50	Some Education After High School	285.5 (1.74)	9/50
Graduated College	271.4 (1.72)	28/50	Graduated College	290.7 (1.45)	22/50
Percent Attaining Achievement Levels			Percent Attaining Achievement Levels		
Below Basic	36.0 (1.31)	23/51	Below Basic	26.0 (1.24)	35/51
Basic or Above	64.0 (1.31)	29/51	Basic or Above	74.0 (1.24)	17/51
Proficient or Above	30.3 (1.37)	29/51	Proficient or Above	30.4 (1.34)	23/51
Advanced or Above	6.8 (0.67)	28/51	Advanced or Above	5.1 (0.59)	27/51

Note: *For an explanation of data, please refer to the User's Guide in the front of the book; n/a indicates data not available*

Adams County

North Adams Community Schools
625 Stadium Dr PO Box 670 · Decatur, IN 46733-0670
(260) 724-7146 · http://www.nadams.k12.in.us/
Grade Span: KG-12; **Agency Type:** 1
Schools: 5
    3 Primary; 1 Middle; 1 High; 0 Other Level
    5 Regular; 0 Special Education; 0 Vocational; 0 Alternative
    0 Magnet; 0 Charter; 4 Title I Eligible; 0 School-wide Title I
Students: 2,302   (50.6% male; 49.3% female)
    Individual Education Program: 353 (15.3%);
    English Language Learner: 38 (1.7%); Migrant: n/a
    Eligible for Free Lunch Program: 466 (20.2%)
    Eligible for Reduced-Price Lunch Program: 112 (4.9%)
Teachers: 141.6 (16.3 to 1)
Librarians/Media Specialists: 2.8 (822.1 to 1)
Guidance Counselors: 8.0 (287.8 to 1)
Current Spending: ($ per student per year):
    Total: $7,554; Instruction: $4,272; Support Services: $2,897
Enrollment, Drop-out Rates and Diploma Recipients by Race/Ethnicity

Category	Total	White	Black	Asian	AIAN	Hisp.
Enrollment (%)	100.0	92.4	0.3	0.4	0.2	6.6
Drop-out Rate (%)	3.2	3.0	0.0	0.0	0.0	8.0
H.S. Diplomas (#)	205	192	1	0	0	12

Allen County

East Allen County Schools
1240 Sr 930 E · New Haven, IN 46774-1732
(260) 446-0100 · http://www.eacs.k12.in.us/
Grade Span: PK-12; **Agency Type:** 1
Schools: 20
    10 Primary; 3 Middle; 5 High; 2 Other Level
    18 Regular; 1 Special Education; 0 Vocational; 1 Alternative
    0 Magnet; 0 Charter; 7 Title I Eligible; 2 School-wide Title I
Students: 9,936   (51.7% male; 48.2% female)
    Individual Education Program: 1,473 (14.8%);
    English Language Learner: 328 (3.3%); Migrant: n/a
    Eligible for Free Lunch Program: 2,391 (24.1%)
    Eligible for Reduced-Price Lunch Program: 807 (8.1%)
Teachers: 585.6 (17.0 to 1)
Librarians/Media Specialists: 7.0 (1,419.4 to 1)
Guidance Counselors: 21.5 (462.1 to 1)
Current Spending: ($ per student per year):
    Total: $8,217; Instruction: $5,042; Support Services: $2,815
Enrollment, Drop-out Rates and Diploma Recipients by Race/Ethnicity

Category	Total	White	Black	Asian	AIAN	Hisp.
Enrollment (%)	100.0	77.2	18.9	0.8	0.2	2.9
Drop-out Rate (%)	0.8	0.4	2.1	0.0	0.0	6.3
H.S. Diplomas (#)	609	529	70	3	2	5

Fort Wayne Community Schools
1200 S Clinton St · Fort Wayne, IN 46802-3594
(260) 467-2025 · http://www.fwcs.k12.in.us/
Grade Span: PK-12; **Agency Type:** 1
Schools: 54
    35 Primary; 11 Middle; 7 High; 1 Other Level
    51 Regular; 1 Special Education; 1 Vocational; 1 Alternative
    6 Magnet; 0 Charter; 28 Title I Eligible; 10 School-wide Title I
Students: 31,815   (51.2% male; 48.7% female)
    Individual Education Program: 5,779 (18.2%);
    English Language Learner: 2,496 (7.8%); Migrant: n/a
    Eligible for Free Lunch Program: 13,201 (41.5%)
    Eligible for Reduced-Price Lunch Program: 2,826 (8.9%)
Teachers: 1,763.1 (18.0 to 1)
Librarians/Media Specialists: 17.5 (1,818.0 to 1)
Guidance Counselors: 31.1 (1,023.0 to 1)
Current Spending: ($ per student per year):
    Total: $8,681; Instruction: $5,296; Support Services: $3,066
Enrollment, Drop-out Rates and Diploma Recipients by Race/Ethnicity

Category	Total	White	Black	Asian	AIAN	Hisp.
Enrollment (%)	100.0	62.2	26.4	2.2	0.5	8.6
Drop-out Rate (%)	2.9	2.2	4.4	2.2	4.2	5.3
H.S. Diplomas (#)	1,596	1,183	312	36	10	55

M S D Southwest Allen County
4824 Homestead Rd · Fort Wayne, IN 46814-5455
(260) 431-2010 · http://www.sacs.k12.in.us/
Grade Span: PK-12; **Agency Type:** 1
Schools: 9
    6 Primary; 2 Middle; 1 High; 0 Other Level
    9 Regular; 0 Special Education; 0 Vocational; 0 Alternative
    0 Magnet; 0 Charter; 0 Title I Eligible; 0 School-wide Title I
Students: 6,149   (52.1% male; 47.8% female)
    Individual Education Program: 952 (15.5%);
    English Language Learner: 281 (4.6%); Migrant: n/a
    Eligible for Free Lunch Program: 183 (3.0%)
    Eligible for Reduced-Price Lunch Program: 90 (1.5%)
Teachers: 337.9 (18.2 to 1)
Librarians/Media Specialists: 4.0 (1,537.3 to 1)
Guidance Counselors: 15.0 (409.9 to 1)
Current Spending: ($ per student per year):
    Total: $8,189; Instruction: $5,444; Support Services: $2,458
Enrollment, Drop-out Rates and Diploma Recipients by Race/Ethnicity

Category	Total	White	Black	Asian	AIAN	Hisp.
Enrollment (%)	100.0	90.8	3.2	3.2	0.4	2.4
Drop-out Rate (%)	1.1	1.2	0.0	1.6	0.0	0.0
H.S. Diplomas (#)	371	345	9	11	2	4

Northwest Allen County Schools
13119 Coldwater Rd · Fort Wayne, IN 46845-9632
(260) 637-3155 · http://www.nacs.k12.in.us/
Grade Span: PK-12; **Agency Type:** 1
Schools: 9
    5 Primary; 2 Middle; 1 High; 1 Other Level
    8 Regular; 0 Special Education; 0 Vocational; 1 Alternative
    0 Magnet; 0 Charter; 3 Title I Eligible; 0 School-wide Title I
Students: 5,247   (50.0% male; 49.9% female)
    Individual Education Program: 649 (12.4%);
    English Language Learner: 55 (1.0%); Migrant: n/a
    Eligible for Free Lunch Program: 257 (4.9%)
    Eligible for Reduced-Price Lunch Program: 176 (3.4%)
Teachers: 262.5 (20.0 to 1)
Librarians/Media Specialists: 3.0 (1,749.0 to 1)
Guidance Counselors: 12.0 (437.3 to 1)
Current Spending: ($ per student per year):
    Total: $6,624; Instruction: $4,069; Support Services: $2,225
Enrollment, Drop-out Rates and Diploma Recipients by Race/Ethnicity

Category	Total	White	Black	Asian	AIAN	Hisp.
Enrollment (%)	100.0	94.6	1.6	2.1	0.4	1.3
Drop-out Rate (%)	0.1	0.1	0.0	0.0	n/a	0.0
H.S. Diplomas (#)	290	279	5	2	0	4

Bartholomew County

Bartholomew Con School Corp
2650 Home Ave · Columbus, IN 47201-3152
(812) 376-4220 · http://www.bcsc.k12.in.us/
Grade Span: PK-12; **Agency Type:** 1
Schools: 16
    11 Primary; 2 Middle; 2 High; 1 Other Level
    15 Regular; 0 Special Education; 1 Vocational; 0 Alternative
    0 Magnet; 0 Charter; 7 Title I Eligible; 2 School-wide Title I
Students: 10,629   (52.1% male; 47.8% female)
    Individual Education Program: 1,658 (15.6%);
    English Language Learner: 401 (3.8%); Migrant: n/a
    Eligible for Free Lunch Program: 2,576 (24.2%)
    Eligible for Reduced-Price Lunch Program: 889 (8.4%)
Teachers: 598.2 (17.8 to 1)
Librarians/Media Specialists: 7.7 (1,380.4 to 1)
Guidance Counselors: 21.0 (506.1 to 1)
Current Spending: ($ per student per year):
    Total: $8,680; Instruction: $5,215; Support Services: $3,169
Enrollment, Drop-out Rates and Diploma Recipients by Race/Ethnicity

Category	Total	White	Black	Asian	AIAN	Hisp.
Enrollment (%)	100.0	92.8	2.0	1.7	0.2	3.4
Drop-out Rate (%)	1.3	1.1	0.0	0.0	3.8	10.9
H.S. Diplomas (#)	620	590	20	7	1	2

Benton County

Benton Community School Corp
405 S Grant Ave · Fowler, IN 47944-1635
Mailing Address: PO Box 512 · Fowler, IN 47944-0512
(765) 884-0850 · http://www.benton.k12.in.us/
Grade Span: KG-12; **Agency Type:** 1
Schools: 5
    4 Primary; 0 Middle; 1 High; 0 Other Level
    5 Regular; 0 Special Education; 0 Vocational; 0 Alternative
    0 Magnet; 0 Charter; 3 Title I Eligible; 0 School-wide Title I
Students: 1,965   (52.5% male; 47.4% female)
    Individual Education Program: 523 (26.6%);
    English Language Learner: 73 (3.7%); Migrant: n/a
    Eligible for Free Lunch Program: 492 (25.0%)
    Eligible for Reduced-Price Lunch Program: 183 (9.3%)
Teachers: 131.5 (14.9 to 1)
Librarians/Media Specialists: 1.0 (1,965.0 to 1)
Guidance Counselors: 5.0 (393.0 to 1)

Current Spending: ($ per student per year):
    Total: $7,657; Instruction: $4,406; Support Services: $2,955
Enrollment, Drop-out Rates and Diploma Recipients by Race/Ethnicity

Category	Total	White	Black	Asian	AIAN	Hisp.
Enrollment (%)	100.0	94.3	0.5	0.1	0.1	5.1
Drop-out Rate (%)	0.0	0.0	n/a	n/a	n/a	0.0
H.S. Diplomas (#)	158	155	0	0	0	3

Blackford County

Blackford County Schools
0668 W 200 S • Hartford City, IN 47348-3018
(765) 348-7550 • http://www.bcs.k12.in.us/
Grade Span: PK-12; **Agency Type:** 1
Schools: 5
    3 Primary; 1 Middle; 1 High; 0 Other Level
    5 Regular; 0 Special Education; 0 Vocational; 0 Alternative
    0 Magnet; 0 Charter; 4 Title I Eligible; 0 School-wide Title I
Students: 2,298   (51.6% male; 48.3% female)
    Individual Education Program: 472 (20.5%);
    English Language Learner: n/a; Migrant: n/a
    Eligible for Free Lunch Program: 643 (28.0%)
    Eligible for Reduced-Price Lunch Program: 201 (8.7%)
Teachers: 143.8 (16.0 to 1)
Librarians/Media Specialists: 2.5 (919.2 to 1)
Guidance Counselors: 4.0 (574.5 to 1)
Current Spending: ($ per student per year):
    Total: $8,274; Instruction: $4,932; Support Services: $2,993
Enrollment, Drop-out Rates and Diploma Recipients by Race/Ethnicity

Category	Total	White	Black	Asian	AIAN	Hisp.
Enrollment (%)	100.0	98.9	0.0	0.2	0.3	0.6
Drop-out Rate (%)	3.0	3.0	n/a	0.0	0.0	0.0
H.S. Diplomas (#)	133	131	0	0	0	2

Boone County

Lebanon Community School Corp
1810 N Grant St • Lebanon, IN 46052-2241
(765) 482-0380 • http://www.bccn.boone.in.us/lcsc/index.html
Grade Span: PK-12; **Agency Type:** 1
Schools: 6
    4 Primary; 1 Middle; 1 High; 0 Other Level
    6 Regular; 0 Special Education; 0 Vocational; 0 Alternative
    0 Magnet; 0 Charter; 4 Title I Eligible; 0 School-wide Title I
Students: 3,352   (50.6% male; 49.3% female)
    Individual Education Program: 628 (18.7%);
    English Language Learner: 34 (1.0%); Migrant: n/a
    Eligible for Free Lunch Program: 747 (22.3%)
    Eligible for Reduced-Price Lunch Program: 234 (7.0%)
Teachers: 199.5 (16.8 to 1)
Librarians/Media Specialists: 6.0 (558.7 to 1)
Guidance Counselors: 8.0 (419.0 to 1)
Current Spending: ($ per student per year):
    Total: $7,268; Instruction: $4,298; Support Services: $2,642
Enrollment, Drop-out Rates and Diploma Recipients by Race/Ethnicity

Category	Total	White	Black	Asian	AIAN	Hisp.
Enrollment (%)	100.0	97.8	0.0	0.4	0.4	1.4
Drop-out Rate (%)	2.0	2.0	50.0	0.0	0.0	0.0
H.S. Diplomas (#)	183	179	1	1	0	2

Western Boone County Com SD
1201 N Sr 75 • Thorntown, IN 46071-9229
(765) 482-6333 • http://www.bccn.boone.in.us/wbsc/index.html
Grade Span: PK-12; **Agency Type:** 1
Schools: 3
    2 Primary; 0 Middle; 1 High; 0 Other Level
    3 Regular; 0 Special Education; 0 Vocational; 0 Alternative
    0 Magnet; 0 Charter; 1 Title I Eligible; 0 School-wide Title I
Students: 1,865   (51.7% male; 48.2% female)
    Individual Education Program: 252 (13.5%);
    English Language Learner: 3 (0.2%); Migrant: n/a
    Eligible for Free Lunch Program: 269 (14.4%)
    Eligible for Reduced-Price Lunch Program: 115 (6.2%)
Teachers: 107.0 (17.4 to 1)
Librarians/Media Specialists: 3.0 (621.7 to 1)
Guidance Counselors: 5.0 (373.0 to 1)
Current Spending: ($ per student per year):
    Total: $6,628; Instruction: $3,819; Support Services: $2,506
Enrollment, Drop-out Rates and Diploma Recipients by Race/Ethnicity

Category	Total	White	Black	Asian	AIAN	Hisp.
Enrollment (%)	100.0	99.2	0.2	0.2	0.2	0.3
Drop-out Rate (%)	1.6	1.6	0.0	0.0	n/a	n/a
H.S. Diplomas (#)	128	128	0	0	0	0

Zionsville Community Schools
900 Mulberry St • Zionsville, IN 46077
(317) 873-2858
Grade Span: PK-12; **Agency Type:** 1
Schools: 7
    5 Primary; 1 Middle; 1 High; 0 Other Level
    7 Regular; 0 Special Education; 0 Vocational; 0 Alternative
    0 Magnet; 0 Charter; 4 Title I Eligible; 0 School-wide Title I
Students: 4,190   (51.9% male; 48.0% female)
    Individual Education Program: 624 (14.9%);
    English Language Learner: 32 (0.8%); Migrant: n/a
    Eligible for Free Lunch Program: 72 (1.7%)
    Eligible for Reduced-Price Lunch Program: 34 (0.8%)
Teachers: 233.7 (17.9 to 1)
Librarians/Media Specialists: 3.0 (1,396.7 to 1)
Guidance Counselors: 10.0 (419.0 to 1)
Current Spending: ($ per student per year):
    Total: $6,959; Instruction: $4,228; Support Services: $2,458
Enrollment, Drop-out Rates and Diploma Recipients by Race/Ethnicity

Category	Total	White	Black	Asian	AIAN	Hisp.
Enrollment (%)	100.0	95.9	0.3	1.8	0.5	1.5
Drop-out Rate (%)	0.0	0.0	0.0	0.0	0.0	0.0
H.S. Diplomas (#)	230	220	2	1	3	4

Brown County

Brown County School Corporation
357 E Main St • Nashville, IN 47448-0038
Mailing Address: PO Box 38 • Nashville, IN 47448-0038
(812) 988-6601 • http://www.brownco.k12.in.us/
Grade Span: PK-12; **Agency Type:** 1
Schools: 6
    4 Primary; 1 Middle; 1 High; 0 Other Level
    6 Regular; 0 Special Education; 0 Vocational; 0 Alternative
    0 Magnet; 0 Charter; 4 Title I Eligible; 0 School-wide Title I
Students: 2,262   (52.5% male; 47.4% female)
    Individual Education Program: 376 (16.6%);
    English Language Learner: 9 (0.4%); Migrant: n/a
    Eligible for Free Lunch Program: 497 (22.0%)
    Eligible for Reduced-Price Lunch Program: 172 (7.6%)
Teachers: 148.2 (15.3 to 1)
Librarians/Media Specialists: 3.3 (685.5 to 1)
Guidance Counselors: 3.0 (754.0 to 1)
Current Spending: ($ per student per year):
    Total: $8,492; Instruction: $4,689; Support Services: $3,468
Enrollment, Drop-out Rates and Diploma Recipients by Race/Ethnicity

Category	Total	White	Black	Asian	AIAN	Hisp.
Enrollment (%)	100.0	98.0	0.4	0.3	0.6	0.8
Drop-out Rate (%)	0.5	0.5	n/a	0.0	0.0	0.0
H.S. Diplomas (#)	131	130	0	0	0	1

Carroll County

Delphi Community School Corp
501 Armory Rd • Delphi, IN 46923-1999
(765) 564-2100 • http://www.delphi.k12.in.us/
Grade Span: PK-12; **Agency Type:** 1
Schools: 4
    2 Primary; 1 Middle; 1 High; 0 Other Level
    4 Regular; 0 Special Education; 0 Vocational; 0 Alternative
    0 Magnet; 0 Charter; 2 Title I Eligible; 1 School-wide Title I
Students: 1,704   (52.7% male; 47.2% female)
    Individual Education Program: 231 (13.6%);
    English Language Learner: 107 (6.3%); Migrant: n/a
    Eligible for Free Lunch Program: 404 (23.7%)
    Eligible for Reduced-Price Lunch Program: 151 (8.9%)
Teachers: 94.5 (18.0 to 1)
Librarians/Media Specialists: 3.0 (568.0 to 1)
Guidance Counselors: 3.0 (568.0 to 1)
Current Spending: ($ per student per year):
    Total: $6,947; Instruction: $3,862; Support Services: $2,816
Enrollment, Drop-out Rates and Diploma Recipients by Race/Ethnicity

Category	Total	White	Black	Asian	AIAN	Hisp.
Enrollment (%)	100.0	93.4	0.2	0.1	0.2	6.1
Drop-out Rate (%)	5.3	5.0	n/a	0.0	n/a	18.2
H.S. Diplomas (#)	91	90	0	0	0	1

Cass County

Logansport Community Sch Corp
2829 George St • Logansport, IN 46947-3997
(574) 722-2911 • http://www.lcsc.k12.in.us/
Grade Span: PK-12; **Agency Type:** 1
Schools: 9
    4 Primary; 2 Middle; 1 High; 2 Other Level

7 Regular; 1 Special Education; 1 Vocational; 0 Alternative
0 Magnet; 0 Charter; 4 Title I Eligible; 3 School-wide Title I
Students: 4,275 (52.0% male; 47.9% female)
Individual Education Program: 622 (14.5%);
English Language Learner: 619 (14.5%); Migrant: n/a
Eligible for Free Lunch Program: 1,559 (36.5%)
Eligible for Reduced-Price Lunch Program: 451 (10.5%)
Teachers: 325.6 (13.1 to 1)
Librarians/Media Specialists: 7.0 (610.7 to 1)
Guidance Counselors: 4.0 (1,068.8 to 1)
Current Spending: ($ per student per year):
Total: $9,737; Instruction: $6,132; Support Services: $3,328
Enrollment, Drop-out Rates and Diploma Recipients by Race/Ethnicity

Category	Total	White	Black	Asian	AIAN	Hisp.
Enrollment (%)	100.0	79.5	1.4	1.0	0.1	18.0
Drop-out Rate (%)	0.3	0.3	0.0	6.3	0.0	0.0
H.S. Diplomas (#)	255	229	2	2	1	21

Southeastern School Corp
6422 E Sr 218 • Walton, IN 46994-0320
(574) 626-2525 • http://www.sesc.k12.in.us/
Grade Span: KG-12; **Agency Type:** 1
Schools: 3
2 Primary; 0 Middle; 1 High; 0 Other Level
3 Regular; 0 Special Education; 0 Vocational; 0 Alternative
0 Magnet; 0 Charter; 1 Title I Eligible; 0 School-wide Title I
Students: 1,651 (51.3% male; 48.6% female)
Individual Education Program: 244 (14.8%);
English Language Learner: 100 (6.1%); Migrant: n/a
Eligible for Free Lunch Program: 232 (14.1%)
Eligible for Reduced-Price Lunch Program: 119 (7.2%)
Teachers: 92.5 (17.8 to 1)
Librarians/Media Specialists: 1.0 (1,651.0 to 1)
Guidance Counselors: 2.0 (825.5 to 1)
Current Spending: ($ per student per year):
Total: $6,573; Instruction: $4,176; Support Services: $2,110
Enrollment, Drop-out Rates and Diploma Recipients by Race/Ethnicity

Category	Total	White	Black	Asian	AIAN	Hisp.
Enrollment (%)	100.0	94.0	0.6	0.2	0.4	4.8
Drop-out Rate (%)	0.8	0.8	0.0	0.0	n/a	0.0
H.S. Diplomas (#)	119	111	1	1	0	6

Clark County

Greater Clark County Schools
2112 Utica-Sellersburg Rd • Jeffersonville, IN 47130-8506
(812) 283-0701 • http://www.gcs.k12.in.us/
Grade Span: PK-12; **Agency Type:** 1
Schools: 20
12 Primary; 3 Middle; 2 High; 3 Other Level
18 Regular; 1 Special Education; 0 Vocational; 1 Alternative
0 Magnet; 0 Charter; 10 Title I Eligible; 4 School-wide Title I
Students: 10,267 (51.2% male; 48.7% female)
Individual Education Program: 2,281 (22.2%);
English Language Learner: 198 (1.9%); Migrant: n/a
Eligible for Free Lunch Program: 2,666 (26.0%)
Eligible for Reduced-Price Lunch Program: 773 (7.5%)
Teachers: 630.6 (16.3 to 1)
Librarians/Media Specialists: 11.0 (933.4 to 1)
Guidance Counselors: 19.0 (540.4 to 1)
Current Spending: ($ per student per year):
Total: $8,531; Instruction: $5,652; Support Services: $2,600
Enrollment, Drop-out Rates and Diploma Recipients by Race/Ethnicity

Category	Total	White	Black	Asian	AIAN	Hisp.
Enrollment (%)	100.0	81.6	14.1	0.7	0.4	3.1
Drop-out Rate (%)	3.6	3.4	5.4	0.0	0.0	2.5
H.S. Diplomas (#)	425	356	56	6	2	5

West Clark Community Schools
601 Renz Ave • Sellersburg, IN 47172-1398
(812) 246-3375 • http://www.wclark.k12.in.us/
Grade Span: KG-12; **Agency Type:** 1
Schools: 7
3 Primary; 1 Middle; 3 High; 0 Other Level
7 Regular; 0 Special Education; 0 Vocational; 0 Alternative
0 Magnet; 0 Charter; 4 Title I Eligible; 0 School-wide Title I
Students: 3,344 (50.1% male; 49.8% female)
Individual Education Program: 544 (16.3%);
English Language Learner: 10 (0.3%); Migrant: n/a
Eligible for Free Lunch Program: 548 (16.4%)
Eligible for Reduced-Price Lunch Program: 189 (5.7%)
Teachers: 183.8 (18.2 to 1)
Librarians/Media Specialists: 3.0 (1,114.7 to 1)
Guidance Counselors: 6.0 (557.3 to 1)
Current Spending: ($ per student per year):
Total: $6,364; Instruction: $4,117; Support Services: $2,015

Enrollment, Drop-out Rates and Diploma Recipients by Race/Ethnicity

Category	Total	White	Black	Asian	AIAN	Hisp.
Enrollment (%)	100.0	98.8	0.3	0.3	0.0	0.6
Drop-out Rate (%)	0.9	0.9	n/a	0.0	0.0	0.0
H.S. Diplomas (#)	175	172	0	0	0	3

Clay County

Clay Community Schools
9750 N Crawford St • Knightsville, IN 47857-0169
Mailing Address: PO Box 169 • Knightsville, IN 47857-0169
(812) 443-4461 • http://www.clay.k12.in.us/
Grade Span: PK-12; **Agency Type:** 1
Schools: 10
7 Primary; 1 Middle; 2 High; 0 Other Level
10 Regular; 0 Special Education; 0 Vocational; 0 Alternative
0 Magnet; 0 Charter; 4 Title I Eligible; 3 School-wide Title I
Students: 4,616 (50.6% male; 49.3% female)
Individual Education Program: 960 (20.8%);
English Language Learner: 7 (0.2%); Migrant: n/a
Eligible for Free Lunch Program: 1,367 (29.6%)
Eligible for Reduced-Price Lunch Program: 504 (10.9%)
Teachers: 289.4 (16.0 to 1)
Librarians/Media Specialists: 6.0 (769.3 to 1)
Guidance Counselors: 8.0 (577.0 to 1)
Current Spending: ($ per student per year):
Total: $7,591; Instruction: $4,895; Support Services: $2,371
Enrollment, Drop-out Rates and Diploma Recipients by Race/Ethnicity

Category	Total	White	Black	Asian	AIAN	Hisp.
Enrollment (%)	100.0	98.5	0.9	0.1	0.1	0.3
Drop-out Rate (%)	0.2	0.2	0.0	0.0	0.0	0.0
H.S. Diplomas (#)	301	299	1	0	1	0

Clinton County

Community Schools of Frankfort
50 S Maish Rd • Frankfort, IN 46041-2824
(765) 654-5585 • http://fhs.frankfort.k12.in.us/
Grade Span: PK-12; **Agency Type:** 1
Schools: 6
4 Primary; 1 Middle; 1 High; 0 Other Level
6 Regular; 0 Special Education; 0 Vocational; 0 Alternative
0 Magnet; 0 Charter; 3 Title I Eligible; 2 School-wide Title I
Students: 3,272 (51.1% male; 48.8% female)
Individual Education Program: 454 (13.9%);
English Language Learner: 538 (16.4%); Migrant: n/a
Eligible for Free Lunch Program: 1,347 (41.2%)
Eligible for Reduced-Price Lunch Program: 387 (11.8%)
Teachers: 193.0 (17.0 to 1)
Librarians/Media Specialists: 4.0 (818.0 to 1)
Guidance Counselors: 5.8 (564.1 to 1)
Current Spending: ($ per student per year):
Total: $6,929; Instruction: $4,403; Support Services: $2,204
Enrollment, Drop-out Rates and Diploma Recipients by Race/Ethnicity

Category	Total	White	Black	Asian	AIAN	Hisp.
Enrollment (%)	100.0	76.5	0.4	0.3	0.0	22.8
Drop-out Rate (%)	4.5	4.3	0.0	0.0	n/a	6.0
H.S. Diplomas (#)	144	129	0	1	0	14

Crawford County

Crawford County Com School Corp
5805 E Administration Rd • Marengo, IN 47140-8415
(812) 365-2135 • http://www.cccs.k12.in.us/
Grade Span: PK-12; **Agency Type:** 1
Schools: 6
5 Primary; 0 Middle; 1 High; 0 Other Level
6 Regular; 0 Special Education; 0 Vocational; 0 Alternative
0 Magnet; 0 Charter; 4 Title I Eligible; 0 School-wide Title I
Students: 1,851 (52.0% male; 47.9% female)
Individual Education Program: 338 (18.3%);
English Language Learner: 17 (0.9%); Migrant: n/a
Eligible for Free Lunch Program: 691 (37.3%)
Eligible for Reduced-Price Lunch Program: 253 (13.7%)
Teachers: 99.4 (18.6 to 1)
Librarians/Media Specialists: 1.0 (1,851.0 to 1)
Guidance Counselors: 3.0 (617.0 to 1)
Current Spending: ($ per student per year):
Total: $7,950; Instruction: $5,301; Support Services: $2,260
Enrollment, Drop-out Rates and Diploma Recipients by Race/Ethnicity

Category	Total	White	Black	Asian	AIAN	Hisp.
Enrollment (%)	100.0	99.8	0.0	0.1	0.0	0.2
Drop-out Rate (%)	1.7	1.7	n/a	0.0	n/a	0.0
H.S. Diplomas (#)	91	91	0	0	0	0

Daviess County

Washington Com Schools Inc
301 E S St • Washington, IN 47501-3294
(812) 254-5536
Grade Span: KG-12; **Agency Type:** 1
Schools: 6
    4 Primary; 1 Middle; 1 High; 0 Other Level
    6 Regular; 0 Special Education; 0 Vocational; 0 Alternative
    0 Magnet; 0 Charter; 3 Title I Eligible; 0 School-wide Title I
Students: 2,475   (53.0% male; 46.9% female)
    Individual Education Program: 518 (20.9%);
    English Language Learner: 130 (5.3%); Migrant: n/a
    Eligible for Free Lunch Program: 836 (33.8%)
    Eligible for Reduced-Price Lunch Program: 224 (9.1%)
Teachers: 140.0 (17.7 to 1)
Librarians/Media Specialists: 2.0 (1,237.5 to 1)
Guidance Counselors: 3.7 (668.9 to 1)
Current Spending: ($ per student per year):
    Total: $6,528; Instruction: $4,035; Support Services: $2,257
Enrollment, Drop-out Rates and Diploma Recipients by Race/Ethnicity

Category	Total	White	Black	Asian	AIAN	Hisp.
Enrollment (%)	100.0	93.0	0.2	0.8	0.2	5.8
Drop-out Rate (%)	2.6	2.7	0.0	0.0	n/a	0.0
H.S. Diplomas (#)	175	170	1	1	0	3

De Kalb County

Dekalb County Ctl United SD
3326 Cr 427 • Waterloo, IN 46793
(260) 925-3914 • http://www.dekalb.k12.in.us/
Grade Span: PK-12; **Agency Type:** 1
Schools: 6
    4 Primary; 1 Middle; 1 High; 0 Other Level
    6 Regular; 0 Special Education; 0 Vocational; 0 Alternative
    0 Magnet; 0 Charter; 6 Title I Eligible; 0 School-wide Title I
Students: 4,137   (51.1% male; 48.8% female)
    Individual Education Program: 598 (14.5%);
    English Language Learner: 55 (1.3%); Migrant: n/a
    Eligible for Free Lunch Program: 646 (15.6%)
    Eligible for Reduced-Price Lunch Program: 319 (7.7%)
Teachers: 207.3 (20.0 to 1)
Librarians/Media Specialists: 3.0 (1,379.0 to 1)
Guidance Counselors: 9.0 (459.7 to 1)
Current Spending: ($ per student per year):
    Total: $7,392; Instruction: $4,517; Support Services: $2,585
Enrollment, Drop-out Rates and Diploma Recipients by Race/Ethnicity

Category	Total	White	Black	Asian	AIAN	Hisp.
Enrollment (%)	100.0	97.2	0.2	0.6	0.2	1.8
Drop-out Rate (%)	3.0	2.9	0.0	0.0	0.0	22.2
H.S. Diplomas (#)	220	216	1	0	0	3

Dekalb County Eastern Com SD
300 E Washington St • Butler, IN 46721-1119
(260) 868-2125
Grade Span: PK-12; **Agency Type:** 1
Schools: 4
    2 Primary; 0 Middle; 0 High; 2 Other Level
    3 Regular; 1 Special Education; 0 Vocational; 0 Alternative
    0 Magnet; 0 Charter; 1 Title I Eligible; 0 School-wide Title I
Students: 1,521   (53.1% male; 46.8% female)
    Individual Education Program: 252 (16.6%);
    English Language Learner: 9 (0.6%); Migrant: n/a
    Eligible for Free Lunch Program: 285 (18.7%)
    Eligible for Reduced-Price Lunch Program: 106 (7.0%)
Teachers: 125.2 (12.1 to 1)
Librarians/Media Specialists: 1.7 (894.7 to 1)
Guidance Counselors: 3.0 (507.0 to 1)
Current Spending: ($ per student per year):
    Total: $11,650; Instruction: $6,719; Support Services: $4,636
Enrollment, Drop-out Rates and Diploma Recipients by Race/Ethnicity

Category	Total	White	Black	Asian	AIAN	Hisp.
Enrollment (%)	100.0	98.4	0.0	0.3	0.1	1.2
Drop-out Rate (%)	1.7	1.7	n/a	0.0	0.0	0.0
H.S. Diplomas (#)	79	76	0	0	0	3

Garrett-Keyser-Butler Com
900 E Warfield • Garrett, IN 46738-1699
Mailing Address: 801 E Houston St • Garrett, IN 46738-1699
(260) 357-3185
Grade Span: KG-12; **Agency Type:** 1
Schools: 4
    1 Primary; 1 Middle; 1 High; 1 Other Level
    3 Regular; 0 Special Education; 1 Vocational; 0 Alternative
    0 Magnet; 0 Charter; 2 Title I Eligible; 0 School-wide Title I

Students: 1,646   (49.1% male; 50.8% female)
    Individual Education Program: 276 (16.8%);
    English Language Learner: 12 (0.7%); Migrant: n/a
    Eligible for Free Lunch Program: 363 (22.1%)
    Eligible for Reduced-Price Lunch Program: 168 (10.2%)
Teachers: 107.9 (15.3 to 1)
Librarians/Media Specialists: 3.0 (548.7 to 1)
Guidance Counselors: 5.0 (329.2 to 1)
Current Spending: ($ per student per year):
    Total: $9,142; Instruction: $5,590; Support Services: $3,192
Enrollment, Drop-out Rates and Diploma Recipients by Race/Ethnicity

Category	Total	White	Black	Asian	AIAN	Hisp.
Enrollment (%)	100.0	98.4	0.3	0.7	0.1	0.5
Drop-out Rate (%)	5.1	5.3	0.0	0.0	n/a	0.0
H.S. Diplomas (#)	109	102	1	4	0	2

Dearborn County

South Dearborn Com School Corp
6109 Squire Pl • Aurora, IN 47001-1499
(812) 926-2090 • http://www.venus.net/~sdearad1/
Grade Span: PK-12; **Agency Type:** 1
Schools: 6
    4 Primary; 1 Middle; 1 High; 0 Other Level
    6 Regular; 0 Special Education; 0 Vocational; 0 Alternative
    0 Magnet; 0 Charter; 3 Title I Eligible; 0 School-wide Title I
Students: 3,030   (50.0% male; 49.9% female)
    Individual Education Program: 617 (20.4%);
    English Language Learner: 4 (0.1%); Migrant: n/a
    Eligible for Free Lunch Program: 478 (15.8%)
    Eligible for Reduced-Price Lunch Program: 136 (4.5%)
Teachers: 179.9 (16.8 to 1)
Librarians/Media Specialists: 3.0 (1,010.0 to 1)
Guidance Counselors: 3.0 (1,010.0 to 1)
Current Spending: ($ per student per year):
    Total: $7,415; Instruction: $4,674; Support Services: $2,444
Enrollment, Drop-out Rates and Diploma Recipients by Race/Ethnicity

Category	Total	White	Black	Asian	AIAN	Hisp.
Enrollment (%)	100.0	99.5	0.0	0.2	0.2	0.1
Drop-out Rate (%)	2.9	2.9	n/a	0.0	n/a	0.0
H.S. Diplomas (#)	199	198	0	1	0	0

Sunman-Dearborn Com Sch Corp
26022 Lawrenceville Rd • Sunman, IN 47041-0210
Mailing Address: PO Box 210 • Sunman, IN 47041-0210
(812) 623-2291 • http://sunmandearborn.k12.in.us/
Grade Span: KG-12; **Agency Type:** 1
Schools: 7
    3 Primary; 2 Middle; 1 High; 1 Other Level
    6 Regular; 1 Special Education; 0 Vocational; 0 Alternative
    0 Magnet; 0 Charter; 4 Title I Eligible; 0 School-wide Title I
Students: 4,242   (52.0% male; 47.9% female)
    Individual Education Program: 749 (17.7%);
    English Language Learner: 25 (0.6%); Migrant: n/a
    Eligible for Free Lunch Program: 376 (8.9%)
    Eligible for Reduced-Price Lunch Program: 122 (2.9%)
Teachers: 212.6 (20.0 to 1)
Librarians/Media Specialists: 5.8 (731.4 to 1)
Guidance Counselors: 9.0 (471.3 to 1)
Current Spending: ($ per student per year):
    Total: $7,640; Instruction: $4,618; Support Services: $2,726
Enrollment, Drop-out Rates and Diploma Recipients by Race/Ethnicity

Category	Total	White	Black	Asian	AIAN	Hisp.
Enrollment (%)	100.0	99.1	0.2	0.3	0.0	0.4
Drop-out Rate (%)	1.8	1.8	0.0	0.0	n/a	0.0
H.S. Diplomas (#)	312	312	0	0	0	0

Decatur County

Decatur County Com Schools
1645 W Sr 46 • Greensburg, IN 47240-9054
(812) 663-4595 • http://www.decaturco.k12.in.us/
Grade Span: PK-12; **Agency Type:** 1
Schools: 4
    2 Primary; 0 Middle; 2 High; 0 Other Level
    4 Regular; 0 Special Education; 0 Vocational; 0 Alternative
    0 Magnet; 0 Charter; 3 Title I Eligible; 0 School-wide Title I
Students: 2,178   (53.2% male; 46.7% female)
    Individual Education Program: 364 (16.7%);
    English Language Learner: 2 (0.1%); Migrant: n/a
    Eligible for Free Lunch Program: 295 (13.5%)
    Eligible for Reduced-Price Lunch Program: 190 (8.7%)
Teachers: 133.9 (16.3 to 1)
Librarians/Media Specialists: 3.7 (588.6 to 1)
Guidance Counselors: 3.5 (622.3 to 1)

Current Spending: ($ per student per year):
Total: $6,860; Instruction: $4,355; Support Services: $2,298
Enrollment, Drop-out Rates and Diploma Recipients by Race/Ethnicity

Category	Total	White	Black	Asian	AIAN	Hisp.
Enrollment (%)	100.0	99.4	0.1	0.0	0.1	0.3
Drop-out Rate (%)	3.6	3.6	n/a	0.0	n/a	0.0
H.S. Diplomas (#)	146	144	0	0	0	2

Greensburg Community Schools
504 E Central Ave • Greensburg, IN 47240-1898
(812) 663-4774 • http://www.treecity.com/community/gschools/grbg.html
Grade Span: KG-12; **Agency Type:** 1
Schools: 5
2 Primary; 2 Middle; 1 High; 0 Other Level
5 Regular; 0 Special Education; 0 Vocational; 0 Alternative
0 Magnet; 0 Charter; 3 Title I Eligible; 0 School-wide Title I
Students: 2,026   (51.4% male; 48.5% female)
Individual Education Program: 305 (15.1%);
English Language Learner: 33 (1.6%); Migrant: n/a
Eligible for Free Lunch Program: 447 (22.1%)
Eligible for Reduced-Price Lunch Program: 136 (6.7%)
Teachers: 118.7 (17.1 to 1)
Librarians/Media Specialists: 2.7 (750.4 to 1)
Guidance Counselors: 2.0 (1,013.0 to 1)
Current Spending: ($ per student per year):
Total: $6,603; Instruction: $3,924; Support Services: $2,263
Enrollment, Drop-out Rates and Diploma Recipients by Race/Ethnicity

Category	Total	White	Black	Asian	AIAN	Hisp.
Enrollment (%)	100.0	98.0	0.0	1.1	0.0	0.9
Drop-out Rate (%)	0.0	0.0	n/a	0.0	n/a	0.0
H.S. Diplomas (#)	106	105	0	1	0	0

Delaware County

Delaware Community School Corp
7821 Sr 3 N • Muncie, IN 47303-9803
(765) 284-5074 • http://www.delcomschools.org/
Grade Span: KG-12; **Agency Type:** 1
Schools: 6
4 Primary; 1 Middle; 1 High; 0 Other Level
6 Regular; 0 Special Education; 0 Vocational; 0 Alternative
0 Magnet; 0 Charter; 3 Title I Eligible; 0 School-wide Title I
Students: 2,879   (51.5% male; 48.4% female)
Individual Education Program: 454 (15.8%);
English Language Learner: 10 (0.3%); Migrant: n/a
Eligible for Free Lunch Program: 448 (15.6%)
Eligible for Reduced-Price Lunch Program: 232 (8.1%)
Teachers: 165.3 (17.4 to 1)
Librarians/Media Specialists: 3.0 (959.7 to 1)
Guidance Counselors: 7.0 (411.3 to 1)
Current Spending: ($ per student per year):
Total: $6,603; Instruction: $3,812; Support Services: $2,487
Enrollment, Drop-out Rates and Diploma Recipients by Race/Ethnicity

Category	Total	White	Black	Asian	AIAN	Hisp.
Enrollment (%)	100.0	98.2	1.1	0.2	0.0	0.4
Drop-out Rate (%)	3.3	3.4	0.0	0.0	0.0	0.0
H.S. Diplomas (#)	199	193	2	2	0	2

Mt Pleasant Twp Com Sch Corp
8800 W Smith St • Yorktown, IN 47396-1399
(765) 759-2720 • http://www.yorktown.k12.in.us/
Grade Span: KG-12; **Agency Type:** 1
Schools: 4
2 Primary; 1 Middle; 1 High; 0 Other Level
4 Regular; 0 Special Education; 0 Vocational; 0 Alternative
0 Magnet; 0 Charter; 3 Title I Eligible; 0 School-wide Title I
Students: 2,246   (51.9% male; 48.0% female)
Individual Education Program: 401 (17.9%);
English Language Learner: 31 (1.4%); Migrant: n/a
Eligible for Free Lunch Program: 198 (8.8%)
Eligible for Reduced-Price Lunch Program: 122 (5.4%)
Teachers: 124.8 (18.0 to 1)
Librarians/Media Specialists: 4.0 (561.5 to 1)
Guidance Counselors: 4.0 (561.5 to 1)
Current Spending: ($ per student per year):
Total: $6,604; Instruction: $3,757; Support Services: $2,566
Enrollment, Drop-out Rates and Diploma Recipients by Race/Ethnicity

Category	Total	White	Black	Asian	AIAN	Hisp.
Enrollment (%)	100.0	97.2	0.9	1.1	0.1	0.7
Drop-out Rate (%)	1.7	1.6	11.1	0.0	n/a	0.0
H.S. Diplomas (#)	141	136	2	1	0	2

Muncie Community Schools
2501 N Oakwood Ave • Muncie, IN 47304-2399
(765) 747-5205 • http://www.muncie.k12.in.us/
Grade Span: PK-12; **Agency Type:** 1
Schools: 18
12 Primary; 2 Middle; 2 High; 2 Other Level
16 Regular; 0 Special Education; 1 Vocational; 1 Alternative
0 Magnet; 0 Charter; 8 Title I Eligible; 7 School-wide Title I
Students: 8,075   (51.3% male; 48.6% female)
Individual Education Program: 1,877 (23.2%);
English Language Learner: 135 (1.7%); Migrant: n/a
Eligible for Free Lunch Program: 3,929 (48.7%)
Eligible for Reduced-Price Lunch Program: 920 (11.4%)
Teachers: 555.0 (14.5 to 1)
Librarians/Media Specialists: 10.0 (807.5 to 1)
Guidance Counselors: 21.0 (384.5 to 1)
Current Spending: ($ per student per year):
Total: $10,467; Instruction: $6,216; Support Services: $3,918
Enrollment, Drop-out Rates and Diploma Recipients by Race/Ethnicity

Category	Total	White	Black	Asian	AIAN	Hisp.
Enrollment (%)	100.0	78.7	18.6	1.1	0.2	1.3
Drop-out Rate (%)	4.4	4.7	2.6	8.7	0.0	13.3
H.S. Diplomas (#)	408	305	93	4	0	6

Dubois County

Greater Jasper Con Schs
1520 St Charles St Ste 1 • Jasper, IN 47546-8228
(812) 482-1801
Grade Span: PK-12; **Agency Type:** 1
Schools: 6
3 Primary; 1 Middle; 1 High; 1 Other Level
5 Regular; 1 Special Education; 0 Vocational; 0 Alternative
0 Magnet; 0 Charter; 2 Title I Eligible; 0 School-wide Title I
Students: 3,128   (50.6% male; 49.3% female)
Individual Education Program: 377 (12.1%);
English Language Learner: 147 (4.7%); Migrant: n/a
Eligible for Free Lunch Program: 352 (11.3%)
Eligible for Reduced-Price Lunch Program: 136 (4.3%)
Teachers: 190.7 (16.4 to 1)
Librarians/Media Specialists: 4.0 (782.0 to 1)
Guidance Counselors: 2.0 (1,564.0 to 1)
Current Spending: ($ per student per year):
Total: $9,904; Instruction: $6,386; Support Services: $3,203
Enrollment, Drop-out Rates and Diploma Recipients by Race/Ethnicity

Category	Total	White	Black	Asian	AIAN	Hisp.
Enrollment (%)	100.0	93.9	0.2	0.6	0.2	5.1
Drop-out Rate (%)	0.9	0.9	0.0	0.0	0.0	0.0
H.S. Diplomas (#)	240	230	1	3	0	6

Southeast Dubois County Sch Corp
432 E 15th St • Ferdinand, IN 47532-9199
(812) 367-1653 • http://www.sedubois.k12.in.us/
Grade Span: KG-12; **Agency Type:** 1
Schools: 4
3 Primary; 0 Middle; 1 High; 0 Other Level
4 Regular; 0 Special Education; 0 Vocational; 0 Alternative
0 Magnet; 0 Charter; 1 Title I Eligible; 0 School-wide Title I
Students: 1,512   (48.0% male; 51.9% female)
Individual Education Program: 179 (11.8%);
English Language Learner: 11 (0.7%); Migrant: n/a
Eligible for Free Lunch Program: 131 (8.7%)
Eligible for Reduced-Price Lunch Program: 65 (4.3%)
Teachers: 83.1 (18.2 to 1)
Librarians/Media Specialists: 1.0 (1,512.0 to 1)
Guidance Counselors: 0.8 (1,890.0 to 1)
Current Spending: ($ per student per year):
Total: $6,286; Instruction: $4,112; Support Services: $1,893
Enrollment, Drop-out Rates and Diploma Recipients by Race/Ethnicity

Category	Total	White	Black	Asian	AIAN	Hisp.
Enrollment (%)	100.0	99.4	0.3	0.3	0.0	0.0
Drop-out Rate (%)	0.0	0.0	n/a	0.0	0.0	n/a
H.S. Diplomas (#)	89	88	0	1	0	0

Southwest Dubois County Sch Corp
113 N Jackson St • Huntingburg, IN 47542-0398
Mailing Address: PO Box 398 • Huntingburg, IN 47542-0398
(812) 683-3971 • http://www.swdubois.k12.in.us/
Grade Span: PK-12; **Agency Type:** 1
Schools: 4
2 Primary; 1 Middle; 1 High; 0 Other Level
4 Regular; 0 Special Education; 0 Vocational; 0 Alternative
0 Magnet; 0 Charter; 1 Title I Eligible; 0 School-wide Title I
Students: 1,889   (49.9% male; 50.0% female)
Individual Education Program: 278 (14.7%);

English Language Learner: 108 (5.7%); Migrant: n/a
Eligible for Free Lunch Program: 325 (17.2%)
Eligible for Reduced-Price Lunch Program: 129 (6.8%)
Teachers: 98.3 (19.2 to 1)
Librarians/Media Specialists: 3.0 (629.7 to 1)
Guidance Counselors: 2.7 (699.6 to 1)
Current Spending: ($ per student per year):
Total: $9,094; Instruction: $4,892; Support Services: $3,864
Enrollment, Drop-out Rates and Diploma Recipients by Race/Ethnicity

Category	Total	White	Black	Asian	AIAN	Hisp.
Enrollment (%)	100.0	91.5	0.1	0.4	0.0	7.9
Drop-out Rate (%)	2.1	1.7	n/a	0.0	n/a	10.5
H.S. Diplomas (#)	122	120	0	0	0	2

Elkhart County

Baugo Community Schools
29125 Cr 22 W • Elkhart, IN 46517-9510
(574) 293-8583 • http://www.baugo.k12.in.us/
Grade Span: KG-12; **Agency Type:** 1
Schools: 5
2 Primary; 2 Middle; 1 High; 0 Other Level
5 Regular; 0 Special Education; 0 Vocational; 0 Alternative
0 Magnet; 0 Charter; 3 Title I Eligible; 0 School-wide Title I
Students: 1,765 (52.0% male; 47.9% female)
Individual Education Program: 317 (18.0%);
English Language Learner: 24 (1.4%); Migrant: n/a
Eligible for Free Lunch Program: 303 (17.2%)
Eligible for Reduced-Price Lunch Program: 145 (8.2%)
Teachers: 99.5 (17.7 to 1)
Librarians/Media Specialists: 1.0 (1,765.0 to 1)
Guidance Counselors: 6.0 (294.2 to 1)
Current Spending: ($ per student per year):
Total: $6,730; Instruction: $4,126; Support Services: $2,367
Enrollment, Drop-out Rates and Diploma Recipients by Race/Ethnicity

Category	Total	White	Black	Asian	AIAN	Hisp.
Enrollment (%)	100.0	92.6	3.3	0.4	0.3	3.4
Drop-out Rate (%)	0.0	0.0	0.0	0.0	n/a	0.0
H.S. Diplomas (#)	118	111	3	0	0	4

Concord Community Schools
59040 Minuteman Way • Elkhart, IN 46517-3499
(574) 875-5161 • http://www.concord.k12.in.us/
Grade Span: KG-12; **Agency Type:** 1
Schools: 6
4 Primary; 1 Middle; 1 High; 0 Other Level
6 Regular; 0 Special Education; 0 Vocational; 0 Alternative
0 Magnet; 0 Charter; 3 Title I Eligible; 0 School-wide Title I
Students: 4,452 (50.5% male; 49.4% female)
Individual Education Program: 659 (14.8%);
English Language Learner: 478 (10.7%); Migrant: n/a
Eligible for Free Lunch Program: 1,058 (23.8%)
Eligible for Reduced-Price Lunch Program: 426 (9.6%)
Teachers: 235.1 (18.9 to 1)
Librarians/Media Specialists: 2.0 (2,226.0 to 1)
Guidance Counselors: 9.0 (494.7 to 1)
Current Spending: ($ per student per year):
Total: $6,614; Instruction: $4,129; Support Services: $2,182
Enrollment, Drop-out Rates and Diploma Recipients by Race/Ethnicity

Category	Total	White	Black	Asian	AIAN	Hisp.
Enrollment (%)	100.0	79.9	7.7	1.1	0.2	11.1
Drop-out Rate (%)	2.5	2.2	1.3	0.0	0.0	8.9
H.S. Diplomas (#)	244	215	11	4	1	13

Elkhart Community Schools
2720 California Rd • Elkhart, IN 46514-1220
(574) 262-5516 • http://www.elkhart.k12.in.us/
Grade Span: PK-12; **Agency Type:** 1
Schools: 20
14 Primary; 3 Middle; 2 High; 1 Other Level
19 Regular; 0 Special Education; 1 Vocational; 0 Alternative
1 Magnet; 0 Charter; 10 Title I Eligible; 4 School-wide Title I
Students: 13,059 (51.3% male; 48.6% female)
Individual Education Program: 2,142 (16.4%);
English Language Learner: 1,958 (15.0%); Migrant: n/a
Eligible for Free Lunch Program: 5,109 (39.1%)
Eligible for Reduced-Price Lunch Program: 1,391 (10.7%)
Teachers: 802.0 (16.3 to 1)
Librarians/Media Specialists: 5.0 (2,611.8 to 1)
Guidance Counselors: 19.0 (687.3 to 1)
Current Spending: ($ per student per year):
Total: $7,525; Instruction: $4,452; Support Services: $2,743

Enrollment, Drop-out Rates and Diploma Recipients by Race/Ethnicity

Category	Total	White	Black	Asian	AIAN	Hisp.
Enrollment (%)	100.0	64.0	16.9	1.6	0.3	17.2
Drop-out Rate (%)	3.9	3.6	4.3	3.1	0.0	5.3
H.S. Diplomas (#)	544	423	82	9	2	28

Fairfield Community Schools
67240 Cr 31 • Goshen, IN 46528-9300
(574) 831-2188 • http://www.fairfield.k12.in.us/
Grade Span: KG-12; **Agency Type:** 1
Schools: 4
3 Primary; 0 Middle; 1 High; 0 Other Level
4 Regular; 0 Special Education; 0 Vocational; 0 Alternative
0 Magnet; 0 Charter; 3 Title I Eligible; 0 School-wide Title I
Students: 2,070 (50.3% male; 49.6% female)
Individual Education Program: 280 (13.5%);
English Language Learner: 327 (15.8%); Migrant: n/a
Eligible for Free Lunch Program: 162 (7.8%)
Eligible for Reduced-Price Lunch Program: 183 (8.8%)
Teachers: 113.6 (18.2 to 1)
Librarians/Media Specialists: 2.0 (1,035.0 to 1)
Guidance Counselors: 3.0 (690.0 to 1)
Current Spending: ($ per student per year):
Total: $6,532; Instruction: $4,194; Support Services: $2,066
Enrollment, Drop-out Rates and Diploma Recipients by Race/Ethnicity

Category	Total	White	Black	Asian	AIAN	Hisp.
Enrollment (%)	100.0	98.6	0.0	0.3	0.0	1.1
Drop-out Rate (%)	0.8	0.8	n/a	n/a	n/a	0.0
H.S. Diplomas (#)	120	120	0	0	0	0

Goshen Community Schools
721 E Madison St • Goshen, IN 46528-3521
(574) 533-8631 • http://www.goshenschools.org/
Grade Span: KG-12; **Agency Type:** 1
Schools: 9
6 Primary; 1 Middle; 1 High; 1 Other Level
8 Regular; 1 Special Education; 0 Vocational; 0 Alternative
0 Magnet; 0 Charter; 6 Title I Eligible; 0 School-wide Title I
Students: 5,824 (51.1% male; 48.8% female)
Individual Education Program: 1,044 (17.9%);
English Language Learner: 1,526 (26.2%); Migrant: n/a
Eligible for Free Lunch Program: 2,082 (35.7%)
Eligible for Reduced-Price Lunch Program: 597 (10.3%)
Teachers: 369.2 (15.8 to 1)
Librarians/Media Specialists: 2.0 (2,912.0 to 1)
Guidance Counselors: 13.0 (448.0 to 1)
Current Spending: ($ per student per year):
Total: $8,626; Instruction: $5,505; Support Services: $2,863
Enrollment, Drop-out Rates and Diploma Recipients by Race/Ethnicity

Category	Total	White	Black	Asian	AIAN	Hisp.
Enrollment (%)	100.0	68.4	1.4	1.3	0.2	28.7
Drop-out Rate (%)	2.5	1.8	0.0	9.5	0.0	5.6
H.S. Diplomas (#)	271	237	1	0	0	33

Middlebury Community Schools
57853 Northridge Dr • Middlebury, IN 46540-9408
(574) 825-9425 • http://www.mcsin-k12.org/
Grade Span: KG-12; **Agency Type:** 1
Schools: 6
4 Primary; 1 Middle; 1 High; 0 Other Level
6 Regular; 0 Special Education; 0 Vocational; 0 Alternative
0 Magnet; 0 Charter; 3 Title I Eligible; 0 School-wide Title I
Students: 3,733 (51.4% male; 48.5% female)
Individual Education Program: 473 (12.7%);
English Language Learner: 227 (6.1%); Migrant: n/a
Eligible for Free Lunch Program: 382 (10.2%)
Eligible for Reduced-Price Lunch Program: 221 (5.9%)
Teachers: 205.5 (18.2 to 1)
Librarians/Media Specialists: 2.0 (1,866.5 to 1)
Guidance Counselors: 8.0 (466.6 to 1)
Current Spending: ($ per student per year):
Total: $8,301; Instruction: $4,857; Support Services: $3,171
Enrollment, Drop-out Rates and Diploma Recipients by Race/Ethnicity

Category	Total	White	Black	Asian	AIAN	Hisp.
Enrollment (%)	100.0	96.4	0.3	1.1	0.4	1.8
Drop-out Rate (%)	0.2	0.2	0.0	0.0	0.0	0.0
H.S. Diplomas (#)	221	210	1	5	1	4

Wa-Nee Community Schools
1300 N Main St • Nappanee, IN 46550-1015
(574) 773-3131 • http://www.wanee.k12.in.us/
Grade Span: KG-12; **Agency Type:** 1
Schools: 5
3 Primary; 1 Middle; 1 High; 0 Other Level
5 Regular; 0 Special Education; 0 Vocational; 0 Alternative

0 Magnet; 0 Charter; 2 Title I Eligible; 0 School-wide Title I
Students: 3,050   (50.4% male; 49.5% female)
   Individual Education Program: 484 (15.9%);
   English Language Learner: 298 (9.8%); Migrant: n/a
   Eligible for Free Lunch Program: 407 (13.3%)
   Eligible for Reduced-Price Lunch Program: 207 (6.8%)
Teachers: 174.7 (17.5 to 1)
Librarians/Media Specialists: 3.0 (1,016.7 to 1)
Guidance Counselors: 7.0 (435.7 to 1)
Current Spending: ($ per student per year):
   Total: $8,083; Instruction: $5,121; Support Services: $2,652
Enrollment, Drop-out Rates and Diploma Recipients by Race/Ethnicity

Category	Total	White	Black	Asian	AIAN	Hisp.
Enrollment (%)	100.0	95.0	0.8	0.4	0.1	3.8
Drop-out Rate (%)	3.0	2.5	0.0	50.0	n/a	30.0
H.S. Diplomas (#)	169	167	0	1	0	1

Fayette County

Fayette County School Corp
1401 Spartan Dr • Connersville, IN 47331-1053
(765) 825-2178 • http://fayette.k12.in.us/admin/
Grade Span: PK-12; **Agency Type:** 1
Schools: 13
   8 Primary; 1 Middle; 2 High; 2 Other Level
   10 Regular; 1 Special Education; 1 Vocational; 1 Alternative
   0 Magnet; 0 Charter; 6 Title I Eligible; 0 School-wide Title I
Students: 3,935   (52.2% male; 47.7% female)
   Individual Education Program: 832 (21.1%);
   English Language Learner: 15 (0.4%); Migrant: n/a
   Eligible for Free Lunch Program: 1,585 (40.3%)
   Eligible for Reduced-Price Lunch Program: 306 (7.8%)
Teachers: 260.1 (15.1 to 1)
Librarians/Media Specialists: 2.0 (1,967.5 to 1)
Guidance Counselors: 9.0 (437.2 to 1)
Current Spending: ($ per student per year):
   Total: $9,604; Instruction: $5,792; Support Services: $3,495
Enrollment, Drop-out Rates and Diploma Recipients by Race/Ethnicity

Category	Total	White	Black	Asian	AIAN	Hisp.
Enrollment (%)	100.0	97.2	2.1	0.2	0.1	0.3
Drop-out Rate (%)	1.8	1.8	0.0	0.0	n/a	0.0
H.S. Diplomas (#)	197	194	2	0	0	1

Floyd County

New Albany-Floyd County Con Sch
PO Box 1087 • New Albany, IN 47151-1087
Mailing Address: 2813 Grant Line PO Box 1087 • New Albany, IN 47150-1087
(812) 949-4200 • http://www.nafcs.k12.in.us/
Grade Span: PK-12; **Agency Type:** 1
Schools: 18
   13 Primary; 2 Middle; 2 High; 1 Other Level
   17 Regular; 0 Special Education; 1 Vocational; 0 Alternative
   0 Magnet; 0 Charter; 11 Title I Eligible; 4 School-wide Title I
Students: 11,253   (51.3% male; 48.6% female)
   Individual Education Program: 2,119 (18.8%);
   English Language Learner: 152 (1.4%); Migrant: n/a
   Eligible for Free Lunch Program: 2,839 (25.2%)
   Eligible for Reduced-Price Lunch Program: 671 (6.0%)
Teachers: 630.3 (17.9 to 1)
Librarians/Media Specialists: 5.0 (2,250.6 to 1)
Guidance Counselors: 32.5 (346.2 to 1)
Current Spending: ($ per student per year):
   Total: $8,176; Instruction: $5,209; Support Services: $2,647
Enrollment, Drop-out Rates and Diploma Recipients by Race/Ethnicity

Category	Total	White	Black	Asian	AIAN	Hisp.
Enrollment (%)	100.0	90.9	7.0	1.0	0.1	1.1
Drop-out Rate (%)	2.8	2.9	1.8	0.0	0.0	0.0
H.S. Diplomas (#)	660	611	42	2	0	5

Franklin County

Franklin County Com Sch Corp
1020 Franklin Ave • Brookville, IN 47012-0309
(765) 647-4128 • http://fcsc.k12.in.us/
Grade Span: PK-12; **Agency Type:** 1
Schools: 5
   3 Primary; 1 Middle; 1 High; 0 Other Level
   5 Regular; 0 Special Education; 0 Vocational; 0 Alternative
   0 Magnet; 0 Charter; 2 Title I Eligible; 1 School-wide Title I
Students: 3,048   (50.5% male; 49.4% female)
   Individual Education Program: 513 (16.8%);
   English Language Learner: n/a; Migrant: n/a
   Eligible for Free Lunch Program: 747 (24.5%)

Eligible for Reduced-Price Lunch Program: 278 (9.1%)
Teachers: 159.2 (19.1 to 1)
Librarians/Media Specialists: 2.7 (1,128.9 to 1)
Guidance Counselors: 5.0 (609.6 to 1)
Current Spending: ($ per student per year):
   Total: $6,943; Instruction: $4,183; Support Services: $2,455
Enrollment, Drop-out Rates and Diploma Recipients by Race/Ethnicity

Category	Total	White	Black	Asian	AIAN	Hisp.
Enrollment (%)	100.0	99.7	0.1	0.1	0.0	0.1
Drop-out Rate (%)	2.4	2.4	n/a	0.0	n/a	0.0
H.S. Diplomas (#)	207	207	0	0	0	0

Fulton County

Rochester Community Sch Corp
690 Zebra Ln • Rochester, IN 46975-0108
Mailing Address: 690 Zebra Ln Box 108 • Rochester, IN 46975-0108
(574) 223-2159 • http://www.rochester.k12.in.us/
Grade Span: PK-12; **Agency Type:** 1
Schools: 4
   2 Primary; 1 Middle; 1 High; 0 Other Level
   4 Regular; 0 Special Education; 0 Vocational; 0 Alternative
   0 Magnet; 0 Charter; 2 Title I Eligible; 0 School-wide Title I
Students: 2,013   (52.6% male; 47.3% female)
   Individual Education Program: 299 (14.9%);
   English Language Learner: 31 (1.5%); Migrant: n/a
   Eligible for Free Lunch Program: 473 (23.5%)
   Eligible for Reduced-Price Lunch Program: 153 (7.6%)
Teachers: 105.0 (19.2 to 1)
Librarians/Media Specialists: 3.0 (671.0 to 1)
Guidance Counselors: 3.0 (671.0 to 1)
Current Spending: ($ per student per year):
   Total: $6,809; Instruction: $4,083; Support Services: $2,371
Enrollment, Drop-out Rates and Diploma Recipients by Race/Ethnicity

Category	Total	White	Black	Asian	AIAN	Hisp.
Enrollment (%)	100.0	96.8	0.9	1.1	0.2	0.9
Drop-out Rate (%)	1.5	1.5	0.0	0.0	0.0	0.0
H.S. Diplomas (#)	135	132	0	1	0	2

Gibson County

North Gibson School Corp
RR 5 Box 49 • Princeton, IN 47670-9405
(812) 385-4851 • http://www.ngsc.k12.in.us/
Grade Span: KG-12; **Agency Type:** 1
Schools: 4
   2 Primary; 1 Middle; 1 High; 0 Other Level
   4 Regular; 0 Special Education; 0 Vocational; 0 Alternative
   0 Magnet; 0 Charter; 3 Title I Eligible; 0 School-wide Title I
Students: 2,080   (50.3% male; 49.6% female)
   Individual Education Program: 407 (19.6%);
   English Language Learner: 12 (0.6%); Migrant: n/a
   Eligible for Free Lunch Program: 518 (24.9%)
   Eligible for Reduced-Price Lunch Program: 193 (9.3%)
Teachers: 116.3 (17.9 to 1)
Librarians/Media Specialists: 1.5 (1,386.7 to 1)
Guidance Counselors: 2.5 (832.0 to 1)
Current Spending: ($ per student per year):
   Total: $7,447; Instruction: $4,327; Support Services: $2,763
Enrollment, Drop-out Rates and Diploma Recipients by Race/Ethnicity

Category	Total	White	Black	Asian	AIAN	Hisp.
Enrollment (%)	100.0	93.9	4.9	0.2	0.3	0.6
Drop-out Rate (%)	3.6	3.9	0.0	0.0	n/a	0.0
H.S. Diplomas (#)	140	129	8	1	0	2

South Gibson School Corp
204 W Vine St • Fort Branch, IN 47648-1099
(812) 753-4230 • http://www.sgibson.k12.in.us/
Grade Span: KG-12; **Agency Type:** 1
Schools: 4
   3 Primary; 0 Middle; 1 High; 0 Other Level
   4 Regular; 0 Special Education; 0 Vocational; 0 Alternative
   0 Magnet; 0 Charter; 2 Title I Eligible; 0 School-wide Title I
Students: 1,857   (49.7% male; 50.2% female)
   Individual Education Program: 313 (16.9%);
   English Language Learner: 2 (0.1%); Migrant: n/a
   Eligible for Free Lunch Program: 171 (9.2%)
   Eligible for Reduced-Price Lunch Program: 105 (5.7%)
Teachers: 99.8 (18.6 to 1)
Librarians/Media Specialists: 1.0 (1,857.0 to 1)
Guidance Counselors: 2.0 (928.5 to 1)
Current Spending: ($ per student per year):
   Total: $6,799; Instruction: $4,428; Support Services: $2,026

Enrollment, Drop-out Rates and Diploma Recipients by Race/Ethnicity

Category	Total	White	Black	Asian	AIAN	Hisp.
Enrollment (%)	100.0	99.3	0.0	0.6	0.1	0.1
Drop-out Rate (%)	2.5	2.5	0.0	n/a	n/a	0.0
H.S. Diplomas (#)	145	144	0	0	0	1

Grant County

Eastbrook Community Sch Corp
Cr 560 S 900 E • Marion, IN 46953-9699
(765) 664-0624 • http://www.eastbrook.k12.in.us/
Grade Span: KG-12; **Agency Type:** 1
Schools: 6
　4 Primary; 1 Middle; 1 High; 0 Other Level
　6 Regular; 0 Special Education; 0 Vocational; 0 Alternative
　0 Magnet; 0 Charter; 3 Title I Eligible; 0 School-wide Title I
Students: 1,784　(49.4% male; 50.5% female)
　Individual Education Program: 299 (16.8%);
　English Language Learner: 7 (0.4%); Migrant: n/a
　Eligible for Free Lunch Program: 299 (16.8%)
　Eligible for Reduced-Price Lunch Program: 165 (9.2%)
Teachers: 104.5 (17.1 to 1)
Librarians/Media Specialists: 2.0 (892.0 to 1)
Guidance Counselors: 4.0 (446.0 to 1)
Current Spending: ($ per student per year):
　Total: $6,273; Instruction: $3,754; Support Services: $2,253
Enrollment, Drop-out Rates and Diploma Recipients by Race/Ethnicity

Category	Total	White	Black	Asian	AIAN	Hisp.
Enrollment (%)	100.0	98.5	0.1	0.3	0.3	0.7
Drop-out Rate (%)	0.0	0.0	n/a	0.0	n/a	0.0
H.S. Diplomas (#)	94	91	0	1	0	2

Madison-Grant United Sch Corp
11580 SE 00 W • Fairmount, IN 46928-9318
(765) 948-4143 • http://www.mgusc.k12.in.us/
Grade Span: PK-12; **Agency Type:** 1
Schools: 5
　3 Primary; 1 Middle; 1 High; 0 Other Level
　5 Regular; 0 Special Education; 0 Vocational; 0 Alternative
　0 Magnet; 0 Charter; 3 Title I Eligible; 0 School-wide Title I
Students: 1,620　(51.2% male; 48.7% female)
　Individual Education Program: 232 (14.3%);
　English Language Learner: 14 (0.9%); Migrant: n/a
　Eligible for Free Lunch Program: 343 (21.2%)
　Eligible for Reduced-Price Lunch Program: 117 (7.2%)
Teachers: 103.2 (15.7 to 1)
Librarians/Media Specialists: 1.7 (952.9 to 1)
Guidance Counselors: 3.0 (540.0 to 1)
Current Spending: ($ per student per year):
　Total: $7,020; Instruction: $4,240; Support Services: $2,435
Enrollment, Drop-out Rates and Diploma Recipients by Race/Ethnicity

Category	Total	White	Black	Asian	AIAN	Hisp.
Enrollment (%)	100.0	98.5	0.1	0.0	0.1	1.3
Drop-out Rate (%)	0.5	0.5	n/a	n/a	0.0	0.0
H.S. Diplomas (#)	81	80	0	0	1	0

Marion Community Schools
1240 S Adams St • Marion, IN 46953-2327
Mailing Address: 1240 S Adams PO Box 2020 • Marion, IN 46952-8420
(765) 662-2546 • http://www.mcslink.net/
Grade Span: PK-12; **Agency Type:** 1
Schools: 14
　7 Primary; 3 Middle; 1 High; 3 Other Level
　10 Regular; 1 Special Education; 1 Vocational; 2 Alternative
　0 Magnet; 0 Charter; 7 Title I Eligible; 5 School-wide Title I
Students: 5,689　(51.0% male; 48.9% female)
　Individual Education Program: 911 (16.0%);
　English Language Learner: 167 (2.9%); Migrant: n/a
　Eligible for Free Lunch Program: 2,454 (43.1%)
　Eligible for Reduced-Price Lunch Program: 425 (7.5%)
Teachers: 373.5 (15.2 to 1)
Librarians/Media Specialists: 3.0 (1,896.3 to 1)
Guidance Counselors: 8.0 (711.1 to 1)
Current Spending: ($ per student per year):
　Total: $8,951; Instruction: $5,316; Support Services: $3,317
Enrollment, Drop-out Rates and Diploma Recipients by Race/Ethnicity

Category	Total	White	Black	Asian	AIAN	Hisp.
Enrollment (%)	100.0	69.8	23.9	0.8	0.2	5.3
Drop-out Rate (%)	6.2	5.8	7.3	0.0	0.0	10.0
H.S. Diplomas (#)	271	198	62	4	0	7

Mississinewa Community School Corp
424 E S 'a' St • Gas City, IN 46933
(765) 674-8528 • http://www.olemiss.k12.in.us/
Grade Span: PK-12; **Agency Type:** 1
Schools: 4
　2 Primary; 1 Middle; 1 High; 0 Other Level
　4 Regular; 0 Special Education; 0 Vocational; 0 Alternative
　0 Magnet; 0 Charter; 3 Title I Eligible; 1 School-wide Title I
Students: 2,172　(53.5% male; 46.4% female)
　Individual Education Program: 370 (17.0%);
　English Language Learner: 11 (0.5%); Migrant: n/a
　Eligible for Free Lunch Program: 662 (30.5%)
　Eligible for Reduced-Price Lunch Program: 244 (11.2%)
Teachers: 135.5 (16.0 to 1)
Librarians/Media Specialists: 2.0 (1,086.0 to 1)
Guidance Counselors: 4.0 (543.0 to 1)
Current Spending: ($ per student per year):
　Total: $7,221; Instruction: $4,422; Support Services: $2,509
Enrollment, Drop-out Rates and Diploma Recipients by Race/Ethnicity

Category	Total	White	Black	Asian	AIAN	Hisp.
Enrollment (%)	100.0	98.2	0.4	0.2	0.2	1.0
Drop-out Rate (%)	1.1	1.1	n/a	0.0	n/a	0.0
H.S. Diplomas (#)	123	122	0	0	0	1

Hamilton County

Carmel Clay Schools
5201 E 131st St • Carmel, IN 46033-9311
(317) 844-9961 • http://www.ccs.k12.in.us/
Grade Span: PK-12; **Agency Type:** 1
Schools: 15
　10 Primary; 2 Middle; 1 High; 2 Other Level
　13 Regular; 2 Special Education; 0 Vocational; 0 Alternative
　0 Magnet; 0 Charter; 5 Title I Eligible; 0 School-wide Title I
Students: 13,514　(50.9% male; 49.0% female)
　Individual Education Program: 1,649 (12.2%);
　English Language Learner: 850 (6.3%); Migrant: n/a
　Eligible for Free Lunch Program: 429 (3.2%)
　Eligible for Reduced-Price Lunch Program: 233 (1.7%)
Teachers: 766.5 (17.6 to 1)
Librarians/Media Specialists: 14.5 (932.0 to 1)
Guidance Counselors: 26.0 (519.8 to 1)
Current Spending: ($ per student per year):
　Total: $7,750; Instruction: $4,917; Support Services: $2,509
Enrollment, Drop-out Rates and Diploma Recipients by Race/Ethnicity

Category	Total	White	Black	Asian	AIAN	Hisp.
Enrollment (%)	100.0	88.7	2.2	7.4	0.0	1.7
Drop-out Rate (%)	0.5	0.5	2.7	0.0	0.0	0.0
H.S. Diplomas (#)	765	699	8	46	2	10

Hamilton Heights School Corp
410 W Main St • Arcadia, IN 46030-0469
Mailing Address: PO Box 469 • Arcadia, IN 46030-0469
(317) 984-3538 • http://www.hhsc.k12.in.us/
Grade Span: PK-12; **Agency Type:** 1
Schools: 4
　2 Primary; 1 Middle; 1 High; 0 Other Level
　4 Regular; 0 Special Education; 0 Vocational; 0 Alternative
　0 Magnet; 0 Charter; 3 Title I Eligible; 0 School-wide Title I
Students: 2,234　(50.7% male; 49.2% female)
　Individual Education Program: 427 (19.1%);
　English Language Learner: 22 (1.0%); Migrant: n/a
　Eligible for Free Lunch Program: 272 (12.2%)
　Eligible for Reduced-Price Lunch Program: 148 (6.6%)
Teachers: 121.8 (18.3 to 1)
Librarians/Media Specialists: 3.0 (744.7 to 1)
Guidance Counselors: 4.7 (475.3 to 1)
Current Spending: ($ per student per year):
　Total: $6,900; Instruction: $4,036; Support Services: $2,550
Enrollment, Drop-out Rates and Diploma Recipients by Race/Ethnicity

Category	Total	White	Black	Asian	AIAN	Hisp.
Enrollment (%)	100.0	98.6	0.3	0.2	0.2	0.8
Drop-out Rate (%)	1.9	1.9	0.0	n/a	0.0	0.0
H.S. Diplomas (#)	145	145	0	0	0	0

Hamilton Southeastern Schools
13485 Cumberland Rd • Fishers, IN 46038-3602
(317) 594-4100 • http://www.hse.k12.in.us/
Grade Span: PK-12; **Agency Type:** 1
Schools: 14
　9 Primary; 4 Middle; 1 High; 0 Other Level
　14 Regular; 0 Special Education; 0 Vocational; 0 Alternative
　0 Magnet; 0 Charter; 8 Title I Eligible; 0 School-wide Title I
Students: 11,710　(51.1% male; 48.8% female)
　Individual Education Program: 1,722 (14.7%);

English Language Learner: 469 (4.0%); Migrant: n/a
Eligible for Free Lunch Program: 520 (4.4%)
Eligible for Reduced-Price Lunch Program: 258 (2.2%)
Teachers: 617.3 (19.0 to 1)
Librarians/Media Specialists: 14.8 (791.2 to 1)
Guidance Counselors: 26.0 (450.4 to 1)
Current Spending: ($ per student per year):
Total: $6,779; Instruction: $3,939; Support Services: $2,541
Enrollment, Drop-out Rates and Diploma Recipients by Race/Ethnicity

Category	Total	White	Black	Asian	AIAN	Hisp.
Enrollment (%)	100.0	89.6	4.6	3.5	0.1	2.1
Drop-out Rate (%)	0.5	0.4	0.0	1.6	0.0	5.8
H.S. Diplomas (#)	434	401	13	11	0	9

Noblesville Schools

1775 Field Dr • Noblesville, IN 46060-1797
(317) 773-3171 • http://www.nobl.k12.in.us/
Grade Span: PK-12; **Agency Type:** 1
Schools: 9
6 Primary; 2 Middle; 1 High; 0 Other Level
9 Regular; 0 Special Education; 0 Vocational; 0 Alternative
0 Magnet; 0 Charter; 5 Title I Eligible; 0 School-wide Title I
Students: 7,144   (51.6% male; 48.3% female)
Individual Education Program: 1,226 (17.2%);
English Language Learner: 109 (1.5%); Migrant: n/a
Eligible for Free Lunch Program: 769 (10.8%)
Eligible for Reduced-Price Lunch Program: 293 (4.1%)
Teachers: 386.3 (18.5 to 1)
Librarians/Media Specialists: 10.0 (714.4 to 1)
Guidance Counselors: 14.5 (492.7 to 1)
Current Spending: ($ per student per year):
Total: $7,114; Instruction: $4,332; Support Services: $2,467
Enrollment, Drop-out Rates and Diploma Recipients by Race/Ethnicity

Category	Total	White	Black	Asian	AIAN	Hisp.
Enrollment (%)	100.0	96.0	1.0	1.1	0.2	1.7
Drop-out Rate (%)	2.0	2.0	5.9	0.0	0.0	0.0
H.S. Diplomas (#)	401	389	1	10	0	1

Westfield-Washington Schools

322 W Main St • Westfield, IN 46074-9384
(317) 867-8000 • http://www.wws.k12.in.us/
Grade Span: PK-12; **Agency Type:** 1
Schools: 7
4 Primary; 2 Middle; 1 High; 0 Other Level
7 Regular; 0 Special Education; 0 Vocational; 0 Alternative
0 Magnet; 0 Charter; 1 Title I Eligible; 0 School-wide Title I
Students: 4,687   (51.5% male; 48.4% female)
Individual Education Program: 737 (15.7%);
English Language Learner: 92 (2.0%); Migrant: n/a
Eligible for Free Lunch Program: 410 (8.7%)
Eligible for Reduced-Price Lunch Program: 250 (5.3%)
Teachers: 258.9 (18.1 to 1)
Librarians/Media Specialists: 7.0 (669.6 to 1)
Guidance Counselors: 9.0 (520.8 to 1)
Current Spending: ($ per student per year):
Total: $7,258; Instruction: $3,813; Support Services: $3,144
Enrollment, Drop-out Rates and Diploma Recipients by Race/Ethnicity

Category	Total	White	Black	Asian	AIAN	Hisp.
Enrollment (%)	100.0	94.1	1.3	1.4	0.1	3.1
Drop-out Rate (%)	0.0	0.0	0.0	0.0	n/a	0.0
H.S. Diplomas (#)	233	221	1	9	0	2

Hancock County

Greenfield-Central Com Schools

110 W N St • Greenfield, IN 46140-2172
(317) 462-4434 • http://gcsc.k12.in.us/
Grade Span: PK-12; **Agency Type:** 1
Schools: 8
4 Primary; 2 Middle; 1 High; 1 Other Level
7 Regular; 1 Special Education; 0 Vocational; 0 Alternative
0 Magnet; 0 Charter; 4 Title I Eligible; 0 School-wide Title I
Students: 4,154   (51.2% male; 48.7% female)
Individual Education Program: 876 (21.1%);
English Language Learner: 7 (0.2%); Migrant: n/a
Eligible for Free Lunch Program: 576 (13.9%)
Eligible for Reduced-Price Lunch Program: 234 (5.6%)
Teachers: 321.0 (12.9 to 1)
Librarians/Media Specialists: 2.0 (2,077.0 to 1)
Guidance Counselors: 6.0 (692.3 to 1)
Current Spending: ($ per student per year):
Total: $8,635; Instruction: $5,547; Support Services: $2,783

Enrollment, Drop-out Rates and Diploma Recipients by Race/Ethnicity

Category	Total	White	Black	Asian	AIAN	Hisp.
Enrollment (%)	100.0	98.7	0.1	0.4	0.1	0.6
Drop-out Rate (%)	1.1	1.1	0.0	0.0	0.0	0.0
H.S. Diplomas (#)	238	238	0	0	0	0

Mt Vernon Community Sch Corp

One Shoppell Blvd • Fortville, IN 46040-9707
Mailing Address: 1 Shoppell Blvd 1776 W Sr 234 • Fortville, IN 46040-9707
(317) 485-3100 • http://www.mvcsc.k12.in.us/
Grade Span: PK-12; **Agency Type:** 1
Schools: 5
2 Primary; 2 Middle; 1 High; 0 Other Level
5 Regular; 0 Special Education; 0 Vocational; 0 Alternative
0 Magnet; 0 Charter; 2 Title I Eligible; 0 School-wide Title I
Students: 3,029   (51.7% male; 48.2% female)
Individual Education Program: 517 (17.1%)
English Language Learner: 15 (0.5%); Migrant: n/a
Eligible for Free Lunch Program: 186 (6.1%)
Eligible for Reduced-Price Lunch Program: 127 (4.2%)
Teachers: 148.5 (20.4 to 1)
Librarians/Media Specialists: 3.0 (1,009.7 to 1)
Guidance Counselors: 6.0 (504.8 to 1)
Current Spending: ($ per student per year):
Total: $6,479; Instruction: $3,993; Support Services: $2,193
Enrollment, Drop-out Rates and Diploma Recipients by Race/Ethnicity

Category	Total	White	Black	Asian	AIAN	Hisp.
Enrollment (%)	100.0	93.5	4.4	0.5	0.2	1.5
Drop-out Rate (%)	1.0	1.0	0.0	0.0	0.0	0.0
H.S. Diplomas (#)	183	179	2	0	0	2

Southern Hancock County Com Sch Corp

4711 S 500 W • New Palestine, IN 46163-0508
Mailing Address: PO Box 508 • New Palestine, IN 46163-0508
(317) 861-4463 • http://www.kiva.net/~shancock/
Grade Span: PK-12; **Agency Type:** 1
Schools: 5
3 Primary; 1 Middle; 1 High; 0 Other Level
5 Regular; 0 Special Education; 0 Vocational; 0 Alternative
0 Magnet; 0 Charter; 2 Title I Eligible; 0 School-wide Title I
Students: 2,945   (50.5% male; 49.4% female)
Individual Education Program: 505 (17.1%);
English Language Learner: 1 (<0.1%); Migrant: n/a
Eligible for Free Lunch Program: 179 (6.1%)
Eligible for Reduced-Price Lunch Program: 59 (2.0%)
Teachers: 143.5 (20.5 to 1)
Librarians/Media Specialists: 3.7 (795.9 to 1)
Guidance Counselors: 4.0 (736.3 to 1)
Current Spending: ($ per student per year):
Total: $6,203; Instruction: $3,600; Support Services: $2,240
Enrollment, Drop-out Rates and Diploma Recipients by Race/Ethnicity

Category	Total	White	Black	Asian	AIAN	Hisp.
Enrollment (%)	100.0	98.6	0.2	0.4	0.2	0.5
Drop-out Rate (%)	1.0	1.0	n/a	0.0	n/a	0.0
H.S. Diplomas (#)	182	179	0	2	0	1

Harrison County

North Harrison Com School Corp

1260 Hwy 64 NW • Ramsey, IN 47166-0008
(812) 347-2407 • http://nhcs.k12.in.us/
Grade Span: KG-12; **Agency Type:** 1
Schools: 5
2 Primary; 1 Middle; 1 High; 1 Other Level
5 Regular; 0 Special Education; 0 Vocational; 0 Alternative
0 Magnet; 0 Charter; 4 Title I Eligible; 0 School-wide Title I
Students: 2,299   (50.9% male; 49.0% female)
Individual Education Program: 405 (17.6%);
English Language Learner: 6 (0.3%); Migrant: n/a
Eligible for Free Lunch Program: 472 (20.5%)
Eligible for Reduced-Price Lunch Program: 199 (8.7%)
Teachers: 129.5 (17.8 to 1)
Librarians/Media Specialists: 3.8 (605.0 to 1)
Guidance Counselors: 5.5 (418.0 to 1)
Current Spending: ($ per student per year):
Total: $7,535; Instruction: $4,657; Support Services: $2,566
Enrollment, Drop-out Rates and Diploma Recipients by Race/Ethnicity

Category	Total	White	Black	Asian	AIAN	Hisp.
Enrollment (%)	100.0	99.0	0.1	0.1	0.3	0.5
Drop-out Rate (%)	1.8	1.9	0.0	n/a	n/a	0.0
H.S. Diplomas (#)	169	169	0	0	0	0

South Harrison Com Schools
315 S Harrison Dr • Corydon, IN 47112-8417
(812) 738-2168 • http://www.shcsc.k12.in.us/
Grade Span: KG-12; **Agency Type:** 1
Schools: 9
  4 Primary; 2 Middle; 2 High; 1 Other Level
  8 Regular; 1 Special Education; 0 Vocational; 0 Alternative
  0 Magnet; 0 Charter; 5 Title I Eligible; 0 School-wide Title I
Students: 3,185 (51.4% male; 48.5% female)
  Individual Education Program: 604 (19.0%);
  English Language Learner: 22 (0.7%); Migrant: n/a
  Eligible for Free Lunch Program: 662 (20.8%)
  Eligible for Reduced-Price Lunch Program: 300 (9.4%)
Teachers: 187.5 (17.0 to 1)
Librarians/Media Specialists: 0.0 (n/a to 1)
Guidance Counselors: 8.0 (398.1 to 1)
Current Spending: ($ per student per year):
  Total: $7,321; Instruction: $4,412; Support Services: $2,592
Enrollment, Drop-out Rates and Diploma Recipients by Race/Ethnicity

Category	Total	White	Black	Asian	AIAN	Hisp.
Enrollment (%)	100.0	98.2	0.3	0.4	0.1	1.0
Drop-out Rate (%)	0.8	0.8	0.0	0.0	n/a	0.0
H.S. Diplomas (#)	193	192	0	0	0	1

Hendricks County

Avon Community School Corp
7203 E US Hwy 36 • Avon, IN 46123
(317) 272-2920 • http://www.avon.k12.in.us/
Grade Span: KG-12; **Agency Type:** 1
Schools: 8
  5 Primary; 2 Middle; 1 High; 0 Other Level
  8 Regular; 0 Special Education; 0 Vocational; 0 Alternative
  0 Magnet; 0 Charter; 4 Title I Eligible; 0 School-wide Title I
Students: 6,350 (51.0% male; 48.9% female)
  Individual Education Program: 977 (15.4%);
  English Language Learner: 92 (1.4%); Migrant: n/a
  Eligible for Free Lunch Program: 488 (7.7%)
  Eligible for Reduced-Price Lunch Program: 233 (3.7%)
Teachers: 330.5 (19.2 to 1)
Librarians/Media Specialists: 8.0 (793.8 to 1)
Guidance Counselors: 14.0 (453.6 to 1)
Current Spending: ($ per student per year):
  Total: $6,974; Instruction: $3,781; Support Services: $2,920
Enrollment, Drop-out Rates and Diploma Recipients by Race/Ethnicity

Category	Total	White	Black	Asian	AIAN	Hisp.
Enrollment (%)	100.0	92.4	3.4	1.7	0.2	2.3
Drop-out Rate (%)	0.0	0.0	0.0	0.0	0.0	0.0
H.S. Diplomas (#)	298	274	4	13	0	7

Brownsburg Community Sch Corp
444 E Tilden Dr • Brownsburg, IN 46112-1498
(317) 852-5726 • http://www.brownsburg.k12.in.us/
Grade Span: PK-12; **Agency Type:** 1
Schools: 7
  5 Primary; 1 Middle; 1 High; 0 Other Level
  7 Regular; 0 Special Education; 0 Vocational; 0 Alternative
  0 Magnet; 0 Charter; 4 Title I Eligible; 0 School-wide Title I
Students: 5,899 (50.8% male; 49.1% female)
  Individual Education Program: 703 (11.9%);
  English Language Learner: 119 (2.0%); Migrant: n/a
  Eligible for Free Lunch Program: 395 (6.7%)
  Eligible for Reduced-Price Lunch Program: 294 (5.0%)
Teachers: 315.0 (18.7 to 1)
Librarians/Media Specialists: 7.0 (842.7 to 1)
Guidance Counselors: 12.0 (491.6 to 1)
Current Spending: ($ per student per year):
  Total: $6,876; Instruction: $3,984; Support Services: $2,559
Enrollment, Drop-out Rates and Diploma Recipients by Race/Ethnicity

Category	Total	White	Black	Asian	AIAN	Hisp.
Enrollment (%)	100.0	94.3	2.6	1.5	0.2	1.5
Drop-out Rate (%)	0.6	0.4	25.0	0.0	n/a	7.7
H.S. Diplomas (#)	378	354	20	3	0	1

Danville Community School Corp
200 Warrior Way • Danville, IN 46122-0469
(317) 745-2212 • http://www.danville.k12.in.us/
Grade Span: PK-12; **Agency Type:** 1
Schools: 4
  1 Primary; 2 Middle; 1 High; 0 Other Level
  4 Regular; 0 Special Education; 0 Vocational; 0 Alternative
  0 Magnet; 0 Charter; 3 Title I Eligible; 0 School-wide Title I
Students: 2,326 (50.1% male; 49.8% female)
  Individual Education Program: 325 (14.0%);
  English Language Learner: 13 (0.6%); Migrant: n/a

Eligible for Free Lunch Program: 235 (10.1%)
Eligible for Reduced-Price Lunch Program: 157 (6.7%)
Teachers: 125.0 (18.6 to 1)
Librarians/Media Specialists: 2.0 (1,163.0 to 1)
Guidance Counselors: 3.0 (775.3 to 1)
Current Spending: ($ per student per year):
  Total: $6,843; Instruction: $3,817; Support Services: $2,686
Enrollment, Drop-out Rates and Diploma Recipients by Race/Ethnicity

Category	Total	White	Black	Asian	AIAN	Hisp.
Enrollment (%)	100.0	98.8	0.1	0.0	0.1	1.0
Drop-out Rate (%)	0.0	0.0	0.0	0.0	n/a	0.0
H.S. Diplomas (#)	151	151	0	0	0	0

Mill Creek Community Sch Corp
6631 S Cr 200 W • Clayton, IN 46118-4906
(317) 539-9200
Grade Span: PK-12; **Agency Type:** 1
Schools: 4
  2 Primary; 1 Middle; 1 High; 0 Other Level
  4 Regular; 0 Special Education; 0 Vocational; 0 Alternative
  0 Magnet; 0 Charter; 3 Title I Eligible; 0 School-wide Title I
Students: 1,567 (50.6% male; 49.3% female)
  Individual Education Program: 288 (18.4%);
  English Language Learner: 3 (0.2%); Migrant: n/a
  Eligible for Free Lunch Program: 187 (11.9%)
  Eligible for Reduced-Price Lunch Program: 86 (5.5%)
Teachers: 94.2 (16.6 to 1)
Librarians/Media Specialists: 1.0 (1,567.0 to 1)
Guidance Counselors: 3.0 (522.3 to 1)
Current Spending: ($ per student per year):
  Total: $6,764; Instruction: $3,829; Support Services: $2,792
Enrollment, Drop-out Rates and Diploma Recipients by Race/Ethnicity

Category	Total	White	Black	Asian	AIAN	Hisp.
Enrollment (%)	100.0	99.6	0.2	0.1	0.0	0.1
Drop-out Rate (%)	1.0	1.0	n/a	0.0	0.0	0.0
H.S. Diplomas (#)	77	77	0	0	0	0

North West Hendricks Schools
104 N Church St • Lizton, IN 46149-0070
Mailing Address: Box 70 • Lizton, IN 46149-0070
(317) 994-4100
Grade Span: PK-12; **Agency Type:** 1
Schools: 4
  2 Primary; 1 Middle; 1 High; 0 Other Level
  4 Regular; 0 Special Education; 0 Vocational; 0 Alternative
  0 Magnet; 0 Charter; 2 Title I Eligible; 0 School-wide Title I
Students: 1,577 (50.0% male; 49.9% female)
  Individual Education Program: 238 (15.1%);
  English Language Learner: n/a; Migrant: n/a
  Eligible for Free Lunch Program: 103 (6.5%)
  Eligible for Reduced-Price Lunch Program: 97 (6.2%)
Teachers: 93.0 (17.0 to 1)
Librarians/Media Specialists: 2.0 (788.5 to 1)
Guidance Counselors: 4.0 (394.3 to 1)
Current Spending: ($ per student per year):
  Total: $7,019; Instruction: $3,783; Support Services: $2,851
Enrollment, Drop-out Rates and Diploma Recipients by Race/Ethnicity

Category	Total	White	Black	Asian	AIAN	Hisp.
Enrollment (%)	100.0	99.0	0.3	0.4	0.1	0.2
Drop-out Rate (%)	1.5	1.5	0.0	n/a	n/a	0.0
H.S. Diplomas (#)	88	86	1	0	0	1

Plainfield Community Sch Corp
985 S Longfellow Dr • Plainfield, IN 46168-1443
(317) 839-2578 • http://www.plainfield.k12.in.us/
Grade Span: PK-12; **Agency Type:** 1
Schools: 6
  4 Primary; 1 Middle; 1 High; 0 Other Level
  6 Regular; 0 Special Education; 0 Vocational; 0 Alternative
  0 Magnet; 0 Charter; 4 Title I Eligible; 0 School-wide Title I
Students: 4,048 (50.5% male; 49.4% female)
  Individual Education Program: 603 (14.9%);
  English Language Learner: 55 (1.4%); Migrant: n/a
  Eligible for Free Lunch Program: 556 (13.7%)
  Eligible for Reduced-Price Lunch Program: 245 (6.1%)
Teachers: 204.8 (19.8 to 1)
Librarians/Media Specialists: 5.0 (809.6 to 1)
Guidance Counselors: 6.0 (674.7 to 1)
Current Spending: ($ per student per year):
  Total: $6,969; Instruction: $4,430; Support Services: $2,223
Enrollment, Drop-out Rates and Diploma Recipients by Race/Ethnicity

Category	Total	White	Black	Asian	AIAN	Hisp.
Enrollment (%)	100.0	96.1	0.8	1.5	0.2	1.4
Drop-out Rate (%)	0.2	0.3	0.0	0.0	n/a	0.0
H.S. Diplomas (#)	272	267	0	3	0	2

Henry County

New Castle Community Sch Corp
322 Elliott Ave • New Castle, IN 47362-4878
(765) 521-7201 • http://nccsc.k12.in.us/
Grade Span: PK-12; **Agency Type:** 1
Schools: 11
  7 Primary; 1 Middle; 2 High; 1 Other Level
  9 Regular; 0 Special Education; 1 Vocational; 1 Alternative
  0 Charter; 6 Title I Eligible; 3 School-wide Title I
Students: 3,882   (50.9% male; 49.0% female)
  Individual Education Program: 997 (25.7%);
  English Language Learner: 5 (0.1%); Migrant: n/a
  Eligible for Free Lunch Program: 1,286 (33.1%)
  Eligible for Reduced-Price Lunch Program: 302 (7.8%)
Teachers: 279.0 (13.9 to 1)
Librarians/Media Specialists: 2.0 (1,941.0 to 1)
Guidance Counselors: 6.0 (647.0 to 1)
Current Spending: ($ per student per year):
  Total: $9,819; Instruction: $6,420; Support Services: $3,044
Enrollment, Drop-out Rates and Diploma Recipients by Race/Ethnicity

Category	Total	White	Black	Asian	AIAN	Hisp.
Enrollment (%)	100.0	96.7	1.6	0.5	0.2	1.0
Drop-out Rate (%)	2.5	2.6	0.0	0.0	n/a	0.0
H.S. Diplomas (#)	235	230	5	0	0	0

Howard County

Kokomo-Center Twp Con Sch Corp
100 W Lincoln • Kokomo, IN 46904-2188
Mailing Address: PO Box 2188 • Kokomo, IN 46904-2188
(765) 455-8000 • http://www.kokomo.k12.in.us/
Grade Span: PK-12; **Agency Type:** 1
Schools: 17
  10 Primary; 4 Middle; 1 High; 2 Other Level
  16 Regular; 0 Special Education; 1 Vocational; 0 Alternative
  0 Magnet; 0 Charter; 9 Title I Eligible; 7 School-wide Title I
Students: 6,987   (50.3% male; 49.6% female)
  Individual Education Program: 1,679 (24.0%);
  English Language Learner: 121 (1.7%); Migrant: n/a
  Eligible for Free Lunch Program: 2,762 (39.5%)
  Eligible for Reduced-Price Lunch Program: 566 (8.1%)
Teachers: 502.0 (13.9 to 1)
Librarians/Media Specialists: 6.0 (1,164.5 to 1)
Guidance Counselors: 10.0 (698.7 to 1)
Current Spending: ($ per student per year):
  Total: $9,765; Instruction: $5,727; Support Services: $3,698
Enrollment, Drop-out Rates and Diploma Recipients by Race/Ethnicity

Category	Total	White	Black	Asian	AIAN	Hisp.
Enrollment (%)	100.0	79.6	16.3	1.1	0.4	2.6
Drop-out Rate (%)	0.0	0.0	0.0	0.0	0.0	0.0
H.S. Diplomas (#)	367	297	55	3	1	11

Northwestern School Corp
4154 W Rd 350 N • Kokomo, IN 46901-9121
(765) 454-2321 • http://www.nwsc.k12.in.us/
Grade Span: KG-12; **Agency Type:** 1
Schools: 4
  2 Primary; 1 Middle; 1 High; 0 Other Level
  4 Regular; 0 Special Education; 0 Vocational; 0 Alternative
  0 Magnet; 0 Charter; 3 Title I Eligible; 0 School-wide Title I
Students: 1,679   (52.8% male; 47.1% female)
  Individual Education Program: 278 (16.6%);
  English Language Learner: 23 (1.4%); Migrant: n/a
  Eligible for Free Lunch Program: 133 (7.9%)
  Eligible for Reduced-Price Lunch Program: 48 (2.9%)
Teachers: 103.9 (16.2 to 1)
Librarians/Media Specialists: 2.0 (839.5 to 1)
Guidance Counselors: 3.0 (559.7 to 1)
Current Spending: ($ per student per year):
  Total: $7,930; Instruction: $4,863; Support Services: $2,763
Enrollment, Drop-out Rates and Diploma Recipients by Race/Ethnicity

Category	Total	White	Black	Asian	AIAN	Hisp.
Enrollment (%)	100.0	95.9	1.3	1.1	0.1	1.5
Drop-out Rate (%)	1.4	1.4	0.0	0.0	n/a	0.0
H.S. Diplomas (#)	127	126	1	0	0	0

Taylor Community School Corp
3750 E Cr 300 S • Kokomo, IN 46902-9509
(765) 453-3035 • http://taylor.in.schoolwebpages.com
Grade Span: KG-12; **Agency Type:** 1
Schools: 4
  2 Primary; 1 Middle; 1 High; 0 Other Level
  4 Regular; 0 Special Education; 0 Vocational; 0 Alternative
  0 Magnet; 0 Charter; 2 Title I Eligible; 0 School-wide Title I
Students: 1,516   (52.0% male; 47.9% female)
  Individual Education Program: 295 (19.5%);
  English Language Learner: 22 (1.5%); Migrant: n/a
  Eligible for Free Lunch Program: 371 (24.5%)
  Eligible for Reduced-Price Lunch Program: 92 (6.1%)
Teachers: 108.5 (14.0 to 1)
Librarians/Media Specialists: 1.0 (1,516.0 to 1)
Guidance Counselors: 2.5 (606.4 to 1)
Current Spending: ($ per student per year):
  Total: $7,859; Instruction: $4,791; Support Services: $2,772
Enrollment, Drop-out Rates and Diploma Recipients by Race/Ethnicity

Category	Total	White	Black	Asian	AIAN	Hisp.
Enrollment (%)	100.0	91.8	4.8	1.6	0.6	1.3
Drop-out Rate (%)	3.8	3.7	0.0	0.0	n/a	20.0
H.S. Diplomas (#)	82	79	1	2	0	0

Western School Corp
600 W 2600 S • Russiaville, IN 46979-0247
(765) 883-5576 • http://www.western.k12.in.us/
Grade Span: KG-12; **Agency Type:** 1
Schools: 4
  2 Primary; 1 Middle; 1 High; 0 Other Level
  4 Regular; 0 Special Education; 0 Vocational; 0 Alternative
  0 Magnet; 0 Charter; 3 Title I Eligible; 0 School-wide Title I
Students: 2,328   (50.6% male; 49.3% female)
  Individual Education Program: 352 (15.1%);
  English Language Learner: 47 (2.0%); Migrant: n/a
  Eligible for Free Lunch Program: 263 (11.3%)
  Eligible for Reduced-Price Lunch Program: 81 (3.5%)
Teachers: 126.2 (18.4 to 1)
Librarians/Media Specialists: 1.0 (2,328.0 to 1)
Guidance Counselors: 4.0 (582.0 to 1)
Current Spending: ($ per student per year):
  Total: $6,202; Instruction: $3,685; Support Services: $2,265
Enrollment, Drop-out Rates and Diploma Recipients by Race/Ethnicity

Category	Total	White	Black	Asian	AIAN	Hisp.
Enrollment (%)	100.0	93.0	3.6	1.4	0.7	1.2
Drop-out Rate (%)	0.9	0.8	0.0	0.0	n/a	12.5
H.S. Diplomas (#)	162	147	10	2	0	3

Huntington County

Huntington County Com Sch Corp
1360 Warren Rd • Huntington, IN 46750-2192
(260) 356-7812 • http://www.hccsc.k12.in.us/
Grade Span: KG-12; **Agency Type:** 1
Schools: 11
  8 Primary; 2 Middle; 1 High; 0 Other Level
  11 Regular; 0 Special Education; 0 Vocational; 0 Alternative
  0 Magnet; 0 Charter; 6 Title I Eligible; 2 School-wide Title I
Students: 6,337   (50.7% male; 49.2% female)
  Individual Education Program: 1,025 (16.2%);
  English Language Learner: 25 (0.4%); Migrant: n/a
  Eligible for Free Lunch Program: 1,156 (18.2%)
  Eligible for Reduced-Price Lunch Program: 577 (9.1%)
Teachers: 387.1 (16.4 to 1)
Librarians/Media Specialists: 3.0 (2,112.3 to 1)
Guidance Counselors: 17.2 (368.4 to 1)
Current Spending: ($ per student per year):
  Total: $7,056; Instruction: $4,495; Support Services: $2,209
Enrollment, Drop-out Rates and Diploma Recipients by Race/Ethnicity

Category	Total	White	Black	Asian	AIAN	Hisp.
Enrollment (%)	100.0	98.5	0.1	0.2	0.4	0.8
Drop-out Rate (%)	0.0	0.0	0.0	0.0	0.0	0.0
H.S. Diplomas (#)	453	452	0	1	0	0

Jackson County

Brownstown Cnt Com Sch Corp
608 W Commerce St • Brownstown, IN 47220
(812) 358-4271 • http://www.btownccs.k12.in.us/
Grade Span: PK-12; **Agency Type:** 1
Schools: 5
  2 Primary; 1 Middle; 1 High; 1 Other Level
  4 Regular; 0 Special Education; 0 Vocational; 1 Alternative
  0 Magnet; 0 Charter; 3 Title I Eligible; 0 School-wide Title I
Students: 1,733   (51.8% male; 48.1% female)
  Individual Education Program: 275 (15.9%);
  English Language Learner: 9 (0.5%); Migrant: n/a
  Eligible for Free Lunch Program: 389 (22.4%)
  Eligible for Reduced-Price Lunch Program: 113 (6.5%)
Teachers: 94.0 (18.4 to 1)
Librarians/Media Specialists: 2.0 (866.5 to 1)
Guidance Counselors: 3.0 (577.7 to 1)

Current Spending: ($ per student per year):
Total: $7,094; Instruction: $4,570; Support Services: $2,253
Enrollment, Drop-out Rates and Diploma Recipients by Race/Ethnicity

Category	Total	White	Black	Asian	AIAN	Hisp.
Enrollment (%)	100.0	99.5	0.1	0.1	0.0	0.3
Drop-out Rate (%)	3.7	3.7	0.0	0.0	n/a	n/a
H.S. Diplomas (#)	115	115	0	0	0	0

Seymour Community Schools
1638 S Walnut St • Seymour, IN 47274-0366
(812) 522-3340 • http://scsc.k12.in.us/
Grade Span: PK-12; **Agency Type:** 1
Schools: 8
　5 Primary; 2 Middle; 1 High; 0 Other Level
　7 Regular; 0 Special Education; 0 Vocational; 1 Alternative
　0 Magnet; 0 Charter; 4 Title I Eligible; 0 School-wide Title I
Students: 3,815　(50.6% male; 49.3% female)
　Individual Education Program: 761 (19.9%);
　English Language Learner: 164 (4.3%); Migrant: n/a
　Eligible for Free Lunch Program: 906 (23.7%)
　Eligible for Reduced-Price Lunch Program: 361 (9.5%)
Teachers: 211.8 (18.0 to 1)
Librarians/Media Specialists: 1.5 (2,543.3 to 1)
Guidance Counselors: 7.0 (545.0 to 1)
Current Spending: ($ per student per year):
Total: $7,615; Instruction: $4,762; Support Services: $2,532
Enrollment, Drop-out Rates and Diploma Recipients by Race/Ethnicity

Category	Total	White	Black	Asian	AIAN	Hisp.
Enrollment (%)	100.0	93.2	1.0	1.6	0.2	4.0
Drop-out Rate (%)	3.8	3.9	0.0	0.0	0.0	8.0
H.S. Diplomas (#)	242	230	1	9	0	2

Jasper County

Kankakee Valley School Corp
12021 N 550 W • Wheatfield, IN 46392-0278
Mailing Address: PO Box 278 • Wheatfield, IN 46392-0278
(219) 987-4711 • http://www.kv.k12.in.us/qguide.htm
Grade Span: KG-12; **Agency Type:** 1
Schools: 5
　2 Primary; 2 Middle; 1 High; 0 Other Level
　5 Regular; 0 Special Education; 0 Vocational; 0 Alternative
　0 Magnet; 0 Charter; 4 Title I Eligible; 0 School-wide Title I
Students: 3,226　(51.6% male; 48.3% female)
　Individual Education Program: 562 (17.4%);
　English Language Learner: 119 (3.7%); Migrant: n/a
　Eligible for Free Lunch Program: 638 (19.8%)
　Eligible for Reduced-Price Lunch Program: 258 (8.0%)
Teachers: 168.0 (19.2 to 1)
Librarians/Media Specialists: 4.0 (806.5 to 1)
Guidance Counselors: 7.0 (460.9 to 1)
Current Spending: ($ per student per year):
Total: $6,944; Instruction: $4,381; Support Services: $2,252
Enrollment, Drop-out Rates and Diploma Recipients by Race/Ethnicity

Category	Total	White	Black	Asian	AIAN	Hisp.
Enrollment (%)	100.0	93.6	0.3	0.5	0.4	5.2
Drop-out Rate (%)	2.4	2.2	0.0	0.0	0.0	9.1
H.S. Diplomas (#)	212	204	1	2	0	5

Rensselaer Central School Corp
605 Grove St • Rensselaer, IN 47978-0069
(219) 866-7822 • http://www.rcsc.k12.in.us/
Grade Span: PK-12; **Agency Type:** 1
Schools: 4
　2 Primary; 1 Middle; 1 High; 0 Other Level
　4 Regular; 0 Special Education; 0 Vocational; 0 Alternative
　0 Magnet; 0 Charter; 3 Title I Eligible; 0 School-wide Title I
Students: 1,781　(53.7% male; 46.2% female)
　Individual Education Program: 350 (19.7%);
　English Language Learner: 38 (2.1%); Migrant: n/a
　Eligible for Free Lunch Program: 388 (21.8%)
　Eligible for Reduced-Price Lunch Program: 158 (8.9%)
Teachers: 107.2 (16.6 to 1)
Librarians/Media Specialists: 1.3 (1,370.0 to 1)
Guidance Counselors: 4.0 (445.3 to 1)
Current Spending: ($ per student per year):
Total: $6,894; Instruction: $4,057; Support Services: $2,510
Enrollment, Drop-out Rates and Diploma Recipients by Race/Ethnicity

Category	Total	White	Black	Asian	AIAN	Hisp.
Enrollment (%)	100.0	96.1	0.4	0.1	0.2	3.2
Drop-out Rate (%)	2.7	2.8	n/a	0.0	0.0	0.0
H.S. Diplomas (#)	98	90	0	3	1	4

Jay County

Jay School Corp
404 E Arch • Portland, IN 47371-3239
Mailing Address: PO Box 1239 • Portland, IN 47371-3239
(260) 726-9341 • http://www.jayschools.k12.in.us/
Grade Span: PK-12; **Agency Type:** 1
Schools: 10
　7 Primary; 2 Middle; 1 High; 0 Other Level
　10 Regular; 0 Special Education; 0 Vocational; 0 Alternative
　0 Magnet; 0 Charter; 5 Title I Eligible; 0 School-wide Title I
Students: 3,888　(52.5% male; 47.4% female)
　Individual Education Program: 653 (16.8%);
　English Language Learner: 98 (2.5%); Migrant: n/a
　Eligible for Free Lunch Program: 1,034 (26.6%)
　Eligible for Reduced-Price Lunch Program: 486 (12.5%)
Teachers: 225.2 (17.3 to 1)
Librarians/Media Specialists: 7.0 (555.4 to 1)
Guidance Counselors: 2.0 (1,944.0 to 1)
Current Spending: ($ per student per year):
Total: $8,590; Instruction: $5,331; Support Services: $2,911
Enrollment, Drop-out Rates and Diploma Recipients by Race/Ethnicity

Category	Total	White	Black	Asian	AIAN	Hisp.
Enrollment (%)	100.0	97.5	0.1	0.4	0.1	2.0
Drop-out Rate (%)	2.2	2.2	n/a	0.0	n/a	5.0
H.S. Diplomas (#)	211	204	0	0	0	7

Jefferson County

Madison Consolidated Schools
2421 Wilson Ave • Madison, IN 47250-2134
(812) 273-8511 • http://www.madisonconsolidatedschools.com/
Grade Span: PK-12; **Agency Type:** 1
Schools: 9
　7 Primary; 1 Middle; 1 High; 0 Other Level
　9 Regular; 0 Special Education; 0 Vocational; 0 Alternative
　0 Magnet; 0 Charter; 6 Title I Eligible; 0 School-wide Title I
Students: 3,503　(51.7% male; 48.2% female)
　Individual Education Program: 843 (24.1%);
　English Language Learner: 37 (1.1%); Migrant: n/a
　Eligible for Free Lunch Program: 1,014 (28.9%)
　Eligible for Reduced-Price Lunch Program: 344 (9.8%)
Teachers: 199.0 (17.6 to 1)
Librarians/Media Specialists: 4.0 (875.8 to 1)
Guidance Counselors: 6.0 (583.8 to 1)
Current Spending: ($ per student per year):
Total: $7,868; Instruction: $4,928; Support Services: $2,615
Enrollment, Drop-out Rates and Diploma Recipients by Race/Ethnicity

Category	Total	White	Black	Asian	AIAN	Hisp.
Enrollment (%)	100.0	97.4	1.3	0.9	0.1	0.4
Drop-out Rate (%)	0.0	0.0	0.0	0.0	0.0	0.0
H.S. Diplomas (#)	176	174	1	1	0	0

Jennings County

Jennings County Schools
34 Main St • North Vernon, IN 47265-1706
(812) 346-4483 • http://www.jcsc.org/
Grade Span: PK-12; **Agency Type:** 1
Schools: 10
　7 Primary; 1 Middle; 2 High; 0 Other Level
　9 Regular; 0 Special Education; 0 Vocational; 1 Alternative
　0 Magnet; 0 Charter; 6 Title I Eligible; 0 School-wide Title I
Students: 5,315　(52.6% male; 47.3% female)
　Individual Education Program: 1,196 (22.5%);
　English Language Learner: 32 (0.6%); Migrant: n/a
　Eligible for Free Lunch Program: 1,617 (30.4%)
　Eligible for Reduced-Price Lunch Program: 564 (10.6%)
Teachers: 280.3 (19.0 to 1)
Librarians/Media Specialists: 2.2 (2,415.9 to 1)
Guidance Counselors: 14.0 (379.6 to 1)
Current Spending: ($ per student per year):
Total: $6,965; Instruction: $4,162; Support Services: $2,513
Enrollment, Drop-out Rates and Diploma Recipients by Race/Ethnicity

Category	Total	White	Black	Asian	AIAN	Hisp.
Enrollment (%)	100.0	97.9	0.6	0.2	0.5	0.8
Drop-out Rate (%)	3.2	3.1	15.4	0.0	11.1	0.0
H.S. Diplomas (#)	234	230	2	1	0	1

Johnson County

Center Grove Com Sch Corp
2929 S Morgantown Rd · Greenwood, IN 46143-9100
(317) 881-9326 · http://www.centergrove.k12.in.us/
Grade Span: KG-12; **Agency Type:** 1
Schools: 9
   6 Primary; 2 Middle; 1 High; 0 Other Level
   9 Regular; 0 Special Education; 0 Vocational; 0 Alternative
   0 Magnet; 0 Charter; 6 Title I Eligible; 0 School-wide Title I
Students: 7,011   (51.4% male; 48.5% female)
   Individual Education Program: 879 (12.5%);
   English Language Learner: 98 (1.4%); Migrant: n/a
   Eligible for Free Lunch Program: 436 (6.2%)
   Eligible for Reduced-Price Lunch Program: 214 (3.1%)
Teachers: 366.6 (19.1 to 1)
Librarians/Media Specialists: 6.0 (1,168.5 to 1)
Guidance Counselors: 15.0 (467.4 to 1)
Current Spending: ($ per student per year):
   Total: $6,406; Instruction: $3,868; Support Services: $2,255
Enrollment, Drop-out Rates and Diploma Recipients by Race/Ethnicity

Category	Total	White	Black	Asian	AIAN	Hisp.
Enrollment (%)	100.0	96.5	0.5	1.6	0.1	1.2
Drop-out Rate (%)	0.8	0.8	0.0	0.0	0.0	0.0
H.S. Diplomas (#)	445	436	1	4	1	3

Clark-Pleasant Com School Corp
50 Center St · Whiteland, IN 46184-1698
(317) 535-7579 · http://www.cpcsc.k12.in.us/
Grade Span: KG-12; **Agency Type:** 1
Schools: 6
   4 Primary; 1 Middle; 1 High; 0 Other Level
   6 Regular; 0 Special Education; 0 Vocational; 0 Alternative
   0 Magnet; 0 Charter; 3 Title I Eligible; 0 School-wide Title I
Students: 3,952   (50.3% male; 49.6% female)
   Individual Education Program: 551 (13.9%);
   English Language Learner: 21 (0.5%); Migrant: n/a
   Eligible for Free Lunch Program: 484 (12.2%)
   Eligible for Reduced-Price Lunch Program: 355 (9.0%)
Teachers: 189.0 (20.9 to 1)
Librarians/Media Specialists: 2.0 (1,976.0 to 1)
Guidance Counselors: 9.0 (439.1 to 1)
Current Spending: ($ per student per year):
   Total: $6,514; Instruction: $3,668; Support Services: $2,538
Enrollment, Drop-out Rates and Diploma Recipients by Race/Ethnicity

Category	Total	White	Black	Asian	AIAN	Hisp.
Enrollment (%)	100.0	97.3	0.2	0.6	0.3	1.6
Drop-out Rate (%)	0.3	0.2	n/a	33.3	0.0	0.0
H.S. Diplomas (#)	178	176	0	0	1	1

Franklin Community School Corp
998 Grizzly Cub Dr · Franklin, IN 46131-1398
(317) 738-5800 · http://fcsc.k12.in.us/
Grade Span: KG-12; **Agency Type:** 1
Schools: 7
   5 Primary; 1 Middle; 1 High; 0 Other Level
   7 Regular; 0 Special Education; 0 Vocational; 0 Alternative
   0 Magnet; 0 Charter; 3 Title I Eligible; 0 School-wide Title I
Students: 4,396   (50.8% male; 49.1% female)
   Individual Education Program: 806 (18.3%);
   English Language Learner: 45 (1.0%); Migrant: n/a
   Eligible for Free Lunch Program: 969 (22.0%)
   Eligible for Reduced-Price Lunch Program: 320 (7.3%)
Teachers: 251.9 (17.5 to 1)
Librarians/Media Specialists: 3.0 (1,465.3 to 1)
Guidance Counselors: 12.0 (366.3 to 1)
Current Spending: ($ per student per year):
   Total: $6,620; Instruction: $4,046; Support Services: $2,226
Enrollment, Drop-out Rates and Diploma Recipients by Race/Ethnicity

Category	Total	White	Black	Asian	AIAN	Hisp.
Enrollment (%)	100.0	96.5	1.2	0.4	0.5	1.5
Drop-out Rate (%)	3.5	3.4	33.3	0.0	0.0	0.0
H.S. Diplomas (#)	208	204	0	1	0	3

Greenwood Community Sch Corp
605 W Smith Valley Rd · Greenwood, IN 46142-0218
(317) 889-4060
Grade Span: KG-12; **Agency Type:** 1
Schools: 6
   4 Primary; 1 Middle; 1 High; 0 Other Level
   6 Regular; 0 Special Education; 0 Vocational; 0 Alternative
   0 Magnet; 0 Charter; 3 Title I Eligible; 0 School-wide Title I
Students: 3,834   (50.6% male; 49.3% female)
   Individual Education Program: 511 (13.3%);
   English Language Learner: 92 (2.4%); Migrant: n/a

   Eligible for Free Lunch Program: 655 (17.1%)
   Eligible for Reduced-Price Lunch Program: 217 (5.7%)
Teachers: 179.5 (21.4 to 1)
Librarians/Media Specialists: 2.0 (1,917.0 to 1)
Guidance Counselors: 5.0 (766.8 to 1)
Current Spending: ($ per student per year):
   Total: $6,584; Instruction: $4,280; Support Services: $2,019
Enrollment, Drop-out Rates and Diploma Recipients by Race/Ethnicity

Category	Total	White	Black	Asian	AIAN	Hisp.
Enrollment (%)	100.0	94.7	1.2	1.5	0.2	2.5
Drop-out Rate (%)	0.5	0.4	0.0	0.0	n/a	10.0
H.S. Diplomas (#)	210	202	0	4	3	1

Nineveh-Hensley-Jackson United
802 S Indian Creek Dr · Trafalgar, IN 46181
(317) 878-2100 · http://www.nhj.k12.in.us/
Grade Span: KG-12; **Agency Type:** 1
Schools: 4
   2 Primary; 1 Middle; 1 High; 0 Other Level
   4 Regular; 0 Special Education; 0 Vocational; 0 Alternative
   0 Magnet; 0 Charter; 2 Title I Eligible; 0 School-wide Title I
Students: 1,828   (52.0% male; 47.9% female)
   Individual Education Program: 254 (13.9%);
   English Language Learner: 3 (0.2%); Migrant: n/a
   Eligible for Free Lunch Program: 184 (10.1%)
   Eligible for Reduced-Price Lunch Program: 81 (4.4%)
Teachers: 103.2 (17.7 to 1)
Librarians/Media Specialists: 3.0 (609.3 to 1)
Guidance Counselors: 4.5 (406.2 to 1)
Current Spending: ($ per student per year):
   Total: $6,595; Instruction: $3,791; Support Services: $2,527
Enrollment, Drop-out Rates and Diploma Recipients by Race/Ethnicity

Category	Total	White	Black	Asian	AIAN	Hisp.
Enrollment (%)	100.0	99.2	0.2	0.3	0.2	0.1
Drop-out Rate (%)	0.6	0.6	n/a	n/a	n/a	n/a
H.S. Diplomas (#)	110	110	0	0	0	0

Knox County

North Knox School Corp
11110 N Sr 159 · Bicknell, IN 47512-9801
(812) 735-4434 · http://www.nknox.k12.in.us/local.htm
Grade Span: KG-12; **Agency Type:** 1
Schools: 5
   3 Primary; 0 Middle; 1 High; 1 Other Level
   4 Regular; 0 Special Education; 0 Vocational; 1 Alternative
   0 Magnet; 0 Charter; 2 Title I Eligible; 1 School-wide Title I
Students: 1,521   (51.4% male; 48.5% female)
   Individual Education Program: 216 (14.2%);
   English Language Learner: n/a; Migrant: n/a
   Eligible for Free Lunch Program: 465 (30.6%)
   Eligible for Reduced-Price Lunch Program: 142 (9.3%)
Teachers: 84.0 (18.1 to 1)
Librarians/Media Specialists: 1.0 (1,521.0 to 1)
Guidance Counselors: 2.0 (760.5 to 1)
Current Spending: ($ per student per year):
   Total: $7,859; Instruction: $5,178; Support Services: $2,371
Enrollment, Drop-out Rates and Diploma Recipients by Race/Ethnicity

Category	Total	White	Black	Asian	AIAN	Hisp.
Enrollment (%)	100.0	99.4	0.2	0.1	0.0	0.3
Drop-out Rate (%)	1.0	1.0	0.0	n/a	n/a	n/a
H.S. Diplomas (#)	103	103	0	0	0	0

Vincennes Community Sch Corp
300 N 6th St · Vincennes, IN 47591-1267
(812) 882-4844 · http://www.vcsc.k12.in.us/
Grade Span: KG-12; **Agency Type:** 1
Schools: 7
   5 Primary; 1 Middle; 1 High; 0 Other Level
   7 Regular; 0 Special Education; 0 Vocational; 0 Alternative
   0 Magnet; 0 Charter; 5 Title I Eligible; 3 School-wide Title I
Students: 3,019   (51.9% male; 48.0% female)
   Individual Education Program: 509 (16.9%);
   English Language Learner: 24 (0.8%); Migrant: n/a
   Eligible for Free Lunch Program: 1,037 (34.3%)
   Eligible for Reduced-Price Lunch Program: 254 (8.4%)
Teachers: 203.9 (14.8 to 1)
Librarians/Media Specialists: 2.0 (1,509.5 to 1)
Guidance Counselors: 4.0 (754.8 to 1)
Current Spending: ($ per student per year):
   Total: $8,050; Instruction: $5,164; Support Services: $2,493

Enrollment, Drop-out Rates and Diploma Recipients by Race/Ethnicity

Category	Total	White	Black	Asian	AIAN	Hisp.
Enrollment (%)	100.0	96.9	1.6	0.7	0.3	0.6
Drop-out Rate (%)	0.0	0.0	0.0	0.0	n/a	0.0
H.S. Diplomas (#)	197	192	2	2	0	1

Kosciusko County

Tippecanoe Valley School Corp
8343 S Sr 19 • Akron, IN 46910
(574) 353-7741 • http://www.tvsc.k12.in.us/
Grade Span: KG-12; **Agency Type:** 1
Schools: 4
  2 Primary; 1 Middle; 1 High; 0 Other Level
  4 Regular; 0 Special Education; 0 Vocational; 0 Alternative
  0 Magnet; 0 Charter; 3 Title I Eligible; 0 School-wide Title I
Students: 2,130 (53.6% male; 46.3% female)
  Individual Education Program: 312 (14.6%);
  English Language Learner: 69 (3.2%); Migrant: n/a
  Eligible for Free Lunch Program: 444 (20.8%)
  Eligible for Reduced-Price Lunch Program: 209 (9.8%)
Teachers: 115.6 (18.4 to 1)
Librarians/Media Specialists: 2.0 (1,065.0 to 1)
Guidance Counselors: 5.0 (426.0 to 1)
Current Spending: ($ per student per year):
  Total: $6,978; Instruction: $4,226; Support Services: $2,414
Enrollment, Drop-out Rates and Diploma Recipients by Race/Ethnicity

Category	Total	White	Black	Asian	AIAN	Hisp.
Enrollment (%)	100.0	95.1	0.2	0.0	0.0	4.7
Drop-out Rate (%)	5.0	4.8	0.0	0.0	n/a	12.5
H.S. Diplomas (#)	135	134	0	0	0	1

Warsaw Community Schools
1 Administration Dr • Warsaw, IN 46581-0288
Mailing Address: 1 Administration Dr Pob 288 • Warsaw, IN 46581-0288
(574) 371-5098 • http://www.warsaw.k12.in.us/
Grade Span: KG-12; **Agency Type:** 1
Schools: 15
  10 Primary; 2 Middle; 2 High; 1 Other Level
  13 Regular; 1 Special Education; 0 Vocational; 1 Alternative
  0 Magnet; 0 Charter; 8 Title I Eligible; 0 School-wide Title I
Students: 6,453 (51.5% male; 48.4% female)
  Individual Education Program: 900 (13.9%);
  English Language Learner: 574 (8.9%); Migrant: n/a
  Eligible for Free Lunch Program: 1,400 (21.7%)
  Eligible for Reduced-Price Lunch Program: 578 (9.0%)
Teachers: 355.2 (18.2 to 1)
Librarians/Media Specialists: 4.0 (1,613.3 to 1)
Guidance Counselors: 6.0 (1,075.5 to 1)
Current Spending: ($ per student per year):
  Total: $8,731; Instruction: $4,984; Support Services: $3,442
Enrollment, Drop-out Rates and Diploma Recipients by Race/Ethnicity

Category	Total	White	Black	Asian	AIAN	Hisp.
Enrollment (%)	100.0	87.2	1.0	1.1	0.1	10.6
Drop-out Rate (%)	3.7	3.9	0.0	0.0	0.0	2.3
H.S. Diplomas (#)	388	362	3	7	2	14

Wawasee Community School Corp
1 Warrior Path - Bldg 2 • Syracuse, IN 46567-9170
(574) 457-3188 • http://www.wawasee.k12.in.us/
Grade Span: KG-12; **Agency Type:** 1
Schools: 5
  3 Primary; 1 Middle; 1 High; 0 Other Level
  5 Regular; 0 Special Education; 0 Vocational; 0 Alternative
  0 Magnet; 0 Charter; 4 Title I Eligible; 0 School-wide Title I
Students: 3,481 (51.1% male; 48.8% female)
  Individual Education Program: 379 (10.9%);
  English Language Learner: 191 (5.5%); Migrant: n/a
  Eligible for Free Lunch Program: 694 (19.9%)
  Eligible for Reduced-Price Lunch Program: 264 (7.6%)
Teachers: 197.0 (17.7 to 1)
Librarians/Media Specialists: 2.0 (1,740.5 to 1)
Guidance Counselors: 8.0 (435.1 to 1)
Current Spending: ($ per student per year):
  Total: $7,584; Instruction: $4,630; Support Services: $2,653
Enrollment, Drop-out Rates and Diploma Recipients by Race/Ethnicity

Category	Total	White	Black	Asian	AIAN	Hisp.
Enrollment (%)	100.0	93.7	0.3	0.4	0.2	5.4
Drop-out Rate (%)	1.7	1.6	0.0	0.0	n/a	n/a
H.S. Diplomas (#)	206	200	0	1	0	5

Whitko Community School Corp
432 S First St • Pierceton, IN 46562-0114
Mailing Address: PO Box 114 • Pierceton, IN 46562-0114
(574) 594-2658 • http://www.whitko.k12.in.us/
Grade Span: PK-12; **Agency Type:** 1
Schools: 4
  2 Primary; 1 Middle; 1 High; 0 Other Level
  4 Regular; 0 Special Education; 0 Vocational; 0 Alternative
  0 Magnet; 0 Charter; 2 Title I Eligible; 0 School-wide Title I
Students: 1,966 (51.1% male; 48.8% female)
  Individual Education Program: 281 (14.3%);
  English Language Learner: 24 (1.2%); Migrant: n/a
  Eligible for Free Lunch Program: 354 (18.0%)
  Eligible for Reduced-Price Lunch Program: 190 (9.7%)
Teachers: 115.5 (17.0 to 1)
Librarians/Media Specialists: 1.0 (1,966.0 to 1)
Guidance Counselors: 6.0 (327.7 to 1)
Current Spending: ($ per student per year):
  Total: $7,229; Instruction: $4,313; Support Services: $2,593
Enrollment, Drop-out Rates and Diploma Recipients by Race/Ethnicity

Category	Total	White	Black	Asian	AIAN	Hisp.
Enrollment (%)	100.0	97.3	0.3	0.3	0.1	2.0
Drop-out Rate (%)	3.2	3.3	0.0	n/a	n/a	0.0
H.S. Diplomas (#)	91	91	0	0	0	0

La Porte County

Laporte Community School Corp
1921 'a' St • Laporte, IN 46350-6697
(219) 362-7056
Grade Span: PK-12; **Agency Type:** 1
Schools: 12
  9 Primary; 2 Middle; 1 High; 0 Other Level
  12 Regular; 0 Special Education; 0 Vocational; 0 Alternative
  0 Magnet; 0 Charter; 7 Title I Eligible; 0 School-wide Title I
Students: 6,301 (52.0% male; 47.9% female)
  Individual Education Program: 820 (13.0%);
  English Language Learner: 271 (4.3%); Migrant: n/a
  Eligible for Free Lunch Program: 1,531 (24.3%)
  Eligible for Reduced-Price Lunch Program: 475 (7.5%)
Teachers: 392.1 (16.1 to 1)
Librarians/Media Specialists: 5.0 (1,260.2 to 1)
Guidance Counselors: 10.5 (600.1 to 1)
Current Spending: ($ per student per year):
  Total: $7,689; Instruction: $4,777; Support Services: $2,573
Enrollment, Drop-out Rates and Diploma Recipients by Race/Ethnicity

Category	Total	White	Black	Asian	AIAN	Hisp.
Enrollment (%)	100.0	92.3	1.9	0.5	0.2	5.1
Drop-out Rate (%)	0.7	0.7	0.0	0.0	0.0	2.0
H.S. Diplomas (#)	401	385	5	1	2	8

Michigan City Area Schools
408 S Carroll Ave • Michigan City, IN 46360-5345
(219) 873-2000 • http://www.mcas.k12.in.us/homepage/
Grade Span: PK-12; **Agency Type:** 1
Schools: 14
  9 Primary; 3 Middle; 1 High; 1 Other Level
  13 Regular; 0 Special Education; 1 Vocational; 0 Alternative
  0 Magnet; 0 Charter; 7 Title I Eligible; 3 School-wide Title I
Students: 6,761 (52.4% male; 47.5% female)
  Individual Education Program: 1,344 (19.9%);
  English Language Learner: 128 (1.9%); Migrant: n/a
  Eligible for Free Lunch Program: 2,968 (43.9%)
  Eligible for Reduced-Price Lunch Program: 580 (8.6%)
Teachers: 420.0 (16.1 to 1)
Librarians/Media Specialists: 5.5 (1,229.3 to 1)
Guidance Counselors: 19.0 (355.8 to 1)
Current Spending: ($ per student per year):
  Total: $8,746; Instruction: $5,197; Support Services: $3,181
Enrollment, Drop-out Rates and Diploma Recipients by Race/Ethnicity

Category	Total	White	Black	Asian	AIAN	Hisp.
Enrollment (%)	100.0	63.8	31.3	0.7	0.8	3.4
Drop-out Rate (%)	0.0	0.0	0.0	0.0	0.0	0.0
H.S. Diplomas (#)	350	266	67	8	0	9

New Prairie United School Corp
5327 N Cougar Rd • New Carlisle, IN 46552-9505
(574) 654-7273
Grade Span: KG-12; **Agency Type:** 1
Schools: 5
  3 Primary; 1 Middle; 1 High; 0 Other Level
  5 Regular; 0 Special Education; 0 Vocational; 0 Alternative
  0 Magnet; 0 Charter; 3 Title I Eligible; 0 School-wide Title I
Students: 2,404 (51.7% male; 48.2% female)
  Individual Education Program: 328 (13.6%);

English Language Learner: 51 (2.1%); Migrant: n/a
Eligible for Free Lunch Program: 328 (13.6%)
Eligible for Reduced-Price Lunch Program: 163 (6.8%)
Teachers: 136.0 (17.7 to 1)
Librarians/Media Specialists: 1.0 (2,404.0 to 1)
Guidance Counselors: 3.0 (801.3 to 1)
Current Spending: ($ per student per year):
Total: $6,317; Instruction: $3,875; Support Services: $2,325
Enrollment, Drop-out Rates and Diploma Recipients by Race/Ethnicity

Category	Total	White	Black	Asian	AIAN	Hisp.
Enrollment (%)	100.0	95.3	0.5	0.3	0.4	3.5
Drop-out Rate (%)	2.3	2.4	0.0	0.0	0.0	0.0
H.S. Diplomas (#)	150	149	0	0	0	1

Lagrange County

Lakeland School Corporation
200 S Cherry St • Lagrange, IN 46761-2099
(260) 499-2400 • http://www.lakeland.k12.in.us/
Grade Span: KG-12; **Agency Type:** 1
Schools: 5
3 Primary; 1 Middle; 1 High; 0 Other Level
5 Regular; 0 Special Education; 0 Vocational; 0 Alternative
0 Magnet; 0 Charter; 4 Title I Eligible; 0 School-wide Title I
Students: 2,264 (53.2% male; 46.7% female)
Individual Education Program: 325 (14.4%);
English Language Learner: 238 (10.5%); Migrant: n/a
Eligible for Free Lunch Program: 530 (23.4%)
Eligible for Reduced-Price Lunch Program: 181 (8.0%)
Teachers: 134.0 (16.9 to 1)
Librarians/Media Specialists: 1.0 (2,264.0 to 1)
Guidance Counselors: 5.0 (452.8 to 1)
Current Spending: ($ per student per year):
Total: $7,452; Instruction: $4,524; Support Services: $2,574
Enrollment, Drop-out Rates and Diploma Recipients by Race/Ethnicity

Category	Total	White	Black	Asian	AIAN	Hisp.
Enrollment (%)	100.0	88.7	0.2	0.3	0.4	10.4
Drop-out Rate (%)	0.0	0.0	0.0	0.0	0.0	0.0
H.S. Diplomas (#)	103	94	0	0	2	7

Prairie Heights Com Sch Corp
0305 S 1150 E • Lagrange, IN 46761-9653
(260) 351-3214
Grade Span: KG-12; **Agency Type:** 1
Schools: 4
2 Primary; 1 Middle; 1 High; 0 Other Level
4 Regular; 0 Special Education; 0 Vocational; 0 Alternative
0 Magnet; 0 Charter; 3 Title I Eligible; 0 School-wide Title I
Students: 1,783 (48.5% male; 51.4% female)
Individual Education Program: 240 (13.5%);
English Language Learner: 71 (4.0%); Migrant: n/a
Eligible for Free Lunch Program: 331 (18.6%)
Eligible for Reduced-Price Lunch Program: 163 (9.1%)
Teachers: 100.4 (17.8 to 1)
Librarians/Media Specialists: 2.0 (891.5 to 1)
Guidance Counselors: 4.7 (379.4 to 1)
Current Spending: ($ per student per year):
Total: $7,956; Instruction: $4,904; Support Services: $2,726
Enrollment, Drop-out Rates and Diploma Recipients by Race/Ethnicity

Category	Total	White	Black	Asian	AIAN	Hisp.
Enrollment (%)	100.0	97.5	0.1	0.2	0.1	2.2
Drop-out Rate (%)	1.1	0.9	n/a	n/a	n/a	9.1
H.S. Diplomas (#)	110	110	0	0	0	0

Westview School Corporation
1545 S 600 W • Topeka, IN 46571-9741
(260) 768-4404 • http://www.westview.k12.in.us/
Grade Span: KG-12; **Agency Type:** 1
Schools: 5
3 Primary; 1 Middle; 1 High; 0 Other Level
5 Regular; 0 Special Education; 0 Vocational; 0 Alternative
0 Magnet; 0 Charter; 5 Title I Eligible; 0 School-wide Title I
Students: 2,214 (52.4% male; 47.5% female)
Individual Education Program: 233 (10.5%);
English Language Learner: 925 (41.8%); Migrant: n/a
Eligible for Free Lunch Program: 236 (10.7%)
Eligible for Reduced-Price Lunch Program: 130 (5.9%)
Teachers: 134.2 (16.5 to 1)
Librarians/Media Specialists: 2.0 (1,107.0 to 1)
Guidance Counselors: 2.0 (1,107.0 to 1)
Current Spending: ($ per student per year):
Total: $8,674; Instruction: $5,016; Support Services: $3,363

Enrollment, Drop-out Rates and Diploma Recipients by Race/Ethnicity

Category	Total	White	Black	Asian	AIAN	Hisp.
Enrollment (%)	100.0	98.6	0.1	0.2	0.1	0.9
Drop-out Rate (%)	0.8	0.8	0.0	0.0	n/a	0.0
H.S. Diplomas (#)	91	90	1	0	0	0

Lake County

Crown Point Community Sch Corp
200 E N St • Crown Point, IN 46307-4078
(219) 663-3371 • http://www.cps.k12.in.us/index.html
Grade Span: PK-12; **Agency Type:** 1
Schools: 9
6 Primary; 2 Middle; 1 High; 0 Other Level
9 Regular; 0 Special Education; 0 Vocational; 0 Alternative
0 Magnet; 0 Charter; 3 Title I Eligible; 0 School-wide Title I
Students: 6,175 (50.6% male; 49.3% female)
Individual Education Program: 732 (11.9%);
English Language Learner: 200 (3.2%); Migrant: n/a
Eligible for Free Lunch Program: 750 (12.1%)
Eligible for Reduced-Price Lunch Program: 242 (3.9%)
Teachers: 263.7 (23.4 to 1)
Librarians/Media Specialists: 2.0 (3,087.5 to 1)
Guidance Counselors: 5.0 (1,235.0 to 1)
Current Spending: ($ per student per year):
Total: $6,141; Instruction: $3,550; Support Services: $2,333
Enrollment, Drop-out Rates and Diploma Recipients by Race/Ethnicity

Category	Total	White	Black	Asian	AIAN	Hisp.
Enrollment (%)	100.0	94.4	0.6	1.0	0.3	3.8
Drop-out Rate (%)	0.1	0.1	0.0	0.0	0.0	0.0
H.S. Diplomas (#)	427	412	2	2	4	7

Gary Community School Corp
620 E 10th Pl • Gary, IN 46402-2731
(219) 881-5401 • http://www.garycsc.k12.in.us/
Grade Span: PK-12; **Agency Type:** 1
Schools: 35
21 Primary; 5 Middle; 6 High; 3 Other Level
32 Regular; 1 Special Education; 1 Vocational; 1 Alternative
0 Magnet; 0 Charter; 30 Title I Eligible; 26 School-wide Title I
Students: 17,381 (50.7% male; 49.2% female)
Individual Education Program: 2,655 (15.3%);
English Language Learner: 129 (0.7%); Migrant: n/a
Eligible for Free Lunch Program: 9,910 (57.0%)
Eligible for Reduced-Price Lunch Program: 417 (2.4%)
Teachers: 1,001.8 (17.3 to 1)
Librarians/Media Specialists: 37.0 (469.6 to 1)
Guidance Counselors: 55.5 (313.1 to 1)
Current Spending: ($ per student per year):
Total: $9,631; Instruction: $5,110; Support Services: $4,225
Enrollment, Drop-out Rates and Diploma Recipients by Race/Ethnicity

Category	Total	White	Black	Asian	AIAN	Hisp.
Enrollment (%)	100.0	0.6	97.9	0.2	0.1	1.2
Drop-out Rate (%)	0.5	0.0	0.5	0.0	0.0	0.0
H.S. Diplomas (#)	706	0	695	1	0	10

Griffith Public Schools
132 N Broad St • Griffith, IN 46319-2289
(219) 924-4250 • http://165.138.244.1/
Grade Span: KG-12; **Agency Type:** 1
Schools: 6
4 Primary; 1 Middle; 1 High; 0 Other Level
6 Regular; 0 Special Education; 0 Vocational; 0 Alternative
0 Magnet; 0 Charter; 2 Title I Eligible; 0 School-wide Title I
Students: 2,694 (50.1% male; 49.8% female)
Individual Education Program: 371 (13.8%);
English Language Learner: 146 (5.4%); Migrant: n/a
Eligible for Free Lunch Program: 404 (15.0%)
Eligible for Reduced-Price Lunch Program: 108 (4.0%)
Teachers: 137.0 (19.7 to 1)
Librarians/Media Specialists: 1.0 (2,694.0 to 1)
Guidance Counselors: 4.0 (673.5 to 1)
Current Spending: ($ per student per year):
Total: $6,206; Instruction: $3,659; Support Services: $2,319
Enrollment, Drop-out Rates and Diploma Recipients by Race/Ethnicity

Category	Total	White	Black	Asian	AIAN	Hisp.
Enrollment (%)	100.0	76.0	13.0	0.2	0.2	10.7
Drop-out Rate (%)	0.1	0.1	0.0	0.0	0.0	0.0
H.S. Diplomas (#)	188	159	6	0	2	21

Hanover Community School Corp
9520 W 133rd Ave • Cedar Lake, IN 46303-0645
Mailing Address: PO Box 645 • Cedar Lake, IN 46303-0645
(219) 374-3500 • http://www.hanover.k12.in.us/
Grade Span: KG-12; **Agency Type:** 1
Schools: 4
  2 Primary; 1 Middle; 1 High; 0 Other Level
  4 Regular; 0 Special Education; 0 Vocational; 0 Alternative
  0 Magnet; 0 Charter; 1 Title I Eligible; 0 School-wide Title I
Students: 1,583 (52.6% male; 47.3% female)
  Individual Education Program: 225 (14.2%);
  English Language Learner: 26 (1.6%); Migrant: n/a
  Eligible for Free Lunch Program: 255 (16.1%)
  Eligible for Reduced-Price Lunch Program: 84 (5.3%)
Teachers: 78.0 (20.3 to 1)
Librarians/Media Specialists: 1.0 (1,583.0 to 1)
Guidance Counselors: 2.0 (791.5 to 1)
Current Spending: ($ per student per year):
  Total: $6,332; Instruction: $3,853; Support Services: $2,213
Enrollment, Drop-out Rates and Diploma Recipients by Race/Ethnicity

Category	Total	White	Black	Asian	AIAN	Hisp.
Enrollment (%)	100.0	94.8	0.5	0.4	0.2	4.2
Drop-out Rate (%)	0.8	0.9	n/a	n/a	n/a	0.0
H.S. Diplomas (#)	102	99	0	0	0	3

Lake Central School Corp
8260 Wicker Ave • Saint John, IN 46373-9711
(219) 365-8507 • http://www.lakecentral.k12.in.us/
Grade Span: PK-12; **Agency Type:** 1
Schools: 10
  6 Primary; 2 Middle; 1 High; 1 Other Level
  9 Regular; 1 Special Education; 0 Vocational; 0 Alternative
  0 Magnet; 0 Charter; 3 Title I Eligible; 0 School-wide Title I
Students: 8,674 (53.5% male; 46.4% female)
  Individual Education Program: 1,501 (17.3%);
  English Language Learner: 534 (6.2%); Migrant: n/a
  Eligible for Free Lunch Program: 550 (6.3%)
  Eligible for Reduced-Price Lunch Program: 271 (3.1%)
Teachers: 450.3 (19.3 to 1)
Librarians/Media Specialists: 3.0 (2,891.3 to 1)
Guidance Counselors: 9.0 (963.8 to 1)
Current Spending: ($ per student per year):
  Total: $7,264; Instruction: $4,787; Support Services: $2,223
Enrollment, Drop-out Rates and Diploma Recipients by Race/Ethnicity

Category	Total	White	Black	Asian	AIAN	Hisp.
Enrollment (%)	100.0	88.2	1.8	2.2	0.4	7.3
Drop-out Rate (%)	0.7	0.6	4.0	6.7	0.0	0.0
H.S. Diplomas (#)	452	418	4	5	2	23

Lake Ridge Schools
6111 W Ridge Rd • Gary, IN 46408-1797
(219) 838-1819 • http://lakeridgeschools.homestead.com/
Grade Span: KG-12; **Agency Type:** 1
Schools: 6
  3 Primary; 1 Middle; 1 High; 1 Other Level
  5 Regular; 0 Special Education; 0 Vocational; 1 Alternative
  0 Magnet; 0 Charter; 3 Title I Eligible; 0 School-wide Title I
Students: 2,393 (49.8% male; 50.1% female)
  Individual Education Program: 328 (13.7%);
  English Language Learner: 32 (1.3%); Migrant: n/a
  Eligible for Free Lunch Program: 1,420 (59.3%)
  Eligible for Reduced-Price Lunch Program: 224 (9.4%)
Teachers: 125.0 (19.1 to 1)
Librarians/Media Specialists: 2.0 (1,196.5 to 1)
Guidance Counselors: 4.7 (509.1 to 1)
Current Spending: ($ per student per year):
  Total: $9,824; Instruction: $5,825; Support Services: $3,521
Enrollment, Drop-out Rates and Diploma Recipients by Race/Ethnicity

Category	Total	White	Black	Asian	AIAN	Hisp.
Enrollment (%)	100.0	64.2	20.4	0.6	0.4	14.4
Drop-out Rate (%)	4.1	4.1	3.9	0.0	12.5	3.6
H.S. Diplomas (#)	133	89	31	0	0	13

Merrillville Community School
6701 Delaware St • Merrillville, IN 46410-3586
(219) 650-5300 • http://www.mvsc.k12.in.us/index.htm
Grade Span: KG-12; **Agency Type:** 1
Schools: 8
  5 Primary; 2 Middle; 1 High; 0 Other Level
  8 Regular; 0 Special Education; 0 Vocational; 0 Alternative
  0 Magnet; 0 Charter; 5 Title I Eligible; 0 School-wide Title I
Students: 6,528 (51.0% male; 48.9% female)
  Individual Education Program: 723 (11.1%);
  English Language Learner: 400 (6.1%); Migrant: n/a
  Eligible for Free Lunch Program: 1,346 (20.6%)

  Eligible for Reduced-Price Lunch Program: 614 (9.4%)
Teachers: 320.6 (20.4 to 1)
Librarians/Media Specialists: 4.0 (1,632.0 to 1)
Guidance Counselors: 9.0 (725.3 to 1)
Current Spending: ($ per student per year):
  Total: $6,831; Instruction: $3,744; Support Services: $2,817
Enrollment, Drop-out Rates and Diploma Recipients by Race/Ethnicity

Category	Total	White	Black	Asian	AIAN	Hisp.
Enrollment (%)	100.0	46.9	41.1	1.3	0.2	10.4
Drop-out Rate (%)	0.5	0.5	0.6	0.0	0.0	0.5
H.S. Diplomas (#)	468	264	141	8	0	55

School City of East Chicago
210 E Columbus Dr • East Chicago, IN 46312-2799
(219) 391-4100 • http://www.ecps.org/
Grade Span: PK-12; **Agency Type:** 1
Schools: 10
  7 Primary; 2 Middle; 1 High; 0 Other Level
  10 Regular; 0 Special Education; 0 Vocational; 0 Alternative
  0 Magnet; 0 Charter; 7 Title I Eligible; 7 School-wide Title I
Students: 6,444 (51.4% male; 48.5% female)
  Individual Education Program: 909 (14.1%);
  English Language Learner: 1,396 (21.7%); Migrant: n/a
  Eligible for Free Lunch Program: 4,924 (76.4%)
  Eligible for Reduced-Price Lunch Program: 551 (8.6%)
Teachers: 374.0 (17.2 to 1)
Librarians/Media Specialists: 4.0 (1,611.0 to 1)
Guidance Counselors: 6.0 (1,074.0 to 1)
Current Spending: ($ per student per year):
  Total: $9,207; Instruction: $4,665; Support Services: $4,089
Enrollment, Drop-out Rates and Diploma Recipients by Race/Ethnicity

Category	Total	White	Black	Asian	AIAN	Hisp.
Enrollment (%)	100.0	3.1	45.6	0.4	0.1	50.8
Drop-out Rate (%)	7.5	31.9	5.8	50.0	n/a	6.3
H.S. Diplomas (#)	256	11	112	2	0	131

School City of Hammond
41 Williams St • Hammond, IN 46320-1948
(219) 933-2400 • http://hammond.k12.in.us/
Grade Span: PK-12; **Agency Type:** 1
Schools: 23
  16 Primary; 2 Middle; 2 High; 3 Other Level
  22 Regular; 0 Special Education; 1 Vocational; 0 Alternative
  0 Magnet; 0 Charter; 10 Title I Eligible; 8 School-wide Title I
Students: 13,696 (52.1% male; 47.8% female)
  Individual Education Program: 2,117 (15.5%);
  English Language Learner: 2,811 (20.5%); Migrant: n/a
  Eligible for Free Lunch Program: 7,983 (58.3%)
  Eligible for Reduced-Price Lunch Program: 1,463 (10.7%)
Teachers: 752.2 (18.2 to 1)
Librarians/Media Specialists: 18.0 (760.9 to 1)
Guidance Counselors: 17.0 (805.6 to 1)
Current Spending: ($ per student per year):
  Total: $8,764; Instruction: $4,928; Support Services: $3,472
Enrollment, Drop-out Rates and Diploma Recipients by Race/Ethnicity

Category	Total	White	Black	Asian	AIAN	Hisp.
Enrollment (%)	100.0	39.9	26.6	0.4	0.3	32.7
Drop-out Rate (%)	1.2	1.4	0.3	0.0	0.0	1.4
H.S. Diplomas (#)	545	314	102	4	0	125

School City of Hobart
32 E 7th St • Hobart, IN 46342-5197
(219) 942-8885 • http://www.hobart.k12.in.us/
Grade Span: KG-12; **Agency Type:** 1
Schools: 6
  4 Primary; 1 Middle; 1 High; 0 Other Level
  6 Regular; 0 Special Education; 0 Vocational; 0 Alternative
  0 Magnet; 0 Charter; 3 Title I Eligible; 0 School-wide Title I
Students: 3,617 (50.8% male; 49.1% female)
  Individual Education Program: 395 (10.9%);
  English Language Learner: 301 (8.3%); Migrant: n/a
  Eligible for Free Lunch Program: 706 (19.5%)
  Eligible for Reduced-Price Lunch Program: 270 (7.5%)
Teachers: 178.0 (20.3 to 1)
Librarians/Media Specialists: 2.0 (1,808.5 to 1)
Guidance Counselors: 4.0 (904.3 to 1)
Current Spending: ($ per student per year):
  Total: $6,837; Instruction: $3,774; Support Services: $2,783
Enrollment, Drop-out Rates and Diploma Recipients by Race/Ethnicity

Category	Total	White	Black	Asian	AIAN	Hisp.
Enrollment (%)	100.0	83.5	2.3	0.8	0.9	12.4
Drop-out Rate (%)	0.6	0.5	0.0	0.0	0.0	0.9
H.S. Diplomas (#)	241	213	3	0	1	24

School Town of Highland
9145 Kennedy Ave • Highland, IN 46322-2796
(219) 922-5615 • http://stoh.highland.k12.in.us/
Grade Span: KG-12; **Agency Type:** 1
Schools: 6
    4 Primary; 1 Middle; 1 High; 0 Other Level
    6 Regular; 0 Special Education; 0 Vocational; 0 Alternative
    0 Magnet; 0 Charter; 4 Title I Eligible; 0 School-wide Title I
Students: 3,360 (51.3% male; 48.6% female)
    Individual Education Program: 398 (11.8%);
    English Language Learner: 170 (5.1%); Migrant: n/a
    Eligible for Free Lunch Program: 279 (8.3%)
    Eligible for Reduced-Price Lunch Program: 99 (2.9%)
Teachers: 151.0 (22.3 to 1)
Librarians/Media Specialists: 2.0 (1,680.0 to 1)
Guidance Counselors: 6.0 (560.0 to 1)
Current Spending: ($ per student per year):
    Total: $6,496; Instruction: $3,641; Support Services: $2,733
Enrollment, Drop-out Rates and Diploma Recipients by Race/Ethnicity

Category	Total	White	Black	Asian	AIAN	Hisp.
Enrollment (%)	100.0	89.8	1.3	1.9	0.1	6.9
Drop-out Rate (%)	0.0	0.0	0.0	0.0	n/a	0.0
H.S. Diplomas (#)	251	248	0	0	0	3

School Town of Munster
8616 Columbia Ave • Munster, IN 46321-2597
(219) 836-9111 • http://www.munster.k12.in.us/
Grade Span: KG-12; **Agency Type:** 1
Schools: 5
    3 Primary; 1 Middle; 1 High; 0 Other Level
    5 Regular; 0 Special Education; 0 Vocational; 0 Alternative
    0 Magnet; 0 Charter; 3 Title I Eligible; 0 School-wide Title I
Students: 3,863 (52.8% male; 47.1% female)
    Individual Education Program: 670 (17.3%);
    English Language Learner: 413 (10.7%); Migrant: n/a
    Eligible for Free Lunch Program: 164 (4.2%)
    Eligible for Reduced-Price Lunch Program: 108 (2.8%)
Teachers: 216.0 (17.9 to 1)
Librarians/Media Specialists: 3.0 (1,287.7 to 1)
Guidance Counselors: 5.0 (772.6 to 1)
Current Spending: ($ per student per year):
    Total: $7,606; Instruction: $4,548; Support Services: $2,756
Enrollment, Drop-out Rates and Diploma Recipients by Race/Ethnicity

Category	Total	White	Black	Asian	AIAN	Hisp.
Enrollment (%)	100.0	84.9	2.5	6.8	0.2	5.7
Drop-out Rate (%)	0.8	0.7	0.0	1.3	0.0	2.7
H.S. Diplomas (#)	281	250	1	14	1	15

Tri-Creek School Corp
195 W Oakley Ave • Lowell, IN 46356-2293
(219) 696-6661 • http://www.tricreek.k12.in.us/
Grade Span: KG-12; **Agency Type:** 1
Schools: 5
    3 Primary; 1 Middle; 1 High; 0 Other Level
    5 Regular; 0 Special Education; 0 Vocational; 0 Alternative
    0 Magnet; 0 Charter; 4 Title I Eligible; 0 School-wide Title I
Students: 3,367 (51.0% male; 48.9% female)
    Individual Education Program: 461 (13.7%);
    English Language Learner: 40 (1.2%); Migrant: n/a
    Eligible for Free Lunch Program: 424 (12.6%)
    Eligible for Reduced-Price Lunch Program: 131 (3.9%)
Teachers: 146.3 (23.0 to 1)
Librarians/Media Specialists: 0.0 (n/a to 1)
Guidance Counselors: 3.5 (962.0 to 1)
Current Spending: ($ per student per year):
    Total: $5,977; Instruction: $3,313; Support Services: $2,229
Enrollment, Drop-out Rates and Diploma Recipients by Race/Ethnicity

Category	Total	White	Black	Asian	AIAN	Hisp.
Enrollment (%)	100.0	97.5	0.1	0.1	0.4	2.0
Drop-out Rate (%)	0.6	0.6	0.0	0.0	0.0	3.3
H.S. Diplomas (#)	224	212	1	1	3	7

Lawrence County

Mitchell Community Schools
441 N 8th St • Mitchell, IN 47446-1020
(812) 849-4481 • http://www.mitchell.k12.in.us/
Grade Span: PK-12; **Agency Type:** 1
Schools: 4
    2 Primary; 1 Middle; 1 High; 0 Other Level
    4 Regular; 0 Special Education; 0 Vocational; 0 Alternative
    0 Magnet; 0 Charter; 3 Title I Eligible; 0 School-wide Title I
Students: 2,064 (50.1% male; 49.8% female)
    Individual Education Program: 366 (17.7%)
    English Language Learner: 17 (0.8%); Migrant: n/a

Eligible for Free Lunch Program: 650 (31.5%)
Eligible for Reduced-Price Lunch Program: 158 (7.7%)
Teachers: 110.3 (18.7 to 1)
Librarians/Media Specialists: 3.0 (688.0 to 1)
Guidance Counselors: 4.0 (516.0 to 1)
Current Spending: ($ per student per year):
    Total: $7,676; Instruction: $4,828; Support Services: $2,564
Enrollment, Drop-out Rates and Diploma Recipients by Race/Ethnicity

Category	Total	White	Black	Asian	AIAN	Hisp.
Enrollment (%)	100.0	98.8	0.4	0.2	0.0	0.5
Drop-out Rate (%)	2.8	2.8	0.0	0.0	n/a	0.0
H.S. Diplomas (#)	118	118	0	0	0	0

North Lawrence Com Schools
460 'w' St • Bedford, IN 47421-0729
Mailing Address: PO Box 729 • Bedford, IN 47421-0729
(812) 279-3521 • http://www.nlcs.k12.in.us/
Grade Span: PK-12; **Agency Type:** 1
Schools: 16
    10 Primary; 3 Middle; 1 High; 2 Other Level
    14 Regular; 1 Special Education; 1 Vocational; 0 Alternative
    0 Magnet; 0 Charter; 8 Title I Eligible; 0 School-wide Title I
Students: 5,442 (52.6% male; 47.3% female)
    Individual Education Program: 958 (17.6%);
    English Language Learner: 52 (1.0%); Migrant: n/a
    Eligible for Free Lunch Program: 1,336 (24.5%)
    Eligible for Reduced-Price Lunch Program: 529 (9.7%)
Teachers: 335.6 (16.2 to 1)
Librarians/Media Specialists: 2.0 (2,721.0 to 1)
Guidance Counselors: 7.5 (725.6 to 1)
Current Spending: ($ per student per year):
    Total: $7,952; Instruction: $4,766; Support Services: $2,875
Enrollment, Drop-out Rates and Diploma Recipients by Race/Ethnicity

Category	Total	White	Black	Asian	AIAN	Hisp.
Enrollment (%)	100.0	98.1	0.6	0.4	0.4	0.5
Drop-out Rate (%)	1.6	1.6	0.0	0.0	0.0	3.6
H.S. Diplomas (#)	352	332	2	8	4	6

Madison County

Alexandria Com School Corp
202 E Washington St • Alexandria, IN 46001-2005
(765) 724-4496 • http://www.alex.k12.in.us/centraloffice/centraloffice.html
Grade Span: PK-12; **Agency Type:** 1
Schools: 4
    2 Primary; 1 Middle; 1 High; 0 Other Level
    4 Regular; 0 Special Education; 0 Vocational; 0 Alternative
    0 Magnet; 0 Charter; 3 Title I Eligible; 0 School-wide Title I
Students: 1,678 (53.2% male; 46.7% female)
    Individual Education Program: 252 (15.0%);
    English Language Learner: 70 (4.2%); Migrant: n/a
    Eligible for Free Lunch Program: 476 (28.4%)
    Eligible for Reduced-Price Lunch Program: 121 (7.2%)
Teachers: 101.8 (16.5 to 1)
Librarians/Media Specialists: 2.0 (839.0 to 1)
Guidance Counselors: 1.0 (1,678.0 to 1)
Current Spending: ($ per student per year):
    Total: $6,919; Instruction: $4,397; Support Services: $2,211
Enrollment, Drop-out Rates and Diploma Recipients by Race/Ethnicity

Category	Total	White	Black	Asian	AIAN	Hisp.
Enrollment (%)	100.0	95.3	0.4	0.1	0.1	4.1
Drop-out Rate (%)	1.6	1.6	0.0	0.0	n/a	0.0
H.S. Diplomas (#)	119	117	2	0	0	0

Anderson Community School Corp
1229 Lincoln St • Anderson, IN 46016-1479
(765) 641-2028 • http://www.acsc.net/
Grade Span: PK-12; **Agency Type:** 1
Schools: 21
    14 Primary; 3 Middle; 3 High; 1 Other Level
    18 Regular; 1 Special Education; 1 Vocational; 1 Alternative
    0 Magnet; 0 Charter; 8 Title I Eligible; 2 School-wide Title I
Students: 10,315 (51.0% male; 48.9% female)
    Individual Education Program: 1,963 (19.0%);
    English Language Learner: 165 (1.6%); Migrant: n/a
    Eligible for Free Lunch Program: 4,390 (42.6%)
    Eligible for Reduced-Price Lunch Program: 926 (9.0%)
Teachers: 674.8 (15.3 to 1)
Librarians/Media Specialists: 13.0 (793.5 to 1)
Guidance Counselors: 14.5 (711.4 to 1)
Current Spending: ($ per student per year):
    Total: $9,308; Instruction: $6,138; Support Services: $2,701

Enrollment, Drop-out Rates and Diploma Recipients by Race/Ethnicity

Category	Total	White	Black	Asian	AIAN	Hisp.
Enrollment (%)	100.0	75.8	21.2	0.5	0.1	2.3
Drop-out Rate (%)	0.0	0.0	0.0	0.0	0.0	0.0
H.S. Diplomas (#)	504	421	63	7	2	11

Elwood Community School Corp
1306 N Anderson St • Elwood, IN 46036-9460
(765) 552-9861 • http://www.elwood.k12.in.us/
Grade Span: PK-12; **Agency Type:** 1
Schools: 5
  2 Primary; 1 Middle; 1 High; 1 Other Level
  4 Regular; 0 Special Education; 1 Vocational; 0 Alternative
  0 Magnet; 0 Charter; 2 Title I Eligible; 2 School-wide Title I
Students: 1,999   (52.0% male; 47.9% female)
  Individual Education Program: 400 (20.0%);
  English Language Learner: 43 (2.2%); Migrant: n/a
  Eligible for Free Lunch Program: 731 (36.6%)
  Eligible for Reduced-Price Lunch Program: 161 (8.1%)
Teachers: 122.5 (16.3 to 1)
Librarians/Media Specialists: 2.0 (999.5 to 1)
Guidance Counselors: 3.0 (666.3 to 1)
Current Spending: ($ per student per year):
  Total: $7,570; Instruction: $4,876; Support Services: $2,322

Enrollment, Drop-out Rates and Diploma Recipients by Race/Ethnicity

Category	Total	White	Black	Asian	AIAN	Hisp.
Enrollment (%)	100.0	96.6	0.1	0.5	0.2	2.7
Drop-out Rate (%)	3.1	3.2	0.0	0.0	n/a	0.0
H.S. Diplomas (#)	119	115	0	2	0	2

Frankton-Lapel Community Schs
7916 W 300 N • Anderson, IN 46011-9129
(765) 734-1261 • http://www.flcs.k12.in.us/
Grade Span: PK-12; **Agency Type:** 1
Schools: 4
  2 Primary; 0 Middle; 2 High; 0 Other Level
  4 Regular; 0 Special Education; 0 Vocational; 0 Alternative
  0 Magnet; 0 Charter; 2 Title I Eligible; 0 School-wide Title I
Students: 2,293   (50.4% male; 49.5% female)
  Individual Education Program: 396 (17.3%);
  English Language Learner: 12 (0.5%); Migrant: n/a
  Eligible for Free Lunch Program: 358 (15.6%)
  Eligible for Reduced-Price Lunch Program: 190 (8.3%)
Teachers: 123.4 (18.6 to 1)
Librarians/Media Specialists: 1.7 (1,348.8 to 1)
Guidance Counselors: 2.0 (1,146.5 to 1)
Current Spending: ($ per student per year):
  Total: $6,298; Instruction: $3,792; Support Services: $2,250

Enrollment, Drop-out Rates and Diploma Recipients by Race/Ethnicity

Category	Total	White	Black	Asian	AIAN	Hisp.
Enrollment (%)	100.0	98.9	0.3	0.2	0.0	0.6
Drop-out Rate (%)	3.0	3.0	n/a	0.0	0.0	0.0
H.S. Diplomas (#)	137	137	0	0	0	0

South Madison Com Sch Corp
201 S E St • Pendleton, IN 46064-1211
(765) 778-2152 • http://www.smadison.k12.in.us/
Grade Span: PK-12; **Agency Type:** 1
Schools: 5
  3 Primary; 1 Middle; 1 High; 0 Other Level
  5 Regular; 0 Special Education; 0 Vocational; 0 Alternative
  0 Magnet; 0 Charter; 0 Title I Eligible; 0 School-wide Title I
Students: 3,506   (50.7% male; 49.2% female)
  Individual Education Program: 774 (22.1%);
  English Language Learner: 9 (0.3%); Migrant: n/a
  Eligible for Free Lunch Program: 423 (12.1%)
  Eligible for Reduced-Price Lunch Program: 120 (3.4%)
Teachers: 181.8 (19.3 to 1)
Librarians/Media Specialists: 5.0 (701.2 to 1)
Guidance Counselors: 5.0 (701.2 to 1)
Current Spending: ($ per student per year):
  Total: $6,944; Instruction: $4,100; Support Services: $2,461

Enrollment, Drop-out Rates and Diploma Recipients by Race/Ethnicity

Category	Total	White	Black	Asian	AIAN	Hisp.
Enrollment (%)	100.0	99.0	0.2	0.4	0.1	0.3
Drop-out Rate (%)	0.0	0.0	0.0	0.0	0.0	0.0
H.S. Diplomas (#)	232	229	0	1	1	1

Marion County

Beech Grove City Schools
5334 Hornet Ave • Beech Grove, IN 46107-2306
(317) 788-4481 • http://www.bgcs.k12.in.us/01default.html
Grade Span: PK-12; **Agency Type:** 1
Schools: 5

  2 Primary; 2 Middle; 1 High; 0 Other Level
  5 Regular; 0 Special Education; 0 Vocational; 0 Alternative
  0 Magnet; 0 Charter; 4 Title I Eligible; 0 School-wide Title I
Students: 2,403   (51.9% male; 48.0% female)
  Individual Education Program: 380 (15.8%);
  English Language Learner: 35 (1.5%); Migrant: n/a
  Eligible for Free Lunch Program: 602 (25.1%)
  Eligible for Reduced-Price Lunch Program: 204 (8.5%)
Teachers: 129.3 (18.6 to 1)
Librarians/Media Specialists: 2.0 (1,201.5 to 1)
Guidance Counselors: 3.0 (801.0 to 1)
Current Spending: ($ per student per year):
  Total: $6,744; Instruction: $4,157; Support Services: $2,237

Enrollment, Drop-out Rates and Diploma Recipients by Race/Ethnicity

Category	Total	White	Black	Asian	AIAN	Hisp.
Enrollment (%)	100.0	94.3	2.4	1.1	0.2	2.0
Drop-out Rate (%)	2.1	1.9	9.1	0.0	0.0	12.5
H.S. Diplomas (#)	145	141	0	3	0	1

Franklin Township Com Sch Corp
6141 S Franklin Rd • Indianapolis, IN 46259-1399
(317) 862-2411 • http://www.ftcsc.k12.in.us/
Grade Span: PK-12; **Agency Type:** 1
Schools: 8
  5 Primary; 2 Middle; 1 High; 0 Other Level
  8 Regular; 0 Special Education; 0 Vocational; 0 Alternative
  0 Magnet; 0 Charter; 4 Title I Eligible; 0 School-wide Title I
Students: 6,875   (51.1% male; 48.8% female)
  Individual Education Program: 989 (14.4%);
  English Language Learner: 126 (1.8%); Migrant: n/a
  Eligible for Free Lunch Program: 950 (13.8%)
  Eligible for Reduced-Price Lunch Program: 411 (6.0%)
Teachers: 332.1 (20.7 to 1)
Librarians/Media Specialists: 5.5 (1,250.0 to 1)
Guidance Counselors: 14.0 (491.1 to 1)
Current Spending: ($ per student per year):
  Total: $6,935; Instruction: $3,953; Support Services: $2,648

Enrollment, Drop-out Rates and Diploma Recipients by Race/Ethnicity

Category	Total	White	Black	Asian	AIAN	Hisp.
Enrollment (%)	100.0	90.6	6.4	1.3	0.2	1.5
Drop-out Rate (%)	1.5	1.5	2.2	0.0	0.0	0.0
H.S. Diplomas (#)	305	285	13	4	0	3

Indianapolis Public Schools
120 E Walnut St • Indianapolis, IN 46204-1389
(317) 226-4411 • http://www.ips.k12.in.us/
Grade Span: PK-12; **Agency Type:** 1
Schools: 92
  57 Primary; 12 Middle; 2 High; 21 Other Level
  78 Regular; 6 Special Education; 0 Vocational; 8 Alternative
  17 Magnet; 0 Charter; 54 Title I Eligible; 19 School-wide Title I
Students: 39,989   (51.1% male; 48.8% female)
  Individual Education Program: 7,425 (18.6%);
  English Language Learner: 2,758 (6.9%); Migrant: n/a
  Eligible for Free Lunch Program: 27,023 (67.6%)
  Eligible for Reduced-Price Lunch Program: 5,014 (12.5%)
Teachers: 2,769.8 (14.4 to 1)
Librarians/Media Specialists: 46.9 (852.4 to 1)
Guidance Counselors: 67.3 (594.0 to 1)
Current Spending: ($ per student per year):
  Total: $9,604; Instruction: $5,204; Support Services: $4,078

Enrollment, Drop-out Rates and Diploma Recipients by Race/Ethnicity

Category	Total	White	Black	Asian	AIAN	Hisp.
Enrollment (%)	100.0	30.6	59.7	0.4	0.2	9.1
Drop-out Rate (%)	2.2	2.1	2.2	1.7	0.0	3.7
H.S. Diplomas (#)	1,203	341	816	0	2	44

M S D Decatur Township
5275 Kentucky Ave • Indianapolis, IN 46221-9616
(317) 856-5265 • http://www.msddecatur.k12.in.us/
Grade Span: KG-12; **Agency Type:** 1
Schools: 7
  5 Primary; 1 Middle; 1 High; 0 Other Level
  7 Regular; 0 Special Education; 0 Vocational; 0 Alternative
  0 Magnet; 0 Charter; 3 Title I Eligible; 3 School-wide Title I
Students: 5,626   (50.7% male; 49.2% female)
  Individual Education Program: 1,005 (17.9%);
  English Language Learner: 81 (1.4%); Migrant: n/a
  Eligible for Free Lunch Program: 1,798 (32.0%)
  Eligible for Reduced-Price Lunch Program: 537 (9.5%)
Teachers: 294.5 (19.1 to 1)
Librarians/Media Specialists: 4.0 (1,406.5 to 1)
Guidance Counselors: 5.0 (1,125.2 to 1)
Current Spending: ($ per student per year):
  Total: $7,691; Instruction: $4,686; Support Services: $2,676

Enrollment, Drop-out Rates and Diploma Recipients by Race/Ethnicity

Category	Total	White	Black	Asian	AIAN	Hisp.
Enrollment (%)	100.0	87.3	9.9	0.3	0.1	2.4
Drop-out Rate (%)	0.0	0.0	0.0	0.0	0.0	0.0
H.S. Diplomas (#)	246	216	20	1	0	9

M S D Lawrence Township

7601 E 56th St • Indianapolis, IN 46226-1306
(317) 423-8200 • http://www.msdlt.k12.in.us/
Grade Span: PK-12; **Agency Type:** 1
Schools: 19
    12 Primary; 3 Middle; 3 High; 1 Other Level
    17 Regular; 0 Special Education; 1 Vocational; 1 Alternative
    2 Magnet; 0 Charter; 9 Title I Eligible; 0 School-wide Title I
Students: 16,201 (51.6% male; 48.3% female)
    Individual Education Program: 2,516 (15.5%);
    English Language Learner: 891 (5.5%); Migrant: n/a
    Eligible for Free Lunch Program: 3,494 (21.6%)
    Eligible for Reduced-Price Lunch Program: 1,227 (7.6%)
Teachers: 922.0 (17.6 to 1)
Librarians/Media Specialists: 16.0 (1,012.6 to 1)
Guidance Counselors: 23.5 (689.4 to 1)
Current Spending: ($ per student per year):
    Total: $8,677; Instruction: $5,747; Support Services: $2,647
Enrollment, Drop-out Rates and Diploma Recipients by Race/Ethnicity

Category	Total	White	Black	Asian	AIAN	Hisp.
Enrollment (%)	100.0	59.2	33.3	1.9	0.2	5.5
Drop-out Rate (%)	1.4	0.9	1.9	0.0	0.0	6.4
H.S. Diplomas (#)	871	609	221	25	0	16

M S D Perry Township

6548 Orinoco Ave • Indianapolis, IN 46227-4820
(317) 789-3700 • http://www.msdpt.k12.in.us/
Grade Span: PK-12; **Agency Type:** 1
Schools: 16
    11 Primary; 2 Middle; 2 High; 1 Other Level
    15 Regular; 1 Special Education; 0 Vocational; 0 Alternative
    0 Magnet; 0 Charter; 7 Title I Eligible; 0 School-wide Title I
Students: 13,209 (51.2% male; 48.7% female)
    Individual Education Program: 1,873 (14.2%);
    English Language Learner: 562 (4.3%); Migrant: n/a
    Eligible for Free Lunch Program: 4,309 (32.6%)
    Eligible for Reduced-Price Lunch Program: 1,096 (8.3%)
Teachers: 766.0 (17.2 to 1)
Librarians/Media Specialists: 14.0 (943.5 to 1)
Guidance Counselors: 18.0 (733.8 to 1)
Current Spending: ($ per student per year):
    Total: $8,191; Instruction: $4,788; Support Services: $3,040
Enrollment, Drop-out Rates and Diploma Recipients by Race/Ethnicity

Category	Total	White	Black	Asian	AIAN	Hisp.
Enrollment (%)	100.0	81.2	12.6	1.2	0.2	4.7
Drop-out Rate (%)	2.6	2.2	5.6	2.3	0.0	5.8
H.S. Diplomas (#)	611	554	35	10	3	9

M S D Pike Township

6901 Zionsville Rd • Indianapolis, IN 46268-2467
(317) 293-0393 • http://www.pike.k12.in.us/
Grade Span: PK-12; **Agency Type:** 1
Schools: 13
    9 Primary; 3 Middle; 1 High; 0 Other Level
    13 Regular; 0 Special Education; 0 Vocational; 0 Alternative
    0 Magnet; 0 Charter; 9 Title I Eligible; 0 School-wide Title I
Students: 10,490 (51.3% male; 48.6% female)
    Individual Education Program: 1,842 (17.6%);
    English Language Learner: 730 (7.0%); Migrant: n/a
    Eligible for Free Lunch Program: 2,930 (27.9%)
    Eligible for Reduced-Price Lunch Program: 611 (5.8%)
Teachers: 585.0 (17.9 to 1)
Librarians/Media Specialists: 14.0 (749.3 to 1)
Guidance Counselors: 21.0 (499.5 to 1)
Current Spending: ($ per student per year):
    Total: $8,227; Instruction: $4,804; Support Services: $3,144
Enrollment, Drop-out Rates and Diploma Recipients by Race/Ethnicity

Category	Total	White	Black	Asian	AIAN	Hisp.
Enrollment (%)	100.0	27.5	60.6	3.6	0.1	8.2
Drop-out Rate (%)	0.0	0.0	0.0	0.0	0.0	0.0
H.S. Diplomas (#)	480	224	217	27	1	11

M S D Warren Township

975 N Post Rd • Indianapolis, IN 46219
(317) 869-4300 • http://www.warren.k12.in.us/
Grade Span: PK-12; **Agency Type:** 1
Schools: 19
    12 Primary; 3 Middle; 1 High; 3 Other Level
    16 Regular; 1 Special Education; 1 Vocational; 1 Alternative

    0 Magnet; 0 Charter; 11 Title I Eligible; 1 School-wide Title I
Students: 11,752 (51.1% male; 48.8% female)
    Individual Education Program: 2,090 (17.8%);
    English Language Learner: 423 (3.6%); Migrant: n/a
    Eligible for Free Lunch Program: 4,072 (34.6%)
    Eligible for Reduced-Price Lunch Program: 1,131 (9.6%)
Teachers: 652.2 (18.0 to 1)
Librarians/Media Specialists: 10.5 (1,119.2 to 1)
Guidance Counselors: 22.0 (534.2 to 1)
Current Spending: ($ per student per year):
    Total: $8,459; Instruction: $4,774; Support Services: $3,384
Enrollment, Drop-out Rates and Diploma Recipients by Race/Ethnicity

Category	Total	White	Black	Asian	AIAN	Hisp.
Enrollment (%)	100.0	56.5	38.2	1.0	0.3	4.1
Drop-out Rate (%)	4.4	4.3	4.6	2.0	n/a	4.3
H.S. Diplomas (#)	550	392	136	7	0	15

M S D Washington Township

8550 Woodfield Crossing Blvd • Indianapolis, IN 46240-2478
(317) 845-9400 • http://www.msdwt.k12.in.us/
Grade Span: PK-12; **Agency Type:** 1
Schools: 14
    9 Primary; 3 Middle; 1 High; 1 Other Level
    13 Regular; 0 Special Education; 1 Vocational; 0 Alternative
    0 Magnet; 0 Charter; 8 Title I Eligible; 0 School-wide Title I
Students: 10,116 (51.0% male; 48.9% female)
    Individual Education Program: 1,495 (14.8%);
    English Language Learner: 999 (9.9%); Migrant: n/a
    Eligible for Free Lunch Program: 2,750 (27.2%)
    Eligible for Reduced-Price Lunch Program: 964 (9.5%)
Teachers: 588.4 (17.2 to 1)
Librarians/Media Specialists: 13.0 (778.2 to 1)
Guidance Counselors: 17.5 (578.1 to 1)
Current Spending: ($ per student per year):
    Total: $8,242; Instruction: $4,973; Support Services: $2,955
Enrollment, Drop-out Rates and Diploma Recipients by Race/Ethnicity

Category	Total	White	Black	Asian	AIAN	Hisp.
Enrollment (%)	100.0	49.8	40.5	1.6	0.2	7.9
Drop-out Rate (%)	0.6	0.3	0.9	0.0	16.7	2.4
H.S. Diplomas (#)	662	432	202	18	2	8

M S D Wayne Township

1220 S High Sch Rd • Indianapolis, IN 46241-3199
(317) 243-8251 • http://www.wayne.k12.in.us/
Grade Span: PK-12; **Agency Type:** 1
Schools: 15
    10 Primary; 3 Middle; 1 High; 1 Other Level
    14 Regular; 1 Special Education; 0 Vocational; 0 Alternative
    0 Magnet; 0 Charter; 8 Title I Eligible; 0 School-wide Title I
Students: 14,174 (51.1% male; 48.8% female)
    Individual Education Program: 2,267 (16.0%);
    English Language Learner: 833 (5.9%); Migrant: n/a
    Eligible for Free Lunch Program: 5,696 (40.5%)
    Eligible for Reduced-Price Lunch Program: 1,357 (9.6%)
Teachers: 831.3 (16.9 to 1)
Librarians/Media Specialists: 14.5 (971.0 to 1)
Guidance Counselors: 21.5 (654.8 to 1)
Current Spending: ($ per student per year):
    Total: $8,518; Instruction: $5,679; Support Services: $2,502
Enrollment, Drop-out Rates and Diploma Recipients by Race/Ethnicity

Category	Total	White	Black	Asian	AIAN	Hisp.
Enrollment (%)	100.0	62.4	29.3	1.4	0.3	6.6
Drop-out Rate (%)	3.8	3.8	3.7	0.0	18.8	3.0
H.S. Diplomas (#)	585	425	138	11	0	11

School Town of Speedway

5335 W 25th St • Speedway, IN 46224-3905
(317) 244-0236 • http://www.speedway.k12.in.us/
Grade Span: KG-12; **Agency Type:** 1
Schools: 6
    4 Primary; 1 Middle; 1 High; 0 Other Level
    6 Regular; 0 Special Education; 0 Vocational; 0 Alternative
    0 Magnet; 0 Charter; 0 Title I Eligible; 0 School-wide Title I
Students: 1,662 (53.1% male; 46.8% female)
    Individual Education Program: 263 (15.8%);
    English Language Learner: 94 (5.7%); Migrant: n/a
    Eligible for Free Lunch Program: 473 (28.5%)
    Eligible for Reduced-Price Lunch Program: 98 (5.9%)
Teachers: 99.5 (16.7 to 1)
Librarians/Media Specialists: 2.0 (831.0 to 1)
Guidance Counselors: 3.0 (554.0 to 1)
Current Spending: ($ per student per year):
    Total: $7,172; Instruction: $4,636; Support Services: $2,141

Enrollment, Drop-out Rates and Diploma Recipients by Race/Ethnicity

Category	Total	White	Black	Asian	AIAN	Hisp.
Enrollment (%)	100.0	70.0	22.8	1.2	0.4	5.6
Drop-out Rate (%)	0.0	0.0	0.0	0.0	0.0	0.0
H.S. Diplomas (#)	84	74	4	5	0	1

Marshall County

Plymouth Community School Corp

611 Berkley St • Plymouth, IN 46563-1817
(574) 936-3115 • http://www.epcsc.k12.in.us/index.htm
Grade Span: PK-12; **Agency Type:** 1
Schools: 6
   4 Primary; 1 Middle; 1 High; 0 Other Level
   6 Regular; 0 Special Education; 0 Vocational; 0 Alternative
   0 Magnet; 0 Charter; 4 Title I Eligible; 0 School-wide Title I
Students: 3,357 (52.2% male; 47.7% female)
   Individual Education Program: 433 (12.9%);
   English Language Learner: 264 (7.9%); Migrant: n/a
   Eligible for Free Lunch Program: 943 (28.1%)
   Eligible for Reduced-Price Lunch Program: 306 (9.1%)
Teachers: 164.2 (20.4 to 1)
Librarians/Media Specialists: 3.0 (1,119.0 to 1)
Guidance Counselors: 5.0 (671.4 to 1)
Current Spending: ($ per student per year):
   Total: $6,980; Instruction: $3,979; Support Services: $2,708
Enrollment, Drop-out Rates and Diploma Recipients by Race/Ethnicity

Category	Total	White	Black	Asian	AIAN	Hisp.
Enrollment (%)	100.0	86.6	0.6	0.5	0.3	12.0
Drop-out Rate (%)	0.8	0.8	0.0	0.0	0.0	1.0
H.S. Diplomas (#)	266	241	0	1	0	24

Miami County

Maconaquah School Corp

7932 S Strawtown Pk • Bunker Hill, IN 46914-9667
(765) 689-9131 • http://www.maconaquah.k12.in.us/
Grade Span: PK-12; **Agency Type:** 1
Schools: 4
   2 Primary; 1 Middle; 1 High; 0 Other Level
   4 Regular; 0 Special Education; 0 Vocational; 0 Alternative
   0 Magnet; 0 Charter; 3 Title I Eligible; 0 School-wide Title I
Students: 2,351 (51.2% male; 48.7% female)
   Individual Education Program: 381 (16.2%);
   English Language Learner: 32 (1.4%); Migrant: n/a
   Eligible for Free Lunch Program: 498 (21.2%)
   Eligible for Reduced-Price Lunch Program: 184 (7.8%)
Teachers: 143.4 (16.4 to 1)
Librarians/Media Specialists: 4.0 (587.8 to 1)
Guidance Counselors: 3.0 (783.7 to 1)
Current Spending: ($ per student per year):
   Total: $8,707; Instruction: $5,212; Support Services: $3,160
Enrollment, Drop-out Rates and Diploma Recipients by Race/Ethnicity

Category	Total	White	Black	Asian	AIAN	Hisp.
Enrollment (%)	100.0	94.7	2.5	0.4	0.8	1.7
Drop-out Rate (%)	0.4	0.5	0.0	0.0	0.0	0.0
H.S. Diplomas (#)	124	120	1	0	2	1

Oak Hill United School Corp

1474 N 800 W 27 PO Box 550 • Converse, IN 46919-0550
(765) 395-3341
Grade Span: PK-12; **Agency Type:** 1
Schools: 5
   3 Primary; 1 Middle; 1 High; 0 Other Level
   5 Regular; 0 Special Education; 0 Vocational; 0 Alternative
   0 Magnet; 0 Charter; 4 Title I Eligible; 0 School-wide Title I
Students: 1,507 (51.7% male; 48.2% female)
   Individual Education Program: 187 (12.4%);
   English Language Learner: 14 (0.9%); Migrant: n/a
   Eligible for Free Lunch Program: 189 (12.5%)
   Eligible for Reduced-Price Lunch Program: 82 (5.4%)
Teachers: 91.7 (16.4 to 1)
Librarians/Media Specialists: 1.0 (1,507.0 to 1)
Guidance Counselors: 1.5 (1,004.7 to 1)
Current Spending: ($ per student per year):
   Total: $7,255; Instruction: $3,959; Support Services: $3,022
Enrollment, Drop-out Rates and Diploma Recipients by Race/Ethnicity

Category	Total	White	Black	Asian	AIAN	Hisp.
Enrollment (%)	100.0	95.8	0.0	0.4	0.9	2.9
Drop-out Rate (%)	2.5	2.6	n/a	n/a	n/a	0.0
H.S. Diplomas (#)	104	101	0	0	0	3

Peru Community Schools

35 W 3rd St • Peru, IN 46970
(765) 473-3081 • http://www.peru.k12.in.us/
Grade Span: PK-12; **Agency Type:** 1
Schools: 6
   4 Primary; 1 Middle; 1 High; 0 Other Level
   6 Regular; 0 Special Education; 0 Vocational; 0 Alternative
   0 Magnet; 0 Charter; 5 Title I Eligible; 0 School-wide Title I
Students: 2,417 (50.9% male; 49.0% female)
   Individual Education Program: 411 (17.0%);
   English Language Learner: 21 (0.9%); Migrant: n/a
   Eligible for Free Lunch Program: 756 (31.3%)
   Eligible for Reduced-Price Lunch Program: 243 (10.1%)
Teachers: 155.5 (15.5 to 1)
Librarians/Media Specialists: 2.0 (1,208.5 to 1)
Guidance Counselors: 4.0 (604.3 to 1)
Current Spending: ($ per student per year):
   Total: $7,065; Instruction: $4,576; Support Services: $2,163
Enrollment, Drop-out Rates and Diploma Recipients by Race/Ethnicity

Category	Total	White	Black	Asian	AIAN	Hisp.
Enrollment (%)	100.0	94.0	2.2	0.8	1.9	1.0
Drop-out Rate (%)	4.9	4.9	5.6	0.0	7.1	0.0
H.S. Diplomas (#)	152	143	4	0	4	1

Monroe County

Monroe County Com Sch Corp

315 N Dr • Bloomington, IN 47401-6595
(812) 330-7700 • http://www.mccsc.edu/
Grade Span: PK-12; **Agency Type:** 1
Schools: 21
   14 Primary; 3 Middle; 3 High; 1 Other Level
   19 Regular; 0 Special Education; 1 Vocational; 1 Alternative
   0 Magnet; 0 Charter; 10 Title I Eligible; 0 School-wide Title I
Students: 10,698 (50.8% male; 49.1% female)
   Individual Education Program: 1,730 (16.2%);
   English Language Learner: 582 (5.4%); Migrant: n/a
   Eligible for Free Lunch Program: 2,346 (21.9%)
   Eligible for Reduced-Price Lunch Program: 729 (6.8%)
Teachers: 632.1 (16.9 to 1)
Librarians/Media Specialists: 16.0 (668.6 to 1)
Guidance Counselors: 17.5 (611.3 to 1)
Current Spending: ($ per student per year):
   Total: $8,454; Instruction: $4,794; Support Services: $3,360
Enrollment, Drop-out Rates and Diploma Recipients by Race/Ethnicity

Category	Total	White	Black	Asian	AIAN	Hisp.
Enrollment (%)	100.0	88.7	4.1	4.7	0.5	1.9
Drop-out Rate (%)	2.7	2.7	4.6	0.0	4.9	0.0
H.S. Diplomas (#)	647	596	20	12	5	14

Richland-Bean Blossom C S C

600 S Edgewood Dr • Ellettsville, IN 47429-1134
(812) 876-7100 • http://www.rbbcsc.k12.in.us/
Grade Span: PK-12; **Agency Type:** 1
Schools: 7
   4 Primary; 1 Middle; 1 High; 1 Other Level
   6 Regular; 1 Special Education; 0 Vocational; 0 Alternative
   0 Magnet; 0 Charter; 2 Title I Eligible; 0 School-wide Title I
Students: 2,751 (52.7% male; 47.2% female)
   Individual Education Program: 510 (18.5%);
   English Language Learner: 9 (0.3%); Migrant: n/a
   Eligible for Free Lunch Program: 427 (15.5%)
   Eligible for Reduced-Price Lunch Program: 186 (6.8%)
Teachers: 169.0 (16.3 to 1)
Librarians/Media Specialists: 3.0 (917.0 to 1)
Guidance Counselors: 5.0 (550.2 to 1)
Current Spending: ($ per student per year):
   Total: $7,397; Instruction: $4,567; Support Services: $2,657
Enrollment, Drop-out Rates and Diploma Recipients by Race/Ethnicity

Category	Total	White	Black	Asian	AIAN	Hisp.
Enrollment (%)	100.0	98.2	0.7	0.7	0.0	0.4
Drop-out Rate (%)	1.0	1.0	0.0	0.0	n/a	0.0
H.S. Diplomas (#)	154	151	1	1	0	1

Montgomery County

Crawfordsville Com Schools

1000 Fairview Ave • Crawfordsville, IN 47933-1511
(765) 362-2342 • http://www.cville.k12.in.us/Cville/Webpages/Start.aspx
Grade Span: PK-12; **Agency Type:** 1
Schools: 8
   5 Primary; 1 Middle; 1 High; 1 Other Level
   6 Regular; 1 Special Education; 0 Vocational; 1 Alternative
   0 Magnet; 0 Charter; 4 Title I Eligible; 1 School-wide Title I
Students: 2,402 (49.7% male; 50.2% female)

Individual Education Program: 401 (16.7%);
English Language Learner: 96 (4.0%); Migrant: n/a
Eligible for Free Lunch Program: 872 (36.3%)
Eligible for Reduced-Price Lunch Program: 182 (7.6%)
Teachers: 156.0 (15.4 to 1)
Librarians/Media Specialists: 4.0 (600.5 to 1)
Guidance Counselors: 5.5 (436.7 to 1)
Current Spending: ($ per student per year):
Total: $8,852; Instruction: $4,854; Support Services: $3,620
Enrollment, Drop-out Rates and Diploma Recipients by Race/Ethnicity

Category	Total	White	Black	Asian	AIAN	Hisp.
Enrollment (%)	100.0	93.1	1.4	0.8	0.2	4.5
Drop-out Rate (%)	0.6	0.5	0.0	0.0	0.0	4.3
H.S. Diplomas (#)	127	120	3	1	0	3

North Montgomery Com Sch Corp
480 W 580 N • Crawfordsville, IN 47933-7306
(765) 359-2112 • http://www.nm.k12.in.us/
Grade Span: KG-12; **Agency Type:** 1
Schools: 5
3 Primary; 1 Middle; 1 High; 0 Other Level
5 Regular; 0 Special Education; 0 Vocational; 0 Alternative
0 Magnet; 0 Charter; 4 Title I Eligible; 0 School-wide Title I
Students: 2,075   (52.0% male; 48.0% female)
Individual Education Program: 354 (17.1%);
English Language Learner: 4 (0.2%); Migrant: n/a
Eligible for Free Lunch Program: 377 (18.2%)
Eligible for Reduced-Price Lunch Program: 118 (5.7%)
Teachers: 118.0 (17.6 to 1)
Librarians/Media Specialists: 1.5 (1,383.3 to 1)
Guidance Counselors: 6.0 (345.8 to 1)
Current Spending: ($ per student per year):
Total: $7,081; Instruction: $3,886; Support Services: $2,900
Enrollment, Drop-out Rates and Diploma Recipients by Race/Ethnicity

Category	Total	White	Black	Asian	AIAN	Hisp.
Enrollment (%)	100.0	99.4	0.1	0.1	0.1	0.2
Drop-out Rate (%)	0.0	0.0	0.0	0.0	0.0	0.0
H.S. Diplomas (#)	108	107	0	1	0	0

South Montgomery Com Sch Corp
200 N 3rd St • New Market, IN 47965-0008
Mailing Address: PO Box 8 • New Market, IN 47965-0008
(765) 866-0203 • http://www.southmont.k12.in.us/
Grade Span: KG-12; **Agency Type:** 1
Schools: 6
4 Primary; 1 Middle; 1 High; 0 Other Level
6 Regular; 0 Special Education; 0 Vocational; 0 Alternative
0 Magnet; 0 Charter; 4 Title I Eligible; 0 School-wide Title I
Students: 2,056   (51.0% male; 48.9% female)
Individual Education Program: 373 (18.1%);
English Language Learner: n/a; Migrant: n/a
Eligible for Free Lunch Program: 357 (17.4%)
Eligible for Reduced-Price Lunch Program: 157 (7.6%)
Teachers: 128.5 (16.0 to 1)
Librarians/Media Specialists: 1.0 (2,056.0 to 1)
Guidance Counselors: 5.0 (411.2 to 1)
Current Spending: ($ per student per year):
Total: $6,598; Instruction: $4,146; Support Services: $2,155
Enrollment, Drop-out Rates and Diploma Recipients by Race/Ethnicity

Category	Total	White	Black	Asian	AIAN	Hisp.
Enrollment (%)	100.0	99.0	0.1	0.2	0.0	0.7
Drop-out Rate (%)	4.5	4.5	n/a	0.0	n/a	0.0
H.S. Diplomas (#)	117	116	0	0	0	1

Morgan County

M S D Martinsville Schools
460 S Main St • Martinsville, IN 46151-1416
Mailing Address: PO Box 1416 • Martinsville, IN 46151-1416
(765) 342-6641 • http://msdadmin.scican.net/
Grade Span: PK-12; **Agency Type:** 1
Schools: 12
8 Primary; 2 Middle; 2 High; 0 Other Level
11 Regular; 0 Special Education; 0 Vocational; 1 Alternative
0 Magnet; 0 Charter; 6 Title I Eligible; 0 School-wide Title I
Students: 5,419   (52.2% male; 47.7% female)
Individual Education Program: 866 (16.0%);
English Language Learner: 20 (0.4%); Migrant: n/a
Eligible for Free Lunch Program: 1,110 (20.5%)
Eligible for Reduced-Price Lunch Program: 430 (7.9%)
Teachers: 308.4 (17.6 to 1)
Librarians/Media Specialists: 4.0 (1,354.8 to 1)
Guidance Counselors: 8.0 (677.4 to 1)
Current Spending: ($ per student per year):
Total: $7,036; Instruction: $4,041; Support Services: $2,693

Enrollment, Drop-out Rates and Diploma Recipients by Race/Ethnicity

Category	Total	White	Black	Asian	AIAN	Hisp.
Enrollment (%)	100.0	99.4	0.0	0.2	0.1	0.3
Drop-out Rate (%)	3.3	3.3	n/a	0.0	n/a	0.0
H.S. Diplomas (#)	312	312	0	0	0	0

Mooresville Con School Corp
11 W Carlisle St • Mooresville, IN 46158-1509
(317) 831-0950 • http://mcsc.k12.in.us/
Grade Span: PK-12; **Agency Type:** 1
Schools: 7
5 Primary; 1 Middle; 1 High; 0 Other Level
7 Regular; 0 Special Education; 0 Vocational; 0 Alternative
0 Magnet; 0 Charter; 3 Title I Eligible; 0 School-wide Title I
Students: 4,341   (51.1% male; 48.8% female)
Individual Education Program: 515 (11.9%);
English Language Learner: 17 (0.4%); Migrant: n/a
Eligible for Free Lunch Program: 646 (14.9%)
Eligible for Reduced-Price Lunch Program: 207 (4.8%)
Teachers: 246.4 (17.6 to 1)
Librarians/Media Specialists: 3.0 (1,447.0 to 1)
Guidance Counselors: 8.0 (542.6 to 1)
Current Spending: ($ per student per year):
Total: $6,591; Instruction: $4,109; Support Services: $2,207
Enrollment, Drop-out Rates and Diploma Recipients by Race/Ethnicity

Category	Total	White	Black	Asian	AIAN	Hisp.
Enrollment (%)	100.0	98.5	0.2	0.4	0.3	0.6
Drop-out Rate (%)	0.7	0.7	n/a	0.0	0.0	0.0
H.S. Diplomas (#)	262	262	0	0	0	0

Newton County

North Newton School Corp
405 W State St • Morocco, IN 47963-0008
Mailing Address: PO Box 8 • Morocco, IN 47963-0008
(219) 285-2228 • http://www.nn.k12.in.us/
Grade Span: KG-12; **Agency Type:** 1
Schools: 4
3 Primary; 0 Middle; 1 High; 0 Other Level
4 Regular; 0 Special Education; 0 Vocational; 0 Alternative
0 Magnet; 0 Charter; 3 Title I Eligible; 0 School-wide Title I
Students: 1,650   (50.4% male; 49.5% female)
Individual Education Program: 293 (17.8%);
English Language Learner: 31 (1.9%); Migrant: n/a
Eligible for Free Lunch Program: 301 (18.2%)
Eligible for Reduced-Price Lunch Program: 137 (8.3%)
Teachers: 104.0 (15.9 to 1)
Librarians/Media Specialists: 1.0 (1,650.0 to 1)
Guidance Counselors: 2.5 (660.0 to 1)
Current Spending: ($ per student per year):
Total: $7,389; Instruction: $4,312; Support Services: $2,812
Enrollment, Drop-out Rates and Diploma Recipients by Race/Ethnicity

Category	Total	White	Black	Asian	AIAN	Hisp.
Enrollment (%)	100.0	96.4	0.2	0.4	0.2	2.9
Drop-out Rate (%)	2.3	2.4	n/a	0.0	0.0	0.0
H.S. Diplomas (#)	75	75	0	0	0	0

Noble County

East Noble School Corp
702 E Dowling St • Kendallville, IN 46755-1298
(260) 347-2502 • http://www.enoble.k12.in.us/
Grade Span: PK-12; **Agency Type:** 1
Schools: 8
6 Primary; 1 Middle; 1 High; 0 Other Level
8 Regular; 0 Special Education; 0 Vocational; 0 Alternative
0 Magnet; 0 Charter; 5 Title I Eligible; 0 School-wide Title I
Students: 3,833   (49.9% male; 50.0% female)
Individual Education Program: 608 (15.9%);
English Language Learner: 71 (1.9%); Migrant: n/a
Eligible for Free Lunch Program: 716 (18.7%)
Eligible for Reduced-Price Lunch Program: 429 (11.2%)
Teachers: 230.7 (16.6 to 1)
Librarians/Media Specialists: 4.0 (958.3 to 1)
Guidance Counselors: 7.0 (547.6 to 1)
Current Spending: ($ per student per year):
Total: $7,530; Instruction: $4,438; Support Services: $2,746
Enrollment, Drop-out Rates and Diploma Recipients by Race/Ethnicity

Category	Total	White	Black	Asian	AIAN	Hisp.
Enrollment (%)	100.0	96.1	0.5	0.7	0.1	2.6
Drop-out Rate (%)	0.0	0.0	0.0	0.0	n/a	0.0
H.S. Diplomas (#)	224	213	0	4	0	7

West Noble School Corporation
5050 N US 33 • Ligonier, IN 46767-9606
(260) 894-3191 • http://westnoble.k12.in.us/
Grade Span: KG-12; **Agency Type:** 1
Schools: 4
  2 Primary; 1 Middle; 1 High; 0 Other Level
  4 Regular; 0 Special Education; 0 Vocational; 0 Alternative
  0 Magnet; 0 Charter; 3 Title I Eligible; 0 School-wide Title I
Students: 2,504 (52.5% male; 47.4% female)
  Individual Education Program: 289 (11.5%);
  English Language Learner: 795 (31.7%); Migrant: n/a
  Eligible for Free Lunch Program: 995 (39.7%)
  Eligible for Reduced-Price Lunch Program: 299 (11.9%)
Teachers: 144.5 (17.3 to 1)
Librarians/Media Specialists: 2.3 (1,088.7 to 1)
Guidance Counselors: 3.3 (758.8 to 1)
Current Spending: ($ per student per year):
  Total: $7,856; Instruction: $4,451; Support Services: $3,078
Enrollment, Drop-out Rates and Diploma Recipients by Race/Ethnicity

Category	Total	White	Black	Asian	AIAN	Hisp.
Enrollment (%)	100.0	66.7	0.2	0.4	0.0	32.7
Drop-out Rate (%)	0.0	0.0	0.0	0.0	n/a	0.0
H.S. Diplomas (#)	119	95	0	2	0	22

Orange County

Paoli Community School Corp
501 Elm St - Ofc Supt • Paoli, IN 47454-1197
(812) 723-4717
Grade Span: KG-12; **Agency Type:** 1
Schools: 2
  1 Primary; 0 Middle; 1 High; 0 Other Level
  2 Regular; 0 Special Education; 0 Vocational; 0 Alternative
  0 Magnet; 0 Charter; 1 Title I Eligible; 0 School-wide Title I
Students: 1,712 (50.7% male; 49.2% female)
  Individual Education Program: 303 (17.7%);
  English Language Learner: 5 (0.3%); Migrant: n/a
  Eligible for Free Lunch Program: 579 (33.8%)
  Eligible for Reduced-Price Lunch Program: 193 (11.3%)
Teachers: 90.2 (19.0 to 1)
Librarians/Media Specialists: 1.0 (1,712.0 to 1)
Guidance Counselors: 3.0 (570.7 to 1)
Current Spending: ($ per student per year):
  Total: $6,787; Instruction: $4,596; Support Services: $1,886
Enrollment, Drop-out Rates and Diploma Recipients by Race/Ethnicity

Category	Total	White	Black	Asian	AIAN	Hisp.
Enrollment (%)	100.0	99.4	0.2	0.1	0.1	0.2
Drop-out Rate (%)	4.3	4.4	0.0	0.0	n/a	n/a
H.S. Diplomas (#)	108	108	0	0	0	0

Owen County

Spencer-Owen Community Schools
205 E Hillside • Spencer, IN 47460-1099
(812) 829-2233 • http://www.socs.k12.in.us/
Grade Span: PK-12; **Agency Type:** 1
Schools: 6
  4 Primary; 1 Middle; 1 High; 0 Other Level
  6 Regular; 0 Special Education; 0 Vocational; 0 Alternative
  0 Magnet; 0 Charter; 5 Title I Eligible; 0 School-wide Title I
Students: 3,140 (50.7% male; 49.2% female)
  Individual Education Program: 669 (21.3%);
  English Language Learner: 2 (0.1%); Migrant: n/a
  Eligible for Free Lunch Program: 933 (29.7%)
  Eligible for Reduced-Price Lunch Program: 247 (7.9%)
Teachers: 191.4 (16.4 to 1)
Librarians/Media Specialists: 2.0 (1,570.0 to 1)
Guidance Counselors: 6.0 (523.3 to 1)
Current Spending: ($ per student per year):
  Total: $7,955; Instruction: $4,878; Support Services: $2,831
Enrollment, Drop-out Rates and Diploma Recipients by Race/Ethnicity

Category	Total	White	Black	Asian	AIAN	Hisp.
Enrollment (%)	100.0	98.7	0.4	0.2	0.4	0.4
Drop-out Rate (%)	5.8	5.7	0.0	0.0	0.0	20.0
H.S. Diplomas (#)	187	187	0	0	0	0

Perry County

Tell City-Troy Twp School Corp
837 17th St • Tell City, IN 47586-1698
(812) 547-3300 • http://www.tellcity.k12.in.us/
Grade Span: PK-12; **Agency Type:** 1
Schools: 3
  1 Primary; 1 Middle; 1 High; 0 Other Level
  3 Regular; 0 Special Education; 0 Vocational; 0 Alternative

---

  0 Magnet; 0 Charter; 1 Title I Eligible; 0 School-wide Title I
Students: 1,688 (51.4% male; 48.5% female)
  Individual Education Program: 228 (13.5%);
  English Language Learner: 6 (0.4%); Migrant: n/a
  Eligible for Free Lunch Program: 408 (24.2%)
  Eligible for Reduced-Price Lunch Program: 133 (7.9%)
Teachers: 92.0 (18.3 to 1)
Librarians/Media Specialists: 3.0 (562.7 to 1)
Guidance Counselors: 4.5 (375.1 to 1)
Current Spending: ($ per student per year):
  Total: $7,097; Instruction: $4,286; Support Services: $2,537
Enrollment, Drop-out Rates and Diploma Recipients by Race/Ethnicity

Category	Total	White	Black	Asian	AIAN	Hisp.
Enrollment (%)	100.0	98.7	0.1	0.7	0.2	0.4
Drop-out Rate (%)	3.9	3.9	n/a	0.0	n/a	n/a
H.S. Diplomas (#)	108	108	0	0	0	0

Pike County

Pike County School Corp
907 Walnut St • Petersburg, IN 47567-1561
(812) 354-8731 • http://www.pcsc.k12.in.us/
Grade Span: PK-12; **Agency Type:** 1
Schools: 5
  3 Primary; 1 Middle; 1 High; 0 Other Level
  5 Regular; 0 Special Education; 0 Vocational; 0 Alternative
  0 Magnet; 0 Charter; 3 Title I Eligible; 0 School-wide Title I
Students: 2,144 (50.2% male; 49.7% female)
  Individual Education Program: 397 (18.5%);
  English Language Learner: 2 (0.1%); Migrant: n/a
  Eligible for Free Lunch Program: 522 (24.3%)
  Eligible for Reduced-Price Lunch Program: 246 (11.5%)
Teachers: 122.5 (17.5 to 1)
Librarians/Media Specialists: 1.0 (2,144.0 to 1)
Guidance Counselors: 3.0 (714.7 to 1)
Current Spending: ($ per student per year):
  Total: $6,780; Instruction: $4,027; Support Services: $2,535
Enrollment, Drop-out Rates and Diploma Recipients by Race/Ethnicity

Category	Total	White	Black	Asian	AIAN	Hisp.
Enrollment (%)	100.0	99.2	0.1	0.4	0.0	0.4
Drop-out Rate (%)	2.6	2.6	n/a	0.0	n/a	n/a
H.S. Diplomas (#)	124	124	0	0	0	0

Porter County

Duneland School Corporation
700 W Porter Ave • Chesterton, IN 46304-2205
(219) 983-3605 • http://www.duneland.k12.in.us/
Grade Span: KG-12; **Agency Type:** 1
Schools: 9
  5 Primary; 3 Middle; 1 High; 0 Other Level
  9 Regular; 0 Special Education; 0 Vocational; 0 Alternative
  0 Magnet; 0 Charter; 5 Title I Eligible; 0 School-wide Title I
Students: 5,421 (52.2% male; 47.7% female)
  Individual Education Program: 920 (17.0%);
  English Language Learner: 72 (1.3%); Migrant: n/a
  Eligible for Free Lunch Program: 801 (14.8%)
  Eligible for Reduced-Price Lunch Program: 297 (5.5%)
Teachers: 266.6 (20.3 to 1)
Librarians/Media Specialists: 11.0 (492.8 to 1)
Guidance Counselors: 11.0 (492.8 to 1)
Current Spending: ($ per student per year):
  Total: $7,715; Instruction: $4,309; Support Services: $3,108
Enrollment, Drop-out Rates and Diploma Recipients by Race/Ethnicity

Category	Total	White	Black	Asian	AIAN	Hisp.
Enrollment (%)	100.0	95.4	0.5	1.1	0.3	2.7
Drop-out Rate (%)	0.6	0.6	0.0	0.0	0.0	0.0
H.S. Diplomas (#)	390	365	1	5	2	17

East Porter County School Corp
502 E College • Kouts, IN 46347
Mailing Address: 502 E College - PO Box 370 • Kouts, IN 46347
(219) 766-2214
Grade Span: KG-12; **Agency Type:** 1
Schools: 6
  3 Primary; 0 Middle; 0 High; 3 Other Level
  6 Regular; 0 Special Education; 0 Vocational; 0 Alternative
  0 Magnet; 0 Charter; 4 Title I Eligible; 0 School-wide Title I
Students: 1,969 (50.1% male; 49.8% female)
  Individual Education Program: 345 (17.5%);
  English Language Learner: 6 (0.3%); Migrant: n/a
  Eligible for Free Lunch Program: 126 (6.4%)
  Eligible for Reduced-Price Lunch Program: 102 (5.2%)
Teachers: 115.5 (17.0 to 1)
Librarians/Media Specialists: 2.0 (984.5 to 1)

Guidance Counselors: 3.0 (656.3 to 1)
Current Spending: ($ per student per year):
   Total: $7,082; Instruction: $4,063; Support Services: $2,744
Enrollment, Drop-out Rates and Diploma Recipients by Race/Ethnicity

Category	Total	White	Black	Asian	AIAN	Hisp.
Enrollment (%)	100.0	98.4	0.1	0.5	0.0	1.0
Drop-out Rate (%)	1.1	1.1	0.0	0.0	n/a	0.0
H.S. Diplomas (#)	138	138	0	0	0	0

Portage Township Schools
6240 US Hwy 6 • Portage, IN 46368-5057
(219) 762-6511 • http://www.portage.k12.in.us/
Grade Span: PK-12; **Agency Type:** 1
Schools: 11
   8 Primary; 2 Middle; 1 High; 0 Other Level
   11 Regular; 0 Special Education; 0 Vocational; 0 Alternative
   0 Magnet; 0 Charter; 8 Title I Eligible; 0 School-wide Title I
Students: 8,021   (51.4% male; 48.5% female)
   Individual Education Program: 1,261 (15.7%);
   English Language Learner: 234 (2.9%); Migrant: n/a
   Eligible for Free Lunch Program: 1,908 (23.8%)
   Eligible for Reduced-Price Lunch Program: 619 (7.7%)
Teachers: 403.6 (19.9 to 1)
Librarians/Media Specialists: 6.0 (1,336.8 to 1)
Guidance Counselors: 10.0 (802.1 to 1)
Current Spending: ($ per student per year):
   Total: $7,085; Instruction: $4,182; Support Services: $2,627
Enrollment, Drop-out Rates and Diploma Recipients by Race/Ethnicity

Category	Total	White	Black	Asian	AIAN	Hisp.
Enrollment (%)	100.0	86.1	3.1	0.8	0.1	9.9
Drop-out Rate (%)	1.7	1.6	8.3	0.0	0.0	2.8
H.S. Diplomas (#)	521	459	8	6	3	45

Porter Township School Corp
248 S 500 W • Valparaiso, IN 46383-9642
(219) 477-4933 • http://www.ptsc.k12.in.us/
Grade Span: KG-12; **Agency Type:** 1
Schools: 4
   2 Primary; 1 Middle; 1 High; 0 Other Level
   4 Regular; 0 Special Education; 0 Vocational; 0 Alternative
   0 Magnet; 0 Charter; 2 Title I Eligible; 0 School-wide Title I
Students: 1,537   (52.2% male; 47.7% female)
   Individual Education Program: 177 (11.5%);
   English Language Learner: 10 (0.7%); Migrant: n/a
   Eligible for Free Lunch Program: 92 (6.0%)
   Eligible for Reduced-Price Lunch Program: 43 (2.8%)
Teachers: 75.5 (20.4 to 1)
Librarians/Media Specialists: 2.0 (768.5 to 1)
Guidance Counselors: 1.0 (1,537.0 to 1)
Current Spending: ($ per student per year):
   Total: $6,765; Instruction: $3,612; Support Services: $2,851
Enrollment, Drop-out Rates and Diploma Recipients by Race/Ethnicity

Category	Total	White	Black	Asian	AIAN	Hisp.
Enrollment (%)	100.0	94.2	0.7	0.7	0.5	4.0
Drop-out Rate (%)	1.7	1.8	0.0	0.0	n/a	0.0
H.S. Diplomas (#)	137	130	0	3	0	4

Union Township School Corp
599 W 300 N Ste A • Valparaiso, IN 46385-9212
(219) 759-2531
Grade Span: KG-12; **Agency Type:** 1
Schools: 4
   2 Primary; 1 Middle; 1 High; 0 Other Level
   4 Regular; 0 Special Education; 0 Vocational; 0 Alternative
   0 Magnet; 0 Charter; 2 Title I Eligible; 0 School-wide Title I
Students: 1,558   (50.3% male; 49.6% female)
   Individual Education Program: 261 (16.8%);
   English Language Learner: 34 (2.2%); Migrant: n/a
   Eligible for Free Lunch Program: 107 (6.9%)
   Eligible for Reduced-Price Lunch Program: 78 (5.0%)
Teachers: 89.0 (17.5 to 1)
Librarians/Media Specialists: 0.0 (n/a to 1)
Guidance Counselors: 1.0 (1,558.0 to 1)
Current Spending: ($ per student per year):
   Total: $7,057; Instruction: $4,250; Support Services: $2,520
Enrollment, Drop-out Rates and Diploma Recipients by Race/Ethnicity

Category	Total	White	Black	Asian	AIAN	Hisp.
Enrollment (%)	100.0	93.1	0.4	0.9	1.0	4.6
Drop-out Rate (%)	1.0	1.1	0.0	0.0	0.0	0.0
H.S. Diplomas (#)	109	100	0	1	3	5

Valparaiso Community Schools
3801 N Campbell St • Valparaiso, IN 46385
(219) 531-3000 • http://www.valpo.k12.in.us/
Grade Span: KG-12; **Agency Type:** 1
Schools: 12
   8 Primary; 2 Middle; 1 High; 1 Other Level
   11 Regular; 0 Special Education; 1 Vocational; 0 Alternative
   0 Magnet; 0 Charter; 5 Title I Eligible; 0 School-wide Title I
Students: 6,057   (49.8% male; 50.1% female)
   Individual Education Program: 818 (13.5%);
   English Language Learner: 181 (3.0%); Migrant: n/a
   Eligible for Free Lunch Program: 689 (11.4%)
   Eligible for Reduced-Price Lunch Program: 291 (4.8%)
Teachers: 313.5 (19.3 to 1)
Librarians/Media Specialists: 4.0 (1,514.3 to 1)
Guidance Counselors: 10.5 (576.9 to 1)
Current Spending: ($ per student per year):
   Total: $7,726; Instruction: $4,972; Support Services: $2,357
Enrollment, Drop-out Rates and Diploma Recipients by Race/Ethnicity

Category	Total	White	Black	Asian	AIAN	Hisp.
Enrollment (%)	100.0	91.6	2.5	2.3	0.1	3.5
Drop-out Rate (%)	0.8	0.8	0.0	0.0	50.0	0.0
H.S. Diplomas (#)	494	468	5	13	1	7

Posey County

M S D Mount Vernon
1000 W 4th St • Mount Vernon, IN 47620-1696
(812) 838-4471
Grade Span: PK-12; **Agency Type:** 1
Schools: 6
   4 Primary; 1 Middle; 1 High; 0 Other Level
   6 Regular; 0 Special Education; 0 Vocational; 0 Alternative
   0 Magnet; 0 Charter; 2 Title I Eligible; 0 School-wide Title I
Students: 2,721   (51.5% male; 48.4% female)
   Individual Education Program: 618 (22.7%);
   English Language Learner: 8 (0.3%); Migrant: n/a
   Eligible for Free Lunch Program: 513 (18.9%)
   Eligible for Reduced-Price Lunch Program: 125 (4.6%)
Teachers: 170.0 (16.0 to 1)
Librarians/Media Specialists: 3.5 (777.4 to 1)
Guidance Counselors: 5.0 (544.2 to 1)
Current Spending: ($ per student per year):
   Total: $8,750; Instruction: $5,230; Support Services: $3,164
Enrollment, Drop-out Rates and Diploma Recipients by Race/Ethnicity

Category	Total	White	Black	Asian	AIAN	Hisp.
Enrollment (%)	100.0	97.2	1.7	0.3	0.3	0.6
Drop-out Rate (%)	2.7	2.7	0.0	n/a	50.0	n/a
H.S. Diplomas (#)	192	188	4	0	0	0

Putnam County

Greencastle Community Sch Corp
PO Box 480 • Greencastle, IN 46135-0480
(765) 653-9771 • http://www.greencastle.k12.in.us/
Grade Span: KG-12; **Agency Type:** 1
Schools: 5
   3 Primary; 1 Middle; 1 High; 0 Other Level
   5 Regular; 0 Special Education; 0 Vocational; 0 Alternative
   0 Magnet; 0 Charter; 3 Title I Eligible; 0 School-wide Title I
Students: 1,959   (52.8% male; 47.1% female)
   Individual Education Program: 421 (21.5%);
   English Language Learner: 18 (0.9%); Migrant: n/a
   Eligible for Free Lunch Program: 417 (21.3%)
   Eligible for Reduced-Price Lunch Program: 161 (8.2%)
Teachers: 106.3 (18.4 to 1)
Librarians/Media Specialists: 2.0 (979.5 to 1)
Guidance Counselors: 6.0 (326.5 to 1)
Current Spending: ($ per student per year):
   Total: $6,763; Instruction: $3,574; Support Services: $2,855
Enrollment, Drop-out Rates and Diploma Recipients by Race/Ethnicity

Category	Total	White	Black	Asian	AIAN	Hisp.
Enrollment (%)	100.0	97.5	1.2	0.7	0.1	0.5
Drop-out Rate (%)	1.4	1.4	0.0	0.0	n/a	0.0
H.S. Diplomas (#)	136	136	0	0	0	0

North Putnam Community Schools
300 N Washington • Bainbridge, IN 46105-0169
Mailing Address: PO Box 169-300 N Washington • Bainbridge, IN 46105-0169
(765) 522-6218 • http://www.nputnam.k12.in.us/
Grade Span: PK-12; **Agency Type:** 1
Schools: 5
   2 Primary; 1 Middle; 1 High; 1 Other Level
   4 Regular; 1 Special Education; 0 Vocational; 0 Alternative

0 Magnet; 0 Charter; 3 Title I Eligible; 0 School-wide Title I
Students: 1,927   (52.8% male; 47.1% female)
   Individual Education Program: 505 (26.2%);
   English Language Learner: n/a; Migrant: n/a
   Eligible for Free Lunch Program: 380 (19.7%)
   Eligible for Reduced-Price Lunch Program: 119 (6.2%)
Teachers: 148.5 (13.0 to 1)
Librarians/Media Specialists: 3.0 (642.3 to 1)
Guidance Counselors: 4.0 (481.8 to 1)
Current Spending: ($ per student per year):
   Total: $9,049; Instruction: $5,844; Support Services: $2,871
Enrollment, Drop-out Rates and Diploma Recipients by Race/Ethnicity

Category	Total	White	Black	Asian	AIAN	Hisp.
Enrollment (%)	100.0	99.1	0.4	0.3	0.0	0.2
Drop-out Rate (%)	3.3	3.4	0.0	n/a	n/a	0.0
H.S. Diplomas (#)	109	109	0	0	0	0

Randolph County

Randolph Central School Corp
103 N E St • Winchester, IN 47394-1604
(765) 584-1401 • http://www.rc.k12.in.us/
Grade Span: KG-12; **Agency Type:** 1
Schools: 5
   3 Primary; 1 Middle; 1 High; 0 Other Level
   5 Regular; 0 Special Education; 0 Vocational; 0 Alternative
   0 Magnet; 0 Charter; 3 Title I Eligible; 0 School-wide Title I
Students: 1,678   (52.2% male; 47.7% female)
   Individual Education Program: 402 (24.0%);
   English Language Learner: 14 (0.8%); Migrant: n/a
   Eligible for Free Lunch Program: 475 (28.3%)
   Eligible for Reduced-Price Lunch Program: 122 (7.3%)
Teachers: 109.2 (15.4 to 1)
Librarians/Media Specialists: 1.5 (1,118.7 to 1)
Guidance Counselors: 3.5 (479.4 to 1)
Current Spending: ($ per student per year):
   Total: $7,119; Instruction: $4,388; Support Services: $2,482
Enrollment, Drop-out Rates and Diploma Recipients by Race/Ethnicity

Category	Total	White	Black	Asian	AIAN	Hisp.
Enrollment (%)	100.0	98.0	0.4	0.4	0.1	1.1
Drop-out Rate (%)	3.0	3.0	0.0	0.0	n/a	0.0
H.S. Diplomas (#)	98	95	1	2	0	0

Ripley County

Batesville Community Sch Corp
626 N Huntersville Rd • Batesville, IN 47006-0121
Mailing Address: PO Box 121 • Batesville, IN 47006-0121
(812) 934-2194 • http://www.batesville.k12.in.us/bcsc/default.html
Grade Span: PK-12; **Agency Type:** 1
Schools: 4
   1 Primary; 2 Middle; 1 High; 0 Other Level
   4 Regular; 0 Special Education; 0 Vocational; 0 Alternative
   0 Magnet; 0 Charter; 2 Title I Eligible; 0 School-wide Title I
Students: 1,913   (50.9% male; 49.0% female)
   Individual Education Program: 313 (16.4%);
   English Language Learner: 35 (1.8%); Migrant: n/a
   Eligible for Free Lunch Program: 122 (6.4%)
   Eligible for Reduced-Price Lunch Program: 73 (3.8%)
Teachers: 112.2 (17.0 to 1)
Librarians/Media Specialists: 3.6 (531.4 to 1)
Guidance Counselors: 4.0 (478.3 to 1)
Current Spending: ($ per student per year):
   Total: $6,989; Instruction: $4,154; Support Services: $2,593
Enrollment, Drop-out Rates and Diploma Recipients by Race/Ethnicity

Category	Total	White	Black	Asian	AIAN	Hisp.
Enrollment (%)	100.0	98.1	0.1	0.7	0.2	1.0
Drop-out Rate (%)	1.2	1.2	n/a	0.0	0.0	0.0
H.S. Diplomas (#)	125	122	0	0	1	2

South Ripley Com Sch Corp
207 W Tyson St • Versailles, IN 47042-0690
Mailing Address: PO Box 690 • Versailles, IN 47042-0690
(812) 689-6282
Grade Span: KG-12; **Agency Type:** 1
Schools: 2
   1 Primary; 0 Middle; 1 High; 0 Other Level
   2 Regular; 0 Special Education; 0 Vocational; 0 Alternative
   0 Magnet; 0 Charter; 1 Title I Eligible; 0 School-wide Title I
Students: 1,513   (51.8% male; 48.1% female)
   Individual Education Program: 246 (16.3%);
   English Language Learner: 7 (0.5%); Migrant: n/a
   Eligible for Free Lunch Program: 356 (23.5%)
   Eligible for Reduced-Price Lunch Program: 127 (8.4%)
Teachers: 80.0 (18.9 to 1)

Librarians/Media Specialists: 2.0 (756.5 to 1)
Guidance Counselors: 4.0 (378.3 to 1)
Current Spending: ($ per student per year):
   Total: $7,038; Instruction: $4,413; Support Services: $2,300
Enrollment, Drop-out Rates and Diploma Recipients by Race/Ethnicity

Category	Total	White	Black	Asian	AIAN	Hisp.
Enrollment (%)	100.0	99.6	0.2	0.0	0.0	0.2
Drop-out Rate (%)	0.2	0.2	0.0	n/a	n/a	n/a
H.S. Diplomas (#)	92	91	0	1	0	0

Rush County

Rush County Schools
330 W 8th St • Rushville, IN 46173-1217
(765) 932-4186 • http://rcs.rushville.k12.in.us/
Grade Span: PK-12; **Agency Type:** 1
Schools: 6
   4 Primary; 1 Middle; 1 High; 0 Other Level
   6 Regular; 0 Special Education; 0 Vocational; 0 Alternative
   0 Magnet; 0 Charter; 2 Title I Eligible; 0 School-wide Title I
Students: 2,703   (50.9% male; 49.0% female)
   Individual Education Program: 382 (14.1%);
   English Language Learner: 19 (0.7%); Migrant: n/a
   Eligible for Free Lunch Program: 591 (21.9%)
   Eligible for Reduced-Price Lunch Program: 217 (8.0%)
Teachers: 167.8 (16.1 to 1)
Librarians/Media Specialists: 4.0 (675.8 to 1)
Guidance Counselors: 4.0 (675.8 to 1)
Current Spending: ($ per student per year):
   Total: $7,071; Instruction: $4,328; Support Services: $2,327
Enrollment, Drop-out Rates and Diploma Recipients by Race/Ethnicity

Category	Total	White	Black	Asian	AIAN	Hisp.
Enrollment (%)	100.0	97.9	0.8	0.4	0.0	1.0
Drop-out Rate (%)	1.2	1.2	0.0	0.0	n/a	0.0
H.S. Diplomas (#)	146	145	0	0	0	1

Scott County

Scott County SD 2
375 E Mcclain Ave • Scottsburg, IN 47170-1798
(812) 752-8946 • http://www.scott1.k12.in.us/
Grade Span: KG-12; **Agency Type:** 1
Schools: 6
   4 Primary; 1 Middle; 1 High; 0 Other Level
   6 Regular; 0 Special Education; 0 Vocational; 0 Alternative
   0 Magnet; 0 Charter; 4 Title I Eligible; 0 School-wide Title I
Students: 2,821   (52.8% male; 47.1% female)
   Individual Education Program: 422 (15.0%);
   English Language Learner: 12 (0.4%); Migrant: n/a
   Eligible for Free Lunch Program: 860 (30.5%)
   Eligible for Reduced-Price Lunch Program: 209 (7.4%)
Teachers: 152.6 (18.5 to 1)
Librarians/Media Specialists: 3.0 (940.3 to 1)
Guidance Counselors: 7.7 (366.4 to 1)
Current Spending: ($ per student per year):
   Total: $6,849; Instruction: $4,141; Support Services: $2,408
Enrollment, Drop-out Rates and Diploma Recipients by Race/Ethnicity

Category	Total	White	Black	Asian	AIAN	Hisp.
Enrollment (%)	100.0	100.0	0.0	0.0	0.0	0.0
Drop-out Rate (%)	2.6	2.7	0.0	0.0	n/a	n/a
H.S. Diplomas (#)	139	139	0	0	0	0

Shelby County

Northwestern Con School Corp
4920 W 600 N • Fairland, IN 46126-9702
(317) 835-7461
Grade Span: KG-12; **Agency Type:** 1
Schools: 3
   1 Primary; 1 Middle; 1 High; 0 Other Level
   3 Regular; 0 Special Education; 0 Vocational; 0 Alternative
   0 Magnet; 0 Charter; 2 Title I Eligible; 0 School-wide Title I
Students: 1,539   (51.5% male; 48.4% female)
   Individual Education Program: 257 (16.7%);
   English Language Learner: n/a; Migrant: n/a
   Eligible for Free Lunch Program: 183 (11.9%)
   Eligible for Reduced-Price Lunch Program: 116 (7.5%)
Teachers: 78.0 (19.7 to 1)
Librarians/Media Specialists: 3.0 (513.0 to 1)
Guidance Counselors: 4.0 (384.8 to 1)
Current Spending: ($ per student per year):
   Total: $6,422; Instruction: $3,918; Support Services: $2,203

Enrollment, Drop-out Rates and Diploma Recipients by Race/Ethnicity

Category	Total	White	Black	Asian	AIAN	Hisp.
Enrollment (%)	100.0	99.2	0.0	0.3	0.2	0.3
Drop-out Rate (%)	0.4	0.4	0.0	0.0	n/a	0.0
H.S. Diplomas (#)	93	92	0	0	0	1

Shelby Eastern Schools
2451 N 600 E • Shelbyville, IN 46176-9113
(765) 544-2246 • http://www.ses.k12.in.us/
Grade Span: KG-12; **Agency Type:** 1
Schools: 4
  2 Primary; 0 Middle; 0 High; 2 Other Level
  4 Regular; 0 Special Education; 0 Vocational; 0 Alternative
  0 Magnet; 0 Charter; 3 Title I Eligible; 0 School-wide Title I
Students: 1,595   (51.0% male; 48.9% female)
  Individual Education Program: 275 (17.2%);
  English Language Learner: n/a; Migrant: n/a
  Eligible for Free Lunch Program: 183 (11.5%)
  Eligible for Reduced-Price Lunch Program: 59 (3.7%)
Teachers: 99.3 (16.1 to 1)
Librarians/Media Specialists: 3.0 (531.7 to 1)
Guidance Counselors: 5.0 (319.0 to 1)
Current Spending: ($ per student per year):
  Total: $6,539; Instruction: $3,958; Support Services: $2,301

Enrollment, Drop-out Rates and Diploma Recipients by Race/Ethnicity

Category	Total	White	Black	Asian	AIAN	Hisp.
Enrollment (%)	100.0	99.4	0.2	0.1	0.0	0.3
Drop-out Rate (%)	1.7	1.7	n/a	0.0	n/a	0.0
H.S. Diplomas (#)	131	127	1	2	0	1

Shelbyville Central Schools
803 St Joseph St • Shelbyville, IN 46176-1295
(317) 392-2505 • http://www.shelbycs.org/
Grade Span: KG-12; **Agency Type:** 1
Schools: 5
  3 Primary; 1 Middle; 1 High; 0 Other Level
  5 Regular; 0 Special Education; 0 Vocational; 0 Alternative
  0 Magnet; 0 Charter; 3 Title I Eligible; 0 School-wide Title I
Students: 3,814   (52.4% male; 47.5% female)
  Individual Education Program: 850 (22.3%);
  English Language Learner: 168 (4.4%); Migrant: n/a
  Eligible for Free Lunch Program: 873 (22.9%)
  Eligible for Reduced-Price Lunch Program: 274 (7.2%)
Teachers: 188.0 (20.3 to 1)
Librarians/Media Specialists: 2.0 (1,907.0 to 1)
Guidance Counselors: 8.0 (476.8 to 1)
Current Spending: ($ per student per year):
  Total: $6,726; Instruction: $4,121; Support Services: $2,230

Enrollment, Drop-out Rates and Diploma Recipients by Race/Ethnicity

Category	Total	White	Black	Asian	AIAN	Hisp.
Enrollment (%)	100.0	93.3	1.5	1.2	0.0	4.1
Drop-out Rate (%)	0.0	0.0	0.0	0.0	n/a	0.0
H.S. Diplomas (#)	170	164	3	2	0	1

Spencer County

North Spencer County Sch Corp
3720 E Sr 162 • Lincoln City, IN 47552-0316
Mailing Address: PO Box 316 • Lincoln City, IN 47552-0316
(812) 937-2400 • http://www.nspencer.k12.in.us/
Grade Span: PK-12; **Agency Type:** 1
Schools: 6
  4 Primary; 1 Middle; 1 High; 0 Other Level
  6 Regular; 0 Special Education; 0 Vocational; 0 Alternative
  0 Magnet; 0 Charter; 2 Title I Eligible; 0 School-wide Title I
Students: 2,307   (49.5% male; 50.4% female)
  Individual Education Program: 294 (12.7%);
  English Language Learner: 66 (2.9%); Migrant: n/a
  Eligible for Free Lunch Program: 246 (10.7%)
  Eligible for Reduced-Price Lunch Program: 164 (7.1%)
Teachers: 129.5 (17.8 to 1)
Librarians/Media Specialists: 3.0 (769.0 to 1)
Guidance Counselors: 3.0 (769.0 to 1)
Current Spending: ($ per student per year):
  Total: $6,925; Instruction: $4,455; Support Services: $2,128

Enrollment, Drop-out Rates and Diploma Recipients by Race/Ethnicity

Category	Total	White	Black	Asian	AIAN	Hisp.
Enrollment (%)	100.0	96.2	0.2	0.4	0.0	3.2
Drop-out Rate (%)	0.4	0.4	0.0	0.0	n/a	0.0
H.S. Diplomas (#)	160	157	1	0	0	2

St. Joseph County

John Glenn School Corporation
101 John Glenn Dr • Walkerton, IN 46574-1288
(574) 586-3129 • http://www.jgsc.k12.in.us/
Grade Span: PK-12; **Agency Type:** 1
Schools: 4
  2 Primary; 1 Middle; 1 High; 0 Other Level
  4 Regular; 0 Special Education; 0 Vocational; 0 Alternative
  0 Magnet; 0 Charter; 1 Title I Eligible; 0 School-wide Title I
Students: 1,734   (51.2% male; 48.7% female)
  Individual Education Program: 243 (14.0%);
  English Language Learner: 23 (1.3%); Migrant: n/a
  Eligible for Free Lunch Program: 280 (16.1%)
  Eligible for Reduced-Price Lunch Program: 159 (9.2%)
Teachers: 90.2 (19.2 to 1)
Librarians/Media Specialists: 3.0 (578.0 to 1)
Guidance Counselors: 4.0 (433.5 to 1)
Current Spending: ($ per student per year):
  Total: $6,821; Instruction: $4,096; Support Services: $2,422

Enrollment, Drop-out Rates and Diploma Recipients by Race/Ethnicity

Category	Total	White	Black	Asian	AIAN	Hisp.
Enrollment (%)	100.0	96.9	0.3	0.1	0.4	2.3
Drop-out Rate (%)	0.4	0.4	0.0	0.0	n/a	0.0
H.S. Diplomas (#)	113	112	0	0	0	1

Penn-Harris-Madison Sch Corp
55900 Bittersweet Rd • Mishawaka, IN 46545-7717
(574) 259-7941 • http://www.phm.k12.in.us/
Grade Span: KG-12; **Agency Type:** 1
Schools: 15
  11 Primary; 3 Middle; 1 High; 0 Other Level
  15 Regular; 0 Special Education; 0 Vocational; 0 Alternative
  0 Magnet; 0 Charter; 7 Title I Eligible; 0 School-wide Title I
Students: 10,056   (50.4% male; 49.5% female)
  Individual Education Program: 1,408 (14.0%);
  English Language Learner: 361 (3.6%); Migrant: n/a
  Eligible for Free Lunch Program: 961 (9.6%)
  Eligible for Reduced-Price Lunch Program: 356 (3.5%)
Teachers: 481.2 (20.9 to 1)
Librarians/Media Specialists: 1.0 (10,056.0 to 1)
Guidance Counselors: 14.0 (718.3 to 1)
Current Spending: ($ per student per year):
  Total: $7,426; Instruction: $4,346; Support Services: $2,822

Enrollment, Drop-out Rates and Diploma Recipients by Race/Ethnicity

Category	Total	White	Black	Asian	AIAN	Hisp.
Enrollment (%)	100.0	92.6	2.4	2.7	0.7	1.6
Drop-out Rate (%)	1.1	1.1	6.7	0.0	0.0	0.0
H.S. Diplomas (#)	619	587	9	15	1	7

School City of Mishawaka
1402 S Main St • Mishawaka, IN 46544-5297
(574) 254-4537
Grade Span: PK-12; **Agency Type:** 1
Schools: 11
  7 Primary; 1 Middle; 1 High; 2 Other Level
  9 Regular; 2 Special Education; 0 Vocational; 0 Alternative
  0 Magnet; 0 Charter; 4 Title I Eligible; 4 School-wide Title I
Students: 5,541   (51.9% male; 48.0% female)
  Individual Education Program: 1,036 (18.7%);
  English Language Learner: 98 (1.8%); Migrant: n/a
  Eligible for Free Lunch Program: 1,641 (29.6%)
  Eligible for Reduced-Price Lunch Program: 746 (13.5%)
Teachers: 381.2 (14.5 to 1)
Librarians/Media Specialists: 2.0 (2,770.5 to 1)
Guidance Counselors: 8.0 (692.6 to 1)
Current Spending: ($ per student per year):
  Total: $8,805; Instruction: $5,812; Support Services: $2,689

Enrollment, Drop-out Rates and Diploma Recipients by Race/Ethnicity

Category	Total	White	Black	Asian	AIAN	Hisp.
Enrollment (%)	100.0	92.0	3.7	0.7	0.4	3.2
Drop-out Rate (%)	2.1	2.3	0.0	0.0	0.0	0.0
H.S. Diplomas (#)	261	248	6	2	1	4

South Bend Community Sch Corp
635 S Main St • South Bend, IN 46601-2295
(574) 283-8000 • http://www.sbcsc.k12.in.us/
Grade Span: PK-12; **Agency Type:** 1
Schools: 38
  20 Primary; 10 Middle; 5 High; 3 Other Level
  34 Regular; 2 Special Education; 0 Vocational; 2 Alternative
  0 Magnet; 0 Charter; 18 Title I Eligible; 5 School-wide Title I
Students: 21,871   (51.3% male; 48.6% female)
  Individual Education Program: 5,084 (23.2%);
  English Language Learner: 2,884 (13.2%); Migrant: n/a

Eligible for Free Lunch Program: 10,886 (49.8%)
Eligible for Reduced-Price Lunch Program: 1,936 (8.9%)
Teachers: 1,342.5 (16.3 to 1)
Librarians/Media Specialists: 19.0 (1,150.1 to 1)
Guidance Counselors: 25.8 (847.0 to 1)
Current Spending: ($ per student per year):
Total: $9,330; Instruction: $5,904; Support Services: $3,067
Enrollment, Drop-out Rates and Diploma Recipients by Race/Ethnicity

Category	Total	White	Black	Asian	AIAN	Hisp.
Enrollment (%)	100.0	48.4	37.6	1.2	0.5	12.4
Drop-out Rate (%)	1.5	0.9	2.3	1.7	0.0	2.4
H.S. Diplomas (#)	1,206	773	305	31	2	95

Starke County

Knox Community School Corp
2 Redskin Trl • Knox, IN 46534-2238
(574) 772-1600 • http://www.niesc.k12.in.us/knox/index.html
Grade Span: KG-12; **Agency Type:** 1
Schools: 3
1 Primary; 1 Middle; 1 High; 0 Other Level
3 Regular; 0 Special Education; 0 Vocational; 0 Alternative
0 Magnet; 0 Charter; 2 Title I Eligible; 0 School-wide Title I
Students: 2,005 (50.3% male; 49.6% female)
Individual Education Program: 293 (14.6%);
English Language Learner: 67 (3.3%); Migrant: n/a
Eligible for Free Lunch Program: 689 (34.4%)
Eligible for Reduced-Price Lunch Program: 217 (10.8%)
Teachers: 105.5 (19.0 to 1)
Librarians/Media Specialists: 3.0 (668.3 to 1)
Guidance Counselors: 4.0 (501.3 to 1)
Current Spending: ($ per student per year):
Total: $7,915; Instruction: $4,635; Support Services: $2,757
Enrollment, Drop-out Rates and Diploma Recipients by Race/Ethnicity

Category	Total	White	Black	Asian	AIAN	Hisp.
Enrollment (%)	100.0	96.9	0.3	0.2	0.1	2.5
Drop-out Rate (%)	2.1	2.2	0.0	0.0	n/a	0.0
H.S. Diplomas (#)	101	96	0	0	0	5

Steuben County

M S D Steuben County
400 S Martha St • Angola, IN 46703-1953
(260) 665-2854 • http://www.msdsteuben.k12.in.us/
Grade Span: KG-12; **Agency Type:** 1
Schools: 6
4 Primary; 1 Middle; 1 High; 0 Other Level
6 Regular; 0 Special Education; 0 Vocational; 0 Alternative
0 Magnet; 0 Charter; 4 Title I Eligible; 0 School-wide Title I
Students: 3,034 (51.0% male; 48.9% female)
Individual Education Program: 378 (12.5%);
English Language Learner: 93 (3.1%); Migrant: n/a
Eligible for Free Lunch Program: 648 (21.4%)
Eligible for Reduced-Price Lunch Program: 245 (8.1%)
Teachers: 162.5 (18.7 to 1)
Librarians/Media Specialists: 3.0 (1,011.3 to 1)
Guidance Counselors: 7.0 (433.4 to 1)
Current Spending: ($ per student per year):
Total: $7,070; Instruction: $3,902; Support Services: $2,735
Enrollment, Drop-out Rates and Diploma Recipients by Race/Ethnicity

Category	Total	White	Black	Asian	AIAN	Hisp.
Enrollment (%)	100.0	94.9	0.5	0.6	0.7	3.4
Drop-out Rate (%)	1.2	1.2	0.0	0.0	0.0	0.0
H.S. Diplomas (#)	178	171	2	0	1	4

Sullivan County

Northeast School Corp
406 N Vine St • Hymera, IN 47855-0493
Mailing Address: PO Box 493 • Hymera, IN 47855-0493
(812) 383-5761 • http://www.nesc.k12.in.us/
Grade Span: PK-12; **Agency Type:** 1
Schools: 6
4 Primary; 0 Middle; 2 High; 0 Other Level
6 Regular; 0 Special Education; 0 Vocational; 0 Alternative
0 Magnet; 0 Charter; 3 Title I Eligible; 0 School-wide Title I
Students: 1,522 (53.2% male; 46.7% female)
Individual Education Program: 341 (22.4%);
English Language Learner: n/a; Migrant: n/a
Eligible for Free Lunch Program: 547 (35.9%)
Eligible for Reduced-Price Lunch Program: 201 (13.2%)
Teachers: 99.5 (15.3 to 1)
Librarians/Media Specialists: 2.0 (761.0 to 1)
Guidance Counselors: 1.5 (1,014.7 to 1)

Current Spending: ($ per student per year):
Total: $8,339; Instruction: $5,417; Support Services: $2,560
Enrollment, Drop-out Rates and Diploma Recipients by Race/Ethnicity

Category	Total	White	Black	Asian	AIAN	Hisp.
Enrollment (%)	100.0	99.1	0.1	0.4	0.3	0.1
Drop-out Rate (%)	1.0	1.0	n/a	0.0	n/a	0.0
H.S. Diplomas (#)	96	96	0	0	0	0

Southwest School Corp
31 N Court St • Sullivan, IN 47882-1509
(812) 268-6311 • http://www.swest.k12.in.us/
Grade Span: PK-12; **Agency Type:** 1
Schools: 4
2 Primary; 0 Middle; 1 High; 1 Other Level
4 Regular; 0 Special Education; 0 Vocational; 0 Alternative
0 Magnet; 0 Charter; 2 Title I Eligible; 0 School-wide Title I
Students: 1,930 (51.2% male; 48.7% female)
Individual Education Program: 463 (24.0%);
English Language Learner: 6 (0.3%); Migrant: n/a
Eligible for Free Lunch Program: 445 (23.1%)
Eligible for Reduced-Price Lunch Program: 191 (9.9%)
Teachers: 108.7 (17.8 to 1)
Librarians/Media Specialists: 1.0 (1,930.0 to 1)
Guidance Counselors: 3.5 (551.4 to 1)
Current Spending: ($ per student per year):
Total: $7,799; Instruction: $4,930; Support Services: $2,541
Enrollment, Drop-out Rates and Diploma Recipients by Race/Ethnicity

Category	Total	White	Black	Asian	AIAN	Hisp.
Enrollment (%)	100.0	99.2	0.2	0.2	0.0	0.4
Drop-out Rate (%)	3.0	3.0	0.0	n/a	n/a	0.0
H.S. Diplomas (#)	136	136	0	0	0	0

Switzerland County

Switzerland County School Corp
305 W Seminary St • Vevay, IN 47043-1141
(812) 427-2611 • http://www.switzerland.k12.in.us/
Grade Span: PK-12; **Agency Type:** 1
Schools: 4
2 Primary; 1 Middle; 1 High; 0 Other Level
4 Regular; 0 Special Education; 0 Vocational; 0 Alternative
0 Magnet; 0 Charter; 2 Title I Eligible; 0 School-wide Title I
Students: 1,563 (52.5% male; 47.4% female)
Individual Education Program: 292 (18.7%);
English Language Learner: 3 (0.2%); Migrant: n/a
Eligible for Free Lunch Program: 490 (31.4%)
Eligible for Reduced-Price Lunch Program: 130 (8.3%)
Teachers: 85.7 (18.2 to 1)
Librarians/Media Specialists: 1.0 (1,563.0 to 1)
Guidance Counselors: 2.5 (625.2 to 1)
Current Spending: ($ per student per year):
Total: $6,437; Instruction: $3,611; Support Services: $2,514
Enrollment, Drop-out Rates and Diploma Recipients by Race/Ethnicity

Category	Total	White	Black	Asian	AIAN	Hisp.
Enrollment (%)	100.0	99.0	0.3	0.3	0.0	0.4
Drop-out Rate (%)	0.0	0.0	0.0	0.0	n/a	n/a
H.S. Diplomas (#)	89	88	1	0	0	0

Tippecanoe County

Lafayette School Corporation
2300 Cason St • Lafayette, IN 47904-2692
(765) 771-6000 • http://www.lsc.k12.in.us/
Grade Span: KG-12; **Agency Type:** 1
Schools: 15
11 Primary; 2 Middle; 1 High; 1 Other Level
14 Regular; 1 Special Education; 0 Vocational; 0 Alternative
0 Magnet; 0 Charter; 10 Title I Eligible; 4 School-wide Title I
Students: 7,315 (50.4% male; 49.5% female)
Individual Education Program: 1,663 (22.7%);
English Language Learner: 1,028 (14.1%); Migrant: n/a
Eligible for Free Lunch Program: 2,742 (37.5%)
Eligible for Reduced-Price Lunch Program: 702 (9.6%)
Teachers: 531.9 (13.8 to 1)
Librarians/Media Specialists: 11.5 (636.1 to 1)
Guidance Counselors: 13.3 (550.0 to 1)
Current Spending: ($ per student per year):
Total: $8,934; Instruction: $5,310; Support Services: $3,351
Enrollment, Drop-out Rates and Diploma Recipients by Race/Ethnicity

Category	Total	White	Black	Asian	AIAN	Hisp.
Enrollment (%)	100.0	76.7	7.3	0.5	0.2	15.3
Drop-out Rate (%)	6.2	4.9	10.3	0.0	n/a	15.1
H.S. Diplomas (#)	357	312	16	0	0	29

Tippecanoe School Corp

21 Elston Rd • Lafayette, IN 47909-2899
(765) 474-2481 • http://tsc.k12.in.us/
Grade Span: KG-12; **Agency Type:** 1
Schools: 17
   9 Primary; 6 Middle; 2 High; 0 Other Level
   17 Regular; 0 Special Education; 0 Vocational; 0 Alternative
   0 Magnet; 0 Charter; 9 Title I Eligible; 0 School-wide Title I
Students: 10,271 (52.2% male; 47.7% female)
   Individual Education Program: 1,527 (14.9%);
   English Language Learner: 547 (5.3%); Migrant: n/a
   Eligible for Free Lunch Program: 1,657 (16.1%)
   Eligible for Reduced-Price Lunch Program: 502 (4.9%)
Teachers: 558.1 (18.4 to 1)
Librarians/Media Specialists: 22.3 (460.6 to 1)
Guidance Counselors: 22.0 (466.9 to 1)
Current Spending: ($ per student per year):
   Total: $6,683; Instruction: $4,080; Support Services: $2,351
Enrollment, Drop-out Rates and Diploma Recipients by Race/Ethnicity

Category	Total	White	Black	Asian	AIAN	Hisp.
Enrollment (%)	100.0	90.2	1.7	2.4	0.8	4.9
Drop-out Rate (%)	1.8	1.8	3.1	0.0	0.0	5.4
H.S. Diplomas (#)	599	576	3	4	9	7

West Lafayette Com School Corp

1130 N Salisbury • West Lafayette, IN 47906-2497
(765) 746-1641 • http://www.wl.k12.in.us/
Grade Span: KG-12; **Agency Type:** 1
Schools: 3
   1 Primary; 1 Middle; 1 High; 0 Other Level
   3 Regular; 0 Special Education; 0 Vocational; 0 Alternative
   0 Magnet; 0 Charter; 2 Title I Eligible; 0 School-wide Title I
Students: 1,980 (49.8% male; 50.1% female)
   Individual Education Program: 216 (10.9%);
   English Language Learner: 326 (16.5%); Migrant: n/a
   Eligible for Free Lunch Program: 104 (5.3%)
   Eligible for Reduced-Price Lunch Program: 52 (2.6%)
Teachers: 112.2 (17.6 to 1)
Librarians/Media Specialists: 3.0 (660.0 to 1)
Guidance Counselors: 3.0 (660.0 to 1)
Current Spending: ($ per student per year):
   Total: $8,607; Instruction: $4,568; Support Services: $3,878
Enrollment, Drop-out Rates and Diploma Recipients by Race/Ethnicity

Category	Total	White	Black	Asian	AIAN	Hisp.
Enrollment (%)	100.0	76.8	2.8	17.5	0.2	2.6
Drop-out Rate (%)	0.0	0.0	0.0	0.0	0.0	0.0
H.S. Diplomas (#)	148	126	3	14	1	4

Tipton County

Tipton Community School Corp

221 N Main St Ste A • Tipton, IN 46072-1698
(765) 675-2147 • http://www.tcsc.k12.in.us/
Grade Span: KG-12; **Agency Type:** 1
Schools: 3
   1 Primary; 1 Middle; 1 High; 0 Other Level
   3 Regular; 0 Special Education; 0 Vocational; 0 Alternative
   0 Magnet; 0 Charter; 2 Title I Eligible; 0 School-wide Title I
Students: 1,875 (52.6% male; 47.3% female)
   Individual Education Program: 290 (15.5%);
   English Language Learner: 43 (2.3%); Migrant: n/a
   Eligible for Free Lunch Program: 243 (13.0%)
   Eligible for Reduced-Price Lunch Program: 111 (5.9%)
Teachers: 111.7 (16.8 to 1)
Librarians/Media Specialists: 3.0 (625.0 to 1)
Guidance Counselors: 4.0 (468.8 to 1)
Current Spending: ($ per student per year):
   Total: $7,141; Instruction: $4,232; Support Services: $2,731
Enrollment, Drop-out Rates and Diploma Recipients by Race/Ethnicity

Category	Total	White	Black	Asian	AIAN	Hisp.
Enrollment (%)	100.0	97.3	0.1	0.7	0.3	1.6
Drop-out Rate (%)	3.1	3.0	0.0	0.0	4.2	7.7
H.S. Diplomas (#)	131	127	0	3	1	0

Union County

Union Co/Clg Corner Joint SD

107 Layman St • Liberty, IN 47353-1203
(765) 458-7471 • http://www.uc.k12.in.us/
Grade Span: KG-12; **Agency Type:** 1
Schools: 4
   2 Primary; 1 Middle; 1 High; 0 Other Level
   4 Regular; 0 Special Education; 0 Vocational; 0 Alternative
   0 Magnet; 0 Charter; 3 Title I Eligible; 0 School-wide Title I
Students: 1,610 (53.6% male; 46.3% female)

Individual Education Program: 304 (18.9%);
English Language Learner: 1 (0.1%); Migrant: n/a
Eligible for Free Lunch Program: 348 (21.6%)
Eligible for Reduced-Price Lunch Program: 145 (9.0%)
Teachers: 104.5 (15.4 to 1)
Librarians/Media Specialists: 1.0 (1,610.0 to 1)
Guidance Counselors: 1.0 (1,610.0 to 1)
Current Spending: ($ per student per year):
   Total: $7,254; Instruction: $4,311; Support Services: $2,560
Enrollment, Drop-out Rates and Diploma Recipients by Race/Ethnicity

Category	Total	White	Black	Asian	AIAN	Hisp.
Enrollment (%)	100.0	99.4	0.2	0.1	0.1	0.1
Drop-out Rate (%)	1.1	1.1	0.0	0.0	0.0	n/a
H.S. Diplomas (#)	109	106	0	3	0	0

Vanderburgh County

Evansville-Vanderburgh Sch Corp

1 SE 9th St • Evansville, IN 47708-1821
(812) 435-8477 • http://www.evsc.k12.in.us/
Grade Span: PK-12; **Agency Type:** 1
Schools: 42
   20 Primary; 10 Middle; 9 High; 3 Other Level
   35 Regular; 3 Special Education; 0 Vocational; 4 Alternative
   0 Magnet; 0 Charter; 20 Title I Eligible; 11 School-wide Title I
Students: 22,408 (50.9% male; 49.0% female)
   Individual Education Program: 4,555 (20.3%);
   English Language Learner: 348 (1.6%); Migrant: n/a
   Eligible for Free Lunch Program: 8,111 (36.3%)
   Eligible for Reduced-Price Lunch Program: 2,076 (9.3%)
Teachers: 1,399.8 (16.0 to 1)
Librarians/Media Specialists: 5.0 (4,472.8 to 1)
Guidance Counselors: 48.0 (465.9 to 1)
Current Spending: ($ per student per year):
   Total: $8,229; Instruction: $5,086; Support Services: $2,775
Enrollment, Drop-out Rates and Diploma Recipients by Race/Ethnicity

Category	Total	White	Black	Asian	AIAN	Hisp.
Enrollment (%)	100.0	82.1	15.7	0.8	0.3	1.2
Drop-out Rate (%)	1.0	0.8	1.8	0.0	0.0	0.0
H.S. Diplomas (#)	1,344	1,186	140	8	2	8

Vermillion County

South Vermillion Com Sch Corp

800 W Wildcat Dr • Clinton, IN 47842-0387
Mailing Address: PO Box 387 • Clinton, IN 47842-0387
(765) 832-2426 • http://www.svcs.k12.in.us/
Grade Span: KG-12; **Agency Type:** 1
Schools: 5
   3 Primary; 0 Middle; 1 High; 1 Other Level
   5 Regular; 0 Special Education; 0 Vocational; 0 Alternative
   0 Magnet; 0 Charter; 2 Title I Eligible; 0 School-wide Title I
Students: 1,973 (51.6% male; 48.3% female)
   Individual Education Program: 365 (18.5%);
   English Language Learner: 12 (0.6%); Migrant: n/a
   Eligible for Free Lunch Program: 566 (28.7%)
   Eligible for Reduced-Price Lunch Program: 234 (11.9%)
Teachers: 123.4 (16.0 to 1)
Librarians/Media Specialists: 3.0 (657.7 to 1)
Guidance Counselors: 4.0 (493.3 to 1)
Current Spending: ($ per student per year):
   Total: $7,436; Instruction: $4,477; Support Services: $2,619
Enrollment, Drop-out Rates and Diploma Recipients by Race/Ethnicity

Category	Total	White	Black	Asian	AIAN	Hisp.
Enrollment (%)	100.0	99.4	0.1	0.3	0.1	0.1
Drop-out Rate (%)	3.0	3.0	n/a	0.0	n/a	0.0
H.S. Diplomas (#)	119	118	0	0	0	1

Vigo County

Vigo County School Corp

686 Wabash Ave • Terre Haute, IN 47807-0703
Mailing Address: PO Box 3703 • Terre Haute, IN 47803-0703
(812) 462-4216 • http://www.vigoco.k12.in.us/
Grade Span: PK-12; **Agency Type:** 1
Schools: 29
   18 Primary; 6 Middle; 4 High; 1 Other Level
   27 Regular; 0 Special Education; 0 Vocational; 2 Alternative
   0 Magnet; 0 Charter; 17 Title I Eligible; 10 School-wide Title I
Students: 16,377 (51.5% male; 48.4% female)
   Individual Education Program: 3,222 (19.7%);
   English Language Learner: 55 (0.3%); Migrant: n/a
   Eligible for Free Lunch Program: 5,527 (33.7%)
   Eligible for Reduced-Price Lunch Program: 1,709 (10.4%)
Teachers: 1,017.1 (16.1 to 1)

Librarians/Media Specialists: 28.6 (572.6 to 1)
Guidance Counselors: 28.8 (568.6 to 1)
Current Spending: ($ per student per year):
    Total: $6,956; Instruction: $4,372; Support Services: $2,280
Enrollment, Drop-out Rates and Diploma Recipients by Race/Ethnicity

Category	Total	White	Black	Asian	AIAN	Hisp.
Enrollment (%)	100.0	91.6	6.6	1.1	0.1	0.6
Drop-out Rate (%)	3.8	3.9	3.4	1.9	0.0	0.0
H.S. Diplomas (#)	997	895	74	20	1	7

Wabash County

M S D Wabash County Schools
204 N 300 W • Wabash, IN 46992-8689
(260) 563-8050 • http://www.msdwc.k12.in.us/
Grade Span: KG-12; **Agency Type:** 1
Schools: 8
    4 Primary; 0 Middle; 2 High; 2 Other Level
    6 Regular; 1 Special Education; 0 Vocational; 1 Alternative
    0 Magnet; 0 Charter; 4 Title I Eligible; 0 School-wide Title I
Students: 2,598   (52.6% male; 47.3% female)
    Individual Education Program: 464 (17.9%);
    English Language Learner: 17 (0.7%); Migrant: n/a
    Eligible for Free Lunch Program: 311 (12.0%)
    Eligible for Reduced-Price Lunch Program: 130 (5.0%)
Teachers: 188.2 (13.8 to 1)
Librarians/Media Specialists: 2.0 (1,299.0 to 1)
Guidance Counselors: 6.2 (419.0 to 1)
Current Spending: ($ per student per year):
    Total: $8,178; Instruction: $5,078; Support Services: $2,814
Enrollment, Drop-out Rates and Diploma Recipients by Race/Ethnicity

Category	Total	White	Black	Asian	AIAN	Hisp.
Enrollment (%)	100.0	97.3	0.7	0.7	0.5	0.7
Drop-out Rate (%)	1.7	1.7	0.0	0.0	n/a	0.0
H.S. Diplomas (#)	137	133	0	3	0	1

Manchester Community Schools
107 S Buffalo • N Manchester, IN 46962-0308
(260) 982-7518 • http://mcs.k12.in.us/welcome.htm
Grade Span: KG-12; **Agency Type:** 1
Schools: 4
    1 Primary; 2 Middle; 1 High; 0 Other Level
    4 Regular; 0 Special Education; 0 Vocational; 0 Alternative
    0 Magnet; 0 Charter; 2 Title I Eligible; 0 School-wide Title I
Students: 1,577   (51.6% male; 48.3% female)
    Individual Education Program: 240 (15.2%);
    English Language Learner: 18 (1.1%); Migrant: n/a
    Eligible for Free Lunch Program: 349 (22.1%)
    Eligible for Reduced-Price Lunch Program: 168 (10.7%)
Teachers: 87.3 (18.1 to 1)
Librarians/Media Specialists: 2.8 (563.2 to 1)
Guidance Counselors: 3.0 (525.7 to 1)
Current Spending: ($ per student per year):
    Total: $6,948; Instruction: $4,144; Support Services: $2,456
Enrollment, Drop-out Rates and Diploma Recipients by Race/Ethnicity

Category	Total	White	Black	Asian	AIAN	Hisp.
Enrollment (%)	100.0	98.0	0.7	0.8	0.2	0.3
Drop-out Rate (%)	0.0	0.0	0.0	0.0	n/a	0.0
H.S. Diplomas (#)	102	100	0	1	0	1

Wabash City Schools
1101 Colerain St Box 744 • Wabash, IN 46992-0744
(260) 563-2151 • http://apaches.k12.in.us/
Grade Span: PK-12; **Agency Type:** 1
Schools: 4
    1 Primary; 2 Middle; 1 High; 0 Other Level
    4 Regular; 0 Special Education; 0 Vocational; 0 Alternative
    0 Magnet; 0 Charter; 2 Title I Eligible; 0 School-wide Title I
Students: 1,540   (52.5% male; 47.4% female)
    Individual Education Program: 314 (20.4%);
    English Language Learner: 10 (0.6%); Migrant: n/a
    Eligible for Free Lunch Program: 456 (29.6%)
    Eligible for Reduced-Price Lunch Program: 189 (12.3%)
Teachers: 95.7 (16.1 to 1)
Librarians/Media Specialists: 2.0 (770.0 to 1)
Guidance Counselors: 1.5 (1,026.7 to 1)
Current Spending: ($ per student per year):
    Total: $7,587; Instruction: $4,824; Support Services: $2,456
Enrollment, Drop-out Rates and Diploma Recipients by Race/Ethnicity

Category	Total	White	Black	Asian	AIAN	Hisp.
Enrollment (%)	100.0	97.3	0.5	0.1	1.2	1.0
Drop-out Rate (%)	1.5	1.3	50.0	n/a	n/a	0.0
H.S. Diplomas (#)	98	98	0	0	0	0

Warrick County

Warrick County School Corp
300 E Gum • Boonville, IN 47601-0809
Mailing Address: PO Box 809 • Boonville, IN 47601-0809
(812) 897-0400 • http://www.warrick.k12.in.us/
Grade Span: KG-12; **Agency Type:** 1
Schools: 16
    10 Primary; 2 Middle; 4 High; 0 Other Level
    15 Regular; 0 Special Education; 0 Vocational; 1 Alternative
    0 Magnet; 0 Charter; 9 Title I Eligible; 0 School-wide Title I
Students: 9,269   (52.4% male; 47.5% female)
    Individual Education Program: 1,763 (19.0%);
    English Language Learner: 85 (0.9%); Migrant: n/a
    Eligible for Free Lunch Program: 1,154 (12.5%)
    Eligible for Reduced-Price Lunch Program: 549 (5.9%)
Teachers: 481.8 (19.2 to 1)
Librarians/Media Specialists: 6.0 (1,544.8 to 1)
Guidance Counselors: 11.3 (820.3 to 1)
Current Spending: ($ per student per year):
    Total: $6,558; Instruction: $4,137; Support Services: $2,124
Enrollment, Drop-out Rates and Diploma Recipients by Race/Ethnicity

Category	Total	White	Black	Asian	AIAN	Hisp.
Enrollment (%)	100.0	96.9	1.2	1.1	0.2	0.6
Drop-out Rate (%)	1.2	1.1	3.2	3.1	n/a	0.0
H.S. Diplomas (#)	596	580	5	9	0	2

Washington County

East Washington School Corp
1050 N Eastern School Rd • Pekin, IN 47165-7901
(812) 967-3926 • http://ewsc.k12.in.us/
Grade Span: KG-12; **Agency Type:** 1
Schools: 3
    1 Primary; 1 Middle; 1 High; 0 Other Level
    3 Regular; 0 Special Education; 0 Vocational; 0 Alternative
    0 Magnet; 0 Charter; 2 Title I Eligible; 0 School-wide Title I
Students: 1,768   (52.2% male; 47.7% female)
    Individual Education Program: 300 (17.0%);
    English Language Learner: 5 (0.3%); Migrant: n/a
    Eligible for Free Lunch Program: 460 (26.0%)
    Eligible for Reduced-Price Lunch Program: 189 (10.7%)
Teachers: 89.0 (19.9 to 1)
Librarians/Media Specialists: 2.0 (884.0 to 1)
Guidance Counselors: 5.0 (353.6 to 1)
Current Spending: ($ per student per year):
    Total: $7,004; Instruction: $4,430; Support Services: $2,275
Enrollment, Drop-out Rates and Diploma Recipients by Race/Ethnicity

Category	Total	White	Black	Asian	AIAN	Hisp.
Enrollment (%)	100.0	99.2	0.2	0.1	0.1	0.5
Drop-out Rate (%)	4.4	4.2	0.0	n/a	n/a	n/a
H.S. Diplomas (#)	85	85	0	0	0	0

Salem Community Schools
500 N Harrison St • Salem, IN 47167-1671
(812) 883-4437 • http://www.salemschools.com/
Grade Span: KG-12; **Agency Type:** 1
Schools: 4
    2 Primary; 1 Middle; 0 High; 1 Other Level
    4 Regular; 0 Special Education; 0 Vocational; 0 Alternative
    0 Magnet; 0 Charter; 2 Title I Eligible; 0 School-wide Title I
Students: 2,109   (50.6% male; 49.3% female)
    Individual Education Program: 315 (14.9%);
    English Language Learner: 13 (0.6%); Migrant: n/a
    Eligible for Free Lunch Program: 551 (26.1%)
    Eligible for Reduced-Price Lunch Program: 129 (6.1%)
Teachers: 108.0 (19.5 to 1)
Librarians/Media Specialists: 3.0 (703.0 to 1)
Guidance Counselors: 2.6 (811.2 to 1)
Current Spending: ($ per student per year):
    Total: $6,622; Instruction: $3,848; Support Services: $2,492
Enrollment, Drop-out Rates and Diploma Recipients by Race/Ethnicity

Category	Total	White	Black	Asian	AIAN	Hisp.
Enrollment (%)	100.0	99.3	0.0	0.1	0.2	0.3
Drop-out Rate (%)	1.4	1.4	n/a	n/a	n/a	0.0
H.S. Diplomas (#)	115	115	0	0	0	0

Wayne County

Centerville-Abington Com Schs
115 W S St • Centerville, IN 47330-1499
(765) 855-3475 • http://www.centerville.k12.in.us/
Grade Span: PK-12; **Agency Type:** 1
Schools: 4
    2 Primary; 1 Middle; 1 High; 0 Other Level

4 Regular; 0 Special Education; 0 Vocational; 0 Alternative
0 Magnet; 0 Charter; 2 Title I Eligible; 0 School-wide Title I
Students: 1,667 (53.4% male; 46.5% female)
Individual Education Program: 246 (14.8%);
English Language Learner: 8 (0.5%); Migrant: n/a
Eligible for Free Lunch Program: 211 (12.7%)
Eligible for Reduced-Price Lunch Program: 122 (7.3%)
Teachers: 100.4 (16.6 to 1)
Librarians/Media Specialists: 2.0 (833.5 to 1)
Guidance Counselors: 5.0 (333.4 to 1)
Current Spending: ($ per student per year):
Total: $7,562; Instruction: $4,580; Support Services: $2,589
Enrollment, Drop-out Rates and Diploma Recipients by Race/Ethnicity

Category	Total	White	Black	Asian	AIAN	Hisp.
Enrollment (%)	100.0	98.7	0.2	0.5	0.3	0.3
Drop-out Rate (%)	2.9	2.9	0.0	0.0	n/a	0.0
H.S. Diplomas (#)	97	96	0	1	0	0

Richmond Community School Corp
300 Hub Etchison Pky • Richmond, IN 47374-5399
(765) 973-3300 • http://www.rcs.k12.in.us/
Grade Span: PK-12; **Agency Type:** 1
Schools: 14
11 Primary; 1 Middle; 1 High; 1 Other Level
13 Regular; 1 Special Education; 0 Vocational; 0 Alternative
0 Magnet; 0 Charter; 9 Title I Eligible; 6 School-wide Title I
Students: 5,837 (51.3% male; 48.6% female)
Individual Education Program: 1,476 (25.3%);
English Language Learner: 101 (1.7%); Migrant: n/a
Eligible for Free Lunch Program: 2,765 (47.4%)
Eligible for Reduced-Price Lunch Program: 568 (9.7%)
Teachers: 390.1 (15.0 to 1)
Librarians/Media Specialists: 14.0 (416.9 to 1)
Guidance Counselors: 8.0 (729.6 to 1)
Current Spending: ($ per student per year):
Total: $8,274; Instruction: $5,110; Support Services: $2,891
Enrollment, Drop-out Rates and Diploma Recipients by Race/Ethnicity

Category	Total	White	Black	Asian	AIAN	Hisp.
Enrollment (%)	100.0	85.6	11.5	0.7	0.3	1.9
Drop-out Rate (%)	5.8	5.7	7.6	0.0	14.3	0.0
H.S. Diplomas (#)	306	250	36	12	1	7

Wells County

M S D Bluffton-Harrison
628 S Bennett St • Bluffton, IN 46714-3399
(260) 824-2620
Grade Span: KG-12; **Agency Type:** 1
Schools: 3
1 Primary; 1 Middle; 1 High; 0 Other Level
3 Regular; 0 Special Education; 0 Vocational; 0 Alternative
0 Magnet; 0 Charter; 2 Title I Eligible; 0 School-wide Title I
Students: 1,529 (49.5% male; 50.4% female)
Individual Education Program: 205 (13.4%);
English Language Learner: 71 (4.6%); Migrant: n/a
Eligible for Free Lunch Program: 262 (17.1%)
Eligible for Reduced-Price Lunch Program: 121 (7.9%)
Teachers: 86.0 (17.8 to 1)
Librarians/Media Specialists: 3.0 (509.7 to 1)
Guidance Counselors: 2.9 (527.2 to 1)
Current Spending: ($ per student per year):
Total: $6,828; Instruction: $4,129; Support Services: $2,390
Enrollment, Drop-out Rates and Diploma Recipients by Race/Ethnicity

Category	Total	White	Black	Asian	AIAN	Hisp.
Enrollment (%)	100.0	95.7	0.6	1.0	0.2	2.6
Drop-out Rate (%)	1.3	1.4	0.0	0.0	0.0	0.0
H.S. Diplomas (#)	112	107	0	1	0	4

Northern Wells Com Schools
312 N Jefferson St • Ossian, IN 46777-0386
Mailing Address: PO Box 386 • Ossian, IN 46777-0386
(260) 622-4125 • http://www.nwcs.k12.in.us/
Grade Span: PK-12; **Agency Type:** 1
Schools: 4
2 Primary; 1 Middle; 1 High; 0 Other Level
4 Regular; 0 Special Education; 0 Vocational; 0 Alternative
0 Magnet; 0 Charter; 3 Title I Eligible; 0 School-wide Title I
Students: 2,602 (51.9% male; 48.0% female)
Individual Education Program: 417 (16.0%);
English Language Learner: 4 (0.2%); Migrant: n/a
Eligible for Free Lunch Program: 325 (12.5%)
Eligible for Reduced-Price Lunch Program: 154 (5.9%)
Teachers: 144.4 (18.0 to 1)
Librarians/Media Specialists: 2.0 (1,301.0 to 1)
Guidance Counselors: 7.0 (371.7 to 1)

Current Spending: ($ per student per year):
Total: $6,625; Instruction: $3,723; Support Services: $2,607
Enrollment, Drop-out Rates and Diploma Recipients by Race/Ethnicity

Category	Total	White	Black	Asian	AIAN	Hisp.
Enrollment (%)	100.0	97.5	0.2	0.6	0.2	1.5
Drop-out Rate (%)	1.2	1.1	0.0	0.0	0.0	9.1
H.S. Diplomas (#)	203	195	1	5	0	2

White County

Twin Lakes School Corp
565 S Main St • Monticello, IN 47960-2446
(574) 583-7211 • http://www.twinlakes.k12.in.us/
Grade Span: PK-12; **Agency Type:** 1
Schools: 6
4 Primary; 1 Middle; 1 High; 0 Other Level
6 Regular; 0 Special Education; 0 Vocational; 0 Alternative
0 Magnet; 0 Charter; 5 Title I Eligible; 0 School-wide Title I
Students: 2,650 (51.0% male; 48.9% female)
Individual Education Program: 425 (16.0%);
English Language Learner: 213 (8.0%); Migrant: n/a
Eligible for Free Lunch Program: 646 (24.4%)
Eligible for Reduced-Price Lunch Program: 268 (10.1%)
Teachers: 143.0 (18.5 to 1)
Librarians/Media Specialists: 3.0 (883.3 to 1)
Guidance Counselors: 7.0 (378.6 to 1)
Current Spending: ($ per student per year):
Total: $7,419; Instruction: $4,520; Support Services: $2,534
Enrollment, Drop-out Rates and Diploma Recipients by Race/Ethnicity

Category	Total	White	Black	Asian	AIAN	Hisp.
Enrollment (%)	100.0	90.6	0.2	0.5	0.0	8.6
Drop-out Rate (%)	1.7	1.6	0.0	0.0	n/a	2.7
H.S. Diplomas (#)	180	173	0	0	0	7

Whitley County

Whitley County Cons Schools
107 N Walnut St Ste A • Columbia City, IN 46725
(260) 244-5772 • http://www.wccs.k12.in.us/
Grade Span: PK-12; **Agency Type:** 1
Schools: 8
5 Primary; 1 Middle; 2 High; 0 Other Level
7 Regular; 0 Special Education; 0 Vocational; 1 Alternative
0 Magnet; 0 Charter; 3 Title I Eligible; 0 School-wide Title I
Students: 3,635 (50.7% male; 49.2% female)
Individual Education Program: 462 (12.7%);
English Language Learner: 22 (0.6%); Migrant: n/a
Eligible for Free Lunch Program: 471 (13.0%)
Eligible for Reduced-Price Lunch Program: 275 (7.6%)
Teachers: 211.1 (17.2 to 1)
Librarians/Media Specialists: 4.0 (908.8 to 1)
Guidance Counselors: 8.5 (427.6 to 1)
Current Spending: ($ per student per year):
Total: $7,635; Instruction: $4,399; Support Services: $2,930
Enrollment, Drop-out Rates and Diploma Recipients by Race/Ethnicity

Category	Total	White	Black	Asian	AIAN	Hisp.
Enrollment (%)	100.0	98.1	0.1	0.4	0.4	0.9
Drop-out Rate (%)	n/a	n/a	n/a	n/a	n/a	n/a
H.S. Diplomas (#)	244	239	0	2	3	0

Number of Schools

Rank	Number	District Name	City
1	92	Indianapolis Public Schools	Indianapolis
2	54	Fort Wayne Community Schools	Fort Wayne
3	42	Evansville-Vanderburgh Sch Corp	Evansville
4	38	South Bend Community Sch Corp	South Bend
5	35	Gary Community School Corp	Gary
6	29	Vigo County School Corp	Terre Haute
7	23	School City of Hammond	Hammond
8	21	Anderson Community School Corp	Anderson
8	21	Monroe County Com Sch Corp	Bloomington
10	20	East Allen County Schools	New Haven
10	20	Elkhart Community Schools	Elkhart
10	20	Greater Clark County Schools	Jeffersonville
13	19	M S D Lawrence Township	Indianapolis
13	19	M S D Warren Township	Indianapolis
15	18	Muncie Community Schools	Muncie
15	18	New Albany-Floyd County Con Sch	New Albany
17	17	Kokomo-Center Twp Con Sch Corp	Kokomo
17	17	Tippecanoe School Corp	Lafayette
19	16	Bartholomew Con School Corp	Columbus
19	16	M S D Perry Township	Indianapolis
19	16	North Lawrence Com Schools	Bedford
19	16	Warrick County School Corp	Boonville
23	15	Carmel Clay Schools	Carmel
23	15	Lafayette School Corporation	Lafayette
23	15	M S D Wayne Township	Indianapolis
23	15	Penn-Harris-Madison Sch Corp	Mishawaka
23	15	Warsaw Community Schools	Warsaw
28	14	Hamilton Southeastern Schools	Fishers
28	14	M S D Washington Township	Indianapolis
28	14	Marion Community Schools	Marion
28	14	Michigan City Area Schools	Michigan City
28	14	Richmond Community School Corp	Richmond
33	13	Fayette County School Corp	Connersville
33	13	M S D Pike Township	Indianapolis
35	12	Laporte Community School Corp	Laporte
35	12	M S D Martinsville Schools	Martinsville
35	12	Valparaiso Community Schools	Valparaiso
38	11	Huntington County Com Sch Corp	Huntington
38	11	New Castle Community Sch Corp	New Castle
38	11	Portage Township Schools	Portage
38	11	School City of Mishawaka	Mishawaka
42	10	Clay Community Schools	Knightsville
42	10	Jay School Corp	Portland
42	10	Jennings County Schools	North Vernon
42	10	Lake Central School Corp	Saint John
42	10	School City of East Chicago	East Chicago
47	9	Center Grove Com Sch Corp	Greenwood
47	9	Crown Point Community Sch Corp	Crown Point
47	9	Duneland School Corporation	Chesterton
47	9	Goshen Community Schools	Goshen
47	9	Logansport Community Sch Corp	Logansport
47	9	M S D Southwest Allen County	Fort Wayne
47	9	Madison Consolidated Schools	Madison
47	9	Noblesville Schools	Noblesville
47	9	Northwest Allen County Schools	Fort Wayne
47	9	South Harrison Com Schools	Corydon
57	8	Avon Community School Corp	Avon
57	8	Crawfordsville Com Schools	Crawfordsville
57	8	East Noble School Corp	Kendallville
57	8	Franklin Township Com Sch Corp	Indianapolis
57	8	Greenfield-Central Com Schools	Greenfield
57	8	M S D Wabash County Schools	Wabash
57	8	Merrillville Community School	Merrillville
57	8	Seymour Community Schools	Seymour
57	8	Whitley County Cons Schools	Columbia City
66	7	Brownsburg Community Sch Corp	Brownsburg
66	7	Franklin Community School Corp	Franklin
66	7	M S D Decatur Township	Indianapolis
66	7	Mooresville Con School Corp	Mooresville
66	7	Richland-Bean Blossom C S C	Ellettsville
66	7	Sunman-Dearborn Com Sch Corp	Sunman
66	7	Vincennes Community Sch Corp	Vincennes
66	7	West Clark Community Schools	Sellersburg
66	7	Westfield-Washington Schools	Westfield
66	7	Zionsville Community Schools	Zionsville
76	6	Brown County School Corporation	Nashville
76	6	Clark-Pleasant Com School Corp	Whiteland
76	6	Community Schools of Frankfort	Frankfort
76	6	Concord Community Schools	Elkhart
76	6	Crawford County Com School Corp	Marengo
76	6	Dekalb County Ctl United SD	Waterloo
76	6	Delaware Community School Corp	Muncie
76	6	East Porter County School Corp	Kouts
76	6	Eastbrook Community Sch Corp	Marion
76	6	Greater Jasper Con Schs	Jasper
76	6	Greenwood Community Sch Corp	Greenwood
76	6	Griffith Public Schools	Griffith
76	6	Lake Ridge Schools	Gary
76	6	Lebanon Community School Corp	Lebanon
76	6	M S D Mount Vernon	Mount Vernon
76	6	M S D Steuben County	Angola
76	6	Middlebury Community Schools	Middlebury
76	6	North Spencer County Sch Corp	Lincoln City
76	6	Northeast School Corp	Hymera
76	6	Peru Community Schools	Peru
76	6	Plainfield Community Sch Corp	Plainfield
76	6	Plymouth Community School Corp	Plymouth
76	6	Rush County Schools	Rushville
76	6	School City of Hobart	Hobart
76	6	School Town of Highland	Highland
76	6	School Town of Speedway	Speedway
76	6	Scott County SD 2	Scottsburg
76	6	South Dearborn Com School Corp	Aurora
76	6	South Montgomery Com Sch Corp	New Market
76	6	Spencer-Owen Community Schools	Spencer
76	6	Twin Lakes School Corp	Monticello
76	6	Washington Com Schools Inc	Washington
108	5	Baugo Community Schools	Elkhart
108	5	Beech Grove City Schools	Beech Grove
108	5	Benton Community School Corp	Fowler
108	5	Blackford County Schools	Hartford City
108	5	Brownstown Cnt Com Sch Corp	Brownstown
108	5	Elwood Community School Corp	Elwood
108	5	Franklin County Com Sch Corp	Brookville
108	5	Greencastle Community Sch Corp	Greencastle
108	5	Greensburg Community Schools	Greensburg
108	5	Kankakee Valley School Corp	Wheatfield
108	5	Lakeland School Corporation	Lagrange
108	5	Madison-Grant United Sch Corp	Fairmount
108	5	Mt Vernon Community Sch Corp	Fortville
108	5	New Prairie United School Corp	New Carlisle
108	5	North Adams Community Schools	Decatur
108	5	North Harrison Com School Corp	Ramsey
108	5	North Knox School Corp	Bicknell
108	5	North Montgomery Com Sch Corp	Crawfordsville
108	5	North Putnam Community Schools	Bainbridge
108	5	Oak Hill United School Corp	Converse
108	5	Pike County School Corp	Petersburg
108	5	Randolph Central School Corp	Winchester
108	5	School Town of Munster	Munster
108	5	Shelbyville Central Schools	Shelbyville
108	5	South Madison Com Sch Corp	Pendleton
108	5	South Vermillion Com Sch Corp	Clinton
108	5	Southern Hancock Co Com Sch Corp	New Palestine
108	5	Tri-Creek School Corp	Lowell
108	5	Wa-Nee Community Schools	Nappanee
108	5	Wawasee Community School Corp	Syracuse
108	5	Westview School Corporation	Topeka
139	4	Alexandria Com School Corp	Alexandria
139	4	Batesville Community Sch Corp	Batesville
139	4	Centerville-Abington Com Schs	Centerville
139	4	Danville Community School Corp	Danville
139	4	Decatur County Com Schools	Greensburg
139	4	Dekalb County Eastern Com SD	Butler
139	4	Delphi Community School Corp	Delphi
139	4	Fairfield Community Schools	Goshen
139	4	Frankton-Lapel Community Schs	Anderson
139	4	Garrett-Keyser-Butler Com	Garrett
139	4	Hamilton Heights School Corp	Arcadia
139	4	Hanover Community School Corp	Cedar Lake
139	4	John Glenn School Corporation	Walkerton
139	4	Maconaquah School Corp	Bunker Hill
139	4	Manchester Community Schools	N Manchester
139	4	Mill Creek Community Sch Corp	Clayton
139	4	Mississinewa Community School Corp	Gas City
139	4	Mitchell Community Schools	Mitchell
139	4	Mt Pleasant Twp Com Sch Corp	Yorktown
139	4	Nineveh-Hensley-Jackson United	Trafalgar
139	4	North Gibson School Corp	Princeton
139	4	North Newton School Corp	Morocco
139	4	North West Hendricks Schools	Lizton
139	4	Northern Wells Com Schools	Ossian
139	4	Northwestern School Corp	Kokomo
139	4	Porter Township School Corp	Valparaiso
139	4	Prairie Heights Com Sch Corp	Lagrange
139	4	Rensselaer Central School Corp	Rensselaer
139	4	Rochester Community Sch Corp	Rochester
139	4	Salem Community Schools	Salem
139	4	Shelby Eastern Schools	Shelbyville
139	4	South Gibson School Corp	Fort Branch
139	4	Southeast Dubois County Sch Corp	Ferdinand
139	4	Southwest Dubois County Sch Corp	Huntingburg
139	4	Southwest School Corp	Sullivan
139	4	Switzerland County School Corp	Vevay
139	4	Taylor Community School Corp	Kokomo
139	4	Tippecanoe Valley School Corp	Akron
139	4	Union Co/Clg Corner Joint SD	Liberty
139	4	Union Township School Corp	Valparaiso
139	4	Wabash City Schools	Wabash
139	4	West Noble School Corporation	Ligonier
139	4	Western School Corp	Russiaville
139	4	Whitko Community School Corp	Pierceton
183	3	East Washington School Corp	Pekin
183	3	Knox Community School Corp	Knox
183	3	M S D Bluffton-Harrison	Bluffton
183	3	Northwestern Con School Corp	Fairland
183	3	Southeastern School Corp	Walton
183	3	Tell City-Troy Twp School Corp	Tell City
183	3	Tipton Community School Corp	Tipton
183	3	West Lafayette Com School Corp	West Lafayette
183	3	Western Boone County Com SD	Thorntown
192	2	Paoli Community School Corp	Paoli
192	2	South Ripley Com Sch Corp	Versailles

Number of Teachers

Rank	Number	District Name	City
1	2,769	Indianapolis Public Schools	Indianapolis
2	1,763	Fort Wayne Community Schools	Fort Wayne
3	1,399	Evansville-Vanderburgh Sch Corp	Evansville
4	1,342	South Bend Community Sch Corp	South Bend
5	1,017	Vigo County School Corp	Terre Haute
6	1,001	Gary Community School Corp	Gary
7	922	M S D Lawrence Township	Indianapolis
8	831	M S D Wayne Township	Indianapolis
9	802	Elkhart Community Schools	Elkhart
10	766	Carmel Clay Schools	Carmel
11	766	M S D Perry Township	Indianapolis
12	752	School City of Hammond	Hammond
13	674	Anderson Community School Corp	Anderson
14	652	M S D Warren Township	Indianapolis
15	632	Monroe County Com Sch Corp	Bloomington
16	630	Greater Clark County Schools	Jeffersonville
17	630	New Albany-Floyd County Con Sch	New Albany
18	617	Hamilton Southeastern Schools	Fishers
19	598	Bartholomew Con School Corp	Columbus
20	588	M S D Washington Township	Indianapolis
21	585	East Allen County Schools	New Haven
22	585	M S D Pike Township	Indianapolis
23	558	Tippecanoe School Corp	Lafayette
24	555	Muncie Community Schools	Muncie
25	531	Lafayette School Corporation	Lafayette
26	502	Kokomo-Center Twp Con Sch Corp	Kokomo
27	481	Warrick County School Corp	Boonville
28	481	Penn-Harris-Madison Sch Corp	Mishawaka
29	450	Lake Central School Corp	Saint John
30	420	Michigan City Area Schools	Michigan City
31	403	Portage Township Schools	Portage
32	392	Laporte Community School Corp	Laporte
33	390	Richmond Community School Corp	Richmond
34	387	Huntington County Com Sch Corp	Huntington
35	386	Noblesville Schools	Noblesville
36	381	School City of Mishawaka	Mishawaka
37	374	School City of East Chicago	East Chicago
38	373	Marion Community Schools	Marion
39	369	Goshen Community Schools	Goshen
40	366	Center Grove Com Sch Corp	Greenwood
41	355	Warsaw Community Schools	Warsaw
42	337	M S D Southwest Allen County	Fort Wayne
43	335	North Lawrence Com Schools	Bedford
44	332	Franklin Township Com Sch Corp	Indianapolis
45	330	Avon Community School Corp	Avon
46	325	Logansport Community Sch Corp	Logansport
47	321	Greenfield-Central Com Schools	Greenfield
48	320	Merrillville Community School	Merrillville
49	315	Brownsburg Community Sch Corp	Brownsburg
50	313	Valparaiso Community Schools	Valparaiso
51	308	M S D Martinsville Schools	Martinsville
52	294	M S D Decatur Township	Indianapolis
53	289	Clay Community Schools	Knightsville
54	280	Jennings County Schools	North Vernon
55	279	New Castle Community Sch Corp	New Castle
56	266	Duneland School Corporation	Chesterton
57	263	Crown Point Community Sch Corp	Crown Point
58	262	Northwest Allen County Schools	Fort Wayne
59	260	Fayette County School Corp	Connersville
60	258	Westfield-Washington Schools	Westfield
61	251	Franklin Community School Corp	Franklin
62	246	Mooresville Con School Corp	Mooresville
63	235	Concord Community Schools	Elkhart
64	233	Zionsville Community Schools	Zionsville
65	230	East Noble School Corp	Kendallville
66	225	Jay School Corp	Portland
67	216	School Town of Munster	Munster
68	212	Sunman-Dearborn Com Sch Corp	Sunman
69	211	Seymour Community Schools	Seymour
70	211	Whitley County Cons Schools	Columbia City
71	207	Dekalb County Ctl United SD	Waterloo
72	205	Middlebury Community Schools	Middlebury
73	204	Plainfield Community Sch Corp	Plainfield
74	203	Vincennes Community Sch Corp	Vincennes
75	199	Lebanon Community School Corp	Lebanon
76	199	Madison Consolidated Schools	Madison
77	197	Wawasee Community School Corp	Syracuse
78	193	Community Schools of Frankfort	Frankfort

79	191	Spencer-Owen Community Schools	Spencer
80	190	Greater Jasper Con Schs	Jasper
81	189	Clark-Pleasant Com School Corp	Whiteland
82	188	M S D Wabash County Schools	Wabash
83	188	Shelbyville Central Schools	Shelbyville
84	187	South Harrison Com Schools	Corydon
85	183	West Clark Community Schools	Sellersburg
86	181	South Madison Com Sch Corp	Pendleton
87	179	South Dearborn Com School Corp	Aurora
88	179	Greenwood Community Sch Corp	Greenwood
89	178	School City of Hobart	Hobart
90	174	Wa-Nee Community Schools	Nappanee
91	170	M S D Mount Vernon	Mount Vernon
92	169	Richland-Bean Blossom C S C	Ellettsville
93	168	Kankakee Valley School Corp	Wheatfield
94	167	Rush County Schools	Rushville
95	165	Delaware Community School Corp	Muncie
96	164	Plymouth Community School Corp	Plymouth
97	162	M S D Steuben County	Angola
98	159	Franklin County Com Sch Corp	Brookville
99	156	Crawfordsville Com Schools	Crawfordsville
100	155	Peru Community Schools	Peru
101	152	Scott County SD 2	Scottsburg
102	151	School Town of Highland	Highland
103	148	Mt Vernon Community Sch Corp	Fortville
103	148	North Putnam Community Schools	Bainbridge
105	148	Brown County School Corporation	Nashville
106	146	Tri-Creek School Corp	Lowell
107	144	West Noble School Corporation	Ligonier
108	144	Northern Wells Com Schools	Ossian
109	143	Blackford County Schools	Hartford City
110	143	Southern Hancock Co Com Sch Corp	New Palestine
111	143	Maconaquah School Corp	Bunker Hill
112	143	Twin Lakes School Corp	Monticello
113	141	North Adams Community Schools	Decatur
114	140	Washington Com Schools Inc	Washington
115	137	Griffith Public Schools	Griffith
116	136	New Prairie United School Corp	New Carlisle
117	135	Mississinewa Community School Corp	Gas City
118	134	Westview School Corporation	Topeka
119	134	Lakeland School Corporation	Lagrange
120	133	Decatur County Com Schools	Greensburg
121	131	Benton Community School Corp	Fowler
122	129	North Harrison Com School Corp	Ramsey
122	129	North Spencer County Sch Corp	Lincoln City
124	129	Beech Grove City Schools	Beech Grove
125	128	South Montgomery Com Sch Corp	New Market
126	126	Western School Corp	Russiaville
127	125	Dekalb County Eastern Com SD	Butler
128	125	Danville Community School Corp	Danville
128	125	Lake Ridge Schools	Gary
130	124	Mt Pleasant Twp Com Sch Corp	Yorktown
131	123	Frankton-Lapel Community Schs	Anderson
131	123	South Vermillion Com Sch Corp	Clinton
133	122	Elwood Community School Corp	Elwood
133	122	Pike County School Corp	Petersburg
135	121	Hamilton Heights School Corp	Arcadia
136	118	Greensburg Community Schools	Greensburg
137	118	North Montgomery Com Sch Corp	Crawfordsville
138	116	North Gibson School Corp	Princeton
139	115	Tippecanoe Valley School Corp	Akron
140	115	East Porter County School Corp	Kouts
140	115	Whitko Community School Corp	Pierceton
142	113	Fairfield Community Schools	Goshen
143	112	Batesville Community Sch Corp	Batesville
143	112	West Lafayette Com School Corp	West Lafayette
145	111	Tipton Community School Corp	Tipton
146	110	Mitchell Community Schools	Mitchell
147	109	Randolph Central School Corp	Winchester
148	108	Southwest School Corp	Sullivan
149	108	Taylor Community School Corp	Kokomo
150	108	Salem Community Schools	Salem
151	107	Garrett-Keyser-Butler Com	Garrett
152	107	Rensselaer Central School Corp	Rensselaer
153	107	Western Boone County Com SD	Thorntown
154	106	Greencastle Community Sch Corp	Greencastle
155	105	Knox Community School Corp	Knox
156	105	Rochester Community Sch Corp	Rochester
157	104	Eastbrook Community Sch Corp	Marion
157	104	Union Co/Clg Corner Joint SD	Liberty
159	104	North Newton School Corp	Morocco
160	103	Northwestern School Corp	Kokomo
161	103	Madison-Grant United Sch Corp	Fairmount
161	103	Nineveh-Hensley-Jackson United	Trafalgar
163	101	Alexandria Com School Corp	Alexandria
164	100	Centerville-Abington Com Schs	Centerville
164	100	Prairie Heights Com Sch Corp	Lagrange
166	99	South Gibson School Corp	Fort Branch
167	99	Baugo Community Schools	Elkhart
167	99	Northeast School Corp	Hymera
167	99	School Town of Speedway	Speedway
170	99	Crawford County Com School Corp	Marengo
171	99	Shelby Eastern Schools	Shelbyville
172	98	Southwest Dubois County Sch Corp	Huntingburg
173	95	Wabash City Schools	Wabash
174	94	Delphi Community School Corp	Delphi
175	94	Mill Creek Community Sch Corp	Clayton
176	94	Brownstown Cnt Com Sch Corp	Brownstown
177	93	North West Hendricks Schools	Lizton
178	92	Southeastern School Corp	Walton
179	92	Tell City-Troy Twp School Corp	Tell City
180	91	Oak Hill United School Corp	Converse
181	90	John Glenn School Corporation	Walkerton
181	90	Paoli Community School Corp	Paoli
183	89	East Washington School Corp	Pekin
183	89	Union Township School Corp	Valparaiso
185	87	Manchester Community Schools	N Manchester
186	86	M S D Bluffton-Harrison	Bluffton
187	85	Switzerland County School Corp	Vevay
188	84	North Knox School Corp	Bicknell
189	83	Southeast Dubois County Sch Corp	Ferdinand
190	80	South Ripley Com Sch Corp	Versailles
191	78	Hanover Community School Corp	Cedar Lake
191	78	Northwestern Con School Corp	Fairland
193	75	Porter Township School Corp	Valparaiso

Number of Students

Rank	Number	District Name	City
1	39,989	Indianapolis Public Schools	Indianapolis
2	31,815	Fort Wayne Community Schools	Fort Wayne
3	22,408	Evansville-Vanderburgh Sch Corp	Evansville
4	21,871	South Bend Community Sch Corp	South Bend
5	17,381	Gary Community School Corp	Gary
6	16,377	Vigo County School Corp	Terre Haute
7	16,201	M S D Lawrence Township	Indianapolis
8	14,174	M S D Wayne Township	Indianapolis
9	13,696	School City of Hammond	Hammond
10	13,514	Carmel Clay Schools	Carmel
11	13,209	M S D Perry Township	Indianapolis
12	13,059	Elkhart Community Schools	Elkhart
13	11,752	M S D Warren Township	Indianapolis
14	11,710	Hamilton Southeastern Schools	Fishers
15	11,253	New Albany-Floyd County Con Sch	New Albany
16	10,698	Monroe County Com Sch Corp	Bloomington
17	10,629	Bartholomew Con School Corp	Columbus
18	10,490	M S D Pike Township	Indianapolis
19	10,315	Anderson Community School Corp	Anderson
20	10,271	Tippecanoe School Corp	Lafayette
21	10,267	Greater Clark County Schools	Jeffersonville
22	10,116	M S D Washington Township	Indianapolis
23	10,056	Penn-Harris-Madison Sch Corp	Mishawaka
24	9,936	East Allen County Schools	New Haven
25	9,269	Warrick County School Corp	Boonville
26	8,674	Lake Central School Corp	Saint John
27	8,075	Muncie Community Schools	Muncie
28	8,021	Portage Township Schools	Portage
29	7,315	Lafayette School Corporation	Lafayette
30	7,144	Noblesville Schools	Noblesville
31	7,011	Center Grove Com Sch Corp	Greenwood
32	6,987	Kokomo-Center Twp Con Sch Corp	Kokomo
33	6,875	Franklin Township Com Sch Corp	Indianapolis
34	6,761	Michigan City Area Schools	Michigan City
35	6,528	Merrillville Community School	Merrillville
36	6,453	Warsaw Community Schools	Warsaw
37	6,444	School City of East Chicago	East Chicago
38	6,350	Avon Community School Corp	Avon
39	6,337	Huntington County Com Sch Corp	Huntington
40	6,301	Laporte Community School Corp	Laporte
41	6,175	Crown Point Community Sch Corp	Crown Point
42	6,149	M S D Southwest Allen County	Fort Wayne
43	6,057	Valparaiso Community Schools	Valparaiso
44	5,899	Brownsburg Community Sch Corp	Brownsburg
45	5,837	Richmond Community School Corp	Richmond
46	5,824	Goshen Community Schools	Goshen
47	5,689	Marion Community Schools	Marion
48	5,626	M S D Decatur Township	Indianapolis
49	5,541	School City of Mishawaka	Mishawaka
50	5,442	North Lawrence Com Schools	Bedford
51	5,421	Duneland School Corporation	Chesterton
52	5,419	M S D Martinsville Schools	Martinsville
53	5,315	Jennings County Schools	North Vernon
54	5,247	Northwest Allen County Schools	Fort Wayne
55	4,687	Westfield-Washington Schools	Westfield
56	4,616	Clay Community Schools	Knightsville
57	4,452	Concord Community Schools	Elkhart
58	4,396	Franklin Community School Corp	Franklin
59	4,341	Mooresville Con School Corp	Mooresville
60	4,275	Logansport Community Sch Corp	Logansport
61	4,242	Sunman-Dearborn Com Sch Corp	Sunman
62	4,190	Zionsville Community Schools	Zionsville
63	4,154	Greenfield-Central Com Schools	Greenfield
64	4,137	Dekalb County Ctl United SD	Waterloo
65	4,048	Plainfield Community Sch Corp	Plainfield
66	3,952	Clark-Pleasant Com School Corp	Whiteland
67	3,935	Fayette County School Corp	Connersville
68	3,888	Jay School Corp	Portland
69	3,882	New Castle Community Sch Corp	New Castle
70	3,863	School Town of Munster	Munster
71	3,834	Greenwood Community Sch Corp	Greenwood
72	3,833	East Noble School Corp	Kendallville
73	3,815	Seymour Community Schools	Seymour
74	3,814	Shelbyville Central Schools	Shelbyville
75	3,733	Middlebury Community Schools	Middlebury
76	3,635	Whitley County Cons Schools	Columbia City
77	3,617	School City of Hobart	Hobart
78	3,506	South Madison Com Sch Corp	Pendleton
79	3,503	Madison Consolidated Schools	Madison
80	3,481	Wawasee Community School Corp	Syracuse
81	3,367	Tri-Creek School Corp	Lowell
82	3,360	School Town of Highland	Highland
83	3,357	Plymouth Community School Corp	Plymouth
84	3,352	Lebanon Community School Corp	Lebanon
85	3,344	West Clark Community Schools	Sellersburg
86	3,272	Community Schools of Frankfort	Frankfort
87	3,226	Kankakee Valley School Corp	Wheatfield
88	3,185	South Harrison Com Schools	Corydon
89	3,140	Spencer-Owen Community Schools	Spencer
90	3,128	Greater Jasper Con Schs	Jasper
91	3,050	Wa-Nee Community Schools	Nappanee
92	3,048	Franklin County Com Sch Corp	Brookville
93	3,034	M S D Steuben County	Angola
94	3,030	South Dearborn Com School Corp	Aurora
95	3,029	Mt Vernon Community Sch Corp	Fortville
96	3,019	Vincennes Community Sch Corp	Vincennes
97	2,945	Southern Hancock Co Com Sch Corp	New Palestine
98	2,879	Delaware Community School Corp	Muncie
99	2,821	Scott County SD 2	Scottsburg
100	2,751	Richland-Bean Blossom C S C	Ellettsville
101	2,721	M S D Mount Vernon	Mount Vernon
102	2,703	Rush County Schools	Rushville
103	2,694	Griffith Public Schools	Griffith
104	2,650	Twin Lakes School Corp	Monticello
105	2,602	Northern Wells Com Schools	Ossian
106	2,598	M S D Wabash County Schools	Wabash
107	2,504	West Noble School Corporation	Ligonier
108	2,475	Washington Com Schools Inc	Washington
109	2,417	Peru Community Schools	Peru
110	2,404	New Prairie United School Corp	New Carlisle
111	2,403	Beech Grove City Schools	Beech Grove
112	2,402	Crawfordsville Com Schools	Crawfordsville
113	2,393	Lake Ridge Schools	Gary
114	2,351	Maconaquah School Corp	Bunker Hill
115	2,328	Western School Corp	Russiaville
116	2,326	Danville Community School Corp	Danville
117	2,307	North Spencer County Sch Corp	Lincoln City
118	2,302	North Adams Community Schools	Decatur
119	2,299	North Harrison Com School Corp	Ramsey
120	2,298	Blackford County Schools	Hartford City
121	2,293	Frankton-Lapel Community Schs	Anderson
122	2,264	Lakeland School Corporation	Lagrange
123	2,262	Brown County School Corporation	Nashville
124	2,246	Mt Pleasant Twp Com Sch Corp	Yorktown
125	2,234	Hamilton Heights School Corp	Arcadia
126	2,214	Westview School Corporation	Topeka
127	2,178	Decatur County Com Schools	Greensburg
128	2,172	Mississinewa Community School Corp	Gas City
129	2,144	Pike County School Corp	Petersburg
130	2,130	Tippecanoe Valley School Corp	Akron
131	2,109	Salem Community Schools	Salem
132	2,080	North Gibson School Corp	Princeton
133	2,075	North Montgomery Com Sch Corp	Crawfordsville
134	2,070	Fairfield Community Schools	Goshen
135	2,064	Mitchell Community Schools	Mitchell
136	2,056	South Montgomery Com Sch Corp	New Market
137	2,026	Greensburg Community Schools	Greensburg
138	2,013	Rochester Community Sch Corp	Rochester
139	2,005	Knox Community School Corp	Knox
140	1,999	Elwood Community School Corp	Elwood
141	1,980	West Lafayette Com School Corp	West Lafayette
142	1,973	South Vermillion Com Sch Corp	Clinton
143	1,969	East Porter County School Corp	Kouts
144	1,966	Whitko Community School Corp	Pierceton
145	1,965	Benton Community School Corp	Fowler
146	1,959	Greencastle Community Sch Corp	Greencastle
147	1,930	Southwest School Corp	Sullivan
148	1,927	North Putnam Community Schools	Bainbridge
149	1,913	Batesville Community Sch Corp	Batesville
150	1,889	Southwest Dubois County Sch Corp	Huntingburg
151	1,875	Tipton Community School Corp	Tipton
152	1,865	Western Boone County Com SD	Thorntown
153	1,857	South Gibson School Corp	Fort Branch
154	1,851	Crawford County Com School Corp	Marengo
155	1,828	Nineveh-Hensley-Jackson United	Trafalgar
156	1,784	Eastbrook Community Sch Corp	Marion
157	1,783	Prairie Heights Com Sch Corp	Lagrange
158	1,781	Rensselaer Central School Corp	Rensselaer

159	1,768	East Washington School Corp	Pekin
160	1,765	Baugo Community Schools	Elkhart
161	1,734	John Glenn School Corporation	Walkerton
162	1,733	Brownstown Cnt Com Sch Corp	Brownstown
163	1,712	Paoli Community School Corp	Paoli
164	1,704	Delphi Community School Corp	Delphi
165	1,688	Tell City-Troy Twp School Corp	Tell City
166	1,679	Northwestern School Corp	Kokomo
167	1,678	Alexandria Com School Corp	Alexandria
167	1,678	Randolph Central School Corp	Winchester
169	1,667	Centerville-Abington Com Schs	Centerville
170	1,662	School Town of Speedway	Speedway
171	1,651	Southeastern School Corp	Walton
172	1,650	North Newton School Corp	Morocco
173	1,646	Garrett-Keyser-Butler Com	Garrett
174	1,620	Madison-Grant United Sch Corp	Fairmount
175	1,610	Union Co/Clg Corner Joint SD	Liberty
176	1,595	Shelby Eastern Schools	Shelbyville
177	1,583	Hanover Community School Corp	Cedar Lake
178	1,577	Manchester Community Schools	N Manchester
178	1,577	North West Hendricks Schools	Lizton
180	1,567	Mill Creek Community Sch Corp	Clayton
181	1,563	Switzerland County School Corp	Vevay
182	1,558	Union Township School Corp	Valparaiso
183	1,540	Wabash City Schools	Wabash
184	1,539	Northwestern Con School Corp	Fairland
185	1,537	Porter Township School Corp	Valparaiso
186	1,529	M S D Bluffton-Harrison	Bluffton
187	1,522	Northeast School Corp	Hymera
188	1,521	Dekalb County Eastern Com SD	Butler
188	1,521	North Knox School Corp	Bicknell
190	1,516	Taylor Community School Corp	Kokomo
191	1,513	South Ripley Com Sch Corp	Versailles
192	1,512	Southeast Dubois County Sch Corp	Ferdinand
193	1,507	Oak Hill United School Corp	Converse

Male Students

Rank	Percent	District Name	City
1	53.7	Rensselaer Central School Corp	Rensselaer
2	53.6	Tippecanoe Valley School Corp	Akron
3	53.6	Union Co/Clg Corner Joint SD	Liberty
4	53.5	Lake Central School Corp	Saint John
5	53.5	Mississinewa Community School Corp	Gas City
6	53.4	Centerville-Abington Com Schs	Centerville
7	53.2	Northeast School Corp	Hymera
8	53.2	Lakeland School Corporation	Lagrange
9	53.2	Alexandria Com School Corp	Alexandria
10	53.2	Decatur County Com Schools	Greensburg
11	53.1	School Town of Speedway	Speedway
12	53.1	Dekalb County Eastern Com SD	Butler
13	53.0	Washington Com Schools Inc	Washington
14	52.8	School Town of Munster	Munster
15	52.8	Greencastle Community Sch Corp	Greencastle
16	52.8	Northwestern School Corp	Kokomo
17	52.8	North Putnam Community Schools	Bainbridge
18	52.8	Scott County SD 2	Scottsburg
19	52.7	Delphi Community School Corp	Delphi
20	52.7	Richland-Bean Blossom C S C	Ellettsville
21	52.6	Tipton Community School Corp	Tipton
22	52.6	Hanover Community School Corp	Cedar Lake
23	52.6	North Lawrence Com Schools	Bedford
24	52.6	Jennings County Schools	North Vernon
25	52.6	M S D Wabash County Schools	Wabash
26	52.6	Rochester Community Sch Corp	Rochester
27	52.5	West Noble School Corporation	Ligonier
28	52.5	Switzerland County School Corp	Vevay
29	52.5	Jay School Corp	Portland
30	52.5	Benton Community School Corp	Fowler
31	52.5	Brown County School Corporation	Nashville
32	52.5	Wabash City Schools	Wabash
33	52.4	Michigan City Area Schools	Michigan City
34	52.4	Westview School Corporation	Topeka
35	52.4	Shelbyville Central Schools	Shelbyville
36	52.4	Warrick County School Corp	Boonville
37	52.2	Duneland School Corporation	Chesterton
38	52.2	Fayette County School Corp	Connersville
38	52.2	Plymouth Community School Corp	Plymouth
40	52.2	Porter Township School Corp	Valparaiso
41	52.2	Tippecanoe School Corp	Lafayette
42	52.2	M S D Martinsville Schools	Martinsville
43	52.2	East Washington School Corp	Pekin
44	52.2	Randolph Central School Corp	Winchester
45	52.1	M S D Southwest Allen County	Fort Wayne
46	52.1	Bartholomew Con School Corp	Columbus
47	52.1	School City of Hammond	Hammond
48	52.0	Logansport Community Sch Corp	Logansport
49	52.0	Crawford County Com School Corp	Marengo
50	52.0	Elwood Community School Corp	Elwood
51	52.0	Sunman-Dearborn Com Sch Corp	Sunman
52	52.0	Baugo Community Schools	Elkhart
53	52.0	Taylor Community School Corp	Kokomo
54	52.0	Nineveh-Hensley-Jackson United	Trafalgar
55	52.0	Laporte Community School Corp	Laporte
56	52.0	North Montgomery Com Sch Corp	Crawfordsville
57	51.9	School City of Mishawaka	Mishawaka
58	51.9	Mt Pleasant Twp Com Sch Corp	Yorktown
59	51.9	Vincennes Community Sch Corp	Vincennes
60	51.9	Beech Grove City Schools	Beech Grove
61	51.9	Northern Wells Com Schools	Ossian
62	51.9	Zionsville Community Schools	Zionsville
63	51.8	Brownstown Cnt Com Sch Corp	Brownstown
64	51.8	South Ripley Com Sch Corp	Versailles
65	51.7	Mt Vernon Community Sch Corp	Fortville
66	51.7	Oak Hill United School Corp	Converse
67	51.7	Western Boone County Com SD	Thorntown
68	51.7	East Allen County Schools	New Haven
69	51.7	Madison Consolidated Schools	Madison
70	51.7	New Prairie United School Corp	New Carlisle
71	51.6	Blackford County Schools	Hartford City
72	51.6	Manchester Community Schools	N Manchester
73	51.6	South Vermillion Com Sch Corp	Clinton
74	51.6	Kankakee Valley School Corp	Wheatfield
75	51.6	Noblesville Schools	Noblesville
76	51.6	M S D Lawrence Township	Indianapolis
77	51.5	Northwestern Con School Corp	Fairland
78	51.5	Delaware Community School Corp	Muncie
79	51.5	Westfield-Washington Schools	Westfield
80	51.5	M S D Mount Vernon	Mount Vernon
81	51.5	Warsaw Community Schools	Warsaw
82	51.5	Vigo County School Corp	Terre Haute
83	51.4	Portage Township Schools	Portage
84	51.4	Tell City-Troy Twp School Corp	Tell City
85	51.4	Greensburg Community Schools	Greensburg
86	51.4	South Harrison Com Schools	Corydon
87	51.4	Center Grove Com Sch Corp	Greenwood
88	51.4	North Knox School Corp	Bicknell
89	51.4	School City of East Chicago	East Chicago
90	51.4	Middlebury Community Schools	Middlebury
91	51.3	School Town of Highland	Highland
92	51.3	Elkhart Community Schools	Elkhart
93	51.3	Richmond Community School Corp	Richmond
94	51.3	M S D Pike Township	Indianapolis
95	51.3	South Bend Community Sch Corp	South Bend
96	51.3	Southeastern School Corp	Walton
97	51.3	New Albany-Floyd County Con Sch	New Albany
98	51.3	Muncie Community Schools	Muncie
99	51.2	M S D Perry Township	Indianapolis
100	51.2	Fort Wayne Community Schools	Fort Wayne
101	51.2	Greater Clark County Schools	Jeffersonville
102	51.2	John Glenn School Corporation	Walkerton
103	51.2	Maconaquah School Corp	Bunker Hill
104	51.2	Southwest School Corp	Sullivan
105	51.2	Madison-Grant United Sch Corp	Fairmount
106	51.2	Greenfield-Central Com Schools	Greenfield
107	51.1	M S D Warren Township	Indianapolis
108	51.1	Community Schools of Frankfort	Frankfort
109	51.1	Indianapolis Public Schools	Indianapolis
110	51.1	Hamilton Southeastern Schools	Fishers
111	51.1	Whitko Community School Corp	Pierceton
112	51.1	Goshen Community Schools	Goshen
113	51.1	Mooresville Con School Corp	Mooresville
114	51.1	Wawasee Community School Corp	Syracuse
115	51.1	M S D Wayne Township	Indianapolis
116	51.1	Franklin Township Com Sch Corp	Indianapolis
117	51.1	Dekalb County Ctl United SD	Waterloo
118	51.0	Marion Community Schools	Marion
119	51.0	Twin Lakes School Corp	Monticello
120	51.0	M S D Steuben County	Angola
121	51.0	Anderson Community School Corp	Anderson
122	51.0	M S D Washington Township	Indianapolis
123	51.0	Shelby Eastern Schools	Shelbyville
124	51.0	Tri-Creek School Corp	Lowell
125	51.0	Avon Community School Corp	Avon
126	51.0	South Montgomery Com Sch Corp	New Market
127	51.0	Merrillville Community School	Merrillville
128	50.9	New Castle Community Sch Corp	New Castle
129	50.9	North Harrison Com School Corp	Ramsey
130	50.9	Peru Community Schools	Peru
131	50.9	Carmel Clay Schools	Carmel
132	50.9	Rush County Schools	Rushville
133	50.9	Evansville-Vanderburgh Sch Corp	Evansville
134	50.9	Batesville Community Sch Corp	Batesville
135	50.8	Monroe County Com Sch Corp	Bloomington
136	50.8	Franklin Community School Corp	Franklin
137	50.8	Brownsburg Community Sch Corp	Brownsburg
138	50.8	School City of Hobart	Hobart
139	50.7	South Madison Com Sch Corp	Pendleton
140	50.7	Huntington County Com Sch Corp	Huntington
141	50.7	M S D Decatur Township	Indianapolis
142	50.7	Spencer-Owen Community Schools	Spencer
143	50.7	Gary Community School Corp	Gary
144	50.7	Whitley County Cons Schools	Columbia City
145	50.7	Hamilton Heights School Corp	Arcadia
146	50.7	Paoli Community School Corp	Paoli
147	50.6	Clay Community Schools	Knightsville
148	50.6	Lebanon Community School Corp	Lebanon
149	50.6	Mill Creek Community Sch Corp	Clayton
150	50.6	Crown Point Community Sch Corp	Crown Point
151	50.6	Greenwood Community Sch Corp	Greenwood
152	50.6	Seymour Community Schools	Seymour
153	50.6	Salem Community Schools	Salem
154	50.6	Greater Jasper Con Schs	Jasper
155	50.6	North Adams Community Schools	Decatur
156	50.6	Western School Corp	Russiaville
157	50.5	Franklin County Com Sch Corp	Brookville
158	50.5	Concord Community Schools	Elkhart
159	50.5	Plainfield Community Sch Corp	Plainfield
160	50.5	Southern Hancock Co Com Sch Corp	New Palestine
161	50.4	Wa-Nee Community Schools	Nappanee
162	50.4	Lafayette School Corporation	Lafayette
163	50.4	Penn-Harris-Madison Sch Corp	Mishawaka
164	50.4	North Newton School Corp	Morocco
165	50.4	Frankton-Lapel Community Schs	Anderson
166	50.3	North Gibson School Corp	Princeton
167	50.3	Clark-Pleasant Com School Corp	Whiteland
168	50.3	Fairfield Community Schools	Goshen
169	50.3	Knox Community School Corp	Knox
170	50.3	Union Township School Corp	Valparaiso
171	50.3	Kokomo-Center Twp Con Sch Corp	Kokomo
172	50.2	Pike County School Corp	Petersburg
173	50.1	Griffith Public Schools	Griffith
174	50.1	West Clark Community Schools	Sellersburg
175	50.1	Danville Community School Corp	Danville
176	50.1	Mitchell Community Schools	Mitchell
177	50.1	East Porter County School Corp	Kouts
178	50.0	North West Hendricks Schools	Lizton
179	50.0	South Dearborn Com School Corp	Aurora
180	50.0	Northwest Allen County Schools	Fort Wayne
181	49.9	Southwest Dubois County Sch Corp	Huntingburg
182	49.9	East Noble School Corp	Kendallville
183	49.8	Lake Ridge Schools	Gary
184	49.8	Valparaiso Community Schools	Valparaiso
185	49.8	West Lafayette Com School Corp	West Lafayette
186	49.7	South Gibson School Corp	Fort Branch
187	49.7	Crawfordsville Com Schools	Crawfordsville
188	49.5	M S D Bluffton-Harrison	Bluffton
189	49.5	North Spencer County Sch Corp	Lincoln City
190	49.4	Eastbrook Community Sch Corp	Marion
191	49.1	Garrett-Keyser-Butler Com	Garrett
192	48.5	Prairie Heights Com Sch Corp	Lagrange
193	48.0	Southeast Dubois County Sch Corp	Ferdinand

Female Students

Rank	Percent	District Name	City
1	51.9	Southeast Dubois County Sch Corp	Ferdinand
2	51.4	Prairie Heights Com Sch Corp	Lagrange
3	50.8	Garrett-Keyser-Butler Com	Garrett
4	50.5	Eastbrook Community Sch Corp	Marion
5	50.4	North Spencer County Sch Corp	Lincoln City
6	50.4	M S D Bluffton-Harrison	Bluffton
7	50.2	Crawfordsville Com Schools	Crawfordsville
8	50.2	South Gibson School Corp	Fort Branch
9	50.1	West Lafayette Com School Corp	West Lafayette
10	50.1	Valparaiso Community Schools	Valparaiso
11	50.1	Lake Ridge Schools	Gary
12	50.0	East Noble School Corp	Kendallville
13	50.0	Southwest Dubois County Sch Corp	Huntingburg
14	49.9	Northwest Allen County Schools	Fort Wayne
15	49.9	South Dearborn Com School Corp	Aurora
16	49.9	North West Hendricks Schools	Lizton
17	49.8	East Porter County School Corp	Kouts
18	49.8	Mitchell Community Schools	Mitchell
19	49.8	Danville Community School Corp	Danville
20	49.8	West Clark Community Schools	Sellersburg
21	49.8	Griffith Public Schools	Griffith
22	49.7	Pike County School Corp	Petersburg
23	49.6	Kokomo-Center Twp Con Sch Corp	Kokomo
24	49.6	Union Township School Corp	Valparaiso
25	49.6	Knox Community School Corp	Knox
26	49.6	Fairfield Community Schools	Goshen
27	49.6	Clark-Pleasant Com School Corp	Whiteland
28	49.6	North Gibson School Corp	Princeton
29	49.5	Frankton-Lapel Community Schs	Anderson
30	49.5	North Newton School Corp	Morocco
31	49.5	Penn-Harris-Madison Sch Corp	Mishawaka
32	49.5	Lafayette School Corporation	Lafayette
33	49.5	Wa-Nee Community Schools	Nappanee
34	49.4	Southern Hancock Co Com Sch Corp	New Palestine
35	49.4	Plainfield Community Sch Corp	Plainfield
36	49.4	Concord Community Schools	Elkhart
37	49.4	Franklin County Com Sch Corp	Brookville
38	49.3	Western School Corp	Russiaville
39	49.3	North Adams Community Schools	Decatur
40	49.3	Greater Jasper Con Schs	Jasper
41	49.3	Salem Community Schools	Salem
42	49.3	Seymour Community Schools	Seymour

43	49.3	Greenwood Community Sch Corp	Greenwood
44	49.3	Crown Point Community Sch Corp	Crown Point
45	49.3	Mill Creek Community Sch Corp	Clayton
46	49.3	Lebanon Community School Corp	Lebanon
47	49.3	Clay Community Schools	Knightsville
48	49.2	Paoli Community School Corp	Paoli
49	49.2	Hamilton Heights School Corp	Arcadia
50	49.2	Whitley County Cons Schools	Columbia City
51	49.2	Gary Community School Corp	Gary
52	49.2	Spencer-Owen Community Schools	Spencer
53	49.2	M S D Decatur Township	Indianapolis
54	49.2	Huntington County Com Sch Corp	Huntington
55	49.2	South Madison Com Sch Corp	Pendleton
56	49.1	School City of Hobart	Hobart
57	49.1	Brownsburg Community Sch Corp	Brownsburg
58	49.1	Franklin Community School Corp	Franklin
59	49.1	Monroe County Com Sch Corp	Bloomington
60	49.0	Batesville Community Sch Corp	Batesville
61	49.0	Evansville-Vanderburgh Sch Corp	Evansville
62	49.0	Rush County Schools	Rushville
63	49.0	Carmel Clay Schools	Carmel
64	49.0	Peru Community Schools	Peru
65	49.0	North Harrison Com School Corp	Ramsey
66	49.0	New Castle Community Sch Corp	New Castle
67	48.9	Merrillville Community School	Merrillville
68	48.9	South Montgomery Com Sch Corp	New Market
69	48.9	Avon Community School Corp	Avon
70	48.9	Tri-Creek School Corp	Lowell
71	48.9	Shelby Eastern Schools	Shelbyville
72	48.9	M S D Washington Township	Indianapolis
73	48.9	Anderson Community School Corp	Anderson
74	48.9	M S D Steuben County	Angola
75	48.9	Twin Lakes School Corp	Monticello
76	48.9	Marion Community Schools	Marion
77	48.8	Dekalb County Ctl United SD	Waterloo
78	48.8	Franklin Township Com Sch Corp	Indianapolis
79	48.8	M S D Wayne Township	Indianapolis
80	48.8	Wawasee Community School Corp	Syracuse
81	48.8	Mooresville Con School Corp	Mooresville
82	48.8	Goshen Community Schools	Goshen
83	48.8	Whitko Community School Corp	Pierceton
84	48.8	Hamilton Southeastern Schools	Fishers
85	48.8	Indianapolis Public Schools	Indianapolis
86	48.8	Community Schools of Frankfort	Frankfort
87	48.8	M S D Warren Township	Indianapolis
88	48.7	Greenfield-Central Com Schools	Greenfield
89	48.7	Madison-Grant United Sch Corp	Fairmount
90	48.7	Southwest School Corp	Sullivan
91	48.7	Maconaquah School Corp	Bunker Hill
92	48.7	John Glenn School Corporation	Walkerton
93	48.7	Greater Clark County Schools	Jeffersonville
94	48.7	Fort Wayne Community Schools	Fort Wayne
95	48.7	M S D Perry Township	Indianapolis
96	48.6	Muncie Community Schools	Muncie
97	48.6	New Albany-Floyd County Con Sch	New Albany
98	48.6	Southeastern School Corp	Walton
99	48.6	South Bend Community Sch Corp	South Bend
100	48.6	M S D Pike Township	Indianapolis
101	48.6	Richmond Community School Corp	Richmond
102	48.6	Elkhart Community Schools	Elkhart
103	48.6	School Town of Highland	Highland
104	48.5	Middlebury Community Schools	Middlebury
105	48.5	School City of East Chicago	East Chicago
106	48.5	North Knox School Corp	Bicknell
107	48.5	Center Grove Com Sch Corp	Greenwood
108	48.5	South Harrison Com Schools	Corydon
109	48.5	Greensburg Community Schools	Greensburg
110	48.5	Tell City-Troy Twp School Corp	Tell City
111	48.5	Portage Township Schools	Portage
112	48.4	Vigo County School Corp	Terre Haute
113	48.4	Warsaw Community Schools	Warsaw
114	48.4	M S D Mount Vernon	Mount Vernon
115	48.4	Westfield-Washington Schools	Westfield
116	48.4	Delaware Community School Corp	Muncie
117	48.4	Northwestern Con School Corp	Fairland
118	48.3	M S D Lawrence Township	Indianapolis
119	48.3	Noblesville Schools	Noblesville
120	48.3	Kankakee Valley School Corp	Wheatfield
121	48.3	South Vermillion Com Sch Corp	Clinton
122	48.3	Manchester Community Schools	N Manchester
123	48.3	Blackford County Schools	Hartford City
124	48.2	New Prairie United School Corp	New Carlisle
125	48.2	Madison Consolidated Schools	Madison
126	48.2	East Allen County Schools	New Haven
127	48.2	Western Boone County Com SD	Thorntown
128	48.2	Oak Hill United School Corp	Converse
129	48.2	Mt Vernon Community Sch Corp	Fortville
130	48.1	South Ripley Com Sch Corp	Versailles
131	48.1	Brownstown Cnt Com Sch Corp	Brownstown
132	48.0	Zionsville Community Schools	Zionsville
133	48.0	Northern Wells Com Schools	Ossian
134	48.0	Beech Grove City Schools	Beech Grove
135	48.0	Vincennes Community Sch Corp	Vincennes
136	48.0	Mt Pleasant Twp Com Sch Corp	Yorktown
137	48.0	School City of Mishawaka	Mishawaka
138	48.0	North Montgomery Com Sch Corp	Crawfordsville
139	47.9	Laporte Community School Corp	Laporte
140	47.9	Nineveh-Hensley-Jackson United	Trafalgar
141	47.9	Taylor Community School Corp	Kokomo
142	47.9	Baugo Community Schools	Elkhart
143	47.9	Sunman-Dearborn Com Sch Corp	Sunman
144	47.9	Elwood Community School Corp	Elwood
145	47.9	Crawford County Com School Corp	Marengo
146	47.9	Logansport Community Sch Corp	Logansport
147	47.8	School City of Hammond	Hammond
148	47.8	Bartholomew Con School Corp	Columbus
149	47.8	M S D Southwest Allen County	Fort Wayne
150	47.7	Randolph Central School Corp	Winchester
151	47.7	East Washington School Corp	Pekin
152	47.7	M S D Martinsville Schools	Martinsville
153	47.7	Tippecanoe School Corp	Lafayette
154	47.7	Porter Township School Corp	Valparaiso
155	47.7	Fayette County School Corp	Connersville
155	47.7	Plymouth Community School Corp	Plymouth
157	47.7	Duneland School Corporation	Chesterton
158	47.5	Warrick County School Corp	Boonville
159	47.5	Shelbyville Central Schools	Shelbyville
160	47.5	Westview School Corporation	Topeka
161	47.5	Michigan City Area Schools	Michigan City
162	47.4	Wabash City Schools	Wabash
163	47.4	Brown County School Corporation	Nashville
164	47.4	Benton Community School Corp	Fowler
165	47.4	Jay School Corp	Portland
166	47.4	Switzerland County School Corp	Vevay
167	47.4	West Noble School Corporation	Ligonier
168	47.3	Rochester Community Sch Corp	Rochester
169	47.3	M S D Wabash County Schools	Wabash
170	47.3	Jennings County Schools	North Vernon
171	47.3	North Lawrence Com Schools	Bedford
172	47.3	Hanover Community School Corp	Cedar Lake
173	47.3	Tipton Community School Corp	Tipton
174	47.2	Richland-Bean Blossom C S C	Ellettsville
175	47.2	Delphi Community School Corp	Delphi
176	47.1	Scott County SD 2	Scottsburg
177	47.1	North Putnam Community Schools	Bainbridge
178	47.1	Northwestern School Corp	Kokomo
179	47.1	Greencastle Community Sch Corp	Greencastle
180	47.1	School Town of Munster	Munster
181	46.9	Washington Com Schools Inc	Washington
182	46.8	Dekalb County Eastern Com SD	Butler
183	46.8	School Town of Speedway	Speedway
184	46.7	Decatur County Com Schools	Greensburg
185	46.7	Alexandria Com School Corp	Alexandria
186	46.7	Lakeland School Corporation	Lagrange
187	46.7	Northeast School Corp	Hymera
188	46.5	Centerville-Abington Com Schs	Centerville
189	46.4	Mississinewa Community School Corp	Gas City
190	46.4	Lake Central School Corp	Saint John
191	46.3	Union Co/Clg Corner Joint SD	Liberty
192	46.3	Tippecanoe Valley School Corp	Akron
193	46.2	Rensselaer Central School Corp	Rensselaer

Individual Education Program Students

Rank	Percent	District Name	City
1	26.6	Benton Community School Corp	Fowler
2	26.2	North Putnam Community Schools	Bainbridge
3	25.7	New Castle Community Sch Corp	New Castle
4	25.3	Richmond Community School Corp	Richmond
5	24.1	Madison Consolidated Schools	Madison
6	24.0	Kokomo-Center Twp Con Sch Corp	Kokomo
6	24.0	Randolph Central School Corp	Winchester
6	24.0	Southwest School Corp	Sullivan
9	23.2	Muncie Community Schools	Muncie
9	23.2	South Bend Community Sch Corp	South Bend
11	22.7	Lafayette School Corporation	Lafayette
11	22.7	M S D Mount Vernon	Mount Vernon
13	22.5	Jennings County Schools	North Vernon
14	22.4	Northeast School Corp	Hymera
15	22.3	Shelbyville Central Schools	Shelbyville
16	22.2	Greater Clark County Schools	Jeffersonville
17	22.1	South Madison Com Sch Corp	Pendleton
18	21.5	Greencastle Community Sch Corp	Greencastle
19	21.3	Spencer-Owen Community Schools	Spencer
20	21.1	Fayette County School Corp	Connersville
20	21.1	Greenfield-Central Com Schools	Greenfield
22	20.9	Washington Com Schools Inc	Washington
23	20.8	Clay Community Schools	Knightsville
24	20.5	Blackford County Schools	Hartford City
25	20.4	South Dearborn Com School Corp	Aurora
25	20.4	Wabash City Schools	Wabash
27	20.3	Evansville-Vanderburgh Sch Corp	Evansville
28	20.0	Elwood Community School Corp	Elwood
29	19.9	Michigan City Area Schools	Michigan City
29	19.9	Seymour Community Schools	Seymour
31	19.7	Rensselaer Central School Corp	Rensselaer
31	19.7	Vigo County School Corp	Terre Haute
33	19.6	North Gibson School Corp	Princeton
34	19.5	Taylor Community School Corp	Kokomo
35	19.1	Hamilton Heights School Corp	Arcadia
36	19.0	Anderson Community School Corp	Anderson
36	19.0	South Harrison Com Schools	Corydon
36	19.0	Warrick County School Corp	Boonville
39	18.9	Union Co/Clg Corner Joint SD	Liberty
40	18.8	New Albany-Floyd County Con Sch	New Albany
41	18.7	Lebanon Community School Corp	Lebanon
41	18.7	School City of Mishawaka	Mishawaka
41	18.7	Switzerland County School Corp	Vevay
44	18.6	Indianapolis Public Schools	Indianapolis
45	18.5	Pike County School Corp	Petersburg
45	18.5	Richland-Bean Blossom C S C	Ellettsville
45	18.5	South Vermillion Com Sch Corp	Clinton
48	18.4	Mill Creek Community Sch Corp	Clayton
49	18.3	Crawford County Com School Corp	Marengo
49	18.3	Franklin Community School Corp	Franklin
51	18.2	Fort Wayne Community Schools	Fort Wayne
52	18.1	South Montgomery Com Sch Corp	New Market
53	18.0	Baugo Community Schools	Elkhart
54	17.9	Goshen Community Schools	Goshen
54	17.9	M S D Decatur Township	Indianapolis
54	17.9	M S D Wabash County Schools	Wabash
54	17.9	Mt Pleasant Twp Com Sch Corp	Yorktown
58	17.8	M S D Warren Township	Indianapolis
58	17.8	North Newton School Corp	Morocco
60	17.7	Mitchell Community Schools	Mitchell
60	17.7	Paoli Community School Corp	Paoli
60	17.7	Sunman-Dearborn Com Sch Corp	Sunman
63	17.6	M S D Pike Township	Indianapolis
63	17.6	North Harrison Com School Corp	Ramsey
63	17.6	North Lawrence Com Schools	Bedford
66	17.5	East Porter County School Corp	Kouts
67	17.4	Kankakee Valley School Corp	Wheatfield
68	17.3	Frankton-Lapel Community Schs	Anderson
68	17.3	Lake Central School Corp	Saint John
68	17.3	School Town of Munster	Munster
71	17.2	Noblesville Schools	Noblesville
71	17.2	Shelby Eastern Schools	Shelbyville
73	17.1	Mt Vernon Community Sch Corp	Fortville
73	17.1	North Montgomery Com Sch Corp	Crawfordsville
73	17.1	Southern Hancock Co Com Sch Corp	New Palestine
76	17.0	Duneland School Corporation	Chesterton
76	17.0	East Washington School Corp	Pekin
76	17.0	Mississinewa Community School Corp	Gas City
76	17.0	Peru Community Schools	Peru
80	16.9	South Gibson School Corp	Fort Branch
80	16.9	Vincennes Community Sch Corp	Vincennes
82	16.8	Eastbrook Community Sch Corp	Marion
82	16.8	Franklin County Com Sch Corp	Brookville
82	16.8	Garrett-Keyser-Butler Com	Garrett
82	16.8	Jay School Corp	Portland
82	16.8	Union Township School Corp	Valparaiso
87	16.7	Crawfordsville Com Schools	Crawfordsville
87	16.7	Decatur County Com Schools	Greensburg
87	16.7	Northwestern Con School Corp	Fairland
90	16.6	Brown County School Corporation	Nashville
90	16.6	Dekalb County Eastern Com SD	Butler
90	16.6	Northwestern School Corp	Kokomo
93	16.4	Batesville Community Sch Corp	Batesville
93	16.4	Elkhart Community Schools	Elkhart
95	16.3	South Ripley Com Sch Corp	Versailles
95	16.3	West Clark Community Schools	Sellersburg
97	16.2	Huntington County Com Sch Corp	Huntington
97	16.2	Maconaquah School Corp	Bunker Hill
97	16.2	Monroe County Com Sch Corp	Bloomington
100	16.0	M S D Martinsville Schools	Martinsville
100	16.0	M S D Wayne Township	Indianapolis
100	16.0	Marion Community Schools	Marion
100	16.0	Northern Wells Com Schools	Ossian
100	16.0	Twin Lakes School Corp	Monticello
105	15.9	Brownstown Cnt Com Sch Corp	Brownstown
105	15.9	East Noble School Corp	Kendallville
105	15.9	Wa-Nee Community Schools	Nappanee
108	15.8	Beech Grove City Schools	Beech Grove
108	15.8	Delaware Community School Corp	Muncie
108	15.8	School Town of Speedway	Speedway
111	15.7	Portage Township Schools	Portage
111	15.7	Westfield-Washington Schools	Westfield
113	15.6	Bartholomew Con School Corp	Columbus
114	15.5	M S D Lawrence Township	Indianapolis
114	15.5	M S D Southwest Allen County	Fort Wayne
114	15.5	School City of Hammond	Hammond
114	15.5	Tipton Community School Corp	Tipton
118	15.4	Avon Community School Corp	Avon
119	15.3	Gary Community School Corp	Gary
119	15.3	North Adams Community Schools	Decatur
121	15.2	Manchester Community Schools	N Manchester
122	15.1	Greensburg Community Schools	Greensburg

122	15.1	North West Hendricks Schools	Lizton
122	15.1	Western School Corp	Russiaville
125	15.0	Alexandria Com School Corp	Alexandria
125	15.0	Scott County SD 2	Scottsburg
127	14.9	Plainfield Community Sch Corp	Plainfield
127	14.9	Rochester Community Sch Corp	Rochester
127	14.9	Salem Community Schools	Salem
127	14.9	Tippecanoe School Corp	Lafayette
127	14.9	Zionsville Community Schools	Zionsville
132	14.8	Centerville-Abington Com Schs	Centerville
132	14.8	Concord Community Schools	Elkhart
132	14.8	East Allen County Schools	New Haven
132	14.8	M S D Washington Township	Indianapolis
132	14.8	Southeastern School Corp	Walton
137	14.7	Hamilton Southeastern Schools	Fishers
137	14.7	Southwest Dubois County Sch Corp	Huntingburg
139	14.6	Knox Community School Corp	Knox
139	14.6	Tippecanoe Valley School Corp	Akron
141	14.5	Dekalb County Ctl United SD	Waterloo
141	14.5	Logansport Community Sch Corp	Logansport
143	14.4	Franklin Township Com Sch Corp	Indianapolis
143	14.4	Lakeland School Corporation	Lagrange
145	14.3	Madison-Grant United Sch Corp	Fairmount
145	14.3	Whitko Community School Corp	Pierceton
147	14.2	Hanover Community School Corp	Cedar Lake
147	14.2	M S D Perry Township	Indianapolis
147	14.2	North Knox School Corp	Bicknell
150	14.1	Rush County Schools	Rushville
150	14.1	School City of East Chicago	East Chicago
152	14.0	Danville Community School Corp	Danville
152	14.0	John Glenn School Corporation	Walkerton
152	14.0	Penn-Harris-Madison Sch Corp	Mishawaka
155	13.9	Clark-Pleasant Com School Corp	Whiteland
155	13.9	Community Schools of Frankfort	Frankfort
155	13.9	Nineveh-Hensley-Jackson United	Trafalgar
155	13.9	Warsaw Community Schools	Warsaw
159	13.8	Griffith Public Schools	Griffith
160	13.7	Lake Ridge Schools	Gary
160	13.7	Tri-Creek School Corp	Lowell
162	13.6	Delphi Community School Corp	Delphi
162	13.6	New Prairie United School Corp	New Carlisle
164	13.5	Fairfield Community Schools	Goshen
164	13.5	Prairie Heights Com Sch Corp	Lagrange
164	13.5	Tell City-Troy Twp School Corp	Tell City
164	13.5	Valparaiso Community Schools	Valparaiso
164	13.5	Western Boone County Com SD	Thorntown
169	13.4	M S D Bluffton-Harrison	Bluffton
170	13.3	Greenwood Community Sch Corp	Greenwood
171	13.0	Laporte Community School Corp	Laporte
172	12.9	Plymouth Community School Corp	Plymouth
173	12.7	Middlebury Community Schools	Middlebury
173	12.7	North Spencer County Sch Corp	Lincoln City
173	12.7	Whitley County Cons Schools	Columbia City
176	12.5	Center Grove Com Sch Corp	Greenwood
176	12.5	M S D Steuben County	Angola
178	12.4	Northwest Allen County Schools	Fort Wayne
178	12.4	Oak Hill United School Corp	Converse
180	12.2	Carmel Clay Schools	Carmel
181	12.1	Greater Jasper Con Schs	Jasper
182	11.9	Brownsburg Community Sch Corp	Brownsburg
182	11.9	Crown Point Community Sch Corp	Crown Point
182	11.9	Mooresville Con School Corp	Mooresville
185	11.8	School Town of Highland	Highland
185	11.8	Southeast Dubois County Sch Corp	Ferdinand
187	11.5	Porter Township School Corp	Valparaiso
187	11.5	West Noble School Corporation	Ligonier
189	11.1	Merrillville Community School	Merrillville
190	10.9	School City of Hobart	Hobart
190	10.9	Wawasee Community School Corp	Syracuse
190	10.9	West Lafayette Com School Corp	West Lafayette
193	10.5	Westview School Corporation	Topeka

English Language Learner Students

Rank	Percent	District Name	City
1	41.8	Westview School Corporation	Topeka
2	31.7	West Noble School Corporation	Ligonier
3	26.2	Goshen Community Schools	Goshen
4	21.7	School City of East Chicago	East Chicago
5	20.5	School City of Hammond	Hammond
6	16.5	West Lafayette Com School Corp	West Lafayette
7	16.4	Community Schools of Frankfort	Frankfort
8	15.8	Fairfield Community Schools	Goshen
9	15.0	Elkhart Community Schools	Elkhart
10	14.5	Logansport Community Sch Corp	Logansport
11	14.1	Lafayette School Corporation	Lafayette
12	13.2	South Bend Community Sch Corp	South Bend
13	10.7	Concord Community Schools	Elkhart
13	10.7	School Town of Munster	Munster
15	10.5	Lakeland School Corporation	Lagrange
16	9.9	M S D Washington Township	Indianapolis
17	9.8	Wa-Nee Community Schools	Nappanee
18	8.9	Warsaw Community Schools	Warsaw
19	8.3	School City of Hobart	Hobart
20	8.0	Twin Lakes School Corp	Monticello
21	7.9	Plymouth Community School Corp	Plymouth
22	7.8	Fort Wayne Community Schools	Fort Wayne
23	7.0	M S D Pike Township	Indianapolis
24	6.9	Indianapolis Public Schools	Indianapolis
25	6.3	Carmel Clay Schools	Carmel
25	6.3	Delphi Community School Corp	Delphi
27	6.2	Lake Central School Corp	Saint John
28	6.1	Merrillville Community School	Merrillville
28	6.1	Middlebury Community Schools	Middlebury
28	6.1	Southeastern School Corp	Walton
31	5.9	M S D Wayne Township	Indianapolis
32	5.7	School Town of Speedway	Speedway
32	5.7	Southwest Dubois County Sch Corp	Huntingburg
34	5.5	M S D Lawrence Township	Indianapolis
34	5.5	Wawasee Community School Corp	Syracuse
36	5.4	Griffith Public Schools	Griffith
36	5.4	Monroe County Com Sch Corp	Bloomington
38	5.3	Tippecanoe School Corp	Lafayette
38	5.3	Washington Com Schools Inc	Washington
40	5.1	School Town of Highland	Highland
41	4.7	Greater Jasper Con Schs	Jasper
42	4.6	M S D Bluffton-Harrison	Bluffton
42	4.6	M S D Southwest Allen County	Fort Wayne
44	4.4	Shelbyville Central Schools	Shelbyville
45	4.3	Laporte Community School Corp	Laporte
45	4.3	M S D Perry Township	Indianapolis
45	4.3	Seymour Community Schools	Seymour
48	4.2	Alexandria Com School Corp	Alexandria
49	4.0	Crawfordsville Com Schools	Crawfordsville
49	4.0	Hamilton Southeastern Schools	Fishers
49	4.0	Prairie Heights Com Sch Corp	Lagrange
52	3.8	Bartholomew Con School Corp	Columbus
53	3.7	Benton Community School Corp	Fowler
53	3.7	Kankakee Valley School Corp	Wheatfield
55	3.6	M S D Warren Township	Indianapolis
55	3.6	Penn-Harris-Madison Sch Corp	Mishawaka
57	3.3	East Allen County Schools	New Haven
57	3.3	Knox Community School Corp	Knox
59	3.2	Crown Point Community Sch Corp	Crown Point
59	3.2	Tippecanoe Valley School Corp	Akron
61	3.1	M S D Steuben County	Angola
62	3.0	Valparaiso Community Schools	Valparaiso
63	2.9	Marion Community Schools	Marion
63	2.9	North Spencer County Sch Corp	Lincoln City
63	2.9	Portage Township Schools	Portage
66	2.5	Jay School Corp	Portland
67	2.4	Greenwood Community Sch Corp	Greenwood
68	2.3	Tipton Community School Corp	Tipton
69	2.2	Elwood Community School Corp	Elwood
69	2.2	Union Township School Corp	Valparaiso
71	2.1	New Prairie United School Corp	New Carlisle
71	2.1	Rensselaer Central School Corp	Rensselaer
73	2.0	Brownsburg Community Sch Corp	Brownsburg
73	2.0	Western School Corp	Russiaville
73	2.0	Westfield-Washington Schools	Westfield
76	1.9	East Noble School Corp	Kendallville
76	1.9	Greater Clark County Schools	Jeffersonville
76	1.9	Michigan City Area Schools	Michigan City
76	1.9	North Newton School Corp	Morocco
80	1.8	Batesville Community Sch Corp	Batesville
80	1.8	Franklin Township Com Sch Corp	Indianapolis
80	1.8	School City of Mishawaka	Mishawaka
83	1.7	Kokomo-Center Twp Con Sch Corp	Kokomo
83	1.7	Muncie Community Schools	Muncie
83	1.7	North Adams Community Schools	Decatur
83	1.7	Richmond Community School Corp	Richmond
87	1.6	Anderson Community School Corp	Anderson
87	1.6	Evansville-Vanderburgh Sch Corp	Evansville
87	1.6	Greensburg Community Schools	Greensburg
87	1.6	Hanover Community School Corp	Cedar Lake
91	1.5	Beech Grove City Schools	Beech Grove
91	1.5	Noblesville Schools	Noblesville
91	1.5	Rochester Community Sch Corp	Rochester
91	1.5	Taylor Community School Corp	Kokomo
95	1.4	Avon Community School Corp	Avon
95	1.4	Baugo Community Schools	Elkhart
95	1.4	Center Grove Com Sch Corp	Greenwood
95	1.4	M S D Decatur Township	Indianapolis
95	1.4	Maconaquah School Corp	Bunker Hill
95	1.4	Mt Pleasant Twp Com Sch Corp	Yorktown
95	1.4	New Albany-Floyd County Con Sch	New Albany
95	1.4	Northwestern School Corp	Kokomo
95	1.4	Plainfield Community Sch Corp	Plainfield
104	1.3	Dekalb County Ctl United SD	Waterloo
104	1.3	Duneland School Corporation	Chesterton
104	1.3	John Glenn School Corporation	Walkerton
104	1.3	Lake Ridge Schools	Gary
108	1.2	Tri-Creek School Corp	Lowell
108	1.2	Whitko Community School Corp	Pierceton
110	1.1	Madison Consolidated Schools	Madison
110	1.1	Manchester Community Schools	N Manchester
112	1.0	Franklin Community School Corp	Franklin
112	1.0	Hamilton Heights School Corp	Arcadia
112	1.0	Lebanon Community School Corp	Lebanon
112	1.0	North Lawrence Com Schools	Bedford
112	1.0	Northwest Allen County Schools	Fort Wayne
117	0.9	Crawford County Com School Corp	Marengo
117	0.9	Greencastle Community Sch Corp	Greencastle
117	0.9	Madison-Grant United Sch Corp	Fairmount
117	0.9	Oak Hill United School Corp	Converse
117	0.9	Peru Community Schools	Peru
117	0.9	Warrick County School Corp	Boonville
123	0.8	Mitchell Community Schools	Mitchell
123	0.8	Randolph Central School Corp	Winchester
123	0.8	Vincennes Community Sch Corp	Vincennes
123	0.8	Zionsville Community Schools	Zionsville
127	0.7	Garrett-Keyser-Butler Com	Garrett
127	0.7	Gary Community School Corp	Gary
127	0.7	M S D Wabash County Schools	Wabash
127	0.7	Porter Township School Corp	Valparaiso
127	0.7	Rush County Schools	Rushville
127	0.7	South Harrison Com Schools	Corydon
127	0.7	Southeast Dubois County Sch Corp	Ferdinand
134	0.6	Danville Community School Corp	Danville
134	0.6	Dekalb County Eastern Com SD	Butler
134	0.6	Jennings County Schools	North Vernon
134	0.6	North Gibson School Corp	Princeton
134	0.6	Salem Community Schools	Salem
134	0.6	South Vermillion Com Sch Corp	Clinton
134	0.6	Sunman-Dearborn Com Sch Corp	Sunman
134	0.6	Wabash City Schools	Wabash
134	0.6	Whitley County Cons Schools	Columbia City
143	0.5	Brownstown Cnt Com Sch Corp	Brownstown
143	0.5	Centerville-Abington Com Schs	Centerville
143	0.5	Clark-Pleasant Com School Corp	Whiteland
143	0.5	Frankton-Lapel Community Schs	Anderson
143	0.5	Mississinewa Community School Corp	Gas City
143	0.5	Mt Vernon Community Sch Corp	Fortville
143	0.5	South Ripley Com Sch Corp	Versailles
150	0.4	Brown County School Corporation	Nashville
150	0.4	Eastbrook Community Sch Corp	Marion
150	0.4	Fayette County School Corp	Connersville
150	0.4	Huntington County Com Sch Corp	Huntington
150	0.4	M S D Martinsville Schools	Martinsville
150	0.4	Mooresville Con School Corp	Mooresville
150	0.4	Scott County SD 2	Scottsburg
150	0.4	Tell City-Troy Twp School Corp	Tell City
158	0.3	Delaware Community School Corp	Muncie
158	0.3	East Porter County School Corp	Kouts
158	0.3	East Washington School Corp	Pekin
158	0.3	M S D Mount Vernon	Mount Vernon
158	0.3	North Harrison Com School Corp	Ramsey
158	0.3	Paoli Community School Corp	Paoli
158	0.3	Richland-Bean Blossom C S C	Ellettsville
158	0.3	South Madison Com Sch Corp	Pendleton
158	0.3	Southwest School Corp	Sullivan
158	0.3	Vigo County School Corp	Terre Haute
158	0.3	West Clark Community Schools	Sellersburg
169	0.2	Clay Community Schools	Knightsville
169	0.2	Greenfield-Central Com Schools	Greenfield
169	0.2	Mill Creek Community Sch Corp	Clayton
169	0.2	Nineveh-Hensley-Jackson United	Trafalgar
169	0.2	North Montgomery Com Sch Corp	Crawfordsville
169	0.2	Northern Wells Com Schools	Ossian
169	0.2	Switzerland County School Corp	Vevay
169	0.2	Western Boone County Com SD	Thorntown
177	0.1	Decatur County Com Schools	Greensburg
177	0.1	New Castle Community Sch Corp	New Castle
177	0.1	Pike County School Corp	Petersburg
177	0.1	South Dearborn Com School Corp	Aurora
177	0.1	South Gibson School Corp	Fort Branch
177	0.1	Spencer-Owen Community Schools	Spencer
177	0.1	Union Co/Clg Corner Joint SD	Liberty
184	0.0	Southern Hancock Co Com Sch Corp	New Palestine
185	n/a	Blackford County Schools	Hartford City
185	n/a	Franklin County Com Sch Corp	Brookville
185	n/a	North Knox School Corp	Bicknell
185	n/a	North Putnam Community Schools	Bainbridge
185	n/a	North West Hendricks Schools	Lizton
185	n/a	Northeast School Corp	Hymera
185	n/a	Northwestern Con School Corp	Fairland
185	n/a	Shelby Eastern Schools	Shelbyville
185	n/a	South Montgomery Com Sch Corp	New Market

Migrant Students

Rank	Percent	District Name	City
1	n/a	Alexandria Com School Corp	Alexandria
1	n/a	Anderson Community School Corp	Anderson
1	n/a	Avon Community School Corp	Avon
1	n/a	Bartholomew Con School Corp	Columbus
1	n/a	Batesville Community Sch Corp	Batesville
1	n/a	Baugo Community Schools	Elkhart

1	n/a	Beech Grove City Schools	Beech Grove
1	n/a	Benton Community School Corp	Fowler
1	n/a	Blackford County Schools	Hartford City
1	n/a	Brown County School Corporation	Nashville
1	n/a	Brownsburg Community Sch Corp	Brownsburg
1	n/a	Brownstown Cnt Com Sch Corp	Brownstown
1	n/a	Carmel Clay Schools	Carmel
1	n/a	Center Grove Com Sch Corp	Greenwood
1	n/a	Centerville-Abington Com Schs	Centerville
1	n/a	Clark-Pleasant Com School Corp	Whiteland
1	n/a	Clay Community Schools	Knightsville
1	n/a	Community Schools of Frankfort	Frankfort
1	n/a	Concord Community Schools	Elkhart
1	n/a	Crawford County Com School Corp	Marengo
1	n/a	Crawfordsville Com Schools	Crawfordsville
1	n/a	Crown Point Community Sch Corp	Crown Point
1	n/a	Danville Community School Corp	Danville
1	n/a	Decatur County Com Schools	Greensburg
1	n/a	Dekalb County Ctl United SD	Waterloo
1	n/a	Dekalb County Eastern Com SD	Butler
1	n/a	Delaware Community School Corp	Muncie
1	n/a	Delphi Community School Corp	Delphi
1	n/a	Duneland School Corporation	Chesterton
1	n/a	East Allen County Schools	New Haven
1	n/a	East Noble School Corp	Kendallville
1	n/a	East Porter County School Corp	Kouts
1	n/a	East Washington School Corp	Pekin
1	n/a	Eastbrook Community Sch Corp	Marion
1	n/a	Elkhart Community Schools	Elkhart
1	n/a	Elwood Community School Corp	Elwood
1	n/a	Evansville-Vanderburgh Sch Corp	Evansville
1	n/a	Fairfield Community Schools	Goshen
1	n/a	Fayette County School Corp	Connersville
1	n/a	Fort Wayne Community Schools	Fort Wayne
1	n/a	Franklin Community School Corp	Franklin
1	n/a	Franklin County Com Sch Corp	Brookville
1	n/a	Franklin Township Com Sch Corp	Indianapolis
1	n/a	Frankton-Lapel Community Schs	Anderson
1	n/a	Garrett-Keyser-Butler Com	Garrett
1	n/a	Gary Community School Corp	Gary
1	n/a	Goshen Community Schools	Goshen
1	n/a	Greater Clark County Schools	Jeffersonville
1	n/a	Greater Jasper Con Schs	Jasper
1	n/a	Greencastle Community Sch Corp	Greencastle
1	n/a	Greenfield-Central Com Schools	Greenfield
1	n/a	Greensburg Community Schools	Greensburg
1	n/a	Greenwood Community Sch Corp	Greenwood
1	n/a	Griffith Public Schools	Griffith
1	n/a	Hamilton Heights School Corp	Arcadia
1	n/a	Hamilton Southeastern Schools	Fishers
1	n/a	Hanover Community School Corp	Cedar Lake
1	n/a	Huntington County Com Sch Corp	Huntington
1	n/a	Indianapolis Public Schools	Indianapolis
1	n/a	Jay School Corp	Portland
1	n/a	Jennings County Schools	North Vernon
1	n/a	John Glenn School Corporation	Walkerton
1	n/a	Kankakee Valley School Corp	Wheatfield
1	n/a	Knox Community School Corp	Knox
1	n/a	Kokomo-Center Twp Con Sch Corp	Kokomo
1	n/a	Lafayette School Corporation	Lafayette
1	n/a	Lake Central School Corp	Saint John
1	n/a	Lake Ridge Schools	Gary
1	n/a	Lakeland School Corporation	Lagrange
1	n/a	Laporte Community School Corp	Laporte
1	n/a	Lebanon Community School Corp	Lebanon
1	n/a	Logansport Community Sch Corp	Logansport
1	n/a	M S D Bluffton-Harrison	Bluffton
1	n/a	M S D Decatur Township	Indianapolis
1	n/a	M S D Lawrence Township	Indianapolis
1	n/a	M S D Martinsville Schools	Martinsville
1	n/a	M S D Mount Vernon	Mount Vernon
1	n/a	M S D Perry Township	Indianapolis
1	n/a	M S D Pike Township	Indianapolis
1	n/a	M S D Southwest Allen County	Fort Wayne
1	n/a	M S D Steuben County	Angola
1	n/a	M S D Wabash County Schools	Wabash
1	n/a	M S D Warren Township	Indianapolis
1	n/a	M S D Washington Township	Indianapolis
1	n/a	M S D Wayne Township	Indianapolis
1	n/a	Maconaquah School Corp	Bunker Hill
1	n/a	Madison Consolidated Schools	Madison
1	n/a	Madison-Grant United Sch Corp	Fairmount
1	n/a	Manchester Community Schools	N Manchester
1	n/a	Marion Community Schools	Marion
1	n/a	Merrillville Community School	Merrillville
1	n/a	Michigan City Area Schools	Michigan City
1	n/a	Middlebury Community Schools	Middlebury
1	n/a	Mill Creek Community Sch Corp	Clayton
1	n/a	Mississinewa Community School Corp	Gas City
1	n/a	Mitchell Community Schools	Mitchell
1	n/a	Monroe County Com Sch Corp	Bloomington
1	n/a	Mooresville Con School Corp	Mooresville
1	n/a	Mt Pleasant Twp Com Sch Corp	Yorktown
1	n/a	Mt Vernon Community Sch Corp	Fortville
1	n/a	Muncie Community Schools	Muncie
1	n/a	New Albany-Floyd County Con Sch	New Albany
1	n/a	New Castle Community Sch Corp	New Castle
1	n/a	New Prairie United School Corp	New Carlisle
1	n/a	Nineveh-Hensley-Jackson United	Trafalgar
1	n/a	Noblesville Schools	Noblesville
1	n/a	North Adams Community Schools	Decatur
1	n/a	North Gibson School Corp	Princeton
1	n/a	North Harrison Com School Corp	Ramsey
1	n/a	North Knox School Corp	Bicknell
1	n/a	North Lawrence Com Schools	Bedford
1	n/a	North Montgomery Com Sch Corp	Crawfordsville
1	n/a	North Newton School Corp	Morocco
1	n/a	North Putnam Community Schools	Bainbridge
1	n/a	North Spencer County Sch Corp	Lincoln City
1	n/a	North West Hendricks Schools	Lizton
1	n/a	Northeast School Corp	Hymera
1	n/a	Northern Wells Com Schools	Ossian
1	n/a	Northwest Allen County Schools	Fort Wayne
1	n/a	Northwestern Con School Corp	Fairland
1	n/a	Northwestern School Corp	Kokomo
1	n/a	Oak Hill United School Corp	Converse
1	n/a	Paoli Community School Corp	Paoli
1	n/a	Penn-Harris-Madison Sch Corp	Mishawaka
1	n/a	Peru Community Schools	Peru
1	n/a	Pike County School Corp	Petersburg
1	n/a	Plainfield Community Sch Corp	Plainfield
1	n/a	Plymouth Community School Corp	Plymouth
1	n/a	Portage Township Schools	Portage
1	n/a	Porter Township School Corp	Valparaiso
1	n/a	Prairie Heights Com Sch Corp	Lagrange
1	n/a	Randolph Central School Corp	Winchester
1	n/a	Rensselaer Central School Corp	Rensselaer
1	n/a	Richland-Bean Blossom C S C	Ellettsville
1	n/a	Richmond Community School Corp	Richmond
1	n/a	Rochester Community Sch Corp	Rochester
1	n/a	Rush County Schools	Rushville
1	n/a	Salem Community Schools	Salem
1	n/a	School City of East Chicago	East Chicago
1	n/a	School City of Hammond	Hammond
1	n/a	School City of Hobart	Hobart
1	n/a	School City of Mishawaka	Mishawaka
1	n/a	School Town of Highland	Highland
1	n/a	School Town of Munster	Munster
1	n/a	School Town of Speedway	Speedway
1	n/a	Scott County SD 2	Scottsburg
1	n/a	Seymour Community Schools	Seymour
1	n/a	Shelby Eastern Schools	Shelbyville
1	n/a	Shelbyville Central Schools	Shelbyville
1	n/a	South Bend Community Sch Corp	South Bend
1	n/a	South Dearborn Com School Corp	Aurora
1	n/a	South Gibson School Corp	Fort Branch
1	n/a	South Harrison Com Schools	Corydon
1	n/a	South Madison Com Sch Corp	Pendleton
1	n/a	South Montgomery Com Sch Corp	New Market
1	n/a	South Ripley Com Sch Corp	Versailles
1	n/a	South Vermillion Com Sch Corp	Clinton
1	n/a	Southeast Dubois County Sch Corp	Ferdinand
1	n/a	Southeastern School Corp	Walton
1	n/a	Southern Hancock Co Com Sch Corp	New Palestine
1	n/a	Southwest Dubois County Sch Corp	Huntingburg
1	n/a	Southwest School Corp	Sullivan
1	n/a	Spencer-Owen Community Schools	Spencer
1	n/a	Sunman-Dearborn Com Sch Corp	Sunman
1	n/a	Switzerland County School Corp	Vevay
1	n/a	Taylor Community School Corp	Kokomo
1	n/a	Tell City-Troy Twp School Corp	Tell City
1	n/a	Tippecanoe School Corp	Lafayette
1	n/a	Tippecanoe Valley School Corp	Akron
1	n/a	Tipton Community School Corp	Tipton
1	n/a	Tri-Creek School Corp	Lowell
1	n/a	Twin Lakes School Corp	Monticello
1	n/a	Union Co/Clg Corner Joint SD	Liberty
1	n/a	Union Township School Corp	Valparaiso
1	n/a	Valparaiso Community Schools	Valparaiso
1	n/a	Vigo County School Corp	Terre Haute
1	n/a	Vincennes Community Sch Corp	Vincennes
1	n/a	Wa-Nee Community Schools	Nappanee
1	n/a	Wabash City Schools	Wabash
1	n/a	Warrick County School Corp	Boonville
1	n/a	Warsaw Community Schools	Warsaw
1	n/a	Washington Com Schools Inc	Washington
1	n/a	Wawasee Community School Corp	Syracuse
1	n/a	West Clark Community Schools	Sellersburg
1	n/a	West Lafayette Com School Corp	West Lafayette
1	n/a	West Noble School Corporation	Ligonier
1	n/a	Western Boone County Com SD	Thorntown
1	n/a	Western School Corp	Russiaville
1	n/a	Westfield-Washington Schools	Westfield
1	n/a	Westview School Corporation	Topeka
1	n/a	Whitko Community School Corp	Pierceton
1	n/a	Whitley County Cons Schools	Columbia City
1	n/a	Zionsville Community Schools	Zionsville

Students Eligible for Free Lunch

Rank	Percent	District Name	City
1	76.4	School City of East Chicago	East Chicago
2	67.6	Indianapolis Public Schools	Indianapolis
3	59.3	Lake Ridge Schools	Gary
4	58.3	School City of Hammond	Hammond
5	57.0	Gary Community School Corp	Gary
6	49.8	South Bend Community Sch Corp	South Bend
7	48.7	Muncie Community Schools	Muncie
8	47.4	Richmond Community School Corp	Richmond
9	43.9	Michigan City Area Schools	Michigan City
10	43.1	Marion Community Schools	Marion
11	42.6	Anderson Community School Corp	Anderson
12	41.5	Fort Wayne Community Schools	Fort Wayne
13	41.2	Community Schools of Frankfort	Frankfort
14	40.5	M S D Wayne Township	Indianapolis
15	40.3	Fayette County School Corp	Connersville
16	39.7	West Noble School Corporation	Ligonier
17	39.5	Kokomo-Center Twp Con Sch Corp	Kokomo
18	39.1	Elkhart Community Schools	Elkhart
19	37.5	Lafayette School Corporation	Lafayette
20	37.3	Crawford County Com School Corp	Marengo
21	36.6	Elwood Community School Corp	Elwood
22	36.5	Logansport Community Sch Corp	Logansport
23	36.3	Crawfordsville Com Schools	Crawfordsville
23	36.3	Evansville-Vanderburgh Sch Corp	Evansville
25	35.9	Northeast School Corp	Hymera
26	35.7	Goshen Community Schools	Goshen
27	34.6	M S D Warren Township	Indianapolis
28	34.4	Knox Community School Corp	Knox
29	34.3	Vincennes Community Sch Corp	Vincennes
30	33.8	Paoli Community School Corp	Paoli
30	33.8	Washington Com Schools Inc	Washington
32	33.7	Vigo County School Corp	Terre Haute
33	33.1	New Castle Community Sch Corp	New Castle
34	32.6	M S D Perry Township	Indianapolis
35	32.0	M S D Decatur Township	Indianapolis
36	31.5	Mitchell Community Schools	Mitchell
37	31.4	Switzerland County School Corp	Vevay
38	31.3	Peru Community Schools	Peru
39	30.6	North Knox School Corp	Bicknell
40	30.5	Mississinewa Community School Corp	Gas City
40	30.5	Scott County SD 2	Scottsburg
42	30.4	Jennings County Schools	North Vernon
43	29.7	Spencer-Owen Community Schools	Spencer
44	29.6	Clay Community Schools	Knightsville
44	29.6	School City of Mishawaka	Mishawaka
44	29.6	Wabash City Schools	Wabash
47	28.9	Madison Consolidated Schools	Madison
48	28.7	South Vermillion Com Sch Corp	Clinton
49	28.5	School Town of Speedway	Speedway
50	28.4	Alexandria Com School Corp	Alexandria
51	28.3	Randolph Central School Corp	Winchester
52	28.1	Plymouth Community School Corp	Plymouth
53	28.0	Blackford County Schools	Hartford City
54	27.9	M S D Pike Township	Indianapolis
55	27.2	M S D Washington Township	Indianapolis
56	26.6	Jay School Corp	Portland
57	26.1	Salem Community Schools	Salem
58	26.0	East Washington School Corp	Pekin
58	26.0	Greater Clark County Schools	Jeffersonville
60	25.2	New Albany-Floyd County Con Sch	New Albany
61	25.1	Beech Grove City Schools	Beech Grove
62	25.0	Benton Community School Corp	Fowler
63	24.9	North Gibson School Corp	Princeton
64	24.5	Franklin County Com Sch Corp	Brookville
64	24.5	North Lawrence Com Schools	Bedford
64	24.5	Taylor Community School Corp	Kokomo
67	24.4	Twin Lakes School Corp	Monticello
68	24.3	Laporte Community School Corp	Laporte
68	24.3	Pike County School Corp	Petersburg
70	24.2	Bartholomew Con School Corp	Columbus
70	24.2	Tell City-Troy Twp School Corp	Tell City
72	24.1	East Allen County Schools	New Haven
73	23.8	Concord Community Schools	Elkhart
73	23.8	Portage Township Schools	Portage
75	23.7	Delphi Community School Corp	Delphi
75	23.7	Seymour Community Schools	Seymour
77	23.5	Rochester Community Sch Corp	Rochester
77	23.5	South Ripley Com Sch Corp	Versailles
79	23.4	Lakeland School Corporation	Lagrange
80	23.1	Southwest School Corp	Sullivan
81	22.9	Shelbyville Central Schools	Shelbyville
82	22.4	Brownstown Cnt Com Sch Corp	Brownstown
83	22.3	Lebanon Community School Corp	Lebanon
84	22.1	Garrett-Keyser-Butler Com	Garrett
84	22.1	Greensburg Community Schools	Greensburg
84	22.1	Manchester Community Schools	N Manchester
87	22.0	Brown County School Corporation	Nashville

87	22.0	Franklin Community School Corp	Franklin
89	21.9	Monroe County Com Sch Corp	Bloomington
89	21.9	Rush County Schools	Rushville
91	21.8	Rensselaer Central School Corp	Rensselaer
92	21.7	Warsaw Community Schools	Warsaw
93	21.6	M S D Lawrence Township	Indianapolis
93	21.6	Union Co/Clg Corner Joint SD	Liberty
95	21.4	M S D Steuben County	Angola
96	21.3	Greencastle Community Sch Corp	Greencastle
97	21.2	Maconaquah School Corp	Bunker Hill
97	21.2	Madison-Grant United Sch Corp	Fairmount
99	20.8	South Harrison Com Schools	Corydon
99	20.8	Tippecanoe Valley School Corp	Akron
101	20.6	Merrillville Community School	Merrillville
102	20.5	M S D Martinsville Schools	Martinsville
102	20.5	North Harrison Com School Corp	Ramsey
104	20.2	North Adams Community Schools	Decatur
105	19.9	Wawasee Community School Corp	Syracuse
106	19.8	Kankakee Valley School Corp	Wheatfield
107	19.7	North Putnam Community Schools	Bainbridge
108	19.5	School City of Hobart	Hobart
109	18.9	M S D Mount Vernon	Mount Vernon
110	18.7	Dekalb County Eastern Com SD	Butler
110	18.7	East Noble School Corp	Kendallville
112	18.6	Prairie Heights Com Sch Corp	Lagrange
113	18.2	Huntington County Com Sch Corp	Huntington
113	18.2	North Montgomery Com Sch Corp	Crawfordsville
113	18.2	North Newton School Corp	Morocco
116	18.0	Whitko Community School Corp	Pierceton
117	17.4	South Montgomery Com Sch Corp	New Market
118	17.2	Baugo Community Schools	Elkhart
118	17.2	Southwest Dubois County Sch Corp	Huntingburg
120	17.1	Greenwood Community Sch Corp	Greenwood
120	17.1	M S D Bluffton-Harrison	Bluffton
122	16.8	Eastbrook Community Sch Corp	Marion
123	16.4	West Clark Community Schools	Sellersburg
124	16.1	Hanover Community School Corp	Cedar Lake
124	16.1	John Glenn School Corporation	Walkerton
124	16.1	Tippecanoe School Corp	Lafayette
127	15.8	South Dearborn Com School Corp	Aurora
128	15.6	Dekalb County Ctl United SD	Waterloo
128	15.6	Delaware Community School Corp	Muncie
128	15.6	Frankton-Lapel Community Schs	Anderson
131	15.5	Richland-Bean Blossom C S C	Ellettsville
132	15.0	Griffith Public Schools	Griffith
133	14.9	Mooresville Con School Corp	Mooresville
134	14.8	Duneland School Corporation	Chesterton
135	14.4	Western Boone County Com SD	Thorntown
136	14.1	Southeastern School Corp	Walton
137	13.9	Greenfield-Central Com Schools	Greenfield
138	13.8	Franklin Township Com Sch Corp	Indianapolis
139	13.7	Plainfield Community Sch Corp	Plainfield
140	13.6	New Prairie United School Corp	New Carlisle
141	13.5	Decatur County Com Schools	Greensburg
142	13.3	Wa-Nee Community Schools	Nappanee
143	13.0	Tipton Community School Corp	Tipton
143	13.0	Whitley County Cons Schools	Columbia City
145	12.7	Centerville-Abington Com Schs	Centerville
146	12.6	Tri-Creek School Corp	Lowell
147	12.5	Northern Wells Com Schools	Ossian
147	12.5	Oak Hill United School Corp	Converse
147	12.5	Warrick County School Corp	Boonville
150	12.2	Clark-Pleasant Com School Corp	Whiteland
150	12.2	Hamilton Heights School Corp	Arcadia
152	12.1	Crown Point Community Sch Corp	Crown Point
152	12.1	South Madison Com Sch Corp	Pendleton
154	12.0	M S D Wabash County Schools	Wabash
155	11.9	Mill Creek Community Sch Corp	Clayton
155	11.9	Northwestern Con School Corp	Fairland
157	11.5	Shelby Eastern Schools	Shelbyville
158	11.4	Valparaiso Community Schools	Valparaiso
159	11.3	Greater Jasper Con Schs	Jasper
159	11.3	Western School Corp	Russiaville
161	10.8	Noblesville Schools	Noblesville
162	10.7	North Spencer County Sch Corp	Lincoln City
162	10.7	Westview School Corporation	Topeka
164	10.2	Middlebury Community Schools	Middlebury
165	10.1	Danville Community School Corp	Danville
165	10.1	Nineveh-Hensley-Jackson United	Trafalgar
167	9.6	Penn-Harris-Madison Sch Corp	Mishawaka
168	9.2	South Gibson School Corp	Fort Branch
169	8.9	Sunman-Dearborn Com Sch Corp	Sunman
170	8.8	Mt Pleasant Twp Com Sch Corp	Yorktown
171	8.7	Southeast Dubois County Sch Corp	Ferdinand
171	8.7	Westfield-Washington Schools	Westfield
173	8.3	School Town of Highland	Highland
174	7.9	Northwestern School Corp	Kokomo
175	7.8	Fairfield Community Schools	Goshen
176	7.7	Avon Community School Corp	Avon
177	6.9	Union Township School Corp	Valparaiso
178	6.7	Brownsburg Community Sch Corp	Brownsburg
179	6.5	North West Hendricks Schools	Lizton
180	6.4	Batesville Community Sch Corp	Batesville
180	6.4	East Porter County School Corp	Kouts
182	6.3	Lake Central School Corp	Saint John
183	6.2	Center Grove Com Sch Corp	Greenwood
184	6.1	Mt Vernon Community Sch Corp	Fortville
184	6.1	Southern Hancock Co Com Sch Corp	New Palestine
186	6.0	Porter Township School Corp	Valparaiso
187	5.3	West Lafayette Com School Corp	West Lafayette
188	4.9	Northwest Allen County Schools	Fort Wayne
189	4.4	Hamilton Southeastern Schools	Fishers
190	4.2	School Town of Munster	Munster
191	3.2	Carmel Clay Schools	Carmel
192	3.0	M S D Southwest Allen County	Fort Wayne
193	1.7	Zionsville Community Schools	Zionsville

Students Eligible for Reduced-Price Lunch

Rank	Percent	District Name	City
1	13.7	Crawford County Com School Corp	Marengo
2	13.5	School City of Mishawaka	Mishawaka
3	13.2	Northeast School Corp	Hymera
4	12.5	Indianapolis Public Schools	Indianapolis
4	12.5	Jay School Corp	Portland
6	12.3	Wabash City Schools	Wabash
7	11.9	South Vermillion Com Sch Corp	Clinton
7	11.9	West Noble School Corporation	Ligonier
9	11.8	Community Schools of Frankfort	Frankfort
10	11.5	Pike County School Corp	Petersburg
11	11.4	Muncie Community Schools	Muncie
12	11.3	Paoli Community School Corp	Paoli
13	11.2	East Noble School Corp	Kendallville
13	11.2	Mississinewa Community School Corp	Gas City
15	10.9	Clay Community Schools	Knightsville
16	10.8	Knox Community School Corp	Knox
17	10.7	East Washington School Corp	Pekin
17	10.7	Elkhart Community Schools	Elkhart
17	10.7	Manchester Community Schools	N Manchester
17	10.7	School City of Hammond	Hammond
21	10.6	Jennings County Schools	North Vernon
22	10.5	Logansport Community Sch Corp	Logansport
23	10.4	Vigo County School Corp	Terre Haute
24	10.3	Goshen Community Schools	Goshen
25	10.2	Garrett-Keyser-Butler Com	Garrett
26	10.1	Peru Community Schools	Peru
26	10.1	Twin Lakes School Corp	Monticello
28	9.9	Southwest School Corp	Sullivan
29	9.8	Madison Consolidated Schools	Madison
29	9.8	Tippecanoe Valley School Corp	Akron
31	9.7	North Lawrence Com Schools	Bedford
31	9.7	Richmond Community School Corp	Richmond
31	9.7	Whitko Community School Corp	Pierceton
34	9.6	Concord Community Schools	Elkhart
34	9.6	Lafayette School Corporation	Lafayette
34	9.6	M S D Warren Township	Indianapolis
34	9.6	M S D Wayne Township	Indianapolis
38	9.5	M S D Decatur Township	Indianapolis
38	9.5	M S D Washington Township	Indianapolis
38	9.5	Seymour Community Schools	Seymour
41	9.4	Lake Ridge Schools	Gary
41	9.4	Merrillville Community School	Merrillville
41	9.4	South Harrison Com Schools	Corydon
44	9.3	Benton Community School Corp	Fowler
44	9.3	Evansville-Vanderburgh Sch Corp	Evansville
44	9.3	North Gibson School Corp	Princeton
44	9.3	North Knox School Corp	Bicknell
48	9.2	Eastbrook Community Sch Corp	Marion
48	9.2	John Glenn School Corporation	Walkerton
50	9.1	Franklin County Com Sch Corp	Brookville
50	9.1	Huntington County Com Sch Corp	Huntington
50	9.1	Plymouth Community School Corp	Plymouth
50	9.1	Prairie Heights Com Sch Corp	Lagrange
50	9.1	Washington Com Schools Inc	Washington
55	9.0	Anderson Community School Corp	Anderson
55	9.0	Clark-Pleasant Com School Corp	Whiteland
55	9.0	Union Co/Clg Corner Joint SD	Liberty
55	9.0	Warsaw Community Schools	Warsaw
59	8.9	Delphi Community School Corp	Delphi
59	8.9	Fort Wayne Community Schools	Fort Wayne
59	8.9	Rensselaer Central School Corp	Rensselaer
59	8.9	South Bend Community Sch Corp	South Bend
63	8.8	Fairfield Community Schools	Goshen
64	8.7	Blackford County Schools	Hartford City
64	8.7	Decatur County Com Schools	Greensburg
64	8.7	North Harrison Com School Corp	Ramsey
67	8.6	Michigan City Area Schools	Michigan City
67	8.6	School City of East Chicago	East Chicago
69	8.5	Beech Grove City Schools	Beech Grove
70	8.4	Bartholomew Con School Corp	Columbus
70	8.4	South Ripley Com Sch Corp	Versailles
70	8.4	Vincennes Community Sch Corp	Vincennes
73	8.3	Frankton-Lapel Community Schs	Anderson
73	8.3	M S D Perry Township	Indianapolis
73	8.3	North Newton School Corp	Morocco
73	8.3	Switzerland County School Corp	Vevay
77	8.2	Baugo Community Schools	Elkhart
77	8.2	Greencastle Community Sch Corp	Greencastle
79	8.1	Delaware Community School Corp	Muncie
79	8.1	East Allen County Schools	New Haven
79	8.1	Elwood Community School Corp	Elwood
79	8.1	Kokomo-Center Twp Con Sch Corp	Kokomo
79	8.1	M S D Steuben County	Angola
84	8.0	Kankakee Valley School Corp	Wheatfield
84	8.0	Lakeland School Corporation	Lagrange
84	8.0	Rush County Schools	Rushville
87	7.9	M S D Bluffton-Harrison	Bluffton
87	7.9	M S D Martinsville Schools	Martinsville
87	7.9	Spencer-Owen Community Schools	Spencer
87	7.9	Tell City-Troy Twp School Corp	Tell City
91	7.8	Fayette County School Corp	Connersville
91	7.8	Maconaquah School Corp	Bunker Hill
91	7.8	New Castle Community Sch Corp	New Castle
94	7.7	Dekalb County Ctl United SD	Waterloo
94	7.7	Mitchell Community Schools	Mitchell
94	7.7	Portage Township Schools	Portage
97	7.6	Brown County School Corporation	Nashville
97	7.6	Crawfordsville Com Schools	Crawfordsville
97	7.6	M S D Lawrence Township	Indianapolis
97	7.6	Rochester Community Sch Corp	Rochester
97	7.6	South Montgomery Com Sch Corp	New Market
97	7.6	Wawasee Community School Corp	Syracuse
97	7.6	Whitley County Cons Schools	Columbia City
104	7.5	Greater Clark County Schools	Jeffersonville
104	7.5	Laporte Community School Corp	Laporte
104	7.5	Marion Community Schools	Marion
104	7.5	Northwestern Con School Corp	Fairland
104	7.5	School City of Hobart	Hobart
109	7.4	Scott County SD 2	Scottsburg
110	7.3	Centerville-Abington Com Schs	Centerville
110	7.3	Franklin Community School Corp	Franklin
110	7.3	Randolph Central School Corp	Winchester
113	7.2	Alexandria Com School Corp	Alexandria
113	7.2	Madison-Grant United Sch Corp	Fairmount
113	7.2	Shelbyville Central Schools	Shelbyville
113	7.2	Southeastern School Corp	Walton
117	7.1	North Spencer County Sch Corp	Lincoln City
118	7.0	Dekalb County Eastern Com SD	Butler
118	7.0	Lebanon Community School Corp	Lebanon
120	6.8	Monroe County Com Sch Corp	Bloomington
120	6.8	New Prairie United School Corp	New Carlisle
120	6.8	Richland-Bean Blossom C S C	Ellettsville
120	6.8	Southwest Dubois County Sch Corp	Huntingburg
120	6.8	Wa-Nee Community Schools	Nappanee
125	6.7	Danville Community School Corp	Danville
125	6.7	Greensburg Community Schools	Greensburg
127	6.6	Hamilton Heights School Corp	Arcadia
128	6.5	Brownstown Cnt Com Sch Corp	Brownstown
129	6.2	North Putnam Community Schools	Bainbridge
129	6.2	North West Hendricks Schools	Lizton
129	6.2	Western Boone County Com SD	Thorntown
132	6.1	Plainfield Community Sch Corp	Plainfield
132	6.1	Salem Community Schools	Salem
132	6.1	Taylor Community School Corp	Kokomo
135	6.0	Franklin Township Com Sch Corp	Indianapolis
135	6.0	New Albany-Floyd County Con Sch	New Albany
137	5.9	Middlebury Community Schools	Middlebury
137	5.9	Northern Wells Com Schools	Ossian
137	5.9	School Town of Speedway	Speedway
137	5.9	Tipton Community School Corp	Tipton
137	5.9	Warrick County School Corp	Boonville
137	5.9	Westview School Corporation	Topeka
143	5.8	M S D Pike Township	Indianapolis
144	5.7	Greenwood Community Sch Corp	Greenwood
144	5.7	North Montgomery Com Sch Corp	Crawfordsville
144	5.7	South Gibson School Corp	Fort Branch
144	5.7	West Clark Community Schools	Sellersburg
148	5.6	Greenfield-Central Com Schools	Greenfield
149	5.5	Duneland School Corporation	Chesterton
149	5.5	Mill Creek Community Sch Corp	Clayton
151	5.4	Mt Pleasant Twp Com Sch Corp	Yorktown
151	5.4	Oak Hill United School Corp	Converse
153	5.3	Hanover Community School Corp	Cedar Lake
153	5.3	Westfield-Washington Schools	Westfield
155	5.2	East Porter County School Corp	Kouts
156	5.0	Brownsburg Community Sch Corp	Brownsburg
156	5.0	M S D Wabash County Schools	Wabash
156	5.0	Union Township School Corp	Valparaiso
159	4.9	North Adams Community Schools	Decatur
159	4.9	Tippecanoe School Corp	Lafayette
161	4.8	Mooresville Con School Corp	Mooresville
161	4.8	Valparaiso Community Schools	Valparaiso
163	4.6	M S D Mount Vernon	Mount Vernon
164	4.5	South Dearborn Com School Corp	Aurora
165	4.4	Nineveh-Hensley-Jackson United	Trafalgar
166	4.3	Greater Jasper Con Schs	Jasper
166	4.3	Southeast Dubois County Sch Corp	Ferdinand

168	4.2	Mt Vernon Community Sch Corp	Fortville
169	4.1	Noblesville Schools	Noblesville
170	4.0	Griffith Public Schools	Griffith
171	3.9	Crown Point Community Sch Corp	Crown Point
171	3.9	Tri-Creek School Corp	Lowell
173	3.8	Batesville Community Sch Corp	Batesville
174	3.7	Avon Community School Corp	Avon
174	3.7	Shelby Eastern Schools	Shelbyville
176	3.5	Penn-Harris-Madison Sch Corp	Mishawaka
176	3.5	Western School Corp	Russiaville
178	3.4	Northwest Allen County Schools	Fort Wayne
178	3.4	South Madison Com Sch Corp	Pendleton
180	3.1	Center Grove Com Sch Corp	Greenwood
180	3.1	Lake Central School Corp	Saint John
182	2.9	Northwestern School Corp	Kokomo
182	2.9	School Town of Highland	Highland
182	2.9	Sunman-Dearborn Com Sch Corp	Sunman
185	2.8	Porter Township School Corp	Valparaiso
185	2.8	School Town of Munster	Munster
187	2.6	West Lafayette Com School Corp	West Lafayette
188	2.4	Gary Community School Corp	Gary
189	2.2	Hamilton Southeastern Schools	Fishers
190	2.0	Southern Hancock Co Com Sch Corp	New Palestine
191	1.7	Carmel Clay Schools	Carmel
192	1.5	M S D Southwest Allen County	Fort Wayne
193	0.8	Zionsville Community Schools	Zionsville

Student/Teacher Ratio

Rank	Ratio	District Name	City
1	23.4	Crown Point Community Sch Corp	Crown Point
2	23.0	Tri-Creek School Corp	Lowell
3	22.3	School Town of Highland	Highland
4	21.4	Greenwood Community Sch Corp	Greenwood
5	20.9	Clark-Pleasant Com School Corp	Whiteland
5	20.9	Penn-Harris-Madison Sch Corp	Mishawaka
7	20.7	Franklin Township Com Sch Corp	Indianapolis
8	20.5	Southern Hancock Co Com Sch Corp	New Palestine
9	20.4	Merrillville Community School	Merrillville
9	20.4	Mt Vernon Community Sch Corp	Fortville
9	20.4	Plymouth Community School Corp	Plymouth
9	20.4	Porter Township School Corp	Valparaiso
13	20.3	Duneland School Corporation	Chesterton
13	20.3	Hanover Community School Corp	Cedar Lake
13	20.3	School City of Hobart	Hobart
13	20.3	Shelbyville Central Schools	Shelbyville
17	20.0	Dekalb County Ctl United SD	Waterloo
17	20.0	Northwest Allen County Schools	Fort Wayne
17	20.0	Sunman-Dearborn Com Sch Corp	Sunman
20	19.9	East Washington School Corp	Pekin
20	19.9	Portage Township Schools	Portage
22	19.8	Plainfield Community Sch Corp	Plainfield
23	19.7	Griffith Public Schools	Griffith
23	19.7	Northwestern Con School Corp	Fairland
25	19.5	Salem Community Schools	Salem
26	19.3	Lake Central School Corp	Saint John
26	19.3	South Madison Com Sch Corp	Pendleton
26	19.3	Valparaiso Community Schools	Valparaiso
29	19.2	Avon Community School Corp	Avon
29	19.2	John Glenn School Corporation	Walkerton
29	19.2	Kankakee Valley School Corp	Wheatfield
29	19.2	Rochester Community Sch Corp	Rochester
29	19.2	Southwest Dubois County Sch Corp	Huntingburg
29	19.2	Warrick County School Corp	Boonville
35	19.1	Center Grove Com Sch Corp	Greenwood
35	19.1	Franklin County Com Sch Corp	Brookville
35	19.1	Lake Ridge Schools	Gary
35	19.1	M S D Decatur Township	Indianapolis
39	19.0	Hamilton Southeastern Schools	Fishers
39	19.0	Jennings County Schools	North Vernon
39	19.0	Knox Community School Corp	Knox
39	19.0	Paoli Community School Corp	Paoli
43	18.9	Concord Community Schools	Elkhart
43	18.9	South Ripley Com Sch Corp	Versailles
45	18.7	Brownsburg Community Sch Corp	Brownsburg
45	18.7	M S D Steuben County	Angola
45	18.7	Mitchell Community Schools	Mitchell
48	18.6	Beech Grove City Schools	Beech Grove
48	18.6	Crawford County Com School Corp	Marengo
48	18.6	Danville Community School Corp	Danville
48	18.6	Frankton-Lapel Community Schs	Anderson
48	18.6	South Gibson School Corp	Fort Branch
53	18.5	Noblesville Schools	Noblesville
53	18.5	Scott County SD 2	Scottsburg
53	18.5	Twin Lakes School Corp	Monticello
56	18.4	Brownstown Cnt Com Sch Corp	Brownstown
56	18.4	Greencastle Community Sch Corp	Greencastle
56	18.4	Tippecanoe School Corp	Lafayette
56	18.4	Tippecanoe Valley School Corp	Akron
56	18.4	Western School Corp	Russiaville
61	18.3	Hamilton Heights School Corp	Arcadia
61	18.3	Tell City-Troy Twp School Corp	Tell City
63	18.2	Fairfield Community Schools	Goshen
63	18.2	M S D Southwest Allen County	Fort Wayne
63	18.2	Middlebury Community Schools	Middlebury
63	18.2	School City of Hammond	Hammond
63	18.2	Southeast Dubois County Sch Corp	Ferdinand
63	18.2	Switzerland County School Corp	Vevay
63	18.2	Warsaw Community Schools	Warsaw
63	18.2	West Clark Community Schools	Sellersburg
71	18.1	Manchester Community Schools	N Manchester
71	18.1	North Knox School Corp	Bicknell
71	18.1	Westfield-Washington Schools	Westfield
74	18.0	Delphi Community School Corp	Delphi
74	18.0	Fort Wayne Community Schools	Fort Wayne
74	18.0	M S D Warren Township	Indianapolis
74	18.0	Mt Pleasant Twp Com Sch Corp	Yorktown
74	18.0	Northern Wells Com Schools	Ossian
74	18.0	Seymour Community Schools	Seymour
80	17.9	M S D Pike Township	Indianapolis
80	17.9	New Albany-Floyd County Con Sch	New Albany
80	17.9	North Gibson School Corp	Princeton
80	17.9	School Town of Munster	Munster
80	17.9	Zionsville Community Schools	Zionsville
85	17.8	Bartholomew Con School Corp	Columbus
85	17.8	M S D Bluffton-Harrison	Bluffton
85	17.8	North Harrison Com School Corp	Ramsey
85	17.8	North Spencer County Sch Corp	Lincoln City
85	17.8	Prairie Heights Com Sch Corp	Lagrange
85	17.8	Southeastern School Corp	Walton
85	17.8	Southwest School Corp	Sullivan
92	17.7	Baugo Community Schools	Elkhart
92	17.7	New Prairie United School Corp	New Carlisle
92	17.7	Nineveh-Hensley-Jackson United	Trafalgar
92	17.7	Washington Com Schools Inc	Washington
92	17.7	Wawasee Community School Corp	Syracuse
97	17.6	Carmel Clay Schools	Carmel
97	17.6	M S D Lawrence Township	Indianapolis
97	17.6	M S D Martinsville Schools	Martinsville
97	17.6	Madison Consolidated Schools	Madison
97	17.6	Mooresville Con School Corp	Mooresville
97	17.6	North Montgomery Com Sch Corp	Crawfordsville
97	17.6	West Lafayette Com School Corp	West Lafayette
104	17.5	Franklin Community School Corp	Franklin
104	17.5	Pike County School Corp	Petersburg
104	17.5	Union Township School Corp	Valparaiso
104	17.5	Wa-Nee Community Schools	Nappanee
108	17.4	Delaware Community School Corp	Muncie
108	17.4	Western Boone County Com SD	Thorntown
110	17.3	Gary Community School Corp	Gary
110	17.3	Jay School Corp	Portland
110	17.3	West Noble School Corporation	Ligonier
113	17.2	M S D Perry Township	Indianapolis
113	17.2	M S D Washington Township	Indianapolis
113	17.2	School City of East Chicago	East Chicago
113	17.2	Whitley County Cons Schools	Columbia City
117	17.1	Eastbrook Community Sch Corp	Marion
117	17.1	Greensburg Community Schools	Greensburg
119	17.0	Batesville Community Sch Corp	Batesville
119	17.0	Community Schools of Frankfort	Frankfort
119	17.0	East Allen County Schools	New Haven
119	17.0	East Porter County School Corp	Kouts
119	17.0	North West Hendricks Schools	Lizton
119	17.0	South Harrison Com Schools	Corydon
119	17.0	Whitko Community School Corp	Pierceton
126	16.9	Lakeland School Corporation	Lagrange
126	16.9	M S D Wayne Township	Indianapolis
126	16.9	Monroe County Com Sch Corp	Bloomington
129	16.8	Lebanon Community School Corp	Lebanon
129	16.8	South Dearborn Com School Corp	Aurora
129	16.8	Tipton Community School Corp	Tipton
132	16.7	School Town of Speedway	Speedway
133	16.6	Centerville-Abington Com Schs	Centerville
133	16.6	East Noble School Corp	Kendallville
133	16.6	Mill Creek Community Sch Corp	Clayton
133	16.6	Rensselaer Central School Corp	Rensselaer
137	16.5	Alexandria Com School Corp	Alexandria
137	16.5	Westview School Corporation	Topeka
139	16.4	Greater Jasper Con Schs	Jasper
139	16.4	Huntington County Com Sch Corp	Huntington
139	16.4	Maconaquah School Corp	Bunker Hill
139	16.4	Oak Hill United School Corp	Converse
139	16.4	Spencer-Owen Community Schools	Spencer
144	16.3	Decatur County Com Schools	Greensburg
144	16.3	Elkhart Community Schools	Elkhart
144	16.3	Elwood Community School Corp	Elwood
144	16.3	Greater Clark County Schools	Jeffersonville
144	16.3	North Adams Community Schools	Decatur
144	16.3	Richland-Bean Blossom C S C	Ellettsville
144	16.3	South Bend Community Sch Corp	South Bend
151	16.2	North Lawrence Com Schools	Bedford
151	16.2	Northwestern School Corp	Kokomo
153	16.1	Laporte Community School Corp	Laporte
153	16.1	Michigan City Area Schools	Michigan City
153	16.1	Rush County Schools	Rushville
153	16.1	Shelby Eastern Schools	Shelbyville
153	16.1	Vigo County School Corp	Terre Haute
153	16.1	Wabash City Schools	Wabash
159	16.0	Blackford County Schools	Hartford City
159	16.0	Clay Community Schools	Knightsville
159	16.0	Evansville-Vanderburgh Sch Corp	Evansville
159	16.0	M S D Mount Vernon	Mount Vernon
159	16.0	Mississinewa Community School Corp	Gas City
159	16.0	South Montgomery Com Sch Corp	New Market
159	16.0	South Vermillion Com Sch Corp	Clinton
166	15.9	North Newton School Corp	Morocco
167	15.8	Goshen Community Schools	Goshen
168	15.7	Madison-Grant United Sch Corp	Fairmount
169	15.5	Peru Community Schools	Peru
170	15.4	Crawfordsville Com Schools	Crawfordsville
170	15.4	Randolph Central School Corp	Winchester
170	15.4	Union Co/Clg Corner Joint SD	Liberty
173	15.3	Anderson Community School Corp	Anderson
173	15.3	Brown County School Corporation	Nashville
173	15.3	Garrett-Keyser-Butler Com	Garrett
173	15.3	Northeast School Corp	Hymera
177	15.2	Marion Community Schools	Marion
178	15.1	Fayette County School Corp	Connersville
179	15.0	Richmond Community School Corp	Richmond
180	14.9	Benton Community School Corp	Fowler
181	14.8	Vincennes Community Sch Corp	Vincennes
182	14.5	Muncie Community Schools	Muncie
182	14.5	School City of Mishawaka	Mishawaka
184	14.4	Indianapolis Public Schools	Indianapolis
185	14.0	Taylor Community School Corp	Kokomo
186	13.9	Kokomo-Center Twp Con Sch Corp	Kokomo
186	13.9	New Castle Community Sch Corp	New Castle
188	13.8	Lafayette School Corporation	Lafayette
188	13.8	M S D Wabash County Schools	Wabash
190	13.1	Logansport Community Sch Corp	Logansport
191	13.0	North Putnam Community Schools	Bainbridge
192	12.9	Greenfield-Central Com Schools	Greenfield
193	12.1	Dekalb County Eastern Com SD	Butler

Student/Librarian Ratio

Rank	Ratio	District Name	City
1	10,056.0	Penn-Harris-Madison Sch Corp	Mishawaka
2	4,472.8	Evansville-Vanderburgh Sch Corp	Evansville
3	3,087.5	Crown Point Community Sch Corp	Crown Point
4	2,912.0	Goshen Community Schools	Goshen
5	2,891.3	Lake Central School Corp	Saint John
6	2,770.5	School City of Mishawaka	Mishawaka
7	2,721.0	North Lawrence Com Schools	Bedford
8	2,694.0	Griffith Public Schools	Griffith
9	2,611.8	Elkhart Community Schools	Elkhart
10	2,543.3	Seymour Community Schools	Seymour
11	2,415.9	Jennings County Schools	North Vernon
12	2,404.0	New Prairie United School Corp	New Carlisle
13	2,328.0	Western School Corp	Russiaville
14	2,264.0	Lakeland School Corporation	Lagrange
15	2,250.6	New Albany-Floyd County Con Sch	New Albany
16	2,226.0	Concord Community Schools	Elkhart
17	2,144.0	Pike County School Corp	Petersburg
18	2,112.3	Huntington County Com Sch Corp	Huntington
19	2,077.0	Greenfield-Central Com Schools	Greenfield
20	2,056.0	South Montgomery Com Sch Corp	New Market
21	1,976.0	Clark-Pleasant Com School Corp	Whiteland
22	1,967.5	Fayette County School Corp	Connersville
23	1,966.0	Whitko Community School Corp	Pierceton
24	1,965.0	Benton Community School Corp	Fowler
25	1,941.0	New Castle Community Sch Corp	New Castle
26	1,930.0	Southwest School Corp	Sullivan
27	1,917.0	Greenwood Community Sch Corp	Greenwood
28	1,907.0	Shelbyville Central Schools	Shelbyville
29	1,896.3	Marion Community Schools	Marion
30	1,866.5	Middlebury Community Schools	Middlebury
31	1,857.0	South Gibson School Corp	Fort Branch
32	1,851.0	Crawford County Com School Corp	Marengo
33	1,818.0	Fort Wayne Community Schools	Fort Wayne
34	1,808.5	School City of Hobart	Hobart
35	1,765.0	Baugo Community Schools	Elkhart
36	1,749.0	Northwest Allen County Schools	Fort Wayne
37	1,740.5	Wawasee Community School Corp	Syracuse
38	1,712.0	Paoli Community School Corp	Paoli
39	1,680.0	School Town of Highland	Highland
40	1,651.0	Southeastern School Corp	Walton
41	1,650.0	North Newton School Corp	Morocco
42	1,632.0	Merrillville Community School	Merrillville
43	1,613.3	Warsaw Community Schools	Warsaw
44	1,611.0	School City of East Chicago	East Chicago
45	1,610.0	Union Co/Clg Corner Joint SD	Liberty
46	1,583.0	Hanover Community School Corp	Cedar Lake
47	1,570.0	Spencer-Owen Community Schools	Spencer
48	1,567.0	Mill Creek Community Sch Corp	Clayton
49	1,563.0	Switzerland County School Corp	Vevay
50	1,544.8	Warrick County School Corp	Boonville
51	1,537.3	M S D Southwest Allen County	Fort Wayne
52	1,521.0	North Knox School Corp	Bicknell

53	1,516.0	Taylor Community School Corp	Kokomo
54	1,514.3	Valparaiso Community Schools	Valparaiso
55	1,512.0	Southeast Dubois County Sch Corp	Ferdinand
56	1,509.5	Vincennes Community Sch Corp	Vincennes
57	1,507.0	Oak Hill United School Corp	Converse
58	1,465.3	Franklin Community School Corp	Franklin
59	1,447.0	Mooresville Con School Corp	Mooresville
60	1,419.4	East Allen County Schools	New Haven
61	1,406.5	M S D Decatur Township	Indianapolis
62	1,396.7	Zionsville Community Schools	Zionsville
63	1,386.7	North Gibson School Corp	Princeton
64	1,383.3	North Montgomery Com Sch Corp	Crawfordsville
65	1,380.4	Bartholomew Con School Corp	Columbus
66	1,379.0	Dekalb County Ctl United SD	Waterloo
67	1,370.0	Rensselaer Central School Corp	Rensselaer
68	1,354.8	M S D Martinsville Schools	Martinsville
69	1,348.8	Frankton-Lapel Community Schs	Anderson
70	1,336.8	Portage Township Schools	Portage
71	1,301.0	Northern Wells Com Schools	Ossian
72	1,299.0	M S D Wabash County Schools	Wabash
73	1,287.7	School Town of Munster	Munster
74	1,260.2	Laporte Community School Corp	Laporte
75	1,250.0	Franklin Township Com Sch Corp	Indianapolis
76	1,237.5	Washington Com Schools Inc	Washington
77	1,229.3	Michigan City Area Schools	Michigan City
78	1,208.5	Peru Community Schools	Peru
79	1,201.5	Beech Grove City Schools	Beech Grove
80	1,196.5	Lake Ridge Schools	Gary
81	1,168.5	Center Grove Com Sch Corp	Greenwood
82	1,164.5	Kokomo-Center Twp Con Sch Corp	Kokomo
83	1,163.0	Danville Community School Corp	Danville
84	1,150.1	South Bend Community Sch Corp	South Bend
85	1,128.9	Franklin County Com Sch Corp	Brookville
86	1,119.2	M S D Warren Township	Indianapolis
87	1,119.0	Plymouth Community School Corp	Plymouth
88	1,118.7	Randolph Central School Corp	Winchester
89	1,114.7	West Clark Community Schools	Sellersburg
90	1,107.0	Westview School Corporation	Topeka
91	1,088.7	West Noble School Corporation	Ligonier
92	1,086.0	Mississinewa Community School Corp	Gas City
93	1,065.0	Tippecanoe Valley School Corp	Akron
94	1,035.0	Fairfield Community Schools	Goshen
95	1,016.7	Wa-Nee Community Schools	Nappanee
96	1,012.6	M S D Lawrence Township	Indianapolis
97	1,011.3	M S D Steuben County	Angola
98	1,010.0	South Dearborn Com School Corp	Aurora
99	1,009.7	Mt Vernon Community Sch Corp	Fortville
100	999.5	Elwood Community School Corp	Elwood
101	984.5	East Porter County School Corp	Kouts
102	979.5	Greencastle Community Sch Corp	Greencastle
103	971.0	M S D Wayne Township	Indianapolis
104	959.7	Delaware Community School Corp	Muncie
105	958.3	East Noble School Corp	Kendallville
106	952.9	Madison-Grant United Sch Corp	Fairmount
107	943.5	M S D Perry Township	Indianapolis
108	940.3	Scott County SD 2	Scottsburg
109	933.4	Greater Clark County Schools	Jeffersonville
110	932.0	Carmel Clay Schools	Carmel
111	919.2	Blackford County Schools	Hartford City
112	917.0	Richland-Bean Blossom C S C	Ellettsville
113	908.8	Whitley County Cons Schools	Columbia City
114	894.7	Dekalb County Eastern Com SD	Butler
115	892.0	Eastbrook Community Sch Corp	Marion
116	891.5	Prairie Heights Com Sch Corp	Lagrange
117	884.0	East Washington School Corp	Pekin
118	883.3	Twin Lakes School Corp	Monticello
119	875.8	Madison Consolidated Schools	Madison
120	866.5	Brownstown Cnt Com Sch Corp	Brownstown
121	852.4	Indianapolis Public Schools	Indianapolis
122	842.7	Brownsburg Community Sch Corp	Brownsburg
123	839.5	Northwestern School Corp	Kokomo
124	839.0	Alexandria Com School Corp	Alexandria
125	833.5	Centerville-Abington Com Schs	Centerville
126	831.0	School Town of Speedway	Speedway
127	822.1	North Adams Community Schools	Decatur
128	818.0	Community Schools of Frankfort	Frankfort
129	809.6	Plainfield Community Sch Corp	Plainfield
130	807.5	Muncie Community Schools	Muncie
131	806.5	Kankakee Valley School Corp	Wheatfield
132	795.9	Southern Hancock Co Com Sch Corp	New Palestine
133	793.8	Avon Community School Corp	Avon
134	793.5	Anderson Community School Corp	Anderson
135	791.2	Hamilton Southeastern Schools	Fishers
136	788.5	North West Hendricks Schools	Lizton
137	782.0	Greater Jasper Con Schs	Jasper
138	778.2	M S D Washington Township	Indianapolis
139	777.4	M S D Mount Vernon	Mount Vernon
140	770.0	Wabash City Schools	Wabash
141	769.3	Clay Community Schools	Knightsville
142	769.0	North Spencer County Sch Corp	Lincoln City
143	768.5	Porter Township School Corp	Valparaiso
144	761.0	Northeast School Corp	Hymera
145	760.9	School City of Hammond	Hammond
146	756.5	South Ripley Com Sch Corp	Versailles
147	750.4	Greensburg Community Schools	Greensburg
148	749.3	M S D Pike Township	Indianapolis
149	744.7	Hamilton Heights School Corp	Arcadia
150	731.4	Sunman-Dearborn Com Sch Corp	Sunman
151	714.4	Noblesville Schools	Noblesville
152	703.0	Salem Community Schools	Salem
153	701.2	South Madison Com Sch Corp	Pendleton
154	688.0	Mitchell Community Schools	Mitchell
155	685.5	Brown County School Corporation	Nashville
156	675.8	Rush County Schools	Rushville
157	671.0	Rochester Community Sch Corp	Rochester
158	669.6	Westfield-Washington Schools	Westfield
159	668.6	Monroe County Com Sch Corp	Bloomington
160	668.3	Knox Community School Corp	Knox
161	660.0	West Lafayette Com School Corp	West Lafayette
162	657.7	South Vermillion Com Sch Corp	Clinton
163	642.3	North Putnam Community Schools	Bainbridge
164	636.1	Lafayette School Corporation	Lafayette
165	629.7	Southwest Dubois County Sch Corp	Huntingburg
166	625.0	Tipton Community School Corp	Tipton
167	621.7	Western Boone County Com SD	Thorntown
168	610.7	Logansport Community Sch Corp	Logansport
169	609.3	Nineveh-Hensley-Jackson United	Trafalgar
170	605.0	North Harrison Com School Corp	Ramsey
171	600.5	Crawfordsville Com Schools	Crawfordsville
172	588.6	Decatur County Com Schools	Greensburg
173	587.8	Maconaquah School Corp	Bunker Hill
174	578.0	John Glenn School Corporation	Walkerton
175	572.6	Vigo County School Corp	Terre Haute
176	568.0	Delphi Community School Corp	Delphi
177	563.2	Manchester Community Schools	N Manchester
178	562.7	Tell City-Troy Twp School Corp	Tell City
179	561.5	Mt Pleasant Twp Com Sch Corp	Yorktown
180	558.7	Lebanon Community School Corp	Lebanon
181	555.4	Jay School Corp	Portland
182	548.7	Garrett-Keyser-Butler Com	Garrett
183	531.7	Shelby Eastern Schools	Shelbyville
184	531.4	Batesville Community Sch Corp	Batesville
185	513.0	Northwestern Con School Corp	Fairland
186	509.7	M S D Bluffton-Harrison	Bluffton
187	492.8	Duneland School Corporation	Chesterton
188	469.6	Gary Community School Corp	Gary
189	460.6	Tippecanoe School Corp	Lafayette
190	416.9	Richmond Community School Corp	Richmond
191	n/a	South Harrison Com Schools	Corydon
191	n/a	Tri-Creek School Corp	Lowell
191	n/a	Union Township School Corp	Valparaiso

Student/Counselor Ratio

Rank	Ratio	District Name	City
1	1,944.0	Jay School Corp	Portland
2	1,890.0	Southeast Dubois County Sch Corp	Ferdinand
3	1,678.0	Alexandria Com School Corp	Alexandria
4	1,610.0	Union Co/Clg Corner Joint SD	Liberty
5	1,564.0	Greater Jasper Con Schs	Jasper
6	1,558.0	Union Township School Corp	Valparaiso
7	1,537.0	Porter Township School Corp	Valparaiso
8	1,235.0	Crown Point Community Sch Corp	Crown Point
9	1,146.5	Frankton-Lapel Community Schs	Anderson
10	1,125.2	M S D Decatur Township	Indianapolis
11	1,107.0	Westview School Corporation	Topeka
12	1,075.5	Warsaw Community Schools	Warsaw
13	1,074.0	School City of East Chicago	East Chicago
14	1,068.8	Logansport Community Sch Corp	Logansport
15	1,026.7	Wabash City Schools	Wabash
16	1,023.0	Fort Wayne Community Schools	Fort Wayne
17	1,014.7	Northeast School Corp	Hymera
18	1,013.0	Greensburg Community Schools	Greensburg
19	1,010.0	South Dearborn Com School Corp	Aurora
20	1,004.7	Oak Hill United School Corp	Converse
21	963.8	Lake Central School Corp	Saint John
22	962.0	Tri-Creek School Corp	Lowell
23	928.5	South Gibson School Corp	Fort Branch
24	904.3	School City of Hobart	Hobart
25	847.0	South Bend Community Sch Corp	South Bend
26	832.0	North Gibson School Corp	Princeton
27	825.5	Southeastern School Corp	Walton
28	820.3	Warrick County School Corp	Boonville
29	811.2	Salem Community Schools	Salem
30	805.6	School City of Hammond	Hammond
31	802.1	Portage Township Schools	Portage
32	801.3	New Prairie United School Corp	New Carlisle
33	801.0	Beech Grove City Schools	Beech Grove
34	791.5	Hanover Community School Corp	Cedar Lake
35	783.7	Maconaquah School Corp	Bunker Hill
36	775.3	Danville Community School Corp	Danville
37	772.6	School Town of Munster	Munster
38	769.0	North Spencer County Sch Corp	Lincoln City
39	766.8	Greenwood Community Sch Corp	Greenwood
40	760.5	North Knox School Corp	Bicknell
41	758.8	West Noble School Corporation	Ligonier
42	754.8	Vincennes Community Sch Corp	Vincennes
43	754.0	Brown County School Corporation	Nashville
44	736.3	Southern Hancock Co Com Sch Corp	New Palestine
45	733.8	M S D Perry Township	Indianapolis
46	729.6	Richmond Community School Corp	Richmond
47	725.6	North Lawrence Com Schools	Bedford
48	725.3	Merrillville Community School	Merrillville
49	718.3	Penn-Harris-Madison Sch Corp	Mishawaka
50	714.7	Pike County School Corp	Petersburg
51	711.4	Anderson Community School Corp	Anderson
52	711.1	Marion Community Schools	Marion
53	701.2	South Madison Com Sch Corp	Pendleton
54	699.6	Southwest Dubois County Sch Corp	Huntingburg
55	698.7	Kokomo-Center Twp Con Sch Corp	Kokomo
56	692.6	School City of Mishawaka	Mishawaka
57	692.3	Greenfield-Central Com Schools	Greenfield
58	690.0	Fairfield Community Schools	Goshen
59	689.4	M S D Lawrence Township	Indianapolis
60	687.3	Elkhart Community Schools	Elkhart
61	677.4	M S D Martinsville Schools	Martinsville
62	675.8	Rush County Schools	Rushville
63	674.7	Plainfield Community Sch Corp	Plainfield
64	673.5	Griffith Public Schools	Griffith
65	671.4	Plymouth Community School Corp	Plymouth
66	671.0	Rochester Community Sch Corp	Rochester
67	668.9	Washington Com Schools Inc	Washington
68	666.3	Elwood Community School Corp	Elwood
69	660.0	North Newton School Corp	Morocco
69	660.0	West Lafayette Com School Corp	West Lafayette
71	656.3	East Porter County School Corp	Kouts
72	654.8	M S D Wayne Township	Indianapolis
73	647.0	New Castle Community Sch Corp	New Castle
74	625.2	Switzerland County School Corp	Vevay
75	622.3	Decatur County Com Schools	Greensburg
76	617.0	Crawford County Com School Corp	Marengo
77	611.3	Monroe County Com Sch Corp	Bloomington
78	609.6	Franklin County Com Sch Corp	Brookville
79	606.4	Taylor Community School Corp	Kokomo
80	604.3	Peru Community Schools	Peru
81	600.1	Laporte Community School Corp	Laporte
82	594.0	Indianapolis Public Schools	Indianapolis
83	583.8	Madison Consolidated Schools	Madison
84	582.0	Western School Corp	Russiaville
85	578.1	M S D Washington Township	Indianapolis
86	577.7	Brownstown Cnt Com Sch Corp	Brownstown
87	577.0	Clay Community Schools	Knightsville
88	576.9	Valparaiso Community Schools	Valparaiso
89	574.5	Blackford County Schools	Hartford City
90	570.7	Paoli Community School Corp	Paoli
91	568.6	Vigo County School Corp	Terre Haute
92	568.0	Delphi Community School Corp	Delphi
93	564.1	Community Schools of Frankfort	Frankfort
94	561.5	Mt Pleasant Twp Com Sch Corp	Yorktown
95	560.0	School Town of Highland	Highland
96	559.7	Northwestern School Corp	Kokomo
97	557.3	West Clark Community Schools	Sellersburg
98	554.0	School Town of Speedway	Speedway
99	551.4	Southwest School Corp	Sullivan
100	550.2	Richland-Bean Blossom C S C	Ellettsville
101	550.0	Lafayette School Corporation	Lafayette
102	547.6	East Noble School Corp	Kendallville
103	545.0	Seymour Community Schools	Seymour
104	544.2	M S D Mount Vernon	Mount Vernon
105	543.0	Mississinewa Community School Corp	Gas City
106	542.6	Mooresville Con School Corp	Mooresville
107	540.4	Greater Clark County Schools	Jeffersonville
108	540.0	Madison-Grant United Sch Corp	Fairmount
109	534.2	M S D Warren Township	Indianapolis
110	527.2	M S D Bluffton-Harrison	Bluffton
111	525.7	Manchester Community Schools	N Manchester
112	523.3	Spencer-Owen Community Schools	Spencer
113	522.3	Mill Creek Community Sch Corp	Clayton
114	520.8	Westfield-Washington Schools	Westfield
115	519.8	Carmel Clay Schools	Carmel
116	516.0	Mitchell Community Schools	Mitchell
117	509.1	Lake Ridge Schools	Gary
118	507.0	Dekalb County Eastern Com SD	Butler
119	506.1	Bartholomew Con School Corp	Columbus
120	504.8	Mt Vernon Community Sch Corp	Fortville
121	501.3	Knox Community School Corp	Knox
122	499.5	M S D Pike Township	Indianapolis
123	494.7	Concord Community Schools	Elkhart
124	493.3	South Vermillion Com Sch Corp	Clinton
125	492.8	Duneland School Corporation	Chesterton
126	492.7	Noblesville Schools	Noblesville
127	491.6	Brownsburg Community Sch Corp	Brownsburg
128	491.1	Franklin Township Com Sch Corp	Indianapolis
129	481.8	North Putnam Community Schools	Bainbridge
130	479.4	Randolph Central School Corp	Winchester
131	478.3	Batesville Community Sch Corp	Batesville
132	476.8	Shelbyville Central Schools	Shelbyville

133	475.3	Hamilton Heights School Corp	Arcadia
134	471.3	Sunman-Dearborn Com Sch Corp	Sunman
135	468.8	Tipton Community School Corp	Tipton
136	467.4	Center Grove Com Sch Corp	Greenwood
137	466.9	Tippecanoe School Corp	Lafayette
138	466.6	Middlebury Community Schools	Middlebury
139	465.9	Evansville-Vanderburgh Sch Corp	Evansville
140	462.1	East Allen County Schools	New Haven
141	460.9	Kankakee Valley School Corp	Wheatfield
142	459.7	Dekalb County Ctl United SD	Waterloo
143	453.6	Avon Community School Corp	Avon
144	452.8	Lakeland School Corporation	Lagrange
145	450.4	Hamilton Southeastern Schools	Fishers
146	448.0	Goshen Community Schools	Goshen
147	446.0	Eastbrook Community Sch Corp	Marion
148	445.3	Rensselaer Central School Corp	Rensselaer
149	439.1	Clark-Pleasant Com School Corp	Whiteland
150	437.3	Northwest Allen County Schools	Fort Wayne
151	437.2	Fayette County School Corp	Connersville
152	436.7	Crawfordsville Com Schools	Crawfordsville
153	435.7	Wa-Nee Community Schools	Nappanee
154	435.1	Wawasee Community School Corp	Syracuse
155	433.5	John Glenn School Corporation	Walkerton
156	433.4	M S D Steuben County	Angola
157	427.6	Whitley County Cons Schools	Columbia City
158	426.0	Tippecanoe Valley School Corp	Akron
159	419.0	Lebanon Community School Corp	Lebanon
159	419.0	M S D Wabash County Schools	Wabash
159	419.0	Zionsville Community Schools	Zionsville
162	418.0	North Harrison Com School Corp	Ramsey
163	411.3	Delaware Community School Corp	Muncie
164	411.2	South Montgomery Com Sch Corp	New Market
165	409.9	M S D Southwest Allen County	Fort Wayne
166	406.2	Nineveh-Hensley-Jackson United	Trafalgar
167	398.1	South Harrison Com Schools	Corydon
168	394.3	North West Hendricks Schools	Lizton
169	393.0	Benton Community School Corp	Fowler
170	384.8	Northwestern Con School Corp	Fairland
171	384.5	Muncie Community Schools	Muncie
172	379.6	Jennings County Schools	North Vernon
173	379.4	Prairie Heights Com Sch Corp	Lagrange
174	378.6	Twin Lakes School Corp	Monticello
175	378.3	South Ripley Com Sch Corp	Versailles
176	375.1	Tell City-Troy Twp School Corp	Tell City
177	373.0	Western Boone County Com SD	Thorntown
178	371.7	Northern Wells Com Schools	Ossian
179	368.4	Huntington County Com Sch Corp	Huntington
180	366.4	Scott County SD 2	Scottsburg
181	366.3	Franklin Community School Corp	Franklin
182	355.8	Michigan City Area Schools	Michigan City
183	353.6	East Washington School Corp	Pekin
184	346.2	New Albany-Floyd County Con Sch	New Albany
185	345.8	North Montgomery Com Sch Corp	Crawfordsville
186	333.4	Centerville-Abington Com Schs	Centerville
187	329.2	Garrett-Keyser-Butler Com	Garrett
188	327.7	Whitko Community School Corp	Pierceton
189	326.5	Greencastle Community Sch Corp	Greencastle
190	319.0	Shelby Eastern Schools	Shelbyville
191	313.1	Gary Community School Corp	Gary
192	294.2	Baugo Community Schools	Elkhart
193	287.8	North Adams Community Schools	Decatur

Current Spending per Student in FY2003

Rank	Dollars	District Name	City
1	11,650	Dekalb County Eastern Com SD	Butler
2	10,467	Muncie Community Schools	Muncie
3	9,904	Greater Jasper Con Schs	Jasper
4	9,824	Lake Ridge Schools	Gary
5	9,819	New Castle Community Sch Corp	New Castle
6	9,765	Kokomo-Center Twp Con Sch Corp	Kokomo
7	9,737	Logansport Community Sch Corp	Logansport
8	9,631	Gary Community School Corp	Gary
9	9,604	Fayette County School Corp	Connersville
9	9,604	Indianapolis Public Schools	Indianapolis
11	9,330	South Bend Community Sch Corp	South Bend
12	9,308	Anderson Community School Corp	Anderson
13	9,207	School City of East Chicago	East Chicago
14	9,142	Garrett-Keyser-Butler Com	Garrett
15	9,094	Southwest Dubois County Sch Corp	Huntingburg
16	9,049	North Putnam Community Schools	Bainbridge
17	8,951	Marion Community Schools	Marion
18	8,934	Lafayette School Corporation	Lafayette
19	8,852	Crawfordsville Com Schools	Crawfordsville
20	8,805	School City of Mishawaka	Mishawaka
21	8,764	School City of Hammond	Hammond
22	8,750	M S D Mount Vernon	Mount Vernon
23	8,746	Michigan City Area Schools	Michigan City
24	8,731	Warsaw Community Schools	Warsaw
25	8,707	Maconaquah School Corp	Bunker Hill
26	8,681	Fort Wayne Community Schools	Fort Wayne
27	8,680	Bartholomew Con School Corp	Columbus
28	8,677	M S D Lawrence Township	Indianapolis
29	8,674	Westview School Corporation	Topeka
30	8,635	Greenfield-Central Com Schools	Greenfield
31	8,626	Goshen Community Schools	Goshen
32	8,607	West Lafayette Com School Corp	West Lafayette
33	8,590	Jay School Corp	Portland
34	8,531	Greater Clark County Schools	Jeffersonville
35	8,518	M S D Wayne Township	Indianapolis
36	8,492	Brown County School Corporation	Nashville
37	8,459	M S D Warren Township	Indianapolis
38	8,454	Monroe County Com Sch Corp	Bloomington
39	8,339	Northeast School Corp	Hymera
40	8,301	Middlebury Community Schools	Middlebury
41	8,274	Blackford County Schools	Hartford City
41	8,274	Richmond Community School Corp	Richmond
43	8,242	M S D Washington Township	Indianapolis
44	8,229	Evansville-Vanderburgh Sch Corp	Evansville
45	8,227	M S D Pike Township	Indianapolis
46	8,217	East Allen County Schools	New Haven
47	8,191	M S D Perry Township	Indianapolis
48	8,189	M S D Southwest Allen County	Fort Wayne
49	8,178	M S D Wabash County Schools	Wabash
50	8,176	New Albany-Floyd County Con Sch	New Albany
51	8,083	Wa-Nee Community Schools	Nappanee
52	8,050	Vincennes Community Sch Corp	Vincennes
53	7,956	Prairie Heights Com Sch Corp	Lagrange
54	7,955	Spencer-Owen Community Schools	Spencer
55	7,952	North Lawrence Com Schools	Bedford
56	7,950	Crawford County Com School Corp	Marengo
57	7,930	Northwestern School Corp	Kokomo
58	7,915	Knox Community School Corp	Knox
59	7,868	Madison Consolidated Schools	Madison
60	7,859	North Knox School Corp	Bicknell
60	7,859	Taylor Community School Corp	Kokomo
62	7,856	West Noble School Corporation	Ligonier
63	7,799	Southwest School Corp	Sullivan
64	7,750	Carmel Clay Schools	Carmel
65	7,726	Valparaiso Community Schools	Valparaiso
66	7,715	Duneland School Corporation	Chesterton
67	7,691	M S D Decatur Township	Indianapolis
68	7,689	Laporte Community School Corp	Laporte
69	7,676	Mitchell Community Schools	Mitchell
70	7,657	Benton Community School Corp	Fowler
71	7,640	Sunman-Dearborn Com Sch Corp	Sunman
72	7,635	Whitley County Cons Schools	Columbia City
73	7,615	Seymour Community Schools	Seymour
74	7,606	School Town of Munster	Munster
75	7,591	Clay Community Schools	Knightsville
76	7,587	Wabash City Schools	Wabash
77	7,584	Wawasee Community School Corp	Syracuse
78	7,570	Elwood Community School Corp	Elwood
79	7,562	Centerville-Abington Com Schs	Centerville
80	7,554	North Adams Community Schools	Decatur
81	7,535	North Harrison Com School Corp	Ramsey
82	7,530	East Noble School Corp	Kendallville
83	7,525	Elkhart Community Schools	Elkhart
84	7,452	Lakeland School Corporation	Lagrange
85	7,447	North Gibson School Corp	Princeton
86	7,436	South Vermillion Com Sch Corp	Clinton
87	7,426	Penn-Harris-Madison Sch Corp	Mishawaka
88	7,419	Twin Lakes School Corp	Monticello
89	7,415	South Dearborn Com School Corp	Aurora
90	7,397	Richland-Bean Blossom C S C	Ellettsville
91	7,392	Dekalb County Ctl United SD	Waterloo
92	7,389	North Newton School Corp	Morocco
93	7,321	South Harrison Com Schools	Corydon
94	7,268	Lebanon Community School Corp	Lebanon
95	7,264	Lake Central School Corp	Saint John
96	7,258	Westfield-Washington Schools	Westfield
97	7,255	Oak Hill United School Corp	Converse
98	7,254	Union Co/Clg Corner Joint SD	Liberty
99	7,229	Whitko Community School Corp	Pierceton
100	7,221	Mississinewa Community School Corp	Gas City
101	7,172	School Town of Speedway	Speedway
102	7,141	Tipton Community School Corp	Tipton
103	7,119	Randolph Central School Corp	Winchester
104	7,114	Noblesville Schools	Noblesville
105	7,097	Tell City-Troy Twp School Corp	Tell City
106	7,094	Brownstown Cnt Com Sch Corp	Brownstown
107	7,085	Portage Township Schools	Portage
108	7,082	East Porter County School Corp	Kouts
109	7,081	North Montgomery Com Sch Corp	Crawfordsville
110	7,071	Rush County Schools	Rushville
111	7,070	M S D Steuben County	Angola
112	7,065	Peru Community Schools	Peru
113	7,057	Union Township School Corp	Valparaiso
114	7,056	Huntington County Com Sch Corp	Huntington
115	7,038	South Ripley Com Sch Corp	Versailles
116	7,036	M S D Martinsville Schools	Martinsville
117	7,020	Madison-Grant United Sch Corp	Fairmount
118	7,019	North West Hendricks Schools	Lizton
119	7,004	East Washington School Corp	Pekin
120	6,989	Batesville Community Sch Corp	Batesville
121	6,980	Plymouth Community School Corp	Plymouth
122	6,978	Tippecanoe Valley School Corp	Akron
123	6,974	Avon Community School Corp	Avon
124	6,969	Plainfield Community Sch Corp	Plainfield
125	6,965	Jennings County Schools	North Vernon
126	6,959	Zionsville Community Schools	Zionsville
127	6,956	Vigo County School Corp	Terre Haute
128	6,948	Manchester Community Schools	N Manchester
129	6,947	Delphi Community School Corp	Delphi
130	6,944	Kankakee Valley School Corp	Wheatfield
130	6,944	South Madison Com Sch Corp	Pendleton
132	6,943	Franklin County Com Sch Corp	Brookville
133	6,935	Franklin Township Com Sch Corp	Indianapolis
134	6,929	Community Schools of Frankfort	Frankfort
135	6,925	North Spencer County Sch Corp	Lincoln City
136	6,919	Alexandria Com School Corp	Alexandria
137	6,900	Hamilton Heights School Corp	Arcadia
138	6,894	Rensselaer Central School Corp	Rensselaer
139	6,876	Brownsburg Community Sch Corp	Brownsburg
140	6,860	Decatur County Com Schools	Greensburg
141	6,849	Scott County SD 2	Scottsburg
142	6,843	Danville Community School Corp	Danville
143	6,837	School City of Hobart	Hobart
144	6,831	Merrillville Community School	Merrillville
145	6,828	M S D Bluffton-Harrison	Bluffton
146	6,821	John Glenn School Corporation	Walkerton
147	6,809	Rochester Community Sch Corp	Rochester
148	6,799	South Gibson School Corp	Fort Branch
149	6,787	Paoli Community School Corp	Paoli
150	6,780	Pike County School Corp	Petersburg
151	6,779	Hamilton Southeastern Schools	Fishers
152	6,765	Porter Township School Corp	Valparaiso
153	6,764	Mill Creek Community Sch Corp	Clayton
154	6,763	Greencastle Community Sch Corp	Greencastle
155	6,744	Beech Grove City Schools	Beech Grove
156	6,730	Baugo Community Schools	Elkhart
157	6,726	Shelbyville Central Schools	Shelbyville
158	6,683	Tippecanoe School Corp	Lafayette
159	6,628	Western Boone County Com SD	Thorntown
160	6,625	Northern Wells Com Schools	Ossian
161	6,624	Northwest Allen County Schools	Fort Wayne
162	6,622	Salem Community Schools	Salem
163	6,620	Franklin Community School Corp	Franklin
164	6,614	Concord Community Schools	Elkhart
165	6,604	Mt Pleasant Twp Com Sch Corp	Yorktown
166	6,603	Delaware Community School Corp	Muncie
166	6,603	Greensburg Community Schools	Greensburg
168	6,598	South Montgomery Com Sch Corp	New Market
169	6,595	Nineveh-Hensley-Jackson United	Trafalgar
170	6,591	Mooresville Con School Corp	Mooresville
171	6,584	Greenwood Community Sch Corp	Greenwood
172	6,573	Southeastern School Corp	Walton
173	6,558	Warrick County School Corp	Boonville
174	6,539	Shelby Eastern Schools	Shelbyville
175	6,532	Fairfield Community Schools	Goshen
176	6,528	Washington Com Schools Inc	Washington
177	6,514	Clark-Pleasant Com School Corp	Whiteland
178	6,496	School Town of Highland	Highland
179	6,479	Mt Vernon Community Sch Corp	Fortville
180	6,437	Switzerland County School Corp	Vevay
181	6,422	Northwestern Con School Corp	Fairland
182	6,406	Center Grove Com Sch Corp	Greenwood
183	6,364	West Clark Community Schools	Sellersburg
184	6,332	Hanover Community School Corp	Cedar Lake
185	6,317	New Prairie United School Corp	New Carlisle
186	6,298	Frankton-Lapel Community Schs	Anderson
187	6,286	Southeast Dubois County Sch Corp	Ferdinand
188	6,273	Eastbrook Community Sch Corp	Marion
189	6,206	Griffith Public Schools	Griffith
190	6,203	Southern Hancock Co Com Sch Corp	New Palestine
191	6,202	Western School Corp	Russiaville
192	6,141	Crown Point Community Sch Corp	Crown Point
193	5,977	Tri-Creek School Corp	Lowell

Number of Diploma Recipients

Rank	Number	District Name	City
1	1,596	Fort Wayne Community Schools	Fort Wayne
2	1,344	Evansville-Vanderburgh Sch Corp	Evansville
3	1,206	South Bend Community Sch Corp	South Bend
4	1,203	Indianapolis Public Schools	Indianapolis
5	997	Vigo County School Corp	Terre Haute
6	871	M S D Lawrence Township	Indianapolis
7	765	Carmel Clay Schools	Carmel
8	706	Gary Community School Corp	Gary
9	662	M S D Washington Township	Indianapolis
10	660	New Albany-Floyd County Con Sch	New Albany
11	647	Monroe County Com Sch Corp	Bloomington
12	620	Bartholomew Con School Corp	Columbus
13	619	Penn-Harris-Madison Sch Corp	Mishawaka
14	611	M S D Perry Township	Indianapolis
15	609	East Allen County Schools	New Haven
16	599	Tippecanoe School Corp	Lafayette

17	596	Warrick County School Corp	Boonville
18	585	M S D Wayne Township	Indianapolis
19	550	M S D Warren Township	Indianapolis
20	545	School City of Hammond	Hammond
21	544	Elkhart Community Schools	Elkhart
22	521	Portage Township Schools	Portage
23	504	Anderson Community School Corp	Anderson
24	494	Valparaiso Community Schools	Valparaiso
25	480	M S D Pike Township	Indianapolis
26	468	Merrillville Community School	Merrillville
27	453	Huntington County Com Sch Corp	Huntington
28	452	Lake Central School Corp	Saint John
29	445	Center Grove Com Sch Corp	Greenwood
30	434	Hamilton Southeastern Schools	Fishers
31	427	Crown Point Community Sch Corp	Crown Point
32	425	Greater Clark County Schools	Jeffersonville
33	408	Muncie Community Schools	Muncie
34	401	Laporte Community School Corp	Laporte
34	401	Noblesville Schools	Noblesville
36	390	Duneland School Corporation	Chesterton
37	388	Warsaw Community Schools	Warsaw
38	378	Brownsburg Community Sch Corp	Brownsburg
39	371	M S D Southwest Allen County	Fort Wayne
40	367	Kokomo-Center Twp Con Sch Corp	Kokomo
41	357	Lafayette School Corporation	Lafayette
42	352	North Lawrence Com Schools	Bedford
43	350	Michigan City Area Schools	Michigan City
44	312	M S D Martinsville Schools	Martinsville
44	312	Sunman-Dearborn Com Sch Corp	Sunman
46	306	Richmond Community School Corp	Richmond
47	305	Franklin Township Com Sch Corp	Indianapolis
48	301	Clay Community Schools	Knightsville
49	298	Avon Community School Corp	Avon
50	290	Northwest Allen County Schools	Fort Wayne
51	281	School Town of Munster	Munster
52	272	Plainfield Community Sch Corp	Plainfield
53	271	Goshen Community Schools	Goshen
53	271	Marion Community Schools	Marion
55	266	Plymouth Community School Corp	Plymouth
56	262	Mooresville Con School Corp	Mooresville
57	261	School City of Mishawaka	Mishawaka
58	256	School City of East Chicago	East Chicago
59	255	Logansport Community Sch Corp	Logansport
60	251	School Town of Highland	Highland
61	246	M S D Decatur Township	Indianapolis
62	244	Concord Community Schools	Elkhart
62	244	Whitley County Cons Schools	Columbia City
64	242	Seymour Community Schools	Seymour
65	241	School City of Hobart	Hobart
66	240	Greater Jasper Con Schs	Jasper
67	238	Greenfield-Central Com Schools	Greenfield
68	235	New Castle Community Sch Corp	New Castle
69	234	Jennings County Schools	North Vernon
70	233	Westfield-Washington Schools	Westfield
71	232	South Madison Com Sch Corp	Pendleton
72	230	Zionsville Community Schools	Zionsville
73	224	East Noble School Corp	Kendallville
73	224	Tri-Creek School Corp	Lowell
75	221	Middlebury Community Schools	Middlebury
76	220	Dekalb County Ctl United SD	Waterloo
77	212	Kankakee Valley School Corp	Wheatfield
78	211	Jay School Corp	Portland
79	210	Greenwood Community Sch Corp	Greenwood
80	208	Franklin Community School Corp	Franklin
81	207	Franklin County Com Sch Corp	Brookville
82	206	Wawasee Community School Corp	Syracuse
83	205	North Adams Community Schools	Decatur
84	203	Northern Wells Com Schools	Ossian
85	199	Delaware Community School Corp	Muncie
85	199	South Dearborn Com School Corp	Aurora
87	197	Fayette County School Corp	Connersville
87	197	Vincennes Community Sch Corp	Vincennes
89	193	South Harrison Com Schools	Corydon
90	192	M S D Mount Vernon	Mount Vernon
91	188	Griffith Public Schools	Griffith
92	187	Spencer-Owen Community Schools	Spencer
93	183	Lebanon Community School Corp	Lebanon
93	183	Mt Vernon Community Sch Corp	Fortville
95	182	Southern Hancock Co Com Sch Corp	New Palestine
96	180	Twin Lakes School Corp	Monticello
97	178	Clark-Pleasant Com School Corp	Whiteland
97	178	M S D Steuben County	Angola
99	176	Madison Consolidated Schools	Madison
100	175	Washington Com Schools Inc	Washington
100	175	West Clark Community Schools	Sellersburg
102	170	Shelbyville Central Schools	Shelbyville
103	169	North Harrison Com School Corp	Ramsey
103	169	Wa-Nee Community Schools	Nappanee
105	162	Western School Corp	Russiaville
106	160	North Spencer County Sch Corp	Lincoln City
107	158	Benton Community School Corp	Fowler
108	154	Richland-Bean Blossom C S C	Ellettsville
109	152	Peru Community Schools	Peru
110	151	Danville Community School Corp	Danville
111	150	New Prairie United School Corp	New Carlisle
112	148	West Lafayette Com School Corp	West Lafayette
113	146	Decatur County Com Schools	Greensburg
113	146	Rush County Schools	Rushville
115	145	Beech Grove City Schools	Beech Grove
115	145	Hamilton Heights School Corp	Arcadia
115	145	South Gibson School Corp	Fort Branch
118	144	Community Schools of Frankfort	Frankfort
119	141	Mt Pleasant Twp Com Sch Corp	Yorktown
120	140	North Gibson School Corp	Princeton
121	139	Scott County SD 2	Scottsburg
122	138	East Porter County School Corp	Kouts
123	137	Frankton-Lapel Community Schs	Anderson
123	137	M S D Wabash County Schools	Wabash
123	137	Porter Township School Corp	Valparaiso
126	136	Greencastle Community Sch Corp	Greencastle
126	136	Southwest School Corp	Sullivan
128	135	Rochester Community Sch Corp	Rochester
128	135	Tippecanoe Valley School Corp	Akron
130	133	Blackford County Schools	Hartford City
130	133	Lake Ridge Schools	Gary
132	131	Brown County School Corporation	Nashville
132	131	Shelby Eastern Schools	Shelbyville
132	131	Tipton Community School Corp	Tipton
135	128	Western Boone County Com SD	Thorntown
136	127	Crawfordsville Com Schools	Crawfordsville
136	127	Northwestern School Corp	Kokomo
138	125	Batesville Community Sch Corp	Batesville
139	124	Maconaquah School Corp	Bunker Hill
139	124	Pike County School Corp	Petersburg
141	123	Mississinewa Community School Corp	Gas City
142	122	Southwest Dubois County Sch Corp	Huntingburg
143	120	Fairfield Community Schools	Goshen
144	119	Alexandria Com School Corp	Alexandria
144	119	Elwood Community School Corp	Elwood
144	119	South Vermillion Com Sch Corp	Clinton
144	119	Southeastern School Corp	Walton
144	119	West Noble School Corporation	Ligonier
149	118	Baugo Community Schools	Elkhart
149	118	Mitchell Community Schools	Mitchell
151	117	South Montgomery Com Sch Corp	New Market
152	115	Brownstown Cnt Com Sch Corp	Brownstown
152	115	Salem Community Schools	Salem
154	113	John Glenn School Corporation	Walkerton
155	112	M S D Bluffton-Harrison	Bluffton
156	110	Nineveh-Hensley-Jackson United	Trafalgar
156	110	Prairie Heights Com Sch Corp	Lagrange
158	109	Garrett-Keyser-Butler Com	Garrett
158	109	North Putnam Community Schools	Bainbridge
158	109	Union Co/Clg Corner Joint SD	Liberty
158	109	Union Township School Corp	Valparaiso
162	108	North Montgomery Com Sch Corp	Crawfordsville
162	108	Paoli Community School Corp	Paoli
162	108	Tell City-Troy Twp School Corp	Tell City
165	106	Greensburg Community Schools	Greensburg
166	104	Oak Hill United School Corp	Converse
167	103	Lakeland School Corporation	Lagrange
167	103	North Knox School Corp	Bicknell
169	102	Hanover Community School Corp	Cedar Lake
169	102	Manchester Community Schools	N Manchester
171	101	Knox Community School Corp	Knox
172	98	Randolph Central School Corp	Winchester
172	98	Rensselaer Central School Corp	Rensselaer
172	98	Wabash City Schools	Wabash
175	97	Centerville-Abington Com Schs	Centerville
176	96	Northeast School Corp	Hymera
177	94	Eastbrook Community Sch Corp	Marion
178	93	Northwestern Con School Corp	Fairland
179	92	South Ripley Com Sch Corp	Versailles
180	91	Crawford County Com School Corp	Marengo
180	91	Delphi Community School Corp	Delphi
180	91	Westview School Corporation	Topeka
180	91	Whitko Community School Corp	Pierceton
184	89	Southeast Dubois County Sch Corp	Ferdinand
184	89	Switzerland County School Corp	Vevay
186	88	North West Hendricks Schools	Lizton
187	85	East Washington School Corp	Pekin
188	84	School Town of Speedway	Speedway
189	82	Taylor Community School Corp	Kokomo
190	81	Madison-Grant United Sch Corp	Fairmount
191	79	Dekalb County Eastern Com SD	Butler
192	77	Mill Creek Community Sch Corp	Clayton
193	75	North Newton School Corp	Morocco

High School Drop-out Rate

Rank	Percent	District Name	City
1	7.5	School City of East Chicago	East Chicago
2	6.2	Lafayette School Corporation	Lafayette
2	6.2	Marion Community Schools	Marion
4	5.8	Richmond Community School Corp	Richmond
4	5.8	Spencer-Owen Community Schools	Spencer
6	5.3	Delphi Community School Corp	Delphi
7	5.1	Garrett-Keyser-Butler Com	Garrett
8	5.0	Tippecanoe Valley School Corp	Akron
9	4.9	Peru Community Schools	Peru
10	4.5	Community Schools of Frankfort	Frankfort
10	4.5	South Montgomery Com Sch Corp	New Market
12	4.4	East Washington School Corp	Pekin
12	4.4	M S D Warren Township	Indianapolis
12	4.4	Muncie Community Schools	Muncie
15	4.3	Paoli Community School Corp	Paoli
16	4.1	Lake Ridge Schools	Gary
17	3.9	Elkhart Community Schools	Elkhart
17	3.9	Tell City-Troy Twp School Corp	Tell City
19	3.8	M S D Wayne Township	Indianapolis
19	3.8	Seymour Community Schools	Seymour
19	3.8	Taylor Community School Corp	Kokomo
19	3.8	Vigo County School Corp	Terre Haute
23	3.7	Brownstown Cnt Com Sch Corp	Brownstown
23	3.7	Warsaw Community Schools	Warsaw
25	3.6	Decatur County Com Schools	Greensburg
25	3.6	Greater Clark County Schools	Jeffersonville
25	3.6	North Gibson School Corp	Princeton
28	3.5	Franklin Community School Corp	Franklin
29	3.3	Delaware Community School Corp	Muncie
29	3.3	M S D Martinsville Schools	Martinsville
29	3.3	North Putnam Community Schools	Bainbridge
32	3.2	Jennings County Schools	North Vernon
32	3.2	North Adams Community Schools	Decatur
32	3.2	Whitko Community School Corp	Pierceton
35	3.1	Elwood Community School Corp	Elwood
35	3.1	Tipton Community School Corp	Tipton
37	3.0	Blackford County Schools	Hartford City
37	3.0	Dekalb County Ctl United SD	Waterloo
37	3.0	Frankton-Lapel Community Schs	Anderson
37	3.0	Randolph Central School Corp	Winchester
37	3.0	South Vermillion Com Sch Corp	Clinton
37	3.0	Southwest School Corp	Sullivan
37	3.0	Wa-Nee Community Schools	Nappanee
44	2.9	Centerville-Abington Com Schs	Centerville
44	2.9	Fort Wayne Community Schools	Fort Wayne
44	2.9	South Dearborn Com School Corp	Aurora
47	2.8	Mitchell Community Schools	Mitchell
47	2.8	New Albany-Floyd County Con Sch	New Albany
49	2.7	M S D Mount Vernon	Mount Vernon
49	2.7	Monroe County Com Sch Corp	Bloomington
49	2.7	Rensselaer Central School Corp	Rensselaer
52	2.6	M S D Perry Township	Indianapolis
52	2.6	Pike County School Corp	Petersburg
52	2.6	Scott County SD 2	Scottsburg
52	2.6	Washington Com Schools Inc	Washington
56	2.5	Concord Community Schools	Elkhart
56	2.5	Goshen Community Schools	Goshen
56	2.5	New Castle Community Sch Corp	New Castle
56	2.5	Oak Hill United School Corp	Converse
56	2.5	South Gibson School Corp	Fort Branch
61	2.4	Franklin County Com Sch Corp	Brookville
61	2.4	Kankakee Valley School Corp	Wheatfield
63	2.3	New Prairie United School Corp	New Carlisle
63	2.3	North Newton School Corp	Morocco
65	2.2	Indianapolis Public Schools	Indianapolis
65	2.2	Jay School Corp	Portland
67	2.1	Beech Grove City Schools	Beech Grove
67	2.1	Knox Community School Corp	Knox
67	2.1	School City of Mishawaka	Mishawaka
67	2.1	Southwest Dubois County Sch Corp	Huntingburg
71	2.0	Lebanon Community School Corp	Lebanon
71	2.0	Noblesville Schools	Noblesville
73	1.9	Hamilton Heights School Corp	Arcadia
74	1.8	Fayette County School Corp	Connersville
74	1.8	North Harrison Com School Corp	Ramsey
74	1.8	Sunman-Dearborn Com Sch Corp	Sunman
74	1.8	Tippecanoe School Corp	Lafayette
78	1.7	Crawford County Com School Corp	Marengo
78	1.7	Dekalb County Eastern Com SD	Butler
78	1.7	M S D Wabash County Schools	Wabash
78	1.7	Mt Pleasant Twp Com Sch Corp	Yorktown
78	1.7	Portage Township Schools	Portage
78	1.7	Porter Township School Corp	Valparaiso
78	1.7	Shelby Eastern Schools	Shelbyville
78	1.7	Twin Lakes School Corp	Monticello
78	1.7	Wawasee Community School Corp	Syracuse
87	1.6	Alexandria Com School Corp	Alexandria
87	1.6	North Lawrence Com Schools	Bedford
87	1.6	Western Boone County Com SD	Thorntown
90	1.5	Franklin Township Com Sch Corp	Indianapolis
90	1.5	North West Hendricks Schools	Lizton
90	1.5	Rochester Community Sch Corp	Rochester
90	1.5	South Bend Community Sch Corp	South Bend
90	1.5	Wabash City Schools	Wabash
95	1.4	Greencastle Community Sch Corp	Greencastle
95	1.4	M S D Lawrence Township	Indianapolis

95	1.4	Northwestern School Corp	Kokomo
95	1.4	Salem Community Schools	Salem
99	1.3	Bartholomew Con School Corp	Columbus
99	1.3	M S D Bluffton-Harrison	Bluffton
101	1.2	Batesville Community Sch Corp	Batesville
101	1.2	M S D Steuben County	Angola
101	1.2	Northern Wells Com Schools	Ossian
101	1.2	Rush County Schools	Rushville
101	1.2	School City of Hammond	Hammond
101	1.2	Warrick County School Corp	Boonville
107	1.1	East Porter County School Corp	Kouts
107	1.1	Greenfield-Central Com Schools	Greenfield
107	1.1	M S D Southwest Allen County	Fort Wayne
107	1.1	Mississinewa Community School Corp	Gas City
107	1.1	Penn-Harris-Madison Sch Corp	Mishawaka
107	1.1	Prairie Heights Com Sch Corp	Lagrange
107	1.1	Union Co/Clg Corner Joint SD	Liberty
114	1.0	Evansville-Vanderburgh Sch Corp	Evansville
114	1.0	Mill Creek Community Sch Corp	Clayton
114	1.0	Mt Vernon Community Sch Corp	Fortville
114	1.0	North Knox School Corp	Bicknell
114	1.0	Northeast School Corp	Hymera
114	1.0	Richland-Bean Blossom C S C	Ellettsville
114	1.0	Southern Hancock Co Com Sch Corp	New Palestine
114	1.0	Union Township School Corp	Valparaiso
122	0.9	Greater Jasper Con Schs	Jasper
122	0.9	West Clark Community Schools	Sellersburg
122	0.9	Western School Corp	Russiaville
125	0.8	Center Grove Com Sch Corp	Greenwood
125	0.8	East Allen County Schools	New Haven
125	0.8	Fairfield Community Schools	Goshen
125	0.8	Hanover Community School Corp	Cedar Lake
125	0.8	Plymouth Community School Corp	Plymouth
125	0.8	School Town of Munster	Munster
125	0.8	South Harrison Com Schools	Corydon
125	0.8	Southeastern School Corp	Walton
125	0.8	Valparaiso Community Schools	Valparaiso
125	0.8	Westview School Corporation	Topeka
135	0.7	Lake Central School Corp	Saint John
135	0.7	Laporte Community School Corp	Laporte
135	0.7	Mooresville Con School Corp	Mooresville
138	0.6	Brownsburg Community Sch Corp	Brownsburg
138	0.6	Crawfordsville Com Schools	Crawfordsville
138	0.6	Duneland School Corporation	Chesterton
138	0.6	M S D Washington Township	Indianapolis
138	0.6	Nineveh-Hensley-Jackson United	Trafalgar
138	0.6	School City of Hobart	Hobart
138	0.6	Tri-Creek School Corp	Lowell
145	0.5	Brown County School Corporation	Nashville
145	0.5	Carmel Clay Schools	Carmel
145	0.5	Gary Community School Corp	Gary
145	0.5	Greenwood Community Sch Corp	Greenwood
145	0.5	Hamilton Southeastern Schools	Fishers
145	0.5	Madison-Grant United Sch Corp	Fairmount
145	0.5	Merrillville Community School	Merrillville
152	0.4	John Glenn School Corporation	Walkerton
152	0.4	Maconaquah School Corp	Bunker Hill
152	0.4	North Spencer County Sch Corp	Lincoln City
152	0.4	Northwestern Con School Corp	Fairland
156	0.3	Clark-Pleasant Com School Corp	Whiteland
156	0.3	Logansport Community Sch Corp	Logansport
158	0.2	Clay Community Schools	Knightsville
158	0.2	Middlebury Community Schools	Middlebury
158	0.2	Plainfield Community Sch Corp	Plainfield
158	0.2	South Ripley Com Sch Corp	Versailles
162	0.1	Crown Point Community Sch Corp	Crown Point
162	0.1	Griffith Public Schools	Griffith
162	0.1	Northwest Allen County Schools	Fort Wayne
165	0.0	Anderson Community School Corp	Anderson
165	0.0	Avon Community School Corp	Avon
165	0.0	Baugo Community Schools	Elkhart
165	0.0	Benton Community School Corp	Fowler
165	0.0	Danville Community School Corp	Danville
165	0.0	East Noble School Corp	Kendallville
165	0.0	Eastbrook Community Sch Corp	Marion
165	0.0	Greensburg Community Schools	Greensburg
165	0.0	Huntington County Com Sch Corp	Huntington
165	0.0	Kokomo-Center Twp Con Sch Corp	Kokomo
165	0.0	Lakeland School Corporation	Lagrange
165	0.0	M S D Decatur Township	Indianapolis
165	0.0	M S D Pike Township	Indianapolis
165	0.0	Madison Consolidated Schools	Madison
165	0.0	Manchester Community Schools	N Manchester
165	0.0	Michigan City Area Schools	Michigan City
165	0.0	North Montgomery Com Sch Corp	Crawfordsville
165	0.0	School Town of Highland	Highland
165	0.0	School Town of Speedway	Speedway
165	0.0	Shelbyville Central Schools	Shelbyville
165	0.0	South Madison Com Sch Corp	Pendleton
165	0.0	Southeast Dubois County Sch Corp	Ferdinand
165	0.0	Switzerland County School Corp	Vevay
165	0.0	Vincennes Community Sch Corp	Vincennes

165	0.0	West Lafayette Com School Corp	West Lafayette
165	0.0	West Noble School Corporation	Ligonier
165	0.0	Westfield-Washington Schools	Westfield
165	0.0	Zionsville Community Schools	Zionsville
193	n/a	Whitley County Cons Schools	Columbia City

Iowa

Iowa Public School Educational Profile

Category	Value	Category	Value
Schools *(2003-2004)*	1,495	**Diploma Recipients** *(2002-2003)*	33,789
Instructional Level		White, Non-Hispanic	31,608
Primary	786	Black, Non-Hispanic	756
Middle	291	Asian/Pacific Islander	657
High	368	American Indian/Alaskan Native	108
Other Level	48	Hispanic	660
Curriculum		**High School Drop-out Rate** (%) *(2001-2002)*	2.4
Regular	1,440	White, Non-Hispanic	2.1
Special Education	10	Black, Non-Hispanic	6.8
Vocational	0	Asian/Pacific Islander	2.7
Alternative	43	American Indian/Alaskan Native	6.6
Type		Hispanic	7.1
Magnet	0	**Staff** *(2003-2004)*	
Charter	0	Teachers	34,784.0
Title I Eligible	694	Average Salary ($)	38,381
School-wide Title I	128	Librarians/Media Specialists	589.0
Students *(2003-2004)*	481,226	Guidance Counselors	1,179.5
Gender (%)		**Ratios** *(2003-2004)*	
Male	51.4	Student/Teacher Ratio	13.8 to 1
Female	48.6	Student/Librarian Ratio	817.0 to 1
Race/Ethnicity (%)		Student/Counselor Ratio	408.0 to 1
White, Non-Hispanic	88.2	**College Entrance Exam Scores** *(2005)*	
Black, Non-Hispanic	4.5	Scholastic Aptitude Test (SAT)	
Asian/Pacific Islander	1.8	Participation Rate (%)	5
American Indian/Alaskan Native	0.6	Mean SAT Reasoning Test Verbal Score	596
Hispanic	4.9	Mean SAT Reasoning Test Math Score	608
Classification (%)		American College Testing Program (ACT)	
Individual Education Program (IEP)	13.3	Participation Rate (%)	66
Migrant *(2002-2003)*	1.1	Average Composite Score	22.0
English Language Learner (ELL)	3.2	Average English Score	21.5
Eligible for Free Lunch Program	22.3	Average Math Score	21.7
Eligible for Reduced-Price Lunch Program	7.7	Average Reading Score	22.4
Current Spending *($ per student in FY 2003)*	7,081	Average Science Score	22.1
Instruction	4,438		
Support Services	2,092		

Note: *For an explanation of data, please refer to the User's Guide in the front of the book*

Iowa NAEP 2005 Test Scores

Reading			Mathematics		
Grade/Category	Value	Rank	Grade/Category	Value	Rank
4th Grade			**4th Grade**		
Average Proficiency	220.8 (0.91)	24/51	Average Proficiency	239.9 (0.72)	22/51
Proficiency by Gender/Race/Ethnicity			Proficiency by Gender/Race/Ethnicity		
Male	217.7 (1.22)	24/51	Male	241.7 (0.96)	20/51
Female	224.0 (1.22)	21/51	Female	237.9 (0.83)	25/51
White, Non-Hispanic	223.5 (0.94)	41/51	White, Non-Hispanic	241.9 (0.66)	38/51
Black, Non-Hispanic	200.7 (3.59)	16/42	Black, Non-Hispanic	223.9 (2.72)	10/42
Asian, Non-Hispanic	224.3 (5.93)	17/27	Asian, Non-Hispanic	n/a	n/a
American Indian, Non-Hispanic	n/a	n/a	American Indian, Non-Hispanic	n/a	n/a
Hispanic	199.7 (2.93)	29/40	Hispanic	222.2 (2.54)	28/41
Proficiency by Class Size			Proficiency by Class Size		
Less than 16 Students	199.4 (4.61)	21/34	Less than 16 Students	230.5 (3.14)	14/35
16 to 18 Students	220.5 (1.91)	12/33	16 to 18 Students	241.3 (1.61)	8/31
19 to 20 Students	n/a	n/a	19 to 20 Students	n/a	n/a
21 to 25 Students	223.6 (1.32)	21/51	21 to 25 Students	241.4 (1.15)	21/51
Greater than 25 Students	224.2 (4.09)	9/36	Greater than 25 Students	240.2 (1.99)	14/33
Percent Attaining Achievement Levels			Percent Attaining Achievement Levels		
Below Basic	32.5 (1.32)	30/51	Below Basic	15.3 (0.96)	39/51
Basic or Above	67.5 (1.32)	22/51	Basic or Above	84.7 (0.96)	13/51
Proficient or Above	33.0 (1.24)	21/51	Proficient or Above	37.3 (1.30)	25/51
Advanced or Above	7.1 (0.54)	23/51	Advanced or Above	4.1 (0.40)	31/51
8th Grade			**8th Grade**		
Average Proficiency	267.0 (0.90)	13/51	Average Proficiency	283.8 (0.85)	14/51
Proficiency by Gender/Race/Ethnicity			Proficiency by Gender/Race/Ethnicity		
Male	261.3 (1.21)	15/51	Male	283.1 (1.14)	17/51
Female	272.9 (1.15)	11/51	Female	284.5 (1.09)	8/51
White, Non-Hispanic	268.9 (0.95)	26/51	White, Non-Hispanic	286.4 (0.88)	28/51
Black, Non-Hispanic	245.6 (3.42)	11/40	Black, Non-Hispanic	256.2 (5.13)	16/41
Asian, Non-Hispanic	n/a	n/a	Asian, Non-Hispanic	n/a	n/a
American Indian, Non-Hispanic	n/a	n/a	American Indian, Non-Hispanic	n/a	n/a
Hispanic	255.6 (3.92)	5/38	Hispanic	264.0 (3.23)	17/38
Proficiency by Parents Highest Level of Ed.			Proficiency by Parents Highest Level of Ed.		
Did Not Finish High School	247.3 (2.94)	17/49	Did Not Finish High School	263.9 (2.64)	17/50
Graduated High School	256.9 (1.83)	15/50	Graduated High School	271.9 (1.71)	17/50
Some Education After High School	268.7 (1.28)	16/50	Some Education After High School	284.8 (1.30)	12/50
Graduated College	275.1 (1.13)	13/50	Graduated College	292.5 (1.02)	19/50
Percent Attaining Achievement Levels			Percent Attaining Achievement Levels		
Below Basic	32.5 (1.32)	30/51	Below Basic	24.5 (1.08)	41/51
Basic or Above	67.5 (1.32)	22/51	Basic or Above	75.5 (1.08)	11/51
Proficient or Above	33.0 (1.24)	21/51	Proficient or Above	33.7 (1.20)	14/51
Advanced or Above	7.1 (0.54)	23/51	Advanced or Above	5.7 (0.59)	21/51

Note: *For an explanation of data, please refer to the User's Guide in the front of the book; n/a indicates data not available*

Appanoose County

Centerville Community SD
634 N Main • Centerville, IA 52544-0370
Mailing Address: Box 370 • Centerville, IA 52544-0370
(641) 856-0601
Grade Span: PK-12; Agency Type: 1
Schools: 10
  6 Primary; 2 Middle; 2 High; 0 Other Level
  8 Regular; 1 Special Education; 0 Vocational; 1 Alternative
  0 Magnet; 0 Charter; 6 Title I Eligible; 4 School-wide Title I
Students: 1,612 (48.8% male; 51.1% female)
  Individual Education Program: 297 (18.4%)
  English Language Learner: 2 (0.1%); Migrant: 0 (0.0%)
  Eligible for Free Lunch Program: 546 (33.9%)
  Eligible for Reduced-Price Lunch Program: 152 (9.4%)
Teachers: 132.0 (12.2 to 1)
Librarians/Media Specialists: 3.0 (537.3 to 1)
Guidance Counselors: 2.0 (806.0 to 1)
Current Spending: ($ per student per year):
  Total: $7,448; Instruction: $4,999; Support Services: $1,912
Enrollment, Drop-out Rates and Diploma Recipients by Race/Ethnicity

Category	Total	White	Black	Asian	AIAN	Hisp.
Enrollment (%)	100.0	96.8	1.6	0.9	0.2	0.6
Drop-out Rate (%)	0.6	0.6	0.0	0.0	0.0	0.0
H.S. Diplomas (#)	118	113	2	1	1	1

Benton County

Benton Community SD
304 1st St • Van Horne, IA 52346
Mailing Address: Box 70 • Van Horne, IA 52346
(319) 228-8701
Grade Span: PK-12; Agency Type: 1
Schools: 6
  4 Primary; 1 Middle; 1 High; 0 Other Level
  6 Regular; 0 Special Education; 0 Vocational; 0 Alternative
  0 Magnet; 0 Charter; 4 Title I Eligible; 0 School-wide Title I
Students: 1,561 (50.6% male; 49.3% female)
  Individual Education Program: 233 (14.9%);
  English Language Learner: 0 (0.0%); Migrant: 0 (0.0%)
  Eligible for Free Lunch Program: 165 (10.6%)
  Eligible for Reduced-Price Lunch Program: 71 (4.5%)
Teachers: 113.0 (13.8 to 1)
Librarians/Media Specialists: 2.0 (780.5 to 1)
Guidance Counselors: 4.0 (390.3 to 1)
Current Spending: ($ per student per year):
  Total: $6,608; Instruction: $4,035; Support Services: $1,914
Enrollment, Drop-out Rates and Diploma Recipients by Race/Ethnicity

Category	Total	White	Black	Asian	AIAN	Hisp.
Enrollment (%)	100.0	98.8	0.2	0.4	0.2	0.4
Drop-out Rate (%)	0.6	0.6	n/a	0.0	0.0	0.0
H.S. Diplomas (#)	135	134	0	1	0	0

Vinton-Shellsburg Community SD
810 W 9th St • Vinton, IA 52349
(319) 436-4728 • http://www.vinton-shellsburg.k12.ia.us
Grade Span: PK-12; Agency Type: 1
Schools: 5
  3 Primary; 1 Middle; 1 High; 0 Other Level
  5 Regular; 0 Special Education; 0 Vocational; 0 Alternative
  0 Magnet; 0 Charter; 3 Title I Eligible; 0 School-wide Title I
Students: 1,822 (52.3% male; 47.6% female)
  Individual Education Program: 265 (14.5%);
  English Language Learner: 1 (0.1%); Migrant: 0 (0.0%)
  Eligible for Free Lunch Program: 447 (24.5%)
  Eligible for Reduced-Price Lunch Program: 123 (6.8%)
Teachers: 135.0 (13.5 to 1)
Librarians/Media Specialists: 4.0 (455.5 to 1)
Guidance Counselors: 5.0 (364.4 to 1)
Current Spending: ($ per student per year):
  Total: $6,835; Instruction: $4,450; Support Services: $1,872
Enrollment, Drop-out Rates and Diploma Recipients by Race/Ethnicity

Category	Total	White	Black	Asian	AIAN	Hisp.
Enrollment (%)	100.0	97.7	0.8	0.8	0.2	0.5
Drop-out Rate (%)	0.4	0.4	0.0	n/a	0.0	0.0
H.S. Diplomas (#)	123	121	1	0	1	0

Black Hawk County

Cedar Falls Community SD
1002 W 1st St • Cedar Falls, IA 50613
(319) 277-8800 • http://www.cedar-falls.k12.ia.us
Grade Span: KG-12; Agency Type: 1
Schools: 9
  6 Primary; 2 Middle; 1 High; 0 Other Level
  9 Regular; 0 Special Education; 0 Vocational; 0 Alternative
  0 Magnet; 0 Charter; 3 Title I Eligible; 1 School-wide Title I
Students: 4,387 (51.1% male; 48.8% female)
  Individual Education Program: 542 (12.4%)
  English Language Learner: 40 (0.9%); Migrant: 0 (0.0%)
  Eligible for Free Lunch Program: 587 (13.4%)
  Eligible for Reduced-Price Lunch Program: 172 (3.9%)
Teachers: 299.5 (14.6 to 1)
Librarians/Media Specialists: 7.0 (626.7 to 1)
Guidance Counselors: 13.0 (337.5 to 1)
Current Spending: ($ per student per year):
  Total: $6,825; Instruction: $4,403; Support Services: $1,921
Enrollment, Drop-out Rates and Diploma Recipients by Race/Ethnicity

Category	Total	White	Black	Asian	AIAN	Hisp.
Enrollment (%)	100.0	91.7	4.3	2.5	0.2	1.3
Drop-out Rate (%)	0.6	0.6	5.0	0.0	0.0	0.0
H.S. Diplomas (#)	369	343	4	17	3	2

Waterloo Community SD
1516 Washington St • Waterloo, IA 50702
(319) 433-1800 • http://www.waterloo.k12.ia.us/home.html
Grade Span: PK-12; Agency Type: 1
Schools: 22
  15 Primary; 4 Middle; 3 High; 0 Other Level
  20 Regular; 0 Special Education; 0 Vocational; 2 Alternative
  0 Magnet; 0 Charter; 14 Title I Eligible; 12 School-wide Title I
Students: 10,407 (51.4% male; 48.5% female)
  Individual Education Program: 1,603 (15.4%)
  English Language Learner: 601 (5.8%); Migrant: 370 (3.6%)
  Eligible for Free Lunch Program: 4,599 (44.2%)
  Eligible for Reduced-Price Lunch Program: 1,149 (11.0%)
Teachers: 719.0 (14.5 to 1)
Librarians/Media Specialists: 18.0 (578.2 to 1)
Guidance Counselors: 24.5 (424.8 to 1)
Current Spending: ($ per student per year):
  Total: $7,430; Instruction: $4,777; Support Services: $2,107
Enrollment, Drop-out Rates and Diploma Recipients by Race/Ethnicity

Category	Total	White	Black	Asian	AIAN	Hisp.
Enrollment (%)	100.0	66.7	26.4	1.1	0.4	5.5
Drop-out Rate (%)	9.2	7.9	14.3	4.3	0.0	5.9
H.S. Diplomas (#)	596	479	101	8	2	6

Boone County

Boone Community SD
500 7th St • Boone, IA 50036
(515) 433-0750 • http://www.boone.k12.ia.us
Grade Span: PK-12; Agency Type: 1
Schools: 9
  6 Primary; 1 Middle; 2 High; 0 Other Level
  8 Regular; 0 Special Education; 0 Vocational; 1 Alternative
  0 Magnet; 0 Charter; 6 Title I Eligible; 0 School-wide Title I
Students: 2,309 (50.4% male; 49.5% female)
  Individual Education Program: 305 (13.2%);
  English Language Learner: 8 (0.3%); Migrant: 0 (0.0%)
  Eligible for Free Lunch Program: 417 (18.1%)
  Eligible for Reduced-Price Lunch Program: 164 (7.1%)
Teachers: 154.0 (15.0 to 1)
Librarians/Media Specialists: 2.5 (923.6 to 1)
Guidance Counselors: 6.0 (384.8 to 1)
Current Spending: ($ per student per year):
  Total: $7,193; Instruction: $4,819; Support Services: $1,964
Enrollment, Drop-out Rates and Diploma Recipients by Race/Ethnicity

Category	Total	White	Black	Asian	AIAN	Hisp.
Enrollment (%)	100.0	97.3	1.0	0.3	0.3	1.1
Drop-out Rate (%)	2.4	2.4	0.0	0.0	0.0	0.0
H.S. Diplomas (#)	191	188	0	2	1	0

Bremer County

Waverly-Shell Rock Community SD
1415 4th Ave SW • Waverly, IA 50677
(319) 352-3630 • http://www.waverly-shellrock.k12.ia.us
Grade Span: PK-12; Agency Type: 1
Schools: 7
  4 Primary; 2 Middle; 1 High; 0 Other Level
  7 Regular; 0 Special Education; 0 Vocational; 0 Alternative
  0 Magnet; 0 Charter; 3 Title I Eligible; 0 School-wide Title I
Students: 2,015 (51.8% male; 48.1% female)
  Individual Education Program: 203 (10.1%);
  English Language Learner: 1 (<0.1%); Migrant: 0 (0.0%)
  Eligible for Free Lunch Program: 267 (13.3%)
  Eligible for Reduced-Price Lunch Program: 93 (4.6%)
Teachers: 116.0 (17.4 to 1)

Librarians/Media Specialists: 2.0 (1,007.5 to 1)
Guidance Counselors: 3.0 (671.7 to 1)
Current Spending: ($ per student per year):
    Total: $5,823; Instruction: $3,349; Support Services: $1,795
Enrollment, Drop-out Rates and Diploma Recipients by Race/Ethnicity

Category	Total	White	Black	Asian	AIAN	Hisp.
Enrollment (%)	100.0	96.9	1.5	1.0	0.1	0.5
Drop-out Rate (%)	0.0	0.0	0.0	0.0	0.0	0.0
H.S. Diplomas (#)	177	176	1	0	0	0

Buchanan County

Independence Community SD
1207 1st St W • Independence, IA 50644
Mailing Address: PO Box 900 • Independence, IA 50644
(319) 334-7400 • http://www.indee.k12.ia.us
Grade Span: PK-12; Agency Type: 1
Schools: 5
    3 Primary; 1 Middle; 1 High; 0 Other Level
    5 Regular; 0 Special Education; 0 Vocational; 0 Alternative
    0 Magnet; 0 Charter; 3 Title I Eligible; 0 School-wide Title I
Students: 1,504 (51.0% male; 48.9% female)
    Individual Education Program: 213 (14.2%);
    English Language Learner: 0 (0.0%); Migrant: 0 (0.0%)
    Eligible for Free Lunch Program: 322 (21.4%)
    Eligible for Reduced-Price Lunch Program: 113 (7.5%)
Teachers: 114.5 (13.1 to 1)
Librarians/Media Specialists: 3.0 (501.3 to 1)
Guidance Counselors: 3.0 (501.3 to 1)
Current Spending: ($ per student per year):
    Total: $7,400; Instruction: $4,852; Support Services: $1,947
Enrollment, Drop-out Rates and Diploma Recipients by Race/Ethnicity

Category	Total	White	Black	Asian	AIAN	Hisp.
Enrollment (%)	100.0	96.7	0.8	1.5	0.1	0.8
Drop-out Rate (%)	0.6	0.6	0.0	0.0	n/a	0.0
H.S. Diplomas (#)	122	121	0	1	0	0

Buena Vista County

Storm Lake Community SD
419 Lake Ave • Storm Lake, IA 50588-0638
Mailing Address: PO Box 638 • Storm Lake, IA 50588-0638
(712) 732-8060 • http://www.storm-lake.k12.ia.us
Grade Span: PK-12; Agency Type: 1
Schools: 6
    4 Primary; 1 Middle; 1 High; 0 Other Level
    6 Regular; 0 Special Education; 0 Vocational; 0 Alternative
    0 Magnet; 0 Charter; 5 Title I Eligible; 5 School-wide Title I
Students: 2,039 (52.7% male; 47.2% female)
    Individual Education Program: 244 (12.0%);
    English Language Learner: 1,015 (49.8%); Migrant: 770 (37.8%)
    Eligible for Free Lunch Program: 741 (36.3%)
    Eligible for Reduced-Price Lunch Program: 270 (13.2%)
Teachers: 140.0 (14.6 to 1)
Librarians/Media Specialists: 1.0 (2,039.0 to 1)
Guidance Counselors: 5.0 (407.8 to 1)
Current Spending: ($ per student per year):
    Total: $7,308; Instruction: $4,971; Support Services: $1,720
Enrollment, Drop-out Rates and Diploma Recipients by Race/Ethnicity

Category	Total	White	Black	Asian	AIAN	Hisp.
Enrollment (%)	100.0	44.7	1.0	11.8	0.1	42.3
Drop-out Rate (%)	2.5	1.7	16.7	4.9	0.0	3.1
H.S. Diplomas (#)	122	82	0	19	0	21

Carroll County

Carroll Community SD
1026 N Adams • Carroll, IA 51401
(712) 792-8001 • http://www.carroll.k12.ia.us
Grade Span: PK-12; Agency Type: 1
Schools: 5
    1 Primary; 2 Middle; 2 High; 0 Other Level
    4 Regular; 0 Special Education; 0 Vocational; 1 Alternative
    0 Magnet; 0 Charter; 1 Title I Eligible; 0 School-wide Title I
Students: 1,778 (48.1% male; 51.8% female)
    Individual Education Program: 224 (12.6%);
    English Language Learner: 26 (1.5%); Migrant: 0 (0.0%)
    Eligible for Free Lunch Program: 317 (17.8%)
    Eligible for Reduced-Price Lunch Program: 136 (7.6%)
Teachers: 121.0 (14.7 to 1)
Librarians/Media Specialists: 3.0 (592.7 to 1)
Guidance Counselors: 5.0 (355.6 to 1)
Current Spending: ($ per student per year):
    Total: $6,871; Instruction: $4,235; Support Services: $2,104

Enrollment, Drop-out Rates and Diploma Recipients by Race/Ethnicity

Category	Total	White	Black	Asian	AIAN	Hisp.
Enrollment (%)	100.0	95.7	1.5	0.5	0.1	2.2
Drop-out Rate (%)	0.5	0.3	0.0	0.0	n/a	20.0
H.S. Diplomas (#)	147	144	0	0	0	3

Cass County

Atlantic Community SD
1100 Linn St • Atlantic, IA 50022
(712) 243-4252 • http://www.atlantic.k12.ia.us
Grade Span: PK-12; Agency Type: 1
Schools: 4
    1 Primary; 2 Middle; 1 High; 0 Other Level
    4 Regular; 0 Special Education; 0 Vocational; 0 Alternative
    0 Magnet; 0 Charter; 1 Title I Eligible; 0 School-wide Title I
Students: 1,513 (53.9% male; 46.0% female)
    Individual Education Program: 183 (12.1%);
    English Language Learner: 0 (0.0%); Migrant: 0 (0.0%)
    Eligible for Free Lunch Program: 367 (24.3%)
    Eligible for Reduced-Price Lunch Program: 165 (10.9%)
Teachers: 105.0 (14.4 to 1)
Librarians/Media Specialists: 2.0 (756.5 to 1)
Guidance Counselors: 3.0 (504.3 to 1)
Current Spending: ($ per student per year):
    Total: $6,609; Instruction: $4,204; Support Services: $1,846
Enrollment, Drop-out Rates and Diploma Recipients by Race/Ethnicity

Category	Total	White	Black	Asian	AIAN	Hisp.
Enrollment (%)	100.0	97.7	0.8	0.5	0.3	0.7
Drop-out Rate (%)	1.0	1.0	0.0	0.0	0.0	0.0
H.S. Diplomas (#)	122	115	1	3	2	1

Cerro Gordo County

Mason City Community SD
1515 S Pennsylvania • Mason City, IA 50401
(641) 421-4400 • http://www.mason-city.k12.ia.us
Grade Span: PK-12; Agency Type: 1
Schools: 10
    5 Primary; 2 Middle; 2 High; 1 Other Level
    8 Regular; 1 Special Education; 0 Vocational; 1 Alternative
    0 Magnet; 0 Charter; 4 Title I Eligible; 0 School-wide Title I
Students: 4,257 (50.0% male; 49.9% female)
    Individual Education Program: 798 (18.7%);
    English Language Learner: 7 (0.2%); Migrant: 0 (0.0%)
    Eligible for Free Lunch Program: 1,001 (23.5%)
    Eligible for Reduced-Price Lunch Program: 344 (8.1%)
Teachers: 289.5 (14.7 to 1)
Librarians/Media Specialists: 5.0 (851.4 to 1)
Guidance Counselors: 10.0 (425.7 to 1)
Current Spending: ($ per student per year):
    Total: $6,787; Instruction: $4,560; Support Services: $1,676
Enrollment, Drop-out Rates and Diploma Recipients by Race/Ethnicity

Category	Total	White	Black	Asian	AIAN	Hisp.
Enrollment (%)	100.0	87.2	4.2	1.9	0.3	6.4
Drop-out Rate (%)	3.8	3.2	12.0	0.0	0.0	11.7
H.S. Diplomas (#)	315	282	7	9	0	17

Clay County

Spencer Community SD
23 E 7th St • Spencer, IA 51301
Mailing Address: Ste A-Box 200 • Spencer, IA 51301
(712) 262-8950 • http://www.spencer.k12.ia.us
Grade Span: PK-12; Agency Type: 1
Schools: 6
    4 Primary; 1 Middle; 1 High; 0 Other Level
    6 Regular; 0 Special Education; 0 Vocational; 0 Alternative
    0 Magnet; 0 Charter; 3 Title I Eligible; 0 School-wide Title I
Students: 2,120 (51.1% male; 48.8% female)
    Individual Education Program: 264 (12.5%);
    English Language Learner: 17 (0.8%); Migrant: 0 (0.0%)
    Eligible for Free Lunch Program: 379 (17.9%)
    Eligible for Reduced-Price Lunch Program: 190 (9.0%)
Teachers: 145.0 (14.6 to 1)
Librarians/Media Specialists: 2.0 (1,060.0 to 1)
Guidance Counselors: 4.0 (530.0 to 1)
Current Spending: ($ per student per year):
    Total: $6,638; Instruction: $4,412; Support Services: $1,715
Enrollment, Drop-out Rates and Diploma Recipients by Race/Ethnicity

Category	Total	White	Black	Asian	AIAN	Hisp.
Enrollment (%)	100.0	94.6	0.8	2.1	0.4	2.2
Drop-out Rate (%)	0.7	0.5	0.0	6.3	0.0	0.0
H.S. Diplomas (#)	174	172	0	2	0	0

Clinton County

Central Clinton Community SD
923 4th Ave E • De Witt, IA 52742-0110
Mailing Address: PO Box 110 • De Witt, IA 52742-0110
(563) 659-0700 • http://www.central-clinton.k12.ia.us
Grade Span: PK-12; Agency Type: 1
Schools: 4
　2 Primary; 1 Middle; 1 High; 0 Other Level
　4 Regular; 0 Special Education; 0 Vocational; 0 Alternative
　0 Magnet; 0 Charter; 2 Title I Eligible; 0 School-wide Title I
Students: 1,623 (53.0% male; 46.9% female)
　Individual Education Program: 222 (13.7%);
　English Language Learner: 0 (0.0%); Migrant: 0 (0.0%)
　Eligible for Free Lunch Program: 232 (14.3%)
　Eligible for Reduced-Price Lunch Program: 85 (5.2%)
Teachers: 124.0 (13.1 to 1)
Librarians/Media Specialists: 2.0 (811.5 to 1)
Guidance Counselors: 4.0 (405.8 to 1)
Current Spending: ($ per student per year):
　Total: $7,009; Instruction: $4,280; Support Services: $2,208
Enrollment, Drop-out Rates and Diploma Recipients by Race/Ethnicity

Category	Total	White	Black	Asian	AIAN	Hisp.
Enrollment (%)	100.0	97.3	1.1	0.7	0.2	0.7
Drop-out Rate (%)	1.6	1.6	0.0	0.0	n/a	0.0
H.S. Diplomas (#)	138	135	1	1	0	1

Clinton Community SD
600 S 4th St • Clinton, IA 52732
(563) 243-9600 • http://www.clinton.k12.ia.us
Grade Span: PK-12; Agency Type: 1
Schools: 9
　5 Primary; 2 Middle; 2 High; 0 Other Level
　8 Regular; 0 Special Education; 0 Vocational; 1 Alternative
　0 Magnet; 0 Charter; 3 Title I Eligible; 2 School-wide Title I
Students: 4,366 (51.6% male; 48.3% female)
　Individual Education Program: 836 (19.1%);
　English Language Learner: 1 (<0.1%); Migrant: 0 (0.0%)
　Eligible for Free Lunch Program: 1,440 (33.0%)
　Eligible for Reduced-Price Lunch Program: 367 (8.4%)
Teachers: 310.0 (14.1 to 1)
Librarians/Media Specialists: 7.0 (623.7 to 1)
Guidance Counselors: 10.5 (415.8 to 1)
Current Spending: ($ per student per year):
　Total: $7,122; Instruction: $4,646; Support Services: $2,042
Enrollment, Drop-out Rates and Diploma Recipients by Race/Ethnicity

Category	Total	White	Black	Asian	AIAN	Hisp.
Enrollment (%)	100.0	88.4	7.5	1.4	0.5	2.2
Drop-out Rate (%)	3.7	3.7	6.1	0.0	0.0	0.0
H.S. Diplomas (#)	326	295	15	4	2	10

Crawford County

Denison Community SD
819 N 16th St • Denison, IA 51442
(712) 263-2176 • http://www.denison.k12.ia.us
Grade Span: PK-12; Agency Type: 1
Schools: 3
　1 Primary; 1 Middle; 1 High; 0 Other Level
　3 Regular; 0 Special Education; 0 Vocational; 0 Alternative
　0 Magnet; 0 Charter; 2 Title I Eligible; 1 School-wide Title I
Students: 1,802 (52.5% male; 47.4% female)
　Individual Education Program: 191 (10.6%)
　English Language Learner: 357 (19.8%); Migrant: 565 (31.4%)
　Eligible for Free Lunch Program: 675 (37.5%)
　Eligible for Reduced-Price Lunch Program: 224 (12.4%)
Teachers: 115.5 (15.6 to 1)
Librarians/Media Specialists: 3.0 (600.7 to 1)
Guidance Counselors: 4.0 (450.5 to 1)
Current Spending: ($ per student per year):
　Total: $7,016; Instruction: $4,424; Support Services: $1,887
Enrollment, Drop-out Rates and Diploma Recipients by Race/Ethnicity

Category	Total	White	Black	Asian	AIAN	Hisp.
Enrollment (%)	100.0	67.1	1.3	1.5	0.7	29.4
Drop-out Rate (%)	2.9	0.9	n/a	0.0	n/a	28.3
H.S. Diplomas (#)	127	120	0	3	0	4

Dallas County

Dallas Center-Grimes Community SD
1414 Walnut St Ste. 200 • Dallas Center, IA 50063
Mailing Address: PO Box 512 • Dallas Center, IA 50063
(515) 992-3866
Grade Span: PK-12; Agency Type: 1
Schools: 4

　2 Primary; 1 Middle; 1 High; 0 Other Level
　4 Regular; 0 Special Education; 0 Vocational; 0 Alternative
　0 Magnet; 0 Charter; 2 Title I Eligible; 0 School-wide Title I
Students: 1,560 (51.7% male; 48.2% female)
　Individual Education Program: 125 (8.0%);
　English Language Learner: 9 (0.6%); Migrant: 0 (0.0%)
　Eligible for Free Lunch Program: 101 (6.5%)
　Eligible for Reduced-Price Lunch Program: 61 (3.9%)
Teachers: 112.0 (13.9 to 1)
Librarians/Media Specialists: 3.0 (520.0 to 1)
Guidance Counselors: 3.0 (520.0 to 1)
Current Spending: ($ per student per year):
　Total: $6,012; Instruction: $3,510; Support Services: $2,025
Enrollment, Drop-out Rates and Diploma Recipients by Race/Ethnicity

Category	Total	White	Black	Asian	AIAN	Hisp.
Enrollment (%)	100.0	97.6	0.8	0.7	0.1	0.8
Drop-out Rate (%)	0.6	0.7	0.0	0.0	0.0	0.0
H.S. Diplomas (#)	90	87	0	1	1	1

Perry Community SD
1219 Warford St • Perry, IA 50220
(515) 465-4656 • http://www.perry.k12.ia.us
Grade Span: PK-12; Agency Type: 1
Schools: 3
　1 Primary; 1 Middle; 1 High; 0 Other Level
　3 Regular; 0 Special Education; 0 Vocational; 0 Alternative
　0 Magnet; 0 Charter; 1 Title I Eligible; 1 School-wide Title I
Students: 1,755 (53.8% male; 46.1% female)
　Individual Education Program: 252 (14.4%);
　English Language Learner: 421 (24.0%); Migrant: 329 (18.7%)
　Eligible for Free Lunch Program: 649 (37.0%)
　Eligible for Reduced-Price Lunch Program: 263 (15.0%)
Teachers: 138.5 (12.7 to 1)
Librarians/Media Specialists: 2.0 (877.5 to 1)
Guidance Counselors: 3.0 (585.0 to 1)
Current Spending: ($ per student per year):
　Total: $7,569; Instruction: $4,647; Support Services: $2,325
Enrollment, Drop-out Rates and Diploma Recipients by Race/Ethnicity

Category	Total	White	Black	Asian	AIAN	Hisp.
Enrollment (%)	100.0	63.6	1.0	1.1	0.0	34.3
Drop-out Rate (%)	3.2	2.5	0.0	0.0	n/a	6.4
H.S. Diplomas (#)	124	97	4	4	0	19

Waukee Community SD
560 SE University Ave • Waukee, IA 50263
(515) 987-5161 • http://www.waukee.k12.ia.us
Grade Span: PK-12; Agency Type: 1
Schools: 5
　3 Primary; 1 Middle; 1 High; 0 Other Level
　5 Regular; 0 Special Education; 0 Vocational; 0 Alternative
　0 Magnet; 0 Charter; 1 Title I Eligible; 0 School-wide Title I
Students: 3,629 (51.3% male; 48.6% female)
　Individual Education Program: 331 (9.1%);
　English Language Learner: 52 (1.4%); Migrant: 0 (0.0%)
　Eligible for Free Lunch Program: 252 (6.9%)
　Eligible for Reduced-Price Lunch Program: 83 (2.3%)
Teachers: 227.0 (16.0 to 1)
Librarians/Media Specialists: 5.0 (725.8 to 1)
Guidance Counselors: 4.0 (907.3 to 1)
Current Spending: ($ per student per year):
　Total: $5,943; Instruction: $3,698; Support Services: $1,752
Enrollment, Drop-out Rates and Diploma Recipients by Race/Ethnicity

Category	Total	White	Black	Asian	AIAN	Hisp.
Enrollment (%)	100.0	93.0	2.6	2.5	0.1	1.8
Drop-out Rate (%)	0.1	0.1	0.0	0.0	n/a	0.0
H.S. Diplomas (#)	130	128	0	2	0	0

Delaware County

West Delaware County Community SD
601 New St • Manchester, IA 52057
(563) 927-3515 • http://www.w-delaware.k12.ia.us
Grade Span: PK-12; Agency Type: 1
Schools: 4
　2 Primary; 1 Middle; 1 High; 0 Other Level
　4 Regular; 0 Special Education; 0 Vocational; 0 Alternative
　0 Magnet; 0 Charter; 1 Title I Eligible; 0 School-wide Title I
Students: 1,723 (48.6% male; 51.3% female)
　Individual Education Program: 158 (9.2%);
　English Language Learner: 0 (0.0%); Migrant: 0 (0.0%)
　Eligible for Free Lunch Program: 263 (15.3%)
　Eligible for Reduced-Price Lunch Program: 107 (6.2%)
Teachers: 118.0 (14.6 to 1)
Librarians/Media Specialists: 3.0 (574.3 to 1)
Guidance Counselors: 5.0 (344.6 to 1)

Current Spending: ($ per student per year):
   Total: $6,756; Instruction: $4,086; Support Services: $2,133
Enrollment, Drop-out Rates and Diploma Recipients by Race/Ethnicity

Category	Total	White	Black	Asian	AIAN	Hisp.
Enrollment (%)	100.0	97.9	0.6	0.5	0.1	0.9
Drop-out Rate (%)	4.5	4.6	0.0	0.0	0.0	0.0
H.S. Diplomas (#)	168	162	0	4	0	2

Des Moines County

Burlington Community SD
1429 W Ave • Burlington, IA 52601
(319) 753-6791 • http://www.burlington.k12.ia.us
Grade Span: PK-12; **Agency Type:** 1
Schools: 11
   6 Primary; 3 Middle; 2 High; 0 Other Level
   10 Regular; 0 Special Education; 0 Vocational; 1 Alternative
   0 Magnet; 0 Charter; 4 Title I Eligible; 4 School-wide Title I
Students: 4,379   (51.3% male; 48.6% female)
   Individual Education Program: 763 (17.4%);
   English Language Learner: 17 (0.4%); Migrant: 0 (0.0%)
   Eligible for Free Lunch Program: 1,496 (34.2%)
   Eligible for Reduced-Price Lunch Program: 362 (8.3%)
Teachers: 325.5 (13.5 to 1)
Librarians/Media Specialists: 7.0 (625.6 to 1)
Guidance Counselors: 13.0 (336.8 to 1)
Current Spending: ($ per student per year):
   Total: $7,187; Instruction: $5,002; Support Services: $1,747
Enrollment, Drop-out Rates and Diploma Recipients by Race/Ethnicity

Category	Total	White	Black	Asian	AIAN	Hisp.
Enrollment (%)	100.0	83.8	11.8	1.1	0.2	3.1
Drop-out Rate (%)	6.5	6.1	8.9	9.5	0.0	11.1
H.S. Diplomas (#)	289	266	10	9	0	4

Dubuque County

Dubuque Community SD
2300 Chaney Rd • Dubuque, IA 52001
(563) 588-5100 • http://www.dubuque.k12.ia.us
Grade Span: PK-12; **Agency Type:** 1
Schools: 18
   12 Primary; 3 Middle; 3 High; 0 Other Level
   17 Regular; 0 Special Education; 0 Vocational; 1 Alternative
   0 Magnet; 0 Charter; 9 Title I Eligible; 0 School-wide Title I
Students: 10,143   (51.2% male; 48.7% female)
   Individual Education Program: 1,700 (16.8%);
   English Language Learner: 99 (1.0%); Migrant: 0 (0.0%)
   Eligible for Free Lunch Program: 2,196 (21.7%)
   Eligible for Reduced-Price Lunch Program: 827 (8.2%)
Teachers: 673.0 (15.1 to 1)
Librarians/Media Specialists: 5.0 (2,028.6 to 1)
Guidance Counselors: 28.0 (362.3 to 1)
Current Spending: ($ per student per year):
   Total: $7,018; Instruction: $4,290; Support Services: $2,252
Enrollment, Drop-out Rates and Diploma Recipients by Race/Ethnicity

Category	Total	White	Black	Asian	AIAN	Hisp.
Enrollment (%)	100.0	93.2	4.3	1.4	0.3	0.8
Drop-out Rate (%)	3.2	3.0	9.5	4.4	0.0	5.0
H.S. Diplomas (#)	702	683	6	8	0	5

Western Dubuque Community SD
405 3rd Ave NE • Farley, IA 52046
(563) 744-3885
Grade Span: PK-12; **Agency Type:** 1
Schools: 8
   5 Primary; 1 Middle; 2 High; 0 Other Level
   8 Regular; 0 Special Education; 0 Vocational; 0 Alternative
   0 Magnet; 0 Charter; 5 Title I Eligible; 0 School-wide Title I
Students: 2,709   (51.6% male; 48.3% female)
   Individual Education Program: 324 (12.0%);
   English Language Learner: 5 (0.2%); Migrant: 0 (0.0%)
   Eligible for Free Lunch Program: 415 (15.3%)
   Eligible for Reduced-Price Lunch Program: 223 (8.2%)
Teachers: 197.5 (13.7 to 1)
Librarians/Media Specialists: 3.0 (903.0 to 1)
Guidance Counselors: 6.0 (451.5 to 1)
Current Spending: ($ per student per year):
   Total: $7,074; Instruction: $4,495; Support Services: $2,004
Enrollment, Drop-out Rates and Diploma Recipients by Race/Ethnicity

Category	Total	White	Black	Asian	AIAN	Hisp.
Enrollment (%)	100.0	98.3	1.0	0.1	0.0	0.5
Drop-out Rate (%)	0.9	0.8	0.0	0.0	n/a	25.0
H.S. Diplomas (#)	270	268	0	1	0	1

Floyd County

Charles City Community SD
500 N Grand Ave • Charles City, IA 50616
(641) 257-6500 • http://comet.charles-city.k12.ia.us
Grade Span: PK-12; **Agency Type:** 1
Schools: 5
   3 Primary; 1 Middle; 1 High; 0 Other Level
   5 Regular; 0 Special Education; 0 Vocational; 0 Alternative
   0 Magnet; 0 Charter; 4 Title I Eligible; 4 School-wide Title I
Students: 1,677   (52.6% male; 47.3% female)
   Individual Education Program: 265 (15.8%);
   English Language Learner: 24 (1.4%); Migrant: 0 (0.0%)
   Eligible for Free Lunch Program: 494 (29.5%)
   Eligible for Reduced-Price Lunch Program: 130 (7.8%)
Teachers: 123.0 (13.6 to 1)
Librarians/Media Specialists: 3.0 (559.0 to 1)
Guidance Counselors: 5.0 (335.4 to 1)
Current Spending: ($ per student per year):
   Total: $7,264; Instruction: $4,641; Support Services: $2,057
Enrollment, Drop-out Rates and Diploma Recipients by Race/Ethnicity

Category	Total	White	Black	Asian	AIAN	Hisp.
Enrollment (%)	100.0	94.3	1.4	1.7	0.1	2.6
Drop-out Rate (%)	1.5	1.4	0.0	8.3	n/a	0.0
H.S. Diplomas (#)	121	117	2	2	0	0

Hamilton County

Webster City Community SD
825 Beach St • Webster City, IA 50595-1948
(515) 832-9200 • http://www.webster-city.k12.ia.us
Grade Span: PK-12; **Agency Type:** 1
Schools: 5
   3 Primary; 1 Middle; 1 High; 0 Other Level
   5 Regular; 0 Special Education; 0 Vocational; 0 Alternative
   0 Magnet; 0 Charter; 2 Title I Eligible; 0 School-wide Title I
Students: 1,770   (50.0% male; 50.0% female)
   Individual Education Program: 223 (12.6%);
   English Language Learner: 83 (4.7%); Migrant: 0 (0.0%)
   Eligible for Free Lunch Program: 375 (21.2%)
   Eligible for Reduced-Price Lunch Program: 141 (8.0%)
Teachers: 113.0 (15.7 to 1)
Librarians/Media Specialists: 2.0 (885.0 to 1)
Guidance Counselors: 6.0 (295.0 to 1)
Current Spending: ($ per student per year):
   Total: $6,478; Instruction: $4,037; Support Services: $1,833
Enrollment, Drop-out Rates and Diploma Recipients by Race/Ethnicity

Category	Total	White	Black	Asian	AIAN	Hisp.
Enrollment (%)	100.0	92.4	0.6	4.2	0.0	2.8
Drop-out Rate (%)	4.4	3.1	25.0	63.6	n/a	9.1
H.S. Diplomas (#)	138	132	0	1	0	5

Henry County

Mount Pleasant Community SD
400 E Madison • Mount Pleasant, IA 52641
(319) 385-7750 • http://www.mtpleasantschools.com
Grade Span: PK-12; **Agency Type:** 1
Schools: 6
   4 Primary; 1 Middle; 1 High; 0 Other Level
   6 Regular; 0 Special Education; 0 Vocational; 0 Alternative
   0 Magnet; 0 Charter; 4 Title I Eligible; 0 School-wide Title I
Students: 2,137   (48.5% male; 51.4% female)
   Individual Education Program: 273 (12.8%);
   English Language Learner: 50 (2.3%); Migrant: 0 (0.0%)
   Eligible for Free Lunch Program: 375 (17.5%)
   Eligible for Reduced-Price Lunch Program: 135 (6.3%)
Teachers: 148.0 (14.4 to 1)
Librarians/Media Specialists: 1.0 (2,137.0 to 1)
Guidance Counselors: 3.0 (712.3 to 1)
Current Spending: ($ per student per year):
   Total: $6,390; Instruction: $4,175; Support Services: $1,747
Enrollment, Drop-out Rates and Diploma Recipients by Race/Ethnicity

Category	Total	White	Black	Asian	AIAN	Hisp.
Enrollment (%)	100.0	89.8	2.7	4.7	0.1	2.7
Drop-out Rate (%)	0.6	0.5	0.0	0.0	n/a	0.0
H.S. Diplomas (#)	163	154	1	6	0	2

Howard County

Howard-Winneshiek Community SD
1000 Schroder Dr • Cresco, IA 52136
(563) 547-2762
Grade Span: PK-12; **Agency Type:** 1
Schools: 6

4 Primary; 1 Middle; 1 High; 0 Other Level
6 Regular; 0 Special Education; 0 Vocational; 0 Alternative
0 Magnet; 0 Charter; 4 Title I Eligible; 0 School-wide Title I
Students: 1,527 (49.5% male; 50.4% female)
Individual Education Program: 232 (15.2%);
English Language Learner: 1 (0.1%); Migrant: 0 (0.0%)
Eligible for Free Lunch Program: 276 (18.1%)
Eligible for Reduced-Price Lunch Program: 145 (9.5%)
Teachers: 111.0 (13.8 to 1)
Librarians/Media Specialists: 2.0 (763.5 to 1)
Guidance Counselors: 3.0 (509.0 to 1)
Current Spending: ($ per student per year):
Total: $7,202; Instruction: $4,194; Support Services: $2,464
Enrollment, Drop-out Rates and Diploma Recipients by Race/Ethnicity

Category	Total	White	Black	Asian	AIAN	Hisp.
Enrollment (%)	100.0	97.1	0.6	1.6	0.1	0.7
Drop-out Rate (%)	2.1	2.2	0.0	0.0	n/a	0.0
H.S. Diplomas (#)	130	128	0	1	0	1

Jackson County

Maquoketa Community SD
612 So Vermont • Maquoketa, IA 52060
(563) 652-4984 • http://www.maquoketa.k12.ia.us
Grade Span: PK-12; **Agency Type:** 1
Schools: 4
2 Primary; 1 Middle; 1 High; 0 Other Level
4 Regular; 0 Special Education; 0 Vocational; 0 Alternative
0 Magnet; 0 Charter; 2 Title I Eligible; 1 School-wide Title I
Students: 1,659 (52.9% male; 47.0% female)
Individual Education Program: 262 (15.8%);
English Language Learner: 1 (0.1%); Migrant: 0 (0.0%)
Eligible for Free Lunch Program: 536 (32.3%)
Eligible for Reduced-Price Lunch Program: 146 (8.8%)
Teachers: 129.5 (12.8 to 1)
Librarians/Media Specialists: 2.0 (829.5 to 1)
Guidance Counselors: 4.5 (368.7 to 1)
Current Spending: ($ per student per year):
Total: $7,634; Instruction: $4,998; Support Services: $2,082
Enrollment, Drop-out Rates and Diploma Recipients by Race/Ethnicity

Category	Total	White	Black	Asian	AIAN	Hisp.
Enrollment (%)	100.0	96.7	1.3	1.2	0.5	0.2
Drop-out Rate (%)	2.7	2.7	0.0	0.0	0.0	0.0
H.S. Diplomas (#)	115	115	0	0	0	0

Jasper County

Newton Community SD
807 S 6th Ave W • Newton, IA 50208
(641) 792-5809 • http://www.newton.k12.ia.us
Grade Span: PK-12; **Agency Type:** 1
Schools: 8
5 Primary; 1 Middle; 2 High; 0 Other Level
7 Regular; 0 Special Education; 0 Vocational; 1 Alternative
0 Magnet; 0 Charter; 3 Title I Eligible; 0 School-wide Title I
Students: 3,340 (51.1% male; 48.8% female)
Individual Education Program: 470 (14.1%);
English Language Learner: 7 (0.2%); Migrant: 0 (0.0%)
Eligible for Free Lunch Program: 609 (18.2%)
Eligible for Reduced-Price Lunch Program: 202 (6.0%)
Teachers: 236.0 (14.2 to 1)
Librarians/Media Specialists: 4.0 (835.0 to 1)
Guidance Counselors: 12.0 (278.3 to 1)
Current Spending: ($ per student per year):
Total: $6,572; Instruction: $4,106; Support Services: $1,996
Enrollment, Drop-out Rates and Diploma Recipients by Race/Ethnicity

Category	Total	White	Black	Asian	AIAN	Hisp.
Enrollment (%)	100.0	96.1	1.3	1.0	0.5	1.2
Drop-out Rate (%)	4.1	4.1	0.0	0.0	0.0	10.0
H.S. Diplomas (#)	261	255	0	3	0	3

Jefferson County

Fairfield Community SD
607 E Broadway • Fairfield, IA 52556
(641) 472-2655 • http://www.aea15.k12.ia.us./fairfld.htm
Grade Span: PK-12; **Agency Type:** 1
Schools: 6
4 Primary; 1 Middle; 1 High; 0 Other Level
6 Regular; 0 Special Education; 0 Vocational; 0 Alternative
0 Magnet; 0 Charter; 5 Title I Eligible; 0 School-wide Title I
Students: 1,968 (51.2% male; 48.7% female)
Individual Education Program: 270 (13.7%);
English Language Learner: 16 (0.8%); Migrant: 0 (0.0%)
Eligible for Free Lunch Program: 422 (21.4%)

Eligible for Reduced-Price Lunch Program: 117 (5.9%)
Teachers: 133.5 (14.7 to 1)
Librarians/Media Specialists: 2.0 (984.0 to 1)
Guidance Counselors: 5.0 (393.6 to 1)
Current Spending: ($ per student per year):
Total: $7,045; Instruction: $4,088; Support Services: $2,418
Enrollment, Drop-out Rates and Diploma Recipients by Race/Ethnicity

Category	Total	White	Black	Asian	AIAN	Hisp.
Enrollment (%)	100.0	92.3	2.0	2.2	0.4	3.0
Drop-out Rate (%)	2.5	2.4	0.0	0.0	0.0	14.3
H.S. Diplomas (#)	133	127	2	2	1	1

Johnson County

Iowa City Community SD
509 S Dubuque St • Iowa City, IA 52240
(319) 688-1000 • http://www.iowa-city.k12.ia.us
Grade Span: PK-12; **Agency Type:** 1
Schools: 21
17 Primary; 2 Middle; 2 High; 0 Other Level
21 Regular; 0 Special Education; 0 Vocational; 0 Alternative
0 Magnet; 0 Charter; 9 Title I Eligible; 0 School-wide Title I
Students: 10,620 (51.9% male; 48.0% female)
Individual Education Program: 1,446 (13.6%);
English Language Learner: 216 (2.0%); Migrant: 0 (0.0%)
Eligible for Free Lunch Program: 1,822 (17.2%)
Eligible for Reduced-Price Lunch Program: 391 (3.7%)
Teachers: 696.0 (15.3 to 1)
Librarians/Media Specialists: 17.0 (624.7 to 1)
Guidance Counselors: 24.5 (433.5 to 1)
Current Spending: ($ per student per year):
Total: $6,971; Instruction: $4,441; Support Services: $2,101
Enrollment, Drop-out Rates and Diploma Recipients by Race/Ethnicity

Category	Total	White	Black	Asian	AIAN	Hisp.
Enrollment (%)	100.0	75.7	11.9	6.7	0.4	5.3
Drop-out Rate (%)	2.2	2.0	5.9	0.6	0.0	4.4
H.S. Diplomas (#)	721	599	45	48	5	24

Lee County

Fort Madison Community SD
1930 Ave M • Fort Madison, IA 52627
Mailing Address: PO Box 1423 • Fort Madison, IA 52627
(319) 372-7252 • http://www.ft-madison.k12.ia.us
Grade Span: PK-12; **Agency Type:** 1
Schools: 6
3 Primary; 1 Middle; 2 High; 0 Other Level
5 Regular; 0 Special Education; 0 Vocational; 1 Alternative
0 Magnet; 0 Charter; 2 Title I Eligible; 0 School-wide Title I
Students: 2,385 (51.1% male; 48.8% female)
Individual Education Program: 375 (15.7%);
English Language Learner: 2 (0.1%); Migrant: 0 (0.0%)
Eligible for Free Lunch Program: 670 (28.1%)
Eligible for Reduced-Price Lunch Program: 172 (7.2%)
Teachers: 162.5 (14.7 to 1)
Librarians/Media Specialists: 1.0 (2,385.0 to 1)
Guidance Counselors: 4.0 (596.3 to 1)
Current Spending: ($ per student per year):
Total: $6,391; Instruction: $4,436; Support Services: $1,533
Enrollment, Drop-out Rates and Diploma Recipients by Race/Ethnicity

Category	Total	White	Black	Asian	AIAN	Hisp.
Enrollment (%)	100.0	88.3	4.3	0.9	0.3	6.1
Drop-out Rate (%)	4.1	4.3	4.8	0.0	0.0	0.0
H.S. Diplomas (#)	186	175	1	0	0	10

Keokuk Community SD
727 Washington St • Keokuk, IA 52632
(319) 524-1402 • http://www.keokuk.k12.ia.us
Grade Span: PK-12; **Agency Type:** 1
Schools: 7
5 Primary; 1 Middle; 1 High; 0 Other Level
7 Regular; 0 Special Education; 0 Vocational; 0 Alternative
0 Magnet; 0 Charter; 4 Title I Eligible; 0 School-wide Title I
Students: 2,264 (50.3% male; 49.6% female)
Individual Education Program: 359 (15.9%);
English Language Learner: 0 (0.0%); Migrant: 0 (0.0%)
Eligible for Free Lunch Program: 1,046 (46.2%)
Eligible for Reduced-Price Lunch Program: 229 (10.1%)
Teachers: 149.5 (15.1 to 1)
Librarians/Media Specialists: 2.0 (1,132.0 to 1)
Guidance Counselors: 4.0 (566.0 to 1)
Current Spending: ($ per student per year):
Total: $7,140; Instruction: $4,488; Support Services: $2,194

Enrollment, Drop-out Rates and Diploma Recipients by Race/Ethnicity

Category	Total	White	Black	Asian	AIAN	Hisp.
Enrollment (%)	100.0	87.8	8.8	1.4	0.4	1.5
Drop-out Rate (%)	5.1	5.1	6.4	8.3	0.0	0.0
H.S. Diplomas (#)	161	150	9	2	0	0

Linn County

Cedar Rapids Community SD
346 2nd Ave SW • Cedar Rapids, IA 52404
(319) 558-2000 • http://www.cr.k12.ia.us
Grade Span: PK-12; **Agency Type:** 1
Schools: 34
24 Primary; 6 Middle; 4 High; 0 Other Level
32 Regular; 0 Special Education; 0 Vocational; 2 Alternative
0 Magnet; 0 Charter; 9 Title I Eligible; 9 School-wide Title I
Students: 17,324 (51.3% male; 48.6% female)
Individual Education Program: 2,999 (17.3%);
English Language Learner: 161 (0.9%); Migrant: 0 (0.0%)
Eligible for Free Lunch Program: 4,707 (27.2%)
Eligible for Reduced-Price Lunch Program: 1,302 (7.5%)
Teachers: 1,126.0 (15.4 to 1)
Librarians/Media Specialists: 30.0 (577.5 to 1)
Guidance Counselors: 43.0 (402.9 to 1)
Current Spending: ($ per student per year):
Total: $7,482; Instruction: $4,745; Support Services: $2,193
Enrollment, Drop-out Rates and Diploma Recipients by Race/Ethnicity

Category	Total	White	Black	Asian	AIAN	Hisp.
Enrollment (%)	100.0	83.0	12.1	2.1	0.4	2.4
Drop-out Rate (%)	2.6	2.4	3.6	2.5	0.0	6.8
H.S. Diplomas (#)	1,013	925	48	25	6	9

College Community SD
401 76th Ave SW • Cedar Rapids, IA 52404
(319) 848-5201 • http://www.prairiepride.org
Grade Span: PK-12; **Agency Type:** 1
Schools: 7
4 Primary; 1 Middle; 1 High; 1 Other Level
6 Regular; 1 Special Education; 0 Vocational; 0 Alternative
0 Magnet; 0 Charter; 4 Title I Eligible; 0 School-wide Title I
Students: 3,697 (51.6% male; 48.3% female)
Individual Education Program: 423 (11.4%);
English Language Learner: 0 (0.0%); Migrant: 0 (0.0%)
Eligible for Free Lunch Program: 608 (16.4%)
Eligible for Reduced-Price Lunch Program: 213 (5.8%)
Teachers: 239.0 (15.5 to 1)
Librarians/Media Specialists: 5.0 (739.4 to 1)
Guidance Counselors: 9.0 (410.8 to 1)
Current Spending: ($ per student per year):
Total: $6,911; Instruction: $4,329; Support Services: $1,955
Enrollment, Drop-out Rates and Diploma Recipients by Race/Ethnicity

Category	Total	White	Black	Asian	AIAN	Hisp.
Enrollment (%)	100.0	93.2	3.3	1.5	0.5	1.4
Drop-out Rate (%)	1.3	1.2	9.5	0.0	0.0	0.0
H.S. Diplomas (#)	228	223	2	1	0	2

Linn-Mar Community SD
3333 N 10th St • Marion, IA 52302
(319) 377-7373 • http://www.linnmar.k12.ia.us
Grade Span: PK-12; **Agency Type:** 1
Schools: 8
6 Primary; 1 Middle; 1 High; 0 Other Level
8 Regular; 0 Special Education; 0 Vocational; 0 Alternative
0 Magnet; 0 Charter; 3 Title I Eligible; 0 School-wide Title I
Students: 4,902 (50.9% male; 49.0% female)
Individual Education Program: 533 (10.9%);
English Language Learner: 0 (0.0%); Migrant: 0 (0.0%)
Eligible for Free Lunch Program: 393 (8.0%)
Eligible for Reduced-Price Lunch Program: 126 (2.6%)
Teachers: 319.0 (15.4 to 1)
Librarians/Media Specialists: 7.5 (653.6 to 1)
Guidance Counselors: 12.0 (408.5 to 1)
Current Spending: ($ per student per year):
Total: $6,567; Instruction: $4,063; Support Services: $2,037
Enrollment, Drop-out Rates and Diploma Recipients by Race/Ethnicity

Category	Total	White	Black	Asian	AIAN	Hisp.
Enrollment (%)	100.0	92.2	2.6	3.3	0.2	1.6
Drop-out Rate (%)	0.9	0.8	11.1	0.0	0.0	5.6
H.S. Diplomas (#)	291	280	1	8	0	2

Marion Independent SD
777 S 15th St • Marion, IA 52302
Mailing Address: PO Box 606 • Marion, IA 52302
(319) 377-4691 • http://www.marion.k12.ia.us
Grade Span: PK-12; **Agency Type:** 1
Schools: 5
2 Primary; 2 Middle; 1 High; 0 Other Level
5 Regular; 0 Special Education; 0 Vocational; 0 Alternative
0 Magnet; 0 Charter; 1 Title I Eligible; 0 School-wide Title I
Students: 1,959 (51.7% male; 48.2% female)
Individual Education Program: 262 (13.4%);
English Language Learner: 7 (0.4%); Migrant: 0 (0.0%)
Eligible for Free Lunch Program: 269 (13.7%)
Eligible for Reduced-Price Lunch Program: 112 (5.7%)
Teachers: 150.5 (13.0 to 1)
Librarians/Media Specialists: 3.5 (559.7 to 1)
Guidance Counselors: 4.5 (435.3 to 1)
Current Spending: ($ per student per year):
Total: $7,100; Instruction: $4,230; Support Services: $2,369
Enrollment, Drop-out Rates and Diploma Recipients by Race/Ethnicity

Category	Total	White	Black	Asian	AIAN	Hisp.
Enrollment (%)	100.0	94.2	2.6	1.6	0.4	1.2
Drop-out Rate (%)	1.9	0.0	40.0	100.0	66.7	75.0
H.S. Diplomas (#)	141	135	3	1	1	1

Madison County

Winterset Community SD
302 W S St • Winterset, IA 50273
Mailing Address: PO Box 30 • Winterset, IA 50273
(515) 462-2718
Grade Span: PK-12; **Agency Type:** 1
Schools: 4
1 Primary; 2 Middle; 1 High; 0 Other Level
4 Regular; 0 Special Education; 0 Vocational; 0 Alternative
0 Magnet; 0 Charter; 1 Title I Eligible; 0 School-wide Title I
Students: 1,614 (50.3% male; 49.6% female)
Individual Education Program: 229 (14.2%);
English Language Learner: 0 (0.0%); Migrant: 0 (0.0%)
Eligible for Free Lunch Program: 270 (16.7%)
Eligible for Reduced-Price Lunch Program: 119 (7.4%)
Teachers: 110.5 (14.6 to 1)
Librarians/Media Specialists: 1.0 (1,614.0 to 1)
Guidance Counselors: 4.0 (403.5 to 1)
Current Spending: ($ per student per year):
Total: $6,553; Instruction: $4,080; Support Services: $1,964
Enrollment, Drop-out Rates and Diploma Recipients by Race/Ethnicity

Category	Total	White	Black	Asian	AIAN	Hisp.
Enrollment (%)	100.0	97.7	0.3	0.8	0.5	0.7
Drop-out Rate (%)	1.3	1.3	n/a	0.0	0.0	0.0
H.S. Diplomas (#)	143	142	0	1	0	0

Mahaska County

Oskaloosa Community SD
1800 N 3rd • Oskaloosa, IA 52577
Mailing Address: PO Box 710 • Oskaloosa, IA 52577
(641) 673-8345
Grade Span: KG-12; **Agency Type:** 1
Schools: 7
5 Primary; 1 Middle; 1 High; 0 Other Level
7 Regular; 0 Special Education; 0 Vocational; 0 Alternative
0 Magnet; 0 Charter; 4 Title I Eligible; 0 School-wide Title I
Students: 2,411 (51.5% male; 48.4% female)
Individual Education Program: 362 (15.0%);
English Language Learner: 21 (0.9%); Migrant: 0 (0.0%)
Eligible for Free Lunch Program: 657 (27.3%)
Eligible for Reduced-Price Lunch Program: 200 (8.3%)
Teachers: 151.5 (15.9 to 1)
Librarians/Media Specialists: 2.0 (1,205.5 to 1)
Guidance Counselors: 10.0 (241.1 to 1)
Current Spending: ($ per student per year):
Total: $6,621; Instruction: $4,067; Support Services: $2,025
Enrollment, Drop-out Rates and Diploma Recipients by Race/Ethnicity

Category	Total	White	Black	Asian	AIAN	Hisp.
Enrollment (%)	100.0	95.7	1.1	1.6	0.5	1.2
Drop-out Rate (%)	2.4	2.4	0.0	0.0	0.0	11.1
H.S. Diplomas (#)	171	164	1	6	0	0

Marion County

Knoxville Community SD
309 W Main • Knoxville, IA 50138
(641) 842-6552 • http://www.knoxville.k12.ia.us
Grade Span: PK-12; **Agency Type:** 1
Schools: 6
  3 Primary; 1 Middle; 2 High; 0 Other Level
  5 Regular; 0 Special Education; 0 Vocational; 1 Alternative
  0 Magnet; 0 Charter; 3 Title I Eligible; 0 School-wide Title I
Students: 2,064   (52.2% male; 47.7% female)
  Individual Education Program: 310 (15.0%);
  English Language Learner: 14 (0.7%); Migrant: 0 (0.0%)
  Eligible for Free Lunch Program: 435 (21.1%)
  Eligible for Reduced-Price Lunch Program: 165 (8.0%)
Teachers: 132.0 (15.6 to 1)
Librarians/Media Specialists: 1.0 (2,064.0 to 1)
Guidance Counselors: 7.0 (294.9 to 1)
Current Spending: ($ per student per year):
  Total: $6,583; Instruction: $3,856; Support Services: $2,194
Enrollment, Drop-out Rates and Diploma Recipients by Race/Ethnicity

Category	Total	White	Black	Asian	AIAN	Hisp.
Enrollment (%)	100.0	95.0	1.4	1.2	0.2	2.2
Drop-out Rate (%)	1.8	1.7	0.0	0.0	0.0	14.3
H.S. Diplomas (#)	158	157	0	0	0	1

Pella Community SD
210 E University St • Pella, IA 50219-0989
(641) 628-1111 • http://www.pella.k12.ia.us
Grade Span: PK-12; **Agency Type:** 1
Schools: 5
  3 Primary; 1 Middle; 1 High; 0 Other Level
  5 Regular; 0 Special Education; 0 Vocational; 0 Alternative
  0 Magnet; 0 Charter; 3 Title I Eligible; 0 School-wide Title I
Students: 2,090   (50.7% male; 49.2% female)
  Individual Education Program: 193 (9.2%);
  English Language Learner: 24 (1.1%); Migrant: 0 (0.0%)
  Eligible for Free Lunch Program: 222 (10.6%)
  Eligible for Reduced-Price Lunch Program: 100 (4.8%)
Teachers: 131.0 (16.0 to 1)
Librarians/Media Specialists: 3.0 (696.7 to 1)
Guidance Counselors: 4.0 (522.5 to 1)
Current Spending: ($ per student per year):
  Total: $6,431; Instruction: $3,888; Support Services: $1,870
Enrollment, Drop-out Rates and Diploma Recipients by Race/Ethnicity

Category	Total	White	Black	Asian	AIAN	Hisp.
Enrollment (%)	100.0	94.2	0.6	3.6	0.1	1.6
Drop-out Rate (%)	1.2	1.2	n/a	0.0	n/a	0.0
H.S. Diplomas (#)	137	127	0	7	0	3

Marshall County

Marshalltown Community SD
317 Columbus Dr • Marshalltown, IA 50158
(641) 754-1000 • http://www.marshalltown.k12.ia.us
Grade Span: PK-12; **Agency Type:** 1
Schools: 9
  6 Primary; 2 Middle; 1 High; 0 Other Level
  9 Regular; 0 Special Education; 0 Vocational; 0 Alternative
  0 Magnet; 0 Charter; 4 Title I Eligible; 3 School-wide Title I
Students: 4,974   (52.0% male; 47.9% female)
  Individual Education Program: 719 (14.5%);
  English Language Learner: 1,076 (21.6%); Migrant: 353 (7.1%)
  Eligible for Free Lunch Program: 1,939 (39.0%)
  Eligible for Reduced-Price Lunch Program: 437 (8.8%)
Teachers: 315.5 (15.8 to 1)
Librarians/Media Specialists: 8.0 (621.8 to 1)
Guidance Counselors: 12.5 (397.9 to 1)
Current Spending: ($ per student per year):
  Total: $7,204; Instruction: $4,421; Support Services: $2,245
Enrollment, Drop-out Rates and Diploma Recipients by Race/Ethnicity

Category	Total	White	Black	Asian	AIAN	Hisp.
Enrollment (%)	100.0	65.2	3.8	2.2	0.7	28.2
Drop-out Rate (%)	4.8	3.9	1.6	5.9	0.0	9.6
H.S. Diplomas (#)	310	273	6	10	0	21

Mills County

Glenwood Community SD
103 Central • Glenwood, IA 51534
Mailing Address: Ste 300 • Glenwood, IA 51534
(712) 527-9034
Grade Span: PK-12; **Agency Type:** 1
Schools: 6
  1 Primary; 2 Middle; 1 High; 2 Other Level

---

  4 Regular; 1 Special Education; 0 Vocational; 1 Alternative
  0 Magnet; 0 Charter; 1 Title I Eligible; 0 School-wide Title I
Students: 2,053   (53.9% male; 46.0% female)
  Individual Education Program: 255 (12.4%);
  English Language Learner: 4 (0.2%); Migrant: 0 (0.0%)
  Eligible for Free Lunch Program: 399 (19.4%)
  Eligible for Reduced-Price Lunch Program: 123 (6.0%)
Teachers: 138.0 (14.9 to 1)
Librarians/Media Specialists: 2.0 (1,026.5 to 1)
Guidance Counselors: 4.0 (513.3 to 1)
Current Spending: ($ per student per year):
  Total: $6,840; Instruction: $4,220; Support Services: $2,094
Enrollment, Drop-out Rates and Diploma Recipients by Race/Ethnicity

Category	Total	White	Black	Asian	AIAN	Hisp.
Enrollment (%)	100.0	96.3	0.9	0.6	0.4	1.8
Drop-out Rate (%)	2.4	2.5	0.0	0.0	0.0	0.0
H.S. Diplomas (#)	147	142	1	1	1	2

Muscatine County

Muscatine Community SD
1403 Park Ave • Muscatine, IA 52761
(563) 263-7223 • http://www.muscatine.k12.ia.us/index2.htm
Grade Span: PK-12; **Agency Type:** 1
Schools: 12
  9 Primary; 2 Middle; 1 High; 0 Other Level
  12 Regular; 0 Special Education; 0 Vocational; 0 Alternative
  0 Magnet; 0 Charter; 6 Title I Eligible; 5 School-wide Title I
Students: 5,224   (53.1% male; 46.8% female)
  Individual Education Program: 741 (14.2%);
  English Language Learner: 311 (6.0%); Migrant: 152 (2.9%)
  Eligible for Free Lunch Program: 1,429 (27.4%)
  Eligible for Reduced-Price Lunch Program: 344 (6.6%)
Teachers: 373.5 (14.0 to 1)
Librarians/Media Specialists: 7.0 (746.3 to 1)
Guidance Counselors: 14.0 (373.1 to 1)
Current Spending: ($ per student per year):
  Total: $6,862; Instruction: $4,781; Support Services: $1,597
Enrollment, Drop-out Rates and Diploma Recipients by Race/Ethnicity

Category	Total	White	Black	Asian	AIAN	Hisp.
Enrollment (%)	100.0	76.8	2.0	1.3	0.5	19.4
Drop-out Rate (%)	4.3	3.0	11.1	4.2	16.7	11.4
H.S. Diplomas (#)	336	287	2	6	0	41

Plymouth County

Le Mars Community SD
921 3rd Ave SW • Le Mars, IA 51031
(712) 546-4155 • http://www.lemars.k12.ia.us
Grade Span: PK-12; **Agency Type:** 1
Schools: 6
  4 Primary; 1 Middle; 1 High; 0 Other Level
  6 Regular; 0 Special Education; 0 Vocational; 0 Alternative
  0 Magnet; 0 Charter; 4 Title I Eligible; 0 School-wide Title I
Students: 2,281   (51.5% male; 48.4% female)
  Individual Education Program: 192 (8.4%);
  English Language Learner: 45 (2.0%); Migrant: 0 (0.0%)
  Eligible for Free Lunch Program: 234 (10.3%)
  Eligible for Reduced-Price Lunch Program: 152 (6.7%)
Teachers: 150.0 (15.2 to 1)
Librarians/Media Specialists: 2.0 (1,140.5 to 1)
Guidance Counselors: 6.0 (380.2 to 1)
Current Spending: ($ per student per year):
  Total: $6,225; Instruction: $3,937; Support Services: $1,791
Enrollment, Drop-out Rates and Diploma Recipients by Race/Ethnicity

Category	Total	White	Black	Asian	AIAN	Hisp.
Enrollment (%)	100.0	93.3	1.5	0.9	0.3	4.0
Drop-out Rate (%)	1.1	1.1	0.0	0.0	0.0	0.0
H.S. Diplomas (#)	181	178	1	1	0	1

Polk County

Ankeny Community SD
306 SW School St • Ankeny, IA 50021
Mailing Address: PO Box 189 • Ankeny, IA 50021
(515) 965-9600 • http://www.ankeny.k12.ia.us
Grade Span: PK-12; **Agency Type:** 1
Schools: 10
  6 Primary; 1 Middle; 1 High; 1 Other Level
  9 Regular; 0 Special Education; 0 Vocational; 0 Alternative
  0 Magnet; 0 Charter; 3 Title I Eligible; 0 School-wide Title I
Students: 6,290   (51.0% male; 48.9% female)
  Individual Education Program: 504 (8.0%);
  English Language Learner: 45 (0.7%); Migrant: 0 (0.0%)
  Eligible for Free Lunch Program: 266 (4.2%)

Eligible for Reduced-Price Lunch Program: 141 (2.2%)
Teachers: 353.5 (17.8 to 1)
Librarians/Media Specialists: 9.0 (698.9 to 1)
Guidance Counselors: 14.0 (449.3 to 1)
Current Spending: ($ per student per year):
  Total: $6,086; Instruction: $3,753; Support Services: $1,869
Enrollment, Drop-out Rates and Diploma Recipients by Race/Ethnicity

Category	Total	White	Black	Asian	AIAN	Hisp.
Enrollment (%)	100.0	95.4	1.6	1.3	0.1	1.6
Drop-out Rate (%)	0.8	0.8	0.0	0.0	0.0	0.0
H.S. Diplomas (#)	386	374	6	2	2	2

Des Moines Independent Community SD
1801 16th St • Des Moines, IA 50314-1992
(515) 242-7911 • http://www.des-moines.k12.ia.us/
Grade Span: PK-12; **Agency Type:** 1
Schools: 61
  40 Primary; 10 Middle; 7 High; 4 Other Level
  56 Regular; 3 Special Education; 0 Vocational; 2 Alternative
  0 Magnet; 0 Charter; 20 Title I Eligible; 19 School-wide Title I
Students: 31,086 (51.3% male; 48.6% female)
  Individual Education Program: 5,509 (17.7%);
  English Language Learner: 3,200 (10.3%); Migrant: 0 (0.0%)
  Eligible for Free Lunch Program: 12,198 (39.2%)
  Eligible for Reduced-Price Lunch Program: 3,271 (10.5%)
Teachers: 2,328.5 (13.4 to 1)
Librarians/Media Specialists: 21.0 (1,480.3 to 1)
Guidance Counselors: 88.5 (351.3 to 1)
Current Spending: ($ per student per year):
  Total: $8,434; Instruction: $5,358; Support Services: $2,610
Enrollment, Drop-out Rates and Diploma Recipients by Race/Ethnicity

Category	Total	White	Black	Asian	AIAN	Hisp.
Enrollment (%)	100.0	66.7	15.9	4.6	0.7	12.2
Drop-out Rate (%)	4.6	4.1	5.7	4.0	2.0	7.7
H.S. Diplomas (#)	1,659	1,280	201	96	3	79

Johnston Community SD
5608 Merle Hay Rd • Johnston, IA 50131
Mailing Address: PO Box 10 • Johnston, IA 50131
(515) 278-0470 • http://www.johnston.k12.ia.us
Grade Span: PK-12; **Agency Type:** 1
Schools: 8
  4 Primary; 1 Middle; 1 High; 1 Other Level
  6 Regular; 0 Special Education; 0 Vocational; 1 Alternative
  0 Magnet; 0 Charter; 1 Title I Eligible; 0 School-wide Title I
Students: 4,724 (52.5% male; 47.4% female)
  Individual Education Program: 394 (8.3%);
  English Language Learner: 68 (1.4%); Migrant: 0 (0.0%)
  Eligible for Free Lunch Program: 197 (4.2%)
  Eligible for Reduced-Price Lunch Program: 64 (1.4%)
Teachers: 288.0 (16.4 to 1)
Librarians/Media Specialists: 6.0 (787.3 to 1)
Guidance Counselors: 7.0 (674.9 to 1)
Current Spending: ($ per student per year):
  Total: $6,829; Instruction: $3,809; Support Services: $2,146
Enrollment, Drop-out Rates and Diploma Recipients by Race/Ethnicity

Category	Total	White	Black	Asian	AIAN	Hisp.
Enrollment (%)	100.0	92.1	2.9	3.3	0.1	1.7
Drop-out Rate (%)	0.4	0.4	0.0	0.0	n/a	0.0
H.S. Diplomas (#)	262	243	4	10	0	5

Southeast Polk Community SD
8379 NE University • Runnells, IA 50237
Mailing Address: RR 2 • Runnells, IA 50237
(515) 967-4294 • http://www.se-polk.k12.ia.us
Grade Span: PK-12; **Agency Type:** 1
Schools: 10
  7 Primary; 1 Middle; 2 High; 0 Other Level
  9 Regular; 0 Special Education; 0 Vocational; 1 Alternative
  0 Magnet; 0 Charter; 4 Title I Eligible; 0 School-wide Title I
Students: 4,837 (51.1% male; 48.8% female)
  Individual Education Program: 630 (13.0%);
  English Language Learner: 30 (0.6%); Migrant: 0 (0.0%)
  Eligible for Free Lunch Program: 569 (11.8%)
  Eligible for Reduced-Price Lunch Program: 222 (4.6%)
Teachers: 317.5 (15.2 to 1)
Librarians/Media Specialists: 4.0 (1,209.3 to 1)
Guidance Counselors: 16.0 (302.3 to 1)
Current Spending: ($ per student per year):
  Total: $6,897; Instruction: $4,138; Support Services: $2,233
Enrollment, Drop-out Rates and Diploma Recipients by Race/Ethnicity

Category	Total	White	Black	Asian	AIAN	Hisp.
Enrollment (%)	100.0	94.8	1.7	1.6	0.1	1.9
Drop-out Rate (%)	0.6	0.6	0.0	0.0	0.0	0.0
H.S. Diplomas (#)	322	313	0	3	2	4

Urbandale Community SD
6200 Aurora Ave • Urbandale, IA 50322
Mailing Address: Merle Hay Ctr 500 W • Urbandale, IA 50322
(515) 457-5000 • http://www.urbandale.k12.ia.us
Grade Span: PK-12; **Agency Type:** 1
Schools: 8
  5 Primary; 1 Middle; 2 High; 0 Other Level
  7 Regular; 0 Special Education; 0 Vocational; 1 Alternative
  0 Magnet; 0 Charter; 1 Title I Eligible; 0 School-wide Title I
Students: 3,365 (51.4% male; 48.5% female)
  Individual Education Program: 312 (9.3%);
  English Language Learner: 289 (8.6%); Migrant: 0 (0.0%)
  Eligible for Free Lunch Program: 228 (6.8%)
  Eligible for Reduced-Price Lunch Program: 104 (3.1%)
Teachers: 211.0 (15.9 to 1)
Librarians/Media Specialists: 3.0 (1,121.7 to 1)
Guidance Counselors: 9.0 (373.9 to 1)
Current Spending: ($ per student per year):
  Total: $6,648; Instruction: $3,857; Support Services: $2,286
Enrollment, Drop-out Rates and Diploma Recipients by Race/Ethnicity

Category	Total	White	Black	Asian	AIAN	Hisp.
Enrollment (%)	100.0	91.5	3.5	2.3	0.2	2.5
Drop-out Rate (%)	0.8	0.8	0.0	0.0	0.0	0.0
H.S. Diplomas (#)	332	320	3	4	1	4

West Des Moines Community SD
3550 Mills Civic Pkwy • West Des Moines, IA 50265
(515) 633-5000 • http://www.wdm.k12.ia.us
Grade Span: PK-12; **Agency Type:** 1
Schools: 15
  10 Primary; 2 Middle; 2 High; 1 Other Level
  14 Regular; 0 Special Education; 0 Vocational; 1 Alternative
  0 Magnet; 0 Charter; 3 Title I Eligible; 1 School-wide Title I
Students: 8,646 (51.8% male; 48.1% female)
  Individual Education Program: 840 (9.7%);
  English Language Learner: 416 (4.8%); Migrant: 0 (0.0%)
  Eligible for Free Lunch Program: 720 (8.3%)
  Eligible for Reduced-Price Lunch Program: 312 (3.6%)
Teachers: 548.0 (15.8 to 1)
Librarians/Media Specialists: 8.0 (1,080.8 to 1)
Guidance Counselors: 18.5 (467.4 to 1)
Current Spending: ($ per student per year):
  Total: $7,124; Instruction: $4,233; Support Services: $2,168
Enrollment, Drop-out Rates and Diploma Recipients by Race/Ethnicity

Category	Total	White	Black	Asian	AIAN	Hisp.
Enrollment (%)	100.0	86.8	3.7	4.5	0.2	4.8
Drop-out Rate (%)	1.6	1.4	0.0	1.1	33.3	6.9
H.S. Diplomas (#)	554	509	8	24	2	11

Pottawattamie County

Council Bluffs Community SD
12 Scott St • Council Bluffs, IA 51503-0782
(712) 328-6446 • http://www.council-bluffs.k12.ia.us
Grade Span: PK-12; **Agency Type:** 1
Schools: 22
  14 Primary; 2 Middle; 4 High; 2 Other Level
  19 Regular; 0 Special Education; 0 Vocational; 3 Alternative
  0 Magnet; 0 Charter; 8 Title I Eligible; 8 School-wide Title I
Students: 10,020 (50.4% male; 49.5% female)
  Individual Education Program: 1,497 (14.9%);
  English Language Learner: 385 (3.8%); Migrant: 0 (0.0%)
  Eligible for Free Lunch Program: 3,456 (34.5%)
  Eligible for Reduced-Price Lunch Program: 820 (8.2%)
Teachers: 658.5 (15.2 to 1)
Librarians/Media Specialists: 7.0 (1,431.4 to 1)
Guidance Counselors: 25.5 (392.9 to 1)
Current Spending: ($ per student per year):
  Total: $7,410; Instruction: $4,842; Support Services: $2,131
Enrollment, Drop-out Rates and Diploma Recipients by Race/Ethnicity

Category	Total	White	Black	Asian	AIAN	Hisp.
Enrollment (%)	100.0	88.8	2.2	0.9	0.9	7.2
Drop-out Rate (%)	5.1	5.3	3.3	0.0	5.9	2.5
H.S. Diplomas (#)	545	505	15	8	4	13

Lewis Central Community SD
1600 E S Omaha Brdg Rd • Council Bluffs, IA 51503
(712) 366-8202 • http://www.lewiscentral.k12.ia.us
Grade Span: PK-12; **Agency Type:** 1
Schools: 5
  2 Primary; 2 Middle; 1 High; 0 Other Level
  5 Regular; 0 Special Education; 0 Vocational; 0 Alternative
  0 Magnet; 0 Charter; 2 Title I Eligible; 0 School-wide Title I
Students: 2,744 (50.8% male; 49.1% female)
  Individual Education Program: 256 (9.3%);

English Language Learner: 126 (4.6%); Migrant: 0 (0.0%)
Eligible for Free Lunch Program: 661 (24.1%)
Eligible for Reduced-Price Lunch Program: 231 (8.4%)
Teachers: 166.5 (16.5 to 1)
Librarians/Media Specialists: 3.5 (784.0 to 1)
Guidance Counselors: 3.0 (914.7 to 1)
Current Spending: ($ per student per year):
Total: $6,633; Instruction: $4,235; Support Services: $1,786
Enrollment, Drop-out Rates and Diploma Recipients by Race/Ethnicity

Category	Total	White	Black	Asian	AIAN	Hisp.
Enrollment (%)	100.0	91.4	1.2	1.1	0.3	6.0
Drop-out Rate (%)	1.8	1.7	0.0	0.0	0.0	7.4
H.S. Diplomas (#)	176	167	4	0	0	5

Poweshiek County

Grinnell-Newburg Community SD
927 4th Ave • Grinnell, IA 50112-2055
(641) 236-2700 • http://www.grinnell.k12.ia.us
Grade Span: PK-12; **Agency Type:** 1
Schools: 5
3 Primary; 1 Middle; 1 High; 0 Other Level
5 Regular; 0 Special Education; 0 Vocational; 0 Alternative
0 Magnet; 0 Charter; 3 Title I Eligible; 0 School-wide Title I
Students: 1,750   (52.3% male; 47.6% female)
Individual Education Program: 248 (14.2%);
English Language Learner: 11 (0.6%); Migrant: 0 (0.0%)
Eligible for Free Lunch Program: 327 (18.7%)
Eligible for Reduced-Price Lunch Program: 136 (7.8%)
Teachers: 125.0 (14.0 to 1)
Librarians/Media Specialists: 3.0 (583.3 to 1)
Guidance Counselors: 5.0 (350.0 to 1)
Current Spending: ($ per student per year):
Total: $7,831; Instruction: $4,950; Support Services: $2,199
Enrollment, Drop-out Rates and Diploma Recipients by Race/Ethnicity

Category	Total	White	Black	Asian	AIAN	Hisp.
Enrollment (%)	100.0	94.3	1.7	1.2	0.7	2.1
Drop-out Rate (%)	1.1	1.1	0.0	0.0	0.0	0.0
H.S. Diplomas (#)	123	115	3	3	0	2

Scott County

Bettendorf Community SD
3311 Central Ave • Bettendorf, IA 52722
(563) 359-3681 • http://www.bettendorf.k12.ia.us
Grade Span: PK-12; **Agency Type:** 1
Schools: 8
6 Primary; 1 Middle; 1 High; 0 Other Level
8 Regular; 0 Special Education; 0 Vocational; 0 Alternative
0 Magnet; 0 Charter; 4 Title I Eligible; 0 School-wide Title I
Students: 4,339   (51.4% male; 48.5% female)
Individual Education Program: 363 (8.4%);
English Language Learner: 32 (0.7%); Migrant: 0 (0.0%)
Eligible for Free Lunch Program: 481 (11.1%)
Eligible for Reduced-Price Lunch Program: 211 (4.9%)
Teachers: 267.5 (16.2 to 1)
Librarians/Media Specialists: 9.0 (482.1 to 1)
Guidance Counselors: 13.0 (333.8 to 1)
Current Spending: ($ per student per year):
Total: $7,035; Instruction: $4,632; Support Services: $1,926
Enrollment, Drop-out Rates and Diploma Recipients by Race/Ethnicity

Category	Total	White	Black	Asian	AIAN	Hisp.
Enrollment (%)	100.0	90.7	4.6	1.8	0.3	2.7
Drop-out Rate (%)	1.8	1.6	4.4	0.0	0.0	4.4
H.S. Diplomas (#)	295	276	8	6	0	5

Davenport Community SD
1606 Brady St • Davenport, IA 52803
(563) 336-5000 • http://www.davenport.k12.ia.us
Grade Span: PK-12; **Agency Type:** 1
Schools: 32
20 Primary; 6 Middle; 4 High; 2 Other Level
29 Regular; 1 Special Education; 0 Vocational; 2 Alternative
0 Magnet; 0 Charter; 7 Title I Eligible; 7 School-wide Title I
Students: 16,366   (51.5% male; 48.4% female)
Individual Education Program: 1,934 (11.8%);
English Language Learner: 335 (2.0%); Migrant: 0 (0.0%)
Eligible for Free Lunch Program: 6,217 (38.0%)
Eligible for Reduced-Price Lunch Program: 1,370 (8.4%)
Teachers: 1,112.0 (14.7 to 1)
Librarians/Media Specialists: 8.0 (2,045.8 to 1)
Guidance Counselors: 29.5 (554.8 to 1)
Current Spending: ($ per student per year):
Total: $7,379; Instruction: $4,938; Support Services: $1,989

Enrollment, Drop-out Rates and Diploma Recipients by Race/Ethnicity

Category	Total	White	Black	Asian	AIAN	Hisp.
Enrollment (%)	100.0	70.9	18.0	2.6	1.1	7.3
Drop-out Rate (%)	4.2	3.8	6.5	0.0	3.4	5.8
H.S. Diplomas (#)	956	768	111	28	9	40

North Scott Community SD
251 E Iowa St • Eldridge, IA 52748
(563) 285-9081 • http://www.north-scott.k12.ia.us
Grade Span: PK-12; **Agency Type:** 1
Schools: 7
5 Primary; 1 Middle; 1 High; 0 Other Level
7 Regular; 0 Special Education; 0 Vocational; 0 Alternative
0 Magnet; 0 Charter; 4 Title I Eligible; 0 School-wide Title I
Students: 2,985   (51.5% male; 48.4% female)
Individual Education Program: 312 (10.5%);
English Language Learner: 0 (0.0%); Migrant: 0 (0.0%)
Eligible for Free Lunch Program: 383 (12.8%)
Eligible for Reduced-Price Lunch Program: 159 (5.3%)
Teachers: 209.5 (14.2 to 1)
Librarians/Media Specialists: 6.0 (497.5 to 1)
Guidance Counselors: 11.0 (271.4 to 1)
Current Spending: ($ per student per year):
Total: $7,173; Instruction: $4,329; Support Services: $2,276
Enrollment, Drop-out Rates and Diploma Recipients by Race/Ethnicity

Category	Total	White	Black	Asian	AIAN	Hisp.
Enrollment (%)	100.0	96.2	1.2	0.6	0.4	1.6
Drop-out Rate (%)	1.3	1.3	0.0	0.0	0.0	0.0
H.S. Diplomas (#)	194	185	1	2	0	6

Pleasant Valley Community SD
525 Belmont Rd • Pleasant Valley, IA 52767
Mailing Address: PO Box 332 • Pleasant Valley, IA 52767
(563) 332-5550 • http://www.pleasval.k12.ia.us/
Grade Span: PK-12; **Agency Type:** 1
Schools: 6
4 Primary; 1 Middle; 1 High; 0 Other Level
6 Regular; 0 Special Education; 0 Vocational; 0 Alternative
0 Magnet; 0 Charter; 2 Title I Eligible; 0 School-wide Title I
Students: 3,196   (50.8% male; 49.1% female)
Individual Education Program: 227 (7.1%);
English Language Learner: 7 (0.2%); Migrant: 0 (0.0%)
Eligible for Free Lunch Program: 206 (6.4%)
Eligible for Reduced-Price Lunch Program: 64 (2.0%)
Teachers: 205.5 (15.6 to 1)
Librarians/Media Specialists: 6.0 (532.7 to 1)
Guidance Counselors: 8.0 (399.5 to 1)
Current Spending: ($ per student per year):
Total: $6,586; Instruction: $4,282; Support Services: $1,812
Enrollment, Drop-out Rates and Diploma Recipients by Race/Ethnicity

Category	Total	White	Black	Asian	AIAN	Hisp.
Enrollment (%)	100.0	93.0	0.9	2.8	1.1	2.3
Drop-out Rate (%)	3.0	3.0	0.0	3.8	0.0	5.0
H.S. Diplomas (#)	241	222	0	8	3	8

Shelby County

Harlan Community SD
2102 Durant • Harlan, IA 51537-1299
(712) 755-2152 • http://www.harlan.k12.ia.us
Grade Span: PK-12; **Agency Type:** 1
Schools: 5
2 Primary; 1 Middle; 2 High; 0 Other Level
4 Regular; 0 Special Education; 0 Vocational; 1 Alternative
0 Magnet; 0 Charter; 2 Title I Eligible; 0 School-wide Title I
Students: 1,644   (50.0% male; 49.9% female)
Individual Education Program: 173 (10.5%);
English Language Learner: 6 (0.4%); Migrant: 0 (0.0%)
Eligible for Free Lunch Program: 316 (19.2%)
Eligible for Reduced-Price Lunch Program: 142 (8.6%)
Teachers: 104.0 (15.8 to 1)
Librarians/Media Specialists: 3.0 (548.0 to 1)
Guidance Counselors: 5.0 (328.8 to 1)
Current Spending: ($ per student per year):
Total: $6,117; Instruction: $3,796; Support Services: $1,795
Enrollment, Drop-out Rates and Diploma Recipients by Race/Ethnicity

Category	Total	White	Black	Asian	AIAN	Hisp.
Enrollment (%)	100.0	97.3	0.9	0.4	0.4	1.2
Drop-out Rate (%)	0.2	0.2	n/a	0.0	0.0	0.0
H.S. Diplomas (#)	153	150	0	3	0	0

Story County

Ames Community SD
415 Stanton Ave • Ames, IA 50014
(515) 268-6600 • http://www.ames.k12.ia.us
Grade Span: PK-12; **Agency Type:** 1
Schools: 11
  9 Primary; 1 Middle; 1 High; 0 Other Level
  11 Regular; 0 Special Education; 0 Vocational; 0 Alternative
  0 Magnet; 0 Charter; 7 Title I Eligible; 0 School-wide Title I
Students: 4,539   (52.3% male; 47.6% female)
  Individual Education Program: 509 (11.2%);
  English Language Learner: 158 (3.5%); Migrant: 0 (0.0%)
  Eligible for Free Lunch Program: 640 (14.1%)
  Eligible for Reduced-Price Lunch Program: 206 (4.5%)
Teachers: 307.0 (14.8 to 1)
Librarians/Media Specialists: 5.0 (907.8 to 1)
Guidance Counselors: 12.0 (378.3 to 1)
Current Spending: ($ per student per year):
  Total: $7,603; Instruction: $5,126; Support Services: $1,985
Enrollment, Drop-out Rates and Diploma Recipients by Race/Ethnicity

Category	Total	White	Black	Asian	AIAN	Hisp.
Enrollment (%)	100.0	80.5	6.9	9.3	0.2	3.1
Drop-out Rate (%)	2.3	2.3	6.0	0.0	0.0	2.9
H.S. Diplomas (#)	397	343	16	31	1	6

Tama County

South Tama County Community SD
1702 Harding St • Tama, IA 52339-1028
(641) 484-4811 • http://www.aea6.k12.ia.us/schools/tama.html
Grade Span: PK-12; **Agency Type:** 1
Schools: 5
  3 Primary; 1 Middle; 1 High; 0 Other Level
  5 Regular; 0 Special Education; 0 Vocational; 0 Alternative
  0 Magnet; 0 Charter; 3 Title I Eligible; 1 School-wide Title I
Students: 1,751   (52.9% male; 47.0% female)
  Individual Education Program: 276 (15.8%);
  English Language Learner: 133 (7.6%); Migrant: 0 (0.0%)
  Eligible for Free Lunch Program: 579 (33.1%)
  Eligible for Reduced-Price Lunch Program: 206 (11.8%)
Teachers: 118.0 (14.8 to 1)
Librarians/Media Specialists: 2.0 (875.5 to 1)
Guidance Counselors: 5.0 (350.2 to 1)
Current Spending: ($ per student per year):
  Total: $6,648; Instruction: $4,049; Support Services: $2,004
Enrollment, Drop-out Rates and Diploma Recipients by Race/Ethnicity

Category	Total	White	Black	Asian	AIAN	Hisp.
Enrollment (%)	100.0	62.3	1.7	0.6	19.0	16.4
Drop-out Rate (%)	4.1	3.5	0.0	0.0	6.2	7.9
H.S. Diplomas (#)	116	96	0	2	8	10

Wapello County

Ottumwa Community SD
422 Mccarroll Dr • Ottumwa, IA 52501
(641) 684-6596
Grade Span: PK-12; **Agency Type:** 1
Schools: 12
  8 Primary; 1 Middle; 2 High; 1 Other Level
  10 Regular; 1 Special Education; 0 Vocational; 1 Alternative
  0 Magnet; 0 Charter; 5 Title I Eligible; 4 School-wide Title I
Students: 4,870   (50.9% male; 49.0% female)
  Individual Education Program: 743 (15.3%);
  English Language Learner: 258 (5.3%); Migrant: 496 (10.2%)
  Eligible for Free Lunch Program: 1,080 (22.2%)
  Eligible for Reduced-Price Lunch Program: 188 (3.9%)
Teachers: 329.0 (14.8 to 1)
Librarians/Media Specialists: 5.0 (974.0 to 1)
Guidance Counselors: 8.0 (608.8 to 1)
Current Spending: ($ per student per year):
  Total: $6,447; Instruction: $4,028; Support Services: $1,914
Enrollment, Drop-out Rates and Diploma Recipients by Race/Ethnicity

Category	Total	White	Black	Asian	AIAN	Hisp.
Enrollment (%)	100.0	85.7	2.2	1.3	0.3	10.5
Drop-out Rate (%)	6.6	6.1	8.0	8.8	0.0	13.8
H.S. Diplomas (#)	291	273	1	10	0	7

Warren County

Indianola Community SD
1304 E 2nd Ave • Indianola, IA 50125
(515) 961-9500 • http://www.indianola.ia.us/k12/
Grade Span: PK-12; **Agency Type:** 1
Schools: 6

  3 Primary; 1 Middle; 2 High; 0 Other Level
  5 Regular; 0 Special Education; 0 Vocational; 1 Alternative
  0 Magnet; 0 Charter; 3 Title I Eligible; 0 School-wide Title I
Students: 3,192   (49.7% male; 50.2% female)
  Individual Education Program: 355 (11.1%)
  English Language Learner: 5 (0.2%); Migrant: 0 (0.0%)
  Eligible for Free Lunch Program: 388 (12.2%)
  Eligible for Reduced-Price Lunch Program: 152 (4.8%)
Teachers: 205.5 (15.5 to 1)
Librarians/Media Specialists: 3.0 (1,064.0 to 1)
Guidance Counselors: 9.0 (354.7 to 1)
Current Spending: ($ per student per year):
  Total: $6,528; Instruction: $3,915; Support Services: $1,941
Enrollment, Drop-out Rates and Diploma Recipients by Race/Ethnicity

Category	Total	White	Black	Asian	AIAN	Hisp.
Enrollment (%)	100.0	97.1	0.9	0.8	0.2	0.9
Drop-out Rate (%)	2.7	2.7	8.3	0.0	n/a	0.0
H.S. Diplomas (#)	218	216	1	1	0	0

Norwalk Community SD
906 School Ave • Norwalk, IA 50211
(515) 981-0676 • http://www.norwalk.k12.ia.us/
Grade Span: PK-12; **Agency Type:** 1
Schools: 5
  2 Primary; 2 Middle; 1 High; 0 Other Level
  5 Regular; 0 Special Education; 0 Vocational; 0 Alternative
  0 Magnet; 0 Charter; 2 Title I Eligible; 0 School-wide Title I
Students: 2,234   (51.8% male; 48.1% female)
  Individual Education Program: 324 (14.5%);
  English Language Learner: 10 (0.4%); Migrant: 0 (0.0%)
  Eligible for Free Lunch Program: 130 (5.8%)
  Eligible for Reduced-Price Lunch Program: 103 (4.6%)
Teachers: 154.0 (14.5 to 1)
Librarians/Media Specialists: 3.0 (744.7 to 1)
Guidance Counselors: 6.0 (372.3 to 1)
Current Spending: ($ per student per year):
  Total: $6,330; Instruction: $3,802; Support Services: $2,047
Enrollment, Drop-out Rates and Diploma Recipients by Race/Ethnicity

Category	Total	White	Black	Asian	AIAN	Hisp.
Enrollment (%)	100.0	96.6	0.5	1.1	0.3	1.5
Drop-out Rate (%)	0.3	0.3	0.0	0.0	0.0	0.0
H.S. Diplomas (#)	129	129	0	0	0	0

Washington County

Washington Community SD
404 W Main • Washington, IA 52353
Mailing Address: Pobox 926 • Washington, IA 52353
(319) 653-6543 • http://www.washington.k12.ia.us
Grade Span: PK-12; **Agency Type:** 1
Schools: 5
  1 Primary; 2 Middle; 2 High; 0 Other Level
  4 Regular; 0 Special Education; 0 Vocational; 1 Alternative
  0 Magnet; 0 Charter; 2 Title I Eligible; 0 School-wide Title I
Students: 1,721   (50.1% male; 49.8% female)
  Individual Education Program: 266 (15.5%);
  English Language Learner: 174 (10.1%); Migrant: 0 (0.0%)
  Eligible for Free Lunch Program: 429 (24.9%)
  Eligible for Reduced-Price Lunch Program: 131 (7.6%)
Teachers: 128.5 (13.4 to 1)
Librarians/Media Specialists: 3.0 (573.7 to 1)
Guidance Counselors: 5.0 (344.2 to 1)
Current Spending: ($ per student per year):
  Total: $7,279; Instruction: $4,092; Support Services: $2,686
Enrollment, Drop-out Rates and Diploma Recipients by Race/Ethnicity

Category	Total	White	Black	Asian	AIAN	Hisp.
Enrollment (%)	100.0	87.0	2.5	0.4	0.0	10.1
Drop-out Rate (%)	3.8	4.3	0.0	0.0	n/a	0.0
H.S. Diplomas (#)	90	82	1	1	0	6

Webster County

Fort Dodge Community SD
104 S 17th St • Fort Dodge, IA 50501
(515) 576-1161 • http://www.fort-dodge.k12.ia.us
Grade Span: PK-12; **Agency Type:** 1
Schools: 10
  6 Primary; 2 Middle; 2 High; 0 Other Level
  9 Regular; 0 Special Education; 0 Vocational; 1 Alternative
  0 Magnet; 0 Charter; 5 Title I Eligible; 0 School-wide Title I
Students: 4,194   (50.9% male; 49.0% female)
  Individual Education Program: 663 (15.8%);
  English Language Learner: 29 (0.7%); Migrant: 0 (0.0%)
  Eligible for Free Lunch Program: 1,410 (33.6%)
  Eligible for Reduced-Price Lunch Program: 314 (7.5%)

Teachers: 287.0 (14.6 to 1)
Librarians/Media Specialists: 5.0 (838.8 to 1)
Guidance Counselors: 13.0 (322.6 to 1)
Current Spending: ($ per student per year):
 Total: $7,358; Instruction: $4,679; Support Services: $2,130
Enrollment, Drop-out Rates and Diploma Recipients by Race/Ethnicity

Category	Total	White	Black	Asian	AIAN	Hisp.
Enrollment (%)	100.0	87.0	7.2	1.9	0.2	3.8
Drop-out Rate (%)	3.3	3.0	8.2	0.0	0.0	4.8
H.S. Diplomas (#)	293	265	15	7	2	4

Winneshiek County

Decorah Community SD
510 Winnebago St • Decorah, IA 52101
(563) 382-4208 • http://www.decorah.k12.ia.us
Grade Span: PK-12; **Agency Type:** 1
Schools: 4
 2 Primary; 1 Middle; 1 High; 0 Other Level
 4 Regular; 0 Special Education; 0 Vocational; 0 Alternative
 0 Magnet; 0 Charter; 1 Title I Eligible; 0 School-wide Title I
Students: 1,713   (49.9% male; 50.0% female)
 Individual Education Program: 184 (10.7%);
 English Language Learner: 0 (0.0%); Migrant: 0 (0.0%)
 Eligible for Free Lunch Program: 199 (11.6%)
 Eligible for Reduced-Price Lunch Program: 104 (6.1%)
Teachers: 119.0 (14.4 to 1)
Librarians/Media Specialists: 3.0 (571.0 to 1)
Guidance Counselors: 3.0 (571.0 to 1)
Current Spending: ($ per student per year):
 Total: $6,899; Instruction: $4,416; Support Services: $1,889
Enrollment, Drop-out Rates and Diploma Recipients by Race/Ethnicity

Category	Total	White	Black	Asian	AIAN	Hisp.
Enrollment (%)	100.0	96.6	0.5	1.8	0.1	1.0
Drop-out Rate (%)	0.6	0.5	0.0	16.7	n/a	n/a
H.S. Diplomas (#)	139	134	1	4	0	0

Woodbury County

Sioux City Community SD
1221 Pierce St • Sioux City, IA 51105
(712) 279-6667 • http://www.sioux-city.k12.ia.us
Grade Span: PK-12; **Agency Type:** 1
Schools: 29
 21 Primary; 4 Middle; 4 High; 0 Other Level
 28 Regular; 0 Special Education; 0 Vocational; 1 Alternative
 0 Magnet; 0 Charter; 13 Title I Eligible; 12 School-wide Title I
Students: 14,089   (51.2% male; 48.7% female)
 Individual Education Program: 1,938 (13.8%);
 English Language Learner: 2,618 (18.6%); Migrant: 699 (5.0%)
 Eligible for Free Lunch Program: 4,852 (34.4%)
 Eligible for Reduced-Price Lunch Program: 1,378 (9.8%)
Teachers: 910.0 (15.5 to 1)
Librarians/Media Specialists: 7.5 (1,878.5 to 1)
Guidance Counselors: 26.0 (541.9 to 1)
Current Spending: ($ per student per year):
 Total: $7,216; Instruction: $5,115; Support Services: $1,733
Enrollment, Drop-out Rates and Diploma Recipients by Race/Ethnicity

Category	Total	White	Black	Asian	AIAN	Hisp.
Enrollment (%)	100.0	65.5	5.6	3.8	5.4	19.7
Drop-out Rate (%)	7.5	6.4	10.1	6.0	16.5	10.4
H.S. Diplomas (#)	834	678	31	40	15	70

Number of Schools

Rank	Number	District Name	City
1	61	Des Moines ICSD	Des Moines
2	34	Cedar Rapids Community SD	Cedar Rapids
3	32	Davenport Community SD	Davenport
4	29	Sioux City Community SD	Sioux City
5	22	Council Bluffs Community SD	Council Bluffs
5	22	Waterloo Community SD	Waterloo
7	21	Iowa City Community SD	Iowa City
8	18	Dubuque Community SD	Dubuque
9	15	West Des Moines Community SD	West Des Moines
10	12	Muscatine Community SD	Muscatine
10	12	Ottumwa Community SD	Ottumwa
12	11	Ames Community SD	Ames
12	11	Burlington Community SD	Burlington
14	10	Ankeny Community SD	Ankeny
14	10	Centerville Community SD	Centerville
14	10	Fort Dodge Community SD	Fort Dodge
14	10	Mason City Community SD	Mason City
14	10	Southeast Polk Community SD	Runnells
19	9	Boone Community SD	Boone
19	9	Cedar Falls Community SD	Cedar Falls
19	9	Clinton Community SD	Clinton
19	9	Marshalltown Community SD	Marshalltown
23	8	Bettendorf Community SD	Bettendorf
23	8	Johnston Community SD	Johnston
23	8	Linn-Mar Community SD	Marion
23	8	Newton Community SD	Newton
23	8	Urbandale Community SD	Urbandale
23	8	Western Dubuque Community SD	Farley
29	7	College Community SD	Cedar Rapids
29	7	Keokuk Community SD	Keokuk
29	7	North Scott Community SD	Eldridge
29	7	Oskaloosa Community SD	Oskaloosa
29	7	Waverly-Shell Rock Community SD	Waverly
34	6	Benton Community SD	Van Horne
34	6	Fairfield Community SD	Fairfield
34	6	Fort Madison Community SD	Fort Madison
34	6	Glenwood Community SD	Glenwood
34	6	Howard-Winneshiek Community SD	Cresco
34	6	Indianola Community SD	Indianola
34	6	Knoxville Community SD	Knoxville
34	6	Le Mars Community SD	Le Mars
34	6	Mount Pleasant Community SD	Mount Pleasant
34	6	Pleasant Valley Community SD	Pleasant Valley
34	6	Spencer Community SD	Spencer
34	6	Storm Lake Community SD	Storm Lake
46	5	Carroll Community SD	Carroll
46	5	Charles City Community SD	Charles City
46	5	Grinnell-Newburg Community SD	Grinnell
46	5	Harlan Community SD	Harlan
46	5	Independence Community SD	Independence
46	5	Lewis Central Community SD	Council Bluffs
46	5	Marion Independent SD	Marion
46	5	Norwalk Community SD	Norwalk
46	5	Pella Community SD	Pella
46	5	South Tama County Community SD	Tama
46	5	Vinton-Shellsburg Community SD	Vinton
46	5	Washington Community SD	Washington
46	5	Waukee Community SD	Waukee
46	5	Webster City Community SD	Webster City
60	4	Atlantic Community SD	Atlantic
60	4	Central Clinton Community SD	De Witt
60	4	Dallas Center-Grimes CSD	Dallas Center
60	4	Decorah Community SD	Decorah
60	4	Maquoketa Community SD	Maquoketa
60	4	West Delaware County CSD	Manchester
60	4	Winterset Community SD	Winterset
67	3	Denison Community SD	Denison
67	3	Perry Community SD	Perry

Number of Teachers

Rank	Number	District Name	City
1	2,328	Des Moines ICSD	Des Moines
2	1,126	Cedar Rapids Community SD	Cedar Rapids
3	1,112	Davenport Community SD	Davenport
4	910	Sioux City Community SD	Sioux City
5	719	Waterloo Community SD	Waterloo
6	696	Iowa City Community SD	Iowa City
7	673	Dubuque Community SD	Dubuque
8	658	Council Bluffs Community SD	Council Bluffs
9	548	West Des Moines Community SD	West Des Moines
10	373	Muscatine Community SD	Muscatine
11	353	Ankeny Community SD	Ankeny
12	329	Ottumwa Community SD	Ottumwa
13	325	Burlington Community SD	Burlington
14	319	Linn-Mar Community SD	Marion
15	317	Southeast Polk Community SD	Runnells
16	315	Marshalltown Community SD	Marshalltown
17	310	Clinton Community SD	Clinton
18	307	Ames Community SD	Ames
19	299	Cedar Falls Community SD	Cedar Falls
20	289	Mason City Community SD	Mason City
21	288	Johnston Community SD	Johnston
22	287	Fort Dodge Community SD	Fort Dodge
23	267	Bettendorf Community SD	Bettendorf
24	239	College Community SD	Cedar Rapids
25	236	Newton Community SD	Newton
26	227	Waukee Community SD	Waukee
27	211	Urbandale Community SD	Urbandale
28	209	North Scott Community SD	Eldridge
29	205	Indianola Community SD	Indianola
29	205	Pleasant Valley Community SD	Pleasant Valley
31	197	Western Dubuque Community SD	Farley
32	166	Lewis Central Community SD	Council Bluffs
33	162	Fort Madison Community SD	Fort Madison
34	154	Boone Community SD	Boone
34	154	Norwalk Community SD	Norwalk
36	151	Oskaloosa Community SD	Oskaloosa
37	150	Marion Independent SD	Marion
38	150	Le Mars Community SD	Le Mars
39	149	Keokuk Community SD	Keokuk
40	148	Mount Pleasant Community SD	Mount Pleasant
41	145	Spencer Community SD	Spencer
42	140	Storm Lake Community SD	Storm Lake
43	138	Perry Community SD	Perry
44	138	Glenwood Community SD	Glenwood
45	135	Vinton-Shellsburg Community SD	Vinton
46	133	Fairfield Community SD	Fairfield
47	132	Centerville Community SD	Centerville
47	132	Knoxville Community SD	Knoxville
49	131	Pella Community SD	Pella
50	129	Maquoketa Community SD	Maquoketa
51	128	Washington Community SD	Washington
52	125	Grinnell-Newburg Community SD	Grinnell
53	124	Central Clinton Community SD	De Witt
54	123	Charles City Community SD	Charles City
55	121	Carroll Community SD	Carroll
56	119	Decorah Community SD	Decorah
57	118	South Tama County Community SD	Tama
57	118	West Delaware County CSD	Manchester
59	116	Waverly-Shell Rock Community SD	Waverly
60	115	Denison Community SD	Denison
61	114	Independence Community SD	Independence
62	113	Benton Community SD	Van Horne
62	113	Webster City Community SD	Webster City
64	112	Dallas Center-Grimes CSD	Dallas Center
65	111	Howard-Winneshiek Community SD	Cresco
66	110	Winterset Community SD	Winterset
67	105	Atlantic Community SD	Atlantic
68	104	Harlan Community SD	Harlan

Number of Students

Rank	Number	District Name	City
1	31,086	Des Moines ICSD	Des Moines
2	17,324	Cedar Rapids Community SD	Cedar Rapids
3	16,366	Davenport Community SD	Davenport
4	14,089	Sioux City Community SD	Sioux City
5	10,620	Iowa City Community SD	Iowa City
6	10,407	Waterloo Community SD	Waterloo
7	10,143	Dubuque Community SD	Dubuque
8	10,020	Council Bluffs Community SD	Council Bluffs
9	8,646	West Des Moines Community SD	West Des Moines
10	6,290	Ankeny Community SD	Ankeny
11	5,224	Muscatine Community SD	Muscatine
12	4,974	Marshalltown Community SD	Marshalltown
13	4,902	Linn-Mar Community SD	Marion
14	4,870	Ottumwa Community SD	Ottumwa
15	4,837	Southeast Polk Community SD	Runnells
16	4,724	Johnston Community SD	Johnston
17	4,539	Ames Community SD	Ames
18	4,387	Cedar Falls Community SD	Cedar Falls
19	4,379	Burlington Community SD	Burlington
20	4,366	Clinton Community SD	Clinton
21	4,339	Bettendorf Community SD	Bettendorf
22	4,257	Mason City Community SD	Mason City
23	4,194	Fort Dodge Community SD	Fort Dodge
24	3,697	College Community SD	Cedar Rapids
25	3,629	Waukee Community SD	Waukee
26	3,365	Urbandale Community SD	Urbandale
27	3,340	Newton Community SD	Newton
28	3,196	Pleasant Valley Community SD	Pleasant Valley
29	3,192	Indianola Community SD	Indianola
30	2,985	North Scott Community SD	Eldridge
31	2,744	Lewis Central Community SD	Council Bluffs
32	2,709	Western Dubuque Community SD	Farley
33	2,411	Oskaloosa Community SD	Oskaloosa
34	2,385	Fort Madison Community SD	Fort Madison
35	2,309	Boone Community SD	Boone
36	2,281	Le Mars Community SD	Le Mars
37	2,264	Keokuk Community SD	Keokuk
38	2,234	Norwalk Community SD	Norwalk
39	2,137	Mount Pleasant Community SD	Mount Pleasant
40	2,120	Spencer Community SD	Spencer
41	2,090	Pella Community SD	Pella
42	2,064	Knoxville Community SD	Knoxville
43	2,053	Glenwood Community SD	Glenwood
44	2,039	Storm Lake Community SD	Storm Lake
45	2,015	Waverly-Shell Rock Community SD	Waverly
46	1,968	Fairfield Community SD	Fairfield
47	1,959	Marion Independent SD	Marion
48	1,822	Vinton-Shellsburg Community SD	Vinton
49	1,802	Denison Community SD	Denison
50	1,778	Carroll Community SD	Carroll
51	1,770	Webster City Community SD	Webster City
52	1,755	Perry Community SD	Perry
53	1,751	South Tama County Community SD	Tama
54	1,750	Grinnell-Newburg Community SD	Grinnell
55	1,723	West Delaware County CSD	Manchester
56	1,721	Washington Community SD	Washington
57	1,713	Decorah Community SD	Decorah
58	1,677	Charles City Community SD	Charles City
59	1,659	Maquoketa Community SD	Maquoketa
60	1,644	Harlan Community SD	Harlan
61	1,623	Central Clinton Community SD	De Witt
62	1,614	Winterset Community SD	Winterset
63	1,612	Centerville Community SD	Centerville
64	1,561	Benton Community SD	Van Horne
65	1,560	Dallas Center-Grimes CSD	Dallas Center
66	1,527	Howard-Winneshiek Community SD	Cresco
67	1,513	Atlantic Community SD	Atlantic
68	1,504	Independence Community SD	Independence

Male Students

Rank	Percent	District Name	City
1	53.9	Atlantic Community SD	Atlantic
2	53.9	Glenwood Community SD	Glenwood
3	53.8	Perry Community SD	Perry
4	53.1	Muscatine Community SD	Muscatine
5	53.0	Central Clinton Community SD	De Witt
6	52.9	South Tama County Community SD	Tama
7	52.9	Maquoketa Community SD	Maquoketa
8	52.7	Storm Lake Community SD	Storm Lake
9	52.6	Charles City Community SD	Charles City
10	52.5	Denison Community SD	Denison
11	52.5	Johnston Community SD	Johnston
12	52.3	Ames Community SD	Ames
13	52.3	Grinnell-Newburg Community SD	Grinnell
14	52.3	Vinton-Shellsburg Community SD	Vinton
15	52.2	Knoxville Community SD	Knoxville
16	52.0	Marshalltown Community SD	Marshalltown
17	51.9	Iowa City Community SD	Iowa City
18	51.8	Norwalk Community SD	Norwalk
19	51.8	Waverly-Shell Rock Community SD	Waverly
20	51.8	West Des Moines Community SD	West Des Moines
21	51.7	Dallas Center-Grimes CSD	Dallas Center
22	51.7	Marion Independent SD	Marion
23	51.6	Clinton Community SD	Clinton
24	51.6	College Community SD	Cedar Rapids
25	51.6	Western Dubuque Community SD	Farley
26	51.5	Oskaloosa Community SD	Oskaloosa
27	51.5	North Scott Community SD	Eldridge
28	51.5	Davenport Community SD	Davenport
29	51.5	Le Mars Community SD	Le Mars
30	51.4	Waterloo Community SD	Waterloo
31	51.4	Bettendorf Community SD	Bettendorf
32	51.4	Urbandale Community SD	Urbandale
33	51.3	Cedar Rapids Community SD	Cedar Rapids
34	51.3	Burlington Community SD	Burlington
35	51.3	Des Moines ICSD	Des Moines
36	51.3	Waukee Community SD	Waukee
37	51.2	Dubuque Community SD	Dubuque
38	51.2	Fairfield Community SD	Fairfield
39	51.2	Sioux City Community SD	Sioux City
40	51.1	Spencer Community SD	Spencer
41	51.1	Newton Community SD	Newton
42	51.1	Fort Madison Community SD	Fort Madison
43	51.1	Southeast Polk Community SD	Runnells
44	51.1	Cedar Falls Community SD	Cedar Falls
45	51.0	Independence Community SD	Independence
46	51.0	Ankeny Community SD	Ankeny
47	50.9	Linn-Mar Community SD	Marion
48	50.9	Ottumwa Community SD	Ottumwa
49	50.9	Fort Dodge Community SD	Fort Dodge
50	50.8	Lewis Central Community SD	Council Bluffs
51	50.8	Pleasant Valley Community SD	Pleasant Valley
52	50.7	Pella Community SD	Pella
53	50.6	Benton Community SD	Van Horne
54	50.4	Boone Community SD	Boone
55	50.4	Council Bluffs Community SD	Council Bluffs
56	50.3	Keokuk Community SD	Keokuk
57	50.3	Winterset Community SD	Winterset
58	50.1	Washington Community SD	Washington
59	50.0	Mason City Community SD	Mason City
60	50.0	Harlan Community SD	Harlan

Rank	Percent	District Name	City
61	50.0	Webster City Community SD	Webster City
62	49.9	Decorah Community SD	Decorah
63	49.7	Indianola Community SD	Indianola
64	49.5	Howard-Winneshiek Community SD	Cresco
65	48.8	Centerville Community SD	Centerville
66	48.6	West Delaware County CSD	Manchester
67	48.5	Mount Pleasant Community SD	Mount Pleasant
68	48.1	Carroll Community SD	Carroll

Female Students

Rank	Percent	District Name	City
1	51.8	Carroll Community SD	Carroll
2	51.4	Mount Pleasant Community SD	Mount Pleasant
3	51.3	West Delaware County CSD	Manchester
4	51.1	Centerville Community SD	Centerville
5	50.4	Howard-Winneshiek Community SD	Cresco
6	50.2	Indianola Community SD	Indianola
7	50.0	Decorah Community SD	Decorah
8	50.0	Webster City Community SD	Webster City
9	49.9	Harlan Community SD	Harlan
10	49.9	Mason City Community SD	Mason City
11	49.8	Washington Community SD	Washington
12	49.6	Winterset Community SD	Winterset
13	49.6	Keokuk Community SD	Keokuk
14	49.5	Council Bluffs Community SD	Council Bluffs
15	49.5	Boone Community SD	Boone
16	49.3	Benton Community SD	Van Horne
17	49.2	Pella Community SD	Pella
18	49.1	Pleasant Valley Community SD	Pleasant Valley
19	49.1	Lewis Central Community SD	Council Bluffs
20	49.0	Fort Dodge Community SD	Fort Dodge
21	49.0	Ottumwa Community SD	Ottumwa
22	49.0	Linn-Mar Community SD	Marion
23	48.9	Ankeny Community SD	Ankeny
24	48.9	Independence Community SD	Independence
25	48.8	Cedar Falls Community SD	Cedar Falls
26	48.8	Southeast Polk Community SD	Runnells
27	48.8	Fort Madison Community SD	Fort Madison
28	48.8	Newton Community SD	Newton
29	48.8	Spencer Community SD	Spencer
30	48.7	Sioux City Community SD	Sioux City
31	48.7	Fairfield Community SD	Fairfield
32	48.7	Dubuque Community SD	Dubuque
33	48.6	Waukee Community SD	Waukee
34	48.6	Des Moines ICSD	Des Moines
35	48.6	Burlington Community SD	Burlington
36	48.6	Cedar Rapids Community SD	Cedar Rapids
37	48.5	Urbandale Community SD	Urbandale
38	48.5	Bettendorf Community SD	Bettendorf
39	48.5	Waterloo Community SD	Waterloo
40	48.4	Le Mars Community SD	Le Mars
41	48.4	Davenport Community SD	Davenport
42	48.4	North Scott Community SD	Eldridge
43	48.4	Oskaloosa Community SD	Oskaloosa
44	48.3	Western Dubuque Community SD	Farley
45	48.3	College Community SD	Cedar Rapids
46	48.3	Clinton Community SD	Clinton
47	48.2	Marion Independent SD	Marion
48	48.2	Dallas Center-Grimes CSD	Dallas Center
49	48.1	West Des Moines Community SD	West Des Moines
50	48.1	Waverly-Shell Rock Community SD	Waverly
51	48.1	Norwalk Community SD	Norwalk
52	48.0	Iowa City Community SD	Iowa City
53	47.9	Marshalltown Community SD	Marshalltown
54	47.7	Knoxville Community SD	Knoxville
55	47.6	Vinton-Shellsburg Community SD	Vinton
56	47.6	Grinnell-Newburg Community SD	Grinnell
57	47.6	Ames Community SD	Ames
58	47.4	Johnston Community SD	Johnston
59	47.4	Denison Community SD	Denison
60	47.3	Charles City Community SD	Charles City
61	47.2	Storm Lake Community SD	Storm Lake
62	47.0	Maquoketa Community SD	Maquoketa
63	47.0	South Tama County Community SD	Tama
64	46.9	Central Clinton Community SD	De Witt
65	46.8	Muscatine Community SD	Muscatine
66	46.1	Perry Community SD	Perry
67	46.0	Glenwood Community SD	Glenwood
68	46.0	Atlantic Community SD	Atlantic

Individual Education Program Students

Rank	Percent	District Name	City
1	19.1	Clinton Community SD	Clinton
2	18.7	Mason City Community SD	Mason City
3	18.4	Centerville Community SD	Centerville
4	17.7	Des Moines ICSD	Des Moines
5	17.4	Burlington Community SD	Burlington
6	17.3	Cedar Rapids Community SD	Cedar Rapids
7	16.8	Dubuque Community SD	Dubuque
8	15.9	Keokuk Community SD	Keokuk
9	15.8	Charles City Community SD	Charles City
9	15.8	Fort Dodge Community SD	Fort Dodge
9	15.8	Maquoketa Community SD	Maquoketa
9	15.8	South Tama County Community SD	Tama
13	15.7	Fort Madison Community SD	Fort Madison
14	15.5	Washington Community SD	Washington
15	15.4	Waterloo Community SD	Waterloo
16	15.3	Ottumwa Community SD	Ottumwa
17	15.2	Howard-Winneshiek Community SD	Cresco
18	15.0	Knoxville Community SD	Knoxville
18	15.0	Oskaloosa Community SD	Oskaloosa
20	14.9	Benton Community SD	Van Horne
20	14.9	Council Bluffs Community SD	Council Bluffs
22	14.5	Marshalltown Community SD	Marshalltown
22	14.5	Norwalk Community SD	Norwalk
22	14.5	Vinton-Shellsburg Community SD	Vinton
25	14.4	Perry Community SD	Perry
26	14.2	Grinnell-Newburg Community SD	Grinnell
26	14.2	Independence Community SD	Independence
26	14.2	Muscatine Community SD	Muscatine
26	14.2	Winterset Community SD	Winterset
30	14.1	Newton Community SD	Newton
31	13.8	Sioux City Community SD	Sioux City
32	13.7	Central Clinton Community SD	De Witt
32	13.7	Fairfield Community SD	Fairfield
34	13.6	Iowa City Community SD	Iowa City
35	13.4	Marion Independent SD	Marion
36	13.2	Boone Community SD	Boone
37	13.0	Southeast Polk Community SD	Runnells
38	12.8	Mount Pleasant Community SD	Mount Pleasant
39	12.6	Carroll Community SD	Carroll
39	12.6	Webster City Community SD	Webster City
41	12.5	Spencer Community SD	Spencer
42	12.4	Cedar Falls Community SD	Cedar Falls
42	12.4	Glenwood Community SD	Glenwood
44	12.1	Atlantic Community SD	Atlantic
45	12.0	Storm Lake Community SD	Storm Lake
45	12.0	Western Dubuque Community SD	Farley
47	11.8	Davenport Community SD	Davenport
48	11.4	College Community SD	Cedar Rapids
49	11.2	Ames Community SD	Ames
50	11.1	Indianola Community SD	Indianola
51	10.9	Linn-Mar Community SD	Marion
52	10.7	Decorah Community SD	Decorah
53	10.6	Denison Community SD	Denison
54	10.5	Harlan Community SD	Harlan
54	10.5	North Scott Community SD	Eldridge
56	10.1	Waverly-Shell Rock Community SD	Waverly
57	9.7	West Des Moines Community SD	West Des Moines
58	9.3	Lewis Central Community SD	Council Bluffs
58	9.3	Urbandale Community SD	Urbandale
60	9.2	Pella Community SD	Pella
60	9.2	West Delaware County CSD	Manchester
62	9.1	Waukee Community SD	Waukee
63	8.4	Bettendorf Community SD	Bettendorf
63	8.4	Le Mars Community SD	Le Mars
65	8.3	Johnston Community SD	Johnston
66	8.0	Ankeny Community SD	Ankeny
66	8.0	Dallas Center-Grimes CSD	Dallas Center
68	7.1	Pleasant Valley Community SD	Pleasant Valley

English Language Learner Students

Rank	Percent	District Name	City
1	49.8	Storm Lake Community SD	Storm Lake
2	24.0	Perry Community SD	Perry
3	21.6	Marshalltown Community SD	Marshalltown
4	19.8	Denison Community SD	Denison
5	18.6	Sioux City Community SD	Sioux City
6	10.3	Des Moines ICSD	Des Moines
7	10.1	Washington Community SD	Washington
8	8.6	Urbandale Community SD	Urbandale
9	7.6	South Tama County Community SD	Tama
10	6.0	Muscatine Community SD	Muscatine
11	5.8	Waterloo Community SD	Waterloo
12	5.3	Ottumwa Community SD	Ottumwa
13	4.8	West Des Moines Community SD	West Des Moines
14	4.7	Webster City Community SD	Webster City
15	4.6	Lewis Central Community SD	Council Bluffs
16	3.8	Council Bluffs Community SD	Council Bluffs
17	3.5	Ames Community SD	Ames
18	2.3	Mount Pleasant Community SD	Mount Pleasant
19	2.0	Davenport Community SD	Davenport
19	2.0	Iowa City Community SD	Iowa City
19	2.0	Le Mars Community SD	Le Mars
22	1.5	Carroll Community SD	Carroll
23	1.4	Charles City Community SD	Charles City
23	1.4	Johnston Community SD	Johnston
23	1.4	Waukee Community SD	Waukee
26	1.1	Pella Community SD	Pella
27	1.0	Dubuque Community SD	Dubuque
28	0.9	Cedar Falls Community SD	Cedar Falls
28	0.9	Cedar Rapids Community SD	Cedar Rapids
28	0.9	Oskaloosa Community SD	Oskaloosa
31	0.8	Fairfield Community SD	Fairfield
31	0.8	Spencer Community SD	Spencer
33	0.7	Ankeny Community SD	Ankeny
33	0.7	Bettendorf Community SD	Bettendorf
33	0.7	Fort Dodge Community SD	Fort Dodge
33	0.7	Knoxville Community SD	Knoxville
37	0.6	Dallas Center-Grimes CSD	Dallas Center
37	0.6	Grinnell-Newburg Community SD	Grinnell
37	0.6	Southeast Polk Community SD	Runnells
40	0.4	Burlington Community SD	Burlington
40	0.4	Harlan Community SD	Harlan
40	0.4	Marion Independent SD	Marion
40	0.4	Norwalk Community SD	Norwalk
44	0.3	Boone Community SD	Boone
45	0.2	Glenwood Community SD	Glenwood
45	0.2	Indianola Community SD	Indianola
45	0.2	Mason City Community SD	Mason City
45	0.2	Newton Community SD	Newton
45	0.2	Pleasant Valley Community SD	Pleasant Valley
45	0.2	Western Dubuque Community SD	Farley
51	0.1	Centerville Community SD	Centerville
51	0.1	Fort Madison Community SD	Fort Madison
51	0.1	Howard-Winneshiek Community SD	Cresco
51	0.1	Maquoketa Community SD	Maquoketa
51	0.1	Vinton-Shellsburg Community SD	Vinton
56	0.0	Clinton Community SD	Clinton
56	0.0	Waverly-Shell Rock Community SD	Waverly
58	0.0	Atlantic Community SD	Atlantic
58	0.0	Benton Community SD	Van Horne
58	0.0	Central Clinton Community SD	De Witt
58	0.0	College Community SD	Cedar Rapids
58	0.0	Decorah Community SD	Decorah
58	0.0	Independence Community SD	Independence
58	0.0	Keokuk Community SD	Keokuk
58	0.0	Linn-Mar Community SD	Marion
58	0.0	North Scott Community SD	Eldridge
58	0.0	West Delaware County CSD	Manchester
58	0.0	Winterset Community SD	Winterset

Migrant Students

Rank	Percent	District Name	City
1	37.8	Storm Lake Community SD	Storm Lake
2	31.4	Denison Community SD	Denison
3	18.7	Perry Community SD	Perry
4	10.2	Ottumwa Community SD	Ottumwa
5	7.1	Marshalltown Community SD	Marshalltown
6	5.0	Sioux City Community SD	Sioux City
7	3.6	Waterloo Community SD	Waterloo
8	2.9	Muscatine Community SD	Muscatine
9	0.0	Ames Community SD	Ames
9	0.0	Ankeny Community SD	Ankeny
9	0.0	Atlantic Community SD	Atlantic
9	0.0	Benton Community SD	Van Horne
9	0.0	Bettendorf Community SD	Bettendorf
9	0.0	Boone Community SD	Boone
9	0.0	Burlington Community SD	Burlington
9	0.0	Carroll Community SD	Carroll
9	0.0	Cedar Falls Community SD	Cedar Falls
9	0.0	Cedar Rapids Community SD	Cedar Rapids
9	0.0	Centerville Community SD	Centerville
9	0.0	Central Clinton Community SD	De Witt
9	0.0	Charles City Community SD	Charles City
9	0.0	Clinton Community SD	Clinton
9	0.0	College Community SD	Cedar Rapids
9	0.0	Council Bluffs Community SD	Council Bluffs
9	0.0	Dallas Center-Grimes CSD	Dallas Center
9	0.0	Davenport Community SD	Davenport
9	0.0	Decorah Community SD	Decorah
9	0.0	Des Moines ICSD	Des Moines
9	0.0	Dubuque Community SD	Dubuque
9	0.0	Fairfield Community SD	Fairfield
9	0.0	Fort Dodge Community SD	Fort Dodge
9	0.0	Fort Madison Community SD	Fort Madison
9	0.0	Glenwood Community SD	Glenwood
9	0.0	Grinnell-Newburg Community SD	Grinnell
9	0.0	Harlan Community SD	Harlan
9	0.0	Howard-Winneshiek Community SD	Cresco
9	0.0	Independence Community SD	Independence
9	0.0	Indianola Community SD	Indianola
9	0.0	Iowa City Community SD	Iowa City
9	0.0	Johnston Community SD	Johnston
9	0.0	Keokuk Community SD	Keokuk
9	0.0	Knoxville Community SD	Knoxville
9	0.0	Le Mars Community SD	Le Mars
9	0.0	Lewis Central Community SD	Council Bluffs
9	0.0	Linn-Mar Community SD	Marion
9	0.0	Maquoketa Community SD	Maquoketa
9	0.0	Marion Independent SD	Marion
9	0.0	Mason City Community SD	Mason City
9	0.0	Mount Pleasant Community SD	Mount Pleasant
9	0.0	Newton Community SD	Newton
9	0.0	North Scott Community SD	Eldridge

9	0.0	Norwalk Community SD	Norwalk
9	0.0	Oskaloosa Community SD	Oskaloosa
9	0.0	Pella Community SD	Pella
9	0.0	Pleasant Valley Community SD	Pleasant Valley
9	0.0	South Tama County Community SD	Tama
9	0.0	Southeast Polk Community SD	Runnells
9	0.0	Spencer Community SD	Spencer
9	0.0	Urbandale Community SD	Urbandale
9	0.0	Vinton-Shellsburg Community SD	Vinton
9	0.0	Washington Community SD	Washington
9	0.0	Waukee Community SD	Waukee
9	0.0	Waverly-Shell Rock Community SD	Waverly
9	0.0	Webster City Community SD	Webster City
9	0.0	West Delaware County CSD	Manchester
9	0.0	West Des Moines Community SD	West Des Moines
9	0.0	Western Dubuque Community SD	Farley
9	0.0	Winterset Community SD	Winterset

Students Eligible for Free Lunch

Rank	Percent	District Name	City
1	46.2	Keokuk Community SD	Keokuk
2	44.2	Waterloo Community SD	Waterloo
3	39.2	Des Moines ICSD	Des Moines
4	39.0	Marshalltown Community SD	Marshalltown
5	38.0	Davenport Community SD	Davenport
6	37.5	Denison Community SD	Denison
7	37.0	Perry Community SD	Perry
8	36.3	Storm Lake Community SD	Storm Lake
9	34.5	Council Bluffs Community SD	Council Bluffs
10	34.4	Sioux City Community SD	Sioux City
11	34.2	Burlington Community SD	Burlington
12	33.9	Centerville Community SD	Centerville
13	33.6	Fort Dodge Community SD	Fort Dodge
14	33.1	South Tama County Community SD	Tama
15	33.0	Clinton Community SD	Clinton
16	32.3	Maquoketa Community SD	Maquoketa
17	29.5	Charles City Community SD	Charles City
18	28.1	Fort Madison Community SD	Fort Madison
19	27.4	Muscatine Community SD	Muscatine
20	27.3	Oskaloosa Community SD	Oskaloosa
21	27.2	Cedar Rapids Community SD	Cedar Rapids
22	24.9	Washington Community SD	Washington
23	24.5	Vinton-Shellsburg Community SD	Vinton
24	24.3	Atlantic Community SD	Atlantic
25	24.1	Lewis Central Community SD	Council Bluffs
26	23.5	Mason City Community SD	Mason City
27	22.2	Ottumwa Community SD	Ottumwa
28	21.7	Dubuque Community SD	Dubuque
29	21.4	Fairfield Community SD	Fairfield
29	21.4	Independence Community SD	Independence
31	21.2	Webster City Community SD	Webster City
32	21.1	Knoxville Community SD	Knoxville
33	19.4	Glenwood Community SD	Glenwood
34	19.2	Harlan Community SD	Harlan
35	18.7	Grinnell-Newburg Community SD	Grinnell
36	18.2	Newton Community SD	Newton
37	18.1	Boone Community SD	Boone
37	18.1	Howard-Winneshiek Community SD	Cresco
39	17.9	Spencer Community SD	Spencer
40	17.8	Carroll Community SD	Carroll
41	17.5	Mount Pleasant Community SD	Mount Pleasant
42	17.2	Iowa City Community SD	Iowa City
43	16.7	Winterset Community SD	Winterset
44	16.4	College Community SD	Cedar Rapids
45	15.3	West Delaware County CSD	Manchester
45	15.3	Western Dubuque Community SD	Farley
47	14.3	Central Clinton Community SD	De Witt
48	14.1	Ames Community SD	Ames
49	13.7	Marion Independent SD	Marion
50	13.4	Cedar Falls Community SD	Cedar Falls
51	13.3	Waverly-Shell Rock Community SD	Waverly
52	12.8	North Scott Community SD	Eldridge
53	12.2	Indianola Community SD	Indianola
54	11.8	Southeast Polk Community SD	Runnells
55	11.6	Decorah Community SD	Decorah
56	11.1	Bettendorf Community SD	Bettendorf
57	10.6	Benton Community SD	Van Horne
57	10.6	Pella Community SD	Pella
59	10.3	Le Mars Community SD	Le Mars
60	8.3	West Des Moines Community SD	West Des Moines
61	8.0	Linn-Mar Community SD	Marion
62	6.9	Waukee Community SD	Waukee
63	6.8	Urbandale Community SD	Urbandale
64	6.5	Dallas Center-Grimes CSD	Dallas Center
65	6.4	Pleasant Valley Community SD	Pleasant Valley
66	5.8	Norwalk Community SD	Norwalk
67	4.2	Ankeny Community SD	Ankeny
67	4.2	Johnston Community SD	Johnston

Students Eligible for Reduced-Price Lunch

Rank	Percent	District Name	City
1	15.0	Perry Community SD	Perry
2	13.2	Storm Lake Community SD	Storm Lake
3	12.4	Denison Community SD	Denison
4	11.8	South Tama County Community SD	Tama
5	11.0	Waterloo Community SD	Waterloo
6	10.9	Atlantic Community SD	Atlantic
7	10.5	Des Moines ICSD	Des Moines
8	10.1	Keokuk Community SD	Keokuk
9	9.8	Sioux City Community SD	Sioux City
10	9.5	Howard-Winneshiek Community SD	Cresco
11	9.4	Centerville Community SD	Centerville
12	9.0	Spencer Community SD	Spencer
13	8.8	Maquoketa Community SD	Maquoketa
13	8.8	Marshalltown Community SD	Marshalltown
15	8.6	Harlan Community SD	Harlan
16	8.4	Clinton Community SD	Clinton
16	8.4	Davenport Community SD	Davenport
16	8.4	Lewis Central Community SD	Council Bluffs
19	8.3	Burlington Community SD	Burlington
19	8.3	Oskaloosa Community SD	Oskaloosa
21	8.2	Council Bluffs Community SD	Council Bluffs
21	8.2	Dubuque Community SD	Dubuque
21	8.2	Western Dubuque Community SD	Farley
24	8.1	Mason City Community SD	Mason City
25	8.0	Knoxville Community SD	Knoxville
25	8.0	Webster City Community SD	Webster City
27	7.8	Charles City Community SD	Charles City
27	7.8	Grinnell-Newburg Community SD	Grinnell
29	7.6	Carroll Community SD	Carroll
29	7.6	Washington Community SD	Washington
31	7.5	Cedar Rapids Community SD	Cedar Rapids
31	7.5	Fort Dodge Community SD	Fort Dodge
31	7.5	Independence Community SD	Independence
34	7.4	Winterset Community SD	Winterset
35	7.2	Fort Madison Community SD	Fort Madison
36	7.1	Boone Community SD	Boone
37	6.8	Vinton-Shellsburg Community SD	Vinton
38	6.7	Le Mars Community SD	Le Mars
39	6.6	Muscatine Community SD	Muscatine
40	6.3	Mount Pleasant Community SD	Mount Pleasant
41	6.2	West Delaware County CSD	Manchester
42	6.1	Decorah Community SD	Decorah
43	6.0	Glenwood Community SD	Glenwood
43	6.0	Newton Community SD	Newton
45	5.9	Fairfield Community SD	Fairfield
46	5.8	College Community SD	Cedar Rapids
47	5.7	Marion Independent SD	Marion
48	5.3	North Scott Community SD	Eldridge
49	5.2	Central Clinton Community SD	De Witt
50	4.9	Bettendorf Community SD	Bettendorf
51	4.8	Indianola Community SD	Indianola
51	4.8	Pella Community SD	Pella
53	4.6	Norwalk Community SD	Norwalk
53	4.6	Southeast Polk Community SD	Runnells
53	4.6	Waverly-Shell Rock Community SD	Waverly
56	4.5	Ames Community SD	Ames
56	4.5	Benton Community SD	Van Horne
58	3.9	Cedar Falls Community SD	Cedar Falls
58	3.9	Dallas Center-Grimes CSD	Dallas Center
58	3.9	Ottumwa Community SD	Ottumwa
61	3.7	Iowa City Community SD	Iowa City
62	3.6	West Des Moines Community SD	West Des Moines
63	3.1	Urbandale Community SD	Urbandale
64	2.6	Linn-Mar Community SD	Marion
65	2.3	Waukee Community SD	Waukee
66	2.2	Ankeny Community SD	Ankeny
67	2.0	Pleasant Valley Community SD	Pleasant Valley
68	1.4	Johnston Community SD	Johnston

Student/Teacher Ratio

Rank	Ratio	District Name	City
1	17.8	Ankeny Community SD	Ankeny
2	17.4	Waverly-Shell Rock Community SD	Waverly
3	16.5	Lewis Central Community SD	Council Bluffs
4	16.4	Johnston Community SD	Johnston
5	16.2	Bettendorf Community SD	Bettendorf
6	16.0	Pella Community SD	Pella
6	16.0	Waukee Community SD	Waukee
8	15.9	Oskaloosa Community SD	Oskaloosa
8	15.9	Urbandale Community SD	Urbandale
10	15.8	Harlan Community SD	Harlan
10	15.8	Marshalltown Community SD	Marshalltown
10	15.8	West Des Moines Community SD	West Des Moines
13	15.7	Webster City Community SD	Webster City
14	15.6	Denison Community SD	Denison
14	15.6	Knoxville Community SD	Knoxville
14	15.6	Pleasant Valley Community SD	Pleasant Valley
17	15.5	College Community SD	Cedar Rapids
17	15.5	Indianola Community SD	Indianola
17	15.5	Sioux City Community SD	Sioux City
20	15.4	Cedar Rapids Community SD	Cedar Rapids
20	15.4	Linn-Mar Community SD	Marion
22	15.3	Iowa City Community SD	Iowa City
23	15.2	Council Bluffs Community SD	Council Bluffs
23	15.2	Le Mars Community SD	Le Mars
23	15.2	Southeast Polk Community SD	Runnells
26	15.1	Dubuque Community SD	Dubuque
26	15.1	Keokuk Community SD	Keokuk
28	15.0	Boone Community SD	Boone
29	14.9	Glenwood Community SD	Glenwood
30	14.8	Ames Community SD	Ames
30	14.8	Ottumwa Community SD	Ottumwa
30	14.8	South Tama County Community SD	Tama
33	14.7	Carroll Community SD	Carroll
33	14.7	Davenport Community SD	Davenport
33	14.7	Fairfield Community SD	Fairfield
33	14.7	Fort Madison Community SD	Fort Madison
33	14.7	Mason City Community SD	Mason City
38	14.6	Cedar Falls Community SD	Cedar Falls
38	14.6	Fort Dodge Community SD	Fort Dodge
38	14.6	Spencer Community SD	Spencer
38	14.6	Storm Lake Community SD	Storm Lake
38	14.6	West Delaware County CSD	Manchester
38	14.6	Winterset Community SD	Winterset
44	14.5	Norwalk Community SD	Norwalk
44	14.5	Waterloo Community SD	Waterloo
46	14.4	Atlantic Community SD	Atlantic
46	14.4	Decorah Community SD	Decorah
46	14.4	Mount Pleasant Community SD	Mount Pleasant
49	14.2	Newton Community SD	Newton
49	14.2	North Scott Community SD	Eldridge
51	14.1	Clinton Community SD	Clinton
52	14.0	Grinnell-Newburg Community SD	Grinnell
52	14.0	Muscatine Community SD	Muscatine
54	13.9	Dallas Center-Grimes CSD	Dallas Center
55	13.8	Benton Community SD	Van Horne
55	13.8	Howard-Winneshiek Community SD	Cresco
57	13.7	Western Dubuque Community SD	Farley
58	13.6	Charles City Community SD	Charles City
59	13.5	Burlington Community SD	Burlington
59	13.5	Vinton-Shellsburg Community SD	Vinton
61	13.4	Des Moines ICSD	Des Moines
61	13.4	Washington Community SD	Washington
63	13.1	Central Clinton Community SD	De Witt
63	13.1	Independence Community SD	Independence
65	13.0	Marion Independent SD	Marion
66	12.8	Maquoketa Community SD	Maquoketa
67	12.7	Perry Community SD	Perry
68	12.2	Centerville Community SD	Centerville

Student/Librarian Ratio

Rank	Ratio	District Name	City
1	2,385.0	Fort Madison Community SD	Fort Madison
2	2,137.0	Mount Pleasant Community SD	Mount Pleasant
3	2,064.0	Knoxville Community SD	Knoxville
4	2,045.8	Davenport Community SD	Davenport
5	2,039.0	Storm Lake Community SD	Storm Lake
6	2,028.6	Dubuque Community SD	Dubuque
7	1,878.5	Sioux City Community SD	Sioux City
8	1,614.0	Winterset Community SD	Winterset
9	1,480.3	Des Moines ICSD	Des Moines
10	1,431.4	Council Bluffs Community SD	Council Bluffs
11	1,209.3	Southeast Polk Community SD	Runnells
12	1,205.5	Oskaloosa Community SD	Oskaloosa
13	1,140.5	Le Mars Community SD	Le Mars
14	1,132.0	Keokuk Community SD	Keokuk
15	1,121.7	Urbandale Community SD	Urbandale
16	1,080.8	West Des Moines Community SD	West Des Moines
17	1,064.0	Indianola Community SD	Indianola
18	1,060.0	Spencer Community SD	Spencer
19	1,026.5	Glenwood Community SD	Glenwood
20	1,007.5	Waverly-Shell Rock Community SD	Waverly
21	984.0	Fairfield Community SD	Fairfield
22	974.0	Ottumwa Community SD	Ottumwa
23	923.6	Boone Community SD	Boone
24	907.8	Ames Community SD	Ames
25	903.0	Western Dubuque Community SD	Farley
26	885.0	Webster City Community SD	Webster City
27	877.5	Perry Community SD	Perry
28	875.5	South Tama County Community SD	Tama
29	851.4	Mason City Community SD	Mason City
30	838.8	Fort Dodge Community SD	Fort Dodge
31	835.0	Newton Community SD	Newton
32	829.5	Maquoketa Community SD	Maquoketa
33	811.5	Central Clinton Community SD	De Witt
34	787.3	Johnston Community SD	Johnston
35	784.0	Lewis Central Community SD	Council Bluffs
36	780.5	Benton Community SD	Van Horne
37	763.5	Howard-Winneshiek Community SD	Cresco
38	756.5	Atlantic Community SD	Atlantic

39	746.3	Muscatine Community SD	Muscatine
40	744.7	Norwalk Community SD	Norwalk
41	739.4	College Community SD	Cedar Rapids
42	725.8	Waukee Community SD	Waukee
43	698.9	Ankeny Community SD	Ankeny
44	696.7	Pella Community SD	Pella
45	653.6	Linn-Mar Community SD	Marion
46	626.7	Cedar Falls Community SD	Cedar Falls
47	625.6	Burlington Community SD	Burlington
48	624.7	Iowa City Community SD	Iowa City
49	623.7	Clinton Community SD	Clinton
50	621.8	Marshalltown Community SD	Marshalltown
51	600.7	Denison Community SD	Denison
52	592.7	Carroll Community SD	Carroll
53	583.3	Grinnell-Newburg Community SD	Grinnell
54	578.2	Waterloo Community SD	Waterloo
55	577.5	Cedar Rapids Community SD	Cedar Rapids
56	574.3	West Delaware County CSD	Manchester
57	573.7	Washington Community SD	Washington
58	571.0	Decorah Community SD	Decorah
59	559.7	Marion Independent SD	Marion
60	559.0	Charles City Community SD	Charles City
61	548.0	Harlan Community SD	Harlan
62	537.3	Centerville Community SD	Centerville
63	532.7	Pleasant Valley Community SD	Pleasant Valley
64	520.0	Dallas Center-Grimes CSD	Dallas Center
65	501.3	Independence Community SD	Independence
66	497.5	North Scott Community SD	Eldridge
67	482.1	Bettendorf Community SD	Bettendorf
68	455.5	Vinton-Shellsburg Community SD	Vinton

Student/Counselor Ratio

Rank	Ratio	District Name	City
1	914.7	Lewis Central Community SD	Council Bluffs
2	907.3	Waukee Community SD	Waukee
3	806.0	Centerville Community SD	Centerville
4	712.3	Mount Pleasant Community SD	Mount Pleasant
5	674.9	Johnston Community SD	Johnston
6	671.7	Waverly-Shell Rock Community SD	Waverly
7	608.8	Ottumwa Community SD	Ottumwa
8	596.3	Fort Madison Community SD	Fort Madison
9	585.0	Perry Community SD	Perry
10	571.0	Decorah Community SD	Decorah
11	566.0	Keokuk Community SD	Keokuk
12	554.8	Davenport Community SD	Davenport
13	541.9	Sioux City Community SD	Sioux City
14	530.0	Spencer Community SD	Spencer
15	522.5	Pella Community SD	Pella
16	520.0	Dallas Center-Grimes CSD	Dallas Center
17	513.3	Glenwood Community SD	Glenwood
18	509.0	Howard-Winneshiek Community SD	Cresco
19	504.3	Atlantic Community SD	Atlantic
20	501.3	Independence Community SD	Independence
21	467.4	West Des Moines Community SD	West Des Moines
22	451.5	Western Dubuque Community SD	Farley
23	450.5	Denison Community SD	Denison
24	449.3	Ankeny Community SD	Ankeny
25	435.3	Marion Independent SD	Marion
26	433.5	Iowa City Community SD	Iowa City
27	425.7	Mason City Community SD	Mason City
28	424.8	Waterloo Community SD	Waterloo
29	415.8	Clinton Community SD	Clinton
30	410.8	College Community SD	Cedar Rapids
31	408.5	Linn-Mar Community SD	Marion
32	407.8	Storm Lake Community SD	Storm Lake
33	405.8	Central Clinton Community SD	De Witt
34	403.5	Winterset Community SD	Winterset
35	402.9	Cedar Rapids Community SD	Cedar Rapids
36	399.5	Pleasant Valley Community SD	Pleasant Valley
37	397.9	Marshalltown Community SD	Marshalltown
38	393.6	Fairfield Community SD	Fairfield
39	392.9	Council Bluffs Community SD	Council Bluffs
40	390.3	Benton Community SD	Van Horne
41	384.8	Boone Community SD	Boone
42	380.2	Le Mars Community SD	Le Mars
43	378.3	Ames Community SD	Ames
44	373.9	Urbandale Community SD	Urbandale
45	373.1	Muscatine Community SD	Muscatine
46	372.3	Norwalk Community SD	Norwalk
47	368.7	Maquoketa Community SD	Maquoketa
48	364.4	Vinton-Shellsburg Community SD	Vinton
49	362.3	Dubuque Community SD	Dubuque
50	355.6	Carroll Community SD	Carroll
51	354.7	Indianola Community SD	Indianola
52	351.3	Des Moines ICSD	Des Moines
53	350.2	South Tama County Community SD	Tama
54	350.0	Grinnell-Newburg Community SD	Grinnell
55	344.6	West Delaware County CSD	Manchester
56	344.2	Washington Community SD	Washington
57	337.5	Cedar Falls Community SD	Cedar Falls
58	336.8	Burlington Community SD	Burlington
59	335.4	Charles City Community SD	Charles City
60	333.8	Bettendorf Community SD	Bettendorf
61	328.8	Harlan Community SD	Harlan
62	322.6	Fort Dodge Community SD	Fort Dodge
63	302.3	Southeast Polk Community SD	Runnells
64	295.0	Webster City Community SD	Webster City
65	294.9	Knoxville Community SD	Knoxville
66	278.3	Newton Community SD	Newton
67	271.4	North Scott Community SD	Eldridge
68	241.1	Oskaloosa Community SD	Oskaloosa

Current Spending per Student in FY2003

Rank	Dollars	District Name	City
1	8,434	Des Moines ICSD	Des Moines
2	7,831	Grinnell-Newburg Community SD	Grinnell
3	7,634	Maquoketa Community SD	Maquoketa
4	7,603	Ames Community SD	Ames
5	7,569	Perry Community SD	Perry
6	7,482	Cedar Rapids Community SD	Cedar Rapids
7	7,448	Centerville Community SD	Centerville
8	7,430	Waterloo Community SD	Waterloo
9	7,410	Council Bluffs Community SD	Council Bluffs
10	7,400	Independence Community SD	Independence
11	7,379	Davenport Community SD	Davenport
12	7,358	Fort Dodge Community SD	Fort Dodge
13	7,308	Storm Lake Community SD	Storm Lake
14	7,279	Washington Community SD	Washington
15	7,264	Charles City Community SD	Charles City
16	7,216	Sioux City Community SD	Sioux City
17	7,204	Marshalltown Community SD	Marshalltown
18	7,202	Howard-Winneshiek Community SD	Cresco
19	7,193	Boone Community SD	Boone
20	7,187	Burlington Community SD	Burlington
21	7,173	North Scott Community SD	Eldridge
22	7,140	Keokuk Community SD	Keokuk
23	7,124	West Des Moines Community SD	West Des Moines
24	7,122	Clinton Community SD	Clinton
25	7,100	Marion Independent SD	Marion
26	7,074	Western Dubuque Community SD	Farley
27	7,045	Fairfield Community SD	Fairfield
28	7,035	Bettendorf Community SD	Bettendorf
29	7,018	Dubuque Community SD	Dubuque
30	7,016	Denison Community SD	Denison
31	7,009	Central Clinton Community SD	De Witt
32	6,971	Iowa City Community SD	Iowa City
33	6,911	College Community SD	Cedar Rapids
34	6,899	Decorah Community SD	Decorah
35	6,897	Southeast Polk Community SD	Runnells
36	6,871	Carroll Community SD	Carroll
37	6,862	Muscatine Community SD	Muscatine
38	6,840	Glenwood Community SD	Glenwood
39	6,835	Vinton-Shellsburg Community SD	Vinton
40	6,829	Johnston Community SD	Johnston
41	6,825	Cedar Falls Community SD	Cedar Falls
42	6,787	Mason City Community SD	Mason City
43	6,756	West Delaware County CSD	Manchester
44	6,648	South Tama County Community SD	Tama
44	6,648	Urbandale Community SD	Urbandale
46	6,638	Spencer Community SD	Spencer
47	6,633	Lewis Central Community SD	Council Bluffs
48	6,621	Oskaloosa Community SD	Oskaloosa
49	6,609	Atlantic Community SD	Atlantic
50	6,608	Benton Community SD	Van Horne
51	6,586	Pleasant Valley Community SD	Pleasant Valley
52	6,583	Knoxville Community SD	Knoxville
53	6,572	Newton Community SD	Newton
54	6,567	Linn-Mar Community SD	Marion
55	6,553	Winterset Community SD	Winterset
56	6,528	Indianola Community SD	Indianola
57	6,478	Webster City Community SD	Webster City
58	6,447	Ottumwa Community SD	Ottumwa
59	6,431	Pella Community SD	Pella
60	6,391	Fort Madison Community SD	Fort Madison
61	6,390	Mount Pleasant Community SD	Mount Pleasant
62	6,330	Norwalk Community SD	Norwalk
63	6,225	Le Mars Community SD	Le Mars
64	6,117	Harlan Community SD	Harlan
65	6,086	Ankeny Community SD	Ankeny
66	6,012	Dallas Center-Grimes CSD	Dallas Center
67	5,943	Waukee Community SD	Waukee
68	5,823	Waverly-Shell Rock Community SD	Waverly

Number of Diploma Recipients

Rank	Number	District Name	City
1	1,659	Des Moines ICSD	Des Moines
2	1,013	Cedar Rapids Community SD	Cedar Rapids
3	956	Davenport Community SD	Davenport
4	834	Sioux City Community SD	Sioux City
5	721	Iowa City Community SD	Iowa City
6	702	Dubuque Community SD	Dubuque
7	596	Waterloo Community SD	Waterloo
8	554	West Des Moines Community SD	West Des Moines
9	545	Council Bluffs Community SD	Council Bluffs
10	397	Ames Community SD	Ames
11	386	Ankeny Community SD	Ankeny
12	369	Cedar Falls Community SD	Cedar Falls
13	336	Muscatine Community SD	Muscatine
14	332	Urbandale Community SD	Urbandale
15	326	Clinton Community SD	Clinton
16	322	Southeast Polk Community SD	Runnells
17	315	Mason City Community SD	Mason City
18	310	Marshalltown Community SD	Marshalltown
19	295	Bettendorf Community SD	Bettendorf
20	293	Fort Dodge Community SD	Fort Dodge
21	291	Linn-Mar Community SD	Marion
21	291	Ottumwa Community SD	Ottumwa
23	289	Burlington Community SD	Burlington
24	270	Western Dubuque Community SD	Farley
25	262	Johnston Community SD	Johnston
26	261	Newton Community SD	Newton
27	241	Pleasant Valley Community SD	Pleasant Valley
28	228	College Community SD	Cedar Rapids
29	218	Indianola Community SD	Indianola
30	194	North Scott Community SD	Eldridge
31	191	Boone Community SD	Boone
32	186	Fort Madison Community SD	Fort Madison
33	181	Le Mars Community SD	Le Mars
34	177	Waverly-Shell Rock Community SD	Waverly
35	176	Lewis Central Community SD	Council Bluffs
36	174	Spencer Community SD	Spencer
37	171	Oskaloosa Community SD	Oskaloosa
38	168	West Delaware County CSD	Manchester
39	163	Mount Pleasant Community SD	Mount Pleasant
40	161	Keokuk Community SD	Keokuk
41	158	Knoxville Community SD	Knoxville
42	153	Harlan Community SD	Harlan
43	147	Carroll Community SD	Carroll
43	147	Glenwood Community SD	Glenwood
45	143	Winterset Community SD	Winterset
46	141	Marion Independent SD	Marion
47	139	Decorah Community SD	Decorah
48	138	Central Clinton Community SD	De Witt
48	138	Webster City Community SD	Webster City
50	137	Pella Community SD	Pella
51	135	Benton Community SD	Van Horne
52	133	Fairfield Community SD	Fairfield
53	130	Howard-Winneshiek Community SD	Cresco
53	130	Waukee Community SD	Waukee
55	129	Norwalk Community SD	Norwalk
56	127	Denison Community SD	Denison
57	124	Perry Community SD	Perry
58	123	Grinnell-Newburg Community SD	Grinnell
58	123	Vinton-Shellsburg Community SD	Vinton
60	122	Atlantic Community SD	Atlantic
60	122	Independence Community SD	Independence
60	122	Storm Lake Community SD	Storm Lake
63	121	Charles City Community SD	Charles City
64	118	Centerville Community SD	Centerville
65	116	South Tama County Community SD	Tama
66	115	Maquoketa Community SD	Maquoketa
67	90	Dallas Center-Grimes CSD	Dallas Center
67	90	Washington Community SD	Washington

High School Drop-out Rate

Rank	Percent	District Name	City
1	9.2	Waterloo Community SD	Waterloo
2	7.5	Sioux City Community SD	Sioux City
3	6.6	Ottumwa Community SD	Ottumwa
4	6.5	Burlington Community SD	Burlington
5	5.1	Council Bluffs Community SD	Council Bluffs
5	5.1	Keokuk Community SD	Keokuk
7	4.8	Marshalltown Community SD	Marshalltown
8	4.6	Des Moines ICSD	Des Moines
9	4.5	West Delaware County CSD	Manchester
10	4.4	Webster City Community SD	Webster City
11	4.3	Muscatine Community SD	Muscatine
12	4.2	Davenport Community SD	Davenport
13	4.1	Fort Madison Community SD	Fort Madison
13	4.1	Newton Community SD	Newton
13	4.1	South Tama County Community SD	Tama
16	3.8	Mason City Community SD	Mason City
16	3.8	Washington Community SD	Washington
18	3.7	Clinton Community SD	Clinton
19	3.3	Fort Dodge Community SD	Fort Dodge
20	3.2	Dubuque Community SD	Dubuque
20	3.2	Perry Community SD	Perry
22	3.0	Pleasant Valley Community SD	Pleasant Valley
23	2.9	Denison Community SD	Denison
24	2.7	Indianola Community SD	Indianola
24	2.7	Maquoketa Community SD	Maquoketa
26	2.6	Cedar Rapids Community SD	Cedar Rapids
27	2.5	Fairfield Community SD	Fairfield
27	2.5	Storm Lake Community SD	Storm Lake
29	2.4	Boone Community SD	Boone

29	2.4	Glenwood Community SD	Glenwood
29	2.4	Oskaloosa Community SD	Oskaloosa
32	2.3	Ames Community SD	Ames
33	2.2	Iowa City Community SD	Iowa City
34	2.1	Howard-Winneshiek Community SD	Cresco
35	1.9	Marion Independent SD	Marion
36	1.8	Bettendorf Community SD	Bettendorf
36	1.8	Knoxville Community SD	Knoxville
36	1.8	Lewis Central Community SD	Council Bluffs
39	1.6	Central Clinton Community SD	De Witt
39	1.6	West Des Moines Community SD	West Des Moines
41	1.5	Charles City Community SD	Charles City
42	1.3	College Community SD	Cedar Rapids
42	1.3	North Scott Community SD	Eldridge
42	1.3	Winterset Community SD	Winterset
45	1.2	Pella Community SD	Pella
46	1.1	Grinnell-Newburg Community SD	Grinnell
46	1.1	Le Mars Community SD	Le Mars
48	1.0	Atlantic Community SD	Atlantic
49	0.9	Linn-Mar Community SD	Marion
49	0.9	Western Dubuque Community SD	Farley
51	0.8	Ankeny Community SD	Ankeny
51	0.8	Urbandale Community SD	Urbandale
53	0.7	Spencer Community SD	Spencer
54	0.6	Benton Community SD	Van Horne
54	0.6	Cedar Falls Community SD	Cedar Falls
54	0.6	Centerville Community SD	Centerville
54	0.6	Dallas Center-Grimes CSD	Dallas Center
54	0.6	Decorah Community SD	Decorah
54	0.6	Independence Community SD	Independence
54	0.6	Mount Pleasant Community SD	Mount Pleasant
54	0.6	Southeast Polk Community SD	Runnells
62	0.5	Carroll Community SD	Carroll
63	0.4	Johnston Community SD	Johnston
63	0.4	Vinton-Shellsburg Community SD	Vinton
65	0.3	Norwalk Community SD	Norwalk
66	0.2	Harlan Community SD	Harlan
67	0.1	Waukee Community SD	Waukee
68	0.0	Waverly-Shell Rock Community SD	Waverly

Kansas

Kansas Public School Educational Profile

Category	Value	Category	Value
Schools (2003-2004)	1,413	**Diploma Recipients** (2002-2003)	29,492
Instructional Level		White, Non-Hispanic	25,170
Primary	782	Black, Non-Hispanic	1,856
Middle	258	Asian/Pacific Islander	685
High	359	American Indian/Alaskan Native	283
Other Level	14	Hispanic	1,498
Curriculum		**High School Drop-out Rate** (%) (2001-2002)	3.1
Regular	1,404	White, Non-Hispanic	2.6
Special Education	4	Black, Non-Hispanic	5.3
Vocational	0	Asian/Pacific Islander	2.4
Alternative	5	American Indian/Alaskan Native	5.4
Type		Hispanic	5.9
Magnet	32	**Staff** (2003-2004)	
Charter	17	Teachers	32,701.9
Title I Eligible	466	Average Salary ($)	38,622
School-wide Title I	241	Librarians/Media Specialists	923.2
Students (2003-2004)	470,500	Guidance Counselors	1,117.9
Gender (%)		**Ratios** (2003-2004)	
Male	51.7	Student/Teacher Ratio	14.4 to 1
Female	48.3	Student/Librarian Ratio	509.6 to 1
Race/Ethnicity (%)		Student/Counselor Ratio	420.9 to 1
White, Non-Hispanic	75.2	**College Entrance Exam Scores** (2005)	
Black, Non-Hispanic	8.7	Scholastic Aptitude Test (SAT)	
Asian/Pacific Islander	2.3	Participation Rate (%)	9
American Indian/Alaskan Native	1.4	Mean SAT Reasoning Test Verbal Score	585
Hispanic	10.8	Mean SAT Reasoning Test Math Score	588
Classification (%)		American College Testing Program (ACT)	
Individual Education Program (IEP)	13.8	Participation Rate (%)	76
Migrant (2002-2003)	2.3	Average Composite Score	21.7
English Language Learner (ELL)	4.8	Average English Score	21.2
Eligible for Free Lunch Program	28.1	Average Math Score	21.4
Eligible for Reduced-Price Lunch Program	9.5	Average Reading Score	22.1
Current Spending ($ per student in FY 2003)	7,285	Average Science Score	21.6
Instruction	4,397		
Support Services	2,543		

Note: For an explanation of data, please refer to the User's Guide in the front of the book

Kansas NAEP 2005 Test Scores

Reading			Mathematics		
Grade/Category	Value	Rank	Grade/Category	Value	Rank
4th Grade			**4th Grade**		
Average Proficiency	220.5 (1.27)	25/51	Average Proficiency	245.8 (0.95)	2/51
Proficiency by Gender/Race/Ethnicity			Proficiency by Gender/Race/Ethnicity		
Male	217.8 (1.22)	23/51	Male	246.9 (1.02)	3/51
Female	223.2 (1.54)	25/51	Female	244.5 (1.16)	3/51
White, Non-Hispanic	225.3 (1.30)	32/51	White, Non-Hispanic	249.4 (1.07)	10/51
Black, Non-Hispanic	196.2 (2.53)	28/42	Black, Non-Hispanic	227.9 (1.77)	3/42
Asian, Non-Hispanic	238.1 (4.88)	6/27	Asian, Non-Hispanic	261.6 (3.60)	3/25
American Indian, Non-Hispanic	n/a	n/a	American Indian, Non-Hispanic	n/a	n/a
Hispanic	203.2 (2.76)	22/40	Hispanic	233.8 (2.08)	5/41
Proficiency by Class Size			Proficiency by Class Size		
Less than 16 Students	211.4 (3.41)	13/34	Less than 16 Students	241.1 (2.34)	3/35
16 to 18 Students	221.2 (2.83)	11/33	16 to 18 Students	244.7 (2.02)	2/31
19 to 20 Students	218.9 (2.35)	22/38	19 to 20 Students	246.2 (1.81)	5/38
21 to 25 Students	222.7 (1.83)	22/51	21 to 25 Students	247.0 (1.48)	2/51
Greater than 25 Students	n/a	n/a	Greater than 25 Students	n/a	n/a
Percent Attaining Achievement Levels			Percent Attaining Achievement Levels		
Below Basic	33.7 (1.46)	27/51	Below Basic	11.9 (0.73)	48/51
Basic or Above	66.3 (1.46)	25/51	Basic or Above	88.1 (0.73)	4/51
Proficient or Above	32.5 (1.34)	25/51	Proficient or Above	46.8 (1.57)	4/51
Advanced or Above	7.7 (0.95)	13/51	Advanced or Above	8.0 (0.82)	3/51
8th Grade			**8th Grade**		
Average Proficiency	266.8 (0.99)	14/51	Average Proficiency	284.0 (1.03)	11/51
Proficiency by Gender/Race/Ethnicity			Proficiency by Gender/Race/Ethnicity		
Male	262.5 (1.19)	11/51	Male	284.6 (1.32)	12/51
Female	271.4 (1.31)	16/51	Female	283.4 (1.37)	11/51
White, Non-Hispanic	271.1 (0.98)	19/51	White, Non-Hispanic	289.5 (0.95)	18/51
Black, Non-Hispanic	246.9 (2.23)	9/40	Black, Non-Hispanic	256.1 (4.45)	17/41
Asian, Non-Hispanic	n/a	n/a	Asian, Non-Hispanic	n/a	n/a
American Indian, Non-Hispanic	n/a	n/a	American Indian, Non-Hispanic	n/a	n/a
Hispanic	248.6 (2.59)	14/38	Hispanic	265.6 (2.51)	8/38
Proficiency by Parents Highest Level of Ed.			Proficiency by Parents Highest Level of Ed.		
Did Not Finish High School	250.5 (3.34)	10/49	Did Not Finish High School	261.3 (2.71)	28/50
Graduated High School	256.4 (2.20)	20/50	Graduated High School	272.9 (1.79)	12/50
Some Education After High School	271.3 (1.50)	4/50	Some Education After High School	286.0 (1.33)	7/50
Graduated College	275.5 (1.31)	9/50	Graduated College	293.7 (1.25)	11/50
Percent Attaining Achievement Levels			Percent Attaining Achievement Levels		
Below Basic	33.7 (1.46)	27/51	Below Basic	23.3 (1.31)	44/51
Basic or Above	66.3 (1.46)	25/51	Basic or Above	76.7 (1.31)	8/51
Proficient or Above	32.5 (1.34)	25/51	Proficient or Above	34.2 (1.37)	13/51
Advanced or Above	7.7 (0.95)	13/51	Advanced or Above	5.2 (0.60)	26/51

Note: For an explanation of data, please refer to the User's Guide in the front of the book; n/a indicates data not available

Allen County

Iola
408 N Cottonwood · Iola, KS 66749-2997
(620) 365-4700 · http://www.iola.com/usd256.htm
Grade Span: KG-12; **Agency Type:** 1
Schools: 6
  4 Primary; 1 Middle; 1 High; 0 Other Level
  6 Regular; 0 Special Education; 0 Vocational; 0 Alternative
  0 Magnet; 0 Charter; 4 Title I Eligible; 2 School-wide Title I
Students: 1,513 (52.4% male; 47.5% female)
  Individual Education Program: 308 (20.4%);
  English Language Learner: 0 (0.0%); Migrant: 0 (0.0%)
  Eligible for Free Lunch Program: 497 (33.0%)
  Eligible for Reduced-Price Lunch Program: 240 (16.0%)
Teachers: 105.1 (14.3 to 1)
Librarians/Media Specialists: 4.0 (376.0 to 1)
Guidance Counselors: 5.0 (300.8 to 1)
Current Spending: ($ per student per year):
  Total: $7,675; Instruction: $4,939; Support Services: $2,296
Enrollment, Drop-out Rates and Diploma Recipients by Race/Ethnicity

Category	Total	White	Black	Asian	AIAN	Hisp.
Enrollment (%)	100.0	91.8	2.9	1.1	1.1	1.5
Drop-out Rate (%)	3.0	3.3	0.0	0.0	0.0	0.0
H.S. Diplomas (#)	117	109	3	1	3	1

Atchison County

Atchison Public Schools
215 N 8th St · Atchison, KS 66002
(913) 367-4384 · http://www.atchison.k12.ks.us
Grade Span: KG-12; **Agency Type:** 1
Schools: 3
  1 Primary; 1 Middle; 1 High; 0 Other Level
  3 Regular; 0 Special Education; 0 Vocational; 0 Alternative
  0 Magnet; 0 Charter; 1 Title I Eligible; 1 School-wide Title I
Students: 1,676 (52.3% male; 47.6% female)
  Individual Education Program: 332 (19.8%);
  English Language Learner: 0 (0.0%); Migrant: 0 (0.0%)
  Eligible for Free Lunch Program: 685 (40.9%)
  Eligible for Reduced-Price Lunch Program: 253 (15.1%)
Teachers: 130.0 (12.9 to 1)
Librarians/Media Specialists: 3.5 (478.9 to 1)
Guidance Counselors: 3.0 (558.7 to 1)
Current Spending: ($ per student per year):
  Total: $8,265; Instruction: $4,900; Support Services: $2,938
Enrollment, Drop-out Rates and Diploma Recipients by Race/Ethnicity

Category	Total	White	Black	Asian	AIAN	Hisp.
Enrollment (%)	100.0	81.9	15.5	0.6	0.4	1.6
Drop-out Rate (%)	3.4	3.8	2.2	0.0	0.0	0.0
H.S. Diplomas (#)	107	90	14	2	0	1

Barton County

Great Bend
201 Patton Rd · Great Bend, KS 67530-4613
(620) 793-1500 · http://www.usd428.org/
Grade Span: PK-12; **Agency Type:** 1
Schools: 7
  5 Primary; 1 Middle; 1 High; 0 Other Level
  7 Regular; 0 Special Education; 0 Vocational; 0 Alternative
  0 Magnet; 0 Charter; 2 Title I Eligible; 2 School-wide Title I
Students: 3,307 (51.7% male; 48.2% female)
  Individual Education Program: 437 (13.2%);
  English Language Learner: 302 (9.1%); Migrant: 615 (18.6%)
  Eligible for Free Lunch Program: 1,405 (42.5%)
  Eligible for Reduced-Price Lunch Program: 266 (8.0%)
Teachers: 238.9 (13.8 to 1)
Librarians/Media Specialists: 5.0 (661.4 to 1)
Guidance Counselors: 7.5 (440.9 to 1)
Current Spending: ($ per student per year):
  Total: $6,852; Instruction: $4,248; Support Services: $2,209
Enrollment, Drop-out Rates and Diploma Recipients by Race/Ethnicity

Category	Total	White	Black	Asian	AIAN	Hisp.
Enrollment (%)	100.0	70.3	3.0	0.4	0.6	24.6
Drop-out Rate (%)	2.6	2.3	0.0	0.0	50.0	3.9
H.S. Diplomas (#)	217	188	6	1	0	22

Bourbon County

Fort Scott
424 S Main · Fort Scott, KS 66701-2097
(620) 223-0800 · http://www.usd234.org/
Grade Span: KG-12; **Agency Type:** 1
Schools: 4

  2 Primary; 1 Middle; 1 High; 0 Other Level
  4 Regular; 0 Special Education; 0 Vocational; 0 Alternative
  0 Magnet; 0 Charter; 1 Title I Eligible; 1 School-wide Title I
Students: 2,046 (50.6% male; 49.3% female)
  Individual Education Program: 216 (10.6%);
  English Language Learner: 10 (0.5%); Migrant: 0 (0.0%)
  Eligible for Free Lunch Program: 745 (36.4%)
  Eligible for Reduced-Price Lunch Program: 253 (12.4%)
Teachers: 145.1 (14.1 to 1)
Librarians/Media Specialists: 4.0 (511.5 to 1)
Guidance Counselors: 4.0 (511.5 to 1)
Current Spending: ($ per student per year):
  Total: $6,019; Instruction: $4,016; Support Services: $1,720
Enrollment, Drop-out Rates and Diploma Recipients by Race/Ethnicity

Category	Total	White	Black	Asian	AIAN	Hisp.
Enrollment (%)	100.0	91.8	5.4	0.4	0.5	1.6
Drop-out Rate (%)	4.2	4.1	0.0	0.0	0.0	23.1
H.S. Diplomas (#)	150	143	1	1	1	4

Butler County

Andover
1432 N Andover Rd · Andover, KS 67002-0248
(316) 733-5017 · http://www.usd385.org
Grade Span: KG-12; **Agency Type:** 1
Schools: 8
  4 Primary; 2 Middle; 2 High; 0 Other Level
  8 Regular; 0 Special Education; 0 Vocational; 0 Alternative
  0 Magnet; 0 Charter; 2 Title I Eligible; 0 School-wide Title I
Students: 3,520 (52.3% male; 47.6% female)
  Individual Education Program: 400 (11.4%);
  English Language Learner: 23 (0.7%); Migrant: 0 (0.0%)
  Eligible for Free Lunch Program: 250 (7.1%)
  Eligible for Reduced-Price Lunch Program: 154 (4.4%)
Teachers: 208.7 (16.9 to 1)
Librarians/Media Specialists: 7.0 (502.6 to 1)
Guidance Counselors: 10.0 (351.8 to 1)
Current Spending: ($ per student per year):
  Total: $6,549; Instruction: $3,966; Support Services: $2,225
Enrollment, Drop-out Rates and Diploma Recipients by Race/Ethnicity

Category	Total	White	Black	Asian	AIAN	Hisp.
Enrollment (%)	100.0	91.6	1.7	2.4	1.2	3.0
Drop-out Rate (%)	1.9	1.8	0.0	9.1	0.0	0.0
H.S. Diplomas (#)	216	209	0	1	0	6

Augusta
2345 Greyhound Dr · Augusta, KS 67010-1699
(316) 775-5484 · http://www.usd402.com/
Grade Span: KG-12; **Agency Type:** 1
Schools: 6
  4 Primary; 1 Middle; 1 High; 0 Other Level
  6 Regular; 0 Special Education; 0 Vocational; 0 Alternative
  0 Magnet; 0 Charter; 1 Title I Eligible; 1 School-wide Title I
Students: 2,171 (52.8% male; 47.1% female)
  Individual Education Program: 266 (12.3%);
  English Language Learner: 0 (0.0%); Migrant: 0 (0.0%)
  Eligible for Free Lunch Program: 452 (20.9%)
  Eligible for Reduced-Price Lunch Program: 152 (7.0%)
Teachers: 130.0 (16.6 to 1)
Librarians/Media Specialists: 6.0 (360.7 to 1)
Guidance Counselors: 6.0 (360.7 to 1)
Current Spending: ($ per student per year):
  Total: $5,956; Instruction: $3,787; Support Services: $1,918
Enrollment, Drop-out Rates and Diploma Recipients by Race/Ethnicity

Category	Total	White	Black	Asian	AIAN	Hisp.
Enrollment (%)	100.0	93.2	0.6	1.1	1.2	3.3
Drop-out Rate (%)	0.6	0.6	0.0	0.0	0.0	0.0
H.S. Diplomas (#)	142	135	1	1	1	4

Circle
901 Main · Towanda, KS 67144-0009
Mailing Address: PO Box 9 · Towanda, KS 67144-0009
(316) 541-2577
Grade Span: KG-12; **Agency Type:** 1
Schools: 5
  3 Primary; 1 Middle; 1 High; 0 Other Level
  5 Regular; 0 Special Education; 0 Vocational; 0 Alternative
  0 Magnet; 0 Charter; 2 Title I Eligible; 0 School-wide Title I
Students: 1,537 (50.7% male; 49.2% female)
  Individual Education Program: 188 (12.2%);
  English Language Learner: 0 (0.0%); Migrant: 0 (0.0%)
  Eligible for Free Lunch Program: 273 (18.3%)
  Eligible for Reduced-Price Lunch Program: 133 (8.9%)
Teachers: 88.8 (16.8 to 1)
Librarians/Media Specialists: 5.0 (298.8 to 1)
Guidance Counselors: 5.5 (271.6 to 1)

Current Spending: ($ per student per year):
Total: $7,024; Instruction: $3,978; Support Services: $2,662
Enrollment, Drop-out Rates and Diploma Recipients by Race/Ethnicity

Category	Total	White	Black	Asian	AIAN	Hisp.
Enrollment (%)	100.0	92.8	1.7	0.7	1.7	2.1
Drop-out Rate (%)	1.6	1.5	0.0	0.0	0.0	16.7
H.S. Diplomas (#)	99	94	2	1	0	2

El Dorado

124 W Central Ave • El Dorado, KS 67042-2138
(316) 322-4800 • http://http://www.eldoradoschools.org
Grade Span: KG-12; **Agency Type:** 1
Schools: 7
5 Primary; 1 Middle; 1 High; 0 Other Level
7 Regular; 0 Special Education; 0 Vocational; 0 Alternative
0 Magnet; 0 Charter; 4 Title I Eligible; 0 School-wide Title I
Students: 2,198 (54.1% male; 45.8% female)
Individual Education Program: 375 (17.1%);
English Language Learner: 0 (0.0%); Migrant: 0 (0.0%)
Eligible for Free Lunch Program: 628 (29.6%)
Eligible for Reduced-Price Lunch Program: 174 (8.2%)
Teachers: 227.0 (9.3 to 1)
Librarians/Media Specialists: 4.5 (471.6 to 1)
Guidance Counselors: 7.0 (303.1 to 1)
Current Spending: ($ per student per year):
Total: $6,030; Instruction: $3,671; Support Services: $2,025
Enrollment, Drop-out Rates and Diploma Recipients by Race/Ethnicity

Category	Total	White	Black	Asian	AIAN	Hisp.
Enrollment (%)	100.0	90.4	3.6	0.5	1.4	4.1
Drop-out Rate (%)	2.5	2.6	0.0	0.0	0.0	3.7
H.S. Diplomas (#)	114	103	4	1	1	5

Rose Hill Public Schools

104 N Rose Hill Rd • Rose Hill, KS 67133-9785
(316) 776-3300
Grade Span: KG-12; **Agency Type:** 1
Schools: 4
2 Primary; 1 Middle; 1 High; 0 Other Level
4 Regular; 0 Special Education; 0 Vocational; 0 Alternative
0 Magnet; 0 Charter; 2 Title I Eligible; 0 School-wide Title I
Students: 1,878 (51.4% male; 48.5% female)
Individual Education Program: 174 (9.3%);
English Language Learner: 0 (0.0%); Migrant: 0 (0.0%)
Eligible for Free Lunch Program: 206 (11.1%)
Eligible for Reduced-Price Lunch Program: 96 (5.2%)
Teachers: 102.0 (18.2 to 1)
Librarians/Media Specialists: 2.0 (927.0 to 1)
Guidance Counselors: 4.0 (463.5 to 1)
Current Spending: ($ per student per year):
Total: $6,212; Instruction: $3,715; Support Services: $2,240
Enrollment, Drop-out Rates and Diploma Recipients by Race/Ethnicity

Category	Total	White	Black	Asian	AIAN	Hisp.
Enrollment (%)	100.0	95.4	0.8	0.7	0.9	1.8
Drop-out Rate (%)	1.4	1.4	0.0	0.0	0.0	0.0
H.S. Diplomas (#)	127	125	0	0	1	1

Cowley County

Arkansas City

119 W Washington • Arkansas City, KS 67005-1028
Mailing Address: PO Box 1028 • Arkansas City, KS 67005-1028
(620) 441-2000 • http://www.arkcity.com
Grade Span: PK-12; **Agency Type:** 1
Schools: 8
6 Primary; 1 Middle; 1 High; 0 Other Level
8 Regular; 0 Special Education; 0 Vocational; 0 Alternative
0 Magnet; 0 Charter; 5 Title I Eligible; 5 School-wide Title I
Students: 3,017 (51.2% male; 48.7% female)
Individual Education Program: 583 (19.3%);
English Language Learner: 245 (8.1%); Migrant: 78 (2.6%)
Eligible for Free Lunch Program: 1,352 (44.9%)
Eligible for Reduced-Price Lunch Program: 343 (11.4%)
Teachers: 179.7 (16.8 to 1)
Librarians/Media Specialists: 6.0 (502.0 to 1)
Guidance Counselors: 8.0 (376.5 to 1)
Current Spending: ($ per student per year):
Total: $6,425; Instruction: $3,892; Support Services: $2,176
Enrollment, Drop-out Rates and Diploma Recipients by Race/Ethnicity

Category	Total	White	Black	Asian	AIAN	Hisp.
Enrollment (%)	100.0	73.0	5.5	0.5	7.8	12.9
Drop-out Rate (%)	5.2	4.4	11.8	0.0	10.9	7.8
H.S. Diplomas (#)	169	147	5	2	9	6

Winfield

920 Millington • Winfield, KS 67156-3691
(620) 221-5100 • http://www.usd465.com/
Grade Span: PK-12; **Agency Type:** 1
Schools: 8
5 Primary; 1 Middle; 1 High; 1 Other Level
8 Regular; 0 Special Education; 0 Vocational; 0 Alternative
0 Magnet; 0 Charter; 4 Title I Eligible; 3 School-wide Title I
Students: 2,706 (52.1% male; 47.8% female)
Individual Education Program: 454 (16.8%)
English Language Learner: 68 (2.5%); Migrant: 0 (0.0%)
Eligible for Free Lunch Program: 780 (28.9%)
Eligible for Reduced-Price Lunch Program: 365 (13.5%)
Teachers: 244.1 (11.1 to 1)
Librarians/Media Specialists: 4.0 (675.3 to 1)
Guidance Counselors: 4.0 (675.3 to 1)
Current Spending: ($ per student per year):
Total: $6,657; Instruction: $4,011; Support Services: $2,301
Enrollment, Drop-out Rates and Diploma Recipients by Race/Ethnicity

Category	Total	White	Black	Asian	AIAN	Hisp.
Enrollment (%)	100.0	85.1	3.3	5.2	1.2	5.0
Drop-out Rate (%)	0.2	0.2	0.0	0.0	0.0	0.0
H.S. Diplomas (#)	217	195	6	10	0	6

Crawford County

Pittsburg

510 Deill St • Pittsburg, KS 66762-0075
Mailing Address: Drawer 75 • Pittsburg, KS 66762-0075
(620) 235-3100 • http://www.usd250.k12.ks.us/
Grade Span: KG-12; **Agency Type:** 1
Schools: 6
4 Primary; 1 Middle; 1 High; 0 Other Level
6 Regular; 0 Special Education; 0 Vocational; 0 Alternative
0 Magnet; 0 Charter; 3 Title I Eligible; 3 School-wide Title I
Students: 2,609 (50.7% male; 49.2% female)
Individual Education Program: 379 (14.5%);
English Language Learner: 126 (4.8%); Migrant: 94 (3.6%)
Eligible for Free Lunch Program: 1,124 (43.5%)
Eligible for Reduced-Price Lunch Program: 222 (8.6%)
Teachers: 159.0 (16.3 to 1)
Librarians/Media Specialists: 6.6 (391.7 to 1)
Guidance Counselors: 8.0 (323.1 to 1)
Current Spending: ($ per student per year):
Total: $6,904; Instruction: $4,181; Support Services: $2,352
Enrollment, Drop-out Rates and Diploma Recipients by Race/Ethnicity

Category	Total	White	Black	Asian	AIAN	Hisp.
Enrollment (%)	100.0	82.3	7.3	2.5	1.0	6.8
Drop-out Rate (%)	4.0	4.0	0.0	0.0	0.0	15.0
H.S. Diplomas (#)	144	132	4	7	0	1

Douglas County

Lawrence

110 Mcdonald Dr • Lawrence, KS 66044-1063
(785) 832-5000 • http://www.usd497.org/
Grade Span: KG-12; **Agency Type:** 1
Schools: 21
15 Primary; 4 Middle; 2 High; 0 Other Level
21 Regular; 0 Special Education; 0 Vocational; 0 Alternative
1 Magnet; 0 Charter; 8 Title I Eligible; 4 School-wide Title I
Students: 10,022 (50.7% male; 49.2% female)
Individual Education Program: 1,578 (15.7%);
English Language Learner: 506 (5.0%); Migrant: 0 (0.0%)
Eligible for Free Lunch Program: 2,024 (20.2%)
Eligible for Reduced-Price Lunch Program: 920 (9.2%)
Teachers: 749.5 (13.4 to 1)
Librarians/Media Specialists: 22.5 (445.4 to 1)
Guidance Counselors: 25.8 (388.4 to 1)
Current Spending: ($ per student per year):
Total: $7,471; Instruction: $4,517; Support Services: $2,619
Enrollment, Drop-out Rates and Diploma Recipients by Race/Ethnicity

Category	Total	White	Black	Asian	AIAN	Hisp.
Enrollment (%)	100.0	74.4	10.0	3.7	4.8	4.3
Drop-out Rate (%)	1.9	1.9	1.4	0.9	2.9	2.7
H.S. Diplomas (#)	772	639	68	27	20	18

Ellis County

Hays

323 W 12th St • Hays, KS 67601-3893
(785) 623-2400 • http://www.hays489.k12.ks.us/
Grade Span: PK-12; **Agency Type:** 1
Schools: 9
6 Primary; 2 Middle; 1 High; 0 Other Level

9 Regular; 0 Special Education; 0 Vocational; 0 Alternative
0 Magnet; 0 Charter; 6 Title I Eligible; 0 School-wide Title I
Students: 3,271 (51.7% male; 48.2% female)
Individual Education Program: 542 (16.6%);
English Language Learner: 44 (1.3%); Migrant: 49 (1.5%)
Eligible for Free Lunch Program: 682 (20.8%)
Eligible for Reduced-Price Lunch Program: 343 (10.5%)
Teachers: 269.7 (12.1 to 1)
Librarians/Media Specialists: 5.9 (554.4 to 1)
Guidance Counselors: 8.0 (408.9 to 1)
Current Spending: ($ per student per year):
Total: $7,456; Instruction: $4,926; Support Services: $2,176
Enrollment, Drop-out Rates and Diploma Recipients by Race/Ethnicity

Category	Total	White	Black	Asian	AIAN	Hisp.
Enrollment (%)	100.0	90.8	2.0	1.0	0.3	5.5
Drop-out Rate (%)	2.6	2.6	10.0	0.0	0.0	1.8
H.S. Diplomas (#)	229	221	1	2	0	5

Finney County

Garden City
1205 Fleming St • Garden City, KS 67846-4751
(620) 276-5100 • http://www.gckschools.com/
Grade Span: PK-12; **Agency Type:** 1
Schools: 16
11 Primary; 4 Middle; 1 High; 0 Other Level
16 Regular; 0 Special Education; 0 Vocational; 0 Alternative
0 Magnet; 0 Charter; 4 Title I Eligible; 4 School-wide Title I
Students: 7,736 (51.2% male; 48.7% female)
Individual Education Program: 925 (12.0%);
English Language Learner: 1,701 (22.0%); Migrant: 678 (8.8%)
Eligible for Free Lunch Program: 3,349 (43.3%)
Eligible for Reduced-Price Lunch Program: 880 (11.4%)
Teachers: 496.4 (15.6 to 1)
Librarians/Media Specialists: 15.0 (515.7 to 1)
Guidance Counselors: 20.0 (386.8 to 1)
Current Spending: ($ per student per year):
Total: $6,838; Instruction: $3,898; Support Services: $2,669
Enrollment, Drop-out Rates and Diploma Recipients by Race/Ethnicity

Category	Total	White	Black	Asian	AIAN	Hisp.
Enrollment (%)	100.0	32.6	1.2	2.6	0.3	58.3
Drop-out Rate (%)	3.7	2.3	3.1	5.5	33.3	4.7
H.S. Diplomas (#)	279	180	6	11	2	80

Ford County

Dodge City
1000 Second Ave • Dodge City, KS 67801-0460
Mailing Address: Box 460 • Dodge City, KS 67801-0460
(620) 227-1620 • http://www.usd443.org/
Grade Span: KG-12; **Agency Type:** 1
Schools: 11
7 Primary; 3 Middle; 1 High; 0 Other Level
11 Regular; 0 Special Education; 0 Vocational; 0 Alternative
0 Magnet; 0 Charter; 7 Title I Eligible; 7 School-wide Title I
Students: 5,960 (51.4% male; 48.5% female)
Individual Education Program: 751 (12.6%);
English Language Learner: 2,954 (49.6%); Migrant: 2,196 (36.8%)
Eligible for Free Lunch Program: 3,073 (51.6%)
Eligible for Reduced-Price Lunch Program: 836 (14.0%)
Teachers: 340.7 (17.5 to 1)
Librarians/Media Specialists: 10.5 (567.6 to 1)
Guidance Counselors: 13.4 (444.8 to 1)
Current Spending: ($ per student per year):
Total: $7,336; Instruction: $4,515; Support Services: $2,363
Enrollment, Drop-out Rates and Diploma Recipients by Race/Ethnicity

Category	Total	White	Black	Asian	AIAN	Hisp.
Enrollment (%)	100.0	32.1	2.6	2.3	0.7	61.1
Drop-out Rate (%)	2.0	1.3	0.0	0.0	0.0	3.1
H.S. Diplomas (#)	303	197	3	17	1	85

Franklin County

Ottawa
123 W 4th St • Ottawa, KS 66067-2223
(785) 229-8010 • http://www.ottawa.k12.ks.us/
Grade Span: KG-12; **Agency Type:** 1
Schools: 7
5 Primary; 1 Middle; 1 High; 0 Other Level
7 Regular; 0 Special Education; 0 Vocational; 0 Alternative
0 Magnet; 0 Charter; 5 Title I Eligible; 5 School-wide Title I
Students: 2,472 (52.4% male; 47.5% female)
Individual Education Program: 368 (14.9%);
English Language Learner: 25 (1.0%); Migrant: 0 (0.0%)
Eligible for Free Lunch Program: 657 (26.6%)

Eligible for Reduced-Price Lunch Program: 205 (8.3%)
Teachers: 166.0 (14.9 to 1)
Librarians/Media Specialists: 4.5 (549.1 to 1)
Guidance Counselors: 9.5 (260.1 to 1)
Current Spending: ($ per student per year):
Total: $6,085; Instruction: $3,956; Support Services: $1,881
Enrollment, Drop-out Rates and Diploma Recipients by Race/Ethnicity

Category	Total	White	Black	Asian	AIAN	Hisp.
Enrollment (%)	100.0	88.7	3.1	0.8	1.5	4.0
Drop-out Rate (%)	1.4	1.3	0.0	0.0	0.0	3.8
H.S. Diplomas (#)	121	115	3	2	0	1

Geary County

Geary County Schools
123 N Eisenhower • Junction City, KS 66441-0370
Mailing Address: PO Box 370 • Junction City, KS 66441-0370
(785) 238-6184 • http://www.usd475.org/
Grade Span: PK-12; **Agency Type:** 1
Schools: 16
13 Primary; 2 Middle; 1 High; 0 Other Level
16 Regular; 0 Special Education; 0 Vocational; 0 Alternative
0 Magnet; 0 Charter; 11 Title I Eligible; 11 School-wide Title I
Students: 6,645 (51.4% male; 48.5% female)
Individual Education Program: 974 (14.7%);
English Language Learner: 309 (4.7%); Migrant: 0 (0.0%)
Eligible for Free Lunch Program: 2,495 (37.5%)
Eligible for Reduced-Price Lunch Program: 1,243 (18.7%)
Teachers: 447.1 (14.9 to 1)
Librarians/Media Specialists: 16.0 (415.3 to 1)
Guidance Counselors: 9.0 (738.3 to 1)
Current Spending: ($ per student per year):
Total: $7,414; Instruction: $4,078; Support Services: $2,994
Enrollment, Drop-out Rates and Diploma Recipients by Race/Ethnicity

Category	Total	White	Black	Asian	AIAN	Hisp.
Enrollment (%)	100.0	51.9	28.8	2.7	0.9	9.0
Drop-out Rate (%)	4.6	4.4	4.8	3.8	8.3	5.2
H.S. Diplomas (#)	226	116	81	12	1	16

Grant County

Ulysses
111 S Baughman • Ulysses, KS 67880-2402
(620) 356-3655 • http://www.ulysses.org
Grade Span: PK-12; **Agency Type:** 1
Schools: 4
2 Primary; 1 Middle; 1 High; 0 Other Level
4 Regular; 0 Special Education; 0 Vocational; 0 Alternative
0 Magnet; 0 Charter; 0 Title I Eligible; 0 School-wide Title I
Students: 1,833 (53.5% male; 46.4% female)
Individual Education Program: 221 (12.1%);
English Language Learner: 226 (12.3%); Migrant: 310 (16.9%)
Eligible for Free Lunch Program: 626 (34.2%)
Eligible for Reduced-Price Lunch Program: 218 (11.9%)
Teachers: 116.0 (15.8 to 1)
Librarians/Media Specialists: 4.0 (458.3 to 1)
Guidance Counselors: 4.0 (458.3 to 1)
Current Spending: ($ per student per year):
Total: $6,704; Instruction: $4,264; Support Services: $2,131
Enrollment, Drop-out Rates and Diploma Recipients by Race/Ethnicity

Category	Total	White	Black	Asian	AIAN	Hisp.
Enrollment (%)	100.0	48.1	0.0	0.2	0.2	51.6
Drop-out Rate (%)	2.0	0.0	0.0	0.0	n/a	4.9
H.S. Diplomas (#)	121	90	0	2	0	29

Harvey County

Newton
308 E First • Newton, KS 67114-3846
(316) 284-6200 • http://www.newton.k12.ks.us/home/
Grade Span: PK-12; **Agency Type:** 1
Schools: 10
5 Primary; 3 Middle; 1 High; 1 Other Level
10 Regular; 0 Special Education; 0 Vocational; 0 Alternative
0 Magnet; 0 Charter; 5 Title I Eligible; 3 School-wide Title I
Students: 3,765 (52.9% male; 47.0% female)
Individual Education Program: 579 (15.4%);
English Language Learner: 175 (4.6%); Migrant: 0 (0.0%)
Eligible for Free Lunch Program: 1,187 (31.5%)
Eligible for Reduced-Price Lunch Program: 467 (12.4%)
Teachers: 256.7 (14.7 to 1)
Librarians/Media Specialists: 8.0 (470.6 to 1)
Guidance Counselors: 7.0 (537.9 to 1)
Current Spending: ($ per student per year):
Total: $6,231; Instruction: $3,653; Support Services: $2,213

Enrollment, Drop-out Rates and Diploma Recipients by Race/Ethnicity

Category	Total	White	Black	Asian	AIAN	Hisp.
Enrollment (%)	100.0	74.7	3.0	0.8	0.8	18.4
Drop-out Rate (%)	2.9	3.1	0.0	0.0	0.0	3.1
H.S. Diplomas (#)	199	166	4	5	2	22

Johnson County

Blue Valley
15020 Metcalf • Overland Park, KS 66223-2200
Mailing Address: Box 23901 • Overland Park, KS 66283-0901
(913) 239-4000 • http://www.bluevalleyk12.org/
Grade Span: PK-12; Agency Type: 1
Schools: 29
  17 Primary; 8 Middle; 4 High; 0 Other Level
  29 Regular; 0 Special Education; 0 Vocational; 0 Alternative
  0 Magnet; 0 Charter; 0 Title I Eligible; 0 School-wide Title I
Students: 19,055 (51.4% male; 48.5% female)
  Individual Education Program: 1,666 (8.7%);
  English Language Learner: 240 (1.3%); Migrant: 0 (0.0%)
  Eligible for Free Lunch Program: 310 (1.6%)
  Eligible for Reduced-Price Lunch Program: 198 (1.0%)
Teachers: 1,249.5 (15.3 to 1)
Librarians/Media Specialists: 34.0 (560.4 to 1)
Guidance Counselors: 54.0 (352.9 to 1)
Current Spending: ($ per student per year):
  Total: $7,236; Instruction: $4,296; Support Services: $2,627
Enrollment, Drop-out Rates and Diploma Recipients by Race/Ethnicity

Category	Total	White	Black	Asian	AIAN	Hisp.
Enrollment (%)	100.0	88.3	3.3	6.2	0.3	1.8
Drop-out Rate (%)	0.7	0.7	2.0	0.4	0.0	2.6
H.S. Diplomas (#)	1,190	1,099	27	44	4	16

De Soto
35200 W 91st St • De Soto, KS 66018-0449
(913) 583-8300 •
http://www.usd232.org/education/district/district.php?sectionid=1
Grade Span: PK-12; Agency Type: 1
Schools: 8
  4 Primary; 2 Middle; 2 High; 0 Other Level
  8 Regular; 0 Special Education; 0 Vocational; 0 Alternative
  0 Magnet; 0 Charter; 0 Title I Eligible; 0 School-wide Title I
Students: 4,545 (51.0% male; 48.9% female)
  Individual Education Program: 430 (9.5%);
  English Language Learner: 103 (2.3%); Migrant: 0 (0.0%)
  Eligible for Free Lunch Program: 393 (8.7%)
  Eligible for Reduced-Price Lunch Program: 167 (3.7%)
Teachers: 320.6 (14.2 to 1)
Librarians/Media Specialists: 8.0 (567.6 to 1)
Guidance Counselors: 9.5 (478.0 to 1)
Current Spending: ($ per student per year):
  Total: $6,868; Instruction: $3,741; Support Services: $2,807
Enrollment, Drop-out Rates and Diploma Recipients by Race/Ethnicity

Category	Total	White	Black	Asian	AIAN	Hisp.
Enrollment (%)	100.0	88.2	2.6	2.3	0.7	5.2
Drop-out Rate (%)	0.9	0.9	0.0	0.0	0.0	2.3
H.S. Diplomas (#)	203	180	7	3	2	11

Gardner Edgerton
231 E Madison • Gardner, KS 66030
Mailing Address: Box 97 • Gardner, KS 66030
(913) 856-2000 • http://usd231.com/
Grade Span: KG-12; Agency Type: 1
Schools: 7
  4 Primary; 2 Middle; 1 High; 0 Other Level
  7 Regular; 0 Special Education; 0 Vocational; 0 Alternative
  0 Magnet; 0 Charter; 3 Title I Eligible; 0 School-wide Title I
Students: 3,401 (51.0% male; 48.9% female)
  Individual Education Program: 444 (13.1%);
  English Language Learner: 7 (0.2%); Migrant: 24 (0.7%)
  Eligible for Free Lunch Program: 450 (13.5%)
  Eligible for Reduced-Price Lunch Program: 239 (7.2%)
Teachers: 232.5 (14.3 to 1)
Librarians/Media Specialists: 5.0 (665.2 to 1)
Guidance Counselors: 9.0 (369.6 to 1)
Current Spending: ($ per student per year):
  Total: $6,788; Instruction: $4,161; Support Services: $2,337
Enrollment, Drop-out Rates and Diploma Recipients by Race/Ethnicity

Category	Total	White	Black	Asian	AIAN	Hisp.
Enrollment (%)	100.0	90.7	3.0	1.7	0.5	3.2
Drop-out Rate (%)	1.9	2.0	0.0	0.0	n/a	0.0
H.S. Diplomas (#)	138	133	2	0	0	3

Olathe
14160 Black Bob Rd • Olathe, KS 66063-2000
Mailing Address: PO Box 2000 • Olathe, KS 66063-2000
(913) 780-7000 • http://www.olathe.k12.ks.us/
Grade Span: PK-12; Agency Type: 1
Schools: 39
  28 Primary; 7 Middle; 4 High; 0 Other Level
  39 Regular; 0 Special Education; 0 Vocational; 0 Alternative
  0 Magnet; 0 Charter; 2 Title I Eligible; 2 School-wide Title I
Students: 22,917 (51.8% male; 48.1% female)
  Individual Education Program: 2,969 (13.0%);
  English Language Learner: 700 (3.1%); Migrant: 294 (1.3%)
  Eligible for Free Lunch Program: 2,067 (9.0%)
  Eligible for Reduced-Price Lunch Program: 936 (4.1%)
Teachers: 1,536.5 (14.9 to 1)
Librarians/Media Specialists: 40.6 (564.4 to 1)
Guidance Counselors: 57.5 (398.5 to 1)
Current Spending: ($ per student per year):
  Total: $6,848; Instruction: $4,319; Support Services: $2,236
Enrollment, Drop-out Rates and Diploma Recipients by Race/Ethnicity

Category	Total	White	Black	Asian	AIAN	Hisp.
Enrollment (%)	100.0	83.1	5.8	3.6	0.4	6.1
Drop-out Rate (%)	1.8	1.7	2.2	0.5	5.0	2.9
H.S. Diplomas (#)	1,319	1,165	65	46	4	39

Shawnee Mission Public Schools
7235 Antioch • Shawnee Mission, KS 66204-1798
(913) 993-6200 • http://www.smsd.org/
Grade Span: KG-12; Agency Type: 1
Schools: 50
  38 Primary; 7 Middle; 5 High; 0 Other Level
  50 Regular; 0 Special Education; 0 Vocational; 0 Alternative
  0 Magnet; 0 Charter; 7 Title I Eligible; 7 School-wide Title I
Students: 29,389 (51.9% male; 48.0% female)
  Individual Education Program: 3,379 (11.5%);
  English Language Learner: 980 (3.3%); Migrant: 0 (0.0%)
  Eligible for Free Lunch Program: 2,908 (9.9%)
  Eligible for Reduced-Price Lunch Program: 1,271 (4.3%)
Teachers: 1,815.4 (16.2 to 1)
Librarians/Media Specialists: 52.1 (564.1 to 1)
Guidance Counselors: 47.9 (613.5 to 1)
Current Spending: ($ per student per year):
  Total: $6,941; Instruction: $4,515; Support Services: $2,134
Enrollment, Drop-out Rates and Diploma Recipients by Race/Ethnicity

Category	Total	White	Black	Asian	AIAN	Hisp.
Enrollment (%)	100.0	82.9	6.7	3.1	0.5	6.8
Drop-out Rate (%)	2.0	1.9	2.4	1.1	0.0	4.1
H.S. Diplomas (#)	2,226	1,964	89	74	10	89

Spring Hill
101 E S St • Spring Hill, KS 66083
(913) 592-7200
Grade Span: PK-12; Agency Type: 1
Schools: 4
  2 Primary; 1 Middle; 1 High; 0 Other Level
  4 Regular; 0 Special Education; 0 Vocational; 0 Alternative
  0 Magnet; 1 Charter; 1 Title I Eligible; 0 School-wide Title I
Students: 1,605 (49.4% male; 50.5% female)
  Individual Education Program: 168 (10.5%);
  English Language Learner: 7 (0.4%); Migrant: 0 (0.0%)
  Eligible for Free Lunch Program: 133 (8.3%)
  Eligible for Reduced-Price Lunch Program: 70 (4.4%)
Teachers: 107.4 (14.9 to 1)
Librarians/Media Specialists: 3.5 (458.0 to 1)
Guidance Counselors: 4.0 (400.8 to 1)
Current Spending: ($ per student per year):
  Total: $7,128; Instruction: $4,265; Support Services: $2,555
Enrollment, Drop-out Rates and Diploma Recipients by Race/Ethnicity

Category	Total	White	Black	Asian	AIAN	Hisp.
Enrollment (%)	100.0	93.6	0.9	0.4	0.9	3.1
Drop-out Rate (%)	1.1	1.1	0.0	0.0	0.0	0.0
H.S. Diplomas (#)	93	90	0	0	2	1

Labette County

Labette County
521 S Huston Ave • Altamont, KS 67330-0188
Mailing Address: Box 188 • Altamont, KS 67330-0188
(620) 784-5326 • http://www.usd506.k12.ks.us/
Grade Span: KG-12; Agency Type: 1
Schools: 6
  5 Primary; 0 Middle; 1 High; 0 Other Level
  6 Regular; 0 Special Education; 0 Vocational; 0 Alternative
  0 Magnet; 0 Charter; 0 Title I Eligible; 0 School-wide Title I
Students: 1,709 (51.3% male; 48.6% female)

Individual Education Program: 181 (10.6%);
English Language Learner: 0 (0.0%); Migrant: 0 (0.0%)
Eligible for Free Lunch Program: 411 (24.2%)
Eligible for Reduced-Price Lunch Program: 213 (12.5%)
Teachers: 108.1 (15.7 to 1)
Librarians/Media Specialists: 3.0 (566.3 to 1)
Guidance Counselors: 1.0 (1,699.0 to 1)
Current Spending: ($ per student per year):
Total: $6,926; Instruction: $4,122; Support Services: $2,453
Enrollment, Drop-out Rates and Diploma Recipients by Race/Ethnicity

Category	Total	White	Black	Asian	AIAN	Hisp.
Enrollment (%)	100.0	74.7	0.9	0.4	13.0	3.1
Drop-out Rate (%)	0.9	1.0	n/a	0.0	0.0	0.0
H.S. Diplomas (#)	152	146	0	1	2	3

Parsons

2900 Southern • Parsons, KS 67357-1056
Mailing Address: Box 1056 • Parsons, KS 67357-1056
(620) 421-5950 • http://www.vikingnet.net/
Grade Span: PK-12; **Agency Type:** 1
Schools: 5
3 Primary; 1 Middle; 1 High; 0 Other Level
5 Regular; 0 Special Education; 0 Vocational; 0 Alternative
0 Magnet; 0 Charter; 3 Title I Eligible; 3 School-wide Title I
Students: 1,630   (52.3% male; 47.6% female)
Individual Education Program: 220 (13.5%);
English Language Learner: 0 (0.0%); Migrant: 0 (0.0%)
Eligible for Free Lunch Program: 686 (42.1%)
Eligible for Reduced-Price Lunch Program: 242 (14.8%)
Teachers: 105.2 (15.5 to 1)
Librarians/Media Specialists: 3.0 (543.3 to 1)
Guidance Counselors: 4.0 (407.5 to 1)
Current Spending: ($ per student per year):
Total: $6,838; Instruction: $4,222; Support Services: $2,217
Enrollment, Drop-out Rates and Diploma Recipients by Race/Ethnicity

Category	Total	White	Black	Asian	AIAN	Hisp.
Enrollment (%)	100.0	73.3	17.7	0.7	1.4	5.0
Drop-out Rate (%)	3.8	3.1	8.5	0.0	0.0	4.3
H.S. Diplomas (#)	106	86	13	2	0	5

Leavenworth County

Basehor-Linwood

2008 N 155th St • Basehor, KS 66007-0282
Mailing Address: PO Box 282 • Basehor, KS 66007-0282
(913) 724-1396 • http://www.usd458.k12.ks.us
Grade Span: KG-12; **Agency Type:** 1
Schools: 5
3 Primary; 1 Middle; 1 High; 0 Other Level
5 Regular; 0 Special Education; 0 Vocational; 0 Alternative
0 Magnet; 0 Charter; 0 Title I Eligible; 0 School-wide Title I
Students: 2,102   (47.4% male; 52.5% female)
Individual Education Program: 222 (10.6%);
English Language Learner: 0 (0.0%); Migrant: 0 (0.0%)
Eligible for Free Lunch Program: 100 (4.8%)
Eligible for Reduced-Price Lunch Program: 79 (3.8%)
Teachers: 97.0 (21.5 to 1)
Librarians/Media Specialists: 3.0 (695.0 to 1)
Guidance Counselors: 6.0 (347.5 to 1)
Current Spending: ($ per student per year):
Total: $6,116; Instruction: $3,258; Support Services: $2,599
Enrollment, Drop-out Rates and Diploma Recipients by Race/Ethnicity

Category	Total	White	Black	Asian	AIAN	Hisp.
Enrollment (%)	100.0	92.5	1.7	0.7	0.1	4.5
Drop-out Rate (%)	6.8	6.4	16.0	11.1	0.0	5.9
H.S. Diplomas (#)	127	125	1	0	1	0

Ft Leavenworth

5 Grant Ave • Fort Leavenworth, KS 66027-2701
(913) 651-7373 • http://www.ftlvn.com/district/index.htm
Grade Span: KG-09; **Agency Type:** 1
Schools: 4
3 Primary; 1 Middle; 0 High; 0 Other Level
4 Regular; 0 Special Education; 0 Vocational; 0 Alternative
0 Magnet; 0 Charter; 1 Title I Eligible; 0 School-wide Title I
Students: 1,915   (50.7% male; 49.2% female)
Individual Education Program: 270 (14.1%);
English Language Learner: 0 (0.0%); Migrant: 0 (0.0%)
Eligible for Free Lunch Program: 59 (3.1%)
Eligible for Reduced-Price Lunch Program: 92 (4.9%)
Teachers: 114.0 (16.6 to 1)
Librarians/Media Specialists: 4.0 (472.5 to 1)
Guidance Counselors: 4.0 (472.5 to 1)
Current Spending: ($ per student per year):
Total: $5,243; Instruction: $3,300; Support Services: $1,671

Enrollment, Drop-out Rates and Diploma Recipients by Race/Ethnicity

Category	Total	White	Black	Asian	AIAN	Hisp.
Enrollment (%)	100.0	72.4	14.3	2.4	1.1	4.9
Drop-out Rate (%)	0.0	0.0	0.0	0.0	n/a	0.0
H.S. Diplomas (#)	n/a	n/a	n/a	n/a	n/a	n/a

Lansing

613 Holiday Plaza • Lansing, KS 66043
(913) 727-1100 • http://usd469.net/
Grade Span: PK-12; **Agency Type:** 1
Schools: 4
1 Primary; 2 Middle; 1 High; 0 Other Level
4 Regular; 0 Special Education; 0 Vocational; 0 Alternative
0 Magnet; 0 Charter; 0 Title I Eligible; 0 School-wide Title I
Students: 2,065   (51.7% male; 48.2% female)
Individual Education Program: 218 (10.6%);
English Language Learner: 0 (0.0%); Migrant: 0 (0.0%)
Eligible for Free Lunch Program: 105 (5.1%)
Eligible for Reduced-Price Lunch Program: 53 (2.6%)
Teachers: 110.9 (18.4 to 1)
Librarians/Media Specialists: 4.0 (511.3 to 1)
Guidance Counselors: 4.0 (511.3 to 1)
Current Spending: ($ per student per year):
Total: $5,848; Instruction: $3,599; Support Services: $1,977
Enrollment, Drop-out Rates and Diploma Recipients by Race/Ethnicity

Category	Total	White	Black	Asian	AIAN	Hisp.
Enrollment (%)	100.0	87.7	5.3	1.5	0.7	3.7
Drop-out Rate (%)	0.3	0.3	0.0	0.0	0.0	0.0
H.S. Diplomas (#)	147	134	5	1	1	6

Leavenworth

200 N 4th • Leavenworth, KS 66048
Mailing Address: PO Box 186 • Leavenworth, KS 66048
(913) 684-1400 • http://www.lvksch.org/
Grade Span: KG-12; **Agency Type:** 1
Schools: 9
6 Primary; 2 Middle; 1 High; 0 Other Level
9 Regular; 0 Special Education; 0 Vocational; 0 Alternative
0 Magnet; 0 Charter; 4 Title I Eligible; 4 School-wide Title I
Students: 4,274   (51.9% male; 48.0% female)
Individual Education Program: 793 (18.6%);
English Language Learner: 141 (3.3%); Migrant: 0 (0.0%)
Eligible for Free Lunch Program: 1,566 (36.9%)
Eligible for Reduced-Price Lunch Program: 423 (10.0%)
Teachers: 453.9 (9.4 to 1)
Librarians/Media Specialists: 9.0 (471.9 to 1)
Guidance Counselors: 11.0 (386.1 to 1)
Current Spending: ($ per student per year):
Total: $6,735; Instruction: $3,975; Support Services: $2,393
Enrollment, Drop-out Rates and Diploma Recipients by Race/Ethnicity

Category	Total	White	Black	Asian	AIAN	Hisp.
Enrollment (%)	100.0	66.2	24.8	2.6	0.5	4.3
Drop-out Rate (%)	4.0	3.9	3.5	0.0	9.1	9.4
H.S. Diplomas (#)	282	196	64	6	3	13

Tonganoxie

330 E 24/40 Hwy • Tonganoxie, KS 66086-0199
Mailing Address: Box 199 • Tonganoxie, KS 66086-0199
(913) 845-2153
Grade Span: KG-12; **Agency Type:** 1
Schools: 3
1 Primary; 1 Middle; 1 High; 0 Other Level
3 Regular; 0 Special Education; 0 Vocational; 0 Alternative
0 Magnet; 0 Charter; 0 Title I Eligible; 0 School-wide Title I
Students: 1,558   (51.3% male; 48.6% female)
Individual Education Program: 217 (13.9%);
English Language Learner: 0 (0.0%); Migrant: 0 (0.0%)
Eligible for Free Lunch Program: 181 (11.6%)
Eligible for Reduced-Price Lunch Program: 105 (6.8%)
Teachers: 92.4 (16.8 to 1)
Librarians/Media Specialists: 2.0 (777.5 to 1)
Guidance Counselors: 4.0 (388.8 to 1)
Current Spending: ($ per student per year):
Total: $6,457; Instruction: $4,234; Support Services: $1,931
Enrollment, Drop-out Rates and Diploma Recipients by Race/Ethnicity

Category	Total	White	Black	Asian	AIAN	Hisp.
Enrollment (%)	100.0	92.4	1.7	1.2	1.0	3.7
Drop-out Rate (%)	1.4	1.4	0.0	0.0	0.0	0.0
H.S. Diplomas (#)	112	110	0	1	1	0

Lyon County

Emporia
501 Merchant • Emporia, KS 66801-7201
Mailing Address: Box 1008 • Emporia, KS 66801-1008
(620) 341-2200 • http://www.usd253.org/
Grade Span: PK-12; **Agency Type:** 1
Schools: 10
  6 Primary; 3 Middle; 1 High; 0 Other Level
  10 Regular; 0 Special Education; 0 Vocational; 0 Alternative
  0 Magnet; 0 Charter; 4 Title I Eligible; 3 School-wide Title I
Students: 4,981   (51.6% male; 48.3% female)
  Individual Education Program: 542 (10.9%);
  English Language Learner: 1,024 (20.6%); Migrant: 414 (8.3%)
  Eligible for Free Lunch Program: 2,060 (41.4%)
  Eligible for Reduced-Price Lunch Program: 629 (12.6%)
Teachers: 381.7 (13.0 to 1)
Librarians/Media Specialists: 6.0 (830.2 to 1)
Guidance Counselors: 11.6 (429.4 to 1)
Current Spending: ($ per student per year):
  Total: $6,787; Instruction: $4,599; Support Services: $1,894
Enrollment, Drop-out Rates and Diploma Recipients by Race/Ethnicity

Category	Total	White	Black	Asian	AIAN	Hisp.
Enrollment (%)	100.0	51.5	3.4	2.8	0.3	39.0
Drop-out Rate (%)	2.9	2.8	6.3	2.3	0.0	2.8
H.S. Diplomas (#)	296	221	12	9	2	52

Mcpherson County

Mcpherson
514 N Main • Mcpherson, KS 67460-3499
(620) 241-9400
Grade Span: KG-12; **Agency Type:** 1
Schools: 6
  4 Primary; 1 Middle; 1 High; 0 Other Level
  6 Regular; 0 Special Education; 0 Vocational; 0 Alternative
  0 Magnet; 0 Charter; 0 Title I Eligible; 0 School-wide Title I
Students: 2,559   (51.9% male; 48.0% female)
  Individual Education Program: 420 (16.4%);
  English Language Learner: 12 (0.5%); Migrant: 0 (0.0%)
  Eligible for Free Lunch Program: 409 (16.5%)
  Eligible for Reduced-Price Lunch Program: 183 (7.4%)
Teachers: 207.4 (12.0 to 1)
Librarians/Media Specialists: 5.0 (497.2 to 1)
Guidance Counselors: 8.0 (310.8 to 1)
Current Spending: ($ per student per year):
  Total: $6,823; Instruction: $4,384; Support Services: $2,101
Enrollment, Drop-out Rates and Diploma Recipients by Race/Ethnicity

Category	Total	White	Black	Asian	AIAN	Hisp.
Enrollment (%)	100.0	92.2	2.2	1.2	0.5	2.5
Drop-out Rate (%)	2.2	2.3	0.0	0.0	0.0	0.0
H.S. Diplomas (#)	234	227	3	2	0	2

Miami County

Paola
202 E Wea • Paola, KS 66071-0268
Mailing Address: Box 268 • Paola, KS 66071-0268
(913) 294-3646 • http://usd368.k12.ks.us/
Grade Span: KG-12; **Agency Type:** 1
Schools: 5
  3 Primary; 1 Middle; 1 High; 0 Other Level
  5 Regular; 0 Special Education; 0 Vocational; 0 Alternative
  0 Magnet; 0 Charter; 0 Title I Eligible; 0 School-wide Title I
Students: 2,167   (51.2% male; 48.7% female)
  Individual Education Program: 299 (13.8%);
  English Language Learner: 0 (0.0%); Migrant: 0 (0.0%)
  Eligible for Free Lunch Program: 387 (17.9%)
  Eligible for Reduced-Price Lunch Program: 136 (6.3%)
Teachers: 190.9 (11.3 to 1)
Librarians/Media Specialists: 4.0 (541.3 to 1)
Guidance Counselors: 5.0 (433.0 to 1)
Current Spending: ($ per student per year):
  Total: $6,772; Instruction: $4,080; Support Services: $2,337
Enrollment, Drop-out Rates and Diploma Recipients by Race/Ethnicity

Category	Total	White	Black	Asian	AIAN	Hisp.
Enrollment (%)	100.0	92.8	3.8	0.3	0.5	1.4
Drop-out Rate (%)	2.0	2.1	0.0	0.0	0.0	0.0
H.S. Diplomas (#)	147	141	4	0	0	2

Montgomery County

Coffeyville
615 Ellis • Coffeyville, KS 67337-3427
(620) 252-6800 • http://cvilleschools.com/
Grade Span: KG-12; **Agency Type:** 1
Schools: 5
  3 Primary; 1 Middle; 1 High; 0 Other Level
  5 Regular; 0 Special Education; 0 Vocational; 0 Alternative
  0 Magnet; 0 Charter; 3 Title I Eligible; 3 School-wide Title I
Students: 1,966   (51.3% male; 48.6% female)
  Individual Education Program: 285 (14.5%);
  English Language Learner: 0 (0.0%); Migrant: 0 (0.0%)
  Eligible for Free Lunch Program: 930 (47.5%)
  Eligible for Reduced-Price Lunch Program: 223 (11.4%)
Teachers: 110.5 (17.7 to 1)
Librarians/Media Specialists: 2.0 (978.5 to 1)
Guidance Counselors: 5.0 (391.4 to 1)
Current Spending: ($ per student per year):
  Total: $7,347; Instruction: $4,564; Support Services: $2,387
Enrollment, Drop-out Rates and Diploma Recipients by Race/Ethnicity

Category	Total	White	Black	Asian	AIAN	Hisp.
Enrollment (%)	100.0	61.0	17.2	1.4	16.2	4.2
Drop-out Rate (%)	2.6	2.8	4.3	0.0	1.0	0.0
H.S. Diplomas (#)	168	106	24	5	31	2

Independence
517 N Tenth • Independence, KS 67301-0487
Mailing Address: PO Drawer 487 • Independence, KS 67301-0487
(620) 332-1800 • http://www.indyschools.com/
Grade Span: KG-12; **Agency Type:** 1
Schools: 5
  2 Primary; 2 Middle; 1 High; 0 Other Level
  5 Regular; 0 Special Education; 0 Vocational; 0 Alternative
  0 Magnet; 0 Charter; 3 Title I Eligible; 3 School-wide Title I
Students: 2,036   (53.8% male; 46.1% female)
  Individual Education Program: 290 (14.2%);
  English Language Learner: 0 (0.0%); Migrant: 0 (0.0%)
  Eligible for Free Lunch Program: 726 (35.7%)
  Eligible for Reduced-Price Lunch Program: 253 (12.4%)
Teachers: 125.5 (16.2 to 1)
Librarians/Media Specialists: 5.0 (406.8 to 1)
Guidance Counselors: 5.5 (369.8 to 1)
Current Spending: ($ per student per year):
  Total: $6,636; Instruction: $4,246; Support Services: $2,006
Enrollment, Drop-out Rates and Diploma Recipients by Race/Ethnicity

Category	Total	White	Black	Asian	AIAN	Hisp.
Enrollment (%)	100.0	84.1	9.5	1.0	1.5	3.9
Drop-out Rate (%)	2.0	2.0	3.3	0.0	0.0	0.0
H.S. Diplomas (#)	162	146	7	2	1	6

Neosho County

Chanute Public Schools
208 N Lincoln • Chanute, KS 66720-1822
(620) 432-2500 • http://www.usd413.k12.ks.us/
Grade Span: KG-12; **Agency Type:** 1
Schools: 7
  4 Primary; 1 Middle; 2 High; 0 Other Level
  7 Regular; 0 Special Education; 0 Vocational; 0 Alternative
  0 Magnet; 2 Charter; 3 Title I Eligible; 3 School-wide Title I
Students: 1,934   (49.6% male; 50.3% female)
  Individual Education Program: 333 (17.2%);
  English Language Learner: 0 (0.0%); Migrant: 0 (0.0%)
  Eligible for Free Lunch Program: 682 (35.3%)
  Eligible for Reduced-Price Lunch Program: 234 (12.1%)
Teachers: 119.6 (16.2 to 1)
Librarians/Media Specialists: 4.4 (439.5 to 1)
Guidance Counselors: 4.0 (483.5 to 1)
Current Spending: ($ per student per year):
  Total: $7,066; Instruction: $4,643; Support Services: $2,054
Enrollment, Drop-out Rates and Diploma Recipients by Race/Ethnicity

Category	Total	White	Black	Asian	AIAN	Hisp.
Enrollment (%)	100.0	91.3	2.0	1.3	1.6	3.9
Drop-out Rate (%)	2.4	2.3	0.0	0.0	0.0	12.5
H.S. Diplomas (#)	117	111	3	1	1	1

Reno County

Buhler
406 W 7th • Buhler, KS 67522-0320
Mailing Address: Box 320 • Buhler, KS 67522-0320
(620) 543-2258 • http://buhler.usd313.k12.ks.us/
Grade Span: PK-12; **Agency Type:** 1
Schools: 6

3 Primary; 2 Middle; 1 High; 0 Other Level
6 Regular; 0 Special Education; 0 Vocational; 0 Alternative
0 Magnet; 0 Charter; 0 Title I Eligible; 0 School-wide Title I
Students: 2,269   (51.6% male; 48.3% female)
    Individual Education Program: 300 (13.2%);
    English Language Learner: 5 (0.2%); Migrant: 0 (0.0%)
    Eligible for Free Lunch Program: 439 (19.7%)
    Eligible for Reduced-Price Lunch Program: 195 (8.8%)
Teachers: 133.9 (16.6 to 1)
Librarians/Media Specialists: 6.0 (370.8 to 1)
Guidance Counselors: 4.0 (556.3 to 1)
Current Spending: ($ per student per year):
    Total: $6,735; Instruction: $4,077; Support Services: $2,286
Enrollment, Drop-out Rates and Diploma Recipients by Race/Ethnicity

Category	Total	White	Black	Asian	AIAN	Hisp.
Enrollment (%)	100.0	92.1	2.0	0.8	0.5	3.9
Drop-out Rate (%)	2.6	2.8	0.0	0.0	0.0	0.0
H.S. Diplomas (#)	167	159	1	4	0	3

Hutchinson Public Schools
1520 N Plum • Hutchinson, KS 67501
Mailing Address: Box 1908 • Hutchinson, KS 67504-1908
(620) 665-4400 • http://www.usd308.com/
Grade Span: PK-12; **Agency Type:** 1
Schools: 10
    8 Primary; 1 Middle; 1 High; 0 Other Level
    10 Regular; 0 Special Education; 0 Vocational; 0 Alternative
    0 Magnet; 0 Charter; 5 Title I Eligible; 4 School-wide Title I
Students: 5,025   (51.4% male; 48.5% female)
    Individual Education Program: 810 (16.1%);
    English Language Learner: 38 (0.8%); Migrant: 0 (0.0%)
    Eligible for Free Lunch Program: 2,030 (40.4%)
    Eligible for Reduced-Price Lunch Program: 508 (10.1%)
Teachers: 330.5 (15.2 to 1)
Librarians/Media Specialists: 8.0 (628.1 to 1)
Guidance Counselors: 9.0 (558.3 to 1)
Current Spending: ($ per student per year):
    Total: $6,507; Instruction: $3,666; Support Services: $2,523
Enrollment, Drop-out Rates and Diploma Recipients by Race/Ethnicity

Category	Total	White	Black	Asian	AIAN	Hisp.
Enrollment (%)	100.0	77.8	6.9	0.8	0.6	13.2
Drop-out Rate (%)	5.3	5.6	2.9	0.0	16.7	4.7
H.S. Diplomas (#)	294	243	19	4	2	26

Riley County

Manhattan
2031 Poyntz • Manhattan, KS 66502
(785) 587-2000 • http://www.usd383.org/
Grade Span: KG-12; **Agency Type:** 1
Schools: 11
    8 Primary; 2 Middle; 1 High; 0 Other Level
    11 Regular; 0 Special Education; 0 Vocational; 0 Alternative
    0 Magnet; 0 Charter; 6 Title I Eligible; 5 School-wide Title I
Students: 5,383   (52.4% male; 47.5% female)
    Individual Education Program: 866 (16.1%);
    English Language Learner: 121 (2.2%); Migrant: 0 (0.0%)
    Eligible for Free Lunch Program: 1,044 (19.4%)
    Eligible for Reduced-Price Lunch Program: 570 (10.6%)
Teachers: 389.0 (13.8 to 1)
Librarians/Media Specialists: 12.5 (430.6 to 1)
Guidance Counselors: 8.5 (633.2 to 1)
Current Spending: ($ per student per year):
    Total: $8,308; Instruction: $4,696; Support Services: $3,185
Enrollment, Drop-out Rates and Diploma Recipients by Race/Ethnicity

Category	Total	White	Black	Asian	AIAN	Hisp.
Enrollment (%)	100.0	78.2	9.3	5.2	0.4	4.2
Drop-out Rate (%)	3.3	3.4	2.5	3.0	0.0	3.2
H.S. Diplomas (#)	417	358	33	11	1	14

Saline County

Salina
1511 Gypsum • Salina, KS 67402-0797
Mailing Address: Box 797 • Salina, KS 67402-0797
(785) 309-4700 • http://www.usd305.com/
Grade Span: KG-12; **Agency Type:** 1
Schools: 12
    8 Primary; 2 Middle; 2 High; 0 Other Level
    12 Regular; 0 Special Education; 0 Vocational; 0 Alternative
    0 Magnet; 0 Charter; 4 Title I Eligible; 4 School-wide Title I
Students: 7,594   (51.4% male; 48.5% female)
    Individual Education Program: 1,118 (14.7%);
    English Language Learner: 276 (3.6%); Migrant: 30 (0.4%)
    Eligible for Free Lunch Program: 2,468 (32.5%)

Eligible for Reduced-Price Lunch Program: 849 (11.2%)
Teachers: 563.0 (13.5 to 1)
Librarians/Media Specialists: 12.0 (632.8 to 1)
Guidance Counselors: 22.3 (340.5 to 1)
Current Spending: ($ per student per year):
    Total: $7,804; Instruction: $4,820; Support Services: $2,593
Enrollment, Drop-out Rates and Diploma Recipients by Race/Ethnicity

Category	Total	White	Black	Asian	AIAN	Hisp.
Enrollment (%)	100.0	76.7	5.4	2.7	0.6	10.6
Drop-out Rate (%)	2.9	2.4	2.8	0.0	13.3	8.6
H.S. Diplomas (#)	462	409	19	13	1	20

Sedgwick County

Derby
120 E Washington • Derby, KS 67037-1489
(316) 788-8400 • http://www.derbyschools.com/
Grade Span: PK-12; **Agency Type:** 1
Schools: 12
    9 Primary; 2 Middle; 1 High; 0 Other Level
    12 Regular; 0 Special Education; 0 Vocational; 0 Alternative
    0 Magnet; 0 Charter; 3 Title I Eligible; 2 School-wide Title I
Students: 6,695   (51.4% male; 48.5% female)
    Individual Education Program: 957 (14.3%);
    English Language Learner: 121 (1.8%); Migrant: 0 (0.0%)
    Eligible for Free Lunch Program: 1,431 (21.4%)
    Eligible for Reduced-Price Lunch Program: 567 (8.5%)
Teachers: 426.1 (15.7 to 1)
Librarians/Media Specialists: 13.0 (514.2 to 1)
Guidance Counselors: 7.0 (954.9 to 1)
Current Spending: ($ per student per year):
    Total: $6,390; Instruction: $3,878; Support Services: $2,218
Enrollment, Drop-out Rates and Diploma Recipients by Race/Ethnicity

Category	Total	White	Black	Asian	AIAN	Hisp.
Enrollment (%)	100.0	81.0	6.3	5.0	1.8	5.9
Drop-out Rate (%)	1.3	1.2	2.5	2.3	0.0	1.1
H.S. Diplomas (#)	420	365	17	16	5	17

Goddard
201 S Main • Goddard, KS 67052-0249
Mailing Address: Box 249 • Goddard, KS 67052-0249
(316) 794-4000 • http://www.goddardusd.com/
Grade Span: KG-12; **Agency Type:** 1
Schools: 8
    3 Primary; 4 Middle; 1 High; 0 Other Level
    8 Regular; 0 Special Education; 0 Vocational; 0 Alternative
    0 Magnet; 0 Charter; 3 Title I Eligible; 0 School-wide Title I
Students: 4,065   (52.1% male; 47.8% female)
    Individual Education Program: 548 (13.5%);
    English Language Learner: 20 (0.5%); Migrant: 0 (0.0%)
    Eligible for Free Lunch Program: 377 (9.4%)
    Eligible for Reduced-Price Lunch Program: 263 (6.5%)
Teachers: 204.0 (19.8 to 1)
Librarians/Media Specialists: 7.0 (575.9 to 1)
Guidance Counselors: 10.0 (403.1 to 1)
Current Spending: ($ per student per year):
    Total: $6,187; Instruction: $3,566; Support Services: $2,281
Enrollment, Drop-out Rates and Diploma Recipients by Race/Ethnicity

Category	Total	White	Black	Asian	AIAN	Hisp.
Enrollment (%)	100.0	89.7	2.1	2.1	1.2	4.4
Drop-out Rate (%)	1.7	1.8	0.0	3.1	0.0	0.0
H.S. Diplomas (#)	247	217	3	12	5	10

Haysville
1745 W Grand Ave • Haysville, KS 67060-1234
(316) 554-2200 • http://www.usd261.com/
Grade Span: PK-12; **Agency Type:** 1
Schools: 7
    5 Primary; 1 Middle; 1 High; 0 Other Level
    7 Regular; 0 Special Education; 0 Vocational; 0 Alternative
    0 Magnet; 0 Charter; 4 Title I Eligible; 0 School-wide Title I
Students: 4,690   (51.7% male; 48.2% female)
    Individual Education Program: 734 (15.7%);
    English Language Learner: 109 (2.3%); Migrant: 9 (0.2%)
    Eligible for Free Lunch Program: 1,206 (25.8%)
    Eligible for Reduced-Price Lunch Program: 483 (10.3%)
Teachers: 287.0 (16.3 to 1)
Librarians/Media Specialists: 7.0 (666.7 to 1)
Guidance Counselors: 11.6 (402.3 to 1)
Current Spending: ($ per student per year):
    Total: $6,486; Instruction: $3,736; Support Services: $2,436

Enrollment, Drop-out Rates and Diploma Recipients by Race/Ethnicity

Category	Total	White	Black	Asian	AIAN	Hisp.
Enrollment (%)	100.0	86.1	1.9	4.1	2.5	5.4
Drop-out Rate (%)	6.9	6.7	21.4	2.3	17.4	7.5
H.S. Diplomas (#)	250	231	4	7	4	4

Maize
201 S Park • Maize, KS 67101-0580
(316) 722-0614 • http://www.usd266.com/
Grade Span: KG-12; **Agency Type:** 1
Schools: 6
  3 Primary; 2 Middle; 1 High; 0 Other Level
  6 Regular; 0 Special Education; 0 Vocational; 0 Alternative
  0 Magnet; 0 Charter; 1 Title I Eligible; 0 School-wide Title I
Students: 5,815 (50.8% male; 49.1% female)
  Individual Education Program: 569 (9.8%);
  English Language Learner: 56 (1.0%); Migrant: 0 (0.0%)
  Eligible for Free Lunch Program: 328 (5.6%)
  Eligible for Reduced-Price Lunch Program: 134 (2.3%)
Teachers: 301.0 (19.3 to 1)
Librarians/Media Specialists: 6.0 (969.2 to 1)
Guidance Counselors: 15.0 (387.7 to 1)
Current Spending: ($ per student per year):
  Total: $6,050; Instruction: $4,160; Support Services: $1,632

Enrollment, Drop-out Rates and Diploma Recipients by Race/Ethnicity

Category	Total	White	Black	Asian	AIAN	Hisp.
Enrollment (%)	100.0	87.9	2.3	3.4	1.1	5.1
Drop-out Rate (%)	2.7	2.6	5.6	4.8	0.0	3.7
H.S. Diplomas (#)	308	285	4	11	1	7

Mulvane
430 E Main • Mulvane, KS 67110
Mailing Address: Box 129 • Mulvane, KS 67110
(316) 777-1102 • http://www.usd263.k12.ks.us/
Grade Span: KG-12; **Agency Type:** 1
Schools: 5
  2 Primary; 2 Middle; 1 High; 0 Other Level
  5 Regular; 0 Special Education; 0 Vocational; 0 Alternative
  0 Magnet; 0 Charter; 3 Title I Eligible; 0 School-wide Title I
Students: 1,937 (50.7% male; 49.2% female)
  Individual Education Program: 191 (9.9%);
  English Language Learner: 0 (0.0%); Migrant: 0 (0.0%)
  Eligible for Free Lunch Program: 316 (16.4%)
  Eligible for Reduced-Price Lunch Program: 125 (6.5%)
Teachers: 123.5 (15.6 to 1)
Librarians/Media Specialists: 3.5 (551.4 to 1)
Guidance Counselors: 6.0 (321.7 to 1)
Current Spending: ($ per student per year):
  Total: $5,694; Instruction: $3,345; Support Services: $1,947

Enrollment, Drop-out Rates and Diploma Recipients by Race/Ethnicity

Category	Total	White	Black	Asian	AIAN	Hisp.
Enrollment (%)	100.0	93.1	1.0	0.5	2.1	3.3
Drop-out Rate (%)	0.9	1.0	0.0	0.0	0.0	0.0
H.S. Diplomas (#)	157	152	0	1	3	1

Renwick
600 W Rush • Andale, KS 67001-0068
Mailing Address: Box 68 • Andale, KS 67001-0068
(316) 444-2165 • http://www.usd267.com/
Grade Span: KG-12; **Agency Type:** 1
Schools: 7
  5 Primary; 0 Middle; 2 High; 0 Other Level
  7 Regular; 0 Special Education; 0 Vocational; 0 Alternative
  0 Magnet; 1 Charter; 2 Title I Eligible; 0 School-wide Title I
Students: 2,070 (53.1% male; 46.8% female)
  Individual Education Program: 197 (9.5%);
  English Language Learner: 0 (0.0%); Migrant: 0 (0.0%)
  Eligible for Free Lunch Program: 168 (8.1%)
  Eligible for Reduced-Price Lunch Program: 173 (8.4%)
Teachers: 126.6 (16.4 to 1)
Librarians/Media Specialists: 4.0 (517.5 to 1)
Guidance Counselors: 3.0 (690.0 to 1)
Current Spending: ($ per student per year):
  Total: $6,425; Instruction: $4,006; Support Services: $2,078

Enrollment, Drop-out Rates and Diploma Recipients by Race/Ethnicity

Category	Total	White	Black	Asian	AIAN	Hisp.
Enrollment (%)	100.0	98.2	0.0	0.1	0.7	0.9
Drop-out Rate (%)	0.2	0.2	n/a	0.0	0.0	0.0
H.S. Diplomas (#)	124	123	0	1	0	0

Valley Center Public Schools
132 S Park • Valley Center, KS 67147-0157
Mailing Address: Box 157 • Valley Center, KS 67147-0157
(316) 755-7100 • http://www.usd262.net/
Grade Span: KG-12; **Agency Type:** 1
Schools: 6
  2 Primary; 2 Middle; 1 High; 1 Other Level
  6 Regular; 0 Special Education; 0 Vocational; 0 Alternative
  0 Magnet; 1 Charter; 2 Title I Eligible; 0 School-wide Title I
Students: 2,394 (52.3% male; 47.6% female)
  Individual Education Program: 328 (13.7%);
  English Language Learner: 0 (0.0%); Migrant: 0 (0.0%)
  Eligible for Free Lunch Program: 322 (13.6%)
  Eligible for Reduced-Price Lunch Program: 167 (7.0%)
Teachers: 130.5 (18.2 to 1)
Librarians/Media Specialists: 4.7 (505.5 to 1)
Guidance Counselors: 4.0 (594.0 to 1)
Current Spending: ($ per student per year):
  Total: $5,743; Instruction: $3,442; Support Services: $1,925

Enrollment, Drop-out Rates and Diploma Recipients by Race/Ethnicity

Category	Total	White	Black	Asian	AIAN	Hisp.
Enrollment (%)	100.0	93.2	1.3	0.4	1.9	3.1
Drop-out Rate (%)	3.9	3.9	25.0	0.0	0.0	0.0
H.S. Diplomas (#)	177	171	1	0	3	2

Wichita
201 N Water • Wichita, KS 67202-1292
(316) 973-4000 • http://www.usd259.com/
Grade Span: PK-12; **Agency Type:** 1
Schools: 90
  59 Primary; 17 Middle; 12 High; 2 Other Level
  90 Regular; 0 Special Education; 0 Vocational; 0 Alternative
  26 Magnet; 0 Charter; 38 Title I Eligible; 36 School-wide Title I
Students: 48,894 (51.0% male; 48.9% female)
  Individual Education Program: 7,087 (14.5%);
  English Language Learner: 5,111 (10.5%); Migrant: 2,745 (5.6%)
  Eligible for Free Lunch Program: 25,583 (52.4%)
  Eligible for Reduced-Price Lunch Program: 5,570 (11.4%)
Teachers: 3,069.4 (15.9 to 1)
Librarians/Media Specialists: 66.8 (730.4 to 1)
Guidance Counselors: 86.6 (563.4 to 1)
Current Spending: ($ per student per year):
  Total: $7,431; Instruction: $4,170; Support Services: $2,978

Enrollment, Drop-out Rates and Diploma Recipients by Race/Ethnicity

Category	Total	White	Black	Asian	AIAN	Hisp.
Enrollment (%)	100.0	47.4	23.0	5.2	2.6	19.2
Drop-out Rate (%)	8.7	7.9	9.6	4.0	10.1	12.1
H.S. Diplomas (#)	2,147	1,325	401	162	36	223

Seward County

Liberal
401 N Kansas • Liberal, KS 67901
Mailing Address: Box 949 • Liberal, KS 67905-0949
(620) 626-3800 • http://www.usd480.net/
Grade Span: PK-12; **Agency Type:** 1
Schools: 12
  7 Primary; 4 Middle; 1 High; 0 Other Level
  12 Regular; 0 Special Education; 0 Vocational; 0 Alternative
  0 Magnet; 0 Charter; 7 Title I Eligible; 7 School-wide Title I
Students: 4,592 (52.6% male; 47.3% female)
  Individual Education Program: 452 (9.8%);
  English Language Learner: 1,322 (28.8%); Migrant: 1,212 (26.4%)
  Eligible for Free Lunch Program: 2,347 (51.1%)
  Eligible for Reduced-Price Lunch Program: 479 (10.4%)
Teachers: 289.0 (15.9 to 1)
Librarians/Media Specialists: 4.0 (1,148.0 to 1)
Guidance Counselors: 9.0 (510.2 to 1)
Current Spending: ($ per student per year):
  Total: $6,558; Instruction: $4,089; Support Services: $2,058

Enrollment, Drop-out Rates and Diploma Recipients by Race/Ethnicity

Category	Total	White	Black	Asian	AIAN	Hisp.
Enrollment (%)	100.0	28.6	4.7	3.3	0.2	62.8
Drop-out Rate (%)	8.3	6.1	4.5	0.0	25.0	11.3
H.S. Diplomas (#)	178	92	14	11	1	60

Shawnee County

Auburn Washburn
5928 SW 53rd • Topeka, KS 66610-9451
(785) 339-4000 • http://www.usd437.net
Grade Span: PK-12; **Agency Type:** 1
Schools: 8
  5 Primary; 2 Middle; 1 High; 0 Other Level
  8 Regular; 0 Special Education; 0 Vocational; 0 Alternative

0 Magnet; 0 Charter; 2 Title I Eligible; 2 School-wide Title I
Students: 5,179   (50.4% male; 49.5% female)
   Individual Education Program: 711 (13.7%);
   English Language Learner: 52 (1.0%); Migrant: 0 (0.0%)
   Eligible for Free Lunch Program: 691 (13.4%)
   Eligible for Reduced-Price Lunch Program: 362 (7.0%)
Teachers: 377.7 (13.6 to 1)
Librarians/Media Specialists: 9.0 (572.2 to 1)
Guidance Counselors: 14.0 (367.9 to 1)
Current Spending: ($ per student per year):
   Total: $6,717; Instruction: $4,076; Support Services: $2,351
Enrollment, Drop-out Rates and Diploma Recipients by Race/Ethnicity

Category	Total	White	Black	Asian	AIAN	Hisp.
Enrollment (%)	100.0	84.6	5.3	2.3	1.4	5.3
Drop-out Rate (%)	2.0	1.9	3.4	2.9	4.5	1.8
H.S. Diplomas (#)	325	295	10	10	2	8

Seaman
901 NW Lyman Rd • Topeka, KS 66608-1900
(785) 575-8600 • http://www.usd345.com/
Grade Span: PK-12; **Agency Type:** 1
Schools: 11
   8 Primary; 2 Middle; 1 High; 0 Other Level
   11 Regular; 0 Special Education; 0 Vocational; 0 Alternative
   0 Magnet; 0 Charter; 0 Title I Eligible; 0 School-wide Title I
Students: 3,426   (52.4% male; 47.5% female)
   Individual Education Program: 477 (13.9%);
   English Language Learner: 0 (0.0%); Migrant: 0 (0.0%)
   Eligible for Free Lunch Program: 471 (13.8%)
   Eligible for Reduced-Price Lunch Program: 245 (7.2%)
Teachers: 257.1 (13.3 to 1)
Librarians/Media Specialists: 7.0 (487.3 to 1)
Guidance Counselors: 9.0 (379.0 to 1)
Current Spending: ($ per student per year):
   Total: $6,533; Instruction: $3,870; Support Services: $2,370
Enrollment, Drop-out Rates and Diploma Recipients by Race/Ethnicity

Category	Total	White	Black	Asian	AIAN	Hisp.
Enrollment (%)	100.0	90.7	1.1	0.6	1.2	2.4
Drop-out Rate (%)	2.4	2.6	0.0	0.0	0.0	2.0
H.S. Diplomas (#)	235	224	1	1	0	9

Shawnee Heights
4401 SE Shawnee Heights Rd • Tecumseh, KS 66542-9799
(785) 379-5800 • http://www.snh450.k12.ks.us/district/index.htm
Grade Span: PK-12; **Agency Type:** 1
Schools: 6
   4 Primary; 1 Middle; 1 High; 0 Other Level
   6 Regular; 0 Special Education; 0 Vocational; 0 Alternative
   0 Magnet; 0 Charter; 1 Title I Eligible; 0 School-wide Title I
Students: 3,465   (51.5% male; 48.4% female)
   Individual Education Program: 488 (14.1%);
   English Language Learner: 15 (0.4%); Migrant: 0 (0.0%)
   Eligible for Free Lunch Program: 482 (14.0%)
   Eligible for Reduced-Price Lunch Program: 227 (6.6%)
Teachers: 222.2 (15.5 to 1)
Librarians/Media Specialists: 7.0 (491.0 to 1)
Guidance Counselors: 10.0 (343.7 to 1)
Current Spending: ($ per student per year):
   Total: $6,830; Instruction: $3,919; Support Services: $2,577
Enrollment, Drop-out Rates and Diploma Recipients by Race/Ethnicity

Category	Total	White	Black	Asian	AIAN	Hisp.
Enrollment (%)	100.0	82.4	6.5	0.6	1.3	6.4
Drop-out Rate (%)	0.6	0.5	0.0	0.0	0.0	3.1
H.S. Diplomas (#)	255	222	10	4	4	15

Topeka Public Schools
624 SW 24th • Topeka, KS 66611-1294
(785) 295-3000 • http://www.topeka.k12.ks.us/
Grade Span: PK-12; **Agency Type:** 1
Schools: 32
   21 Primary; 6 Middle; 4 High; 1 Other Level
   32 Regular; 0 Special Education; 0 Vocational; 0 Alternative
   2 Magnet; 1 Charter; 21 Title I Eligible; 19 School-wide Title I
Students: 14,049   (51.6% male; 48.3% female)
   Individual Education Program: 2,466 (17.6%);
   English Language Learner: 329 (2.3%); Migrant: 325 (2.3%)
   Eligible for Free Lunch Program: 6,892 (49.1%)
   Eligible for Reduced-Price Lunch Program: 1,373 (9.8%)
Teachers: 1,071.4 (13.1 to 1)
Librarians/Media Specialists: 31.5 (446.0 to 1)
Guidance Counselors: 35.5 (395.7 to 1)
Current Spending: ($ per student per year):
   Total: $8,196; Instruction: $5,128; Support Services: $2,756

Enrollment, Drop-out Rates and Diploma Recipients by Race/Ethnicity

Category	Total	White	Black	Asian	AIAN	Hisp.
Enrollment (%)	100.0	48.5	22.3	0.8	2.0	14.8
Drop-out Rate (%)	5.1	4.7	5.7	5.2	7.8	5.5
H.S. Diplomas (#)	769	496	148	17	28	80

Sumner County

Wellington
221 S Washington • Wellington, KS 67152-0648
Mailing Address: Box 648 • Wellington, KS 67152-0648
(620) 326-4300 • http://www.usd353.com/
Grade Span: KG-12; **Agency Type:** 1
Schools: 7
   4 Primary; 2 Middle; 1 High; 0 Other Level
   7 Regular; 0 Special Education; 0 Vocational; 0 Alternative
   0 Magnet; 0 Charter; 3 Title I Eligible; 0 School-wide Title I
Students: 1,775   (50.9% male; 49.0% female)
   Individual Education Program: 298 (16.8%);
   English Language Learner: 0 (0.0%); Migrant: 0 (0.0%)
   Eligible for Free Lunch Program: 611 (34.4%)
   Eligible for Reduced-Price Lunch Program: 215 (12.1%)
Teachers: 125.7 (14.1 to 1)
Librarians/Media Specialists: 2.0 (887.5 to 1)
Guidance Counselors: 3.8 (467.1 to 1)
Current Spending: ($ per student per year):
   Total: $6,890; Instruction: $4,605; Support Services: $2,028
Enrollment, Drop-out Rates and Diploma Recipients by Race/Ethnicity

Category	Total	White	Black	Asian	AIAN	Hisp.
Enrollment (%)	100.0	87.0	3.4	0.6	0.4	8.6
Drop-out Rate (%)	3.8	4.1	10.0	0.0	0.0	1.5
H.S. Diplomas (#)	140	127	2	0	0	11

Wyandotte County

Bonner Springs
2200 S 138th St • Bonner Springs, KS 66012-0435
Mailing Address: PO Box 435 • Bonner Springs, KS 66012-0435
(913) 422-5600 • http://www.usd204.k12.ks.us/
Grade Span: KG-12; **Agency Type:** 1
Schools: 4
   2 Primary; 1 Middle; 1 High; 0 Other Level
   4 Regular; 0 Special Education; 0 Vocational; 0 Alternative
   0 Magnet; 0 Charter; 0 Title I Eligible; 0 School-wide Title I
Students: 2,294   (51.6% male; 48.3% female)
   Individual Education Program: 261 (11.4%);
   English Language Learner: 0 (0.0%); Migrant: 297 (13.1%)
   Eligible for Free Lunch Program: 519 (22.8%)
   Eligible for Reduced-Price Lunch Program: 192 (8.4%)
Teachers: 136.8 (16.6 to 1)
Librarians/Media Specialists: 4.0 (568.5 to 1)
Guidance Counselors: 5.0 (454.8 to 1)
Current Spending: ($ per student per year):
   Total: $6,919; Instruction: $4,445; Support Services: $2,134
Enrollment, Drop-out Rates and Diploma Recipients by Race/Ethnicity

Category	Total	White	Black	Asian	AIAN	Hisp.
Enrollment (%)	100.0	81.1	8.2	0.9	1.1	8.7
Drop-out Rate (%)	2.2	2.0	0.0	0.0	14.3	5.7
H.S. Diplomas (#)	150	126	12	2	1	9

Kansas City
625 Minnesota Ave • Kansas City, KS 66101-2805
(913) 551-3200 • http://www.kckps.k12.ks.us/
Grade Span: KG-12; **Agency Type:** 1
Schools: 42
   28 Primary; 8 Middle; 6 High; 0 Other Level
   42 Regular; 0 Special Education; 0 Vocational; 0 Alternative
   3 Magnet; 0 Charter; 28 Title I Eligible; 26 School-wide Title I
Students: 20,868   (51.9% male; 48.0% female)
   Individual Education Program: 2,686 (12.9%);
   English Language Learner: 2,508 (12.0%); Migrant: 170 (0.8%)
   Eligible for Free Lunch Program: 13,196 (63.2%)
   Eligible for Reduced-Price Lunch Program: 2,449 (11.7%)
Teachers: 1,475.5 (14.1 to 1)
Librarians/Media Specialists: 30.0 (695.5 to 1)
Guidance Counselors: 37.0 (563.9 to 1)
Current Spending: ($ per student per year):
   Total: $7,827; Instruction: $4,485; Support Services: $2,931
Enrollment, Drop-out Rates and Diploma Recipients by Race/Ethnicity

Category	Total	White	Black	Asian	AIAN	Hisp.
Enrollment (%)	100.0	20.3	48.2	3.3	0.5	27.7
Drop-out Rate (%)	4.8	6.5	3.9	4.0	11.1	5.4
H.S. Diplomas (#)	938	227	548	34	2	127

Turner-Kansas City
800 S 55th St • Kansas City, KS 66106-1566
(913) 288-4100 • http://www.turnerusd202.org/
Grade Span: KG-12; **Agency Type:** 1
Schools: 8
6 Primary; 1 Middle; 1 High; 0 Other Level
8 Regular; 0 Special Education; 0 Vocational; 0 Alternative
0 Magnet; 0 Charter; 6 Title I Eligible; 6 School-wide Title I
Students: 3,864   (50.4% male; 49.5% female)
Individual Education Program: 536 (13.9%);
English Language Learner: 142 (3.7%); Migrant: 0 (0.0%)
Eligible for Free Lunch Program: 1,281 (33.2%)
Eligible for Reduced-Price Lunch Program: 521 (13.5%)
Teachers: 199.0 (19.4 to 1)
Librarians/Media Specialists: 7.0 (552.0 to 1)
Guidance Counselors: 7.0 (552.0 to 1)
Current Spending: ($ per student per year):
Total: $6,651; Instruction: $3,814; Support Services: $2,508
Enrollment, Drop-out Rates and Diploma Recipients by Race/Ethnicity

Category	Total	White	Black	Asian	AIAN	Hisp.
Enrollment (%)	100.0	68.0	10.6	2.5	1.0	15.9
Drop-out Rate (%)	6.0	6.5	1.6	3.1	0.0	6.3
H.S. Diplomas (#)	161	128	11	7	1	14

Number of Schools

Rank	Number	District Name	City
1	90	Wichita	Wichita
2	50	Shawnee Mission Public Schools	Shawnee Mission
3	42	Kansas City	Kansas City
4	39	Olathe	Olathe
5	32	Topeka Public Schools	Topeka
6	29	Blue Valley	Overland Park
7	21	Lawrence	Lawrence
8	16	Garden City	Garden City
8	16	Geary County Schools	Junction City
10	12	Derby	Derby
10	12	Liberal	Liberal
10	12	Salina	Salina
13	11	Dodge City	Dodge City
13	11	Manhattan	Manhattan
13	11	Seaman	Topeka
16	10	Emporia	Emporia
16	10	Hutchinson Public Schools	Hutchinson
16	10	Newton	Newton
19	9	Hays	Hays
19	9	Leavenworth	Leavenworth
21	8	Andover	Andover
21	8	Arkansas City	Arkansas City
21	8	Auburn Washburn	Topeka
21	8	De Soto	De Soto
21	8	Goddard	Goddard
21	8	Turner-Kansas City	Kansas City
21	8	Winfield	Winfield
28	7	Chanute Public Schools	Chanute
28	7	El Dorado	El Dorado
28	7	Gardner Edgerton	Gardner
28	7	Great Bend	Great Bend
28	7	Haysville	Haysville
28	7	Ottawa	Ottawa
28	7	Renwick	Andale
28	7	Wellington	Wellington
36	6	Augusta	Augusta
36	6	Buhler	Buhler
36	6	Iola	Iola
36	6	Labette County	Altamont
36	6	Maize	Maize
36	6	Mcpherson	Mcpherson
36	6	Pittsburg	Pittsburg
36	6	Shawnee Heights	Tecumseh
36	6	Valley Center Public Schools	Valley Center
45	5	Basehor-Linwood	Basehor
45	5	Circle	Towanda
45	5	Coffeyville	Coffeyville
45	5	Independence	Independence
45	5	Mulvane	Mulvane
45	5	Paola	Paola
45	5	Parsons	Parsons
52	4	Bonner Springs	Bonner Springs
52	4	Fort Scott	Fort Scott
52	4	Ft Leavenworth	Ft Leavenworth
52	4	Lansing	Lansing
52	4	Rose Hill Public Schools	Rose Hill
52	4	Spring Hill	Spring Hill
52	4	Ulysses	Ulysses
59	3	Atchison Public Schools	Atchison
59	3	Tonganoxie	Tonganoxie

Number of Teachers

Rank	Number	District Name	City
1	3,069	Wichita	Wichita
2	1,815	Shawnee Mission Public Schools	Shawnee Mission
3	1,536	Olathe	Olathe
4	1,475	Kansas City	Kansas City
5	1,249	Blue Valley	Overland Park
6	1,071	Topeka Public Schools	Topeka
7	749	Lawrence	Lawrence
8	563	Salina	Salina
9	496	Garden City	Garden City
10	453	Leavenworth	Leavenworth
11	447	Geary County Schools	Junction City
12	426	Derby	Derby
13	389	Manhattan	Manhattan
14	381	Emporia	Emporia
15	377	Auburn Washburn	Topeka
16	340	Dodge City	Dodge City
17	330	Hutchinson Public Schools	Hutchinson
18	320	De Soto	De Soto
19	301	Maize	Maize
20	289	Liberal	Liberal
21	287	Haysville	Haysville
22	269	Hays	Hays
23	257	Seaman	Topeka
24	256	Newton	Newton
25	244	Winfield	Winfield
26	238	Great Bend	Great Bend

Rank	Number	District Name	City
27	232	Gardner Edgerton	Gardner
28	227	El Dorado	El Dorado
29	222	Shawnee Heights	Tecumseh
30	208	Andover	Andover
31	207	Mcpherson	Mcpherson
32	204	Goddard	Goddard
33	199	Turner-Kansas City	Kansas City
34	190	Paola	Paola
35	179	Arkansas City	Arkansas City
36	166	Ottawa	Ottawa
37	159	Pittsburg	Pittsburg
38	145	Fort Scott	Fort Scott
39	136	Bonner Springs	Bonner Springs
40	133	Buhler	Buhler
41	130	Valley Center Public Schools	Valley Center
42	130	Atchison Public Schools	Atchison
42	130	Augusta	Augusta
44	126	Renwick	Andale
45	125	Wellington	Wellington
46	125	Independence	Independence
47	123	Mulvane	Mulvane
48	119	Chanute Public Schools	Chanute
49	116	Ulysses	Ulysses
50	114	Ft Leavenworth	Ft Leavenworth
51	110	Lansing	Lansing
52	110	Coffeyville	Coffeyville
53	108	Labette County	Altamont
54	107	Spring Hill	Spring Hill
55	105	Parsons	Parsons
56	105	Iola	Iola
57	102	Rose Hill Public Schools	Rose Hill
58	97	Basehor-Linwood	Basehor
59	92	Tonganoxie	Tonganoxie
60	88	Circle	Towanda

Number of Students

Rank	Number	District Name	City
1	48,894	Wichita	Wichita
2	29,389	Shawnee Mission Public Schools	Shawnee Mission
3	22,917	Olathe	Olathe
4	20,868	Kansas City	Kansas City
5	19,055	Blue Valley	Overland Park
6	14,049	Topeka Public Schools	Topeka
7	10,022	Lawrence	Lawrence
8	7,736	Garden City	Garden City
9	7,594	Salina	Salina
10	6,695	Derby	Derby
11	6,645	Geary County Schools	Junction City
12	5,960	Dodge City	Dodge City
13	5,815	Maize	Maize
14	5,383	Manhattan	Manhattan
15	5,179	Auburn Washburn	Topeka
16	5,025	Hutchinson Public Schools	Hutchinson
17	4,981	Emporia	Emporia
18	4,690	Haysville	Haysville
19	4,592	Liberal	Liberal
20	4,545	De Soto	De Soto
21	4,274	Leavenworth	Leavenworth
22	4,065	Goddard	Goddard
23	3,864	Turner-Kansas City	Kansas City
24	3,765	Newton	Newton
25	3,520	Andover	Andover
26	3,465	Shawnee Heights	Tecumseh
27	3,426	Seaman	Topeka
28	3,401	Gardner Edgerton	Gardner
29	3,307	Great Bend	Great Bend
30	3,271	Hays	Hays
31	3,017	Arkansas City	Arkansas City
32	2,706	Winfield	Winfield
33	2,609	Pittsburg	Pittsburg
34	2,559	Mcpherson	Mcpherson
35	2,472	Ottawa	Ottawa
36	2,394	Valley Center Public Schools	Valley Center
37	2,294	Bonner Springs	Bonner Springs
38	2,269	Buhler	Buhler
39	2,198	El Dorado	El Dorado
40	2,171	Augusta	Augusta
41	2,167	Paola	Paola
42	2,102	Basehor-Linwood	Basehor
43	2,070	Renwick	Andale
44	2,065	Lansing	Lansing
45	2,046	Fort Scott	Fort Scott
46	2,036	Independence	Independence
47	1,966	Coffeyville	Coffeyville
48	1,937	Mulvane	Mulvane
49	1,934	Chanute Public Schools	Chanute
50	1,915	Ft Leavenworth	Ft Leavenworth
51	1,878	Rose Hill Public Schools	Rose Hill
52	1,833	Ulysses	Ulysses
53	1,775	Wellington	Wellington
54	1,709	Labette County	Altamont
55	1,676	Atchison Public Schools	Atchison
56	1,630	Parsons	Parsons
57	1,605	Spring Hill	Spring Hill
58	1,558	Tonganoxie	Tonganoxie
59	1,537	Circle	Towanda
60	1,513	Iola	Iola

Male Students

Rank	Percent	District Name	City
1	54.1	El Dorado	El Dorado
2	53.8	Independence	Independence
3	53.5	Ulysses	Ulysses
4	53.1	Renwick	Andale
5	52.9	Newton	Newton
6	52.8	Augusta	Augusta
7	52.6	Liberal	Liberal
8	52.4	Manhattan	Manhattan
9	52.4	Ottawa	Ottawa
10	52.4	Seaman	Topeka
11	52.4	Iola	Iola
12	52.3	Valley Center Public Schools	Valley Center
13	52.3	Atchison Public Schools	Atchison
14	52.3	Andover	Andover
15	52.3	Parsons	Parsons
16	52.1	Goddard	Goddard
17	52.1	Winfield	Winfield
18	51.9	Shawnee Mission Public Schools	Shawnee Mission
19	51.9	Kansas City	Kansas City
20	51.9	Leavenworth	Leavenworth
21	51.9	Mcpherson	Mcpherson
22	51.8	Olathe	Olathe
23	51.7	Hays	Hays
24	51.7	Haysville	Haysville
25	51.7	Great Bend	Great Bend
26	51.7	Lansing	Lansing
27	51.6	Emporia	Emporia
28	51.6	Buhler	Buhler
29	51.6	Topeka Public Schools	Topeka
30	51.6	Bonner Springs	Bonner Springs
31	51.5	Shawnee Heights	Tecumseh
32	51.4	Hutchinson Public Schools	Hutchinson
33	51.4	Derby	Derby
34	51.4	Geary County Schools	Junction City
35	51.4	Salina	Salina
36	51.4	Dodge City	Dodge City
37	51.4	Blue Valley	Overland Park
38	51.4	Rose Hill Public Schools	Rose Hill
39	51.3	Labette County	Altamont
40	51.3	Coffeyville	Coffeyville
41	51.3	Tonganoxie	Tonganoxie
42	51.2	Paola	Paola
43	51.2	Garden City	Garden City
44	51.2	Arkansas City	Arkansas City
45	51.0	Gardner Edgerton	Gardner
46	51.0	Wichita	Wichita
47	51.0	De Soto	De Soto
48	50.9	Wellington	Wellington
49	50.8	Maize	Maize
50	50.7	Pittsburg	Pittsburg
51	50.7	Ft Leavenworth	Ft Leavenworth
52	50.7	Circle	Towanda
53	50.7	Lawrence	Lawrence
54	50.7	Mulvane	Mulvane
55	50.6	Fort Scott	Fort Scott
56	50.4	Auburn Washburn	Topeka
57	50.4	Turner-Kansas City	Kansas City
58	49.6	Chanute Public Schools	Chanute
59	49.4	Spring Hill	Spring Hill
60	47.4	Basehor-Linwood	Basehor

Female Students

Rank	Percent	District Name	City
1	52.5	Basehor-Linwood	Basehor
2	50.5	Spring Hill	Spring Hill
3	50.3	Chanute Public Schools	Chanute
4	49.5	Turner-Kansas City	Kansas City
5	49.5	Auburn Washburn	Topeka
6	49.3	Fort Scott	Fort Scott
7	49.2	Mulvane	Mulvane
8	49.2	Lawrence	Lawrence
9	49.2	Circle	Towanda
10	49.2	Ft Leavenworth	Ft Leavenworth
11	49.2	Pittsburg	Pittsburg
12	49.1	Maize	Maize
13	49.0	Wellington	Wellington
14	48.9	De Soto	De Soto
15	48.9	Wichita	Wichita
16	48.9	Gardner Edgerton	Gardner
17	48.7	Arkansas City	Arkansas City
18	48.7	Garden City	Garden City
19	48.7	Paola	Paola
20	48.6	Tonganoxie	Tonganoxie

21	48.6	Coffeyville	Coffeyville
22	48.6	Labette County	Altamont
23	48.5	Rose Hill Public Schools	Rose Hill
24	48.5	Blue Valley	Overland Park
25	48.5	Dodge City	Dodge City
26	48.5	Salina	Salina
27	48.5	Geary County Schools	Junction City
28	48.5	Derby	Derby
29	48.5	Hutchinson Public Schools	Hutchinson
30	48.4	Shawnee Heights	Tecumseh
31	48.3	Bonner Springs	Bonner Springs
32	48.3	Topeka Public Schools	Topeka
33	48.3	Buhler	Buhler
34	48.3	Emporia	Emporia
35	48.2	Lansing	Lansing
36	48.2	Great Bend	Great Bend
37	48.2	Haysville	Haysville
38	48.2	Hays	Hays
39	48.1	Olathe	Olathe
40	48.0	Mcpherson	Mcpherson
41	48.0	Leavenworth	Leavenworth
42	48.0	Kansas City	Kansas City
43	48.0	Shawnee Mission Public Schools	Shawnee Mission
44	47.8	Winfield	Winfield
45	47.8	Goddard	Goddard
46	47.6	Parsons	Parsons
47	47.6	Andover	Andover
48	47.6	Atchison Public Schools	Atchison
49	47.6	Valley Center Public Schools	Valley Center
50	47.5	Iola	Iola
51	47.5	Seaman	Topeka
52	47.5	Ottawa	Ottawa
53	47.5	Manhattan	Manhattan
54	47.3	Liberal	Liberal
55	47.1	Augusta	Augusta
56	47.0	Newton	Newton
57	46.8	Renwick	Andale
58	46.4	Ulysses	Ulysses
59	46.1	Independence	Independence
60	45.8	El Dorado	El Dorado

Individual Education Program Students

Rank	Percent	District Name	City
1	20.4	Iola	Iola
2	19.8	Atchison Public Schools	Atchison
3	19.3	Arkansas City	Arkansas City
4	18.6	Leavenworth	Leavenworth
5	17.6	Topeka Public Schools	Topeka
6	17.2	Chanute Public Schools	Chanute
7	17.1	El Dorado	El Dorado
8	16.8	Wellington	Wellington
8	16.8	Winfield	Winfield
10	16.6	Hays	Hays
11	16.4	Mcpherson	Mcpherson
12	16.1	Hutchinson Public Schools	Hutchinson
12	16.1	Manhattan	Manhattan
14	15.7	Haysville	Haysville
14	15.7	Lawrence	Lawrence
16	15.4	Newton	Newton
17	14.9	Ottawa	Ottawa
18	14.7	Geary County Schools	Junction City
18	14.7	Salina	Salina
20	14.5	Coffeyville	Coffeyville
20	14.5	Pittsburg	Pittsburg
20	14.5	Wichita	Wichita
23	14.3	Derby	Derby
24	14.2	Independence	Independence
25	14.1	Ft Leavenworth	Ft Leavenworth
25	14.1	Shawnee Heights	Tecumseh
27	13.9	Seaman	Topeka
27	13.9	Tonganoxie	Tonganoxie
27	13.9	Turner-Kansas City	Kansas City
30	13.8	Paola	Paola
31	13.7	Auburn Washburn	Topeka
31	13.7	Valley Center Public Schools	Valley Center
33	13.5	Goddard	Goddard
33	13.5	Parsons	Parsons
35	13.2	Buhler	Buhler
35	13.2	Great Bend	Great Bend
37	13.1	Gardner Edgerton	Gardner
38	13.0	Olathe	Olathe
39	12.9	Kansas City	Kansas City
40	12.6	Dodge City	Dodge City
41	12.3	Augusta	Augusta
42	12.2	Circle	Towanda
43	12.1	Ulysses	Ulysses
44	12.0	Garden City	Garden City
45	11.5	Shawnee Mission Public Schools	Shawnee Mission
46	11.4	Andover	Andover
46	11.4	Bonner Springs	Bonner Springs
48	10.9	Emporia	Emporia
49	10.6	Basehor-Linwood	Basehor
49	10.6	Fort Scott	Fort Scott
49	10.6	Labette County	Altamont
49	10.6	Lansing	Lansing
53	10.5	Spring Hill	Spring Hill
54	9.9	Mulvane	Mulvane
55	9.8	Liberal	Liberal
55	9.8	Maize	Maize
57	9.5	De Soto	De Soto
57	9.5	Renwick	Andale
59	9.3	Rose Hill Public Schools	Rose Hill
60	8.7	Blue Valley	Overland Park

English Language Learner Students

Rank	Percent	District Name	City
1	49.6	Dodge City	Dodge City
2	28.8	Liberal	Liberal
3	22.0	Garden City	Garden City
4	20.6	Emporia	Emporia
5	12.3	Ulysses	Ulysses
6	12.0	Kansas City	Kansas City
7	10.5	Wichita	Wichita
8	9.1	Great Bend	Great Bend
9	8.1	Arkansas City	Arkansas City
10	5.0	Lawrence	Lawrence
11	4.8	Pittsburg	Pittsburg
12	4.7	Geary County Schools	Junction City
13	4.6	Newton	Newton
14	3.7	Turner-Kansas City	Kansas City
15	3.6	Salina	Salina
16	3.3	Leavenworth	Leavenworth
16	3.3	Shawnee Mission Public Schools	Shawnee Mission
18	3.1	Olathe	Olathe
19	2.5	Winfield	Winfield
20	2.3	De Soto	De Soto
20	2.3	Haysville	Haysville
20	2.3	Topeka Public Schools	Topeka
23	2.2	Manhattan	Manhattan
24	1.8	Derby	Derby
25	1.3	Blue Valley	Overland Park
25	1.3	Hays	Hays
27	1.0	Auburn Washburn	Topeka
27	1.0	Maize	Maize
27	1.0	Ottawa	Ottawa
30	0.8	Hutchinson Public Schools	Hutchinson
31	0.7	Andover	Andover
32	0.5	Fort Scott	Fort Scott
32	0.5	Goddard	Goddard
32	0.5	Mcpherson	Mcpherson
35	0.4	Shawnee Heights	Tecumseh
35	0.4	Spring Hill	Spring Hill
37	0.2	Buhler	Buhler
37	0.2	Gardner Edgerton	Gardner
39	0.0	Atchison Public Schools	Atchison
39	0.0	Augusta	Augusta
39	0.0	Basehor-Linwood	Basehor
39	0.0	Bonner Springs	Bonner Springs
39	0.0	Chanute Public Schools	Chanute
39	0.0	Circle	Towanda
39	0.0	Coffeyville	Coffeyville
39	0.0	El Dorado	El Dorado
39	0.0	Ft Leavenworth	Ft Leavenworth
39	0.0	Independence	Independence
39	0.0	Iola	Iola
39	0.0	Labette County	Altamont
39	0.0	Lansing	Lansing
39	0.0	Mulvane	Mulvane
39	0.0	Paola	Paola
39	0.0	Parsons	Parsons
39	0.0	Renwick	Andale
39	0.0	Rose Hill Public Schools	Rose Hill
39	0.0	Seaman	Topeka
39	0.0	Tonganoxie	Tonganoxie
39	0.0	Valley Center Public Schools	Valley Center
39	0.0	Wellington	Wellington

Migrant Students

Rank	Percent	District Name	City
1	36.8	Dodge City	Dodge City
2	26.4	Liberal	Liberal
3	18.6	Great Bend	Great Bend
4	16.9	Ulysses	Ulysses
5	13.1	Bonner Springs	Bonner Springs
6	8.8	Garden City	Garden City
7	8.3	Emporia	Emporia
8	5.6	Wichita	Wichita
9	3.6	Pittsburg	Pittsburg
10	2.6	Arkansas City	Arkansas City
11	2.3	Topeka Public Schools	Topeka
12	1.5	Hays	Hays
13	1.3	Olathe	Olathe
14	0.8	Kansas City	Kansas City
15	0.7	Gardner Edgerton	Gardner
16	0.4	Salina	Salina
17	0.2	Haysville	Haysville
18	0.0	Andover	Andover
18	0.0	Atchison Public Schools	Atchison
18	0.0	Auburn Washburn	Topeka
18	0.0	Augusta	Augusta
18	0.0	Basehor-Linwood	Basehor
18	0.0	Blue Valley	Overland Park
18	0.0	Buhler	Buhler
18	0.0	Chanute Public Schools	Chanute
18	0.0	Circle	Towanda
18	0.0	Coffeyville	Coffeyville
18	0.0	De Soto	De Soto
18	0.0	Derby	Derby
18	0.0	El Dorado	El Dorado
18	0.0	Fort Scott	Fort Scott
18	0.0	Ft Leavenworth	Ft Leavenworth
18	0.0	Geary County Schools	Junction City
18	0.0	Goddard	Goddard
18	0.0	Hutchinson Public Schools	Hutchinson
18	0.0	Independence	Independence
18	0.0	Iola	Iola
18	0.0	Labette County	Altamont
18	0.0	Lansing	Lansing
18	0.0	Lawrence	Lawrence
18	0.0	Leavenworth	Leavenworth
18	0.0	Maize	Maize
18	0.0	Manhattan	Manhattan
18	0.0	Mcpherson	Mcpherson
18	0.0	Mulvane	Mulvane
18	0.0	Newton	Newton
18	0.0	Ottawa	Ottawa
18	0.0	Paola	Paola
18	0.0	Parsons	Parsons
18	0.0	Renwick	Andale
18	0.0	Rose Hill Public Schools	Rose Hill
18	0.0	Seaman	Topeka
18	0.0	Shawnee Heights	Tecumseh
18	0.0	Shawnee Mission Public Schools	Shawnee Mission
18	0.0	Spring Hill	Spring Hill
18	0.0	Tonganoxie	Tonganoxie
18	0.0	Turner-Kansas City	Kansas City
18	0.0	Valley Center Public Schools	Valley Center
18	0.0	Wellington	Wellington
18	0.0	Winfield	Winfield

Students Eligible for Free Lunch

Rank	Percent	District Name	City
1	63.2	Kansas City	Kansas City
2	52.4	Wichita	Wichita
3	51.6	Dodge City	Dodge City
4	51.1	Liberal	Liberal
5	49.1	Topeka Public Schools	Topeka
6	47.5	Coffeyville	Coffeyville
7	44.9	Arkansas City	Arkansas City
8	43.5	Pittsburg	Pittsburg
9	43.3	Garden City	Garden City
10	42.5	Great Bend	Great Bend
11	42.1	Parsons	Parsons
12	41.4	Emporia	Emporia
13	40.9	Atchison Public Schools	Atchison
14	40.4	Hutchinson Public Schools	Hutchinson
15	37.5	Geary County Schools	Junction City
16	36.9	Leavenworth	Leavenworth
17	36.4	Fort Scott	Fort Scott
18	35.7	Independence	Independence
19	35.3	Chanute Public Schools	Chanute
20	34.4	Wellington	Wellington
21	34.2	Ulysses	Ulysses
22	33.2	Turner-Kansas City	Kansas City
23	33.0	Iola	Iola
24	32.5	Salina	Salina
25	31.5	Newton	Newton
26	29.6	El Dorado	El Dorado
27	28.9	Winfield	Winfield
28	26.6	Ottawa	Ottawa
29	25.8	Haysville	Haysville
30	24.2	Labette County	Altamont
31	22.8	Bonner Springs	Bonner Springs
32	21.4	Derby	Derby
33	20.9	Augusta	Augusta
34	20.8	Hays	Hays
35	20.2	Lawrence	Lawrence
36	19.7	Buhler	Buhler
37	19.4	Manhattan	Manhattan
38	18.3	Circle	Towanda
39	17.9	Paola	Paola
40	16.5	Mcpherson	Mcpherson
41	16.4	Mulvane	Mulvane
42	14.0	Shawnee Heights	Tecumseh
43	13.8	Seaman	Topeka

Rank		District Name	City
44	13.6	Valley Center Public Schools	Valley Center
45	13.5	Gardner Edgerton	Gardner
46	13.4	Auburn Washburn	Topeka
47	11.6	Tonganoxie	Tonganoxie
48	11.1	Rose Hill Public Schools	Rose Hill
49	9.9	Shawnee Mission Public Schools	Shawnee Mission
50	9.4	Goddard	Goddard
51	9.0	Olathe	Olathe
52	8.7	De Soto	De Soto
53	8.3	Spring Hill	Spring Hill
54	8.1	Renwick	Andale
55	7.1	Andover	Andover
56	5.6	Maize	Maize
57	5.1	Lansing	Lansing
58	4.8	Basehor-Linwood	Basehor
59	3.1	Ft Leavenworth	Ft Leavenworth
60	1.6	Blue Valley	Overland Park

Students Eligible for Reduced-Price Lunch

Rank	Percent	District Name	City
1	18.7	Geary County Schools	Junction City
2	16.0	Iola	Iola
3	15.1	Atchison Public Schools	Atchison
4	14.8	Parsons	Parsons
5	14.0	Dodge City	Dodge City
6	13.5	Turner-Kansas City	Kansas City
6	13.5	Winfield	Winfield
8	12.6	Emporia	Emporia
9	12.5	Labette County	Altamont
10	12.4	Fort Scott	Fort Scott
10	12.4	Independence	Independence
10	12.4	Newton	Newton
13	12.1	Chanute Public Schools	Chanute
13	12.1	Wellington	Wellington
15	11.9	Ulysses	Ulysses
16	11.7	Kansas City	Kansas City
17	11.4	Arkansas City	Arkansas City
17	11.4	Coffeyville	Coffeyville
17	11.4	Garden City	Garden City
17	11.4	Wichita	Wichita
21	11.2	Salina	Salina
22	10.6	Manhattan	Manhattan
23	10.5	Hays	Hays
24	10.4	Liberal	Liberal
25	10.3	Haysville	Haysville
26	10.1	Hutchinson Public Schools	Hutchinson
27	10.0	Leavenworth	Leavenworth
28	9.8	Topeka Public Schools	Topeka
29	9.2	Lawrence	Lawrence
30	8.9	Circle	Towanda
31	8.8	Buhler	Buhler
32	8.6	Pittsburg	Pittsburg
33	8.5	Derby	Derby
34	8.4	Bonner Springs	Bonner Springs
34	8.4	Renwick	Andale
36	8.3	Ottawa	Ottawa
37	8.2	El Dorado	El Dorado
38	8.0	Great Bend	Great Bend
39	7.4	Mcpherson	Mcpherson
40	7.2	Gardner Edgerton	Gardner
40	7.2	Seaman	Topeka
42	7.0	Auburn Washburn	Topeka
42	7.0	Augusta	Augusta
42	7.0	Valley Center Public Schools	Valley Center
45	6.8	Tonganoxie	Tonganoxie
46	6.6	Shawnee Heights	Tecumseh
47	6.5	Goddard	Goddard
47	6.5	Mulvane	Mulvane
49	6.3	Paola	Paola
50	5.2	Rose Hill Public Schools	Rose Hill
51	4.9	Ft Leavenworth	Ft Leavenworth
52	4.4	Andover	Andover
52	4.4	Spring Hill	Spring Hill
54	4.3	Shawnee Mission Public Schools	Shawnee Mission
55	4.1	Olathe	Olathe
56	3.8	Basehor-Linwood	Basehor
57	3.7	De Soto	De Soto
58	2.6	Lansing	Lansing
59	2.3	Maize	Maize
60	1.0	Blue Valley	Overland Park

Student/Teacher Ratio

Rank	Ratio	District Name	City
1	21.5	Basehor-Linwood	Basehor
2	19.8	Goddard	Goddard
3	19.4	Turner-Kansas City	Kansas City
4	19.3	Maize	Maize
5	18.4	Lansing	Lansing
6	18.2	Rose Hill Public Schools	Rose Hill
6	18.2	Valley Center Public Schools	Valley Center

Rank		District Name	City
8	17.7	Coffeyville	Coffeyville
9	17.5	Dodge City	Dodge City
10	16.9	Andover	Andover
11	16.8	Arkansas City	Arkansas City
11	16.8	Circle	Towanda
11	16.8	Tonganoxie	Tonganoxie
14	16.6	Augusta	Augusta
14	16.6	Bonner Springs	Bonner Springs
14	16.6	Buhler	Buhler
14	16.6	Ft Leavenworth	Ft Leavenworth
18	16.4	Andale	Andale
19	16.3	Haysville	Haysville
19	16.3	Pittsburg	Pittsburg
21	16.2	Chanute Public Schools	Chanute
21	16.2	Independence	Independence
21	16.2	Shawnee Mission Public Schools	Shawnee Mission
24	15.9	Liberal	Liberal
24	15.9	Wichita	Wichita
26	15.8	Ulysses	Ulysses
27	15.7	Derby	Derby
27	15.7	Labette County	Altamont
29	15.6	Garden City	Garden City
29	15.6	Mulvane	Mulvane
31	15.5	Parsons	Parsons
31	15.5	Shawnee Heights	Tecumseh
33	15.3	Blue Valley	Overland Park
34	15.2	Hutchinson Public Schools	Hutchinson
35	14.9	Geary County Schools	Junction City
35	14.9	Olathe	Olathe
35	14.9	Ottawa	Ottawa
35	14.9	Spring Hill	Spring Hill
39	14.7	Newton	Newton
40	14.3	Gardner Edgerton	Gardner
40	14.3	Iola	Iola
42	14.2	De Soto	De Soto
43	14.1	Fort Scott	Fort Scott
43	14.1	Kansas City	Kansas City
43	14.1	Wellington	Wellington
46	13.8	Great Bend	Great Bend
46	13.8	Manhattan	Manhattan
48	13.6	Auburn Washburn	Topeka
49	13.5	Salina	Salina
50	13.4	Lawrence	Lawrence
51	13.3	Seaman	Topeka
52	13.1	Topeka Public Schools	Topeka
53	13.0	Emporia	Emporia
54	12.9	Atchison Public Schools	Atchison
55	12.1	Hays	Hays
56	12.0	Mcpherson	Mcpherson
57	11.3	Paola	Paola
58	11.1	Winfield	Winfield
59	9.4	Leavenworth	Leavenworth
60	9.3	El Dorado	El Dorado

Student/Librarian Ratio

Rank	Ratio	District Name	City
1	1,148.0	Liberal	Liberal
2	978.5	Coffeyville	Coffeyville
3	969.2	Maize	Maize
4	927.0	Rose Hill Public Schools	Rose Hill
5	887.5	Wellington	Wellington
6	830.2	Emporia	Emporia
7	777.5	Tonganoxie	Tonganoxie
8	730.4	Wichita	Wichita
9	695.5	Kansas City	Kansas City
10	695.0	Basehor-Linwood	Basehor
11	675.3	Winfield	Winfield
12	666.7	Haysville	Haysville
13	665.2	Gardner Edgerton	Gardner
14	661.4	Great Bend	Great Bend
15	632.8	Salina	Salina
16	628.1	Hutchinson Public Schools	Hutchinson
17	575.9	Goddard	Goddard
18	572.2	Auburn Washburn	Topeka
19	568.5	Bonner Springs	Bonner Springs
20	567.6	De Soto	De Soto
20	567.6	Dodge City	Dodge City
22	566.3	Labette County	Altamont
23	564.4	Olathe	Olathe
24	564.1	Shawnee Mission Public Schools	Shawnee Mission
25	560.4	Blue Valley	Overland Park
26	554.4	Hays	Hays
27	552.0	Turner-Kansas City	Kansas City
28	551.4	Mulvane	Mulvane
29	549.1	Ottawa	Ottawa
30	543.3	Parsons	Parsons
31	541.3	Paola	Paola
32	517.5	Renwick	Andale
33	515.7	Garden City	Garden City
34	514.2	Derby	Derby
35	511.5	Fort Scott	Fort Scott
36	511.3	Lansing	Lansing

Rank		District Name	City
37	505.5	Valley Center Public Schools	Valley Center
38	502.6	Andover	Andover
39	502.0	Arkansas City	Arkansas City
40	497.2	Mcpherson	Mcpherson
41	491.0	Shawnee Heights	Tecumseh
42	487.3	Seaman	Topeka
43	478.9	Atchison Public Schools	Atchison
44	472.5	Ft Leavenworth	Ft Leavenworth
45	471.9	Leavenworth	Leavenworth
46	471.6	El Dorado	El Dorado
47	470.6	Newton	Newton
48	458.3	Ulysses	Ulysses
49	458.0	Spring Hill	Spring Hill
50	446.0	Topeka Public Schools	Topeka
51	445.4	Lawrence	Lawrence
52	439.5	Chanute Public Schools	Chanute
53	430.6	Manhattan	Manhattan
54	415.3	Geary County Schools	Junction City
55	406.8	Independence	Independence
56	391.7	Pittsburg	Pittsburg
57	376.0	Iola	Iola
58	370.8	Buhler	Buhler
59	360.7	Augusta	Augusta
60	298.8	Circle	Towanda

Student/Counselor Ratio

Rank	Ratio	District Name	City
1	1,699.0	Labette County	Altamont
2	954.9	Derby	Derby
3	738.3	Geary County Schools	Junction City
4	690.0	Renwick	Andale
5	675.3	Winfield	Winfield
6	633.2	Manhattan	Manhattan
7	613.5	Shawnee Mission Public Schools	Shawnee Mission
8	594.0	Valley Center Public Schools	Valley Center
9	563.9	Kansas City	Kansas City
10	563.4	Wichita	Wichita
11	558.7	Atchison Public Schools	Atchison
12	558.3	Hutchinson Public Schools	Hutchinson
13	556.3	Buhler	Buhler
14	552.0	Turner-Kansas City	Kansas City
15	537.9	Newton	Newton
16	511.5	Fort Scott	Fort Scott
17	511.3	Lansing	Lansing
18	510.2	Liberal	Liberal
19	483.5	Chanute Public Schools	Chanute
20	478.0	De Soto	De Soto
21	472.5	Ft Leavenworth	Ft Leavenworth
22	467.1	Wellington	Wellington
23	463.5	Rose Hill Public Schools	Rose Hill
24	458.3	Ulysses	Ulysses
25	454.8	Bonner Springs	Bonner Springs
26	444.8	Dodge City	Dodge City
27	440.9	Great Bend	Great Bend
28	433.0	Paola	Paola
29	429.4	Emporia	Emporia
30	408.9	Hays	Hays
31	407.5	Parsons	Parsons
32	403.1	Goddard	Goddard
33	402.3	Haysville	Haysville
34	400.8	Spring Hill	Spring Hill
35	398.5	Olathe	Olathe
36	395.7	Topeka Public Schools	Topeka
37	391.4	Coffeyville	Coffeyville
38	388.8	Tonganoxie	Tonganoxie
39	388.4	Lawrence	Lawrence
40	387.7	Maize	Maize
41	386.8	Garden City	Garden City
42	386.1	Leavenworth	Leavenworth
43	379.0	Seaman	Topeka
44	376.5	Arkansas City	Arkansas City
45	369.8	Independence	Independence
46	369.6	Gardner Edgerton	Gardner
47	367.9	Auburn Washburn	Topeka
48	360.7	Augusta	Augusta
49	352.9	Blue Valley	Overland Park
50	351.8	Andover	Andover
51	347.5	Basehor-Linwood	Basehor
52	343.7	Shawnee Heights	Tecumseh
53	340.5	Salina	Salina
54	323.1	Pittsburg	Pittsburg
55	321.7	Mulvane	Mulvane
56	310.8	Mcpherson	Mcpherson
57	303.1	El Dorado	El Dorado
58	300.8	Iola	Iola
59	271.6	Circle	Towanda
60	260.1	Ottawa	Ottawa

Current Spending per Student in FY2003

Rank	Dollars	District Name	City
1	8,308	Manhattan	Manhattan

Rank		District Name	City
2	8,265	Atchison Public Schools	Atchison
3	8,196	Topeka Public Schools	Topeka
4	7,827	Kansas City	Kansas City
5	7,804	Salina	Salina
6	7,675	Iola	Iola
7	7,471	Lawrence	Lawrence
8	7,456	Hays	Hays
9	7,431	Wichita	Wichita
10	7,414	Geary County Schools	Junction City
11	7,347	Coffeyville	Coffeyville
12	7,336	Dodge City	Dodge City
13	7,236	Blue Valley	Overland Park
14	7,128	Spring Hill	Spring Hill
15	7,066	Chanute Public Schools	Chanute
16	7,024	Circle	Towanda
17	6,941	Shawnee Mission Public Schools	Shawnee Mission
18	6,926	Labette County	Altamont
19	6,919	Bonner Springs	Bonner Springs
20	6,904	Pittsburg	Pittsburg
21	6,890	Wellington	Wellington
22	6,868	De Soto	De Soto
23	6,852	Great Bend	Great Bend
24	6,848	Olathe	Olathe
25	6,838	Garden City	Garden City
25	6,838	Parsons	Parsons
27	6,830	Shawnee Heights	Tecumseh
28	6,823	Mcpherson	Mcpherson
29	6,788	Gardner Edgerton	Gardner
30	6,787	Emporia	Emporia
31	6,772	Paola	Paola
32	6,735	Buhler	Buhler
32	6,735	Leavenworth	Leavenworth
34	6,717	Auburn Washburn	Topeka
35	6,704	Ulysses	Ulysses
36	6,657	Winfield	Winfield
37	6,651	Turner-Kansas City	Kansas City
38	6,636	Independence	Independence
39	6,558	Liberal	Liberal
40	6,549	Andover	Andover
41	6,533	Seaman	Topeka
42	6,507	Hutchinson Public Schools	Hutchinson
43	6,486	Haysville	Haysville
44	6,457	Tonganoxie	Tonganoxie
45	6,425	Arkansas City	Arkansas City
45	6,425	Renwick	Andale
47	6,390	Derby	Derby
48	6,231	Newton	Newton
49	6,212	Rose Hill Public Schools	Rose Hill
50	6,187	Goddard	Goddard
51	6,116	Basehor-Linwood	Basehor
52	6,085	Ottawa	Ottawa
53	6,050	Maize	Maize
54	6,030	El Dorado	El Dorado
55	6,019	Fort Scott	Fort Scott
56	5,956	Augusta	Augusta
57	5,848	Lansing	Lansing
58	5,743	Valley Center Public Schools	Valley Center
59	5,694	Mulvane	Mulvane
60	5,243	Ft Leavenworth	Ft Leavenworth

Number of Diploma Recipients

Rank	Number	District Name	City
1	2,226	Shawnee Mission Public Schools	Shawnee Mission
2	2,147	Wichita	Wichita
3	1,319	Olathe	Olathe
4	1,190	Blue Valley	Overland Park
5	938	Kansas City	Kansas City
6	772	Lawrence	Lawrence
7	769	Topeka Public Schools	Topeka
8	462	Salina	Salina
9	420	Derby	Derby
10	417	Manhattan	Manhattan
11	325	Auburn Washburn	Topeka
12	308	Maize	Maize
13	303	Dodge City	Dodge City
14	296	Emporia	Emporia
15	294	Hutchinson Public Schools	Hutchinson
16	282	Leavenworth	Leavenworth
17	279	Garden City	Garden City
18	255	Shawnee Heights	Tecumseh
19	250	Haysville	Haysville
20	247	Goddard	Goddard
21	235	Seaman	Topeka
22	234	Mcpherson	Mcpherson
23	229	Hays	Hays
24	226	Geary County Schools	Junction City
25	217	Great Bend	Great Bend
25	217	Winfield	Winfield
27	216	Andover	Andover
28	203	De Soto	De Soto
29	199	Newton	Newton
30	178	Liberal	Liberal
31	177	Valley Center Public Schools	Valley Center
32	169	Arkansas City	Arkansas City
33	168	Coffeyville	Coffeyville
34	167	Buhler	Buhler
35	162	Independence	Independence
36	161	Turner-Kansas City	Kansas City
37	157	Mulvane	Mulvane
38	152	Labette County	Altamont
39	150	Bonner Springs	Bonner Springs
39	150	Fort Scott	Fort Scott
41	147	Lansing	Lansing
41	147	Paola	Paola
43	144	Pittsburg	Pittsburg
44	142	Augusta	Augusta
45	140	Wellington	Wellington
46	138	Gardner Edgerton	Gardner
47	127	Basehor-Linwood	Basehor
47	127	Rose Hill Public Schools	Rose Hill
49	124	Renwick	Andale
50	121	Ottawa	Ottawa
50	121	Ulysses	Ulysses
52	117	Chanute Public Schools	Chanute
52	117	Iola	Iola
54	114	El Dorado	El Dorado
55	112	Tonganoxie	Tonganoxie
56	107	Atchison Public Schools	Atchison
57	106	Parsons	Parsons
58	99	Circle	Towanda
59	93	Spring Hill	Spring Hill
60	n/a	Ft Leavenworth	Ft Leavenworth

High School Drop-out Rate

Rank	Percent	District Name	City
1	8.7	Wichita	Wichita
2	8.3	Liberal	Liberal
3	6.9	Haysville	Haysville
4	6.8	Basehor-Linwood	Basehor
5	6.0	Turner-Kansas City	Kansas City
6	5.3	Hutchinson Public Schools	Hutchinson
7	5.2	Arkansas City	Arkansas City
8	5.1	Topeka Public Schools	Topeka
9	4.8	Kansas City	Kansas City
10	4.6	Geary County Schools	Junction City
11	4.2	Fort Scott	Fort Scott
12	4.0	Leavenworth	Leavenworth
12	4.0	Pittsburg	Pittsburg
14	3.9	Valley Center Public Schools	Valley Center
15	3.8	Parsons	Parsons
15	3.8	Wellington	Wellington
17	3.7	Garden City	Garden City
18	3.4	Atchison Public Schools	Atchison
19	3.3	Manhattan	Manhattan
20	3.0	Iola	Iola
21	2.9	Emporia	Emporia
21	2.9	Newton	Newton
21	2.9	Salina	Salina
24	2.7	Maize	Maize
25	2.6	Buhler	Buhler
25	2.6	Coffeyville	Coffeyville
25	2.6	Great Bend	Great Bend
25	2.6	Hays	Hays
29	2.5	El Dorado	El Dorado
30	2.4	Chanute Public Schools	Chanute
30	2.4	Seaman	Topeka
32	2.2	Bonner Springs	Bonner Springs
32	2.2	Mcpherson	Mcpherson
34	2.0	Auburn Washburn	Topeka
34	2.0	Dodge City	Dodge City
34	2.0	Independence	Independence
34	2.0	Paola	Paola
34	2.0	Shawnee Mission Public Schools	Shawnee Mission
34	2.0	Ulysses	Ulysses
40	1.9	Andover	Andover
40	1.9	Gardner Edgerton	Gardner
40	1.9	Lawrence	Lawrence
43	1.8	Olathe	Olathe
44	1.7	Goddard	Goddard
45	1.6	Circle	Towanda
46	1.4	Ottawa	Ottawa
46	1.4	Rose Hill Public Schools	Rose Hill
46	1.4	Tonganoxie	Tonganoxie
49	1.3	Derby	Derby
50	1.1	Spring Hill	Spring Hill
51	0.9	De Soto	De Soto
51	0.9	Labette County	Altamont
51	0.9	Mulvane	Mulvane
54	0.7	Blue Valley	Overland Park
55	0.6	Augusta	Augusta
55	0.6	Shawnee Heights	Tecumseh
57	0.3	Lansing	Lansing
58	0.2	Renwick	Andale
58	0.2	Winfield	Winfield
60	0.0	Ft Leavenworth	Ft Leavenworth

Kentucky

Kentucky Public School Educational Profile

Category	Value	Category	Value
Schools *(2003-2004)*	1,438	**Diploma Recipients** *(2002-2003)*	36,337
Instructional Level		White, Non-Hispanic	32,556
Primary	800	Black, Non-Hispanic	3,151
Middle	236	Asian/Pacific Islander	350
High	309	American Indian/Alaskan Native	31
Other Level	91	Hispanic	249
Curriculum		**High School Drop-out Rate** (%) *(2001-2002)*	4.0
Regular	1,257	White, Non-Hispanic	3.8
Special Education	11	Black, Non-Hispanic	5.3
Vocational	10	Asian/Pacific Islander	1.7
Alternative	158	American Indian/Alaskan Native	n/a
Type		Hispanic	4.0
Magnet	36	**Staff** *(2003-2004)*	
Charter	0	Teachers	41,202.8
Title I Eligible	901	Average Salary ($)	39,831
School-wide Title I	785	Librarians/Media Specialists	1,147.0
Students *(2003-2004)*	663,886	Guidance Counselors	1,471.0
Gender (%)		**Ratios** *(2003-2004)*	
Male	51.9	Student/Teacher Ratio	16.1 to 1
Female	48.1	Student/Librarian Ratio	578.8 to 1
Race/Ethnicity (%)		Student/Counselor Ratio	451.3 to 1
White, Non-Hispanic	87.0	**College Entrance Exam Scores** *(2005)*	
Black, Non-Hispanic	10.4	Scholastic Aptitude Test (SAT)	
Asian/Pacific Islander	0.8	Participation Rate (%)	12
American Indian/Alaskan Native	0.2	Mean SAT Reasoning Test Verbal Score	561
Hispanic	1.5	Mean SAT Reasoning Test Math Score	559
Classification (%)		American College Testing Program (ACT)	
Individual Education Program (IEP)	15.6	Participation Rate (%)	76
Migrant *(2002-2003)*	2.3	Average Composite Score	20.4
English Language Learner (ELL)	1.3	Average English Score	20.0
Eligible for Free Lunch Program	0.0	Average Math Score	19.7
Eligible for Reduced-Price Lunch Program	0.0	Average Reading Score	20.8
Current Spending *($ per student in FY 2003)*	6,647	Average Science Score	20.4
Instruction	4,069		
Support Services	2,230		

Note: *For an explanation of data, please refer to the User's Guide in the front of the book*

Kentucky NAEP 2005 Test Scores

Reading			Mathematics		
Grade/Category	Value	Rank	Grade/Category	Value	Rank
4th Grade			**4th Grade**		
Average Proficiency	219.9 (1.07)	27/51	Average Proficiency	231.5 (0.85)	41/51
Proficiency by Gender/Race/Ethnicity			Proficiency by Gender/Race/Ethnicity		
Male	217.5 (1.40)	25/51	Male	233.2 (1.12)	40/51
Female	222.5 (1.33)	27/51	Female	229.7 (1.07)	42/51
White, Non-Hispanic	221.9 (1.14)	45/51	White, Non-Hispanic	233.7 (0.93)	50/51
Black, Non-Hispanic	203.3 (2.28)	11/42	Black, Non-Hispanic	217.0 (1.68)	27/42
Asian, Non-Hispanic	n/a	n/a	Asian, Non-Hispanic	n/a	n/a
American Indian, Non-Hispanic	n/a	n/a	American Indian, Non-Hispanic	n/a	n/a
Hispanic	n/a	n/a	Hispanic	n/a	n/a
Proficiency by Class Size			Proficiency by Class Size		
Less than 16 Students	212.3 (3.93)	12/34	Less than 16 Students	n/a	n/a
16 to 18 Students	216.0 (2.83)	21/33	16 to 18 Students	229.9 (3.12)	25/31
19 to 20 Students	218.3 (3.07)	23/38	19 to 20 Students	n/a	n/a
21 to 25 Students	221.4 (1.44)	27/51	21 to 25 Students	234.0 (1.37)	40/51
Greater than 25 Students	223.4 (2.32)	13/36	Greater than 25 Students	233.9 (1.98)	25/33
Percent Attaining Achievement Levels			Percent Attaining Achievement Levels		
Below Basic	35.1 (1.46)	26/51	Below Basic	25.0 (1.15)	12/51
Basic or Above	64.9 (1.46)	26/51	Basic or Above	75.0 (1.15)	40/51
Proficient or Above	30.8 (1.24)	28/51	Proficient or Above	26.1 (1.42)	44/51
Advanced or Above	7.5 (0.76)	17/51	Advanced or Above	2.5 (0.46)	44/51
8th Grade			**8th Grade**		
Average Proficiency	263.9 (1.14)	25/51	Average Proficiency	274.0 (1.22)	36/51
Proficiency by Gender/Race/Ethnicity			Proficiency by Gender/Race/Ethnicity		
Male	258.1 (1.42)	26/51	Male	275.0 (1.45)	36/51
Female	269.7 (1.34)	22/51	Female	273.0 (1.30)	36/51
White, Non-Hispanic	265.7 (1.20)	37/51	White, Non-Hispanic	276.2 (1.17)	49/51
Black, Non-Hispanic	247.7 (3.07)	8/40	Black, Non-Hispanic	255.2 (2.42)	20/41
Asian, Non-Hispanic	n/a	n/a	Asian, Non-Hispanic	n/a	n/a
American Indian, Non-Hispanic	n/a	n/a	American Indian, Non-Hispanic	n/a	n/a
Hispanic	n/a	n/a	Hispanic	n/a	n/a
Proficiency by Parents Highest Level of Ed.			Proficiency by Parents Highest Level of Ed.		
Did Not Finish High School	249.7 (2.54)	12/49	Did Not Finish High School	255.7 (1.93)	35/50
Graduated High School	256.5 (1.81)	19/50	Graduated High School	264.3 (1.40)	34/50
Some Education After High School	268.9 (1.57)	14/50	Some Education After High School	277.3 (1.76)	36/50
Graduated College	273.5 (1.37)	20/50	Graduated College	285.3 (1.62)	34/50
Percent Attaining Achievement Levels			Percent Attaining Achievement Levels		
Below Basic	35.1 (1.46)	26/51	Below Basic	35.7 (1.61)	16/51
Basic or Above	64.9 (1.46)	26/51	Basic or Above	64.3 (1.61)	36/51
Proficient or Above	30.8 (1.24)	28/51	Proficient or Above	22.5 (1.43)	39/51
Advanced or Above	7.5 (0.76)	17/51	Advanced or Above	3.4 (0.55)	39/51

Note: *For an explanation of data, please refer to the User's Guide in the front of the book; n/a indicates data not available*

Adair County

Adair County
1204 Greensburg St • Columbia, KY 42728-1811
(270) 384-2476 • http://www.adair.k12.ky.us/
Grade Span: PK-12; **Agency Type:** 1
Schools: 8
    4 Primary; 2 Middle; 1 High; 1 Other Level
    7 Regular; 0 Special Education; 0 Vocational; 1 Alternative
    0 Magnet; 0 Charter; 6 Title I Eligible; 6 School-wide Title I
Students: 2,743   (50.3% male; 49.6% female)
    Individual Education Program: 472 (17.2%);
    English Language Learner: 10 (0.4%); Migrant: 177 (6.8%)
    Eligible for Free Lunch Program: n/a
    Eligible for Reduced-Price Lunch Program: n/a
Teachers: 195.0 (13.3 to 1)
Librarians/Media Specialists: 7.0 (370.9 to 1)
Guidance Counselors: 6.0 (432.7 to 1)
Current Spending: ($ per student per year):
    Total: $6,644; Instruction: $4,374; Support Services: $1,920
Enrollment, Drop-out Rates and Diploma Recipients by Race/Ethnicity

Category	Total	White	Black	Asian	AIAN	Hisp.
Enrollment (%)	100.0	95.3	3.3	0.3	0.2	1.0
Drop-out Rate (%)	5.0	4.9	0.0	0.0	0.0	n/a
H.S. Diplomas (#)	127	123	4	0	0	0

Allen County

Allen County
238 Blgn Rd • Scottsville, KY 42164-9650
(270) 237-3181 • http://www.allen.k12.ky.us/
Grade Span: PK-12; **Agency Type:** 1
Schools: 4
    1 Primary; 2 Middle; 1 High; 0 Other Level
    4 Regular; 0 Special Education; 0 Vocational; 0 Alternative
    0 Magnet; 0 Charter; 3 Title I Eligible; 0 School-wide Title I
Students: 3,065   (51.3% male; 48.6% female)
    Individual Education Program: 399 (13.0%);
    English Language Learner: 0 (0.0%); Migrant: 54 (1.8%)
    Eligible for Free Lunch Program: n/a
    Eligible for Reduced-Price Lunch Program: n/a
Teachers: 172.1 (17.3 to 1)
Librarians/Media Specialists: 5.0 (596.4 to 1)
Guidance Counselors: 4.0 (745.5 to 1)
Current Spending: ($ per student per year):
    Total: $5,434; Instruction: $3,399; Support Services: $1,698
Enrollment, Drop-out Rates and Diploma Recipients by Race/Ethnicity

Category	Total	White	Black	Asian	AIAN	Hisp.
Enrollment (%)	100.0	98.7	0.8	0.1	0.0	0.3
Drop-out Rate (%)	4.2	4.1	0.0	0.0	n/a	0.0
H.S. Diplomas (#)	184	180	2	1	0	1

Anderson County

Anderson County
103 N Main • Lawrenceburg, KY 40342-1013
(502) 839-3406 • http://www.anderson.k12.ky.us/
Grade Span: PK-12; **Agency Type:** 1
Schools: 6
    4 Primary; 1 Middle; 1 High; 0 Other Level
    6 Regular; 0 Special Education; 0 Vocational; 0 Alternative
    0 Magnet; 0 Charter; 3 Title I Eligible; 0 School-wide Title I
Students: 3,987   (51.2% male; 48.7% female)
    Individual Education Program: 773 (19.4%);
    English Language Learner: 10 (0.3%); Migrant: 4 (0.1%)
    Eligible for Free Lunch Program: n/a
    Eligible for Reduced-Price Lunch Program: n/a
Teachers: 212.4 (17.4 to 1)
Librarians/Media Specialists: 5.5 (670.9 to 1)
Guidance Counselors: 6.5 (567.7 to 1)
Current Spending: ($ per student per year):
    Total: $5,284; Instruction: $3,424; Support Services: $1,569
Enrollment, Drop-out Rates and Diploma Recipients by Race/Ethnicity

Category	Total	White	Black	Asian	AIAN	Hisp.
Enrollment (%)	100.0	96.4	2.6	0.1	0.1	0.7
Drop-out Rate (%)	4.0	4.1	0.0	0.0	n/a	0.0
H.S. Diplomas (#)	189	184	3	0	0	2

Ballard County

Ballard County
Rt 1 3465 Paducah Rd • Barlow, KY 42024-9529
(270) 665-8400
Grade Span: PK-12; **Agency Type:** 1
Schools: 4

---

    2 Primary; 1 Middle; 1 High; 0 Other Level
    4 Regular; 0 Special Education; 0 Vocational; 0 Alternative
    0 Magnet; 0 Charter; 2 Title I Eligible; 2 School-wide Title I
Students: 1,537   (51.8% male; 48.1% female)
    Individual Education Program: 319 (20.8%);
    English Language Learner: 2 (0.1%); Migrant: 147 (10.7%)
    Eligible for Free Lunch Program: n/a
    Eligible for Reduced-Price Lunch Program: n/a
Teachers: 88.9 (15.4 to 1)
Librarians/Media Specialists: 2.0 (685.0 to 1)
Guidance Counselors: 3.0 (456.7 to 1)
Current Spending: ($ per student per year):
    Total: $5,850; Instruction: $3,412; Support Services: $2,069
Enrollment, Drop-out Rates and Diploma Recipients by Race/Ethnicity

Category	Total	White	Black	Asian	AIAN	Hisp.
Enrollment (%)	100.0	95.3	4.2	0.0	0.1	0.4
Drop-out Rate (%)	2.3	2.4	0.0	n/a	n/a	0.0
H.S. Diplomas (#)	101	96	3	2	0	0

Barren County

Barren County
PO Box 879 • Glasgow, KY 42141
(270) 651-3787 • http://www.bchs.barren.k12.ky.us/
Grade Span: PK-12; **Agency Type:** 1
Schools: 10
    6 Primary; 1 Middle; 2 High; 1 Other Level
    8 Regular; 0 Special Education; 0 Vocational; 2 Alternative
    0 Magnet; 0 Charter; 6 Title I Eligible; 6 School-wide Title I
Students: 4,204   (50.6% male; 49.3% female)
    Individual Education Program: 629 (15.0%);
    English Language Learner: 7 (0.2%); Migrant: 391 (9.6%)
    Eligible for Free Lunch Program: n/a
    Eligible for Reduced-Price Lunch Program: n/a
Teachers: 260.1 (15.6 to 1)
Librarians/Media Specialists: 8.1 (501.7 to 1)
Guidance Counselors: 11.0 (369.5 to 1)
Current Spending: ($ per student per year):
    Total: $6,510; Instruction: $4,174; Support Services: $1,918
Enrollment, Drop-out Rates and Diploma Recipients by Race/Ethnicity

Category	Total	White	Black	Asian	AIAN	Hisp.
Enrollment (%)	100.0	98.3	0.8	0.3	0.1	0.5
Drop-out Rate (%)	4.5	4.5	0.0	0.0	0.0	0.0
H.S. Diplomas (#)	208	205	2	0	0	1

Glasgow Independent
1108 Cleveland Ave • Glasgow, KY 42142-1239
(270) 651-6757 •
http://www.glasgowbarren.com/commun/edu/glas_sch/index.htm
Grade Span: PK-12; **Agency Type:** 1
Schools: 6
    4 Primary; 1 Middle; 1 High; 0 Other Level
    6 Regular; 0 Special Education; 0 Vocational; 0 Alternative
    0 Magnet; 0 Charter; 4 Title I Eligible; 4 School-wide Title I
Students: 2,051   (52.7% male; 47.2% female)
    Individual Education Program: 327 (15.9%);
    English Language Learner: 17 (0.8%); Migrant: 229 (11.8%)
    Eligible for Free Lunch Program: n/a
    Eligible for Reduced-Price Lunch Program: n/a
Teachers: 139.0 (13.9 to 1)
Librarians/Media Specialists: 3.0 (646.0 to 1)
Guidance Counselors: 3.0 (646.0 to 1)
Current Spending: ($ per student per year):
    Total: $6,510; Instruction: $4,229; Support Services: $1,884
Enrollment, Drop-out Rates and Diploma Recipients by Race/Ethnicity

Category	Total	White	Black	Asian	AIAN	Hisp.
Enrollment (%)	100.0	84.0	13.1	1.0	0.2	1.8
Drop-out Rate (%)	2.8	3.0	1.6	0.0	0.0	0.0
H.S. Diplomas (#)	118	99	18	1	0	0

Bath County

Bath County
405 W Main St • Owingsv, KY 40360-0409
(606) 674-6314 • http://www.bath.k12.ky.us/
Grade Span: PK-12; **Agency Type:** 1
Schools: 5
    3 Primary; 1 Middle; 1 High; 0 Other Level
    5 Regular; 0 Special Education; 0 Vocational; 0 Alternative
    0 Magnet; 0 Charter; 4 Title I Eligible; 4 School-wide Title I
Students: 2,017   (52.8% male; 47.1% female)
    Individual Education Program: 284 (14.1%);
    English Language Learner: 0 (0.0%); Migrant: 201 (10.5%)
    Eligible for Free Lunch Program: n/a
    Eligible for Reduced-Price Lunch Program: n/a

Teachers: 123.0 (15.6 to 1)
Librarians/Media Specialists: 4.0 (478.3 to 1)
Guidance Counselors: 3.5 (546.6 to 1)
Current Spending: ($ per student per year):
  Total: $6,104; Instruction: $3,701; Support Services: $1,972
Enrollment, Drop-out Rates and Diploma Recipients by Race/Ethnicity

Category	Total	White	Black	Asian	AIAN	Hisp.
Enrollment (%)	100.0	97.9	1.6	0.1	0.2	0.3
Drop-out Rate (%)	5.8	5.3	0.0	n/a	n/a	0.0
H.S. Diplomas (#)	107	105	0	1	0	1

Bell County

Bell County
211 Virginia Ave • Pineville, KY 40977-0340
(606) 337-7051 •
http://www.bellcountyschools.bell.k12.ky.us/education/district/district.php?sectionid=1
Grade Span: PK-12; **Agency Type:** 1
Schools: 8
  6 Primary; 0 Middle; 1 High; 1 Other Level
  7 Regular; 0 Special Education; 0 Vocational; 1 Alternative
  0 Magnet; 0 Charter; 6 Title I Eligible; 6 School-wide Title I
Students: 3,188 (51.3% male; 48.6% female)
  Individual Education Program: 556 (17.4%);
  English Language Learner: 0 (0.0%); Migrant: 0 (0.0%)
  Eligible for Free Lunch Program: n/a
  Eligible for Reduced-Price Lunch Program: n/a
Teachers: 233.0 (13.2 to 1)
Librarians/Media Specialists: 7.0 (438.1 to 1)
Guidance Counselors: 7.0 (438.1 to 1)
Current Spending: ($ per student per year):
  Total: $6,873; Instruction: $4,047; Support Services: $2,357
Enrollment, Drop-out Rates and Diploma Recipients by Race/Ethnicity

Category	Total	White	Black	Asian	AIAN	Hisp.
Enrollment (%)	100.0	99.6	0.3	0.0	0.1	0.0
Drop-out Rate (%)	8.1	8.2	0.0	n/a	n/a	n/a
H.S. Diplomas (#)	195	194	1	0	0	0

Middlesboro Independent
220 N 20th St • Middlesboro, KY 40965-0959
(606) 242-8800 • http://www.mboro.k12.ky.us/
Grade Span: PK-12; **Agency Type:** 1
Schools: 5
  1 Primary; 2 Middle; 2 High; 0 Other Level
  4 Regular; 0 Special Education; 0 Vocational; 1 Alternative
  0 Magnet; 0 Charter; 4 Title I Eligible; 4 School-wide Title I
Students: 1,841 (52.2% male; 47.7% female)
  Individual Education Program: 312 (16.9%);
  English Language Learner: 2 (0.1%); Migrant: 0 (0.0%)
  Eligible for Free Lunch Program: n/a
  Eligible for Reduced-Price Lunch Program: n/a
Teachers: 116.0 (15.1 to 1)
Librarians/Media Specialists: 4.0 (437.5 to 1)
Guidance Counselors: 4.0 (437.5 to 1)
Current Spending: ($ per student per year):
  Total: $6,169; Instruction: $3,979; Support Services: $1,798
Enrollment, Drop-out Rates and Diploma Recipients by Race/Ethnicity

Category	Total	White	Black	Asian	AIAN	Hisp.
Enrollment (%)	100.0	93.0	6.3	0.1	0.5	0.1
Drop-out Rate (%)	3.8	4.1	0.0	0.0	0.0	0.0
H.S. Diplomas (#)	97	91	5	1	0	0

Boone County

Boone County
8330 US 42 • Florence, KY 41042-9286
(859) 283-1003 • http://www.boone.k12.ky.us/
Grade Span: PK-12; **Agency Type:** 1
Schools: 18
  11 Primary; 4 Middle; 3 High; 0 Other Level
  18 Regular; 0 Special Education; 0 Vocational; 0 Alternative
  0 Magnet; 0 Charter; 9 Title I Eligible; 3 School-wide Title I
Students: 15,406 (51.7% male; 48.2% female)
  Individual Education Program: 2,081 (13.5%);
  English Language Learner: 354 (2.3%); Migrant: 0 (0.0%)
  Eligible for Free Lunch Program: n/a
  Eligible for Reduced-Price Lunch Program: n/a
Teachers: 894.9 (16.8 to 1)
Librarians/Media Specialists: 19.5 (771.3 to 1)
Guidance Counselors: 24.3 (619.0 to 1)
Current Spending: ($ per student per year):
  Total: $5,821; Instruction: $3,629; Support Services: $1,922

Enrollment, Drop-out Rates and Diploma Recipients by Race/Ethnicity

Category	Total	White	Black	Asian	AIAN	Hisp.
Enrollment (%)	100.0	93.9	2.2	1.5	0.1	2.2
Drop-out Rate (%)	2.1	2.1	0.0	0.0	0.0	0.0
H.S. Diplomas (#)	722	702	8	6	0	6

Bourbon County

Bourbon County
3343 Lexington Rd • Paris, KY 40361-1000
(859) 987-2180 • http://www.bourbon.k12.ky.us/boco/
Grade Span: PK-12; **Agency Type:** 1
Schools: 7
  5 Primary; 1 Middle; 1 High; 0 Other Level
  7 Regular; 0 Special Education; 0 Vocational; 0 Alternative
  0 Magnet; 0 Charter; 4 Title I Eligible; 2 School-wide Title I
Students: 2,946 (51.4% male; 48.5% female)
  Individual Education Program: 434 (14.7%);
  English Language Learner: 12 (0.4%); Migrant: 146 (5.5%)
  Eligible for Free Lunch Program: n/a
  Eligible for Reduced-Price Lunch Program: n/a
Teachers: 174.9 (15.3 to 1)
Librarians/Media Specialists: 5.0 (533.8 to 1)
Guidance Counselors: 4.0 (667.3 to 1)
Current Spending: ($ per student per year):
  Total: $6,731; Instruction: $4,497; Support Services: $1,917
Enrollment, Drop-out Rates and Diploma Recipients by Race/Ethnicity

Category	Total	White	Black	Asian	AIAN	Hisp.
Enrollment (%)	100.0	92.2	4.2	0.2	0.1	3.3
Drop-out Rate (%)	2.3	2.4	0.0	0.0	0.0	0.0
H.S. Diplomas (#)	182	174	6	0	0	2

Boyd County

Ashland Ind
1420 Central Ave • Ashland, KY 41101-7552
(606) 327-2706 • http://www.ashland.k12.ky.us/
Grade Span: PK-12; **Agency Type:** 1
Schools: 9
  6 Primary; 1 Middle; 2 High; 0 Other Level
  8 Regular; 0 Special Education; 0 Vocational; 1 Alternative
  0 Magnet; 0 Charter; 6 Title I Eligible; 6 School-wide Title I
Students: 3,402 (50.9% male; 49.0% female)
  Individual Education Program: 544 (16.0%);
  English Language Learner: 3 (0.1%); Migrant: 110 (3.4%)
  Eligible for Free Lunch Program: n/a
  Eligible for Reduced-Price Lunch Program: n/a
Teachers: 208.7 (15.6 to 1)
Librarians/Media Specialists: 9.0 (361.8 to 1)
Guidance Counselors: 7.0 (465.1 to 1)
Current Spending: ($ per student per year):
  Total: $6,604; Instruction: $3,920; Support Services: $2,306
Enrollment, Drop-out Rates and Diploma Recipients by Race/Ethnicity

Category	Total	White	Black	Asian	AIAN	Hisp.
Enrollment (%)	100.0	94.1	4.4	0.7	0.3	0.5
Drop-out Rate (%)	2.4	2.4	2.3	0.0	0.0	0.0
H.S. Diplomas (#)	205	193	8	3	1	0

Boyd County
1104 Bob Mccullough • Ashland, KY 41102-9275
(606) 928-4141 • http://www.boyd.k12.ky.us/
Grade Span: PK-12; **Agency Type:** 1
Schools: 9
  5 Primary; 1 Middle; 3 High; 0 Other Level
  7 Regular; 0 Special Education; 1 Vocational; 1 Alternative
  0 Magnet; 0 Charter; 5 Title I Eligible; 5 School-wide Title I
Students: 3,627 (52.0% male; 47.9% female)
  Individual Education Program: 702 (19.4%);
  English Language Learner: 4 (0.1%); Migrant: 63 (1.9%)
  Eligible for Free Lunch Program: n/a
  Eligible for Reduced-Price Lunch Program: n/a
Teachers: 249.3 (13.6 to 1)
Librarians/Media Specialists: 5.8 (582.9 to 1)
Guidance Counselors: 9.0 (375.7 to 1)
Current Spending: ($ per student per year):
  Total: $7,298; Instruction: $4,844; Support Services: $2,083
Enrollment, Drop-out Rates and Diploma Recipients by Race/Ethnicity

Category	Total	White	Black	Asian	AIAN	Hisp.
Enrollment (%)	100.0	97.8	1.7	0.1	0.1	0.3
Drop-out Rate (%)	2.4	2.4	3.2	0.0	0.0	0.0
H.S. Diplomas (#)	198	194	1	1	1	1

Boyle County

Boyle County
PO Box 520 • Danville, KY 40422
(859) 236-6634 • http://www.boyle.k12.ky.us/
Grade Span: PK-12; **Agency Type:** 1
Schools: 6
   3 Primary; 1 Middle; 1 High; 1 Other Level
   5 Regular; 0 Special Education; 0 Vocational; 1 Alternative
   0 Magnet; 0 Charter; 2 Title I Eligible; 1 School-wide Title I
Students: 2,881 (52.2% male; 47.7% female)
   Individual Education Program: 627 (21.8%);
   English Language Learner: 12 (0.4%); Migrant: 56 (2.0%)
   Eligible for Free Lunch Program: n/a
   Eligible for Reduced-Price Lunch Program: n/a
Teachers: 191.6 (14.3 to 1)
Librarians/Media Specialists: 5.0 (549.0 to 1)
Guidance Counselors: 9.3 (295.2 to 1)
Current Spending: ($ per student per year):
   Total: $7,186; Instruction: $4,907; Support Services: $1,976
Enrollment, Drop-out Rates and Diploma Recipients by Race/Ethnicity

Category	Total	White	Black	Asian	AIAN	Hisp.
Enrollment (%)	100.0	97.3	0.9	0.5	0.1	1.1
Drop-out Rate (%)	2.5	2.6	0.0	0.0	0.0	0.0
H.S. Diplomas (#)	182	178	1	1	1	1

Danville Independent
359 Proctor St • Danville, KY 40422-1577
(859) 936-8500 • http://www.danville.k12.ky.us/
Grade Span: PK-12; **Agency Type:** 1
Schools: 6
   4 Primary; 1 Middle; 1 High; 0 Other Level
   5 Regular; 0 Special Education; 0 Vocational; 1 Alternative
   0 Magnet; 0 Charter; 4 Title I Eligible; 3 School-wide Title I
Students: 1,851 (53.7% male; 46.2% female)
   Individual Education Program: 363 (19.6%);
   English Language Learner: 19 (1.0%); Migrant: 33 (1.9%)
   Eligible for Free Lunch Program: n/a
   Eligible for Reduced-Price Lunch Program: n/a
Teachers: 123.6 (14.2 to 1)
Librarians/Media Specialists: 5.0 (350.6 to 1)
Guidance Counselors: 5.9 (297.1 to 1)
Current Spending: ($ per student per year):
   Total: $8,544; Instruction: $5,466; Support Services: $2,610
Enrollment, Drop-out Rates and Diploma Recipients by Race/Ethnicity

Category	Total	White	Black	Asian	AIAN	Hisp.
Enrollment (%)	100.0	71.8	23.5	1.1	0.2	3.4
Drop-out Rate (%)	2.1	1.2	4.7	0.0	0.0	0.0
H.S. Diplomas (#)	108	82	23	1	0	2

Breathitt County

Breathitt County
PO Box 750 • Jackson, KY 41339-0750
(606) 666-2491 • http://www.breathitt.k12.ky.us/
Grade Span: PK-12; **Agency Type:** 1
Schools: 9
   4 Primary; 1 Middle; 3 High; 1 Other Level
   6 Regular; 0 Special Education; 0 Vocational; 3 Alternative
   0 Magnet; 0 Charter; 6 Title I Eligible; 6 School-wide Title I
Students: 2,321 (54.6% male; 45.3% female)
   Individual Education Program: 528 (22.7%);
   English Language Learner: 0 (0.0%); Migrant: 120 (5.6%)
   Eligible for Free Lunch Program: n/a
   Eligible for Reduced-Price Lunch Program: n/a
Teachers: 155.0 (13.9 to 1)
Librarians/Media Specialists: 6.0 (359.2 to 1)
Guidance Counselors: 5.0 (431.0 to 1)
Current Spending: ($ per student per year):
   Total: $7,273; Instruction: $4,397; Support Services: $2,417
Enrollment, Drop-out Rates and Diploma Recipients by Race/Ethnicity

Category	Total	White	Black	Asian	AIAN	Hisp.
Enrollment (%)	100.0	98.5	1.3	0.0	0.0	0.1
Drop-out Rate (%)	4.9	5.0	0.0	0.0	0.0	n/a
H.S. Diplomas (#)	117	117	0	0	0	0

Breckinridge County

Breckinridge County
PO Box 148 • Hardinsburg, KY 40143-0148
(270) 756-3000 • http://www.breck.k12.ky.us/
Grade Span: PK-12; **Agency Type:** 1
Schools: 6
   4 Primary; 1 Middle; 1 High; 0 Other Level
   6 Regular; 0 Special Education; 0 Vocational; 0 Alternative

---

   0 Magnet; 0 Charter; 5 Title I Eligible; 5 School-wide Title I
Students: 2,769 (51.7% male; 48.2% female)
   Individual Education Program: 439 (15.9%);
   English Language Learner: 4 (0.1%); Migrant: 70 (2.7%)
   Eligible for Free Lunch Program: n/a
   Eligible for Reduced-Price Lunch Program: n/a
Teachers: 147.8 (17.7 to 1)
Librarians/Media Specialists: 5.0 (522.8 to 1)
Guidance Counselors: 5.2 (502.7 to 1)
Current Spending: ($ per student per year):
   Total: $6,407; Instruction: $3,852; Support Services: $2,121
Enrollment, Drop-out Rates and Diploma Recipients by Race/Ethnicity

Category	Total	White	Black	Asian	AIAN	Hisp.
Enrollment (%)	100.0	96.1	2.9	0.2	0.2	0.7
Drop-out Rate (%)	2.4	2.3	0.0	n/a	0.0	0.0
H.S. Diplomas (#)	175	167	7	0	0	1

Bullitt County

Bullitt County
1040 Hw44e • Shepherdsville, KY 40165-6168
(502) 543-2271 • http://www.bullitt.k12.ky.us/
Grade Span: PK-12; **Agency Type:** 1
Schools: 20
   11 Primary; 4 Middle; 4 High; 1 Other Level
   18 Regular; 0 Special Education; 0 Vocational; 2 Alternative
   0 Magnet; 0 Charter; 12 Title I Eligible; 8 School-wide Title I
Students: 11,538 (51.4% male; 48.5% female)
   Individual Education Program: 1,630 (14.1%);
   English Language Learner: 11 (0.1%); Migrant: 78 (0.7%)
   Eligible for Free Lunch Program: n/a
   Eligible for Reduced-Price Lunch Program: n/a
Teachers: 645.5 (17.3 to 1)
Librarians/Media Specialists: 18.0 (621.2 to 1)
Guidance Counselors: 21.5 (520.1 to 1)
Current Spending: ($ per student per year):
   Total: $5,536; Instruction: $3,707; Support Services: $1,540
Enrollment, Drop-out Rates and Diploma Recipients by Race/Ethnicity

Category	Total	White	Black	Asian	AIAN	Hisp.
Enrollment (%)	100.0	98.4	0.5	0.3	0.2	0.5
Drop-out Rate (%)	4.2	4.3	0.0	0.0	0.0	0.0
H.S. Diplomas (#)	630	620	6	1	0	3

Butler County

Butler County
PO Box 339 • Morgantown, KY 42261-0339
(270) 526-5624 • http://www.butler.k12.ky.us/
Grade Span: PK-12; **Agency Type:** 1
Schools: 6
   3 Primary; 1 Middle; 2 High; 0 Other Level
   5 Regular; 0 Special Education; 0 Vocational; 1 Alternative
   0 Magnet; 0 Charter; 5 Title I Eligible; 5 School-wide Title I
Students: 2,255 (51.8% male; 48.1% female)
   Individual Education Program: 370 (16.4%);
   English Language Learner: 2 (0.1%); Migrant: 22 (1.0%)
   Eligible for Free Lunch Program: n/a
   Eligible for Reduced-Price Lunch Program: n/a
Teachers: 138.5 (15.7 to 1)
Librarians/Media Specialists: 4.0 (543.3 to 1)
Guidance Counselors: 5.0 (434.6 to 1)
Current Spending: ($ per student per year):
   Total: $6,432; Instruction: $4,040; Support Services: $1,967
Enrollment, Drop-out Rates and Diploma Recipients by Race/Ethnicity

Category	Total	White	Black	Asian	AIAN	Hisp.
Enrollment (%)	100.0	98.5	0.8	0.2	0.1	0.4
Drop-out Rate (%)	2.1	2.2	0.0	0.0	n/a	0.0
H.S. Diplomas (#)	138	136	1	0	0	1

Caldwell County

Caldwell County
PO Box 229 • Princeton, KY 42445-0229
(270) 365-8000 • http://www.caldwell.k12.ky.us/
Grade Span: PK-12; **Agency Type:** 1
Schools: 4
   2 Primary; 1 Middle; 1 High; 0 Other Level
   4 Regular; 0 Special Education; 0 Vocational; 0 Alternative
   0 Magnet; 0 Charter; 3 Title I Eligible; 3 School-wide Title I
Students: 2,092 (51.4% male; 48.5% female)
   Individual Education Program: 308 (14.7%);
   English Language Learner: 0 (0.0%); Migrant: 258 (12.9%)
   Eligible for Free Lunch Program: n/a
   Eligible for Reduced-Price Lunch Program: n/a
Teachers: 141.0 (14.2 to 1)

Librarians/Media Specialists: 4.0 (499.3 to 1)
Guidance Counselors: 4.0 (499.3 to 1)
Current Spending: ($ per student per year):
    Total: $6,043; Instruction: $3,433; Support Services: $2,295
Enrollment, Drop-out Rates and Diploma Recipients by Race/Ethnicity

Category	Total	White	Black	Asian	AIAN	Hisp.
Enrollment (%)	100.0	92.4	6.7	0.3	0.6	0.1
Drop-out Rate (%)	2.5	2.3	5.1	0.0	n/a	n/a
H.S. Diplomas (#)	132	121	10	1	0	0

Calloway County

Calloway County
PO Box 800 • Murray, KY 42071-0800
(270) 762-7300 • http://www.calloway.k12.ky.us/
Grade Span: PK-12; Agency Type: 1
Schools: 6
    4 Primary; 1 Middle; 1 High; 0 Other Level
    6 Regular; 0 Special Education; 0 Vocational; 0 Alternative
    0 Magnet; 0 Charter; 5 Title I Eligible; 4 School-wide Title I
Students: 3,043   (52.0% male; 47.9% female)
    Individual Education Program: 556 (18.3%);
    English Language Learner: 17 (0.6%); Migrant: 142 (5.0%)
    Eligible for Free Lunch Program: n/a
    Eligible for Reduced-Price Lunch Program: n/a
Teachers: 200.7 (14.3 to 1)
Librarians/Media Specialists: 5.0 (572.6 to 1)
Guidance Counselors: 9.4 (304.6 to 1)
Current Spending: ($ per student per year):
    Total: $6,473; Instruction: $4,326; Support Services: $1,733
Enrollment, Drop-out Rates and Diploma Recipients by Race/Ethnicity

Category	Total	White	Black	Asian	AIAN	Hisp.
Enrollment (%)	100.0	97.1	1.2	0.3	0.3	1.0
Drop-out Rate (%)	1.8	1.6	0.0	0.0	0.0	0.0
H.S. Diplomas (#)	218	213	3	0	0	2

Murray Independent
208 S 13th St • Murray, KY 42071-2302
(270) 753-4363
Grade Span: PK-12; Agency Type: 1
Schools: 4
    2 Primary; 1 Middle; 1 High; 0 Other Level
    4 Regular; 0 Special Education; 0 Vocational; 0 Alternative
    0 Magnet; 0 Charter; 2 Title I Eligible; 0 School-wide Title I
Students: 1,799   (49.8% male; 50.1% female)
    Individual Education Program: 284 (15.8%);
    English Language Learner: 27 (1.5%); Migrant: 58 (3.4%)
    Eligible for Free Lunch Program: n/a
    Eligible for Reduced-Price Lunch Program: n/a
Teachers: 104.0 (16.4 to 1)
Librarians/Media Specialists: 3.0 (569.3 to 1)
Guidance Counselors: 4.0 (427.0 to 1)
Current Spending: ($ per student per year):
    Total: $5,543; Instruction: $3,497; Support Services: $1,719
Enrollment, Drop-out Rates and Diploma Recipients by Race/Ethnicity

Category	Total	White	Black	Asian	AIAN	Hisp.
Enrollment (%)	100.0	85.8	9.7	1.8	0.3	2.5
Drop-out Rate (%)	1.1	1.3	0.0	0.0	0.0	0.0
H.S. Diplomas (#)	127	111	13	2	0	1

Campbell County

Campbell County
101 Orchard • Alexandria, KY 41001-1223
(859) 635-2173 • http://www.campbell.k12.ky.us/
Grade Span: PK-12; Agency Type: 1
Schools: 10
    6 Primary; 1 Middle; 1 High; 2 Other Level
    8 Regular; 0 Special Education; 0 Vocational; 2 Alternative
    0 Magnet; 0 Charter; 2 Title I Eligible; 1 School-wide Title I
Students: 4,688   (53.2% male; 46.7% female)
    Individual Education Program: 863 (18.4%);
    English Language Learner: 31 (0.7%); Migrant: 3 (0.1%)
    Eligible for Free Lunch Program: n/a
    Eligible for Reduced-Price Lunch Program: n/a
Teachers: 283.0 (16.0 to 1)
Librarians/Media Specialists: 6.0 (754.5 to 1)
Guidance Counselors: 12.0 (377.3 to 1)
Current Spending: ($ per student per year):
    Total: $6,236; Instruction: $3,493; Support Services: $2,442
Enrollment, Drop-out Rates and Diploma Recipients by Race/Ethnicity

Category	Total	White	Black	Asian	AIAN	Hisp.
Enrollment (%)	100.0	98.1	0.9	0.6	0.0	0.4
Drop-out Rate (%)	2.4	2.4	0.0	0.0	n/a	0.0
H.S. Diplomas (#)	322	321	0	0	0	1

Fort Thomas Independent
28 N Ft Thomas Ave • Ft Thomas, KY 41075-1527
(859) 781-3333 • http://www.ft-thomas.k12.ky.us/
Grade Span: PK-12; Agency Type: 1
Schools: 5
    3 Primary; 1 Middle; 1 High; 0 Other Level
    5 Regular; 0 Special Education; 0 Vocational; 0 Alternative
    0 Magnet; 0 Charter; 2 Title I Eligible; 0 School-wide Title I
Students: 2,328   (52.0% male; 47.9% female)
    Individual Education Program: 242 (10.4%);
    English Language Learner: 3 (0.1%); Migrant: 0 (0.0%)
    Eligible for Free Lunch Program: n/a
    Eligible for Reduced-Price Lunch Program: n/a
Teachers: 147.5 (15.6 to 1)
Librarians/Media Specialists: 5.0 (458.8 to 1)
Guidance Counselors: 5.8 (395.5 to 1)
Current Spending: ($ per student per year):
    Total: $6,636; Instruction: $3,969; Support Services: $2,390
Enrollment, Drop-out Rates and Diploma Recipients by Race/Ethnicity

Category	Total	White	Black	Asian	AIAN	Hisp.
Enrollment (%)	100.0	98.5	0.6	0.4	0.1	0.3
Drop-out Rate (%)	0.9	0.9	0.0	0.0	0.0	n/a
H.S. Diplomas (#)	193	191	1	1	0	0

Newport Independent
301 E 8th St • Newport, KY 41071-1963
Mailing Address: 301 E Eighth St • Newport, KY 41071-1963
(859) 292-3004 • http://www.newportwildcats.org/
Grade Span: PK-12; Agency Type: 1
Schools: 7
    3 Primary; 1 Middle; 2 High; 1 Other Level
    5 Regular; 0 Special Education; 0 Vocational; 2 Alternative
    0 Magnet; 0 Charter; 4 Title I Eligible; 4 School-wide Title I
Students: 2,560   (51.4% male; 48.5% female)
    Individual Education Program: 426 (16.6%);
    English Language Learner: 19 (0.7%); Migrant: 0 (0.0%)
    Eligible for Free Lunch Program: n/a
    Eligible for Reduced-Price Lunch Program: n/a
Teachers: 166.3 (14.4 to 1)
Librarians/Media Specialists: 5.0 (478.6 to 1)
Guidance Counselors: 4.5 (531.8 to 1)
Current Spending: ($ per student per year):
    Total: $7,847; Instruction: $5,469; Support Services: $1,978
Enrollment, Drop-out Rates and Diploma Recipients by Race/Ethnicity

Category	Total	White	Black	Asian	AIAN	Hisp.
Enrollment (%)	100.0	88.4	9.9	0.3	0.0	1.4
Drop-out Rate (%)	2.8	2.8	3.4	0.0	n/a	0.0
H.S. Diplomas (#)	106	98	6	2	0	0

Carroll County

Carroll County
813 Hawkins St • Carrollton, KY 41008-0090
(502) 732-7070 • http://www.carroll.k12.ky.us/
Grade Span: PK-12; Agency Type: 1
Schools: 5
    1 Primary; 2 Middle; 1 High; 1 Other Level
    4 Regular; 0 Special Education; 0 Vocational; 1 Alternative
    0 Magnet; 0 Charter; 3 Title I Eligible; 3 School-wide Title I
Students: 1,934   (52.9% male; 47.0% female)
    Individual Education Program: 272 (14.1%);
    English Language Learner: 44 (2.3%); Migrant: 92 (5.1%)
    Eligible for Free Lunch Program: n/a
    Eligible for Reduced-Price Lunch Program: n/a
Teachers: 114.0 (15.9 to 1)
Librarians/Media Specialists: 4.0 (452.3 to 1)
Guidance Counselors: 7.9 (229.0 to 1)
Current Spending: ($ per student per year):
    Total: $6,735; Instruction: $4,176; Support Services: $2,176
Enrollment, Drop-out Rates and Diploma Recipients by Race/Ethnicity

Category	Total	White	Black	Asian	AIAN	Hisp.
Enrollment (%)	100.0	93.9	1.9	0.1	0.3	3.9
Drop-out Rate (%)	4.8	5.0	0.0	0.0	0.0	0.0
H.S. Diplomas (#)	116	108	6	0	2	0

Carter County

Carter County
228 S Carol Malone • Grayson, KY 41143-1345
Mailing Address: 228 S Carol Malone Blvd • Grayson, KY 41143-1345
(606) 474-6696 • http://www.carter.k12.ky.us/
Grade Span: PK-12; Agency Type: 1
Schools: 11
    6 Primary; 2 Middle; 3 High; 0 Other Level
    10 Regular; 0 Special Education; 1 Vocational; 0 Alternative

0 Magnet; 0 Charter; 10 Title I Eligible; 10 School-wide Title I
Students: 5,101 (50.6% male; 49.3% female)
Individual Education Program: 918 (18.0%);
English Language Learner: 0 (0.0%); Migrant: 185 (3.9%)
Eligible for Free Lunch Program: n/a
Eligible for Reduced-Price Lunch Program: n/a
Teachers: 340.8 (14.1 to 1)
Librarians/Media Specialists: 8.0 (600.5 to 1)
Guidance Counselors: 16.0 (300.3 to 1)
Current Spending: ($ per student per year):
Total: $6,043; Instruction: $3,808; Support Services: $1,927
Enrollment, Drop-out Rates and Diploma Recipients by Race/Ethnicity

Category	Total	White	Black	Asian	AIAN	Hisp.
Enrollment (%)	100.0	99.5	0.2	0.1	0.1	0.1
Drop-out Rate (%)	3.0	3.0	0.0	0.0	0.0	0.0
H.S. Diplomas (#)	227	226	0	0	1	0

Casey County

Casey County
1922 N US 127 • Liberty, KY 42539-9705
(606) 787-6941 • http://www.casey.k12.ky.us/
Grade Span: PK-12; **Agency Type:** 1
Schools: 8
6 Primary; 1 Middle; 1 High; 0 Other Level
8 Regular; 0 Special Education; 0 Vocational; 0 Alternative
0 Magnet; 0 Charter; 7 Title I Eligible; 7 School-wide Title I
Students: 2,489 (51.0% male; 48.9% female)
Individual Education Program: 389 (15.6%);
English Language Learner: 0 (0.0%); Migrant: 110 (4.6%)
Eligible for Free Lunch Program: n/a
Eligible for Reduced-Price Lunch Program: n/a
Teachers: 157.6 (15.0 to 1)
Librarians/Media Specialists: 4.4 (538.9 to 1)
Guidance Counselors: 5.0 (474.2 to 1)
Current Spending: ($ per student per year):
Total: $6,327; Instruction: $4,006; Support Services: $1,957
Enrollment, Drop-out Rates and Diploma Recipients by Race/Ethnicity

Category	Total	White	Black	Asian	AIAN	Hisp.
Enrollment (%)	100.0	97.6	0.3	0.3	0.2	1.7
Drop-out Rate (%)	5.0	5.1	0.0	n/a	0.0	0.0
H.S. Diplomas (#)	119	119	0	0	0	0

Christian County

Christian County
200 Glass St • Hopkinsville, KY 42240-0609
(270) 887-1300 • http://www.christian.k12.ky.us/
Grade Span: PK-12; **Agency Type:** 1
Schools: 20
11 Primary; 3 Middle; 4 High; 2 Other Level
16 Regular; 0 Special Education; 1 Vocational; 3 Alternative
0 Magnet; 0 Charter; 14 Title I Eligible; 14 School-wide Title I
Students: 9,474 (51.9% male; 48.0% female)
Individual Education Program: 1,508 (15.9%);
English Language Learner: 87 (0.9%); Migrant: 292 (3.3%)
Eligible for Free Lunch Program: n/a
Eligible for Reduced-Price Lunch Program: n/a
Teachers: 553.5 (16.2 to 1)
Librarians/Media Specialists: 16.0 (558.8 to 1)
Guidance Counselors: 26.0 (343.9 to 1)
Current Spending: ($ per student per year):
Total: $5,975; Instruction: $3,756; Support Services: $1,886
Enrollment, Drop-out Rates and Diploma Recipients by Race/Ethnicity

Category	Total	White	Black	Asian	AIAN	Hisp.
Enrollment (%)	100.0	61.3	35.3	0.8	0.4	2.2
Drop-out Rate (%)	4.5	4.1	5.0	0.0	0.0	0.0
H.S. Diplomas (#)	416	264	141	4	1	6

Clark County

Clark County
1600 W Lexington • Winchester, KY 40391-1145
Mailing Address: 1600 W Lexington Ave • Winchester, KY 40391-1145
(859) 744-4545 • http://www.clark.k12.ky.us/
Grade Span: KG-12; **Agency Type:** 1
Schools: 13
8 Primary; 3 Middle; 1 High; 1 Other Level
11 Regular; 0 Special Education; 0 Vocational; 2 Alternative
1 Magnet; 0 Charter; 10 Title I Eligible; 7 School-wide Title I
Students: 5,507 (51.9% male; 48.0% female)
Individual Education Program: 826 (15.0%);
English Language Learner: 28 (0.5%); Migrant: 139 (2.6%)
Eligible for Free Lunch Program: n/a
Eligible for Reduced-Price Lunch Program: n/a

Teachers: 333.5 (15.7 to 1)
Librarians/Media Specialists: 10.0 (524.8 to 1)
Guidance Counselors: 16.0 (328.0 to 1)
Current Spending: ($ per student per year):
Total: $5,711; Instruction: $3,673; Support Services: $1,704
Enrollment, Drop-out Rates and Diploma Recipients by Race/Ethnicity

Category	Total	White	Black	Asian	AIAN	Hisp.
Enrollment (%)	100.0	91.9	6.0	0.3	0.3	1.4
Drop-out Rate (%)	6.5	6.4	4.4	0.0	0.0	0.0
H.S. Diplomas (#)	299	284	15	0	0	0

Clay County

Clay County
128 Richmond Rd • Manchester, KY 40962-1207
(606) 598-2168 • http://www.clay.k12.ky.us/
Grade Span: PK-12; **Agency Type:** 1
Schools: 12
9 Primary; 1 Middle; 1 High; 1 Other Level
11 Regular; 0 Special Education; 0 Vocational; 1 Alternative
0 Magnet; 0 Charter; 10 Title I Eligible; 10 School-wide Title I
Students: 4,230 (52.5% male; 47.4% female)
Individual Education Program: 958 (22.6%);
English Language Learner: 0 (0.0%); Migrant: 0 (0.0%)
Eligible for Free Lunch Program: n/a
Eligible for Reduced-Price Lunch Program: n/a
Teachers: 313.0 (12.6 to 1)
Librarians/Media Specialists: 12.0 (328.8 to 1)
Guidance Counselors: 4.0 (986.5 to 1)
Current Spending: ($ per student per year):
Total: $7,240; Instruction: $4,252; Support Services: $2,572
Enrollment, Drop-out Rates and Diploma Recipients by Race/Ethnicity

Category	Total	White	Black	Asian	AIAN	Hisp.
Enrollment (%)	100.0	99.0	0.7	0.2	0.1	0.1
Drop-out Rate (%)	8.8	8.8	0.0	0.0	0.0	n/a
H.S. Diplomas (#)	161	159	2	0	0	0

Clinton County

Clinton County
Rt 4 Box 100 • Albany, KY 42602-9304
Mailing Address: Rt 4 Box 100 Hwy 127 • Albany, KY 42602-9304
(606) 387-6480 • http://www.clinton.k12.ky.us/
Grade Span: PK-12; **Agency Type:** 1
Schools: 3
1 Primary; 1 Middle; 1 High; 0 Other Level
3 Regular; 0 Special Education; 0 Vocational; 0 Alternative
0 Magnet; 0 Charter; 3 Title I Eligible; 3 School-wide Title I
Students: 1,708 (50.6% male; 49.3% female)
Individual Education Program: 347 (20.3%);
English Language Learner: 13 (0.8%); Migrant: 89 (5.7%)
Eligible for Free Lunch Program: n/a
Eligible for Reduced-Price Lunch Program: n/a
Teachers: 105.6 (14.7 to 1)
Librarians/Media Specialists: 1.2 (1,295.8 to 1)
Guidance Counselors: 7.0 (222.1 to 1)
Current Spending: ($ per student per year):
Total: $7,329; Instruction: $4,475; Support Services: $2,374
Enrollment, Drop-out Rates and Diploma Recipients by Race/Ethnicity

Category	Total	White	Black	Asian	AIAN	Hisp.
Enrollment (%)	100.0	98.3	0.2	0.1	0.0	1.4
Drop-out Rate (%)	4.8	4.5	n/a	0.0	n/a	0.0
H.S. Diplomas (#)	79	79	0	0	0	0

Daviess County

Daviess County
1622 Southeastern Pkwy • Owensboro, KY 42304-1510
(270) 852-7000 • http://www.daviess.k12.ky.us/
Grade Span: PK-12; **Agency Type:** 1
Schools: 22
13 Primary; 3 Middle; 5 High; 0 Other Level
17 Regular; 0 Special Education; 0 Vocational; 4 Alternative
0 Magnet; 0 Charter; 10 Title I Eligible; 6 School-wide Title I
Students: 11,084 (51.8% male; 48.1% female)
Individual Education Program: 1,720 (15.5%);
English Language Learner: 55 (0.5%); Migrant: 202 (1.9%)
Eligible for Free Lunch Program: n/a
Eligible for Reduced-Price Lunch Program: n/a
Teachers: 659.3 (16.0 to 1)
Librarians/Media Specialists: 17.4 (604.7 to 1)
Guidance Counselors: 28.0 (375.8 to 1)
Current Spending: ($ per student per year):
Total: $7,200; Instruction: $4,754; Support Services: $2,048

Enrollment, Drop-out Rates and Diploma Recipients by Race/Ethnicity

Category	Total	White	Black	Asian	AIAN	Hisp.
Enrollment (%)	100.0	95.1	3.2	0.7	0.1	0.8
Drop-out Rate (%)	1.9	1.9	1.1	0.0	0.0	0.0
H.S. Diplomas (#)	720	702	11	1	1	5

Owensboro Independent
1335 W 11th St • Owensboro, KY 42302-0249
(270) 686-1000 • http://www.owensboro.k12.ky.us/
Grade Span: PK-12; **Agency Type:** 1
Schools: 12
   7 Primary; 2 Middle; 2 High; 1 Other Level
   10 Regular; 0 Special Education; 0 Vocational; 2 Alternative
   0 Magnet; 0 Charter; 9 Title I Eligible; 9 School-wide Title I
Students: 4,261 (52.6% male; 47.3% female)
   Individual Education Program: 832 (19.5%);
   English Language Learner: 18 (0.4%); Migrant: 157 (4.0%)
   Eligible for Free Lunch Program: n/a
   Eligible for Reduced-Price Lunch Program: n/a
Teachers: 296.3 (13.3 to 1)
Librarians/Media Specialists: 8.5 (464.1 to 1)
Guidance Counselors: 13.0 (303.5 to 1)
Current Spending: ($ per student per year):
   Total: $7,922; Instruction: $4,819; Support Services: $2,695
Enrollment, Drop-out Rates and Diploma Recipients by Race/Ethnicity

Category	Total	White	Black	Asian	AIAN	Hisp.
Enrollment (%)	100.0	81.9	16.1	0.5	0.3	1.2
Drop-out Rate (%)	2.7	2.3	3.9	0.0	0.0	0.0
H.S. Diplomas (#)	215	180	33	0	0	2

Edmonson County

Edmonson County
100 High School Rd • Brownsville, KY 42210-0129
(270) 597-2101 • http://www.edmonson.k12.ky.us/
Grade Span: PK-12; **Agency Type:** 1
Schools: 5
   3 Primary; 1 Middle; 1 High; 0 Other Level
   5 Regular; 0 Special Education; 0 Vocational; 0 Alternative
   0 Magnet; 0 Charter; 3 Title I Eligible; 3 School-wide Title I
Students: 2,156 (53.4% male; 46.5% female)
   Individual Education Program: 417 (19.3%);
   English Language Learner: 0 (0.0%); Migrant: 21 (1.0%)
   Eligible for Free Lunch Program: n/a
   Eligible for Reduced-Price Lunch Program: n/a
Teachers: 135.0 (15.0 to 1)
Librarians/Media Specialists: 4.0 (505.3 to 1)
Guidance Counselors: 5.0 (404.2 to 1)
Current Spending: ($ per student per year):
   Total: $6,653; Instruction: $4,290; Support Services: $1,964
Enrollment, Drop-out Rates and Diploma Recipients by Race/Ethnicity

Category	Total	White	Black	Asian	AIAN	Hisp.
Enrollment (%)	100.0	97.7	1.9	0.0	0.2	0.1
Drop-out Rate (%)	4.6	4.6	0.0	0.0	0.0	0.0
H.S. Diplomas (#)	99	98	0	0	1	0

Estill County

Estill County
253 Main St • Irvine, KY 40336-0391
(606) 723-2181 • http://www.estill.k12.ky.us/
Grade Span: PK-12; **Agency Type:** 1
Schools: 7
   3 Primary; 1 Middle; 1 High; 2 Other Level
   5 Regular; 0 Special Education; 0 Vocational; 2 Alternative
   0 Magnet; 0 Charter; 4 Title I Eligible; 4 School-wide Title I
Students: 2,592 (51.3% male; 48.6% female)
   Individual Education Program: 489 (18.9%);
   English Language Learner: 2 (0.1%); Migrant: 43 (1.7%)
   Eligible for Free Lunch Program: n/a
   Eligible for Reduced-Price Lunch Program: n/a
Teachers: 179.4 (13.8 to 1)
Librarians/Media Specialists: 5.0 (495.0 to 1)
Guidance Counselors: 6.0 (412.5 to 1)
Current Spending: ($ per student per year):
   Total: $6,324; Instruction: $3,995; Support Services: $1,984
Enrollment, Drop-out Rates and Diploma Recipients by Race/Ethnicity

Category	Total	White	Black	Asian	AIAN	Hisp.
Enrollment (%)	100.0	99.1	0.5	0.2	0.1	0.1
Drop-out Rate (%)	4.8	4.8	0.0	0.0	0.0	0.0
H.S. Diplomas (#)	154	154	0	0	0	0

Fayette County

Fayette County
701 E Main St • Lexington, KY 40502-1601
(859) 381-4000 • http://www.fayette.k12.ky.us/
Grade Span: PK-12; **Agency Type:** 1
Schools: 61
   35 Primary; 11 Middle; 8 High; 6 Other Level
   50 Regular; 0 Special Education; 2 Vocational; 8 Alternative
   21 Magnet; 0 Charter; 29 Title I Eligible; 25 School-wide Title I
Students: 34,259 (51.6% male; 48.3% female)
   Individual Education Program: 3,574 (10.4%);
   English Language Learner: 1,230 (3.6%); Migrant: 342 (1.0%)
   Eligible for Free Lunch Program: n/a
   Eligible for Reduced-Price Lunch Program: n/a
Teachers: 2,534.2 (13.1 to 1)
Librarians/Media Specialists: 60.5 (548.3 to 1)
Guidance Counselors: 78.6 (422.0 to 1)
Current Spending: ($ per student per year):
   Total: $7,255; Instruction: $4,403; Support Services: $2,540
Enrollment, Drop-out Rates and Diploma Recipients by Race/Ethnicity

Category	Total	White	Black	Asian	AIAN	Hisp.
Enrollment (%)	100.0	68.5	23.3	2.9	0.2	5.1
Drop-out Rate (%)	5.0	4.2	7.8	0.9	0.0	8.5
H.S. Diplomas (#)	1,643	1,244	313	53	3	30

Fleming County

Fleming County
211 W Water St • Flemingsburg, KY 41041-1022
(606) 845-5851 • http://www.fleming.k12.ky.us/
Grade Span: KG-12; **Agency Type:** 1
Schools: 6
   4 Primary; 1 Middle; 1 High; 0 Other Level
   6 Regular; 0 Special Education; 0 Vocational; 0 Alternative
   0 Magnet; 0 Charter; 6 Title I Eligible; 6 School-wide Title I
Students: 2,687 (50.6% male; 49.3% female)
   Individual Education Program: 367 (13.7%);
   English Language Learner: 9 (0.3%); Migrant: 49 (2.0%)
   Eligible for Free Lunch Program: n/a
   Eligible for Reduced-Price Lunch Program: n/a
Teachers: 162.2 (15.5 to 1)
Librarians/Media Specialists: 5.0 (501.8 to 1)
Guidance Counselors: 5.0 (501.8 to 1)
Current Spending: ($ per student per year):
   Total: $6,355; Instruction: $4,035; Support Services: $1,969
Enrollment, Drop-out Rates and Diploma Recipients by Race/Ethnicity

Category	Total	White	Black	Asian	AIAN	Hisp.
Enrollment (%)	100.0	96.4	2.3	0.2	0.0	1.1
Drop-out Rate (%)	4.6	4.6	0.0	0.0	n/a	0.0
H.S. Diplomas (#)	131	129	1	1	0	0

Floyd County

Floyd County
106 N Front Ave • Prestons, KY 41653-1209
(606) 886-2354 • http://www.floyd.k12.ky.us/
Grade Span: PK-12; **Agency Type:** 1
Schools: 17
   9 Primary; 3 Middle; 5 High; 0 Other Level
   16 Regular; 0 Special Education; 0 Vocational; 1 Alternative
   0 Magnet; 0 Charter; 17 Title I Eligible; 17 School-wide Title I
Students: 7,080 (51.7% male; 48.2% female)
   Individual Education Program: 1,312 (18.5%);
   English Language Learner: 0 (0.0%); Migrant: 0 (0.0%)
   Eligible for Free Lunch Program: n/a
   Eligible for Reduced-Price Lunch Program: n/a
Teachers: 463.0 (14.5 to 1)
Librarians/Media Specialists: 12.0 (560.6 to 1)
Guidance Counselors: 16.0 (420.4 to 1)
Current Spending: ($ per student per year):
   Total: $6,624; Instruction: $4,048; Support Services: $2,170
Enrollment, Drop-out Rates and Diploma Recipients by Race/Ethnicity

Category	Total	White	Black	Asian	AIAN	Hisp.
Enrollment (%)	100.0	99.5	0.3	0.0	0.1	0.1
Drop-out Rate (%)	6.1	6.1	0.0	0.0	n/a	0.0
H.S. Diplomas (#)	407	405	1	1	0	0

Franklin County

Franklin County
916 E Main St • Frankfort, KY 40601-2521
(502) 695-6700 • http://www.franklin.k12.ky.us/
Grade Span: PK-12; **Agency Type:** 1
Schools: 12

6 Primary; 2 Middle; 3 High; 1 Other Level
10 Regular; 0 Special Education; 1 Vocational; 1 Alternative
0 Magnet; 0 Charter; 5 Title I Eligible; 0 School-wide Title I
Students: 6,026　(52.5% male; 47.4% female)
　Individual Education Program: 806 (13.4%);
　English Language Learner: 59 (1.0%); Migrant: 0 (0.0%)
　Eligible for Free Lunch Program: n/a
　Eligible for Reduced-Price Lunch Program: n/a
Teachers: 365.1 (15.8 to 1)
Librarians/Media Specialists: 9.5 (608.4 to 1)
Guidance Counselors: 10.0 (578.0 to 1)
Current Spending: ($ per student per year):
　Total: $5,959; Instruction: $3,516; Support Services: $2,151
Enrollment, Drop-out Rates and Diploma Recipients by Race/Ethnicity

Category	Total	White	Black	Asian	AIAN	Hisp.
Enrollment (%)	100.0	88.6	8.9	0.5	0.2	1.8
Drop-out Rate (%)	3.3	3.2	3.9	0.0	0.0	0.0
H.S. Diplomas (#)	361	324	30	5	0	2

Gallatin County

Gallatin County
600 Main St • Warsaw, KY 41095-0146
(859) 567-2828
Grade Span: PK-12; **Agency Type:** 1
Schools: 5
　1 Primary; 2 Middle; 1 High; 1 Other Level
　4 Regular; 0 Special Education; 0 Vocational; 1 Alternative
　0 Magnet; 0 Charter; 2 Title I Eligible; 2 School-wide Title I
Students: 1,621　(50.3% male; 49.6% female)
　Individual Education Program: 282 (17.4%);
　English Language Learner: 25 (1.5%); Migrant: 33 (2.1%)
　Eligible for Free Lunch Program: n/a
　Eligible for Reduced-Price Lunch Program: n/a
Teachers: 88.2 (17.5 to 1)
Librarians/Media Specialists: 3.0 (514.7 to 1)
Guidance Counselors: 4.0 (386.0 to 1)
Current Spending: ($ per student per year):
　Total: $6,365; Instruction: $3,491; Support Services: $2,518
Enrollment, Drop-out Rates and Diploma Recipients by Race/Ethnicity

Category	Total	White	Black	Asian	AIAN	Hisp.
Enrollment (%)	100.0	96.6	1.0	0.1	0.4	1.9
Drop-out Rate (%)	2.8	2.6	0.0	n/a	n/a	0.0
H.S. Diplomas (#)	71	70	1	0	0	0

Garrard County

Garrard County
322 W Maple • Lancaster, KY 40444-1064
Mailing Address: 322 W Maple St • Lancaster, KY 40444-1064
(859) 792-3018 • http://www.garrard.k12.ky.us/
Grade Span: PK-12; **Agency Type:** 1
Schools: 6
　3 Primary; 1 Middle; 1 High; 1 Other Level
　5 Regular; 0 Special Education; 0 Vocational; 1 Alternative
　0 Magnet; 0 Charter; 4 Title I Eligible; 2 School-wide Title I
Students: 2,572　(53.4% male; 46.5% female)
　Individual Education Program: 399 (15.5%);
　English Language Learner: 59 (2.3%); Migrant: 213 (8.6%)
　Eligible for Free Lunch Program: n/a
　Eligible for Reduced-Price Lunch Program: n/a
Teachers: 171.6 (14.4 to 1)
Librarians/Media Specialists: 5.0 (493.8 to 1)
Guidance Counselors: 5.5 (448.9 to 1)
Current Spending: ($ per student per year):
　Total: $5,981; Instruction: $3,840; Support Services: $1,802
Enrollment, Drop-out Rates and Diploma Recipients by Race/Ethnicity

Category	Total	White	Black	Asian	AIAN	Hisp.
Enrollment (%)	100.0	95.4	3.0	0.0	0.1	1.5
Drop-out Rate (%)	4.5	4.5	0.0	n/a	n/a	0.0
H.S. Diplomas (#)	136	132	1	0	1	2

Grant County

Grant County
505 S Main St • Williamsto, KY 41097-0369
(859) 824-3323
Grade Span: KG-12; **Agency Type:** 1
Schools: 6
　3 Primary; 1 Middle; 1 High; 1 Other Level
　5 Regular; 0 Special Education; 0 Vocational; 1 Alternative
　0 Magnet; 0 Charter; 4 Title I Eligible; 3 School-wide Title I
Students: 3,840　(51.4% male; 48.5% female)
　Individual Education Program: 538 (14.0%);
　English Language Learner: 24 (0.6%); Migrant: 108 (2.9%)

　Eligible for Free Lunch Program: n/a
　Eligible for Reduced-Price Lunch Program: n/a
Teachers: 214.9 (17.4 to 1)
Librarians/Media Specialists: 5.0 (747.2 to 1)
Guidance Counselors: 8.0 (467.0 to 1)
Current Spending: ($ per student per year):
　Total: $5,560; Instruction: $3,420; Support Services: $1,807
Enrollment, Drop-out Rates and Diploma Recipients by Race/Ethnicity

Category	Total	White	Black	Asian	AIAN	Hisp.
Enrollment (%)	100.0	98.5	0.3	0.2	0.3	0.7
Drop-out Rate (%)	3.2	3.1	0.0	0.0	n/a	0.0
H.S. Diplomas (#)	169	168	0	1	0	0

Graves County

Graves County
2290 State Rt 121 N • Mayfield, KY 42066-3267
(270) 247-2656 • http://www.graves.k12.ky.us/
Grade Span: KG-12; **Agency Type:** 1
Schools: 12
　7 Primary; 1 Middle; 4 High; 0 Other Level
　9 Regular; 0 Special Education; 0 Vocational; 3 Alternative
　0 Magnet; 0 Charter; 7 Title I Eligible; 0 School-wide Title I
Students: 4,642　(51.4% male; 48.5% female)
　Individual Education Program: 691 (14.9%);
　English Language Learner: 63 (1.4%); Migrant: 328 (7.4%)
　Eligible for Free Lunch Program: n/a
　Eligible for Reduced-Price Lunch Program: n/a
Teachers: 274.3 (16.1 to 1)
Librarians/Media Specialists: 6.0 (735.8 to 1)
Guidance Counselors: 9.0 (490.6 to 1)
Current Spending: ($ per student per year):
　Total: $5,595; Instruction: $3,489; Support Services: $1,737
Enrollment, Drop-out Rates and Diploma Recipients by Race/Ethnicity

Category	Total	White	Black	Asian	AIAN	Hisp.
Enrollment (%)	100.0	95.4	1.8	0.3	2.1	0.3
Drop-out Rate (%)	2.0	2.0	0.0	0.0	0.0	0.0
H.S. Diplomas (#)	271	267	3	1	0	0

Mayfield Independent
709 S 8th St • Mayfiel, KY 42066-3037
Mailing Address: 709 S Eighth St • Mayfield, KY 42066-3037
(270) 247-3868
Grade Span: PK-12; **Agency Type:** 1
Schools: 5
　2 Primary; 2 Middle; 1 High; 0 Other Level
　5 Regular; 0 Special Education; 0 Vocational; 0 Alternative
　0 Magnet; 0 Charter; 3 Title I Eligible; 3 School-wide Title I
Students: 1,612　(53.9% male; 46.0% female)
　Individual Education Program: 254 (15.8%);
　English Language Learner: 119 (7.4%); Migrant: 194 (13.0%)
　Eligible for Free Lunch Program: n/a
　Eligible for Reduced-Price Lunch Program: n/a
Teachers: 95.5 (15.6 to 1)
Librarians/Media Specialists: 4.0 (372.5 to 1)
Guidance Counselors: 3.0 (496.7 to 1)
Current Spending: ($ per student per year):
　Total: $6,577; Instruction: $4,179; Support Services: $1,952
Enrollment, Drop-out Rates and Diploma Recipients by Race/Ethnicity

Category	Total	White	Black	Asian	AIAN	Hisp.
Enrollment (%)	100.0	63.0	21.7	0.8	0.3	14.2
Drop-out Rate (%)	3.9	2.8	3.0	0.0	n/a	4.2
H.S. Diplomas (#)	83	64	17	0	0	2

Grayson County

Grayson County
909 Brandenburg Rd • Leitchfield, KY 42754-4009
(270) 259-4011 • http://www.grayson.k12.ky.us/
Grade Span: PK-12; **Agency Type:** 1
Schools: 7
　4 Primary; 1 Middle; 1 High; 1 Other Level
　6 Regular; 0 Special Education; 0 Vocational; 1 Alternative
　0 Magnet; 0 Charter; 5 Title I Eligible; 5 School-wide Title I
Students: 4,376　(52.0% male; 47.9% female)
　Individual Education Program: 620 (14.2%);
　English Language Learner: 3 (0.1%); Migrant: 126 (3.1%)
　Eligible for Free Lunch Program: n/a
　Eligible for Reduced-Price Lunch Program: n/a
Teachers: 267.2 (15.4 to 1)
Librarians/Media Specialists: 6.0 (684.7 to 1)
Guidance Counselors: 12.0 (342.3 to 1)
Current Spending: ($ per student per year):
　Total: $5,817; Instruction: $3,804; Support Services: $1,647

Enrollment, Drop-out Rates and Diploma Recipients by Race/Ethnicity

Category	Total	White	Black	Asian	AIAN	Hisp.
Enrollment (%)	100.0	98.9	0.6	0.0	0.0	0.4
Drop-out Rate (%)	4.5	4.5	0.0	n/a	n/a	0.0
H.S. Diplomas (#)	252	252	0	0	0	0

Green County

Green County

206 W Court St • Greensburg, KY 42743-0369
(270) 932-5231 • http://www.green.k12.ky.us/
Grade Span: KG-12; **Agency Type:** 1
Schools: 5
   3 Primary; 1 Middle; 1 High; 0 Other Level
   5 Regular; 0 Special Education; 0 Vocational; 0 Alternative
   0 Magnet; 0 Charter; 4 Title I Eligible; 4 School-wide Title I
Students: 1,732   (51.1% male; 48.8% female)
   Individual Education Program: 282 (16.3%);
   English Language Learner: 0 (0.0%); Migrant: 75 (4.5%)
   Eligible for Free Lunch Program: n/a
   Eligible for Reduced-Price Lunch Program: n/a
Teachers: 113.5 (14.6 to 1)
Librarians/Media Specialists: 3.6 (460.3 to 1)
Guidance Counselors: 3.0 (552.3 to 1)
Current Spending: ($ per student per year):
   Total: $6,264; Instruction: $3,782; Support Services: $2,147

Enrollment, Drop-out Rates and Diploma Recipients by Race/Ethnicity

Category	Total	White	Black	Asian	AIAN	Hisp.
Enrollment (%)	100.0	96.6	2.2	0.3	0.4	0.5
Drop-out Rate (%)	1.6	1.7	0.0	0.0	0.0	0.0
H.S. Diplomas (#)	119	115	3	0	0	1

Greenup County

8000 US 23 N • Greenup, KY 41144-9618
(606) 473-9819 • http://www.greenup.k12.ky.us/
Grade Span: PK-12; **Agency Type:** 1
Schools: 8
   4 Primary; 3 Middle; 1 High; 0 Other Level
   8 Regular; 0 Special Education; 0 Vocational; 0 Alternative
   0 Magnet; 0 Charter; 7 Title I Eligible; 7 School-wide Title I
Students: 3,261   (50.6% male; 49.3% female)
   Individual Education Program: 545 (16.7%);
   English Language Learner: 1 (<0.1%); Migrant: 102 (3.3%)
   Eligible for Free Lunch Program: n/a
   Eligible for Reduced-Price Lunch Program: n/a
Teachers: 199.0 (15.6 to 1)
Librarians/Media Specialists: 8.0 (387.1 to 1)
Guidance Counselors: 8.0 (387.1 to 1)
Current Spending: ($ per student per year):
   Total: $6,403; Instruction: $3,497; Support Services: $2,511

Enrollment, Drop-out Rates and Diploma Recipients by Race/Ethnicity

Category	Total	White	Black	Asian	AIAN	Hisp.
Enrollment (%)	100.0	98.1	1.2	0.1	0.4	0.3
Drop-out Rate (%)	5.1	5.0	0.0	0.0	0.0	0.0
H.S. Diplomas (#)	182	180	1	1	0	0

Russell Independent

409 Belfont St • Russell, KY 41169-1320
(606) 836-9679 • http://www.russell.k12.ky.us/
Grade Span: PK-12; **Agency Type:** 1
Schools: 4
   1 Primary; 2 Middle; 1 High; 0 Other Level
   4 Regular; 0 Special Education; 0 Vocational; 0 Alternative
   0 Magnet; 0 Charter; 3 Title I Eligible; 0 School-wide Title I
Students: 2,173   (51.2% male; 48.7% female)
   Individual Education Program: 272 (12.5%);
   English Language Learner: 0 (0.0%); Migrant: 21 (1.0%)
   Eligible for Free Lunch Program: n/a
   Eligible for Reduced-Price Lunch Program: n/a
Teachers: 120.6 (17.4 to 1)
Librarians/Media Specialists: 4.0 (525.8 to 1)
Guidance Counselors: 6.0 (350.5 to 1)
Current Spending: ($ per student per year):
   Total: $5,834; Instruction: $3,515; Support Services: $2,012

Enrollment, Drop-out Rates and Diploma Recipients by Race/Ethnicity

Category	Total	White	Black	Asian	AIAN	Hisp.
Enrollment (%)	100.0	97.7	1.0	0.9	0.0	0.4
Drop-out Rate (%)	0.4	0.4	0.0	0.0	0.0	0.0
H.S. Diplomas (#)	152	151	0	1	0	0

Hancock County

Hancock County

83 State Rt 271 N • Hawesville, KY 42348-6809
(270) 927-6914 • http://www.hancock.k12.ky.us/hcboe/
Grade Span: KG-12; **Agency Type:** 1
Schools: 5
   3 Primary; 1 Middle; 1 High; 0 Other Level
   5 Regular; 0 Special Education; 0 Vocational; 0 Alternative
   0 Magnet; 0 Charter; 4 Title I Eligible; 2 School-wide Title I
Students: 1,623   (52.3% male; 47.6% female)
   Individual Education Program: 225 (13.9%);
   English Language Learner: 0 (0.0%); Migrant: 0 (0.0%)
   Eligible for Free Lunch Program: n/a
   Eligible for Reduced-Price Lunch Program: n/a
Teachers: 96.4 (16.0 to 1)
Librarians/Media Specialists: 3.0 (515.3 to 1)
Guidance Counselors: 3.0 (515.3 to 1)
Current Spending: ($ per student per year):
   Total: $6,527; Instruction: $3,687; Support Services: $2,482

Enrollment, Drop-out Rates and Diploma Recipients by Race/Ethnicity

Category	Total	White	Black	Asian	AIAN	Hisp.
Enrollment (%)	100.0	98.1	1.0	0.0	0.1	0.8
Drop-out Rate (%)	0.0	0.0	0.0	0.0	n/a	0.0
H.S. Diplomas (#)	109	107	1	1	0	0

Hardin County

Elizabethtown Independent

219 Helm St • Elizabethtow, KY 42701-0605
(270) 765-6146 • http://www.etown.k12.ky.us/
Grade Span: KG-12; **Agency Type:** 1
Schools: 4
   2 Primary; 1 Middle; 1 High; 0 Other Level
   4 Regular; 0 Special Education; 0 Vocational; 0 Alternative
   0 Magnet; 0 Charter; 2 Title I Eligible; 2 School-wide Title I
Students: 2,310   (51.5% male; 48.4% female)
   Individual Education Program: 261 (11.3%);
   English Language Learner: 15 (0.6%); Migrant: 5 (0.2%)
   Eligible for Free Lunch Program: n/a
   Eligible for Reduced-Price Lunch Program: n/a
Teachers: 142.5 (15.9 to 1)
Librarians/Media Specialists: 4.0 (566.5 to 1)
Guidance Counselors: 4.5 (503.6 to 1)
Current Spending: ($ per student per year):
   Total: $6,628; Instruction: $4,272; Support Services: $2,026

Enrollment, Drop-out Rates and Diploma Recipients by Race/Ethnicity

Category	Total	White	Black	Asian	AIAN	Hisp.
Enrollment (%)	100.0	79.7	13.8	3.5	1.0	1.9
Drop-out Rate (%)	3.6	3.9	2.2	0.0	0.0	0.0
H.S. Diplomas (#)	146	120	19	3	0	4

Hardin County

65 W.A. Jenkins Rd • Elizabe, KY 42701-1419
Mailing Address: 65 W A Jenkins Rd • Elizabethtown, KY 42701-1419
(270) 769-8800 • http://www.hardin.k12.ky.us/
Grade Span: PK-12; **Agency Type:** 1
Schools: 24
   12 Primary; 5 Middle; 3 High; 4 Other Level
   20 Regular; 0 Special Education; 0 Vocational; 4 Alternative
   0 Magnet; 0 Charter; 19 Title I Eligible; 19 School-wide Title I
Students: 13,466   (52.2% male; 47.7% female)
   Individual Education Program: 2,148 (16.0%);
   English Language Learner: 108 (0.8%); Migrant: 72 (0.6%)
   Eligible for Free Lunch Program: n/a
   Eligible for Reduced-Price Lunch Program: n/a
Teachers: 815.0 (15.9 to 1)
Librarians/Media Specialists: 24.0 (541.6 to 1)
Guidance Counselors: 32.0 (406.2 to 1)
Current Spending: ($ per student per year):
   Total: $6,206; Instruction: $3,805; Support Services: $2,008

Enrollment, Drop-out Rates and Diploma Recipients by Race/Ethnicity

Category	Total	White	Black	Asian	AIAN	Hisp.
Enrollment (%)	100.0	79.6	15.0	2.2	0.5	2.7
Drop-out Rate (%)	3.4	3.4	2.9	1.7	0.0	5.7
H.S. Diplomas (#)	817	632	130	29	3	23

Harlan County

Harlan County

251 Ball Park Rd • Harlan, KY 40831-1756
(606) 573-4330 • http://www.harlan.k12.ky.us/
Grade Span: PK-12; **Agency Type:** 1
Schools: 11
   8 Primary; 0 Middle; 3 High; 0 Other Level

11 Regular; 0 Special Education; 0 Vocational; 0 Alternative
0 Magnet; 0 Charter; 11 Title I Eligible; 11 School-wide Title I
Students: 5,014   (52.3% male; 47.6% female)
    Individual Education Program: 847 (16.9%);
    English Language Learner: 0 (0.0%); Migrant: 0 (0.0%)
    Eligible for Free Lunch Program: n/a
    Eligible for Reduced-Price Lunch Program: n/a
Teachers: 332.5 (14.1 to 1)
Librarians/Media Specialists: 12.0 (389.4 to 1)
Guidance Counselors: 12.0 (389.4 to 1)
Current Spending: ($ per student per year):
    Total: $6,529; Instruction: $4,042; Support Services: $2,101
Enrollment, Drop-out Rates and Diploma Recipients by Race/Ethnicity

Category	Total	White	Black	Asian	AIAN	Hisp.
Enrollment (%)	100.0	97.4	2.4	0.0	0.1	0.1
Drop-out Rate (%)	6.8	6.8	0.0	0.0	n/a	0.0
H.S. Diplomas (#)	265	258	6	0	0	1

Harrison County

Harrison County
324 Webster Ave • Cynthiana, KY 41031-8803
(859) 234-7110 • http://www.harrison.k12.ky.us/
Grade Span: KG-12; **Agency Type:** 1
Schools: 6
    4 Primary; 1 Middle; 1 High; 0 Other Level
    6 Regular; 0 Special Education; 0 Vocational; 0 Alternative
    0 Magnet; 0 Charter; 4 Title I Eligible; 2 School-wide Title I
Students: 3,277   (51.7% male; 48.2% female)
    Individual Education Program: 508 (15.5%)
    English Language Learner: 13 (0.4%); Migrant: 125 (4.0%)
    Eligible for Free Lunch Program: n/a
    Eligible for Reduced-Price Lunch Program: n/a
Teachers: 179.5 (17.5 to 1)
Librarians/Media Specialists: 7.0 (448.3 to 1)
Guidance Counselors: 5.0 (627.6 to 1)
Current Spending: ($ per student per year):
    Total: $5,815; Instruction: $3,530; Support Services: $1,898
Enrollment, Drop-out Rates and Diploma Recipients by Race/Ethnicity

Category	Total	White	Black	Asian	AIAN	Hisp.
Enrollment (%)	100.0	95.1	3.3	0.2	0.3	1.1
Drop-out Rate (%)	2.9	2.9	0.0	0.0	n/a	0.0
H.S. Diplomas (#)	192	187	4	0	0	1

Hart County

Hart County
511 W Union St • Munfordville, KY 42765-0068
(270) 524-2631 • http://www.hart.k12.ky.us/
Grade Span: PK-12; **Agency Type:** 1
Schools: 6
    5 Primary; 0 Middle; 1 High; 0 Other Level
    6 Regular; 0 Special Education; 0 Vocational; 0 Alternative
    0 Magnet; 0 Charter; 5 Title I Eligible; 5 School-wide Title I
Students: 2,519   (53.5% male; 46.4% female)
    Individual Education Program: 435 (17.3%);
    English Language Learner: 5 (0.2%); Migrant: 119 (5.0%)
    Eligible for Free Lunch Program: n/a
    Eligible for Reduced-Price Lunch Program: n/a
Teachers: 162.0 (14.6 to 1)
Librarians/Media Specialists: 5.0 (474.6 to 1)
Guidance Counselors: 7.0 (339.0 to 1)
Current Spending: ($ per student per year):
    Total: $7,056; Instruction: $4,162; Support Services: $2,425
Enrollment, Drop-out Rates and Diploma Recipients by Race/Ethnicity

Category	Total	White	Black	Asian	AIAN	Hisp.
Enrollment (%)	100.0	94.7	4.2	0.2	0.2	0.8
Drop-out Rate (%)	4.8	4.9	0.0	n/a	n/a	0.0
H.S. Diplomas (#)	133	122	10	0	0	1

Henderson County

Henderson County
1805 2nd St • Henderson, KY 42420-3367
Mailing Address: 1805 Second St • Henderson, KY 42420-3367
(270) 831-5000 • http://www.henderson.k12.ky.us/
Grade Span: PK-12; **Agency Type:** 1
Schools: 12
    8 Primary; 2 Middle; 1 High; 1 Other Level
    11 Regular; 0 Special Education; 0 Vocational; 1 Alternative
    0 Magnet; 0 Charter; 10 Title I Eligible; 6 School-wide Title I
Students: 7,037   (51.5% male; 48.4% female)
    Individual Education Program: 1,145 (16.3%);
    English Language Learner: 33 (0.5%); Migrant: 152 (2.2%)
    Eligible for Free Lunch Program: n/a

Eligible for Reduced-Price Lunch Program: n/a
Teachers: 428.7 (15.8 to 1)
Librarians/Media Specialists: 12.0 (563.4 to 1)
Guidance Counselors: 23.7 (285.3 to 1)
Current Spending: ($ per student per year):
    Total: $6,292; Instruction: $3,855; Support Services: $2,071
Enrollment, Drop-out Rates and Diploma Recipients by Race/Ethnicity

Category	Total	White	Black	Asian	AIAN	Hisp.
Enrollment (%)	100.0	89.0	9.9	0.2	0.8	0.1
Drop-out Rate (%)	4.8	5.0	3.5	0.0	0.0	0.0
H.S. Diplomas (#)	455	411	42	2	0	0

Henry County

Henry County
326 S Main St • New Castle, KY 40050-0299
(502) 845-8600 • http://www.henry.k12.ky.us/
Grade Span: PK-12; **Agency Type:** 1
Schools: 5
    3 Primary; 1 Middle; 1 High; 0 Other Level
    5 Regular; 0 Special Education; 0 Vocational; 0 Alternative
    0 Magnet; 0 Charter; 3 Title I Eligible; 3 School-wide Title I
Students: 2,199   (52.9% male; 47.0% female)
    Individual Education Program: 269 (12.2%);
    English Language Learner: 23 (1.0%); Migrant: 53 (2.5%)
    Eligible for Free Lunch Program: n/a
    Eligible for Reduced-Price Lunch Program: n/a
Teachers: 130.0 (16.2 to 1)
Librarians/Media Specialists: 3.5 (603.1 to 1)
Guidance Counselors: 3.5 (603.1 to 1)
Current Spending: ($ per student per year):
    Total: $5,964; Instruction: $3,555; Support Services: $1,989
Enrollment, Drop-out Rates and Diploma Recipients by Race/Ethnicity

Category	Total	White	Black	Asian	AIAN	Hisp.
Enrollment (%)	100.0	96.3	1.5	0.3	0.0	1.9
Drop-out Rate (%)	3.8	3.8	0.0	0.0	n/a	0.0
H.S. Diplomas (#)	107	103	3	0	0	1

Hopkins County

Hopkins County
320 S Seminary • Madisonvi, KY 42431-0509
Mailing Address: 320 S Seminary St • Madisonville, KY 42431-0509
(270) 825-6000 • http://www.hopkins.k12.ky.us/
Grade Span: PK-12; **Agency Type:** 1
Schools: 14
    8 Primary; 3 Middle; 2 High; 1 Other Level
    13 Regular; 0 Special Education; 0 Vocational; 1 Alternative
    0 Magnet; 0 Charter; 9 Title I Eligible; 8 School-wide Title I
Students: 7,405   (50.7% male; 49.2% female)
    Individual Education Program: 1,433 (19.4%);
    English Language Learner: 0 (0.0%); Migrant: 304 (4.4%)
    Eligible for Free Lunch Program: n/a
    Eligible for Reduced-Price Lunch Program: n/a
Teachers: 477.8 (14.6 to 1)
Librarians/Media Specialists: 14.0 (498.6 to 1)
Guidance Counselors: 19.0 (367.4 to 1)
Current Spending: ($ per student per year):
    Total: $6,132; Instruction: $3,815; Support Services: $1,988
Enrollment, Drop-out Rates and Diploma Recipients by Race/Ethnicity

Category	Total	White	Black	Asian	AIAN	Hisp.
Enrollment (%)	100.0	87.7	10.7	0.7	0.2	0.8
Drop-out Rate (%)	4.4	4.5	3.0	0.0	n/a	0.0
H.S. Diplomas (#)	375	338	34	2	0	1

Jackson County

Jackson County
Hwy 421 • Mckee, KY 40447-0217
(606) 287-7181
Grade Span: PK-12; **Agency Type:** 1
Schools: 6
    3 Primary; 1 Middle; 1 High; 1 Other Level
    5 Regular; 0 Special Education; 0 Vocational; 1 Alternative
    0 Magnet; 0 Charter; 5 Title I Eligible; 4 School-wide Title I
Students: 2,444   (53.5% male; 46.4% female)
    Individual Education Program: 471 (19.3%);
    English Language Learner: 0 (0.0%); Migrant: 25 (1.1%)
    Eligible for Free Lunch Program: n/a
    Eligible for Reduced-Price Lunch Program: n/a
Teachers: 165.0 (13.8 to 1)
Librarians/Media Specialists: 7.0 (325.1 to 1)
Guidance Counselors: 6.0 (379.3 to 1)
Current Spending: ($ per student per year):
    Total: $7,201; Instruction: $4,214; Support Services: $2,535

Enrollment, Drop-out Rates and Diploma Recipients by Race/Ethnicity

Category	Total	White	Black	Asian	AIAN	Hisp.
Enrollment (%)	100.0	99.8	0.1	0.0	0.0	0.1
Drop-out Rate (%)	4.7	4.8	0.0	0.0	0.0	0.0
H.S. Diplomas (#)	122	122	0	0	0	0

Jefferson County

Jefferson County
3332 Newburg Rd • Louisville, KY 40232-4020
(502) 485-3011 • http://www.jefferson.k12.ky.us/
Grade Span: PK-12; Agency Type: 1
Schools: 173
   98 Primary; 25 Middle; 36 High; 14 Other Level
   138 Regular; 7 Special Education; 1 Vocational; 27 Alternative
   14 Magnet; 0 Charter; 83 Title I Eligible; 83 School-wide Title I
Students: 95,582 (51.3% male; 48.6% female)
   Individual Education Program: 13,598 (14.2%);
   English Language Learner: 3,301 (3.5%); Migrant: 151 (0.2%)
   Eligible for Free Lunch Program: n/a
   Eligible for Reduced-Price Lunch Program: n/a
Teachers: 5,656.4 (16.2 to 1)
Librarians/Media Specialists: 148.1 (618.3 to 1)
Guidance Counselors: 247.6 (369.8 to 1)
Current Spending: ($ per student per year):
   Total: $7,663; Instruction: $4,218; Support Services: $3,152

Enrollment, Drop-out Rates and Diploma Recipients by Race/Ethnicity

Category	Total	White	Black	Asian	AIAN	Hisp.
Enrollment (%)	100.0	59.9	35.0	1.9	0.4	2.7
Drop-out Rate (%)	5.9	5.5	6.9	4.8	0.0	8.2
H.S. Diplomas (#)	4,932	3,347	1,400	126	0	59

Jessamine County

Jessamine County
501 E Maple • Nicholasville, KY 40356-1642
(859) 885-4179 • http://www.jessamine.k12.ky.us/
Grade Span: PK-12; Agency Type: 1
Schools: 11
   6 Primary; 2 Middle; 2 High; 1 Other Level
   10 Regular; 0 Special Education; 0 Vocational; 1 Alternative
   0 Magnet; 0 Charter; 8 Title I Eligible; 8 School-wide Title I
Students: 7,150 (51.6% male; 48.3% female)
   Individual Education Program: 1,190 (16.6%);
   English Language Learner: 82 (1.1%); Migrant: 129 (1.9%)
   Eligible for Free Lunch Program: n/a
   Eligible for Reduced-Price Lunch Program: n/a
Teachers: 455.2 (15.1 to 1)
Librarians/Media Specialists: 8.5 (811.3 to 1)
Guidance Counselors: 16.0 (431.0 to 1)
Current Spending: ($ per student per year):
   Total: $6,082; Instruction: $3,838; Support Services: $1,974

Enrollment, Drop-out Rates and Diploma Recipients by Race/Ethnicity

Category	Total	White	Black	Asian	AIAN	Hisp.
Enrollment (%)	100.0	94.8	3.5	0.6	0.2	0.9
Drop-out Rate (%)	5.3	5.4	2.6	0.0	0.0	0.0
H.S. Diplomas (#)	322	294	22	3	1	2

Johnson County

Johnson County
253 N Mayo • Paintsville, KY 41240-1803
Mailing Address: 253 N Mayo Tr • Paintsville, KY 41240-1803
(606) 789-2530 • http://www.johnson.k12.ky.us/
Grade Span: PK-12; Agency Type: 1
Schools: 9
   6 Primary; 1 Middle; 2 High; 0 Other Level
   8 Regular; 0 Special Education; 0 Vocational; 1 Alternative
   0 Magnet; 0 Charter; 9 Title I Eligible; 9 School-wide Title I
Students: 3,825 (51.4% male; 48.5% female)
   Individual Education Program: 638 (16.7%);
   English Language Learner: 0 (0.0%); Migrant: 0 (0.0%)
   Eligible for Free Lunch Program: n/a
   Eligible for Reduced-Price Lunch Program: n/a
Teachers: 240.5 (15.3 to 1)
Librarians/Media Specialists: 5.0 (733.8 to 1)
Guidance Counselors: 7.0 (524.1 to 1)
Current Spending: ($ per student per year):
   Total: $6,376; Instruction: $4,298; Support Services: $1,693

Enrollment, Drop-out Rates and Diploma Recipients by Race/Ethnicity

Category	Total	White	Black	Asian	AIAN	Hisp.
Enrollment (%)	100.0	99.7	0.2	0.1	0.0	0.1
Drop-out Rate (%)	3.0	3.0	0.0	0.0	n/a	n/a
H.S. Diplomas (#)	213	213	0	0	0	0

Kenton County

Covington Independent
25 E 7th St • Covington, KY 41011-2401
Mailing Address: 25 E Seventh St • Covington, KY 41011-2401
(859) 392-1000 • http://www.covington.k12.ky.us/
Grade Span: PK-12; Agency Type: 1
Schools: 11
   7 Primary; 1 Middle; 3 High; 0 Other Level
   9 Regular; 0 Special Education; 0 Vocational; 2 Alternative
   0 Magnet; 0 Charter; 8 Title I Eligible; 8 School-wide Title I
Students: 4,507 (53.3% male; 46.6% female)
   Individual Education Program: 868 (19.3%);
   English Language Learner: 15 (0.3%); Migrant: 0 (0.0%)
   Eligible for Free Lunch Program: n/a
   Eligible for Reduced-Price Lunch Program: n/a
Teachers: 309.7 (13.2 to 1)
Librarians/Media Specialists: 6.0 (681.0 to 1)
Guidance Counselors: 10.9 (374.9 to 1)
Current Spending: ($ per student per year):
   Total: $8,492; Instruction: $4,968; Support Services: $3,114

Enrollment, Drop-out Rates and Diploma Recipients by Race/Ethnicity

Category	Total	White	Black	Asian	AIAN	Hisp.
Enrollment (%)	100.0	72.8	25.6	0.1	1.3	0.1
Drop-out Rate (%)	1.0	1.0	1.2	0.0	0.0	0.0
H.S. Diplomas (#)	200	153	45	2	0	0

Erlanger-Elsmere Independent
500 Graves Ave • Erlanger, KY 41018-1620
(859) 727-2009 • http://www.erlanger.k12.ky.us/
Grade Span: PK-12; Agency Type: 1
Schools: 6
   4 Primary; 1 Middle; 1 High; 0 Other Level
   6 Regular; 0 Special Education; 0 Vocational; 0 Alternative
   0 Magnet; 0 Charter; 3 Title I Eligible; 2 School-wide Title I
Students: 2,240 (53.5% male; 46.4% female)
   Individual Education Program: 373 (16.7%);
   English Language Learner: 61 (2.7%); Migrant: 0 (0.0%)
   Eligible for Free Lunch Program: n/a
   Eligible for Reduced-Price Lunch Program: n/a
Teachers: 140.7 (15.4 to 1)
Librarians/Media Specialists: 4.0 (540.0 to 1)
Guidance Counselors: 5.5 (392.7 to 1)
Current Spending: ($ per student per year):
   Total: $5,865; Instruction: $3,561; Support Services: $2,026

Enrollment, Drop-out Rates and Diploma Recipients by Race/Ethnicity

Category	Total	White	Black	Asian	AIAN	Hisp.
Enrollment (%)	100.0	85.6	10.1	0.4	0.2	3.6
Drop-out Rate (%)	1.9	1.6	4.2	0.0	0.0	0.0
H.S. Diplomas (#)	123	113	8	0	0	2

Kenton County
20 Kenton Lands • Erlanger, KY 41018-1878
Mailing Address: 20 Kenton Lands Rd • Erlanger, KY 41018-1878
(859) 344-8888 • http://www.kenton.k12.ky.us/
Grade Span: PK-12; Agency Type: 1
Schools: 20
   11 Primary; 4 Middle; 5 High; 0 Other Level
   18 Regular; 1 Special Education; 0 Vocational; 1 Alternative
   0 Magnet; 0 Charter; 7 Title I Eligible; 2 School-wide Title I
Students: 12,752 (53.4% male; 46.5% female)
   Individual Education Program: 1,754 (13.8%);
   English Language Learner: 120 (0.9%); Migrant: 0 (0.0%)
   Eligible for Free Lunch Program: n/a
   Eligible for Reduced-Price Lunch Program: n/a
Teachers: 701.8 (17.6 to 1)
Librarians/Media Specialists: 18.1 (682.2 to 1)
Guidance Counselors: 25.0 (493.9 to 1)
Current Spending: ($ per student per year):
   Total: $5,841; Instruction: $3,583; Support Services: $2,002

Enrollment, Drop-out Rates and Diploma Recipients by Race/Ethnicity

Category	Total	White	Black	Asian	AIAN	Hisp.
Enrollment (%)	100.0	97.4	1.1	0.7	0.1	0.8
Drop-out Rate (%)	2.7	2.6	2.2	0.0	0.0	0.0
H.S. Diplomas (#)	758	741	5	3	0	9

Knott County

Knott County
Rt 160 • Hindman, KY 41822-0869
(606) 785-3153 • http://www.knott.k12.ky.us/
Grade Span: PK-12; Agency Type: 1
Schools: 11
   8 Primary; 0 Middle; 3 High; 0 Other Level
   10 Regular; 0 Special Education; 0 Vocational; 1 Alternative

0 Magnet; 0 Charter; 10 Title I Eligible; 10 School-wide Title I
Students: 3,016   (53.7% male; 46.2% female)
  Individual Education Program: 569 (18.9%);
  English Language Learner: 0 (0.0%); Migrant: 0 (0.0%)
  Eligible for Free Lunch Program: n/a
  Eligible for Reduced-Price Lunch Program: n/a
Teachers: 194.2 (14.2 to 1)
Librarians/Media Specialists: 6.9 (399.3 to 1)
Guidance Counselors: 4.0 (688.8 to 1)
Current Spending: ($ per student per year):
  Total: $7,657; Instruction: $5,288; Support Services: $1,956
Enrollment, Drop-out Rates and Diploma Recipients by Race/Ethnicity

Category	Total	White	Black	Asian	AIAN	Hisp.
Enrollment (%)	100.0	98.9	1.0	0.0	0.1	0.0
Drop-out Rate (%)	4.5	4.5	0.0	n/a	n/a	n/a
H.S. Diplomas (#)	178	173	5	0	0	0

Knox County

Knox County
200 Daniel Boone • Barbourvill, KY 40906-1104
Mailing Address: 200 Daniel Boone Dr • Barbourville, KY 40906-1104
(606) 546-3157 • http://www.knox.k12.ky.us/
Grade Span: PK-12; **Agency Type:** 1
Schools: 11
  8 Primary; 0 Middle; 2 High; 1 Other Level
  10 Regular; 0 Special Education; 0 Vocational; 1 Alternative
  0 Magnet; 0 Charter; 8 Title I Eligible; 8 School-wide Title I
Students: 5,197   (52.7% male; 47.2% female)
  Individual Education Program: 880 (16.9%);
  English Language Learner: 0 (0.0%); Migrant: 0 (0.0%)
  Eligible for Free Lunch Program: n/a
  Eligible for Reduced-Price Lunch Program: n/a
Teachers: 320.0 (14.8 to 1)
Librarians/Media Specialists: 10.0 (473.7 to 1)
Guidance Counselors: 8.0 (592.1 to 1)
Current Spending: ($ per student per year):
  Total: $7,073; Instruction: $4,532; Support Services: $2,100
Enrollment, Drop-out Rates and Diploma Recipients by Race/Ethnicity

Category	Total	White	Black	Asian	AIAN	Hisp.
Enrollment (%)	100.0	98.9	0.9	0.1	0.1	0.0
Drop-out Rate (%)	5.6	5.6	0.0	n/a	n/a	0.0
H.S. Diplomas (#)	224	222	2	0	0	0

Larue County

Larue County
2375 Lincoln Farm Rd • Hodgenville, KY 42748-0039
(270) 358-4111 • http://www.larue.k12.ky.us/
Grade Span: KG-12; **Agency Type:** 1
Schools: 6
  3 Primary; 2 Middle; 1 High; 0 Other Level
  6 Regular; 0 Special Education; 0 Vocational; 0 Alternative
  0 Magnet; 0 Charter; 4 Title I Eligible; 4 School-wide Title I
Students: 2,411   (52.5% male; 47.4% female)
  Individual Education Program: 448 (18.6%);
  English Language Learner: 21 (0.9%); Migrant: 58 (2.5%)
  Eligible for Free Lunch Program: n/a
  Eligible for Reduced-Price Lunch Program: n/a
Teachers: 143.6 (16.2 to 1)
Librarians/Media Specialists: 5.0 (464.4 to 1)
Guidance Counselors: 8.0 (290.3 to 1)
Current Spending: ($ per student per year):
  Total: $6,150; Instruction: $3,878; Support Services: $1,918
Enrollment, Drop-out Rates and Diploma Recipients by Race/Ethnicity

Category	Total	White	Black	Asian	AIAN	Hisp.
Enrollment (%)	100.0	93.7	4.5	0.2	0.5	1.2
Drop-out Rate (%)	4.1	3.7	0.0	0.0	0.0	0.0
H.S. Diplomas (#)	168	164	4	0	0	0

Laurel County

Laurel County
275 S Laurel Rd • London, KY 40744-7914
(606) 862-4600 • http://www.laurel.k12.ky.us/
Grade Span: PK-12; **Agency Type:** 1
Schools: 18
  11 Primary; 2 Middle; 2 High; 3 Other Level
  15 Regular; 0 Special Education; 0 Vocational; 3 Alternative
  0 Magnet; 0 Charter; 12 Title I Eligible; 12 School-wide Title I
Students: 9,022   (51.8% male; 48.1% female)
  Individual Education Program: 1,502 (16.6%);
  English Language Learner: 54 (0.6%); Migrant: 0 (0.0%)
  Eligible for Free Lunch Program: n/a
  Eligible for Reduced-Price Lunch Program: n/a

Teachers: 494.5 (17.7 to 1)
Librarians/Media Specialists: 17.0 (514.7 to 1)
Guidance Counselors: 18.2 (480.8 to 1)
Current Spending: ($ per student per year):
  Total: $5,876; Instruction: $3,662; Support Services: $1,868
Enrollment, Drop-out Rates and Diploma Recipients by Race/Ethnicity

Category	Total	White	Black	Asian	AIAN	Hisp.
Enrollment (%)	100.0	98.0	1.0	0.5	0.1	0.3
Drop-out Rate (%)	5.7	5.7	0.0	0.0	0.0	0.0
H.S. Diplomas (#)	458	454	2	0	1	1

Lawrence County

Lawrence County
Hwy 644 • Louisa, KY 41230-0607
(606) 638-9671 • http://www.lawrence.k12.ky.us/
Grade Span: PK-12; **Agency Type:** 1
Schools: 5
  3 Primary; 1 Middle; 1 High; 0 Other Level
  5 Regular; 0 Special Education; 0 Vocational; 0 Alternative
  0 Magnet; 0 Charter; 4 Title I Eligible; 4 School-wide Title I
Students: 2,705   (53.4% male; 46.5% female)
  Individual Education Program: 450 (16.6%);
  English Language Learner: 0 (0.0%); Migrant: 146 (5.6%)
  Eligible for Free Lunch Program: n/a
  Eligible for Reduced-Price Lunch Program: n/a
Teachers: 184.6 (14.1 to 1)
Librarians/Media Specialists: 4.0 (650.3 to 1)
Guidance Counselors: 6.5 (400.2 to 1)
Current Spending: ($ per student per year):
  Total: $6,573; Instruction: $4,239; Support Services: $1,988
Enrollment, Drop-out Rates and Diploma Recipients by Race/Ethnicity

Category	Total	White	Black	Asian	AIAN	Hisp.
Enrollment (%)	100.0	99.6	0.2	0.0	0.1	0.1
Drop-out Rate (%)	3.4	3.4	0.0	n/a	n/a	n/a
H.S. Diplomas (#)	168	166	1	1	0	0

Leslie County

Leslie County
108 Maple St • Hyden, KY 41749-0949
(606) 672-2397 • http://leslie.k12.ky.us/
Grade Span: PK-12; **Agency Type:** 1
Schools: 7
  5 Primary; 1 Middle; 1 High; 0 Other Level
  7 Regular; 0 Special Education; 0 Vocational; 0 Alternative
  0 Magnet; 0 Charter; 6 Title I Eligible; 6 School-wide Title I
Students: 2,250   (53.2% male; 46.7% female)
  Individual Education Program: 407 (18.1%);
  English Language Learner: 0 (0.0%); Migrant: 0 (0.0%)
  Eligible for Free Lunch Program: n/a
  Eligible for Reduced-Price Lunch Program: n/a
Teachers: 135.0 (15.5 to 1)
Librarians/Media Specialists: 5.0 (418.0 to 1)
Guidance Counselors: 4.0 (522.5 to 1)
Current Spending: ($ per student per year):
  Total: $7,262; Instruction: $4,268; Support Services: $2,586
Enrollment, Drop-out Rates and Diploma Recipients by Race/Ethnicity

Category	Total	White	Black	Asian	AIAN	Hisp.
Enrollment (%)	100.0	99.6	0.2	0.0	0.0	0.1
Drop-out Rate (%)	3.0	3.0	n/a	n/a	n/a	n/a
H.S. Diplomas (#)	139	138	0	1	0	0

Letcher County

Letcher County
224 Parks St • Whitesburg, KY 41858-0788
(606) 633-4455 • http://www.letcher.k12.ky.us/
Grade Span: PK-12; **Agency Type:** 1
Schools: 13
  8 Primary; 1 Middle; 4 High; 0 Other Level
  12 Regular; 0 Special Education; 0 Vocational; 1 Alternative
  0 Magnet; 0 Charter; 9 Title I Eligible; 9 School-wide Title I
Students: 3,774   (53.3% male; 46.6% female)
  Individual Education Program: 770 (20.4%);
  English Language Learner: 0 (0.0%); Migrant: 175 (5.0%)
  Eligible for Free Lunch Program: n/a
  Eligible for Reduced-Price Lunch Program: n/a
Teachers: 235.1 (14.8 to 1)
Librarians/Media Specialists: 8.0 (435.1 to 1)
Guidance Counselors: 11.0 (316.5 to 1)
Current Spending: ($ per student per year):
  Total: $7,363; Instruction: $4,266; Support Services: $2,722

Enrollment, Drop-out Rates and Diploma Recipients by Race/Ethnicity

Category	Total	White	Black	Asian	AIAN	Hisp.
Enrollment (%)	100.0	98.9	0.2	0.1	0.8	0.0
Drop-out Rate (%)	5.1	5.2	0.0	0.0	0.0	n/a
H.S. Diplomas (#)	196	196	0	0	0	0

Lewis County

Lewis County
520 Plummer Ln • Vanceburg, KY 41179-0159
(606) 796-2811 • http://www.lewis.k12.ky.us/
Grade Span: PK-12; **Agency Type:** 1
Schools: 7
    4 Primary; 1 Middle; 2 High; 0 Other Level
    6 Regular; 0 Special Education; 1 Vocational; 0 Alternative
    0 Magnet; 0 Charter; 5 Title I Eligible; 5 School-wide Title I
Students: 2,655   (52.9% male; 47.0% female)
    Individual Education Program: 427 (16.1%);
    English Language Learner: 0 (0.0%); Migrant: 138 (5.7%)
    Eligible for Free Lunch Program: n/a
    Eligible for Reduced-Price Lunch Program: n/a
Teachers: 172.1 (14.0 to 1)
Librarians/Media Specialists: 3.5 (687.1 to 1)
Guidance Counselors: 4.0 (601.3 to 1)
Current Spending: ($ per student per year):
    Total: $6,663; Instruction: $4,101; Support Services: $2,176
Enrollment, Drop-out Rates and Diploma Recipients by Race/Ethnicity

Category	Total	White	Black	Asian	AIAN	Hisp.
Enrollment (%)	100.0	99.5	0.2	0.0	0.2	0.0
Drop-out Rate (%)	4.0	4.0	0.0	n/a	0.0	n/a
H.S. Diplomas (#)	142	142	0	0	0	0

Lincoln County

Lincoln County
305 Danville Ave • Stanford, KY 40484-0265
(606) 365-2124 • http://www.lincoln.k12.ky.us/
Grade Span: PK-12; **Agency Type:** 1
Schools: 10
    7 Primary; 1 Middle; 2 High; 0 Other Level
    9 Regular; 0 Special Education; 0 Vocational; 1 Alternative
    0 Magnet; 0 Charter; 7 Title I Eligible; 7 School-wide Title I
Students: 4,537   (52.5% male; 47.4% female)
    Individual Education Program: 949 (20.9%);
    English Language Learner: 14 (0.3%); Migrant: 101 (2.4%)
    Eligible for Free Lunch Program: n/a
    Eligible for Reduced-Price Lunch Program: n/a
Teachers: 297.6 (14.2 to 1)
Librarians/Media Specialists: 8.0 (529.9 to 1)
Guidance Counselors: 7.0 (605.6 to 1)
Current Spending: ($ per student per year):
    Total: $7,733; Instruction: $5,406; Support Services: $1,903
Enrollment, Drop-out Rates and Diploma Recipients by Race/Ethnicity

Category	Total	White	Black	Asian	AIAN	Hisp.
Enrollment (%)	100.0	96.3	2.7	0.0	0.1	0.9
Drop-out Rate (%)	6.8	6.9	0.0	0.0	n/a	0.0
H.S. Diplomas (#)	214	205	8	0	0	1

Logan County

Logan County
2222 Bowling Green Rd • Russellville, KY 42276-0417
(270) 726-2436 • http://www.logan.k12.ky.us/
Grade Span: PK-12; **Agency Type:** 1
Schools: 6
    5 Primary; 0 Middle; 1 High; 0 Other Level
    6 Regular; 0 Special Education; 0 Vocational; 0 Alternative
    0 Magnet; 0 Charter; 5 Title I Eligible; 5 School-wide Title I
Students: 3,532   (50.7% male; 49.2% female)
    Individual Education Program: 643 (18.2%);
    English Language Learner: 0 (0.0%); Migrant: 80 (2.4%)
    Eligible for Free Lunch Program: n/a
    Eligible for Reduced-Price Lunch Program: n/a
Teachers: 215.7 (15.5 to 1)
Librarians/Media Specialists: 6.0 (555.5 to 1)
Guidance Counselors: 6.0 (555.5 to 1)
Current Spending: ($ per student per year):
    Total: $6,852; Instruction: $4,549; Support Services: $1,915
Enrollment, Drop-out Rates and Diploma Recipients by Race/Ethnicity

Category	Total	White	Black	Asian	AIAN	Hisp.
Enrollment (%)	100.0	96.3	3.2	0.1	0.0	0.4
Drop-out Rate (%)	2.2	2.2	0.0	0.0	0.0	0.0
H.S. Diplomas (#)	225	212	11	0	0	2

Madison County

Madison County
550 S Keeneland Dr • Richmond, KY 40475-0768
(859) 624-4500 • http://www.madison.k12.ky.us/
Grade Span: PK-12; **Agency Type:** 1
Schools: 18
    10 Primary; 4 Middle; 3 High; 1 Other Level
    17 Regular; 0 Special Education; 0 Vocational; 1 Alternative
    0 Magnet; 0 Charter; 12 Title I Eligible; 12 School-wide Title I
Students: 10,067   (51.2% male; 48.7% female)
    Individual Education Program: 2,009 (20.0%);
    English Language Learner: 47 (0.5%); Migrant: 490 (5.1%)
    Eligible for Free Lunch Program: n/a
    Eligible for Reduced-Price Lunch Program: n/a
Teachers: 578.6 (16.6 to 1)
Librarians/Media Specialists: 15.0 (640.9 to 1)
Guidance Counselors: 19.4 (495.5 to 1)
Current Spending: ($ per student per year):
    Total: $5,943; Instruction: $3,886; Support Services: $1,767
Enrollment, Drop-out Rates and Diploma Recipients by Race/Ethnicity

Category	Total	White	Black	Asian	AIAN	Hisp.
Enrollment (%)	100.0	92.3	5.8	0.7	0.2	1.0
Drop-out Rate (%)	1.6	1.4	0.0	0.0	0.0	0.0
H.S. Diplomas (#)	442	412	25	1	0	4

Magoffin County

Magoffin County
Gardner Tr • Salyersville, KY 41465-0109
(606) 349-6117 • http://www.magoffin.k12.ky.us/
Grade Span: PK-12; **Agency Type:** 1
Schools: 8
    6 Primary; 1 Middle; 1 High; 0 Other Level
    8 Regular; 0 Special Education; 0 Vocational; 0 Alternative
    0 Magnet; 0 Charter; 7 Title I Eligible; 7 School-wide Title I
Students: 2,542   (51.7% male; 48.2% female)
    Individual Education Program: 430 (16.9%);
    English Language Learner: 0 (0.0%); Migrant: 0 (0.0%)
    Eligible for Free Lunch Program: n/a
    Eligible for Reduced-Price Lunch Program: n/a
Teachers: 166.5 (14.3 to 1)
Librarians/Media Specialists: 6.5 (365.1 to 1)
Guidance Counselors: 4.0 (593.3 to 1)
Current Spending: ($ per student per year):
    Total: $7,151; Instruction: $4,223; Support Services: $2,474
Enrollment, Drop-out Rates and Diploma Recipients by Race/Ethnicity

Category	Total	White	Black	Asian	AIAN	Hisp.
Enrollment (%)	100.0	99.8	0.0	0.0	0.0	0.1
Drop-out Rate (%)	5.3	5.3	n/a	n/a	n/a	n/a
H.S. Diplomas (#)	160	160	0	0	0	0

Marion County

Marion County
755 E Main St • Lebanon, KY 40033-1518
(270) 692-3721 • http://www.marion.k12.ky.us/
Grade Span: PK-12; **Agency Type:** 1
Schools: 7
    4 Primary; 2 Middle; 1 High; 0 Other Level
    7 Regular; 0 Special Education; 0 Vocational; 0 Alternative
    0 Magnet; 0 Charter; 6 Title I Eligible; 6 School-wide Title I
Students: 3,182   (51.7% male; 48.2% female)
    Individual Education Program: 535 (16.8%);
    English Language Learner: 32 (1.0%); Migrant: 91 (3.0%)
    Eligible for Free Lunch Program: n/a
    Eligible for Reduced-Price Lunch Program: n/a
Teachers: 200.3 (15.1 to 1)
Librarians/Media Specialists: 5.0 (604.0 to 1)
Guidance Counselors: 8.0 (377.5 to 1)
Current Spending: ($ per student per year):
    Total: $6,628; Instruction: $4,215; Support Services: $1,967
Enrollment, Drop-out Rates and Diploma Recipients by Race/Ethnicity

Category	Total	White	Black	Asian	AIAN	Hisp.
Enrollment (%)	100.0	90.1	7.8	0.8	0.0	1.2
Drop-out Rate (%)	4.1	4.3	2.7	0.0	n/a	0.0
H.S. Diplomas (#)	202	181	19	2	0	0

Marshall County

Marshall County
86 High School Rd • Benton, KY 42025-7017
(270) 527-8628 • http://www.marshall.k12.ky.us/
Grade Span: PK-12; **Agency Type:** 1
Schools: 11

6 Primary; 3 Middle; 2 High; 0 Other Level
10 Regular; 0 Special Education; 1 Vocational; 0 Alternative
0 Magnet; 0 Charter; 7 Title I Eligible; 6 School-wide Title I
Students: 4,782   (51.7% male; 48.2% female)
   Individual Education Program: 620 (13.0%);
   English Language Learner: 8 (0.2%); Migrant: 122 (2.7%)
   Eligible for Free Lunch Program: n/a
   Eligible for Reduced-Price Lunch Program: n/a
Teachers: 307.2 (15.0 to 1)
Librarians/Media Specialists: 9.0 (510.7 to 1)
Guidance Counselors: 13.0 (353.5 to 1)
Current Spending: ($ per student per year):
   Total: $6,029; Instruction: $4,012; Support Services: $1,674
Enrollment, Drop-out Rates and Diploma Recipients by Race/Ethnicity

Category	Total	White	Black	Asian	AIAN	Hisp.
Enrollment (%)	100.0	99.6	0.1	0.1	0.0	0.2
Drop-out Rate (%)	2.5	2.5	n/a	0.0	0.0	0.0
H.S. Diplomas (#)	272	271	0	1	0	0

Martin County

Martin County
Rt 40 • Inez, KY 41224-0366
(606) 298-3572 • http://www.martin.k12.ky.us/
Grade Span: PK-12; **Agency Type:** 1
Schools: 8
   5 Primary; 2 Middle; 1 High; 0 Other Level
   8 Regular; 0 Special Education; 0 Vocational; 0 Alternative
   0 Magnet; 0 Charter; 7 Title I Eligible; 7 School-wide Title I
Students: 2,494   (56.1% male; 43.8% female)
   Individual Education Program: 491 (19.7%);
   English Language Learner: 0 (0.0%); Migrant: 64 (2.7%)
   Eligible for Free Lunch Program: n/a
   Eligible for Reduced-Price Lunch Program: n/a
Teachers: 163.0 (14.4 to 1)
Librarians/Media Specialists: 4.0 (585.0 to 1)
Guidance Counselors: 6.5 (360.0 to 1)
Current Spending: ($ per student per year):
   Total: $7,370; Instruction: $4,341; Support Services: $2,608
Enrollment, Drop-out Rates and Diploma Recipients by Race/Ethnicity

Category	Total	White	Black	Asian	AIAN	Hisp.
Enrollment (%)	100.0	99.4	0.5	0.0	0.0	0.0
Drop-out Rate (%)	5.7	5.7	0.0	n/a	n/a	n/a
H.S. Diplomas (#)	154	153	0	1	0	0

Mason County

Mason County
2nd And Limestone • Maysville, KY 41056-0099
(606) 564-5563 • http://www.mason.k12.ky.us/
Grade Span: PK-12; **Agency Type:** 1
Schools: 4
   1 Primary; 2 Middle; 1 High; 0 Other Level
   4 Regular; 0 Special Education; 0 Vocational; 0 Alternative
   0 Magnet; 0 Charter; 3 Title I Eligible; 3 School-wide Title I
Students: 2,955   (53.5% male; 46.4% female)
   Individual Education Program: 424 (14.3%);
   English Language Learner: 15 (0.5%); Migrant: 100 (3.7%)
   Eligible for Free Lunch Program: n/a
   Eligible for Reduced-Price Lunch Program: n/a
Teachers: 177.8 (15.2 to 1)
Librarians/Media Specialists: 4.0 (677.0 to 1)
Guidance Counselors: 8.0 (338.5 to 1)
Current Spending: ($ per student per year):
   Total: $6,226; Instruction: $4,044; Support Services: $1,863
Enrollment, Drop-out Rates and Diploma Recipients by Race/Ethnicity

Category	Total	White	Black	Asian	AIAN	Hisp.
Enrollment (%)	100.0	89.1	9.1	0.8	0.2	0.7
Drop-out Rate (%)	2.8	2.8	2.3	0.0	0.0	0.0
H.S. Diplomas (#)	171	148	22	0	0	1

Mccracken County

Mccracken County
260 Bleich Rd • Paducah, KY 42003-5573
(270) 744-4000 • http://www.mccracken.k12.ky.us/
Grade Span: PK-12; **Agency Type:** 1
Schools: 15
   6 Primary; 3 Middle; 3 High; 3 Other Level
   12 Regular; 0 Special Education; 0 Vocational; 3 Alternative
   0 Magnet; 0 Charter; 9 Title I Eligible; 6 School-wide Title I
Students: 6,902   (52.0% male; 47.9% female)
   Individual Education Program: 1,010 (14.6%);
   English Language Learner: 23 (0.3%); Migrant: 261 (3.9%)
   Eligible for Free Lunch Program: n/a

Eligible for Reduced-Price Lunch Program: n/a
Teachers: 381.8 (17.4 to 1)
Librarians/Media Specialists: 12.0 (554.3 to 1)
Guidance Counselors: 15.0 (443.5 to 1)
Current Spending: ($ per student per year):
   Total: $6,080; Instruction: $3,924; Support Services: $1,778
Enrollment, Drop-out Rates and Diploma Recipients by Race/Ethnicity

Category	Total	White	Black	Asian	AIAN	Hisp.
Enrollment (%)	100.0	94.3	3.5	0.5	0.4	1.3
Drop-out Rate (%)	1.7	1.7	1.8	0.0	0.0	0.0
H.S. Diplomas (#)	436	426	5	2	1	2

Paducah Independent
800 Caldwell St • Paducah, KY 42002-2550
(270) 444-5600 • http://www.paducah.k12.ky.us/
Grade Span: PK-12; **Agency Type:** 1
Schools: 7
   5 Primary; 1 Middle; 1 High; 0 Other Level
   7 Regular; 0 Special Education; 0 Vocational; 0 Alternative
   0 Magnet; 0 Charter; 6 Title I Eligible; 6 School-wide Title I
Students: 3,201   (50.8% male; 49.1% female)
   Individual Education Program: 427 (13.3%);
   English Language Learner: 39 (1.2%); Migrant: 23 (0.8%)
   Eligible for Free Lunch Program: n/a
   Eligible for Reduced-Price Lunch Program: n/a
Teachers: 232.2 (12.6 to 1)
Librarians/Media Specialists: 6.2 (472.4 to 1)
Guidance Counselors: 7.0 (418.4 to 1)
Current Spending: ($ per student per year):
   Total: $7,798; Instruction: $4,749; Support Services: $2,608
Enrollment, Drop-out Rates and Diploma Recipients by Race/Ethnicity

Category	Total	White	Black	Asian	AIAN	Hisp.
Enrollment (%)	100.0	47.5	49.8	0.6	1.8	0.3
Drop-out Rate (%)	6.0	6.0	6.3	0.0	0.0	0.0
H.S. Diplomas (#)	153	96	52	3	0	2

Mccreary County

Mccreary County
120 Raider Way • Stearns, KY 42647-9715
(606) 376-2591 • http://www.mccreary.k12.ky.us/
Grade Span: PK-12; **Agency Type:** 1
Schools: 11
   6 Primary; 2 Middle; 2 High; 1 Other Level
   9 Regular; 0 Special Education; 0 Vocational; 2 Alternative
   0 Magnet; 0 Charter; 6 Title I Eligible; 6 School-wide Title I
Students: 3,412   (51.4% male; 48.5% female)
   Individual Education Program: 622 (18.2%);
   English Language Learner: 0 (0.0%); Migrant: 0 (0.0%)
   Eligible for Free Lunch Program: n/a
   Eligible for Reduced-Price Lunch Program: n/a
Teachers: 235.5 (13.8 to 1)
Librarians/Media Specialists: 6.0 (541.2 to 1)
Guidance Counselors: 7.0 (463.9 to 1)
Current Spending: ($ per student per year):
   Total: $7,256; Instruction: $4,610; Support Services: $2,249
Enrollment, Drop-out Rates and Diploma Recipients by Race/Ethnicity

Category	Total	White	Black	Asian	AIAN	Hisp.
Enrollment (%)	100.0	98.6	1.0	0.0	0.1	0.2
Drop-out Rate (%)	4.3	4.5	0.0	n/a	n/a	0.0
H.S. Diplomas (#)	170	170	0	0	0	0

Mclean County

Mclean County
283 Main St • Calhoun, KY 42327-0245
(270) 273-5257 • http://www.mclean.k12.ky.us/
Grade Span: KG-12; **Agency Type:** 1
Schools: 5
   3 Primary; 1 Middle; 1 High; 0 Other Level
   5 Regular; 0 Special Education; 0 Vocational; 0 Alternative
   0 Magnet; 0 Charter; 3 Title I Eligible; 3 School-wide Title I
Students: 1,672   (51.1% male; 48.8% female)
   Individual Education Program: 249 (14.9%);
   English Language Learner: 0 (0.0%); Migrant: 111 (7.1%)
   Eligible for Free Lunch Program: n/a
   Eligible for Reduced-Price Lunch Program: n/a
Teachers: 105.6 (14.9 to 1)
Librarians/Media Specialists: 3.0 (524.3 to 1)
Guidance Counselors: 2.5 (629.2 to 1)
Current Spending: ($ per student per year):
   Total: $5,988; Instruction: $3,481; Support Services: $2,126

Enrollment, Drop-out Rates and Diploma Recipients by Race/Ethnicity

Category	Total	White	Black	Asian	AIAN	Hisp.
Enrollment (%)	100.0	99.4	0.3	0.0	0.0	0.4
Drop-out Rate (%)	2.2	2.2	n/a	n/a	0.0	n/a
H.S. Diplomas (#)	93	93	0	0	0	0

Meade County

Meade County
1155 Old Ekron Rd • Brandenburg, KY 40108-0337
(270) 422-7500 • http://www.meade.k12.ky.us/
Grade Span: PK-12; **Agency Type:** 1
Schools: 10
  7 Primary; 1 Middle; 2 High; 0 Other Level
  9 Regular; 0 Special Education; 0 Vocational; 1 Alternative
  0 Magnet; 0 Charter; 7 Title I Eligible; 7 School-wide Title I
Students: 4,809 (51.8% male; 48.1% female)
  Individual Education Program: 748 (15.6%);
  English Language Learner: 3 (0.1%); Migrant: 38 (0.8%)
  Eligible for Free Lunch Program: n/a
  Eligible for Reduced-Price Lunch Program: n/a
Teachers: 265.3 (17.3 to 1)
Librarians/Media Specialists: 7.0 (657.1 to 1)
Guidance Counselors: 10.6 (434.0 to 1)
Current Spending: ($ per student per year):
  Total: $5,772; Instruction: $3,686; Support Services: $1,742

Enrollment, Drop-out Rates and Diploma Recipients by Race/Ethnicity

Category	Total	White	Black	Asian	AIAN	Hisp.
Enrollment (%)	100.0	95.6	2.4	0.7	0.4	0.8
Drop-out Rate (%)	3.2	3.2	2.2	0.0	0.0	0.0
H.S. Diplomas (#)	336	319	11	3	2	1

Mercer County

Mercer County
961 Moberly Rd • Harrodsburg, KY 40330-9104
(859) 734-4364 • http://www.mercer.k12.ky.us/
Grade Span: PK-12; **Agency Type:** 1
Schools: 4
  1 Primary; 1 Middle; 1 High; 1 Other Level
  3 Regular; 0 Special Education; 0 Vocational; 1 Alternative
  0 Magnet; 0 Charter; 2 Title I Eligible; 0 School-wide Title I
Students: 2,318 (54.4% male; 45.5% female)
  Individual Education Program: 376 (16.2%);
  English Language Learner: 10 (0.4%); Migrant: 7 (0.3%)
  Eligible for Free Lunch Program: n/a
  Eligible for Reduced-Price Lunch Program: n/a
Teachers: 145.2 (15.6 to 1)
Librarians/Media Specialists: 3.0 (752.7 to 1)
Guidance Counselors: 4.0 (564.5 to 1)
Current Spending: ($ per student per year):
  Total: $5,681; Instruction: $3,544; Support Services: $1,875

Enrollment, Drop-out Rates and Diploma Recipients by Race/Ethnicity

Category	Total	White	Black	Asian	AIAN	Hisp.
Enrollment (%)	100.0	98.0	0.6	1.0	0.0	0.4
Drop-out Rate (%)	1.4	1.4	0.0	n/a	n/a	0.0
H.S. Diplomas (#)	149	149	0	0	0	0

Metcalfe County

Metcalfe County
1007 W Stockton • Edmonton, KY 42129-8127
(270) 432-3171 • http://www.metcalfe.k12.ky.us/
Grade Span: PK-12; **Agency Type:** 1
Schools: 5
  3 Primary; 1 Middle; 1 High; 0 Other Level
  5 Regular; 0 Special Education; 0 Vocational; 0 Alternative
  0 Magnet; 0 Charter; 3 Title I Eligible; 3 School-wide Title I
Students: 1,709 (53.5% male; 46.4% female)
  Individual Education Program: 265 (15.5%);
  English Language Learner: 0 (0.0%); Migrant: 214 (13.0%)
  Eligible for Free Lunch Program: n/a
  Eligible for Reduced-Price Lunch Program: n/a
Teachers: 119.9 (13.7 to 1)
Librarians/Media Specialists: 3.3 (497.6 to 1)
Guidance Counselors: 4.0 (410.5 to 1)
Current Spending: ($ per student per year):
  Total: $7,143; Instruction: $4,233; Support Services: $2,479

Enrollment, Drop-out Rates and Diploma Recipients by Race/Ethnicity

Category	Total	White	Black	Asian	AIAN	Hisp.
Enrollment (%)	100.0	98.3	1.4	0.1	0.1	0.2
Drop-out Rate (%)	3.0	2.8	0.0	n/a	n/a	0.0
H.S. Diplomas (#)	87	83	4	0	0	0

Monroe County

Monroe County
1209 N Main St • Tompkinsville, KY 42167-0518
(270) 487-5456 • http://www.monroe.k12.ky.us/
Grade Span: PK-12; **Agency Type:** 1
Schools: 5
  3 Primary; 1 Middle; 1 High; 0 Other Level
  5 Regular; 0 Special Education; 0 Vocational; 0 Alternative
  0 Magnet; 0 Charter; 4 Title I Eligible; 3 School-wide Title I
Students: 2,090 (54.3% male; 45.6% female)
  Individual Education Program: 312 (14.9%);
  English Language Learner: 23 (1.1%); Migrant: 219 (11.0%)
  Eligible for Free Lunch Program: n/a
  Eligible for Reduced-Price Lunch Program: n/a
Teachers: 142.6 (13.9 to 1)
Librarians/Media Specialists: 5.3 (374.3 to 1)
Guidance Counselors: 4.7 (422.1 to 1)
Current Spending: ($ per student per year):
  Total: $6,586; Instruction: $4,034; Support Services: $2,141

Enrollment, Drop-out Rates and Diploma Recipients by Race/Ethnicity

Category	Total	White	Black	Asian	AIAN	Hisp.
Enrollment (%)	100.0	93.9	4.5	0.0	0.1	1.6
Drop-out Rate (%)	2.6	2.8	0.0	n/a	n/a	0.0
H.S. Diplomas (#)	128	120	7	0	0	1

Montgomery County

Montgomery County
212 N Maysville • Mt Sterling, KY 40353-9504
Mailing Address: 212 N Maysville St • Mt Sterling, KY 40353-9504
(859) 497-8760 • http://www.montgomery.k12.ky.us/
Grade Span: PK-12; **Agency Type:** 1
Schools: 9
  4 Primary; 1 Middle; 2 High; 2 Other Level
  6 Regular; 0 Special Education; 0 Vocational; 3 Alternative
  0 Magnet; 0 Charter; 4 Title I Eligible; 4 School-wide Title I
Students: 4,231 (51.1% male; 48.8% female)
  Individual Education Program: 580 (13.7%);
  English Language Learner: 33 (0.8%); Migrant: 389 (9.7%)
  Eligible for Free Lunch Program: n/a
  Eligible for Reduced-Price Lunch Program: n/a
Teachers: 266.3 (15.1 to 1)
Librarians/Media Specialists: 5.0 (801.6 to 1)
Guidance Counselors: 11.0 (364.4 to 1)
Current Spending: ($ per student per year):
  Total: $5,969; Instruction: $3,861; Support Services: $1,763

Enrollment, Drop-out Rates and Diploma Recipients by Race/Ethnicity

Category	Total	White	Black	Asian	AIAN	Hisp.
Enrollment (%)	100.0	95.6	2.5	0.3	0.0	1.5
Drop-out Rate (%)	3.4	3.6	0.0	n/a	n/a	0.0
H.S. Diplomas (#)	221	211	8	0	0	2

Morgan County

Morgan County
496 Prestonsburg St • West Liberty, KY 41472-0489
(606) 743-8002 • http://www.morgan.k12.ky.us/
Grade Span: KG-12; **Agency Type:** 1
Schools: 8
  5 Primary; 1 Middle; 2 High; 0 Other Level
  7 Regular; 0 Special Education; 0 Vocational; 1 Alternative
  0 Magnet; 0 Charter; 7 Title I Eligible; 7 School-wide Title I
Students: 2,441 (53.2% male; 46.7% female)
  Individual Education Program: 457 (18.7%);
  English Language Learner: 2 (0.1%); Migrant: 76 (3.4%)
  Eligible for Free Lunch Program: n/a
  Eligible for Reduced-Price Lunch Program: n/a
Teachers: 163.2 (13.6 to 1)
Librarians/Media Specialists: 4.6 (481.7 to 1)
Guidance Counselors: 2.0 (1,108.0 to 1)
Current Spending: ($ per student per year):
  Total: $6,268; Instruction: $3,804; Support Services: $2,041

Enrollment, Drop-out Rates and Diploma Recipients by Race/Ethnicity

Category	Total	White	Black	Asian	AIAN	Hisp.
Enrollment (%)	100.0	99.1	0.7	0.1	0.0	0.0
Drop-out Rate (%)	4.6	4.7	0.0	n/a	n/a	n/a
H.S. Diplomas (#)	126	126	0	0	0	0

Muhlenberg County

Muhlenberg County
510 W Main St • Greenville, KY 42345-0167
(270) 338-2871 • http://www.mberg.k12.ky.us/
Grade Span: PK-12; **Agency Type:** 1
Schools: 14
   8 Primary; 2 Middle; 3 High; 1 Other Level
   12 Regular; 0 Special Education; 0 Vocational; 2 Alternative
   0 Magnet; 0 Charter; 8 Title I Eligible; 8 School-wide Title I
Students: 5,376   (51.2% male; 48.7% female)
   Individual Education Program: 967 (18.0%);
   English Language Learner: 4 (0.1%); Migrant: 205 (4.1%)
   Eligible for Free Lunch Program: n/a
   Eligible for Reduced-Price Lunch Program: n/a
Teachers: 361.0 (14.0 to 1)
Librarians/Media Specialists: 11.5 (439.7 to 1)
Guidance Counselors: 13.5 (374.6 to 1)
Current Spending: ($ per student per year):
   Total: $6,545; Instruction: $4,280; Support Services: $1,896
Enrollment, Drop-out Rates and Diploma Recipients by Race/Ethnicity

Category	Total	White	Black	Asian	AIAN	Hisp.
Enrollment (%)	100.0	94.9	4.5	0.2	0.0	0.4
Drop-out Rate (%)	3.5	3.7	0.0	0.0	n/a	0.0
H.S. Diplomas (#)	321	307	12	1	0	1

Nelson County

Bardstown Ind
308 N 5th • Bardstown, KY 40004-1406
(502) 331-8800 • http://www.btown.k12.ky.us/
Grade Span: PK-12; **Agency Type:** 1
Schools: 6
   4 Primary; 1 Middle; 1 High; 0 Other Level
   6 Regular; 0 Special Education; 0 Vocational; 0 Alternative
   0 Magnet; 0 Charter; 1 Title I Eligible; 1 School-wide Title I
Students: 2,110   (51.4% male; 48.5% female)
   Individual Education Program: 322 (15.3%);
   English Language Learner: 11 (0.5%); Migrant: 0 (0.0%)
   Eligible for Free Lunch Program: n/a
   Eligible for Reduced-Price Lunch Program: n/a
Teachers: 127.0 (15.6 to 1)
Librarians/Media Specialists: 3.0 (661.7 to 1)
Guidance Counselors: 5.0 (397.0 to 1)
Current Spending: ($ per student per year):
   Total: $6,638; Instruction: $4,123; Support Services: $2,151
Enrollment, Drop-out Rates and Diploma Recipients by Race/Ethnicity

Category	Total	White	Black	Asian	AIAN	Hisp.
Enrollment (%)	100.0	74.8	22.3	1.4	0.3	1.3
Drop-out Rate (%)	3.9	4.5	2.3	0.0	0.0	0.0
H.S. Diplomas (#)	111	70	40	1	0	0

Nelson County
1200 Cardinal • Bardstown, KY 40004-1740
Mailing Address: 1200 Cardinal Dr • Bardstown, KY 40004-5277
(502) 349-7000 • http://www.nelson.k12.ky.us/
Grade Span: PK-12; **Agency Type:** 1
Schools: 10
   6 Primary; 2 Middle; 2 High; 0 Other Level
   9 Regular; 0 Special Education; 0 Vocational; 1 Alternative
   0 Magnet; 0 Charter; 6 Title I Eligible; 4 School-wide Title I
Students: 4,888   (51.0% male; 48.9% female)
   Individual Education Program: 769 (15.7%);
   English Language Learner: 0 (0.0%); Migrant: 0 (0.0%)
   Eligible for Free Lunch Program: n/a
   Eligible for Reduced-Price Lunch Program: n/a
Teachers: 284.7 (16.5 to 1)
Librarians/Media Specialists: 8.8 (534.7 to 1)
Guidance Counselors: 10.5 (448.1 to 1)
Current Spending: ($ per student per year):
   Total: $5,861; Instruction: $3,541; Support Services: $1,998
Enrollment, Drop-out Rates and Diploma Recipients by Race/Ethnicity

Category	Total	White	Black	Asian	AIAN	Hisp.
Enrollment (%)	100.0	97.2	1.8	0.4	0.0	0.6
Drop-out Rate (%)	2.0	2.1	0.0	0.0	0.0	0.0
H.S. Diplomas (#)	312	304	6	2	0	0

Ohio County

Ohio County
315 E Union St • Hartford, KY 42347-0070
(270) 298-3249 • http://www.ohio.k12.ky.us/
Grade Span: PK-12; **Agency Type:** 1
Schools: 10
   6 Primary; 1 Middle; 3 High; 0 Other Level
   8 Regular; 0 Special Education; 0 Vocational; 2 Alternative
   0 Magnet; 0 Charter; 7 Title I Eligible; 7 School-wide Title I
Students: 4,188   (52.3% male; 47.6% female)
   Individual Education Program: 699 (16.7%);
   English Language Learner: 32 (0.8%); Migrant: 171 (4.3%)
   Eligible for Free Lunch Program: n/a
   Eligible for Reduced-Price Lunch Program: n/a
Teachers: 252.5 (15.6 to 1)
Librarians/Media Specialists: 6.0 (655.8 to 1)
Guidance Counselors: 4.5 (874.4 to 1)
Current Spending: ($ per student per year):
   Total: $7,128; Instruction: $4,338; Support Services: $2,367
Enrollment, Drop-out Rates and Diploma Recipients by Race/Ethnicity

Category	Total	White	Black	Asian	AIAN	Hisp.
Enrollment (%)	100.0	98.1	0.6	0.1	0.0	1.2
Drop-out Rate (%)	2.6	2.7	0.0	n/a	0.0	0.0
H.S. Diplomas (#)	254	248	1	1	1	3

Oldham County

Oldham County
1350 N Hwy 393 • Buckner, KY 40010-0218
(502) 222-8880 • http://www.oldham.k12.ky.us/
Grade Span: PK-12; **Agency Type:** 1
Schools: 17
   9 Primary; 3 Middle; 4 High; 1 Other Level
   14 Regular; 0 Special Education; 1 Vocational; 2 Alternative
   0 Magnet; 0 Charter; 4 Title I Eligible; 1 School-wide Title I
Students: 10,204   (51.4% male; 48.5% female)
   Individual Education Program: 1,458 (14.3%);
   English Language Learner: 225 (2.2%); Migrant: 68 (0.7%)
   Eligible for Free Lunch Program: n/a
   Eligible for Reduced-Price Lunch Program: n/a
Teachers: 582.3 (17.1 to 1)
Librarians/Media Specialists: 16.5 (602.7 to 1)
Guidance Counselors: 23.5 (423.2 to 1)
Current Spending: ($ per student per year):
   Total: $5,894; Instruction: $3,698; Support Services: $1,947
Enrollment, Drop-out Rates and Diploma Recipients by Race/Ethnicity

Category	Total	White	Black	Asian	AIAN	Hisp.
Enrollment (%)	100.0	94.6	2.8	0.6	0.2	1.7
Drop-out Rate (%)	1.1	1.1	2.4	0.0	0.0	0.0
H.S. Diplomas (#)	606	584	17	2	0	3

Owen County

Owen County
1600 Hwy 22e • Owenton, KY 40359-9042
Mailing Address: 1600 Hwy 22 E • Owenton, KY 40359-9042
(502) 484-3934 • http://www.owen.k12.ky.us/
Grade Span: PK-12; **Agency Type:** 1
Schools: 4
   2 Primary; 1 Middle; 1 High; 0 Other Level
   4 Regular; 0 Special Education; 0 Vocational; 0 Alternative
   0 Magnet; 0 Charter; 3 Title I Eligible; 3 School-wide Title I
Students: 1,992   (53.5% male; 46.4% female)
   Individual Education Program: 248 (12.4%);
   English Language Learner: 11 (0.6%); Migrant: 121 (6.3%)
   Eligible for Free Lunch Program: n/a
   Eligible for Reduced-Price Lunch Program: n/a
Teachers: 106.0 (18.0 to 1)
Librarians/Media Specialists: 4.0 (476.8 to 1)
Guidance Counselors: 3.0 (635.7 to 1)
Current Spending: ($ per student per year):
   Total: $5,941; Instruction: $3,475; Support Services: $2,104
Enrollment, Drop-out Rates and Diploma Recipients by Race/Ethnicity

Category	Total	White	Black	Asian	AIAN	Hisp.
Enrollment (%)	100.0	97.4	0.8	0.1	0.4	1.3
Drop-out Rate (%)	6.9	6.4	0.0	0.0	0.0	0.0
H.S. Diplomas (#)	104	100	2	0	0	2

Pendleton County

Pendleton County
2525 Hwy 27 N • Falmouth, KY 41040-9805
(859) 654-6911
Grade Span: PK-12; **Agency Type:** 1
Schools: 4
   2 Primary; 1 Middle; 1 High; 0 Other Level
   4 Regular; 0 Special Education; 0 Vocational; 0 Alternative
   0 Magnet; 0 Charter; 2 Title I Eligible; 1 School-wide Title I
Students: 2,972   (52.3% male; 47.6% female)
   Individual Education Program: 413 (13.9%);
   English Language Learner: 12 (0.4%); Migrant: 453 (16.0%)
   Eligible for Free Lunch Program: n/a

Eligible for Reduced-Price Lunch Program: n/a
Teachers: 178.7 (15.8 to 1)
Librarians/Media Specialists: 4.0 (707.8 to 1)
Guidance Counselors: 5.0 (566.2 to 1)
Current Spending: ($ per student per year):
  Total: $5,691; Instruction: $3,504; Support Services: $1,849
Enrollment, Drop-out Rates and Diploma Recipients by Race/Ethnicity

Category	Total	White	Black	Asian	AIAN	Hisp.
Enrollment (%)	100.0	98.5	0.9	0.0	0.1	0.5
Drop-out Rate (%)	1.9	1.9	0.0	n/a	0.0	0.0
H.S. Diplomas (#)	155	155	0	0	0	0

Perry County

Perry County
315 Park Ave • Hazard, KY 41701-9548
(606) 439-5814 • http://www.perry.k12.ky.us/
Grade Span: PK-12; **Agency Type:** 1
Schools: 14
  11 Primary; 0 Middle; 3 High; 0 Other Level
  13 Regular; 0 Special Education; 0 Vocational; 1 Alternative
  0 Magnet; 0 Charter; 12 Title I Eligible; 12 School-wide Title I
Students: 4,804   (52.2% male; 47.7% female)
  Individual Education Program: 905 (18.8%);
  English Language Learner: 0 (0.0%); Migrant: 0 (0.0%)
  Eligible for Free Lunch Program: n/a
  Eligible for Reduced-Price Lunch Program: n/a
Teachers: 314.2 (14.4 to 1)
Librarians/Media Specialists: 12.0 (378.2 to 1)
Guidance Counselors: 7.0 (648.3 to 1)
Current Spending: ($ per student per year):
  Total: $6,889; Instruction: $4,386; Support Services: $2,120
Enrollment, Drop-out Rates and Diploma Recipients by Race/Ethnicity

Category	Total	White	Black	Asian	AIAN	Hisp.
Enrollment (%)	100.0	99.0	0.6	0.0	0.1	0.2
Drop-out Rate (%)	4.7	4.8	0.0	0.0	n/a	0.0
H.S. Diplomas (#)	242	237	1	0	1	3

Pike County

Pike County
314 S Mayo Tr • Pikeville, KY 41501-3097
(606) 432-7724 • http://lvillage.pike.k12.ky.us/lt/district.nsf
Grade Span: PK-12; **Agency Type:** 1
Schools: 26
  16 Primary; 3 Middle; 6 High; 1 Other Level
  24 Regular; 0 Special Education; 0 Vocational; 2 Alternative
  0 Magnet; 0 Charter; 17 Title I Eligible; 17 School-wide Title I
Students: 10,533   (53.1% male; 46.8% female)
  Individual Education Program: 1,459 (13.9%);
  English Language Learner: 0 (0.0%); Migrant: 364 (3.6%)
  Eligible for Free Lunch Program: n/a
  Eligible for Reduced-Price Lunch Program: n/a
Teachers: 682.5 (14.7 to 1)
Librarians/Media Specialists: 22.0 (455.5 to 1)
Guidance Counselors: 13.0 (770.8 to 1)
Current Spending: ($ per student per year):
  Total: $6,842; Instruction: $3,986; Support Services: $2,438
Enrollment, Drop-out Rates and Diploma Recipients by Race/Ethnicity

Category	Total	White	Black	Asian	AIAN	Hisp.
Enrollment (%)	100.0	99.3	0.3	0.2	0.1	0.1
Drop-out Rate (%)	4.2	4.2	0.0	0.0	0.0	0.0
H.S. Diplomas (#)	602	599	2	0	0	1

Powell County

Powell County
691 Breckinridge St • Stanton, KY 40380-0430
(606) 663-3300 • http://www.powell.k12.ky.us/
Grade Span: PK-12; **Agency Type:** 1
Schools: 5
  3 Primary; 1 Middle; 1 High; 0 Other Level
  5 Regular; 0 Special Education; 0 Vocational; 0 Alternative
  0 Magnet; 0 Charter; 4 Title I Eligible; 4 School-wide Title I
Students: 2,667   (51.6% male; 48.3% female)
  Individual Education Program: 485 (18.2%);
  English Language Learner: 8 (0.3%); Migrant: 329 (13.1%)
  Eligible for Free Lunch Program: n/a
  Eligible for Reduced-Price Lunch Program: n/a
Teachers: 180.0 (14.0 to 1)
Librarians/Media Specialists: 5.0 (503.2 to 1)
Guidance Counselors: 6.0 (419.3 to 1)
Current Spending: ($ per student per year):
  Total: $6,421; Instruction: $3,905; Support Services: $2,168

Enrollment, Drop-out Rates and Diploma Recipients by Race/Ethnicity

Category	Total	White	Black	Asian	AIAN	Hisp.
Enrollment (%)	100.0	98.6	0.7	0.1	0.2	0.4
Drop-out Rate (%)	6.5	6.6	0.0	n/a	0.0	0.0
H.S. Diplomas (#)	136	135	0	0	0	1

Pulaski County

Pulaski County
501 University Dr • Somerset, KY 42502-1055
(606) 679-1123 • http://www.pulaski.net/
Grade Span: PK-12; **Agency Type:** 1
Schools: 14
  8 Primary; 2 Middle; 4 High; 0 Other Level
  12 Regular; 0 Special Education; 0 Vocational; 2 Alternative
  0 Magnet; 0 Charter; 8 Title I Eligible; 8 School-wide Title I
Students: 7,961   (52.0% male; 47.9% female)
  Individual Education Program: 1,205 (15.1%);
  English Language Learner: 10 (0.1%); Migrant: 226 (3.0%)
  Eligible for Free Lunch Program: n/a
  Eligible for Reduced-Price Lunch Program: n/a
Teachers: 469.0 (16.0 to 1)
Librarians/Media Specialists: 13.0 (578.9 to 1)
Guidance Counselors: 18.0 (418.1 to 1)
Current Spending: ($ per student per year):
  Total: $7,141; Instruction: $4,719; Support Services: $2,051
Enrollment, Drop-out Rates and Diploma Recipients by Race/Ethnicity

Category	Total	White	Black	Asian	AIAN	Hisp.
Enrollment (%)	100.0	98.1	0.6	0.3	0.3	0.7
Drop-out Rate (%)	3.8	3.7	0.0	0.0	0.0	0.0
H.S. Diplomas (#)	462	456	2	1	0	3

Somerset Independent
305 N College St • Somerset, KY 42502-1311
(606) 679-4451 • http://www.somerset.k12.ky.us/
Grade Span: PK-12; **Agency Type:** 1
Schools: 3
  1 Primary; 1 Middle; 1 High; 0 Other Level
  3 Regular; 0 Special Education; 0 Vocational; 0 Alternative
  0 Magnet; 0 Charter; 1 Title I Eligible; 1 School-wide Title I
Students: 1,546   (51.8% male; 48.1% female)
  Individual Education Program: 195 (12.6%);
  English Language Learner: 26 (1.7%); Migrant: 25 (1.6%)
  Eligible for Free Lunch Program: n/a
  Eligible for Reduced-Price Lunch Program: n/a
Teachers: 105.2 (14.4 to 1)
Librarians/Media Specialists: 3.0 (506.3 to 1)
Guidance Counselors: 4.0 (379.8 to 1)
Current Spending: ($ per student per year):
  Total: $5,922; Instruction: $3,823; Support Services: $1,790
Enrollment, Drop-out Rates and Diploma Recipients by Race/Ethnicity

Category	Total	White	Black	Asian	AIAN	Hisp.
Enrollment (%)	100.0	89.1	6.6	2.4	0.3	1.6
Drop-out Rate (%)	3.6	3.7	0.0	0.0	0.0	0.0
H.S. Diplomas (#)	98	86	10	2	0	0

Rockcastle County

Rockcastle County
245 Richmond St • Mt Verno, KY 40456-2705
(606) 256-2125 • http://www.rockcastle.k12.ky.us/
Grade Span: PK-12; **Agency Type:** 1
Schools: 6
  3 Primary; 1 Middle; 1 High; 1 Other Level
  5 Regular; 0 Special Education; 0 Vocational; 1 Alternative
  0 Magnet; 0 Charter; 3 Title I Eligible; 3 School-wide Title I
Students: 3,037   (52.4% male; 47.5% female)
  Individual Education Program: 535 (17.6%);
  English Language Learner: 0 (0.0%); Migrant: 413 (14.1%)
  Eligible for Free Lunch Program: n/a
  Eligible for Reduced-Price Lunch Program: n/a
Teachers: 198.5 (14.7 to 1)
Librarians/Media Specialists: 5.0 (584.6 to 1)
Guidance Counselors: 6.0 (487.2 to 1)
Current Spending: ($ per student per year):
  Total: $6,513; Instruction: $4,149; Support Services: $1,998
Enrollment, Drop-out Rates and Diploma Recipients by Race/Ethnicity

Category	Total	White	Black	Asian	AIAN	Hisp.
Enrollment (%)	100.0	99.8	0.1	0.0	0.1	0.1
Drop-out Rate (%)	4.5	4.5	n/a	n/a	n/a	0.0
H.S. Diplomas (#)	184	183	1	0	0	0

Rowan County

Rowan County
121 E Second St • Morehead, KY 40351-1669
(606) 784-8928 • http://www.rowan.k12.ky.us/
Grade Span: PK-12; **Agency Type:** 1
Schools: 7
    4 Primary; 1 Middle; 2 High; 0 Other Level
    6 Regular; 0 Special Education; 0 Vocational; 1 Alternative
    0 Magnet; 0 Charter; 6 Title I Eligible; 6 School-wide Title I
Students: 3,113   (50.5% male; 49.4% female)
    Individual Education Program: 563 (18.1%);
    English Language Learner: 8 (0.3%); Migrant: 64 (2.2%)
    Eligible for Free Lunch Program: n/a
    Eligible for Reduced-Price Lunch Program: n/a
Teachers: 208.7 (14.1 to 1)
Librarians/Media Specialists: 6.0 (489.2 to 1)
Guidance Counselors: 8.0 (366.9 to 1)
Current Spending: ($ per student per year):
    Total: $6,489; Instruction: $4,159; Support Services: $1,984
Enrollment, Drop-out Rates and Diploma Recipients by Race/Ethnicity

Category	Total	White	Black	Asian	AIAN	Hisp.
Enrollment (%)	100.0	96.8	1.6	0.6	0.5	0.5
Drop-out Rate (%)	3.4	3.5	0.0	0.0	0.0	0.0
H.S. Diplomas (#)	183	181	1	1	0	0

Russell County

Russell County
404 S Main St • Jamestown, KY 42629-2148
(270) 343-3191 • http://russell-ind.k12.ky.us/
Grade Span: PK-12; **Agency Type:** 1
Schools: 6
    4 Primary; 1 Middle; 1 High; 0 Other Level
    6 Regular; 0 Special Education; 0 Vocational; 0 Alternative
    0 Magnet; 0 Charter; 5 Title I Eligible; 5 School-wide Title I
Students: 2,935   (51.4% male; 48.5% female)
    Individual Education Program: 544 (18.5%);
    English Language Learner: 7 (0.2%); Migrant: 145 (5.1%)
    Eligible for Free Lunch Program: n/a
    Eligible for Reduced-Price Lunch Program: n/a
Teachers: 209.0 (13.5 to 1)
Librarians/Media Specialists: 6.0 (469.7 to 1)
Guidance Counselors: 6.0 (469.7 to 1)
Current Spending: ($ per student per year):
    Total: $7,627; Instruction: $4,707; Support Services: $2,483
Enrollment, Drop-out Rates and Diploma Recipients by Race/Ethnicity

Category	Total	White	Black	Asian	AIAN	Hisp.
Enrollment (%)	100.0	98.7	0.6	0.1	0.0	0.5
Drop-out Rate (%)	5.7	5.5	0.0	0.0	0.0	n/a
H.S. Diplomas (#)	140	137	1	2	0	0

Scott County

Scott County
2168 Frankfort Pk • Georgetown, KY 40324-0561
(502) 863-3663 • http://www.scott.k12.ky.us/
Grade Span: PK-12; **Agency Type:** 1
Schools: 11
    7 Primary; 2 Middle; 1 High; 1 Other Level
    11 Regular; 0 Special Education; 0 Vocational; 0 Alternative
    0 Magnet; 0 Charter; 6 Title I Eligible; 0 School-wide Title I
Students: 7,161   (53.0% male; 46.9% female)
    Individual Education Program: 910 (12.7%);
    English Language Learner: 39 (0.5%); Migrant: 150 (2.4%)
    Eligible for Free Lunch Program: n/a
    Eligible for Reduced-Price Lunch Program: n/a
Teachers: 400.0 (15.9 to 1)
Librarians/Media Specialists: 12.0 (529.7 to 1)
Guidance Counselors: 14.0 (454.0 to 1)
Current Spending: ($ per student per year):
    Total: $6,256; Instruction: $4,023; Support Services: $1,934
Enrollment, Drop-out Rates and Diploma Recipients by Race/Ethnicity

Category	Total	White	Black	Asian	AIAN	Hisp.
Enrollment (%)	100.0	91.8	5.9	0.5	0.1	1.6
Drop-out Rate (%)	3.4	3.4	3.5	0.0	0.0	0.0
H.S. Diplomas (#)	334	307	23	0	1	3

Shelby County

Shelby County
403 Washington St • Shelbyville, KY 40066-0159
(502) 633-2375 • http://www.shelby.k12.ky.us/
Grade Span: PK-12; **Agency Type:** 1
Schools: 10

    6 Primary; 2 Middle; 1 High; 1 Other Level
    9 Regular; 0 Special Education; 0 Vocational; 1 Alternative
    0 Magnet; 0 Charter; 7 Title I Eligible; 0 School-wide Title I
Students: 5,537   (51.6% male; 48.3% female)
    Individual Education Program: 766 (13.8%);
    English Language Learner: 242 (4.4%); Migrant: 196 (3.6%)
    Eligible for Free Lunch Program: n/a
    Eligible for Reduced-Price Lunch Program: n/a
Teachers: 339.6 (15.8 to 1)
Librarians/Media Specialists: 9.0 (597.4 to 1)
Guidance Counselors: 10.0 (537.7 to 1)
Current Spending: ($ per student per year):
    Total: $5,938; Instruction: $3,614; Support Services: $1,972
Enrollment, Drop-out Rates and Diploma Recipients by Race/Ethnicity

Category	Total	White	Black	Asian	AIAN	Hisp.
Enrollment (%)	100.0	80.9	9.6	0.5	0.3	8.7
Drop-out Rate (%)	3.9	3.9	4.3	0.0	0.0	2.2
H.S. Diplomas (#)	306	267	28	5	1	5

Simpson County

Simpson County
430 S College St • Franklin, KY 42135-0467
(270) 586-8877 • http://www.simpson.k12.ky.us/
Grade Span: PK-12; **Agency Type:** 1
Schools: 6
    2 Primary; 2 Middle; 2 High; 0 Other Level
    5 Regular; 0 Special Education; 0 Vocational; 1 Alternative
    0 Magnet; 0 Charter; 3 Title I Eligible; 0 School-wide Title I
Students: 3,110   (52.6% male; 47.3% female)
    Individual Education Program: 376 (12.1%);
    English Language Learner: 4 (0.1%); Migrant: 26 (0.9%)
    Eligible for Free Lunch Program: n/a
    Eligible for Reduced-Price Lunch Program: n/a
Teachers: 184.6 (16.0 to 1)
Librarians/Media Specialists: 5.0 (592.4 to 1)
Guidance Counselors: 6.0 (493.7 to 1)
Current Spending: ($ per student per year):
    Total: $6,160; Instruction: $4,083; Support Services: $1,751
Enrollment, Drop-out Rates and Diploma Recipients by Race/Ethnicity

Category	Total	White	Black	Asian	AIAN	Hisp.
Enrollment (%)	100.0	86.2	12.4	0.4	0.3	0.8
Drop-out Rate (%)	3.4	3.9	0.0	0.0	n/a	0.0
H.S. Diplomas (#)	201	166	30	5	0	0

Spencer County

Spencer County
207 W Main St • Taylorsvil, KY 40071-0339
(502) 477-3250 • http://www.spencer.k12.ky.us/
Grade Span: PK-12; **Agency Type:** 1
Schools: 5
    2 Primary; 1 Middle; 1 High; 1 Other Level
    4 Regular; 0 Special Education; 0 Vocational; 1 Alternative
    0 Magnet; 0 Charter; 2 Title I Eligible; 1 School-wide Title I
Students: 2,469   (52.2% male; 47.7% female)
    Individual Education Program: 433 (17.5%);
    English Language Learner: 5 (0.2%); Migrant: 10 (0.4%)
    Eligible for Free Lunch Program: n/a
    Eligible for Reduced-Price Lunch Program: n/a
Teachers: 134.4 (16.9 to 1)
Librarians/Media Specialists: 3.0 (756.7 to 1)
Guidance Counselors: 3.0 (756.7 to 1)
Current Spending: ($ per student per year):
    Total: $6,098; Instruction: $3,820; Support Services: $1,916
Enrollment, Drop-out Rates and Diploma Recipients by Race/Ethnicity

Category	Total	White	Black	Asian	AIAN	Hisp.
Enrollment (%)	100.0	97.1	2.1	0.3	0.0	0.5
Drop-out Rate (%)	3.2	3.2	0.0	0.0	n/a	0.0
H.S. Diplomas (#)	113	112	1	0	0	0

Taylor County

Taylor County
1209 E Brdway • Campbellsville, KY 42718-1500
Mailing Address: 1209 E Broadway • Campbellsville, KY 42718-1549
(270) 465-5371 • http://www.taylor.k12.ky.us/
Grade Span: PK-12; **Agency Type:** 1
Schools: 3
    1 Primary; 1 Middle; 1 High; 0 Other Level
    3 Regular; 0 Special Education; 0 Vocational; 0 Alternative
    0 Magnet; 0 Charter; 1 Title I Eligible; 1 School-wide Title I
Students: 2,643   (50.8% male; 49.1% female)
    Individual Education Program: 392 (14.8%);
    English Language Learner: 16 (0.6%); Migrant: 48 (1.9%)

Eligible for Free Lunch Program: n/a
Eligible for Reduced-Price Lunch Program: n/a
Teachers: 159.0 (15.9 to 1)
Librarians/Media Specialists: 3.0 (844.7 to 1)
Guidance Counselors: 6.0 (422.3 to 1)
Current Spending: ($ per student per year):
    Total: $5,864; Instruction: $3,720; Support Services: $1,848
Enrollment, Drop-out Rates and Diploma Recipients by Race/Ethnicity

Category	Total	White	Black	Asian	AIAN	Hisp.
Enrollment (%)	100.0	97.6	1.2	0.1	0.2	0.9
Drop-out Rate (%)	2.3	2.3	0.0	0.0	n/a	n/a
H.S. Diplomas (#)	162	157	5	0	0	0

Todd County

Todd County
804 S Main • Elkton, KY 42220-8812
(270) 265-2436 • http://www.todd.k12.ky.us/
Grade Span: PK-12; **Agency Type:** 1
Schools: 4
    2 Primary; 1 Middle; 1 High; 0 Other Level
    4 Regular; 0 Special Education; 0 Vocational; 0 Alternative
    0 Magnet; 0 Charter; 2 Title I Eligible; 2 School-wide Title I
Students: 2,109 (50.4% male; 49.5% female)
    Individual Education Program: 427 (20.2%);
    English Language Learner: 0 (0.0%); Migrant: 132 (6.9%)
    Eligible for Free Lunch Program: n/a
    Eligible for Reduced-Price Lunch Program: n/a
Teachers: 120.0 (15.9 to 1)
Librarians/Media Specialists: 4.0 (478.3 to 1)
Guidance Counselors: 4.0 (478.3 to 1)
Current Spending: ($ per student per year):
    Total: $6,771; Instruction: $3,878; Support Services: $2,443
Enrollment, Drop-out Rates and Diploma Recipients by Race/Ethnicity

Category	Total	White	Black	Asian	AIAN	Hisp.
Enrollment (%)	100.0	86.5	11.0	0.2	0.2	2.0
Drop-out Rate (%)	4.1	4.1	4.4	0.0	0.0	0.0
H.S. Diplomas (#)	115	102	13	0	0	0

Trigg County

Trigg County
202 Main St • Cadiz, KY 42211-6124
(270) 522-6075 • http://www.rowan.k12.ky.us/
Grade Span: PK-12; **Agency Type:** 1
Schools: 3
    1 Primary; 1 Middle; 1 High; 0 Other Level
    3 Regular; 0 Special Education; 0 Vocational; 0 Alternative
    0 Magnet; 0 Charter; 2 Title I Eligible; 2 School-wide Title I
Students: 2,135 (51.9% male; 48.0% female)
    Individual Education Program: 374 (17.5%);
    English Language Learner: 0 (0.0%); Migrant: 62 (3.1%)
    Eligible for Free Lunch Program: n/a
    Eligible for Reduced-Price Lunch Program: n/a
Teachers: 131.6 (15.4 to 1)
Librarians/Media Specialists: 3.0 (676.3 to 1)
Guidance Counselors: 4.0 (507.3 to 1)
Current Spending: ($ per student per year):
    Total: $6,223; Instruction: $3,738; Support Services: $2,187
Enrollment, Drop-out Rates and Diploma Recipients by Race/Ethnicity

Category	Total	White	Black	Asian	AIAN	Hisp.
Enrollment (%)	100.0	85.1	13.8	0.2	0.1	0.8
Drop-out Rate (%)	7.7	8.6	2.6	0.0	n/a	0.0
H.S. Diplomas (#)	111	94	17	0	0	0

Trimble County

Trimble County
68 Wentworth Ave • Bedford, KY 40006-0275
(502) 255-3201
Grade Span: KG-12; **Agency Type:** 1
Schools: 4
    2 Primary; 1 Middle; 1 High; 0 Other Level
    4 Regular; 0 Special Education; 0 Vocational; 0 Alternative
    0 Magnet; 0 Charter; 3 Title I Eligible; 3 School-wide Title I
Students: 1,634 (50.8% male; 49.1% female)
    Individual Education Program: 250 (15.3%);
    English Language Learner: 17 (1.0%); Migrant: 77 (4.9%)
    Eligible for Free Lunch Program: n/a
    Eligible for Reduced-Price Lunch Program: n/a
Teachers: 97.8 (15.9 to 1)
Librarians/Media Specialists: 3.4 (457.6 to 1)
Guidance Counselors: 3.2 (486.3 to 1)
Current Spending: ($ per student per year):
    Total: $6,100; Instruction: $3,898; Support Services: $1,852

Enrollment, Drop-out Rates and Diploma Recipients by Race/Ethnicity

Category	Total	White	Black	Asian	AIAN	Hisp.
Enrollment (%)	100.0	98.0	0.3	0.0	0.3	1.4
Drop-out Rate (%)	3.0	2.8	0.0	n/a	n/a	33.3
H.S. Diplomas (#)	102	102	0	0	0	0

Union County

Union County
510 S Mart St • Morganfiel, KY 42437-1724
(270) 389-1694 • http://www.union.k12.ky.us/
Grade Span: PK-12; **Agency Type:** 1
Schools: 9
    4 Primary; 1 Middle; 3 High; 1 Other Level
    6 Regular; 0 Special Education; 0 Vocational; 3 Alternative
    0 Magnet; 0 Charter; 4 Title I Eligible; 4 School-wide Title I
Students: 2,459 (50.9% male; 49.0% female)
    Individual Education Program: 568 (23.1%);
    English Language Learner: 0 (0.0%); Migrant: 66 (2.8%)
    Eligible for Free Lunch Program: n/a
    Eligible for Reduced-Price Lunch Program: n/a
Teachers: 159.0 (14.8 to 1)
Librarians/Media Specialists: 5.0 (470.6 to 1)
Guidance Counselors: 6.0 (392.2 to 1)
Current Spending: ($ per student per year):
    Total: $6,700; Instruction: $4,178; Support Services: $2,166
Enrollment, Drop-out Rates and Diploma Recipients by Race/Ethnicity

Category	Total	White	Black	Asian	AIAN	Hisp.
Enrollment (%)	100.0	85.3	14.1	0.2	0.0	0.4
Drop-out Rate (%)	3.6	3.6	4.2	0.0	0.0	0.0
H.S. Diplomas (#)	156	138	17	0	0	1

Warren County

Bowling Green Ind
1211 Center St • Bowling Green, KY 42101-6801
(270) 746-2200 • http://www.b-g.k12.ky.us/
Grade Span: PK-12; **Agency Type:** 1
Schools: 10
    5 Primary; 1 Middle; 3 High; 1 Other Level
    7 Regular; 0 Special Education; 0 Vocational; 3 Alternative
    0 Magnet; 0 Charter; 4 Title I Eligible; 4 School-wide Title I
Students: 3,664 (52.1% male; 47.8% female)
    Individual Education Program: 456 (12.4%);
    English Language Learner: 475 (13.0%); Migrant: 41 (1.2%)
    Eligible for Free Lunch Program: n/a
    Eligible for Reduced-Price Lunch Program: n/a
Teachers: 231.6 (15.0 to 1)
Librarians/Media Specialists: 7.0 (496.6 to 1)
Guidance Counselors: 12.0 (289.7 to 1)
Current Spending: ($ per student per year):
    Total: $8,119; Instruction: $5,194; Support Services: $2,445
Enrollment, Drop-out Rates and Diploma Recipients by Race/Ethnicity

Category	Total	White	Black	Asian	AIAN	Hisp.
Enrollment (%)	100.0	68.9	21.7	2.8	0.1	6.4
Drop-out Rate (%)	4.7	4.0	7.7	0.0	0.0	2.5
H.S. Diplomas (#)	222	173	33	10	0	6

Warren County
303 Lover's Ln • Bowling Gre, KY 42101-2310
(270) 781-5150 • http://www.warren.k12.ky.us/
Grade Span: PK-12; **Agency Type:** 1
Schools: 24
    13 Primary; 4 Middle; 6 High; 1 Other Level
    18 Regular; 0 Special Education; 0 Vocational; 6 Alternative
    0 Magnet; 0 Charter; 11 Title I Eligible; 10 School-wide Title I
Students: 11,710 (52.3% male; 47.6% female)
    Individual Education Program: 1,471 (12.6%);
    English Language Learner: 511 (4.4%); Migrant: 73 (0.7%)
    Eligible for Free Lunch Program: n/a
    Eligible for Reduced-Price Lunch Program: n/a
Teachers: 684.0 (16.3 to 1)
Librarians/Media Specialists: 20.0 (558.8 to 1)
Guidance Counselors: 24.5 (456.1 to 1)
Current Spending: ($ per student per year):
    Total: $5,624; Instruction: $3,660; Support Services: $1,592
Enrollment, Drop-out Rates and Diploma Recipients by Race/Ethnicity

Category	Total	White	Black	Asian	AIAN	Hisp.
Enrollment (%)	100.0	86.4	9.6	1.5	0.1	2.5
Drop-out Rate (%)	1.9	1.8	3.7	0.0	0.0	2.2
H.S. Diplomas (#)	706	631	54	12	2	7

Washington County

Washington County
120 Mackville Hill • Springfie, KY 40069-0192
(859) 336-5470
Grade Span: PK-12; **Agency Type:** 1
Schools: 6
   3 Primary; 1 Middle; 2 High; 0 Other Level
   5 Regular; 0 Special Education; 0 Vocational; 1 Alternative
   0 Magnet; 0 Charter; 3 Title I Eligible; 3 School-wide Title I
Students: 1,925   (51.3% male; 48.6% female)
   Individual Education Program: 351 (18.2%);
   English Language Learner: 32 (1.7%); Migrant: 43 (2.4%)
   Eligible for Free Lunch Program: n/a
   Eligible for Reduced-Price Lunch Program: n/a
Teachers: 113.7 (16.1 to 1)
Librarians/Media Specialists: 3.1 (589.7 to 1)
Guidance Counselors: 2.0 (914.0 to 1)
Current Spending: ($ per student per year):
   Total: $6,183; Instruction: $3,714; Support Services: $2,085

Enrollment, Drop-out Rates and Diploma Recipients by Race/Ethnicity

Category	Total	White	Black	Asian	AIAN	Hisp.
Enrollment (%)	100.0	86.4	10.2	0.6	0.0	2.7
Drop-out Rate (%)	3.7	3.9	2.1	0.0	n/a	0.0
H.S. Diplomas (#)	108	97	10	1	0	0

Wayne County

Wayne County
534 Albany Rd • Monticello, KY 42633-0437
(606) 348-8484 • http://www.wayne.k12.ky.us/
Grade Span: PK-12; **Agency Type:** 1
Schools: 7
   3 Primary; 2 Middle; 2 High; 0 Other Level
   6 Regular; 0 Special Education; 0 Vocational; 1 Alternative
   0 Magnet; 0 Charter; 4 Title I Eligible; 4 School-wide Title I
Students: 2,752   (53.2% male; 46.7% female)
   Individual Education Program: 434 (15.8%);
   English Language Learner: 0 (0.0%); Migrant: 215 (8.4%)
   Eligible for Free Lunch Program: n/a
   Eligible for Reduced-Price Lunch Program: n/a
Teachers: 160.8 (15.9 to 1)
Librarians/Media Specialists: 5.0 (512.2 to 1)
Guidance Counselors: 6.0 (426.8 to 1)
Current Spending: ($ per student per year):
   Total: $6,415; Instruction: $3,919; Support Services: $2,109

Enrollment, Drop-out Rates and Diploma Recipients by Race/Ethnicity

Category	Total	White	Black	Asian	AIAN	Hisp.
Enrollment (%)	100.0	96.8	2.4	0.0	0.1	0.7
Drop-out Rate (%)	4.1	4.2	0.0	0.0	n/a	0.0
H.S. Diplomas (#)	140	134	4	0	0	2

Webster County

Webster County
28 State Rt. 1340 • Dixon, KY 42409-0420
(270) 639-5083 • http://proxy.atc.webster.k12.ky.us/
Grade Span: PK-12; **Agency Type:** 1
Schools: 6
   4 Primary; 0 Middle; 1 High; 1 Other Level
   5 Regular; 0 Special Education; 0 Vocational; 1 Alternative
   0 Magnet; 0 Charter; 4 Title I Eligible; 3 School-wide Title I
Students: 1,995   (49.1% male; 50.8% female)
   Individual Education Program: 313 (15.7%);
   English Language Learner: 0 (0.0%); Migrant: 76 (4.0%)
   Eligible for Free Lunch Program: n/a
   Eligible for Reduced-Price Lunch Program: n/a
Teachers: 114.6 (16.4 to 1)
Librarians/Media Specialists: 4.5 (418.7 to 1)
Guidance Counselors: 4.5 (418.7 to 1)
Current Spending: ($ per student per year):
   Total: $5,653; Instruction: $3,185; Support Services: $2,098

Enrollment, Drop-out Rates and Diploma Recipients by Race/Ethnicity

Category	Total	White	Black	Asian	AIAN	Hisp.
Enrollment (%)	100.0	96.2	1.3	0.1	0.0	2.4
Drop-out Rate (%)	2.2	2.1	0.0	0.0	n/a	0.0
H.S. Diplomas (#)	137	135	2	0	0	0

Whitley County

Corbin Independent
108 E Center St • Corbin, KY 40701-1302
Mailing Address: 108 Roy Kidd Ave • Corbin, KY 40701-1302
(606) 528-1303 • http://www.corbinschools.org/
Grade Span: PK-12; **Agency Type:** 1
Schools: 9
   2 Primary; 2 Middle; 3 High; 2 Other Level
   4 Regular; 0 Special Education; 0 Vocational; 5 Alternative
   0 Magnet; 0 Charter; 3 Title I Eligible; 3 School-wide Title I
Students: 2,221   (51.1% male; 48.8% female)
   Individual Education Program: 293 (13.2%);
   English Language Learner: 0 (0.0%); Migrant: 0 (0.0%)
   Eligible for Free Lunch Program: n/a
   Eligible for Reduced-Price Lunch Program: n/a
Teachers: 138.2 (15.7 to 1)
Librarians/Media Specialists: 3.9 (555.6 to 1)
Guidance Counselors: 6.0 (361.2 to 1)
Current Spending: ($ per student per year):
   Total: $6,813; Instruction: $4,704; Support Services: $1,675

Enrollment, Drop-out Rates and Diploma Recipients by Race/Ethnicity

Category	Total	White	Black	Asian	AIAN	Hisp.
Enrollment (%)	100.0	98.6	0.3	0.7	0.0	0.4
Drop-out Rate (%)	4.3	4.4	n/a	0.0	0.0	0.0
H.S. Diplomas (#)	150	148	0	1	0	1

Whitley County
116 N 4th • Williamsburg, KY 40769-1115
Mailing Address: 116 N 4th St • Williamsburg, KY 40769-1115
(606) 549-7000 • http://whitley.k12.ky.us/
Grade Span: PK-12; **Agency Type:** 1
Schools: 11
   7 Primary; 2 Middle; 2 High; 0 Other Level
   10 Regular; 0 Special Education; 0 Vocational; 1 Alternative
   0 Magnet; 0 Charter; 10 Title I Eligible; 10 School-wide Title I
Students: 4,821   (51.4% male; 48.5% female)
   Individual Education Program: 867 (18.0%);
   English Language Learner: 0 (0.0%); Migrant: 0 (0.0%)
   Eligible for Free Lunch Program: n/a
   Eligible for Reduced-Price Lunch Program: n/a
Teachers: 312.5 (14.7 to 1)
Librarians/Media Specialists: 8.0 (572.5 to 1)
Guidance Counselors: 5.0 (916.0 to 1)
Current Spending: ($ per student per year):
   Total: $7,285; Instruction: $4,594; Support Services: $2,300

Enrollment, Drop-out Rates and Diploma Recipients by Race/Ethnicity

Category	Total	White	Black	Asian	AIAN	Hisp.
Enrollment (%)	100.0	99.7	0.1	0.1	0.0	0.0
Drop-out Rate (%)	4.4	4.4	n/a	n/a	0.0	n/a
H.S. Diplomas (#)	225	225	0	0	0	0

Woodford County

Woodford County
330 Pisgah Pike • Versailles, KY 40383-1418
(859) 873-4701 • http://www.woodford.k12.ky.us/
Grade Span: PK-12; **Agency Type:** 1
Schools: 8
   5 Primary; 1 Middle; 2 High; 0 Other Level
   7 Regular; 0 Special Education; 0 Vocational; 1 Alternative
   0 Magnet; 0 Charter; 3 Title I Eligible; 0 School-wide Title I
Students: 3,833   (49.4% male; 50.5% female)
   Individual Education Program: 425 (11.1%);
   English Language Learner: 97 (2.5%); Migrant: 64 (1.7%)
   Eligible for Free Lunch Program: n/a
   Eligible for Reduced-Price Lunch Program: n/a
Teachers: 236.0 (15.9 to 1)
Librarians/Media Specialists: 7.0 (535.3 to 1)
Guidance Counselors: 6.7 (559.3 to 1)
Current Spending: ($ per student per year):
   Total: $5,968; Instruction: $3,971; Support Services: $1,643

Enrollment, Drop-out Rates and Diploma Recipients by Race/Ethnicity

Category	Total	White	Black	Asian	AIAN	Hisp.
Enrollment (%)	100.0	89.7	6.3	0.3	0.1	3.5
Drop-out Rate (%)	2.5	2.4	4.7	0.0	n/a	0.0
H.S. Diplomas (#)	222	205	11	2	0	4

Number of Schools

Rank	Number	District Name	City
1	173	Jefferson County	Louisville
2	61	Fayette County	Lexington
3	26	Pike County	Pikeville
4	24	Hardin County	Elizabe
4	24	Warren County	Bowling Gre
6	22	Daviess County	Owensboro
7	20	Bullitt County	Shepherdsville
7	20	Christian County	Hopkinsville
7	20	Kenton County	Erlanger
10	18	Boone County	Florence
10	18	Laurel County	London
10	18	Madison County	Richmond
13	17	Floyd County	Prestons
13	17	Oldham County	Buckner
15	15	Mccracken County	Paducah
16	14	Hopkins County	Madisonvi
16	14	Muhlenberg County	Greenville
16	14	Perry County	Hazard
16	14	Pulaski County	Somerset
20	13	Clark County	Winchester
20	13	Letcher County	Whitesburg
22	12	Clay County	Manchester
22	12	Franklin County	Frankfort
22	12	Graves County	Mayfield
22	12	Henderson County	Henderson
22	12	Owensboro Independent	Owensboro
27	11	Carter County	Grayson
27	11	Covington Independent	Covington
27	11	Harlan County	Harlan
27	11	Jessamine County	Nicholasville
27	11	Knott County	Hindman
27	11	Knox County	Barbourvill
27	11	Marshall County	Benton
27	11	Mccreary County	Stearns
27	11	Scott County	Georgetown
27	11	Whitley County	Williamsburg
37	10	Barren County	Glasgow
37	10	Bowling Green Ind	Bowling Green
37	10	Campbell County	Alexandria
37	10	Lincoln County	Stanford
37	10	Meade County	Brandenburg
37	10	Nelson County	Bardstown
37	10	Ohio County	Hartford
37	10	Shelby County	Shelbyville
45	9	Ashland Ind	Ashland
45	9	Boyd County	Ashland
45	9	Breathitt County	Jackson
45	9	Corbin Independent	Corbin
45	9	Johnson County	Paintsville
45	9	Montgomery County	Mt Sterling
45	9	Union County	Morganfiel
52	8	Adair County	Columbia
52	8	Bell County	Pineville
52	8	Casey County	Liberty
52	8	Greenup County	Greenup
52	8	Magoffin County	Salyersville
52	8	Martin County	Inez
52	8	Morgan County	West Liberty
52	8	Woodford County	Versailles
60	7	Bourbon County	Paris
60	7	Estill County	Irvine
60	7	Grayson County	Leitchfield
60	7	Leslie County	Hyden
60	7	Lewis County	Vanceburg
60	7	Marion County	Lebanon
60	7	Newport Independent	Newport
60	7	Paducah Independent	Paducah
60	7	Rowan County	Morehead
60	7	Wayne County	Monticello
70	6	Anderson County	Lawrenceburg
70	6	Bardstown Ind	Bardstown
70	6	Boyle County	Danville
70	6	Breckinridge County	Hardinsburg
70	6	Butler County	Morgantown
70	6	Calloway County	Murray
70	6	Danville Independent	Danville
70	6	Erlanger-Elsmere Independent	Erlanger
70	6	Fleming County	Flemingsburg
70	6	Garrard County	Lancaster
70	6	Glasgow Independent	Glasgow
70	6	Grant County	Williamsto
70	6	Harrison County	Cynthiana
70	6	Hart County	Munfordville
70	6	Jackson County	Mckee
70	6	Larue County	Hodgenville
70	6	Logan County	Russellville
70	6	Rockcastle County	Mt Verno
70	6	Russell County	Jamestown
70	6	Simpson County	Franklin
70	6	Washington County	Springfie
70	6	Webster County	Dixon
92	5	Bath County	Owingsv
92	5	Carroll County	Carrollton
92	5	Edmonson County	Brownsville
92	5	Fort Thomas Independent	Ft Thomas
92	5	Gallatin County	Warsaw
92	5	Green County	Greensburg
92	5	Hancock County	Hawesville
92	5	Henry County	New Castle
92	5	Lawrence County	Louisa
92	5	Mayfield Independent	Mayfiel
92	5	Mclean County	Calhoun
92	5	Metcalfe County	Edmonton
92	5	Middlesboro Independent	Middlesboro
92	5	Monroe County	Tompkinsville
92	5	Powell County	Stanton
92	5	Spencer County	Taylorsvil
108	4	Allen County	Scottsville
108	4	Ballard County	Barlow
108	4	Caldwell County	Princeton
108	4	Elizabethtown Independent	Elizabethtow
108	4	Mason County	Maysville
108	4	Mercer County	Harrodsburg
108	4	Murray Independent	Murray
108	4	Owen County	Owenton
108	4	Pendleton County	Falmouth
108	4	Russell Independent	Russell
108	4	Todd County	Elkton
108	4	Trimble County	Bedford
120	3	Clinton County	Albany
120	3	Somerset Independent	Somerset
120	3	Taylor County	Campbellsville
120	3	Trigg County	Cadiz

Number of Teachers

Rank	Number	District Name	City
1	5,656	Jefferson County	Louisville
2	2,534	Fayette County	Lexington
3	894	Boone County	Florence
4	815	Hardin County	Elizabe
5	701	Kenton County	Erlanger
6	684	Warren County	Bowling Gre
7	682	Pike County	Pikeville
8	659	Daviess County	Owensboro
9	645	Bullitt County	Shepherdsville
10	582	Oldham County	Buckner
11	578	Madison County	Richmond
12	553	Christian County	Hopkinsville
13	494	Laurel County	London
14	477	Hopkins County	Madisonvi
15	469	Pulaski County	Somerset
16	463	Floyd County	Prestons
17	455	Jessamine County	Nicholasville
18	428	Henderson County	Henderson
19	400	Scott County	Georgetown
20	381	Mccracken County	Paducah
21	365	Franklin County	Frankfort
22	361	Muhlenberg County	Greenville
23	340	Carter County	Grayson
24	339	Shelby County	Shelbyville
25	333	Clark County	Winchester
26	332	Harlan County	Harlan
27	320	Knox County	Barbourvill
28	314	Perry County	Hazard
29	313	Clay County	Manchester
30	312	Whitley County	Williamsburg
31	309	Covington Independent	Covington
32	307	Marshall County	Benton
33	297	Lincoln County	Stanford
34	296	Owensboro Independent	Owensboro
35	284	Nelson County	Bardstown
36	283	Campbell County	Alexandria
37	274	Graves County	Mayfield
38	267	Grayson County	Leitchfield
39	266	Montgomery County	Mt Sterling
40	265	Meade County	Brandenburg
41	260	Barren County	Glasgow
42	252	Ohio County	Hartford
43	249	Boyd County	Ashland
44	240	Johnson County	Paintsville
45	236	Woodford County	Versailles
46	235	Mccreary County	Stearns
47	235	Letcher County	Whitesburg
48	233	Bell County	Pineville
49	232	Paducah Independent	Paducah
50	231	Bowling Green Ind	Bowling Green
51	215	Logan County	Russellville
52	214	Grant County	Williamsto
53	212	Anderson County	Lawrenceburg
54	209	Russell County	Jamestown
55	208	Ashland Ind	Ashland
55	208	Rowan County	Morehead

Number of Students

Rank	Number	District Name	City
57	200	Calloway County	Murray
58	200	Marion County	Lebanon
59	199	Greenup County	Greenup
60	198	Rockcastle County	Mt Verno
61	195	Adair County	Columbia
62	194	Knott County	Hindman
63	191	Boyle County	Danville
64	184	Lawrence County	Louisa
64	184	Simpson County	Franklin
66	180	Powell County	Stanton
67	179	Harrison County	Cynthiana
68	179	Estill County	Irvine
69	178	Pendleton County	Falmouth
70	177	Mason County	Maysville
71	174	Bourbon County	Paris
72	172	Allen County	Scottsville
72	172	Lewis County	Vanceburg
74	171	Garrard County	Lancaster
75	166	Magoffin County	Salyersville
76	166	Newport Independent	Newport
77	165	Jackson County	Mckee
78	163	Morgan County	West Liberty
79	163	Martin County	Inez
80	162	Fleming County	Flemingsburg
81	162	Hart County	Munfordville
82	160	Wayne County	Monticello
83	159	Taylor County	Campbellsville
83	159	Union County	Morganfiel
85	157	Casey County	Liberty
86	155	Breathitt County	Jackson
87	147	Breckinridge County	Hardinsburg
88	147	Fort Thomas Independent	Ft Thomas
89	145	Mercer County	Harrodsburg
90	143	Larue County	Hodgenville
91	142	Monroe County	Tompkinsville
92	142	Elizabethtown Independent	Elizabethtow
93	141	Caldwell County	Princeton
94	140	Erlanger-Elsmere Independent	Erlanger
95	139	Glasgow Independent	Glasgow
96	138	Butler County	Morgantown
97	138	Corbin Independent	Corbin
98	135	Edmonson County	Brownsville
98	135	Leslie County	Hyden
100	134	Spencer County	Taylorsvil
101	131	Trigg County	Cadiz
102	130	Henry County	New Castle
103	127	Bardstown Ind	Bardstown
104	123	Danville Independent	Danville
105	123	Bath County	Owingsv
106	120	Russell Independent	Russell
107	120	Todd County	Elkton
108	119	Metcalfe County	Edmonton
109	116	Middlesboro Independent	Middlesboro
110	114	Webster County	Dixon
111	114	Carroll County	Carrollton
112	113	Washington County	Springfie
113	113	Green County	Greensburg
114	106	Owen County	Owenton
115	105	Clinton County	Albany
115	105	Mclean County	Calhoun
117	105	Somerset Independent	Somerset
118	104	Murray Independent	Murray
119	97	Trimble County	Bedford
120	96	Hancock County	Hawesville
121	95	Mayfield Independent	Mayfiel
122	88	Ballard County	Barlow
123	88	Gallatin County	Warsaw

Number of Students

Rank	Number	District Name	City
1	95,582	Jefferson County	Louisville
2	34,259	Fayette County	Lexington
3	15,406	Boone County	Florence
4	13,466	Hardin County	Elizabe
5	12,752	Kenton County	Erlanger
6	11,710	Warren County	Bowling Gre
7	11,538	Bullitt County	Shepherdsville
8	11,084	Daviess County	Owensboro
9	10,533	Pike County	Pikeville
10	10,204	Oldham County	Buckner
11	10,067	Madison County	Richmond
12	9,474	Christian County	Hopkinsville
13	9,022	Laurel County	London
14	7,961	Pulaski County	Somerset
15	7,405	Hopkins County	Madisonvi
16	7,161	Scott County	Georgetown
17	7,150	Jessamine County	Nicholasville
18	7,080	Floyd County	Prestons
19	7,037	Henderson County	Henderson
20	6,902	Mccracken County	Paducah
21	6,026	Franklin County	Frankfort
22	5,537	Shelby County	Shelbyville

Rank	Number	District Name	City
23	5,507	Clark County	Winchester
24	5,376	Muhlenberg County	Greenville
25	5,197	Knox County	Barbourvill
26	5,101	Carter County	Grayson
27	5,014	Harlan County	Harlan
28	4,888	Nelson County	Bardstown
29	4,821	Whitley County	Williamsburg
30	4,809	Meade County	Brandenburg
31	4,804	Perry County	Hazard
32	4,782	Marshall County	Benton
33	4,688	Campbell County	Alexandria
34	4,642	Graves County	Mayfield
35	4,537	Lincoln County	Stanford
36	4,507	Covington Independent	Covington
37	4,376	Grayson County	Leitchfield
38	4,261	Owensboro Independent	Owensboro
39	4,231	Montgomery County	Mt Sterling
40	4,230	Clay County	Manchester
41	4,204	Barren County	Glasgow
42	4,188	Ohio County	Hartford
43	3,987	Anderson County	Lawrenceburg
44	3,840	Grant County	Williamsto
45	3,833	Woodford County	Versailles
46	3,825	Johnson County	Paintsville
47	3,774	Letcher County	Whitesburg
48	3,664	Bowling Green Ind	Bowling Green
49	3,627	Boyd County	Ashland
50	3,532	Logan County	Russellville
51	3,412	Mccreary County	Stearns
52	3,402	Ashland Ind	Ashland
53	3,277	Harrison County	Cynthiana
54	3,261	Greenup County	Greenup
55	3,201	Paducah Independent	Paducah
56	3,188	Bell County	Pineville
57	3,182	Marion County	Lebanon
58	3,113	Rowan County	Morehead
59	3,110	Simpson County	Franklin
60	3,065	Allen County	Scottsville
61	3,043	Calloway County	Murray
62	3,037	Rockcastle County	Mt Verno
63	3,016	Knott County	Hindman
64	2,972	Pendleton County	Falmouth
65	2,955	Mason County	Maysville
66	2,946	Bourbon County	Paris
67	2,935	Russell County	Jamestown
68	2,881	Boyle County	Danville
69	2,769	Breckinridge County	Hardinsburg
70	2,752	Wayne County	Monticello
71	2,743	Adair County	Columbia
72	2,705	Lawrence County	Louisa
73	2,687	Fleming County	Flemingsburg
74	2,667	Powell County	Stanton
75	2,655	Lewis County	Vanceburg
76	2,643	Taylor County	Campbellsville
77	2,592	Estill County	Irvine
78	2,572	Garrard County	Lancaster
79	2,560	Newport Independent	Newport
80	2,542	Magoffin County	Salyersville
81	2,519	Hart County	Munfordville
82	2,494	Martin County	Inez
83	2,489	Casey County	Liberty
84	2,469	Spencer County	Taylorsvil
85	2,459	Union County	Morganfiel
86	2,444	Jackson County	Mckee
87	2,441	Morgan County	West Liberty
88	2,411	Larue County	Hodgenville
89	2,328	Fort Thomas Independent	Ft Thomas
90	2,321	Breathitt County	Jackson
91	2,318	Mercer County	Harrodsburg
92	2,310	Elizabethtown Independent	Elizabethtow
93	2,255	Butler County	Morgantown
94	2,250	Leslie County	Hyden
95	2,240	Erlanger-Elsmere Independent	Erlanger
96	2,221	Corbin Independent	Corbin
97	2,199	Henry County	New Castle
98	2,173	Russell Independent	Russell
99	2,156	Edmonson County	Brownsville
100	2,135	Trigg County	Cadiz
101	2,110	Bardstown Ind	Bardstown
102	2,109	Todd County	Elkton
103	2,092	Caldwell County	Princeton
104	2,090	Monroe County	Tompkinsville
105	2,051	Glasgow Independent	Glasgow
106	2,017	Bath County	Owingsv
107	1,995	Webster County	Dixon
108	1,992	Owen County	Owenton
109	1,934	Carroll County	Carrollton
110	1,925	Washington County	Springfie
111	1,851	Danville Independent	Danville
112	1,841	Middlesboro Independent	Middlesboro
113	1,799	Murray Independent	Murray
114	1,732	Green County	Greensburg
115	1,709	Metcalfe County	Edmonton
116	1,708	Clinton County	Albany
117	1,672	Mclean County	Calhoun
118	1,634	Trimble County	Bedford
119	1,623	Hancock County	Hawesville
120	1,621	Gallatin County	Warsaw
121	1,612	Mayfield Independent	Mayfiel
122	1,546	Somerset Independent	Somerset
123	1,537	Ballard County	Barlow

Male Students

Rank	Percent	District Name	City
1	56.1	Martin County	Inez
2	54.6	Breathitt County	Jackson
3	54.4	Mercer County	Harrodsburg
4	54.3	Monroe County	Tompkinsville
5	53.9	Mayfield Independent	Mayfiel
6	53.7	Danville Independent	Danville
7	53.7	Knott County	Hindman
8	53.5	Owen County	Owenton
9	53.5	Erlanger-Elsmere Independent	Erlanger
10	53.5	Hart County	Munfordville
11	53.5	Jackson County	Mckee
12	53.5	Metcalfe County	Edmonton
13	53.5	Mason County	Maysville
14	53.4	Lawrence County	Louisa
15	53.4	Kenton County	Erlanger
16	53.4	Edmonson County	Brownsville
17	53.4	Garrard County	Lancaster
18	53.3	Covington Independent	Covington
19	53.3	Letcher County	Whitesburg
20	53.2	Wayne County	Monticello
21	53.2	Morgan County	West Liberty
22	53.2	Campbell County	Alexandria
23	53.2	Leslie County	Hyden
24	53.1	Pike County	Pikeville
25	53.0	Scott County	Georgetown
26	52.9	Lewis County	Vanceburg
27	52.9	Henry County	New Castle
28	52.9	Carroll County	Carrollton
29	52.8	Bath County	Owingsv
30	52.7	Knox County	Barbourvill
31	52.7	Glasgow Independent	Glasgow
32	52.6	Owensboro Independent	Owensboro
33	52.6	Simpson County	Franklin
34	52.5	Larue County	Hodgenville
35	52.5	Franklin County	Frankfort
36	52.5	Clay County	Manchester
37	52.5	Lincoln County	Stanford
38	52.3	Rockcastle County	Mt Verno
39	52.3	Hancock County	Hawesville
40	52.3	Warren County	Bowling Gre
41	52.3	Ohio County	Hartford
42	52.3	Pendleton County	Falmouth
43	52.3	Harlan County	Harlan
44	52.2	Hardin County	Elizabe
45	52.2	Boyle County	Danville
46	52.2	Middlesboro Independent	Middlesboro
47	52.2	Perry County	Hazard
48	52.2	Spencer County	Taylorsvil
49	52.1	Bowling Green Ind	Bowling Green
50	52.0	Mccracken County	Paducah
51	52.0	Boyd County	Ashland
52	52.0	Fort Thomas Independent	Ft Thomas
53	52.0	Grayson County	Leitchfield
54	52.0	Pulaski County	Somerset
55	52.0	Calloway County	Murray
56	51.9	Trigg County	Cadiz
57	51.9	Clark County	Winchester
58	51.9	Christian County	Hopkinsville
59	51.8	Somerset Independent	Somerset
60	51.8	Butler County	Morgantown
61	51.8	Daviess County	Owensboro
62	51.8	Laurel County	London
63	51.8	Meade County	Brandenburg
64	51.8	Ballard County	Barlow
65	51.7	Boone County	Florence
66	51.7	Harrison County	Cynthiana
67	51.7	Floyd County	Prestons
68	51.7	Marshall County	Benton
69	51.7	Marion County	Lebanon
70	51.7	Breckinridge County	Hardinsburg
71	51.7	Magoffin County	Salyersville
72	51.6	Fayette County	Lexington
73	51.6	Jessamine County	Nicholasville
74	51.6	Shelby County	Shelbyville
75	51.6	Powell County	Stanton
76	51.5	Henderson County	Henderson
77	51.5	Elizabethtown Independent	Elizabethtow
78	51.4	Oldham County	Buckner
79	51.4	Russell County	Jamestown
80	51.4	Bardstown Ind	Bardstown
81	51.4	Graves County	Mayfield
82	51.4	Bourbon County	Paris
83	51.4	Caldwell County	Princeton
84	51.4	Whitley County	Williamsburg
85	51.4	Johnson County	Paintsville
86	51.4	Bullitt County	Shepherdsville
87	51.4	Newport Independent	Newport
88	51.4	Grant County	Williamsto
89	51.4	Mccreary County	Stearns
90	51.3	Jefferson County	Louisville
91	51.3	Allen County	Scottsville
92	51.3	Washington County	Springfie
93	51.3	Estill County	Irvine
94	51.3	Bell County	Pineville
95	51.2	Russell Independent	Russell
96	51.2	Muhlenberg County	Greenville
97	51.2	Madison County	Richmond
98	51.2	Anderson County	Lawrenceburg
99	51.1	Mclean County	Calhoun
100	51.1	Montgomery County	Mt Sterling
101	51.1	Corbin Independent	Corbin
102	51.1	Green County	Greensburg
103	51.0	Casey County	Liberty
104	51.0	Nelson County	Bardstown
105	50.9	Ashland Ind	Ashland
106	50.9	Union County	Morganfiel
107	50.8	Trimble County	Bedford
108	50.8	Paducah Independent	Paducah
109	50.8	Taylor County	Campbellsville
110	50.7	Logan County	Russellville
111	50.7	Hopkins County	Madisonvi
112	50.6	Barren County	Glasgow
113	50.6	Carter County	Grayson
114	50.6	Greenup County	Greenup
115	50.6	Fleming County	Flemingsburg
116	50.6	Clinton County	Albany
117	50.5	Rowan County	Morehead
118	50.4	Todd County	Elkton
119	50.3	Gallatin County	Warsaw
120	50.3	Adair County	Columbia
121	49.8	Murray Independent	Murray
122	49.4	Woodford County	Versailles
123	49.1	Webster County	Dixon

Female Students

Rank	Percent	District Name	City
1	50.8	Webster County	Dixon
2	50.5	Woodford County	Versailles
3	50.1	Murray Independent	Murray
4	49.6	Adair County	Columbia
5	49.6	Gallatin County	Warsaw
6	49.5	Todd County	Elkton
7	49.4	Rowan County	Morehead
8	49.3	Clinton County	Albany
9	49.3	Fleming County	Flemingsburg
10	49.3	Greenup County	Greenup
11	49.3	Carter County	Grayson
12	49.3	Barren County	Glasgow
13	49.2	Hopkins County	Madisonvi
14	49.2	Logan County	Russellville
15	49.1	Taylor County	Campbellsville
16	49.1	Paducah Independent	Paducah
17	49.1	Trimble County	Bedford
18	49.0	Union County	Morganfiel
19	49.0	Ashland Ind	Ashland
20	48.9	Nelson County	Bardstown
21	48.9	Casey County	Liberty
22	48.8	Green County	Greensburg
23	48.8	Corbin Independent	Corbin
24	48.8	Montgomery County	Mt Sterling
25	48.8	Mclean County	Calhoun
26	48.7	Anderson County	Lawrenceburg
27	48.7	Madison County	Richmond
28	48.7	Muhlenberg County	Greenville
29	48.7	Russell Independent	Russell
30	48.6	Bell County	Pineville
31	48.6	Estill County	Irvine
32	48.6	Washington County	Springfie
33	48.6	Allen County	Scottsville
34	48.6	Jefferson County	Louisville
35	48.5	Mccreary County	Stearns
36	48.5	Grant County	Williamsto
37	48.5	Newport Independent	Newport
38	48.5	Bullitt County	Shepherdsville
39	48.5	Johnson County	Paintsville
40	48.5	Whitley County	Williamsburg
41	48.5	Caldwell County	Princeton
42	48.5	Bourbon County	Paris
43	48.5	Graves County	Mayfield
44	48.5	Bardstown Ind	Bardstown
45	48.5	Russell County	Jamestown
46	48.5	Oldham County	Buckner

Rank	Percent	District Name	City
47	48.4	Elizabethtown Independent	Elizabethtow
48	48.4	Henderson County	Henderson
49	48.3	Powell County	Stanton
50	48.3	Shelby County	Shelbyville
51	48.3	Jessamine County	Nicholasville
52	48.3	Fayette County	Lexington
53	48.2	Magoffin County	Salyersville
54	48.2	Breckinridge County	Hardinsburg
55	48.2	Marion County	Lebanon
56	48.2	Marshall County	Benton
57	48.2	Floyd County	Prestons
58	48.2	Harrison County	Cynthiana
59	48.2	Boone County	Florence
60	48.1	Ballard County	Barlow
61	48.1	Meade County	Brandenburg
62	48.1	Laurel County	London
63	48.1	Daviess County	Owensboro
64	48.1	Butler County	Morgantown
65	48.1	Somerset Independent	Somerset
66	48.0	Christian County	Hopkinsville
67	48.0	Clark County	Winchester
68	48.0	Trigg County	Cadiz
69	47.9	Calloway County	Murray
70	47.9	Pulaski County	Somerset
71	47.9	Grayson County	Leitchfield
72	47.9	Fort Thomas Independent	Ft Thomas
73	47.9	Boyd County	Ashland
74	47.9	Mccracken County	Paducah
75	47.8	Bowling Green Ind	Bowling Green
76	47.7	Spencer County	Taylorsvil
77	47.7	Perry County	Hazard
78	47.7	Middlesboro Independent	Middlesboro
79	47.7	Boyle County	Danville
80	47.7	Hardin County	Elizabe
81	47.6	Harlan County	Harlan
82	47.6	Pendleton County	Falmouth
83	47.6	Ohio County	Hartford
84	47.6	Warren County	Bowling Gre
85	47.6	Hancock County	Hawesville
86	47.5	Rockcastle County	Mt Verno
87	47.4	Lincoln County	Stanford
88	47.4	Clay County	Manchester
89	47.4	Franklin County	Frankfort
90	47.4	Larue County	Hodgenville
91	47.3	Simpson County	Franklin
92	47.3	Owensboro Independent	Owensboro
93	47.2	Glasgow Independent	Glasgow
94	47.2	Knox County	Barbourvill
95	47.1	Bath County	Owingsv
96	47.0	Carroll County	Carrollton
97	47.0	Henry County	New Castle
98	47.0	Lewis County	Vanceburg
99	46.9	Scott County	Georgetown
100	46.8	Pike County	Pikeville
101	46.7	Leslie County	Hyden
102	46.7	Campbell County	Alexandria
103	46.7	Morgan County	West Liberty
104	46.7	Wayne County	Monticello
105	46.6	Letcher County	Whitesburg
106	46.6	Covington Independent	Covington
107	46.5	Garrard County	Lancaster
108	46.5	Edmonson County	Brownsville
109	46.5	Kenton County	Erlanger
110	46.5	Lawrence County	Louisa
111	46.4	Mason County	Maysville
112	46.4	Metcalfe County	Edmonton
113	46.4	Jackson County	Mckee
114	46.4	Hart County	Munfordville
115	46.4	Erlanger-Elsmere Independent	Erlanger
116	46.4	Owen County	Owenton
117	46.2	Knott County	Hindman
118	46.2	Danville Independent	Danville
119	46.0	Mayfield Independent	Mayfiel
120	45.6	Monroe County	Tompkinsville
121	45.5	Mercer County	Harrodsburg
122	45.3	Breathitt County	Jackson
123	43.8	Martin County	Inez

Individual Education Program Students

Rank	Percent	District Name	City
1	23.1	Union County	Morganfiel
2	22.7	Breathitt County	Jackson
3	22.6	Clay County	Manchester
4	21.8	Boyle County	Danville
5	20.9	Lincoln County	Stanford
6	20.8	Ballard County	Barlow
7	20.4	Letcher County	Whitesburg
8	20.3	Clinton County	Albany
9	20.2	Todd County	Elkton
10	20.0	Madison County	Richmond
11	19.7	Martin County	Inez
12	19.6	Danville Independent	Danville
13	19.5	Owensboro Independent	Owensboro
14	19.4	Anderson County	Lawrenceburg
14	19.4	Boyd County	Ashland
14	19.4	Hopkins County	Madisonvi
17	19.3	Covington Independent	Covington
17	19.3	Edmonson County	Brownsville
17	19.3	Jackson County	Mckee
20	18.9	Estill County	Irvine
20	18.9	Knott County	Hindman
22	18.8	Perry County	Hazard
23	18.7	Morgan County	West Liberty
24	18.6	Larue County	Hodgenville
25	18.5	Floyd County	Prestons
25	18.5	Russell County	Jamestown
27	18.4	Campbell County	Alexandria
28	18.3	Calloway County	Murray
29	18.2	Logan County	Russellville
29	18.2	Mccreary County	Stearns
29	18.2	Powell County	Stanton
29	18.2	Washington County	Springfie
33	18.1	Leslie County	Hyden
33	18.1	Rowan County	Morehead
35	18.0	Carter County	Grayson
35	18.0	Muhlenberg County	Greenville
35	18.0	Whitley County	Williamsburg
38	17.6	Rockcastle County	Mt Verno
39	17.5	Spencer County	Taylorsvil
39	17.5	Trigg County	Cadiz
41	17.4	Bell County	Pineville
41	17.4	Gallatin County	Warsaw
43	17.3	Hart County	Munfordville
44	17.2	Adair County	Columbia
45	16.9	Harlan County	Harlan
45	16.9	Knox County	Barbourvill
45	16.9	Magoffin County	Salyersville
45	16.9	Middlesboro Independent	Middlesboro
49	16.8	Marion County	Lebanon
50	16.7	Erlanger-Elsmere Independent	Erlanger
50	16.7	Greenup County	Greenup
50	16.7	Johnson County	Paintsville
50	16.7	Ohio County	Hartford
54	16.6	Jessamine County	Nicholasville
54	16.6	Laurel County	London
54	16.6	Lawrence County	Louisa
54	16.6	Newport Independent	Newport
58	16.4	Butler County	Morgantown
59	16.3	Green County	Greensburg
59	16.3	Henderson County	Henderson
61	16.2	Mercer County	Harrodsburg
62	16.1	Lewis County	Vanceburg
63	16.0	Ashland Ind	Ashland
63	16.0	Hardin County	Elizabe
65	15.9	Breckinridge County	Hardinsburg
65	15.9	Christian County	Hopkinsville
65	15.9	Glasgow Independent	Glasgow
68	15.8	Mayfield Independent	Mayfiel
68	15.8	Murray Independent	Murray
68	15.8	Wayne County	Monticello
71	15.7	Nelson County	Bardstown
71	15.7	Webster County	Dixon
73	15.6	Casey County	Liberty
73	15.6	Meade County	Brandenburg
75	15.5	Daviess County	Owensboro
75	15.5	Garrard County	Lancaster
75	15.5	Harrison County	Cynthiana
75	15.5	Metcalfe County	Edmonton
79	15.3	Bardstown Ind	Bardstown
79	15.3	Trimble County	Bedford
81	15.1	Pulaski County	Somerset
82	15.0	Barren County	Glasgow
82	15.0	Clark County	Winchester
84	14.9	Graves County	Mayfield
84	14.9	Mclean County	Calhoun
84	14.9	Monroe County	Tompkinsville
87	14.8	Taylor County	Campbellsville
88	14.7	Bourbon County	Paris
88	14.7	Caldwell County	Princeton
90	14.6	Mccracken County	Paducah
91	14.3	Mason County	Maysville
91	14.3	Oldham County	Buckner
93	14.2	Grayson County	Leitchfield
93	14.2	Jefferson County	Louisville
95	14.1	Bath County	Owingsv
95	14.1	Bullitt County	Shepherdsville
95	14.1	Carroll County	Carrollton
98	14.0	Grant County	Williamsto
99	13.9	Hancock County	Hawesville
99	13.9	Pendleton County	Falmouth
99	13.9	Pike County	Pikeville
102	13.8	Kenton County	Erlanger
102	13.8	Shelby County	Shelbyville
104	13.7	Fleming County	Flemingsburg
104	13.7	Montgomery County	Mt Sterling
106	13.5	Boone County	Florence
107	13.4	Franklin County	Frankfort
108	13.3	Paducah Independent	Paducah
109	13.2	Corbin Independent	Corbin
110	13.0	Allen County	Scottsville
110	13.0	Marshall County	Benton
112	12.7	Scott County	Georgetown
113	12.6	Somerset Independent	Somerset
113	12.6	Warren County	Bowling Gre
115	12.5	Russell Independent	Russell
116	12.4	Bowling Green Ind	Bowling Green
116	12.4	Owen County	Owenton
118	12.2	Henry County	New Castle
119	12.1	Simpson County	Franklin
120	11.3	Elizabethtown Independent	Elizabethtow
121	11.1	Woodford County	Versailles
122	10.4	Fayette County	Lexington
122	10.4	Fort Thomas Independent	Ft Thomas

English Language Learner Students

Rank	Percent	District Name	City
1	13.0	Bowling Green Ind	Bowling Green
2	7.4	Mayfield Independent	Mayfiel
3	4.4	Shelby County	Shelbyville
3	4.4	Warren County	Bowling Gre
5	3.6	Fayette County	Lexington
6	3.5	Jefferson County	Louisville
7	2.7	Erlanger-Elsmere Independent	Erlanger
8	2.5	Woodford County	Versailles
9	2.3	Boone County	Florence
9	2.3	Carroll County	Carrollton
9	2.3	Garrard County	Lancaster
12	2.2	Oldham County	Buckner
13	1.7	Somerset Independent	Somerset
13	1.7	Washington County	Springfie
15	1.5	Gallatin County	Warsaw
15	1.5	Murray Independent	Murray
17	1.4	Graves County	Mayfield
18	1.2	Paducah Independent	Paducah
19	1.1	Jessamine County	Nicholasville
19	1.1	Monroe County	Tompkinsville
21	1.0	Danville Independent	Danville
21	1.0	Franklin County	Frankfort
21	1.0	Henry County	New Castle
21	1.0	Marion County	Lebanon
21	1.0	Trimble County	Bedford
26	0.9	Christian County	Hopkinsville
26	0.9	Kenton County	Erlanger
26	0.9	Larue County	Hodgenville
29	0.8	Clinton County	Albany
29	0.8	Glasgow Independent	Glasgow
29	0.8	Hardin County	Elizabe
29	0.8	Montgomery County	Mt Sterling
29	0.8	Ohio County	Hartford
34	0.7	Campbell County	Alexandria
34	0.7	Newport Independent	Newport
36	0.6	Calloway County	Murray
36	0.6	Elizabethtown Independent	Elizabethtow
36	0.6	Grant County	Williamsto
36	0.6	Laurel County	London
36	0.6	Owen County	Owenton
36	0.6	Taylor County	Campbellsville
42	0.5	Bardstown Ind	Bardstown
42	0.5	Clark County	Winchester
42	0.5	Daviess County	Owensboro
42	0.5	Henderson County	Henderson
42	0.5	Madison County	Richmond
42	0.5	Mason County	Maysville
42	0.5	Scott County	Georgetown
49	0.4	Adair County	Columbia
49	0.4	Bourbon County	Paris
49	0.4	Boyle County	Danville
49	0.4	Harrison County	Cynthiana
49	0.4	Mercer County	Harrodsburg
49	0.4	Owensboro Independent	Owensboro
49	0.4	Pendleton County	Falmouth
56	0.3	Anderson County	Lawrenceburg
56	0.3	Covington Independent	Covington
56	0.3	Fleming County	Flemingsburg
56	0.3	Lincoln County	Stanford
56	0.3	Mccracken County	Paducah
56	0.3	Powell County	Stanton
56	0.3	Rowan County	Morehead
63	0.2	Barren County	Glasgow
63	0.2	Hart County	Munfordville
63	0.2	Marshall County	Benton
63	0.2	Russell County	Jamestown
63	0.2	Spencer County	Taylorsvil
68	0.1	Ashland Ind	Ashland
68	0.1	Ballard County	Barlow
68	0.1	Boyd County	Ashland

Rank	Percent	District Name	City
68	0.1	Breckinridge County	Hardinsburg
68	0.1	Bullitt County	Shepherdsville
68	0.1	Butler County	Morgantown
68	0.1	Estill County	Irvine
68	0.1	Fort Thomas Independent	Ft Thomas
68	0.1	Grayson County	Leitchfield
68	0.1	Meade County	Brandenburg
68	0.1	Middlesboro Independent	Middlesboro
68	0.1	Morgan County	West Liberty
68	0.1	Muhlenberg County	Greenville
68	0.1	Pulaski County	Somerset
68	0.1	Simpson County	Franklin
83	0.0	Greenup County	Greenup
84	0.0	Allen County	Scottsville
84	0.0	Bath County	Owingsv
84	0.0	Bell County	Pineville
84	0.0	Breathitt County	Jackson
84	0.0	Caldwell County	Princeton
84	0.0	Carter County	Grayson
84	0.0	Casey County	Liberty
84	0.0	Clay County	Manchester
84	0.0	Corbin Independent	Corbin
84	0.0	Edmonson County	Brownsville
84	0.0	Floyd County	Prestons
84	0.0	Green County	Greensburg
84	0.0	Hancock County	Hawesville
84	0.0	Harlan County	Harlan
84	0.0	Hopkins County	Madisonvi
84	0.0	Jackson County	Mckee
84	0.0	Johnson County	Paintsville
84	0.0	Knott County	Hindman
84	0.0	Knox County	Barbourvill
84	0.0	Lawrence County	Louisa
84	0.0	Leslie County	Hyden
84	0.0	Letcher County	Whitesburg
84	0.0	Lewis County	Vanceburg
84	0.0	Logan County	Russellville
84	0.0	Magoffin County	Salyersville
84	0.0	Martin County	Inez
84	0.0	Mccreary County	Stearns
84	0.0	Mclean County	Calhoun
84	0.0	Metcalfe County	Edmonton
84	0.0	Nelson County	Bardstown
84	0.0	Perry County	Hazard
84	0.0	Pike County	Pikeville
84	0.0	Rockcastle County	Mt Verno
84	0.0	Russell Independent	Russell
84	0.0	Todd County	Elkton
84	0.0	Trigg County	Cadiz
84	0.0	Union County	Morganfiel
84	0.0	Wayne County	Monticello
84	0.0	Webster County	Dixon
84	0.0	Whitley County	Williamsburg

Migrant Students

Rank	Percent	District Name	City
1	16.0	Pendleton County	Falmouth
2	14.1	Rockcastle County	Mt Verno
3	13.1	Powell County	Stanton
4	13.0	Mayfield Independent	Mayfiel
4	13.0	Metcalfe County	Edmonton
6	12.9	Caldwell County	Princeton
7	11.8	Glasgow Independent	Glasgow
8	11.0	Monroe County	Tompkinsville
9	10.7	Ballard County	Barlow
10	10.5	Bath County	Owingsv
11	9.7	Montgomery County	Mt Sterling
12	9.6	Barren County	Glasgow
13	8.6	Garrard County	Lancaster
14	8.4	Wayne County	Monticello
15	7.4	Graves County	Mayfield
16	7.1	Mclean County	Calhoun
17	6.9	Todd County	Elkton
18	6.8	Adair County	Columbia
19	6.3	Owen County	Owenton
20	5.7	Clinton County	Albany
20	5.7	Lewis County	Vanceburg
22	5.6	Breathitt County	Jackson
22	5.6	Lawrence County	Louisa
24	5.5	Bourbon County	Paris
25	5.1	Carroll County	Carrollton
25	5.1	Madison County	Richmond
25	5.1	Russell County	Jamestown
28	5.0	Calloway County	Murray
28	5.0	Hart County	Munfordville
28	5.0	Letcher County	Whitesburg
31	4.9	Trimble County	Bedford
32	4.6	Casey County	Liberty
33	4.5	Green County	Greensburg
34	4.4	Hopkins County	Madisonvi
35	4.3	Ohio County	Hartford
36	4.1	Muhlenberg County	Greenville
37	4.0	Harrison County	Cynthiana
37	4.0	Owensboro Independent	Owensboro
37	4.0	Webster County	Dixon
40	3.9	Carter County	Grayson
40	3.9	Mccracken County	Paducah
42	3.7	Mason County	Maysville
43	3.6	Pike County	Pikeville
43	3.6	Shelby County	Shelbyville
45	3.4	Ashland Ind	Ashland
45	3.4	Morgan County	West Liberty
45	3.4	Murray Independent	Murray
48	3.3	Christian County	Hopkinsville
48	3.3	Greenup County	Greenup
50	3.1	Grayson County	Leitchfield
50	3.1	Trigg County	Cadiz
52	3.0	Marion County	Lebanon
52	3.0	Pulaski County	Somerset
54	2.9	Grant County	Williamsto
55	2.8	Union County	Morganfiel
56	2.7	Breckinridge County	Hardinsburg
56	2.7	Marshall County	Benton
56	2.7	Martin County	Inez
59	2.6	Clark County	Winchester
60	2.5	Henry County	New Castle
60	2.5	Larue County	Hodgenville
62	2.4	Lincoln County	Stanford
62	2.4	Logan County	Russellville
62	2.4	Scott County	Georgetown
62	2.4	Washington County	Springfie
66	2.2	Henderson County	Henderson
66	2.2	Rowan County	Morehead
68	2.1	Gallatin County	Warsaw
69	2.0	Boyle County	Danville
69	2.0	Fleming County	Flemingsburg
71	1.9	Boyd County	Ashland
71	1.9	Danville Independent	Danville
71	1.9	Daviess County	Owensboro
71	1.9	Jessamine County	Nicholasville
71	1.9	Taylor County	Campbellsville
76	1.8	Allen County	Scottsville
77	1.7	Estill County	Irvine
77	1.7	Woodford County	Versailles
79	1.6	Somerset Independent	Somerset
80	1.2	Bowling Green Ind	Bowling Green
81	1.1	Jackson County	Mckee
82	1.0	Butler County	Morgantown
82	1.0	Edmonson County	Brownsville
82	1.0	Fayette County	Lexington
82	1.0	Russell Independent	Russell
86	0.9	Simpson County	Franklin
87	0.8	Meade County	Brandenburg
87	0.8	Paducah Independent	Paducah
89	0.7	Bullitt County	Shepherdsville
89	0.7	Oldham County	Buckner
89	0.7	Warren County	Bowling Gre
92	0.6	Hardin County	Elizabe
93	0.4	Spencer County	Taylorsvil
94	0.3	Mercer County	Harrodsburg
95	0.2	Elizabethtown Independent	Elizabethtow
95	0.2	Jefferson County	Louisville
97	0.1	Anderson County	Lawrenceburg
97	0.1	Campbell County	Alexandria
99	0.0	Bardstown Ind	Bardstown
99	0.0	Bell County	Pineville
99	0.0	Boone County	Florence
99	0.0	Clay County	Manchester
99	0.0	Corbin Independent	Corbin
99	0.0	Covington Independent	Covington
99	0.0	Erlanger-Elsmere Independent	Erlanger
99	0.0	Floyd County	Prestons
99	0.0	Fort Thomas Independent	Ft Thomas
99	0.0	Franklin County	Frankfort
99	0.0	Hancock County	Hawesville
99	0.0	Harlan County	Harlan
99	0.0	Johnson County	Paintsville
99	0.0	Kenton County	Erlanger
99	0.0	Knott County	Hindman
99	0.0	Knox County	Barbourvill
99	0.0	Laurel County	London
99	0.0	Leslie County	Hyden
99	0.0	Magoffin County	Salyersville
99	0.0	Mccreary County	Stearns
99	0.0	Middlesboro Independent	Middlesboro
99	0.0	Nelson County	Bardstown
99	0.0	Newport Independent	Newport
99	0.0	Perry County	Hazard
99	0.0	Whitley County	Williamsburg

Students Eligible for Free Lunch

Rank	Percent	District Name	City
1	n/a	Adair County	Columbia
1	n/a	Allen County	Scottsville
1	n/a	Anderson County	Lawrenceburg
1	n/a	Ashland Ind	Ashland
1	n/a	Ballard County	Barlow
1	n/a	Bardstown Ind	Bardstown
1	n/a	Barren County	Glasgow
1	n/a	Bath County	Owingsv
1	n/a	Bell County	Pineville
1	n/a	Boone County	Florence
1	n/a	Bourbon County	Paris
1	n/a	Bowling Green Ind	Bowling Green
1	n/a	Boyd County	Ashland
1	n/a	Boyle County	Danville
1	n/a	Breathitt County	Jackson
1	n/a	Breckinridge County	Hardinsburg
1	n/a	Bullitt County	Shepherdsville
1	n/a	Butler County	Morgantown
1	n/a	Caldwell County	Princeton
1	n/a	Calloway County	Murray
1	n/a	Campbell County	Alexandria
1	n/a	Carroll County	Carrollton
1	n/a	Carter County	Grayson
1	n/a	Casey County	Liberty
1	n/a	Christian County	Hopkinsville
1	n/a	Clark County	Winchester
1	n/a	Clay County	Manchester
1	n/a	Clinton County	Albany
1	n/a	Corbin Independent	Corbin
1	n/a	Covington Independent	Covington
1	n/a	Danville Independent	Danville
1	n/a	Daviess County	Owensboro
1	n/a	Edmonson County	Brownsville
1	n/a	Elizabethtown Independent	Elizabethtow
1	n/a	Erlanger-Elsmere Independent	Erlanger
1	n/a	Estill County	Irvine
1	n/a	Fayette County	Lexington
1	n/a	Fleming County	Flemingsburg
1	n/a	Floyd County	Prestons
1	n/a	Fort Thomas Independent	Ft Thomas
1	n/a	Franklin County	Frankfort
1	n/a	Gallatin County	Warsaw
1	n/a	Garrard County	Lancaster
1	n/a	Glasgow Independent	Glasgow
1	n/a	Grant County	Williamsto
1	n/a	Graves County	Mayfield
1	n/a	Grayson County	Leitchfield
1	n/a	Green County	Greensburg
1	n/a	Greenup County	Greenup
1	n/a	Hancock County	Hawesville
1	n/a	Hardin County	Elizabe
1	n/a	Harlan County	Harlan
1	n/a	Harrison County	Cynthiana
1	n/a	Hart County	Munfordville
1	n/a	Henderson County	Henderson
1	n/a	Henry County	New Castle
1	n/a	Hopkins County	Madisonvi
1	n/a	Jackson County	Mckee
1	n/a	Jefferson County	Louisville
1	n/a	Jessamine County	Nicholasville
1	n/a	Johnson County	Paintsville
1	n/a	Kenton County	Erlanger
1	n/a	Knott County	Hindman
1	n/a	Knox County	Barbourvill
1	n/a	Larue County	Hodgenville
1	n/a	Laurel County	London
1	n/a	Lawrence County	Louisa
1	n/a	Leslie County	Hyden
1	n/a	Letcher County	Whitesburg
1	n/a	Lewis County	Vanceburg
1	n/a	Lincoln County	Stanford
1	n/a	Logan County	Russellville
1	n/a	Madison County	Richmond
1	n/a	Magoffin County	Salyersville
1	n/a	Marion County	Lebanon
1	n/a	Marshall County	Benton
1	n/a	Martin County	Inez
1	n/a	Mason County	Maysville
1	n/a	Mayfield Independent	Mayfiel
1	n/a	Mccracken County	Paducah
1	n/a	Mccreary County	Stearns
1	n/a	Mclean County	Calhoun
1	n/a	Meade County	Brandenburg
1	n/a	Mercer County	Harrodsburg
1	n/a	Metcalfe County	Edmonton
1	n/a	Middlesboro Independent	Middlesboro
1	n/a	Monroe County	Tompkinsville
1	n/a	Montgomery County	Mt Sterling
1	n/a	Morgan County	West Liberty
1	n/a	Muhlenberg County	Greenville
1	n/a	Murray Independent	Murray
1	n/a	Nelson County	Bardstown
1	n/a	Newport Independent	Newport
1	n/a	Ohio County	Hartford
1	n/a	Oldham County	Buckner

Rank	Percent	District Name	City
1	n/a	Owen County	Owenton
1	n/a	Owensboro Independent	Owensboro
1	n/a	Paducah Independent	Paducah
1	n/a	Pendleton County	Falmouth
1	n/a	Perry County	Hazard
1	n/a	Pike County	Pikeville
1	n/a	Powell County	Stanton
1	n/a	Pulaski County	Somerset
1	n/a	Rockcastle County	Mt Verno
1	n/a	Rowan County	Morehead
1	n/a	Russell County	Jamestown
1	n/a	Russell Independent	Russell
1	n/a	Scott County	Georgetown
1	n/a	Shelby County	Shelbyville
1	n/a	Simpson County	Franklin
1	n/a	Somerset Independent	Somerset
1	n/a	Spencer County	Taylorsvil
1	n/a	Taylor County	Campbellsville
1	n/a	Todd County	Elkton
1	n/a	Trigg County	Cadiz
1	n/a	Trimble County	Bedford
1	n/a	Union County	Morganfiel
1	n/a	Warren County	Bowling Gre
1	n/a	Washington County	Springfie
1	n/a	Wayne County	Monticello
1	n/a	Webster County	Dixon
1	n/a	Whitley County	Williamsburg
1	n/a	Woodford County	Versailles

Students Eligible for Reduced-Price Lunch

Rank	Percent	District Name	City
1	n/a	Adair County	Columbia
1	n/a	Allen County	Scottsville
1	n/a	Anderson County	Lawrenceburg
1	n/a	Ashland Ind	Ashland
1	n/a	Ballard County	Barlow
1	n/a	Bardstown Ind	Bardstown
1	n/a	Barren County	Glasgow
1	n/a	Bath County	Owingsv
1	n/a	Bell County	Pineville
1	n/a	Boone County	Florence
1	n/a	Bourbon County	Paris
1	n/a	Bowling Green Ind	Bowling Green
1	n/a	Boyd County	Ashland
1	n/a	Boyle County	Danville
1	n/a	Breathitt County	Jackson
1	n/a	Breckinridge County	Hardinsburg
1	n/a	Bullitt County	Shepherdsville
1	n/a	Butler County	Morgantown
1	n/a	Caldwell County	Princeton
1	n/a	Calloway County	Murray
1	n/a	Campbell County	Alexandria
1	n/a	Carroll County	Carrollton
1	n/a	Carter County	Grayson
1	n/a	Casey County	Liberty
1	n/a	Christian County	Hopkinsville
1	n/a	Clark County	Winchester
1	n/a	Clay County	Manchester
1	n/a	Clinton County	Albany
1	n/a	Corbin Independent	Corbin
1	n/a	Covington Independent	Covington
1	n/a	Danville Independent	Danville
1	n/a	Daviess County	Owensboro
1	n/a	Edmonson County	Brownsville
1	n/a	Elizabethtown Independent	Elizabethtow
1	n/a	Erlanger-Elsmere Independent	Erlanger
1	n/a	Estill County	Irvine
1	n/a	Fayette County	Lexington
1	n/a	Fleming County	Flemingsburg
1	n/a	Floyd County	Prestons
1	n/a	Fort Thomas Independent	Ft Thomas
1	n/a	Franklin County	Frankfort
1	n/a	Gallatin County	Warsaw
1	n/a	Garrard County	Lancaster
1	n/a	Glasgow Independent	Glasgow
1	n/a	Grant County	Williamsto
1	n/a	Graves County	Mayfield
1	n/a	Grayson County	Leitchfield
1	n/a	Green County	Greensburg
1	n/a	Greenup County	Greenup
1	n/a	Hancock County	Hawesville
1	n/a	Hardin County	Elizabe
1	n/a	Harlan County	Harlan
1	n/a	Harrison County	Cynthiana
1	n/a	Hart County	Munfordville
1	n/a	Henderson County	Henderson
1	n/a	Henry County	New Castle
1	n/a	Hopkins County	Madisonvi
1	n/a	Jackson County	Mckee
1	n/a	Jefferson County	Louisville
1	n/a	Jessamine County	Nicholasville
1	n/a	Johnson County	Paintsville
1	n/a	Kenton County	Erlanger
1	n/a	Knott County	Hindman
1	n/a	Knox County	Barbourvill
1	n/a	Larue County	Hodgenville
1	n/a	Laurel County	London
1	n/a	Lawrence County	Louisa
1	n/a	Leslie County	Hyden
1	n/a	Letcher County	Whitesburg
1	n/a	Lewis County	Vanceburg
1	n/a	Lincoln County	Stanford
1	n/a	Logan County	Russellville
1	n/a	Madison County	Richmond
1	n/a	Magoffin County	Salyersville
1	n/a	Marion County	Lebanon
1	n/a	Marshall County	Benton
1	n/a	Martin County	Inez
1	n/a	Mason County	Maysville
1	n/a	Mayfield Independent	Mayfiel
1	n/a	Mccracken County	Paducah
1	n/a	Mccreary County	Stearns
1	n/a	Mclean County	Calhoun
1	n/a	Meade County	Brandenburg
1	n/a	Mercer County	Harrodsburg
1	n/a	Metcalfe County	Edmonton
1	n/a	Middlesboro Independent	Middlesboro
1	n/a	Monroe County	Tompkinsville
1	n/a	Montgomery County	Mt Sterling
1	n/a	Morgan County	West Liberty
1	n/a	Muhlenberg County	Greenville
1	n/a	Murray Independent	Murray
1	n/a	Nelson County	Bardstown
1	n/a	Newport Independent	Newport
1	n/a	Ohio County	Hartford
1	n/a	Oldham County	Buckner
1	n/a	Owen County	Owenton
1	n/a	Owensboro Independent	Owensboro
1	n/a	Paducah Independent	Paducah
1	n/a	Pendleton County	Falmouth
1	n/a	Perry County	Hazard
1	n/a	Pike County	Pikeville
1	n/a	Powell County	Stanton
1	n/a	Pulaski County	Somerset
1	n/a	Rockcastle County	Mt Verno
1	n/a	Rowan County	Morehead
1	n/a	Russell County	Jamestown
1	n/a	Russell Independent	Russell
1	n/a	Scott County	Georgetown
1	n/a	Shelby County	Shelbyville
1	n/a	Simpson County	Franklin
1	n/a	Somerset Independent	Somerset
1	n/a	Spencer County	Taylorsvil
1	n/a	Taylor County	Campbellsville
1	n/a	Todd County	Elkton
1	n/a	Trigg County	Cadiz
1	n/a	Trimble County	Bedford
1	n/a	Union County	Morganfiel
1	n/a	Warren County	Bowling Gre
1	n/a	Washington County	Springfie
1	n/a	Wayne County	Monticello
1	n/a	Webster County	Dixon
1	n/a	Whitley County	Williamsburg
1	n/a	Woodford County	Versailles

Student/Teacher Ratio

Rank	Ratio	District Name	City
1	18.0	Owen County	Owenton
2	17.7	Breckinridge County	Hardinsburg
2	17.7	Laurel County	London
4	17.6	Kenton County	Erlanger
5	17.5	Gallatin County	Warsaw
5	17.5	Harrison County	Cynthiana
7	17.4	Anderson County	Lawrenceburg
7	17.4	Grant County	Williamsto
7	17.4	Mccracken County	Paducah
7	17.4	Russell Independent	Russell
11	17.3	Allen County	Scottsville
11	17.3	Bullitt County	Shepherdsville
11	17.3	Meade County	Brandenburg
14	17.1	Oldham County	Buckner
15	16.9	Spencer County	Taylorsvil
16	16.8	Boone County	Florence
17	16.6	Madison County	Richmond
18	16.5	Nelson County	Bardstown
19	16.4	Murray Independent	Murray
19	16.4	Webster County	Dixon
21	16.3	Warren County	Bowling Gre
22	16.2	Christian County	Hopkinsville
22	16.2	Henry County	New Castle
22	16.2	Jefferson County	Louisville
22	16.2	Larue County	Hodgenville
26	16.1	Graves County	Mayfield
26	16.1	Washington County	Springfie
28	16.0	Campbell County	Alexandria
28	16.0	Daviess County	Owensboro
28	16.0	Hancock County	Hawesville
28	16.0	Pulaski County	Somerset
28	16.0	Simpson County	Franklin
33	15.9	Carroll County	Carrollton
33	15.9	Elizabethtown Independent	Elizabethtow
33	15.9	Hardin County	Elizabe
33	15.9	Scott County	Georgetown
33	15.9	Taylor County	Campbellsville
33	15.9	Todd County	Elkton
33	15.9	Trimble County	Bedford
33	15.9	Wayne County	Monticello
33	15.9	Woodford County	Versailles
42	15.8	Franklin County	Frankfort
42	15.8	Henderson County	Henderson
42	15.8	Pendleton County	Falmouth
42	15.8	Shelby County	Shelbyville
46	15.7	Butler County	Morgantown
46	15.7	Clark County	Winchester
46	15.7	Corbin Independent	Corbin
49	15.6	Ashland Ind	Ashland
49	15.6	Bardstown Ind	Bardstown
49	15.6	Barren County	Glasgow
49	15.6	Bath County	Owingsv
49	15.6	Fort Thomas Independent	Ft Thomas
49	15.6	Greenup County	Greenup
49	15.6	Mayfield Independent	Mayfiel
49	15.6	Mercer County	Harrodsburg
49	15.6	Ohio County	Hartford
58	15.5	Fleming County	Flemingsburg
58	15.5	Leslie County	Hyden
58	15.5	Logan County	Russellville
61	15.4	Ballard County	Barlow
61	15.4	Erlanger-Elsmere Independent	Erlanger
61	15.4	Grayson County	Leitchfield
61	15.4	Trigg County	Cadiz
65	15.3	Bourbon County	Paris
65	15.3	Johnson County	Paintsville
67	15.2	Mason County	Maysville
68	15.1	Jessamine County	Nicholasville
68	15.1	Marion County	Lebanon
68	15.1	Middlesboro Independent	Middlesboro
68	15.1	Montgomery County	Mt Sterling
72	15.0	Bowling Green Ind	Bowling Green
72	15.0	Casey County	Liberty
72	15.0	Edmonson County	Brownsville
72	15.0	Marshall County	Benton
76	14.9	Mclean County	Calhoun
77	14.8	Knox County	Barbourvill
77	14.8	Letcher County	Whitesburg
77	14.8	Union County	Morganfiel
80	14.7	Clinton County	Albany
80	14.7	Pike County	Pikeville
80	14.7	Rockcastle County	Mt Verno
80	14.7	Whitley County	Williamsburg
84	14.6	Green County	Greensburg
84	14.6	Hart County	Munfordville
84	14.6	Hopkins County	Madisonvi
87	14.5	Floyd County	Prestons
88	14.4	Garrard County	Lancaster
88	14.4	Martin County	Inez
88	14.4	Newport Independent	Newport
88	14.4	Perry County	Hazard
88	14.4	Somerset Independent	Somerset
93	14.3	Boyle County	Danville
93	14.3	Calloway County	Murray
93	14.3	Magoffin County	Salyersville
96	14.2	Caldwell County	Princeton
96	14.2	Danville Independent	Danville
96	14.2	Knott County	Hindman
96	14.2	Lincoln County	Stanford
100	14.1	Carter County	Grayson
100	14.1	Harlan County	Harlan
100	14.1	Lawrence County	Louisa
100	14.1	Rowan County	Morehead
104	14.0	Lewis County	Vanceburg
104	14.0	Muhlenberg County	Greenville
104	14.0	Powell County	Stanton
107	13.9	Breathitt County	Jackson
107	13.9	Glasgow Independent	Glasgow
107	13.9	Monroe County	Tompkinsville
110	13.8	Estill County	Irvine
110	13.8	Jackson County	Mckee
110	13.8	Mccreary County	Stearns
113	13.7	Metcalfe County	Edmonton
114	13.6	Boyd County	Ashland
114	13.6	Morgan County	West Liberty
116	13.5	Russell County	Jamestown
117	13.3	Adair County	Columbia
117	13.3	Owensboro Independent	Owensboro

119	13.2	Bell County	Pineville
119	13.2	Covington Independent	Covington
121	13.1	Fayette County	Lexington
122	12.6	Clay County	Manchester
122	12.6	Paducah Independent	Paducah

Student/Librarian Ratio

Rank	Ratio	District Name	City
1	1,295.8	Clinton County	Albany
2	844.7	Taylor County	Campbellsville
3	811.3	Jessamine County	Nicholasville
4	801.6	Montgomery County	Mt Sterling
5	771.3	Boone County	Florence
6	756.7	Spencer County	Taylorsvil
7	754.5	Campbell County	Alexandria
8	752.7	Mercer County	Harrodsburg
9	747.2	Grant County	Williamsto
10	735.8	Graves County	Mayfield
11	733.8	Johnson County	Paintsville
12	707.8	Pendleton County	Falmouth
13	687.1	Lewis County	Vanceburg
14	685.0	Ballard County	Barlow
15	684.7	Grayson County	Leitchfield
16	682.2	Kenton County	Erlanger
17	681.0	Covington Independent	Covington
18	677.0	Mason County	Maysville
19	676.3	Trigg County	Cadiz
20	670.9	Anderson County	Lawrenceburg
21	661.7	Bardstown Ind	Bardstown
22	657.1	Meade County	Brandenburg
23	655.8	Ohio County	Hartford
24	650.3	Lawrence County	Louisa
25	646.0	Glasgow Independent	Glasgow
26	640.9	Madison County	Richmond
27	621.2	Bullitt County	Shepherdsville
28	618.3	Jefferson County	Louisville
29	608.4	Franklin County	Frankfort
30	604.7	Daviess County	Owensboro
31	604.0	Marion County	Lebanon
32	603.1	Henry County	New Castle
33	602.7	Oldham County	Buckner
34	600.5	Carter County	Grayson
35	597.4	Shelby County	Shelbyville
36	596.4	Allen County	Scottsville
37	592.4	Simpson County	Franklin
38	589.7	Washington County	Springfie
39	585.0	Martin County	Inez
40	584.6	Rockcastle County	Mt Verno
41	582.9	Boyd County	Ashland
42	578.9	Pulaski County	Somerset
43	572.6	Calloway County	Murray
44	572.5	Whitley County	Williamsburg
45	569.3	Murray Independent	Murray
46	566.5	Elizabethtown Independent	Elizabethtow
47	563.4	Henderson County	Henderson
48	560.6	Floyd County	Prestons
49	558.8	Christian County	Hopkinsville
49	558.8	Warren County	Bowling Gre
51	555.6	Corbin Independent	Corbin
52	555.5	Logan County	Russellville
53	554.3	Mccracken County	Paducah
54	549.0	Boyle County	Danville
55	548.3	Fayette County	Lexington
56	543.3	Butler County	Morgantown
57	541.6	Hardin County	Elizabe
58	541.2	Mccreary County	Stearns
59	540.0	Erlanger-Elsmere Independent	Erlanger
60	538.9	Casey County	Liberty
61	535.3	Woodford County	Versailles
62	534.7	Nelson County	Bardstown
63	533.8	Bourbon County	Paris
64	529.9	Lincoln County	Stanford
65	529.7	Scott County	Georgetown
66	525.8	Russell Independent	Russell
67	524.8	Clark County	Winchester
68	524.3	Mclean County	Calhoun
69	522.8	Breckinridge County	Hardinsburg
70	515.3	Hancock County	Hawesville
71	514.7	Gallatin County	Warsaw
71	514.7	Laurel County	London
73	512.2	Wayne County	Monticello
74	510.7	Marshall County	Benton
75	506.3	Somerset Independent	Somerset
76	505.3	Edmonson County	Brownsville
77	503.2	Powell County	Stanton
78	501.8	Fleming County	Flemingsburg
79	501.7	Barren County	Glasgow
80	499.3	Caldwell County	Princeton
81	498.6	Hopkins County	Madisonvi
82	497.6	Metcalfe County	Edmonton
83	496.6	Bowling Green Ind	Bowling Green
84	495.0	Estill County	Irvine
85	493.8	Garrard County	Lancaster
86	489.2	Rowan County	Morehead
87	481.7	Morgan County	West Liberty
88	478.6	Newport Independent	Newport
89	478.3	Bath County	Owingsv
89	478.3	Todd County	Elkton
91	476.8	Owen County	Owenton
92	474.6	Hart County	Munfordville
93	473.7	Knox County	Barbourvill
94	472.4	Paducah Independent	Paducah
95	470.6	Union County	Morganfiel
96	469.7	Russell County	Jamestown
97	464.4	Larue County	Hodgenville
98	464.1	Owensboro Independent	Owensboro
99	460.3	Green County	Greensburg
100	458.8	Fort Thomas Independent	Ft Thomas
101	457.6	Trimble County	Bedford
102	455.5	Pike County	Pikeville
103	452.3	Carroll County	Carrollton
104	448.3	Harrison County	Cynthiana
105	439.7	Muhlenberg County	Greenville
106	438.1	Bell County	Pineville
107	437.5	Middlesboro Independent	Middlesboro
108	435.1	Letcher County	Whitesburg
109	418.7	Webster County	Dixon
110	418.0	Leslie County	Hyden
111	399.3	Knott County	Hindman
112	389.4	Harlan County	Harlan
113	387.1	Greenup County	Greenup
114	378.2	Perry County	Hazard
115	374.3	Monroe County	Tompkinsville
116	372.5	Mayfield Independent	Mayfiel
117	370.9	Adair County	Columbia
118	365.1	Magoffin County	Salyersville
119	361.8	Ashland Ind	Ashland
120	359.2	Breathitt County	Jackson
121	350.6	Danville Independent	Danville
122	328.8	Clay County	Manchester
123	325.1	Jackson County	Mckee

Student/Counselor Ratio

Rank	Ratio	District Name	City
1	1,108.0	Morgan County	West Liberty
2	986.5	Clay County	Manchester
3	916.0	Whitley County	Williamsburg
4	914.0	Washington County	Springfie
5	874.4	Ohio County	Hartford
6	770.8	Pike County	Pikeville
7	756.7	Spencer County	Taylorsvil
8	745.5	Allen County	Scottsville
9	688.8	Knott County	Hindman
10	667.3	Bourbon County	Paris
11	648.3	Perry County	Hazard
12	646.0	Glasgow Independent	Glasgow
13	635.7	Owen County	Owenton
14	629.2	Mclean County	Calhoun
15	627.6	Harrison County	Cynthiana
16	619.0	Boone County	Florence
17	605.6	Lincoln County	Stanford
18	603.1	Henry County	New Castle
19	601.3	Lewis County	Vanceburg
20	593.3	Magoffin County	Salyersville
21	592.1	Knox County	Barbourvill
22	578.0	Franklin County	Frankfort
23	567.7	Anderson County	Lawrenceburg
24	566.2	Pendleton County	Falmouth
25	564.5	Mercer County	Harrodsburg
26	559.3	Woodford County	Versailles
27	555.5	Logan County	Russellville
28	552.3	Green County	Greensburg
29	546.6	Bath County	Owingsv
30	537.7	Shelby County	Shelbyville
31	531.8	Newport Independent	Newport
32	524.1	Johnson County	Paintsville
33	522.5	Leslie County	Hyden
34	520.1	Bullitt County	Shepherdsville
35	515.3	Hancock County	Hawesville
36	507.3	Trigg County	Cadiz
37	503.6	Elizabethtown Independent	Elizabethtow
38	502.7	Breckinridge County	Hardinsburg
39	501.8	Fleming County	Flemingsburg
40	499.3	Caldwell County	Princeton
41	496.7	Mayfield Independent	Mayfiel
42	495.5	Madison County	Richmond
43	493.9	Kenton County	Erlanger
44	493.7	Simpson County	Franklin
45	490.6	Graves County	Mayfield
46	487.2	Rockcastle County	Mt Verno
47	486.3	Trimble County	Bedford
48	480.8	Laurel County	London
49	478.3	Todd County	Elkton
50	474.2	Casey County	Liberty
51	469.7	Russell County	Jamestown
52	467.0	Grant County	Williamsto
53	465.1	Ashland Ind	Ashland
54	463.9	Mccreary County	Stearns
55	456.7	Ballard County	Barlow
56	456.1	Warren County	Bowling Gre
57	454.0	Scott County	Georgetown
58	448.9	Garrard County	Lancaster
59	448.1	Nelson County	Bardstown
60	443.5	Mccracken County	Paducah
61	438.1	Bell County	Pineville
62	437.5	Middlesboro Independent	Middlesboro
63	434.6	Butler County	Morgantown
64	434.0	Meade County	Brandenburg
65	432.7	Adair County	Columbia
66	431.0	Breathitt County	Jackson
66	431.0	Jessamine County	Nicholasville
68	427.0	Murray Independent	Murray
69	426.8	Wayne County	Monticello
70	423.2	Oldham County	Buckner
71	422.3	Taylor County	Campbellsville
72	422.1	Monroe County	Tompkinsville
73	422.0	Fayette County	Lexington
74	420.4	Floyd County	Prestons
75	419.3	Powell County	Stanton
76	418.7	Webster County	Dixon
77	418.4	Paducah Independent	Paducah
78	418.1	Pulaski County	Somerset
79	412.5	Estill County	Irvine
80	410.5	Metcalfe County	Edmonton
81	406.2	Hardin County	Elizabe
82	404.2	Edmonson County	Brownsville
83	400.2	Lawrence County	Louisa
84	397.0	Bardstown Ind	Bardstown
85	395.5	Fort Thomas Independent	Ft Thomas
86	392.7	Erlanger-Elsmere Independent	Erlanger
87	392.2	Union County	Morganfiel
88	389.4	Harlan County	Harlan
89	387.1	Greenup County	Greenup
90	386.0	Gallatin County	Warsaw
91	379.8	Somerset Independent	Somerset
92	379.3	Jackson County	Mckee
93	377.5	Marion County	Lebanon
94	377.3	Campbell County	Alexandria
95	375.8	Daviess County	Owensboro
96	375.7	Boyd County	Ashland
97	374.9	Covington Independent	Covington
98	374.6	Muhlenberg County	Greenville
99	369.8	Jefferson County	Louisville
100	369.5	Barren County	Glasgow
101	367.4	Hopkins County	Madisonvi
102	366.9	Rowan County	Morehead
103	364.4	Montgomery County	Mt Sterling
104	361.2	Corbin Independent	Corbin
105	360.0	Martin County	Inez
106	353.5	Marshall County	Benton
107	350.5	Russell Independent	Russell
108	343.9	Christian County	Hopkinsville
109	342.3	Grayson County	Leitchfield
110	339.0	Hart County	Munfordville
111	338.5	Mason County	Maysville
112	328.0	Clark County	Winchester
113	316.5	Letcher County	Whitesburg
114	304.6	Calloway County	Murray
115	303.5	Owensboro Independent	Owensboro
116	300.3	Carter County	Grayson
117	297.1	Danville Independent	Danville
118	295.2	Boyle County	Danville
119	290.3	Larue County	Hodgenville
120	289.7	Bowling Green Ind	Bowling Green
121	285.3	Henderson County	Henderson
122	229.0	Carroll County	Carrollton
123	222.1	Clinton County	Albany

Current Spending per Student in FY2003

Rank	Dollars	District Name	City
1	8,544	Danville Independent	Danville
2	8,492	Covington Independent	Covington
3	8,119	Bowling Green Ind	Bowling Green
4	7,922	Owensboro Independent	Owensboro
5	7,847	Newport Independent	Newport
6	7,798	Paducah Independent	Paducah
7	7,733	Lincoln County	Stanford
8	7,663	Jefferson County	Louisville
9	7,657	Knott County	Hindman
10	7,627	Russell County	Jamestown
11	7,370	Martin County	Inez
12	7,363	Letcher County	Whitesburg
13	7,329	Clinton County	Albany
14	7,298	Boyd County	Ashland
15	7,285	Whitley County	Williamsburg
16	7,273	Breathitt County	Jackson

Rank	Number	District Name	City
17	7,262	Leslie County	Hyden
18	7,256	Mccreary County	Stearns
19	7,255	Fayette County	Lexington
20	7,240	Clay County	Manchester
21	7,201	Jackson County	Mckee
22	7,200	Daviess County	Owensboro
23	7,186	Boyle County	Danville
24	7,151	Magoffin County	Salyersville
25	7,143	Metcalfe County	Edmonton
26	7,141	Pulaski County	Somerset
27	7,128	Ohio County	Hartford
28	7,073	Knox County	Barbourvill
29	7,056	Hart County	Munfordville
30	6,889	Perry County	Hazard
31	6,873	Bell County	Pineville
32	6,852	Logan County	Russellville
33	6,842	Pike County	Pikeville
34	6,813	Corbin Independent	Corbin
35	6,771	Todd County	Elkton
36	6,735	Carroll County	Carrollton
37	6,731	Bourbon County	Paris
38	6,700	Union County	Morganfiel
39	6,663	Lewis County	Vanceburg
40	6,653	Edmonson County	Brownsville
41	6,644	Adair County	Columbia
42	6,638	Bardstown Ind	Bardstown
43	6,636	Fort Thomas Independent	Ft Thomas
44	6,628	Elizabethtown Independent	Elizabethtow
44	6,628	Marion County	Lebanon
46	6,624	Floyd County	Prestons
47	6,604	Ashland Ind	Ashland
48	6,586	Monroe County	Tompkinsville
49	6,577	Mayfield Independent	Mayfiel
50	6,573	Lawrence County	Louisa
51	6,545	Muhlenberg County	Greenville
52	6,529	Harlan County	Harlan
53	6,527	Hancock County	Hawesville
54	6,513	Rockcastle County	Mt Verno
55	6,510	Barren County	Glasgow
55	6,510	Glasgow Independent	Glasgow
57	6,489	Rowan County	Morehead
58	6,473	Calloway County	Murray
59	6,432	Butler County	Morgantown
60	6,421	Powell County	Stanton
61	6,415	Wayne County	Monticello
62	6,407	Breckinridge County	Hardinsburg
63	6,403	Greenup County	Greenup
64	6,376	Johnson County	Paintsville
65	6,365	Gallatin County	Warsaw
66	6,355	Fleming County	Flemingsburg
67	6,327	Casey County	Liberty
68	6,324	Estill County	Irvine
69	6,292	Henderson County	Henderson
70	6,268	Morgan County	West Liberty
71	6,264	Green County	Greensburg
72	6,256	Scott County	Georgetown
73	6,236	Campbell County	Alexandria
74	6,226	Mason County	Maysville
75	6,223	Trigg County	Cadiz
76	6,206	Hardin County	Elizabe
77	6,183	Washington County	Springfie
78	6,169	Middlesboro Independent	Middlesboro
79	6,160	Simpson County	Franklin
80	6,150	Larue County	Hodgenville
81	6,132	Hopkins County	Madisonvi
82	6,104	Bath County	Owingsv
83	6,100	Trimble County	Bedford
84	6,098	Spencer County	Taylorsvil
85	6,082	Jessamine County	Nicholasville
86	6,080	Mccracken County	Paducah
87	6,043	Caldwell County	Princeton
87	6,043	Carter County	Grayson
89	6,029	Marshall County	Benton
90	5,988	Mclean County	Calhoun
91	5,981	Garrard County	Lancaster
92	5,975	Christian County	Hopkinsville
93	5,969	Montgomery County	Mt Sterling
94	5,968	Woodford County	Versailles
95	5,964	Henry County	New Castle
96	5,959	Franklin County	Frankfort
97	5,943	Madison County	Richmond
98	5,941	Owen County	Owenton
99	5,938	Shelby County	Shelbyville
100	5,922	Somerset Independent	Somerset
101	5,894	Oldham County	Buckner
102	5,876	Laurel County	London
103	5,865	Erlanger-Elsmere Independent	Erlanger
104	5,864	Taylor County	Campbellsville
105	5,861	Nelson County	Bardstown
106	5,850	Ballard County	Barlow
107	5,841	Kenton County	Erlanger
108	5,834	Russell Independent	Russell
109	5,821	Boone County	Florence
110	5,817	Grayson County	Leitchfield
111	5,815	Harrison County	Cynthiana
112	5,772	Meade County	Brandenburg
113	5,711	Clark County	Winchester
114	5,691	Pendleton County	Falmouth
115	5,681	Mercer County	Harrodsburg
116	5,653	Webster County	Dixon
117	5,624	Warren County	Bowling Gre
118	5,595	Graves County	Mayfield
119	5,560	Grant County	Williamsto
120	5,543	Murray Independent	Murray
121	5,536	Bullitt County	Shepherdsville
122	5,434	Allen County	Scottsville
123	5,284	Anderson County	Lawrenceburg

Number of Diploma Recipients

Rank	Number	District Name	City
1	4,932	Jefferson County	Louisville
2	1,643	Fayette County	Lexington
3	817	Hardin County	Elizabe
4	758	Kenton County	Erlanger
5	722	Boone County	Florence
6	720	Daviess County	Owensboro
7	706	Warren County	Bowling Gre
8	630	Bullitt County	Shepherdsville
9	606	Oldham County	Buckner
10	602	Pike County	Pikeville
11	462	Pulaski County	Somerset
12	458	Laurel County	London
13	455	Henderson County	Henderson
14	442	Madison County	Richmond
15	436	Mccracken County	Paducah
16	416	Christian County	Hopkinsville
17	407	Floyd County	Prestons
18	375	Hopkins County	Madisonvi
19	361	Franklin County	Frankfort
20	336	Meade County	Brandenburg
21	334	Scott County	Georgetown
22	322	Campbell County	Alexandria
22	322	Jessamine County	Nicholasville
24	321	Muhlenberg County	Greenville
25	312	Nelson County	Bardstown
26	306	Shelby County	Shelbyville
27	299	Clark County	Winchester
28	272	Marshall County	Benton
29	271	Graves County	Mayfield
30	265	Harlan County	Harlan
31	254	Ohio County	Hartford
32	252	Grayson County	Leitchfield
33	242	Perry County	Hazard
34	227	Carter County	Grayson
35	225	Logan County	Russellville
35	225	Whitley County	Williamsburg
37	224	Knox County	Barbourvill
38	222	Bowling Green Ind	Bowling Green
38	222	Woodford County	Versailles
40	221	Montgomery County	Mt Sterling
41	218	Calloway County	Murray
42	215	Owensboro Independent	Owensboro
43	214	Lincoln County	Stanford
44	213	Johnson County	Paintsville
45	208	Barren County	Glasgow
46	205	Ashland Ind	Ashland
47	202	Marion County	Lebanon
48	201	Simpson County	Franklin
49	200	Covington Independent	Covington
50	198	Boyd County	Ashland
51	196	Letcher County	Whitesburg
52	195	Bell County	Pineville
53	193	Fort Thomas Independent	Ft Thomas
54	192	Harrison County	Cynthiana
55	189	Anderson County	Lawrenceburg
56	184	Allen County	Scottsville
56	184	Rockcastle County	Mt Verno
58	183	Rowan County	Morehead
59	182	Bourbon County	Paris
59	182	Boyle County	Danville
59	182	Greenup County	Greenup
62	178	Knott County	Hindman
63	175	Breckinridge County	Hardinsburg
64	171	Mason County	Maysville
65	170	Mccreary County	Stearns
66	169	Grant County	Williamsto
67	168	Larue County	Hodgenville
67	168	Lawrence County	Louisa
69	162	Taylor County	Campbellsville
70	161	Clay County	Manchester
71	160	Magoffin County	Salyersville
72	156	Union County	Morganfiel
73	155	Pendleton County	Falmouth
74	154	Estill County	Irvine
74	154	Martin County	Inez
76	153	Paducah Independent	Paducah
77	152	Russell Independent	Russell
78	150	Corbin Independent	Corbin
79	149	Mercer County	Harrodsburg
80	146	Elizabethtown Independent	Elizabethtow
81	142	Lewis County	Vanceburg
82	140	Russell County	Jamestown
82	140	Wayne County	Monticello
84	139	Leslie County	Hyden
85	138	Butler County	Morgantown
86	137	Webster County	Dixon
87	136	Garrard County	Lancaster
87	136	Powell County	Stanton
89	133	Hart County	Munfordville
90	132	Caldwell County	Princeton
91	131	Fleming County	Flemingsburg
92	128	Monroe County	Tompkinsville
93	127	Adair County	Columbia
93	127	Murray Independent	Murray
95	126	Morgan County	West Liberty
96	123	Erlanger-Elsmere Independent	Erlanger
97	122	Jackson County	Mckee
98	119	Casey County	Liberty
98	119	Green County	Greensburg
100	118	Glasgow Independent	Glasgow
101	117	Breathitt County	Jackson
102	116	Carroll County	Carrollton
103	115	Todd County	Elkton
104	113	Spencer County	Taylorsvil
105	111	Bardstown Ind	Bardstown
105	111	Trigg County	Cadiz
107	109	Hancock County	Hawesville
108	108	Danville Independent	Danville
108	108	Washington County	Springfie
110	107	Bath County	Owingsv
110	107	Henry County	New Castle
112	106	Newport Independent	Newport
113	102	Owen County	Owenton
114	102	Trimble County	Bedford
115	101	Ballard County	Barlow
116	99	Edmonson County	Brownsville
117	98	Somerset Independent	Somerset
118	97	Middlesboro Independent	Middlesboro
119	93	Mclean County	Calhoun
120	87	Metcalfe County	Edmonton
121	83	Mayfield Independent	Mayfiel
122	79	Clinton County	Albany
123	71	Gallatin County	Warsaw

High School Drop-out Rate

Rank	Percent	District Name	City
1	8.8	Clay County	Manchester
2	8.1	Bell County	Pineville
3	7.7	Trigg County	Cadiz
4	6.9	Owen County	Owenton
5	6.8	Harlan County	Harlan
5	6.8	Lincoln County	Stanford
7	6.5	Clark County	Winchester
7	6.5	Powell County	Stanton
9	6.1	Floyd County	Prestons
10	6.0	Paducah Independent	Paducah
11	5.9	Jefferson County	Louisville
12	5.8	Bath County	Owingsv
13	5.7	Laurel County	London
13	5.7	Martin County	Inez
13	5.7	Russell County	Jamestown
16	5.6	Knox County	Barbourvill
17	5.3	Jessamine County	Nicholasville
17	5.3	Magoffin County	Salyersville
19	5.1	Greenup County	Greenup
19	5.1	Letcher County	Whitesburg
21	5.0	Adair County	Columbia
21	5.0	Casey County	Liberty
21	5.0	Fayette County	Lexington
24	4.9	Breathitt County	Jackson
25	4.8	Carroll County	Carrollton
25	4.8	Clinton County	Albany
25	4.8	Estill County	Irvine
25	4.8	Hart County	Munfordville
25	4.8	Henderson County	Henderson
30	4.7	Bowling Green Ind	Bowling Green
30	4.7	Jackson County	Mckee
30	4.7	Perry County	Hazard
33	4.6	Edmonson County	Brownsville
33	4.6	Fleming County	Flemingsburg
33	4.6	Morgan County	West Liberty
36	4.5	Barren County	Glasgow
36	4.5	Christian County	Hopkinsville
36	4.5	Garrard County	Lancaster
36	4.5	Grayson County	Leitchfield
36	4.5	Knott County	Hindman

36	4.5	Rockcastle County	Mt Verno
42	4.4	Hopkins County	Madisonvi
42	4.4	Whitley County	Williamsburg
44	4.3	Corbin Independent	Corbin
44	4.3	Mccreary County	Stearns
46	4.2	Allen County	Scottsville
46	4.2	Bullitt County	Shepherdsville
46	4.2	Pike County	Pikeville
49	4.1	Larue County	Hodgenville
49	4.1	Marion County	Lebanon
49	4.1	Todd County	Elkton
49	4.1	Wayne County	Monticello
53	4.0	Anderson County	Lawrenceburg
53	4.0	Lewis County	Vanceburg
55	3.9	Bardstown Ind	Bardstown
55	3.9	Mayfield Independent	Mayfiel
55	3.9	Shelby County	Shelbyville
58	3.8	Henry County	New Castle
58	3.8	Middlesboro Independent	Middlesboro
58	3.8	Pulaski County	Somerset
61	3.7	Washington County	Springfie
62	3.6	Elizabethtown Independent	Elizabethtow
62	3.6	Somerset Independent	Somerset
62	3.6	Union County	Morganfiel
65	3.5	Muhlenberg County	Greenville
66	3.4	Hardin County	Elizabe
66	3.4	Lawrence County	Louisa
66	3.4	Montgomery County	Mt Sterling
66	3.4	Rowan County	Morehead
66	3.4	Scott County	Georgetown
66	3.4	Simpson County	Franklin
72	3.3	Franklin County	Frankfort
73	3.2	Grant County	Williamsto
73	3.2	Meade County	Brandenburg
73	3.2	Spencer County	Taylorsvil
76	3.0	Carter County	Grayson
76	3.0	Johnson County	Paintsville
76	3.0	Leslie County	Hyden
76	3.0	Metcalfe County	Edmonton
76	3.0	Trimble County	Bedford
81	2.9	Harrison County	Cynthiana
82	2.8	Gallatin County	Warsaw
82	2.8	Glasgow Independent	Glasgow
82	2.8	Mason County	Maysville
82	2.8	Newport Independent	Newport
86	2.7	Kenton County	Erlanger
86	2.7	Owensboro Independent	Owensboro
88	2.6	Monroe County	Tompkinsville
88	2.6	Ohio County	Hartford
90	2.5	Boyle County	Danville
90	2.5	Caldwell County	Princeton
90	2.5	Marshall County	Benton
90	2.5	Woodford County	Versailles
94	2.4	Ashland Ind	Ashland
94	2.4	Boyd County	Ashland
94	2.4	Breckinridge County	Hardinsburg
94	2.4	Campbell County	Alexandria
98	2.3	Ballard County	Barlow
98	2.3	Bourbon County	Paris
98	2.3	Taylor County	Campbellsville
101	2.2	Logan County	Russellville
101	2.2	Mclean County	Calhoun
101	2.2	Webster County	Dixon
104	2.1	Boone County	Florence
104	2.1	Butler County	Morgantown
104	2.1	Danville Independent	Danville
107	2.0	Graves County	Mayfield
107	2.0	Nelson County	Bardstown
109	1.9	Daviess County	Owensboro
109	1.9	Erlanger-Elsmere Independent	Erlanger
109	1.9	Pendleton County	Falmouth
109	1.9	Warren County	Bowling Gre
113	1.8	Calloway County	Murray
114	1.7	Mccracken County	Paducah
115	1.6	Green County	Greensburg
115	1.6	Madison County	Richmond
117	1.4	Mercer County	Harrodsburg
118	1.1	Murray Independent	Murray
118	1.1	Oldham County	Buckner
120	1.0	Covington Independent	Covington
121	0.9	Fort Thomas Independent	Ft Thomas
122	0.4	Russell Independent	Russell
123	0.0	Hancock County	Hawesville

Louisiana

Louisiana Public School Educational Profile

Category	Value	Category	Value
Schools *(2003-2004)*	1,551	**Diploma Recipients** *(2002-2003)*	37,843
Instructional Level		White, Non-Hispanic	21,237
Primary	800	Black, Non-Hispanic	15,275
Middle	288	Asian/Pacific Islander	622
High	258	American Indian/Alaskan Native	225
Other Level	198	Hispanic	484
Curriculum		**High School Drop-out Rate** (%) *(2001-2002)*	6.9
Regular	1,384	White, Non-Hispanic	5.0
Special Education	39	Black, Non-Hispanic	9.4
Vocational	9	Asian/Pacific Islander	5.1
Alternative	112	American Indian/Alaskan Native	7.3
Type		Hispanic	6.8
Magnet	70	**Staff** *(2003-2004)*	
Charter	16	Teachers	50,495.7
Title I Eligible	951	Average Salary ($)	37,123
School-wide Title I	797	Librarians/Media Specialists	1,233.2
Students *(2003-2004)*	727,709	Guidance Counselors	3,154.9
Gender (%)		**Ratios** *(2003-2004)*	
Male	51.2	Student/Teacher Ratio	14.4 to 1
Female	48.8	Student/Librarian Ratio	590.1 to 1
Race/Ethnicity (%)		Student/Counselor Ratio	230.7 to 1
White, Non-Hispanic	48.5	**College Entrance Exam Scores** *(2005)*	
Black, Non-Hispanic	47.7	Scholastic Aptitude Test (SAT)	
Asian/Pacific Islander	1.3	Participation Rate (%)	8
American Indian/Alaskan Native	0.7	Mean SAT Reasoning Test Verbal Score	565
Hispanic	1.8	Mean SAT Reasoning Test Math Score	562
Classification (%)		American College Testing Program (ACT)	
Individual Education Program (IEP)	13.9	Participation Rate (%)	85
Migrant *(2002-2003)*	0.6	Average Composite Score	19.8
English Language Learner (ELL)	1.7	Average English Score	19.9
Eligible for Free Lunch Program	53.2	Average Math Score	19.2
Eligible for Reduced-Price Lunch Program	8.3	Average Reading Score	19.8
Current Spending *($ per student in FY 2003)*	6,868	Average Science Score	19.7
Instruction	4,161		
Support Services	2,275		

Note: For an explanation of data, please refer to the User's Guide in the front of the book

Louisiana NAEP 2005 Test Scores

Reading			Mathematics		
Grade/Category	Value	Rank	Grade/Category	Value	Rank
4th Grade			**4th Grade**		
Average Proficiency	209.2 (1.31)	44/51	Average Proficiency	230.2 (0.88)	44/51
Proficiency by Gender/Race/Ethnicity			Proficiency by Gender/Race/Ethnicity		
Male	207.8 (1.50)	42/51	Male	231.3 (1.09)	45/51
Female	210.6 (1.55)	47/51	Female	229.1 (1.08)	45/51
White, Non-Hispanic	222.8 (1.07)	44/51	White, Non-Hispanic	241.1 (0.96)	40/51
Black, Non-Hispanic	194.9 (1.74)	30/42	Black, Non-Hispanic	218.8 (1.19)	24/42
Asian, Non-Hispanic	n/a	n/a	Asian, Non-Hispanic	n/a	n/a
American Indian, Non-Hispanic	n/a	n/a	American Indian, Non-Hispanic	n/a	n/a
Hispanic	n/a	n/a	Hispanic	n/a	n/a
Proficiency by Class Size			Proficiency by Class Size		
Less than 16 Students	196.4 (3.58)	25/34	Less than 16 Students	219.8 (2.95)	26/35
16 to 18 Students	212.1 (2.81)	25/33	16 to 18 Students	233.1 (3.16)	21/31
19 to 20 Students	n/a	n/a	19 to 20 Students	n/a	n/a
21 to 25 Students	211.4 (2.00)	43/51	21 to 25 Students	231.8 (1.73)	43/51
Greater than 25 Students	215.3 (3.41)	28/36	Greater than 25 Students	n/a	n/a
Percent Attaining Achievement Levels			Percent Attaining Achievement Levels		
Below Basic	47.0 (1.82)	9/51	Below Basic	26.0 (1.33)	11/51
Basic or Above	53.0 (1.82)	43/51	Basic or Above	74.0 (1.33)	41/51
Proficient or Above	20.4 (1.39)	49/51	Proficient or Above	23.9 (1.27)	47/51
Advanced or Above	3.5 (0.55)	49/51	Advanced or Above	2.1 (0.40)	46/51
8th Grade			**8th Grade**		
Average Proficiency	252.7 (1.58)	45/51	Average Proficiency	267.8 (1.39)	46/51
Proficiency by Gender/Race/Ethnicity			Proficiency by Gender/Race/Ethnicity		
Male	246.7 (1.85)	46/51	Male	267.3 (1.50)	46/51
Female	258.6 (1.67)	45/51	Female	268.3 (1.59)	45/51
White, Non-Hispanic	263.6 (1.73)	47/51	White, Non-Hispanic	280.7 (1.25)	42/51
Black, Non-Hispanic	239.8 (1.93)	28/40	Black, Non-Hispanic	251.8 (1.64)	22/41
Asian, Non-Hispanic	n/a	n/a	Asian, Non-Hispanic	n/a	n/a
American Indian, Non-Hispanic	n/a	n/a	American Indian, Non-Hispanic	n/a	n/a
Hispanic	n/a	n/a	Hispanic	n/a	n/a
Proficiency by Parents Highest Level of Ed.			Proficiency by Parents Highest Level of Ed.		
Did Not Finish High School	239.8 (3.67)	38/49	Did Not Finish High School	260.3 (2.55)	29/50
Graduated High School	245.4 (2.16)	45/50	Graduated High School	259.5 (2.29)	44/50
Some Education After High School	260.8 (1.95)	42/50	Some Education After High School	274.0 (1.64)	44/50
Graduated College	260.0 (1.66)	47/50	Graduated College	274.9 (1.73)	46/50
Percent Attaining Achievement Levels			Percent Attaining Achievement Levels		
Below Basic	47.0 (1.82)	9/51	Below Basic	41.1 (2.05)	7/51
Basic or Above	53.0 (1.82)	43/51	Basic or Above	58.9 (2.05)	45/51
Proficient or Above	20.4 (1.39)	49/51	Proficient or Above	16.1 (1.40)	47/51
Advanced or Above	3.5 (0.55)	49/51	Advanced or Above	1.7 (0.43)	48/51

Note: *For an explanation of data, please refer to the User's Guide in the front of the book; n/a indicates data not available*

Acadia Parish

Acadia Parish School Board
2402 N Parkerson Ave • Crowley, LA 70526
Mailing Address: PO Drawer 309 • Crowley, LA 70527-0309
(337) 783-3664 • http://www.acadia.k12.la.us/
Grade Span: PK-12; **Agency Type:** 1
Schools: 27
  16 Primary; 5 Middle; 5 High; 1 Other Level
  26 Regular; 0 Special Education; 0 Vocational; 1 Alternative
  0 Magnet; 0 Charter; 21 Title I Eligible; 21 School-wide Title I
Students: 9,650   (51.2% male; 48.7% female)
  Individual Education Program: 1,829 (19.0%);
  English Language Learner: 55 (0.6%); Migrant: 62 (0.6%)
  Eligible for Free Lunch Program: 5,301 (54.9%)
  Eligible for Reduced-Price Lunch Program: 1,052 (10.9%)
Teachers: 651.1 (14.8 to 1)
Librarians/Media Specialists: 16.0 (603.1 to 1)
Guidance Counselors: 50.0 (193.0 to 1)
Current Spending: ($ per student per year):
  Total: $6,482; Instruction: $4,032; Support Services: $2,023
Enrollment, Drop-out Rates and Diploma Recipients by Race/Ethnicity

Category	Total	White	Black	Asian	AIAN	Hisp.
Enrollment (%)	100.0	70.6	28.4	0.2	0.1	0.6
Drop-out Rate (%)	7.1	6.0	10.8	0.0	0.0	8.3
H.S. Diplomas (#)	444	356	83	2	0	3

Allen Parish

Allen Parish School Board
417 W Court St • Oberlin, LA 70655
Mailing Address: PO Drawer C • Oberlin, LA 70655
(337) 639-4311 • http://www.allen.k12.la.us/
Grade Span: PK-12; **Agency Type:** 1
Schools: 12
  3 Primary; 2 Middle; 3 High; 4 Other Level
  11 Regular; 0 Special Education; 0 Vocational; 1 Alternative
  0 Magnet; 0 Charter; 8 Title I Eligible; 0 School-wide Title I
Students: 4,281   (52.0% male; 47.9% female)
  Individual Education Program: 516 (12.1%);
  English Language Learner: 2 (<0.1%); Migrant: 17 (0.4%)
  Eligible for Free Lunch Program: 2,052 (47.9%)
  Eligible for Reduced-Price Lunch Program: 561 (13.1%)
Teachers: 338.0 (12.7 to 1)
Librarians/Media Specialists: 10.0 (428.1 to 1)
Guidance Counselors: 20.0 (214.1 to 1)
Current Spending: ($ per student per year):
  Total: $6,621; Instruction: $3,703; Support Services: $2,461
Enrollment, Drop-out Rates and Diploma Recipients by Race/Ethnicity

Category	Total	White	Black	Asian	AIAN	Hisp.
Enrollment (%)	100.0	73.3	24.6	0.4	0.7	1.1
Drop-out Rate (%)	2.2	1.4	4.9	0.0	0.0	0.0
H.S. Diplomas (#)	218	161	52	1	1	3

Ascension Parish

Ascension Parish School Board
1100 Webster St • Donaldsonville, LA 70346-0189
Mailing Address: PO Box 189 • Donaldsonville, LA 70346-0189
(225) 473-7981 • http://www.apsb.org/
Grade Span: PK-12; **Agency Type:** 1
Schools: 23
  13 Primary; 5 Middle; 4 High; 1 Other Level
  22 Regular; 0 Special Education; 0 Vocational; 1 Alternative
  0 Magnet; 0 Charter; 13 Title I Eligible; 7 School-wide Title I
Students: 15,810   (51.5% male; 48.4% female)
  Individual Education Program: 2,442 (15.4%);
  English Language Learner: 316 (2.0%); Migrant: 1 (<0.1%)
  Eligible for Free Lunch Program: 5,643 (35.7%)
  Eligible for Reduced-Price Lunch Program: 1,219 (7.7%)
Teachers: 1,105.1 (14.3 to 1)
Librarians/Media Specialists: 23.0 (687.4 to 1)
Guidance Counselors: 98.0 (161.3 to 1)
Current Spending: ($ per student per year):
  Total: $6,892; Instruction: $4,389; Support Services: $2,133
Enrollment, Drop-out Rates and Diploma Recipients by Race/Ethnicity

Category	Total	White	Black	Asian	AIAN	Hisp.
Enrollment (%)	100.0	67.7	28.6	0.6	0.3	2.9
Drop-out Rate (%)	4.7	3.7	7.3	0.0	12.5	7.3
H.S. Diplomas (#)	772	580	178	4	1	9

Assumption Parish

Assumption Parish School Board
4901 Hwy 308 • Napoleonville, LA 70390
(985) 369-7251 • http://www.assumption.k12.la.us/home.htm
Grade Span: PK-12; **Agency Type:** 1
Schools: 10
  5 Primary; 4 Middle; 1 High; 0 Other Level
  10 Regular; 0 Special Education; 0 Vocational; 0 Alternative
  0 Magnet; 0 Charter; 9 Title I Eligible; 8 School-wide Title I
Students: 4,431   (50.7% male; 49.2% female)
  Individual Education Program: 641 (14.5%);
  English Language Learner: 45 (1.0%); Migrant: 85 (1.9%)
  Eligible for Free Lunch Program: 2,330 (52.6%)
  Eligible for Reduced-Price Lunch Program: 418 (9.4%)
Teachers: 318.0 (13.9 to 1)
Librarians/Media Specialists: 2.0 (2,215.5 to 1)
Guidance Counselors: 6.0 (738.5 to 1)
Current Spending: ($ per student per year):
  Total: $7,518; Instruction: $4,601; Support Services: $2,492
Enrollment, Drop-out Rates and Diploma Recipients by Race/Ethnicity

Category	Total	White	Black	Asian	AIAN	Hisp.
Enrollment (%)	100.0	56.7	41.9	0.3	0.0	1.1
Drop-out Rate (%)	7.3	3.0	13.5	50.0	0.0	66.7
H.S. Diplomas (#)	201	128	71	2	0	0

Avoyelles Parish

Avoyelles Parish School Board
221 Tunica Dr W • Marksville, LA 71351
(318) 240-0201 • http://www.avoyellespsb.com/
Grade Span: PK-12; **Agency Type:** 1
Schools: 14
  6 Primary; 3 Middle; 3 High; 2 Other Level
  12 Regular; 0 Special Education; 0 Vocational; 2 Alternative
  1 Magnet; 1 Charter; 10 Title I Eligible; 9 School-wide Title I
Students: 6,585   (51.7% male; 48.2% female)
  Individual Education Program: 751 (11.4%);
  English Language Learner: 16 (0.2%); Migrant: 56 (0.9%)
  Eligible for Free Lunch Program: 4,445 (67.5%)
  Eligible for Reduced-Price Lunch Program: 610 (9.3%)
Teachers: 419.0 (15.7 to 1)
Librarians/Media Specialists: 10.0 (658.5 to 1)
Guidance Counselors: 12.0 (548.8 to 1)
Current Spending: ($ per student per year):
  Total: $6,331; Instruction: $3,626; Support Services: $2,212
Enrollment, Drop-out Rates and Diploma Recipients by Race/Ethnicity

Category	Total	White	Black	Asian	AIAN	Hisp.
Enrollment (%)	100.0	55.4	42.7	0.3	1.0	0.6
Drop-out Rate (%)	6.7	5.2	9.8	0.0	0.0	0.0
H.S. Diplomas (#)	399	281	116	0	2	0

Beauregard Parish

Beauregard Parish School Board
202 W Third St • Deridder, LA 70634-0938
Mailing Address: PO Drawer 938 • Deridder, LA 70634-0938
(337) 463-5551 • http://www.beau.k12.la.us/
Grade Span: PK-12; **Agency Type:** 1
Schools: 14
  4 Primary; 2 Middle; 1 High; 7 Other Level
  12 Regular; 0 Special Education; 0 Vocational; 2 Alternative
  0 Magnet; 0 Charter; 8 Title I Eligible; 2 School-wide Title I
Students: 6,127   (51.9% male; 48.0% female)
  Individual Education Program: 804 (13.1%);
  English Language Learner: 23 (0.4%); Migrant: 30 (0.5%)
  Eligible for Free Lunch Program: 2,312 (37.7%)
  Eligible for Reduced-Price Lunch Program: 583 (9.5%)
Teachers: 404.5 (15.1 to 1)
Librarians/Media Specialists: 13.0 (471.3 to 1)
Guidance Counselors: 26.0 (235.7 to 1)
Current Spending: ($ per student per year):
  Total: $6,267; Instruction: $3,591; Support Services: $2,288
Enrollment, Drop-out Rates and Diploma Recipients by Race/Ethnicity

Category	Total	White	Black	Asian	AIAN	Hisp.
Enrollment (%)	100.0	82.1	15.5	0.6	0.6	1.2
Drop-out Rate (%)	2.0	2.1	1.9	0.0	0.0	0.0
H.S. Diplomas (#)	371	299	64	2	1	5

Bienville Parish

Bienville Parish School Board
1956 First St • Arcadia, LA 71001-0418
Mailing Address: PO Box 418 • Arcadia, LA 71001-0418
(318) 263-9416 • http://bienville.nls.k12.la.us/
Grade Span: PK-12; Agency Type: 1
Schools: 8
   2 Primary; 0 Middle; 2 High; 4 Other Level
   8 Regular; 0 Special Education; 0 Vocational; 0 Alternative
   0 Magnet; 0 Charter; 8 Title I Eligible; 8 School-wide Title I
Students: 2,498 (50.5% male; 49.4% female)
   Individual Education Program: 341 (13.7%);
   English Language Learner: 1 (<0.1%); Migrant: 23 (0.9%)
   Eligible for Free Lunch Program: 1,464 (58.7%)
   Eligible for Reduced-Price Lunch Program: 180 (7.2%)
Teachers: 206.0 (12.1 to 1)
Librarians/Media Specialists: 4.0 (623.0 to 1)
Guidance Counselors: 5.8 (429.7 to 1)
Current Spending: ($ per student per year):
   Total: $8,220; Instruction: $4,828; Support Services: $2,829

Enrollment, Drop-out Rates and Diploma Recipients by Race/Ethnicity

Category	Total	White	Black	Asian	AIAN	Hisp.
Enrollment (%)	100.0	39.6	59.6	0.1	0.3	0.4
Drop-out Rate (%)	7.7	10.0	6.2	n/a	0.0	0.0
H.S. Diplomas (#)	138	57	81	0	0	0

Bossier Parish

Bossier Parish School Board
316 Sibley St • Benton, LA 71006-2000
Mailing Address: PO Box 2000 • Benton, LA 71006-2000
(318) 549-5000 • http://www.bossier.k12.la.us/
Grade Span: PK-12; Agency Type: 1
Schools: 35
   14 Primary; 9 Middle; 8 High; 4 Other Level
   29 Regular; 1 Special Education; 1 Vocational; 4 Alternative
   0 Magnet; 0 Charter; 8 Title I Eligible; 8 School-wide Title I
Students: 18,771 (50.7% male; 49.2% female)
   Individual Education Program: 2,256 (12.0%);
   English Language Learner: 609 (3.2%); Migrant: 46 (0.2%)
   Eligible for Free Lunch Program: 6,459 (34.4%)
   Eligible for Reduced-Price Lunch Program: 1,268 (6.8%)
Teachers: 1,169.7 (16.0 to 1)
Librarians/Media Specialists: 32.0 (586.6 to 1)
Guidance Counselors: 78.9 (237.9 to 1)
Current Spending: ($ per student per year):
   Total: $6,183; Instruction: $3,654; Support Services: $2,124

Enrollment, Drop-out Rates and Diploma Recipients by Race/Ethnicity

Category	Total	White	Black	Asian	AIAN	Hisp.
Enrollment (%)	100.0	64.9	30.5	1.4	0.3	2.9
Drop-out Rate (%)	4.6	3.5	7.5	4.8	0.0	3.9
H.S. Diplomas (#)	983	704	230	25	1	23

Caddo Parish

Caddo Parish School Board
1961 Midway St • Shreveport, LA 71108
Mailing Address: PO Box 32000 • Shreveport, LA 71130-2000
(318) 603-6509 • http://www.caddo.k12.la.us/
Grade Span: PK-12; Agency Type: 1
Schools: 75
   46 Primary; 11 Middle; 11 High; 7 Other Level
   67 Regular; 1 Special Education; 1 Vocational; 6 Alternative
   19 Magnet; 0 Charter; 37 Title I Eligible; 30 School-wide Title I
Students: 44,473 (50.7% male; 49.2% female)
   Individual Education Program: 6,092 (13.7%);
   English Language Learner: 543 (1.2%); Migrant: 10 (<0.1%)
   Eligible for Free Lunch Program: 23,256 (52.3%)
   Eligible for Reduced-Price Lunch Program: 2,282 (5.1%)
Teachers: 2,927.5 (15.2 to 1)
Librarians/Media Specialists: 82.0 (542.4 to 1)
Guidance Counselors: 265.0 (167.8 to 1)
Current Spending: ($ per student per year):
   Total: $7,270; Instruction: $4,456; Support Services: $2,409

Enrollment, Drop-out Rates and Diploma Recipients by Race/Ethnicity

Category	Total	White	Black	Asian	AIAN	Hisp.
Enrollment (%)	100.0	35.4	62.8	0.8	0.2	0.9
Drop-out Rate (%)	10.0	4.9	13.8	1.1	17.4	5.9
H.S. Diplomas (#)	2,223	996	1,183	18	3	23

Calcasieu Parish

Calcasieu Parish School Board
1724 Kirkman St • Lake Charles, LA 70601-6299
Mailing Address: PO Box 800 • Lake Charles, LA 70602-0800
(337) 491-1600 • http://www.cpsb.org/
Grade Span: PK-12; Agency Type: 1
Schools: 59
   34 Primary; 11 Middle; 10 High; 4 Other Level
   57 Regular; 1 Special Education; 0 Vocational; 1 Alternative
   1 Magnet; 0 Charter; 30 Title I Eligible; 27 School-wide Title I
Students: 32,149 (51.2% male; 48.7% female)
   Individual Education Program: 4,926 (15.3%);
   English Language Learner: 7 (<0.1%); Migrant: 7 (<0.1%)
   Eligible for Free Lunch Program: 13,674 (42.5%)
   Eligible for Reduced-Price Lunch Program: 2,239 (7.0%)
Teachers: 2,184.7 (14.7 to 1)
Librarians/Media Specialists: 64.0 (502.3 to 1)
Guidance Counselors: 125.6 (256.0 to 1)
Current Spending: ($ per student per year):
   Total: $6,471; Instruction: $3,850; Support Services: $2,226

Enrollment, Drop-out Rates and Diploma Recipients by Race/Ethnicity

Category	Total	White	Black	Asian	AIAN	Hisp.
Enrollment (%)	100.0	64.5	33.8	0.7	0.2	0.7
Drop-out Rate (%)	4.8	3.4	8.0	8.2	0.0	5.1
H.S. Diplomas (#)	1,747	1,238	493	9	0	7

Caldwell Parish

Caldwell Parish School Board
219 Main St - Courthouse Sq • Columbia, LA 71418-1019
Mailing Address: PO Box 1019 • Columbia, LA 71418-1019
(318) 649-2689 • http://caldwell.nls.k12.la.us/
Grade Span: PK-12; Agency Type: 1
Schools: 6
   4 Primary; 1 Middle; 0 High; 1 Other Level
   6 Regular; 0 Special Education; 0 Vocational; 0 Alternative
   0 Magnet; 0 Charter; 4 Title I Eligible; 4 School-wide Title I
Students: 1,841 (53.7% male; 46.2% female)
   Individual Education Program: 260 (14.1%);
   English Language Learner: 0 (0.0%); Migrant: 17 (0.9%)
   Eligible for Free Lunch Program: 848 (46.1%)
   Eligible for Reduced-Price Lunch Program: 202 (11.0%)
Teachers: 136.7 (13.5 to 1)
Librarians/Media Specialists: 1.0 (1,841.0 to 1)
Guidance Counselors: 5.0 (368.2 to 1)
Current Spending: ($ per student per year):
   Total: $6,560; Instruction: $3,920; Support Services: $2,096

Enrollment, Drop-out Rates and Diploma Recipients by Race/Ethnicity

Category	Total	White	Black	Asian	AIAN	Hisp.
Enrollment (%)	100.0	79.6	19.2	0.2	0.0	0.9
Drop-out Rate (%)	4.8	3.9	7.1	50.0	n/a	25.0
H.S. Diplomas (#)	66	60	5	0	0	1

Cameron Parish

Cameron Parish School Board
246 Dewey St • Cameron, LA 70631
Mailing Address: PO Box 1548 • Cameron, LA 70631
(337) 775-5784 • http://www.cameron.k12.la.us/
Grade Span: PK-12; Agency Type: 1
Schools: 6
   2 Primary; 0 Middle; 1 High; 3 Other Level
   6 Regular; 0 Special Education; 0 Vocational; 0 Alternative
   0 Magnet; 0 Charter; 6 Title I Eligible; 0 School-wide Title I
Students: 1,819 (51.4% male; 48.5% female)
   Individual Education Program: 334 (18.4%);
   English Language Learner: 16 (0.9%); Migrant: 59 (3.2%)
   Eligible for Free Lunch Program: 534 (29.4%)
   Eligible for Reduced-Price Lunch Program: 248 (13.6%)
Teachers: 159.0 (11.4 to 1)
Librarians/Media Specialists: 6.0 (303.2 to 1)
Guidance Counselors: 8.5 (214.0 to 1)
Current Spending: ($ per student per year):
   Total: $8,529; Instruction: $4,739; Support Services: $3,281

Enrollment, Drop-out Rates and Diploma Recipients by Race/Ethnicity

Category	Total	White	Black	Asian	AIAN	Hisp.
Enrollment (%)	100.0	92.5	5.0	0.4	0.1	2.0
Drop-out Rate (%)	2.1	2.2	0.0	0.0	n/a	0.0
H.S. Diplomas (#)	109	104	4	1	0	0

Catahoula Parish

Catahoula Parish School Board
200 Bushley St • Harrisonburg, LA 71340-0290
Mailing Address: PO Box 290 • Harrisonburg, LA 71340-0290
(318) 744-5727 • http://catahoula.nls.k12.la.us/
Grade Span: PK-12; **Agency Type:** 1
Schools: 10
    4 Primary; 1 Middle; 4 High; 1 Other Level
    9 Regular; 0 Special Education; 0 Vocational; 1 Alternative
    0 Magnet; 0 Charter; 6 Title I Eligible; 6 School-wide Title I
Students: 1,800 (52.1% male; 47.8% female)
    Individual Education Program: 202 (11.2%);
    English Language Learner: 0 (0.0%); Migrant: 34 (1.9%)
    Eligible for Free Lunch Program: 972 (54.0%)
    Eligible for Reduced-Price Lunch Program: 188 (10.4%)
Teachers: 137.9 (13.1 to 1)
Librarians/Media Specialists: 2.7 (666.7 to 1)
Guidance Counselors: 4.4 (409.1 to 1)
Current Spending: ($ per student per year):
    Total: $7,177; Instruction: $3,793; Support Services: $2,861
Enrollment, Drop-out Rates and Diploma Recipients by Race/Ethnicity

Category	Total	White	Black	Asian	AIAN	Hisp.
Enrollment (%)	100.0	62.5	36.8	0.0	0.1	0.6
Drop-out Rate (%)	6.3	5.6	7.8	n/a	n/a	0.0
H.S. Diplomas (#)	94	63	29	0	0	2

Claiborne Parish

Claiborne Parish School Board
415 E Main St • Homer, LA 71040-0600
Mailing Address: PO Box 600 • Homer, LA 71040-0600
(318) 927-3502
Grade Span: PK-12; **Agency Type:** 1
Schools: 9
    2 Primary; 1 Middle; 1 High; 5 Other Level
    8 Regular; 0 Special Education; 0 Vocational; 1 Alternative
    0 Magnet; 0 Charter; 5 Title I Eligible; 5 School-wide Title I
Students: 2,833 (51.2% male; 48.7% female)
    Individual Education Program: 478 (16.9%);
    English Language Learner: 0 (0.0%); Migrant: 13 (0.5%)
    Eligible for Free Lunch Program: 1,576 (57.9%)
    Eligible for Reduced-Price Lunch Program: 208 (7.6%)
Teachers: 228.0 (11.9 to 1)
Librarians/Media Specialists: 0.0 (n/a to 1)
Guidance Counselors: 8.6 (316.7 to 1)
Current Spending: ($ per student per year):
    Total: $7,428; Instruction: $4,433; Support Services: $2,431
Enrollment, Drop-out Rates and Diploma Recipients by Race/Ethnicity

Category	Total	White	Black	Asian	AIAN	Hisp.
Enrollment (%)	100.0	32.5	67.0	0.1	0.1	0.3
Drop-out Rate (%)	2.5	2.1	2.8	0.0	0.0	0.0
H.S. Diplomas (#)	149	57	92	0	0	0

Concordia Parish

Concordia Parish School Board
4358 Hwy 84 W • Vidalia, LA 71373-0950
Mailing Address: PO Box 950 • Vidalia, LA 71373-0950
(318) 336-4226 • http://nls.k12.la.us/~ccps/
Grade Span: PK-12; **Agency Type:** 1
Schools: 11
    5 Primary; 2 Middle; 2 High; 2 Other Level
    10 Regular; 0 Special Education; 0 Vocational; 1 Alternative
    0 Magnet; 0 Charter; 10 Title I Eligible; 6 School-wide Title I
Students: 3,798 (51.1% male; 48.8% female)
    Individual Education Program: 414 (10.9%);
    English Language Learner: 3 (0.1%); Migrant: 53 (1.4%)
    Eligible for Free Lunch Program: 2,582 (68.0%)
    Eligible for Reduced-Price Lunch Program: 226 (6.0%)
Teachers: 269.3 (14.1 to 1)
Librarians/Media Specialists: 10.0 (379.8 to 1)
Guidance Counselors: 11.5 (330.3 to 1)
Current Spending: ($ per student per year):
    Total: $6,841; Instruction: $4,048; Support Services: $2,331
Enrollment, Drop-out Rates and Diploma Recipients by Race/Ethnicity

Category	Total	White	Black	Asian	AIAN	Hisp.
Enrollment (%)	100.0	48.7	51.1	0.1	0.0	0.1
Drop-out Rate (%)	6.2	3.7	8.5	0.0	n/a	0.0
H.S. Diplomas (#)	205	102	103	0	0	0

De Soto Parish

Desoto Parish School Board
201 Crosby St • Mansfield, LA 71052
(318) 872-2836 • http://www.desoto.k12.la.us/
Grade Span: PK-12; **Agency Type:** 1
Schools: 13
    4 Primary; 2 Middle; 3 High; 4 Other Level
    11 Regular; 0 Special Education; 0 Vocational; 2 Alternative
    0 Magnet; 0 Charter; 9 Title I Eligible; 8 School-wide Title I
Students: 4,924 (50.9% male; 49.0% female)
    Individual Education Program: 779 (15.8%);
    English Language Learner: 63 (1.3%); Migrant: 36 (0.7%)
    Eligible for Free Lunch Program: 2,836 (57.6%)
    Eligible for Reduced-Price Lunch Program: 400 (8.1%)
Teachers: 371.0 (13.3 to 1)
Librarians/Media Specialists: 11.0 (447.6 to 1)
Guidance Counselors: 14.0 (351.7 to 1)
Current Spending: ($ per student per year):
    Total: $8,021; Instruction: $4,714; Support Services: $2,789
Enrollment, Drop-out Rates and Diploma Recipients by Race/Ethnicity

Category	Total	White	Black	Asian	AIAN	Hisp.
Enrollment (%)	100.0	42.6	55.8	0.2	0.2	1.3
Drop-out Rate (%)	4.5	3.3	5.5	0.0	0.0	10.0
H.S. Diplomas (#)	248	128	117	0	0	3

East Baton Rouge Parish

City of Baker SD
3033 Ray Weiland Dr • Baker, LA 70714
Mailing Address: PO Box 680 • Baker, LA 70704-0680
(225) 774-5795
Grade Span: N -N ; **Agency Type:** 1
Schools: 5
    3 Primary; 1 Middle; 1 High; 0 Other Level
    5 Regular; 0 Special Education; 0 Vocational; 0 Alternative
    0 Magnet; 0 Charter; 0 Title I Eligible; 0 School-wide Title I
Students: 2,253 (50.9% male; 49.0% female)
    Individual Education Program: 228 (10.1%);
    English Language Learner: 9 (0.4%); Migrant: 0 (0.0%)
    Eligible for Free Lunch Program: 1,321 (58.6%)
    Eligible for Reduced-Price Lunch Program: 313 (13.9%)
Teachers: 144.6 (15.6 to 1)
Librarians/Media Specialists: 0.0 (n/a to 1)
Guidance Counselors: 7.0 (321.9 to 1)
Current Spending: ($ per student per year):
    Total: n/a; Instruction: n/a; Support Services: n/a
Enrollment, Drop-out Rates and Diploma Recipients by Race/Ethnicity

Category	Total	White	Black	Asian	AIAN	Hisp.
Enrollment (%)	100.0	14.9	84.5	0.4	0.0	0.3
Drop-out Rate (%)	n/a	n/a	n/a	n/a	n/a	n/a
H.S. Diplomas (#)	n/a	n/a	n/a	n/a	n/a	n/a

East Baton Rouge Parish School Board
1050 S Foster Dr • Baton Rouge, LA 70806
Mailing Address: PO Box 2950 • Baton Rouge, LA 70821-2950
(225) 922-5618
Grade Span: PK-12; **Agency Type:** 1
Schools: 98
    60 Primary; 18 Middle; 17 High; 3 Other Level
    87 Regular; 2 Special Education; 0 Vocational; 9 Alternative
    26 Magnet; 3 Charter; 58 Title I Eligible; 58 School-wide Title I
Students: 46,644 (50.9% male; 49.0% female)
    Individual Education Program: 4,737 (10.2%);
    English Language Learner: 1,446 (3.1%); Migrant: 1 (<0.1%)
    Eligible for Free Lunch Program: 30,227 (64.8%)
    Eligible for Reduced-Price Lunch Program: 3,335 (7.1%)
Teachers: 3,137.0 (14.9 to 1)
Librarians/Media Specialists: 97.0 (480.9 to 1)
Guidance Counselors: 312.0 (149.5 to 1)
Current Spending: ($ per student per year):
    Total: $7,633; Instruction: $4,221; Support Services: $2,886
Enrollment, Drop-out Rates and Diploma Recipients by Race/Ethnicity

Category	Total	White	Black	Asian	AIAN	Hisp.
Enrollment (%)	100.0	20.5	75.8	2.3	0.1	1.3
Drop-out Rate (%)	8.5	6.5	9.8	7.1	11.1	7.8
H.S. Diplomas (#)	2,815	1,199	1,527	65	2	22

Zachary Community SD
4656 Main St • Zachary, LA 70791
(225) 658-4969
Grade Span: N -N ; **Agency Type:** 1
Schools: 4
    2 Primary; 1 Middle; 1 High; 0 Other Level
    4 Regular; 0 Special Education; 0 Vocational; 0 Alternative

0 Magnet; 0 Charter; 3 Title I Eligible; 2 School-wide Title I
Students: 3,250   (49.5% male; 50.4% female)
  Individual Education Program: 299 (9.2%);
  English Language Learner: 15 (0.5%); Migrant: 0 (0.0%)
  Eligible for Free Lunch Program: 897 (27.6%)
  Eligible for Reduced-Price Lunch Program: 212 (6.5%)
Teachers: 175.0 (18.6 to 1)
Librarians/Media Specialists: 5.0 (650.0 to 1)
Guidance Counselors: 12.0 (270.8 to 1)
Current Spending: ($ per student per year):
  Total: n/a; Instruction: n/a; Support Services: n/a
Enrollment, Drop-out Rates and Diploma Recipients by Race/Ethnicity

Category	Total	White	Black	Asian	AIAN	Hisp.
Enrollment (%)	100.0	59.8	39.2	0.6	0.1	0.3
Drop-out Rate (%)	n/a	n/a	n/a	n/a	n/a	n/a
H.S. Diplomas (#)	n/a	n/a	n/a	n/a	n/a	n/a

East Carroll Parish

East Carroll Parish School Board
504 Third St • Lake Providence, LA 71254-0792
Mailing Address: PO Box 792 • Lake Providence, LA 71254-0792
(318) 559-2222 • http://www.e-carrollschools.org/
Grade Span: PK-12; **Agency Type:** 1
Schools: 6
  3 Primary; 1 Middle; 1 High; 1 Other Level
  6 Regular; 0 Special Education; 0 Vocational; 0 Alternative
  0 Magnet; 0 Charter; 6 Title I Eligible; 6 School-wide Title I
Students: 1,675   (48.6% male; 51.3% female)
  Individual Education Program: 239 (14.3%)
  English Language Learner: 2 (0.1%); Migrant: 31 (1.9%)
  Eligible for Free Lunch Program: 1,456 (86.9%)
  Eligible for Reduced-Price Lunch Program: 56 (3.3%)
Teachers: 142.1 (11.8 to 1)
Librarians/Media Specialists: 2.0 (837.5 to 1)
Guidance Counselors: 4.0 (418.8 to 1)
Current Spending: ($ per student per year):
  Total: $7,557; Instruction: $4,572; Support Services: $2,248
Enrollment, Drop-out Rates and Diploma Recipients by Race/Ethnicity

Category	Total	White	Black	Asian	AIAN	Hisp.
Enrollment (%)	100.0	7.8	91.8	0.1	0.1	0.2
Drop-out Rate (%)	7.6	0.0	8.4	n/a	n/a	0.0
H.S. Diplomas (#)	83	4	79	0	0	0

East Feliciana Parish

East Feliciana Parish School Board
12732 Silliman St • Clinton, LA 70722-0397
Mailing Address: PO Box 397 • Clinton, LA 70722-0397
(225) 683-3040
Grade Span: PK-12; **Agency Type:** 1
Schools: 8
  3 Primary; 2 Middle; 2 High; 1 Other Level
  7 Regular; 0 Special Education; 0 Vocational; 1 Alternative
  0 Magnet; 0 Charter; 7 Title I Eligible; 0 School-wide Title I
Students: 2,369   (52.3% male; 47.6% female)
  Individual Education Program: 384 (16.2%);
  English Language Learner: 6 (0.3%); Migrant: 0 (0.0%)
  Eligible for Free Lunch Program: 1,788 (75.5%)
  Eligible for Reduced-Price Lunch Program: 196 (8.3%)
Teachers: 156.9 (15.1 to 1)
Librarians/Media Specialists: 5.0 (473.8 to 1)
Guidance Counselors: 12.0 (197.4 to 1)
Current Spending: ($ per student per year):
  Total: $7,156; Instruction: $4,128; Support Services: $2,545
Enrollment, Drop-out Rates and Diploma Recipients by Race/Ethnicity

Category	Total	White	Black	Asian	AIAN	Hisp.
Enrollment (%)	100.0	19.7	80.2	0.1	0.0	0.0
Drop-out Rate (%)	5.4	8.8	4.9	n/a	n/a	n/a
H.S. Diplomas (#)	142	13	129	0	0	0

Evangeline Parish

Evangeline Parish School Board
1123 Te Mamou Rd • Ville Platte, LA 70586
(337) 363-6651 • http://www.epsb.com/index3.htm
Grade Span: PK-12; **Agency Type:** 1
Schools: 15
  6 Primary; 1 Middle; 2 High; 5 Other Level
  14 Regular; 0 Special Education; 0 Vocational; 0 Alternative
  0 Magnet; 0 Charter; 14 Title I Eligible; 14 School-wide Title I
Students: 6,289   (52.0% male; 47.9% female)
  Individual Education Program: 1,085 (17.3%);
  English Language Learner: 27 (0.4%); Migrant: 33 (0.5%)
  Eligible for Free Lunch Program: 3,717 (59.1%)

Eligible for Reduced-Price Lunch Program: 713 (11.3%)
Teachers: 431.0 (14.6 to 1)
Librarians/Media Specialists: 11.0 (571.7 to 1)
Guidance Counselors: 20.0 (314.5 to 1)
Current Spending: ($ per student per year):
  Total: $6,460; Instruction: $3,975; Support Services: $2,063
Enrollment, Drop-out Rates and Diploma Recipients by Race/Ethnicity

Category	Total	White	Black	Asian	AIAN	Hisp.
Enrollment (%)	100.0	59.2	40.0	0.2	0.1	0.4
Drop-out Rate (%)	6.6	4.9	9.9	0.0	0.0	0.0
H.S. Diplomas (#)	286	175	110	0	0	1

Franklin Parish

Franklin Parish School Board
7293 Prairie Rd • Winnsboro, LA 71295
(318) 435-9046 • http://www.franklin.k12.la.us/
Grade Span: PK-12; **Agency Type:** 1
Schools: 11
  6 Primary; 2 Middle; 2 High; 1 Other Level
  10 Regular; 0 Special Education; 0 Vocational; 1 Alternative
  0 Magnet; 0 Charter; 7 Title I Eligible; 7 School-wide Title I
Students: 3,851   (51.3% male; 48.6% female)
  Individual Education Program: 450 (11.7%);
  English Language Learner: 0 (0.0%); Migrant: 112 (2.9%)
  Eligible for Free Lunch Program: 2,427 (63.0%)
  Eligible for Reduced-Price Lunch Program: 329 (8.5%)
Teachers: 321.4 (12.0 to 1)
Librarians/Media Specialists: 0.0 (n/a to 1)
Guidance Counselors: 6.6 (583.5 to 1)
Current Spending: ($ per student per year):
  Total: $6,235; Instruction: $3,961; Support Services: $1,782
Enrollment, Drop-out Rates and Diploma Recipients by Race/Ethnicity

Category	Total	White	Black	Asian	AIAN	Hisp.
Enrollment (%)	100.0	51.5	47.8	0.3	0.1	0.4
Drop-out Rate (%)	7.2	5.6	9.4	0.0	0.0	50.0
H.S. Diplomas (#)	199	108	88	3	0	0

Grant Parish

Grant Parish School Board
512 Main St • Colfax, LA 71417-0208
Mailing Address: PO Box 208 • Colfax, LA 71417-0208
(318) 627-3274
Grade Span: PK-12; **Agency Type:** 1
Schools: 9
  4 Primary; 1 Middle; 3 High; 1 Other Level
  8 Regular; 0 Special Education; 0 Vocational; 1 Alternative
  0 Magnet; 0 Charter; 7 Title I Eligible; 7 School-wide Title I
Students: 3,621   (51.6% male; 48.3% female)
  Individual Education Program: 556 (15.4%);
  English Language Learner: 0 (0.0%); Migrant: 38 (1.0%)
  Eligible for Free Lunch Program: 1,771 (48.9%)
  Eligible for Reduced-Price Lunch Program: 439 (12.1%)
Teachers: 245.7 (14.7 to 1)
Librarians/Media Specialists: 6.0 (603.5 to 1)
Guidance Counselors: 11.0 (329.2 to 1)
Current Spending: ($ per student per year):
  Total: $6,385; Instruction: $3,557; Support Services: $2,318
Enrollment, Drop-out Rates and Diploma Recipients by Race/Ethnicity

Category	Total	White	Black	Asian	AIAN	Hisp.
Enrollment (%)	100.0	83.8	14.7	0.3	0.3	0.9
Drop-out Rate (%)	6.0	6.0	6.3	n/a	0.0	0.0
H.S. Diplomas (#)	184	152	29	0	2	1

Iberia Parish

Iberia Parish School Board
1500 Jane St • New Iberia, LA 70560
Mailing Address: PO Box 200 • New Iberia, LA 70562-0200
(337) 365-2341 • http://www.iberia.k12.la.us/
Grade Span: PK-12; **Agency Type:** 1
Schools: 32
  22 Primary; 4 Middle; 4 High; 2 Other Level
  31 Regular; 0 Special Education; 0 Vocational; 1 Alternative
  0 Magnet; 0 Charter; 21 Title I Eligible; 20 School-wide Title I
Students: 14,201   (50.9% male; 49.0% female)
  Individual Education Program: 2,354 (16.6%);
  English Language Learner: 253 (1.8%); Migrant: 123 (0.9%)
  Eligible for Free Lunch Program: 7,861 (55.4%)
  Eligible for Reduced-Price Lunch Program: 1,228 (8.6%)
Teachers: 1,027.0 (13.8 to 1)
Librarians/Media Specialists: 29.0 (489.7 to 1)
Guidance Counselors: 62.0 (229.0 to 1)

Current Spending: ($ per student per year):
    Total: $6,802; Instruction: $4,190; Support Services: $2,168

Enrollment, Drop-out Rates and Diploma Recipients by Race/Ethnicity

Category	Total	White	Black	Asian	AIAN	Hisp.
Enrollment (%)	100.0	53.0	43.2	2.8	0.2	0.8
Drop-out Rate (%)	5.9	5.3	7.0	6.1	0.0	0.0
H.S. Diplomas (#)	637	395	218	22	1	1

Iberville Parish

Iberville Parish School Board
58030 Plaquemine St • Plaquemine, LA 70764
Mailing Address: PO Box 151 • Plaquemine, LA 70765-0151
(225) 687-4341 • http://www.ipsb.net/
Grade Span: PK-12; **Agency Type:** 1
Schools: 9
    3 Primary; 1 Middle; 2 High; 3 Other Level
    8 Regular; 0 Special Education; 0 Vocational; 1 Alternative
    0 Magnet; 0 Charter; 8 Title I Eligible; 0 School-wide Title I
Students: 4,395   (50.8% male; 49.1% female)
    Individual Education Program: 678 (15.4%);
    English Language Learner: 14 (0.3%); Migrant: 4 (0.1%)
    Eligible for Free Lunch Program: 3,350 (76.2%)
    Eligible for Reduced-Price Lunch Program: 329 (7.5%)
Teachers: 333.6 (13.2 to 1)
Librarians/Media Specialists: 8.0 (549.4 to 1)
Guidance Counselors: 17.0 (258.5 to 1)
Current Spending: ($ per student per year):
    Total: $8,756; Instruction: $4,434; Support Services: $3,717

Enrollment, Drop-out Rates and Diploma Recipients by Race/Ethnicity

Category	Total	White	Black	Asian	AIAN	Hisp.
Enrollment (%)	100.0	22.6	76.5	0.0	0.1	0.8
Drop-out Rate (%)	7.5	5.8	8.0	0.0	n/a	0.0
H.S. Diplomas (#)	253	67	185	1	0	0

Jackson Parish

Jackson Parish School Board
315 Pershing Hwy • Jonesboro, LA 71251-0705
Mailing Address: PO Box 705 • Jonesboro, LA 71251-0705
(318) 259-4456
Grade Span: PK-12; **Agency Type:** 1
Schools: 7
    2 Primary; 1 Middle; 1 High; 3 Other Level
    7 Regular; 0 Special Education; 0 Vocational; 0 Alternative
    0 Magnet; 0 Charter; 4 Title I Eligible; 4 School-wide Title I
Students: 2,389   (51.1% male; 48.8% female)
    Individual Education Program: 279 (11.7%);
    English Language Learner: 0 (0.0%); Migrant: 27 (1.1%)
    Eligible for Free Lunch Program: 1,132 (47.4%)
    Eligible for Reduced-Price Lunch Program: 249 (10.4%)
Teachers: 177.0 (13.5 to 1)
Librarians/Media Specialists: 4.0 (597.3 to 1)
Guidance Counselors: 7.0 (341.3 to 1)
Current Spending: ($ per student per year):
    Total: $8,251; Instruction: $4,722; Support Services: $3,002

Enrollment, Drop-out Rates and Diploma Recipients by Race/Ethnicity

Category	Total	White	Black	Asian	AIAN	Hisp.
Enrollment (%)	100.0	62.2	36.8	0.3	0.0	0.8
Drop-out Rate (%)	6.0	6.7	5.1	0.0	n/a	0.0
H.S. Diplomas (#)	169	83	83	2	0	1

Jefferson Parish

Jefferson Parish School Board
501 Manhattan Blvd • Harvey, LA 70058-4495
(504) 349-7802 • http://www.jppss.k12.la.us/
Grade Span: PK-12; **Agency Type:** 1
Schools: 84
    57 Primary; 17 Middle; 9 High; 1 Other Level
    79 Regular; 2 Special Education; 1 Vocational; 2 Alternative
    0 Magnet; 1 Charter; 48 Title I Eligible; 48 School-wide Title I
Students: 51,453   (51.6% male; 48.3% female)
    Individual Education Program: 7,891 (15.3%);
    English Language Learner: 3,303 (6.4%); Migrant: 240 (0.5%)
    Eligible for Free Lunch Program: 31,387 (61.0%)
    Eligible for Reduced-Price Lunch Program: 5,303 (10.3%)
Teachers: 3,371.7 (15.3 to 1)
Librarians/Media Specialists: 53.0 (970.8 to 1)
Guidance Counselors: 239.7 (214.7 to 1)
Current Spending: ($ per student per year):
    Total: $6,645; Instruction: $4,129; Support Services: $2,180

Enrollment, Drop-out Rates and Diploma Recipients by Race/Ethnicity

Category	Total	White	Black	Asian	AIAN	Hisp.
Enrollment (%)	100.0	35.3	51.1	4.2	0.7	8.7
Drop-out Rate (%)	9.7	10.0	10.0	6.0	7.8	8.9
H.S. Diplomas (#)	2,261	976	973	132	11	169

Jefferson Davis Parish School Board
203 E Plaquemine St • Jennings, LA 70546-0640
Mailing Address: PO Box 640 • Jennings, LA 70546-0640
(337) 824-1834
Grade Span: PK-12; **Agency Type:** 1
Schools: 14
    6 Primary; 2 Middle; 3 High; 3 Other Level
    14 Regular; 0 Special Education; 0 Vocational; 0 Alternative
    0 Magnet; 0 Charter; 8 Title I Eligible; 8 School-wide Title I
Students: 5,748   (51.6% male; 48.3% female)
    Individual Education Program: 993 (17.3%);
    English Language Learner: 9 (0.2%); Migrant: 50 (0.9%)
    Eligible for Free Lunch Program: 2,478 (43.1%)
    Eligible for Reduced-Price Lunch Program: 801 (13.9%)
Teachers: 370.0 (15.5 to 1)
Librarians/Media Specialists: 14.0 (410.6 to 1)
Guidance Counselors: 26.0 (221.1 to 1)
Current Spending: ($ per student per year):
    Total: $7,025; Instruction: $4,007; Support Services: $2,470

Enrollment, Drop-out Rates and Diploma Recipients by Race/Ethnicity

Category	Total	White	Black	Asian	AIAN	Hisp.
Enrollment (%)	100.0	73.6	24.4	0.3	1.5	0.2
Drop-out Rate (%)	3.6	2.9	6.1	0.0	5.3	25.0
H.S. Diplomas (#)	318	266	45	0	4	3

La Salle Parish

Lasalle Parish School Board
3012 N First St • Jena, LA 71342-0090
Mailing Address: PO Drawer 90 • Jena, LA 71342-0090
(318) 992-2161 • http://www.lpsb.org/
Grade Span: PK-12; **Agency Type:** 1
Schools: 10
    4 Primary; 3 Middle; 2 High; 1 Other Level
    9 Regular; 0 Special Education; 0 Vocational; 1 Alternative
    0 Magnet; 0 Charter; 6 Title I Eligible; 4 School-wide Title I
Students: 2,699   (50.3% male; 49.6% female)
    Individual Education Program: 228 (8.4%);
    English Language Learner: 0 (0.0%); Migrant: 22 (0.8%)
    Eligible for Free Lunch Program: 1,104 (40.9%)
    Eligible for Reduced-Price Lunch Program: 343 (12.7%)
Teachers: 191.7 (14.1 to 1)
Librarians/Media Specialists: 7.0 (385.6 to 1)
Guidance Counselors: 5.0 (539.8 to 1)
Current Spending: ($ per student per year):
    Total: $6,844; Instruction: $4,105; Support Services: $2,240

Enrollment, Drop-out Rates and Diploma Recipients by Race/Ethnicity

Category	Total	White	Black	Asian	AIAN	Hisp.
Enrollment (%)	100.0	85.5	12.9	0.2	0.8	0.6
Drop-out Rate (%)	3.9	3.6	5.9	0.0	0.0	n/a
H.S. Diplomas (#)	163	150	13	0	0	0

Lafayette Parish

Lafayette Parish School Board
113 Chaplin Dr • Lafayette, LA 70508
Mailing Address: PO Drawer 2158 • Lafayette, LA 70502-2158
(337) 236-6800 • http://www.lft.k12.la.us/
Grade Span: PK-12; **Agency Type:** 1
Schools: 45
    24 Primary; 11 Middle; 5 High; 5 Other Level
    41 Regular; 0 Special Education; 0 Vocational; 4 Alternative
    0 Magnet; 1 Charter; 23 Title I Eligible; 23 School-wide Title I
Students: 29,813   (50.8% male; 49.1% female)
    Individual Education Program: 3,431 (11.5%);
    English Language Learner: 546 (1.8%); Migrant: 93 (0.3%)
    Eligible for Free Lunch Program: 13,420 (45.0%)
    Eligible for Reduced-Price Lunch Program: 2,803 (9.4%)
Teachers: 2,117.7 (14.1 to 1)
Librarians/Media Specialists: 50.0 (596.3 to 1)
Guidance Counselors: 140.5 (212.2 to 1)
Current Spending: ($ per student per year):
    Total: $6,623; Instruction: $4,359; Support Services: $1,952

Enrollment, Drop-out Rates and Diploma Recipients by Race/Ethnicity

Category	Total	White	Black	Asian	AIAN	Hisp.
Enrollment (%)	100.0	56.9	40.2	1.3	0.3	1.4
Drop-out Rate (%)	7.8	6.9	9.5	9.5	30.8	10.7
H.S. Diplomas (#)	1,624	1,153	438	21	1	11

Lafourche Parish

Lafourche Parish School Board
805 E Seventh St • Thibodaux, LA 70301
Mailing Address: PO Box 879 • Thibodaux, LA 70302-0879
(985) 446-5631 • http://lafourche.k12.la.us/
Grade Span: PK-12; **Agency Type:** 1
Schools: 29
    14 Primary; 10 Middle; 3 High; 2 Other Level
    27 Regular; 0 Special Education; 0 Vocational; 2 Alternative
    0 Magnet; 0 Charter; 18 Title I Eligible; 17 School-wide Title I
Students: 14,872 (51.8% male; 48.1% female)
    Individual Education Program: 2,057 (13.8%);
    English Language Learner: 378 (2.5%); Migrant: 252 (1.7%)
    Eligible for Free Lunch Program: 6,712 (45.1%)
    Eligible for Reduced-Price Lunch Program: 1,623 (10.9%)
Teachers: 1,152.9 (12.9 to 1)
Librarians/Media Specialists: 31.0 (479.7 to 1)
Guidance Counselors: 91.2 (163.1 to 1)
Current Spending: ($ per student per year):
    Total: $7,091; Instruction: $4,326; Support Services: $2,343

Enrollment, Drop-out Rates and Diploma Recipients by Race/Ethnicity

Category	Total	White	Black	Asian	AIAN	Hisp.
Enrollment (%)	100.0	71.2	22.3	0.9	3.9	1.7
Drop-out Rate (%)	5.8	4.5	11.0	3.4	9.4	2.0
H.S. Diplomas (#)	810	656	110	13	24	7

Lincoln Parish

Lincoln Parish School Board
410 S Farmerville St • Ruston, LA 71270-4699
(318) 255-1430 • http://www.lincolnschools.org/
Grade Span: PK-12; **Agency Type:** 1
Schools: 19
    9 Primary; 3 Middle; 5 High; 2 Other Level
    16 Regular; 0 Special Education; 0 Vocational; 3 Alternative
    0 Magnet; 0 Charter; 9 Title I Eligible; 9 School-wide Title I
Students: 6,596 (50.6% male; 49.3% female)
    Individual Education Program: 856 (13.0%);
    English Language Learner: 28 (0.4%); Migrant: 35 (0.5%)
    Eligible for Free Lunch Program: 3,189 (48.3%)
    Eligible for Reduced-Price Lunch Program: 445 (6.7%)
Teachers: 478.8 (13.8 to 1)
Librarians/Media Specialists: 18.0 (366.4 to 1)
Guidance Counselors: 26.1 (252.7 to 1)
Current Spending: ($ per student per year):
    Total: $6,575; Instruction: $4,047; Support Services: $2,046

Enrollment, Drop-out Rates and Diploma Recipients by Race/Ethnicity

Category	Total	White	Black	Asian	AIAN	Hisp.
Enrollment (%)	100.0	49.0	49.2	0.8	0.0	1.1
Drop-out Rate (%)	6.4	4.8	8.7	0.0	0.0	0.0
H.S. Diplomas (#)	418	236	172	6	0	4

Livingston Parish

Livingston Parish School Board
13909 Florida Blvd • Livingston, LA 70754-1130
Mailing Address: PO Box 1130 • Livingston, LA 70754-1130
(225) 686-7044 • http://www.nls.k12.la.us/~mpsb/
Grade Span: PK-12; **Agency Type:** 1
Schools: 39
    19 Primary; 7 Middle; 7 High; 4 Other Level
    36 Regular; 1 Special Education; 0 Vocational; 0 Alternative
    0 Magnet; 0 Charter; 19 Title I Eligible; 19 School-wide Title I
Students: 20,743 (51.5% male; 48.4% female)
    Individual Education Program: 2,478 (11.9%);
    English Language Learner: 93 (0.4%); Migrant: 29 (0.1%)
    Eligible for Free Lunch Program: 6,443 (31.1%)
    Eligible for Reduced-Price Lunch Program: 2,542 (12.3%)
Teachers: 1,353.5 (15.3 to 1)
Librarians/Media Specialists: 23.0 (901.9 to 1)
Guidance Counselors: 71.0 (292.2 to 1)
Current Spending: ($ per student per year):
    Total: $5,641; Instruction: $3,611; Support Services: $1,608

Enrollment, Drop-out Rates and Diploma Recipients by Race/Ethnicity

Category	Total	White	Black	Asian	AIAN	Hisp.
Enrollment (%)	100.0	93.7	5.2	0.2	0.2	0.7
Drop-out Rate (%)	1.2	1.3	0.4	0.0	0.0	0.0
H.S. Diplomas (#)	1,056	997	50	4	0	5

Madison Parish

Madison Parish School Board
301 S Chestnut St • Tallulah, LA 71282
Mailing Address: PO Box 1620 • Tallulah, LA 71284-1620
(318) 574-3616 • http://nls.k12.la.us/~mpsb/
Grade Span: PK-12; **Agency Type:** 1
Schools: 7
    2 Primary; 2 Middle; 2 High; 1 Other Level
    6 Regular; 0 Special Education; 0 Vocational; 1 Alternative
    0 Magnet; 0 Charter; 7 Title I Eligible; 7 School-wide Title I
Students: 2,319 (52.4% male; 47.5% female)
    Individual Education Program: 299 (12.9%);
    English Language Learner: 1 (<0.1%); Migrant: 45 (1.9%)
    Eligible for Free Lunch Program: 1,878 (81.0%)
    Eligible for Reduced-Price Lunch Program: 66 (2.8%)
Teachers: 159.1 (14.6 to 1)
Librarians/Media Specialists: 5.0 (463.8 to 1)
Guidance Counselors: 5.9 (393.1 to 1)
Current Spending: ($ per student per year):
    Total: $6,703; Instruction: $3,475; Support Services: $2,626

Enrollment, Drop-out Rates and Diploma Recipients by Race/Ethnicity

Category	Total	White	Black	Asian	AIAN	Hisp.
Enrollment (%)	100.0	9.1	89.9	0.2	0.0	0.8
Drop-out Rate (%)	10.9	19.3	9.5	50.0	n/a	20.0
H.S. Diplomas (#)	111	11	97	1	0	2

Morehouse Parish

Morehouse Parish School Board
714 S Washington St • Bastrop, LA 71220
Mailing Address: PO Box 872 • Bastrop, LA 71221-0872
(318) 281-5784 • http://www.mpsb.us/
Grade Span: PK-12; **Agency Type:** 1
Schools: 16
    11 Primary; 2 Middle; 1 High; 2 Other Level
    14 Regular; 0 Special Education; 0 Vocational; 2 Alternative
    1 Magnet; 0 Charter; 9 Title I Eligible; 9 School-wide Title I
Students: 5,153 (51.2% male; 48.7% female)
    Individual Education Program: 830 (16.1%);
    English Language Learner: 14 (0.3%); Migrant: 13 (0.3%)
    Eligible for Free Lunch Program: 3,331 (64.6%)
    Eligible for Reduced-Price Lunch Program: 429 (8.3%)
Teachers: 377.3 (13.7 to 1)
Librarians/Media Specialists: 6.6 (780.8 to 1)
Guidance Counselors: 17.8 (289.5 to 1)
Current Spending: ($ per student per year):
    Total: $6,810; Instruction: $4,194; Support Services: $2,122

Enrollment, Drop-out Rates and Diploma Recipients by Race/Ethnicity

Category	Total	White	Black	Asian	AIAN	Hisp.
Enrollment (%)	100.0	35.0	64.5	0.1	0.0	0.4
Drop-out Rate (%)	9.2	7.4	10.3	n/a	0.0	0.0
H.S. Diplomas (#)	230	93	137	0	0	0

Natchitoches Parish

Natchitoches Parish School Board
310 Royal St • Natchitoches, LA 71457-5709
Mailing Address: PO Box 16 • Natchitoches, LA 71458-0016
(318) 352-2358 • http://www.nat.k12.la.us/
Grade Span: PK-12; **Agency Type:** 1
Schools: 15
    9 Primary; 3 Middle; 0 High; 3 Other Level
    14 Regular; 0 Special Education; 0 Vocational; 1 Alternative
    0 Magnet; 0 Charter; 11 Title I Eligible; 11 School-wide Title I
Students: 6,963 (51.1% male; 48.8% female)
    Individual Education Program: 839 (12.0%);
    English Language Learner: 19 (0.3%); Migrant: 208 (3.0%)
    Eligible for Free Lunch Program: 4,235 (60.8%)
    Eligible for Reduced-Price Lunch Program: 595 (8.5%)
Teachers: 481.6 (14.5 to 1)
Librarians/Media Specialists: 14.0 (497.4 to 1)
Guidance Counselors: 14.0 (497.4 to 1)
Current Spending: ($ per student per year):
    Total: $6,802; Instruction: $4,103; Support Services: $2,225

Enrollment, Drop-out Rates and Diploma Recipients by Race/Ethnicity

Category	Total	White	Black	Asian	AIAN	Hisp.
Enrollment (%)	100.0	42.4	55.6	0.5	0.6	0.9
Drop-out Rate (%)	7.9	6.3	9.6	0.0	0.0	0.0
H.S. Diplomas (#)	353	185	159	1	3	5

Orleans Parish

Orleans Parish School Board
3510 General Degaulle Dr • New Orleans, LA 70114
(504) 304-5702 • http://www.nops.k12.la.us/
Grade Span: PK-12; **Agency Type:** 1
Schools: 129
  77 Primary; 24 Middle; 23 High; 4 Other Level
  116 Regular; 0 Special Education; 1 Vocational; 11 Alternative
  6 Magnet; 2 Charter; 112 Title I Eligible; 112 School-wide Title I
Students: 67,922 (50.3% male; 49.6% female)
  Individual Education Program: 7,174 (10.6%);
  English Language Learner: 1,227 (1.8%); Migrant: 115 (0.2%)
  Eligible for Free Lunch Program: 48,826 (71.9%)
  Eligible for Reduced-Price Lunch Program: 2,439 (3.6%)
Teachers: 4,656.5 (14.6 to 1)
Librarians/Media Specialists: 76.5 (887.9 to 1)
Guidance Counselors: 166.0 (409.2 to 1)
Current Spending: ($ per student per year):
  Total: $6,560; Instruction: $4,059; Support Services: $2,129
Enrollment, Drop-out Rates and Diploma Recipients by Race/Ethnicity

Category	Total	White	Black	Asian	AIAN	Hisp.
Enrollment (%)	100.0	3.4	93.6	1.9	0.1	1.1
Drop-out Rate (%)	9.1	2.9	9.6	4.4	14.3	5.0
H.S. Diplomas (#)	3,471	162	3,131	136	2	40

Ouachita Parish

City of Monroe School Board
2101 Roselawn Ave • Monroe, LA 71201
Mailing Address: PO Box 4180 • Monroe, LA 71211-4180
(318) 325-0601 • http://www.monroe.k12.la.us/mcs/
Grade Span: PK-12; **Agency Type:** 1
Schools: 20
  12 Primary; 3 Middle; 4 High; 1 Other Level
  18 Regular; 0 Special Education; 0 Vocational; 2 Alternative
  3 Magnet; 0 Charter; 15 Title I Eligible; 12 School-wide Title I
Students: 9,548 (50.1% male; 49.8% female)
  Individual Education Program: 1,386 (14.5%);
  English Language Learner: 22 (0.2%); Migrant: 8 (0.1%)
  Eligible for Free Lunch Program: 6,898 (72.2%)
  Eligible for Reduced-Price Lunch Program: 407 (4.3%)
Teachers: 671.1 (14.2 to 1)
Librarians/Media Specialists: 19.0 (502.5 to 1)
Guidance Counselors: 42.0 (227.3 to 1)
Current Spending: ($ per student per year):
  Total: $7,018; Instruction: $4,323; Support Services: $2,221
Enrollment, Drop-out Rates and Diploma Recipients by Race/Ethnicity

Category	Total	White	Black	Asian	AIAN	Hisp.
Enrollment (%)	100.0	10.5	88.8	0.4	0.0	0.3
Drop-out Rate (%)	12.5	6.8	13.5	0.0	n/a	40.0
H.S. Diplomas (#)	469	83	384	0	0	2

Ouachita Parish School Board
100 Bry St • Monroe, LA 71201
Mailing Address: PO Box 1642 • Monroe, LA 71210-1642
(318) 338-5300 • http://www.opsb.net/
Grade Span: PK-12; **Agency Type:** 1
Schools: 35
  22 Primary; 7 Middle; 5 High; 1 Other Level
  33 Regular; 0 Special Education; 0 Vocational; 2 Alternative
  0 Magnet; 0 Charter; 10 Title I Eligible; 10 School-wide Title I
Students: 18,324 (50.5% male; 49.4% female)
  Individual Education Program: 2,362 (12.9%);
  English Language Learner: 168 (0.9%); Migrant: 29 (0.2%)
  Eligible for Free Lunch Program: 7,317 (39.9%)
  Eligible for Reduced-Price Lunch Program: 1,486 (8.1%)
Teachers: 1,282.9 (14.3 to 1)
Librarians/Media Specialists: 36.0 (509.0 to 1)
Guidance Counselors: 67.3 (272.3 to 1)
Current Spending: ($ per student per year):
  Total: $6,871; Instruction: $4,289; Support Services: $2,149
Enrollment, Drop-out Rates and Diploma Recipients by Race/Ethnicity

Category	Total	White	Black	Asian	AIAN	Hisp.
Enrollment (%)	100.0	70.7	27.8	0.6	0.1	0.8
Drop-out Rate (%)	7.1	6.5	9.1	4.3	0.0	0.0
H.S. Diplomas (#)	923	720	188	7	1	7

Plaquemines Parish

Plaquemines Parish School Board
26138 Hwy 23 S • Port Sulphur, LA 70083-0070
Mailing Address: PO Box 70 • Port Sulphur, LA 70083-0070
(985) 564-2743 • http://www.ppsb.org/
Grade Span: PK-12; **Agency Type:** 1
Schools: 9
  1 Primary; 2 Middle; 2 High; 4 Other Level
  8 Regular; 0 Special Education; 0 Vocational; 1 Alternative
  0 Magnet; 0 Charter; 5 Title I Eligible; 4 School-wide Title I
Students: 4,967 (51.9% male; 48.0% female)
  Individual Education Program: 635 (12.8%);
  English Language Learner: 98 (2.0%); Migrant: 198 (4.0%)
  Eligible for Free Lunch Program: 2,603 (52.4%)
  Eligible for Reduced-Price Lunch Program: 432 (8.7%)
Teachers: 332.0 (15.0 to 1)
Librarians/Media Specialists: 12.0 (413.9 to 1)
Guidance Counselors: 23.0 (216.0 to 1)
Current Spending: ($ per student per year):
  Total: $8,079; Instruction: $4,467; Support Services: $3,111
Enrollment, Drop-out Rates and Diploma Recipients by Race/Ethnicity

Category	Total	White	Black	Asian	AIAN	Hisp.
Enrollment (%)	100.0	59.1	33.0	4.9	1.6	1.4
Drop-out Rate (%)	5.9	7.0	4.5	4.1	5.6	0.0
H.S. Diplomas (#)	278	166	95	9	3	5

Pointe Coupee Parish

Pointe Coupee Parish School Board
1662 Morganza Hwy • New Roads, LA 70760-0579
Mailing Address: PO Drawer 579 • New Roads, LA 70760-0579
(225) 638-8674
Grade Span: PK-12; **Agency Type:** 1
Schools: 9
  6 Primary; 0 Middle; 2 High; 1 Other Level
  8 Regular; 0 Special Education; 0 Vocational; 1 Alternative
  1 Magnet; 0 Charter; 6 Title I Eligible; 6 School-wide Title I
Students: 3,182 (49.4% male; 50.5% female)
  Individual Education Program: 694 (21.8%);
  English Language Learner: 2 (0.1%); Migrant: 5 (0.2%)
  Eligible for Free Lunch Program: 2,249 (70.7%)
  Eligible for Reduced-Price Lunch Program: 270 (8.5%)
Teachers: 230.0 (13.8 to 1)
Librarians/Media Specialists: 4.0 (795.5 to 1)
Guidance Counselors: 14.0 (227.3 to 1)
Current Spending: ($ per student per year):
  Total: $7,939; Instruction: $4,640; Support Services: $2,731
Enrollment, Drop-out Rates and Diploma Recipients by Race/Ethnicity

Category	Total	White	Black	Asian	AIAN	Hisp.
Enrollment (%)	100.0	35.3	63.8	0.2	0.0	0.8
Drop-out Rate (%)	11.6	11.2	11.5	n/a	50.0	n/a
H.S. Diplomas (#)	167	46	120	0	1	0

Rapides Parish

Rapides Parish School Board
619 Sixth St • Alexandria, LA 71301
Mailing Address: PO Box 1230 • Alexandria, LA 71309-1230
(318) 487-0888 • http://www.rapides.k12.la.us/
Grade Span: PK-12; **Agency Type:** 1
Schools: 53
  29 Primary; 8 Middle; 9 High; 7 Other Level
  48 Regular; 2 Special Education; 0 Vocational; 3 Alternative
  7 Magnet; 0 Charter; 33 Title I Eligible; 25 School-wide Title I
Students: 22,646 (51.0% male; 48.9% female)
  Individual Education Program: 3,288 (14.5%);
  English Language Learner: 338 (1.5%); Migrant: 141 (0.6%)
  Eligible for Free Lunch Program: 12,340 (54.5%)
  Eligible for Reduced-Price Lunch Program: 2,044 (9.0%)
Teachers: 1,572.5 (14.4 to 1)
Librarians/Media Specialists: 41.0 (552.3 to 1)
Guidance Counselors: 113.2 (200.1 to 1)
Current Spending: ($ per student per year):
  Total: $6,989; Instruction: $4,078; Support Services: $2,348
Enrollment, Drop-out Rates and Diploma Recipients by Race/Ethnicity

Category	Total	White	Black	Asian	AIAN	Hisp.
Enrollment (%)	100.0	53.9	42.9	1.2	0.9	1.1
Drop-out Rate (%)	8.7	6.3	12.7	4.5	11.3	6.3
H.S. Diplomas (#)	1,294	799	450	14	29	2

Red River Parish

Red River Parish School Board
1922 Alonzo St • Coushatta, LA 71019-1369
Mailing Address: PO Box 1369 • Coushatta, LA 71019-1369
(318) 932-4081
Grade Span: PK-12; **Agency Type:** 1
Schools: 5
  1 Primary; 1 Middle; 1 High; 2 Other Level
  3 Regular; 0 Special Education; 0 Vocational; 2 Alternative
  0 Magnet; 0 Charter; 3 Title I Eligible; 3 School-wide Title I
Students: 1,631   (51.5% male; 48.4% female)
  Individual Education Program: 214 (13.1%);
  English Language Learner: 0 (0.0%); Migrant: 0 (0.0%)
  Eligible for Free Lunch Program: 1,264 (77.5%)
  Eligible for Reduced-Price Lunch Program: 139 (8.5%)
Teachers: 129.5 (12.6 to 1)
Librarians/Media Specialists: 2.0 (815.5 to 1)
Guidance Counselors: 7.0 (233.0 to 1)
Current Spending: ($ per student per year):
  Total: $8,071; Instruction: $4,861; Support Services: $2,628
Enrollment, Drop-out Rates and Diploma Recipients by Race/Ethnicity

Category	Total	White	Black	Asian	AIAN	Hisp.
Enrollment (%)	100.0	32.2	67.4	0.1	0.2	0.1
Drop-out Rate (%)	20.5	28.8	16.4	n/a	n/a	0.0
H.S. Diplomas (#)	75	26	49	0	0	0

Richland Parish

Richland Parish School Board
411 Foster St • Rayville, LA 71269-0599
Mailing Address: PO Box 599 • Rayville, LA 71269-0599
(318) 728-5964 • http://www.nls.k12.la.us/~richland/
Grade Span: PK-12; **Agency Type:** 1
Schools: 12
  6 Primary; 2 Middle; 3 High; 1 Other Level
  11 Regular; 0 Special Education; 0 Vocational; 1 Alternative
  0 Magnet; 0 Charter; 9 Title I Eligible; 8 School-wide Title I
Students: 3,477   (51.7% male; 48.2% female)
  Individual Education Program: 473 (13.6%);
  English Language Learner: 0 (0.0%); Migrant: 18 (0.5%)
  Eligible for Free Lunch Program: 2,276 (65.5%)
  Eligible for Reduced-Price Lunch Program: 210 (6.0%)
Teachers: 279.4 (12.4 to 1)
Librarians/Media Specialists: 0.0 (n/a to 1)
Guidance Counselors: 8.0 (434.6 to 1)
Current Spending: ($ per student per year):
  Total: $7,010; Instruction: $4,325; Support Services: $2,174
Enrollment, Drop-out Rates and Diploma Recipients by Race/Ethnicity

Category	Total	White	Black	Asian	AIAN	Hisp.
Enrollment (%)	100.0	42.9	56.1	0.1	0.1	0.8
Drop-out Rate (%)	7.3	7.9	7.0	n/a	n/a	0.0
H.S. Diplomas (#)	175	70	105	0	0	0

Sabine Parish

Sabine Parish School Board
695 Peterson St • Many, LA 71449-1079
Mailing Address: PO Box 1079 • Many, LA 71449-1079
(318) 256-9228 • http://www.sabine.k12.la.us/
Grade Span: PK-12; **Agency Type:** 1
Schools: 14
  4 Primary; 2 Middle; 3 High; 5 Other Level
  13 Regular; 0 Special Education; 0 Vocational; 1 Alternative
  0 Magnet; 0 Charter; 10 Title I Eligible; 10 School-wide Title I
Students: 4,269   (52.3% male; 47.6% female)
  Individual Education Program: 694 (16.3%);
  English Language Learner: 37 (0.9%); Migrant: 6 (0.1%)
  Eligible for Free Lunch Program: 2,226 (52.1%)
  Eligible for Reduced-Price Lunch Program: 538 (12.6%)
Teachers: 300.0 (14.2 to 1)
Librarians/Media Specialists: 11.0 (388.1 to 1)
Guidance Counselors: 9.0 (474.3 to 1)
Current Spending: ($ per student per year):
  Total: $6,232; Instruction: $3,533; Support Services: $2,253
Enrollment, Drop-out Rates and Diploma Recipients by Race/Ethnicity

Category	Total	White	Black	Asian	AIAN	Hisp.
Enrollment (%)	100.0	51.0	25.9	0.2	19.0	3.9
Drop-out Rate (%)	5.0	5.4	5.9	0.0	2.6	5.5
H.S. Diplomas (#)	257	148	62	1	35	11

St. Bernard Parish

Saint Bernard Parish School Board
200 E Saint Bernard Hwy • Chalmette, LA 70043
(504) 301-2000 • http://www.gnofn.org/~sbpsb/
Grade Span: PK-12; **Agency Type:** 1
Schools: 14
  7 Primary; 3 Middle; 3 High; 1 Other Level
  13 Regular; 0 Special Education; 0 Vocational; 1 Alternative
  1 Magnet; 0 Charter; 8 Title I Eligible; 0 School-wide Title I
Students: 8,869   (50.9% male; 49.0% female)
  Individual Education Program: 1,295 (14.6%);
  English Language Learner: 52 (0.6%); Migrant: 0 (0.0%)
  Eligible for Free Lunch Program: 4,367 (49.2%)
  Eligible for Reduced-Price Lunch Program: 934 (10.5%)
Teachers: 623.0 (14.2 to 1)
Librarians/Media Specialists: 14.0 (633.5 to 1)
Guidance Counselors: 22.0 (403.1 to 1)
Current Spending: ($ per student per year):
  Total: $6,832; Instruction: $4,199; Support Services: $2,239
Enrollment, Drop-out Rates and Diploma Recipients by Race/Ethnicity

Category	Total	White	Black	Asian	AIAN	Hisp.
Enrollment (%)	100.0	75.9	16.5	2.4	1.1	4.0
Drop-out Rate (%)	6.3	6.1	5.9	9.1	8.0	9.9
H.S. Diplomas (#)	382	325	38	5	3	11

St. Charles Parish

Saint Charles Parish School Board
13855 River Rd • Luling, LA 70070-0046
Mailing Address: PO Box 46 • Luling, LA 70070-0046
(985) 785-6289 • http://www.stcharles.k12.la.us/
Grade Span: PK-12; **Agency Type:** 1
Schools: 21
  13 Primary; 6 Middle; 2 High; 0 Other Level
  21 Regular; 0 Special Education; 0 Vocational; 0 Alternative
  0 Magnet; 0 Charter; 4 Title I Eligible; 0 School-wide Title I
Students: 9,685   (51.2% male; 48.7% female)
  Individual Education Program: 1,195 (12.3%);
  English Language Learner: 108 (1.1%); Migrant: 5 (0.1%)
  Eligible for Free Lunch Program: 3,738 (38.6%)
  Eligible for Reduced-Price Lunch Program: 764 (7.9%)
Teachers: 774.0 (12.5 to 1)
Librarians/Media Specialists: 18.0 (538.1 to 1)
Guidance Counselors: 31.0 (312.4 to 1)
Current Spending: ($ per student per year):
  Total: $8,600; Instruction: $5,063; Support Services: $3,152
Enrollment, Drop-out Rates and Diploma Recipients by Race/Ethnicity

Category	Total	White	Black	Asian	AIAN	Hisp.
Enrollment (%)	100.0	59.6	36.8	0.9	0.4	2.4
Drop-out Rate (%)	3.4	2.7	5.2	0.0	0.0	4.0
H.S. Diplomas (#)	628	438	172	5	0	13

St. James Parish

Saint James Parish School Board
1876 W Main St • Lutcher, LA 70071-0338
Mailing Address: PO Box 338 • Lutcher, LA 70071-0338
(225) 869-5375
Grade Span: PK-12; **Agency Type:** 1
Schools: 10
  7 Primary; 1 Middle; 2 High; 0 Other Level
  10 Regular; 0 Special Education; 0 Vocational; 0 Alternative
  0 Magnet; 0 Charter; 10 Title I Eligible; 0 School-wide Title I
Students: 4,062   (50.9% male; 49.0% female)
  Individual Education Program: 574 (14.1%);
  English Language Learner: 4 (0.1%); Migrant: 12 (0.3%)
  Eligible for Free Lunch Program: 2,651 (65.3%)
  Eligible for Reduced-Price Lunch Program: 279 (6.9%)
Teachers: 284.3 (14.3 to 1)
Librarians/Media Specialists: 9.0 (451.3 to 1)
Guidance Counselors: 13.9 (292.2 to 1)
Current Spending: ($ per student per year):
  Total: $7,725; Instruction: $4,181; Support Services: $3,040
Enrollment, Drop-out Rates and Diploma Recipients by Race/Ethnicity

Category	Total	White	Black	Asian	AIAN	Hisp.
Enrollment (%)	100.0	30.6	69.0	0.0	0.0	0.4
Drop-out Rate (%)	7.0	4.1	8.6	n/a	n/a	n/a
H.S. Diplomas (#)	230	95	135	0	0	0

St. John The Baptist Parish

Saint John the Baptist Parish School Board

118 W Tenth St • Reserve, LA 70084
Mailing Address: PO Drawer AI • Reserve, LA 70084
(985) 536-3797 • http://www.stjohn.k12.la.us/
Grade Span: PK-12; **Agency Type:** 1
Schools: 12
  8 Primary; 1 Middle; 2 High; 1 Other Level
  10 Regular; 0 Special Education; 0 Vocational; 2 Alternative
  2 Magnet; 0 Charter; 10 Title I Eligible; 10 School-wide Title I
Students: 6,338   (51.0% male; 48.9% female)
  Individual Education Program: 1,245 (19.6%);
  English Language Learner: 94 (1.5%); Migrant: 0 (0.0%)
  Eligible for Free Lunch Program: 4,778 (75.4%)
  Eligible for Reduced-Price Lunch Program: 420 (6.6%)
Teachers: 462.4 (13.7 to 1)
Librarians/Media Specialists: 3.0 (2,112.7 to 1)
Guidance Counselors: 35.9 (176.5 to 1)
Current Spending: ($ per student per year):
  Total: $8,235; Instruction: $5,284; Support Services: $2,549

Enrollment, Drop-out Rates and Diploma Recipients by Race/Ethnicity

Category	Total	White	Black	Asian	AIAN	Hisp.
Enrollment (%)	100.0	21.3	75.5	0.6	0.1	2.5
Drop-out Rate (%)	8.5	8.0	8.7	12.5	33.3	2.5
H.S. Diplomas (#)	276	61	207	2	2	4

St. Landry Parish

Saint Landry Parish School Board

1013 E Creswell Ln • Opelousas, LA 70570
Mailing Address: PO Box 310 • Opelousas, LA 70571-0310
(337) 948-3657 • http://www.slp.k12.la.us/
Grade Span: PK-12; **Agency Type:** 1
Schools: 39
  25 Primary; 5 Middle; 8 High; 0 Other Level
  36 Regular; 0 Special Education; 2 Vocational; 0 Alternative
  0 Magnet; 0 Charter; 32 Title I Eligible; 10 School-wide Title I
Students: 15,231   (51.0% male; 48.9% female)
  Individual Education Program: 2,331 (15.3%);
  English Language Learner: 85 (0.6%); Migrant: 178 (1.2%)
  Eligible for Free Lunch Program: 9,970 (65.5%)
  Eligible for Reduced-Price Lunch Program: 1,534 (10.1%)
Teachers: 1,045.6 (14.6 to 1)
Librarians/Media Specialists: 20.0 (761.6 to 1)
Guidance Counselors: 53.7 (283.6 to 1)
Current Spending: ($ per student per year):
  Total: $6,605; Instruction: $4,131; Support Services: $1,975

Enrollment, Drop-out Rates and Diploma Recipients by Race/Ethnicity

Category	Total	White	Black	Asian	AIAN	Hisp.
Enrollment (%)	100.0	43.5	55.7	0.3	0.1	0.4
Drop-out Rate (%)	5.0	3.5	6.5	9.1	0.0	0.0
H.S. Diplomas (#)	805	417	383	3	0	2

St. Martin Parish

Saint Martin Parish School Board

305 Washington St • St. Martinville, LA 70582-0859
Mailing Address: PO Box 859 • Saint Martinville, LA 70582-0859
(337) 394-6261 • http://www.stmartin.k12.la.us/
Grade Span: PK-12; **Agency Type:** 1
Schools: 18
  7 Primary; 7 Middle; 3 High; 1 Other Level
  17 Regular; 0 Special Education; 0 Vocational; 1 Alternative
  0 Magnet; 0 Charter; 11 Title I Eligible; 11 School-wide Title I
Students: 8,637   (51.7% male; 48.2% female)
  Individual Education Program: 1,262 (14.6%);
  English Language Learner: 82 (0.9%); Migrant: 83 (1.0%)
  Eligible for Free Lunch Program: 5,274 (61.1%)
  Eligible for Reduced-Price Lunch Program: 858 (9.9%)
Teachers: 590.1 (14.6 to 1)
Librarians/Media Specialists: 17.0 (508.1 to 1)
Guidance Counselors: 33.0 (261.7 to 1)
Current Spending: ($ per student per year):
  Total: $6,471; Instruction: $3,990; Support Services: $2,037

Enrollment, Drop-out Rates and Diploma Recipients by Race/Ethnicity

Category	Total	White	Black	Asian	AIAN	Hisp.
Enrollment (%)	100.0	50.7	47.5	1.3	0.2	0.3
Drop-out Rate (%)	6.4	5.1	8.0	7.7	100.0	0.0
H.S. Diplomas (#)	460	274	181	3	0	2

St. Mary Parish

Saint Mary Parish School Board

474 Hwy 317 • Centerville, LA 70522-0170
Mailing Address: PO Box 170 • Centerville, LA 70522-0170
(337) 836-9661 • http://www.stmary.k12.la.us/
Grade Span: PK-12; **Agency Type:** 1
Schools: 27
  15 Primary; 5 Middle; 5 High; 2 Other Level
  26 Regular; 0 Special Education; 0 Vocational; 1 Alternative
  0 Magnet; 0 Charter; 12 Title I Eligible; 12 School-wide Title I
Students: 10,193   (50.4% male; 49.5% female)
  Individual Education Program: 1,563 (15.3%);
  English Language Learner: 328 (3.2%); Migrant: 92 (0.9%)
  Eligible for Free Lunch Program: 5,918 (58.1%)
  Eligible for Reduced-Price Lunch Program: 1,009 (9.9%)
Teachers: 723.3 (14.1 to 1)
Librarians/Media Specialists: 23.0 (443.2 to 1)
Guidance Counselors: 45.0 (226.5 to 1)
Current Spending: ($ per student per year):
  Total: $6,806; Instruction: $4,008; Support Services: $2,301

Enrollment, Drop-out Rates and Diploma Recipients by Race/Ethnicity

Category	Total	White	Black	Asian	AIAN	Hisp.
Enrollment (%)	100.0	48.3	46.8	2.3	0.8	1.8
Drop-out Rate (%)	4.9	4.3	6.1	1.1	2.9	0.0
H.S. Diplomas (#)	614	332	249	15	7	11

St. Tammany Parish

Saint Tammany Parish School Board

212 W Seventeenth Ave • Covington, LA 70433
Mailing Address: PO Box 940 • Covington, LA 70434-0940
(985) 892-3216 • http://www.stpsb.org.
Grade Span: PK-12; **Agency Type:** 1
Schools: 51
  23 Primary; 18 Middle; 7 High; 3 Other Level
  48 Regular; 2 Special Education; 0 Vocational; 1 Alternative
  0 Magnet; 0 Charter; 28 Title I Eligible; 20 School-wide Title I
Students: 34,750   (51.8% male; 48.1% female)
  Individual Education Program: 6,127 (17.6%);
  English Language Learner: 600 (1.7%); Migrant: 13 (<0.1%)
  Eligible for Free Lunch Program: 9,262 (26.7%)
  Eligible for Reduced-Price Lunch Program: 2,358 (6.8%)
Teachers: 2,491.6 (13.9 to 1)
Librarians/Media Specialists: 54.0 (643.5 to 1)
Guidance Counselors: 209.8 (165.6 to 1)
Current Spending: ($ per student per year):
  Total: $7,246; Instruction: $4,612; Support Services: $2,245

Enrollment, Drop-out Rates and Diploma Recipients by Race/Ethnicity

Category	Total	White	Black	Asian	AIAN	Hisp.
Enrollment (%)	100.0	79.5	17.1	1.1	0.4	1.8
Drop-out Rate (%)	4.0	3.4	8.1	3.0	13.6	4.0
H.S. Diplomas (#)	1,834	1,595	195	19	5	20

Tangipahoa Parish

Tangipahoa Parish School Board

59656 Puleston Rd • Amite, LA 70422-0457
(985) 748-7153 • http://www.tangischools.org/
Grade Span: PK-12; **Agency Type:** 1
Schools: 37
  17 Primary; 10 Middle; 9 High; 1 Other Level
  33 Regular; 0 Special Education; 0 Vocational; 4 Alternative
  0 Magnet; 0 Charter; 9 Title I Eligible; 9 School-wide Title I
Students: 18,465   (51.2% male; 48.7% female)
  Individual Education Program: 2,686 (14.5%);
  English Language Learner: 122 (0.7%); Migrant: 246 (1.3%)
  Eligible for Free Lunch Program: 10,913 (59.1%)
  Eligible for Reduced-Price Lunch Program: 1,551 (8.4%)
Teachers: 1,058.3 (17.4 to 1)
Librarians/Media Specialists: 24.8 (744.6 to 1)
Guidance Counselors: 58.9 (313.5 to 1)
Current Spending: ($ per student per year):
  Total: $5,888; Instruction: $3,788; Support Services: $1,694

Enrollment, Drop-out Rates and Diploma Recipients by Race/Ethnicity

Category	Total	White	Black	Asian	AIAN	Hisp.
Enrollment (%)	100.0	52.8	45.4	0.5	0.1	1.3
Drop-out Rate (%)	7.0	6.2	8.2	3.3	0.0	3.8
H.S. Diplomas (#)	1,030	611	404	6	3	6

Terrebonne Parish

Terrebonne Parish School Board
201 Stadium Dr • Houma, LA 70360
Mailing Address: PO Box 5097 • Houma, LA 70361-5097
(985) 876-7400 • http://www.tpsd.org/99-00/
Grade Span: PK-12; **Agency Type:** 1
Schools: 41
  21 Primary; 11 Middle; 5 High; 4 Other Level
  36 Regular; 1 Special Education; 1 Vocational; 3 Alternative
  0 Magnet; 0 Charter; 24 Title I Eligible; 23 School-wide Title I
Students: 19,256 (51.1% male; 48.8% female)
  Individual Education Program: 3,105 (16.1%);
  English Language Learner: 411 (2.1%); Migrant: 722 (3.7%)
  Eligible for Free Lunch Program: 9,506 (49.4%)
  Eligible for Reduced-Price Lunch Program: 2,174 (11.3%)
Teachers: 1,385.6 (13.9 to 1)
Librarians/Media Specialists: 42.1 (457.4 to 1)
Guidance Counselors: 92.2 (208.9 to 1)
Current Spending: ($ per student per year):
  Total: $6,551; Instruction: $4,105; Support Services: $2,051
Enrollment, Drop-out Rates and Diploma Recipients by Race/Ethnicity

Category	Total	White	Black	Asian	AIAN	Hisp.
Enrollment (%)	100.0	61.1	27.8	1.3	8.4	1.3
Drop-out Rate (%)	8.3	7.2	11.3	5.8	9.0	6.3
H.S. Diplomas (#)	1,007	691	232	14	64	6

Union Parish

Union Parish School Board
1206 Marion Hwy • Farmerville, LA 71241-0308
Mailing Address: PO Box 308 • Farmerville, LA 71241-0308
(318) 368-9715 • http://www.unionparishschools.org/
Grade Span: PK-12; **Agency Type:** 1
Schools: 10
  2 Primary; 2 Middle; 1 High; 5 Other Level
  10 Regular; 0 Special Education; 0 Vocational; 0 Alternative
  0 Magnet; 0 Charter; 9 Title I Eligible; 7 School-wide Title I
Students: 3,360 (50.5% male; 49.4% female)
  Individual Education Program: 450 (13.4%);
  English Language Learner: 87 (2.6%); Migrant: 69 (2.1%)
  Eligible for Free Lunch Program: 1,869 (55.6%)
  Eligible for Reduced-Price Lunch Program: 376 (11.2%)
Teachers: 218.6 (15.4 to 1)
Librarians/Media Specialists: 7.0 (480.0 to 1)
Guidance Counselors: 7.0 (480.0 to 1)
Current Spending: ($ per student per year):
  Total: $6,125; Instruction: $3,648; Support Services: $1,926
Enrollment, Drop-out Rates and Diploma Recipients by Race/Ethnicity

Category	Total	White	Black	Asian	AIAN	Hisp.
Enrollment (%)	100.0	55.4	40.8	0.3	0.1	3.4
Drop-out Rate (%)	4.1	3.9	4.2	0.0	0.0	14.3
H.S. Diplomas (#)	217	131	81	1	1	3

Vermilion Parish

Vermilion Parish School Board
220 S Jefferson St • Abbeville, LA 70510
Mailing Address: PO Drawer 520 • Abbeville, LA 70511-0520
(337) 898-5770 • http://www.vrml.k12.la.us/
Grade Span: PK-12; **Agency Type:** 1
Schools: 20
  11 Primary; 3 Middle; 4 High; 2 Other Level
  20 Regular; 0 Special Education; 0 Vocational; 0 Alternative
  0 Magnet; 0 Charter; 12 Title I Eligible; 11 School-wide Title I
Students: 8,912 (50.7% male; 49.2% female)
  Individual Education Program: 1,437 (16.1%);
  English Language Learner: 131 (1.5%); Migrant: 86 (1.0%)
  Eligible for Free Lunch Program: 3,976 (44.6%)
  Eligible for Reduced-Price Lunch Program: 844 (9.5%)
Teachers: 592.4 (15.0 to 1)
Librarians/Media Specialists: 19.0 (469.1 to 1)
Guidance Counselors: 48.1 (185.3 to 1)
Current Spending: ($ per student per year):
  Total: $6,294; Instruction: $3,740; Support Services: $2,188
Enrollment, Drop-out Rates and Diploma Recipients by Race/Ethnicity

Category	Total	White	Black	Asian	AIAN	Hisp.
Enrollment (%)	100.0	75.0	21.3	2.8	0.1	0.9
Drop-out Rate (%)	4.0	3.4	6.8	3.4	n/a	25.0
H.S. Diplomas (#)	480	395	75	10	0	0

Vernon Parish

Vernon Parish School Board
201 Belview Rd • Leesville, LA 71446
(337) 239-3401 • http://www.vpsb.k12.la.us/
Grade Span: PK-12; **Agency Type:** 1
Schools: 20
  8 Primary; 2 Middle; 5 High; 5 Other Level
  19 Regular; 0 Special Education; 0 Vocational; 1 Alternative
  0 Magnet; 0 Charter; 13 Title I Eligible; 11 School-wide Title I
Students: 9,874 (50.8% male; 49.1% female)
  Individual Education Program: 1,304 (13.2%);
  English Language Learner: 167 (1.7%); Migrant: 10 (0.1%)
  Eligible for Free Lunch Program: 3,428 (34.7%)
  Eligible for Reduced-Price Lunch Program: 1,596 (16.2%)
Teachers: 677.8 (14.6 to 1)
Librarians/Media Specialists: 18.0 (548.6 to 1)
Guidance Counselors: 29.0 (340.5 to 1)
Current Spending: ($ per student per year):
  Total: $6,800; Instruction: $4,163; Support Services: $2,206
Enrollment, Drop-out Rates and Diploma Recipients by Race/Ethnicity

Category	Total	White	Black	Asian	AIAN	Hisp.
Enrollment (%)	100.0	71.4	20.5	2.0	1.3	4.7
Drop-out Rate (%)	4.1	3.7	6.0	3.5	0.0	2.6
H.S. Diplomas (#)	455	327	94	10	9	15

Washington Parish

City of Bogalusa School Board
1705 Sullivan Dr • Bogalusa, LA 70427
Mailing Address: PO Box 310 • Bogalusa, LA 70429-0310
(985) 735-1392
Grade Span: PK-12; **Agency Type:** 1
Schools: 10
  6 Primary; 2 Middle; 2 High; 0 Other Level
  9 Regular; 0 Special Education; 0 Vocational; 1 Alternative
  0 Magnet; 0 Charter; 8 Title I Eligible; 8 School-wide Title I
Students: 2,995 (50.0% male; 49.9% female)
  Individual Education Program: 663 (22.1%);
  English Language Learner: 43 (1.4%); Migrant: 3 (0.1%)
  Eligible for Free Lunch Program: 2,296 (76.7%)
  Eligible for Reduced-Price Lunch Program: 242 (8.1%)
Teachers: 229.4 (13.1 to 1)
Librarians/Media Specialists: 2.0 (1,497.5 to 1)
Guidance Counselors: 18.9 (158.5 to 1)
Current Spending: ($ per student per year):
  Total: $7,380; Instruction: $4,470; Support Services: $2,429
Enrollment, Drop-out Rates and Diploma Recipients by Race/Ethnicity

Category	Total	White	Black	Asian	AIAN	Hisp.
Enrollment (%)	100.0	45.2	53.4	0.6	0.0	0.8
Drop-out Rate (%)	4.6	6.1	3.0	0.0	0.0	0.0
H.S. Diplomas (#)	164	90	73	0	0	1

Washington Parish School Board
800 Main St • Franklinton, LA 70438-0587
Mailing Address: PO Box 587 • Franklinton, LA 70438-0587
(985) 839-3436 • http://www.wpsb.org/
Grade Span: PK-12; **Agency Type:** 1
Schools: 13
  6 Primary; 2 Middle; 3 High; 2 Other Level
  12 Regular; 0 Special Education; 1 Vocational; 0 Alternative
  0 Magnet; 0 Charter; 12 Title I Eligible; 12 School-wide Title I
Students: 4,712 (51.6% male; 48.3% female)
  Individual Education Program: 791 (16.8%);
  English Language Learner: 6 (0.1%); Migrant: 24 (0.5%)
  Eligible for Free Lunch Program: 3,422 (72.6%)
  Eligible for Reduced-Price Lunch Program: 396 (8.4%)
Teachers: 360.0 (13.1 to 1)
Librarians/Media Specialists: 12.0 (392.7 to 1)
Guidance Counselors: 27.2 (173.2 to 1)
Current Spending: ($ per student per year):
  Total: $7,104; Instruction: $4,372; Support Services: $2,198
Enrollment, Drop-out Rates and Diploma Recipients by Race/Ethnicity

Category	Total	White	Black	Asian	AIAN	Hisp.
Enrollment (%)	100.0	62.5	36.9	0.3	0.1	0.2
Drop-out Rate (%)	3.6	2.8	5.1	0.0	n/a	0.0
H.S. Diplomas (#)	270	170	98	0	0	2

Webster Parish

Webster Parish School Board
1422 Sheppard St • Minden, LA 71055
Mailing Address: PO Box 520 • Minden, LA 71058-0520
(318) 377-7052 • http://www.webster.k12.la.us/
Grade Span: PK-12; **Agency Type:** 1
Schools: 22
    10 Primary; 2 Middle; 3 High; 7 Other Level
    19 Regular; 0 Special Education; 0 Vocational; 3 Alternative
    0 Magnet; 0 Charter; 12 Title I Eligible; 12 School-wide Title I
Students: 7,678   (51.2% male; 48.7% female)
    Individual Education Program: 1,111 (14.5%);
    English Language Learner: 9 (0.1%); Migrant: 20 (0.3%)
    Eligible for Free Lunch Program: 3,472 (45.2%)
    Eligible for Reduced-Price Lunch Program: 711 (9.3%)
Teachers: 492.0 (15.6 to 1)
Librarians/Media Specialists: 19.0 (404.1 to 1)
Guidance Counselors: 41.0 (187.3 to 1)
Current Spending: ($ per student per year):
    Total: $6,253; Instruction: $3,811; Support Services: $1,946

Enrollment, Drop-out Rates and Diploma Recipients by Race/Ethnicity

Category	Total	White	Black	Asian	AIAN	Hisp.
Enrollment (%)	100.0	55.4	43.6	0.2	0.1	0.7
Drop-out Rate (%)	3.8	3.3	4.5	0.0	0.0	0.0
H.S. Diplomas (#)	369	219	146	2	2	0

West Baton Rouge Parish

West Baton Rouge Parish School Board
3761 Rosedale Rd • Port Allen, LA 70767
(225) 343-8309
Grade Span: PK-12; **Agency Type:** 1
Schools: 11
    5 Primary; 3 Middle; 3 High; 0 Other Level
    10 Regular; 0 Special Education; 1 Vocational; 0 Alternative
    0 Magnet; 0 Charter; 6 Title I Eligible; 0 School-wide Title I
Students: 3,539   (52.0% male; 47.9% female)
    Individual Education Program: 452 (12.8%);
    English Language Learner: 1 (<0.1%); Migrant: 0 (0.0%)
    Eligible for Free Lunch Program: 1,906 (53.9%)
    Eligible for Reduced-Price Lunch Program: 317 (9.0%)
Teachers: 254.5 (13.9 to 1)
Librarians/Media Specialists: 10.0 (353.9 to 1)
Guidance Counselors: 12.0 (294.9 to 1)
Current Spending: ($ per student per year):
    Total: $7,040; Instruction: $3,952; Support Services: $2,522

Enrollment, Drop-out Rates and Diploma Recipients by Race/Ethnicity

Category	Total	White	Black	Asian	AIAN	Hisp.
Enrollment (%)	100.0	49.6	49.6	0.2	0.0	0.6
Drop-out Rate (%)	6.8	4.9	9.2	0.0	0.0	11.1
H.S. Diplomas (#)	243	147	93	1	0	2

West Carroll Parish

West Carroll Parish School Board
314 E Main St • Oak Grove, LA 71263-1318
(318) 428-2378
Grade Span: PK-12; **Agency Type:** 1
Schools: 8
    4 Primary; 0 Middle; 1 High; 3 Other Level
    8 Regular; 0 Special Education; 0 Vocational; 0 Alternative
    0 Magnet; 0 Charter; 8 Title I Eligible; 0 School-wide Title I
Students: 2,371   (53.1% male; 46.9% female)
    Individual Education Program: 291 (12.3%);
    English Language Learner: 12 (0.5%); Migrant: 28 (1.2%)
    Eligible for Free Lunch Program: 1,373 (57.9%)
    Eligible for Reduced-Price Lunch Program: 278 (11.7%)
Teachers: 170.7 (13.9 to 1)
Librarians/Media Specialists: 4.0 (592.8 to 1)
Guidance Counselors: 6.4 (370.5 to 1)
Current Spending: ($ per student per year):
    Total: $5,963; Instruction: $3,577; Support Services: $1,869

Enrollment, Drop-out Rates and Diploma Recipients by Race/Ethnicity

Category	Total	White	Black	Asian	AIAN	Hisp.
Enrollment (%)	100.0	78.1	20.2	0.2	0.1	1.4
Drop-out Rate (%)	5.6	3.7	12.2	n/a	n/a	50.0
H.S. Diplomas (#)	131	113	18	0	0	0

West Feliciana Parish

West Feliciana Parish School Board
4727 Fidelity St • St. Francisville, LA 70775-1910
Mailing Address: PO Box 1910 • Saint Francisville, LA 70775-1910
(225) 635-3891
Grade Span: PK-12; **Agency Type:** 1
Schools: 5
    3 Primary; 1 Middle; 1 High; 0 Other Level
    5 Regular; 0 Special Education; 0 Vocational; 0 Alternative
    0 Magnet; 0 Charter; 3 Title I Eligible; 0 School-wide Title I
Students: 2,434   (52.1% male; 47.8% female)
    Individual Education Program: 355 (14.6%);
    English Language Learner: 7 (0.3%); Migrant: 0 (0.0%)
    Eligible for Free Lunch Program: 920 (37.8%)
    Eligible for Reduced-Price Lunch Program: 260 (10.7%)
Teachers: 200.0 (12.2 to 1)
Librarians/Media Specialists: 5.0 (486.8 to 1)
Guidance Counselors: 9.0 (270.4 to 1)
Current Spending: ($ per student per year):
    Total: $9,175; Instruction: $5,314; Support Services: $3,421

Enrollment, Drop-out Rates and Diploma Recipients by Race/Ethnicity

Category	Total	White	Black	Asian	AIAN	Hisp.
Enrollment (%)	100.0	55.6	43.6	0.3	0.2	0.2
Drop-out Rate (%)	3.4	2.6	4.1	50.0	n/a	n/a
H.S. Diplomas (#)	122	65	56	1	0	0

Winn Parish

Winn Parish School Board
304 E Court St • Winnfield, LA 71483-0430
Mailing Address: PO Box 430 • Winnfield, LA 71483-0430
(318) 628-6936 • http://www.winnpsb.org/
Grade Span: PK-12; **Agency Type:** 1
Schools: 8
    2 Primary; 2 Middle; 1 High; 3 Other Level
    8 Regular; 0 Special Education; 0 Vocational; 0 Alternative
    0 Magnet; 0 Charter; 6 Title I Eligible; 5 School-wide Title I
Students: 2,782   (50.7% male; 49.2% female)
    Individual Education Program: 331 (11.9%);
    English Language Learner: 2 (0.1%); Migrant: 67 (2.4%)
    Eligible for Free Lunch Program: 1,598 (57.4%)
    Eligible for Reduced-Price Lunch Program: 242 (8.7%)
Teachers: 207.0 (13.4 to 1)
Librarians/Media Specialists: 7.0 (397.4 to 1)
Guidance Counselors: 10.5 (265.0 to 1)
Current Spending: ($ per student per year):
    Total: $7,288; Instruction: $4,205; Support Services: $2,497

Enrollment, Drop-out Rates and Diploma Recipients by Race/Ethnicity

Category	Total	White	Black	Asian	AIAN	Hisp.
Enrollment (%)	100.0	62.4	36.5	0.4	0.1	0.5
Drop-out Rate (%)	5.5	4.8	6.3	0.0	n/a	20.0
H.S. Diplomas (#)	150	102	46	0	0	2

Number of Schools

Rank	Number	District Name	City
1	129	Orleans Parish School Board	New Orleans
2	98	E Baton Rouge Parish SB	Baton Rouge
3	84	Jefferson Parish School Board	Harvey
4	75	Caddo Parish School Board	Shreveport
5	59	Calcasieu Parish School Board	Lake Charles
6	53	Rapides Parish School Board	Alexandria
7	51	Saint Tammany Parish School Board	Covington
8	45	Lafayette Parish School Board	Lafayette
9	41	Terrebonne Parish School Board	Houma
10	39	Livingston Parish School Board	Livingston
10	39	Saint Landry Parish School Board	Opelousas
12	37	Tangipahoa Parish School Board	Amite
13	35	Bossier Parish School Board	Benton
13	35	Ouachita Parish School Board	Monroe
15	32	Iberia Parish School Board	New Iberia
16	29	Lafourche Parish School Board	Thibodaux
17	27	Acadia Parish School Board	Crowley
17	27	Saint Mary Parish School Board	Centerville
19	23	Ascension Parish School Board	Donaldsonville
20	22	Webster Parish School Board	Minden
21	21	Saint Charles Parish School Board	Luling
22	20	City of Monroe School Board	Monroe
22	20	Vermilion Parish School Board	Abbeville
22	20	Vernon Parish School Board	Leesville
25	19	Lincoln Parish School Board	Ruston
26	18	Saint Martin Parish School Board	St Martinville
27	16	Morehouse Parish School Board	Bastrop
28	15	Evangeline Parish School Board	Ville Platte
28	15	Natchitoches Parish School Board	Natchitoches
30	14	Avoyelles Parish School Board	Marksville
30	14	Beauregard Parish School Board	Deridder
30	14	Jefferson Davis Parish SB	Jennings
30	14	Sabine Parish School Board	Many
30	14	Saint Bernard Parish School Board	Chalmette
35	13	Desoto Parish School Board	Mansfield
35	13	Washington Parish School Board	Franklinton
37	12	Allen Parish School Board	Oberlin
37	12	Richland Parish School Board	Rayville
37	12	Saint John the Baptist Parish SB	Reserve
40	11	Concordia Parish School Board	Vidalia
40	11	Franklin Parish School Board	Winnsboro
40	11	W Baton Rouge Parish SB	Port Allen
43	10	Assumption Parish School Board	Napoleonville
43	10	Catahoula Parish School Board	Harrisonburg
43	10	City of Bogalusa School Board	Bogalusa
43	10	Lasalle Parish School Board	Jena
43	10	Saint James Parish School Board	Lutcher
43	10	Union Parish School Board	Farmerville
49	9	Claiborne Parish School Board	Homer
49	9	Grant Parish School Board	Colfax
49	9	Iberville Parish School Board	Plaquemine
49	9	Plaquemines Parish School Board	Port Sulphur
49	9	Pointe Coupee Parish School Board	New Roads
54	8	Bienville Parish School Board	Arcadia
54	8	East Feliciana Parish School Board	Clinton
54	8	West Carroll Parish School Board	Oak Grove
54	8	Winn Parish School Board	Winnfield
58	7	Jackson Parish School Board	Jonesboro
58	7	Madison Parish School Board	Tallulah
60	6	Caldwell Parish School Board	Columbia
60	6	Cameron Parish School Board	Cameron
60	6	East Carroll Parish School Board	Lake Providence
63	5	City of Baker SD	Baker
63	5	Red River Parish School Board	Coushatta
63	5	West Feliciana Parish School Board	St Francisville
66	4	Zachary Community SD	Zachary

Number of Teachers

Rank	Number	District Name	City
1	4,656	Orleans Parish School Board	New Orleans
2	3,371	Jefferson Parish School Board	Harvey
3	3,137	E Baton Rouge Parish SB	Baton Rouge
4	2,927	Caddo Parish School Board	Shreveport
5	2,491	Saint Tammany Parish School Board	Covington
6	2,184	Calcasieu Parish School Board	Lake Charles
7	2,117	Lafayette Parish School Board	Lafayette
8	1,572	Rapides Parish School Board	Alexandria
9	1,385	Terrebonne Parish School Board	Houma
10	1,353	Livingston Parish School Board	Livingston
11	1,282	Ouachita Parish School Board	Monroe
12	1,169	Bossier Parish School Board	Benton
13	1,152	Lafourche Parish School Board	Thibodaux
14	1,105	Ascension Parish School Board	Donaldsonville
15	1,058	Tangipahoa Parish School Board	Amite
16	1,045	Saint Landry Parish School Board	Opelousas
17	1,027	Iberia Parish School Board	New Iberia
18	774	Saint Charles Parish School Board	Luling
19	723	Saint Mary Parish School Board	Centerville
20	677	Vernon Parish School Board	Leesville
21	671	City of Monroe School Board	Monroe
22	651	Acadia Parish School Board	Crowley
23	623	Saint Bernard Parish School Board	Chalmette
24	592	Vermilion Parish School Board	Abbeville
25	590	Saint Martin Parish School Board	St Martinville
26	492	Webster Parish School Board	Minden
27	481	Natchitoches Parish School Board	Natchitoches
28	478	Lincoln Parish School Board	Ruston
29	462	Saint John the Baptist Parish SB	Reserve
30	431	Evangeline Parish School Board	Ville Platte
31	419	Avoyelles Parish School Board	Marksville
32	404	Beauregard Parish School Board	Deridder
33	377	Morehouse Parish School Board	Bastrop
34	371	Desoto Parish School Board	Mansfield
35	370	Jefferson Davis Parish SB	Jennings
36	360	Washington Parish School Board	Franklinton
37	338	Allen Parish School Board	Oberlin
38	333	Iberville Parish School Board	Plaquemine
39	332	Plaquemines Parish School Board	Port Sulphur
40	321	Franklin Parish School Board	Winnsboro
41	318	Assumption Parish School Board	Napoleonville
42	300	Sabine Parish School Board	Many
43	284	Saint James Parish School Board	Lutcher
44	279	Richland Parish School Board	Rayville
45	269	Concordia Parish School Board	Vidalia
46	254	W Baton Rouge Parish SB	Port Allen
47	245	Grant Parish School Board	Colfax
48	230	Pointe Coupee Parish School Board	New Roads
49	229	City of Bogalusa School Board	Bogalusa
50	228	Claiborne Parish School Board	Homer
51	218	Union Parish School Board	Farmerville
52	207	Winn Parish School Board	Winnfield
53	206	Bienville Parish School Board	Arcadia
54	200	West Feliciana Parish School Board	St Francisville
55	191	Lasalle Parish School Board	Jena
56	177	Jackson Parish School Board	Jonesboro
57	175	Zachary Community SD	Zachary
58	170	West Carroll Parish School Board	Oak Grove
59	159	Madison Parish School Board	Tallulah
60	159	Cameron Parish School Board	Cameron
61	156	East Feliciana Parish School Board	Clinton
62	144	City of Baker SD	Baker
63	142	East Carroll Parish School Board	Lake Providence
64	137	Catahoula Parish School Board	Harrisonburg
65	136	Caldwell Parish School Board	Columbia
66	129	Red River Parish School Board	Coushatta

Number of Students

Rank	Number	District Name	City
1	67,922	Orleans Parish School Board	New Orleans
2	51,453	Jefferson Parish School Board	Harvey
3	46,644	E Baton Rouge Parish SB	Baton Rouge
4	44,473	Caddo Parish School Board	Shreveport
5	34,750	Saint Tammany Parish School Board	Covington
6	32,149	Calcasieu Parish School Board	Lake Charles
7	29,813	Lafayette Parish School Board	Lafayette
8	22,646	Rapides Parish School Board	Alexandria
9	20,743	Livingston Parish School Board	Livingston
10	19,256	Terrebonne Parish School Board	Houma
11	18,771	Bossier Parish School Board	Benton
12	18,465	Tangipahoa Parish School Board	Amite
13	18,324	Ouachita Parish School Board	Monroe
14	15,810	Ascension Parish School Board	Donaldsonville
15	15,231	Saint Landry Parish School Board	Opelousas
16	14,872	Lafourche Parish School Board	Thibodaux
17	14,201	Iberia Parish School Board	New Iberia
18	10,193	Saint Mary Parish School Board	Centerville
19	9,874	Vernon Parish School Board	Leesville
20	9,685	Saint Charles Parish School Board	Luling
21	9,650	Acadia Parish School Board	Crowley
22	9,548	City of Monroe School Board	Monroe
23	8,912	Vermilion Parish School Board	Abbeville
24	8,869	Saint Bernard Parish School Board	Chalmette
25	8,637	Saint Martin Parish School Board	St Martinville
26	7,678	Webster Parish School Board	Minden
27	6,963	Natchitoches Parish School Board	Natchitoches
28	6,596	Lincoln Parish School Board	Ruston
29	6,585	Avoyelles Parish School Board	Marksville
30	6,338	Saint John the Baptist Parish SB	Reserve
31	6,289	Evangeline Parish School Board	Ville Platte
32	6,127	Beauregard Parish School Board	Deridder
33	5,748	Jefferson Davis Parish SB	Jennings
34	5,153	Morehouse Parish School Board	Bastrop
35	4,967	Plaquemines Parish School Board	Port Sulphur
36	4,924	Desoto Parish School Board	Mansfield
37	4,712	Washington Parish School Board	Franklinton
38	4,431	Assumption Parish School Board	Napoleonville
39	4,395	Iberville Parish School Board	Plaquemine
40	4,281	Allen Parish School Board	Oberlin
41	4,269	Sabine Parish School Board	Many
42	4,062	Saint James Parish School Board	Lutcher
43	3,851	Franklin Parish School Board	Winnsboro
44	3,798	Concordia Parish School Board	Vidalia
45	3,621	Grant Parish School Board	Colfax
46	3,539	W Baton Rouge Parish SB	Port Allen
47	3,477	Richland Parish School Board	Rayville
48	3,360	Union Parish School Board	Farmerville
49	3,250	Zachary Community SD	Zachary
50	3,182	Pointe Coupee Parish School Board	New Roads
51	2,995	City of Bogalusa School Board	Bogalusa
52	2,833	Claiborne Parish School Board	Homer
53	2,782	Winn Parish School Board	Winnfield
54	2,699	Lasalle Parish School Board	Jena
55	2,498	Bienville Parish School Board	Arcadia
56	2,434	West Feliciana Parish School Board	St Francisville
57	2,389	Jackson Parish School Board	Jonesboro
58	2,371	West Carroll Parish School Board	Oak Grove
59	2,369	East Feliciana Parish School Board	Clinton
60	2,319	Madison Parish School Board	Tallulah
61	2,253	City of Baker SD	Baker
62	1,841	Caldwell Parish School Board	Columbia
63	1,819	Cameron Parish School Board	Cameron
64	1,800	Catahoula Parish School Board	Harrisonburg
65	1,675	East Carroll Parish School Board	Lake Providence
66	1,631	Red River Parish School Board	Coushatta

Male Students

Rank	Percent	District Name	City
1	53.7	Caldwell Parish School Board	Columbia
2	53.1	West Carroll Parish School Board	Oak Grove
3	52.4	Madison Parish School Board	Tallulah
4	52.3	East Feliciana Parish School Board	Clinton
5	52.3	Sabine Parish School Board	Many
6	52.1	West Feliciana Parish School Board	St Francisville
7	52.1	Catahoula Parish School Board	Harrisonburg
8	52.0	Allen Parish School Board	Oberlin
9	52.0	W Baton Rouge Parish SB	Port Allen
10	52.0	Evangeline Parish School Board	Ville Platte
11	51.9	Plaquemines Parish School Board	Port Sulphur
12	51.9	Beauregard Parish School Board	Deridder
13	51.8	Saint Tammany Parish School Board	Covington
14	51.8	Lafourche Parish School Board	Thibodaux
15	51.7	Avoyelles Parish School Board	Marksville
16	51.7	Richland Parish School Board	Rayville
17	51.7	Saint Martin Parish School Board	St Martinville
18	51.6	Jefferson Parish School Board	Harvey
19	51.6	Grant Parish School Board	Colfax
20	51.6	Washington Parish School Board	Franklinton
21	51.6	Jefferson Davis Parish SB	Jennings
22	51.5	Red River Parish School Board	Coushatta
23	51.5	Ascension Parish School Board	Donaldsonville
24	51.5	Livingston Parish School Board	Livingston
25	51.4	Cameron Parish School Board	Cameron
26	51.3	Franklin Parish School Board	Winnsboro
27	51.2	Saint Charles Parish School Board	Luling
28	51.2	Calcasieu Parish School Board	Lake Charles
29	51.2	Acadia Parish School Board	Crowley
30	51.2	Tangipahoa Parish School Board	Amite
31	51.2	Morehouse Parish School Board	Bastrop
32	51.2	Webster Parish School Board	Minden
33	51.2	Claiborne Parish School Board	Homer
34	51.1	Natchitoches Parish School Board	Natchitoches
35	51.1	Terrebonne Parish School Board	Houma
36	51.1	Concordia Parish School Board	Vidalia
37	51.1	Jackson Parish School Board	Jonesboro
38	51.0	Saint John the Baptist Parish SB	Reserve
39	51.0	Rapides Parish School Board	Alexandria
40	51.0	Saint Landry Parish School Board	Opelousas
41	50.9	E Baton Rouge Parish SB	Baton Rouge
42	50.9	Iberia Parish School Board	New Iberia
43	50.9	Desoto Parish School Board	Mansfield
44	50.9	Saint James Parish School Board	Lutcher
45	50.9	Saint Bernard Parish School Board	Chalmette
46	50.9	City of Baker SD	Baker
47	50.8	Lafayette Parish School Board	Lafayette
48	50.8	Vernon Parish School Board	Leesville
49	50.8	Iberville Parish School Board	Plaquemine
50	50.7	Bossier Parish School Board	Benton
51	50.7	Winn Parish School Board	Winnfield
52	50.7	Vermilion Parish School Board	Abbeville
53	50.7	Caddo Parish School Board	Shreveport
54	50.7	Assumption Parish School Board	Napoleonville
55	50.6	Lincoln Parish School Board	Ruston
56	50.5	Bienville Parish School Board	Arcadia
57	50.5	Ouachita Parish School Board	Monroe
58	50.5	Union Parish School Board	Farmerville
59	50.4	Saint Mary Parish School Board	Centerville
60	50.3	Orleans Parish School Board	New Orleans
61	50.3	Lasalle Parish School Board	Jena
62	50.1	City of Monroe School Board	Monroe
63	50.0	City of Bogalusa School Board	Bogalusa
64	49.5	Zachary Community SD	Zachary
65	49.4	Pointe Coupee Parish School Board	New Roads
66	48.6	East Carroll Parish School Board	Lake Providence

Female Students

Rank	Percent	District Name	City
1	51.3	East Carroll Parish School Board	Lake Providence
2	50.5	Pointe Coupee Parish School Board	New Roads
3	50.4	Zachary Community SD	Zachary
4	49.9	City of Bogalusa School Board	Bogalusa
5	49.8	City of Monroe School Board	Monroe
6	49.6	Lasalle Parish School Board	Jena
7	49.6	Orleans Parish School Board	New Orleans
8	49.5	Saint Mary Parish School Board	Centerville
9	49.4	Union Parish School Board	Farmerville
10	49.4	Ouachita Parish School Board	Monroe
11	49.4	Bienville Parish School Board	Arcadia
12	49.3	Lincoln Parish School Board	Ruston
13	49.2	Assumption Parish School Board	Napoleonville
14	49.2	Caddo Parish School Board	Shreveport
15	49.2	Vermilion Parish School Board	Abbeville
16	49.2	Winn Parish School Board	Winnfield
17	49.2	Bossier Parish School Board	Benton
18	49.1	Iberville Parish School Board	Plaquemine
19	49.1	Vernon Parish School Board	Leesville
20	49.1	Lafayette Parish School Board	Lafayette
21	49.0	City of Baker SD	Baker
22	49.0	Saint Bernard Parish School Board	Chalmette
23	49.0	Saint James Parish School Board	Lutcher
24	49.0	Desoto Parish School Board	Mansfield
25	49.0	Iberia Parish School Board	New Iberia
26	49.0	E Baton Rouge Parish SB	Baton Rouge
27	48.9	Saint Landry Parish School Board	Opelousas
28	48.9	Rapides Parish School Board	Alexandria
29	48.9	Saint John the Baptist Parish SB	Reserve
30	48.8	Jackson Parish School Board	Jonesboro
31	48.8	Concordia Parish School Board	Vidalia
32	48.8	Terrebonne Parish School Board	Houma
33	48.8	Natchitoches Parish School Board	Natchitoches
34	48.7	Claiborne Parish School Board	Homer
35	48.7	Webster Parish School Board	Minden
36	48.7	Morehouse Parish School Board	Bastrop
37	48.7	Tangipahoa Parish School Board	Amite
38	48.7	Acadia Parish School Board	Crowley
39	48.7	Calcasieu Parish School Board	Lake Charles
40	48.7	Saint Charles Parish School Board	Luling
41	48.6	Franklin Parish School Board	Winnsboro
42	48.5	Cameron Parish School Board	Cameron
43	48.4	Livingston Parish School Board	Livingston
44	48.4	Ascension Parish School Board	Donaldsonville
45	48.4	Red River Parish School Board	Coushatta
46	48.3	Jefferson Davis Parish SB	Jennings
47	48.3	Washington Parish School Board	Franklinton
48	48.3	Grant Parish School Board	Colfax
49	48.3	Jefferson Parish School Board	Harvey
50	48.2	Saint Martin Parish School Board	St Martinville
51	48.2	Richland Parish School Board	Rayville
52	48.2	Avoyelles Parish School Board	Marksville
53	48.1	Lafourche Parish School Board	Thibodaux
54	48.1	Saint Tammany Parish School Board	Covington
55	48.0	Beauregard Parish School Board	Deridder
56	48.0	Plaquemines Parish School Board	Port Sulphur
57	47.9	Evangeline Parish School Board	Ville Platte
58	47.9	W Baton Rouge Parish SB	Port Allen
59	47.9	Allen Parish School Board	Oberlin
60	47.8	Catahoula Parish School Board	Harrisonburg
61	47.8	West Feliciana Parish School Board	St Francisville
62	47.6	Sabine Parish School Board	Many
63	47.6	East Feliciana Parish School Board	Clinton
64	47.5	Madison Parish School Board	Tallulah
65	46.9	West Carroll Parish School Board	Oak Grove
66	46.2	Caldwell Parish School Board	Columbia

Individual Education Program Students

Rank	Percent	District Name	City
1	22.1	City of Bogalusa School Board	Bogalusa
2	21.8	Pointe Coupee Parish School Board	New Roads
3	19.6	Saint John the Baptist Parish SB	Reserve
4	19.0	Acadia Parish School Board	Crowley
5	18.4	Cameron Parish School Board	Cameron
6	17.6	Saint Tammany Parish School Board	Covington
7	17.3	Evangeline Parish School Board	Ville Platte
7	17.3	Jefferson Davis Parish SB	Jennings
9	16.9	Claiborne Parish School Board	Homer
10	16.8	Washington Parish School Board	Franklinton
11	16.6	Iberia Parish School Board	New Iberia
12	16.3	Sabine Parish School Board	Many
13	16.2	East Feliciana Parish School Board	Clinton
14	16.1	Morehouse Parish School Board	Bastrop
14	16.1	Terrebonne Parish School Board	Houma
14	16.1	Vermilion Parish School Board	Abbeville
17	15.8	Desoto Parish School Board	Mansfield
18	15.4	Ascension Parish School Board	Donaldsonville
18	15.4	Grant Parish School Board	Colfax
18	15.4	Iberville Parish School Board	Plaquemine
21	15.3	Calcasieu Parish School Board	Lake Charles
21	15.3	Jefferson Parish School Board	Harvey
21	15.3	Saint Landry Parish School Board	Opelousas
21	15.3	Saint Mary Parish School Board	Centerville
25	14.6	Saint Bernard Parish School Board	Chalmette
25	14.6	Saint Martin Parish School Board	St Martinville
25	14.6	West Feliciana Parish School Board	St Francisville
28	14.5	Assumption Parish School Board	Napoleonville
28	14.5	City of Monroe School Board	Monroe
28	14.5	Rapides Parish School Board	Alexandria
28	14.5	Tangipahoa Parish School Board	Amite
28	14.5	Webster Parish School Board	Minden
33	14.3	East Carroll Parish School Board	Lake Providence
34	14.1	Caldwell Parish School Board	Columbia
34	14.1	Saint James Parish School Board	Lutcher
36	13.8	Lafourche Parish School Board	Thibodaux
37	13.7	Bienville Parish School Board	Arcadia
37	13.7	Caddo Parish School Board	Shreveport
39	13.6	Richland Parish School Board	Rayville
40	13.4	Union Parish School Board	Farmerville
41	13.2	Vernon Parish School Board	Leesville
42	13.1	Beauregard Parish School Board	Deridder
42	13.1	Red River Parish School Board	Coushatta
44	13.0	Lincoln Parish School Board	Ruston
45	12.9	Madison Parish School Board	Tallulah
45	12.9	Ouachita Parish School Board	Monroe
47	12.8	Plaquemines Parish School Board	Port Sulphur
47	12.8	W Baton Rouge Parish SB	Port Allen
49	12.3	Saint Charles Parish School Board	Luling
49	12.3	West Carroll Parish School Board	Oak Grove
51	12.1	Allen Parish School Board	Oberlin
52	12.0	Bossier Parish School Board	Benton
52	12.0	Natchitoches Parish School Board	Natchitoches
54	11.9	Livingston Parish School Board	Livingston
54	11.9	Winn Parish School Board	Winnfield
56	11.7	Franklin Parish School Board	Winnsboro
56	11.7	Jackson Parish School Board	Jonesboro
58	11.5	Lafayette Parish School Board	Lafayette
59	11.4	Avoyelles Parish School Board	Marksville
60	11.2	Catahoula Parish School Board	Harrisonburg
61	10.9	Concordia Parish School Board	Vidalia
62	10.6	Orleans Parish School Board	New Orleans
63	10.2	E Baton Rouge Parish SB	Baton Rouge
64	10.1	City of Baker SD	Baker
65	9.2	Zachary Community SD	Zachary
66	8.4	Lasalle Parish School Board	Jena

English Language Learner Students

Rank	Percent	District Name	City
1	6.4	Jefferson Parish School Board	Harvey
2	3.2	Bossier Parish School Board	Benton
2	3.2	Saint Mary Parish School Board	Centerville
4	3.1	E Baton Rouge Parish SB	Baton Rouge
5	2.6	Union Parish School Board	Farmerville
6	2.5	Lafourche Parish School Board	Thibodaux
7	2.1	Terrebonne Parish School Board	Houma
8	2.0	Ascension Parish School Board	Donaldsonville
8	2.0	Plaquemines Parish School Board	Port Sulphur
10	1.8	Iberia Parish School Board	New Iberia
10	1.8	Lafayette Parish School Board	Lafayette
10	1.8	Orleans Parish School Board	New Orleans
13	1.7	Saint Tammany Parish School Board	Covington
13	1.7	Vernon Parish School Board	Leesville
15	1.5	Rapides Parish School Board	Alexandria
15	1.5	Saint John the Baptist Parish SB	Reserve
15	1.5	Vermilion Parish School Board	Abbeville
18	1.4	City of Bogalusa School Board	Bogalusa
19	1.3	Desoto Parish School Board	Mansfield
20	1.2	Caddo Parish School Board	Shreveport
21	1.1	Saint Charles Parish School Board	Luling
22	1.0	Assumption Parish School Board	Napoleonville
23	0.9	Cameron Parish School Board	Cameron
23	0.9	Ouachita Parish School Board	Monroe
23	0.9	Sabine Parish School Board	Many
23	0.9	Saint Martin Parish School Board	St Martinville
27	0.7	Tangipahoa Parish School Board	Amite
28	0.6	Acadia Parish School Board	Crowley
28	0.6	Saint Bernard Parish School Board	Chalmette
28	0.6	Saint Landry Parish School Board	Opelousas
31	0.5	West Carroll Parish School Board	Oak Grove
31	0.5	Zachary Community SD	Zachary
33	0.4	Beauregard Parish School Board	Deridder
33	0.4	City of Baker SD	Baker
33	0.4	Evangeline Parish School Board	Ville Platte
33	0.4	Lincoln Parish School Board	Ruston
33	0.4	Livingston Parish School Board	Livingston
38	0.3	East Feliciana Parish School Board	Clinton
38	0.3	Iberville Parish School Board	Plaquemine
38	0.3	Morehouse Parish School Board	Bastrop
38	0.3	Natchitoches Parish School Board	Natchitoches
38	0.3	West Feliciana Parish School Board	St Francisville
43	0.2	Avoyelles Parish School Board	Marksville
43	0.2	City of Monroe School Board	Monroe
43	0.2	Jefferson Davis Parish SB	Jennings
46	0.1	Concordia Parish School Board	Vidalia
46	0.1	East Carroll Parish School Board	Lake Providence
46	0.1	Pointe Coupee Parish School Board	New Roads
46	0.1	Saint James Parish School Board	Lutcher
46	0.1	Washington Parish School Board	Franklinton
46	0.1	Webster Parish School Board	Minden
46	0.1	Winn Parish School Board	Winnfield
53	0.0	Allen Parish School Board	Oberlin
53	0.0	Bienville Parish School Board	Arcadia
53	0.0	Calcasieu Parish School Board	Lake Charles
53	0.0	Madison Parish School Board	Tallulah
53	0.0	W Baton Rouge Parish SB	Port Allen
58	0.0	Caldwell Parish School Board	Columbia
58	0.0	Catahoula Parish School Board	Harrisonburg
58	0.0	Claiborne Parish School Board	Homer
58	0.0	Franklin Parish School Board	Winnsboro
58	0.0	Grant Parish School Board	Colfax
58	0.0	Jackson Parish School Board	Jonesboro
58	0.0	Lasalle Parish School Board	Jena
58	0.0	Red River Parish School Board	Coushatta
58	0.0	Richland Parish School Board	Rayville

Migrant Students

Rank	Percent	District Name	City
1	4.0	Plaquemines Parish School Board	Port Sulphur
2	3.7	Terrebonne Parish School Board	Houma
3	3.2	Cameron Parish School Board	Cameron
4	3.0	Natchitoches Parish School Board	Natchitoches
5	2.9	Franklin Parish School Board	Winnsboro
6	2.4	Winn Parish School Board	Winnfield
7	2.1	Union Parish School Board	Farmerville
8	1.9	Assumption Parish School Board	Napoleonville
8	1.9	Catahoula Parish School Board	Harrisonburg
8	1.9	East Carroll Parish School Board	Lake Providence
8	1.9	Madison Parish School Board	Tallulah
12	1.7	Lafourche Parish School Board	Thibodaux
13	1.4	Concordia Parish School Board	Vidalia
14	1.3	Tangipahoa Parish School Board	Amite
15	1.2	Saint Landry Parish School Board	Opelousas
15	1.2	West Carroll Parish School Board	Oak Grove
17	1.1	Jackson Parish School Board	Jonesboro
18	1.0	Grant Parish School Board	Colfax
18	1.0	Saint Martin Parish School Board	St Martinville
18	1.0	Vermilion Parish School Board	Abbeville
21	0.9	Avoyelles Parish School Board	Marksville
21	0.9	Bienville Parish School Board	Arcadia
21	0.9	Caldwell Parish School Board	Columbia
21	0.9	Iberia Parish School Board	New Iberia
21	0.9	Jefferson Davis Parish SB	Jennings
21	0.9	Saint Mary Parish School Board	Centerville
27	0.8	Lasalle Parish School Board	Jena
28	0.7	Desoto Parish School Board	Mansfield
29	0.6	Acadia Parish School Board	Crowley
29	0.6	Rapides Parish School Board	Alexandria
31	0.5	Beauregard Parish School Board	Deridder
31	0.5	Claiborne Parish School Board	Homer
31	0.5	Evangeline Parish School Board	Ville Platte
31	0.5	Jefferson Parish School Board	Harvey
31	0.5	Lincoln Parish School Board	Ruston
31	0.5	Richland Parish School Board	Rayville
31	0.5	Washington Parish School Board	Franklinton
38	0.4	Allen Parish School Board	Oberlin
39	0.3	Lafayette Parish School Board	Lafayette
39	0.3	Morehouse Parish School Board	Bastrop
39	0.3	Saint James Parish School Board	Lutcher
39	0.3	Webster Parish School Board	Minden
43	0.2	Bossier Parish School Board	Benton
43	0.2	Orleans Parish School Board	New Orleans
43	0.2	Ouachita Parish School Board	Monroe
43	0.2	Pointe Coupee Parish School Board	New Roads
47	0.1	City of Bogalusa School Board	Bogalusa
47	0.1	City of Monroe School Board	Monroe
47	0.1	Iberville Parish School Board	Plaquemine
47	0.1	Livingston Parish School Board	Livingston
47	0.1	Sabine Parish School Board	Many
47	0.1	Saint Charles Parish School Board	Luling
47	0.1	Vernon Parish School Board	Leesville
54	0.0	Ascension Parish School Board	Donaldsonville
54	0.0	Caddo Parish School Board	Shreveport
54	0.0	Calcasieu Parish School Board	Lake Charles
54	0.0	E Baton Rouge Parish SB	Baton Rouge
54	0.0	Saint Tammany Parish School Board	Covington
59	0.0	City of Baker SD	Baker
59	0.0	East Feliciana Parish School Board	Clinton
59	0.0	Red River Parish School Board	Coushatta
59	0.0	Saint Bernard Parish School Board	Chalmette
59	0.0	Saint John the Baptist Parish SB	Reserve
59	0.0	W Baton Rouge Parish SB	Port Allen
59	0.0	West Feliciana Parish School Board	St Francisville
59	0.0	Zachary Community SD	Zachary

Students Eligible for Free Lunch

Rank	Percent	District Name	City
1	86.9	East Carroll Parish School Board	Lake Providence
2	81.0	Madison Parish School Board	Tallulah
3	77.5	Red River Parish School Board	Coushatta
4	76.7	City of Bogalusa School Board	Bogalusa
5	76.2	Iberville Parish School Board	Plaquemine
6	75.5	East Feliciana Parish School Board	Clinton
7	75.4	Saint John the Baptist Parish SB	Reserve
8	72.6	Washington Parish School Board	Franklinton
9	72.2	City of Monroe School Board	Monroe
10	71.9	Orleans Parish School Board	New Orleans
11	70.7	Pointe Coupee Parish School Board	New Roads
12	68.0	Concordia Parish School Board	Vidalia
13	67.5	Avoyelles Parish School Board	Marksville
14	65.5	Richland Parish School Board	Rayville
14	65.5	Saint Landry Parish School Board	Opelousas
16	65.3	Saint James Parish School Board	Lutcher
17	64.8	E Baton Rouge Parish SB	Baton Rouge
18	64.6	Morehouse Parish School Board	Bastrop
19	63.0	Franklin Parish School Board	Winnsboro
20	61.1	Saint Martin Parish School Board	St Martinville
21	61.0	Jefferson Parish School Board	Harvey
22	60.8	Natchitoches Parish School Board	Natchitoches
23	59.1	Evangeline Parish School Board	Ville Platte
23	59.1	Tangipahoa Parish School Board	Amite
25	58.7	Bienville Parish School Board	Arcadia
26	58.6	City of Baker SD	Baker
27	58.1	Saint Mary Parish School Board	Centerville
28	57.9	Claiborne Parish School Board	Homer
28	57.9	West Carroll Parish School Board	Oak Grove
30	57.6	Desoto Parish School Board	Mansfield
31	57.4	Winn Parish School Board	Winnfield
32	55.6	Union Parish School Board	Farmerville
33	55.4	Iberia Parish School Board	New Iberia
34	54.9	Acadia Parish School Board	Crowley
35	54.5	Rapides Parish School Board	Alexandria
36	54.0	Catahoula Parish School Board	Harrisonburg
37	53.9	W Baton Rouge Parish SB	Port Allen
38	52.6	Assumption Parish School Board	Napoleonville
39	52.4	Plaquemines Parish School Board	Port Sulphur
40	52.3	Caddo Parish School Board	Shreveport
41	52.1	Sabine Parish School Board	Many
42	49.4	Terrebonne Parish School Board	Houma
43	49.2	Saint Bernard Parish School Board	Chalmette
44	48.9	Grant Parish School Board	Colfax
45	48.3	Lincoln Parish School Board	Ruston
46	47.9	Allen Parish School Board	Oberlin
47	47.4	Jackson Parish School Board	Jonesboro
48	46.1	Caldwell Parish School Board	Columbia
49	45.2	Webster Parish School Board	Minden
50	45.1	Lafourche Parish School Board	Thibodaux
51	45.0	Lafayette Parish School Board	Lafayette
52	44.6	Vermilion Parish School Board	Abbeville
53	43.1	Jefferson Davis Parish SB	Jennings
54	42.5	Calcasieu Parish School Board	Lake Charles
55	40.9	Lasalle Parish School Board	Jena
56	39.9	Ouachita Parish School Board	Monroe
57	38.6	Saint Charles Parish School Board	Luling
58	37.8	West Feliciana Parish School Board	St Francisville
59	37.7	Beauregard Parish School Board	Deridder
60	35.7	Ascension Parish School Board	Donaldsonville
61	34.7	Vernon Parish School Board	Leesville
62	34.4	Bossier Parish School Board	Benton
63	31.1	Livingston Parish School Board	Livingston
64	29.4	Cameron Parish School Board	Cameron
65	27.6	Zachary Community SD	Zachary
66	26.7	Saint Tammany Parish School Board	Covington

Students Eligible for Reduced-Price Lunch

Rank	Percent	District Name	City
1	16.2	Vernon Parish School Board	Leesville
2	13.9	City of Baker SD	Baker
2	13.9	Jefferson Davis Parish SB	Jennings
4	13.6	Cameron Parish School Board	Cameron
5	13.1	Allen Parish School Board	Oberlin
6	12.7	Lasalle Parish School Board	Jena
7	12.6	Sabine Parish School Board	Many
8	12.3	Livingston Parish School Board	Livingston
9	12.1	Grant Parish School Board	Colfax
10	11.7	West Carroll Parish School Board	Oak Grove
11	11.3	Evangeline Parish School Board	Ville Platte
11	11.3	Terrebonne Parish School Board	Houma
13	11.2	Union Parish School Board	Farmerville
14	11.0	Caldwell Parish School Board	Columbia
15	10.9	Acadia Parish School Board	Crowley
15	10.9	Lafourche Parish School Board	Thibodaux
17	10.7	West Feliciana Parish School Board	St Francisville
18	10.5	Saint Bernard Parish School Board	Chalmette
19	10.4	Catahoula Parish School Board	Harrisonburg
19	10.4	Jackson Parish School Board	Jonesboro
21	10.3	Jefferson Parish School Board	Harvey
22	10.1	Saint Landry Parish School Board	Opelousas
23	9.9	Saint Martin Parish School Board	St Martinville
23	9.9	Saint Mary Parish School Board	Centerville
25	9.5	Beauregard Parish School Board	Deridder
25	9.5	Vermilion Parish School Board	Abbeville
27	9.4	Assumption Parish School Board	Napoleonville
27	9.4	Lafayette Parish School Board	Lafayette
29	9.3	Avoyelles Parish School Board	Marksville
29	9.3	Webster Parish School Board	Minden
31	9.0	Rapides Parish School Board	Alexandria
31	9.0	W Baton Rouge Parish SB	Port Allen
33	8.7	Plaquemines Parish School Board	Port Sulphur
33	8.7	Winn Parish School Board	Winnfield
35	8.6	Iberia Parish School Board	New Iberia
36	8.5	Franklin Parish School Board	Winnsboro
36	8.5	Natchitoches Parish School Board	Natchitoches
36	8.5	Pointe Coupee Parish School Board	New Roads
36	8.5	Red River Parish School Board	Coushatta
40	8.4	Tangipahoa Parish School Board	Amite
40	8.4	Washington Parish School Board	Franklinton
42	8.3	East Feliciana Parish School Board	Clinton
42	8.3	Morehouse Parish School Board	Bastrop
44	8.1	City of Bogalusa School Board	Bogalusa
44	8.1	Desoto Parish School Board	Mansfield
44	8.1	Ouachita Parish School Board	Monroe
47	7.9	Saint Charles Parish School Board	Luling
48	7.7	Ascension Parish School Board	Donaldsonville
49	7.6	Claiborne Parish School Board	Homer
50	7.5	Iberville Parish School Board	Plaquemine
51	7.2	Bienville Parish School Board	Arcadia
52	7.1	E Baton Rouge Parish SB	Baton Rouge
53	7.0	Calcasieu Parish School Board	Lake Charles
54	6.9	Saint James Parish School Board	Lutcher
55	6.8	Bossier Parish School Board	Benton
55	6.8	Saint Tammany Parish School Board	Covington
57	6.7	Lincoln Parish School Board	Ruston
58	6.6	Saint John the Baptist Parish SB	Reserve
59	6.5	Zachary Community SD	Zachary
60	6.0	Concordia Parish School Board	Vidalia
60	6.0	Richland Parish School Board	Rayville
62	5.1	Caddo Parish School Board	Shreveport
63	4.3	City of Monroe School Board	Monroe
64	3.6	Orleans Parish School Board	New Orleans
65	3.3	East Carroll Parish School Board	Lake Providence
66	2.8	Madison Parish School Board	Tallulah

Student/Teacher Ratio

Rank	Ratio	District Name	City
1	18.6	Zachary Community SD	Zachary
2	17.4	Tangipahoa Parish School Board	Amite
3	16.0	Bossier Parish School Board	Benton
4	15.7	Avoyelles Parish School Board	Marksville
5	15.6	City of Baker SD	Baker
5	15.6	Webster Parish School Board	Minden
7	15.5	Jefferson Davis Parish SB	Jennings
8	15.4	Union Parish School Board	Farmerville
9	15.3	Jefferson Parish School Board	Harvey
9	15.3	Livingston Parish School Board	Livingston
11	15.2	Caddo Parish School Board	Shreveport
12	15.1	Beauregard Parish School Board	Deridder
12	15.1	East Feliciana Parish School Board	Clinton
14	15.0	Plaquemines Parish School Board	Port Sulphur
14	15.0	Vermilion Parish School Board	Abbeville
16	14.9	E Baton Rouge Parish SB	Baton Rouge
17	14.8	Acadia Parish School Board	Crowley
18	14.7	Calcasieu Parish School Board	Lake Charles
18	14.7	Grant Parish School Board	Colfax
20	14.6	Evangeline Parish School Board	Ville Platte
20	14.6	Madison Parish School Board	Tallulah
20	14.6	Orleans Parish School Board	New Orleans
20	14.6	Saint Landry Parish School Board	Opelousas
20	14.6	Saint Martin Parish School Board	St Martinville
20	14.6	Vernon Parish School Board	Leesville
26	14.5	Natchitoches Parish School Board	Natchitoches
27	14.4	Rapides Parish School Board	Alexandria
28	14.3	Ascension Parish School Board	Donaldsonville
28	14.3	Ouachita Parish School Board	Monroe
28	14.3	Saint James Parish School Board	Lutcher
31	14.2	City of Monroe School Board	Monroe
31	14.2	Sabine Parish School Board	Many
31	14.2	Saint Bernard Parish School Board	Chalmette
34	14.1	Concordia Parish School Board	Vidalia
34	14.1	Lafayette Parish School Board	Lafayette
34	14.1	Lasalle Parish School Board	Jena
34	14.1	Saint Mary Parish School Board	Centerville
38	13.9	Assumption Parish School Board	Napoleonville
38	13.9	Saint Tammany Parish School Board	Covington
38	13.9	Terrebonne Parish School Board	Houma
38	13.9	W Baton Rouge Parish SB	Port Allen
38	13.9	West Carroll Parish School Board	Oak Grove
43	13.8	Iberia Parish School Board	New Iberia
43	13.8	Lincoln Parish School Board	Ruston
43	13.8	Pointe Coupee Parish School Board	New Roads
46	13.7	Morehouse Parish School Board	Bastrop
46	13.7	Saint John the Baptist Parish SB	Reserve
48	13.5	Caldwell Parish School Board	Columbia
48	13.5	Jackson Parish School Board	Jonesboro
50	13.4	Winn Parish School Board	Winnfield
51	13.3	Desoto Parish School Board	Mansfield
52	13.2	Iberville Parish School Board	Plaquemine
53	13.1	Catahoula Parish School Board	Harrisonburg
53	13.1	City of Bogalusa School Board	Bogalusa
53	13.1	Washington Parish School Board	Franklinton
56	12.9	Lafourche Parish School Board	Thibodaux
57	12.7	Allen Parish School Board	Oberlin
58	12.6	Red River Parish School Board	Coushatta
59	12.5	Saint Charles Parish School Board	Luling
60	12.4	Richland Parish School Board	Rayville
61	12.2	West Feliciana Parish School Board	St Francisville
62	12.1	Bienville Parish School Board	Arcadia
63	12.0	Franklin Parish School Board	Winnsboro
64	11.9	Claiborne Parish School Board	Homer
65	11.8	East Carroll Parish School Board	Lake Providence
66	11.4	Cameron Parish School Board	Cameron

Student/Librarian Ratio

Rank	Ratio	District Name	City
1	2,215.5	Assumption Parish School Board	Napoleonville
2	2,112.7	Saint John the Baptist Parish SB	Reserve
3	1,841.0	Caldwell Parish School Board	Columbia
4	1,497.5	City of Bogalusa School Board	Bogalusa
5	970.8	Jefferson Parish School Board	Harvey
6	901.9	Livingston Parish School Board	Livingston
7	887.9	Orleans Parish School Board	New Orleans
8	837.5	East Carroll Parish School Board	Lake Providence
9	815.5	Red River Parish School Board	Coushatta
10	795.5	Pointe Coupee Parish School Board	New Roads
11	780.8	Morehouse Parish School Board	Bastrop
12	761.6	Saint Landry Parish School Board	Opelousas
13	744.6	Tangipahoa Parish School Board	Amite
14	687.4	Ascension Parish School Board	Donaldsonville
15	666.7	Catahoula Parish School Board	Harrisonburg
16	658.5	Avoyelles Parish School Board	Marksville
17	650.0	Zachary Community SD	Zachary
18	643.5	Saint Tammany Parish School Board	Covington
19	633.5	Saint Bernard Parish School Board	Chalmette
20	623.0	Bienville Parish School Board	Arcadia
21	603.5	Grant Parish School Board	Colfax
22	603.1	Acadia Parish School Board	Crowley
23	597.3	Jackson Parish School Board	Jonesboro
24	596.3	Lafayette Parish School Board	Lafayette
25	592.8	West Carroll Parish School Board	Oak Grove
26	586.6	Bossier Parish School Board	Benton
27	571.7	Evangeline Parish School Board	Ville Platte
28	552.3	Rapides Parish School Board	Alexandria
29	549.4	Iberville Parish School Board	Plaquemine
30	548.6	Vernon Parish School Board	Leesville
31	542.4	Caddo Parish School Board	Shreveport
32	538.1	Saint Charles Parish School Board	Luling
33	509.0	Ouachita Parish School Board	Monroe
34	508.1	Saint Martin Parish School Board	St Martinville
35	502.5	City of Monroe School Board	Monroe
36	502.3	Calcasieu Parish School Board	Lake Charles
37	497.4	Natchitoches Parish School Board	Natchitoches
38	489.7	Iberia Parish School Board	New Iberia
39	486.8	West Feliciana Parish School Board	St Francisville
40	480.9	E Baton Rouge Parish SB	Baton Rouge
41	480.0	Union Parish School Board	Farmerville
42	479.7	Lafourche Parish School Board	Thibodaux
43	473.8	East Feliciana Parish School Board	Clinton
44	471.3	Beauregard Parish School Board	Deridder
45	469.1	Vermilion Parish School Board	Abbeville
46	463.8	Madison Parish School Board	Tallulah
47	457.4	Terrebonne Parish School Board	Houma
48	451.3	Saint James Parish School Board	Lutcher
49	447.6	Desoto Parish School Board	Mansfield
50	443.2	Saint Mary Parish School Board	Centerville
51	428.1	Allen Parish School Board	Oberlin
52	413.9	Plaquemines Parish School Board	Port Sulphur
53	410.6	Jefferson Davis Parish SB	Jennings
54	404.1	Webster Parish School Board	Minden
55	397.4	Winn Parish School Board	Winnfield
56	392.7	Washington Parish School Board	Franklinton
57	388.1	Sabine Parish School Board	Many
58	385.6	Lasalle Parish School Board	Jena
59	379.8	Concordia Parish School Board	Vidalia
60	366.4	Lincoln Parish School Board	Ruston
61	353.9	W Baton Rouge Parish SB	Port Allen
62	303.2	Cameron Parish School Board	Cameron
63	n/a	City of Baker SD	Baker
63	n/a	Claiborne Parish School Board	Homer
63	n/a	Franklin Parish School Board	Winnsboro

| 63 | n/a | Richland Parish School Board | Rayville |

Student/Counselor Ratio

Rank	Ratio	District Name	City
1	738.5	Assumption Parish School Board	Napoleonville
2	583.5	Franklin Parish School Board	Winnsboro
3	548.8	Avoyelles Parish School Board	Marksville
4	539.8	Lasalle Parish School Board	Jena
5	497.4	Natchitoches Parish School Board	Natchitoches
6	480.0	Union Parish School Board	Farmerville
7	474.3	Sabine Parish School Board	Many
8	434.6	Richland Parish School Board	Rayville
9	429.7	Bienville Parish School Board	Arcadia
10	418.8	East Carroll Parish School Board	Lake Providence
11	409.2	Orleans Parish School Board	New Orleans
12	409.1	Catahoula Parish School Board	Harrisonburg
13	403.1	Saint Bernard Parish School Board	Chalmette
14	393.1	Madison Parish School Board	Tallulah
15	370.5	West Carroll Parish School Board	Oak Grove
16	368.2	Caldwell Parish School Board	Columbia
17	351.7	Desoto Parish School Board	Mansfield
18	341.3	Jackson Parish School Board	Jonesboro
19	340.5	Vernon Parish School Board	Leesville
20	330.3	Concordia Parish School Board	Vidalia
21	329.2	Grant Parish School Board	Colfax
22	321.9	City of Baker SD	Baker
23	316.7	Claiborne Parish School Board	Homer
24	314.5	Evangeline Parish School Board	Ville Platte
25	313.5	Tangipahoa Parish School Board	Amite
26	312.4	Saint Charles Parish School Board	Luling
27	294.9	W Baton Rouge Parish SB	Port Allen
28	292.2	Livingston Parish School Board	Livingston
28	292.2	Saint James Parish School Board	Lutcher
30	289.5	Morehouse Parish School Board	Bastrop
31	283.6	Saint Landry Parish School Board	Opelousas
32	272.3	Ouachita Parish School Board	Monroe
33	270.8	Zachary Community SD	Zachary
34	270.4	West Feliciana Parish School Board	St Francisville
35	265.0	Winn Parish School Board	Winnfield
36	261.7	Saint Martin Parish School Board	St Martinville
37	258.5	Iberville Parish School Board	Plaquemine
38	256.0	Calcasieu Parish School Board	Lake Charles
39	252.7	Lincoln Parish School Board	Ruston
40	237.9	Bossier Parish School Board	Benton
41	235.7	Beauregard Parish School Board	Deridder
42	233.0	Red River Parish School Board	Coushatta
43	229.0	Iberia Parish School Board	New Iberia
44	227.3	City of Monroe School Board	Monroe
44	227.3	Pointe Coupee Parish School Board	New Roads
46	226.5	Saint Mary Parish School Board	Centerville
47	221.1	Jefferson Davis Parish SB	Jennings
48	216.0	Plaquemines Parish School Board	Port Sulphur
49	214.7	Jefferson Parish School Board	Harvey
50	214.1	Allen Parish School Board	Oberlin
51	214.0	Cameron Parish School Board	Cameron
52	212.2	Lafayette Parish School Board	Lafayette
53	208.9	Terrebonne Parish School Board	Houma
54	200.1	Rapides Parish School Board	Alexandria
55	197.4	East Feliciana Parish School Board	Clinton
56	193.0	Acadia Parish School Board	Crowley
57	187.3	Webster Parish School Board	Minden
58	185.3	Vermilion Parish School Board	Abbeville
59	176.5	Saint John the Baptist Parish SB	Reserve
60	173.2	Washington Parish School Board	Franklinton
61	167.8	Caddo Parish School Board	Shreveport
62	165.6	Saint Tammany Parish School Board	Covington
63	163.1	Lafourche Parish School Board	Thibodaux
64	161.3	Ascension Parish School Board	Donaldsonville
65	158.5	City of Bogalusa School Board	Bogalusa
66	149.5	E Baton Rouge Parish SB	Baton Rouge

Current Spending per Student in FY2003

Rank	Dollars	District Name	City
1	9,175	West Feliciana Parish School Board	St Francisville
2	8,756	Iberville Parish School Board	Plaquemine
3	8,600	Saint Charles Parish School Board	Luling
4	8,529	Cameron Parish School Board	Cameron
5	8,251	Jackson Parish School Board	Jonesboro
6	8,235	Saint John the Baptist Parish SB	Reserve
7	8,220	Bienville Parish School Board	Arcadia
8	8,079	Plaquemines Parish School Board	Port Sulphur
9	8,071	Red River Parish School Board	Coushatta
10	8,021	Desoto Parish School Board	Mansfield
11	7,939	Pointe Coupee Parish School Board	New Roads
12	7,725	Saint James Parish School Board	Lutcher
13	7,633	E Baton Rouge Parish SB	Baton Rouge
14	7,557	East Carroll Parish School Board	Lake Providence
15	7,518	Assumption Parish School Board	Napoleonville
16	7,428	Claiborne Parish School Board	Homer
17	7,380	City of Bogalusa School Board	Bogalusa
18	7,288	Winn Parish School Board	Winnfield

19	7,270	Caddo Parish School Board	Shreveport
20	7,246	Saint Tammany Parish School Board	Covington
21	7,177	Catahoula Parish School Board	Harrisonburg
22	7,156	East Feliciana Parish School Board	Clinton
23	7,104	Washington Parish School Board	Franklinton
24	7,091	Lafourche Parish School Board	Thibodaux
25	7,040	W Baton Rouge Parish SB	Port Allen
26	7,025	Jefferson Davis Parish SB	Jennings
27	7,018	City of Monroe School Board	Monroe
28	7,010	Richland Parish School Board	Rayville
29	6,989	Rapides Parish School Board	Alexandria
30	6,892	Ascension Parish School Board	Donaldsonville
31	6,871	Ouachita Parish School Board	Monroe
32	6,844	Lasalle Parish School Board	Jena
33	6,841	Concordia Parish School Board	Vidalia
34	6,832	Saint Bernard Parish School Board	Chalmette
35	6,810	Morehouse Parish School Board	Bastrop
36	6,806	Saint Mary Parish School Board	Centerville
37	6,802	Iberia Parish School Board	New Iberia
37	6,802	Natchitoches Parish School Board	Natchitoches
39	6,800	Vernon Parish School Board	Leesville
40	6,703	Madison Parish School Board	Tallulah
41	6,645	Jefferson Parish School Board	Harvey
42	6,623	Lafayette Parish School Board	Lafayette
43	6,621	Allen Parish School Board	Oberlin
44	6,605	Saint Landry Parish School Board	Opelousas
45	6,575	Lincoln Parish School Board	Ruston
46	6,560	Caldwell Parish School Board	Columbia
46	6,560	Orleans Parish School Board	New Orleans
48	6,551	Terrebonne Parish School Board	Houma
49	6,482	Acadia Parish School Board	Crowley
50	6,471	Calcasieu Parish School Board	Lake Charles
50	6,471	Saint Martin Parish School Board	St Martinville
52	6,460	Evangeline Parish School Board	Ville Platte
53	6,385	Grant Parish School Board	Colfax
54	6,331	Avoyelles Parish School Board	Marksville
55	6,294	Vermilion Parish School Board	Abbeville
56	6,267	Beauregard Parish School Board	Deridder
57	6,253	Webster Parish School Board	Minden
58	6,235	Franklin Parish School Board	Winnsboro
59	6,232	Sabine Parish School Board	Many
60	6,183	Bossier Parish School Board	Benton
61	6,125	Union Parish School Board	Farmerville
62	5,963	West Carroll Parish School Board	Oak Grove
63	5,888	Tangipahoa Parish School Board	Amite
64	5,641	Livingston Parish School Board	Livingston
65	n/a	City of Baker SD	Baker
65	n/a	Zachary Community SD	Zachary

Number of Diploma Recipients

Rank	Number	District Name	City
1	3,471	Orleans Parish School Board	New Orleans
2	2,815	E Baton Rouge Parish SB	Baton Rouge
3	2,261	Jefferson Parish School Board	Harvey
4	2,223	Caddo Parish School Board	Shreveport
5	1,834	Saint Tammany Parish School Board	Covington
6	1,747	Calcasieu Parish School Board	Lake Charles
7	1,624	Lafayette Parish School Board	Lafayette
8	1,294	Rapides Parish School Board	Alexandria
9	1,056	Livingston Parish School Board	Livingston
10	1,030	Tangipahoa Parish School Board	Amite
11	1,007	Terrebonne Parish School Board	Houma
12	983	Bossier Parish School Board	Benton
13	923	Ouachita Parish School Board	Monroe
14	810	Lafourche Parish School Board	Thibodaux
15	805	Saint Landry Parish School Board	Opelousas
16	772	Ascension Parish School Board	Donaldsonville
17	637	Iberia Parish School Board	New Iberia
18	628	Saint Charles Parish School Board	Luling
19	614	Saint Mary Parish School Board	Centerville
20	480	Vermilion Parish School Board	Abbeville
21	469	City of Monroe School Board	Monroe
22	460	Saint Martin Parish School Board	St Martinville
23	455	Vernon Parish School Board	Leesville
24	444	Acadia Parish School Board	Crowley
25	418	Lincoln Parish School Board	Ruston
26	399	Avoyelles Parish School Board	Marksville
27	382	Saint Bernard Parish School Board	Chalmette
28	371	Beauregard Parish School Board	Deridder
29	369	Webster Parish School Board	Minden
30	353	Natchitoches Parish School Board	Natchitoches
31	318	Jefferson Davis Parish SB	Jennings
32	286	Evangeline Parish School Board	Ville Platte
33	278	Plaquemines Parish School Board	Port Sulphur
34	276	Saint John the Baptist Parish SB	Reserve
35	270	Washington Parish School Board	Franklinton
36	257	Sabine Parish School Board	Many
37	253	Iberville Parish School Board	Plaquemine
38	248	Desoto Parish School Board	Mansfield
39	243	W Baton Rouge Parish SB	Port Allen
40	230	Morehouse Parish School Board	Bastrop
40	230	Saint James Parish School Board	Lutcher

42	218	Allen Parish School Board	Oberlin
43	217	Union Parish School Board	Farmerville
44	205	Concordia Parish School Board	Vidalia
45	201	Assumption Parish School Board	Napoleonville
46	199	Franklin Parish School Board	Winnsboro
47	184	Grant Parish School Board	Colfax
48	175	Richland Parish School Board	Rayville
49	169	Jackson Parish School Board	Jonesboro
50	167	Pointe Coupee Parish School Board	New Roads
51	164	City of Bogalusa School Board	Bogalusa
52	163	Lasalle Parish School Board	Jena
53	150	Winn Parish School Board	Winnfield
54	149	Claiborne Parish School Board	Homer
55	142	East Feliciana Parish School Board	Clinton
56	138	Bienville Parish School Board	Arcadia
57	131	West Carroll Parish School Board	Oak Grove
58	122	West Feliciana Parish School Board	St Francisville
59	111	Madison Parish School Board	Tallulah
60	109	Cameron Parish School Board	Cameron
61	94	Catahoula Parish School Board	Harrisonburg
62	83	East Carroll Parish School Board	Lake Providence
63	75	Red River Parish School Board	Coushatta
64	66	Caldwell Parish School Board	Columbia
65	n/a	City of Baker SD	Baker
65	n/a	Zachary Community SD	Zachary

High School Drop-out Rate

Rank	Percent	District Name	City
1	20.5	Red River Parish School Board	Coushatta
2	12.5	City of Monroe School Board	Monroe
3	11.6	Pointe Coupee Parish School Board	New Roads
4	10.9	Madison Parish School Board	Tallulah
5	10.0	Caddo Parish School Board	Shreveport
6	9.7	Jefferson Parish School Board	Harvey
7	9.2	Morehouse Parish School Board	Bastrop
8	9.1	Orleans Parish School Board	New Orleans
9	8.7	Rapides Parish School Board	Alexandria
10	8.5	E Baton Rouge Parish SB	Baton Rouge
10	8.5	Saint John the Baptist Parish SB	Reserve
12	8.3	Terrebonne Parish School Board	Houma
13	7.9	Natchitoches Parish School Board	Natchitoches
14	7.8	Lafayette Parish School Board	Lafayette
15	7.7	Bienville Parish School Board	Arcadia
16	7.6	East Carroll Parish School Board	Lake Providence
17	7.5	Iberville Parish School Board	Plaquemine
18	7.3	Assumption Parish School Board	Napoleonville
18	7.3	Richland Parish School Board	Rayville
20	7.2	Franklin Parish School Board	Winnsboro
21	7.1	Acadia Parish School Board	Crowley
21	7.1	Ouachita Parish School Board	Monroe
23	7.0	Saint James Parish School Board	Lutcher
23	7.0	Tangipahoa Parish School Board	Amite
25	6.8	W Baton Rouge Parish SB	Port Allen
26	6.7	Avoyelles Parish School Board	Marksville
27	6.6	Evangeline Parish School Board	Ville Platte
28	6.4	Lincoln Parish School Board	Ruston
28	6.4	Saint Martin Parish School Board	St Martinville
30	6.3	Catahoula Parish School Board	Harrisonburg
30	6.3	Saint Bernard Parish School Board	Chalmette
32	6.2	Concordia Parish School Board	Vidalia
33	6.0	Grant Parish School Board	Colfax
33	6.0	Jackson Parish School Board	Jonesboro
35	5.9	Iberia Parish School Board	New Iberia
35	5.9	Plaquemines Parish School Board	Port Sulphur
37	5.8	Lafourche Parish School Board	Thibodaux
38	5.6	West Carroll Parish School Board	Oak Grove
39	5.5	Winn Parish School Board	Winnfield
40	5.4	East Feliciana Parish School Board	Clinton
41	5.0	Sabine Parish School Board	Many
41	5.0	Saint Landry Parish School Board	Opelousas
43	4.9	Saint Mary Parish School Board	Centerville
44	4.8	Calcasieu Parish School Board	Lake Charles
44	4.8	Caldwell Parish School Board	Columbia
46	4.7	Ascension Parish School Board	Donaldsonville
47	4.6	Bossier Parish School Board	Benton
47	4.6	City of Bogalusa School Board	Bogalusa
49	4.5	Desoto Parish School Board	Mansfield
50	4.1	Union Parish School Board	Farmerville
50	4.1	Vernon Parish School Board	Leesville
52	4.0	Saint Tammany Parish School Board	Covington
52	4.0	Vermilion Parish School Board	Abbeville
54	3.9	Lasalle Parish School Board	Jena
55	3.8	Webster Parish School Board	Minden
56	3.6	Jefferson Davis Parish SB	Jennings
56	3.6	Washington Parish School Board	Franklinton
58	3.4	Saint Charles Parish School Board	Luling
58	3.4	West Feliciana Parish School Board	St Francisville
60	2.5	Claiborne Parish School Board	Homer
61	2.2	Allen Parish School Board	Oberlin
62	2.1	Cameron Parish School Board	Cameron
63	2.0	Beauregard Parish School Board	Deridder
64	1.2	Livingston Parish School Board	Livingston

| 65 | n/a | City of Baker SD | Baker |
| 65 | n/a | Zachary Community SD | Zachary |

Maine

Maine Public School Educational Profile

Category	Value	Category	Value
Schools *(2003-2004)*	694	**Diploma Recipients** *(2002-2003)*	12,166
Instructional Level		White, Non-Hispanic	11,841
Primary	414	Black, Non-Hispanic	79
Middle	121	Asian/Pacific Islander	112
High	138	American Indian/Alaskan Native	77
Other Level	21	Hispanic	57
Curriculum		**High School Drop-out Rate** (%) *(2001-2002)*	2.8
Regular	663	White, Non-Hispanic	2.8
Special Education	4	Black, Non-Hispanic	4.4
Vocational	27	Asian/Pacific Islander	2.7
Alternative	0	American Indian/Alaskan Native	5.0
Type		Hispanic	3.7
Magnet	1	**Staff** *(2003-2004)*	
Charter	0	Teachers	17,620.8
Title I Eligible	517	Average Salary ($)	39,864
School-wide Title I	49	Librarians/Media Specialists	250.5
Students *(2003-2004)*	201,549	Guidance Counselors	627.8
Gender (%)		**Ratios** *(2003-2004)*	
Male	51.6	Student/Teacher Ratio	11.4 to 1
Female	48.4	Student/Librarian Ratio	804.6 to 1
Race/Ethnicity (%)		Student/Counselor Ratio	321.0 to 1
White, Non-Hispanic	95.8	**College Entrance Exam Scores** *(2005)*	
Black, Non-Hispanic	1.7	Scholastic Aptitude Test (SAT)	
Asian/Pacific Islander	1.2	Participation Rate (%)	75
American Indian/Alaskan Native	0.5	Mean SAT Reasoning Test Verbal Score	509
Hispanic	0.8	Mean SAT Reasoning Test Math Score	505
Classification (%)		American College Testing Program (ACT)	
Individual Education Program (IEP)	16.6	Participation Rate (%)	10
Migrant *(2002-2003)*	0.0	Average Composite Score	22.4
English Language Learner (ELL)	1.4	Average English Score	22.1
Eligible for Free Lunch Program	23.0	Average Math Score	22.0
Eligible for Reduced-Price Lunch Program	7.2	Average Reading Score	23.1
Current Spending *($ per student in FY 2003)*	9,122	Average Science Score	21.9
Instruction	6,083		
Support Services	2,749		

Note: *For an explanation of data, please refer to the User's Guide in the front of the book*

Maine NAEP 2005 Test Scores

Reading			Mathematics		
Grade/Category	Value	Rank	Grade/Category	Value	Rank
4th Grade			**4th Grade**		
Average Proficiency	224.6 (0.94)	9/51	Average Proficiency	240.7 (0.82)	16/51
Proficiency by Gender/Race/Ethnicity			Proficiency by Gender/Race/Ethnicity		
Male	221.4 (1.22)	9/51	Male	242.7 (0.88)	13/51
Female	227.6 (1.21)	9/51	Female	238.7 (1.06)	20/51
White, Non-Hispanic	224.8 (1.00)	34/51	White, Non-Hispanic	240.8 (0.87)	41/51
Black, Non-Hispanic	n/a	n/a	Black, Non-Hispanic	n/a	n/a
Asian, Non-Hispanic	n/a	n/a	Asian, Non-Hispanic	n/a	n/a
American Indian, Non-Hispanic	n/a	n/a	American Indian, Non-Hispanic	n/a	n/a
Hispanic	n/a	n/a	Hispanic	n/a	n/a
Proficiency by Class Size			Proficiency by Class Size		
Less than 16 Students	221.2 (2.62)	3/34	Less than 16 Students	237.7 (1.32)	7/35
16 to 18 Students	223.4 (1.45)	7/33	16 to 18 Students	237.0 (1.73)	17/31
19 to 20 Students	225.5 (2.16)	13/38	19 to 20 Students	240.4 (1.60)	16/38
21 to 25 Students	227.0 (1.61)	9/51	21 to 25 Students	245.7 (1.69)	3/51
Greater than 25 Students	n/a	n/a	Greater than 25 Students	n/a	n/a
Percent Attaining Achievement Levels			Percent Attaining Achievement Levels		
Below Basic	29.0 (1.16)	43/51	Below Basic	15.7 (0.92)	37/51
Basic or Above	71.0 (1.16)	9/51	Basic or Above	84.3 (0.92)	14/51
Proficient or Above	35.2 (1.27)	13/51	Proficient or Above	38.8 (1.42)	19/51
Advanced or Above	8.6 (0.77)	8/51	Advanced or Above	5.2 (0.57)	18/51
8th Grade			**8th Grade**		
Average Proficiency	270.0 (0.95)	3/51	Average Proficiency	281.1 (0.84)	21/51
Proficiency by Gender/Race/Ethnicity			Proficiency by Gender/Race/Ethnicity		
Male	263.8 (1.07)	8/51	Male	281.7 (1.20)	22/51
Female	276.4 (1.14)	2/51	Female	280.4 (1.00)	23/51
White, Non-Hispanic	270.5 (0.98)	20/51	White, Non-Hispanic	281.5 (0.87)	39/51
Black, Non-Hispanic	n/a	n/a	Black, Non-Hispanic	n/a	n/a
Asian, Non-Hispanic	n/a	n/a	Asian, Non-Hispanic	n/a	n/a
American Indian, Non-Hispanic	n/a	n/a	American Indian, Non-Hispanic	n/a	n/a
Hispanic	n/a	n/a	Hispanic	n/a	n/a
Proficiency by Parents Highest Level of Ed.			Proficiency by Parents Highest Level of Ed.		
Did Not Finish High School	250.3 (3.50)	11/49	Did Not Finish High School	264.0 (3.07)	15/50
Graduated High School	264.4 (1.53)	1/50	Graduated High School	270.5 (1.71)	22/50
Some Education After High School	271.2 (1.92)	5/50	Some Education After High School	283.7 (1.69)	16/50
Graduated College	276.8 (1.20)	5/50	Graduated College	290.0 (1.07)	26/50
Percent Attaining Achievement Levels			Percent Attaining Achievement Levels		
Below Basic	29.0 (1.16)	43/51	Below Basic	26.2 (1.02)	34/51
Basic or Above	71.0 (1.16)	9/51	Basic or Above	73.8 (1.02)	18/51
Proficient or Above	35.2 (1.27)	13/51	Proficient or Above	29.9 (1.10)	25/51
Advanced or Above	8.6 (0.77)	8/51	Advanced or Above	5.0 (0.49)	28/51

Note: For an explanation of data, please refer to the User's Guide in the front of the book; n/a indicates data not available

Androscoggin County

Auburn School Department
23 High St PO Box 800 • Auburn, ME 04212-0800
(207) 784-6431 • http://www.auburnschl.edu/default.html
Grade Span: KG-12; **Agency Type:** 1
Schools: 12
  6 Primary; 2 Middle; 2 High; 2 Other Level
  11 Regular; 1 Special Education; 0 Vocational; 0 Alternative
  0 Magnet; 0 Charter; 5 Title I Eligible; 0 School-wide Title I
Students: 3,613   (52.4% male; 47.5% female)
  Individual Education Program: 716 (19.8%);
  English Language Learner: 113 (3.1%); Migrant: n/a
  Eligible for Free Lunch Program: 830 (22.7%)
  Eligible for Reduced-Price Lunch Program: 202 (5.5%)
Teachers: 355.7 (10.3 to 1)
Librarians/Media Specialists: 3.4 (1,074.7 to 1)
Guidance Counselors: 16.7 (218.8 to 1)
Current Spending: ($ per student per year):
  Total: $8,449; Instruction: $5,817; Support Services: $2,448
Enrollment, Drop-out Rates and Diploma Recipients by Race/Ethnicity

Category	Total	White	Black	Asian	AIAN	Hisp.
Enrollment (%)	100.0	92.9	4.3	1.2	0.6	1.0
Drop-out Rate (%)	4.0	4.1	4.5	0.0	n/a	0.0
H.S. Diplomas (#)	228	223	1	3	1	0

Lewiston School Department
Dingley Bldg 36 Oak St • Lewiston, ME 04240-7190
(207) 795-4100 • http://www.lewiston.k12.me.us/
Grade Span: KG-12; **Agency Type:** 1
Schools: 9
  6 Primary; 1 Middle; 2 High; 0 Other Level
  8 Regular; 0 Special Education; 1 Vocational; 0 Alternative
  0 Magnet; 0 Charter; 6 Title I Eligible; 1 School-wide Title I
Students: 4,550   (51.8% male; 48.1% female)
  Individual Education Program: 842 (18.5%);
  English Language Learner: 304 (6.7%); Migrant: n/a
  Eligible for Free Lunch Program: 1,852 (40.7%)
  Eligible for Reduced-Price Lunch Program: 319 (7.0%)
Teachers: 376.1 (12.1 to 1)
Librarians/Media Specialists: 3.0 (1,516.7 to 1)
Guidance Counselors: 16.9 (269.2 to 1)
Current Spending: ($ per student per year):
  Total: $8,139; Instruction: $5,293; Support Services: $2,524
Enrollment, Drop-out Rates and Diploma Recipients by Race/Ethnicity

Category	Total	White	Black	Asian	AIAN	Hisp.
Enrollment (%)	100.0	87.1	9.4	1.4	0.8	1.3
Drop-out Rate (%)	3.7	3.8	3.2	0.0	0.0	0.0
H.S. Diplomas (#)	270	255	9	5	1	0

MSAD 52 Turner
98 Matthews Way • Turner, ME 04282-9778
(207) 225-3795 • http://www.yarmouth.k12.me.us/
Grade Span: PK-12; **Agency Type:** 1
Schools: 6
  3 Primary; 2 Middle; 1 High; 0 Other Level
  6 Regular; 0 Special Education; 0 Vocational; 0 Alternative
  0 Magnet; 0 Charter; 4 Title I Eligible; 0 School-wide Title I
Students: 2,256   (51.6% male; 48.3% female)
  Individual Education Program: 321 (14.2%);
  English Language Learner: 69 (3.1%); Migrant: n/a
  Eligible for Free Lunch Program: 347 (15.5%)
  Eligible for Reduced-Price Lunch Program: 104 (4.7%)
Teachers: 199.9 (11.2 to 1)
Librarians/Media Specialists: 3.0 (745.0 to 1)
Guidance Counselors: 10.0 (223.5 to 1)
Current Spending: ($ per student per year):
  Total: $7,980; Instruction: $5,183; Support Services: $2,562
Enrollment, Drop-out Rates and Diploma Recipients by Race/Ethnicity

Category	Total	White	Black	Asian	AIAN	Hisp.
Enrollment (%)	100.0	96.8	0.9	0.4	0.3	1.7
Drop-out Rate (%)	1.6	1.6	0.0	0.0	n/a	0.0
H.S. Diplomas (#)	150	148	0	1	0	1

Aroostook County

Caribou School Department
628 Main St • Caribou, ME 04736-4421
(207) 496-6311
Grade Span: KG-12; **Agency Type:** 1
Schools: 6
  2 Primary; 1 Middle; 3 High; 0 Other Level
  5 Regular; 0 Special Education; 1 Vocational; 0 Alternative
  0 Magnet; 0 Charter; 3 Title I Eligible; 2 School-wide Title I
Students: 1,667   (51.3% male; 48.6% female)

  Individual Education Program: 181 (10.9%);
  English Language Learner: 19 (1.1%); Migrant: n/a
  Eligible for Free Lunch Program: 540 (32.9%)
  Eligible for Reduced-Price Lunch Program: 150 (9.1%)
Teachers: 143.6 (11.4 to 1)
Librarians/Media Specialists: 2.0 (820.5 to 1)
Guidance Counselors: 4.9 (334.9 to 1)
Current Spending: ($ per student per year):
  Total: $8,323; Instruction: $5,382; Support Services: $2,659
Enrollment, Drop-out Rates and Diploma Recipients by Race/Ethnicity

Category	Total	White	Black	Asian	AIAN	Hisp.
Enrollment (%)	100.0	94.6	1.2	1.5	2.0	0.7
Drop-out Rate (%)	1.5	1.4	0.0	12.5	0.0	0.0
H.S. Diplomas (#)	120	116	0	1	3	0

MSAD 01 Presque Isle
79 Blake St Ste 1 PO Box 1118 • Presque Isle, ME 04769-2484
(207) 764-4101 • http://www.sad1.k12.me.us/
Grade Span: PK-12; **Agency Type:** 1
Schools: 9
  4 Primary; 2 Middle; 3 High; 0 Other Level
  8 Regular; 0 Special Education; 1 Vocational; 0 Alternative
  0 Magnet; 0 Charter; 4 Title I Eligible; 0 School-wide Title I
Students: 2,133   (51.2% male; 48.7% female)
  Individual Education Program: 266 (12.5%);
  English Language Learner: 7 (0.3%); Migrant: n/a
  Eligible for Free Lunch Program: 520 (24.4%)
  Eligible for Reduced-Price Lunch Program: 187 (8.8%)
Teachers: 188.5 (11.3 to 1)
Librarians/Media Specialists: 1.0 (2,130.0 to 1)
Guidance Counselors: 3.9 (546.2 to 1)
Current Spending: ($ per student per year):
  Total: $8,695; Instruction: $5,282; Support Services: $3,040
Enrollment, Drop-out Rates and Diploma Recipients by Race/Ethnicity

Category	Total	White	Black	Asian	AIAN	Hisp.
Enrollment (%)	100.0	94.8	1.0	0.8	2.9	0.5
Drop-out Rate (%)	2.9	2.6	33.3	12.5	0.0	0.0
H.S. Diplomas (#)	128	120	0	1	5	2

Cumberland County

Brunswick School Department
35 Union St • Brunswick, ME 04011-1922
(207) 729-4148 • http://www.brunswick.k12.me.us/
Grade Span: KG-12; **Agency Type:** 1
Schools: 6
  4 Primary; 1 Middle; 1 High; 0 Other Level
  6 Regular; 0 Special Education; 0 Vocational; 0 Alternative
  0 Magnet; 0 Charter; 4 Title I Eligible; 0 School-wide Title I
Students: 3,356   (52.3% male; 47.6% female)
  Individual Education Program: 476 (14.2%);
  English Language Learner: 31 (0.9%); Migrant: n/a
  Eligible for Free Lunch Program: 312 (9.3%)
  Eligible for Reduced-Price Lunch Program: 167 (5.0%)
Teachers: 247.9 (13.5 to 1)
Librarians/Media Specialists: 5.5 (610.4 to 1)
Guidance Counselors: 11.5 (291.9 to 1)
Current Spending: ($ per student per year):
  Total: $7,731; Instruction: $5,129; Support Services: $2,358
Enrollment, Drop-out Rates and Diploma Recipients by Race/Ethnicity

Category	Total	White	Black	Asian	AIAN	Hisp.
Enrollment (%)	100.0	92.4	2.7	2.4	0.3	2.1
Drop-out Rate (%)	1.9	1.9	7.1	0.0	0.0	0.0
H.S. Diplomas (#)	230	223	3	2	1	1

Cape Elizabeth School Department
PO Box 6267 • Cape Elizabeth, ME 04107-0067
(207) 799-2217 • http://www.cape.k12.me.us/
Grade Span: KG-12; **Agency Type:** 1
Schools: 3
  1 Primary; 1 Middle; 1 High; 0 Other Level
  3 Regular; 0 Special Education; 0 Vocational; 0 Alternative
  0 Magnet; 0 Charter; 1 Title I Eligible; 0 School-wide Title I
Students: 1,807   (52.4% male; 47.5% female)
  Individual Education Program: 222 (12.3%);
  English Language Learner: 4 (0.2%); Migrant: n/a
  Eligible for Free Lunch Program: n/a
  Eligible for Reduced-Price Lunch Program: n/a
Teachers: 136.4 (13.2 to 1)
Librarians/Media Specialists: 3.0 (600.0 to 1)
Guidance Counselors: 6.1 (295.1 to 1)
Current Spending: ($ per student per year):
  Total: $8,768; Instruction: $6,121; Support Services: $2,377

Enrollment, Drop-out Rates and Diploma Recipients by Race/Ethnicity

Category	Total	White	Black	Asian	AIAN	Hisp.
Enrollment (%)	100.0	96.2	0.8	1.9	0.0	1.1
Drop-out Rate (%)	0.2	0.2	0.0	0.0	n/a	n/a
H.S. Diplomas (#)	107	107	0	0	0	0

Falmouth School Department
51 Woodville Rd • Falmouth, ME 04105-1105
(207) 781-3200 • http://www.falmouthschools.org/
Grade Span: KG-12; Agency Type: 1
Schools: 4
  2 Primary; 1 Middle; 1 High; 0 Other Level
  4 Regular; 0 Special Education; 0 Vocational; 0 Alternative
  0 Magnet; 0 Charter; 1 Title I Eligible; 0 School-wide Title I
Students: 2,183 (52.4% male; 47.5% female)
  Individual Education Program: 254 (11.6%);
  English Language Learner: 9 (0.4%); Migrant: n/a
  Eligible for Free Lunch Program: 29 (1.3%)
  Eligible for Reduced-Price Lunch Program: 16 (0.7%)
Teachers: 171.9 (12.7 to 1)
Librarians/Media Specialists: 3.0 (727.0 to 1)
Guidance Counselors: 6.9 (316.1 to 1)
Current Spending: ($ per student per year):
  Total: $9,319; Instruction: $6,097; Support Services: $3,004

Enrollment, Drop-out Rates and Diploma Recipients by Race/Ethnicity

Category	Total	White	Black	Asian	AIAN	Hisp.
Enrollment (%)	100.0	95.8	0.8	2.3	0.1	1.0
Drop-out Rate (%)	0.5	0.5	0.0	0.0	n/a	0.0
H.S. Diplomas (#)	113	107	1	1	1	3

Gorham School Department
381 Main St • Gorham, ME 04038-1309
(207) 222-1000 • http://www.gorhamschools.org/
Grade Span: KG-12; Agency Type: 1
Schools: 5
  3 Primary; 1 Middle; 1 High; 0 Other Level
  5 Regular; 0 Special Education; 0 Vocational; 0 Alternative
  0 Magnet; 0 Charter; 3 Title I Eligible; 0 School-wide Title I
Students: 2,751 (51.1% male; 48.8% female)
  Individual Education Program: 387 (14.1%);
  English Language Learner: 11 (0.4%); Migrant: n/a
  Eligible for Free Lunch Program: 235 (8.5%)
  Eligible for Reduced-Price Lunch Program: 78 (2.8%)
Teachers: 194.0 (14.2 to 1)
Librarians/Media Specialists: 5.0 (550.2 to 1)
Guidance Counselors: 7.0 (393.0 to 1)
Current Spending: ($ per student per year):
  Total: $8,111; Instruction: $5,350; Support Services: $2,463

Enrollment, Drop-out Rates and Diploma Recipients by Race/Ethnicity

Category	Total	White	Black	Asian	AIAN	Hisp.
Enrollment (%)	100.0	96.9	1.2	1.1	0.2	0.5
Drop-out Rate (%)	1.8	1.7	20.0	0.0	0.0	0.0
H.S. Diplomas (#)	149	146	0	3	0	0

MSAD 15 Gray
14 Shaker Rd • Gray, ME 04039-1080
(207) 657-3335 • http://www.msad15.org
Grade Span: KG-12; Agency Type: 1
Schools: 5
  3 Primary; 1 Middle; 1 High; 0 Other Level
  5 Regular; 0 Special Education; 0 Vocational; 0 Alternative
  0 Magnet; 0 Charter; 4 Title I Eligible; 0 School-wide Title I
Students: 2,069 (53.3% male; 46.6% female)
  Individual Education Program: 314 (15.2%);
  English Language Learner: 3 (0.1%); Migrant: n/a
  Eligible for Free Lunch Program: 351 (16.9%)
  Eligible for Reduced-Price Lunch Program: 133 (6.4%)
Teachers: 159.3 (13.1 to 1)
Librarians/Media Specialists: 1.0 (2,079.0 to 1)
Guidance Counselors: 8.0 (259.9 to 1)
Current Spending: ($ per student per year):
  Total: $8,295; Instruction: $5,131; Support Services: $2,910

Enrollment, Drop-out Rates and Diploma Recipients by Race/Ethnicity

Category	Total	White	Black	Asian	AIAN	Hisp.
Enrollment (%)	100.0	97.0	1.9	0.1	0.4	0.6
Drop-out Rate (%)	1.1	1.1	0.0	n/a	n/a	n/a
H.S. Diplomas (#)	117	116	1	0	0	0

MSAD 51 Cumberland
357 Tuttle Rd PO Box 6a • Cumberland Ctr., ME 04021-0606
(207) 829-4800
Grade Span: KG-12; Agency Type: 1
Schools: 6
  2 Primary; 3 Middle; 1 High; 0 Other Level
  6 Regular; 0 Special Education; 0 Vocational; 0 Alternative

  0 Magnet; 0 Charter; 5 Title I Eligible; 0 School-wide Title I
Students: 2,341 (48.9% male; 51.0% female)
  Individual Education Program: 151 (6.5%);
  English Language Learner: 5 (0.2%); Migrant: n/a
  Eligible for Free Lunch Program: 52 (2.2%)
  Eligible for Reduced-Price Lunch Program: 16 (0.7%)
Teachers: 182.0 (12.9 to 1)
Librarians/Media Specialists: 1.0 (2,341.0 to 1)
Guidance Counselors: 7.4 (316.4 to 1)
Current Spending: ($ per student per year):
  Total: $9,101; Instruction: $6,145; Support Services: $2,695

Enrollment, Drop-out Rates and Diploma Recipients by Race/Ethnicity

Category	Total	White	Black	Asian	AIAN	Hisp.
Enrollment (%)	100.0	98.2	0.5	1.0	0.0	0.3
Drop-out Rate (%)	1.1	1.1	0.0	0.0	n/a	0.0
H.S. Diplomas (#)	148	147	0	1	0	0

MSAD 61 Bridgton
RR 2 Box 554 • Bridgton, ME 04009-9802
(207) 647-3048 • http://www.yorkschools.org/
Grade Span: KG-12; Agency Type: 1
Schools: 7
  3 Primary; 2 Middle; 2 High; 0 Other Level
  6 Regular; 0 Special Education; 1 Vocational; 0 Alternative
  0 Magnet; 0 Charter; 5 Title I Eligible; 0 School-wide Title I
Students: 2,206 (53.1% male; 46.8% female)
  Individual Education Program: 481 (21.8%);
  English Language Learner: 1 (<0.1%); Migrant: n/a
  Eligible for Free Lunch Program: 624 (28.3%)
  Eligible for Reduced-Price Lunch Program: 176 (8.0%)
Teachers: 225.8 (9.8 to 1)
Librarians/Media Specialists: 1.8 (1,226.7 to 1)
Guidance Counselors: 6.4 (345.0 to 1)
Current Spending: ($ per student per year):
  Total: $10,181; Instruction: $6,424; Support Services: $3,484

Enrollment, Drop-out Rates and Diploma Recipients by Race/Ethnicity

Category	Total	White	Black	Asian	AIAN	Hisp.
Enrollment (%)	100.0	98.0	0.8	0.4	0.4	0.5
Drop-out Rate (%)	1.7	1.8	0.0	0.0	0.0	0.0
H.S. Diplomas (#)	128	123	1	2	2	0

Portland Public Schools
331 Veranda St • Portland, ME 04103-5535
(207) 874-8100 • http://www.portlandschools.org/
Grade Span: KG-12; Agency Type: 1
Schools: 17
  10 Primary; 3 Middle; 3 High; 1 Other Level
  16 Regular; 0 Special Education; 1 Vocational; 0 Alternative
  0 Magnet; 0 Charter; 8 Title I Eligible; 2 School-wide Title I
Students: 7,555 (50.6% male; 49.3% female)
  Individual Education Program: 1,135 (15.0%);
  English Language Learner: 1,110 (14.7%); Migrant: n/a
  Eligible for Free Lunch Program: 2,648 (35.1%)
  Eligible for Reduced-Price Lunch Program: 310 (4.1%)
Teachers: 642.4 (11.7 to 1)
Librarians/Media Specialists: 7.9 (953.9 to 1)
Guidance Counselors: 15.6 (483.1 to 1)
Current Spending: ($ per student per year):
  Total: $11,042; Instruction: $7,307; Support Services: $3,455

Enrollment, Drop-out Rates and Diploma Recipients by Race/Ethnicity

Category	Total	White	Black	Asian	AIAN	Hisp.
Enrollment (%)	100.0	77.1	11.6	7.9	0.6	2.9
Drop-out Rate (%)	7.7	7.4	7.2	8.8	13.3	18.6
H.S. Diplomas (#)	288	275	6	3	1	3

Scarborough School Department
PO Box 370 • Scarborough, ME 04070-0370
(207) 883-4315 • http://www.scarborough.k12.me.us/
Grade Span: KG-12; Agency Type: 1
Schools: 6
  4 Primary; 1 Middle; 1 High; 0 Other Level
  6 Regular; 0 Special Education; 0 Vocational; 0 Alternative
  0 Magnet; 0 Charter; 3 Title I Eligible; 0 School-wide Title I
Students: 3,240 (51.1% male; 48.8% female)
  Individual Education Program: 424 (13.1%);
  English Language Learner: 50 (1.5%); Migrant: n/a
  Eligible for Free Lunch Program: 218 (6.7%)
  Eligible for Reduced-Price Lunch Program: 98 (3.0%)
Teachers: 256.6 (12.6 to 1)
Librarians/Media Specialists: 2.9 (1,117.2 to 1)
Guidance Counselors: 6.8 (476.5 to 1)
Current Spending: ($ per student per year):
  Total: $7,632; Instruction: $5,221; Support Services: $2,092

Enrollment, Drop-out Rates and Diploma Recipients by Race/Ethnicity

Category	Total	White	Black	Asian	AIAN	Hisp.
Enrollment (%)	100.0	97.2	0.4	1.3	0.2	1.0
Drop-out Rate (%)	0.0	0.0	0.0	0.0	n/a	0.0
H.S. Diplomas (#)	178	176	0	1	0	1

South Portland School Department
130 Wescott Rd • South Portland, ME 04106-3420
(207) 871-0555 • http://www.spsd.org/
Grade Span: KG-12; **Agency Type:** 1
Schools: 8
   5 Primary; 2 Middle; 1 High; 0 Other Level
   8 Regular; 0 Special Education; 0 Vocational; 0 Alternative
   0 Magnet; 0 Charter; 5 Title I Eligible; 0 School-wide Title I
Students: 3,113   (52.2% male; 47.7% female)
   Individual Education Program: 593 (19.0%);
   English Language Learner: 71 (2.3%); Migrant: n/a
   Eligible for Free Lunch Program: 466 (14.8%)
   Eligible for Reduced-Price Lunch Program: 126 (4.0%)
Teachers: 286.1 (11.0 to 1)
Librarians/Media Specialists: 3.0 (1,047.7 to 1)
Guidance Counselors: 13.6 (231.1 to 1)
Current Spending: ($ per student per year):
   Total: $10,814; Instruction: $7,583; Support Services: $2,968
Enrollment, Drop-out Rates and Diploma Recipients by Race/Ethnicity

Category	Total	White	Black	Asian	AIAN	Hisp.
Enrollment (%)	100.0	93.1	2.2	3.2	0.1	1.4
Drop-out Rate (%)	2.4	2.4	6.7	0.0	0.0	0.0
H.S. Diplomas (#)	228	220	1	3	0	4

Westbrook School Department
117 Stroudwater St • Westbrook, ME 04092-4130
(207) 854-0800 • http://www.westbrookschools.org/
Grade Span: KG-12; **Agency Type:** 1
Schools: 7
   4 Primary; 1 Middle; 2 High; 0 Other Level
   6 Regular; 0 Special Education; 1 Vocational; 0 Alternative
   0 Magnet; 0 Charter; 4 Title I Eligible; 0 School-wide Title I
Students: 2,722   (52.8% male; 47.1% female)
   Individual Education Program: 324 (11.9%);
   English Language Learner: 28 (1.0%); Migrant: n/a
   Eligible for Free Lunch Program: 758 (28.4%)
   Eligible for Reduced-Price Lunch Program: 161 (6.0%)
Teachers: 255.4 (10.5 to 1)
Librarians/Media Specialists: 2.0 (1,336.0 to 1)
Guidance Counselors: 8.0 (334.0 to 1)
Current Spending: ($ per student per year):
   Total: $9,969; Instruction: $6,339; Support Services: $3,285
Enrollment, Drop-out Rates and Diploma Recipients by Race/Ethnicity

Category	Total	White	Black	Asian	AIAN	Hisp.
Enrollment (%)	100.0	94.7	2.8	1.4	0.1	0.9
Drop-out Rate (%)	1.0	1.0	0.0	0.0	0.0	9.1
H.S. Diplomas (#)	153	147	2	3	0	1

Windham School Department
228 Windham Center Rd • Windham, ME 04062-4862
(207) 892-1800 • http://www.windham.k12.me.us/
Grade Span: KG-12; **Agency Type:** 1
Schools: 5
   1 Primary; 2 Middle; 2 High; 0 Other Level
   5 Regular; 0 Special Education; 0 Vocational; 0 Alternative
   0 Magnet; 0 Charter; 2 Title I Eligible; 0 School-wide Title I
Students: 2,829   (52.6% male; 47.3% female)
   Individual Education Program: 299 (10.6%);
   English Language Learner: 18 (0.6%); Migrant: n/a
   Eligible for Free Lunch Program: 307 (10.9%)
   Eligible for Reduced-Price Lunch Program: 106 (3.8%)
Teachers: 205.9 (13.7 to 1)
Librarians/Media Specialists: 1.9 (1,486.8 to 1)
Guidance Counselors: 8.8 (321.0 to 1)
Current Spending: ($ per student per year):
   Total: $7,996; Instruction: $5,385; Support Services: $2,341
Enrollment, Drop-out Rates and Diploma Recipients by Race/Ethnicity

Category	Total	White	Black	Asian	AIAN	Hisp.
Enrollment (%)	100.0	97.3	1.1	0.7	0.4	0.6
Drop-out Rate (%)	1.9	2.0	0.0	0.0	0.0	0.0
H.S. Diplomas (#)	4	1	0	1	2	0

Franklin County

MSAD 09 Farmington
11 School Ln • New Sharon, ME 04955-9739
(207) 778-6571 • http://www.route2.com/msad9.htm
Grade Span: KG-12; **Agency Type:** 1
Schools: 9

   5 Primary; 2 Middle; 2 High; 0 Other Level
   8 Regular; 0 Special Education; 1 Vocational; 0 Alternative
   0 Magnet; 0 Charter; 6 Title I Eligible; 0 School-wide Title I
Students: 2,666   (52.0% male; 47.9% female)
   Individual Education Program: 343 (12.9%);
   English Language Learner: 4 (0.2%); Migrant: n/a
   Eligible for Free Lunch Program: 747 (28.0%)
   Eligible for Reduced-Price Lunch Program: 309 (11.6%)
Teachers: 264.0 (10.1 to 1)
Librarians/Media Specialists: 4.9 (544.3 to 1)
Guidance Counselors: 6.9 (386.5 to 1)
Current Spending: ($ per student per year):
   Total: $8,511; Instruction: $5,303; Support Services: $2,992
Enrollment, Drop-out Rates and Diploma Recipients by Race/Ethnicity

Category	Total	White	Black	Asian	AIAN	Hisp.
Enrollment (%)	100.0	97.5	0.4	0.9	0.2	0.9
Drop-out Rate (%)	5.1	5.1	33.3	0.0	0.0	0.0
H.S. Diplomas (#)	197	193	0	2	1	1

Kennebec County

Augusta Public Schools
40 Pierce Dr Ste 3 • Augusta, ME 04330-9105
(207) 626-2468 • http://www.cony-hs.augusta.k12.me.us/
Grade Span: PK-12; **Agency Type:** 1
Schools: 7
   4 Primary; 1 Middle; 2 High; 0 Other Level
   6 Regular; 0 Special Education; 1 Vocational; 0 Alternative
   0 Magnet; 0 Charter; 4 Title I Eligible; 0 School-wide Title I
Students: 2,611   (51.8% male; 48.1% female)
   Individual Education Program: 569 (21.8%);
   English Language Learner: 74 (2.8%); Migrant: n/a
   Eligible for Free Lunch Program: 671 (25.7%)
   Eligible for Reduced-Price Lunch Program: 200 (7.7%)
Teachers: 244.7 (10.7 to 1)
Librarians/Media Specialists: 2.0 (1,306.5 to 1)
Guidance Counselors: 10.0 (261.3 to 1)
Current Spending: ($ per student per year):
   Total: $10,403; Instruction: $6,663; Support Services: $3,384
Enrollment, Drop-out Rates and Diploma Recipients by Race/Ethnicity

Category	Total	White	Black	Asian	AIAN	Hisp.
Enrollment (%)	100.0	95.9	0.9	2.5	0.2	0.5
Drop-out Rate (%)	1.0	1.1	0.0	0.0	0.0	0.0
H.S. Diplomas (#)	183	173	2	3	1	4

MSAD 11 Gardiner
150 Highland Ave • Gardiner, ME 04345-1812
(207) 582-5346 • http://www.sad11.k12.me.us/
Grade Span: KG-12; **Agency Type:** 1
Schools: 8
   6 Primary; 1 Middle; 1 High; 0 Other Level
   8 Regular; 0 Special Education; 0 Vocational; 0 Alternative
   0 Magnet; 0 Charter; 8 Title I Eligible; 0 School-wide Title I
Students: 2,382   (53.5% male; 46.4% female)
   Individual Education Program: 373 (15.7%);
   English Language Learner: 1 (<0.1%); Migrant: n/a
   Eligible for Free Lunch Program: 546 (22.9%)
   Eligible for Reduced-Price Lunch Program: 173 (7.3%)
Teachers: 181.3 (13.1 to 1)
Librarians/Media Specialists: 1.9 (1,253.2 to 1)
Guidance Counselors: 7.8 (305.3 to 1)
Current Spending: ($ per student per year):
   Total: $7,916; Instruction: $4,906; Support Services: $2,698
Enrollment, Drop-out Rates and Diploma Recipients by Race/Ethnicity

Category	Total	White	Black	Asian	AIAN	Hisp.
Enrollment (%)	100.0	96.6	0.8	0.8	1.1	0.6
Drop-out Rate (%)	4.0	4.0	0.0	0.0	0.0	0.0
H.S. Diplomas (#)	169	159	1	2	4	3

MSAD 47 Oakland
47 Heath St • Oakland, ME 04963-1102
(207) 465-7384 • http://www.sad47.me.us/
Grade Span: KG-12; **Agency Type:** 1
Schools: 6
   4 Primary; 1 Middle; 1 High; 0 Other Level
   6 Regular; 0 Special Education; 0 Vocational; 0 Alternative
   0 Magnet; 0 Charter; 3 Title I Eligible; 0 School-wide Title I
Students: 2,687   (50.7% male; 49.2% female)
   Individual Education Program: 336 (12.5%);
   English Language Learner: 3 (0.1%); Migrant: n/a
   Eligible for Free Lunch Program: 369 (13.7%)
   Eligible for Reduced-Price Lunch Program: 137 (5.1%)
Teachers: 215.0 (12.5 to 1)
Librarians/Media Specialists: 3.0 (898.3 to 1)
Guidance Counselors: 8.9 (302.8 to 1)

Current Spending: ($ per student per year):
    Total: $8,003; Instruction: $5,246; Support Services: $2,513
Enrollment, Drop-out Rates and Diploma Recipients by Race/Ethnicity

Category	Total	White	Black	Asian	AIAN	Hisp.
Enrollment (%)	100.0	98.4	0.4	0.7	0.2	0.3
Drop-out Rate (%)	1.5	1.5	0.0	0.0	0.0	0.0
H.S. Diplomas (#)	197	194	0	3	0	0

Waterville Public Schools
21 Gilman St • Waterville, ME 04901-5437
(207) 873-4281 • http://web.wtvl.k12.me.us/
Grade Span: KG-12; **Agency Type:** 1
Schools: 5
    1 Primary; 2 Middle; 2 High; 0 Other Level
    4 Regular; 0 Special Education; 1 Vocational; 0 Alternative
    0 Magnet; 0 Charter; 4 Title I Eligible; 2 School-wide Title I
Students: 1,934   (50.6% male; 49.3% female)
    Individual Education Program: 406 (21.0%);
    English Language Learner: 19 (1.0%); Migrant: n/a
    Eligible for Free Lunch Program: 741 (38.3%)
    Eligible for Reduced-Price Lunch Program: 145 (7.5%)
Teachers: 173.0 (11.2 to 1)
Librarians/Media Specialists: 1.5 (1,289.3 to 1)
Guidance Counselors: 8.9 (217.3 to 1)
Current Spending: ($ per student per year):
    Total: $9,580; Instruction: $6,198; Support Services: $3,090
Enrollment, Drop-out Rates and Diploma Recipients by Race/Ethnicity

Category	Total	White	Black	Asian	AIAN	Hisp.
Enrollment (%)	100.0	95.0	2.1	1.1	0.2	1.5
Drop-out Rate (%)	3.6	3.8	0.0	0.0	n/a	0.0
H.S. Diplomas (#)	141	136	1	2	0	2

MSAD 05 Rockland
28 Lincoln St • Rockland, ME 04841-2881
(207) 596-6620 • http://www.msad5.org/
Grade Span: KG-12; **Agency Type:** 1
Schools: 6
    4 Primary; 1 Middle; 1 High; 0 Other Level
    6 Regular; 0 Special Education; 0 Vocational; 0 Alternative
    0 Magnet; 0 Charter; 3 Title I Eligible; 0 School-wide Title I
Students: 1,507   (48.3% male; 51.6% female)
    Individual Education Program: 205 (13.6%);
    English Language Learner: 8 (0.5%); Migrant: n/a
    Eligible for Free Lunch Program: 412 (27.5%)
    Eligible for Reduced-Price Lunch Program: 132 (8.8%)
Teachers: 126.8 (11.8 to 1)
Librarians/Media Specialists: 1.9 (787.9 to 1)
Guidance Counselors: 5.8 (258.1 to 1)
Current Spending: ($ per student per year):
    Total: $9,480; Instruction: $6,000; Support Services: $3,192
Enrollment, Drop-out Rates and Diploma Recipients by Race/Ethnicity

Category	Total	White	Black	Asian	AIAN	Hisp.
Enrollment (%)	100.0	98.1	0.6	1.1	0.0	0.3
Drop-out Rate (%)	0.0	0.0	0.0	0.0	n/a	n/a
H.S. Diplomas (#)	103	99	1	3	0	0

MSAD 40 Waldoboro
44 School St • Warren, ME 04864-0913
(207) 273-4070
Grade Span: KG-12; **Agency Type:** 1
Schools: 7
    5 Primary; 1 Middle; 1 High; 0 Other Level
    7 Regular; 0 Special Education; 0 Vocational; 0 Alternative
    0 Magnet; 0 Charter; 5 Title I Eligible; 0 School-wide Title I
Students: 2,095   (50.0% male; 49.9% female)
    Individual Education Program: 367 (17.5%);
    English Language Learner: 0 (0.0%); Migrant: n/a
    Eligible for Free Lunch Program: 606 (28.9%)
    Eligible for Reduced-Price Lunch Program: 232 (11.1%)
Teachers: 196.9 (10.6 to 1)
Librarians/Media Specialists: 6.0 (349.2 to 1)
Guidance Counselors: 8.4 (249.4 to 1)
Current Spending: ($ per student per year):
    Total: $9,128; Instruction: $6,740; Support Services: $2,190
Enrollment, Drop-out Rates and Diploma Recipients by Race/Ethnicity

Category	Total	White	Black	Asian	AIAN	Hisp.
Enrollment (%)	100.0	98.9	0.5	0.1	0.0	0.4
Drop-out Rate (%)	2.1	2.1	0.0	0.0	0.0	0.0
H.S. Diplomas (#)	158	157	0	1	0	0

MSAD 17 Oxford
1570 Main St Ste 11 • Oxford, ME 04270-3390
(207) 743-8972
Grade Span: KG-12; **Agency Type:** 1
Schools: 12
    9 Primary; 2 Middle; 1 High; 0 Other Level
    12 Regular; 0 Special Education; 0 Vocational; 0 Alternative
    0 Magnet; 0 Charter; 10 Title I Eligible; 0 School-wide Title I
Students: 3,735   (51.3% male; 48.6% female)
    Individual Education Program: 414 (11.1%);
    English Language Learner: 5 (0.1%); Migrant: n/a
    Eligible for Free Lunch Program: 1,004 (26.7%)
    Eligible for Reduced-Price Lunch Program: 350 (9.3%)
Teachers: 304.1 (12.4 to 1)
Librarians/Media Specialists: 2.9 (1,295.9 to 1)
Guidance Counselors: 14.3 (262.8 to 1)
Current Spending: ($ per student per year):
    Total: $7,784; Instruction: $4,955; Support Services: $2,555
Enrollment, Drop-out Rates and Diploma Recipients by Race/Ethnicity

Category	Total	White	Black	Asian	AIAN	Hisp.
Enrollment (%)	100.0	97.3	0.9	1.1	0.2	0.6
Drop-out Rate (%)	4.4	4.5	0.0	0.0	n/a	0.0
H.S. Diplomas (#)	245	238	3	4	0	0

MSAD 43 Mexico
3 Recreation Dr • Mexico, ME 04257-1531
(207) 364-7896 • http://valnet.mtvalleyhs.sad43.k12.me.us/
Grade Span: PK-12; **Agency Type:** 1
Schools: 5
    3 Primary; 1 Middle; 1 High; 0 Other Level
    5 Regular; 0 Special Education; 0 Vocational; 0 Alternative
    0 Magnet; 0 Charter; 4 Title I Eligible; 2 School-wide Title I
Students: 1,598   (53.7% male; 46.2% female)
    Individual Education Program: 325 (20.3%);
    English Language Learner: 0 (0.0%); Migrant: n/a
    Eligible for Free Lunch Program: 666 (41.3%)
    Eligible for Reduced-Price Lunch Program: 177 (11.0%)
Teachers: 149.4 (10.8 to 1)
Librarians/Media Specialists: 3.9 (413.3 to 1)
Guidance Counselors: 6.9 (233.6 to 1)
Current Spending: ($ per student per year):
    Total: $9,061; Instruction: $5,735; Support Services: $2,998
Enrollment, Drop-out Rates and Diploma Recipients by Race/Ethnicity

Category	Total	White	Black	Asian	AIAN	Hisp.
Enrollment (%)	100.0	98.2	0.5	0.8	0.2	0.3
Drop-out Rate (%)	2.6	2.7	0.0	0.0	0.0	0.0
H.S. Diplomas (#)	108	106	1	0	0	1

Bangor School Department
73 Harlow St • Bangor, ME 04401-5118
(207) 945-4400 • http://www.bangorschools.net/
Grade Span: KG-12; **Agency Type:** 1
Schools: 10
    5 Primary; 4 Middle; 1 High; 0 Other Level
    10 Regular; 0 Special Education; 0 Vocational; 0 Alternative
    0 Magnet; 0 Charter; 5 Title I Eligible; 0 School-wide Title I
Students: 4,104   (51.6% male; 48.3% female)
    Individual Education Program: 556 (13.5%);
    English Language Learner: 47 (1.1%); Migrant: n/a
    Eligible for Free Lunch Program: 1,074 (26.2%)
    Eligible for Reduced-Price Lunch Program: 189 (4.6%)
Teachers: 349.4 (11.7 to 1)
Librarians/Media Specialists: 2.5 (1,641.6 to 1)
Guidance Counselors: 12.9 (318.1 to 1)
Current Spending: ($ per student per year):
    Total: $8,609; Instruction: $6,051; Support Services: $2,306
Enrollment, Drop-out Rates and Diploma Recipients by Race/Ethnicity

Category	Total	White	Black	Asian	AIAN	Hisp.
Enrollment (%)	100.0	93.6	2.3	2.0	0.8	1.3
Drop-out Rate (%)	2.1	2.1	0.0	0.0	0.0	0.0
H.S. Diplomas (#)	298	289	3	4	1	1

Brewer School Department
49 Capri St • Brewer, ME 04412-1362
(207) 989-3160
Grade Span: KG-12; **Agency Type:** 1
Schools: 6
    3 Primary; 2 Middle; 1 High; 0 Other Level
    6 Regular; 0 Special Education; 0 Vocational; 0 Alternative
    0 Magnet; 0 Charter; 6 Title I Eligible; 0 School-wide Title I
Students: 1,790   (54.5% male; 45.4% female)

Individual Education Program: 229 (12.8%);
English Language Learner: 4 (0.2%); Migrant: n/a
Eligible for Free Lunch Program: 338 (18.7%)
Eligible for Reduced-Price Lunch Program: 67 (3.7%)
Teachers: 141.7 (12.8 to 1)
Librarians/Media Specialists: 1.7 (1,064.7 to 1)
Guidance Counselors: 8.0 (226.3 to 1)
Current Spending: ($ per student per year):
Total: $8,162; Instruction: $5,906; Support Services: $1,972
Enrollment, Drop-out Rates and Diploma Recipients by Race/Ethnicity

Category	Total	White	Black	Asian	AIAN	Hisp.
Enrollment (%)	100.0	97.0	1.2	0.7	0.8	0.4
Drop-out Rate (%)	4.4	4.4	0.0	n/a	n/a	0.0
H.S. Diplomas (#)	178	172	0	2	4	0

MSAD 22 Hampden
24 Main Rd N • Hampden, ME 04444-0279
(207) 862-3255 • http://www.sad22.us/
Grade Span: KG-12; **Agency Type:** 1
Schools: 7
4 Primary; 2 Middle; 1 High; 0 Other Level
7 Regular; 0 Special Education; 0 Vocational; 0 Alternative
0 Magnet; 0 Charter; 3 Title I Eligible; 0 School-wide Title I
Students: 2,301 (53.4% male; 46.5% female)
Individual Education Program: 361 (15.7%);
English Language Learner: 6 (0.3%); Migrant: n/a
Eligible for Free Lunch Program: 323 (14.1%)
Eligible for Reduced-Price Lunch Program: 103 (4.5%)
Teachers: 193.3 (11.9 to 1)
Librarians/Media Specialists: 3.0 (765.7 to 1)
Guidance Counselors: 8.2 (280.1 to 1)
Current Spending: ($ per student per year):
Total: $8,494; Instruction: $5,740; Support Services: $2,483
Enrollment, Drop-out Rates and Diploma Recipients by Race/Ethnicity

Category	Total	White	Black	Asian	AIAN	Hisp.
Enrollment (%)	100.0	97.2	1.0	1.0	0.3	0.6
Drop-out Rate (%)	2.2	2.2	0.0	0.0	n/a	0.0
H.S. Diplomas (#)	174	169	0	0	4	1

MSAD 48 Newport
PO Box 40 • Newport, ME 04953-0040
(207) 368-5091 • http://www.msad48.org/mainfrm.cfm
Grade Span: PK-12; **Agency Type:** 1
Schools: 8
5 Primary; 2 Middle; 1 High; 0 Other Level
8 Regular; 0 Special Education; 0 Vocational; 0 Alternative
0 Magnet; 0 Charter; 5 Title I Eligible; 0 School-wide Title I
Students: 2,139 (51.2% male; 48.7% female)
Individual Education Program: 393 (18.4%);
English Language Learner: 0 (0.0%); Migrant: n/a
Eligible for Free Lunch Program: 745 (34.8%)
Eligible for Reduced-Price Lunch Program: 287 (13.4%)
Teachers: 177.8 (12.1 to 1)
Librarians/Media Specialists: 2.0 (1,071.5 to 1)
Guidance Counselors: 7.0 (306.1 to 1)
Current Spending: ($ per student per year):
Total: $7,959; Instruction: $4,914; Support Services: $2,741
Enrollment, Drop-out Rates and Diploma Recipients by Race/Ethnicity

Category	Total	White	Black	Asian	AIAN	Hisp.
Enrollment (%)	100.0	98.0	0.9	0.4	0.4	0.2
Drop-out Rate (%)	0.5	0.5	0.0	0.0	0.0	0.0
H.S. Diplomas (#)	154	153	0	1	0	0

Old Town School Department
156 Oak St • Old Town, ME 04468-1623
(207) 827-7171
Grade Span: KG-12; **Agency Type:** 1
Schools: 4
1 Primary; 1 Middle; 1 High; 1 Other Level
3 Regular; 1 Special Education; 0 Vocational; 0 Alternative
0 Magnet; 0 Charter; 1 Title I Eligible; 0 School-wide Title I
Students: 1,569 (49.9% male; 50.0% female)
Individual Education Program: 214 (13.6%);
English Language Learner: 7 (0.4%); Migrant: n/a
Eligible for Free Lunch Program: 184 (11.7%)
Eligible for Reduced-Price Lunch Program: 62 (4.0%)
Teachers: 132.2 (11.9 to 1)
Librarians/Media Specialists: 2.9 (541.0 to 1)
Guidance Counselors: 3.8 (412.9 to 1)
Current Spending: ($ per student per year):
Total: $7,824; Instruction: $5,159; Support Services: $2,399

Enrollment, Drop-out Rates and Diploma Recipients by Race/Ethnicity

Category	Total	White	Black	Asian	AIAN	Hisp.
Enrollment (%)	100.0	94.1	1.7	1.4	2.3	0.5
Drop-out Rate (%)	3.4	3.4	0.0	0.0	5.0	0.0
H.S. Diplomas (#)	157	144	0	1	11	1

Sagadahoc County

Bath School Department
39 Andrews Rd • Bath, ME 04530-2125
(207) 443-6601
Grade Span: KG-12; **Agency Type:** 1
Schools: 6
3 Primary; 1 Middle; 2 High; 0 Other Level
5 Regular; 0 Special Education; 1 Vocational; 0 Alternative
0 Magnet; 0 Charter; 4 Title I Eligible; 0 School-wide Title I
Students: 1,813 (50.1% male; 49.8% female)
Individual Education Program: 235 (13.0%);
English Language Learner: 9 (0.5%); Migrant: n/a
Eligible for Free Lunch Program: 484 (26.6%)
Eligible for Reduced-Price Lunch Program: 164 (9.0%)
Teachers: 175.3 (10.4 to 1)
Librarians/Media Specialists: 2.0 (909.5 to 1)
Guidance Counselors: 4.0 (454.8 to 1)
Current Spending: ($ per student per year):
Total: $9,326; Instruction: $6,119; Support Services: $2,963
Enrollment, Drop-out Rates and Diploma Recipients by Race/Ethnicity

Category	Total	White	Black	Asian	AIAN	Hisp.
Enrollment (%)	100.0	93.9	3.6	0.9	0.1	1.4
Drop-out Rate (%)	4.5	4.6	0.0	n/a	n/a	n/a
H.S. Diplomas (#)	154	153	1	0	0	0

MSAD 75 Topsham
50 Republic Ave • Topsham, ME 04086-0475
(207) 729-9961
Grade Span: KG-12; **Agency Type:** 1
Schools: 8
6 Primary; 1 Middle; 1 High; 0 Other Level
8 Regular; 0 Special Education; 0 Vocational; 0 Alternative
0 Magnet; 0 Charter; 5 Title I Eligible; 0 School-wide Title I
Students: 3,333 (52.6% male; 47.3% female)
Individual Education Program: 682 (20.5%);
English Language Learner: 39 (1.2%); Migrant: n/a
Eligible for Free Lunch Program: 465 (13.7%)
Eligible for Reduced-Price Lunch Program: 169 (5.0%)
Teachers: 292.9 (11.6 to 1)
Librarians/Media Specialists: 6.1 (554.6 to 1)
Guidance Counselors: 9.9 (341.7 to 1)
Current Spending: ($ per student per year):
Total: $9,156; Instruction: $5,938; Support Services: $2,923
Enrollment, Drop-out Rates and Diploma Recipients by Race/Ethnicity

Category	Total	White	Black	Asian	AIAN	Hisp.
Enrollment (%)	100.0	95.8	1.6	0.9	0.6	1.1
Drop-out Rate (%)	1.9	1.8	18.2	0.0	0.0	0.0
H.S. Diplomas (#)	252	231	3	7	1	10

Somerset County

MSAD 49 Fairfield
8 School St • Fairfield, ME 04937-1370
(207) 453-4200 • http://www.lhs.sad49.k12.me.us/
Grade Span: PK-12; **Agency Type:** 1
Schools: 6
4 Primary; 1 Middle; 1 High; 0 Other Level
6 Regular; 0 Special Education; 0 Vocational; 0 Alternative
0 Magnet; 0 Charter; 6 Title I Eligible; 0 School-wide Title I
Students: 2,699 (50.8% male; 49.1% female)
Individual Education Program: 497 (18.4%);
English Language Learner: 0 (0.0%); Migrant: n/a
Eligible for Free Lunch Program: 816 (30.3%)
Eligible for Reduced-Price Lunch Program: 297 (11.0%)
Teachers: 223.5 (12.1 to 1)
Librarians/Media Specialists: 3.0 (899.0 to 1)
Guidance Counselors: 8.1 (333.0 to 1)
Current Spending: ($ per student per year):
Total: $8,151; Instruction: $5,544; Support Services: $2,562
Enrollment, Drop-out Rates and Diploma Recipients by Race/Ethnicity

Category	Total	White	Black	Asian	AIAN	Hisp.
Enrollment (%)	100.0	97.8	1.3	0.5	0.0	0.3
Drop-out Rate (%)	1.2	1.2	0.0	0.0	n/a	0.0
H.S. Diplomas (#)	174	173	1	0	0	0

MSAD 54 Skowhegan

196 W Front St • Skowhegan, ME 04976-9739
(207) 474-9508 • http://www.msad54.k12.me.us/
Grade Span: KG-12; **Agency Type:** 1
Schools: 11
  6 Primary; 3 Middle; 2 High; 0 Other Level
  10 Regular; 0 Special Education; 1 Vocational; 0 Alternative
  0 Magnet; 0 Charter; 8 Title I Eligible; 3 School-wide Title I
Students: 2,947 (51.5% male; 48.4% female)
  Individual Education Program: 522 (17.7%)
  English Language Learner: 10 (0.3%); Migrant: n/a
  Eligible for Free Lunch Program: 940 (31.9%)
  Eligible for Reduced-Price Lunch Program: 275 (9.3%)
Teachers: 263.9 (11.2 to 1)
Librarians/Media Specialists: 2.0 (1,473.5 to 1)
Guidance Counselors: 6.7 (439.9 to 1)
Current Spending: ($ per student per year):
  Total: $9,225; Instruction: $6,448; Support Services: $2,537
Enrollment, Drop-out Rates and Diploma Recipients by Race/Ethnicity

Category	Total	White	Black	Asian	AIAN	Hisp.
Enrollment (%)	100.0	97.4	0.8	1.1	0.1	0.5
Drop-out Rate (%)	1.1	1.2	0.0	0.0	0.0	0.0
H.S. Diplomas (#)	213	206	2	5	0	0

Waldo County

MSAD 03 Unity

74 School St • Unity, ME 04988-9734
(207) 948-6136
Grade Span: KG-12; **Agency Type:** 1
Schools: 8
  6 Primary; 1 Middle; 1 High; 0 Other Level
  8 Regular; 0 Special Education; 0 Vocational; 0 Alternative
  0 Magnet; 0 Charter; 7 Title I Eligible; 0 School-wide Title I
Students: 1,624 (52.2% male; 47.7% female)
  Individual Education Program: 292 (18.0%)
  English Language Learner: 0 (0.0%); Migrant: n/a
  Eligible for Free Lunch Program: 675 (41.6%)
  Eligible for Reduced-Price Lunch Program: 216 (13.3%)
Teachers: 150.1 (10.8 to 1)
Librarians/Media Specialists: 1.0 (1,624.0 to 1)
Guidance Counselors: 8.4 (193.3 to 1)
Current Spending: ($ per student per year):
  Total: $9,020; Instruction: $5,743; Support Services: $2,891
Enrollment, Drop-out Rates and Diploma Recipients by Race/Ethnicity

Category	Total	White	Black	Asian	AIAN	Hisp.
Enrollment (%)	100.0	98.4	0.5	0.2	0.1	0.7
Drop-out Rate (%)	3.9	4.0	0.0	0.0	n/a	0.0
H.S. Diplomas (#)	115	115	0	0	0	0

MSAD 34 Belfast

PO Box 363 • Belfast, ME 04915-0363
(207) 338-1960 • http://www.sad34.net/
Grade Span: PK-12; **Agency Type:** 1
Schools: 10
  8 Primary; 1 Middle; 1 High; 0 Other Level
  10 Regular; 0 Special Education; 0 Vocational; 0 Alternative
  0 Magnet; 0 Charter; 6 Title I Eligible; 0 School-wide Title I
Students: 2,008 (51.4% male; 48.5% female)
  Individual Education Program: 435 (21.7%)
  English Language Learner: 3 (0.1%); Migrant: n/a
  Eligible for Free Lunch Program: 646 (32.2%)
  Eligible for Reduced-Price Lunch Program: 157 (7.8%)
Teachers: 201.2 (10.0 to 1)
Librarians/Media Specialists: 2.0 (1,003.5 to 1)
Guidance Counselors: 9.1 (220.5 to 1)
Current Spending: ($ per student per year):
  Total: $9,868; Instruction: $6,861; Support Services: $2,647
Enrollment, Drop-out Rates and Diploma Recipients by Race/Ethnicity

Category	Total	White	Black	Asian	AIAN	Hisp.
Enrollment (%)	100.0	98.6	0.6	0.2	0.0	0.4
Drop-out Rate (%)	0.0	0.0	0.0	0.0	n/a	0.0
H.S. Diplomas (#)	136	135	0	1	0	0

York County

Biddeford School Department

205 Main St PO Box 1865 • Biddeford, ME 04005-1865
(207) 282-8280 • http://www.biddschools.org/
Grade Span: PK-12; **Agency Type:** 1
Schools: 5
  2 Primary; 1 Middle; 2 High; 0 Other Level
  4 Regular; 0 Special Education; 1 Vocational; 0 Alternative
  0 Magnet; 0 Charter; 3 Title I Eligible; 0 School-wide Title I
Students: 2,958 (51.1% male; 48.8% female)

  Individual Education Program: 466 (15.8%);
  English Language Learner: 27 (0.9%); Migrant: n/a
  Eligible for Free Lunch Program: 883 (29.7%)
  Eligible for Reduced-Price Lunch Program: 167 (5.6%)
Teachers: 231.1 (12.9 to 1)
Librarians/Media Specialists: 3.8 (783.7 to 1)
Guidance Counselors: 7.8 (381.8 to 1)
Current Spending: ($ per student per year):
  Total: $8,226; Instruction: $5,915; Support Services: $2,051
Enrollment, Drop-out Rates and Diploma Recipients by Race/Ethnicity

Category	Total	White	Black	Asian	AIAN	Hisp.
Enrollment (%)	100.0	96.1	1.9	1.2	0.3	0.5
Drop-out Rate (%)	1.0	1.0	0.0	0.0	n/a	0.0
H.S. Diplomas (#)	163	157	0	5	0	1

MSAD 06 Buxton

100 Main St PO Box 38 • Bar Mills, ME 04004-0038
(207) 929-3831 • http://www.sad6.k12.me.us/
Grade Span: KG-12; **Agency Type:** 1
Schools: 11
  7 Primary; 3 Middle; 1 High; 0 Other Level
  11 Regular; 0 Special Education; 0 Vocational; 0 Alternative
  0 Magnet; 0 Charter; 9 Title I Eligible; 1 School-wide Title I
Students: 3,990 (53.4% male; 46.5% female)
  Individual Education Program: 642 (16.1%)
  English Language Learner: 3 (0.1%); Migrant: n/a
  Eligible for Free Lunch Program: 759 (19.0%)
  Eligible for Reduced-Price Lunch Program: 407 (10.2%)
Teachers: 331.8 (12.0 to 1)
Librarians/Media Specialists: 6.8 (587.2 to 1)
Guidance Counselors: 11.9 (335.5 to 1)
Current Spending: ($ per student per year):
  Total: $8,276; Instruction: $5,386; Support Services: $2,530
Enrollment, Drop-out Rates and Diploma Recipients by Race/Ethnicity

Category	Total	White	Black	Asian	AIAN	Hisp.
Enrollment (%)	100.0	97.8	0.9	0.7	0.2	0.4
Drop-out Rate (%)	3.3	3.3	0.0	0.0	n/a	0.0
H.S. Diplomas (#)	282	281	1	0	0	0

MSAD 35 So. Berwick

64 Depot Rd • Eliot, ME 03903
(207) 439-2438 • http://web.mhs.sad35.k12.me.us/msad35/current.htm
Grade Span: PK-12; **Agency Type:** 1
Schools: 5
  2 Primary; 2 Middle; 1 High; 0 Other Level
  5 Regular; 0 Special Education; 0 Vocational; 0 Alternative
  0 Magnet; 0 Charter; 4 Title I Eligible; 0 School-wide Title I
Students: 2,734 (50.9% male; 49.0% female)
  Individual Education Program: 351 (12.8%)
  English Language Learner: 8 (0.3%); Migrant: n/a
  Eligible for Free Lunch Program: 170 (6.2%)
  Eligible for Reduced-Price Lunch Program: 65 (2.4%)
Teachers: 184.8 (14.8 to 1)
Librarians/Media Specialists: 1.0 (2,738.0 to 1)
Guidance Counselors: 8.4 (326.0 to 1)
Current Spending: ($ per student per year):
  Total: $6,939; Instruction: $4,611; Support Services: $2,153
Enrollment, Drop-out Rates and Diploma Recipients by Race/Ethnicity

Category	Total	White	Black	Asian	AIAN	Hisp.
Enrollment (%)	100.0	98.8	0.7	0.3	0.1	0.2
Drop-out Rate (%)	2.2	2.2	0.0	0.0	0.0	0.0
H.S. Diplomas (#)	204	202	1	0	1	0

MSAD 57 Waterboro

PO Box 499 • Waterboro, ME 04087-0499
(207) 247-3221 • http://www.sad57.k12.me.us/
Grade Span: KG-12; **Agency Type:** 1
Schools: 7
  5 Primary; 1 Middle; 1 High; 0 Other Level
  7 Regular; 0 Special Education; 0 Vocational; 0 Alternative
  0 Magnet; 0 Charter; 5 Title I Eligible; 0 School-wide Title I
Students: 3,732 (52.0% male; 47.9% female)
  Individual Education Program: 570 (15.3%);
  English Language Learner: 11 (0.3%); Migrant: n/a
  Eligible for Free Lunch Program: 608 (16.3%)
  Eligible for Reduced-Price Lunch Program: 317 (8.5%)
Teachers: 280.8 (13.3 to 1)
Librarians/Media Specialists: 3.0 (1,240.3 to 1)
Guidance Counselors: 10.7 (347.8 to 1)
Current Spending: ($ per student per year):
  Total: $6,914; Instruction: $4,413; Support Services: $2,210

Enrollment, Drop-out Rates and Diploma Recipients by Race/Ethnicity

Category	Total	White	Black	Asian	AIAN	Hisp.
Enrollment (%)	100.0	97.7	0.6	0.8	0.4	0.5
Drop-out Rate (%)	1.9	1.9	0.0	0.0	0.0	0.0
H.S. Diplomas (#)	206	199	2	2	2	1

MSAD 60 North Berwick
PO Box 819 • North Berwick, ME 03906-0819
(207) 676-2234 • http://www.sad60.k12.me.us/
Grade Span: KG-12; **Agency Type:** 1
Schools: 7
   3 Primary; 3 Middle; 1 High; 0 Other Level
   7 Regular; 0 Special Education; 0 Vocational; 0 Alternative
   0 Magnet; 0 Charter; 4 Title I Eligible; 0 School-wide Title I
Students: 3,268   (50.4% male; 49.5% female)
   Individual Education Program: 645 (19.7%);
   English Language Learner: 32 (1.0%); Migrant: n/a
   Eligible for Free Lunch Program: 487 (15.2%)
   Eligible for Reduced-Price Lunch Program: 401 (12.5%)
Teachers: 272.6 (11.7 to 1)
Librarians/Media Specialists: 3.0 (1,067.0 to 1)
Guidance Counselors: 13.0 (246.2 to 1)
Current Spending: ($ per student per year):
   Total: $8,881; Instruction: $5,803; Support Services: $2,726
Enrollment, Drop-out Rates and Diploma Recipients by Race/Ethnicity

Category	Total	White	Black	Asian	AIAN	Hisp.
Enrollment (%)	100.0	98.0	0.7	1.0	0.0	0.3
Drop-out Rate (%)	5.2	5.2	0.0	20.0	n/a	0.0
H.S. Diplomas (#)	191	188	1	2	0	0

MSAD 71 Kennebunk
1 Storer St • Kennebunk, ME 04043-6830
(207) 985-1100 • http://www.msad71.net/
Grade Span: PK-12; **Agency Type:** 1
Schools: 6
   3 Primary; 2 Middle; 1 High; 0 Other Level
   6 Regular; 0 Special Education; 0 Vocational; 0 Alternative
   0 Magnet; 0 Charter; 2 Title I Eligible; 0 School-wide Title I
Students: 2,527   (50.6% male; 49.3% female)
   Individual Education Program: 406 (16.1%);
   English Language Learner: 36 (1.4%); Migrant: n/a
   Eligible for Free Lunch Program: 136 (5.4%)
   Eligible for Reduced-Price Lunch Program: 79 (3.1%)
Teachers: 202.3 (12.5 to 1)
Librarians/Media Specialists: 3.0 (842.3 to 1)
Guidance Counselors: 10.1 (250.2 to 1)
Current Spending: ($ per student per year):
   Total: $10,101; Instruction: $6,733; Support Services: $3,128
Enrollment, Drop-out Rates and Diploma Recipients by Race/Ethnicity

Category	Total	White	Black	Asian	AIAN	Hisp.
Enrollment (%)	100.0	97.9	0.6	1.2	0.0	0.3
Drop-out Rate (%)	1.1	1.1	0.0	0.0	0.0	0.0
H.S. Diplomas (#)	162	162	0	0	0	0

Saco School Department
90 Beach St • Saco, ME 04072-1878
(207) 284-4505 • http://www.saco.org/admin/index.html
Grade Span: KG-08; **Agency Type:** 2
Schools: 5
   3 Primary; 1 Middle; 0 High; 1 Other Level
   4 Regular; 1 Special Education; 0 Vocational; 0 Alternative
   0 Magnet; 0 Charter; 2 Title I Eligible; 0 School-wide Title I
Students: 1,955   (51.5% male; 48.4% female)
   Individual Education Program: 470 (24.0%);
   English Language Learner: 8 (0.4%); Migrant: n/a
   Eligible for Free Lunch Program: 357 (18.3%)
   Eligible for Reduced-Price Lunch Program: 88 (4.5%)
Teachers: 137.4 (14.2 to 1)
Librarians/Media Specialists: 0.0 (n/a to 1)
Guidance Counselors: 6.2 (315.3 to 1)
Current Spending: ($ per student per year):
   Total: $11,170; Instruction: $8,990; Support Services: $2,019
Enrollment, Drop-out Rates and Diploma Recipients by Race/Ethnicity

Category	Total	White	Black	Asian	AIAN	Hisp.
Enrollment (%)	100.0	95.0	1.9	1.5	0.5	1.0
Drop-out Rate (%)	n/a	n/a	n/a	n/a	n/a	n/a
H.S. Diplomas (#)	n/a	n/a	n/a	n/a	n/a	n/a

Sanford School Department
917 Main St Ste 200 • Sanford, ME 04073-3545
(207) 324-2810 • http://www.sanford.org/
Grade Span: KG-12; **Agency Type:** 1
Schools: 8
   4 Primary; 2 Middle; 2 High; 0 Other Level
   7 Regular; 0 Special Education; 1 Vocational; 0 Alternative

   0 Magnet; 0 Charter; 4 Title I Eligible; 0 School-wide Title I
Students: 3,732   (51.8% male; 48.1% female)
   Individual Education Program: 676 (18.1%);
   English Language Learner: 97 (2.6%); Migrant: n/a
   Eligible for Free Lunch Program: 1,175 (31.6%)
   Eligible for Reduced-Price Lunch Program: 277 (7.5%)
Teachers: 297.2 (12.5 to 1)
Librarians/Media Specialists: 4.9 (758.8 to 1)
Guidance Counselors: 12.9 (288.2 to 1)
Current Spending: ($ per student per year):
   Total: $7,786; Instruction: $5,218; Support Services: $2,277
Enrollment, Drop-out Rates and Diploma Recipients by Race/Ethnicity

Category	Total	White	Black	Asian	AIAN	Hisp.
Enrollment (%)	100.0	95.2	1.5	2.5	0.1	0.8
Drop-out Rate (%)	2.2	2.3	0.0	0.0	n/a	n/a
H.S. Diplomas (#)	219	212	0	6	0	1

Wells-Ogunquit CSD
PO Box 578 • Wells, ME 04090-0578
(207) 646-8331 • http://wocsd.maine.org/
Grade Span: KG-12; **Agency Type:** 1
Schools: 4
   2 Primary; 1 Middle; 1 High; 0 Other Level
   4 Regular; 0 Special Education; 0 Vocational; 0 Alternative
   0 Magnet; 0 Charter; 2 Title I Eligible; 0 School-wide Title I
Students: 1,542   (51.2% male; 48.7% female)
   Individual Education Program: 220 (14.3%);
   English Language Learner: 15 (1.0%); Migrant: n/a
   Eligible for Free Lunch Program: 122 (7.9%)
   Eligible for Reduced-Price Lunch Program: 14 (0.9%)
Teachers: 141.5 (10.9 to 1)
Librarians/Media Specialists: 2.7 (571.9 to 1)
Guidance Counselors: 4.9 (315.1 to 1)
Current Spending: ($ per student per year):
   Total: $10,492; Instruction: $6,975; Support Services: $3,180
Enrollment, Drop-out Rates and Diploma Recipients by Race/Ethnicity

Category	Total	White	Black	Asian	AIAN	Hisp.
Enrollment (%)	100.0	97.4	0.5	0.7	0.1	1.2
Drop-out Rate (%)	2.7	2.7	0.0	0.0	0.0	0.0
H.S. Diplomas (#)	126	126	0	0	0	0

York School Department
469 U.S Route 1 • York, ME 03909-1006
(207) 363-3403 • http://www.yorkschools.org/
Grade Span: KG-12; **Agency Type:** 1
Schools: 4
   2 Primary; 1 Middle; 1 High; 0 Other Level
   4 Regular; 0 Special Education; 0 Vocational; 0 Alternative
   0 Magnet; 0 Charter; 2 Title I Eligible; 0 School-wide Title I
Students: 2,162   (51.3% male; 48.6% female)
   Individual Education Program: 308 (14.2%);
   English Language Learner: 13 (0.6%); Migrant: n/a
   Eligible for Free Lunch Program: 120 (5.6%)
   Eligible for Reduced-Price Lunch Program: 68 (3.1%)
Teachers: 160.5 (13.5 to 1)
Librarians/Media Specialists: 2.0 (1,081.0 to 1)
Guidance Counselors: 7.2 (300.3 to 1)
Current Spending: ($ per student per year):
   Total: $8,907; Instruction: $5,913; Support Services: $2,731
Enrollment, Drop-out Rates and Diploma Recipients by Race/Ethnicity

Category	Total	White	Black	Asian	AIAN	Hisp.
Enrollment (%)	100.0	97.7	0.8	0.7	0.0	0.7
Drop-out Rate (%)	1.5	1.5	0.0	n/a	n/a	0.0
H.S. Diplomas (#)	137	133	4	0	0	0

Number of Schools

Rank	Number	District Name	City
1	17	Portland Public Schools	Portland
2	12	Auburn School Department	Auburn
2	12	MSAD 17 Oxford	Oxford
4	11	MSAD 06 Buxton	Bar Mills
4	11	MSAD 54 Skowhegan	Skowhegan
6	10	Bangor School Department	Bangor
6	10	MSAD 34 Belfast	Belfast
8	9	Lewiston School Department	Lewiston
8	9	MSAD 01 Presque Isle	Presque Isle
8	9	MSAD 09 Farmington	New Sharon
11	8	MSAD 03 Unity	Unity
11	8	MSAD 11 Gardiner	Gardiner
11	8	MSAD 48 Newport	Newport
11	8	MSAD 75 Topsham	Topsham
11	8	Sanford School Department	Sanford
11	8	South Portland School Department	South Portland
17	7	Augusta Public Schools	Augusta
17	7	MSAD 22 Hampden	Hampden
17	7	MSAD 40 Waldoboro	Warren
17	7	MSAD 57 Waterboro	Waterboro
17	7	MSAD 60 North Berwick	North Berwick
17	7	MSAD 61 Bridgton	Bridgton
17	7	Westbrook School Department	Westbrook
24	6	Bath School Department	Bath
24	6	Brewer School Department	Brewer
24	6	Brunswick School Department	Brunswick
24	6	Caribou School Department	Caribou
24	6	MSAD 05 Rockland	Rockland
24	6	MSAD 47 Oakland	Oakland
24	6	MSAD 49 Fairfield	Fairfield
24	6	MSAD 51 Cumberland	Cumberland Ctr
24	6	MSAD 52 Turner	Turner
24	6	MSAD 71 Kennebunk	Kennebunk
24	6	Scarborough School Department	Scarborough
35	5	Biddeford School Department	Biddeford
35	5	Gorham School Department	Gorham
35	5	MSAD 15 Gray	Gray
35	5	MSAD 35 So. Berwick	Eliot
35	5	MSAD 43 Mexico	Mexico
35	5	Saco School Department	Saco
35	5	Waterville Public Schools	Waterville
35	5	Windham School Department	Windham
43	4	Falmouth School Department	Falmouth
43	4	Old Town School Department	Old Town
43	4	Wells-Ogunquit CSD	Wells
43	4	York School Department	York
47	3	Cape Elizabeth School Department	Cape Elizabeth

Number of Teachers

Rank	Number	District Name	City
1	642	Portland Public Schools	Portland
2	376	Lewiston School Department	Lewiston
3	355	Auburn School Department	Auburn
4	349	Bangor School Department	Bangor
5	331	MSAD 06 Buxton	Bar Mills
6	304	MSAD 17 Oxford	Oxford
7	297	Sanford School Department	Sanford
8	292	MSAD 75 Topsham	Topsham
9	286	South Portland School Department	South Portland
10	280	MSAD 57 Waterboro	Waterboro
11	272	MSAD 60 North Berwick	North Berwick
12	264	MSAD 09 Farmington	New Sharon
13	263	MSAD 54 Skowhegan	Skowhegan
14	256	Scarborough School Department	Scarborough
15	255	Westbrook School Department	Westbrook
16	247	Brunswick School Department	Brunswick
17	244	Augusta Public Schools	Augusta
18	231	Biddeford School Department	Biddeford
19	225	MSAD 61 Bridgton	Bridgton
20	223	MSAD 49 Fairfield	Fairfield
21	215	MSAD 47 Oakland	Oakland
22	205	Windham School Department	Windham
23	202	MSAD 71 Kennebunk	Kennebunk
24	201	MSAD 34 Belfast	Belfast
25	199	MSAD 52 Turner	Turner
26	196	MSAD 40 Waldoboro	Warren
27	194	Gorham School Department	Gorham
28	193	MSAD 22 Hampden	Hampden
29	188	MSAD 01 Presque Isle	Presque Isle
30	184	MSAD 35 So. Berwick	Eliot
31	182	MSAD 51 Cumberland	Cumberland Ctr
32	181	MSAD 11 Gardiner	Gardiner
33	177	MSAD 48 Newport	Newport
34	175	Bath School Department	Bath
35	173	Waterville Public Schools	Waterville
36	171	Falmouth School Department	Falmouth
37	160	York School Department	York
38	159	MSAD 15 Gray	Gray
39	150	MSAD 03 Unity	Unity
40	149	MSAD 43 Mexico	Mexico
41	143	Caribou School Department	Caribou
42	141	Brewer School Department	Brewer
43	141	Wells-Ogunquit CSD	Wells
44	137	Saco School Department	Saco
45	136	Cape Elizabeth School Department	Cape Elizabeth
46	132	Old Town School Department	Old Town
47	126	MSAD 05 Rockland	Rockland

Number of Students

Rank	Number	District Name	City
1	7,555	Portland Public Schools	Portland
2	4,550	Lewiston School Department	Lewiston
3	4,104	Bangor School Department	Bangor
4	3,990	MSAD 06 Buxton	Bar Mills
5	3,735	MSAD 17 Oxford	Oxford
6	3,732	MSAD 57 Waterboro	Waterboro
6	3,732	Sanford School Department	Sanford
8	3,613	Auburn School Department	Auburn
9	3,356	Brunswick School Department	Brunswick
10	3,333	MSAD 75 Topsham	Topsham
11	3,268	MSAD 60 North Berwick	North Berwick
12	3,240	Scarborough School Department	Scarborough
13	3,113	South Portland School Department	South Portland
14	2,958	Biddeford School Department	Biddeford
15	2,947	MSAD 54 Skowhegan	Skowhegan
16	2,829	Windham School Department	Windham
17	2,751	Gorham School Department	Gorham
18	2,734	MSAD 35 So. Berwick	Eliot
19	2,722	Westbrook School Department	Westbrook
20	2,699	MSAD 49 Fairfield	Fairfield
21	2,687	MSAD 47 Oakland	Oakland
22	2,666	MSAD 09 Farmington	New Sharon
23	2,611	Augusta Public Schools	Augusta
24	2,527	MSAD 71 Kennebunk	Kennebunk
25	2,382	MSAD 11 Gardiner	Gardiner
26	2,341	MSAD 51 Cumberland	Cumberland Ctr
27	2,301	MSAD 22 Hampden	Hampden
28	2,256	MSAD 52 Turner	Turner
29	2,206	MSAD 61 Bridgton	Bridgton
30	2,183	Falmouth School Department	Falmouth
31	2,162	York School Department	York
32	2,139	MSAD 48 Newport	Newport
33	2,133	MSAD 01 Presque Isle	Presque Isle
34	2,095	MSAD 40 Waldoboro	Warren
35	2,069	MSAD 15 Gray	Gray
36	2,008	MSAD 34 Belfast	Belfast
37	1,955	Saco School Department	Saco
38	1,934	Waterville Public Schools	Waterville
39	1,813	Bath School Department	Bath
40	1,807	Cape Elizabeth School Department	Cape Elizabeth
41	1,790	Brewer School Department	Brewer
42	1,667	Caribou School Department	Caribou
43	1,624	MSAD 03 Unity	Unity
44	1,598	MSAD 43 Mexico	Mexico
45	1,569	Old Town School Department	Old Town
46	1,542	Wells-Ogunquit CSD	Wells
47	1,507	MSAD 05 Rockland	Rockland

Male Students

Rank	Percent	District Name	City
1	54.5	Brewer School Department	Brewer
2	53.7	MSAD 43 Mexico	Mexico
3	53.5	MSAD 11 Gardiner	Gardiner
4	53.4	MSAD 22 Hampden	Hampden
5	53.4	MSAD 06 Buxton	Bar Mills
6	53.3	MSAD 15 Gray	Gray
7	53.1	MSAD 61 Bridgton	Bridgton
8	52.8	Westbrook School Department	Westbrook
9	52.6	MSAD 75 Topsham	Topsham
10	52.6	Windham School Department	Windham
11	52.4	Falmouth School Department	Falmouth
12	52.4	Cape Elizabeth School Department	Cape Elizabeth
13	52.4	Auburn School Department	Auburn
14	52.3	Brunswick School Department	Brunswick
15	52.2	MSAD 03 Unity	Unity
16	52.2	South Portland School Department	South Portland
17	52.0	MSAD 57 Waterboro	Waterboro
18	52.0	MSAD 09 Farmington	New Sharon
19	51.8	Lewiston School Department	Lewiston
20	51.8	Sanford School Department	Sanford
21	51.8	Augusta Public Schools	Augusta
22	51.6	Bangor School Department	Bangor
23	51.6	MSAD 52 Turner	Turner
24	51.5	MSAD 54 Skowhegan	Skowhegan
25	51.5	Saco School Department	Saco
26	51.4	MSAD 34 Belfast	Belfast
27	51.3	York School Department	York
28	51.3	Caribou School Department	Caribou
29	51.3	MSAD 17 Oxford	Oxford
30	51.2	Wells-Ogunquit CSD	Wells
31	51.2	MSAD 48 Newport	Newport
32	51.2	MSAD 01 Presque Isle	Presque Isle
33	51.1	Gorham School Department	Gorham
34	51.1	Scarborough School Department	Scarborough
35	51.1	Biddeford School Department	Biddeford
36	50.9	MSAD 35 So. Berwick	Eliot
37	50.8	MSAD 49 Fairfield	Fairfield
38	50.7	MSAD 47 Oakland	Oakland
39	50.6	Waterville Public Schools	Waterville
40	50.6	MSAD 71 Kennebunk	Kennebunk
41	50.6	Portland Public Schools	Portland
42	50.4	MSAD 60 North Berwick	North Berwick
43	50.1	Bath School Department	Bath
44	50.0	MSAD 40 Waldoboro	Warren
45	49.9	Old Town School Department	Old Town
46	48.9	MSAD 51 Cumberland	Cumberland Ctr
47	48.3	MSAD 05 Rockland	Rockland

Female Students

Rank	Percent	District Name	City
1	51.6	MSAD 05 Rockland	Rockland
2	51.0	MSAD 51 Cumberland	Cumberland Ctr
3	50.0	Old Town School Department	Old Town
4	49.9	MSAD 40 Waldoboro	Warren
5	49.8	Bath School Department	Bath
6	49.5	MSAD 60 North Berwick	North Berwick
7	49.3	Portland Public Schools	Portland
8	49.3	MSAD 71 Kennebunk	Kennebunk
9	49.3	Waterville Public Schools	Waterville
10	49.2	MSAD 47 Oakland	Oakland
11	49.1	MSAD 49 Fairfield	Fairfield
12	49.0	MSAD 35 So. Berwick	Eliot
13	48.8	Biddeford School Department	Biddeford
14	48.8	Scarborough School Department	Scarborough
15	48.8	Gorham School Department	Gorham
16	48.7	MSAD 01 Presque Isle	Presque Isle
17	48.7	MSAD 48 Newport	Newport
18	48.7	Wells-Ogunquit CSD	Wells
19	48.6	MSAD 17 Oxford	Oxford
20	48.6	Caribou School Department	Caribou
21	48.6	York School Department	York
22	48.5	MSAD 34 Belfast	Belfast
23	48.4	Saco School Department	Saco
24	48.4	MSAD 54 Skowhegan	Skowhegan
25	48.3	MSAD 52 Turner	Turner
26	48.3	Bangor School Department	Bangor
27	48.1	Augusta Public Schools	Augusta
28	48.1	Sanford School Department	Sanford
29	48.1	Lewiston School Department	Lewiston
30	47.9	MSAD 09 Farmington	New Sharon
31	47.9	MSAD 57 Waterboro	Waterboro
32	47.7	South Portland School Department	South Portland
33	47.7	MSAD 03 Unity	Unity
34	47.6	Brunswick School Department	Brunswick
35	47.5	Auburn School Department	Auburn
36	47.5	Cape Elizabeth School Department	Cape Elizabeth
37	47.5	Falmouth School Department	Falmouth
38	47.3	Windham School Department	Windham
39	47.3	MSAD 75 Topsham	Topsham
40	47.1	Westbrook School Department	Westbrook
41	46.8	MSAD 61 Bridgton	Bridgton
42	46.6	MSAD 15 Gray	Gray
43	46.5	MSAD 06 Buxton	Bar Mills
44	46.5	MSAD 22 Hampden	Hampden
45	46.4	MSAD 11 Gardiner	Gardiner
46	46.2	MSAD 43 Mexico	Mexico
47	45.4	Brewer School Department	Brewer

Individual Education Program Students

Rank	Percent	District Name	City
1	24.0	Saco School Department	Saco
2	21.8	Augusta Public Schools	Augusta
2	21.8	MSAD 61 Bridgton	Bridgton
4	21.7	MSAD 34 Belfast	Belfast
5	21.0	Waterville Public Schools	Waterville
6	20.5	MSAD 75 Topsham	Topsham
7	20.3	MSAD 43 Mexico	Mexico
8	19.8	Auburn School Department	Auburn
9	19.7	MSAD 60 North Berwick	North Berwick
10	19.0	South Portland School Department	South Portland
11	18.5	Lewiston School Department	Lewiston
12	18.4	MSAD 48 Newport	Newport
12	18.4	MSAD 49 Fairfield	Fairfield
14	18.1	Sanford School Department	Sanford
15	18.0	MSAD 03 Unity	Unity
16	17.7	MSAD 54 Skowhegan	Skowhegan
17	17.5	MSAD 40 Waldoboro	Warren
18	16.1	MSAD 06 Buxton	Bar Mills
18	16.1	MSAD 71 Kennebunk	Kennebunk
20	15.8	Biddeford School Department	Biddeford
21	15.7	MSAD 11 Gardiner	Gardiner

21	15.7	MSAD 22 Hampden	Hampden
23	15.3	MSAD 57 Waterboro	Waterboro
24	15.2	MSAD 15 Gray	Gray
25	15.0	Portland Public Schools	Portland
26	14.3	Wells-Ogunquit CSD	Wells
27	14.2	Brunswick School Department	Brunswick
27	14.2	MSAD 52 Turner	Turner
27	14.2	York School Department	York
30	14.1	Gorham School Department	Gorham
31	13.6	MSAD 05 Rockland	Rockland
31	13.6	Old Town School Department	Old Town
33	13.5	Bangor School Department	Bangor
34	13.1	Scarborough School Department	Scarborough
35	13.0	Bath School Department	Bath
36	12.9	MSAD 09 Farmington	New Sharon
37	12.8	Brewer School Department	Brewer
37	12.8	MSAD 35 So. Berwick	Eliot
39	12.5	MSAD 01 Presque Isle	Presque Isle
39	12.5	MSAD 47 Oakland	Oakland
41	12.3	Cape Elizabeth School Department	Cape Elizabeth
42	11.9	Westbrook School Department	Westbrook
43	11.6	Falmouth School Department	Falmouth
44	11.1	MSAD 17 Oxford	Oxford
45	10.9	Caribou School Department	Caribou
46	10.6	Windham School Department	Windham
47	6.5	MSAD 51 Cumberland	Cumberland Ctr

English Language Learner Students

Rank	Percent	District Name	City
1	14.7	Portland Public Schools	Portland
2	6.7	Lewiston School Department	Lewiston
3	3.1	Auburn School Department	Auburn
3	3.1	MSAD 52 Turner	Turner
5	2.8	Augusta Public Schools	Augusta
6	2.6	Sanford School Department	Sanford
7	2.3	South Portland School Department	South Portland
8	1.5	Scarborough School Department	Scarborough
9	1.4	MSAD 71 Kennebunk	Kennebunk
10	1.2	MSAD 75 Topsham	Topsham
11	1.1	Bangor School Department	Bangor
11	1.1	Caribou School Department	Caribou
13	1.0	MSAD 60 North Berwick	North Berwick
13	1.0	Waterville Public Schools	Waterville
13	1.0	Wells-Ogunquit CSD	Wells
13	1.0	Westbrook School Department	Westbrook
17	0.9	Biddeford School Department	Biddeford
17	0.9	Brunswick School Department	Brunswick
19	0.6	Windham School Department	Windham
19	0.6	York School Department	York
21	0.5	Bath School Department	Bath
21	0.5	MSAD 05 Rockland	Rockland
23	0.4	Falmouth School Department	Falmouth
23	0.4	Gorham School Department	Gorham
23	0.4	Old Town School Department	Old Town
23	0.4	Saco School Department	Saco
27	0.3	MSAD 01 Presque Isle	Presque Isle
27	0.3	MSAD 22 Hampden	Hampden
27	0.3	MSAD 35 So. Berwick	Eliot
27	0.3	MSAD 54 Skowhegan	Skowhegan
27	0.3	MSAD 57 Waterboro	Waterboro
32	0.2	Brewer School Department	Brewer
32	0.2	Cape Elizabeth School Department	Cape Elizabeth
32	0.2	MSAD 09 Farmington	New Sharon
32	0.2	MSAD 51 Cumberland	Cumberland Ctr
36	0.1	MSAD 06 Buxton	Bar Mills
36	0.1	MSAD 15 Gray	Gray
36	0.1	MSAD 17 Oxford	Oxford
36	0.1	MSAD 34 Belfast	Belfast
36	0.1	MSAD 47 Oakland	Oakland
41	0.0	MSAD 11 Gardiner	Gardiner
41	0.0	MSAD 61 Bridgton	Bridgton
43	0.0	MSAD 03 Unity	Unity
43	0.0	MSAD 40 Waldoboro	Warren
43	0.0	MSAD 43 Mexico	Mexico
43	0.0	MSAD 48 Newport	Newport
43	0.0	MSAD 49 Fairfield	Fairfield

Migrant Students

Rank	Percent	District Name	City
1	n/a	Auburn School Department	Auburn
1	n/a	Augusta Public Schools	Augusta
1	n/a	Bangor School Department	Bangor
1	n/a	Bath School Department	Bath
1	n/a	Biddeford School Department	Biddeford
1	n/a	Brewer School Department	Brewer
1	n/a	Brunswick School Department	Brunswick
1	n/a	Cape Elizabeth School Department	Cape Elizabeth
1	n/a	Caribou School Department	Caribou
1	n/a	Falmouth School Department	Falmouth
1	n/a	Gorham School Department	Gorham
1	n/a	Lewiston School Department	Lewiston
1	n/a	MSAD 01 Presque Isle	Presque Isle
1	n/a	MSAD 03 Unity	Unity
1	n/a	MSAD 05 Rockland	Rockland
1	n/a	MSAD 06 Buxton	Bar Mills
1	n/a	MSAD 09 Farmington	New Sharon
1	n/a	MSAD 11 Gardiner	Gardiner
1	n/a	MSAD 15 Gray	Gray
1	n/a	MSAD 17 Oxford	Oxford
1	n/a	MSAD 22 Hampden	Hampden
1	n/a	MSAD 34 Belfast	Belfast
1	n/a	MSAD 35 So. Berwick	Eliot
1	n/a	MSAD 40 Waldoboro	Warren
1	n/a	MSAD 43 Mexico	Mexico
1	n/a	MSAD 47 Oakland	Oakland
1	n/a	MSAD 48 Newport	Newport
1	n/a	MSAD 49 Fairfield	Fairfield
1	n/a	MSAD 51 Cumberland	Cumberland Ctr
1	n/a	MSAD 52 Turner	Turner
1	n/a	MSAD 54 Skowhegan	Skowhegan
1	n/a	MSAD 57 Waterboro	Waterboro
1	n/a	MSAD 60 North Berwick	North Berwick
1	n/a	MSAD 61 Bridgton	Bridgton
1	n/a	MSAD 71 Kennebunk	Kennebunk
1	n/a	MSAD 75 Topsham	Topsham
1	n/a	Old Town School Department	Old Town
1	n/a	Portland Public Schools	Portland
1	n/a	Saco School Department	Saco
1	n/a	Sanford School Department	Sanford
1	n/a	Scarborough School Department	Scarborough
1	n/a	South Portland School Department	South Portland
1	n/a	Waterville Public Schools	Waterville
1	n/a	Wells-Ogunquit CSD	Wells
1	n/a	Westbrook School Department	Westbrook
1	n/a	Windham School Department	Windham
1	n/a	York School Department	York

Students Eligible for Free Lunch

Rank	Percent	District Name	City
1	41.6	MSAD 03 Unity	Unity
2	41.3	MSAD 43 Mexico	Mexico
3	40.7	Lewiston School Department	Lewiston
4	38.3	Waterville Public Schools	Waterville
5	35.1	Portland Public Schools	Portland
6	34.8	MSAD 48 Newport	Newport
7	32.9	Caribou School Department	Caribou
8	32.2	MSAD 34 Belfast	Belfast
9	31.9	MSAD 54 Skowhegan	Skowhegan
10	31.6	Sanford School Department	Sanford
11	30.3	MSAD 49 Fairfield	Fairfield
12	29.7	Biddeford School Department	Biddeford
13	28.9	MSAD 40 Waldoboro	Warren
14	28.4	Westbrook School Department	Westbrook
15	28.3	MSAD 61 Bridgton	Bridgton
16	28.0	MSAD 09 Farmington	New Sharon
17	27.5	MSAD 05 Rockland	Rockland
18	26.7	MSAD 17 Oxford	Oxford
19	26.6	Bath School Department	Bath
20	26.2	Bangor School Department	Bangor
21	25.7	Augusta Public Schools	Augusta
22	24.4	MSAD 01 Presque Isle	Presque Isle
23	22.9	MSAD 11 Gardiner	Gardiner
24	22.7	Auburn School Department	Auburn
25	19.0	MSAD 06 Buxton	Bar Mills
26	18.7	Brewer School Department	Brewer
27	18.3	Saco School Department	Saco
28	16.9	MSAD 15 Gray	Gray
29	16.3	MSAD 57 Waterboro	Waterboro
30	15.5	MSAD 52 Turner	Turner
31	15.2	MSAD 60 North Berwick	North Berwick
32	14.8	South Portland School Department	South Portland
33	14.1	MSAD 22 Hampden	Hampden
34	13.7	MSAD 47 Oakland	Oakland
34	13.7	MSAD 75 Topsham	Topsham
36	11.7	Old Town School Department	Old Town
37	10.9	Windham School Department	Windham
38	9.3	Brunswick School Department	Brunswick
39	8.5	Gorham School Department	Gorham
40	7.9	Wells-Ogunquit CSD	Wells
41	6.7	Scarborough School Department	Scarborough
42	6.2	MSAD 35 So. Berwick	Eliot
43	5.6	York School Department	York
44	5.4	MSAD 71 Kennebunk	Kennebunk
45	2.2	MSAD 51 Cumberland	Cumberland Ctr
46	1.3	Falmouth School Department	Falmouth
47	n/a	Cape Elizabeth School Department	Cape Elizabeth

Students Eligible for Reduced-Price Lunch

Rank	Percent	District Name	City
1	13.4	MSAD 48 Newport	Newport
2	13.3	MSAD 03 Unity	Unity
3	12.5	MSAD 60 North Berwick	North Berwick
4	11.6	MSAD 09 Farmington	New Sharon
5	11.1	MSAD 40 Waldoboro	Warren
6	11.0	MSAD 43 Mexico	Mexico
6	11.0	MSAD 49 Fairfield	Fairfield
8	10.2	MSAD 06 Buxton	Bar Mills
9	9.3	MSAD 17 Oxford	Oxford
9	9.3	MSAD 54 Skowhegan	Skowhegan
11	9.1	Caribou School Department	Caribou
12	9.0	Bath School Department	Bath
13	8.8	MSAD 01 Presque Isle	Presque Isle
13	8.8	MSAD 05 Rockland	Rockland
15	8.5	MSAD 57 Waterboro	Waterboro
16	8.0	MSAD 61 Bridgton	Bridgton
17	7.8	MSAD 34 Belfast	Belfast
18	7.7	Augusta Public Schools	Augusta
19	7.5	Sanford School Department	Sanford
19	7.5	Waterville Public Schools	Waterville
21	7.3	MSAD 11 Gardiner	Gardiner
22	7.0	Lewiston School Department	Lewiston
23	6.4	MSAD 15 Gray	Gray
24	6.0	Westbrook School Department	Westbrook
25	5.6	Biddeford School Department	Biddeford
26	5.5	Auburn School Department	Auburn
27	5.1	MSAD 47 Oakland	Oakland
28	5.0	Brunswick School Department	Brunswick
28	5.0	MSAD 75 Topsham	Topsham
30	4.7	MSAD 52 Turner	Turner
31	4.6	Bangor School Department	Bangor
32	4.5	MSAD 22 Hampden	Hampden
32	4.5	Saco School Department	Saco
34	4.1	Portland Public Schools	Portland
35	4.0	Old Town School Department	Old Town
35	4.0	South Portland School Department	South Portland
37	3.8	Windham School Department	Windham
38	3.7	Brewer School Department	Brewer
39	3.1	MSAD 71 Kennebunk	Kennebunk
39	3.1	York School Department	York
41	3.0	Scarborough School Department	Scarborough
42	2.8	Gorham School Department	Gorham
43	2.4	MSAD 35 So. Berwick	Eliot
44	0.9	Wells-Ogunquit CSD	Wells
45	0.7	Falmouth School Department	Falmouth
45	0.7	MSAD 51 Cumberland	Cumberland Ctr
47	n/a	Cape Elizabeth School Department	Cape Elizabeth

Student/Teacher Ratio

Rank	Ratio	District Name	City
1	14.8	MSAD 35 So. Berwick	Eliot
2	14.2	Gorham School Department	Gorham
2	14.2	Saco School Department	Saco
4	13.7	Windham School Department	Windham
5	13.5	Brunswick School Department	Brunswick
5	13.5	York School Department	York
7	13.3	MSAD 57 Waterboro	Waterboro
8	13.2	Cape Elizabeth School Department	Cape Elizabeth
9	13.1	MSAD 11 Gardiner	Gardiner
9	13.1	MSAD 15 Gray	Gray
11	12.9	Biddeford School Department	Biddeford
11	12.9	MSAD 51 Cumberland	Cumberland Ctr
13	12.8	Brewer School Department	Brewer
14	12.7	Falmouth School Department	Falmouth
15	12.6	Scarborough School Department	Scarborough
16	12.5	MSAD 47 Oakland	Oakland
16	12.5	MSAD 71 Kennebunk	Kennebunk
16	12.5	Sanford School Department	Sanford
19	12.4	MSAD 17 Oxford	Oxford
20	12.1	Lewiston School Department	Lewiston
20	12.1	MSAD 48 Newport	Newport
20	12.1	MSAD 49 Fairfield	Fairfield
23	12.0	MSAD 06 Buxton	Bar Mills
24	11.9	MSAD 22 Hampden	Hampden
24	11.9	Old Town School Department	Old Town
26	11.8	MSAD 05 Rockland	Rockland
27	11.7	Bangor School Department	Bangor
27	11.7	MSAD 60 North Berwick	North Berwick
27	11.7	Portland Public Schools	Portland
30	11.6	MSAD 75 Topsham	Topsham
31	11.4	Caribou School Department	Caribou
32	11.3	MSAD 01 Presque Isle	Presque Isle
33	11.2	MSAD 52 Turner	Turner
33	11.2	MSAD 54 Skowhegan	Skowhegan
33	11.2	Waterville Public Schools	Waterville
36	11.0	South Portland School Department	South Portland
37	10.9	Wells-Ogunquit CSD	Wells
38	10.8	MSAD 03 Unity	Unity
38	10.8	MSAD 43 Mexico	Mexico
40	10.7	Augusta Public Schools	Augusta
41	10.6	MSAD 40 Waldoboro	Warren
42	10.5	Westbrook School Department	Westbrook
43	10.4	Bath School Department	Bath
44	10.3	Auburn School Department	Auburn

45	10.1	MSAD 09 Farmington	New Sharon
46	10.0	MSAD 34 Belfast	Belfast
47	9.8	MSAD 61 Bridgton	Bridgton

Student/Librarian Ratio

Rank	Ratio	District Name	City
1	2,738.0	MSAD 35 So. Berwick	Eliot
2	2,341.0	MSAD 51 Cumberland	Cumberland Ctr
3	2,130.0	MSAD 01 Presque Isle	Presque Isle
4	2,079.0	MSAD 15 Gray	Gray
5	1,641.6	Bangor School Department	Bangor
6	1,624.0	MSAD 03 Unity	Unity
7	1,516.7	Lewiston School Department	Lewiston
8	1,486.8	Windham School Department	Windham
9	1,473.5	MSAD 54 Skowhegan	Skowhegan
10	1,336.0	Westbrook School Department	Westbrook
11	1,306.5	Augusta Public Schools	Augusta
12	1,295.9	MSAD 17 Oxford	Oxford
13	1,289.3	Waterville Public Schools	Waterville
14	1,253.2	MSAD 11 Gardiner	Gardiner
15	1,240.3	MSAD 57 Waterboro	Waterboro
16	1,226.7	MSAD 61 Bridgton	Bridgton
17	1,117.2	Scarborough School Department	Scarborough
18	1,081.0	York School Department	York
19	1,074.7	Auburn School Department	Auburn
20	1,071.5	MSAD 48 Newport	Newport
21	1,067.0	MSAD 60 North Berwick	North Berwick
22	1,064.7	Brewer School Department	Brewer
23	1,047.7	South Portland School Department	South Portland
24	1,003.5	MSAD 34 Belfast	Belfast
25	953.9	Portland Public Schools	Portland
26	909.5	Bath School Department	Bath
27	899.0	MSAD 49 Fairfield	Fairfield
28	898.3	MSAD 47 Oakland	Oakland
29	842.3	MSAD 71 Kennebunk	Kennebunk
30	820.5	Caribou School Department	Caribou
31	787.9	MSAD 05 Rockland	Rockland
32	783.7	Biddeford School Department	Biddeford
33	765.7	MSAD 22 Hampden	Hampden
34	758.8	Sanford School Department	Sanford
35	745.0	MSAD 52 Turner	Turner
36	727.0	Falmouth School Department	Falmouth
37	610.4	Brunswick School Department	Brunswick
38	600.0	Cape Elizabeth School Department	Cape Elizabeth
39	587.2	MSAD 06 Buxton	Bar Mills
40	571.9	Wells-Ogunquit CSD	Wells
41	554.6	MSAD 75 Topsham	Topsham
42	550.2	Gorham School Department	Gorham
43	544.3	MSAD 09 Farmington	New Sharon
44	541.0	Old Town School Department	Old Town
45	413.3	MSAD 43 Mexico	Mexico
46	349.2	MSAD 40 Waldoboro	Warren
47	n/a	Saco School Department	Saco

Student/Counselor Ratio

Rank	Ratio	District Name	City
1	546.2	MSAD 01 Presque Isle	Presque Isle
2	483.1	Portland Public Schools	Portland
3	476.5	Scarborough School Department	Scarborough
4	454.8	Bath School Department	Bath
5	439.9	MSAD 54 Skowhegan	Skowhegan
6	412.9	Old Town School Department	Old Town
7	393.0	Gorham School Department	Gorham
8	386.5	MSAD 09 Farmington	New Sharon
9	381.8	Biddeford School Department	Biddeford
10	347.8	MSAD 57 Waterboro	Waterboro
11	345.0	MSAD 61 Bridgton	Bridgton
12	341.7	MSAD 75 Topsham	Topsham
13	335.5	MSAD 06 Buxton	Bar Mills
14	334.9	Caribou School Department	Caribou
15	334.0	Westbrook School Department	Westbrook
16	333.0	MSAD 49 Fairfield	Fairfield
17	326.0	MSAD 35 So. Berwick	Eliot
18	321.0	Windham School Department	Windham
19	318.1	Bangor School Department	Bangor
20	316.4	MSAD 51 Cumberland	Cumberland Ctr
21	316.1	Falmouth School Department	Falmouth
22	315.3	Saco School Department	Saco
23	315.1	Wells-Ogunquit CSD	Wells
24	306.1	MSAD 48 Newport	Newport
25	305.3	MSAD 11 Gardiner	Gardiner
26	302.8	MSAD 47 Oakland	Oakland
27	300.3	York School Department	York
28	295.1	Cape Elizabeth School Department	Cape Elizabeth
29	291.9	Brunswick School Department	Brunswick
30	288.2	Sanford School Department	Sanford
31	280.1	MSAD 22 Hampden	Hampden
32	269.2	Lewiston School Department	Lewiston
33	262.8	MSAD 17 Oxford	Oxford
34	261.3	Augusta Public Schools	Augusta
35	259.9	MSAD 15 Gray	Gray
36	258.1	MSAD 05 Rockland	Rockland
37	250.2	MSAD 71 Kennebunk	Kennebunk
38	249.4	MSAD 40 Waldoboro	Warren
39	246.2	MSAD 60 North Berwick	North Berwick
40	233.6	MSAD 43 Mexico	Mexico
41	231.1	South Portland School Department	South Portland
42	226.3	Brewer School Department	Brewer
43	223.5	MSAD 52 Turner	Turner
44	220.5	MSAD 34 Belfast	Belfast
45	218.8	Auburn School Department	Auburn
46	217.3	Waterville Public Schools	Waterville
47	193.3	MSAD 03 Unity	Unity

Current Spending per Student in FY2003

Rank	Dollars	District Name	City
1	11,170	Saco School Department	Saco
2	11,042	Portland Public Schools	Portland
3	10,814	South Portland School Department	South Portland
4	10,492	Wells-Ogunquit CSD	Wells
5	10,403	Augusta Public Schools	Augusta
6	10,181	MSAD 61 Bridgton	Bridgton
7	10,101	MSAD 71 Kennebunk	Kennebunk
8	9,969	Westbrook School Department	Westbrook
9	9,868	MSAD 34 Belfast	Belfast
10	9,580	Waterville Public Schools	Waterville
11	9,480	MSAD 05 Rockland	Rockland
12	9,326	Bath School Department	Bath
13	9,319	Falmouth School Department	Falmouth
14	9,225	MSAD 54 Skowhegan	Skowhegan
15	9,156	MSAD 75 Topsham	Topsham
16	9,128	MSAD 40 Waldoboro	Warren
17	9,101	MSAD 51 Cumberland	Cumberland Ctr
18	9,061	MSAD 43 Mexico	Mexico
19	9,020	MSAD 03 Unity	Unity
20	8,907	York School Department	York
21	8,881	MSAD 60 North Berwick	North Berwick
22	8,768	Cape Elizabeth School Department	Cape Elizabeth
23	8,695	MSAD 01 Presque Isle	Presque Isle
24	8,609	Bangor School Department	Bangor
25	8,511	MSAD 09 Farmington	New Sharon
26	8,494	MSAD 22 Hampden	Hampden
27	8,449	Auburn School Department	Auburn
28	8,323	Caribou School Department	Caribou
29	8,295	MSAD 15 Gray	Gray
30	8,276	MSAD 06 Buxton	Bar Mills
31	8,226	Biddeford School Department	Biddeford
32	8,162	Brewer School Department	Brewer
33	8,151	MSAD 49 Fairfield	Fairfield
34	8,139	Lewiston School Department	Lewiston
35	8,111	Gorham School Department	Gorham
36	8,003	MSAD 47 Oakland	Oakland
37	7,996	Windham School Department	Windham
38	7,980	MSAD 52 Turner	Turner
39	7,959	MSAD 48 Newport	Newport
40	7,916	MSAD 11 Gardiner	Gardiner
41	7,824	Old Town School Department	Old Town
42	7,786	Sanford School Department	Sanford
43	7,784	MSAD 17 Oxford	Oxford
44	7,731	Brunswick School Department	Brunswick
45	7,632	Scarborough School Department	Scarborough
46	6,939	MSAD 35 So. Berwick	Eliot
47	6,914	MSAD 57 Waterboro	Waterboro

Number of Diploma Recipients

Rank	Number	District Name	City
1	298	Bangor School Department	Bangor
2	288	Portland Public Schools	Portland
3	282	MSAD 06 Buxton	Bar Mills
4	270	Lewiston School Department	Lewiston
5	252	MSAD 75 Topsham	Topsham
6	245	MSAD 17 Oxford	Oxford
7	230	Brunswick School Department	Brunswick
8	228	Auburn School Department	Auburn
8	228	South Portland School Department	South Portland
10	219	Sanford School Department	Sanford
11	213	MSAD 54 Skowhegan	Skowhegan
12	206	MSAD 57 Waterboro	Waterboro
13	204	MSAD 35 So. Berwick	Eliot
14	197	MSAD 09 Farmington	New Sharon
14	197	MSAD 47 Oakland	Oakland
16	191	MSAD 60 North Berwick	North Berwick
17	183	Augusta Public Schools	Augusta
18	178	Brewer School Department	Brewer
18	178	Scarborough School Department	Scarborough
20	174	MSAD 22 Hampden	Hampden
20	174	MSAD 49 Fairfield	Fairfield
22	169	MSAD 11 Gardiner	Gardiner
23	163	Biddeford School Department	Biddeford
24	162	MSAD 71 Kennebunk	Kennebunk
25	158	MSAD 40 Waldoboro	Warren
26	157	Old Town School Department	Old Town
27	154	Bath School Department	Bath
27	154	MSAD 48 Newport	Newport
29	153	Westbrook School Department	Westbrook
30	150	MSAD 52 Turner	Turner
31	149	Gorham School Department	Gorham
32	148	MSAD 51 Cumberland	Cumberland Ctr
33	141	Waterville Public Schools	Waterville
34	137	York School Department	York
35	136	MSAD 34 Belfast	Belfast
36	128	MSAD 01 Presque Isle	Presque Isle
36	128	MSAD 61 Bridgton	Bridgton
38	126	Wells-Ogunquit CSD	Wells
39	120	Caribou School Department	Caribou
40	117	MSAD 15 Gray	Gray
41	115	MSAD 03 Unity	Unity
42	113	Falmouth School Department	Falmouth
43	108	MSAD 43 Mexico	Mexico
44	107	Cape Elizabeth School Department	Cape Elizabeth
45	103	MSAD 05 Rockland	Rockland
46	4	Windham School Department	Windham
47	n/a	Saco School Department	Saco

High School Drop-out Rate

Rank	Percent	District Name	City
1	7.7	Portland Public Schools	Portland
2	5.2	MSAD 60 North Berwick	North Berwick
3	5.1	MSAD 09 Farmington	New Sharon
4	4.5	Bath School Department	Bath
5	4.4	Brewer School Department	Brewer
5	4.4	MSAD 17 Oxford	Oxford
7	4.0	Auburn School Department	Auburn
7	4.0	MSAD 11 Gardiner	Gardiner
9	3.9	MSAD 03 Unity	Unity
10	3.7	Lewiston School Department	Lewiston
11	3.6	Waterville Public Schools	Waterville
12	3.4	Old Town School Department	Old Town
13	3.3	MSAD 06 Buxton	Bar Mills
14	2.9	MSAD 01 Presque Isle	Presque Isle
15	2.7	Wells-Ogunquit CSD	Wells
16	2.6	MSAD 43 Mexico	Mexico
17	2.4	South Portland School Department	South Portland
18	2.2	MSAD 22 Hampden	Hampden
18	2.2	MSAD 35 So. Berwick	Eliot
18	2.2	Sanford School Department	Sanford
21	2.1	Bangor School Department	Bangor
21	2.1	MSAD 40 Waldoboro	Warren
23	1.9	Brunswick School Department	Brunswick
23	1.9	MSAD 57 Waterboro	Waterboro
23	1.9	MSAD 75 Topsham	Topsham
23	1.9	Windham School Department	Windham
27	1.8	Gorham School Department	Gorham
28	1.7	MSAD 61 Bridgton	Bridgton
29	1.6	MSAD 52 Turner	Turner
30	1.5	Caribou School Department	Caribou
30	1.5	MSAD 47 Oakland	Oakland
30	1.5	York School Department	York
33	1.2	MSAD 49 Fairfield	Fairfield
34	1.1	MSAD 15 Gray	Gray
34	1.1	MSAD 51 Cumberland	Cumberland Ctr
34	1.1	MSAD 54 Skowhegan	Skowhegan
34	1.1	MSAD 71 Kennebunk	Kennebunk
38	1.0	Augusta Public Schools	Augusta
38	1.0	Biddeford School Department	Biddeford
38	1.0	Westbrook School Department	Westbrook
41	0.5	Falmouth School Department	Falmouth
41	0.5	MSAD 48 Newport	Newport
43	0.2	Cape Elizabeth School Department	Cape Elizabeth
44	0.0	MSAD 05 Rockland	Rockland
44	0.0	MSAD 34 Belfast	Belfast
44	0.0	Scarborough School Department	Scarborough
47	n/a	Saco School Department	Saco

Maryland

Maryland Public School Educational Profile

Category	Value	Category	Value
Schools *(2003-2004)*	1,408	**Diploma Recipients** *(2002-2003)*	50,883
Instructional Level		White, Non-Hispanic	29,364
Primary	866	Black, Non-Hispanic	16,746
Middle	240	Asian/Pacific Islander	2,725
High	237	American Indian/Alaskan Native	158
Other Level	65	Hispanic	1,890
Curriculum		**High School Drop-out Rate** *(%) (2001-2002)*	3.9
Regular	1,261	White, Non-Hispanic	3.0
Special Education	50	Black, Non-Hispanic	5.5
Vocational	25	Asian/Pacific Islander	1.4
Alternative	72	American Indian/Alaskan Native	4.1
Type		Hispanic	3.7
Magnet	0	**Staff** *(2003-2004)*	
Charter	1	Teachers	55,125.9
Title I Eligible	401	Average Salary ($)	50,303
School-wide Title I	320	Librarians/Media Specialists	1,116.0
Students *(2003-2004)*	869,113	Guidance Counselors	2,230.0
Gender (%)		**Ratios** *(2003-2004)*	
Male	51.3	Student/Teacher Ratio	15.8 to 1
Female	48.7	Student/Librarian Ratio	778.8 to 1
Race/Ethnicity (%)		Student/Counselor Ratio	389.7 to 1
White, Non-Hispanic	50.4	**College Entrance Exam Scores** *(2005)*	
Black, Non-Hispanic	37.9	Scholastic Aptitude Test (SAT)	
Asian/Pacific Islander	4.9	Participation Rate (%)	71
American Indian/Alaskan Native	0.4	Mean SAT Reasoning Test Verbal Score	511
Hispanic	6.4	Mean SAT Reasoning Test Math Score	515
Classification (%)		American College Testing Program (ACT)	
Individual Education Program (IEP)	12.4	Participation Rate (%)	12
Migrant *(2002-2003)*	0.0	Average Composite Score	21.0
English Language Learner (ELL)	3.2	Average English Score	20.5
Eligible for Free Lunch Program	24.0	Average Math Score	20.8
Eligible for Reduced-Price Lunch Program	7.4	Average Reading Score	21.5
Current Spending *($ per student in FY 2003)*	8,921	Average Science Score	20.7
Instruction	5,467		
Support Services	3,035		

Note: For an explanation of data, please refer to the User's Guide in the front of the book

Maryland NAEP 2005 Test Scores

Reading			Mathematics		
Grade/Category	Value	Rank	Grade/Category	Value	Rank
4th Grade			**4th Grade**		
Average Proficiency	220.0 (1.26)	26/51	Average Proficiency	238.4 (1.03)	27/51
Proficiency by Gender/Race/Ethnicity			Proficiency by Gender/Race/Ethnicity		
Male	217.0 (1.33)	27/51	Male	239.7 (1.15)	28/51
Female	222.9 (1.49)	26/51	Female	237.1 (1.22)	29/51
White, Non-Hispanic	232.5 (1.52)	6/51	White, Non-Hispanic	250.1 (1.16)	6/51
Black, Non-Hispanic	200.9 (1.50)	15/42	Black, Non-Hispanic	220.0 (1.29)	21/42
Asian, Non-Hispanic	239.0 (3.55)	3/27	Asian, Non-Hispanic	256.0 (2.34)	9/25
American Indian, Non-Hispanic	n/a	n/a	American Indian, Non-Hispanic	n/a	n/a
Hispanic	209.8 (2.70)	10/40	Hispanic	231.7 (2.47)	8/41
Proficiency by Class Size			Proficiency by Class Size		
Less than 16 Students	n/a	n/a	Less than 16 Students	n/a	n/a
16 to 18 Students	n/a	n/a	16 to 18 Students	n/a	n/a
19 to 20 Students	223.5 (4.22)	18/38	19 to 20 Students	235.0 (3.08)	28/38
21 to 25 Students	220.1 (2.29)	31/51	21 to 25 Students	238.6 (1.91)	34/51
Greater than 25 Students	224.7 (2.95)	7/36	Greater than 25 Students	240.6 (2.58)	10/33
Percent Attaining Achievement Levels			Percent Attaining Achievement Levels		
Below Basic	35.4 (1.36)	24/51	Below Basic	21.2 (1.25)	19/51
Basic or Above	64.6 (1.36)	28/51	Basic or Above	78.8 (1.25)	33/51
Proficient or Above	32.3 (1.51)	26/51	Proficient or Above	38.0 (1.48)	23/51
Advanced or Above	8.3 (0.74)	9/51	Advanced or Above	6.9 (0.96)	5/51
8th Grade			**8th Grade**		
Average Proficiency	260.8 (1.22)	32/51	Average Proficiency	277.9 (1.08)	31/51
Proficiency by Gender/Race/Ethnicity			Proficiency by Gender/Race/Ethnicity		
Male	255.8 (1.49)	30/51	Male	277.8 (1.35)	34/51
Female	265.8 (1.30)	31/51	Female	278.1 (1.27)	30/51
White, Non-Hispanic	272.4 (1.51)	10/51	White, Non-Hispanic	291.9 (1.19)	9/51
Black, Non-Hispanic	243.8 (1.78)	14/40	Black, Non-Hispanic	258.5 (1.37)	12/41
Asian, Non-Hispanic	282.9 (2.90)	2/24	Asian, Non-Hispanic	304.3 (4.04)	5/23
American Indian, Non-Hispanic	n/a	n/a	American Indian, Non-Hispanic	n/a	n/a
Hispanic	256.5 (4.77)	3/38	Hispanic	262.1 (4.86)	20/38
Proficiency by Parents Highest Level of Ed.			Proficiency by Parents Highest Level of Ed.		
Did Not Finish High School	243.7 (4.49)	32/49	Did Not Finish High School	255.0 (4.17)	38/50
Graduated High School	249.7 (1.97)	35/50	Graduated High School	267.9 (2.24)	28/50
Some Education After High School	262.2 (2.97)	39/50	Some Education After High School	277.1 (1.86)	38/50
Graduated College	269.8 (1.35)	31/50	Graduated College	287.9 (1.47)	32/50
Percent Attaining Achievement Levels			Percent Attaining Achievement Levels		
Below Basic	35.4 (1.36)	24/51	Below Basic	33.8 (1.47)	18/51
Basic or Above	64.6 (1.36)	28/51	Basic or Above	66.2 (1.47)	34/51
Proficient or Above	32.3 (1.51)	26/51	Proficient or Above	29.6 (1.27)	28/51
Advanced or Above	8.3 (0.74)	9/51	Advanced or Above	6.8 (0.71)	10/51

Note: For an explanation of data, please refer to the User's Guide in the front of the book; n/a indicates data not available

Allegany County

Board of Educ Allegany County
108 Washington St • Cumberland, MD 21502-2931
Mailing Address: PO Box 1724 • Cumberland, MD 21502-1724
(301) 759-2038 • http://boe.allconet.org/
Grade Span: PK-12; **Agency Type:** 1
Schools: 27
   14 Primary; 4 Middle; 8 High; 1 Other Level
   22 Regular; 0 Special Education; 1 Vocational; 4 Alternative
   0 Magnet; 0 Charter; 11 Title I Eligible; 11 School-wide Title I
Students: 9,926   (52.1% male; 47.8% female)
   Individual Education Program: 1,587 (16.0%);
   English Language Learner: 15 (0.2%); Migrant: n/a
   Eligible for Free Lunch Program: 3,514 (35.4%)
   Eligible for Reduced-Price Lunch Program: 1,209 (12.2%)
Teachers: 690.0 (14.4 to 1)
Librarians/Media Specialists: 23.0 (431.6 to 1)
Guidance Counselors: 23.0 (431.6 to 1)
Current Spending: ($ per student per year):
   Total: $8,813; Instruction: $5,409; Support Services: $2,668
Enrollment, Drop-out Rates and Diploma Recipients by Race/Ethnicity

Category	Total	White	Black	Asian	AIAN	Hisp.
Enrollment (%)	100.0	94.3	4.4	0.7	0.2	0.4
Drop-out Rate (%)	4.1	4.0	8.9	0.0	0.0	0.0
H.S. Diplomas (#)	733	710	12	9	1	1

Anne Arundel County

Anne Arundel County Pub Schls
2644 Riva Rd • Annapolis, MD 21401-7305
(410) 222-5304 • http://www.aacps.org/
Grade Span: PK-12; **Agency Type:** 1
Schools: 119
   77 Primary; 20 Middle; 17 High; 5 Other Level
   108 Regular; 4 Special Education; 2 Vocational; 5 Alternative
   0 Magnet; 0 Charter; 19 Title I Eligible; 10 School-wide Title I
Students: 74,508   (51.3% male; 48.6% female)
   Individual Education Program: 9,930 (13.3%);
   English Language Learner: 1,161 (1.6%); Migrant: n/a
   Eligible for Free Lunch Program: 9,888 (13.3%)
   Eligible for Reduced-Price Lunch Program: 3,353 (4.5%)
Teachers: 4,501.1 (16.6 to 1)
Librarians/Media Specialists: 107.8 (691.2 to 1)
Guidance Counselors: 196.1 (379.9 to 1)
Current Spending: ($ per student per year):
   Total: $8,361; Instruction: $5,146; Support Services: $2,991
Enrollment, Drop-out Rates and Diploma Recipients by Race/Ethnicity

Category	Total	White	Black	Asian	AIAN	Hisp.
Enrollment (%)	100.0	72.2	20.9	3.1	0.3	3.4
Drop-out Rate (%)	4.4	4.1	6.1	1.7	2.9	3.6
H.S. Diplomas (#)	4,466	3,502	734	148	10	72

Baltimore County

Baltimore County Public Schls
6901 N Charles St • Towson, MD 21204-3711
(410) 887-4281 • http://www.bcps.org/
Grade Span: PK-12; **Agency Type:** 1
Schools: 167
   105 Primary; 27 Middle; 28 High; 7 Other Level
   147 Regular; 9 Special Education; 4 Vocational; 7 Alternative
   0 Magnet; 0 Charter; 43 Title I Eligible; 37 School-wide Title I
Students: 108,523 (51.3% male; 48.6% female)
   Individual Education Program: 13,482 (12.4%);
   English Language Learner: 2,209 (2.0%); Migrant: n/a
   Eligible for Free Lunch Program: 23,621 (21.8%)
   Eligible for Reduced-Price Lunch Program: 8,662 (8.0%)
Teachers: 7,291.6 (14.9 to 1)
Librarians/Media Specialists: 165.9 (654.1 to 1)
Guidance Counselors: 302.0 (359.3 to 1)
Current Spending: ($ per student per year):
   Total: $8,744; Instruction: $5,232; Support Services: $3,097
Enrollment, Drop-out Rates and Diploma Recipients by Race/Ethnicity

Category	Total	White	Black	Asian	AIAN	Hisp.
Enrollment (%)	100.0	56.0	36.7	4.3	0.5	2.5
Drop-out Rate (%)	3.0	3.1	2.8	2.2	4.1	4.8
H.S. Diplomas (#)	6,859	4,482	1,973	275	32	97

Baltimore City Public Schools System
200 E N Ave • Baltimore, MD 21202-5910
(410) 396-8803 • http://www.bcps.k12.md.us/
Grade Span: PK-12; **Agency Type:** 1
Schools: 189
   121 Primary; 26 Middle; 26 High; 16 Other Level
   158 Regular; 10 Special Education; 3 Vocational; 18 Alternative
   0 Magnet; 0 Charter; 100 Title I Eligible; 98 School-wide Title I
Students: 94,049   (50.3% male; 49.6% female)
   Individual Education Program: 14,472 (15.4%);
   English Language Learner: 1,284 (1.4%); Migrant: n/a
   Eligible for Free Lunch Program: 58,565 (62.3%)
   Eligible for Reduced-Price Lunch Program: 8,499 (9.0%)
Teachers: 6,268.0 (15.0 to 1)
Librarians/Media Specialists: 70.0 (1,343.6 to 1)
Guidance Counselors: 166.0 (566.6 to 1)
Current Spending: ($ per student per year):
   Total: $9,639; Instruction: $6,036; Support Services: $3,232
Enrollment, Drop-out Rates and Diploma Recipients by Race/Ethnicity

Category	Total	White	Black	Asian	AIAN	Hisp.
Enrollment (%)	100.0	9.1	88.6	0.6	0.3	1.4
Drop-out Rate (%)	11.5	12.3	11.5	4.7	8.8	6.3
H.S. Diplomas (#)	4,524	362	4,090	35	21	16

Calvert County

Calvert County Public Schools
1305 Dares Beach Rd • Prince Frederick, MD 20678
(410) 535-7207 • http://www.calvertnet.k12.md.us/
Grade Span: PK-12; **Agency Type:** 1
Schools: 25
   12 Primary; 6 Middle; 5 High; 2 Other Level
   21 Regular; 1 Special Education; 1 Vocational; 2 Alternative
   0 Magnet; 0 Charter; 8 Title I Eligible; 0 School-wide Title I
Students: 17,423   (51.3% male; 48.6% female)
   Individual Education Program: 2,320 (13.3%);
   English Language Learner: 101 (0.6%); Migrant: n/a
   Eligible for Free Lunch Program: 1,697 (9.7%)
   Eligible for Reduced-Price Lunch Program: 564 (3.2%)
Teachers: 1,042.3 (16.7 to 1)
Librarians/Media Specialists: 21.0 (829.7 to 1)
Guidance Counselors: 39.0 (446.7 to 1)
Current Spending: ($ per student per year):
   Total: $8,112; Instruction: $5,077; Support Services: $2,603
Enrollment, Drop-out Rates and Diploma Recipients by Race/Ethnicity

Category	Total	White	Black	Asian	AIAN	Hisp.
Enrollment (%)	100.0	81.7	15.7	1.2	0.2	1.2
Drop-out Rate (%)	3.3	3.3	3.9	0.0	0.0	1.6
H.S. Diplomas (#)	1,043	878	146	5	1	13

Caroline County

Caroline County Board of Ed
204 Franklin St • Denton, MD 21629-1035
(410) 479-3250 • http://cl.k12.md.us/
Grade Span: PK-12; **Agency Type:** 1
Schools: 10
   5 Primary; 2 Middle; 3 High; 0 Other Level
   9 Regular; 0 Special Education; 1 Vocational; 0 Alternative
   0 Magnet; 0 Charter; 5 Title I Eligible; 4 School-wide Title I
Students: 5,400   (51.6% male; 48.3% female)
   Individual Education Program: 705 (13.1%);
   English Language Learner: 109 (2.0%); Migrant: n/a
   Eligible for Free Lunch Program: 1,747 (32.4%)
   Eligible for Reduced-Price Lunch Program: 610 (11.3%)
Teachers: 352.0 (15.3 to 1)
Librarians/Media Specialists: 9.0 (600.0 to 1)
Guidance Counselors: 18.0 (300.0 to 1)
Current Spending: ($ per student per year):
   Total: $7,964; Instruction: $4,774; Support Services: $2,687
Enrollment, Drop-out Rates and Diploma Recipients by Race/Ethnicity

Category	Total	White	Black	Asian	AIAN	Hisp.
Enrollment (%)	100.0	76.2	19.6	0.9	0.3	3.0
Drop-out Rate (%)	5.8	5.7	6.7	0.0	0.0	0.0
H.S. Diplomas (#)	341	276	61	3	0	1

Carroll County

Carroll County Public Schools
55 N Court St • Westminster, MD 21157-5155
(410) 751-3128 • http://www.carr.org/ccps
Grade Span: PK-12; **Agency Type:** 1
Schools: 42
   21 Primary; 9 Middle; 8 High; 4 Other Level
   37 Regular; 1 Special Education; 1 Vocational; 3 Alternative
   0 Magnet; 0 Charter; 15 Title I Eligible; 0 School-wide Title I
Students: 28,832   (51.5% male; 48.4% female)
   Individual Education Program: 3,604 (12.5%);
   English Language Learner: 76 (0.3%); Migrant: n/a
   Eligible for Free Lunch Program: 1,976 (6.9%)
   Eligible for Reduced-Price Lunch Program: 744 (2.6%)

Teachers: 1,709.3 (16.9 to 1)
Librarians/Media Specialists: 34.0 (848.0 to 1)
Guidance Counselors: 77.5 (372.0 to 1)
Current Spending: ($ per student per year):
Total: $7,769; Instruction: $4,666; Support Services: $2,772
Enrollment, Drop-out Rates and Diploma Recipients by Race/Ethnicity

Category	Total	White	Black	Asian	AIAN	Hisp.
Enrollment (%)	100.0	94.4	2.8	1.3	0.3	1.3
Drop-out Rate (%)	2.0	2.0	2.0	0.0	0.0	6.3
H.S. Diplomas (#)	1,910	1,831	42	29	0	8

Cecil County

Board of Ed of Cecil County
201 Booth St • Elkton, MD 21921-5684
(410) 996-5499 • http://www.ccps.org/
Grade Span: PK-12; **Agency Type:** 1
Schools: 31
17 Primary; 6 Middle; 7 High; 1 Other Level
28 Regular; 0 Special Education; 1 Vocational; 2 Alternative
0 Magnet; 0 Charter; 11 Title I Eligible; 6 School-wide Title I
Students: 16,475   (51.6% male; 48.3% female)
Individual Education Program: 2,495 (15.1%);
English Language Learner: 93 (0.6%); Migrant: n/a
Eligible for Free Lunch Program: 3,013 (18.3%)
Eligible for Reduced-Price Lunch Program: 980 (5.9%)
Teachers: 1,043.6 (15.8 to 1)
Librarians/Media Specialists: 27.5 (599.1 to 1)
Guidance Counselors: 49.5 (332.8 to 1)
Current Spending: ($ per student per year):
Total: $7,879; Instruction: $4,820; Support Services: $2,617
Enrollment, Drop-out Rates and Diploma Recipients by Race/Ethnicity

Category	Total	White	Black	Asian	AIAN	Hisp.
Enrollment (%)	100.0	89.0	7.5	0.8	0.3	2.3
Drop-out Rate (%)	3.0	3.0	3.9	0.0	0.0	3.1
H.S. Diplomas (#)	878	815	45	9	1	8

Charles County

Board of Educ Charles County
5980 Radio Station Rd • La Plata, MD 20646-0170
Mailing Address: PO Box 2770 • La Plata, MD 20646-2770
(301) 934-7223 • http://www.ccboe.com/
Grade Span: PK-12; **Agency Type:** 1
Schools: 34
19 Primary; 7 Middle; 6 High; 2 Other Level
31 Regular; 0 Special Education; 1 Vocational; 2 Alternative
0 Magnet; 0 Charter; 9 Title I Eligible; 9 School-wide Title I
Students: 25,610   (51.1% male; 48.8% female)
Individual Education Program: 2,430 (9.5%);
English Language Learner: 189 (0.7%); Migrant: n/a
Eligible for Free Lunch Program: 4,154 (16.2%)
Eligible for Reduced-Price Lunch Program: 1,285 (5.0%)
Teachers: 1,446.8 (17.7 to 1)
Librarians/Media Specialists: 31.0 (826.1 to 1)
Guidance Counselors: 58.6 (437.0 to 1)
Current Spending: ($ per student per year):
Total: $7,955; Instruction: $4,631; Support Services: $2,845
Enrollment, Drop-out Rates and Diploma Recipients by Race/Ethnicity

Category	Total	White	Black	Asian	AIAN	Hisp.
Enrollment (%)	100.0	52.6	41.1	2.8	0.9	2.7
Drop-out Rate (%)	3.3	2.9	4.2	2.1	6.1	1.8
H.S. Diplomas (#)	1,481	935	453	49	12	32

Dorchester County

Dorchester County Board of Ed
700 Glasgow St • Cambridge, MD 21613-1738
Mailing Address: PO Box 619 • Cambridge, MD 21613-0619
(410) 221-5230 • http://www.dcps.k12.md.us/
Grade Span: PK-12; **Agency Type:** 1
Schools: 13
7 Primary; 2 Middle; 3 High; 1 Other Level
11 Regular; 0 Special Education; 1 Vocational; 1 Alternative
0 Magnet; 0 Charter; 4 Title I Eligible; 4 School-wide Title I
Students: 4,803   (50.1% male; 49.8% female)
Individual Education Program: 571 (11.9%);
English Language Learner: 88 (1.8%); Migrant: n/a
Eligible for Free Lunch Program: 1,927 (40.1%)
Eligible for Reduced-Price Lunch Program: 380 (7.9%)
Teachers: 308.4 (15.6 to 1)
Librarians/Media Specialists: 9.0 (533.7 to 1)
Guidance Counselors: 14.0 (343.1 to 1)
Current Spending: ($ per student per year):
Total: $8,913; Instruction: $5,110; Support Services: $3,225

Enrollment, Drop-out Rates and Diploma Recipients by Race/Ethnicity

Category	Total	White	Black	Asian	AIAN	Hisp.
Enrollment (%)	100.0	55.0	41.4	1.2	0.3	2.1
Drop-out Rate (%)	5.8	5.0	7.2	0.0	0.0	0.0
H.S. Diplomas (#)	283	177	98	4	0	4

Frederick County

Frederick County Board of Ed
115 E Church St • Frederick, MD 21701-5403
(301) 696-6910 • http://www.fcps.org/
Grade Span: PK-12; **Agency Type:** 1
Schools: 59
34 Primary; 12 Middle; 12 High; 1 Other Level
54 Regular; 3 Special Education; 1 Vocational; 1 Alternative
0 Magnet; 1 Charter; 9 Title I Eligible; 3 School-wide Title I
Students: 38,950   (51.1% male; 48.8% female)
Individual Education Program: 4,691 (12.0%);
English Language Learner: 537 (1.4%); Migrant: n/a
Eligible for Free Lunch Program: 3,930 (10.1%)
Eligible for Reduced-Price Lunch Program: 1,464 (3.8%)
Teachers: 2,408.3 (16.2 to 1)
Librarians/Media Specialists: 52.3 (744.7 to 1)
Guidance Counselors: 91.8 (424.3 to 1)
Current Spending: ($ per student per year):
Total: $7,944; Instruction: $4,854; Support Services: $2,722
Enrollment, Drop-out Rates and Diploma Recipients by Race/Ethnicity

Category	Total	White	Black	Asian	AIAN	Hisp.
Enrollment (%)	100.0	82.8	9.9	2.9	0.3	4.1
Drop-out Rate (%)	1.8	1.7	3.4	0.4	0.0	3.7
H.S. Diplomas (#)	2,465	2,201	164	48	3	49

Garrett County

Board of Educ Garrett County
40 S 2nd St • Oakland, MD 21550-1506
(301) 334-8901 • http://www.ga.k12.md.us/
Grade Span: PK-12; **Agency Type:** 1
Schools: 18
11 Primary; 2 Middle; 4 High; 1 Other Level
15 Regular; 0 Special Education; 0 Vocational; 3 Alternative
0 Magnet; 0 Charter; 8 Title I Eligible; 8 School-wide Title I
Students: 4,810   (52.0% male; 47.9% female)
Individual Education Program: 678 (14.1%);
English Language Learner: 0 (0.0%); Migrant: n/a
Eligible for Free Lunch Program: 1,435 (29.8%)
Eligible for Reduced-Price Lunch Program: 710 (14.8%)
Teachers: 360.0 (13.4 to 1)
Librarians/Media Specialists: 2.0 (2,405.0 to 1)
Guidance Counselors: 12.0 (400.8 to 1)
Current Spending: ($ per student per year):
Total: $8,815; Instruction: $5,287; Support Services: $2,950
Enrollment, Drop-out Rates and Diploma Recipients by Race/Ethnicity

Category	Total	White	Black	Asian	AIAN	Hisp.
Enrollment (%)	100.0	99.4	0.2	0.2	0.0	0.1
Drop-out Rate (%)	4.8	4.8	0.0	0.0	n/a	0.0
H.S. Diplomas (#)	293	291	2	0	0	0

Harford County

Harford County Public Schools
45 E Gordon St • Bel Air, MD 21014-2915
(410) 588-5204 • http://www.co.ha.md.us/harford_schools/
Grade Span: PK-12; **Agency Type:** 1
Schools: 51
32 Primary; 8 Middle; 10 High; 1 Other Level
48 Regular; 1 Special Education; 1 Vocational; 1 Alternative
0 Magnet; 0 Charter; 13 Title I Eligible; 5 School-wide Title I
Students: 40,200   (51.4% male; 48.5% female)
Individual Education Program: 6,038 (15.0%);
English Language Learner: 289 (0.7%); Migrant: n/a
Eligible for Free Lunch Program: 5,372 (13.4%)
Eligible for Reduced-Price Lunch Program: 1,913 (4.8%)
Teachers: 2,296.6 (17.5 to 1)
Librarians/Media Specialists: 54.5 (737.6 to 1)
Guidance Counselors: 75.0 (536.0 to 1)
Current Spending: ($ per student per year):
Total: $7,641; Instruction: $4,741; Support Services: $2,535
Enrollment, Drop-out Rates and Diploma Recipients by Race/Ethnicity

Category	Total	White	Black	Asian	AIAN	Hisp.
Enrollment (%)	100.0	78.1	16.3	2.3	0.5	2.7
Drop-out Rate (%)	3.4	3.2	5.1	2.0	8.9	3.7
H.S. Diplomas (#)	2,425	2,028	272	53	9	63

Howard County

Howard County Pub Schls System
10910 State Route 108 • Ellicott City, MD 21042-6198
(410) 313-6674 • http://www.howard.k12.md.us/
Grade Span: PK-12; **Agency Type:** 1
Schools: 71
    38 Primary; 19 Middle; 11 High; 3 Other Level
    68 Regular; 1 Special Education; 0 Vocational; 2 Alternative
    0 Magnet; 0 Charter; 9 Title I Eligible; 1 School-wide Title I
Students: 47,833   (52.1% male; 47.8% female)
    Individual Education Program: 4,939 (10.3%);
    English Language Learner: 1,354 (2.8%); Migrant: n/a
    Eligible for Free Lunch Program: 3,505 (7.3%)
    Eligible for Reduced-Price Lunch Program: 1,486 (3.1%)
Teachers: 3,323.6 (14.4 to 1)
Librarians/Media Specialists: 81.0 (590.5 to 1)
Guidance Counselors: 122.5 (390.5 to 1)
Current Spending: ($ per student per year):
    Total: $9,420; Instruction: $5,982; Support Services: $2,986
Enrollment, Drop-out Rates and Diploma Recipients by Race/Ethnicity

Category	Total	White	Black	Asian	AIAN	Hisp.
Enrollment (%)	100.0	65.9	18.4	11.8	0.2	3.6
Drop-out Rate (%)	2.0	1.6	3.4	1.5	0.0	5.1
H.S. Diplomas (#)	2,990	2,098	490	337	3	62

Kent County

Board of Ed of Kent County
215 Washington Ave • Chestertown, MD 21620-1668
(410) 778-7113 • http://www.kent.k12.md.us/
Grade Span: PK-12; **Agency Type:** 1
Schools: 8
    4 Primary; 3 Middle; 1 High; 0 Other Level
    8 Regular; 0 Special Education; 0 Vocational; 0 Alternative
    0 Magnet; 0 Charter; 4 Title I Eligible; 4 School-wide Title I
Students: 2,565   (51.8% male; 48.1% female)
    Individual Education Program: 332 (12.9%);
    English Language Learner: 58 (2.3%); Migrant: n/a
    Eligible for Free Lunch Program: 764 (29.8%)
    Eligible for Reduced-Price Lunch Program: 286 (11.2%)
Teachers: 166.5 (15.4 to 1)
Librarians/Media Specialists: 1.0 (2,565.0 to 1)
Guidance Counselors: 11.0 (233.2 to 1)
Current Spending: ($ per student per year):
    Total: $10,189; Instruction: $5,993; Support Services: $3,719
Enrollment, Drop-out Rates and Diploma Recipients by Race/Ethnicity

Category	Total	White	Black	Asian	AIAN	Hisp.
Enrollment (%)	100.0	69.7	25.5	0.5	0.4	3.9
Drop-out Rate (%)	6.3	5.0	10.6	0.0	0.0	0.0
H.S. Diplomas (#)	185	128	53	0	1	3

Montgomery County

Montgomery County Public Schls
850 Hungerford Dr • Rockville, MD 20850-1718
(301) 279-3301 • http://www.mcps.k12.md.us/
Grade Span: PK-12; **Agency Type:** 1
Schools: 194
    126 Primary; 36 Middle; 27 High; 5 Other Level
    184 Regular; 7 Special Education; 1 Vocational; 2 Alternative
    0 Magnet; 0 Charter; 18 Title I Eligible; 18 School-wide Title I
Students: 139,201   (51.4% male; 48.5% female)
    Individual Education Program: 16,699 (12.0%);
    English Language Learner: 11,860 (8.5%); Migrant: n/a
    Eligible for Free Lunch Program: 21,536 (15.5%)
    Eligible for Reduced-Price Lunch Program: 9,861 (7.1%)
Teachers: 9,007.4 (15.5 to 1)
Librarians/Media Specialists: 192.0 (725.0 to 1)
Guidance Counselors: 422.1 (329.8 to 1)
Current Spending: ($ per student per year):
    Total: $10,580; Instruction: $6,783; Support Services: $3,328
Enrollment, Drop-out Rates and Diploma Recipients by Race/Ethnicity

Category	Total	White	Black	Asian	AIAN	Hisp.
Enrollment (%)	100.0	44.6	22.1	14.3	0.3	18.7
Drop-out Rate (%)	1.9	1.4	2.5	1.0	2.6	3.5
H.S. Diplomas (#)	8,282	4,286	1,624	1,336	21	1,015

Prince George's County

Prince Georges County Public Schools
14201 School Ln • Upper Marlboro, MD 20772-2866
(301) 952-6008 • http://www.pgcps.pg.k12.md.us/
Grade Span: PK-12; **Agency Type:** 1
Schools: 203

    140 Primary; 27 Middle; 30 High; 6 Other Level
    183 Regular; 9 Special Education; 2 Vocational; 9 Alternative
    0 Magnet; 0 Charter; 74 Title I Eligible; 74 School-wide Title I
Students: 137,285   (51.2% male; 48.7% female)
    Individual Education Program: 14,048 (10.2%);
    English Language Learner: 7,368 (5.4%); Migrant: n/a
    Eligible for Free Lunch Program: 44,369 (32.3%)
    Eligible for Reduced-Price Lunch Program: 17,218 (12.5%)
Teachers: 8,119.3 (16.9 to 1)
Librarians/Media Specialists: 129.5 (1,060.1 to 1)
Guidance Counselors: 346.9 (395.7 to 1)
Current Spending: ($ per student per year):
    Total: $8,621; Instruction: $4,983; Support Services: $3,173
Enrollment, Drop-out Rates and Diploma Recipients by Race/Ethnicity

Category	Total	White	Black	Asian	AIAN	Hisp.
Enrollment (%)	100.0	8.0	77.6	3.1	0.6	10.8
Drop-out Rate (%)	3.1	4.6	2.9	1.8	3.8	4.2
H.S. Diplomas (#)	7,552	972	5,847	307	38	388

Queen Anne's County

Board of Edqueen Annes County
202 Chesterfield Ave • Centreville, MD 21617-0080
(410) 758-2403 • http://www.boe.qacps.k12.md.us/
Grade Span: PK-12; **Agency Type:** 1
Schools: 14
    8 Primary; 3 Middle; 3 High; 0 Other Level
    13 Regular; 0 Special Education; 0 Vocational; 1 Alternative
    0 Magnet; 0 Charter; 3 Title I Eligible; 0 School-wide Title I
Students: 7,526   (51.1% male; 48.8% female)
    Individual Education Program: 1,027 (13.6%);
    English Language Learner: 50 (0.7%); Migrant: n/a
    Eligible for Free Lunch Program: 820 (10.9%)
    Eligible for Reduced-Price Lunch Program: 338 (4.5%)
Teachers: 443.2 (17.0 to 1)
Librarians/Media Specialists: 11.0 (684.2 to 1)
Guidance Counselors: 17.0 (442.7 to 1)
Current Spending: ($ per student per year):
    Total: $8,025; Instruction: $4,842; Support Services: $2,839
Enrollment, Drop-out Rates and Diploma Recipients by Race/Ethnicity

Category	Total	White	Black	Asian	AIAN	Hisp.
Enrollment (%)	100.0	88.7	9.2	0.8	0.3	1.1
Drop-out Rate (%)	3.3	2.9	6.7	0.0	0.0	0.0
H.S. Diplomas (#)	393	348	40	3	2	0

Somerset County

Somerset County Public Schools
7982a Crisfield Hwy • Princess Anne, MD 21871
(410) 651-1616 • http://www.somerset.k12.md.us/
Grade Span: PK-12; **Agency Type:** 1
Schools: 11
    6 Primary; 2 Middle; 3 High; 0 Other Level
    10 Regular; 0 Special Education; 1 Vocational; 0 Alternative
    0 Magnet; 0 Charter; 5 Title I Eligible; 5 School-wide Title I
Students: 2,951   (51.3% male; 48.6% female)
    Individual Education Program: 355 (12.0%);
    English Language Learner: 50 (1.7%); Migrant: n/a
    Eligible for Free Lunch Program: 1,413 (47.9%)
    Eligible for Reduced-Price Lunch Program: 291 (9.9%)
Teachers: 214.6 (13.8 to 1)
Librarians/Media Specialists: 4.0 (737.8 to 1)
Guidance Counselors: 9.0 (327.9 to 1)
Current Spending: ($ per student per year):
    Total: $9,623; Instruction: $5,469; Support Services: $3,506
Enrollment, Drop-out Rates and Diploma Recipients by Race/Ethnicity

Category	Total	White	Black	Asian	AIAN	Hisp.
Enrollment (%)	100.0	50.8	45.5	0.9	0.0	2.8
Drop-out Rate (%)	5.3	4.7	6.4	0.0	0.0	0.0
H.S. Diplomas (#)	163	101	57	4	0	1

St. Mary's County

Saint Marys County Public Schools
23160 Moakley St • Leonardtown, MD 20650-0641
Mailing Address: PO Box 641 • Leonardtown, MD 20650-0641
(301) 475-4250 • http://www.smcps.k12.md.us/
Grade Span: PK-12; **Agency Type:** 1
Schools: 27
    16 Primary; 4 Middle; 6 High; 1 Other Level
    22 Regular; 1 Special Education; 1 Vocational; 3 Alternative
    0 Magnet; 0 Charter; 3 Title I Eligible; 3 School-wide Title I
Students: 16,261   (51.0% male; 48.9% female)
    Individual Education Program: 2,208 (13.6%);
    English Language Learner: 136 (0.8%); Migrant: n/a

Eligible for Free Lunch Program: 2,704 (16.6%)
Eligible for Reduced-Price Lunch Program: 854 (5.3%)
Teachers: 1,003.5 (16.2 to 1)
Librarians/Media Specialists: 28.0 (580.8 to 1)
Guidance Counselors: 38.0 (427.9 to 1)
Current Spending: ($ per student per year):
Total: $7,963; Instruction: $4,637; Support Services: $2,875
Enrollment, Drop-out Rates and Diploma Recipients by Race/Ethnicity

Category	Total	White	Black	Asian	AIAN	Hisp.
Enrollment (%)	100.0	76.5	18.6	2.1	0.6	2.1
Drop-out Rate (%)	3.1	2.8	5.1	1.1	0.0	0.0
H.S. Diplomas (#)	845	707	108	15	2	13

Talbot County

Talbot County Public Schools
12 Magnolia St • Easton, MD 21601-1029
Mailing Address: PO Box 1029 • Easton, MD 21601-1029
(410) 822-0330 • http://www.tcps.k12.md.us/
Grade Span: PK-12; **Agency Type:** 1
Schools: 8
5 Primary; 1 Middle; 2 High; 0 Other Level
8 Regular; 0 Special Education; 0 Vocational; 0 Alternative
0 Magnet; 0 Charter; 2 Title I Eligible; 0 School-wide Title I
Students: 4,459 (51.8% male; 48.1% female)
Individual Education Program: 400 (9.0%);
English Language Learner: 114 (2.6%); Migrant: n/a
Eligible for Free Lunch Program: 864 (19.4%)
Eligible for Reduced-Price Lunch Program: 248 (5.6%)
Teachers: 307.2 (14.5 to 1)
Librarians/Media Specialists: 5.0 (891.8 to 1)
Guidance Counselors: 15.5 (287.7 to 1)
Current Spending: ($ per student per year):
Total: $8,743; Instruction: $5,500; Support Services: $2,751
Enrollment, Drop-out Rates and Diploma Recipients by Race/Ethnicity

Category	Total	White	Black	Asian	AIAN	Hisp.
Enrollment (%)	100.0	72.6	22.2	1.7	0.2	3.2
Drop-out Rate (%)	3.3	2.8	5.0	0.0	0.0	5.3
H.S. Diplomas (#)	272	216	52	1	0	3

Washington County

Board of Ed Washington County
820 Commonwealth Ave • Hagerstown, MD 21741-0730
Mailing Address: PO Box 730 • Hagerstown, MD 21741-0730
(301) 766-2817 • http://www.wcboe.k12.md.us/
Grade Span: PK-12; **Agency Type:** 1
Schools: 46
26 Primary; 7 Middle; 9 High; 4 Other Level
40 Regular; 2 Special Education; 1 Vocational; 3 Alternative
0 Magnet; 0 Charter; 10 Title I Eligible; 10 School-wide Title I
Students: 20,338 (51.4% male; 48.5% female)
Individual Education Program: 2,663 (13.1%);
English Language Learner: 155 (0.8%); Migrant: n/a
Eligible for Free Lunch Program: 4,685 (23.0%)
Eligible for Reduced-Price Lunch Program: 1,942 (9.5%)
Teachers: 1,292.0 (15.7 to 1)
Librarians/Media Specialists: 37.5 (542.3 to 1)
Guidance Counselors: 50.5 (402.7 to 1)
Current Spending: ($ per student per year):
Total: $7,984; Instruction: $4,970; Support Services: $2,532
Enrollment, Drop-out Rates and Diploma Recipients by Race/Ethnicity

Category	Total	White	Black	Asian	AIAN	Hisp.
Enrollment (%)	100.0	87.1	9.5	1.1	0.2	2.0
Drop-out Rate (%)	3.1	2.9	7.6	1.1	0.0	1.4
H.S. Diplomas (#)	1,234	1,130	61	22	0	21

Wicomico County

Wicomico County Board of Ed
101 Long Ave • Salisbury, MD 21802-1538
Mailing Address: PO Box 1538 • Salisbury, MD 21802-1538
(410) 677-4596 • http://www.wcboe.org/
Grade Span: PK-12; **Agency Type:** 1
Schools: 27
17 Primary; 3 Middle; 4 High; 3 Other Level
24 Regular; 0 Special Education; 0 Vocational; 3 Alternative
0 Magnet; 0 Charter; 13 Title I Eligible; 5 School-wide Title I
Students: 14,402 (51.7% male; 48.2% female)
Individual Education Program: 1,702 (11.8%);
English Language Learner: 276 (1.9%); Migrant: n/a
Eligible for Free Lunch Program: 4,944 (34.3%)
Eligible for Reduced-Price Lunch Program: 1,197 (8.3%)
Teachers: 1,018.3 (14.1 to 1)
Librarians/Media Specialists: 8.0 (1,800.3 to 1)

Guidance Counselors: 52.6 (273.8 to 1)
Current Spending: ($ per student per year):
Total: $8,261; Instruction: $5,105; Support Services: $2,710
Enrollment, Drop-out Rates and Diploma Recipients by Race/Ethnicity

Category	Total	White	Black	Asian	AIAN	Hisp.
Enrollment (%)	100.0	58.0	36.1	3.0	0.2	2.8
Drop-out Rate (%)	6.2	4.6	10.1	2.5	0.0	3.3
H.S. Diplomas (#)	780	527	211	26	1	15

Worcester County

Board of Ed Worcester County
6270 Worcester Hwy • Newark, MD 21841-2224
(410) 632-2582 • http://www.co.worcester.md.us/
Grade Span: PK-12; **Agency Type:** 1
Schools: 14
5 Primary; 4 Middle; 4 High; 1 Other Level
12 Regular; 1 Special Education; 1 Vocational; 0 Alternative
0 Magnet; 0 Charter; 5 Title I Eligible; 5 School-wide Title I
Students: 6,783 (51.4% male; 48.5% female)
Individual Education Program: 765 (11.3%);
English Language Learner: 123 (1.8%); Migrant: n/a
Eligible for Free Lunch Program: 1,828 (26.9%)
Eligible for Reduced-Price Lunch Program: 457 (6.7%)
Teachers: 512.3 (13.2 to 1)
Librarians/Media Specialists: 12.0 (565.3 to 1)
Guidance Counselors: 22.4 (302.8 to 1)
Current Spending: ($ per student per year):
Total: $10,085; Instruction: $6,270; Support Services: $3,239
Enrollment, Drop-out Rates and Diploma Recipients by Race/Ethnicity

Category	Total	White	Black	Asian	AIAN	Hisp.
Enrollment (%)	100.0	71.7	25.0	0.9	0.3	2.1
Drop-out Rate (%)	3.2	3.2	3.1	0.0	n/a	0.0
H.S. Diplomas (#)	486	363	111	7	0	5

Number of Schools

Rank	Number	District Name	City
1	203	Prince Georges Co Public Schools	Upper Marlboro
2	194	Montgomery County Public Schls	Rockville
3	189	Baltimore City Public Schools Sys	Baltimore
4	167	Baltimore County Public Schls	Towson
5	119	Anne Arundel County Pub Schls	Annapolis
6	71	Howard County Pub Schls System	Ellicott City
7	59	Frederick County Board of Ed	Frederick
8	51	Harford County Public Schools	Bel Air
9	46	Board of Ed Washington County	Hagerstown
10	42	Carroll County Public Schools	Westminster
11	34	Board of Educ Charles County	La Plata
12	31	Board of Ed of Cecil County	Elkton
13	27	Board of Educ Allegany County	Cumberland
13	27	Saint Marys County Public Schools	Leonardtown
13	27	Wicomico County Board of Ed	Salisbury
16	25	Calvert County Public Schools	Prince Frederick
17	18	Board of Educ Garrett County	Oakland
18	14	Board of Ed Worcester County	Newark
18	14	Board of Edqueen Annes County	Centreville
20	13	Dorchester County Board of Ed	Cambridge
21	11	Somerset County Public Schools	Princess Anne
22	10	Caroline County Board of Ed	Denton
23	8	Board of Ed of Kent County	Chestertown
23	8	Talbot County Public Schools	Easton

Number of Teachers

Rank	Number	District Name	City
1	9,007	Montgomery County Public Schls	Rockville
2	8,119	Prince Georges Co Public Schools	Upper Marlboro
3	7,291	Baltimore County Public Schls	Towson
4	6,268	Baltimore City Public Schools Sys	Baltimore
5	4,501	Anne Arundel County Pub Schls	Annapolis
6	3,323	Howard County Pub Schls System	Ellicott City
7	2,408	Frederick County Board of Ed	Frederick
8	2,296	Harford County Public Schools	Bel Air
9	1,709	Carroll County Public Schools	Westminster
10	1,446	Board of Educ Charles County	La Plata
11	1,292	Board of Ed Washington County	Hagerstown
12	1,043	Board of Ed of Cecil County	Elkton
13	1,042	Calvert County Public Schools	Prince Frederick
14	1,018	Wicomico County Board of Ed	Salisbury
15	1,003	Saint Marys County Public Schools	Leonardtown
16	690	Board of Educ Allegany County	Cumberland
17	512	Board of Ed Worcester County	Newark
18	443	Board of Edqueen Annes County	Centreville
19	360	Board of Educ Garrett County	Oakland
20	352	Caroline County Board of Ed	Denton
21	308	Dorchester County Board of Ed	Cambridge
22	307	Talbot County Public Schools	Easton
23	214	Somerset County Public Schools	Princess Anne
24	166	Board of Ed of Kent County	Chestertown

Number of Students

Rank	Number	District Name	City
1	139,201	Montgomery County Public Schls	Rockville
2	137,285	Prince Georges Co Public Schools	Upper Marlboro
3	108,523	Baltimore County Public Schls	Towson
4	94,049	Baltimore City Public Schools Sys	Baltimore
5	74,508	Anne Arundel County Pub Schls	Annapolis
6	47,833	Howard County Pub Schls System	Ellicott City
7	40,200	Harford County Public Schools	Bel Air
8	38,950	Frederick County Board of Ed	Frederick
9	28,832	Carroll County Public Schools	Westminster
10	25,610	Board of Educ Charles County	La Plata
11	20,338	Board of Ed Washington County	Hagerstown
12	17,423	Calvert County Public Schools	Prince Frederick
13	16,475	Board of Ed of Cecil County	Elkton
14	16,261	Saint Marys County Public Schools	Leonardtown
15	14,402	Wicomico County Board of Ed	Salisbury
16	9,926	Board of Educ Allegany County	Cumberland
17	7,526	Board of Edqueen Annes County	Centreville
18	6,783	Board of Ed Worcester County	Newark
19	5,400	Caroline County Board of Ed	Denton
20	4,810	Board of Educ Garrett County	Oakland
21	4,803	Dorchester County Board of Ed	Cambridge
22	4,459	Talbot County Public Schools	Easton
23	2,951	Somerset County Public Schools	Princess Anne
24	2,565	Board of Ed of Kent County	Chestertown

Male Students

Rank	Percent	District Name	City
1	52.1	Board of Educ Allegany County	Cumberland
2	52.1	Howard County Pub Schls System	Ellicott City
3	52.0	Board of Educ Garrett County	Oakland
4	51.8	Talbot County Public Schools	Easton
5	51.8	Board of Ed of Kent County	Chestertown
6	51.7	Wicomico County Board of Ed	Salisbury
7	51.6	Board of Ed of Cecil County	Elkton
8	51.6	Caroline County Board of Ed	Denton
9	51.5	Carroll County Public Schools	Westminster
10	51.4	Montgomery County Public Schls	Rockville
11	51.4	Board of Ed Worcester County	Newark
12	51.4	Board of Ed Washington County	Hagerstown
13	51.4	Harford County Public Schools	Bel Air
14	51.3	Somerset County Public Schools	Princess Anne
15	51.3	Anne Arundel County Pub Schls	Annapolis
16	51.3	Baltimore County Public Schls	Towson
17	51.3	Calvert County Public Schools	Prince Frederick
18	51.2	Prince Georges Co Public Schools	Upper Marlboro
19	51.1	Frederick County Board of Ed	Frederick
20	51.1	Board of Edqueen Annes County	Centreville
21	51.1	Board of Educ Charles County	La Plata
22	51.0	Saint Marys County Public Schools	Leonardtown
23	50.3	Baltimore City Public Schools Sys	Baltimore
24	50.1	Dorchester County Board of Ed	Cambridge

Female Students

Rank	Percent	District Name	City
1	49.8	Dorchester County Board of Ed	Cambridge
2	49.6	Baltimore City Public Schools Sys	Baltimore
3	48.9	Saint Marys County Public Schools	Leonardtown
4	48.8	Board of Educ Charles County	La Plata
5	48.8	Board of Edqueen Annes County	Centreville
6	48.8	Frederick County Board of Ed	Frederick
7	48.7	Prince Georges Co Public Schools	Upper Marlboro
8	48.6	Calvert County Public Schools	Prince Frederick
9	48.6	Baltimore County Public Schls	Towson
10	48.6	Anne Arundel County Pub Schls	Annapolis
11	48.6	Somerset County Public Schools	Princess Anne
12	48.5	Harford County Public Schools	Bel Air
13	48.5	Board of Ed Washington County	Hagerstown
14	48.5	Board of Ed Worcester County	Newark
15	48.5	Montgomery County Public Schls	Rockville
16	48.4	Carroll County Public Schools	Westminster
17	48.3	Caroline County Board of Ed	Denton
18	48.3	Board of Ed of Cecil County	Elkton
19	48.2	Wicomico County Board of Ed	Salisbury
20	48.1	Board of Ed of Kent County	Chestertown
21	48.1	Talbot County Public Schools	Easton
22	47.9	Board of Educ Garrett County	Oakland
23	47.8	Howard County Pub Schls System	Ellicott City
24	47.8	Board of Educ Allegany County	Cumberland

Individual Education Program Students

Rank	Percent	District Name	City
1	16.0	Board of Educ Allegany County	Cumberland
2	15.4	Baltimore City Public Schools Sys	Baltimore
3	15.1	Board of Ed of Cecil County	Elkton
4	15.0	Harford County Public Schools	Bel Air
5	14.1	Board of Educ Garrett County	Oakland
6	13.6	Board of Edqueen Annes County	Centreville
6	13.6	Saint Marys County Public Schools	Leonardtown
8	13.3	Anne Arundel County Pub Schls	Annapolis
8	13.3	Calvert County Public Schools	Prince Frederick
10	13.1	Board of Ed Washington County	Hagerstown
10	13.1	Caroline County Board of Ed	Denton
12	12.9	Board of Ed of Kent County	Chestertown
13	12.5	Carroll County Public Schools	Westminster
14	12.4	Baltimore County Public Schls	Towson
15	12.0	Frederick County Board of Ed	Frederick
15	12.0	Montgomery County Public Schls	Rockville
15	12.0	Somerset County Public Schools	Princess Anne
18	11.9	Dorchester County Board of Ed	Cambridge
19	11.8	Wicomico County Board of Ed	Salisbury
20	11.3	Board of Ed Worcester County	Newark
21	10.3	Howard County Pub Schls System	Ellicott City
22	10.2	Prince Georges Co Public Schools	Upper Marlboro
23	9.5	Board of Educ Charles County	La Plata
24	9.0	Talbot County Public Schools	Easton

English Language Learner Students

Rank	Percent	District Name	City
1	8.5	Montgomery County Public Schls	Rockville
2	5.4	Prince Georges Co Public Schools	Upper Marlboro
3	2.8	Howard County Pub Schls System	Ellicott City
4	2.6	Talbot County Public Schools	Easton
5	2.3	Board of Ed of Kent County	Chestertown
6	2.0	Baltimore County Public Schls	Towson
6	2.0	Caroline County Board of Ed	Denton
8	1.9	Wicomico County Board of Ed	Salisbury
9	1.8	Board of Ed Worcester County	Newark
9	1.8	Dorchester County Board of Ed	Cambridge
11	1.7	Somerset County Public Schools	Princess Anne
12	1.6	Anne Arundel County Pub Schls	Annapolis
13	1.4	Baltimore City Public Schools Sys	Baltimore
13	1.4	Frederick County Board of Ed	Frederick
15	0.8	Board of Ed Washington County	Hagerstown
15	0.8	Saint Marys County Public Schools	Leonardtown
17	0.7	Board of Edqueen Annes County	Centreville
17	0.7	Board of Educ Charles County	La Plata
17	0.7	Harford County Public Schools	Bel Air
20	0.6	Board of Ed of Cecil County	Elkton
20	0.6	Calvert County Public Schools	Prince Frederick
22	0.3	Carroll County Public Schools	Westminster
23	0.2	Board of Educ Allegany County	Cumberland
24	0.0	Board of Educ Garrett County	Oakland

Migrant Students

Rank	Percent	District Name	City
1	n/a	Anne Arundel County Pub Schls	Annapolis
1	n/a	Baltimore City Public Schools Sys	Baltimore
1	n/a	Baltimore County Public Schls	Towson
1	n/a	Board of Ed Washington County	Hagerstown
1	n/a	Board of Ed Worcester County	Newark
1	n/a	Board of Ed of Cecil County	Elkton
1	n/a	Board of Ed of Kent County	Chestertown
1	n/a	Board of Edqueen Annes County	Centreville
1	n/a	Board of Educ Allegany County	Cumberland
1	n/a	Board of Educ Charles County	La Plata
1	n/a	Board of Educ Garrett County	Oakland
1	n/a	Calvert County Public Schools	Prince Frederick
1	n/a	Caroline County Board of Ed	Denton
1	n/a	Carroll County Public Schools	Westminster
1	n/a	Dorchester County Board of Ed	Cambridge
1	n/a	Frederick County Board of Ed	Frederick
1	n/a	Harford County Public Schools	Bel Air
1	n/a	Howard County Pub Schls System	Ellicott City
1	n/a	Montgomery County Public Schls	Rockville
1	n/a	Prince Georges Co Public Schools	Upper Marlboro
1	n/a	Saint Marys County Public Schools	Leonardtown
1	n/a	Somerset County Public Schools	Princess Anne
1	n/a	Talbot County Public Schools	Easton
1	n/a	Wicomico County Board of Ed	Salisbury

Students Eligible for Free Lunch

Rank	Percent	District Name	City
1	62.3	Baltimore City Public Schools Sys	Baltimore
2	47.9	Somerset County Public Schools	Princess Anne
3	40.1	Dorchester County Board of Ed	Cambridge
4	35.4	Board of Educ Allegany County	Cumberland
5	34.3	Wicomico County Board of Ed	Salisbury
6	32.4	Caroline County Board of Ed	Denton
7	32.3	Prince Georges Co Public Schools	Upper Marlboro
8	29.8	Board of Ed of Kent County	Chestertown
8	29.8	Board of Educ Garrett County	Oakland
10	26.9	Board of Ed Worcester County	Newark
11	23.0	Board of Ed Washington County	Hagerstown
12	21.8	Baltimore County Public Schls	Towson
13	19.4	Talbot County Public Schools	Easton
14	18.3	Board of Ed of Cecil County	Elkton
15	16.6	Saint Marys County Public Schools	Leonardtown
16	16.2	Board of Educ Charles County	La Plata
17	15.5	Montgomery County Public Schls	Rockville
18	13.4	Harford County Public Schools	Bel Air
19	13.3	Anne Arundel County Pub Schls	Annapolis
20	10.9	Board of Edqueen Annes County	Centreville
21	10.1	Frederick County Board of Ed	Frederick
22	9.7	Calvert County Public Schools	Prince Frederick
23	7.3	Howard County Pub Schls System	Ellicott City
24	6.9	Carroll County Public Schools	Westminster

Students Eligible for Reduced-Price Lunch

Rank	Percent	District Name	City
1	14.8	Board of Educ Garrett County	Oakland
2	12.5	Prince Georges Co Public Schools	Upper Marlboro
3	12.2	Board of Educ Allegany County	Cumberland
4	11.3	Caroline County Board of Ed	Denton
5	11.2	Board of Ed of Kent County	Chestertown
6	9.9	Somerset County Public Schools	Princess Anne
7	9.5	Board of Ed Washington County	Hagerstown
8	9.0	Baltimore City Public Schools Sys	Baltimore
9	8.3	Wicomico County Board of Ed	Salisbury
10	8.0	Baltimore County Public Schls	Towson
11	7.9	Dorchester County Board of Ed	Cambridge
12	7.1	Montgomery County Public Schls	Rockville
13	6.7	Board of Ed Worcester County	Newark
14	5.9	Board of Ed of Cecil County	Elkton
15	5.6	Talbot County Public Schools	Easton
16	5.3	Saint Marys County Public Schools	Leonardtown
17	5.0	Board of Educ Charles County	La Plata
18	4.8	Harford County Public Schools	Bel Air
19	4.5	Anne Arundel County Pub Schls	Annapolis
19	4.5	Board of Edqueen Annes County	Centreville
21	3.8	Frederick County Board of Ed	Frederick
22	3.2	Calvert County Public Schools	Prince Frederick
23	3.1	Howard County Pub Schls System	Ellicott City

24	2.6	Carroll County Public Schools	Westminster

Student/Teacher Ratio

Rank	Ratio	District Name	City
1	17.7	Board of Educ Charles County	La Plata
2	17.5	Harford County Public Schools	Bel Air
3	17.0	Board of Edqueen Annes County	Centreville
4	16.9	Carroll County Public Schools	Westminster
4	16.9	Prince Georges Co Public Schools	Upper Marlboro
6	16.7	Calvert County Public Schools	Prince Frederick
7	16.6	Anne Arundel County Pub Schls	Annapolis
8	16.2	Frederick County Board of Ed	Frederick
8	16.2	Saint Marys County Public Schools	Leonardtown
10	15.8	Board of Ed of Cecil County	Elkton
11	15.7	Board of Ed Washington County	Hagerstown
12	15.6	Dorchester County Board of Ed	Cambridge
13	15.5	Montgomery County Public Schls	Rockville
14	15.4	Board of Ed of Kent County	Chestertown
15	15.3	Caroline County Board of Ed	Denton
16	15.0	Baltimore City Public Schools Sys	Baltimore
17	14.9	Baltimore County Public Schls	Towson
18	14.5	Talbot County Public Schools	Easton
19	14.4	Board of Educ Allegany County	Cumberland
19	14.4	Howard County Pub Schls System	Ellicott City
21	14.1	Wicomico County Board of Ed	Salisbury
22	13.8	Somerset County Public Schools	Princess Anne
23	13.4	Board of Educ Garrett County	Oakland
24	13.2	Board of Ed Worcester County	Newark

Student/Librarian Ratio

Rank	Ratio	District Name	City
1	2,565.0	Board of Ed of Kent County	Chestertown
2	2,405.0	Board of Educ Garrett County	Oakland
3	1,800.3	Wicomico County Board of Ed	Salisbury
4	1,343.6	Baltimore City Public Schools Sys	Baltimore
5	1,060.1	Prince Georges Co Public Schools	Upper Marlboro
6	891.8	Talbot County Public Schools	Easton
7	848.0	Carroll County Public Schools	Westminster
8	829.7	Calvert County Public Schools	Prince Frederick
9	826.1	Board of Educ Charles County	La Plata
10	744.7	Frederick County Board of Ed	Frederick
11	737.8	Somerset County Public Schools	Princess Anne
12	737.6	Harford County Public Schools	Bel Air
13	725.0	Montgomery County Public Schls	Rockville
14	691.2	Anne Arundel County Pub Schls	Annapolis
15	684.2	Board of Edqueen Annes County	Centreville
16	654.1	Baltimore County Public Schls	Towson
17	600.0	Caroline County Board of Ed	Denton
18	599.1	Board of Ed of Cecil County	Elkton
19	590.5	Howard County Pub Schls System	Ellicott City
20	580.8	Saint Marys County Public Schools	Leonardtown
21	565.3	Board of Ed Worcester County	Newark
22	542.3	Board of Ed Washington County	Hagerstown
23	533.7	Dorchester County Board of Ed	Cambridge
24	431.6	Board of Educ Allegany County	Cumberland

Student/Counselor Ratio

Rank	Ratio	District Name	City
1	566.6	Baltimore City Public Schools Sys	Baltimore
2	536.0	Harford County Public Schools	Bel Air
3	446.7	Calvert County Public Schools	Prince Frederick
4	442.7	Board of Edqueen Annes County	Centreville
5	437.0	Board of Educ Charles County	La Plata
6	431.6	Board of Educ Allegany County	Cumberland
7	427.9	Saint Marys County Public Schools	Leonardtown
8	424.3	Frederick County Board of Ed	Frederick
9	402.7	Board of Ed Washington County	Hagerstown
10	400.8	Board of Educ Garrett County	Oakland
11	395.7	Prince Georges Co Public Schools	Upper Marlboro
12	390.5	Howard County Pub Schls System	Ellicott City
13	379.9	Anne Arundel County Pub Schls	Annapolis
14	372.0	Carroll County Public Schools	Westminster
15	359.3	Baltimore County Public Schls	Towson
16	343.1	Dorchester County Board of Ed	Cambridge
17	332.8	Board of Ed of Cecil County	Elkton
18	329.8	Montgomery County Public Schls	Rockville
19	327.9	Somerset County Public Schools	Princess Anne
20	302.8	Board of Ed Worcester County	Newark
21	300.0	Caroline County Board of Ed	Denton
22	287.7	Talbot County Public Schools	Easton
23	273.8	Wicomico County Board of Ed	Salisbury
24	233.2	Board of Ed of Kent County	Chestertown

Current Spending per Student in FY2003

Rank	Dollars	District Name	City
1	10,580	Montgomery County Public Schls	Rockville
2	10,189	Board of Ed of Kent County	Chestertown
3	10,085	Board of Ed Worcester County	Newark
4	9,639	Baltimore City Public Schools Sys	Baltimore
5	9,623	Somerset County Public Schools	Princess Anne
6	9,420	Howard County Pub Schls System	Ellicott City
7	8,913	Dorchester County Board of Ed	Cambridge
8	8,815	Board of Educ Garrett County	Oakland
9	8,813	Board of Educ Allegany County	Cumberland
10	8,744	Baltimore County Public Schls	Towson
11	8,743	Talbot County Public Schools	Easton
12	8,621	Prince Georges Co Public Schools	Upper Marlboro
13	8,361	Anne Arundel County Pub Schls	Annapolis
14	8,261	Wicomico County Board of Ed	Salisbury
15	8,112	Calvert County Public Schools	Prince Frederick
16	8,025	Board of Edqueen Annes County	Centreville
17	7,984	Board of Ed Washington County	Hagerstown
18	7,964	Caroline County Board of Ed	Denton
19	7,963	Saint Marys County Public Schools	Leonardtown
20	7,955	Board of Educ Charles County	La Plata
21	7,944	Frederick County Board of Ed	Frederick
22	7,879	Board of Ed of Cecil County	Elkton
23	7,769	Carroll County Public Schools	Westminster
24	7,641	Harford County Public Schools	Bel Air

Number of Diploma Recipients

Rank	Number	District Name	City
1	8,282	Montgomery County Public Schls	Rockville
2	7,552	Prince Georges Co Public Schools	Upper Marlboro
3	6,859	Baltimore County Public Schls	Towson
4	4,524	Baltimore City Public Schools Sys	Baltimore
5	4,466	Anne Arundel County Pub Schls	Annapolis
6	2,990	Howard County Pub Schls System	Ellicott City
7	2,465	Frederick County Board of Ed	Frederick
8	2,425	Harford County Public Schools	Bel Air
9	1,910	Carroll County Public Schools	Westminster
10	1,481	Board of Educ Charles County	La Plata
11	1,234	Board of Ed Washington County	Hagerstown
12	1,043	Calvert County Public Schools	Prince Frederick
13	878	Board of Ed of Cecil County	Elkton
14	845	Saint Marys County Public Schools	Leonardtown
15	780	Wicomico County Board of Ed	Salisbury
16	733	Board of Educ Allegany County	Cumberland
17	486	Board of Ed Worcester County	Newark
18	393	Board of Edqueen Annes County	Centreville
19	341	Caroline County Board of Ed	Denton
20	293	Board of Educ Garrett County	Oakland
21	283	Dorchester County Board of Ed	Cambridge
22	272	Talbot County Public Schools	Easton
23	185	Board of Ed of Kent County	Chestertown
24	163	Somerset County Public Schools	Princess Anne

High School Drop-out Rate

Rank	Percent	District Name	City
1	11.5	Baltimore City Public Schools Sys	Baltimore
2	6.3	Board of Ed of Kent County	Chestertown
3	6.2	Wicomico County Board of Ed	Salisbury
4	5.8	Caroline County Board of Ed	Denton
4	5.8	Dorchester County Board of Ed	Cambridge
6	5.3	Somerset County Public Schools	Princess Anne
7	4.8	Board of Educ Garrett County	Oakland
8	4.4	Anne Arundel County Pub Schls	Annapolis
9	4.1	Board of Educ Allegany County	Cumberland
10	3.4	Harford County Public Schools	Bel Air
11	3.3	Board of Edqueen Annes County	Centreville
11	3.3	Board of Educ Charles County	La Plata
11	3.3	Calvert County Public Schools	Prince Frederick
11	3.3	Talbot County Public Schools	Easton
15	3.2	Board of Ed Worcester County	Newark
16	3.1	Board of Ed Washington County	Hagerstown
16	3.1	Prince Georges Co Public Schools	Upper Marlboro
16	3.1	Saint Marys County Public Schools	Leonardtown
19	3.0	Baltimore County Public Schls	Towson
19	3.0	Board of Ed of Cecil County	Elkton
21	2.0	Carroll County Public Schools	Westminster
21	2.0	Howard County Pub Schls System	Ellicott City
23	1.9	Montgomery County Public Schls	Rockville
24	1.8	Frederick County Board of Ed	Frederick

Massachusetts

Massachusetts Public School Educational Profile

Category	Value	Category	Value
Schools (2003-2004)	1,867	**Diploma Recipients** (2002-2003)	55,272
Instructional Level		White, Non-Hispanic	44,973
Primary	1,171	Black, Non-Hispanic	3,944
Middle	329	Asian/Pacific Islander	2,693
High	296	American Indian/Alaskan Native	136
Other Level	71	Hispanic	3,526
Curriculum		**High School Drop-out Rate** (%) (2001-2002)	n/a
Regular	1,795	White, Non-Hispanic	n/a
Special Education	5	Black, Non-Hispanic	n/a
Vocational	40	Asian/Pacific Islander	n/a
Alternative	27	American Indian/Alaskan Native	n/a
Type		Hispanic	n/a
Magnet	5	**Staff** (2003-2004)	
Charter	51	Teachers	72,061.8
Title I Eligible	1,145	Average Salary ($)	53,274
School-wide Title I	452	Librarians/Media Specialists	946.6
Students (2003-2004)	980,459	Guidance Counselors	2,117.7
Gender (%)		**Ratios** (2003-2004)	
Male	51.5	Student/Teacher Ratio	13.6 to 1
Female	48.5	Student/Librarian Ratio	1,035.8 to 1
Race/Ethnicity (%)		Student/Counselor Ratio	463.0 to 1
White, Non-Hispanic	74.6	**College Entrance Exam Scores** (2005)	
Black, Non-Hispanic	8.8	Scholastic Aptitude Test (SAT)	
Asian/Pacific Islander	4.7	Participation Rate (%)	86
American Indian/Alaskan Native	0.3	Mean SAT Reasoning Test Verbal Score	520
Hispanic	11.5	Mean SAT Reasoning Test Math Score	527
Classification (%)		American College Testing Program (ACT)	
Individual Education Program (IEP)	15.7	Participation Rate (%)	12
Migrant (2002-2003)	0.2	Average Composite Score	22.8
English Language Learner (ELL)	5.0	Average English Score	22.5
Eligible for Free Lunch Program	22.3	Average Math Score	22.8
Eligible for Reduced-Price Lunch Program	4.9	Average Reading Score	23.4
Current Spending ($ per student in FY 2003)	10,627	Average Science Score	22.0
Instruction	6,742		
Support Services	3,559		

Note: For an explanation of data, please refer to the User's Guide in the front of the book

Massachusetts NAEP 2005 Test Scores

Reading			Mathematics		
Grade/Category	Value	Rank	Grade/Category	Value	Rank
4th Grade			**4th Grade**		
Average Proficiency	231.3 (0.88)	1/51	Average Proficiency	247.3 (0.82)	1/51
Proficiency by Gender/Race/Ethnicity			Proficiency by Gender/Race/Ethnicity		
Male	229.9 (1.11)	1/51	Male	248.2 (0.88)	1/51
Female	232.7 (1.12)	1/51	Female	246.5 (0.95)	1/51
White, Non-Hispanic	237.4 (0.93)	2/51	White, Non-Hispanic	252.2 (0.89)	3/51
Black, Non-Hispanic	211.3 (1.89)	4/42	Black, Non-Hispanic	227.8 (1.15)	4/42
Asian, Non-Hispanic	233.6 (4.14)	10/27	Asian, Non-Hispanic	257.5 (3.39)	7/25
American Indian, Non-Hispanic	n/a	n/a	American Indian, Non-Hispanic	n/a	n/a
Hispanic	202.9 (2.37)	25/40	Hispanic	225.4 (1.68)	22/41
Proficiency by Class Size			Proficiency by Class Size		
Less than 16 Students	n/a	n/a	Less than 16 Students	n/a	n/a
16 to 18 Students	222.8 (2.43)	8/33	16 to 18 Students	241.0 (2.53)	9/31
19 to 20 Students	231.4 (2.30)	1/38	19 to 20 Students	248.7 (1.96)	1/38
21 to 25 Students	235.7 (1.27)	1/51	21 to 25 Students	250.3 (1.21)	1/51
Greater than 25 Students	n/a	n/a	Greater than 25 Students	n/a	n/a
Percent Attaining Achievement Levels			Percent Attaining Achievement Levels		
Below Basic	22.1 (1.18)	51/51	Below Basic	9.4 (0.67)	51/51
Basic or Above	77.9 (1.18)	1/51	Basic or Above	90.6 (0.67)	1/51
Proficient or Above	43.7 (1.35)	1/51	Proficient or Above	48.8 (1.54)	1/51
Advanced or Above	11.7 (0.92)	1/51	Advanced or Above	8.2 (0.74)	2/51
8th Grade			**8th Grade**		
Average Proficiency	273.7 (1.00)	1/51	Average Proficiency	291.5 (0.88)	1/51
Proficiency by Gender/Race/Ethnicity			Proficiency by Gender/Race/Ethnicity		
Male	268.8 (1.13)	1/51	Male	290.7 (1.23)	2/51
Female	278.5 (1.15)	1/51	Female	292.3 (1.23)	1/51
White, Non-Hispanic	278.9 (1.15)	2/51	White, Non-Hispanic	297.0 (0.88)	2/51
Black, Non-Hispanic	253.1 (1.99)	3/40	Black, Non-Hispanic	262.5 (2.65)	8/41
Asian, Non-Hispanic	281.6 (3.06)	4/24	Asian, Non-Hispanic	313.6 (4.24)	1/23
American Indian, Non-Hispanic	n/a	n/a	American Indian, Non-Hispanic	n/a	n/a
Hispanic	246.4 (2.59)	24/38	Hispanic	264.7 (1.49)	14/38
Proficiency by Parents Highest Level of Ed.			Proficiency by Parents Highest Level of Ed.		
Did Not Finish High School	251.6 (3.38)	6/49	Did Not Finish High School	271.2 (3.15)	1/50
Graduated High School	262.5 (1.68)	2/50	Graduated High School	277.7 (1.73)	1/50
Some Education After High School	271.5 (1.52)	3/50	Some Education After High School	285.5 (1.56)	9/50
Graduated College	282.7 (1.29)	1/50	Graduated College	301.5 (1.10)	1/50
Percent Attaining Achievement Levels			Percent Attaining Achievement Levels		
Below Basic	22.1 (1.18)	51/51	Below Basic	19.9 (1.13)	49/51
Basic or Above	77.9 (1.18)	1/51	Basic or Above	80.1 (1.13)	3/51
Proficient or Above	43.7 (1.35)	1/51	Proficient or Above	43.3 (1.38)	1/51
Advanced or Above	11.7 (0.92)	1/51	Advanced or Above	11.4 (0.84)	1/51

Note: *For an explanation of data, please refer to the User's Guide in the front of the book; n/a indicates data not available*

Barnstable County

Barnstable
PO Box 955 · Hyannis, MA 02601-0955
(508) 790-9802 · http://www.barnstable.k12.ma.us/
Grade Span: PK-12; **Agency Type:** 1
Schools: 11
  9 Primary; 1 Middle; 1 High; 0 Other Level
  11 Regular; 0 Special Education; 0 Vocational; 0 Alternative
  0 Magnet; 0 Charter; 7 Title I Eligible; 2 School-wide Title I
Students: 5,586 (51.0% male; 48.9% female)
  Individual Education Program: 704 (12.6%);
  English Language Learner: 235 (4.2%); Migrant: 6 (0.1%)
  Eligible for Free Lunch Program: 1,004 (18.0%)
  Eligible for Reduced-Price Lunch Program: 389 (7.0%)
Teachers: 436.9 (12.8 to 1)
Librarians/Media Specialists: 3.3 (1,692.7 to 1)
Guidance Counselors: 15.5 (360.4 to 1)
Current Spending: ($ per student per year):
  Total: $9,255; Instruction: $5,864; Support Services: $2,978
Enrollment, Drop-out Rates and Diploma Recipients by Race/Ethnicity

Category	Total	White	Black	Asian	AIAN	Hisp.
Enrollment (%)	100.0	85.7	5.2	2.1	1.4	5.5
Drop-out Rate (%)	n/a	n/a	n/a	n/a	n/a	n/a
H.S. Diplomas (#)	393	342	22	5	2	22

Bourne
36 Sandwich Rd · Bourne, MA 02532-3609
(508) 759-0660 · http://www.bourne.k12.ma.us/
Grade Span: PK-12; **Agency Type:** 1
Schools: 5
  3 Primary; 1 Middle; 1 High; 0 Other Level
  5 Regular; 0 Special Education; 0 Vocational; 0 Alternative
  0 Magnet; 0 Charter; 3 Title I Eligible; 0 School-wide Title I
Students: 2,530 (50.7% male; 49.2% female)
  Individual Education Program: 316 (12.5%);
  English Language Learner: 3 (0.1%); Migrant: 5 (0.2%)
  Eligible for Free Lunch Program: 257 (10.2%)
  Eligible for Reduced-Price Lunch Program: 126 (5.0%)
Teachers: 162.7 (15.6 to 1)
Librarians/Media Specialists: 2.0 (1,265.0 to 1)
Guidance Counselors: 5.0 (506.0 to 1)
Current Spending: ($ per student per year):
  Total: $9,490; Instruction: $5,957; Support Services: $3,258
Enrollment, Drop-out Rates and Diploma Recipients by Race/Ethnicity

Category	Total	White	Black	Asian	AIAN	Hisp.
Enrollment (%)	100.0	93.3	3.6	0.9	0.3	1.9
Drop-out Rate (%)	n/a	n/a	n/a	n/a	n/a	n/a
H.S. Diplomas (#)	113	108	1	2	1	1

Dennis-Yarmouth
296 Station Ave · South Yarmouth, MA 02664-1898
(508) 398-7600 · http://dy-regional.k12.ma.us/
Grade Span: PK-12; **Agency Type:** 3
Schools: 8
  5 Primary; 2 Middle; 1 High; 0 Other Level
  8 Regular; 0 Special Education; 0 Vocational; 0 Alternative
  0 Magnet; 0 Charter; 6 Title I Eligible; 1 School-wide Title I
Students: 4,205 (52.1% male; 47.8% female)
  Individual Education Program: 585 (13.9%);
  English Language Learner: 166 (3.9%); Migrant: 0 (0.0%)
  Eligible for Free Lunch Program: 1,163 (27.7%)
  Eligible for Reduced-Price Lunch Program: 188 (4.5%)
Teachers: 359.8 (11.7 to 1)
Librarians/Media Specialists: 7.2 (584.0 to 1)
Guidance Counselors: 4.5 (934.4 to 1)
Current Spending: ($ per student per year):
  Total: $10,155; Instruction: $6,812; Support Services: $3,018
Enrollment, Drop-out Rates and Diploma Recipients by Race/Ethnicity

Category	Total	White	Black	Asian	AIAN	Hisp.
Enrollment (%)	100.0	89.5	4.8	1.4	1.0	3.3
Drop-out Rate (%)	n/a	n/a	n/a	n/a	n/a	n/a
H.S. Diplomas (#)	269	251	5	5	0	8

Falmouth
340 Teaticket Hwy · East Falmouth, MA 02536-6527
(508) 548-0151 · http://www.falmouth.k12.ma.us/
Grade Span: PK-12; **Agency Type:** 1
Schools: 7
  4 Primary; 2 Middle; 1 High; 0 Other Level
  7 Regular; 0 Special Education; 0 Vocational; 0 Alternative
  0 Magnet; 0 Charter; 3 Title I Eligible; 0 School-wide Title I
Students: 4,444 (50.6% male; 49.3% female)
  Individual Education Program: 629 (14.2%);
  English Language Learner: 39 (0.9%); Migrant: 2 (<0.1%)
  Eligible for Free Lunch Program: 500 (11.3%)
  Eligible for Reduced-Price Lunch Program: 156 (3.5%)
Teachers: 347.4 (12.8 to 1)
Librarians/Media Specialists: 8.0 (555.5 to 1)
Guidance Counselors: 8.0 (555.5 to 1)
Current Spending: ($ per student per year):
  Total: $10,076; Instruction: $6,539; Support Services: $3,317
Enrollment, Drop-out Rates and Diploma Recipients by Race/Ethnicity

Category	Total	White	Black	Asian	AIAN	Hisp.
Enrollment (%)	100.0	91.9	3.4	1.0	1.4	2.3
Drop-out Rate (%)	n/a	n/a	n/a	n/a	n/a	n/a
H.S. Diplomas (#)	238	231	1	1	2	3

Harwich
81 Oak St · Harwich, MA 02645-2701
(508) 430-7200 · http://www.harwich.edu/
Grade Span: PK-12; **Agency Type:** 1
Schools: 3
  1 Primary; 1 Middle; 1 High; 0 Other Level
  3 Regular; 0 Special Education; 0 Vocational; 0 Alternative
  0 Magnet; 0 Charter; 2 Title I Eligible; 0 School-wide Title I
Students: 1,522 (52.3% male; 47.6% female)
  Individual Education Program: 242 (15.9%);
  English Language Learner: 7 (0.5%); Migrant: 0 (0.0%)
  Eligible for Free Lunch Program: 138 (9.1%)
  Eligible for Reduced-Price Lunch Program: 52 (3.4%)
Teachers: 117.3 (13.0 to 1)
Librarians/Media Specialists: 3.0 (507.3 to 1)
Guidance Counselors: 3.0 (507.3 to 1)
Current Spending: ($ per student per year):
  Total: $11,316; Instruction: $7,093; Support Services: $3,937
Enrollment, Drop-out Rates and Diploma Recipients by Race/Ethnicity

Category	Total	White	Black	Asian	AIAN	Hisp.
Enrollment (%)	100.0	95.3	2.2	0.7	0.4	1.4
Drop-out Rate (%)	n/a	n/a	n/a	n/a	n/a	n/a
H.S. Diplomas (#)	91	88	1	0	0	2

Mashpee
150-A Old Barnstable Rd · Mashpee, MA 02649-3130
(508) 539-1500 · http://www.mashpee.k12.ma.us/
Grade Span: PK-12; **Agency Type:** 1
Schools: 3
  2 Primary; 0 Middle; 1 High; 0 Other Level
  3 Regular; 0 Special Education; 0 Vocational; 0 Alternative
  0 Magnet; 0 Charter; 2 Title I Eligible; 0 School-wide Title I
Students: 2,164 (50.6% male; 49.3% female)
  Individual Education Program: 415 (19.2%);
  English Language Learner: 6 (0.3%); Migrant: 3 (0.1%)
  Eligible for Free Lunch Program: 260 (12.0%)
  Eligible for Reduced-Price Lunch Program: 102 (4.7%)
Teachers: 171.0 (12.7 to 1)
Librarians/Media Specialists: 3.0 (721.3 to 1)
Guidance Counselors: 7.5 (288.5 to 1)
Current Spending: ($ per student per year):
  Total: $9,372; Instruction: $6,300; Support Services: $2,854
Enrollment, Drop-out Rates and Diploma Recipients by Race/Ethnicity

Category	Total	White	Black	Asian	AIAN	Hisp.
Enrollment (%)	100.0	85.9	5.0	1.0	6.1	1.9
Drop-out Rate (%)	n/a	n/a	n/a	n/a	n/a	n/a
H.S. Diplomas (#)	117	101	7	0	7	2

Nauset
78 Eldredge Pkwy · Orleans, MA 02653-3326
(508) 255-8800 · http://www.nausetschools.org
Grade Span: PK-12; **Agency Type:** 3
Schools: 2
  1 Primary; 0 Middle; 1 High; 0 Other Level
  2 Regular; 0 Special Education; 0 Vocational; 0 Alternative
  0 Magnet; 0 Charter; 2 Title I Eligible; 0 School-wide Title I
Students: 1,825 (50.1% male; 49.8% female)
  Individual Education Program: 275 (15.1%);
  English Language Learner: 8 (0.4%); Migrant: 0 (0.0%)
  Eligible for Free Lunch Program: 98 (5.4%)
  Eligible for Reduced-Price Lunch Program: 57 (3.1%)
Teachers: 145.8 (12.5 to 1)
Librarians/Media Specialists: 2.0 (912.5 to 1)
Guidance Counselors: 8.0 (228.1 to 1)
Current Spending: ($ per student per year):
  Total: $12,405; Instruction: $8,701; Support Services: $3,377
Enrollment, Drop-out Rates and Diploma Recipients by Race/Ethnicity

Category	Total	White	Black	Asian	AIAN	Hisp.
Enrollment (%)	100.0	96.2	0.9	1.2	0.3	1.5
Drop-out Rate (%)	n/a	n/a	n/a	n/a	n/a	n/a
H.S. Diplomas (#)	212	202	1	5	2	2

Sandwich
16 Dewey Ave • Sandwich, MA 02563-2096
(508) 888-1054 • http://www.sandwich.k12.ma.us/
Grade Span: PK-12; **Agency Type:** 1
Schools: 4
   3 Primary; 0 Middle; 1 High; 0 Other Level
   4 Regular; 0 Special Education; 0 Vocational; 0 Alternative
   0 Magnet; 0 Charter; 3 Title I Eligible; 0 School-wide Title I
Students: 4,148 (51.3% male; 48.6% female)
   Individual Education Program: 623 (15.0%);
   English Language Learner: 4 (0.1%); Migrant: 0 (0.0%)
   Eligible for Free Lunch Program: 195 (4.7%)
   Eligible for Reduced-Price Lunch Program: 0 (0.0%)
Teachers: 252.5 (16.4 to 1)
Librarians/Media Specialists: 5.0 (829.6 to 1)
Guidance Counselors: 4.0 (1,037.0 to 1)
Current Spending: ($ per student per year):
   Total: $7,777; Instruction: $5,277; Support Services: $2,299
Enrollment, Drop-out Rates and Diploma Recipients by Race/Ethnicity

Category	Total	White	Black	Asian	AIAN	Hisp.
Enrollment (%)	100.0	97.7	0.6	1.2	0.1	0.4
Drop-out Rate (%)	n/a	n/a	n/a	n/a	n/a	n/a
H.S. Diplomas (#)	237	232	2	2	0	1

Berkshire County

Adams-Cheshire
125 Savoy Rd • Cheshire, MA 01225-9522
(413) 743-2939
Grade Span: PK-12; **Agency Type:** 3
Schools: 4
   2 Primary; 1 Middle; 1 High; 0 Other Level
   4 Regular; 0 Special Education; 0 Vocational; 0 Alternative
   0 Magnet; 0 Charter; 1 Title I Eligible; 1 School-wide Title I
Students: 1,844 (51.0% male; 48.9% female)
   Individual Education Program: 301 (16.3%);
   English Language Learner: 2 (0.1%); Migrant: 0 (0.0%)
   Eligible for Free Lunch Program: 383 (20.8%)
   Eligible for Reduced-Price Lunch Program: 158 (8.6%)
Teachers: 149.2 (12.4 to 1)
Librarians/Media Specialists: 2.0 (922.0 to 1)
Guidance Counselors: 4.0 (461.0 to 1)
Current Spending: ($ per student per year):
   Total: $9,449; Instruction: $6,216; Support Services: $2,878
Enrollment, Drop-out Rates and Diploma Recipients by Race/Ethnicity

Category	Total	White	Black	Asian	AIAN	Hisp.
Enrollment (%)	100.0	95.1	2.3	0.9	0.5	1.2
Drop-out Rate (%)	n/a	n/a	n/a	n/a	n/a	n/a
H.S. Diplomas (#)	112	109	1	2	0	0

Central Berkshire
254 Hinsdale Rd • Dalton, MA 01227-0299
Mailing Address: PO Box 299 • Dalton, MA 01227-0299
(413) 684-0320 • http://www.cbrsd.org/
Grade Span: PK-12; **Agency Type:** 3
Schools: 6
   4 Primary; 1 Middle; 1 High; 0 Other Level
   6 Regular; 0 Special Education; 0 Vocational; 0 Alternative
   0 Magnet; 0 Charter; 5 Title I Eligible; 0 School-wide Title I
Students: 2,286 (52.1% male; 47.8% female)
   Individual Education Program: 362 (15.8%);
   English Language Learner: 0 (0.0%); Migrant: 0 (0.0%)
   Eligible for Free Lunch Program: 268 (11.7%)
   Eligible for Reduced-Price Lunch Program: 183 (8.0%)
Teachers: 146.6 (15.6 to 1)
Librarians/Media Specialists: 1.3 (1,758.5 to 1)
Guidance Counselors: 5.0 (457.2 to 1)
Current Spending: ($ per student per year):
   Total: $9,948; Instruction: $6,134; Support Services: $3,492
Enrollment, Drop-out Rates and Diploma Recipients by Race/Ethnicity

Category	Total	White	Black	Asian	AIAN	Hisp.
Enrollment (%)	100.0	96.9	1.2	1.1	0.1	0.6
Drop-out Rate (%)	n/a	n/a	n/a	n/a	n/a	n/a
H.S. Diplomas (#)	171	170	0	1	0	0

North Adams
191 E Main St • North Adams, MA 01247-4434
(413) 662-3225 • http://www.northadamsschools.com
Grade Span: PK-12; **Agency Type:** 1
Schools: 5
   3 Primary; 1 Middle; 1 High; 0 Other Level
   5 Regular; 0 Special Education; 0 Vocational; 0 Alternative
   0 Magnet; 0 Charter; 3 Title I Eligible; 3 School-wide Title I
Students: 2,070 (46.9% male; 53.0% female)
   Individual Education Program: 332 (16.0%);

   English Language Learner: 35 (1.7%); Migrant: 1 (<0.1%)
   Eligible for Free Lunch Program: 816 (39.4%)
   Eligible for Reduced-Price Lunch Program: 62 (3.0%)
Teachers: 178.7 (11.6 to 1)
Librarians/Media Specialists: 1.0 (2,070.0 to 1)
Guidance Counselors: 3.0 (690.0 to 1)
Current Spending: ($ per student per year):
   Total: $11,252; Instruction: $6,058; Support Services: $4,886
Enrollment, Drop-out Rates and Diploma Recipients by Race/Ethnicity

Category	Total	White	Black	Asian	AIAN	Hisp.
Enrollment (%)	100.0	89.9	4.4	1.4	0.7	3.6
Drop-out Rate (%)	n/a	n/a	n/a	n/a	n/a	n/a
H.S. Diplomas (#)	105	99	1	4	0	1

Pittsfield
269 First St • Pittsfield, MA 01201-4727
(413) 499-9512 • http://www.pittsfield.net/
Grade Span: PK-12; **Agency Type:** 1
Schools: 13
   8 Primary; 2 Middle; 2 High; 1 Other Level
   12 Regular; 0 Special Education; 0 Vocational; 1 Alternative
   0 Magnet; 0 Charter; 3 Title I Eligible; 2 School-wide Title I
Students: 6,605 (51.3% male; 48.6% female)
   Individual Education Program: 996 (15.1%);
   English Language Learner: 166 (2.5%); Migrant: 0 (0.0%)
   Eligible for Free Lunch Program: 1,705 (25.8%)
   Eligible for Reduced-Price Lunch Program: 670 (10.1%)
Teachers: 502.8 (13.1 to 1)
Librarians/Media Specialists: 11.0 (600.5 to 1)
Guidance Counselors: 12.0 (550.4 to 1)
Current Spending: ($ per student per year):
   Total: $10,017; Instruction: $6,390; Support Services: $3,295
Enrollment, Drop-out Rates and Diploma Recipients by Race/Ethnicity

Category	Total	White	Black	Asian	AIAN	Hisp.
Enrollment (%)	100.0	84.4	9.3	2.2	0.3	3.8
Drop-out Rate (%)	n/a	n/a	n/a	n/a	n/a	n/a
H.S. Diplomas (#)	316	291	13	6	0	6

Bristol County

Attleboro
100 Rathbun Willard Dr • Attleboro, MA 02703-2799
(508) 222-0012 • http://www.attleboroschools.com/
Grade Span: PK-12; **Agency Type:** 1
Schools: 10
   6 Primary; 3 Middle; 1 High; 0 Other Level
   10 Regular; 0 Special Education; 0 Vocational; 0 Alternative
   0 Magnet; 0 Charter; 6 Title I Eligible; 0 School-wide Title I
Students: 6,531 (51.1% male; 48.8% female)
   Individual Education Program: 1,048 (16.0%);
   English Language Learner: 312 (4.8%); Migrant: 3 (<0.1%)
   Eligible for Free Lunch Program: 946 (14.5%)
   Eligible for Reduced-Price Lunch Program: 366 (5.6%)
Teachers: 465.6 (14.0 to 1)
Librarians/Media Specialists: 1.8 (3,628.3 to 1)
Guidance Counselors: 8.5 (768.4 to 1)
Current Spending: ($ per student per year):
   Total: $8,605; Instruction: $5,470; Support Services: $2,862
Enrollment, Drop-out Rates and Diploma Recipients by Race/Ethnicity

Category	Total	White	Black	Asian	AIAN	Hisp.
Enrollment (%)	100.0	84.2	3.8	5.5	0.3	6.1
Drop-out Rate (%)	n/a	n/a	n/a	n/a	n/a	n/a
H.S. Diplomas (#)	342	308	5	18	0	11

Bridgewater-Raynham
687 Pleasant St • Raynham, MA 02767-1534
Mailing Address: 777 Pleasant St • Raynham, MA 02767-1534
(508) 824-2730 • http://bridge-rayn.org/
Grade Span: PK-12; **Agency Type:** 3
Schools: 7
   4 Primary; 2 Middle; 1 High; 0 Other Level
   7 Regular; 0 Special Education; 0 Vocational; 0 Alternative
   0 Magnet; 0 Charter; 2 Title I Eligible; 0 School-wide Title I
Students: 6,061 (51.0% male; 48.9% female)
   Individual Education Program: 933 (15.4%);
   English Language Learner: 2 (<0.1%); Migrant: 0 (0.0%)
   Eligible for Free Lunch Program: 324 (5.3%)
   Eligible for Reduced-Price Lunch Program: 92 (1.5%)
Teachers: 338.4 (17.9 to 1)
Librarians/Media Specialists: 2.3 (2,635.2 to 1)
Guidance Counselors: 7.0 (865.9 to 1)
Current Spending: ($ per student per year):
   Total: $8,144; Instruction: $5,372; Support Services: $2,514

Enrollment, Drop-out Rates and Diploma Recipients by Race/Ethnicity

Category	Total	White	Black	Asian	AIAN	Hisp.
Enrollment (%)	100.0	95.2	2.4	1.2	0.3	1.0
Drop-out Rate (%)	n/a	n/a	n/a	n/a	n/a	n/a
H.S. Diplomas (#)	331	320	3	5	0	3

Dartmouth
8 Bush St • South Dartmouth, MA 02748-3102
(508) 997-3391 • http://dartmouth.mec.edu/
Grade Span: PK-12; **Agency Type:** 1
Schools: 7
    5 Primary; 1 Middle; 1 High; 0 Other Level
    7 Regular; 0 Special Education; 0 Vocational; 0 Alternative
    0 Magnet; 0 Charter; 4 Title I Eligible; 0 School-wide Title I
Students: 4,267 (51.0% male; 48.9% female)
    Individual Education Program: 603 (14.1%);
    English Language Learner: 39 (0.9%); Migrant: 0 (0.0%)
    Eligible for Free Lunch Program: 248 (5.8%)
    Eligible for Reduced-Price Lunch Program: 162 (3.8%)
Teachers: 260.2 (16.4 to 1)
Librarians/Media Specialists: 2.0 (2,133.5 to 1)
Guidance Counselors: 8.3 (514.1 to 1)
Current Spending: ($ per student per year):
    Total: $8,147; Instruction: $5,110; Support Services: $2,761

Enrollment, Drop-out Rates and Diploma Recipients by Race/Ethnicity

Category	Total	White	Black	Asian	AIAN	Hisp.
Enrollment (%)	100.0	95.3	1.4	2.2	0.4	0.7
Drop-out Rate (%)	n/a	n/a	n/a	n/a	n/a	n/a
H.S. Diplomas (#)	303	291	2	4	2	4

Dighton-Rehoboth
340 Anawan St • Rehoboth, MA 02769-2617
(508) 252-5000
Grade Span: PK-12; **Agency Type:** 3
Schools: 5
    2 Primary; 2 Middle; 1 High; 0 Other Level
    5 Regular; 0 Special Education; 0 Vocational; 0 Alternative
    0 Magnet; 0 Charter; 4 Title I Eligible; 1 School-wide Title I
Students: 3,390 (52.0% male; 47.9% female)
    Individual Education Program: 337 (9.9%);
    English Language Learner: 1 (<0.1%); Migrant: 0 (0.0%)
    Eligible for Free Lunch Program: 77 (2.3%)
    Eligible for Reduced-Price Lunch Program: 25 (0.7%)
Teachers: 214.2 (15.8 to 1)
Librarians/Media Specialists: 4.0 (847.5 to 1)
Guidance Counselors: 6.0 (565.0 to 1)
Current Spending: ($ per student per year):
    Total: $8,038; Instruction: $5,315; Support Services: $2,534

Enrollment, Drop-out Rates and Diploma Recipients by Race/Ethnicity

Category	Total	White	Black	Asian	AIAN	Hisp.
Enrollment (%)	100.0	97.4	0.7	1.1	0.1	0.7
Drop-out Rate (%)	n/a	n/a	n/a	n/a	n/a	n/a
H.S. Diplomas (#)	205	199	4	2	0	0

Easton
Pob 359 • North Easton, MA 02356-0359
(508) 230-3200 • http://www.easton.k12.ma.us/
Grade Span: PK-12; **Agency Type:** 1
Schools: 7
    4 Primary; 2 Middle; 1 High; 0 Other Level
    7 Regular; 0 Special Education; 0 Vocational; 0 Alternative
    0 Magnet; 0 Charter; 3 Title I Eligible; 0 School-wide Title I
Students: 3,826 (51.5% male; 48.4% female)
    Individual Education Program: 668 (17.5%);
    English Language Learner: 8 (0.2%); Migrant: 0 (0.0%)
    Eligible for Free Lunch Program: 60 (1.6%)
    Eligible for Reduced-Price Lunch Program: 43 (1.1%)
Teachers: 245.6 (15.6 to 1)
Librarians/Media Specialists: 4.5 (850.2 to 1)
Guidance Counselors: 6.0 (637.7 to 1)
Current Spending: ($ per student per year):
    Total: $7,806; Instruction: $5,109; Support Services: $2,505

Enrollment, Drop-out Rates and Diploma Recipients by Race/Ethnicity

Category	Total	White	Black	Asian	AIAN	Hisp.
Enrollment (%)	100.0	92.9	2.7	2.5	0.1	1.7
Drop-out Rate (%)	n/a	n/a	n/a	n/a	n/a	n/a
H.S. Diplomas (#)	271	251	9	7	0	4

Fairhaven
128 Washington St • Fairhaven, MA 02719-4037
(508) 979-4000 • http://www.fairhavenps.org/
Grade Span: PK-12; **Agency Type:** 1
Schools: 6
    4 Primary; 1 Middle; 1 High; 0 Other Level
    6 Regular; 0 Special Education; 0 Vocational; 0 Alternative

0 Magnet; 0 Charter; 5 Title I Eligible; 0 School-wide Title I
Students: 2,257 (50.8% male; 49.1% female)
    Individual Education Program: 323 (14.3%);
    English Language Learner: 1 (<0.1%); Migrant: 0 (0.0%)
    Eligible for Free Lunch Program: 256 (11.3%)
    Eligible for Reduced-Price Lunch Program: 107 (4.7%)
Teachers: 153.6 (14.7 to 1)
Librarians/Media Specialists: 2.0 (1,128.5 to 1)
Guidance Counselors: 5.0 (451.4 to 1)
Current Spending: ($ per student per year):
    Total: $8,630; Instruction: $5,375; Support Services: $2,887

Enrollment, Drop-out Rates and Diploma Recipients by Race/Ethnicity

Category	Total	White	Black	Asian	AIAN	Hisp.
Enrollment (%)	100.0	97.1	1.8	0.4	0.3	0.5
Drop-out Rate (%)	n/a	n/a	n/a	n/a	n/a	n/a
H.S. Diplomas (#)	129	125	2	1	0	1

Fall River
417 Rock St • Fall River, MA 02720-3344
(508) 675-8420 • http://www.fallriver.k12.ma.us/
Grade Span: PK-12; **Agency Type:** 1
Schools: 31
    25 Primary; 5 Middle; 1 High; 0 Other Level
    29 Regular; 0 Special Education; 0 Vocational; 2 Alternative
    0 Magnet; 0 Charter; 22 Title I Eligible; 22 School-wide Title I
Students: 11,697 (51.3% male; 48.6% female)
    Individual Education Program: 1,643 (14.0%);
    English Language Learner: 550 (4.7%); Migrant: 204 (1.7%)
    Eligible for Free Lunch Program: 5,200 (44.5%)
    Eligible for Reduced-Price Lunch Program: 1,091 (9.3%)
Teachers: 874.3 (13.4 to 1)
Librarians/Media Specialists: 4.0 (2,924.3 to 1)
Guidance Counselors: 18.1 (646.2 to 1)
Current Spending: ($ per student per year):
    Total: $10,688; Instruction: $7,152; Support Services: $3,230

Enrollment, Drop-out Rates and Diploma Recipients by Race/Ethnicity

Category	Total	White	Black	Asian	AIAN	Hisp.
Enrollment (%)	100.0	76.7	8.3	4.9	0.5	9.6
Drop-out Rate (%)	n/a	n/a	n/a	n/a	n/a	n/a
H.S. Diplomas (#)	499	422	18	38	3	18

Freetown-Lakeville
98 Howland Rd • Lakeville, MA 02347-2230
(508) 923-2000 • http://www.freelake.mec.edu/
Grade Span: 05-12; **Agency Type:** 3
Schools: 2
    0 Primary; 1 Middle; 1 High; 0 Other Level
    2 Regular; 0 Special Education; 0 Vocational; 0 Alternative
    0 Magnet; 0 Charter; 1 Title I Eligible; 0 School-wide Title I
Students: 1,896 (50.3% male; 49.6% female)
    Individual Education Program: 247 (13.0%);
    English Language Learner: 0 (0.0%); Migrant: 0 (0.0%)
    Eligible for Free Lunch Program: 109 (5.7%)
    Eligible for Reduced-Price Lunch Program: 50 (2.6%)
Teachers: 126.6 (15.0 to 1)
Librarians/Media Specialists: 2.0 (948.0 to 1)
Guidance Counselors: 5.0 (379.2 to 1)
Current Spending: ($ per student per year):
    Total: $9,226; Instruction: $5,697; Support Services: $3,244

Enrollment, Drop-out Rates and Diploma Recipients by Race/Ethnicity

Category	Total	White	Black	Asian	AIAN	Hisp.
Enrollment (%)	100.0	98.2	1.1	0.2	0.1	0.4
Drop-out Rate (%)	n/a	n/a	n/a	n/a	n/a	n/a
H.S. Diplomas (#)	148	145	2	0	0	1

Greater New Bedford
1121 Ashley Blvd • New Bedford, MA 02745-2419
(508) 998-3321 • http://www.gnbvt.edu/
Grade Span: 09-12; **Agency Type:** 4
Schools: 1
    0 Primary; 0 Middle; 1 High; 0 Other Level
    0 Regular; 0 Special Education; 1 Vocational; 0 Alternative
    0 Magnet; 0 Charter; 1 Title I Eligible; 0 School-wide Title I
Students: 1,856 (54.6% male; 45.3% female)
    Individual Education Program: 186 (10.0%);
    English Language Learner: 43 (2.3%); Migrant: 2 (0.1%)
    Eligible for Free Lunch Program: 672 (36.2%)
    Eligible for Reduced-Price Lunch Program: 0 (0.0%)
Teachers: 187.0 (9.9 to 1)
Librarians/Media Specialists: 1.0 (1,856.0 to 1)
Guidance Counselors: 8.0 (232.0 to 1)
Current Spending: ($ per student per year):
    Total: $13,609; Instruction: $8,570; Support Services: $4,723

Enrollment, Drop-out Rates and Diploma Recipients by Race/Ethnicity

Category	Total	White	Black	Asian	AIAN	Hisp.
Enrollment (%)	100.0	82.6	8.2	0.5	0.5	8.1
Drop-out Rate (%)	n/a	n/a	n/a	n/a	n/a	n/a
H.S. Diplomas (#)	258	228	13	3	1	13

Mansfield
2 Park Row • Mansfield, MA 02048-2433
(508) 261-7500 • http://www.mansfieldschools.com/
Grade Span: PK-12; **Agency Type:** 1
Schools: 5
   3 Primary; 1 Middle; 1 High; 0 Other Level
   5 Regular; 0 Special Education; 0 Vocational; 0 Alternative
   0 Magnet; 0 Charter; 1 Title I Eligible; 0 School-wide Title I
Students: 4,742 (52.7% male; 47.2% female)
   Individual Education Program: 816 (17.2%);
   English Language Learner: 9 (0.2%); Migrant: 0 (0.0%)
   Eligible for Free Lunch Program: 216 (4.6%)
   Eligible for Reduced-Price Lunch Program: 58 (1.2%)
Teachers: 308.0 (15.4 to 1)
Librarians/Media Specialists: 2.7 (1,756.3 to 1)
Guidance Counselors: 8.0 (592.8 to 1)
Current Spending: ($ per student per year):
   Total: $8,453; Instruction: $5,419; Support Services: $2,828

Enrollment, Drop-out Rates and Diploma Recipients by Race/Ethnicity

Category	Total	White	Black	Asian	AIAN	Hisp.
Enrollment (%)	100.0	94.2	2.9	1.8	0.2	0.9
Drop-out Rate (%)	n/a	n/a	n/a	n/a	n/a	n/a
H.S. Diplomas (#)	209	197	8	2	0	2

New Bedford
455 County St • New Bedford, MA 02740-5194
Mailing Address: Prab • New Bedford, MA 02740-5194
(508) 997-4511 • http://www.newbedford.k12.ma.us/
Grade Span: PK-12; **Agency Type:** 1
Schools: 28
   23 Primary; 3 Middle; 1 High; 1 Other Level
   28 Regular; 0 Special Education; 0 Vocational; 0 Alternative
   0 Magnet; 0 Charter; 25 Title I Eligible; 23 School-wide Title I
Students: 14,546 (51.5% male; 48.4% female)
   Individual Education Program: 2,617 (18.0%);
   English Language Learner: 442 (3.0%); Migrant: 96 (0.7%)
   Eligible for Free Lunch Program: 7,275 (50.0%)
   Eligible for Reduced-Price Lunch Program: 1,737 (11.9%)
Teachers: 1,085.2 (13.4 to 1)
Librarians/Media Specialists: 2.0 (7,273.0 to 1)
Guidance Counselors: 24.0 (606.1 to 1)
Current Spending: ($ per student per year):
   Total: $10,542; Instruction: $6,444; Support Services: $3,651

Enrollment, Drop-out Rates and Diploma Recipients by Race/Ethnicity

Category	Total	White	Black	Asian	AIAN	Hisp.
Enrollment (%)	100.0	64.0	15.9	0.9	0.4	18.7
Drop-out Rate (%)	n/a	n/a	n/a	n/a	n/a	n/a
H.S. Diplomas (#)	565	428	83	6	0	48

North Attleborough
6 Morse St • North Attleborough, MA 02760-2702
(508) 643-2100 • http://www.naschools.net/
Grade Span: PK-12; **Agency Type:** 1
Schools: 9
   7 Primary; 1 Middle; 1 High; 0 Other Level
   9 Regular; 0 Special Education; 0 Vocational; 0 Alternative
   0 Magnet; 0 Charter; 2 Title I Eligible; 0 School-wide Title I
Students: 4,668 (52.8% male; 47.1% female)
   Individual Education Program: 732 (15.7%);
   English Language Learner: 35 (0.7%); Migrant: 0 (0.0%)
   Eligible for Free Lunch Program: 265 (5.7%)
   Eligible for Reduced-Price Lunch Program: 107 (2.3%)
Teachers: 322.0 (14.5 to 1)
Librarians/Media Specialists: 4.9 (952.7 to 1)
Guidance Counselors: 6.5 (718.2 to 1)
Current Spending: ($ per student per year):
   Total: $8,751; Instruction: $5,872; Support Services: $2,600

Enrollment, Drop-out Rates and Diploma Recipients by Race/Ethnicity

Category	Total	White	Black	Asian	AIAN	Hisp.
Enrollment (%)	100.0	95.1	1.4	2.4	0.2	1.0
Drop-out Rate (%)	n/a	n/a	n/a	n/a	n/a	n/a
H.S. Diplomas (#)	263	242	4	10	0	7

Norton
64 W Main St • Norton, MA 02766-2713
(508) 285-0100 • http://www.norton.mec.edu/index.htm
Grade Span: PK-12; **Agency Type:** 1
Schools: 5
   2 Primary; 2 Middle; 1 High; 0 Other Level

   5 Regular; 0 Special Education; 0 Vocational; 0 Alternative
   0 Magnet; 0 Charter; 3 Title I Eligible; 0 School-wide Title I
Students: 3,182 (52.5% male; 47.4% female)
   Individual Education Program: 663 (20.8%);
   English Language Learner: 0 (0.0%); Migrant: 0 (0.0%)
   Eligible for Free Lunch Program: 236 (7.4%)
   Eligible for Reduced-Price Lunch Program: 64 (2.0%)
Teachers: 204.8 (15.5 to 1)
Librarians/Media Specialists: 2.0 (1,591.0 to 1)
Guidance Counselors: 7.0 (454.6 to 1)
Current Spending: ($ per student per year):
   Total: $7,843; Instruction: $5,005; Support Services: $2,618

Enrollment, Drop-out Rates and Diploma Recipients by Race/Ethnicity

Category	Total	White	Black	Asian	AIAN	Hisp.
Enrollment (%)	100.0	96.6	1.6	1.1	0.1	0.6
Drop-out Rate (%)	n/a	n/a	n/a	n/a	n/a	n/a
H.S. Diplomas (#)	128	125	2	1	0	0

Seekonk
69 School St • Seekonk, MA 02771-5992
(508) 336-7711 • http://seekonkschools.lucasproject.com/controller.action
Grade Span: PK-12; **Agency Type:** 1
Schools: 5
   3 Primary; 1 Middle; 1 High; 0 Other Level
   5 Regular; 0 Special Education; 0 Vocational; 0 Alternative
   0 Magnet; 0 Charter; 3 Title I Eligible; 0 School-wide Title I
Students: 2,328 (51.2% male; 48.7% female)
   Individual Education Program: 225 (9.7%);
   English Language Learner: 0 (0.0%); Migrant: 0 (0.0%)
   Eligible for Free Lunch Program: 94 (4.0%)
   Eligible for Reduced-Price Lunch Program: 61 (2.6%)
Teachers: 159.0 (14.6 to 1)
Librarians/Media Specialists: 3.0 (776.0 to 1)
Guidance Counselors: 5.0 (465.6 to 1)
Current Spending: ($ per student per year):
   Total: $9,085; Instruction: $5,683; Support Services: $3,162

Enrollment, Drop-out Rates and Diploma Recipients by Race/Ethnicity

Category	Total	White	Black	Asian	AIAN	Hisp.
Enrollment (%)	100.0	96.2	1.3	1.3	0.4	0.7
Drop-out Rate (%)	n/a	n/a	n/a	n/a	n/a	n/a
H.S. Diplomas (#)	128	123	3	2	0	0

Somerset
580 Whetstone Hill Rd • Somerset, MA 02726-3702
(508) 324-3100 • http://www.somerset.k12.ma.us/SchoolFrontEnd/
Grade Span: PK-12; **Agency Type:** 1
Schools: 6
   4 Primary; 1 Middle; 1 High; 0 Other Level
   6 Regular; 0 Special Education; 0 Vocational; 0 Alternative
   0 Magnet; 0 Charter; 4 Title I Eligible; 0 School-wide Title I
Students: 2,886 (50.7% male; 49.2% female)
   Individual Education Program: 251 (8.7%);
   English Language Learner: 0 (0.0%); Migrant: 0 (0.0%)
   Eligible for Free Lunch Program: 189 (6.5%)
   Eligible for Reduced-Price Lunch Program: 56 (1.9%)
Teachers: 223.0 (12.9 to 1)
Librarians/Media Specialists: 3.8 (759.5 to 1)
Guidance Counselors: 5.3 (544.5 to 1)
Current Spending: ($ per student per year):
   Total: $10,401; Instruction: $6,732; Support Services: $3,433

Enrollment, Drop-out Rates and Diploma Recipients by Race/Ethnicity

Category	Total	White	Black	Asian	AIAN	Hisp.
Enrollment (%)	100.0	97.1	1.1	1.2	0.2	0.4
Drop-out Rate (%)	n/a	n/a	n/a	n/a	n/a	n/a
H.S. Diplomas (#)	211	210	1	0	0	0

Swansea
1 Gardner's Neck Rd • Swansea, MA 02777-3201
(508) 675-1195
Grade Span: PK-12; **Agency Type:** 1
Schools: 6
   4 Primary; 1 Middle; 1 High; 0 Other Level
   6 Regular; 0 Special Education; 0 Vocational; 0 Alternative
   0 Magnet; 0 Charter; 4 Title I Eligible; 0 School-wide Title I
Students: 2,188 (51.9% male; 48.0% female)
   Individual Education Program: 301 (13.8%);
   English Language Learner: 1 (<0.1%); Migrant: 0 (0.0%)
   Eligible for Free Lunch Program: 140 (6.4%)
   Eligible for Reduced-Price Lunch Program: 92 (4.2%)
Teachers: 171.1 (12.8 to 1)
Librarians/Media Specialists: 1.0 (2,188.0 to 1)
Guidance Counselors: 5.5 (397.8 to 1)
Current Spending: ($ per student per year):
   Total: $8,776; Instruction: $5,635; Support Services: $3,141

Enrollment, Drop-out Rates and Diploma Recipients by Race/Ethnicity

Category	Total	White	Black	Asian	AIAN	Hisp.
Enrollment (%)	100.0	97.3	1.2	1.0	0.2	0.2
Drop-out Rate (%)	n/a	n/a	n/a	n/a	n/a	n/a
H.S. Diplomas (#)	148	146	0	1	0	1

Taunton
50 Williams St • Taunton, MA 02780-2747
(508) 821-1201 • http://www.tauntonschools.org/
Grade Span: PK-12; **Agency Type:** 1
Schools: 16
  11 Primary; 4 Middle; 1 High; 0 Other Level
  16 Regular; 0 Special Education; 0 Vocational; 0 Alternative
  0 Magnet; 0 Charter; 7 Title I Eligible; 7 School-wide Title I
Students: 8,388   (51.4% male; 48.5% female)
  Individual Education Program: 1,452 (17.3%);
  English Language Learner: 220 (2.6%); Migrant: 8 (0.1%)
  Eligible for Free Lunch Program: 1,896 (22.6%)
  Eligible for Reduced-Price Lunch Program: 616 (7.3%)
Teachers: 493.5 (17.0 to 1)
Librarians/Media Specialists: 3.5 (2,396.6 to 1)
Guidance Counselors: 18.8 (446.2 to 1)
Current Spending: ($ per student per year):
  Total: $9,010; Instruction: $5,878; Support Services: $2,775

Enrollment, Drop-out Rates and Diploma Recipients by Race/Ethnicity

Category	Total	White	Black	Asian	AIAN	Hisp.
Enrollment (%)	100.0	85.5	6.9	1.0	0.2	6.4
Drop-out Rate (%)	n/a	n/a	n/a	n/a	n/a	n/a
H.S. Diplomas (#)	316	275	16	5	0	20

Westport
17 Main Rd • Westport, MA 02790-4201
(508) 636-1137 • http://www.westportschools.org/
Grade Span: PK-12; **Agency Type:** 1
Schools: 4
  2 Primary; 1 Middle; 1 High; 0 Other Level
  4 Regular; 0 Special Education; 0 Vocational; 0 Alternative
  0 Magnet; 0 Charter; 2 Title I Eligible; 0 School-wide Title I
Students: 1,901   (51.9% male; 48.0% female)
  Individual Education Program: 286 (15.0%);
  English Language Learner: 2 (0.1%); Migrant: 0 (0.0%)
  Eligible for Free Lunch Program: 202 (10.6%)
  Eligible for Reduced-Price Lunch Program: 113 (5.9%)
Teachers: 123.0 (15.5 to 1)
Librarians/Media Specialists: 2.0 (950.5 to 1)
Guidance Counselors: 3.5 (543.1 to 1)
Current Spending: ($ per student per year):
  Total: $8,281; Instruction: $4,887; Support Services: $3,120

Enrollment, Drop-out Rates and Diploma Recipients by Race/Ethnicity

Category	Total	White	Black	Asian	AIAN	Hisp.
Enrollment (%)	100.0	97.7	0.7	0.5	0.1	0.9
Drop-out Rate (%)	n/a	n/a	n/a	n/a	n/a	n/a
H.S. Diplomas (#)	81	79	1	1	0	n/a

Essex County

Amesbury
10 Congress St • Amesbury, MA 01913-2812
(978) 388-0507 •
http://www.ci.amesbury.ma.us/home.nfs?a=amesbury&s=1091469238:185
25&group=2
Grade Span: PK-12; **Agency Type:** 1
Schools: 4
  2 Primary; 1 Middle; 1 High; 0 Other Level
  4 Regular; 0 Special Education; 0 Vocational; 0 Alternative
  0 Magnet; 0 Charter; 2 Title I Eligible; 0 School-wide Title I
Students: 2,720   (51.9% male; 48.0% female)
  Individual Education Program: 469 (17.2%);
  English Language Learner: 10 (0.4%); Migrant: 0 (0.0%)
  Eligible for Free Lunch Program: 236 (8.7%)
  Eligible for Reduced-Price Lunch Program: 137 (5.0%)
Teachers: 195.0 (13.9 to 1)
Librarians/Media Specialists: 4.0 (680.0 to 1)
Guidance Counselors: 6.0 (453.3 to 1)
Current Spending: ($ per student per year):
  Total: $9,048; Instruction: $6,274; Support Services: $2,774

Enrollment, Drop-out Rates and Diploma Recipients by Race/Ethnicity

Category	Total	White	Black	Asian	AIAN	Hisp.
Enrollment (%)	100.0	95.3	1.4	0.8	0.3	2.2
Drop-out Rate (%)	n/a	n/a	n/a	n/a	n/a	n/a
H.S. Diplomas (#)	174	172	1	0	1	0

Andover
36 Bartlet St • Andover, MA 01810-3813
(978) 623-8501 • http://www.aps1.net/
Grade Span: PK-12; **Agency Type:** 1
Schools: 10
  6 Primary; 3 Middle; 1 High; 0 Other Level
  10 Regular; 0 Special Education; 0 Vocational; 0 Alternative
  0 Magnet; 0 Charter; 2 Title I Eligible; 0 School-wide Title I
Students: 5,939   (51.4% male; 48.5% female)
  Individual Education Program: 899 (15.1%);
  English Language Learner: 30 (0.5%); Migrant: 2 (<0.1%)
  Eligible for Free Lunch Program: 184 (3.1%)
  Eligible for Reduced-Price Lunch Program: 0 (0.0%)
Teachers: 425.9 (13.9 to 1)
Librarians/Media Specialists: 8.6 (690.6 to 1)
Guidance Counselors: 10.0 (593.9 to 1)
Current Spending: ($ per student per year):
  Total: $10,764; Instruction: $7,007; Support Services: $3,548

Enrollment, Drop-out Rates and Diploma Recipients by Race/Ethnicity

Category	Total	White	Black	Asian	AIAN	Hisp.
Enrollment (%)	100.0	88.2	1.0	8.3	0.2	2.4
Drop-out Rate (%)	n/a	n/a	n/a	n/a	n/a	n/a
H.S. Diplomas (#)	383	337	5	36	0	5

Beverly
20 Colon St • Beverly, MA 01915-3444
(978) 921-6100 • http://www.beverlyschools.org/index2.shtm
Grade Span: PK-12; **Agency Type:** 1
Schools: 9
  6 Primary; 2 Middle; 1 High; 0 Other Level
  9 Regular; 0 Special Education; 0 Vocational; 0 Alternative
  0 Magnet; 0 Charter; 3 Title I Eligible; 0 School-wide Title I
Students: 4,557   (50.2% male; 49.7% female)
  Individual Education Program: 932 (20.5%);
  English Language Learner: 73 (1.6%); Migrant: 4 (0.1%)
  Eligible for Free Lunch Program: 657 (14.4%)
  Eligible for Reduced-Price Lunch Program: 188 (4.1%)
Teachers: 343.5 (13.3 to 1)
Librarians/Media Specialists: 8.1 (562.6 to 1)
Guidance Counselors: 10.7 (425.9 to 1)
Current Spending: ($ per student per year):
  Total: $9,737; Instruction: $6,325; Support Services: $3,110

Enrollment, Drop-out Rates and Diploma Recipients by Race/Ethnicity

Category	Total	White	Black	Asian	AIAN	Hisp.
Enrollment (%)	100.0	91.7	2.6	1.3	0.1	4.2
Drop-out Rate (%)	n/a	n/a	n/a	n/a	n/a	n/a
H.S. Diplomas (#)	285	276	2	2	0	5

Danvers
64 Cabot Rd • Danvers, MA 01923-2355
(978) 777-4539 • http://www.danvers.mec.edu/
Grade Span: PK-12; **Agency Type:** 1
Schools: 7
  5 Primary; 1 Middle; 1 High; 0 Other Level
  7 Regular; 0 Special Education; 0 Vocational; 0 Alternative
  0 Magnet; 0 Charter; 4 Title I Eligible; 0 School-wide Title I
Students: 3,657   (47.6% male; 52.3% female)
  Individual Education Program: 453 (12.4%);
  English Language Learner: 13 (0.4%); Migrant: 0 (0.0%)
  Eligible for Free Lunch Program: 164 (4.5%)
  Eligible for Reduced-Price Lunch Program: 84 (2.3%)
Teachers: 262.7 (13.9 to 1)
Librarians/Media Specialists: 1.0 (3,657.0 to 1)
Guidance Counselors: 7.0 (522.4 to 1)
Current Spending: ($ per student per year):
  Total: $9,581; Instruction: $6,132; Support Services: $3,226

Enrollment, Drop-out Rates and Diploma Recipients by Race/Ethnicity

Category	Total	White	Black	Asian	AIAN	Hisp.
Enrollment (%)	100.0	96.3	0.5	1.3	0.2	1.7
Drop-out Rate (%)	n/a	n/a	n/a	n/a	n/a	n/a
H.S. Diplomas (#)	238	234	0	3	0	1

Georgetown
51 N St • Georgetown, MA 01833-1699
(978) 352-5777
Grade Span: PK-12; **Agency Type:** 1
Schools: 3
  2 Primary; 0 Middle; 0 High; 1 Other Level
  3 Regular; 0 Special Education; 0 Vocational; 0 Alternative
  0 Magnet; 0 Charter; 2 Title I Eligible; 0 School-wide Title I
Students: 1,617   (50.8% male; 49.1% female)
  Individual Education Program: 169 (10.5%);
  English Language Learner: 0 (0.0%); Migrant: 0 (0.0%)
  Eligible for Free Lunch Program: 45 (2.8%)
  Eligible for Reduced-Price Lunch Program: 16 (1.0%)

Teachers: 109.7 (14.7 to 1)
Librarians/Media Specialists: 1.0 (1,617.0 to 1)
Guidance Counselors: 3.2 (505.3 to 1)
Current Spending: ($ per student per year):
Total: $7,820; Instruction: $5,273; Support Services: $2,264
Enrollment, Drop-out Rates and Diploma Recipients by Race/Ethnicity

Category	Total	White	Black	Asian	AIAN	Hisp.
Enrollment (%)	100.0	96.9	0.4	1.2	0.2	1.3
Drop-out Rate (%)	n/a	n/a	n/a	n/a	n/a	n/a
H.S. Diplomas (#)	94	92	0	0	1	1

Gloucester

6 School House Rd • Gloucester, MA 01930-2702
(978) 281-9800 • http://www.gloucester.k12.ma.us/
Grade Span: PK-12; **Agency Type:** 1
Schools: 8
6 Primary; 1 Middle; 1 High; 0 Other Level
8 Regular; 0 Special Education; 0 Vocational; 0 Alternative
0 Magnet; 0 Charter; 2 Title I Eligible; 0 School-wide Title I
Students: 4,019 (51.9% male; 48.0% female)
Individual Education Program: 744 (18.5%);
English Language Learner: 42 (1.0%); Migrant: 33 (0.8%)
Eligible for Free Lunch Program: 736 (18.3%)
Eligible for Reduced-Price Lunch Program: 178 (4.4%)
Teachers: 307.3 (13.1 to 1)
Librarians/Media Specialists: 1.0 (4,019.0 to 1)
Guidance Counselors: 9.0 (446.6 to 1)
Current Spending: ($ per student per year):
Total: $9,496; Instruction: $6,213; Support Services: $2,911
Enrollment, Drop-out Rates and Diploma Recipients by Race/Ethnicity

Category	Total	White	Black	Asian	AIAN	Hisp.
Enrollment (%)	100.0	94.8	1.3	1.0	0.1	2.8
Drop-out Rate (%)	n/a	n/a	n/a	n/a	n/a	n/a
H.S. Diplomas (#)	290	285	2	1	0	2

Hamilton-Wenham

5 School St • Wenham, MA 01984-1053
(978) 468-5310
Grade Span: PK-12; **Agency Type:** 3
Schools: 5
3 Primary; 1 Middle; 1 High; 0 Other Level
5 Regular; 0 Special Education; 0 Vocational; 0 Alternative
0 Magnet; 0 Charter; 3 Title I Eligible; 0 School-wide Title I
Students: 2,213 (50.1% male; 49.8% female)
Individual Education Program: 307 (13.9%);
English Language Learner: 3 (0.1%); Migrant: 1 (<0.1%)
Eligible for Free Lunch Program: 68 (3.1%)
Eligible for Reduced-Price Lunch Program: 19 (0.9%)
Teachers: 156.2 (14.2 to 1)
Librarians/Media Specialists: 1.8 (1,229.4 to 1)
Guidance Counselors: 2.6 (851.2 to 1)
Current Spending: ($ per student per year):
Total: $10,154; Instruction: $6,940; Support Services: $2,957
Enrollment, Drop-out Rates and Diploma Recipients by Race/Ethnicity

Category	Total	White	Black	Asian	AIAN	Hisp.
Enrollment (%)	100.0	95.7	0.8	2.7	0.1	0.7
Drop-out Rate (%)	n/a	n/a	n/a	n/a	n/a	n/a
H.S. Diplomas (#)	158	145	1	5	5	2

Haverhill

4 Summer St • Haverhill, MA 01830-5877
(978) 374-3400 • http://www.haverhill-ma.com/
Grade Span: PK-12; **Agency Type:** 1
Schools: 17
10 Primary; 4 Middle; 1 High; 2 Other Level
17 Regular; 0 Special Education; 0 Vocational; 0 Alternative
0 Magnet; 0 Charter; 7 Title I Eligible; 4 School-wide Title I
Students: 8,043 (51.6% male; 48.3% female)
Individual Education Program: 1,282 (15.9%);
English Language Learner: 357 (4.4%); Migrant: 23 (0.3%)
Eligible for Free Lunch Program: 1,879 (23.4%)
Eligible for Reduced-Price Lunch Program: 676 (8.4%)
Teachers: 550.4 (14.6 to 1)
Librarians/Media Specialists: 4.0 (2,010.8 to 1)
Guidance Counselors: 12.0 (670.3 to 1)
Current Spending: ($ per student per year):
Total: $9,607; Instruction: $6,022; Support Services: $3,170
Enrollment, Drop-out Rates and Diploma Recipients by Race/Ethnicity

Category	Total	White	Black	Asian	AIAN	Hisp.
Enrollment (%)	100.0	78.6	2.9	1.8	0.0	16.7
Drop-out Rate (%)	n/a	n/a	n/a	n/a	n/a	n/a
H.S. Diplomas (#)	377	311	12	6	0	48

Ipswich

1 Lord Square • Ipswich, MA 01938-1909
(978) 356-2935 • http://www.ipswichschools.org/
Grade Span: PK-12; **Agency Type:** 1
Schools: 4
2 Primary; 1 Middle; 1 High; 0 Other Level
4 Regular; 0 Special Education; 0 Vocational; 0 Alternative
0 Magnet; 0 Charter; 2 Title I Eligible; 0 School-wide Title I
Students: 2,094 (49.1% male; 50.8% female)
Individual Education Program: 279 (13.3%);
English Language Learner: 12 (0.6%); Migrant: 1 (<0.1%)
Eligible for Free Lunch Program: 172 (8.2%)
Eligible for Reduced-Price Lunch Program: 23 (1.1%)
Teachers: 149.1 (14.0 to 1)
Librarians/Media Specialists: 1.5 (1,396.0 to 1)
Guidance Counselors: 4.3 (487.0 to 1)
Current Spending: ($ per student per year):
Total: $8,999; Instruction: $5,880; Support Services: $2,832
Enrollment, Drop-out Rates and Diploma Recipients by Race/Ethnicity

Category	Total	White	Black	Asian	AIAN	Hisp.
Enrollment (%)	100.0	95.4	1.2	1.9	0.1	1.3
Drop-out Rate (%)	n/a	n/a	n/a	n/a	n/a	n/a
H.S. Diplomas (#)	116	113	0	1	1	1

Lawrence

255 Essex St • Lawrence, MA 01840-1492
(978) 975-5900 • http://www.lawrence.k12.ma.us/
Grade Span: PK-12; **Agency Type:** 1
Schools: 16
13 Primary; 1 Middle; 1 High; 1 Other Level
16 Regular; 0 Special Education; 0 Vocational; 0 Alternative
0 Magnet; 0 Charter; 16 Title I Eligible; 16 School-wide Title I
Students: 12,508 (51.4% male; 48.5% female)
Individual Education Program: 1,946 (15.6%);
English Language Learner: 2,065 (16.5%); Migrant: 82 (0.7%)
Eligible for Free Lunch Program: 8,712 (69.7%)
Eligible for Reduced-Price Lunch Program: 1,632 (13.0%)
Teachers: 898.9 (13.9 to 1)
Librarians/Media Specialists: 7.0 (1,786.9 to 1)
Guidance Counselors: 21.0 (595.6 to 1)
Current Spending: ($ per student per year):
Total: $11,381; Instruction: $6,529; Support Services: $4,367
Enrollment, Drop-out Rates and Diploma Recipients by Race/Ethnicity

Category	Total	White	Black	Asian	AIAN	Hisp.
Enrollment (%)	100.0	9.8	2.3	3.0	0.1	84.8
Drop-out Rate (%)	n/a	n/a	n/a	n/a	n/a	n/a
H.S. Diplomas (#)	270	10	11	21	0	228

Lynn

90 Commercial St • Lynn, MA 01905-1201
(781) 593-1680 • http://www.lynnschools.org/
Grade Span: PK-12; **Agency Type:** 1
Schools: 28
19 Primary; 4 Middle; 4 High; 1 Other Level
23 Regular; 0 Special Education; 1 Vocational; 4 Alternative
0 Magnet; 0 Charter; 19 Title I Eligible; 19 School-wide Title I
Students: 14,618 (51.7% male; 48.2% female)
Individual Education Program: 2,169 (14.8%);
English Language Learner: 2,772 (19.0%); Migrant: 31 (0.2%)
Eligible for Free Lunch Program: 8,428 (57.7%)
Eligible for Reduced-Price Lunch Program: 1,551 (10.6%)
Teachers: 1,080.6 (13.5 to 1)
Librarians/Media Specialists: 12.5 (1,169.4 to 1)
Guidance Counselors: 25.0 (584.7 to 1)
Current Spending: ($ per student per year):
Total: $11,119; Instruction: $6,412; Support Services: $4,261
Enrollment, Drop-out Rates and Diploma Recipients by Race/Ethnicity

Category	Total	White	Black	Asian	AIAN	Hisp.
Enrollment (%)	100.0	38.1	15.4	12.0	0.3	34.2
Drop-out Rate (%)	n/a	n/a	n/a	n/a	n/a	n/a
H.S. Diplomas (#)	676	333	89	98	1	155

Lynnfield

55 Summer St • Lynnfield, MA 01940-1789
Mailing Address: Lynnfield Public Schools • Lynnfield, MA 01940-1789
(781) 334-5800 •
http://www.lynnfield.k12.ma.us/education/district/district.php?sectionid=1
Grade Span: PK-12; **Agency Type:** 1
Schools: 4
2 Primary; 1 Middle; 1 High; 0 Other Level
4 Regular; 0 Special Education; 0 Vocational; 0 Alternative
0 Magnet; 0 Charter; 1 Title I Eligible; 0 School-wide Title I
Students: 2,031 (51.5% male; 48.4% female)
Individual Education Program: 207 (10.2%);
English Language Learner: 3 (0.1%); Migrant: 0 (0.0%)

Eligible for Free Lunch Program: 20 (1.0%)
Eligible for Reduced-Price Lunch Program: 20 (1.0%)
Teachers: 142.7 (14.2 to 1)
Librarians/Media Specialists: 4.0 (507.8 to 1)
Guidance Counselors: 3.6 (564.2 to 1)
Current Spending: ($ per student per year):
   Total: $9,157; Instruction: $6,163; Support Services: $2,826
Enrollment, Drop-out Rates and Diploma Recipients by Race/Ethnicity

Category	Total	White	Black	Asian	AIAN	Hisp.
Enrollment (%)	100.0	93.7	1.7	3.0	0.4	1.2
Drop-out Rate (%)	n/a	n/a	n/a	n/a	n/a	n/a
H.S. Diplomas (#)	106	102	1	0	1	2

Marblehead

9 Widger Rd • Marblehead, MA 01945-1920
(781) 639-3141 • http://www.marblehead.com/schools/
Grade Span: PK-12; **Agency Type:** 1
Schools: 7
   5 Primary; 1 Middle; 1 High; 0 Other Level
   7 Regular; 0 Special Education; 0 Vocational; 0 Alternative
   0 Magnet; 0 Charter; 4 Title I Eligible; 0 School-wide Title I
Students: 3,016 (51.0% male; 48.9% female)
   Individual Education Program: 474 (15.7%);
   English Language Learner: 7 (0.2%); Migrant: 8 (0.3%)
   Eligible for Free Lunch Program: 151 (5.0%)
   Eligible for Reduced-Price Lunch Program: 27 (0.9%)
Teachers: 218.1 (13.8 to 1)
Librarians/Media Specialists: 4.6 (655.7 to 1)
Guidance Counselors: 10.0 (301.6 to 1)
Current Spending: ($ per student per year):
   Total: $10,225; Instruction: $7,075; Support Services: $2,915
Enrollment, Drop-out Rates and Diploma Recipients by Race/Ethnicity

Category	Total	White	Black	Asian	AIAN	Hisp.
Enrollment (%)	100.0	91.7	3.3	1.4	2.3	1.3
Drop-out Rate (%)	n/a	n/a	n/a	n/a	n/a	n/a
H.S. Diplomas (#)	208	201	4	2	0	1

Masconomet

20 Endicott Rd • Topsfield, MA 01983-2009
(978) 887-2323 • http://www.masconomet.org/
Grade Span: 07-12; **Agency Type:** 4
Schools: 2
   0 Primary; 1 Middle; 1 High; 0 Other Level
   2 Regular; 0 Special Education; 0 Vocational; 0 Alternative
   0 Magnet; 0 Charter; 2 Title I Eligible; 0 School-wide Title I
Students: 1,993 (48.8% male; 51.1% female)
   Individual Education Program: 287 (14.4%);
   English Language Learner: 0 (0.0%); Migrant: 0 (0.0%)
   Eligible for Free Lunch Program: 20 (1.0%)
   Eligible for Reduced-Price Lunch Program: 0 (0.0%)
Teachers: 124.6 (16.0 to 1)
Librarians/Media Specialists: 2.0 (996.5 to 1)
Guidance Counselors: 9.6 (207.6 to 1)
Current Spending: ($ per student per year):
   Total: $10,910; Instruction: $6,871; Support Services: $3,832
Enrollment, Drop-out Rates and Diploma Recipients by Race/Ethnicity

Category	Total	White	Black	Asian	AIAN	Hisp.
Enrollment (%)	100.0	97.7	0.6	0.8	0.1	0.9
Drop-out Rate (%)	n/a	n/a	n/a	n/a	n/a	n/a
H.S. Diplomas (#)	269	260	0	6	0	3

Methuen

10 Ditson Place • Methuen, MA 01844-6117
(978) 681-1317 • http://www.methuen.k12.ma.us/
Grade Span: PK-12; **Agency Type:** 1
Schools: 6
   5 Primary; 0 Middle; 1 High; 0 Other Level
   6 Regular; 0 Special Education; 0 Vocational; 0 Alternative
   0 Magnet; 0 Charter; 4 Title I Eligible; 0 School-wide Title I
Students: 7,230 (51.7% male; 48.2% female)
   Individual Education Program: 912 (12.6%);
   English Language Learner: 406 (5.6%); Migrant: 0 (0.0%)
   Eligible for Free Lunch Program: 1,434 (19.8%)
   Eligible for Reduced-Price Lunch Program: 427 (5.9%)
Teachers: 470.1 (15.4 to 1)
Librarians/Media Specialists: 6.0 (1,205.0 to 1)
Guidance Counselors: 25.0 (289.2 to 1)
Current Spending: ($ per student per year):
   Total: $8,974; Instruction: $5,498; Support Services: $3,207
Enrollment, Drop-out Rates and Diploma Recipients by Race/Ethnicity

Category	Total	White	Black	Asian	AIAN	Hisp.
Enrollment (%)	100.0	78.0	1.8	2.7	0.5	17.1
Drop-out Rate (%)	n/a	n/a	n/a	n/a	n/a	n/a
H.S. Diplomas (#)	354	297	8	11	1	37

Newburyport

70 Low St • Newburyport, MA 01950-4049
(978) 465-4457 • http://www.newburyport.k12.ma.us
Grade Span: PK-12; **Agency Type:** 1
Schools: 5
   3 Primary; 1 Middle; 1 High; 0 Other Level
   5 Regular; 0 Special Education; 0 Vocational; 0 Alternative
   0 Magnet; 0 Charter; 2 Title I Eligible; 0 School-wide Title I
Students: 2,381 (52.6% male; 47.3% female)
   Individual Education Program: 362 (15.2%);
   English Language Learner: 12 (0.5%); Migrant: 0 (0.0%)
   Eligible for Free Lunch Program: 77 (3.2%)
   Eligible for Reduced-Price Lunch Program: 42 (1.8%)
Teachers: 180.3 (13.2 to 1)
Librarians/Media Specialists: 3.0 (793.7 to 1)
Guidance Counselors: 4.0 (595.3 to 1)
Current Spending: ($ per student per year):
   Total: $11,167; Instruction: $7,258; Support Services: $3,603
Enrollment, Drop-out Rates and Diploma Recipients by Race/Ethnicity

Category	Total	White	Black	Asian	AIAN	Hisp.
Enrollment (%)	100.0	96.6	1.0	1.1	0.3	1.0
Drop-out Rate (%)	n/a	n/a	n/a	n/a	n/a	n/a
H.S. Diplomas (#)	130	128	0	1	1	0

North Andover

43 High St • North Andover, MA 01845-1901
(978) 794-1503 • http://www.nandover.mec.edu
Grade Span: PK-12; **Agency Type:** 1
Schools: 8
   6 Primary; 1 Middle; 1 High; 0 Other Level
   8 Regular; 0 Special Education; 0 Vocational; 0 Alternative
   0 Magnet; 0 Charter; 2 Title I Eligible; 0 School-wide Title I
Students: 4,358 (53.0% male; 46.9% female)
   Individual Education Program: 487 (11.2%);
   English Language Learner: 30 (0.7%); Migrant: 10 (0.2%)
   Eligible for Free Lunch Program: 118 (2.7%)
   Eligible for Reduced-Price Lunch Program: 41 (0.9%)
Teachers: 288.9 (15.1 to 1)
Librarians/Media Specialists: 3.0 (1,452.7 to 1)
Guidance Counselors: 11.8 (369.3 to 1)
Current Spending: ($ per student per year):
   Total: $9,206; Instruction: $5,599; Support Services: $3,298
Enrollment, Drop-out Rates and Diploma Recipients by Race/Ethnicity

Category	Total	White	Black	Asian	AIAN	Hisp.
Enrollment (%)	100.0	90.3	0.8	5.9	0.6	2.4
Drop-out Rate (%)	n/a	n/a	n/a	n/a	n/a	n/a
H.S. Diplomas (#)	248	232	0	11	0	5

Peabody

70 Endicott St • Peabody, MA 01960-8199
(978) 536-6500 • http://www.peabody.k12.ma.us/
Grade Span: PK-12; **Agency Type:** 1
Schools: 10
   8 Primary; 1 Middle; 1 High; 0 Other Level
   10 Regular; 0 Special Education; 0 Vocational; 0 Alternative
   0 Magnet; 0 Charter; 4 Title I Eligible; 0 School-wide Title I
Students: 6,625 (50.6% male; 49.3% female)
   Individual Education Program: 957 (14.4%);
   English Language Learner: 142 (2.1%); Migrant: 46 (0.7%)
   Eligible for Free Lunch Program: 851 (12.8%)
   Eligible for Reduced-Price Lunch Program: 189 (2.9%)
Teachers: 465.5 (14.2 to 1)
Librarians/Media Specialists: 2.0 (3,312.5 to 1)
Guidance Counselors: 18.0 (368.1 to 1)
Current Spending: ($ per student per year):
   Total: $9,605; Instruction: $6,210; Support Services: $3,099
Enrollment, Drop-out Rates and Diploma Recipients by Race/Ethnicity

Category	Total	White	Black	Asian	AIAN	Hisp.
Enrollment (%)	100.0	89.5	1.5	1.7	0.1	7.2
Drop-out Rate (%)	n/a	n/a	n/a	n/a	n/a	n/a
H.S. Diplomas (#)	384	363	1	6	0	14

Pentucket

22 Main St • West Newbury, MA 01985-1897
(978) 363-2280 • http://www.prsd.org/
Grade Span: PK-12; **Agency Type:** 3
Schools: 6
   4 Primary; 1 Middle; 1 High; 0 Other Level
   6 Regular; 0 Special Education; 0 Vocational; 0 Alternative
   0 Magnet; 0 Charter; 2 Title I Eligible; 0 School-wide Title I
Students: 3,488 (50.5% male; 49.4% female)
   Individual Education Program: 461 (13.2%);
   English Language Learner: 0 (0.0%); Migrant: 0 (0.0%)
   Eligible for Free Lunch Program: 92 (2.6%)
   Eligible for Reduced-Price Lunch Program: 41 (1.2%)

Teachers: 239.6 (14.6 to 1)
Librarians/Media Specialists: 4.0 (872.0 to 1)
Guidance Counselors: 4.0 (872.0 to 1)
Current Spending: ($ per student per year):
Total: $8,770; Instruction: $5,745; Support Services: $2,761
Enrollment, Drop-out Rates and Diploma Recipients by Race/Ethnicity

Category	Total	White	Black	Asian	AIAN	Hisp.
Enrollment (%)	100.0	97.8	0.6	0.8	0.0	0.8
Drop-out Rate (%)	n/a	n/a	n/a	n/a	n/a	n/a
H.S. Diplomas (#)	197	192	1	2	0	2

Salem

29 Highland Ave • Salem, MA 01970-2116
(978) 740-1212 • http://salem.k12.ma.us/
Grade Span: PK-12; **Agency Type:** 1
Schools: 10
8 Primary; 1 Middle; 1 High; 0 Other Level
10 Regular; 0 Special Education; 0 Vocational; 0 Alternative
0 Magnet; 0 Charter; 8 Title I Eligible; 3 School-wide Title I
Students: 4,923 (50.2% male; 49.7% female)
Individual Education Program: 938 (19.1%);
English Language Learner: 386 (7.8%); Migrant: 29 (0.6%)
Eligible for Free Lunch Program: 1,604 (32.6%)
Eligible for Reduced-Price Lunch Program: 243 (4.9%)
Teachers: 408.5 (12.1 to 1)
Librarians/Media Specialists: 2.2 (2,237.7 to 1)
Guidance Counselors: 6.0 (820.5 to 1)
Current Spending: ($ per student per year):
Total: $11,265; Instruction: $7,044; Support Services: $3,882
Enrollment, Drop-out Rates and Diploma Recipients by Race/Ethnicity

Category	Total	White	Black	Asian	AIAN	Hisp.
Enrollment (%)	100.0	63.9	4.7	2.6	0.3	28.5
Drop-out Rate (%)	n/a	n/a	n/a	n/a	n/a	n/a
H.S. Diplomas (#)	217	136	10	7	0	64

Saugus

23 Main St • Saugus, MA 01906-2347
(781) 231-5000
Grade Span: PK-12; **Agency Type:** 1
Schools: 6
4 Primary; 1 Middle; 0 High; 1 Other Level
6 Regular; 0 Special Education; 0 Vocational; 0 Alternative
0 Magnet; 0 Charter; 3 Title I Eligible; 0 School-wide Title I
Students: 3,306 (50.8% male; 49.1% female)
Individual Education Program: 398 (12.0%);
English Language Learner: 0 (0.0%); Migrant: 0 (0.0%)
Eligible for Free Lunch Program: 259 (7.8%)
Eligible for Reduced-Price Lunch Program: 75 (2.3%)
Teachers: 221.8 (14.9 to 1)
Librarians/Media Specialists: 1.0 (3,306.0 to 1)
Guidance Counselors: 5.0 (661.2 to 1)
Current Spending: ($ per student per year):
Total: $9,291; Instruction: $5,951; Support Services: $3,020
Enrollment, Drop-out Rates and Diploma Recipients by Race/Ethnicity

Category	Total	White	Black	Asian	AIAN	Hisp.
Enrollment (%)	100.0	93.1	1.7	2.4	0.2	2.6
Drop-out Rate (%)	n/a	n/a	n/a	n/a	n/a	n/a
H.S. Diplomas (#)	175	170	1	3	0	1

Swampscott

207 Forest Ave • Swampscott, MA 01907-2293
(781) 596-8800
Grade Span: PK-12; **Agency Type:** 1
Schools: 6
4 Primary; 1 Middle; 0 High; 1 Other Level
6 Regular; 0 Special Education; 0 Vocational; 0 Alternative
0 Magnet; 0 Charter; 2 Title I Eligible; 0 School-wide Title I
Students: 2,382 (50.5% male; 49.4% female)
Individual Education Program: 348 (14.6%);
English Language Learner: 17 (0.7%); Migrant: 0 (0.0%)
Eligible for Free Lunch Program: 75 (3.1%)
Eligible for Reduced-Price Lunch Program: 8 (0.3%)
Teachers: 168.5 (14.1 to 1)
Librarians/Media Specialists: 3.5 (680.6 to 1)
Guidance Counselors: 6.0 (397.0 to 1)
Current Spending: ($ per student per year):
Total: $10,261; Instruction: $6,853; Support Services: $3,078
Enrollment, Drop-out Rates and Diploma Recipients by Race/Ethnicity

Category	Total	White	Black	Asian	AIAN	Hisp.
Enrollment (%)	100.0	94.5	2.1	1.7	0.2	1.5
Drop-out Rate (%)	n/a	n/a	n/a	n/a	n/a	n/a
H.S. Diplomas (#)	171	167	2	1	0	1

Triton

112 Elm St • Byfield, MA 01922-2814
(978) 465-2397 • http://www.triton1.org/district/
Grade Span: PK-12; **Agency Type:** 3
Schools: 5
3 Primary; 1 Middle; 1 High; 0 Other Level
5 Regular; 0 Special Education; 0 Vocational; 0 Alternative
0 Magnet; 0 Charter; 1 Title I Eligible; 0 School-wide Title I
Students: 3,551 (51.9% male; 48.0% female)
Individual Education Program: 378 (10.6%);
English Language Learner: 14 (0.4%); Migrant: 1 (<0.1%)
Eligible for Free Lunch Program: 316 (8.9%)
Eligible for Reduced-Price Lunch Program: 75 (2.1%)
Teachers: 211.9 (16.8 to 1)
Librarians/Media Specialists: 3.0 (1,183.7 to 1)
Guidance Counselors: 6.0 (591.8 to 1)
Current Spending: ($ per student per year):
Total: $8,788; Instruction: $5,643; Support Services: $2,868
Enrollment, Drop-out Rates and Diploma Recipients by Race/Ethnicity

Category	Total	White	Black	Asian	AIAN	Hisp.
Enrollment (%)	100.0	96.5	0.9	0.7	0.8	1.1
Drop-out Rate (%)	n/a	n/a	n/a	n/a	n/a	n/a
H.S. Diplomas (#)	198	195	1	1	0	1

Franklin County

Greenfield

141 Davis St • Greenfield, MA 01301-2504
(413) 772-1311 • http://gpsk12.org/
Grade Span: PK-12; **Agency Type:** 1
Schools: 7
5 Primary; 1 Middle; 1 High; 0 Other Level
7 Regular; 0 Special Education; 0 Vocational; 0 Alternative
0 Magnet; 0 Charter; 6 Title I Eligible; 3 School-wide Title I
Students: 2,120 (51.6% male; 48.3% female)
Individual Education Program: 357 (16.8%);
English Language Learner: 106 (5.0%); Migrant: 0 (0.0%)
Eligible for Free Lunch Program: 756 (35.7%)
Eligible for Reduced-Price Lunch Program: 174 (8.2%)
Teachers: 163.5 (13.0 to 1)
Librarians/Media Specialists: 1.0 (2,120.0 to 1)
Guidance Counselors: 5.0 (424.0 to 1)
Current Spending: ($ per student per year):
Total: $10,841; Instruction: $6,766; Support Services: $3,612
Enrollment, Drop-out Rates and Diploma Recipients by Race/Ethnicity

Category	Total	White	Black	Asian	AIAN	Hisp.
Enrollment (%)	100.0	86.1	3.4	2.2	0.3	7.9
Drop-out Rate (%)	n/a	n/a	n/a	n/a	n/a	n/a
H.S. Diplomas (#)	124	117	2	3	0	2

Mohawk Trail

24 Ashfield Rd • Shelburne Falls, MA 01370-9416
(413) 625-0192 • http://www.mohawk.k14.mass.edu/
Grade Span: PK-12; **Agency Type:** 3
Schools: 5
4 Primary; 0 Middle; 1 High; 0 Other Level
5 Regular; 0 Special Education; 0 Vocational; 0 Alternative
0 Magnet; 0 Charter; 3 Title I Eligible; 0 School-wide Title I
Students: 1,529 (53.1% male; 46.8% female)
Individual Education Program: 286 (18.7%);
English Language Learner: 1 (0.1%); Migrant: 1 (0.1%)
Eligible for Free Lunch Program: 347 (22.7%)
Eligible for Reduced-Price Lunch Program: 97 (6.3%)
Teachers: 119.1 (12.8 to 1)
Librarians/Media Specialists: 5.2 (294.0 to 1)
Guidance Counselors: 3.8 (402.4 to 1)
Current Spending: ($ per student per year):
Total: $11,184; Instruction: $6,997; Support Services: $3,785
Enrollment, Drop-out Rates and Diploma Recipients by Race/Ethnicity

Category	Total	White	Black	Asian	AIAN	Hisp.
Enrollment (%)	100.0	96.6	1.3	0.7	0.5	0.9
Drop-out Rate (%)	n/a	n/a	n/a	n/a	n/a	n/a
H.S. Diplomas (#)	96	95	0	1	0	0

Hampden County

Agawam

1305 Springfield St • Feeding Hills, MA 01030-2198
Mailing Address: 1305 Springfield St-Ste 1 • Feeding Hills, MA 01030-2198
(413) 821-0548 • http://www.agawampublicschools.org/
Grade Span: PK-12; **Agency Type:** 1
Schools: 8
5 Primary; 2 Middle; 1 High; 0 Other Level
8 Regular; 0 Special Education; 0 Vocational; 0 Alternative
0 Magnet; 0 Charter; 5 Title I Eligible; 0 School-wide Title I

Students: 4,335   (51.7% male; 48.2% female)
   Individual Education Program: 717 (16.5%);
   English Language Learner: 64 (1.5%); Migrant: 0 (0.0%)
   Eligible for Free Lunch Program: 400 (9.2%)
   Eligible for Reduced-Price Lunch Program: 181 (4.2%)
Teachers: 325.7 (13.3 to 1)
Librarians/Media Specialists: 4.0 (1,083.8 to 1)
Guidance Counselors: 8.0 (541.9 to 1)
Current Spending: ($ per student per year):
   Total: $8,852; Instruction: $5,597; Support Services: $3,006
Enrollment, Drop-out Rates and Diploma Recipients by Race/Ethnicity

Category	Total	White	Black	Asian	AIAN	Hisp.
Enrollment (%)	100.0	95.4	1.2	1.2	0.2	2.0
Drop-out Rate (%)	n/a	n/a	n/a	n/a	n/a	n/a
H.S. Diplomas (#)	245	236	0	6	2	1

Chicopee
180 Broadway • Chicopee, MA 01020-2638
(413) 594-3410 • http://www.chicopee.mec.edu/
Grade Span: PK-12; **Agency Type:** 1
Schools: 15
   10 Primary; 2 Middle; 3 High; 0 Other Level
   14 Regular; 0 Special Education; 0 Vocational; 1 Alternative
   0 Magnet; 0 Charter; 9 Title I Eligible; 5 School-wide Title I
Students: 7,528   (51.1% male; 48.8% female)
   Individual Education Program: 1,160 (15.4%);
   English Language Learner: 393 (5.2%); Migrant: 14 (0.2%)
   Eligible for Free Lunch Program: 2,878 (38.2%)
   Eligible for Reduced-Price Lunch Program: 771 (10.2%)
Teachers: 582.0 (12.9 to 1)
Librarians/Media Specialists: 4.0 (1,882.0 to 1)
Guidance Counselors: 22.0 (342.2 to 1)
Current Spending: ($ per student per year):
   Total: $9,261; Instruction: $5,985; Support Services: $3,271
Enrollment, Drop-out Rates and Diploma Recipients by Race/Ethnicity

Category	Total	White	Black	Asian	AIAN	Hisp.
Enrollment (%)	100.0	76.4	3.3	1.1	0.1	19.1
Drop-out Rate (%)	n/a	n/a	n/a	n/a	n/a	n/a
H.S. Diplomas (#)	426	389	8	0	2	27

East Longmeadow
180 Maple St • East Longmeadow, MA 01028-2721
(413) 525-5450 • http://www.eastlongmeadow.org/Schools/Schools.htm
Grade Span: PK-12; **Agency Type:** 1
Schools: 5
   3 Primary; 1 Middle; 1 High; 0 Other Level
   5 Regular; 0 Special Education; 0 Vocational; 0 Alternative
   0 Magnet; 0 Charter; 2 Title I Eligible; 0 School-wide Title I
Students: 2,748   (50.6% male; 49.3% female)
   Individual Education Program: 614 (22.3%);
   English Language Learner: 0 (0.0%); Migrant: 0 (0.0%)
   Eligible for Free Lunch Program: 150 (5.5%)
   Eligible for Reduced-Price Lunch Program: 0 (0.0%)
Teachers: 193.9 (14.2 to 1)
Librarians/Media Specialists: 1.0 (2,748.0 to 1)
Guidance Counselors: 9.0 (305.3 to 1)
Current Spending: ($ per student per year):
   Total: $8,758; Instruction: $5,586; Support Services: $2,911
Enrollment, Drop-out Rates and Diploma Recipients by Race/Ethnicity

Category	Total	White	Black	Asian	AIAN	Hisp.
Enrollment (%)	100.0	95.2	2.7	1.2	0.1	0.9
Drop-out Rate (%)	n/a	n/a	n/a	n/a	n/a	n/a
H.S. Diplomas (#)	186	180	4	2	0	0

Hampden-Wilbraham
621 Main St • Wilbraham, MA 01095-1689
(413) 596-3884 • http://www.hwrsd.org/
Grade Span: PK-12; **Agency Type:** 3
Schools: 8
   5 Primary; 2 Middle; 1 High; 0 Other Level
   8 Regular; 0 Special Education; 0 Vocational; 0 Alternative
   0 Magnet; 0 Charter; 3 Title I Eligible; 0 School-wide Title I
Students: 3,852   (51.9% male; 48.0% female)
   Individual Education Program: 625 (16.2%);
   English Language Learner: 18 (0.5%); Migrant: 1 (<0.1%)
   Eligible for Free Lunch Program: 190 (4.9%)
   Eligible for Reduced-Price Lunch Program: 46 (1.2%)
Teachers: 258.0 (14.9 to 1)
Librarians/Media Specialists: 2.0 (1,926.0 to 1)
Guidance Counselors: 7.0 (550.3 to 1)
Current Spending: ($ per student per year):
   Total: $8,694; Instruction: $5,375; Support Services: $2,998

Enrollment, Drop-out Rates and Diploma Recipients by Race/Ethnicity

Category	Total	White	Black	Asian	AIAN	Hisp.
Enrollment (%)	100.0	94.7	2.1	2.0	0.1	1.1
Drop-out Rate (%)	n/a	n/a	n/a	n/a	n/a	n/a
H.S. Diplomas (#)	303	287	5	9	0	2

Holyoke
57 Suffolk St • Holyoke, MA 01040-5015
(413) 534-2005 • http://www.hps.holyoke.ma.us/
Grade Span: PK-12; **Agency Type:** 1
Schools: 13
   8 Primary; 2 Middle; 2 High; 1 Other Level
   11 Regular; 0 Special Education; 1 Vocational; 1 Alternative
   0 Magnet; 0 Charter; 13 Title I Eligible; 12 School-wide Title I
Students: 7,245   (51.6% male; 48.3% female)
   Individual Education Program: 1,605 (22.2%);
   English Language Learner: 1,562 (21.6%); Migrant: 42 (0.6%)
   Eligible for Free Lunch Program: 4,924 (68.0%)
   Eligible for Reduced-Price Lunch Program: 589 (8.1%)
Teachers: 647.5 (11.2 to 1)
Librarians/Media Specialists: 10.0 (724.5 to 1)
Guidance Counselors: 19.0 (381.3 to 1)
Current Spending: ($ per student per year):
   Total: $12,951; Instruction: $6,134; Support Services: $6,350
Enrollment, Drop-out Rates and Diploma Recipients by Race/Ethnicity

Category	Total	White	Black	Asian	AIAN	Hisp.
Enrollment (%)	100.0	22.8	3.5	0.9	0.0	72.6
Drop-out Rate (%)	n/a	n/a	n/a	n/a	n/a	n/a
H.S. Diplomas (#)	275	141	15	1	1	117

Longmeadow
127 Grassy Gutter Rd • Longmeadow, MA 01106-2238
(413) 565-4200 • http://www.longmeadow.k12.ma.us/
Grade Span: PK-12; **Agency Type:** 1
Schools: 6
   3 Primary; 2 Middle; 0 High; 1 Other Level
   6 Regular; 0 Special Education; 0 Vocational; 0 Alternative
   0 Magnet; 0 Charter; 1 Title I Eligible; 0 School-wide Title I
Students: 3,389   (52.6% male; 47.3% female)
   Individual Education Program: 409 (12.1%);
   English Language Learner: 18 (0.5%); Migrant: 4 (0.1%)
   Eligible for Free Lunch Program: 96 (2.8%)
   Eligible for Reduced-Price Lunch Program: 31 (0.9%)
Teachers: 229.8 (14.7 to 1)
Librarians/Media Specialists: 3.0 (1,129.7 to 1)
Guidance Counselors: 6.9 (491.2 to 1)
Current Spending: ($ per student per year):
   Total: $8,967; Instruction: $5,786; Support Services: $2,835
Enrollment, Drop-out Rates and Diploma Recipients by Race/Ethnicity

Category	Total	White	Black	Asian	AIAN	Hisp.
Enrollment (%)	100.0	91.1	2.7	5.2	0.1	0.9
Drop-out Rate (%)	n/a	n/a	n/a	n/a	n/a	n/a
H.S. Diplomas (#)	246	233	1	11	0	1

Ludlow
63 Chestnut St • Ludlow, MA 01056-3468
(413) 583-5662
Grade Span: PK-12; **Agency Type:** 1
Schools: 6
   4 Primary; 1 Middle; 1 High; 0 Other Level
   6 Regular; 0 Special Education; 0 Vocational; 0 Alternative
   0 Magnet; 0 Charter; 3 Title I Eligible; 0 School-wide Title I
Students: 3,077   (51.6% male; 48.3% female)
   Individual Education Program: 511 (16.6%);
   English Language Learner: 27 (0.9%); Migrant: 1 (<0.1%)
   Eligible for Free Lunch Program: 288 (9.4%)
   Eligible for Reduced-Price Lunch Program: 171 (5.6%)
Teachers: 221.8 (13.9 to 1)
Librarians/Media Specialists: 2.8 (1,098.9 to 1)
Guidance Counselors: 6.6 (466.2 to 1)
Current Spending: ($ per student per year):
   Total: $8,533; Instruction: $5,218; Support Services: $2,961
Enrollment, Drop-out Rates and Diploma Recipients by Race/Ethnicity

Category	Total	White	Black	Asian	AIAN	Hisp.
Enrollment (%)	100.0	95.6	1.1	0.8	0.1	2.3
Drop-out Rate (%)	n/a	n/a	n/a	n/a	n/a	n/a
H.S. Diplomas (#)	195	190	1	1	1	2

Monson
PO Box 159 • Monson, MA 01057-0159
(413) 267-4150
Grade Span: PK-12; **Agency Type:** 1
Schools: 3
   1 Primary; 1 Middle; 1 High; 0 Other Level
   3 Regular; 0 Special Education; 0 Vocational; 0 Alternative

0 Magnet; 0 Charter; 1 Title I Eligible; 0 School-wide Title I
Students: 1,544   (49.1% male; 50.8% female)
  Individual Education Program: 199 (12.9%);
  English Language Learner: 0 (0.0%); Migrant: 0 (0.0%)
  Eligible for Free Lunch Program: 144 (9.3%)
  Eligible for Reduced-Price Lunch Program: 60 (3.9%)
Teachers: 105.8 (14.6 to 1)
Librarians/Media Specialists: 2.0 (772.0 to 1)
Guidance Counselors: 4.5 (343.1 to 1)
Current Spending: ($ per student per year):
  Total: $8,252; Instruction: $5,024; Support Services: $2,969
Enrollment, Drop-out Rates and Diploma Recipients by Race/Ethnicity

Category	Total	White	Black	Asian	AIAN	Hisp.
Enrollment (%)	100.0	96.5	1.3	0.7	0.0	1.5
Drop-out Rate (%)	n/a	n/a	n/a	n/a	n/a	n/a
H.S. Diplomas (#)	77	72	1	4	0	0

Palmer
24 Converse St • Palmer, MA 01069-1770
(413) 283-2650 • http://www.palmerschools.org/main.htm
Grade Span: PK-12; **Agency Type:** 1
Schools: 3
  1 Primary; 1 Middle; 1 High; 0 Other Level
  3 Regular; 0 Special Education; 0 Vocational; 0 Alternative
  0 Magnet; 0 Charter; 2 Title I Eligible; 0 School-wide Title I
Students: 2,090   (51.1% male; 48.8% female)
  Individual Education Program: 371 (17.8%);
  English Language Learner: 0 (0.0%); Migrant: 7 (0.3%)
  Eligible for Free Lunch Program: 322 (15.4%)
  Eligible for Reduced-Price Lunch Program: 72 (3.4%)
Teachers: 160.3 (13.0 to 1)
Librarians/Media Specialists: 3.0 (696.7 to 1)
Guidance Counselors: 5.0 (418.0 to 1)
Current Spending: ($ per student per year):
  Total: $9,478; Instruction: $6,587; Support Services: $2,571
Enrollment, Drop-out Rates and Diploma Recipients by Race/Ethnicity

Category	Total	White	Black	Asian	AIAN	Hisp.
Enrollment (%)	100.0	96.4	1.0	1.2	0.2	1.2
Drop-out Rate (%)	n/a	n/a	n/a	n/a	n/a	n/a
H.S. Diplomas (#)	102	101	1	0	0	0

Southwick-Tolland
86 Powder Mill Rd • Southwick, MA 01077-9326
(413) 569-5391 • http://strsd.southwick.ma.us/
Grade Span: PK-12; **Agency Type:** 3
Schools: 3
  1 Primary; 1 Middle; 1 High; 0 Other Level
  3 Regular; 0 Special Education; 0 Vocational; 0 Alternative
  0 Magnet; 0 Charter; 2 Title I Eligible; 0 School-wide Title I
Students: 1,923   (51.2% male; 48.7% female)
  Individual Education Program: 272 (14.1%);
  English Language Learner: 0 (0.0%); Migrant: 0 (0.0%)
  Eligible for Free Lunch Program: 166 (8.6%)
  Eligible for Reduced-Price Lunch Program: 79 (4.1%)
Teachers: 127.7 (15.1 to 1)
Librarians/Media Specialists: 3.0 (641.0 to 1)
Guidance Counselors: 6.9 (278.7 to 1)
Current Spending: ($ per student per year):
  Total: $8,444; Instruction: $5,448; Support Services: $2,778
Enrollment, Drop-out Rates and Diploma Recipients by Race/Ethnicity

Category	Total	White	Black	Asian	AIAN	Hisp.
Enrollment (%)	100.0	97.4	1.3	0.6	0.1	0.6
Drop-out Rate (%)	n/a	n/a	n/a	n/a	n/a	n/a
H.S. Diplomas (#)	134	131	1	0	1	1

Springfield
195 State Box 1410 • Springfield, MA 01102-1410
Mailing Address: 195 State St Box 1410 • Springfield, MA 01102-1410
(413) 787-7000 • http://sps.springfield.ma.us/
Grade Span: PK-12; **Agency Type:** 1
Schools: 48
  33 Primary; 6 Middle; 5 High; 4 Other Level
  42 Regular; 0 Special Education; 1 Vocational; 5 Alternative
  0 Magnet; 0 Charter; 48 Title I Eligible; 44 School-wide Title I
Students: 26,132   (51.5% male; 48.4% female)
  Individual Education Program: 5,301 (20.3%);
  English Language Learner: 3,021 (11.6%); Migrant: 307 (1.2%)
  Eligible for Free Lunch Program: 17,682 (67.7%)
  Eligible for Reduced-Price Lunch Program: 2,475 (9.5%)
Teachers: 2,302.2 (11.4 to 1)
Librarians/Media Specialists: 29.0 (901.1 to 1)
Guidance Counselors: 39.0 (670.1 to 1)
Current Spending: ($ per student per year):
  Total: $12,014; Instruction: $7,730; Support Services: $3,705

Enrollment, Drop-out Rates and Diploma Recipients by Race/Ethnicity

Category	Total	White	Black	Asian	AIAN	Hisp.
Enrollment (%)	100.0	20.7	28.3	2.4	0.2	48.5
Drop-out Rate (%)	n/a	n/a	n/a	n/a	n/a	n/a
H.S. Diplomas (#)	839	268	289	36	1	245

West Springfield
26 Central St • West Springfield, MA 01089-2753
(413) 263-3290 • http://www.wsps.org/
Grade Span: PK-12; **Agency Type:** 1
Schools: 8
  6 Primary; 1 Middle; 1 High; 0 Other Level
  8 Regular; 0 Special Education; 0 Vocational; 0 Alternative
  0 Magnet; 0 Charter; 5 Title I Eligible; 2 School-wide Title I
Students: 3,965   (52.7% male; 47.2% female)
  Individual Education Program: 554 (14.0%);
  English Language Learner: 215 (5.4%); Migrant: 5 (0.1%)
  Eligible for Free Lunch Program: 991 (25.0%)
  Eligible for Reduced-Price Lunch Program: 261 (6.6%)
Teachers: 304.4 (13.0 to 1)
Librarians/Media Specialists: 2.2 (1,802.3 to 1)
Guidance Counselors: 8.0 (495.6 to 1)
Current Spending: ($ per student per year):
  Total: $9,930; Instruction: $6,042; Support Services: $3,588
Enrollment, Drop-out Rates and Diploma Recipients by Race/Ethnicity

Category	Total	White	Black	Asian	AIAN	Hisp.
Enrollment (%)	100.0	83.7	2.8	2.5	0.2	10.9
Drop-out Rate (%)	n/a	n/a	n/a	n/a	n/a	n/a
H.S. Diplomas (#)	222	196	3	9	1	13

Westfield
22 Ashley St • Westfield, MA 01085-3899
(413) 572-6403 • http://www.westfield.k12.wi.us/
Grade Span: PK-12; **Agency Type:** 1
Schools: 14
  10 Primary; 2 Middle; 2 High; 0 Other Level
  13 Regular; 0 Special Education; 1 Vocational; 0 Alternative
  0 Magnet; 0 Charter; 7 Title I Eligible; 3 School-wide Title I
Students: 6,574   (52.8% male; 47.1% female)
  Individual Education Program: 1,156 (17.6%);
  English Language Learner: 261 (4.0%); Migrant: 1 (<0.1%)
  Eligible for Free Lunch Program: 1,333 (20.3%)
  Eligible for Reduced-Price Lunch Program: 482 (7.3%)
Teachers: 523.2 (12.6 to 1)
Librarians/Media Specialists: 7.0 (939.1 to 1)
Guidance Counselors: 11.0 (597.6 to 1)
Current Spending: ($ per student per year):
  Total: $10,091; Instruction: $6,338; Support Services: $3,498
Enrollment, Drop-out Rates and Diploma Recipients by Race/Ethnicity

Category	Total	White	Black	Asian	AIAN	Hisp.
Enrollment (%)	100.0	89.8	1.2	1.1	0.1	7.8
Drop-out Rate (%)	n/a	n/a	n/a	n/a	n/a	n/a
H.S. Diplomas (#)	412	375	6	4	1	26

Hampshire County

Amherst-Pelham
170 Chestnut St • Amherst, MA 01002-1825
(413) 362-1810 • http://www.arps.org/
Grade Span: 07-12; **Agency Type:** 3
Schools: 2
  0 Primary; 1 Middle; 1 High; 0 Other Level
  2 Regular; 0 Special Education; 0 Vocational; 0 Alternative
  0 Magnet; 0 Charter; 2 Title I Eligible; 0 School-wide Title I
Students: 2,041   (51.2% male; 48.7% female)
  Individual Education Program: 347 (17.0%);
  English Language Learner: 93 (4.6%); Migrant: 4 (0.2%)
  Eligible for Free Lunch Program: 336 (16.5%)
  Eligible for Reduced-Price Lunch Program: 0 (0.0%)
Teachers: 167.3 (12.2 to 1)
Librarians/Media Specialists: 2.0 (1,020.5 to 1)
Guidance Counselors: 10.0 (204.1 to 1)
Current Spending: ($ per student per year):
  Total: $12,551; Instruction: $7,924; Support Services: $4,326
Enrollment, Drop-out Rates and Diploma Recipients by Race/Ethnicity

Category	Total	White	Black	Asian	AIAN	Hisp.
Enrollment (%)	100.0	72.4	10.1	9.5	0.9	7.1
Drop-out Rate (%)	n/a	n/a	n/a	n/a	n/a	n/a
H.S. Diplomas (#)	298	226	26	32	1	13

Belchertown
14 Maple St • Belchertown, MA 01007-0841
Mailing Address: PO Box 841 • Belchertown, MA 01007-0841
(413) 323-0456 • http://www.belchertownps.org/
Grade Span: PK-12; **Agency Type:** 1
Schools: 6
    4 Primary; 0 Middle; 1 High; 1 Other Level
    6 Regular; 0 Special Education; 0 Vocational; 0 Alternative
    0 Magnet; 0 Charter; 3 Title I Eligible; 0 School-wide Title I
Students: 2,513   (49.9% male; 50.0% female)
    Individual Education Program: 351 (14.0%);
    English Language Learner: 9 (0.4%); Migrant: 0 (0.0%)
    Eligible for Free Lunch Program: 218 (8.7%)
    Eligible for Reduced-Price Lunch Program: 37 (1.5%)
Teachers: 152.0 (16.5 to 1)
Librarians/Media Specialists: 3.0 (837.7 to 1)
Guidance Counselors: 7.0 (359.0 to 1)
Current Spending: ($ per student per year):
    Total: $8,614; Instruction: $5,231; Support Services: $3,099
Enrollment, Drop-out Rates and Diploma Recipients by Race/Ethnicity

Category	Total	White	Black	Asian	AIAN	Hisp.
Enrollment (%)	100.0	95.9	1.0	1.2	0.1	1.8
Drop-out Rate (%)	n/a	n/a	n/a	n/a	n/a	n/a
H.S. Diplomas (#)	126	122	0	1	0	3

Easthampton
130 Main St • Easthampton, MA 01027-2023
Mailing Address: 50 Payson Ave • Easthampton, MA 01027-2023
(413) 529-1500 • http://www.easthampton.k12.ma.us/
Grade Span: PK-12; **Agency Type:** 1
Schools: 5
    3 Primary; 1 Middle; 1 High; 0 Other Level
    5 Regular; 0 Special Education; 0 Vocational; 0 Alternative
    0 Magnet; 0 Charter; 4 Title I Eligible; 0 School-wide Title I
Students: 1,634   (50.8% male; 49.1% female)
    Individual Education Program: 284 (17.4%);
    English Language Learner: 33 (2.0%); Migrant: 1 (0.1%)
    Eligible for Free Lunch Program: 255 (15.6%)
    Eligible for Reduced-Price Lunch Program: 142 (8.7%)
Teachers: 132.8 (12.3 to 1)
Librarians/Media Specialists: 0.0 (n/a to 1)
Guidance Counselors: 3.0 (544.7 to 1)
Current Spending: ($ per student per year):
    Total: $9,674; Instruction: $6,112; Support Services: $3,221
Enrollment, Drop-out Rates and Diploma Recipients by Race/Ethnicity

Category	Total	White	Black	Asian	AIAN	Hisp.
Enrollment (%)	100.0	91.0	1.4	4.0	0.2	3.3
Drop-out Rate (%)	n/a	n/a	n/a	n/a	n/a	n/a
H.S. Diplomas (#)	130	119	1	9	0	1

Northampton
212 Main St • Northampton, MA 01060-3112
(413) 587-1328 • http://www.nps.northampton.ma.us/
Grade Span: PK-12; **Agency Type:** 1
Schools: 6
    4 Primary; 1 Middle; 1 High; 0 Other Level
    6 Regular; 0 Special Education; 0 Vocational; 0 Alternative
    0 Magnet; 0 Charter; 4 Title I Eligible; 0 School-wide Title I
Students: 2,978   (50.7% male; 49.2% female)
    Individual Education Program: 505 (17.0%);
    English Language Learner: 64 (2.1%); Migrant: 3 (0.1%)
    Eligible for Free Lunch Program: 470 (15.8%)
    Eligible for Reduced-Price Lunch Program: 224 (7.5%)
Teachers: 217.6 (13.7 to 1)
Librarians/Media Specialists: 1.5 (1,985.3 to 1)
Guidance Counselors: 9.0 (330.9 to 1)
Current Spending: ($ per student per year):
    Total: $10,612; Instruction: $6,779; Support Services: $3,585
Enrollment, Drop-out Rates and Diploma Recipients by Race/Ethnicity

Category	Total	White	Black	Asian	AIAN	Hisp.
Enrollment (%)	100.0	80.0	3.6	4.5	0.5	11.5
Drop-out Rate (%)	n/a	n/a	n/a	n/a	n/a	n/a
H.S. Diplomas (#)	181	166	3	5	1	6

South Hadley
116 Main St • South Hadley, MA 01075-2898
(413) 538-5060 • http://www.shschools.com/
Grade Span: PK-12; **Agency Type:** 1
Schools: 4
    2 Primary; 1 Middle; 1 High; 0 Other Level
    4 Regular; 0 Special Education; 0 Vocational; 0 Alternative
    0 Magnet; 0 Charter; 3 Title I Eligible; 0 School-wide Title I
Students: 2,303   (51.4% male; 48.5% female)
    Individual Education Program: 390 (16.9%);
    English Language Learner: 0 (0.0%); Migrant: 0 (0.0%)

    Eligible for Free Lunch Program: 391 (17.0%)
    Eligible for Reduced-Price Lunch Program: 0 (0.0%)
Teachers: 161.8 (14.2 to 1)
Librarians/Media Specialists: 1.0 (2,303.0 to 1)
Guidance Counselors: 2.5 (921.2 to 1)
Current Spending: ($ per student per year):
    Total: $9,164; Instruction: $5,762; Support Services: $3,128
Enrollment, Drop-out Rates and Diploma Recipients by Race/Ethnicity

Category	Total	White	Black	Asian	AIAN	Hisp.
Enrollment (%)	100.0	91.5	2.3	1.7	0.2	4.3
Drop-out Rate (%)	n/a	n/a	n/a	n/a	n/a	n/a
H.S. Diplomas (#)	160	154	2	2	0	2

Middlesex County

Acton
16 Charter Rd • Acton, MA 01720-2931
(978) 264-4700 • http://ab.mec.edu/
Grade Span: PK-06; **Agency Type:** 2
Schools: 5
    5 Primary; 0 Middle; 0 High; 0 Other Level
    5 Regular; 0 Special Education; 0 Vocational; 0 Alternative
    0 Magnet; 0 Charter; 3 Title I Eligible; 0 School-wide Title I
Students: 2,522   (51.7% male; 48.2% female)
    Individual Education Program: 359 (14.2%);
    English Language Learner: 51 (2.0%); Migrant: 20 (0.8%)
    Eligible for Free Lunch Program: 35 (1.4%)
    Eligible for Reduced-Price Lunch Program: 14 (0.6%)
Teachers: 145.9 (17.3 to 1)
Librarians/Media Specialists: 0.0 (n/a to 1)
Guidance Counselors: 5.0 (504.4 to 1)
Current Spending: ($ per student per year):
    Total: $8,368; Instruction: $5,450; Support Services: $2,673
Enrollment, Drop-out Rates and Diploma Recipients by Race/Ethnicity

Category	Total	White	Black	Asian	AIAN	Hisp.
Enrollment (%)	100.0	78.6	0.7	18.5	0.1	2.1
Drop-out Rate (%)	n/a	n/a	n/a	n/a	n/a	n/a
H.S. Diplomas (#)	n/a	n/a	n/a	n/a	n/a	n/a

Acton-Boxborough
16 Charter Rd • Acton, MA 01720-2931
(978) 264-4700 • http://ab.mec.edu/
Grade Span: 07-12; **Agency Type:** 3
Schools: 2
    0 Primary; 1 Middle; 1 High; 0 Other Level
    2 Regular; 0 Special Education; 0 Vocational; 0 Alternative
    0 Magnet; 0 Charter; 1 Title I Eligible; 0 School-wide Title I
Students: 2,611   (51.0% male; 48.9% female)
    Individual Education Program: 391 (15.0%);
    English Language Learner: 21 (0.8%); Migrant: 0 (0.0%)
    Eligible for Free Lunch Program: 56 (2.1%)
    Eligible for Reduced-Price Lunch Program: 8 (0.3%)
Teachers: 157.1 (16.6 to 1)
Librarians/Media Specialists: 3.0 (870.3 to 1)
Guidance Counselors: 11.6 (225.1 to 1)
Current Spending: ($ per student per year):
    Total: $10,813; Instruction: $6,908; Support Services: $3,607
Enrollment, Drop-out Rates and Diploma Recipients by Race/Ethnicity

Category	Total	White	Black	Asian	AIAN	Hisp.
Enrollment (%)	100.0	84.1	1.2	13.0	0.2	1.5
Drop-out Rate (%)	n/a	n/a	n/a	n/a	n/a	n/a
H.S. Diplomas (#)	350	307	2	32	1	8

Arlington
869 Massachusetts Ave • Arlington, MA 02476-0002
(781) 316-3501 • http://www.arlington.k12.ma.us/
Grade Span: PK-12; **Agency Type:** 1
Schools: 10
    8 Primary; 1 Middle; 1 High; 0 Other Level
    10 Regular; 0 Special Education; 0 Vocational; 0 Alternative
    0 Magnet; 0 Charter; 4 Title I Eligible; 0 School-wide Title I
Students: 4,425   (50.4% male; 49.5% female)
    Individual Education Program: 620 (14.0%);
    English Language Learner: 229 (5.2%); Migrant: 0 (0.0%)
    Eligible for Free Lunch Program: 277 (6.3%)
    Eligible for Reduced-Price Lunch Program: 96 (2.2%)
Teachers: 304.1 (14.6 to 1)
Librarians/Media Specialists: 2.0 (2,212.5 to 1)
Guidance Counselors: 10.0 (442.5 to 1)
Current Spending: ($ per student per year):
    Total: $9,938; Instruction: $6,277; Support Services: $3,327

Enrollment, Drop-out Rates and Diploma Recipients by Race/Ethnicity

Category	Total	White	Black	Asian	AIAN	Hisp.
Enrollment (%)	100.0	85.2	4.9	7.3	0.1	2.5
Drop-out Rate (%)	n/a	n/a	n/a	n/a	n/a	n/a
H.S. Diplomas (#)	260	226	14	15	0	5

Ashland

90 Concord St • Ashland, MA 01721-1699
(508) 881-0150 • http://www.ashlandhs.org/
Grade Span: PK-12; **Agency Type:** 1
Schools: 5
    2 Primary; 2 Middle; 1 High; 0 Other Level
    5 Regular; 0 Special Education; 0 Vocational; 0 Alternative
    0 Magnet; 0 Charter; 1 Title I Eligible; 0 School-wide Title I
Students: 2,590   (50.4% male; 49.5% female)
    Individual Education Program: 319 (12.3%);
    English Language Learner: 49 (1.9%); Migrant: 0 (0.0%)
    Eligible for Free Lunch Program: 121 (4.7%)
    Eligible for Reduced-Price Lunch Program: 28 (1.1%)
Teachers: 176.2 (14.7 to 1)
Librarians/Media Specialists: 2.0 (1,295.0 to 1)
Guidance Counselors: 7.0 (370.0 to 1)
Current Spending: ($ per student per year):
    Total: $9,495; Instruction: $6,115; Support Services: $3,089

Enrollment, Drop-out Rates and Diploma Recipients by Race/Ethnicity

Category	Total	White	Black	Asian	AIAN	Hisp.
Enrollment (%)	100.0	89.6	2.9	4.0	0.2	3.3
Drop-out Rate (%)	n/a	n/a	n/a	n/a	n/a	n/a
H.S. Diplomas (#)	135	123	4	6	0	2

Bedford

11 Mudge Way • Bedford, MA 01730-2166
Mailing Address: 97 Mcmahon Rd • Bedford, MA 01730-2166
(781) 275-7588 • http://www.bedford.k12.ma.us/
Grade Span: PK-12; **Agency Type:** 1
Schools: 4
    2 Primary; 1 Middle; 1 High; 0 Other Level
    4 Regular; 0 Special Education; 0 Vocational; 0 Alternative
    0 Magnet; 0 Charter; 4 Title I Eligible; 0 School-wide Title I
Students: 2,246   (49.4% male; 50.5% female)
    Individual Education Program: 375 (16.7%);
    English Language Learner: 25 (1.1%); Migrant: 2 (0.1%)
    Eligible for Free Lunch Program: 33 (1.5%)
    Eligible for Reduced-Price Lunch Program: 22 (1.0%)
Teachers: 188.1 (11.9 to 1)
Librarians/Media Specialists: 4.0 (561.5 to 1)
Guidance Counselors: 7.4 (303.5 to 1)
Current Spending: ($ per student per year):
    Total: $12,200; Instruction: $7,574; Support Services: $4,328

Enrollment, Drop-out Rates and Diploma Recipients by Race/Ethnicity

Category	Total	White	Black	Asian	AIAN	Hisp.
Enrollment (%)	100.0	82.5	5.7	9.3	0.5	2.0
Drop-out Rate (%)	n/a	n/a	n/a	n/a	n/a	n/a
H.S. Diplomas (#)	154	139	9	5	1	0

Belmont

644 Pleasant St • Belmont, MA 02478-2589
(617) 484-2642 • http://www.belmont.k12.ma.us/
Grade Span: PK-12; **Agency Type:** 1
Schools: 6
    4 Primary; 1 Middle; 1 High; 0 Other Level
    6 Regular; 0 Special Education; 0 Vocational; 0 Alternative
    0 Magnet; 0 Charter; 2 Title I Eligible; 0 School-wide Title I
Students: 3,713   (51.2% male; 48.7% female)
    Individual Education Program: 480 (12.9%);
    English Language Learner: 108 (2.9%); Migrant: 0 (0.0%)
    Eligible for Free Lunch Program: 107 (2.9%)
    Eligible for Reduced-Price Lunch Program: 55 (1.5%)
Teachers: 250.8 (14.8 to 1)
Librarians/Media Specialists: 2.0 (1,856.5 to 1)
Guidance Counselors: 11.5 (322.9 to 1)
Current Spending: ($ per student per year):
    Total: $9,614; Instruction: $6,254; Support Services: $3,144

Enrollment, Drop-out Rates and Diploma Recipients by Race/Ethnicity

Category	Total	White	Black	Asian	AIAN	Hisp.
Enrollment (%)	100.0	79.9	4.7	12.4	0.2	2.9
Drop-out Rate (%)	n/a	n/a	n/a	n/a	n/a	n/a
H.S. Diplomas (#)	203	163	10	24	1	5

Billerica

365 Boston Rd • Billerica, MA 01821-1888
(978) 436-9500 • http://www.billerica.mec.edu
Grade Span: PK-12; **Agency Type:** 1
Schools: 9
    6 Primary; 2 Middle; 0 High; 1 Other Level

9 Regular; 0 Special Education; 0 Vocational; 0 Alternative
    0 Magnet; 0 Charter; 2 Title I Eligible; 0 School-wide Title I
Students: 6,395   (51.6% male; 48.3% female)
    Individual Education Program: 1,094 (17.1%);
    English Language Learner: 46 (0.7%); Migrant: 3 (<0.1%)
    Eligible for Free Lunch Program: 243 (3.8%)
    Eligible for Reduced-Price Lunch Program: 108 (1.7%)
Teachers: 434.2 (14.7 to 1)
Librarians/Media Specialists: 6.5 (983.8 to 1)
Guidance Counselors: 9.0 (710.6 to 1)
Current Spending: ($ per student per year):
    Total: $9,419; Instruction: $6,363; Support Services: $2,758

Enrollment, Drop-out Rates and Diploma Recipients by Race/Ethnicity

Category	Total	White	Black	Asian	AIAN	Hisp.
Enrollment (%)	100.0	94.9	0.8	2.1	0.4	1.8
Drop-out Rate (%)	n/a	n/a	n/a	n/a	n/a	n/a
H.S. Diplomas (#)	335	311	3	15	2	4

Burlington

123 Cambridge St • Burlington, MA 01803-3755
(781) 270-1801 • http://www.burlington.mec.edu/
Grade Span: PK-12; **Agency Type:** 1
Schools: 6
    4 Primary; 1 Middle; 0 High; 1 Other Level
    6 Regular; 0 Special Education; 0 Vocational; 0 Alternative
    0 Magnet; 0 Charter; 4 Title I Eligible; 0 School-wide Title I
Students: 3,486   (51.3% male; 48.6% female)
    Individual Education Program: 543 (15.6%);
    English Language Learner: 65 (1.9%); Migrant: 0 (0.0%)
    Eligible for Free Lunch Program: 170 (4.9%)
    Eligible for Reduced-Price Lunch Program: 0 (0.0%)
Teachers: 273.6 (12.7 to 1)
Librarians/Media Specialists: 6.0 (581.0 to 1)
Guidance Counselors: 13.3 (262.1 to 1)
Current Spending: ($ per student per year):
    Total: $11,041; Instruction: $7,374; Support Services: $3,443

Enrollment, Drop-out Rates and Diploma Recipients by Race/Ethnicity

Category	Total	White	Black	Asian	AIAN	Hisp.
Enrollment (%)	100.0	85.5	2.4	10.8	0.1	1.2
Drop-out Rate (%)	n/a	n/a	n/a	n/a	n/a	n/a
H.S. Diplomas (#)	202	170	2	29	0	1

Cambridge

159 Thorndike St • Cambridge, MA 02141-1528
(617) 349-6494 • http://www.cpsd.us/index.cfm
Grade Span: PK-12; **Agency Type:** 1
Schools: 13
    9 Primary; 0 Middle; 1 High; 3 Other Level
    13 Regular; 0 Special Education; 0 Vocational; 0 Alternative
    0 Magnet; 0 Charter; 8 Title I Eligible; 4 School-wide Title I
Students: 6,437   (51.6% male; 48.3% female)
    Individual Education Program: 1,427 (22.2%);
    English Language Learner: 649 (10.1%); Migrant: 0 (0.0%)
    Eligible for Free Lunch Program: 2,122 (33.0%)
    Eligible for Reduced-Price Lunch Program: 490 (7.6%)
Teachers: 651.1 (9.9 to 1)
Librarians/Media Specialists: 14.0 (459.8 to 1)
Guidance Counselors: 17.0 (378.6 to 1)
Current Spending: ($ per student per year):
    Total: $20,835; Instruction: $12,802; Support Services: $7,452

Enrollment, Drop-out Rates and Diploma Recipients by Race/Ethnicity

Category	Total	White	Black	Asian	AIAN	Hisp.
Enrollment (%)	100.0	36.4	38.2	10.3	0.7	14.5
Drop-out Rate (%)	n/a	n/a	n/a	n/a	n/a	n/a
H.S. Diplomas (#)	338	145	122	28	0	43

Chelmsford

190 Richardson Rd • North Chelmsford, MA 01863-2323
(978) 251-5100 • http://www.chelmsford.k12.ma.us/
Grade Span: PK-12; **Agency Type:** 1
Schools: 8
    5 Primary; 2 Middle; 1 High; 0 Other Level
    8 Regular; 0 Special Education; 0 Vocational; 0 Alternative
    0 Magnet; 0 Charter; 5 Title I Eligible; 0 School-wide Title I
Students: 5,773   (51.3% male; 48.6% female)
    Individual Education Program: 733 (12.7%);
    English Language Learner: 37 (0.6%); Migrant: 3 (0.1%)
    Eligible for Free Lunch Program: 108 (1.9%)
    Eligible for Reduced-Price Lunch Program: 59 (1.0%)
Teachers: 377.9 (15.3 to 1)
Librarians/Media Specialists: 5.0 (1,154.6 to 1)
Guidance Counselors: 17.5 (329.9 to 1)
Current Spending: ($ per student per year):
    Total: $8,962; Instruction: $5,931; Support Services: $2,777

Enrollment, Drop-out Rates and Diploma Recipients by Race/Ethnicity

Category	Total	White	Black	Asian	AIAN	Hisp.
Enrollment (%)	100.0	90.9	1.1	7.0	0.1	1.0
Drop-out Rate (%)	n/a	n/a	n/a	n/a	n/a	n/a
H.S. Diplomas (#)	401	359	3	36	1	2

Concord

120 Meriam Rd • Concord, MA 01742-2699
(978) 318-1510 • http://www.colonial.net/
Grade Span: PK-08; **Agency Type:** 2
Schools: 4
   3 Primary; 1 Middle; 0 High; 0 Other Level
   4 Regular; 0 Special Education; 0 Vocational; 0 Alternative
   0 Magnet; 0 Charter; 2 Title I Eligible; 0 School-wide Title I
Students: 1,974 (48.0% male; 51.9% female)
   Individual Education Program: 374 (18.9%);
   English Language Learner: 27 (1.4%); Migrant: 4 (0.2%)
   Eligible for Free Lunch Program: 60 (3.0%)
   Eligible for Reduced-Price Lunch Program: 34 (1.7%)
Teachers: 150.0 (13.2 to 1)
Librarians/Media Specialists: 4.0 (493.5 to 1)
Guidance Counselors: 4.0 (493.5 to 1)
Current Spending: ($ per student per year):
   Total: $12,557; Instruction: $7,986; Support Services: $4,400

Enrollment, Drop-out Rates and Diploma Recipients by Race/Ethnicity

Category	Total	White	Black	Asian	AIAN	Hisp.
Enrollment (%)	100.0	84.9	5.4	6.7	0.6	2.4
Drop-out Rate (%)	n/a	n/a	n/a	n/a	n/a	n/a
H.S. Diplomas (#)	n/a	n/a	n/a	n/a	n/a	n/a

Dracut

2063 Lakeview Ave • Dracut, MA 01826-3005
(978) 957-2660 • http://www.dracut.k12.ma.us/
Grade Span: PK-12; **Agency Type:** 1
Schools: 7
   4 Primary; 2 Middle; 1 High; 0 Other Level
   7 Regular; 0 Special Education; 0 Vocational; 0 Alternative
   0 Magnet; 0 Charter; 2 Title I Eligible; 0 School-wide Title I
Students: 4,263 (52.4% male; 47.5% female)
   Individual Education Program: 488 (11.4%)
   English Language Learner: 60 (1.4%); Migrant: 2 (<0.1%)
   Eligible for Free Lunch Program: 352 (8.3%)
   Eligible for Reduced-Price Lunch Program: 91 (2.1%)
Teachers: 259.1 (16.5 to 1)
Librarians/Media Specialists: 2.0 (2,131.5 to 1)
Guidance Counselors: 7.0 (609.0 to 1)
Current Spending: ($ per student per year):
   Total: $7,925; Instruction: $5,064; Support Services: $2,560

Enrollment, Drop-out Rates and Diploma Recipients by Race/Ethnicity

Category	Total	White	Black	Asian	AIAN	Hisp.
Enrollment (%)	100.0	93.6	1.1	3.3	0.2	1.7
Drop-out Rate (%)	n/a	n/a	n/a	n/a	n/a	n/a
H.S. Diplomas (#)	246	232	0	12	0	2

Everett

121 Vine St • Everett, MA 02149-4827
(617) 389-7950 • http://www.everett.k12.ma.us/
Grade Span: PK-12; **Agency Type:** 1
Schools: 6
   5 Primary; 0 Middle; 0 High; 1 Other Level
   6 Regular; 0 Special Education; 0 Vocational; 0 Alternative
   0 Magnet; 0 Charter; 5 Title I Eligible; 5 School-wide Title I
Students: 5,321 (50.1% male; 49.8% female)
   Individual Education Program: 758 (14.2%)
   English Language Learner: 571 (10.7%); Migrant: 0 (0.0%)
   Eligible for Free Lunch Program: 1,835 (34.5%)
   Eligible for Reduced-Price Lunch Program: 570 (10.7%)
Teachers: 366.0 (14.5 to 1)
Librarians/Media Specialists: 5.0 (1,064.2 to 1)
Guidance Counselors: 10.0 (532.1 to 1)
Current Spending: ($ per student per year):
   Total: $9,447; Instruction: $6,321; Support Services: $2,824

Enrollment, Drop-out Rates and Diploma Recipients by Race/Ethnicity

Category	Total	White	Black	Asian	AIAN	Hisp.
Enrollment (%)	100.0	68.7	9.9	5.9	0.1	15.4
Drop-out Rate (%)	n/a	n/a	n/a	n/a	n/a	n/a
H.S. Diplomas (#)	294	231	30	11	0	22

Framingham

14 Vernon St Ste 201 • Framingham, MA 01701-7433
(508) 626-9117 • http://www.framingham.k12.ma.us/
Grade Span: PK-12; **Agency Type:** 1
Schools: 13
   9 Primary; 3 Middle; 1 High; 0 Other Level
   13 Regular; 0 Special Education; 0 Vocational; 0 Alternative

0 Magnet; 0 Charter; 6 Title I Eligible; 2 School-wide Title I
Students: 8,102 (49.9% male; 50.0% female)
   Individual Education Program: 1,388 (17.1%);
   English Language Learner: 1,200 (14.8%); Migrant: 0 (0.0%)
   Eligible for Free Lunch Program: 2,242 (27.7%)
   Eligible for Reduced-Price Lunch Program: 0 (0.0%)
Teachers: 642.8 (12.6 to 1)
Librarians/Media Specialists: 5.0 (1,620.4 to 1)
Guidance Counselors: 21.0 (385.8 to 1)
Current Spending: ($ per student per year):
   Total: $12,550; Instruction: $8,195; Support Services: $4,061

Enrollment, Drop-out Rates and Diploma Recipients by Race/Ethnicity

Category	Total	White	Black	Asian	AIAN	Hisp.
Enrollment (%)	100.0	68.1	7.4	6.2	0.3	18.0
Drop-out Rate (%)	n/a	n/a	n/a	n/a	n/a	n/a
H.S. Diplomas (#)	395	311	27	23	0	34

Greater Lowell Voc Tec

250 Pawtucket Blvd • Tyngsborough, MA 01879-2199
Mailing Address: 2590 Pawtucket Blvd • Tyngsborough, MA 01879-2199
(978) 441-4800 • http://www.gltech.org/
Grade Span: 09-12; **Agency Type:** 4
Schools: 1
   0 Primary; 0 Middle; 1 High; 0 Other Level
   0 Regular; 0 Special Education; 1 Vocational; 0 Alternative
   0 Magnet; 0 Charter; 1 Title I Eligible; 1 School-wide Title I
Students: 1,893 (52.1% male; 47.8% female)
   Individual Education Program: 476 (25.1%);
   English Language Learner: 31 (1.6%); Migrant: 0 (0.0%)
   Eligible for Free Lunch Program: 648 (34.2%)
   Eligible for Reduced-Price Lunch Program: 178 (9.4%)
Teachers: 180.5 (10.5 to 1)
Librarians/Media Specialists: 1.0 (1,893.0 to 1)
Guidance Counselors: 6.0 (315.5 to 1)
Current Spending: ($ per student per year):
   Total: $13,773; Instruction: $7,939; Support Services: $5,464

Enrollment, Drop-out Rates and Diploma Recipients by Race/Ethnicity

Category	Total	White	Black	Asian	AIAN	Hisp.
Enrollment (%)	100.0	62.2	2.6	12.3	0.3	22.6
Drop-out Rate (%)	n/a	n/a	n/a	n/a	n/a	n/a
H.S. Diplomas (#)	337	250	9	19	2	57

Groton-Dunstable

PO Box 729 • Groton, MA 01450-0729
(978) 448-5505 • http://www.gdrsd.org/
Grade Span: PK-12; **Agency Type:** 3
Schools: 6
   4 Primary; 1 Middle; 1 High; 0 Other Level
   6 Regular; 0 Special Education; 0 Vocational; 0 Alternative
   0 Magnet; 0 Charter; 3 Title I Eligible; 0 School-wide Title I
Students: 2,895 (52.9% male; 47.0% female)
   Individual Education Program: 321 (11.1%);
   English Language Learner: 6 (0.2%); Migrant: 0 (0.0%)
   Eligible for Free Lunch Program: 44 (1.5%)
   Eligible for Reduced-Price Lunch Program: 13 (0.4%)
Teachers: 170.4 (17.0 to 1)
Librarians/Media Specialists: 2.5 (1,158.0 to 1)
Guidance Counselors: 8.3 (348.8 to 1)
Current Spending: ($ per student per year):
   Total: $8,218; Instruction: $4,875; Support Services: $3,092

Enrollment, Drop-out Rates and Diploma Recipients by Race/Ethnicity

Category	Total	White	Black	Asian	AIAN	Hisp.
Enrollment (%)	100.0	96.5	0.4	2.5	0.1	0.5
Drop-out Rate (%)	n/a	n/a	n/a	n/a	n/a	n/a
H.S. Diplomas (#)	118	115	0	1	0	2

Holliston

370 Hollis St • Holliston, MA 01746-1803
(508) 429-0654 • http://www.holliston.k12.ma.us/
Grade Span: PK-12; **Agency Type:** 1
Schools: 4
   2 Primary; 1 Middle; 1 High; 0 Other Level
   4 Regular; 0 Special Education; 0 Vocational; 0 Alternative
   0 Magnet; 0 Charter; 0 Title I Eligible; 0 School-wide Title I
Students: 3,117 (51.0% male; 48.9% female)
   Individual Education Program: 352 (11.3%);
   English Language Learner: 2 (0.1%); Migrant: 0 (0.0%)
   Eligible for Free Lunch Program: 35 (1.1%)
   Eligible for Reduced-Price Lunch Program: 20 (0.6%)
Teachers: 213.4 (14.6 to 1)
Librarians/Media Specialists: 2.0 (1,558.5 to 1)
Guidance Counselors: 11.0 (283.4 to 1)
Current Spending: ($ per student per year):
   Total: $9,812; Instruction: $6,201; Support Services: $3,423

Enrollment, Drop-out Rates and Diploma Recipients by Race/Ethnicity

Category	Total	White	Black	Asian	AIAN	Hisp.
Enrollment (%)	100.0	95.7	1.2	1.9	0.1	1.2
Drop-out Rate (%)	n/a	n/a	n/a	n/a	n/a	n/a
H.S. Diplomas (#)	187	180	2	2	0	3

Hopkinton
88-A Hayden Rowe St • Hopkinton, MA 01748-2533
(508) 497-9800 • http://www.hopkinton.k12.ma.us/
Grade Span: PK-12; **Agency Type:** 1
Schools: 6
  4 Primary; 1 Middle; 1 High; 0 Other Level
  6 Regular; 0 Special Education; 0 Vocational; 0 Alternative
  0 Magnet; 0 Charter; 1 Title I Eligible; 0 School-wide Title I
Students: 3,355 (50.8% male; 49.1% female)
  Individual Education Program: 419 (12.5%);
  English Language Learner: 9 (0.3%); Migrant: 0 (0.0%)
  Eligible for Free Lunch Program: 29 (0.9%)
  Eligible for Reduced-Price Lunch Program: 0 (0.0%)
Teachers: 232.3 (14.4 to 1)
Librarians/Media Specialists: 4.5 (745.6 to 1)
Guidance Counselors: 9.0 (372.8 to 1)
Current Spending: ($ per student per year):
  Total: $10,846; Instruction: $6,990; Support Services: $3,633

Enrollment, Drop-out Rates and Diploma Recipients by Race/Ethnicity

Category	Total	White	Black	Asian	AIAN	Hisp.
Enrollment (%)	100.0	95.9	0.8	2.4	0.0	0.8
Drop-out Rate (%)	n/a	n/a	n/a	n/a	n/a	n/a
H.S. Diplomas (#)	162	151	3	6	1	1

Hudson
155 Apsley St • Hudson, MA 01749-1645
(978) 567-6100 • http://www.hudson.k12.ma.us/
Grade Span: PK-12; **Agency Type:** 1
Schools: 6
  4 Primary; 1 Middle; 0 High; 1 Other Level
  6 Regular; 0 Special Education; 0 Vocational; 0 Alternative
  0 Magnet; 0 Charter; 3 Title I Eligible; 0 School-wide Title I
Students: 2,769 (52.2% male; 47.7% female)
  Individual Education Program: 496 (17.9%);
  English Language Learner: 136 (4.9%); Migrant: 0 (0.0%)
  Eligible for Free Lunch Program: 310 (11.2%)
  Eligible for Reduced-Price Lunch Program: 54 (2.0%)
Teachers: 210.6 (13.1 to 1)
Librarians/Media Specialists: 3.0 (923.0 to 1)
Guidance Counselors: 8.5 (325.8 to 1)
Current Spending: ($ per student per year):
  Total: $9,829; Instruction: $6,280; Support Services: $3,326

Enrollment, Drop-out Rates and Diploma Recipients by Race/Ethnicity

Category	Total	White	Black	Asian	AIAN	Hisp.
Enrollment (%)	100.0	93.5	1.4	1.5	0.3	3.2
Drop-out Rate (%)	n/a	n/a	n/a	n/a	n/a	n/a
H.S. Diplomas (#)	177	175	0	0	0	2

Lexington
1557 Mass Ave • Lexington, MA 02420-3801
(781) 861-2550 • http://lps.lexingtonma.org/
Grade Span: PK-12; **Agency Type:** 1
Schools: 9
  6 Primary; 2 Middle; 1 High; 0 Other Level
  9 Regular; 0 Special Education; 0 Vocational; 0 Alternative
  0 Magnet; 0 Charter; 4 Title I Eligible; 0 School-wide Title I
Students: 6,175 (50.6% male; 49.3% female)
  Individual Education Program: 1,005 (16.3%);
  English Language Learner: 211 (3.4%); Migrant: 0 (0.0%)
  Eligible for Free Lunch Program: 161 (2.6%)
  Eligible for Reduced-Price Lunch Program: 79 (1.3%)
Teachers: 495.5 (12.5 to 1)
Librarians/Media Specialists: 10.0 (617.5 to 1)
Guidance Counselors: 24.3 (254.1 to 1)
Current Spending: ($ per student per year):
  Total: $11,389; Instruction: $7,786; Support Services: $3,604

Enrollment, Drop-out Rates and Diploma Recipients by Race/Ethnicity

Category	Total	White	Black	Asian	AIAN	Hisp.
Enrollment (%)	100.0	75.3	4.9	17.9	0.1	1.8
Drop-out Rate (%)	n/a	n/a	n/a	n/a	n/a	n/a
H.S. Diplomas (#)	396	308	18	64	1	5

Littleton
PO Box 1486 • Littleton, MA 01460-4486
(978) 486-8951
Grade Span: PK-12; **Agency Type:** 1
Schools: 4
  2 Primary; 1 Middle; 1 High; 0 Other Level
  4 Regular; 0 Special Education; 0 Vocational; 0 Alternative

0 Magnet; 0 Charter; 3 Title I Eligible; 0 School-wide Title I
Students: 1,564 (48.7% male; 51.2% female)
  Individual Education Program: 275 (17.6%);
  English Language Learner: 0 (0.0%); Migrant: 0 (0.0%)
  Eligible for Free Lunch Program: 43 (2.7%)
  Eligible for Reduced-Price Lunch Program: 1 (0.1%)
Teachers: 106.3 (14.7 to 1)
Librarians/Media Specialists: 2.0 (782.0 to 1)
Guidance Counselors: 4.0 (391.0 to 1)
Current Spending: ($ per student per year):
  Total: $10,736; Instruction: $6,780; Support Services: $3,771

Enrollment, Drop-out Rates and Diploma Recipients by Race/Ethnicity

Category	Total	White	Black	Asian	AIAN	Hisp.
Enrollment (%)	100.0	96.1	0.3	2.2	0.0	1.4
Drop-out Rate (%)	n/a	n/a	n/a	n/a	n/a	n/a
H.S. Diplomas (#)	82	78	1	2	0	1

Lowell
155 Merrimack St • Lowell, MA 01852-1723
(978) 937-7647 • http://www.lowell.k12.ma.us
Grade Span: PK-12; **Agency Type:** 1
Schools: 25
  17 Primary; 7 Middle; 1 High; 0 Other Level
  24 Regular; 0 Special Education; 0 Vocational; 1 Alternative
  1 Magnet; 0 Charter; 24 Title I Eligible; 24 School-wide Title I
Students: 15,105 (51.9% male; 48.0% female)
  Individual Education Program: 1,912 (12.7%);
  English Language Learner: 3,559 (23.6%); Migrant: 273 (1.8%)
  Eligible for Free Lunch Program: 7,911 (52.4%)
  Eligible for Reduced-Price Lunch Program: 2,320 (15.4%)
Teachers: 1,110.9 (13.6 to 1)
Librarians/Media Specialists: 16.5 (915.5 to 1)
Guidance Counselors: 24.0 (629.4 to 1)
Current Spending: ($ per student per year):
  Total: $11,413; Instruction: $7,504; Support Services: $3,462

Enrollment, Drop-out Rates and Diploma Recipients by Race/Ethnicity

Category	Total	White	Black	Asian	AIAN	Hisp.
Enrollment (%)	100.0	43.5	5.7	29.4	0.2	21.2
Drop-out Rate (%)	n/a	n/a	n/a	n/a	n/a	n/a
H.S. Diplomas (#)	732	319	38	285	0	90

Malden
77 Salem St • Malden, MA 02148-5289
(781) 397-7204 • http://www.malden.mec.edu/
Grade Span: PK-12; **Agency Type:** 1
Schools: 7
  6 Primary; 0 Middle; 1 High; 0 Other Level
  7 Regular; 0 Special Education; 0 Vocational; 0 Alternative
  0 Magnet; 0 Charter; 4 Title I Eligible; 1 School-wide Title I
Students: 6,135 (51.3% male; 48.6% female)
  Individual Education Program: 979 (16.0%);
  English Language Learner: 481 (7.8%); Migrant: 0 (0.0%)
  Eligible for Free Lunch Program: 1,922 (31.3%)
  Eligible for Reduced-Price Lunch Program: 644 (10.5%)
Teachers: 454.8 (13.5 to 1)
Librarians/Media Specialists: 4.4 (1,394.3 to 1)
Guidance Counselors: 9.0 (681.7 to 1)
Current Spending: ($ per student per year):
  Total: $11,580; Instruction: $7,959; Support Services: $3,377

Enrollment, Drop-out Rates and Diploma Recipients by Race/Ethnicity

Category	Total	White	Black	Asian	AIAN	Hisp.
Enrollment (%)	100.0	52.9	17.1	20.1	0.3	9.6
Drop-out Rate (%)	n/a	n/a	n/a	n/a	n/a	n/a
H.S. Diplomas (#)	308	131	53	91	1	32

Marlborough
17 Washington St • Marlborough, MA 01752-2225
Mailing Address: District Education Center • Marlborough, MA 01752-2225
(508) 460-3509 • http://www.marlborough.k12.ma.us/
Grade Span: PK-12; **Agency Type:** 1
Schools: 7
  4 Primary; 2 Middle; 1 High; 0 Other Level
  7 Regular; 0 Special Education; 0 Vocational; 0 Alternative
  0 Magnet; 0 Charter; 5 Title I Eligible; 0 School-wide Title I
Students: 4,851 (51.5% male; 48.4% female)
  Individual Education Program: 991 (20.4%);
  English Language Learner: 638 (13.2%); Migrant: 5 (0.1%)
  Eligible for Free Lunch Program: 804 (16.6%)
  Eligible for Reduced-Price Lunch Program: 303 (6.2%)
Teachers: 370.4 (13.1 to 1)
Librarians/Media Specialists: 2.0 (2,425.5 to 1)
Guidance Counselors: 12.6 (385.0 to 1)
Current Spending: ($ per student per year):
  Total: $11,348; Instruction: $7,282; Support Services: $3,820

Enrollment, Drop-out Rates and Diploma Recipients by Race/Ethnicity

Category	Total	White	Black	Asian	AIAN	Hisp.
Enrollment (%)	100.0	69.9	3.2	3.7	0.4	22.9
Drop-out Rate (%)	n/a	n/a	n/a	n/a	n/a	n/a
H.S. Diplomas (#)	188	145	4	9	1	29

Medford

489 Winthrop St • Medford, MA 02155-2349
(781) 393-2442 • http://www.medford.k12.ma.us/
Grade Span: PK-12; **Agency Type:** 1
Schools: 9
    4 Primary; 2 Middle; 2 High; 1 Other Level
    8 Regular; 0 Special Education; 1 Vocational; 0 Alternative
    0 Magnet; 0 Charter; 4 Title I Eligible; 0 School-wide Title I
Students: 4,716 (51.8% male; 48.1% female)
    Individual Education Program: 790 (16.8%);
    English Language Learner: 302 (6.4%); Migrant: 24 (0.5%)
    Eligible for Free Lunch Program: 826 (17.5%)
    Eligible for Reduced-Price Lunch Program: 184 (3.9%)
Teachers: 426.5 (11.1 to 1)
Librarians/Media Specialists: 6.0 (786.0 to 1)
Guidance Counselors: 10.0 (471.6 to 1)
Current Spending: ($ per student per year):
    Total: $12,968; Instruction: $8,250; Support Services: $4,534

Enrollment, Drop-out Rates and Diploma Recipients by Race/Ethnicity

Category	Total	White	Black	Asian	AIAN	Hisp.
Enrollment (%)	100.0	72.1	14.7	5.9	0.7	6.7
Drop-out Rate (%)	n/a	n/a	n/a	n/a	n/a	n/a
H.S. Diplomas (#)	283	200	43	13	5	22

Melrose

360 Lynn Fells Pkwy • Melrose, MA 02176-2244
(781) 662-2000 • http://www.melroseschools.com/
Grade Span: PK-12; **Agency Type:** 1
Schools: 7
    5 Primary; 1 Middle; 1 High; 0 Other Level
    7 Regular; 0 Special Education; 0 Vocational; 0 Alternative
    0 Magnet; 0 Charter; 0 Title I Eligible; 0 School-wide Title I
Students: 3,572 (50.7% male; 49.2% female)
    Individual Education Program: 584 (16.3%);
    English Language Learner: 60 (1.7%); Migrant: 0 (0.0%)
    Eligible for Free Lunch Program: 537 (15.0%)
    Eligible for Reduced-Price Lunch Program: 0 (0.0%)
Teachers: 221.2 (16.1 to 1)
Librarians/Media Specialists: 0.0 (n/a to 1)
Guidance Counselors: 3.0 (1,190.7 to 1)
Current Spending: ($ per student per year):
    Total: $9,694; Instruction: $6,211; Support Services: $3,178

Enrollment, Drop-out Rates and Diploma Recipients by Race/Ethnicity

Category	Total	White	Black	Asian	AIAN	Hisp.
Enrollment (%)	100.0	90.9	4.9	2.5	0.2	1.5
Drop-out Rate (%)	n/a	n/a	n/a	n/a	n/a	n/a
H.S. Diplomas (#)	213	192	15	5	0	1

Natick

13 E Central St • Natick, MA 01760-4629
Mailing Address: Natick Public Schools • Natick, MA 01760-4629
(508) 647-6500 • http://www.natick.k12.ma.us/
Grade Span: PK-12; **Agency Type:** 1
Schools: 8
    5 Primary; 2 Middle; 1 High; 0 Other Level
    8 Regular; 0 Special Education; 0 Vocational; 0 Alternative
    0 Magnet; 0 Charter; 3 Title I Eligible; 0 School-wide Title I
Students: 4,604 (52.3% male; 47.6% female)
    Individual Education Program: 719 (15.6%);
    English Language Learner: 77 (1.7%); Migrant: 3 (0.1%)
    Eligible for Free Lunch Program: 191 (4.1%)
    Eligible for Reduced-Price Lunch Program: 74 (1.6%)
Teachers: 336.1 (13.7 to 1)
Librarians/Media Specialists: 4.0 (1,151.0 to 1)
Guidance Counselors: 15.1 (304.9 to 1)
Current Spending: ($ per student per year):
    Total: $10,559; Instruction: $6,725; Support Services: $3,269

Enrollment, Drop-out Rates and Diploma Recipients by Race/Ethnicity

Category	Total	White	Black	Asian	AIAN	Hisp.
Enrollment (%)	100.0	90.3	2.8	4.8	0.3	1.8
Drop-out Rate (%)	n/a	n/a	n/a	n/a	n/a	n/a
H.S. Diplomas (#)	257	237	9	7	0	4

Newton

100 Walnut St • Newtonville, MA 02460-1314
(617) 559-6100 • http://newton.mec.edu
Grade Span: PK-12; **Agency Type:** 1
Schools: 22
    16 Primary; 4 Middle; 2 High; 0 Other Level

    22 Regular; 0 Special Education; 0 Vocational; 0 Alternative
    0 Magnet; 0 Charter; 7 Title I Eligible; 0 School-wide Title I
Students: 11,415 (51.1% male; 48.8% female)
    Individual Education Program: 2,105 (18.4%);
    English Language Learner: 550 (4.8%); Migrant: 0 (0.0%)
    Eligible for Free Lunch Program: 550 (4.8%)
    Eligible for Reduced-Price Lunch Program: 255 (2.2%)
Teachers: 967.1 (11.8 to 1)
Librarians/Media Specialists: 24.4 (467.8 to 1)
Guidance Counselors: 41.0 (278.4 to 1)
Current Spending: ($ per student per year):
    Total: $13,566; Instruction: $8,787; Support Services: $4,453

Enrollment, Drop-out Rates and Diploma Recipients by Race/Ethnicity

Category	Total	White	Black	Asian	AIAN	Hisp.
Enrollment (%)	100.0	79.7	5.3	11.6	0.1	3.2
Drop-out Rate (%)	n/a	n/a	n/a	n/a	n/a	n/a
H.S. Diplomas (#)	848	716	39	74	0	19

North Middlesex

23 Main St • Townsend, MA 01469-1356
(978) 597-8713 • http://www.nmiddlesex.mec.edu/
Grade Span: PK-12; **Agency Type:** 3
Schools: 8
    5 Primary; 2 Middle; 1 High; 0 Other Level
    8 Regular; 0 Special Education; 0 Vocational; 0 Alternative
    0 Magnet; 0 Charter; 4 Title I Eligible; 0 School-wide Title I
Students: 4,678   (50.9% male; 49.0% female)
    Individual Education Program: 523 (11.2%);
    English Language Learner: 3 (0.1%); Migrant: 1 (<0.1%)
    Eligible for Free Lunch Program: 211 (4.5%)
    Eligible for Reduced-Price Lunch Program: 110 (2.4%)
Teachers: 327.7 (14.3 to 1)
Librarians/Media Specialists: 8.0 (584.8 to 1)
Guidance Counselors: 12.0 (389.8 to 1)
Current Spending: ($ per student per year):
    Total: $8,622; Instruction: $5,762; Support Services: $2,670

Enrollment, Drop-out Rates and Diploma Recipients by Race/Ethnicity

Category	Total	White	Black	Asian	AIAN	Hisp.
Enrollment (%)	100.0	98.0	0.6	0.7	0.0	0.7
Drop-out Rate (%)	n/a	n/a	n/a	n/a	n/a	n/a
H.S. Diplomas (#)	241	239	0	0	2	0

North Reading

19 Sherman Rd • North Reading, MA 01864-2398
(978) 664-7810
Grade Span: PK-12; **Agency Type:** 1
Schools: 5
    3 Primary; 1 Middle; 1 High; 0 Other Level
    5 Regular; 0 Special Education; 0 Vocational; 0 Alternative
    0 Magnet; 0 Charter; 2 Title I Eligible; 0 School-wide Title I
Students: 2,664   (50.9% male; 49.0% female)
    Individual Education Program: 365 (13.7%);
    English Language Learner: 5 (0.2%); Migrant: 0 (0.0%)
    Eligible for Free Lunch Program: 56 (2.1%)
    Eligible for Reduced-Price Lunch Program: 30 (1.1%)
Teachers: 164.0 (16.2 to 1)
Librarians/Media Specialists: 1.0 (2,664.0 to 1)
Guidance Counselors: 3.5 (761.1 to 1)
Current Spending: ($ per student per year):
    Total: $7,920; Instruction: $5,162; Support Services: $2,535

Enrollment, Drop-out Rates and Diploma Recipients by Race/Ethnicity

Category	Total	White	Black	Asian	AIAN	Hisp.
Enrollment (%)	100.0	96.2	0.5	2.0	0.8	0.6
Drop-out Rate (%)	n/a	n/a	n/a	n/a	n/a	n/a
H.S. Diplomas (#)	90	88	1	1	0	0

Reading

82 Oakland Rd • Reading, MA 01867-1613
(781) 944-5800 • http://www.reading.k12.ma.us/
Grade Span: PK-12; **Agency Type:** 1
Schools: 7
    5 Primary; 1 Middle; 0 High; 1 Other Level
    7 Regular; 0 Special Education; 0 Vocational; 0 Alternative
    0 Magnet; 0 Charter; 3 Title I Eligible; 0 School-wide Title I
Students: 4,260   (51.0% male; 48.9% female)
    Individual Education Program: 617 (14.5%);
    English Language Learner: 26 (0.6%); Migrant: 1 (<0.1%)
    Eligible for Free Lunch Program: 73 (1.7%)
    Eligible for Reduced-Price Lunch Program: 33 (0.8%)
Teachers: 281.9 (15.1 to 1)
Librarians/Media Specialists: 6.5 (655.4 to 1)
Guidance Counselors: 4.6 (926.1 to 1)
Current Spending: ($ per student per year):
    Total: $8,460; Instruction: $5,833; Support Services: $2,385

Enrollment, Drop-out Rates and Diploma Recipients by Race/Ethnicity

Category	Total	White	Black	Asian	AIAN	Hisp.
Enrollment (%)	100.0	94.3	1.3	3.5	0.2	0.7
Drop-out Rate (%)	n/a	n/a	n/a	n/a	n/a	n/a
H.S. Diplomas (#)	288	269	8	9	0	2

Somerville
181 Washington St • Somerville, MA 02143-1717
(617) 625-6600 •
**http://www.somerville.k12.ma.us/education/district/district.php?sectionid
=1**
Grade Span: PK-12; **Agency Type:** 1
Schools: 13
   10 Primary; 1 Middle; 2 High; 0 Other Level
   11 Regular; 0 Special Education; 0 Vocational; 2 Alternative
   0 Magnet; 0 Charter; 9 Title I Eligible; 9 School-wide Title I
Students: 5,616 (50.8% male; 49.1% female)
   Individual Education Program: 1,206 (21.5%);
   English Language Learner: 856 (15.2%); Migrant: 7 (0.1%)
   Eligible for Free Lunch Program: 2,431 (43.3%)
   Eligible for Reduced-Price Lunch Program: 980 (17.5%)
Teachers: 445.6 (12.6 to 1)
Librarians/Media Specialists: 10.4 (540.0 to 1)
Guidance Counselors: 14.5 (387.3 to 1)
Current Spending: ($ per student per year):
   Total: $14,672; Instruction: $9,194; Support Services: $4,803

Enrollment, Drop-out Rates and Diploma Recipients by Race/Ethnicity

Category	Total	White	Black	Asian	AIAN	Hisp.
Enrollment (%)	100.0	45.8	16.6	7.8	0.4	29.5
Drop-out Rate (%)	n/a	n/a	n/a	n/a	n/a	n/a
H.S. Diplomas (#)	334	152	76	30	0	76

Stoneham
149 Franklin St • Stoneham, MA 02180-1513
(781) 279-3826
Grade Span: PK-12; **Agency Type:** 1
Schools: 6
   4 Primary; 1 Middle; 1 High; 0 Other Level
   6 Regular; 0 Special Education; 0 Vocational; 0 Alternative
   0 Magnet; 0 Charter; 4 Title I Eligible; 0 School-wide Title I
Students: 2,990 (50.4% male; 49.5% female)
   Individual Education Program: 475 (15.9%);
   English Language Learner: 58 (1.9%); Migrant: 0 (0.0%)
   Eligible for Free Lunch Program: 188 (6.3%)
   Eligible for Reduced-Price Lunch Program: 62 (2.1%)
Teachers: 195.1 (15.3 to 1)
Librarians/Media Specialists: 4.0 (747.5 to 1)
Guidance Counselors: 6.4 (467.2 to 1)
Current Spending: ($ per student per year):
   Total: $9,072; Instruction: $5,381; Support Services: $3,447

Enrollment, Drop-out Rates and Diploma Recipients by Race/Ethnicity

Category	Total	White	Black	Asian	AIAN	Hisp.
Enrollment (%)	100.0	92.8	1.4	3.3	0.0	2.4
Drop-out Rate (%)	n/a	n/a	n/a	n/a	n/a	n/a
H.S. Diplomas (#)	203	193	1	4	0	5

Sudbury
40 Fairbank Rd • Sudbury, MA 01776-1681
(978) 443-1058 • http://www.sudbury-k8.org/
Grade Span: PK-08; **Agency Type:** 1
Schools: 5
   4 Primary; 1 Middle; 0 High; 0 Other Level
   5 Regular; 0 Special Education; 0 Vocational; 0 Alternative
   0 Magnet; 0 Charter; 0 Title I Eligible; 0 School-wide Title I
Students: 3,101 (50.4% male; 49.5% female)
   Individual Education Program: 442 (14.3%);
   English Language Learner: 26 (0.8%); Migrant: 0 (0.0%)
   Eligible for Free Lunch Program: 73 (2.4%)
   Eligible for Reduced-Price Lunch Program: 6 (0.2%)
Teachers: 211.5 (14.7 to 1)
Librarians/Media Specialists: 4.6 (674.1 to 1)
Guidance Counselors: 6.9 (449.4 to 1)
Current Spending: ($ per student per year):
   Total: $9,454; Instruction: $5,727; Support Services: $3,496

Enrollment, Drop-out Rates and Diploma Recipients by Race/Ethnicity

Category	Total	White	Black	Asian	AIAN	Hisp.
Enrollment (%)	100.0	90.7	2.5	5.4	0.1	1.3
Drop-out Rate (%)	n/a	n/a	n/a	n/a	n/a	n/a
H.S. Diplomas (#)	n/a	n/a	n/a	n/a	n/a	n/a

Tewksbury
1469 Andover St • Tewksbury, MA 01876-2725
(978) 640-7800 • http://www.tewksbury.mec.edu/
Grade Span: PK-12; **Agency Type:** 1
Schools: 8

   5 Primary; 2 Middle; 1 High; 0 Other Level
   8 Regular; 0 Special Education; 0 Vocational; 0 Alternative
   0 Magnet; 0 Charter; 3 Title I Eligible; 0 School-wide Title I
Students: 4,765 (50.5% male; 49.4% female)
   Individual Education Program: 676 (14.2%);
   English Language Learner: 0 (0.0%); Migrant: 0 (0.0%)
   Eligible for Free Lunch Program: 213 (4.5%)
   Eligible for Reduced-Price Lunch Program: 59 (1.2%)
Teachers: 279.3 (17.1 to 1)
Librarians/Media Specialists: 4.0 (1,191.3 to 1)
Guidance Counselors: 6.0 (794.2 to 1)
Current Spending: ($ per student per year):
   Total: $8,218; Instruction: $5,265; Support Services: $2,692

Enrollment, Drop-out Rates and Diploma Recipients by Race/Ethnicity

Category	Total	White	Black	Asian	AIAN	Hisp.
Enrollment (%)	100.0	95.1	0.8	2.2	0.0	1.8
Drop-out Rate (%)	n/a	n/a	n/a	n/a	n/a	n/a
H.S. Diplomas (#)	181	173	1	4	0	3

Tyngsborough
50 Norris Rd • Tyngsborough, MA 01879-1228
(978) 649-7488
Grade Span: PK-12; **Agency Type:** 1
Schools: 4
   2 Primary; 1 Middle; 1 High; 0 Other Level
   4 Regular; 0 Special Education; 0 Vocational; 0 Alternative
   0 Magnet; 0 Charter; 2 Title I Eligible; 0 School-wide Title I
Students: 2,269 (50.8% male; 49.1% female)
   Individual Education Program: 230 (10.1%);
   English Language Learner: 10 (0.4%); Migrant: 0 (0.0%)
   Eligible for Free Lunch Program: 68 (3.0%)
   Eligible for Reduced-Price Lunch Program: 36 (1.6%)
Teachers: 158.7 (14.3 to 1)
Librarians/Media Specialists: 3.0 (756.3 to 1)
Guidance Counselors: 6.8 (333.7 to 1)
Current Spending: ($ per student per year):
   Total: $8,943; Instruction: $5,602; Support Services: $3,093

Enrollment, Drop-out Rates and Diploma Recipients by Race/Ethnicity

Category	Total	White	Black	Asian	AIAN	Hisp.
Enrollment (%)	100.0	94.7	0.2	3.4	0.0	1.7
Drop-out Rate (%)	n/a	n/a	n/a	n/a	n/a	n/a
H.S. Diplomas (#)	127	122	1	4	0	0

Wakefield
60 Farm St • Wakefield, MA 01880-3502
(781) 246-6400 • http://www.wakefield.k12.ma.us/
Grade Span: PK-12; **Agency Type:** 1
Schools: 6
   4 Primary; 1 Middle; 1 High; 0 Other Level
   6 Regular; 0 Special Education; 0 Vocational; 0 Alternative
   0 Magnet; 0 Charter; 2 Title I Eligible; 0 School-wide Title I
Students: 3,453 (50.0% male; 49.9% female)
   Individual Education Program: 587 (17.0%);
   English Language Learner: 23 (0.7%); Migrant: 17 (0.5%)
   Eligible for Free Lunch Program: 109 (3.2%)
   Eligible for Reduced-Price Lunch Program: 38 (1.1%)
Teachers: 265.5 (13.0 to 1)
Librarians/Media Specialists: 5.0 (690.6 to 1)
Guidance Counselors: 5.0 (690.6 to 1)
Current Spending: ($ per student per year):
   Total: $10,313; Instruction: $6,773; Support Services: $3,265

Enrollment, Drop-out Rates and Diploma Recipients by Race/Ethnicity

Category	Total	White	Black	Asian	AIAN	Hisp.
Enrollment (%)	100.0	96.1	1.4	1.4	0.1	1.1
Drop-out Rate (%)	n/a	n/a	n/a	n/a	n/a	n/a
H.S. Diplomas (#)	213	206	2	1	0	4

Waltham
617 Lexington St • Waltham, MA 02452-3099
(781) 314-5440 •
http://www.city.waltham.ma.us/SCHOOL/WebPAge/tofc.htm
Grade Span: PK-12; **Agency Type:** 1
Schools: 10
   7 Primary; 2 Middle; 1 High; 0 Other Level
   10 Regular; 0 Special Education; 0 Vocational; 0 Alternative
   0 Magnet; 0 Charter; 6 Title I Eligible; 0 School-wide Title I
Students: 4,667 (51.8% male; 48.1% female)
   Individual Education Program: 942 (20.2%);
   English Language Learner: 185 (4.0%); Migrant: 0 (0.0%)
   Eligible for Free Lunch Program: 1,028 (22.0%)
   Eligible for Reduced-Price Lunch Program: 158 (3.4%)
Teachers: 444.7 (10.5 to 1)
Librarians/Media Specialists: 10.3 (453.1 to 1)
Guidance Counselors: 8.9 (524.4 to 1)
Current Spending: ($ per student per year):
   Total: $14,959; Instruction: $9,714; Support Services: $4,833

Enrollment, Drop-out Rates and Diploma Recipients by Race/Ethnicity

Category	Total	White	Black	Asian	AIAN	Hisp.
Enrollment (%)	100.0	63.3	9.6	7.0	0.1	20.1
Drop-out Rate (%)	n/a	n/a	n/a	n/a	n/a	n/a
H.S. Diplomas (#)	328	244	31	19	0	34

Watertown
30 Common St • Watertown, MA 02472-3492
(617) 926-7700 • http://www.watertown.k12.ma.us/
Grade Span: PK-12; Agency Type: 1
Schools: 5
   3 Primary; 1 Middle; 1 High; 0 Other Level
   5 Regular; 0 Special Education; 0 Vocational; 0 Alternative
   0 Magnet; 0 Charter; 3 Title I Eligible; 0 School-wide Title I
Students: 2,394   (51.4% male; 48.5% female)
   Individual Education Program: 423 (17.7%);
   English Language Learner: 200 (8.4%); Migrant: 0 (0.0%)
   Eligible for Free Lunch Program: 320 (13.4%)
   Eligible for Reduced-Price Lunch Program: 117 (4.9%)
Teachers: 286.0 (8.4 to 1)
Librarians/Media Specialists: 3.5 (684.0 to 1)
Guidance Counselors: 9.8 (244.3 to 1)
Current Spending: ($ per student per year):
   Total: $14,734; Instruction: $9,515; Support Services: $4,839

Enrollment, Drop-out Rates and Diploma Recipients by Race/Ethnicity

Category	Total	White	Black	Asian	AIAN	Hisp.
Enrollment (%)	100.0	85.1	2.9	5.9	0.5	5.6
Drop-out Rate (%)	n/a	n/a	n/a	n/a	n/a	n/a
H.S. Diplomas (#)	200	177	7	11	0	5

Wayland
41 Cochituate Rd • Wayland, MA 01778-2018
(508) 358-3774 • http://www.wayland.k12.ma.us/index.html
Grade Span: KG-12; Agency Type: 1
Schools: 5
   3 Primary; 1 Middle; 1 High; 0 Other Level
   5 Regular; 0 Special Education; 0 Vocational; 0 Alternative
   0 Magnet; 0 Charter; 2 Title I Eligible; 0 School-wide Title I
Students: 2,985   (51.4% male; 48.5% female)
   Individual Education Program: 504 (16.9%);
   English Language Learner: 13 (0.4%); Migrant: 0 (0.0%)
   Eligible for Free Lunch Program: 98 (3.3%)
   Eligible for Reduced-Price Lunch Program: 6 (0.2%)
Teachers: 203.4 (14.7 to 1)
Librarians/Media Specialists: 4.2 (710.7 to 1)
Guidance Counselors: 8.1 (368.5 to 1)
Current Spending: ($ per student per year):
   Total: $11,578; Instruction: $7,438; Support Services: $3,868

Enrollment, Drop-out Rates and Diploma Recipients by Race/Ethnicity

Category	Total	White	Black	Asian	AIAN	Hisp.
Enrollment (%)	100.0	84.0	4.2	8.9	0.0	2.9
Drop-out Rate (%)	n/a	n/a	n/a	n/a	n/a	n/a
H.S. Diplomas (#)	187	163	6	14	0	4

Westford
35 Town Farm Rd • Westford, MA 01886-2338
Mailing Address: 23 Depot St • Westford, MA 01886-2338
(978) 692-5560 • http://westford.mec.edu/schools/index.html
Grade Span: PK-12; Agency Type: 1
Schools: 10
   7 Primary; 2 Middle; 1 High; 0 Other Level
   10 Regular; 0 Special Education; 0 Vocational; 0 Alternative
   0 Magnet; 0 Charter; 4 Title I Eligible; 0 School-wide Title I
Students: 5,112   (52.3% male; 47.6% female)
   Individual Education Program: 473 (9.3%);
   English Language Learner: 18 (0.4%); Migrant: 0 (0.0%)
   Eligible for Free Lunch Program: 72 (1.4%)
   Eligible for Reduced-Price Lunch Program: 48 (0.9%)
Teachers: 368.3 (13.9 to 1)
Librarians/Media Specialists: 7.5 (681.6 to 1)
Guidance Counselors: 17.0 (300.7 to 1)
Current Spending: ($ per student per year):
   Total: $8,617; Instruction: $5,281; Support Services: $3,001

Enrollment, Drop-out Rates and Diploma Recipients by Race/Ethnicity

Category	Total	White	Black	Asian	AIAN	Hisp.
Enrollment (%)	100.0	90.7	0.4	8.0	0.1	0.8
Drop-out Rate (%)	n/a	n/a	n/a	n/a	n/a	n/a
H.S. Diplomas (#)	312	289	2	17	2	2

Weston
89 Wellesley St • Weston, MA 02493-2509
(781) 529-8080 • http://www.westonschools.org/
Grade Span: PK-12; Agency Type: 1
Schools: 5
   2 Primary; 2 Middle; 1 High; 0 Other Level

   5 Regular; 0 Special Education; 0 Vocational; 0 Alternative
   0 Magnet; 0 Charter; 3 Title I Eligible; 0 School-wide Title I
Students: 2,370   (51.3% male; 48.6% female)
   Individual Education Program: 343 (14.5%);
   English Language Learner: 23 (1.0%); Migrant: 0 (0.0%)
   Eligible for Free Lunch Program: 47 (2.0%)
   Eligible for Reduced-Price Lunch Program: 20 (0.8%)
Teachers: 187.9 (12.6 to 1)
Librarians/Media Specialists: 3.0 (790.0 to 1)
Guidance Counselors: 10.1 (234.7 to 1)
Current Spending: ($ per student per year):
   Total: $13,746; Instruction: $8,394; Support Services: $4,971

Enrollment, Drop-out Rates and Diploma Recipients by Race/Ethnicity

Category	Total	White	Black	Asian	AIAN	Hisp.
Enrollment (%)	100.0	81.5	6.3	10.4	0.2	1.7
Drop-out Rate (%)	n/a	n/a	n/a	n/a	n/a	n/a
H.S. Diplomas (#)	139	107	12	17	1	2

Wilmington
161 Church St • Wilmington, MA 01887-2736
(978) 694-6000 • http://www.wilmington.k12.ma.us/
Grade Span: PK-12; Agency Type: 1
Schools: 8
   4 Primary; 3 Middle; 1 High; 0 Other Level
   8 Regular; 0 Special Education; 0 Vocational; 0 Alternative
   0 Magnet; 0 Charter; 2 Title I Eligible; 0 School-wide Title I
Students: 3,792   (51.2% male; 48.7% female)
   Individual Education Program: 493 (13.0%);
   English Language Learner: 0 (0.0%); Migrant: 0 (0.0%)
   Eligible for Free Lunch Program: 93 (2.5%)
   Eligible for Reduced-Price Lunch Program: 45 (1.2%)
Teachers: 256.3 (14.8 to 1)
Librarians/Media Specialists: 5.6 (677.1 to 1)
Guidance Counselors: 7.0 (541.7 to 1)
Current Spending: ($ per student per year):
   Total: $9,145; Instruction: $5,954; Support Services: $2,886

Enrollment, Drop-out Rates and Diploma Recipients by Race/Ethnicity

Category	Total	White	Black	Asian	AIAN	Hisp.
Enrollment (%)	100.0	95.3	0.6	2.6	0.7	0.8
Drop-out Rate (%)	n/a	n/a	n/a	n/a	n/a	n/a
H.S. Diplomas (#)	193	181	2	6	1	3

Winchester
154 Horn Pond Brk Rd • Winchester, MA 01890-1887
(781) 721-7004 • http://www.winchester.k12.ma.us/
Grade Span: PK-12; Agency Type: 1
Schools: 7
   5 Primary; 1 Middle; 1 High; 0 Other Level
   7 Regular; 0 Special Education; 0 Vocational; 0 Alternative
   0 Magnet; 0 Charter; 2 Title I Eligible; 0 School-wide Title I
Students: 3,571   (50.1% male; 49.8% female)
   Individual Education Program: 474 (13.3%);
   English Language Learner: 23 (0.6%); Migrant: 0 (0.0%)
   Eligible for Free Lunch Program: 56 (1.6%)
   Eligible for Reduced-Price Lunch Program: 0 (0.0%)
Teachers: 263.9 (13.5 to 1)
Librarians/Media Specialists: 6.0 (595.2 to 1)
Guidance Counselors: 7.5 (476.1 to 1)
Current Spending: ($ per student per year):
   Total: $10,246; Instruction: $6,807; Support Services: $3,182

Enrollment, Drop-out Rates and Diploma Recipients by Race/Ethnicity

Category	Total	White	Black	Asian	AIAN	Hisp.
Enrollment (%)	100.0	90.3	1.0	6.1	0.1	2.5
Drop-out Rate (%)	n/a	n/a	n/a	n/a	n/a	n/a
H.S. Diplomas (#)	216	196	3	14	0	3

Woburn
55 Locust St • Woburn, MA 01801-3841
(781) 937-8200 • http://www.woburnpublicschools.com/
Grade Span: PK-12; Agency Type: 1
Schools: 12
   9 Primary; 2 Middle; 1 High; 0 Other Level
   12 Regular; 0 Special Education; 0 Vocational; 0 Alternative
   0 Magnet; 0 Charter; 7 Title I Eligible; 1 School-wide Title I
Students: 4,702   (50.4% male; 49.5% female)
   Individual Education Program: 543 (11.5%);
   English Language Learner: 143 (3.0%); Migrant: 0 (0.0%)
   Eligible for Free Lunch Program: 529 (11.3%)
   Eligible for Reduced-Price Lunch Program: 141 (3.0%)
Teachers: 358.5 (13.1 to 1)
Librarians/Media Specialists: 3.8 (1,237.4 to 1)
Guidance Counselors: 8.8 (534.3 to 1)
Current Spending: ($ per student per year):
   Total: $11,415; Instruction: $7,185; Support Services: $3,842

Enrollment, Drop-out Rates and Diploma Recipients by Race/Ethnicity

Category	Total	White	Black	Asian	AIAN	Hisp.
Enrollment (%)	100.0	85.4	3.6	4.9	0.0	6.2
Drop-out Rate (%)	n/a	n/a	n/a	n/a	n/a	n/a
H.S. Diplomas (#)	291	260	6	12	0	13

Norfolk County

Bellingham
60 Harpin St • Bellingham, MA 02019-2011
(508) 883-1706 • http://www.bellingham.k12.ma.us/
Grade Span: PK-12; **Agency Type:** 1
Schools: 7
    4 Primary; 1 Middle; 2 High; 0 Other Level
    7 Regular; 0 Special Education; 0 Vocational; 0 Alternative
    0 Magnet; 0 Charter; 3 Title I Eligible; 0 School-wide Title I
Students: 2,729   (49.7% male; 50.2% female)
    Individual Education Program: 364 (13.3%);
    English Language Learner: 14 (0.5%); Migrant: 1 (<0.1%)
    Eligible for Free Lunch Program: 212 (7.8%)
    Eligible for Reduced-Price Lunch Program: 30 (1.1%)
Teachers: 190.3 (14.3 to 1)
Librarians/Media Specialists: 1.0 (2,729.0 to 1)
Guidance Counselors: 3.5 (779.7 to 1)
Current Spending: ($ per student per year):
    Total: $8,528; Instruction: $5,333; Support Services: $2,988
Enrollment, Drop-out Rates and Diploma Recipients by Race/Ethnicity

Category	Total	White	Black	Asian	AIAN	Hisp.
Enrollment (%)	100.0	95.6	0.6	1.5	0.3	2.1
Drop-out Rate (%)	n/a	n/a	n/a	n/a	n/a	n/a
H.S. Diplomas (#)	161	149	3	5	1	3

Braintree
348 Pond St • Braintree, MA 02184-5310
(781) 380-0130 • http://www.braintreeschools.org/
Grade Span: PK-12; **Agency Type:** 1
Schools: 9
    6 Primary; 2 Middle; 0 High; 1 Other Level
    9 Regular; 0 Special Education; 0 Vocational; 0 Alternative
    0 Magnet; 0 Charter; 4 Title I Eligible; 0 School-wide Title I
Students: 4,999   (51.4% male; 48.5% female)
    Individual Education Program: 909 (18.2%);
    English Language Learner: 66 (1.3%); Migrant: 0 (0.0%)
    Eligible for Free Lunch Program: 390 (7.8%)
    Eligible for Reduced-Price Lunch Program: 124 (2.5%)
Teachers: 333.0 (15.0 to 1)
Librarians/Media Specialists: 5.4 (925.7 to 1)
Guidance Counselors: 8.7 (574.6 to 1)
Current Spending: ($ per student per year):
    Total: $10,307; Instruction: $6,737; Support Services: $3,289
Enrollment, Drop-out Rates and Diploma Recipients by Race/Ethnicity

Category	Total	White	Black	Asian	AIAN	Hisp.
Enrollment (%)	100.0	89.1	3.5	5.2	0.2	1.9
Drop-out Rate (%)	n/a	n/a	n/a	n/a	n/a	n/a
H.S. Diplomas (#)	322	294	6	18	0	4

Brookline
333 Washington St • Brookline, MA 02445-6853
(617) 730-2403 • http://bec.brookline.mec.edu/publicschools/
Grade Span: PK-12; **Agency Type:** 1
Schools: 10
    9 Primary; 0 Middle; 0 High; 1 Other Level
    10 Regular; 0 Special Education; 0 Vocational; 0 Alternative
    0 Magnet; 0 Charter; 4 Title I Eligible; 0 School-wide Title I
Students: 6,018   (50.6% male; 49.3% female)
    Individual Education Program: 1,064 (17.7%);
    English Language Learner: 397 (6.6%); Migrant: 3 (<0.1%)
    Eligible for Free Lunch Program: 421 (7.0%)
    Eligible for Reduced-Price Lunch Program: 155 (2.6%)
Teachers: 511.9 (11.8 to 1)
Librarians/Media Specialists: 11.4 (527.9 to 1)
Guidance Counselors: 21.8 (276.1 to 1)
Current Spending: ($ per student per year):
    Total: $13,723; Instruction: $8,552; Support Services: $4,925
Enrollment, Drop-out Rates and Diploma Recipients by Race/Ethnicity

Category	Total	White	Black	Asian	AIAN	Hisp.
Enrollment (%)	100.0	66.0	9.9	17.7	0.2	6.1
Drop-out Rate (%)	n/a	n/a	n/a	n/a	n/a	n/a
H.S. Diplomas (#)	390	274	39	62	0	15

Canton
960 Washington St • Canton, MA 02021-2574
(781) 821-5060 • http://www.cantonma.org/
Grade Span: PK-12; **Agency Type:** 1
Schools: 5

    3 Primary; 1 Middle; 1 High; 0 Other Level
    5 Regular; 0 Special Education; 0 Vocational; 0 Alternative
    0 Magnet; 0 Charter; 4 Title I Eligible; 0 School-wide Title I
Students: 3,006   (50.5% male; 49.4% female)
    Individual Education Program: 465 (15.5%);
    English Language Learner: 41 (1.4%); Migrant: 0 (0.0%)
    Eligible for Free Lunch Program: 165 (5.5%)
    Eligible for Reduced-Price Lunch Program: 49 (1.6%)
Teachers: 214.4 (14.0 to 1)
Librarians/Media Specialists: 5.0 (601.2 to 1)
Guidance Counselors: 4.2 (715.7 to 1)
Current Spending: ($ per student per year):
    Total: $10,100; Instruction: $6,620; Support Services: $3,210
Enrollment, Drop-out Rates and Diploma Recipients by Race/Ethnicity

Category	Total	White	Black	Asian	AIAN	Hisp.
Enrollment (%)	100.0	84.5	7.2	5.7	0.3	2.3
Drop-out Rate (%)	n/a	n/a	n/a	n/a	n/a	n/a
H.S. Diplomas (#)	172	153	9	9	0	1

Dedham
30 Whiting Ave • Dedham, MA 02026
Mailing Address: 1106 High St • Dedham, MA 02027-0246
(781) 326-5622 • http://www.dedham.k12.ma.us/
Grade Span: PK-12; **Agency Type:** 1
Schools: 7
    5 Primary; 1 Middle; 1 High; 0 Other Level
    7 Regular; 0 Special Education; 0 Vocational; 0 Alternative
    0 Magnet; 0 Charter; 3 Title I Eligible; 0 School-wide Title I
Students: 2,996   (49.8% male; 50.1% female)
    Individual Education Program: 537 (17.9%);
    English Language Learner: 104 (3.5%); Migrant: 20 (0.7%)
    Eligible for Free Lunch Program: 249 (8.3%)
    Eligible for Reduced-Price Lunch Program: 76 (2.5%)
Teachers: 238.7 (12.6 to 1)
Librarians/Media Specialists: 5.0 (599.2 to 1)
Guidance Counselors: 5.0 (599.2 to 1)
Current Spending: ($ per student per year):
    Total: $11,159; Instruction: $7,104; Support Services: $3,818
Enrollment, Drop-out Rates and Diploma Recipients by Race/Ethnicity

Category	Total	White	Black	Asian	AIAN	Hisp.
Enrollment (%)	100.0	88.7	3.8	2.5	0.6	4.4
Drop-out Rate (%)	n/a	n/a	n/a	n/a	n/a	n/a
H.S. Diplomas (#)	144	132	2	1	2	7

Foxborough
Igo Administration Building • Foxborough, MA 02035-2317
(508) 543-1660 • http://foxborough.k12.ma.us/fpsweb/index.html
Grade Span: PK-12; **Agency Type:** 1
Schools: 5
    3 Primary; 1 Middle; 1 High; 0 Other Level
    5 Regular; 0 Special Education; 0 Vocational; 0 Alternative
    0 Magnet; 0 Charter; 3 Title I Eligible; 0 School-wide Title I
Students: 2,887   (50.5% male; 49.4% female)
    Individual Education Program: 550 (19.1%);
    English Language Learner: 0 (0.0%); Migrant: 0 (0.0%)
    Eligible for Free Lunch Program: 109 (3.8%)
    Eligible for Reduced-Price Lunch Program: 55 (1.9%)
Teachers: 209.2 (13.8 to 1)
Librarians/Media Specialists: 1.0 (2,887.0 to 1)
Guidance Counselors: 5.5 (524.9 to 1)
Current Spending: ($ per student per year):
    Total: $10,077; Instruction: $6,501; Support Services: $3,278
Enrollment, Drop-out Rates and Diploma Recipients by Race/Ethnicity

Category	Total	White	Black	Asian	AIAN	Hisp.
Enrollment (%)	100.0	94.7	2.3	1.8	0.0	1.2
Drop-out Rate (%)	n/a	n/a	n/a	n/a	n/a	n/a
H.S. Diplomas (#)	191	175	5	8	0	3

Franklin
397 E Central St • Franklin, MA 02038-1304
(508) 541-5243 • http://www.franklin.ma.us/auto/schools/FPS/
Grade Span: PK-12; **Agency Type:** 1
Schools: 10
    7 Primary; 2 Middle; 1 High; 0 Other Level
    10 Regular; 0 Special Education; 0 Vocational; 0 Alternative
    0 Magnet; 0 Charter; 2 Title I Eligible; 0 School-wide Title I
Students: 5,826   (50.7% male; 49.2% female)
    Individual Education Program: 785 (13.5%);
    English Language Learner: 0 (0.0%); Migrant: 0 (0.0%)
    Eligible for Free Lunch Program: 230 (3.9%)
    Eligible for Reduced-Price Lunch Program: 0 (0.0%)
Teachers: 407.5 (14.3 to 1)
Librarians/Media Specialists: 2.0 (2,913.0 to 1)
Guidance Counselors: 5.0 (1,165.2 to 1)
Current Spending: ($ per student per year):
    Total: $8,683; Instruction: $6,264; Support Services: $2,201

Enrollment, Drop-out Rates and Diploma Recipients by Race/Ethnicity

Category	Total	White	Black	Asian	AIAN	Hisp.
Enrollment (%)	100.0	95.4	1.0	2.3	0.4	0.9
Drop-out Rate (%)	n/a	n/a	n/a	n/a	n/a	n/a
H.S. Diplomas (#)	305	295	0	7	2	1

King Philip
201 Franklin St • Wrentham, MA 02093-0049
(508) 384-3144 • http://www.kingphilip.org/homekp.html
Grade Span: 07-12; Agency Type: 4
Schools: 2
  0 Primary; 1 Middle; 1 High; 0 Other Level
  2 Regular; 0 Special Education; 0 Vocational; 0 Alternative
  0 Magnet; 0 Charter; 1 Title I Eligible; 0 School-wide Title I
Students: 1,922   (48.0% male; 51.9% female)
  Individual Education Program: 270 (14.0%);
  English Language Learner: 0 (0.0%); Migrant: 0 (0.0%)
  Eligible for Free Lunch Program: 53 (2.8%)
  Eligible for Reduced-Price Lunch Program: 2 (0.1%)
Teachers: 119.3 (16.1 to 1)
Librarians/Media Specialists: 1.0 (1,922.0 to 1)
Guidance Counselors: 6.0 (320.3 to 1)
Current Spending: ($ per student per year):
  Total: $9,029; Instruction: $5,759; Support Services: $2,955

Enrollment, Drop-out Rates and Diploma Recipients by Race/Ethnicity

Category	Total	White	Black	Asian	AIAN	Hisp.
Enrollment (%)	100.0	96.8	0.9	1.8	0.0	0.5
Drop-out Rate (%)	n/a	n/a	n/a	n/a	n/a	n/a
H.S. Diplomas (#)	217	205	2	5	1	4

Medfield
459 Main St 3rd Fl • Medfield, MA 02052-1606
(508) 359-2302 • http://medfield.net/
Grade Span: PK-12; Agency Type: 1
Schools: 5
  2 Primary; 2 Middle; 1 High; 0 Other Level
  5 Regular; 0 Special Education; 0 Vocational; 0 Alternative
  0 Magnet; 0 Charter; 0 Title I Eligible; 0 School-wide Title I
Students: 3,047   (50.9% male; 49.0% female)
  Individual Education Program: 337 (11.1%);
  English Language Learner: 0 (0.0%); Migrant: 0 (0.0%)
  Eligible for Free Lunch Program: 44 (1.4%)
  Eligible for Reduced-Price Lunch Program: 24 (0.8%)
Teachers: 227.3 (13.4 to 1)
Librarians/Media Specialists: 4.5 (677.1 to 1)
Guidance Counselors: 5.4 (564.3 to 1)
Current Spending: ($ per student per year):
  Total: $7,927; Instruction: $5,022; Support Services: $2,650

Enrollment, Drop-out Rates and Diploma Recipients by Race/Ethnicity

Category	Total	White	Black	Asian	AIAN	Hisp.
Enrollment (%)	100.0	96.4	0.6	2.3	0.1	0.6
Drop-out Rate (%)	n/a	n/a	n/a	n/a	n/a	n/a
H.S. Diplomas (#)	155	151	0	2	0	2

Medway
45 Holliston St • Medway, MA 02053-1404
(508) 533-3222 • http://www.medway.k12.ma.us/
Grade Span: PK-12; Agency Type: 1
Schools: 5
  3 Primary; 1 Middle; 1 High; 0 Other Level
  5 Regular; 0 Special Education; 0 Vocational; 0 Alternative
  0 Magnet; 0 Charter; 2 Title I Eligible; 0 School-wide Title I
Students: 2,886   (50.5% male; 49.4% female)
  Individual Education Program: 423 (14.7%);
  English Language Learner: 1 (<0.1%); Migrant: 0 (0.0%)
  Eligible for Free Lunch Program: 59 (2.0%)
  Eligible for Reduced-Price Lunch Program: 13 (0.5%)
Teachers: 169.4 (17.0 to 1)
Librarians/Media Specialists: 1.0 (2,886.0 to 1)
Guidance Counselors: 4.0 (721.5 to 1)
Current Spending: ($ per student per year):
  Total: $8,195; Instruction: $5,399; Support Services: $2,619

Enrollment, Drop-out Rates and Diploma Recipients by Race/Ethnicity

Category	Total	White	Black	Asian	AIAN	Hisp.
Enrollment (%)	100.0	96.8	1.0	1.4	0.1	0.7
Drop-out Rate (%)	n/a	n/a	n/a	n/a	n/a	n/a
H.S. Diplomas (#)	154	148	2	2	0	2

Milton
1372 Brush Hill Rd • Milton, MA 02186-2845
Mailing Address: 25 Gile Rd • Milton, MA 02186-2845
(617) 696-4808 • http://www.miltonps.org/
Grade Span: PK-12; Agency Type: 1
Schools: 6
  4 Primary; 1 Middle; 0 High; 1 Other Level

  6 Regular; 0 Special Education; 0 Vocational; 0 Alternative
  0 Magnet; 0 Charter; 2 Title I Eligible; 0 School-wide Title I
Students: 3,572   (51.2% male; 48.7% female)
  Individual Education Program: 576 (16.1%);
  English Language Learner: 6 (0.2%); Migrant: 0 (0.0%)
  Eligible for Free Lunch Program: 158 (4.4%)
  Eligible for Reduced-Price Lunch Program: 55 (1.5%)
Teachers: 242.0 (14.8 to 1)
Librarians/Media Specialists: 3.0 (1,190.7 to 1)
Guidance Counselors: 11.4 (313.3 to 1)
Current Spending: ($ per student per year):
  Total: $9,793; Instruction: $6,528; Support Services: $3,027

Enrollment, Drop-out Rates and Diploma Recipients by Race/Ethnicity

Category	Total	White	Black	Asian	AIAN	Hisp.
Enrollment (%)	100.0	76.0	17.7	3.8	0.0	2.5
Drop-out Rate (%)	n/a	n/a	n/a	n/a	n/a	n/a
H.S. Diplomas (#)	220	171	38	6	0	5

Needham
1330 Highland Ave • Needham, MA 02492-2613
(781) 455-0400 • http://www.needham.k12.ma.us/
Grade Span: PK-12; Agency Type: 1
Schools: 7
  5 Primary; 1 Middle; 1 High; 0 Other Level
  7 Regular; 0 Special Education; 0 Vocational; 0 Alternative
  0 Magnet; 0 Charter; 2 Title I Eligible; 0 School-wide Title I
Students: 4,722   (52.3% male; 47.6% female)
  Individual Education Program: 516 (10.9%);
  English Language Learner: 33 (0.7%); Migrant: 2 (<0.1%)
  Eligible for Free Lunch Program: 105 (2.2%)
  Eligible for Reduced-Price Lunch Program: 43 (0.9%)
Teachers: 364.6 (13.0 to 1)
Librarians/Media Specialists: 7.0 (674.6 to 1)
Guidance Counselors: 18.3 (258.0 to 1)
Current Spending: ($ per student per year):
  Total: $10,940; Instruction: $7,091; Support Services: $3,517

Enrollment, Drop-out Rates and Diploma Recipients by Race/Ethnicity

Category	Total	White	Black	Asian	AIAN	Hisp.
Enrollment (%)	100.0	88.5	3.7	5.6	0.0	2.1
Drop-out Rate (%)	n/a	n/a	n/a	n/a	n/a	n/a
H.S. Diplomas (#)	302	277	10	12	0	3

Norwood
100 Westover Pkwy • Norwood, MA 02062-0067
Mailing Address: Box 67 • Norwood, MA 02062-0067
(781) 762-6804 • http://www.norwood.k12.ma.us/
Grade Span: PK-12; Agency Type: 1
Schools: 8
  6 Primary; 1 Middle; 1 High; 0 Other Level
  8 Regular; 0 Special Education; 0 Vocational; 0 Alternative
  0 Magnet; 0 Charter; 4 Title I Eligible; 0 School-wide Title I
Students: 3,727   (50.6% male; 49.3% female)
  Individual Education Program: 630 (16.9%);
  English Language Learner: 209 (5.6%); Migrant: 2 (0.1%)
  Eligible for Free Lunch Program: 399 (10.7%)
  Eligible for Reduced-Price Lunch Program: 153 (4.1%)
Teachers: 281.6 (13.2 to 1)
Librarians/Media Specialists: 5.0 (745.4 to 1)
Guidance Counselors: 8.0 (465.9 to 1)
Current Spending: ($ per student per year):
  Total: $10,028; Instruction: $6,019; Support Services: $3,696

Enrollment, Drop-out Rates and Diploma Recipients by Race/Ethnicity

Category	Total	White	Black	Asian	AIAN	Hisp.
Enrollment (%)	100.0	82.8	6.6	7.0	0.1	3.5
Drop-out Rate (%)	n/a	n/a	n/a	n/a	n/a	n/a
H.S. Diplomas (#)	234	217	6	7	0	4

Quincy
70 Coddington St • Quincy, MA 02169-4501
(617) 984-8700 • http://QuincyPublicSchools.com/qpshome.htm
Grade Span: PK-12; Agency Type: 1
Schools: 18
  11 Primary; 5 Middle; 1 High; 1 Other Level
  18 Regular; 0 Special Education; 0 Vocational; 0 Alternative
  0 Magnet; 0 Charter; 3 Title I Eligible; 1 School-wide Title I
Students: 8,897   (51.7% male; 48.2% female)
  Individual Education Program: 1,383 (15.5%);
  English Language Learner: 1,216 (13.7%); Migrant: 5 (0.1%)
  Eligible for Free Lunch Program: 2,053 (23.1%)
  Eligible for Reduced-Price Lunch Program: 660 (7.4%)
Teachers: 670.9 (13.3 to 1)
Librarians/Media Specialists: 14.3 (622.2 to 1)
Guidance Counselors: 35.4 (251.3 to 1)
Current Spending: ($ per student per year):
  Total: $10,543; Instruction: $6,761; Support Services: $3,489

Enrollment, Drop-out Rates and Diploma Recipients by Race/Ethnicity

Category	Total	White	Black	Asian	AIAN	Hisp.
Enrollment (%)	100.0	66.1	4.0	26.5	0.4	3.1
Drop-out Rate (%)	n/a	n/a	n/a	n/a	n/a	n/a
H.S. Diplomas (#)	591	409	19	148	2	13

Randolph
40 Highland Ave • Randolph, MA 02368-4513
(781) 961-6205 • http://www.randolph.mec.edu/
Grade Span: PK-12; **Agency Type:** 1
Schools: 8
  6 Primary; 1 Middle; 1 High; 0 Other Level
  8 Regular; 0 Special Education; 0 Vocational; 0 Alternative
  0 Magnet; 0 Charter; 6 Title I Eligible; 0 School-wide Title I
Students: 3,811 (52.8% male; 47.1% female)
  Individual Education Program: 786 (20.6%);
  English Language Learner: 277 (7.3%); Migrant: 0 (0.0%)
  Eligible for Free Lunch Program: 797 (20.9%)
  Eligible for Reduced-Price Lunch Program: 330 (8.7%)
Teachers: 266.1 (14.3 to 1)
Librarians/Media Specialists: 2.0 (1,905.5 to 1)
Guidance Counselors: 3.0 (1,270.3 to 1)
Current Spending: ($ per student per year):
  Total: $9,628; Instruction: $6,314; Support Services: $2,981

Enrollment, Drop-out Rates and Diploma Recipients by Race/Ethnicity

Category	Total	White	Black	Asian	AIAN	Hisp.
Enrollment (%)	100.0	37.4	41.8	13.2	0.3	7.2
Drop-out Rate (%)	n/a	n/a	n/a	n/a	n/a	n/a
H.S. Diplomas (#)	196	88	64	34	0	10

Sharon
1 School St • Sharon, MA 02067-1298
(781) 784-1570 • http://www.sharonschools.com/
Grade Span: PK-12; **Agency Type:** 1
Schools: 5
  3 Primary; 1 Middle; 0 High; 1 Other Level
  5 Regular; 0 Special Education; 0 Vocational; 0 Alternative
  0 Magnet; 0 Charter; 3 Title I Eligible; 0 School-wide Title I
Students: 3,561 (49.3% male; 50.6% female)
  Individual Education Program: 516 (14.5%);
  English Language Learner: 40 (1.1%); Migrant: 38 (1.1%)
  Eligible for Free Lunch Program: 106 (3.0%)
  Eligible for Reduced-Price Lunch Program: 29 (0.8%)
Teachers: 314.4 (11.3 to 1)
Librarians/Media Specialists: 3.6 (989.2 to 1)
Guidance Counselors: 8.7 (409.3 to 1)
Current Spending: ($ per student per year):
  Total: $9,949; Instruction: $6,540; Support Services: $3,200

Enrollment, Drop-out Rates and Diploma Recipients by Race/Ethnicity

Category	Total	White	Black	Asian	AIAN	Hisp.
Enrollment (%)	100.0	86.7	4.8	7.1	0.1	1.3
Drop-out Rate (%)	n/a	n/a	n/a	n/a	n/a	n/a
H.S. Diplomas (#)	254	226	14	10	0	4

Stoughton
232 Pearl St • Stoughton, MA 02072-2397
(781) 344-4000 • http://www.stoughton.k12.ma.us/
Grade Span: PK-12; **Agency Type:** 1
Schools: 8
  6 Primary; 1 Middle; 1 High; 0 Other Level
  8 Regular; 0 Special Education; 0 Vocational; 0 Alternative
  0 Magnet; 0 Charter; 4 Title I Eligible; 0 School-wide Title I
Students: 4,067 (52.0% male; 47.9% female)
  Individual Education Program: 657 (16.2%);
  English Language Learner: 61 (1.5%); Migrant: 0 (0.0%)
  Eligible for Free Lunch Program: 412 (10.1%)
  Eligible for Reduced-Price Lunch Program: 198 (4.9%)
Teachers: 279.4 (14.6 to 1)
Librarians/Media Specialists: 3.0 (1,355.7 to 1)
Guidance Counselors: 11.6 (350.6 to 1)
Current Spending: ($ per student per year):
  Total: $9,205; Instruction: $5,984; Support Services: $2,876

Enrollment, Drop-out Rates and Diploma Recipients by Race/Ethnicity

Category	Total	White	Black	Asian	AIAN	Hisp.
Enrollment (%)	100.0	83.3	10.7	3.4	0.1	2.5
Drop-out Rate (%)	n/a	n/a	n/a	n/a	n/a	n/a
H.S. Diplomas (#)	219	189	21	8	0	1

Walpole
135 School St • Walpole, MA 02081
(508) 660-7200 • http://www.walpole.ma.us/walpoleschools.htm
Grade Span: PK-12; **Agency Type:** 1
Schools: 7
  4 Primary; 2 Middle; 1 High; 0 Other Level
  7 Regular; 0 Special Education; 0 Vocational; 0 Alternative

0 Magnet; 0 Charter; 3 Title I Eligible; 0 School-wide Title I
Students: 3,629 (49.9% male; 50.0% female)
  Individual Education Program: 626 (17.2%);
  English Language Learner: 1 (<0.1%); Migrant: 0 (0.0%)
  Eligible for Free Lunch Program: 144 (4.0%)
  Eligible for Reduced-Price Lunch Program: 66 (1.8%)
Teachers: 244.2 (14.9 to 1)
Librarians/Media Specialists: 5.0 (725.8 to 1)
Guidance Counselors: 8.8 (412.4 to 1)
Current Spending: ($ per student per year):
  Total: $9,251; Instruction: $5,873; Support Services: $3,118

Enrollment, Drop-out Rates and Diploma Recipients by Race/Ethnicity

Category	Total	White	Black	Asian	AIAN	Hisp.
Enrollment (%)	100.0	95.8	1.8	1.4	0.1	0.9
Drop-out Rate (%)	n/a	n/a	n/a	n/a	n/a	n/a
H.S. Diplomas (#)	206	203	3	0	0	0

Wellesley
40 Kingsbury St • Wellesley, MA 02481-4827
(781) 446-6210 • http://www.wellesley.mec.edu/
Grade Span: PK-12; **Agency Type:** 1
Schools: 9
  8 Primary; 0 Middle; 1 High; 0 Other Level
  9 Regular; 0 Special Education; 0 Vocational; 0 Alternative
  0 Magnet; 0 Charter; 3 Title I Eligible; 0 School-wide Title I
Students: 4,252 (49.8% male; 50.1% female)
  Individual Education Program: 610 (14.3%);
  English Language Learner: 49 (1.2%); Migrant: 0 (0.0%)
  Eligible for Free Lunch Program: 95 (2.2%)
  Eligible for Reduced-Price Lunch Program: 40 (0.9%)
Teachers: 324.0 (13.1 to 1)
Librarians/Media Specialists: 7.8 (545.1 to 1)
Guidance Counselors: 10.0 (425.2 to 1)
Current Spending: ($ per student per year):
  Total: $12,184; Instruction: $7,793; Support Services: $4,158

Enrollment, Drop-out Rates and Diploma Recipients by Race/Ethnicity

Category	Total	White	Black	Asian	AIAN	Hisp.
Enrollment (%)	100.0	87.3	3.9	6.3	0.2	2.2
Drop-out Rate (%)	n/a	n/a	n/a	n/a	n/a	n/a
H.S. Diplomas (#)	244	210	9	16	0	9

Westwood
660 High St • Westwood, MA 02090-1687
(781) 326-7500 • http://www.westwood.k12.ma.us/
Grade Span: PK-12; **Agency Type:** 1
Schools: 7
  5 Primary; 1 Middle; 1 High; 0 Other Level
  7 Regular; 0 Special Education; 0 Vocational; 0 Alternative
  0 Magnet; 0 Charter; 4 Title I Eligible; 0 School-wide Title I
Students: 2,761 (50.1% male; 49.8% female)
  Individual Education Program: 388 (14.1%);
  English Language Learner: 0 (0.0%); Migrant: 0 (0.0%)
  Eligible for Free Lunch Program: 0 (0.0%)
  Eligible for Reduced-Price Lunch Program: 0 (0.0%)
Teachers: 218.5 (12.6 to 1)
Librarians/Media Specialists: 7.0 (394.4 to 1)
Guidance Counselors: 9.0 (306.8 to 1)
Current Spending: ($ per student per year):
  Total: $12,037; Instruction: $7,047; Support Services: $4,697

Enrollment, Drop-out Rates and Diploma Recipients by Race/Ethnicity

Category	Total	White	Black	Asian	AIAN	Hisp.
Enrollment (%)	100.0	92.6	2.0	4.3	0.2	0.9
Drop-out Rate (%)	n/a	n/a	n/a	n/a	n/a	n/a
H.S. Diplomas (#)	151	140	4	5	0	2

Weymouth
111 Middle St • Weymouth, MA 02189-1332
(781) 335-1460 • http://www.weymouth.ma.us/schools/
Grade Span: PK-12; **Agency Type:** 1
Schools: 12
  9 Primary; 2 Middle; 1 High; 0 Other Level
  12 Regular; 0 Special Education; 0 Vocational; 0 Alternative
  0 Magnet; 0 Charter; 3 Title I Eligible; 1 School-wide Title I
Students: 6,890 (51.5% male; 48.4% female)
  Individual Education Program: 1,313 (19.1%);
  English Language Learner: 53 (0.8%); Migrant: 3 (<0.1%)
  Eligible for Free Lunch Program: 790 (11.5%)
  Eligible for Reduced-Price Lunch Program: 209 (3.0%)
Teachers: 504.9 (13.6 to 1)
Librarians/Media Specialists: 3.0 (2,296.7 to 1)
Guidance Counselors: 11.5 (599.1 to 1)
Current Spending: ($ per student per year):
  Total: $9,154; Instruction: $5,962; Support Services: $2,941

Enrollment, Drop-out Rates and Diploma Recipients by Race/Ethnicity

Category	Total	White	Black	Asian	AIAN	Hisp.
Enrollment (%)	100.0	90.7	3.0	2.6	0.4	3.4
Drop-out Rate (%)	n/a	n/a	n/a	n/a	n/a	n/a
H.S. Diplomas (#)	383	366	6	5	0	6

Plymouth County

Abington
1 Ralph Hamlin Ln • Abington, MA 02351-2003
(781) 982-2150 • http://www.abington.k12.ma.us/
Grade Span: PK-12; **Agency Type:** 1
Schools: 6
  4 Primary; 1 Middle; 1 High; 0 Other Level
  6 Regular; 0 Special Education; 0 Vocational; 0 Alternative
  0 Magnet; 0 Charter; 4 Title I Eligible; 1 School-wide Title I
Students: 2,454 (51.5% male; 48.4% female)
  Individual Education Program: 312 (12.7%);
  English Language Learner: 2 (0.1%); Migrant: 0 (0.0%)
  Eligible for Free Lunch Program: 155 (6.3%)
  Eligible for Reduced-Price Lunch Program: 26 (1.1%)
Teachers: 129.7 (18.9 to 1)
Librarians/Media Specialists: 1.8 (1,363.3 to 1)
Guidance Counselors: 3.6 (681.7 to 1)
Current Spending: ($ per student per year):
  Total: $7,947; Instruction: $5,263; Support Services: $2,452
Enrollment, Drop-out Rates and Diploma Recipients by Race/Ethnicity

Category	Total	White	Black	Asian	AIAN	Hisp.
Enrollment (%)	100.0	96.0	1.8	0.7	0.0	1.5
Drop-out Rate (%)	n/a	n/a	n/a	n/a	n/a	n/a
H.S. Diplomas (#)	115	111	1	2	0	1

Brockton
43 Crescent St • Brockton, MA 02301-4376
(508) 580-7511 • http://www.brocktonpublicschools.com/
Grade Span: PK-12; **Agency Type:** 1
Schools: 25
  18 Primary; 4 Middle; 1 High; 2 Other Level
  24 Regular; 0 Special Education; 1 Vocational; 0 Alternative
  0 Magnet; 0 Charter; 16 Title I Eligible; 16 School-wide Title I
Students: 16,454 (51.6% male; 48.3% female)
  Individual Education Program: 2,096 (12.7%);
  English Language Learner: 1,213 (7.4%); Migrant: 52 (0.3%)
  Eligible for Free Lunch Program: 7,908 (48.1%)
  Eligible for Reduced-Price Lunch Program: 1,683 (10.2%)
Teachers: 1,147.5 (14.3 to 1)
Librarians/Media Specialists: 15.0 (1,096.9 to 1)
Guidance Counselors: 25.5 (645.3 to 1)
Current Spending: ($ per student per year):
  Total: $11,212; Instruction: $6,907; Support Services: $3,947
Enrollment, Drop-out Rates and Diploma Recipients by Race/Ethnicity

Category	Total	White	Black	Asian	AIAN	Hisp.
Enrollment (%)	100.0	37.8	45.9	2.9	0.9	12.4
Drop-out Rate (%)	n/a	n/a	n/a	n/a	n/a	n/a
H.S. Diplomas (#)	689	279	309	32	2	67

Carver
3 Carver Square Blvd • Carver, MA 02330-0972
(508) 866-6160 • http://www.carver.org/
Grade Span: PK-12; **Agency Type:** 1
Schools: 4
  2 Primary; 1 Middle; 1 High; 0 Other Level
  4 Regular; 0 Special Education; 0 Vocational; 0 Alternative
  0 Magnet; 0 Charter; 2 Title I Eligible; 0 School-wide Title I
Students: 2,094 (50.8% male; 49.1% female)
  Individual Education Program: 287 (13.7%);
  English Language Learner: 0 (0.0%); Migrant: 0 (0.0%)
  Eligible for Free Lunch Program: 183 (8.7%)
  Eligible for Reduced-Price Lunch Program: 128 (6.1%)
Teachers: 158.3 (13.2 to 1)
Librarians/Media Specialists: 2.3 (910.4 to 1)
Guidance Counselors: 3.0 (698.0 to 1)
Current Spending: ($ per student per year):
  Total: $9,101; Instruction: $5,636; Support Services: $3,186
Enrollment, Drop-out Rates and Diploma Recipients by Race/Ethnicity

Category	Total	White	Black	Asian	AIAN	Hisp.
Enrollment (%)	100.0	96.4	3.0	0.0	0.3	0.2
Drop-out Rate (%)	n/a	n/a	n/a	n/a	n/a	n/a
H.S. Diplomas (#)	108	103	5	0	0	0

Duxbury
130 St George St • Duxbury, MA 02332-3871
(781) 934-7600 • http://www.duxbury.k12.ma.us/
Grade Span: PK-12; **Agency Type:** 1
Schools: 4

  2 Primary; 1 Middle; 1 High; 0 Other Level
  4 Regular; 0 Special Education; 0 Vocational; 0 Alternative
  0 Magnet; 0 Charter; 2 Title I Eligible; 2 School-wide Title I
Students: 3,293 (52.4% male; 47.5% female)
  Individual Education Program: 388 (11.8%);
  English Language Learner: 0 (0.0%); Migrant: 0 (0.0%)
  Eligible for Free Lunch Program: 0 (0.0%)
  Eligible for Reduced-Price Lunch Program: 0 (0.0%)
Teachers: 216.0 (15.2 to 1)
Librarians/Media Specialists: 4.0 (823.3 to 1)
Guidance Counselors: 6.3 (522.7 to 1)
Current Spending: ($ per student per year):
  Total: $8,646; Instruction: $5,552; Support Services: $3,093
Enrollment, Drop-out Rates and Diploma Recipients by Race/Ethnicity

Category	Total	White	Black	Asian	AIAN	Hisp.
Enrollment (%)	100.0	97.9	0.5	0.9	0.1	0.6
Drop-out Rate (%)	n/a	n/a	n/a	n/a	n/a	n/a
H.S. Diplomas (#)	236	229	1	5	0	1

East Bridgewater
11 Plymouth St • East Bridgewater, MA 02333-1995
(508) 378-8200 • http://ebps.net/
Grade Span: PK-12; **Agency Type:** 1
Schools: 3
  1 Primary; 1 Middle; 1 High; 0 Other Level
  3 Regular; 0 Special Education; 0 Vocational; 0 Alternative
  0 Magnet; 0 Charter; 2 Title I Eligible; 0 School-wide Title I
Students: 2,422 (50.5% male; 49.4% female)
  Individual Education Program: 220 (9.1%);
  English Language Learner: 0 (0.0%); Migrant: 0 (0.0%)
  Eligible for Free Lunch Program: 93 (3.8%)
  Eligible for Reduced-Price Lunch Program: 48 (2.0%)
Teachers: 148.2 (16.3 to 1)
Librarians/Media Specialists: 1.0 (2,422.0 to 1)
Guidance Counselors: 7.0 (346.0 to 1)
Current Spending: ($ per student per year):
  Total: $7,840; Instruction: $5,098; Support Services: $2,567
Enrollment, Drop-out Rates and Diploma Recipients by Race/Ethnicity

Category	Total	White	Black	Asian	AIAN	Hisp.
Enrollment (%)	100.0	97.3	1.8	0.4	0.0	0.5
Drop-out Rate (%)	n/a	n/a	n/a	n/a	n/a	n/a
H.S. Diplomas (#)	156	153	2	0	0	1

Hanover
188 Broadway • Hanover, MA 02339-1572
(781) 878-0786 • http://hanoverschools.org/
Grade Span: PK-12; **Agency Type:** 1
Schools: 5
  3 Primary; 1 Middle; 1 High; 0 Other Level
  5 Regular; 0 Special Education; 0 Vocational; 0 Alternative
  0 Magnet; 0 Charter; 2 Title I Eligible; 0 School-wide Title I
Students: 2,775 (50.3% male; 49.6% female)
  Individual Education Program: 479 (17.3%);
  English Language Learner: 2 (0.1%); Migrant: 0 (0.0%)
  Eligible for Free Lunch Program: 44 (1.6%)
  Eligible for Reduced-Price Lunch Program: 15 (0.5%)
Teachers: 216.4 (12.8 to 1)
Librarians/Media Specialists: 4.0 (693.8 to 1)
Guidance Counselors: 4.0 (693.8 to 1)
Current Spending: ($ per student per year):
  Total: $8,524; Instruction: $5,764; Support Services: $2,540
Enrollment, Drop-out Rates and Diploma Recipients by Race/Ethnicity

Category	Total	White	Black	Asian	AIAN	Hisp.
Enrollment (%)	100.0	97.5	0.9	1.2	0.0	0.4
Drop-out Rate (%)	n/a	n/a	n/a	n/a	n/a	n/a
H.S. Diplomas (#)	150	148	2	0	0	0

Hingham
220 Central St • Hingham, MA 02043-2745
(781) 741-1500 • http://www.hinghamschools.com/
Grade Span: PK-12; **Agency Type:** 1
Schools: 5
  3 Primary; 1 Middle; 1 High; 0 Other Level
  5 Regular; 0 Special Education; 0 Vocational; 0 Alternative
  0 Magnet; 0 Charter; 3 Title I Eligible; 0 School-wide Title I
Students: 3,590 (50.6% male; 49.3% female)
  Individual Education Program: 454 (12.6%);
  English Language Learner: 0 (0.0%); Migrant: 0 (0.0%)
  Eligible for Free Lunch Program: 71 (2.0%)
  Eligible for Reduced-Price Lunch Program: 28 (0.8%)
Teachers: 249.3 (14.4 to 1)
Librarians/Media Specialists: 6.0 (598.3 to 1)
Guidance Counselors: 7.4 (485.1 to 1)
Current Spending: ($ per student per year):
  Total: $8,927; Instruction: $5,789; Support Services: $2,939

Enrollment, Drop-out Rates and Diploma Recipients by Race/Ethnicity

Category	Total	White	Black	Asian	AIAN	Hisp.
Enrollment (%)	100.0	95.9	1.1	1.9	0.0	1.1
Drop-out Rate (%)	n/a	n/a	n/a	n/a	n/a	n/a
H.S. Diplomas (#)	232	225	1	4	0	2

Marshfield
76 S River St • Marshfield, MA 02050-2499
(781) 834-5000 • http://www.mpsd.org/
Grade Span: PK-12; Agency Type: 1
Schools: 7
  5 Primary; 1 Middle; 1 High; 0 Other Level
  7 Regular; 0 Special Education; 0 Vocational; 0 Alternative
  0 Magnet; 0 Charter; 4 Title I Eligible; 0 School-wide Title I
Students: 4,598 (51.8% male; 48.1% female)
  Individual Education Program: 668 (14.5%);
  English Language Learner: 2 (<0.1%); Migrant: 1 (<0.1%)
  Eligible for Free Lunch Program: 250 (5.4%)
  Eligible for Reduced-Price Lunch Program: 19 (0.4%)
Teachers: 333.8 (13.8 to 1)
Librarians/Media Specialists: 2.0 (2,299.0 to 1)
Guidance Counselors: 9.0 (510.9 to 1)
Current Spending: ($ per student per year):
  Total: $8,803; Instruction: $5,924; Support Services: $2,624

Enrollment, Drop-out Rates and Diploma Recipients by Race/Ethnicity

Category	Total	White	Black	Asian	AIAN	Hisp.
Enrollment (%)	100.0	97.7	0.5	0.7	0.3	0.8
Drop-out Rate (%)	n/a	n/a	n/a	n/a	n/a	n/a
H.S. Diplomas (#)	277	269	3	2	0	3

Middleborough
30 Forest St • Middleborough, MA 02346-4012
(508) 946-2000 • http://www.middleboro.k12.ma.us/
Grade Span: PK-12; Agency Type: 1
Schools: 6
  4 Primary; 1 Middle; 1 High; 0 Other Level
  6 Regular; 0 Special Education; 0 Vocational; 0 Alternative
  0 Magnet; 0 Charter; 2 Title I Eligible; 0 School-wide Title I
Students: 3,686 (52.2% male; 47.7% female)
  Individual Education Program: 523 (14.2%);
  English Language Learner: 5 (0.1%); Migrant: 0 (0.0%)
  Eligible for Free Lunch Program: 435 (11.8%)
  Eligible for Reduced-Price Lunch Program: 175 (4.7%)
Teachers: 231.9 (15.9 to 1)
Librarians/Media Specialists: 3.0 (1,228.7 to 1)
Guidance Counselors: 5.9 (624.7 to 1)
Current Spending: ($ per student per year):
  Total: $8,141; Instruction: $5,079; Support Services: $2,736

Enrollment, Drop-out Rates and Diploma Recipients by Race/Ethnicity

Category	Total	White	Black	Asian	AIAN	Hisp.
Enrollment (%)	100.0	95.3	2.5	0.8	0.1	1.2
Drop-out Rate (%)	n/a	n/a	n/a	n/a	n/a	n/a
H.S. Diplomas (#)	189	184	2	2	0	1

Norwell
322 Main St • Norwell, MA 02061-2420
(781) 659-8800 • http://www.norwellschools.org/
Grade Span: PK-12; Agency Type: 1
Schools: 4
  2 Primary; 1 Middle; 1 High; 0 Other Level
  4 Regular; 0 Special Education; 0 Vocational; 0 Alternative
  0 Magnet; 0 Charter; 2 Title I Eligible; 0 School-wide Title I
Students: 2,063 (51.7% male; 48.2% female)
  Individual Education Program: 312 (15.1%);
  English Language Learner: 0 (0.0%); Migrant: 0 (0.0%)
  Eligible for Free Lunch Program: 31 (1.5%)
  Eligible for Reduced-Price Lunch Program: 3 (0.1%)
Teachers: 143.6 (14.4 to 1)
Librarians/Media Specialists: 2.0 (1,031.5 to 1)
Guidance Counselors: 6.4 (322.3 to 1)
Current Spending: ($ per student per year):
  Total: $9,728; Instruction: $6,015; Support Services: $3,445

Enrollment, Drop-out Rates and Diploma Recipients by Race/Ethnicity

Category	Total	White	Black	Asian	AIAN	Hisp.
Enrollment (%)	100.0	96.3	0.9	2.1	0.0	0.7
Drop-out Rate (%)	n/a	n/a	n/a	n/a	n/a	n/a
H.S. Diplomas (#)	131	128	0	2	0	1

Pembroke
72 Pilgrim Rd • Pembroke, MA 02359
Mailing Address: Office Of The Superintendent • Pembroke, MA 02359
(781) 829-1178
Grade Span: KG-06; Agency Type: 2
Schools: 3
  3 Primary; 0 Middle; 0 High; 0 Other Level

  3 Regular; 0 Special Education; 0 Vocational; 0 Alternative
  0 Magnet; 0 Charter; 1 Title I Eligible; 0 School-wide Title I
Students: 1,903 (51.2% male; 48.7% female)
  Individual Education Program: 227 (11.9%);
  English Language Learner: 0 (0.0%); Migrant: 0 (0.0%)
  Eligible for Free Lunch Program: 78 (4.1%)
  Eligible for Reduced-Price Lunch Program: 17 (0.9%)
Teachers: 79.0 (24.1 to 1)
Librarians/Media Specialists: 1.0 (1,903.0 to 1)
Guidance Counselors: 0.0 (n/a to 1)
Current Spending: ($ per student per year):
  Total: $7,972; Instruction: $4,835; Support Services: $3,101

Enrollment, Drop-out Rates and Diploma Recipients by Race/Ethnicity

Category	Total	White	Black	Asian	AIAN	Hisp.
Enrollment (%)	100.0	97.5	0.5	1.6	0.0	0.4
Drop-out Rate (%)	n/a	n/a	n/a	n/a	n/a	n/a
H.S. Diplomas (#)	n/a	n/a	n/a	n/a	n/a	n/a

Plymouth
253 S Meadow Rd • Plymouth, MA 02360-4739
(508) 830-4300 • http://plymouthschools.com/
Grade Span: PK-12; Agency Type: 1
Schools: 14
  9 Primary; 2 Middle; 3 High; 0 Other Level
  13 Regular; 0 Special Education; 1 Vocational; 0 Alternative
  0 Magnet; 0 Charter; 6 Title I Eligible; 1 School-wide Title I
Students: 8,754 (52.2% male; 47.7% female)
  Individual Education Program: 1,358 (15.5%);
  English Language Learner: 50 (0.6%); Migrant: 0 (0.0%)
  Eligible for Free Lunch Program: 989 (11.3%)
  Eligible for Reduced-Price Lunch Program: 407 (4.6%)
Teachers: 628.9 (13.9 to 1)
Librarians/Media Specialists: 11.0 (795.8 to 1)
Guidance Counselors: 25.5 (343.3 to 1)
Current Spending: ($ per student per year):
  Total: $9,641; Instruction: $6,437; Support Services: $2,924

Enrollment, Drop-out Rates and Diploma Recipients by Race/Ethnicity

Category	Total	White	Black	Asian	AIAN	Hisp.
Enrollment (%)	100.0	94.0	3.0	1.0	0.3	1.7
Drop-out Rate (%)	n/a	n/a	n/a	n/a	n/a	n/a
H.S. Diplomas (#)	534	509	14	6	2	3

Rockland
34 Mackinlay Way • Rockland, MA 02370-2374
(781) 878-3893 • http://www.rockland.mec.edu/
Grade Span: PK-12; Agency Type: 1
Schools: 5
  3 Primary; 1 Middle; 1 High; 0 Other Level
  5 Regular; 0 Special Education; 0 Vocational; 0 Alternative
  0 Magnet; 0 Charter; 4 Title I Eligible; 0 School-wide Title I
Students: 2,722 (52.5% male; 47.4% female)
  Individual Education Program: 400 (14.7%);
  English Language Learner: 0 (0.0%); Migrant: 0 (0.0%)
  Eligible for Free Lunch Program: 326 (12.0%)
  Eligible for Reduced-Price Lunch Program: 92 (3.4%)
Teachers: 170.7 (15.9 to 1)
Librarians/Media Specialists: 0.5 (5,444.0 to 1)
Guidance Counselors: 3.0 (907.3 to 1)
Current Spending: ($ per student per year):
  Total: $8,787; Instruction: $5,440; Support Services: $3,045

Enrollment, Drop-out Rates and Diploma Recipients by Race/Ethnicity

Category	Total	White	Black	Asian	AIAN	Hisp.
Enrollment (%)	100.0	91.4	3.5	1.7	0.4	3.0
Drop-out Rate (%)	n/a	n/a	n/a	n/a	n/a	n/a
H.S. Diplomas (#)	177	163	4	7	2	1

Scituate
606 C J Cushing Hwy • Scituate, MA 02066-3296
(781) 545-8759 • http://www.scituate.k12.ma.us/
Grade Span: PK-12; Agency Type: 1
Schools: 6
  4 Primary; 1 Middle; 0 High; 1 Other Level
  6 Regular; 0 Special Education; 0 Vocational; 0 Alternative
  0 Magnet; 0 Charter; 3 Title I Eligible; 0 School-wide Title I
Students: 3,143 (50.2% male; 49.7% female)
  Individual Education Program: 391 (12.4%);
  English Language Learner: 40 (1.3%); Migrant: 2 (0.1%)
  Eligible for Free Lunch Program: 116 (3.7%)
  Eligible for Reduced-Price Lunch Program: 22 (0.7%)
Teachers: 219.4 (14.3 to 1)
Librarians/Media Specialists: 2.0 (1,571.5 to 1)
Guidance Counselors: 9.6 (327.4 to 1)
Current Spending: ($ per student per year):
  Total: $8,653; Instruction: $5,557; Support Services: $2,872

Enrollment, Drop-out Rates and Diploma Recipients by Race/Ethnicity

Category	Total	White	Black	Asian	AIAN	Hisp.
Enrollment (%)	100.0	95.8	3.0	0.5	0.1	0.7
Drop-out Rate (%)	n/a	n/a	n/a	n/a	n/a	n/a
H.S. Diplomas (#)	176	169	6	0	0	1

Silver Lake
250 Pembroke St • Kingston, MA 02364-1153
(781) 585-4313 • http://www.silverlake.mec.edu/
Grade Span: 07-12; **Agency Type:** 3
Schools: 2
    0 Primary; 1 Middle; 0 High; 1 Other Level
    2 Regular; 0 Special Education; 0 Vocational; 0 Alternative
    0 Magnet; 0 Charter; 2 Title I Eligible; 0 School-wide Title I
Students: 2,949 (51.4% male; 48.5% female)
    Individual Education Program: 357 (12.1%);
    English Language Learner: 5 (0.2%); Migrant: 0 (0.0%)
    Eligible for Free Lunch Program: 111 (3.8%)
    Eligible for Reduced-Price Lunch Program: 33 (1.1%)
Teachers: 221.6 (13.3 to 1)
Librarians/Media Specialists: 2.0 (1,474.5 to 1)
Guidance Counselors: 11.0 (268.1 to 1)
Current Spending: ($ per student per year):
    Total: $9,882; Instruction: $6,397; Support Services: $3,169

Enrollment, Drop-out Rates and Diploma Recipients by Race/Ethnicity

Category	Total	White	Black	Asian	AIAN	Hisp.
Enrollment (%)	100.0	98.3	0.9	0.6	0.0	0.2
Drop-out Rate (%)	n/a	n/a	n/a	n/a	n/a	n/a
H.S. Diplomas (#)	352	350	1	1	0	0

Wareham
54 Marion Rd • Wareham, MA 02571-1428
(508) 291-3500 • http://www.wareham.mec.edu/
Grade Span: PK-12; **Agency Type:** 1
Schools: 7
    5 Primary; 1 Middle; 1 High; 0 Other Level
    7 Regular; 0 Special Education; 0 Vocational; 0 Alternative
    0 Magnet; 0 Charter; 6 Title I Eligible; 6 School-wide Title I
Students: 3,484 (52.1% male; 47.8% female)
    Individual Education Program: 558 (16.0%);
    English Language Learner: 1 (<0.1%); Migrant: 3 (0.1%)
    Eligible for Free Lunch Program: 897 (25.7%)
    Eligible for Reduced-Price Lunch Program: 339 (9.7%)
Teachers: 244.0 (14.3 to 1)
Librarians/Media Specialists: 3.4 (1,024.7 to 1)
Guidance Counselors: 6.0 (580.7 to 1)
Current Spending: ($ per student per year):
    Total: $9,273; Instruction: $5,694; Support Services: $3,260

Enrollment, Drop-out Rates and Diploma Recipients by Race/Ethnicity

Category	Total	White	Black	Asian	AIAN	Hisp.
Enrollment (%)	100.0	84.0	12.3	0.7	1.1	1.9
Drop-out Rate (%)	n/a	n/a	n/a	n/a	n/a	n/a
H.S. Diplomas (#)	164	140	17	3	2	2

Whitman-Hanson
600 Franklin St • Whitman, MA 02382-2599
(781) 618-7412 • http://www.whrsd.k12.ma.us/
Grade Span: PK-12; **Agency Type:** 3
Schools: 8
    5 Primary; 2 Middle; 1 High; 0 Other Level
    8 Regular; 0 Special Education; 0 Vocational; 0 Alternative
    0 Magnet; 0 Charter; 3 Title I Eligible; 0 School-wide Title I
Students: 4,452 (51.4% male; 48.5% female)
    Individual Education Program: 639 (14.4%);
    English Language Learner: 4 (0.1%); Migrant: 0 (0.0%)
    Eligible for Free Lunch Program: 312 (7.0%)
    Eligible for Reduced-Price Lunch Program: 114 (2.6%)
Teachers: 287.4 (15.5 to 1)
Librarians/Media Specialists: 7.0 (636.0 to 1)
Guidance Counselors: 8.0 (556.5 to 1)
Current Spending: ($ per student per year):
    Total: $8,492; Instruction: $5,667; Support Services: $2,530

Enrollment, Drop-out Rates and Diploma Recipients by Race/Ethnicity

Category	Total	White	Black	Asian	AIAN	Hisp.
Enrollment (%)	100.0	96.0	2.1	0.3	0.1	1.5
Drop-out Rate (%)	n/a	n/a	n/a	n/a	n/a	n/a
H.S. Diplomas (#)	258	250	3	4	0	1

Suffolk County

Boston
26 Court St • Boston, MA 02108-2581
(617) 635-9050 • http://www.boston.k12.ma.us/
Grade Span: PK-12; **Agency Type:** 1
Schools: 136

    83 Primary; 19 Middle; 27 High; 7 Other Level
    126 Regular; 1 Special Education; 0 Vocational; 9 Alternative
    0 Magnet; 0 Charter; 127 Title I Eligible; 127 School-wide Title I
Students: 60,150 (51.6% male; 48.3% female)
    Individual Education Program: 11,827 (19.7%);
    English Language Learner: 11,403 (19.0%); Migrant: 31 (0.1%)
    Eligible for Free Lunch Program: 39,179 (65.1%)
    Eligible for Reduced-Price Lunch Program: 4,964 (8.3%)
Teachers: 3,926.3 (15.3 to 1)
Librarians/Media Specialists: 20.5 (2,934.1 to 1)
Guidance Counselors: 85.1 (706.8 to 1)
Current Spending: ($ per student per year):
    Total: $14,602; Instruction: $8,709; Support Services: $5,367

Enrollment, Drop-out Rates and Diploma Recipients by Race/Ethnicity

Category	Total	White	Black	Asian	AIAN	Hisp.
Enrollment (%)	100.0	14.0	46.4	8.8	0.4	30.4
Drop-out Rate (%)	n/a	n/a	n/a	n/a	n/a	n/a
H.S. Diplomas (#)	2,816	525	1,372	345	10	564

Chelsea
500 Broadway • Chelsea, MA 02150
Mailing Address: City Hall Room 216 • Chelsea, MA 02150
(617) 889-8415 • http://www.chelseaschools.com/
Grade Span: PK-12; **Agency Type:** 1
Schools: 9
    5 Primary; 2 Middle; 1 High; 1 Other Level
    8 Regular; 0 Special Education; 0 Vocational; 1 Alternative
    0 Magnet; 0 Charter; 9 Title I Eligible; 9 School-wide Title I
Students: 5,672 (51.0% male; 48.9% female)
    Individual Education Program: 833 (14.7%);
    English Language Learner: 923 (16.3%); Migrant: 0 (0.0%)
    Eligible for Free Lunch Program: 4,562 (80.4%)
    Eligible for Reduced-Price Lunch Program: 0 (0.0%)
Teachers: 467.4 (12.1 to 1)
Librarians/Media Specialists: 5.0 (1,134.4 to 1)
Guidance Counselors: 9.0 (630.2 to 1)
Current Spending: ($ per student per year):
    Total: $11,853; Instruction: $7,527; Support Services: $3,826

Enrollment, Drop-out Rates and Diploma Recipients by Race/Ethnicity

Category	Total	White	Black	Asian	AIAN	Hisp.
Enrollment (%)	100.0	15.2	7.0	4.2	0.2	73.4
Drop-out Rate (%)	n/a	n/a	n/a	n/a	n/a	n/a
H.S. Diplomas (#)	161	28	14	21	0	98

Revere
101 School St • Revere, MA 02151-3001
(781) 286-8226 • http://www.revereps.mec.edu/
Grade Span: PK-12; **Agency Type:** 1
Schools: 8
    6 Primary; 0 Middle; 2 High; 0 Other Level
    8 Regular; 0 Special Education; 0 Vocational; 0 Alternative
    1 Magnet; 0 Charter; 6 Title I Eligible; 2 School-wide Title I
Students: 5,711 (52.7% male; 47.2% female)
    Individual Education Program: 748 (13.1%);
    English Language Learner: 401 (7.0%); Migrant: 0 (0.0%)
    Eligible for Free Lunch Program: 2,365 (41.4%)
    Eligible for Reduced-Price Lunch Program: 656 (11.5%)
Teachers: 380.1 (15.0 to 1)
Librarians/Media Specialists: 2.0 (2,855.5 to 1)
Guidance Counselors: 7.0 (815.9 to 1)
Current Spending: ($ per student per year):
    Total: $9,377; Instruction: $5,897; Support Services: $3,116

Enrollment, Drop-out Rates and Diploma Recipients by Race/Ethnicity

Category	Total	White	Black	Asian	AIAN	Hisp.
Enrollment (%)	100.0	62.3	5.8	9.2	0.4	22.4
Drop-out Rate (%)	n/a	n/a	n/a	n/a	n/a	n/a
H.S. Diplomas (#)	236	158	15	36	3	24

Winthrop
45 Pauline St • Winthrop, MA 02152-3011
(617) 846-5500 • http://www.winthrop.k12.ma.us/
Grade Span: PK-12; **Agency Type:** 1
Schools: 4
    2 Primary; 1 Middle; 1 High; 0 Other Level
    4 Regular; 0 Special Education; 0 Vocational; 0 Alternative
    0 Magnet; 0 Charter; 2 Title I Eligible; 0 School-wide Title I
Students: 2,149 (49.3% male; 50.6% female)
    Individual Education Program: 346 (16.1%);
    English Language Learner: 16 (0.7%); Migrant: 0 (0.0%)
    Eligible for Free Lunch Program: 319 (14.8%)
    Eligible for Reduced-Price Lunch Program: 77 (3.6%)
Teachers: 153.0 (14.0 to 1)
Librarians/Media Specialists: 0.0 (n/a to 1)
Guidance Counselors: 4.0 (537.3 to 1)
Current Spending: ($ per student per year):
    Total: $9,348; Instruction: $6,372; Support Services: $2,731

Enrollment, Drop-out Rates and Diploma Recipients by Race/Ethnicity

Category	Total	White	Black	Asian	AIAN	Hisp.
Enrollment (%)	100.0	93.4	2.1	0.7	0.0	3.8
Drop-out Rate (%)	n/a	n/a	n/a	n/a	n/a	n/a
H.S. Diplomas (#)	90	88	0	1	0	1

Worcester County

Ashburnham-Westminster

2 Narrows Rd / Ste 101 • Westminster, MA 01473-1619
Mailing Address: Office Of The Superintendent • Ashburnham, MA 01430-1670
(978) 827-1434 • http://www.awrsd.org/
Grade Span: PK-12; **Agency Type:** 3
Schools: 5
   3 Primary; 1 Middle; 1 High; 0 Other Level
   5 Regular; 0 Special Education; 0 Vocational; 0 Alternative
   0 Magnet; 0 Charter; 2 Title I Eligible; 0 School-wide Title I
Students: 2,433   (52.8% male; 47.1% female)
   Individual Education Program: 444 (18.2%);
   English Language Learner: 0 (0.0%); Migrant: 0 (0.0%)
   Eligible for Free Lunch Program: 103 (4.2%)
   Eligible for Reduced-Price Lunch Program: 98 (4.0%)
Teachers: 153.4 (15.9 to 1)
Librarians/Media Specialists: 4.0 (608.3 to 1)
Guidance Counselors: 6.0 (405.5 to 1)
Current Spending: ($ per student per year):
   Total: $8,921; Instruction: $5,492; Support Services: $3,191
Enrollment, Drop-out Rates and Diploma Recipients by Race/Ethnicity

Category	Total	White	Black	Asian	AIAN	Hisp.
Enrollment (%)	100.0	96.3	1.1	1.2	0.1	1.3
Drop-out Rate (%)	n/a	n/a	n/a	n/a	n/a	n/a
H.S. Diplomas (#)	174	169	0	2	0	3

Athol-Royalston

1062 Pleasant St • Athol, MA 01331-3526
Mailing Address: PO Box 968 • Athol, MA 01331-3526
(978) 249-2400 • http://www.athol-royalstonschools.org/
Grade Span: PK-12; **Agency Type:** 3
Schools: 8
   5 Primary; 1 Middle; 1 High; 1 Other Level
   8 Regular; 0 Special Education; 0 Vocational; 0 Alternative
   0 Magnet; 0 Charter; 6 Title I Eligible; 0 School-wide Title I
Students: 2,200   (53.2% male; 46.7% female)
   Individual Education Program: 346 (15.7%);
   English Language Learner: 8 (0.4%); Migrant: 0 (0.0%)
   Eligible for Free Lunch Program: 459 (20.9%)
   Eligible for Reduced-Price Lunch Program: 238 (10.8%)
Teachers: 153.3 (14.4 to 1)
Librarians/Media Specialists: 1.0 (2,200.0 to 1)
Guidance Counselors: 5.9 (372.9 to 1)
Current Spending: ($ per student per year):
   Total: $10,996; Instruction: $6,863; Support Services: $3,782
Enrollment, Drop-out Rates and Diploma Recipients by Race/Ethnicity

Category	Total	White	Black	Asian	AIAN	Hisp.
Enrollment (%)	100.0	93.2	1.6	0.9	0.5	3.8
Drop-out Rate (%)	n/a	n/a	n/a	n/a	n/a	n/a
H.S. Diplomas (#)	108	103	3	0	0	2

Auburn

5 W St • Auburn, MA 01501-1301
(508) 832-7755 • http://www.auburn.mec.edu/
Grade Span: PK-12; **Agency Type:** 1
Schools: 6
   4 Primary; 1 Middle; 1 High; 0 Other Level
   6 Regular; 0 Special Education; 0 Vocational; 0 Alternative
   0 Magnet; 0 Charter; 5 Title I Eligible; 0 School-wide Title I
Students: 2,371   (51.2% male; 48.7% female)
   Individual Education Program: 262 (11.1%);
   English Language Learner: 8 (0.3%); Migrant: 2 (0.1%)
   Eligible for Free Lunch Program: 213 (9.0%)
   Eligible for Reduced-Price Lunch Program: 21 (0.9%)
Teachers: 163.5 (14.5 to 1)
Librarians/Media Specialists: 1.0 (2,371.0 to 1)
Guidance Counselors: 7.5 (316.1 to 1)
Current Spending: ($ per student per year):
   Total: $9,898; Instruction: $6,732; Support Services: $2,910
Enrollment, Drop-out Rates and Diploma Recipients by Race/Ethnicity

Category	Total	White	Black	Asian	AIAN	Hisp.
Enrollment (%)	100.0	92.9	1.4	2.4	0.9	2.3
Drop-out Rate (%)	n/a	n/a	n/a	n/a	n/a	n/a
H.S. Diplomas (#)	151	144	3	3	0	1

Blackstone-Millville

175 Lincoln St • Blackstone, MA 01504-1202
(508) 883-4400 • http://www.bmrsd.net/
Grade Span: PK-12; **Agency Type:** 3
Schools: 5
   2 Primary; 2 Middle; 1 High; 0 Other Level
   5 Regular; 0 Special Education; 0 Vocational; 0 Alternative
   0 Magnet; 0 Charter; 3 Title I Eligible; 0 School-wide Title I
Students: 2,294   (50.3% male; 49.6% female)
   Individual Education Program: 340 (14.8%);
   English Language Learner: 0 (0.0%); Migrant: 0 (0.0%)
   Eligible for Free Lunch Program: 115 (5.0%)
   Eligible for Reduced-Price Lunch Program: 81 (3.5%)
Teachers: 155.8 (14.7 to 1)
Librarians/Media Specialists: 0.4 (5,735.0 to 1)
Guidance Counselors: 4.0 (573.5 to 1)
Current Spending: ($ per student per year):
   Total: $8,644; Instruction: $5,845; Support Services: $2,517
Enrollment, Drop-out Rates and Diploma Recipients by Race/Ethnicity

Category	Total	White	Black	Asian	AIAN	Hisp.
Enrollment (%)	100.0	96.3	1.0	1.2	0.0	1.4
Drop-out Rate (%)	n/a	n/a	n/a	n/a	n/a	n/a
H.S. Diplomas (#)	143	141	1	0	0	1

Clinton

500 Main St • Clinton, MA 01510-2504
Mailing Address: 150 School St • Clinton, MA 01510-2504
(978) 365-4200 • http://www.clinton.k12.ma.us/
Grade Span: PK-12; **Agency Type:** 1
Schools: 3
   1 Primary; 1 Middle; 1 High; 0 Other Level
   3 Regular; 0 Special Education; 0 Vocational; 0 Alternative
   0 Magnet; 0 Charter; 1 Title I Eligible; 0 School-wide Title I
Students: 2,020   (51.7% male; 48.2% female)
   Individual Education Program: 303 (15.0%);
   English Language Learner: 45 (2.2%); Migrant: 4 (0.2%)
   Eligible for Free Lunch Program: 466 (23.1%)
   Eligible for Reduced-Price Lunch Program: 181 (9.0%)
Teachers: 140.8 (14.3 to 1)
Librarians/Media Specialists: 2.0 (1,010.0 to 1)
Guidance Counselors: 4.0 (505.0 to 1)
Current Spending: ($ per student per year):
   Total: $9,972; Instruction: $7,082; Support Services: $2,743
Enrollment, Drop-out Rates and Diploma Recipients by Race/Ethnicity

Category	Total	White	Black	Asian	AIAN	Hisp.
Enrollment (%)	100.0	75.2	3.4	1.1	0.0	20.2
Drop-out Rate (%)	n/a	n/a	n/a	n/a	n/a	n/a
H.S. Diplomas (#)	131	111	0	1	0	19

Douglas

21 Davis St • Douglas, MA 01516-2311
(508) 476-7901
Grade Span: PK-12; **Agency Type:** 1
Schools: 4
   2 Primary; 1 Middle; 1 High; 0 Other Level
   4 Regular; 0 Special Education; 0 Vocational; 0 Alternative
   0 Magnet; 0 Charter; 1 Title I Eligible; 0 School-wide Title I
Students: 1,585   (50.6% male; 49.3% female)
   Individual Education Program: 128 (8.1%);
   English Language Learner: 1 (0.1%); Migrant: 0 (0.0%)
   Eligible for Free Lunch Program: 93 (5.9%)
   Eligible for Reduced-Price Lunch Program: 35 (2.2%)
Teachers: 98.6 (16.1 to 1)
Librarians/Media Specialists: 3.0 (528.3 to 1)
Guidance Counselors: 3.6 (440.3 to 1)
Current Spending: ($ per student per year):
   Total: $7,731; Instruction: $4,875; Support Services: $2,695
Enrollment, Drop-out Rates and Diploma Recipients by Race/Ethnicity

Category	Total	White	Black	Asian	AIAN	Hisp.
Enrollment (%)	100.0	98.4	0.4	0.4	0.0	0.7
Drop-out Rate (%)	n/a	n/a	n/a	n/a	n/a	n/a
H.S. Diplomas (#)	67	67	0	0	0	0

Dudley-Charlton Reg

68 Dudley Oxford Rd • Dudley, MA 01571-6116
(508) 943-6888 • http://www.dc-regional.k12.ma.us/
Grade Span: PK-12; **Agency Type:** 3
Schools: 7
   4 Primary; 2 Middle; 1 High; 0 Other Level
   7 Regular; 0 Special Education; 0 Vocational; 0 Alternative
   0 Magnet; 0 Charter; 6 Title I Eligible; 0 School-wide Title I
Students: 4,334   (49.9% male; 50.0% female)
   Individual Education Program: 546 (12.6%);
   English Language Learner: 1 (<0.1%); Migrant: 0 (0.0%)
   Eligible for Free Lunch Program: 260 (6.0%)

Eligible for Reduced-Price Lunch Program: 122 (2.8%)
Teachers: 282.2 (15.4 to 1)
Librarians/Media Specialists: 5.0 (866.8 to 1)
Guidance Counselors: 7.3 (593.7 to 1)
Current Spending: ($ per student per year):
   Total: $8,073; Instruction: $5,244; Support Services: $2,609
Enrollment, Drop-out Rates and Diploma Recipients by Race/Ethnicity

Category	Total	White	Black	Asian	AIAN	Hisp.
Enrollment (%)	100.0	98.5	0.3	0.2	0.1	0.9
Drop-out Rate (%)	n/a	n/a	n/a	n/a	n/a	n/a
H.S. Diplomas (#)	221	219	0	0	0	2

Fitchburg
376 S St • Fitchburg, MA 01420-7942
(978) 345-3200 • http://www.fitchburg.k12.ma.us/
Grade Span: PK-12; **Agency Type:** 1
Schools: 10
   6 Primary; 3 Middle; 0 High; 1 Other Level
   10 Regular; 0 Special Education; 0 Vocational; 0 Alternative
   0 Magnet; 0 Charter; 10 Title I Eligible; 6 School-wide Title I
Students: 5,757   (50.1% male; 49.8% female)
   Individual Education Program: 966 (16.8%);
   English Language Learner: 1,082 (18.8%); Migrant: 2 (<0.1%)
   Eligible for Free Lunch Program: 2,295 (39.9%)
   Eligible for Reduced-Price Lunch Program: 600 (10.4%)
Teachers: 437.2 (13.2 to 1)
Librarians/Media Specialists: 6.6 (872.3 to 1)
Guidance Counselors: 19.0 (303.0 to 1)
Current Spending: ($ per student per year):
   Total: $10,229; Instruction: $6,836; Support Services: $2,846
Enrollment, Drop-out Rates and Diploma Recipients by Race/Ethnicity

Category	Total	White	Black	Asian	AIAN	Hisp.
Enrollment (%)	100.0	51.0	6.6	9.5	0.4	32.5
Drop-out Rate (%)	n/a	n/a	n/a	n/a	n/a	n/a
H.S. Diplomas (#)	300	221	22	25	0	32

Gardner
130 Elm/ Sauter Sch • Gardner, MA 01440-2373
(978) 632-1000 • http://www.gardnerk12.org/
Grade Span: PK-12; **Agency Type:** 1
Schools: 6
   3 Primary; 1 Middle; 1 High; 1 Other Level
   6 Regular; 0 Special Education; 0 Vocational; 0 Alternative
   0 Magnet; 0 Charter; 5 Title I Eligible; 0 School-wide Title I
Students: 3,259   (49.8% male; 50.1% female)
   Individual Education Program: 631 (19.4%);
   English Language Learner: 17 (0.5%); Migrant: 0 (0.0%)
   Eligible for Free Lunch Program: 668 (20.5%)
   Eligible for Reduced-Price Lunch Program: 167 (5.1%)
Teachers: 211.0 (15.4 to 1)
Librarians/Media Specialists: 2.0 (1,629.5 to 1)
Guidance Counselors: 13.0 (250.7 to 1)
Current Spending: ($ per student per year):
   Total: $8,394; Instruction: $5,177; Support Services: $2,963
Enrollment, Drop-out Rates and Diploma Recipients by Race/Ethnicity

Category	Total	White	Black	Asian	AIAN	Hisp.
Enrollment (%)	100.0	86.8	3.3	2.5	0.6	6.8
Drop-out Rate (%)	n/a	n/a	n/a	n/a	n/a	n/a
H.S. Diplomas (#)	172	162	3	5	0	2

Grafton
30 Providence Rd • Grafton, MA 01519-1178
(508) 839-5421 • http://www.grafton.k12.ma.us/district/index.cfm
Grade Span: PK-12; **Agency Type:** 1
Schools: 5
   3 Primary; 1 Middle; 1 High; 0 Other Level
   5 Regular; 0 Special Education; 0 Vocational; 0 Alternative
   0 Magnet; 0 Charter; 2 Title I Eligible; 0 School-wide Title I
Students: 2,453   (52.0% male; 47.9% female)
   Individual Education Program: 366 (14.9%);
   English Language Learner: 1 (<0.1%); Migrant: 0 (0.0%)
   Eligible for Free Lunch Program: 128 (5.2%)
   Eligible for Reduced-Price Lunch Program: 58 (2.4%)
Teachers: 161.8 (15.2 to 1)
Librarians/Media Specialists: 2.0 (1,226.5 to 1)
Guidance Counselors: 5.0 (490.6 to 1)
Current Spending: ($ per student per year):
   Total: $8,533; Instruction: $5,501; Support Services: $2,796
Enrollment, Drop-out Rates and Diploma Recipients by Race/Ethnicity

Category	Total	White	Black	Asian	AIAN	Hisp.
Enrollment (%)	100.0	93.4	1.1	2.8	0.9	1.9
Drop-out Rate (%)	n/a	n/a	n/a	n/a	n/a	n/a
H.S. Diplomas (#)	119	112	2	4	0	1

Leicester
1078 Main St • Leicester, MA 01524-1349
(508) 892-7040 • http://www.leicester.k12.ma.us/
Grade Span: PK-12; **Agency Type:** 1
Schools: 4
   2 Primary; 1 Middle; 1 High; 0 Other Level
   4 Regular; 0 Special Education; 0 Vocational; 0 Alternative
   0 Magnet; 0 Charter; 2 Title I Eligible; 0 School-wide Title I
Students: 1,940   (51.3% male; 48.6% female)
   Individual Education Program: 287 (14.8%);
   English Language Learner: 2 (0.1%); Migrant: 0 (0.0%)
   Eligible for Free Lunch Program: 154 (7.9%)
   Eligible for Reduced-Price Lunch Program: 75 (3.9%)
Teachers: 136.9 (14.2 to 1)
Librarians/Media Specialists: 3.0 (646.7 to 1)
Guidance Counselors: 4.0 (485.0 to 1)
Current Spending: ($ per student per year):
   Total: $8,610; Instruction: $5,459; Support Services: $2,843
Enrollment, Drop-out Rates and Diploma Recipients by Race/Ethnicity

Category	Total	White	Black	Asian	AIAN	Hisp.
Enrollment (%)	100.0	94.2	2.1	1.6	0.3	1.8
Drop-out Rate (%)	n/a	n/a	n/a	n/a	n/a	n/a
H.S. Diplomas (#)	106	99	1	3	0	3

Leominster
24 Church St • Leominster, MA 01453-3102
(978) 534-7700 • http://www.leominster.mec.edu/
Grade Span: PK-12; **Agency Type:** 1
Schools: 10
   5 Primary; 3 Middle; 2 High; 0 Other Level
   9 Regular; 0 Special Education; 1 Vocational; 0 Alternative
   0 Magnet; 0 Charter; 3 Title I Eligible; 0 School-wide Title I
Students: 6,228   (51.7% male; 48.2% female)
   Individual Education Program: 951 (15.3%);
   English Language Learner: 670 (10.8%); Migrant: 2 (<0.1%)
   Eligible for Free Lunch Program: 1,288 (20.7%)
   Eligible for Reduced-Price Lunch Program: 482 (7.7%)
Teachers: 390.4 (16.0 to 1)
Librarians/Media Specialists: 7.0 (889.7 to 1)
Guidance Counselors: 17.0 (366.4 to 1)
Current Spending: ($ per student per year):
   Total: $9,422; Instruction: $6,358; Support Services: $2,764
Enrollment, Drop-out Rates and Diploma Recipients by Race/Ethnicity

Category	Total	White	Black	Asian	AIAN	Hisp.
Enrollment (%)	100.0	70.8	5.1	3.8	0.2	20.0
Drop-out Rate (%)	n/a	n/a	n/a	n/a	n/a	n/a
H.S. Diplomas (#)	350	284	11	13	0	42

Lunenburg
1033 Mass Ave • Lunenburg, MA 01462-1479
(978) 582-4100
Grade Span: PK-12; **Agency Type:** 1
Schools: 3
   1 Primary; 1 Middle; 1 High; 0 Other Level
   3 Regular; 0 Special Education; 0 Vocational; 0 Alternative
   0 Magnet; 0 Charter; 2 Title I Eligible; 0 School-wide Title I
Students: 1,830   (52.2% male; 47.7% female)
   Individual Education Program: 244 (13.3%);
   English Language Learner: 0 (0.0%); Migrant: 0 (0.0%)
   Eligible for Free Lunch Program: 79 (4.3%)
   Eligible for Reduced-Price Lunch Program: 42 (2.3%)
Teachers: 118.9 (15.4 to 1)
Librarians/Media Specialists: 1.5 (1,220.0 to 1)
Guidance Counselors: 5.0 (366.0 to 1)
Current Spending: ($ per student per year):
   Total: $8,703; Instruction: $5,706; Support Services: $2,704
Enrollment, Drop-out Rates and Diploma Recipients by Race/Ethnicity

Category	Total	White	Black	Asian	AIAN	Hisp.
Enrollment (%)	100.0	95.1	1.0	1.6	0.3	2.0
Drop-out Rate (%)	n/a	n/a	n/a	n/a	n/a	n/a
H.S. Diplomas (#)	128	123	1	2	1	1

Mendon-Upton
150 N Ave PO Box 5 • Mendon, MA 01756-0176
(508) 634-1585 • http://www.mu-regional.k12.ma.us/
Grade Span: PK-12; **Agency Type:** 3
Schools: 4
   3 Primary; 0 Middle; 1 High; 0 Other Level
   4 Regular; 0 Special Education; 0 Vocational; 0 Alternative
   0 Magnet; 0 Charter; 3 Title I Eligible; 0 School-wide Title I
Students: 2,574   (50.6% male; 49.3% female)
   Individual Education Program: 246 (9.6%);
   English Language Learner: 0 (0.0%); Migrant: 0 (0.0%)
   Eligible for Free Lunch Program: 41 (1.6%)
   Eligible for Reduced-Price Lunch Program: 19 (0.7%)

Teachers: 174.0 (14.8 to 1)
Librarians/Media Specialists: 0.0 (n/a to 1)
Guidance Counselors: 6.0 (429.0 to 1)
Current Spending: ($ per student per year):
    Total: $7,918; Instruction: $5,052; Support Services: $2,611
Enrollment, Drop-out Rates and Diploma Recipients by Race/Ethnicity

Category	Total	White	Black	Asian	AIAN	Hisp.
Enrollment (%)	100.0	97.5	0.3	0.9	0.6	0.7
Drop-out Rate (%)	n/a	n/a	n/a	n/a	n/a	n/a
H.S. Diplomas (#)	111	111	0	0	0	0

Milford

31 W Fountain St • Milford, MA 01757-4098
(508) 478-1100 • http://mail.milfordma.com/schools/
Grade Span: PK-12; **Agency Type:** 1
Schools: 7
    4 Primary; 1 Middle; 0 High; 2 Other Level
    7 Regular; 0 Special Education; 0 Vocational; 0 Alternative
    0 Magnet; 0 Charter; 4 Title I Eligible; 0 School-wide Title I
Students: 4,185   (51.3% male; 48.6% female)
    Individual Education Program: 586 (14.0%);
    English Language Learner: 157 (3.8%); Migrant: 20 (0.5%)
    Eligible for Free Lunch Program: 459 (11.0%)
    Eligible for Reduced-Price Lunch Program: 128 (3.1%)
Teachers: 322.3 (13.0 to 1)
Librarians/Media Specialists: 0.1 (41,850.0 to 1)
Guidance Counselors: 8.0 (523.1 to 1)
Current Spending: ($ per student per year):
    Total: $10,094; Instruction: $6,676; Support Services: $3,114
Enrollment, Drop-out Rates and Diploma Recipients by Race/Ethnicity

Category	Total	White	Black	Asian	AIAN	Hisp.
Enrollment (%)	100.0	86.9	2.2	2.6	0.2	8.1
Drop-out Rate (%)	n/a	n/a	n/a	n/a	n/a	n/a
H.S. Diplomas (#)	227	186	6	5	0	30

Millbury

12 Martin St • Millbury, MA 01527-2014
(508) 865-9501 • http://www.millbury.k12.ma.us/
Grade Span: PK-12; **Agency Type:** 1
Schools: 3
    1 Primary; 1 Middle; 1 High; 0 Other Level
    3 Regular; 0 Special Education; 0 Vocational; 0 Alternative
    0 Magnet; 0 Charter; 2 Title I Eligible; 0 School-wide Title I
Students: 2,008   (53.0% male; 46.9% female)
    Individual Education Program: 306 (15.2%);
    English Language Learner: 6 (0.3%); Migrant: 0 (0.0%)
    Eligible for Free Lunch Program: 201 (10.0%)
    Eligible for Reduced-Price Lunch Program: 72 (3.6%)
Teachers: 125.3 (16.0 to 1)
Librarians/Media Specialists: 1.0 (2,008.0 to 1)
Guidance Counselors: 5.0 (401.6 to 1)
Current Spending: ($ per student per year):
    Total: $8,653; Instruction: $5,759; Support Services: $2,650
Enrollment, Drop-out Rates and Diploma Recipients by Race/Ethnicity

Category	Total	White	Black	Asian	AIAN	Hisp.
Enrollment (%)	100.0	94.0	1.8	1.5	0.3	2.3
Drop-out Rate (%)	n/a	n/a	n/a	n/a	n/a	n/a
H.S. Diplomas (#)	92	89	1	0	1	1

Narragansett

462 Baldwinville Rd • Baldwinville, MA 01436-1225
(978) 939-5661 • http://www.nrsd.org/
Grade Span: PK-12; **Agency Type:** 3
Schools: 6
    4 Primary; 1 Middle; 1 High; 0 Other Level
    6 Regular; 0 Special Education; 0 Vocational; 0 Alternative
    0 Magnet; 0 Charter; 4 Title I Eligible; 0 School-wide Title I
Students: 1,635   (50.8% male; 49.1% female)
    Individual Education Program: 242 (14.8%);
    English Language Learner: 0 (0.0%); Migrant: 0 (0.0%)
    Eligible for Free Lunch Program: 191 (11.7%)
    Eligible for Reduced-Price Lunch Program: 73 (4.5%)
Teachers: 112.6 (14.5 to 1)
Librarians/Media Specialists: 1.0 (1,635.0 to 1)
Guidance Counselors: 5.0 (327.0 to 1)
Current Spending: ($ per student per year):
    Total: $8,759; Instruction: $5,637; Support Services: $2,842
Enrollment, Drop-out Rates and Diploma Recipients by Race/Ethnicity

Category	Total	White	Black	Asian	AIAN	Hisp.
Enrollment (%)	100.0	97.7	1.1	0.5	0.1	0.6
Drop-out Rate (%)	n/a	n/a	n/a	n/a	n/a	n/a
H.S. Diplomas (#)	79	78	0	1	0	0

Nashoba

50 Mechanic St • Bolton, MA 01740-3300
(978) 779-0539 • http://www.nrsd.net/
Grade Span: PK-12; **Agency Type:** 3
Schools: 7
    4 Primary; 2 Middle; 1 High; 0 Other Level
    7 Regular; 0 Special Education; 0 Vocational; 0 Alternative
    0 Magnet; 0 Charter; 2 Title I Eligible; 0 School-wide Title I
Students: 3,063   (51.5% male; 48.4% female)
    Individual Education Program: 384 (12.5%);
    English Language Learner: 8 (0.3%); Migrant: 0 (0.0%)
    Eligible for Free Lunch Program: 88 (2.9%)
    Eligible for Reduced-Price Lunch Program: 26 (0.8%)
Teachers: 217.6 (14.1 to 1)
Librarians/Media Specialists: 1.8 (1,701.7 to 1)
Guidance Counselors: 9.8 (312.6 to 1)
Current Spending: ($ per student per year):
    Total: $10,517; Instruction: $6,848; Support Services: $3,418
Enrollment, Drop-out Rates and Diploma Recipients by Race/Ethnicity

Category	Total	White	Black	Asian	AIAN	Hisp.
Enrollment (%)	100.0	94.7	1.2	1.5	0.1	2.5
Drop-out Rate (%)	n/a	n/a	n/a	n/a	n/a	n/a
H.S. Diplomas (#)	190	176	4	7	0	3

Northborough

44 Bearfoot Rd • Northborough, MA 01532-1657
(508) 351-7000 • http://www.nsboro.k12.ma.us/
Grade Span: PK-08; **Agency Type:** 2
Schools: 5
    4 Primary; 1 Middle; 0 High; 0 Other Level
    5 Regular; 0 Special Education; 0 Vocational; 0 Alternative
    0 Magnet; 0 Charter; 5 Title I Eligible; 0 School-wide Title I
Students: 1,936   (52.7% male; 47.2% female)
    Individual Education Program: 224 (11.6%);
    English Language Learner: 13 (0.7%); Migrant: 1 (0.1%)
    Eligible for Free Lunch Program: 33 (1.7%)
    Eligible for Reduced-Price Lunch Program: 43 (2.2%)
Teachers: 137.1 (14.1 to 1)
Librarians/Media Specialists: 5.0 (387.2 to 1)
Guidance Counselors: 2.0 (968.0 to 1)
Current Spending: ($ per student per year):
    Total: $8,715; Instruction: $6,140; Support Services: $2,335
Enrollment, Drop-out Rates and Diploma Recipients by Race/Ethnicity

Category	Total	White	Black	Asian	AIAN	Hisp.
Enrollment (%)	100.0	90.4	1.0	5.7	0.3	2.6
Drop-out Rate (%)	n/a	n/a	n/a	n/a	n/a	n/a
H.S. Diplomas (#)	n/a	n/a	n/a	n/a	n/a	n/a

Northbridge

87 Linwood Ave • Whitinsville, MA 01588-2309
(508) 234-8156 • http://www.northbridge.k12.ma.us/
Grade Span: PK-12; **Agency Type:** 1
Schools: 5
    3 Primary; 1 Middle; 1 High; 0 Other Level
    5 Regular; 0 Special Education; 0 Vocational; 0 Alternative
    0 Magnet; 0 Charter; 2 Title I Eligible; 0 School-wide Title I
Students: 2,544   (51.4% male; 48.5% female)
    Individual Education Program: 299 (11.8%);
    English Language Learner: 29 (1.1%); Migrant: 0 (0.0%)
    Eligible for Free Lunch Program: 381 (15.0%)
    Eligible for Reduced-Price Lunch Program: 176 (6.9%)
Teachers: 178.6 (14.2 to 1)
Librarians/Media Specialists: 4.0 (636.0 to 1)
Guidance Counselors: 4.0 (636.0 to 1)
Current Spending: ($ per student per year):
    Total: $9,399; Instruction: $6,065; Support Services: $3,014
Enrollment, Drop-out Rates and Diploma Recipients by Race/Ethnicity

Category	Total	White	Black	Asian	AIAN	Hisp.
Enrollment (%)	100.0	94.3	1.8	0.5	0.3	3.1
Drop-out Rate (%)	n/a	n/a	n/a	n/a	n/a	n/a
H.S. Diplomas (#)	102	96	2	0	0	4

Oxford

5 Sigourney St • Oxford, MA 01540-1998
(508) 987-6050 • http://www.oxps.org/
Grade Span: PK-12; **Agency Type:** 1
Schools: 4
    2 Primary; 1 Middle; 1 High; 0 Other Level
    4 Regular; 0 Special Education; 0 Vocational; 0 Alternative
    0 Magnet; 0 Charter; 2 Title I Eligible; 0 School-wide Title I
Students: 2,241   (52.7% male; 47.2% female)
    Individual Education Program: 281 (12.5%);
    English Language Learner: 10 (0.4%); Migrant: 1 (<0.1%)
    Eligible for Free Lunch Program: 209 (9.3%)
    Eligible for Reduced-Price Lunch Program: 101 (4.5%)

Teachers: 131.6 (17.0 to 1)
Librarians/Media Specialists: 2.0 (1,120.5 to 1)
Guidance Counselors: 1.0 (2,241.0 to 1)
Current Spending: ($ per student per year):
    Total: $8,860; Instruction: $5,546; Support Services: $3,104
Enrollment, Drop-out Rates and Diploma Recipients by Race/Ethnicity

Category	Total	White	Black	Asian	AIAN	Hisp.
Enrollment (%)	100.0	92.9	1.9	1.7	0.3	3.2
Drop-out Rate (%)	n/a	n/a	n/a	n/a	n/a	n/a
H.S. Diplomas (#)	151	145	2	0	0	4

Quabbin
872 S St • Barre, MA 01005
(978) 355-4668 • http://www.quabbin.k12.ma.us/
Grade Span: PK-12; **Agency Type:** 3
Schools: 6
    5 Primary; 0 Middle; 1 High; 0 Other Level
    6 Regular; 0 Special Education; 0 Vocational; 0 Alternative
    0 Magnet; 0 Charter; 3 Title I Eligible; 0 School-wide Title I
Students: 3,224   (50.3% male; 49.6% female)
    Individual Education Program: 353 (10.9%);
    English Language Learner: 2 (0.1%); Migrant: 0 (0.0%)
    Eligible for Free Lunch Program: 237 (7.4%)
    Eligible for Reduced-Price Lunch Program: 128 (4.0%)
Teachers: 216.1 (14.9 to 1)
Librarians/Media Specialists: 3.0 (1,074.7 to 1)
Guidance Counselors: 9.1 (354.3 to 1)
Current Spending: ($ per student per year):
    Total: $8,837; Instruction: $5,493; Support Services: $3,109
Enrollment, Drop-out Rates and Diploma Recipients by Race/Ethnicity

Category	Total	White	Black	Asian	AIAN	Hisp.
Enrollment (%)	100.0	96.1	1.3	0.7	0.3	1.6
Drop-out Rate (%)	n/a	n/a	n/a	n/a	n/a	n/a
H.S. Diplomas (#)	161	158	1	0	0	2

Shrewsbury
100 Maple Ave • Shrewsbury, MA 01545-5398
(508) 841-8400 • http://www.shrewsbury-ma.gov/schools/index.asp
Grade Span: PK-12; **Agency Type:** 1
Schools: 8
    6 Primary; 1 Middle; 1 High; 0 Other Level
    8 Regular; 0 Special Education; 0 Vocational; 0 Alternative
    0 Magnet; 0 Charter; 5 Title I Eligible; 0 School-wide Title I
Students: 5,557   (50.3% male; 49.6% female)
    Individual Education Program: 770 (13.9%);
    English Language Learner: 75 (1.3%); Migrant: 0 (0.0%)
    Eligible for Free Lunch Program: 298 (5.4%)
    Eligible for Reduced-Price Lunch Program: 90 (1.6%)
Teachers: 346.8 (16.0 to 1)
Librarians/Media Specialists: 6.0 (926.2 to 1)
Guidance Counselors: 6.4 (868.3 to 1)
Current Spending: ($ per student per year):
    Total: $8,422; Instruction: $5,384; Support Services: $2,758
Enrollment, Drop-out Rates and Diploma Recipients by Race/Ethnicity

Category	Total	White	Black	Asian	AIAN	Hisp.
Enrollment (%)	100.0	84.3	2.1	10.7	0.3	2.6
Drop-out Rate (%)	n/a	n/a	n/a	n/a	n/a	n/a
H.S. Diplomas (#)	259	225	5	23	2	4

Southborough
44 Bearfoot Rd • Northborough, MA 01532-1657
(508) 351-7000
Grade Span: PK-08; **Agency Type:** 2
Schools: 3
    2 Primary; 1 Middle; 0 High; 0 Other Level
    3 Regular; 0 Special Education; 0 Vocational; 0 Alternative
    0 Magnet; 0 Charter; 0 Title I Eligible; 0 School-wide Title I
Students: 1,607   (50.3% male; 49.6% female)
    Individual Education Program: 188 (11.7%);
    English Language Learner: 8 (0.5%); Migrant: 0 (0.0%)
    Eligible for Free Lunch Program: 12 (0.7%)
    Eligible for Reduced-Price Lunch Program: 12 (0.7%)
Teachers: 114.6 (14.0 to 1)
Librarians/Media Specialists: 3.0 (535.7 to 1)
Guidance Counselors: 3.5 (459.1 to 1)
Current Spending: ($ per student per year):
    Total: $8,541; Instruction: $5,701; Support Services: $2,711
Enrollment, Drop-out Rates and Diploma Recipients by Race/Ethnicity

Category	Total	White	Black	Asian	AIAN	Hisp.
Enrollment (%)	100.0	92.2	1.1	5.0	0.4	1.2
Drop-out Rate (%)	n/a	n/a	n/a	n/a	n/a	n/a
H.S. Diplomas (#)	n/a	n/a	n/a	n/a	n/a	n/a

Southbridge
41 Elm St • Southbridge, MA 01550-0665
(508) 764-5414
Grade Span: PK-12; **Agency Type:** 1
Schools: 5
    3 Primary; 1 Middle; 1 High; 0 Other Level
    5 Regular; 0 Special Education; 0 Vocational; 0 Alternative
    0 Magnet; 0 Charter; 4 Title I Eligible; 3 School-wide Title I
Students: 2,592   (52.0% male; 47.9% female)
    Individual Education Program: 450 (17.4%);
    English Language Learner: 92 (3.5%); Migrant: 0 (0.0%)
    Eligible for Free Lunch Program: 1,094 (42.2%)
    Eligible for Reduced-Price Lunch Program: 155 (6.0%)
Teachers: 208.9 (12.4 to 1)
Librarians/Media Specialists: 5.0 (518.4 to 1)
Guidance Counselors: 9.0 (288.0 to 1)
Current Spending: ($ per student per year):
    Total: $9,949; Instruction: $6,640; Support Services: $2,971
Enrollment, Drop-out Rates and Diploma Recipients by Race/Ethnicity

Category	Total	White	Black	Asian	AIAN	Hisp.
Enrollment (%)	100.0	60.3	2.5	2.1	0.0	35.1
Drop-out Rate (%)	n/a	n/a	n/a	n/a	n/a	n/a
H.S. Diplomas (#)	92	60	4	1	0	27

Spencer-E Brookfield
306 Main St • Spencer, MA 01562-1856
(508) 885-8500 • http://www.seb.k12.ma.us/
Grade Span: PK-12; **Agency Type:** 3
Schools: 7
    3 Primary; 3 Middle; 1 High; 0 Other Level
    7 Regular; 0 Special Education; 0 Vocational; 0 Alternative
    0 Magnet; 0 Charter; 4 Title I Eligible; 0 School-wide Title I
Students: 2,253   (52.0% male; 47.9% female)
    Individual Education Program: 427 (19.0%);
    English Language Learner: 2 (0.1%); Migrant: 75 (3.3%)
    Eligible for Free Lunch Program: 273 (12.1%)
    Eligible for Reduced-Price Lunch Program: 161 (7.1%)
Teachers: 155.3 (14.5 to 1)
Librarians/Media Specialists: 3.0 (751.0 to 1)
Guidance Counselors: 3.0 (751.0 to 1)
Current Spending: ($ per student per year):
    Total: $9,251; Instruction: $5,824; Support Services: $3,122
Enrollment, Drop-out Rates and Diploma Recipients by Race/Ethnicity

Category	Total	White	Black	Asian	AIAN	Hisp.
Enrollment (%)	100.0	95.7	1.1	0.4	0.7	2.1
Drop-out Rate (%)	n/a	n/a	n/a	n/a	n/a	n/a
H.S. Diplomas (#)	128	126	1	1	0	0

Sutton
Boston Rd • Sutton, MA 01590-1804
Mailing Address: 383 Boston Rd • Sutton, MA 01590-1804
(508) 581-1600
Grade Span: PK-12; **Agency Type:** 1
Schools: 4
    2 Primary; 1 Middle; 1 High; 0 Other Level
    4 Regular; 0 Special Education; 0 Vocational; 0 Alternative
    0 Magnet; 0 Charter; 2 Title I Eligible; 0 School-wide Title I
Students: 1,660   (49.7% male; 50.2% female)
    Individual Education Program: 227 (13.7%);
    English Language Learner: 0 (0.0%); Migrant: 2 (0.1%)
    Eligible for Free Lunch Program: 50 (3.0%)
    Eligible for Reduced-Price Lunch Program: 10 (0.6%)
Teachers: 99.5 (16.7 to 1)
Librarians/Media Specialists: 1.0 (1,660.0 to 1)
Guidance Counselors: 4.7 (353.2 to 1)
Current Spending: ($ per student per year):
    Total: $8,148; Instruction: $5,029; Support Services: $2,916
Enrollment, Drop-out Rates and Diploma Recipients by Race/Ethnicity

Category	Total	White	Black	Asian	AIAN	Hisp.
Enrollment (%)	100.0	97.2	0.8	0.8	0.1	1.0
Drop-out Rate (%)	n/a	n/a	n/a	n/a	n/a	n/a
H.S. Diplomas (#)	107	106	0	0	0	1

Tantasqua
320 Brookfield Rd • Fiskdale, MA 01518-1098
(508) 347-3077 • http://www.tantasqua.org/
Grade Span: 07-12; **Agency Type:** 3
Schools: 3
    0 Primary; 1 Middle; 2 High; 0 Other Level
    2 Regular; 0 Special Education; 1 Vocational; 0 Alternative
    0 Magnet; 0 Charter; 2 Title I Eligible; 0 School-wide Title I
Students: 1,761   (50.9% male; 49.0% female)
    Individual Education Program: 251 (14.3%);
    English Language Learner: 0 (0.0%); Migrant: 2 (0.1%)
    Eligible for Free Lunch Program: 143 (8.1%)

Eligible for Reduced-Price Lunch Program: 60 (3.4%)
Teachers: 137.6 (12.8 to 1)
Librarians/Media Specialists: 1.0 (1,761.0 to 1)
Guidance Counselors: 5.5 (320.2 to 1)
Current Spending: ($ per student per year):
    Total: $10,155; Instruction: $6,571; Support Services: $3,350
Enrollment, Drop-out Rates and Diploma Recipients by Race/Ethnicity

Category	Total	White	Black	Asian	AIAN	Hisp.
Enrollment (%)	100.0	96.0	0.6	0.7	1.0	1.8
Drop-out Rate (%)	n/a	n/a	n/a	n/a	n/a	n/a
H.S. Diplomas (#)	212	210	0	0	1	1

Uxbridge

62 Capron St · Uxbridge, MA 01569-1530
(508) 278-8648 · http://www.uxbridge.mec.edu/
Grade Span: PK-12; **Agency Type:** 1
Schools: 3
    1 Primary; 1 Middle; 1 High; 0 Other Level
    3 Regular; 0 Special Education; 0 Vocational; 0 Alternative
    0 Magnet; 0 Charter; 1 Title I Eligible; 0 School-wide Title I
Students: 2,236   (53.6% male; 46.3% female)
    Individual Education Program: 335 (15.0%);
    English Language Learner: 8 (0.4%); Migrant: 1 (<0.1%)
    Eligible for Free Lunch Program: 134 (6.0%)
    Eligible for Reduced-Price Lunch Program: 118 (5.3%)
Teachers: 154.6 (14.5 to 1)
Librarians/Media Specialists: 1.0 (2,236.0 to 1)
Guidance Counselors: 5.0 (447.2 to 1)
Current Spending: ($ per student per year):
    Total: $8,319; Instruction: $5,301; Support Services: $2,752
Enrollment, Drop-out Rates and Diploma Recipients by Race/Ethnicity

Category	Total	White	Black	Asian	AIAN	Hisp.
Enrollment (%)	100.0	96.0	0.8	0.6	0.4	2.1
Drop-out Rate (%)	n/a	n/a	n/a	n/a	n/a	n/a
H.S. Diplomas (#)	118	116	1	1	0	0

Wachusett

1745 Main St · Jefferson, MA 01522-1097
Mailing Address: Jefferson School · Jefferson, MA 01522-1097
(508) 829-1670 · http://www.wrsd.net/
Grade Span: PK-12; **Agency Type:** 3
Schools: 11
    7 Primary; 3 Middle; 1 High; 0 Other Level
    11 Regular; 0 Special Education; 0 Vocational; 0 Alternative
    0 Magnet; 0 Charter; 8 Title I Eligible; 0 School-wide Title I
Students: 6,987   (51.5% male; 48.4% female)
    Individual Education Program: 890 (12.7%);
    English Language Learner: 19 (0.3%); Migrant: 0 (0.0%)
    Eligible for Free Lunch Program: 177 (2.5%)
    Eligible for Reduced-Price Lunch Program: 63 (0.9%)
Teachers: 434.6 (16.1 to 1)
Librarians/Media Specialists: 1.0 (6,987.0 to 1)
Guidance Counselors: 6.0 (1,164.5 to 1)
Current Spending: ($ per student per year):
    Total: $8,556; Instruction: $5,627; Support Services: $2,638
Enrollment, Drop-out Rates and Diploma Recipients by Race/Ethnicity

Category	Total	White	Black	Asian	AIAN	Hisp.
Enrollment (%)	100.0	95.9	1.2	1.5	0.2	1.1
Drop-out Rate (%)	n/a	n/a	n/a	n/a	n/a	n/a
H.S. Diplomas (#)	363	359	1	2	1	0

Webster

41 E Main St · Webster, MA 01570-0430
Mailing Address: PO Box 430 · Webster, MA 01570-0430
(508) 943-0104
Grade Span: PK-12; **Agency Type:** 1
Schools: 3
    2 Primary; 0 Middle; 0 High; 1 Other Level
    3 Regular; 0 Special Education; 0 Vocational; 0 Alternative
    0 Magnet; 0 Charter; 2 Title I Eligible; 2 School-wide Title I
Students: 1,818   (50.5% male; 49.4% female)
    Individual Education Program: 269 (14.8%);
    English Language Learner: 50 (2.8%); Migrant: 0 (0.0%)
    Eligible for Free Lunch Program: 534 (29.4%)
    Eligible for Reduced-Price Lunch Program: 143 (7.9%)
Teachers: 142.4 (12.8 to 1)
Librarians/Media Specialists: 1.0 (1,818.0 to 1)
Guidance Counselors: 5.0 (363.6 to 1)
Current Spending: ($ per student per year):
    Total: $10,196; Instruction: $6,491; Support Services: $3,304
Enrollment, Drop-out Rates and Diploma Recipients by Race/Ethnicity

Category	Total	White	Black	Asian	AIAN	Hisp.
Enrollment (%)	100.0	85.5	3.6	1.5	1.0	8.4
Drop-out Rate (%)	n/a	n/a	n/a	n/a	n/a	n/a
H.S. Diplomas (#)	99	90	3	0	0	6

Westborough

45 W Main St P.O.B 1152 · Westborough, MA 01581-6152
Mailing Address: PO Box 1152 · Westborough, MA 01581-6152
(508) 836-7700 · http://www.westborough.org
Grade Span: PK-12; **Agency Type:** 1
Schools: 6
    3 Primary; 2 Middle; 1 High; 0 Other Level
    6 Regular; 0 Special Education; 0 Vocational; 0 Alternative
    0 Magnet; 0 Charter; 3 Title I Eligible; 0 School-wide Title I
Students: 3,507   (50.5% male; 49.4% female)
    Individual Education Program: 382 (10.9%);
    English Language Learner: 135 (3.8%); Migrant: 123 (3.5%)
    Eligible for Free Lunch Program: 156 (4.4%)
    Eligible for Reduced-Price Lunch Program: 40 (1.1%)
Teachers: 279.6 (12.5 to 1)
Librarians/Media Specialists: 4.0 (876.8 to 1)
Guidance Counselors: 12.5 (280.6 to 1)
Current Spending: ($ per student per year):
    Total: $10,719; Instruction: $6,760; Support Services: $3,709
Enrollment, Drop-out Rates and Diploma Recipients by Race/Ethnicity

Category	Total	White	Black	Asian	AIAN	Hisp.
Enrollment (%)	100.0	84.4	1.1	10.7	0.1	3.8
Drop-out Rate (%)	n/a	n/a	n/a	n/a	n/a	n/a
H.S. Diplomas (#)	224	195	2	23	0	4

Winchendon

175 Grove St · Winchendon, MA 01475-1198
(978) 297-0031 · http://www.winchendonk12.org
Grade Span: PK-12; **Agency Type:** 1
Schools: 3
    1 Primary; 1 Middle; 1 High; 0 Other Level
    3 Regular; 0 Special Education; 0 Vocational; 0 Alternative
    0 Magnet; 0 Charter; 2 Title I Eligible; 0 School-wide Title I
Students: 1,877   (50.5% male; 49.4% female)
    Individual Education Program: 342 (18.2%);
    English Language Learner: 3 (0.2%); Migrant: 2 (0.1%)
    Eligible for Free Lunch Program: 337 (18.0%)
    Eligible for Reduced-Price Lunch Program: 106 (5.6%)
Teachers: 148.5 (12.6 to 1)
Librarians/Media Specialists: 3.0 (625.7 to 1)
Guidance Counselors: 5.0 (375.4 to 1)
Current Spending: ($ per student per year):
    Total: $9,121; Instruction: $6,313; Support Services: $2,575
Enrollment, Drop-out Rates and Diploma Recipients by Race/Ethnicity

Category	Total	White	Black	Asian	AIAN	Hisp.
Enrollment (%)	100.0	93.5	1.9	1.7	0.1	2.9
Drop-out Rate (%)	n/a	n/a	n/a	n/a	n/a	n/a
H.S. Diplomas (#)	89	83	0	2	0	4

Worcester

20 Irving St · Worcester, MA 01609-2432
(508) 799-3116 · http://www.wpsweb.com/default2.asp
Grade Span: PK-12; **Agency Type:** 1
Schools: 47
    36 Primary; 4 Middle; 6 High; 1 Other Level
    46 Regular; 0 Special Education; 1 Vocational; 0 Alternative
    3 Magnet; 0 Charter; 33 Title I Eligible; 33 School-wide Title I
Students: 25,028   (51.5% male; 48.4% female)
    Individual Education Program: 4,648 (18.6%);
    English Language Learner: 3,379 (13.5%); Migrant: 0 (0.0%)
    Eligible for Free Lunch Program: 13,060 (52.2%)
    Eligible for Reduced-Price Lunch Program: 2,082 (8.3%)
Teachers: 1,891.5 (13.2 to 1)
Librarians/Media Specialists: 13.6 (1,840.3 to 1)
Guidance Counselors: 43.6 (574.0 to 1)
Current Spending: ($ per student per year):
    Total: $11,397; Instruction: $7,884; Support Services: $3,136
Enrollment, Drop-out Rates and Diploma Recipients by Race/Ethnicity

Category	Total	White	Black	Asian	AIAN	Hisp.
Enrollment (%)	100.0	48.2	12.2	8.2	0.6	30.8
Drop-out Rate (%)	n/a	n/a	n/a	n/a	n/a	n/a
H.S. Diplomas (#)	1,087	624	144	104	4	211

Number of Schools

Rank	Number	District Name	City
1	136	Boston	Boston
2	48	Springfield	Springfield
3	47	Worcester	Worcester
4	31	Fall River	Fall River
5	28	Lynn	Lynn
5	28	New Bedford	New Bedford
7	25	Brockton	Brockton
7	25	Lowell	Lowell
9	22	Newton	Newtonville
10	18	Quincy	Quincy
11	17	Haverhill	Haverhill
12	16	Lawrence	Lawrence
12	16	Taunton	Taunton
14	15	Chicopee	Chicopee
15	14	Plymouth	Plymouth
15	14	Westfield	Westfield
17	13	Cambridge	Cambridge
17	13	Framingham	Framingham
17	13	Holyoke	Holyoke
17	13	Pittsfield	Pittsfield
17	13	Somerville	Somerville
22	12	Weymouth	Weymouth
22	12	Woburn	Woburn
24	11	Barnstable	Hyannis
24	11	Wachusett	Jefferson
26	10	Andover	Andover
26	10	Arlington	Arlington
26	10	Attleboro	Attleboro
26	10	Brookline	Brookline
26	10	Fitchburg	Fitchburg
26	10	Franklin	Franklin
26	10	Leominster	Leominster
26	10	Peabody	Peabody
26	10	Salem	Salem
26	10	Waltham	Waltham
26	10	Westford	Westford
37	9	Beverly	Beverly
37	9	Billerica	Billerica
37	9	Braintree	Braintree
37	9	Chelsea	Chelsea
37	9	Lexington	Lexington
37	9	Medford	Medford
37	9	North Attleborough	N Attleborough
37	9	Wellesley	Wellesley
45	8	Agawam	Feeding Hills
45	8	Athol-Royalston	Athol
45	8	Chelmsford	N Chelmsford
45	8	Dennis-Yarmouth	South Yarmouth
45	8	Gloucester	Gloucester
45	8	Hampden-Wilbraham	Wilbraham
45	8	Natick	Natick
45	8	North Andover	North Andover
45	8	North Middlesex	Townsend
45	8	Norwood	Norwood
45	8	Randolph	Randolph
45	8	Revere	Revere
45	8	Shrewsbury	Shrewsbury
45	8	Stoughton	Stoughton
45	8	Tewksbury	Tewksbury
45	8	West Springfield	W Springfield
45	8	Whitman-Hanson	Whitman
45	8	Wilmington	Wilmington
63	7	Bellingham	Bellingham
63	7	Bridgewater-Raynham	Raynham
63	7	Danvers	Danvers
63	7	Dartmouth	South Dartmouth
63	7	Dedham	Dedham
63	7	Dracut	Dracut
63	7	Dudley-Charlton Reg	Dudley
63	7	Easton	North Easton
63	7	Falmouth	East Falmouth
63	7	Greenfield	Greenfield
63	7	Malden	Malden
63	7	Marblehead	Marblehead
63	7	Marlborough	Marlborough
63	7	Marshfield	Marshfield
63	7	Melrose	Melrose
63	7	Milford	Milford
63	7	Nashoba	Bolton
63	7	Needham	Needham
63	7	Reading	Reading
63	7	Spencer-E Brookfield	Spencer
63	7	Walpole	Walpole
63	7	Wareham	Wareham
63	7	Westwood	Westwood
63	7	Winchester	Winchester
87	6	Abington	Abington
87	6	Auburn	Auburn
87	6	Belchertown	Belchertown
87	6	Belmont	Belmont
87	6	Burlington	Burlington
87	6	Central Berkshire	Dalton
87	6	Everett	Everett
87	6	Fairhaven	Fairhaven
87	6	Gardner	Gardner
87	6	Groton-Dunstable	Groton
87	6	Hopkinton	Hopkinton
87	6	Hudson	Hudson
87	6	Longmeadow	Longmeadow
87	6	Ludlow	Ludlow
87	6	Methuen	Methuen
87	6	Middleborough	Middleborough
87	6	Milton	Milton
87	6	Narragansett	Baldwinville
87	6	Northampton	Northampton
87	6	Pentucket	West Newbury
87	6	Quabbin	Barre
87	6	Saugus	Saugus
87	6	Scituate	Scituate
87	6	Somerset	Somerset
87	6	Stoneham	Stoneham
87	6	Swampscott	Swampscott
87	6	Swansea	Swansea
87	6	Wakefield	Wakefield
87	6	Westborough	Westborough
116	5	Acton	Acton
116	5	Ashburnham-Westminster	Westminster
116	5	Ashland	Ashland
116	5	Blackstone-Millville	Blackstone
116	5	Bourne	Bourne
116	5	Canton	Canton
116	5	Dighton-Rehoboth	Rehoboth
116	5	East Longmeadow	E Longmeadow
116	5	Easthampton	Easthampton
116	5	Foxborough	Foxborough
116	5	Grafton	Grafton
116	5	Hamilton-Wenham	Wenham
116	5	Hanover	Hanover
116	5	Hingham	Hingham
116	5	Mansfield	Mansfield
116	5	Medfield	Medfield
116	5	Medway	Medway
116	5	Mohawk Trail	Shelburne Falls
116	5	Newburyport	Newburyport
116	5	North Adams	North Adams
116	5	North Reading	North Reading
116	5	Northborough	Northborough
116	5	Northbridge	Whitinsville
116	5	Norton	Norton
116	5	Rockland	Rockland
116	5	Seekonk	Seekonk
116	5	Sharon	Sharon
116	5	Southbridge	Southbridge
116	5	Sudbury	Sudbury
116	5	Triton	Byfield
116	5	Watertown	Watertown
116	5	Wayland	Wayland
116	5	Weston	Weston
149	4	Adams-Cheshire	Cheshire
149	4	Amesbury	Amesbury
149	4	Bedford	Bedford
149	4	Carver	Carver
149	4	Concord	Concord
149	4	Douglas	Douglas
149	4	Duxbury	Duxbury
149	4	Holliston	Holliston
149	4	Ipswich	Ipswich
149	4	Leicester	Leicester
149	4	Littleton	Littleton
149	4	Lynnfield	Lynnfield
149	4	Mendon-Upton	Mendon
149	4	Norwell	Norwell
149	4	Oxford	Oxford
149	4	Sandwich	Sandwich
149	4	South Hadley	South Hadley
149	4	Sutton	Sutton
149	4	Tyngsborough	Tyngsborough
149	4	Westport	Westport
149	4	Winthrop	Winthrop
170	3	Clinton	Clinton
170	3	East Bridgewater	E Bridgewater
170	3	Georgetown	Georgetown
170	3	Harwich	Harwich
170	3	Lunenburg	Lunenburg
170	3	Mashpee	Mashpee
170	3	Millbury	Millbury
170	3	Monson	Monson
170	3	Palmer	Palmer
170	3	Pembroke	Pembroke
170	3	Southborough	Northborough
170	3	Southwick-Tolland	Southwick
170	3	Tantasqua	Fiskdale
170	3	Uxbridge	Uxbridge
170	3	Webster	Webster
170	3	Winchendon	Winchendon
186	2	Acton-Boxborough	Acton
186	2	Amherst-Pelham	Amherst
186	2	Freetown-Lakeville	Lakeville
186	2	King Philip	Wrentham
186	2	Masconomet	Topsfield
186	2	Nauset	Orleans
186	2	Silver Lake	Kingston
193	1	Greater Lowell Voc Tec	Tyngsborough
193	1	Greater New Bedford	New Bedford

Number of Teachers

Rank	Number	District Name	City
1	3,926	Boston	Boston
2	2,302	Springfield	Springfield
3	1,891	Worcester	Worcester
4	1,147	Brockton	Brockton
5	1,110	Lowell	Lowell
6	1,085	New Bedford	New Bedford
7	1,080	Lynn	Lynn
8	967	Newton	Newtonville
9	898	Lawrence	Lawrence
10	874	Fall River	Fall River
11	670	Quincy	Quincy
12	651	Cambridge	Cambridge
13	647	Holyoke	Holyoke
14	642	Framingham	Framingham
15	628	Plymouth	Plymouth
16	582	Chicopee	Chicopee
17	550	Haverhill	Haverhill
18	523	Westfield	Westfield
19	511	Brookline	Brookline
20	504	Weymouth	Weymouth
21	502	Pittsfield	Pittsfield
22	495	Lexington	Lexington
23	493	Taunton	Taunton
24	470	Methuen	Methuen
25	467	Chelsea	Chelsea
26	465	Attleboro	Attleboro
27	465	Peabody	Peabody
28	454	Malden	Malden
29	445	Somerville	Somerville
30	444	Waltham	Waltham
31	437	Fitchburg	Fitchburg
32	436	Barnstable	Hyannis
33	434	Wachusett	Jefferson
34	434	Billerica	Billerica
35	426	Medford	Medford
36	425	Andover	Andover
37	408	Salem	Salem
38	407	Franklin	Franklin
39	390	Leominster	Leominster
40	380	Revere	Revere
41	377	Chelmsford	N Chelmsford
42	370	Marlborough	Marlborough
43	368	Westford	Westford
44	366	Everett	Everett
45	364	Needham	Needham
46	359	Dennis-Yarmouth	South Yarmouth
47	358	Woburn	Woburn
48	347	Falmouth	East Falmouth
49	346	Shrewsbury	Shrewsbury
50	343	Beverly	Beverly
51	338	Bridgewater-Raynham	Raynham
52	336	Natick	Natick
53	333	Marshfield	Marshfield
54	333	Braintree	Braintree
55	327	North Middlesex	Townsend
56	325	Agawam	Feeding Hills
57	324	Wellesley	Wellesley
58	322	Milford	Milford
59	322	North Attleborough	N Attleborough
60	314	Sharon	Sharon
61	308	Mansfield	Mansfield
62	307	Gloucester	Gloucester
63	304	West Springfield	W Springfield
64	304	Arlington	Arlington
65	288	North Andover	North Andover
66	287	Whitman-Hanson	Whitman
67	286	Watertown	Watertown
68	282	Dudley-Charlton Reg	Dudley
69	281	Reading	Reading
70	281	Norwood	Norwood
71	279	Westborough	Westborough
72	279	Stoughton	Stoughton
73	279	Tewksbury	Tewksbury
74	273	Burlington	Burlington
75	266	Randolph	Randolph
76	265	Wakefield	Wakefield
77	263	Winchester	Winchester

Rank	Number	District Name	City
78	262	Danvers	Danvers
79	260	Dartmouth	South Dartmouth
80	259	Dracut	Dracut
81	258	Hampden-Wilbraham	Wilbraham
82	256	Wilmington	Wilmington
83	252	Sandwich	Sandwich
84	250	Belmont	Belmont
85	249	Hingham	Hingham
86	245	Easton	North Easton
87	244	Walpole	Walpole
88	244	Wareham	Wareham
89	242	Milton	Milton
90	239	Pentucket	West Newbury
91	238	Dedham	Dedham
92	232	Hopkinton	Hopkinton
93	231	Middleborough	Middleborough
94	229	Longmeadow	Longmeadow
95	227	Medfield	Medfield
96	223	Somerset	Somerset
97	221	Ludlow	Ludlow
97	221	Saugus	Saugus
99	221	Silver Lake	Kingston
100	221	Melrose	Melrose
101	219	Scituate	Scituate
102	218	Westwood	Westwood
103	218	Marblehead	Marblehead
104	217	Nashoba	Bolton
104	217	Northampton	Northampton
106	216	Hanover	Hanover
107	216	Quabbin	Barre
108	216	Duxbury	Duxbury
109	214	Canton	Canton
110	214	Dighton-Rehoboth	Rehoboth
111	213	Holliston	Holliston
112	211	Triton	Byfield
113	211	Sudbury	Sudbury
114	211	Gardner	Gardner
115	210	Hudson	Hudson
116	209	Foxborough	Foxborough
117	208	Southbridge	Southbridge
118	204	Norton	Norton
119	203	Wayland	Wayland
120	195	Stoneham	Stoneham
121	195	Amesbury	Amesbury
122	193	East Longmeadow	E Longmeadow
123	190	Bellingham	Bellingham
124	188	Bedford	Bedford
125	187	Weston	Weston
126	187	Greater New Bedford	New Bedford
127	180	Greater Lowell Voc Tec	Tyngsborough
128	180	Newburyport	Newburyport
129	178	North Adams	North Adams
130	178	Northbridge	Whitinsville
131	176	Ashland	Ashland
132	174	Mendon-Upton	Mendon
133	171	Swansea	Swansea
134	171	Mashpee	Mashpee
135	170	Rockland	Rockland
136	170	Groton-Dunstable	Groton
137	169	Medway	Medway
138	168	Swampscott	Swampscott
139	167	Amherst-Pelham	Amherst
140	164	North Reading	North Reading
141	163	Auburn	Auburn
141	163	Greenfield	Greenfield
143	162	Bourne	Bourne
144	161	Grafton	Grafton
144	161	South Hadley	South Hadley
146	160	Palmer	Palmer
147	159	Seekonk	Seekonk
148	158	Tyngsborough	Tyngsborough
149	158	Carver	Carver
150	157	Acton-Boxborough	Acton
151	156	Hamilton-Wenham	Wenham
152	155	Blackstone-Millville	Blackstone
153	155	Spencer-E Brookfield	Spencer
154	154	Uxbridge	Uxbridge
155	153	Fairhaven	Fairhaven
156	153	Ashburnham-Westminster	Westminster
157	153	Athol-Royalston	Athol
158	153	Winthrop	Winthrop
159	152	Belchertown	Belchertown
160	150	Concord	Concord
161	149	Adams-Cheshire	Cheshire
162	149	Ipswich	Ipswich
163	148	Winchendon	Winchendon
164	148	East Bridgewater	E Bridgewater
165	146	Central Berkshire	Dalton
166	145	Acton	Acton
167	145	Nauset	Orleans
168	143	Norwell	Norwell
169	142	Lynnfield	Lynnfield
170	142	Webster	Webster
171	140	Clinton	Clinton
172	137	Tantasqua	Fiskdale
173	137	Northborough	Northborough
174	136	Leicester	Leicester
175	132	Easthampton	Easthampton
176	131	Oxford	Oxford
177	129	Abington	Abington
178	127	Southwick-Tolland	Southwick
179	126	Freetown-Lakeville	Lakeville
180	125	Millbury	Millbury
181	124	Masconomet	Topsfield
182	123	Westport	Westport
183	119	King Philip	Wrentham
184	119	Mohawk Trail	Shelburne Falls
185	118	Lunenburg	Lunenburg
186	117	Harwich	Harwich
187	114	Southborough	Northborough
188	112	Narragansett	Baldwinville
189	109	Georgetown	Georgetown
190	106	Littleton	Littleton
191	105	Monson	Monson
192	99	Sutton	Sutton
193	98	Douglas	Douglas
194	79	Pembroke	Pembroke

Number of Students

Rank	Number	District Name	City
1	60,150	Boston	Boston
2	26,132	Springfield	Springfield
3	25,028	Worcester	Worcester
4	16,454	Brockton	Brockton
5	15,105	Lowell	Lowell
6	14,618	Lynn	Lynn
7	14,546	New Bedford	New Bedford
8	12,508	Lawrence	Lawrence
9	11,697	Fall River	Fall River
10	11,415	Newton	Newtonville
11	8,897	Quincy	Quincy
12	8,754	Plymouth	Plymouth
13	8,388	Taunton	Taunton
14	8,102	Framingham	Framingham
15	8,043	Haverhill	Haverhill
16	7,528	Chicopee	Chicopee
17	7,245	Holyoke	Holyoke
18	7,230	Methuen	Methuen
19	6,987	Wachusett	Jefferson
20	6,890	Weymouth	Weymouth
21	6,625	Peabody	Peabody
22	6,605	Pittsfield	Pittsfield
23	6,574	Westfield	Westfield
24	6,531	Attleboro	Attleboro
25	6,437	Cambridge	Cambridge
26	6,395	Billerica	Billerica
27	6,228	Leominster	Leominster
28	6,175	Lexington	Lexington
29	6,135	Malden	Malden
30	6,061	Bridgewater-Raynham	Raynham
31	6,018	Brookline	Brookline
32	5,939	Andover	Andover
33	5,826	Franklin	Franklin
34	5,773	Chelmsford	N Chelmsford
35	5,757	Fitchburg	Fitchburg
36	5,711	Revere	Revere
37	5,672	Chelsea	Chelsea
38	5,616	Somerville	Somerville
39	5,586	Barnstable	Hyannis
40	5,557	Shrewsbury	Shrewsbury
41	5,321	Everett	Everett
42	5,112	Westford	Westford
43	4,999	Braintree	Braintree
44	4,923	Salem	Salem
45	4,851	Marlborough	Marlborough
46	4,765	Tewksbury	Tewksbury
47	4,742	Mansfield	Mansfield
48	4,722	Needham	Needham
49	4,716	Medford	Medford
50	4,702	Woburn	Woburn
51	4,678	North Middlesex	Townsend
52	4,668	North Attleborough	N Attleborough
53	4,667	Waltham	Waltham
54	4,604	Natick	Natick
55	4,598	Marshfield	Marshfield
56	4,557	Beverly	Beverly
57	4,452	Whitman-Hanson	Whitman
58	4,444	Falmouth	East Falmouth
59	4,425	Arlington	Arlington
60	4,358	North Andover	North Andover
61	4,335	Agawam	Feeding Hills
62	4,334	Dudley-Charlton Reg	Dudley
63	4,267	Dartmouth	South Dartmouth
64	4,263	Dracut	Dracut
65	4,260	Reading	Reading
66	4,252	Wellesley	Wellesley
67	4,205	Dennis-Yarmouth	South Yarmouth
68	4,185	Milford	Milford
69	4,148	Sandwich	Sandwich
70	4,067	Stoughton	Stoughton
71	4,019	Gloucester	Gloucester
72	3,965	West Springfield	W Springfield
73	3,852	Hampden-Wilbraham	Wilbraham
74	3,826	Easton	North Easton
75	3,811	Randolph	Randolph
76	3,792	Wilmington	Wilmington
77	3,727	Norwood	Norwood
78	3,713	Belmont	Belmont
79	3,686	Middleborough	Middleborough
80	3,657	Danvers	Danvers
81	3,629	Walpole	Walpole
82	3,590	Hingham	Hingham
83	3,572	Melrose	Melrose
83	3,572	Milton	Milton
85	3,571	Winchester	Winchester
86	3,561	Sharon	Sharon
87	3,551	Triton	Byfield
88	3,507	Westborough	Westborough
89	3,488	Pentucket	West Newbury
90	3,486	Burlington	Burlington
91	3,484	Wareham	Wareham
92	3,453	Wakefield	Wakefield
93	3,390	Dighton-Rehoboth	Rehoboth
94	3,389	Longmeadow	Longmeadow
95	3,355	Hopkinton	Hopkinton
96	3,306	Saugus	Saugus
97	3,293	Duxbury	Duxbury
98	3,259	Gardner	Gardner
99	3,224	Quabbin	Barre
100	3,182	Norton	Norton
101	3,143	Scituate	Scituate
102	3,117	Holliston	Holliston
103	3,101	Sudbury	Sudbury
104	3,077	Ludlow	Ludlow
105	3,063	Nashoba	Bolton
106	3,047	Medfield	Medfield
107	3,016	Marblehead	Marblehead
108	3,006	Canton	Canton
109	2,996	Dedham	Dedham
110	2,990	Stoneham	Stoneham
111	2,985	Wayland	Wayland
112	2,978	Northampton	Northampton
113	2,949	Silver Lake	Kingston
114	2,895	Groton-Dunstable	Groton
115	2,887	Foxborough	Foxborough
116	2,886	Medway	Medway
116	2,886	Somerset	Somerset
118	2,775	Hanover	Hanover
119	2,769	Hudson	Hudson
120	2,761	Westwood	Westwood
121	2,748	East Longmeadow	E Longmeadow
122	2,729	Bellingham	Bellingham
123	2,722	Rockland	Rockland
124	2,720	Amesbury	Amesbury
125	2,664	North Reading	North Reading
126	2,611	Acton-Boxborough	Acton
127	2,592	Southbridge	Southbridge
128	2,590	Ashland	Ashland
129	2,574	Mendon-Upton	Mendon
130	2,544	Northbridge	Whitinsville
131	2,530	Bourne	Bourne
132	2,522	Acton	Acton
133	2,513	Belchertown	Belchertown
134	2,454	Abington	Abington
135	2,453	Grafton	Grafton
136	2,433	Ashburnham-Westminster	Westminster
137	2,422	East Bridgewater	E Bridgewater
138	2,394	Watertown	Watertown
139	2,382	Swampscott	Swampscott
140	2,381	Newburyport	Newburyport
141	2,371	Auburn	Auburn
142	2,370	Weston	Weston
143	2,328	Seekonk	Seekonk
144	2,303	South Hadley	South Hadley
145	2,294	Blackstone-Millville	Blackstone
146	2,286	Central Berkshire	Dalton
147	2,269	Tyngsborough	Tyngsborough
148	2,257	Fairhaven	Fairhaven
149	2,253	Spencer-E Brookfield	Spencer
150	2,246	Bedford	Bedford
151	2,241	Oxford	Oxford
152	2,236	Uxbridge	Uxbridge
153	2,213	Hamilton-Wenham	Wenham
154	2,200	Athol-Royalston	Athol
155	2,188	Swansea	Swansea
156	2,164	Mashpee	Mashpee

157	2,149	Winthrop	Winthrop
158	2,120	Greenfield	Greenfield
159	2,094	Carver	Carver
159	2,094	Ipswich	Ipswich
161	2,090	Palmer	Palmer
162	2,070	North Adams	North Adams
163	2,063	Norwell	Norwell
164	2,041	Amherst-Pelham	Amherst
165	2,031	Lynnfield	Lynnfield
166	2,020	Clinton	Clinton
167	2,008	Millbury	Millbury
168	1,993	Masconomet	Topsfield
169	1,974	Concord	Concord
170	1,940	Leicester	Leicester
171	1,936	Northborough	Northborough
172	1,923	Southwick-Tolland	Southwick
173	1,922	King Philip	Wrentham
174	1,903	Pembroke	Pembroke
175	1,901	Westport	Westport
176	1,896	Freetown-Lakeville	Lakeville
177	1,893	Greater Lowell Voc Tec	Tyngsborough
178	1,877	Winchendon	Winchendon
179	1,856	Greater New Bedford	New Bedford
180	1,844	Adams-Cheshire	Cheshire
181	1,830	Lunenburg	Lunenburg
182	1,825	Nauset	Orleans
183	1,818	Webster	Webster
184	1,761	Tantasqua	Fiskdale
185	1,660	Sutton	Sutton
186	1,635	Narragansett	Baldwinville
187	1,634	Easthampton	Easthampton
188	1,617	Georgetown	Georgetown
189	1,607	Southborough	Northborough
190	1,585	Douglas	Douglas
191	1,564	Littleton	Littleton
192	1,544	Monson	Monson
193	1,529	Mohawk Trail	Shelburne Falls
194	1,522	Harwich	Harwich

Male Students

Rank	Percent	District Name	City
1	54.6	Greater New Bedford	New Bedford
2	53.6	Uxbridge	Uxbridge
3	53.2	Athol-Royalston	Athol
4	53.1	Mohawk Trail	Shelburne Falls
5	53.0	Millbury	Millbury
6	53.0	North Andover	North Andover
7	52.9	Groton-Dunstable	Groton
8	52.8	Ashburnham-Westminster	Westminster
9	52.8	Westfield	Westfield
10	52.8	North Attleborough	N Attleborough
11	52.8	Randolph	Randolph
12	52.7	Mansfield	Mansfield
13	52.7	Oxford	Oxford
14	52.7	Northborough	Northborough
15	52.7	Revere	Revere
16	52.7	West Springfield	W Springfield
17	52.6	Longmeadow	Longmeadow
18	52.6	Newburyport	Newburyport
19	52.5	Norton	Norton
20	52.5	Rockland	Rockland
21	52.4	Dracut	Dracut
22	52.4	Duxbury	Duxbury
23	52.3	Needham	Needham
24	52.3	Westford	Westford
25	52.3	Harwich	Harwich
26	52.3	Natick	Natick
27	52.2	Middleborough	Middleborough
28	52.2	Lunenburg	Lunenburg
29	52.2	Plymouth	Plymouth
30	52.2	Hudson	Hudson
31	52.1	Central Berkshire	Dalton
32	52.1	Wareham	Wareham
33	52.1	Dennis-Yarmouth	South Yarmouth
34	52.1	Greater Lowell Voc Tec	Tyngsborough
35	52.0	Grafton	Grafton
36	52.0	Dighton-Rehoboth	Rehoboth
37	52.0	Stoughton	Stoughton
38	52.0	Southbridge	Southbridge
39	52.0	Spencer-E Brookfield	Spencer
40	51.9	Gloucester	Gloucester
41	51.9	Swansea	Swansea
42	51.9	Triton	Byfield
43	51.9	Lowell	Lowell
44	51.9	Hampden-Wilbraham	Wilbraham
45	51.9	Westport	Westport
46	51.9	Amesbury	Amesbury
47	51.8	Medford	Medford
48	51.8	Waltham	Waltham
49	51.8	Marshfield	Marshfield
50	51.7	Lynn	Lynn
51	51.7	Agawam	Feeding Hills
52	51.7	Leominster	Leominster
53	51.7	Clinton	Clinton
54	51.7	Methuen	Methuen
55	51.7	Quincy	Quincy
56	51.7	Norwell	Norwell
57	51.7	Acton	Acton
58	51.6	Billerica	Billerica
59	51.6	Brockton	Brockton
60	51.6	Boston	Boston
61	51.6	Holyoke	Holyoke
62	51.6	Haverhill	Haverhill
63	51.6	Ludlow	Ludlow
64	51.6	Cambridge	Cambridge
65	51.6	Greenfield	Greenfield
66	51.5	Springfield	Springfield
67	51.5	Worcester	Worcester
68	51.5	New Bedford	New Bedford
69	51.5	Weymouth	Weymouth
70	51.5	Lynnfield	Lynnfield
71	51.5	Wachusett	Jefferson
72	51.5	Nashoba	Bolton
73	51.5	Easton	North Easton
74	51.5	Marlborough	Marlborough
75	51.5	Abington	Abington
76	51.4	South Hadley	South Hadley
77	51.4	Northbridge	Whitinsville
78	51.4	Wayland	Wayland
79	51.4	Braintree	Braintree
80	51.4	Andover	Andover
81	51.4	Lawrence	Lawrence
82	51.4	Whitman-Hanson	Whitman
83	51.4	Watertown	Watertown
84	51.4	Silver Lake	Kingston
85	51.4	Taunton	Taunton
86	51.3	Sandwich	Sandwich
87	51.3	Chelmsford	N Chelmsford
88	51.3	Malden	Malden
89	51.3	Leicester	Leicester
90	51.3	Burlington	Burlington
91	51.3	Fall River	Fall River
92	51.3	Pittsfield	Pittsfield
93	51.3	Weston	Weston
94	51.3	Milford	Milford
95	51.2	Seekonk	Seekonk
96	51.2	Milton	Milton
97	51.2	Belmont	Belmont
98	51.2	Amherst-Pelham	Amherst
99	51.2	Auburn	Auburn
100	51.2	Pembroke	Pembroke
101	51.2	Southwick-Tolland	Southwick
102	51.2	Wilmington	Wilmington
103	51.1	Attleboro	Attleboro
104	51.1	Newton	Newtonville
105	51.1	Chicopee	Chicopee
106	51.1	Palmer	Palmer
107	51.0	Bridgewater-Raynham	Raynham
108	51.0	Adams-Cheshire	Cheshire
109	51.0	Reading	Reading
110	51.0	Holliston	Holliston
111	51.0	Barnstable	Hyannis
112	51.0	Dartmouth	South Dartmouth
113	51.0	Marblehead	Marblehead
114	51.0	Chelsea	Chelsea
115	51.0	Acton-Boxborough	Acton
116	50.9	North Middlesex	Townsend
117	50.9	North Reading	North Reading
118	50.9	Medfield	Medfield
119	50.8	Tantasqua	Fiskdale
120	50.8	Georgetown	Georgetown
121	50.8	Narragansett	Baldwinville
122	50.8	Somerville	Somerville
123	50.8	Carver	Carver
124	50.8	Tyngsborough	Tyngsborough
125	50.8	Easthampton	Easthampton
126	50.8	Hopkinton	Hopkinton
127	50.8	Saugus	Saugus
128	50.8	Fairhaven	Fairhaven
129	50.7	Melrose	Melrose
130	50.7	Somerset	Somerset
131	50.7	Bourne	Bourne
132	50.7	Franklin	Franklin
133	50.7	Northampton	Northampton
134	50.6	Hingham	Hingham
135	50.6	Falmouth	East Falmouth
136	50.6	Douglas	Douglas
137	50.6	East Longmeadow	E Longmeadow
138	50.6	Peabody	Peabody
139	50.6	Lexington	Lexington
140	50.6	Mendon-Upton	Mendon
141	50.6	Brookline	Brookline
142	50.6	Norwood	Norwood
143	50.6	Mashpee	Mashpee
144	50.5	Swampscott	Swampscott
145	50.5	East Bridgewater	E Bridgewater
146	50.5	Tewksbury	Tewksbury
147	50.5	Pentucket	West Newbury
148	50.5	Canton	Canton
149	50.5	Winchendon	Winchendon
150	50.5	Westborough	Westborough
151	50.5	Medway	Medway
152	50.5	Webster	Webster
153	50.5	Foxborough	Foxborough
154	50.4	Woburn	Woburn
155	50.4	Sudbury	Sudbury
156	50.4	Arlington	Arlington
157	50.4	Stoneham	Stoneham
158	50.4	Ashland	Ashland
159	50.3	Freetown-Lakeville	Lakeville
160	50.3	Shrewsbury	Shrewsbury
161	50.3	Blackstone-Millville	Blackstone
162	50.3	Southborough	Northborough
163	50.3	Quabbin	Barre
164	50.3	Hanover	Hanover
165	50.2	Salem	Salem
166	50.2	Beverly	Beverly
167	50.2	Scituate	Scituate
168	50.1	Everett	Everett
169	50.1	Fitchburg	Fitchburg
170	50.1	Westwood	Westwood
171	50.1	Winchester	Winchester
172	50.1	Nauset	Orleans
173	50.1	Hamilton-Wenham	Wenham
174	50.0	Wakefield	Wakefield
175	49.9	Walpole	Walpole
176	49.9	Belchertown	Belchertown
177	49.9	Dudley-Charlton Reg	Dudley
178	49.9	Framingham	Framingham
179	49.8	Dedham	Dedham
180	49.8	Gardner	Gardner
181	49.8	Wellesley	Wellesley
182	49.7	Bellingham	Bellingham
183	49.7	Sutton	Sutton
184	49.4	Bedford	Bedford
185	49.3	Winthrop	Winthrop
186	49.3	Sharon	Sharon
187	49.1	Ipswich	Ipswich
188	49.1	Monson	Monson
189	48.8	Masconomet	Topsfield
190	48.7	Littleton	Littleton
191	48.0	King Philip	Wrentham
192	48.0	Concord	Concord
193	47.6	Danvers	Danvers
194	46.9	North Adams	North Adams

Female Students

Rank	Percent	District Name	City
1	53.0	North Adams	North Adams
2	52.3	Danvers	Danvers
3	51.9	Concord	Concord
4	51.9	King Philip	Wrentham
5	51.2	Littleton	Littleton
6	51.1	Masconomet	Topsfield
7	50.8	Monson	Monson
8	50.8	Ipswich	Ipswich
9	50.6	Sharon	Sharon
10	50.6	Winthrop	Winthrop
11	50.5	Bedford	Bedford
12	50.2	Sutton	Sutton
13	50.2	Bellingham	Bellingham
14	50.1	Wellesley	Wellesley
15	50.1	Gardner	Gardner
16	50.1	Dedham	Dedham
17	50.0	Framingham	Framingham
18	50.0	Dudley-Charlton Reg	Dudley
19	50.0	Belchertown	Belchertown
20	50.0	Walpole	Walpole
21	49.9	Wakefield	Wakefield
22	49.8	Hamilton-Wenham	Wenham
23	49.8	Nauset	Orleans
24	49.8	Winchester	Winchester
25	49.8	Westwood	Westwood
26	49.8	Fitchburg	Fitchburg
27	49.8	Everett	Everett
28	49.7	Scituate	Scituate
29	49.7	Beverly	Beverly
30	49.7	Salem	Salem
31	49.6	Hanover	Hanover
32	49.6	Quabbin	Barre
33	49.6	Southborough	Northborough
34	49.6	Blackstone-Millville	Blackstone
35	49.6	Shrewsbury	Shrewsbury
36	49.6	Freetown-Lakeville	Lakeville
37	49.5	Ashland	Ashland
38	49.5	Stoneham	Stoneham
39	49.5	Arlington	Arlington

Rank	Percent	District Name	City
40	49.5	Sudbury	Sudbury
41	49.5	Woburn	Woburn
42	49.4	Foxborough	Foxborough
43	49.4	Webster	Webster
44	49.4	Medway	Medway
45	49.4	Westborough	Westborough
46	49.4	Winchendon	Winchendon
47	49.4	Canton	Canton
48	49.4	Pentucket	West Newbury
49	49.4	Tewksbury	Tewksbury
50	49.4	East Bridgewater	E Bridgewater
51	49.4	Swampscott	Swampscott
52	49.3	Mashpee	Mashpee
53	49.3	Norwood	Norwood
54	49.3	Brookline	Brookline
55	49.3	Mendon-Upton	Mendon
56	49.3	Lexington	Lexington
57	49.3	Peabody	Peabody
58	49.3	East Longmeadow	E Longmeadow
59	49.3	Douglas	Douglas
60	49.3	Falmouth	East Falmouth
61	49.3	Hingham	Hingham
62	49.2	Northampton	Northampton
63	49.2	Franklin	Franklin
64	49.2	Bourne	Bourne
65	49.2	Somerset	Somerset
66	49.2	Melrose	Melrose
67	49.1	Fairhaven	Fairhaven
68	49.1	Saugus	Saugus
69	49.1	Hopkinton	Hopkinton
70	49.1	Easthampton	Easthampton
71	49.1	Tyngsborough	Tyngsborough
72	49.1	Carver	Carver
73	49.1	Somerville	Somerville
74	49.1	Narragansett	Baldwinville
75	49.1	Georgetown	Georgetown
76	49.0	Tantasqua	Fiskdale
77	49.0	Medfield	Medfield
78	49.0	North Reading	North Reading
79	49.0	North Middlesex	Townsend
80	48.9	Acton-Boxborough	Acton
81	48.9	Chelsea	Chelsea
82	48.9	Marblehead	Marblehead
83	48.9	Dartmouth	South Dartmouth
84	48.9	Barnstable	Hyannis
85	48.9	Holliston	Holliston
86	48.9	Reading	Reading
87	48.9	Adams-Cheshire	Cheshire
88	48.9	Bridgewater-Raynham	Raynham
89	48.8	Palmer	Palmer
90	48.8	Chicopee	Chicopee
91	48.8	Newton	Newtonville
92	48.8	Attleboro	Attleboro
93	48.7	Wilmington	Wilmington
94	48.7	Southwick-Tolland	Southwick
95	48.7	Pembroke	Pembroke
96	48.7	Auburn	Auburn
97	48.7	Amherst-Pelham	Amherst
98	48.7	Belmont	Belmont
99	48.7	Milton	Milton
100	48.7	Seekonk	Seekonk
101	48.6	Milford	Milford
102	48.6	Weston	Weston
103	48.6	Pittsfield	Pittsfield
104	48.6	Fall River	Fall River
105	48.6	Burlington	Burlington
106	48.6	Leicester	Leicester
107	48.6	Malden	Malden
108	48.6	Chelmsford	N Chelmsford
109	48.6	Sandwich	Sandwich
110	48.5	Taunton	Taunton
111	48.5	Silver Lake	Kingston
112	48.5	Watertown	Watertown
113	48.5	Whitman-Hanson	Whitman
114	48.5	Lawrence	Lawrence
115	48.5	Andover	Andover
116	48.5	Braintree	Braintree
117	48.5	Wayland	Wayland
118	48.5	Northbridge	Whitinsville
119	48.5	South Hadley	South Hadley
120	48.4	Abington	Abington
121	48.4	Marlborough	Marlborough
122	48.4	Easton	North Easton
123	48.4	Nashoba	Bolton
124	48.4	Wachusett	Jefferson
125	48.4	Lynnfield	Lynnfield
126	48.4	Weymouth	Weymouth
127	48.4	New Bedford	New Bedford
128	48.4	Worcester	Worcester
129	48.4	Springfield	Springfield
130	48.3	Greenfield	Greenfield
131	48.3	Cambridge	Cambridge
132	48.3	Ludlow	Ludlow
133	48.3	Haverhill	Haverhill
134	48.3	Holyoke	Holyoke
135	48.3	Boston	Boston
136	48.3	Brockton	Brockton
137	48.3	Billerica	Billerica
138	48.2	Acton	Acton
139	48.2	Norwell	Norwell
140	48.2	Quincy	Quincy
141	48.2	Methuen	Methuen
142	48.2	Clinton	Clinton
143	48.2	Leominster	Leominster
144	48.2	Agawam	Feeding Hills
145	48.2	Lynn	Lynn
146	48.1	Marshfield	Marshfield
147	48.1	Waltham	Waltham
148	48.1	Medford	Medford
149	48.0	Amesbury	Amesbury
150	48.0	Westport	Westport
151	48.0	Hampden-Wilbraham	Wilbraham
152	48.0	Lowell	Lowell
153	48.0	Triton	Byfield
154	48.0	Swansea	Swansea
155	48.0	Gloucester	Gloucester
156	47.9	Spencer-E Brookfield	Spencer
157	47.9	Southbridge	Southbridge
158	47.9	Stoughton	Stoughton
159	47.9	Dighton-Rehoboth	Rehoboth
160	47.9	Grafton	Grafton
161	47.8	Greater Lowell Voc Tec	Tyngsborough
162	47.8	Dennis-Yarmouth	South Yarmouth
163	47.8	Wareham	Wareham
164	47.8	Central Berkshire	Dalton
165	47.7	Hudson	Hudson
166	47.7	Plymouth	Plymouth
167	47.7	Lunenburg	Lunenburg
168	47.7	Middleborough	Middleborough
169	47.6	Natick	Natick
170	47.6	Harwich	Harwich
171	47.6	Westford	Westford
172	47.6	Needham	Needham
173	47.5	Duxbury	Duxbury
174	47.5	Dracut	Dracut
175	47.4	Rockland	Rockland
176	47.4	Norton	Norton
177	47.3	Newburyport	Newburyport
178	47.3	Longmeadow	Longmeadow
179	47.2	West Springfield	W Springfield
180	47.2	Revere	Revere
181	47.2	Northborough	Northborough
182	47.2	Oxford	Oxford
183	47.2	Mansfield	Mansfield
184	47.1	Randolph	Randolph
185	47.1	North Attleborough	N Attleborough
186	47.1	Westfield	Westfield
187	47.1	Ashburnham-Westminster	Westminster
188	47.0	Groton-Dunstable	Groton
189	46.9	North Andover	North Andover
190	46.9	Millbury	Millbury
191	46.8	Mohawk Trail	Shelburne Falls
192	46.7	Athol-Royalston	Athol
193	46.3	Uxbridge	Uxbridge
194	45.3	Greater New Bedford	New Bedford

Individual Education Program Students

Rank	Percent	District Name	City
1	25.1	Greater Lowell Voc Tec	Tyngsborough
2	22.3	East Longmeadow	E Longmeadow
3	22.2	Cambridge	Cambridge
3	22.2	Holyoke	Holyoke
5	21.5	Somerville	Somerville
6	20.8	Norton	Norton
7	20.6	Randolph	Randolph
8	20.5	Beverly	Beverly
9	20.4	Marlborough	Marlborough
10	20.3	Springfield	Springfield
11	20.2	Waltham	Waltham
12	19.7	Boston	Boston
13	19.4	Gardner	Gardner
14	19.1	Mashpee	Mashpee
15	19.1	Foxborough	Foxborough
15	19.1	Salem	Salem
15	19.1	Weymouth	Weymouth
18	19.0	Spencer-E Brookfield	Spencer
19	18.9	Concord	Concord
20	18.7	Mohawk Trail	Shelburne Falls
21	18.6	Worcester	Worcester
22	18.5	Gloucester	Gloucester
23	18.4	Newton	Newtonville
24	18.2	Ashburnham-Westminster	Westminster
24	18.2	Braintree	Braintree
24	18.2	Winchendon	Winchendon
27	18.0	New Bedford	New Bedford
28	17.9	Dedham	Dedham
28	17.9	Hudson	Hudson
30	17.8	Palmer	Palmer
31	17.7	Brookline	Brookline
31	17.7	Watertown	Watertown
33	17.6	Littleton	Littleton
33	17.6	Westfield	Westfield
35	17.5	Easton	North Easton
36	17.4	Easthampton	Easthampton
36	17.4	Southbridge	Southbridge
38	17.3	Hanover	Hanover
38	17.3	Taunton	Taunton
40	17.2	Amesbury	Amesbury
40	17.2	Mansfield	Mansfield
40	17.2	Walpole	Walpole
43	17.1	Billerica	Billerica
43	17.1	Framingham	Framingham
45	17.0	Amherst-Pelham	Amherst
45	17.0	Northampton	Northampton
45	17.0	Wakefield	Wakefield
48	16.9	Norwood	Norwood
48	16.9	South Hadley	South Hadley
48	16.9	Wayland	Wayland
51	16.8	Fitchburg	Fitchburg
51	16.8	Greenfield	Greenfield
51	16.8	Medford	Medford
54	16.7	Bedford	Bedford
55	16.6	Ludlow	Ludlow
56	16.5	Agawam	Feeding Hills
57	16.3	Adams-Cheshire	Cheshire
57	16.3	Lexington	Lexington
57	16.3	Melrose	Melrose
60	16.2	Hampden-Wilbraham	Wilbraham
60	16.2	Stoughton	Stoughton
62	16.1	Milton	Milton
62	16.1	Winthrop	Winthrop
64	16.0	Attleboro	Attleboro
64	16.0	Malden	Malden
64	16.0	North Adams	North Adams
64	16.0	Wareham	Wareham
68	15.9	Harwich	Harwich
68	15.9	Haverhill	Haverhill
68	15.9	Stoneham	Stoneham
71	15.8	Central Berkshire	Dalton
72	15.7	Athol-Royalston	Athol
72	15.7	Marblehead	Marblehead
72	15.7	North Attleborough	N Attleborough
75	15.6	Burlington	Burlington
75	15.6	Lawrence	Lawrence
75	15.6	Natick	Natick
78	15.5	Canton	Canton
78	15.5	Plymouth	Plymouth
78	15.5	Quincy	Quincy
81	15.4	Bridgewater-Raynham	Raynham
81	15.4	Chicopee	Chicopee
83	15.3	Leominster	Leominster
84	15.2	Millbury	Millbury
84	15.2	Newburyport	Newburyport
86	15.1	Andover	Andover
86	15.1	Nauset	Orleans
86	15.1	Norwell	Norwell
86	15.1	Pittsfield	Pittsfield
90	15.0	Acton-Boxborough	Acton
90	15.0	Clinton	Clinton
90	15.0	Sandwich	Sandwich
90	15.0	Uxbridge	Uxbridge
90	15.0	Westport	Westport
95	14.9	Grafton	Grafton
96	14.8	Blackstone-Millville	Blackstone
96	14.8	Leicester	Leicester
96	14.8	Lynn	Lynn
96	14.8	Narragansett	Baldwinville
96	14.8	Webster	Webster
101	14.7	Chelsea	Chelsea
101	14.7	Medway	Medway
101	14.7	Rockland	Rockland
104	14.6	Swampscott	Swampscott
105	14.5	Marshfield	Marshfield
105	14.5	Reading	Reading
105	14.5	Sharon	Sharon
105	14.5	Weston	Weston
109	14.4	Masconomet	Topsfield
109	14.4	Peabody	Peabody
109	14.4	Whitman-Hanson	Whitman
112	14.3	Fairhaven	Fairhaven
112	14.3	Sudbury	Sudbury
112	14.3	Tantasqua	Fiskdale
112	14.3	Wellesley	Wellesley
116	14.2	Acton	Acton
116	14.2	Everett	Everett
116	14.2	Falmouth	East Falmouth
116	14.2	Middleborough	Middleborough
116	14.2	Tewksbury	Tewksbury

Rank	Percent	District Name	City
121	14.1	Dartmouth	South Dartmouth
121	14.1	Southwick-Tolland	Southwick
121	14.1	Westwood	Westwood
124	14.0	Arlington	Arlington
124	14.0	Belchertown	Belchertown
124	14.0	Fall River	Fall River
124	14.0	King Philip	Wrentham
124	14.0	Milford	Milford
124	14.0	West Springfield	W Springfield
130	13.9	Dennis-Yarmouth	South Yarmouth
130	13.9	Hamilton-Wenham	Wenham
130	13.9	Shrewsbury	Shrewsbury
133	13.8	Swansea	Swansea
134	13.7	Carver	Carver
134	13.7	North Reading	North Reading
134	13.7	Sutton	Sutton
137	13.5	Franklin	Franklin
138	13.3	Bellingham	Bellingham
138	13.3	Ipswich	Ipswich
138	13.3	Lunenburg	Lunenburg
138	13.3	Winchester	Winchester
142	13.2	Pentucket	West Newbury
143	13.1	Revere	Revere
144	13.0	Freetown-Lakeville	Lakeville
144	13.0	Wilmington	Wilmington
146	12.9	Belmont	Belmont
146	12.9	Monson	Monson
148	12.7	Abington	Abington
148	12.7	Brockton	Brockton
148	12.7	Chelmsford	N Chelmsford
148	12.7	Lowell	Lowell
148	12.7	Wachusett	Jefferson
153	12.6	Barnstable	Hyannis
153	12.6	Dudley-Charlton Reg	Dudley
153	12.6	Hingham	Hingham
153	12.6	Methuen	Methuen
157	12.5	Bourne	Bourne
157	12.5	Hopkinton	Hopkinton
157	12.5	Nashoba	Bolton
157	12.5	Oxford	Oxford
161	12.4	Danvers	Danvers
161	12.4	Scituate	Scituate
163	12.3	Ashland	Ashland
164	12.1	Longmeadow	Longmeadow
164	12.1	Silver Lake	Kingston
166	12.0	Saugus	Saugus
167	11.9	Pembroke	Pembroke
168	11.8	Duxbury	Duxbury
168	11.8	Northbridge	Whitinsville
170	11.7	Southborough	Northborough
171	11.6	Northborough	Northborough
172	11.5	Woburn	Woburn
173	11.4	Dracut	Dracut
174	11.3	Holliston	Holliston
175	11.2	North Andover	North Andover
175	11.2	North Middlesex	Townsend
177	11.1	Auburn	Auburn
177	11.1	Groton-Dunstable	Groton
177	11.1	Medfield	Medfield
180	10.9	Needham	Needham
180	10.9	Quabbin	Barre
180	10.9	Westborough	Westborough
183	10.6	Triton	Byfield
184	10.5	Georgetown	Georgetown
185	10.2	Lynnfield	Lynnfield
186	10.1	Tyngsborough	Tyngsborough
187	10.0	Greater New Bedford	New Bedford
188	9.9	Dighton-Rehoboth	Rehoboth
189	9.7	Seekonk	Seekonk
190	9.6	Mendon-Upton	Mendon
191	9.3	Westford	Westford
192	9.1	East Bridgewater	E Bridgewater
193	8.7	Somerset	Somerset
194	8.1	Douglas	Douglas

English Language Learner Students

Rank	Percent	District Name	City
1	23.6	Lowell	Lowell
2	21.6	Holyoke	Holyoke
3	19.0	Boston	Boston
3	19.0	Lynn	Lynn
5	18.8	Fitchburg	Fitchburg
6	16.5	Lawrence	Lawrence
7	16.3	Chelsea	Chelsea
8	15.2	Somerville	Somerville
9	14.8	Framingham	Framingham
10	13.7	Quincy	Quincy
11	13.5	Worcester	Worcester
12	13.2	Marlborough	Marlborough
13	11.6	Springfield	Springfield
14	10.8	Leominster	Leominster
15	10.7	Everett	Everett
16	10.1	Cambridge	Cambridge
17	8.4	Watertown	Watertown
18	7.8	Malden	Malden
18	7.8	Salem	Salem
20	7.4	Brockton	Brockton
21	7.3	Randolph	Randolph
22	7.0	Revere	Revere
23	6.6	Brookline	Brookline
24	6.4	Medford	Medford
25	5.6	Methuen	Methuen
25	5.6	Norwood	Norwood
27	5.4	West Springfield	W Springfield
28	5.2	Arlington	Arlington
28	5.2	Chicopee	Chicopee
30	5.0	Greenfield	Greenfield
31	4.9	Hudson	Hudson
32	4.8	Attleboro	Attleboro
32	4.8	Newton	Newtonville
34	4.7	Fall River	Fall River
35	4.6	Amherst-Pelham	Amherst
36	4.4	Haverhill	Haverhill
37	4.2	Barnstable	Hyannis
38	4.0	Waltham	Waltham
38	4.0	Westfield	Westfield
40	3.9	Dennis-Yarmouth	South Yarmouth
41	3.8	Milford	Milford
41	3.8	Westborough	Westborough
43	3.5	Dedham	Dedham
43	3.5	Southbridge	Southbridge
45	3.4	Lexington	Lexington
46	3.0	New Bedford	New Bedford
46	3.0	Woburn	Woburn
48	2.9	Belmont	Belmont
49	2.8	Webster	Webster
50	2.6	Taunton	Taunton
51	2.5	Pittsfield	Pittsfield
52	2.3	Greater New Bedford	New Bedford
53	2.2	Clinton	Clinton
54	2.1	Northampton	Northampton
54	2.1	Peabody	Peabody
56	2.0	Acton	Acton
56	2.0	Easthampton	Easthampton
58	1.9	Ashland	Ashland
58	1.9	Burlington	Burlington
58	1.9	Stoneham	Stoneham
61	1.7	Melrose	Melrose
61	1.7	Natick	Natick
61	1.7	North Adams	North Adams
64	1.6	Beverly	Beverly
64	1.6	Greater Lowell Voc Tec	Tyngsborough
66	1.5	Agawam	Feeding Hills
66	1.5	Stoughton	Stoughton
68	1.4	Canton	Canton
68	1.4	Concord	Concord
68	1.4	Dracut	Dracut
71	1.3	Braintree	Braintree
71	1.3	Scituate	Scituate
71	1.3	Shrewsbury	Shrewsbury
74	1.2	Wellesley	Wellesley
75	1.1	Bedford	Bedford
75	1.1	Northbridge	Whitinsville
75	1.1	Sharon	Sharon
78	1.0	Gloucester	Gloucester
78	1.0	Weston	Weston
80	0.9	Dartmouth	South Dartmouth
80	0.9	Falmouth	East Falmouth
80	0.9	Ludlow	Ludlow
83	0.8	Acton-Boxborough	Acton
83	0.8	Sudbury	Sudbury
83	0.8	Weymouth	Weymouth
86	0.7	Billerica	Billerica
86	0.7	Needham	Needham
86	0.7	North Andover	North Andover
86	0.7	North Attleborough	N Attleborough
86	0.7	Northborough	Northborough
86	0.7	Swampscott	Swampscott
86	0.7	Wakefield	Wakefield
86	0.7	Winthrop	Winthrop
94	0.6	Chelmsford	N Chelmsford
94	0.6	Ipswich	Ipswich
94	0.6	Plymouth	Plymouth
94	0.6	Reading	Reading
94	0.6	Winchester	Winchester
99	0.5	Andover	Andover
99	0.5	Bellingham	Bellingham
99	0.5	Gardner	Gardner
99	0.5	Hampden-Wilbraham	Wilbraham
99	0.5	Harwich	Harwich
99	0.5	Longmeadow	Longmeadow
99	0.5	Newburyport	Newburyport
99	0.5	Southborough	Northborough
107	0.4	Amesbury	Amesbury
107	0.4	Athol-Royalston	Athol
107	0.4	Belchertown	Belchertown
107	0.4	Danvers	Danvers
107	0.4	Nauset	Orleans
107	0.4	Oxford	Oxford
107	0.4	Triton	Byfield
107	0.4	Tyngsborough	Tyngsborough
107	0.4	Uxbridge	Uxbridge
107	0.4	Wayland	Wayland
107	0.4	Westford	Westford
118	0.3	Auburn	Auburn
118	0.3	Hopkinton	Hopkinton
118	0.3	Mashpee	Mashpee
118	0.3	Millbury	Millbury
118	0.3	Nashoba	Bolton
118	0.3	Wachusett	Jefferson
124	0.2	Easton	North Easton
124	0.2	Groton-Dunstable	Groton
124	0.2	Mansfield	Mansfield
124	0.2	Marblehead	Marblehead
124	0.2	Milton	Milton
124	0.2	North Reading	North Reading
124	0.2	Silver Lake	Kingston
124	0.2	Winchendon	Winchendon
132	0.1	Abington	Abington
132	0.1	Adams-Cheshire	Cheshire
132	0.1	Bourne	Bourne
132	0.1	Douglas	Douglas
132	0.1	Hamilton-Wenham	Wenham
132	0.1	Hanover	Hanover
132	0.1	Holliston	Holliston
132	0.1	Leicester	Leicester
132	0.1	Lynnfield	Lynnfield
132	0.1	Middleborough	Middleborough
132	0.1	Mohawk Trail	Shelburne Falls
132	0.1	North Middlesex	Townsend
132	0.1	Quabbin	Barre
132	0.1	Sandwich	Sandwich
132	0.1	Spencer-E Brookfield	Spencer
132	0.1	Westport	Westport
132	0.1	Whitman-Hanson	Whitman
149	0.0	Bridgewater-Raynham	Raynham
149	0.0	Dighton-Rehoboth	Rehoboth
149	0.0	Dudley-Charlton Reg	Dudley
149	0.0	Fairhaven	Fairhaven
149	0.0	Grafton	Grafton
149	0.0	Marshfield	Marshfield
149	0.0	Medway	Medway
149	0.0	Swansea	Swansea
149	0.0	Walpole	Walpole
149	0.0	Wareham	Wareham
159	0.0	Ashburnham-Westminster	Westminster
159	0.0	Blackstone-Millville	Blackstone
159	0.0	Carver	Carver
159	0.0	Central Berkshire	Dalton
159	0.0	Duxbury	Duxbury
159	0.0	East Bridgewater	E Bridgewater
159	0.0	East Longmeadow	E Longmeadow
159	0.0	Foxborough	Foxborough
159	0.0	Franklin	Franklin
159	0.0	Freetown-Lakeville	Lakeville
159	0.0	Georgetown	Georgetown
159	0.0	Hingham	Hingham
159	0.0	King Philip	Wrentham
159	0.0	Littleton	Littleton
159	0.0	Lunenburg	Lunenburg
159	0.0	Masconomet	Topsfield
159	0.0	Medfield	Medfield
159	0.0	Mendon-Upton	Mendon
159	0.0	Monson	Monson
159	0.0	Narragansett	Baldwinville
159	0.0	Norton	Norton
159	0.0	Norwell	Norwell
159	0.0	Palmer	Palmer
159	0.0	Pembroke	Pembroke
159	0.0	Pentucket	West Newbury
159	0.0	Rockland	Rockland
159	0.0	Saugus	Saugus
159	0.0	Seekonk	Seekonk
159	0.0	Somerset	Somerset
159	0.0	South Hadley	South Hadley
159	0.0	Southwick-Tolland	Southwick
159	0.0	Sutton	Sutton
159	0.0	Tantasqua	Fiskdale
159	0.0	Tewksbury	Tewksbury
159	0.0	Westwood	Westwood
159	0.0	Wilmington	Wilmington

Migrant Students

Rank	Percent	District Name	City
1	3.5	Westborough	Westborough
2	3.3	Spencer-E Brookfield	Spencer
3	1.8	Lowell	Lowell

Rank	Percent	District Name	City
4	1.7	Fall River	Fall River
5	1.2	Springfield	Springfield
6	1.1	Sharon	Sharon
7	0.8	Acton	Acton
7	0.8	Gloucester	Gloucester
9	0.7	Dedham	Dedham
9	0.7	Lawrence	Lawrence
9	0.7	New Bedford	New Bedford
9	0.7	Peabody	Peabody
13	0.6	Holyoke	Holyoke
13	0.6	Salem	Salem
15	0.5	Medford	Medford
15	0.5	Milford	Milford
15	0.5	Wakefield	Wakefield
18	0.3	Brockton	Brockton
18	0.3	Haverhill	Haverhill
18	0.3	Marblehead	Marblehead
18	0.3	Palmer	Palmer
22	0.2	Amherst-Pelham	Amherst
22	0.2	Bourne	Bourne
22	0.2	Chicopee	Chicopee
22	0.2	Clinton	Clinton
22	0.2	Concord	Concord
22	0.2	Lynn	Lynn
22	0.2	North Andover	North Andover
29	0.1	Auburn	Auburn
29	0.1	Barnstable	Hyannis
29	0.1	Bedford	Bedford
29	0.1	Beverly	Beverly
29	0.1	Boston	Boston
29	0.1	Chelmsford	N Chelmsford
29	0.1	Easthampton	Easthampton
29	0.1	Greater New Bedford	New Bedford
29	0.1	Longmeadow	Longmeadow
29	0.1	Marlborough	Marlborough
29	0.1	Mashpee	Mashpee
29	0.1	Mohawk Trail	Shelburne Falls
29	0.1	Natick	Natick
29	0.1	Northampton	Northampton
29	0.1	Northborough	Northborough
29	0.1	Norwood	Norwood
29	0.1	Quincy	Quincy
29	0.1	Scituate	Scituate
29	0.1	Somerville	Somerville
29	0.1	Sutton	Sutton
29	0.1	Tantasqua	Fiskdale
29	0.1	Taunton	Taunton
29	0.1	Wareham	Wareham
29	0.1	West Springfield	W Springfield
29	0.1	Winchendon	Winchendon
54	0.0	Andover	Andover
54	0.0	Attleboro	Attleboro
54	0.0	Bellingham	Bellingham
54	0.0	Billerica	Billerica
54	0.0	Brookline	Brookline
54	0.0	Dracut	Dracut
54	0.0	Falmouth	East Falmouth
54	0.0	Fitchburg	Fitchburg
54	0.0	Hamilton-Wenham	Wenham
54	0.0	Hampden-Wilbraham	Wilbraham
54	0.0	Ipswich	Ipswich
54	0.0	Leominster	Leominster
54	0.0	Ludlow	Ludlow
54	0.0	Marshfield	Marshfield
54	0.0	Needham	Needham
54	0.0	North Adams	North Adams
54	0.0	North Middlesex	Townsend
54	0.0	Oxford	Oxford
54	0.0	Reading	Reading
54	0.0	Triton	Byfield
54	0.0	Uxbridge	Uxbridge
54	0.0	Westfield	Westfield
54	0.0	Weymouth	Weymouth
77	0.0	Abington	Abington
77	0.0	Acton-Boxborough	Acton
77	0.0	Adams-Cheshire	Cheshire
77	0.0	Agawam	Feeding Hills
77	0.0	Amesbury	Amesbury
77	0.0	Arlington	Arlington
77	0.0	Ashburnham-Westminster	Westminster
77	0.0	Ashland	Ashland
77	0.0	Athol-Royalston	Athol
77	0.0	Belchertown	Belchertown
77	0.0	Belmont	Belmont
77	0.0	Blackstone-Millville	Blackstone
77	0.0	Braintree	Braintree
77	0.0	Bridgewater-Raynham	Raynham
77	0.0	Burlington	Burlington
77	0.0	Cambridge	Cambridge
77	0.0	Canton	Canton
77	0.0	Carver	Carver
77	0.0	Central Berkshire	Dalton
77	0.0	Chelsea	Chelsea
77	0.0	Danvers	Danvers
77	0.0	Dartmouth	South Dartmouth
77	0.0	Dennis-Yarmouth	South Yarmouth
77	0.0	Dighton-Rehoboth	Rehoboth
77	0.0	Douglas	Douglas
77	0.0	Dudley-Charlton Reg	Dudley
77	0.0	Duxbury	Duxbury
77	0.0	East Bridgewater	E Bridgewater
77	0.0	East Longmeadow	E Longmeadow
77	0.0	Easton	North Easton
77	0.0	Everett	Everett
77	0.0	Fairhaven	Fairhaven
77	0.0	Foxborough	Foxborough
77	0.0	Framingham	Framingham
77	0.0	Franklin	Franklin
77	0.0	Freetown-Lakeville	Lakeville
77	0.0	Gardner	Gardner
77	0.0	Georgetown	Georgetown
77	0.0	Grafton	Grafton
77	0.0	Greater Lowell Voc Tec	Tyngsborough
77	0.0	Greenfield	Greenfield
77	0.0	Groton-Dunstable	Groton
77	0.0	Hanover	Hanover
77	0.0	Harwich	Harwich
77	0.0	Hingham	Hingham
77	0.0	Holliston	Holliston
77	0.0	Hopkinton	Hopkinton
77	0.0	Hudson	Hudson
77	0.0	King Philip	Wrentham
77	0.0	Leicester	Leicester
77	0.0	Lexington	Lexington
77	0.0	Littleton	Littleton
77	0.0	Lunenburg	Lunenburg
77	0.0	Lynnfield	Lynnfield
77	0.0	Malden	Malden
77	0.0	Mansfield	Mansfield
77	0.0	Masconomet	Topsfield
77	0.0	Medfield	Medfield
77	0.0	Medway	Medway
77	0.0	Melrose	Melrose
77	0.0	Mendon-Upton	Mendon
77	0.0	Methuen	Methuen
77	0.0	Middleborough	Middleborough
77	0.0	Millbury	Millbury
77	0.0	Milton	Milton
77	0.0	Monson	Monson
77	0.0	Narragansett	Baldwinville
77	0.0	Nashoba	Bolton
77	0.0	Nauset	Orleans
77	0.0	Newburyport	Newburyport
77	0.0	Newton	Newtonville
77	0.0	North Attleborough	N Attleborough
77	0.0	North Reading	North Reading
77	0.0	Northbridge	Whitinsville
77	0.0	Norton	Norton
77	0.0	Norwell	Norwell
77	0.0	Pembroke	Pembroke
77	0.0	Pentucket	West Newbury
77	0.0	Pittsfield	Pittsfield
77	0.0	Plymouth	Plymouth
77	0.0	Quabbin	Barre
77	0.0	Randolph	Randolph
77	0.0	Revere	Revere
77	0.0	Rockland	Rockland
77	0.0	Sandwich	Sandwich
77	0.0	Saugus	Saugus
77	0.0	Seekonk	Seekonk
77	0.0	Shrewsbury	Shrewsbury
77	0.0	Silver Lake	Kingston
77	0.0	Somerset	Somerset
77	0.0	South Hadley	South Hadley
77	0.0	Southborough	Northborough
77	0.0	Southbridge	Southbridge
77	0.0	Southwick-Tolland	Southwick
77	0.0	Stoneham	Stoneham
77	0.0	Stoughton	Stoughton
77	0.0	Sudbury	Sudbury
77	0.0	Swampscott	Swampscott
77	0.0	Swansea	Swansea
77	0.0	Tewksbury	Tewksbury
77	0.0	Tyngsborough	Tyngsborough
77	0.0	Wachusett	Jefferson
77	0.0	Walpole	Walpole
77	0.0	Waltham	Waltham
77	0.0	Watertown	Watertown
77	0.0	Wayland	Wayland
77	0.0	Webster	Webster
77	0.0	Wellesley	Wellesley
77	0.0	Westford	Westford
77	0.0	Weston	Weston
77	0.0	Westport	Westport
77	0.0	Westwood	Westwood
77	0.0	Whitman-Hanson	Whitman
77	0.0	Wilmington	Wilmington
77	0.0	Winchester	Winchester
77	0.0	Winthrop	Winthrop
77	0.0	Woburn	Woburn
77	0.0	Worcester	Worcester

Students Eligible for Free Lunch

Rank	Percent	District Name	City
1	80.4	Chelsea	Chelsea
2	69.7	Lawrence	Lawrence
3	68.0	Holyoke	Holyoke
4	67.7	Springfield	Springfield
5	65.1	Boston	Boston
6	57.7	Lynn	Lynn
7	52.4	Lowell	Lowell
8	52.2	Worcester	Worcester
9	50.0	New Bedford	New Bedford
10	48.1	Brockton	Brockton
11	44.5	Fall River	Fall River
12	43.3	Somerville	Somerville
13	42.2	Southbridge	Southbridge
14	41.4	Revere	Revere
15	39.9	Fitchburg	Fitchburg
16	39.4	North Adams	North Adams
17	38.2	Chicopee	Chicopee
18	36.2	Greater New Bedford	New Bedford
19	35.7	Greenfield	Greenfield
20	34.5	Everett	Everett
21	34.2	Greater Lowell Voc Tec	Tyngsborough
22	33.0	Cambridge	Cambridge
23	32.6	Salem	Salem
24	31.3	Malden	Malden
25	29.4	Webster	Webster
26	27.7	Dennis-Yarmouth	South Yarmouth
26	27.7	Framingham	Framingham
28	25.8	Pittsfield	Pittsfield
29	25.7	Wareham	Wareham
30	25.0	West Springfield	W Springfield
31	23.4	Haverhill	Haverhill
32	23.1	Clinton	Clinton
32	23.1	Quincy	Quincy
34	22.7	Mohawk Trail	Shelburne Falls
35	22.6	Taunton	Taunton
36	22.0	Waltham	Waltham
37	20.9	Athol-Royalston	Athol
37	20.9	Randolph	Randolph
39	20.8	Adams-Cheshire	Cheshire
40	20.7	Leominster	Leominster
41	20.5	Gardner	Gardner
42	20.3	Westfield	Westfield
43	19.8	Methuen	Methuen
44	18.3	Gloucester	Gloucester
45	18.0	Barnstable	Hyannis
45	18.0	Winchendon	Winchendon
47	17.5	Medford	Medford
48	17.0	South Hadley	South Hadley
49	16.6	Marlborough	Marlborough
50	16.5	Amherst-Pelham	Amherst
51	15.8	Northampton	Northampton
52	15.6	Easthampton	Easthampton
53	15.4	Palmer	Palmer
54	15.0	Melrose	Melrose
54	15.0	Northbridge	Whitinsville
56	14.8	Winthrop	Winthrop
57	14.5	Attleboro	Attleboro
58	14.4	Beverly	Beverly
59	13.4	Watertown	Watertown
60	12.8	Peabody	Peabody
61	12.1	Spencer-E Brookfield	Spencer
62	12.0	Mashpee	Mashpee
62	12.0	Rockland	Rockland
64	11.8	Middleborough	Middleborough
65	11.7	Central Berkshire	Dalton
65	11.7	Narragansett	Baldwinville
67	11.5	Weymouth	Weymouth
68	11.3	Fairhaven	Fairhaven
68	11.3	Falmouth	East Falmouth
68	11.3	Plymouth	Plymouth
68	11.3	Woburn	Woburn
72	11.2	Hudson	Hudson
73	11.0	Milford	Milford
74	10.7	Norwood	Norwood
75	10.6	Westport	Westport
76	10.2	Bourne	Bourne
77	10.1	Stoughton	Stoughton
78	10.0	Millbury	Millbury
79	9.4	Ludlow	Ludlow
80	9.3	Monson	Monson
80	9.3	Oxford	Oxford
82	9.2	Agawam	Feeding Hills
83	9.1	Harwich	Harwich

Rank	Percent	District	City
84	9.0	Auburn	Auburn
85	8.9	Triton	Byfield
86	8.7	Amesbury	Amesbury
86	8.7	Belchertown	Belchertown
86	8.7	Carver	Carver
89	8.6	Southwick-Tolland	Southwick
90	8.3	Dedham	Dedham
90	8.3	Dracut	Dracut
92	8.2	Ipswich	Ipswich
93	8.1	Tantasqua	Fiskdale
94	7.9	Leicester	Leicester
95	7.8	Bellingham	Bellingham
95	7.8	Braintree	Braintree
95	7.8	Saugus	Saugus
98	7.4	Norton	Norton
98	7.4	Quabbin	Barre
100	7.0	Brookline	Brookline
100	7.0	Whitman-Hanson	Whitman
102	6.5	Somerset	Somerset
103	6.4	Swansea	Swansea
104	6.3	Abington	Abington
104	6.3	Arlington	Arlington
104	6.3	Stoneham	Stoneham
107	6.0	Dudley-Charlton Reg	Dudley
107	6.0	Uxbridge	Uxbridge
109	5.9	Douglas	Douglas
110	5.8	Dartmouth	South Dartmouth
111	5.7	Freetown-Lakeville	Lakeville
111	5.7	North Attleborough	N Attleborough
113	5.5	Canton	Canton
113	5.5	East Longmeadow	E Longmeadow
115	5.4	Marshfield	Marshfield
115	5.4	Nauset	Orleans
115	5.4	Shrewsbury	Shrewsbury
118	5.3	Bridgewater-Raynham	Raynham
119	5.2	Grafton	Grafton
120	5.0	Blackstone-Millville	Blackstone
120	5.0	Marblehead	Marblehead
122	4.9	Burlington	Burlington
122	4.9	Hampden-Wilbraham	Wilbraham
124	4.8	Newton	Newtonville
125	4.7	Ashland	Ashland
125	4.7	Sandwich	Sandwich
127	4.6	Mansfield	Mansfield
128	4.5	Danvers	Danvers
128	4.5	North Middlesex	Townsend
128	4.5	Tewksbury	Tewksbury
131	4.4	Milton	Milton
131	4.4	Westborough	Westborough
133	4.3	Lunenburg	Lunenburg
134	4.2	Ashburnham-Westminster	Westminster
135	4.1	Natick	Natick
135	4.1	Pembroke	Pembroke
137	4.0	Seekonk	Seekonk
137	4.0	Walpole	Walpole
139	3.9	Franklin	Franklin
140	3.8	Billerica	Billerica
140	3.8	East Bridgewater	E Bridgewater
140	3.8	Foxborough	Foxborough
140	3.8	Silver Lake	Kingston
144	3.7	Scituate	Scituate
145	3.3	Wayland	Wayland
146	3.2	Newburyport	Newburyport
146	3.2	Wakefield	Wakefield
148	3.1	Andover	Andover
148	3.1	Hamilton-Wenham	Wenham
148	3.1	Swampscott	Swampscott
151	3.0	Concord	Concord
151	3.0	Sharon	Sharon
151	3.0	Sutton	Sutton
151	3.0	Tyngsborough	Tyngsborough
155	2.9	Belmont	Belmont
155	2.9	Nashoba	Bolton
157	2.8	Georgetown	Georgetown
157	2.8	King Philip	Wrentham
157	2.8	Longmeadow	Longmeadow
160	2.7	Littleton	Littleton
160	2.7	North Andover	North Andover
162	2.6	Lexington	Lexington
162	2.6	Pentucket	West Newbury
164	2.5	Wachusett	Jefferson
164	2.5	Wilmington	Wilmington
166	2.4	Sudbury	Sudbury
167	2.3	Dighton-Rehoboth	Rehoboth
168	2.2	Needham	Needham
168	2.2	Wellesley	Wellesley
170	2.1	Acton-Boxborough	Acton
170	2.1	North Reading	North Reading
172	2.0	Hingham	Hingham
172	2.0	Medway	Medway
172	2.0	Weston	Weston
175	1.9	Chelmsford	N Chelmsford
176	1.7	Northborough	Northborough
176	1.7	Reading	Reading
178	1.6	Easton	North Easton
178	1.6	Hanover	Hanover
178	1.6	Mendon-Upton	Mendon
178	1.6	Winchester	Winchester
182	1.5	Bedford	Bedford
182	1.5	Groton-Dunstable	Groton
182	1.5	Norwell	Norwell
185	1.4	Acton	Acton
185	1.4	Medfield	Medfield
185	1.4	Westford	Westford
188	1.1	Holliston	Holliston
189	1.0	Lynnfield	Lynnfield
189	1.0	Masconomet	Topsfield
191	0.9	Hopkinton	Hopkinton
192	0.7	Southborough	Northborough
193	0.0	Duxbury	Duxbury
193	0.0	Westwood	Westwood

Students Eligible for Reduced-Price Lunch

Rank	Percent	District Name	City
1	17.5	Somerville	Somerville
2	15.4	Lowell	Lowell
3	13.0	Lawrence	Lawrence
4	11.9	New Bedford	New Bedford
5	11.5	Revere	Revere
6	10.8	Athol-Royalston	Athol
7	10.7	Everett	Everett
8	10.6	Lynn	Lynn
9	10.5	Malden	Malden
10	10.4	Fitchburg	Fitchburg
11	10.2	Brockton	Brockton
11	10.2	Chicopee	Chicopee
13	10.1	Pittsfield	Pittsfield
14	9.7	Wareham	Wareham
15	9.5	Springfield	Springfield
16	9.4	Greater Lowell Voc Tec	Tyngsborough
17	9.3	Fall River	Fall River
18	9.0	Clinton	Clinton
19	8.7	Easthampton	Easthampton
19	8.7	Randolph	Randolph
21	8.6	Adams-Cheshire	Cheshire
22	8.4	Haverhill	Haverhill
23	8.3	Boston	Boston
23	8.3	Worcester	Worcester
25	8.2	Greenfield	Greenfield
26	8.1	Holyoke	Holyoke
27	8.0	Central Berkshire	Dalton
28	7.9	Webster	Webster
29	7.7	Leominster	Leominster
30	7.6	Cambridge	Cambridge
31	7.5	Northampton	Northampton
32	7.4	Quincy	Quincy
33	7.3	Taunton	Taunton
33	7.3	Westfield	Westfield
35	7.1	Spencer-E Brookfield	Spencer
36	7.0	Barnstable	Hyannis
37	6.9	Northbridge	Whitinsville
38	6.6	West Springfield	W Springfield
39	6.3	Mohawk Trail	Shelburne Falls
40	6.2	Marlborough	Marlborough
41	6.1	Carver	Carver
42	6.0	Southbridge	Southbridge
43	5.9	Methuen	Methuen
43	5.9	Westport	Westport
45	5.6	Attleboro	Attleboro
45	5.6	Ludlow	Ludlow
45	5.6	Winchendon	Winchendon
48	5.3	Uxbridge	Uxbridge
49	5.1	Gardner	Gardner
50	5.0	Amesbury	Amesbury
50	5.0	Bourne	Bourne
52	4.9	Salem	Salem
52	4.9	Stoughton	Stoughton
52	4.9	Watertown	Watertown
55	4.7	Fairhaven	Fairhaven
55	4.7	Mashpee	Mashpee
55	4.7	Middleborough	Middleborough
58	4.6	Plymouth	Plymouth
59	4.5	Dennis-Yarmouth	South Yarmouth
59	4.5	Narragansett	Baldwinville
59	4.5	Oxford	Oxford
62	4.4	Gloucester	Gloucester
63	4.2	Agawam	Feeding Hills
63	4.2	Swansea	Swansea
65	4.1	Beverly	Beverly
65	4.1	Norwood	Norwood
65	4.1	Southwick-Tolland	Southwick
68	4.0	Ashburnham-Westminster	Westminster
68	4.0	Quabbin	Barre
70	3.9	Leicester	Leicester
70	3.9	Medford	Medford
70	3.9	Monson	Monson
73	3.8	Dartmouth	South Dartmouth
74	3.6	Millbury	Millbury
74	3.6	Winthrop	Winthrop
76	3.5	Blackstone-Millville	Blackstone
76	3.5	Falmouth	East Falmouth
78	3.4	Harwich	Harwich
78	3.4	Palmer	Palmer
78	3.4	Rockland	Rockland
78	3.4	Tantasqua	Fiskdale
78	3.4	Waltham	Waltham
83	3.1	Milford	Milford
83	3.1	Nauset	Orleans
85	3.0	North Adams	North Adams
85	3.0	Weymouth	Weymouth
85	3.0	Woburn	Woburn
88	2.9	Peabody	Peabody
89	2.8	Dudley-Charlton Reg	Dudley
90	2.6	Brookline	Brookline
90	2.6	Freetown-Lakeville	Lakeville
90	2.6	Seekonk	Seekonk
90	2.6	Whitman-Hanson	Whitman
94	2.5	Braintree	Braintree
94	2.5	Dedham	Dedham
96	2.4	Grafton	Grafton
96	2.4	North Middlesex	Townsend
98	2.3	Danvers	Danvers
98	2.3	Lunenburg	Lunenburg
98	2.3	North Attleborough	N Attleborough
98	2.3	Saugus	Saugus
102	2.2	Arlington	Arlington
102	2.2	Douglas	Douglas
102	2.2	Newton	Newtonville
102	2.2	Northborough	Northborough
106	2.1	Dracut	Dracut
106	2.1	Stoneham	Stoneham
106	2.1	Triton	Byfield
109	2.0	East Bridgewater	E Bridgewater
109	2.0	Hudson	Hudson
109	2.0	Norton	Norton
112	1.9	Foxborough	Foxborough
112	1.9	Somerset	Somerset
114	1.8	Newburyport	Newburyport
114	1.8	Walpole	Walpole
116	1.7	Billerica	Billerica
116	1.7	Concord	Concord
118	1.6	Canton	Canton
118	1.6	Natick	Natick
118	1.6	Shrewsbury	Shrewsbury
118	1.6	Tyngsborough	Tyngsborough
122	1.5	Belchertown	Belchertown
122	1.5	Belmont	Belmont
122	1.5	Bridgewater-Raynham	Raynham
122	1.5	Milton	Milton
126	1.3	Lexington	Lexington
127	1.2	Hampden-Wilbraham	Wilbraham
127	1.2	Mansfield	Mansfield
127	1.2	Pentucket	West Newbury
127	1.2	Tewksbury	Tewksbury
127	1.2	Wilmington	Wilmington
132	1.1	Abington	Abington
132	1.1	Ashland	Ashland
132	1.1	Bellingham	Bellingham
132	1.1	Easton	North Easton
132	1.1	Ipswich	Ipswich
132	1.1	North Reading	North Reading
132	1.1	Silver Lake	Kingston
132	1.1	Wakefield	Wakefield
132	1.1	Westborough	Westborough
141	1.0	Bedford	Bedford
141	1.0	Chelmsford	N Chelmsford
141	1.0	Georgetown	Georgetown
141	1.0	Lynnfield	Lynnfield
145	0.9	Auburn	Auburn
145	0.9	Hamilton-Wenham	Wenham
145	0.9	Longmeadow	Longmeadow
145	0.9	Marblehead	Marblehead
145	0.9	Needham	Needham
145	0.9	North Andover	North Andover
145	0.9	Pembroke	Pembroke
145	0.9	Wachusett	Jefferson
145	0.9	Wellesley	Wellesley
145	0.9	Westford	Westford
155	0.8	Hingham	Hingham
155	0.8	Medfield	Medfield
155	0.8	Nashoba	Bolton
155	0.8	Reading	Reading
155	0.8	Sharon	Sharon
155	0.8	Weston	Weston
161	0.7	Dighton-Rehoboth	Rehoboth

Rank	Ratio	District Name	City
161	0.7	Mendon-Upton	Mendon
161	0.7	Scituate	Scituate
161	0.7	Southborough	Northborough
165	0.6	Acton	Acton
165	0.6	Holliston	Holliston
165	0.6	Sutton	Sutton
168	0.5	Hanover	Hanover
168	0.5	Medway	Medway
170	0.4	Groton-Dunstable	Groton
170	0.4	Marshfield	Marshfield
172	0.3	Acton-Boxborough	Acton
172	0.3	Swampscott	Swampscott
174	0.2	Sudbury	Sudbury
174	0.2	Wayland	Wayland
176	0.1	King Philip	Wrentham
176	0.1	Littleton	Littleton
176	0.1	Norwell	Norwell
179	0.0	Amherst-Pelham	Amherst
179	0.0	Andover	Andover
179	0.0	Burlington	Burlington
179	0.0	Chelsea	Chelsea
179	0.0	Duxbury	Duxbury
179	0.0	East Longmeadow	E Longmeadow
179	0.0	Framingham	Framingham
179	0.0	Franklin	Franklin
179	0.0	Greater New Bedford	New Bedford
179	0.0	Hopkinton	Hopkinton
179	0.0	Masconomet	Topsfield
179	0.0	Melrose	Melrose
179	0.0	Sandwich	Sandwich
179	0.0	South Hadley	South Hadley
179	0.0	Westwood	Westwood
179	0.0	Winchester	Winchester

Student/Teacher Ratio

Rank	Ratio	District Name	City
1	24.1	Pembroke	Pembroke
2	18.9	Abington	Abington
3	17.9	Bridgewater-Raynham	Raynham
4	17.3	Acton	Acton
5	17.1	Tewksbury	Tewksbury
6	17.0	Groton-Dunstable	Groton
6	17.0	Medway	Medway
6	17.0	Oxford	Oxford
6	17.0	Taunton	Taunton
10	16.8	Triton	Byfield
11	16.7	Sutton	Sutton
12	16.6	Acton-Boxborough	Acton
13	16.5	Belchertown	Belchertown
13	16.5	Dracut	Dracut
15	16.4	Dartmouth	South Dartmouth
15	16.4	Sandwich	Sandwich
17	16.3	East Bridgewater	E Bridgewater
18	16.2	North Reading	North Reading
19	16.1	Douglas	Douglas
19	16.1	King Philip	Wrentham
19	16.1	Melrose	Melrose
19	16.1	Wachusett	Jefferson
23	16.0	Leominster	Leominster
23	16.0	Masconomet	Topsfield
23	16.0	Millbury	Millbury
23	16.0	Shrewsbury	Shrewsbury
27	15.9	Ashburnham-Westminster	Westminster
27	15.9	Middleborough	Middleborough
27	15.9	Rockland	Rockland
30	15.8	Dighton-Rehoboth	Rehoboth
31	15.6	Bourne	Bourne
31	15.6	Central Berkshire	Dalton
31	15.6	Easton	North Easton
34	15.5	Norton	Norton
34	15.5	Westport	Westport
34	15.5	Whitman-Hanson	Whitman
37	15.4	Dudley-Charlton Reg	Dudley
37	15.4	Gardner	Gardner
37	15.4	Lunenburg	Lunenburg
37	15.4	Mansfield	Mansfield
37	15.4	Methuen	Methuen
42	15.3	Boston	Boston
42	15.3	Chelmsford	N Chelmsford
42	15.3	Stoneham	Stoneham
45	15.2	Duxbury	Duxbury
45	15.2	Grafton	Grafton
47	15.1	North Andover	North Andover
47	15.1	Reading	Reading
47	15.1	Southwick-Tolland	Southwick
50	15.0	Braintree	Braintree
50	15.0	Freetown-Lakeville	Lakeville
50	15.0	Revere	Revere
53	14.9	Hampden-Wilbraham	Wilbraham
53	14.9	Quabbin	Barre
53	14.9	Saugus	Saugus
53	14.9	Walpole	Walpole
57	14.8	Belmont	Belmont
57	14.8	Mendon-Upton	Mendon
57	14.8	Milton	Milton
57	14.8	Wilmington	Wilmington
61	14.7	Ashland	Ashland
61	14.7	Billerica	Billerica
61	14.7	Blackstone-Millville	Blackstone
61	14.7	Fairhaven	Fairhaven
61	14.7	Georgetown	Georgetown
61	14.7	Littleton	Littleton
61	14.7	Longmeadow	Longmeadow
61	14.7	Sudbury	Sudbury
61	14.7	Wayland	Wayland
70	14.6	Arlington	Arlington
70	14.6	Haverhill	Haverhill
70	14.6	Holliston	Holliston
70	14.6	Monson	Monson
70	14.6	Pentucket	West Newbury
70	14.6	Seekonk	Seekonk
70	14.6	Stoughton	Stoughton
77	14.5	Auburn	Auburn
77	14.5	Everett	Everett
77	14.5	Narragansett	Baldwinville
77	14.5	North Attleborough	N Attleborough
77	14.5	Spencer-E Brookfield	Spencer
77	14.5	Uxbridge	Uxbridge
83	14.4	Athol-Royalston	Athol
83	14.4	Hingham	Hingham
83	14.4	Hopkinton	Hopkinton
83	14.4	Norwell	Norwell
87	14.3	Bellingham	Bellingham
87	14.3	Brockton	Brockton
87	14.3	Clinton	Clinton
87	14.3	Franklin	Franklin
87	14.3	North Middlesex	Townsend
87	14.3	Randolph	Randolph
87	14.3	Scituate	Scituate
87	14.3	Tyngsborough	Tyngsborough
87	14.3	Wareham	Wareham
96	14.2	East Longmeadow	E Longmeadow
96	14.2	Hamilton-Wenham	Wenham
96	14.2	Leicester	Leicester
96	14.2	Lynnfield	Lynnfield
96	14.2	Northbridge	Whitinsville
96	14.2	Peabody	Peabody
96	14.2	South Hadley	South Hadley
103	14.1	Nashoba	Bolton
103	14.1	Northborough	Northborough
103	14.1	Swampscott	Swampscott
106	14.0	Attleboro	Attleboro
106	14.0	Canton	Canton
106	14.0	Ipswich	Ipswich
106	14.0	Southborough	Northborough
106	14.0	Winthrop	Winthrop
111	13.9	Amesbury	Amesbury
111	13.9	Andover	Andover
111	13.9	Danvers	Danvers
111	13.9	Lawrence	Lawrence
111	13.9	Ludlow	Ludlow
111	13.9	Plymouth	Plymouth
111	13.9	Westford	Westford
118	13.8	Foxborough	Foxborough
118	13.8	Marblehead	Marblehead
118	13.8	Marshfield	Marshfield
121	13.7	Natick	Natick
121	13.7	Northampton	Northampton
123	13.6	Lowell	Lowell
123	13.6	Weymouth	Weymouth
125	13.5	Lynn	Lynn
125	13.5	Malden	Malden
125	13.5	Winchester	Winchester
128	13.4	Fall River	Fall River
128	13.4	Medfield	Medfield
128	13.4	New Bedford	New Bedford
131	13.3	Agawam	Feeding Hills
131	13.3	Beverly	Beverly
131	13.3	Quincy	Quincy
131	13.3	Silver Lake	Kingston
135	13.2	Carver	Carver
135	13.2	Concord	Concord
135	13.2	Fitchburg	Fitchburg
135	13.2	Newburyport	Newburyport
135	13.2	Norwood	Norwood
135	13.2	Worcester	Worcester
141	13.1	Gloucester	Gloucester
141	13.1	Hudson	Hudson
141	13.1	Marlborough	Marlborough
141	13.1	Pittsfield	Pittsfield
141	13.1	Wellesley	Wellesley
141	13.1	Woburn	Woburn
147	13.0	Greenfield	Greenfield
147	13.0	Harwich	Harwich
147	13.0	Milford	Milford
147	13.0	Needham	Needham
147	13.0	Palmer	Palmer
147	13.0	Wakefield	Wakefield
147	13.0	West Springfield	W Springfield
154	12.9	Chicopee	Chicopee
154	12.9	Somerset	Somerset
156	12.8	Barnstable	Hyannis
156	12.8	Falmouth	East Falmouth
156	12.8	Hanover	Hanover
156	12.8	Mohawk Trail	Shelburne Falls
156	12.8	Swansea	Swansea
156	12.8	Tantasqua	Fiskdale
156	12.8	Webster	Webster
163	12.7	Burlington	Burlington
163	12.7	Mashpee	Mashpee
165	12.6	Dedham	Dedham
165	12.6	Framingham	Framingham
165	12.6	Somerville	Somerville
165	12.6	Westfield	Westfield
165	12.6	Weston	Weston
165	12.6	Westwood	Westwood
165	12.6	Winchendon	Winchendon
172	12.5	Lexington	Lexington
172	12.5	Nauset	Orleans
172	12.5	Westborough	Westborough
175	12.4	Adams-Cheshire	Cheshire
175	12.4	Southbridge	Southbridge
177	12.3	Easthampton	Easthampton
178	12.2	Amherst-Pelham	Amherst
179	12.1	Chelsea	Chelsea
179	12.1	Salem	Salem
181	11.9	Bedford	Bedford
182	11.8	Brookline	Brookline
182	11.8	Newton	Newtonville
184	11.7	Dennis-Yarmouth	South Yarmouth
185	11.6	North Adams	North Adams
186	11.4	Springfield	Springfield
187	11.3	Sharon	Sharon
188	11.2	Holyoke	Holyoke
189	11.1	Medford	Medford
190	10.5	Greater Lowell Voc Tec	Tyngsborough
190	10.5	Waltham	Waltham
192	9.9	Cambridge	Cambridge
192	9.9	Greater New Bedford	New Bedford
194	8.4	Watertown	Watertown

Student/Librarian Ratio

Rank	Ratio	District Name	City
1	41,850.0	Milford	Milford
2	7,273.0	New Bedford	New Bedford
3	6,987.0	Wachusett	Jefferson
4	5,735.0	Blackstone-Millville	Blackstone
5	5,444.0	Rockland	Rockland
6	4,019.0	Gloucester	Gloucester
7	3,657.0	Danvers	Danvers
8	3,628.3	Attleboro	Attleboro
9	3,312.5	Peabody	Peabody
10	3,306.0	Saugus	Saugus
11	2,934.1	Boston	Boston
12	2,924.3	Fall River	Fall River
13	2,913.0	Franklin	Franklin
14	2,887.0	Foxborough	Foxborough
15	2,886.0	Medway	Medway
16	2,855.5	Revere	Revere
17	2,748.0	East Longmeadow	E Longmeadow
18	2,729.0	Bellingham	Bellingham
19	2,664.0	North Reading	North Reading
20	2,635.2	Bridgewater-Raynham	Raynham
21	2,425.5	Marlborough	Marlborough
22	2,422.0	East Bridgewater	E Bridgewater
23	2,396.6	Taunton	Taunton
24	2,371.0	Auburn	Auburn
25	2,303.0	South Hadley	South Hadley
26	2,299.0	Marshfield	Marshfield
27	2,296.7	Weymouth	Weymouth
28	2,237.7	Salem	Salem
29	2,236.0	Uxbridge	Uxbridge
30	2,212.5	Arlington	Arlington
31	2,200.0	Athol-Royalston	Athol
32	2,188.0	Swansea	Swansea
33	2,133.5	Dartmouth	South Dartmouth
34	2,131.5	Dracut	Dracut
35	2,120.0	Greenfield	Greenfield
36	2,070.0	North Adams	North Adams
37	2,010.8	Haverhill	Haverhill
38	2,008.0	Millbury	Millbury
39	1,985.3	Northampton	Northampton
40	1,926.0	Hampden-Wilbraham	Wilbraham
41	1,922.0	King Philip	Wrentham
42	1,905.5	Randolph	Randolph
43	1,903.0	Pembroke	Pembroke
44	1,893.0	Greater Lowell Voc Tec	Tyngsborough

Rank		District	City
45	1,882.0	Chicopee	Chicopee
46	1,856.5	Belmont	Belmont
47	1,856.0	Greater New Bedford	New Bedford
48	1,840.3	Worcester	Worcester
49	1,818.0	Webster	Webster
50	1,802.3	West Springfield	W Springfield
51	1,786.9	Lawrence	Lawrence
52	1,761.0	Tantasqua	Fiskdale
53	1,758.5	Central Berkshire	Dalton
54	1,756.3	Mansfield	Mansfield
55	1,701.7	Nashoba	Bolton
56	1,692.7	Barnstable	Hyannis
57	1,660.0	Sutton	Sutton
58	1,635.0	Narragansett	Baldwinville
59	1,629.5	Gardner	Gardner
60	1,620.4	Framingham	Framingham
61	1,617.0	Georgetown	Georgetown
62	1,591.0	Norton	Norton
63	1,571.5	Scituate	Scituate
64	1,558.5	Holliston	Holliston
65	1,474.5	Silver Lake	Kingston
66	1,452.7	North Andover	North Andover
67	1,396.0	Ipswich	Ipswich
68	1,394.3	Malden	Malden
69	1,363.3	Abington	Abington
70	1,355.7	Stoughton	Stoughton
71	1,295.0	Ashland	Ashland
72	1,265.0	Bourne	Bourne
73	1,237.4	Woburn	Woburn
74	1,229.4	Hamilton-Wenham	Wenham
75	1,228.7	Middleborough	Middleborough
76	1,226.5	Grafton	Grafton
77	1,220.0	Lunenburg	Lunenburg
78	1,205.0	Methuen	Methuen
79	1,191.3	Tewksbury	Tewksbury
80	1,190.7	Milton	Milton
81	1,183.7	Triton	Byfield
82	1,169.4	Lynn	Lynn
83	1,158.0	Groton-Dunstable	Groton
84	1,154.6	Chelmsford	N Chelmsford
85	1,151.0	Natick	Natick
86	1,134.4	Chelsea	Chelsea
87	1,129.7	Longmeadow	Longmeadow
88	1,128.5	Fairhaven	Fairhaven
89	1,120.5	Oxford	Oxford
90	1,098.9	Ludlow	Ludlow
91	1,096.9	Brockton	Brockton
92	1,083.8	Agawam	Feeding Hills
93	1,074.7	Quabbin	Barre
94	1,064.2	Everett	Everett
95	1,031.5	Norwell	Norwell
96	1,024.7	Wareham	Wareham
97	1,020.5	Amherst-Pelham	Amherst
98	1,010.0	Clinton	Clinton
99	996.5	Masconomet	Topsfield
100	989.2	Sharon	Sharon
101	983.8	Billerica	Billerica
102	952.7	North Attleborough	N Attleborough
103	950.5	Westport	Westport
104	948.0	Freetown-Lakeville	Lakeville
105	939.1	Westfield	Westfield
106	926.2	Shrewsbury	Shrewsbury
107	925.7	Braintree	Braintree
108	923.0	Hudson	Hudson
109	922.0	Adams-Cheshire	Cheshire
110	915.5	Lowell	Lowell
111	912.5	Nauset	Orleans
112	910.4	Carver	Carver
113	901.1	Springfield	Springfield
114	889.7	Leominster	Leominster
115	876.8	Westborough	Westborough
116	872.3	Fitchburg	Fitchburg
117	872.0	Pentucket	West Newbury
118	870.3	Acton-Boxborough	Acton
119	866.8	Dudley-Charlton Reg	Dudley
120	850.2	Easton	North Easton
121	847.5	Dighton-Rehoboth	Rehoboth
122	837.7	Belchertown	Belchertown
123	829.6	Sandwich	Sandwich
124	823.3	Duxbury	Duxbury
125	795.8	Plymouth	Plymouth
126	793.7	Newburyport	Newburyport
127	790.0	Weston	Weston
128	786.0	Medford	Medford
129	782.0	Littleton	Littleton
130	776.0	Seekonk	Seekonk
131	772.0	Monson	Monson
132	759.5	Somerset	Somerset
133	756.3	Tyngsborough	Tyngsborough
134	751.0	Spencer-E Brookfield	Spencer
135	747.5	Stoneham	Stoneham
136	745.6	Hopkinton	Hopkinton
137	745.4	Norwood	Norwood
138	725.8	Walpole	Walpole
139	724.5	Holyoke	Holyoke
140	721.3	Mashpee	Mashpee
141	710.7	Wayland	Wayland
142	696.7	Palmer	Palmer
143	693.8	Hanover	Hanover
144	690.6	Andover	Andover
144	690.6	Wakefield	Wakefield
146	684.0	Watertown	Watertown
147	681.6	Westford	Westford
148	680.6	Swampscott	Swampscott
149	680.0	Amesbury	Amesbury
150	677.1	Medfield	Medfield
150	677.1	Wilmington	Wilmington
152	674.6	Needham	Needham
153	674.1	Sudbury	Sudbury
154	655.5	Marblehead	Marblehead
155	655.4	Reading	Reading
156	646.7	Leicester	Leicester
157	641.0	Southwick-Tolland	Southwick
158	636.0	Northbridge	Whitinsville
158	636.0	Whitman-Hanson	Whitman
160	625.7	Winchendon	Winchendon
161	622.2	Quincy	Quincy
162	617.5	Lexington	Lexington
163	608.3	Ashburnham-Westminster	Westminster
164	601.2	Canton	Canton
165	600.5	Pittsfield	Pittsfield
166	599.2	Dedham	Dedham
167	598.3	Hingham	Hingham
168	595.2	Winchester	Winchester
169	584.8	North Middlesex	Townsend
170	584.0	Dennis-Yarmouth	South Yarmouth
171	581.0	Burlington	Burlington
172	562.6	Beverly	Beverly
173	561.5	Bedford	Bedford
174	555.5	Falmouth	East Falmouth
175	545.1	Wellesley	Wellesley
176	540.0	Somerville	Somerville
177	535.7	Southborough	Northborough
178	528.3	Douglas	Douglas
179	527.9	Brookline	Brookline
180	518.4	Southbridge	Southbridge
181	507.8	Lynnfield	Lynnfield
182	507.3	Harwich	Harwich
183	493.5	Concord	Concord
184	467.8	Newton	Newtonville
185	459.8	Cambridge	Cambridge
186	453.1	Waltham	Waltham
187	394.4	Westwood	Westwood
188	387.2	Northborough	Northborough
189	294.0	Mohawk Trail	Shelburne Falls
190	n/a	Acton	Acton
190	n/a	Easthampton	Easthampton
190	n/a	Melrose	Melrose
190	n/a	Mendon-Upton	Mendon
190	n/a	Winthrop	Winthrop

Student/Counselor Ratio

Rank	Ratio	District Name	City
1	2,241.0	Oxford	Oxford
2	1,270.3	Randolph	Randolph
3	1,190.7	Melrose	Melrose
4	1,165.2	Franklin	Franklin
5	1,164.5	Wachusett	Jefferson
6	1,037.0	Sandwich	Sandwich
7	968.0	Northborough	Northborough
8	934.4	Dennis-Yarmouth	South Yarmouth
9	926.1	Reading	Reading
10	921.2	South Hadley	South Hadley
11	907.3	Rockland	Rockland
12	872.0	Pentucket	West Newbury
13	868.3	Shrewsbury	Shrewsbury
14	865.9	Bridgewater-Raynham	Raynham
15	851.2	Hamilton-Wenham	Wenham
16	820.5	Salem	Salem
17	815.9	Revere	Revere
18	794.2	Tewksbury	Tewksbury
19	779.7	Bellingham	Bellingham
20	768.4	Attleboro	Attleboro
21	761.1	North Reading	North Reading
22	751.0	Spencer-E Brookfield	Spencer
23	721.5	Medway	Medway
24	718.2	North Attleborough	N Attleborough
25	715.7	Canton	Canton
26	710.6	Billerica	Billerica
27	706.8	Boston	Boston
28	698.0	Carver	Carver
29	693.8	Hanover	Hanover
30	690.6	Wakefield	Wakefield
31	690.0	North Adams	North Adams
32	681.7	Abington	Abington
32	681.7	Malden	Malden
34	670.3	Haverhill	Haverhill
35	670.1	Springfield	Springfield
36	661.2	Saugus	Saugus
37	646.2	Fall River	Fall River
38	645.3	Brockton	Brockton
39	637.7	Easton	North Easton
40	636.0	Northbridge	Whitinsville
41	630.2	Chelsea	Chelsea
42	629.4	Lowell	Lowell
43	624.7	Middleborough	Middleborough
44	609.0	Dracut	Dracut
45	606.1	New Bedford	New Bedford
46	599.2	Dedham	Dedham
47	599.1	Weymouth	Weymouth
48	597.6	Westfield	Westfield
49	595.6	Lawrence	Lawrence
50	595.3	Newburyport	Newburyport
51	593.9	Andover	Andover
52	593.7	Dudley-Charlton Reg	Dudley
53	592.8	Mansfield	Mansfield
54	591.8	Triton	Byfield
55	584.7	Lynn	Lynn
56	580.7	Wareham	Wareham
57	574.6	Braintree	Braintree
58	574.0	Worcester	Worcester
59	573.5	Blackstone-Millville	Blackstone
60	565.0	Dighton-Rehoboth	Rehoboth
61	564.3	Medfield	Medfield
62	564.2	Lynnfield	Lynnfield
63	556.5	Whitman-Hanson	Whitman
64	555.5	Falmouth	East Falmouth
65	550.4	Pittsfield	Pittsfield
66	550.3	Hampden-Wilbraham	Wilbraham
67	544.7	Easthampton	Easthampton
68	544.5	Somerset	Somerset
69	543.1	Westport	Westport
70	541.9	Agawam	Feeding Hills
71	541.7	Wilmington	Wilmington
72	537.3	Winthrop	Winthrop
73	534.3	Woburn	Woburn
74	532.1	Everett	Everett
75	524.9	Foxborough	Foxborough
76	524.4	Waltham	Waltham
77	523.1	Milford	Milford
78	522.7	Duxbury	Duxbury
79	522.4	Danvers	Danvers
80	514.1	Dartmouth	South Dartmouth
81	510.9	Marshfield	Marshfield
82	507.3	Harwich	Harwich
83	506.0	Bourne	Bourne
84	505.3	Georgetown	Georgetown
85	505.0	Clinton	Clinton
86	504.4	Acton	Acton
87	495.6	West Springfield	W Springfield
88	493.5	Concord	Concord
89	491.2	Longmeadow	Longmeadow
90	490.6	Grafton	Grafton
91	487.0	Ipswich	Ipswich
92	485.1	Hingham	Hingham
93	485.0	Leicester	Leicester
94	476.1	Winchester	Winchester
95	471.6	Medford	Medford
96	467.2	Stoneham	Stoneham
97	466.2	Ludlow	Ludlow
98	465.9	Norwood	Norwood
99	465.6	Seekonk	Seekonk
100	461.0	Adams-Cheshire	Cheshire
101	459.1	Southborough	Northborough
102	457.2	Central Berkshire	Dalton
103	454.6	Norton	Norton
104	453.3	Amesbury	Amesbury
105	451.4	Fairhaven	Fairhaven
106	449.4	Sudbury	Sudbury
107	447.2	Uxbridge	Uxbridge
108	446.6	Gloucester	Gloucester
109	446.2	Taunton	Taunton
110	442.5	Arlington	Arlington
111	440.3	Douglas	Douglas
112	429.0	Mendon-Upton	Mendon
113	425.9	Beverly	Beverly
114	425.2	Wellesley	Wellesley
115	424.0	Greenfield	Greenfield
116	418.0	Palmer	Palmer
117	412.4	Walpole	Walpole
118	409.3	Sharon	Sharon
119	405.6	Ashburnham-Westminster	Westminster
120	402.4	Mohawk Trail	Shelburne Falls
121	401.6	Millbury	Millbury
122	397.8	Swansea	Swansea
123	397.0	Swampscott	Swampscott
124	391.0	Littleton	Littleton
125	389.8	North Middlesex	Townsend

Rank		District Name	City
126	387.3	Somerville	Somerville
127	385.8	Framingham	Framingham
128	385.0	Marlborough	Marlborough
129	381.3	Holyoke	Holyoke
130	379.2	Freetown-Lakeville	Lakeville
131	378.6	Cambridge	Cambridge
132	375.4	Winchendon	Winchendon
133	372.9	Athol-Royalston	Athol
134	372.8	Hopkinton	Hopkinton
135	370.0	Ashland	Ashland
136	369.3	North Andover	North Andover
137	368.5	Wayland	Wayland
138	368.1	Peabody	Peabody
139	366.4	Leominster	Leominster
140	366.0	Lunenburg	Lunenburg
141	363.6	Webster	Webster
142	360.4	Barnstable	Hyannis
143	359.0	Belchertown	Belchertown
144	354.3	Quabbin	Barre
145	353.2	Sutton	Sutton
146	350.6	Stoughton	Stoughton
147	348.8	Groton-Dunstable	Groton
148	346.0	East Bridgewater	E Bridgewater
149	343.3	Plymouth	Plymouth
150	343.1	Monson	Monson
151	342.2	Chicopee	Chicopee
152	333.7	Tyngsborough	Tyngsborough
153	330.9	Northampton	Northampton
154	329.9	Chelmsford	N Chelmsford
155	327.4	Scituate	Scituate
156	327.0	Narragansett	Baldwinville
157	325.8	Hudson	Hudson
158	322.9	Belmont	Belmont
159	322.3	Norwell	Norwell
160	320.3	King Philip	Wrentham
161	320.2	Tantasqua	Fiskdale
162	316.1	Auburn	Auburn
163	315.5	Greater Lowell Voc Tec	Tyngsborough
164	313.3	Milton	Milton
165	312.6	Nashoba	Bolton
166	306.8	Westwood	Westwood
167	305.3	East Longmeadow	E Longmeadow
168	304.9	Natick	Natick
169	303.5	Bedford	Bedford
170	303.0	Fitchburg	Fitchburg
171	301.6	Marblehead	Marblehead
172	300.7	Westford	Westford
173	289.2	Methuen	Methuen
174	288.5	Mashpee	Mashpee
175	288.0	Southbridge	Southbridge
176	283.4	Holliston	Holliston
177	280.6	Westborough	Westborough
178	278.7	Southwick-Tolland	Southwick
179	278.4	Newton	Newtonville
180	276.1	Brookline	Brookline
181	268.1	Silver Lake	Kingston
182	262.1	Burlington	Burlington
183	258.0	Needham	Needham
184	254.1	Lexington	Lexington
185	251.3	Quincy	Quincy
186	250.7	Gardner	Gardner
187	244.3	Watertown	Watertown
188	234.7	Weston	Weston
189	232.0	Greater New Bedford	New Bedford
190	228.1	Nauset	Orleans
191	225.1	Acton-Boxborough	Acton
192	207.6	Masconomet	Topsfield
193	204.1	Amherst-Pelham	Amherst
194	n/a	Pembroke	Pembroke

Current Spending per Student in FY2003

Rank	Dollars	District Name	City
1	20,835	Cambridge	Cambridge
2	14,959	Waltham	Waltham
3	14,734	Watertown	Watertown
4	14,672	Somerville	Somerville
5	14,602	Boston	Boston
6	13,773	Greater Lowell Voc Tec	Tyngsborough
7	13,746	Weston	Weston
8	13,723	Brookline	Brookline
9	13,609	Greater New Bedford	New Bedford
10	13,566	Newton	Newtonville
11	12,968	Medford	Medford
12	12,951	Holyoke	Holyoke
13	12,557	Concord	Concord
14	12,551	Amherst-Pelham	Amherst
15	12,550	Framingham	Framingham
16	12,405	Nauset	Orleans
17	12,200	Bedford	Bedford
18	12,184	Wellesley	Wellesley
19	12,037	Westwood	Westwood
20	12,014	Springfield	Springfield
21	11,853	Chelsea	Chelsea
22	11,580	Malden	Malden
23	11,578	Wayland	Wayland
24	11,415	Woburn	Woburn
25	11,413	Lowell	Lowell
26	11,397	Worcester	Worcester
27	11,389	Lexington	Lexington
28	11,381	Lawrence	Lawrence
29	11,348	Marlborough	Marlborough
30	11,316	Harwich	Harwich
31	11,265	Salem	Salem
32	11,252	North Adams	North Adams
33	11,212	Brockton	Brockton
34	11,184	Mohawk Trail	Shelburne Falls
35	11,167	Newburyport	Newburyport
36	11,159	Dedham	Dedham
37	11,119	Lynn	Lynn
38	11,041	Burlington	Burlington
39	10,996	Athol-Royalston	Athol
40	10,940	Needham	Needham
41	10,910	Masconomet	Topsfield
42	10,846	Hopkinton	Hopkinton
43	10,841	Greenfield	Greenfield
44	10,813	Acton-Boxborough	Acton
45	10,764	Andover	Andover
46	10,736	Littleton	Littleton
47	10,719	Westborough	Westborough
48	10,688	Fall River	Fall River
49	10,612	Northampton	Northampton
50	10,559	Natick	Natick
51	10,543	Quincy	Quincy
52	10,542	New Bedford	New Bedford
53	10,517	Nashoba	Bolton
54	10,401	Somerset	Somerset
55	10,313	Wakefield	Wakefield
56	10,307	Braintree	Braintree
57	10,261	Swampscott	Swampscott
58	10,246	Winchester	Winchester
59	10,229	Fitchburg	Fitchburg
60	10,225	Marblehead	Marblehead
61	10,196	Webster	Webster
62	10,155	Dennis-Yarmouth	South Yarmouth
62	10,155	Tantasqua	Fiskdale
64	10,154	Hamilton-Wenham	Wenham
65	10,100	Canton	Canton
66	10,094	Milford	Milford
67	10,091	Westfield	Westfield
68	10,077	Foxborough	Foxborough
69	10,076	Falmouth	East Falmouth
70	10,028	Norwood	Norwood
71	10,017	Pittsfield	Pittsfield
72	9,972	Clinton	Clinton
73	9,949	Sharon	Sharon
73	9,949	Southbridge	Southbridge
75	9,948	Central Berkshire	Dalton
76	9,938	Arlington	Arlington
77	9,930	West Springfield	W Springfield
78	9,898	Auburn	Auburn
79	9,882	Silver Lake	Kingston
80	9,829	Hudson	Hudson
81	9,812	Holliston	Holliston
82	9,793	Milton	Milton
83	9,737	Beverly	Beverly
84	9,728	Norwell	Norwell
85	9,694	Melrose	Melrose
86	9,674	Easthampton	Easthampton
87	9,641	Plymouth	Plymouth
88	9,628	Randolph	Randolph
89	9,614	Belmont	Belmont
90	9,607	Haverhill	Haverhill
91	9,605	Peabody	Peabody
92	9,581	Danvers	Danvers
93	9,496	Gloucester	Gloucester
94	9,495	Ashland	Ashland
95	9,490	Bourne	Bourne
96	9,478	Palmer	Palmer
97	9,454	Sudbury	Sudbury
98	9,449	Adams-Cheshire	Cheshire
99	9,447	Everett	Everett
100	9,422	Leominster	Leominster
101	9,419	Billerica	Billerica
102	9,399	Northbridge	Whitinsville
103	9,377	Revere	Revere
104	9,372	Mashpee	Mashpee
105	9,348	Winthrop	Winthrop
106	9,291	Saugus	Saugus
107	9,273	Wareham	Wareham
108	9,261	Chicopee	Chicopee
109	9,255	Barnstable	Hyannis
110	9,251	Spencer-E Brookfield	Spencer
110	9,251	Walpole	Walpole
112	9,226	Freetown-Lakeville	Lakeville
113	9,206	North Andover	North Andover
114	9,205	Stoughton	Stoughton
115	9,164	South Hadley	South Hadley
116	9,157	Lynnfield	Lynnfield
117	9,154	Weymouth	Weymouth
118	9,145	Wilmington	Wilmington
119	9,121	Winchendon	Winchendon
120	9,101	Carver	Carver
121	9,085	Seekonk	Seekonk
122	9,072	Stoneham	Stoneham
123	9,048	Amesbury	Amesbury
124	9,029	King Philip	Wrentham
125	9,010	Taunton	Taunton
126	8,999	Ipswich	Ipswich
127	8,974	Methuen	Methuen
128	8,967	Longmeadow	Longmeadow
129	8,962	Chelmsford	N Chelmsford
130	8,943	Tyngsborough	Tyngsborough
131	8,927	Hingham	Hingham
132	8,921	Ashburnham-Westminster	Westminster
133	8,860	Oxford	Oxford
134	8,852	Agawam	Feeding Hills
135	8,837	Quabbin	Barre
136	8,803	Marshfield	Marshfield
137	8,788	Triton	Byfield
138	8,787	Rockland	Rockland
139	8,776	Swansea	Swansea
140	8,770	Pentucket	West Newbury
141	8,759	Narragansett	Baldwinville
142	8,758	East Longmeadow	E Longmeadow
143	8,751	North Attleborough	N Attleborough
144	8,715	Northborough	Northborough
145	8,703	Lunenburg	Lunenburg
146	8,694	Hampden-Wilbraham	Wilbraham
147	8,683	Franklin	Franklin
148	8,653	Millbury	Millbury
148	8,653	Scituate	Scituate
150	8,646	Duxbury	Duxbury
151	8,644	Blackstone-Millville	Blackstone
152	8,630	Fairhaven	Fairhaven
153	8,622	North Middlesex	Townsend
154	8,617	Westford	Westford
155	8,614	Belchertown	Belchertown
156	8,610	Leicester	Leicester
157	8,605	Attleboro	Attleboro
158	8,556	Wachusett	Jefferson
159	8,541	Southborough	Northborough
160	8,533	Grafton	Grafton
160	8,533	Ludlow	Ludlow
162	8,528	Bellingham	Bellingham
163	8,524	Hanover	Hanover
164	8,492	Whitman-Hanson	Whitman
165	8,460	Reading	Reading
166	8,453	Mansfield	Mansfield
167	8,444	Southwick-Tolland	Southwick
168	8,422	Shrewsbury	Shrewsbury
169	8,394	Gardner	Gardner
170	8,368	Acton	Acton
171	8,319	Uxbridge	Uxbridge
172	8,281	Westport	Westport
173	8,252	Monson	Monson
174	8,218	Groton-Dunstable	Groton
174	8,218	Tewksbury	Tewksbury
176	8,195	Medway	Medway
177	8,148	Sutton	Sutton
178	8,147	Dartmouth	South Dartmouth
179	8,144	Bridgewater-Raynham	Raynham
180	8,141	Middleborough	Middleborough
181	8,073	Dudley-Charlton Reg	Dudley
182	8,038	Dighton-Rehoboth	Rehoboth
183	7,972	Pembroke	Pembroke
184	7,947	Abington	Abington
185	7,927	Medfield	Medfield
186	7,925	Dracut	Dracut
187	7,920	North Reading	North Reading
188	7,918	Mendon-Upton	Mendon
189	7,843	Norton	Norton
190	7,840	East Bridgewater	E Bridgewater
191	7,820	Georgetown	Georgetown
192	7,806	Easton	North Easton
193	7,777	Sandwich	Sandwich
194	7,731	Douglas	Douglas

Number of Diploma Recipients

Rank	Number	District Name	City
1	2,816	Boston	Boston
2	1,087	Worcester	Worcester
3	848	Newton	Newtonville
4	839	Springfield	Springfield
5	732	Lowell	Lowell
6	689	Brockton	Brockton
7	676	Lynn	Lynn
8	591	Quincy	Quincy

Rank		District Name	City
9	565	New Bedford	New Bedford
10	534	Plymouth	Plymouth
11	499	Fall River	Fall River
12	426	Chicopee	Chicopee
13	412	Westfield	Westfield
14	401	Chelmsford	N Chelmsford
15	396	Lexington	Lexington
16	395	Framingham	Framingham
17	393	Barnstable	Hyannis
18	390	Brookline	Brookline
19	384	Peabody	Peabody
20	383	Andover	Andover
20	383	Weymouth	Weymouth
22	377	Haverhill	Haverhill
23	363	Wachusett	Jefferson
24	354	Methuen	Methuen
25	352	Silver Lake	Kingston
26	350	Acton-Boxborough	Acton
26	350	Leominster	Leominster
28	342	Attleboro	Attleboro
29	338	Cambridge	Cambridge
30	337	Greater Lowell Voc Tec	Tyngsborough
31	335	Billerica	Billerica
32	334	Somerville	Somerville
33	331	Bridgewater-Raynham	Raynham
34	328	Waltham	Waltham
35	322	Braintree	Braintree
36	316	Pittsfield	Pittsfield
36	316	Taunton	Taunton
38	312	Westford	Westford
39	308	Malden	Malden
40	305	Franklin	Franklin
41	303	Dartmouth	South Dartmouth
41	303	Hampden-Wilbraham	Wilbraham
43	302	Needham	Needham
44	300	Fitchburg	Fitchburg
45	298	Amherst-Pelham	Amherst
46	294	Everett	Everett
47	291	Woburn	Woburn
48	290	Gloucester	Gloucester
49	288	Reading	Reading
50	285	Beverly	Beverly
51	283	Medford	Medford
52	277	Marshfield	Marshfield
53	275	Holyoke	Holyoke
54	271	Easton	North Easton
55	270	Lawrence	Lawrence
56	269	Dennis-Yarmouth	South Yarmouth
56	269	Masconomet	Topsfield
58	263	North Attleborough	N Attleborough
59	260	Arlington	Arlington
60	259	Shrewsbury	Shrewsbury
61	258	Greater New Bedford	New Bedford
61	258	Whitman-Hanson	Whitman
63	257	Natick	Natick
64	254	Sharon	Sharon
65	248	North Andover	North Andover
66	246	Dracut	Dracut
66	246	Longmeadow	Longmeadow
68	245	Agawam	Feeding Hills
69	244	Wellesley	Wellesley
70	241	North Middlesex	Townsend
71	238	Danvers	Danvers
71	238	Falmouth	East Falmouth
73	237	Sandwich	Sandwich
74	236	Duxbury	Duxbury
74	236	Revere	Revere
76	234	Norwood	Norwood
77	232	Hingham	Hingham
78	227	Milford	Milford
79	224	Westborough	Westborough
80	222	West Springfield	W Springfield
81	221	Dudley-Charlton Reg	Dudley
82	220	Milton	Milton
83	219	Stoughton	Stoughton
84	217	King Philip	Wrentham
84	217	Salem	Salem
86	216	Winchester	Winchester
87	213	Melrose	Melrose
87	213	Wakefield	Wakefield
89	212	Nauset	Orleans
89	212	Tantasqua	Fiskdale
91	211	Somerset	Somerset
92	209	Mansfield	Mansfield
93	208	Marblehead	Marblehead
94	206	Walpole	Walpole
95	205	Dighton-Rehoboth	Rehoboth
96	203	Belmont	Belmont
96	203	Stoneham	Stoneham
98	202	Burlington	Burlington
99	200	Watertown	Watertown
100	198	Triton	Byfield
101	197	Pentucket	West Newbury

Rank		District Name	City
102	196	Randolph	Randolph
103	195	Ludlow	Ludlow
104	193	Wilmington	Wilmington
105	191	Foxborough	Foxborough
106	190	Nashoba	Bolton
107	189	Middleborough	Middleborough
108	188	Marlborough	Marlborough
109	187	Holliston	Holliston
109	187	Wayland	Wayland
111	186	East Longmeadow	E Longmeadow
112	181	Northampton	Northampton
112	181	Tewksbury	Tewksbury
114	177	Hudson	Hudson
114	177	Rockland	Rockland
116	176	Scituate	Scituate
117	175	Saugus	Saugus
118	174	Amesbury	Amesbury
118	174	Ashburnham-Westminster	Westminster
120	172	Canton	Canton
120	172	Gardner	Gardner
122	171	Central Berkshire	Dalton
122	171	Swampscott	Swampscott
124	164	Wareham	Wareham
125	162	Hopkinton	Hopkinton
126	161	Bellingham	Bellingham
126	161	Chelsea	Chelsea
126	161	Quabbin	Barre
129	160	South Hadley	South Hadley
130	158	Hamilton-Wenham	Wenham
131	156	East Bridgewater	E Bridgewater
132	155	Medfield	Medfield
133	154	Bedford	Bedford
133	154	Medway	Medway
135	151	Auburn	Auburn
135	151	Oxford	Oxford
135	151	Westwood	Westwood
138	150	Hanover	Hanover
139	148	Freetown-Lakeville	Lakeville
139	148	Swansea	Swansea
141	144	Dedham	Dedham
142	143	Blackstone-Millville	Blackstone
143	139	Weston	Weston
144	135	Ashland	Ashland
145	134	Southwick-Tolland	Southwick
146	131	Clinton	Clinton
146	131	Norwell	Norwell
148	130	Easthampton	Easthampton
148	130	Newburyport	Newburyport
150	129	Fairhaven	Fairhaven
151	128	Lunenburg	Lunenburg
151	128	Norton	Norton
151	128	Seekonk	Seekonk
151	128	Spencer-E Brookfield	Spencer
155	127	Tyngsborough	Tyngsborough
156	126	Belchertown	Belchertown
157	124	Greenfield	Greenfield
158	119	Grafton	Grafton
159	118	Groton-Dunstable	Groton
159	118	Uxbridge	Uxbridge
161	117	Mashpee	Mashpee
162	116	Ipswich	Ipswich
163	115	Abington	Abington
164	113	Bourne	Bourne
165	112	Adams-Cheshire	Cheshire
166	111	Mendon-Upton	Mendon
167	108	Athol-Royalston	Athol
167	108	Carver	Carver
169	107	Sutton	Sutton
170	106	Leicester	Leicester
170	106	Lynnfield	Lynnfield
172	105	North Adams	North Adams
173	102	Northbridge	Whitinsville
173	102	Palmer	Palmer
175	99	Webster	Webster
176	96	Mohawk Trail	Shelburne Falls
177	94	Georgetown	Georgetown
178	92	Millbury	Millbury
178	92	Southbridge	Southbridge
180	91	Harwich	Harwich
181	90	North Reading	North Reading
181	90	Winthrop	Winthrop
183	89	Winchendon	Winchendon
184	82	Littleton	Littleton
185	81	Westport	Westport
186	79	Narragansett	Baldwinville
187	77	Monson	Monson
188	67	Douglas	Douglas
189	n/a	Acton	Acton
189	n/a	Concord	Concord
189	n/a	Northborough	Northborough
189	n/a	Pembroke	Pembroke
189	n/a	Southborough	Northborough
189	n/a	Sudbury	Sudbury

High School Drop-out Rate

Rank	Percent	District Name	City
1	n/a	Abington	Abington
1	n/a	Acton	Acton
1	n/a	Acton-Boxborough	Acton
1	n/a	Adams-Cheshire	Cheshire
1	n/a	Agawam	Feeding Hills
1	n/a	Amesbury	Amesbury
1	n/a	Amherst-Pelham	Amherst
1	n/a	Andover	Andover
1	n/a	Arlington	Arlington
1	n/a	Ashburnham-Westminster	Westminster
1	n/a	Ashland	Ashland
1	n/a	Athol-Royalston	Athol
1	n/a	Attleboro	Attleboro
1	n/a	Auburn	Auburn
1	n/a	Barnstable	Hyannis
1	n/a	Bedford	Bedford
1	n/a	Belchertown	Belchertown
1	n/a	Bellingham	Bellingham
1	n/a	Belmont	Belmont
1	n/a	Beverly	Beverly
1	n/a	Billerica	Billerica
1	n/a	Blackstone-Millville	Blackstone
1	n/a	Boston	Boston
1	n/a	Bourne	Bourne
1	n/a	Braintree	Braintree
1	n/a	Bridgewater-Raynham	Raynham
1	n/a	Brockton	Brockton
1	n/a	Brookline	Brookline
1	n/a	Burlington	Burlington
1	n/a	Cambridge	Cambridge
1	n/a	Canton	Canton
1	n/a	Carver	Carver
1	n/a	Central Berkshire	Dalton
1	n/a	Chelmsford	N Chelmsford
1	n/a	Chelsea	Chelsea
1	n/a	Chicopee	Chicopee
1	n/a	Clinton	Clinton
1	n/a	Concord	Concord
1	n/a	Danvers	Danvers
1	n/a	Dartmouth	South Dartmouth
1	n/a	Dedham	Dedham
1	n/a	Dennis-Yarmouth	South Yarmouth
1	n/a	Dighton-Rehoboth	Rehoboth
1	n/a	Douglas	Douglas
1	n/a	Dracut	Dracut
1	n/a	Dudley-Charlton Reg	Dudley
1	n/a	Duxbury	Duxbury
1	n/a	East Bridgewater	E Bridgewater
1	n/a	East Longmeadow	E Longmeadow
1	n/a	Easthampton	Easthampton
1	n/a	Easton	North Easton
1	n/a	Everett	Everett
1	n/a	Fairhaven	Fairhaven
1	n/a	Fall River	Fall River
1	n/a	Falmouth	East Falmouth
1	n/a	Fitchburg	Fitchburg
1	n/a	Foxborough	Foxborough
1	n/a	Framingham	Framingham
1	n/a	Franklin	Franklin
1	n/a	Freetown-Lakeville	Lakeville
1	n/a	Gardner	Gardner
1	n/a	Georgetown	Georgetown
1	n/a	Gloucester	Gloucester
1	n/a	Grafton	Grafton
1	n/a	Greater Lowell Voc Tec	Tyngsborough
1	n/a	Greater New Bedford	New Bedford
1	n/a	Greenfield	Greenfield
1	n/a	Groton-Dunstable	Groton
1	n/a	Hamilton-Wenham	Wenham
1	n/a	Hampden-Wilbraham	Wilbraham
1	n/a	Hanover	Hanover
1	n/a	Harwich	Harwich
1	n/a	Haverhill	Haverhill
1	n/a	Hingham	Hingham
1	n/a	Holliston	Holliston
1	n/a	Holyoke	Holyoke
1	n/a	Hopkinton	Hopkinton
1	n/a	Hudson	Hudson
1	n/a	Ipswich	Ipswich
1	n/a	King Philip	Wrentham
1	n/a	Lawrence	Lawrence
1	n/a	Leicester	Leicester
1	n/a	Leominster	Leominster
1	n/a	Lexington	Lexington
1	n/a	Littleton	Littleton
1	n/a	Longmeadow	Longmeadow
1	n/a	Lowell	Lowell
1	n/a	Ludlow	Ludlow

1	n/a	Lunenburg	Lunenburg
1	n/a	Lynn	Lynn
1	n/a	Lynnfield	Lynnfield
1	n/a	Malden	Malden
1	n/a	Mansfield	Mansfield
1	n/a	Marblehead	Marblehead
1	n/a	Marlborough	Marlborough
1	n/a	Marshfield	Marshfield
1	n/a	Masconomet	Topsfield
1	n/a	Mashpee	Mashpee
1	n/a	Medfield	Medfield
1	n/a	Medford	Medford
1	n/a	Medway	Medway
1	n/a	Melrose	Melrose
1	n/a	Mendon-Upton	Mendon
1	n/a	Methuen	Methuen
1	n/a	Middleborough	Middleborough
1	n/a	Milford	Milford
1	n/a	Millbury	Millbury
1	n/a	Milton	Milton
1	n/a	Mohawk Trail	Shelburne Falls
1	n/a	Monson	Monson
1	n/a	Narragansett	Baldwinville
1	n/a	Nashoba	Bolton
1	n/a	Natick	Natick
1	n/a	Nauset	Orleans
1	n/a	Needham	Needham
1	n/a	New Bedford	New Bedford
1	n/a	Newburyport	Newburyport
1	n/a	Newton	Newtonville
1	n/a	North Adams	North Adams
1	n/a	North Andover	North Andover
1	n/a	North Attleborough	N Attleborough
1	n/a	North Middlesex	Townsend
1	n/a	North Reading	North Reading
1	n/a	Northampton	Northampton
1	n/a	Northborough	Northborough
1	n/a	Northbridge	Whitinsville
1	n/a	Norton	Norton
1	n/a	Norwell	Norwell
1	n/a	Norwood	Norwood
1	n/a	Oxford	Oxford
1	n/a	Palmer	Palmer
1	n/a	Peabody	Peabody
1	n/a	Pembroke	Pembroke
1	n/a	Pentucket	West Newbury
1	n/a	Pittsfield	Pittsfield
1	n/a	Plymouth	Plymouth
1	n/a	Quabbin	Barre
1	n/a	Quincy	Quincy
1	n/a	Randolph	Randolph
1	n/a	Reading	Reading
1	n/a	Revere	Revere
1	n/a	Rockland	Rockland
1	n/a	Salem	Salem
1	n/a	Sandwich	Sandwich
1	n/a	Saugus	Saugus
1	n/a	Scituate	Scituate
1	n/a	Seekonk	Seekonk
1	n/a	Sharon	Sharon
1	n/a	Shrewsbury	Shrewsbury
1	n/a	Silver Lake	Kingston
1	n/a	Somerset	Somerset
1	n/a	Somerville	Somerville
1	n/a	South Hadley	South Hadley
1	n/a	Southborough	Northborough
1	n/a	Southbridge	Southbridge
1	n/a	Southwick-Tolland	Southwick
1	n/a	Spencer-E Brookfield	Spencer
1	n/a	Springfield	Springfield
1	n/a	Stoneham	Stoneham
1	n/a	Stoughton	Stoughton
1	n/a	Sudbury	Sudbury
1	n/a	Sutton	Sutton
1	n/a	Swampscott	Swampscott
1	n/a	Swansea	Swansea
1	n/a	Tantasqua	Fiskdale
1	n/a	Taunton	Taunton
1	n/a	Tewksbury	Tewksbury
1	n/a	Triton	Byfield
1	n/a	Tyngsborough	Tyngsborough
1	n/a	Uxbridge	Uxbridge
1	n/a	Wachusett	Jefferson
1	n/a	Wakefield	Wakefield
1	n/a	Walpole	Walpole
1	n/a	Waltham	Waltham
1	n/a	Wareham	Wareham
1	n/a	Watertown	Watertown
1	n/a	Wayland	Wayland
1	n/a	Webster	Webster
1	n/a	Wellesley	Wellesley
1	n/a	West Springfield	W Springfield

1	n/a	Westborough	Westborough
1	n/a	Westfield	Westfield
1	n/a	Westford	Westford
1	n/a	Weston	Weston
1	n/a	Westport	Westport
1	n/a	Westwood	Westwood
1	n/a	Weymouth	Weymouth
1	n/a	Whitman-Hanson	Whitman
1	n/a	Wilmington	Wilmington
1	n/a	Winchendon	Winchendon
1	n/a	Winchester	Winchester
1	n/a	Winthrop	Winthrop
1	n/a	Woburn	Woburn
1	n/a	Worcester	Worcester

Michigan

Michigan Public School Educational Profile

Category	Value	Category	Value
Schools (2003-2004)	4,008	**Diploma Recipients** (2002-2003)	94,990
Instructional Level		White, Non-Hispanic	77,939
Primary	2,158	Black, Non-Hispanic	11,617
Middle	659	Asian/Pacific Islander	2,249
High	687	American Indian/Alaskan Native	901
Other Level	496	Hispanic	2,284
Curriculum		**High School Drop-out Rate** (%) (2001-2002)	n/a
Regular	3,532	White, Non-Hispanic	n/a
Special Education	179	Black, Non-Hispanic	n/a
Vocational	45	Asian/Pacific Islander	n/a
Alternative	244	American Indian/Alaskan Native	n/a
Type		Hispanic	n/a
Magnet	300	**Staff** (2003-2004)	
Charter	212	Teachers	95,563.0
Title I Eligible	769	Average Salary[1] ($)	54,474
School-wide Title I	769	Librarians/Media Specialists	1,405.0
Students (2003-2004)	1,757,604	Guidance Counselors	2,708.0
Gender (%)		**Ratios** (2003-2004)	
Male	51.6	Student/Teacher Ratio	18.4 to 1
Female	48.4	Student/Librarian Ratio	1,251.0 to 1
Race/Ethnicity (%)		Student/Counselor Ratio	649.0 to 1
White, Non-Hispanic	72.7	**College Entrance Exam Scores** (2005)	
Black, Non-Hispanic	20.0	Scholastic Aptitude Test (SAT)	
Asian/Pacific Islander	2.2	Participation Rate (%)	10
American Indian/Alaskan Native	1.0	Mean SAT Reasoning Test Verbal Score	568
Hispanic	4.0	Mean SAT Reasoning Test Math Score	579
Classification (%)		American College Testing Program (ACT)	
Individual Education Program (IEP)	13.9	Participation Rate (%)	69
Migrant (2002-2003)	0.4	Average Composite Score	21.4
English Language Learner (ELL)	3.5	Average English Score	20.7
Eligible for Free Lunch Program	26.5	Average Math Score	21.2
Eligible for Reduced-Price Lunch Program	6.1	Average Reading Score	21.8
Current Spending ($ per student in FY 2003)	8,126	Average Science Score	21.6
Instruction	4,777		
Support Services	3,092		

Note: For an explanation of data, please refer to the User's Guide in the front of the book; (1) AFT estimate

Michigan NAEP 2005 Test Scores

Reading			Mathematics		
Grade/Category	Value	Rank	Grade/Category	Value	Rank
4th Grade			**4th Grade**		
Average Proficiency	218.3 (1.49)	30/51	Average Proficiency	237.7 (1.20)	31/51
Proficiency by Gender/Race/Ethnicity			Proficiency by Gender/Race/Ethnicity		
Male	215.7 (1.80)	29/51	Male	239.8 (1.27)	27/51
Female	220.8 (1.55)	33/51	Female	235.5 (1.41)	32/51
White, Non-Hispanic	226.3 (1.44)	26/51	White, Non-Hispanic	245.5 (1.04)	21/51
Black, Non-Hispanic	190.1 (2.66)	39/42	Black, Non-Hispanic	210.6 (1.78)	39/42
Asian, Non-Hispanic	n/a	n/a	Asian, Non-Hispanic	n/a	n/a
American Indian, Non-Hispanic	n/a	n/a	American Indian, Non-Hispanic	n/a	n/a
Hispanic	n/a	n/a	Hispanic	n/a	n/a
Proficiency by Class Size			Proficiency by Class Size		
Less than 16 Students	n/a	n/a	Less than 16 Students	n/a	n/a
16 to 18 Students	n/a	n/a	16 to 18 Students	n/a	n/a
19 to 20 Students	n/a	n/a	19 to 20 Students	n/a	n/a
21 to 25 Students	220.4 (1.72)	30/51	21 to 25 Students	238.7 (1.61)	32/51
Greater than 25 Students	217.8 (2.65)	25/36	Greater than 25 Students	239.4 (2.69)	16/33
Percent Attaining Achievement Levels			Percent Attaining Achievement Levels		
Below Basic	37.1 (1.66)	21/51	Below Basic	20.9 (1.46)	21/51
Basic or Above	62.9 (1.66)	31/51	Basic or Above	79.1 (1.46)	31/51
Proficient or Above	31.7 (1.43)	27/51	Proficient or Above	37.7 (1.65)	24/51
Advanced or Above	7.4 (0.85)	19/51	Advanced or Above	5.3 (0.67)	17/51
8th Grade			**8th Grade**		
Average Proficiency	261.1 (1.16)	29/51	Average Proficiency	277.3 (1.53)	33/51
Proficiency by Gender/Race/Ethnicity			Proficiency by Gender/Race/Ethnicity		
Male	256.5 (1.54)	28/51	Male	279.4 (1.71)	31/51
Female	265.9 (1.29)	30/51	Female	275.3 (1.76)	33/51
White, Non-Hispanic	267.7 (1.20)	31/51	White, Non-Hispanic	285.5 (1.62)	32/51
Black, Non-Hispanic	238.6 (2.10)	33/40	Black, Non-Hispanic	247.5 (2.02)	32/41
Asian, Non-Hispanic	n/a	n/a	Asian, Non-Hispanic	n/a	n/a
American Indian, Non-Hispanic	n/a	n/a	American Indian, Non-Hispanic	n/a	n/a
Hispanic	249.8 (4.15)	13/38	Hispanic	265.0 (3.78)	12/38
Proficiency by Parents Highest Level of Ed.			Proficiency by Parents Highest Level of Ed.		
Did Not Finish High School	247.3 (3.44)	17/49	Did Not Finish High School	253.6 (3.99)	41/50
Graduated High School	250.6 (1.80)	31/50	Graduated High School	264.9 (2.41)	33/50
Some Education After High School	261.7 (2.09)	41/50	Some Education After High School	280.6 (1.72)	27/50
Graduated College	269.6 (1.46)	32/50	Graduated College	286.0 (1.86)	33/50
Percent Attaining Achievement Levels			Percent Attaining Achievement Levels		
Below Basic	37.1 (1.66)	21/51	Below Basic	32.3 (1.55)	19/51
Basic or Above	62.9 (1.66)	31/51	Basic or Above	67.7 (1.55)	33/51
Proficient or Above	31.7 (1.43)	27/51	Proficient or Above	29.3 (1.79)	30/51
Advanced or Above	7.4 (0.85)	19/51	Advanced or Above	5.5 (0.83)	23/51

Note: *For an explanation of data, please refer to the User's Guide in the front of the book; n/a indicates data not available*

Allegan Public Schools
550 Fifth St · Allegan, MI 49010-1670
(269) 673-5431 · http://www.accn.org/~aps/
Grade Span: KG-12; **Agency Type:** 1
Schools: 7
　4 Primary; 1 Middle; 2 High; 0 Other Level
　6 Regular; 0 Special Education; 0 Vocational; 1 Alternative
　0 Magnet; 0 Charter; 0 Title I Eligible; 0 School-wide Title I
Students: 3,025　(50.6% male; 49.3% female)
　Individual Education Program: 403 (13.3%);
　English Language Learner: 5 (0.2%); Migrant: n/a
　Eligible for Free Lunch Program: 641 (21.2%)
　Eligible for Reduced-Price Lunch Program: 194 (6.4%)
Teachers: 171.0 (17.7 to 1)
Librarians/Media Specialists: 1.0 (3,025.0 to 1)
Guidance Counselors: 7.0 (432.1 to 1)
Current Spending: ($ per student per year):
　Total: $7,300; Instruction: $4,513; Support Services: $2,535
Enrollment, Drop-out Rates and Diploma Recipients by Race/Ethnicity

Category	Total	White	Black	Asian	AIAN	Hisp.
Enrollment (%)	100.0	92.8	3.7	0.7	0.3	2.3
Drop-out Rate (%)	n/a	n/a	n/a	n/a	n/a	n/a
H.S. Diplomas (#)	150	145	2	2	0	1

Hamilton Community Schools
4815 136th Ave · Hamilton, MI 49419-9604
Mailing Address: PO Box 300 · Hamilton, MI 49419-0300
(269) 751-5148 · http://www.remc7.k12.mi.us/hamilton/
Grade Span: KG-12; **Agency Type:** 1
Schools: 6
　4 Primary; 1 Middle; 1 High; 0 Other Level
　6 Regular; 0 Special Education; 0 Vocational; 0 Alternative
　6 Magnet; 0 Charter; 0 Title I Eligible; 0 School-wide Title I
Students: 2,551　(52.6% male; 47.3% female)
　Individual Education Program: 276 (10.8%);
　English Language Learner: 23 (0.9%); Migrant: n/a
　Eligible for Free Lunch Program: 220 (8.6%)
　Eligible for Reduced-Price Lunch Program: 123 (4.8%)
Teachers: 134.0 (19.0 to 1)
Librarians/Media Specialists: 4.0 (637.8 to 1)
Guidance Counselors: 4.0 (637.8 to 1)
Current Spending: ($ per student per year):
　Total: $6,482; Instruction: $3,827; Support Services: $2,432
Enrollment, Drop-out Rates and Diploma Recipients by Race/Ethnicity

Category	Total	White	Black	Asian	AIAN	Hisp.
Enrollment (%)	100.0	94.3	0.7	1.5	0.2	3.3
Drop-out Rate (%)	n/a	n/a	n/a	n/a	n/a	n/a
H.S. Diplomas (#)	131	127	0	2	1	1

Otsego Public Schools
313 W Allegan St · Otsego, MI 49078-1011
(269) 692-6066 · http://www.accn.org/~roo/
Grade Span: PK-12; **Agency Type:** 1
Schools: 5
　3 Primary; 1 Middle; 1 High; 0 Other Level
　5 Regular; 0 Special Education; 0 Vocational; 0 Alternative
　0 Magnet; 0 Charter; 0 Title I Eligible; 0 School-wide Title I
Students: 2,297　(52.4% male; 47.5% female)
　Individual Education Program: 263 (11.4%);
　English Language Learner: 18 (0.8%); Migrant: n/a
　Eligible for Free Lunch Program: 319 (13.9%)
　Eligible for Reduced-Price Lunch Program: 170 (7.4%)
Teachers: 130.0 (17.7 to 1)
Librarians/Media Specialists: 3.0 (765.7 to 1)
Guidance Counselors: 6.0 (382.8 to 1)
Current Spending: ($ per student per year):
　Total: $6,953; Instruction: $4,375; Support Services: $2,318
Enrollment, Drop-out Rates and Diploma Recipients by Race/Ethnicity

Category	Total	White	Black	Asian	AIAN	Hisp.
Enrollment (%)	100.0	97.3	0.9	0.4	0.2	0.6
Drop-out Rate (%)	n/a	n/a	n/a	n/a	n/a	n/a
H.S. Diplomas (#)	168	161	4	1	0	2

Plainwell Community Schools
600 School Dr · Plainwell, MI 49080-1582
(269) 685-5823 · http://www.plainwellschools.org
Grade Span: PK-12; **Agency Type:** 1
Schools: 6
　3 Primary; 1 Middle; 1 High; 1 Other Level
　5 Regular; 0 Special Education; 0 Vocational; 1 Alternative
　0 Magnet; 0 Charter; 0 Title I Eligible; 0 School-wide Title I
Students: 2,867　(51.6% male; 48.3% female)
　Individual Education Program: 311 (10.8%);

　English Language Learner: 0 (0.0%); Migrant: n/a
　Eligible for Free Lunch Program: 385 (13.4%)
　Eligible for Reduced-Price Lunch Program: 192 (6.7%)
Teachers: 157.0 (18.3 to 1)
Librarians/Media Specialists: 3.0 (955.7 to 1)
Guidance Counselors: 5.0 (573.4 to 1)
Current Spending: ($ per student per year):
　Total: $6,717; Instruction: $4,280; Support Services: $2,222
Enrollment, Drop-out Rates and Diploma Recipients by Race/Ethnicity

Category	Total	White	Black	Asian	AIAN	Hisp.
Enrollment (%)	100.0	96.7	1.3	0.7	0.1	1.1
Drop-out Rate (%)	n/a	n/a	n/a	n/a	n/a	n/a
H.S. Diplomas (#)	187	180	2	4	0	1

Wayland Union Schools
835 E Superior St · Wayland, MI 49348-9505
(269) 792-2181 · http://wayland.k12.mi.us/
Grade Span: PK-12; **Agency Type:** 1
Schools: 6
　3 Primary; 2 Middle; 1 High; 0 Other Level
　6 Regular; 0 Special Education; 0 Vocational; 0 Alternative
　0 Magnet; 0 Charter; 0 Title I Eligible; 0 School-wide Title I
Students: 3,326　(50.6% male; 49.3% female)
　Individual Education Program: 512 (15.4%);
　English Language Learner: 0 (0.0%); Migrant: n/a
　Eligible for Free Lunch Program: 535 (16.2%)
　Eligible for Reduced-Price Lunch Program: 280 (8.5%)
Teachers: 170.0 (19.4 to 1)
Librarians/Media Specialists: 3.0 (1,100.0 to 1)
Guidance Counselors: 3.0 (1,100.0 to 1)
Current Spending: ($ per student per year):
　Total: $6,842; Instruction: $3,764; Support Services: $2,786
Enrollment, Drop-out Rates and Diploma Recipients by Race/Ethnicity

Category	Total	White	Black	Asian	AIAN	Hisp.
Enrollment (%)	100.0	95.2	1.0	0.7	1.0	2.1
Drop-out Rate (%)	n/a	n/a	n/a	n/a	n/a	n/a
H.S. Diplomas (#)	209	206	0	1	0	2

Alpena Public Schools
2373 Gordon Rd · Alpena, MI 49707-4627
(989) 358-5040 · http://www.alpenaschools.com/
Grade Span: PK-12; **Agency Type:** 1
Schools: 11
　8 Primary; 1 Middle; 1 High; 1 Other Level
　10 Regular; 0 Special Education; 0 Vocational; 1 Alternative
　0 Magnet; 0 Charter; 10 Title I Eligible; 10 School-wide Title I
Students: 5,123　(50.6% male; 49.3% female)
　Individual Education Program: 551 (10.8%);
　English Language Learner: 0 (0.0%); Migrant: n/a
　Eligible for Free Lunch Program: 1,419 (27.7%)
　Eligible for Reduced-Price Lunch Program: 548 (10.7%)
Teachers: 264.0 (19.4 to 1)
Librarians/Media Specialists: 3.0 (1,707.7 to 1)
Guidance Counselors: 8.0 (640.4 to 1)
Current Spending: ($ per student per year):
　Total: $7,484; Instruction: $4,348; Support Services: $2,792
Enrollment, Drop-out Rates and Diploma Recipients by Race/Ethnicity

Category	Total	White	Black	Asian	AIAN	Hisp.
Enrollment (%)	100.0	98.1	0.4	0.7	0.5	0.2
Drop-out Rate (%)	n/a	n/a	n/a	n/a	n/a	n/a
H.S. Diplomas (#)	383	372	4	4	1	2

Elk Rapids Schools
707 E 3rd St · Elk Rapids, MI 49629-9402
(231) 264-8692 · http://www.erschools.com/
Grade Span: PK-12; **Agency Type:** 1
Schools: 4
　2 Primary; 1 Middle; 1 High; 0 Other Level
　4 Regular; 0 Special Education; 0 Vocational; 0 Alternative
　0 Magnet; 0 Charter; 0 Title I Eligible; 0 School-wide Title I
Students: 1,548　(51.7% male; 48.2% female)
　Individual Education Program: 176 (11.4%);
　English Language Learner: 0 (0.0%); Migrant: 7 (0.5%)
　Eligible for Free Lunch Program: 255 (16.5%)
　Eligible for Reduced-Price Lunch Program: 103 (6.7%)
Teachers: 81.0 (19.1 to 1)
Librarians/Media Specialists: 4.0 (387.0 to 1)
Guidance Counselors: 2.0 (774.0 to 1)
Current Spending: ($ per student per year):
　Total: $7,297; Instruction: $4,634; Support Services: $2,399

Enrollment, Drop-out Rates and Diploma Recipients by Race/Ethnicity

Category	Total	White	Black	Asian	AIAN	Hisp.
Enrollment (%)	100.0	93.5	0.5	0.7	1.9	3.5
Drop-out Rate (%)	n/a	n/a	n/a	n/a	n/a	n/a
H.S. Diplomas (#)	119	115	0	0	0	4

Arenac County

Standish-Sterling Community Schools
3789 W Wyatt Rd • Standish, MI 48658-9120
Mailing Address: 3789 Wyatt Rd • Standish, MI 48658-9120
(989) 846-3670 • http://www.standish-sterling.org/
Grade Span: PK-12; Agency Type: 1
Schools: 4
   2 Primary; 1 Middle; 1 High; 0 Other Level
   4 Regular; 0 Special Education; 0 Vocational; 0 Alternative
   0 Magnet; 0 Charter; 0 Title I Eligible; 0 School-wide Title I
Students: 1,939 (51.3% male; 48.6% female)
   Individual Education Program: 250 (12.9%);
   English Language Learner: 0 (0.0%); Migrant: n/a
   Eligible for Free Lunch Program: 650 (33.5%)
   Eligible for Reduced-Price Lunch Program: 201 (10.4%)
Teachers: 103.0 (18.8 to 1)
Librarians/Media Specialists: 1.0 (1,939.0 to 1)
Guidance Counselors: 3.0 (646.3 to 1)
Current Spending: ($ per student per year):
   Total: $7,104; Instruction: $4,228; Support Services: $2,551

Enrollment, Drop-out Rates and Diploma Recipients by Race/Ethnicity

Category	Total	White	Black	Asian	AIAN	Hisp.
Enrollment (%)	100.0	97.3	0.3	0.5	1.1	0.8
Drop-out Rate (%)	n/a	n/a	n/a	n/a	n/a	n/a
H.S. Diplomas (#)	129	125	0	0	2	2

Barry County

Delton-Kellogg SD
327 N Grove St • Delton, MI 49046-9771
(616) 623-9246 • http://delton-kellogg.k12.mi.us/
Grade Span: PK-12; Agency Type: 1
Schools: 4
   1 Primary; 1 Middle; 1 High; 1 Other Level
   3 Regular; 0 Special Education; 0 Vocational; 1 Alternative
   0 Magnet; 0 Charter; 0 Title I Eligible; 0 School-wide Title I
Students: 2,059 (53.1% male; 46.8% female)
   Individual Education Program: 255 (12.4%);
   English Language Learner: 0 (0.0%); Migrant: n/a
   Eligible for Free Lunch Program: 463 (22.5%)
   Eligible for Reduced-Price Lunch Program: 148 (7.2%)
Teachers: 115.0 (17.9 to 1)
Librarians/Media Specialists: 1.0 (2,059.0 to 1)
Guidance Counselors: 5.0 (411.8 to 1)
Current Spending: ($ per student per year):
   Total: $7,282; Instruction: $4,773; Support Services: $2,156

Enrollment, Drop-out Rates and Diploma Recipients by Race/Ethnicity

Category	Total	White	Black	Asian	AIAN	Hisp.
Enrollment (%)	100.0	96.1	0.8	0.5	0.7	1.9
Drop-out Rate (%)	n/a	n/a	n/a	n/a	n/a	n/a
H.S. Diplomas (#)	142	137	1	0	1	3

Hastings Area SD
232 W Grand St • Hastings, MI 49058-2225
(269) 948-4400 •
http://www.hassk12.org/education/district/district.php?sectionid=1
Grade Span: PK-12; Agency Type: 1
Schools: 7
   5 Primary; 1 Middle; 1 High; 0 Other Level
   7 Regular; 0 Special Education; 0 Vocational; 0 Alternative
   0 Magnet; 0 Charter; 0 Title I Eligible; 0 School-wide Title I
Students: 3,360 (49.8% male; 50.1% female)
   Individual Education Program: 389 (11.6%);
   English Language Learner: 4 (0.1%); Migrant: n/a
   Eligible for Free Lunch Program: 512 (15.2%)
   Eligible for Reduced-Price Lunch Program: 268 (8.0%)
Teachers: 191.0 (17.6 to 1)
Librarians/Media Specialists: 5.0 (672.0 to 1)
Guidance Counselors: 4.0 (840.0 to 1)
Current Spending: ($ per student per year):
   Total: $7,168; Instruction: $4,867; Support Services: $2,083

Enrollment, Drop-out Rates and Diploma Recipients by Race/Ethnicity

Category	Total	White	Black	Asian	AIAN	Hisp.
Enrollment (%)	100.0	97.4	0.7	0.4	0.4	1.2
Drop-out Rate (%)	n/a	n/a	n/a	n/a	n/a	n/a
H.S. Diplomas (#)	192	184	1	3	2	2

Thornapple Kellogg SD
10051 Green Lake Rd • Middleville, MI 49333-9274
(269) 795-3313 • http://www.tk.k12.mi.us/
Grade Span: PK-12; Agency Type: 1
Schools: 6
   2 Primary; 2 Middle; 1 High; 1 Other Level
   5 Regular; 0 Special Education; 0 Vocational; 1 Alternative
   0 Magnet; 0 Charter; 0 Title I Eligible; 0 School-wide Title I
Students: 2,902 (52.3% male; 47.6% female)
   Individual Education Program: 285 (9.8%);
   English Language Learner: 32 (1.1%); Migrant: n/a
   Eligible for Free Lunch Program: 346 (11.9%)
   Eligible for Reduced-Price Lunch Program: 170 (5.9%)
Teachers: 147.0 (19.7 to 1)
Librarians/Media Specialists: 2.0 (1,451.0 to 1)
Guidance Counselors: 4.0 (725.5 to 1)
Current Spending: ($ per student per year):
   Total: $7,036; Instruction: $4,216; Support Services: $2,549

Enrollment, Drop-out Rates and Diploma Recipients by Race/Ethnicity

Category	Total	White	Black	Asian	AIAN	Hisp.
Enrollment (%)	100.0	94.9	0.7	1.5	0.8	2.2
Drop-out Rate (%)	n/a	n/a	n/a	n/a	n/a	n/a
H.S. Diplomas (#)	209	200	1	1	1	6

Bay County

Bangor Township Schools
3520 Old Kawkawlin Rd • Bay City, MI 48706-2039
(989) 684-8121 • http://www.bangorschools.org/
Grade Span: PK-12; Agency Type: 1
Schools: 6
   4 Primary; 1 Middle; 1 High; 0 Other Level
   6 Regular; 0 Special Education; 0 Vocational; 0 Alternative
   0 Magnet; 0 Charter; 0 Title I Eligible; 0 School-wide Title I
Students: 2,528 (51.1% male; 48.8% female)
   Individual Education Program: 330 (13.1%);
   English Language Learner: 0 (0.0%); Migrant: n/a
   Eligible for Free Lunch Program: 611 (24.2%)
   Eligible for Reduced-Price Lunch Program: 146 (5.8%)
Teachers: 126.0 (20.1 to 1)
Librarians/Media Specialists: 2.0 (1,264.0 to 1)
Guidance Counselors: 4.0 (632.0 to 1)
Current Spending: ($ per student per year):
   Total: $7,413; Instruction: $4,450; Support Services: $2,687

Enrollment, Drop-out Rates and Diploma Recipients by Race/Ethnicity

Category	Total	White	Black	Asian	AIAN	Hisp.
Enrollment (%)	100.0	89.6	3.5	4.3	0.4	2.2
Drop-out Rate (%)	n/a	n/a	n/a	n/a	n/a	n/a
H.S. Diplomas (#)	175	159	1	5	0	10

Bay City SD
910 N Walnut St • Bay City, MI 48706-3773
(989) 686-9700 • http://www.bcschools.net/
Grade Span: PK-12; Agency Type: 1
Schools: 18
   12 Primary; 3 Middle; 2 High; 1 Other Level
   16 Regular; 1 Special Education; 0 Vocational; 1 Alternative
   0 Magnet; 0 Charter; 8 Title I Eligible; 8 School-wide Title I
Students: 9,887 (52.6% male; 47.3% female)
   Individual Education Program: 1,296 (13.1%);
   English Language Learner: 568 (5.7%); Migrant: 39 (0.4%)
   Eligible for Free Lunch Program: 2,903 (29.5%)
   Eligible for Reduced-Price Lunch Program: 710 (7.2%)
Teachers: 513.0 (19.2 to 1)
Librarians/Media Specialists: 11.0 (893.6 to 1)
Guidance Counselors: 18.0 (546.1 to 1)
Current Spending: ($ per student per year):
   Total: $7,545; Instruction: $4,745; Support Services: $2,546

Enrollment, Drop-out Rates and Diploma Recipients by Race/Ethnicity

Category	Total	White	Black	Asian	AIAN	Hisp.
Enrollment (%)	100.0	86.5	5.1	0.8	1.3	6.2
Drop-out Rate (%)	n/a	n/a	n/a	n/a	n/a	n/a
H.S. Diplomas (#)	590	554	9	5	5	17

Essexville-Hampton Public Schools
303 Pine St • Essexville, MI 48732-1584
(989) 894-9700 • http://www.e-hps.net/
Grade Span: KG-12; Agency Type: 1
Schools: 5
   3 Primary; 1 Middle; 1 High; 0 Other Level
   5 Regular; 0 Special Education; 0 Vocational; 0 Alternative
   0 Magnet; 0 Charter; 0 Title I Eligible; 0 School-wide Title I
Students: 1,958 (49.9% male; 50.0% female)
   Individual Education Program: 222 (11.3%);
   English Language Learner: 0 (0.0%); Migrant: n/a

Eligible for Free Lunch Program: 353 (18.0%)
Eligible for Reduced-Price Lunch Program: 108 (5.5%)
Teachers: 105.0 (18.6 to 1)
Librarians/Media Specialists: 2.0 (979.0 to 1)
Guidance Counselors: 5.0 (391.6 to 1)
Current Spending: ($ per student per year):
Total: $7,652; Instruction: $4,725; Support Services: $2,702
Enrollment, Drop-out Rates and Diploma Recipients by Race/Ethnicity

Category	Total	White	Black	Asian	AIAN	Hisp.
Enrollment (%)	100.0	95.3	1.9	0.9	0.1	1.8
Drop-out Rate (%)	n/a	n/a	n/a	n/a	n/a	n/a
H.S. Diplomas (#)	137	125	1	1	1	9

Pinconning Area Schools
605 W 5th St • Pinconning, MI 48650-8712
(989) 879-4556 • http://www.pasd.org/
Grade Span: PK-12; **Agency Type:** 1
Schools: 6
3 Primary; 1 Middle; 1 High; 1 Other Level
5 Regular; 0 Special Education; 0 Vocational; 1 Alternative
0 Magnet; 0 Charter; 6 Title I Eligible; 6 School-wide Title I
Students: 1,974   (50.4% male; 49.5% female)
Individual Education Program: 220 (11.1%);
English Language Learner: 1 (0.1%); Migrant: n/a
Eligible for Free Lunch Program: 595 (30.1%)
Eligible for Reduced-Price Lunch Program: 209 (10.6%)
Teachers: 106.0 (18.6 to 1)
Librarians/Media Specialists: 1.0 (1,974.0 to 1)
Guidance Counselors: 3.0 (658.0 to 1)
Current Spending: ($ per student per year):
Total: $7,424; Instruction: $4,421; Support Services: $2,740
Enrollment, Drop-out Rates and Diploma Recipients by Race/Ethnicity

Category	Total	White	Black	Asian	AIAN	Hisp.
Enrollment (%)	100.0	93.1	1.5	0.2	0.4	4.6
Drop-out Rate (%)	n/a	n/a	n/a	n/a	n/a	n/a
H.S. Diplomas (#)	163	156	0	0	3	4

Benzie County

Benzie County Central Schools
9222 Homestead Rd • Benzonia, MI 49616-9660
Mailing Address: PO Box 240 • Benzonia, MI 49616-0240
(231) 882-9654 • http://www.benzie.k12.mi.us/
Grade Span: KG-12; **Agency Type:** 1
Schools: 6
4 Primary; 1 Middle; 1 High; 0 Other Level
6 Regular; 0 Special Education; 0 Vocational; 0 Alternative
6 Magnet; 0 Charter; 0 Title I Eligible; 0 School-wide Title I
Students: 2,004   (52.9% male; 47.0% female)
Individual Education Program: 262 (13.1%);
English Language Learner: 0 (0.0%); Migrant: n/a
Eligible for Free Lunch Program: 533 (26.6%)
Eligible for Reduced-Price Lunch Program: 247 (12.3%)
Teachers: 111.0 (18.1 to 1)
Librarians/Media Specialists: 0.0 (n/a to 1)
Guidance Counselors: 4.0 (501.0 to 1)
Current Spending: ($ per student per year):
Total: $7,347; Instruction: $4,428; Support Services: $2,598
Enrollment, Drop-out Rates and Diploma Recipients by Race/Ethnicity

Category	Total	White	Black	Asian	AIAN	Hisp.
Enrollment (%)	100.0	92.2	0.8	0.3	3.2	3.3
Drop-out Rate (%)	n/a	n/a	n/a	n/a	n/a	n/a
H.S. Diplomas (#)	111	110	0	0	0	1

Berrien County

Benton Harbor Area Schools
777 Riverview Dr Bldg B • Benton Harbor, MI 49023-5065
Mailing Address: PO Box 1107 • Benton Harbor, MI 49023-1107
(269) 927-0600 • http://www.remc11.k12.mi.us/bhas/
Grade Span: PK-12; **Agency Type:** 1
Schools: 16
10 Primary; 3 Middle; 2 High; 1 Other Level
14 Regular; 0 Special Education; 1 Vocational; 1 Alternative
1 Magnet; 0 Charter; 0 Title I Eligible; 0 School-wide Title I
Students: 5,064   (49.9% male; 50.0% female)
Individual Education Program: 713 (14.1%);
English Language Learner: 0 (0.0%); Migrant: n/a
Eligible for Free Lunch Program: 4,082 (80.6%)
Eligible for Reduced-Price Lunch Program: 313 (6.2%)
Teachers: n/a
Librarians/Media Specialists: 0.0 (n/a to 1)
Guidance Counselors: 1.0 (5,064.0 to 1)
Current Spending: ($ per student per year):
Total: $9,153; Instruction: $4,934; Support Services: $3,783

Enrollment, Drop-out Rates and Diploma Recipients by Race/Ethnicity

Category	Total	White	Black	Asian	AIAN	Hisp.
Enrollment (%)	100.0	3.7	94.0	0.0	0.0	2.1
Drop-out Rate (%)	n/a	n/a	n/a	n/a	n/a	n/a
H.S. Diplomas (#)	201	12	187	0	0	2

Berrien Springs Public Schools
One Sylvester Ave • Berrien Springs, MI 49103-1126
(269) 471-2891 • http://www.remc11.k12.mi.us/bsps/bsp/
Grade Span: PK-12; **Agency Type:** 1
Schools: 5
2 Primary; 1 Middle; 1 High; 1 Other Level
4 Regular; 0 Special Education; 0 Vocational; 1 Alternative
3 Magnet; 0 Charter; 3 Title I Eligible; 3 School-wide Title I
Students: 1,606   (52.8% male; 47.1% female)
Individual Education Program: 231 (14.4%);
English Language Learner: 123 (7.7%); Migrant: 77 (4.8%)
Eligible for Free Lunch Program: 589 (36.7%)
Eligible for Reduced-Price Lunch Program: 183 (11.4%)
Teachers: 97.0 (16.6 to 1)
Librarians/Media Specialists: 1.0 (1,606.0 to 1)
Guidance Counselors: 3.0 (535.3 to 1)
Current Spending: ($ per student per year):
Total: $8,521; Instruction: $4,904; Support Services: $3,336
Enrollment, Drop-out Rates and Diploma Recipients by Race/Ethnicity

Category	Total	White	Black	Asian	AIAN	Hisp.
Enrollment (%)	100.0	61.6	22.3	4.9	0.4	10.8
Drop-out Rate (%)	n/a	n/a	n/a	n/a	n/a	n/a
H.S. Diplomas (#)	93	68	19	3	0	3

Brandywine Public SD
1830 S Third St • Niles, MI 49120-4002
(269) 684-7150 • http://www.remc11.k12.mi.us/brandy/
Grade Span: PK-12; **Agency Type:** 1
Schools: 5
2 Primary; 1 Middle; 1 High; 1 Other Level
4 Regular; 0 Special Education; 0 Vocational; 1 Alternative
0 Magnet; 0 Charter; 0 Title I Eligible; 0 School-wide Title I
Students: 1,537   (53.3% male; 46.6% female)
Individual Education Program: 222 (14.4%);
English Language Learner: 0 (0.0%); Migrant: n/a
Eligible for Free Lunch Program: 369 (24.0%)
Eligible for Reduced-Price Lunch Program: 150 (9.8%)
Teachers: 93.0 (16.5 to 1)
Librarians/Media Specialists: 1.0 (1,537.0 to 1)
Guidance Counselors: 4.0 (384.3 to 1)
Current Spending: ($ per student per year):
Total: $7,051; Instruction: $3,856; Support Services: $2,926
Enrollment, Drop-out Rates and Diploma Recipients by Race/Ethnicity

Category	Total	White	Black	Asian	AIAN	Hisp.
Enrollment (%)	100.0	91.0	3.6	0.7	0.8	2.7
Drop-out Rate (%)	n/a	n/a	n/a	n/a	n/a	n/a
H.S. Diplomas (#)	97	90	3	1	0	3

Buchanan Community Schools
401 W Chicago St • Buchanan, MI 49107-1044
(269) 695-8401 • http://www.buchanan.k12.mi.us/
Grade Span: PK-12; **Agency Type:** 1
Schools: 5
3 Primary; 1 Middle; 1 High; 0 Other Level
5 Regular; 0 Special Education; 0 Vocational; 0 Alternative
0 Magnet; 0 Charter; 0 Title I Eligible; 0 School-wide Title I
Students: 1,747   (53.8% male; 46.1% female)
Individual Education Program: 289 (16.5%);
English Language Learner: 0 (0.0%); Migrant: n/a
Eligible for Free Lunch Program: 427 (24.4%)
Eligible for Reduced-Price Lunch Program: 167 (9.6%)
Teachers: 98.0 (17.8 to 1)
Librarians/Media Specialists: 3.0 (582.3 to 1)
Guidance Counselors: 6.0 (291.2 to 1)
Current Spending: ($ per student per year):
Total: $6,820; Instruction: $3,929; Support Services: $2,614
Enrollment, Drop-out Rates and Diploma Recipients by Race/Ethnicity

Category	Total	White	Black	Asian	AIAN	Hisp.
Enrollment (%)	100.0	86.5	9.7	0.6	0.5	2.6
Drop-out Rate (%)	n/a	n/a	n/a	n/a	n/a	n/a
H.S. Diplomas (#)	93	85	7	0	0	1

Coloma Community Schools
2518 Boyer Rd • Coloma, MI 49038-9743
Mailing Address: PO Box 550 • Coloma, MI 49038-0550
(269) 468-2424 • http://www.remc11.k12.mi.us/coloma/
Grade Span: PK-12; **Agency Type:** 1
Schools: 6
3 Primary; 1 Middle; 1 High; 1 Other Level

6 Regular; 0 Special Education; 0 Vocational; 0 Alternative
0 Magnet; 0 Charter; 3 Title I Eligible; 3 School-wide Title I
Students: 2,174 (52.8% male; 47.1% female)
Individual Education Program: 337 (15.5%);
English Language Learner: 0 (0.0%); Migrant: 56 (2.6%)
Eligible for Free Lunch Program: 733 (33.7%)
Eligible for Reduced-Price Lunch Program: 225 (10.3%)
Teachers: 132.0 (16.5 to 1)
Librarians/Media Specialists: 2.0 (1,087.0 to 1)
Guidance Counselors: 6.0 (362.3 to 1)
Current Spending: ($ per student per year):
Total: $7,454; Instruction: $4,338; Support Services: $2,792
Enrollment, Drop-out Rates and Diploma Recipients by Race/Ethnicity

Category	Total	White	Black	Asian	AIAN	Hisp.
Enrollment (%)	100.0	79.4	14.6	0.2	0.4	5.3
Drop-out Rate (%)	n/a	n/a	n/a	n/a	n/a	n/a
H.S. Diplomas (#)	132	93	34	0	0	5

Lakeshore SD (Berrien)
5771 Cleveland Ave • Stevensville, MI 49127-9481
(269) 428-1400 • http://www.remc11.k12.mi.us/bcisd/
Grade Span: PK-12; **Agency Type:** 1
Schools: 5
3 Primary; 1 Middle; 1 High; 0 Other Level
5 Regular; 0 Special Education; 0 Vocational; 0 Alternative
0 Magnet; 0 Charter; 0 Title I Eligible; 0 School-wide Title I
Students: 2,855 (52.4% male; 47.5% female)
Individual Education Program: 347 (12.2%);
English Language Learner: 0 (0.0%); Migrant: 1 (<0.1%)
Eligible for Free Lunch Program: 238 (8.3%)
Eligible for Reduced-Price Lunch Program: 96 (3.4%)
Teachers: 155.0 (18.4 to 1)
Librarians/Media Specialists: 3.0 (951.7 to 1)
Guidance Counselors: 7.0 (407.9 to 1)
Current Spending: ($ per student per year):
Total: $6,853; Instruction: $4,180; Support Services: $2,443
Enrollment, Drop-out Rates and Diploma Recipients by Race/Ethnicity

Category	Total	White	Black	Asian	AIAN	Hisp.
Enrollment (%)	100.0	94.3	2.3	1.1	0.2	2.0
Drop-out Rate (%)	n/a	n/a	n/a	n/a	n/a	n/a
H.S. Diplomas (#)	237	223	6	8	0	0

Niles Community SD
111 Spruce St • Niles, MI 49120-2963
(269) 683-0732
Grade Span: PK-12; **Agency Type:** 1
Schools: 10
6 Primary; 1 Middle; 1 High; 2 Other Level
8 Regular; 1 Special Education; 0 Vocational; 1 Alternative
0 Magnet; 0 Charter; 4 Title I Eligible; 4 School-wide Title I
Students: 4,221 (53.7% male; 46.2% female)
Individual Education Program: 732 (17.3%);
English Language Learner: 0 (0.0%); Migrant: n/a
Eligible for Free Lunch Program: 1,312 (31.5%)
Eligible for Reduced-Price Lunch Program: 377 (9.1%)
Teachers: 254.0 (16.4 to 1)
Librarians/Media Specialists: 1.0 (4,165.0 to 1)
Guidance Counselors: 6.0 (694.2 to 1)
Current Spending: ($ per student per year):
Total: $7,477; Instruction: $4,644; Support Services: $2,555
Enrollment, Drop-out Rates and Diploma Recipients by Race/Ethnicity

Category	Total	White	Black	Asian	AIAN	Hisp.
Enrollment (%)	100.0	79.5	15.3	0.6	0.4	3.9
Drop-out Rate (%)	n/a	n/a	n/a	n/a	n/a	n/a
H.S. Diplomas (#)	160	134	18	2	3	3

St. Joseph Public Schools
2214 S State St • St. Joseph, MI 49085-1910
(269) 982-4621 • http://www.remc11.k12.mi.us/stjoe/
Grade Span: PK-12; **Agency Type:** 1
Schools: 6
4 Primary; 1 Middle; 1 High; 0 Other Level
6 Regular; 0 Special Education; 0 Vocational; 0 Alternative
0 Magnet; 0 Charter; 0 Title I Eligible; 0 School-wide Title I
Students: 2,852 (51.6% male; 48.3% female)
Individual Education Program: 240 (8.4%);
English Language Learner: 0 (0.0%); Migrant: n/a
Eligible for Free Lunch Program: 177 (6.2%)
Eligible for Reduced-Price Lunch Program: 93 (3.3%)
Teachers: 153.0 (18.6 to 1)
Librarians/Media Specialists: 3.0 (950.7 to 1)
Guidance Counselors: 5.0 (570.4 to 1)
Current Spending: ($ per student per year):
Total: $7,461; Instruction: $4,228; Support Services: $2,927

Category	Total	White	Black	Asian	AIAN	Hisp.
Enrollment (%)	100.0	90.7	3.2	3.8	0.4	1.9
Drop-out Rate (%)	n/a	n/a	n/a	n/a	n/a	n/a
H.S. Diplomas (#)	210	195	3	10	0	2

Branch County

Coldwater Community Schools
401 Sauk River Dr • Coldwater, MI 49036-2067
(517) 279-5910 • http://www.coldwater.k12.mi.us/
Grade Span: PK-12; **Agency Type:** 1
Schools: 8
5 Primary; 1 Middle; 1 High; 1 Other Level
7 Regular; 0 Special Education; 0 Vocational; 1 Alternative
7 Magnet; 0 Charter; 2 Title I Eligible; 2 School-wide Title I
Students: 3,365 (52.4% male; 47.5% female)
Individual Education Program: 50 (1.5%);
English Language Learner: 296 (8.8%); Migrant: n/a
Eligible for Free Lunch Program: 875 (26.0%)
Eligible for Reduced-Price Lunch Program: 200 (5.9%)
Teachers: 179.0 (18.8 to 1)
Librarians/Media Specialists: 4.0 (841.3 to 1)
Guidance Counselors: 6.0 (560.8 to 1)
Current Spending: ($ per student per year):
Total: $6,180; Instruction: $3,935; Support Services: $2,002
Enrollment, Drop-out Rates and Diploma Recipients by Race/Ethnicity

Category	Total	White	Black	Asian	AIAN	Hisp.
Enrollment (%)	100.0	92.3	0.8	1.2	0.5	5.1
Drop-out Rate (%)	n/a	n/a	n/a	n/a	n/a	n/a
H.S. Diplomas (#)	211	206	2	0	0	3

Quincy Community SD
1 Educational Pkwy • Quincy, MI 49082-1173
(517) 639-7141
Grade Span: KG-12; **Agency Type:** 1
Schools: 3
1 Primary; 1 Middle; 1 High; 0 Other Level
3 Regular; 0 Special Education; 0 Vocational; 0 Alternative
0 Magnet; 0 Charter; 0 Title I Eligible; 0 School-wide Title I
Students: 1,539 (51.1% male; 48.8% female)
Individual Education Program: 42 (2.7%);
English Language Learner: 0 (0.0%); Migrant: n/a
Eligible for Free Lunch Program: 317 (20.6%)
Eligible for Reduced-Price Lunch Program: 116 (7.5%)
Teachers: 85.0 (18.1 to 1)
Librarians/Media Specialists: 2.0 (769.5 to 1)
Guidance Counselors: 3.0 (513.0 to 1)
Current Spending: ($ per student per year):
Total: $6,080; Instruction: $4,138; Support Services: $1,754
Enrollment, Drop-out Rates and Diploma Recipients by Race/Ethnicity

Category	Total	White	Black	Asian	AIAN	Hisp.
Enrollment (%)	100.0	98.1	0.4	0.7	0.3	0.6
Drop-out Rate (%)	n/a	n/a	n/a	n/a	n/a	n/a
H.S. Diplomas (#)	87	87	0	0	0	0

Calhoun County

Albion Public Schools
1418 Cooper St • Albion, MI 49224-1083
(517) 629-9166 • http://www.albion.k12.mi.us/
Grade Span: PK-12; **Agency Type:** 1
Schools: 5
2 Primary; 1 Middle; 1 High; 1 Other Level
4 Regular; 0 Special Education; 0 Vocational; 1 Alternative
0 Magnet; 0 Charter; 3 Title I Eligible; 3 School-wide Title I
Students: 1,748 (51.6% male; 48.3% female)
Individual Education Program: 227 (13.0%);
English Language Learner: 0 (0.0%); Migrant: n/a
Eligible for Free Lunch Program: 855 (48.9%)
Eligible for Reduced-Price Lunch Program: 149 (8.5%)
Teachers: 96.0 (18.2 to 1)
Librarians/Media Specialists: 2.0 (874.0 to 1)
Guidance Counselors: 3.0 (582.7 to 1)
Current Spending: ($ per student per year):
Total: $8,124; Instruction: $4,776; Support Services: $3,013
Enrollment, Drop-out Rates and Diploma Recipients by Race/Ethnicity

Category	Total	White	Black	Asian	AIAN	Hisp.
Enrollment (%)	100.0	43.8	52.1	0.6	0.1	3.5
Drop-out Rate (%)	n/a	n/a	n/a	n/a	n/a	n/a
H.S. Diplomas (#)	101	53	40	0	0	8

Battle Creek Public Schools
3 W Van Buren St • Battle Creek, MI 49017-3009
(269) 965-9465 • http://www.woburn.k12.ma.us/
Grade Span: PK-12; **Agency Type:** 1
Schools: 25
    15 Primary; 4 Middle; 5 High; 1 Other Level
    21 Regular; 0 Special Education; 1 Vocational; 3 Alternative
    1 Magnet; 0 Charter; 20 Title I Eligible; 20 School-wide Title I
Students: 7,945 (51.9% male; 48.0% female)
    Individual Education Program: 1,210 (15.2%);
    English Language Learner: 190 (2.4%); Migrant: 26 (0.3%)
    Eligible for Free Lunch Program: 3,912 (49.2%)
    Eligible for Reduced-Price Lunch Program: 432 (5.4%)
Teachers: 556.0 (14.3 to 1)
Librarians/Media Specialists: 2.0 (3,972.5 to 1)
Guidance Counselors: 23.0 (345.4 to 1)
Current Spending: ($ per student per year):
    Total: $8,912; Instruction: $5,278; Support Services: $3,316
Enrollment, Drop-out Rates and Diploma Recipients by Race/Ethnicity

Category	Total	White	Black	Asian	AIAN	Hisp.
Enrollment (%)	100.0	55.3	35.8	0.7	1.7	6.6
Drop-out Rate (%)	n/a	n/a	n/a	n/a	n/a	n/a
H.S. Diplomas (#)	278	147	113	3	3	12

Harper Creek Community Schools
201 Crosby Dr • Battle Creek, MI 49014-8270
(269) 979-1136 • http://www.harpercreek.net/
Grade Span: PK-12; **Agency Type:** 1
Schools: 5
    3 Primary; 1 Middle; 1 High; 0 Other Level
    5 Regular; 0 Special Education; 0 Vocational; 0 Alternative
    0 Magnet; 0 Charter; 2 Title I Eligible; 2 School-wide Title I
Students: 2,687 (51.9% male; 48.0% female)
    Individual Education Program: 327 (12.2%);
    English Language Learner: 0 (0.0%); Migrant: n/a
    Eligible for Free Lunch Program: 419 (15.6%)
    Eligible for Reduced-Price Lunch Program: 162 (6.0%)
Teachers: 159.0 (16.9 to 1)
Librarians/Media Specialists: 1.0 (2,687.0 to 1)
Guidance Counselors: 4.0 (671.8 to 1)
Current Spending: ($ per student per year):
    Total: $7,039; Instruction: $4,315; Support Services: $2,461
Enrollment, Drop-out Rates and Diploma Recipients by Race/Ethnicity

Category	Total	White	Black	Asian	AIAN	Hisp.
Enrollment (%)	100.0	93.3	1.7	1.7	0.6	2.8
Drop-out Rate (%)	n/a	n/a	n/a	n/a	n/a	n/a
H.S. Diplomas (#)	156	151	0	1	1	3

Lakeview SD (Calhoun)
15 Arbor St • Battle Creek, MI 49015-2903
(269) 565-2411 • http://www.lakeviewspartans.org/index.taf
Grade Span: PK-12; **Agency Type:** 1
Schools: 8
    5 Primary; 2 Middle; 1 High; 0 Other Level
    8 Regular; 0 Special Education; 0 Vocational; 0 Alternative
    0 Magnet; 0 Charter; 0 Title I Eligible; 0 School-wide Title I
Students: 3,315 (51.0% male; 48.9% female)
    Individual Education Program: 375 (11.3%);
    English Language Learner: 0 (0.0%); Migrant: n/a
    Eligible for Free Lunch Program: 414 (12.5%)
    Eligible for Reduced-Price Lunch Program: 138 (4.2%)
Teachers: 191.0 (17.4 to 1)
Librarians/Media Specialists: 3.0 (1,105.0 to 1)
Guidance Counselors: 7.0 (473.6 to 1)
Current Spending: ($ per student per year):
    Total: $7,389; Instruction: $4,306; Support Services: $2,843
Enrollment, Drop-out Rates and Diploma Recipients by Race/Ethnicity

Category	Total	White	Black	Asian	AIAN	Hisp.
Enrollment (%)	100.0	83.0	5.7	6.8	1.1	3.4
Drop-out Rate (%)	n/a	n/a	n/a	n/a	n/a	n/a
H.S. Diplomas (#)	238	215	8	10	0	5

Marshall Public Schools
100 E Green St • Marshall, MI 49068-1533
(269) 781-1256 • http://www.marshallschools.com/
Grade Span: KG-12; **Agency Type:** 1
Schools: 7
    3 Primary; 1 Middle; 2 High; 1 Other Level
    6 Regular; 0 Special Education; 0 Vocational; 1 Alternative
    0 Magnet; 0 Charter; 0 Title I Eligible; 0 School-wide Title I
Students: 2,563 (52.8% male; 47.1% female)
    Individual Education Program: 282 (11.0%);
    English Language Learner: 0 (0.0%); Migrant: n/a
    Eligible for Free Lunch Program: 262 (10.2%)
    Eligible for Reduced-Price Lunch Program: 74 (2.9%)

Teachers: 145.0 (17.7 to 1)
Librarians/Media Specialists: 1.0 (2,563.0 to 1)
Guidance Counselors: 6.0 (427.2 to 1)
Current Spending: ($ per student per year):
    Total: $7,224; Instruction: $4,489; Support Services: $2,542
Enrollment, Drop-out Rates and Diploma Recipients by Race/Ethnicity

Category	Total	White	Black	Asian	AIAN	Hisp.
Enrollment (%)	100.0	93.4	1.5	1.1	1.0	3.1
Drop-out Rate (%)	n/a	n/a	n/a	n/a	n/a	n/a
H.S. Diplomas (#)	203	186	0	4	1	12

Pennfield SD
8587 Q Dr N • Battle Creek, MI 49017-8104
(269) 961-9781 • http://www.pennfield.k12.mi.us/
Grade Span: PK-12; **Agency Type:** 1
Schools: 6
    3 Primary; 2 Middle; 1 High; 0 Other Level
    6 Regular; 0 Special Education; 0 Vocational; 0 Alternative
    0 Magnet; 0 Charter; 0 Title I Eligible; 0 School-wide Title I
Students: 1,926 (49.2% male; 50.7% female)
    Individual Education Program: 184 (9.6%);
    English Language Learner: 0 (0.0%); Migrant: n/a
    Eligible for Free Lunch Program: 359 (18.6%)
    Eligible for Reduced-Price Lunch Program: 93 (4.8%)
Teachers: 101.0 (19.1 to 1)
Librarians/Media Specialists: 2.0 (963.0 to 1)
Guidance Counselors: 4.0 (481.5 to 1)
Current Spending: ($ per student per year):
    Total: $6,709; Instruction: $4,148; Support Services: $2,342
Enrollment, Drop-out Rates and Diploma Recipients by Race/Ethnicity

Category	Total	White	Black	Asian	AIAN	Hisp.
Enrollment (%)	100.0	92.2	4.9	0.7	0.6	1.7
Drop-out Rate (%)	n/a	n/a	n/a	n/a	n/a	n/a
H.S. Diplomas (#)	114	109	3	2	0	0

Cass County

Dowagiac Union SD
206 Main St • Dowagiac, MI 49047-1743
(269) 782-4402 • http://www.remc11.k12.mi.us/dowagiac/
Grade Span: PK-12; **Agency Type:** 1
Schools: 8
    4 Primary; 2 Middle; 2 High; 0 Other Level
    7 Regular; 0 Special Education; 0 Vocational; 1 Alternative
    0 Magnet; 0 Charter; 0 Title I Eligible; 0 School-wide Title I
Students: 2,771 (51.3% male; 48.6% female)
    Individual Education Program: 373 (13.5%);
    English Language Learner: 0 (0.0%); Migrant: 256 (9.2%)
    Eligible for Free Lunch Program: 1,088 (39.3%)
    Eligible for Reduced-Price Lunch Program: 266 (9.6%)
Teachers: 154.0 (18.0 to 1)
Librarians/Media Specialists: 2.0 (1,385.5 to 1)
Guidance Counselors: 6.0 (461.8 to 1)
Current Spending: ($ per student per year):
    Total: $7,091; Instruction: $4,193; Support Services: $2,661
Enrollment, Drop-out Rates and Diploma Recipients by Race/Ethnicity

Category	Total	White	Black	Asian	AIAN	Hisp.
Enrollment (%)	100.0	75.2	11.3	0.4	1.3	11.8
Drop-out Rate (%)	n/a	n/a	n/a	n/a	n/a	n/a
H.S. Diplomas (#)	140	115	15	2	0	8

Edwardsburg Public Schools
69410 Section St • Edwardsburg, MI 49112-8603
(269) 663-1053 • http://www.remc11.k12.mi.us/edward/
Grade Span: PK-12; **Agency Type:** 1
Schools: 6
    2 Primary; 2 Middle; 1 High; 1 Other Level
    5 Regular; 0 Special Education; 0 Vocational; 1 Alternative
    0 Magnet; 0 Charter; 0 Title I Eligible; 0 School-wide Title I
Students: 2,311 (51.8% male; 48.1% female)
    Individual Education Program: 235 (10.2%);
    English Language Learner: 0 (0.0%); Migrant: n/a
    Eligible for Free Lunch Program: 422 (18.3%)
    Eligible for Reduced-Price Lunch Program: 164 (7.1%)
Teachers: 114.0 (20.3 to 1)
Librarians/Media Specialists: 3.0 (770.3 to 1)
Guidance Counselors: 3.0 (770.3 to 1)
Current Spending: ($ per student per year):
    Total: $6,347; Instruction: $3,334; Support Services: $2,730
Enrollment, Drop-out Rates and Diploma Recipients by Race/Ethnicity

Category	Total	White	Black	Asian	AIAN	Hisp.
Enrollment (%)	100.0	96.2	1.0	1.0	0.6	1.2
Drop-out Rate (%)	n/a	n/a	n/a	n/a	n/a	n/a
H.S. Diplomas (#)	114	111	1	0	0	2

Cheboygan County

Cheboygan Area Schools
504 Division St • Cheboygan, MI 49721-1537
Mailing Address: PO Box 100 • Cheboygan, MI 49721-0100
(231) 627-4436
Grade Span: PK-12; **Agency Type:** 1
Schools: 7
    3 Primary; 1 Middle; 1 High; 2 Other Level
    6 Regular; 0 Special Education; 0 Vocational; 1 Alternative
    0 Magnet; 0 Charter; 0 Title I Eligible; 0 School-wide Title I
Students: 2,279 (51.2% male; 48.7% female)
    Individual Education Program: 285 (12.5%);
    English Language Learner: 0 (0.0%); Migrant: n/a
    Eligible for Free Lunch Program: 790 (34.7%)
    Eligible for Reduced-Price Lunch Program: 195 (8.6%)
Teachers: 134.0 (17.0 to 1)
Librarians/Media Specialists: 1.0 (2,279.0 to 1)
Guidance Counselors: 5.0 (455.8 to 1)
Current Spending: ($ per student per year):
    Total: $7,367; Instruction: $4,734; Support Services: $2,384
Enrollment, Drop-out Rates and Diploma Recipients by Race/Ethnicity

Category	Total	White	Black	Asian	AIAN	Hisp.
Enrollment (%)	100.0	93.1	1.3	0.9	4.4	0.4
Drop-out Rate (%)	n/a	n/a	n/a	n/a	n/a	n/a
H.S. Diplomas (#)	164	161	0	2	0	1

Chippewa County

Sault Ste. Marie Area Schools
876 Marquette Ave • Sault Ste. Marie, MI 49783-1800
(906) 635-6609
Grade Span: PK-12; **Agency Type:** 1
Schools: 8
    5 Primary; 1 Middle; 2 High; 0 Other Level
    7 Regular; 0 Special Education; 0 Vocational; 1 Alternative
    8 Magnet; 0 Charter; 4 Title I Eligible; 4 School-wide Title I
Students: 2,897 (52.3% male; 47.6% female)
    Individual Education Program: 411 (14.2%);
    English Language Learner: 31 (1.1%); Migrant: n/a
    Eligible for Free Lunch Program: 825 (28.5%)
    Eligible for Reduced-Price Lunch Program: 306 (10.6%)
Teachers: 178.0 (16.3 to 1)
Librarians/Media Specialists: 2.0 (1,448.5 to 1)
Guidance Counselors: 5.0 (579.4 to 1)
Current Spending: ($ per student per year):
    Total: $7,444; Instruction: $4,402; Support Services: $2,724
Enrollment, Drop-out Rates and Diploma Recipients by Race/Ethnicity

Category	Total	White	Black	Asian	AIAN	Hisp.
Enrollment (%)	100.0	63.4	1.0	0.7	34.3	0.7
Drop-out Rate (%)	n/a	n/a	n/a	n/a	n/a	n/a
H.S. Diplomas (#)	213	138	0	0	73	2

Clare County

Clare Public Schools
201 E State St • Clare, MI 48617-1317
(989) 386-9945 • http://www.clare.k12.mi.us/district/index.php
Grade Span: KG-12; **Agency Type:** 1
Schools: 4
    1 Primary; 1 Middle; 1 High; 1 Other Level
    3 Regular; 0 Special Education; 0 Vocational; 1 Alternative
    0 Magnet; 0 Charter; 2 Title I Eligible; 2 School-wide Title I
Students: 1,598 (48.8% male; 51.1% female)
    Individual Education Program: 173 (10.8%);
    English Language Learner: 2 (0.1%); Migrant: n/a
    Eligible for Free Lunch Program: 345 (21.6%)
    Eligible for Reduced-Price Lunch Program: 145 (9.1%)
Teachers: 84.0 (19.0 to 1)
Librarians/Media Specialists: 3.0 (532.7 to 1)
Guidance Counselors: 3.0 (532.7 to 1)
Current Spending: ($ per student per year):
    Total: $7,072; Instruction: $4,602; Support Services: $2,187
Enrollment, Drop-out Rates and Diploma Recipients by Race/Ethnicity

Category	Total	White	Black	Asian	AIAN	Hisp.
Enrollment (%)	100.0	98.5	0.4	0.2	0.3	0.7
Drop-out Rate (%)	n/a	n/a	n/a	n/a	n/a	n/a
H.S. Diplomas (#)	107	106	0	0	1	0

Farwell Area Schools
371 E Main St • Farwell, MI 48622-9463
(989) 588-9917 • http://farwell.edzone.net/
Grade Span: KG-12; **Agency Type:** 1
Schools: 3
    1 Primary; 1 Middle; 1 High; 0 Other Level

    3 Regular; 0 Special Education; 0 Vocational; 0 Alternative
    3 Magnet; 0 Charter; 0 Title I Eligible; 0 School-wide Title I
Students: 1,628 (51.1% male; 48.8% female)
    Individual Education Program: 202 (12.4%);
    English Language Learner: 0 (0.0%); Migrant: n/a
    Eligible for Free Lunch Program: 689 (42.3%)
    Eligible for Reduced-Price Lunch Program: 253 (15.5%)
Teachers: 91.0 (17.9 to 1)
Librarians/Media Specialists: 3.0 (542.7 to 1)
Guidance Counselors: 4.0 (407.0 to 1)
Current Spending: ($ per student per year):
    Total: $7,355; Instruction: $4,945; Support Services: $2,142
Enrollment, Drop-out Rates and Diploma Recipients by Race/Ethnicity

Category	Total	White	Black	Asian	AIAN	Hisp.
Enrollment (%)	100.0	96.5	0.6	0.2	1.5	1.3
Drop-out Rate (%)	n/a	n/a	n/a	n/a	n/a	n/a
H.S. Diplomas (#)	87	83	2	2	0	0

Harrison Community Schools
224 S Main St • Harrison, MI 48625-9765
Mailing Address: PO Box 529 • Harrison, MI 48625-0529
(989) 539-7871 • http://www.hcs.cgresd.net/
Grade Span: KG-12; **Agency Type:** 1
Schools: 5
    2 Primary; 1 Middle; 1 High; 1 Other Level
    4 Regular; 0 Special Education; 0 Vocational; 1 Alternative
    0 Magnet; 0 Charter; 3 Title I Eligible; 3 School-wide Title I
Students: 2,122 (51.4% male; 48.5% female)
    Individual Education Program: 426 (20.1%);
    English Language Learner: 4 (0.2%); Migrant: n/a
    Eligible for Free Lunch Program: 1,060 (50.0%)
    Eligible for Reduced-Price Lunch Program: 164 (7.7%)
Teachers: 116.0 (18.3 to 1)
Librarians/Media Specialists: 1.0 (2,122.0 to 1)
Guidance Counselors: 2.0 (1,061.0 to 1)
Current Spending: ($ per student per year):
    Total: $7,907; Instruction: $4,941; Support Services: $2,636
Enrollment, Drop-out Rates and Diploma Recipients by Race/Ethnicity

Category	Total	White	Black	Asian	AIAN	Hisp.
Enrollment (%)	100.0	95.9	0.8	0.7	1.8	0.8
Drop-out Rate (%)	n/a	n/a	n/a	n/a	n/a	n/a
H.S. Diplomas (#)	108	104	0	1	1	2

Clinton County

Dewitt Public Schools
2957 W Herbison Rd • Dewitt, MI 48820-0800
Mailing Address: PO Box 800 • Dewitt, MI 48820-0800
(517) 668-3000 • http://dewitt.k12.mi.us/
Grade Span: PK-12; **Agency Type:** 1
Schools: 6
    3 Primary; 2 Middle; 1 High; 0 Other Level
    6 Regular; 0 Special Education; 0 Vocational; 0 Alternative
    0 Magnet; 0 Charter; 0 Title I Eligible; 0 School-wide Title I
Students: 2,780 (52.8% male; 47.1% female)
    Individual Education Program: 235 (8.5%);
    English Language Learner: 0 (0.0%); Migrant: n/a
    Eligible for Free Lunch Program: 131 (4.7%)
    Eligible for Reduced-Price Lunch Program: 62 (2.2%)
Teachers: 144.0 (19.3 to 1)
Librarians/Media Specialists: 4.0 (695.0 to 1)
Guidance Counselors: 4.0 (695.0 to 1)
Current Spending: ($ per student per year):
    Total: $7,115; Instruction: $4,640; Support Services: $2,261
Enrollment, Drop-out Rates and Diploma Recipients by Race/Ethnicity

Category	Total	White	Black	Asian	AIAN	Hisp.
Enrollment (%)	100.0	92.6	1.4	0.8	1.3	3.3
Drop-out Rate (%)	n/a	n/a	n/a	n/a	n/a	n/a
H.S. Diplomas (#)	194	186	1	1	0	6

Ovid-Elsie Area Schools
8989 Colony Rd • Elsie, MI 48831-9724
(989) 834-2271 • http://www.oe.k12.mi.us/
Grade Span: KG-12; **Agency Type:** 1
Schools: 6
    2 Primary; 2 Middle; 1 High; 1 Other Level
    5 Regular; 0 Special Education; 0 Vocational; 1 Alternative
    0 Magnet; 0 Charter; 0 Title I Eligible; 0 School-wide Title I
Students: 1,803 (53.1% male; 46.8% female)
    Individual Education Program: 246 (13.6%);
    English Language Learner: 0 (0.0%); Migrant: n/a
    Eligible for Free Lunch Program: 386 (21.4%)
    Eligible for Reduced-Price Lunch Program: 132 (7.3%)
Teachers: 89.0 (20.3 to 1)
Librarians/Media Specialists: 0.0 (n/a to 1)
Guidance Counselors: 3.0 (601.0 to 1)

Current Spending: ($ per student per year):
    Total: $7,270; Instruction: $4,119; Support Services: $2,869
Enrollment, Drop-out Rates and Diploma Recipients by Race/Ethnicity

Category	Total	White	Black	Asian	AIAN	Hisp.
Enrollment (%)	100.0	94.8	0.8	1.0	0.4	3.1
Drop-out Rate (%)	n/a	n/a	n/a	n/a	n/a	n/a
H.S. Diplomas (#)	125	122	0	1	0	2

St. Johns Public Schools
501 W Sickels St • St. Johns, MI 48879-0230
Mailing Address: PO Box 230 • St. Johns, MI 48879-0230
(989) 227-4050 • http://stjohns.edzone.net/
Grade Span: KG-12; **Agency Type:** 1
Schools: 8
    6 Primary; 1 Middle; 1 High; 0 Other Level
    8 Regular; 0 Special Education; 0 Vocational; 0 Alternative
    8 Magnet; 0 Charter; 0 Title I Eligible; 0 School-wide Title I
Students: 3,383 (52.3% male; 47.6% female)
    Individual Education Program: 455 (13.4%);
    English Language Learner: 0 (0.0%); Migrant: n/a
    Eligible for Free Lunch Program: 292 (9.0%)
    Eligible for Reduced-Price Lunch Program: 208 (6.4%)
Teachers: 185.0 (17.6 to 1)
Librarians/Media Specialists: 1.0 (3,249.0 to 1)
Guidance Counselors: 8.0 (406.1 to 1)
Current Spending: ($ per student per year):
    Total: $7,423; Instruction: $4,529; Support Services: $2,638
Enrollment, Drop-out Rates and Diploma Recipients by Race/Ethnicity

Category	Total	White	Black	Asian	AIAN	Hisp.
Enrollment (%)	100.0	93.5	1.0	1.2	0.6	3.7
Drop-out Rate (%)	n/a	n/a	n/a	n/a	n/a	n/a
H.S. Diplomas (#)	238	228	0	2	0	8

Crawford County

Crawford Ausable Schools
403 E Michigan Ave • Grayling, MI 49738-1644
(989) 344-3500 • http://www.casdk12.net/
Grade Span: PK-12; **Agency Type:** 1
Schools: 5
    2 Primary; 1 Middle; 1 High; 1 Other Level
    5 Regular; 0 Special Education; 0 Vocational; 0 Alternative
    0 Magnet; 0 Charter; 5 Title I Eligible; 5 School-wide Title I
Students: 2,103 (53.3% male; 46.6% female)
    Individual Education Program: 341 (16.2%);
    English Language Learner: 0 (0.0%); Migrant: n/a
    Eligible for Free Lunch Program: 738 (35.1%)
    Eligible for Reduced-Price Lunch Program: 238 (11.3%)
Teachers: 119.0 (17.7 to 1)
Librarians/Media Specialists: 2.0 (1,051.5 to 1)
Guidance Counselors: 4.0 (525.8 to 1)
Current Spending: ($ per student per year):
    Total: $7,553; Instruction: $4,287; Support Services: $2,894
Enrollment, Drop-out Rates and Diploma Recipients by Race/Ethnicity

Category	Total	White	Black	Asian	AIAN	Hisp.
Enrollment (%)	100.0	97.0	0.9	1.0	0.3	0.8
Drop-out Rate (%)	n/a	n/a	n/a	n/a	n/a	n/a
H.S. Diplomas (#)	122	122	0	0	0	0

Delta County

Escanaba Area Public Schools
111 N 5th St • Escanaba, MI 49829-3944
(906) 786-5411 • http://www.escanabaschools.com/
Grade Span: KG-12; **Agency Type:** 1
Schools: 7
    5 Primary; 1 Middle; 1 High; 0 Other Level
    7 Regular; 0 Special Education; 0 Vocational; 0 Alternative
    0 Magnet; 0 Charter; 0 Title I Eligible; 0 School-wide Title I
Students: 3,061 (51.8% male; 48.1% female)
    Individual Education Program: 376 (12.3%);
    English Language Learner: 1 (<0.1%); Migrant: n/a
    Eligible for Free Lunch Program: 838 (27.4%)
    Eligible for Reduced-Price Lunch Program: 289 (9.4%)
Teachers: 157.0 (19.5 to 1)
Librarians/Media Specialists: 1.0 (3,061.0 to 1)
Guidance Counselors: 3.0 (1,020.3 to 1)
Current Spending: ($ per student per year):
    Total: $7,645; Instruction: $4,898; Support Services: $2,479
Enrollment, Drop-out Rates and Diploma Recipients by Race/Ethnicity

Category	Total	White	Black	Asian	AIAN	Hisp.
Enrollment (%)	100.0	95.2	0.1	0.3	3.9	0.1
Drop-out Rate (%)	n/a	n/a	n/a	n/a	n/a	n/a
H.S. Diplomas (#)	263	246	1	5	11	0

Gladstone Area Schools
400 S 10th St • Gladstone, MI 49837-1534
(906) 428-2417 • http://www.gladstoneschools.com/
Grade Span: KG-12; **Agency Type:** 1
Schools: 4
    2 Primary; 1 Middle; 1 High; 0 Other Level
    4 Regular; 0 Special Education; 0 Vocational; 0 Alternative
    2 Magnet; 0 Charter; 0 Title I Eligible; 0 School-wide Title I
Students: 1,744 (51.9% male; 48.0% female)
    Individual Education Program: 216 (12.4%);
    English Language Learner: 0 (0.0%); Migrant: n/a
    Eligible for Free Lunch Program: 425 (24.4%)
    Eligible for Reduced-Price Lunch Program: 208 (11.9%)
Teachers: 99.0 (17.6 to 1)
Librarians/Media Specialists: 0.0 (n/a to 1)
Guidance Counselors: 0.0 (n/a to 1)
Current Spending: ($ per student per year):
    Total: $7,130; Instruction: $4,545; Support Services: $2,322
Enrollment, Drop-out Rates and Diploma Recipients by Race/Ethnicity

Category	Total	White	Black	Asian	AIAN	Hisp.
Enrollment (%)	100.0	95.9	0.2	0.4	3.3	0.2
Drop-out Rate (%)	n/a	n/a	n/a	n/a	n/a	n/a
H.S. Diplomas (#)	149	132	1	3	13	0

Dickinson County

Breitung Township Schools
2000 W Pyle Dr • Kingsford, MI 49802-4250
(906) 779-2650 • http://www.kingsford.org/
Grade Span: KG-12; **Agency Type:** 1
Schools: 3
    1 Primary; 1 Middle; 1 High; 0 Other Level
    3 Regular; 0 Special Education; 0 Vocational; 0 Alternative
    0 Magnet; 0 Charter; 0 Title I Eligible; 0 School-wide Title I
Students: 2,020 (53.1% male; 46.8% female)
    Individual Education Program: 251 (12.4%);
    English Language Learner: 0 (0.0%); Migrant: n/a
    Eligible for Free Lunch Program: 346 (17.1%)
    Eligible for Reduced-Price Lunch Program: 183 (9.1%)
Teachers: 114.0 (17.7 to 1)
Librarians/Media Specialists: 2.0 (1,010.0 to 1)
Guidance Counselors: 2.0 (1,010.0 to 1)
Current Spending: ($ per student per year):
    Total: $6,913; Instruction: $4,396; Support Services: $2,197
Enrollment, Drop-out Rates and Diploma Recipients by Race/Ethnicity

Category	Total	White	Black	Asian	AIAN	Hisp.
Enrollment (%)	100.0	98.8	0.0	0.7	0.1	0.1
Drop-out Rate (%)	n/a	n/a	n/a	n/a	n/a	n/a
H.S. Diplomas (#)	171	166	0	3	2	0

Eaton County

Charlotte Public Schools
378 State St • Charlotte, MI 48813-1704
(517) 541-5100 • http://scnc.cps.k12.mi.us/
Grade Span: PK-12; **Agency Type:** 1
Schools: 7
    4 Primary; 1 Middle; 1 High; 1 Other Level
    6 Regular; 0 Special Education; 0 Vocational; 1 Alternative
    6 Magnet; 0 Charter; 0 Title I Eligible; 0 School-wide Title I
Students: 3,347 (51.0% male; 48.9% female)
    Individual Education Program: 559 (16.7%);
    English Language Learner: 0 (0.0%); Migrant: n/a
    Eligible for Free Lunch Program: 671 (20.0%)
    Eligible for Reduced-Price Lunch Program: 225 (6.7%)
Teachers: 199.0 (16.8 to 1)
Librarians/Media Specialists: 3.0 (1,115.7 to 1)
Guidance Counselors: 7.0 (478.1 to 1)
Current Spending: ($ per student per year):
    Total: $7,187; Instruction: $4,374; Support Services: $2,563
Enrollment, Drop-out Rates and Diploma Recipients by Race/Ethnicity

Category	Total	White	Black	Asian	AIAN	Hisp.
Enrollment (%)	100.0	94.9	1.2	0.4	0.0	3.5
Drop-out Rate (%)	n/a	n/a	n/a	n/a	n/a	n/a
H.S. Diplomas (#)	189	183	2	1	0	3

Eaton Rapids Public Schools
501 King St • Eaton Rapids, MI 48827-1251
(517) 663-8155 • http://scnc.erps.k12.mi.us/
Grade Span: KG-12; **Agency Type:** 1
Schools: 6
    3 Primary; 2 Middle; 1 High; 0 Other Level
    6 Regular; 0 Special Education; 0 Vocational; 0 Alternative
    0 Magnet; 0 Charter; 0 Title I Eligible; 0 School-wide Title I
Students: 3,179 (52.0% male; 47.9% female)

Individual Education Program: 521 (16.4%);
English Language Learner: 0 (0.0%); Migrant: n/a
Eligible for Free Lunch Program: 465 (15.0%)
Eligible for Reduced-Price Lunch Program: 216 (6.9%)
Teachers: 166.0 (18.7 to 1)
Librarians/Media Specialists: 4.0 (777.0 to 1)
Guidance Counselors: 6.0 (518.0 to 1)
Current Spending: ($ per student per year):
Total: $7,212; Instruction: $4,446; Support Services: $2,508
Enrollment, Drop-out Rates and Diploma Recipients by Race/Ethnicity

Category	Total	White	Black	Asian	AIAN	Hisp.
Enrollment (%)	100.0	95.1	1.3	0.8	0.2	2.6
Drop-out Rate (%)	n/a	n/a	n/a	n/a	n/a	n/a
H.S. Diplomas (#)	237	222	0	1	5	9

Grand Ledge Public Schools
220 Lamson St • Grand Ledge, MI 48837-1760
(517) 627-3241 • http://scnc.glps.k12.mi.us/
Grade Span: KG-12; **Agency Type:** 1
Schools: 10
6 Primary; 2 Middle; 2 High; 0 Other Level
9 Regular; 0 Special Education; 0 Vocational; 1 Alternative
0 Magnet; 0 Charter; 0 Title I Eligible; 0 School-wide Title I
Students: 5,368 (51.5% male; 48.4% female)
Individual Education Program: 864 (16.1%);
English Language Learner: 0 (0.0%); Migrant: n/a
Eligible for Free Lunch Program: 528 (9.8%)
Eligible for Reduced-Price Lunch Program: 220 (4.1%)
Teachers: 304.0 (17.7 to 1)
Librarians/Media Specialists: 4.0 (1,342.0 to 1)
Guidance Counselors: 7.0 (766.9 to 1)
Current Spending: ($ per student per year):
Total: $7,156; Instruction: $4,395; Support Services: $2,504
Enrollment, Drop-out Rates and Diploma Recipients by Race/Ethnicity

Category	Total	White	Black	Asian	AIAN	Hisp.
Enrollment (%)	100.0	92.3	3.6	2.1	0.4	1.6
Drop-out Rate (%)	n/a	n/a	n/a	n/a	n/a	n/a
H.S. Diplomas (#)	386	365	10	3	1	7

Maple Valley Schools
11090 Nashville Hwy • Vermontville, MI 49096-8578
(517) 852-9699 • http://scnc.mvs.k12.mi.us/
Grade Span: PK-12; **Agency Type:** 1
Schools: 5
1 Primary; 1 Middle; 1 High; 2 Other Level
3 Regular; 0 Special Education; 0 Vocational; 2 Alternative
4 Magnet; 0 Charter; 2 Title I Eligible; 2 School-wide Title I
Students: 1,735 (52.0% male; 47.9% female)
Individual Education Program: 242 (13.9%);
English Language Learner: 0 (0.0%); Migrant: n/a
Eligible for Free Lunch Program: 478 (27.6%)
Eligible for Reduced-Price Lunch Program: 170 (9.8%)
Teachers: 98.0 (17.7 to 1)
Librarians/Media Specialists: 1.0 (1,735.0 to 1)
Guidance Counselors: 2.0 (867.5 to 1)
Current Spending: ($ per student per year):
Total: $6,825; Instruction: $4,487; Support Services: $2,061
Enrollment, Drop-out Rates and Diploma Recipients by Race/Ethnicity

Category	Total	White	Black	Asian	AIAN	Hisp.
Enrollment (%)	100.0	96.6	0.6	0.7	0.2	1.8
Drop-out Rate (%)	n/a	n/a	n/a	n/a	n/a	n/a
H.S. Diplomas (#)	93	90	0	2	0	1

Emmet County

Public Schools of Petoskey
1130 Howard St • Petoskey, MI 49770-3026
Mailing Address: PO Box 247 • Petoskey, MI 49770-3026
(231) 348-2100 • http://www.petoskeyschools.org/
Grade Span: KG-12; **Agency Type:** 1
Schools: 7
5 Primary; 1 Middle; 1 High; 0 Other Level
7 Regular; 0 Special Education; 0 Vocational; 0 Alternative
7 Magnet; 0 Charter; 0 Title I Eligible; 0 School-wide Title I
Students: 3,092 (52.5% male; 47.4% female)
Individual Education Program: 302 (9.8%);
English Language Learner: 6 (0.2%); Migrant: n/a
Eligible for Free Lunch Program: 414 (13.4%)
Eligible for Reduced-Price Lunch Program: 276 (8.9%)
Teachers: 163.0 (19.0 to 1)
Librarians/Media Specialists: 3.0 (1,030.7 to 1)
Guidance Counselors: 5.0 (618.4 to 1)
Current Spending: ($ per student per year):
Total: $7,490; Instruction: $4,801; Support Services: $2,399

Enrollment, Drop-out Rates and Diploma Recipients by Race/Ethnicity

Category	Total	White	Black	Asian	AIAN	Hisp.
Enrollment (%)	100.0	93.6	0.8	0.7	4.0	0.8
Drop-out Rate (%)	n/a	n/a	n/a	n/a	n/a	n/a
H.S. Diplomas (#)	0	0	0	0	0	0

Genesee County

Beecher Community SD
1020 W Coldwater Rd • Flint, MI 48505-4831
(810) 591-9200 • http://www.beecherschools.org/
Grade Span: PK-12; **Agency Type:** 1
Schools: 7
5 Primary; 1 Middle; 1 High; 0 Other Level
7 Regular; 0 Special Education; 0 Vocational; 0 Alternative
0 Magnet; 0 Charter; 5 Title I Eligible; 5 School-wide Title I
Students: 2,423 (49.9% male; 50.0% female)
Individual Education Program: 215 (8.9%);
English Language Learner: 0 (0.0%); Migrant: n/a
Eligible for Free Lunch Program: 1,655 (72.5%)
Eligible for Reduced-Price Lunch Program: 138 (6.0%)
Teachers: 115.0 (19.9 to 1)
Librarians/Media Specialists: 2.0 (1,142.0 to 1)
Guidance Counselors: 2.0 (1,142.0 to 1)
Current Spending: ($ per student per year):
Total: $11,595; Instruction: $5,709; Support Services: $5,243
Enrollment, Drop-out Rates and Diploma Recipients by Race/Ethnicity

Category	Total	White	Black	Asian	AIAN	Hisp.
Enrollment (%)	100.0	10.2	87.5	0.0	0.1	2.1
Drop-out Rate (%)	n/a	n/a	n/a	n/a	n/a	n/a
H.S. Diplomas (#)	63	8	52	0	0	3

Bendle Public Schools
2283 E Scottwood Ave • Burton, MI 48529-1721
(810) 591-2501 • http://www.bendleschools.org/
Grade Span: PK-12; **Agency Type:** 1
Schools: 5
3 Primary; 1 Middle; 1 High; 0 Other Level
5 Regular; 0 Special Education; 0 Vocational; 0 Alternative
4 Magnet; 0 Charter; 5 Title I Eligible; 5 School-wide Title I
Students: 1,590 (52.5% male; 47.4% female)
Individual Education Program: 205 (12.9%);
English Language Learner: 0 (0.0%); Migrant: n/a
Eligible for Free Lunch Program: 558 (45.1%)
Eligible for Reduced-Price Lunch Program: 76 (6.1%)
Teachers: 91.0 (13.6 to 1)
Librarians/Media Specialists: 1.0 (1,236.0 to 1)
Guidance Counselors: 3.0 (412.0 to 1)
Current Spending: ($ per student per year):
Total: $6,440; Instruction: $3,922; Support Services: $2,357
Enrollment, Drop-out Rates and Diploma Recipients by Race/Ethnicity

Category	Total	White	Black	Asian	AIAN	Hisp.
Enrollment (%)	100.0	92.4	2.2	0.5	1.5	3.4
Drop-out Rate (%)	n/a	n/a	n/a	n/a	n/a	n/a
H.S. Diplomas (#)	65	61	0	0	3	1

Carman-Ainsworth Community Schools
G-3475 W Court St • Flint, MI 48532-4742
(810) 591-3205 • http://www.carman.k12.mi.us/
Grade Span: PK-12; **Agency Type:** 1
Schools: 10
7 Primary; 2 Middle; 1 High; 0 Other Level
10 Regular; 0 Special Education; 0 Vocational; 0 Alternative
0 Magnet; 0 Charter; 5 Title I Eligible; 5 School-wide Title I
Students: 5,363 (50.8% male; 49.1% female)
Individual Education Program: 719 (13.4%);
English Language Learner: 16 (0.3%); Migrant: n/a
Eligible for Free Lunch Program: 1,839 (34.3%)
Eligible for Reduced-Price Lunch Program: 401 (7.5%)
Teachers: 315.0 (17.0 to 1)
Librarians/Media Specialists: 6.0 (893.8 to 1)
Guidance Counselors: 12.0 (446.9 to 1)
Current Spending: ($ per student per year):
Total: $9,045; Instruction: $5,379; Support Services: $3,340
Enrollment, Drop-out Rates and Diploma Recipients by Race/Ethnicity

Category	Total	White	Black	Asian	AIAN	Hisp.
Enrollment (%)	100.0	62.4	25.7	2.3	6.2	2.7
Drop-out Rate (%)	n/a	n/a	n/a	n/a	n/a	n/a
H.S. Diplomas (#)	272	189	55	7	18	3

Clio Area SD
430 N Mill St • Clio, MI 48420-1227
(810) 591-0502 • http://www.hs.clio.k12.mi.us/
Grade Span: PK-12; **Agency Type:** 1
Schools: 5

3 Primary; 1 Middle; 1 High; 0 Other Level
5 Regular; 0 Special Education; 0 Vocational; 0 Alternative
0 Magnet; 0 Charter; 0 Title I Eligible; 0 School-wide Title I
Students: 3,603 (54.2% male; 45.7% female)
Individual Education Program: 406 (11.3%);
English Language Learner: 3 (0.1%); Migrant: n/a
Eligible for Free Lunch Program: 753 (21.3%)
Eligible for Reduced-Price Lunch Program: 196 (5.5%)
Teachers: 178.0 (19.9 to 1)
Librarians/Media Specialists: 2.0 (1,768.0 to 1)
Guidance Counselors: 3.0 (1,178.7 to 1)
Current Spending: ($ per student per year):
Total: $6,937; Instruction: $4,181; Support Services: $2,523
Enrollment, Drop-out Rates and Diploma Recipients by Race/Ethnicity

Category	Total	White	Black	Asian	AIAN	Hisp.
Enrollment (%)	100.0	95.8	1.2	0.6	0.7	1.5
Drop-out Rate (%)	n/a	n/a	n/a	n/a	n/a	n/a
H.S. Diplomas (#)	185	180	0	3	0	2

Davison Community Schools
1490 N Oak Rd • Davison, MI 48423-9101
Mailing Address: PO Box 319 • Davison, MI 48423-0319
(810) 591-0801 • http://www.davison.k12.mi.us
Grade Span: PK-12; **Agency Type:** 1
Schools: 9
5 Primary; 2 Middle; 1 High; 1 Other Level
8 Regular; 0 Special Education; 0 Vocational; 1 Alternative
0 Magnet; 0 Charter; 0 Title I Eligible; 0 School-wide Title I
Students: 5,365 (50.0% male; 49.9% female)
Individual Education Program: 563 (10.5%);
English Language Learner: 0 (0.0%); Migrant: n/a
Eligible for Free Lunch Program: 723 (13.5%)
Eligible for Reduced-Price Lunch Program: 317 (5.9%)
Teachers: 260.0 (20.6 to 1)
Librarians/Media Specialists: 3.0 (1,788.3 to 1)
Guidance Counselors: 9.0 (596.1 to 1)
Current Spending: ($ per student per year):
Total: $6,961; Instruction: $4,193; Support Services: $2,541
Enrollment, Drop-out Rates and Diploma Recipients by Race/Ethnicity

Category	Total	White	Black	Asian	AIAN	Hisp.
Enrollment (%)	100.0	92.1	1.7	1.0	2.7	1.9
Drop-out Rate (%)	n/a	n/a	n/a	n/a	n/a	n/a
H.S. Diplomas (#)	296	274	5	2	13	2

Fenton Area Public Schools
3100 Owen Rd • Fenton, MI 48430-1754
(810) 591-4700 • http://www.fenton.k12.mi.us/
Grade Span: PK-12; **Agency Type:** 1
Schools: 7
3 Primary; 2 Middle; 2 High; 0 Other Level
6 Regular; 0 Special Education; 0 Vocational; 1 Alternative
0 Magnet; 0 Charter; 3 Title I Eligible; 3 School-wide Title I
Students: 3,753 (50.3% male; 49.6% female)
Individual Education Program: 452 (12.0%);
English Language Learner: 2 (0.1%); Migrant: 3 (0.1%)
Eligible for Free Lunch Program: 384 (10.2%)
Eligible for Reduced-Price Lunch Program: 98 (2.6%)
Teachers: 192.0 (19.5 to 1)
Librarians/Media Specialists: 1.0 (3,753.0 to 1)
Guidance Counselors: 5.0 (750.6 to 1)
Current Spending: ($ per student per year):
Total: $7,099; Instruction: $4,140; Support Services: $2,696
Enrollment, Drop-out Rates and Diploma Recipients by Race/Ethnicity

Category	Total	White	Black	Asian	AIAN	Hisp.
Enrollment (%)	100.0	97.1	0.7	1.0	0.3	0.8
Drop-out Rate (%)	n/a	n/a	n/a	n/a	n/a	n/a
H.S. Diplomas (#)	229	229	0	0	0	0

Flint City SD
923 E Kearsley St • Flint, MI 48503-1974
(810) 760-1249 • http://www.flintschools.org/
Grade Span: PK-12; **Agency Type:** 1
Schools: 39
28 Primary; 4 Middle; 6 High; 1 Other Level
37 Regular; 0 Special Education; 1 Vocational; 1 Alternative
0 Magnet; 0 Charter; 26 Title I Eligible; 26 School-wide Title I
Students: 20,465 (50.3% male; 49.6% female)
Individual Education Program: 2,623 (12.8%);
English Language Learner: 832 (4.1%); Migrant: 2,067 (10.3%)
Eligible for Free Lunch Program: 13,095 (65.4%)
Eligible for Reduced-Price Lunch Program: 633 (3.2%)
Teachers: 1,209.0 (16.6 to 1)
Librarians/Media Specialists: 9.0 (2,224.0 to 1)
Guidance Counselors: 30.0 (667.2 to 1)
Current Spending: ($ per student per year):
Total: $9,475; Instruction: $5,222; Support Services: $3,915

Enrollment, Drop-out Rates and Diploma Recipients by Race/Ethnicity

Category	Total	White	Black	Asian	AIAN	Hisp.
Enrollment (%)	100.0	18.7	77.9	0.3	0.4	2.7
Drop-out Rate (%)	n/a	n/a	n/a	n/a	n/a	n/a
H.S. Diplomas (#)	714	152	538	1	2	21

Flushing Community Schools
522 N Mckinley Rd • Flushing, MI 48433-1353
(810) 591-1180 • http://www.flushing.k12.mi.us/
Grade Span: PK-12; **Agency Type:** 1
Schools: 6
4 Primary; 1 Middle; 1 High; 0 Other Level
6 Regular; 0 Special Education; 0 Vocational; 0 Alternative
0 Magnet; 0 Charter; 0 Title I Eligible; 0 School-wide Title I
Students: 4,801 (49.5% male; 50.4% female)
Individual Education Program: 498 (10.4%);
English Language Learner: 0 (0.0%); Migrant: n/a
Eligible for Free Lunch Program: 377 (7.9%)
Eligible for Reduced-Price Lunch Program: 114 (2.4%)
Teachers: 213.0 (22.5 to 1)
Librarians/Media Specialists: 3.0 (1,600.3 to 1)
Guidance Counselors: 5.0 (960.2 to 1)
Current Spending: ($ per student per year):
Total: $5,866; Instruction: $3,727; Support Services: $1,977
Enrollment, Drop-out Rates and Diploma Recipients by Race/Ethnicity

Category	Total	White	Black	Asian	AIAN	Hisp.
Enrollment (%)	100.0	92.7	3.4	1.7	0.5	1.5
Drop-out Rate (%)	n/a	n/a	n/a	n/a	n/a	n/a
H.S. Diplomas (#)	315	301	5	5	0	4

Goodrich Area Schools
8029 S Gale Rd • Goodrich, MI 48438-9260
(810) 591-2201 • http://www.goodrich.k12.mi.us/
Grade Span: KG-12; **Agency Type:** 1
Schools: 4
2 Primary; 1 Middle; 1 High; 0 Other Level
4 Regular; 0 Special Education; 0 Vocational; 0 Alternative
0 Magnet; 0 Charter; 0 Title I Eligible; 0 School-wide Title I
Students: 2,087 (52.3% male; 47.6% female)
Individual Education Program: 208 (10.0%);
English Language Learner: 0 (0.0%); Migrant: n/a
Eligible for Free Lunch Program: 65 (3.1%)
Eligible for Reduced-Price Lunch Program: 22 (1.1%)
Teachers: 105.0 (19.9 to 1)
Librarians/Media Specialists: 1.0 (2,087.0 to 1)
Guidance Counselors: 3.0 (695.7 to 1)
Current Spending: ($ per student per year):
Total: $6,939; Instruction: $4,321; Support Services: $2,292
Enrollment, Drop-out Rates and Diploma Recipients by Race/Ethnicity

Category	Total	White	Black	Asian	AIAN	Hisp.
Enrollment (%)	100.0	97.3	0.9	0.9	0.4	0.6
Drop-out Rate (%)	n/a	n/a	n/a	n/a	n/a	n/a
H.S. Diplomas (#)	129	128	0	0	0	1

Grand Blanc Community Schools
G-11920 S Saginaw St • Grand Blanc, MI 48439-1402
(810) 591-6014 • http://www.grand-blanc.k12.mi.us/
Grade Span: KG-12; **Agency Type:** 1
Schools: 11
9 Primary; 1 Middle; 1 High; 0 Other Level
11 Regular; 0 Special Education; 0 Vocational; 0 Alternative
0 Magnet; 0 Charter; 0 Title I Eligible; 0 School-wide Title I
Students: 7,322 (50.8% male; 49.1% female)
Individual Education Program: 727 (9.9%);
English Language Learner: 51 (0.7%); Migrant: n/a
Eligible for Free Lunch Program: 718 (9.8%)
Eligible for Reduced-Price Lunch Program: 279 (3.8%)
Teachers: 367.0 (20.0 to 1)
Librarians/Media Specialists: 4.0 (1,830.5 to 1)
Guidance Counselors: 8.0 (915.3 to 1)
Current Spending: ($ per student per year):
Total: $6,855; Instruction: $4,213; Support Services: $2,401
Enrollment, Drop-out Rates and Diploma Recipients by Race/Ethnicity

Category	Total	White	Black	Asian	AIAN	Hisp.
Enrollment (%)	100.0	84.3	8.2	3.3	0.2	1.7
Drop-out Rate (%)	n/a	n/a	n/a	n/a	n/a	n/a
H.S. Diplomas (#)	416	351	39	19	1	6

Kearsley Community Schools
4396 Underhill Dr • Flint, MI 48506-1534
(810) 591-8000 • http://www.kearsley.k12.mi.us/
Grade Span: KG-12; **Agency Type:** 1
Schools: 7
4 Primary; 1 Middle; 1 High; 1 Other Level
6 Regular; 0 Special Education; 0 Vocational; 1 Alternative

0 Magnet; 0 Charter; 0 Title I Eligible; 0 School-wide Title I
Students: 3,904   (51.6% male; 48.3% female)
   Individual Education Program: 387 (9.9%);
   English Language Learner: 0 (0.0%); Migrant: n/a
   Eligible for Free Lunch Program: 750 (19.2%)
   Eligible for Reduced-Price Lunch Program: 239 (6.1%)
Teachers: 185.0 (21.1 to 1)
Librarians/Media Specialists: 2.0 (1,952.0 to 1)
Guidance Counselors: 10.0 (390.4 to 1)
Current Spending: ($ per student per year):
   Total: $7,068; Instruction: $4,035; Support Services: $2,803

Enrollment, Drop-out Rates and Diploma Recipients by Race/Ethnicity

Category	Total	White	Black	Asian	AIAN	Hisp.
Enrollment (%)	100.0	92.7	2.7	0.7	0.8	1.9
Drop-out Rate (%)	n/a	n/a	n/a	n/a	n/a	n/a
H.S. Diplomas (#)	247	233	3	5	0	6

Lake Fenton Community Schools
11425 Torrey Rd • Fenton, MI 48430-9622
(810) 591-1004
Grade Span: KG-12; **Agency Type:** 1
Schools: 3
   1 Primary; 1 Middle; 1 High; 0 Other Level
   3 Regular; 0 Special Education; 0 Vocational; 0 Alternative
   3 Magnet; 0 Charter; 0 Title I Eligible; 0 School-wide Title I
Students: 1,502   (51.4% male; 48.5% female)
   Individual Education Program: 140 (9.3%);
   English Language Learner: 5 (0.3%); Migrant: n/a
   Eligible for Free Lunch Program: 110 (7.3%)
   Eligible for Reduced-Price Lunch Program: 19 (1.3%)
Teachers: 70.0 (21.5 to 1)
Librarians/Media Specialists: 1.0 (1,502.0 to 1)
Guidance Counselors: 2.0 (751.0 to 1)
Current Spending: ($ per student per year):
   Total: $7,280; Instruction: $4,359; Support Services: $2,660

Enrollment, Drop-out Rates and Diploma Recipients by Race/Ethnicity

Category	Total	White	Black	Asian	AIAN	Hisp.
Enrollment (%)	100.0	96.2	0.5	1.0	1.3	1.0
Drop-out Rate (%)	n/a	n/a	n/a	n/a	n/a	n/a
H.S. Diplomas (#)	85	82	0	0	0	3

Lakeville Community Schools
11107 Washburn Rd • Otisville, MI 48463-9630
(810) 591-3980 • http://www.lakeville.k12.mi.us/
Grade Span: KG-12; **Agency Type:** 1
Schools: 7
   4 Primary; 1 Middle; 2 High; 0 Other Level
   6 Regular; 0 Special Education; 0 Vocational; 1 Alternative
   0 Magnet; 0 Charter; 0 Title I Eligible; 0 School-wide Title I
Students: 2,139   (50.6% male; 49.3% female)
   Individual Education Program: 209 (9.8%);
   English Language Learner: 0 (0.0%); Migrant: n/a
   Eligible for Free Lunch Program: 469 (21.9%)
   Eligible for Reduced-Price Lunch Program: 139 (6.5%)
Teachers: 113.0 (18.9 to 1)
Librarians/Media Specialists: 1.0 (2,139.0 to 1)
Guidance Counselors: 2.0 (1,069.5 to 1)
Current Spending: ($ per student per year):
   Total: $7,279; Instruction: $4,247; Support Services: $2,726

Enrollment, Drop-out Rates and Diploma Recipients by Race/Ethnicity

Category	Total	White	Black	Asian	AIAN	Hisp.
Enrollment (%)	100.0	96.9	1.0	0.4	0.2	1.5
Drop-out Rate (%)	n/a	n/a	n/a	n/a	n/a	n/a
H.S. Diplomas (#)	141	138	0	0	1	2

Linden Community Schools
7205 W Silver Lake Rd • Linden, MI 48451-8710
(810) 591-7821 • http://www.lindenschools.org/
Grade Span: PK-12; **Agency Type:** 1
Schools: 6
   3 Primary; 1 Middle; 1 High; 0 Other Level
   5 Regular; 0 Special Education; 0 Vocational; 0 Alternative
   0 Magnet; 0 Charter; 0 Title I Eligible; 0 School-wide Title I
Students: 2,980   (51.4% male; 48.5% female)
   Individual Education Program: 400 (13.4%);
   English Language Learner: 1 (<0.1%); Migrant: n/a
   Eligible for Free Lunch Program: 205 (6.9%)
   Eligible for Reduced-Price Lunch Program: 88 (3.0%)
Teachers: 129.0 (23.1 to 1)
Librarians/Media Specialists: 2.0 (1,490.0 to 1)
Guidance Counselors: 3.0 (993.3 to 1)
Current Spending: ($ per student per year):
   Total: $6,738; Instruction: $3,857; Support Services: $2,563

Enrollment, Drop-out Rates and Diploma Recipients by Race/Ethnicity

Category	Total	White	Black	Asian	AIAN	Hisp.
Enrollment (%)	100.0	98.8	0.2	0.2	0.3	0.6
Drop-out Rate (%)	n/a	n/a	n/a	n/a	n/a	n/a
H.S. Diplomas (#)	151	143	0	4	1	3

Montrose Community Schools
300 Nanita Dr • Montrose, MI 48457-9149
Mailing Address: PO Box 3129 • Montrose, MI 48457-0829
(810) 591-7267 • http://www.montrose.k12.mi.us/Default.asp?Res=746
Grade Span: PK-12; **Agency Type:** 1
Schools: 3
   1 Primary; 1 Middle; 1 High; 0 Other Level
   3 Regular; 0 Special Education; 0 Vocational; 0 Alternative
   0 Magnet; 0 Charter; 0 Title I Eligible; 0 School-wide Title I
Students: 1,752   (53.4% male; 46.5% female)
   Individual Education Program: 230 (13.1%);
   English Language Learner: 0 (0.0%); Migrant: n/a
   Eligible for Free Lunch Program: 475 (27.1%)
   Eligible for Reduced-Price Lunch Program: 168 (9.6%)
Teachers: n/a
Librarians/Media Specialists: n/a
Guidance Counselors: n/a
Current Spending: ($ per student per year):
   Total: $7,922; Instruction: $4,846; Support Services: $2,773

Enrollment, Drop-out Rates and Diploma Recipients by Race/Ethnicity

Category	Total	White	Black	Asian	AIAN	Hisp.
Enrollment (%)	100.0	91.2	2.2	0.5	2.5	3.7
Drop-out Rate (%)	n/a	n/a	n/a	n/a	n/a	n/a
H.S. Diplomas (#)	98	93	1	0	0	4

Mt. Morris Consolidated Schools
12356 Walter St • Mt. Morris, MI 48458-1749
(810) 591-8760 • http://www.mtmorrisschools.org/
Grade Span: KG-12; **Agency Type:** 1
Schools: 7
   3 Primary; 2 Middle; 1 High; 1 Other Level
   6 Regular; 0 Special Education; 0 Vocational; 1 Alternative
   1 Magnet; 0 Charter; 4 Title I Eligible; 4 School-wide Title I
Students: 3,675   (52.7% male; 47.2% female)
   Individual Education Program: 529 (14.4%);
   English Language Learner: 3 (0.1%); Migrant: n/a
   Eligible for Free Lunch Program: 1,133 (30.8%)
   Eligible for Reduced-Price Lunch Program: 315 (8.6%)
Teachers: 188.0 (19.5 to 1)
Librarians/Media Specialists: 3.0 (1,225.0 to 1)
Guidance Counselors: 5.0 (735.0 to 1)
Current Spending: ($ per student per year):
   Total: $7,224; Instruction: $4,372; Support Services: $2,635

Enrollment, Drop-out Rates and Diploma Recipients by Race/Ethnicity

Category	Total	White	Black	Asian	AIAN	Hisp.
Enrollment (%)	100.0	72.3	17.8	0.4	6.9	2.7
Drop-out Rate (%)	n/a	n/a	n/a	n/a	n/a	n/a
H.S. Diplomas (#)	164	124	3	2	35	0

Swartz Creek Community Schools
8354 Cappy Ln • Swartz Creek, MI 48473-1242
(810) 591-2300 • http://www.swartzcreek.org/
Grade Span: PK-12; **Agency Type:** 1
Schools: 8
   5 Primary; 1 Middle; 2 High; 0 Other Level
   7 Regular; 0 Special Education; 0 Vocational; 1 Alternative
   0 Magnet; 0 Charter; 0 Title I Eligible; 0 School-wide Title I
Students: 4,180   (51.6% male; 48.3% female)
   Individual Education Program: 533 (12.8%);
   English Language Learner: 0 (0.0%); Migrant: n/a
   Eligible for Free Lunch Program: 590 (14.1%)
   Eligible for Reduced-Price Lunch Program: 190 (4.5%)
Teachers: 247.0 (16.9 to 1)
Librarians/Media Specialists: 2.0 (2,090.0 to 1)
Guidance Counselors: 7.0 (597.1 to 1)
Current Spending: ($ per student per year):
   Total: $6,664; Instruction: $4,229; Support Services: $2,244

Enrollment, Drop-out Rates and Diploma Recipients by Race/Ethnicity

Category	Total	White	Black	Asian	AIAN	Hisp.
Enrollment (%)	100.0	92.3	2.5	0.8	2.3	2.0
Drop-out Rate (%)	n/a	n/a	n/a	n/a	n/a	n/a
H.S. Diplomas (#)	268	242	5	7	10	4

Gladwin County

Beaverton Rural Schools
468 S Ross St • Beaverton, MI 48612-9101
Mailing Address: PO Box 529 • Beaverton, MI 48612-0529
(989) 246-3000 • http://beaverton.k12.mi.us
Grade Span: KG-12; **Agency Type:** 1
Schools: 4
   2 Primary; 1 Middle; 1 High; 0 Other Level
   4 Regular; 0 Special Education; 0 Vocational; 0 Alternative
   4 Magnet; 0 Charter; 0 Title I Eligible; 0 School-wide Title I
Students: 1,675   (52.6% male; 47.3% female)
   Individual Education Program: 266 (15.9%);
   English Language Learner: 0 (0.0%); Migrant: n/a
   Eligible for Free Lunch Program: 560 (33.4%)
   Eligible for Reduced-Price Lunch Program: 126 (7.5%)
Teachers: 96.0 (17.4 to 1)
Librarians/Media Specialists: 3.0 (558.3 to 1)
Guidance Counselors: 3.0 (558.3 to 1)
Current Spending: ($ per student per year):
   Total: $7,324; Instruction: $4,422; Support Services: $2,622
Enrollment, Drop-out Rates and Diploma Recipients by Race/Ethnicity

Category	Total	White	Black	Asian	AIAN	Hisp.
Enrollment (%)	100.0	96.7	1.0	0.1	1.1	1.1
Drop-out Rate (%)	n/a	n/a	n/a	n/a	n/a	n/a
H.S. Diplomas (#)	118	115	0	0	1	2

Gladwin Community Schools
1206 N Spring St • Gladwin, MI 48624-1041
(989) 426-9255 • http://www.gladwin.k12.mi.us/
Grade Span: PK-12; **Agency Type:** 1
Schools: 5
   2 Primary; 1 Middle; 1 High; 1 Other Level
   4 Regular; 0 Special Education; 0 Vocational; 1 Alternative
   0 Magnet; 0 Charter; 5 Title I Eligible; 5 School-wide Title I
Students: 2,092   (51.7% male; 48.2% female)
   Individual Education Program: 365 (17.4%);
   English Language Learner: 0 (0.0%); Migrant: n/a
   Eligible for Free Lunch Program: 591 (28.3%)
   Eligible for Reduced-Price Lunch Program: 212 (10.1%)
Teachers: 116.0 (18.0 to 1)
Librarians/Media Specialists: 1.0 (2,092.0 to 1)
Guidance Counselors: 1.0 (2,092.0 to 1)
Current Spending: ($ per student per year):
   Total: $7,494; Instruction: $4,730; Support Services: $2,537
Enrollment, Drop-out Rates and Diploma Recipients by Race/Ethnicity

Category	Total	White	Black	Asian	AIAN	Hisp.
Enrollment (%)	100.0	96.7	0.6	0.6	0.5	1.1
Drop-out Rate (%)	n/a	n/a	n/a	n/a	n/a	n/a
H.S. Diplomas (#)	141	138	1	1	0	1

Grand Traverse County

Traverse City Area Public Schools
412 Webster St • Traverse City, MI 49685-2650
Mailing Address: PO Box 32 • Traverse City, MI 49685-0032
(231) 933-1727 • http://www.tcaps.net/
Grade Span: PK-12; **Agency Type:** 1
Schools: 22
   17 Primary; 2 Middle; 3 High; 0 Other Level
   21 Regular; 0 Special Education; 0 Vocational; 1 Alternative
   0 Magnet; 0 Charter; 1 Title I Eligible; 1 School-wide Title I
Students: 11,133   (51.0% male; 48.9% female)
   Individual Education Program: 1,464 (13.2%);
   English Language Learner: 116 (1.0%); Migrant: 74 (0.7%)
   Eligible for Free Lunch Program: 2,022 (18.2%)
   Eligible for Reduced-Price Lunch Program: 1,003 (9.0%)
Teachers: 595.0 (18.7 to 1)
Librarians/Media Specialists: 5.0 (2,226.6 to 1)
Guidance Counselors: 14.0 (795.2 to 1)
Current Spending: ($ per student per year):
   Total: $7,076; Instruction: $4,131; Support Services: $2,578
Enrollment, Drop-out Rates and Diploma Recipients by Race/Ethnicity

Category	Total	White	Black	Asian	AIAN	Hisp.
Enrollment (%)	100.0	94.2	0.6	1.1	1.7	2.5
Drop-out Rate (%)	n/a	n/a	n/a	n/a	n/a	n/a
H.S. Diplomas (#)	760	732	0	11	9	8

Gratiot County

Alma Public Schools
1500 N Pine Ave • Alma, MI 48801-1275
(989) 463-3111 • http://www.esu11.k12.ne.us/alma/home.html
Grade Span: PK-12; **Agency Type:** 1
Schools: 5

   3 Primary; 0 Middle; 1 High; 1 Other Level
   5 Regular; 0 Special Education; 0 Vocational; 0 Alternative
   0 Magnet; 0 Charter; 5 Title I Eligible; 5 School-wide Title I
Students: 2,549   (50.9% male; 49.0% female)
   Individual Education Program: 370 (14.5%);
   English Language Learner: 0 (0.0%); Migrant: n/a
   Eligible for Free Lunch Program: 753 (30.4%)
   Eligible for Reduced-Price Lunch Program: 237 (9.6%)
Teachers: 152.0 (16.3 to 1)
Librarians/Media Specialists: 2.0 (1,239.0 to 1)
Guidance Counselors: 4.0 (619.5 to 1)
Current Spending: ($ per student per year):
   Total: $7,037; Instruction: $4,209; Support Services: $2,570
Enrollment, Drop-out Rates and Diploma Recipients by Race/Ethnicity

Category	Total	White	Black	Asian	AIAN	Hisp.
Enrollment (%)	100.0	94.2	0.4	0.5	0.6	4.3
Drop-out Rate (%)	n/a	n/a	n/a	n/a	n/a	n/a
H.S. Diplomas (#)	147	131	2	1	1	12

Hillsdale County

Hillsdale Community Schools
30 S Norwood Ave • Hillsdale, MI 49242-1802
(517) 437-4401 •
http://hillsdale-isd.org/Directory/Hillsdale%20Schools.htm
Grade Span: PK-12; **Agency Type:** 1
Schools: 5
   3 Primary; 1 Middle; 1 High; 0 Other Level
   5 Regular; 0 Special Education; 0 Vocational; 0 Alternative
   0 Magnet; 0 Charter; 3 Title I Eligible; 3 School-wide Title I
Students: 1,896   (51.6% male; 48.3% female)
   Individual Education Program: 219 (11.6%);
   English Language Learner: 0 (0.0%); Migrant: n/a
   Eligible for Free Lunch Program: 617 (32.5%)
   Eligible for Reduced-Price Lunch Program: 257 (13.6%)
Teachers: 104.0 (18.2 to 1)
Librarians/Media Specialists: 1.0 (1,896.0 to 1)
Guidance Counselors: 4.0 (474.0 to 1)
Current Spending: ($ per student per year):
   Total: $7,576; Instruction: $5,030; Support Services: $2,223
Enrollment, Drop-out Rates and Diploma Recipients by Race/Ethnicity

Category	Total	White	Black	Asian	AIAN	Hisp.
Enrollment (%)	100.0	97.1	0.7	0.7	0.3	1.2
Drop-out Rate (%)	n/a	n/a	n/a	n/a	n/a	n/a
H.S. Diplomas (#)	117	111	1	3	0	2

Houghton County

Public Schools of Calumet
57070 Mine St • Calumet, MI 49913-2949
(906) 337-0311 • http://www.clk.k12.mi.us/
Grade Span: KG-12; **Agency Type:** 1
Schools: 4
   2 Primary; 1 Middle; 1 High; 0 Other Level
   4 Regular; 0 Special Education; 0 Vocational; 0 Alternative
   0 Magnet; 0 Charter; 0 Title I Eligible; 0 School-wide Title I
Students: 1,580   (50.8% male; 49.1% female)
   Individual Education Program: 140 (8.9%);
   English Language Learner: 0 (0.0%); Migrant: n/a
   Eligible for Free Lunch Program: 557 (35.3%)
   Eligible for Reduced-Price Lunch Program: 238 (15.1%)
Teachers: 91.0 (17.4 to 1)
Librarians/Media Specialists: 1.0 (1,580.0 to 1)
Guidance Counselors: 2.0 (790.0 to 1)
Current Spending: ($ per student per year):
   Total: $7,431; Instruction: $4,673; Support Services: $2,387
Enrollment, Drop-out Rates and Diploma Recipients by Race/Ethnicity

Category	Total	White	Black	Asian	AIAN	Hisp.
Enrollment (%)	100.0	98.4	0.3	0.6	0.4	0.3
Drop-out Rate (%)	n/a	n/a	n/a	n/a	n/a	n/a
H.S. Diplomas (#)	108	107	0	0	0	1

Ingham County

East Lansing SD
841 Timberlane Ste A • East Lansing, MI 48823-3791
(517) 333-7424 • http://scnc.elps.k12.mi.us/
Grade Span: KG-12; **Agency Type:** 1
Schools: 8
   4 Primary; 3 Middle; 1 High; 0 Other Level
   8 Regular; 0 Special Education; 0 Vocational; 0 Alternative
   0 Magnet; 0 Charter; 0 Title I Eligible; 0 School-wide Title I
Students: 3,553   (50.8% male; 49.1% female)
   Individual Education Program: 396 (11.1%);
   English Language Learner: 572 (16.1%); Migrant: n/a

Eligible for Free Lunch Program: 610 (17.2%)
Eligible for Reduced-Price Lunch Program: 185 (5.2%)
Teachers: 207.0 (17.2 to 1)
Librarians/Media Specialists: 2.0 (1,776.5 to 1)
Guidance Counselors: 7.0 (507.6 to 1)
Current Spending: ($ per student per year):
Total: $8,758; Instruction: $5,231; Support Services: $3,308
Enrollment, Drop-out Rates and Diploma Recipients by Race/Ethnicity

Category	Total	White	Black	Asian	AIAN	Hisp.
Enrollment (%)	100.0	63.9	16.0	12.0	0.4	5.5
Drop-out Rate (%)	n/a	n/a	n/a	n/a	n/a	n/a
H.S. Diplomas (#)	273	190	39	24	1	19

Haslett Public Schools
5593 Franklin St • Haslett, MI 48840-8434
(517) 339-8242 • http://scnc.haslett.k12.mi.us/
Grade Span: PK-12; **Agency Type:** 1
Schools: 6
3 Primary; 1 Middle; 2 High; 0 Other Level
5 Regular; 0 Special Education; 0 Vocational; 1 Alternative
0 Magnet; 0 Charter; 2 Title I Eligible; 2 School-wide Title I
Students: 2,941 (52.3% male; 47.6% female)
Individual Education Program: 437 (14.9%);
English Language Learner: 16 (0.5%); Migrant: n/a
Eligible for Free Lunch Program: 275 (9.4%)
Eligible for Reduced-Price Lunch Program: 69 (2.3%)
Teachers: 172.0 (17.1 to 1)
Librarians/Media Specialists: 2.0 (1,470.5 to 1)
Guidance Counselors: 6.0 (490.2 to 1)
Current Spending: ($ per student per year):
Total: $7,401; Instruction: $4,309; Support Services: $2,836
Enrollment, Drop-out Rates and Diploma Recipients by Race/Ethnicity

Category	Total	White	Black	Asian	AIAN	Hisp.
Enrollment (%)	100.0	88.3	4.7	3.7	0.3	2.9
Drop-out Rate (%)	n/a	n/a	n/a	n/a	n/a	n/a
H.S. Diplomas (#)	216	198	8	3	2	5

Holt Public Schools
5780 W Holt Rd • Holt, MI 48842-9696
(517) 694-5715 • http://www.holt.k12.mi.us/
Grade Span: PK-12; **Agency Type:** 1
Schools: 12
6 Primary; 3 Middle; 2 High; 1 Other Level
11 Regular; 0 Special Education; 0 Vocational; 1 Alternative
0 Magnet; 0 Charter; 0 Title I Eligible; 0 School-wide Title I
Students: 5,840 (51.0% male; 48.9% female)
Individual Education Program: 968 (16.6%);
English Language Learner: 0 (0.0%); Migrant: n/a
Eligible for Free Lunch Program: 686 (11.7%)
Eligible for Reduced-Price Lunch Program: 266 (4.6%)
Teachers: 318.0 (18.4 to 1)
Librarians/Media Specialists: 4.0 (1,460.0 to 1)
Guidance Counselors: 8.0 (730.0 to 1)
Current Spending: ($ per student per year):
Total: $7,294; Instruction: $4,442; Support Services: $2,683
Enrollment, Drop-out Rates and Diploma Recipients by Race/Ethnicity

Category	Total	White	Black	Asian	AIAN	Hisp.
Enrollment (%)	100.0	86.0	5.8	2.1	0.9	5.3
Drop-out Rate (%)	n/a	n/a	n/a	n/a	n/a	n/a
H.S. Diplomas (#)	301	267	4	9	7	14

Lansing Public SD
519 W Kalamazoo St • Lansing, MI 48933-2008
(517) 325-6007 • http://scnc.lsd.k12.mi.us/
Grade Span: PK-12; **Agency Type:** 1
Schools: 42
29 Primary; 6 Middle; 4 High; 3 Other Level
38 Regular; 1 Special Education; 2 Vocational; 1 Alternative
5 Magnet; 0 Charter; 0 Title I Eligible; 0 School-wide Title I
Students: 16,979 (51.8% male; 48.1% female)
Individual Education Program: 3,306 (19.5%);
English Language Learner: 1,588 (9.4%); Migrant: 1 (<0.1%)
Eligible for Free Lunch Program: 8,582 (52.1%)
Eligible for Reduced-Price Lunch Program: 1,527 (9.3%)
Teachers: 304.0 (54.2 to 1)
Librarians/Media Specialists: 1.0 (16,463.0 to 1)
Guidance Counselors: 2.0 (8,231.5 to 1)
Current Spending: ($ per student per year):
Total: $10,430; Instruction: $5,787; Support Services: $4,315
Enrollment, Drop-out Rates and Diploma Recipients by Race/Ethnicity

Category	Total	White	Black	Asian	AIAN	Hisp.
Enrollment (%)	100.0	37.6	41.1	5.0	1.2	15.2
Drop-out Rate (%)	n/a	n/a	n/a	n/a	n/a	n/a
H.S. Diplomas (#)	778	331	301	63	7	76

Mason Public Schools (Ingham)
118 W Oak St • Mason, MI 48854-1618
(517) 676-2484 • http://www.mason.k12.mi.us/
Grade Span: PK-12; **Agency Type:** 1
Schools: 6
4 Primary; 1 Middle; 1 High; 0 Other Level
6 Regular; 0 Special Education; 0 Vocational; 0 Alternative
0 Magnet; 0 Charter; 0 Title I Eligible; 0 School-wide Title I
Students: 3,170 (49.8% male; 50.1% female)
Individual Education Program: 431 (13.6%);
English Language Learner: 0 (0.0%); Migrant: n/a
Eligible for Free Lunch Program: 302 (9.5%)
Eligible for Reduced-Price Lunch Program: 159 (5.0%)
Teachers: 173.0 (18.3 to 1)
Librarians/Media Specialists: 2.0 (1,585.0 to 1)
Guidance Counselors: 4.0 (792.5 to 1)
Current Spending: ($ per student per year):
Total: $7,267; Instruction: $4,526; Support Services: $2,431
Enrollment, Drop-out Rates and Diploma Recipients by Race/Ethnicity

Category	Total	White	Black	Asian	AIAN	Hisp.
Enrollment (%)	100.0	91.7	1.7	2.1	0.9	3.6
Drop-out Rate (%)	n/a	n/a	n/a	n/a	n/a	n/a
H.S. Diplomas (#)	235	219	2	4	0	10

Okemos Public Schools
4406 N Okemos Rd • Okemos, MI 48864-1781
(517) 349-9460 • http://okemos.k12.mi.us/
Grade Span: PK-12; **Agency Type:** 1
Schools: 9
6 Primary; 2 Middle; 1 High; 0 Other Level
9 Regular; 0 Special Education; 0 Vocational; 0 Alternative
0 Magnet; 0 Charter; 0 Title I Eligible; 0 School-wide Title I
Students: 4,046 (51.2% male; 48.7% female)
Individual Education Program: 465 (11.5%);
English Language Learner: 0 (0.0%); Migrant: n/a
Eligible for Free Lunch Program: 246 (6.1%)
Eligible for Reduced-Price Lunch Program: 31 (0.8%)
Teachers: 127.0 (31.9 to 1)
Librarians/Media Specialists: 2.0 (2,023.0 to 1)
Guidance Counselors: 10.0 (404.6 to 1)
Current Spending: ($ per student per year):
Total: $8,668; Instruction: $5,121; Support Services: $3,225
Enrollment, Drop-out Rates and Diploma Recipients by Race/Ethnicity

Category	Total	White	Black	Asian	AIAN	Hisp.
Enrollment (%)	100.0	75.6	5.1	14.0	0.5	2.0
Drop-out Rate (%)	n/a	n/a	n/a	n/a	n/a	n/a
H.S. Diplomas (#)	351	286	17	40	5	3

Stockbridge Community Schools
305 W Elizabeth St • Stockbridge, MI 49285-9791
(517) 851-7188 • http://scs.k12.mi.us/
Grade Span: KG-12; **Agency Type:** 1
Schools: 7
4 Primary; 1 Middle; 1 High; 0 Other Level
6 Regular; 0 Special Education; 0 Vocational; 0 Alternative
0 Magnet; 0 Charter; 0 Title I Eligible; 0 School-wide Title I
Students: 1,750 (51.8% male; 48.1% female)
Individual Education Program: 273 (15.6%);
English Language Learner: 5 (0.3%); Migrant: n/a
Eligible for Free Lunch Program: 270 (15.4%)
Eligible for Reduced-Price Lunch Program: 114 (6.5%)
Teachers: 100.0 (17.5 to 1)
Librarians/Media Specialists: 2.0 (875.0 to 1)
Guidance Counselors: 3.0 (583.3 to 1)
Current Spending: ($ per student per year):
Total: $7,505; Instruction: $4,409; Support Services: $2,780
Enrollment, Drop-out Rates and Diploma Recipients by Race/Ethnicity

Category	Total	White	Black	Asian	AIAN	Hisp.
Enrollment (%)	100.0	95.7	1.0	0.6	0.1	2.6
Drop-out Rate (%)	n/a	n/a	n/a	n/a	n/a	n/a
H.S. Diplomas (#)	106	102	0	1	0	3

Waverly Community Schools
515 Snow Rd • Lansing, MI 48917-4501
(517) 321-7265 • http://web.waverly.k12.mi.us/intro.cfm
Grade Span: KG-12; **Agency Type:** 1
Schools: 7
4 Primary; 2 Middle; 1 High; 0 Other Level
7 Regular; 0 Special Education; 0 Vocational; 0 Alternative
0 Magnet; 0 Charter; 7 Title I Eligible; 7 School-wide Title I
Students: 3,406 (51.8% male; 48.1% female)
Individual Education Program: 435 (12.8%);
English Language Learner: 59 (1.7%); Migrant: n/a
Eligible for Free Lunch Program: 625 (18.4%)
Eligible for Reduced-Price Lunch Program: 113 (3.3%)

Teachers: 206.0 (16.5 to 1)
Librarians/Media Specialists: 0.0 (n/a to 1)
Guidance Counselors: 5.0 (681.2 to 1)
Current Spending: ($ per student per year):
  Total: $8,987; Instruction: $5,199; Support Services: $3,561
Enrollment, Drop-out Rates and Diploma Recipients by Race/Ethnicity

Category	Total	White	Black	Asian	AIAN	Hisp.
Enrollment (%)	100.0	60.3	25.5	4.7	0.9	8.5
Drop-out Rate (%)	n/a	n/a	n/a	n/a	n/a	n/a
H.S. Diplomas (#)	255	188	46	11	0	10

Williamston Community Schools

418 Highland St • Williamston, MI 48895-1133
(517) 655-4361 • http://www.wmston.k12.mi.us/
Grade Span: KG-12; **Agency Type:** 1
Schools: 4
  2 Primary; 1 Middle; 1 High; 0 Other Level
  4 Regular; 0 Special Education; 0 Vocational; 0 Alternative
  0 Magnet; 0 Charter; 0 Title I Eligible; 0 School-wide Title I
Students: 2,090 (50.4% male; 49.5% female)
  Individual Education Program: 234 (11.2%);
  English Language Learner: 0 (0.0%); Migrant: n/a
  Eligible for Free Lunch Program: 191 (9.1%)
  Eligible for Reduced-Price Lunch Program: 76 (3.6%)
Teachers: 114.0 (18.3 to 1)
Librarians/Media Specialists: 1.0 (2,090.0 to 1)
Guidance Counselors: 6.0 (348.3 to 1)
Current Spending: ($ per student per year):
  Total: $7,016; Instruction: $4,018; Support Services: $2,802
Enrollment, Drop-out Rates and Diploma Recipients by Race/Ethnicity

Category	Total	White	Black	Asian	AIAN	Hisp.
Enrollment (%)	100.0	94.2	1.7	1.6	0.5	1.9
Drop-out Rate (%)	n/a	n/a	n/a	n/a	n/a	n/a
H.S. Diplomas (#)	130	125	3	2	0	0

Ionia County

Belding Area SD

321 Wilson St • Belding, MI 48809-1744
(616) 794-4444 • http://www.belding.k12.mi.us/
Grade Span: PK-12; **Agency Type:** 1
Schools: 7
  4 Primary; 1 Middle; 2 High; 0 Other Level
  6 Regular; 0 Special Education; 0 Vocational; 1 Alternative
  0 Magnet; 0 Charter; 4 Title I Eligible; 4 School-wide Title I
Students: 2,500 (49.0% male; 50.9% female)
  Individual Education Program: 400 (16.0%);
  English Language Learner: 359 (14.4%); Migrant: 84 (3.4%)
  Eligible for Free Lunch Program: 714 (28.6%)
  Eligible for Reduced-Price Lunch Program: 285 (11.4%)
Teachers: 147.0 (17.0 to 1)
Librarians/Media Specialists: 2.0 (1,250.0 to 1)
Guidance Counselors: 3.0 (833.3 to 1)
Current Spending: ($ per student per year):
  Total: $7,007; Instruction: $4,399; Support Services: $2,369
Enrollment, Drop-out Rates and Diploma Recipients by Race/Ethnicity

Category	Total	White	Black	Asian	AIAN	Hisp.
Enrollment (%)	100.0	91.5	0.7	0.6	0.4	5.4
Drop-out Rate (%)	n/a	n/a	n/a	n/a	n/a	n/a
H.S. Diplomas (#)	152	148	0	1	1	2

Ionia Public Schools

250 E Tuttle Rd • Ionia, MI 48846-8605
(616) 527-9280 • http://www.ionia.k12.mi.us/
Grade Span: PK-12; **Agency Type:** 1
Schools: 8
  5 Primary; 1 Middle; 1 High; 1 Other Level
  7 Regular; 0 Special Education; 0 Vocational; 1 Alternative
  0 Magnet; 0 Charter; 8 Title I Eligible; 8 School-wide Title I
Students: 3,427 (51.7% male; 48.2% female)
  Individual Education Program: 613 (17.9%);
  English Language Learner: 0 (0.0%); Migrant: n/a
  Eligible for Free Lunch Program: 1,111 (32.4%)
  Eligible for Reduced-Price Lunch Program: 344 (10.0%)
Teachers: 211.0 (16.2 to 1)
Librarians/Media Specialists: 1.0 (3,427.0 to 1)
Guidance Counselors: 6.0 (571.2 to 1)
Current Spending: ($ per student per year):
  Total: $7,665; Instruction: $4,711; Support Services: $2,650
Enrollment, Drop-out Rates and Diploma Recipients by Race/Ethnicity

Category	Total	White	Black	Asian	AIAN	Hisp.
Enrollment (%)	100.0	91.1	1.3	0.8	0.3	4.5
Drop-out Rate (%)	n/a	n/a	n/a	n/a	n/a	n/a
H.S. Diplomas (#)	207	197	3	1	0	6

Lakewood Public Schools

639 Jordan Lake St • Lake Odessa, MI 48849-6203
(616) 374-8043 • http://www.lakewood.k12.mi.us/
Grade Span: PK-12; **Agency Type:** 1
Schools: 7
  4 Primary; 1 Middle; 1 High; 1 Other Level
  6 Regular; 0 Special Education; 0 Vocational; 1 Alternative
  0 Magnet; 0 Charter; 0 Title I Eligible; 0 School-wide Title I
Students: 2,530 (50.6% male; 49.3% female)
  Individual Education Program: 398 (15.7%);
  English Language Learner: 8 (0.3%); Migrant: n/a
  Eligible for Free Lunch Program: 469 (18.5%)
  Eligible for Reduced-Price Lunch Program: 191 (7.5%)
Teachers: 133.0 (19.0 to 1)
Librarians/Media Specialists: 0.0 (n/a to 1)
Guidance Counselors: 3.0 (843.3 to 1)
Current Spending: ($ per student per year):
  Total: $7,186; Instruction: $4,313; Support Services: $2,571
Enrollment, Drop-out Rates and Diploma Recipients by Race/Ethnicity

Category	Total	White	Black	Asian	AIAN	Hisp.
Enrollment (%)	100.0	94.2	0.7	0.8	0.5	3.9
Drop-out Rate (%)	n/a	n/a	n/a	n/a	n/a	n/a
H.S. Diplomas (#)	182	178	0	0	2	2

Portland Public SD

1100 Ionia Rd • Portland, MI 48875-1035
(517) 647-4161 • http://www.portlandpublicschools.cc/
Grade Span: PK-12; **Agency Type:** 1
Schools: 5
  2 Primary; 1 Middle; 1 High; 1 Other Level
  4 Regular; 0 Special Education; 0 Vocational; 1 Alternative
  0 Magnet; 0 Charter; 0 Title I Eligible; 0 School-wide Title I
Students: 2,086 (51.0% male; 48.9% female)
  Individual Education Program: 329 (15.8%);
  English Language Learner: 0 (0.0%); Migrant: n/a
  Eligible for Free Lunch Program: 206 (9.9%)
  Eligible for Reduced-Price Lunch Program: 103 (4.9%)
Teachers: 107.0 (19.5 to 1)
Librarians/Media Specialists: 0.0 (n/a to 1)
Guidance Counselors: 3.0 (695.3 to 1)
Current Spending: ($ per student per year):
  Total: $6,800; Instruction: $4,168; Support Services: $2,415
Enrollment, Drop-out Rates and Diploma Recipients by Race/Ethnicity

Category	Total	White	Black	Asian	AIAN	Hisp.
Enrollment (%)	100.0	97.6	0.8	0.7	0.3	0.6
Drop-out Rate (%)	n/a	n/a	n/a	n/a	n/a	n/a
H.S. Diplomas (#)	153	151	0	2	0	0

Iosco County

Oscoda Area Schools

3550 E River Rd • Oscoda, MI 48750-9025
(989) 739-2033 • http://www.oscodaschools.org/
Grade Span: PK-12; **Agency Type:** 1
Schools: 6
  3 Primary; 1 Middle; 1 High; 1 Other Level
  5 Regular; 0 Special Education; 0 Vocational; 1 Alternative
  0 Magnet; 0 Charter; 0 Title I Eligible; 0 School-wide Title I
Students: 1,855 (52.2% male; 47.7% female)
  Individual Education Program: 313 (16.9%);
  English Language Learner: 0 (0.0%); Migrant: n/a
  Eligible for Free Lunch Program: 816 (44.0%)
  Eligible for Reduced-Price Lunch Program: 276 (14.9%)
Teachers: 103.0 (18.0 to 1)
Librarians/Media Specialists: 2.0 (927.5 to 1)
Guidance Counselors: 4.0 (463.8 to 1)
Current Spending: ($ per student per year):
  Total: $7,490; Instruction: $4,381; Support Services: $2,775
Enrollment, Drop-out Rates and Diploma Recipients by Race/Ethnicity

Category	Total	White	Black	Asian	AIAN	Hisp.
Enrollment (%)	100.0	95.4	1.6	0.6	1.1	1.1
Drop-out Rate (%)	n/a	n/a	n/a	n/a	n/a	n/a
H.S. Diplomas (#)	133	123	1	3	2	4

Tawas Area Schools

245 M-55 W • Tawas City, MI 48763-9252
(989) 984-2250 • http://www.tawas.net/
Grade Span: PK-12; **Agency Type:** 1
Schools: 4
  1 Primary; 2 Middle; 1 High; 0 Other Level
  4 Regular; 0 Special Education; 0 Vocational; 0 Alternative
  0 Magnet; 0 Charter; 0 Title I Eligible; 0 School-wide Title I
Students: 1,529 (50.6% male; 49.3% female)
  Individual Education Program: 218 (14.3%);
  English Language Learner: 0 (0.0%); Migrant: n/a

Eligible for Free Lunch Program: 370 (24.2%)
Eligible for Reduced-Price Lunch Program: 134 (8.8%)
Teachers: 87.0 (17.6 to 1)
Librarians/Media Specialists: 1.0 (1,529.0 to 1)
Guidance Counselors: 2.0 (764.5 to 1)
Current Spending: ($ per student per year):
Total: $7,064; Instruction: $4,498; Support Services: $2,295
Enrollment, Drop-out Rates and Diploma Recipients by Race/Ethnicity

Category	Total	White	Black	Asian	AIAN	Hisp.
Enrollment (%)	100.0	97.6	0.9	0.3	0.5	0.8
Drop-out Rate (%)	n/a	n/a	n/a	n/a	n/a	n/a
H.S. Diplomas (#)	134	127	0	4	1	2

Isabella County

Mt. Pleasant City SD
201 S University St • Mt. Pleasant, MI 48858-2527
(989) 775-2301 • http://www.edzone.net/mpps/
Grade Span: PK-12; **Agency Type:** 1
Schools: 11
5 Primary; 3 Middle; 2 High; 1 Other Level
9 Regular; 0 Special Education; 0 Vocational; 2 Alternative
0 Magnet; 0 Charter; 0 Title I Eligible; 0 School-wide Title I
Students: 3,936   (51.5% male; 48.4% female)
Individual Education Program: 584 (14.8%);
English Language Learner: 5 (0.1%); Migrant: n/a
Eligible for Free Lunch Program: 818 (20.8%)
Eligible for Reduced-Price Lunch Program: 252 (6.4%)
Teachers: 223.0 (17.7 to 1)
Librarians/Media Specialists: 4.0 (984.0 to 1)
Guidance Counselors: 4.0 (984.0 to 1)
Current Spending: ($ per student per year):
Total: $8,716; Instruction: $4,852; Support Services: $3,569
Enrollment, Drop-out Rates and Diploma Recipients by Race/Ethnicity

Category	Total	White	Black	Asian	AIAN	Hisp.
Enrollment (%)	100.0	84.2	3.0	2.7	7.3	2.0
Drop-out Rate (%)	n/a	n/a	n/a	n/a	n/a	n/a
H.S. Diplomas (#)	270	240	8	11	6	5

Shepherd Public SD
258 W Wright • Shepherd, MI 48883-2502
Mailing Address: PO Box 219 • Shepherd, MI 48883-0219
(989) 828-5520 • http://shepherd.edzone.net/
Grade Span: KG-12; **Agency Type:** 1
Schools: 5
2 Primary; 1 Middle; 2 High; 0 Other Level
4 Regular; 0 Special Education; 0 Vocational; 1 Alternative
0 Magnet; 0 Charter; 2 Title I Eligible; 2 School-wide Title I
Students: 1,768   (53.4% male; 46.5% female)
Individual Education Program: 279 (15.8%);
English Language Learner: 0 (0.0%); Migrant: n/a
Eligible for Free Lunch Program: 368 (20.8%)
Eligible for Reduced-Price Lunch Program: 158 (8.9%)
Teachers: 104.0 (17.0 to 1)
Librarians/Media Specialists: 1.0 (1,768.0 to 1)
Guidance Counselors: 3.0 (589.3 to 1)
Current Spending: ($ per student per year):
Total: $7,649; Instruction: $4,772; Support Services: $2,578
Enrollment, Drop-out Rates and Diploma Recipients by Race/Ethnicity

Category	Total	White	Black	Asian	AIAN	Hisp.
Enrollment (%)	100.0	92.6	1.0	0.6	3.2	2.7
Drop-out Rate (%)	n/a	n/a	n/a	n/a	n/a	n/a
H.S. Diplomas (#)	116	111	0	1	2	2

Jackson County

Columbia SD
11775 Hewitt Rd • Brooklyn, MI 49230-8961
(517) 592-6641 • http://scnc.csd.k12.mi.us/
Grade Span: KG-12; **Agency Type:** 1
Schools: 5
2 Primary; 1 Middle; 1 High; 1 Other Level
4 Regular; 0 Special Education; 0 Vocational; 1 Alternative
0 Magnet; 0 Charter; 0 Title I Eligible; 0 School-wide Title I
Students: 1,912   (52.3% male; 47.6% female)
Individual Education Program: 254 (13.3%);
English Language Learner: 0 (0.0%); Migrant: n/a
Eligible for Free Lunch Program: 252 (13.2%)
Eligible for Reduced-Price Lunch Program: 104 (5.4%)
Teachers: 95.0 (20.1 to 1)
Librarians/Media Specialists: 1.0 (1,912.0 to 1)
Guidance Counselors: 3.0 (637.3 to 1)
Current Spending: ($ per student per year):
Total: $6,932; Instruction: $4,313; Support Services: $2,371

Enrollment, Drop-out Rates and Diploma Recipients by Race/Ethnicity

Category	Total	White	Black	Asian	AIAN	Hisp.
Enrollment (%)	100.0	95.9	0.9	0.5	1.2	1.5
Drop-out Rate (%)	n/a	n/a	n/a	n/a	n/a	n/a
H.S. Diplomas (#)	115	111	1	0	1	2

East Jackson Community Schools
1404 N Sutton Rd • Jackson, MI 49202-2822
(517) 764-2090 • http://www.ejs.k12.mi.us/MAIN%20PAGE/links_page.htm
Grade Span: KG-12; **Agency Type:** 1
Schools: 4
2 Primary; 1 Middle; 1 High; 0 Other Level
4 Regular; 0 Special Education; 0 Vocational; 0 Alternative
1 Magnet; 0 Charter; 1 Title I Eligible; 1 School-wide Title I
Students: 1,628   (50.8% male; 49.1% female)
Individual Education Program: 225 (13.8%);
English Language Learner: 0 (0.0%); Migrant: n/a
Eligible for Free Lunch Program: 538 (33.0%)
Eligible for Reduced-Price Lunch Program: 105 (6.4%)
Teachers: 89.0 (18.3 to 1)
Librarians/Media Specialists: 2.0 (814.0 to 1)
Guidance Counselors: 4.0 (407.0 to 1)
Current Spending: ($ per student per year):
Total: $7,124; Instruction: $4,590; Support Services: $2,268
Enrollment, Drop-out Rates and Diploma Recipients by Race/Ethnicity

Category	Total	White	Black	Asian	AIAN	Hisp.
Enrollment (%)	100.0	92.3	4.1	1.1	0.9	1.7
Drop-out Rate (%)	n/a	n/a	n/a	n/a	n/a	n/a
H.S. Diplomas (#)	88	86	2	0	0	0

Jackson Public Schools
522 Wildwood Ave • Jackson, MI 49201-1013
(517) 841-2200 • http://scnc.jps.k12.mi.us/
Grade Span: PK-12; **Agency Type:** 1
Schools: 14
10 Primary; 2 Middle; 1 High; 1 Other Level
12 Regular; 0 Special Education; 0 Vocational; 2 Alternative
0 Magnet; 0 Charter; 14 Title I Eligible; 14 School-wide Title I
Students: 7,247   (51.4% male; 48.5% female)
Individual Education Program: 1,162 (16.0%);
English Language Learner: 185 (2.6%); Migrant: n/a
Eligible for Free Lunch Program: 3,965 (54.7%)
Eligible for Reduced-Price Lunch Program: 564 (7.8%)
Teachers: 198.0 (36.6 to 1)
Librarians/Media Specialists: 1.0 (7,247.0 to 1)
Guidance Counselors: 0.0 (n/a to 1)
Current Spending: ($ per student per year):
Total: $8,958; Instruction: $5,267; Support Services: $3,349
Enrollment, Drop-out Rates and Diploma Recipients by Race/Ethnicity

Category	Total	White	Black	Asian	AIAN	Hisp.
Enrollment (%)	100.0	56.5	37.1	1.3	1.2	3.9
Drop-out Rate (%)	n/a	n/a	n/a	n/a	n/a	n/a
H.S. Diplomas (#)	333	227	85	7	1	13

Michigan Center SD
400 S State St • Michigan Center, MI 49254-1237
(517) 764-5778
Grade Span: PK-12; **Agency Type:** 1
Schools: 4
2 Primary; 0 Middle; 2 High; 0 Other Level
3 Regular; 0 Special Education; 0 Vocational; 1 Alternative
0 Magnet; 0 Charter; 0 Title I Eligible; 0 School-wide Title I
Students: 1,595   (52.3% male; 47.6% female)
Individual Education Program: 211 (13.2%);
English Language Learner: 0 (0.0%); Migrant: n/a
Eligible for Free Lunch Program: 419 (26.3%)
Eligible for Reduced-Price Lunch Program: 134 (8.4%)
Teachers: 77.0 (20.7 to 1)
Librarians/Media Specialists: 2.0 (797.5 to 1)
Guidance Counselors: 3.0 (531.7 to 1)
Current Spending: ($ per student per year):
Total: $6,511; Instruction: $3,960; Support Services: $2,244
Enrollment, Drop-out Rates and Diploma Recipients by Race/Ethnicity

Category	Total	White	Black	Asian	AIAN	Hisp.
Enrollment (%)	100.0	96.4	1.4	0.5	0.4	1.2
Drop-out Rate (%)	n/a	n/a	n/a	n/a	n/a	n/a
H.S. Diplomas (#)	70	69	0	1	0	0

Napoleon Community Schools
200 W Ave • Napoleon, MI 49261-0308
Mailing Address: PO Box 308 • Napoleon, MI 49261-0308
(517) 536-8667 • http://scnc.ncs.k12.mi.us/
Grade Span: KG-12; **Agency Type:** 1
Schools: 4
1 Primary; 1 Middle; 1 High; 1 Other Level

3 Regular; 0 Special Education; 0 Vocational; 1 Alternative
0 Magnet; 0 Charter; 1 Title I Eligible; 1 School-wide Title I
Students: 1,767 (53.0% male; 46.9% female)
Individual Education Program: 178 (10.1%);
English Language Learner: 0 (0.0%); Migrant: n/a
Eligible for Free Lunch Program: 291 (16.5%)
Eligible for Reduced-Price Lunch Program: 64 (3.6%)
Teachers: 96.0 (18.4 to 1)
Librarians/Media Specialists: 2.0 (883.5 to 1)
Guidance Counselors: 3.0 (589.0 to 1)
Current Spending: ($ per student per year):
Total: $6,538; Instruction: $4,159; Support Services: $2,151
Enrollment, Drop-out Rates and Diploma Recipients by Race/Ethnicity

Category	Total	White	Black	Asian	AIAN	Hisp.
Enrollment (%)	100.0	97.2	0.8	0.3	0.3	1.0
Drop-out Rate (%)	n/a	n/a	n/a	n/a	n/a	n/a
H.S. Diplomas (#)	94	91	0	2	0	1

Northwest Community Schools
4000 Van Horn Rd • Jackson, MI 49201-7449
(517) 569-2247 • http://nsd.k12.mi.us/
Grade Span: PK-12; **Agency Type:** 1
Schools: 6
3 Primary; 1 Middle; 1 High; 1 Other Level
5 Regular; 0 Special Education; 0 Vocational; 1 Alternative
0 Magnet; 0 Charter; 0 Title I Eligible; 0 School-wide Title I
Students: 3,667 (50.3% male; 49.6% female)
Individual Education Program: 489 (13.3%);
English Language Learner: 0 (0.0%); Migrant: n/a
Eligible for Free Lunch Program: 799 (21.8%)
Eligible for Reduced-Price Lunch Program: 291 (7.9%)
Teachers: 193.0 (19.0 to 1)
Librarians/Media Specialists: 3.0 (1,222.3 to 1)
Guidance Counselors: 8.0 (458.4 to 1)
Current Spending: ($ per student per year):
Total: $7,029; Instruction: $4,352; Support Services: $2,403
Enrollment, Drop-out Rates and Diploma Recipients by Race/Ethnicity

Category	Total	White	Black	Asian	AIAN	Hisp.
Enrollment (%)	100.0	92.4	3.1	1.3	0.9	2.3
Drop-out Rate (%)	n/a	n/a	n/a	n/a	n/a	n/a
H.S. Diplomas (#)	206	195	2	4	1	4

Western SD
1400 S Dearing Rd • Parma, MI 49269-9712
(517) 841-8100 • http://scnc.western.k12.mi.us/
Grade Span: KG-12; **Agency Type:** 1
Schools: 6
3 Primary; 1 Middle; 2 High; 0 Other Level
5 Regular; 0 Special Education; 0 Vocational; 1 Alternative
0 Magnet; 0 Charter; 3 Title I Eligible; 3 School-wide Title I
Students: 2,819 (50.5% male; 49.4% female)
Individual Education Program: 346 (12.3%);
English Language Learner: 0 (0.0%); Migrant: n/a
Eligible for Free Lunch Program: 473 (16.9%)
Eligible for Reduced-Price Lunch Program: 156 (5.6%)
Teachers: 143.0 (19.6 to 1)
Librarians/Media Specialists: 2.0 (1,401.0 to 1)
Guidance Counselors: 3.0 (934.0 to 1)
Current Spending: ($ per student per year):
Total: $6,947; Instruction: $4,233; Support Services: $2,491
Enrollment, Drop-out Rates and Diploma Recipients by Race/Ethnicity

Category	Total	White	Black	Asian	AIAN	Hisp.
Enrollment (%)	100.0	93.6	2.5	1.1	0.7	1.9
Drop-out Rate (%)	n/a	n/a	n/a	n/a	n/a	n/a
H.S. Diplomas (#)	148	146	1	0	0	1

Kalamazoo County

Comstock Public Schools
301 N 26th St • Kalamazoo, MI 49048-9223
(269) 388-9461 • http://www.remc12.k12.mi.us/comstock/
Grade Span: PK-12; **Agency Type:** 1
Schools: 7
4 Primary; 1 Middle; 1 High; 1 Other Level
6 Regular; 0 Special Education; 0 Vocational; 1 Alternative
0 Magnet; 0 Charter; 2 Title I Eligible; 2 School-wide Title I
Students: 2,916 (52.7% male; 47.2% female)
Individual Education Program: 413 (14.2%);
English Language Learner: 0 (0.0%); Migrant: n/a
Eligible for Free Lunch Program: 960 (34.5%)
Eligible for Reduced-Price Lunch Program: 325 (11.7%)
Teachers: 186.0 (14.9 to 1)
Librarians/Media Specialists: 5.0 (555.8 to 1)
Guidance Counselors: 3.0 (926.3 to 1)
Current Spending: ($ per student per year):
Total: $7,640; Instruction: $4,455; Support Services: $2,938

Category	Total	White	Black	Asian	AIAN	Hisp.
Enrollment (%)	100.0	85.6	9.9	0.8	0.9	2.3
Drop-out Rate (%)	n/a	n/a	n/a	n/a	n/a	n/a
H.S. Diplomas (#)	143	125	12	3	2	1

Gull Lake Community Schools
11775 E D Ave • Richland, MI 49083-9669
(269) 629-5880 • http://www.gull-lake.k12.mi.us/
Grade Span: PK-12; **Agency Type:** 1
Schools: 6
3 Primary; 2 Middle; 1 High; 0 Other Level
6 Regular; 0 Special Education; 0 Vocational; 0 Alternative
0 Magnet; 0 Charter; 0 Title I Eligible; 0 School-wide Title I
Students: 3,034 (50.6% male; 49.3% female)
Individual Education Program: 276 (9.1%);
English Language Learner: 0 (0.0%); Migrant: n/a
Eligible for Free Lunch Program: 233 (7.7%)
Eligible for Reduced-Price Lunch Program: 133 (4.4%)
Teachers: 176.0 (17.2 to 1)
Librarians/Media Specialists: 2.0 (1,509.5 to 1)
Guidance Counselors: 5.0 (603.8 to 1)
Current Spending: ($ per student per year):
Total: $6,523; Instruction: $4,057; Support Services: $2,280
Enrollment, Drop-out Rates and Diploma Recipients by Race/Ethnicity

Category	Total	White	Black	Asian	AIAN	Hisp.
Enrollment (%)	100.0	96.2	1.9	0.9	0.3	0.8
Drop-out Rate (%)	n/a	n/a	n/a	n/a	n/a	n/a
H.S. Diplomas (#)	210	203	1	2	0	4

Kalamazoo Public SD
1220 Howard St • Kalamazoo, MI 49008-1871
(269) 337-0123 • http://63.241.176.180/
Grade Span: PK-12; **Agency Type:** 1
Schools: 26
17 Primary; 3 Middle; 5 High; 1 Other Level
24 Regular; 1 Special Education; 0 Vocational; 1 Alternative
8 Magnet; 0 Charter; 17 Title I Eligible; 17 School-wide Title I
Students: 11,099 (51.8% male; 48.1% female)
Individual Education Program: 1,496 (13.5%);
English Language Learner: 830 (7.5%); Migrant: 148 (1.3%)
Eligible for Free Lunch Program: 5,768 (52.1%)
Eligible for Reduced-Price Lunch Program: 896 (8.1%)
Teachers: 768.0 (14.4 to 1)
Librarians/Media Specialists: 2.0 (5,531.0 to 1)
Guidance Counselors: 3.0 (3,687.3 to 1)
Current Spending: ($ per student per year):
Total: $9,310; Instruction: $5,597; Support Services: $3,389
Enrollment, Drop-out Rates and Diploma Recipients by Race/Ethnicity

Category	Total	White	Black	Asian	AIAN	Hisp.
Enrollment (%)	100.0	41.9	46.8	1.8	1.4	8.2
Drop-out Rate (%)	n/a	n/a	n/a	n/a	n/a	n/a
H.S. Diplomas (#)	434	255	90	61	4	24

Parchment SD
520 N Orient St • Parchment, MI 49004-1757
(269) 488-1050 • http://www.remc12.k12.mi.us/parchment/
Grade Span: PK-12; **Agency Type:** 1
Schools: 6
3 Primary; 1 Middle; 1 High; 1 Other Level
5 Regular; 0 Special Education; 0 Vocational; 1 Alternative
0 Magnet; 0 Charter; 0 Title I Eligible; 0 School-wide Title I
Students: 2,025 (51.3% male; 48.6% female)
Individual Education Program: 191 (9.4%);
English Language Learner: 0 (0.0%); Migrant: n/a
Eligible for Free Lunch Program: 610 (30.1%)
Eligible for Reduced-Price Lunch Program: 155 (7.7%)
Teachers: 110.0 (18.4 to 1)
Librarians/Media Specialists: 3.0 (675.0 to 1)
Guidance Counselors: 3.0 (675.0 to 1)
Current Spending: ($ per student per year):
Total: $7,185; Instruction: $4,412; Support Services: $2,536
Enrollment, Drop-out Rates and Diploma Recipients by Race/Ethnicity

Category	Total	White	Black	Asian	AIAN	Hisp.
Enrollment (%)	100.0	86.5	8.7	0.8	0.3	3.1
Drop-out Rate (%)	n/a	n/a	n/a	n/a	n/a	n/a
H.S. Diplomas (#)	107	99	2	2	0	4

Portage Public Schools
8111 S Westnedge Ave • Portage, MI 49002-5433
(269) 323-5000 • http://www.portageps.org/
Grade Span: PK-12; **Agency Type:** 1
Schools: 14
8 Primary; 3 Middle; 2 High; 1 Other Level
13 Regular; 0 Special Education; 0 Vocational; 1 Alternative

0 Magnet; 0 Charter; 0 Title I Eligible; 0 School-wide Title I
Students: 9,145   (51.3% male; 48.6% female)
   Individual Education Program: 828 (9.1%);
   English Language Learner: 0 (0.0%); Migrant: n/a
   Eligible for Free Lunch Program: 922 (10.1%)
   Eligible for Reduced-Price Lunch Program: 345 (3.8%)
Teachers: 528.0 (17.3 to 1)
Librarians/Media Specialists: 13.0 (703.5 to 1)
Guidance Counselors: 17.0 (537.9 to 1)
Current Spending: ($ per student per year):
   Total: $7,181; Instruction: $4,329; Support Services: $2,659
Enrollment, Drop-out Rates and Diploma Recipients by Race/Ethnicity

Category	Total	White	Black	Asian	AIAN	Hisp.
Enrollment (%)	100.0	87.9	5.1	4.5	0.3	1.7
Drop-out Rate (%)	n/a	n/a	n/a	n/a	n/a	n/a
H.S. Diplomas (#)	616	576	16	22	2	0

Vicksburg Community Schools
301 S Kalamazoo Ave • Vicksburg, MI 49097-1308
Mailing Address: PO Box 158 • Vicksburg, MI 49097-0158
(269) 321-1000 • http://www.remc.k12.mi.us/vicksburg/
Grade Span: KG-12; **Agency Type:** 1
Schools: 5
   3 Primary; 1 Middle; 1 High; 0 Other Level
   5 Regular; 0 Special Education; 0 Vocational; 0 Alternative
   0 Magnet; 0 Charter; 3 Title I Eligible; 3 School-wide Title I
Students: 2,729   (50.0% male; 50.0% female)
   Individual Education Program: 243 (8.9%);
   English Language Learner: 0 (0.0%); Migrant: n/a
   Eligible for Free Lunch Program: 365 (13.4%)
   Eligible for Reduced-Price Lunch Program: 135 (5.0%)
Teachers: 160.0 (17.0 to 1)
Librarians/Media Specialists: 4.0 (680.3 to 1)
Guidance Counselors: 7.0 (388.7 to 1)
Current Spending: ($ per student per year):
   Total: $7,054; Instruction: $4,110; Support Services: $2,675
Enrollment, Drop-out Rates and Diploma Recipients by Race/Ethnicity

Category	Total	White	Black	Asian	AIAN	Hisp.
Enrollment (%)	100.0	95.1	1.1	1.2	0.1	1.7
Drop-out Rate (%)	n/a	n/a	n/a	n/a	n/a	n/a
H.S. Diplomas (#)	209	203	3	1	0	2

Kalkaska County

Kalkaska Public Schools
315 S Coral St • Kalkaska, MI 49646-0580
Mailing Address: PO Box 580 • Kalkaska, MI 49646-0580
(231) 258-9109 • http://tcnet.org/schools/kk/kps.htm
Grade Span: KG-12; **Agency Type:** 1
Schools: 6
   2 Primary; 2 Middle; 2 High; 0 Other Level
   5 Regular; 0 Special Education; 0 Vocational; 1 Alternative
   0 Magnet; 0 Charter; 1 Title I Eligible; 1 School-wide Title I
Students: 1,797   (51.1% male; 48.8% female)
   Individual Education Program: 288 (16.0%);
   English Language Learner: 0 (0.0%); Migrant: n/a
   Eligible for Free Lunch Program: 570 (31.7%)
   Eligible for Reduced-Price Lunch Program: 284 (15.8%)
Teachers: 105.0 (17.1 to 1)
Librarians/Media Specialists: 2.0 (898.5 to 1)
Guidance Counselors: 4.0 (449.3 to 1)
Current Spending: ($ per student per year):
   Total: $7,939; Instruction: $4,738; Support Services: $2,934
Enrollment, Drop-out Rates and Diploma Recipients by Race/Ethnicity

Category	Total	White	Black	Asian	AIAN	Hisp.
Enrollment (%)	100.0	96.5	0.3	0.8	1.9	0.4
Drop-out Rate (%)	n/a	n/a	n/a	n/a	n/a	n/a
H.S. Diplomas (#)	132	126	1	1	2	2

Kent County

Byron Center Public Schools
2475 84th St SW • Byron Center, MI 49315-8120
(616) 878-6100 • http://www.remc8.k12.mi.us/byroncen/
Grade Span: PK-12; **Agency Type:** 1
Schools: 8
   5 Primary; 2 Middle; 1 High; 0 Other Level
   7 Regular; 1 Special Education; 0 Vocational; 0 Alternative
   0 Magnet; 0 Charter; 0 Title I Eligible; 0 School-wide Title I
Students: 2,915   (52.9% male; 47.0% female)
   Individual Education Program: 396 (13.6%);
   English Language Learner: 0 (0.0%); Migrant: n/a
   Eligible for Free Lunch Program: 334 (11.5%)
   Eligible for Reduced-Price Lunch Program: 200 (6.9%)
Teachers: 159.0 (18.3 to 1)

Librarians/Media Specialists: 1.0 (2,915.0 to 1)
Guidance Counselors: 4.0 (728.8 to 1)
Current Spending: ($ per student per year):
   Total: $7,442; Instruction: $4,357; Support Services: $2,801
Enrollment, Drop-out Rates and Diploma Recipients by Race/Ethnicity

Category	Total	White	Black	Asian	AIAN	Hisp.
Enrollment (%)	100.0	92.3	1.8	2.4	0.4	3.1
Drop-out Rate (%)	n/a	n/a	n/a	n/a	n/a	n/a
H.S. Diplomas (#)	165	160	1	2	0	2

Caledonia Community Schools
203 E Main St SE • Caledonia, MI 49316-9101
(616) 891-8185 • http://www.caledonia.k12.mi.us/
Grade Span: PK-12; **Agency Type:** 1
Schools: 7
   4 Primary; 1 Middle; 2 High; 0 Other Level
   6 Regular; 0 Special Education; 0 Vocational; 1 Alternative
   0 Magnet; 0 Charter; 0 Title I Eligible; 0 School-wide Title I
Students: 3,407   (53.9% male; 46.0% female)
   Individual Education Program: 449 (13.2%);
   English Language Learner: 0 (0.0%); Migrant: n/a
   Eligible for Free Lunch Program: 199 (5.8%)
   Eligible for Reduced-Price Lunch Program: 108 (3.2%)
Teachers: 190.0 (17.9 to 1)
Librarians/Media Specialists: 1.0 (3,407.0 to 1)
Guidance Counselors: 2.0 (1,703.5 to 1)
Current Spending: ($ per student per year):
   Total: $8,200; Instruction: $4,868; Support Services: $3,024
Enrollment, Drop-out Rates and Diploma Recipients by Race/Ethnicity

Category	Total	White	Black	Asian	AIAN	Hisp.
Enrollment (%)	100.0	97.4	0.5	1.2	0.2	0.7
Drop-out Rate (%)	n/a	n/a	n/a	n/a	n/a	n/a
H.S. Diplomas (#)	202	197	2	1	1	1

Cedar Springs Public Schools
204 E Muskegon St • Cedar Springs, MI 49319-9326
(616) 696-1204 • http://www.cedar-springs.k12.mi.us/
Grade Span: PK-12; **Agency Type:** 1
Schools: 6
   2 Primary; 2 Middle; 2 High; 0 Other Level
   5 Regular; 0 Special Education; 0 Vocational; 1 Alternative
   0 Magnet; 0 Charter; 1 Title I Eligible; 1 School-wide Title I
Students: 3,407   (50.1% male; 49.8% female)
   Individual Education Program: 474 (13.9%);
   English Language Learner: 33 (1.0%); Migrant: n/a
   Eligible for Free Lunch Program: 642 (18.8%)
   Eligible for Reduced-Price Lunch Program: 342 (10.0%)
Teachers: 187.0 (18.2 to 1)
Librarians/Media Specialists: 1.0 (3,407.0 to 1)
Guidance Counselors: 5.0 (681.4 to 1)
Current Spending: ($ per student per year):
   Total: $7,063; Instruction: $4,243; Support Services: $2,580
Enrollment, Drop-out Rates and Diploma Recipients by Race/Ethnicity

Category	Total	White	Black	Asian	AIAN	Hisp.
Enrollment (%)	100.0	94.7	1.1	0.8	1.0	2.3
Drop-out Rate (%)	n/a	n/a	n/a	n/a	n/a	n/a
H.S. Diplomas (#)	132	126	2	4	0	0

Comstock Park Public Schools
101 School St NE • Comstock Park, MI 49321-9114
Mailing Address: PO Box 800 • Comstock Park, MI 49321-0800
(616) 254-5001 • http://www.cppschools.com
Grade Span: PK-12; **Agency Type:** 1
Schools: 6
   3 Primary; 1 Middle; 1 High; 1 Other Level
   5 Regular; 0 Special Education; 0 Vocational; 1 Alternative
   0 Magnet; 0 Charter; 0 Title I Eligible; 0 School-wide Title I
Students: 2,344   (53.0% male; 46.9% female)
   Individual Education Program: 372 (15.9%);
   English Language Learner: 0 (0.0%); Migrant: n/a
   Eligible for Free Lunch Program: 306 (13.1%)
   Eligible for Reduced-Price Lunch Program: 109 (4.7%)
Teachers: 129.0 (18.2 to 1)
Librarians/Media Specialists: 2.0 (1,172.0 to 1)
Guidance Counselors: 5.0 (468.8 to 1)
Current Spending: ($ per student per year):
   Total: $7,302; Instruction: $4,488; Support Services: $2,655
Enrollment, Drop-out Rates and Diploma Recipients by Race/Ethnicity

Category	Total	White	Black	Asian	AIAN	Hisp.
Enrollment (%)	100.0	86.6	6.2	1.4	0.6	5.2
Drop-out Rate (%)	n/a	n/a	n/a	n/a	n/a	n/a
H.S. Diplomas (#)	104	92	1	3	1	7

East Grand Rapids Public Schools
2915 Hall St SE • East Grand Rapids, MI 49506-3111
(616) 235-3535 • http://remc8.k12.mi.us/eastgr/egrps.html
Grade Span: KG-12; **Agency Type:** 1
Schools: 5
   3 Primary; 1 Middle; 1 High; 0 Other Level
   5 Regular; 0 Special Education; 0 Vocational; 0 Alternative
   0 Magnet; 0 Charter; 0 Title I Eligible; 0 School-wide Title I
Students: 2,884 (50.9% male; 49.0% female)
   Individual Education Program: 340 (11.8%);
   English Language Learner: 0 (0.0%); Migrant: n/a
   Eligible for Free Lunch Program: 84 (2.9%)
   Eligible for Reduced-Price Lunch Program: 27 (0.9%)
Teachers: 160.0 (18.0 to 1)
Librarians/Media Specialists: 1.0 (2,884.0 to 1)
Guidance Counselors: 5.0 (576.8 to 1)
Current Spending: ($ per student per year):
   Total: $7,975; Instruction: $4,642; Support Services: $3,079

Enrollment, Drop-out Rates and Diploma Recipients by Race/Ethnicity

Category	Total	White	Black	Asian	AIAN	Hisp.
Enrollment (%)	100.0	94.4	2.6	1.5	0.1	1.4
Drop-out Rate (%)	n/a	n/a	n/a	n/a	n/a	n/a
H.S. Diplomas (#)	218	202	4	8	0	4

Forest Hills Public Schools
6590 Cascade Rd SE • Grand Rapids, MI 49546-6428
(616) 493-8800 • http://www.fhps.k12.mi.us/
Grade Span: PK-12; **Agency Type:** 1
Schools: 17
   8 Primary; 5 Middle; 2 High; 0 Other Level
   15 Regular; 0 Special Education; 0 Vocational; 0 Alternative
   2 Magnet; 0 Charter; 0 Title I Eligible; 0 School-wide Title I
Students: 9,112 (51.6% male; 48.3% female)
   Individual Education Program: 1,123 (12.3%);
   English Language Learner: 179 (2.0%); Migrant: n/a
   Eligible for Free Lunch Program: 274 (3.0%)
   Eligible for Reduced-Price Lunch Program: 158 (1.7%)
Teachers: 533.0 (17.1 to 1)
Librarians/Media Specialists: 4.0 (2,278.0 to 1)
Guidance Counselors: 19.0 (479.6 to 1)
Current Spending: ($ per student per year):
   Total: $8,467; Instruction: $5,172; Support Services: $3,094

Enrollment, Drop-out Rates and Diploma Recipients by Race/Ethnicity

Category	Total	White	Black	Asian	AIAN	Hisp.
Enrollment (%)	100.0	94.2	1.9	2.9	0.2	0.8
Drop-out Rate (%)	n/a	n/a	n/a	n/a	n/a	n/a
H.S. Diplomas (#)	659	618	5	26	1	9

Godfrey-Lee Public Schools
963 Joosten SW • Wyoming, MI 49509-1464
(616) 241-4722
Grade Span: PK-12; **Agency Type:** 1
Schools: 6
   2 Primary; 1 Middle; 1 High; 2 Other Level
   4 Regular; 0 Special Education; 0 Vocational; 2 Alternative
   0 Magnet; 0 Charter; 0 Title I Eligible; 0 School-wide Title I
Students: 1,597 (49.7% male; 50.2% female)
   Individual Education Program: 218 (13.7%);
   English Language Learner: 534 (33.4%); Migrant: n/a
   Eligible for Free Lunch Program: 856 (53.6%)
   Eligible for Reduced-Price Lunch Program: 166 (10.4%)
Teachers: 95.0 (16.8 to 1)
Librarians/Media Specialists: 1.0 (1,597.0 to 1)
Guidance Counselors: 2.0 (798.5 to 1)
Current Spending: ($ per student per year):
   Total: $7,520; Instruction: $5,058; Support Services: $2,204

Enrollment, Drop-out Rates and Diploma Recipients by Race/Ethnicity

Category	Total	White	Black	Asian	AIAN	Hisp.
Enrollment (%)	100.0	35.6	13.8	1.3	0.6	48.8
Drop-out Rate (%)	n/a	n/a	n/a	n/a	n/a	n/a
H.S. Diplomas (#)	46	24	4	3	0	15

Godwin Heights Public Schools
15 36th St SW • Wyoming, MI 49548-2101
(616) 252-2090 • http://fp.remc8.k12.mi.us/godwin/
Grade Span: PK-12; **Agency Type:** 1
Schools: 6
   3 Primary; 1 Middle; 1 High; 1 Other Level
   5 Regular; 0 Special Education; 0 Vocational; 1 Alternative
   0 Magnet; 0 Charter; 0 Title I Eligible; 0 School-wide Title I
Students: 2,300 (53.0% male; 47.0% female)
   Individual Education Program: 337 (14.7%);
   English Language Learner: 284 (12.3%); Migrant: n/a
   Eligible for Free Lunch Program: 1,070 (46.5%)
   Eligible for Reduced-Price Lunch Program: 308 (13.4%)

Teachers: 148.0 (15.5 to 1)
Librarians/Media Specialists: 2.0 (1,150.0 to 1)
Guidance Counselors: 3.0 (766.7 to 1)
Current Spending: ($ per student per year):
   Total: $8,550; Instruction: $5,373; Support Services: $2,846

Enrollment, Drop-out Rates and Diploma Recipients by Race/Ethnicity

Category	Total	White	Black	Asian	AIAN	Hisp.
Enrollment (%)	100.0	57.1	15.3	4.3	1.0	22.3
Drop-out Rate (%)	n/a	n/a	n/a	n/a	n/a	n/a
H.S. Diplomas (#)	114	74	16	6	1	17

Grand Rapids Public Schools
1331 Franklin St SE • Grand Rapids, MI 49501-2634
Mailing Address: PO Box 117 • Grand Rapids, MI 49501-0117
(616) 771-2000 • http://www.grps.k12.mi.us/
Grade Span: PK-12; **Agency Type:** 1
Schools: 88
   42 Primary; 8 Middle; 6 High; 32 Other Level
   54 Regular; 15 Special Education; 0 Vocational; 19 Alternative
   8 Magnet; 0 Charter; 44 Title I Eligible; 44 School-wide Title I
Students: 24,166 (52.0% male; 47.9% female)
   Individual Education Program: 5,920 (24.5%);
   English Language Learner: 4,818 (19.9%); Migrant: 843 (3.5%)
   Eligible for Free Lunch Program: 15,570 (64.4%)
   Eligible for Reduced-Price Lunch Program: 1,897 (7.8%)
Teachers: 1,633.0 (14.8 to 1)
Librarians/Media Specialists: 11.0 (2,196.9 to 1)
Guidance Counselors: 35.0 (690.5 to 1)
Current Spending: ($ per student per year):
   Total: $10,501; Instruction: $5,934; Support Services: $4,251

Enrollment, Drop-out Rates and Diploma Recipients by Race/Ethnicity

Category	Total	White	Black	Asian	AIAN	Hisp.
Enrollment (%)	100.0	27.8	44.0	1.4	1.5	25.4
Drop-out Rate (%)	n/a	n/a	n/a	n/a	n/a	n/a
H.S. Diplomas (#)	708	259	308	21	9	111

Grandville Public Schools
3131 Barrett Ave SW • Grandville, MI 49418-1688
(616) 254-6570 • http://www.grandville.k12.mi.us/home/home.asp
Grade Span: KG-12; **Agency Type:** 1
Schools: 12
   9 Primary; 1 Middle; 2 High; 0 Other Level
   11 Regular; 0 Special Education; 0 Vocational; 1 Alternative
   0 Magnet; 0 Charter; 0 Title I Eligible; 0 School-wide Title I
Students: 6,118 (51.3% male; 48.6% female)
   Individual Education Program: 749 (12.2%);
   English Language Learner: 0 (0.0%); Migrant: n/a
   Eligible for Free Lunch Program: 647 (10.6%)
   Eligible for Reduced-Price Lunch Program: 290 (4.7%)
Teachers: 325.0 (18.8 to 1)
Librarians/Media Specialists: 4.0 (1,529.5 to 1)
Guidance Counselors: 8.0 (764.8 to 1)
Current Spending: ($ per student per year):
   Total: $6,956; Instruction: $4,349; Support Services: $2,443

Enrollment, Drop-out Rates and Diploma Recipients by Race/Ethnicity

Category	Total	White	Black	Asian	AIAN	Hisp.
Enrollment (%)	100.0	89.2	3.3	2.7	0.3	4.4
Drop-out Rate (%)	n/a	n/a	n/a	n/a	n/a	n/a
H.S. Diplomas (#)	371	350	1	10	1	9

Kelloggsville Public Schools
242 52nd St SE • Grand Rapids, MI 49548-5829
(616) 538-7460 • http://www.kelloggsville.k12.mi.us/
Grade Span: PK-12; **Agency Type:** 1
Schools: 7
   4 Primary; 1 Middle; 1 High; 1 Other Level
   6 Regular; 0 Special Education; 0 Vocational; 1 Alternative
   0 Magnet; 0 Charter; 3 Title I Eligible; 3 School-wide Title I
Students: 2,217 (50.8% male; 49.1% female)
   Individual Education Program: 234 (10.6%);
   English Language Learner: 315 (14.2%); Migrant: n/a
   Eligible for Free Lunch Program: 858 (38.7%)
   Eligible for Reduced-Price Lunch Program: 245 (11.1%)
Teachers: 108.0 (20.5 to 1)
Librarians/Media Specialists: 2.0 (1,108.5 to 1)
Guidance Counselors: 4.0 (554.3 to 1)
Current Spending: ($ per student per year):
   Total: $7,455; Instruction: $4,754; Support Services: $2,394

Enrollment, Drop-out Rates and Diploma Recipients by Race/Ethnicity

Category	Total	White	Black	Asian	AIAN	Hisp.
Enrollment (%)	100.0	60.2	14.9	5.8	1.7	17.3
Drop-out Rate (%)	n/a	n/a	n/a	n/a	n/a	n/a
H.S. Diplomas (#)	115	87	8	5	11	4

Kenowa Hills Public Schools
2325 4 Mile Rd NW • Grand Rapids, MI 49544-9703
(616) 784-2511 • http://www.remc8.k12.mi.us/kenowa/
Grade Span: PK-12; **Agency Type:** 1
Schools: 9
   6 Primary; 2 Middle; 1 High; 0 Other Level
   9 Regular; 0 Special Education; 0 Vocational; 0 Alternative
   0 Magnet; 0 Charter; 0 Title I Eligible; 0 School-wide Title I
Students: 3,702   (51.3% male; 48.6% female)
   Individual Education Program: 497 (13.4%);
   English Language Learner: 123 (3.3%); Migrant: 86 (2.3%)
   Eligible for Free Lunch Program: 646 (17.5%)
   Eligible for Reduced-Price Lunch Program: 232 (6.3%)
Teachers: 174.0 (21.3 to 1)
Librarians/Media Specialists: 4.0 (925.5 to 1)
Guidance Counselors: 5.0 (740.4 to 1)
Current Spending: ($ per student per year):
   Total: $7,717; Instruction: $4,608; Support Services: $2,812
Enrollment, Drop-out Rates and Diploma Recipients by Race/Ethnicity

Category	Total	White	Black	Asian	AIAN	Hisp.
Enrollment (%)	100.0	87.8	2.7	1.2	1.1	7.1
Drop-out Rate (%)	n/a	n/a	n/a	n/a	n/a	n/a
H.S. Diplomas (#)	217	209	4	1	2	1

Kentwood Public Schools
5820 Eastern Ave SE • Kentwood, MI 49508-6213
(616) 455-4400 • http://www.kentwoodps.org/
Grade Span: PK-12; **Agency Type:** 1
Schools: 17
   10 Primary; 3 Middle; 2 High; 2 Other Level
   15 Regular; 1 Special Education; 0 Vocational; 1 Alternative
   0 Magnet; 0 Charter; 8 Title I Eligible; 8 School-wide Title I
Students: 9,419   (51.5% male; 48.4% female)
   Individual Education Program: 1,236 (13.1%);
   English Language Learner: 290 (3.1%); Migrant: n/a
   Eligible for Free Lunch Program: 2,473 (26.3%)
   Eligible for Reduced-Price Lunch Program: 700 (7.4%)
Teachers: 501.0 (18.8 to 1)
Librarians/Media Specialists: 4.0 (2,354.8 to 1)
Guidance Counselors: 17.0 (554.1 to 1)
Current Spending: ($ per student per year):
   Total: $7,860; Instruction: $4,973; Support Services: $2,648
Enrollment, Drop-out Rates and Diploma Recipients by Race/Ethnicity

Category	Total	White	Black	Asian	AIAN	Hisp.
Enrollment (%)	100.0	59.8	26.5	6.0	0.9	6.5
Drop-out Rate (%)	n/a	n/a	n/a	n/a	n/a	n/a
H.S. Diplomas (#)	570	406	85	60	3	16

Lowell Area Schools
300 High St • Lowell, MI 49331-1478
(616) 897-8415 • http://www.lowell.k12.mi.us/
Grade Span: KG-12; **Agency Type:** 1
Schools: 7
   3 Primary; 1 Middle; 1 High; 1 Other Level
   5 Regular; 0 Special Education; 0 Vocational; 1 Alternative
   0 Magnet; 0 Charter; 0 Title I Eligible; 0 School-wide Title I
Students: 3,931   (51.4% male; 48.5% female)
   Individual Education Program: 507 (12.9%);
   English Language Learner: 0 (0.0%); Migrant: n/a
   Eligible for Free Lunch Program: 491 (12.5%)
   Eligible for Reduced-Price Lunch Program: 205 (5.2%)
Teachers: 214.0 (18.4 to 1)
Librarians/Media Specialists: 3.0 (1,310.3 to 1)
Guidance Counselors: 5.0 (786.2 to 1)
Current Spending: ($ per student per year):
   Total: $7,184; Instruction: $4,309; Support Services: $2,613
Enrollment, Drop-out Rates and Diploma Recipients by Race/Ethnicity

Category	Total	White	Black	Asian	AIAN	Hisp.
Enrollment (%)	100.0	96.5	0.9	0.8	0.2	1.6
Drop-out Rate (%)	n/a	n/a	n/a	n/a	n/a	n/a
H.S. Diplomas (#)	224	216	0	3	4	1

Northview Public SD
4365 Hunsberger Dr NE • Grand Rapids, MI 49525-6128
(616) 363-6861 • http://www.nvps.net/
Grade Span: PK-12; **Agency Type:** 1
Schools: 7
   3 Primary; 2 Middle; 2 High; 0 Other Level
   6 Regular; 0 Special Education; 0 Vocational; 1 Alternative
   0 Magnet; 0 Charter; 0 Title I Eligible; 0 School-wide Title I
Students: 3,435   (52.9% male; 47.0% female)
   Individual Education Program: 485 (14.1%);
   English Language Learner: 0 (0.0%); Migrant: n/a
   Eligible for Free Lunch Program: 387 (11.3%)
   Eligible for Reduced-Price Lunch Program: 200 (5.8%)

Teachers: 35.0 (98.1 to 1)
Librarians/Media Specialists: 0.0 (n/a to 1)
Guidance Counselors: 0.0 (n/a to 1)
Current Spending: ($ per student per year):
   Total: $7,178; Instruction: $4,515; Support Services: $2,444
Enrollment, Drop-out Rates and Diploma Recipients by Race/Ethnicity

Category	Total	White	Black	Asian	AIAN	Hisp.
Enrollment (%)	100.0	91.8	4.6	1.1	0.4	2.0
Drop-out Rate (%)	n/a	n/a	n/a	n/a	n/a	n/a
H.S. Diplomas (#)	258	242	3	5	0	8

Rockford Public Schools
350 N Main St • Rockford, MI 49341-1020
(616) 866-6557 • http://www.rockfordschools.org/
Grade Span: KG-12; **Agency Type:** 1
Schools: 13
   8 Primary; 2 Middle; 1 High; 2 Other Level
   12 Regular; 0 Special Education; 0 Vocational; 1 Alternative
   0 Magnet; 0 Charter; 0 Title I Eligible; 0 School-wide Title I
Students: 7,750   (52.6% male; 47.3% female)
   Individual Education Program: 791 (10.2%);
   English Language Learner: 0 (0.0%); Migrant: n/a
   Eligible for Free Lunch Program: 357 (4.6%)
   Eligible for Reduced-Price Lunch Program: 142 (1.8%)
Teachers: 389.0 (19.9 to 1)
Librarians/Media Specialists: 3.0 (2,583.3 to 1)
Guidance Counselors: 10.0 (775.0 to 1)
Current Spending: ($ per student per year):
   Total: $7,255; Instruction: $4,391; Support Services: $2,648
Enrollment, Drop-out Rates and Diploma Recipients by Race/Ethnicity

Category	Total	White	Black	Asian	AIAN	Hisp.
Enrollment (%)	100.0	96.6	1.0	0.9	0.2	1.3
Drop-out Rate (%)	n/a	n/a	n/a	n/a	n/a	n/a
H.S. Diplomas (#)	559	537	3	9	1	9

Sparta Area Schools
465 S Union St • Sparta, MI 49345-1503
(616) 887-8253 • http://www.spartaschools.org/
Grade Span: PK-12; **Agency Type:** 1
Schools: 6
   3 Primary; 1 Middle; 2 High; 0 Other Level
   5 Regular; 0 Special Education; 0 Vocational; 1 Alternative
   0 Magnet; 0 Charter; 0 Title I Eligible; 0 School-wide Title I
Students: 3,084   (51.0% male; 48.9% female)
   Individual Education Program: 479 (15.5%);
   English Language Learner: 245 (7.9%); Migrant: 150 (5.2%)
   Eligible for Free Lunch Program: 575 (20.0%)
   Eligible for Reduced-Price Lunch Program: 204 (7.1%)
Teachers: 155.0 (18.5 to 1)
Librarians/Media Specialists: 1.0 (2,871.0 to 1)
Guidance Counselors: 5.0 (574.2 to 1)
Current Spending: ($ per student per year):
   Total: $7,552; Instruction: $4,908; Support Services: $2,430
Enrollment, Drop-out Rates and Diploma Recipients by Race/Ethnicity

Category	Total	White	Black	Asian	AIAN	Hisp.
Enrollment (%)	100.0	89.6	1.0	1.0	0.0	8.2
Drop-out Rate (%)	n/a	n/a	n/a	n/a	n/a	n/a
H.S. Diplomas (#)	190	181	1	5	0	3

Wyoming Public Schools
3575 Gladiola St SW • Wyoming, MI 49509-3264
(616) 530-7555 • http://www.remc8.k12.mi.us/wyoming/
Grade Span: PK-12; **Agency Type:** 1
Schools: 13
   8 Primary; 2 Middle; 2 High; 1 Other Level
   12 Regular; 1 Special Education; 0 Vocational; 0 Alternative
   0 Magnet; 0 Charter; 6 Title I Eligible; 6 School-wide Title I
Students: 5,914   (51.2% male; 48.7% female)
   Individual Education Program: 856 (14.5%);
   English Language Learner: 391 (6.6%); Migrant: n/a
   Eligible for Free Lunch Program: 1,633 (30.2%)
   Eligible for Reduced-Price Lunch Program: 690 (12.8%)
Teachers: 262.0 (20.6 to 1)
Librarians/Media Specialists: 4.0 (1,351.0 to 1)
Guidance Counselors: 8.0 (675.5 to 1)
Current Spending: ($ per student per year):
   Total: $7,681; Instruction: $4,675; Support Services: $2,746
Enrollment, Drop-out Rates and Diploma Recipients by Race/Ethnicity

Category	Total	White	Black	Asian	AIAN	Hisp.
Enrollment (%)	100.0	66.0	10.9	5.5	0.8	16.8
Drop-out Rate (%)	n/a	n/a	n/a	n/a	n/a	n/a
H.S. Diplomas (#)	347	292	11	16	1	27

Almont Community Schools
401 Church St • Almont, MI 48003-1030
(810) 798-8561 • http://www.almont.k12.mi.us/
Grade Span: KG-12; **Agency Type:** 1
Schools: 3
   2 Primary; 0 Middle; 1 High; 0 Other Level
   3 Regular; 0 Special Education; 0 Vocational; 0 Alternative
   0 Magnet; 0 Charter; 0 Title I Eligible; 0 School-wide Title I
Students: 1,799   (52.5% male; 47.4% female)
   Individual Education Program: 147 (8.2%);
   English Language Learner: 0 (0.0%); Migrant: 46 (2.6%)
   Eligible for Free Lunch Program: 155 (8.6%)
   Eligible for Reduced-Price Lunch Program: 44 (2.4%)
Teachers: 89.0 (20.2 to 1)
Librarians/Media Specialists: 0.0 (n/a to 1)
Guidance Counselors: 3.0 (599.7 to 1)
Current Spending: ($ per student per year):
   Total: $6,430; Instruction: $3,868; Support Services: $2,374
Enrollment, Drop-out Rates and Diploma Recipients by Race/Ethnicity

Category	Total	White	Black	Asian	AIAN	Hisp.
Enrollment (%)	100.0	94.4	0.5	0.5	0.6	4.0
Drop-out Rate (%)	n/a	n/a	n/a	n/a	n/a	n/a
H.S. Diplomas (#)	88	86	0	1	1	0

Imlay City Community Schools
634 W Borland Rd • Imlay City, MI 48444-1416
Mailing Address: PO Box 128 • Imlay City, MI 48444-0128
(810) 724-9861 • http://imlay.imlay.k12.mi.us/
Grade Span: PK-12; **Agency Type:** 1
Schools: 5
   2 Primary; 1 Middle; 1 High; 1 Other Level
   4 Regular; 0 Special Education; 0 Vocational; 1 Alternative
   5 Magnet; 0 Charter; 0 Title I Eligible; 0 School-wide Title I
Students: 2,336   (50.3% male; 49.6% female)
   Individual Education Program: 234 (10.0%);
   English Language Learner: 170 (7.3%); Migrant: 287 (12.3%)
   Eligible for Free Lunch Program: 579 (24.8%)
   Eligible for Reduced-Price Lunch Program: 233 (10.0%)
Teachers: 117.0 (20.0 to 1)
Librarians/Media Specialists: 1.0 (2,336.0 to 1)
Guidance Counselors: 3.0 (778.7 to 1)
Current Spending: ($ per student per year):
   Total: $6,708; Instruction: $4,011; Support Services: $2,474
Enrollment, Drop-out Rates and Diploma Recipients by Race/Ethnicity

Category	Total	White	Black	Asian	AIAN	Hisp.
Enrollment (%)	100.0	81.2	0.7	1.3	0.1	16.5
Drop-out Rate (%)	n/a	n/a	n/a	n/a	n/a	n/a
H.S. Diplomas (#)	140	130	0	1	0	9

Lapeer Community Schools
1025 W Nepessing St • Lapeer, MI 48446-1873
(810) 667-2401 • http://www.lapeerschools.net/
Grade Span: PK-12; **Agency Type:** 1
Schools: 16
   11 Primary; 2 Middle; 2 High; 1 Other Level
   15 Regular; 0 Special Education; 0 Vocational; 1 Alternative
   0 Magnet; 0 Charter; 0 Title I Eligible; 0 School-wide Title I
Students: 7,472   (52.0% male; 47.9% female)
   Individual Education Program: 961 (12.9%);
   English Language Learner: 10 (0.1%); Migrant: n/a
   Eligible for Free Lunch Program: 1,212 (16.2%)
   Eligible for Reduced-Price Lunch Program: 579 (7.7%)
Teachers: 378.0 (19.8 to 1)
Librarians/Media Specialists: 3.0 (2,490.7 to 1)
Guidance Counselors: 10.0 (747.2 to 1)
Current Spending: ($ per student per year):
   Total: $6,740; Instruction: $4,283; Support Services: $2,207
Enrollment, Drop-out Rates and Diploma Recipients by Race/Ethnicity

Category	Total	White	Black	Asian	AIAN	Hisp.
Enrollment (%)	100.0	95.8	0.6	0.7	0.6	2.2
Drop-out Rate (%)	n/a	n/a	n/a	n/a	n/a	n/a
H.S. Diplomas (#)	475	452	1	7	2	13

North Branch Area Schools
6600 Brush St • North Branch, MI 48461-6114
Mailing Address: PO Box 3620 • North Branch, MI 48461-0620
(810) 688-3570
Grade Span: KG-12; **Agency Type:** 1
Schools: 5
   2 Primary; 2 Middle; 1 High; 0 Other Level
   5 Regular; 0 Special Education; 0 Vocational; 0 Alternative
   0 Magnet; 0 Charter; 0 Title I Eligible; 0 School-wide Title I
Students: 2,678   (52.1% male; 47.8% female)

Individual Education Program: 315 (11.8%);
   English Language Learner: 0 (0.0%); Migrant: n/a
   Eligible for Free Lunch Program: 505 (18.9%)
   Eligible for Reduced-Price Lunch Program: 272 (10.2%)
Teachers: 61.0 (43.9 to 1)
Librarians/Media Specialists: 1.0 (2,678.0 to 1)
Guidance Counselors: 0.0 (n/a to 1)
Current Spending: ($ per student per year):
   Total: $6,814; Instruction: $4,281; Support Services: $2,273
Enrollment, Drop-out Rates and Diploma Recipients by Race/Ethnicity

Category	Total	White	Black	Asian	AIAN	Hisp.
Enrollment (%)	100.0	98.0	0.2	0.2	0.3	1.3
Drop-out Rate (%)	n/a	n/a	n/a	n/a	n/a	n/a
H.S. Diplomas (#)	169	164	1	1	0	3

Adrian City SD
227 N Winter St • Adrian, MI 49221-2066
(517) 264-6641 • http://www.adrian.k12.mi.us/
Grade Span: PK-12; **Agency Type:** 1
Schools: 9
   6 Primary; 2 Middle; 1 High; 0 Other Level
   9 Regular; 0 Special Education; 0 Vocational; 0 Alternative
   0 Magnet; 0 Charter; 4 Title I Eligible; 4 School-wide Title I
Students: 3,997   (51.1% male; 48.8% female)
   Individual Education Program: 731 (18.3%);
   English Language Learner: 598 (15.0%); Migrant: n/a
   Eligible for Free Lunch Program: 1,466 (37.1%)
   Eligible for Reduced-Price Lunch Program: 302 (7.6%)
Teachers: 227.0 (17.4 to 1)
Librarians/Media Specialists: 1.0 (3,952.0 to 1)
Guidance Counselors: 5.0 (790.4 to 1)
Current Spending: ($ per student per year):
   Total: $8,588; Instruction: $5,057; Support Services: $3,189
Enrollment, Drop-out Rates and Diploma Recipients by Race/Ethnicity

Category	Total	White	Black	Asian	AIAN	Hisp.
Enrollment (%)	100.0	67.7	6.6	0.9	0.4	23.8
Drop-out Rate (%)	n/a	n/a	n/a	n/a	n/a	n/a
H.S. Diplomas (#)	246	199	8	4	1	34

Onsted Community Schools
10109 Slee Rd • Onsted, MI 49265-9701
Mailing Address: PO Box 220 • Onsted, MI 49265-0220
(517) 467-2174 • http://www.onsted.k12.mi.us/
Grade Span: KG-12; **Agency Type:** 1
Schools: 5
   2 Primary; 1 Middle; 2 High; 0 Other Level
   4 Regular; 0 Special Education; 0 Vocational; 1 Alternative
   0 Magnet; 0 Charter; 5 Title I Eligible; 5 School-wide Title I
Students: 1,862   (52.5% male; 47.4% female)
   Individual Education Program: 209 (11.2%);
   English Language Learner: 1 (0.1%); Migrant: n/a
   Eligible for Free Lunch Program: 172 (9.2%)
   Eligible for Reduced-Price Lunch Program: 79 (4.2%)
Teachers: 102.0 (18.3 to 1)
Librarians/Media Specialists: 3.0 (620.7 to 1)
Guidance Counselors: 4.0 (465.5 to 1)
Current Spending: ($ per student per year):
   Total: $6,826; Instruction: $4,187; Support Services: $2,349
Enrollment, Drop-out Rates and Diploma Recipients by Race/Ethnicity

Category	Total	White	Black	Asian	AIAN	Hisp.
Enrollment (%)	100.0	95.2	0.3	0.4	0.8	1.3
Drop-out Rate (%)	n/a	n/a	n/a	n/a	n/a	n/a
H.S. Diplomas (#)	120	114	1	0	1	4

Tecumseh Public Schools
212 N Ottawa St • Tecumseh, MI 49286-1306
(517) 424-7318 • http://www.tps.k12.mi.us/
Grade Span: KG-12; **Agency Type:** 1
Schools: 7
   4 Primary; 1 Middle; 2 High; 0 Other Level
   6 Regular; 0 Special Education; 0 Vocational; 1 Alternative
   0 Magnet; 0 Charter; 0 Title I Eligible; 0 School-wide Title I
Students: 3,460   (50.9% male; 49.0% female)
   Individual Education Program: 480 (13.9%);
   English Language Learner: 0 (0.0%); Migrant: n/a
   Eligible for Free Lunch Program: 294 (8.5%)
   Eligible for Reduced-Price Lunch Program: 157 (4.5%)
Teachers: 185.0 (18.7 to 1)
Librarians/Media Specialists: 1.0 (3,460.0 to 1)
Guidance Counselors: 5.0 (692.0 to 1)
Current Spending: ($ per student per year):
   Total: $6,838; Instruction: $4,321; Support Services: $2,285

Enrollment, Drop-out Rates and Diploma Recipients by Race/Ethnicity

Category	Total	White	Black	Asian	AIAN	Hisp.
Enrollment (%)	100.0	95.7	0.6	0.4	0.4	2.5
Drop-out Rate (%)	n/a	n/a	n/a	n/a	n/a	n/a
H.S. Diplomas (#)	214	197	1	3	4	9

Livingston County

Brighton Area Schools
125 S Church St • Brighton, MI 48116-1652
(810) 299-4000 • http://bas.k12.mi.us/
Grade Span: KG-12; **Agency Type:** 1
Schools: 9
  6 Primary; 2 Middle; 0 High; 1 Other Level
  9 Regular; 0 Special Education; 0 Vocational; 0 Alternative
  0 Magnet; 0 Charter; 0 Title I Eligible; 0 School-wide Title I
Students: 7,300 (52.0% male; 47.9% female)
  Individual Education Program: 1,008 (13.8%)
  English Language Learner: 0 (0.0%); Migrant: n/a
  Eligible for Free Lunch Program: 246 (3.4%)
  Eligible for Reduced-Price Lunch Program: 107 (1.5%)
Teachers: 371.0 (19.7 to 1)
Librarians/Media Specialists: 6.0 (1,216.7 to 1)
Guidance Counselors: 9.0 (811.1 to 1)
Current Spending: ($ per student per year):
  Total: $7,071; Instruction: $4,463; Support Services: $2,373

Enrollment, Drop-out Rates and Diploma Recipients by Race/Ethnicity

Category	Total	White	Black	Asian	AIAN	Hisp.
Enrollment (%)	100.0	95.1	0.6	1.3	1.5	1.4
Drop-out Rate (%)	n/a	n/a	n/a	n/a	n/a	n/a
H.S. Diplomas (#)	485	459	0	10	14	2

Fowlerville Community Schools
735 N Grand • Fowlerville, MI 48836-0769
Mailing Address: PO Box 769 • Fowlerville, MI 48836-0769
(517) 223-6015 • http://scnc.fvl.k12.mi.us/
Grade Span: KG-12; **Agency Type:** 1
Schools: 5
  2 Primary; 2 Middle; 1 High; 0 Other Level
  5 Regular; 0 Special Education; 0 Vocational; 0 Alternative
  0 Magnet; 0 Charter; 0 Title I Eligible; 0 School-wide Title I
Students: 3,191 (52.7% male; 47.2% female)
  Individual Education Program: 443 (13.9%)
  English Language Learner: 0 (0.0%); Migrant: n/a
  Eligible for Free Lunch Program: 385 (12.4%)
  Eligible for Reduced-Price Lunch Program: 181 (5.8%)
Teachers: 159.0 (19.6 to 1)
Librarians/Media Specialists: 5.0 (623.4 to 1)
Guidance Counselors: 6.0 (519.5 to 1)
Current Spending: ($ per student per year):
  Total: $7,033; Instruction: $4,322; Support Services: $2,411

Enrollment, Drop-out Rates and Diploma Recipients by Race/Ethnicity

Category	Total	White	Black	Asian	AIAN	Hisp.
Enrollment (%)	100.0	96.9	0.2	0.5	1.3	1.2
Drop-out Rate (%)	n/a	n/a	n/a	n/a	n/a	n/a
H.S. Diplomas (#)	206	197	0	3	2	4

Hartland Consolidated Schools
3642 Washington St • Hartland, MI 48353-0900
Mailing Address: PO Box 900 • Hartland, MI 48353-0900
(810) 632-7481 • http://hartland.k12.mi.us/
Grade Span: PK-12; **Agency Type:** 1
Schools: 8
  4 Primary; 2 Middle; 1 High; 1 Other Level
  7 Regular; 0 Special Education; 0 Vocational; 1 Alternative
  0 Magnet; 0 Charter; 0 Title I Eligible; 0 School-wide Title I
Students: 5,285 (52.0% male; 47.9% female)
  Individual Education Program: 626 (11.8%)
  English Language Learner: 0 (0.0%); Migrant: n/a
  Eligible for Free Lunch Program: 159 (3.0%)
  Eligible for Reduced-Price Lunch Program: 103 (1.9%)
Teachers: 263.0 (20.1 to 1)
Librarians/Media Specialists: 7.0 (755.0 to 1)
Guidance Counselors: 5.0 (1,057.0 to 1)
Current Spending: ($ per student per year):
  Total: $6,869; Instruction: $4,224; Support Services: $2,464

Enrollment, Drop-out Rates and Diploma Recipients by Race/Ethnicity

Category	Total	White	Black	Asian	AIAN	Hisp.
Enrollment (%)	100.0	91.6	0.5	0.7	6.5	0.7
Drop-out Rate (%)	n/a	n/a	n/a	n/a	n/a	n/a
H.S. Diplomas (#)	285	276	1	2	3	3

Howell Public Schools
411 N Highlander Way • Howell, MI 48843-1021
(517) 548-6234 • http://hps.k12.mi.us/
Grade Span: KG-12; **Agency Type:** 1
Schools: 10
  7 Primary; 2 Middle; 1 High; 0 Other Level
  10 Regular; 0 Special Education; 0 Vocational; 0 Alternative
  0 Magnet; 0 Charter; 0 Title I Eligible; 0 School-wide Title I
Students: 8,345 (51.9% male; 48.0% female)
  Individual Education Program: 1,258 (15.1%)
  English Language Learner: 0 (0.0%); Migrant: n/a
  Eligible for Free Lunch Program: 614 (7.4%)
  Eligible for Reduced-Price Lunch Program: 300 (3.6%)
Teachers: 435.0 (19.0 to 1)
Librarians/Media Specialists: 2.0 (4,128.0 to 1)
Guidance Counselors: 7.0 (1,179.4 to 1)
Current Spending: ($ per student per year):
  Total: $7,017; Instruction: $4,403; Support Services: $2,392

Enrollment, Drop-out Rates and Diploma Recipients by Race/Ethnicity

Category	Total	White	Black	Asian	AIAN	Hisp.
Enrollment (%)	100.0	96.1	0.4	1.1	0.9	1.5
Drop-out Rate (%)	n/a	n/a	n/a	n/a	n/a	n/a
H.S. Diplomas (#)	437	426	0	4	5	2

Macomb County

Anchor Bay SD
52801 Ashley St • New Baltimore, MI 48047-3277
(586) 725-2861 • http://www.anchorbay.misd.net
Grade Span: PK-12; **Agency Type:** 1
Schools: 13
  9 Primary; 2 Middle; 1 High; 1 Other Level
  12 Regular; 0 Special Education; 0 Vocational; 1 Alternative
  0 Magnet; 0 Charter; 0 Title I Eligible; 0 School-wide Title I
Students: 6,615 (51.5% male; 48.4% female)
  Individual Education Program: 835 (12.6%)
  English Language Learner: 0 (0.0%); Migrant: n/a
  Eligible for Free Lunch Program: 680 (10.3%)
  Eligible for Reduced-Price Lunch Program: 336 (5.1%)
Teachers: 349.0 (19.0 to 1)
Librarians/Media Specialists: 3.0 (2,205.0 to 1)
Guidance Counselors: 5.0 (1,323.0 to 1)
Current Spending: ($ per student per year):
  Total: $6,894; Instruction: $4,180; Support Services: $2,499

Enrollment, Drop-out Rates and Diploma Recipients by Race/Ethnicity

Category	Total	White	Black	Asian	AIAN	Hisp.
Enrollment (%)	100.0	92.2	3.8	0.7	0.4	2.8
Drop-out Rate (%)	n/a	n/a	n/a	n/a	n/a	n/a
H.S. Diplomas (#)	276	267	5	2	1	1

Armada Area Schools
74500 Burk St • Armada, MI 48005-3314
(586) 784-4511 •
http://www.macomb.k12.mi.us/armada/armada/armada.htm
Grade Span: PK-12; **Agency Type:** 1
Schools: 5
  2 Primary; 1 Middle; 2 High; 0 Other Level
  5 Regular; 0 Special Education; 0 Vocational; 0 Alternative
  0 Magnet; 0 Charter; 0 Title I Eligible; 0 School-wide Title I
Students: 2,249 (52.6% male; 47.3% female)
  Individual Education Program: 261 (11.6%)
  English Language Learner: 0 (0.0%); Migrant: n/a
  Eligible for Free Lunch Program: 100 (4.4%)
  Eligible for Reduced-Price Lunch Program: 38 (1.7%)
Teachers: 106.0 (21.2 to 1)
Librarians/Media Specialists: 3.0 (749.7 to 1)
Guidance Counselors: 3.0 (749.7 to 1)
Current Spending: ($ per student per year):
  Total: $7,078; Instruction: $4,307; Support Services: $2,601

Enrollment, Drop-out Rates and Diploma Recipients by Race/Ethnicity

Category	Total	White	Black	Asian	AIAN	Hisp.
Enrollment (%)	100.0	97.8	0.3	0.4	0.3	1.2
Drop-out Rate (%)	n/a	n/a	n/a	n/a	n/a	n/a
H.S. Diplomas (#)	131	130	0	0	0	1

Center Line Public Schools
26400 Arsenal St • Center Line, MI 48015-1600
(586) 510-2000 • http://www.clps.org/
Grade Span: PK-12; **Agency Type:** 1
Schools: 7
  5 Primary; 1 Middle; 1 High; 0 Other Level
  7 Regular; 0 Special Education; 0 Vocational; 0 Alternative
  0 Magnet; 0 Charter; 4 Title I Eligible; 4 School-wide Title I
Students: 2,987 (51.7% male; 48.2% female)
  Individual Education Program: 479 (16.0%)

English Language Learner: 0 (0.0%); Migrant: n/a
Eligible for Free Lunch Program: 762 (25.5%)
Eligible for Reduced-Price Lunch Program: 262 (8.8%)
Teachers: 177.0 (16.9 to 1)
Librarians/Media Specialists: 2.0 (1,493.5 to 1)
Guidance Counselors: 7.0 (426.7 to 1)
Current Spending: ($ per student per year):
    Total: $9,587; Instruction: $5,551; Support Services: $3,813
Enrollment, Drop-out Rates and Diploma Recipients by Race/Ethnicity

Category	Total	White	Black	Asian	AIAN	Hisp.
Enrollment (%)	100.0	87.3	4.2	5.3	1.5	1.8
Drop-out Rate (%)	n/a	n/a	n/a	n/a	n/a	n/a
H.S. Diplomas (#)	154	139	3	7	3	2

Chippewa Valley Schools
19120 Cass Ave • Clinton Township, MI 48038-2301
(586) 723-2000 • http://www.chippewavalleyschools.org/
Grade Span: KG-12; **Agency Type:** 1
Schools: 17
    11 Primary; 4 Middle; 2 High; 0 Other Level
    17 Regular; 0 Special Education; 0 Vocational; 0 Alternative
    17 Magnet; 0 Charter; 0 Title I Eligible; 0 School-wide Title I
Students: 13,906   (51.2% male; 48.7% female)
    Individual Education Program: 1,340 (9.6%);
    English Language Learner: 325 (2.3%); Migrant: n/a
    Eligible for Free Lunch Program: 1,447 (10.4%)
    Eligible for Reduced-Price Lunch Program: 373 (2.7%)
Teachers: 667.0 (20.8 to 1)
Librarians/Media Specialists: 8.0 (1,738.3 to 1)
Guidance Counselors: 25.0 (556.2 to 1)
Current Spending: ($ per student per year):
    Total: $7,320; Instruction: $4,526; Support Services: $2,624
Enrollment, Drop-out Rates and Diploma Recipients by Race/Ethnicity

Category	Total	White	Black	Asian	AIAN	Hisp.
Enrollment (%)	100.0	93.1	2.7	2.5	0.2	1.4
Drop-out Rate (%)	n/a	n/a	n/a	n/a	n/a	n/a
H.S. Diplomas (#)	762	742	2	9	2	7

Clintondale Community Schools
35100 Little Mack Ave • Clinton Township, MI 48035-2633
(586) 791-6300 • http://www.clintondale.k12.mi.us/
Grade Span: PK-12; **Agency Type:** 1
Schools: 5
    3 Primary; 1 Middle; 1 High; 0 Other Level
    5 Regular; 0 Special Education; 0 Vocational; 0 Alternative
    0 Magnet; 0 Charter; 0 Title I Eligible; 0 School-wide Title I
Students: 4,002   (53.5% male; 46.4% female)
    Individual Education Program: 528 (13.2%);
    English Language Learner: 0 (0.0%); Migrant: n/a
    Eligible for Free Lunch Program: 883 (32.0%)
    Eligible for Reduced-Price Lunch Program: 192 (7.0%)
Teachers: 156.0 (17.7 to 1)
Librarians/Media Specialists: 1.0 (2,758.0 to 1)
Guidance Counselors: 3.0 (919.3 to 1)
Current Spending: ($ per student per year):
    Total: $8,561; Instruction: $5,291; Support Services: $2,994
Enrollment, Drop-out Rates and Diploma Recipients by Race/Ethnicity

Category	Total	White	Black	Asian	AIAN	Hisp.
Enrollment (%)	100.0	61.5	33.1	3.7	0.1	1.6
Drop-out Rate (%)	n/a	n/a	n/a	n/a	n/a	n/a
H.S. Diplomas (#)	119	84	33	2	0	0

East Detroit Public Schools
15115 Deerfield Ave • Eastpointe, MI 48021-1515
(586) 445-4410 • http://www.macomb.k12.mi.us/eastdet/scheast.htm
Grade Span: PK-12; **Agency Type:** 1
Schools: 12
    8 Primary; 2 Middle; 1 High; 1 Other Level
    11 Regular; 0 Special Education; 0 Vocational; 1 Alternative
    0 Magnet; 0 Charter; 2 Title I Eligible; 2 School-wide Title I
Students: 6,137   (50.5% male; 49.4% female)
    Individual Education Program: 889 (14.5%);
    English Language Learner: 99 (1.6%); Migrant: n/a
    Eligible for Free Lunch Program: 1,812 (30.2%)
    Eligible for Reduced-Price Lunch Program: 763 (12.7%)
Teachers: 340.0 (17.7 to 1)
Librarians/Media Specialists: 10.0 (600.7 to 1)
Guidance Counselors: 10.0 (600.7 to 1)
Current Spending: ($ per student per year):
    Total: $7,780; Instruction: $4,709; Support Services: $2,833
Enrollment, Drop-out Rates and Diploma Recipients by Race/Ethnicity

Category	Total	White	Black	Asian	AIAN	Hisp.
Enrollment (%)	100.0	79.7	14.2	2.4	2.3	1.3
Drop-out Rate (%)	n/a	n/a	n/a	n/a	n/a	n/a
H.S. Diplomas (#)	342	303	21	8	10	0

Fitzgerald Public Schools
23200 Ryan Rd • Warren, MI 48091-4551
(586) 757-1750 • http://www.fitz.k12.mi.us/
Grade Span: PK-12; **Agency Type:** 1
Schools: 7
    4 Primary; 1 Middle; 2 High; 0 Other Level
    6 Regular; 0 Special Education; 0 Vocational; 1 Alternative
    0 Magnet; 0 Charter; 0 Title I Eligible; 0 School-wide Title I
Students: 3,282   (53.7% male; 46.2% female)
    Individual Education Program: 485 (14.8%);
    English Language Learner: 162 (4.9%); Migrant: n/a
    Eligible for Free Lunch Program: 1,183 (36.0%)
    Eligible for Reduced-Price Lunch Program: 370 (11.3%)
Teachers: 163.0 (20.1 to 1)
Librarians/Media Specialists: 4.0 (820.5 to 1)
Guidance Counselors: 4.0 (820.5 to 1)
Current Spending: ($ per student per year):
    Total: $8,807; Instruction: $4,743; Support Services: $3,838
Enrollment, Drop-out Rates and Diploma Recipients by Race/Ethnicity

Category	Total	White	Black	Asian	AIAN	Hisp.
Enrollment (%)	100.0	75.9	13.1	8.6	0.8	1.6
Drop-out Rate (%)	n/a	n/a	n/a	n/a	n/a	n/a
H.S. Diplomas (#)	169	133	6	24	4	2

Fraser Public Schools
33466 Garfield Rd • Fraser, MI 48026-1850
(586) 293-5100 • http://www.macomb.k12.mi.us/fraser/schfras.htm
Grade Span: PK-12; **Agency Type:** 1
Schools: 10
    8 Primary; 1 Middle; 1 High; 0 Other Level
    10 Regular; 0 Special Education; 0 Vocational; 0 Alternative
    0 Magnet; 0 Charter; 0 Title I Eligible; 0 School-wide Title I
Students: 4,940   (51.5% male; 48.4% female)
    Individual Education Program: 533 (10.8%);
    English Language Learner: 0 (0.0%); Migrant: n/a
    Eligible for Free Lunch Program: 566 (11.5%)
    Eligible for Reduced-Price Lunch Program: 207 (4.2%)
Teachers: 286.0 (17.3 to 1)
Librarians/Media Specialists: 2.0 (2,470.0 to 1)
Guidance Counselors: 6.0 (823.3 to 1)
Current Spending: ($ per student per year):
    Total: $8,608; Instruction: $5,212; Support Services: $3,161
Enrollment, Drop-out Rates and Diploma Recipients by Race/Ethnicity

Category	Total	White	Black	Asian	AIAN	Hisp.
Enrollment (%)	100.0	92.6	4.2	1.5	1.1	0.6
Drop-out Rate (%)	n/a	n/a	n/a	n/a	n/a	n/a
H.S. Diplomas (#)	300	283	1	9	4	3

L'anse Creuse Public Schools
36727 Jefferson Ave • Harrison Township, MI 48045-2917
(586) 783-6300 • http://www.lc-ps.org/
Grade Span: PK-12; **Agency Type:** 1
Schools: 20
    11 Primary; 4 Middle; 2 High; 3 Other Level
    18 Regular; 1 Special Education; 1 Vocational; 0 Alternative
    15 Magnet; 0 Charter; 1 Title I Eligible; 1 School-wide Title I
Students: 12,220   (50.5% male; 49.4% female)
    Individual Education Program: 1,325 (10.8%);
    English Language Learner: 264 (2.2%); Migrant: n/a
    Eligible for Free Lunch Program: 1,458 (12.3%)
    Eligible for Reduced-Price Lunch Program: 520 (4.4%)
Teachers: 609.0 (19.5 to 1)
Librarians/Media Specialists: 9.0 (1,316.2 to 1)
Guidance Counselors: 17.0 (696.8 to 1)
Current Spending: ($ per student per year):
    Total: $7,270; Instruction: $4,319; Support Services: $2,751
Enrollment, Drop-out Rates and Diploma Recipients by Race/Ethnicity

Category	Total	White	Black	Asian	AIAN	Hisp.
Enrollment (%)	100.0	90.4	5.9	1.2	0.3	2.2
Drop-out Rate (%)	n/a	n/a	n/a	n/a	n/a	n/a
H.S. Diplomas (#)	615	576	21	10	3	5

Lake Shore Public Schools (Macomb)
28850 Harper Ave • St. Clair Shores, MI 48081-1249
(586) 285-8480 • http://www.lakeshoreschools.org/
Grade Span: KG-12; **Agency Type:** 1
Schools: 6
    3 Primary; 1 Middle; 1 High; 1 Other Level
    5 Regular; 0 Special Education; 0 Vocational; 1 Alternative
    0 Magnet; 0 Charter; 0 Title I Eligible; 0 School-wide Title I
Students: 3,378   (52.1% male; 47.8% female)
    Individual Education Program: 385 (11.4%);
    English Language Learner: 0 (0.0%); Migrant: n/a
    Eligible for Free Lunch Program: 373 (11.0%)
    Eligible for Reduced-Price Lunch Program: 195 (5.8%)

Teachers: 181.0 (18.7 to 1)
Librarians/Media Specialists: 5.0 (675.6 to 1)
Guidance Counselors: 5.0 (675.6 to 1)
Current Spending: ($ per student per year):
   Total: $8,047; Instruction: $4,235; Support Services: $3,576
Enrollment, Drop-out Rates and Diploma Recipients by Race/Ethnicity

Category	Total	White	Black	Asian	AIAN	Hisp.
Enrollment (%)	100.0	91.0	3.0	1.0	3.8	1.2
Drop-out Rate (%)	n/a	n/a	n/a	n/a	n/a	n/a
H.S. Diplomas (#)	194	175	5	2	9	3

Lakeview Public Schools (Macomb)
20300 Statler St · St. Clair Shores, MI 48081-2181
(586) 445-4015 · http://www.lakeview.misd.net/
Grade Span: PK-12; **Agency Type:** 1
Schools: 6
   4 Primary; 1 Middle; 1 High; 0 Other Level
   6 Regular; 0 Special Education; 0 Vocational; 0 Alternative
   0 Magnet; 0 Charter; 0 Title I Eligible; 0 School-wide Title I
Students: 2,876 (50.5% male; 49.4% female)
   Individual Education Program: 378 (13.1%);
   English Language Learner: 0 (0.0%); Migrant: n/a
   Eligible for Free Lunch Program: 216 (7.5%)
   Eligible for Reduced-Price Lunch Program: 110 (3.8%)
Teachers: 160.0 (18.0 to 1)
Librarians/Media Specialists: 2.0 (1,438.0 to 1)
Guidance Counselors: 5.0 (575.2 to 1)
Current Spending: ($ per student per year):
   Total: $6,705; Instruction: $3,791; Support Services: $2,779
Enrollment, Drop-out Rates and Diploma Recipients by Race/Ethnicity

Category	Total	White	Black	Asian	AIAN	Hisp.
Enrollment (%)	100.0	95.3	1.6	0.5	2.0	0.6
Drop-out Rate (%)	n/a	n/a	n/a	n/a	n/a	n/a
H.S. Diplomas (#)	218	210	0	2	5	1

Macomb ISD
44001 Garfield Rd · Clinton Township, MI 48038-1100
(586) 228-3300
Grade Span: 06-09; **Agency Type:** 4
Schools: 10
   0 Primary; 1 Middle; 0 High; 9 Other Level
   0 Regular; 10 Special Education; 0 Vocational; 0 Alternative
   0 Magnet; 0 Charter; 0 Title I Eligible; 0 School-wide Title I
Students: 1,523 (71.4% male; 28.5% female)
   Individual Education Program: n/a
   English Language Learner: 846 (55.5%); Migrant: n/a
   Eligible for Free Lunch Program: n/a
   Eligible for Reduced-Price Lunch Program: n/a
Teachers: 206.0 (7.4 to 1)
Librarians/Media Specialists: 0.0 (n/a to 1)
Guidance Counselors: 0.0 (n/a to 1)
Current Spending: ($ per student per year):
   Total: n/a; Instruction: n/a; Support Services: n/a
Enrollment, Drop-out Rates and Diploma Recipients by Race/Ethnicity

Category	Total	White	Black	Asian	AIAN	Hisp.
Enrollment (%)	100.0	90.4	5.2	1.6	1.1	0.9
Drop-out Rate (%)	n/a	n/a	n/a	n/a	n/a	n/a
H.S. Diplomas (#)	n/a	n/a	n/a	n/a	n/a	n/a

Mt. Clemens Community SD
167 Cass Ave · Mt. Clemens, MI 48043-2203
(586) 469-6100 · http://www.mtclemens.k12.mi.us
Grade Span: PK-12; **Agency Type:** 1
Schools: 7
   5 Primary; 1 Middle; 1 High; 0 Other Level
   7 Regular; 0 Special Education; 0 Vocational; 0 Alternative
   0 Magnet; 0 Charter; 7 Title I Eligible; 7 School-wide Title I
Students: 3,051 (50.3% male; 49.6% female)
   Individual Education Program: 572 (18.7%);
   English Language Learner: 0 (0.0%); Migrant: n/a
   Eligible for Free Lunch Program: 1,565 (51.3%)
   Eligible for Reduced-Price Lunch Program: 317 (10.4%)
Teachers: 190.0 (16.1 to 1)
Librarians/Media Specialists: 4.0 (762.8 to 1)
Guidance Counselors: 4.0 (762.8 to 1)
Current Spending: ($ per student per year):
   Total: $9,559; Instruction: $6,114; Support Services: $3,068
Enrollment, Drop-out Rates and Diploma Recipients by Race/Ethnicity

Category	Total	White	Black	Asian	AIAN	Hisp.
Enrollment (%)	100.0	47.8	47.6	1.1	0.5	2.4
Drop-out Rate (%)	n/a	n/a	n/a	n/a	n/a	n/a
H.S. Diplomas (#)	89	56	30	1	1	1

Richmond Community Schools
68931 S Main St · Richmond, MI 48062-1527
(586) 727-3565 · http://www.rcs.k12.in.us/default.asp
Grade Span: PK-12; **Agency Type:** 1
Schools: 3
   1 Primary; 1 Middle; 1 High; 0 Other Level
   3 Regular; 0 Special Education; 0 Vocational; 0 Alternative
   0 Magnet; 0 Charter; 0 Title I Eligible; 0 School-wide Title I
Students: 2,074 (51.2% male; 48.7% female)
   Individual Education Program: 352 (17.0%);
   English Language Learner: 0 (0.0%); Migrant: n/a
   Eligible for Free Lunch Program: 202 (9.7%)
   Eligible for Reduced-Price Lunch Program: 103 (5.0%)
Teachers: 108.0 (19.2 to 1)
Librarians/Media Specialists: 2.0 (1,037.0 to 1)
Guidance Counselors: 2.0 (1,037.0 to 1)
Current Spending: ($ per student per year):
   Total: $7,074; Instruction: $3,960; Support Services: $2,886
Enrollment, Drop-out Rates and Diploma Recipients by Race/Ethnicity

Category	Total	White	Black	Asian	AIAN	Hisp.
Enrollment (%)	100.0	94.0	0.9	1.1	0.4	3.6
Drop-out Rate (%)	n/a	n/a	n/a	n/a	n/a	n/a
H.S. Diplomas (#)	145	144	0	1	0	0

Romeo Community Schools
316 N Main St · Romeo, MI 48065-4621
(586) 752-0200 · http://www.romeo.k12.mi.us/
Grade Span: PK-12; **Agency Type:** 1
Schools: 11
   6 Primary; 2 Middle; 1 High; 2 Other Level
   9 Regular; 0 Special Education; 1 Vocational; 1 Alternative
   0 Magnet; 0 Charter; 0 Title I Eligible; 0 School-wide Title I
Students: 5,580 (50.3% male; 49.6% female)
   Individual Education Program: 699 (12.5%);
   English Language Learner: 0 (0.0%); Migrant: n/a
   Eligible for Free Lunch Program: 470 (8.4%)
   Eligible for Reduced-Price Lunch Program: 243 (4.4%)
Teachers: 299.0 (18.7 to 1)
Librarians/Media Specialists: 8.0 (697.5 to 1)
Guidance Counselors: 10.0 (558.0 to 1)
Current Spending: ($ per student per year):
   Total: $7,597; Instruction: $4,241; Support Services: $3,183
Enrollment, Drop-out Rates and Diploma Recipients by Race/Ethnicity

Category	Total	White	Black	Asian	AIAN	Hisp.
Enrollment (%)	100.0	94.3	1.5	0.8	0.3	3.0
Drop-out Rate (%)	n/a	n/a	n/a	n/a	n/a	n/a
H.S. Diplomas (#)	343	326	5	8	2	2

Roseville Community Schools
18975 Church St · Roseville, MI 48066-3952
(586) 445-5505 · http://www.rcs.misd.net/
Grade Span: PK-12; **Agency Type:** 1
Schools: 14
   10 Primary; 2 Middle; 1 High; 1 Other Level
   13 Regular; 0 Special Education; 0 Vocational; 1 Alternative
   0 Magnet; 0 Charter; 0 Title I Eligible; 0 School-wide Title I
Students: 6,560 (52.2% male; 47.7% female)
   Individual Education Program: 967 (14.7%);
   English Language Learner: 0 (0.0%); Migrant: n/a
   Eligible for Free Lunch Program: 1,607 (24.5%)
   Eligible for Reduced-Price Lunch Program: 705 (10.7%)
Teachers: 348.0 (18.9 to 1)
Librarians/Media Specialists: 8.0 (820.0 to 1)
Guidance Counselors: 8.0 (820.0 to 1)
Current Spending: ($ per student per year):
   Total: $8,246; Instruction: $4,636; Support Services: $3,358
Enrollment, Drop-out Rates and Diploma Recipients by Race/Ethnicity

Category	Total	White	Black	Asian	AIAN	Hisp.
Enrollment (%)	100.0	83.8	9.1	2.9	2.6	1.5
Drop-out Rate (%)	n/a	n/a	n/a	n/a	n/a	n/a
H.S. Diplomas (#)	308	286	5	11	4	2

South Lake Schools
23101 Stadium Blvd · St. Clair Shores, MI 48080-3208
(586) 435-1600
Grade Span: KG-12; **Agency Type:** 1
Schools: 6
   4 Primary; 1 Middle; 1 High; 0 Other Level
   6 Regular; 0 Special Education; 0 Vocational; 0 Alternative
   0 Magnet; 0 Charter; 0 Title I Eligible; 0 School-wide Title I
Students: 2,467 (51.2% male; 48.7% female)
   Individual Education Program: 347 (14.1%);
   English Language Learner: 0 (0.0%); Migrant: n/a
   Eligible for Free Lunch Program: 264 (10.7%)
   Eligible for Reduced-Price Lunch Program: 149 (6.0%)

Teachers: 147.0 (16.8 to 1)
Librarians/Media Specialists: 5.0 (493.4 to 1)
Guidance Counselors: 8.0 (308.4 to 1)
Current Spending: ($ per student per year):
    Total: $9,069; Instruction: $4,736; Support Services: $4,144
Enrollment, Drop-out Rates and Diploma Recipients by Race/Ethnicity

Category	Total	White	Black	Asian	AIAN	Hisp.
Enrollment (%)	100.0	83.2	11.3	1.8	1.4	1.5
Drop-out Rate (%)	n/a	n/a	n/a	n/a	n/a	n/a
H.S. Diplomas (#)	155	138	8	2	6	1

Utica Community Schools
11303 Greendale Dr • Sterling Heights, MI 48312-2925
(586) 797-1000 • http://www.macomb.k12.mi.us/utica/schutic.htm
Grade Span: PK-12; **Agency Type:** 1
Schools: 43
    30 Primary; 7 Middle; 6 High; 0 Other Level
    42 Regular; 0 Special Education; 0 Vocational; 1 Alternative
    0 Magnet; 0 Charter; 0 Title I Eligible; 0 School-wide Title I
Students: 28,935   (51.9% male; 48.0% female)
    Individual Education Program: 3,540 (12.2%);
    English Language Learner: 608 (2.1%); Migrant: n/a
    Eligible for Free Lunch Program: 2,151 (7.4%)
    Eligible for Reduced-Price Lunch Program: 736 (2.5%)
Teachers: 1,546.0 (18.7 to 1)
Librarians/Media Specialists: 40.0 (723.4 to 1)
Guidance Counselors: 44.0 (657.6 to 1)
Current Spending: ($ per student per year):
    Total: $7,683; Instruction: $4,707; Support Services: $2,823
Enrollment, Drop-out Rates and Diploma Recipients by Race/Ethnicity

Category	Total	White	Black	Asian	AIAN	Hisp.
Enrollment (%)	100.0	92.6	1.8	3.1	0.1	2.3
Drop-out Rate (%)	n/a	n/a	n/a	n/a	n/a	n/a
H.S. Diplomas (#)	1,867	1,763	18	61	3	22

Van Dyke Public Schools
23500 Macarthur • Warren, MI 48089-1741
(586) 758-8333 • http://www.macomb.k12.mi.us/vandyke/vandyke.htm
Grade Span: PK-12; **Agency Type:** 1
Schools: 11
    7 Primary; 2 Middle; 2 High; 0 Other Level
    9 Regular; 0 Special Education; 0 Vocational; 2 Alternative
    0 Magnet; 0 Charter; 8 Title I Eligible; 8 School-wide Title I
Students: 4,276   (53.0% male; 46.9% female)
    Individual Education Program: 712 (16.7%)
    English Language Learner: 0 (0.0%); Migrant: n/a
    Eligible for Free Lunch Program: 2,106 (49.3%)
    Eligible for Reduced-Price Lunch Program: 653 (15.3%)
Teachers: 221.0 (19.3 to 1)
Librarians/Media Specialists: 6.0 (712.7 to 1)
Guidance Counselors: 5.0 (855.2 to 1)
Current Spending: ($ per student per year):
    Total: $9,417; Instruction: $5,079; Support Services: $3,986
Enrollment, Drop-out Rates and Diploma Recipients by Race/Ethnicity

Category	Total	White	Black	Asian	AIAN	Hisp.
Enrollment (%)	100.0	75.0	14.9	6.5	1.3	1.8
Drop-out Rate (%)	n/a	n/a	n/a	n/a	n/a	n/a
H.S. Diplomas (#)	155	118	10	19	6	2

Warren Consolidated Schools
31300 Anita St • Warren, MI 48093-1646
(586) 825-2400 • http://www.wcs.k12.mi.us/
Grade Span: PK-12; **Agency Type:** 1
Schools: 26
    15 Primary; 5 Middle; 3 High; 3 Other Level
    23 Regular; 1 Special Education; 1 Vocational; 1 Alternative
    0 Magnet; 0 Charter; 0 Title I Eligible; 0 School-wide Title I
Students: 15,421   (50.9% male; 49.0% female)
    Individual Education Program: 1,562 (10.1%);
    English Language Learner: 3,882 (25.2%); Migrant: n/a
    Eligible for Free Lunch Program: 2,895 (18.8%)
    Eligible for Reduced-Price Lunch Program: 802 (5.2%)
Teachers: 802.0 (19.2 to 1)
Librarians/Media Specialists: 19.0 (811.6 to 1)
Guidance Counselors: 36.0 (428.4 to 1)
Current Spending: ($ per student per year):
    Total: $9,369; Instruction: $5,229; Support Services: $3,925
Enrollment, Drop-out Rates and Diploma Recipients by Race/Ethnicity

Category	Total	White	Black	Asian	AIAN	Hisp.
Enrollment (%)	100.0	88.7	5.3	4.5	0.7	0.8
Drop-out Rate (%)	n/a	n/a	n/a	n/a	n/a	n/a
H.S. Diplomas (#)	970	905	19	39	0	7

Warren Woods Public Schools
27100 Schoenherr Rd • Warren, MI 48088-4738
(586) 439-4401 • http://www.macomb.k12.mi.us/warrenw/home/home.htm
Grade Span: PK-12; **Agency Type:** 1
Schools: 6
    3 Primary; 1 Middle; 2 High; 0 Other Level
    5 Regular; 0 Special Education; 0 Vocational; 1 Alternative
    0 Magnet; 0 Charter; 0 Title I Eligible; 0 School-wide Title I
Students: 3,272   (51.1% male; 48.8% female)
    Individual Education Program: 465 (14.2%);
    English Language Learner: 0 (0.0%); Migrant: n/a
    Eligible for Free Lunch Program: 378 (11.8%)
    Eligible for Reduced-Price Lunch Program: 154 (4.8%)
Teachers: 173.0 (18.5 to 1)
Librarians/Media Specialists: 5.0 (640.0 to 1)
Guidance Counselors: 4.0 (800.0 to 1)
Current Spending: ($ per student per year):
    Total: $9,607; Instruction: $5,472; Support Services: $3,907
Enrollment, Drop-out Rates and Diploma Recipients by Race/Ethnicity

Category	Total	White	Black	Asian	AIAN	Hisp.
Enrollment (%)	100.0	88.4	4.5	5.4	1.2	0.4
Drop-out Rate (%)	n/a	n/a	n/a	n/a	n/a	n/a
H.S. Diplomas (#)	191	184	0	7	0	0

Manistee County

Manistee Area Schools
550 Maple St • Manistee, MI 49660-1896
(231) 723-3521 • http://www.honoredstudents.org/maps/html/
Grade Span: KG-12; **Agency Type:** 1
Schools: 6
    3 Primary; 2 Middle; 1 High; 0 Other Level
    6 Regular; 0 Special Education; 0 Vocational; 0 Alternative
    0 Magnet; 0 Charter; 0 Title I Eligible; 0 School-wide Title I
Students: 1,772   (50.7% male; 49.2% female)
    Individual Education Program: 150 (8.5%)
    English Language Learner: 0 (0.0%); Migrant: n/a
    Eligible for Free Lunch Program: 405 (22.9%)
    Eligible for Reduced-Price Lunch Program: 183 (10.3%)
Teachers: n/a
Librarians/Media Specialists: n/a
Guidance Counselors: n/a
Current Spending: ($ per student per year):
    Total: $8,099; Instruction: $5,088; Support Services: $2,731
Enrollment, Drop-out Rates and Diploma Recipients by Race/Ethnicity

Category	Total	White	Black	Asian	AIAN	Hisp.
Enrollment (%)	100.0	89.7	1.6	1.7	4.6	2.3
Drop-out Rate (%)	n/a	n/a	n/a	n/a	n/a	n/a
H.S. Diplomas (#)	135	129	0	2	1	3

Marquette County

Gwinn Area Community Schools
50 W M-35 • Gwinn, MI 49841-9180
Mailing Address: PO Box 447 • Gwinn, MI 49841-9180
(906) 346-9283
Grade Span: PK-12; **Agency Type:** 1
Schools: 5
    3 Primary; 1 Middle; 1 High; 0 Other Level
    5 Regular; 0 Special Education; 0 Vocational; 0 Alternative
    0 Magnet; 0 Charter; 0 Title I Eligible; 0 School-wide Title I
Students: 1,509   (52.1% male; 47.8% female)
    Individual Education Program: 278 (18.4%);
    English Language Learner: 1 (0.1%); Migrant: n/a
    Eligible for Free Lunch Program: 541 (35.9%)
    Eligible for Reduced-Price Lunch Program: 175 (11.6%)
Teachers: 91.0 (16.6 to 1)
Librarians/Media Specialists: 1.0 (1,509.0 to 1)
Guidance Counselors: 3.0 (503.0 to 1)
Current Spending: ($ per student per year):
    Total: $8,135; Instruction: $4,790; Support Services: $3,065
Enrollment, Drop-out Rates and Diploma Recipients by Race/Ethnicity

Category	Total	White	Black	Asian	AIAN	Hisp.
Enrollment (%)	100.0	94.2	0.5	0.3	0.8	0.2
Drop-out Rate (%)	n/a	n/a	n/a	n/a	n/a	n/a
H.S. Diplomas (#)	91	90	1	0	0	0

Marquette Area Public Schools
1201 W Fair Ave • Marquette, MI 49855-2668
(906) 225-4200 • http://www.wpsweb.com
Grade Span: KG-12; **Agency Type:** 1
Schools: 7
    4 Primary; 2 Middle; 1 High; 0 Other Level
    7 Regular; 0 Special Education; 0 Vocational; 0 Alternative
    0 Magnet; 0 Charter; 0 Title I Eligible; 0 School-wide Title I

Students: 3,679 (52.1% male; 47.8% female)
Individual Education Program: 577 (15.7%);
English Language Learner: 11 (0.3%); Migrant: n/a
Eligible for Free Lunch Program: 538 (14.8%)
Eligible for Reduced-Price Lunch Program: 163 (4.5%)
Teachers: 192.0 (19.0 to 1)
Librarians/Media Specialists: 1.0 (3,646.0 to 1)
Guidance Counselors: 7.0 (520.9 to 1)
Current Spending: ($ per student per year):
Total: $7,057; Instruction: $4,437; Support Services: $2,428
Enrollment, Drop-out Rates and Diploma Recipients by Race/Ethnicity

Category	Total	White	Black	Asian	AIAN	Hisp.
Enrollment (%)	100.0	91.8	1.3	1.3	5.2	0.5
Drop-out Rate (%)	n/a	n/a	n/a	n/a	n/a	n/a
H.S. Diplomas (#)	331	311	5	2	13	0

Mason County

Ludington Area SD
809 E Tinkham Ave • Ludington, MI 49431-1536
(231) 845-7303 • http://www.lasd.net
Grade Span: PK-12; **Agency Type:** 1
Schools: 8
6 Primary; 1 Middle; 1 High; 0 Other Level
8 Regular; 0 Special Education; 0 Vocational; 0 Alternative
8 Magnet; 0 Charter; 0 Title I Eligible; 0 School-wide Title I
Students: 2,553 (51.0% male; 48.9% female)
Individual Education Program: 339 (13.3%);
English Language Learner: 0 (0.0%); Migrant: n/a
Eligible for Free Lunch Program: 684 (26.8%)
Eligible for Reduced-Price Lunch Program: 196 (7.7%)
Teachers: 149.0 (17.1 to 1)
Librarians/Media Specialists: 0.0 (n/a to 1)
Guidance Counselors: 4.0 (638.3 to 1)
Current Spending: ($ per student per year):
Total: $7,935; Instruction: $5,466; Support Services: $2,275
Enrollment, Drop-out Rates and Diploma Recipients by Race/Ethnicity

Category	Total	White	Black	Asian	AIAN	Hisp.
Enrollment (%)	100.0	93.2	0.0	0.4	0.0	0.5
Drop-out Rate (%)	n/a	n/a	n/a	n/a	n/a	n/a
H.S. Diplomas (#)	178	167	2	3	0	6

Mason County Central Schools
300 W Broadway St • Scottville, MI 49454-1019
(231) 757-3713 • http://www.masoncountycentral.com/main/main.asp
Grade Span: KG-12; **Agency Type:** 1
Schools: 6
3 Primary; 1 Middle; 2 High; 0 Other Level
5 Regular; 0 Special Education; 0 Vocational; 1 Alternative
0 Magnet; 0 Charter; 4 Title I Eligible; 4 School-wide Title I
Students: 1,671 (54.6% male; 45.3% female)
Individual Education Program: 225 (13.5%);
English Language Learner: 0 (0.0%); Migrant: 54 (3.2%)
Eligible for Free Lunch Program: 584 (34.9%)
Eligible for Reduced-Price Lunch Program: 141 (8.4%)
Teachers: 93.0 (18.0 to 1)
Librarians/Media Specialists: 0.0 (n/a to 1)
Guidance Counselors: 3.0 (557.0 to 1)
Current Spending: ($ per student per year):
Total: $7,856; Instruction: $5,217; Support Services: $2,121
Enrollment, Drop-out Rates and Diploma Recipients by Race/Ethnicity

Category	Total	White	Black	Asian	AIAN	Hisp.
Enrollment (%)	100.0	89.0	2.1	0.2	1.8	6.8
Drop-out Rate (%)	n/a	n/a	n/a	n/a	n/a	n/a
H.S. Diplomas (#)	114	111	0	1	0	2

Mecosta County

Big Rapids Public Schools
21034 15 Mile Rd • Big Rapids, MI 49307-8845
(231) 796-2627 • http://www.brps.k12.mi.us/
Grade Span: PK-12; **Agency Type:** 1
Schools: 7
4 Primary; 1 Middle; 2 High; 0 Other Level
6 Regular; 0 Special Education; 0 Vocational; 1 Alternative
0 Magnet; 0 Charter; 0 Title I Eligible; 0 School-wide Title I
Students: 2,172 (51.1% male; 48.8% female)
Individual Education Program: 331 (15.2%);
English Language Learner: 0 (0.0%); Migrant: n/a
Eligible for Free Lunch Program: 749 (34.5%)
Eligible for Reduced-Price Lunch Program: 178 (8.2%)
Teachers: 114.0 (19.1 to 1)
Librarians/Media Specialists: 2.0 (1,086.0 to 1)
Guidance Counselors: 3.0 (724.0 to 1)

Current Spending: ($ per student per year):
Total: $7,206; Instruction: $4,252; Support Services: $2,550
Enrollment, Drop-out Rates and Diploma Recipients by Race/Ethnicity

Category	Total	White	Black	Asian	AIAN	Hisp.
Enrollment (%)	100.0	88.3	8.2	1.7	0.6	1.2
Drop-out Rate (%)	n/a	n/a	n/a	n/a	n/a	n/a
H.S. Diplomas (#)	170	163	1	6	0	0

Chippewa Hills SD
3226 Arthur Rd • Remus, MI 49340-9329
(989) 967-2000 • http://www.chippewa-hills.k12.mi.us/
Grade Span: PK-12; **Agency Type:** 1
Schools: 7
4 Primary; 1 Middle; 2 High; 0 Other Level
6 Regular; 0 Special Education; 0 Vocational; 1 Alternative
1 Magnet; 0 Charter; 3 Title I Eligible; 3 School-wide Title I
Students: 2,673 (50.8% male; 49.1% female)
Individual Education Program: 420 (15.7%);
English Language Learner: 0 (0.0%); Migrant: n/a
Eligible for Free Lunch Program: 1,129 (42.2%)
Eligible for Reduced-Price Lunch Program: 305 (11.4%)
Teachers: 154.0 (17.4 to 1)
Librarians/Media Specialists: 2.0 (1,336.5 to 1)
Guidance Counselors: 3.0 (891.0 to 1)
Current Spending: ($ per student per year):
Total: $7,992; Instruction: $4,900; Support Services: $2,754
Enrollment, Drop-out Rates and Diploma Recipients by Race/Ethnicity

Category	Total	White	Black	Asian	AIAN	Hisp.
Enrollment (%)	100.0	90.4	1.9	0.4	6.5	0.8
Drop-out Rate (%)	n/a	n/a	n/a	n/a	n/a	n/a
H.S. Diplomas (#)	143	135	2	1	3	2

Morley Stanwood Community Schools
4700 Northland Dr • Morley, MI 49336-9522
(231) 856-4392 • http://www.moisd.k12.mi.us/
Grade Span: KG-12; **Agency Type:** 1
Schools: 4
2 Primary; 1 Middle; 1 High; 0 Other Level
4 Regular; 0 Special Education; 0 Vocational; 0 Alternative
0 Magnet; 0 Charter; 4 Title I Eligible; 4 School-wide Title I
Students: 1,636 (50.5% male; 49.4% female)
Individual Education Program: 233 (14.2%);
English Language Learner: 0 (0.0%); Migrant: n/a
Eligible for Free Lunch Program: 552 (33.7%)
Eligible for Reduced-Price Lunch Program: 190 (11.6%)
Teachers: 94.0 (17.4 to 1)
Librarians/Media Specialists: 1.0 (1,636.0 to 1)
Guidance Counselors: 2.0 (818.0 to 1)
Current Spending: ($ per student per year):
Total: $7,582; Instruction: $4,871; Support Services: $2,407
Enrollment, Drop-out Rates and Diploma Recipients by Race/Ethnicity

Category	Total	White	Black	Asian	AIAN	Hisp.
Enrollment (%)	100.0	95.4	1.2	0.4	1.4	1.6
Drop-out Rate (%)	n/a	n/a	n/a	n/a	n/a	n/a
H.S. Diplomas (#)	86	83	1	0	1	1

Menominee County

Menominee Area Public Schools
1230 13th St • Menominee, MI 49858-2763
(906) 863-9951 • http://www.menominee.k12.mi.us/
Grade Span: PK-12; **Agency Type:** 1
Schools: 6
3 Primary; 1 Middle; 2 High; 0 Other Level
5 Regular; 0 Special Education; 0 Vocational; 1 Alternative
0 Magnet; 0 Charter; 1 Title I Eligible; 1 School-wide Title I
Students: 2,012 (51.3% male; 48.6% female)
Individual Education Program: 245 (12.2%);
English Language Learner: 0 (0.0%); Migrant: n/a
Eligible for Free Lunch Program: 434 (21.6%)
Eligible for Reduced-Price Lunch Program: 165 (8.2%)
Teachers: 107.0 (18.8 to 1)
Librarians/Media Specialists: 2.0 (1,006.0 to 1)
Guidance Counselors: 6.0 (335.3 to 1)
Current Spending: ($ per student per year):
Total: $7,076; Instruction: $4,469; Support Services: $2,331
Enrollment, Drop-out Rates and Diploma Recipients by Race/Ethnicity

Category	Total	White	Black	Asian	AIAN	Hisp.
Enrollment (%)	100.0	96.7	0.4	0.3	0.2	0.3
Drop-out Rate (%)	n/a	n/a	n/a	n/a	n/a	n/a
H.S. Diplomas (#)	144	142	0	0	0	2

Midland County

Bullock Creek SD
1420 S Badour Rd · Midland, MI 48640-9543
(989) 631-9022 · http://www.bullockcreekschools.com/
Grade Span: KG-12; **Agency Type:** 1
Schools: 5
  3 Primary; 1 Middle; 1 High; 0 Other Level
  5 Regular; 0 Special Education; 0 Vocational; 0 Alternative
  0 Magnet; 0 Charter; 1 Title I Eligible; 1 School-wide Title I
Students: 2,078 (51.1% male; 48.8% female)
  Individual Education Program: 339 (16.3%);
  English Language Learner: 1 (<0.1%); Migrant: n/a
  Eligible for Free Lunch Program: 523 (25.2%)
  Eligible for Reduced-Price Lunch Program: 155 (7.5%)
Teachers: 122.0 (17.0 to 1)
Librarians/Media Specialists: 2.0 (1,039.0 to 1)
Guidance Counselors: 5.0 (415.6 to 1)
Current Spending: ($ per student per year):
  Total: $7,020; Instruction: $4,105; Support Services: $2,688
Enrollment, Drop-out Rates and Diploma Recipients by Race/Ethnicity

Category	Total	White	Black	Asian	AIAN	Hisp.
Enrollment (%)	100.0	96.9	1.3	0.4	0.5	0.9
Drop-out Rate (%)	n/a	n/a	n/a	n/a	n/a	n/a
H.S. Diplomas (#)	118	115	0	0	1	2

Meridian Public Schools
3361 N M-30 · Sanford, MI 48657-9533
Mailing Address: 3361 N M-30 · Sanford, MI 48657-9533
(989) 687-3200 · http://www.merps.k12.mi.us/
Grade Span: PK-12; **Agency Type:** 1
Schools: 4
  2 Primary; 1 Middle; 1 High; 0 Other Level
  4 Regular; 0 Special Education; 0 Vocational; 0 Alternative
  2 Magnet; 0 Charter; 0 Title I Eligible; 0 School-wide Title I
Students: 1,573 (49.3% male; 50.6% female)
  Individual Education Program: 242 (15.4%);
  English Language Learner: 0 (0.0%); Migrant: n/a
  Eligible for Free Lunch Program: 436 (28.4%)
  Eligible for Reduced-Price Lunch Program: 127 (8.3%)
Teachers: 84.0 (18.3 to 1)
Librarians/Media Specialists: 2.0 (768.5 to 1)
Guidance Counselors: 2.0 (768.5 to 1)
Current Spending: ($ per student per year):
  Total: $7,426; Instruction: $4,545; Support Services: $2,560
Enrollment, Drop-out Rates and Diploma Recipients by Race/Ethnicity

Category	Total	White	Black	Asian	AIAN	Hisp.
Enrollment (%)	100.0	98.1	0.6	0.3	0.4	0.6
Drop-out Rate (%)	n/a	n/a	n/a	n/a	n/a	n/a
H.S. Diplomas (#)	91	91	0	0	0	0

Midland Public Schools
600 E Carpenter St · Midland, MI 48640-5417
(989) 923-5001 · http://www.mps.k12.mi.us/
Grade Span: KG-12; **Agency Type:** 1
Schools: 20
  12 Primary; 3 Middle; 2 High; 3 Other Level
  17 Regular; 1 Special Education; 0 Vocational; 2 Alternative
  0 Magnet; 0 Charter; 1 Title I Eligible; 1 School-wide Title I
Students: 9,608 (51.9% male; 48.0% female)
  Individual Education Program: 1,356 (14.1%);
  English Language Learner: 46 (0.5%); Migrant: n/a
  Eligible for Free Lunch Program: 1,158 (12.1%)
  Eligible for Reduced-Price Lunch Program: 381 (4.0%)
Teachers: 532.0 (18.1 to 1)
Librarians/Media Specialists: 17.0 (565.2 to 1)
Guidance Counselors: 21.0 (457.5 to 1)
Current Spending: ($ per student per year):
  Total: $8,447; Instruction: $5,183; Support Services: $3,061
Enrollment, Drop-out Rates and Diploma Recipients by Race/Ethnicity

Category	Total	White	Black	Asian	AIAN	Hisp.
Enrollment (%)	100.0	91.7	2.4	3.3	0.6	1.9
Drop-out Rate (%)	n/a	n/a	n/a	n/a	n/a	n/a
H.S. Diplomas (#)	678	637	8	19	2	12

Monroe County

Airport Community SD
11270 Grafton Rd · Carleton, MI 48117-9392
(734) 654-2414 · http://airport.k12.mi.us/
Grade Span: KG-12; **Agency Type:** 1
Schools: 6
  4 Primary; 1 Middle; 1 High; 0 Other Level
  6 Regular; 0 Special Education; 0 Vocational; 0 Alternative
  0 Magnet; 0 Charter; 0 Title I Eligible; 0 School-wide Title I

Students: 3,432 (52.5% male; 47.4% female)
  Individual Education Program: 424 (12.4%);
  English Language Learner: 0 (0.0%); Migrant: n/a
  Eligible for Free Lunch Program: 717 (20.9%)
  Eligible for Reduced-Price Lunch Program: 218 (6.4%)
Teachers: 175.0 (19.6 to 1)
Librarians/Media Specialists: 2.0 (1,716.0 to 1)
Guidance Counselors: 5.0 (686.4 to 1)
Current Spending: ($ per student per year):
  Total: $7,023; Instruction: $4,199; Support Services: $2,564
Enrollment, Drop-out Rates and Diploma Recipients by Race/Ethnicity

Category	Total	White	Black	Asian	AIAN	Hisp.
Enrollment (%)	100.0	93.4	3.7	0.4	0.6	1.9
Drop-out Rate (%)	n/a	n/a	n/a	n/a	n/a	n/a
H.S. Diplomas (#)	171	165	3	1	0	2

Bedford Public Schools
1623 W Sterns Rd · Temperance, MI 48182-1597
(734) 850-6000 · http://www.bedford.k12.mi.us/
Grade Span: KG-12; **Agency Type:** 1
Schools: 7
  5 Primary; 1 Middle; 0 High; 1 Other Level
  7 Regular; 0 Special Education; 0 Vocational; 0 Alternative
  0 Magnet; 0 Charter; 0 Title I Eligible; 0 School-wide Title I
Students: 5,475 (50.4% male; 49.5% female)
  Individual Education Program: 761 (13.9%);
  English Language Learner: 8 (0.1%); Migrant: n/a
  Eligible for Free Lunch Program: 422 (7.7%)
  Eligible for Reduced-Price Lunch Program: 220 (4.0%)
Teachers: 285.0 (19.2 to 1)
Librarians/Media Specialists: 6.0 (912.5 to 1)
Guidance Counselors: 7.0 (782.1 to 1)
Current Spending: ($ per student per year):
  Total: $7,068; Instruction: $4,166; Support Services: $2,664
Enrollment, Drop-out Rates and Diploma Recipients by Race/Ethnicity

Category	Total	White	Black	Asian	AIAN	Hisp.
Enrollment (%)	100.0	94.9	1.4	0.9	0.3	2.5
Drop-out Rate (%)	n/a	n/a	n/a	n/a	n/a	n/a
H.S. Diplomas (#)	392	388	1	0	0	3

Dundee Community Schools
420 Ypsilanti St · Dundee, MI 48131-1152
(734) 529-2350 · http://www.dundee.k12.mi.us/
Grade Span: PK-12; **Agency Type:** 1
Schools: 4
  1 Primary; 1 Middle; 1 High; 1 Other Level
  3 Regular; 0 Special Education; 0 Vocational; 1 Alternative
  0 Magnet; 0 Charter; 0 Title I Eligible; 0 School-wide Title I
Students: 1,668 (52.8% male; 47.1% female)
  Individual Education Program: 163 (9.8%);
  English Language Learner: 0 (0.0%); Migrant: n/a
  Eligible for Free Lunch Program: 168 (10.1%)
  Eligible for Reduced-Price Lunch Program: 52 (3.1%)
Teachers: n/a
Librarians/Media Specialists: n/a
Guidance Counselors: n/a
Current Spending: ($ per student per year):
  Total: $6,494; Instruction: $3,920; Support Services: $2,309
Enrollment, Drop-out Rates and Diploma Recipients by Race/Ethnicity

Category	Total	White	Black	Asian	AIAN	Hisp.
Enrollment (%)	100.0	97.1	1.8	0.2	0.1	0.8
Drop-out Rate (%)	n/a	n/a	n/a	n/a	n/a	n/a
H.S. Diplomas (#)	91	91	0	0	0	0

Ida Public SD
3145 Prairie St · Ida, MI 48140-9600
(734) 269-9003 · http://www.idaschools.org/
Grade Span: PK-12; **Agency Type:** 1
Schools: 3
  1 Primary; 1 Middle; 1 High; 0 Other Level
  3 Regular; 0 Special Education; 0 Vocational; 0 Alternative
  0 Magnet; 0 Charter; 0 Title I Eligible; 0 School-wide Title I
Students: 1,737 (52.4% male; 47.5% female)
  Individual Education Program: 275 (15.8%);
  English Language Learner: 12 (0.7%); Migrant: n/a
  Eligible for Free Lunch Program: 139 (8.0%)
  Eligible for Reduced-Price Lunch Program: 47 (2.7%)
Teachers: 97.0 (17.9 to 1)
Librarians/Media Specialists: 1.0 (1,737.0 to 1)
Guidance Counselors: 2.0 (868.5 to 1)
Current Spending: ($ per student per year):
  Total: $7,400; Instruction: $4,360; Support Services: $2,725

Enrollment, Drop-out Rates and Diploma Recipients by Race/Ethnicity

Category	Total	White	Black	Asian	AIAN	Hisp.
Enrollment (%)	100.0	98.8	0.3	0.1	0.1	0.7
Drop-out Rate (%)	n/a	n/a	n/a	n/a	n/a	n/a
H.S. Diplomas (#)	128	126	1	0	0	1

Jefferson Schools (Monroe)

2400 N Dixie Hwy • Monroe, MI 48162-5213
(734) 289-5550 • http://jefferson.k12.mi.us
Grade Span: PK-12; **Agency Type:** 1
Schools: 6
    3 Primary; 1 Middle; 2 High; 0 Other Level
    5 Regular; 0 Special Education; 0 Vocational; 1 Alternative
    0 Magnet; 0 Charter; 0 Title I Eligible; 0 School-wide Title I
Students: 2,634 (51.3% male; 48.6% female)
    Individual Education Program: 395 (15.0%);
    English Language Learner: 0 (0.0%); Migrant: n/a
    Eligible for Free Lunch Program: 415 (15.8%)
    Eligible for Reduced-Price Lunch Program: 142 (5.4%)
Teachers: 137.0 (19.2 to 1)
Librarians/Media Specialists: 4.0 (658.5 to 1)
Guidance Counselors: 4.0 (658.5 to 1)
Current Spending: ($ per student per year):
    Total: $9,025; Instruction: $5,439; Support Services: $3,308

Enrollment, Drop-out Rates and Diploma Recipients by Race/Ethnicity

Category	Total	White	Black	Asian	AIAN	Hisp.
Enrollment (%)	100.0	96.1	0.8	0.4	0.8	2.0
Drop-out Rate (%)	n/a	n/a	n/a	n/a	n/a	n/a
H.S. Diplomas (#)	178	168	0	0	5	5

Mason Consolidated Schools (Monroe)

2400 Mason Eagles Dr • Erie, MI 48133-9318
(734) 848-9304 • http://scnc.eriemason.k12.mi.us
Grade Span: KG-12; **Agency Type:** 1
Schools: 4
    2 Primary; 1 Middle; 1 High; 0 Other Level
    4 Regular; 0 Special Education; 0 Vocational; 0 Alternative
    0 Magnet; 0 Charter; 0 Title I Eligible; 0 School-wide Title I
Students: 1,522 (51.0% male; 48.9% female)
    Individual Education Program: 256 (16.8%);
    English Language Learner: 0 (0.0%); Migrant: n/a
    Eligible for Free Lunch Program: 311 (20.4%)
    Eligible for Reduced-Price Lunch Program: 127 (8.3%)
Teachers: 16.0 (95.1 to 1)
Librarians/Media Specialists: 1.0 (1,522.0 to 1)
Guidance Counselors: 0.0 (n/a to 1)
Current Spending: ($ per student per year):
    Total: $7,540; Instruction: $4,149; Support Services: $3,104

Enrollment, Drop-out Rates and Diploma Recipients by Race/Ethnicity

Category	Total	White	Black	Asian	AIAN	Hisp.
Enrollment (%)	100.0	87.2	1.1	0.3	5.7	5.6
Drop-out Rate (%)	n/a	n/a	n/a	n/a	n/a	n/a
H.S. Diplomas (#)	113	108	1	0	0	4

Monroe Public Schools

1275 N Macomb St • Monroe, MI 48162-3128
Mailing Address: PO Box 733 • Monroe, MI 48162-0733
(734) 241-0330 • http://www.monroe.k12.mi.us/
Grade Span: KG-12; **Agency Type:** 1
Schools: 13
    9 Primary; 2 Middle; 1 High; 1 Other Level
    12 Regular; 0 Special Education; 0 Vocational; 1 Alternative
    0 Magnet; 0 Charter; 3 Title I Eligible; 3 School-wide Title I
Students: 7,199 (51.7% male; 48.2% female)
    Individual Education Program: 979 (13.6%);
    English Language Learner: 74 (1.0%); Migrant: n/a
    Eligible for Free Lunch Program: 1,936 (26.9%)
    Eligible for Reduced-Price Lunch Program: 394 (5.5%)
Teachers: 365.0 (19.7 to 1)
Librarians/Media Specialists: 4.0 (1,799.8 to 1)
Guidance Counselors: 18.0 (399.9 to 1)
Current Spending: ($ per student per year):
    Total: $7,509; Instruction: $4,393; Support Services: $2,819

Enrollment, Drop-out Rates and Diploma Recipients by Race/Ethnicity

Category	Total	White	Black	Asian	AIAN	Hisp.
Enrollment (%)	100.0	87.2	8.4	1.0	0.0	3.4
Drop-out Rate (%)	n/a	n/a	n/a	n/a	n/a	n/a
H.S. Diplomas (#)	386	364	15	0	0	7

Montcalm County

Central Montcalm Public Schools

621 New St • Stanton, MI 48888-9459
Mailing Address: PO Box 9 • Stanton, MI 48888-0009
(989) 831-5243 • http://www.maisd.com/cms/
Grade Span: PK-12; **Agency Type:** 1
Schools: 6
    2 Primary; 2 Middle; 1 High; 1 Other Level
    5 Regular; 0 Special Education; 0 Vocational; 1 Alternative
    0 Magnet; 0 Charter; 0 Title I Eligible; 0 School-wide Title I
Students: 2,127 (49.2% male; 50.7% female)
    Individual Education Program: 290 (13.6%);
    English Language Learner: 0 (0.0%); Migrant: n/a
    Eligible for Free Lunch Program: 606 (28.5%)
    Eligible for Reduced-Price Lunch Program: 190 (8.9%)
Teachers: 114.0 (18.7 to 1)
Librarians/Media Specialists: 2.0 (1,063.5 to 1)
Guidance Counselors: 5.0 (425.4 to 1)
Current Spending: ($ per student per year):
    Total: $7,090; Instruction: $4,138; Support Services: $2,679

Enrollment, Drop-out Rates and Diploma Recipients by Race/Ethnicity

Category	Total	White	Black	Asian	AIAN	Hisp.
Enrollment (%)	100.0	95.3	0.4	0.6	0.2	3.6
Drop-out Rate (%)	n/a	n/a	n/a	n/a	n/a	n/a
H.S. Diplomas (#)	122	122	0	0	0	0

Greenville Public Schools

1414 W Chase Rd • Greenville, MI 48838-7147
(616) 754-3686 • http://www.greenville.k12.mi.us/
Grade Span: PK-12; **Agency Type:** 1
Schools: 6
    4 Primary; 1 Middle; 1 High; 0 Other Level
    6 Regular; 0 Special Education; 0 Vocational; 0 Alternative
    0 Magnet; 0 Charter; 2 Title I Eligible; 2 School-wide Title I
Students: 3,914 (51.7% male; 48.2% female)
    Individual Education Program: 592 (15.1%);
    English Language Learner: 13 (0.3%); Migrant: n/a
    Eligible for Free Lunch Program: 815 (20.8%)
    Eligible for Reduced-Price Lunch Program: 286 (7.3%)
Teachers: 212.0 (18.5 to 1)
Librarians/Media Specialists: 3.0 (1,304.7 to 1)
Guidance Counselors: 8.0 (489.3 to 1)
Current Spending: ($ per student per year):
    Total: $7,216; Instruction: $4,420; Support Services: $2,554

Enrollment, Drop-out Rates and Diploma Recipients by Race/Ethnicity

Category	Total	White	Black	Asian	AIAN	Hisp.
Enrollment (%)	100.0	95.5	0.4	0.4	0.1	3.6
Drop-out Rate (%)	n/a	n/a	n/a	n/a	n/a	n/a
H.S. Diplomas (#)	242	235	1	2	0	4

Lakeview Community Schools (Montcalm)

123 5th St • Lakeview, MI 48850-9153
(989) 352-6226
Grade Span: PK-12; **Agency Type:** 1
Schools: 5
    3 Primary; 1 Middle; 1 High; 0 Other Level
    5 Regular; 0 Special Education; 0 Vocational; 0 Alternative
    0 Magnet; 0 Charter; 0 Title I Eligible; 0 School-wide Title I
Students: 1,910 (51.4% male; 48.5% female)
    Individual Education Program: 315 (16.5%);
    English Language Learner: 0 (0.0%); Migrant: n/a
    Eligible for Free Lunch Program: 582 (30.5%)
    Eligible for Reduced-Price Lunch Program: 183 (9.6%)
Teachers: 103.0 (18.5 to 1)
Librarians/Media Specialists: 2.0 (955.0 to 1)
Guidance Counselors: 5.0 (382.0 to 1)
Current Spending: ($ per student per year):
    Total: $6,965; Instruction: $4,088; Support Services: $2,613

Enrollment, Drop-out Rates and Diploma Recipients by Race/Ethnicity

Category	Total	White	Black	Asian	AIAN	Hisp.
Enrollment (%)	100.0	96.0	0.6	1.2	0.8	1.5
Drop-out Rate (%)	n/a	n/a	n/a	n/a	n/a	n/a
H.S. Diplomas (#)	115	110	0	1	2	2

Tri County Area Schools

94 Cherry St • Sand Lake, MI 49343-0079
Mailing Address: 94 Cherry St PO Box 79 • Sand Lake, MI 49343-0079
(616) 636-5454 • http://www.tricountyschools.com/
Grade Span: PK-12; **Agency Type:** 1
Schools: 6
    2 Primary; 2 Middle; 1 High; 1 Other Level
    5 Regular; 0 Special Education; 0 Vocational; 1 Alternative
    0 Magnet; 0 Charter; 0 Title I Eligible; 0 School-wide Title I
Students: 2,422 (52.6% male; 47.3% female)

Individual Education Program: 332 (13.7%);
English Language Learner: 0 (0.0%); Migrant: n/a
Eligible for Free Lunch Program: 509 (21.0%)
Eligible for Reduced-Price Lunch Program: 289 (11.9%)
Teachers: 133.0 (18.2 to 1)
Librarians/Media Specialists: 5.0 (484.4 to 1)
Guidance Counselors: 2.0 (1,211.0 to 1)
Current Spending: ($ per student per year):
Total: $6,669; Instruction: $4,086; Support Services: $2,329
Enrollment, Drop-out Rates and Diploma Recipients by Race/Ethnicity

Category	Total	White	Black	Asian	AIAN	Hisp.
Enrollment (%)	100.0	96.2	0.3	0.3	0.6	2.0
Drop-out Rate (%)	n/a	n/a	n/a	n/a	n/a	n/a
H.S. Diplomas (#)	69	69	0	0	0	0

Muskegon County

Fruitport Community Schools
3255 Pontaluna Rd • Fruitport, MI 49415-9600
(231) 865-3154 • http://remc4.k12.mi.us/fport/home.htm
Grade Span: PK-12; **Agency Type:** 1
Schools: 6
2 Primary; 1 Middle; 1 High; 2 Other Level
5 Regular; 0 Special Education; 0 Vocational; 1 Alternative
0 Magnet; 0 Charter; 2 Title I Eligible; 2 School-wide Title I
Students: 3,303   (51.4% male; 48.5% female)
Individual Education Program: 555 (16.8%);
English Language Learner: 0 (0.0%); Migrant: 2 (0.1%)
Eligible for Free Lunch Program: 827 (25.0%)
Eligible for Reduced-Price Lunch Program: 341 (10.3%)
Teachers: 184.0 (18.0 to 1)
Librarians/Media Specialists: 0.0 (n/a to 1)
Guidance Counselors: 7.0 (471.9 to 1)
Current Spending: ($ per student per year):
Total: $7,555; Instruction: $4,163; Support Services: $3,170
Enrollment, Drop-out Rates and Diploma Recipients by Race/Ethnicity

Category	Total	White	Black	Asian	AIAN	Hisp.
Enrollment (%)	100.0	93.9	1.7	0.7	0.5	3.2
Drop-out Rate (%)	n/a	n/a	n/a	n/a	n/a	n/a
H.S. Diplomas (#)	201	197	2	1	0	1

Mona Shores Public SD
3374 Mccracken St • Norton Shores, MI 49441-3657
(231) 780-4751 • http://www.mona-shores.k12.mi.us/
Grade Span: PK-12; **Agency Type:** 1
Schools: 6
4 Primary; 1 Middle; 1 High; 0 Other Level
6 Regular; 0 Special Education; 0 Vocational; 0 Alternative
0 Magnet; 0 Charter; 0 Title I Eligible; 0 School-wide Title I
Students: 4,226   (50.7% male; 49.2% female)
Individual Education Program: 498 (11.8%);
English Language Learner: 0 (0.0%); Migrant: n/a
Eligible for Free Lunch Program: 552 (13.2%)
Eligible for Reduced-Price Lunch Program: 287 (6.8%)
Teachers: 218.0 (19.2 to 1)
Librarians/Media Specialists: 3.0 (1,397.0 to 1)
Guidance Counselors: 5.0 (838.2 to 1)
Current Spending: ($ per student per year):
Total: $7,022; Instruction: $4,025; Support Services: $2,755
Enrollment, Drop-out Rates and Diploma Recipients by Race/Ethnicity

Category	Total	White	Black	Asian	AIAN	Hisp.
Enrollment (%)	100.0	88.2	4.9	1.8	1.2	3.9
Drop-out Rate (%)	n/a	n/a	n/a	n/a	n/a	n/a
H.S. Diplomas (#)	303	282	9	4	1	7

Montague Area Public Schools
4882 Stanton Blvd • Montague, MI 49437-1040
(231) 893-1515 • http://www.montague.k12.mi.us/
Grade Span: PK-12; **Agency Type:** 1
Schools: 3
1 Primary; 1 Middle; 1 High; 0 Other Level
3 Regular; 0 Special Education; 0 Vocational; 0 Alternative
0 Magnet; 0 Charter; 0 Title I Eligible; 0 School-wide Title I
Students: 1,500   (52.7% male; 47.2% female)
Individual Education Program: 239 (15.9%);
English Language Learner: 10 (0.7%); Migrant: n/a
Eligible for Free Lunch Program: 494 (32.9%)
Eligible for Reduced-Price Lunch Program: 150 (10.0%)
Teachers: 84.0 (17.9 to 1)
Librarians/Media Specialists: 0.0 (n/a to 1)
Guidance Counselors: 4.0 (375.0 to 1)
Current Spending: ($ per student per year):
Total: $6,876; Instruction: $4,371; Support Services: $2,214

Enrollment, Drop-out Rates and Diploma Recipients by Race/Ethnicity

Category	Total	White	Black	Asian	AIAN	Hisp.
Enrollment (%)	100.0	93.0	1.4	0.5	0.1	4.9
Drop-out Rate (%)	n/a	n/a	n/a	n/a	n/a	n/a
H.S. Diplomas (#)	104	99	0	1	0	4

Muskegon City SD
349 W Webster Ave • Muskegon, MI 49440-1208
(231) 720-2000 • http://www.muskegon.k12.mi.us/
Grade Span: PK-12; **Agency Type:** 1
Schools: 16
10 Primary; 2 Middle; 1 High; 3 Other Level
13 Regular; 1 Special Education; 0 Vocational; 2 Alternative
0 Magnet; 0 Charter; 10 Title I Eligible; 10 School-wide Title I
Students: 7,028   (52.4% male; 47.5% female)
Individual Education Program: 1,329 (18.9%);
English Language Learner: 322 (4.6%); Migrant: n/a
Eligible for Free Lunch Program: 4,103 (58.4%)
Eligible for Reduced-Price Lunch Program: 570 (8.1%)
Teachers: 379.0 (18.5 to 1)
Librarians/Media Specialists: 4.0 (1,757.0 to 1)
Guidance Counselors: 10.0 (702.8 to 1)
Current Spending: ($ per student per year):
Total: $8,408; Instruction: $4,490; Support Services: $3,663
Enrollment, Drop-out Rates and Diploma Recipients by Race/Ethnicity

Category	Total	White	Black	Asian	AIAN	Hisp.
Enrollment (%)	100.0	42.5	44.7	1.8	1.4	9.6
Drop-out Rate (%)	n/a	n/a	n/a	n/a	n/a	n/a
H.S. Diplomas (#)	247	102	128	2	1	14

Muskegon Heights SD
2603 Leahy St • Muskegon Heights, MI 49444-2121
(231) 830-3221 • http://www.muskegon-heights.k12.mi.us/
Grade Span: PK-12; **Agency Type:** 1
Schools: 8
6 Primary; 1 Middle; 1 High; 0 Other Level
8 Regular; 0 Special Education; 0 Vocational; 0 Alternative
0 Magnet; 0 Charter; 6 Title I Eligible; 6 School-wide Title I
Students: 2,281   (49.8% male; 50.1% female)
Individual Education Program: 456 (20.0%);
English Language Learner: 0 (0.0%); Migrant: n/a
Eligible for Free Lunch Program: 1,750 (80.6%)
Eligible for Reduced-Price Lunch Program: 121 (5.6%)
Teachers: 145.0 (15.0 to 1)
Librarians/Media Specialists: 1.0 (2,171.0 to 1)
Guidance Counselors: 1.0 (2,171.0 to 1)
Current Spending: ($ per student per year):
Total: $10,360; Instruction: $5,539; Support Services: $4,209
Enrollment, Drop-out Rates and Diploma Recipients by Race/Ethnicity

Category	Total	White	Black	Asian	AIAN	Hisp.
Enrollment (%)	100.0	2.1	93.5	1.9	0.3	2.3
Drop-out Rate (%)	n/a	n/a	n/a	n/a	n/a	n/a
H.S. Diplomas (#)	73	0	72	0	0	1

Oakridge Public Schools
275 S Wolf Lake Rd • Muskegon, MI 49442-3029
(231) 788-7100 • http://www.oakridge.k12.mi.us/
Grade Span: PK-12; **Agency Type:** 1
Schools: 5
1 Primary; 2 Middle; 1 High; 1 Other Level
5 Regular; 0 Special Education; 0 Vocational; 0 Alternative
0 Magnet; 0 Charter; 5 Title I Eligible; 5 School-wide Title I
Students: 2,003   (52.9% male; 47.0% female)
Individual Education Program: 251 (12.5%);
English Language Learner: 2 (0.1%); Migrant: n/a
Eligible for Free Lunch Program: 639 (31.9%)
Eligible for Reduced-Price Lunch Program: 246 (12.3%)
Teachers: 117.0 (17.1 to 1)
Librarians/Media Specialists: 2.0 (1,001.5 to 1)
Guidance Counselors: 2.0 (1,001.5 to 1)
Current Spending: ($ per student per year):
Total: $7,295; Instruction: $4,458; Support Services: $2,505
Enrollment, Drop-out Rates and Diploma Recipients by Race/Ethnicity

Category	Total	White	Black	Asian	AIAN	Hisp.
Enrollment (%)	100.0	91.2	1.1	0.8	0.6	6.3
Drop-out Rate (%)	n/a	n/a	n/a	n/a	n/a	n/a
H.S. Diplomas (#)	106	99	2	0	1	4

Orchard View Schools
2310 Marquette Ave • Muskegon, MI 49442-1409
(231) 760-1309 • http://www.orchardview.k12.mi.us/
Grade Span: PK-12; **Agency Type:** 1
Schools: 6
3 Primary; 1 Middle; 2 High; 0 Other Level
5 Regular; 0 Special Education; 0 Vocational; 1 Alternative

0 Magnet; 0 Charter; 5 Title I Eligible; 5 School-wide Title I
Students: 2,858   (50.3% male; 49.6% female)
  Individual Education Program: 320 (11.2%);
  English Language Learner: 0 (0.0%); Migrant: n/a
  Eligible for Free Lunch Program: 1,149 (42.6%)
  Eligible for Reduced-Price Lunch Program: 358 (13.3%)
Teachers: 151.0 (17.9 to 1)
Librarians/Media Specialists: 4.0 (674.5 to 1)
Guidance Counselors: 4.0 (674.5 to 1)
Current Spending: ($ per student per year):
  Total: $6,921; Instruction: $4,339; Support Services: $2,311
Enrollment, Drop-out Rates and Diploma Recipients by Race/Ethnicity

Category	Total	White	Black	Asian	AIAN	Hisp.
Enrollment (%)	100.0	84.2	8.5	0.3	1.5	5.5
Drop-out Rate (%)	n/a	n/a	n/a	n/a	n/a	n/a
H.S. Diplomas (#)	126	106	12	3	0	5

Reeths-Puffer Schools
991 W Giles Rd • Muskegon, MI 49445-1329
(231) 744-4736 • http://www.reeths-puffer.k12.mi.us/
Grade Span: PK-12; **Agency Type:** 1
Schools: 9
  5 Primary; 1 Middle; 2 High; 1 Other Level
  8 Regular; 0 Special Education; 0 Vocational; 1 Alternative
  0 Magnet; 0 Charter; 0 Title I Eligible; 0 School-wide Title I
Students: 4,349   (51.1% male; 48.8% female)
  Individual Education Program: 766 (17.6%);
  English Language Learner: 0 (0.0%); Migrant: n/a
  Eligible for Free Lunch Program: 993 (22.8%)
  Eligible for Reduced-Price Lunch Program: 387 (8.9%)
Teachers: 239.0 (18.2 to 1)
Librarians/Media Specialists: 2.0 (2,174.5 to 1)
Guidance Counselors: 5.0 (869.8 to 1)
Current Spending: ($ per student per year):
  Total: $7,757; Instruction: $4,485; Support Services: $2,997
Enrollment, Drop-out Rates and Diploma Recipients by Race/Ethnicity

Category	Total	White	Black	Asian	AIAN	Hisp.
Enrollment (%)	100.0	91.0	5.7	0.6	0.6	2.1
Drop-out Rate (%)	n/a	n/a	n/a	n/a	n/a	n/a
H.S. Diplomas (#)	279	257	13	2	5	2

Whitehall District Schools
541 E Slocum St • Whitehall, MI 49461-1199
(231) 893-1005 • http://www.whitehallsd.k12.wi.us/
Grade Span: PK-12; **Agency Type:** 1
Schools: 4
  1 Primary; 2 Middle; 1 High; 0 Other Level
  4 Regular; 0 Special Education; 0 Vocational; 0 Alternative
  3 Magnet; 0 Charter; 0 Title I Eligible; 0 School-wide Title I
Students: 2,281   (52.8% male; 47.1% female)
  Individual Education Program: 271 (11.9%);
  English Language Learner: 4 (0.2%); Migrant: n/a
  Eligible for Free Lunch Program: 526 (24.4%)
  Eligible for Reduced-Price Lunch Program: 114 (5.3%)
Teachers: 118.0 (18.3 to 1)
Librarians/Media Specialists: 2.0 (1,077.5 to 1)
Guidance Counselors: 5.0 (431.0 to 1)
Current Spending: ($ per student per year):
  Total: $6,906; Instruction: $4,505; Support Services: $2,182
Enrollment, Drop-out Rates and Diploma Recipients by Race/Ethnicity

Category	Total	White	Black	Asian	AIAN	Hisp.
Enrollment (%)	100.0	90.7	5.6	0.7	0.9	2.0
Drop-out Rate (%)	n/a	n/a	n/a	n/a	n/a	n/a
H.S. Diplomas (#)	132	118	7	0	4	3

Newaygo County

Fremont Public SD
220 W Pine St • Fremont, MI 49412-1532
(231) 924-2350 • http://www.fpsweb.org/
Grade Span: KG-12; **Agency Type:** 1
Schools: 6
  2 Primary; 2 Middle; 1 High; 1 Other Level
  5 Regular; 0 Special Education; 0 Vocational; 1 Alternative
  0 Magnet; 0 Charter; 1 Title I Eligible; 1 School-wide Title I
Students: 2,622   (51.2% male; 48.7% female)
  Individual Education Program: 426 (16.2%);
  English Language Learner: 0 (0.0%); Migrant: n/a
  Eligible for Free Lunch Program: 735 (28.0%)
  Eligible for Reduced-Price Lunch Program: 250 (9.5%)
Teachers: 148.0 (17.7 to 1)
Librarians/Media Specialists: 3.0 (874.0 to 1)
Guidance Counselors: 5.0 (524.4 to 1)
Current Spending: ($ per student per year):
  Total: $7,511; Instruction: $5,198; Support Services: $2,070

Category	Total	White	Black	Asian	AIAN	Hisp.
Enrollment (%)	100.0	92.2	1.0	1.0	0.3	5.6
Drop-out Rate (%)	n/a	n/a	n/a	n/a	n/a	n/a
H.S. Diplomas (#)	193	179	1	0	8	5

Grant Public SD
12192 S Elder Ave • Grant, MI 49327-8506
(231) 834-5621 • http://www.grantps.net/
Grade Span: KG-12; **Agency Type:** 1
Schools: 4
  2 Primary; 1 Middle; 1 High; 0 Other Level
  4 Regular; 0 Special Education; 0 Vocational; 0 Alternative
  0 Magnet; 0 Charter; 0 Title I Eligible; 0 School-wide Title I
Students: 2,502   (52.5% male; 47.4% female)
  Individual Education Program: 345 (13.8%);
  English Language Learner: 252 (10.1%); Migrant: 89 (3.9%)
  Eligible for Free Lunch Program: 705 (30.8%)
  Eligible for Reduced-Price Lunch Program: 187 (8.2%)
Teachers: 131.0 (17.5 to 1)
Librarians/Media Specialists: 1.0 (2,292.0 to 1)
Guidance Counselors: 3.0 (764.0 to 1)
Current Spending: ($ per student per year):
  Total: $6,767; Instruction: $4,244; Support Services: $2,266
Enrollment, Drop-out Rates and Diploma Recipients by Race/Ethnicity

Category	Total	White	Black	Asian	AIAN	Hisp.
Enrollment (%)	100.0	82.5	0.7	0.3	0.2	16.2
Drop-out Rate (%)	n/a	n/a	n/a	n/a	n/a	n/a
H.S. Diplomas (#)	137	125	0	1	0	11

Newaygo Public SD
360 S Mill St • Newaygo, MI 49337-8545
Mailing Address: PO Box 820 • Newaygo, MI 49337-0820
(231) 652-6984 • http://www.newaygo.net/
Grade Span: PK-12; **Agency Type:** 1
Schools: 5
  1 Primary; 2 Middle; 1 High; 1 Other Level
  4 Regular; 0 Special Education; 0 Vocational; 1 Alternative
  0 Magnet; 0 Charter; 2 Title I Eligible; 2 School-wide Title I
Students: 2,378   (49.0% male; 50.9% female)
  Individual Education Program: 270 (11.4%);
  English Language Learner: 0 (0.0%); Migrant: n/a
  Eligible for Free Lunch Program: 574 (25.4%)
  Eligible for Reduced-Price Lunch Program: 178 (7.9%)
Teachers: 111.0 (20.4 to 1)
Librarians/Media Specialists: 2.0 (1,130.5 to 1)
Guidance Counselors: 4.0 (565.3 to 1)
Current Spending: ($ per student per year):
  Total: $6,163; Instruction: $4,012; Support Services: $1,980
Enrollment, Drop-out Rates and Diploma Recipients by Race/Ethnicity

Category	Total	White	Black	Asian	AIAN	Hisp.
Enrollment (%)	100.0	91.2	0.6	0.4	0.4	6.6
Drop-out Rate (%)	n/a	n/a	n/a	n/a	n/a	n/a
H.S. Diplomas (#)	91	88	1	0	0	2

White Cloud Public Schools
553 Wilcox Ave • White Cloud, MI 49349-9701
Mailing Address: PO Box 1003 • White Cloud, MI 49349-1003
(231) 689-6591 • http://www.whitecloud.net/
Grade Span: KG-12; **Agency Type:** 1
Schools: 4
  1 Primary; 2 Middle; 1 High; 0 Other Level
  4 Regular; 0 Special Education; 0 Vocational; 0 Alternative
  0 Magnet; 0 Charter; 2 Title I Eligible; 2 School-wide Title I
Students: 1,530   (51.5% male; 48.4% female)
  Individual Education Program: 276 (18.0%);
  English Language Learner: 0 (0.0%); Migrant: n/a
  Eligible for Free Lunch Program: 809 (52.9%)
  Eligible for Reduced-Price Lunch Program: 195 (12.7%)
Teachers: 92.0 (16.6 to 1)
Librarians/Media Specialists: 1.0 (1,530.0 to 1)
Guidance Counselors: 2.0 (765.0 to 1)
Current Spending: ($ per student per year):
  Total: $7,813; Instruction: $5,181; Support Services: $2,281
Enrollment, Drop-out Rates and Diploma Recipients by Race/Ethnicity

Category	Total	White	Black	Asian	AIAN	Hisp.
Enrollment (%)	100.0	91.0	4.4	0.8	1.8	2.0
Drop-out Rate (%)	n/a	n/a	n/a	n/a	n/a	n/a
H.S. Diplomas (#)	73	70	2	0	0	1

Oakland County

Avondale SD
260 S Squirrel Rd • Auburn Hills, MI 48326-3255
(248) 852-4411 • http://www.avondale.k12.mi.us/
Grade Span: PK-12; **Agency Type:** 1
Schools: 8
   4 Primary; 2 Middle; 1 High; 1 Other Level
   7 Regular; 1 Special Education; 0 Vocational; 0 Alternative
   0 Magnet; 0 Charter; 3 Title I Eligible; 3 School-wide Title I
Students: 3,868 (51.2% male; 48.7% female)
   Individual Education Program: 364 (9.4%);
   English Language Learner: 0 (0.0%); Migrant: n/a
   Eligible for Free Lunch Program: 253 (6.5%)
   Eligible for Reduced-Price Lunch Program: 111 (2.9%)
Teachers: 246.0 (15.7 to 1)
Librarians/Media Specialists: 4.0 (967.0 to 1)
Guidance Counselors: 8.0 (483.5 to 1)
Current Spending: ($ per student per year):
   Total: $9,309; Instruction: $5,660; Support Services: $3,436
Enrollment, Drop-out Rates and Diploma Recipients by Race/Ethnicity

Category	Total	White	Black	Asian	AIAN	Hisp.
Enrollment (%)	100.0	75.2	13.2	7.5	0.5	3.3
Drop-out Rate (%)	n/a	n/a	n/a	n/a	n/a	n/a
H.S. Diplomas (#)	207	174	27	4	0	2

Berkley SD
2211 Oakshire St • Berkley, MI 48072-1290
(248) 837-8004 • http://www.berkley.k12.mi.us/
Grade Span: PK-12; **Agency Type:** 1
Schools: 10
   7 Primary; 1 Middle; 1 High; 1 Other Level
   9 Regular; 0 Special Education; 0 Vocational; 1 Alternative
   0 Magnet; 0 Charter; 0 Title I Eligible; 0 School-wide Title I
Students: 4,483 (50.7% male; 49.2% female)
   Individual Education Program: 494 (11.0%);
   English Language Learner: 149 (3.3%); Migrant: n/a
   Eligible for Free Lunch Program: 392 (8.7%)
   Eligible for Reduced-Price Lunch Program: 116 (2.6%)
Teachers: 266.0 (16.9 to 1)
Librarians/Media Specialists: 6.0 (747.2 to 1)
Guidance Counselors: 8.0 (560.4 to 1)
Current Spending: ($ per student per year):
   Total: $8,402; Instruction: $5,057; Support Services: $3,206
Enrollment, Drop-out Rates and Diploma Recipients by Race/Ethnicity

Category	Total	White	Black	Asian	AIAN	Hisp.
Enrollment (%)	100.0	83.0	14.0	1.7	0.4	0.9
Drop-out Rate (%)	n/a	n/a	n/a	n/a	n/a	n/a
H.S. Diplomas (#)	296	278	10	7	1	0

Birmingham City SD
550 W Merrill St • Birmingham, MI 48009-1443
(248) 203-3004 • http://www.birmingham.k12.mi.us/
Grade Span: PK-12; **Agency Type:** 1
Schools: 14
   10 Primary; 2 Middle; 2 High; 0 Other Level
   14 Regular; 0 Special Education; 0 Vocational; 0 Alternative
   13 Magnet; 0 Charter; 0 Title I Eligible; 0 School-wide Title I
Students: 7,934 (51.7% male; 48.2% female)
   Individual Education Program: 865 (10.9%);
   English Language Learner: 180 (2.3%); Migrant: n/a
   Eligible for Free Lunch Program: 156 (2.0%)
   Eligible for Reduced-Price Lunch Program: 69 (0.9%)
Teachers: 395.0 (20.1 to 1)
Librarians/Media Specialists: 12.0 (661.2 to 1)
Guidance Counselors: 12.0 (661.2 to 1)
Current Spending: ($ per student per year):
   Total: $11,769; Instruction: $6,675; Support Services: $4,831
Enrollment, Drop-out Rates and Diploma Recipients by Race/Ethnicity

Category	Total	White	Black	Asian	AIAN	Hisp.
Enrollment (%)	100.0	89.7	6.9	2.3	0.2	1.0
Drop-out Rate (%)	n/a	n/a	n/a	n/a	n/a	n/a
H.S. Diplomas (#)	503	461	29	12	1	0

Bloomfield Hills SD
4175 Andover Rd • Bloomfield Hills, MI 48302-1903
Mailing Address: PO Box 816 • Bloomfield Hills, MI 48303-0816
(248) 341-5405 • http://www.bloomfield.org/
Grade Span: PK-12; **Agency Type:** 1
Schools: 14
   7 Primary; 3 Middle; 3 High; 1 Other Level
   12 Regular; 2 Special Education; 0 Vocational; 0 Alternative
   0 Magnet; 0 Charter; 0 Title I Eligible; 0 School-wide Title I
Students: 6,000 (51.6% male; 48.3% female)
   Individual Education Program: 920 (15.3%);

   English Language Learner: 259 (4.3%); Migrant: n/a
   Eligible for Free Lunch Program: 141 (2.4%)
   Eligible for Reduced-Price Lunch Program: 30 (0.5%)
Teachers: 430.0 (14.0 to 1)
Librarians/Media Specialists: 10.0 (600.0 to 1)
Guidance Counselors: 17.0 (352.9 to 1)
Current Spending: ($ per student per year):
   Total: $12,759; Instruction: $7,589; Support Services: $4,843
Enrollment, Drop-out Rates and Diploma Recipients by Race/Ethnicity

Category	Total	White	Black	Asian	AIAN	Hisp.
Enrollment (%)	100.0	81.1	7.8	9.3	0.5	1.3
Drop-out Rate (%)	n/a	n/a	n/a	n/a	n/a	n/a
H.S. Diplomas (#)	442	360	27	52	0	3

Brandon SD
1025 S Ortonville Rd • Ortonville, MI 48462-8547
(248) 627-1802 • http://www.brandon.k12.mi.us/splash.htm
Grade Span: PK-12; **Agency Type:** 1
Schools: 7
   3 Primary; 2 Middle; 1 High; 1 Other Level
   6 Regular; 0 Special Education; 0 Vocational; 1 Alternative
   0 Magnet; 0 Charter; 0 Title I Eligible; 0 School-wide Title I
Students: 3,682 (51.4% male; 48.5% female)
   Individual Education Program: 504 (13.7%);
   English Language Learner: 12 (0.3%); Migrant: n/a
   Eligible for Free Lunch Program: 422 (11.5%)
   Eligible for Reduced-Price Lunch Program: 118 (3.2%)
Teachers: 194.0 (19.0 to 1)
Librarians/Media Specialists: 1.0 (3,682.0 to 1)
Guidance Counselors: 4.0 (920.5 to 1)
Current Spending: ($ per student per year):
   Total: $7,053; Instruction: $3,972; Support Services: $2,877
Enrollment, Drop-out Rates and Diploma Recipients by Race/Ethnicity

Category	Total	White	Black	Asian	AIAN	Hisp.
Enrollment (%)	100.0	95.6	1.4	0.9	0.4	1.8
Drop-out Rate (%)	n/a	n/a	n/a	n/a	n/a	n/a
H.S. Diplomas (#)	237	232	1	1	1	2

Clarenceville SD
20210 Middlebelt Rd • Livonia, MI 48152-2002
(248) 473-8900 • http://www.clarenceville.k12.mi.us/
Grade Span: PK-12; **Agency Type:** 1
Schools: 4
   2 Primary; 1 Middle; 1 High; 0 Other Level
   4 Regular; 0 Special Education; 0 Vocational; 0 Alternative
   0 Magnet; 0 Charter; 0 Title I Eligible; 0 School-wide Title I
Students: 2,007 (51.2% male; 48.7% female)
   Individual Education Program: 291 (14.5%);
   English Language Learner: 0 (0.0%); Migrant: n/a
   Eligible for Free Lunch Program: 468 (23.3%)
   Eligible for Reduced-Price Lunch Program: 112 (5.6%)
Teachers: 112.0 (17.9 to 1)
Librarians/Media Specialists: 4.0 (501.8 to 1)
Guidance Counselors: 2.0 (1,003.5 to 1)
Current Spending: ($ per student per year):
   Total: $8,655; Instruction: $4,831; Support Services: $3,605
Enrollment, Drop-out Rates and Diploma Recipients by Race/Ethnicity

Category	Total	White	Black	Asian	AIAN	Hisp.
Enrollment (%)	100.0	82.7	10.5	3.4	1.5	1.9
Drop-out Rate (%)	n/a	n/a	n/a	n/a	n/a	n/a
H.S. Diplomas (#)	94	80	8	2	0	4

Clarkston Community SD
6389 Clarkston Rd • Clarkston, MI 48347-1613
Mailing Address: PO Box 1050 • Clarkston, MI 48347-1050
(248) 623-5408 • http://www.clarkston.k12.mi.us/
Grade Span: PK-12; **Agency Type:** 1
Schools: 13
   8 Primary; 2 Middle; 2 High; 1 Other Level
   11 Regular; 1 Special Education; 0 Vocational; 1 Alternative
   0 Magnet; 0 Charter; 0 Title I Eligible; 0 School-wide Title I
Students: 7,951 (51.5% male; 48.4% female)
   Individual Education Program: 1,015 (12.8%);
   English Language Learner: 0 (0.0%); Migrant: n/a
   Eligible for Free Lunch Program: 366 (4.6%)
   Eligible for Reduced-Price Lunch Program: 112 (1.4%)
Teachers: 438.0 (18.2 to 1)
Librarians/Media Specialists: 10.0 (795.1 to 1)
Guidance Counselors: 10.0 (795.1 to 1)
Current Spending: ($ per student per year):
   Total: $7,466; Instruction: $4,597; Support Services: $2,651

Enrollment, Drop-out Rates and Diploma Recipients by Race/Ethnicity

Category	Total	White	Black	Asian	AIAN	Hisp.
Enrollment (%)	100.0	93.7	1.9	1.6	0.2	2.4
Drop-out Rate (%)	n/a	n/a	n/a	n/a	n/a	n/a
H.S. Diplomas (#)	501	475	3	3	3	17

Farmington Public SD

32500 Shiawassee St • Farmington, MI 48336-2363
(248) 489-3300 • http://www.farmington.k12.mi.us/
Grade Span: PK-12; **Agency Type:** 1
Schools: 27
  15 Primary; 4 Middle; 3 High; 5 Other Level
  22 Regular; 4 Special Education; 0 Vocational; 1 Alternative
  0 Magnet; 0 Charter; 0 Title I Eligible; 0 School-wide Title I
Students: 12,307 (52.0% male; 47.9% female)
  Individual Education Program: 1,509 (12.3%);
  English Language Learner: 2,496 (20.3%); Migrant: n/a
  Eligible for Free Lunch Program: 787 (6.4%)
  Eligible for Reduced-Price Lunch Program: 279 (2.3%)
Teachers: 768.0 (16.0 to 1)
Librarians/Media Specialists: 21.0 (586.0 to 1)
Guidance Counselors: 21.0 (586.0 to 1)
Current Spending: ($ per student per year):
  Total: $10,888; Instruction: $6,196; Support Services: $4,446

Enrollment, Drop-out Rates and Diploma Recipients by Race/Ethnicity

Category	Total	White	Black	Asian	AIAN	Hisp.
Enrollment (%)	100.0	76.6	12.5	9.5	0.1	1.3
Drop-out Rate (%)	n/a	n/a	n/a	n/a	n/a	n/a
H.S. Diplomas (#)	847	704	81	56	0	6

Ferndale Public Schools

2920 Burdette • Ferndale, MI 48220-1055
(248) 586-8653 • http://www.ferndaleschools.org/
Grade Span: PK-12; **Agency Type:** 1
Schools: 7
  4 Primary; 2 Middle; 1 High; 0 Other Level
  7 Regular; 0 Special Education; 0 Vocational; 0 Alternative
  0 Magnet; 0 Charter; 1 Title I Eligible; 1 School-wide Title I
Students: 3,951 (51.6% male; 48.3% female)
  Individual Education Program: 351 (8.9%);
  English Language Learner: 0 (0.0%); Migrant: n/a
  Eligible for Free Lunch Program: 1,042 (33.2%)
  Eligible for Reduced-Price Lunch Program: 324 (10.3%)
Teachers: 233.0 (13.5 to 1)
Librarians/Media Specialists: 1.0 (3,142.0 to 1)
Guidance Counselors: 9.0 (349.1 to 1)
Current Spending: ($ per student per year):
  Total: $9,683; Instruction: $4,359; Support Services: $5,062

Enrollment, Drop-out Rates and Diploma Recipients by Race/Ethnicity

Category	Total	White	Black	Asian	AIAN	Hisp.
Enrollment (%)	100.0	53.3	42.8	1.9	0.9	1.0
Drop-out Rate (%)	n/a	n/a	n/a	n/a	n/a	n/a
H.S. Diplomas (#)	202	118	78	5	0	1

Hazel Park City SD

23136 Hughes Ave • Hazel Park, MI 48030-1500
(248) 542-3910 • http://www.oakland.k12.mi.us/district/hazel.htm
Grade Span: PK-12; **Agency Type:** 1
Schools: 13
  7 Primary; 2 Middle; 2 High; 2 Other Level
  10 Regular; 2 Special Education; 0 Vocational; 1 Alternative
  0 Magnet; 0 Charter; 0 Title I Eligible; 0 School-wide Title I
Students: 4,944 (53.7% male; 46.2% female)
  Individual Education Program: 824 (16.7%);
  English Language Learner: 379 (7.7%); Migrant: n/a
  Eligible for Free Lunch Program: 1,532 (36.0%)
  Eligible for Reduced-Price Lunch Program: 472 (11.1%)
Teachers: 287.0 (14.8 to 1)
Librarians/Media Specialists: 6.0 (709.2 to 1)
Guidance Counselors: 5.0 (851.0 to 1)
Current Spending: ($ per student per year):
  Total: $9,882; Instruction: $5,743; Support Services: $3,861

Enrollment, Drop-out Rates and Diploma Recipients by Race/Ethnicity

Category	Total	White	Black	Asian	AIAN	Hisp.
Enrollment (%)	100.0	82.2	12.1	1.4	2.8	1.5
Drop-out Rate (%)	n/a	n/a	n/a	n/a	n/a	n/a
H.S. Diplomas (#)	157	132	2	2	17	4

Holly Area SD

111 College St • Holly, MI 48442-1720
(248) 328-3140 • http://www.hollyareaschools.com
Grade Span: PK-12; **Agency Type:** 1
Schools: 7
  4 Primary; 1 Middle; 1 High; 1 Other Level
  6 Regular; 1 Special Education; 0 Vocational; 0 Alternative

0 Magnet; 0 Charter; 0 Title I Eligible; 0 School-wide Title I
Students: 4,419 (52.2% male; 47.7% female)
  Individual Education Program: 851 (19.3%);
  English Language Learner: 0 (0.0%); Migrant: n/a
  Eligible for Free Lunch Program: 780 (17.7%)
  Eligible for Reduced-Price Lunch Program: 266 (6.0%)
Teachers: 241.0 (18.3 to 1)
Librarians/Media Specialists: 2.0 (2,209.5 to 1)
Guidance Counselors: 9.0 (491.0 to 1)
Current Spending: ($ per student per year):
  Total: $7,741; Instruction: $4,223; Support Services: $3,260

Enrollment, Drop-out Rates and Diploma Recipients by Race/Ethnicity

Category	Total	White	Black	Asian	AIAN	Hisp.
Enrollment (%)	100.0	93.8	3.2	0.9	0.1	1.8
Drop-out Rate (%)	n/a	n/a	n/a	n/a	n/a	n/a
H.S. Diplomas (#)	257	245	4	1	3	4

Huron Valley Schools

2390 S Milford Rd • Highland, MI 48357-4934
(248) 684-8000 • http://www.huronvalley.k12.mi.us/winindex.html
Grade Span: PK-12; **Agency Type:** 1
Schools: 18
  11 Primary; 4 Middle; 3 High; 0 Other Level
  18 Regular; 0 Special Education; 0 Vocational; 0 Alternative
  0 Magnet; 0 Charter; 0 Title I Eligible; 0 School-wide Title I
Students: 10,877 (51.7% male; 48.2% female)
  Individual Education Program: 1,395 (12.8%);
  English Language Learner: 0 (0.0%); Migrant: n/a
  Eligible for Free Lunch Program: 1,060 (9.8%)
  Eligible for Reduced-Price Lunch Program: 399 (3.7%)
Teachers: 558.0 (19.4 to 1)
Librarians/Media Specialists: 7.0 (1,546.1 to 1)
Guidance Counselors: 15.0 (721.5 to 1)
Current Spending: ($ per student per year):
  Total: $7,647; Instruction: $4,257; Support Services: $3,183

Enrollment, Drop-out Rates and Diploma Recipients by Race/Ethnicity

Category	Total	White	Black	Asian	AIAN	Hisp.
Enrollment (%)	100.0	95.5	0.7	0.9	1.6	1.3
Drop-out Rate (%)	n/a	n/a	n/a	n/a	n/a	n/a
H.S. Diplomas (#)	622	597	2	6	9	8

Lake Orion Community Schools

315 N Lapeer St • Lake Orion, MI 48362-3165
(248) 693-5413 • http://www.lakeorion.k12.mi.us/
Grade Span: PK-12; **Agency Type:** 1
Schools: 12
  7 Primary; 3 Middle; 2 High; 0 Other Level
  11 Regular; 0 Special Education; 0 Vocational; 1 Alternative
  0 Magnet; 0 Charter; 0 Title I Eligible; 0 School-wide Title I
Students: 7,890 (52.1% male; 47.8% female)
  Individual Education Program: 839 (10.6%);
  English Language Learner: 281 (3.6%); Migrant: n/a
  Eligible for Free Lunch Program: 455 (6.1%)
  Eligible for Reduced-Price Lunch Program: 231 (3.1%)
Teachers: 397.0 (18.8 to 1)
Librarians/Media Specialists: 11.0 (679.5 to 1)
Guidance Counselors: 11.0 (679.5 to 1)
Current Spending: ($ per student per year):
  Total: $8,184; Instruction: $4,846; Support Services: $3,107

Enrollment, Drop-out Rates and Diploma Recipients by Race/Ethnicity

Category	Total	White	Black	Asian	AIAN	Hisp.
Enrollment (%)	100.0	93.5	1.9	1.3	0.9	2.1
Drop-out Rate (%)	n/a	n/a	n/a	n/a	n/a	n/a
H.S. Diplomas (#)	402	384	7	5	0	6

Lamphere Public Schools

31201 Dorchester St • Madison Heights, MI 48071-1075
(248) 589-1990 • http://www.lamphere.k12.mi.us/education/district/
Grade Span: PK-12; **Agency Type:** 1
Schools: 9
  4 Primary; 1 Middle; 1 High; 3 Other Level
  6 Regular; 2 Special Education; 0 Vocational; 1 Alternative
  0 Magnet; 0 Charter; 0 Title I Eligible; 0 School-wide Title I
Students: 2,469 (52.2% male; 47.7% female)
  Individual Education Program: 386 (15.6%);
  English Language Learner: 236 (9.6%); Migrant: n/a
  Eligible for Free Lunch Program: 508 (20.6%)
  Eligible for Reduced-Price Lunch Program: 102 (4.1%)
Teachers: 154.0 (16.0 to 1)
Librarians/Media Specialists: 2.0 (1,234.5 to 1)
Guidance Counselors: 5.0 (493.8 to 1)
Current Spending: ($ per student per year):
  Total: $11,607; Instruction: $6,607; Support Services: $4,712

Enrollment, Drop-out Rates and Diploma Recipients by Race/Ethnicity

Category	Total	White	Black	Asian	AIAN	Hisp.
Enrollment (%)	100.0	89.8	4.6	4.6	0.2	0.9
Drop-out Rate (%)	n/a	n/a	n/a	n/a	n/a	n/a
H.S. Diplomas (#)	167	162	2	1	0	2

Madison Public Schools (Oakland)
25421 Alger St • Madison Heights, MI 48071-3921
(248) 399-7800 • http://www.madisonschools.k12.mi.us/
Grade Span: PK-12; **Agency Type:** 1
Schools: 6
    3 Primary; 1 Middle; 2 High; 0 Other Level
    5 Regular; 0 Special Education; 0 Vocational; 1 Alternative
    0 Magnet; 0 Charter; 3 Title I Eligible; 3 School-wide Title I
Students: 2,033   (51.6% male; 48.3% female)
    Individual Education Program: 369 (18.2%);
    English Language Learner: 232 (11.4%); Migrant: n/a
    Eligible for Free Lunch Program: 580 (28.5%)
    Eligible for Reduced-Price Lunch Program: 181 (8.9%)
Teachers: 126.0 (16.1 to 1)
Librarians/Media Specialists: 1.0 (2,033.0 to 1)
Guidance Counselors: 4.0 (508.3 to 1)
Current Spending: ($ per student per year):
    Total: $8,259; Instruction: $4,485; Support Services: $3,471

Enrollment, Drop-out Rates and Diploma Recipients by Race/Ethnicity

Category	Total	White	Black	Asian	AIAN	Hisp.
Enrollment (%)	100.0	85.9	11.4	1.7	0.1	0.9
Drop-out Rate (%)	n/a	n/a	n/a	n/a	n/a	n/a
H.S. Diplomas (#)	86	81	5	0	0	0

Novi Community SD
25345 Taft Rd • Novi, MI 48374-2423
(248) 449-1200 • http://itc.novi.k12.mi.us/
Grade Span: PK-12; **Agency Type:** 1
Schools: 9
    6 Primary; 2 Middle; 1 High; 0 Other Level
    9 Regular; 0 Special Education; 0 Vocational; 0 Alternative
    7 Magnet; 0 Charter; 0 Title I Eligible; 0 School-wide Title I
Students: 6,315   (52.1% male; 47.8% female)
    Individual Education Program: 626 (9.9%);
    English Language Learner: 0 (0.0%); Migrant: n/a
    Eligible for Free Lunch Program: 78 (1.2%)
    Eligible for Reduced-Price Lunch Program: 29 (0.5%)
Teachers: 396.0 (15.9 to 1)
Librarians/Media Specialists: 8.0 (787.0 to 1)
Guidance Counselors: 10.0 (629.6 to 1)
Current Spending: ($ per student per year):
    Total: $9,313; Instruction: $5,860; Support Services: $3,135

Enrollment, Drop-out Rates and Diploma Recipients by Race/Ethnicity

Category	Total	White	Black	Asian	AIAN	Hisp.
Enrollment (%)	100.0	79.0	2.6	16.4	0.1	2.0
Drop-out Rate (%)	n/a	n/a	n/a	n/a	n/a	n/a
H.S. Diplomas (#)	389	345	5	34	0	5

Oak Park City SD
13900 Granzon St • Oak Park, MI 48237-2756
(248) 691-8400 • http://www.oakparkschools.org/
Grade Span: PK-12; **Agency Type:** 1
Schools: 8
    6 Primary; 1 Middle; 1 High; 0 Other Level
    8 Regular; 0 Special Education; 0 Vocational; 0 Alternative
    0 Magnet; 0 Charter; 1 Title I Eligible; 1 School-wide Title I
Students: 4,156   (51.5% male; 48.4% female)
    Individual Education Program: 393 (9.5%);
    English Language Learner: 255 (6.1%); Migrant: n/a
    Eligible for Free Lunch Program: 1,632 (39.3%)
    Eligible for Reduced-Price Lunch Program: 299 (7.2%)
Teachers: 219.0 (19.0 to 1)
Librarians/Media Specialists: 4.0 (1,039.0 to 1)
Guidance Counselors: 4.0 (1,039.0 to 1)
Current Spending: ($ per student per year):
    Total: $9,636; Instruction: $5,678; Support Services: $3,658

Enrollment, Drop-out Rates and Diploma Recipients by Race/Ethnicity

Category	Total	White	Black	Asian	AIAN	Hisp.
Enrollment (%)	100.0	8.2	90.0	0.8	0.5	0.5
Drop-out Rate (%)	n/a	n/a	n/a	n/a	n/a	n/a
H.S. Diplomas (#)	238	17	217	1	0	3

Oxford Area Community Schools
105 Pontiac St • Oxford, MI 48371-4847
(248) 969-5000 • http://www.oxford.k12.mi.us/
Grade Span: PK-12; **Agency Type:** 1
Schools: 8
    5 Primary; 1 Middle; 1 High; 1 Other Level
    7 Regular; 0 Special Education; 0 Vocational; 1 Alternative

    0 Magnet; 0 Charter; 0 Title I Eligible; 0 School-wide Title I
Students: 4,069   (52.7% male; 47.2% female)
    Individual Education Program: 449 (11.0%);
    English Language Learner: 0 (0.0%); Migrant: n/a
    Eligible for Free Lunch Program: 297 (7.3%)
    Eligible for Reduced-Price Lunch Program: 164 (4.0%)
Teachers: 171.0 (23.8 to 1)
Librarians/Media Specialists: 5.0 (813.8 to 1)
Guidance Counselors: 2.0 (2,034.5 to 1)
Current Spending: ($ per student per year):
    Total: $7,672; Instruction: $4,519; Support Services: $2,952

Enrollment, Drop-out Rates and Diploma Recipients by Race/Ethnicity

Category	Total	White	Black	Asian	AIAN	Hisp.
Enrollment (%)	100.0	94.9	1.8	0.8	0.7	1.7
Drop-out Rate (%)	n/a	n/a	n/a	n/a	n/a	n/a
H.S. Diplomas (#)	235	225	3	5	1	1

Pontiac City SD
47200 Woodwrd • Pontiac, MI 48342-5008
Mailing Address: 47200 Woodward • Pontiac, MI 48342-5008
(248) 451-6883 • http://www.pontiac.k12.mi.us/
Grade Span: PK-12; **Agency Type:** 1
Schools: 24
    13 Primary; 4 Middle; 3 High; 4 Other Level
    20 Regular; 2 Special Education; 0 Vocational; 2 Alternative
    1 Magnet; 0 Charter; 23 Title I Eligible; 23 School-wide Title I
Students: 11,490   (51.4% male; 48.5% female)
    Individual Education Program: 1,946 (16.9%);
    English Language Learner: 1,832 (15.9%); Migrant: n/a
    Eligible for Free Lunch Program: 6,417 (55.8%)
    Eligible for Reduced-Price Lunch Program: 665 (5.8%)
Teachers: 736.0 (15.6 to 1)
Librarians/Media Specialists: 14.0 (820.7 to 1)
Guidance Counselors: 14.0 (820.7 to 1)
Current Spending: ($ per student per year):
    Total: $9,787; Instruction: $5,489; Support Services: $3,915

Enrollment, Drop-out Rates and Diploma Recipients by Race/Ethnicity

Category	Total	White	Black	Asian	AIAN	Hisp.
Enrollment (%)	100.0	15.2	62.5	5.0	0.5	16.8
Drop-out Rate (%)	n/a	n/a	n/a	n/a	n/a	n/a
H.S. Diplomas (#)	416	60	284	17	12	43

Rochester Community SD
501 W University Dr • Rochester, MI 48307-1944
(248) 726-3000 • http://www.rochester.k12.mi.us/
Grade Span: KG-12; **Agency Type:** 1
Schools: 21
    13 Primary; 4 Middle; 4 High; 0 Other Level
    20 Regular; 0 Special Education; 0 Vocational; 1 Alternative
    0 Magnet; 0 Charter; 0 Title I Eligible; 0 School-wide Title I
Students: 14,461   (51.0% male; 48.9% female)
    Individual Education Program: 1,513 (10.5%);
    English Language Learner: 907 (6.3%); Migrant: n/a
    Eligible for Free Lunch Program: 475 (3.3%)
    Eligible for Reduced-Price Lunch Program: 207 (1.4%)
Teachers: 712.0 (20.2 to 1)
Librarians/Media Specialists: 18.0 (798.1 to 1)
Guidance Counselors: 25.0 (574.6 to 1)
Current Spending: ($ per student per year):
    Total: $8,431; Instruction: $4,840; Support Services: $3,370

Enrollment, Drop-out Rates and Diploma Recipients by Race/Ethnicity

Category	Total	White	Black	Asian	AIAN	Hisp.
Enrollment (%)	100.0	90.7	2.5	5.3	0.1	1.4
Drop-out Rate (%)	n/a	n/a	n/a	n/a	n/a	n/a
H.S. Diplomas (#)	1,009	894	28	72	1	14

SD of the City of Royal Oak
1123 Lexington Blvd • Royal Oak, MI 48073-2438
(248) 435-8400 • http://www.rosd.k12.mi.us/
Grade Span: PK-12; **Agency Type:** 1
Schools: 13
    9 Primary; 2 Middle; 2 High; 0 Other Level
    13 Regular; 0 Special Education; 0 Vocational; 0 Alternative
    0 Magnet; 0 Charter; 0 Title I Eligible; 0 School-wide Title I
Students: 6,477   (52.4% male; 47.5% female)
    Individual Education Program: 893 (13.8%);
    English Language Learner: 189 (2.9%); Migrant: n/a
    Eligible for Free Lunch Program: 523 (8.3%)
    Eligible for Reduced-Price Lunch Program: 232 (3.7%)
Teachers: 398.0 (15.8 to 1)
Librarians/Media Specialists: 4.0 (1,575.3 to 1)
Guidance Counselors: 10.0 (630.1 to 1)
Current Spending: ($ per student per year):
    Total: $9,466; Instruction: $5,451; Support Services: $3,850

Enrollment, Drop-out Rates and Diploma Recipients by Race/Ethnicity

Category	Total	White	Black	Asian	AIAN	Hisp.
Enrollment (%)	100.0	92.2	5.4	1.3	0.1	0.7
Drop-out Rate (%)	n/a	n/a	n/a	n/a	n/a	n/a
H.S. Diplomas (#)	475	458	11	5	0	1

South Lyon Community Schools
345 S Warren St • South Lyon, MI 48178-1317
(248) 573-8100 • http://www.southlyon.k12.mi.us/portal.htm
Grade Span: PK-12; **Agency Type:** 1
Schools: 11
 7 Primary; 2 Middle; 1 High; 0 Other Level
 10 Regular; 0 Special Education; 0 Vocational; 0 Alternative
 2 Magnet; 0 Charter; 0 Title I Eligible; 0 School-wide Title I
Students: 6,748   (51.7% male; 48.2% female)
 Individual Education Program: 807 (12.0%);
 English Language Learner: 0 (0.0%); Migrant: n/a
 Eligible for Free Lunch Program: 487 (7.4%)
 Eligible for Reduced-Price Lunch Program: 235 (3.6%)
Teachers: 351.0 (18.8 to 1)
Librarians/Media Specialists: 7.0 (945.1 to 1)
Guidance Counselors: 9.0 (735.1 to 1)
Current Spending: ($ per student per year):
 Total: $6,856; Instruction: $3,848; Support Services: $2,820
Enrollment, Drop-out Rates and Diploma Recipients by Race/Ethnicity

Category	Total	White	Black	Asian	AIAN	Hisp.
Enrollment (%)	100.0	95.1	1.6	1.3	0.5	1.5
Drop-out Rate (%)	n/a	n/a	n/a	n/a	n/a	n/a
H.S. Diplomas (#)	345	332	0	3	4	6

Southfield Public SD
24661 Lahser Rd • Southfield, MI 48034-3238
(248) 746-8550 • http://www.southfield.k12.mi.us/
Grade Span: PK-12; **Agency Type:** 1
Schools: 18
 12 Primary; 3 Middle; 3 High; 0 Other Level
 18 Regular; 0 Special Education; 0 Vocational; 0 Alternative
 2 Magnet; 0 Charter; 13 Title I Eligible; 13 School-wide Title I
Students: 10,300   (50.5% male; 49.4% female)
 Individual Education Program: 1,197 (11.6%);
 English Language Learner: 549 (5.3%); Migrant: n/a
 Eligible for Free Lunch Program: 2,613 (25.4%)
 Eligible for Reduced-Price Lunch Program: 937 (9.1%)
Teachers: 615.0 (16.7 to 1)
Librarians/Media Specialists: 17.0 (605.9 to 1)
Guidance Counselors: 20.0 (515.0 to 1)
Current Spending: ($ per student per year):
 Total: $11,444; Instruction: $6,679; Support Services: $4,535
Enrollment, Drop-out Rates and Diploma Recipients by Race/Ethnicity

Category	Total	White	Black	Asian	AIAN	Hisp.
Enrollment (%)	100.0	7.4	88.9	1.5	0.1	0.4
Drop-out Rate (%)	n/a	n/a	n/a	n/a	n/a	n/a
H.S. Diplomas (#)	534	61	457	9	0	7

Troy SD
4400 Livernois Rd • Troy, MI 48098-4777
(248) 823-4000 • http://www.troy.k12.mi.us/
Grade Span: PK-12; **Agency Type:** 1
Schools: 19
 12 Primary; 4 Middle; 2 High; 1 Other Level
 18 Regular; 0 Special Education; 0 Vocational; 1 Alternative
 0 Magnet; 0 Charter; 0 Title I Eligible; 0 School-wide Title I
Students: 12,093   (52.0% male; 47.9% female)
 Individual Education Program: 951 (7.9%);
 English Language Learner: 1,806 (14.9%); Migrant: n/a
 Eligible for Free Lunch Program: 327 (2.7%)
 Eligible for Reduced-Price Lunch Program: 104 (0.9%)
Teachers: 727.0 (16.6 to 1)
Librarians/Media Specialists: 20.0 (602.0 to 1)
Guidance Counselors: 23.0 (523.4 to 1)
Current Spending: ($ per student per year):
 Total: $9,818; Instruction: $6,055; Support Services: $3,532
Enrollment, Drop-out Rates and Diploma Recipients by Race/Ethnicity

Category	Total	White	Black	Asian	AIAN	Hisp.
Enrollment (%)	100.0	75.0	3.5	19.5	0.3	1.5
Drop-out Rate (%)	n/a	n/a	n/a	n/a	n/a	n/a
H.S. Diplomas (#)	967	767	32	161	2	5

Walled Lake Consolidated Schools
850 Ladd Rd Building D • Walled Lake, MI 48390-3019
(248) 956-2000 • http://www.walledlake.k12.mi.us/
Grade Span: PK-12; **Agency Type:** 1
Schools: 24
 14 Primary; 4 Middle; 3 High; 3 Other Level
 22 Regular; 1 Special Education; 0 Vocational; 1 Alternative

 0 Magnet; 0 Charter; 0 Title I Eligible; 0 School-wide Title I
Students: 15,205   (52.5% male; 47.4% female)
 Individual Education Program: 1,820 (12.0%);
 English Language Learner: 935 (6.1%); Migrant: 46 (0.3%)
 Eligible for Free Lunch Program: 967 (6.4%)
 Eligible for Reduced-Price Lunch Program: 376 (2.5%)
Teachers: 888.0 (17.1 to 1)
Librarians/Media Specialists: 4.0 (3,801.3 to 1)
Guidance Counselors: 39.0 (389.9 to 1)
Current Spending: ($ per student per year):
 Total: $9,196; Instruction: $5,210; Support Services: $3,792
Enrollment, Drop-out Rates and Diploma Recipients by Race/Ethnicity

Category	Total	White	Black	Asian	AIAN	Hisp.
Enrollment (%)	100.0	89.2	3.4	5.2	0.5	1.7
Drop-out Rate (%)	n/a	n/a	n/a	n/a	n/a	n/a
H.S. Diplomas (#)	811	761	16	16	9	9

Waterford SD
6020 Pontiac Lake Rd • Waterford, MI 48327-1847
(248) 666-2222 • http://www.waterford.k12.mi.us/
Grade Span: PK-12; **Agency Type:** 1
Schools: 25
 15 Primary; 4 Middle; 2 High; 4 Other Level
 22 Regular; 2 Special Education; 0 Vocational; 1 Alternative
 0 Magnet; 0 Charter; 0 Title I Eligible; 0 School-wide Title I
Students: 12,264   (52.0% male; 47.9% female)
 Individual Education Program: 1,854 (15.1%);
 English Language Learner: 416 (3.4%); Migrant: n/a
 Eligible for Free Lunch Program: 1,972 (16.1%)
 Eligible for Reduced-Price Lunch Program: 714 (5.8%)
Teachers: 537.0 (22.8 to 1)
Librarians/Media Specialists: 5.0 (2,452.8 to 1)
Guidance Counselors: 17.0 (721.4 to 1)
Current Spending: ($ per student per year):
 Total: $8,476; Instruction: $4,825; Support Services: $3,352
Enrollment, Drop-out Rates and Diploma Recipients by Race/Ethnicity

Category	Total	White	Black	Asian	AIAN	Hisp.
Enrollment (%)	100.0	87.4	4.4	2.6	0.3	5.3
Drop-out Rate (%)	n/a	n/a	n/a	n/a	n/a	n/a
H.S. Diplomas (#)	555	513	17	13	0	12

West Bloomfield SD
5810 Commerce Rd • West Bloomfield, MI 48324-3200
(248) 865-6420 • http://www.westbloomfield.k12.mi.us/
Grade Span: PK-12; **Agency Type:** 1
Schools: 11
 6 Primary; 2 Middle; 2 High; 1 Other Level
 10 Regular; 0 Special Education; 0 Vocational; 1 Alternative
 1 Magnet; 0 Charter; 0 Title I Eligible; 0 School-wide Title I
Students: 7,235   (52.5% male; 47.4% female)
 Individual Education Program: 791 (10.9%);
 English Language Learner: 474 (6.6%); Migrant: n/a
 Eligible for Free Lunch Program: 423 (5.8%)
 Eligible for Reduced-Price Lunch Program: 216 (3.0%)
Teachers: 409.0 (17.7 to 1)
Librarians/Media Specialists: 5.0 (1,447.0 to 1)
Guidance Counselors: 12.0 (602.9 to 1)
Current Spending: ($ per student per year):
 Total: $9,187; Instruction: $5,532; Support Services: $3,413
Enrollment, Drop-out Rates and Diploma Recipients by Race/Ethnicity

Category	Total	White	Black	Asian	AIAN	Hisp.
Enrollment (%)	100.0	73.4	14.7	10.1	0.4	1.4
Drop-out Rate (%)	n/a	n/a	n/a	n/a	n/a	n/a
H.S. Diplomas (#)	418	340	34	43	1	0

Oceana County

Shelby Public Schools
525 N State St • Shelby, MI 49455-8201
(231) 861-5211 • http://hs.shelby.k12.mi.us/main/
Grade Span: PK-12; **Agency Type:** 1
Schools: 7
 4 Primary; 1 Middle; 2 High; 0 Other Level
 6 Regular; 0 Special Education; 0 Vocational; 1 Alternative
 0 Magnet; 0 Charter; 3 Title I Eligible; 3 School-wide Title I
Students: 1,963   (52.6% male; 47.3% female)
 Individual Education Program: 256 (13.0%);
 English Language Learner: 231 (11.8%); Migrant: 191 (9.9%)
 Eligible for Free Lunch Program: 788 (40.7%)
 Eligible for Reduced-Price Lunch Program: 216 (11.2%)
Teachers: 108.0 (17.9 to 1)
Librarians/Media Specialists: 1.0 (1,936.0 to 1)
Guidance Counselors: 3.0 (645.3 to 1)
Current Spending: ($ per student per year):
 Total: $6,869; Instruction: $4,431; Support Services: $2,210

Enrollment, Drop-out Rates and Diploma Recipients by Race/Ethnicity

Category	Total	White	Black	Asian	AIAN	Hisp.
Enrollment (%)	100.0	72.9	0.5	2.0	0.5	24.1
Drop-out Rate (%)	n/a	n/a	n/a	n/a	n/a	n/a
H.S. Diplomas (#)	91	80	0	2	0	9

Ogemaw County

West Branch-Rose City Area Schools
836 S M-33 • West Branch, MI 48661-9079
Mailing Address: PO Box 308 • West Branch, MI 48661-0308
(989) 343-2000 • http://www.westbranch.com/wb_rcschool.htm
Grade Span: PK-12; **Agency Type:** 1
Schools: 5
   2 Primary; 2 Middle; 1 High; 0 Other Level
   5 Regular; 0 Special Education; 0 Vocational; 0 Alternative
   0 Magnet; 0 Charter; 4 Title I Eligible; 4 School-wide Title I
Students: 2,663 (51.7% male; 48.2% female)
   Individual Education Program: 400 (15.0%);
   English Language Learner: 0 (0.0%); Migrant: n/a
   Eligible for Free Lunch Program: 921 (34.6%)
   Eligible for Reduced-Price Lunch Program: 280 (10.5%)
Teachers: 158.0 (16.9 to 1)
Librarians/Media Specialists: 3.0 (887.7 to 1)
Guidance Counselors: 6.0 (443.8 to 1)
Current Spending: ($ per student per year):
   Total: $7,836; Instruction: $4,842; Support Services: $2,644
Enrollment, Drop-out Rates and Diploma Recipients by Race/Ethnicity

Category	Total	White	Black	Asian	AIAN	Hisp.
Enrollment (%)	100.0	97.6	0.4	0.9	0.5	0.6
Drop-out Rate (%)	n/a	n/a	n/a	n/a	n/a	n/a
H.S. Diplomas (#)	181	173	0	2	2	4

Osceola County

Reed City Area Public Schools
829 S Chestnut St • Reed City, MI 49677-1384
(231) 832-2201 • http://www.reedcity.k12.mi.us/
Grade Span: KG-12; **Agency Type:** 1
Schools: 6
   2 Primary; 2 Middle; 1 High; 1 Other Level
   5 Regular; 0 Special Education; 0 Vocational; 1 Alternative
   0 Magnet; 0 Charter; 0 Title I Eligible; 0 School-wide Title I
Students: 1,981 (50.4% male; 49.5% female)
   Individual Education Program: 290 (14.6%);
   English Language Learner: 0 (0.0%); Migrant: n/a
   Eligible for Free Lunch Program: 571 (29.3%)
   Eligible for Reduced-Price Lunch Program: 212 (10.9%)
Teachers: 113.0 (17.3 to 1)
Librarians/Media Specialists: 3.0 (650.0 to 1)
Guidance Counselors: 3.0 (650.0 to 1)
Current Spending: ($ per student per year):
   Total: $6,817; Instruction: $4,237; Support Services: $2,303
Enrollment, Drop-out Rates and Diploma Recipients by Race/Ethnicity

Category	Total	White	Black	Asian	AIAN	Hisp.
Enrollment (%)	100.0	95.8	2.7	0.1	0.8	0.6
Drop-out Rate (%)	n/a	n/a	n/a	n/a	n/a	n/a
H.S. Diplomas (#)	145	137	3	4	0	1

Otsego County

Gaylord Community Schools
615 S Elm St • Gaylord, MI 49735-1253
(989) 705-3080 • http://www.gaylordschools.com/
Grade Span: KG-12; **Agency Type:** 1
Schools: 7
   3 Primary; 2 Middle; 1 High; 1 Other Level
   6 Regular; 0 Special Education; 0 Vocational; 1 Alternative
   6 Magnet; 0 Charter; 0 Title I Eligible; 0 School-wide Title I
Students: 3,497 (50.2% male; 49.7% female)
   Individual Education Program: 432 (12.4%);
   English Language Learner: 0 (0.0%); Migrant: n/a
   Eligible for Free Lunch Program: 922 (26.4%)
   Eligible for Reduced-Price Lunch Program: 302 (8.6%)
Teachers: 188.0 (18.6 to 1)
Librarians/Media Specialists: 3.0 (1,165.7 to 1)
Guidance Counselors: 6.0 (582.8 to 1)
Current Spending: ($ per student per year):
   Total: $7,498; Instruction: $4,930; Support Services: $2,276
Enrollment, Drop-out Rates and Diploma Recipients by Race/Ethnicity

Category	Total	White	Black	Asian	AIAN	Hisp.
Enrollment (%)	100.0	97.3	0.3	0.5	1.0	0.9
Drop-out Rate (%)	n/a	n/a	n/a	n/a	n/a	n/a
H.S. Diplomas (#)	206	202	0	0	3	1

Ottawa County

Allendale Public SD
6561 Lake Michigan Dr • Allendale, MI 49401-9574
Mailing Address: PO Box 30 • Allendale, MI 49401-0030
(616) 892-5570 • http://www.allendale.k12.mi.us/
Grade Span: PK-12; **Agency Type:** 1
Schools: 5
   2 Primary; 1 Middle; 1 High; 1 Other Level
   4 Regular; 0 Special Education; 0 Vocational; 1 Alternative
   0 Magnet; 0 Charter; 0 Title I Eligible; 0 School-wide Title I
Students: 2,035 (51.1% male; 48.8% female)
   Individual Education Program: 240 (11.8%);
   English Language Learner: 42 (2.1%); Migrant: n/a
   Eligible for Free Lunch Program: 306 (15.0%)
   Eligible for Reduced-Price Lunch Program: 143 (7.0%)
Teachers: 120.0 (17.0 to 1)
Librarians/Media Specialists: 2.0 (1,017.5 to 1)
Guidance Counselors: 1.0 (2,035.0 to 1)
Current Spending: ($ per student per year):
   Total: $7,208; Instruction: $4,520; Support Services: $2,461
Enrollment, Drop-out Rates and Diploma Recipients by Race/Ethnicity

Category	Total	White	Black	Asian	AIAN	Hisp.
Enrollment (%)	100.0	92.2	1.6	1.2	0.4	4.6
Drop-out Rate (%)	n/a	n/a	n/a	n/a	n/a	n/a
H.S. Diplomas (#)	110	101	1	6	0	2

Coopersville Public SD
198 E St • Coopersville, MI 49404-1211
(616) 997-3200 • http://www.coopersvillebroncos.org/
Grade Span: PK-12; **Agency Type:** 1
Schools: 4
   2 Primary; 1 Middle; 1 High; 0 Other Level
   4 Regular; 0 Special Education; 0 Vocational; 0 Alternative
   0 Magnet; 0 Charter; 0 Title I Eligible; 0 School-wide Title I
Students: 2,374 (51.6% male; 48.3% female)
   Individual Education Program: 288 (12.1%);
   English Language Learner: 0 (0.0%); Migrant: 82 (3.5%)
   Eligible for Free Lunch Program: 392 (16.6%)
   Eligible for Reduced-Price Lunch Program: 159 (6.7%)
Teachers: 115.0 (20.5 to 1)
Librarians/Media Specialists: 0.0 (n/a to 1)
Guidance Counselors: 1.0 (2,363.0 to 1)
Current Spending: ($ per student per year):
   Total: $7,480; Instruction: $4,686; Support Services: $2,572
Enrollment, Drop-out Rates and Diploma Recipients by Race/Ethnicity

Category	Total	White	Black	Asian	AIAN	Hisp.
Enrollment (%)	100.0	94.0	0.4	0.7	0.2	4.6
Drop-out Rate (%)	n/a	n/a	n/a	n/a	n/a	n/a
H.S. Diplomas (#)	156	153	0	2	0	1

Grand Haven Area Public Schools
1415 S Beechtree St • Grand Haven, MI 49417-2843
(616) 850-5015 • http://www.ghaps.org/
Grade Span: PK-12; **Agency Type:** 1
Schools: 12
   8 Primary; 2 Middle; 2 High; 0 Other Level
   11 Regular; 0 Special Education; 0 Vocational; 1 Alternative
   0 Magnet; 0 Charter; 1 Title I Eligible; 1 School-wide Title I
Students: 6,095 (52.9% male; 47.0% female)
   Individual Education Program: 638 (10.5%);
   English Language Learner: 0 (0.0%); Migrant: 111 (1.8%)
   Eligible for Free Lunch Program: 736 (12.1%)
   Eligible for Reduced-Price Lunch Program: 396 (6.5%)
Teachers: 316.0 (19.3 to 1)
Librarians/Media Specialists: 8.0 (761.9 to 1)
Guidance Counselors: 14.0 (435.4 to 1)
Current Spending: ($ per student per year):
   Total: $7,832; Instruction: $4,678; Support Services: $2,911
Enrollment, Drop-out Rates and Diploma Recipients by Race/Ethnicity

Category	Total	White	Black	Asian	AIAN	Hisp.
Enrollment (%)	100.0	93.1	0.8	1.3	0.7	3.3
Drop-out Rate (%)	n/a	n/a	n/a	n/a	n/a	n/a
H.S. Diplomas (#)	446	429	2	8	3	4

Holland City SD
372 S River Ave • Holland, MI 49423-3356
(616) 494-2000 • http://www.holland.k12.mi.us/
Grade Span: PK-12; **Agency Type:** 1
Schools: 11
   5 Primary; 4 Middle; 1 High; 1 Other Level
   10 Regular; 0 Special Education; 0 Vocational; 1 Alternative
   0 Magnet; 0 Charter; 0 Title I Eligible; 0 School-wide Title I
Students: 5,340 (51.9% male; 48.0% female)
   Individual Education Program: 765 (14.3%);

English Language Learner: 1,140 (21.3%); Migrant: 42 (0.8%)
Eligible for Free Lunch Program: 1,747 (32.7%)
Eligible for Reduced-Price Lunch Program: 384 (7.2%)
Teachers: 312.0 (17.1 to 1)
Librarians/Media Specialists: 7.0 (762.9 to 1)
Guidance Counselors: 8.0 (667.5 to 1)
Current Spending: ($ per student per year):
Total: $8,296; Instruction: $5,147; Support Services: $2,890
Enrollment, Drop-out Rates and Diploma Recipients by Race/Ethnicity

Category	Total	White	Black	Asian	AIAN	Hisp.
Enrollment (%)	100.0	51.9	5.4	5.4	0.5	36.9
Drop-out Rate (%)	n/a	n/a	n/a	n/a	n/a	n/a
H.S. Diplomas (#)	292	195	9	14	1	73

Hudsonville Public SD
3886 Van Buren St • Hudsonville, MI 49426-1038
(616) 669-1740 • http://www.hudsonville.k12.mi.us
Grade Span: KG-12; **Agency Type:** 1
Schools: 10
6 Primary; 2 Middle; 1 High; 1 Other Level
10 Regular; 0 Special Education; 0 Vocational; 0 Alternative
0 Magnet; 0 Charter; 5 Title I Eligible; 5 School-wide Title I
Students: 4,877 (51.0% male; 48.9% female)
Individual Education Program: 615 (12.6%);
English Language Learner: 5 (0.1%); Migrant: n/a
Eligible for Free Lunch Program: 326 (6.7%)
Eligible for Reduced-Price Lunch Program: 250 (5.1%)
Teachers: 271.0 (18.0 to 1)
Librarians/Media Specialists: 3.0 (1,625.7 to 1)
Guidance Counselors: 11.0 (443.4 to 1)
Current Spending: ($ per student per year):
Total: $7,038; Instruction: $4,474; Support Services: $2,565
Enrollment, Drop-out Rates and Diploma Recipients by Race/Ethnicity

Category	Total	White	Black	Asian	AIAN	Hisp.
Enrollment (%)	100.0	95.4	1.0	1.3	0.3	1.9
Drop-out Rate (%)	n/a	n/a	n/a	n/a	n/a	n/a
H.S. Diplomas (#)	260	253	2	3	0	2

Jenison Public Schools
8375 20th Ave • Jenison, MI 49428-9230
(616) 457-8890 • http://www.remc7.k12.mi.us/jps/
Grade Span: PK-12; **Agency Type:** 1
Schools: 8
6 Primary; 1 Middle; 1 High; 0 Other Level
8 Regular; 0 Special Education; 0 Vocational; 0 Alternative
0 Magnet; 0 Charter; 8 Title I Eligible; 8 School-wide Title I
Students: 4,787 (51.8% male; 48.1% female)
Individual Education Program: 821 (17.2%);
English Language Learner: 29 (0.6%); Migrant: n/a
Eligible for Free Lunch Program: 284 (5.9%)
Eligible for Reduced-Price Lunch Program: 235 (4.9%)
Teachers: 268.0 (17.9 to 1)
Librarians/Media Specialists: 7.0 (683.9 to 1)
Guidance Counselors: 9.0 (531.9 to 1)
Current Spending: ($ per student per year):
Total: $7,879; Instruction: $5,124; Support Services: $2,373
Enrollment, Drop-out Rates and Diploma Recipients by Race/Ethnicity

Category	Total	White	Black	Asian	AIAN	Hisp.
Enrollment (%)	100.0	92.9	1.3	1.9	0.8	3.1
Drop-out Rate (%)	n/a	n/a	n/a	n/a	n/a	n/a
H.S. Diplomas (#)	357	343	3	6	0	5

Spring Lake Public Schools
345 Hammond St • Spring Lake, MI 49456-2064
(616) 847-7919 • http://www.spring-lake.k12.mi.us
Grade Span: PK-12; **Agency Type:** 1
Schools: 6
2 Primary; 2 Middle; 2 High; 0 Other Level
5 Regular; 0 Special Education; 0 Vocational; 1 Alternative
0 Magnet; 0 Charter; 0 Title I Eligible; 0 School-wide Title I
Students: 2,237 (53.2% male; 46.7% female)
Individual Education Program: 262 (11.7%);
English Language Learner: 3 (0.1%); Migrant: n/a
Eligible for Free Lunch Program: 228 (10.2%)
Eligible for Reduced-Price Lunch Program: 138 (6.2%)
Teachers: 120.0 (18.6 to 1)
Librarians/Media Specialists: 1.0 (2,237.0 to 1)
Guidance Counselors: 4.0 (559.3 to 1)
Current Spending: ($ per student per year):
Total: $7,693; Instruction: $4,832; Support Services: $2,602
Enrollment, Drop-out Rates and Diploma Recipients by Race/Ethnicity

Category	Total	White	Black	Asian	AIAN	Hisp.
Enrollment (%)	100.0	97.1	0.6	0.7	0.1	0.8
Drop-out Rate (%)	n/a	n/a	n/a	n/a	n/a	n/a
H.S. Diplomas (#)	144	142	0	2	0	0

West Ottawa Public SD
1138 136th Ave • Holland, MI 49424-8418
(616) 738-5795 • http://www.westottawa.k12.mi.us/
Grade Span: PK-12; **Agency Type:** 1
Schools: 13
9 Primary; 1 Middle; 1 High; 2 Other Level
12 Regular; 0 Special Education; 0 Vocational; 1 Alternative
0 Magnet; 0 Charter; 0 Title I Eligible; 0 School-wide Title I
Students: 7,999 (51.4% male; 48.5% female)
Individual Education Program: 987 (12.3%);
English Language Learner: 999 (12.5%); Migrant: n/a
Eligible for Free Lunch Program: 1,896 (23.7%)
Eligible for Reduced-Price Lunch Program: 519 (6.5%)
Teachers: 403.0 (19.8 to 1)
Librarians/Media Specialists: 9.0 (888.8 to 1)
Guidance Counselors: 12.0 (666.6 to 1)
Current Spending: ($ per student per year):
Total: $7,690; Instruction: $4,777; Support Services: $2,606
Enrollment, Drop-out Rates and Diploma Recipients by Race/Ethnicity

Category	Total	White	Black	Asian	AIAN	Hisp.
Enrollment (%)	100.0	62.6	3.5	9.1	0.3	20.7
Drop-out Rate (%)	n/a	n/a	n/a	n/a	n/a	n/a
H.S. Diplomas (#)	416	328	8	39	3	38

Zeeland Public Schools
183 W Roosevelt • Zeeland, MI 49464-1155
Mailing Address: PO Box 110 • Zeeland, MI 49464-0110
(616) 748-3000 • http://www.zeeland.k12.mi.us/
Grade Span: PK-12; **Agency Type:** 1
Schools: 11
5 Primary; 2 Middle; 3 High; 0 Other Level
9 Regular; 0 Special Education; 0 Vocational; 1 Alternative
0 Magnet; 0 Charter; 1 Title I Eligible; 1 School-wide Title I
Students: 5,008 (51.0% male; 48.9% female)
Individual Education Program: 529 (10.6%);
English Language Learner: 111 (2.2%); Migrant: n/a
Eligible for Free Lunch Program: 411 (8.3%)
Eligible for Reduced-Price Lunch Program: 254 (5.1%)
Teachers: 274.0 (18.1 to 1)
Librarians/Media Specialists: 5.0 (992.2 to 1)
Guidance Counselors: 6.0 (826.8 to 1)
Current Spending: ($ per student per year):
Total: $7,069; Instruction: $4,367; Support Services: $2,428
Enrollment, Drop-out Rates and Diploma Recipients by Race/Ethnicity

Category	Total	White	Black	Asian	AIAN	Hisp.
Enrollment (%)	100.0	86.2	1.2	4.3	0.2	8.0
Drop-out Rate (%)	n/a	n/a	n/a	n/a	n/a	n/a
H.S. Diplomas (#)	286	261	0	8	0	17

Roscommon County

Gerrish-Higgins SD
702 Lake St • Roscommon, MI 48653-8653
Mailing Address: PO Box 825 • Roscommon, MI 48653-0825
(989) 275-6600 • http://www.ghsd.k12.mi.us/
Grade Span: KG-12; **Agency Type:** 1
Schools: 5
2 Primary; 1 Middle; 1 High; 1 Other Level
4 Regular; 0 Special Education; 0 Vocational; 1 Alternative
0 Magnet; 0 Charter; 0 Title I Eligible; 0 School-wide Title I
Students: 1,841 (53.3% male; 46.6% female)
Individual Education Program: 259 (14.1%);
English Language Learner: 0 (0.0%); Migrant: n/a
Eligible for Free Lunch Program: 720 (39.1%)
Eligible for Reduced-Price Lunch Program: 173 (9.4%)
Teachers: 93.0 (19.8 to 1)
Librarians/Media Specialists: 1.0 (1,841.0 to 1)
Guidance Counselors: 3.0 (613.7 to 1)
Current Spending: ($ per student per year):
Total: $7,338; Instruction: $4,648; Support Services: $2,331
Enrollment, Drop-out Rates and Diploma Recipients by Race/Ethnicity

Category	Total	White	Black	Asian	AIAN	Hisp.
Enrollment (%)	100.0	97.3	1.1	0.7	0.5	0.4
Drop-out Rate (%)	n/a	n/a	n/a	n/a	n/a	n/a
H.S. Diplomas (#)	102	102	0	0	0	0

Houghton Lake Community Schools
6001 W Houghton Lake Dr • Houghton Lake, MI 48629-9704
(989) 366-2000 • http://www.hlcs.k12.mi.us
Grade Span: PK-12; **Agency Type:** 1
Schools: 7
3 Primary; 1 Middle; 1 High; 2 Other Level
5 Regular; 0 Special Education; 0 Vocational; 2 Alternative
0 Magnet; 0 Charter; 4 Title I Eligible; 4 School-wide Title I
Students: 2,128 (52.2% male; 47.7% female)

Individual Education Program: 310 (14.6%);
English Language Learner: 0 (0.0%); Migrant: n/a
Eligible for Free Lunch Program: 873 (41.0%)
Eligible for Reduced-Price Lunch Program: 171 (8.0%)
Teachers: 134.0 (15.9 to 1)
Librarians/Media Specialists: 1.0 (2,128.0 to 1)
Guidance Counselors: 5.0 (425.6 to 1)
Current Spending: ($ per student per year):
Total: $7,963; Instruction: $5,193; Support Services: $2,484
Enrollment, Drop-out Rates and Diploma Recipients by Race/Ethnicity

Category	Total	White	Black	Asian	AIAN	Hisp.
Enrollment (%)	100.0	96.5	1.3	0.4	0.9	0.8
Drop-out Rate (%)	n/a	n/a	n/a	n/a	n/a	n/a
H.S. Diplomas (#)	121	120	0	1	0	0

Saginaw County

Birch Run Area SD
12400 Church St • Birch Run, MI 48415-8759
(989) 624-9307 • http://www.birchrun.k12.mi.us/
Grade Span: PK-12; **Agency Type:** 1
Schools: 4
2 Primary; 1 Middle; 1 High; 0 Other Level
4 Regular; 0 Special Education; 0 Vocational; 0 Alternative
0 Magnet; 0 Charter; 0 Title I Eligible; 0 School-wide Title I
Students: 1,898   (52.2% male; 47.7% female)
Individual Education Program: 209 (11.0%);
English Language Learner: 2 (0.1%); Migrant: n/a
Eligible for Free Lunch Program: 371 (19.5%)
Eligible for Reduced-Price Lunch Program: 146 (7.7%)
Teachers: 101.0 (18.8 to 1)
Librarians/Media Specialists: 3.0 (632.7 to 1)
Guidance Counselors: 2.0 (949.0 to 1)
Current Spending: ($ per student per year):
Total: $6,920; Instruction: $4,047; Support Services: $2,612
Enrollment, Drop-out Rates and Diploma Recipients by Race/Ethnicity

Category	Total	White	Black	Asian	AIAN	Hisp.
Enrollment (%)	100.0	95.2	0.7	0.7	0.5	2.9
Drop-out Rate (%)	n/a	n/a	n/a	n/a	n/a	n/a
H.S. Diplomas (#)	112	106	2	2	2	0

Bridgeport-Spaulding Community SD
3878 Sherman St • Bridgeport, MI 48722-0657
Mailing Address: PO Box 657 • Bridgeport, MI 48722-0657
(989) 777-1770 • http://www.bscs.k12.mi.us/
Grade Span: KG-12; **Agency Type:** 1
Schools: 7
4 Primary; 1 Middle; 2 High; 0 Other Level
6 Regular; 0 Special Education; 0 Vocational; 1 Alternative
0 Magnet; 0 Charter; 1 Title I Eligible; 1 School-wide Title I
Students: 2,349   (50.7% male; 49.2% female)
Individual Education Program: 392 (16.7%);
English Language Learner: 0 (0.0%); Migrant: 70 (3.0%)
Eligible for Free Lunch Program: 1,161 (49.4%)
Eligible for Reduced-Price Lunch Program: 225 (9.6%)
Teachers: 149.0 (15.8 to 1)
Librarians/Media Specialists: 1.0 (2,349.0 to 1)
Guidance Counselors: 4.0 (587.3 to 1)
Current Spending: ($ per student per year):
Total: $7,923; Instruction: $4,603; Support Services: $3,019
Enrollment, Drop-out Rates and Diploma Recipients by Race/Ethnicity

Category	Total	White	Black	Asian	AIAN	Hisp.
Enrollment (%)	100.0	50.9	31.9	0.8	1.1	15.3
Drop-out Rate (%)	n/a	n/a	n/a	n/a	n/a	n/a
H.S. Diplomas (#)	118	61	41	4	0	12

Carrollton SD
3211 Carla • Saginaw, MI 48604-1750
Mailing Address: PO Box 517 • Carrollton, MI 48724-0517
(989) 754-1475
Grade Span: KG-12; **Agency Type:** 1
Schools: 4
1 Primary; 1 Middle; 1 High; 1 Other Level
3 Regular; 1 Special Education; 0 Vocational; 0 Alternative
0 Magnet; 0 Charter; 2 Title I Eligible; 2 School-wide Title I
Students: 1,517   (52.0% male; 47.9% female)
Individual Education Program: 240 (15.8%);
English Language Learner: 0 (0.0%); Migrant: n/a
Eligible for Free Lunch Program: 479 (32.6%)
Eligible for Reduced-Price Lunch Program: 159 (10.8%)
Teachers: 95.0 (15.5 to 1)
Librarians/Media Specialists: 1.0 (1,471.0 to 1)
Guidance Counselors: 3.0 (490.3 to 1)
Current Spending: ($ per student per year):
Total: $7,604; Instruction: $4,813; Support Services: $2,501

Enrollment, Drop-out Rates and Diploma Recipients by Race/Ethnicity

Category	Total	White	Black	Asian	AIAN	Hisp.
Enrollment (%)	100.0	64.2	17.7	6.1	0.7	11.2
Drop-out Rate (%)	n/a	n/a	n/a	n/a	n/a	n/a
H.S. Diplomas (#)	80	67	7	0	0	6

Chesaning Union Schools
850 N 4th St • Chesaning, MI 48616-1056
(989) 845-7020 • http://www.chesaning.k12.mi.us/
Grade Span: PK-12; **Agency Type:** 1
Schools: 5
3 Primary; 1 Middle; 1 High; 0 Other Level
5 Regular; 0 Special Education; 0 Vocational; 0 Alternative
0 Magnet; 0 Charter; 3 Title I Eligible; 3 School-wide Title I
Students: 2,056   (50.6% male; 49.3% female)
Individual Education Program: 348 (16.9%);
English Language Learner: 0 (0.0%); Migrant: n/a
Eligible for Free Lunch Program: 421 (20.5%)
Eligible for Reduced-Price Lunch Program: 169 (8.2%)
Teachers: 113.0 (18.2 to 1)
Librarians/Media Specialists: 0.0 (n/a to 1)
Guidance Counselors: 4.0 (514.0 to 1)
Current Spending: ($ per student per year):
Total: $7,610; Instruction: $4,977; Support Services: $2,389
Enrollment, Drop-out Rates and Diploma Recipients by Race/Ethnicity

Category	Total	White	Black	Asian	AIAN	Hisp.
Enrollment (%)	100.0	94.0	1.3	0.3	0.2	4.2
Drop-out Rate (%)	n/a	n/a	n/a	n/a	n/a	n/a
H.S. Diplomas (#)	139	133	0	2	0	4

Freeland Community SD
710 Powley Dr • Freeland, MI 48623-8106
(989) 695-5527 • http://www.freeland.k12.mi.us/
Grade Span: KG-12; **Agency Type:** 1
Schools: 3
2 Primary; 0 Middle; 1 High; 0 Other Level
3 Regular; 0 Special Education; 0 Vocational; 0 Alternative
0 Magnet; 0 Charter; 0 Title I Eligible; 0 School-wide Title I
Students: 1,696   (52.9% male; 47.0% female)
Individual Education Program: 191 (11.3%);
English Language Learner: 0 (0.0%); Migrant: n/a
Eligible for Free Lunch Program: 87 (5.1%)
Eligible for Reduced-Price Lunch Program: 37 (2.2%)
Teachers: 90.0 (18.8 to 1)
Librarians/Media Specialists: 2.0 (848.0 to 1)
Guidance Counselors: 2.0 (848.0 to 1)
Current Spending: ($ per student per year):
Total: $6,306; Instruction: $3,753; Support Services: $2,351
Enrollment, Drop-out Rates and Diploma Recipients by Race/Ethnicity

Category	Total	White	Black	Asian	AIAN	Hisp.
Enrollment (%)	100.0	95.1	1.5	1.2	0.1	2.0
Drop-out Rate (%)	n/a	n/a	n/a	n/a	n/a	n/a
H.S. Diplomas (#)	86	80	2	2	0	2

Saginaw City SD
550 Millard St • Saginaw, MI 48607-1140
(989) 399-6500 • http://www.saginaw-city.k12.mi.us/
Grade Span: PK-12; **Agency Type:** 1
Schools: 33
23 Primary; 3 Middle; 3 High; 4 Other Level
30 Regular; 2 Special Education; 1 Vocational; 0 Alternative
2 Magnet; 0 Charter; 14 Title I Eligible; 14 School-wide Title I
Students: 12,353   (50.7% male; 49.2% female)
Individual Education Program: 2,488 (20.1%);
English Language Learner: 698 (5.7%); Migrant: n/a
Eligible for Free Lunch Program: 8,335 (67.5%)
Eligible for Reduced-Price Lunch Program: 686 (5.6%)
Teachers: 811.0 (15.2 to 1)
Librarians/Media Specialists: 8.0 (1,544.1 to 1)
Guidance Counselors: 19.0 (650.2 to 1)
Current Spending: ($ per student per year):
Total: $8,423; Instruction: $4,876; Support Services: $3,251
Enrollment, Drop-out Rates and Diploma Recipients by Race/Ethnicity

Category	Total	White	Black	Asian	AIAN	Hisp.
Enrollment (%)	100.0	23.2	62.5	1.0	0.2	13.1
Drop-out Rate (%)	n/a	n/a	n/a	n/a	n/a	n/a
H.S. Diplomas (#)	462	153	254	7	3	45

Saginaw ISD
6235 Gratiot Rd • Saginaw, MI 48603-5987
(989) 249-8704
Grade Span: 07-12; **Agency Type:** 4
Schools: 4
0 Primary; 0 Middle; 1 High; 3 Other Level
0 Regular; 2 Special Education; 0 Vocational; 2 Alternative

0 Magnet; 0 Charter; 1 Title I Eligible; 1 School-wide Title I
Students: 2,511 (52.9% male; 47.0% female)
 Individual Education Program: 271 (10.8%);
 English Language Learner: 0 (0.0%); Migrant: n/a
 Eligible for Free Lunch Program: n/a
 Eligible for Reduced-Price Lunch Program: n/a
Teachers: 73.0 (34.4 to 1)
Librarians/Media Specialists: 0.0 (n/a to 1)
Guidance Counselors: 0.0 (n/a to 1)
Current Spending: ($ per student per year):
 Total: n/a; Instruction: n/a; Support Services: n/a
Enrollment, Drop-out Rates and Diploma Recipients by Race/Ethnicity

Category	Total	White	Black	Asian	AIAN	Hisp.
Enrollment (%)	100.0	58.2	31.7	1.3	0.3	8.6
Drop-out Rate (%)	n/a	n/a	n/a	n/a	n/a	n/a
H.S. Diplomas (#)	n/a	n/a	n/a	n/a	n/a	n/a

Saginaw Township Community Schools
3465 N Center Rd • Saginaw, MI 48603-1863
Mailing Address: PO Box 6278 • Saginaw, MI 48608-6278
(989) 797-1800 • http://www.saginaw-twp.k12.mi.us/
Grade Span: KG-12; **Agency Type:** 1
Schools: 9
 6 Primary; 1 Middle; 1 High; 1 Other Level
 8 Regular; 0 Special Education; 0 Vocational; 1 Alternative
 0 Magnet; 0 Charter; 0 Title I Eligible; 0 School-wide Title I
Students: 5,189 (50.2% male; 49.7% female)
 Individual Education Program: 711 (13.7%);
 English Language Learner: 0 (0.0%); Migrant: n/a
 Eligible for Free Lunch Program: 1,074 (20.7%)
 Eligible for Reduced-Price Lunch Program: 256 (4.9%)
Teachers: 282.0 (18.4 to 1)
Librarians/Media Specialists: 2.0 (2,594.5 to 1)
Guidance Counselors: 11.0 (471.7 to 1)
Current Spending: ($ per student per year):
 Total: $6,939; Instruction: $4,230; Support Services: $2,350
Enrollment, Drop-out Rates and Diploma Recipients by Race/Ethnicity

Category	Total	White	Black	Asian	AIAN	Hisp.
Enrollment (%)	100.0	76.5	12.1	3.0	0.7	7.7
Drop-out Rate (%)	n/a	n/a	n/a	n/a	n/a	n/a
H.S. Diplomas (#)	350	292	26	18	1	13

Swan Valley SD
8380 O'hern Rd • Saginaw, MI 48609-5118
(989) 921-3701 • http://www.swanvalley.k12.mi.us/
Grade Span: PK-12; **Agency Type:** 1
Schools: 4
 2 Primary; 1 Middle; 1 High; 0 Other Level
 4 Regular; 0 Special Education; 0 Vocational; 0 Alternative
 0 Magnet; 0 Charter; 0 Title I Eligible; 0 School-wide Title I
Students: 1,717 (49.5% male; 50.4% female)
 Individual Education Program: 273 (15.9%);
 English Language Learner: 0 (0.0%); Migrant: n/a
 Eligible for Free Lunch Program: 243 (14.2%)
 Eligible for Reduced-Price Lunch Program: 78 (4.5%)
Teachers: 94.0 (18.3 to 1)
Librarians/Media Specialists: 2.0 (858.5 to 1)
Guidance Counselors: 3.0 (572.3 to 1)
Current Spending: ($ per student per year):
 Total: $6,657; Instruction: $4,128; Support Services: $2,518
Enrollment, Drop-out Rates and Diploma Recipients by Race/Ethnicity

Category	Total	White	Black	Asian	AIAN	Hisp.
Enrollment (%)	100.0	92.9	2.6	1.3	0.2	3.0
Drop-out Rate (%)	n/a	n/a	n/a	n/a	n/a	n/a
H.S. Diplomas (#)	113	107	6	0	0	0

Sanilac County

Croswell-Lexington Community Schools
5407 E Peck Rd • Croswell, MI 48422-8317
(810) 679-1000 • http://www.cros-lex.k12.mi.us/
Grade Span: PK-12; **Agency Type:** 1
Schools: 5
 2 Primary; 2 Middle; 1 High; 0 Other Level
 5 Regular; 0 Special Education; 0 Vocational; 0 Alternative
 0 Magnet; 0 Charter; 0 Title I Eligible; 0 School-wide Title I
Students: 2,522 (53.0% male; 46.9% female)
 Individual Education Program: 297 (11.8%);
 English Language Learner: 0 (0.0%); Migrant: n/a
 Eligible for Free Lunch Program: 539 (21.4%)
 Eligible for Reduced-Price Lunch Program: 216 (8.6%)
Teachers: 136.0 (18.5 to 1)
Librarians/Media Specialists: 2.0 (1,261.0 to 1)
Guidance Counselors: 5.0 (504.4 to 1)
Current Spending: ($ per student per year):
 Total: $6,733; Instruction: $4,001; Support Services: $2,459

Enrollment, Drop-out Rates and Diploma Recipients by Race/Ethnicity

Category	Total	White	Black	Asian	AIAN	Hisp.
Enrollment (%)	100.0	96.2	0.2	0.2	0.1	3.3
Drop-out Rate (%)	n/a	n/a	n/a	n/a	n/a	n/a
H.S. Diplomas (#)	158	152	0	0	1	5

Shiawassee County

Corunna Public SD
106 S Shiawassee St • Corunna, MI 48817-1359
(989) 743-6338 • http://corunna.k12.mi.us
Grade Span: PK-12; **Agency Type:** 1
Schools: 6
 4 Primary; 1 Middle; 1 High; 0 Other Level
 6 Regular; 0 Special Education; 0 Vocational; 0 Alternative
 0 Magnet; 0 Charter; 0 Title I Eligible; 0 School-wide Title I
Students: 2,317 (51.5% male; 48.4% female)
 Individual Education Program: 251 (10.8%);
 English Language Learner: 0 (0.0%); Migrant: n/a
 Eligible for Free Lunch Program: 406 (17.5%)
 Eligible for Reduced-Price Lunch Program: 180 (7.8%)
Teachers: 115.0 (20.1 to 1)
Librarians/Media Specialists: 2.0 (1,158.5 to 1)
Guidance Counselors: 3.0 (772.3 to 1)
Current Spending: ($ per student per year):
 Total: $6,932; Instruction: $4,203; Support Services: $2,417
Enrollment, Drop-out Rates and Diploma Recipients by Race/Ethnicity

Category	Total	White	Black	Asian	AIAN	Hisp.
Enrollment (%)	100.0	96.8	0.5	0.4	0.9	1.3
Drop-out Rate (%)	n/a	n/a	n/a	n/a	n/a	n/a
H.S. Diplomas (#)	144	142	0	1	0	1

Durand Area Schools
310 N Saginaw St • Durand, MI 48429-1237
(989) 288-2681 • http://scnc.durand.k12.mi.us/
Grade Span: PK-12; **Agency Type:** 1
Schools: 6
 4 Primary; 1 Middle; 1 High; 0 Other Level
 6 Regular; 0 Special Education; 0 Vocational; 0 Alternative
 0 Magnet; 0 Charter; 0 Title I Eligible; 0 School-wide Title I
Students: 2,061 (50.7% male; 49.2% female)
 Individual Education Program: 247 (12.0%);
 English Language Learner: 0 (0.0%); Migrant: n/a
 Eligible for Free Lunch Program: 412 (20.0%)
 Eligible for Reduced-Price Lunch Program: 189 (9.2%)
Teachers: 106.0 (19.4 to 1)
Librarians/Media Specialists: 1.0 (2,061.0 to 1)
Guidance Counselors: 3.0 (687.0 to 1)
Current Spending: ($ per student per year):
 Total: $6,979; Instruction: $4,632; Support Services: $2,080
Enrollment, Drop-out Rates and Diploma Recipients by Race/Ethnicity

Category	Total	White	Black	Asian	AIAN	Hisp.
Enrollment (%)	100.0	97.8	0.4	0.6	0.2	0.9
Drop-out Rate (%)	n/a	n/a	n/a	n/a	n/a	n/a
H.S. Diplomas (#)	100	98	1	0	0	1

Owosso Public Schools
1405 W N St • Owosso, MI 48867-1445
Mailing Address: PO Box 340 • Owosso, MI 48867-0340
(989) 723-8131 • http://www.owosso.k12.mi.us/
Grade Span: PK-12; **Agency Type:** 1
Schools: 8
 6 Primary; 1 Middle; 1 High; 0 Other Level
 8 Regular; 0 Special Education; 0 Vocational; 0 Alternative
 0 Magnet; 0 Charter; 0 Title I Eligible; 0 School-wide Title I
Students: 4,132 (53.1% male; 46.8% female)
 Individual Education Program: 570 (13.8%);
 English Language Learner: 0 (0.0%); Migrant: n/a
 Eligible for Free Lunch Program: 1,100 (26.6%)
 Eligible for Reduced-Price Lunch Program: 312 (7.6%)
Teachers: 227.0 (18.2 to 1)
Librarians/Media Specialists: 4.0 (1,033.0 to 1)
Guidance Counselors: 5.0 (826.4 to 1)
Current Spending: ($ per student per year):
 Total: $6,998; Instruction: $4,610; Support Services: $2,140
Enrollment, Drop-out Rates and Diploma Recipients by Race/Ethnicity

Category	Total	White	Black	Asian	AIAN	Hisp.
Enrollment (%)	100.0	95.4	0.9	0.8	0.2	2.7
Drop-out Rate (%)	n/a	n/a	n/a	n/a	n/a	n/a
H.S. Diplomas (#)	244	234	0	4	0	6

Perry Public SD
2775 Britton Rd • Perry, MI 48872-9604
Mailing Address: PO Box 900 • Perry, MI 48872-0900
(517) 625-3108 • http://scnc.perry.k12.mi.us/main.html
Grade Span: PK-12; Agency Type: 1
Schools: 5
   3 Primary; 1 Middle; 1 High; 0 Other Level
   5 Regular; 0 Special Education; 0 Vocational; 0 Alternative
   0 Magnet; 0 Charter; 0 Title I Eligible; 0 School-wide Title I
Students: 1,997 (50.8% male; 49.1% female)
   Individual Education Program: 269 (13.5%);
   English Language Learner: 0 (0.0%); Migrant: n/a
   Eligible for Free Lunch Program: 336 (16.8%)
   Eligible for Reduced-Price Lunch Program: 138 (6.9%)
Teachers: 109.0 (18.3 to 1)
Librarians/Media Specialists: 2.0 (998.5 to 1)
Guidance Counselors: 5.0 (399.4 to 1)
Current Spending: ($ per student per year):
   Total: $7,096; Instruction: $4,357; Support Services: $2,538
Enrollment, Drop-out Rates and Diploma Recipients by Race/Ethnicity

Category	Total	White	Black	Asian	AIAN	Hisp.
Enrollment (%)	100.0	98.6	0.5	0.4	0.1	0.5
Drop-out Rate (%)	n/a	n/a	n/a	n/a	n/a	n/a
H.S. Diplomas (#)	111	105	1	1	0	4

St. Clair County

Algonac Community SD
1216 St Clair Blvd • Algonac, MI 48001-1435
(810) 794-9364 • http://algonac.k12.mi.us/
Grade Span: PK-12; Agency Type: 1
Schools: 7
   5 Primary; 1 Middle; 1 High; 0 Other Level
   7 Regular; 0 Special Education; 0 Vocational; 0 Alternative
   0 Magnet; 0 Charter; 2 Title I Eligible; 2 School-wide Title I
Students: 2,671 (51.7% male; 48.2% female)
   Individual Education Program: 304 (11.4%);
   English Language Learner: 0 (0.0%); Migrant: n/a
   Eligible for Free Lunch Program: 425 (15.9%)
   Eligible for Reduced-Price Lunch Program: 202 (7.6%)
Teachers: 137.0 (19.5 to 1)
Librarians/Media Specialists: 3.0 (890.3 to 1)
Guidance Counselors: 3.0 (890.3 to 1)
Current Spending: ($ per student per year):
   Total: $6,510; Instruction: $3,874; Support Services: $2,330
Enrollment, Drop-out Rates and Diploma Recipients by Race/Ethnicity

Category	Total	White	Black	Asian	AIAN	Hisp.
Enrollment (%)	100.0	94.7	0.4	0.7	2.9	1.2
Drop-out Rate (%)	n/a	n/a	n/a	n/a	n/a	n/a
H.S. Diplomas (#)	145	139	0	0	6	0

Capac Community SD
403 N Glassford St • Capac, MI 48014-3016
Mailing Address: PO Box 700 • Capac, MI 48014-0700
(810) 395-4321 • http://www.capac.k12.mi.us/
Grade Span: PK-12; Agency Type: 1
Schools: 3
   1 Primary; 1 Middle; 1 High; 0 Other Level
   3 Regular; 0 Special Education; 0 Vocational; 0 Alternative
   0 Magnet; 0 Charter; 0 Title I Eligible; 0 School-wide Title I
Students: 1,950 (52.4% male; 47.5% female)
   Individual Education Program: 280 (14.4%);
   English Language Learner: 0 (0.0%); Migrant: n/a
   Eligible for Free Lunch Program: 264 (13.8%)
   Eligible for Reduced-Price Lunch Program: 131 (6.9%)
Teachers: 104.0 (18.4 to 1)
Librarians/Media Specialists: 2.0 (956.0 to 1)
Guidance Counselors: 3.0 (637.3 to 1)
Current Spending: ($ per student per year):
   Total: $6,669; Instruction: $4,030; Support Services: $2,404
Enrollment, Drop-out Rates and Diploma Recipients by Race/Ethnicity

Category	Total	White	Black	Asian	AIAN	Hisp.
Enrollment (%)	100.0	89.6	0.7	0.9	0.2	8.5
Drop-out Rate (%)	n/a	n/a	n/a	n/a	n/a	n/a
H.S. Diplomas (#)	118	111	1	0	1	5

East China SD
1585 Meisner Rd • East China, MI 48054-4143
(810) 676-1018 • http://www.east-china.k12.mi.us/
Grade Span: PK-12; Agency Type: 1
Schools: 11
   6 Primary; 2 Middle; 3 High; 0 Other Level
   10 Regular; 0 Special Education; 0 Vocational; 1 Alternative
   11 Magnet; 0 Charter; 1 Title I Eligible; 1 School-wide Title I
Students: 5,978 (51.6% male; 48.3% female)

   Individual Education Program: 637 (10.7%);
   English Language Learner: 0 (0.0%); Migrant: n/a
   Eligible for Free Lunch Program: 669 (11.2%)
   Eligible for Reduced-Price Lunch Program: 313 (5.2%)
Teachers: 306.0 (19.5 to 1)
Librarians/Media Specialists: 8.0 (747.3 to 1)
Guidance Counselors: 9.0 (664.2 to 1)
Current Spending: ($ per student per year):
   Total: $7,658; Instruction: $4,379; Support Services: $3,089
Enrollment, Drop-out Rates and Diploma Recipients by Race/Ethnicity

Category	Total	White	Black	Asian	AIAN	Hisp.
Enrollment (%)	100.0	97.3	0.5	0.6	0.8	0.7
Drop-out Rate (%)	n/a	n/a	n/a	n/a	n/a	n/a
H.S. Diplomas (#)	404	394	1	1	3	5

Marysville Public Schools
1111 Delaware Ave • Marysville, MI 48040-1566
(810) 364-7731 • http://www.marysville.k12.mi.us/
Grade Span: PK-12; Agency Type: 1
Schools: 5
   3 Primary; 1 Middle; 1 High; 0 Other Level
   5 Regular; 0 Special Education; 0 Vocational; 0 Alternative
   0 Magnet; 0 Charter; 3 Title I Eligible; 3 School-wide Title I
Students: 2,887 (51.8% male; 48.1% female)
   Individual Education Program: 281 (9.7%);
   English Language Learner: 0 (0.0%); Migrant: n/a
   Eligible for Free Lunch Program: 198 (6.9%)
   Eligible for Reduced-Price Lunch Program: 109 (3.8%)
Teachers: 136.0 (21.2 to 1)
Librarians/Media Specialists: 2.0 (1,443.5 to 1)
Guidance Counselors: 4.0 (721.8 to 1)
Current Spending: ($ per student per year):
   Total: $6,197; Instruction: $3,619; Support Services: $2,435
Enrollment, Drop-out Rates and Diploma Recipients by Race/Ethnicity

Category	Total	White	Black	Asian	AIAN	Hisp.
Enrollment (%)	100.0	96.4	0.6	0.7	1.1	1.1
Drop-out Rate (%)	n/a	n/a	n/a	n/a	n/a	n/a
H.S. Diplomas (#)	172	161	1	2	4	4

Port Huron Area SD
1925 Lapeer Ave • Port Huron, MI 48061-4153
Mailing Address: PO Box 5013 • Port Huron, MI 48061-5013
(810) 984-3101 • http://www.port-huron.k12.mi.us/phasd/
Grade Span: PK-12; Agency Type: 1
Schools: 22
   14 Primary; 4 Middle; 3 High; 1 Other Level
   20 Regular; 0 Special Education; 0 Vocational; 2 Alternative
   0 Magnet; 0 Charter; 2 Title I Eligible; 2 School-wide Title I
Students: 12,754 (51.7% male; 48.2% female)
   Individual Education Program: 1,781 (14.0%);
   English Language Learner: 32 (0.3%); Migrant: n/a
   Eligible for Free Lunch Program: 3,711 (29.6%)
   Eligible for Reduced-Price Lunch Program: 975 (7.8%)
Teachers: 735.0 (17.0 to 1)
Librarians/Media Specialists: 9.0 (1,391.9 to 1)
Guidance Counselors: 20.0 (626.4 to 1)
Current Spending: ($ per student per year):
   Total: $6,912; Instruction: $4,436; Support Services: $2,288
Enrollment, Drop-out Rates and Diploma Recipients by Race/Ethnicity

Category	Total	White	Black	Asian	AIAN	Hisp.
Enrollment (%)	100.0	85.4	9.1	0.8	2.0	2.5
Drop-out Rate (%)	n/a	n/a	n/a	n/a	n/a	n/a
H.S. Diplomas (#)	691	609	49	7	13	13

Yale Public Schools
198 School Dr • Yale, MI 48097-3342
(810) 387-4274 • http://www.yale.k12.mi.us/
Grade Span: PK-12; Agency Type: 1
Schools: 6
   3 Primary; 1 Middle; 2 High; 0 Other Level
   5 Regular; 0 Special Education; 0 Vocational; 1 Alternative
   4 Magnet; 0 Charter; 0 Title I Eligible; 0 School-wide Title I
Students: 2,490 (52.5% male; 47.4% female)
   Individual Education Program: 262 (10.5%);
   English Language Learner: 5 (0.2%); Migrant: n/a
   Eligible for Free Lunch Program: 401 (16.1%)
   Eligible for Reduced-Price Lunch Program: 148 (5.9%)
Teachers: 114.0 (21.8 to 1)
Librarians/Media Specialists: 1.0 (2,490.0 to 1)
Guidance Counselors: 5.0 (498.0 to 1)
Current Spending: ($ per student per year):
   Total: $6,345; Instruction: $3,552; Support Services: $2,566

Enrollment, Drop-out Rates and Diploma Recipients by Race/Ethnicity

Category	Total	White	Black	Asian	AIAN	Hisp.
Enrollment (%)	100.0	97.0	0.9	0.4	0.7	0.8
Drop-out Rate (%)	n/a	n/a	n/a	n/a	n/a	n/a
H.S. Diplomas (#)	143	137	2	0	3	1

St. Joseph County

Constantine Public SD
260 W 6th St • Constantine, MI 49042-1306
(269) 435-8900 • http://home.constps.org/
Grade Span: PK-12; **Agency Type:** 1
Schools: 4
    2 Primary; 1 Middle; 1 High; 0 Other Level
    4 Regular; 0 Special Education; 0 Vocational; 0 Alternative
    0 Magnet; 0 Charter; 1 Title I Eligible; 1 School-wide Title I
Students: 1,556 (52.2% male; 47.7% female)
    Individual Education Program: 177 (11.4%);
    English Language Learner: 0 (0.0%); Migrant: n/a
    Eligible for Free Lunch Program: 293 (18.8%)
    Eligible for Reduced-Price Lunch Program: 127 (8.2%)
Teachers: 93.0 (16.7 to 1)
Librarians/Media Specialists: 1.0 (1,556.0 to 1)
Guidance Counselors: 3.0 (518.7 to 1)
Current Spending: ($ per student per year):
    Total: $7,341; Instruction: $4,976; Support Services: $2,098
Enrollment, Drop-out Rates and Diploma Recipients by Race/Ethnicity

Category	Total	White	Black	Asian	AIAN	Hisp.
Enrollment (%)	100.0	95.8	1.5	1.2	0.1	1.3
Drop-out Rate (%)	n/a	n/a	n/a	n/a	n/a	n/a
H.S. Diplomas (#)	101	100	1	0	0	0

Sturgis Public Schools
216 Vinewood Ave • Sturgis, MI 49091-8426
(269) 659-1500 • http://www.sturgis.k12.mi.us/
Grade Span: PK-12; **Agency Type:** 1
Schools: 9
    5 Primary; 1 Middle; 1 High; 2 Other Level
    8 Regular; 0 Special Education; 0 Vocational; 1 Alternative
    0 Magnet; 0 Charter; 5 Title I Eligible; 5 School-wide Title I
Students: 3,126 (50.6% male; 49.3% female)
    Individual Education Program: 333 (10.7%);
    English Language Learner: 250 (8.0%); Migrant: 94 (3.1%)
    Eligible for Free Lunch Program: 1,046 (34.1%)
    Eligible for Reduced-Price Lunch Program: 277 (9.0%)
Teachers: 170.0 (18.0 to 1)
Librarians/Media Specialists: 4.0 (767.0 to 1)
Guidance Counselors: 7.0 (438.3 to 1)
Current Spending: ($ per student per year):
    Total: $7,170; Instruction: $4,403; Support Services: $2,488
Enrollment, Drop-out Rates and Diploma Recipients by Race/Ethnicity

Category	Total	White	Black	Asian	AIAN	Hisp.
Enrollment (%)	100.0	80.5	1.8	1.0	0.1	16.5
Drop-out Rate (%)	n/a	n/a	n/a	n/a	n/a	n/a
H.S. Diplomas (#)	184	167	2	2	0	13

Three Rivers Community Schools
851 6th Ave • Three Rivers, MI 49093-9406
(269) 279-1100 • http://www.trschools.org/
Grade Span: PK-12; **Agency Type:** 1
Schools: 9
    6 Primary; 1 Middle; 1 High; 1 Other Level
    8 Regular; 0 Special Education; 0 Vocational; 1 Alternative
    1 Magnet; 0 Charter; 0 Title I Eligible; 0 School-wide Title I
Students: 3,105 (53.8% male; 46.1% female)
    Individual Education Program: 440 (14.2%);
    English Language Learner: 0 (0.0%); Migrant: n/a
    Eligible for Free Lunch Program: 903 (29.8%)
    Eligible for Reduced-Price Lunch Program: 238 (7.9%)
Teachers: n/a
Librarians/Media Specialists: n/a
Guidance Counselors: n/a
Current Spending: ($ per student per year):
    Total: $7,062; Instruction: $4,299; Support Services: $2,469
Enrollment, Drop-out Rates and Diploma Recipients by Race/Ethnicity

Category	Total	White	Black	Asian	AIAN	Hisp.
Enrollment (%)	100.0	82.8	12.8	1.3	0.1	2.8
Drop-out Rate (%)	n/a	n/a	n/a	n/a	n/a	n/a
H.S. Diplomas (#)	159	143	9	2	2	3

Tuscola County

Caro Community Schools
301 N Hooper St • Caro, MI 48723-1474
(989) 673-3160 • http://www.caro.k12.mi.us/
Grade Span: KG-12; **Agency Type:** 1
Schools: 5
    2 Primary; 1 Middle; 2 High; 0 Other Level
    4 Regular; 0 Special Education; 0 Vocational; 1 Alternative
    5 Magnet; 0 Charter; 0 Title I Eligible; 0 School-wide Title I
Students: 2,267 (52.0% male; 47.9% female)
    Individual Education Program: 343 (15.1%);
    English Language Learner: 0 (0.0%); Migrant: n/a
    Eligible for Free Lunch Program: 596 (26.3%)
    Eligible for Reduced-Price Lunch Program: 201 (8.9%)
Teachers: 130.0 (17.4 to 1)
Librarians/Media Specialists: 3.0 (755.7 to 1)
Guidance Counselors: 4.0 (566.8 to 1)
Current Spending: ($ per student per year):
    Total: $6,861; Instruction: $4,676; Support Services: $1,902
Enrollment, Drop-out Rates and Diploma Recipients by Race/Ethnicity

Category	Total	White	Black	Asian	AIAN	Hisp.
Enrollment (%)	100.0	94.6	0.6	0.7	0.3	3.8
Drop-out Rate (%)	n/a	n/a	n/a	n/a	n/a	n/a
H.S. Diplomas (#)	143	137	0	1	0	5

Millington Community Schools
8780 Dean Dr • Millington, MI 48746-9601
(989) 871-5201 • http://www.mcsdistrict.com/
Grade Span: KG-12; **Agency Type:** 1
Schools: 5
    2 Primary; 1 Middle; 2 High; 0 Other Level
    4 Regular; 0 Special Education; 0 Vocational; 1 Alternative
    0 Magnet; 0 Charter; 0 Title I Eligible; 0 School-wide Title I
Students: 1,772 (51.2% male; 48.7% female)
    Individual Education Program: 236 (13.3%);
    English Language Learner: 0 (0.0%); Migrant: n/a
    Eligible for Free Lunch Program: 418 (23.6%)
    Eligible for Reduced-Price Lunch Program: 140 (7.9%)
Teachers: 81.0 (21.9 to 1)
Librarians/Media Specialists: 1.0 (1,772.0 to 1)
Guidance Counselors: 3.0 (590.7 to 1)
Current Spending: ($ per student per year):
    Total: $7,212; Instruction: $4,571; Support Services: $2,305
Enrollment, Drop-out Rates and Diploma Recipients by Race/Ethnicity

Category	Total	White	Black	Asian	AIAN	Hisp.
Enrollment (%)	100.0	97.8	0.6	0.3	0.3	1.0
Drop-out Rate (%)	n/a	n/a	n/a	n/a	n/a	n/a
H.S. Diplomas (#)	137	136	0	0	0	1

Vassar Public Schools
220 Athletic St • Vassar, MI 48768-1205
(989) 823-8535 • http://www.vassar.k12.mi.us/
Grade Span: KG-12; **Agency Type:** 1
Schools: 5
    2 Primary; 1 Middle; 2 High; 0 Other Level
    4 Regular; 0 Special Education; 0 Vocational; 1 Alternative
    0 Magnet; 0 Charter; 0 Title I Eligible; 0 School-wide Title I
Students: 1,861 (58.0% male; 41.9% female)
    Individual Education Program: 354 (19.0%);
    English Language Learner: 0 (0.0%); Migrant: n/a
    Eligible for Free Lunch Program: 406 (21.8%)
    Eligible for Reduced-Price Lunch Program: 179 (9.6%)
Teachers: 85.0 (21.9 to 1)
Librarians/Media Specialists: 2.0 (930.5 to 1)
Guidance Counselors: 5.0 (372.2 to 1)
Current Spending: ($ per student per year):
    Total: $6,735; Instruction: $4,445; Support Services: $2,028
Enrollment, Drop-out Rates and Diploma Recipients by Race/Ethnicity

Category	Total	White	Black	Asian	AIAN	Hisp.
Enrollment (%)	100.0	86.4	11.5	0.5	0.0	1.7
Drop-out Rate (%)	n/a	n/a	n/a	n/a	n/a	n/a
H.S. Diplomas (#)	93	87	5	1	0	0

Van Buren County

Bangor Public Schools (Van Buren)
801 W Arlington St • Bangor, MI 49013-1108
(616) 427-6800 • http://www.bangorvikings.org/
Grade Span: KG-12; **Agency Type:** 1
Schools: 5
    2 Primary; 1 Middle; 1 High; 1 Other Level
    4 Regular; 0 Special Education; 0 Vocational; 1 Alternative
    0 Magnet; 0 Charter; 5 Title I Eligible; 5 School-wide Title I
Students: 1,527 (53.6% male; 46.3% female)

Individual Education Program: 104 (6.8%);
English Language Learner: 0 (0.0%); Migrant: 191 (12.5%)
Eligible for Free Lunch Program: 946 (62.0%)
Eligible for Reduced-Price Lunch Program: 120 (7.9%)
Teachers: 87.0 (17.6 to 1)
Librarians/Media Specialists: 1.0 (1,527.0 to 1)
Guidance Counselors: 2.0 (763.5 to 1)
Current Spending: ($ per student per year):
Total: $8,738; Instruction: $5,262; Support Services: $3,077
Enrollment, Drop-out Rates and Diploma Recipients by Race/Ethnicity

Category	Total	White	Black	Asian	AIAN	Hisp.
Enrollment (%)	100.0	69.7	8.9	0.1	1.0	18.5
Drop-out Rate (%)	n/a	n/a	n/a	n/a	n/a	n/a
H.S. Diplomas (#)	103	81	6	0	0	16

Hartford Public SD
115-B School St • Hartford, MI 49057-1183
(269) 621-7000
Grade Span: PK-12; **Agency Type:** 1
Schools: 4
2 Primary; 1 Middle; 1 High; 0 Other Level
4 Regular; 0 Special Education; 0 Vocational; 0 Alternative
0 Magnet; 0 Charter; 3 Title I Eligible; 3 School-wide Title I
Students: 1,513   (51.4% male; 48.5% female)
Individual Education Program: 112 (7.4%)
English Language Learner: 214 (14.1%); Migrant: 163 (10.8%)
Eligible for Free Lunch Program: 539 (35.6%)
Eligible for Reduced-Price Lunch Program: 192 (12.7%)
Teachers: 96.0 (15.8 to 1)
Librarians/Media Specialists: 2.0 (756.5 to 1)
Guidance Counselors: 4.0 (378.3 to 1)
Current Spending: ($ per student per year):
Total: $7,462; Instruction: $4,584; Support Services: $2,537
Enrollment, Drop-out Rates and Diploma Recipients by Race/Ethnicity

Category	Total	White	Black	Asian	AIAN	Hisp.
Enrollment (%)	100.0	67.7	1.4	0.2	1.7	27.6
Drop-out Rate (%)	n/a	n/a	n/a	n/a	n/a	n/a
H.S. Diplomas (#)	90	63	3	3	1	20

Mattawan Consolidated School
56720 Murray St • Mattawan, MI 49071-9567
(269) 668-3361 • http://www.mattawan.k12.mi.us/
Grade Span: KG-12; **Agency Type:** 1
Schools: 4
2 Primary; 1 Middle; 1 High; 0 Other Level
4 Regular; 0 Special Education; 0 Vocational; 0 Alternative
0 Magnet; 0 Charter; 0 Title I Eligible; 0 School-wide Title I
Students: 3,512   (51.6% male; 48.3% female)
Individual Education Program: 120 (3.4%);
English Language Learner: 0 (0.0%); Migrant: 5 (0.1%)
Eligible for Free Lunch Program: 303 (8.6%)
Eligible for Reduced-Price Lunch Program: 119 (3.4%)
Teachers: 184.0 (19.1 to 1)
Librarians/Media Specialists: 5.0 (702.4 to 1)
Guidance Counselors: 6.0 (585.3 to 1)
Current Spending: ($ per student per year):
Total: $6,818; Instruction: $4,202; Support Services: $2,399
Enrollment, Drop-out Rates and Diploma Recipients by Race/Ethnicity

Category	Total	White	Black	Asian	AIAN	Hisp.
Enrollment (%)	100.0	93.7	2.3	1.2	0.9	1.4
Drop-out Rate (%)	n/a	n/a	n/a	n/a	n/a	n/a
H.S. Diplomas (#)	217	198	7	6	4	2

Paw Paw Public SD
119 Johnson St • Paw Paw, MI 49079-1093
(269) 657-8800 • http://www.pawpaw.k12.mi.us/
Grade Span: PK-12; **Agency Type:** 1
Schools: 5
2 Primary; 1 Middle; 1 High; 1 Other Level
4 Regular; 0 Special Education; 0 Vocational; 1 Alternative
0 Magnet; 0 Charter; 0 Title I Eligible; 0 School-wide Title I
Students: 2,400   (51.9% male; 48.0% female)
Individual Education Program: 233 (9.7%);
English Language Learner: 0 (0.0%); Migrant: 20 (0.8%)
Eligible for Free Lunch Program: 599 (25.0%)
Eligible for Reduced-Price Lunch Program: 148 (6.2%)
Teachers: 133.0 (18.0 to 1)
Librarians/Media Specialists: 3.0 (800.0 to 1)
Guidance Counselors: 4.0 (600.0 to 1)
Current Spending: ($ per student per year):
Total: $6,945; Instruction: $4,296; Support Services: $2,363

Category	Total	White	Black	Asian	AIAN	Hisp.
Enrollment (%)	100.0	93.6	1.8	0.8	0.2	3.1
Drop-out Rate (%)	n/a	n/a	n/a	n/a	n/a	n/a
H.S. Diplomas (#)	156	145	4	2	1	4

South Haven Public Schools
554 Green St • South Haven, MI 49090-1432
(269) 637-0520 • http://www.shps.org/
Grade Span: PK-12; **Agency Type:** 1
Schools: 5
3 Primary; 1 Middle; 1 High; 0 Other Level
5 Regular; 0 Special Education; 0 Vocational; 0 Alternative
0 Magnet; 0 Charter; 0 Title I Eligible; 0 School-wide Title I
Students: 2,490   (50.8% male; 49.1% female)
Individual Education Program: 225 (9.0%);
English Language Learner: 134 (5.4%); Migrant: 162 (6.5%)
Eligible for Free Lunch Program: 893 (35.9%)
Eligible for Reduced-Price Lunch Program: 210 (8.4%)
Teachers: 139.0 (17.9 to 1)
Librarians/Media Specialists: 1.0 (2,490.0 to 1)
Guidance Counselors: 3.0 (830.0 to 1)
Current Spending: ($ per student per year):
Total: $7,169; Instruction: $4,437; Support Services: $2,371
Enrollment, Drop-out Rates and Diploma Recipients by Race/Ethnicity

Category	Total	White	Black	Asian	AIAN	Hisp.
Enrollment (%)	100.0	76.3	12.9	0.5	0.7	9.1
Drop-out Rate (%)	n/a	n/a	n/a	n/a	n/a	n/a
H.S. Diplomas (#)	152	129	19	2	0	2

Washtenaw County

Ann Arbor Public Schools
2555 S State Rd • Ann Arbor, MI 48104-6145
Mailing Address: PO Box 1188 • Ann Arbor, MI 48106-1188
(734) 994-2230 • http://aaps.k12.mi.us/
Grade Span: KG-12; **Agency Type:** 1
Schools: 33
21 Primary; 5 Middle; 6 High; 1 Other Level
29 Regular; 1 Special Education; 0 Vocational; 3 Alternative
0 Magnet; 0 Charter; 1 Title I Eligible; 1 School-wide Title I
Students: 16,701   (51.2% male; 48.7% female)
Individual Education Program: 2,075 (12.4%);
English Language Learner: 1,230 (7.4%); Migrant: n/a
Eligible for Free Lunch Program: 2,262 (13.5%)
Eligible for Reduced-Price Lunch Program: 724 (4.3%)
Teachers: 1,055.0 (15.8 to 1)
Librarians/Media Specialists: 33.0 (506.1 to 1)
Guidance Counselors: 40.0 (417.5 to 1)
Current Spending: ($ per student per year):
Total: $9,731; Instruction: $5,669; Support Services: $3,841
Enrollment, Drop-out Rates and Diploma Recipients by Race/Ethnicity

Category	Total	White	Black	Asian	AIAN	Hisp.
Enrollment (%)	100.0	68.1	15.4	12.5	0.5	3.6
Drop-out Rate (%)	n/a	n/a	n/a	n/a	n/a	n/a
H.S. Diplomas (#)	1,141	843	145	117	6	30

Chelsea SD
500 E Washington St • Chelsea, MI 48118-1144
(734) 433-2208 • http://chelsea.k12.mi.us/
Grade Span: PK-12; **Agency Type:** 1
Schools: 6
3 Primary; 2 Middle; 1 High; 0 Other Level
6 Regular; 0 Special Education; 0 Vocational; 0 Alternative
0 Magnet; 0 Charter; 0 Title I Eligible; 0 School-wide Title I
Students: 3,160   (51.9% male; 48.0% female)
Individual Education Program: 469 (14.8%);
English Language Learner: 0 (0.0%); Migrant: n/a
Eligible for Free Lunch Program: 108 (3.5%)
Eligible for Reduced-Price Lunch Program: 76 (2.5%)
Teachers: 163.0 (18.8 to 1)
Librarians/Media Specialists: 3.0 (1,023.7 to 1)
Guidance Counselors: 5.0 (614.2 to 1)
Current Spending: ($ per student per year):
Total: $7,485; Instruction: $4,055; Support Services: $3,143
Enrollment, Drop-out Rates and Diploma Recipients by Race/Ethnicity

Category	Total	White	Black	Asian	AIAN	Hisp.
Enrollment (%)	100.0	96.4	0.6	1.4	0.6	1.0
Drop-out Rate (%)	n/a	n/a	n/a	n/a	n/a	n/a
H.S. Diplomas (#)	240	235	2	1	0	2

Dexter Community SD
7714 Ann Arbor St • Dexter, MI 48130-1322
(734) 424-4100 • http://web.dexter.k12.mi.us/
Grade Span: KG-12; **Agency Type:** 1
Schools: 6
  3 Primary; 2 Middle; 1 High; 0 Other Level
  6 Regular; 0 Special Education; 0 Vocational; 0 Alternative
  0 Magnet; 0 Charter; 6 Title I Eligible; 6 School-wide Title I
Students: 3,489 (51.2% male; 48.7% female)
  Individual Education Program: 449 (12.9%);
  English Language Learner: 9 (0.3%); Migrant: n/a
  Eligible for Free Lunch Program: 111 (3.2%)
  Eligible for Reduced-Price Lunch Program: 69 (2.0%)
Teachers: 188.0 (18.6 to 1)
Librarians/Media Specialists: 6.0 (581.5 to 1)
Guidance Counselors: 6.0 (581.5 to 1)
Current Spending: ($ per student per year):
  Total: $8,552; Instruction: $4,408; Support Services: $3,713
Enrollment, Drop-out Rates and Diploma Recipients by Race/Ethnicity

Category	Total	White	Black	Asian	AIAN	Hisp.
Enrollment (%)	100.0	97.6	0.5	1.3	0.2	0.3
Drop-out Rate (%)	n/a	n/a	n/a	n/a	n/a	n/a
H.S. Diplomas (#)	193	191	0	1	1	0

Lincoln Consolidated SD
8970 Whittaker Rd • Ypsilanti, MI 48197-9440
(734) 484-7001 • http://lincoln.k12.mi.us/
Grade Span: PK-12; **Agency Type:** 1
Schools: 7
  5 Primary; 1 Middle; 1 High; 0 Other Level
  7 Regular; 0 Special Education; 0 Vocational; 0 Alternative
  6 Magnet; 0 Charter; 0 Title I Eligible; 0 School-wide Title I
Students: 4,952 (51.3% male; 48.6% female)
  Individual Education Program: 770 (15.5%);
  English Language Learner: 0 (0.0%); Migrant: n/a
  Eligible for Free Lunch Program: 908 (18.3%)
  Eligible for Reduced-Price Lunch Program: 285 (5.8%)
Teachers: 275.0 (18.0 to 1)
Librarians/Media Specialists: 5.0 (990.4 to 1)
Guidance Counselors: 5.0 (990.4 to 1)
Current Spending: ($ per student per year):
  Total: $7,664; Instruction: $4,353; Support Services: $3,060
Enrollment, Drop-out Rates and Diploma Recipients by Race/Ethnicity

Category	Total	White	Black	Asian	AIAN	Hisp.
Enrollment (%)	100.0	70.0	25.2	2.0	0.4	2.4
Drop-out Rate (%)	n/a	n/a	n/a	n/a	n/a	n/a
H.S. Diplomas (#)	212	156	51	2	0	3

Milan Area Schools
100 Big Red Dr • Milan, MI 48160-1582
(734) 439-5050 • http://scnc.milan.k12.mi.us/
Grade Span: KG-12; **Agency Type:** 1
Schools: 4
  2 Primary; 1 Middle; 1 High; 0 Other Level
  4 Regular; 0 Special Education; 0 Vocational; 0 Alternative
  0 Magnet; 0 Charter; 0 Title I Eligible; 0 School-wide Title I
Students: 2,201 (52.5% male; 47.4% female)
  Individual Education Program: 345 (15.7%);
  English Language Learner: 0 (0.0%); Migrant: n/a
  Eligible for Free Lunch Program: 263 (11.9%)
  Eligible for Reduced-Price Lunch Program: 82 (3.7%)
Teachers: 130.0 (16.9 to 1)
Librarians/Media Specialists: 2.0 (1,100.5 to 1)
Guidance Counselors: 4.0 (550.3 to 1)
Current Spending: ($ per student per year):
  Total: $7,801; Instruction: $4,605; Support Services: $2,880
Enrollment, Drop-out Rates and Diploma Recipients by Race/Ethnicity

Category	Total	White	Black	Asian	AIAN	Hisp.
Enrollment (%)	100.0	88.1	7.2	1.1	1.0	2.5
Drop-out Rate (%)	n/a	n/a	n/a	n/a	n/a	n/a
H.S. Diplomas (#)	125	111	9	2	0	3

SD of Ypsilanti
1885 Packard Rd • Ypsilanti, MI 48197-1846
(734) 714-1218 • http://scnc.yps.k12.mi.us/
Grade Span: PK-12; **Agency Type:** 1
Schools: 12
  7 Primary; 2 Middle; 1 High; 2 Other Level
  11 Regular; 0 Special Education; 0 Vocational; 1 Alternative
  2 Magnet; 0 Charter; 0 Title I Eligible; 0 School-wide Title I
Students: 4,754 (52.3% male; 47.6% female)
  Individual Education Program: 954 (20.1%);
  English Language Learner: 335 (7.0%); Migrant: n/a
  Eligible for Free Lunch Program: 2,247 (47.3%)
  Eligible for Reduced-Price Lunch Program: 406 (8.5%)

Teachers: 277.0 (17.2 to 1)
Librarians/Media Specialists: 8.0 (594.3 to 1)
Guidance Counselors: 8.0 (594.3 to 1)
Current Spending: ($ per student per year):
  Total: $10,209; Instruction: $5,489; Support Services: $4,429
Enrollment, Drop-out Rates and Diploma Recipients by Race/Ethnicity

Category	Total	White	Black	Asian	AIAN	Hisp.
Enrollment (%)	100.0	36.2	59.2	1.5	0.1	3.0
Drop-out Rate (%)	n/a	n/a	n/a	n/a	n/a	n/a
H.S. Diplomas (#)	235	120	102	7	1	5

Saline Area Schools
200 N Ann Arbor St • Saline, MI 48176-1139
(734) 429-8000 • http://www.salineschools.com/
Grade Span: KG-12; **Agency Type:** 1
Schools: 7
  4 Primary; 2 Middle; 1 High; 0 Other Level
  7 Regular; 0 Special Education; 0 Vocational; 0 Alternative
  0 Magnet; 0 Charter; 0 Title I Eligible; 0 School-wide Title I
Students: 5,364 (51.5% male; 48.4% female)
  Individual Education Program: 551 (10.3%);
  English Language Learner: 43 (0.8%); Migrant: n/a
  Eligible for Free Lunch Program: 145 (2.7%)
  Eligible for Reduced-Price Lunch Program: 81 (1.5%)
Teachers: 286.0 (18.8 to 1)
Librarians/Media Specialists: 6.0 (894.0 to 1)
Guidance Counselors: 11.0 (487.6 to 1)
Current Spending: ($ per student per year):
  Total: $8,034; Instruction: $4,882; Support Services: $2,896
Enrollment, Drop-out Rates and Diploma Recipients by Race/Ethnicity

Category	Total	White	Black	Asian	AIAN	Hisp.
Enrollment (%)	100.0	93.8	1.1	3.4	0.2	1.5
Drop-out Rate (%)	n/a	n/a	n/a	n/a	n/a	n/a
H.S. Diplomas (#)	359	339	1	7	0	12

Washtenaw ISD
1819 S Wagner Rd • Ann Arbor, MI 48106-9715
Mailing Address: PO Box 1406 • Ann Arbor, MI 48106-1406
(734) 994-8100
Grade Span: PK-12; **Agency Type:** 4
Schools: 5
  1 Primary; 0 Middle; 1 High; 3 Other Level
  1 Regular; 3 Special Education; 0 Vocational; 1 Alternative
  0 Magnet; 0 Charter; 0 Title I Eligible; 0 School-wide Title I
Students: 2,188 (55.5% male; 44.4% female)
  Individual Education Program: 276 (12.6%);
  English Language Learner: 0 (0.0%); Migrant: n/a
  Eligible for Free Lunch Program: n/a
  Eligible for Reduced-Price Lunch Program: n/a
Teachers: 51.0 (42.6 to 1)
Librarians/Media Specialists: 0.0 (n/a to 1)
Guidance Counselors: 0.0 (n/a to 1)
Current Spending: ($ per student per year):
  Total: n/a; Instruction: n/a; Support Services: n/a
Enrollment, Drop-out Rates and Diploma Recipients by Race/Ethnicity

Category	Total	White	Black	Asian	AIAN	Hisp.
Enrollment (%)	100.0	63.3	9.5	8.3	0.0	4.5
Drop-out Rate (%)	n/a	n/a	n/a	n/a	n/a	n/a
H.S. Diplomas (#)	n/a	n/a	n/a	n/a	n/a	n/a

Willow Run Community Schools
2171 E Michigan Ave • Ypsilanti, MI 48198-6049
(734) 481-8200 • http://wrcs.k12.mi.us/splash.htm
Grade Span: PK-12; **Agency Type:** 1
Schools: 8
  6 Primary; 1 Middle; 1 High; 0 Other Level
  8 Regular; 0 Special Education; 0 Vocational; 0 Alternative
  0 Magnet; 0 Charter; 0 Title I Eligible; 0 School-wide Title I
Students: 2,673 (52.6% male; 47.3% female)
  Individual Education Program: 532 (19.9%);
  English Language Learner: 0 (0.0%); Migrant: n/a
  Eligible for Free Lunch Program: 1,469 (55.0%)
  Eligible for Reduced-Price Lunch Program: 256 (9.6%)
Teachers: 158.0 (16.9 to 1)
Librarians/Media Specialists: 0.0 (n/a to 1)
Guidance Counselors: 3.0 (891.0 to 1)
Current Spending: ($ per student per year):
  Total: $10,930; Instruction: $5,570; Support Services: $4,928
Enrollment, Drop-out Rates and Diploma Recipients by Race/Ethnicity

Category	Total	White	Black	Asian	AIAN	Hisp.
Enrollment (%)	100.0	40.8	56.3	1.2	0.4	1.3
Drop-out Rate (%)	n/a	n/a	n/a	n/a	n/a	n/a
H.S. Diplomas (#)	127	64	57	4	1	1

Wayne County

Allen Park Public Schools
9601 Vine Ave • Allen Park, MI 48101-4300
(313) 928-4667 • http://www.apps.k12.mi.us/
Grade Span: KG-12; **Agency Type:** 1
Schools: 6
  3 Primary; 1 Middle; 1 High; 1 Other Level
  5 Regular; 0 Special Education; 0 Vocational; 1 Alternative
  0 Magnet; 0 Charter; 0 Title I Eligible; 0 School-wide Title I
Students: 3,638 (51.2% male; 48.7% female)
  Individual Education Program: 392 (10.8%);
  English Language Learner: 0 (0.0%); Migrant: n/a
  Eligible for Free Lunch Program: 268 (7.4%)
  Eligible for Reduced-Price Lunch Program: 136 (3.7%)
Teachers: 165.0 (22.0 to 1)
Librarians/Media Specialists: 4.0 (909.5 to 1)
Guidance Counselors: 5.0 (727.6 to 1)
Current Spending: ($ per student per year):
  Total: $7,411; Instruction: $4,674; Support Services: $2,494
Enrollment, Drop-out Rates and Diploma Recipients by Race/Ethnicity

Category	Total	White	Black	Asian	AIAN	Hisp.
Enrollment (%)	100.0	94.1	0.9	0.3	0.1	4.5
Drop-out Rate (%)	n/a	n/a	n/a	n/a	n/a	n/a
H.S. Diplomas (#)	198	182	1	3	0	12

Crestwood SD
1501 N Beech Daly Rd • Dearborn Heights, MI 48127-3403
(313) 278-0903 • http://www.crestwoodhigh.org/
Grade Span: PK-12; **Agency Type:** 1
Schools: 5
  3 Primary; 1 Middle; 1 High; 0 Other Level
  5 Regular; 0 Special Education; 0 Vocational; 0 Alternative
  5 Magnet; 0 Charter; 0 Title I Eligible; 0 School-wide Title I
Students: 3,555 (51.9% male; 48.0% female)
  Individual Education Program: 325 (9.1%);
  English Language Learner: 141 (4.0%); Migrant: n/a
  Eligible for Free Lunch Program: 644 (18.1%)
  Eligible for Reduced-Price Lunch Program: 258 (7.3%)
Teachers: 180.0 (19.8 to 1)
Librarians/Media Specialists: 3.0 (1,185.0 to 1)
Guidance Counselors: 6.0 (592.5 to 1)
Current Spending: ($ per student per year):
  Total: $6,945; Instruction: $4,117; Support Services: $2,567
Enrollment, Drop-out Rates and Diploma Recipients by Race/Ethnicity

Category	Total	White	Black	Asian	AIAN	Hisp.
Enrollment (%)	100.0	91.9	2.7	2.5	0.2	2.7
Drop-out Rate (%)	n/a	n/a	n/a	n/a	n/a	n/a
H.S. Diplomas (#)	216	197	1	6	2	10

Dearborn City SD
18700 Audette St • Dearborn, MI 48124-4222
(313) 730-3242 • http://www.dearbornschools.org/
Grade Span: PK-12; **Agency Type:** 1
Schools: 32
  20 Primary; 6 Middle; 3 High; 3 Other Level
  28 Regular; 2 Special Education; 0 Vocational; 2 Alternative
  0 Magnet; 0 Charter; 14 Title I Eligible; 14 School-wide Title I
Students: 18,083 (51.8% male; 48.1% female)
  Individual Education Program: 1,993 (11.0%);
  English Language Learner: 6,472 (35.8%); Migrant: n/a
  Eligible for Free Lunch Program: 6,069 (33.6%)
  Eligible for Reduced-Price Lunch Program: 748 (4.1%)
Teachers: 1,072.0 (16.9 to 1)
Librarians/Media Specialists: 24.0 (753.5 to 1)
Guidance Counselors: 30.0 (602.8 to 1)
Current Spending: ($ per student per year):
  Total: $9,521; Instruction: $5,592; Support Services: $3,715
Enrollment, Drop-out Rates and Diploma Recipients by Race/Ethnicity

Category	Total	White	Black	Asian	AIAN	Hisp.
Enrollment (%)	100.0	93.5	3.0	0.8	0.6	2.1
Drop-out Rate (%)	n/a	n/a	n/a	n/a	n/a	n/a
H.S. Diplomas (#)	1,014	983	5	7	3	16

Dearborn Heights SD #7
20629 Annapolis St • Dearborn Heights, MI 48125-2904
(313) 278-1900 • http://www.resa.net/district7/
Grade Span: KG-12; **Agency Type:** 1
Schools: 6
  4 Primary; 1 Middle; 1 High; 0 Other Level
  6 Regular; 0 Special Education; 0 Vocational; 0 Alternative
  0 Magnet; 0 Charter; 1 Title I Eligible; 1 School-wide Title I
Students: 2,986 (50.2% male; 49.7% female)
  Individual Education Program: 384 (12.9%);
  English Language Learner: 0 (0.0%); Migrant: n/a

Eligible for Free Lunch Program: 754 (25.3%)
  Eligible for Reduced-Price Lunch Program: 328 (11.0%)
Teachers: 152.0 (19.6 to 1)
Librarians/Media Specialists: 5.0 (597.2 to 1)
Guidance Counselors: 5.0 (597.2 to 1)
Current Spending: ($ per student per year):
  Total: $6,590; Instruction: $3,989; Support Services: $2,251
Enrollment, Drop-out Rates and Diploma Recipients by Race/Ethnicity

Category	Total	White	Black	Asian	AIAN	Hisp.
Enrollment (%)	100.0	87.2	6.3	1.0	0.6	4.9
Drop-out Rate (%)	n/a	n/a	n/a	n/a	n/a	n/a
H.S. Diplomas (#)	100	95	0	2	0	3

Detroit Academy of Arts and Sciences
2985 E Jefferson Ave • Detroit, MI 48207-4288
(313) 259-1744
Grade Span: KG-11; **Agency Type:** 7
Schools: 2
  0 Primary; 0 Middle; 0 High; 2 Other Level
  2 Regular; 0 Special Education; 0 Vocational; 0 Alternative
  0 Magnet; 2 Charter; 1 Title I Eligible; 1 School-wide Title I
Students: 2,254 (46.4% male; 53.5% female)
  Individual Education Program: 106 (4.7%);
  English Language Learner: 0 (0.0%); Migrant: n/a
  Eligible for Free Lunch Program: 455 (20.2%)
  Eligible for Reduced-Price Lunch Program: 64 (2.8%)
Teachers: 104.0 (21.7 to 1)
Librarians/Media Specialists: 1.0 (2,254.0 to 1)
Guidance Counselors: 2.0 (1,127.0 to 1)
Current Spending: ($ per student per year):
  Total: $5,117; Instruction: $2,561; Support Services: $2,399
Enrollment, Drop-out Rates and Diploma Recipients by Race/Ethnicity

Category	Total	White	Black	Asian	AIAN	Hisp.
Enrollment (%)	100.0	0.4	99.6	0.0	0.0	0.0
Drop-out Rate (%)	n/a	n/a	n/a	n/a	n/a	n/a
H.S. Diplomas (#)	n/a	n/a	n/a	n/a	n/a	n/a

Detroit City SD
3011 W Grand Blvdfisher 14th • Detroit, MI 48202-3096
(313) 873-7450 • http://www.detroit.k12.mi.us/
Grade Span: PK-12; **Agency Type:** 1
Schools: 261
  179 Primary; 34 Middle; 36 High; 12 Other Level
  242 Regular; 7 Special Education; 4 Vocational; 8 Alternative
  0 Magnet; 0 Charter; 0 Title I Eligible; 0 School-wide Title I
Students: 153,034 (50.7% male; 49.2% female)
  Individual Education Program: 20,645 (13.5%);
  English Language Learner: 8,216 (5.4%); Migrant: 554 (0.4%)
  Eligible for Free Lunch Program: 97,874 (64.2%)
  Eligible for Reduced-Price Lunch Program: 6,057 (4.0%)
Teachers: 6,719.0 (22.7 to 1)
Librarians/Media Specialists: 73.0 (2,087.6 to 1)
Guidance Counselors: 267.0 (570.8 to 1)
Current Spending: ($ per student per year):
  Total: $9,063; Instruction: $5,089; Support Services: $3,723
Enrollment, Drop-out Rates and Diploma Recipients by Race/Ethnicity

Category	Total	White	Black	Asian	AIAN	Hisp.
Enrollment (%)	100.0	3.0	90.8	0.8	0.3	5.1
Drop-out Rate (%)	n/a	n/a	n/a	n/a	n/a	n/a
H.S. Diplomas (#)	5,540	174	5,096	47	23	200

Flat Rock Community Schools
28639 Division • Flat Rock, MI 48134-1515
(734) 782-2451 • http://www.resa.net/flatrock/
Grade Span: PK-12; **Agency Type:** 1
Schools: 5
  2 Primary; 2 Middle; 1 High; 0 Other Level
  5 Regular; 0 Special Education; 0 Vocational; 0 Alternative
  0 Magnet; 0 Charter; 1 Title I Eligible; 1 School-wide Title I
Students: 1,779 (49.5% male; 50.4% female)
  Individual Education Program: 283 (15.9%);
  English Language Learner: 0 (0.0%); Migrant: n/a
  Eligible for Free Lunch Program: 362 (20.3%)
  Eligible for Reduced-Price Lunch Program: 102 (5.7%)
Teachers: 89.0 (20.0 to 1)
Librarians/Media Specialists: 1.0 (1,779.0 to 1)
Guidance Counselors: 2.0 (889.5 to 1)
Current Spending: ($ per student per year):
  Total: $8,041; Instruction: $4,416; Support Services: $3,374
Enrollment, Drop-out Rates and Diploma Recipients by Race/Ethnicity

Category	Total	White	Black	Asian	AIAN	Hisp.
Enrollment (%)	100.0	95.1	2.4	0.7	0.2	1.6
Drop-out Rate (%)	n/a	n/a	n/a	n/a	n/a	n/a
H.S. Diplomas (#)	92	91	1	0	0	0

Garden City SD

1333 Radcliff St • Garden City, MI 48135-1126
(734) 762-8300 • http://www.resa.net/gardencity/
Grade Span: PK-12; Agency Type: 1
Schools: 10
  5 Primary; 1 Middle; 2 High; 2 Other Level
  7 Regular; 1 Special Education; 0 Vocational; 2 Alternative
  0 Magnet; 0 Charter; 0 Title I Eligible; 0 School-wide Title I
Students: 5,152 (53.1% male; 46.8% female)
  Individual Education Program: 1,123 (21.8%);
  English Language Learner: 0 (0.0%); Migrant: n/a
  Eligible for Free Lunch Program: 655 (13.2%)
  Eligible for Reduced-Price Lunch Program: 268 (5.4%)
Teachers: 346.0 (14.4 to 1)
Librarians/Media Specialists: 1.0 (4,981.0 to 1)
Guidance Counselors: 6.0 (830.2 to 1)
Current Spending: ($ per student per year):
  Total: $10,163; Instruction: $6,569; Support Services: $3,594
Enrollment, Drop-out Rates and Diploma Recipients by Race/Ethnicity

Category	Total	White	Black	Asian	AIAN	Hisp.
Enrollment (%)	100.0	94.2	3.9	0.5	0.3	1.1
Drop-out Rate (%)	n/a	n/a	n/a	n/a	n/a	n/a
H.S. Diplomas (#)	275	269	2	1	0	3

Gibraltar SD

19370 Vreeland Rd • Woodhaven, MI 48183-4430
(734) 692-4002 • http://www.resa.net/gibraltar/
Grade Span: PK-12; Agency Type: 1
Schools: 8
  5 Primary; 1 Middle; 2 High; 0 Other Level
  7 Regular; 0 Special Education; 0 Vocational; 1 Alternative
  0 Magnet; 0 Charter; 4 Title I Eligible; 4 School-wide Title I
Students: 3,306 (50.9% male; 49.0% female)
  Individual Education Program: 464 (14.0%);
  English Language Learner: 0 (0.0%); Migrant: n/a
  Eligible for Free Lunch Program: 430 (13.0%)
  Eligible for Reduced-Price Lunch Program: 135 (4.1%)
Teachers: 154.0 (21.5 to 1)
Librarians/Media Specialists: 2.0 (1,653.0 to 1)
Guidance Counselors: 4.0 (826.5 to 1)
Current Spending: ($ per student per year):
  Total: $7,910; Instruction: $4,418; Support Services: $3,171
Enrollment, Drop-out Rates and Diploma Recipients by Race/Ethnicity

Category	Total	White	Black	Asian	AIAN	Hisp.
Enrollment (%)	100.0	87.4	3.2	1.1	4.4	3.9
Drop-out Rate (%)	n/a	n/a	n/a	n/a	n/a	n/a
H.S. Diplomas (#)	200	182	1	2	11	4

Grosse Ile Township Schools

23276 E River Rd • Grosse Ile, MI 48138-1535
(734) 362-2555 • http://www.gischools.org/
Grade Span: KG-12; Agency Type: 1
Schools: 4
  2 Primary; 1 Middle; 1 High; 0 Other Level
  4 Regular; 0 Special Education; 0 Vocational; 0 Alternative
  0 Magnet; 0 Charter; 0 Title I Eligible; 0 School-wide Title I
Students: 2,023 (49.7% male; 50.2% female)
  Individual Education Program: 181 (8.9%);
  English Language Learner: 0 (0.0%); Migrant: n/a
  Eligible for Free Lunch Program: 31 (1.5%)
  Eligible for Reduced-Price Lunch Program: 32 (1.6%)
Teachers: 108.0 (18.7 to 1)
Librarians/Media Specialists: 3.0 (674.3 to 1)
Guidance Counselors: 3.0 (674.3 to 1)
Current Spending: ($ per student per year):
  Total: $8,799; Instruction: $5,171; Support Services: $3,382
Enrollment, Drop-out Rates and Diploma Recipients by Race/Ethnicity

Category	Total	White	Black	Asian	AIAN	Hisp.
Enrollment (%)	100.0	93.8	0.2	2.7	2.0	1.3
Drop-out Rate (%)	n/a	n/a	n/a	n/a	n/a	n/a
H.S. Diplomas (#)	175	165	0	5	2	3

Grosse Pointe Public Schools

389 St Clair Ave • Grosse Pointe, MI 48230-1501
(313) 432-3000 • http://www.gp.k12.mi.us/
Grade Span: PK-12; Agency Type: 1
Schools: 16
  10 Primary; 3 Middle; 2 High; 1 Other Level
  15 Regular; 1 Special Education; 0 Vocational; 0 Alternative
  0 Magnet; 0 Charter; 0 Title I Eligible; 0 School-wide Title I
Students: 8,938 (50.7% male; 49.2% female)
  Individual Education Program: 1,074 (12.0%);
  English Language Learner: 255 (2.9%); Migrant: n/a
  Eligible for Free Lunch Program: 236 (2.6%)
  Eligible for Reduced-Price Lunch Program: 81 (0.9%)

Teachers: 574.0 (15.6 to 1)
Librarians/Media Specialists: 12.0 (744.8 to 1)
Guidance Counselors: 17.0 (525.8 to 1)
Current Spending: ($ per student per year):
  Total: $9,996; Instruction: $6,166; Support Services: $3,681
Enrollment, Drop-out Rates and Diploma Recipients by Race/Ethnicity

Category	Total	White	Black	Asian	AIAN	Hisp.
Enrollment (%)	100.0	90.4	6.6	1.9	0.2	0.8
Drop-out Rate (%)	n/a	n/a	n/a	n/a	n/a	n/a
H.S. Diplomas (#)	720	679	18	15	1	7

Hamtramck Public Schools

3201 Roosevelt • Hamtramck, MI 48212-3753
Mailing Address: PO Box 12012 • Hamtramck, MI 48212-0012
(313) 872-9270 • http://www.hamtramck.k12.mi.us/
Grade Span: PK-12; Agency Type: 1
Schools: 7
  4 Primary; 1 Middle; 2 High; 0 Other Level
  6 Regular; 0 Special Education; 0 Vocational; 1 Alternative
  0 Magnet; 0 Charter; 7 Title I Eligible; 7 School-wide Title I
Students: 3,802 (55.0% male; 44.9% female)
  Individual Education Program: 310 (8.2%);
  English Language Learner: 2,555 (67.2%); Migrant: n/a
  Eligible for Free Lunch Program: 2,466 (64.9%)
  Eligible for Reduced-Price Lunch Program: 394 (10.4%)
Teachers: 224.0 (17.0 to 1)
Librarians/Media Specialists: 3.0 (1,267.3 to 1)
Guidance Counselors: 3.0 (1,267.3 to 1)
Current Spending: ($ per student per year):
  Total: $8,263; Instruction: $4,687; Support Services: $3,275
Enrollment, Drop-out Rates and Diploma Recipients by Race/Ethnicity

Category	Total	White	Black	Asian	AIAN	Hisp.
Enrollment (%)	100.0	55.6	17.6	25.8	0.3	0.7
Drop-out Rate (%)	n/a	n/a	n/a	n/a	n/a	n/a
H.S. Diplomas (#)	162	102	12	47	1	0

Highland Park City Schools

20 Bartlett St • Highland Park, MI 48203-3720
(313) 957-3000 • http://www.resa.net/highlandpark/index.htm
Grade Span: KG-12; Agency Type: 1
Schools: 6
  4 Primary; 0 Middle; 1 High; 1 Other Level
  5 Regular; 0 Special Education; 0 Vocational; 1 Alternative
  0 Magnet; 0 Charter; 4 Title I Eligible; 4 School-wide Title I
Students: 3,417 (48.9% male; 51.0% female)
  Individual Education Program: 434 (12.7%);
  English Language Learner: 0 (0.0%); Migrant: n/a
  Eligible for Free Lunch Program: 2,012 (58.9%)
  Eligible for Reduced-Price Lunch Program: 103 (3.0%)
Teachers: 100.0 (34.2 to 1)
Librarians/Media Specialists: 6.0 (569.5 to 1)
Guidance Counselors: 3.0 (1,139.0 to 1)
Current Spending: ($ per student per year):
  Total: $9,118; Instruction: $4,633; Support Services: $4,208
Enrollment, Drop-out Rates and Diploma Recipients by Race/Ethnicity

Category	Total	White	Black	Asian	AIAN	Hisp.
Enrollment (%)	100.0	0.4	99.3	0.1	0.2	0.0
Drop-out Rate (%)	n/a	n/a	n/a	n/a	n/a	n/a
H.S. Diplomas (#)	81	1	80	0	0	0

Huron SD

32044 Huron River Dr • New Boston, MI 48164-9282
(734) 782-2441 • http://www.resa.net/huron/
Grade Span: KG-12; Agency Type: 1
Schools: 5
  3 Primary; 1 Middle; 1 High; 0 Other Level
  5 Regular; 0 Special Education; 0 Vocational; 0 Alternative
  0 Magnet; 0 Charter; 1 Title I Eligible; 1 School-wide Title I
Students: 2,124 (52.3% male; 47.6% female)
  Individual Education Program: 321 (15.1%);
  English Language Learner: 0 (0.0%); Migrant: n/a
  Eligible for Free Lunch Program: 253 (11.9%)
  Eligible for Reduced-Price Lunch Program: 90 (4.2%)
Teachers: 114.0 (18.6 to 1)
Librarians/Media Specialists: 2.0 (1,062.0 to 1)
Guidance Counselors: 4.0 (531.0 to 1)
Current Spending: ($ per student per year):
  Total: $7,949; Instruction: $4,834; Support Services: $2,887
Enrollment, Drop-out Rates and Diploma Recipients by Race/Ethnicity

Category	Total	White	Black	Asian	AIAN	Hisp.
Enrollment (%)	100.0	95.1	1.1	0.6	1.0	2.2
Drop-out Rate (%)	n/a	n/a	n/a	n/a	n/a	n/a
H.S. Diplomas (#)	113	106	2	0	3	2

Lincoln Park Public Schools
1650 Champaign Rd • Lincoln Park, MI 48146-3202
(313) 389-0200 • http://www.resa.net/lincolnpark/index.htm
Grade Span: PK-12; **Agency Type:** 1
Schools: 13
    9 Primary; 1 Middle; 2 High; 1 Other Level
    10 Regular; 2 Special Education; 0 Vocational; 1 Alternative
    0 Magnet; 0 Charter; 0 Title I Eligible; 0 School-wide Title I
Students: 5,226   (52.6% male; 47.3% female)
    Individual Education Program: 644 (12.3%);
    English Language Learner: 0 (0.0%); Migrant: n/a
    Eligible for Free Lunch Program: 1,518 (29.0%)
    Eligible for Reduced-Price Lunch Program: 573 (11.0%)
Teachers: 303.0 (17.2 to 1)
Librarians/Media Specialists: 4.0 (1,306.5 to 1)
Guidance Counselors: 8.0 (653.3 to 1)
Current Spending: ($ per student per year):
    Total: $8,368; Instruction: $5,226; Support Services: $2,874
Enrollment, Drop-out Rates and Diploma Recipients by Race/Ethnicity

Category	Total	White	Black	Asian	AIAN	Hisp.
Enrollment (%)	100.0	87.1	3.1	0.7	0.5	8.6
Drop-out Rate (%)	n/a	n/a	n/a	n/a	n/a	n/a
H.S. Diplomas (#)	260	237	7	2	1	13

Livonia Public Schools
15125 Farmington Rd • Livonia, MI 48154-5413
(734) 744-2525 • http://www.livonia.k12.mi.us/
Grade Span: PK-12; **Agency Type:** 1
Schools: 34
    22 Primary; 4 Middle; 3 High; 5 Other Level
    29 Regular; 2 Special Education; 2 Vocational; 1 Alternative
    0 Magnet; 0 Charter; 4 Title I Eligible; 4 School-wide Title I
Students: 18,379   (51.8% male; 48.1% female)
    Individual Education Program: 2,266 (12.3%);
    English Language Learner: 149 (0.8%); Migrant: n/a
    Eligible for Free Lunch Program: 958 (5.2%)
    Eligible for Reduced-Price Lunch Program: 464 (2.5%)
Teachers: 1,035.0 (17.8 to 1)
Librarians/Media Specialists: 31.0 (592.9 to 1)
Guidance Counselors: 34.0 (540.6 to 1)
Current Spending: ($ per student per year):
    Total: $9,204; Instruction: $5,195; Support Services: $3,782
Enrollment, Drop-out Rates and Diploma Recipients by Race/Ethnicity

Category	Total	White	Black	Asian	AIAN	Hisp.
Enrollment (%)	100.0	91.8	3.7	2.7	0.3	1.5
Drop-out Rate (%)	n/a	n/a	n/a	n/a	n/a	n/a
H.S. Diplomas (#)	1,315	1,258	16	27	2	12

Melvindale-North Allen Park Schools
18530 Prospect St • Melvindale, MI 48122-1508
(313) 389-3300 • http://www.melnap.k12.mi.us/
Grade Span: KG-12; **Agency Type:** 1
Schools: 6
    4 Primary; 1 Middle; 1 High; 0 Other Level
    6 Regular; 0 Special Education; 0 Vocational; 0 Alternative
    0 Magnet; 0 Charter; 4 Title I Eligible; 4 School-wide Title I
Students: 2,600   (49.7% male; 50.2% female)
    Individual Education Program: 337 (13.0%);
    English Language Learner: 100 (3.8%); Migrant: n/a
    Eligible for Free Lunch Program: 879 (33.8%)
    Eligible for Reduced-Price Lunch Program: 312 (12.0%)
Teachers: 131.0 (19.8 to 1)
Librarians/Media Specialists: 3.0 (866.7 to 1)
Guidance Counselors: 2.0 (1,300.0 to 1)
Current Spending: ($ per student per year):
    Total: $8,010; Instruction: $4,350; Support Services: $3,407
Enrollment, Drop-out Rates and Diploma Recipients by Race/Ethnicity

Category	Total	White	Black	Asian	AIAN	Hisp.
Enrollment (%)	100.0	80.2	6.8	0.3	0.8	12.0
Drop-out Rate (%)	n/a	n/a	n/a	n/a	n/a	n/a
H.S. Diplomas (#)	123	109	6	0	0	8

Northville Public Schools
501 W Main St • Northville, MI 48167-1576
(248) 349-3400 • http://www.northville.k12.mi.us/
Grade Span: PK-12; **Agency Type:** 1
Schools: 11
    6 Primary; 2 Middle; 1 High; 2 Other Level
    9 Regular; 2 Special Education; 0 Vocational; 0 Alternative
    0 Magnet; 0 Charter; 0 Title I Eligible; 0 School-wide Title I
Students: 6,370   (50.6% male; 49.3% female)
    Individual Education Program: 628 (9.9%);
    English Language Learner: 101 (1.6%); Migrant: n/a
    Eligible for Free Lunch Program: 137 (2.2%)
    Eligible for Reduced-Price Lunch Program: 25 (0.4%)

Teachers: 376.0 (16.9 to 1)
Librarians/Media Specialists: 9.0 (704.8 to 1)
Guidance Counselors: 9.0 (704.8 to 1)
Current Spending: ($ per student per year):
    Total: $10,055; Instruction: $6,066; Support Services: $3,682
Enrollment, Drop-out Rates and Diploma Recipients by Race/Ethnicity

Category	Total	White	Black	Asian	AIAN	Hisp.
Enrollment (%)	100.0	89.0	2.2	7.5	0.1	1.2
Drop-out Rate (%)	n/a	n/a	n/a	n/a	n/a	n/a
H.S. Diplomas (#)	331	303	2	24	0	2

Plymouth-Canton Community Schools
454 S Harvey St • Plymouth, MI 48170-1717
(734) 416-2700 • http://www.pccs.k12.mi.us/
Grade Span: PK-12; **Agency Type:** 1
Schools: 25
    16 Primary; 5 Middle; 3 High; 1 Other Level
    24 Regular; 1 Special Education; 0 Vocational; 0 Alternative
    0 Magnet; 0 Charter; 0 Title I Eligible; 0 School-wide Title I
Students: 18,121   (50.2% male; 49.7% female)
    Individual Education Program: 1,843 (10.2%);
    English Language Learner: 712 (3.9%); Migrant: n/a
    Eligible for Free Lunch Program: 958 (5.3%)
    Eligible for Reduced-Price Lunch Program: 283 (1.6%)
Teachers: 890.0 (20.1 to 1)
Librarians/Media Specialists: 18.0 (995.1 to 1)
Guidance Counselors: 28.0 (639.7 to 1)
Current Spending: ($ per student per year):
    Total: $7,248; Instruction: $4,281; Support Services: $2,782
Enrollment, Drop-out Rates and Diploma Recipients by Race/Ethnicity

Category	Total	White	Black	Asian	AIAN	Hisp.
Enrollment (%)	100.0	81.8	5.1	10.8	0.5	1.8
Drop-out Rate (%)	n/a	n/a	n/a	n/a	n/a	n/a
H.S. Diplomas (#)	1,008	887	37	72	3	9

Redford Union SD
18499 Beech Daly Rd • Redford, MI 48240-1804
(313) 242-6000 • http://www.steve-hatfield.com/redfordunion.htm
Grade Span: PK-12; **Agency Type:** 1
Schools: 11
    6 Primary; 1 Middle; 2 High; 2 Other Level
    8 Regular; 3 Special Education; 0 Vocational; 0 Alternative
    0 Magnet; 0 Charter; 0 Title I Eligible; 0 School-wide Title I
Students: 4,573   (53.5% male; 46.4% female)
    Individual Education Program: 1,137 (24.9%);
    English Language Learner: 0 (0.0%); Migrant: n/a
    Eligible for Free Lunch Program: 1,182 (25.8%)
    Eligible for Reduced-Price Lunch Program: 456 (10.0%)
Teachers: 272.0 (16.8 to 1)
Librarians/Media Specialists: 1.0 (4,573.0 to 1)
Guidance Counselors: 3.0 (1,524.3 to 1)
Current Spending: ($ per student per year):
    Total: $9,084; Instruction: $5,360; Support Services: $3,445
Enrollment, Drop-out Rates and Diploma Recipients by Race/Ethnicity

Category	Total	White	Black	Asian	AIAN	Hisp.
Enrollment (%)	100.0	78.5	18.7	0.9	0.3	1.6
Drop-out Rate (%)	n/a	n/a	n/a	n/a	n/a	n/a
H.S. Diplomas (#)	205	181	18	1	1	4

River Rouge SD
1460 W Coolidge Hwy • River Rouge, MI 48218-1118
(313) 297-9600 • http://www.resa.net/riverrouge/
Grade Span: PK-12; **Agency Type:** 1
Schools: 5
    2 Primary; 2 Middle; 1 High; 0 Other Level
    5 Regular; 0 Special Education; 0 Vocational; 0 Alternative
    0 Magnet; 0 Charter; 4 Title I Eligible; 4 School-wide Title I
Students: 2,327   (53.2% male; 46.7% female)
    Individual Education Program: 359 (15.4%);
    English Language Learner: 0 (0.0%); Migrant: n/a
    Eligible for Free Lunch Program: 1,645 (70.7%)
    Eligible for Reduced-Price Lunch Program: 236 (10.1%)
Teachers: 146.0 (15.9 to 1)
Librarians/Media Specialists: 1.0 (2,327.0 to 1)
Guidance Counselors: 5.0 (465.4 to 1)
Current Spending: ($ per student per year):
    Total: $9,583; Instruction: $5,211; Support Services: $3,902
Enrollment, Drop-out Rates and Diploma Recipients by Race/Ethnicity

Category	Total	White	Black	Asian	AIAN	Hisp.
Enrollment (%)	100.0	26.4	68.5	0.0	0.9	4.2
Drop-out Rate (%)	n/a	n/a	n/a	n/a	n/a	n/a
H.S. Diplomas (#)	136	32	97	0	0	7

Riverview Community SD

13425 Colvin St • Riverview, MI 48192-6674
(734) 285-9660 • http://www.resa.net/riverview/index.htm
Grade Span: KG-12; **Agency Type:** 1
Schools: 5
   3 Primary; 1 Middle; 1 High; 0 Other Level
   5 Regular; 0 Special Education; 0 Vocational; 0 Alternative
   0 Magnet; 0 Charter; 0 Title I Eligible; 0 School-wide Title I
Students: 2,596 (50.8% male; 49.1% female)
   Individual Education Program: 228 (8.8%);
   English Language Learner: 0 (0.0%); Migrant: n/a
   Eligible for Free Lunch Program: 255 (9.8%)
   Eligible for Reduced-Price Lunch Program: 140 (5.4%)
Teachers: 130.0 (20.0 to 1)
Librarians/Media Specialists: 3.0 (865.3 to 1)
Guidance Counselors: 5.0 (519.2 to 1)
Current Spending: ($ per student per year):
   Total: $7,279; Instruction: $4,420; Support Services: $2,717
Enrollment, Drop-out Rates and Diploma Recipients by Race/Ethnicity

Category	Total	White	Black	Asian	AIAN	Hisp.
Enrollment (%)	100.0	94.1	2.1	0.9	0.1	2.8
Drop-out Rate (%)	n/a	n/a	n/a	n/a	n/a	n/a
H.S. Diplomas (#)	171	168	2	0	0	1

Romulus Community Schools

36540 Grant Rd • Romulus, MI 48174-1445
(734) 532-1600 • http://www.romulus.net/
Grade Span: PK-12; **Agency Type:** 1
Schools: 10
   6 Primary; 1 Middle; 1 High; 2 Other Level
   8 Regular; 0 Special Education; 0 Vocational; 2 Alternative
   3 Magnet; 0 Charter; 6 Title I Eligible; 6 School-wide Title I
Students: 4,301 (50.5% male; 49.4% female)
   Individual Education Program: 611 (14.2%);
   English Language Learner: 0 (0.0%); Migrant: n/a
   Eligible for Free Lunch Program: 1,619 (37.6%)
   Eligible for Reduced-Price Lunch Program: 325 (7.6%)
Teachers: 227.0 (18.9 to 1)
Librarians/Media Specialists: 2.0 (2,150.5 to 1)
Guidance Counselors: 6.0 (716.8 to 1)
Current Spending: ($ per student per year):
   Total: $9,500; Instruction: $4,813; Support Services: $4,391
Enrollment, Drop-out Rates and Diploma Recipients by Race/Ethnicity

Category	Total	White	Black	Asian	AIAN	Hisp.
Enrollment (%)	100.0	45.1	52.5	0.2	0.6	1.6
Drop-out Rate (%)	n/a	n/a	n/a	n/a	n/a	n/a
H.S. Diplomas (#)	201	107	94	0	0	0

South Redford SD

26141 Schoolcraft • Redford, MI 48239-2775
(313) 535-4000 • http://southredford.net/
Grade Span: PK-12; **Agency Type:** 1
Schools: 7
   5 Primary; 1 Middle; 1 High; 0 Other Level
   7 Regular; 0 Special Education; 0 Vocational; 0 Alternative
   0 Magnet; 0 Charter; 0 Title I Eligible; 0 School-wide Title I
Students: 3,396 (49.7% male; 50.2% female)
   Individual Education Program: 422 (12.4%);
   English Language Learner: 0 (0.0%); Migrant: n/a
   Eligible for Free Lunch Program: 572 (16.8%)
   Eligible for Reduced-Price Lunch Program: 218 (6.4%)
Teachers: 186.0 (18.3 to 1)
Librarians/Media Specialists: 5.0 (679.2 to 1)
Guidance Counselors: 4.0 (849.0 to 1)
Current Spending: ($ per student per year):
   Total: $7,941; Instruction: $4,018; Support Services: $3,688
Enrollment, Drop-out Rates and Diploma Recipients by Race/Ethnicity

Category	Total	White	Black	Asian	AIAN	Hisp.
Enrollment (%)	100.0	61.3	34.6	0.8	0.4	2.9
Drop-out Rate (%)	n/a	n/a	n/a	n/a	n/a	n/a
H.S. Diplomas (#)	199	148	37	4	0	10

Southgate Community SD

13201 Trenton Rd • Southgate, MI 48195-1891
(734) 246-4600 • http://www.southgateschools.com/
Grade Span: PK-12; **Agency Type:** 1
Schools: 11
   6 Primary; 1 Middle; 1 High; 3 Other Level
   9 Regular; 2 Special Education; 0 Vocational; 0 Alternative
   0 Magnet; 0 Charter; 0 Title I Eligible; 0 School-wide Title I
Students: 5,306 (51.9% male; 48.0% female)
   Individual Education Program: 787 (14.8%);
   English Language Learner: 0 (0.0%); Migrant: n/a
   Eligible for Free Lunch Program: 815 (16.6%)
   Eligible for Reduced-Price Lunch Program: 336 (6.8%)

Teachers: 290.0 (17.0 to 1)
Librarians/Media Specialists: 2.0 (2,459.0 to 1)
Guidance Counselors: 3.0 (1,639.3 to 1)
Current Spending: ($ per student per year):
   Total: $8,335; Instruction: $4,739; Support Services: $3,376
Enrollment, Drop-out Rates and Diploma Recipients by Race/Ethnicity

Category	Total	White	Black	Asian	AIAN	Hisp.
Enrollment (%)	100.0	89.1	3.4	1.2	1.1	5.0
Drop-out Rate (%)	n/a	n/a	n/a	n/a	n/a	n/a
H.S. Diplomas (#)	284	262	4	2	2	14

Taylor SD

23033 Northline Rd • Taylor, MI 48180-4625
(734) 374-1200 • http://www.taylorschools.net/
Grade Span: PK-12; **Agency Type:** 1
Schools: 21
   14 Primary; 3 Middle; 3 High; 1 Other Level
   19 Regular; 0 Special Education; 1 Vocational; 1 Alternative
   0 Magnet; 0 Charter; 18 Title I Eligible; 18 School-wide Title I
Students: 10,890 (50.5% male; 49.4% female)
   Individual Education Program: 1,849 (17.0%);
   English Language Learner: 0 (0.0%); Migrant: n/a
   Eligible for Free Lunch Program: 3,152 (28.9%)
   Eligible for Reduced-Price Lunch Program: 1,032 (9.5%)
Teachers: 614.0 (17.7 to 1)
Librarians/Media Specialists: 4.0 (2,722.5 to 1)
Guidance Counselors: 20.0 (544.5 to 1)
Current Spending: ($ per student per year):
   Total: $8,315; Instruction: $4,510; Support Services: $3,540
Enrollment, Drop-out Rates and Diploma Recipients by Race/Ethnicity

Category	Total	White	Black	Asian	AIAN	Hisp.
Enrollment (%)	100.0	77.1	18.2	1.2	0.9	2.5
Drop-out Rate (%)	n/a	n/a	n/a	n/a	n/a	n/a
H.S. Diplomas (#)	567	488	47	20	1	11

Trenton Public Schools

2603 Charlton Rd • Trenton, MI 48183-2446
(734) 676-8600 • http://www.trenton-mi.com/schools/schools.html
Grade Span: KG-12; **Agency Type:** 1
Schools: 6
   4 Primary; 1 Middle; 1 High; 0 Other Level
   6 Regular; 0 Special Education; 0 Vocational; 0 Alternative
   0 Magnet; 0 Charter; 0 Title I Eligible; 0 School-wide Title I
Students: 3,082 (52.0% male; 47.9% female)
   Individual Education Program: 513 (16.6%);
   English Language Learner: 0 (0.0%); Migrant: n/a
   Eligible for Free Lunch Program: 206 (6.7%)
   Eligible for Reduced-Price Lunch Program: 56 (1.8%)
Teachers: 200.0 (15.4 to 1)
Librarians/Media Specialists: 5.0 (616.4 to 1)
Guidance Counselors: 4.0 (770.5 to 1)
Current Spending: ($ per student per year):
   Total: $9,779; Instruction: $6,053; Support Services: $3,538
Enrollment, Drop-out Rates and Diploma Recipients by Race/Ethnicity

Category	Total	White	Black	Asian	AIAN	Hisp.
Enrollment (%)	100.0	96.3	0.9	1.4	0.1	1.3
Drop-out Rate (%)	n/a	n/a	n/a	n/a	n/a	n/a
H.S. Diplomas (#)	216	214	0	0	0	2

Van Buren Public Schools

555 W Columbia Ave • Belleville, MI 48111-2611
(734) 697-9123 • http://www.resa.net/vanburen/
Grade Span: PK-12; **Agency Type:** 1
Schools: 10
   6 Primary; 2 Middle; 1 High; 1 Other Level
   9 Regular; 0 Special Education; 0 Vocational; 1 Alternative
   0 Magnet; 0 Charter; 1 Title I Eligible; 1 School-wide Title I
Students: 6,110 (50.7% male; 49.2% female)
   Individual Education Program: 844 (13.8%);
   English Language Learner: 0 (0.0%); Migrant: n/a
   Eligible for Free Lunch Program: 1,306 (21.4%)
   Eligible for Reduced-Price Lunch Program: 359 (5.9%)
Teachers: 342.0 (17.9 to 1)
Librarians/Media Specialists: 10.0 (611.0 to 1)
Guidance Counselors: 6.0 (1,018.3 to 1)
Current Spending: ($ per student per year):
   Total: $7,878; Instruction: $4,509; Support Services: $3,116
Enrollment, Drop-out Rates and Diploma Recipients by Race/Ethnicity

Category	Total	White	Black	Asian	AIAN	Hisp.
Enrollment (%)	100.0	67.5	29.1	1.1	0.3	2.0
Drop-out Rate (%)	n/a	n/a	n/a	n/a	n/a	n/a
H.S. Diplomas (#)	363	264	90	6	1	2

Wayne-Westland Community SD
36745 Marquette St • Westland, MI 48185-3235
(734) 419-2000 • http://wwcsd.net/
Grade Span: PK-12; **Agency Type:** 1
Schools: 26
   18 Primary; 4 Middle; 2 High; 2 Other Level
   24 Regular; 0 Special Education; 1 Vocational; 1 Alternative
   0 Magnet; 0 Charter; 15 Title I Eligible; 15 School-wide Title I
Students: 14,296 (51.1% male; 48.8% female)
   Individual Education Program: 2,363 (16.5%);
   English Language Learner: 0 (0.0%); Migrant: n/a
   Eligible for Free Lunch Program: 3,769 (26.4%)
   Eligible for Reduced-Price Lunch Program: 1,233 (8.6%)
Teachers: 787.0 (18.2 to 1)
Librarians/Media Specialists: 13.0 (1,099.7 to 1)
Guidance Counselors: 30.0 (476.5 to 1)
Current Spending: ($ per student per year):
   Total: $8,732; Instruction: $4,781; Support Services: $3,697
Enrollment, Drop-out Rates and Diploma Recipients by Race/Ethnicity

Category	Total	White	Black	Asian	AIAN	Hisp.
Enrollment (%)	100.0	75.9	19.0	1.6	1.0	2.5
Drop-out Rate (%)	n/a	n/a	n/a	n/a	n/a	n/a
H.S. Diplomas (#)	716	565	118	17	9	7

Westwood Community Schools
3335 S Beech Daly Rd • Dearborn Heights, MI 48125-1189
(313) 565-1900 • http://www.westwood.k12.mi.us/
Grade Span: KG-12; **Agency Type:** 1
Schools: 4
   3 Primary; 0 Middle; 1 High; 0 Other Level
   4 Regular; 0 Special Education; 0 Vocational; 0 Alternative
   0 Magnet; 0 Charter; 3 Title I Eligible; 3 School-wide Title I
Students: 2,357 (53.5% male; 46.4% female)
   Individual Education Program: 458 (19.4%);
   English Language Learner: 0 (0.0%); Migrant: n/a
   Eligible for Free Lunch Program: 1,670 (70.9%)
   Eligible for Reduced-Price Lunch Program: 390 (16.5%)
Teachers: 130.0 (18.1 to 1)
Librarians/Media Specialists: 3.0 (785.7 to 1)
Guidance Counselors: 6.0 (392.8 to 1)
Current Spending: ($ per student per year):
   Total: $9,773; Instruction: $5,552; Support Services: $3,759
Enrollment, Drop-out Rates and Diploma Recipients by Race/Ethnicity

Category	Total	White	Black	Asian	AIAN	Hisp.
Enrollment (%)	100.0	23.9	73.3	1.0	0.3	1.4
Drop-out Rate (%)	n/a	n/a	n/a	n/a	n/a	n/a
H.S. Diplomas (#)	67	16	48	3	0	0

Woodhaven-Brownstown SD
24975 Van Horn Rd • Brownstown, MI 48134-9232
(734) 783-3300 • http://warrior.woodhaven.k12.mi.us/
Grade Span: KG-12; **Agency Type:** 1
Schools: 9
   5 Primary; 1 Middle; 1 High; 2 Other Level
   8 Regular; 1 Special Education; 0 Vocational; 0 Alternative
   0 Magnet; 0 Charter; 0 Title I Eligible; 0 School-wide Title I
Students: 5,213 (51.6% male; 48.3% female)
   Individual Education Program: 862 (16.5%);
   English Language Learner: 0 (0.0%); Migrant: n/a
   Eligible for Free Lunch Program: 812 (15.6%)
   Eligible for Reduced-Price Lunch Program: 220 (4.2%)
Teachers: 273.0 (19.1 to 1)
Librarians/Media Specialists: 4.0 (1,303.3 to 1)
Guidance Counselors: 7.0 (744.7 to 1)
Current Spending: ($ per student per year):
   Total: $8,076; Instruction: $4,967; Support Services: $2,840
Enrollment, Drop-out Rates and Diploma Recipients by Race/Ethnicity

Category	Total	White	Black	Asian	AIAN	Hisp.
Enrollment (%)	100.0	82.1	6.3	4.5	2.0	5.1
Drop-out Rate (%)	n/a	n/a	n/a	n/a	n/a	n/a
H.S. Diplomas (#)	274	237	9	17	1	10

Wyandotte City SD
639 Oak St • Wyandotte, MI 48192-5024
Mailing Address: PO Box 130 • Wyandotte, MI 48192-0130
(734) 246-1000 • http://www.wyandotte.org/
Grade Span: PK-12; **Agency Type:** 1
Schools: 11
   6 Primary; 1 Middle; 1 High; 3 Other Level
   8 Regular; 3 Special Education; 0 Vocational; 0 Alternative
   0 Magnet; 0 Charter; 0 Title I Eligible; 0 School-wide Title I
Students: 4,957 (51.1% male; 48.8% female)
   Individual Education Program: 1,077 (21.7%);
   English Language Learner: 0 (0.0%); Migrant: n/a
   Eligible for Free Lunch Program: 969 (19.5%)

Eligible for Reduced-Price Lunch Program: 357 (7.2%)
Teachers: 278.0 (17.8 to 1)
Librarians/Media Specialists: 2.0 (2,478.5 to 1)
Guidance Counselors: 5.0 (991.4 to 1)
Current Spending: ($ per student per year):
   Total: $9,551; Instruction: $6,315; Support Services: $3,043
Enrollment, Drop-out Rates and Diploma Recipients by Race/Ethnicity

Category	Total	White	Black	Asian	AIAN	Hisp.
Enrollment (%)	100.0	93.3	2.5	0.5	0.5	3.1
Drop-out Rate (%)	n/a	n/a	n/a	n/a	n/a	n/a
H.S. Diplomas (#)	264	246	1	1	4	12

Wexford County

Cadillac Area Public Schools
421 S Mitchell St • Cadillac, MI 49601-2571
(231) 876-5000 • http://www.vikingnet.org/
Grade Span: KG-12; **Agency Type:** 1
Schools: 9
   5 Primary; 1 Middle; 2 High; 1 Other Level
   8 Regular; 0 Special Education; 0 Vocational; 1 Alternative
   0 Magnet; 0 Charter; 5 Title I Eligible; 5 School-wide Title I
Students: 3,387 (52.3% male; 47.6% female)
   Individual Education Program: 377 (11.1%);
   English Language Learner: 0 (0.0%); Migrant: n/a
   Eligible for Free Lunch Program: 1,067 (31.5%)
   Eligible for Reduced-Price Lunch Program: 303 (8.9%)
Teachers: 148.0 (22.9 to 1)
Librarians/Media Specialists: 2.0 (1,693.5 to 1)
Guidance Counselors: 6.0 (564.5 to 1)
Current Spending: ($ per student per year):
   Total: $7,667; Instruction: $4,485; Support Services: $2,882
Enrollment, Drop-out Rates and Diploma Recipients by Race/Ethnicity

Category	Total	White	Black	Asian	AIAN	Hisp.
Enrollment (%)	100.0	96.5	1.1	0.6	0.7	1.1
Drop-out Rate (%)	n/a	n/a	n/a	n/a	n/a	n/a
H.S. Diplomas (#)	235	232	3	0	0	0

Number of Schools

Rank	Number	District Name	City
1	261	Detroit City SD	Detroit
2	88	Grand Rapids Public Schools	Grand Rapids
3	43	Utica Community Schools	Sterling Hgts
4	42	Lansing Public SD	Lansing
5	39	Flint City SD	Flint
6	34	Livonia Public Schools	Livonia
7	33	Ann Arbor Public Schools	Ann Arbor
7	33	Saginaw City SD	Saginaw
9	32	Dearborn City SD	Dearborn
10	27	Farmington Public SD	Farmington
11	26	Kalamazoo Public SD	Kalamazoo
11	26	Warren Consolidated Schools	Warren
11	26	Wayne-Westland Community SD	Westland
14	25	Battle Creek Public Schools	Battle Creek
14	25	Plymouth-Canton Community Schls	Plymouth
14	25	Waterford SD	Waterford
17	24	Pontiac City SD	Pontiac
17	24	Walled Lake Consolidated Schools	Walled Lake
19	22	Port Huron Area SD	Port Huron
19	22	Traverse City Area Public Schls	Traverse City
21	21	Rochester Community SD	Rochester
21	21	Taylor SD	Taylor
23	20	L'anse Creuse Public Schools	Harrison Twp
23	20	Midland Public Schools	Midland
25	19	Troy SD	Troy
26	18	Bay City SD	Bay City
26	18	Huron Valley Schools	Highland
26	18	Southfield Public SD	Southfield
29	17	Chippewa Valley Schools	Clinton Twp
29	17	Forest Hills Public Schools	Grand Rapids
29	17	Kentwood Public Schools	Kentwood
32	16	Benton Harbor Area Schools	Benton Harbor
32	16	Grosse Pointe Public Schools	Grosse Pointe
32	16	Lapeer Community Schools	Lapeer
32	16	Muskegon City SD	Muskegon
36	14	Birmingham City SD	Birmingham
36	14	Bloomfield Hills SD	Bloomfield Hls
36	14	Jackson Public Schools	Jackson
36	14	Portage Public Schools	Portage
36	14	Roseville Community Schools	Roseville
41	13	Anchor Bay SD	New Baltimore
41	13	Clarkston Community SD	Clarkston
41	13	Hazel Park City SD	Hazel Park
41	13	Lincoln Park Public Schools	Lincoln Park
41	13	Monroe Public Schools	Monroe
41	13	Rockford Public Schools	Rockford
41	13	SD of the City of Royal Oak	Royal Oak
41	13	West Ottawa Public SD	Holland
41	13	Wyoming Public Schools	Wyoming
50	12	East Detroit Public Schools	Eastpointe
50	12	Grand Haven Area Public Schools	Grand Haven
50	12	Grandville Public Schools	Grandville
50	12	Holt Public Schools	Holt
50	12	Lake Orion Community Schools	Lake Orion
50	12	SD of Ypsilanti	Ypsilanti
56	11	Alpena Public Schools	Alpena
56	11	East China SD	East China
56	11	Grand Blanc Community Schools	Grand Blanc
56	11	Holland City SD	Holland
56	11	Mt. Pleasant City SD	Mt. Pleasant
56	11	Northville Public Schools	Northville
56	11	Redford Union SD	Redford
56	11	Romeo Community Schools	Romeo
56	11	South Lyon Community Schools	South Lyon
56	11	Southgate Community SD	Southgate
56	11	Van Dyke Public Schools	Warren
56	11	West Bloomfield SD	West Bloomfield
56	11	Wyandotte City SD	Wyandotte
56	11	Zeeland Public Schools	Zeeland
70	10	Berkley SD	Berkley
70	10	Carman-Ainsworth Comm Schools	Flint
70	10	Fraser Public Schools	Fraser
70	10	Garden City SD	Garden City
70	10	Grand Ledge Public Schools	Grand Ledge
70	10	Howell Public Schools	Howell
70	10	Hudsonville Public SD	Hudsonville
70	10	Macomb ISD	Clinton Twp
70	10	Niles Community SD	Niles
70	10	Romulus Community Schools	Romulus
70	10	Van Buren Public Schools	Belleville
81	9	Adrian City SD	Adrian
81	9	Brighton Area Schools	Brighton
81	9	Cadillac Area Public Schools	Cadillac
81	9	Davison Community Schools	Davison
81	9	Kenowa Hills Public Schools	Grand Rapids
81	9	Lamphere Public Schools	Madison Heights
81	9	Novi Community SD	Novi
81	9	Okemos Public Schools	Okemos
81	9	Reeths-Puffer Schools	Muskegon
81	9	Saginaw Twp Community Schools	Saginaw
81	9	Sturgis Public Schools	Sturgis
81	9	Three Rivers Community Schools	Three Rivers
81	9	Woodhaven-Brownstown SD	Brownstown
94	8	Avondale SD	Auburn Hills
94	8	Byron Center Public Schools	Byron Center
94	8	Coldwater Community Schools	Coldwater
94	8	Dowagiac Union SD	Dowagiac
94	8	East Lansing SD	East Lansing
94	8	Gibraltar SD	Woodhaven
94	8	Hartland Consolidated Schools	Hartland
94	8	Ionia Public Schools	Ionia
94	8	Jenison Public Schools	Jenison
94	8	Lakeview SD (Calhoun)	Battle Creek
94	8	Ludington Area SD	Ludington
94	8	Muskegon Heights SD	Muskegon Hgts
94	8	Oak Park City SD	Oak Park
94	8	Owosso Public Schools	Owosso
94	8	Oxford Area Community Schools	Oxford
94	8	Sault Ste. Marie Area Schools	Sault Ste Marie
94	8	St. Johns Public Schools	St. Johns
94	8	Swartz Creek Community Schools	Swartz Creek
94	8	Willow Run Community Schools	Ypsilanti
113	7	Algonac Community SD	Algonac
113	7	Allegan Public Schools	Allegan
113	7	Bedford Public Schools	Temperance
113	7	Beecher Community SD	Flint
113	7	Belding Area SD	Belding
113	7	Big Rapids Public Schools	Big Rapids
113	7	Brandon SD	Ortonville
113	7	Bridgeport-Spaulding CSD	Bridgeport
113	7	Caledonia Community Schools	Caledonia
113	7	Center Line Public Schools	Center Line
113	7	Charlotte Public Schools	Charlotte
113	7	Cheboygan Area Schools	Cheboygan
113	7	Chippewa Hills SD	Remus
113	7	Comstock Public Schools	Kalamazoo
113	7	Escanaba Area Public Schools	Escanaba
113	7	Fenton Area Public Schools	Fenton
113	7	Ferndale Public Schools	Ferndale
113	7	Fitzgerald Public Schools	Warren
113	7	Gaylord Community Schools	Gaylord
113	7	Hamtramck Public Schools	Hamtramck
113	7	Hastings Area SD	Hastings
113	7	Holly Area SD	Holly
113	7	Houghton Lake Community Schools	Houghton Lake
113	7	Kearsley Community Schools	Flint
113	7	Kelloggsville Public Schools	Grand Rapids
113	7	Lakeville Community Schools	Otisville
113	7	Lakewood Public Schools	Lake Odessa
113	7	Lincoln Consolidated SD	Ypsilanti
113	7	Lowell Area Schools	Lowell
113	7	Marquette Area Public Schools	Marquette
113	7	Marshall Public Schools	Marshall
113	7	Mt. Clemens Community SD	Mt. Clemens
113	7	Mt. Morris Consolidated Schools	Mt. Morris
113	7	Northview Public SD	Grand Rapids
113	7	Public Schools of Petoskey	Petoskey
113	7	Saline Area Schools	Saline
113	7	Shelby Public Schools	Shelby
113	7	South Redford SD	Redford
113	7	Stockbridge Community Schools	Stockbridge
113	7	Tecumseh Public Schools	Tecumseh
113	7	Waverly Community Schools	Lansing
154	6	Airport Community SD	Carleton
154	6	Allen Park Public Schools	Allen Park
154	6	Bangor Township Schools	Bay City
154	6	Benzie County Central Schools	Benzonia
154	6	Cedar Springs Public Schools	Cedar Springs
154	6	Central Montcalm Public Schools	Stanton
154	6	Chelsea SD	Chelsea
154	6	Coloma Community Schools	Coloma
154	6	Comstock Park Public Schools	Comstock Park
154	6	Corunna Public SD	Corunna
154	6	Dearborn Heights SD #7	Dearborn Hgts
154	6	Dewitt Public Schools	Dewitt
154	6	Dexter Community SD	Dexter
154	6	Durand Area Schools	Durand
154	6	Eaton Rapids Public Schools	Eaton Rapids
154	6	Edwardsburg Public Schools	Edwardsburg
154	6	Flushing Community Schools	Flushing
154	6	Fremont Public SD	Fremont
154	6	Fruitport Community Schools	Fruitport
154	6	Godfrey-Lee Public Schools	Wyoming
154	6	Godwin Heights Public Schools	Wyoming
154	6	Greenville Public Schools	Greenville
154	6	Gull Lake Community Schools	Richland
154	6	Hamilton Community Schools	Hamilton
154	6	Haslett Public Schools	Haslett
154	6	Highland Park City Schools	Highland Park
154	6	Jefferson Schools (Monroe)	Monroe
154	6	Kalkaska Public Schools	Kalkaska
154	6	Lake Shore Pub Schools (Macomb)	St Clair Shores
154	6	Lakeview Public Schools (Macomb)	St Clair Shores
154	6	Linden Community Schools	Linden
154	6	Madison Public Schools (Oakland)	Madison Heights
154	6	Manistee Area Schools	Manistee
154	6	Mason County Central Schools	Scottville
154	6	Mason Public Schools (Ingham)	Mason
154	6	Melvindale-N Allen Park Schools	Melvindale
154	6	Menominee Area Public Schools	Menominee
154	6	Mona Shores Public SD	Norton Shores
154	6	Northwest Community Schools	Jackson
154	6	Orchard View Schools	Muskegon
154	6	Oscoda Area Schools	Oscoda
154	6	Ovid-Elsie Area Schools	Elsie
154	6	Parchment SD	Parchment
154	6	Pennfield SD	Battle Creek
154	6	Pinconning Area Schools	Pinconning
154	6	Plainwell Community Schools	Plainwell
154	6	Reed City Area Public Schools	Reed City
154	6	South Lake Schools	St Clair Shores
154	6	Sparta Area Schools	Sparta
154	6	Spring Lake Public Schools	Spring Lake
154	6	St. Joseph Public Schools	St. Joseph
154	6	Thornapple Kellogg SD	Middleville
154	6	Trenton Public Schools	Trenton
154	6	Tri County Area Schools	Sand Lake
154	6	Warren Woods Public Schools	Warren
154	6	Wayland Union Schools	Wayland
154	6	Western SD	Parma
154	6	Yale Public Schools	Yale
212	5	Albion Public Schools	Albion
212	5	Allendale Public SD	Allendale
212	5	Alma Public Schools	Alma
212	5	Armada Area Schools	Armada
212	5	Bangor Public Schls (Van Buren)	Bangor
212	5	Bendle Public Schools	Burton
212	5	Berrien Springs Public Schools	Berrien Springs
212	5	Brandywine Public SD	Niles
212	5	Buchanan Community Schools	Buchanan
212	5	Bullock Creek SD	Midland
212	5	Caro Community Schools	Caro
212	5	Chesaning Union Schools	Chesaning
212	5	Clintondale Community Schools	Clinton Twp
212	5	Clio Area SD	Clio
212	5	Columbia SD	Brooklyn
212	5	Crawford Ausable Schools	Grayling
212	5	Crestwood SD	Dearborn Hgts
212	5	Croswell-Lexington Comm Schools	Croswell
212	5	East Grand Rapids Public Schools	E Grand Rapids
212	5	Essexville-Hampton Public Schls	Essexville
212	5	Flat Rock Community Schools	Flat Rock
212	5	Fowlerville Community Schools	Fowlerville
212	5	Gerrish-Higgins SD	Roscommon
212	5	Gladwin Community Schools	Gladwin
212	5	Gwinn Area Community Schools	Gwinn
212	5	Harper Creek Community Schools	Battle Creek
212	5	Harrison Community Schools	Harrison
212	5	Hillsdale Community Schools	Hillsdale
212	5	Huron SD	New Boston
212	5	Imlay City Community Schools	Imlay City
212	5	Lakeshore SD (Berrien)	Stevensville
212	5	Lakeview Comm Schools (Montcalm)	Lakeview
212	5	Maple Valley Schools	Vermontville
212	5	Marysville Public Schools	Marysville
212	5	Millington Community Schools	Millington
212	5	Newaygo Public SD	Newaygo
212	5	North Branch Area Schools	North Branch
212	5	Oakridge Public Schools	Muskegon
212	5	Onsted Community Schools	Onsted
212	5	Otsego Public Schools	Otsego
212	5	Paw Paw Public SD	Paw Paw
212	5	Perry Public SD	Perry
212	5	Portland Public SD	Portland
212	5	River Rouge SD	River Rouge
212	5	Riverview Community SD	Riverview
212	5	Shepherd Public SD	Shepherd
212	5	South Haven Public Schools	South Haven
212	5	Vassar Public Schools	Vassar
212	5	Vicksburg Community Schools	Vicksburg
212	5	Washtenaw ISD	Ann Arbor
212	5	W Branch-Rose City Area Schools	West Branch
263	4	Beaverton Rural Schools	Beaverton
263	4	Birch Run Area SD	Birch Run
263	4	Carrollton SD	Saginaw
263	4	Clare Public Schools	Clare
263	4	Clarenceville SD	Livonia
263	4	Constantine Public SD	Constantine
263	4	Coopersville Public SD	Coopersville
263	4	Delton-Kellogg SD	Delton
263	4	Dundee Community Schools	Dundee
263	4	East Jackson Community Schools	Jackson
263	4	Elk Rapids Schools	Elk Rapids
263	4	Gladstone Area Schools	Gladstone
263	4	Goodrich Area Schools	Goodrich

263	4	Grant Public SD	Grant
263	4	Grosse Ile Township Schools	Grosse Ile
263	4	Hartford Public SD	Hartford
263	4	Mason Consol Schools (Monroe)	Erie
263	4	Mattawan Consolidated School	Mattawan
263	4	Meridian Public Schools	Sanford
263	4	Michigan Center SD	Michigan Center
263	4	Milan Area Schools	Milan
263	4	Morley Stanwood Community Schls	Morley
263	4	Napoleon Community Schools	Napoleon
263	4	Public Schools of Calumet	Calumet
263	4	Saginaw ISD	Saginaw
263	4	Standish-Sterling Comm Schools	Standish
263	4	Swan Valley SD	Saginaw
263	4	Tawas Area Schools	Tawas City
263	4	Westwood Community Schools	Dearborn Hgts
263	4	White Cloud Public Schools	White Cloud
263	4	Whitehall District Schools	Whitehall
263	4	Williamston Community Schools	Williamston
295	3	Almont Community Schools	Almont
295	3	Breitung Township Schools	Kingsford
295	3	Capac Community SD	Capac
295	3	Farwell Area Schools	Farwell
295	3	Freeland Community SD	Freeland
295	3	Ida Public SD	Ida
295	3	Lake Fenton Community Schools	Fenton
295	3	Montague Area Public Schools	Montague
295	3	Montrose Community Schools	Montrose
295	3	Quincy Community SD	Quincy
295	3	Richmond Community Schools	Richmond
306	2	Detroit Acad of Arts & Sciences	Detroit

Number of Teachers

Rank	Number	District Name	City
1	6,719	Detroit City SD	Detroit
2	1,633	Grand Rapids Public Schools	Grand Rapids
3	1,546	Utica Community Schools	Sterling Hgts
4	1,209	Flint City SD	Flint
5	1,072	Dearborn City SD	Dearborn
6	1,055	Ann Arbor Public Schools	Ann Arbor
7	1,035	Livonia Public Schools	Livonia
8	890	Plymouth-Canton Community Schls	Plymouth
9	888	Walled Lake Consolidated Schools	Walled Lake
10	811	Saginaw City SD	Saginaw
11	802	Warren Consolidated Schools	Warren
12	787	Wayne-Westland Community SD	Westland
13	768	Farmington Public SD	Farmington
13	768	Kalamazoo Public SD	Kalamazoo
15	736	Pontiac City SD	Pontiac
16	735	Port Huron Area SD	Port Huron
17	727	Troy SD	Troy
18	712	Rochester Community SD	Rochester
19	667	Chippewa Valley Schools	Clinton Twp
20	615	Southfield Public SD	Southfield
21	614	Taylor SD	Taylor
22	609	L'anse Creuse Public Schools	Harrison Twp
23	595	Traverse City Area Public Schls	Traverse City
24	574	Grosse Pointe Public Schools	Grosse Pointe
25	558	Huron Valley Schools	Highland
26	556	Battle Creek Public Schools	Battle Creek
27	537	Waterford SD	Waterford
28	533	Forest Hills Public Schools	Grand Rapids
29	532	Midland Public Schools	Midland
30	528	Portage Public Schools	Portage
31	513	Bay City SD	Bay City
32	501	Kentwood Public Schools	Kentwood
33	438	Clarkston Community SD	Clarkston
34	435	Howell Public Schools	Howell
35	430	Bloomfield Hills SD	Bloomfield Hls
36	409	West Bloomfield SD	West Bloomfield
37	403	West Ottawa Public SD	Holland
38	398	SD of the City of Royal Oak	Royal Oak
39	397	Lake Orion Community Schools	Lake Orion
40	396	Novi Community SD	Novi
41	395	Birmingham City SD	Birmingham
42	389	Rockford Public Schools	Rockford
43	379	Muskegon City SD	Muskegon
44	378	Lapeer Community Schools	Lapeer
45	376	Northville Public Schools	Northville
46	371	Brighton Area Schools	Brighton
47	367	Grand Blanc Community Schools	Grand Blanc
48	365	Monroe Public Schools	Monroe
49	351	South Lyon Community Schools	South Lyon
50	349	Anchor Bay SD	New Baltimore
51	348	Roseville Community Schools	Roseville
52	346	Garden City SD	Garden City
53	342	Van Buren Public Schools	Belleville
54	340	East Detroit Public Schools	Eastpointe
55	325	Grandville Public Schools	Grandville
56	318	Holt Public Schools	Holt
57	316	Grand Haven Area Public Schools	Grand Haven
58	315	Carman-Ainsworth Comm Schools	Flint
59	312	Holland City SD	Holland
60	306	East China SD	East China
61	304	Grand Ledge Public Schools	Grand Ledge
61	304	Lansing Public SD	Lansing
63	303	Lincoln Park Public Schools	Lincoln Park
64	299	Romeo Community Schools	Romeo
65	290	Southgate Community SD	Southgate
66	287	Hazel Park City SD	Hazel Park
67	286	Fraser Public Schools	Fraser
67	286	Saline Area Schools	Saline
69	285	Bedford Public Schools	Temperance
70	282	Saginaw Twp Community Schools	Saginaw
71	278	Wyandotte City SD	Wyandotte
72	277	SD of Ypsilanti	Ypsilanti
73	275	Lincoln Consolidated SD	Ypsilanti
74	274	Zeeland Public Schools	Zeeland
75	273	Woodhaven-Brownstown SD	Brownstown
76	272	Redford Union SD	Redford
77	271	Hudsonville Public SD	Hudsonville
78	268	Jenison Public Schools	Jenison
79	266	Berkley SD	Berkley
80	264	Alpena Public Schools	Alpena
81	263	Hartland Consolidated Schools	Hartland
82	262	Wyoming Public Schools	Wyoming
83	260	Davison Community Schools	Davison
84	254	Niles Community SD	Niles
85	247	Swartz Creek Community Schools	Swartz Creek
86	246	Avondale SD	Auburn Hills
87	241	Holly Area SD	Holly
88	239	Reeths-Puffer Schools	Muskegon
89	233	Ferndale Public Schools	Ferndale
90	227	Adrian City SD	Adrian
90	227	Owosso Public Schools	Owosso
90	227	Romulus Community Schools	Romulus
93	224	Hamtramck Public Schools	Hamtramck
94	223	Mt. Pleasant City SD	Mt. Pleasant
95	221	Van Dyke Public Schools	Warren
96	219	Oak Park City SD	Oak Park
97	218	Mona Shores Public SD	Norton Shores
98	214	Lowell Area Schools	Lowell
99	213	Flushing Community Schools	Flushing
100	212	Greenville Public Schools	Greenville
101	211	Ionia Public Schools	Ionia
102	207	East Lansing SD	East Lansing
103	206	Macomb ISD	Clinton Twp
103	206	Waverly Community Schools	Lansing
105	200	Trenton Public Schools	Trenton
106	199	Charlotte Public Schools	Charlotte
107	198	Jackson Public Schools	Jackson
108	194	Brandon SD	Ortonville
109	193	Northwest Community Schools	Jackson
110	192	Fenton Area Public Schools	Fenton
110	192	Marquette Area Public Schools	Marquette
112	191	Hastings Area SD	Hastings
112	191	Lakeview SD (Calhoun)	Battle Creek
114	190	Caledonia Community Schools	Caledonia
114	190	Mt. Clemens Community SD	Mt. Clemens
116	188	Dexter Community SD	Dexter
116	188	Gaylord Community Schools	Gaylord
116	188	Mt. Morris Consolidated Schools	Mt. Morris
119	187	Cedar Springs Public Schools	Cedar Springs
120	186	Comstock Public Schools	Kalamazoo
120	186	South Redford SD	Redford
122	185	Kearsley Community Schools	Flint
122	185	St. Johns Public Schools	St. Johns
122	185	Tecumseh Public Schools	Tecumseh
125	184	Fruitport Community Schools	Fruitport
125	184	Mattawan Consolidated School	Mattawan
127	181	Lake Shore Pub Schools (Macomb)	St Clair Shores
128	180	Crestwood SD	Dearborn Hgts
129	179	Coldwater Community Schools	Coldwater
130	178	Clio Area SD	Clio
130	178	Sault Ste. Marie Area Schools	Sault Ste Marie
132	177	Center Line Public Schools	Center Line
133	176	Gull Lake Community Schools	Richland
134	175	Airport Community SD	Carleton
135	174	Kenowa Hills Public Schools	Grand Rapids
136	173	Mason Public Schools (Ingham)	Mason
136	173	Warren Woods Public Schools	Warren
138	172	Haslett Public Schools	Haslett
139	171	Allegan Public Schools	Allegan
139	171	Oxford Area Community Schools	Oxford
141	170	Sturgis Public Schools	Sturgis
141	170	Wayland Union Schools	Wayland
143	166	Eaton Rapids Public Schools	Eaton Rapids
144	165	Allen Park Public Schools	Allen Park
145	163	Chelsea SD	Chelsea
145	163	Fitzgerald Public Schools	Warren
145	163	Public Schools of Petoskey	Petoskey
148	160	East Grand Rapids Public Schools	E Grand Rapids
148	160	Lakeview Public Schools (Macomb)	St Clair Shores
148	160	Vicksburg Community Schools	Vicksburg
151	159	Byron Center Public Schools	Byron Center
151	159	Fowlerville Community Schools	Fowlerville
151	159	Harper Creek Community Schools	Battle Creek
154	158	W Branch-Rose City Area Schools	West Branch
154	158	Willow Run Community Schools	Ypsilanti
156	157	Escanaba Area Public Schools	Escanaba
156	157	Plainwell Community Schools	Plainwell
158	156	Clintondale Community Schools	Clinton Twp
159	155	Lakeshore SD (Berrien)	Stevensville
159	155	Sparta Area Schools	Sparta
161	154	Chippewa Hills SD	Remus
161	154	Dowagiac Union SD	Dowagiac
161	154	Gibraltar SD	Woodhaven
161	154	Lamphere Public Schools	Madison Heights
165	153	St. Joseph Public Schools	St. Joseph
166	152	Alma Public Schools	Alma
166	152	Dearborn Heights SD #7	Dearborn Hgts
168	151	Orchard View Schools	Muskegon
169	149	Bridgeport-Spaulding CSD	Bridgeport
169	149	Ludington Area SD	Ludington
171	148	Cadillac Area Public Schools	Cadillac
171	148	Fremont Public SD	Fremont
171	148	Godwin Heights Public Schools	Wyoming
174	147	Belding Area SD	Belding
174	147	South Lake Schools	St Clair Shores
174	147	Thornapple Kellogg SD	Middleville
177	146	River Rouge SD	River Rouge
178	145	Marshall Public Schools	Marshall
178	145	Muskegon Heights SD	Muskegon Hgts
180	144	Dewitt Public Schools	Dewitt
181	143	Western SD	Parma
182	139	South Haven Public Schools	South Haven
183	137	Algonac Community SD	Algonac
183	137	Jefferson Schools (Monroe)	Monroe
185	136	Croswell-Lexington Comm Schools	Croswell
185	136	Marysville Public Schools	Marysville
187	134	Cheboygan Area Schools	Cheboygan
187	134	Hamilton Community Schools	Hamilton
187	134	Houghton Lake Community Schools	Houghton Lake
190	133	Lakewood Public Schools	Lake Odessa
190	133	Paw Paw Public SD	Paw Paw
190	133	Tri County Area Schools	Sand Lake
193	132	Coloma Community Schools	Coloma
194	131	Grant Public SD	Grant
194	131	Melvindale-N Allen Park Schools	Melvindale
196	130	Caro Community Schools	Caro
196	130	Milan Area Schools	Milan
196	130	Otsego Public Schools	Otsego
196	130	Riverview Community SD	Riverview
196	130	Westwood Community Schools	Dearborn Hgts
201	129	Comstock Park Public Schools	Comstock Park
201	129	Linden Community Schools	Linden
203	127	Okemos Public Schools	Okemos
204	126	Bangor Township Schools	Bay City
204	126	Madison Public Schools (Oakland)	Madison Heights
206	122	Bullock Creek SD	Midland
207	120	Allendale Public SD	Allendale
207	120	Spring Lake Public Schools	Spring Lake
209	119	Crawford Ausable Schools	Grayling
210	118	Whitehall District Schools	Whitehall
211	117	Imlay City Community Schools	Imlay City
211	117	Oakridge Public Schools	Muskegon
213	116	Gladwin Community Schools	Gladwin
213	116	Harrison Community Schools	Harrison
215	115	Beecher Community SD	Flint
215	115	Coopersville Public SD	Coopersville
215	115	Corunna Public SD	Corunna
215	115	Delton-Kellogg SD	Delton
219	114	Big Rapids Public Schools	Big Rapids
219	114	Breitung Township Schools	Kingsford
219	114	Central Montcalm Public Schools	Stanton
219	114	Edwardsburg Public Schools	Edwardsburg
219	114	Huron SD	New Boston
219	114	Williamston Community Schools	Williamston
219	114	Yale Public Schools	Yale
226	113	Chesaning Union Schools	Chesaning
226	113	Lakeville Community Schools	Otisville
226	113	Reed City Area Public Schools	Reed City
229	112	Clarenceville SD	Livonia
230	111	Benzie County Central Schools	Benzonia
230	111	Newaygo Public SD	Newaygo
232	110	Parchment SD	Parchment
233	109	Perry Public SD	Perry
234	108	Grosse Ile Township Schools	Grosse Ile
234	108	Kelloggsville Public Schools	Grand Rapids
234	108	Richmond Community Schools	Richmond
234	108	Shelby Public Schools	Shelby
238	107	Menominee Area Public Schools	Menominee
238	107	Portland Public SD	Portland
240	106	Armada Area Schools	Armada
240	106	Durand Area Schools	Durand
240	106	Pinconning Area Schools	Pinconning

243	105	Essexville-Hampton Public Schls	Essexville
243	105	Goodrich Area Schools	Goodrich
243	105	Kalkaska Public Schools	Kalkaska
246	104	Capac Community SD	Capac
246	104	Detroit Acad of Arts & Sciences	Detroit
246	104	Hillsdale Community Schools	Hillsdale
246	104	Shepherd Public SD	Shepherd
250	103	Lakeview Comm Schools (Montcalm)	Lakeview
250	103	Oscoda Area Schools	Oscoda
250	103	Standish-Sterling Comm Schools	Standish
253	102	Onsted Community Schools	Onsted
254	101	Birch Run Area SD	Birch Run
254	101	Pennfield SD	Battle Creek
256	100	Highland Park City Schools	Highland Park
256	100	Stockbridge Community Schools	Stockbridge
258	99	Gladstone Area Schools	Gladstone
259	98	Buchanan Community Schools	Buchanan
259	98	Maple Valley Schools	Vermontville
261	97	Berrien Springs Public Schools	Berrien Springs
261	97	Ida Public SD	Ida
263	96	Albion Public Schools	Albion
263	96	Beaverton Rural Schools	Beaverton
263	96	Hartford Public SD	Hartford
263	96	Napoleon Community Schools	Napoleon
267	95	Carrollton SD	Saginaw
267	95	Columbia SD	Brooklyn
267	95	Godfrey-Lee Public Schools	Wyoming
270	94	Morley Stanwood Community Schls	Morley
270	94	Swan Valley SD	Saginaw
272	93	Brandywine Public SD	Niles
272	93	Constantine Public SD	Constantine
272	93	Gerrish-Higgins SD	Roscommon
272	93	Mason County Central Schools	Scottville
276	92	White Cloud Public Schools	White Cloud
277	91	Bendle Public Schools	Burton
277	91	Farwell Area Schools	Farwell
277	91	Gwinn Area Community Schools	Gwinn
277	91	Public Schools of Calumet	Calumet
281	90	Freeland Community SD	Freeland
282	89	Almont Community Schools	Almont
282	89	East Jackson Community Schools	Jackson
282	89	Flat Rock Community Schools	Flat Rock
282	89	Ovid-Elsie Area Schools	Elsie
286	87	Bangor Public Schls (Van Buren)	Bangor
286	87	Tawas Area Schools	Tawas City
288	85	Quincy Community SD	Quincy
288	85	Vassar Public Schools	Vassar
290	84	Clare Public Schools	Clare
290	84	Meridian Public Schools	Sanford
290	84	Montague Area Public Schools	Montague
293	81	Elk Rapids Schools	Elk Rapids
293	81	Millington Community Schools	Millington
295	77	Michigan Center SD	Michigan Center
296	73	Saginaw ISD	Saginaw
297	70	Lake Fenton Community Schools	Fenton
298	61	North Branch Area Schools	North Branch
299	51	Washtenaw ISD	Ann Arbor
300	35	Northview Public SD	Grand Rapids
301	16	Mason Consol Schools (Monroe)	Erie
302	n/a	Benton Harbor Area Schools	Benton Harbor
302	n/a	Dundee Community Schools	Dundee
302	n/a	Manistee Area Schools	Manistee
302	n/a	Montrose Community Schools	Montrose
302	n/a	Three Rivers Community Schools	Three Rivers

Number of Students

Rank	Number	District Name	City
1	153,034	Detroit City SD	Detroit
2	28,935	Utica Community Schools	Sterling Hgts
3	24,166	Grand Rapids Public Schools	Grand Rapids
4	20,465	Flint City SD	Flint
5	18,379	Livonia Public Schools	Livonia
6	18,121	Plymouth-Canton Community Schls	Plymouth
7	18,083	Dearborn City SD	Dearborn
8	16,979	Lansing Public SD	Lansing
9	16,701	Ann Arbor Public Schools	Ann Arbor
10	15,421	Warren Consolidated Schools	Warren
11	15,205	Walled Lake Consolidated Schools	Walled Lake
12	14,461	Rochester Community SD	Rochester
13	14,296	Wayne-Westland Community SD	Westland
14	13,906	Chippewa Valley Schools	Clinton Twp
15	12,754	Port Huron Area SD	Port Huron
16	12,353	Saginaw City SD	Saginaw
17	12,307	Farmington Public SD	Farmington
18	12,264	Waterford SD	Waterford
19	12,220	L'anse Creuse Public Schools	Harrison Twp
20	12,093	Troy SD	Troy
21	11,490	Pontiac City SD	Pontiac
22	11,133	Traverse City Area Public Schls	Traverse City
23	11,099	Kalamazoo Public SD	Kalamazoo
24	10,890	Taylor SD	Taylor
25	10,877	Huron Valley Schools	Highland
26	10,300	Southfield Public SD	Southfield
27	9,887	Bay City SD	Bay City
28	9,608	Midland Public Schools	Midland
29	9,419	Kentwood Public Schools	Kentwood
30	9,145	Portage Public Schools	Portage
31	9,112	Forest Hills Public Schools	Grand Rapids
32	8,938	Grosse Pointe Public Schools	Grosse Pointe
33	8,345	Howell Public Schools	Howell
34	7,999	West Ottawa Public SD	Holland
35	7,951	Clarkston Community SD	Clarkston
36	7,945	Battle Creek Public Schools	Battle Creek
37	7,934	Birmingham City SD	Birmingham
38	7,890	Lake Orion Community Schools	Lake Orion
39	7,750	Rockford Public Schools	Rockford
40	7,472	Lapeer Community Schools	Lapeer
41	7,322	Grand Blanc Community Schools	Grand Blanc
42	7,300	Brighton Area Schools	Brighton
43	7,247	Jackson Public Schools	Jackson
44	7,235	West Bloomfield SD	West Bloomfield
45	7,199	Monroe Public Schools	Monroe
46	7,028	Muskegon City SD	Muskegon
47	6,748	South Lyon Community Schools	South Lyon
48	6,615	Anchor Bay SD	New Baltimore
49	6,560	Roseville Community Schools	Roseville
50	6,477	SD of the City of Royal Oak	Royal Oak
51	6,370	Northville Public Schools	Northville
52	6,315	Novi Community SD	Novi
53	6,137	East Detroit Public Schools	Eastpointe
54	6,118	Grandville Public Schools	Grandville
55	6,110	Van Buren Public Schools	Belleville
56	6,095	Grand Haven Area Public Schools	Grand Haven
57	6,000	Bloomfield Hills SD	Bloomfield Hls
58	5,978	East China SD	East China
59	5,914	Wyoming Public Schools	Wyoming
60	5,840	Holt Public Schools	Holt
61	5,580	Romeo Community Schools	Romeo
62	5,475	Bedford Public Schools	Temperance
63	5,368	Grand Ledge Public Schools	Grand Ledge
64	5,365	Davison Community Schools	Davison
65	5,364	Saline Area Schools	Saline
66	5,363	Carman-Ainsworth Comm Schools	Flint
67	5,340	Holland City SD	Holland
68	5,306	Southgate Community SD	Southgate
69	5,285	Hartland Consolidated Schools	Hartland
70	5,226	Lincoln Park Public Schools	Lincoln Park
71	5,213	Woodhaven-Brownstown SD	Brownstown
72	5,189	Saginaw Twp Community Schools	Saginaw
73	5,152	Garden City SD	Garden City
74	5,123	Alpena Public Schools	Alpena
75	5,064	Benton Harbor Area Schools	Benton Harbor
76	5,008	Zeeland Public Schools	Zeeland
77	4,957	Wyandotte City SD	Wyandotte
78	4,952	Lincoln Consolidated SD	Ypsilanti
79	4,944	Hazel Park City SD	Hazel Park
80	4,940	Fraser Public Schools	Fraser
81	4,877	Hudsonville Public SD	Hudsonville
82	4,801	Flushing Community Schools	Flushing
83	4,787	Jenison Public Schools	Jenison
84	4,754	SD of Ypsilanti	Ypsilanti
85	4,573	Redford Union SD	Redford
86	4,483	Berkley SD	Berkley
87	4,419	Holly Area SD	Holly
88	4,349	Reeths-Puffer Schools	Muskegon
89	4,301	Romulus Community Schools	Romulus
90	4,276	Van Dyke Public Schools	Warren
91	4,226	Mona Shores Public SD	Norton Shores
92	4,221	Niles Community SD	Niles
93	4,180	Swartz Creek Community Schools	Swartz Creek
94	4,156	Oak Park City SD	Oak Park
95	4,132	Owosso Public Schools	Owosso
96	4,069	Oxford Area Community Schools	Oxford
97	4,046	Okemos Public Schools	Okemos
98	4,002	Clintondale Community Schools	Clinton Twp
99	3,997	Adrian City SD	Adrian
100	3,951	Ferndale Public Schools	Ferndale
101	3,936	Mt. Pleasant City SD	Mt. Pleasant
102	3,931	Lowell Area Schools	Lowell
103	3,914	Greenville Public Schools	Greenville
104	3,904	Kearsley Community Schools	Flint
105	3,868	Avondale SD	Auburn Hills
106	3,802	Hamtramck Public Schools	Hamtramck
107	3,753	Fenton Area Public Schools	Fenton
108	3,702	Kenowa Hills Public Schools	Grand Rapids
109	3,682	Brandon SD	Ortonville
110	3,679	Marquette Area Public Schools	Marquette
111	3,675	Mt. Morris Consolidated Schools	Mt. Morris
112	3,667	Northwest Community Schools	Jackson
113	3,638	Allen Park Public Schools	Allen Park
114	3,603	Clio Area SD	Clio
115	3,555	Crestwood SD	Dearborn Hgts
116	3,553	East Lansing SD	East Lansing
117	3,512	Mattawan Consolidated School	Mattawan
118	3,497	Gaylord Community Schools	Gaylord
119	3,489	Dexter Community SD	Dexter
120	3,460	Tecumseh Public Schools	Tecumseh
121	3,435	Northview Public SD	Grand Rapids
122	3,432	Airport Community SD	Carleton
123	3,427	Ionia Public Schools	Ionia
124	3,417	Highland Park City Schools	Highland Park
125	3,407	Caledonia Community Schools	Caledonia
125	3,407	Cedar Springs Public Schools	Cedar Springs
127	3,406	Waverly Community Schools	Lansing
128	3,396	South Redford SD	Redford
129	3,387	Cadillac Area Public Schools	Cadillac
130	3,383	St. Johns Public Schools	St. Johns
131	3,378	Lake Shore Pub Schools (Macomb)	St Clair Shores
132	3,365	Coldwater Community Schools	Coldwater
133	3,360	Hastings Area SD	Hastings
134	3,347	Charlotte Public Schools	Charlotte
135	3,326	Wayland Union Schools	Wayland
136	3,315	Lakeview SD (Calhoun)	Battle Creek
137	3,306	Gibraltar SD	Woodhaven
138	3,303	Fruitport Community Schools	Fruitport
139	3,282	Fitzgerald Public Schools	Warren
140	3,272	Warren Woods Public Schools	Warren
141	3,191	Fowlerville Community Schools	Fowlerville
142	3,179	Eaton Rapids Public Schools	Eaton Rapids
143	3,170	Mason Public Schools (Ingham)	Mason
144	3,160	Chelsea SD	Chelsea
145	3,126	Sturgis Public Schools	Sturgis
146	3,105	Three Rivers Community Schools	Three Rivers
147	3,092	Public Schools of Petoskey	Petoskey
148	3,084	Sparta Area Schools	Sparta
149	3,082	Trenton Public Schools	Trenton
150	3,061	Escanaba Area Public Schools	Escanaba
151	3,051	Mt. Clemens Community SD	Mt. Clemens
152	3,034	Gull Lake Community Schools	Richland
153	3,025	Allegan Public Schools	Allegan
154	2,987	Center Line Public Schools	Center Line
155	2,986	Dearborn Heights SD #7	Dearborn Hgts
156	2,980	Linden Community Schools	Linden
157	2,941	Haslett Public Schools	Haslett
158	2,916	Comstock Public Schools	Kalamazoo
159	2,915	Byron Center Public Schools	Byron Center
160	2,902	Thornapple Kellogg SD	Middleville
161	2,897	Sault Ste. Marie Area Schools	Sault Ste Marie
162	2,887	Marysville Public Schools	Marysville
163	2,884	East Grand Rapids Public Schools	E Grand Rapids
164	2,876	Lakeview Public Schools (Macomb)	St Clair Shores
165	2,867	Plainwell Community Schools	Plainwell
166	2,858	Orchard View Schools	Muskegon
167	2,855	Lakeshore SD (Berrien)	Stevensville
168	2,852	St. Joseph Public Schools	St. Joseph
169	2,819	Western SD	Parma
170	2,780	Dewitt Public Schools	Dewitt
171	2,771	Dowagiac Union SD	Dowagiac
172	2,729	Vicksburg Community Schools	Vicksburg
173	2,687	Harper Creek Community Schools	Battle Creek
174	2,678	North Branch Area Schools	North Branch
175	2,673	Chippewa Hills SD	Remus
175	2,673	Willow Run Community Schools	Ypsilanti
177	2,671	Algonac Community SD	Algonac
178	2,663	W Branch-Rose City Area Schools	West Branch
179	2,634	Jefferson Schools (Monroe)	Monroe
180	2,622	Fremont Public SD	Fremont
181	2,600	Melvindale-N Allen Park Schools	Melvindale
182	2,596	Riverview Community SD	Riverview
183	2,563	Marshall Public Schools	Marshall
184	2,553	Ludington Area SD	Ludington
185	2,551	Hamilton Community Schools	Hamilton
186	2,549	Alma Public Schools	Alma
187	2,530	Lakewood Public Schools	Lake Odessa
188	2,528	Bangor Township Schools	Bay City
189	2,522	Croswell-Lexington Comm Schools	Croswell
190	2,511	Saginaw ISD	Saginaw
191	2,502	Grant Public SD	Grant
192	2,500	Belding Area SD	Belding
193	2,490	South Haven Public Schools	South Haven
193	2,490	Yale Public Schools	Yale
195	2,469	Lamphere Public Schools	Madison Heights
196	2,467	South Lake Schools	St Clair Shores
197	2,423	Beecher Community SD	Flint
198	2,422	Tri County Area Schools	Sand Lake
199	2,400	Paw Paw Public SD	Paw Paw
200	2,378	Newaygo Public SD	Newaygo
201	2,374	Coopersville Public SD	Coopersville
202	2,357	Westwood Community Schools	Dearborn Hgts
203	2,349	Bridgeport-Spaulding CSD	Bridgeport
204	2,344	Comstock Park Public Schools	Comstock Park
205	2,336	Imlay City Community Schools	Imlay City
206	2,327	River Rouge SD	River Rouge
207	2,317	Corunna Public SD	Corunna
208	2,311	Edwardsburg Public Schools	Edwardsburg
209	2,300	Godwin Heights Public Schools	Wyoming
210	2,297	Otsego Public Schools	Otsego

211	2,281	Muskegon Heights SD	Muskegon Hgts
211	2,281	Whitehall District Schools	Whitehall
213	2,279	Cheboygan Area Schools	Cheboygan
214	2,267	Caro Community Schools	Caro
215	2,254	Detroit Acad of Arts & Sciences	Detroit
216	2,249	Armada Area Schools	Armada
217	2,237	Spring Lake Public Schools	Spring Lake
218	2,217	Kelloggsville Public Schools	Grand Rapids
219	2,201	Milan Area Schools	Milan
220	2,188	Washtenaw ISD	Ann Arbor
221	2,174	Coloma Community Schools	Coloma
222	2,172	Big Rapids Public Schools	Big Rapids
223	2,139	Lakeville Community Schools	Otisville
224	2,128	Houghton Lake Community Schools	Houghton Lake
225	2,127	Central Montcalm Public Schools	Stanton
226	2,124	Huron SD	New Boston
227	2,122	Harrison Community Schools	Harrison
228	2,103	Crawford Ausable Schools	Grayling
229	2,092	Gladwin Community Schools	Gladwin
230	2,090	Williamston Community Schools	Williamston
231	2,087	Goodrich Area Schools	Goodrich
232	2,086	Portland Public SD	Portland
233	2,078	Bullock Creek SD	Midland
234	2,074	Richmond Community Schools	Richmond
235	2,061	Durand Area Schools	Durand
236	2,059	Delton-Kellogg SD	Delton
237	2,056	Chesaning Union Schools	Chesaning
238	2,035	Allendale Public SD	Allendale
239	2,033	Madison Public Schools (Oakland)	Madison Heights
240	2,025	Parchment SD	Parchment
241	2,023	Grosse Ile Township Schools	Grosse Ile
242	2,020	Breitung Township Schools	Kingsford
243	2,012	Menominee Area Public Schools	Menominee
244	2,007	Clarenceville SD	Livonia
245	2,004	Benzie County Central Schools	Benzonia
246	2,003	Oakridge Public Schools	Muskegon
247	1,997	Perry Public SD	Perry
248	1,981	Reed City Area Public Schools	Reed City
249	1,974	Pinconning Area Schools	Pinconning
250	1,963	Shelby Public Schools	Shelby
251	1,958	Essexville-Hampton Public Schls	Essexville
252	1,950	Capac Community SD	Capac
253	1,939	Standish-Sterling Comm Schools	Standish
254	1,926	Pennfield SD	Battle Creek
255	1,912	Columbia SD	Brooklyn
256	1,910	Lakeview Comm Schools (Montcalm)	Lakeview
257	1,898	Birch Run Area SD	Birch Run
258	1,896	Hillsdale Community Schools	Hillsdale
259	1,862	Onsted Community Schools	Onsted
260	1,861	Vassar Public Schools	Vassar
261	1,855	Oscoda Area Schools	Oscoda
262	1,841	Gerrish-Higgins SD	Roscommon
263	1,803	Ovid-Elsie Area Schools	Elsie
264	1,799	Almont Community Schools	Almont
265	1,797	Kalkaska Public Schools	Kalkaska
266	1,779	Flat Rock Community Schools	Flat Rock
267	1,772	Manistee Area Schools	Manistee
267	1,772	Millington Community Schools	Millington
269	1,768	Shepherd Public SD	Shepherd
270	1,767	Napoleon Community Schools	Napoleon
271	1,752	Montrose Community Schools	Montrose
272	1,750	Stockbridge Community Schools	Stockbridge
273	1,748	Albion Public Schools	Albion
274	1,747	Buchanan Community Schools	Buchanan
275	1,744	Gladstone Area Schools	Gladstone
276	1,737	Ida Public SD	Ida
277	1,735	Maple Valley Schools	Vermontville
278	1,717	Swan Valley SD	Saginaw
279	1,696	Freeland Community SD	Freeland
280	1,675	Beaverton Rural Schools	Beaverton
281	1,671	Mason County Central Schools	Scottville
282	1,668	Dundee Community Schools	Dundee
283	1,636	Morley Stanwood Community Schls	Morley
284	1,628	East Jackson Community Schools	Jackson
284	1,628	Farwell Area Schools	Farwell
286	1,606	Berrien Springs Public Schools	Berrien Springs
287	1,598	Clare Public Schools	Clare
288	1,597	Godfrey-Lee Public Schools	Wyoming
289	1,595	Michigan Center SD	Michigan Center
290	1,590	Bendle Public Schools	Burton
291	1,580	Public Schools of Calumet	Calumet
292	1,573	Meridian Public Schools	Sanford
293	1,556	Constantine Public SD	Constantine
294	1,548	Elk Rapids Schools	Elk Rapids
295	1,539	Quincy Community SD	Quincy
296	1,537	Brandywine Public SD	Niles
297	1,530	White Cloud Public Schools	White Cloud
298	1,529	Tawas Area Schools	Tawas City
299	1,527	Bangor Public Schls (Van Buren)	Bangor
300	1,523	Macomb ISD	Clinton Twp
301	1,522	Mason Consol Schools (Monroe)	Erie
302	1,517	Carrollton SD	Saginaw
303	1,513	Hartford Public SD	Hartford
304	1,509	Gwinn Area Community Schools	Gwinn
305	1,502	Lake Fenton Community Schools	Fenton
306	1,500	Montague Area Public Schools	Montague

Male Students

Rank	Percent	District Name	City
1	71.4	Macomb ISD	Clinton Twp
2	58.0	Vassar Public Schools	Vassar
3	55.5	Washtenaw ISD	Ann Arbor
4	55.0	Hamtramck Public Schools	Hamtramck
5	54.6	Mason County Central Schools	Scottville
6	54.2	Clio Area SD	Clio
7	53.9	Caledonia Community Schools	Caledonia
8	53.8	Buchanan Community Schools	Buchanan
9	53.8	Three Rivers Community Schools	Three Rivers
10	53.7	Niles Community SD	Niles
11	53.7	Fitzgerald Public Schools	Warren
12	53.7	Hazel Park City SD	Hazel Park
13	53.6	Bangor Public Schls (Van Buren)	Bangor
14	53.5	Westwood Community Schools	Dearborn Hgts
15	53.5	Redford Union SD	Redford
16	53.5	Clintondale Community Schools	Clinton Twp
17	53.4	Shepherd Public SD	Shepherd
18	53.4	Montrose Community Schools	Montrose
19	53.3	Crawford Ausable Schools	Grayling
20	53.3	Gerrish-Higgins SD	Roscommon
21	53.3	Brandywine Public SD	Niles
22	53.2	Spring Lake Public Schools	Spring Lake
23	53.2	River Rouge SD	River Rouge
24	53.1	Ovid-Elsie Area Schools	Elsie
25	53.1	Delton-Kellogg SD	Delton
26	53.1	Breitung Township Schools	Kingsford
27	53.1	Garden City SD	Garden City
28	53.1	Owosso Public Schools	Owosso
29	53.0	Comstock Park Public Schools	Comstock Park
30	53.0	Van Dyke Public Schools	Warren
31	53.0	Napoleon Community Schools	Napoleon
32	53.0	Croswell-Lexington Comm Schools	Croswell
33	53.0	Godwin Heights Public Schools	Wyoming
34	52.9	Benzie County Central Schools	Benzonia
35	52.9	Grand Haven Area Public Schools	Grand Haven
36	52.9	Byron Center Public Schools	Byron Center
37	52.9	Northview Public SD	Grand Rapids
38	52.9	Freeland Community SD	Freeland
39	52.9	Saginaw ISD	Saginaw
40	52.9	Oakridge Public Schools	Muskegon
41	52.8	Dewitt Public Schools	Dewitt
42	52.8	Dundee Community Schools	Dundee
43	52.8	Coloma Community Schools	Coloma
44	52.8	Berrien Springs Public Schools	Berrien Springs
45	52.8	Whitehall District Schools	Whitehall
46	52.8	Marshall Public Schools	Marshall
47	52.7	Oxford Area Community Schools	Oxford
48	52.7	Fowlerville Community Schools	Fowlerville
49	52.7	Comstock Public Schools	Kalamazoo
50	52.7	Montague Area Public Schools	Montague
51	52.7	Mt. Morris Consolidated Schools	Mt. Morris
52	52.6	Armada Area Schools	Armada
53	52.6	Shelby Public Schools	Shelby
54	52.6	Willow Run Community Schools	Ypsilanti
55	52.6	Beaverton Rural Schools	Beaverton
56	52.6	Tri County Area Schools	Sand Lake
57	52.6	Rockford Public Schools	Rockford
58	52.6	Lincoln Park Public Schools	Lincoln Park
59	52.6	Bay City SD	Bay City
60	52.6	Hamilton Community Schools	Hamilton
61	52.5	West Bloomfield SD	West Bloomfield
62	52.5	Bendle Public Schools	Burton
63	52.5	Almont Community Schools	Almont
64	52.5	Grant Public SD	Grant
65	52.5	Public Schools of Petoskey	Petoskey
66	52.5	Airport Community SD	Carleton
67	52.5	Milan Area Schools	Milan
68	52.5	Yale Public Schools	Yale
69	52.5	Onsted Community Schools	Onsted
70	52.5	Walled Lake Consolidated Schools	Walled Lake
71	52.4	Capac Community SD	Capac
72	52.4	Otsego Public Schools	Otsego
73	52.4	Coldwater Community Schools	Coldwater
74	52.4	Ida Public SD	Ida
74	52.4	Lakeshore SD (Berrien)	Stevensville
76	52.4	Muskegon City SD	Muskegon
77	52.4	SD of the City of Royal Oak	Royal Oak
78	52.3	Sault Ste. Marie Area Schools	Sault Ste Marie
79	52.3	Thornapple Kellogg SD	Middleville
80	52.3	Haslett Public Schools	Haslett
81	52.3	St. Johns Public Schools	St. Johns
82	52.3	Huron SD	New Boston
82	52.3	Michigan Center SD	Michigan Center
84	52.3	Columbia SD	Brooklyn
85	52.3	Goodrich Area Schools	Goodrich
86	52.3	Cadillac Area Public Schools	Cadillac
87	52.3	SD of Ypsilanti	Ypsilanti
88	52.2	Lamphere Public Schools	Madison Heights
89	52.2	Constantine Public SD	Constantine
90	52.2	Roseville Community Schools	Roseville
91	52.2	Oscoda Area Schools	Oscoda
92	52.2	Holly Area SD	Holly
93	52.2	Birch Run Area SD	Birch Run
94	52.2	Houghton Lake Community Schools	Houghton Lake
95	52.1	Lake Shore Pub Schools (Macomb)	St Clair Shores
96	52.1	Lake Orion Community Schools	Lake Orion
97	52.1	Novi Community SD	Novi
98	52.1	Gwinn Area Community Schools	Gwinn
99	52.1	North Branch Area Schools	North Branch
100	52.1	Marquette Area Public Schools	Marquette
101	52.0	Carrollton SD	Saginaw
102	52.0	Brighton Area Schools	Brighton
103	52.0	Eaton Rapids Public Schools	Eaton Rapids
104	52.0	Grand Rapids Public Schools	Grand Rapids
105	52.0	Lapeer Community Schools	Lapeer
106	52.0	Waterford SD	Waterford
107	52.0	Maple Valley Schools	Vermontville
108	52.0	Hartland Consolidated Schools	Hartland
109	52.0	Troy SD	Troy
110	52.0	Farmington Public SD	Farmington
111	52.0	Trenton Public Schools	Trenton
112	52.0	Caro Community Schools	Caro
113	51.9	Harper Creek Community Schools	Battle Creek
114	51.9	Paw Paw Public SD	Paw Paw
115	51.9	Holland City SD	Holland
116	51.9	Southgate Community SD	Southgate
117	51.9	Crestwood SD	Dearborn Hgts
118	51.9	Gladstone Area Schools	Gladstone
119	51.9	Battle Creek Public Schools	Battle Creek
120	51.9	Midland Public Schools	Midland
121	51.9	Utica Community Schools	Sterling Hgts
122	51.9	Chelsea SD	Chelsea
123	51.9	Howell Public Schools	Howell
124	51.8	Dearborn City SD	Dearborn
125	51.8	Kalamazoo Public SD	Kalamazoo
126	51.8	Waverly Community Schools	Lansing
127	51.8	Marysville Public Schools	Marysville
128	51.8	Livonia Public Schools	Livonia
129	51.8	Escanaba Area Public Schools	Escanaba
130	51.8	Edwardsburg Public Schools	Edwardsburg
131	51.8	Stockbridge Community Schools	Stockbridge
132	51.8	Jenison Public Schools	Jenison
133	51.8	Lansing Public SD	Lansing
134	51.7	Center Line Public Schools	Center Line
135	51.7	Ionia Public Schools	Ionia
136	51.7	Port Huron Area SD	Port Huron
137	51.7	W Branch-Rose City Area Schools	West Branch
138	51.7	Monroe Public Schools	Monroe
139	51.7	Greenville Public Schools	Greenville
140	51.7	Elk Rapids Schools	Elk Rapids
141	51.7	Algonac Community SD	Algonac
142	51.7	Gladwin Community Schools	Gladwin
143	51.7	Huron Valley Schools	Highland
144	51.7	Birmingham City SD	Birmingham
145	51.7	South Lyon Community Schools	South Lyon
146	51.6	Plainwell Community Schools	Plainwell
147	51.6	Hillsdale Community Schools	Hillsdale
148	51.6	Bloomfield Hills SD	Bloomfield Hls
149	51.6	St. Joseph Public Schools	St. Joseph
150	51.6	Mattawan Consolidated School	Mattawan
151	51.6	Kearsley Community Schools	Flint
152	51.6	Ferndale Public Schools	Ferndale
153	51.6	East China SD	East China
154	51.6	Madison Public Schools (Oakland)	Madison Heights
155	51.6	Forest Hills Public Schools	Grand Rapids
156	51.6	Woodhaven-Brownstown SD	Brownstown
157	51.6	Coopersville Public SD	Coopersville
158	51.6	Swartz Creek Community Schools	Swartz Creek
159	51.6	Albion Public Schools	Albion
160	51.5	Fraser Public Schools	Fraser
161	51.5	Mt. Pleasant City SD	Mt. Pleasant
162	51.5	Saline Area Schools	Saline
163	51.5	Anchor Bay SD	New Baltimore
164	51.5	Corunna Public SD	Corunna
165	51.5	Grand Ledge Public Schools	Grand Ledge
166	51.5	Oak Park City SD	Oak Park
167	51.5	Clarkston Community SD	Clarkston
168	51.5	Kentwood Public Schools	Kentwood
169	51.5	White Cloud Public Schools	White Cloud
170	51.4	Fruitport Community Schools	Fruitport
171	51.4	Brandon SD	Ortonville
172	51.4	Lake Fenton Community Schools	Fenton
173	51.4	Lowell Area Schools	Lowell
174	51.4	Harrison Community Schools	Harrison
175	51.4	Linden Community Schools	Linden
176	51.4	Hartford Public SD	Hartford
177	51.4	Pontiac City SD	Pontiac
178	51.4	West Ottawa Public SD	Holland

179	51.4	Lakeview Comm Schools (Montcalm)	Lakeview
180	51.4	Jackson Public Schools	Jackson
181	51.3	Grandville Public Schools	Grandville
182	51.3	Parchment SD	Parchment
183	51.3	Portage Public Schools	Portage
184	51.3	Dowagiac Union SD	Dowagiac
185	51.3	Lincoln Consolidated SD	Ypsilanti
186	51.3	Menominee Area Public Schools	Menominee
187	51.3	Jefferson Schools (Monroe)	Monroe
188	51.3	Standish-Sterling Comm Schools	Standish
189	51.3	Kenowa Hills Public Schools	Grand Rapids
190	51.2	Avondale SD	Auburn Hills
191	51.2	Allen Park Public Schools	Allen Park
192	51.2	Chippewa Valley Schools	Clinton Twp
193	51.2	Fremont Public SD	Fremont
194	51.2	Cheboygan Area Schools	Cheboygan
195	51.2	Millington Community Schools	Millington
196	51.2	Ann Arbor Public Schools	Ann Arbor
197	51.2	Wyoming Public Schools	Wyoming
198	51.2	Clarenceville SD	Livonia
199	51.2	Dexter Community SD	Dexter
200	51.2	Okemos Public Schools	Okemos
201	51.2	South Lake Schools	St Clair Shores
202	51.2	Richmond Community Schools	Richmond
203	51.1	Adrian City SD	Adrian
204	51.1	Big Rapids Public Schools	Big Rapids
205	51.1	Kalkaska Public Schools	Kalkaska
206	51.1	Wayne-Westland Community SD	Westland
207	51.1	Bangor Township Schools	Bay City
208	51.1	Quincy Community SD	Quincy
209	51.1	Warren Woods Public Schools	Warren
210	51.1	Wyandotte City SD	Wyandotte
211	51.1	Reeths-Puffer Schools	Muskegon
212	51.1	Bullock Creek SD	Midland
213	51.1	Allendale Public SD	Allendale
213	51.1	Farwell Area Schools	Farwell
215	51.0	Traverse City Area Public Schls	Traverse City
216	51.0	Charlotte Public Schools	Charlotte
217	51.0	Hudsonville Public SD	Hudsonville
218	51.0	Lakeview SD (Calhoun)	Battle Creek
219	51.0	Zeeland Public Schools	Zeeland
220	51.0	Ludington Area SD	Ludington
221	51.0	Rochester Community SD	Rochester
222	51.0	Portland Public SD	Portland
223	51.0	Mason Consol Schools (Monroe)	Erie
224	51.0	Sparta Area Schools	Sparta
225	51.0	Holt Public Schools	Holt
226	50.9	Tecumseh Public Schools	Tecumseh
227	50.9	Alma Public Schools	Alma
228	50.9	Warren Consolidated Schools	Warren
229	50.9	East Grand Rapids Public Schools	E Grand Rapids
230	50.9	Gibraltar SD	Woodhaven
231	50.8	Riverview Community SD	Riverview
232	50.8	Carman-Ainsworth Comm Schools	Flint
233	50.8	Kelloggsville Public Schools	Grand Rapids
234	50.8	South Haven Public Schools	South Haven
235	50.8	East Jackson Community Schools	Jackson
236	50.8	Grand Blanc Community Schools	Grand Blanc
237	50.8	Perry Public SD	Perry
238	50.8	Public Schools of Calumet	Calumet
239	50.8	East Lansing SD	East Lansing
240	50.8	Chippewa Hills SD	Remus
241	50.7	Grosse Pointe Public Schools	Grosse Pointe
242	50.7	Manistee Area Schools	Manistee
243	50.7	Van Buren Public Schools	Belleville
244	50.7	Detroit City SD	Detroit
245	50.7	Berkley SD	Berkley
246	50.7	Saginaw City SD	Saginaw
247	50.7	Mona Shores Public SD	Norton Shores
248	50.7	Durand Area Schools	Durand
249	50.7	Bridgeport-Spaulding CSD	Bridgeport
250	50.6	Tawas Area Schools	Tawas City
251	50.6	Chesaning Union Schools	Chesaning
252	50.6	Sturgis Public Schools	Sturgis
253	50.6	Alpena Public Schools	Alpena
254	50.6	Northville Public Schools	Northville
255	50.6	Lakewood Public Schools	Lake Odessa
256	50.6	Lakeville Community Schools	Otisville
257	50.6	Allegan Public Schools	Allegan
257	50.6	Gull Lake Community Schools	Richland
259	50.6	Wayland Union Schools	Wayland
260	50.5	Southfield Public SD	Southfield
261	50.5	East Detroit Public Schools	Eastpointe
262	50.5	Morley Stanwood Community Schls	Morley
263	50.5	L'anse Creuse Public Schools	Harrison Twp
264	50.5	Lakeview Public Schools (Macomb)	St Clair Shores
265	50.5	Taylor SD	Taylor
266	50.5	Romulus Community Schools	Romulus
267	50.5	Western SD	Parma
268	50.4	Bedford Public Schools	Temperance
269	50.4	Reed City Area Public Schools	Reed City
270	50.4	Williamston Community Schools	Williamston
271	50.4	Pinconning Area Schools	Pinconning
272	50.3	Northwest Community Schools	Jackson
273	50.3	Imlay City Community Schools	Imlay City
274	50.3	Orchard View Schools	Muskegon
275	50.3	Mt. Clemens Community SD	Mt. Clemens
276	50.3	Fenton Area Public Schools	Fenton
277	50.3	Romeo Community Schools	Romeo
278	50.3	Flint City SD	Flint
279	50.2	Plymouth-Canton Community Schls	Plymouth
280	50.2	Gaylord Community Schools	Gaylord
281	50.2	Saginaw Twp Community Schools	Saginaw
282	50.2	Dearborn Heights SD #7	Dearborn Hgts
283	50.1	Cedar Springs Public Schools	Cedar Springs
284	50.0	Davison Community Schools	Davison
285	50.0	Vicksburg Community Schools	Vicksburg
286	49.9	Beecher Community SD	Flint
287	49.9	Essexville-Hampton Public Schls	Essexville
288	49.9	Benton Harbor Area Schools	Benton Harbor
289	49.8	Muskegon Heights SD	Muskegon Hgts
290	49.8	Hastings Area SD	Hastings
291	49.8	Mason Public Schools (Ingham)	Mason
292	49.7	Melvindale-N Allen Park Schools	Melvindale
293	49.7	Grosse Ile Township Schools	Grosse Ile
294	49.7	Godfrey-Lee Public Schools	Wyoming
295	49.7	South Redford SD	Redford
296	49.5	Flat Rock Community Schools	Flat Rock
297	49.5	Flushing Community Schools	Flushing
298	49.5	Swan Valley SD	Saginaw
299	49.3	Meridian Public Schools	Sanford
300	49.2	Central Montcalm Public Schools	Stanton
301	49.2	Pennfield SD	Battle Creek
302	49.0	Newaygo Public SD	Newaygo
303	49.0	Belding Area SD	Belding
304	48.9	Highland Park City Schools	Highland Park
305	48.8	Clare Public Schools	Clare
306	46.4	Detroit Acad of Arts & Sciences	Detroit

Female Students

Rank	Percent	District Name	City
1	53.5	Detroit Acad of Arts & Sciences	Detroit
2	51.1	Clare Public Schools	Clare
3	51.0	Highland Park City Schools	Highland Park
4	50.9	Belding Area SD	Belding
5	50.9	Newaygo Public SD	Newaygo
6	50.7	Pennfield SD	Battle Creek
7	50.7	Central Montcalm Public Schools	Stanton
8	50.6	Meridian Public Schools	Sanford
9	50.4	Swan Valley SD	Saginaw
10	50.4	Flushing Community Schools	Flushing
11	50.4	Flat Rock Community Schools	Flat Rock
12	50.2	South Redford SD	Redford
13	50.2	Godfrey-Lee Public Schools	Wyoming
14	50.2	Grosse Ile Township Schools	Grosse Ile
15	50.2	Melvindale-N Allen Park Schools	Melvindale
16	50.1	Mason Public Schools (Ingham)	Mason
17	50.1	Hastings Area SD	Hastings
18	50.1	Muskegon Heights SD	Muskegon Hgts
19	50.0	Benton Harbor Area Schools	Benton Harbor
20	50.0	Essexville-Hampton Public Schls	Essexville
21	50.0	Beecher Community SD	Flint
22	50.0	Vicksburg Community Schools	Vicksburg
23	49.9	Davison Community Schools	Davison
24	49.8	Cedar Springs Public Schools	Cedar Springs
25	49.7	Dearborn Heights SD #7	Dearborn Hgts
26	49.7	Saginaw Twp Community Schools	Saginaw
27	49.7	Gaylord Community Schools	Gaylord
28	49.7	Plymouth-Canton Community Schls	Plymouth
29	49.6	Flint City SD	Flint
30	49.6	Romeo Community Schools	Romeo
31	49.6	Fenton Area Public Schools	Fenton
32	49.6	Mt. Clemens Community SD	Mt. Clemens
33	49.6	Orchard View Schools	Muskegon
34	49.6	Imlay City Community Schools	Imlay City
35	49.6	Northwest Community Schools	Jackson
36	49.5	Pinconning Area Schools	Pinconning
37	49.5	Williamston Community Schools	Williamston
38	49.5	Reed City Area Public Schools	Reed City
39	49.5	Bedford Public Schools	Temperance
40	49.4	Western SD	Parma
41	49.4	Romulus Community Schools	Romulus
42	49.4	Taylor SD	Taylor
43	49.4	Lakeview Public Schools (Macomb)	St Clair Shores
44	49.4	L'anse Creuse Public Schools	Harrison Twp
45	49.4	Morley Stanwood Community Schls	Morley
46	49.4	East Detroit Public Schools	Eastpointe
47	49.4	Southfield Public SD	Southfield
48	49.3	Wayland Union Schools	Wayland
49	49.3	Allegan Public Schools	Allegan
49	49.3	Gull Lake Community Schools	Richland
51	49.3	Lakeville Community Schools	Otisville
52	49.3	Lakewood Public Schools	Lake Odessa
53	49.3	Northville Public Schools	Northville
54	49.3	Alpena Public Schools	Alpena
55	49.3	Sturgis Public Schools	Sturgis
56	49.3	Chesaning Union Schools	Chesaning
57	49.3	Tawas Area Schools	Tawas City
58	49.2	Bridgeport-Spaulding CSD	Bridgeport
59	49.2	Durand Area Schools	Durand
60	49.2	Mona Shores Public SD	Norton Shores
61	49.2	Saginaw City SD	Saginaw
62	49.2	Berkley SD	Berkley
63	49.2	Detroit City SD	Detroit
64	49.2	Van Buren Public Schools	Belleville
65	49.2	Manistee Area Schools	Manistee
66	49.2	Grosse Pointe Public Schools	Grosse Pointe
67	49.1	Chippewa Hills SD	Remus
68	49.1	East Lansing SD	East Lansing
69	49.1	Public Schools of Calumet	Calumet
70	49.1	Perry Public SD	Perry
71	49.1	Grand Blanc Community Schools	Grand Blanc
72	49.1	East Jackson Community Schools	Jackson
73	49.1	South Haven Public Schools	South Haven
74	49.1	Kelloggsville Public Schools	Grand Rapids
75	49.1	Carman-Ainsworth Comm Schools	Flint
76	49.1	Riverview Community SD	Riverview
77	49.0	Gibraltar SD	Woodhaven
78	49.0	East Grand Rapids Public Schools	E Grand Rapids
79	49.0	Warren Consolidated Schools	Warren
80	49.0	Alma Public Schools	Alma
81	49.0	Tecumseh Public Schools	Tecumseh
82	48.9	Holt Public Schools	Holt
83	48.9	Sparta Area Schools	Sparta
84	48.9	Mason Consol Schools (Monroe)	Erie
85	48.9	Portland Public SD	Portland
86	48.9	Rochester Community SD	Rochester
87	48.9	Ludington Area SD	Ludington
88	48.9	Zeeland Public Schools	Zeeland
89	48.9	Lakeview SD (Calhoun)	Battle Creek
90	48.9	Hudsonville Public SD	Hudsonville
91	48.9	Charlotte Public Schools	Charlotte
92	48.9	Traverse City Area Public Schls	Traverse City
93	48.8	Allendale Public SD	Allendale
93	48.8	Farwell Area Schools	Farwell
95	48.8	Bullock Creek SD	Midland
96	48.8	Reeths-Puffer Schools	Muskegon
97	48.8	Wyandotte City SD	Wyandotte
98	48.8	Warren Woods Public Schools	Warren
99	48.8	Quincy Community SD	Quincy
100	48.8	Bangor Township Schools	Bay City
101	48.8	Wayne-Westland Community SD	Westland
102	48.8	Kalkaska Public Schools	Kalkaska
103	48.8	Big Rapids Public Schools	Big Rapids
104	48.8	Adrian City SD	Adrian
105	48.7	Richmond Community Schools	Richmond
106	48.7	South Lake Schools	St Clair Shores
107	48.7	Okemos Public Schools	Okemos
108	48.7	Dexter Community SD	Dexter
109	48.7	Clarenceville SD	Livonia
110	48.7	Wyoming Public Schools	Wyoming
111	48.7	Ann Arbor Public Schools	Ann Arbor
112	48.7	Millington Community Schools	Millington
113	48.7	Cheboygan Area Schools	Cheboygan
114	48.7	Fremont Public SD	Fremont
115	48.7	Chippewa Valley Schools	Clinton Twp
116	48.7	Allen Park Public Schools	Allen Park
117	48.7	Avondale SD	Auburn Hills
118	48.6	Kenowa Hills Public Schools	Grand Rapids
119	48.6	Standish-Sterling Comm Schools	Standish
120	48.6	Jefferson Schools (Monroe)	Monroe
121	48.6	Menominee Area Public Schools	Menominee
122	48.6	Lincoln Consolidated SD	Ypsilanti
123	48.6	Dowagiac Union SD	Dowagiac
124	48.6	Portage Public Schools	Portage
125	48.6	Parchment SD	Parchment
126	48.6	Grandville Public Schools	Grandville
127	48.5	Jackson Public Schools	Jackson
128	48.5	Lakeview Comm Schools (Montcalm)	Lakeview
129	48.5	West Ottawa Public SD	Holland
130	48.5	Pontiac City SD	Pontiac
131	48.5	Hartford Public SD	Hartford
132	48.5	Linden Community Schools	Linden
133	48.5	Harrison Community Schools	Harrison
134	48.5	Lowell Area Schools	Lowell
135	48.5	Lake Fenton Community Schools	Fenton
136	48.5	Brandon SD	Ortonville
137	48.5	Fruitport Community Schools	Fruitport
138	48.4	White Cloud Public Schools	White Cloud
139	48.4	Kentwood Public Schools	Kentwood
140	48.4	Clarkston Community SD	Clarkston
141	48.4	Oak Park City SD	Oak Park
142	48.4	Grand Ledge Public Schools	Grand Ledge
143	48.4	Corunna Public SD	Corunna
144	48.4	Anchor Bay SD	New Baltimore
145	48.4	Saline Area Schools	Saline

146	48.4	Mt. Pleasant City SD	Mt. Pleasant
147	48.4	Fraser Public Schools	Fraser
148	48.3	Albion Public Schools	Albion
149	48.3	Swartz Creek Community Schools	Swartz Creek
150	48.3	Coopersville Public SD	Coopersville
151	48.3	Woodhaven-Brownstown SD	Brownstown
152	48.3	Forest Hills Public Schools	Grand Rapids
153	48.3	Madison Public Schools (Oakland)	Madison Heights
154	48.3	East China SD	East China
155	48.3	Ferndale Public Schools	Ferndale
156	48.3	Kearsley Community Schools	Flint
157	48.3	Mattawan Consolidated School	Mattawan
158	48.3	St. Joseph Public Schools	St. Joseph
159	48.3	Bloomfield Hills SD	Bloomfield Hls
160	48.3	Hillsdale Community Schools	Hillsdale
161	48.3	Plainwell Community Schools	Plainwell
162	48.2	South Lyon Community Schools	South Lyon
163	48.2	Birmingham City SD	Birmingham
164	48.2	Huron Valley Schools	Highland
165	48.2	Gladwin Community Schools	Gladwin
166	48.2	Algonac Community SD	Algonac
167	48.2	Elk Rapids Schools	Elk Rapids
168	48.2	Greenville Public Schools	Greenville
169	48.2	Monroe Public Schools	Monroe
170	48.2	W Branch-Rose City Area Schools	West Branch
171	48.2	Port Huron Area SD	Port Huron
172	48.2	Ionia Public Schools	Ionia
173	48.2	Center Line Public Schools	Center Line
174	48.1	Lansing Public SD	Lansing
175	48.1	Jenison Public Schools	Jenison
176	48.1	Stockbridge Community Schools	Stockbridge
177	48.1	Edwardsburg Public Schools	Edwardsburg
178	48.1	Escanaba Area Public Schools	Escanaba
179	48.1	Livonia Public Schools	Livonia
180	48.1	Marysville Public Schools	Marysville
181	48.1	Waverly Community Schools	Lansing
182	48.1	Kalamazoo Public SD	Kalamazoo
183	48.1	Dearborn City SD	Dearborn
184	48.0	Howell Public Schools	Howell
185	48.0	Chelsea SD	Chelsea
186	48.0	Utica Community Schools	Sterling Hgts
187	48.0	Midland Public Schools	Midland
188	48.0	Battle Creek Public Schools	Battle Creek
189	48.0	Gladstone Area Schools	Gladstone
190	48.0	Crestwood SD	Dearborn Hgts
191	48.0	Southgate Community SD	Southgate
192	48.0	Holland City SD	Holland
193	48.0	Paw Paw Public SD	Paw Paw
194	48.0	Harper Creek Community Schools	Battle Creek
195	47.9	Caro Community Schools	Caro
196	47.9	Trenton Public Schools	Trenton
197	47.9	Farmington Public SD	Farmington
198	47.9	Troy SD	Troy
199	47.9	Hartland Consolidated Schools	Hartland
200	47.9	Maple Valley Schools	Vermontville
201	47.9	Waterford SD	Waterford
202	47.9	Lapeer Community Schools	Lapeer
203	47.9	Grand Rapids Public Schools	Grand Rapids
204	47.9	Eaton Rapids Public Schools	Eaton Rapids
205	47.9	Brighton Area Schools	Brighton
206	47.9	Carrollton SD	Saginaw
207	47.8	Marquette Area Public Schools	Marquette
208	47.8	North Branch Area Schools	North Branch
209	47.8	Gwinn Area Community Schools	Gwinn
210	47.8	Novi Community SD	Novi
211	47.8	Lake Orion Community Schools	Lake Orion
212	47.8	Lake Shore Pub Schools (Macomb)	St Clair Shores
213	47.7	Houghton Lake Community Schools	Houghton Lake
214	47.7	Birch Run Area SD	Birch Run
215	47.7	Holly Area SD	Holly
216	47.7	Oscoda Area Schools	Oscoda
217	47.7	Roseville Community Schools	Roseville
218	47.7	Constantine Public SD	Constantine
219	47.7	Lamphere Public Schools	Madison Heights
220	47.6	SD of Ypsilanti	Ypsilanti
221	47.6	Cadillac Area Public Schools	Cadillac
222	47.6	Goodrich Area Schools	Goodrich
223	47.6	Columbia SD	Brooklyn
224	47.6	Huron SD	New Boston
224	47.6	Michigan Center SD	Michigan Center
226	47.6	St. Johns Public Schools	St. Johns
227	47.6	Haslett Public Schools	Haslett
228	47.6	Thornapple Kellogg SD	Middleville
229	47.6	Sault Ste. Marie Area Schools	Sault Ste Marie
230	47.5	SD of the City of Royal Oak	Royal Oak
231	47.5	Muskegon City SD	Muskegon
232	47.5	Ida Public SD	Ida
232	47.5	Lakeshore SD (Berrien)	Stevensville
234	47.5	Coldwater Community Schools	Coldwater
235	47.5	Otsego Public Schools	Otsego
236	47.5	Capac Community SD	Capac
237	47.4	Walled Lake Consolidated Schools	Walled Lake
238	47.4	Onsted Community Schools	Onsted
239	47.4	Yale Public Schools	Yale
240	47.4	Milan Area Schools	Milan
241	47.4	Airport Community SD	Carleton
242	47.4	Public Schools of Petoskey	Petoskey
243	47.4	Grant Public SD	Grant
244	47.4	Almont Community Schools	Almont
245	47.4	Bendle Public Schools	Burton
246	47.4	West Bloomfield SD	West Bloomfield
247	47.3	Hamilton Community Schools	Hamilton
248	47.3	Bay City SD	Bay City
249	47.3	Lincoln Park Public Schools	Lincoln Park
250	47.3	Rockford Public Schools	Rockford
251	47.3	Tri County Area Schools	Sand Lake
252	47.3	Beaverton Rural Schools	Beaverton
253	47.3	Willow Run Community Schools	Ypsilanti
254	47.3	Shelby Public Schools	Shelby
255	47.3	Armada Area Schools	Armada
256	47.2	Mt. Morris Consolidated Schools	Mt. Morris
257	47.2	Montague Area Public Schools	Montague
258	47.2	Comstock Public Schools	Kalamazoo
259	47.2	Fowlerville Community Schools	Fowlerville
260	47.2	Oxford Area Community Schools	Oxford
261	47.1	Marshall Public Schools	Marshall
262	47.1	Whitehall District Schools	Whitehall
263	47.1	Berrien Springs Public Schools	Berrien Springs
264	47.1	Coloma Community Schools	Coloma
265	47.1	Dundee Community Schools	Dundee
266	47.1	Dewitt Public Schools	Dewitt
267	47.0	Oakridge Public Schools	Muskegon
268	47.0	Saginaw ISD	Saginaw
269	47.0	Freeland Community SD	Freeland
270	47.0	Northview Public SD	Grand Rapids
271	47.0	Byron Center Public Schools	Byron Center
272	47.0	Grand Haven Area Public Schools	Grand Haven
273	47.0	Benzie County Central Schools	Benzonia
274	47.0	Godwin Heights Public Schools	Wyoming
275	46.9	Croswell-Lexington Comm Schools	Croswell
276	46.9	Napoleon Community Schools	Napoleon
277	46.9	Van Dyke Public Schools	Warren
278	46.9	Comstock Park Public Schools	Comstock Park
279	46.8	Owosso Public Schools	Owosso
280	46.8	Garden City SD	Garden City
281	46.8	Breitung Township Schools	Kingsford
282	46.8	Delton-Kellogg SD	Delton
283	46.8	Ovid-Elsie Area Schools	Elsie
284	46.7	River Rouge SD	River Rouge
285	46.7	Spring Lake Public Schools	Spring Lake
286	46.6	Brandywine Public SD	Niles
287	46.6	Gerrish-Higgins SD	Roscommon
288	46.6	Crawford Ausable Schools	Grayling
289	46.5	Montrose Community Schools	Montrose
290	46.5	Shepherd Public SD	Shepherd
291	46.4	Clintondale Community Schools	Clinton Twp
292	46.4	Redford Union SD	Redford
293	46.4	Westwood Community Schools	Dearborn Hgts
294	46.3	Bangor Public Schls (Van Buren)	Bangor
295	46.2	Hazel Park City SD	Hazel Park
296	46.2	Fitzgerald Public Schools	Warren
297	46.2	Niles Community SD	Niles
298	46.1	Three Rivers Community Schools	Three Rivers
299	46.1	Buchanan Community Schools	Buchanan
300	46.0	Caledonia Community Schools	Caledonia
301	45.7	Clio Area SD	Clio
302	45.3	Mason County Central Schools	Scottville
303	44.9	Hamtramck Public Schools	Hamtramck
304	44.4	Washtenaw ISD	Ann Arbor
305	41.9	Vassar Public Schools	Vassar
306	28.5	Macomb ISD	Clinton Twp

Individual Education Program Students

Rank	Percent	District Name	City
1	24.9	Redford Union SD	Redford
2	24.5	Grand Rapids Public Schools	Grand Rapids
3	21.8	Garden City SD	Garden City
4	21.7	Wyandotte City SD	Wyandotte
5	20.1	Harrison Community Schools	Harrison
5	20.1	SD of Ypsilanti	Ypsilanti
5	20.1	Saginaw City SD	Saginaw
8	20.0	Muskegon Heights SD	Muskegon Hgts
9	19.9	Willow Run Community Schools	Ypsilanti
10	19.5	Lansing Public SD	Lansing
11	19.4	Westwood Community Schools	Dearborn Hgts
12	19.3	Holly Area SD	Holly
13	19.0	Vassar Public Schools	Vassar
14	18.9	Muskegon City SD	Muskegon
15	18.7	Mt. Clemens Community SD	Mt. Clemens
16	18.4	Gwinn Area Community Schools	Gwinn
17	18.3	Adrian City SD	Adrian
18	18.2	Madison Public Schools (Oakland)	Madison Heights
19	18.0	White Cloud Public Schools	White Cloud
20	17.9	Ionia Public Schools	Ionia
21	17.6	Reeths-Puffer Schools	Muskegon
22	17.4	Gladwin Community Schools	Gladwin
23	17.3	Niles Community SD	Niles
24	17.2	Jenison Public Schools	Jenison
25	17.0	Richmond Community Schools	Richmond
25	17.0	Taylor SD	Taylor
27	16.9	Chesaning Union Schools	Chesaning
27	16.9	Oscoda Area Schools	Oscoda
27	16.9	Pontiac City SD	Pontiac
30	16.8	Fruitport Community Schools	Fruitport
30	16.8	Mason Consol Schools (Monroe)	Erie
32	16.7	Bridgeport-Spaulding CSD	Bridgeport
32	16.7	Charlotte Public Schools	Charlotte
32	16.7	Hazel Park City SD	Hazel Park
32	16.7	Van Dyke Public Schools	Warren
36	16.6	Holt Public Schools	Holt
36	16.6	Trenton Public Schools	Trenton
38	16.5	Buchanan Community Schools	Buchanan
38	16.5	Lakeview Comm Schools (Montcalm)	Lakeview
38	16.5	Wayne-Westland Community SD	Westland
38	16.5	Woodhaven-Brownstown SD	Brownstown
42	16.4	Eaton Rapids Public Schools	Eaton Rapids
43	16.3	Bullock Creek SD	Midland
44	16.2	Crawford Ausable Schools	Grayling
44	16.2	Fremont Public SD	Fremont
46	16.1	Grand Ledge Public Schools	Grand Ledge
47	16.0	Belding Area SD	Belding
47	16.0	Center Line Public Schools	Center Line
47	16.0	Jackson Public Schools	Jackson
47	16.0	Kalkaska Public Schools	Kalkaska
51	15.9	Beaverton Rural Schools	Beaverton
51	15.9	Comstock Park Public Schools	Comstock Park
51	15.9	Flat Rock Community Schools	Flat Rock
51	15.9	Montague Area Public Schools	Montague
51	15.9	Swan Valley SD	Saginaw
56	15.8	Carrollton SD	Saginaw
56	15.8	Ida Public SD	Ida
56	15.8	Portland Public SD	Portland
56	15.8	Shepherd Public SD	Shepherd
60	15.7	Chippewa Hills SD	Remus
60	15.7	Lakewood Public Schools	Lake Odessa
60	15.7	Marquette Area Public Schools	Marquette
60	15.7	Milan Area Schools	Milan
64	15.6	Lamphere Public Schools	Madison Heights
64	15.6	Stockbridge Community Schools	Stockbridge
66	15.5	Coloma Community Schools	Coloma
66	15.5	Lincoln Consolidated SD	Ypsilanti
66	15.5	Sparta Area Schools	Sparta
69	15.4	Meridian Public Schools	Sanford
69	15.4	River Rouge SD	River Rouge
69	15.4	Wayland Union Schools	Wayland
72	15.3	Bloomfield Hills SD	Bloomfield Hls
73	15.2	Battle Creek Public Schools	Battle Creek
73	15.2	Big Rapids Public Schools	Big Rapids
75	15.1	Caro Community Schools	Caro
75	15.1	Greenville Public Schools	Greenville
75	15.1	Howell Public Schools	Howell
75	15.1	Huron SD	New Boston
75	15.1	Waterford SD	Waterford
80	15.0	Jefferson Schools (Monroe)	Monroe
80	15.0	W Branch-Rose City Area Schools	West Branch
82	14.9	Haslett Public Schools	Haslett
83	14.8	Chelsea SD	Chelsea
83	14.8	Fitzgerald Public Schools	Warren
83	14.8	Mt. Pleasant City SD	Mt. Pleasant
83	14.8	Southgate Community SD	Southgate
87	14.7	Godwin Heights Public Schools	Wyoming
87	14.7	Roseville Community Schools	Roseville
89	14.6	Houghton Lake Community Schools	Houghton Lake
89	14.6	Reed City Area Public Schools	Reed City
91	14.5	Alma Public Schools	Alma
91	14.5	Clarenceville SD	Livonia
91	14.5	East Detroit Public Schools	Eastpointe
91	14.5	Wyoming Public Schools	Wyoming
95	14.4	Berrien Springs Public Schools	Berrien Springs
95	14.4	Brandywine Public SD	Niles
95	14.4	Capac Community SD	Capac
95	14.4	Mt. Morris Consolidated Schools	Mt. Morris
99	14.3	Holland City SD	Holland
99	14.3	Tawas Area Schools	Tawas City
101	14.2	Comstock Public Schools	Kalamazoo
101	14.2	Morley Stanwood Community Schls	Morley
101	14.2	Romulus Community Schools	Romulus
101	14.2	Sault Ste. Marie Area Schools	Sault Ste Marie
101	14.2	Three Rivers Community Schools	Three Rivers
101	14.2	Warren Woods Public Schools	Warren
107	14.1	Benton Harbor Area Schools	Benton Harbor
107	14.1	Gerrish-Higgins SD	Roscommon
107	14.1	Midland Public Schools	Midland
107	14.1	Northview Public SD	Grand Rapids
107	14.1	South Lake Schools	St Clair Shores
112	14.0	Gibraltar SD	Woodhaven
112	14.0	Port Huron Area SD	Port Huron
114	13.9	Bedford Public Schools	Temperance

114	13.9	Cedar Springs Public Schools	Cedar Springs
114	13.9	Fowlerville Community Schools	Fowlerville
114	13.9	Maple Valley Schools	Vermontville
114	13.9	Tecumseh Public Schools	Tecumseh
119	13.8	Brighton Area Schools	Brighton
119	13.8	East Jackson Community Schools	Jackson
119	13.8	Grant Public SD	Grant
119	13.8	Owosso Public Schools	Owosso
119	13.8	SD of the City of Royal Oak	Royal Oak
119	13.8	Van Buren Public Schools	Belleville
125	13.7	Brandon SD	Ortonville
125	13.7	Godfrey-Lee Public Schools	Wyoming
125	13.7	Saginaw Twp Community Schools	Saginaw
125	13.7	Tri County Area Schools	Sand Lake
129	13.6	Byron Center Public Schools	Byron Center
129	13.6	Central Montcalm Public Schools	Stanton
129	13.6	Mason Public Schools (Ingham)	Mason
129	13.6	Monroe Public Schools	Monroe
129	13.6	Ovid-Elsie Area Schools	Elsie
134	13.5	Detroit City SD	Detroit
134	13.5	Dowagiac Union SD	Dowagiac
134	13.5	Kalamazoo Public SD	Kalamazoo
134	13.5	Mason County Central Schools	Scottville
134	13.5	Perry Public SD	Perry
139	13.4	Carman-Ainsworth Comm Schools	Flint
139	13.4	Kenowa Hills Public Schools	Grand Rapids
139	13.4	Linden Community Schools	Linden
139	13.4	St. Johns Public Schools	St. Johns
143	13.3	Allegan Public Schools	Allegan
143	13.3	Columbia SD	Brooklyn
143	13.3	Ludington Area SD	Ludington
143	13.3	Millington Community Schools	Millington
143	13.3	Northwest Community Schools	Jackson
148	13.2	Caledonia Community Schools	Caledonia
148	13.2	Clintondale Community Schools	Clinton Twp
148	13.2	Michigan Center SD	Michigan Center
148	13.2	Traverse City Area Public Schls	Traverse City
152	13.1	Bangor Township Schools	Bay City
152	13.1	Bay City SD	Bay City
152	13.1	Benzie County Central Schools	Benzonia
152	13.1	Kentwood Public Schools	Kentwood
152	13.1	Lakeview Public Schools (Macomb)	St Clair Shores
152	13.1	Montrose Community Schools	Montrose
158	13.0	Albion Public Schools	Albion
158	13.0	Melvindale-N Allen Park Schools	Melvindale
158	13.0	Shelby Public Schools	Shelby
161	12.9	Bendle Public Schools	Burton
161	12.9	Dearborn Heights SD #7	Dearborn Hgts
161	12.9	Dexter Community SD	Dexter
161	12.9	Lapeer Community Schools	Lapeer
161	12.9	Lowell Area Schools	Lowell
161	12.9	Standish-Sterling Comm Schools	Standish
167	12.8	Clarkston Community SD	Clarkston
167	12.8	Flint City SD	Flint
167	12.8	Huron Valley Schools	Highland
167	12.8	Swartz Creek Community Schools	Swartz Creek
167	12.8	Waverly Community Schools	Lansing
172	12.7	Highland Park City Schools	Highland Park
173	12.6	Anchor Bay SD	New Baltimore
173	12.6	Hudsonville Public SD	Hudsonville
173	12.6	Washtenaw ISD	Ann Arbor
176	12.5	Cheboygan Area Schools	Cheboygan
176	12.5	Oakridge Public Schools	Muskegon
176	12.5	Romeo Community Schools	Romeo
179	12.4	Airport Community SD	Carleton
179	12.4	Ann Arbor Public Schools	Ann Arbor
179	12.4	Breitung Township Schools	Kingsford
179	12.4	Delton-Kellogg SD	Delton
179	12.4	Farwell Area Schools	Farwell
179	12.4	Gaylord Community Schools	Gaylord
179	12.4	Gladstone Area Schools	Gladstone
179	12.4	South Redford SD	Redford
187	12.3	Escanaba Area Public Schools	Escanaba
187	12.3	Farmington Public SD	Farmington
187	12.3	Forest Hills Public Schools	Grand Rapids
187	12.3	Lincoln Park Public Schools	Lincoln Park
187	12.3	Livonia Public Schools	Livonia
187	12.3	West Ottawa Public SD	Holland
187	12.3	Western SD	Parma
194	12.2	Grandville Public Schools	Grandville
194	12.2	Harper Creek Community Schools	Battle Creek
194	12.2	Lakeshore SD (Berrien)	Stevensville
194	12.2	Menominee Area Public Schools	Menominee
194	12.2	Utica Community Schools	Sterling Hgts
199	12.1	Coopersville Public SD	Coopersville
200	12.0	Durand Area Schools	Durand
200	12.0	Fenton Area Public Schools	Fenton
200	12.0	Grosse Pointe Public Schools	Grosse Pointe
200	12.0	South Lyon Community Schools	South Lyon
200	12.0	Walled Lake Consolidated Schools	Walled Lake
205	11.9	Whitehall District Schools	Whitehall
206	11.8	Allendale Public SD	Allendale
206	11.8	Croswell-Lexington Comm Schools	Croswell
206	11.8	East Grand Rapids Public Schools	E Grand Rapids
206	11.8	Hartland Consolidated Schools	Hartland
206	11.8	Mona Shores Public SD	Norton Shores
206	11.8	North Branch Area Schools	North Branch
212	11.7	Spring Lake Public Schools	Spring Lake
213	11.6	Armada Area Schools	Armada
213	11.6	Hastings Area SD	Hastings
213	11.6	Hillsdale Community Schools	Hillsdale
213	11.6	Southfield Public SD	Southfield
217	11.5	Okemos Public Schools	Okemos
218	11.4	Algonac Community SD	Algonac
218	11.4	Constantine Public SD	Constantine
218	11.4	Elk Rapids Schools	Elk Rapids
218	11.4	Lake Shore Pub Schools (Macomb)	St Clair Shores
218	11.4	Newaygo Public SD	Newaygo
218	11.4	Otsego Public Schools	Otsego
224	11.3	Clio Area SD	Clio
224	11.3	Essexville-Hampton Public Schls	Essexville
224	11.3	Freeland Community SD	Freeland
224	11.3	Lakeview SD (Calhoun)	Battle Creek
228	11.2	Onsted Community Schools	Onsted
228	11.2	Orchard View Schools	Muskegon
228	11.2	Williamston Community Schools	Williamston
231	11.1	Cadillac Area Public Schools	Cadillac
231	11.1	East Lansing SD	East Lansing
231	11.1	Pinconning Area Schools	Pinconning
234	11.0	Berkley SD	Berkley
234	11.0	Birch Run Area SD	Birch Run
234	11.0	Dearborn City SD	Dearborn
234	11.0	Marshall Public Schools	Marshall
234	11.0	Oxford Area Community Schools	Oxford
239	10.9	Birmingham City SD	Birmingham
239	10.9	West Bloomfield SD	West Bloomfield
241	10.8	Allen Park Public Schools	Allen Park
241	10.8	Alpena Public Schools	Alpena
241	10.8	Clare Public Schools	Clare
241	10.8	Corunna Public SD	Corunna
241	10.8	Fraser Public Schools	Fraser
241	10.8	Hamilton Community Schools	Hamilton
241	10.8	L'anse Creuse Public Schools	Harrison Twp
241	10.8	Plainwell Community Schools	Plainwell
241	10.8	Saginaw ISD	Saginaw
250	10.7	East China SD	East China
250	10.7	Sturgis Public Schools	Sturgis
252	10.6	Kelloggsville Public Schools	Grand Rapids
252	10.6	Lake Orion Community Schools	Lake Orion
252	10.6	Zeeland Public Schools	Zeeland
255	10.5	Davison Community Schools	Davison
255	10.5	Grand Haven Area Public Schools	Grand Haven
255	10.5	Rochester Community SD	Rochester
255	10.5	Yale Public Schools	Yale
259	10.4	Flushing Community Schools	Flushing
260	10.3	Saline Area Schools	Saline
261	10.2	Edwardsburg Public Schools	Edwardsburg
261	10.2	Plymouth-Canton Community Schls	Plymouth
261	10.2	Rockford Public Schools	Rockford
264	10.1	Napoleon Community Schools	Napoleon
264	10.1	Warren Consolidated Schools	Warren
266	10.0	Goodrich Area Schools	Goodrich
266	10.0	Imlay City Community Schools	Imlay City
268	9.9	Grand Blanc Community Schools	Grand Blanc
268	9.9	Kearsley Community Schools	Flint
268	9.9	Northville Public Schools	Northville
268	9.9	Novi Community SD	Novi
272	9.8	Dundee Community Schools	Dundee
272	9.8	Lakeville Community Schools	Otisville
272	9.8	Public Schools of Petoskey	Petoskey
272	9.8	Thornapple Kellogg SD	Middleville
276	9.7	Marysville Public Schools	Marysville
276	9.7	Paw Paw Public SD	Paw Paw
278	9.6	Chippewa Valley Schools	Clinton Twp
278	9.6	Pennfield SD	Battle Creek
280	9.5	Oak Park City SD	Oak Park
281	9.4	Avondale SD	Auburn Hills
281	9.4	Parchment SD	Parchment
283	9.3	Lake Fenton Community Schools	Fenton
284	9.1	Crestwood SD	Dearborn Hgts
284	9.1	Gull Lake Community Schools	Richland
284	9.1	Portage Public Schools	Portage
287	9.0	South Haven Public Schools	South Haven
288	8.9	Beecher Community SD	Flint
288	8.9	Ferndale Public Schools	Ferndale
288	8.9	Grosse Ile Township Schools	Grosse Ile
288	8.9	Public Schools of Calumet	Calumet
288	8.9	Vicksburg Community Schools	Vicksburg
293	8.8	Riverview Community SD	Riverview
294	8.5	Dewitt Public Schools	Dewitt
294	8.5	Manistee Area Schools	Manistee
296	8.4	St. Joseph Public Schools	St. Joseph
297	8.2	Almont Community Schools	Almont
297	8.2	Hamtramck Public Schools	Hamtramck
299	7.9	Troy SD	Troy
300	7.4	Hartford Public SD	Hartford
301	6.8	Bangor Public Schls (Van Buren)	Bangor
302	4.7	Detroit Acad of Arts & Sciences	Detroit
303	3.4	Mattawan Consolidated School	Mattawan
304	2.7	Quincy Community SD	Quincy
305	1.5	Coldwater Community Schools	Coldwater
306	n/a	Macomb ISD	Clinton Twp

English Language Learner Students

Rank	Percent	District Name	City
1	67.2	Hamtramck Public Schools	Hamtramck
2	55.5	Macomb ISD	Clinton Twp
3	35.8	Dearborn City SD	Dearborn
4	33.4	Godfrey-Lee Public Schools	Wyoming
5	25.2	Warren Consolidated Schools	Warren
6	21.3	Holland City SD	Holland
7	20.3	Farmington Public SD	Farmington
8	19.9	Grand Rapids Public Schools	Grand Rapids
9	16.1	East Lansing SD	East Lansing
10	15.9	Pontiac City SD	Pontiac
11	15.0	Adrian City SD	Adrian
12	14.9	Troy SD	Troy
13	14.4	Belding Area SD	Belding
14	14.2	Kelloggsville Public Schools	Grand Rapids
15	14.1	Hartford Public SD	Hartford
16	12.5	West Ottawa Public SD	Holland
17	12.3	Godwin Heights Public Schools	Wyoming
18	11.8	Shelby Public Schools	Shelby
19	11.4	Madison Public Schools (Oakland)	Madison Heights
20	10.1	Grant Public SD	Grant
21	9.6	Lamphere Public Schools	Madison Heights
22	9.4	Lansing Public SD	Lansing
23	8.8	Coldwater Community Schools	Coldwater
24	8.0	Sturgis Public Schools	Sturgis
25	7.9	Sparta Area Schools	Sparta
26	7.7	Berrien Springs Public Schools	Berrien Springs
26	7.7	Hazel Park City SD	Hazel Park
28	7.5	Kalamazoo Public SD	Kalamazoo
29	7.4	Ann Arbor Public Schools	Ann Arbor
30	7.3	Imlay City Community Schools	Imlay City
31	7.0	SD of Ypsilanti	Ypsilanti
32	6.6	West Bloomfield SD	West Bloomfield
32	6.6	Wyoming Public Schools	Wyoming
34	6.3	Rochester Community SD	Rochester
35	6.1	Oak Park City SD	Oak Park
35	6.1	Walled Lake Consolidated Schools	Walled Lake
37	5.7	Bay City SD	Bay City
37	5.7	Saginaw City SD	Saginaw
39	5.4	Detroit City SD	Detroit
39	5.4	South Haven Public Schools	South Haven
41	5.3	Southfield Public SD	Southfield
42	4.9	Fitzgerald Public Schools	Warren
43	4.6	Muskegon City SD	Muskegon
44	4.3	Bloomfield Hills SD	Bloomfield Hls
45	4.1	Flint City SD	Flint
46	4.0	Crestwood SD	Dearborn Hgts
47	3.9	Plymouth-Canton Community Schls	Plymouth
48	3.8	Melvindale-N Allen Park Schools	Melvindale
49	3.6	Lake Orion Community Schools	Lake Orion
50	3.4	Waterford SD	Waterford
51	3.3	Berkley SD	Berkley
51	3.3	Kenowa Hills Public Schools	Grand Rapids
53	3.1	Kentwood Public Schools	Kentwood
54	2.9	Grosse Pointe Public Schools	Grosse Pointe
54	2.9	SD of the City of Royal Oak	Royal Oak
56	2.6	Jackson Public Schools	Jackson
57	2.4	Battle Creek Public Schools	Battle Creek
58	2.3	Birmingham City SD	Birmingham
58	2.3	Chippewa Valley Schools	Clinton Twp
60	2.2	L'anse Creuse Public Schools	Harrison Twp
60	2.2	Zeeland Public Schools	Zeeland
62	2.1	Allendale Public SD	Allendale
62	2.1	Utica Community Schools	Sterling Hgts
64	2.0	Forest Hills Public Schools	Grand Rapids
65	1.7	Waverly Community Schools	Lansing
66	1.6	East Detroit Public Schools	Eastpointe
66	1.6	Northville Public Schools	Northville
68	1.1	Sault Ste. Marie Area Schools	Sault Ste Marie
68	1.1	Thornapple Kellogg SD	Middleville
70	1.0	Cedar Springs Public Schools	Cedar Springs
70	1.0	Monroe Public Schools	Monroe
70	1.0	Traverse City Area Public Schls	Traverse City
73	0.9	Hamilton Community Schools	Hamilton
74	0.8	Livonia Public Schools	Livonia
74	0.8	Otsego Public Schools	Otsego
74	0.8	Saline Area Schools	Saline
77	0.7	Grand Blanc Community Schools	Grand Blanc
77	0.7	Ida Public SD	Ida
77	0.7	Montague Area Public Schools	Montague
80	0.6	Jenison Public Schools	Jenison
81	0.5	Haslett Public Schools	Haslett
81	0.5	Midland Public Schools	Midland

83	0.3	Brandon SD	Ortonville
83	0.3	Carman-Ainsworth Comm Schools	Flint
83	0.3	Dexter Community SD	Dexter
83	0.3	Greenville Public Schools	Greenville
83	0.3	Lake Fenton Community Schools	Fenton
83	0.3	Lakewood Public Schools	Lake Odessa
83	0.3	Marquette Area Public Schools	Marquette
83	0.3	Port Huron Area SD	Port Huron
83	0.3	Stockbridge Community Schools	Stockbridge
92	0.2	Allegan Public Schools	Allegan
92	0.2	Harrison Community Schools	Harrison
92	0.2	Public Schools of Petoskey	Petoskey
92	0.2	Whitehall District Schools	Whitehall
92	0.2	Yale Public Schools	Yale
97	0.1	Bedford Public Schools	Temperance
97	0.1	Birch Run Area SD	Birch Run
97	0.1	Clare Public Schools	Clare
97	0.1	Clio Area SD	Clio
97	0.1	Fenton Area Public Schools	Fenton
97	0.1	Gwinn Area Community Schools	Gwinn
97	0.1	Hastings Area SD	Hastings
97	0.1	Hudsonville Public SD	Hudsonville
97	0.1	Lapeer Community Schools	Lapeer
97	0.1	Mt. Morris Consolidated Schools	Mt. Morris
97	0.1	Mt. Pleasant City SD	Mt. Pleasant
97	0.1	Oakridge Public Schools	Muskegon
97	0.1	Onsted Community Schools	Onsted
97	0.1	Pinconning Area Schools	Pinconning
97	0.1	Spring Lake Public Schools	Spring Lake
112	0.0	Bullock Creek SD	Midland
112	0.0	Escanaba Area Public Schools	Escanaba
112	0.0	Linden Community Schools	Linden
115	0.0	Airport Community SD	Carleton
115	0.0	Albion Public Schools	Albion
115	0.0	Algonac Community SD	Algonac
115	0.0	Allen Park Public Schools	Allen Park
115	0.0	Alma Public Schools	Alma
115	0.0	Almont Community Schools	Almont
115	0.0	Alpena Public Schools	Alpena
115	0.0	Anchor Bay SD	New Baltimore
115	0.0	Armada Area Schools	Armada
115	0.0	Avondale SD	Auburn Hills
115	0.0	Bangor Public Schls (Van Buren)	Bangor
115	0.0	Bangor Township Schools	Bay City
115	0.0	Beaverton Rural Schools	Beaverton
115	0.0	Beecher Community SD	Flint
115	0.0	Bendle Public Schools	Burton
115	0.0	Benton Harbor Area Schools	Benton Harbor
115	0.0	Benzie County Central Schools	Benzonia
115	0.0	Big Rapids Public Schools	Big Rapids
115	0.0	Brandywine Public SD	Niles
115	0.0	Breitung Township Schools	Kingsford
115	0.0	Bridgeport-Spaulding CSD	Bridgeport
115	0.0	Brighton Area Schools	Brighton
115	0.0	Buchanan Community Schools	Buchanan
115	0.0	Byron Center Public Schools	Byron Center
115	0.0	Cadillac Area Public Schools	Cadillac
115	0.0	Caledonia Community Schools	Caledonia
115	0.0	Capac Community SD	Capac
115	0.0	Caro Community Schools	Caro
115	0.0	Carrollton SD	Saginaw
115	0.0	Center Line Public Schools	Center Line
115	0.0	Central Montcalm Public Schools	Stanton
115	0.0	Charlotte Public Schools	Charlotte
115	0.0	Cheboygan Area Schools	Cheboygan
115	0.0	Chelsea SD	Chelsea
115	0.0	Chesaning Union Schools	Chesaning
115	0.0	Chippewa Hills SD	Remus
115	0.0	Clarenceville SD	Livonia
115	0.0	Clarkston Community SD	Clarkston
115	0.0	Clintondale Community Schools	Clinton Twp
115	0.0	Coloma Community Schools	Coloma
115	0.0	Columbia SD	Brooklyn
115	0.0	Comstock Park Public Schools	Comstock Park
115	0.0	Comstock Public Schools	Kalamazoo
115	0.0	Constantine Public SD	Constantine
115	0.0	Coopersville Public SD	Coopersville
115	0.0	Corunna Public SD	Corunna
115	0.0	Crawford Ausable Schools	Grayling
115	0.0	Croswell-Lexington Comm Schools	Croswell
115	0.0	Davison Community Schools	Davison
115	0.0	Dearborn Heights SD #7	Dearborn Hgts
115	0.0	Delton-Kellogg SD	Delton
115	0.0	Detroit Acad of Arts & Sciences	Detroit
115	0.0	Dewitt Public Schools	Dewitt
115	0.0	Dowagiac Union SD	Dowagiac
115	0.0	Dundee Community Schools	Dundee
115	0.0	Durand Area Schools	Durand
115	0.0	East China SD	East China
115	0.0	East Grand Rapids Public Schools	E Grand Rapids
115	0.0	East Jackson Community Schools	Jackson
115	0.0	Eaton Rapids Public Schools	Eaton Rapids
115	0.0	Edwardsburg Public Schools	Edwardsburg
115	0.0	Elk Rapids Schools	Elk Rapids
115	0.0	Essexville-Hampton Public Schls	Essexville
115	0.0	Farwell Area Schools	Farwell
115	0.0	Ferndale Public Schools	Ferndale
115	0.0	Flat Rock Community Schools	Flat Rock
115	0.0	Flushing Community Schools	Flushing
115	0.0	Fowlerville Community Schools	Fowlerville
115	0.0	Fraser Public Schools	Fraser
115	0.0	Freeland Community SD	Freeland
115	0.0	Fremont Public SD	Fremont
115	0.0	Fruitport Community Schools	Fruitport
115	0.0	Garden City SD	Garden City
115	0.0	Gaylord Community Schools	Gaylord
115	0.0	Gerrish-Higgins SD	Roscommon
115	0.0	Gibraltar SD	Woodhaven
115	0.0	Gladstone Area Schools	Gladstone
115	0.0	Gladwin Community Schools	Gladwin
115	0.0	Goodrich Area Schools	Goodrich
115	0.0	Grand Haven Area Public Schools	Grand Haven
115	0.0	Grand Ledge Public Schools	Grand Ledge
115	0.0	Grandville Public Schools	Grandville
115	0.0	Grosse Ile Township Schools	Grosse Ile
115	0.0	Gull Lake Community Schools	Richland
115	0.0	Harper Creek Community Schools	Battle Creek
115	0.0	Hartland Consolidated Schools	Hartland
115	0.0	Highland Park City Schools	Highland Park
115	0.0	Hillsdale Community Schools	Hillsdale
115	0.0	Holly Area SD	Holly
115	0.0	Holt Public Schools	Holt
115	0.0	Houghton Lake Community Schools	Houghton Lake
115	0.0	Howell Public Schools	Howell
115	0.0	Huron SD	New Boston
115	0.0	Huron Valley Schools	Highland
115	0.0	Ionia Public Schools	Ionia
115	0.0	Jefferson Schools (Monroe)	Monroe
115	0.0	Kalkaska Public Schools	Kalkaska
115	0.0	Kearsley Community Schools	Flint
115	0.0	Lake Shore Pub Schools (Macomb)	St Clair Shores
115	0.0	Lakeshore SD (Berrien)	Stevensville
115	0.0	Lakeview Comm Schools (Montcalm)	Lakeview
115	0.0	Lakeview Public Schools (Macomb)	St Clair Shores
115	0.0	Lakeview SD (Calhoun)	Battle Creek
115	0.0	Lakeville Community Schools	Otisville
115	0.0	Lincoln Consolidated SD	Ypsilanti
115	0.0	Lincoln Park Public Schools	Lincoln Park
115	0.0	Lowell Area Schools	Lowell
115	0.0	Ludington Area SD	Ludington
115	0.0	Manistee Area Schools	Manistee
115	0.0	Maple Valley Schools	Vermontville
115	0.0	Marshall Public Schools	Marshall
115	0.0	Marysville Public Schools	Marysville
115	0.0	Mason Consol Schools (Monroe)	Erie
115	0.0	Mason County Central Schools	Scottville
115	0.0	Mason Public Schools (Ingham)	Mason
115	0.0	Mattawan Consolidated School	Mattawan
115	0.0	Menominee Area Public Schools	Menominee
115	0.0	Meridian Public Schools	Sanford
115	0.0	Michigan Center SD	Michigan Center
115	0.0	Milan Area Schools	Milan
115	0.0	Millington Community Schools	Millington
115	0.0	Mona Shores Public SD	Norton Shores
115	0.0	Montrose Community Schools	Montrose
115	0.0	Morley Stanwood Community Schls	Morley
115	0.0	Mt. Clemens Community SD	Mt. Clemens
115	0.0	Muskegon Heights SD	Muskegon Hgts
115	0.0	Napoleon Community Schools	Napoleon
115	0.0	Newaygo Public SD	Newaygo
115	0.0	Niles Community SD	Niles
115	0.0	North Branch Area Schools	North Branch
115	0.0	Northview Public SD	Grand Rapids
115	0.0	Northwest Community Schools	Jackson
115	0.0	Novi Community SD	Novi
115	0.0	Okemos Public Schools	Okemos
115	0.0	Orchard View Schools	Muskegon
115	0.0	Oscoda Area Schools	Oscoda
115	0.0	Ovid-Elsie Area Schools	Elsie
115	0.0	Owosso Public Schools	Owosso
115	0.0	Oxford Area Community Schools	Oxford
115	0.0	Parchment SD	Parchment
115	0.0	Paw Paw Public SD	Paw Paw
115	0.0	Pennfield SD	Battle Creek
115	0.0	Perry Public SD	Perry
115	0.0	Plainwell Community Schools	Plainwell
115	0.0	Portage Public Schools	Portage
115	0.0	Portland Public SD	Portland
115	0.0	Public Schools of Calumet	Calumet
115	0.0	Quincy Community SD	Quincy
115	0.0	Redford Union SD	Redford
115	0.0	Reed City Area Public Schools	Reed City
115	0.0	Reeths-Puffer Schools	Muskegon
115	0.0	Richmond Community Schools	Richmond
115	0.0	River Rouge SD	River Rouge
115	0.0	Riverview Community SD	Riverview
115	0.0	Rockford Public Schools	Rockford
115	0.0	Romeo Community Schools	Romeo
115	0.0	Romulus Community Schools	Romulus
115	0.0	Roseville Community Schools	Roseville
115	0.0	Saginaw ISD	Saginaw
115	0.0	Saginaw Twp Community Schools	Saginaw
115	0.0	Shepherd Public SD	Shepherd
115	0.0	South Lake Schools	St Clair Shores
115	0.0	South Lyon Community Schools	South Lyon
115	0.0	South Redford SD	Redford
115	0.0	Southgate Community SD	Southgate
115	0.0	St. Johns Public Schools	St. Johns
115	0.0	St. Joseph Public Schools	St. Joseph
115	0.0	Standish-Sterling Comm Schools	Standish
115	0.0	Swan Valley SD	Saginaw
115	0.0	Swartz Creek Community Schools	Swartz Creek
115	0.0	Tawas Area Schools	Tawas City
115	0.0	Taylor SD	Taylor
115	0.0	Tecumseh Public Schools	Tecumseh
115	0.0	Three Rivers Community Schools	Three Rivers
115	0.0	Trenton Public Schools	Trenton
115	0.0	Tri County Area Schools	Sand Lake
115	0.0	Van Buren Public Schools	Belleville
115	0.0	Van Dyke Public Schools	Warren
115	0.0	Vassar Public Schools	Vassar
115	0.0	Vicksburg Community Schools	Vicksburg
115	0.0	Warren Woods Public Schools	Warren
115	0.0	Washtenaw ISD	Ann Arbor
115	0.0	Wayland Union Schools	Wayland
115	0.0	Wayne-Westland Community SD	Westland
115	0.0	W Branch-Rose City Area Schools	West Branch
115	0.0	Western SD	Parma
115	0.0	Westwood Community Schools	Dearborn Hgts
115	0.0	White Cloud Public Schools	White Cloud
115	0.0	Williamston Community Schools	Williamston
115	0.0	Willow Run Community Schools	Ypsilanti
115	0.0	Woodhaven-Brownstown SD	Brownstown
115	0.0	Wyandotte City SD	Wyandotte

Migrant Students

Rank	Percent	District Name	City
1	12.5	Bangor Public Schls (Van Buren)	Bangor
2	12.3	Imlay City Community Schools	Imlay City
3	10.8	Hartford Public SD	Hartford
4	10.3	Flint City SD	Flint
5	9.9	Shelby Public Schools	Shelby
6	9.2	Dowagiac Union SD	Dowagiac
7	6.5	South Haven Public Schools	South Haven
8	5.2	Sparta Area Schools	Sparta
9	4.8	Berrien Springs Public Schools	Berrien Springs
10	3.9	Grant Public SD	Grant
11	3.5	Coopersville Public SD	Coopersville
11	3.5	Grand Rapids Public Schools	Grand Rapids
13	3.4	Belding Area SD	Belding
14	3.2	Mason County Central Schools	Scottville
15	3.1	Sturgis Public Schools	Sturgis
16	3.0	Bridgeport-Spaulding CSD	Bridgeport
17	2.6	Almont Community Schools	Almont
17	2.6	Coloma Community Schools	Coloma
19	2.3	Kenowa Hills Public Schools	Grand Rapids
20	1.8	Grand Haven Area Public Schools	Grand Haven
21	1.3	Kalamazoo Public SD	Kalamazoo
22	0.8	Holland City SD	Holland
22	0.8	Paw Paw Public SD	Paw Paw
24	0.7	Traverse City Area Public Schls	Traverse City
25	0.5	Elk Rapids Schools	Elk Rapids
26	0.4	Bay City SD	Bay City
26	0.4	Detroit City SD	Detroit
28	0.3	Battle Creek Public Schools	Battle Creek
28	0.3	Walled Lake Consolidated Schools	Walled Lake
30	0.1	Fenton Area Public Schools	Fenton
30	0.1	Fruitport Community Schools	Fruitport
30	0.1	Mattawan Consolidated School	Mattawan
33	0.0	Lakeshore SD (Berrien)	Stevensville
33	0.0	Lansing Public SD	Lansing
35	n/a	Adrian City SD	Adrian
35	n/a	Airport Community SD	Carleton
35	n/a	Albion Public Schools	Albion
35	n/a	Algonac Community SD	Algonac
35	n/a	Allegan Public Schools	Allegan
35	n/a	Allen Park Public Schools	Allen Park
35	n/a	Allendale Public SD	Allendale
35	n/a	Alma Public Schools	Alma
35	n/a	Alpena Public Schools	Alpena
35	n/a	Anchor Bay SD	New Baltimore
35	n/a	Ann Arbor Public Schools	Ann Arbor
35	n/a	Armada Area Schools	Armada
35	n/a	Avondale SD	Auburn Hills
35	n/a	Bangor Township Schools	Bay City
35	n/a	Beaverton Rural Schools	Beaverton

35	n/a	Bedford Public Schools	Temperance
35	n/a	Beecher Community SD	Flint
35	n/a	Bendle Public Schools	Burton
35	n/a	Benton Harbor Area Schools	Benton Harbor
35	n/a	Benzie County Central Schools	Benzonia
35	n/a	Berkley SD	Berkley
35	n/a	Big Rapids Public Schools	Big Rapids
35	n/a	Birch Run Area SD	Birch Run
35	n/a	Birmingham City SD	Birmingham
35	n/a	Bloomfield Hills SD	Bloomfield Hls
35	n/a	Brandon SD	Ortonville
35	n/a	Brandywine Public SD	Niles
35	n/a	Breitung Township Schools	Kingsford
35	n/a	Brighton Area Schools	Brighton
35	n/a	Buchanan Community Schools	Buchanan
35	n/a	Bullock Creek SD	Midland
35	n/a	Byron Center Public Schools	Byron Center
35	n/a	Cadillac Area Public Schools	Cadillac
35	n/a	Caledonia Community Schools	Caledonia
35	n/a	Capac Community SD	Capac
35	n/a	Carman-Ainsworth Comm Schools	Flint
35	n/a	Caro Community Schools	Caro
35	n/a	Carrollton SD	Saginaw
35	n/a	Cedar Springs Public Schools	Cedar Springs
35	n/a	Center Line Public Schools	Center Line
35	n/a	Central Montcalm Public Schools	Stanton
35	n/a	Charlotte Public Schools	Charlotte
35	n/a	Cheboygan Area Schools	Cheboygan
35	n/a	Chelsea SD	Chelsea
35	n/a	Chesaning Union Schools	Chesaning
35	n/a	Chippewa Hills SD	Remus
35	n/a	Chippewa Valley Schools	Clinton Twp
35	n/a	Clare Public Schools	Clare
35	n/a	Clarenceville SD	Livonia
35	n/a	Clarkston Community SD	Clarkston
35	n/a	Clintondale Community Schools	Clinton Twp
35	n/a	Clio Area SD	Clio
35	n/a	Coldwater Community Schools	Coldwater
35	n/a	Columbia SD	Brooklyn
35	n/a	Comstock Park Public Schools	Comstock Park
35	n/a	Comstock Public Schools	Kalamazoo
35	n/a	Constantine Public SD	Constantine
35	n/a	Corunna Public SD	Corunna
35	n/a	Crawford Ausable Schools	Grayling
35	n/a	Crestwood SD	Dearborn Hgts
35	n/a	Croswell-Lexington Comm Schools	Croswell
35	n/a	Davison Community Schools	Davison
35	n/a	Dearborn City SD	Dearborn
35	n/a	Dearborn Heights SD #7	Dearborn Hgts
35	n/a	Delton-Kellogg SD	Delton
35	n/a	Detroit Acad of Arts & Sciences	Detroit
35	n/a	Dewitt Public Schools	Dewitt
35	n/a	Dexter Community SD	Dexter
35	n/a	Dundee Community Schools	Dundee
35	n/a	Durand Area Schools	Durand
35	n/a	East China SD	East China
35	n/a	East Detroit Public Schools	Eastpointe
35	n/a	East Grand Rapids Public Schools	E Grand Rapids
35	n/a	East Jackson Community Schools	Jackson
35	n/a	East Lansing SD	East Lansing
35	n/a	Eaton Rapids Public Schools	Eaton Rapids
35	n/a	Edwardsburg Public Schools	Edwardsburg
35	n/a	Escanaba Area Public Schools	Escanaba
35	n/a	Essexville-Hampton Public Schls	Essexville
35	n/a	Farmington Public SD	Farmington
35	n/a	Farwell Area Schools	Farwell
35	n/a	Ferndale Public Schools	Ferndale
35	n/a	Fitzgerald Public Schools	Warren
35	n/a	Flat Rock Community Schools	Flat Rock
35	n/a	Flushing Community Schools	Flushing
35	n/a	Forest Hills Public Schools	Grand Rapids
35	n/a	Fowlerville Community Schools	Fowlerville
35	n/a	Fraser Public Schools	Fraser
35	n/a	Freeland Community SD	Freeland
35	n/a	Fremont Public SD	Fremont
35	n/a	Garden City SD	Garden City
35	n/a	Gaylord Community Schools	Gaylord
35	n/a	Gerrish-Higgins SD	Roscommon
35	n/a	Gibraltar SD	Woodhaven
35	n/a	Gladstone Area Schools	Gladstone
35	n/a	Gladwin Community Schools	Gladwin
35	n/a	Godfrey-Lee Public Schools	Wyoming
35	n/a	Godwin Heights Public Schools	Wyoming
35	n/a	Goodrich Area Schools	Goodrich
35	n/a	Grand Blanc Community Schools	Grand Blanc
35	n/a	Grand Ledge Public Schools	Grand Ledge
35	n/a	Grandville Public Schools	Grandville
35	n/a	Greenville Public Schools	Greenville
35	n/a	Grosse Ile Township Schools	Grosse Ile
35	n/a	Grosse Pointe Public Schools	Grosse Pointe
35	n/a	Gull Lake Community Schools	Richland
35	n/a	Gwinn Area Community Schools	Gwinn
35	n/a	Hamilton Community Schools	Hamilton
35	n/a	Hamtramck Public Schools	Hamtramck
35	n/a	Harper Creek Community Schools	Battle Creek
35	n/a	Harrison Community Schools	Harrison
35	n/a	Hartland Consolidated Schools	Hartland
35	n/a	Haslett Public Schools	Haslett
35	n/a	Hastings Area SD	Hastings
35	n/a	Hazel Park City SD	Hazel Park
35	n/a	Highland Park City Schools	Highland Park
35	n/a	Hillsdale Community Schools	Hillsdale
35	n/a	Holly Area SD	Holly
35	n/a	Holt Public Schools	Holt
35	n/a	Houghton Lake Community Schools	Houghton Lake
35	n/a	Howell Public Schools	Howell
35	n/a	Hudsonville Public SD	Hudsonville
35	n/a	Huron SD	New Boston
35	n/a	Huron Valley Schools	Highland
35	n/a	Ida Public SD	Ida
35	n/a	Ionia Public Schools	Ionia
35	n/a	Jackson Public Schools	Jackson
35	n/a	Jefferson Schools (Monroe)	Monroe
35	n/a	Jenison Public Schools	Jenison
35	n/a	Kalkaska Public Schools	Kalkaska
35	n/a	Kearsley Community Schools	Flint
35	n/a	Kelloggsville Public Schools	Grand Rapids
35	n/a	Kentwood Public Schools	Kentwood
35	n/a	L'anse Creuse Public Schools	Harrison Twp
35	n/a	Lake Fenton Community Schools	Fenton
35	n/a	Lake Orion Community Schools	Lake Orion
35	n/a	Lake Shore Pub Schools (Macomb)	St Clair Shores
35	n/a	Lakeview Comm Schools (Montcalm)	Lakeview
35	n/a	Lakeview Public Schools (Macomb)	St Clair Shores
35	n/a	Lakeview SD (Calhoun)	Battle Creek
35	n/a	Lakeville Community Schools	Otisville
35	n/a	Lakewood Public Schools	Lake Odessa
35	n/a	Lamphere Public Schools	Madison Heights
35	n/a	Lapeer Community Schools	Lapeer
35	n/a	Lincoln Consolidated SD	Ypsilanti
35	n/a	Lincoln Park Public Schools	Lincoln Park
35	n/a	Linden Community Schools	Linden
35	n/a	Livonia Public Schools	Livonia
35	n/a	Lowell Area Schools	Lowell
35	n/a	Ludington Area SD	Ludington
35	n/a	Macomb ISD	Clinton Twp
35	n/a	Madison Public Schools (Oakland)	Madison Heights
35	n/a	Manistee Area Schools	Manistee
35	n/a	Maple Valley Schools	Vermontville
35	n/a	Marquette Area Public Schools	Marquette
35	n/a	Marshall Public Schools	Marshall
35	n/a	Marysville Public Schools	Marysville
35	n/a	Mason Consol Schools (Monroe)	Erie
35	n/a	Mason Public Schools (Ingham)	Mason
35	n/a	Melvindale-N Allen Park Schools	Melvindale
35	n/a	Menominee Area Public Schools	Menominee
35	n/a	Meridian Public Schools	Sanford
35	n/a	Michigan Center SD	Michigan Center
35	n/a	Midland Public Schools	Midland
35	n/a	Milan Area Schools	Milan
35	n/a	Millington Community Schools	Millington
35	n/a	Mona Shores Public SD	Norton Shores
35	n/a	Monroe Public Schools	Monroe
35	n/a	Montague Area Public Schools	Montague
35	n/a	Montrose Community Schools	Montrose
35	n/a	Morley Stanwood Community Schls	Morley
35	n/a	Mt. Clemens Community SD	Mt. Clemens
35	n/a	Mt. Morris Consolidated Schools	Mt. Morris
35	n/a	Mt. Pleasant City SD	Mt. Pleasant
35	n/a	Muskegon City SD	Muskegon
35	n/a	Muskegon Heights SD	Muskegon Hgts
35	n/a	Napoleon Community Schools	Napoleon
35	n/a	Newaygo Public SD	Newaygo
35	n/a	Niles Community SD	Niles
35	n/a	North Branch Area Schools	North Branch
35	n/a	Northview Public SD	Grand Rapids
35	n/a	Northville Public Schools	Northville
35	n/a	Northwest Community Schools	Jackson
35	n/a	Novi Community SD	Novi
35	n/a	Oak Park City SD	Oak Park
35	n/a	Oakridge Public Schools	Muskegon
35	n/a	Okemos Public Schools	Okemos
35	n/a	Onsted Community Schools	Onsted
35	n/a	Orchard View Schools	Muskegon
35	n/a	Oscoda Area Schools	Oscoda
35	n/a	Otsego Public Schools	Otsego
35	n/a	Ovid-Elsie Area Schools	Elsie
35	n/a	Owosso Public Schools	Owosso
35	n/a	Oxford Area Community Schools	Oxford
35	n/a	Parchment SD	Parchment
35	n/a	Pennfield SD	Battle Creek
35	n/a	Perry Public SD	Perry
35	n/a	Pinconning Area Schools	Pinconning
35	n/a	Plainwell Community Schools	Plainwell
35	n/a	Plymouth-Canton Community Schls	Plymouth
35	n/a	Pontiac City SD	Pontiac
35	n/a	Port Huron Area SD	Port Huron
35	n/a	Portage Public Schools	Portage
35	n/a	Portland Public SD	Portland
35	n/a	Public Schools of Calumet	Calumet
35	n/a	Public Schools of Petoskey	Petoskey
35	n/a	Quincy Community SD	Quincy
35	n/a	Redford Union SD	Redford
35	n/a	Reed City Area Public Schools	Reed City
35	n/a	Reeths-Puffer Schools	Muskegon
35	n/a	Richmond Community Schools	Richmond
35	n/a	River Rouge SD	River Rouge
35	n/a	Riverview Community SD	Riverview
35	n/a	Rochester Community SD	Rochester
35	n/a	Rockford Public Schools	Rockford
35	n/a	Romeo Community Schools	Romeo
35	n/a	Romulus Community Schools	Romulus
35	n/a	Roseville Community Schools	Roseville
35	n/a	SD of Ypsilanti	Ypsilanti
35	n/a	SD of the City of Royal Oak	Royal Oak
35	n/a	Saginaw City SD	Saginaw
35	n/a	Saginaw ISD	Saginaw
35	n/a	Saginaw Twp Community Schools	Saginaw
35	n/a	Saline Area Schools	Saline
35	n/a	Sault Ste. Marie Area Schools	Sault Ste Marie
35	n/a	Shepherd Public SD	Shepherd
35	n/a	South Lake Schools	St Clair Shores
35	n/a	South Lyon Community Schools	South Lyon
35	n/a	South Redford SD	Redford
35	n/a	Southfield Public SD	Southfield
35	n/a	Southgate Community SD	Southgate
35	n/a	Spring Lake Public Schools	Spring Lake
35	n/a	St. Johns Public Schools	St. Johns
35	n/a	St. Joseph Public Schools	St. Joseph
35	n/a	Standish-Sterling Comm Schools	Standish
35	n/a	Stockbridge Community Schools	Stockbridge
35	n/a	Swan Valley SD	Saginaw
35	n/a	Swartz Creek Community Schools	Swartz Creek
35	n/a	Tawas Area Schools	Tawas City
35	n/a	Taylor SD	Taylor
35	n/a	Tecumseh Public Schools	Tecumseh
35	n/a	Thornapple Kellogg SD	Middleville
35	n/a	Three Rivers Community Schools	Three Rivers
35	n/a	Trenton Public Schools	Trenton
35	n/a	Tri County Area Schools	Sand Lake
35	n/a	Troy SD	Troy
35	n/a	Utica Community Schools	Sterling Hgts
35	n/a	Van Buren Public Schools	Belleville
35	n/a	Van Dyke Public Schools	Warren
35	n/a	Vassar Public Schools	Vassar
35	n/a	Vicksburg Community Schools	Vicksburg
35	n/a	Warren Consolidated Schools	Warren
35	n/a	Warren Woods Public Schools	Warren
35	n/a	Washtenaw ISD	Ann Arbor
35	n/a	Waterford SD	Waterford
35	n/a	Waverly Community Schools	Lansing
35	n/a	Wayland Union Schools	Wayland
35	n/a	Wayne-Westland Community SD	Westland
35	n/a	West Bloomfield SD	West Bloomfield
35	n/a	W Branch-Rose City Area Schools	West Branch
35	n/a	West Ottawa Public SD	Holland
35	n/a	Western SD	Parma
35	n/a	Westwood Community Schools	Dearborn Hgts
35	n/a	White Cloud Public Schools	White Cloud
35	n/a	Whitehall District Schools	Whitehall
35	n/a	Williamston Community Schools	Williamston
35	n/a	Willow Run Community Schools	Ypsilanti
35	n/a	Woodhaven-Brownstown SD	Brownstown
35	n/a	Wyandotte City SD	Wyandotte
35	n/a	Wyoming Public Schools	Wyoming
35	n/a	Yale Public Schools	Yale
35	n/a	Zeeland Public Schools	Zeeland

Students Eligible for Free Lunch

Rank	Percent	District Name	City
1	80.6	Benton Harbor Area Schools	Benton Harbor
1	80.6	Muskegon Heights SD	Muskegon Hgts
3	72.5	Beecher Community SD	Flint
4	70.9	Westwood Community Schools	Dearborn Hgts
5	70.7	River Rouge SD	River Rouge
6	67.5	Saginaw City SD	Saginaw
7	65.4	Flint City SD	Flint
8	64.9	Hamtramck Public Schools	Hamtramck
9	64.4	Grand Rapids Public Schools	Grand Rapids
10	64.2	Detroit City SD	Detroit
11	62.0	Bangor Public Schls (Van Buren)	Bangor
12	58.9	Highland Park City Schools	Highland Park
13	58.4	Muskegon City SD	Muskegon
14	55.8	Pontiac City SD	Pontiac
15	55.0	Willow Run Community Schools	Ypsilanti
16	54.7	Jackson Public Schools	Jackson
17	53.6	Godfrey-Lee Public Schools	Wyoming

18	52.9	White Cloud Public Schools	White Cloud
19	52.1	Kalamazoo Public SD	Kalamazoo
19	52.1	Lansing Public SD	Lansing
21	51.3	Mt. Clemens Community SD	Mt. Clemens
22	50.0	Harrison Community Schools	Harrison
23	49.4	Bridgeport-Spaulding CSD	Bridgeport
24	49.3	Van Dyke Public Schools	Warren
25	49.2	Battle Creek Public Schools	Battle Creek
26	48.9	Albion Public Schools	Albion
27	47.3	SD of Ypsilanti	Ypsilanti
28	46.5	Godwin Heights Public Schools	Wyoming
29	45.1	Bendle Public Schools	Burton
30	44.0	Oscoda Area Schools	Oscoda
31	42.6	Orchard View Schools	Muskegon
32	42.3	Farwell Area Schools	Farwell
33	42.2	Chippewa Hills SD	Remus
34	41.0	Houghton Lake Community Schools	Houghton Lake
35	40.7	Shelby Public Schools	Shelby
36	39.3	Dowagiac Union SD	Dowagiac
36	39.3	Oak Park City SD	Oak Park
38	39.1	Gerrish-Higgins SD	Roscommon
39	38.7	Kelloggsville Public Schools	Grand Rapids
40	37.6	Romulus Community Schools	Romulus
41	37.1	Adrian City SD	Adrian
42	36.7	Berrien Springs Public Schools	Berrien Springs
43	36.0	Fitzgerald Public Schools	Warren
43	36.0	Hazel Park City SD	Hazel Park
45	35.9	Gwinn Area Community Schools	Gwinn
45	35.9	South Haven Public Schools	South Haven
47	35.6	Hartford Public SD	Hartford
48	35.3	Public Schools of Calumet	Calumet
49	35.1	Crawford Ausable Schools	Grayling
50	34.9	Mason County Central Schools	Scottville
51	34.7	Cheboygan Area Schools	Cheboygan
52	34.6	W Branch-Rose City Area Schools	West Branch
53	34.5	Big Rapids Public Schools	Big Rapids
53	34.5	Comstock Public Schools	Kalamazoo
55	34.3	Carman-Ainsworth Comm Schools	Flint
56	34.1	Sturgis Public Schools	Sturgis
57	33.8	Melvindale-N Allen Park Schools	Melvindale
58	33.7	Coloma Community Schools	Coloma
58	33.7	Morley Stanwood Community Schls	Morley
60	33.6	Dearborn City SD	Dearborn
61	33.5	Standish-Sterling Comm Schools	Standish
62	33.4	Beaverton Rural Schools	Beaverton
63	33.2	Ferndale Public Schools	Ferndale
64	33.0	East Jackson Community Schools	Jackson
65	32.9	Montague Area Public Schools	Montague
66	32.7	Holland City SD	Holland
67	32.6	Carrollton SD	Saginaw
68	32.5	Hillsdale Community Schools	Hillsdale
69	32.4	Ionia Public Schools	Ionia
70	32.0	Clintondale Community Schools	Clinton Twp
71	31.9	Oakridge Public Schools	Muskegon
72	31.7	Kalkaska Public Schools	Kalkaska
73	31.5	Cadillac Area Public Schools	Cadillac
73	31.5	Niles Community SD	Niles
75	30.8	Grant Public SD	Grant
75	30.8	Mt. Morris Consolidated Schools	Mt. Morris
77	30.5	Lakeview Comm Schools (Montcalm)	Lakeview
78	30.4	Alma Public Schools	Alma
79	30.2	East Detroit Public Schools	Eastpointe
79	30.2	Wyoming Public Schools	Wyoming
81	30.1	Parchment SD	Parchment
81	30.1	Pinconning Area Schools	Pinconning
83	29.8	Three Rivers Community Schools	Three Rivers
84	29.6	Port Huron Area SD	Port Huron
85	29.5	Bay City SD	Bay City
86	29.3	Reed City Area Public Schools	Reed City
87	29.0	Lincoln Park Public Schools	Lincoln Park
88	28.9	Taylor SD	Taylor
89	28.6	Belding Area SD	Belding
90	28.5	Central Montcalm Public Schools	Stanton
90	28.5	Madison Public Schools (Oakland)	Madison Heights
90	28.5	Sault Ste. Marie Area Schools	Sault Ste Marie
93	28.4	Meridian Public Schools	Sanford
94	28.3	Gladwin Community Schools	Gladwin
95	28.0	Fremont Public SD	Fremont
96	27.7	Alpena Public Schools	Alpena
97	27.6	Maple Valley Schools	Vermontville
98	27.4	Escanaba Area Public Schools	Escanaba
99	27.1	Montrose Community Schools	Montrose
100	26.9	Monroe Public Schools	Monroe
101	26.8	Ludington Area SD	Ludington
102	26.6	Benzie County Central Schools	Benzonia
102	26.6	Owosso Public Schools	Owosso
104	26.4	Gaylord Community Schools	Gaylord
104	26.4	Wayne-Westland Community SD	Westland
106	26.3	Caro Community Schools	Caro
106	26.3	Kentwood Public Schools	Kentwood
106	26.3	Michigan Center SD	Michigan Center
109	26.0	Coldwater Community Schools	Coldwater
110	25.8	Redford Union SD	Redford
111	25.5	Center Line Public Schools	Center Line
112	25.4	Newaygo Public SD	Newaygo
112	25.4	Southfield Public SD	Southfield
114	25.3	Dearborn Heights SD #7	Dearborn Hgts
115	25.2	Bullock Creek SD	Midland
116	25.0	Fruitport Community Schools	Fruitport
116	25.0	Paw Paw Public SD	Paw Paw
118	24.8	Imlay City Community Schools	Imlay City
119	24.5	Roseville Community Schools	Roseville
120	24.4	Buchanan Community Schools	Buchanan
120	24.4	Gladstone Area Schools	Gladstone
120	24.4	Whitehall District Schools	Whitehall
123	24.2	Bangor Township Schools	Bay City
123	24.2	Tawas Area Schools	Tawas City
125	24.0	Brandywine Public SD	Niles
126	23.7	West Ottawa Public SD	Holland
127	23.6	Millington Community Schools	Millington
128	23.3	Clarenceville SD	Livonia
129	22.9	Manistee Area Schools	Manistee
130	22.8	Reeths-Puffer Schools	Muskegon
131	22.5	Delton-Kellogg SD	Delton
132	21.9	Lakeville Community Schools	Otisville
133	21.8	Northwest Community Schools	Jackson
133	21.8	Vassar Public Schools	Vassar
135	21.6	Clare Public Schools	Clare
135	21.6	Menominee Area Public Schools	Menominee
137	21.4	Croswell-Lexington Comm Schools	Croswell
137	21.4	Ovid-Elsie Area Schools	Elsie
137	21.4	Van Buren Public Schools	Belleville
140	21.3	Clio Area SD	Clio
141	21.2	Allegan Public Schools	Allegan
142	21.0	Tri County Area Schools	Sand Lake
143	20.9	Airport Community SD	Carleton
144	20.8	Greenville Public Schools	Greenville
144	20.8	Mt. Pleasant City SD	Mt. Pleasant
144	20.8	Shepherd Public SD	Shepherd
147	20.7	Saginaw Twp Community Schools	Saginaw
148	20.6	Lamphere Public Schools	Madison Heights
148	20.6	Quincy Community SD	Quincy
150	20.5	Chesaning Union Schools	Chesaning
151	20.4	Mason Consol Schools (Monroe)	Erie
152	20.3	Flat Rock Community Schools	Flat Rock
153	20.2	Detroit Acad of Arts & Sciences	Detroit
154	20.0	Charlotte Public Schools	Charlotte
154	20.0	Durand Area Schools	Durand
154	20.0	Sparta Area Schools	Sparta
157	19.5	Birch Run Area SD	Birch Run
157	19.5	Wyandotte City SD	Wyandotte
159	19.2	Kearsley Community Schools	Flint
160	18.9	North Branch Area Schools	North Branch
161	18.8	Cedar Springs Public Schools	Cedar Springs
161	18.8	Constantine Public SD	Constantine
161	18.8	Warren Consolidated Schools	Warren
164	18.6	Pennfield SD	Battle Creek
165	18.5	Lakewood Public Schools	Lake Odessa
166	18.4	Waverly Community Schools	Lansing
167	18.3	Edwardsburg Public Schools	Edwardsburg
167	18.3	Lincoln Consolidated SD	Ypsilanti
169	18.2	Traverse City Area Public Schls	Traverse City
170	18.1	Crestwood SD	Dearborn Hgts
171	18.0	Essexville-Hampton Public Schls	Essexville
172	17.7	Holly Area SD	Holly
173	17.5	Corunna Public SD	Corunna
173	17.5	Kenowa Hills Public Schools	Grand Rapids
175	17.2	East Lansing SD	East Lansing
176	17.1	Breitung Township Schools	Kingsford
177	16.9	Western SD	Parma
178	16.8	Perry Public SD	Perry
178	16.8	South Redford SD	Redford
180	16.6	Coopersville Public SD	Coopersville
180	16.6	Southgate Community SD	Southgate
182	16.5	Elk Rapids Schools	Elk Rapids
182	16.5	Napoleon Community Schools	Napoleon
184	16.2	Lapeer Community Schools	Lapeer
184	16.2	Wayland Union Schools	Wayland
186	16.1	Waterford SD	Waterford
186	16.1	Yale Public Schools	Yale
188	15.9	Algonac Community SD	Algonac
189	15.8	Jefferson Schools (Monroe)	Monroe
190	15.6	Harper Creek Community Schools	Battle Creek
190	15.6	Woodhaven-Brownstown SD	Brownstown
192	15.4	Stockbridge Community Schools	Stockbridge
193	15.2	Hastings Area SD	Hastings
194	15.0	Allendale Public SD	Allendale
194	15.0	Eaton Rapids Public Schools	Eaton Rapids
196	14.8	Marquette Area Public Schools	Marquette
197	14.2	Swan Valley SD	Saginaw
198	14.1	Swartz Creek Community Schools	Swartz Creek
199	13.9	Otsego Public Schools	Otsego
200	13.8	Capac Community SD	Capac
201	13.5	Ann Arbor Public Schools	Ann Arbor
201	13.5	Davison Community Schools	Davison
203	13.4	Plainwell Community Schools	Plainwell
203	13.4	Public Schools of Petoskey	Petoskey
203	13.4	Vicksburg Community Schools	Vicksburg
206	13.2	Columbia SD	Brooklyn
206	13.2	Garden City SD	Garden City
206	13.2	Mona Shores Public SD	Norton Shores
209	13.1	Comstock Park Public Schools	Comstock Park
210	13.0	Gibraltar SD	Woodhaven
211	12.5	Lakeview SD (Calhoun)	Battle Creek
211	12.5	Lowell Area Schools	Lowell
213	12.4	Fowlerville Community Schools	Fowlerville
214	12.3	L'anse Creuse Public Schools	Harrison Twp
215	12.1	Grand Haven Area Public Schools	Grand Haven
215	12.1	Midland Public Schools	Midland
217	11.9	Huron SD	New Boston
217	11.9	Milan Area Schools	Milan
217	11.9	Thornapple Kellogg SD	Middleville
220	11.8	Warren Woods Public Schools	Warren
221	11.7	Holt Public Schools	Holt
222	11.5	Brandon SD	Ortonville
222	11.5	Byron Center Public Schools	Byron Center
222	11.5	Fraser Public Schools	Fraser
225	11.3	Northview Public SD	Grand Rapids
226	11.2	East China SD	East China
227	11.0	Lake Shore Pub Schools (Macomb)	St Clair Shores
228	10.7	South Lake Schools	St Clair Shores
229	10.6	Grandville Public Schools	Grandville
230	10.4	Chippewa Valley Schools	Clinton Twp
231	10.3	Anchor Bay SD	New Baltimore
232	10.2	Fenton Area Public Schools	Fenton
232	10.2	Marshall Public Schools	Marshall
232	10.2	Spring Lake Public Schools	Spring Lake
235	10.1	Dundee Community Schools	Dundee
235	10.1	Portage Public Schools	Portage
237	9.9	Portland Public SD	Portland
238	9.8	Grand Blanc Community Schools	Grand Blanc
238	9.8	Grand Ledge Public Schools	Grand Ledge
238	9.8	Huron Valley Schools	Highland
238	9.8	Riverview Community SD	Riverview
242	9.7	Richmond Community Schools	Richmond
243	9.5	Mason Public Schools (Ingham)	Mason
244	9.4	Haslett Public Schools	Haslett
245	9.2	Onsted Community Schools	Onsted
246	9.1	Williamston Community Schools	Williamston
247	9.0	St. Johns Public Schools	St. Johns
248	8.7	Berkley SD	Berkley
249	8.6	Almont Community Schools	Almont
249	8.6	Hamilton Community Schools	Hamilton
249	8.6	Mattawan Consolidated School	Mattawan
252	8.5	Tecumseh Public Schools	Tecumseh
253	8.4	Romeo Community Schools	Romeo
254	8.3	Lakeshore SD (Berrien)	Stevensville
254	8.3	SD of the City of Royal Oak	Royal Oak
254	8.3	Zeeland Public Schools	Zeeland
257	8.0	Ida Public SD	Ida
258	7.9	Flushing Community Schools	Flushing
259	7.7	Bedford Public Schools	Temperance
259	7.7	Gull Lake Community Schools	Richland
261	7.5	Lakeview Public Schools (Macomb)	St Clair Shores
262	7.4	Allen Park Public Schools	Allen Park
262	7.4	Howell Public Schools	Howell
262	7.4	South Lyon Community Schools	South Lyon
262	7.4	Utica Community Schools	Sterling Hgts
266	7.3	Lake Fenton Community Schools	Fenton
266	7.3	Oxford Area Community Schools	Oxford
268	6.9	Linden Community Schools	Linden
268	6.9	Marysville Public Schools	Marysville
270	6.7	Hudsonville Public SD	Hudsonville
270	6.7	Trenton Public Schools	Trenton
272	6.5	Avondale SD	Auburn Hills
273	6.4	Farmington Public SD	Farmington
273	6.4	Walled Lake Consolidated Schools	Walled Lake
275	6.2	St. Joseph Public Schools	St. Joseph
276	6.1	Lake Orion Community Schools	Lake Orion
276	6.1	Okemos Public Schools	Okemos
278	5.9	Jenison Public Schools	Jenison
279	5.8	Caledonia Community Schools	Caledonia
279	5.8	West Bloomfield SD	West Bloomfield
281	5.3	Plymouth-Canton Community Schls	Plymouth
282	5.2	Livonia Public Schools	Livonia
283	5.1	Freeland Community SD	Freeland
284	4.7	Dewitt Public Schools	Dewitt
285	4.6	Clarkston Community SD	Clarkston
285	4.6	Rockford Public Schools	Rockford
287	4.4	Armada Area Schools	Armada
288	3.5	Chelsea SD	Chelsea
289	3.4	Brighton Area Schools	Brighton
290	3.3	Rochester Community SD	Rochester
291	3.2	Dexter Community SD	Dexter
292	3.1	Goodrich Area Schools	Goodrich
293	3.0	Forest Hills Public Schools	Grand Rapids
293	3.0	Hartland Consolidated Schools	Hartland

295	2.9	East Grand Rapids Public Schools	E Grand Rapids
296	2.7	Saline Area Schools	Saline
296	2.7	Troy SD	Troy
298	2.6	Grosse Pointe Public Schools	Grosse Pointe
299	2.4	Bloomfield Hills SD	Bloomfield Hls
300	2.2	Northville Public Schools	Northville
301	2.0	Birmingham City SD	Birmingham
302	1.5	Grosse Ile Township Schools	Grosse Ile
303	1.2	Novi Community SD	Novi
304	n/a	Macomb ISD	Clinton Twp
304	n/a	Saginaw ISD	Saginaw
304	n/a	Washtenaw ISD	Ann Arbor

Students Eligible for Reduced-Price Lunch

Rank	Percent	District Name	City
1	16.5	Westwood Community Schools	Dearborn Hgts
2	15.8	Kalkaska Public Schools	Kalkaska
3	15.5	Farwell Area Schools	Farwell
4	15.3	Van Dyke Public Schools	Warren
5	15.1	Public Schools of Calumet	Calumet
6	14.9	Oscoda Area Schools	Oscoda
7	13.6	Hillsdale Community Schools	Hillsdale
8	13.4	Godwin Heights Public Schools	Wyoming
9	13.3	Orchard View Schools	Muskegon
10	12.8	Wyoming Public Schools	Wyoming
11	12.7	East Detroit Public Schools	Eastpointe
11	12.7	Hartford Public SD	Hartford
11	12.7	White Cloud Public Schools	White Cloud
14	12.3	Benzie County Central Schools	Benzonia
14	12.3	Oakridge Public Schools	Muskegon
16	12.0	Melvindale-N Allen Park Schools	Melvindale
17	11.9	Gladstone Area Schools	Gladstone
17	11.9	Tri County Area Schools	Sand Lake
19	11.7	Comstock Public Schools	Kalamazoo
20	11.6	Gwinn Area Community Schools	Gwinn
20	11.6	Morley Stanwood Community Schls	Morley
22	11.4	Belding Area SD	Belding
22	11.4	Berrien Springs Public Schools	Berrien Springs
22	11.4	Chippewa Hills SD	Remus
25	11.3	Crawford Ausable Schools	Grayling
25	11.3	Fitzgerald Public Schools	Warren
27	11.2	Shelby Public Schools	Shelby
28	11.1	Hazel Park City SD	Hazel Park
28	11.1	Kelloggsville Public Schools	Grand Rapids
30	11.0	Dearborn Heights SD #7	Dearborn Hgts
30	11.0	Lincoln Park Public Schools	Lincoln Park
32	10.9	Reed City Area Public Schools	Reed City
33	10.8	Carrollton SD	Saginaw
34	10.7	Alpena Public Schools	Alpena
34	10.7	Roseville Community Schools	Roseville
36	10.6	Pinconning Area Schools	Pinconning
36	10.6	Sault Ste. Marie Area Schools	Sault Ste Marie
38	10.5	W Branch-Rose City Area Schools	West Branch
39	10.4	Godfrey-Lee Public Schools	Wyoming
39	10.4	Hamtramck Public Schools	Hamtramck
39	10.4	Mt. Clemens Community SD	Mt. Clemens
39	10.4	Standish-Sterling Comm Schools	Standish
43	10.3	Coloma Community Schools	Coloma
43	10.3	Ferndale Public Schools	Ferndale
43	10.3	Fruitport Community Schools	Fruitport
43	10.3	Manistee Area Schools	Manistee
47	10.2	North Branch Area Schools	North Branch
48	10.1	Gladwin Community Schools	Gladwin
48	10.1	River Rouge SD	River Rouge
50	10.0	Cedar Springs Public Schools	Cedar Springs
50	10.0	Imlay City Community Schools	Imlay City
50	10.0	Ionia Public Schools	Ionia
50	10.0	Montague Area Public Schools	Montague
50	10.0	Redford Union SD	Redford
55	9.8	Brandywine Public SD	Niles
55	9.8	Maple Valley Schools	Vermontville
57	9.6	Alma Public Schools	Alma
57	9.6	Bridgeport-Spaulding CSD	Bridgeport
57	9.6	Buchanan Community Schools	Buchanan
57	9.6	Dowagiac Union SD	Dowagiac
57	9.6	Lakeview Comm Schools (Montcalm)	Lakeview
57	9.6	Montrose Community Schools	Montrose
57	9.6	Vassar Public Schools	Vassar
57	9.6	Willow Run Community Schools	Ypsilanti
65	9.5	Fremont Public SD	Fremont
65	9.5	Taylor SD	Taylor
67	9.4	Escanaba Area Public Schools	Escanaba
67	9.4	Gerrish-Higgins SD	Roscommon
69	9.3	Lansing Public SD	Lansing
70	9.2	Durand Area Schools	Durand
71	9.1	Breitung Township Schools	Kingsford
71	9.1	Clare Public Schools	Clare
71	9.1	Niles Community SD	Niles
71	9.1	Southfield Public SD	Southfield
75	9.0	Sturgis Public Schools	Sturgis
75	9.0	Traverse City Area Public Schls	Traverse City
77	8.9	Cadillac Area Public Schools	Cadillac
77	8.9	Caro Community Schools	Caro
77	8.9	Central Montcalm Public Schools	Stanton
77	8.9	Madison Public Schools (Oakland)	Madison Heights
77	8.9	Public Schools of Petoskey	Petoskey
77	8.9	Reeths-Puffer Schools	Muskegon
77	8.9	Shepherd Public SD	Shepherd
84	8.8	Center Line Public Schools	Center Line
84	8.8	Tawas Area Schools	Tawas City
86	8.6	Cheboygan Area Schools	Cheboygan
86	8.6	Croswell-Lexington Comm Schools	Croswell
86	8.6	Gaylord Community Schools	Gaylord
86	8.6	Mt. Morris Consolidated Schools	Mt. Morris
86	8.6	Wayne-Westland Community SD	Westland
91	8.5	Albion Public Schools	Albion
91	8.5	SD of Ypsilanti	Ypsilanti
91	8.5	Wayland Union Schools	Wayland
94	8.4	Mason County Central Schools	Scottville
94	8.4	Michigan Center SD	Michigan Center
94	8.4	South Haven Public Schools	South Haven
97	8.3	Mason Consol Schools (Monroe)	Erie
97	8.3	Meridian Public Schools	Sanford
99	8.2	Big Rapids Public Schools	Big Rapids
99	8.2	Chesaning Union Schools	Chesaning
99	8.2	Constantine Public SD	Constantine
99	8.2	Grant Public SD	Grant
99	8.2	Menominee Area Public Schools	Menominee
104	8.1	Kalamazoo Public SD	Kalamazoo
104	8.1	Muskegon City SD	Muskegon
106	8.0	Hastings Area SD	Hastings
106	8.0	Houghton Lake Community Schools	Houghton Lake
108	7.9	Bangor Public Schls (Van Buren)	Bangor
108	7.9	Millington Community Schools	Millington
108	7.9	Newaygo Public SD	Newaygo
108	7.9	Northwest Community Schools	Jackson
108	7.9	Three Rivers Community Schools	Three Rivers
113	7.8	Corunna Public SD	Corunna
113	7.8	Grand Rapids Public Schools	Grand Rapids
113	7.8	Jackson Public Schools	Jackson
113	7.8	Port Huron Area SD	Port Huron
117	7.7	Birch Run Area SD	Birch Run
117	7.7	Harrison Community Schools	Harrison
117	7.7	Lapeer Community Schools	Lapeer
117	7.7	Ludington Area SD	Ludington
117	7.7	Parchment SD	Parchment
122	7.6	Adrian City SD	Adrian
122	7.6	Algonac Community SD	Algonac
122	7.6	Owosso Public Schools	Owosso
122	7.6	Romulus Community Schools	Romulus
126	7.5	Beaverton Rural Schools	Beaverton
126	7.5	Bullock Creek SD	Midland
126	7.5	Carman-Ainsworth Comm Schools	Flint
126	7.5	Lakewood Public Schools	Lake Odessa
126	7.5	Quincy Community SD	Quincy
131	7.4	Kentwood Public Schools	Kentwood
131	7.4	Otsego Public Schools	Otsego
133	7.3	Crestwood SD	Dearborn Hgts
133	7.3	Greenville Public Schools	Greenville
133	7.3	Ovid-Elsie Area Schools	Elsie
136	7.2	Bay City SD	Bay City
136	7.2	Delton-Kellogg SD	Delton
136	7.2	Holland City SD	Holland
136	7.2	Oak Park City SD	Oak Park
136	7.2	Wyandotte City SD	Wyandotte
141	7.1	Edwardsburg Public Schools	Edwardsburg
141	7.1	Sparta Area Schools	Sparta
143	7.0	Allendale Public SD	Allendale
143	7.0	Clintondale Community Schools	Clinton Twp
145	6.9	Byron Center Public Schools	Byron Center
145	6.9	Capac Community SD	Capac
145	6.9	Eaton Rapids Public Schools	Eaton Rapids
145	6.9	Perry Public SD	Perry
149	6.8	Mona Shores Public SD	Norton Shores
149	6.8	Southgate Community SD	Southgate
151	6.7	Charlotte Public Schools	Charlotte
151	6.7	Coopersville Public SD	Coopersville
151	6.7	Elk Rapids Schools	Elk Rapids
151	6.7	Plainwell Community Schools	Plainwell
155	6.5	Grand Haven Area Public Schools	Grand Haven
155	6.5	Lakeville Community Schools	Otisville
155	6.5	Stockbridge Community Schools	Stockbridge
155	6.5	West Ottawa Public SD	Holland
159	6.4	Airport Community SD	Carleton
159	6.4	Allegan Public Schools	Allegan
159	6.4	East Jackson Community Schools	Jackson
159	6.4	Mt. Pleasant City SD	Mt. Pleasant
159	6.4	South Redford SD	Redford
159	6.4	St. Johns Public Schools	St. Johns
165	6.3	Kenowa Hills Public Schools	Grand Rapids
166	6.2	Benton Harbor Area Schools	Benton Harbor
166	6.2	Paw Paw Public SD	Paw Paw
166	6.2	Spring Lake Public Schools	Spring Lake
169	6.1	Bendle Public Schools	Burton
169	6.1	Kearsley Community Schools	Flint
171	6.0	Beecher Community SD	Flint
171	6.0	Harper Creek Community Schools	Battle Creek
171	6.0	Holly Area SD	Holly
171	6.0	South Lake Schools	St Clair Shores
175	5.9	Coldwater Community Schools	Coldwater
175	5.9	Davison Community Schools	Davison
175	5.9	Thornapple Kellogg SD	Middleville
175	5.9	Van Buren Public Schools	Belleville
175	5.9	Yale Public Schools	Yale
180	5.8	Bangor Township Schools	Bay City
180	5.8	Fowlerville Community Schools	Fowlerville
180	5.8	Lake Shore Pub Schools (Macomb)	St Clair Shores
180	5.8	Lincoln Consolidated SD	Ypsilanti
180	5.8	Northview Public SD	Grand Rapids
180	5.8	Pontiac City SD	Pontiac
180	5.8	Waterford SD	Waterford
187	5.7	Flat Rock Community Schools	Flat Rock
188	5.6	Clarenceville SD	Livonia
188	5.6	Muskegon Heights SD	Muskegon Hgts
188	5.6	Saginaw City SD	Saginaw
188	5.6	Western SD	Parma
192	5.5	Clio Area SD	Clio
192	5.5	Essexville-Hampton Public Schls	Essexville
192	5.5	Monroe Public Schools	Monroe
195	5.4	Battle Creek Public Schools	Battle Creek
195	5.4	Columbia SD	Brooklyn
195	5.4	Garden City SD	Garden City
195	5.4	Jefferson Schools (Monroe)	Monroe
195	5.4	Riverview Community SD	Riverview
200	5.3	Whitehall District Schools	Whitehall
201	5.2	East China SD	East China
201	5.2	East Lansing SD	East Lansing
201	5.2	Lowell Area Schools	Lowell
201	5.2	Warren Consolidated Schools	Warren
205	5.1	Anchor Bay SD	New Baltimore
205	5.1	Hudsonville Public SD	Hudsonville
205	5.1	Zeeland Public Schools	Zeeland
208	5.0	Mason Public Schools (Ingham)	Mason
208	5.0	Richmond Community Schools	Richmond
208	5.0	Vicksburg Community Schools	Vicksburg
211	4.9	Jenison Public Schools	Jenison
211	4.9	Portland Public SD	Portland
211	4.9	Saginaw Twp Community Schools	Saginaw
214	4.8	Hamilton Community Schools	Hamilton
214	4.8	Pennfield SD	Battle Creek
214	4.8	Warren Woods Public Schools	Warren
217	4.7	Comstock Park Public Schools	Comstock Park
217	4.7	Grandville Public Schools	Grandville
219	4.6	Holt Public Schools	Holt
220	4.5	Marquette Area Public Schools	Marquette
220	4.5	Swan Valley SD	Saginaw
220	4.5	Swartz Creek Community Schools	Swartz Creek
220	4.5	Tecumseh Public Schools	Tecumseh
224	4.4	Gull Lake Community Schools	Richland
224	4.4	L'anse Creuse Public Schools	Harrison Twp
224	4.4	Romeo Community Schools	Romeo
227	4.3	Ann Arbor Public Schools	Ann Arbor
228	4.2	Fraser Public Schools	Fraser
228	4.2	Huron SD	New Boston
228	4.2	Lakeview SD (Calhoun)	Battle Creek
228	4.2	Onsted Community Schools	Onsted
228	4.2	Woodhaven-Brownstown SD	Brownstown
233	4.1	Dearborn City SD	Dearborn
233	4.1	Gibraltar SD	Woodhaven
233	4.1	Grand Ledge Public Schools	Grand Ledge
233	4.1	Lamphere Public Schools	Madison Heights
237	4.0	Bedford Public Schools	Temperance
237	4.0	Detroit City SD	Detroit
237	4.0	Midland Public Schools	Midland
237	4.0	Oxford Area Community Schools	Oxford
241	3.8	Grand Blanc Community Schools	Grand Blanc
241	3.8	Lakeview Public Schools (Macomb)	St Clair Shores
241	3.8	Marysville Public Schools	Marysville
241	3.8	Portage Public Schools	Portage
245	3.7	Allen Park Public Schools	Allen Park
245	3.7	Huron Valley Schools	Highland
245	3.7	Milan Area Schools	Milan
245	3.7	SD of the City of Royal Oak	Royal Oak
249	3.6	Howell Public Schools	Howell
249	3.6	Napoleon Community Schools	Napoleon
249	3.6	South Lyon Community Schools	South Lyon
249	3.6	Williamston Community Schools	Williamston
253	3.4	Lakeshore SD (Berrien)	Stevensville
253	3.4	Mattawan Consolidated School	Mattawan
255	3.3	St. Joseph Public Schools	St. Joseph
255	3.3	Waverly Community Schools	Lansing
257	3.2	Brandon SD	Ortonville
257	3.2	Caledonia Community Schools	Caledonia
257	3.2	Flint City SD	Flint
260	3.1	Dundee Community Schools	Dundee

260	3.1	Lake Orion Community Schools	Lake Orion
262	3.0	Highland Park City Schools	Highland Park
262	3.0	Linden Community Schools	Linden
262	3.0	West Bloomfield SD	West Bloomfield
265	2.9	Avondale SD	Auburn Hills
265	2.9	Marshall Public Schools	Marshall
267	2.8	Detroit Acad of Arts & Sciences	Detroit
268	2.7	Chippewa Valley Schools	Clinton Twp
268	2.7	Ida Public SD	Ida
270	2.6	Berkley SD	Berkley
270	2.6	Fenton Area Public Schools	Fenton
272	2.5	Chelsea SD	Chelsea
272	2.5	Livonia Public Schools	Livonia
272	2.5	Utica Community Schools	Sterling Hgts
272	2.5	Walled Lake Consolidated Schools	Walled Lake
276	2.4	Almont Community Schools	Almont
276	2.4	Flushing Community Schools	Flushing
278	2.3	Farmington Public SD	Farmington
278	2.3	Haslett Public Schools	Haslett
280	2.2	Dewitt Public Schools	Dewitt
280	2.2	Freeland Community SD	Freeland
282	2.0	Dexter Community SD	Dexter
283	1.9	Hartland Consolidated Schools	Hartland
284	1.8	Rockford Public Schools	Rockford
284	1.8	Trenton Public Schools	Trenton
286	1.7	Armada Area Schools	Armada
286	1.7	Forest Hills Public Schools	Grand Rapids
288	1.6	Grosse Ile Township Schools	Grosse Ile
288	1.6	Plymouth-Canton Community Schls	Plymouth
290	1.5	Brighton Area Schools	Brighton
290	1.5	Saline Area Schools	Saline
292	1.4	Clarkston Community SD	Clarkston
292	1.4	Rochester Community SD	Rochester
294	1.3	Lake Fenton Community Schools	Fenton
295	1.1	Goodrich Area Schools	Goodrich
296	0.9	Birmingham City SD	Birmingham
296	0.9	East Grand Rapids Public Schools	E Grand Rapids
296	0.9	Grosse Pointe Public Schools	Grosse Pointe
296	0.9	Troy SD	Troy
300	0.8	Okemos Public Schools	Okemos
301	0.5	Bloomfield Hills SD	Bloomfield Hls
301	0.5	Novi Community SD	Novi
303	0.4	Northville Public Schools	Northville
304	n/a	Macomb ISD	Clinton Twp
304	n/a	Saginaw ISD	Saginaw
304	n/a	Washtenaw ISD	Ann Arbor

Student/Teacher Ratio

Rank	Ratio	District Name	City
1	98.1	Northview Public SD	Grand Rapids
2	95.1	Mason Consol Schools (Monroe)	Erie
3	54.2	Lansing Public SD	Lansing
4	43.9	North Branch Area Schools	North Branch
5	42.6	Washtenaw ISD	Ann Arbor
6	36.6	Jackson Public Schools	Jackson
7	34.4	Saginaw ISD	Saginaw
8	34.2	Highland Park City Schools	Highland Park
9	31.9	Okemos Public Schools	Okemos
10	23.8	Oxford Area Community Schools	Oxford
11	23.1	Linden Community Schools	Linden
12	22.9	Cadillac Area Public Schools	Cadillac
13	22.8	Waterford SD	Waterford
14	22.7	Detroit City SD	Detroit
15	22.5	Flushing Community Schools	Flushing
16	22.0	Allen Park Public Schools	Allen Park
17	21.9	Millington Community Schools	Millington
17	21.9	Vassar Public Schools	Vassar
19	21.8	Yale Public Schools	Yale
20	21.7	Detroit Acad of Arts & Sciences	Detroit
21	21.5	Gibraltar SD	Woodhaven
21	21.5	Lake Fenton Community Schools	Fenton
23	21.3	Kenowa Hills Public Schools	Grand Rapids
24	21.2	Armada Area Schools	Armada
24	21.2	Marysville Public Schools	Marysville
26	21.1	Kearsley Community Schools	Flint
27	20.8	Chippewa Valley Schools	Clinton Twp
28	20.7	Michigan Center SD	Michigan Center
29	20.6	Davison Community Schools	Davison
29	20.6	Wyoming Public Schools	Wyoming
31	20.5	Coopersville Public SD	Coopersville
31	20.5	Kelloggsville Public Schools	Grand Rapids
33	20.4	Newaygo Public SD	Newaygo
34	20.3	Edwardsburg Public Schools	Edwardsburg
34	20.3	Ovid-Elsie Area Schools	Elsie
36	20.2	Almont Community Schools	Almont
36	20.2	Rochester Community SD	Rochester
38	20.1	Bangor Township Schools	Bay City
38	20.1	Birmingham City SD	Birmingham
38	20.1	Columbia SD	Brooklyn
38	20.1	Corunna Public SD	Corunna
38	20.1	Fitzgerald Public Schools	Warren
38	20.1	Hartland Consolidated Schools	Hartland
38	20.1	Plymouth-Canton Community Schls	Plymouth
45	20.0	Flat Rock Community Schools	Flat Rock
45	20.0	Grand Blanc Community Schools	Grand Blanc
45	20.0	Imlay City Community Schools	Imlay City
45	20.0	Riverview Community SD	Riverview
49	19.9	Beecher Community SD	Flint
49	19.9	Clio Area SD	Clio
49	19.9	Goodrich Area Schools	Goodrich
49	19.9	Rockford Public Schools	Rockford
53	19.8	Crestwood SD	Dearborn Hgts
53	19.8	Gerrish-Higgins SD	Roscommon
53	19.8	Lapeer Community Schools	Lapeer
53	19.8	Melvindale-N Allen Park Schools	Melvindale
53	19.8	West Ottawa Public SD	Holland
58	19.7	Brighton Area Schools	Brighton
58	19.7	Monroe Public Schools	Monroe
58	19.7	Thornapple Kellogg SD	Middleville
61	19.6	Airport Community SD	Carleton
61	19.6	Dearborn Heights SD #7	Dearborn Hgts
61	19.6	Fowlerville Community Schools	Fowlerville
61	19.6	Western SD	Parma
65	19.5	Algonac Community SD	Algonac
65	19.5	East China SD	East China
65	19.5	Escanaba Area Public Schools	Escanaba
65	19.5	Fenton Area Public Schools	Fenton
65	19.5	L'anse Creuse Public Schools	Harrison Twp
65	19.5	Mt. Morris Consolidated Schools	Mt. Morris
65	19.5	Portland Public SD	Portland
72	19.4	Alpena Public Schools	Alpena
72	19.4	Durand Area Schools	Durand
72	19.4	Huron Valley Schools	Highland
72	19.4	Wayland Union Schools	Wayland
76	19.3	Dewitt Public Schools	Dewitt
76	19.3	Grand Haven Area Public Schools	Grand Haven
76	19.3	Van Dyke Public Schools	Warren
79	19.2	Bay City SD	Bay City
79	19.2	Bedford Public Schools	Temperance
79	19.2	Jefferson Schools (Monroe)	Monroe
79	19.2	Mona Shores Public SD	Norton Shores
79	19.2	Richmond Community Schools	Richmond
79	19.2	Warren Consolidated Schools	Warren
85	19.1	Big Rapids Public Schools	Big Rapids
85	19.1	Elk Rapids Schools	Elk Rapids
85	19.1	Mattawan Consolidated School	Mattawan
85	19.1	Pennfield SD	Battle Creek
85	19.1	Woodhaven-Brownstown SD	Brownstown
90	19.0	Anchor Bay SD	New Baltimore
90	19.0	Brandon SD	Ortonville
90	19.0	Clare Public Schools	Clare
90	19.0	Hamilton Community Schools	Hamilton
90	19.0	Howell Public Schools	Howell
90	19.0	Lakewood Public Schools	Lake Odessa
90	19.0	Marquette Area Public Schools	Marquette
90	19.0	Northwest Community Schools	Jackson
90	19.0	Oak Park City SD	Oak Park
90	19.0	Public Schools of Petoskey	Petoskey
100	18.9	Lakeville Community Schools	Otisville
100	18.9	Romulus Community Schools	Romulus
100	18.9	Roseville Community Schools	Roseville
103	18.8	Birch Run Area SD	Birch Run
103	18.8	Chelsea SD	Chelsea
103	18.8	Coldwater Community Schools	Coldwater
103	18.8	Freeland Community SD	Freeland
103	18.8	Grandville Public Schools	Grandville
103	18.8	Kentwood Public Schools	Kentwood
103	18.8	Lake Orion Community Schools	Lake Orion
103	18.8	Menominee Area Public Schools	Menominee
103	18.8	Saline Area Schools	Saline
103	18.8	South Lyon Community Schools	South Lyon
103	18.8	Standish-Sterling Comm Schools	Standish
114	18.7	Central Montcalm Public Schools	Stanton
114	18.7	Eaton Rapids Public Schools	Eaton Rapids
114	18.7	Grosse Ile Township Schools	Grosse Ile
114	18.7	Lake Shore Pub Schools (Macomb)	St Clair Shores
114	18.7	Romeo Community Schools	Romeo
114	18.7	Tecumseh Public Schools	Tecumseh
114	18.7	Traverse City Area Public Schls	Traverse City
114	18.7	Utica Community Schools	Sterling Hgts
122	18.6	Dexter Community SD	Dexter
122	18.6	Essexville-Hampton Public Schls	Essexville
122	18.6	Gaylord Community Schools	Gaylord
122	18.6	Huron SD	New Boston
122	18.6	Pinconning Area Schools	Pinconning
122	18.6	Spring Lake Public Schools	Spring Lake
122	18.6	St. Joseph Public Schools	St. Joseph
129	18.5	Croswell-Lexington Comm Schools	Croswell
129	18.5	Greenville Public Schools	Greenville
129	18.5	Lakeview Comm Schools (Montcalm)	Lakeview
129	18.5	Muskegon City SD	Muskegon
129	18.5	Sparta Area Schools	Sparta
129	18.5	Warren Woods Public Schools	Warren
135	18.4	Capac Community SD	Capac
135	18.4	Holt Public Schools	Holt
135	18.4	Lakeshore SD (Berrien)	Stevensville
135	18.4	Lowell Area Schools	Lowell
135	18.4	Napoleon Community Schools	Napoleon
135	18.4	Parchment SD	Parchment
135	18.4	Saginaw Twp Community Schools	Saginaw
142	18.3	Byron Center Public Schools	Byron Center
142	18.3	East Jackson Community Schools	Jackson
142	18.3	Harrison Community Schools	Harrison
142	18.3	Holly Area SD	Holly
142	18.3	Mason Public Schools (Ingham)	Mason
142	18.3	Meridian Public Schools	Sanford
142	18.3	Onsted Community Schools	Onsted
142	18.3	Perry Public SD	Perry
142	18.3	Plainwell Community Schools	Plainwell
142	18.3	South Redford SD	Redford
142	18.3	Swan Valley SD	Saginaw
142	18.3	Whitehall District Schools	Whitehall
142	18.3	Williamston Community Schools	Williamston
155	18.2	Albion Public Schools	Albion
155	18.2	Cedar Springs Public Schools	Cedar Springs
155	18.2	Chesaning Union Schools	Chesaning
155	18.2	Clarkston Community SD	Clarkston
155	18.2	Comstock Park Public Schools	Comstock Park
155	18.2	Hillsdale Community Schools	Hillsdale
155	18.2	Owosso Public Schools	Owosso
155	18.2	Reeths-Puffer Schools	Muskegon
155	18.2	Tri County Area Schools	Sand Lake
155	18.2	Wayne-Westland Community SD	Westland
165	18.1	Benzie County Central Schools	Benzonia
165	18.1	Midland Public Schools	Midland
165	18.1	Quincy Community SD	Quincy
165	18.1	Westwood Community Schools	Dearborn Hgts
165	18.1	Zeeland Public Schools	Zeeland
170	18.0	Dowagiac Union SD	Dowagiac
170	18.0	East Grand Rapids Public Schools	E Grand Rapids
170	18.0	Fruitport Community Schools	Fruitport
170	18.0	Gladwin Community Schools	Gladwin
170	18.0	Hudsonville Public SD	Hudsonville
170	18.0	Lakeview Public Schools (Macomb)	St Clair Shores
170	18.0	Lincoln Consolidated SD	Ypsilanti
170	18.0	Mason County Central Schools	Scottville
170	18.0	Oscoda Area Schools	Oscoda
170	18.0	Paw Paw Public SD	Paw Paw
170	18.0	Sturgis Public Schools	Sturgis
181	17.9	Caledonia Community Schools	Caledonia
181	17.9	Clarenceville SD	Livonia
181	17.9	Delton-Kellogg SD	Delton
181	17.9	Farwell Area Schools	Farwell
181	17.9	Ida Public SD	Ida
181	17.9	Jenison Public Schools	Jenison
181	17.9	Montague Area Public Schools	Montague
181	17.9	Orchard View Schools	Muskegon
181	17.9	Shelby Public Schools	Shelby
181	17.9	South Haven Public Schools	South Haven
181	17.9	Van Buren Public Schools	Belleville
192	17.8	Buchanan Community Schools	Buchanan
192	17.8	Livonia Public Schools	Livonia
192	17.8	Wyandotte City SD	Wyandotte
195	17.7	Allegan Public Schools	Allegan
195	17.7	Breitung Township Schools	Kingsford
195	17.7	Clintondale Community Schools	Clinton Twp
195	17.7	Crawford Ausable Schools	Grayling
195	17.7	East Detroit Public Schools	Eastpointe
195	17.7	Fremont Public SD	Fremont
195	17.7	Grand Ledge Public Schools	Grand Ledge
195	17.7	Maple Valley Schools	Vermontville
195	17.7	Marshall Public Schools	Marshall
195	17.7	Mt. Pleasant City SD	Mt. Pleasant
195	17.7	Otsego Public Schools	Otsego
195	17.7	Taylor SD	Taylor
195	17.7	West Bloomfield SD	West Bloomfield
208	17.6	Bangor Public Schls (Van Buren)	Bangor
208	17.6	Gladstone Area Schools	Gladstone
208	17.6	Hastings Area SD	Hastings
208	17.6	St. Johns Public Schools	St. Johns
208	17.6	Tawas Area Schools	Tawas City
213	17.5	Grant Public SD	Grant
213	17.5	Stockbridge Community Schools	Stockbridge
215	17.4	Adrian City SD	Adrian
215	17.4	Beaverton Rural Schools	Beaverton
215	17.4	Caro Community Schools	Caro
215	17.4	Chippewa Hills SD	Remus
215	17.4	Lakeview SD (Calhoun)	Battle Creek
215	17.4	Morley Stanwood Community Schls	Morley
215	17.4	Public Schools of Calumet	Calumet
222	17.3	Fraser Public Schools	Fraser
222	17.3	Portage Public Schools	Portage
222	17.3	Reed City Area Public Schools	Reed City
225	17.2	East Lansing SD	East Lansing
225	17.2	Gull Lake Community Schools	Richland
225	17.2	Lincoln Park Public Schools	Lincoln Park
225	17.2	SD of Ypsilanti	Ypsilanti

229	17.1	Forest Hills Public Schools	Grand Rapids
229	17.1	Haslett Public Schools	Haslett
229	17.1	Holland City SD	Holland
229	17.1	Kalkaska Public Schools	Kalkaska
229	17.1	Ludington Area SD	Ludington
229	17.1	Oakridge Public Schools	Muskegon
229	17.1	Walled Lake Consolidated Schools	Walled Lake
236	17.0	Allendale Public SD	Allendale
236	17.0	Belding Area SD	Belding
236	17.0	Bullock Creek SD	Midland
236	17.0	Carman-Ainsworth Comm Schools	Flint
236	17.0	Cheboygan Area Schools	Cheboygan
236	17.0	Hamtramck Public Schools	Hamtramck
236	17.0	Port Huron Area SD	Port Huron
236	17.0	Shepherd Public SD	Shepherd
236	17.0	Southgate Community SD	Southgate
236	17.0	Vicksburg Community Schools	Vicksburg
246	16.9	Berkley SD	Berkley
246	16.9	Center Line Public Schools	Center Line
246	16.9	Dearborn City SD	Dearborn
246	16.9	Harper Creek Community Schools	Battle Creek
246	16.9	Milan Area Schools	Milan
246	16.9	Northville Public Schools	Northville
246	16.9	Swartz Creek Community Schools	Swartz Creek
246	16.9	W Branch-Rose City Area Schools	West Branch
246	16.9	Willow Run Community Schools	Ypsilanti
255	16.8	Charlotte Public Schools	Charlotte
255	16.8	Godfrey-Lee Public Schools	Wyoming
255	16.8	Redford Union SD	Redford
255	16.8	South Lake Schools	St Clair Shores
259	16.7	Constantine Public SD	Constantine
259	16.7	Southfield Public SD	Southfield
261	16.6	Berrien Springs Public Schools	Berrien Springs
261	16.6	Flint City SD	Flint
261	16.6	Gwinn Area Community Schools	Gwinn
261	16.6	Troy SD	Troy
261	16.6	White Cloud Public Schools	White Cloud
266	16.5	Brandywine Public SD	Niles
266	16.5	Coloma Community Schools	Coloma
266	16.5	Waverly Community Schools	Lansing
269	16.4	Niles Community SD	Niles
270	16.3	Alma Public Schools	Alma
270	16.3	Sault Ste. Marie Area Schools	Sault Ste Marie
272	16.2	Ionia Public Schools	Ionia
273	16.1	Madison Public Schools (Oakland)	Madison Heights
273	16.1	Mt. Clemens Community SD	Mt. Clemens
275	16.0	Farmington Public SD	Farmington
275	16.0	Lamphere Public Schools	Madison Heights
277	15.9	Houghton Lake Community Schools	Houghton Lake
277	15.9	Novi Community SD	Novi
277	15.9	River Rouge SD	River Rouge
280	15.8	Ann Arbor Public Schools	Ann Arbor
280	15.8	Bridgeport-Spaulding CSD	Bridgeport
280	15.8	Hartford Public SD	Hartford
280	15.8	SD of the City of Royal Oak	Royal Oak
284	15.7	Avondale SD	Auburn Hills
285	15.6	Grosse Pointe Public Schools	Grosse Pointe
285	15.6	Pontiac City SD	Pontiac
287	15.5	Carrollton SD	Saginaw
287	15.5	Godwin Heights Public Schools	Wyoming
289	15.4	Trenton Public Schools	Trenton
290	15.2	Saginaw City SD	Saginaw
291	15.0	Muskegon Heights SD	Muskegon Hgts
292	14.9	Comstock Public Schools	Kalamazoo
293	14.8	Grand Rapids Public Schools	Grand Rapids
293	14.8	Hazel Park City SD	Hazel Park
295	14.4	Garden City SD	Garden City
295	14.4	Kalamazoo Public SD	Kalamazoo
297	14.3	Battle Creek Public Schools	Battle Creek
298	14.0	Bloomfield Hills SD	Bloomfield Hls
299	13.6	Bendle Public Schools	Burton
300	13.5	Ferndale Public Schools	Ferndale
301	7.4	Macomb ISD	Clinton Twp
302	n/a	Benton Harbor Area Schools	Benton Harbor
302	n/a	Dundee Community Schools	Dundee
302	n/a	Manistee Area Schools	Manistee
302	n/a	Montrose Community Schools	Montrose
302	n/a	Three Rivers Community Schools	Three Rivers

Student/Librarian Ratio

Rank	Ratio	District Name	City
1	16,463.0	Lansing Public SD	Lansing
2	7,247.0	Jackson Public Schools	Jackson
3	5,531.0	Kalamazoo Public SD	Kalamazoo
4	4,981.0	Garden City SD	Garden City
5	4,573.0	Redford Union SD	Redford
6	4,165.0	Niles Community SD	Niles
7	4,128.0	Howell Public Schools	Howell
8	3,972.5	Battle Creek Public Schools	Battle Creek
9	3,952.0	Adrian City SD	Adrian
10	3,801.3	Walled Lake Consolidated Schools	Walled Lake
11	3,753.0	Fenton Area Public Schools	Fenton
12	3,682.0	Brandon SD	Ortonville
13	3,646.0	Marquette Area Public Schools	Marquette
14	3,460.0	Tecumseh Public Schools	Tecumseh
15	3,427.0	Ionia Public Schools	Ionia
16	3,407.0	Caledonia Community Schools	Caledonia
16	3,407.0	Cedar Springs Public Schools	Cedar Springs
18	3,249.0	St. Johns Public Schools	St. Johns
19	3,142.0	Ferndale Public Schools	Ferndale
20	3,061.0	Escanaba Area Public Schools	Escanaba
21	3,025.0	Allegan Public Schools	Allegan
22	2,915.0	Byron Center Public Schools	Byron Center
23	2,884.0	East Grand Rapids Public Schools	E Grand Rapids
24	2,871.0	Sparta Area Schools	Sparta
25	2,758.0	Clintondale Community Schools	Clinton Twp
26	2,722.5	Taylor SD	Taylor
27	2,687.0	Harper Creek Community Schools	Battle Creek
28	2,678.0	North Branch Area Schools	North Branch
29	2,594.5	Saginaw Twp Community Schools	Saginaw
30	2,583.3	Rockford Public Schools	Rockford
31	2,563.0	Marshall Public Schools	Marshall
32	2,490.7	Lapeer Community Schools	Lapeer
33	2,490.0	South Haven Public Schools	South Haven
33	2,490.0	Yale Public Schools	Yale
35	2,478.5	Wyandotte City SD	Wyandotte
36	2,470.0	Fraser Public Schools	Fraser
37	2,459.0	Southgate Community SD	Southgate
38	2,452.8	Waterford SD	Waterford
39	2,354.8	Kentwood Public Schools	Kentwood
40	2,349.0	Bridgeport-Spaulding CSD	Bridgeport
41	2,336.0	Imlay City Community Schools	Imlay City
42	2,327.0	River Rouge SD	River Rouge
43	2,292.0	Grant Public SD	Grant
44	2,279.0	Cheboygan Area Schools	Cheboygan
45	2,278.0	Forest Hills Public Schools	Grand Rapids
46	2,254.0	Detroit Acad of Arts & Sciences	Detroit
47	2,237.0	Spring Lake Public Schools	Spring Lake
48	2,226.6	Traverse City Area Public Schls	Traverse City
49	2,224.0	Flint City SD	Flint
50	2,209.5	Holly Area SD	Holly
51	2,205.0	Anchor Bay SD	New Baltimore
52	2,196.9	Grand Rapids Public Schools	Grand Rapids
53	2,174.5	Reeths-Puffer Schools	Muskegon
54	2,171.0	Muskegon Heights SD	Muskegon Hgts
55	2,150.5	Romulus Community Schools	Romulus
56	2,139.0	Lakeville Community Schools	Otisville
57	2,128.0	Houghton Lake Community Schools	Houghton Lake
58	2,122.0	Harrison Community Schools	Harrison
59	2,092.0	Gladwin Community Schools	Gladwin
60	2,090.0	Swartz Creek Community Schools	Swartz Creek
60	2,090.0	Williamston Community Schools	Williamston
62	2,087.6	Detroit City SD	Detroit
63	2,087.0	Goodrich Area Schools	Goodrich
64	2,061.0	Durand Area Schools	Durand
65	2,059.0	Delton-Kellogg SD	Delton
66	2,033.0	Madison Public Schools (Oakland)	Madison Heights
67	2,023.0	Okemos Public Schools	Okemos
68	1,974.0	Pinconning Area Schools	Pinconning
69	1,952.0	Kearsley Community Schools	Flint
70	1,939.0	Standish-Sterling Comm Schools	Standish
71	1,936.0	Shelby Public Schools	Shelby
72	1,912.0	Columbia SD	Brooklyn
73	1,896.0	Hillsdale Community Schools	Hillsdale
74	1,841.0	Gerrish-Higgins SD	Roscommon
75	1,830.5	Grand Blanc Community Schools	Grand Blanc
76	1,799.8	Monroe Public Schools	Monroe
77	1,788.3	Davison Community Schools	Davison
78	1,779.0	Flat Rock Community Schools	Flat Rock
79	1,776.5	East Lansing SD	East Lansing
80	1,772.0	Millington Community Schools	Millington
81	1,768.0	Clio Area SD	Clio
81	1,768.0	Shepherd Public SD	Shepherd
83	1,757.0	Muskegon City SD	Muskegon
84	1,738.3	Chippewa Valley Schools	Clinton Twp
85	1,737.0	Ida Public SD	Ida
86	1,735.0	Maple Valley Schools	Vermontville
87	1,716.0	Airport Community SD	Carleton
88	1,707.7	Alpena Public Schools	Alpena
89	1,693.5	Cadillac Area Public Schools	Cadillac
90	1,653.0	Gibraltar SD	Woodhaven
91	1,636.0	Morley Stanwood Community Schls	Morley
92	1,625.7	Hudsonville Public SD	Hudsonville
93	1,606.0	Berrien Springs Public Schools	Berrien Springs
94	1,600.3	Flushing Community Schools	Flushing
95	1,597.0	Godfrey-Lee Public Schools	Wyoming
96	1,585.0	Mason Public Schools (Ingham)	Mason
97	1,580.0	Public Schools of Calumet	Calumet
98	1,575.3	SD of the City of Royal Oak	Royal Oak
99	1,556.0	Constantine Public SD	Constantine
100	1,546.1	Huron Valley Schools	Highland
101	1,544.1	Saginaw City SD	Saginaw
102	1,537.0	Brandywine Public SD	Niles
103	1,530.0	White Cloud Public Schools	White Cloud
104	1,529.5	Grandville Public Schools	Grandville
105	1,529.0	Tawas Area Schools	Tawas City
106	1,527.0	Bangor Public Schls (Van Buren)	Bangor
107	1,522.0	Mason Consol Schools (Monroe)	Erie
108	1,509.5	Gull Lake Community Schools	Richland
109	1,509.0	Gwinn Area Community Schools	Gwinn
110	1,502.0	Lake Fenton Community Schools	Fenton
111	1,493.5	Center Line Public Schools	Center Line
112	1,490.0	Linden Community Schools	Linden
113	1,471.0	Carrollton SD	Saginaw
114	1,470.5	Haslett Public Schools	Haslett
115	1,460.0	Holt Public Schools	Holt
116	1,451.0	Thornapple Kellogg SD	Middleville
117	1,448.5	Sault Ste. Marie Area Schools	Sault Ste Marie
118	1,447.0	West Bloomfield SD	West Bloomfield
119	1,443.5	Marysville Public Schools	Marysville
120	1,438.0	Lakeview Public Schools (Macomb)	St Clair Shores
121	1,401.0	Western SD	Parma
122	1,397.0	Mona Shores Public SD	Norton Shores
123	1,391.9	Port Huron Area SD	Port Huron
124	1,385.5	Dowagiac Union SD	Dowagiac
125	1,351.0	Wyoming Public Schools	Wyoming
126	1,342.0	Grand Ledge Public Schools	Grand Ledge
127	1,336.5	Chippewa Hills SD	Remus
128	1,316.2	L'anse Creuse Public Schools	Harrison Twp
129	1,310.3	Lowell Area Schools	Lowell
130	1,306.5	Lincoln Park Public Schools	Lincoln Park
131	1,304.7	Greenville Public Schools	Greenville
132	1,303.3	Woodhaven-Brownstown SD	Brownstown
133	1,267.3	Hamtramck Public Schools	Hamtramck
134	1,264.0	Bangor Township Schools	Bay City
135	1,261.0	Croswell-Lexington Comm Schools	Croswell
136	1,250.0	Belding Area SD	Belding
137	1,239.0	Alma Public Schools	Alma
138	1,236.0	Bendle Public Schools	Burton
139	1,234.5	Lamphere Public Schools	Madison Heights
140	1,225.0	Mt. Morris Consolidated Schools	Mt. Morris
141	1,222.3	Northwest Community Schools	Jackson
142	1,216.7	Brighton Area Schools	Brighton
143	1,185.0	Crestwood SD	Dearborn Hgts
144	1,172.0	Comstock Park Public Schools	Comstock Park
145	1,165.7	Gaylord Community Schools	Gaylord
146	1,158.5	Corunna Public SD	Corunna
147	1,150.0	Godwin Heights Public Schools	Wyoming
148	1,142.0	Beecher Community SD	Flint
149	1,130.5	Newaygo Public SD	Newaygo
150	1,115.7	Charlotte Public Schools	Charlotte
151	1,108.5	Kelloggsville Public Schools	Grand Rapids
152	1,105.0	Lakeview SD (Calhoun)	Battle Creek
153	1,100.5	Milan Area Schools	Milan
154	1,100.0	Wayland Union Schools	Wayland
155	1,099.7	Wayne-Westland Community SD	Westland
156	1,087.0	Coloma Community Schools	Coloma
157	1,086.0	Big Rapids Public Schools	Big Rapids
158	1,077.5	Whitehall District Schools	Whitehall
159	1,063.5	Central Montcalm Public Schools	Stanton
160	1,062.0	Huron SD	New Boston
161	1,051.5	Crawford Ausable Schools	Grayling
162	1,039.0	Bullock Creek SD	Midland
162	1,039.0	Oak Park City SD	Oak Park
164	1,037.0	Richmond Community Schools	Richmond
165	1,033.0	Owosso Public Schools	Owosso
166	1,030.7	Public Schools of Petoskey	Petoskey
167	1,023.7	Chelsea SD	Chelsea
168	1,017.5	Allendale Public SD	Allendale
169	1,010.0	Breitung Township Schools	Kingsford
170	1,006.0	Menominee Area Public Schools	Menominee
171	1,001.5	Oakridge Public Schools	Muskegon
172	998.5	Perry Public SD	Perry
173	995.1	Plymouth-Canton Community Schls	Plymouth
174	992.2	Zeeland Public Schools	Zeeland
175	990.4	Lincoln Consolidated SD	Ypsilanti
176	984.0	Mt. Pleasant City SD	Mt. Pleasant
177	979.0	Essexville-Hampton Public Schls	Essexville
178	967.0	Avondale SD	Auburn Hills
179	963.0	Pennfield SD	Battle Creek
180	956.0	Capac Community SD	Capac
181	955.7	Plainwell Community Schools	Plainwell
182	955.0	Lakeview Comm Schools (Montcalm)	Lakeview
183	951.7	Lakeshore SD (Berrien)	Stevensville
184	950.7	St. Joseph Public Schools	St. Joseph
185	945.1	South Lyon Community Schools	South Lyon
186	930.5	Vassar Public Schools	Vassar
187	927.5	Oscoda Area Schools	Oscoda
188	925.5	Kenowa Hills Public Schools	Grand Rapids
189	912.5	Bedford Public Schools	Temperance
190	909.5	Allen Park Public Schools	Allen Park
191	898.5	Kalkaska Public Schools	Kalkaska
192	894.0	Saline Area Schools	Saline
193	893.8	Carman-Ainsworth Comm Schools	Flint
194	893.6	Bay City SD	Bay City
195	890.3	Algonac Community SD	Algonac
196	888.8	West Ottawa Public SD	Holland

197	887.7	W Branch-Rose City Area Schools	West Branch
198	883.5	Napoleon Community Schools	Napoleon
199	875.0	Stockbridge Community Schools	Stockbridge
200	874.0	Albion Public Schools	Albion
200	874.0	Fremont Public SD	Fremont
202	866.7	Melvindale-N Allen Park Schools	Melvindale
203	865.3	Riverview Community SD	Riverview
204	858.5	Swan Valley SD	Saginaw
205	848.0	Freeland Community SD	Freeland
206	841.3	Coldwater Community Schools	Coldwater
207	820.7	Pontiac City SD	Pontiac
208	820.5	Fitzgerald Public Schools	Warren
209	820.0	Roseville Community Schools	Roseville
210	814.0	East Jackson Community Schools	Jackson
211	813.8	Oxford Area Community Schools	Oxford
212	811.6	Warren Consolidated Schools	Warren
213	800.0	Paw Paw Public SD	Paw Paw
214	798.1	Rochester Community SD	Rochester
215	797.5	Michigan Center SD	Michigan Center
216	795.1	Clarkston Community SD	Clarkston
217	787.0	Novi Community SD	Novi
218	785.7	Westwood Community Schools	Dearborn Hgts
219	777.0	Eaton Rapids Public Schools	Eaton Rapids
220	770.3	Edwardsburg Public Schools	Edwardsburg
221	769.5	Quincy Community SD	Quincy
222	768.5	Meridian Public Schools	Sanford
223	767.0	Sturgis Public Schools	Sturgis
224	765.7	Otsego Public Schools	Otsego
225	762.9	Holland City SD	Holland
226	762.8	Mt. Clemens Community SD	Mt. Clemens
227	761.9	Grand Haven Area Public Schools	Grand Haven
228	756.5	Hartford Public SD	Hartford
229	755.7	Caro Community Schools	Caro
230	755.0	Hartland Consolidated Schools	Hartland
231	753.5	Dearborn City SD	Dearborn
232	749.7	Armada Area Schools	Armada
233	747.3	East China SD	East China
234	747.2	Berkley SD	Berkley
235	744.8	Grosse Pointe Public Schools	Grosse Pointe
236	723.4	Utica Community Schools	Sterling Hgts
237	712.7	Van Dyke Public Schools	Warren
238	709.2	Hazel Park City SD	Hazel Park
239	704.8	Northville Public Schools	Northville
240	703.5	Portage Public Schools	Portage
241	702.4	Mattawan Consolidated School	Mattawan
242	697.5	Romeo Community Schools	Romeo
243	695.0	Dewitt Public Schools	Dewitt
244	683.9	Jenison Public Schools	Jenison
245	680.3	Vicksburg Community Schools	Vicksburg
246	679.5	Lake Orion Community Schools	Lake Orion
247	679.2	South Redford SD	Redford
248	675.6	Lake Shore Pub Schools (Macomb)	St Clair Shores
249	675.0	Parchment SD	Parchment
250	674.5	Orchard View Schools	Muskegon
251	674.3	Grosse Ile Township Schools	Grosse Ile
252	672.0	Hastings Area SD	Hastings
253	661.2	Birmingham City SD	Birmingham
254	658.5	Jefferson Schools (Monroe)	Monroe
255	650.0	Reed City Area Public Schools	Reed City
256	640.0	Warren Woods Public Schools	Warren
257	637.8	Hamilton Community Schools	Hamilton
258	632.7	Birch Run Area SD	Birch Run
259	623.4	Fowlerville Community Schools	Fowlerville
260	620.7	Onsted Community Schools	Onsted
261	616.4	Trenton Public Schools	Trenton
262	611.0	Van Buren Public Schools	Belleville
263	605.9	Southfield Public SD	Southfield
264	602.0	Troy SD	Troy
265	600.7	East Detroit Public Schools	Eastpointe
266	600.0	Bloomfield Hills SD	Bloomfield Hls
267	597.2	Dearborn Heights SD #7	Dearborn Hgts
268	594.3	SD of Ypsilanti	Ypsilanti
269	592.9	Livonia Public Schools	Livonia
270	586.0	Farmington Public SD	Farmington
271	582.3	Buchanan Community Schools	Buchanan
272	581.5	Dexter Community SD	Dexter
273	569.5	Highland Park City Schools	Highland Park
274	565.2	Midland Public Schools	Midland
275	558.3	Beaverton Rural Schools	Beaverton
276	555.8	Comstock Public Schools	Kalamazoo
277	542.7	Farwell Area Schools	Farwell
278	532.7	Clare Public Schools	Clare
279	506.1	Ann Arbor Public Schools	Ann Arbor
280	501.8	Clarenceville SD	Livonia
281	493.4	South Lake Schools	St Clair Shores
282	484.4	Tri County Area Schools	Sand Lake
283	387.0	Elk Rapids Schools	Elk Rapids
284	n/a	Almont Community Schools	Almont
284	n/a	Benton Harbor Area Schools	Benton Harbor
284	n/a	Benzie County Central Schools	Benzonia
284	n/a	Chesaning Union Schools	Chesaning
284	n/a	Coopersville Public SD	Coopersville
284	n/a	Dundee Community Schools	Dundee
284	n/a	Fruitport Community Schools	Fruitport
284	n/a	Gladstone Area Schools	Gladstone
284	n/a	Lakewood Public Schools	Lake Odessa
284	n/a	Ludington Area SD	Ludington
284	n/a	Macomb ISD	Clinton Twp
284	n/a	Manistee Area Schools	Manistee
284	n/a	Mason County Central Schools	Scottville
284	n/a	Montague Area Public Schools	Montague
284	n/a	Montrose Community Schools	Montrose
284	n/a	Northview Public SD	Grand Rapids
284	n/a	Ovid-Elsie Area Schools	Elsie
284	n/a	Portland Public SD	Portland
284	n/a	Saginaw ISD	Saginaw
284	n/a	Three Rivers Community Schools	Three Rivers
284	n/a	Washtenaw ISD	Ann Arbor
284	n/a	Waverly Community Schools	Lansing
284	n/a	Willow Run Community Schools	Ypsilanti

Student/Counselor Ratio

Rank	Ratio	District Name	City
1	8,231.5	Lansing Public SD	Lansing
2	5,064.0	Benton Harbor Area Schools	Benton Harbor
3	3,687.3	Kalamazoo Public SD	Kalamazoo
4	2,363.0	Coopersville Public SD	Coopersville
5	2,171.0	Muskegon Heights SD	Muskegon Hgts
6	2,092.0	Gladwin Community Schools	Gladwin
7	2,035.0	Allendale Public SD	Allendale
8	2,034.5	Oxford Area Community Schools	Oxford
9	1,703.5	Caledonia Community Schools	Caledonia
10	1,639.3	Southgate Community SD	Southgate
11	1,524.3	Redford Union SD	Redford
12	1,323.0	Anchor Bay SD	New Baltimore
13	1,300.0	Melvindale-N Allen Park Schools	Melvindale
14	1,267.3	Hamtramck Public Schools	Hamtramck
15	1,211.0	Tri County Area Schools	Sand Lake
16	1,179.4	Howell Public Schools	Howell
17	1,178.7	Clio Area SD	Clio
18	1,142.0	Beecher Community SD	Flint
19	1,139.0	Highland Park City Schools	Highland Park
20	1,127.0	Detroit Acad of Arts & Sciences	Detroit
21	1,100.0	Wayland Union Schools	Wayland
22	1,069.5	Lakeville Community Schools	Otisville
23	1,061.0	Harrison Community Schools	Harrison
24	1,057.0	Hartland Consolidated Schools	Hartland
25	1,039.0	Oak Park City SD	Oak Park
26	1,037.0	Richmond Community Schools	Richmond
27	1,020.3	Escanaba Area Public Schools	Escanaba
28	1,018.3	Van Buren Public Schools	Belleville
29	1,010.0	Breitung Township Schools	Kingsford
30	1,003.5	Clarenceville SD	Livonia
31	1,001.5	Oakridge Public Schools	Muskegon
32	993.3	Linden Community Schools	Linden
33	991.4	Wyandotte City SD	Wyandotte
34	990.4	Lincoln Consolidated SD	Ypsilanti
35	984.0	Mt. Pleasant City SD	Mt. Pleasant
36	960.2	Flushing Community Schools	Flushing
37	949.0	Birch Run Area SD	Birch Run
38	934.0	Western SD	Parma
39	926.3	Comstock Public Schools	Kalamazoo
40	920.5	Brandon SD	Ortonville
41	919.3	Clintondale Community Schools	Clinton Twp
42	915.3	Grand Blanc Community Schools	Grand Blanc
43	891.0	Chippewa Hills SD	Remus
43	891.0	Willow Run Community Schools	Ypsilanti
45	890.3	Algonac Community SD	Algonac
46	889.5	Flat Rock Community Schools	Flat Rock
47	869.8	Reeths-Puffer Schools	Muskegon
48	868.5	Ida Public SD	Ida
49	867.5	Maple Valley Schools	Vermontville
50	855.2	Van Dyke Public Schools	Warren
51	851.0	Hazel Park City SD	Hazel Park
52	849.0	South Redford SD	Redford
53	848.0	Freeland Community SD	Freeland
54	843.3	Lakewood Public Schools	Lake Odessa
55	840.0	Hastings Area SD	Hastings
56	838.2	Mona Shores Public SD	Norton Shores
57	833.3	Belding Area SD	Belding
58	830.2	Garden City SD	Garden City
59	830.0	South Haven Public Schools	South Haven
60	826.8	Zeeland Public Schools	Zeeland
61	826.5	Gibraltar SD	Woodhaven
62	826.4	Owosso Public Schools	Owosso
63	823.3	Fraser Public Schools	Fraser
64	820.7	Pontiac City SD	Pontiac
65	820.5	Fitzgerald Public Schools	Warren
66	820.0	Roseville Community Schools	Roseville
67	818.0	Morley Stanwood Community Schls	Morley
68	811.1	Brighton Area Schools	Brighton
69	800.0	Warren Woods Public Schools	Warren
70	798.5	Godfrey-Lee Public Schools	Wyoming
71	795.2	Traverse City Area Public Schls	Traverse City
72	795.1	Clarkston Community SD	Clarkston
73	792.5	Mason Public Schools (Ingham)	Mason
74	790.4	Adrian City SD	Adrian
75	790.0	Public Schools of Calumet	Calumet
76	786.2	Lowell Area Schools	Lowell
77	782.1	Bedford Public Schools	Temperance
78	778.7	Imlay City Community Schools	Imlay City
79	775.0	Rockford Public Schools	Rockford
80	774.0	Elk Rapids Schools	Elk Rapids
81	772.3	Corunna Public SD	Corunna
82	770.5	Trenton Public Schools	Trenton
83	770.3	Edwardsburg Public Schools	Edwardsburg
84	768.5	Meridian Public Schools	Sanford
85	766.9	Grand Ledge Public Schools	Grand Ledge
86	766.7	Godwin Heights Public Schools	Wyoming
87	765.0	White Cloud Public Schools	White Cloud
88	764.8	Grandville Public Schools	Grandville
89	764.5	Tawas Area Schools	Tawas City
90	764.0	Grant Public SD	Grant
91	763.5	Bangor Public Schls (Van Buren)	Bangor
92	762.8	Mt. Clemens Community SD	Mt. Clemens
93	751.0	Lake Fenton Community Schools	Fenton
94	750.6	Fenton Area Public Schools	Fenton
95	749.7	Armada Area Schools	Armada
96	747.2	Lapeer Community Schools	Lapeer
97	744.7	Woodhaven-Brownstown SD	Brownstown
98	740.4	Kenowa Hills Public Schools	Grand Rapids
99	735.1	South Lyon Community Schools	South Lyon
100	735.0	Mt. Morris Consolidated Schools	Mt. Morris
101	730.0	Holt Public Schools	Holt
102	728.8	Byron Center Public Schools	Byron Center
103	727.6	Allen Park Public Schools	Allen Park
104	725.5	Thornapple Kellogg SD	Middleville
105	724.0	Big Rapids Public Schools	Big Rapids
106	721.8	Marysville Public Schools	Marysville
107	721.5	Huron Valley Schools	Highland
108	721.4	Waterford SD	Waterford
109	716.8	Romulus Community Schools	Romulus
110	704.8	Northville Public Schools	Northville
111	702.8	Muskegon City SD	Muskegon
112	696.8	L'anse Creuse Public Schools	Harrison Twp
113	695.7	Goodrich Area Schools	Goodrich
114	695.3	Portland Public SD	Portland
115	695.0	Dewitt Public Schools	Dewitt
116	694.2	Niles Community SD	Niles
117	692.0	Tecumseh Public Schools	Tecumseh
118	690.5	Grand Rapids Public Schools	Grand Rapids
119	687.0	Durand Area Schools	Durand
120	686.4	Airport Community SD	Carleton
121	681.4	Cedar Springs Public Schools	Cedar Springs
122	681.2	Waverly Community Schools	Lansing
123	679.5	Lake Orion Community Schools	Lake Orion
124	675.6	Lake Shore Pub Schools (Macomb)	St Clair Shores
125	675.5	Wyoming Public Schools	Wyoming
126	675.0	Parchment SD	Parchment
127	674.5	Orchard View Schools	Muskegon
128	674.3	Grosse Ile Township Schools	Grosse Ile
129	671.8	Harper Creek Community Schools	Battle Creek
130	667.5	Holland City SD	Holland
131	667.2	Flint City SD	Flint
132	666.6	West Ottawa Public SD	Holland
133	664.2	East China SD	East China
134	661.2	Birmingham City SD	Birmingham
135	658.5	Jefferson Schools (Monroe)	Monroe
136	658.0	Pinconning Area Schools	Pinconning
137	657.6	Utica Community Schools	Sterling Hgts
138	653.3	Lincoln Park Public Schools	Lincoln Park
139	650.2	Saginaw City SD	Saginaw
140	650.0	Reed City Area Public Schools	Reed City
141	646.3	Standish-Sterling Comm Schools	Standish
142	645.3	Shelby Public Schools	Shelby
143	640.4	Alpena Public Schools	Alpena
144	639.7	Plymouth-Canton Community Schls	Plymouth
145	638.3	Ludington Area SD	Ludington
146	637.8	Hamilton Community Schools	Hamilton
147	637.3	Capac Community SD	Capac
147	637.3	Columbia SD	Brooklyn
149	632.0	Bangor Township Schools	Bay City
150	630.1	SD of the City of Royal Oak	Royal Oak
151	629.6	Novi Community SD	Novi
152	626.4	Port Huron Area SD	Port Huron
153	619.5	Alma Public Schools	Alma
154	618.4	Public Schools of Petoskey	Petoskey
155	614.2	Chelsea SD	Chelsea
156	613.7	Gerrish-Higgins SD	Roscommon
157	603.8	Gull Lake Community Schools	Richland
158	602.9	West Bloomfield SD	West Bloomfield
159	602.8	Dearborn City SD	Dearborn
160	601.0	Ovid-Elsie Area Schools	Elsie
161	600.7	East Detroit Public Schools	Eastpointe
162	600.0	Paw Paw Public SD	Paw Paw
163	599.7	Almont Community Schools	Almont

164	597.2	Dearborn Heights SD #7	Dearborn Hgts
165	597.1	Swartz Creek Community Schools	Swartz Creek
166	596.1	Davison Community Schools	Davison
167	594.3	SD of Ypsilanti	Ypsilanti
168	592.5	Crestwood SD	Dearborn Hgts
169	590.7	Millington Community Schools	Millington
170	589.3	Shepherd Public SD	Shepherd
171	589.0	Napoleon Community Schools	Napoleon
172	587.3	Bridgeport-Spaulding CSD	Bridgeport
173	586.0	Farmington Public SD	Farmington
174	585.3	Mattawan Consolidated School	Mattawan
175	583.3	Stockbridge Community Schools	Stockbridge
176	582.8	Gaylord Community Schools	Gaylord
177	582.7	Albion Public Schools	Albion
178	581.5	Dexter Community SD	Dexter
179	579.4	Sault Ste. Marie Area Schools	Sault Ste Marie
180	576.8	East Grand Rapids Public Schools	E Grand Rapids
181	575.2	Lakeview Public Schools (Macomb)	St Clair Shores
182	574.6	Rochester Community SD	Rochester
183	574.2	Sparta Area Schools	Sparta
184	573.4	Plainwell Community Schools	Plainwell
185	572.3	Swan Valley SD	Saginaw
186	571.2	Ionia Public Schools	Ionia
187	570.8	Detroit City SD	Detroit
188	570.4	St. Joseph Public Schools	St. Joseph
189	566.8	Caro Community Schools	Caro
190	565.3	Newaygo Public SD	Newaygo
191	564.5	Cadillac Area Public Schools	Cadillac
192	560.8	Coldwater Community Schools	Coldwater
193	560.4	Berkley SD	Berkley
194	559.3	Spring Lake Public Schools	Spring Lake
195	558.3	Beaverton Rural Schools	Beaverton
196	558.0	Romeo Community Schools	Romeo
197	557.0	Mason County Central Schools	Scottville
198	556.2	Chippewa Valley Schools	Clinton Twp
199	554.3	Kelloggsville Public Schools	Grand Rapids
200	554.1	Kentwood Public Schools	Kentwood
201	550.3	Milan Area Schools	Milan
202	546.1	Bay City SD	Bay City
203	544.5	Taylor SD	Taylor
204	540.6	Livonia Public Schools	Livonia
205	537.9	Portage Public Schools	Portage
206	535.3	Berrien Springs Public Schools	Berrien Springs
207	532.7	Clare Public Schools	Clare
208	531.9	Jenison Public Schools	Jenison
209	531.7	Michigan Center SD	Michigan Center
210	531.0	Huron SD	New Boston
211	525.8	Crawford Ausable Schools	Grayling
211	525.8	Grosse Pointe Public Schools	Grosse Pointe
213	524.4	Fremont Public SD	Fremont
214	523.4	Troy SD	Troy
215	520.9	Marquette Area Public Schools	Marquette
216	519.5	Fowlerville Community Schools	Fowlerville
217	519.2	Riverview Community SD	Riverview
218	518.7	Constantine Public SD	Constantine
219	518.0	Eaton Rapids Public Schools	Eaton Rapids
220	515.0	Southfield Public SD	Southfield
221	514.0	Chesaning Union Schools	Chesaning
222	513.0	Quincy Community SD	Quincy
223	508.3	Madison Public Schools (Oakland)	Madison Heights
224	507.6	East Lansing SD	East Lansing
225	504.4	Croswell-Lexington Comm Schools	Croswell
226	503.0	Gwinn Area Community Schools	Gwinn
227	501.0	Benzie County Central Schools	Benzonia
228	498.0	Yale Public Schools	Yale
229	493.8	Lamphere Public Schools	Madison Heights
230	491.0	Holly Area SD	Holly
231	490.3	Carrollton SD	Saginaw
232	490.2	Haslett Public Schools	Haslett
233	489.3	Greenville Public Schools	Greenville
234	487.6	Saline Area Schools	Saline
235	483.5	Avondale SD	Auburn Hills
236	481.5	Pennfield SD	Battle Creek
237	479.6	Forest Hills Public Schools	Grand Rapids
238	478.1	Charlotte Public Schools	Charlotte
239	476.5	Wayne-Westland Community SD	Westland
240	474.0	Hillsdale Community Schools	Hillsdale
241	473.6	Lakeview SD (Calhoun)	Battle Creek
242	471.9	Fruitport Community Schools	Fruitport
243	471.7	Saginaw Twp Community Schools	Saginaw
244	468.8	Comstock Park Public Schools	Comstock Park
245	465.5	Onsted Community Schools	Onsted
246	465.4	River Rouge SD	River Rouge
247	463.8	Oscoda Area Schools	Oscoda
248	461.8	Dowagiac Union SD	Dowagiac
249	458.4	Northwest Community Schools	Jackson
250	457.5	Midland Public Schools	Midland
251	455.8	Cheboygan Area Schools	Cheboygan
252	449.3	Kalkaska Public Schools	Kalkaska
253	446.9	Carman-Ainsworth Comm Schools	Flint
254	443.8	W Branch-Rose City Area Schools	West Branch
255	443.4	Hudsonville Public SD	Hudsonville
256	438.3	Sturgis Public Schools	Sturgis
257	435.4	Grand Haven Area Public Schools	Grand Haven
258	432.1	Allegan Public Schools	Allegan
259	431.0	Whitehall District Schools	Whitehall
260	428.4	Warren Consolidated Schools	Warren
261	427.2	Marshall Public Schools	Marshall
262	426.7	Center Line Public Schools	Center Line
263	425.6	Houghton Lake Community Schools	Houghton Lake
264	425.4	Central Montcalm Public Schools	Stanton
265	417.5	Ann Arbor Public Schools	Ann Arbor
266	415.6	Bullock Creek SD	Midland
267	412.0	Bendle Public Schools	Burton
268	411.8	Delton-Kellogg SD	Delton
269	407.9	Lakeshore SD (Berrien)	Stevensville
270	407.0	East Jackson Community Schools	Jackson
270	407.0	Farwell Area Schools	Farwell
272	406.1	St. Johns Public Schools	St. Johns
273	404.6	Okemos Public Schools	Okemos
274	399.9	Monroe Public Schools	Monroe
275	399.4	Perry Public SD	Perry
276	392.8	Westwood Community Schools	Dearborn Hgts
277	391.6	Essexville-Hampton Public Schls	Essexville
278	390.4	Kearsley Community Schools	Flint
279	389.9	Walled Lake Consolidated Schools	Walled Lake
280	388.7	Vicksburg Community Schools	Vicksburg
281	384.3	Brandywine Public SD	Niles
282	382.8	Otsego Public Schools	Otsego
283	382.0	Lakeview Comm Schools (Montcalm)	Lakeview
284	378.3	Hartford Public SD	Hartford
285	375.0	Montague Area Public Schools	Montague
286	372.2	Vassar Public Schools	Vassar
287	362.3	Coloma Community Schools	Coloma
288	352.9	Bloomfield Hills SD	Bloomfield Hls
289	349.1	Ferndale Public Schools	Ferndale
290	348.3	Williamston Community Schools	Williamston
291	345.4	Battle Creek Public Schools	Battle Creek
292	335.3	Menominee Area Public Schools	Menominee
293	308.4	South Lake Schools	St Clair Shores
294	291.2	Buchanan Community Schools	Buchanan
295	n/a	Dundee Community Schools	Dundee
295	n/a	Gladstone Area Schools	Gladstone
295	n/a	Jackson Public Schools	Jackson
295	n/a	Macomb ISD	Clinton Twp
295	n/a	Manistee Area Schools	Manistee
295	n/a	Mason Consol Schools (Monroe)	Erie
295	n/a	Montrose Community Schools	Montrose
295	n/a	North Branch Area Schools	North Branch
295	n/a	Northview Public SD	Grand Rapids
295	n/a	Saginaw ISD	Saginaw
295	n/a	Three Rivers Community Schools	Three Rivers
295	n/a	Washtenaw ISD	Ann Arbor

Current Spending per Student in FY2003

Rank	Dollars	District Name	City
1	12,759	Bloomfield Hills SD	Bloomfield Hls
2	11,769	Birmingham City SD	Birmingham
3	11,607	Lamphere Public Schools	Madison Heights
4	11,595	Beecher Community SD	Flint
5	11,444	Southfield Public SD	Southfield
6	10,930	Willow Run Community Schools	Ypsilanti
7	10,888	Farmington Public SD	Farmington
8	10,501	Grand Rapids Public Schools	Grand Rapids
9	10,430	Lansing Public SD	Lansing
10	10,360	Muskegon Heights SD	Muskegon Hgts
11	10,209	SD of Ypsilanti	Ypsilanti
12	10,163	Garden City SD	Garden City
13	10,055	Northville Public Schools	Northville
14	9,996	Grosse Pointe Public Schools	Grosse Pointe
15	9,882	Hazel Park City SD	Hazel Park
16	9,818	Troy SD	Troy
17	9,787	Pontiac City SD	Pontiac
18	9,779	Trenton Public Schools	Trenton
19	9,773	Westwood Community Schools	Dearborn Hgts
20	9,731	Ann Arbor Public Schools	Ann Arbor
21	9,683	Ferndale Public Schools	Ferndale
22	9,636	Oak Park City SD	Oak Park
23	9,607	Warren Woods Public Schools	Warren
24	9,587	Center Line Public Schools	Center Line
25	9,583	River Rouge SD	River Rouge
26	9,559	Mt. Clemens Community SD	Mt. Clemens
27	9,551	Wyandotte City SD	Wyandotte
28	9,521	Dearborn City SD	Dearborn
29	9,500	Romulus Community Schools	Romulus
30	9,475	Flint City SD	Flint
31	9,466	SD of the City of Royal Oak	Royal Oak
32	9,417	Van Dyke Public Schools	Warren
33	9,369	Warren Consolidated Schools	Warren
34	9,313	Novi Community SD	Novi
35	9,310	Kalamazoo Public SD	Kalamazoo
36	9,309	Avondale SD	Auburn Hills
37	9,204	Livonia Public Schools	Livonia
38	9,196	Walled Lake Consolidated Schools	Walled Lake
39	9,187	West Bloomfield SD	West Bloomfield
40	9,153	Benton Harbor Area Schools	Benton Harbor
41	9,118	Highland Park City Schools	Highland Park
42	9,084	Redford Union SD	Redford
43	9,069	South Lake Schools	St Clair Shores
44	9,063	Detroit City SD	Detroit
45	9,045	Carman-Ainsworth Comm Schools	Flint
46	9,025	Jefferson Schools (Monroe)	Monroe
47	8,987	Waverly Community Schools	Lansing
48	8,958	Jackson Public Schools	Jackson
49	8,912	Battle Creek Public Schools	Battle Creek
50	8,807	Fitzgerald Public Schools	Warren
51	8,799	Grosse Ile Township Schools	Grosse Ile
52	8,758	East Lansing SD	East Lansing
53	8,738	Bangor Public Schls (Van Buren)	Bangor
54	8,732	Wayne-Westland Community SD	Westland
55	8,716	Mt. Pleasant City SD	Mt. Pleasant
56	8,668	Okemos Public Schools	Okemos
57	8,655	Clarenceville SD	Livonia
58	8,608	Fraser Public Schools	Fraser
59	8,588	Adrian City SD	Adrian
60	8,561	Clintondale Community Schools	Clinton Twp
61	8,552	Dexter Community SD	Dexter
62	8,550	Godwin Heights Public Schools	Wyoming
63	8,521	Berrien Springs Public Schools	Berrien Springs
64	8,476	Waterford SD	Waterford
65	8,467	Forest Hills Public Schools	Grand Rapids
66	8,447	Midland Public Schools	Midland
67	8,431	Rochester Community SD	Rochester
68	8,423	Saginaw City SD	Saginaw
69	8,408	Muskegon City SD	Muskegon
70	8,402	Berkley SD	Berkley
71	8,368	Lincoln Park Public Schools	Lincoln Park
72	8,335	Southgate Community SD	Southgate
73	8,315	Taylor SD	Taylor
74	8,296	Holland City SD	Holland
75	8,263	Hamtramck Public Schools	Hamtramck
76	8,259	Madison Public Schools (Oakland)	Madison Heights
77	8,246	Roseville Community Schools	Roseville
78	8,200	Caledonia Community Schools	Caledonia
79	8,184	Lake Orion Community Schools	Lake Orion
80	8,135	Gwinn Area Community Schools	Gwinn
81	8,124	Albion Public Schools	Albion
82	8,099	Manistee Area Schools	Manistee
83	8,076	Woodhaven-Brownstown SD	Brownstown
84	8,047	Lake Shore Pub Schools (Macomb)	St Clair Shores
85	8,041	Flat Rock Community Schools	Flat Rock
86	8,034	Saline Area Schools	Saline
87	8,010	Melvindale-N Allen Park Schools	Melvindale
88	7,992	Chippewa Hills SD	Remus
89	7,975	East Grand Rapids Public Schools	E Grand Rapids
90	7,963	Houghton Lake Community Schools	Houghton Lake
91	7,949	Huron SD	New Boston
92	7,941	South Redford SD	Redford
93	7,939	Kalkaska Public Schools	Kalkaska
94	7,935	Ludington Area SD	Ludington
95	7,923	Bridgeport-Spaulding CSD	Bridgeport
96	7,922	Montrose Community Schools	Montrose
97	7,910	Gibraltar SD	Woodhaven
98	7,907	Harrison Community Schools	Harrison
99	7,879	Jenison Public Schools	Jenison
100	7,878	Van Buren Public Schools	Belleville
101	7,860	Kentwood Public Schools	Kentwood
102	7,856	Mason County Central Schools	Scottville
103	7,836	W Branch-Rose City Area Schools	West Branch
104	7,832	Grand Haven Area Public Schools	Grand Haven
105	7,813	White Cloud Public Schools	White Cloud
106	7,801	Milan Area Schools	Milan
107	7,780	East Detroit Public Schools	Eastpointe
108	7,757	Reeths-Puffer Schools	Muskegon
109	7,741	Holly Area SD	Holly
110	7,717	Kenowa Hills Public Schools	Grand Rapids
111	7,693	Spring Lake Public Schools	Spring Lake
112	7,690	West Ottawa Public SD	Holland
113	7,683	Utica Community Schools	Sterling Hgts
114	7,681	Wyoming Public Schools	Wyoming
115	7,672	Oxford Area Community Schools	Oxford
116	7,667	Cadillac Area Public Schools	Cadillac
117	7,665	Ionia Public Schools	Ionia
118	7,664	Lincoln Consolidated SD	Ypsilanti
119	7,658	East China SD	East China
120	7,652	Essexville-Hampton Public Schls	Essexville
121	7,649	Shepherd Public SD	Shepherd
122	7,647	Huron Valley Schools	Highland
123	7,645	Escanaba Area Public Schools	Escanaba
124	7,640	Comstock Public Schools	Kalamazoo
125	7,610	Chesaning Union Schools	Chesaning
126	7,604	Carrollton SD	Saginaw
127	7,597	Romeo Community Schools	Romeo
128	7,582	Morley Stanwood Community Schls	Morley
129	7,576	Hillsdale Community Schools	Hillsdale
130	7,555	Fruitport Community Schools	Fruitport
131	7,553	Crawford Ausable Schools	Grayling
132	7,552	Sparta Area Schools	Sparta

133	7,545	Bay City SD	Bay City
134	7,540	Mason Consol Schools (Monroe)	Erie
135	7,520	Godfrey-Lee Public Schools	Wyoming
136	7,511	Fremont Public SD	Fremont
137	7,509	Monroe Public Schools	Monroe
138	7,505	Stockbridge Community Schools	Stockbridge
139	7,498	Gaylord Community Schools	Gaylord
140	7,494	Gladwin Community Schools	Gladwin
141	7,490	Oscoda Area Schools	Oscoda
141	7,490	Public Schools of Petoskey	Petoskey
143	7,485	Chelsea SD	Chelsea
144	7,484	Alpena Public Schools	Alpena
145	7,480	Coopersville Public SD	Coopersville
146	7,477	Niles Community SD	Niles
147	7,466	Clarkston Community SD	Clarkston
148	7,462	Hartford Public SD	Hartford
149	7,461	St. Joseph Public Schools	St. Joseph
150	7,455	Kelloggsville Public Schools	Grand Rapids
151	7,454	Coloma Community Schools	Coloma
152	7,444	Sault Ste. Marie Area Schools	Sault Ste Marie
153	7,442	Byron Center Public Schools	Byron Center
154	7,431	Public Schools of Calumet	Calumet
155	7,426	Meridian Public Schools	Sanford
156	7,424	Pinconning Area Schools	Pinconning
157	7,423	St. Johns Public Schools	St. Johns
158	7,413	Bangor Township Schools	Bay City
159	7,411	Allen Park Public Schools	Allen Park
160	7,401	Haslett Public Schools	Haslett
161	7,400	Ida Public SD	Ida
162	7,389	Lakeview SD (Calhoun)	Battle Creek
163	7,367	Cheboygan Area Schools	Cheboygan
164	7,355	Farwell Area Schools	Farwell
165	7,347	Benzie County Central Schools	Benzonia
166	7,341	Constantine Public SD	Constantine
167	7,338	Gerrish-Higgins SD	Roscommon
168	7,324	Beaverton Rural Schools	Beaverton
169	7,320	Chippewa Valley Schools	Clinton Twp
170	7,302	Comstock Park Public Schools	Comstock Park
171	7,300	Allegan Public Schools	Allegan
172	7,297	Elk Rapids Schools	Elk Rapids
173	7,295	Oakridge Public Schools	Muskegon
174	7,294	Holt Public Schools	Holt
175	7,282	Delton-Kellogg SD	Delton
176	7,280	Lake Fenton Community Schools	Fenton
177	7,279	Lakeville Community Schools	Otisville
177	7,279	Riverview Community SD	Riverview
179	7,270	L'anse Creuse Public Schools	Harrison Twp
179	7,270	Ovid-Elsie Area Schools	Elsie
181	7,267	Mason Public Schools (Ingham)	Mason
182	7,255	Rockford Public Schools	Rockford
183	7,248	Plymouth-Canton Community Schls	Plymouth
184	7,224	Marshall Public Schools	Marshall
184	7,224	Mt. Morris Consolidated Schools	Mt. Morris
186	7,216	Greenville Public Schools	Greenville
187	7,212	Eaton Rapids Public Schools	Eaton Rapids
187	7,212	Millington Community Schools	Millington
189	7,208	Allendale Public SD	Allendale
190	7,206	Big Rapids Public Schools	Big Rapids
191	7,187	Charlotte Public Schools	Charlotte
192	7,186	Lakewood Public Schools	Lake Odessa
193	7,185	Parchment SD	Parchment
194	7,184	Lowell Area Schools	Lowell
195	7,181	Portage Public Schools	Portage
196	7,178	Northview Public SD	Grand Rapids
197	7,170	Sturgis Public Schools	Sturgis
198	7,169	South Haven Public Schools	South Haven
199	7,168	Hastings Area SD	Hastings
200	7,156	Grand Ledge Public Schools	Grand Ledge
201	7,130	Gladstone Area Schools	Gladstone
202	7,124	East Jackson Community Schools	Jackson
203	7,115	Dewitt Public Schools	Dewitt
204	7,104	Standish-Sterling Comm Schools	Standish
205	7,099	Fenton Area Public Schools	Fenton
206	7,096	Perry Public SD	Perry
207	7,091	Dowagiac Union SD	Dowagiac
208	7,090	Central Montcalm Public Schools	Stanton
209	7,078	Armada Area Schools	Armada
210	7,076	Menominee Area Public Schools	Menominee
210	7,076	Traverse City Area Public Schls	Traverse City
212	7,074	Richmond Community Schools	Richmond
213	7,072	Clare Public Schools	Clare
214	7,071	Brighton Area Schools	Brighton
215	7,069	Zeeland Public Schools	Zeeland
216	7,068	Bedford Public Schools	Temperance
216	7,068	Kearsley Community Schools	Flint
218	7,064	Tawas Area Schools	Tawas City
219	7,063	Cedar Springs Public Schools	Cedar Springs
220	7,062	Three Rivers Community Schools	Three Rivers
221	7,057	Marquette Area Public Schools	Marquette
222	7,054	Vicksburg Community Schools	Vicksburg
223	7,053	Brandon SD	Ortonville
224	7,051	Brandywine Public SD	Niles
225	7,039	Harper Creek Community Schools	Battle Creek
226	7,038	Hudsonville Public SD	Hudsonville
227	7,037	Alma Public Schools	Alma
228	7,036	Thornapple Kellogg SD	Middleville
229	7,033	Fowlerville Community Schools	Fowlerville
230	7,029	Northwest Community Schools	Jackson
231	7,023	Airport Community SD	Carleton
232	7,022	Mona Shores Public SD	Norton Shores
233	7,020	Bullock Creek SD	Midland
234	7,017	Howell Public Schools	Howell
235	7,016	Williamston Community Schools	Williamston
236	7,007	Belding Area SD	Belding
237	6,998	Owosso Public Schools	Owosso
238	6,979	Durand Area Schools	Durand
239	6,965	Lakeview Comm Schools (Montcalm)	Lakeview
240	6,961	Davison Community Schools	Davison
241	6,956	Grandville Public Schools	Grandville
242	6,953	Otsego Public Schools	Otsego
243	6,947	Western SD	Parma
244	6,945	Crestwood SD	Dearborn Hgts
244	6,945	Paw Paw Public SD	Paw Paw
246	6,939	Goodrich Area Schools	Goodrich
246	6,939	Saginaw Twp Community Schools	Saginaw
248	6,937	Clio Area SD	Clio
249	6,932	Columbia SD	Brooklyn
249	6,932	Corunna Public SD	Corunna
251	6,921	Orchard View Schools	Muskegon
252	6,920	Birch Run Area SD	Birch Run
253	6,913	Breitung Township Schools	Kingsford
254	6,912	Port Huron Area SD	Port Huron
255	6,906	Whitehall District Schools	Whitehall
256	6,894	Anchor Bay SD	New Baltimore
257	6,876	Montague Area Public Schools	Montague
258	6,869	Hartland Consolidated Schools	Hartland
258	6,869	Shelby Public Schools	Shelby
260	6,861	Caro Community Schools	Caro
261	6,856	South Lyon Community Schools	South Lyon
262	6,855	Grand Blanc Community Schools	Grand Blanc
263	6,853	Lakeshore SD (Berrien)	Stevensville
264	6,842	Wayland Union Schools	Wayland
265	6,838	Tecumseh Public Schools	Tecumseh
266	6,826	Onsted Community Schools	Onsted
267	6,825	Maple Valley Schools	Vermontville
268	6,820	Buchanan Community Schools	Buchanan
269	6,818	Mattawan Consolidated School	Mattawan
270	6,817	Reed City Area Public Schools	Reed City
271	6,814	North Branch Area Schools	North Branch
272	6,800	Portland Public SD	Portland
273	6,767	Grant Public SD	Grant
274	6,740	Lapeer Community Schools	Lapeer
275	6,738	Linden Community Schools	Linden
276	6,735	Vassar Public Schools	Vassar
277	6,733	Croswell-Lexington Comm Schools	Croswell
278	6,717	Plainwell Community Schools	Plainwell
279	6,709	Pennfield SD	Battle Creek
280	6,708	Imlay City Community Schools	Imlay City
281	6,705	Lakeview Public Schools (Macomb)	St Clair Shores
282	6,669	Capac Community SD	Capac
282	6,669	Tri County Area Schools	Sand Lake
284	6,664	Swartz Creek Community Schools	Swartz Creek
285	6,657	Swan Valley SD	Saginaw
286	6,590	Dearborn Heights SD #7	Dearborn Hgts
287	6,538	Napoleon Community Schools	Napoleon
288	6,523	Gull Lake Community Schools	Richland
289	6,511	Michigan Center SD	Michigan Center
290	6,510	Algonac Community SD	Algonac
291	6,494	Dundee Community Schools	Dundee
292	6,482	Hamilton Community Schools	Hamilton
293	6,440	Bendle Public Schools	Burton
294	6,430	Almont Community Schools	Almont
295	6,347	Edwardsburg Public Schools	Edwardsburg
296	6,345	Yale Public Schools	Yale
297	6,306	Freeland Community SD	Freeland
298	6,197	Marysville Public Schools	Marysville
299	6,180	Coldwater Community Schools	Coldwater
300	6,163	Newaygo Public SD	Newaygo
301	6,080	Quincy Community SD	Quincy
302	5,866	Flushing Community Schools	Flushing
303	5,117	Detroit Acad of Arts & Sciences	Detroit
304	n/a	Macomb ISD	Clinton Twp
304	n/a	Saginaw ISD	Saginaw
304	n/a	Washtenaw ISD	Ann Arbor

Number of Diploma Recipients

Rank	Number	District Name	City
1	5,540	Detroit City SD	Detroit
2	1,867	Utica Community Schools	Sterling Hgts
3	1,315	Livonia Public Schools	Livonia
4	1,141	Ann Arbor Public Schools	Ann Arbor
5	1,014	Dearborn City SD	Dearborn
6	1,009	Rochester Community SD	Rochester
7	1,008	Plymouth-Canton Community Schls	Plymouth
8	970	Warren Consolidated Schools	Warren
9	967	Troy SD	Troy
10	847	Farmington Public SD	Farmington
11	811	Walled Lake Consolidated Schools	Walled Lake
12	778	Lansing Public SD	Lansing
13	762	Chippewa Valley Schools	Clinton Twp
14	760	Traverse City Area Public Schls	Traverse City
15	720	Grosse Pointe Public Schools	Grosse Pointe
16	716	Wayne-Westland Community SD	Westland
17	714	Flint City SD	Flint
18	708	Grand Rapids Public Schools	Grand Rapids
19	691	Port Huron Area SD	Port Huron
20	678	Midland Public Schools	Midland
21	659	Forest Hills Public Schools	Grand Rapids
22	622	Huron Valley Schools	Highland
23	616	Portage Public Schools	Portage
24	615	L'anse Creuse Public Schools	Harrison Twp
25	590	Bay City SD	Bay City
26	570	Kentwood Public Schools	Kentwood
27	567	Taylor SD	Taylor
28	559	Rockford Public Schools	Rockford
29	555	Waterford SD	Waterford
30	534	Southfield Public SD	Southfield
31	503	Birmingham City SD	Birmingham
32	501	Clarkston Community SD	Clarkston
33	485	Brighton Area Schools	Brighton
34	475	Lapeer Community Schools	Lapeer
34	475	SD of the City of Royal Oak	Royal Oak
36	462	Saginaw City SD	Saginaw
37	446	Grand Haven Area Public Schools	Grand Haven
38	442	Bloomfield Hills SD	Bloomfield Hls
39	437	Howell Public Schools	Howell
40	434	Kalamazoo Public SD	Kalamazoo
41	418	West Bloomfield SD	West Bloomfield
42	416	Grand Blanc Community Schools	Grand Blanc
42	416	Pontiac City SD	Pontiac
42	416	West Ottawa Public SD	Holland
45	404	East China SD	East China
46	402	Lake Orion Community Schools	Lake Orion
47	392	Bedford Public Schools	Temperance
48	389	Novi Community SD	Novi
49	386	Grand Ledge Public Schools	Grand Ledge
49	386	Monroe Public Schools	Monroe
51	383	Alpena Public Schools	Alpena
52	371	Grandville Public Schools	Grandville
53	363	Van Buren Public Schools	Belleville
54	359	Saline Area Schools	Saline
55	357	Jenison Public Schools	Jenison
56	351	Okemos Public Schools	Okemos
57	350	Saginaw Twp Community Schools	Saginaw
58	347	Wyoming Public Schools	Wyoming
59	345	South Lyon Community Schools	South Lyon
60	343	Romeo Community Schools	Romeo
61	342	East Detroit Public Schools	Eastpointe
62	333	Jackson Public Schools	Jackson
63	331	Marquette Area Public Schools	Marquette
63	331	Northville Public Schools	Northville
65	315	Flushing Community Schools	Flushing
66	308	Roseville Community Schools	Roseville
67	303	Mona Shores Public SD	Norton Shores
68	301	Holt Public Schools	Holt
69	300	Fraser Public Schools	Fraser
70	296	Berkley SD	Berkley
70	296	Davison Community Schools	Davison
72	292	Holland City SD	Holland
73	286	Zeeland Public Schools	Zeeland
74	285	Hartland Consolidated Schools	Hartland
75	284	Southgate Community SD	Southgate
76	279	Reeths-Puffer Schools	Muskegon
77	278	Battle Creek Public Schools	Battle Creek
78	276	Anchor Bay SD	New Baltimore
79	275	Garden City SD	Garden City
80	274	Woodhaven-Brownstown SD	Brownstown
81	273	East Lansing SD	East Lansing
82	272	Carman-Ainsworth Comm Schools	Flint
83	270	Mt. Pleasant City SD	Mt. Pleasant
84	268	Swartz Creek Community Schools	Swartz Creek
85	264	Wyandotte City SD	Wyandotte
86	263	Escanaba Area Public Schools	Escanaba
87	260	Hudsonville Public SD	Hudsonville
87	260	Lincoln Park Public Schools	Lincoln Park
89	258	Northview Public SD	Grand Rapids
90	257	Holly Area SD	Holly
91	255	Waverly Community Schools	Lansing
92	247	Kearsley Community Schools	Flint
92	247	Muskegon City SD	Muskegon
94	246	Adrian City SD	Adrian
95	244	Owosso Public Schools	Owosso
96	242	Greenville Public Schools	Greenville
97	240	Chelsea SD	Chelsea
98	238	Lakeview SD (Calhoun)	Battle Creek
98	238	Oak Park City SD	Oak Park
98	238	St. Johns Public Schools	St. Johns

101	237	Brandon SD	Ortonville
101	237	Eaton Rapids Public Schools	Eaton Rapids
101	237	Lakeshore SD (Berrien)	Stevensville
104	235	Cadillac Area Public Schools	Cadillac
104	235	Mason Public Schools (Ingham)	Mason
104	235	Oxford Area Community Schools	Oxford
104	235	SD of Ypsilanti	Ypsilanti
108	229	Fenton Area Public Schools	Fenton
109	224	Lowell Area Schools	Lowell
110	218	East Grand Rapids Public Schools	E Grand Rapids
110	218	Lakeview Public Schools (Macomb)	St Clair Shores
112	217	Kenowa Hills Public Schools	Grand Rapids
112	217	Mattawan Consolidated School	Mattawan
114	216	Crestwood SD	Dearborn Hgts
114	216	Haslett Public Schools	Haslett
114	216	Trenton Public Schools	Trenton
117	214	Tecumseh Public Schools	Tecumseh
118	213	Sault Ste. Marie Area Schools	Sault Ste Marie
119	212	Lincoln Consolidated SD	Ypsilanti
120	211	Coldwater Community Schools	Coldwater
121	210	Gull Lake Community Schools	Richland
121	210	St. Joseph Public Schools	St. Joseph
123	209	Thornapple Kellogg SD	Middleville
123	209	Vicksburg Community Schools	Vicksburg
123	209	Wayland Union Schools	Wayland
126	207	Avondale SD	Auburn Hills
126	207	Ionia Public Schools	Ionia
128	206	Fowlerville Community Schools	Fowlerville
128	206	Gaylord Community Schools	Gaylord
128	206	Northwest Community Schools	Jackson
131	205	Redford Union SD	Redford
132	203	Marshall Public Schools	Marshall
133	202	Caledonia Community Schools	Caledonia
133	202	Ferndale Public Schools	Ferndale
135	201	Benton Harbor Area Schools	Benton Harbor
135	201	Fruitport Community Schools	Fruitport
135	201	Romulus Community Schools	Romulus
138	200	Gibraltar SD	Woodhaven
139	199	South Redford SD	Redford
140	198	Allen Park Public Schools	Allen Park
141	194	Dewitt Public Schools	Dewitt
141	194	Lake Shore Pub Schools (Macomb)	St Clair Shores
143	193	Dexter Community SD	Dexter
143	193	Fremont Public SD	Fremont
145	192	Hastings Area SD	Hastings
146	191	Warren Woods Public Schools	Warren
147	190	Sparta Area Schools	Sparta
148	189	Charlotte Public Schools	Charlotte
149	187	Plainwell Community Schools	Plainwell
150	185	Clio Area SD	Clio
151	184	Sturgis Public Schools	Sturgis
152	182	Lakewood Public Schools	Lake Odessa
153	181	W Branch-Rose City Area Schools	West Branch
154	178	Jefferson Schools (Monroe)	Monroe
154	178	Ludington Area SD	Ludington
156	175	Bangor Township Schools	Bay City
156	175	Grosse Ile Township Schools	Grosse Ile
158	172	Marysville Public Schools	Marysville
159	171	Airport Community SD	Carleton
159	171	Breitung Township Schools	Kingsford
159	171	Riverview Community SD	Riverview
162	170	Big Rapids Public Schools	Big Rapids
163	169	Fitzgerald Public Schools	Warren
163	169	North Branch Area Schools	North Branch
165	168	Otsego Public Schools	Otsego
166	167	Lamphere Public Schools	Madison Heights
167	165	Byron Center Public Schools	Byron Center
168	164	Cheboygan Area Schools	Cheboygan
168	164	Mt. Morris Consolidated Schools	Mt. Morris
170	163	Pinconning Area Schools	Pinconning
171	162	Hamtramck Public Schools	Hamtramck
172	160	Niles Community SD	Niles
173	159	Three Rivers Community Schools	Three Rivers
174	158	Croswell-Lexington Comm Schools	Croswell
175	157	Hazel Park City SD	Hazel Park
176	156	Coopersville Public SD	Coopersville
176	156	Harper Creek Community Schools	Battle Creek
176	156	Paw Paw Public SD	Paw Paw
179	155	South Lake Schools	St Clair Shores
179	155	Van Dyke Public Schools	Warren
181	154	Center Line Public Schools	Center Line
182	153	Portland Public SD	Portland
183	152	Belding Area SD	Belding
183	152	South Haven Public Schools	South Haven
185	151	Linden Community Schools	Linden
186	150	Allegan Public Schools	Allegan
187	149	Gladstone Area Schools	Gladstone
188	148	Western SD	Parma
189	147	Alma Public Schools	Alma
190	145	Algonac Community SD	Algonac
190	145	Reed City Area Public Schools	Reed City
190	145	Richmond Community Schools	Richmond
193	144	Corunna Public SD	Corunna
193	144	Menominee Area Public Schools	Menominee
193	144	Spring Lake Public Schools	Spring Lake
196	143	Caro Community Schools	Caro
196	143	Chippewa Hills SD	Remus
196	143	Comstock Public Schools	Kalamazoo
196	143	Yale Public Schools	Yale
200	142	Delton-Kellogg SD	Delton
201	141	Gladwin Community Schools	Gladwin
201	141	Lakeville Community Schools	Otisville
203	140	Dowagiac Union SD	Dowagiac
203	140	Imlay City Community Schools	Imlay City
205	139	Chesaning Union Schools	Chesaning
206	137	Essexville-Hampton Public Schls	Essexville
206	137	Grant Public SD	Grant
206	137	Millington Community Schools	Millington
209	136	River Rouge SD	River Rouge
210	135	Manistee Area Schools	Manistee
211	134	Tawas Area Schools	Tawas City
212	133	Oscoda Area Schools	Oscoda
213	132	Cedar Springs Public Schools	Cedar Springs
213	132	Coloma Community Schools	Coloma
213	132	Kalkaska Public Schools	Kalkaska
213	132	Whitehall District Schools	Whitehall
217	131	Armada Area Schools	Armada
217	131	Hamilton Community Schools	Hamilton
219	130	Williamston Community Schools	Williamston
220	129	Goodrich Area Schools	Goodrich
220	129	Standish-Sterling Comm Schools	Standish
222	128	Ida Public SD	Ida
223	127	Willow Run Community Schools	Ypsilanti
224	126	Orchard View Schools	Muskegon
225	125	Milan Area Schools	Milan
225	125	Ovid-Elsie Area Schools	Elsie
227	123	Melvindale-N Allen Park Schools	Melvindale
228	122	Central Montcalm Public Schools	Stanton
228	122	Crawford Ausable Schools	Grayling
230	121	Houghton Lake Community Schools	Houghton Lake
231	120	Onsted Community Schools	Onsted
232	119	Clintondale Community Schools	Clinton Twp
232	119	Elk Rapids Schools	Elk Rapids
234	118	Beaverton Rural Schools	Beaverton
234	118	Bridgeport-Spaulding CSD	Bridgeport
234	118	Bullock Creek SD	Midland
234	118	Capac Community SD	Capac
238	117	Hillsdale Community Schools	Hillsdale
239	116	Shepherd Public SD	Shepherd
240	115	Columbia SD	Brooklyn
240	115	Kelloggsville Public Schools	Grand Rapids
240	115	Lakeview Comm Schools (Montcalm)	Lakeview
243	114	Edwardsburg Public Schools	Edwardsburg
243	114	Godwin Heights Public Schools	Wyoming
243	114	Mason County Central Schools	Scottville
243	114	Pennfield SD	Battle Creek
247	113	Huron SD	New Boston
247	113	Mason Consol Schools (Monroe)	Erie
247	113	Swan Valley SD	Saginaw
250	112	Birch Run Area SD	Birch Run
251	111	Benzie County Central Schools	Benzonia
251	111	Perry Public SD	Perry
253	110	Allendale Public SD	Allendale
254	108	Harrison Community Schools	Harrison
254	108	Public Schools of Calumet	Calumet
256	107	Clare Public Schools	Clare
256	107	Parchment SD	Parchment
258	106	Oakridge Public Schools	Muskegon
258	106	Stockbridge Community Schools	Stockbridge
260	104	Comstock Park Public Schools	Comstock Park
260	104	Montague Area Public Schools	Montague
262	103	Bangor Public Schls (Van Buren)	Bangor
263	102	Gerrish-Higgins SD	Roscommon
264	101	Albion Public Schools	Albion
264	101	Constantine Public SD	Constantine
266	100	Dearborn Heights SD #7	Dearborn Hgts
266	100	Durand Area Schools	Durand
268	98	Montrose Community Schools	Montrose
269	97	Brandywine Public SD	Niles
270	94	Clarenceville SD	Livonia
270	94	Napoleon Community Schools	Napoleon
272	93	Berrien Springs Public Schools	Berrien Springs
272	93	Buchanan Community Schools	Buchanan
272	93	Maple Valley Schools	Vermontville
272	93	Vassar Public Schools	Vassar
276	92	Flat Rock Community Schools	Flat Rock
277	91	Dundee Community Schools	Dundee
277	91	Gwinn Area Community Schools	Gwinn
277	91	Meridian Public Schools	Sanford
277	91	Newaygo Public SD	Newaygo
277	91	Shelby Public Schools	Shelby
282	90	Hartford Public SD	Hartford
283	89	Mt. Clemens Community SD	Mt. Clemens
284	88	Almont Community Schools	Almont
284	88	East Jackson Community Schools	Jackson
286	87	Farwell Area Schools	Farwell
286	87	Quincy Community SD	Quincy
288	86	Freeland Community SD	Freeland
288	86	Madison Public Schools (Oakland)	Madison Heights
288	86	Morley Stanwood Community Schls	Morley
291	85	Lake Fenton Community Schools	Fenton
292	81	Highland Park City Schools	Highland Park
293	80	Carrollton SD	Saginaw
294	73	Muskegon Heights SD	Muskegon Hgts
294	73	White Cloud Public Schools	White Cloud
296	70	Michigan Center SD	Michigan Center
297	69	Tri County Area Schools	Sand Lake
298	67	Westwood Community Schools	Dearborn Hgts
299	65	Bendle Public Schools	Burton
300	63	Beecher Community SD	Flint
301	46	Godfrey-Lee Public Schools	Wyoming
302	0	Public Schools of Petoskey	Petoskey
303	n/a	Saginaw ISD	Saginaw
303	n/a	Washtenaw ISD	Ann Arbor
305	n/a	Detroit Acad of Arts & Sciences	Detroit
305	n/a	Macomb ISD	Clinton Twp

High School Drop-out Rate

Rank	Percent	District Name	City
1	n/a	Adrian City SD	Adrian
1	n/a	Airport Community SD	Carleton
1	n/a	Albion Public Schools	Albion
1	n/a	Algonac Community SD	Algonac
1	n/a	Allegan Public Schools	Allegan
1	n/a	Allen Park Public Schools	Allen Park
1	n/a	Allendale Public SD	Allendale
1	n/a	Alma Public Schools	Alma
1	n/a	Almont Community Schools	Almont
1	n/a	Alpena Public Schools	Alpena
1	n/a	Anchor Bay SD	New Baltimore
1	n/a	Ann Arbor Public Schools	Ann Arbor
1	n/a	Armada Area Schools	Armada
1	n/a	Avondale SD	Auburn Hills
1	n/a	Bangor Public Schls (Van Buren)	Bangor
1	n/a	Bangor Township Schools	Bay City
1	n/a	Battle Creek Public Schools	Battle Creek
1	n/a	Bay City SD	Bay City
1	n/a	Beaverton Rural Schools	Beaverton
1	n/a	Bedford Public Schools	Temperance
1	n/a	Beecher Community SD	Flint
1	n/a	Belding Area SD	Belding
1	n/a	Bendle Public Schools	Burton
1	n/a	Benton Harbor Area Schools	Benton Harbor
1	n/a	Benzie County Central Schools	Benzonia
1	n/a	Berkley SD	Berkley
1	n/a	Berrien Springs Public Schools	Berrien Springs
1	n/a	Big Rapids Public Schools	Big Rapids
1	n/a	Birch Run Area SD	Birch Run
1	n/a	Birmingham City SD	Birmingham
1	n/a	Bloomfield Hills SD	Bloomfield Hls
1	n/a	Brandon SD	Ortonville
1	n/a	Brandywine Public SD	Niles
1	n/a	Breitung Township Schools	Kingsford
1	n/a	Bridgeport-Spaulding CSD	Bridgeport
1	n/a	Brighton Area Schools	Brighton
1	n/a	Buchanan Community Schools	Buchanan
1	n/a	Bullock Creek SD	Midland
1	n/a	Byron Center Public Schools	Byron Center
1	n/a	Cadillac Area Public Schools	Cadillac
1	n/a	Caledonia Community Schools	Caledonia
1	n/a	Capac Community SD	Capac
1	n/a	Carman-Ainsworth Comm Schools	Flint
1	n/a	Caro Community Schools	Caro
1	n/a	Carrollton SD	Saginaw
1	n/a	Cedar Springs Public Schools	Cedar Springs
1	n/a	Center Line Public Schools	Center Line
1	n/a	Central Montcalm Public Schools	Stanton
1	n/a	Charlotte Public Schools	Charlotte
1	n/a	Cheboygan Area Schools	Cheboygan
1	n/a	Chelsea SD	Chelsea
1	n/a	Chesaning Union Schools	Chesaning
1	n/a	Chippewa Hills SD	Remus
1	n/a	Chippewa Valley Schools	Clinton Twp
1	n/a	Clare Public Schools	Clare
1	n/a	Clarenceville SD	Livonia
1	n/a	Clarkston Community SD	Clarkston
1	n/a	Clintondale Community Schools	Clinton Twp
1	n/a	Clio Area SD	Clio
1	n/a	Coldwater Community Schools	Coldwater
1	n/a	Coloma Community Schools	Coloma
1	n/a	Columbia SD	Brooklyn
1	n/a	Comstock Park Public Schools	Comstock Park
1	n/a	Comstock Public Schools	Kalamazoo
1	n/a	Constantine Public SD	Constantine
1	n/a	Coopersville Public SD	Coopersville
1	n/a	Corunna Public SD	Corunna

1	n/a	Crawford Ausable Schools	Grayling
1	n/a	Crestwood SD	Dearborn Hgts
1	n/a	Croswell-Lexington Comm Schools	Croswell
1	n/a	Davison Community Schools	Davison
1	n/a	Dearborn City SD	Dearborn
1	n/a	Dearborn Heights SD #7	Dearborn Hgts
1	n/a	Delton-Kellogg SD	Delton
1	n/a	Detroit Acad of Arts & Sciences	Detroit
1	n/a	Detroit City SD	Detroit
1	n/a	Dewitt Public Schools	Dewitt
1	n/a	Dexter Community SD	Dexter
1	n/a	Dowagiac Union SD	Dowagiac
1	n/a	Dundee Community Schools	Dundee
1	n/a	Durand Area Schools	Durand
1	n/a	East China SD	East China
1	n/a	East Detroit Public Schools	Eastpointe
1	n/a	East Grand Rapids Public Schools	E Grand Rapids
1	n/a	East Jackson Community Schools	Jackson
1	n/a	East Lansing SD	East Lansing
1	n/a	Eaton Rapids Public Schools	Eaton Rapids
1	n/a	Edwardsburg Public Schools	Edwardsburg
1	n/a	Elk Rapids Schools	Elk Rapids
1	n/a	Escanaba Area Public Schools	Escanaba
1	n/a	Essexville-Hampton Public Schls	Essexville
1	n/a	Farmington Public SD	Farmington
1	n/a	Farwell Area Schools	Farwell
1	n/a	Fenton Area Public Schools	Fenton
1	n/a	Ferndale Public Schools	Ferndale
1	n/a	Fitzgerald Public Schools	Warren
1	n/a	Flat Rock Community Schools	Flat Rock
1	n/a	Flint City SD	Flint
1	n/a	Flushing Community Schools	Flushing
1	n/a	Forest Hills Public Schools	Grand Rapids
1	n/a	Fowlerville Community Schools	Fowlerville
1	n/a	Fraser Public Schools	Fraser
1	n/a	Freeland Community SD	Freeland
1	n/a	Fremont Public SD	Fremont
1	n/a	Fruitport Community Schools	Fruitport
1	n/a	Garden City SD	Garden City
1	n/a	Gaylord Community Schools	Gaylord
1	n/a	Gerrish-Higgins SD	Roscommon
1	n/a	Gibraltar SD	Woodhaven
1	n/a	Gladstone Area Schools	Gladstone
1	n/a	Gladwin Community Schools	Gladwin
1	n/a	Godfrey-Lee Public Schools	Wyoming
1	n/a	Godwin Heights Public Schools	Wyoming
1	n/a	Goodrich Area Schools	Goodrich
1	n/a	Grand Blanc Community Schools	Grand Blanc
1	n/a	Grand Haven Area Public Schools	Grand Haven
1	n/a	Grand Ledge Public Schools	Grand Ledge
1	n/a	Grand Rapids Public Schools	Grand Rapids
1	n/a	Grandville Public Schools	Grandville
1	n/a	Grant Public SD	Grant
1	n/a	Greenville Public Schools	Greenville
1	n/a	Grosse Ile Township Schools	Grosse Ile
1	n/a	Grosse Pointe Public Schools	Grosse Pointe
1	n/a	Gull Lake Community Schools	Richland
1	n/a	Gwinn Area Community Schools	Gwinn
1	n/a	Hamilton Community Schools	Hamilton
1	n/a	Hamtramck Public Schools	Hamtramck
1	n/a	Harper Creek Community Schools	Battle Creek
1	n/a	Harrison Community Schools	Harrison
1	n/a	Hartford Public SD	Hartford
1	n/a	Hartland Consolidated Schools	Hartland
1	n/a	Haslett Public Schools	Haslett
1	n/a	Hastings Area SD	Hastings
1	n/a	Hazel Park City SD	Hazel Park
1	n/a	Highland Park City Schools	Highland Park
1	n/a	Hillsdale Community Schools	Hillsdale
1	n/a	Holland City SD	Holland
1	n/a	Holly Area SD	Holly
1	n/a	Holt Public Schools	Holt
1	n/a	Houghton Lake Community Schools	Houghton Lake
1	n/a	Howell Public Schools	Howell
1	n/a	Hudsonville Public SD	Hudsonville
1	n/a	Huron SD	New Boston
1	n/a	Huron Valley Schools	Highland
1	n/a	Ida Public SD	Ida
1	n/a	Imlay City Community Schools	Imlay City
1	n/a	Ionia Public Schools	Ionia
1	n/a	Jackson Public Schools	Jackson
1	n/a	Jefferson Schools (Monroe)	Monroe
1	n/a	Jenison Public Schools	Jenison
1	n/a	Kalamazoo Public SD	Kalamazoo
1	n/a	Kalkaska Public Schools	Kalkaska
1	n/a	Kearsley Community Schools	Flint
1	n/a	Kelloggsville Public Schools	Grand Rapids
1	n/a	Kenowa Hills Public Schools	Grand Rapids
1	n/a	Kentwood Public Schools	Kentwood
1	n/a	L'anse Creuse Public Schools	Harrison Twp
1	n/a	Lake Fenton Community Schools	Fenton
1	n/a	Lake Orion Community Schools	Lake Orion
1	n/a	Lake Shore Pub Schools (Macomb)	St Clair Shores

1	n/a	Lakeshore SD (Berrien)	Stevensville
1	n/a	Lakeview Comm Schools (Montcalm)	Lakeview
1	n/a	Lakeview Public Schools (Macomb)	St Clair Shores
1	n/a	Lakeview SD (Calhoun)	Battle Creek
1	n/a	Lakeville Community Schools	Otisville
1	n/a	Lakewood Public Schools	Lake Odessa
1	n/a	Lamphere Public Schools	Madison Heights
1	n/a	Lansing Public SD	Lansing
1	n/a	Lapeer Community Schools	Lapeer
1	n/a	Lincoln Consolidated SD	Ypsilanti
1	n/a	Lincoln Park Public Schools	Lincoln Park
1	n/a	Linden Community Schools	Linden
1	n/a	Livonia Public Schools	Livonia
1	n/a	Lowell Area Schools	Lowell
1	n/a	Ludington Area SD	Ludington
1	n/a	Macomb ISD	Clinton Twp
1	n/a	Madison Public Schools (Oakland)	Madison Heights
1	n/a	Manistee Area Schools	Manistee
1	n/a	Maple Valley Schools	Vermontville
1	n/a	Marquette Area Public Schools	Marquette
1	n/a	Marshall Public Schools	Marshall
1	n/a	Marysville Public Schools	Marysville
1	n/a	Mason Consol Schools (Monroe)	Erie
1	n/a	Mason County Central Schools	Scottville
1	n/a	Mason Public Schools (Ingham)	Mason
1	n/a	Mattawan Consolidated School	Mattawan
1	n/a	Melvindale-N Allen Park Schools	Melvindale
1	n/a	Menominee Area Public Schools	Menominee
1	n/a	Meridian Public Schools	Sanford
1	n/a	Michigan Center SD	Michigan Center
1	n/a	Midland Public Schools	Midland
1	n/a	Milan Area Schools	Milan
1	n/a	Millington Community Schools	Millington
1	n/a	Mona Shores Public SD	Norton Shores
1	n/a	Monroe Public Schools	Monroe
1	n/a	Montague Area Public Schools	Montague
1	n/a	Montrose Community Schools	Montrose
1	n/a	Morley Stanwood Community Schls	Morley
1	n/a	Mt. Clemens Community SD	Mt. Clemens
1	n/a	Mt. Morris Consolidated Schools	Mt. Morris
1	n/a	Mt. Pleasant City SD	Mt. Pleasant
1	n/a	Muskegon City SD	Muskegon
1	n/a	Muskegon Heights SD	Muskegon Hgts
1	n/a	Napoleon Community Schools	Napoleon
1	n/a	Newaygo Public SD	Newaygo
1	n/a	Niles Community SD	Niles
1	n/a	North Branch Area Schools	North Branch
1	n/a	Northview Public SD	Grand Rapids
1	n/a	Northville Public Schools	Northville
1	n/a	Northwest Community Schools	Jackson
1	n/a	Novi Community SD	Novi
1	n/a	Oak Park City SD	Oak Park
1	n/a	Oakridge Public Schools	Muskegon
1	n/a	Okemos Public Schools	Okemos
1	n/a	Onsted Community Schools	Onsted
1	n/a	Orchard View Schools	Muskegon
1	n/a	Oscoda Area Schools	Oscoda
1	n/a	Otsego Public Schools	Otsego
1	n/a	Ovid-Elsie Area Schools	Elsie
1	n/a	Owosso Public Schools	Owosso
1	n/a	Oxford Area Community Schools	Oxford
1	n/a	Parchment SD	Parchment
1	n/a	Paw Paw Public SD	Paw Paw
1	n/a	Pennfield SD	Battle Creek
1	n/a	Perry Public SD	Perry
1	n/a	Pinconning Area Schools	Pinconning
1	n/a	Plainwell Community Schools	Plainwell
1	n/a	Plymouth-Canton Community Schls	Plymouth
1	n/a	Pontiac City SD	Pontiac
1	n/a	Port Huron Area SD	Port Huron
1	n/a	Portage Public Schools	Portage
1	n/a	Portland Public SD	Portland
1	n/a	Public Schools of Calumet	Calumet
1	n/a	Public Schools of Petoskey	Petoskey
1	n/a	Quincy Community SD	Quincy
1	n/a	Redford Union SD	Redford
1	n/a	Reed City Area Public Schools	Reed City
1	n/a	Reeths-Puffer Schools	Muskegon
1	n/a	Richmond Community Schools	Richmond
1	n/a	River Rouge SD	River Rouge
1	n/a	Riverview Community SD	Riverview
1	n/a	Rochester Community SD	Rochester
1	n/a	Rockford Public Schools	Rockford
1	n/a	Romeo Community Schools	Romeo
1	n/a	Romulus Community Schools	Romulus
1	n/a	Roseville Community Schools	Roseville
1	n/a	SD of Ypsilanti	Ypsilanti
1	n/a	SD of the City of Royal Oak	Royal Oak
1	n/a	Saginaw City SD	Saginaw
1	n/a	Saginaw ISD	Saginaw
1	n/a	Saginaw Twp Community Schools	Saginaw
1	n/a	Saline Area Schools	Saline

1	n/a	Sault Ste. Marie Area Schools	Sault Ste Marie
1	n/a	Shelby Public Schools	Shelby
1	n/a	Shepherd Public SD	Shepherd
1	n/a	South Haven Public Schools	South Haven
1	n/a	South Lake Schools	St Clair Shores
1	n/a	South Lyon Community Schools	South Lyon
1	n/a	South Redford SD	Redford
1	n/a	Southfield Public SD	Southfield
1	n/a	Southgate Community SD	Southgate
1	n/a	Sparta Area Schools	Sparta
1	n/a	Spring Lake Public Schools	Spring Lake
1	n/a	St. Johns Public Schools	St. Johns
1	n/a	St. Joseph Public Schools	St. Joseph
1	n/a	Standish-Sterling Comm Schools	Standish
1	n/a	Stockbridge Community Schools	Stockbridge
1	n/a	Sturgis Public Schools	Sturgis
1	n/a	Swan Valley SD	Saginaw
1	n/a	Swartz Creek Community Schools	Swartz Creek
1	n/a	Tawas Area Schools	Tawas City
1	n/a	Taylor SD	Taylor
1	n/a	Tecumseh Public Schools	Tecumseh
1	n/a	Thornapple Kellogg SD	Middleville
1	n/a	Three Rivers Community Schools	Three Rivers
1	n/a	Traverse City Area Public Schls	Traverse City
1	n/a	Trenton Public Schools	Trenton
1	n/a	Tri County Area Schools	Sand Lake
1	n/a	Troy SD	Troy
1	n/a	Utica Community Schools	Sterling Hgts
1	n/a	Van Buren Public Schools	Belleville
1	n/a	Van Dyke Public Schools	Warren
1	n/a	Vassar Public Schools	Vassar
1	n/a	Vicksburg Community Schools	Vicksburg
1	n/a	Walled Lake Consolidated Schools	Walled Lake
1	n/a	Warren Consolidated Schools	Warren
1	n/a	Warren Woods Public Schools	Warren
1	n/a	Washtenaw ISD	Ann Arbor
1	n/a	Waterford SD	Waterford
1	n/a	Waverly Community Schools	Lansing
1	n/a	Wayland Union Schools	Wayland
1	n/a	Wayne-Westland Community SD	Westland
1	n/a	West Bloomfield SD	West Bloomfield
1	n/a	W Branch-Rose City Area Schools	West Branch
1	n/a	West Ottawa Public SD	Holland
1	n/a	Western SD	Parma
1	n/a	Westwood Community Schools	Dearborn Hgts
1	n/a	White Cloud Public Schools	White Cloud
1	n/a	Whitehall District Schools	Whitehall
1	n/a	Williamston Community Schools	Williamston
1	n/a	Willow Run Community Schools	Ypsilanti
1	n/a	Woodhaven-Brownstown SD	Brownstown
1	n/a	Wyandotte City SD	Wyandotte
1	n/a	Wyoming Public Schools	Wyoming
1	n/a	Yale Public Schools	Yale
1	n/a	Zeeland Public Schools	Zeeland

Minnesota

Minnesota Public School Educational Profile

Category	Value	Category	Value
Schools *(2003-2004)*	2,552	**Diploma Recipients** *(2002-2003)*	57,431
Instructional Level		White, Non-Hispanic	51,050
Primary	1,046	Black, Non-Hispanic	2,121
Middle	291	Asian/Pacific Islander	2,573
High	699	American Indian/Alaskan Native	660
Other Level	509	Hispanic	1,027
Curriculum		**High School Drop-out Rate** (%) *(2001-2002)*	3.8
Regular	1,620	White, Non-Hispanic	2.7
Special Education	275	Black, Non-Hispanic	9.9
Vocational	12	Asian/Pacific Islander	4.4
Alternative	638	American Indian/Alaskan Native	14.2
Type		Hispanic	14.6
Magnet	62	**Staff** *(2003-2004)*	
Charter	105	Teachers	51,611.4
Title I Eligible	1,005	Average Salary[1] ($)	45,010
School-wide Title I	235	Librarians/Media Specialists	941.9
Students *(2003-2004)*	842,915	Guidance Counselors	1,063.9
Gender (%)		**Ratios** *(2003-2004)*	
Male	51.5	Student/Teacher Ratio	16.3 to 1
Female	48.5	Student/Librarian Ratio	894.9 to 1
Race/Ethnicity (%)		Student/Counselor Ratio	792.3 to 1
White, Non-Hispanic	80.2	**College Entrance Exam Scores** *(2005)*	
Black, Non-Hispanic	7.8	Scholastic Aptitude Test (SAT)	
Asian/Pacific Islander	5.4	Participation Rate (%)	11
American Indian/Alaskan Native	2.1	Mean SAT Reasoning Test Verbal Score	592
Hispanic	4.6	Mean SAT Reasoning Test Math Score	597
Classification (%)		American College Testing Program (ACT)	
Individual Education Program (IEP)	13.5	Participation Rate (%)	68
Migrant *(2002-2003)*	0.1	Average Composite Score	22.3
English Language Learner (ELL)	6.3	Average English Score	21.6
Eligible for Free Lunch Program	21.0	Average Math Score	22.1
Eligible for Reduced-Price Lunch Program	7.2	Average Reading Score	22.7
Current Spending *($ per student in FY 2003)*	7,795	Average Science Score	22.4
Instruction	5,037		
Support Services	2,415		

Note: For an explanation of data, please refer to the User's Guide in the front of the book; (1) Includes extra-duty pay

Minnesota NAEP 2005 Test Scores

Reading			Mathematics		
Grade/Category	Value	Rank	Grade/Category	Value	Rank
4th Grade			**4th Grade**		
Average Proficiency	225.2 (1.28)	7/51	Average Proficiency	245.7 (0.96)	3/51
Proficiency by Gender/Race/Ethnicity			Proficiency by Gender/Race/Ethnicity		
Male	221.2 (1.58)	10/51	Male	246.9 (1.19)	3/51
Female	229.2 (1.47)	5/51	Female	244.6 (1.13)	2/51
White, Non-Hispanic	230.5 (1.29)	11/51	White, Non-Hispanic	250.9 (1.03)	4/51
Black, Non-Hispanic	191.9 (3.83)	37/42	Black, Non-Hispanic	218.9 (2.11)	23/42
Asian, Non-Hispanic	215.9 (4.56)	24/27	Asian, Non-Hispanic	241.8 (3.18)	18/25
American Indian, Non-Hispanic	n/a	n/a	American Indian, Non-Hispanic	n/a	n/a
Hispanic	204.3 (3.64)	18/40	Hispanic	223.0 (2.37)	26/41
Proficiency by Class Size			Proficiency by Class Size		
Less than 16 Students	188.9 (7.17)	31/34	Less than 16 Students	224.8 (3.97)	18/35
16 to 18 Students	n/a	n/a	16 to 18 Students	n/a	n/a
19 to 20 Students	n/a	n/a	19 to 20 Students	n/a	n/a
21 to 25 Students	225.8 (2.51)	14/51	21 to 25 Students	245.6 (1.68)	4/51
Greater than 25 Students	229.5 (1.57)	1/36	Greater than 25 Students	247.0 (1.59)	1/33
Percent Attaining Achievement Levels			Percent Attaining Achievement Levels		
Below Basic	28.6 (1.62)	45/51	Below Basic	12.4 (0.87)	47/51
Basic or Above	71.4 (1.62)	7/51	Basic or Above	87.6 (0.87)	5/51
Proficient or Above	38.0 (1.74)	5/51	Proficient or Above	47.3 (1.72)	2/51
Advanced or Above	10.5 (0.87)	3/51	Advanced or Above	8.3 (0.77)	1/51
8th Grade			**8th Grade**		
Average Proficiency	268.4 (1.19)	9/51	Average Proficiency	290.1 (1.19)	2/51
Proficiency by Gender/Race/Ethnicity			Proficiency by Gender/Race/Ethnicity		
Male	262.9 (1.43)	9/51	Male	290.8 (1.46)	1/51
Female	274.0 (1.27)	6/51	Female	289.3 (1.28)	2/51
White, Non-Hispanic	273.1 (1.11)	7/51	White, Non-Hispanic	296.3 (1.06)	3/51
Black, Non-Hispanic	239.1 (4.05)	32/40	Black, Non-Hispanic	250.7 (1.98)	25/41
Asian, Non-Hispanic	261.6 (4.19)	20/24	Asian, Non-Hispanic	284.7 (3.90)	18/23
American Indian, Non-Hispanic	n/a	n/a	American Indian, Non-Hispanic	n/a	n/a
Hispanic	244.1 (5.12)	32/38	Hispanic	262.6 (4.07)	18/38
Proficiency by Parents Highest Level of Ed.			Proficiency by Parents Highest Level of Ed.		
Did Not Finish High School	240.0 (5.21)	36/49	Did Not Finish High School	263.4 (4.35)	19/50
Graduated High School	259.9 (2.28)	9/50	Graduated High School	274.6 (2.50)	7/50
Some Education After High School	268.4 (2.01)	17/50	Some Education After High School	290.6 (1.88)	1/50
Graduated College	276.4 (1.08)	6/50	Graduated College	300.0 (1.23)	2/50
Percent Attaining Achievement Levels			Percent Attaining Achievement Levels		
Below Basic	28.6 (1.62)	45/51	Below Basic	21.0 (1.26)	47/51
Basic or Above	71.4 (1.62)	7/51	Basic or Above	79.0 (1.26)	5/51
Proficient or Above	38.0 (1.74)	5/51	Proficient or Above	42.7 (1.57)	2/51
Advanced or Above	10.5 (0.87)	3/51	Advanced or Above	10.8 (0.91)	2/51

Note: For an explanation of data, please refer to the User's Guide in the front of the book; n/a indicates data not available

Anoka County

Anoka-Hennepin
11299 Hanson Blvd NW • Coon Rapids, MN 55433-3799
(763) 506-1000 • http://www.anoka.k12.mn.us/
Grade Span: PK-12; **Agency Type:** 1
Schools: 60
   31 Primary; 8 Middle; 14 High; 7 Other Level
   42 Regular; 4 Special Education; 1 Vocational; 13 Alternative
   0 Magnet; 0 Charter; 20 Title I Eligible; 0 School-wide Title I
Students: 41,254   (51.2% male; 48.7% female)
   Individual Education Program: 5,489 (13.3%);
   English Language Learner: 1,926 (4.7%); Migrant: 0 (0.0%)
   Eligible for Free Lunch Program: 5,319 (12.9%)
   Eligible for Reduced-Price Lunch Program: 2,595 (6.3%)
Teachers: 2,256.0 (18.3 to 1)
Librarians/Media Specialists: 30.3 (1,361.5 to 1)
Guidance Counselors: 33.9 (1,216.9 to 1)
Current Spending: ($ per student per year):
   Total: $7,159; Instruction: $4,714; Support Services: $2,089
Enrollment, Drop-out Rates and Diploma Recipients by Race/Ethnicity

Category	Total	White	Black	Asian	AIAN	Hisp.
Enrollment (%)	100.0	87.0	4.8	4.6	1.4	2.1
Drop-out Rate (%)	3.9	3.6	8.3	3.8	11.7	7.2
H.S. Diplomas (#)	2,372	2,184	36	84	39	29

Centennial
4707 N Rd • Circle Pines, MN 55014-1545
(763) 792-6000 • http://www.centennial.k12.mn.us/
Grade Span: PK-12; **Agency Type:** 1
Schools: 11
   6 Primary; 1 Middle; 2 High; 2 Other Level
   7 Regular; 1 Special Education; 0 Vocational; 3 Alternative
   0 Magnet; 0 Charter; 6 Title I Eligible; 0 School-wide Title I
Students: 7,051   (50.9% male; 49.0% female)
   Individual Education Program: 886 (12.6%);
   English Language Learner: 68 (1.0%); Migrant: 0 (0.0%)
   Eligible for Free Lunch Program: 491 (7.0%)
   Eligible for Reduced-Price Lunch Program: 236 (3.3%)
Teachers: 375.8 (18.8 to 1)
Librarians/Media Specialists: 6.0 (1,175.2 to 1)
Guidance Counselors: 11.0 (641.0 to 1)
Current Spending: ($ per student per year):
   Total: $6,848; Instruction: $4,358; Support Services: $2,173
Enrollment, Drop-out Rates and Diploma Recipients by Race/Ethnicity

Category	Total	White	Black	Asian	AIAN	Hisp.
Enrollment (%)	100.0	93.2	1.2	2.6	1.6	1.4
Drop-out Rate (%)	1.5	1.4	0.0	0.0	9.5	0.0
H.S. Diplomas (#)	340	326	1	5	3	5

Columbia Heights
1400 49th Ave NE • Columbia Heights, MN 55421-1992
(763) 528-4505 • http://www.colheights.k12.mn.us/
Grade Span: PK-12; **Agency Type:** 1
Schools: 6
   4 Primary; 1 Middle; 1 High; 0 Other Level
   5 Regular; 1 Special Education; 0 Vocational; 0 Alternative
   0 Magnet; 0 Charter; 3 Title I Eligible; 0 School-wide Title I
Students: 2,971   (49.7% male; 50.2% female)
   Individual Education Program: 352 (11.8%);
   English Language Learner: 519 (17.5%); Migrant: 0 (0.0%)
   Eligible for Free Lunch Program: 1,092 (36.8%)
   Eligible for Reduced-Price Lunch Program: 259 (8.7%)
Teachers: 182.4 (16.3 to 1)
Librarians/Media Specialists: 4.6 (645.9 to 1)
Guidance Counselors: 3.7 (803.0 to 1)
Current Spending: ($ per student per year):
   Total: $7,176; Instruction: $4,563; Support Services: $2,302
Enrollment, Drop-out Rates and Diploma Recipients by Race/Ethnicity

Category	Total	White	Black	Asian	AIAN	Hisp.
Enrollment (%)	100.0	61.9	17.7	7.0	3.3	10.1
Drop-out Rate (%)	8.9	7.3	12.8	3.8	18.8	24.4
H.S. Diplomas (#)	213	161	25	11	7	9

Fridley
6000 W Moore Lake Dr • Fridley, MN 55432-5698
(763) 502-5000 • http://www.fridley.k12.mn.us/
Grade Span: PK-12; **Agency Type:** 1
Schools: 8
   2 Primary; 2 Middle; 3 High; 1 Other Level
   4 Regular; 1 Special Education; 0 Vocational; 3 Alternative
   0 Magnet; 0 Charter; 1 Title I Eligible; 0 School-wide Title I
Students: 2,581   (51.5% male; 48.4% female)
   Individual Education Program: 328 (12.7%);
   English Language Learner: 161 (6.2%); Migrant: 0 (0.0%)

   Eligible for Free Lunch Program: 678 (26.3%)
   Eligible for Reduced-Price Lunch Program: 227 (8.8%)
Teachers: 155.1 (16.6 to 1)
Librarians/Media Specialists: 3.9 (661.8 to 1)
Guidance Counselors: 6.0 (430.2 to 1)
Current Spending: ($ per student per year):
   Total: $7,722; Instruction: $5,159; Support Services: $2,196
Enrollment, Drop-out Rates and Diploma Recipients by Race/Ethnicity

Category	Total	White	Black	Asian	AIAN	Hisp.
Enrollment (%)	100.0	73.3	13.4	7.4	2.7	3.2
Drop-out Rate (%)	5.5	5.3	1.7	2.2	25.0	5.3
H.S. Diplomas (#)	158	129	9	12	2	6

Spring Lake Park
8000 Hwy 65 NE • Spring Lake Park, MN 55432-2071
(763) 786-5570 • http://www.splkpark.k12.mn.us/mainsite/default.htm
Grade Span: PK-12; **Agency Type:** 1
Schools: 12
   5 Primary; 1 Middle; 2 High; 4 Other Level
   6 Regular; 1 Special Education; 0 Vocational; 5 Alternative
   0 Magnet; 0 Charter; 4 Title I Eligible; 0 School-wide Title I
Students: 4,319   (51.3% male; 48.6% female)
   Individual Education Program: 515 (11.9%);
   English Language Learner: 168 (3.9%); Migrant: 0 (0.0%)
   Eligible for Free Lunch Program: 563 (13.0%)
   Eligible for Reduced-Price Lunch Program: 204 (4.7%)
Teachers: 210.8 (20.5 to 1)
Librarians/Media Specialists: 4.0 (1,079.8 to 1)
Guidance Counselors: 7.0 (617.0 to 1)
Current Spending: ($ per student per year):
   Total: $6,975; Instruction: $4,343; Support Services: $2,322
Enrollment, Drop-out Rates and Diploma Recipients by Race/Ethnicity

Category	Total	White	Black	Asian	AIAN	Hisp.
Enrollment (%)	100.0	82.9	4.4	6.1	1.9	4.7
Drop-out Rate (%)	9.3	8.9	17.2	4.1	24.0	17.6
H.S. Diplomas (#)	275	252	5	13	0	5

St. Francis
4115 Ambassador Blvd • St. Francis, MN 55070-9668
(763) 753-7059 • http://www.stfrancissd.com/
Grade Span: PK-12; **Agency Type:** 1
Schools: 9
   4 Primary; 2 Middle; 2 High; 1 Other Level
   6 Regular; 2 Special Education; 0 Vocational; 1 Alternative
   0 Magnet; 0 Charter; 5 Title I Eligible; 0 School-wide Title I
Students: 5,946   (52.0% male; 47.9% female)
   Individual Education Program: 627 (10.5%);
   English Language Learner: 59 (1.0%); Migrant: 0 (0.0%)
   Eligible for Free Lunch Program: 669 (11.3%)
   Eligible for Reduced-Price Lunch Program: 348 (5.9%)
Teachers: 283.9 (20.9 to 1)
Librarians/Media Specialists: 0.0 (n/a to 1)
Guidance Counselors: 5.8 (1,025.2 to 1)
Current Spending: ($ per student per year):
   Total: $6,566; Instruction: $4,460; Support Services: $1,753
Enrollment, Drop-out Rates and Diploma Recipients by Race/Ethnicity

Category	Total	White	Black	Asian	AIAN	Hisp.
Enrollment (%)	100.0	93.8	1.4	2.0	1.5	1.3
Drop-out Rate (%)	1.3	1.3	0.0	0.0	4.8	0.0
H.S. Diplomas (#)	297	273	6	6	6	6

Becker County

Detroit Lakes
702 Lake Ave • Detroit Lakes, MN 56501-3026
Mailing Address: Box 766 702 Lake Ave • Detroit Lakes, MN 56501-3026
(218) 847-9271 • http://www.detroitlakes.com/schools/index2.html
Grade Span: PK-12; **Agency Type:** 1
Schools: 14
   3 Primary; 0 Middle; 3 High; 8 Other Level
   5 Regular; 0 Special Education; 0 Vocational; 9 Alternative
   0 Magnet; 0 Charter; 3 Title I Eligible; 1 School-wide Title I
Students: 2,784   (50.3% male; 49.6% female)
   Individual Education Program: 482 (17.3%);
   English Language Learner: 3 (0.1%); Migrant: 0 (0.0%)
   Eligible for Free Lunch Program: 671 (24.1%)
   Eligible for Reduced-Price Lunch Program: 290 (10.4%)
Teachers: 200.2 (13.9 to 1)
Librarians/Media Specialists: 2.9 (960.0 to 1)
Guidance Counselors: 5.5 (506.2 to 1)
Current Spending: ($ per student per year):
   Total: $7,423; Instruction: $4,896; Support Services: $2,220

Enrollment, Drop-out Rates and Diploma Recipients by Race/Ethnicity

Category	Total	White	Black	Asian	AIAN	Hisp.
Enrollment (%)	100.0	85.5	0.8	0.7	11.7	1.3
Drop-out Rate (%)	4.5	4.4	8.3	0.0	6.8	0.0
H.S. Diplomas (#)	213	201	0	1	9	2

Beltrami County

Bemidji
3300 Gillett Dr NW · Bemidji, MN 56601-5668
(218) 333-3110 · http://www.bemidji.k12.mn.us/
Grade Span: PK-12; **Agency Type:** 1
Schools: 17
  6 Primary; 1 Middle; 3 High; 7 Other Level
  8 Regular; 4 Special Education; 0 Vocational; 5 Alternative
  0 Magnet; 0 Charter; 8 Title I Eligible; 0 School-wide Title I
Students: 4,901 (52.6% male; 47.3% female)
  Individual Education Program: 789 (16.1%);
  English Language Learner: 4 (0.1%); Migrant: 0 (0.0%)
  Eligible for Free Lunch Program: 1,748 (36.1%)
  Eligible for Reduced-Price Lunch Program: 371 (7.7%)
Teachers: 321.5 (15.1 to 1)
Librarians/Media Specialists: 5.0 (968.0 to 1)
Guidance Counselors: 3.0 (1,613.3 to 1)
Current Spending: ($ per student per year):
  Total: $7,779; Instruction: $5,203; Support Services: $2,207

Enrollment, Drop-out Rates and Diploma Recipients by Race/Ethnicity

Category	Total	White	Black	Asian	AIAN	Hisp.
Enrollment (%)	100.0	81.1	1.2	0.9	15.8	1.0
Drop-out Rate (%)	4.3	3.0	0.0	0.0	12.7	6.3
H.S. Diplomas (#)	340	313	2	4	18	3

Red Lake
Box 99 Hwy 1 · Red Lake, MN 56671
(218) 679-3353
Grade Span: PK-12; **Agency Type:** 1
Schools: 8
  2 Primary; 2 Middle; 3 High; 1 Other Level
  5 Regular; 1 Special Education; 0 Vocational; 2 Alternative
  0 Magnet; 0 Charter; 8 Title I Eligible; 8 School-wide Title I
Students: 1,503 (51.6% male; 48.3% female)
  Individual Education Program: 247 (16.4%);
  English Language Learner: 382 (25.4%); Migrant: 0 (0.0%)
  Eligible for Free Lunch Program: 1,141 (75.9%)
  Eligible for Reduced-Price Lunch Program: 117 (7.8%)
Teachers: 161.1 (9.3 to 1)
Librarians/Media Specialists: 4.0 (375.8 to 1)
Guidance Counselors: 2.0 (751.5 to 1)
Current Spending: ($ per student per year):
  Total: $14,843; Instruction: $9,226; Support Services: $4,869

Enrollment, Drop-out Rates and Diploma Recipients by Race/Ethnicity

Category	Total	White	Black	Asian	AIAN	Hisp.
Enrollment (%)	100.0	0.0	0.0	0.0	100.0	0.0
Drop-out Rate (%)	12.1	n/a	n/a	n/a	12.1	n/a
H.S. Diplomas (#)	39	0	0	0	39	0

Benton County

Foley
840 Norman Ave N · Foley, MN 56329
Mailing Address: Box 297 · Foley, MN 56329
(320) 968-7175 · http://www.foley.k12.mn.us/
Grade Span: PK-12; **Agency Type:** 1
Schools: 3
  1 Primary; 1 Middle; 1 High; 0 Other Level
  3 Regular; 0 Special Education; 0 Vocational; 0 Alternative
  0 Magnet; 0 Charter; 2 Title I Eligible; 0 School-wide Title I
Students: 1,677 (51.0% male; 48.9% female)
  Individual Education Program: 245 (14.6%);
  English Language Learner: 1 (0.1%); Migrant: 0 (0.0%)
  Eligible for Free Lunch Program: 221 (13.2%)
  Eligible for Reduced-Price Lunch Program: 162 (9.7%)
Teachers: 104.2 (16.1 to 1)
Librarians/Media Specialists: 2.0 (838.5 to 1)
Guidance Counselors: 2.0 (838.5 to 1)
Current Spending: ($ per student per year):
  Total: $6,957; Instruction: $4,554; Support Services: $2,024

Enrollment, Drop-out Rates and Diploma Recipients by Race/Ethnicity

Category	Total	White	Black	Asian	AIAN	Hisp.
Enrollment (%)	100.0	98.0	0.8	0.3	0.5	0.4
Drop-out Rate (%)	2.4	2.4	0.0	0.0	n/a	0.0
H.S. Diplomas (#)	136	136	0	0	0	0

Sauk Rapids
1833 Osauka Rd NE · Sauk Rapids, MN 56379-1916
(320) 253-4703 · http://www.isd47.org/
Grade Span: PK-12; **Agency Type:** 1
Schools: 6
  2 Primary; 2 Middle; 1 High; 1 Other Level
  5 Regular; 0 Special Education; 0 Vocational; 1 Alternative
  0 Magnet; 0 Charter; 3 Title I Eligible; 0 School-wide Title I
Students: 3,605 (51.4% male; 48.5% female)
  Individual Education Program: 492 (13.6%);
  English Language Learner: 9 (0.2%); Migrant: 0 (0.0%)
  Eligible for Free Lunch Program: 487 (13.5%)
  Eligible for Reduced-Price Lunch Program: 334 (9.3%)
Teachers: 213.2 (16.9 to 1)
Librarians/Media Specialists: 5.0 (721.0 to 1)
Guidance Counselors: 5.0 (721.0 to 1)
Current Spending: ($ per student per year):
  Total: $6,898; Instruction: $4,211; Support Services: $2,327

Enrollment, Drop-out Rates and Diploma Recipients by Race/Ethnicity

Category	Total	White	Black	Asian	AIAN	Hisp.
Enrollment (%)	100.0	96.0	1.3	1.7	0.2	0.8
Drop-out Rate (%)	0.7	0.5	0.0	18.2	0.0	0.0
H.S. Diplomas (#)	230	224	2	2	1	1

Blue Earth County

Mankato
10 Civic Center Plaza Ste 1 · Mankato, MN 56001-8741
Mailing Address: Box 8741 10 Civic Cntr Plaza · Mankato, MN 56002-8741
(507) 387-1868 · http://www.isd77.k12.mn.us/index.php3
Grade Span: PK-12; **Agency Type:** 1
Schools: 19
  9 Primary; 3 Middle; 4 High; 3 Other Level
  14 Regular; 1 Special Education; 0 Vocational; 4 Alternative
  0 Magnet; 0 Charter; 8 Title I Eligible; 0 School-wide Title I
Students: 7,087 (51.2% male; 48.7% female)
  Individual Education Program: 1,046 (14.8%);
  English Language Learner: 232 (3.3%); Migrant: 0 (0.0%)
  Eligible for Free Lunch Program: 1,380 (19.5%)
  Eligible for Reduced-Price Lunch Program: 661 (9.3%)
Teachers: 421.9 (16.8 to 1)
Librarians/Media Specialists: 11.6 (610.9 to 1)
Guidance Counselors: 15.3 (463.2 to 1)
Current Spending: ($ per student per year):
  Total: $7,036; Instruction: $4,874; Support Services: $1,872

Enrollment, Drop-out Rates and Diploma Recipients by Race/Ethnicity

Category	Total	White	Black	Asian	AIAN	Hisp.
Enrollment (%)	100.0	88.4	5.3	2.4	0.4	3.5
Drop-out Rate (%)	3.3	3.0	5.6	5.8	0.0	10.0
H.S. Diplomas (#)	606	560	14	21	2	9

Brown County

New Ulm
400 S Payne · New Ulm, MN 56073-3296
(507) 359-8401 · http://www.newulm.k12.mn.us/
Grade Span: PK-12; **Agency Type:** 1
Schools: 5
  1 Primary; 2 Middle; 1 High; 1 Other Level
  4 Regular; 0 Special Education; 0 Vocational; 1 Alternative
  0 Magnet; 0 Charter; 2 Title I Eligible; 0 School-wide Title I
Students: 2,379 (52.3% male; 47.6% female)
  Individual Education Program: 295 (12.4%);
  English Language Learner: 16 (0.7%); Migrant: 0 (0.0%)
  Eligible for Free Lunch Program: 305 (12.8%)
  Eligible for Reduced-Price Lunch Program: 151 (6.3%)
Teachers: 157.1 (15.1 to 1)
Librarians/Media Specialists: 4.0 (594.8 to 1)
Guidance Counselors: 6.0 (396.5 to 1)
Current Spending: ($ per student per year):
  Total: $7,490; Instruction: $4,786; Support Services: $2,427

Enrollment, Drop-out Rates and Diploma Recipients by Race/Ethnicity

Category	Total	White	Black	Asian	AIAN	Hisp.
Enrollment (%)	100.0	96.3	0.7	0.8	0.3	1.8
Drop-out Rate (%)	2.3	2.2	n/a	20.0	0.0	6.7
H.S. Diplomas (#)	215	210	0	0	0	5

Carlton County

Cloquet
302 14th St · Cloquet, MN 55720-1757
(218) 879-6721 · http://www.cloquet.k12.mn.us/
Grade Span: PK-12; **Agency Type:** 1
Schools: 8
  4 Primary; 1 Middle; 2 High; 1 Other Level

4 Regular; 1 Special Education; 0 Vocational; 3 Alternative
0 Magnet; 0 Charter; 3 Title I Eligible; 0 School-wide Title I
Students: 2,348   (50.8% male; 49.1% female)
Individual Education Program: 301 (12.8%);
English Language Learner: 4 (0.2%); Migrant: 0 (0.0%)
Eligible for Free Lunch Program: 510 (21.7%)
Eligible for Reduced-Price Lunch Program: 216 (9.2%)
Teachers: 129.7 (18.1 to 1)
Librarians/Media Specialists: 2.8 (838.6 to 1)
Guidance Counselors: 5.4 (434.8 to 1)
Current Spending: ($ per student per year):
Total: $8,049; Instruction: $5,588; Support Services: $2,175
Enrollment, Drop-out Rates and Diploma Recipients by Race/Ethnicity

Category	Total	White	Black	Asian	AIAN	Hisp.
Enrollment (%)	100.0	82.4	0.8	0.9	15.1	0.8
Drop-out Rate (%)	4.9	4.4	0.0	0.0	9.3	0.0
H.S. Diplomas (#)	197	168	2	1	26	0

Carver County

Chaska
11 Peavey Rd • Chaska, MN 55318-2321
(952) 556-6100 • http://www.district112.org/
Grade Span: PK-12; **Agency Type:** 1
Schools: 12
8 Primary; 2 Middle; 1 High; 1 Other Level
11 Regular; 1 Special Education; 0 Vocational; 0 Alternative
0 Magnet; 0 Charter; 6 Title I Eligible; 0 School-wide Title I
Students: 8,036   (51.6% male; 48.3% female)
Individual Education Program: 870 (10.8%);
English Language Learner: 475 (5.9%); Migrant: 0 (0.0%)
Eligible for Free Lunch Program: 636 (7.9%)
Eligible for Reduced-Price Lunch Program: 303 (3.8%)
Teachers: 458.0 (17.5 to 1)
Librarians/Media Specialists: 9.5 (845.9 to 1)
Guidance Counselors: 14.0 (574.0 to 1)
Current Spending: ($ per student per year):
Total: $7,331; Instruction: $4,239; Support Services: $2,727
Enrollment, Drop-out Rates and Diploma Recipients by Race/Ethnicity

Category	Total	White	Black	Asian	AIAN	Hisp.
Enrollment (%)	100.0	89.1	2.2	3.1	0.2	5.5
Drop-out Rate (%)	0.9	0.7	3.3	1.8	0.0	6.3
H.S. Diplomas (#)	390	369	5	8	2	6

Waconia
24 S Walnut St • Waconia, MN 55387
(952) 442-0600 • http://www.waconia.k12.mn.us/waconia/
Grade Span: PK-12; **Agency Type:** 1
Schools: 4
2 Primary; 1 Middle; 1 High; 0 Other Level
4 Regular; 0 Special Education; 0 Vocational; 0 Alternative
0 Magnet; 0 Charter; 2 Title I Eligible; 0 School-wide Title I
Students: 2,419   (52.2% male; 47.7% female)
Individual Education Program: 307 (12.7%);
English Language Learner: 12 (0.5%); Migrant: 0 (0.0%)
Eligible for Free Lunch Program: 135 (5.6%)
Eligible for Reduced-Price Lunch Program: 73 (3.0%)
Teachers: 132.1 (18.3 to 1)
Librarians/Media Specialists: 1.7 (1,422.9 to 1)
Guidance Counselors: 3.0 (806.3 to 1)
Current Spending: ($ per student per year):
Total: $6,797; Instruction: $3,787; Support Services: $2,609
Enrollment, Drop-out Rates and Diploma Recipients by Race/Ethnicity

Category	Total	White	Black	Asian	AIAN	Hisp.
Enrollment (%)	100.0	94.4	1.6	1.6	0.5	2.0
Drop-out Rate (%)	0.0	0.0	0.0	0.0	0.0	0.0
H.S. Diplomas (#)	134	131	0	1	0	2

Chisago County

Chisago Lakes
13750 Lake Blvd • Lindstrom, MN 55045-0187
(651) 213-2096 • http://www.chisagolakes.k12.mn.us/
Grade Span: PK-12; **Agency Type:** 1
Schools: 7
3 Primary; 1 Middle; 2 High; 1 Other Level
5 Regular; 1 Special Education; 0 Vocational; 1 Alternative
0 Magnet; 0 Charter; 2 Title I Eligible; 0 School-wide Title I
Students: 3,623   (52.7% male; 47.2% female)
Individual Education Program: 347 (9.6%);
English Language Learner: 42 (1.2%); Migrant: 0 (0.0%)
Eligible for Free Lunch Program: 350 (9.7%)
Eligible for Reduced-Price Lunch Program: 200 (5.5%)
Teachers: 192.8 (18.8 to 1)
Librarians/Media Specialists: 5.0 (724.6 to 1)

Guidance Counselors: 3.7 (979.2 to 1)
Current Spending: ($ per student per year):
Total: $6,621; Instruction: $4,393; Support Services: $1,928
Enrollment, Drop-out Rates and Diploma Recipients by Race/Ethnicity

Category	Total	White	Black	Asian	AIAN	Hisp.
Enrollment (%)	100.0	95.4	1.2	1.8	0.5	1.1
Drop-out Rate (%)	1.4	1.4	0.0	0.0	0.0	11.1
H.S. Diplomas (#)	240	233	2	4	0	1

North Branch
6644 Main St • North Branch, MN 55056-0370
Mailing Address: Box 370 6644 Main St • North Branch, MN 55056-0370
(651) 674-1000 • http://www.northbranch.k12.mn.us/
Grade Span: PK-12; **Agency Type:** 1
Schools: 7
2 Primary; 1 Middle; 2 High; 2 Other Level
4 Regular; 1 Special Education; 0 Vocational; 2 Alternative
0 Magnet; 0 Charter; 2 Title I Eligible; 0 School-wide Title I
Students: 3,972   (51.0% male; 48.9% female)
Individual Education Program: 485 (12.2%);
English Language Learner: 92 (2.3%); Migrant: 17 (0.4%)
Eligible for Free Lunch Program: 501 (12.6%)
Eligible for Reduced-Price Lunch Program: 296 (7.5%)
Teachers: 202.3 (19.6 to 1)
Librarians/Media Specialists: 3.0 (1,324.0 to 1)
Guidance Counselors: 3.0 (1,324.0 to 1)
Current Spending: ($ per student per year):
Total: $6,749; Instruction: $4,183; Support Services: $2,218
Enrollment, Drop-out Rates and Diploma Recipients by Race/Ethnicity

Category	Total	White	Black	Asian	AIAN	Hisp.
Enrollment (%)	100.0	95.4	0.5	1.8	0.8	1.6
Drop-out Rate (%)	2.9	2.9	0.0	5.6	0.0	0.0
H.S. Diplomas (#)	259	248	2	6	1	2

Clay County

Moorhead
810 4th Ave S • Moorhead, MN 56560
(218) 284-3335 • http://www.moorhead.k12.mn.us/
Grade Span: PK-12; **Agency Type:** 1
Schools: 12
4 Primary; 2 Middle; 3 High; 3 Other Level
7 Regular; 1 Special Education; 0 Vocational; 4 Alternative
0 Magnet; 0 Charter; 7 Title I Eligible; 1 School-wide Title I
Students: 5,365   (52.5% male; 47.4% female)
Individual Education Program: 942 (17.6%);
English Language Learner: 356 (6.6%); Migrant: 85 (1.6%)
Eligible for Free Lunch Program: 1,234 (23.0%)
Eligible for Reduced-Price Lunch Program: 268 (5.0%)
Teachers: 345.1 (15.5 to 1)
Librarians/Media Specialists: 6.0 (894.2 to 1)
Guidance Counselors: 10.0 (536.5 to 1)
Current Spending: ($ per student per year):
Total: $7,487; Instruction: $5,244; Support Services: $1,992
Enrollment, Drop-out Rates and Diploma Recipients by Race/Ethnicity

Category	Total	White	Black	Asian	AIAN	Hisp.
Enrollment (%)	100.0	84.6	2.5	1.5	3.1	8.3
Drop-out Rate (%)	3.6	2.4	3.8	0.0	37.1	11.8
H.S. Diplomas (#)	399	366	6	4	4	19

Crow Wing County

Brainerd
300 Quince St • Brainerd, MN 56401-4095
(218) 828-5300 • http://www.brainerd.k12.mn.us/
Grade Span: PK-12; **Agency Type:** 1
Schools: 19
9 Primary; 2 Middle; 1 High; 6 Other Level
12 Regular; 1 Special Education; 0 Vocational; 5 Alternative
1 Magnet; 0 Charter; 7 Title I Eligible; 0 School-wide Title I
Students: 7,258   (51.4% male; 48.5% female)
Individual Education Program: 1,080 (14.9%);
English Language Learner: 0 (0.0%); Migrant: 0 (0.0%)
Eligible for Free Lunch Program: 1,647 (22.7%)
Eligible for Reduced-Price Lunch Program: 748 (10.3%)
Teachers: 433.3 (16.8 to 1)
Librarians/Media Specialists: 11.0 (659.8 to 1)
Guidance Counselors: 8.0 (907.3 to 1)
Current Spending: ($ per student per year):
Total: $8,004; Instruction: $5,332; Support Services: $2,301
Enrollment, Drop-out Rates and Diploma Recipients by Race/Ethnicity

Category	Total	White	Black	Asian	AIAN	Hisp.
Enrollment (%)	100.0	96.3	1.2	0.6	1.4	0.5
Drop-out Rate (%)	6.8	6.2	17.6	5.6	32.4	20.0
H.S. Diplomas (#)	498	485	0	3	2	8

Dakota County

Burnsville
100 River Ridge Court • Burnsville, MN 55337-1613
Mailing Address: 100 River Ridge Ct. • Burnsville, MN 55337-1613
(952) 707-2000 • http://www.rschooltoday.com/
Grade Span: PK-12; **Agency Type:** 1
Schools: 24
　13 Primary; 4 Middle; 4 High; 3 Other Level
　14 Regular; 3 Special Education; 0 Vocational; 7 Alternative
　0 Magnet; 0 Charter; 9 Title I Eligible; 0 School-wide Title I
Students: 11,220　(51.8% male; 48.1% female)
　Individual Education Program: 1,428 (12.7%);
　English Language Learner: 788 (7.0%); Migrant: 0 (0.0%)
　Eligible for Free Lunch Program: 1,332 (11.9%)
　Eligible for Reduced-Price Lunch Program: 605 (5.4%)
Teachers: 698.1 (16.1 to 1)
Librarians/Media Specialists: 9.5 (1,181.1 to 1)
Guidance Counselors: 10.8 (1,038.9 to 1)
Current Spending: ($ per student per year):
　Total: $7,762; Instruction: $5,103; Support Services: $2,337
Enrollment, Drop-out Rates and Diploma Recipients by Race/Ethnicity

Category	Total	White	Black	Asian	AIAN	Hisp.
Enrollment (%)	100.0	76.1	11.5	7.5	0.6	4.3
Drop-out Rate (%)	3.2	2.6	6.6	3.6	25.0	7.7
H.S. Diplomas (#)	751	641	41	56	1	12

Farmington
510 Walnut St • Farmington, MN 55024-1284
(651) 463-5011 • http://www.farmington.k12.mn.us/
Grade Span: PK-12; **Agency Type:** 1
Schools: 9
　4 Primary; 1 Middle; 2 High; 2 Other Level
　7 Regular; 0 Special Education; 0 Vocational; 2 Alternative
　0 Magnet; 0 Charter; 4 Title I Eligible; 0 School-wide Title I
Students: 5,451　(51.8% male; 48.1% female)
　Individual Education Program: 688 (12.6%);
　English Language Learner: 116 (2.1%); Migrant: 0 (0.0%)
　Eligible for Free Lunch Program: 286 (5.2%)
　Eligible for Reduced-Price Lunch Program: 197 (3.6%)
Teachers: 308.5 (17.7 to 1)
Librarians/Media Specialists: 6.0 (908.5 to 1)
Guidance Counselors: 7.5 (726.8 to 1)
Current Spending: ($ per student per year):
　Total: $6,579; Instruction: $3,804; Support Services: $2,460
Enrollment, Drop-out Rates and Diploma Recipients by Race/Ethnicity

Category	Total	White	Black	Asian	AIAN	Hisp.
Enrollment (%)	100.0	93.7	1.5	2.5	0.2	2.1
Drop-out Rate (%)	2.6	2.3	16.7	8.7	100.0	0.0
H.S. Diplomas (#)	283	271	4	6	0	2

Hastings
1000 W 10th St • Hastings, MN 55033-2597
Mailing Address: 1000 11th St W • Hastings, MN 55033-2597
(651) 437-6111 • http://www.hastings.k12.mn.us/
Grade Span: PK-12; **Agency Type:** 1
Schools: 11
　6 Primary; 1 Middle; 3 High; 1 Other Level
　6 Regular; 1 Special Education; 0 Vocational; 4 Alternative
　0 Magnet; 0 Charter; 4 Title I Eligible; 0 School-wide Title I
Students: 5,146　(52.1% male; 47.8% female)
　Individual Education Program: 648 (12.6%);
　English Language Learner: 25 (0.5%); Migrant: 0 (0.0%)
　Eligible for Free Lunch Program: 468 (9.1%)
　Eligible for Reduced-Price Lunch Program: 231 (4.5%)
Teachers: 253.7 (20.3 to 1)
Librarians/Media Specialists: 5.0 (1,029.2 to 1)
Guidance Counselors: 7.0 (735.1 to 1)
Current Spending: ($ per student per year):
　Total: $6,935; Instruction: $4,313; Support Services: $2,276
Enrollment, Drop-out Rates and Diploma Recipients by Race/Ethnicity

Category	Total	White	Black	Asian	AIAN	Hisp.
Enrollment (%)	100.0	93.5	1.7	1.3	1.3	2.2
Drop-out Rate (%)	1.2	1.1	9.1	0.0	0.0	9.7
H.S. Diplomas (#)	431	419	2	4	1	5

Inver Grove Heights Schools
2990 80th St E • Inver Grove Heights, MN 55076-3235
(651) 306-7825 • http://www.invergrove.k12.mn.us/
Grade Span: PK-12; **Agency Type:** 1
Schools: 9
　6 Primary; 1 Middle; 2 High; 0 Other Level
　7 Regular; 1 Special Education; 0 Vocational; 1 Alternative
　0 Magnet; 0 Charter; 4 Title I Eligible; 0 School-wide Title I
Students: 3,878　(51.2% male; 48.7% female)

　Individual Education Program: 592 (15.3%);
　English Language Learner: 133 (3.4%); Migrant: 0 (0.0%)
　Eligible for Free Lunch Program: 542 (14.0%)
　Eligible for Reduced-Price Lunch Program: 233 (6.0%)
Teachers: 219.1 (17.7 to 1)
Librarians/Media Specialists: 6.0 (646.3 to 1)
Guidance Counselors: 5.0 (775.6 to 1)
Current Spending: ($ per student per year):
　Total: $7,482; Instruction: $4,855; Support Services: $2,251
Enrollment, Drop-out Rates and Diploma Recipients by Race/Ethnicity

Category	Total	White	Black	Asian	AIAN	Hisp.
Enrollment (%)	100.0	84.5	4.8	3.3	0.8	6.7
Drop-out Rate (%)	1.7	1.6	5.0	0.0	0.0	2.9
H.S. Diplomas (#)	265	242	6	6	0	11

Lakeville
8670 210th St W • Lakeville, MN 55044-8501
(952) 469-7100 • http://www.isd194.k12.mn.us/
Grade Span: PK-12; **Agency Type:** 1
Schools: 16
　10 Primary; 3 Middle; 2 High; 1 Other Level
　13 Regular; 1 Special Education; 0 Vocational; 2 Alternative
　0 Magnet; 0 Charter; 5 Title I Eligible; 0 School-wide Title I
Students: 10,512　(50.9% male; 49.0% female)
　Individual Education Program: 1,186 (11.3%);
　English Language Learner: 146 (1.4%); Migrant: 0 (0.0%)
　Eligible for Free Lunch Program: 367 (3.5%)
　Eligible for Reduced-Price Lunch Program: 183 (1.7%)
Teachers: 599.2 (17.5 to 1)
Librarians/Media Specialists: 13.0 (808.6 to 1)
Guidance Counselors: 9.0 (1,168.0 to 1)
Current Spending: ($ per student per year):
　Total: $6,820; Instruction: $4,262; Support Services: $2,234
Enrollment, Drop-out Rates and Diploma Recipients by Race/Ethnicity

Category	Total	White	Black	Asian	AIAN	Hisp.
Enrollment (%)	100.0	94.5	1.8	1.8	0.3	1.6
Drop-out Rate (%)	2.2	2.2	0.0	1.8	0.0	15.4
H.S. Diplomas (#)	655	628	5	15	0	7

Rosemount-Apple Valley-Eagan
14445 Diamond Path • Rosemount, MN 55068-4199
Mailing Address: 14445 Diamond Path W • Rosemount, MN 55068-4199
(651) 423-7700 • http://www.isd196.k12.mn.us/
Grade Span: PK-12; **Agency Type:** 1
Schools: 37
　19 Primary; 6 Middle; 9 High; 3 Other Level
　29 Regular; 4 Special Education; 0 Vocational; 4 Alternative
　0 Magnet; 0 Charter; 9 Title I Eligible; 0 School-wide Title I
Students: 28,561　(51.1% male; 48.8% female)
　Individual Education Program: 4,106 (14.4%);
　English Language Learner: 1,022 (3.6%); Migrant: 0 (0.0%)
　Eligible for Free Lunch Program: 1,887 (6.6%)
　Eligible for Reduced-Price Lunch Program: 733 (2.6%)
Teachers: 1,749.6 (16.3 to 1)
Librarians/Media Specialists: 28.0 (1,020.0 to 1)
Guidance Counselors: 30.1 (948.9 to 1)
Current Spending: ($ per student per year):
　Total: $7,271; Instruction: $5,062; Support Services: $1,931
Enrollment, Drop-out Rates and Diploma Recipients by Race/Ethnicity

Category	Total	White	Black	Asian	AIAN	Hisp.
Enrollment (%)	100.0	85.0	5.8	5.7	0.6	3.0
Drop-out Rate (%)	1.9	1.7	4.6	1.8	10.5	3.3
H.S. Diplomas (#)	1,865	1,684	48	97	7	29

South St. Paul
104 5th Ave S • South St. Paul, MN 55075-2332
(651) 457-9400
Grade Span: PK-12; **Agency Type:** 1
Schools: 7
　2 Primary; 0 Middle; 2 High; 3 Other Level
　3 Regular; 0 Special Education; 0 Vocational; 4 Alternative
　0 Magnet; 0 Charter; 4 Title I Eligible; 0 School-wide Title I
Students: 3,369　(51.7% male; 48.2% female)
　Individual Education Program: 435 (12.9%);
　English Language Learner: 175 (5.2%); Migrant: 0 (0.0%)
　Eligible for Free Lunch Program: 663 (19.7%)
　Eligible for Reduced-Price Lunch Program: 284 (8.4%)
Teachers: 179.9 (18.7 to 1)
Librarians/Media Specialists: 2.0 (1,684.5 to 1)
Guidance Counselors: 0.0 (n/a to 1)
Current Spending: ($ per student per year):
　Total: $7,138; Instruction: $4,658; Support Services: $2,126

Enrollment, Drop-out Rates and Diploma Recipients by Race/Ethnicity

Category	Total	White	Black	Asian	AIAN	Hisp.
Enrollment (%)	100.0	82.7	4.2	1.3	0.9	10.9
Drop-out Rate (%)	7.3	6.2	8.7	16.7	33.3	19.2
H.S. Diplomas (#)	263	250	3	4	0	6

West St. Paul-Mendota Hts.-Eagan
1897 Delaware • Mendota Heights, MN 55118-4338
Mailing Address: 1897 Delaware Ave • Mendota Heights, MN 55118-4338
(651) 681-2396 •
http://rschooltoday.com/se3bin/clientschool.cgi?schoolname=school157
Grade Span: PK-12; **Agency Type:** 1
Schools: 10
   6 Primary; 2 Middle; 1 High; 1 Other Level
   8 Regular; 1 Special Education; 0 Vocational; 1 Alternative
   0 Magnet; 0 Charter; 4 Title I Eligible; 0 School-wide Title I
Students: 4,789   (51.4% male; 48.5% female)
   Individual Education Program: 765 (16.0%);
   English Language Learner: 342 (7.1%); Migrant: 0 (0.0%)
   Eligible for Free Lunch Program: 809 (16.9%)
   Eligible for Reduced-Price Lunch Program: 357 (7.5%)
Teachers: 273.2 (17.5 to 1)
Librarians/Media Specialists: 6.6 (725.6 to 1)
Guidance Counselors: 9.5 (504.1 to 1)
Current Spending: ($ per student per year):
   Total: $8,073; Instruction: $5,142; Support Services: $2,553
Enrollment, Drop-out Rates and Diploma Recipients by Race/Ethnicity

Category	Total	White	Black	Asian	AIAN	Hisp.
Enrollment (%)	100.0	73.6	7.4	4.9	0.8	13.3
Drop-out Rate (%)	1.8	1.5	1.9	5.2	0.0	3.7
H.S. Diplomas (#)	315	270	9	15	1	20

Dodge County

Kasson-Mantorville
101 16th St NE • Kasson, MN 55944-1610
(507) 634-1100 • http://komets.k12.mn.us/
Grade Span: PK-12; **Agency Type:** 1
Schools: 5
   1 Primary; 2 Middle; 2 High; 0 Other Level
   4 Regular; 0 Special Education; 0 Vocational; 1 Alternative
   0 Magnet; 0 Charter; 1 Title I Eligible; 0 School-wide Title I
Students: 1,895   (51.2% male; 48.7% female)
   Individual Education Program: 140 (7.4%);
   English Language Learner: 14 (0.7%); Migrant: 0 (0.0%)
   Eligible for Free Lunch Program: 147 (7.8%)
   Eligible for Reduced-Price Lunch Program: 70 (3.7%)
Teachers: 110.1 (17.2 to 1)
Librarians/Media Specialists: 2.0 (947.5 to 1)
Guidance Counselors: 4.0 (473.8 to 1)
Current Spending: ($ per student per year):
   Total: $6,294; Instruction: $4,011; Support Services: $1,966
Enrollment, Drop-out Rates and Diploma Recipients by Race/Ethnicity

Category	Total	White	Black	Asian	AIAN	Hisp.
Enrollment (%)	100.0	96.1	0.5	0.9	0.4	2.2
Drop-out Rate (%)	2.2	1.9	33.3	0.0	n/a	12.5
H.S. Diplomas (#)	98	95	1	0	0	2

Douglas County

Alexandria
14th & Jefferson St • Alexandria, MN 56308-0308
Mailing Address: Box 308 • Alexandria, MN 56308-0308
(320) 762-2141 • http://www.alexandria.k12.mn.us/
Grade Span: PK-12; **Agency Type:** 1
Schools: 8
   6 Primary; 1 Middle; 1 High; 0 Other Level
   8 Regular; 0 Special Education; 0 Vocational; 0 Alternative
   1 Magnet; 0 Charter; 5 Title I Eligible; 0 School-wide Title I
Students: 4,153   (51.6% male; 48.3% female)
   Individual Education Program: 644 (15.5%);
   English Language Learner: 11 (0.3%); Migrant: 0 (0.0%)
   Eligible for Free Lunch Program: 549 (13.2%)
   Eligible for Reduced-Price Lunch Program: 399 (9.6%)
Teachers: 255.0 (16.3 to 1)
Librarians/Media Specialists: 5.9 (703.9 to 1)
Guidance Counselors: 5.0 (830.6 to 1)
Current Spending: ($ per student per year):
   Total: $7,077; Instruction: $4,721; Support Services: $2,008
Enrollment, Drop-out Rates and Diploma Recipients by Race/Ethnicity

Category	Total	White	Black	Asian	AIAN	Hisp.
Enrollment (%)	100.0	97.2	1.0	0.7	0.2	0.8
Drop-out Rate (%)	0.8	0.8	16.7	0.0	0.0	0.0
H.S. Diplomas (#)	335	330	0	4	0	1

Freeborn County

Albert Lea
211 W Richway Dr • Albert Lea, MN 56007-2477
(507) 379-4800 • http://albertlea.k12.mn.us/
Grade Span: PK-12; **Agency Type:** 1
Schools: 8
   4 Primary; 1 Middle; 2 High; 1 Other Level
   6 Regular; 0 Special Education; 0 Vocational; 2 Alternative
   0 Magnet; 0 Charter; 5 Title I Eligible; 0 School-wide Title I
Students: 3,644   (50.3% male; 49.6% female)
   Individual Education Program: 653 (17.9%);
   English Language Learner: 203 (5.6%); Migrant: 0 (0.0%)
   Eligible for Free Lunch Program: 883 (24.2%)
   Eligible for Reduced-Price Lunch Program: 380 (10.4%)
Teachers: 223.7 (16.3 to 1)
Librarians/Media Specialists: 3.5 (1,041.1 to 1)
Guidance Counselors: 4.0 (911.0 to 1)
Current Spending: ($ per student per year):
   Total: $7,278; Instruction: $4,828; Support Services: $2,107
Enrollment, Drop-out Rates and Diploma Recipients by Race/Ethnicity

Category	Total	White	Black	Asian	AIAN	Hisp.
Enrollment (%)	100.0	85.3	1.0	1.2	0.2	12.3
Drop-out Rate (%)	2.8	2.4	0.0	0.0	n/a	8.6
H.S. Diplomas (#)	275	255	0	4	0	16

Goodhue County

Red Wing
2451 Eagle Ridge Dr • Red Wing, MN 55066-7444
(651) 385-4500 • http://www.redwing.k12.mn.us/
Grade Span: PK-12; **Agency Type:** 1
Schools: 9
   3 Primary; 1 Middle; 3 High; 2 Other Level
   4 Regular; 1 Special Education; 0 Vocational; 4 Alternative
   0 Magnet; 0 Charter; 2 Title I Eligible; 0 School-wide Title I
Students: 3,011   (50.1% male; 49.8% female)
   Individual Education Program: 391 (13.0%);
   English Language Learner: 39 (1.3%); Migrant: 0 (0.0%)
   Eligible for Free Lunch Program: 449 (14.9%)
   Eligible for Reduced-Price Lunch Program: 134 (4.5%)
Teachers: 156.0 (19.3 to 1)
Librarians/Media Specialists: 3.0 (1,003.7 to 1)
Guidance Counselors: 0.0 (n/a to 1)
Current Spending: ($ per student per year):
   Total: $7,622; Instruction: $4,888; Support Services: $2,363
Enrollment, Drop-out Rates and Diploma Recipients by Race/Ethnicity

Category	Total	White	Black	Asian	AIAN	Hisp.
Enrollment (%)	100.0	88.9	3.2	1.8	3.5	2.7
Drop-out Rate (%)	5.1	4.8	0.0	0.0	20.0	14.3
H.S. Diplomas (#)	263	254	4	2	2	1

Hennepin County

Bloomington
1350 W 106th St • Bloomington, MN 55431
(952) 681-6400 • http://www.bloomington.k12.mn.us/
Grade Span: PK-12; **Agency Type:** 1
Schools: 16
   10 Primary; 3 Middle; 2 High; 1 Other Level
   15 Regular; 1 Special Education; 0 Vocational; 0 Alternative
   0 Magnet; 0 Charter; 3 Title I Eligible; 1 School-wide Title I
Students: 10,653   (51.8% male; 48.1% female)
   Individual Education Program: 1,279 (12.0%);
   English Language Learner: 720 (6.8%); Migrant: 0 (0.0%)
   Eligible for Free Lunch Program: 1,808 (17.0%)
   Eligible for Reduced-Price Lunch Program: 815 (7.7%)
Teachers: 589.8 (18.1 to 1)
Librarians/Media Specialists: 16.4 (649.6 to 1)
Guidance Counselors: 16.0 (665.8 to 1)
Current Spending: ($ per student per year):
   Total: $7,962; Instruction: $4,826; Support Services: $2,775
Enrollment, Drop-out Rates and Diploma Recipients by Race/Ethnicity

Category	Total	White	Black	Asian	AIAN	Hisp.
Enrollment (%)	100.0	71.7	11.6	8.8	1.0	7.0
Drop-out Rate (%)	1.1	0.8	3.3	1.7	0.0	3.3
H.S. Diplomas (#)	662	568	18	60	4	12

Brooklyn Center
6500 Humboldt Ave N • Brooklyn Center, MN 55430-1897
(763) 561-2120
Grade Span: PK-12; **Agency Type:** 1
Schools: 2
   1 Primary; 0 Middle; 1 High; 0 Other Level
   2 Regular; 0 Special Education; 0 Vocational; 0 Alternative

0 Magnet; 0 Charter; 1 Title I Eligible; 1 School-wide Title I
Students: 1,732 (53.1% male; 46.8% female)
Individual Education Program: 188 (10.9%);
English Language Learner: 511 (29.5%); Migrant: 0 (0.0%)
Eligible for Free Lunch Program: 778 (44.9%)
Eligible for Reduced-Price Lunch Program: 270 (15.6%)
Teachers: 102.4 (16.9 to 1)
Librarians/Media Specialists: 2.0 (866.0 to 1)
Guidance Counselors: 1.0 (1,732.0 to 1)
Current Spending: ($ per student per year):
Total: $8,512; Instruction: $5,140; Support Services: $2,934

Enrollment, Drop-out Rates and Diploma Recipients by Race/Ethnicity

Category	Total	White	Black	Asian	AIAN	Hisp.
Enrollment (%)	100.0	38.1	34.7	18.6	1.4	7.2
Drop-out Rate (%)	4.9	4.4	6.7	1.9	16.7	7.1
H.S. Diplomas (#)	121	55	35	27	0	4

Eden Prairie

8100 School Rd • Eden Prairie, MN 55344-2292
(952) 975-7000 • http://www.edenpr.k12.mn.us/
Grade Span: PK-12; **Agency Type:** 1
Schools: 11
6 Primary; 2 Middle; 1 High; 2 Other Level
8 Regular; 2 Special Education; 0 Vocational; 1 Alternative
0 Magnet; 0 Charter; 3 Title I Eligible; 0 School-wide Title I
Students: 10,326 (51.8% male; 48.1% female)
Individual Education Program: 1,063 (10.3%);
English Language Learner: 405 (3.9%); Migrant: 0 (0.0%)
Eligible for Free Lunch Program: 613 (5.9%)
Eligible for Reduced-Price Lunch Program: 199 (1.9%)
Teachers: 546.0 (18.9 to 1)
Librarians/Media Specialists: 8.0 (1,290.8 to 1)
Guidance Counselors: 11.8 (875.1 to 1)
Current Spending: ($ per student per year):
Total: $6,993; Instruction: $4,150; Support Services: $2,473

Enrollment, Drop-out Rates and Diploma Recipients by Race/Ethnicity

Category	Total	White	Black	Asian	AIAN	Hisp.
Enrollment (%)	100.0	86.1	5.5	6.2	1.0	1.3
Drop-out Rate (%)	0.6	0.3	3.6	0.0	9.1	12.2
H.S. Diplomas (#)	706	651	19	27	4	5

Edina

5701 Normandale Rd • Edina, MN 55435
(952) 848-3900 • http://www.edina.k12.mn.us/
Grade Span: PK-12; **Agency Type:** 1
Schools: 11
7 Primary; 2 Middle; 1 High; 1 Other Level
9 Regular; 2 Special Education; 0 Vocational; 0 Alternative
0 Magnet; 0 Charter; 4 Title I Eligible; 0 School-wide Title I
Students: 7,313 (50.4% male; 49.5% female)
Individual Education Program: 768 (10.5%);
English Language Learner: 166 (2.3%); Migrant: 0 (0.0%)
Eligible for Free Lunch Program: 281 (3.8%)
Eligible for Reduced-Price Lunch Program: 133 (1.8%)
Teachers: 414.2 (17.7 to 1)
Librarians/Media Specialists: 9.0 (812.6 to 1)
Guidance Counselors: 9.0 (812.6 to 1)
Current Spending: ($ per student per year):
Total: $7,986; Instruction: $4,985; Support Services: $2,664

Enrollment, Drop-out Rates and Diploma Recipients by Race/Ethnicity

Category	Total	White	Black	Asian	AIAN	Hisp.
Enrollment (%)	100.0	89.7	3.6	4.8	0.2	1.7
Drop-out Rate (%)	0.0	0.1	0.0	0.0	n/a	0.0
H.S. Diplomas (#)	499	469	4	21	1	4

Hopkins

1001 State Hwy 7 • Hopkins, MN 55343
Mailing Address: 1001 Hwy 7 • Hopkins, MN 55305-7294
(952) 988-4000 • http://www.hopkins.k12.mn.us/
Grade Span: PK-12; **Agency Type:** 1
Schools: 17
8 Primary; 2 Middle; 6 High; 1 Other Level
10 Regular; 1 Special Education; 0 Vocational; 6 Alternative
0 Magnet; 0 Charter; 7 Title I Eligible; 1 School-wide Title I
Students: 8,320 (52.3% male; 47.6% female)
Individual Education Program: 1,029 (12.4%);
English Language Learner: 529 (6.4%); Migrant: 0 (0.0%)
Eligible for Free Lunch Program: 1,073 (12.9%)
Eligible for Reduced-Price Lunch Program: 276 (3.3%)
Teachers: 503.8 (16.5 to 1)
Librarians/Media Specialists: 10.6 (784.9 to 1)
Guidance Counselors: 17.0 (489.4 to 1)
Current Spending: ($ per student per year):
Total: $9,359; Instruction: $5,622; Support Services: $3,356

Enrollment, Drop-out Rates and Diploma Recipients by Race/Ethnicity

Category	Total	White	Black	Asian	AIAN	Hisp.
Enrollment (%)	100.0	79.7	11.6	3.6	0.6	4.5
Drop-out Rate (%)	0.7	0.5	1.6	0.0	3.0	5.2
H.S. Diplomas (#)	656	580	33	28	3	12

Intermediate SD 287

1820 N Xenium Ln • Plymouth, MN 55441-3790
(763) 559-3535 • http://www.int287.k12.mn.us/
Grade Span: PK-12; **Agency Type:** 4
Schools: 180
3 Primary; 4 Middle; 48 High; 125 Other Level
0 Regular; 32 Special Education; 2 Vocational; 146 Alternative
0 Magnet; 0 Charter; 0 Title I Eligible; 0 School-wide Title I
Students: 2,026 (57.7% male; 42.2% female)
Individual Education Program: 709 (35.0%);
English Language Learner: 22 (1.1%); Migrant: 0 (0.0%)
Eligible for Free Lunch Program: 213 (10.5%)
Eligible for Reduced-Price Lunch Program: 44 (2.2%)
Teachers: 238.1 (8.5 to 1)
Librarians/Media Specialists: 0.0 (n/a to 1)
Guidance Counselors: 2.0 (1,013.0 to 1)
Current Spending: ($ per student per year):
Total: n/a; Instruction: n/a; Support Services: n/a

Enrollment, Drop-out Rates and Diploma Recipients by Race/Ethnicity

Category	Total	White	Black	Asian	AIAN	Hisp.
Enrollment (%)	100.0	69.4	19.2	6.5	1.5	3.4
Drop-out Rate (%)	13.9	12.1	23.1	16.8	18.2	19.7
H.S. Diplomas (#)	132	113	11	7	0	1

Minneapolis

807 NE Broadway • Minneapolis, MN 55413-2398
Mailing Address: 807 NE Broadway • Minneapolis, MN 55413-2398
(612) 668-0200 • http://www.mpls.k12.mn.us/
Grade Span: PK-12; **Agency Type:** 1
Schools: 142
73 Primary; 13 Middle; 37 High; 19 Other Level
80 Regular; 10 Special Education; 0 Vocational; 52 Alternative
19 Magnet; 0 Charter; 72 Title I Eligible; 72 School-wide Title I
Students: 43,397 (51.4% male; 48.5% female)
Individual Education Program: 6,191 (14.3%);
English Language Learner: 9,839 (22.7%); Migrant: 9 (<0.1%)
Eligible for Free Lunch Program: 25,937 (59.8%)
Eligible for Reduced-Price Lunch Program: 3,469 (8.0%)
Teachers: 3,024.7 (14.3 to 1)
Librarians/Media Specialists: 70.7 (613.8 to 1)
Guidance Counselors: 42.1 (1,030.8 to 1)
Current Spending: ($ per student per year):
Total: $11,304; Instruction: $7,451; Support Services: $3,510

Enrollment, Drop-out Rates and Diploma Recipients by Race/Ethnicity

Category	Total	White	Black	Asian	AIAN	Hisp.
Enrollment (%)	100.0	27.1	42.1	13.1	4.2	13.5
Drop-out Rate (%)	12.5	6.9	12.9	7.0	21.7	32.0
H.S. Diplomas (#)	2,180	835	842	350	48	105

Minnetonka

5621 Hwy 101 • Minnetonka, MN 55345-4214
(952) 401-5000 • http://www.minnetonka.k12.mn.us/
Grade Span: PK-12; **Agency Type:** 1
Schools: 11
7 Primary; 3 Middle; 1 High; 0 Other Level
9 Regular; 0 Special Education; 0 Vocational; 2 Alternative
0 Magnet; 0 Charter; 0 Title I Eligible; 0 School-wide Title I
Students: 7,646 (50.8% male; 49.1% female)
Individual Education Program: 908 (11.9%);
English Language Learner: 117 (1.5%); Migrant: 0 (0.0%)
Eligible for Free Lunch Program: 166 (2.2%)
Eligible for Reduced-Price Lunch Program: 76 (1.0%)
Teachers: 458.3 (16.7 to 1)
Librarians/Media Specialists: 9.0 (849.6 to 1)
Guidance Counselors: 10.0 (764.6 to 1)
Current Spending: ($ per student per year):
Total: $7,957; Instruction: $5,072; Support Services: $2,501

Enrollment, Drop-out Rates and Diploma Recipients by Race/Ethnicity

Category	Total	White	Black	Asian	AIAN	Hisp.
Enrollment (%)	100.0	92.3	1.9	3.6	0.5	1.8
Drop-out Rate (%)	0.5	0.5	0.0	0.0	0.0	0.0
H.S. Diplomas (#)	492	472	4	8	1	7

Orono

685 Old Crystal Bay Rd • Long Lake, MN 55356-0046
Mailing Address: Box 46 685 Old Crystal Bay Rd • Long Lake, MN
55356-0046
(952) 449-8300 • http://www.orono.k12.mn.us/
Grade Span: PK-12; Agency Type: 1
Schools: 5
   3 Primary; 1 Middle; 1 High; 0 Other Level
   4 Regular; 0 Special Education; 0 Vocational; 1 Alternative
   0 Magnet; 0 Charter; 1 Title I Eligible; 0 School-wide Title I
Students: 2,532 (50.2% male; 49.7% female)
   Individual Education Program: 249 (9.8%);
   English Language Learner: 15 (0.6%); Migrant: 0 (0.0%)
   Eligible for Free Lunch Program: 66 (2.6%)
   Eligible for Reduced-Price Lunch Program: 43 (1.7%)
Teachers: 137.6 (18.4 to 1)
Librarians/Media Specialists: 2.6 (973.8 to 1)
Guidance Counselors: 3.5 (723.4 to 1)
Current Spending: ($ per student per year):
   Total: $7,594; Instruction: $4,839; Support Services: $2,352
Enrollment, Drop-out Rates and Diploma Recipients by Race/Ethnicity

Category	Total	White	Black	Asian	AIAN	Hisp.
Enrollment (%)	100.0	95.0	0.8	2.1	0.4	1.8
Drop-out Rate (%)	0.3	0.4	0.0	0.0	0.0	0.0
H.S. Diplomas (#)	185	174	0	7	1	3

Osseo

11200 93rd Ave N • Osseo, MN 55369-6605
(763) 391-7000 • http://www.osseo.k12.mn.us/
Grade Span: PK-12; Agency Type: 1
Schools: 31
   20 Primary; 4 Middle; 4 High; 3 Other Level
   26 Regular; 2 Special Education; 0 Vocational; 3 Alternative
   0 Magnet; 0 Charter; 6 Title I Eligible; 1 School-wide Title I
Students: 21,698 (51.4% male; 48.5% female)
   Individual Education Program: 2,487 (11.5%);
   English Language Learner: 1,925 (8.9%); Migrant: 0 (0.0%)
   Eligible for Free Lunch Program: 3,890 (17.9%)
   Eligible for Reduced-Price Lunch Program: 1,362 (6.3%)
Teachers: 997.5 (21.8 to 1)
Librarians/Media Specialists: 27.8 (780.5 to 1)
Guidance Counselors: 31.9 (680.2 to 1)
Current Spending: ($ per student per year):
   Total: $7,522; Instruction: $5,047; Support Services: $2,125
Enrollment, Drop-out Rates and Diploma Recipients by Race/Ethnicity

Category	Total	White	Black	Asian	AIAN	Hisp.
Enrollment (%)	100.0	67.1	16.9	11.8	0.8	3.4
Drop-out Rate (%)	2.3	1.1	5.2	6.5	8.6	6.8
H.S. Diplomas (#)	1,342	1,099	100	118	3	22

Richfield

7001 Harriet Ave S • Richfield, MN 55423-3000
(612) 798-6000 • http://www.richfield.k12.mn.us/
Grade Span: PK-12; Agency Type: 1
Schools: 7
   4 Primary; 1 Middle; 2 High; 0 Other Level
   5 Regular; 2 Special Education; 0 Vocational; 0 Alternative
   0 Magnet; 0 Charter; 2 Title I Eligible; 0 School-wide Title I
Students: 4,105 (52.7% male; 47.2% female)
   Individual Education Program: 515 (12.5%);
   English Language Learner: 656 (16.0%); Migrant: 0 (0.0%)
   Eligible for Free Lunch Program: 1,293 (31.5%)
   Eligible for Reduced-Price Lunch Program: 323 (7.9%)
Teachers: 260.5 (15.8 to 1)
Librarians/Media Specialists: 3.0 (1,368.3 to 1)
Guidance Counselors: 5.0 (821.0 to 1)
Current Spending: ($ per student per year):
   Total: $8,207; Instruction: $5,041; Support Services: $2,895
Enrollment, Drop-out Rates and Diploma Recipients by Race/Ethnicity

Category	Total	White	Black	Asian	AIAN	Hisp.
Enrollment (%)	100.0	54.4	18.9	9.0	1.4	16.3
Drop-out Rate (%)	7.9	5.1	12.0	10.3	18.8	18.2
H.S. Diplomas (#)	261	198	29	23	1	10

Robbinsdale

4148 Winnetka Ave N • New Hope, MN 55427-1288
(763) 504-8011 • http://www.rdale.k12.mn.us/dist/
Grade Span: PK-12; Agency Type: 1
Schools: 25
   15 Primary; 3 Middle; 2 High; 5 Other Level
   18 Regular; 3 Special Education; 0 Vocational; 4 Alternative
   2 Magnet; 0 Charter; 6 Title I Eligible; 0 School-wide Title I
Students: 13,762 (51.0% male; 48.9% female)
   Individual Education Program: 1,426 (10.4%);
   English Language Learner: 1,296 (9.4%); Migrant: 0 (0.0%)

   Eligible for Free Lunch Program: 2,839 (20.6%)
   Eligible for Reduced-Price Lunch Program: 1,238 (9.0%)
Teachers: 760.8 (18.1 to 1)
Librarians/Media Specialists: 16.0 (860.1 to 1)
Guidance Counselors: 17.0 (809.5 to 1)
Current Spending: ($ per student per year):
   Total: $8,059; Instruction: $4,854; Support Services: $2,833
Enrollment, Drop-out Rates and Diploma Recipients by Race/Ethnicity

Category	Total	White	Black	Asian	AIAN	Hisp.
Enrollment (%)	100.0	66.9	18.0	7.1	1.4	6.6
Drop-out Rate (%)	1.9	1.2	4.4	2.2	7.3	5.3
H.S. Diplomas (#)	693	581	48	47	3	14

St. Anthony-New Brighton

3303 33rd Ave NE • St. Anthony, MN 55418-9971
(612) 706-1000
Grade Span: PK-12; Agency Type: 1
Schools: 3
   1 Primary; 1 Middle; 1 High; 0 Other Level
   3 Regular; 0 Special Education; 0 Vocational; 0 Alternative
   0 Magnet; 0 Charter; 1 Title I Eligible; 0 School-wide Title I
Students: 1,645 (51.6% male; 48.3% female)
   Individual Education Program: 146 (8.9%);
   English Language Learner: 27 (1.6%); Migrant: 0 (0.0%)
   Eligible for Free Lunch Program: 57 (3.5%)
   Eligible for Reduced-Price Lunch Program: 37 (2.2%)
Teachers: 91.0 (18.1 to 1)
Librarians/Media Specialists: 2.0 (822.5 to 1)
Guidance Counselors: 2.2 (747.7 to 1)
Current Spending: ($ per student per year):
   Total: $7,632; Instruction: $4,675; Support Services: $2,613
Enrollment, Drop-out Rates and Diploma Recipients by Race/Ethnicity

Category	Total	White	Black	Asian	AIAN	Hisp.
Enrollment (%)	100.0	82.9	4.9	8.0	1.2	3.0
Drop-out Rate (%)	1.5	1.3	5.3	0.0	0.0	16.7
H.S. Diplomas (#)	116	103	7	5	0	1

St. Louis Park

6425 W 33rd St • St. Louis Park, MN 55426-3498
(952) 928-6003 • http://www.stlpark.k12.mn.us/index.html
Grade Span: PK-12; Agency Type: 1
Schools: 10
   4 Primary; 3 Middle; 3 High; 0 Other Level
   7 Regular; 2 Special Education; 0 Vocational; 1 Alternative
   0 Magnet; 0 Charter; 3 Title I Eligible; 0 School-wide Title I
Students: 4,348 (51.9% male; 48.0% female)
   Individual Education Program: 730 (16.8%);
   English Language Learner: 294 (6.8%); Migrant: 0 (0.0%)
   Eligible for Free Lunch Program: 825 (19.0%)
   Eligible for Reduced-Price Lunch Program: 221 (5.1%)
Teachers: 290.1 (15.0 to 1)
Librarians/Media Specialists: 7.4 (587.6 to 1)
Guidance Counselors: 7.5 (579.7 to 1)
Current Spending: ($ per student per year):
   Total: $9,842; Instruction: $5,740; Support Services: $3,711
Enrollment, Drop-out Rates and Diploma Recipients by Race/Ethnicity

Category	Total	White	Black	Asian	AIAN	Hisp.
Enrollment (%)	100.0	72.6	15.5	5.1	1.1	5.6
Drop-out Rate (%)	1.9	1.7	2.6	0.0	0.0	8.9
H.S. Diplomas (#)	259	224	18	11	1	5

Wayzata

210 County Rd 101 N • Wayzata, MN 55391-0660
Mailing Address: Box 660 • Wayzata, MN 55391-0660
(763) 745-5000 • http://www.wayzata.k12.mn.us/communications/
Grade Span: PK-12; Agency Type: 1
Schools: 11
   7 Primary; 3 Middle; 1 High; 0 Other Level
   11 Regular; 0 Special Education; 0 Vocational; 0 Alternative
   0 Magnet; 0 Charter; 0 Title I Eligible; 0 School-wide Title I
Students: 9,718 (50.7% male; 49.2% female)
   Individual Education Program: 895 (9.2%);
   English Language Learner: 178 (1.8%); Migrant: 0 (0.0%)
   Eligible for Free Lunch Program: 609 (6.3%)
   Eligible for Reduced-Price Lunch Program: 196 (2.0%)
Teachers: 480.7 (20.2 to 1)
Librarians/Media Specialists: 12.0 (809.8 to 1)
Guidance Counselors: 7.0 (1,388.3 to 1)
Current Spending: ($ per student per year):
   Total: $7,825; Instruction: $4,911; Support Services: $2,557
Enrollment, Drop-out Rates and Diploma Recipients by Race/Ethnicity

Category	Total	White	Black	Asian	AIAN	Hisp.
Enrollment (%)	100.0	87.1	4.8	6.0	0.4	1.7
Drop-out Rate (%)	0.6	0.5	2.4	0.0	0.0	4.5
H.S. Diplomas (#)	642	585	8	35	1	13

Westonka

5901 Sunnyfield Rd E • Minnetrista, MN 55364-1697
Mailing Address: 5901 Sunneyfield Rd E • Mound, MN 55364-1697
(952) 491-8001 • http://www.westonka.k12.mn.us/
Grade Span: PK-12; **Agency Type:** 1
Schools: 5
   3 Primary; 1 Middle; 1 High; 0 Other Level
   4 Regular; 1 Special Education; 0 Vocational; 0 Alternative
   0 Magnet; 0 Charter; 2 Title I Eligible; 0 School-wide Title I
Students: 2,270 (54.7% male; 45.2% female)
   Individual Education Program: 284 (12.5%);
   English Language Learner: 32 (1.4%); Migrant: 0 (0.0%)
   Eligible for Free Lunch Program: 217 (9.6%)
   Eligible for Reduced-Price Lunch Program: 94 (4.1%)
Teachers: 131.5 (17.3 to 1)
Librarians/Media Specialists: 4.0 (567.5 to 1)
Guidance Counselors: 4.0 (567.5 to 1)
Current Spending: ($ per student per year):
   Total: $7,811; Instruction: $4,698; Support Services: $2,743
Enrollment, Drop-out Rates and Diploma Recipients by Race/Ethnicity

Category	Total	White	Black	Asian	AIAN	Hisp.
Enrollment (%)	100.0	96.1	1.4	1.1	0.6	0.8
Drop-out Rate (%)	1.0	1.0	0.0	0.0	0.0	0.0
H.S. Diplomas (#)	154	148	1	4	0	1

Houston County

Lacrescent-Hokah

703 S 11th St • Lacrescent, MN 55947-1315
(507) 895-4484 • http://www.isd300.k12.mn.us
Grade Span: PK-12; **Agency Type:** 1
Schools: 5
   2 Primary; 0 Middle; 1 High; 2 Other Level
   3 Regular; 0 Special Education; 0 Vocational; 2 Alternative
   0 Magnet; 0 Charter; 2 Title I Eligible; 0 School-wide Title I
Students: 1,609 (49.5% male; 50.4% female)
   Individual Education Program: 187 (11.6%);
   English Language Learner: 0 (0.0%); Migrant: 0 (0.0%)
   Eligible for Free Lunch Program: 162 (10.1%)
   Eligible for Reduced-Price Lunch Program: 76 (4.7%)
Teachers: 88.4 (18.2 to 1)
Librarians/Media Specialists: 1.6 (1,005.6 to 1)
Guidance Counselors: 2.6 (618.8 to 1)
Current Spending: ($ per student per year):
   Total: $6,882; Instruction: $4,364; Support Services: $2,156
Enrollment, Drop-out Rates and Diploma Recipients by Race/Ethnicity

Category	Total	White	Black	Asian	AIAN	Hisp.
Enrollment (%)	100.0	95.6	2.3	1.3	0.2	0.6
Drop-out Rate (%)	2.1	2.0	16.7	0.0	0.0	0.0
H.S. Diplomas (#)	162	159	1	2	0	0

Hubbard County

Park Rapids

301 Huntsinger Ave • Park Rapids, MN 56470-0591
(218) 237-6500 • http://www.parkrapids.k12.mn.us/
Grade Span: PK-12; **Agency Type:** 1
Schools: 4
   1 Primary; 1 Middle; 2 High; 0 Other Level
   3 Regular; 0 Special Education; 0 Vocational; 1 Alternative
   0 Magnet; 0 Charter; 2 Title I Eligible; 0 School-wide Title I
Students: 1,755 (53.2% male; 46.7% female)
   Individual Education Program: 336 (19.1%);
   English Language Learner: 0 (0.0%); Migrant: 0 (0.0%)
   Eligible for Free Lunch Program: 483 (27.5%)
   Eligible for Reduced-Price Lunch Program: 245 (14.0%)
Teachers: 109.5 (16.0 to 1)
Librarians/Media Specialists: 2.0 (877.5 to 1)
Guidance Counselors: 2.0 (877.5 to 1)
Current Spending: ($ per student per year):
   Total: $7,702; Instruction: $5,025; Support Services: $2,334
Enrollment, Drop-out Rates and Diploma Recipients by Race/Ethnicity

Category	Total	White	Black	Asian	AIAN	Hisp.
Enrollment (%)	100.0	90.6	0.6	0.6	6.7	1.5
Drop-out Rate (%)	5.6	4.9	0.0	0.0	19.4	0.0
H.S. Diplomas (#)	129	122	0	2	3	2

Isanti County

Cambridge-Isanti

315 7th Ln NE • Cambridge, MN 55008-1269
(763) 689-6188 • http://www.cambridge.k12.mn.us/
Grade Span: PK-12; **Agency Type:** 1
Schools: 7
   3 Primary; 3 Middle; 1 High; 0 Other Level

   7 Regular; 0 Special Education; 0 Vocational; 0 Alternative
   0 Magnet; 0 Charter; 4 Title I Eligible; 0 School-wide Title I
Students: 4,913 (51.6% male; 48.3% female)
   Individual Education Program: 495 (10.1%);
   English Language Learner: 56 (1.1%); Migrant: 0 (0.0%)
   Eligible for Free Lunch Program: 756 (15.4%)
   Eligible for Reduced-Price Lunch Program: 351 (7.1%)
Teachers: 267.2 (18.4 to 1)
Librarians/Media Specialists: 5.0 (982.6 to 1)
Guidance Counselors: 4.9 (1,002.7 to 1)
Current Spending: ($ per student per year):
   Total: $7,046; Instruction: $4,830; Support Services: $1,966
Enrollment, Drop-out Rates and Diploma Recipients by Race/Ethnicity

Category	Total	White	Black	Asian	AIAN	Hisp.
Enrollment (%)	100.0	94.8	1.1	1.4	1.5	1.3
Drop-out Rate (%)	1.6	1.6	0.0	0.0	5.6	0.0
H.S. Diplomas (#)	334	319	2	7	6	0

Itasca County

Grand Rapids

820 NW First Ave • Grand Rapids, MN 55744-2687
Mailing Address: 820 NW First Ave • Grand Rapids, MN 55744-2687
(218) 327-5704 • http://www.isd318.org/
Grade Span: PK-12; **Agency Type:** 1
Schools: 19
   8 Primary; 2 Middle; 7 High; 2 Other Level
   10 Regular; 1 Special Education; 0 Vocational; 8 Alternative
   0 Magnet; 0 Charter; 11 Title I Eligible; 1 School-wide Title I
Students: 4,034 (52.1% male; 47.8% female)
   Individual Education Program: 552 (13.7%);
   English Language Learner: 0 (0.0%); Migrant: 0 (0.0%)
   Eligible for Free Lunch Program: 867 (21.5%)
   Eligible for Reduced-Price Lunch Program: 384 (9.5%)
Teachers: 229.8 (17.6 to 1)
Librarians/Media Specialists: 2.4 (1,680.8 to 1)
Guidance Counselors: 6.4 (630.3 to 1)
Current Spending: ($ per student per year):
   Total: $7,952; Instruction: $5,301; Support Services: $2,390
Enrollment, Drop-out Rates and Diploma Recipients by Race/Ethnicity

Category	Total	White	Black	Asian	AIAN	Hisp.
Enrollment (%)	100.0	92.7	0.8	0.6	5.3	0.6
Drop-out Rate (%)	8.7	7.5	55.6	16.7	18.2	50.0
H.S. Diplomas (#)	356	339	0	2	13	2

Kanabec County

Mora

400 E Maple • Mora, MN 55051-1387
(320) 679-6200 • http://www.mora.k12.mn.us/
Grade Span: PK-12; **Agency Type:** 1
Schools: 4
   1 Primary; 1 Middle; 2 High; 0 Other Level
   3 Regular; 0 Special Education; 0 Vocational; 1 Alternative
   0 Magnet; 0 Charter; 2 Title I Eligible; 0 School-wide Title I
Students: 1,927 (51.4% male; 48.5% female)
   Individual Education Program: 188 (9.8%);
   English Language Learner: 3 (0.2%); Migrant: 0 (0.0%)
   Eligible for Free Lunch Program: 460 (23.9%)
   Eligible for Reduced-Price Lunch Program: 186 (9.7%)
Teachers: 114.9 (16.8 to 1)
Librarians/Media Specialists: 2.7 (713.7 to 1)
Guidance Counselors: 2.0 (963.5 to 1)
Current Spending: ($ per student per year):
   Total: $6,582; Instruction: $4,512; Support Services: $1,769
Enrollment, Drop-out Rates and Diploma Recipients by Race/Ethnicity

Category	Total	White	Black	Asian	AIAN	Hisp.
Enrollment (%)	100.0	94.6	0.7	1.1	2.0	1.6
Drop-out Rate (%)	4.8	4.6	0.0	0.0	10.0	15.4
H.S. Diplomas (#)	146	142	0	1	1	2

Kandiyohi County

New London-Spicer

101 4th Ave SW • New London, MN 56273
Mailing Address: Box 430 • New London, MN 56273
(320) 354-2252 • http://nls.k12.mn.us/
Grade Span: PK-12; **Agency Type:** 1
Schools: 6
   2 Primary; 2 Middle; 2 High; 0 Other Level
   4 Regular; 0 Special Education; 0 Vocational; 2 Alternative
   0 Magnet; 0 Charter; 4 Title I Eligible; 0 School-wide Title I
Students: 1,726 (52.2% male; 47.7% female)
   Individual Education Program: 224 (13.0%);
   English Language Learner: 9 (0.5%); Migrant: 0 (0.0%)

Eligible for Free Lunch Program: 235 (13.6%)
Eligible for Reduced-Price Lunch Program: 111 (6.4%)
Teachers: 104.8 (16.5 to 1)
Librarians/Media Specialists: 2.0 (863.0 to 1)
Guidance Counselors: 1.8 (958.9 to 1)
Current Spending: ($ per student per year):
Total: $6,785; Instruction: $4,388; Support Services: $2,042

Enrollment, Drop-out Rates and Diploma Recipients by Race/Ethnicity

Category	Total	White	Black	Asian	AIAN	Hisp.
Enrollment (%)	100.0	98.8	0.3	0.2	0.2	0.4
Drop-out Rate (%)	1.5	1.3	0.0	0.0	0.0	n/a
H.S. Diplomas (#)	125	123	1	1	0	0

Willmar
611 5th St SW • Willmar, MN 56201-3297
(320) 231-8500 • http://www.willmar.k12.mn.us
Grade Span: PK-12; **Agency Type:** 1
Schools: 14
4 Primary; 2 Middle; 3 High; 5 Other Level
6 Regular; 3 Special Education; 0 Vocational; 5 Alternative
1 Magnet; 0 Charter; 7 Title I Eligible; 1 School-wide Title I
Students: 4,285 (51.4% male; 48.5% female)
Individual Education Program: 603 (14.1%);
English Language Learner: 680 (15.9%); Migrant: 211 (4.9%)
Eligible for Free Lunch Program: 1,446 (33.7%)
Eligible for Reduced-Price Lunch Program: 341 (8.0%)
Teachers: 305.3 (14.0 to 1)
Librarians/Media Specialists: 3.5 (1,224.3 to 1)
Guidance Counselors: 5.0 (857.0 to 1)
Current Spending: ($ per student per year):
Total: $7,571; Instruction: $5,004; Support Services: $2,199

Enrollment, Drop-out Rates and Diploma Recipients by Race/Ethnicity

Category	Total	White	Black	Asian	AIAN	Hisp.
Enrollment (%)	100.0	70.9	2.2	0.7	0.6	25.7
Drop-out Rate (%)	5.7	2.9	18.5	0.0	20.0	19.4
H.S. Diplomas (#)	269	244	2	3	0	20

Lake County

Lake Superior
405 4th Ave • Two Harbors, MN 55616
(218) 834-8216 • http://www.isd381.k12.mn.us/
Grade Span: PK-12; **Agency Type:** 1
Schools: 6
2 Primary; 1 Middle; 2 High; 1 Other Level
5 Regular; 0 Special Education; 0 Vocational; 1 Alternative
0 Magnet; 0 Charter; 3 Title I Eligible; 0 School-wide Title I
Students: 1,625 (51.3% male; 48.6% female)
Individual Education Program: 213 (13.1%);
English Language Learner: 0 (0.0%); Migrant: 0 (0.0%)
Eligible for Free Lunch Program: 258 (15.9%)
Eligible for Reduced-Price Lunch Program: 130 (8.0%)
Teachers: 97.1 (16.7 to 1)
Librarians/Media Specialists: 1.0 (1,625.0 to 1)
Guidance Counselors: 3.0 (541.7 to 1)
Current Spending: ($ per student per year):
Total: $8,266; Instruction: $5,050; Support Services: $2,963

Enrollment, Drop-out Rates and Diploma Recipients by Race/Ethnicity

Category	Total	White	Black	Asian	AIAN	Hisp.
Enrollment (%)	100.0	97.8	0.7	0.4	0.9	0.2
Drop-out Rate (%)	3.2	3.2	0.0	0.0	0.0	0.0
H.S. Diplomas (#)	140	139	0	0	0	1

Lyon County

Marshall
401 S Saratoga St • Marshall, MN 56258-1799
(507) 537-6924 • http://www.marshall.k12.mn.us/
Grade Span: PK-12; **Agency Type:** 1
Schools: 6
3 Primary; 1 Middle; 2 High; 0 Other Level
5 Regular; 0 Special Education; 0 Vocational; 1 Alternative
0 Magnet; 0 Charter; 3 Title I Eligible; 0 School-wide Title I
Students: 2,235 (49.3% male; 50.6% female)
Individual Education Program: 271 (12.1%);
English Language Learner: 100 (4.5%); Migrant: 0 (0.0%)
Eligible for Free Lunch Program: 389 (17.4%)
Eligible for Reduced-Price Lunch Program: 190 (8.5%)
Teachers: 157.7 (14.2 to 1)
Librarians/Media Specialists: 1.7 (1,314.7 to 1)
Guidance Counselors: 4.0 (558.8 to 1)
Current Spending: ($ per student per year):
Total: $7,894; Instruction: $5,256; Support Services: $2,218

Enrollment, Drop-out Rates and Diploma Recipients by Race/Ethnicity

Category	Total	White	Black	Asian	AIAN	Hisp.
Enrollment (%)	100.0	84.5	3.8	3.0	0.3	8.4
Drop-out Rate (%)	3.7	3.1	6.0	0.0	50.0	8.7
H.S. Diplomas (#)	243	220	10	6	0	7

Martin County

Fairmont Area Schools
115 S Park St • Fairmont, MN 56031-2287
(507) 238-4234 • http://fairmont.k12.mn.us/
Grade Span: KG-12; **Agency Type:** 1
Schools: 3
2 Primary; 0 Middle; 1 High; 0 Other Level
3 Regular; 0 Special Education; 0 Vocational; 0 Alternative
0 Magnet; 0 Charter; 2 Title I Eligible; 0 School-wide Title I
Students: 1,793 (52.0% male; 47.9% female)
Individual Education Program: 249 (13.9%);
English Language Learner: 64 (3.6%); Migrant: 0 (0.0%)
Eligible for Free Lunch Program: 445 (24.8%)
Eligible for Reduced-Price Lunch Program: 161 (9.0%)
Teachers: 111.2 (16.1 to 1)
Librarians/Media Specialists: 2.0 (896.5 to 1)
Guidance Counselors: 2.0 (896.5 to 1)
Current Spending: ($ per student per year):
Total: $6,984; Instruction: $4,037; Support Services: $2,462

Enrollment, Drop-out Rates and Diploma Recipients by Race/Ethnicity

Category	Total	White	Black	Asian	AIAN	Hisp.
Enrollment (%)	100.0	92.4	0.9	0.8	0.2	5.7
Drop-out Rate (%)	3.0	2.3	33.3	0.0	0.0	26.3
H.S. Diplomas (#)	167	161	0	4	0	2

Mcleod County

Glencoe-Silver Lake
1621 E 16th St • Glencoe, MN 55336-1799
(320) 864-2498 • http://gsl.k12.mn.us/
Grade Span: PK-12; **Agency Type:** 1
Schools: 5
2 Primary; 1 Middle; 1 High; 1 Other Level
4 Regular; 0 Special Education; 0 Vocational; 1 Alternative
0 Magnet; 0 Charter; 2 Title I Eligible; 0 School-wide Title I
Students: 1,771 (51.3% male; 48.6% female)
Individual Education Program: 191 (10.8%);
English Language Learner: 138 (7.8%); Migrant: 0 (0.0%)
Eligible for Free Lunch Program: 297 (16.8%)
Eligible for Reduced-Price Lunch Program: 153 (8.6%)
Teachers: 111.9 (15.8 to 1)
Librarians/Media Specialists: 1.0 (1,771.0 to 1)
Guidance Counselors: 2.0 (885.5 to 1)
Current Spending: ($ per student per year):
Total: $6,859; Instruction: $4,294; Support Services: $2,154

Enrollment, Drop-out Rates and Diploma Recipients by Race/Ethnicity

Category	Total	White	Black	Asian	AIAN	Hisp.
Enrollment (%)	100.0	84.2	0.1	0.3	0.2	15.2
Drop-out Rate (%)	3.4	2.4	0.0	0.0	n/a	15.4
H.S. Diplomas (#)	138	132	0	1	0	5

Hutchinson
30 Glen St N • Hutchinson, MN 55350-1696
(320) 587-2860 • http://www.hutch.k12.mn.us/tigers/html/indexnojava.html
Grade Span: PK-12; **Agency Type:** 1
Schools: 6
2 Primary; 1 Middle; 2 High; 1 Other Level
4 Regular; 1 Special Education; 0 Vocational; 1 Alternative
0 Magnet; 0 Charter; 2 Title I Eligible; 0 School-wide Title I
Students: 3,072 (51.7% male; 48.2% female)
Individual Education Program: 317 (10.3%);
English Language Learner: 83 (2.7%); Migrant: 0 (0.0%)
Eligible for Free Lunch Program: 370 (12.0%)
Eligible for Reduced-Price Lunch Program: 141 (4.6%)
Teachers: 180.2 (17.0 to 1)
Librarians/Media Specialists: 2.0 (1,536.0 to 1)
Guidance Counselors: 6.0 (512.0 to 1)
Current Spending: ($ per student per year):
Total: $6,603; Instruction: $4,131; Support Services: $2,172

Enrollment, Drop-out Rates and Diploma Recipients by Race/Ethnicity

Category	Total	White	Black	Asian	AIAN	Hisp.
Enrollment (%)	100.0	93.6	1.0	1.0	0.4	4.0
Drop-out Rate (%)	4.1	3.6	28.6	0.0	n/a	26.7
H.S. Diplomas (#)	228	226	0	2	0	0

Meeker County

Dassel-Cokato
4852 Reardon Ave SW • Cokato, MN 55321
Mailing Address: Box 1700 • Cokato, MN 55321
(320) 286-4100 • http://www.dc.k12.mn.us/
Grade Span: PK-12; **Agency Type:** 1
Schools: 6
  2 Primary; 1 Middle; 2 High; 1 Other Level
  4 Regular; 0 Special Education; 0 Vocational; 2 Alternative
  0 Magnet; 0 Charter; 3 Title I Eligible; 0 School-wide Title I
Students: 2,270   (51.3% male; 48.6% female)
  Individual Education Program: 216 (9.5%);
  English Language Learner: 13 (0.6%); Migrant: 0 (0.0%)
  Eligible for Free Lunch Program: 381 (16.8%)
  Eligible for Reduced-Price Lunch Program: 198 (8.7%)
Teachers: 129.6 (17.5 to 1)
Librarians/Media Specialists: 4.0 (567.5 to 1)
Guidance Counselors: 1.0 (2,270.0 to 1)
Current Spending: ($ per student per year):
  Total: $6,298; Instruction: $4,103; Support Services: $1,909
Enrollment, Drop-out Rates and Diploma Recipients by Race/Ethnicity

Category	Total	White	Black	Asian	AIAN	Hisp.
Enrollment (%)	100.0	96.4	0.4	0.8	0.4	2.1
Drop-out Rate (%)	4.1	3.8	0.0	0.0	0.0	25.0
H.S. Diplomas (#)	199	192	2	2	0	3

Litchfield
114 N Holcomb • Litchfield, MN 55355-1409
Mailing Address: 114 N Holcombe • Litchfield, MN 55355-1409
(320) 693-2444 • http://www.litchfield.k12.mn.us
Grade Span: PK-12; **Agency Type:** 1
Schools: 5
  1 Primary; 2 Middle; 2 High; 0 Other Level
  4 Regular; 0 Special Education; 0 Vocational; 1 Alternative
  0 Magnet; 0 Charter; 2 Title I Eligible; 0 School-wide Title I
Students: 1,950   (51.5% male; 48.4% female)
  Individual Education Program: 271 (13.9%);
  English Language Learner: 33 (1.7%); Migrant: 0 (0.0%)
  Eligible for Free Lunch Program: 377 (19.3%)
  Eligible for Reduced-Price Lunch Program: 162 (8.3%)
Teachers: 121.9 (16.0 to 1)
Librarians/Media Specialists: 2.0 (975.0 to 1)
Guidance Counselors: 2.0 (975.0 to 1)
Current Spending: ($ per student per year):
  Total: $7,022; Instruction: $4,536; Support Services: $2,171
Enrollment, Drop-out Rates and Diploma Recipients by Race/Ethnicity

Category	Total	White	Black	Asian	AIAN	Hisp.
Enrollment (%)	100.0	91.9	0.8	0.7	0.3	6.3
Drop-out Rate (%)	1.8	1.8	12.5	0.0	n/a	0.0
H.S. Diplomas (#)	162	151	1	3	0	7

Mille Lacs County

Milaca
500 Hwy 23 W • Milaca, MN 56353-1147
(320) 982-7210 • http://www.milaca.k12.mn.us/
Grade Span: PK-12; **Agency Type:** 1
Schools: 5
  1 Primary; 0 Middle; 2 High; 2 Other Level
  2 Regular; 1 Special Education; 0 Vocational; 2 Alternative
  0 Magnet; 0 Charter; 2 Title I Eligible; 0 School-wide Title I
Students: 1,928   (53.5% male; 46.4% female)
  Individual Education Program: 222 (11.5%);
  English Language Learner: 3 (0.2%); Migrant: 0 (0.0%)
  Eligible for Free Lunch Program: 408 (21.2%)
  Eligible for Reduced-Price Lunch Program: 163 (8.5%)
Teachers: 125.0 (15.4 to 1)
Librarians/Media Specialists: 2.0 (964.0 to 1)
Guidance Counselors: 1.0 (1,928.0 to 1)
Current Spending: ($ per student per year):
  Total: $6,668; Instruction: $4,294; Support Services: $1,986
Enrollment, Drop-out Rates and Diploma Recipients by Race/Ethnicity

Category	Total	White	Black	Asian	AIAN	Hisp.
Enrollment (%)	100.0	95.4	0.4	1.0	2.3	0.9
Drop-out Rate (%)	2.8	2.9	0.0	0.0	0.0	n/a
H.S. Diplomas (#)	119	117	2	0	0	0

Princeton
706 1st. St • Princeton, MN 55371-1820
Mailing Address: 706 1st St • Princeton, MN 55371-1820
(763) 389-2422 • http://www.princeton.k12.mn.us/
Grade Span: PK-12; **Agency Type:** 1
Schools: 4
  2 Primary; 1 Middle; 1 High; 0 Other Level

---

  4 Regular; 0 Special Education; 0 Vocational; 0 Alternative
  0 Magnet; 0 Charter; 2 Title I Eligible; 0 School-wide Title I
Students: 3,439   (51.9% male; 48.0% female)
  Individual Education Program: 401 (11.7%);
  English Language Learner: 0 (0.0%); Migrant: 0 (0.0%)
  Eligible for Free Lunch Program: 479 (13.9%)
  Eligible for Reduced-Price Lunch Program: 206 (6.0%)
Teachers: 190.7 (18.0 to 1)
Librarians/Media Specialists: 4.0 (859.8 to 1)
Guidance Counselors: 4.0 (859.8 to 1)
Current Spending: ($ per student per year):
  Total: $6,310; Instruction: $3,902; Support Services: $2,132
Enrollment, Drop-out Rates and Diploma Recipients by Race/Ethnicity

Category	Total	White	Black	Asian	AIAN	Hisp.
Enrollment (%)	100.0	96.6	0.9	0.7	0.9	0.9
Drop-out Rate (%)	1.0	0.9	0.0	33.3	0.0	0.0
H.S. Diplomas (#)	202	196	2	1	2	1

Morrison County

Little Falls
1001 SE 5th Ave • Little Falls, MN 56475
(320) 632-2002 • http://www.lfalls.k12.mn.us/
Grade Span: PK-12; **Agency Type:** 1
Schools: 6
  3 Primary; 1 Middle; 2 High; 0 Other Level
  5 Regular; 0 Special Education; 0 Vocational; 1 Alternative
  0 Magnet; 0 Charter; 3 Title I Eligible; 0 School-wide Title I
Students: 2,973   (50.3% male; 49.6% female)
  Individual Education Program: 500 (16.8%);
  English Language Learner: 15 (0.5%); Migrant: 0 (0.0%)
  Eligible for Free Lunch Program: 733 (24.7%)
  Eligible for Reduced-Price Lunch Program: 380 (12.8%)
Teachers: 178.8 (16.6 to 1)
Librarians/Media Specialists: 2.5 (1,189.2 to 1)
Guidance Counselors: 2.5 (1,189.2 to 1)
Current Spending: ($ per student per year):
  Total: $7,036; Instruction: $4,454; Support Services: $2,233
Enrollment, Drop-out Rates and Diploma Recipients by Race/Ethnicity

Category	Total	White	Black	Asian	AIAN	Hisp.
Enrollment (%)	100.0	96.6	1.0	0.9	0.5	0.9
Drop-out Rate (%)	2.2	2.2	0.0	0.0	0.0	0.0
H.S. Diplomas (#)	302	301	0	0	1	0

Mower County

Austin
401 NW Third Ave • Austin, MN 55912
(507) 433-0966 • http://www.austin.k12.mn.us/
Grade Span: PK-12; **Agency Type:** 1
Schools: 15
  5 Primary; 1 Middle; 2 High; 7 Other Level
  6 Regular; 2 Special Education; 0 Vocational; 7 Alternative
  0 Magnet; 0 Charter; 7 Title I Eligible; 0 School-wide Title I
Students: 4,086   (51.6% male; 48.3% female)
  Individual Education Program: 586 (14.3%);
  English Language Learner: 324 (7.9%); Migrant: 0 (0.0%)
  Eligible for Free Lunch Program: 1,186 (29.0%)
  Eligible for Reduced-Price Lunch Program: 356 (8.7%)
Teachers: 248.3 (16.5 to 1)
Librarians/Media Specialists: 3.0 (1,362.0 to 1)
Guidance Counselors: 4.0 (1,021.5 to 1)
Current Spending: ($ per student per year):
  Total: $7,356; Instruction: $4,871; Support Services: $2,136
Enrollment, Drop-out Rates and Diploma Recipients by Race/Ethnicity

Category	Total	White	Black	Asian	AIAN	Hisp.
Enrollment (%)	100.0	81.2	3.5	3.0	0.4	11.9
Drop-out Rate (%)	5.1	4.5	4.2	9.8	25.0	12.9
H.S. Diplomas (#)	274	256	2	7	0	9

Nicollet County

St. Peter
803 Davis St • St. Peter, MN 56082-1657
(507) 934-5703 • http://www.stpeterschools.org/
Grade Span: PK-12; **Agency Type:** 1
Schools: 8
  2 Primary; 1 Middle; 2 High; 3 Other Level
  4 Regular; 0 Special Education; 0 Vocational; 4 Alternative
  0 Magnet; 0 Charter; 3 Title I Eligible; 0 School-wide Title I
Students: 1,880   (52.7% male; 47.2% female)
  Individual Education Program: 289 (15.4%);
  English Language Learner: 85 (4.5%); Migrant: 0 (0.0%)
  Eligible for Free Lunch Program: 364 (19.4%)
  Eligible for Reduced-Price Lunch Program: 111 (5.9%)

Teachers: 124.7 (15.1 to 1)
Librarians/Media Specialists: 2.5 (752.0 to 1)
Guidance Counselors: 2.5 (752.0 to 1)
Current Spending: ($ per student per year):
    Total: $7,650; Instruction: $4,982; Support Services: $2,321
Enrollment, Drop-out Rates and Diploma Recipients by Race/Ethnicity

Category	Total	White	Black	Asian	AIAN	Hisp.
Enrollment (%)	100.0	90.0	2.6	1.4	0.5	5.6
Drop-out Rate (%)	1.7	1.5	5.3	0.0	0.0	9.1
H.S. Diplomas (#)	151	144	2	0	2	3

Nobles County

Worthington
1117 Marine Ave • Worthington, MN 56187-1610
(507) 372-2172 • http://www.isd518.net/
Grade Span: PK-12; **Agency Type:** 1
Schools: 8
    2 Primary; 1 Middle; 2 High; 3 Other Level
    3 Regular; 2 Special Education; 0 Vocational; 3 Alternative
    0 Magnet; 0 Charter; 1 Title I Eligible; 0 School-wide Title I
Students: 2,296 (50.9% male; 49.0% female)
    Individual Education Program: 329 (14.3%);
    English Language Learner: 458 (19.9%); Migrant: 1 (<0.1%)
    Eligible for Free Lunch Program: 846 (36.8%)
    Eligible for Reduced-Price Lunch Program: 220 (9.6%)
Teachers: 162.9 (14.1 to 1)
Librarians/Media Specialists: 3.0 (765.3 to 1)
Guidance Counselors: 4.0 (574.0 to 1)
Current Spending: ($ per student per year):
    Total: $7,973; Instruction: $5,192; Support Services: $2,432
Enrollment, Drop-out Rates and Diploma Recipients by Race/Ethnicity

Category	Total	White	Black	Asian	AIAN	Hisp.
Enrollment (%)	100.0	59.0	2.1	10.4	0.3	28.2
Drop-out Rate (%)	9.5	6.0	16.7	11.0	33.3	25.9
H.S. Diplomas (#)	192	156	4	18	0	14

Olmsted County

Byron
501 10th Ave NE • Byron, MN 55920
(507) 775-2383
Grade Span: PK-12; **Agency Type:** 1
Schools: 3
    1 Primary; 1 Middle; 1 High; 0 Other Level
    3 Regular; 0 Special Education; 0 Vocational; 0 Alternative
    0 Magnet; 0 Charter; 1 Title I Eligible; 0 School-wide Title I
Students: 1,551 (51.7% male; 48.2% female)
    Individual Education Program: 167 (10.8%);
    English Language Learner: 0 (0.0%); Migrant: 0 (0.0%)
    Eligible for Free Lunch Program: 73 (4.7%)
    Eligible for Reduced-Price Lunch Program: 55 (3.5%)
Teachers: 89.2 (17.4 to 1)
Librarians/Media Specialists: 1.0 (1,551.0 to 1)
Guidance Counselors: 3.0 (517.0 to 1)
Current Spending: ($ per student per year):
    Total: $6,460; Instruction: $4,228; Support Services: $1,941
Enrollment, Drop-out Rates and Diploma Recipients by Race/Ethnicity

Category	Total	White	Black	Asian	AIAN	Hisp.
Enrollment (%)	100.0	97.5	0.5	0.9	0.1	0.9
Drop-out Rate (%)	0.9	0.7	0.0	0.0	n/a	n/a
H.S. Diplomas (#)	106	102	1	3	0	0

Rochester
615 SW 7th St • Rochester, MN 55902
Mailing Address: 615 SW 7th St • Rochester, MN 55902
(507) 285-8551 • http://www.rochester.k12.mn.us/
Grade Span: PK-12; **Agency Type:** 1
Schools: 40
    19 Primary; 5 Middle; 10 High; 6 Other Level
    23 Regular; 4 Special Education; 0 Vocational; 13 Alternative
    1 Magnet; 0 Charter; 11 Title I Eligible; 2 School-wide Title I
Students: 16,470 (51.7% male; 48.2% female)
    Individual Education Program: 1,940 (11.8%);
    English Language Learner: 2,119 (12.9%); Migrant: 11 (0.1%)
    Eligible for Free Lunch Program: 3,296 (20.0%)
    Eligible for Reduced-Price Lunch Program: 802 (4.9%)
Teachers: 938.4 (17.6 to 1)
Librarians/Media Specialists: 17.7 (930.5 to 1)
Guidance Counselors: 30.4 (541.8 to 1)
Current Spending: ($ per student per year):
    Total: $7,515; Instruction: $4,859; Support Services: $2,354

Enrollment, Drop-out Rates and Diploma Recipients by Race/Ethnicity

Category	Total	White	Black	Asian	AIAN	Hisp.
Enrollment (%)	100.0	76.7	9.9	8.5	0.4	4.7
Drop-out Rate (%)	2.9	2.4	5.1	3.5	5.9	9.0
H.S. Diplomas (#)	1,068	926	47	82	2	11

Stewartville
500 4th St SW • Stewartville, MN 55976-1198
(507) 533-1438 • http://stewartville.k12.mn.us/
Grade Span: PK-12; **Agency Type:** 1
Schools: 4
    1 Primary; 2 Middle; 1 High; 0 Other Level
    4 Regular; 0 Special Education; 0 Vocational; 0 Alternative
    0 Magnet; 0 Charter; 1 Title I Eligible; 0 School-wide Title I
Students: 1,771 (49.1% male; 50.8% female)
    Individual Education Program: 181 (10.2%);
    English Language Learner: 3 (0.2%); Migrant: 0 (0.0%)
    Eligible for Free Lunch Program: 107 (6.0%)
    Eligible for Reduced-Price Lunch Program: 146 (8.2%)
Teachers: 101.3 (17.5 to 1)
Librarians/Media Specialists: 1.8 (983.9 to 1)
Guidance Counselors: 3.0 (590.3 to 1)
Current Spending: ($ per student per year):
    Total: $6,280; Instruction: $3,980; Support Services: $1,961
Enrollment, Drop-out Rates and Diploma Recipients by Race/Ethnicity

Category	Total	White	Black	Asian	AIAN	Hisp.
Enrollment (%)	100.0	96.7	1.0	0.8	0.3	1.2
Drop-out Rate (%)	1.6	1.6	0.0	0.0	0.0	0.0
H.S. Diplomas (#)	129	127	0	0	1	1

Otter Tail County

Fergus Falls
4b E Dr • Fergus Falls, MN 56537-4104
(218) 998-0544 • http://www.fergusfalls.k12.mn.us/
Grade Span: KG-12; **Agency Type:** 1
Schools: 7
    3 Primary; 1 Middle; 2 High; 1 Other Level
    5 Regular; 0 Special Education; 0 Vocational; 2 Alternative
    0 Magnet; 0 Charter; 4 Title I Eligible; 0 School-wide Title I
Students: 2,801 (51.3% male; 48.6% female)
    Individual Education Program: 403 (14.4%);
    English Language Learner: 0 (0.0%); Migrant: 0 (0.0%)
    Eligible for Free Lunch Program: 432 (15.4%)
    Eligible for Reduced-Price Lunch Program: 150 (5.4%)
Teachers: 188.3 (14.9 to 1)
Librarians/Media Specialists: 2.9 (965.9 to 1)
Guidance Counselors: 4.9 (571.6 to 1)
Current Spending: ($ per student per year):
    Total: $7,422; Instruction: $4,661; Support Services: $2,509
Enrollment, Drop-out Rates and Diploma Recipients by Race/Ethnicity

Category	Total	White	Black	Asian	AIAN	Hisp.
Enrollment (%)	100.0	94.8	1.9	1.0	1.2	1.0
Drop-out Rate (%)	5.2	5.1	14.3	0.0	0.0	12.5
H.S. Diplomas (#)	251	245	1	1	0	4

Perham
200 5th St SE • Perham, MN 56573-1797
Mailing Address: 200 5th St SE Room D • Perham, MN 56573-1797
(218) 346-4501 • http://www.perham.k12.mn.us/
Grade Span: PK-12; **Agency Type:** 1
Schools: 7
    2 Primary; 1 Middle; 2 High; 2 Other Level
    4 Regular; 0 Special Education; 0 Vocational; 3 Alternative
    0 Magnet; 0 Charter; 2 Title I Eligible; 1 School-wide Title I
Students: 1,639 (53.2% male; 46.7% female)
    Individual Education Program: 213 (13.0%);
    English Language Learner: 19 (1.2%); Migrant: 0 (0.0%)
    Eligible for Free Lunch Program: 371 (22.6%)
    Eligible for Reduced-Price Lunch Program: 180 (11.0%)
Teachers: 112.0 (14.6 to 1)
Librarians/Media Specialists: 2.4 (682.9 to 1)
Guidance Counselors: 2.0 (819.5 to 1)
Current Spending: ($ per student per year):
    Total: $7,486; Instruction: $4,478; Support Services: $2,649
Enrollment, Drop-out Rates and Diploma Recipients by Race/Ethnicity

Category	Total	White	Black	Asian	AIAN	Hisp.
Enrollment (%)	100.0	94.6	1.2	0.5	1.0	2.6
Drop-out Rate (%)	4.7	4.7	20.0	0.0	0.0	0.0
H.S. Diplomas (#)	138	136	0	1	0	1

Pennington County

Thief River Falls
230 S Labree • Thief River Falls, MN 56701-2800
(218) 681-8711 • http://www.trf.k12.mn.us/
Grade Span: PK-12; Agency Type: 1
Schools: 4
  1 Primary; 1 Middle; 2 High; 0 Other Level
  3 Regular; 0 Special Education; 0 Vocational; 1 Alternative
  0 Magnet; 0 Charter; 1 Title I Eligible; 0 School-wide Title I
Students: 2,095 (53.2% male; 46.7% female)
  Individual Education Program: 304 (14.5%);
  English Language Learner: 27 (1.3%); Migrant: 0 (0.0%)
  Eligible for Free Lunch Program: 401 (19.1%)
  Eligible for Reduced-Price Lunch Program: 214 (10.2%)
Teachers: 137.4 (15.2 to 1)
Librarians/Media Specialists: 3.0 (698.3 to 1)
Guidance Counselors: 4.0 (523.8 to 1)
Current Spending: ($ per student per year):
  Total: $7,411; Instruction: $4,843; Support Services: $2,250
Enrollment, Drop-out Rates and Diploma Recipients by Race/Ethnicity

Category	Total	White	Black	Asian	AIAN	Hisp.
Enrollment (%)	100.0	92.9	1.0	0.5	2.6	3.1
Drop-out Rate (%)	1.7	1.4	0.0	0.0	8.3	22.2
H.S. Diplomas (#)	189	177	1	5	3	3

Pine County

Pine City
1400 6th St S • Pine City, MN 55063-2064
Mailing Address: 1400 Main St S • Pine City, MN 55063-2064
(320) 629-4000 • http://www.pinecity.k12.mn.us/
Grade Span: PK-12; Agency Type: 1
Schools: 4
  1 Primary; 0 Middle; 2 High; 1 Other Level
  2 Regular; 0 Special Education; 0 Vocational; 2 Alternative
  0 Magnet; 0 Charter; 1 Title I Eligible; 0 School-wide Title I
Students: 1,717 (51.1% male; 48.8% female)
  Individual Education Program: 130 (7.6%);
  English Language Learner: 1 (0.1%); Migrant: 0 (0.0%)
  Eligible for Free Lunch Program: 399 (23.2%)
  Eligible for Reduced-Price Lunch Program: 122 (7.1%)
Teachers: 105.3 (16.3 to 1)
Librarians/Media Specialists: 2.0 (858.5 to 1)
Guidance Counselors: 1.7 (1,010.0 to 1)
Current Spending: ($ per student per year):
  Total: $6,834; Instruction: $4,485; Support Services: $1,985
Enrollment, Drop-out Rates and Diploma Recipients by Race/Ethnicity

Category	Total	White	Black	Asian	AIAN	Hisp.
Enrollment (%)	100.0	97.7	0.7	0.2	0.9	0.5
Drop-out Rate (%)	5.7	5.8	0.0	0.0	9.1	0.0
H.S. Diplomas (#)	147	143	0	1	3	0

Polk County

Crookston
402 Fisher Ave #593 • Crookston, MN 56716-2099
(218) 281-5313 • http://www.crookston.k12.mn.us/
Grade Span: PK-12; Agency Type: 1
Schools: 6
  3 Primary; 0 Middle; 3 High; 0 Other Level
  4 Regular; 0 Special Education; 0 Vocational; 2 Alternative
  0 Magnet; 0 Charter; 3 Title I Eligible; 0 School-wide Title I
Students: 1,517 (48.9% male; 51.0% female)
  Individual Education Program: 248 (16.3%);
  English Language Learner: 144 (9.5%); Migrant: 14 (0.9%)
  Eligible for Free Lunch Program: 447 (29.5%)
  Eligible for Reduced-Price Lunch Program: 148 (9.8%)
Teachers: 97.9 (15.5 to 1)
Librarians/Media Specialists: 0.0 (n/a to 1)
Guidance Counselors: 1.0 (1,517.0 to 1)
Current Spending: ($ per student per year):
  Total: $7,172; Instruction: $4,782; Support Services: $1,954
Enrollment, Drop-out Rates and Diploma Recipients by Race/Ethnicity

Category	Total	White	Black	Asian	AIAN	Hisp.
Enrollment (%)	100.0	80.4	0.7	0.3	2.8	15.8
Drop-out Rate (%)	5.9	4.1	0.0	0.0	20.8	14.5
H.S. Diplomas (#)	139	132	1	0	0	6

East Grand Forks
1420 4th Ave NW • East Grand Forks, MN 56721-0151
Mailing Address: Box 151 • East Grand Forks, MN 56721-0151
(218) 773-3494 • http://www.ci.east-grand-forks.mn.us/schools.htm
Grade Span: PK-12; Agency Type: 1
Schools: 4

  2 Primary; 1 Middle; 1 High; 0 Other Level
  4 Regular; 0 Special Education; 0 Vocational; 0 Alternative
  0 Magnet; 0 Charter; 2 Title I Eligible; 0 School-wide Title I
Students: 1,801 (53.1% male; 46.8% female)
  Individual Education Program: 246 (13.7%);
  English Language Learner: 42 (2.3%); Migrant: 0 (0.0%)
  Eligible for Free Lunch Program: 380 (21.1%)
  Eligible for Reduced-Price Lunch Program: 179 (9.9%)
Teachers: 125.6 (14.3 to 1)
Librarians/Media Specialists: 3.2 (562.8 to 1)
Guidance Counselors: 3.3 (545.8 to 1)
Current Spending: ($ per student per year):
  Total: $7,278; Instruction: $4,649; Support Services: $2,225
Enrollment, Drop-out Rates and Diploma Recipients by Race/Ethnicity

Category	Total	White	Black	Asian	AIAN	Hisp.
Enrollment (%)	100.0	86.7	0.8	0.4	1.6	10.5
Drop-out Rate (%)	2.1	1.1	n/a	0.0	0.0	15.6
H.S. Diplomas (#)	116	108	0	4	2	2

Ramsey County

Mounds View
2959 Hamline Ave N • Roseville, MN 55113-1664
(651) 639-6118 • http://www.moundsviewschools.org
Grade Span: PK-12; Agency Type: 1
Schools: 29
  12 Primary; 5 Middle; 7 High; 5 Other Level
  13 Regular; 10 Special Education; 0 Vocational; 6 Alternative
  0 Magnet; 0 Charter; 5 Title I Eligible; 0 School-wide Title I
Students: 10,764 (52.3% male; 47.6% female)
  Individual Education Program: 1,273 (11.8%);
  English Language Learner: 180 (1.7%); Migrant: 0 (0.0%)
  Eligible for Free Lunch Program: 1,212 (11.3%)
  Eligible for Reduced-Price Lunch Program: 567 (5.3%)
Teachers: 545.8 (19.7 to 1)
Librarians/Media Specialists: 7.6 (1,416.3 to 1)
Guidance Counselors: 12.5 (861.1 to 1)
Current Spending: ($ per student per year):
  Total: $7,575; Instruction: $4,899; Support Services: $2,276
Enrollment, Drop-out Rates and Diploma Recipients by Race/Ethnicity

Category	Total	White	Black	Asian	AIAN	Hisp.
Enrollment (%)	100.0	84.1	5.1	7.1	1.0	2.7
Drop-out Rate (%)	2.6	2.2	9.7	1.5	20.9	5.4
H.S. Diplomas (#)	918	813	21	65	6	13

North St Paul-Maplewood
2520 E 12th Ave • Maplewood, MN 55109
(651) 748-7410 • http://www.isd622.org/
Grade Span: PK-12; Agency Type: 1
Schools: 19
  10 Primary; 3 Middle; 4 High; 2 Other Level
  14 Regular; 2 Special Education; 0 Vocational; 3 Alternative
  0 Magnet; 0 Charter; 7 Title I Eligible; 0 School-wide Title I
Students: 11,365 (51.2% male; 48.7% female)
  Individual Education Program: 1,413 (12.4%);
  English Language Learner: 523 (4.6%); Migrant: 0 (0.0%)
  Eligible for Free Lunch Program: 1,799 (15.8%)
  Eligible for Reduced-Price Lunch Program: 711 (6.3%)
Teachers: 600.0 (18.9 to 1)
Librarians/Media Specialists: 13.7 (829.6 to 1)
Guidance Counselors: 19.2 (591.9 to 1)
Current Spending: ($ per student per year):
  Total: $7,119; Instruction: $4,627; Support Services: $2,124
Enrollment, Drop-out Rates and Diploma Recipients by Race/Ethnicity

Category	Total	White	Black	Asian	AIAN	Hisp.
Enrollment (%)	100.0	78.7	8.1	8.2	1.2	3.9
Drop-out Rate (%)	1.1	0.9	2.3	1.8	3.4	2.4
H.S. Diplomas (#)	709	632	26	36	2	13

Roseville
1251 W County Rd B-2 • Roseville, MN 55113-3299
(651) 635-1600 • http://www.roseville.k12.mn.us/
Grade Span: PK-12; Agency Type: 1
Schools: 13
  8 Primary; 1 Middle; 1 High; 3 Other Level
  9 Regular; 1 Special Education; 0 Vocational; 3 Alternative
  0 Magnet; 0 Charter; 4 Title I Eligible; 0 School-wide Title I
Students: 6,389 (50.8% male; 49.1% female)
  Individual Education Program: 711 (11.1%);
  English Language Learner: 451 (7.1%); Migrant: 0 (0.0%)
  Eligible for Free Lunch Program: 953 (14.9%)
  Eligible for Reduced-Price Lunch Program: 374 (5.9%)
Teachers: 364.1 (17.5 to 1)
Librarians/Media Specialists: 8.0 (798.6 to 1)
Guidance Counselors: 7.0 (912.7 to 1)

Current Spending: ($ per student per year):
   Total: $8,465; Instruction: $5,109; Support Services: $3,010
Enrollment, Drop-out Rates and Diploma Recipients by Race/Ethnicity

Category	Total	White	Black	Asian	AIAN	Hisp.
Enrollment (%)	100.0	75.6	7.7	11.4	0.9	4.4
Drop-out Rate (%)	0.8	0.7	3.2	0.0	0.0	0.0
H.S. Diplomas (#)	498	419	23	43	5	8

St. Paul
360 Colborne St • St. Paul, MN 55102-3299
(651) 293-5100 • http://www.stpaul.k12.mn.us/
Grade Span: PK-12; **Agency Type:** 1
Schools: 123
   71 Primary; 11 Middle; 22 High; 19 Other Level
   70 Regular; 29 Special Education; 0 Vocational; 24 Alternative
   31 Magnet; 0 Charter; 59 Title I Eligible; 49 School-wide Title I
Students: 42,510   (51.4% male; 48.5% female)
   Individual Education Program: 7,308 (17.2%);
   English Language Learner: 14,257 (33.5%); Migrant: 72 (0.2%)
   Eligible for Free Lunch Program: 23,245 (54.7%)
   Eligible for Reduced-Price Lunch Program: 4,619 (10.9%)
Teachers: 2,754.0 (15.4 to 1)
Librarians/Media Specialists: 45.4 (936.3 to 1)
Guidance Counselors: 81.4 (522.2 to 1)
Current Spending: ($ per student per year):
   Total: $10,112; Instruction: $6,714; Support Services: $3,034
Enrollment, Drop-out Rates and Diploma Recipients by Race/Ethnicity

Category	Total	White	Black	Asian	AIAN	Hisp.
Enrollment (%)	100.0	29.4	28.1	28.9	1.8	11.8
Drop-out Rate (%)	6.6	4.7	9.0	4.9	10.9	12.5
H.S. Diplomas (#)	2,127	920	329	711	15	152

White Bear Lake
4855 Bloom Ave Ste. 300 • White Bear Lake, MN 55110-2731
(651) 407-7500 • http://wblwww.whitebear.k12.mn.us/
Grade Span: PK-12; **Agency Type:** 1
Schools: 20
   10 Primary; 4 Middle; 2 High; 4 Other Level
   12 Regular; 2 Special Education; 0 Vocational; 6 Alternative
   0 Magnet; 0 Charter; 7 Title I Eligible; 0 School-wide Title I
Students: 8,921   (52.0% male; 47.9% female)
   Individual Education Program: 1,165 (13.1%);
   English Language Learner: 279 (3.1%); Migrant: 0 (0.0%)
   Eligible for Free Lunch Program: 939 (10.5%)
   Eligible for Reduced-Price Lunch Program: 473 (5.3%)
Teachers: 458.3 (19.5 to 1)
Librarians/Media Specialists: 9.0 (991.2 to 1)
Guidance Counselors: 8.3 (1,074.8 to 1)
Current Spending: ($ per student per year):
   Total: $7,269; Instruction: $4,918; Support Services: $2,000
Enrollment, Drop-out Rates and Diploma Recipients by Race/Ethnicity

Category	Total	White	Black	Asian	AIAN	Hisp.
Enrollment (%)	100.0	89.4	2.4	5.8	0.6	1.9
Drop-out Rate (%)	1.7	1.6	8.9	1.5	4.2	0.0
H.S. Diplomas (#)	831	775	10	34	2	10

Rice County

Faribault
930 4th Ave NW • Faribault, MN 55021-0618
Mailing Address: Box 618 • Faribault, MN 55021-1908
(507) 333-6000 • http://www.faribault.k12.mn.us/
Grade Span: PK-12; **Agency Type:** 1
Schools: 12
   4 Primary; 2 Middle; 2 High; 4 Other Level
   5 Regular; 1 Special Education; 0 Vocational; 6 Alternative
   0 Magnet; 0 Charter; 4 Title I Eligible; 0 School-wide Title I
Students: 4,057   (50.9% male; 49.0% female)
   Individual Education Program: 630 (15.5%);
   English Language Learner: 557 (13.7%); Migrant: 0 (0.0%)
   Eligible for Free Lunch Program: 1,123 (27.7%)
   Eligible for Reduced-Price Lunch Program: 361 (8.9%)
Teachers: 248.8 (16.3 to 1)
Librarians/Media Specialists: 4.5 (901.6 to 1)
Guidance Counselors: 5.0 (811.4 to 1)
Current Spending: ($ per student per year):
   Total: $8,192; Instruction: $5,290; Support Services: $2,508
Enrollment, Drop-out Rates and Diploma Recipients by Race/Ethnicity

Category	Total	White	Black	Asian	AIAN	Hisp.
Enrollment (%)	100.0	79.7	2.2	2.0	0.2	15.9
Drop-out Rate (%)	4.7	3.4	3.3	14.9	50.0	17.6
H.S. Diplomas (#)	376	348	3	12	0	13

Northfield
1400 S Division • Northfield, MN 55057
(507) 663-0629 • http://www.nfld.k12.mn.us/
Grade Span: PK-12; **Agency Type:** 1
Schools: 8
   4 Primary; 1 Middle; 2 High; 1 Other Level
   6 Regular; 0 Special Education; 0 Vocational; 2 Alternative
   0 Magnet; 0 Charter; 4 Title I Eligible; 0 School-wide Title I
Students: 3,822   (50.5% male; 49.4% female)
   Individual Education Program: 470 (12.3%);
   English Language Learner: 82 (2.1%); Migrant: 0 (0.0%)
   Eligible for Free Lunch Program: 397 (10.4%)
   Eligible for Reduced-Price Lunch Program: 165 (4.3%)
Teachers: 259.6 (14.7 to 1)
Librarians/Media Specialists: 4.6 (830.9 to 1)
Guidance Counselors: 5.8 (659.0 to 1)
Current Spending: ($ per student per year):
   Total: $7,566; Instruction: $4,988; Support Services: $2,219
Enrollment, Drop-out Rates and Diploma Recipients by Race/Ethnicity

Category	Total	White	Black	Asian	AIAN	Hisp.
Enrollment (%)	100.0	90.4	1.2	1.5	0.3	6.6
Drop-out Rate (%)	4.7	4.1	0.0	3.3	0.0	27.8
H.S. Diplomas (#)	297	280	1	8	1	7

Scott County

New Prague Area Schools
301 Lexington Ave S • New Prague, MN 56071-1439
(952) 758-1700 • http://www.np.k12.mn.us/
Grade Span: PK-12; **Agency Type:** 1
Schools: 5
   2 Primary; 1 Middle; 1 High; 1 Other Level
   4 Regular; 0 Special Education; 0 Vocational; 1 Alternative
   0 Magnet; 0 Charter; 1 Title I Eligible; 0 School-wide Title I
Students: 2,872   (50.2% male; 49.7% female)
   Individual Education Program: 258 (9.0%);
   English Language Learner: 10 (0.3%); Migrant: 0 (0.0%)
   Eligible for Free Lunch Program: 125 (4.4%)
   Eligible for Reduced-Price Lunch Program: 88 (3.1%)
Teachers: 159.2 (18.0 to 1)
Librarians/Media Specialists: 4.0 (718.0 to 1)
Guidance Counselors: 3.0 (957.3 to 1)
Current Spending: ($ per student per year):
   Total: $6,375; Instruction: $3,789; Support Services: $2,255
Enrollment, Drop-out Rates and Diploma Recipients by Race/Ethnicity

Category	Total	White	Black	Asian	AIAN	Hisp.
Enrollment (%)	100.0	97.8	0.3	1.0	0.1	0.9
Drop-out Rate (%)	1.2	1.1	0.0	0.0	0.0	20.0
H.S. Diplomas (#)	208	206	0	0	2	0

Prior Lake-Savage Area Schools
5300 Westwood Dr • Prior Lake, MN 55372-0539
Mailing Address: Box 539 • Prior Lake, MN 55372-0539
(952) 226-0000 • http://www.priorlake-savage.k12.mn.us/welcome.htm
Grade Span: PK-12; **Agency Type:** 1
Schools: 11
   6 Primary; 1 Middle; 2 High; 2 Other Level
   8 Regular; 2 Special Education; 0 Vocational; 1 Alternative
   0 Magnet; 0 Charter; 3 Title I Eligible; 0 School-wide Title I
Students: 5,545   (51.0% male; 48.9% female)
   Individual Education Program: 413 (7.4%);
   English Language Learner: 154 (2.8%); Migrant: 0 (0.0%)
   Eligible for Free Lunch Program: 212 (3.8%)
   Eligible for Reduced-Price Lunch Program: 144 (2.6%)
Teachers: 310.3 (17.9 to 1)
Librarians/Media Specialists: 7.2 (770.1 to 1)
Guidance Counselors: 5.0 (1,109.0 to 1)
Current Spending: ($ per student per year):
   Total: $6,525; Instruction: $3,949; Support Services: $2,278
Enrollment, Drop-out Rates and Diploma Recipients by Race/Ethnicity

Category	Total	White	Black	Asian	AIAN	Hisp.
Enrollment (%)	100.0	91.2	1.8	4.2	1.4	1.4
Drop-out Rate (%)	0.7	0.7	0.0	0.0	0.0	0.0
H.S. Diplomas (#)	282	271	0	9	1	1

Shakopee
505 S Holmes • Shakopee, MN 55379-1384
Mailing Address: 505 Holmes St S • Shakopee, MN 55379-1384
(952) 496-5000 • http://www.shakopee.k12.mn.us/shakopee/default.htm
Grade Span: PK-12; **Agency Type:** 1
Schools: 7
   4 Primary; 2 Middle; 1 High; 0 Other Level
   6 Regular; 1 Special Education; 0 Vocational; 0 Alternative
   0 Magnet; 0 Charter; 4 Title I Eligible; 0 School-wide Title I
Students: 4,893   (52.2% male; 47.7% female)

Individual Education Program: 542 (11.1%);
English Language Learner: 582 (11.9%); Migrant: 0 (0.0%)
Eligible for Free Lunch Program: 894 (18.3%)
Eligible for Reduced-Price Lunch Program: 314 (6.4%)
Teachers: 248.9 (19.7 to 1)
Librarians/Media Specialists: 6.0 (815.5 to 1)
Guidance Counselors: 4.0 (1,223.3 to 1)
Current Spending: ($ per student per year):
Total: $7,015; Instruction: $4,713; Support Services: $1,989
Enrollment, Drop-out Rates and Diploma Recipients by Race/Ethnicity

Category	Total	White	Black	Asian	AIAN	Hisp.
Enrollment (%)	100.0	79.1	3.1	6.0	2.1	9.8
Drop-out Rate (%)	3.6	3.0	0.0	2.2	19.2	7.9
H.S. Diplomas (#)	201	194	1	2	1	3

Sherburne County

Becker
12000 Hancock St • Becker, MN 55308-9585
(763) 261-4502 • http://www.becker.k12.mn.us/
Grade Span: PK-12; **Agency Type:** 1
Schools: 4
2 Primary; 1 Middle; 1 High; 0 Other Level
4 Regular; 0 Special Education; 0 Vocational; 0 Alternative
0 Magnet; 0 Charter; 2 Title I Eligible; 0 School-wide Title I
Students: 2,455   (52.1% male; 47.8% female)
Individual Education Program: 334 (13.6%)
English Language Learner: 12 (0.5%); Migrant: 0 (0.0%)
Eligible for Free Lunch Program: 168 (6.8%)
Eligible for Reduced-Price Lunch Program: 104 (4.2%)
Teachers: 139.9 (17.5 to 1)
Librarians/Media Specialists: 4.0 (613.8 to 1)
Guidance Counselors: 2.0 (1,227.5 to 1)
Current Spending: ($ per student per year):
Total: $6,725; Instruction: $4,288; Support Services: $2,181
Enrollment, Drop-out Rates and Diploma Recipients by Race/Ethnicity

Category	Total	White	Black	Asian	AIAN	Hisp.
Enrollment (%)	100.0	97.4	0.6	0.9	0.4	0.7
Drop-out Rate (%)	1.0	1.0	0.0	0.0	0.0	0.0
H.S. Diplomas (#)	117	111	2	2	1	1

Big Lake
501 Minnesota Ave • Big Lake, MN 55309-0407
Mailing Address: Box 407 501 Minnesota Ave • Big Lake, MN 55309-0407
(763) 262-2536 • http://www.biglake.k12.mn.us/
Grade Span: PK-12; **Agency Type:** 1
Schools: 4
2 Primary; 1 Middle; 1 High; 0 Other Level
4 Regular; 0 Special Education; 0 Vocational; 0 Alternative
0 Magnet; 0 Charter; 2 Title I Eligible; 0 School-wide Title I
Students: 3,211   (50.5% male; 49.4% female)
Individual Education Program: 388 (12.1%);
English Language Learner: 44 (1.4%); Migrant: 0 (0.0%)
Eligible for Free Lunch Program: 378 (11.8%)
Eligible for Reduced-Price Lunch Program: 235 (7.3%)
Teachers: 178.0 (18.0 to 1)
Librarians/Media Specialists: 4.0 (802.8 to 1)
Guidance Counselors: 3.0 (1,070.3 to 1)
Current Spending: ($ per student per year):
Total: $6,052; Instruction: $3,835; Support Services: $1,959
Enrollment, Drop-out Rates and Diploma Recipients by Race/Ethnicity

Category	Total	White	Black	Asian	AIAN	Hisp.
Enrollment (%)	100.0	94.4	1.2	1.2	1.2	2.0
Drop-out Rate (%)	1.7	1.7	0.0	0.0	0.0	0.0
H.S. Diplomas (#)	125	123	2	0	0	0

Elk River
327 King Ave • Elk River, MN 55330-1391
(763) 241-3400 • http://www.elkriver.k12.mn.us/
Grade Span: PK-12; **Agency Type:** 1
Schools: 18
8 Primary; 3 Middle; 2 High; 5 Other Level
13 Regular; 2 Special Education; 0 Vocational; 3 Alternative
0 Magnet; 0 Charter; 5 Title I Eligible; 0 School-wide Title I
Students: 10,466   (51.1% male; 48.8% female)
Individual Education Program: 1,332 (12.7%);
English Language Learner: 212 (2.0%); Migrant: 0 (0.0%)
Eligible for Free Lunch Program: 726 (6.9%)
Eligible for Reduced-Price Lunch Program: 391 (3.7%)
Teachers: 458.2 (22.8 to 1)
Librarians/Media Specialists: 8.1 (1,292.1 to 1)
Guidance Counselors: 10.5 (996.8 to 1)
Current Spending: ($ per student per year):
Total: $6,727; Instruction: $4,407; Support Services: $2,001

Enrollment, Drop-out Rates and Diploma Recipients by Race/Ethnicity

Category	Total	White	Black	Asian	AIAN	Hisp.
Enrollment (%)	100.0	95.3	0.9	1.5	0.9	1.4
Drop-out Rate (%)	5.2	5.1	10.0	5.1	10.3	4.0
H.S. Diplomas (#)	595	574	1	5	8	7

St. Louis County

Duluth
215 No. 1st Ave E • Duluth, MN 55802-2069
(218) 723-4100 • http://www.duluth.k12.mn.us/
Grade Span: PK-12; **Agency Type:** 1
Schools: 40
14 Primary; 4 Middle; 7 High; 15 Other Level
19 Regular; 8 Special Education; 1 Vocational; 12 Alternative
3 Magnet; 0 Charter; 13 Title I Eligible; 4 School-wide Title I
Students: 11,272   (52.0% male; 47.9% female)
Individual Education Program: 1,530 (13.6%);
English Language Learner: 86 (0.8%); Migrant: 0 (0.0%)
Eligible for Free Lunch Program: 3,086 (27.4%)
Eligible for Reduced-Price Lunch Program: 888 (7.9%)
Teachers: 568.9 (19.8 to 1)
Librarians/Media Specialists: 14.1 (799.4 to 1)
Guidance Counselors: 17.4 (647.8 to 1)
Current Spending: ($ per student per year):
Total: $8,357; Instruction: $5,595; Support Services: $2,506
Enrollment, Drop-out Rates and Diploma Recipients by Race/Ethnicity

Category	Total	White	Black	Asian	AIAN	Hisp.
Enrollment (%)	100.0	86.7	4.6	2.4	5.0	1.2
Drop-out Rate (%)	7.7	6.6	22.6	4.9	23.1	8.3
H.S. Diplomas (#)	915	854	15	19	18	9

Hermantown
4307 Ugstad Rd • Hermantown, MN 55811-1335
(218) 729-9313 • http://www.hermantown.k12.mn.us/
Grade Span: PK-12; **Agency Type:** 1
Schools: 4
2 Primary; 1 Middle; 1 High; 0 Other Level
3 Regular; 1 Special Education; 0 Vocational; 0 Alternative
0 Magnet; 0 Charter; 1 Title I Eligible; 0 School-wide Title I
Students: 1,984   (51.7% male; 48.2% female)
Individual Education Program: 223 (11.2%);
English Language Learner: 0 (0.0%); Migrant: 0 (0.0%)
Eligible for Free Lunch Program: 138 (7.0%)
Eligible for Reduced-Price Lunch Program: 100 (5.0%)
Teachers: 106.9 (18.6 to 1)
Librarians/Media Specialists: 2.0 (992.0 to 1)
Guidance Counselors: 3.6 (551.1 to 1)
Current Spending: ($ per student per year):
Total: $6,487; Instruction: $4,080; Support Services: $2,156
Enrollment, Drop-out Rates and Diploma Recipients by Race/Ethnicity

Category	Total	White	Black	Asian	AIAN	Hisp.
Enrollment (%)	100.0	96.6	0.2	1.3	1.2	0.7
Drop-out Rate (%)	0.5	0.5	0.0	0.0	0.0	0.0
H.S. Diplomas (#)	149	144	1	0	1	3

Hibbing
800 E 21st St • Hibbing, MN 55746-1803
Mailing Address: 800 E 21st. St • Hibbing, MN 55746-1803
(218) 263-4850 • http://www.hibbing.k12.mn.us/
Grade Span: PK-12; **Agency Type:** 1
Schools: 6
3 Primary; 1 Middle; 2 High; 0 Other Level
4 Regular; 1 Special Education; 0 Vocational; 1 Alternative
0 Magnet; 0 Charter; 3 Title I Eligible; 0 School-wide Title I
Students: 2,723   (51.4% male; 48.5% female)
Individual Education Program: 328 (12.0%);
English Language Learner: 6 (0.2%); Migrant: 0 (0.0%)
Eligible for Free Lunch Program: 641 (23.5%)
Eligible for Reduced-Price Lunch Program: 220 (8.1%)
Teachers: 149.4 (18.2 to 1)
Librarians/Media Specialists: 4.0 (680.8 to 1)
Guidance Counselors: 3.0 (907.7 to 1)
Current Spending: ($ per student per year):
Total: $7,780; Instruction: $4,940; Support Services: $2,552
Enrollment, Drop-out Rates and Diploma Recipients by Race/Ethnicity

Category	Total	White	Black	Asian	AIAN	Hisp.
Enrollment (%)	100.0	96.6	0.5	0.3	2.2	0.5
Drop-out Rate (%)	2.6	2.7	0.0	0.0	0.0	0.0
H.S. Diplomas (#)	208	206	1	1	0	0

Proctor

131 9th Ave • Proctor, MN 55810-2797
(218) 628-4934 • http://www.proctor.k12.mn.us/
Grade Span: PK-12; Agency Type: 1
Schools: 6
   3 Primary; 1 Middle; 1 High; 1 Other Level
   5 Regular; 0 Special Education; 0 Vocational; 1 Alternative
   0 Magnet; 0 Charter; 2 Title I Eligible; 0 School-wide Title I
Students: 1,864 (49.1% male; 50.8% female)
   Individual Education Program: 220 (11.8%);
   English Language Learner: 2 (0.1%); Migrant: 0 (0.0%)
   Eligible for Free Lunch Program: 230 (12.3%)
   Eligible for Reduced-Price Lunch Program: 158 (8.5%)
Teachers: 113.2 (16.5 to 1)
Librarians/Media Specialists: 2.0 (932.0 to 1)
Guidance Counselors: 2.0 (932.0 to 1)
Current Spending: ($ per student per year):
   Total: $7,040; Instruction: $4,689; Support Services: $2,103

Enrollment, Drop-out Rates and Diploma Recipients by Race/Ethnicity

Category	Total	White	Black	Asian	AIAN	Hisp.
Enrollment (%)	100.0	98.4	0.4	0.4	0.5	0.2
Drop-out Rate (%)	2.0	2.1	n/a	0.0	0.0	0.0
H.S. Diplomas (#)	167	167	0	0	0	0

St. Louis County

1701 N 9th Ave • Virginia, MN 55792-2172
(218) 749-8130 • http://www.isd2142.k12.mn.us/
Grade Span: PK-12; Agency Type: 1
Schools: 14
   7 Primary; 0 Middle; 7 High; 0 Other Level
   14 Regular; 0 Special Education; 0 Vocational; 0 Alternative
   0 Magnet; 0 Charter; 7 Title I Eligible; 0 School-wide Title I
Students: 2,416 (52.9% male; 47.0% female)
   Individual Education Program: 421 (17.4%);
   English Language Learner: 3 (0.1%); Migrant: 0 (0.0%)
   Eligible for Free Lunch Program: 719 (29.8%)
   Eligible for Reduced-Price Lunch Program: 294 (12.2%)
Teachers: 178.4 (13.5 to 1)
Librarians/Media Specialists: 5.2 (464.6 to 1)
Guidance Counselors: 3.7 (653.0 to 1)
Current Spending: ($ per student per year):
   Total: $9,597; Instruction: $6,318; Support Services: $2,920

Enrollment, Drop-out Rates and Diploma Recipients by Race/Ethnicity

Category	Total	White	Black	Asian	AIAN	Hisp.
Enrollment (%)	100.0	88.0	0.6	0.5	10.7	0.2
Drop-out Rate (%)	2.3	2.3	n/a	0.0	2.3	0.0
H.S. Diplomas (#)	211	193	0	1	15	2

Virginia

411 5th Ave S • Virginia, MN 55792-2734
(218) 749-5437 • http://www.virginia.k12.mn.us/
Grade Span: PK-12; Agency Type: 1
Schools: 3
   1 Primary; 1 Middle; 1 High; 0 Other Level
   3 Regular; 0 Special Education; 0 Vocational; 0 Alternative
   0 Magnet; 0 Charter; 2 Title I Eligible; 0 School-wide Title I
Students: 1,677 (50.0% male; 49.9% female)
   Individual Education Program: 183 (10.9%);
   English Language Learner: 2 (0.1%); Migrant: 0 (0.0%)
   Eligible for Free Lunch Program: 404 (24.1%)
   Eligible for Reduced-Price Lunch Program: 118 (7.0%)
Teachers: 86.5 (19.4 to 1)
Librarians/Media Specialists: 1.5 (1,118.0 to 1)
Guidance Counselors: 2.0 (838.5 to 1)
Current Spending: ($ per student per year):
   Total: $7,565; Instruction: $5,140; Support Services: $2,111

Enrollment, Drop-out Rates and Diploma Recipients by Race/Ethnicity

Category	Total	White	Black	Asian	AIAN	Hisp.
Enrollment (%)	100.0	92.2	1.8	1.0	4.0	1.0
Drop-out Rate (%)	2.2	2.1	0.0	0.0	0.0	16.7
H.S. Diplomas (#)	130	124	0	2	4	0

Stearns County

Albany

30 Forest Ave • Albany, MN 56307-0330
Mailing Address: Box 330 • Albany, MN 56307-0330
(320) 845-2171 • http://www.albany.k12.mn.us
Grade Span: PK-12; Agency Type: 1
Schools: 4
   2 Primary; 1 Middle; 1 High; 0 Other Level
   4 Regular; 0 Special Education; 0 Vocational; 0 Alternative
   0 Magnet; 0 Charter; 1 Title I Eligible; 0 School-wide Title I
Students: 1,598 (50.8% male; 49.1% female)
   Individual Education Program: 223 (14.0%);

   English Language Learner: 10 (0.6%); Migrant: 0 (0.0%)
   Eligible for Free Lunch Program: 170 (10.6%)
   Eligible for Reduced-Price Lunch Program: 125 (7.8%)
Teachers: 100.3 (15.9 to 1)
Librarians/Media Specialists: 2.0 (799.0 to 1)
Guidance Counselors: 2.0 (799.0 to 1)
Current Spending: ($ per student per year):
   Total: $6,642; Instruction: $4,414; Support Services: $1,914

Enrollment, Drop-out Rates and Diploma Recipients by Race/Ethnicity

Category	Total	White	Black	Asian	AIAN	Hisp.
Enrollment (%)	100.0	98.1	0.4	0.2	0.3	1.0
Drop-out Rate (%)	0.5	0.5	0.0	0.0	n/a	0.0
H.S. Diplomas (#)	146	144	1	1	0	0

Rocori

534 N 5th Ave.Ool • Cold Spring, MN 56320-1409
Mailing Address: 534 N 5th Ave • Cold Spring, MN 56320-1409
(320) 685-4901 • http://rocori.k12.mn.us/
Grade Span: PK-12; Agency Type: 1
Schools: 5
   3 Primary; 1 Middle; 1 High; 0 Other Level
   5 Regular; 0 Special Education; 0 Vocational; 0 Alternative
   0 Magnet; 0 Charter; 2 Title I Eligible; 0 School-wide Title I
Students: 2,355 (53.8% male; 46.1% female)
   Individual Education Program: 245 (10.4%);
   English Language Learner: 12 (0.5%); Migrant: 0 (0.0%)
   Eligible for Free Lunch Program: 298 (12.7%)
   Eligible for Reduced-Price Lunch Program: 143 (6.1%)
Teachers: 133.7 (17.6 to 1)
Librarians/Media Specialists: 4.7 (501.1 to 1)
Guidance Counselors: 4.2 (560.7 to 1)
Current Spending: ($ per student per year):
   Total: $7,309; Instruction: $4,859; Support Services: $2,079

Enrollment, Drop-out Rates and Diploma Recipients by Race/Ethnicity

Category	Total	White	Black	Asian	AIAN	Hisp.
Enrollment (%)	100.0	96.0	0.6	0.6	0.0	2.8
Drop-out Rate (%)	0.5	0.4	n/a	0.0	n/a	n/a
H.S. Diplomas (#)	192	189	0	2	0	1

Sartell

212 Thrid Ave N • Sartell, MN 56377-0328
Mailing Address: 212 Third Ave N • Sartell, MN 56377-0328
(320) 656-3715 • http://www.sartell.k12.mn.us/
Grade Span: PK-12; Agency Type: 1
Schools: 5
   2 Primary; 1 Middle; 1 High; 0 Other Level
   4 Regular; 0 Special Education; 0 Vocational; 0 Alternative
   0 Magnet; 0 Charter; 2 Title I Eligible; 0 School-wide Title I
Students: 2,776 (51.5% male; 48.4% female)
   Individual Education Program: 292 (10.5%);
   English Language Learner: 7 (0.3%); Migrant: 0 (0.0%)
   Eligible for Free Lunch Program: 146 (5.3%)
   Eligible for Reduced-Price Lunch Program: 120 (4.3%)
Teachers: 160.8 (17.3 to 1)
Librarians/Media Specialists: 3.0 (925.3 to 1)
Guidance Counselors: 3.0 (925.3 to 1)
Current Spending: ($ per student per year):
   Total: $6,652; Instruction: $4,406; Support Services: $1,862

Enrollment, Drop-out Rates and Diploma Recipients by Race/Ethnicity

Category	Total	White	Black	Asian	AIAN	Hisp.
Enrollment (%)	100.0	96.8	0.4	2.1	0.1	0.6
Drop-out Rate (%)	0.5	0.5	0.0	0.0	n/a	0.0
H.S. Diplomas (#)	189	185	0	4	0	0

St. Cloud

628 Roosevelt Rd • St. Cloud, MN 56301-4898
(320) 253-9333 • http://isd742.org/
Grade Span: PK-12; Agency Type: 1
Schools: 17
   9 Primary; 2 Middle; 4 High; 2 Other Level
   12 Regular; 3 Special Education; 0 Vocational; 2 Alternative
   0 Magnet; 0 Charter; 6 Title I Eligible; 0 School-wide Title I
Students: 9,832 (51.9% male; 48.0% female)
   Individual Education Program: 1,809 (18.4%);
   English Language Learner: 579 (5.9%); Migrant: 0 (0.0%)
   Eligible for Free Lunch Program: 2,492 (25.3%)
   Eligible for Reduced-Price Lunch Program: 852 (8.7%)
Teachers: 610.6 (16.1 to 1)
Librarians/Media Specialists: 11.8 (833.2 to 1)
Guidance Counselors: 24.8 (396.5 to 1)
Current Spending: ($ per student per year):
   Total: $8,404; Instruction: $5,520; Support Services: $2,551

Enrollment, Drop-out Rates and Diploma Recipients by Race/Ethnicity

Category	Total	White	Black	Asian	AIAN	Hisp.
Enrollment (%)	100.0	85.5	6.7	4.1	1.0	2.6
Drop-out Rate (%)	4.8	4.7	9.8	4.0	5.9	7.0
H.S. Diplomas (#)	834	790	12	23	4	5

Steele County

Owatonna
515 W Bridge • Owatonna, MN 55060-2816
Mailing Address: 515 W Bridge St • Owatonna, MN 55060-2816
(507) 444-8601 • http://www.owatonna.k12.mn.us/
Grade Span: PK-12; **Agency Type:** 1
Schools: 16
 5 Primary; 2 Middle; 3 High; 6 Other Level
 7 Regular; 1 Special Education; 0 Vocational; 8 Alternative
 0 Magnet; 0 Charter; 13 Title I Eligible; 0 School-wide Title I
Students: 4,973 (51.8% male; 48.1% female)
 Individual Education Program: 640 (12.9%);
 English Language Learner: 349 (7.0%); Migrant: 12 (0.2%)
 Eligible for Free Lunch Program: 825 (16.6%)
 Eligible for Reduced-Price Lunch Program: 298 (6.0%)
Teachers: 285.7 (17.4 to 1)
Librarians/Media Specialists: 2.0 (2,486.5 to 1)
Guidance Counselors: 5.0 (994.6 to 1)
Current Spending: ($ per student per year):
 Total: $7,040; Instruction: $4,504; Support Services: $2,162
Enrollment, Drop-out Rates and Diploma Recipients by Race/Ethnicity

Category	Total	White	Black	Asian	AIAN	Hisp.
Enrollment (%)	100.0	85.5	5.4	1.2	0.1	7.8
Drop-out Rate (%)	3.4	2.2	16.3	5.6	n/a	13.0
H.S. Diplomas (#)	359	344	6	3	0	6

Waseca County

Waseca
501 Elm Ave E • Waseca, MN 56093-3399
(507) 835-2500 • http://www.waseca.k12.mn.us/
Grade Span: PK-12; **Agency Type:** 1
Schools: 9
 2 Primary; 1 Middle; 3 High; 3 Other Level
 4 Regular; 1 Special Education; 0 Vocational; 4 Alternative
 0 Magnet; 0 Charter; 2 Title I Eligible; 0 School-wide Title I
Students: 2,166 (51.7% male; 48.2% female)
 Individual Education Program: 358 (16.5%);
 English Language Learner: 115 (5.3%); Migrant: 0 (0.0%)
 Eligible for Free Lunch Program: 429 (19.8%)
 Eligible for Reduced-Price Lunch Program: 144 (6.6%)
Teachers: 132.1 (16.4 to 1)
Librarians/Media Specialists: 2.5 (866.4 to 1)
Guidance Counselors: 3.2 (676.9 to 1)
Current Spending: ($ per student per year):
 Total: $7,476; Instruction: $4,984; Support Services: $2,086
Enrollment, Drop-out Rates and Diploma Recipients by Race/Ethnicity

Category	Total	White	Black	Asian	AIAN	Hisp.
Enrollment (%)	100.0	88.7	2.8	1.0	0.6	6.9
Drop-out Rate (%)	5.3	4.8	2.5	0.0	66.7	21.7
H.S. Diplomas (#)	151	143	3	4	0	1

Washington County

Forest Lake
6100 210th St N • Forest Lake, MN 55025-9796
(651) 982-8100 • http://www.forestlake.k12.mn.us/
Grade Span: PK-12; **Agency Type:** 1
Schools: 16
 9 Primary; 1 Middle; 2 High; 4 Other Level
 11 Regular; 2 Special Education; 0 Vocational; 3 Alternative
 1 Magnet; 0 Charter; 5 Title I Eligible; 0 School-wide Title I
Students: 7,750 (52.4% male; 47.5% female)
 Individual Education Program: 912 (11.8%);
 English Language Learner: 56 (0.7%); Migrant: 0 (0.0%)
 Eligible for Free Lunch Program: 694 (9.0%)
 Eligible for Reduced-Price Lunch Program: 399 (5.1%)
Teachers: 427.1 (18.1 to 1)
Librarians/Media Specialists: 10.0 (775.0 to 1)
Guidance Counselors: 10.0 (775.0 to 1)
Current Spending: ($ per student per year):
 Total: $7,172; Instruction: $4,560; Support Services: $2,235
Enrollment, Drop-out Rates and Diploma Recipients by Race/Ethnicity

Category	Total	White	Black	Asian	AIAN	Hisp.
Enrollment (%)	100.0	95.7	0.8	2.0	0.6	0.9
Drop-out Rate (%)	3.1	3.0	0.0	5.4	5.0	0.0
H.S. Diplomas (#)	570	548	5	9	4	4

Mahtomedi
1520 Mahtomedi Ave • Mahtomedi, MN 55115-1900
(651) 407-2000 • http://www.mahtomedi.k12.mn.us/
Grade Span: PK-12; **Agency Type:** 1
Schools: 6
 3 Primary; 1 Middle; 2 High; 0 Other Level
 4 Regular; 1 Special Education; 0 Vocational; 1 Alternative
 0 Magnet; 0 Charter; 2 Title I Eligible; 0 School-wide Title I
Students: 3,078 (52.2% male; 47.7% female)
 Individual Education Program: 285 (9.3%);
 English Language Learner: 28 (0.9%); Migrant: 0 (0.0%)
 Eligible for Free Lunch Program: 113 (3.7%)
 Eligible for Reduced-Price Lunch Program: 60 (1.9%)
Teachers: 172.0 (17.9 to 1)
Librarians/Media Specialists: 4.0 (769.5 to 1)
Guidance Counselors: 4.5 (684.0 to 1)
Current Spending: ($ per student per year):
 Total: $7,434; Instruction: $4,764; Support Services: $2,332
Enrollment, Drop-out Rates and Diploma Recipients by Race/Ethnicity

Category	Total	White	Black	Asian	AIAN	Hisp.
Enrollment (%)	100.0	94.2	1.9	2.3	0.2	1.4
Drop-out Rate (%)	1.0	1.0	0.0	0.0	0.0	0.0
H.S. Diplomas (#)	236	229	1	3	0	3

South Washington County
7362 E Point Douglas Rd S • Cottage Grove, MN 55016-3025
(651) 458-6301 • http://www.sowashco.k12.mn.us/
Grade Span: PK-12; **Agency Type:** 1
Schools: 24
 15 Primary; 4 Middle; 4 High; 1 Other Level
 20 Regular; 1 Special Education; 0 Vocational; 3 Alternative
 0 Magnet; 1 Charter; 3 Title I Eligible; 0 School-wide Title I
Students: 15,629 (51.0% male; 48.9% female)
 Individual Education Program: 1,940 (12.4%);
 English Language Learner: 176 (1.1%); Migrant: 0 (0.0%)
 Eligible for Free Lunch Program: 1,110 (7.1%)
 Eligible for Reduced-Price Lunch Program: 470 (3.0%)
Teachers: 864.2 (18.1 to 1)
Librarians/Media Specialists: 21.0 (744.2 to 1)
Guidance Counselors: 20.7 (755.0 to 1)
Current Spending: ($ per student per year):
 Total: $7,403; Instruction: $4,973; Support Services: $2,114
Enrollment, Drop-out Rates and Diploma Recipients by Race/Ethnicity

Category	Total	White	Black	Asian	AIAN	Hisp.
Enrollment (%)	100.0	84.7	5.1	6.2	0.6	3.4
Drop-out Rate (%)	2.5	2.4	4.4	2.1	3.6	5.4
H.S. Diplomas (#)	1,031	941	31	41	6	12

Stillwater
1875 S Greeley St • Stillwater, MN 55082-6094
Mailing Address: 1875 Greeley St S • Stillwater, MN 55082-6094
(651) 351-8301 • http://www.stillwater.k12.mn.us/
Grade Span: PK-12; **Agency Type:** 1
Schools: 20
 10 Primary; 2 Middle; 4 High; 4 Other Level
 12 Regular; 2 Special Education; 0 Vocational; 6 Alternative
 0 Magnet; 0 Charter; 4 Title I Eligible; 0 School-wide Title I
Students: 8,993 (52.1% male; 47.8% female)
 Individual Education Program: 1,049 (11.7%);
 English Language Learner: 53 (0.6%); Migrant: 0 (0.0%)
 Eligible for Free Lunch Program: 512 (5.7%)
 Eligible for Reduced-Price Lunch Program: 234 (2.6%)
Teachers: 462.2 (19.5 to 1)
Librarians/Media Specialists: 7.0 (1,284.7 to 1)
Guidance Counselors: 11.0 (817.5 to 1)
Current Spending: ($ per student per year):
 Total: $7,339; Instruction: $4,895; Support Services: $2,171
Enrollment, Drop-out Rates and Diploma Recipients by Race/Ethnicity

Category	Total	White	Black	Asian	AIAN	Hisp.
Enrollment (%)	100.0	95.3	1.1	2.4	0.2	1.1
Drop-out Rate (%)	0.7	0.7	0.0	1.3	0.0	6.9
H.S. Diplomas (#)	704	671	5	21	1	6

Winona County

Winona Area Public Schools
654 Huff St • Winona, MN 55987-3320
(507) 494-0861 • http://www.winona.k12.mn.us/
Grade Span: PK-12; **Agency Type:** 1
Schools: 13
 8 Primary; 1 Middle; 2 High; 2 Other Level
 9 Regular; 1 Special Education; 0 Vocational; 3 Alternative
 0 Magnet; 0 Charter; 3 Title I Eligible; 0 School-wide Title I
Students: 4,051 (51.9% male; 48.0% female)
 Individual Education Program: 660 (16.3%);

English Language Learner: 143 (3.5%); Migrant: 0 (0.0%)
Eligible for Free Lunch Program: 995 (24.6%)
Eligible for Reduced-Price Lunch Program: 307 (7.6%)
Teachers: 268.2 (15.1 to 1)
Librarians/Media Specialists: 2.0 (2,025.5 to 1)
Guidance Counselors: 9.0 (450.1 to 1)
Current Spending: ($ per student per year):
   Total: $7,928; Instruction: $5,203; Support Services: $2,399
Enrollment, Drop-out Rates and Diploma Recipients by Race/Ethnicity

Category	Total	White	Black	Asian	AIAN	Hisp.
Enrollment (%)	100.0	90.7	2.5	4.4	0.2	2.1
Drop-out Rate (%)	2.9	2.7	21.4	4.0	0.0	5.9
H.S. Diplomas (#)	348	333	4	8	2	1

Wright County

Annandale
Box 190 · Annandale, MN 55302-0190
(320) 274-5602 · http://www.annandale.k12.mn.us/
Grade Span: PK-12; **Agency Type:** 1
Schools: 3
   1 Primary; 1 Middle; 1 High; 0 Other Level
   3 Regular; 0 Special Education; 0 Vocational; 0 Alternative
   0 Magnet; 0 Charter; 2 Title I Eligible; 0 School-wide Title I
Students: 1,821   (50.9% male; 49.0% female)
   Individual Education Program: 227 (12.5%);
   English Language Learner: 3 (0.2%); Migrant: 0 (0.0%)
   Eligible for Free Lunch Program: 231 (12.7%)
   Eligible for Reduced-Price Lunch Program: 160 (8.8%)
Teachers: 108.0 (16.9 to 1)
Librarians/Media Specialists: 1.0 (1,821.0 to 1)
Guidance Counselors: 2.0 (910.5 to 1)
Current Spending: ($ per student per year):
   Total: $6,956; Instruction: $4,483; Support Services: $2,164
Enrollment, Drop-out Rates and Diploma Recipients by Race/Ethnicity

Category	Total	White	Black	Asian	AIAN	Hisp.
Enrollment (%)	100.0	97.5	1.1	0.5	0.3	0.5
Drop-out Rate (%)	2.9	2.8	0.0	20.0	n/a	0.0
H.S. Diplomas (#)	117	116	1	0	0	0

Buffalo
214 NE 1st Ave · Buffalo, MN 55313-1697
Mailing Address: 214 NE 1st Ave · Buffalo, MN 55313-1697
(612) 682-5200 · http://www.buffalo.k12.mn.us/
Grade Span: PK-12; **Agency Type:** 1
Schools: 10
   6 Primary; 1 Middle; 2 High; 0 Other Level
   7 Regular; 1 Special Education; 0 Vocational; 1 Alternative
   0 Magnet; 0 Charter; 4 Title I Eligible; 0 School-wide Title I
Students: 5,274   (51.2% male; 48.7% female)
   Individual Education Program: 672 (12.7%);
   English Language Learner: 51 (1.0%); Migrant: 0 (0.0%)
   Eligible for Free Lunch Program: 731 (13.9%)
   Eligible for Reduced-Price Lunch Program: 405 (7.7%)
Teachers: 296.6 (17.8 to 1)
Librarians/Media Specialists: 5.5 (958.9 to 1)
Guidance Counselors: 6.0 (879.0 to 1)
Current Spending: ($ per student per year):
   Total: $6,572; Instruction: $4,291; Support Services: $1,922
Enrollment, Drop-out Rates and Diploma Recipients by Race/Ethnicity

Category	Total	White	Black	Asian	AIAN	Hisp.
Enrollment (%)	100.0	95.5	1.3	1.0	0.7	1.6
Drop-out Rate (%)	1.6	1.5	0.0	0.0	0.0	11.1
H.S. Diplomas (#)	341	334	3	2	1	1

Delano
700 Elm Ave E · Delano, MN 55328-9183
(763) 972-3365 · http://www.delano.k12.mn.us/
Grade Span: PK-12; **Agency Type:** 1
Schools: 3
   1 Primary; 1 Middle; 1 High; 0 Other Level
   3 Regular; 0 Special Education; 0 Vocational; 0 Alternative
   0 Magnet; 0 Charter; 1 Title I Eligible; 0 School-wide Title I
Students: 1,927   (51.0% male; 48.9% female)
   Individual Education Program: 235 (12.2%);
   English Language Learner: 0 (0.0%); Migrant: 0 (0.0%)
   Eligible for Free Lunch Program: 132 (6.9%)
   Eligible for Reduced-Price Lunch Program: 47 (2.4%)
Teachers: 107.5 (17.9 to 1)
Librarians/Media Specialists: 3.0 (642.3 to 1)
Guidance Counselors: 2.0 (963.5 to 1)
Current Spending: ($ per student per year):
   Total: $6,450; Instruction: $4,041; Support Services: $2,085

Enrollment, Drop-out Rates and Diploma Recipients by Race/Ethnicity

Category	Total	White	Black	Asian	AIAN	Hisp.
Enrollment (%)	100.0	96.6	1.0	1.1	0.5	0.8
Drop-out Rate (%)	1.2	1.1	0.0	0.0	0.0	50.0
H.S. Diplomas (#)	119	116	1	0	1	1

Monticello
302 Washington St · Monticello, MN 55362
(763) 271-0300 · http://www.monticello.k12.mn.us/
Grade Span: PK-12; **Agency Type:** 1
Schools: 6
   3 Primary; 1 Middle; 2 High; 0 Other Level
   4 Regular; 0 Special Education; 0 Vocational; 1 Alternative
   0 Magnet; 0 Charter; 3 Title I Eligible; 0 School-wide Title I
Students: 3,965   (49.3% male; 50.6% female)
   Individual Education Program: 654 (16.5%);
   English Language Learner: 61 (1.5%); Migrant: 0 (0.0%)
   Eligible for Free Lunch Program: 413 (10.4%)
   Eligible for Reduced-Price Lunch Program: 202 (5.1%)
Teachers: 228.7 (17.3 to 1)
Librarians/Media Specialists: 5.0 (793.0 to 1)
Guidance Counselors: 4.0 (991.3 to 1)
Current Spending: ($ per student per year):
   Total: $6,871; Instruction: $4,682; Support Services: $1,875
Enrollment, Drop-out Rates and Diploma Recipients by Race/Ethnicity

Category	Total	White	Black	Asian	AIAN	Hisp.
Enrollment (%)	100.0	96.5	0.8	0.9	0.2	1.7
Drop-out Rate (%)	3.0	2.9	25.0	0.0	100.0	0.0
H.S. Diplomas (#)	237	234	1	2	0	0

Rockford
6051 Ash St · Rockford, MN 55373-0009
Mailing Address: Box 9 · Rockford, MN 55373-0009
(763) 477-9165 · http://www.rockford.k12.mn.us/
Grade Span: PK-12; **Agency Type:** 1
Schools: 5
   1 Primary; 1 Middle; 1 High; 2 Other Level
   3 Regular; 0 Special Education; 0 Vocational; 2 Alternative
   0 Magnet; 0 Charter; 1 Title I Eligible; 0 School-wide Title I
Students: 1,758   (53.0% male; 46.9% female)
   Individual Education Program: 254 (14.4%);
   English Language Learner: 36 (2.0%); Migrant: 0 (0.0%)
   Eligible for Free Lunch Program: 204 (11.6%)
   Eligible for Reduced-Price Lunch Program: 155 (8.8%)
Teachers: 101.2 (17.4 to 1)
Librarians/Media Specialists: 2.0 (879.0 to 1)
Guidance Counselors: 1.5 (1,172.0 to 1)
Current Spending: ($ per student per year):
   Total: $6,829; Instruction: $4,253; Support Services: $2,261
Enrollment, Drop-out Rates and Diploma Recipients by Race/Ethnicity

Category	Total	White	Black	Asian	AIAN	Hisp.
Enrollment (%)	100.0	95.1	1.1	1.8	0.8	1.2
Drop-out Rate (%)	1.1	1.2	0.0	0.0	0.0	0.0
H.S. Diplomas (#)	105	97	0	5	1	2

St. Michael-Albertville
11343 50th St NE · St. Michael, MN 55301-9769
(763) 497-3180 · http://www.stma.k12.mn.us/
Grade Span: PK-12; **Agency Type:** 1
Schools: 6
   2 Primary; 1 Middle; 2 High; 0 Other Level
   4 Regular; 0 Special Education; 0 Vocational; 1 Alternative
   0 Magnet; 0 Charter; 2 Title I Eligible; 0 School-wide Title I
Students: 3,625   (50.6% male; 49.3% female)
   Individual Education Program: 364 (10.0%);
   English Language Learner: 39 (1.1%); Migrant: 0 (0.0%)
   Eligible for Free Lunch Program: 156 (4.3%)
   Eligible for Reduced-Price Lunch Program: 113 (3.1%)
Teachers: 190.9 (19.0 to 1)
Librarians/Media Specialists: 4.0 (906.3 to 1)
Guidance Counselors: 4.0 (906.3 to 1)
Current Spending: ($ per student per year):
   Total: $5,971; Instruction: $3,538; Support Services: $2,154
Enrollment, Drop-out Rates and Diploma Recipients by Race/Ethnicity

Category	Total	White	Black	Asian	AIAN	Hisp.
Enrollment (%)	100.0	95.3	1.1	2.5	0.2	0.9
Drop-out Rate (%)	1.1	0.8	0.0	13.3	n/a	0.0
H.S. Diplomas (#)	166	164	0	2	0	0

Number of Schools

Rank	Number	District Name	City
1	180	Intermediate SD 287	Plymouth
2	142	Minneapolis	Minneapolis
3	123	St. Paul	St. Paul
4	60	Anoka-Hennepin	Coon Rapids
5	40	Duluth	Duluth
5	40	Rochester	Rochester
7	37	Rosemount-Apple Valley-Eagan	Rosemount
8	31	Osseo	Osseo
9	29	Mounds View	Roseville
10	25	Robbinsdale	New Hope
11	24	Burnsville	Burnsville
11	24	South Washington County	Cottage Grove
13	20	Stillwater	Stillwater
13	20	White Bear Lake	White Bear Lake
15	19	Brainerd	Brainerd
15	19	Grand Rapids	Grand Rapids
15	19	Mankato	Mankato
15	19	North St Paul-Maplewood	Maplewood
19	18	Elk River	Elk River
20	17	Bemidji	Bemidji
20	17	Hopkins	Hopkins
20	17	St. Cloud	St. Cloud
23	16	Bloomington	Bloomington
23	16	Forest Lake	Forest Lake
23	16	Lakeville	Lakeville
23	16	Owatonna	Owatonna
27	15	Austin	Austin
28	14	Detroit Lakes	Detroit Lakes
28	14	St. Louis County	Virginia
28	14	Willmar	Willmar
31	13	Roseville	Roseville
31	13	Winona Area Public Schools	Winona
33	12	Chaska	Chaska
33	12	Faribault	Faribault
33	12	Moorhead	Moorhead
33	12	Spring Lake Park	Spring Lake Pk
37	11	Centennial	Circle Pines
37	11	Eden Prairie	Eden Prairie
37	11	Edina	Edina
37	11	Hastings	Hastings
37	11	Minnetonka	Minnetonka
37	11	Prior Lake-Savage Area Schools	Prior Lake
37	11	Wayzata	Wayzata
44	10	Buffalo	Buffalo
44	10	St. Louis Park	St Louis Park
44	10	West St. Paul-Mendota Hts.-Eagan	Mendota Heights
47	9	Farmington	Farmington
47	9	Inver Grove Heights Schools	Inver Grove Hgts
47	9	Red Wing	Red Wing
47	9	St. Francis	St. Francis
47	9	Waseca	Waseca
52	8	Albert Lea	Albert Lea
52	8	Alexandria	Alexandria
52	8	Cloquet	Cloquet
52	8	Fridley	Fridley
52	8	Northfield	Northfield
52	8	Red Lake	Red Lake
52	8	St. Peter	St. Peter
52	8	Worthington	Worthington
60	7	Cambridge-Isanti	Cambridge
60	7	Chisago Lakes	Lindstrom
60	7	Fergus Falls	Fergus Falls
60	7	North Branch	North Branch
60	7	Perham	Perham
60	7	Richfield	Richfield
60	7	Shakopee	Shakopee
60	7	South St. Paul	S Saint Paul
68	6	Columbia Heights	Columbia Hgts
68	6	Crookston	Crookston
68	6	Dassel-Cokato	Cokato
68	6	Hibbing	Hibbing
68	6	Hutchinson	Hutchinson
68	6	Lake Superior	Two Harbors
68	6	Little Falls	Little Falls
68	6	Mahtomedi	Mahtomedi
68	6	Marshall	Marshall
68	6	Monticello	Monticello
68	6	New London-Spicer	New London
68	6	Proctor	Proctor
68	6	Sauk Rapids	Sauk Rapids
68	6	St. Michael-Albertville	St. Michael
82	5	Glencoe-Silver Lake	Glencoe
82	5	Kasson-Mantorville	Kasson
82	5	Lacrescent-Hokah	Lacrescent
82	5	Litchfield	Litchfield
82	5	Milaca	Milaca
82	5	New Prague Area Schools	New Prague
82	5	New Ulm	New Ulm
82	5	Orono	Long Lake
82	5	Rockford	Rockford
82	5	Rocori	Cold Spring
82	5	Sartell	Sartell
82	5	Westonka	Minnetrista
94	4	Albany	Albany
94	4	Becker	Becker
94	4	Big Lake	Big Lake
94	4	East Grand Forks	E Grand Forks
94	4	Hermantown	Hermantown
94	4	Mora	Mora
94	4	Park Rapids	Park Rapids
94	4	Pine City	Pine City
94	4	Princeton	Princeton
94	4	Stewartville	Stewartville
94	4	Thief River Falls	Thief River Fls
94	4	Waconia	Waconia
106	3	Annandale	Annandale
106	3	Byron	Byron
106	3	Delano	Delano
106	3	Fairmont Area Schools	Fairmont
106	3	Foley	Foley
106	3	St. Anthony-New Brighton	St. Anthony
106	3	Virginia	Virginia
113	2	Brooklyn Center	Brooklyn Center

Number of Teachers

Rank	Number	District Name	City
1	3,024	Minneapolis	Minneapolis
2	2,754	St. Paul	St. Paul
3	2,256	Anoka-Hennepin	Coon Rapids
4	1,749	Rosemount-Apple Valley-Eagan	Rosemount
5	997	Osseo	Osseo
6	938	Rochester	Rochester
7	864	South Washington County	Cottage Grove
8	760	Robbinsdale	New Hope
9	698	Burnsville	Burnsville
10	610	St. Cloud	St. Cloud
11	600	North St Paul-Maplewood	Maplewood
12	599	Lakeville	Lakeville
13	589	Bloomington	Bloomington
14	568	Duluth	Duluth
15	546	Eden Prairie	Eden Prairie
16	545	Mounds View	Roseville
17	503	Hopkins	Hopkins
18	480	Wayzata	Wayzata
19	462	Stillwater	Stillwater
20	458	Minnetonka	Minnetonka
20	458	White Bear Lake	White Bear Lake
22	458	Elk River	Elk River
23	458	Chaska	Chaska
24	433	Brainerd	Brainerd
25	427	Forest Lake	Forest Lake
26	421	Mankato	Mankato
27	414	Edina	Edina
28	375	Centennial	Circle Pines
29	364	Roseville	Roseville
30	345	Moorhead	Moorhead
31	321	Bemidji	Bemidji
32	310	Prior Lake-Savage Area Schools	Prior Lake
33	308	Farmington	Farmington
34	305	Willmar	Willmar
35	296	Buffalo	Buffalo
36	290	St. Louis Park	St Louis Park
37	285	Owatonna	Owatonna
38	283	St. Francis	St. Francis
39	273	West St. Paul-Mendota Hts.-Eagan	Mendota Heights
40	268	Winona Area Public Schools	Winona
41	267	Cambridge-Isanti	Cambridge
42	260	Richfield	Richfield
43	259	Northfield	Northfield
44	255	Alexandria	Alexandria
45	253	Hastings	Hastings
46	248	Shakopee	Shakopee
47	248	Faribault	Faribault
48	248	Austin	Austin
49	238	Intermediate SD 287	Plymouth
50	229	Grand Rapids	Grand Rapids
51	228	Monticello	Monticello
52	223	Albert Lea	Albert Lea
53	219	Inver Grove Heights Schools	Inver Grove Hgts
54	213	Sauk Rapids	Sauk Rapids
55	210	Spring Lake Park	Spring Lake Pk
56	202	North Branch	North Branch
57	200	Detroit Lakes	Detroit Lakes
58	192	Chisago Lakes	Lindstrom
59	190	St. Michael-Albertville	St. Michael
60	190	Princeton	Princeton
61	188	Fergus Falls	Fergus Falls
62	182	Columbia Heights	Columbia Hgts
63	180	Hutchinson	Hutchinson
64	179	South St. Paul	S Saint Paul
65	178	Little Falls	Little Falls
66	178	St. Louis County	Virginia
67	178	Big Lake	Big Lake
68	172	Mahtomedi	Mahtomedi
69	162	Worthington	Worthington
70	161	Red Lake	Red Lake
71	160	Sartell	Sartell
72	159	New Prague Area Schools	New Prague
73	157	Marshall	Marshall
74	157	New Ulm	New Ulm
75	156	Red Wing	Red Wing
76	155	Fridley	Fridley
77	149	Hibbing	Hibbing
78	139	Becker	Becker
79	137	Orono	Long Lake
80	137	Thief River Falls	Thief River Fls
81	133	Rocori	Cold Spring
82	132	Waconia	Waconia
82	132	Waseca	Waseca
84	131	Westonka	Minnetrista
85	129	Cloquet	Cloquet
86	129	Dassel-Cokato	Cokato
87	125	East Grand Forks	E Grand Forks
88	125	Milaca	Milaca
89	124	St. Peter	St. Peter
90	121	Litchfield	Litchfield
91	114	Mora	Mora
92	113	Proctor	Proctor
93	112	Perham	Perham
94	111	Glencoe-Silver Lake	Glencoe
95	111	Fairmont Area Schools	Fairmont
96	110	Kasson-Mantorville	Kasson
97	109	Park Rapids	Park Rapids
98	108	Annandale	Annandale
99	107	Delano	Delano
100	106	Hermantown	Hermantown
101	105	Pine City	Pine City
102	104	New London-Spicer	New London
103	104	Foley	Foley
104	102	Brooklyn Center	Brooklyn Center
105	101	Stewartville	Stewartville
106	101	Rockford	Rockford
107	100	Albany	Albany
108	97	Crookston	Crookston
109	97	Lake Superior	Two Harbors
110	91	St. Anthony-New Brighton	St. Anthony
111	89	Byron	Byron
112	88	Lacrescent-Hokah	Lacrescent
113	86	Virginia	Virginia

Number of Students

Rank	Number	District Name	City
1	43,397	Minneapolis	Minneapolis
2	42,510	St. Paul	St. Paul
3	41,254	Anoka-Hennepin	Coon Rapids
4	28,561	Rosemount-Apple Valley-Eagan	Rosemount
5	21,698	Osseo	Osseo
6	16,470	Rochester	Rochester
7	15,629	South Washington County	Cottage Grove
8	13,762	Robbinsdale	New Hope
9	11,365	North St Paul-Maplewood	Maplewood
10	11,272	Duluth	Duluth
11	11,220	Burnsville	Burnsville
12	10,764	Mounds View	Roseville
13	10,653	Bloomington	Bloomington
14	10,512	Lakeville	Lakeville
15	10,466	Elk River	Elk River
16	10,326	Eden Prairie	Eden Prairie
17	9,832	St. Cloud	St. Cloud
18	9,718	Wayzata	Wayzata
19	8,993	Stillwater	Stillwater
20	8,921	White Bear Lake	White Bear Lake
21	8,320	Hopkins	Hopkins
22	8,036	Chaska	Chaska
23	7,750	Forest Lake	Forest Lake
24	7,646	Minnetonka	Minnetonka
25	7,313	Edina	Edina
26	7,258	Brainerd	Brainerd
27	7,087	Mankato	Mankato
28	7,051	Centennial	Circle Pines
29	6,389	Roseville	Roseville
30	5,946	St. Francis	St. Francis
31	5,545	Prior Lake-Savage Area Schools	Prior Lake
32	5,451	Farmington	Farmington
33	5,365	Moorhead	Moorhead
34	5,274	Buffalo	Buffalo
35	5,146	Hastings	Hastings
36	4,973	Owatonna	Owatonna
37	4,913	Cambridge-Isanti	Cambridge
38	4,901	Bemidji	Bemidji
39	4,893	Shakopee	Shakopee
40	4,789	West St. Paul-Mendota Hts.-Eagan	Mendota Heights
41	4,348	St. Louis Park	St Louis Park
42	4,319	Spring Lake Park	Spring Lake Pk

Rank		District Name	City
43	4,285	Willmar	Willmar
44	4,153	Alexandria	Alexandria
45	4,105	Richfield	Richfield
46	4,086	Austin	Austin
47	4,057	Faribault	Faribault
48	4,051	Winona Area Public Schools	Winona
49	4,034	Grand Rapids	Grand Rapids
50	3,972	North Branch	North Branch
51	3,965	Monticello	Monticello
52	3,878	Inver Grove Heights Schools	Inver Grove Hgts
53	3,822	Northfield	Northfield
54	3,644	Albert Lea	Albert Lea
55	3,625	St. Michael-Albertville	St. Michael
56	3,623	Chisago Lakes	Lindstrom
57	3,605	Sauk Rapids	Sauk Rapids
58	3,439	Princeton	Princeton
59	3,369	South St. Paul	S Saint Paul
60	3,211	Big Lake	Big Lake
61	3,078	Mahtomedi	Mahtomedi
62	3,072	Hutchinson	Hutchinson
63	3,011	Red Wing	Red Wing
64	2,973	Little Falls	Little Falls
65	2,971	Columbia Heights	Columbia Hgts
66	2,872	New Prague Area Schools	New Prague
67	2,801	Fergus Falls	Fergus Falls
68	2,784	Detroit Lakes	Detroit Lakes
69	2,776	Sartell	Sartell
70	2,723	Hibbing	Hibbing
71	2,581	Fridley	Fridley
72	2,532	Orono	Long Lake
73	2,455	Becker	Becker
74	2,419	Waconia	Waconia
75	2,416	St. Louis County	Virginia
76	2,379	New Ulm	New Ulm
77	2,355	Rocori	Cold Spring
78	2,348	Cloquet	Cloquet
79	2,296	Worthington	Worthington
80	2,270	Dassel-Cokato	Cokato
80	2,270	Westonka	Minnetrista
82	2,235	Marshall	Marshall
83	2,166	Waseca	Waseca
84	2,095	Thief River Falls	Thief River Fls
85	2,026	Intermediate SD 287	Plymouth
86	1,984	Hermantown	Hermantown
87	1,950	Litchfield	Litchfield
88	1,928	Milaca	Milaca
89	1,927	Delano	Delano
89	1,927	Mora	Mora
91	1,895	Kasson-Mantorville	Kasson
92	1,880	St. Peter	St. Peter
93	1,864	Proctor	Proctor
94	1,821	Annandale	Annandale
95	1,801	East Grand Forks	E Grand Forks
96	1,793	Fairmont Area Schools	Fairmont
97	1,771	Glencoe-Silver Lake	Glencoe
97	1,771	Stewartville	Stewartville
99	1,758	Rockford	Rockford
100	1,755	Park Rapids	Park Rapids
101	1,732	Brooklyn Center	Brooklyn Center
102	1,726	New London-Spicer	New London
103	1,717	Pine City	Pine City
104	1,677	Foley	Foley
104	1,677	Virginia	Virginia
106	1,645	St. Anthony-New Brighton	St. Anthony
107	1,639	Perham	Perham
108	1,625	Lake Superior	Two Harbors
109	1,609	Lacrescent-Hokah	Lacrescent
110	1,598	Albany	Albany
111	1,551	Byron	Byron
112	1,517	Crookston	Crookston
113	1,503	Red Lake	Red Lake

Male Students

Rank	Percent	District Name	City
1	57.7	Intermediate SD 287	Plymouth
2	54.7	Westonka	Minnetrista
3	53.8	Rocori	Cold Spring
4	53.5	Milaca	Milaca
5	53.2	Park Rapids	Park Rapids
6	53.2	Thief River Falls	Thief River Fls
7	53.2	Perham	Perham
8	53.1	East Grand Forks	E Grand Forks
9	53.1	Brooklyn Center	Brooklyn Center
10	53.0	Rockford	Rockford
11	52.9	St. Louis County	Virginia
12	52.7	St. Peter	St. Peter
13	52.7	Richfield	Richfield
14	52.7	Chisago Lakes	Lindstrom
15	52.6	Bemidji	Bemidji
16	52.5	Moorhead	Moorhead
17	52.4	Forest Lake	Forest Lake
18	52.3	New Ulm	New Ulm
19	52.3	Mounds View	Roseville
20	52.3	Hopkins	Hopkins
21	52.2	Shakopee	Shakopee
22	52.2	Waconia	Waconia
23	52.2	Mahtomedi	Mahtomedi
24	52.2	New London-Spicer	New London
25	52.1	Hastings	Hastings
26	52.1	Becker	Becker
27	52.1	Stillwater	Stillwater
28	52.1	Grand Rapids	Grand Rapids
29	52.0	Duluth	Duluth
30	52.0	White Bear Lake	White Bear Lake
31	52.0	St. Francis	St. Francis
32	52.0	Fairmont Area Schools	Fairmont
33	51.9	Winona Area Public Schools	Winona
34	51.9	St. Cloud	St. Cloud
35	51.9	St. Louis Park	St Louis Park
36	51.9	Princeton	Princeton
37	51.8	Burnsville	Burnsville
38	51.8	Bloomington	Bloomington
39	51.8	Farmington	Farmington
40	51.8	Eden Prairie	Eden Prairie
41	51.8	Owatonna	Owatonna
42	51.7	South St. Paul	S Saint Paul
43	51.7	Hermantown	Hermantown
44	51.7	Hutchinson	Hutchinson
45	51.7	Rochester	Rochester
46	51.7	Byron	Byron
47	51.7	Waseca	Waseca
48	51.6	Chaska	Chaska
49	51.6	Cambridge-Isanti	Cambridge
50	51.6	St. Anthony-New Brighton	St. Anthony
51	51.6	Alexandria	Alexandria
52	51.6	Austin	Austin
53	51.6	Red Lake	Red Lake
54	51.5	Fridley	Fridley
55	51.5	Sartell	Sartell
56	51.5	Litchfield	Litchfield
57	51.4	St. Paul	St. Paul
58	51.4	West St. Paul-Mendota Hts.-Eagan	Mendota Heights
59	51.4	Hibbing	Hibbing
60	51.4	Brainerd	Brainerd
61	51.4	Osseo	Osseo
62	51.4	Willmar	Willmar
63	51.4	Minneapolis	Minneapolis
64	51.4	Mora	Mora
65	51.4	Sauk Rapids	Sauk Rapids
66	51.3	Lake Superior	Two Harbors
67	51.3	Glencoe-Silver Lake	Glencoe
68	51.3	Spring Lake Park	Spring Lake Pk
69	51.3	Dassel-Cokato	Cokato
70	51.3	Fergus Falls	Fergus Falls
71	51.3	Kasson-Mantorville	Kasson
72	51.2	Buffalo	Buffalo
73	51.2	Mankato	Mankato
74	51.2	Anoka-Hennepin	Coon Rapids
74	51.2	Inver Grove Heights Schools	Inver Grove Hgts
76	51.2	North St Paul-Maplewood	Maplewood
77	51.1	Pine City	Pine City
78	51.1	Rosemount-Apple Valley-Eagan	Rosemount
79	51.1	Elk River	Elk River
80	51.0	Prior Lake-Savage Area Schools	Prior Lake
81	51.0	South Washington County	Cottage Grove
82	51.0	Foley	Foley
83	51.0	Robbinsdale	New Hope
84	51.0	Delano	Delano
85	51.0	North Branch	North Branch
86	50.9	Faribault	Faribault
87	50.9	Centennial	Circle Pines
88	50.9	Lakeville	Lakeville
89	50.9	Annandale	Annandale
90	50.9	Worthington	Worthington
91	50.8	Cloquet	Cloquet
92	50.8	Albany	Albany
93	50.8	Minnetonka	Minnetonka
94	50.8	Roseville	Roseville
95	50.7	Wayzata	Wayzata
96	50.6	St. Michael-Albertville	St. Michael
97	50.5	Big Lake	Big Lake
98	50.5	Northfield	Northfield
99	50.4	Edina	Edina
100	50.3	Detroit Lakes	Detroit Lakes
101	50.3	Little Falls	Little Falls
102	50.3	Albert Lea	Albert Lea
103	50.2	New Prague Area Schools	New Prague
104	50.2	Orono	Long Lake
105	50.1	Red Wing	Red Wing
106	50.0	Virginia	Virginia
107	49.7	Columbia Heights	Columbia Hgts
108	49.5	Lacrescent-Hokah	Lacrescent
109	49.3	Monticello	Monticello
110	49.3	Marshall	Marshall
111	49.1	Proctor	Proctor
112	49.1	Stewartville	Stewartville
113	48.9	Crookston	Crookston

Female Students

Rank	Percent	District Name	City
1	51.0	Crookston	Crookston
2	50.8	Stewartville	Stewartville
3	50.8	Proctor	Proctor
4	50.6	Marshall	Marshall
5	50.6	Monticello	Monticello
6	50.4	Lacrescent-Hokah	Lacrescent
7	50.2	Columbia Heights	Columbia Hgts
8	49.9	Virginia	Virginia
9	49.8	Red Wing	Red Wing
10	49.7	Orono	Long Lake
11	49.7	New Prague Area Schools	New Prague
12	49.6	Albert Lea	Albert Lea
13	49.6	Little Falls	Little Falls
14	49.6	Detroit Lakes	Detroit Lakes
15	49.5	Edina	Edina
16	49.4	Northfield	Northfield
17	49.4	Big Lake	Big Lake
18	49.3	St. Michael-Albertville	St. Michael
19	49.1	Wayzata	Wayzata
20	49.1	Roseville	Roseville
21	49.1	Minnetonka	Minnetonka
22	49.1	Albany	Albany
23	49.1	Cloquet	Cloquet
24	49.0	Worthington	Worthington
25	49.0	Annandale	Annandale
26	49.0	Lakeville	Lakeville
27	49.0	Centennial	Circle Pines
28	49.0	Faribault	Faribault
29	48.9	North Branch	North Branch
30	48.9	Delano	Delano
31	48.9	Robbinsdale	New Hope
32	48.9	Foley	Foley
33	48.9	South Washington County	Cottage Grove
34	48.9	Prior Lake-Savage Area Schools	Prior Lake
35	48.8	Elk River	Elk River
36	48.8	Rosemount-Apple Valley-Eagan	Rosemount
37	48.8	Pine City	Pine City
38	48.8	North St Paul-Maplewood	Maplewood
39	48.7	Anoka-Hennepin	Coon Rapids
39	48.7	Inver Grove Heights Schools	Inver Grove Hgts
41	48.7	Mankato	Mankato
42	48.7	Buffalo	Buffalo
43	48.7	Kasson-Mantorville	Kasson
44	48.6	Fergus Falls	Fergus Falls
45	48.6	Dassel-Cokato	Cokato
46	48.6	Spring Lake Park	Spring Lake Pk
47	48.6	Glencoe-Silver Lake	Glencoe
48	48.6	Lake Superior	Two Harbors
49	48.5	Sauk Rapids	Sauk Rapids
50	48.5	Mora	Mora
51	48.5	Minneapolis	Minneapolis
52	48.5	Willmar	Willmar
53	48.5	Osseo	Osseo
54	48.5	Brainerd	Brainerd
55	48.5	Hibbing	Hibbing
56	48.5	West St. Paul-Mendota Hts.-Eagan	Mendota Heights
57	48.5	St. Paul	St. Paul
58	48.4	Litchfield	Litchfield
59	48.4	Sartell	Sartell
60	48.4	Fridley	Fridley
61	48.3	Red Lake	Red Lake
62	48.3	Austin	Austin
63	48.3	Alexandria	Alexandria
64	48.3	St. Anthony-New Brighton	St. Anthony
65	48.3	Cambridge-Isanti	Cambridge
66	48.3	Chaska	Chaska
67	48.2	Waseca	Waseca
68	48.2	Byron	Byron
69	48.2	Rochester	Rochester
70	48.2	Hutchinson	Hutchinson
71	48.2	Hermantown	Hermantown
72	48.2	South St. Paul	S Saint Paul
73	48.1	Owatonna	Owatonna
74	48.1	Eden Prairie	Eden Prairie
75	48.1	Farmington	Farmington
76	48.1	Bloomington	Bloomington
77	48.1	Burnsville	Burnsville
78	48.1	Princeton	Princeton
79	48.0	St. Louis Park	St Louis Park
80	48.0	St. Cloud	St. Cloud
81	48.0	Winona Area Public Schools	Winona
82	47.9	Fairmont Area Schools	Fairmont
83	47.9	St. Francis	St. Francis
84	47.9	White Bear Lake	White Bear Lake
85	47.9	Duluth	Duluth
86	47.8	Grand Rapids	Grand Rapids

87	47.8	Stillwater	Stillwater
88	47.8	Becker	Becker
89	47.8	Hastings	Hastings
90	47.7	New London-Spicer	New London
91	47.7	Mahtomedi	Mahtomedi
92	47.7	Waconia	Waconia
93	47.7	Shakopee	Shakopee
94	47.6	Hopkins	Hopkins
95	47.6	Mounds View	Roseville
96	47.6	New Ulm	New Ulm
97	47.5	Forest Lake	Forest Lake
98	47.4	Moorhead	Moorhead
99	47.3	Bemidji	Bemidji
100	47.2	Chisago Lakes	Lindstrom
101	47.2	Richfield	Richfield
102	47.2	St. Peter	St. Peter
103	47.0	St. Louis County	Virginia
104	46.9	Rockford	Rockford
105	46.8	Brooklyn Center	Brooklyn Center
106	46.8	East Grand Forks	E Grand Forks
107	46.7	Perham	Perham
108	46.7	Thief River Falls	Thief River Fls
109	46.7	Park Rapids	Park Rapids
110	46.4	Milaca	Milaca
111	46.1	Rocori	Cold Spring
112	45.2	Westonka	Minnetrista
113	42.2	Intermediate SD 287	Plymouth

Individual Education Program Students

Rank	Percent	District Name	City
1	35.0	Intermediate SD 287	Plymouth
2	19.1	Park Rapids	Park Rapids
3	18.4	St. Cloud	St. Cloud
4	17.9	Albert Lea	Albert Lea
5	17.6	Moorhead	Moorhead
6	17.4	St. Louis County	Virginia
7	17.3	Detroit Lakes	Detroit Lakes
8	17.2	St. Paul	St. Paul
9	16.8	Little Falls	Little Falls
9	16.8	St. Louis Park	St Louis Park
11	16.5	Monticello	Monticello
11	16.5	Waseca	Waseca
13	16.4	Red Lake	Red Lake
14	16.3	Crookston	Crookston
14	16.3	Winona Area Public Schools	Winona
16	16.1	Bemidji	Bemidji
17	16.0	West St. Paul-Mendota Hts.-Eagan	Mendota Heights
18	15.5	Alexandria	Alexandria
18	15.5	Faribault	Faribault
20	15.4	St. Peter	St. Peter
21	15.3	Inver Grove Heights Schools	Inver Grove Hgts
22	14.9	Brainerd	Brainerd
23	14.8	Mankato	Mankato
24	14.6	Foley	Foley
25	14.5	Thief River Falls	Thief River Fls
26	14.4	Fergus Falls	Fergus Falls
26	14.4	Rockford	Rockford
26	14.4	Rosemount-Apple Valley-Eagan	Rosemount
29	14.3	Austin	Austin
29	14.3	Minneapolis	Minneapolis
29	14.3	Worthington	Worthington
32	14.1	Willmar	Willmar
33	14.0	Albany	Albany
34	13.9	Fairmont Area Schools	Fairmont
34	13.9	Litchfield	Litchfield
36	13.7	East Grand Forks	E Grand Forks
36	13.7	Grand Rapids	Grand Rapids
38	13.6	Becker	Becker
38	13.6	Duluth	Duluth
38	13.6	Sauk Rapids	Sauk Rapids
41	13.3	Anoka-Hennepin	Coon Rapids
42	13.1	Lake Superior	Two Harbors
42	13.1	White Bear Lake	White Bear Lake
44	13.0	New London-Spicer	New London
44	13.0	Perham	Perham
44	13.0	Red Wing	Red Wing
47	12.9	Owatonna	Owatonna
47	12.9	South St. Paul	S Saint Paul
49	12.8	Cloquet	Cloquet
50	12.7	Buffalo	Buffalo
50	12.7	Burnsville	Burnsville
50	12.7	Elk River	Elk River
50	12.7	Fridley	Fridley
50	12.7	Waconia	Waconia
55	12.6	Centennial	Circle Pines
55	12.6	Farmington	Farmington
55	12.6	Hastings	Hastings
58	12.5	Annandale	Annandale
58	12.5	Richfield	Richfield
58	12.5	Westonka	Minnetrista
61	12.4	Hopkins	Hopkins
61	12.4	New Ulm	New Ulm
61	12.4	North St Paul-Maplewood	Maplewood
61	12.4	South Washington County	Cottage Grove
65	12.3	Northfield	Northfield
66	12.2	Delano	Delano
66	12.2	North Branch	North Branch
68	12.1	Big Lake	Big Lake
68	12.1	Marshall	Marshall
70	12.0	Bloomington	Bloomington
70	12.0	Hibbing	Hibbing
72	11.9	Minnetonka	Minnetonka
72	11.9	Spring Lake Park	Spring Lake Pk
74	11.8	Columbia Heights	Columbia Hgts
74	11.8	Forest Lake	Forest Lake
74	11.8	Mounds View	Roseville
74	11.8	Proctor	Proctor
74	11.8	Rochester	Rochester
79	11.7	Princeton	Princeton
79	11.7	Stillwater	Stillwater
81	11.6	Lacrescent-Hokah	Lacrescent
82	11.5	Milaca	Milaca
82	11.5	Osseo	Osseo
84	11.3	Lakeville	Lakeville
85	11.2	Hermantown	Hermantown
86	11.1	Roseville	Roseville
86	11.1	Shakopee	Shakopee
88	10.9	Brooklyn Center	Brooklyn Center
88	10.9	Virginia	Virginia
90	10.8	Byron	Byron
90	10.8	Chaska	Chaska
90	10.8	Glencoe-Silver Lake	Glencoe
93	10.5	Edina	Edina
93	10.5	Sartell	Sartell
93	10.5	St. Francis	St. Francis
96	10.4	Robbinsdale	New Hope
96	10.4	Rocori	Cold Spring
98	10.3	Eden Prairie	Eden Prairie
98	10.3	Hutchinson	Hutchinson
100	10.2	Stewartville	Stewartville
101	10.1	Cambridge-Isanti	Cambridge
102	10.0	St. Michael-Albertville	St. Michael
103	9.8	Mora	Mora
103	9.8	Orono	Long Lake
105	9.6	Chisago Lakes	Lindstrom
106	9.5	Dassel-Cokato	Cokato
107	9.3	Mahtomedi	Mahtomedi
108	9.2	Wayzata	Wayzata
109	9.0	New Prague Area Schools	New Prague
110	8.9	St. Anthony-New Brighton	St. Anthony
111	7.6	Pine City	Pine City
112	7.4	Kasson-Mantorville	Kasson
112	7.4	Prior Lake-Savage Area Schools	Prior Lake

English Language Learner Students

Rank	Percent	District Name	City
1	33.5	St. Paul	St. Paul
2	29.5	Brooklyn Center	Brooklyn Center
3	25.4	Red Lake	Red Lake
4	22.7	Minneapolis	Minneapolis
5	19.9	Worthington	Worthington
6	17.5	Columbia Heights	Columbia Hgts
7	16.0	Richfield	Richfield
8	15.9	Willmar	Willmar
9	13.7	Faribault	Faribault
10	12.9	Rochester	Rochester
11	11.9	Shakopee	Shakopee
12	9.5	Crookston	Crookston
13	9.4	Robbinsdale	New Hope
14	8.9	Osseo	Osseo
15	7.9	Austin	Austin
16	7.8	Glencoe-Silver Lake	Glencoe
17	7.1	Roseville	Roseville
17	7.1	West St. Paul-Mendota Hts.-Eagan	Mendota Heights
19	7.0	Burnsville	Burnsville
19	7.0	Owatonna	Owatonna
21	6.8	Bloomington	Bloomington
21	6.8	St. Louis Park	St Louis Park
23	6.6	Moorhead	Moorhead
24	6.4	Hopkins	Hopkins
25	6.2	Fridley	Fridley
26	5.9	Chaska	Chaska
26	5.9	St. Cloud	St. Cloud
28	5.6	Albert Lea	Albert Lea
29	5.3	Waseca	Waseca
30	5.2	South St. Paul	S Saint Paul
31	4.7	Anoka-Hennepin	Coon Rapids
32	4.6	North St Paul-Maplewood	Maplewood
33	4.5	Marshall	Marshall
33	4.5	St. Peter	St. Peter
35	3.9	Eden Prairie	Eden Prairie
35	3.9	Spring Lake Park	Spring Lake Pk
37	3.6	Fairmont Area Schools	Fairmont
37	3.6	Rosemount-Apple Valley-Eagan	Rosemount
39	3.5	Winona Area Public Schools	Winona
40	3.4	Inver Grove Heights Schools	Inver Grove Hgts
41	3.3	Mankato	Mankato
42	3.1	White Bear Lake	White Bear Lake
43	2.8	Prior Lake-Savage Area Schools	Prior Lake
44	2.7	Hutchinson	Hutchinson
45	2.3	East Grand Forks	E Grand Forks
45	2.3	Edina	Edina
45	2.3	North Branch	North Branch
48	2.1	Farmington	Farmington
48	2.1	Northfield	Northfield
50	2.0	Elk River	Elk River
50	2.0	Rockford	Rockford
52	1.8	Wayzata	Wayzata
53	1.7	Litchfield	Litchfield
53	1.7	Mounds View	Roseville
55	1.6	St. Anthony-New Brighton	St. Anthony
56	1.5	Minnetonka	Minnetonka
56	1.5	Monticello	Monticello
58	1.4	Big Lake	Big Lake
58	1.4	Lakeville	Lakeville
58	1.4	Westonka	Minnetrista
61	1.3	Red Wing	Red Wing
61	1.3	Thief River Falls	Thief River Fls
63	1.2	Chisago Lakes	Lindstrom
63	1.2	Perham	Perham
65	1.1	Cambridge-Isanti	Cambridge
65	1.1	Intermediate SD 287	Plymouth
65	1.1	South Washington County	Cottage Grove
65	1.1	St. Michael-Albertville	St. Michael
69	1.0	Buffalo	Buffalo
69	1.0	Centennial	Circle Pines
69	1.0	St. Francis	St. Francis
72	0.9	Mahtomedi	Mahtomedi
73	0.8	Duluth	Duluth
74	0.7	Forest Lake	Forest Lake
74	0.7	Kasson-Mantorville	Kasson
74	0.7	New Ulm	New Ulm
77	0.6	Albany	Albany
77	0.6	Dassel-Cokato	Cokato
77	0.6	Orono	Long Lake
77	0.6	Stillwater	Stillwater
81	0.5	Becker	Becker
81	0.5	Hastings	Hastings
81	0.5	Little Falls	Little Falls
81	0.5	New London-Spicer	New London
81	0.5	Rocori	Cold Spring
81	0.5	Waconia	Waconia
87	0.3	Alexandria	Alexandria
87	0.3	New Prague Area Schools	New Prague
87	0.3	Sartell	Sartell
90	0.2	Annandale	Annandale
90	0.2	Cloquet	Cloquet
90	0.2	Hibbing	Hibbing
90	0.2	Milaca	Milaca
90	0.2	Mora	Mora
90	0.2	Sauk Rapids	Sauk Rapids
90	0.2	Stewartville	Stewartville
97	0.1	Bemidji	Bemidji
97	0.1	Detroit Lakes	Detroit Lakes
97	0.1	Foley	Foley
97	0.1	Pine City	Pine City
97	0.1	Proctor	Proctor
97	0.1	St. Louis County	Virginia
97	0.1	Virginia	Virginia
104	0.0	Brainerd	Brainerd
104	0.0	Byron	Byron
104	0.0	Delano	Delano
104	0.0	Fergus Falls	Fergus Falls
104	0.0	Grand Rapids	Grand Rapids
104	0.0	Hermantown	Hermantown
104	0.0	Lacrescent-Hokah	Lacrescent
104	0.0	Lake Superior	Two Harbors
104	0.0	Park Rapids	Park Rapids
104	0.0	Princeton	Princeton

Migrant Students

Rank	Percent	District Name	City
1	4.9	Willmar	Willmar
2	1.6	Moorhead	Moorhead
3	0.9	Crookston	Crookston
4	0.4	North Branch	North Branch
5	0.2	Owatonna	Owatonna
5	0.2	St. Paul	St. Paul
7	0.1	Rochester	Rochester
8	0.0	Minneapolis	Minneapolis
8	0.0	Worthington	Worthington
10	0.0	Albany	Albany
10	0.0	Albert Lea	Albert Lea
10	0.0	Alexandria	Alexandria
10	0.0	Annandale	Annandale
10	0.0	Anoka-Hennepin	Coon Rapids

		District Name	City
10	0.0	Austin	Austin
10	0.0	Becker	Becker
10	0.0	Bemidji	Bemidji
10	0.0	Big Lake	Big Lake
10	0.0	Bloomington	Bloomington
10	0.0	Brainerd	Brainerd
10	0.0	Brooklyn Center	Brooklyn Center
10	0.0	Buffalo	Buffalo
10	0.0	Burnsville	Burnsville
10	0.0	Byron	Byron
10	0.0	Cambridge-Isanti	Cambridge
10	0.0	Centennial	Circle Pines
10	0.0	Chaska	Chaska
10	0.0	Chisago Lakes	Lindstrom
10	0.0	Cloquet	Cloquet
10	0.0	Columbia Heights	Columbia Hgts
10	0.0	Dassel-Cokato	Cokato
10	0.0	Delano	Delano
10	0.0	Detroit Lakes	Detroit Lakes
10	0.0	Duluth	Duluth
10	0.0	East Grand Forks	E Grand Forks
10	0.0	Eden Prairie	Eden Prairie
10	0.0	Edina	Edina
10	0.0	Elk River	Elk River
10	0.0	Fairmont Area Schools	Fairmont
10	0.0	Faribault	Faribault
10	0.0	Farmington	Farmington
10	0.0	Fergus Falls	Fergus Falls
10	0.0	Foley	Foley
10	0.0	Forest Lake	Forest Lake
10	0.0	Fridley	Fridley
10	0.0	Glencoe-Silver Lake	Glencoe
10	0.0	Grand Rapids	Grand Rapids
10	0.0	Hastings	Hastings
10	0.0	Hermantown	Hermantown
10	0.0	Hibbing	Hibbing
10	0.0	Hopkins	Hopkins
10	0.0	Hutchinson	Hutchinson
10	0.0	Intermediate SD 287	Plymouth
10	0.0	Inver Grove Heights Schools	Inver Grove Hgts
10	0.0	Kasson-Mantorville	Kasson
10	0.0	Lacrescent-Hokah	Lacrescent
10	0.0	Lake Superior	Two Harbors
10	0.0	Lakeville	Lakeville
10	0.0	Litchfield	Litchfield
10	0.0	Little Falls	Little Falls
10	0.0	Mahtomedi	Mahtomedi
10	0.0	Mankato	Mankato
10	0.0	Marshall	Marshall
10	0.0	Milaca	Milaca
10	0.0	Minnetonka	Minnetonka
10	0.0	Monticello	Monticello
10	0.0	Mora	Mora
10	0.0	Mounds View	Roseville
10	0.0	New London-Spicer	New London
10	0.0	New Prague Area Schools	New Prague
10	0.0	New Ulm	New Ulm
10	0.0	North St Paul-Maplewood	Maplewood
10	0.0	Northfield	Northfield
10	0.0	Orono	Long Lake
10	0.0	Osseo	Osseo
10	0.0	Park Rapids	Park Rapids
10	0.0	Perham	Perham
10	0.0	Pine City	Pine City
10	0.0	Princeton	Princeton
10	0.0	Prior Lake-Savage Area Schools	Prior Lake
10	0.0	Proctor	Proctor
10	0.0	Red Lake	Red Lake
10	0.0	Red Wing	Red Wing
10	0.0	Richfield	Richfield
10	0.0	Robbinsdale	New Hope
10	0.0	Rockford	Rockford
10	0.0	Rocori	Cold Spring
10	0.0	Rosemount-Apple Valley-Eagan	Rosemount
10	0.0	Roseville	Roseville
10	0.0	Sartell	Sartell
10	0.0	Sauk Rapids	Sauk Rapids
10	0.0	Shakopee	Shakopee
10	0.0	South St. Paul	S Saint Paul
10	0.0	South Washington County	Cottage Grove
10	0.0	Spring Lake Park	Spring Lake Pk
10	0.0	St. Anthony-New Brighton	St. Anthony
10	0.0	St. Cloud	St. Cloud
10	0.0	St. Francis	St. Francis
10	0.0	St. Louis County	Virginia
10	0.0	St. Louis Park	St Louis Park
10	0.0	St. Michael-Albertville	St. Michael
10	0.0	St. Peter	St. Peter
10	0.0	Stewartville	Stewartville
10	0.0	Stillwater	Stillwater
10	0.0	Thief River Falls	Thief River Fls
10	0.0	Virginia	Virginia
10	0.0	Waconia	Waconia
10	0.0	Waseca	Waseca
10	0.0	Wayzata	Wayzata
10	0.0	West St. Paul-Mendota Hts.-Eagan	Mendota Heights
10	0.0	Westonka	Minnetrista
10	0.0	White Bear Lake	White Bear Lake
10	0.0	Winona Area Public Schools	Winona

Students Eligible for Free Lunch

Rank	Percent	District Name	City
1	75.9	Red Lake	Red Lake
2	59.8	Minneapolis	Minneapolis
3	54.7	St. Paul	St. Paul
4	44.9	Brooklyn Center	Brooklyn Center
5	36.8	Columbia Heights	Columbia Hgts
5	36.8	Worthington	Worthington
7	36.1	Bemidji	Bemidji
8	33.7	Willmar	Willmar
9	31.5	Richfield	Richfield
10	29.8	St. Louis County	Virginia
11	29.5	Crookston	Crookston
12	29.0	Austin	Austin
13	27.7	Faribault	Faribault
14	27.5	Park Rapids	Park Rapids
15	27.4	Duluth	Duluth
16	26.3	Fridley	Fridley
17	25.3	St. Cloud	St. Cloud
18	24.8	Fairmont Area Schools	Fairmont
19	24.7	Little Falls	Little Falls
20	24.6	Winona Area Public Schools	Winona
21	24.2	Albert Lea	Albert Lea
22	24.1	Detroit Lakes	Detroit Lakes
22	24.1	Virginia	Virginia
24	23.9	Mora	Mora
25	23.5	Hibbing	Hibbing
26	23.2	Pine City	Pine City
27	23.0	Moorhead	Moorhead
28	22.7	Brainerd	Brainerd
29	22.6	Perham	Perham
30	21.7	Cloquet	Cloquet
31	21.5	Grand Rapids	Grand Rapids
32	21.2	Milaca	Milaca
33	21.1	East Grand Forks	E Grand Forks
34	20.6	Robbinsdale	New Hope
35	20.0	Rochester	Rochester
36	19.8	Waseca	Waseca
37	19.7	South St. Paul	S Saint Paul
38	19.5	Mankato	Mankato
39	19.4	St. Peter	St. Peter
40	19.3	Litchfield	Litchfield
41	19.1	Thief River Falls	Thief River Fls
42	19.0	St. Louis Park	St Louis Park
43	18.3	Shakopee	Shakopee
44	17.9	Osseo	Osseo
45	17.4	Marshall	Marshall
46	17.0	Bloomington	Bloomington
47	16.9	West St. Paul-Mendota Hts.-Eagan	Mendota Heights
48	16.8	Dassel-Cokato	Cokato
48	16.8	Glencoe-Silver Lake	Glencoe
50	16.6	Owatonna	Owatonna
51	15.9	Lake Superior	Two Harbors
52	15.8	North St Paul-Maplewood	Maplewood
53	15.4	Cambridge-Isanti	Cambridge
53	15.4	Fergus Falls	Fergus Falls
55	14.9	Red Wing	Red Wing
55	14.9	Roseville	Roseville
57	14.0	Inver Grove Heights Schools	Inver Grove Hgts
58	13.9	Buffalo	Buffalo
58	13.9	Princeton	Princeton
60	13.6	New London-Spicer	New London
61	13.5	Sauk Rapids	Sauk Rapids
62	13.2	Alexandria	Alexandria
62	13.2	Foley	Foley
64	13.0	Spring Lake Park	Spring Lake Pk
65	12.9	Anoka-Hennepin	Coon Rapids
65	12.9	Hopkins	Hopkins
67	12.8	New Ulm	New Ulm
68	12.7	Annandale	Annandale
68	12.7	Rocori	Cold Spring
70	12.6	North Branch	North Branch
71	12.3	Proctor	Proctor
72	12.0	Hutchinson	Hutchinson
73	11.9	Burnsville	Burnsville
74	11.8	Big Lake	Big Lake
75	11.6	Rockford	Rockford
76	11.3	Mounds View	Roseville
76	11.3	St. Francis	St. Francis
78	10.6	Albany	Albany
79	10.5	Intermediate SD 287	Plymouth
79	10.5	White Bear Lake	White Bear Lake
81	10.4	Monticello	Monticello
81	10.4	Northfield	Northfield
83	10.1	Lacrescent-Hokah	Lacrescent
84	9.7	Chisago Lakes	Lindstrom
85	9.6	Westonka	Minnetrista
86	9.1	Hastings	Hastings
87	9.0	Forest Lake	Forest Lake
88	7.9	Chaska	Chaska
89	7.8	Kasson-Mantorville	Kasson
90	7.1	South Washington County	Cottage Grove
91	7.0	Centennial	Circle Pines
91	7.0	Hermantown	Hermantown
93	6.9	Delano	Delano
93	6.9	Elk River	Elk River
95	6.8	Becker	Becker
96	6.6	Rosemount-Apple Valley-Eagan	Rosemount
97	6.3	Wayzata	Wayzata
98	6.0	Stewartville	Stewartville
99	5.9	Eden Prairie	Eden Prairie
100	5.7	Stillwater	Stillwater
101	5.6	Waconia	Waconia
102	5.3	Sartell	Sartell
103	5.2	Farmington	Farmington
104	4.7	Byron	Byron
105	4.4	New Prague Area Schools	New Prague
106	4.3	St. Michael-Albertville	St. Michael
107	3.8	Edina	Edina
107	3.8	Prior Lake-Savage Area Schools	Prior Lake
109	3.7	Mahtomedi	Mahtomedi
110	3.5	Lakeville	Lakeville
110	3.5	St. Anthony-New Brighton	St. Anthony
112	2.6	Orono	Long Lake
113	2.2	Minnetonka	Minnetonka

Students Eligible for Reduced-Price Lunch

Rank	Percent	District Name	City
1	15.6	Brooklyn Center	Brooklyn Center
2	14.0	Park Rapids	Park Rapids
3	12.8	Little Falls	Little Falls
4	12.2	St. Louis County	Virginia
5	11.0	Perham	Perham
6	10.9	St. Paul	St. Paul
7	10.4	Albert Lea	Albert Lea
7	10.4	Detroit Lakes	Detroit Lakes
9	10.3	Brainerd	Brainerd
10	10.2	Thief River Falls	Thief River Fls
11	9.9	East Grand Forks	E Grand Forks
12	9.8	Crookston	Crookston
13	9.7	Foley	Foley
13	9.7	Mora	Mora
15	9.6	Alexandria	Alexandria
15	9.6	Worthington	Worthington
17	9.5	Grand Rapids	Grand Rapids
18	9.3	Mankato	Mankato
18	9.3	Sauk Rapids	Sauk Rapids
20	9.2	Cloquet	Cloquet
21	9.0	Fairmont Area Schools	Fairmont
21	9.0	Robbinsdale	New Hope
23	8.9	Faribault	Faribault
24	8.8	Annandale	Annandale
24	8.8	Fridley	Fridley
24	8.8	Rockford	Rockford
27	8.7	Austin	Austin
27	8.7	Columbia Heights	Columbia Hgts
27	8.7	Dassel-Cokato	Cokato
27	8.7	St. Cloud	St. Cloud
31	8.6	Glencoe-Silver Lake	Glencoe
32	8.5	Marshall	Marshall
32	8.5	Milaca	Milaca
32	8.5	Proctor	Proctor
35	8.4	South St. Paul	S Saint Paul
36	8.3	Litchfield	Litchfield
37	8.2	Stewartville	Stewartville
38	8.1	Hibbing	Hibbing
39	8.0	Lake Superior	Two Harbors
39	8.0	Minneapolis	Minneapolis
39	8.0	Willmar	Willmar
42	7.9	Duluth	Duluth
42	7.9	Richfield	Richfield
44	7.8	Albany	Albany
44	7.8	Red Lake	Red Lake
46	7.7	Bemidji	Bemidji
46	7.7	Bloomington	Bloomington
46	7.7	Buffalo	Buffalo
49	7.6	Winona Area Public Schools	Winona
50	7.5	North Branch	North Branch
50	7.5	West St. Paul-Mendota Hts.-Eagan	Mendota Heights
52	7.1	Big Lake	Big Lake
53	7.1	Cambridge-Isanti	Cambridge
53	7.1	Pine City	Pine City
55	7.0	Virginia	Virginia
56	6.6	Waseca	Waseca
57	6.4	New London-Spicer	New London

Rank		District Name	City
57	6.4	Shakopee	Shakopee
59	6.3	Anoka-Hennepin	Coon Rapids
59	6.3	New Ulm	New Ulm
59	6.3	North St Paul-Maplewood	Maplewood
59	6.3	Osseo	Osseo
63	6.1	Rocori	Cold Spring
64	6.0	Inver Grove Heights Schools	Inver Grove Hgts
64	6.0	Owatonna	Owatonna
64	6.0	Princeton	Princeton
67	5.9	Roseville	Roseville
67	5.9	St. Francis	St. Francis
67	5.9	St. Peter	St. Peter
70	5.5	Chisago Lakes	Lindstrom
71	5.4	Burnsville	Burnsville
71	5.4	Fergus Falls	Fergus Falls
73	5.3	Mounds View	Roseville
73	5.3	White Bear Lake	White Bear Lake
75	5.1	Forest Lake	Forest Lake
75	5.1	Monticello	Monticello
75	5.1	St. Louis Park	St Louis Park
78	5.0	Hermantown	Hermantown
78	5.0	Moorhead	Moorhead
80	4.9	Rochester	Rochester
81	4.7	Lacrescent-Hokah	Lacrescent
81	4.7	Spring Lake Park	Spring Lake Pk
83	4.6	Hutchinson	Hutchinson
84	4.5	Hastings	Hastings
84	4.5	Red Wing	Red Wing
86	4.3	Northfield	Northfield
86	4.3	Sartell	Sartell
88	4.2	Becker	Becker
89	4.1	Westonka	Minnetrista
90	3.8	Chaska	Chaska
91	3.7	Elk River	Elk River
91	3.7	Kasson-Mantorville	Kasson
93	3.6	Farmington	Farmington
94	3.5	Byron	Byron
95	3.3	Centennial	Circle Pines
95	3.3	Hopkins	Hopkins
97	3.1	New Prague Area Schools	New Prague
97	3.1	St. Michael-Albertville	St. Michael
99	3.0	South Washington County	Cottage Grove
99	3.0	Waconia	Waconia
101	2.6	Prior Lake-Savage Area Schools	Prior Lake
101	2.6	Rosemount-Apple Valley-Eagan	Rosemount
101	2.6	Stillwater	Stillwater
104	2.4	Delano	Delano
105	2.2	Intermediate SD 287	Plymouth
105	2.2	St. Anthony-New Brighton	St. Anthony
107	2.0	Wayzata	Wayzata
108	1.9	Eden Prairie	Eden Prairie
108	1.9	Mahtomedi	Mahtomedi
110	1.8	Edina	Edina
111	1.7	Lakeville	Lakeville
111	1.7	Orono	Long Lake
113	1.0	Minnetonka	Minnetonka

Student/Teacher Ratio

Rank	Ratio	District Name	City
1	22.8	Elk River	Elk River
2	21.8	Osseo	Osseo
3	20.9	St. Francis	St. Francis
4	20.5	Spring Lake Park	Spring Lake Pk
5	20.3	Hastings	Hastings
6	20.2	Wayzata	Wayzata
7	19.8	Duluth	Duluth
8	19.7	Mounds View	Roseville
8	19.7	Shakopee	Shakopee
10	19.6	North Branch	North Branch
11	19.5	Stillwater	Stillwater
11	19.5	White Bear Lake	White Bear Lake
13	19.4	Virginia	Virginia
14	19.3	Red Wing	Red Wing
15	19.0	St. Michael-Albertville	St. Michael
16	18.9	Eden Prairie	Eden Prairie
16	18.9	North St Paul-Maplewood	Maplewood
18	18.8	Centennial	Circle Pines
18	18.8	Chisago Lakes	Lindstrom
20	18.7	South St. Paul	S Saint Paul
21	18.6	Hermantown	Hermantown
22	18.4	Cambridge-Isanti	Cambridge
22	18.4	Orono	Long Lake
24	18.3	Anoka-Hennepin	Coon Rapids
24	18.3	Waconia	Waconia
26	18.2	Hibbing	Hibbing
26	18.2	Lacrescent-Hokah	Lacrescent
28	18.1	Bloomington	Bloomington
28	18.1	Cloquet	Cloquet
28	18.1	Forest Lake	Forest Lake
28	18.1	Robbinsdale	New Hope
28	18.1	South Washington County	Cottage Grove
28	18.1	St. Anthony-New Brighton	St. Anthony
34	18.0	Big Lake	Big Lake
34	18.0	New Prague Area Schools	New Prague
34	18.0	Princeton	Princeton
37	17.9	Delano	Delano
37	17.9	Mahtomedi	Mahtomedi
37	17.9	Prior Lake-Savage Area Schools	Prior Lake
40	17.8	Buffalo	Buffalo
41	17.7	Edina	Edina
41	17.7	Farmington	Farmington
41	17.7	Inver Grove Heights Schools	Inver Grove Hgts
44	17.6	Grand Rapids	Grand Rapids
44	17.6	Rochester	Rochester
44	17.6	Rocori	Cold Spring
47	17.5	Becker	Becker
47	17.5	Chaska	Chaska
47	17.5	Dassel-Cokato	Cokato
47	17.5	Lakeville	Lakeville
47	17.5	Roseville	Roseville
47	17.5	Stewartville	Stewartville
47	17.5	West St. Paul-Mendota Hts.-Eagan	Mendota Heights
54	17.4	Byron	Byron
54	17.4	Owatonna	Owatonna
54	17.4	Rockford	Rockford
57	17.3	Monticello	Monticello
57	17.3	Sartell	Sartell
57	17.3	Westonka	Minnetrista
60	17.2	Kasson-Mantorville	Kasson
61	17.0	Hutchinson	Hutchinson
62	16.9	Annandale	Annandale
62	16.9	Brooklyn Center	Brooklyn Center
62	16.9	Sauk Rapids	Sauk Rapids
65	16.8	Brainerd	Brainerd
65	16.8	Mankato	Mankato
65	16.8	Mora	Mora
68	16.7	Lake Superior	Two Harbors
68	16.7	Minnetonka	Minnetonka
70	16.6	Fridley	Fridley
70	16.6	Little Falls	Little Falls
72	16.5	Austin	Austin
72	16.5	Hopkins	Hopkins
72	16.5	New London-Spicer	New London
72	16.5	Proctor	Proctor
76	16.4	Waseca	Waseca
77	16.3	Albert Lea	Albert Lea
77	16.3	Alexandria	Alexandria
77	16.3	Columbia Heights	Columbia Hgts
77	16.3	Faribault	Faribault
77	16.3	Pine City	Pine City
77	16.3	Rosemount-Apple Valley-Eagan	Rosemount
83	16.1	Burnsville	Burnsville
83	16.1	Fairmont Area Schools	Fairmont
83	16.1	Foley	Foley
83	16.1	St. Cloud	St. Cloud
87	16.0	Litchfield	Litchfield
87	16.0	Park Rapids	Park Rapids
89	15.9	Albany	Albany
90	15.8	Glencoe-Silver Lake	Glencoe
90	15.8	Richfield	Richfield
92	15.5	Crookston	Crookston
92	15.5	Moorhead	Moorhead
94	15.4	Milaca	Milaca
94	15.4	St. Paul	St. Paul
96	15.2	Thief River Falls	Thief River Fls
97	15.1	Bemidji	Bemidji
97	15.1	New Ulm	New Ulm
97	15.1	St. Peter	St. Peter
97	15.1	Winona Area Public Schools	Winona
101	15.0	St. Louis Park	St Louis Park
102	14.9	Fergus Falls	Fergus Falls
103	14.7	Northfield	Northfield
104	14.6	Perham	Perham
105	14.3	East Grand Forks	E Grand Forks
105	14.3	Minneapolis	Minneapolis
107	14.2	Marshall	Marshall
108	14.1	Worthington	Worthington
109	14.0	Willmar	Willmar
110	13.9	Detroit Lakes	Detroit Lakes
111	13.5	St. Louis County	Virginia
112	9.3	Red Lake	Red Lake
113	8.5	Intermediate SD 287	Plymouth

Student/Librarian Ratio

Rank	Ratio	District Name	City
1	2,486.5	Owatonna	Owatonna
2	2,025.5	Winona Area Public Schools	Winona
3	1,821.0	Annandale	Annandale
4	1,771.0	Glencoe-Silver Lake	Glencoe
5	1,684.5	South St. Paul	S Saint Paul
6	1,680.8	Grand Rapids	Grand Rapids
7	1,625.0	Lake Superior	Two Harbors
8	1,551.0	Byron	Byron
9	1,536.0	Hutchinson	Hutchinson
10	1,422.9	Waconia	Waconia
11	1,416.3	Mounds View	Roseville
12	1,368.3	Richfield	Richfield
13	1,362.0	Austin	Austin
14	1,361.5	Anoka-Hennepin	Coon Rapids
15	1,324.0	North Branch	North Branch
16	1,314.7	Marshall	Marshall
17	1,292.1	Elk River	Elk River
18	1,290.8	Eden Prairie	Eden Prairie
19	1,284.7	Stillwater	Stillwater
20	1,224.3	Willmar	Willmar
21	1,189.2	Little Falls	Little Falls
22	1,181.1	Burnsville	Burnsville
23	1,175.2	Centennial	Circle Pines
24	1,118.0	Virginia	Virginia
25	1,079.8	Spring Lake Park	Spring Lake Pk
26	1,041.1	Albert Lea	Albert Lea
27	1,029.2	Hastings	Hastings
28	1,020.0	Rosemount-Apple Valley-Eagan	Rosemount
29	1,005.6	Lacrescent-Hokah	Lacrescent
30	1,003.7	Red Wing	Red Wing
31	992.0	Hermantown	Hermantown
32	991.2	White Bear Lake	White Bear Lake
33	983.9	Stewartville	Stewartville
34	982.6	Cambridge-Isanti	Cambridge
35	975.0	Litchfield	Litchfield
36	973.8	Orono	Long Lake
37	968.0	Bemidji	Bemidji
38	965.9	Fergus Falls	Fergus Falls
39	964.0	Milaca	Milaca
40	960.0	Detroit Lakes	Detroit Lakes
41	958.9	Buffalo	Buffalo
42	947.5	Kasson-Mantorville	Kasson
43	936.3	St. Paul	St. Paul
44	932.0	Proctor	Proctor
45	930.5	Rochester	Rochester
46	925.3	Sartell	Sartell
47	908.5	Farmington	Farmington
48	906.3	St. Michael-Albertville	St. Michael
49	901.6	Faribault	Faribault
50	896.5	Fairmont Area Schools	Fairmont
51	894.2	Moorhead	Moorhead
52	879.0	Rockford	Rockford
53	877.5	Park Rapids	Park Rapids
54	866.4	Waseca	Waseca
55	866.0	Brooklyn Center	Brooklyn Center
56	863.0	New London-Spicer	New London
57	860.1	Robbinsdale	New Hope
58	859.8	Princeton	Princeton
59	858.5	Pine City	Pine City
60	849.6	Minnetonka	Minnetonka
61	845.9	Chaska	Chaska
62	838.6	Cloquet	Cloquet
63	838.5	Foley	Foley
64	833.2	St. Cloud	St. Cloud
65	830.9	Northfield	Northfield
66	829.6	North St Paul-Maplewood	Maplewood
67	822.5	St. Anthony-New Brighton	St. Anthony
68	815.5	Shakopee	Shakopee
69	812.6	Edina	Edina
70	809.8	Wayzata	Wayzata
71	808.5	Lakeville	Lakeville
72	802.8	Big Lake	Big Lake
73	799.4	Duluth	Duluth
74	799.0	Albany	Albany
75	798.6	Roseville	Roseville
76	793.0	Monticello	Monticello
77	784.9	Hopkins	Hopkins
78	780.5	Osseo	Osseo
79	775.0	Forest Lake	Forest Lake
80	770.1	Prior Lake-Savage Area Schools	Prior Lake
81	769.5	Mahtomedi	Mahtomedi
82	765.3	Worthington	Worthington
83	752.0	St. Peter	St. Peter
84	744.2	South Washington County	Cottage Grove
85	725.6	West St. Paul-Mendota Hts.-Eagan	Mendota Heights
86	724.6	Chisago Lakes	Lindstrom
87	721.0	Sauk Rapids	Sauk Rapids
88	718.0	New Prague Area Schools	New Prague
89	713.7	Mora	Mora
90	703.9	Alexandria	Alexandria
91	698.3	Thief River Falls	Thief River Fls
92	682.9	Perham	Perham
93	680.8	Hibbing	Hibbing
94	661.8	Fridley	Fridley
95	659.8	Brainerd	Brainerd
96	649.6	Bloomington	Bloomington
97	646.3	Inver Grove Heights Schools	Inver Grove Hgts
98	645.9	Columbia Heights	Columbia Hgts
99	642.3	Delano	Delano
100	613.8	Becker	Becker
100	613.8	Minneapolis	Minneapolis
102	610.9	Mankato	Mankato

Rank		District Name	City
103	594.8	New Ulm	New Ulm
104	587.6	St. Louis Park	St Louis Park
105	567.5	Dassel-Cokato	Cokato
105	567.5	Westonka	Minnetrista
107	562.8	East Grand Forks	E Grand Forks
108	501.1	Rocori	Cold Spring
109	464.6	St. Louis County	Virginia
110	375.8	Red Lake	Red Lake
111	n/a	Crookston	Crookston
111	n/a	Intermediate SD 287	Plymouth
111	n/a	St. Francis	St. Francis

Rank		District Name	City
79	647.8	Duluth	Duluth
80	641.0	Centennial	Circle Pines
81	630.3	Grand Rapids	Grand Rapids
82	618.8	Lacrescent-Hokah	Lacrescent
83	617.0	Spring Lake Park	Spring Lake Pk
84	591.9	North St Paul-Maplewood	Maplewood
85	590.3	Stewartville	Stewartville
86	579.7	St. Louis Park	St Louis Park
87	574.0	Chaska	Chaska
87	574.0	Worthington	Worthington
89	571.6	Fergus Falls	Fergus Falls
90	567.5	Westonka	Minnetrista
91	560.7	Rocori	Cold Spring
92	558.8	Marshall	Marshall
93	551.1	Hermantown	Hermantown
94	545.8	East Grand Forks	E Grand Forks
95	541.8	Rochester	Rochester
96	541.7	Lake Superior	Two Harbors
97	536.5	Moorhead	Moorhead
98	523.8	Thief River Falls	Thief River Fls
99	522.2	St. Paul	St. Paul
100	517.0	Byron	Byron
101	512.0	Hutchinson	Hutchinson
102	506.2	Detroit Lakes	Detroit Lakes
103	504.1	West St. Paul-Mendota Hts.-Eagan	Mendota Heights
104	489.4	Hopkins	Hopkins
105	473.8	Kasson-Mantorville	Kasson
106	463.2	Mankato	Mankato
107	450.1	Winona Area Public Schools	Winona
108	434.8	Cloquet	Cloquet
109	430.2	Fridley	Fridley
110	396.5	New Ulm	New Ulm
110	396.5	St. Cloud	St. Cloud
112	n/a	Red Wing	Red Wing
112	n/a	South St. Paul	S Saint Paul

Rank		District Name	City
55	7,309	Rocori	Cold Spring
56	7,278	Albert Lea	Albert Lea
56	7,278	East Grand Forks	E Grand Forks
58	7,271	Rosemount-Apple Valley-Eagan	Rosemount
59	7,269	White Bear Lake	White Bear Lake
60	7,176	Columbia Heights	Columbia Hgts
61	7,172	Crookston	Crookston
61	7,172	Forest Lake	Forest Lake
63	7,159	Anoka-Hennepin	Coon Rapids
64	7,138	South St. Paul	S Saint Paul
65	7,119	North St Paul-Maplewood	Maplewood
66	7,077	Alexandria	Alexandria
67	7,046	Cambridge-Isanti	Cambridge
68	7,040	Owatonna	Owatonna
68	7,040	Proctor	Proctor
70	7,036	Little Falls	Little Falls
70	7,036	Mankato	Mankato
72	7,022	Litchfield	Litchfield
73	7,015	Shakopee	Shakopee
74	6,993	Eden Prairie	Eden Prairie
75	6,984	Fairmont Area Schools	Fairmont
76	6,975	Spring Lake Park	Spring Lake Pk
77	6,957	Foley	Foley
78	6,956	Annandale	Annandale
79	6,935	Hastings	Hastings
80	6,898	Sauk Rapids	Sauk Rapids
81	6,882	Lacrescent-Hokah	Lacrescent
82	6,871	Monticello	Monticello
83	6,859	Glencoe-Silver Lake	Glencoe
84	6,848	Centennial	Circle Pines
85	6,834	Pine City	Pine City
86	6,829	Rockford	Rockford
87	6,820	Lakeville	Lakeville
88	6,797	Waconia	Waconia
89	6,785	New London-Spicer	New London
90	6,749	North Branch	North Branch
91	6,727	Elk River	Elk River
92	6,725	Becker	Becker
93	6,668	Milaca	Milaca
94	6,652	Sartell	Sartell
95	6,642	Albany	Albany
96	6,621	Chisago Lakes	Lindstrom
97	6,603	Hutchinson	Hutchinson
98	6,582	Mora	Mora
99	6,579	Farmington	Farmington
100	6,572	Buffalo	Buffalo
101	6,566	St. Francis	St. Francis
102	6,525	Prior Lake-Savage Area Schools	Prior Lake
103	6,487	Hermantown	Hermantown
104	6,460	Byron	Byron
105	6,450	Delano	Delano
106	6,375	New Prague Area Schools	New Prague
107	6,310	Princeton	Princeton
108	6,298	Dassel-Cokato	Cokato
109	6,294	Kasson-Mantorville	Kasson
110	6,280	Stewartville	Stewartville
111	6,052	Big Lake	Big Lake
112	5,971	St. Michael-Albertville	St. Michael
113	n/a	Intermediate SD 287	Plymouth

Student/Counselor Ratio

Rank	Ratio	District Name	City
1	2,270.0	Dassel-Cokato	Cokato
2	1,928.0	Milaca	Milaca
3	1,732.0	Brooklyn Center	Brooklyn Center
4	1,613.3	Bemidji	Bemidji
5	1,517.0	Crookston	Crookston
6	1,388.3	Wayzata	Wayzata
7	1,324.0	North Branch	North Branch
8	1,227.5	Becker	Becker
9	1,223.3	Shakopee	Shakopee
10	1,216.9	Anoka-Hennepin	Coon Rapids
11	1,189.2	Little Falls	Little Falls
12	1,172.0	Rockford	Rockford
13	1,168.0	Lakeville	Lakeville
14	1,109.0	Prior Lake-Savage Area Schools	Prior Lake
15	1,074.8	White Bear Lake	White Bear Lake
16	1,070.3	Big Lake	Big Lake
17	1,038.9	Burnsville	Burnsville
18	1,030.8	Minneapolis	Minneapolis
19	1,025.2	St. Francis	St. Francis
20	1,021.5	Austin	Austin
21	1,013.0	Intermediate SD 287	Plymouth
22	1,010.0	Pine City	Pine City
23	1,002.7	Cambridge-Isanti	Cambridge
24	996.8	Elk River	Elk River
25	994.6	Owatonna	Owatonna
26	991.3	Monticello	Monticello
27	979.2	Chisago Lakes	Lindstrom
28	975.0	Litchfield	Litchfield
29	963.5	Delano	Delano
29	963.5	Mora	Mora
31	958.9	New London-Spicer	New London
32	957.3	New Prague Area Schools	New Prague
33	948.9	Rosemount-Apple Valley-Eagan	Rosemount
34	932.0	Proctor	Proctor
35	925.3	Sartell	Sartell
36	912.7	Roseville	Roseville
37	911.0	Albert Lea	Albert Lea
38	910.5	Annandale	Annandale
39	907.7	Hibbing	Hibbing
40	907.3	Brainerd	Brainerd
41	906.3	St. Michael-Albertville	St. Michael
42	896.5	Fairmont Area Schools	Fairmont
43	885.5	Glencoe-Silver Lake	Glencoe
44	879.0	Buffalo	Buffalo
45	877.5	Park Rapids	Park Rapids
46	875.1	Eden Prairie	Eden Prairie
47	861.1	Mounds View	Roseville
48	859.8	Princeton	Princeton
49	857.0	Willmar	Willmar
50	838.5	Foley	Foley
50	838.5	Virginia	Virginia
52	830.6	Alexandria	Alexandria
53	821.0	Richfield	Richfield
54	819.5	Perham	Perham
55	817.5	Stillwater	Stillwater
56	812.6	Edina	Edina
57	811.4	Faribault	Faribault
58	809.5	Robbinsdale	New Hope
59	806.3	Waconia	Waconia
60	803.0	Columbia Heights	Columbia Hgts
61	799.0	Albany	Albany
62	775.6	Inver Grove Heights Schools	Inver Grove Hgts
63	775.0	Forest Lake	Forest Lake
64	764.6	Minnetonka	Minnetonka
65	755.0	South Washington County	Cottage Grove
66	752.0	St. Peter	St. Peter
67	751.5	Red Lake	Red Lake
68	747.7	St. Anthony-New Brighton	St. Anthony
69	735.1	Hastings	Hastings
70	726.8	Farmington	Farmington
71	723.4	Orono	Long Lake
72	721.0	Sauk Rapids	Sauk Rapids
73	684.0	Mahtomedi	Mahtomedi
74	680.2	Osseo	Osseo
75	676.9	Waseca	Waseca
76	665.8	Bloomington	Bloomington
77	659.0	Northfield	Northfield
78	653.0	St. Louis County	Virginia

Current Spending per Student in FY2003

Rank	Dollars	District Name	City
1	14,843	Red Lake	Red Lake
2	11,304	Minneapolis	Minneapolis
3	10,112	St. Paul	St. Paul
4	9,842	St. Louis Park	St Louis Park
5	9,597	St. Louis County	Virginia
6	9,359	Hopkins	Hopkins
7	8,512	Brooklyn Center	Brooklyn Center
8	8,465	Roseville	Roseville
9	8,404	St. Cloud	St. Cloud
10	8,357	Duluth	Duluth
11	8,266	Lake Superior	Two Harbors
12	8,207	Richfield	Richfield
13	8,192	Faribault	Faribault
14	8,073	West St. Paul-Mendota Hts.-Eagan	Mendota Heights
15	8,059	Robbinsdale	New Hope
16	8,049	Cloquet	Cloquet
17	8,004	Brainerd	Brainerd
18	7,986	Edina	Edina
19	7,973	Worthington	Worthington
20	7,962	Bloomington	Bloomington
21	7,957	Minnetonka	Minnetonka
22	7,952	Grand Rapids	Grand Rapids
23	7,928	Winona Area Public Schools	Winona
24	7,894	Marshall	Marshall
25	7,825	Wayzata	Wayzata
26	7,811	Westonka	Minnetrista
27	7,780	Hibbing	Hibbing
28	7,779	Bemidji	Bemidji
29	7,762	Burnsville	Burnsville
30	7,722	Fridley	Fridley
31	7,702	Park Rapids	Park Rapids
32	7,650	St. Peter	St. Peter
33	7,632	St. Anthony-New Brighton	St. Anthony
34	7,622	Red Wing	Red Wing
35	7,594	Orono	Long Lake
36	7,575	Mounds View	Roseville
37	7,571	Willmar	Willmar
38	7,566	Northfield	Northfield
39	7,565	Virginia	Virginia
40	7,522	Osseo	Osseo
41	7,515	Rochester	Rochester
42	7,490	New Ulm	New Ulm
43	7,487	Moorhead	Moorhead
44	7,486	Perham	Perham
45	7,482	Inver Grove Heights Schools	Inver Grove Hgts
46	7,476	Waseca	Waseca
47	7,434	Mahtomedi	Mahtomedi
48	7,423	Detroit Lakes	Detroit Lakes
49	7,422	Fergus Falls	Fergus Falls
50	7,411	Thief River Falls	Thief River Fls
51	7,403	South Washington County	Cottage Grove
52	7,356	Austin	Austin
53	7,339	Stillwater	Stillwater
54	7,331	Chaska	Chaska

Number of Diploma Recipients

Rank	Number	District Name	City
1	2,372	Anoka-Hennepin	Coon Rapids
2	2,180	Minneapolis	Minneapolis
3	2,127	St. Paul	St. Paul
4	1,865	Rosemount-Apple Valley-Eagan	Rosemount
5	1,342	Osseo	Osseo
6	1,068	Rochester	Rochester
7	1,031	South Washington County	Cottage Grove
8	918	Mounds View	Roseville
9	915	Duluth	Duluth
10	834	St. Cloud	St. Cloud
11	831	White Bear Lake	White Bear Lake
12	751	Burnsville	Burnsville
13	709	North St Paul-Maplewood	Maplewood
14	706	Eden Prairie	Eden Prairie
15	704	Stillwater	Stillwater
16	693	Robbinsdale	New Hope
17	662	Bloomington	Bloomington
18	656	Hopkins	Hopkins
19	655	Lakeville	Lakeville
20	642	Wayzata	Wayzata
21	606	Mankato	Mankato
22	595	Elk River	Elk River
23	570	Forest Lake	Forest Lake
24	499	Edina	Edina
25	498	Brainerd	Brainerd
25	498	Roseville	Roseville
27	492	Minnetonka	Minnetonka
28	431	Hastings	Hastings
29	399	Moorhead	Moorhead
30	390	Chaska	Chaska

Rank		District Name	City
31	376	Faribault	Faribault
32	359	Owatonna	Owatonna
33	356	Grand Rapids	Grand Rapids
34	348	Winona Area Public Schools	Winona
35	341	Buffalo	Buffalo
36	340	Bemidji	Bemidji
36	340	Centennial	Circle Pines
38	335	Alexandria	Alexandria
39	334	Cambridge-Isanti	Cambridge
40	315	West St. Paul-Mendota Hts.-Eagan	Mendota Heights
41	302	Little Falls	Little Falls
42	297	Northfield	Northfield
42	297	St. Francis	St. Francis
44	283	Farmington	Farmington
45	282	Prior Lake-Savage Area Schools	Prior Lake
46	275	Albert Lea	Albert Lea
46	275	Spring Lake Park	Spring Lake Pk
48	274	Austin	Austin
49	269	Willmar	Willmar
50	265	Inver Grove Heights Schools	Inver Grove Hgts
51	263	Red Wing	Red Wing
51	263	South St. Paul	S Saint Paul
53	261	Richfield	Richfield
54	259	North Branch	North Branch
54	259	St. Louis Park	St Louis Park
56	251	Fergus Falls	Fergus Falls
57	243	Marshall	Marshall
58	240	Chisago Lakes	Lindstrom
59	237	Monticello	Monticello
60	236	Mahtomedi	Mahtomedi
61	230	Sauk Rapids	Sauk Rapids
62	228	Hutchinson	Hutchinson
63	215	New Ulm	New Ulm
64	213	Columbia Heights	Columbia Hgts
64	213	Detroit Lakes	Detroit Lakes
66	211	St. Louis County	Virginia
67	208	Hibbing	Hibbing
67	208	New Prague Area Schools	New Prague
69	202	Princeton	Princeton
70	201	Shakopee	Shakopee
71	199	Dassel-Cokato	Cokato
72	197	Cloquet	Cloquet
73	192	Rocori	Cold Spring
73	192	Worthington	Worthington
75	189	Sartell	Sartell
75	189	Thief River Falls	Thief River Fls
77	185	Orono	Long Lake
78	167	Fairmont Area Schools	Fairmont
78	167	Proctor	Proctor
80	166	St. Michael-Albertville	St. Michael
81	162	Lacrescent-Hokah	Lacrescent
81	162	Litchfield	Litchfield
83	158	Fridley	Fridley
84	154	Westonka	Minnetrista
85	151	St. Peter	St. Peter
85	151	Waseca	Waseca
87	149	Hermantown	Hermantown
88	147	Pine City	Pine City
89	146	Albany	Albany
89	146	Mora	Mora
91	140	Lake Superior	Two Harbors
92	139	Crookston	Crookston
93	138	Glencoe-Silver Lake	Glencoe
93	138	Perham	Perham
95	136	Foley	Foley
96	134	Waconia	Waconia
97	132	Intermediate SD 287	Plymouth
98	130	Virginia	Virginia
99	129	Park Rapids	Park Rapids
99	129	Stewartville	Stewartville
101	125	Big Lake	Big Lake
101	125	New London-Spicer	New London
103	121	Brooklyn Center	Brooklyn Center
104	119	Delano	Delano
104	119	Milaca	Milaca
106	117	Annandale	Annandale
106	117	Becker	Becker
108	116	East Grand Forks	E Grand Forks
108	116	St. Anthony-New Brighton	St. Anthony
110	106	Byron	Byron
111	105	Rockford	Rockford
112	98	Kasson-Mantorville	Kasson
113	39	Red Lake	Red Lake

High School Drop-out Rate

Rank	Percent	District Name	City
1	13.9	Intermediate SD 287	Plymouth
2	12.5	Minneapolis	Minneapolis
3	12.1	Red Lake	Red Lake
4	9.5	Worthington	Worthington
5	9.3	Spring Lake Park	Spring Lake Pk
6	8.9	Columbia Heights	Columbia Hgts
7	8.7	Grand Rapids	Grand Rapids
8	7.9	Richfield	Richfield
9	7.7	Duluth	Duluth
10	7.3	South St. Paul	S Saint Paul
11	6.8	Brainerd	Brainerd
12	6.6	St. Paul	St. Paul
13	5.9	Crookston	Crookston
14	5.7	Pine City	Pine City
14	5.7	Willmar	Willmar
16	5.6	Park Rapids	Park Rapids
17	5.5	Fridley	Fridley
18	5.3	Waseca	Waseca
19	5.2	Elk River	Elk River
19	5.2	Fergus Falls	Fergus Falls
21	5.1	Austin	Austin
21	5.1	Red Wing	Red Wing
23	4.9	Brooklyn Center	Brooklyn Center
23	4.9	Cloquet	Cloquet
25	4.8	Mora	Mora
25	4.8	St. Cloud	St. Cloud
27	4.7	Faribault	Faribault
27	4.7	Northfield	Northfield
27	4.7	Perham	Perham
30	4.5	Detroit Lakes	Detroit Lakes
31	4.3	Bemidji	Bemidji
32	4.1	Dassel-Cokato	Cokato
32	4.1	Hutchinson	Hutchinson
34	3.9	Anoka-Hennepin	Coon Rapids
35	3.7	Marshall	Marshall
36	3.6	Moorhead	Moorhead
36	3.6	Shakopee	Shakopee
38	3.4	Glencoe-Silver Lake	Glencoe
38	3.4	Owatonna	Owatonna
40	3.3	Mankato	Mankato
41	3.2	Burnsville	Burnsville
41	3.2	Lake Superior	Two Harbors
43	3.1	Forest Lake	Forest Lake
44	3.0	Fairmont Area Schools	Fairmont
44	3.0	Monticello	Monticello
46	2.9	Annandale	Annandale
46	2.9	North Branch	North Branch
46	2.9	Rochester	Rochester
46	2.9	Winona Area Public Schools	Winona
50	2.8	Albert Lea	Albert Lea
50	2.8	Milaca	Milaca
52	2.6	Farmington	Farmington
52	2.6	Hibbing	Hibbing
52	2.6	Mounds View	Roseville
55	2.5	South Washington County	Cottage Grove
56	2.4	Foley	Foley
57	2.3	New Ulm	New Ulm
57	2.3	Osseo	Osseo
57	2.3	St. Louis County	Virginia
60	2.2	Kasson-Mantorville	Kasson
60	2.2	Lakeville	Lakeville
60	2.2	Little Falls	Little Falls
60	2.2	Virginia	Virginia
64	2.1	East Grand Forks	E Grand Forks
64	2.1	Lacrescent-Hokah	Lacrescent
66	2.0	Proctor	Proctor
67	1.9	Robbinsdale	New Hope
67	1.9	Rosemount-Apple Valley-Eagan	Rosemount
67	1.9	St. Louis Park	St Louis Park
70	1.8	Litchfield	Litchfield
70	1.8	West St. Paul-Mendota Hts.-Eagan	Mendota Heights
72	1.7	Big Lake	Big Lake
72	1.7	Inver Grove Heights Schools	Inver Grove Hgts
72	1.7	St. Peter	St. Peter
72	1.7	Thief River Falls	Thief River Fls
72	1.7	White Bear Lake	White Bear Lake
77	1.6	Buffalo	Buffalo
77	1.6	Cambridge-Isanti	Cambridge
77	1.6	Stewartville	Stewartville
80	1.5	Centennial	Circle Pines
80	1.5	New London-Spicer	New London
80	1.5	St. Anthony-New Brighton	St. Anthony
83	1.4	Chisago Lakes	Lindstrom
84	1.3	St. Francis	St. Francis
85	1.2	Delano	Delano
85	1.2	Hastings	Hastings
85	1.2	New Prague Area Schools	New Prague
88	1.1	Bloomington	Bloomington
88	1.1	North St Paul-Maplewood	Maplewood
88	1.1	Rockford	Rockford
88	1.1	St. Michael-Albertville	St. Michael
92	1.0	Becker	Becker
92	1.0	Mahtomedi	Mahtomedi
92	1.0	Princeton	Princeton
92	1.0	Westonka	Minnetrista
96	0.9	Byron	Byron
96	0.9	Chaska	Chaska
98	0.8	Alexandria	Alexandria
98	0.8	Roseville	Roseville
100	0.7	Hopkins	Hopkins
100	0.7	Prior Lake-Savage Area Schools	Prior Lake
100	0.7	Sauk Rapids	Sauk Rapids
100	0.7	Stillwater	Stillwater
104	0.6	Eden Prairie	Eden Prairie
104	0.6	Wayzata	Wayzata
106	0.5	Albany	Albany
106	0.5	Hermantown	Hermantown
106	0.5	Minnetonka	Minnetonka
106	0.5	Rocori	Cold Spring
106	0.5	Sartell	Sartell
111	0.3	Orono	Long Lake
112	0.0	Edina	Edina
112	0.0	Waconia	Waconia

Mississippi

Mississippi Public School Educational Profile

Category	Value	Category	Value
Schools *(2003-2004)*	1,051	**Diploma Recipients** *(2002-2003)*	23,740
Instructional Level		White, Non-Hispanic	12,174
Primary	447	Black, Non-Hispanic	11,195
Middle	189	Asian/Pacific Islander	219
High	282	American Indian/Alaskan Native	32
Other Level	133	Hispanic	120
Curriculum		**High School Drop-out Rate** (%) *(2001-2002)*	3.9
Regular	901	White, Non-Hispanic	3.1
Special Education	0	Black, Non-Hispanic	4.7
Vocational	89	Asian/Pacific Islander	2.2
Alternative	61	American Indian/Alaskan Native	2.2
Type		Hispanic	4.1
Magnet	6	**Staff** *(2003-2004)*	
Charter	1	Teachers	32,991.0
Title I Eligible	688	Average Salary ($)	36,217
School-wide Title I	629	Librarians/Media Specialists	969.8
Students *(2003-2004)*	493,540	Guidance Counselors	1,007.3
Gender (%)		**Ratios** *(2003-2004)*	
Male	51.0	Student/Teacher Ratio	15.0 to 1
Female	49.0	Student/Librarian Ratio	508.9 to 1
Race/Ethnicity (%)		Student/Counselor Ratio	490.0 to 1
White, Non-Hispanic	47.3	**College Entrance Exam Scores** *(2005)*	
Black, Non-Hispanic	50.7	Scholastic Aptitude Test (SAT)	
Asian/Pacific Islander	0.7	Participation Rate (%)	4
American Indian/Alaskan Native	0.2	Mean SAT Reasoning Test Verbal Score	564
Hispanic	1.1	Mean SAT Reasoning Test Math Score	554
Classification (%)		American College Testing Program (ACT)	
Individual Education Program (IEP)	13.5	Participation Rate (%)	94
Migrant *(2002-2003)*	0.5	Average Composite Score	18.7
English Language Learner (ELL)	0.6	Average English Score	18.8
Eligible for Free Lunch Program	56.3	Average Math Score	17.8
Eligible for Reduced-Price Lunch Program	8.0	Average Reading Score	18.9
Current Spending *($ per student in FY 2003)*	5,816	Average Science Score	18.6
Instruction	3,462		
Support Services	1,963		

Note: *For an explanation of data, please refer to the User's Guide in the front of the book*

Mississippi NAEP 2005 Test Scores

Reading			Mathematics		
Grade/Category	Value	Rank	Grade/Category	Value	Rank
4th Grade			**4th Grade**		
Average Proficiency	204.4 (1.35)	50/51	Average Proficiency	226.7 (0.90)	48/51
Proficiency by Gender/Race/Ethnicity			Proficiency by Gender/Race/Ethnicity		
Male	200.3 (1.63)	50/51	Male	227.4 (0.99)	48/51
Female	208.2 (1.56)	50/51	Female	226.0 (1.06)	48/51
White, Non-Hispanic	219.6 (1.36)	48/51	White, Non-Hispanic	238.2 (0.81)	47/51
Black, Non-Hispanic	190.0 (1.61)	40/42	Black, Non-Hispanic	215.6 (1.14)	29/42
Asian, Non-Hispanic	n/a	n/a	Asian, Non-Hispanic	n/a	n/a
American Indian, Non-Hispanic	n/a	n/a	American Indian, Non-Hispanic	n/a	n/a
Hispanic	n/a	n/a	Hispanic	n/a	n/a
Proficiency by Class Size			Proficiency by Class Size		
Less than 16 Students	n/a	n/a	Less than 16 Students	n/a	n/a
16 to 18 Students	n/a	n/a	16 to 18 Students	n/a	n/a
19 to 20 Students	198.3 (3.73)	37/38	19 to 20 Students	222.5 (2.64)	37/38
21 to 25 Students	203.9 (1.70)	49/51	21 to 25 Students	227.6 (1.27)	47/51
Greater than 25 Students	216.3 (3.34)	27/36	Greater than 25 Students	n/a	n/a
Percent Attaining Achievement Levels			Percent Attaining Achievement Levels		
Below Basic	52.2 (1.73)	2/51	Below Basic	30.7 (1.37)	4/51
Basic or Above	47.8 (1.73)	50/51	Basic or Above	69.3 (1.37)	48/51
Proficient or Above	18.2 (1.35)	50/51	Proficient or Above	19.4 (1.17)	49/51
Advanced or Above	2.8 (0.54)	50/51	Advanced or Above	1.3 (0.25)	50/51
8th Grade			**8th Grade**		
Average Proficiency	250.5 (1.25)	48/51	Average Proficiency	262.5 (1.18)	49/51
Proficiency by Gender/Race/Ethnicity			Proficiency by Gender/Race/Ethnicity		
Male	245.9 (1.36)	47/51	Male	262.8 (1.41)	49/51
Female	254.9 (1.52)	50/51	Female	262.2 (1.31)	50/51
White, Non-Hispanic	264.4 (1.33)	44/51	White, Non-Hispanic	278.9 (1.00)	45/51
Black, Non-Hispanic	236.9 (1.48)	35/40	Black, Non-Hispanic	247.2 (1.32)	34/41
Asian, Non-Hispanic	n/a	n/a	Asian, Non-Hispanic	n/a	n/a
American Indian, Non-Hispanic	n/a	n/a	American Indian, Non-Hispanic	n/a	n/a
Hispanic	n/a	n/a	Hispanic	n/a	n/a
Proficiency by Parents Highest Level of Ed.			Proficiency by Parents Highest Level of Ed.		
Did Not Finish High School	244.1 (2.59)	29/49	Did Not Finish High School	254.1 (2.04)	40/50
Graduated High School	244.0 (1.69)	46/50	Graduated High School	252.5 (1.59)	49/50
Some Education After High School	255.0 (2.13)	49/50	Some Education After High School	268.5 (1.75)	48/50
Graduated College	255.1 (1.65)	49/50	Graduated College	268.5 (1.49)	49/50
Percent Attaining Achievement Levels			Percent Attaining Achievement Levels		
Below Basic	52.2 (1.73)	2/51	Below Basic	48.3 (1.66)	2/51
Basic or Above	47.8 (1.73)	50/51	Basic or Above	51.7 (1.66)	50/51
Proficient or Above	18.2 (1.35)	50/51	Proficient or Above	13.5 (0.88)	50/51
Advanced or Above	2.8 (0.54)	50/51	Advanced or Above	1.3 (0.33)	51/51

Note: *For an explanation of data, please refer to the User's Guide in the front of the book; n/a indicates data not available*

Adams County

Natchez-Adams SD
10 Homochitto St • Natchez, MS 39121-1188
Mailing Address: Pob 1188 • Natchez, MS 39121-1188
(601) 445-2800 • http://natchez.k12.ms.us/
Grade Span: PK-12; Agency Type: 1
Schools: 8
  4 Primary; 1 Middle; 2 High; 1 Other Level
  6 Regular; 0 Special Education; 1 Vocational; 1 Alternative
  0 Magnet; 0 Charter; 6 Title I Eligible; 5 School-wide Title I
Students: 4,653 (50.7% male; 49.2% female)
  Individual Education Program: 537 (11.5%);
  English Language Learner: 21 (0.5%); Migrant: 0 (0.0%)
  Eligible for Free Lunch Program: 3,875 (83.3%)
  Eligible for Reduced-Price Lunch Program: 300 (6.4%)
Teachers: 319.0 (14.6 to 1)
Librarians/Media Specialists: 8.0 (581.6 to 1)
Guidance Counselors: 13.0 (357.9 to 1)
Current Spending: ($ per student per year):
  Total: $6,304; Instruction: $3,664; Support Services: $2,230
Enrollment, Drop-out Rates and Diploma Recipients by Race/Ethnicity

Category	Total	White	Black	Asian	AIAN	Hisp.
Enrollment (%)	100.0	12.0	87.5	0.2	0.0	0.3
Drop-out Rate (%)	3.6	6.7	3.1	0.0	n/a	n/a
H.S. Diplomas (#)	283	42	241	0	0	0

Alcorn County

Alcorn SD
Alcorn County Courthouse • Corinth, MS 38835-1420
Mailing Address: PO Box 1420 • Corinth, MS 38835-1420
(662) 286-5591 • http://www.alcorn.k12.ms.us/
Grade Span: KG-12; Agency Type: 1
Schools: 12
  5 Primary; 2 Middle; 4 High; 1 Other Level
  9 Regular; 0 Special Education; 2 Vocational; 1 Alternative
  0 Magnet; 0 Charter; 8 Title I Eligible; 0 School-wide Title I
Students: 3,779 (51.6% male; 48.3% female)
  Individual Education Program: 646 (17.1%);
  English Language Learner: 23 (0.6%); Migrant: 3 (0.1%)
  Eligible for Free Lunch Program: 1,286 (34.0%)
  Eligible for Reduced-Price Lunch Program: 473 (12.5%)
Teachers: 266.2 (14.2 to 1)
Librarians/Media Specialists: 7.5 (503.9 to 1)
Guidance Counselors: 7.2 (524.9 to 1)
Current Spending: ($ per student per year):
  Total: $5,647; Instruction: $3,732; Support Services: $1,587
Enrollment, Drop-out Rates and Diploma Recipients by Race/Ethnicity

Category	Total	White	Black	Asian	AIAN	Hisp.
Enrollment (%)	100.0	94.9	4.2	0.2	0.0	0.6
Drop-out Rate (%)	3.2	3.4	0.0	0.0	n/a	0.0
H.S. Diplomas (#)	223	214	7	1	0	1

Corinth SD
1204 N Harper Rd • Corinth, MS 38834-4500
(662) 287-2425 • http://www.corinth.k12.ms.us/
Grade Span: PK-12; Agency Type: 1
Schools: 5
  2 Primary; 2 Middle; 1 High; 0 Other Level
  5 Regular; 0 Special Education; 0 Vocational; 0 Alternative
  0 Magnet; 0 Charter; 5 Title I Eligible; 5 School-wide Title I
Students: 1,808 (52.1% male; 47.8% female)
  Individual Education Program: 254 (14.0%);
  English Language Learner: 40 (2.2%); Migrant: 1 (0.1%)
  Eligible for Free Lunch Program: 887 (49.1%)
  Eligible for Reduced-Price Lunch Program: 116 (6.4%)
Teachers: 148.0 (12.2 to 1)
Librarians/Media Specialists: 2.9 (623.4 to 1)
Guidance Counselors: 3.0 (602.7 to 1)
Current Spending: ($ per student per year):
  Total: $6,396; Instruction: $4,040; Support Services: $1,988
Enrollment, Drop-out Rates and Diploma Recipients by Race/Ethnicity

Category	Total	White	Black	Asian	AIAN	Hisp.
Enrollment (%)	100.0	53.5	42.9	1.0	0.1	2.5
Drop-out Rate (%)	4.9	2.4	9.2	0.0	0.0	0.0
H.S. Diplomas (#)	94	72	22	0	0	0

Attala County

Kosciusko SD
206 S Huntington • Kosciusko, MS 39090-3718
Mailing Address: 206 S Huntington St • Kosciusko, MS 39090-3718
(662) 289-4771 • http://www2.mde.k12.ms.us/0420/stc.htm
Grade Span: KG-12; Agency Type: 1
Schools: 6
  2 Primary; 2 Middle; 1 High; 1 Other Level
  5 Regular; 0 Special Education; 0 Vocational; 1 Alternative
  0 Magnet; 0 Charter; 3 Title I Eligible; 2 School-wide Title I
Students: 2,085 (51.6% male; 48.3% female)
  Individual Education Program: 378 (18.1%);
  English Language Learner: 4 (0.2%); Migrant: 0 (0.0%)
  Eligible for Free Lunch Program: 1,041 (49.9%)
  Eligible for Reduced-Price Lunch Program: 226 (10.8%)
Teachers: 135.5 (15.4 to 1)
Librarians/Media Specialists: 6.0 (347.5 to 1)
Guidance Counselors: 3.5 (595.7 to 1)
Current Spending: ($ per student per year):
  Total: $5,359; Instruction: $3,320; Support Services: $1,703
Enrollment, Drop-out Rates and Diploma Recipients by Race/Ethnicity

Category	Total	White	Black	Asian	AIAN	Hisp.
Enrollment (%)	100.0	49.4	49.4	0.4	0.0	0.8
Drop-out Rate (%)	0.0	0.0	0.0	0.0	n/a	0.0
H.S. Diplomas (#)	123	76	46	1	0	0

Bolivar County

Cleveland SD
305 Merritt Dr • Cleveland, MS 38732-2247
(601) 843-3529 • http://www2.mde.k12.ms.us/csd/index_htm.html
Grade Span: PK-12; Agency Type: 1
Schools: 12
  6 Primary; 2 Middle; 3 High; 1 Other Level
  10 Regular; 0 Special Education; 1 Vocational; 1 Alternative
  0 Magnet; 1 Charter; 6 Title I Eligible; 6 School-wide Title I
Students: 3,666 (50.5% male; 49.4% female)
  Individual Education Program: 477 (13.0%);
  English Language Learner: 16 (0.4%); Migrant: 0 (0.0%)
  Eligible for Free Lunch Program: 2,413 (65.8%)
  Eligible for Reduced-Price Lunch Program: 161 (4.4%)
Teachers: 257.6 (14.2 to 1)
Librarians/Media Specialists: 11.2 (327.3 to 1)
Guidance Counselors: 9.3 (394.2 to 1)
Current Spending: ($ per student per year):
  Total: $6,025; Instruction: $3,602; Support Services: $2,026
Enrollment, Drop-out Rates and Diploma Recipients by Race/Ethnicity

Category	Total	White	Black	Asian	AIAN	Hisp.
Enrollment (%)	100.0	30.9	67.2	0.6	0.0	1.3
Drop-out Rate (%)	0.9	0.6	1.1	0.0	n/a	0.0
H.S. Diplomas (#)	200	66	131	0	0	3

Calhoun County

Calhoun County SD
119 W Main • Pittsboro, MS 38951-0058
Mailing Address: PO Box 58 • Pittsboro, MS 38951-0058
(662) 412-3152 • http://www2.mde.k12.ms.us/0700/index.htm
Grade Span: PK-12; Agency Type: 1
Schools: 7
  3 Primary; 1 Middle; 2 High; 1 Other Level
  7 Regular; 0 Special Education; 0 Vocational; 0 Alternative
  0 Magnet; 0 Charter; 3 Title I Eligible; 3 School-wide Title I
Students: 2,546 (50.3% male; 49.6% female)
  Individual Education Program: 438 (17.2%);
  English Language Learner: 87 (3.4%); Migrant: 86 (3.4%)
  Eligible for Free Lunch Program: 1,505 (59.1%)
  Eligible for Reduced-Price Lunch Program: 314 (12.3%)
Teachers: 154.2 (16.5 to 1)
Librarians/Media Specialists: 6.5 (391.7 to 1)
Guidance Counselors: 5.0 (509.2 to 1)
Current Spending: ($ per student per year):
  Total: $5,630; Instruction: $3,371; Support Services: $1,820
Enrollment, Drop-out Rates and Diploma Recipients by Race/Ethnicity

Category	Total	White	Black	Asian	AIAN	Hisp.
Enrollment (%)	100.0	52.6	42.1	0.0	0.0	5.2
Drop-out Rate (%)	2.9	2.8	3.2	0.0	n/a	0.0
H.S. Diplomas (#)	131	75	54	0	1	1

Chickasaw County

Houston SD
636 Starkville Rd • Houston, MS 38851-9303
Mailing Address: PO Drawer 351 • Houston, MS 38851-9303
(601) 456-3332 • http://www.houston.k12.ms.us/
Grade Span: KG-12; Agency Type: 1
Schools: 5
   2 Primary; 1 Middle; 2 High; 0 Other Level
   4 Regular; 0 Special Education; 1 Vocational; 0 Alternative
   0 Magnet; 0 Charter; 4 Title I Eligible; 4 School-wide Title I
Students: 1,974   (50.1% male; 49.8% female)
   Individual Education Program: 266 (13.5%);
   English Language Learner: 59 (3.0%); Migrant: 8 (0.4%)
   Eligible for Free Lunch Program: 1,169 (59.2%)
   Eligible for Reduced-Price Lunch Program: 192 (9.7%)
Teachers: 139.1 (14.2 to 1)
Librarians/Media Specialists: 3.7 (533.5 to 1)
Guidance Counselors: 4.0 (493.5 to 1)
Current Spending: ($ per student per year):
   Total: $5,205; Instruction: $3,194; Support Services: $1,671
Enrollment, Drop-out Rates and Diploma Recipients by Race/Ethnicity

Category	Total	White	Black	Asian	AIAN	Hisp.
Enrollment (%)	100.0	49.3	45.9	0.6	0.1	4.1
Drop-out Rate (%)	6.1	8.4	4.0	0.0	n/a	0.0
H.S. Diplomas (#)	77	44	33	0	0	0

Choctaw County

Choctaw County SD
1260e. Quinn St • Ackerman, MS 39735-9768
Mailing Address: PO Drawer 398 126 E Quinn St • Ackerman, MS 39735-9768
(662) 285-6239 • http://www2.mde.k12.ms.us/1000/index.htm
Grade Span: PK-12; Agency Type: 1
Schools: 5
   2 Primary; 0 Middle; 2 High; 1 Other Level
   4 Regular; 0 Special Education; 1 Vocational; 0 Alternative
   0 Magnet; 0 Charter; 3 Title I Eligible; 3 School-wide Title I
Students: 1,787   (50.4% male; 49.5% female)
   Individual Education Program: 238 (13.3%);
   English Language Learner: 0 (0.0%); Migrant: 3 (0.2%)
   Eligible for Free Lunch Program: 1,051 (58.8%)
   Eligible for Reduced-Price Lunch Program: 204 (11.4%)
Teachers: 135.3 (13.2 to 1)
Librarians/Media Specialists: 5.7 (313.5 to 1)
Guidance Counselors: 5.8 (308.1 to 1)
Current Spending: ($ per student per year):
   Total: $5,778; Instruction: $3,545; Support Services: $1,815
Enrollment, Drop-out Rates and Diploma Recipients by Race/Ethnicity

Category	Total	White	Black	Asian	AIAN	Hisp.
Enrollment (%)	100.0	58.4	40.5	0.2	0.3	0.6
Drop-out Rate (%)	4.0	2.4	4.5	0.0	n/a	300.0
H.S. Diplomas (#)	96	55	41	0	0	0

Claiborne County

Claiborne County SD
404 Market St • Port Gibson, MS 39150
Mailing Address: P. O.Box 337 • Port Gibson, MS 39150
(601) 437-4232 • http://www2.mde.k12.ms.us/1100/index.htm
Grade Span: PK-12; Agency Type: 1
Schools: 4
   1 Primary; 1 Middle; 2 High; 0 Other Level
   3 Regular; 0 Special Education; 1 Vocational; 0 Alternative
   0 Magnet; 0 Charter; 2 Title I Eligible; 2 School-wide Title I
Students: 1,600   (48.8% male; 51.1% female)
   Individual Education Program: 128 (8.0%);
   English Language Learner: 0 (0.0%); Migrant: 0 (0.0%)
   Eligible for Free Lunch Program: 1,591 (99.4%)
   Eligible for Reduced-Price Lunch Program: 0 (0.0%)
Teachers: 123.7 (12.9 to 1)
Librarians/Media Specialists: 3.0 (533.3 to 1)
Guidance Counselors: 3.0 (533.3 to 1)
Current Spending: ($ per student per year):
   Total: $7,128; Instruction: $4,073; Support Services: $2,596
Enrollment, Drop-out Rates and Diploma Recipients by Race/Ethnicity

Category	Total	White	Black	Asian	AIAN	Hisp.
Enrollment (%)	100.0	0.3	99.7	0.1	0.0	0.0
Drop-out Rate (%)	3.4	0.0	3.5	0.0	n/a	n/a
H.S. Diplomas (#)	122	1	121	0	0	0

Clarke County

Quitman SD
104 E Franklin St • Quitman, MS 39355-2510
(601) 776-2186 • http://www.qsd.k12.ms.us/
Grade Span: KG-12; Agency Type: 1
Schools: 6
   2 Primary; 1 Middle; 2 High; 1 Other Level
   4 Regular; 0 Special Education; 1 Vocational; 1 Alternative
   0 Magnet; 0 Charter; 3 Title I Eligible; 3 School-wide Title I
Students: 2,368   (51.0% male; 48.9% female)
   Individual Education Program: 343 (14.5%);
   English Language Learner: 0 (0.0%); Migrant: 0 (0.0%)
   Eligible for Free Lunch Program: 1,444 (61.0%)
   Eligible for Reduced-Price Lunch Program: 217 (9.2%)
Teachers: 161.2 (14.7 to 1)
Librarians/Media Specialists: 4.8 (493.3 to 1)
Guidance Counselors: 2.9 (816.6 to 1)
Current Spending: ($ per student per year):
   Total: $5,432; Instruction: $3,129; Support Services: $1,915
Enrollment, Drop-out Rates and Diploma Recipients by Race/Ethnicity

Category	Total	White	Black	Asian	AIAN	Hisp.
Enrollment (%)	100.0	45.1	54.7	0.1	0.0	0.1
Drop-out Rate (%)	7.1	6.9	7.4	0.0	n/a	n/a
H.S. Diplomas (#)	122	51	71	0	0	0

Clay County

West Point SD
429 Commerce St • West Point, MS 39773-2924
Mailing Address: PO Box 656 • West Point, MS 39773-2924
(662) 494-4242 • http://westpoint.k12.ms.us/
Grade Span: PK-12; Agency Type: 1
Schools: 9
   4 Primary; 3 Middle; 2 High; 0 Other Level
   8 Regular; 0 Special Education; 1 Vocational; 0 Alternative
   0 Magnet; 0 Charter; 6 Title I Eligible; 6 School-wide Title I
Students: 3,715   (49.7% male; 50.2% female)
   Individual Education Program: 392 (10.6%);
   English Language Learner: 15 (0.4%); Migrant: 0 (0.0%)
   Eligible for Free Lunch Program: 2,701 (72.7%)
   Eligible for Reduced-Price Lunch Program: 322 (8.7%)
Teachers: 221.8 (16.7 to 1)
Librarians/Media Specialists: 7.4 (502.0 to 1)
Guidance Counselors: 7.8 (476.3 to 1)
Current Spending: ($ per student per year):
   Total: $5,289; Instruction: $3,122; Support Services: $1,754
Enrollment, Drop-out Rates and Diploma Recipients by Race/Ethnicity

Category	Total	White	Black	Asian	AIAN	Hisp.
Enrollment (%)	100.0	21.5	78.0	0.2	0.0	0.4
Drop-out Rate (%)	4.7	2.2	5.5	0.0	n/a	0.0
H.S. Diplomas (#)	153	37	114	0	0	2

Coahoma County

Clarksdale Municipal SD
101 Mcguire Rd • Clarksdale, MS 38614-2733
Mailing Address: PO Box 1088 • Clarksdale, MS 38614-2733
(662) 627-8500 • http://www.cdps.k12.ms.us/default.htm
Grade Span: KG-12; Agency Type: 1
Schools: 12
   6 Primary; 3 Middle; 2 High; 1 Other Level
   10 Regular; 0 Special Education; 1 Vocational; 1 Alternative
   0 Magnet; 0 Charter; 8 Title I Eligible; 8 School-wide Title I
Students: 3,703   (49.3% male; 50.6% female)
   Individual Education Program: 423 (11.4%);
   English Language Learner: 22 (0.6%); Migrant: 1 (<0.1%)
   Eligible for Free Lunch Program: 2,863 (77.3%)
   Eligible for Reduced-Price Lunch Program: 195 (5.3%)
Teachers: 247.7 (14.9 to 1)
Librarians/Media Specialists: 8.2 (451.6 to 1)
Guidance Counselors: 6.6 (561.1 to 1)
Current Spending: ($ per student per year):
   Total: $5,715; Instruction: $3,107; Support Services: $2,146
Enrollment, Drop-out Rates and Diploma Recipients by Race/Ethnicity

Category	Total	White	Black	Asian	AIAN	Hisp.
Enrollment (%)	100.0	8.9	90.4	0.5	0.0	0.1
Drop-out Rate (%)	2.0	3.2	1.9	0.0	n/a	0.0
H.S. Diplomas (#)	121	19	102	0	0	0

Coahoma County SD
1555 Lee Dr • Clarksdale, MS 38614-2915
Mailing Address: PO Box 820 • Clarksdale, MS 38614-2915
(662) 624-5448 • http://www.coahoma.k12.ms.us/
Grade Span: KG-12; **Agency Type:** 1
Schools: 6
    4 Primary; 1 Middle; 1 High; 0 Other Level
    6 Regular; 0 Special Education; 0 Vocational; 0 Alternative
    0 Magnet; 0 Charter; 6 Title I Eligible; 6 School-wide Title I
Students: 1,923 (50.5% male; 49.4% female)
    Individual Education Program: 403 (21.0%);
    English Language Learner: 15 (0.8%); Migrant: 18 (0.9%)
    Eligible for Free Lunch Program: 1,897 (98.6%)
    Eligible for Reduced-Price Lunch Program: 0 (0.0%)
Teachers: 143.5 (13.4 to 1)
Librarians/Media Specialists: 6.2 (310.2 to 1)
Guidance Counselors: 3.9 (493.1 to 1)
Current Spending: ($ per student per year):
    Total: $7,059; Instruction: $4,006; Support Services: $2,603
Enrollment, Drop-out Rates and Diploma Recipients by Race/Ethnicity

Category	Total	White	Black	Asian	AIAN	Hisp.
Enrollment (%)	100.0	1.2	97.5	0.0	0.0	1.2
Drop-out Rate (%)	8.3	20.0	8.1	n/a	n/a	0.0
H.S. Diplomas (#)	63	1	61	0	0	1

Copiah County SD
254 W Gallatin St • Hazlehurst, MS 39083-3026
(601) 894-1341 • http://www2.mde.k12.ms.us/1500/
Grade Span: KG-12; **Agency Type:** 1
Schools: 4
    1 Primary; 1 Middle; 1 High; 1 Other Level
    4 Regular; 0 Special Education; 0 Vocational; 0 Alternative
    0 Magnet; 0 Charter; 4 Title I Eligible; 4 School-wide Title I
Students: 3,069 (51.9% male; 48.0% female)
    Individual Education Program: 225 (7.3%);
    English Language Learner: 0 (0.0%); Migrant: 1 (<0.1%)
    Eligible for Free Lunch Program: 2,203 (71.8%)
    Eligible for Reduced-Price Lunch Program: 161 (5.2%)
Teachers: 194.3 (15.8 to 1)
Librarians/Media Specialists: 6.0 (511.5 to 1)
Guidance Counselors: 2.9 (1,058.3 to 1)
Current Spending: ($ per student per year):
    Total: $5,101; Instruction: $2,745; Support Services: $1,836
Enrollment, Drop-out Rates and Diploma Recipients by Race/Ethnicity

Category	Total	White	Black	Asian	AIAN	Hisp.
Enrollment (%)	100.0	39.4	59.3	0.2	0.0	1.1
Drop-out Rate (%)	11.2	9.4	12.4	n/a	n/a	0.0
H.S. Diplomas (#)	157	62	95	0	0	0

Hazlehurst City SD
119 Robert Mcdaniel Dr • Hazlehurst, MS 39083-3407
(601) 894-1152 • http://www.hazlehurst.k12.ms.us/
Grade Span: PK-12; **Agency Type:** 1
Schools: 2
    1 Primary; 0 Middle; 1 High; 0 Other Level
    2 Regular; 0 Special Education; 0 Vocational; 0 Alternative
    0 Magnet; 0 Charter; 2 Title I Eligible; 2 School-wide Title I
Students: 1,712 (51.9% male; 48.0% female)
    Individual Education Program: 199 (11.6%);
    English Language Learner: 22 (1.3%); Migrant: 0 (0.0%)
    Eligible for Free Lunch Program: 1,534 (89.6%)
    Eligible for Reduced-Price Lunch Program: 96 (5.6%)
Teachers: 112.7 (15.2 to 1)
Librarians/Media Specialists: 3.0 (570.7 to 1)
Guidance Counselors: 1.8 (951.1 to 1)
Current Spending: ($ per student per year):
    Total: $5,766; Instruction: $3,572; Support Services: $1,692
Enrollment, Drop-out Rates and Diploma Recipients by Race/Ethnicity

Category	Total	White	Black	Asian	AIAN	Hisp.
Enrollment (%)	100.0	2.0	95.6	0.2	0.0	2.1
Drop-out Rate (%)	4.3	7.7	4.2	n/a	n/a	0.0
H.S. Diplomas (#)	97	3	94	0	0	0

Covington County Schools
1211 S Dogwood St • Collins, MS 39428-1269
Mailing Address: PO Box 1269 • Collins, MS 39428-1269
(601) 765-8247 • http://www2.mde.k12.ms.us/1600/index.htm
Grade Span: KG-12; **Agency Type:** 1
Schools: 8
    2 Primary; 1 Middle; 2 High; 3 Other Level
    6 Regular; 0 Special Education; 1 Vocational; 1 Alternative

0 Magnet; 0 Charter; 6 Title I Eligible; 6 School-wide Title I
Students: 3,514 (50.6% male; 49.3% female)
    Individual Education Program: 617 (17.6%);
    English Language Learner: 0 (0.0%); Migrant: 35 (1.0%)
    Eligible for Free Lunch Program: 2,459 (70.0%)
    Eligible for Reduced-Price Lunch Program: 343 (9.8%)
Teachers: 230.2 (15.3 to 1)
Librarians/Media Specialists: 8.9 (394.8 to 1)
Guidance Counselors: 7.3 (481.4 to 1)
Current Spending: ($ per student per year):
    Total: $5,643; Instruction: $3,431; Support Services: $1,803
Enrollment, Drop-out Rates and Diploma Recipients by Race/Ethnicity

Category	Total	White	Black	Asian	AIAN	Hisp.
Enrollment (%)	100.0	48.4	51.3	0.0	0.0	0.2
Drop-out Rate (%)	3.9	2.7	4.8	n/a	n/a	100.0
H.S. Diplomas (#)	161	73	88	0	0	0

Desoto County SD
Five E S St • Hernando, MS 38632-2348
(662) 429-5271 • http://www.desoto.k12.ms.us/
Grade Span: KG-12; **Agency Type:** 1
Schools: 26
    12 Primary; 7 Middle; 5 High; 2 Other Level
    24 Regular; 0 Special Education; 1 Vocational; 1 Alternative
    0 Magnet; 0 Charter; 8 Title I Eligible; 8 School-wide Title I
Students: 23,672 (51.8% male; 48.1% female)
    Individual Education Program: 2,812 (11.9%);
    English Language Learner: 365 (1.5%); Migrant: 78 (0.3%)
    Eligible for Free Lunch Program: 4,984 (21.1%)
    Eligible for Reduced-Price Lunch Program: 1,698 (7.2%)
Teachers: 1,266.4 (18.7 to 1)
Librarians/Media Specialists: 29.0 (816.3 to 1)
Guidance Counselors: 41.9 (565.0 to 1)
Current Spending: ($ per student per year):
    Total: $4,444; Instruction: $2,734; Support Services: $1,522
Enrollment, Drop-out Rates and Diploma Recipients by Race/Ethnicity

Category	Total	White	Black	Asian	AIAN	Hisp.
Enrollment (%)	100.0	75.1	20.5	1.0	0.2	3.2
Drop-out Rate (%)	0.9	0.7	2.3	0.0	0.0	1.2
H.S. Diplomas (#)	862	722	119	9	0	12

Forrest County SD
400 Forrest St • Hattiesburg, MS 39403-1977
Mailing Address: PO Box 1977 • Hattiesburg, MS 39403-1977
(601) 545-6055 • http://www2.mde.k12.ms.us/1800/index.html
Grade Span: PK-12; **Agency Type:** 1
Schools: 6
    5 Primary; 0 Middle; 1 High; 0 Other Level
    6 Regular; 0 Special Education; 0 Vocational; 0 Alternative
    0 Magnet; 0 Charter; 5 Title I Eligible; 5 School-wide Title I
Students: 2,482 (51.3% male; 48.6% female)
    Individual Education Program: 389 (15.7%);
    English Language Learner: 21 (0.8%); Migrant: 2 (0.1%)
    Eligible for Free Lunch Program: 1,374 (55.4%)
    Eligible for Reduced-Price Lunch Program: 246 (9.9%)
Teachers: 195.1 (12.7 to 1)
Librarians/Media Specialists: 6.4 (387.8 to 1)
Guidance Counselors: 2.0 (1,241.0 to 1)
Current Spending: ($ per student per year):
    Total: $6,114; Instruction: $3,808; Support Services: $1,989
Enrollment, Drop-out Rates and Diploma Recipients by Race/Ethnicity

Category	Total	White	Black	Asian	AIAN	Hisp.
Enrollment (%)	100.0	59.5	39.6	0.2	0.0	0.6
Drop-out Rate (%)	7.2	7.9	6.5	0.0	0.0	0.0
H.S. Diplomas (#)	57	32	24	0	0	1

Hattiesburg Public SD
301 Mamie St • Hattiesburg, MS 39401
Mailing Address: PO Box 1569 • Hattiesburg, MS 39403-1569
(601) 582-5078 • http://www.hpsd.k12.ms.us/home.htm
Grade Span: KG-12; **Agency Type:** 1
Schools: 10
    6 Primary; 1 Middle; 1 High; 2 Other Level
    9 Regular; 0 Special Education; 0 Vocational; 1 Alternative
    0 Magnet; 0 Charter; 9 Title I Eligible; 9 School-wide Title I
Students: 4,761 (50.3% male; 49.6% female)
    Individual Education Program: 703 (14.8%);
    English Language Learner: 14 (0.3%); Migrant: 24 (0.5%)
    Eligible for Free Lunch Program: 3,539 (74.3%)
    Eligible for Reduced-Price Lunch Program: 217 (4.6%)
Teachers: 394.6 (12.1 to 1)

Librarians/Media Specialists: 9.0 (529.0 to 1)
Guidance Counselors: 11.0 (432.8 to 1)
Current Spending: ($ per student per year):
    Total: $7,199; Instruction: $4,157; Support Services: $2,594
Enrollment, Drop-out Rates and Diploma Recipients by Race/Ethnicity

Category	Total	White	Black	Asian	AIAN	Hisp.
Enrollment (%)	100.0	10.3	88.4	0.4	0.1	0.8
Drop-out Rate (%)	4.2	3.3	4.5	0.0	0.0	0.0
H.S. Diplomas (#)	226	52	171	2	1	0

Petal SD
115 Hwy 42 E • Petal, MS 39465
Mailing Address: PO Drawer 523 • Petal, MS 39465
(601) 545-3002 • http://www.petalschools.com/
Grade Span: KG-12; **Agency Type:** 1
Schools: 4
    2 Primary; 1 Middle; 1 High; 0 Other Level
    4 Regular; 0 Special Education; 0 Vocational; 0 Alternative
    0 Magnet; 0 Charter; 2 Title I Eligible; 2 School-wide Title I
Students: 3,701   (50.2% male; 49.7% female)
    Individual Education Program: 659 (17.8%);
    English Language Learner: 27 (0.7%); Migrant: 0 (0.0%)
    Eligible for Free Lunch Program: 1,312 (35.4%)
    Eligible for Reduced-Price Lunch Program: 457 (12.3%)
Teachers: 252.7 (14.6 to 1)
Librarians/Media Specialists: 4.6 (804.6 to 1)
Guidance Counselors: 4.6 (804.6 to 1)
Current Spending: ($ per student per year):
    Total: $5,575; Instruction: $3,317; Support Services: $1,786
Enrollment, Drop-out Rates and Diploma Recipients by Race/Ethnicity

Category	Total	White	Black	Asian	AIAN	Hisp.
Enrollment (%)	100.0	87.1	11.5	0.3	0.2	0.9
Drop-out Rate (%)	3.3	2.6	9.4	0.0	0.0	0.0
H.S. Diplomas (#)	158	152	6	0	0	0

Franklin County

Franklin County SD
41 First St • Meadville, MS 39653-0605
Mailing Address: PO Box 605 • Meadville, MS 39653-0605
(601) 384-2340 • http://www2.mde.k12.ms.us/1900/index.htm
Grade Span: PK-12; **Agency Type:** 1
Schools: 5
    2 Primary; 1 Middle; 2 High; 0 Other Level
    4 Regular; 0 Special Education; 1 Vocational; 0 Alternative
    0 Magnet; 0 Charter; 4 Title I Eligible; 4 School-wide Title I
Students: 1,568   (54.4% male; 45.5% female)
    Individual Education Program: 298 (19.0%);
    English Language Learner: 1 (0.1%); Migrant: 0 (0.0%)
    Eligible for Free Lunch Program: 943 (60.1%)
    Eligible for Reduced-Price Lunch Program: 172 (11.0%)
Teachers: 120.7 (13.0 to 1)
Librarians/Media Specialists: 3.9 (402.1 to 1)
Guidance Counselors: 3.9 (402.1 to 1)
Current Spending: ($ per student per year):
    Total: $6,960; Instruction: $4,206; Support Services: $2,373
Enrollment, Drop-out Rates and Diploma Recipients by Race/Ethnicity

Category	Total	White	Black	Asian	AIAN	Hisp.
Enrollment (%)	100.0	50.1	49.8	0.0	0.1	0.0
Drop-out Rate (%)	2.1	1.1	3.1	n/a	n/a	n/a
H.S. Diplomas (#)	95	63	32	0	0	0

George County

George County SD
5152 Main St • Lucedale, MS 39452-6533
(601) 947-6993 • http://www.george.k12.ms.us/
Grade Span: PK-12; **Agency Type:** 1
Schools: 8
    5 Primary; 2 Middle; 1 High; 0 Other Level
    8 Regular; 0 Special Education; 0 Vocational; 0 Alternative
    0 Magnet; 0 Charter; 7 Title I Eligible; 7 School-wide Title I
Students: 4,066   (51.6% male; 48.3% female)
    Individual Education Program: 662 (16.3%);
    English Language Learner: 4 (0.1%); Migrant: 9 (0.2%)
    Eligible for Free Lunch Program: 1,716 (42.2%)
    Eligible for Reduced-Price Lunch Program: 394 (9.7%)
Teachers: 256.5 (15.9 to 1)
Librarians/Media Specialists: 7.0 (580.9 to 1)
Guidance Counselors: 6.1 (666.6 to 1)
Current Spending: ($ per student per year):
    Total: $4,985; Instruction: $3,172; Support Services: $1,388

Enrollment, Drop-out Rates and Diploma Recipients by Race/Ethnicity

Category	Total	White	Black	Asian	AIAN	Hisp.
Enrollment (%)	100.0	87.3	11.8	0.1	0.1	0.8
Drop-out Rate (%)	0.5	0.4	0.7	n/a	n/a	0.0
H.S. Diplomas (#)	207	174	32	0	0	1

Greene County

Greene County SD
528 Oak St • Leakesville, MS 39451-1329
Mailing Address: PO Box 1329 • Leakesville, MS 39451-1329
(601) 394-2364 • http://www.schooltree.org/MS-GREENE.html
Grade Span: KG-12; **Agency Type:** 1
Schools: 6
    3 Primary; 1 Middle; 2 High; 0 Other Level
    5 Regular; 0 Special Education; 1 Vocational; 0 Alternative
    0 Magnet; 0 Charter; 4 Title I Eligible; 4 School-wide Title I
Students: 1,949   (49.1% male; 50.8% female)
    Individual Education Program: 312 (16.0%);
    English Language Learner: 0 (0.0%); Migrant: 0 (0.0%)
    Eligible for Free Lunch Program: 1,196 (61.4%)
    Eligible for Reduced-Price Lunch Program: 226 (11.6%)
Teachers: 139.5 (14.0 to 1)
Librarians/Media Specialists: 3.6 (541.4 to 1)
Guidance Counselors: 3.6 (541.4 to 1)
Current Spending: ($ per student per year):
    Total: $6,381; Instruction: $3,870; Support Services: $2,003
Enrollment, Drop-out Rates and Diploma Recipients by Race/Ethnicity

Category	Total	White	Black	Asian	AIAN	Hisp.
Enrollment (%)	100.0	80.0	19.8	0.2	0.0	0.1
Drop-out Rate (%)	6.0	6.9	3.7	n/a	n/a	0.0
H.S. Diplomas (#)	91	63	28	0	0	0

Grenada County

Grenada SD
1855 Jackson Ave • Grenada, MS 38902-1940
Mailing Address: PO Box 1940 • Grenada, MS 38902-1940
(662) 226-1606 • http://www.gsd.k12.ms.us/
Grade Span: PK-12; **Agency Type:** 1
Schools: 6
    1 Primary; 2 Middle; 2 High; 1 Other Level
    5 Regular; 0 Special Education; 1 Vocational; 0 Alternative
    0 Magnet; 0 Charter; 2 Title I Eligible; 2 School-wide Title I
Students: 4,715   (49.7% male; 50.2% female)
    Individual Education Program: 630 (13.4%);
    English Language Learner: 1 (<0.1%); Migrant: 0 (0.0%)
    Eligible for Free Lunch Program: 2,528 (53.6%)
    Eligible for Reduced-Price Lunch Program: 309 (6.6%)
Teachers: 288.5 (16.3 to 1)
Librarians/Media Specialists: 6.0 (785.8 to 1)
Guidance Counselors: 8.1 (582.1 to 1)
Current Spending: ($ per student per year):
    Total: $5,107; Instruction: $3,095; Support Services: $1,698
Enrollment, Drop-out Rates and Diploma Recipients by Race/Ethnicity

Category	Total	White	Black	Asian	AIAN	Hisp.
Enrollment (%)	100.0	45.7	53.9	0.2	0.1	0.1
Drop-out Rate (%)	3.8	3.3	4.2	0.0	n/a	0.0
H.S. Diplomas (#)	180	89	89	0	0	2

Hancock County

Bay St Louis Waveland SD
201 Carroll Ave • Bay St Louis, MS 39520-4513
(228) 467-6621 • http://www.bwsd.org/
Grade Span: KG-12; **Agency Type:** 1
Schools: 5
    2 Primary; 2 Middle; 1 High; 0 Other Level
    5 Regular; 0 Special Education; 0 Vocational; 0 Alternative
    0 Magnet; 0 Charter; 4 Title I Eligible; 4 School-wide Title I
Students: 2,253   (50.4% male; 49.5% female)
    Individual Education Program: 359 (15.9%);
    English Language Learner: 13 (0.6%); Migrant: 8 (0.4%)
    Eligible for Free Lunch Program: 1,229 (54.5%)
    Eligible for Reduced-Price Lunch Program: 264 (11.7%)
Teachers: 160.0 (14.1 to 1)
Librarians/Media Specialists: 6.0 (375.5 to 1)
Guidance Counselors: 5.3 (425.1 to 1)
Current Spending: ($ per student per year):
    Total: $6,567; Instruction: $3,620; Support Services: $2,539

Enrollment, Drop-out Rates and Diploma Recipients by Race/Ethnicity

Category	Total	White	Black	Asian	AIAN	Hisp.
Enrollment (%)	100.0	75.6	20.8	1.8	0.4	1.4
Drop-out Rate (%)	3.9	4.0	4.1	0.0	0.0	0.0
H.S. Diplomas (#)	121	94	21	3	2	1

Hancock County SD
17304 Hwy 603 • Kiln, MS 39556-8210
(228) 255-0376 • http://www.hancock.k12.ms.us/
Grade Span: KG-12; **Agency Type:** 1
Schools: 7
    4 Primary; 1 Middle; 2 High; 0 Other Level
    6 Regular; 0 Special Education; 1 Vocational; 0 Alternative
    0 Magnet; 0 Charter; 4 Title I Eligible; 4 School-wide Title I
Students: 4,391 (50.9% male; 49.0% female)
    Individual Education Program: 671 (15.3%);
    English Language Learner: 1 (<0.1%); Migrant: 15 (0.3%)
    Eligible for Free Lunch Program: 2,171 (49.4%)
    Eligible for Reduced-Price Lunch Program: 584 (13.3%)
Teachers: 275.5 (15.9 to 1)
Librarians/Media Specialists: 5.5 (798.4 to 1)
Guidance Counselors: 7.9 (555.8 to 1)
Current Spending: ($ per student per year):
    Total: $5,433; Instruction: $3,185; Support Services: $1,898
Enrollment, Drop-out Rates and Diploma Recipients by Race/Ethnicity

Category	Total	White	Black	Asian	AIAN	Hisp.
Enrollment (%)	100.0	94.4	3.6	0.6	0.3	1.1
Drop-out Rate (%)	5.4	5.7	1.6	0.0	0.0	0.0
H.S. Diplomas (#)	170	161	6	1	1	1

Harrison County

Biloxi Public SD
160 St Peters Ave • Biloxi, MS 39530
Mailing Address: PO Box 168 • Biloxi, MS 39533-3404
(228) 374-1810 • http://www.biloxischools.net/
Grade Span: KG-12; **Agency Type:** 1
Schools: 12
    7 Primary; 1 Middle; 2 High; 2 Other Level
    10 Regular; 0 Special Education; 1 Vocational; 1 Alternative
    0 Magnet; 0 Charter; 8 Title I Eligible; 8 School-wide Title I
Students: 6,228 (51.6% male; 48.3% female)
    Individual Education Program: 993 (15.9%);
    English Language Learner: 312 (5.0%); Migrant: 270 (4.3%)
    Eligible for Free Lunch Program: 2,762 (44.3%)
    Eligible for Reduced-Price Lunch Program: 718 (11.5%)
Teachers: 414.6 (15.0 to 1)
Librarians/Media Specialists: 14.0 (444.9 to 1)
Guidance Counselors: 5.2 (1,197.7 to 1)
Current Spending: ($ per student per year):
    Total: $7,024; Instruction: $4,303; Support Services: $2,351
Enrollment, Drop-out Rates and Diploma Recipients by Race/Ethnicity

Category	Total	White	Black	Asian	AIAN	Hisp.
Enrollment (%)	100.0	54.7	33.4	8.4	0.2	3.4
Drop-out Rate (%)	3.2	2.2	3.9	7.7	0.0	0.0
H.S. Diplomas (#)	265	157	74	29	0	5

Gulfport SD
2001 Pass Rd • Gulfport, MS 39501
Mailing Address: PO Box 220 • Gulfport, MS 39502-0220
(228) 865-4600 • http://www.gulfport.k12.datasync.com/
Grade Span: KG-12; **Agency Type:** 1
Schools: 12
    7 Primary; 2 Middle; 2 High; 1 Other Level
    10 Regular; 0 Special Education; 1 Vocational; 1 Alternative
    0 Magnet; 0 Charter; 10 Title I Eligible; 10 School-wide Title I
Students: 6,243 (49.9% male; 50.0% female)
    Individual Education Program: 922 (14.8%);
    English Language Learner: 43 (0.7%); Migrant: 69 (1.1%)
    Eligible for Free Lunch Program: 3,553 (56.9%)
    Eligible for Reduced-Price Lunch Program: 518 (8.3%)
Teachers: 456.2 (13.7 to 1)
Librarians/Media Specialists: 12.0 (520.3 to 1)
Guidance Counselors: 16.8 (371.6 to 1)
Current Spending: ($ per student per year):
    Total: $6,952; Instruction: $3,962; Support Services: $2,602
Enrollment, Drop-out Rates and Diploma Recipients by Race/Ethnicity

Category	Total	White	Black	Asian	AIAN	Hisp.
Enrollment (%)	100.0	45.8	50.6	1.3	0.2	2.0
Drop-out Rate (%)	4.0	2.9	5.3	3.1	0.0	8.3
H.S. Diplomas (#)	336	180	142	7	2	5

Harrison County SD
11072 Hwy 49 • Gulfport, MS 39503-2983
(228) 539-6500 • http://www.harrison.k12.ms.us/site2/DesktopDefault.aspx
Grade Span: KG-12; **Agency Type:** 1
Schools: 20
    11 Primary; 3 Middle; 4 High; 2 Other Level
    18 Regular; 0 Special Education; 1 Vocational; 1 Alternative
    0 Magnet; 0 Charter; 13 Title I Eligible; 13 School-wide Title I
Students: 13,049 (51.4% male; 48.5% female)
    Individual Education Program: 1,799 (13.8%);
    English Language Learner: 49 (0.4%); Migrant: 160 (1.2%)
    Eligible for Free Lunch Program: 5,721 (43.8%)
    Eligible for Reduced-Price Lunch Program: 1,453 (11.1%)
Teachers: 816.5 (16.0 to 1)
Librarians/Media Specialists: 19.2 (679.6 to 1)
Guidance Counselors: 14.0 (932.1 to 1)
Current Spending: ($ per student per year):
    Total: $5,331; Instruction: $3,255; Support Services: $1,751
Enrollment, Drop-out Rates and Diploma Recipients by Race/Ethnicity

Category	Total	White	Black	Asian	AIAN	Hisp.
Enrollment (%)	100.0	70.0	26.1	2.4	0.3	1.3
Drop-out Rate (%)	4.5	4.5	4.9	2.7	0.0	2.8
H.S. Diplomas (#)	534	391	108	26	0	9

Long Beach SD
19148 Commission Rd • Long Beach, MS 39560-2618
(228) 864-1146 • http://www.lbsd.k12.ms.us/
Grade Span: KG-12; **Agency Type:** 1
Schools: 5
    3 Primary; 1 Middle; 1 High; 0 Other Level
    5 Regular; 0 Special Education; 0 Vocational; 0 Alternative
    0 Magnet; 0 Charter; 2 Title I Eligible; 2 School-wide Title I
Students: 3,323 (50.1% male; 49.8% female)
    Individual Education Program: 381 (11.5%);
    English Language Learner: 0 (0.0%); Migrant: 26 (0.8%)
    Eligible for Free Lunch Program: 1,004 (30.2%)
    Eligible for Reduced-Price Lunch Program: 354 (10.7%)
Teachers: 223.5 (14.9 to 1)
Librarians/Media Specialists: 6.0 (553.8 to 1)
Guidance Counselors: 9.0 (369.2 to 1)
Current Spending: ($ per student per year):
    Total: $5,614; Instruction: $3,444; Support Services: $1,912
Enrollment, Drop-out Rates and Diploma Recipients by Race/Ethnicity

Category	Total	White	Black	Asian	AIAN	Hisp.
Enrollment (%)	100.0	80.2	14.5	2.9	0.4	1.9
Drop-out Rate (%)	4.1	4.4	2.7	2.0	0.0	5.9
H.S. Diplomas (#)	218	192	13	7	0	6

Pass Christian Public SD
257 Davis Ave • Pass Christian, MS 39571-3522
(228) 452-7271 • http://welcome.to/pcps
Grade Span: KG-12; **Agency Type:** 1
Schools: 4
    2 Primary; 1 Middle; 1 High; 0 Other Level
    4 Regular; 0 Special Education; 0 Vocational; 0 Alternative
    0 Magnet; 0 Charter; 3 Title I Eligible; 3 School-wide Title I
Students: 1,954 (50.4% male; 49.5% female)
    Individual Education Program: 297 (15.2%);
    English Language Learner: 0 (0.0%); Migrant: 52 (2.7%)
    Eligible for Free Lunch Program: 1,055 (54.0%)
    Eligible for Reduced-Price Lunch Program: 231 (11.8%)
Teachers: 130.0 (15.0 to 1)
Librarians/Media Specialists: 4.5 (434.2 to 1)
Guidance Counselors: 3.5 (558.3 to 1)
Current Spending: ($ per student per year):
    Total: $6,796; Instruction: $4,142; Support Services: $2,240
Enrollment, Drop-out Rates and Diploma Recipients by Race/Ethnicity

Category	Total	White	Black	Asian	AIAN	Hisp.
Enrollment (%)	100.0	58.7	36.2	3.1	0.1	1.9
Drop-out Rate (%)	2.0	1.2	2.6	4.2	n/a	25.0
H.S. Diplomas (#)	109	65	37	7	0	0

Hinds County

Clinton Public SD
203 Easthaven Dr • Clinton, MS 39056-0300
Mailing Address: PO Box 300 • Clinton, MS 39060-0300
(601) 924-7533 • http://www2.mde.k12.ms.us/2521/district/index.htm
Grade Span: KG-12; **Agency Type:** 1
Schools: 9
    2 Primary; 3 Middle; 2 High; 2 Other Level
    7 Regular; 0 Special Education; 1 Vocational; 1 Alternative
    0 Magnet; 0 Charter; 3 Title I Eligible; 0 School-wide Title I
Students: 4,899 (50.7% male; 49.2% female)
    Individual Education Program: 457 (9.3%);

English Language Learner: 32 (0.7%); Migrant: 0 (0.0%)
Eligible for Free Lunch Program: 1,292 (26.4%)
Eligible for Reduced-Price Lunch Program: 375 (7.7%)
Teachers: 305.2 (16.1 to 1)
Librarians/Media Specialists: 8.0 (612.4 to 1)
Guidance Counselors: 12.9 (379.8 to 1)
Current Spending: ($ per student per year):
Total: $5,352; Instruction: $3,352; Support Services: $1,723
Enrollment, Drop-out Rates and Diploma Recipients by Race/Ethnicity

Category	Total	White	Black	Asian	AIAN	Hisp.
Enrollment (%)	100.0	55.4	41.8	2.1	0.1	0.6
Drop-out Rate (%)	3.2	1.6	6.4	0.0	0.0	0.0
H.S. Diplomas (#)	306	228	73	5	0	0

Hinds County SD
13192 Hwy 18 • Raymond, MS 39154-0100
(601) 857-5222 • http://www2.mde.k12.ms.us/hinds/
Grade Span: KG-12; **Agency Type:** 1
Schools: 11
5 Primary; 2 Middle; 3 High; 1 Other Level
9 Regular; 0 Special Education; 1 Vocational; 1 Alternative
0 Magnet; 0 Charter; 9 Title I Eligible; 9 School-wide Title I
Students: 5,776 (50.8% male; 49.1% female)
Individual Education Program: 590 (10.2%);
English Language Learner: 0 (0.0%); Migrant: 0 (0.0%)
Eligible for Free Lunch Program: 2,489 (43.1%)
Eligible for Reduced-Price Lunch Program: 474 (8.2%)
Teachers: 388.5 (14.9 to 1)
Librarians/Media Specialists: 6.2 (931.6 to 1)
Guidance Counselors: 15.5 (372.6 to 1)
Current Spending: ($ per student per year):
Total: $5,413; Instruction: $3,090; Support Services: $1,979
Enrollment, Drop-out Rates and Diploma Recipients by Race/Ethnicity

Category	Total	White	Black	Asian	AIAN	Hisp.
Enrollment (%)	100.0	42.5	56.6	0.2	0.0	0.7
Drop-out Rate (%)	4.0	3.5	4.4	0.0	0.0	0.0
H.S. Diplomas (#)	282	143	138	0	0	1

Jackson Public SD
662 S President St • Jackson, MS 39225-2338
(601) 960-8725 • http://www.jackson.k12.ms.us/
Grade Span: PK-12; **Agency Type:** 1
Schools: 61
37 Primary; 12 Middle; 9 High; 3 Other Level
57 Regular; 0 Special Education; 1 Vocational; 3 Alternative
4 Magnet; 0 Charter; 57 Title I Eligible; 57 School-wide Title I
Students: 31,640 (49.8% male; 50.1% female)
Individual Education Program: 3,256 (10.3%);
English Language Learner: 117 (0.4%); Migrant: 6 (<0.1%)
Eligible for Free Lunch Program: 21,467 (67.8%)
Eligible for Reduced-Price Lunch Program: 2,148 (6.8%)
Teachers: 1,900.8 (16.6 to 1)
Librarians/Media Specialists: 63.2 (500.6 to 1)
Guidance Counselors: 88.2 (358.7 to 1)
Current Spending: ($ per student per year):
Total: $6,106; Instruction: $3,439; Support Services: $2,234
Enrollment, Drop-out Rates and Diploma Recipients by Race/Ethnicity

Category	Total	White	Black	Asian	AIAN	Hisp.
Enrollment (%)	100.0	3.2	96.2	0.2	0.0	0.3
Drop-out Rate (%)	7.0	8.8	6.9	4.2	0.0	33.3
H.S. Diplomas (#)	1,239	81	1,149	9	0	0

Holmes County

Holmes County SD
313 Olive St • Lexington, MS 39095-0630
Mailing Address: PO Box 630 • Lexington, MS 39095-0630
(662) 834-2175 • http://www2.mde.k12.ms.us/2600/HCSD.html
Grade Span: KG-12; **Agency Type:** 1
Schools: 7
3 Primary; 0 Middle; 1 High; 3 Other Level
6 Regular; 0 Special Education; 1 Vocational; 0 Alternative
0 Magnet; 0 Charter; 6 Title I Eligible; 6 School-wide Title I
Students: 3,557 (50.1% male; 49.8% female)
Individual Education Program: 349 (9.8%);
English Language Learner: 0 (0.0%); Migrant: 1 (<0.1%)
Eligible for Free Lunch Program: 3,395 (95.4%)
Eligible for Reduced-Price Lunch Program: 91 (2.6%)
Teachers: 194.7 (18.3 to 1)
Librarians/Media Specialists: 9.0 (395.2 to 1)
Guidance Counselors: 7.1 (501.0 to 1)
Current Spending: ($ per student per year):
Total: $5,578; Instruction: $2,969; Support Services: $1,912

Category	Total	White	Black	Asian	AIAN	Hisp.
Enrollment (%)	100.0	0.1	99.9	0.0	0.0	0.1
Drop-out Rate (%)	2.9	0.0	2.9	0.0	n/a	0.0
H.S. Diplomas (#)	251	0	251	0	0	0

Humphreys County

Humphreys County SD
401 4th St • Belzoni, MS 39038-0678
Mailing Address: PO Box 678 • Belzoni, MS 39038-0678
(662) 247-6000 • http://www.mde.k12.ms.us/Districts/Humpreys.htm
Grade Span: KG-12; **Agency Type:** 1
Schools: 5
1 Primary; 2 Middle; 2 High; 0 Other Level
4 Regular; 0 Special Education; 1 Vocational; 0 Alternative
0 Magnet; 0 Charter; 4 Title I Eligible; 4 School-wide Title I
Students: 1,918 (50.6% male; 49.3% female)
Individual Education Program: 164 (8.6%);
English Language Learner: 0 (0.0%); Migrant: 10 (0.5%)
Eligible for Free Lunch Program: 1,812 (94.5%)
Eligible for Reduced-Price Lunch Program: 39 (2.0%)
Teachers: 114.0 (16.8 to 1)
Librarians/Media Specialists: 4.0 (479.5 to 1)
Guidance Counselors: 4.0 (479.5 to 1)
Current Spending: ($ per student per year):
Total: $5,571; Instruction: $2,951; Support Services: $2,115
Enrollment, Drop-out Rates and Diploma Recipients by Race/Ethnicity

Category	Total	White	Black	Asian	AIAN	Hisp.
Enrollment (%)	100.0	2.5	97.2	0.0	0.0	0.3
Drop-out Rate (%)	5.8	20.0	5.7	n/a	n/a	0.0
H.S. Diplomas (#)	74	0	74	0	0	0

Itawamba County

Itawamba County SD
605 S S Cummings St • Fulton, MS 38843-1846
Mailing Address: 605 S Cummings St • Fulton, MS 38843-1846
(662) 862-2159 • http://www2.mde.k12.ms.us/2900/index.htm
Grade Span: KG-12; **Agency Type:** 1
Schools: 8
3 Primary; 0 Middle; 2 High; 3 Other Level
6 Regular; 0 Special Education; 1 Vocational; 1 Alternative
0 Magnet; 0 Charter; 6 Title I Eligible; 4 School-wide Title I
Students: 3,823 (50.2% male; 49.7% female)
Individual Education Program: 547 (14.3%);
English Language Learner: 2 (0.1%); Migrant: 0 (0.0%)
Eligible for Free Lunch Program: 1,705 (44.6%)
Eligible for Reduced-Price Lunch Program: 443 (11.6%)
Teachers: 262.4 (14.6 to 1)
Librarians/Media Specialists: 8.5 (449.8 to 1)
Guidance Counselors: 6.5 (588.2 to 1)
Current Spending: ($ per student per year):
Total: $5,141; Instruction: $3,375; Support Services: $1,415
Enrollment, Drop-out Rates and Diploma Recipients by Race/Ethnicity

Category	Total	White	Black	Asian	AIAN	Hisp.
Enrollment (%)	100.0	91.7	7.5	0.2	0.0	0.6
Drop-out Rate (%)	4.9	4.9	5.5	0.0	n/a	0.0
H.S. Diplomas (#)	194	174	20	0	0	0

Jackson County

Jackson County SD
12210 Colonel Vickrey Rd • Vancleave, MS 39565-5069
Mailing Address: PO Box 5069 • Vancleave, MS 39565-5069
(228) 826-1757 • http://www2.mde.k12.ms.us/3000/index.htm
Grade Span: PK-12; **Agency Type:** 1
Schools: 15
6 Primary; 4 Middle; 4 High; 1 Other Level
13 Regular; 0 Special Education; 1 Vocational; 1 Alternative
0 Magnet; 0 Charter; 7 Title I Eligible; 3 School-wide Title I
Students: 8,509 (51.5% male; 48.4% female)
Individual Education Program: 855 (10.0%);
English Language Learner: 48 (0.6%); Migrant: 210 (2.5%)
Eligible for Free Lunch Program: 2,574 (30.3%)
Eligible for Reduced-Price Lunch Program: 881 (10.4%)
Teachers: 520.6 (16.3 to 1)
Librarians/Media Specialists: 16.4 (518.8 to 1)
Guidance Counselors: 17.8 (478.0 to 1)
Current Spending: ($ per student per year):
Total: $5,043; Instruction: $2,988; Support Services: $1,772

Enrollment, Drop-out Rates and Diploma Recipients by Race/Ethnicity

Category	Total	White	Black	Asian	AIAN	Hisp.
Enrollment (%)	100.0	88.3	7.1	3.4	0.2	1.0
Drop-out Rate (%)	2.4	2.5	1.8	0.0	0.0	0.0
H.S. Diplomas (#)	466	420	32	12	1	1

Moss Point Separate SD
4924 Church St • Moss Point, MS 39563-2600
(228) 475-0691 • http://www.mphs.edu/
Grade Span: KG-12; **Agency Type:** 1
Schools: 11
  6 Primary; 2 Middle; 3 High; 0 Other Level
  9 Regular; 0 Special Education; 1 Vocational; 1 Alternative
  0 Magnet; 0 Charter; 9 Title I Eligible; 9 School-wide Title I
Students: 4,003 (50.7% male; 49.2% female)
  Individual Education Program: 693 (17.3%);
  English Language Learner: 8 (0.2%); Migrant: 65 (1.6%)
  Eligible for Free Lunch Program: 2,803 (70.0%)
  Eligible for Reduced-Price Lunch Program: 319 (8.0%)
Teachers: 284.6 (14.1 to 1)
Librarians/Media Specialists: 11.0 (363.9 to 1)
Guidance Counselors: 10.0 (400.3 to 1)
Current Spending: ($ per student per year):
  Total: $6,919; Instruction: $3,851; Support Services: $2,609
Enrollment, Drop-out Rates and Diploma Recipients by Race/Ethnicity

Category	Total	White	Black	Asian	AIAN	Hisp.
Enrollment (%)	100.0	31.1	67.8	0.3	0.0	0.7
Drop-out Rate (%)	4.9	4.1	5.2	0.0	n/a	0.0
H.S. Diplomas (#)	205	59	143	3	0	0

Ocean Springs SD
2300 Government St • Ocean Springs, MS 39564-7002
Mailing Address: PO Box 7002 • Ocean Springs, MS 39566-7002
(228) 875-7706 • http://www2.mde.k12.ms.us/ossd/
Grade Span: PK-12; **Agency Type:** 1
Schools: 7
  3 Primary; 2 Middle; 2 High; 0 Other Level
  6 Regular; 0 Special Education; 1 Vocational; 0 Alternative
  0 Magnet; 0 Charter; 3 Title I Eligible; 0 School-wide Title I
Students: 5,252 (50.9% male; 49.0% female)
  Individual Education Program: 698 (13.3%);
  English Language Learner: 9 (0.2%); Migrant: 49 (0.9%)
  Eligible for Free Lunch Program: 788 (15.0%)
  Eligible for Reduced-Price Lunch Program: 329 (6.3%)
Teachers: 305.5 (17.2 to 1)
Librarians/Media Specialists: 8.0 (656.5 to 1)
Guidance Counselors: 10.8 (486.3 to 1)
Current Spending: ($ per student per year):
  Total: $5,211; Instruction: $3,220; Support Services: $1,729
Enrollment, Drop-out Rates and Diploma Recipients by Race/Ethnicity

Category	Total	White	Black	Asian	AIAN	Hisp.
Enrollment (%)	100.0	85.7	9.1	3.1	0.2	2.0
Drop-out Rate (%)	2.4	2.5	1.7	0.0	0.0	3.8
H.S. Diplomas (#)	251	214	26	6	0	5

Pascagoula SD
1006 Communy Ave • Pascagoula, MS 39568-0250
Mailing Address: PO Box 250 • Pascagoula, MS 39568-0250
(228) 938-6491 • http://www.pascagoula.k12.ms.us/
Grade Span: KG-12; **Agency Type:** 1
Schools: 19
  11 Primary; 3 Middle; 3 High; 2 Other Level
  17 Regular; 0 Special Education; 1 Vocational; 1 Alternative
  0 Magnet; 0 Charter; 17 Title I Eligible; 15 School-wide Title I
Students: 7,496 (51.8% male; 48.1% female)
  Individual Education Program: 1,158 (15.4%);
  English Language Learner: 203 (2.7%); Migrant: 94 (1.3%)
  Eligible for Free Lunch Program: 4,130 (55.1%)
  Eligible for Reduced-Price Lunch Program: 635 (8.5%)
Teachers: 496.0 (15.1 to 1)
Librarians/Media Specialists: 17.9 (418.8 to 1)
Guidance Counselors: 13.1 (572.2 to 1)
Current Spending: ($ per student per year):
  Total: $6,765; Instruction: $3,969; Support Services: $2,415
Enrollment, Drop-out Rates and Diploma Recipients by Race/Ethnicity

Category	Total	White	Black	Asian	AIAN	Hisp.
Enrollment (%)	100.0	51.4	44.1	1.6	0.2	2.6
Drop-out Rate (%)	4.0	4.0	4.3	0.0	0.0	2.9
H.S. Diplomas (#)	365	234	116	10	1	4

Jasper County

West Jasper Consolidated Schools
510 Hwy 18 • Bay Springs, MS 39422-0610
Mailing Address: PO Box 610 • Bay Springs, MS 39422-0610
(601) 764-2280 • http://www.westjasper.k12.ms.us/
Grade Span: PK-12; **Agency Type:** 1
Schools: 5
  1 Primary; 1 Middle; 2 High; 1 Other Level
  4 Regular; 0 Special Education; 1 Vocational; 0 Alternative
  0 Magnet; 0 Charter; 2 Title I Eligible; 2 School-wide Title I
Students: 1,793 (49.9% male; 50.0% female)
  Individual Education Program: 297 (16.6%);
  English Language Learner: 0 (0.0%); Migrant: 25 (1.4%)
  Eligible for Free Lunch Program: 1,208 (67.4%)
  Eligible for Reduced-Price Lunch Program: 174 (9.7%)
Teachers: 121.1 (14.8 to 1)
Librarians/Media Specialists: 3.0 (597.7 to 1)
Guidance Counselors: 3.0 (597.7 to 1)
Current Spending: ($ per student per year):
  Total: $5,630; Instruction: $3,096; Support Services: $2,127
Enrollment, Drop-out Rates and Diploma Recipients by Race/Ethnicity

Category	Total	White	Black	Asian	AIAN	Hisp.
Enrollment (%)	100.0	39.7	59.8	0.1	0.2	0.2
Drop-out Rate (%)	1.8	1.8	1.9	0.0	0.0	0.0
H.S. Diplomas (#)	92	39	53	0	0	0

Jefferson County

Jefferson County SD
942 Main St • Fayette, MS 39069
Mailing Address: PO Box 157 • Fayette, MS 39069
(601) 786-3721 • http://www2.mde.k12.ms.us/
Grade Span: PK-12; **Agency Type:** 1
Schools: 5
  1 Primary; 1 Middle; 3 High; 0 Other Level
  3 Regular; 0 Special Education; 1 Vocational; 1 Alternative
  0 Magnet; 0 Charter; 3 Title I Eligible; 3 School-wide Title I
Students: 1,593 (50.5% male; 49.4% female)
  Individual Education Program: 214 (13.4%);
  English Language Learner: 0 (0.0%); Migrant: 0 (0.0%)
  Eligible for Free Lunch Program: 1,584 (99.4%)
  Eligible for Reduced-Price Lunch Program: 0 (0.0%)
Teachers: 110.7 (14.4 to 1)
Librarians/Media Specialists: 3.9 (408.5 to 1)
Guidance Counselors: 3.8 (419.2 to 1)
Current Spending: ($ per student per year):
  Total: $6,307; Instruction: $3,848; Support Services: $2,016
Enrollment, Drop-out Rates and Diploma Recipients by Race/Ethnicity

Category	Total	White	Black	Asian	AIAN	Hisp.
Enrollment (%)	100.0	0.1	99.9	0.0	0.0	0.0
Drop-out Rate (%)	0.4	n/a	0.4	n/a	n/a	n/a
H.S. Diplomas (#)	92	0	92	0	0	0

Jefferson Davis County SD
909 Leo St • Prentiss, MS 39474-1197
Mailing Address: PO Box 1197 • Prentiss, MS 39474-1197
(601) 792-4267 • http://www.mde.k12.ms.us/Districts/Jffdavis.htm
Grade Span: KG-12; **Agency Type:** 1
Schools: 5
  2 Primary; 0 Middle; 2 High; 1 Other Level
  4 Regular; 0 Special Education; 1 Vocational; 0 Alternative
  0 Magnet; 0 Charter; 4 Title I Eligible; 4 School-wide Title I
Students: 2,273 (52.5% male; 47.4% female)
  Individual Education Program: 451 (19.8%);
  English Language Learner: 0 (0.0%); Migrant: 3 (0.1%)
  Eligible for Free Lunch Program: 2,261 (99.5%)
  Eligible for Reduced-Price Lunch Program: 0 (0.0%)
Teachers: 156.7 (14.5 to 1)
Librarians/Media Specialists: 5.7 (398.8 to 1)
Guidance Counselors: 5.0 (454.6 to 1)
Current Spending: ($ per student per year):
  Total: $6,357; Instruction: $3,659; Support Services: $1,984
Enrollment, Drop-out Rates and Diploma Recipients by Race/Ethnicity

Category	Total	White	Black	Asian	AIAN	Hisp.
Enrollment (%)	100.0	12.7	87.1	0.1	0.0	0.0
Drop-out Rate (%)	4.8	9.7	4.1	n/a	n/a	n/a
H.S. Diplomas (#)	114	11	103	0	0	0

Jones County

Jones County SD
5204 Hwy 11 N • Ellisville, MS 39437-5049
(601) 649-5201 • http://jones.k12.ms.us/
Grade Span: KG-12; **Agency Type:** 1
Schools: 14
    8 Primary; 1 Middle; 4 High; 1 Other Level
    12 Regular; 0 Special Education; 1 Vocational; 1 Alternative
    0 Charter; 8 Title I Eligible; 8 School-wide Title I
Students: 7,811 (52.3% male; 47.6% female)
    Individual Education Program: 1,174 (15.0%);
    English Language Learner: 43 (0.6%); Migrant: 240 (3.1%)
    Eligible for Free Lunch Program: 3,583 (45.9%)
    Eligible for Reduced-Price Lunch Program: 898 (11.5%)
Teachers: 546.2 (14.3 to 1)
Librarians/Media Specialists: 15.8 (494.4 to 1)
Guidance Counselors: 16.0 (488.2 to 1)
Current Spending: ($ per student per year):
    Total: $5,595; Instruction: $3,492; Support Services: $1,751
Enrollment, Drop-out Rates and Diploma Recipients by Race/Ethnicity

Category	Total	White	Black	Asian	AIAN	Hisp.
Enrollment (%)	100.0	75.9	21.4	0.4	0.7	1.5
Drop-out Rate (%)	3.0	2.7	4.3	0.0	0.0	0.0
H.S. Diplomas (#)	437	331	102	1	2	1

Laurel SD
600 S 16th Ave • Laurel, MS 39440-4922
Mailing Address: P. O. Drawer 288 • Laurel, MS 39441-0288
(601) 649-6391 • http://www2.mde.k12.ms.us/3420/index.htm
Grade Span: PK-12; **Agency Type:** 1
Schools: 8
    4 Primary; 1 Middle; 1 High; 2 Other Level
    6 Regular; 0 Special Education; 1 Vocational; 1 Alternative
    1 Magnet; 0 Charter; 6 Title I Eligible; 6 School-wide Title I
Students: 3,137 (50.5% male; 49.4% female)
    Individual Education Program: 409 (13.0%);
    English Language Learner: 43 (1.4%); Migrant: 127 (4.0%)
    Eligible for Free Lunch Program: 2,509 (80.0%)
    Eligible for Reduced-Price Lunch Program: 156 (5.0%)
Teachers: 263.7 (11.9 to 1)
Librarians/Media Specialists: 2.5 (1,254.8 to 1)
Guidance Counselors: 9.0 (348.6 to 1)
Current Spending: ($ per student per year):
    Total: $6,555; Instruction: $3,847; Support Services: $2,262
Enrollment, Drop-out Rates and Diploma Recipients by Race/Ethnicity

Category	Total	White	Black	Asian	AIAN	Hisp.
Enrollment (%)	100.0	11.2	86.9	0.0	0.1	1.8
Drop-out Rate (%)	2.0	0.0	2.6	n/a	n/a	0.0
H.S. Diplomas (#)	172	45	126	0	0	1

Lafayette County

Lafayette County SD
100 Commodore Dr • Oxford, MS 38655-0110
(662) 234-3271 • http://www.lafayette.k12.ms.us/index.php?id=main
Grade Span: KG-12; **Agency Type:** 1
Schools: 4
    1 Primary; 1 Middle; 2 High; 0 Other Level
    3 Regular; 0 Special Education; 1 Vocational; 0 Alternative
    0 Magnet; 0 Charter; 2 Title I Eligible; 2 School-wide Title I
Students: 2,193 (52.1% male; 47.8% female)
    Individual Education Program: 471 (21.5%);
    English Language Learner: 6 (0.3%); Migrant: 0 (0.0%)
    Eligible for Free Lunch Program: 968 (44.1%)
    Eligible for Reduced-Price Lunch Program: 202 (9.2%)
Teachers: 163.9 (13.4 to 1)
Librarians/Media Specialists: 4.0 (548.3 to 1)
Guidance Counselors: 6.0 (365.5 to 1)
Current Spending: ($ per student per year):
    Total: $6,817; Instruction: $4,051; Support Services: $2,415
Enrollment, Drop-out Rates and Diploma Recipients by Race/Ethnicity

Category	Total	White	Black	Asian	AIAN	Hisp.
Enrollment (%)	100.0	69.7	29.1	0.1	0.0	1.0
Drop-out Rate (%)	1.4	1.3	1.5	n/a	n/a	n/a
H.S. Diplomas (#)	95	64	31	0	0	0

Oxford SD
224 Bramlett Blvd • Oxford, MS 38655-3416
(662) 234-3541 • http://www.oxford.k12.ms.us/
Grade Span: PK-12; **Agency Type:** 1
Schools: 7
    2 Primary; 2 Middle; 1 High; 2 Other Level
    6 Regular; 0 Special Education; 0 Vocational; 1 Alternative
    0 Magnet; 0 Charter; 5 Title I Eligible; 5 School-wide Title I

Students: 3,118 (50.6% male; 49.3% female)
    Individual Education Program: 340 (10.9%);
    English Language Learner: 26 (0.8%); Migrant: 0 (0.0%)
    Eligible for Free Lunch Program: 1,192 (38.2%)
    Eligible for Reduced-Price Lunch Program: 238 (7.6%)
Teachers: 225.2 (13.8 to 1)
Librarians/Media Specialists: 5.0 (623.6 to 1)
Guidance Counselors: 7.0 (445.4 to 1)
Current Spending: ($ per student per year):
    Total: $5,831; Instruction: $3,737; Support Services: $1,763
Enrollment, Drop-out Rates and Diploma Recipients by Race/Ethnicity

Category	Total	White	Black	Asian	AIAN	Hisp.
Enrollment (%)	100.0	50.1	44.7	3.4	0.2	1.6
Drop-out Rate (%)	3.1	1.3	5.6	0.0	n/a	0.0
H.S. Diplomas (#)	150	91	57	2	0	0

Lamar County

Lamar County SD
300 N St • Purvis, MS 39475-0609
Mailing Address: PO Box 609 • Purvis, MS 39475-0609
(601) 794-1030 • http://www.lamar.k12.ms.us/
Grade Span: KG-12; **Agency Type:** 1
Schools: 13
    4 Primary; 3 Middle; 3 High; 3 Other Level
    10 Regular; 0 Special Education; 1 Vocational; 2 Alternative
    0 Magnet; 0 Charter; 6 Title I Eligible; 4 School-wide Title I
Students: 7,021 (52.2% male; 47.7% female)
    Individual Education Program: 1,112 (15.8%);
    English Language Learner: 51 (0.7%); Migrant: 0 (0.0%)
    Eligible for Free Lunch Program: 2,068 (29.5%)
    Eligible for Reduced-Price Lunch Program: 629 (9.0%)
Teachers: 481.6 (14.6 to 1)
Librarians/Media Specialists: 11.2 (626.9 to 1)
Guidance Counselors: 12.8 (548.5 to 1)
Current Spending: ($ per student per year):
    Total: $5,683; Instruction: $3,429; Support Services: $1,974
Enrollment, Drop-out Rates and Diploma Recipients by Race/Ethnicity

Category	Total	White	Black	Asian	AIAN	Hisp.
Enrollment (%)	100.0	83.3	14.5	0.9	0.1	1.3
Drop-out Rate (%)	2.9	3.0	2.2	0.0	0.0	0.0
H.S. Diplomas (#)	348	313	28	5	1	1

Lauderdale County

Lauderdale County SD
410 Constitution Ave • Meridian, MS 39302-5498
Mailing Address: PO Box 5498 • Meridian, MS 39302-5498
(601) 693-1683 • http://www.lauderdale.k12.ms.us/
Grade Span: KG-12; **Agency Type:** 1
Schools: 10
    3 Primary; 2 Middle; 2 High; 3 Other Level
    9 Regular; 0 Special Education; 0 Vocational; 1 Alternative
    0 Magnet; 0 Charter; 6 Title I Eligible; 6 School-wide Title I
Students: 6,595 (51.7% male; 48.2% female)
    Individual Education Program: 1,031 (15.6%);
    English Language Learner: 0 (0.0%); Migrant: 4 (0.1%)
    Eligible for Free Lunch Program: 2,242 (34.0%)
    Eligible for Reduced-Price Lunch Program: 505 (7.7%)
Teachers: 417.2 (15.8 to 1)
Librarians/Media Specialists: 7.8 (845.5 to 1)
Guidance Counselors: 10.0 (659.5 to 1)
Current Spending: ($ per student per year):
    Total: $5,167; Instruction: $3,230; Support Services: $1,642
Enrollment, Drop-out Rates and Diploma Recipients by Race/Ethnicity

Category	Total	White	Black	Asian	AIAN	Hisp.
Enrollment (%)	100.0	69.5	29.0	0.5	0.1	1.0
Drop-out Rate (%)	5.3	5.3	5.1	12.5	0.0	6.7
H.S. Diplomas (#)	338	240	94	1	0	3

Meridian Public SD
1019 25th Ave • Meridian, MS 39301
Mailing Address: PO Box 31 • Meridian, MS 39302-4926
(601) 483-6271 • http://www.mpsd.k12.ms.us/
Grade Span: KG-12; **Agency Type:** 1
Schools: 15
    7 Primary; 3 Middle; 2 High; 3 Other Level
    13 Regular; 0 Special Education; 1 Vocational; 1 Alternative
    0 Magnet; 0 Charter; 6 Title I Eligible; 6 School-wide Title I
Students: 6,742 (50.2% male; 49.7% female)
    Individual Education Program: 845 (12.5%);
    English Language Learner: 20 (0.3%); Migrant: 7 (0.1%)
    Eligible for Free Lunch Program: 4,704 (69.8%)
    Eligible for Reduced-Price Lunch Program: 351 (5.2%)
Teachers: 432.2 (15.6 to 1)

Librarians/Media Specialists: 10.5 (642.1 to 1)
Guidance Counselors: 23.0 (293.1 to 1)
Current Spending: ($ per student per year):
  Total: $6,697; Instruction: $3,974; Support Services: $2,229
Enrollment, Drop-out Rates and Diploma Recipients by Race/Ethnicity

Category	Total	White	Black	Asian	AIAN	Hisp.
Enrollment (%)	100.0	18.6	80.1	0.4	0.0	0.9
Drop-out Rate (%)	3.6	1.1	4.6	0.0	0.0	0.0
H.S. Diplomas (#)	336	97	232	5	1	1

Lawrence County

Lawrence County SD
346 Thomas E Jolly Dr • Monticello, MS 39654-9301
(601) 587-2506 • http://www.lawrence.k12.ms.us/
Grade Span: KG-12; **Agency Type:** 1
Schools: 6
  3 Primary; 1 Middle; 2 High; 0 Other Level
  5 Regular; 0 Special Education; 1 Vocational; 0 Alternative
  0 Magnet; 0 Charter; 5 Title I Eligible; 5 School-wide Title I
Students: 2,400 (50.1% male; 49.8% female)
  Individual Education Program: 286 (11.9%);
  English Language Learner: 0 (0.0%); Migrant: 0 (0.0%)
  Eligible for Free Lunch Program: 1,172 (48.8%)
  Eligible for Reduced-Price Lunch Program: 257 (10.7%)
Teachers: 174.2 (13.8 to 1)
Librarians/Media Specialists: 4.0 (600.0 to 1)
Guidance Counselors: 1.9 (1,263.2 to 1)
Current Spending: ($ per student per year):
  Total: $5,989; Instruction: $3,735; Support Services: $1,788
Enrollment, Drop-out Rates and Diploma Recipients by Race/Ethnicity

Category	Total	White	Black	Asian	AIAN	Hisp.
Enrollment (%)	100.0	58.3	41.0	0.3	0.0	0.5
Drop-out Rate (%)	5.4	5.1	5.9	n/a	n/a	0.0
H.S. Diplomas (#)	120	80	40	0	0	0

Leake County

Leake County SD
123 Main St • Carthage, MS 39051-0478
Mailing Address: PO Drawer 478 • Carthage, MS 39051-0478
(601) 267-4579 • http://www.leakesd.k12.ms.us/
Grade Span: KG-12; **Agency Type:** 1
Schools: 8
  2 Primary; 1 Middle; 3 High; 2 Other Level
  7 Regular; 0 Special Education; 1 Vocational; 0 Alternative
  0 Magnet; 0 Charter; 6 Title I Eligible; 6 School-wide Title I
Students: 3,345 (52.3% male; 47.6% female)
  Individual Education Program: 487 (14.6%);
  English Language Learner: 49 (1.5%); Migrant: 28 (0.8%)
  Eligible for Free Lunch Program: 2,116 (63.3%)
  Eligible for Reduced-Price Lunch Program: 337 (10.1%)
Teachers: 196.7 (17.0 to 1)
Librarians/Media Specialists: 4.9 (682.7 to 1)
Guidance Counselors: 8.0 (418.1 to 1)
Current Spending: ($ per student per year):
  Total: $5,091; Instruction: $2,962; Support Services: $1,748
Enrollment, Drop-out Rates and Diploma Recipients by Race/Ethnicity

Category	Total	White	Black	Asian	AIAN	Hisp.
Enrollment (%)	100.0	38.5	58.0	0.3	1.3	1.8
Drop-out Rate (%)	5.1	3.9	5.4	0.0	25.0	33.3
H.S. Diplomas (#)	151	62	87	0	2	0

Lee County

Lee County SD
1280 College View Dr • Tupelo, MS 38804
Mailing Address: PO Box 832 • Tupelo, MS 38802-0832
(662) 841-9144 • http://www.lcs.k12.ms.us/default.asp
Grade Span: PK-12; **Agency Type:** 1
Schools: 9
  5 Primary; 1 Middle; 1 High; 2 Other Level
  9 Regular; 0 Special Education; 0 Vocational; 0 Alternative
  0 Magnet; 0 Charter; 6 Title I Eligible; 3 School-wide Title I
Students: 6,245 (51.3% male; 48.6% female)
  Individual Education Program: 1,076 (17.2%);
  English Language Learner: 11 (0.2%); Migrant: 0 (0.0%)
  Eligible for Free Lunch Program: 2,752 (44.1%)
  Eligible for Reduced-Price Lunch Program: 596 (9.5%)
Teachers: 396.4 (15.8 to 1)
Librarians/Media Specialists: 11.5 (543.0 to 1)
Guidance Counselors: 11.3 (552.7 to 1)
Current Spending: ($ per student per year):
  Total: $5,250; Instruction: $3,327; Support Services: $1,628

Enrollment, Drop-out Rates and Diploma Recipients by Race/Ethnicity

Category	Total	White	Black	Asian	AIAN	Hisp.
Enrollment (%)	100.0	69.7	29.2	0.3	0.0	0.8
Drop-out Rate (%)	7.6	8.2	6.2	33.3	n/a	10.0
H.S. Diplomas (#)	260	185	74	1	0	0

Tupelo Public SD
72 S Green St • Tupelo, MS 38804
Mailing Address: PO Box 557 • Tupelo, MS 38802-0557
(662) 841-8850 • http://www.tupeloschools.com/
Grade Span: PK-12; **Agency Type:** 1
Schools: 16
  8 Primary; 4 Middle; 2 High; 2 Other Level
  14 Regular; 0 Special Education; 1 Vocational; 1 Alternative
  0 Magnet; 0 Charter; 7 Title I Eligible; 0 School-wide Title I
Students: 7,264 (51.0% male; 48.9% female)
  Individual Education Program: 1,063 (14.6%);
  English Language Learner: 96 (1.3%); Migrant: 0 (0.0%)
  Eligible for Free Lunch Program: 2,954 (40.7%)
  Eligible for Reduced-Price Lunch Program: 379 (5.2%)
Teachers: 563.6 (12.9 to 1)
Librarians/Media Specialists: 12.0 (605.3 to 1)
Guidance Counselors: 19.0 (382.3 to 1)
Current Spending: ($ per student per year):
  Total: $6,502; Instruction: $4,050; Support Services: $2,119
Enrollment, Drop-out Rates and Diploma Recipients by Race/Ethnicity

Category	Total	White	Black	Asian	AIAN	Hisp.
Enrollment (%)	100.0	54.6	42.9	1.3	0.0	1.2
Drop-out Rate (%)	3.1	1.9	6.0	0.0	n/a	0.0
H.S. Diplomas (#)	353	264	85	4	0	0

Leflore County

Greenwood Public SD
401 Howard St • Greenwood, MS 38935-1497
Mailing Address: PO Box 1497 • Greenwood, MS 38935-1497
(662) 453-4231 • http://www2.mde.k12.ms.us/4220/
Grade Span: PK-12; **Agency Type:** 1
Schools: 8
  4 Primary; 1 Middle; 2 High; 1 Other Level
  6 Regular; 0 Special Education; 1 Vocational; 1 Alternative
  0 Magnet; 0 Charter; 6 Title I Eligible; 6 School-wide Title I
Students: 3,422 (51.0% male; 48.9% female)
  Individual Education Program: 360 (10.5%);
  English Language Learner: 1 (<0.1%); Migrant: 5 (0.1%)
  Eligible for Free Lunch Program: 3,404 (99.5%)
  Eligible for Reduced-Price Lunch Program: 0 (0.0%)
Teachers: 248.7 (13.8 to 1)
Librarians/Media Specialists: 7.0 (488.9 to 1)
Guidance Counselors: 8.0 (427.8 to 1)
Current Spending: ($ per student per year):
  Total: $6,069; Instruction: $3,580; Support Services: $2,030
Enrollment, Drop-out Rates and Diploma Recipients by Race/Ethnicity

Category	Total	White	Black	Asian	AIAN	Hisp.
Enrollment (%)	100.0	10.7	88.8	0.3	0.1	0.1
Drop-out Rate (%)	3.6	21.1	3.2	0.0	n/a	100.0
H.S. Diplomas (#)	150	3	147	0	0	0

Leflore County SD
1901 Hwy 82 W • Greenwood, MS 38930-2722
(662) 453-8566 • http://www.mde.k12.ms.us/Districts/Leflore.htm
Grade Span: KG-12; **Agency Type:** 1
Schools: 8
  4 Primary; 1 Middle; 3 High; 0 Other Level
  7 Regular; 0 Special Education; 1 Vocational; 0 Alternative
  0 Magnet; 0 Charter; 7 Title I Eligible; 7 School-wide Title I
Students: 2,996 (50.5% male; 49.4% female)
  Individual Education Program: 563 (18.8%);
  English Language Learner: 30 (1.0%); Migrant: 58 (1.9%)
  Eligible for Free Lunch Program: 2,975 (99.3%)
  Eligible for Reduced-Price Lunch Program: 0 (0.0%)
Teachers: 171.0 (17.5 to 1)
Librarians/Media Specialists: 6.5 (460.9 to 1)
Guidance Counselors: 4.6 (651.3 to 1)
Current Spending: ($ per student per year):
  Total: $5,911; Instruction: $3,375; Support Services: $1,966
Enrollment, Drop-out Rates and Diploma Recipients by Race/Ethnicity

Category	Total	White	Black	Asian	AIAN	Hisp.
Enrollment (%)	100.0	1.7	96.8	0.0	0.0	1.4
Drop-out Rate (%)	10.6	50.0	10.0	n/a	n/a	16.7
H.S. Diplomas (#)	116	0	115	0	0	1

Lincoln County

Brookhaven SD

326 E Court St • Brookhaven, MS 39601
Mailing Address: PO Box 540 • Brookhaven, MS 39602
(601) 833-6661 • http://www.telapex.com/~bschool/index.html
Grade Span: KG-12; Agency Type: 1
Schools: 7
   2 Primary; 2 Middle; 2 High; 1 Other Level
   5 Regular; 0 Special Education; 1 Vocational; 1 Alternative
   0 Magnet; 0 Charter; 4 Title I Eligible; 4 School-wide Title I
Students: 2,967   (49.7% male; 50.2% female)
   Individual Education Program: 308 (10.4%);
   English Language Learner: 2 (0.1%); Migrant: 0 (0.0%)
   Eligible for Free Lunch Program: 1,640 (55.3%)
   Eligible for Reduced-Price Lunch Program: 231 (7.8%)
Teachers: 224.9 (13.2 to 1)
Librarians/Media Specialists: 5.1 (581.8 to 1)
Guidance Counselors: 8.0 (370.9 to 1)
Current Spending: ($ per student per year):
   Total: $6,138; Instruction: $3,597; Support Services: $2,136
Enrollment, Drop-out Rates and Diploma Recipients by Race/Ethnicity

Category	Total	White	Black	Asian	AIAN	Hisp.
Enrollment (%)	100.0	39.9	59.4	0.4	0.1	0.3
Drop-out Rate (%)	3.5	3.0	4.0	0.0	0.0	n/a
H.S. Diplomas (#)	166	79	87	0	0	0

Lincoln County SD

233 E Monticello St • Brookhaven, MS 39602-0826
Mailing Address: PO Box 826 • Brookhaven, MS 39602-0826
(601) 835-0011 • http://lcsd.k12.ms.us/index2.asp
Grade Span: PK-12; Agency Type: 1
Schools: 5
   0 Primary; 0 Middle; 0 High; 5 Other Level
   4 Regular; 0 Special Education; 0 Vocational; 1 Alternative
   0 Magnet; 0 Charter; 4 Title I Eligible; 0 School-wide Title I
Students: 2,867   (52.7% male; 47.2% female)
   Individual Education Program: 369 (12.9%);
   English Language Learner: 0 (0.0%); Migrant: 0 (0.0%)
   Eligible for Free Lunch Program: 1,185 (41.3%)
   Eligible for Reduced-Price Lunch Program: 408 (14.2%)
Teachers: 175.1 (16.4 to 1)
Librarians/Media Specialists: 8.0 (358.4 to 1)
Guidance Counselors: 4.0 (716.8 to 1)
Current Spending: ($ per student per year):
   Total: $4,916; Instruction: $2,998; Support Services: $1,558
Enrollment, Drop-out Rates and Diploma Recipients by Race/Ethnicity

Category	Total	White	Black	Asian	AIAN	Hisp.
Enrollment (%)	100.0	83.4	16.1	0.2	0.1	0.3
Drop-out Rate (%)	3.3	3.1	4.1	0.0	0.0	0.0
H.S. Diplomas (#)	170	131	36	0	1	2

Lowndes County

Columbus Municipal SD

2630 Mcarthur Dr • Columbus, MS 39705
Mailing Address: PO Box 1308 • Columbus, MS 39703-1810
(662) 241-7400 • http://www2.mde.k12.ms.us/4420/
Grade Span: PK-12; Agency Type: 1
Schools: 13
   8 Primary; 2 Middle; 2 High; 1 Other Level
   11 Regular; 0 Special Education; 1 Vocational; 1 Alternative
   0 Magnet; 0 Charter; 9 Title I Eligible; 9 School-wide Title I
Students: 4,975   (50.8% male; 49.1% female)
   Individual Education Program: 650 (13.1%);
   English Language Learner: 7 (0.1%); Migrant: 0 (0.0%)
   Eligible for Free Lunch Program: 3,374 (67.8%)
   Eligible for Reduced-Price Lunch Program: 373 (7.5%)
Teachers: 387.4 (12.8 to 1)
Librarians/Media Specialists: 12.7 (391.7 to 1)
Guidance Counselors: 13.5 (368.5 to 1)
Current Spending: ($ per student per year):
   Total: $6,565; Instruction: $3,831; Support Services: $2,306
Enrollment, Drop-out Rates and Diploma Recipients by Race/Ethnicity

Category	Total	White	Black	Asian	AIAN	Hisp.
Enrollment (%)	100.0	15.6	82.7	0.8	0.2	0.7
Drop-out Rate (%)	3.6	2.1	4.1	0.0	0.0	0.0
H.S. Diplomas (#)	265	82	178	3	1	1

Lowndes County SD

1053 Hwy 45 S • Columbus, MS 39701-8480
(662) 244-5000 • http://www2.mde.k12.ms.us/4400/
Grade Span: KG-12; Agency Type: 1
Schools: 9
   3 Primary; 3 Middle; 3 High; 0 Other Level

   9 Regular; 0 Special Education; 0 Vocational; 0 Alternative
   0 Magnet; 0 Charter; 7 Title I Eligible; 6 School-wide Title I
Students: 5,383   (50.4% male; 49.5% female)
   Individual Education Program: 589 (10.9%);
   English Language Learner: 26 (0.5%); Migrant: 0 (0.0%)
   Eligible for Free Lunch Program: 2,125 (39.5%)
   Eligible for Reduced-Price Lunch Program: 440 (8.2%)
Teachers: 345.7 (15.6 to 1)
Librarians/Media Specialists: 10.7 (503.1 to 1)
Guidance Counselors: 9.4 (572.7 to 1)
Current Spending: ($ per student per year):
   Total: $5,242; Instruction: $3,290; Support Services: $1,628
Enrollment, Drop-out Rates and Diploma Recipients by Race/Ethnicity

Category	Total	White	Black	Asian	AIAN	Hisp.
Enrollment (%)	100.0	59.8	39.2	0.5	0.1	0.4
Drop-out Rate (%)	5.8	6.0	5.5	0.0	n/a	100.0
H.S. Diplomas (#)	268	178	88	2	0	0

Madison County

Canton Public SD

403 E Lincoln St • Canton, MS 39046-3215
(601) 859-4110 • http://www2.mde.k12.ms.us/4520/canton/main_index.htm
Grade Span: KG-12; Agency Type: 1
Schools: 6
   2 Primary; 1 Middle; 2 High; 1 Other Level
   4 Regular; 0 Special Education; 1 Vocational; 1 Alternative
   0 Magnet; 0 Charter; 4 Title I Eligible; 4 School-wide Title I
Students: 3,393   (48.6% male; 51.3% female)
   Individual Education Program: 403 (11.9%);
   English Language Learner: 4 (0.1%); Migrant: 0 (0.0%)
   Eligible for Free Lunch Program: 3,186 (93.9%)
   Eligible for Reduced-Price Lunch Program: 87 (2.6%)
Teachers: 202.4 (16.8 to 1)
Librarians/Media Specialists: 4.9 (692.4 to 1)
Guidance Counselors: 7.6 (446.4 to 1)
Current Spending: ($ per student per year):
   Total: $4,845; Instruction: $2,673; Support Services: $1,671
Enrollment, Drop-out Rates and Diploma Recipients by Race/Ethnicity

Category	Total	White	Black	Asian	AIAN	Hisp.
Enrollment (%)	100.0	0.2	99.5	0.1	0.0	0.2
Drop-out Rate (%)	6.2	0.0	6.2	n/a	n/a	n/a
H.S. Diplomas (#)	108	0	108	0	0	0

Madison County SD

117 Fourth St • Flora, MS 39071-9761
Mailing Address: PO Box 159 • Flora, MS 39071-9761
(601) 879-3025 • http://www.madison.k12.ms.us/
Grade Span: PK-12; Agency Type: 1
Schools: 17
   8 Primary; 4 Middle; 4 High; 1 Other Level
   15 Regular; 0 Special Education; 1 Vocational; 1 Alternative
   1 Magnet; 0 Charter; 6 Title I Eligible; 6 School-wide Title I
Students: 9,891   (51.2% male; 48.7% female)
   Individual Education Program: 813 (8.2%);
   English Language Learner: 78 (0.8%); Migrant: 0 (0.0%)
   Eligible for Free Lunch Program: 2,165 (21.9%)
   Eligible for Reduced-Price Lunch Program: 528 (5.3%)
Teachers: 639.2 (15.5 to 1)
Librarians/Media Specialists: 16.8 (588.8 to 1)
Guidance Counselors: 23.2 (426.3 to 1)
Current Spending: ($ per student per year):
   Total: $5,577; Instruction: $3,338; Support Services: $1,944
Enrollment, Drop-out Rates and Diploma Recipients by Race/Ethnicity

Category	Total	White	Black	Asian	AIAN	Hisp.
Enrollment (%)	100.0	58.8	37.9	2.3	0.1	1.0
Drop-out Rate (%)	1.3	1.2	1.3	0.0	0.0	14.3
H.S. Diplomas (#)	500	334	158	7	1	0

Marion County

Columbia SD

613 Bryan Ave • Columbia, MS 39429-3135
Mailing Address: PO Box 271 • Columbia, MS 39429-3135
(601) 736-2366 • http://www.columbiaschools.org/
Grade Span: PK-12; Agency Type: 1
Schools: 4
   1 Primary; 2 Middle; 1 High; 0 Other Level
   4 Regular; 0 Special Education; 0 Vocational; 0 Alternative
   0 Magnet; 0 Charter; 2 Title I Eligible; 2 School-wide Title I
Students: 1,873   (50.4% male; 49.5% female)
   Individual Education Program: 341 (18.2%);
   English Language Learner: 0 (0.0%); Migrant: 0 (0.0%)
   Eligible for Free Lunch Program: 1,136 (60.7%)
   Eligible for Reduced-Price Lunch Program: 165 (8.8%)

Teachers: 113.5 (16.5 to 1)
Librarians/Media Specialists: 5.0 (374.6 to 1)
Guidance Counselors: 4.4 (425.7 to 1)
Current Spending: ($ per student per year):
  Total: $6,087; Instruction: $3,593; Support Services: $2,145
Enrollment, Drop-out Rates and Diploma Recipients by Race/Ethnicity

Category	Total	White	Black	Asian	AIAN	Hisp.
Enrollment (%)	100.0	51.6	47.3	0.7	0.1	0.4
Drop-out Rate (%)	1.5	1.5	1.4	0.0	n/a	0.0
H.S. Diplomas (#)	108	68	40	0	0	0

Marion County SD
600 Broad St • Columbia, MS 39429-3009
(601) 736-7193 • http://www2.mde.k12.ms.us/4600/index.htm
Grade Span: KG-12; **Agency Type:** 1
Schools: 9
  3 Primary; 3 Middle; 3 High; 0 Other Level
  8 Regular; 0 Special Education; 1 Vocational; 0 Alternative
  0 Magnet; 0 Charter; 8 Title I Eligible; 8 School-wide Title I
Students: 2,523 (52.0% male; 47.9% female)
  Individual Education Program: 463 (18.4%);
  English Language Learner: 0 (0.0%); Migrant: 5 (0.2%)
  Eligible for Free Lunch Program: 1,853 (73.4%)
  Eligible for Reduced-Price Lunch Program: 263 (10.4%)
Teachers: 198.5 (12.7 to 1)
Librarians/Media Specialists: 4.0 (630.8 to 1)
Guidance Counselors: 3.0 (841.0 to 1)
Current Spending: ($ per student per year):
  Total: $5,953; Instruction: $3,524; Support Services: $1,998
Enrollment, Drop-out Rates and Diploma Recipients by Race/Ethnicity

Category	Total	White	Black	Asian	AIAN	Hisp.
Enrollment (%)	100.0	54.3	45.0	0.0	0.0	0.7
Drop-out Rate (%)	4.9	2.7	7.1	n/a	n/a	0.0
H.S. Diplomas (#)	130	62	68	0	0	0

Marshall County

Holly Springs SD
840 Hwy 178 E • Holly Springs, MS 38635-2633
(662) 252-2183 • http://www2.mde.k12.ms.us/4720/
Grade Span: PK-12; **Agency Type:** 1
Schools: 5
  2 Primary; 0 Middle; 2 High; 1 Other Level
  3 Regular; 0 Special Education; 1 Vocational; 1 Alternative
  0 Magnet; 0 Charter; 3 Title I Eligible; 3 School-wide Title I
Students: 1,816 (50.0% male; 49.9% female)
  Individual Education Program: 343 (18.9%);
  English Language Learner: 7 (0.4%); Migrant: 0 (0.0%)
  Eligible for Free Lunch Program: 1,807 (99.5%)
  Eligible for Reduced-Price Lunch Program: 0 (0.0%)
Teachers: 131.9 (13.8 to 1)
Librarians/Media Specialists: 3.0 (605.3 to 1)
Guidance Counselors: 4.9 (370.6 to 1)
Current Spending: ($ per student per year):
  Total: $5,529; Instruction: $3,300; Support Services: $1,875
Enrollment, Drop-out Rates and Diploma Recipients by Race/Ethnicity

Category	Total	White	Black	Asian	AIAN	Hisp.
Enrollment (%)	100.0	2.4	97.1	0.1	0.0	0.5
Drop-out Rate (%)	4.2	5.3	4.1	0.0	n/a	n/a
H.S. Diplomas (#)	106	1	105	0	0	0

Marshall County SD
158 E College Ave • Holly Springs, MS 38635-3003
Mailing Address: PO Box 38 • Holly Springs, MS 38635-3003
(662) 252-4271 •
http://www.mde.k12.ms.us/Districts/Marshall.htm#MARSHALL
Grade Span: PK-12; **Agency Type:** 1
Schools: 6
  3 Primary; 0 Middle; 1 High; 2 Other Level
  6 Regular; 0 Special Education; 0 Vocational; 0 Alternative
  0 Magnet; 0 Charter; 6 Title I Eligible; 6 School-wide Title I
Students: 3,463 (50.8% male; 49.1% female)
  Individual Education Program: 443 (12.8%);
  English Language Learner: 32 (0.9%); Migrant: 1 (<0.1%)
  Eligible for Free Lunch Program: 2,492 (72.0%)
  Eligible for Reduced-Price Lunch Program: 313 (9.0%)
Teachers: 192.3 (18.0 to 1)
Librarians/Media Specialists: 4.0 (865.8 to 1)
Guidance Counselors: 2.9 (1,194.1 to 1)
Current Spending: ($ per student per year):
  Total: $4,660; Instruction: $2,828; Support Services: $1,424

Enrollment, Drop-out Rates and Diploma Recipients by Race/Ethnicity

Category	Total	White	Black	Asian	AIAN	Hisp.
Enrollment (%)	100.0	36.2	62.1	0.2	0.0	1.4
Drop-out Rate (%)	3.6	4.1	3.2	0.0	n/a	10.0
H.S. Diplomas (#)	122	31	88	1	0	2

Monroe County

Aberdeen SD
205 Hwy 145 N • Aberdeen, MS 39730
Mailing Address: PO Box 607 • Aberdeen, MS 39730
(662) 369-4682 • http://www.aberdeen.k12.ms.us/
Grade Span: PK-12; **Agency Type:** 1
Schools: 7
  2 Primary; 3 Middle; 2 High; 0 Other Level
  6 Regular; 0 Special Education; 0 Vocational; 1 Alternative
  0 Magnet; 0 Charter; 5 Title I Eligible; 5 School-wide Title I
Students: 1,667 (50.8% male; 49.1% female)
  Individual Education Program: 274 (16.4%);
  English Language Learner: 0 (0.0%); Migrant: 4 (0.2%)
  Eligible for Free Lunch Program: 1,419 (85.1%)
  Eligible for Reduced-Price Lunch Program: 92 (5.5%)
Teachers: 156.5 (10.7 to 1)
Librarians/Media Specialists: 6.0 (277.8 to 1)
Guidance Counselors: 2.5 (666.8 to 1)
Current Spending: ($ per student per year):
  Total: $6,684; Instruction: $4,066; Support Services: $2,176
Enrollment, Drop-out Rates and Diploma Recipients by Race/Ethnicity

Category	Total	White	Black	Asian	AIAN	Hisp.
Enrollment (%)	100.0	8.5	90.9	0.1	0.1	0.4
Drop-out Rate (%)	3.6	1.1	4.1	0.0	n/a	n/a
H.S. Diplomas (#)	97	24	73	0	0	0

Amory SD
124 N Main St • Amory, MS 38821-0330
Mailing Address: PO Box 330 • Amory, MS 38821-0330
(662) 256-5991 • http://www.amoryschools.com/
Grade Span: KG-12; **Agency Type:** 1
Schools: 5
  2 Primary; 1 Middle; 2 High; 0 Other Level
  4 Regular; 0 Special Education; 1 Vocational; 0 Alternative
  0 Magnet; 0 Charter; 4 Title I Eligible; 3 School-wide Title I
Students: 1,832 (50.8% male; 49.1% female)
  Individual Education Program: 262 (14.3%);
  English Language Learner: 2 (0.1%); Migrant: 0 (0.0%)
  Eligible for Free Lunch Program: 803 (43.8%)
  Eligible for Reduced-Price Lunch Program: 178 (9.7%)
Teachers: 127.7 (14.3 to 1)
Librarians/Media Specialists: 4.0 (458.0 to 1)
Guidance Counselors: 4.0 (458.0 to 1)
Current Spending: ($ per student per year):
  Total: $5,441; Instruction: $3,330; Support Services: $1,606
Enrollment, Drop-out Rates and Diploma Recipients by Race/Ethnicity

Category	Total	White	Black	Asian	AIAN	Hisp.
Enrollment (%)	100.0	63.8	35.5	0.3	0.0	0.4
Drop-out Rate (%)	2.6	1.5	4.3	n/a	n/a	0.0
H.S. Diplomas (#)	107	70	35	0	0	2

Monroe County SD
1619 Hwy 25 N • Amory, MS 38821-2181
Mailing Address: PO Box 209 • Amory, MS 38821-2181
(662) 257-2176 • http://www.monroe.k12.ms.us/
Grade Span: KG-12; **Agency Type:** 1
Schools: 5
  1 Primary; 0 Middle; 1 High; 3 Other Level
  4 Regular; 0 Special Education; 1 Vocational; 0 Alternative
  0 Magnet; 0 Charter; 4 Title I Eligible; 4 School-wide Title I
Students: 2,602 (52.1% male; 47.8% female)
  Individual Education Program: 398 (15.3%);
  English Language Learner: 0 (0.0%); Migrant: 37 (1.4%)
  Eligible for Free Lunch Program: 951 (36.5%)
  Eligible for Reduced-Price Lunch Program: 367 (14.1%)
Teachers: 170.5 (15.3 to 1)
Librarians/Media Specialists: 6.3 (413.0 to 1)
Guidance Counselors: 4.5 (578.2 to 1)
Current Spending: ($ per student per year):
  Total: $5,267; Instruction: $3,338; Support Services: $1,535
Enrollment, Drop-out Rates and Diploma Recipients by Race/Ethnicity

Category	Total	White	Black	Asian	AIAN	Hisp.
Enrollment (%)	100.0	89.1	9.9	0.2	0.1	0.7
Drop-out Rate (%)	6.2	6.7	2.7	0.0	n/a	0.0
H.S. Diplomas (#)	128	102	22	0	0	4

Neshoba County

Neshoba County SD
Main & Beacon St Courthouse S • Philadelphia, MS 39350-0338
Mailing Address: Courthouse PO Box 338 • Philadelphia, MS 39350-0338
(601) 656-3752 • http://www.neshoba.k12.ms.us/
Grade Span: KG-12; **Agency Type:** 1
Schools: 3
   1 Primary; 1 Middle; 1 High; 0 Other Level
   3 Regular; 0 Special Education; 0 Vocational; 0 Alternative
   0 Magnet; 0 Charter; 2 Title I Eligible; 2 School-wide Title I
Students: 2,975 (49.4% male; 50.5% female)
   Individual Education Program: 354 (11.9%);
   English Language Learner: 0 (0.0%); Migrant: 8 (0.3%)
   Eligible for Free Lunch Program: 1,232 (41.4%)
   Eligible for Reduced-Price Lunch Program: 370 (12.4%)
Teachers: 202.3 (14.7 to 1)
Librarians/Media Specialists: 4.0 (743.8 to 1)
Guidance Counselors: 2.9 (1,025.9 to 1)
Current Spending: ($ per student per year):
   Total: $5,222; Instruction: $3,442; Support Services: $1,380
Enrollment, Drop-out Rates and Diploma Recipients by Race/Ethnicity

Category	Total	White	Black	Asian	AIAN	Hisp.
Enrollment (%)	100.0	72.7	19.2	0.2	7.6	0.4
Drop-out Rate (%)	5.3	4.1	11.0	0.0	0.0	0.0
H.S. Diplomas (#)	125	94	20	1	10	0

Newton County

Newton County SD
15305 Hwy 15 S • Decatur, MS 39327-0097
Mailing Address: PO Box 97 • Decatur, MS 39327-0097
(601) 635-2317 • http://www.newton.k12.ms.us/index.html
Grade Span: PK-12; **Agency Type:** 1
Schools: 4
   1 Primary; 0 Middle; 1 High; 2 Other Level
   2 Regular; 0 Special Education; 1 Vocational; 1 Alternative
   0 Magnet; 0 Charter; 1 Title I Eligible; 1 School-wide Title I
Students: 1,749 (51.4% male; 48.5% female)
   Individual Education Program: 221 (12.6%);
   English Language Learner: 8 (0.5%); Migrant: 3 (0.2%)
   Eligible for Free Lunch Program: 741 (42.4%)
   Eligible for Reduced-Price Lunch Program: 158 (9.0%)
Teachers: 120.2 (14.6 to 1)
Librarians/Media Specialists: 2.0 (874.5 to 1)
Guidance Counselors: 4.0 (437.3 to 1)
Current Spending: ($ per student per year):
   Total: $5,745; Instruction: $3,473; Support Services: $1,874
Enrollment, Drop-out Rates and Diploma Recipients by Race/Ethnicity

Category	Total	White	Black	Asian	AIAN	Hisp.
Enrollment (%)	100.0	70.7	26.1	0.1	2.1	1.0
Drop-out Rate (%)	4.5	5.0	2.4	0.0	11.8	0.0
H.S. Diplomas (#)	74	56	18	0	0	0

Noxubee County

Noxubee County SD
505 S Jefferson • Macon, MS 39341-3007
Mailing Address: PO Box 540 • Macon, MS 39341-3007
(662) 726-4527
Grade Span: KG-12; **Agency Type:** 1
Schools: 6
   3 Primary; 1 Middle; 2 High; 0 Other Level
   5 Regular; 0 Special Education; 1 Vocational; 0 Alternative
   0 Magnet; 0 Charter; 5 Title I Eligible; 5 School-wide Title I
Students: 2,220 (50.0% male; 49.9% female)
   Individual Education Program: 329 (14.8%);
   English Language Learner: 0 (0.0%); Migrant: 0 (0.0%)
   Eligible for Free Lunch Program: 2,205 (99.3%)
   Eligible for Reduced-Price Lunch Program: 0 (0.0%)
Teachers: 148.6 (14.9 to 1)
Librarians/Media Specialists: 3.0 (740.0 to 1)
Guidance Counselors: 2.7 (822.2 to 1)
Current Spending: ($ per student per year):
   Total: $5,869; Instruction: $3,243; Support Services: $2,221
Enrollment, Drop-out Rates and Diploma Recipients by Race/Ethnicity

Category	Total	White	Black	Asian	AIAN	Hisp.
Enrollment (%)	100.0	0.1	99.6	0.1	0.0	0.1
Drop-out Rate (%)	4.8	n/a	4.8	n/a	n/a	n/a
H.S. Diplomas (#)	127	0	127	0	0	0

Oktibbeha County

Starkville SD
401 Greensboro St • Starkville, MS 39759-2803
(662) 324-4050 • http://www2.mde.k12.ms.us/5320/
Grade Span: KG-12; **Agency Type:** 1
Schools: 9
   2 Primary; 3 Middle; 3 High; 1 Other Level
   7 Regular; 0 Special Education; 1 Vocational; 1 Alternative
   0 Magnet; 0 Charter; 0 Title I Eligible; 0 School-wide Title I
Students: 3,886 (50.7% male; 49.2% female)
   Individual Education Program: 538 (13.8%);
   English Language Learner: 4 (0.1%); Migrant: 0 (0.0%)
   Eligible for Free Lunch Program: 2,217 (57.1%)
   Eligible for Reduced-Price Lunch Program: 309 (8.0%)
Teachers: 315.9 (12.3 to 1)
Librarians/Media Specialists: 8.0 (485.8 to 1)
Guidance Counselors: 10.8 (359.8 to 1)
Current Spending: ($ per student per year):
   Total: $7,027; Instruction: $4,064; Support Services: $2,582
Enrollment, Drop-out Rates and Diploma Recipients by Race/Ethnicity

Category	Total	White	Black	Asian	AIAN	Hisp.
Enrollment (%)	100.0	31.8	64.4	2.5	0.3	1.0
Drop-out Rate (%)	4.8	2.1	6.8	0.0	0.0	0.0
H.S. Diplomas (#)	231	104	119	8	0	0

Panola County

North Panola Schools
470 Hwy 51 N • Sardis, MS 38666
Mailing Address: PO Box 334 • Sardis, MS 38666
(662) 487-2305 • http://www2.mde.k12.ms.us/5411/
Grade Span: PK-12; **Agency Type:** 1
Schools: 7
   3 Primary; 1 Middle; 1 High; 2 Other Level
   5 Regular; 0 Special Education; 1 Vocational; 1 Alternative
   0 Magnet; 0 Charter; 5 Title I Eligible; 5 School-wide Title I
Students: 1,751 (50.8% male; 49.1% female)
   Individual Education Program: 231 (13.2%);
   English Language Learner: 1 (0.1%); Migrant: 0 (0.0%)
   Eligible for Free Lunch Program: 1,478 (84.4%)
   Eligible for Reduced-Price Lunch Program: 102 (5.8%)
Teachers: 133.7 (13.1 to 1)
Librarians/Media Specialists: 4.9 (357.3 to 1)
Guidance Counselors: 3.5 (500.3 to 1)
Current Spending: ($ per student per year):
   Total: $6,406; Instruction: $3,676; Support Services: $2,267
Enrollment, Drop-out Rates and Diploma Recipients by Race/Ethnicity

Category	Total	White	Black	Asian	AIAN	Hisp.
Enrollment (%)	100.0	2.3	97.5	0.1	0.0	0.1
Drop-out Rate (%)	3.7	0.0	3.7	n/a	n/a	0.0
H.S. Diplomas (#)	53	0	53	0	0	0

South Panola SD
209 Boothe St • Batesville, MS 38606-2118
(662) 563-9361 • http://www.southpanola.k12.ms.us/
Grade Span: KG-12; **Agency Type:** 1
Schools: 7
   3 Primary; 3 Middle; 1 High; 0 Other Level
   6 Regular; 0 Special Education; 0 Vocational; 1 Alternative
   0 Magnet; 0 Charter; 4 Title I Eligible; 4 School-wide Title I
Students: 4,665 (51.2% male; 48.7% female)
   Individual Education Program: 590 (12.6%);
   English Language Learner: 0 (0.0%); Migrant: 0 (0.0%)
   Eligible for Free Lunch Program: 2,826 (60.6%)
   Eligible for Reduced-Price Lunch Program: 471 (10.1%)
Teachers: 300.9 (15.5 to 1)
Librarians/Media Specialists: 6.8 (686.0 to 1)
Guidance Counselors: 10.8 (431.9 to 1)
Current Spending: ($ per student per year):
   Total: $5,680; Instruction: $3,487; Support Services: $1,819
Enrollment, Drop-out Rates and Diploma Recipients by Race/Ethnicity

Category	Total	White	Black	Asian	AIAN	Hisp.
Enrollment (%)	100.0	43.3	55.6	0.3	0.0	0.8
Drop-out Rate (%)	5.0	2.2	7.3	0.0	n/a	0.0
H.S. Diplomas (#)	191	90	100	0	0	1

Pearl River County

Pearl River County SD
7306 Hwy 11 • Carriere, MS 39426-9231
(601) 798-7744 • http://207.43.239.87/
Grade Span: KG-12; **Agency Type:** 1
Schools: 3
   1 Primary; 1 Middle; 1 High; 0 Other Level

3 Regular; 0 Special Education; 0 Vocational; 0 Alternative
0 Magnet; 0 Charter; 3 Title I Eligible; 2 School-wide Title I
Students: 2,793 (52.2% male; 47.7% female)
Individual Education Program: 246 (8.8%);
English Language Learner: 0 (0.0%); Migrant: 0 (0.0%)
Eligible for Free Lunch Program: 1,144 (41.0%)
Eligible for Reduced-Price Lunch Program: 374 (13.4%)
Teachers: 174.1 (16.0 to 1)
Librarians/Media Specialists: 3.0 (931.0 to 1)
Guidance Counselors: 2.6 (1,074.2 to 1)
Current Spending: ($ per student per year):
Total: $4,733; Instruction: $2,991; Support Services: $1,414
Enrollment, Drop-out Rates and Diploma Recipients by Race/Ethnicity

Category	Total	White	Black	Asian	AIAN	Hisp.
Enrollment (%)	100.0	95.0	3.7	0.4	0.4	0.6
Drop-out Rate (%)	4.2	4.3	3.8	0.0	0.0	0.0
H.S. Diplomas (#)	115	105	6	3	1	0

Picayune SD
706 Goodyear Blvd • Picayune, MS 39466-3220
(601) 798-3230 • http://picayuneschools.datastar.net/
Grade Span: KG-12; **Agency Type:** 1
Schools: 10
6 Primary; 1 Middle; 2 High; 1 Other Level
8 Regular; 0 Special Education; 1 Vocational; 1 Alternative
0 Magnet; 0 Charter; 6 Title I Eligible; 0 School-wide Title I
Students: 3,814 (50.5% male; 49.4% female)
Individual Education Program: 527 (13.8%);
English Language Learner: 0 (0.0%); Migrant: 2 (0.1%)
Eligible for Free Lunch Program: 2,146 (56.3%)
Eligible for Reduced-Price Lunch Program: 234 (6.1%)
Teachers: 294.9 (12.9 to 1)
Librarians/Media Specialists: 7.0 (544.9 to 1)
Guidance Counselors: 4.7 (811.5 to 1)
Current Spending: ($ per student per year):
Total: $6,223; Instruction: $3,519; Support Services: $2,330
Enrollment, Drop-out Rates and Diploma Recipients by Race/Ethnicity

Category	Total	White	Black	Asian	AIAN	Hisp.
Enrollment (%)	100.0	67.2	30.6	0.3	0.4	1.6
Drop-out Rate (%)	2.8	2.4	3.5	0.0	0.0	7.7
H.S. Diplomas (#)	166	130	33	1	1	1

Poplarville Separate SD
804 S Julia St • Poplarville, MS 39470-3017
(601) 795-8477 • http://poplarville.k12.ms.us/testing/home.asp
Grade Span: KG-12; **Agency Type:** 1
Schools: 6
2 Primary; 1 Middle; 3 High; 0 Other Level
4 Regular; 0 Special Education; 1 Vocational; 1 Alternative
0 Magnet; 0 Charter; 3 Title I Eligible; 3 School-wide Title I
Students: 2,039 (51.3% male; 48.6% female)
Individual Education Program: 290 (14.2%);
English Language Learner: 0 (0.0%); Migrant: 0 (0.0%)
Eligible for Free Lunch Program: 820 (40.2%)
Eligible for Reduced-Price Lunch Program: 256 (12.6%)
Teachers: 139.1 (14.7 to 1)
Librarians/Media Specialists: 5.0 (407.8 to 1)
Guidance Counselors: 2.0 (1,019.5 to 1)
Current Spending: ($ per student per year):
Total: $5,753; Instruction: $3,287; Support Services: $2,062
Enrollment, Drop-out Rates and Diploma Recipients by Race/Ethnicity

Category	Total	White	Black	Asian	AIAN	Hisp.
Enrollment (%)	100.0	86.0	13.2	0.4	0.1	0.3
Drop-out Rate (%)	2.0	1.9	2.7	n/a	n/a	0.0
H.S. Diplomas (#)	111	98	13	0	0	0

Pike County

Mccomb SD
695 Minnesota Ave • Mccomb, MS 39648
Mailing Address: PO Box 868 • Mccomb, MS 39649
(601) 684-4661
Grade Span: KG-12; **Agency Type:** 1
Schools: 7
2 Primary; 2 Middle; 3 High; 0 Other Level
5 Regular; 0 Special Education; 1 Vocational; 1 Alternative
0 Magnet; 0 Charter; 3 Title I Eligible; 3 School-wide Title I
Students: 2,869 (50.2% male; 49.7% female)
Individual Education Program: 399 (13.9%);
English Language Learner: 2 (0.1%); Migrant: 0 (0.0%)
Eligible for Free Lunch Program: 2,592 (90.3%)
Eligible for Reduced-Price Lunch Program: 64 (2.2%)
Teachers: 222.0 (12.9 to 1)
Librarians/Media Specialists: 5.0 (573.8 to 1)
Guidance Counselors: 7.8 (367.8 to 1)

Current Spending: ($ per student per year):
Total: $7,004; Instruction: $3,912; Support Services: $2,625
Enrollment, Drop-out Rates and Diploma Recipients by Race/Ethnicity

Category	Total	White	Black	Asian	AIAN	Hisp.
Enrollment (%)	100.0	20.1	79.3	0.5	0.1	0.1
Drop-out Rate (%)	1.3	0.5	1.6	0.0	0.0	0.0
H.S. Diplomas (#)	161	40	120	1	0	0

North Pike SD
1036 Jaguar Tr • Summit, MS 39666-9196
(601) 276-2216
Grade Span: KG-12; **Agency Type:** 1
Schools: 3
1 Primary; 1 Middle; 1 High; 0 Other Level
3 Regular; 0 Special Education; 0 Vocational; 0 Alternative
0 Magnet; 0 Charter; 2 Title I Eligible; 2 School-wide Title I
Students: 1,788 (49.8% male; 50.1% female)
Individual Education Program: 197 (11.0%);
English Language Learner: 0 (0.0%); Migrant: 0 (0.0%)
Eligible for Free Lunch Program: 790 (44.2%)
Eligible for Reduced-Price Lunch Program: 211 (11.8%)
Teachers: 106.5 (16.8 to 1)
Librarians/Media Specialists: 3.0 (596.0 to 1)
Guidance Counselors: 2.3 (777.4 to 1)
Current Spending: ($ per student per year):
Total: $4,606; Instruction: $2,830; Support Services: $1,487
Enrollment, Drop-out Rates and Diploma Recipients by Race/Ethnicity

Category	Total	White	Black	Asian	AIAN	Hisp.
Enrollment (%)	100.0	66.9	32.2	0.8	0.0	0.2
Drop-out Rate (%)	2.6	2.6	2.5	0.0	0.0	n/a
H.S. Diplomas (#)	70	51	19	0	0	0

South Pike SD
250 W Bay St • Magnolia, MS 39652-2716
(601) 783-3742 • http://www.spike.k12.ms.us/
Grade Span: PK-12; **Agency Type:** 1
Schools: 7
2 Primary; 2 Middle; 2 High; 1 Other Level
5 Regular; 0 Special Education; 1 Vocational; 1 Alternative
0 Magnet; 0 Charter; 5 Title I Eligible; 5 School-wide Title I
Students: 2,081 (51.8% male; 48.1% female)
Individual Education Program: 256 (12.3%);
English Language Learner: 2 (0.1%); Migrant: 0 (0.0%)
Eligible for Free Lunch Program: 2,066 (99.3%)
Eligible for Reduced-Price Lunch Program: 0 (0.0%)
Teachers: 127.2 (16.4 to 1)
Librarians/Media Specialists: 6.0 (346.8 to 1)
Guidance Counselors: 4.8 (433.5 to 1)
Current Spending: ($ per student per year):
Total: $5,713; Instruction: $3,454; Support Services: $1,845
Enrollment, Drop-out Rates and Diploma Recipients by Race/Ethnicity

Category	Total	White	Black	Asian	AIAN	Hisp.
Enrollment (%)	100.0	19.8	80.2	0.0	0.0	0.0
Drop-out Rate (%)	10.9	20.6	8.2	0.0	n/a	n/a
H.S. Diplomas (#)	105	23	82	0	0	0

Pontotoc County

Pontotoc City Schools
140 Education Dr • Pontotoc, MS 38863-2108
(662) 489-3336 • http://www.pontotoc.k12.ms.us/
Grade Span: KG-12; **Agency Type:** 1
Schools: 4
2 Primary; 1 Middle; 1 High; 0 Other Level
4 Regular; 0 Special Education; 0 Vocational; 0 Alternative
0 Magnet; 0 Charter; 2 Title I Eligible; 2 School-wide Title I
Students: 2,275 (50.4% male; 49.5% female)
Individual Education Program: 325 (14.3%);
English Language Learner: 25 (1.1%); Migrant: 2 (0.1%)
Eligible for Free Lunch Program: 866 (38.1%)
Eligible for Reduced-Price Lunch Program: 183 (8.0%)
Teachers: 153.5 (14.8 to 1)
Librarians/Media Specialists: 4.7 (484.0 to 1)
Guidance Counselors: 3.0 (758.3 to 1)
Current Spending: ($ per student per year):
Total: $5,288; Instruction: $3,344; Support Services: $1,627
Enrollment, Drop-out Rates and Diploma Recipients by Race/Ethnicity

Category	Total	White	Black	Asian	AIAN	Hisp.
Enrollment (%)	100.0	69.6	27.5	0.3	0.0	2.6
Drop-out Rate (%)	0.4	0.5	0.0	0.0	n/a	0.0
H.S. Diplomas (#)	106	79	25	1	0	1

Pontotoc County SD

285 Hwy 15 Bypass S • Pontotoc, MS 38863-3527
(601) 489-3932 • http://www2.mde.k12.ms.us/5800/default.htm
Grade Span: KG-12; **Agency Type:** 1
Schools: 7
   2 Primary; 2 Middle; 3 High; 0 Other Level
   6 Regular; 0 Special Education; 1 Vocational; 0 Alternative
   0 Magnet; 0 Charter; 2 Title I Eligible; 2 School-wide Title I
Students: 3,125   (50.5% male; 49.4% female)
   Individual Education Program: 422 (13.5%);
   English Language Learner: 52 (1.7%); Migrant: 4 (0.1%)
   Eligible for Free Lunch Program: 1,172 (37.5%)
   Eligible for Reduced-Price Lunch Program: 382 (12.2%)
Teachers: 206.0 (15.2 to 1)
Librarians/Media Specialists: 6.0 (520.8 to 1)
Guidance Counselors: 6.0 (520.8 to 1)
Current Spending: ($ per student per year):
   Total: $5,333; Instruction: $3,419; Support Services: $1,565
Enrollment, Drop-out Rates and Diploma Recipients by Race/Ethnicity

Category	Total	White	Black	Asian	AIAN	Hisp.
Enrollment (%)	100.0	86.6	10.3	0.1	0.1	3.0
Drop-out Rate (%)	1.3	0.9	5.1	n/a	n/a	0.0
H.S. Diplomas (#)	128	110	15	0	0	3

Prentiss County

Prentiss County SD

105 N College St • Booneville, MS 38829-0179
Mailing Address: PO Box 179 • Booneville, MS 38829-0179
(662) 728-4911 • http://www2.mde.k12.ms.us/5900/index.html
Grade Span: KG-12; **Agency Type:** 1
Schools: 8
   2 Primary; 0 Middle; 2 High; 4 Other Level
   6 Regular; 0 Special Education; 1 Vocational; 1 Alternative
   0 Magnet; 0 Charter; 6 Title I Eligible; 1 School-wide Title I
Students: 2,279   (50.3% male; 49.6% female)
   Individual Education Program: 578 (25.4%);
   English Language Learner: 0 (0.0%); Migrant: 0 (0.0%)
   Eligible for Free Lunch Program: 1,113 (48.8%)
   Eligible for Reduced-Price Lunch Program: 331 (14.5%)
Teachers: 210.3 (10.8 to 1)
Librarians/Media Specialists: 7.2 (316.5 to 1)
Guidance Counselors: 5.9 (386.3 to 1)
Current Spending: ($ per student per year):
   Total: $7,013; Instruction: $4,357; Support Services: $2,032
Enrollment, Drop-out Rates and Diploma Recipients by Race/Ethnicity

Category	Total	White	Black	Asian	AIAN	Hisp.
Enrollment (%)	100.0	93.1	6.4	0.1	0.1	0.3
Drop-out Rate (%)	0.6	0.5	2.9	0.0	n/a	0.0
H.S. Diplomas (#)	122	119	3	0	0	0

Quitman County

Quitman County SD

Courthouse Annex Building • Marks, MS 38646
Mailing Address: PO Drawer E • Marks, MS 38646
(662) 326-5451 • http://www2.mde.k12.ms.us/6000/
Grade Span: KG-12; **Agency Type:** 1
Schools: 4
   1 Primary; 1 Middle; 2 High; 0 Other Level
   3 Regular; 0 Special Education; 1 Vocational; 0 Alternative
   0 Magnet; 0 Charter; 3 Title I Eligible; 3 School-wide Title I
Students: 1,604   (51.8% male; 48.1% female)
   Individual Education Program: 271 (16.9%);
   English Language Learner: 0 (0.0%); Migrant: 0 (0.0%)
   Eligible for Free Lunch Program: 1,589 (99.1%)
   Eligible for Reduced-Price Lunch Program: 0 (0.0%)
Teachers: 110.5 (14.5 to 1)
Librarians/Media Specialists: 3.7 (433.5 to 1)
Guidance Counselors: 5.0 (320.8 to 1)
Current Spending: ($ per student per year):
   Total: $6,499; Instruction: $3,880; Support Services: $1,996
Enrollment, Drop-out Rates and Diploma Recipients by Race/Ethnicity

Category	Total	White	Black	Asian	AIAN	Hisp.
Enrollment (%)	100.0	1.7	97.6	0.0	0.0	0.7
Drop-out Rate (%)	2.0	100.0	1.8	n/a	n/a	n/a
H.S. Diplomas (#)	65	0	65	0	0	0

Rankin County

Pearl Public SD

3375 Hwy 80 E • Pearl, MS 39208
Mailing Address: PO Box 5750 • Pearl, MS 39288-5750
(601) 932-7916 • http://www.pearl.k12.ms.us/
Grade Span: KG-12; **Agency Type:** 1
Schools: 5
   2 Primary; 2 Middle; 1 High; 0 Other Level
   5 Regular; 0 Special Education; 0 Vocational; 0 Alternative
   0 Magnet; 0 Charter; 2 Title I Eligible; 2 School-wide Title I
Students: 3,647   (50.9% male; 49.0% female)
   Individual Education Program: 397 (10.9%);
   English Language Learner: 48 (1.3%); Migrant: 0 (0.0%)
   Eligible for Free Lunch Program: 1,387 (38.0%)
   Eligible for Reduced-Price Lunch Program: 350 (9.6%)
Teachers: 224.8 (16.2 to 1)
Librarians/Media Specialists: 6.0 (607.8 to 1)
Guidance Counselors: 8.0 (455.9 to 1)
Current Spending: ($ per student per year):
   Total: $5,577; Instruction: $3,444; Support Services: $1,733
Enrollment, Drop-out Rates and Diploma Recipients by Race/Ethnicity

Category	Total	White	Black	Asian	AIAN	Hisp.
Enrollment (%)	100.0	70.4	26.6	0.7	0.1	2.2
Drop-out Rate (%)	1.3	1.4	1.4	0.0	0.0	0.0
H.S. Diplomas (#)	173	124	43	1	0	5

Rankin County SD

1220 Apple Park Place • Brandon, MS 39042
Mailing Address: PO Box 1359 • Brandon, MS 39042
(601) 825-5590 • http://www.rcsd.k12.ms.us/
Grade Span: PK-12; **Agency Type:** 1
Schools: 23
   10 Primary; 4 Middle; 7 High; 2 Other Level
   22 Regular; 0 Special Education; 0 Vocational; 1 Alternative
   0 Magnet; 0 Charter; 7 Title I Eligible; 7 School-wide Title I
Students: 16,014   (51.4% male; 48.5% female)
   Individual Education Program: 1,706 (10.7%);
   English Language Learner: 165 (1.0%); Migrant: 54 (0.3%)
   Eligible for Free Lunch Program: 4,364 (27.3%)
   Eligible for Reduced-Price Lunch Program: 1,272 (7.9%)
Teachers: 1,047.0 (15.3 to 1)
Librarians/Media Specialists: 30.0 (533.8 to 1)
Guidance Counselors: 38.1 (420.3 to 1)
Current Spending: ($ per student per year):
   Total: $5,342; Instruction: $3,249; Support Services: $1,726
Enrollment, Drop-out Rates and Diploma Recipients by Race/Ethnicity

Category	Total	White	Black	Asian	AIAN	Hisp.
Enrollment (%)	100.0	76.7	21.5	0.8	0.1	0.9
Drop-out Rate (%)	1.6	1.6	1.6	4.0	0.0	4.8
H.S. Diplomas (#)	795	633	151	6	1	4

Scott County

Forest Municipal SD

325 Cleveland St • Forest, MS 39074-3215
(601) 469-3250 • http://www2.mde.k12.ms.us/6220/
Grade Span: KG-12; **Agency Type:** 1
Schools: 3
   1 Primary; 1 Middle; 1 High; 0 Other Level
   3 Regular; 0 Special Education; 0 Vocational; 0 Alternative
   0 Magnet; 0 Charter; 2 Title I Eligible; 2 School-wide Title I
Students: 1,623   (51.8% male; 48.1% female)
   Individual Education Program: 248 (15.3%);
   English Language Learner: 87 (5.4%); Migrant: 5 (0.3%)
   Eligible for Free Lunch Program: 1,151 (70.9%)
   Eligible for Reduced-Price Lunch Program: 136 (8.4%)
Teachers: 105.1 (15.4 to 1)
Librarians/Media Specialists: 3.7 (438.6 to 1)
Guidance Counselors: 3.0 (541.0 to 1)
Current Spending: ($ per student per year):
   Total: $5,653; Instruction: $3,360; Support Services: $1,869
Enrollment, Drop-out Rates and Diploma Recipients by Race/Ethnicity

Category	Total	White	Black	Asian	AIAN	Hisp.
Enrollment (%)	100.0	24.7	64.2	0.4	0.0	10.7
Drop-out Rate (%)	3.5	3.0	3.8	0.0	n/a	4.3
H.S. Diplomas (#)	58	22	34	0	0	2

Scott County SD

100 E First St • Forest, MS 39074
(601) 469-3861 • http://scott.k12.ms.us/
Grade Span: KG-12; **Agency Type:** 1
Schools: 8
   1 Primary; 2 Middle; 2 High; 3 Other Level
   7 Regular; 0 Special Education; 1 Vocational; 0 Alternative

0 Magnet; 0 Charter; 6 Title I Eligible; 6 School-wide Title I
Students: 3,883 (51.5% male; 48.4% female)
   Individual Education Program: 515 (13.3%);
   English Language Learner: 50 (1.3%); Migrant: 167 (4.3%)
   Eligible for Free Lunch Program: 2,411 (62.1%)
   Eligible for Reduced-Price Lunch Program: 445 (11.5%)
Teachers: 247.6 (15.7 to 1)
Librarians/Media Specialists: 10.9 (356.2 to 1)
Guidance Counselors: 9.0 (431.4 to 1)
Current Spending: ($ per student per year):
   Total: $5,061; Instruction: $3,230; Support Services: $1,425
Enrollment, Drop-out Rates and Diploma Recipients by Race/Ethnicity

Category	Total	White	Black	Asian	AIAN	Hisp.
Enrollment (%)	100.0	53.3	42.7	0.2	0.2	3.6
Drop-out Rate (%)	5.7	6.8	4.5	n/a	0.0	5.9
H.S. Diplomas (#)	163	92	69	0	0	2

Simpson County

Simpson County SD
111 Education Ln • Mendenhall, MS 39114-3636
(601) 847-1562 • http://www2.mde.k12.ms.us/6400/index.htm
Grade Span: KG-12; **Agency Type:** 1
Schools: 9
   3 Primary; 2 Middle; 3 High; 1 Other Level
   7 Regular; 0 Special Education; 1 Vocational; 1 Alternative
   0 Magnet; 0 Charter; 5 Title I Eligible; 5 School-wide Title I
Students: 4,249 (51.6% male; 48.3% female)
   Individual Education Program: 521 (12.3%);
   English Language Learner: 10 (0.2%); Migrant: 25 (0.6%)
   Eligible for Free Lunch Program: 2,725 (64.1%)
   Eligible for Reduced-Price Lunch Program: 434 (10.2%)
Teachers: 276.2 (15.4 to 1)
Librarians/Media Specialists: 9.0 (472.1 to 1)
Guidance Counselors: 8.3 (511.9 to 1)
Current Spending: ($ per student per year):
   Total: $5,455; Instruction: $3,356; Support Services: $1,699
Enrollment, Drop-out Rates and Diploma Recipients by Race/Ethnicity

Category	Total	White	Black	Asian	AIAN	Hisp.
Enrollment (%)	100.0	47.4	51.9	0.1	0.1	0.5
Drop-out Rate (%)	5.4	5.0	5.8	0.0	0.0	0.0
H.S. Diplomas (#)	218	108	110	0	0	0

Smith County

Smith County SD
212 Sylvarena Ave • Raleigh, MS 39153
Mailing Address: PO Box 308 • Raleigh, MS 39153
(601) 782-4296 • http://www2.mde.k12.ms.us/6500/index.html
Grade Span: PK-12; **Agency Type:** 1
Schools: 6
   1 Primary; 0 Middle; 3 High; 2 Other Level
   4 Regular; 0 Special Education; 1 Vocational; 1 Alternative
   0 Magnet; 0 Charter; 0 Title I Eligible; 0 School-wide Title I
Students: 3,103 (51.5% male; 48.4% female)
   Individual Education Program: 514 (16.6%);
   English Language Learner: 7 (0.2%); Migrant: 29 (0.9%)
   Eligible for Free Lunch Program: 1,502 (48.4%)
   Eligible for Reduced-Price Lunch Program: 370 (11.9%)
Teachers: 207.6 (14.9 to 1)
Librarians/Media Specialists: 5.5 (564.2 to 1)
Guidance Counselors: 7.8 (397.8 to 1)
Current Spending: ($ per student per year):
   Total: $5,188; Instruction: $3,196; Support Services: $1,661
Enrollment, Drop-out Rates and Diploma Recipients by Race/Ethnicity

Category	Total	White	Black	Asian	AIAN	Hisp.
Enrollment (%)	100.0	67.5	32.2	0.1	0.0	0.3
Drop-out Rate (%)	2.2	2.7	1.2	0.0	n/a	n/a
H.S. Diplomas (#)	147	102	44	1	0	0

Stone County

Stone County SD
214 Critz St • Wiggins, MS 39577-3218
(601) 928-7247 • http://www2.mde.k12.ms.us/6600/
Grade Span: KG-12; **Agency Type:** 1
Schools: 4
   2 Primary; 1 Middle; 1 High; 0 Other Level
   4 Regular; 0 Special Education; 0 Vocational; 0 Alternative
   0 Magnet; 0 Charter; 3 Title I Eligible; 3 School-wide Title I
Students: 2,638 (50.9% male; 49.0% female)
   Individual Education Program: 323 (12.2%);
   English Language Learner: 0 (0.0%); Migrant: 4 (0.2%)
   Eligible for Free Lunch Program: 1,214 (46.0%)
   Eligible for Reduced-Price Lunch Program: 255 (9.7%)

Teachers: 183.1 (14.4 to 1)
Librarians/Media Specialists: 3.2 (824.4 to 1)
Guidance Counselors: 3.5 (753.7 to 1)
Current Spending: ($ per student per year):
   Total: $5,688; Instruction: $3,440; Support Services: $1,891
Enrollment, Drop-out Rates and Diploma Recipients by Race/Ethnicity

Category	Total	White	Black	Asian	AIAN	Hisp.
Enrollment (%)	100.0	75.0	24.4	0.3	0.2	0.2
Drop-out Rate (%)	0.4	0.5	0.0	0.0	n/a	0.0
H.S. Diplomas (#)	125	94	31	0	0	0

Sunflower County

Indianola SD
702 Hwy 82 E • Indianola, MS 38751-2397
(662) 887-2654 • http://www2.mde.k12.ms.us/6721/
Grade Span: KG-12; **Agency Type:** 1
Schools: 6
   3 Primary; 1 Middle; 1 High; 1 Other Level
   6 Regular; 0 Special Education; 0 Vocational; 0 Alternative
   0 Magnet; 0 Charter; 4 Title I Eligible; 4 School-wide Title I
Students: 2,815 (52.0% male; 47.9% female)
   Individual Education Program: 344 (12.2%);
   English Language Learner: 3 (0.1%); Migrant: 0 (0.0%)
   Eligible for Free Lunch Program: 2,395 (85.1%)
   Eligible for Reduced-Price Lunch Program: 191 (6.8%)
Teachers: 171.7 (16.4 to 1)
Librarians/Media Specialists: 5.0 (563.0 to 1)
Guidance Counselors: 4.7 (598.9 to 1)
Current Spending: ($ per student per year):
   Total: $5,625; Instruction: $3,119; Support Services: $2,092
Enrollment, Drop-out Rates and Diploma Recipients by Race/Ethnicity

Category	Total	White	Black	Asian	AIAN	Hisp.
Enrollment (%)	100.0	5.3	93.6	0.2	0.0	0.9
Drop-out Rate (%)	2.0	0.0	2.1	0.0	n/a	0.0
H.S. Diplomas (#)	183	1	181	1	0	0

Sunflower County SD
Courthouse-200 Main St • Indianola, MS 38751
Mailing Address: PO Box 70 • Indianola, MS 38751
(662) 887-4919 • http://www2.mde.k12.ms.us/6700/scsd.html
Grade Span: KG-12; **Agency Type:** 1
Schools: 7
   4 Primary; 2 Middle; 1 High; 0 Other Level
   7 Regular; 0 Special Education; 0 Vocational; 0 Alternative
   0 Magnet; 0 Charter; 7 Title I Eligible; 7 School-wide Title I
Students: 1,915 (51.6% male; 48.3% female)
   Individual Education Program: 243 (12.7%);
   English Language Learner: 30 (1.6%); Migrant: 30 (1.6%)
   Eligible for Free Lunch Program: 1,604 (83.8%)
   Eligible for Reduced-Price Lunch Program: 118 (6.2%)
Teachers: 120.8 (15.9 to 1)
Librarians/Media Specialists: 5.1 (375.5 to 1)
Guidance Counselors: 3.3 (580.3 to 1)
Current Spending: ($ per student per year):
   Total: $6,382; Instruction: $3,975; Support Services: $1,978
Enrollment, Drop-out Rates and Diploma Recipients by Race/Ethnicity

Category	Total	White	Black	Asian	AIAN	Hisp.
Enrollment (%)	100.0	2.4	96.1	0.1	0.0	1.5
Drop-out Rate (%)	3.2	0.0	3.3	n/a	n/a	0.0
H.S. Diplomas (#)	56	0	56	0	0	0

Tallahatchie County

East Tallahatchie Consol SD
411 Chestnut St • Charleston, MS 38921
(662) 647-5524 • http://www2.mde.k12.ms.us/6811/index.htm
Grade Span: KG-12; **Agency Type:** 1
Schools: 4
   1 Primary; 1 Middle; 2 High; 0 Other Level
   3 Regular; 0 Special Education; 1 Vocational; 0 Alternative
   0 Magnet; 0 Charter; 2 Title I Eligible; 2 School-wide Title I
Students: 1,664 (49.9% male; 50.0% female)
   Individual Education Program: 251 (15.1%);
   English Language Learner: 0 (0.0%); Migrant: 0 (0.0%)
   Eligible for Free Lunch Program: 1,288 (77.4%)
   Eligible for Reduced-Price Lunch Program: 136 (8.2%)
Teachers: 115.8 (14.4 to 1)
Librarians/Media Specialists: 3.7 (449.7 to 1)
Guidance Counselors: 2.0 (832.0 to 1)
Current Spending: ($ per student per year):
   Total: $5,751; Instruction: $3,630; Support Services: $1,760

Enrollment, Drop-out Rates and Diploma Recipients by Race/Ethnicity

Category	Total	White	Black	Asian	AIAN	Hisp.
Enrollment (%)	100.0	31.9	67.8	0.1	0.0	0.2
Drop-out Rate (%)	7.1	8.1	6.7	n/a	n/a	n/a
H.S. Diplomas (#)	53	19	34	0	0	0

Tate County

Senatobia Municipal SD
104 Mckie St • Senatobia, MS 38668-2109
(662) 562-4897 • http://www.senatobia.k12.ms.us/
Grade Span: KG-12; **Agency Type:** 1
Schools: 4
  1 Primary; 1 Middle; 1 High; 1 Other Level
  3 Regular; 0 Special Education; 0 Vocational; 1 Alternative
  0 Magnet; 0 Charter; 2 Title I Eligible; 2 School-wide Title I
Students: 1,738 (52.1% male; 47.8% female)
  Individual Education Program: 311 (17.9%);
  English Language Learner: 0 (0.0%); Migrant: 4 (0.2%)
  Eligible for Free Lunch Program: 714 (41.1%)
  Eligible for Reduced-Price Lunch Program: 122 (7.0%)
Teachers: 104.8 (16.6 to 1)
Librarians/Media Specialists: 4.0 (434.5 to 1)
Guidance Counselors: 2.8 (620.7 to 1)
Current Spending: ($ per student per year):
  Total: $5,190; Instruction: $3,144; Support Services: $1,763
Enrollment, Drop-out Rates and Diploma Recipients by Race/Ethnicity

Category	Total	White	Black	Asian	AIAN	Hisp.
Enrollment (%)	100.0	62.0	37.1	0.2	0.0	0.8
Drop-out Rate (%)	2.4	2.3	2.5	0.0	n/a	0.0
H.S. Diplomas (#)	117	82	32	1	0	2

Tate County SD
107 Court • Senatobia, MS 38668-2639
(662) 562-5861 • http://www.tcsd.k12.ms.us/
Grade Span: KG-12; **Agency Type:** 1
Schools: 6
  3 Primary; 0 Middle; 3 High; 0 Other Level
  5 Regular; 0 Special Education; 1 Vocational; 0 Alternative
  0 Magnet; 0 Charter; 4 Title I Eligible; 4 School-wide Title I
Students: 2,863 (50.6% male; 49.3% female)
  Individual Education Program: 376 (13.1%);
  English Language Learner: 13 (0.5%); Migrant: 46 (1.6%)
  Eligible for Free Lunch Program: 1,703 (59.5%)
  Eligible for Reduced-Price Lunch Program: 340 (11.9%)
Teachers: 185.2 (15.5 to 1)
Librarians/Media Specialists: 7.0 (409.0 to 1)
Guidance Counselors: 5.0 (572.6 to 1)
Current Spending: ($ per student per year):
  Total: $5,393; Instruction: $3,162; Support Services: $1,801
Enrollment, Drop-out Rates and Diploma Recipients by Race/Ethnicity

Category	Total	White	Black	Asian	AIAN	Hisp.
Enrollment (%)	100.0	52.1	46.7	0.0	0.0	1.2
Drop-out Rate (%)	4.8	5.6	4.1	n/a	n/a	0.0
H.S. Diplomas (#)	111	42	69	0	0	0

Tippah County

South Tippah SD
402 Greenlee Ave • Ripley, MS 38663-2609
Mailing Address: PO Box 439 • Ripley, MS 38663-2609
(662) 837-7156 • http://ww2.dixie-net.com/Ripley-HS/
Grade Span: PK-12; **Agency Type:** 1
Schools: 6
  1 Primary; 1 Middle; 2 High; 2 Other Level
  5 Regular; 0 Special Education; 1 Vocational; 0 Alternative
  0 Magnet; 0 Charter; 3 Title I Eligible; 3 School-wide Title I
Students: 2,709 (50.1% male; 49.8% female)
  Individual Education Program: 371 (13.7%);
  English Language Learner: 49 (1.8%); Migrant: 0 (0.0%)
  Eligible for Free Lunch Program: 1,264 (46.7%)
  Eligible for Reduced-Price Lunch Program: 300 (11.1%)
Teachers: 174.7 (15.5 to 1)
Librarians/Media Specialists: 6.5 (416.8 to 1)
Guidance Counselors: 5.2 (521.0 to 1)
Current Spending: ($ per student per year):
  Total: $5,208; Instruction: $3,299; Support Services: $1,469
Enrollment, Drop-out Rates and Diploma Recipients by Race/Ethnicity

Category	Total	White	Black	Asian	AIAN	Hisp.
Enrollment (%)	100.0	71.9	23.6	0.1	0.0	4.3
Drop-out Rate (%)	3.5	3.2	5.0	0.0	n/a	0.0
H.S. Diplomas (#)	137	111	23	0	0	3

Tishomingo County

Tishomingo County Sp Mun SD
1620 Paul Edmondson Dr • Iuka, MS 38852-1904
(662) 423-3206 • http://www.tishomingo.k12.ms.us/
Grade Span: PK-12; **Agency Type:** 1
Schools: 9
  3 Primary; 1 Middle; 2 High; 3 Other Level
  7 Regular; 0 Special Education; 1 Vocational; 1 Alternative
  0 Magnet; 0 Charter; 5 Title I Eligible; 5 School-wide Title I
Students: 3,219 (51.1% male; 48.8% female)
  Individual Education Program: 435 (13.5%);
  English Language Learner: 46 (1.4%); Migrant: 0 (0.0%)
  Eligible for Free Lunch Program: 1,360 (42.2%)
  Eligible for Reduced-Price Lunch Program: 392 (12.2%)
Teachers: 208.2 (15.5 to 1)
Librarians/Media Specialists: 5.7 (564.7 to 1)
Guidance Counselors: 8.9 (361.7 to 1)
Current Spending: ($ per student per year):
  Total: $5,398; Instruction: $3,365; Support Services: $1,628
Enrollment, Drop-out Rates and Diploma Recipients by Race/Ethnicity

Category	Total	White	Black	Asian	AIAN	Hisp.
Enrollment (%)	100.0	94.8	3.0	0.1	0.1	2.0
Drop-out Rate (%)	2.0	2.1	0.0	0.0	0.0	0.0
H.S. Diplomas (#)	135	128	7	0	0	0

Tunica County

Tunica County SD
744 School St • Tunica, MS 38676-0758
Mailing Address: PO Box 758 • Tunica, MS 38676-0758
(662) 363-2811 • http://www2.mde.k12.ms.us/7200/tcsd/
Grade Span: PK-12; **Agency Type:** 1
Schools: 7
  3 Primary; 1 Middle; 2 High; 1 Other Level
  5 Regular; 0 Special Education; 1 Vocational; 1 Alternative
  0 Magnet; 0 Charter; 5 Title I Eligible; 5 School-wide Title I
Students: 2,243 (49.3% male; 50.6% female)
  Individual Education Program: 193 (8.6%);
  English Language Learner: 5 (0.2%); Migrant: 19 (0.8%)
  Eligible for Free Lunch Program: 1,964 (87.6%)
  Eligible for Reduced-Price Lunch Program: 112 (5.0%)
Teachers: 148.3 (15.1 to 1)
Librarians/Media Specialists: 6.0 (373.8 to 1)
Guidance Counselors: 7.0 (320.4 to 1)
Current Spending: ($ per student per year):
  Total: $9,270; Instruction: $4,301; Support Services: $4,401
Enrollment, Drop-out Rates and Diploma Recipients by Race/Ethnicity

Category	Total	White	Black	Asian	AIAN	Hisp.
Enrollment (%)	100.0	1.5	97.3	0.0	0.0	1.2
Drop-out Rate (%)	5.0	20.0	4.9	n/a	n/a	n/a
H.S. Diplomas (#)	65	2	63	0	0	0

Union County

New Albany Public Schools
301 Hwy 15 N • New Albany, MS 38652-5519
(662) 534-1800 • http://www2.mde.k12.ms.us/7320/
Grade Span: PK-12; **Agency Type:** 1
Schools: 5
  1 Primary; 1 Middle; 2 High; 1 Other Level
  3 Regular; 0 Special Education; 1 Vocational; 1 Alternative
  0 Magnet; 0 Charter; 1 Title I Eligible; 1 School-wide Title I
Students: 2,034 (52.3% male; 47.6% female)
  Individual Education Program: 304 (14.9%);
  English Language Learner: 61 (3.0%); Migrant: 10 (0.5%)
  Eligible for Free Lunch Program: 822 (40.4%)
  Eligible for Reduced-Price Lunch Program: 279 (13.7%)
Teachers: 146.9 (13.8 to 1)
Librarians/Media Specialists: 4.0 (508.5 to 1)
Guidance Counselors: 2.0 (1,017.0 to 1)
Current Spending: ($ per student per year):
  Total: $6,461; Instruction: $3,914; Support Services: $2,085
Enrollment, Drop-out Rates and Diploma Recipients by Race/Ethnicity

Category	Total	White	Black	Asian	AIAN	Hisp.
Enrollment (%)	100.0	60.3	35.3	0.1	0.0	4.3
Drop-out Rate (%)	1.3	1.3	1.2	0.0	n/a	0.0
H.S. Diplomas (#)	92	66	23	1	0	2

Union County SD
250 Carter Ave • New Albany, MS 38652
Mailing Address: PO Box 939 • New Albany, MS 38652
(662) 534-1960 • http://www.union.k12.ms.us/
Grade Span: KG-12; **Agency Type:** 1
Schools: 4

0 Primary; 0 Middle; 0 High; 4 Other Level
4 Regular; 0 Special Education; 0 Vocational; 0 Alternative
0 Magnet; 0 Charter; 2 Title I Eligible; 2 School-wide Title I
Students: 2,738   (50.5% male; 49.4% female)
Individual Education Program: 402 (14.7%);
English Language Learner: 0 (0.0%); Migrant: 10 (0.4%)
Eligible for Free Lunch Program: 1,047 (38.2%)
Eligible for Reduced-Price Lunch Program: 370 (13.5%)
Teachers: 162.9 (16.8 to 1)
Librarians/Media Specialists: 7.7 (355.6 to 1)
Guidance Counselors: 4.0 (684.5 to 1)
Current Spending: ($ per student per year):
Total: $4,979; Instruction: $2,997; Support Services: $1,462
Enrollment, Drop-out Rates and Diploma Recipients by Race/Ethnicity

Category	Total	White	Black	Asian	AIAN	Hisp.
Enrollment (%)	100.0	90.5	8.7	0.1	0.0	0.7
Drop-out Rate (%)	1.9	2.0	0.0	n/a	n/a	0.0
H.S. Diplomas (#)	112	107	4	0	0	1

Walthall County

Walthall County SD
814a Morse Ave • Tylertown, MS 39667-2130
(601) 876-3401 • http://www2.mde.k12.ms.us/7400/
Grade Span: KG-12; **Agency Type:** 1
Schools: 6
2 Primary; 0 Middle; 2 High; 2 Other Level
5 Regular; 0 Special Education; 1 Vocational; 0 Alternative
0 Magnet; 0 Charter; 5 Title I Eligible; 5 School-wide Title I
Students: 2,685   (53.2% male; 46.7% female)
Individual Education Program: 425 (15.8%);
English Language Learner: 5 (0.2%); Migrant: 0 (0.0%)
Eligible for Free Lunch Program: 1,918 (71.4%)
Eligible for Reduced-Price Lunch Program: 271 (10.1%)
Teachers: 180.2 (14.9 to 1)
Librarians/Media Specialists: 7.0 (383.6 to 1)
Guidance Counselors: 3.9 (688.5 to 1)
Current Spending: ($ per student per year):
Total: $5,952; Instruction: $3,773; Support Services: $1,749
Enrollment, Drop-out Rates and Diploma Recipients by Race/Ethnicity

Category	Total	White	Black	Asian	AIAN	Hisp.
Enrollment (%)	100.0	35.8	63.6	0.1	0.1	0.3
Drop-out Rate (%)	5.1	5.5	4.9	n/a	n/a	0.0
H.S. Diplomas (#)	148	54	94	0	0	0

Warren County

Vicksburg Warren SD
1500 Mission 66 • Vicksburg, MS 39180
(601) 638-5122 • http://www.vwsd.k12.ms.us/
Grade Span: PK-12; **Agency Type:** 1
Schools: 15
7 Primary; 4 Middle; 3 High; 1 Other Level
13 Regular; 0 Special Education; 1 Vocational; 1 Alternative
0 Magnet; 0 Charter; 9 Title I Eligible; 9 School-wide Title I
Students: 8,940   (50.2% male; 49.7% female)
Individual Education Program: 1,179 (13.2%);
English Language Learner: 17 (0.2%); Migrant: 0 (0.0%)
Eligible for Free Lunch Program: 5,103 (57.1%)
Eligible for Reduced-Price Lunch Program: 726 (8.1%)
Teachers: 574.9 (15.6 to 1)
Librarians/Media Specialists: 18.0 (496.7 to 1)
Guidance Counselors: 20.0 (447.0 to 1)
Current Spending: ($ per student per year):
Total: $5,962; Instruction: $3,390; Support Services: $2,168
Enrollment, Drop-out Rates and Diploma Recipients by Race/Ethnicity

Category	Total	White	Black	Asian	AIAN	Hisp.
Enrollment (%)	100.0	38.1	60.1	0.7	0.1	1.0
Drop-out Rate (%)	5.8	4.5	7.0	0.0	0.0	7.7
H.S. Diplomas (#)	441	207	225	7	0	2

Washington County

Greenville Public Schools
412 S Main St • Greenville, MS 38701-4747
Mailing Address: PO Box 1619 • Greenville, MS 38702-1619
(662) 334-7000 • http://members.tripod.com/gpsweb/
Grade Span: PK-12; **Agency Type:** 1
Schools: 16
11 Primary; 2 Middle; 2 High; 1 Other Level
14 Regular; 0 Special Education; 1 Vocational; 1 Alternative
0 Magnet; 0 Charter; 14 Title I Eligible; 14 School-wide Title I
Students: 7,383   (50.5% male; 49.4% female)
Individual Education Program: 907 (12.3%);
English Language Learner: 3 (<0.1%); Migrant: 6 (0.1%)

Eligible for Free Lunch Program: 6,219 (84.2%)
Eligible for Reduced-Price Lunch Program: 326 (4.4%)
Teachers: 501.3 (14.7 to 1)
Librarians/Media Specialists: 10.0 (738.3 to 1)
Guidance Counselors: 12.0 (615.3 to 1)
Current Spending: ($ per student per year):
Total: $5,964; Instruction: $3,469; Support Services: $2,071
Enrollment, Drop-out Rates and Diploma Recipients by Race/Ethnicity

Category	Total	White	Black	Asian	AIAN	Hisp.
Enrollment (%)	100.0	3.7	96.1	0.1	0.0	0.1
Drop-out Rate (%)	6.2	0.0	6.2	n/a	0.0	0.0
H.S. Diplomas (#)	300	0	300	0	0	0

Western Line SD
102 Maddox Rd • Avon, MS 38723-0050
Mailing Address: PO Box 50 • Avon, MS 38723-0050
(662) 335-7186 • http://www2.mde.k12.ms.us/7613/
Grade Span: KG-12; **Agency Type:** 1
Schools: 5
3 Primary; 0 Middle; 2 High; 0 Other Level
5 Regular; 0 Special Education; 0 Vocational; 0 Alternative
0 Magnet; 0 Charter; 3 Title I Eligible; 3 School-wide Title I
Students: 2,050   (53.7% male; 46.2% female)
Individual Education Program: 264 (12.9%);
English Language Learner: 2 (0.1%); Migrant: 26 (1.3%)
Eligible for Free Lunch Program: 1,793 (87.5%)
Eligible for Reduced-Price Lunch Program: 164 (8.0%)
Teachers: 134.4 (15.3 to 1)
Librarians/Media Specialists: 6.9 (297.1 to 1)
Guidance Counselors: 1.8 (1,138.9 to 1)
Current Spending: ($ per student per year):
Total: $6,181; Instruction: $3,587; Support Services: $2,208
Enrollment, Drop-out Rates and Diploma Recipients by Race/Ethnicity

Category	Total	White	Black	Asian	AIAN	Hisp.
Enrollment (%)	100.0	47.2	50.8	0.5	0.0	1.5
Drop-out Rate (%)	5.2	6.3	4.3	n/a	n/a	0.0
H.S. Diplomas (#)	115	44	70	0	0	1

Wayne County

Wayne County SD
810 Chickasawhay St • Waynesboro, MS 39367-2692
(601) 735-4871 • http://www2.mde.k12.ms.us/7700/
Grade Span: KG-12; **Agency Type:** 1
Schools: 8
4 Primary; 1 Middle; 2 High; 1 Other Level
6 Regular; 0 Special Education; 1 Vocational; 1 Alternative
0 Magnet; 0 Charter; 5 Title I Eligible; 5 School-wide Title I
Students: 3,969   (50.1% male; 49.8% female)
Individual Education Program: 544 (13.7%);
English Language Learner: 4 (0.1%); Migrant: 3 (0.1%)
Eligible for Free Lunch Program: 2,596 (65.4%)
Eligible for Reduced-Price Lunch Program: 427 (10.8%)
Teachers: 254.8 (15.6 to 1)
Librarians/Media Specialists: 6.0 (661.5 to 1)
Guidance Counselors: 3.0 (1,323.0 to 1)
Current Spending: ($ per student per year):
Total: $5,592; Instruction: $3,501; Support Services: $1,625
Enrollment, Drop-out Rates and Diploma Recipients by Race/Ethnicity

Category	Total	White	Black	Asian	AIAN	Hisp.
Enrollment (%)	100.0	46.4	53.1	0.3	0.1	0.1
Drop-out Rate (%)	4.6	4.0	5.2	0.0	n/a	0.0
H.S. Diplomas (#)	220	106	114	0	0	0

Webster County

Webster County SD
212 W Clark Ave • Eupora, MS 39744
(662) 258-5921
Grade Span: KG-12; **Agency Type:** 1
Schools: 5
2 Primary; 0 Middle; 3 High; 0 Other Level
4 Regular; 0 Special Education; 1 Vocational; 0 Alternative
0 Magnet; 0 Charter; 4 Title I Eligible; 4 School-wide Title I
Students: 1,880   (51.9% male; 48.0% female)
Individual Education Program: 248 (13.2%);
English Language Learner: 17 (0.9%); Migrant: 3 (0.2%)
Eligible for Free Lunch Program: 889 (47.3%)
Eligible for Reduced-Price Lunch Program: 224 (11.9%)
Teachers: 127.5 (14.7 to 1)
Librarians/Media Specialists: 5.0 (376.0 to 1)
Guidance Counselors: 3.0 (626.7 to 1)
Current Spending: ($ per student per year):
Total: $5,568; Instruction: $3,549; Support Services: $1,655

Enrollment, Drop-out Rates and Diploma Recipients by Race/Ethnicity

Category	Total	White	Black	Asian	AIAN	Hisp.
Enrollment (%)	100.0	70.3	27.9	0.3	0.1	1.4
Drop-out Rate (%)	3.2	2.6	4.4	n/a	n/a	0.0
H.S. Diplomas (#)	93	68	23	0	0	2

Wilkinson County

Wilkinson County SD
488 Main St • Woodville, MS 39669-0785
Mailing Address: PO Box 785 • Woodville, MS 39669-0785
(601) 888-6085 • http://www2.mde.k12.ms.us/7900/default.htm
Grade Span: PK-12; **Agency Type:** 1
Schools: 5
 2 Primary; 1 Middle; 2 High; 0 Other Level
 4 Regular; 0 Special Education; 1 Vocational; 0 Alternative
 0 Magnet; 0 Charter; 4 Title I Eligible; 4 School-wide Title I
Students: 1,563 (51.8% male; 48.1% female)
 Individual Education Program: 281 (18.0%);
 English Language Learner: 0 (0.0%); Migrant: 0 (0.0%)
 Eligible for Free Lunch Program: 1,551 (99.2%)
 Eligible for Reduced-Price Lunch Program: 0 (0.0%)
Teachers: 106.5 (14.7 to 1)
Librarians/Media Specialists: 5.0 (312.6 to 1)
Guidance Counselors: 3.0 (521.0 to 1)
Current Spending: ($ per student per year):
 Total: $6,427; Instruction: $3,507; Support Services: $2,399

Enrollment, Drop-out Rates and Diploma Recipients by Race/Ethnicity

Category	Total	White	Black	Asian	AIAN	Hisp.
Enrollment (%)	100.0	1.5	98.5	0.0	0.0	0.0
Drop-out Rate (%)	4.1	0.0	4.1	n/a	n/a	n/a
H.S. Diplomas (#)	72	0	72	0	0	0

Winston County

Louisville Municipal SD
112 S Columbus Ave • Louisville, MS 39339-0909
Mailing Address: PO Box 909 • Louisville, MS 39339-0909
(662) 773-3411 • http://www2.mde.k12.ms.us/8020/
Grade Span: KG-12; **Agency Type:** 1
Schools: 7
 1 Primary; 2 Middle; 2 High; 2 Other Level
 6 Regular; 0 Special Education; 1 Vocational; 0 Alternative
 0 Magnet; 0 Charter; 6 Title I Eligible; 6 School-wide Title I
Students: 2,965 (52.0% male; 47.9% female)
 Individual Education Program: 378 (12.7%);
 English Language Learner: 0 (0.0%); Migrant: 0 (0.0%)
 Eligible for Free Lunch Program: 1,988 (67.0%)
 Eligible for Reduced-Price Lunch Program: 313 (10.6%)
Teachers: 223.4 (13.3 to 1)
Librarians/Media Specialists: 8.7 (340.8 to 1)
Guidance Counselors: 6.0 (494.2 to 1)
Current Spending: ($ per student per year):
 Total: $6,058; Instruction: $3,844; Support Services: $1,779

Enrollment, Drop-out Rates and Diploma Recipients by Race/Ethnicity

Category	Total	White	Black	Asian	AIAN	Hisp.
Enrollment (%)	100.0	35.0	63.1	0.3	1.4	0.2
Drop-out Rate (%)	2.6	2.2	2.9	0.0	0.0	n/a
H.S. Diplomas (#)	186	64	120	1	1	0

Yazoo County

Yazoo City Municipal SD
1133 Calhoun Ave • Yazoo City, MS 39194-2939
(662) 746-2125 • http://www.yazoocity.k12.ms.us/
Grade Span: PK-12; **Agency Type:** 1
Schools: 6
 2 Primary; 1 Middle; 2 High; 1 Other Level
 4 Regular; 0 Special Education; 1 Vocational; 1 Alternative
 0 Magnet; 0 Charter; 4 Title I Eligible; 4 School-wide Title I
Students: 2,893 (50.2% male; 49.7% female)
 Individual Education Program: 337 (11.6%);
 English Language Learner: 1 (<0.1%); Migrant: 3 (0.1%)
 Eligible for Free Lunch Program: 2,605 (90.0%)
 Eligible for Reduced-Price Lunch Program: 111 (3.8%)
Teachers: 167.3 (17.3 to 1)
Librarians/Media Specialists: 5.0 (578.6 to 1)
Guidance Counselors: 4.0 (723.3 to 1)
Current Spending: ($ per student per year):
 Total: $5,034; Instruction: $3,003; Support Services: $1,627

Enrollment, Drop-out Rates and Diploma Recipients by Race/Ethnicity

Category	Total	White	Black	Asian	AIAN	Hisp.
Enrollment (%)	100.0	1.2	98.3	0.3	0.1	0.1
Drop-out Rate (%)	5.0	4.5	5.0	0.0	n/a	0.0
H.S. Diplomas (#)	90	6	84	0	0	0

Yazoo County SD
119 W Jefferson St • Yazoo City, MS 39194-4005
Mailing Address: PO Box 1088 • Yazoo City, MS 39194-4005
(662) 746-4672 • http://www.yazoo.k12.ms.us/
Grade Span: KG-12; **Agency Type:** 1
Schools: 4
 2 Primary; 1 Middle; 1 High; 0 Other Level
 4 Regular; 0 Special Education; 0 Vocational; 0 Alternative
 0 Magnet; 0 Charter; 4 Title I Eligible; 4 School-wide Title I
Students: 1,873 (51.0% male; 48.9% female)
 Individual Education Program: 315 (16.8%);
 English Language Learner: 6 (0.3%); Migrant: 4 (0.2%)
 Eligible for Free Lunch Program: 1,374 (73.4%)
 Eligible for Reduced-Price Lunch Program: 174 (9.3%)
Teachers: 131.8 (14.2 to 1)
Librarians/Media Specialists: 3.0 (624.3 to 1)
Guidance Counselors: 4.3 (435.6 to 1)
Current Spending: ($ per student per year):
 Total: $6,382; Instruction: $3,515; Support Services: $2,415

Enrollment, Drop-out Rates and Diploma Recipients by Race/Ethnicity

Category	Total	White	Black	Asian	AIAN	Hisp.
Enrollment (%)	100.0	43.8	55.5	0.4	0.0	0.3
Drop-out Rate (%)	5.3	5.7	5.2	n/a	n/a	0.0
H.S. Diplomas (#)	89	31	58	0	0	0

Number of Schools

Rank	Number	District Name	City
1	61	Jackson Public SD	Jackson
2	26	Desoto County SD	Hernando
3	23	Rankin County SD	Brandon
4	20	Harrison County SD	Gulfport
5	19	Pascagoula SD	Pascagoula
6	17	Madison County SD	Flora
7	16	Greenville Public Schools	Greenville
7	16	Tupelo Public SD	Tupelo
9	15	Jackson County SD	Vancleave
9	15	Meridian Public SD	Meridian
9	15	Vicksburg Warren SD	Vicksburg
12	14	Jones County SD	Ellisville
13	13	Columbus Municipal SD	Columbus
13	13	Lamar County SD	Purvis
15	12	Alcorn SD	Corinth
15	12	Biloxi Public SD	Biloxi
15	12	Clarksdale Municipal SD	Clarksdale
15	12	Cleveland SD	Cleveland
15	12	Gulfport SD	Gulfport
20	11	Hinds County SD	Raymond
20	11	Moss Point Separate SD	Moss Point
22	10	Hattiesburg Public SD	Hattiesburg
22	10	Lauderdale County SD	Meridian
22	10	Picayune SD	Picayune
25	9	Clinton Public SD	Clinton
25	9	Lee County SD	Tupelo
25	9	Lowndes County SD	Columbus
25	9	Marion County SD	Columbia
25	9	Simpson County SD	Mendenhall
25	9	Starkville SD	Starkville
25	9	Tishomingo County Sp Mun SD	Iuka
25	9	West Point SD	West Point
33	8	Covington County Schools	Collins
33	8	George County SD	Lucedale
33	8	Greenwood Public SD	Greenwood
33	8	Itawamba County SD	Fulton
33	8	Laurel SD	Laurel
33	8	Leake County SD	Carthage
33	8	Leflore County SD	Greenwood
33	8	Natchez-Adams SD	Natchez
33	8	Prentiss County SD	Booneville
33	8	Scott County SD	Forest
33	8	Wayne County SD	Waynesboro
44	7	Aberdeen SD	Aberdeen
44	7	Brookhaven SD	Brookhaven
44	7	Calhoun County SD	Pittsboro
44	7	Hancock County SD	Kiln
44	7	Holmes County SD	Lexington
44	7	Louisville Municipal SD	Louisville
44	7	Mccomb SD	Mccomb
44	7	North Panola Schools	Sardis
44	7	Ocean Springs SD	Ocean Springs
44	7	Oxford SD	Oxford
44	7	Pontotoc County SD	Pontotoc
44	7	South Panola SD	Batesville
44	7	South Pike SD	Magnolia
44	7	Sunflower County SD	Indianola
44	7	Tunica County SD	Tunica
59	6	Canton Public SD	Canton
59	6	Coahoma County SD	Clarksdale
59	6	Forrest County SD	Hattiesburg
59	6	Greene County SD	Leakesville
59	6	Grenada SD	Grenada
59	6	Indianola SD	Indianola
59	6	Kosciusko SD	Kosciusko
59	6	Lawrence County SD	Monticello
59	6	Marshall County SD	Holly Springs
59	6	Noxubee County SD	Macon
59	6	Poplarville Separate SD	Poplarville
59	6	Quitman SD	Quitman
59	6	Smith County SD	Raleigh
59	6	South Tippah SD	Ripley
59	6	Tate County SD	Senatobia
59	6	Walthall County SD	Tylertown
59	6	Yazoo City Municipal SD	Yazoo City
76	5	Amory SD	Amory
76	5	Bay St Louis Waveland SD	Bay St Louis
76	5	Choctaw County SD	Ackerman
76	5	Corinth SD	Corinth
76	5	Franklin County SD	Meadville
76	5	Holly Springs SD	Holly Springs
76	5	Houston SD	Houston
76	5	Humphreys County SD	Belzoni
76	5	Jefferson County SD	Fayette
76	5	Jefferson Davis County SD	Prentiss
76	5	Lincoln County SD	Brookhaven
76	5	Long Beach SD	Long Beach
76	5	Monroe County SD	Amory
76	5	New Albany Public Schools	New Albany
76	5	Pearl Public SD	Pearl
76	5	Webster County SD	Eupora
76	5	West Jasper Consolidated Schools	Bay Springs
76	5	Western Line SD	Avon
76	5	Wilkinson County SD	Woodville
95	4	Claiborne County SD	Port Gibson
95	4	Columbia SD	Columbia
95	4	Copiah County SD	Hazlehurst
95	4	East Tallahatchie Consol SD	Charleston
95	4	Lafayette County SD	Oxford
95	4	Newton County SD	Decatur
95	4	Pass Christian Public SD	Pass Christian
95	4	Petal SD	Petal
95	4	Pontotoc City Schools	Pontotoc
95	4	Quitman County SD	Marks
95	4	Senatobia Municipal SD	Senatobia
95	4	Stone County SD	Wiggins
95	4	Union County SD	New Albany
95	4	Yazoo County SD	Yazoo City
109	3	Forest Municipal SD	Forest
109	3	Neshoba County SD	Philadelphia
109	3	North Pike SD	Summit
109	3	Pearl River County SD	Carriere
113	2	Hazlehurst City SD	Hazlehurst

Number of Teachers

Rank	Number	District Name	City
1	1,900	Jackson Public SD	Jackson
2	1,266	Desoto County SD	Hernando
3	1,047	Rankin County SD	Brandon
4	816	Harrison County SD	Gulfport
5	639	Madison County SD	Flora
6	574	Vicksburg Warren SD	Vicksburg
7	563	Tupelo Public SD	Tupelo
8	546	Jones County SD	Ellisville
9	520	Jackson County SD	Vancleave
10	501	Greenville Public Schools	Greenville
11	496	Pascagoula SD	Pascagoula
12	481	Lamar County SD	Purvis
13	456	Gulfport SD	Gulfport
14	432	Meridian Public SD	Meridian
15	417	Lauderdale County SD	Meridian
16	414	Biloxi Public SD	Biloxi
17	396	Lee County SD	Tupelo
18	394	Hattiesburg Public SD	Hattiesburg
19	388	Hinds County SD	Raymond
20	387	Columbus Municipal SD	Columbus
21	345	Lowndes County SD	Columbus
22	319	Natchez-Adams SD	Natchez
23	315	Starkville SD	Starkville
24	305	Ocean Springs SD	Ocean Springs
25	305	Clinton Public SD	Clinton
26	300	South Panola SD	Batesville
27	294	Picayune SD	Picayune
28	288	Grenada SD	Grenada
29	284	Moss Point Separate SD	Moss Point
30	276	Simpson County SD	Mendenhall
31	275	Hancock County SD	Kiln
32	266	Alcorn SD	Corinth
33	263	Laurel SD	Laurel
34	262	Itawamba County SD	Fulton
35	257	Cleveland SD	Cleveland
36	256	George County SD	Lucedale
37	254	Wayne County SD	Waynesboro
38	252	Petal SD	Petal
39	248	Greenwood Public SD	Greenwood
40	247	Clarksdale Municipal SD	Clarksdale
41	247	Scott County SD	Forest
42	230	Covington County Schools	Collins
43	225	Oxford SD	Oxford
44	224	Brookhaven SD	Brookhaven
45	224	Pearl Public SD	Pearl
46	223	Long Beach SD	Long Beach
47	223	Louisville Municipal SD	Louisville
48	222	Mccomb SD	Mccomb
49	221	West Point SD	West Point
50	210	Prentiss County SD	Booneville
51	208	Tishomingo County Sp Mun SD	Iuka
52	207	Smith County SD	Raleigh
53	206	Pontotoc County SD	Pontotoc
54	202	Canton Public SD	Canton
55	202	Neshoba County SD	Philadelphia
56	198	Marion County SD	Columbia
57	196	Leake County SD	Carthage
58	195	Forrest County SD	Hattiesburg
59	194	Holmes County SD	Lexington
60	194	Copiah County SD	Hazlehurst
61	192	Marshall County SD	Holly Springs
62	185	Tate County SD	Senatobia
63	183	Stone County SD	Wiggins
64	180	Walthall County SD	Tylertown
65	175	Lincoln County SD	Brookhaven
66	174	South Tippah SD	Ripley
67	174	Lawrence County SD	Monticello
68	174	Pearl River County SD	Carriere
69	171	Indianola SD	Indianola
70	171	Leflore County SD	Greenwood
71	170	Monroe County SD	Amory
72	167	Yazoo City Municipal SD	Yazoo City
73	163	Lafayette County SD	Oxford
74	162	Union County SD	New Albany
75	161	Quitman SD	Quitman
76	160	Bay St Louis Waveland SD	Bay St Louis
77	156	Jefferson Davis County SD	Prentiss
78	156	Aberdeen SD	Aberdeen
79	154	Calhoun County SD	Pittsboro
80	153	Pontotoc City Schools	Pontotoc
81	148	Noxubee County SD	Macon
82	148	Tunica County SD	Tunica
83	148	Corinth SD	Corinth
84	146	New Albany Public Schools	New Albany
85	143	Coahoma County SD	Clarksdale
86	139	Greene County SD	Leakesville
87	139	Houston SD	Houston
87	139	Poplarville Separate SD	Poplarville
89	135	Kosciusko SD	Kosciusko
90	135	Choctaw County SD	Ackerman
91	134	Western Line SD	Avon
92	133	North Panola Schools	Sardis
93	131	Holly Springs SD	Holly Springs
94	131	Yazoo County SD	Yazoo City
95	130	Pass Christian Public SD	Pass Christian
96	127	Amory SD	Amory
97	127	Webster County SD	Eupora
98	127	South Pike SD	Magnolia
99	123	Claiborne County SD	Port Gibson
100	121	West Jasper Consolidated Schools	Bay Springs
101	120	Sunflower County SD	Indianola
102	120	Franklin County SD	Meadville
103	120	Newton County SD	Decatur
104	115	East Tallahatchie Consol SD	Charleston
105	114	Humphreys County SD	Belzoni
106	113	Columbia SD	Columbia
107	112	Hazlehurst City SD	Hazlehurst
108	110	Jefferson County SD	Fayette
109	110	Quitman County SD	Marks
110	106	North Pike SD	Summit
110	106	Wilkinson County SD	Woodville
112	105	Forest Municipal SD	Forest
113	104	Senatobia Municipal SD	Senatobia

Number of Students

Rank	Number	District Name	City
1	31,640	Jackson Public SD	Jackson
2	23,672	Desoto County SD	Hernando
3	16,014	Rankin County SD	Brandon
4	13,049	Harrison County SD	Gulfport
5	9,891	Madison County SD	Flora
6	8,940	Vicksburg Warren SD	Vicksburg
7	8,509	Jackson County SD	Vancleave
8	7,811	Jones County SD	Ellisville
9	7,496	Pascagoula SD	Pascagoula
10	7,383	Greenville Public Schools	Greenville
11	7,264	Tupelo Public SD	Tupelo
12	7,021	Lamar County SD	Purvis
13	6,742	Meridian Public SD	Meridian
14	6,595	Lauderdale County SD	Meridian
15	6,245	Lee County SD	Tupelo
16	6,243	Gulfport SD	Gulfport
17	6,228	Biloxi Public SD	Biloxi
18	5,776	Hinds County SD	Raymond
19	5,383	Lowndes County SD	Columbus
20	5,252	Ocean Springs SD	Ocean Springs
21	4,975	Columbus Municipal SD	Columbus
22	4,899	Clinton Public SD	Clinton
23	4,761	Hattiesburg Public SD	Hattiesburg
24	4,715	Grenada SD	Grenada
25	4,665	South Panola SD	Batesville
26	4,653	Natchez-Adams SD	Natchez
27	4,391	Hancock County SD	Kiln
28	4,249	Simpson County SD	Mendenhall
29	4,066	George County SD	Lucedale
30	4,003	Moss Point Separate SD	Moss Point
31	3,969	Wayne County SD	Waynesboro
32	3,886	Starkville SD	Starkville
33	3,883	Scott County SD	Forest
34	3,823	Itawamba County SD	Fulton
35	3,814	Picayune SD	Picayune
36	3,779	Alcorn SD	Corinth
37	3,715	West Point SD	West Point
38	3,703	Clarksdale Municipal SD	Clarksdale
39	3,701	Petal SD	Petal
40	3,666	Cleveland SD	Cleveland
41	3,647	Pearl Public SD	Pearl
42	3,557	Holmes County SD	Lexington

43	3,514	Covington County Schools	Collins
44	3,463	Marshall County SD	Holly Springs
45	3,422	Greenwood Public SD	Greenwood
46	3,393	Canton Public SD	Canton
47	3,345	Leake County SD	Carthage
48	3,323	Long Beach SD	Long Beach
49	3,219	Tishomingo County Sp Mun SD	Iuka
50	3,137	Laurel SD	Laurel
51	3,125	Pontotoc County SD	Pontotoc
52	3,118	Oxford SD	Oxford
53	3,103	Smith County SD	Raleigh
54	3,069	Copiah County SD	Hazlehurst
55	2,996	Leflore County SD	Greenwood
56	2,975	Neshoba County SD	Philadelphia
57	2,967	Brookhaven SD	Brookhaven
58	2,965	Louisville Municipal SD	Louisville
59	2,893	Yazoo City Municipal SD	Yazoo City
60	2,869	Mccomb SD	Mccomb
61	2,867	Lincoln County SD	Brookhaven
62	2,863	Tate County SD	Senatobia
63	2,815	Indianola SD	Indianola
64	2,793	Pearl River County SD	Carriere
65	2,738	Union County SD	New Albany
66	2,709	South Tippah SD	Ripley
67	2,685	Walthall County SD	Tylertown
68	2,638	Stone County SD	Wiggins
69	2,602	Monroe County SD	Amory
70	2,546	Calhoun County SD	Pittsboro
71	2,523	Marion County SD	Columbia
72	2,482	Forrest County SD	Hattiesburg
73	2,400	Lawrence County SD	Monticello
74	2,368	Quitman SD	Quitman
75	2,279	Prentiss County SD	Booneville
76	2,275	Pontotoc City Schools	Pontotoc
77	2,273	Jefferson Davis County SD	Prentiss
78	2,253	Bay St Louis Waveland SD	Bay St Louis
79	2,243	Tunica County SD	Tunica
80	2,220	Noxubee County SD	Macon
81	2,193	Lafayette County SD	Oxford
82	2,085	Kosciusko SD	Kosciusko
83	2,081	South Pike SD	Magnolia
84	2,050	Western Line SD	Avon
85	2,039	Poplarville Separate SD	Poplarville
86	2,034	New Albany Public Schools	New Albany
87	1,974	Houston SD	Houston
88	1,954	Pass Christian Public SD	Pass Christian
89	1,949	Greene County SD	Leakesville
90	1,923	Coahoma County SD	Clarksdale
91	1,918	Humphreys County SD	Belzoni
92	1,915	Sunflower County SD	Indianola
93	1,880	Webster County SD	Eupora
94	1,873	Columbia SD	Columbia
94	1,873	Yazoo County SD	Yazoo City
96	1,832	Amory SD	Amory
97	1,816	Holly Springs SD	Holly Springs
98	1,808	Corinth SD	Corinth
99	1,793	West Jasper Consolidated Schools	Bay Springs
100	1,788	North Pike SD	Summit
101	1,787	Choctaw County SD	Ackerman
102	1,751	North Panola Schools	Sardis
103	1,749	Newton County SD	Decatur
104	1,738	Senatobia Municipal SD	Senatobia
105	1,712	Hazlehurst City SD	Hazlehurst
106	1,667	Aberdeen SD	Aberdeen
107	1,664	East Tallahatchie Consol SD	Charleston
108	1,623	Forest Municipal SD	Forest
109	1,604	Quitman County SD	Marks
110	1,600	Claiborne County SD	Port Gibson
111	1,593	Jefferson County SD	Fayette
112	1,568	Franklin County SD	Meadville
113	1,563	Wilkinson County SD	Woodville

Male Students

Rank	Percent	District Name	City
1	54.4	Franklin County SD	Meadville
2	53.7	Western Line SD	Avon
3	53.2	Walthall County SD	Tylertown
4	52.7	Lincoln County SD	Brookhaven
5	52.5	Jefferson Davis County SD	Prentiss
6	52.3	Leake County SD	Carthage
7	52.3	Jones County SD	Ellisville
8	52.3	New Albany Public Schools	New Albany
9	52.2	Pearl River County SD	Carriere
10	52.2	Lamar County SD	Purvis
11	52.1	Monroe County SD	Amory
12	52.1	Lafayette County SD	Oxford
13	52.1	Senatobia Municipal SD	Senatobia
14	52.1	Corinth SD	Corinth
15	52.0	Marion County SD	Columbia
16	52.0	Indianola SD	Indianola
17	52.0	Louisville Municipal SD	Louisville
18	51.9	Hazlehurst City SD	Hazlehurst
19	51.9	Webster County SD	Eupora
20	51.9	Copiah County SD	Hazlehurst
21	51.8	South Pike SD	Magnolia
22	51.8	Quitman County SD	Marks
23	51.8	Desoto County SD	Hernando
24	51.8	Wilkinson County SD	Woodville
25	51.8	Forest Municipal SD	Forest
26	51.8	Pascagoula SD	Pascagoula
27	51.7	Lauderdale County SD	Meridian
28	51.6	Alcorn SD	Corinth
29	51.6	George County SD	Lucedale
30	51.6	Sunflower County SD	Indianola
31	51.6	Simpson County SD	Mendenhall
32	51.6	Biloxi Public SD	Biloxi
33	51.6	Kosciusko SD	Kosciusko
34	51.5	Smith County SD	Raleigh
35	51.5	Scott County SD	Forest
36	51.5	Jackson County SD	Vancleave
37	51.4	Rankin County SD	Brandon
38	51.4	Harrison County SD	Gulfport
39	51.4	Newton County SD	Decatur
40	51.3	Poplarville Separate SD	Poplarville
41	51.3	Forrest County SD	Hattiesburg
42	51.3	Lee County SD	Tupelo
43	51.2	South Panola SD	Batesville
44	51.2	Madison County SD	Flora
45	51.1	Tishomingo County Sp Mun SD	Iuka
46	51.0	Yazoo County SD	Yazoo City
47	51.0	Quitman SD	Quitman
48	51.0	Tupelo Public SD	Tupelo
49	51.0	Greenwood Public SD	Greenwood
50	50.9	Ocean Springs SD	Ocean Springs
51	50.9	Pearl Public SD	Pearl
52	50.9	Hancock County SD	Kiln
53	50.9	Stone County SD	Wiggins
54	50.8	North Panola Schools	Sardis
55	50.8	Amory SD	Amory
56	50.8	Marshall County SD	Holly Springs
57	50.8	Columbus Municipal SD	Columbus
58	50.8	Hinds County SD	Raymond
59	50.8	Aberdeen SD	Aberdeen
60	50.7	Moss Point Separate SD	Moss Point
61	50.7	Clinton Public SD	Clinton
62	50.7	Natchez-Adams SD	Natchez
63	50.7	Starkville SD	Starkville
64	50.6	Oxford SD	Oxford
65	50.6	Covington County Schools	Collins
66	50.6	Humphreys County SD	Belzoni
67	50.6	Tate County SD	Senatobia
68	50.5	Laurel SD	Laurel
69	50.5	Picayune SD	Picayune
70	50.5	Union County SD	New Albany
71	50.5	Coahoma County SD	Clarksdale
72	50.5	Cleveland SD	Cleveland
73	50.5	Jefferson County SD	Fayette
74	50.5	Pontotoc County SD	Pontotoc
75	50.5	Greenville Public Schools	Greenville
76	50.5	Leflore County SD	Greenwood
77	50.4	Choctaw County SD	Ackerman
78	50.4	Lowndes County SD	Columbus
79	50.4	Bay St Louis Waveland SD	Bay St Louis
80	50.4	Columbia SD	Columbia
81	50.4	Pontotoc City Schools	Pontotoc
82	50.4	Pass Christian Public SD	Pass Christian
83	50.3	Prentiss County SD	Booneville
84	50.3	Hattiesburg Public SD	Hattiesburg
85	50.3	Calhoun County SD	Pittsboro
86	50.2	Meridian Public SD	Meridian
87	50.2	Mccomb SD	Mccomb
88	50.2	Yazoo City Municipal SD	Yazoo City
89	50.2	Vicksburg Warren SD	Vicksburg
90	50.2	Itawamba County SD	Fulton
91	50.2	Petal SD	Petal
92	50.1	Wayne County SD	Waynesboro
93	50.1	Holmes County SD	Lexington
94	50.1	South Tippah SD	Ripley
95	50.1	Long Beach SD	Long Beach
96	50.1	Lawrence County SD	Monticello
97	50.1	Houston SD	Houston
98	50.0	Holly Springs SD	Holly Springs
99	50.0	Noxubee County SD	Macon
100	49.9	West Jasper Consolidated Schools	Bay Springs
101	49.9	Gulfport SD	Gulfport
102	49.9	East Tallahatchie Consol SD	Charleston
103	49.8	North Pike SD	Summit
104	49.8	Jackson Public SD	Jackson
105	49.7	Brookhaven SD	Brookhaven
106	49.7	West Point SD	West Point
107	49.7	Grenada SD	Grenada
108	49.4	Neshoba County SD	Philadelphia
109	49.3	Tunica County SD	Tunica
110	49.3	Clarksdale Municipal SD	Clarksdale
111	49.1	Greene County SD	Leakesville
112	48.8	Claiborne County SD	Port Gibson
113	48.6	Canton Public SD	Canton

Female Students

Rank	Percent	District Name	City
1	51.3	Canton Public SD	Canton
2	51.1	Claiborne County SD	Port Gibson
3	50.8	Greene County SD	Leakesville
4	50.6	Clarksdale Municipal SD	Clarksdale
5	50.6	Tunica County SD	Tunica
6	50.5	Neshoba County SD	Philadelphia
7	50.2	Grenada SD	Grenada
8	50.2	West Point SD	West Point
9	50.2	Brookhaven SD	Brookhaven
10	50.1	Jackson Public SD	Jackson
11	50.1	North Pike SD	Summit
12	50.0	East Tallahatchie Consol SD	Charleston
13	50.0	Gulfport SD	Gulfport
14	50.0	West Jasper Consolidated Schools	Bay Springs
15	49.9	Noxubee County SD	Macon
16	49.9	Holly Springs SD	Holly Springs
17	49.8	Houston SD	Houston
18	49.8	Lawrence County SD	Monticello
19	49.8	Long Beach SD	Long Beach
20	49.8	South Tippah SD	Ripley
21	49.8	Holmes County SD	Lexington
22	49.8	Wayne County SD	Waynesboro
23	49.7	Petal SD	Petal
24	49.7	Itawamba County SD	Fulton
25	49.7	Vicksburg Warren SD	Vicksburg
26	49.7	Yazoo City Municipal SD	Yazoo City
27	49.7	Mccomb SD	Mccomb
28	49.7	Meridian Public SD	Meridian
29	49.6	Calhoun County SD	Pittsboro
30	49.6	Hattiesburg Public SD	Hattiesburg
31	49.6	Prentiss County SD	Booneville
32	49.5	Pass Christian Public SD	Pass Christian
33	49.5	Pontotoc City Schools	Pontotoc
34	49.5	Columbia SD	Columbia
35	49.5	Bay St Louis Waveland SD	Bay St Louis
36	49.5	Lowndes County SD	Columbus
37	49.5	Choctaw County SD	Ackerman
38	49.4	Leflore County SD	Greenwood
39	49.4	Greenville Public Schools	Greenville
40	49.4	Pontotoc County SD	Pontotoc
41	49.4	Jefferson County SD	Fayette
42	49.4	Cleveland SD	Cleveland
43	49.4	Coahoma County SD	Clarksdale
44	49.4	Union County SD	New Albany
45	49.4	Picayune SD	Picayune
46	49.4	Laurel SD	Laurel
47	49.3	Tate County SD	Senatobia
48	49.3	Humphreys County SD	Belzoni
49	49.3	Covington County Schools	Collins
50	49.3	Oxford SD	Oxford
51	49.2	Starkville SD	Starkville
52	49.2	Natchez-Adams SD	Natchez
53	49.2	Clinton Public SD	Clinton
54	49.2	Moss Point Separate SD	Moss Point
55	49.1	Aberdeen SD	Aberdeen
56	49.1	Hinds County SD	Raymond
57	49.1	Columbus Municipal SD	Columbus
58	49.1	Marshall County SD	Holly Springs
59	49.1	Amory SD	Amory
60	49.1	North Panola Schools	Sardis
61	49.0	Stone County SD	Wiggins
62	49.0	Hancock County SD	Kiln
63	49.0	Pearl Public SD	Pearl
64	49.0	Ocean Springs SD	Ocean Springs
65	48.9	Greenwood Public SD	Greenwood
66	48.9	Tupelo Public SD	Tupelo
67	48.9	Quitman SD	Quitman
68	48.9	Yazoo County SD	Yazoo City
69	48.8	Tishomingo County Sp Mun SD	Iuka
70	48.7	Madison County SD	Flora
71	48.7	South Panola SD	Batesville
72	48.6	Lee County SD	Tupelo
73	48.6	Forrest County SD	Hattiesburg
74	48.6	Poplarville Separate SD	Poplarville
75	48.5	Newton County SD	Decatur
76	48.5	Harrison County SD	Gulfport
77	48.5	Rankin County SD	Brandon
78	48.4	Jackson County SD	Vancleave
79	48.4	Scott County SD	Forest
80	48.4	Smith County SD	Raleigh
81	48.3	Kosciusko SD	Kosciusko
82	48.3	Biloxi Public SD	Biloxi
83	48.3	Simpson County SD	Mendenhall
84	48.3	Sunflower County SD	Indianola
85	48.3	George County SD	Lucedale
86	48.3	Alcorn SD	Corinth

87	48.2	Lauderdale County SD	Meridian
88	48.1	Pascagoula SD	Pascagoula
89	48.1	Forest Municipal SD	Forest
90	48.1	Wilkinson County SD	Woodville
91	48.1	Desoto County SD	Hernando
92	48.1	Quitman County SD	Marks
93	48.1	South Pike SD	Magnolia
94	48.0	Copiah County SD	Hazlehurst
95	48.0	Webster County SD	Eupora
96	48.0	Hazlehurst City SD	Hazlehurst
97	47.9	Louisville Municipal SD	Louisville
98	47.9	Indianola SD	Indianola
99	47.9	Marion County SD	Columbia
100	47.8	Corinth SD	Corinth
101	47.8	Senatobia Municipal SD	Senatobia
102	47.8	Lafayette County SD	Oxford
103	47.8	Monroe County SD	Amory
104	47.7	Lamar County SD	Purvis
105	47.7	Pearl River County SD	Carriere
106	47.6	New Albany Public Schools	New Albany
107	47.6	Jones County SD	Ellisville
108	47.6	Leake County SD	Carthage
109	47.4	Jefferson Davis County SD	Prentiss
110	47.2	Lincoln County SD	Brookhaven
111	46.7	Walthall County SD	Tylertown
112	46.2	Western Line SD	Avon
113	45.5	Franklin County SD	Meadville

Individual Education Program Students

Rank	Percent	District Name	City
1	25.4	Prentiss County SD	Booneville
2	21.5	Lafayette County SD	Oxford
3	21.0	Coahoma County SD	Clarksdale
4	19.8	Jefferson Davis County SD	Prentiss
5	19.0	Franklin County SD	Meadville
6	18.9	Holly Springs SD	Holly Springs
7	18.8	Leflore County SD	Greenwood
8	18.4	Marion County SD	Columbia
9	18.2	Columbia SD	Columbia
10	18.1	Kosciusko SD	Kosciusko
11	18.0	Wilkinson County SD	Woodville
12	17.9	Senatobia Municipal SD	Senatobia
13	17.8	Petal SD	Petal
14	17.6	Covington County Schools	Collins
15	17.3	Moss Point Separate SD	Moss Point
16	17.2	Calhoun County SD	Pittsboro
16	17.2	Lee County SD	Tupelo
18	17.1	Alcorn SD	Corinth
19	16.9	Quitman County SD	Marks
20	16.8	Yazoo County SD	Yazoo City
21	16.6	Smith County SD	Raleigh
21	16.6	West Jasper Consolidated Schools	Bay Springs
23	16.4	Aberdeen SD	Aberdeen
24	16.3	George County SD	Lucedale
25	16.0	Greene County SD	Leakesville
26	15.9	Bay St Louis Waveland SD	Bay St Louis
26	15.9	Biloxi Public SD	Biloxi
28	15.8	Lamar County SD	Purvis
28	15.8	Walthall County SD	Tylertown
30	15.7	Forrest County SD	Hattiesburg
31	15.6	Lauderdale County SD	Meridian
32	15.4	Pascagoula SD	Pascagoula
33	15.3	Forest Municipal SD	Forest
33	15.3	Hancock County SD	Kiln
33	15.3	Monroe County SD	Amory
36	15.2	Pass Christian Public SD	Pass Christian
37	15.1	East Tallahatchie Consol SD	Charleston
38	15.0	Jones County SD	Ellisville
39	14.9	New Albany Public Schools	New Albany
40	14.8	Gulfport SD	Gulfport
40	14.8	Hattiesburg Public SD	Hattiesburg
40	14.8	Noxubee County SD	Macon
43	14.7	Union County SD	New Albany
44	14.6	Leake County SD	Carthage
44	14.6	Tupelo Public SD	Tupelo
46	14.5	Quitman SD	Quitman
47	14.3	Amory SD	Amory
47	14.3	Itawamba County SD	Fulton
47	14.3	Pontotoc City Schools	Pontotoc
50	14.2	Poplarville Separate SD	Poplarville
51	14.0	Corinth SD	Corinth
52	13.9	Mccomb SD	Mccomb
53	13.8	Harrison County SD	Gulfport
53	13.8	Picayune SD	Picayune
53	13.8	Starkville SD	Starkville
56	13.7	South Tippah SD	Ripley
56	13.7	Wayne County SD	Waynesboro
58	13.5	Houston SD	Houston
58	13.5	Pontotoc County SD	Pontotoc
58	13.5	Tishomingo County Sp Mun SD	Iuka
61	13.4	Grenada SD	Grenada
61	13.4	Jefferson County SD	Fayette
63	13.3	Choctaw County SD	Ackerman
63	13.3	Ocean Springs SD	Ocean Springs
63	13.3	Scott County SD	Forest
66	13.2	North Panola Schools	Sardis
66	13.2	Vicksburg Warren SD	Vicksburg
66	13.2	Webster County SD	Eupora
69	13.1	Columbus Municipal SD	Columbus
69	13.1	Tate County SD	Senatobia
71	13.0	Cleveland SD	Cleveland
71	13.0	Laurel SD	Laurel
73	12.9	Lincoln County SD	Brookhaven
73	12.9	Western Line SD	Avon
75	12.8	Marshall County SD	Holly Springs
76	12.7	Louisville Municipal SD	Louisville
76	12.7	Sunflower County SD	Indianola
78	12.6	Newton County SD	Decatur
78	12.6	South Panola SD	Batesville
80	12.5	Meridian Public SD	Meridian
81	12.3	Greenville Public Schools	Greenville
81	12.3	Simpson County SD	Mendenhall
81	12.3	South Pike SD	Magnolia
84	12.2	Indianola SD	Indianola
84	12.2	Stone County SD	Wiggins
86	11.9	Canton Public SD	Canton
86	11.9	Desoto County SD	Hernando
86	11.9	Lawrence County SD	Monticello
86	11.9	Neshoba County SD	Philadelphia
90	11.6	Hazlehurst City SD	Hazlehurst
90	11.6	Yazoo City Municipal SD	Yazoo City
92	11.5	Long Beach SD	Long Beach
92	11.5	Natchez-Adams SD	Natchez
94	11.4	Clarksdale Municipal SD	Clarksdale
95	11.0	North Pike SD	Summit
96	10.9	Lowndes County SD	Columbus
96	10.9	Oxford SD	Oxford
96	10.9	Pearl Public SD	Pearl
99	10.7	Rankin County SD	Brandon
100	10.6	West Point SD	West Point
101	10.5	Greenwood Public SD	Greenwood
102	10.4	Brookhaven SD	Brookhaven
103	10.3	Jackson Public SD	Jackson
104	10.2	Hinds County SD	Raymond
105	10.0	Jackson County SD	Vancleave
106	9.8	Holmes County SD	Lexington
107	9.3	Clinton Public SD	Clinton
108	8.8	Pearl River County SD	Carriere
109	8.6	Humphreys County SD	Belzoni
109	8.6	Tunica County SD	Tunica
111	8.2	Madison County SD	Flora
112	8.0	Claiborne County SD	Port Gibson
113	7.3	Copiah County SD	Hazlehurst

English Language Learner Students

Rank	Percent	District Name	City
1	5.4	Forest Municipal SD	Forest
2	5.0	Biloxi Public SD	Biloxi
3	3.4	Calhoun County SD	Pittsboro
4	3.0	Houston SD	Houston
4	3.0	New Albany Public Schools	New Albany
6	2.7	Pascagoula SD	Pascagoula
7	2.2	Corinth SD	Corinth
8	1.8	South Tippah SD	Ripley
9	1.7	Pontotoc County SD	Pontotoc
10	1.6	Sunflower County SD	Indianola
11	1.5	Desoto County SD	Hernando
11	1.5	Leake County SD	Carthage
13	1.4	Laurel SD	Laurel
13	1.4	Tishomingo County Sp Mun SD	Iuka
15	1.3	Hazlehurst City SD	Hazlehurst
15	1.3	Pearl Public SD	Pearl
15	1.3	Scott County SD	Forest
15	1.3	Tupelo Public SD	Tupelo
19	1.1	Pontotoc City Schools	Pontotoc
20	1.0	Leflore County SD	Greenwood
20	1.0	Rankin County SD	Brandon
22	0.9	Marshall County SD	Holly Springs
22	0.9	Webster County SD	Eupora
24	0.8	Coahoma County SD	Clarksdale
24	0.8	Forrest County SD	Hattiesburg
24	0.8	Madison County SD	Flora
24	0.8	Oxford SD	Oxford
28	0.7	Clinton Public SD	Clinton
28	0.7	Gulfport SD	Gulfport
28	0.7	Lamar County SD	Purvis
28	0.7	Petal SD	Petal
32	0.6	Alcorn SD	Corinth
32	0.6	Bay St Louis Waveland SD	Bay St Louis
32	0.6	Clarksdale Municipal SD	Clarksdale
32	0.6	Jackson County SD	Vancleave
32	0.6	Jones County SD	Ellisville
37	0.5	Lowndes County SD	Columbus
37	0.5	Natchez-Adams SD	Natchez
37	0.5	Newton County SD	Decatur
37	0.5	Tate County SD	Senatobia
41	0.4	Cleveland SD	Cleveland
41	0.4	Harrison County SD	Gulfport
41	0.4	Holly Springs SD	Holly Springs
41	0.4	Jackson Public SD	Jackson
41	0.4	West Point SD	West Point
46	0.3	Hattiesburg Public SD	Hattiesburg
46	0.3	Lafayette County SD	Oxford
46	0.3	Meridian Public SD	Meridian
46	0.3	Yazoo County SD	Yazoo City
50	0.2	Kosciusko SD	Kosciusko
50	0.2	Lee County SD	Tupelo
50	0.2	Moss Point Separate SD	Moss Point
50	0.2	Ocean Springs SD	Ocean Springs
50	0.2	Simpson County SD	Mendenhall
50	0.2	Smith County SD	Raleigh
50	0.2	Tunica County SD	Tunica
50	0.2	Vicksburg Warren SD	Vicksburg
50	0.2	Walthall County SD	Tylertown
59	0.1	Amory SD	Amory
59	0.1	Brookhaven SD	Brookhaven
59	0.1	Canton Public SD	Canton
59	0.1	Columbus Municipal SD	Columbus
59	0.1	Franklin County SD	Meadville
59	0.1	George County SD	Lucedale
59	0.1	Indianola SD	Indianola
59	0.1	Itawamba County SD	Fulton
59	0.1	Mccomb SD	Mccomb
59	0.1	North Panola Schools	Sardis
59	0.1	South Pike SD	Magnolia
59	0.1	Starkville SD	Starkville
59	0.1	Wayne County SD	Waynesboro
59	0.1	Western Line SD	Avon
73	0.0	Greenville Public Schools	Greenville
73	0.0	Greenwood Public SD	Greenwood
73	0.0	Grenada SD	Grenada
73	0.0	Hancock County SD	Kiln
73	0.0	Yazoo City Municipal SD	Yazoo City
78	0.0	Aberdeen SD	Aberdeen
78	0.0	Choctaw County SD	Ackerman
78	0.0	Claiborne County SD	Port Gibson
78	0.0	Columbia SD	Columbia
78	0.0	Copiah County SD	Hazlehurst
78	0.0	Covington County Schools	Collins
78	0.0	East Tallahatchie Consol SD	Charleston
78	0.0	Greene County SD	Leakesville
78	0.0	Hinds County SD	Raymond
78	0.0	Holmes County SD	Lexington
78	0.0	Humphreys County SD	Belzoni
78	0.0	Jefferson County SD	Fayette
78	0.0	Jefferson Davis County SD	Prentiss
78	0.0	Lauderdale County SD	Meridian
78	0.0	Lawrence County SD	Monticello
78	0.0	Lincoln County SD	Brookhaven
78	0.0	Long Beach SD	Long Beach
78	0.0	Louisville Municipal SD	Louisville
78	0.0	Marion County SD	Columbia
78	0.0	Monroe County SD	Amory
78	0.0	Neshoba County SD	Philadelphia
78	0.0	North Pike SD	Summit
78	0.0	Noxubee County SD	Macon
78	0.0	Pass Christian Public SD	Pass Christian
78	0.0	Pearl River County SD	Carriere
78	0.0	Picayune SD	Picayune
78	0.0	Poplarville Separate SD	Poplarville
78	0.0	Prentiss County SD	Booneville
78	0.0	Quitman County SD	Marks
78	0.0	Quitman SD	Quitman
78	0.0	Senatobia Municipal SD	Senatobia
78	0.0	South Panola SD	Batesville
78	0.0	Stone County SD	Wiggins
78	0.0	Union County SD	New Albany
78	0.0	West Jasper Consolidated Schools	Bay Springs
78	0.0	Wilkinson County SD	Woodville

Migrant Students

Rank	Percent	District Name	City
1	4.3	Biloxi Public SD	Biloxi
1	4.3	Scott County SD	Forest
3	4.0	Laurel SD	Laurel
4	3.4	Calhoun County SD	Pittsboro
5	3.1	Jones County SD	Ellisville
6	2.7	Pass Christian Public SD	Pass Christian
7	2.5	Jackson County SD	Vancleave
8	1.9	Leflore County SD	Greenwood
9	1.6	Moss Point Separate SD	Moss Point
9	1.6	Sunflower County SD	Indianola
9	1.6	Tate County SD	Senatobia
12	1.4	Monroe County SD	Amory
12	1.4	West Jasper Consolidated Schools	Bay Springs
14	1.3	Pascagoula SD	Pascagoula

14	1.3	Western Line SD	Avon
16	1.2	Harrison County SD	Gulfport
17	1.1	Gulfport SD	Gulfport
18	1.0	Covington County Schools	Collins
19	0.9	Coahoma County SD	Clarksdale
19	0.9	Ocean Springs SD	Ocean Springs
19	0.9	Smith County SD	Raleigh
22	0.8	Leake County SD	Carthage
22	0.8	Long Beach SD	Long Beach
22	0.8	Tunica County SD	Tunica
25	0.6	Simpson County SD	Mendenhall
26	0.5	Hattiesburg Public SD	Hattiesburg
26	0.5	Humphreys County SD	Belzoni
26	0.5	New Albany Public Schools	New Albany
29	0.4	Bay St Louis Waveland SD	Bay St Louis
29	0.4	Houston SD	Houston
29	0.4	Union County SD	New Albany
32	0.3	Desoto County SD	Hernando
32	0.3	Forest Municipal SD	Forest
32	0.3	Hancock County SD	Kiln
32	0.3	Neshoba County SD	Philadelphia
32	0.3	Rankin County SD	Brandon
37	0.2	Aberdeen SD	Aberdeen
37	0.2	Choctaw County SD	Ackerman
37	0.2	George County SD	Lucedale
37	0.2	Marion County SD	Columbia
37	0.2	Newton County SD	Decatur
37	0.2	Senatobia Municipal SD	Senatobia
37	0.2	Stone County SD	Wiggins
37	0.2	Webster County SD	Eupora
37	0.2	Yazoo County SD	Yazoo City
46	0.1	Alcorn SD	Corinth
46	0.1	Corinth SD	Corinth
46	0.1	Forrest County SD	Hattiesburg
46	0.1	Greenville Public Schools	Greenville
46	0.1	Greenwood Public SD	Greenwood
46	0.1	Jefferson Davis County SD	Prentiss
46	0.1	Lauderdale County SD	Meridian
46	0.1	Meridian Public SD	Meridian
46	0.1	Picayune SD	Picayune
46	0.1	Pontotoc City Schools	Pontotoc
46	0.1	Pontotoc County SD	Pontotoc
46	0.1	Wayne County SD	Waynesboro
46	0.1	Yazoo City Municipal SD	Yazoo City
59	0.0	Clarksdale Municipal SD	Clarksdale
59	0.0	Copiah County SD	Hazlehurst
59	0.0	Holmes County SD	Lexington
59	0.0	Jackson Public SD	Jackson
59	0.0	Marshall County SD	Holly Springs
64	0.0	Amory SD	Amory
64	0.0	Brookhaven SD	Brookhaven
64	0.0	Canton Public SD	Canton
64	0.0	Claiborne County SD	Port Gibson
64	0.0	Cleveland SD	Cleveland
64	0.0	Clinton Public SD	Clinton
64	0.0	Columbia SD	Columbia
64	0.0	Columbus Municipal SD	Columbus
64	0.0	East Tallahatchie Consol SD	Charleston
64	0.0	Franklin County SD	Meadville
64	0.0	Greene County SD	Leakesville
64	0.0	Grenada SD	Grenada
64	0.0	Hazlehurst City SD	Hazlehurst
64	0.0	Hinds County SD	Raymond
64	0.0	Holly Springs SD	Holly Springs
64	0.0	Indianola SD	Indianola
64	0.0	Itawamba County SD	Fulton
64	0.0	Jefferson County SD	Fayette
64	0.0	Kosciusko SD	Kosciusko
64	0.0	Lafayette County SD	Oxford
64	0.0	Lamar County SD	Purvis
64	0.0	Lawrence County SD	Monticello
64	0.0	Lee County SD	Tupelo
64	0.0	Lincoln County SD	Brookhaven
64	0.0	Louisville Municipal SD	Louisville
64	0.0	Lowndes County SD	Columbus
64	0.0	Madison County SD	Flora
64	0.0	Mccomb SD	Mccomb
64	0.0	Natchez-Adams SD	Natchez
64	0.0	North Panola Schools	Sardis
64	0.0	North Pike SD	Summit
64	0.0	Noxubee County SD	Macon
64	0.0	Oxford SD	Oxford
64	0.0	Pearl Public SD	Pearl
64	0.0	Pearl River County SD	Carriere
64	0.0	Petal SD	Petal
64	0.0	Poplarville Separate SD	Poplarville
64	0.0	Prentiss County SD	Booneville
64	0.0	Quitman County SD	Marks
64	0.0	Quitman SD	Quitman
64	0.0	South Panola SD	Batesville
64	0.0	South Pike SD	Magnolia
64	0.0	South Tippah SD	Ripley
64	0.0	Starkville SD	Starkville
64	0.0	Tishomingo County Sp Mun SD	Iuka
64	0.0	Tupelo Public SD	Tupelo
64	0.0	Vicksburg Warren SD	Vicksburg
64	0.0	Walthall County SD	Tylertown
64	0.0	West Point SD	West Point
64	0.0	Wilkinson County SD	Woodville

Students Eligible for Free Lunch

Rank	Percent	District Name	City
1	99.5	Greenwood Public SD	Greenwood
1	99.5	Holly Springs SD	Holly Springs
1	99.5	Jefferson Davis County SD	Prentiss
4	99.4	Claiborne County SD	Port Gibson
4	99.4	Jefferson County SD	Fayette
6	99.3	Leflore County SD	Greenwood
6	99.3	Noxubee County SD	Macon
6	99.3	South Pike SD	Magnolia
9	99.2	Wilkinson County SD	Woodville
10	99.1	Quitman County SD	Marks
11	98.6	Coahoma County SD	Clarksdale
12	95.4	Holmes County SD	Lexington
13	94.5	Humphreys County SD	Belzoni
14	93.9	Canton Public SD	Canton
15	90.3	Mccomb SD	Mccomb
16	90.0	Yazoo City Municipal SD	Yazoo City
17	89.6	Hazlehurst City SD	Hazlehurst
18	87.6	Tunica County SD	Tunica
19	87.5	Western Line SD	Avon
20	85.1	Aberdeen SD	Aberdeen
20	85.1	Indianola SD	Indianola
22	84.4	North Panola Schools	Sardis
23	84.2	Greenville Public Schools	Greenville
24	83.8	Sunflower County SD	Indianola
25	83.3	Natchez-Adams SD	Natchez
26	80.0	Laurel SD	Laurel
27	77.4	East Tallahatchie Consol SD	Charleston
28	77.3	Clarksdale Municipal SD	Clarksdale
29	74.3	Hattiesburg Public SD	Hattiesburg
30	73.4	Marion County SD	Columbia
30	73.4	Yazoo County SD	Yazoo City
32	72.7	West Point SD	West Point
33	72.0	Marshall County SD	Holly Springs
34	71.8	Copiah County SD	Hazlehurst
35	71.4	Walthall County SD	Tylertown
36	70.9	Forest Municipal SD	Forest
37	70.0	Covington County Schools	Collins
37	70.0	Moss Point Separate SD	Moss Point
39	69.8	Meridian Public SD	Meridian
40	67.8	Columbus Municipal SD	Columbus
40	67.8	Jackson Public SD	Jackson
42	67.4	West Jasper Consolidated Schools	Bay Springs
43	67.0	Louisville Municipal SD	Louisville
44	65.8	Cleveland SD	Cleveland
45	65.4	Wayne County SD	Waynesboro
46	64.1	Simpson County SD	Mendenhall
47	63.3	Leake County SD	Carthage
48	62.1	Scott County SD	Forest
49	61.4	Greene County SD	Leakesville
50	61.0	Quitman SD	Quitman
51	60.7	Columbia SD	Columbia
52	60.6	South Panola SD	Batesville
53	60.1	Franklin County SD	Meadville
54	59.5	Tate County SD	Senatobia
55	59.2	Houston SD	Houston
56	59.1	Calhoun County SD	Pittsboro
57	58.8	Choctaw County SD	Ackerman
58	57.1	Starkville SD	Starkville
58	57.1	Vicksburg Warren SD	Vicksburg
60	56.9	Gulfport SD	Gulfport
61	56.3	Picayune SD	Picayune
62	55.4	Forrest County SD	Hattiesburg
63	55.3	Brookhaven SD	Brookhaven
64	55.1	Pascagoula SD	Pascagoula
65	54.5	Bay St Louis Waveland SD	Bay St Louis
66	54.0	Pass Christian Public SD	Pass Christian
67	53.6	Grenada SD	Grenada
68	49.9	Kosciusko SD	Kosciusko
69	49.4	Hancock County SD	Kiln
70	49.1	Corinth SD	Corinth
71	48.8	Lawrence County SD	Monticello
71	48.8	Prentiss County SD	Booneville
73	48.4	Smith County SD	Raleigh
74	47.3	Webster County SD	Eupora
75	46.7	South Tippah SD	Ripley
76	46.0	Stone County SD	Wiggins
77	45.9	Jones County SD	Ellisville
78	44.6	Itawamba County SD	Fulton
79	44.3	Biloxi Public SD	Biloxi
80	44.2	North Pike SD	Summit
81	44.1	Lafayette County SD	Oxford
81	44.1	Lee County SD	Tupelo
83	43.8	Amory SD	Amory
83	43.8	Harrison County SD	Gulfport
85	43.1	Hinds County SD	Raymond
86	42.4	Newton County SD	Decatur
87	42.2	George County SD	Lucedale
87	42.2	Tishomingo County Sp Mun SD	Iuka
89	41.4	Neshoba County SD	Philadelphia
90	41.3	Lincoln County SD	Brookhaven
91	41.1	Senatobia Municipal SD	Senatobia
92	41.0	Pearl River County SD	Carriere
93	40.7	Tupelo Public SD	Tupelo
94	40.4	New Albany Public Schools	New Albany
95	40.2	Poplarville Separate SD	Poplarville
96	39.5	Lowndes County SD	Columbus
97	38.2	Oxford SD	Oxford
97	38.2	Union County SD	New Albany
99	38.1	Pontotoc City Schools	Pontotoc
100	38.0	Pearl Public SD	Pearl
101	37.5	Pontotoc County SD	Pontotoc
102	36.5	Monroe County SD	Amory
103	35.4	Petal SD	Petal
104	34.0	Alcorn SD	Corinth
104	34.0	Lauderdale County SD	Meridian
106	30.3	Jackson County SD	Vancleave
107	30.2	Long Beach SD	Long Beach
108	29.5	Lamar County SD	Purvis
109	27.3	Rankin County SD	Brandon
110	26.4	Clinton Public SD	Clinton
111	21.9	Madison County SD	Flora
112	21.1	Desoto County SD	Hernando
113	15.0	Ocean Springs SD	Ocean Springs

Students Eligible for Reduced-Price Lunch

Rank	Percent	District Name	City
1	14.5	Prentiss County SD	Booneville
2	14.2	Lincoln County SD	Brookhaven
3	14.1	Monroe County SD	Amory
4	13.7	New Albany Public Schools	New Albany
5	13.5	Union County SD	New Albany
6	13.4	Pearl River County SD	Carriere
7	13.3	Hancock County SD	Kiln
8	12.6	Poplarville Separate SD	Poplarville
9	12.5	Alcorn SD	Corinth
10	12.4	Neshoba County SD	Philadelphia
11	12.3	Calhoun County SD	Pittsboro
11	12.3	Petal SD	Petal
13	12.2	Pontotoc County SD	Pontotoc
13	12.2	Tishomingo County Sp Mun SD	Iuka
15	11.9	Smith County SD	Raleigh
15	11.9	Tate County SD	Senatobia
15	11.9	Webster County SD	Eupora
18	11.8	North Pike SD	Summit
18	11.8	Pass Christian Public SD	Pass Christian
20	11.7	Bay St Louis Waveland SD	Bay St Louis
21	11.6	Greene County SD	Leakesville
21	11.6	Itawamba County SD	Fulton
23	11.5	Biloxi Public SD	Biloxi
23	11.5	Jones County SD	Ellisville
23	11.5	Scott County SD	Forest
26	11.4	Choctaw County SD	Ackerman
27	11.1	Harrison County SD	Gulfport
27	11.1	South Tippah SD	Ripley
29	11.0	Franklin County SD	Meadville
30	10.8	Kosciusko SD	Kosciusko
30	10.8	Wayne County SD	Waynesboro
32	10.7	Lawrence County SD	Monticello
32	10.7	Long Beach SD	Long Beach
34	10.6	Louisville Municipal SD	Louisville
35	10.4	Jackson County SD	Vancleave
35	10.4	Marion County SD	Columbia
37	10.2	Simpson County SD	Mendenhall
38	10.1	Leake County SD	Carthage
38	10.1	South Panola SD	Batesville
38	10.1	Walthall County SD	Tylertown
41	9.9	Forrest County SD	Hattiesburg
42	9.8	Covington County Schools	Collins
43	9.7	Amory SD	Amory
43	9.7	George County SD	Lucedale
43	9.7	Houston SD	Houston
43	9.7	Stone County SD	Wiggins
43	9.7	West Jasper Consolidated Schools	Bay Springs
48	9.6	Pearl Public SD	Pearl
49	9.5	Lee County SD	Tupelo
50	9.3	Yazoo County SD	Yazoo City
51	9.2	Lafayette County SD	Oxford
51	9.2	Quitman SD	Quitman
53	9.0	Lamar County SD	Purvis
53	9.0	Marshall County SD	Holly Springs
53	9.0	Newton County SD	Decatur
56	8.8	Columbia SD	Columbia
57	8.7	West Point SD	West Point

58	8.5	Pascagoula SD	Pascagoula
59	8.4	Forest Municipal SD	Forest
60	8.3	Gulfport SD	Gulfport
61	8.2	East Tallahatchie Consol SD	Charleston
61	8.2	Hinds County SD	Raymond
61	8.2	Lowndes County SD	Columbus
64	8.1	Vicksburg Warren SD	Vicksburg
65	8.0	Moss Point Separate SD	Moss Point
65	8.0	Pontotoc City Schools	Pontotoc
65	8.0	Starkville SD	Starkville
65	8.0	Western Line SD	Avon
69	7.9	Rankin County SD	Brandon
70	7.8	Brookhaven SD	Brookhaven
71	7.7	Clinton Public SD	Clinton
71	7.7	Lauderdale County SD	Meridian
73	7.6	Oxford SD	Oxford
74	7.5	Columbus Municipal SD	Columbus
75	7.2	Desoto County SD	Hernando
76	7.0	Senatobia Municipal SD	Senatobia
77	6.8	Indianola SD	Indianola
77	6.8	Jackson Public SD	Jackson
79	6.6	Grenada SD	Grenada
80	6.4	Corinth SD	Corinth
80	6.4	Natchez-Adams SD	Natchez
82	6.3	Ocean Springs SD	Ocean Springs
83	6.2	Sunflower County SD	Indianola
84	6.1	Picayune SD	Picayune
85	5.8	North Panola Schools	Sardis
86	5.6	Hazlehurst City SD	Hazlehurst
87	5.5	Aberdeen SD	Aberdeen
88	5.3	Clarksdale Municipal SD	Clarksdale
88	5.3	Madison County SD	Flora
90	5.2	Copiah County SD	Hazlehurst
90	5.2	Meridian Public SD	Meridian
90	5.2	Tupelo Public SD	Tupelo
93	5.0	Laurel SD	Laurel
93	5.0	Tunica County SD	Tunica
95	4.6	Hattiesburg Public SD	Hattiesburg
96	4.4	Cleveland SD	Cleveland
96	4.4	Greenville Public Schools	Greenville
98	3.8	Yazoo City Municipal SD	Yazoo City
99	2.6	Canton Public SD	Canton
99	2.6	Holmes County SD	Lexington
101	2.2	Mccomb SD	Mccomb
102	2.0	Humphreys County SD	Belzoni
103	0.0	Claiborne County SD	Port Gibson
103	0.0	Coahoma County SD	Clarksdale
103	0.0	Greenwood Public SD	Greenwood
103	0.0	Holly Springs SD	Holly Springs
103	0.0	Jefferson County SD	Fayette
103	0.0	Jefferson Davis County SD	Prentiss
103	0.0	Leflore County SD	Greenwood
103	0.0	Noxubee County SD	Macon
103	0.0	Quitman County SD	Marks
103	0.0	South Pike SD	Magnolia
103	0.0	Wilkinson County SD	Woodville

Student/Teacher Ratio

Rank	Ratio	District Name	City
1	18.7	Desoto County SD	Hernando
2	18.3	Holmes County SD	Lexington
3	18.0	Marshall County SD	Holly Springs
4	17.5	Leflore County SD	Greenwood
5	17.3	Yazoo City Municipal SD	Yazoo City
6	17.2	Ocean Springs SD	Ocean Springs
7	17.0	Leake County SD	Carthage
8	16.8	Canton Public SD	Canton
8	16.8	Humphreys County SD	Belzoni
8	16.8	North Pike SD	Summit
8	16.8	Union County SD	New Albany
12	16.7	West Point SD	West Point
13	16.6	Jackson Public SD	Jackson
13	16.6	Senatobia Municipal SD	Senatobia
15	16.5	Calhoun County SD	Pittsboro
15	16.5	Columbia SD	Columbia
17	16.4	Indianola SD	Indianola
17	16.4	Lincoln County SD	Brookhaven
17	16.4	South Pike SD	Magnolia
20	16.3	Grenada SD	Grenada
20	16.3	Jackson County SD	Vancleave
22	16.2	Pearl Public SD	Pearl
23	16.1	Clinton Public SD	Clinton
24	16.0	Harrison County SD	Gulfport
24	16.0	Pearl River County SD	Carriere
26	15.9	George County SD	Lucedale
26	15.9	Hancock County SD	Kiln
26	15.9	Sunflower County SD	Indianola
29	15.8	Copiah County SD	Hazlehurst
29	15.8	Lauderdale County SD	Meridian
29	15.8	Lee County SD	Tupelo
32	15.7	Scott County SD	Forest
33	15.6	Lowndes County SD	Columbus
33	15.6	Meridian Public SD	Meridian
33	15.6	Vicksburg Warren SD	Vicksburg
33	15.6	Wayne County SD	Waynesboro
37	15.5	Madison County SD	Flora
37	15.5	South Panola SD	Batesville
37	15.5	South Tippah SD	Ripley
37	15.5	Tate County SD	Senatobia
37	15.5	Tishomingo County Sp Mun SD	Iuka
42	15.4	Forest Municipal SD	Forest
42	15.4	Kosciusko SD	Kosciusko
42	15.4	Simpson County SD	Mendenhall
45	15.3	Covington County Schools	Collins
45	15.3	Monroe County SD	Amory
45	15.3	Rankin County SD	Brandon
45	15.3	Western Line SD	Avon
49	15.2	Hazlehurst City SD	Hazlehurst
49	15.2	Pontotoc County SD	Pontotoc
51	15.1	Pascagoula SD	Pascagoula
51	15.1	Tunica County SD	Tunica
53	15.0	Biloxi Public SD	Biloxi
53	15.0	Pass Christian Public SD	Pass Christian
55	14.9	Clarksdale Municipal SD	Clarksdale
55	14.9	Hinds County SD	Raymond
55	14.9	Long Beach SD	Long Beach
55	14.9	Noxubee County SD	Macon
55	14.9	Smith County SD	Raleigh
55	14.9	Walthall County SD	Tylertown
61	14.8	Pontotoc City Schools	Pontotoc
61	14.8	West Jasper Consolidated Schools	Bay Springs
63	14.7	Greenville Public Schools	Greenville
63	14.7	Neshoba County SD	Philadelphia
63	14.7	Poplarville Separate SD	Poplarville
63	14.7	Quitman SD	Quitman
63	14.7	Webster County SD	Eupora
63	14.7	Wilkinson County SD	Woodville
69	14.6	Itawamba County SD	Fulton
69	14.6	Lamar County SD	Purvis
69	14.6	Natchez-Adams SD	Natchez
69	14.6	Newton County SD	Decatur
69	14.6	Petal SD	Petal
74	14.5	Jefferson Davis County SD	Prentiss
74	14.5	Quitman County SD	Marks
76	14.4	East Tallahatchie Consol SD	Charleston
76	14.4	Jefferson County SD	Fayette
76	14.4	Stone County SD	Wiggins
79	14.3	Amory SD	Amory
79	14.3	Jones County SD	Ellisville
81	14.2	Alcorn SD	Corinth
81	14.2	Cleveland SD	Cleveland
81	14.2	Houston SD	Houston
81	14.2	Yazoo County SD	Yazoo City
85	14.1	Bay St Louis Waveland SD	Bay St Louis
85	14.1	Moss Point Separate SD	Moss Point
87	14.0	Greene County SD	Leakesville
88	13.8	Greenwood Public SD	Greenwood
88	13.8	Holly Springs SD	Holly Springs
88	13.8	Lawrence County SD	Monticello
88	13.8	New Albany Public Schools	New Albany
88	13.8	Oxford SD	Oxford
93	13.7	Gulfport SD	Gulfport
94	13.4	Coahoma County SD	Clarksdale
94	13.4	Lafayette County SD	Oxford
96	13.3	Louisville Municipal SD	Louisville
97	13.2	Brookhaven SD	Brookhaven
97	13.2	Choctaw County SD	Ackerman
99	13.1	North Panola Schools	Sardis
100	13.0	Franklin County SD	Meadville
101	12.9	Claiborne County SD	Port Gibson
101	12.9	Mccomb SD	Mccomb
101	12.9	Picayune SD	Picayune
101	12.9	Tupelo Public SD	Tupelo
105	12.8	Columbus Municipal SD	Columbus
106	12.7	Forrest County SD	Hattiesburg
106	12.7	Marion County SD	Columbia
108	12.3	Starkville SD	Starkville
109	12.2	Corinth SD	Corinth
110	12.1	Hattiesburg Public SD	Hattiesburg
111	11.9	Laurel SD	Laurel
112	10.8	Prentiss County SD	Booneville
113	10.7	Aberdeen SD	Aberdeen

Student/Librarian Ratio

Rank	Ratio	District Name	City
1	1,254.8	Laurel SD	Laurel
2	931.6	Hinds County SD	Raymond
3	931.0	Pearl River County SD	Carriere
4	874.5	Newton County SD	Decatur
5	865.8	Marshall County SD	Holly Springs
6	845.5	Lauderdale County SD	Meridian
7	824.4	Stone County SD	Wiggins
8	816.3	Desoto County SD	Hernando
9	804.6	Petal SD	Petal
10	798.4	Hancock County SD	Kiln
11	785.8	Grenada SD	Grenada
12	743.8	Neshoba County SD	Philadelphia
13	740.0	Noxubee County SD	Macon
14	738.3	Greenville Public Schools	Greenville
15	692.4	Canton Public SD	Canton
16	686.0	South Panola SD	Batesville
17	682.7	Leake County SD	Carthage
18	679.6	Harrison County SD	Gulfport
19	661.5	Wayne County SD	Waynesboro
20	656.5	Ocean Springs SD	Ocean Springs
21	642.1	Meridian Public SD	Meridian
22	630.8	Marion County SD	Columbia
23	626.9	Lamar County SD	Purvis
24	624.3	Yazoo County SD	Yazoo City
25	623.6	Oxford SD	Oxford
26	623.4	Corinth SD	Corinth
27	612.4	Clinton Public SD	Clinton
28	607.8	Pearl Public SD	Pearl
29	605.3	Holly Springs SD	Holly Springs
29	605.3	Tupelo Public SD	Tupelo
31	600.0	Lawrence County SD	Monticello
32	597.7	West Jasper Consolidated Schools	Bay Springs
33	596.0	North Pike SD	Summit
34	588.8	Madison County SD	Flora
35	581.8	Brookhaven SD	Brookhaven
36	581.6	Natchez-Adams SD	Natchez
37	580.9	George County SD	Lucedale
38	578.6	Yazoo City Municipal SD	Yazoo City
39	573.8	Mccomb SD	Mccomb
40	570.7	Hazlehurst City SD	Hazlehurst
41	564.7	Tishomingo County Sp Mun SD	Iuka
42	564.2	Smith County SD	Raleigh
43	563.0	Indianola SD	Indianola
44	553.8	Long Beach SD	Long Beach
45	548.3	Lafayette County SD	Oxford
46	544.9	Picayune SD	Picayune
47	543.0	Lee County SD	Tupelo
48	541.4	Greene County SD	Leakesville
49	533.8	Rankin County SD	Brandon
50	533.5	Houston SD	Houston
51	533.3	Claiborne County SD	Port Gibson
52	529.0	Hattiesburg Public SD	Hattiesburg
53	520.8	Pontotoc County SD	Pontotoc
54	520.3	Gulfport SD	Gulfport
55	518.8	Jackson County SD	Vancleave
56	511.5	Copiah County SD	Hazlehurst
57	508.5	New Albany Public Schools	New Albany
58	503.9	Alcorn SD	Corinth
59	503.1	Lowndes County SD	Columbus
60	502.0	West Point SD	West Point
61	500.6	Jackson Public SD	Jackson
62	496.7	Vicksburg Warren SD	Vicksburg
63	494.4	Jones County SD	Ellisville
64	493.3	Quitman SD	Quitman
65	488.9	Greenwood Public SD	Greenwood
66	485.8	Starkville SD	Starkville
67	484.0	Pontotoc City Schools	Pontotoc
68	479.5	Humphreys County SD	Belzoni
69	472.1	Simpson County SD	Mendenhall
70	460.9	Leflore County SD	Greenwood
71	458.0	Amory SD	Amory
72	451.6	Clarksdale Municipal SD	Clarksdale
73	449.8	Itawamba County SD	Fulton
74	449.7	East Tallahatchie Consol SD	Charleston
75	444.9	Biloxi Public SD	Biloxi
76	438.6	Forest Municipal SD	Forest
77	434.5	Senatobia Municipal SD	Senatobia
78	434.2	Pass Christian Public SD	Pass Christian
79	433.5	Quitman County SD	Marks
80	418.8	Pascagoula SD	Pascagoula
81	416.8	South Tippah SD	Ripley
82	413.0	Monroe County SD	Amory
83	409.0	Tate County SD	Senatobia
84	408.5	Jefferson County SD	Fayette
85	407.8	Poplarville Separate SD	Poplarville
86	402.1	Franklin County SD	Meadville
87	398.8	Jefferson Davis County SD	Prentiss
88	395.2	Holmes County SD	Lexington
89	394.8	Covington County Schools	Collins
90	391.7	Calhoun County SD	Pittsboro
90	391.7	Columbus Municipal SD	Columbus
92	387.8	Forrest County SD	Hattiesburg
93	383.6	Walthall County SD	Tylertown
94	376.0	Webster County SD	Eupora
95	375.5	Bay St Louis Waveland SD	Bay St Louis
95	375.5	Sunflower County SD	Indianola
97	374.6	Columbia SD	Columbia
98	373.8	Tunica County SD	Tunica
99	363.9	Moss Point Separate SD	Moss Point
100	358.4	Lincoln County SD	Brookhaven
101	357.3	North Panola Schools	Sardis
102	356.2	Scott County SD	Forest

103	355.6	Union County SD	New Albany
104	347.5	Kosciusko SD	Kosciusko
105	346.8	South Pike SD	Magnolia
106	340.8	Louisville Municipal SD	Louisville
107	327.3	Cleveland SD	Cleveland
108	316.5	Prentiss County SD	Booneville
109	313.5	Choctaw County SD	Ackerman
110	312.6	Wilkinson County SD	Woodville
111	310.2	Coahoma County SD	Clarksdale
112	297.1	Western Line SD	Avon
113	277.8	Aberdeen SD	Aberdeen

Student/Counselor Ratio

Rank	Ratio	District Name	City
1	1,323.0	Wayne County SD	Waynesboro
2	1,263.2	Lawrence County SD	Monticello
3	1,241.0	Forrest County SD	Hattiesburg
4	1,197.7	Biloxi Public SD	Biloxi
5	1,194.1	Marshall County SD	Holly Springs
6	1,138.9	Western Line SD	Avon
7	1,074.2	Pearl River County SD	Carriere
8	1,058.3	Copiah County SD	Hazlehurst
9	1,025.9	Neshoba County SD	Philadelphia
10	1,019.5	Poplarville Separate SD	Poplarville
11	1,017.0	New Albany Public Schools	New Albany
12	951.1	Hazlehurst City SD	Hazlehurst
13	932.1	Harrison County SD	Gulfport
14	841.0	Marion County SD	Columbia
15	832.0	East Tallahatchie Consol SD	Charleston
16	822.2	Noxubee County SD	Macon
17	816.6	Quitman SD	Quitman
18	811.5	Picayune SD	Picayune
19	804.6	Petal SD	Petal
20	777.4	North Pike SD	Summit
21	758.3	Pontotoc City Schools	Pontotoc
22	753.7	Stone County SD	Wiggins
23	723.3	Yazoo City Municipal SD	Yazoo City
24	716.8	Lincoln County SD	Brookhaven
25	688.5	Walthall County SD	Tylertown
26	684.5	Union County SD	New Albany
27	666.8	Aberdeen SD	Aberdeen
28	666.6	George County SD	Lucedale
29	659.5	Lauderdale County SD	Meridian
30	651.3	Leflore County SD	Greenwood
31	626.7	Webster County SD	Eupora
32	620.7	Senatobia Municipal SD	Senatobia
33	615.3	Greenville Public Schools	Greenville
34	602.7	Corinth SD	Corinth
35	598.9	Indianola SD	Indianola
36	597.7	West Jasper Consolidated Schools	Bay Springs
37	595.7	Kosciusko SD	Kosciusko
38	588.2	Itawamba County SD	Fulton
39	582.1	Grenada SD	Grenada
40	580.3	Sunflower County SD	Indianola
41	578.2	Monroe County SD	Amory
42	572.7	Lowndes County SD	Columbus
43	572.6	Tate County SD	Senatobia
44	572.2	Pascagoula SD	Pascagoula
45	565.0	Desoto County SD	Hernando
46	561.1	Clarksdale Municipal SD	Clarksdale
47	558.3	Pass Christian Public SD	Pass Christian
48	555.8	Hancock County SD	Kiln
49	552.7	Lee County SD	Tupelo
50	548.5	Lamar County SD	Purvis
51	541.4	Greene County SD	Leakesville
52	541.0	Forest Municipal SD	Forest
53	533.3	Claiborne County SD	Port Gibson
54	524.9	Alcorn SD	Corinth
55	521.0	South Tippah SD	Ripley
55	521.0	Wilkinson County SD	Woodville
57	520.8	Pontotoc County SD	Pontotoc
58	511.9	Simpson County SD	Mendenhall
59	509.2	Calhoun County SD	Pittsboro
60	501.0	Holmes County SD	Lexington
61	500.3	North Panola Schools	Sardis
62	494.2	Louisville Municipal SD	Louisville
63	493.5	Houston SD	Houston
64	493.1	Coahoma County SD	Clarksdale
65	488.2	Jones County SD	Ellisville
66	486.3	Ocean Springs SD	Ocean Springs
67	481.4	Covington County Schools	Collins
68	479.5	Humphreys County SD	Belzoni
69	478.0	Jackson County SD	Vancleave
70	476.3	West Point SD	West Point
71	458.0	Amory SD	Amory
72	455.9	Pearl Public SD	Pearl
73	454.6	Jefferson Davis County SD	Prentiss
74	447.0	Vicksburg Warren SD	Vicksburg
75	446.4	Canton Public SD	Canton
76	445.4	Oxford SD	Oxford
77	437.3	Newton County SD	Decatur
78	435.6	Yazoo County SD	Yazoo City
79	433.5	South Pike SD	Magnolia
80	432.8	Hattiesburg Public SD	Hattiesburg
81	431.9	South Panola SD	Batesville
82	431.4	Scott County SD	Forest
83	427.8	Greenwood Public SD	Greenwood
84	426.3	Madison County SD	Flora
85	425.7	Columbia SD	Columbia
86	425.1	Bay St Louis Waveland SD	Bay St Louis
87	420.3	Rankin County SD	Brandon
88	419.2	Jefferson County SD	Fayette
89	418.1	Leake County SD	Carthage
90	402.1	Franklin County SD	Meadville
91	400.3	Moss Point Separate SD	Moss Point
92	397.8	Smith County SD	Raleigh
93	394.2	Cleveland SD	Cleveland
94	386.3	Prentiss County SD	Booneville
95	382.3	Tupelo Public SD	Tupelo
96	379.8	Clinton Public SD	Clinton
97	372.6	Hinds County SD	Raymond
98	371.6	Gulfport SD	Gulfport
99	370.9	Brookhaven SD	Brookhaven
100	370.6	Holly Springs SD	Holly Springs
101	369.2	Long Beach SD	Long Beach
102	368.5	Columbus Municipal SD	Columbus
103	367.8	Mccomb SD	Mccomb
104	365.5	Lafayette County SD	Oxford
105	361.7	Tishomingo County Sp Mun SD	Iuka
106	359.8	Starkville SD	Starkville
107	358.7	Jackson Public SD	Jackson
108	357.9	Natchez-Adams SD	Natchez
109	348.6	Laurel SD	Laurel
110	320.8	Quitman County SD	Marks
111	320.4	Tunica County SD	Tunica
112	308.1	Choctaw County SD	Ackerman
113	293.1	Meridian Public SD	Meridian

Current Spending per Student in FY2003

Rank	Dollars	District Name	City
1	9,270	Tunica County SD	Tunica
2	7,199	Hattiesburg Public SD	Hattiesburg
3	7,128	Claiborne County SD	Port Gibson
4	7,059	Coahoma County SD	Clarksdale
5	7,027	Starkville SD	Starkville
6	7,024	Biloxi Public SD	Biloxi
7	7,013	Prentiss County SD	Booneville
8	7,004	Mccomb SD	Mccomb
9	6,960	Franklin County SD	Meadville
10	6,952	Gulfport SD	Gulfport
11	6,919	Moss Point Separate SD	Moss Point
12	6,817	Lafayette County SD	Oxford
13	6,796	Pass Christian Public SD	Pass Christian
14	6,765	Pascagoula SD	Pascagoula
15	6,697	Meridian Public SD	Meridian
16	6,684	Aberdeen SD	Aberdeen
17	6,567	Bay St Louis Waveland SD	Bay St Louis
18	6,565	Columbus Municipal SD	Columbus
19	6,555	Laurel SD	Laurel
20	6,502	Tupelo Public SD	Tupelo
21	6,499	Quitman County SD	Marks
22	6,461	New Albany Public Schools	New Albany
23	6,427	Wilkinson County SD	Woodville
24	6,406	North Panola Schools	Sardis
25	6,396	Corinth SD	Corinth
26	6,382	Sunflower County SD	Indianola
26	6,382	Yazoo County SD	Yazoo City
28	6,381	Greene County SD	Leakesville
29	6,357	Jefferson Davis County SD	Prentiss
30	6,307	Jefferson County SD	Fayette
31	6,304	Natchez-Adams SD	Natchez
32	6,223	Picayune SD	Picayune
33	6,181	Western Line SD	Avon
34	6,138	Brookhaven SD	Brookhaven
35	6,114	Forrest County SD	Hattiesburg
36	6,106	Jackson Public SD	Jackson
37	6,087	Columbia SD	Columbia
38	6,069	Greenwood Public SD	Greenwood
39	6,058	Louisville Municipal SD	Louisville
40	6,025	Cleveland SD	Cleveland
41	5,989	Lawrence County SD	Monticello
42	5,964	Greenville Public Schools	Greenville
43	5,962	Vicksburg Warren SD	Vicksburg
44	5,953	Marion County SD	Columbia
45	5,952	Walthall County SD	Tylertown
46	5,911	Leflore County SD	Greenwood
47	5,869	Noxubee County SD	Macon
48	5,831	Oxford SD	Oxford
49	5,778	Choctaw County SD	Ackerman
50	5,766	Hazlehurst City SD	Hazlehurst
51	5,753	Poplarville Separate SD	Poplarville
52	5,751	East Tallahatchie Consol SD	Charleston
53	5,745	Newton County SD	Decatur
54	5,715	Clarksdale Municipal SD	Clarksdale
55	5,713	South Pike SD	Magnolia
56	5,688	Stone County SD	Wiggins
57	5,683	Lamar County SD	Purvis
58	5,680	South Panola SD	Batesville
59	5,653	Forest Municipal SD	Forest
60	5,647	Alcorn SD	Corinth
61	5,643	Covington County Schools	Collins
62	5,630	Calhoun County SD	Pittsboro
62	5,630	West Jasper Consolidated Schools	Bay Springs
64	5,625	Indianola SD	Indianola
65	5,614	Long Beach SD	Long Beach
66	5,595	Jones County SD	Ellisville
67	5,592	Wayne County SD	Waynesboro
68	5,578	Holmes County SD	Lexington
69	5,577	Madison County SD	Flora
69	5,577	Pearl Public SD	Pearl
71	5,575	Petal SD	Petal
72	5,571	Humphreys County SD	Belzoni
73	5,568	Webster County SD	Eupora
74	5,529	Holly Springs SD	Holly Springs
75	5,455	Simpson County SD	Mendenhall
76	5,441	Amory SD	Amory
77	5,433	Hancock County SD	Kiln
78	5,432	Quitman SD	Quitman
79	5,413	Hinds County SD	Raymond
80	5,398	Tishomingo County Sp Mun SD	Iuka
81	5,393	Tate County SD	Senatobia
82	5,359	Kosciusko SD	Kosciusko
83	5,352	Clinton Public SD	Clinton
84	5,342	Rankin County SD	Brandon
85	5,333	Pontotoc County SD	Pontotoc
86	5,331	Harrison County SD	Gulfport
87	5,289	West Point SD	West Point
88	5,288	Pontotoc City Schools	Pontotoc
89	5,267	Monroe County SD	Amory
90	5,250	Lee County SD	Tupelo
91	5,242	Lowndes County SD	Columbus
92	5,222	Neshoba County SD	Philadelphia
93	5,211	Ocean Springs SD	Ocean Springs
94	5,208	South Tippah SD	Ripley
95	5,205	Houston SD	Houston
96	5,190	Senatobia Municipal SD	Senatobia
97	5,188	Smith County SD	Raleigh
98	5,167	Lauderdale County SD	Meridian
99	5,141	Itawamba County SD	Fulton
100	5,107	Grenada SD	Grenada
101	5,101	Copiah County SD	Hazlehurst
102	5,091	Leake County SD	Carthage
103	5,061	Scott County SD	Forest
104	5,043	Jackson County SD	Vancleave
105	5,034	Yazoo City Municipal SD	Yazoo City
106	4,985	George County SD	Lucedale
107	4,979	Union County SD	New Albany
108	4,916	Lincoln County SD	Brookhaven
109	4,845	Canton Public SD	Canton
110	4,733	Pearl River County SD	Carriere
111	4,660	Marshall County SD	Holly Springs
112	4,606	North Pike SD	Summit
113	4,444	Desoto County SD	Hernando

Number of Diploma Recipients

Rank	Number	District Name	City
1	1,239	Jackson Public SD	Jackson
2	862	Desoto County SD	Hernando
3	795	Rankin County SD	Brandon
4	534	Harrison County SD	Gulfport
5	500	Madison County SD	Flora
6	466	Jackson County SD	Vancleave
7	441	Vicksburg Warren SD	Vicksburg
8	437	Jones County SD	Ellisville
9	365	Pascagoula SD	Pascagoula
10	353	Tupelo Public SD	Tupelo
11	348	Lamar County SD	Purvis
12	338	Lauderdale County SD	Meridian
13	336	Gulfport SD	Gulfport
13	336	Meridian Public SD	Meridian
15	306	Clinton Public SD	Clinton
16	300	Greenville Public Schools	Greenville
17	283	Natchez-Adams SD	Natchez
18	282	Hinds County SD	Raymond
19	268	Lowndes County SD	Columbus
20	265	Biloxi Public SD	Biloxi
20	265	Columbus Municipal SD	Columbus
22	260	Lee County SD	Tupelo
23	251	Holmes County SD	Lexington
23	251	Ocean Springs SD	Ocean Springs
25	231	Starkville SD	Starkville
26	226	Hattiesburg Public SD	Hattiesburg
27	223	Alcorn SD	Corinth
28	220	Wayne County SD	Waynesboro
29	218	Long Beach SD	Long Beach
29	218	Simpson County SD	Mendenhall

Rank	Value	District Name	City
31	207	George County SD	Lucedale
32	205	Moss Point Separate SD	Moss Point
33	200	Cleveland SD	Cleveland
34	194	Itawamba County SD	Fulton
35	191	South Panola SD	Batesville
36	186	Louisville Municipal SD	Louisville
37	183	Indianola SD	Indianola
38	180	Grenada SD	Grenada
39	173	Pearl Public SD	Pearl
40	172	Laurel SD	Laurel
41	170	Hancock County SD	Kiln
41	170	Lincoln County SD	Brookhaven
43	166	Brookhaven SD	Brookhaven
43	166	Picayune SD	Picayune
45	163	Scott County SD	Forest
46	161	Covington County Schools	Collins
46	161	Mccomb SD	Mccomb
48	158	Petal SD	Petal
49	157	Copiah County SD	Hazlehurst
50	153	West Point SD	West Point
51	151	Leake County SD	Carthage
52	150	Greenwood Public SD	Greenwood
52	150	Oxford SD	Oxford
54	148	Walthall County SD	Tylertown
55	147	Smith County SD	Raleigh
56	137	South Tippah SD	Ripley
57	135	Tishomingo County Sp Mun SD	Iuka
58	131	Calhoun County SD	Pittsboro
59	130	Marion County SD	Columbia
60	128	Monroe County SD	Amory
60	128	Pontotoc County SD	Pontotoc
62	127	Noxubee County SD	Macon
63	125	Neshoba County SD	Philadelphia
63	125	Stone County SD	Wiggins
65	123	Kosciusko SD	Kosciusko
66	122	Claiborne County SD	Port Gibson
66	122	Marshall County SD	Holly Springs
66	122	Prentiss County SD	Booneville
66	122	Quitman SD	Quitman
70	121	Bay St Louis Waveland SD	Bay St Louis
70	121	Clarksdale Municipal SD	Clarksdale
72	120	Lawrence County SD	Monticello
73	117	Senatobia Municipal SD	Senatobia
74	116	Leflore County SD	Greenwood
75	115	Pearl River County SD	Carriere
75	115	Western Line SD	Avon
77	114	Jefferson Davis County SD	Prentiss
78	112	Union County SD	New Albany
79	111	Poplarville Separate SD	Poplarville
79	111	Tate County SD	Senatobia
81	109	Pass Christian Public SD	Pass Christian
82	108	Canton Public SD	Canton
82	108	Columbia SD	Columbia
84	107	Amory SD	Amory
85	106	Holly Springs SD	Holly Springs
85	106	Pontotoc City Schools	Pontotoc
87	105	South Pike SD	Magnolia
88	97	Aberdeen SD	Aberdeen
88	97	Hazlehurst City SD	Hazlehurst
90	96	Choctaw County SD	Ackerman
91	95	Franklin County SD	Meadville
91	95	Lafayette County SD	Oxford
93	94	Corinth SD	Corinth
94	93	Webster County SD	Eupora
95	92	Jefferson County SD	Fayette
95	92	New Albany Public Schools	New Albany
95	92	West Jasper Consolidated Schools	Bay Springs
98	91	Greene County SD	Leakesville
99	90	Yazoo City Municipal SD	Yazoo City
100	89	Yazoo County SD	Yazoo City
101	77	Houston SD	Houston
102	74	Humphreys County SD	Belzoni
102	74	Newton County SD	Decatur
104	72	Wilkinson County SD	Woodville
105	70	North Pike SD	Summit
106	65	Quitman County SD	Marks
106	65	Tunica County SD	Tunica
108	63	Coahoma County SD	Clarksdale
109	58	Forest Municipal SD	Forest
110	57	Forrest County SD	Hattiesburg
111	56	Sunflower County SD	Indianola
112	53	East Tallahatchie Consol SD	Charleston
112	53	North Panola Schools	Sardis

High School Drop-out Rate

Rank	Percent	District Name	City
1	11.2	Copiah County SD	Hazlehurst
2	10.9	South Pike SD	Magnolia
3	10.6	Leflore County SD	Greenwood
4	8.3	Coahoma County SD	Clarksdale
5	7.6	Lee County SD	Tupelo
6	7.2	Forrest County SD	Hattiesburg
7	7.1	East Tallahatchie Consol SD	Charleston
7	7.1	Quitman SD	Quitman
9	7.0	Jackson Public SD	Jackson
10	6.2	Canton Public SD	Canton
10	6.2	Greenville Public Schools	Greenville
10	6.2	Monroe County SD	Amory
13	6.1	Houston SD	Houston
14	6.0	Greene County SD	Leakesville
15	5.8	Humphreys County SD	Belzoni
15	5.8	Lowndes County SD	Columbus
15	5.8	Vicksburg Warren SD	Vicksburg
18	5.7	Scott County SD	Forest
19	5.4	Hancock County SD	Kiln
19	5.4	Lawrence County SD	Monticello
19	5.4	Simpson County SD	Mendenhall
22	5.3	Lauderdale County SD	Meridian
22	5.3	Neshoba County SD	Philadelphia
22	5.3	Yazoo County SD	Yazoo City
25	5.2	Western Line SD	Avon
26	5.1	Leake County SD	Carthage
26	5.1	Walthall County SD	Tylertown
28	5.0	South Panola SD	Batesville
28	5.0	Tunica County SD	Tunica
28	5.0	Yazoo City Municipal SD	Yazoo City
31	4.9	Corinth SD	Corinth
31	4.9	Itawamba County SD	Fulton
31	4.9	Marion County SD	Columbia
31	4.9	Moss Point Separate SD	Moss Point
35	4.8	Jefferson Davis County SD	Prentiss
35	4.8	Noxubee County SD	Macon
35	4.8	Starkville SD	Starkville
35	4.8	Tate County SD	Senatobia
39	4.7	West Point SD	West Point
40	4.6	Wayne County SD	Waynesboro
41	4.5	Harrison County SD	Gulfport
41	4.5	Newton County SD	Decatur
43	4.3	Hazlehurst City SD	Hazlehurst
44	4.2	Hattiesburg Public SD	Hattiesburg
44	4.2	Holly Springs SD	Holly Springs
44	4.2	Pearl River County SD	Carriere
47	4.1	Long Beach SD	Long Beach
47	4.1	Wilkinson County SD	Woodville
49	4.0	Choctaw County SD	Ackerman
49	4.0	Gulfport SD	Gulfport
49	4.0	Hinds County SD	Raymond
49	4.0	Pascagoula SD	Pascagoula
53	3.9	Bay St Louis Waveland SD	Bay St Louis
53	3.9	Covington County Schools	Collins
55	3.8	Grenada SD	Grenada
56	3.7	North Panola Schools	Sardis
57	3.6	Aberdeen SD	Aberdeen
57	3.6	Columbus Municipal SD	Columbus
57	3.6	Greenwood Public SD	Greenwood
57	3.6	Marshall County SD	Holly Springs
57	3.6	Meridian Public SD	Meridian
57	3.6	Natchez-Adams SD	Natchez
63	3.5	Brookhaven SD	Brookhaven
63	3.5	Forest Municipal SD	Forest
63	3.5	South Tippah SD	Ripley
66	3.4	Claiborne County SD	Port Gibson
67	3.3	Lincoln County SD	Brookhaven
67	3.3	Petal SD	Petal
69	3.2	Alcorn SD	Corinth
69	3.2	Biloxi Public SD	Biloxi
69	3.2	Clinton Public SD	Clinton
69	3.2	Sunflower County SD	Indianola
69	3.2	Webster County SD	Eupora
74	3.1	Oxford SD	Oxford
74	3.1	Tupelo Public SD	Tupelo
76	3.0	Jones County SD	Ellisville
77	2.9	Calhoun County SD	Pittsboro
77	2.9	Holmes County SD	Lexington
77	2.9	Lamar County SD	Purvis
80	2.8	Picayune SD	Picayune
81	2.6	Amory SD	Amory
81	2.6	Louisville Municipal SD	Louisville
81	2.6	North Pike SD	Summit
84	2.4	Jackson County SD	Vancleave
84	2.4	Ocean Springs SD	Ocean Springs
84	2.4	Senatobia Municipal SD	Senatobia
87	2.2	Smith County SD	Raleigh
88	2.1	Franklin County SD	Meadville
89	2.0	Clarksdale Municipal SD	Clarksdale
89	2.0	Indianola SD	Indianola
89	2.0	Laurel SD	Laurel
89	2.0	Pass Christian Public SD	Pass Christian
89	2.0	Poplarville Separate SD	Poplarville
89	2.0	Quitman County SD	Marks
89	2.0	Tishomingo County Sp Mun SD	Iuka
96	1.9	Union County SD	New Albany
97	1.8	West Jasper Consolidated Schools	Bay Springs
98	1.6	Rankin County SD	Brandon
99	1.5	Columbia SD	Columbia
100	1.4	Lafayette County SD	Oxford
101	1.3	Madison County SD	Flora
101	1.3	Mccomb SD	Mccomb
101	1.3	New Albany Public Schools	New Albany
101	1.3	Pearl Public SD	Pearl
101	1.3	Pontotoc County SD	Pontotoc
106	0.9	Cleveland SD	Cleveland
106	0.9	Desoto County SD	Hernando
108	0.6	Prentiss County SD	Booneville
109	0.5	George County SD	Lucedale
110	0.4	Jefferson County SD	Fayette
110	0.4	Pontotoc City Schools	Pontotoc
110	0.4	Stone County SD	Wiggins
113	0.0	Kosciusko SD	Kosciusko

Missouri

Missouri Public School Educational Profile

Category	Value	Category	Value
Schools *(2003-2004)*	2,372	**Diploma Recipients** *(2002-2003)*	54,400
Instructional Level		White, Non-Hispanic	45,569
Primary	1,244	Black, Non-Hispanic	7,171
Middle	380	Asian/Pacific Islander	820
High	569	American Indian/Alaskan Native	147
Other Level	179	Hispanic	693
Curriculum		**High School Drop-out Rate** (%) *(2001-2002)*	3.7
Regular	2,204	White, Non-Hispanic	3.2
Special Education	23	Black, Non-Hispanic	5.8
Vocational	61	Asian/Pacific Islander	1.6
Alternative	84	American Indian/Alaskan Native	4.8
Type		Hispanic	5.9
Magnet	45	**Staff** *(2003-2004)*	
Charter	26	Teachers	65,369.5
Title I Eligible	1,277	Average Salary ($)	38,247
School-wide Title I	370	Librarians/Media Specialists	1,618.0
Students *(2003-2004)*	918,038	Guidance Counselors	2,589.6
Gender (%)		**Ratios** *(2003-2004)*	
Male	51.4	Student/Teacher Ratio	14.0 to 1
Female	48.6	Student/Librarian Ratio	567.4 to 1
Race/Ethnicity (%)		Student/Counselor Ratio	354.5 to 1
White, Non-Hispanic	77.7	**College Entrance Exam Scores** *(2005)*	
Black, Non-Hispanic	18.0	Scholastic Aptitude Test (SAT)	
Asian/Pacific Islander	1.4	Participation Rate (%)	7
American Indian/Alaskan Native	0.4	Mean SAT Reasoning Test Verbal Score	588
Hispanic	2.6	Mean SAT Reasoning Test Math Score	588
Classification (%)		American College Testing Program (ACT)	
Individual Education Program (IEP)	15.8	Participation Rate (%)	70
Migrant *(2002-2003)*	0.5	Average Composite Score	21.6
English Language Learner (ELL)	1.6	Average English Score	21.4
Eligible for Free Lunch Program	30.5	Average Math Score	20.9
Eligible for Reduced-Price Lunch Program	7.1	Average Reading Score	21.9
Current Spending *($ per student in FY 2003)*	6,990	Average Science Score	21.5
Instruction	4,240		
Support Services	2,436		

Note: For an explanation of data, please refer to the User's Guide in the front of the book

Missouri NAEP 2005 Test Scores

Reading			Mathematics		
Grade/Category	Value	Rank	Grade/Category	Value	Rank
4th Grade			**4th Grade**		
Average Proficiency	221.2 (0.93)	22/51	Average Proficiency	235.0 (0.87)	35/51
Proficiency by Gender/Race/Ethnicity			Proficiency by Gender/Race/Ethnicity		
Male	218.3 (1.43)	21/51	Male	236.7 (1.12)	33/51
Female	224.0 (1.13)	21/51	Female	233.3 (0.92)	35/51
White, Non-Hispanic	226.4 (0.88)	25/51	White, Non-Hispanic	239.9 (0.74)	44/51
Black, Non-Hispanic	200.4 (2.60)	18/42	Black, Non-Hispanic	215.2 (1.75)	31/42
Asian, Non-Hispanic	n/a	n/a	Asian, Non-Hispanic	n/a	n/a
American Indian, Non-Hispanic	n/a	n/a	American Indian, Non-Hispanic	n/a	n/a
Hispanic	209.9 (4.78)	9/40	Hispanic	221.3 (2.98)	29/41
Proficiency by Class Size			Proficiency by Class Size		
Less than 16 Students	209.6 (4.18)	17/34	Less than 16 Students	220.4 (3.13)	25/35
16 to 18 Students	n/a	n/a	16 to 18 Students	n/a	n/a
19 to 20 Students	226.5 (2.88)	7/38	19 to 20 Students	238.9 (2.07)	22/38
21 to 25 Students	222.0 (1.46)	24/51	21 to 25 Students	236.5 (1.24)	37/51
Greater than 25 Students	n/a	n/a	Greater than 25 Students	n/a	n/a
Percent Attaining Achievement Levels			Percent Attaining Achievement Levels		
Below Basic	33.0 (1.17)	28/51	Below Basic	21.4 (1.26)	18/51
Basic or Above	67.0 (1.17)	24/51	Basic or Above	78.6 (1.26)	34/51
Proficient or Above	32.7 (1.27)	24/51	Proficient or Above	31.1 (1.26)	36/51
Advanced or Above	7.3 (0.80)	20/51	Advanced or Above	3.2 (0.51)	40/51
8th Grade			**8th Grade**		
Average Proficiency	264.7 (1.03)	21/51	Average Proficiency	276.4 (1.31)	34/51
Proficiency by Gender/Race/Ethnicity			Proficiency by Gender/Race/Ethnicity		
Male	259.5 (1.31)	22/51	Male	278.0 (1.62)	33/51
Female	269.6 (1.23)	23/51	Female	274.8 (1.36)	34/51
White, Non-Hispanic	269.7 (1.12)	24/51	White, Non-Hispanic	283.9 (1.30)	36/51
Black, Non-Hispanic	242.1 (1.82)	22/40	Black, Non-Hispanic	247.4 (1.88)	33/41
Asian, Non-Hispanic	n/a	n/a	Asian, Non-Hispanic	n/a	n/a
American Indian, Non-Hispanic	n/a	n/a	American Indian, Non-Hispanic	n/a	n/a
Hispanic	257.6 (6.01)	2/38	Hispanic	n/a	n/a
Proficiency by Parents Highest Level of Ed.			Proficiency by Parents Highest Level of Ed.		
Did Not Finish High School	250.6 (2.52)	9/49	Did Not Finish High School	262.9 (2.95)	22/50
Graduated High School	256.8 (2.11)	17/50	Graduated High School	269.5 (1.80)	25/50
Some Education After High School	267.8 (1.99)	22/50	Some Education After High School	277.3 (1.89)	36/50
Graduated College	273.0 (1.45)	23/50	Graduated College	284.6 (1.77)	35/50
Percent Attaining Achievement Levels			Percent Attaining Achievement Levels		
Below Basic	33.0 (1.17)	28/51	Below Basic	31.9 (1.84)	20/51
Basic or Above	67.0 (1.17)	24/51	Basic or Above	68.1 (1.84)	32/51
Proficient or Above	32.7 (1.27)	24/51	Proficient or Above	26.0 (1.43)	34/51
Advanced or Above	7.3 (0.80)	20/51	Advanced or Above	4.1 (0.55)	37/51

Note: For an explanation of data, please refer to the User's Guide in the front of the book; n/a indicates data not available

Adair County

Kirksville R-III
1901 E Hamilton St • Kirksville, MO 63501-3904
(660) 665-7774 • http://www.kirksville.k12.mo.us/
Grade Span: PK-12; **Agency Type:** 1
Schools: 5
    2 Primary; 1 Middle; 2 High; 0 Other Level
    4 Regular; 0 Special Education; 1 Vocational; 0 Alternative
    0 Magnet; 0 Charter; 3 Title I Eligible; 0 School-wide Title I
Students: 2,471 (51.9% male; 48.0% female)
    Individual Education Program: 432 (17.5%);
    English Language Learner: 5 (0.2%); Migrant: 3 (0.1%)
    Eligible for Free Lunch Program: 655 (26.5%)
    Eligible for Reduced-Price Lunch Program: 131 (5.3%)
Teachers: 190.5 (13.0 to 1)
Librarians/Media Specialists: 4.0 (617.8 to 1)
Guidance Counselors: 7.0 (353.0 to 1)
Current Spending: ($ per student per year):
    Total: $6,349; Instruction: $4,021; Support Services: $2,027
Enrollment, Drop-out Rates and Diploma Recipients by Race/Ethnicity

Category	Total	White	Black	Asian	AIAN	Hisp.
Enrollment (%)	100.0	94.8	2.2	1.0	0.4	1.5
Drop-out Rate (%)	3.1	3.2	0.0	0.0	0.0	0.0
H.S. Diplomas (#)	171	166	1	2	0	2

Andrew County

Savannah R-III
507 1/2 W Main • Savannah, MO 64485-0151
Mailing Address: PO Box 151 • Savannah, MO 64485-0151
(816) 324-3144 • http://www.savannah.k12.mo.us
Grade Span: PK-12; **Agency Type:** 1
Schools: 6
    4 Primary; 1 Middle; 1 High; 0 Other Level
    6 Regular; 0 Special Education; 0 Vocational; 0 Alternative
    0 Magnet; 0 Charter; 2 Title I Eligible; 1 School-wide Title I
Students: 2,387 (51.6% male; 48.3% female)
    Individual Education Program: 309 (12.9%);
    English Language Learner: 1 (<0.1%); Migrant: 0 (0.0%)
    Eligible for Free Lunch Program: 499 (20.9%)
    Eligible for Reduced-Price Lunch Program: 188 (7.9%)
Teachers: 160.7 (14.9 to 1)
Librarians/Media Specialists: 3.2 (745.9 to 1)
Guidance Counselors: 4.1 (582.2 to 1)
Current Spending: ($ per student per year):
    Total: $5,897; Instruction: $3,779; Support Services: $1,810
Enrollment, Drop-out Rates and Diploma Recipients by Race/Ethnicity

Category	Total	White	Black	Asian	AIAN	Hisp.
Enrollment (%)	100.0	96.9	1.2	0.2	0.4	1.4
Drop-out Rate (%)	2.7	2.7	0.0	0.0	0.0	0.0
H.S. Diplomas (#)	164	161	1	0	1	1

Audrain County

Mexico 59
920 S Jefferson • Mexico, MO 65265-2599
(573) 581-3773 • http://www.mexicoschools.net/
Grade Span: PK-12; **Agency Type:** 1
Schools: 6
    3 Primary; 1 Middle; 2 High; 0 Other Level
    5 Regular; 0 Special Education; 1 Vocational; 0 Alternative
    0 Magnet; 0 Charter; 2 Title I Eligible; 1 School-wide Title I
Students: 2,433 (51.8% male; 48.1% female)
    Individual Education Program: 346 (14.2%);
    English Language Learner: 14 (0.6%); Migrant: 18 (0.7%)
    Eligible for Free Lunch Program: 827 (34.0%)
    Eligible for Reduced-Price Lunch Program: 245 (10.1%)
Teachers: 171.0 (14.2 to 1)
Librarians/Media Specialists: 4.5 (540.7 to 1)
Guidance Counselors: 9.1 (267.4 to 1)
Current Spending: ($ per student per year):
    Total: $6,465; Instruction: $4,040; Support Services: $2,055
Enrollment, Drop-out Rates and Diploma Recipients by Race/Ethnicity

Category	Total	White	Black	Asian	AIAN	Hisp.
Enrollment (%)	100.0	87.0	10.4	0.9	0.1	1.6
Drop-out Rate (%)	3.2	2.6	9.1	0.0	0.0	0.0
H.S. Diplomas (#)	184	157	20	1	3	3

Barry County

Cassville R-IV
1501 Main • Cassville, MO 65625-1154
(417) 847-2221 • http://wildcats.cassville.k12.mo.us/
Grade Span: PK-12; **Agency Type:** 1
Schools: 4
    2 Primary; 1 Middle; 1 High; 0 Other Level
    4 Regular; 0 Special Education; 0 Vocational; 0 Alternative
    0 Magnet; 0 Charter; 3 Title I Eligible; 0 School-wide Title I
Students: 2,095 (52.8% male; 47.1% female)
    Individual Education Program: 324 (15.5%);
    English Language Learner: 50 (2.4%); Migrant: 70 (3.3%)
    Eligible for Free Lunch Program: 747 (35.7%)
    Eligible for Reduced-Price Lunch Program: 224 (10.7%)
Teachers: 123.4 (17.0 to 1)
Librarians/Media Specialists: 3.4 (616.2 to 1)
Guidance Counselors: 5.0 (419.0 to 1)
Current Spending: ($ per student per year):
    Total: $5,372; Instruction: $3,425; Support Services: $1,631
Enrollment, Drop-out Rates and Diploma Recipients by Race/Ethnicity

Category	Total	White	Black	Asian	AIAN	Hisp.
Enrollment (%)	100.0	93.7	0.3	0.3	0.8	4.9
Drop-out Rate (%)	3.5	3.7	0.0	0.0	0.0	0.0
H.S. Diplomas (#)	135	130	0	1	2	2

Monett R-I
800 E Scott St • Monett, MO 65708-1741
(417) 235-7422 • http://hs1.monett.k12.mo.us/
Grade Span: PK-12; **Agency Type:** 1
Schools: 5
    1 Primary; 2 Middle; 2 High; 0 Other Level
    4 Regular; 0 Special Education; 1 Vocational; 0 Alternative
    0 Magnet; 0 Charter; 3 Title I Eligible; 0 School-wide Title I
Students: 1,975 (51.0% male; 48.9% female)
    Individual Education Program: 321 (16.3%);
    English Language Learner: 273 (13.8%); Migrant: 319 (16.2%)
    Eligible for Free Lunch Program: 745 (37.7%)
    Eligible for Reduced-Price Lunch Program: 177 (9.0%)
Teachers: 151.8 (13.0 to 1)
Librarians/Media Specialists: 4.0 (493.8 to 1)
Guidance Counselors: 8.0 (246.9 to 1)
Current Spending: ($ per student per year):
    Total: $6,549; Instruction: $4,547; Support Services: $1,714
Enrollment, Drop-out Rates and Diploma Recipients by Race/Ethnicity

Category	Total	White	Black	Asian	AIAN	Hisp.
Enrollment (%)	100.0	80.5	0.1	0.5	0.9	18.0
Drop-out Rate (%)	3.4	2.8	n/a	0.0	0.0	7.7
H.S. Diplomas (#)	123	112	0	0	0	11

Benton County

Warsaw R-IX
1 Wildcat Dr • Warsaw, MO 65355-0248
Mailing Address: PO Box 248 • Warsaw, MO 65355-0248
(660) 438-7120
Grade Span: PK-12; **Agency Type:** 1
Schools: 5
    3 Primary; 1 Middle; 1 High; 0 Other Level
    5 Regular; 0 Special Education; 0 Vocational; 0 Alternative
    0 Magnet; 0 Charter; 2 Title I Eligible; 2 School-wide Title I
Students: 1,530 (50.0% male; 49.9% female)
    Individual Education Program: 255 (16.7%);
    English Language Learner: 0 (0.0%); Migrant: 10 (0.7%)
    Eligible for Free Lunch Program: 700 (45.8%)
    Eligible for Reduced-Price Lunch Program: 179 (11.7%)
Teachers: 91.0 (16.8 to 1)
Librarians/Media Specialists: 2.0 (765.0 to 1)
Guidance Counselors: 3.1 (493.5 to 1)
Current Spending: ($ per student per year):
    Total: $5,533; Instruction: $3,380; Support Services: $1,847
Enrollment, Drop-out Rates and Diploma Recipients by Race/Ethnicity

Category	Total	White	Black	Asian	AIAN	Hisp.
Enrollment (%)	100.0	97.1	1.0	0.1	0.4	1.4
Drop-out Rate (%)	3.5	3.6	0.0	0.0	n/a	0.0
H.S. Diplomas (#)	102	99	0	1	0	2

Boone County

Columbia 93
1818 W Worley St • Columbia, MO 65203-1038
(573) 886-2100 • http://www.columbia.k12.mo.us/
Grade Span: PK-12; **Agency Type:** 1
Schools: 31
    20 Primary; 3 Middle; 3 High; 5 Other Level

29 Regular; 0 Special Education; 1 Vocational; 1 Alternative
0 Magnet; 0 Charter; 12 Title I Eligible; 0 School-wide Title I
Students: 16,498 (50.8% male; 49.1% female)
Individual Education Program: 2,566 (15.6%);
English Language Learner: 354 (2.1%); Migrant: 0 (0.0%)
Eligible for Free Lunch Program: 4,109 (24.9%)
Eligible for Reduced-Price Lunch Program: 695 (4.2%)
Teachers: 1,234.0 (13.4 to 1)
Librarians/Media Specialists: 31.2 (528.8 to 1)
Guidance Counselors: 50.9 (324.1 to 1)
Current Spending: ($ per student per year):
Total: $7,410; Instruction: $4,602; Support Services: $2,519

Enrollment, Drop-out Rates and Diploma Recipients by Race/Ethnicity

Category	Total	White	Black	Asian	AIAN	Hisp.
Enrollment (%)	100.0	71.4	21.1	4.6	0.4	2.6
Drop-out Rate (%)	4.5	3.9	7.8	1.1	7.1	7.1
H.S. Diplomas (#)	1,039	834	135	55	1	14

Buchanan County

St. Joseph
925 Felix • St Joseph, MO 64501-2706
(816) 671-4000 • http://www.sjsd.k12.mo.us/
Grade Span: PK-12; **Agency Type:** 1
Schools: 29
18 Primary; 4 Middle; 4 High; 3 Other Level
27 Regular; 1 Special Education; 1 Vocational; 0 Alternative
0 Magnet; 0 Charter; 8 Title I Eligible; 6 School-wide Title I
Students: 12,015 (51.0% male; 48.9% female)
Individual Education Program: 1,564 (13.0%);
English Language Learner: 52 (0.4%); Migrant: 0 (0.0%)
Eligible for Free Lunch Program: 4,641 (38.6%)
Eligible for Reduced-Price Lunch Program: 1,193 (9.9%)
Teachers: 792.9 (15.2 to 1)
Librarians/Media Specialists: 9.6 (1,251.6 to 1)
Guidance Counselors: 31.8 (377.8 to 1)
Current Spending: ($ per student per year):
Total: $6,515; Instruction: $4,153; Support Services: $2,013

Enrollment, Drop-out Rates and Diploma Recipients by Race/Ethnicity

Category	Total	White	Black	Asian	AIAN	Hisp.
Enrollment (%)	100.0	88.7	7.1	0.8	0.5	2.9
Drop-out Rate (%)	3.4	3.3	6.3	0.0	0.0	3.5
H.S. Diplomas (#)	711	659	31	9	2	10

Butler County

Poplar Bluff R-I
1110 N Westwood Blvd • Poplar Bluff, MO 63901-3336
(573) 785-7751 • http://www.pb.k12.mo.us/index.htm
Grade Span: PK-12; **Agency Type:** 1
Schools: 11
6 Primary; 2 Middle; 2 High; 1 Other Level
10 Regular; 0 Special Education; 1 Vocational; 0 Alternative
0 Magnet; 0 Charter; 7 Title I Eligible; 4 School-wide Title I
Students: 4,853 (51.5% male; 48.4% female)
Individual Education Program: 768 (15.8%);
English Language Learner: 2 (<0.1%); Migrant: 0 (0.0%)
Eligible for Free Lunch Program: 2,099 (43.3%)
Eligible for Reduced-Price Lunch Program: 363 (7.5%)
Teachers: 295.3 (16.4 to 1)
Librarians/Media Specialists: 7.0 (693.3 to 1)
Guidance Counselors: 9.9 (490.2 to 1)
Current Spending: ($ per student per year):
Total: $5,670; Instruction: $3,524; Support Services: $1,842

Enrollment, Drop-out Rates and Diploma Recipients by Race/Ethnicity

Category	Total	White	Black	Asian	AIAN	Hisp.
Enrollment (%)	100.0	87.2	10.8	0.7	0.5	0.8
Drop-out Rate (%)	5.2	5.0	6.1	0.0	0.0	27.3
H.S. Diplomas (#)	312	272	36	0	2	2

Callaway County

Fulton 58
2 Hornet Dr • Fulton, MO 65251-2731
(573) 642-2206 • http://www.fulton.k12.mo.us/
Grade Span: PK-12; **Agency Type:** 1
Schools: 5
3 Primary; 1 Middle; 1 High; 0 Other Level
5 Regular; 0 Special Education; 0 Vocational; 0 Alternative
0 Magnet; 0 Charter; 3 Title I Eligible; 0 School-wide Title I
Students: 2,278 (51.0% male; 48.9% female)
Individual Education Program: 273 (12.0%);
English Language Learner: 4 (0.2%); Migrant: 0 (0.0%)
Eligible for Free Lunch Program: 693 (30.4%)
Eligible for Reduced-Price Lunch Program: 201 (8.8%)

Teachers: 169.7 (13.4 to 1)
Librarians/Media Specialists: 5.0 (455.6 to 1)
Guidance Counselors: 6.8 (335.0 to 1)
Current Spending: ($ per student per year):
Total: $6,629; Instruction: $3,891; Support Services: $2,379

Enrollment, Drop-out Rates and Diploma Recipients by Race/Ethnicity

Category	Total	White	Black	Asian	AIAN	Hisp.
Enrollment (%)	100.0	84.4	14.3	0.6	0.1	0.7
Drop-out Rate (%)	5.8	4.5	12.5	11.1	0.0	50.0
H.S. Diplomas (#)	131	118	11	2	0	0

Camden County

Camdenton R-III
Township Rd • Camdenton, MO 65020-1409
Mailing Address: PO Box 1409 • Camdenton, MO 65020-1409
(573) 346-9208 • http://schoolweb.missouri.edu/camdenton.k12.mo.us/
Grade Span: PK-12; **Agency Type:** 1
Schools: 8
3 Primary; 2 Middle; 2 High; 1 Other Level
6 Regular; 0 Special Education; 1 Vocational; 1 Alternative
0 Magnet; 0 Charter; 3 Title I Eligible; 0 School-wide Title I
Students: 4,010 (52.9% male; 47.0% female)
Individual Education Program: 532 (13.3%);
English Language Learner: 18 (0.4%); Migrant: 0 (0.0%)
Eligible for Free Lunch Program: 1,304 (32.5%)
Eligible for Reduced-Price Lunch Program: 385 (9.6%)
Teachers: 286.0 (14.0 to 1)
Librarians/Media Specialists: 5.0 (802.0 to 1)
Guidance Counselors: 14.0 (286.4 to 1)
Current Spending: ($ per student per year):
Total: $6,740; Instruction: $4,193; Support Services: $2,262

Enrollment, Drop-out Rates and Diploma Recipients by Race/Ethnicity

Category	Total	White	Black	Asian	AIAN	Hisp.
Enrollment (%)	100.0	97.1	0.5	0.7	0.3	1.3
Drop-out Rate (%)	2.3	2.2	25.0	12.5	0.0	0.0
H.S. Diplomas (#)	289	288	0	0	1	0

Cape Girardeau County

Cape Girardeau 63
301 N Clark St • Cape Girardeau, MO 63701-5101
(573) 335-1867 • http://www.cape.k12.mo.us/
Grade Span: PK-12; **Agency Type:** 1
Schools: 9
5 Primary; 2 Middle; 2 High; 0 Other Level
8 Regular; 0 Special Education; 1 Vocational; 0 Alternative
0 Magnet; 0 Charter; 5 Title I Eligible; 5 School-wide Title I
Students: 4,049 (50.3% male; 49.6% female)
Individual Education Program: 745 (18.4%);
English Language Learner: 32 (0.8%); Migrant: 0 (0.0%)
Eligible for Free Lunch Program: 1,495 (36.9%)
Eligible for Reduced-Price Lunch Program: 233 (5.8%)
Teachers: 318.3 (12.7 to 1)
Librarians/Media Specialists: 8.0 (506.1 to 1)
Guidance Counselors: 15.0 (269.9 to 1)
Current Spending: ($ per student per year):
Total: $7,097; Instruction: $4,406; Support Services: $2,392

Enrollment, Drop-out Rates and Diploma Recipients by Race/Ethnicity

Category	Total	White	Black	Asian	AIAN	Hisp.
Enrollment (%)	100.0	72.8	24.3	1.3	0.1	1.6
Drop-out Rate (%)	1.8	2.0	1.3	0.0	0.0	0.0
H.S. Diplomas (#)	275	236	34	3	1	1

Jackson R-II
614 E Adams St • Jackson, MO 63755-2150
(573) 243-9501 • http://www.jackson.k12.mo.us/
Grade Span: PK-12; **Agency Type:** 1
Schools: 10
6 Primary; 2 Middle; 1 High; 1 Other Level
10 Regular; 0 Special Education; 0 Vocational; 0 Alternative
0 Magnet; 0 Charter; 5 Title I Eligible; 0 School-wide Title I
Students: 4,585 (51.8% male; 48.1% female)
Individual Education Program: 605 (13.2%);
English Language Learner: 5 (0.1%); Migrant: 0 (0.0%)
Eligible for Free Lunch Program: 800 (17.4%)
Eligible for Reduced-Price Lunch Program: 267 (5.8%)
Teachers: 270.7 (16.9 to 1)
Librarians/Media Specialists: 7.8 (587.8 to 1)
Guidance Counselors: 11.0 (416.8 to 1)
Current Spending: ($ per student per year):
Total: $5,230; Instruction: $3,263; Support Services: $1,749

Enrollment, Drop-out Rates and Diploma Recipients by Race/Ethnicity

Category	Total	White	Black	Asian	AIAN	Hisp.
Enrollment (%)	100.0	96.9	1.9	0.5	0.0	0.6
Drop-out Rate (%)	2.2	2.0	8.3	50.0	n/a	0.0
H.S. Diplomas (#)	343	338	4	0	0	1

Cass County

Belton 124
110 W Walnut • Belton, MO 64012-4808
(816) 348-1000 • http://www.beltonschools.org/
Grade Span: PK-12; **Agency Type:** 1
Schools: 10
   5 Primary; 2 Middle; 1 High; 2 Other Level
   9 Regular; 1 Special Education; 0 Vocational; 0 Alternative
   0 Magnet; 0 Charter; 4 Title I Eligible; 0 School-wide Title I
Students: 5,099 (51.9% male; 48.0% female)
   Individual Education Program: 591 (11.6%);
   English Language Learner: 105 (2.1%); Migrant: 17 (0.3%)
   Eligible for Free Lunch Program: 1,024 (20.1%)
   Eligible for Reduced-Price Lunch Program: 365 (7.2%)
Teachers: 295.5 (17.3 to 1)
Librarians/Media Specialists: 8.8 (579.4 to 1)
Guidance Counselors: 11.5 (443.4 to 1)
Current Spending: ($ per student per year):
   Total: $6,246; Instruction: $3,781; Support Services: $2,172
Enrollment, Drop-out Rates and Diploma Recipients by Race/Ethnicity

Category	Total	White	Black	Asian	AIAN	Hisp.
Enrollment (%)	100.0	86.4	6.2	1.0	0.4	6.0
Drop-out Rate (%)	3.6	3.7	0.0	0.0	11.1	3.1
H.S. Diplomas (#)	261	232	8	4	2	15

Harrisonville R-IX
503 S Lexington • Harrisonville, MO 64701-2415
(816) 380-2727 • http://www.harrisonvilleschools.org/
Grade Span: PK-12; **Agency Type:** 1
Schools: 7
   3 Primary; 1 Middle; 2 High; 1 Other Level
   5 Regular; 0 Special Education; 1 Vocational; 1 Alternative
   0 Magnet; 0 Charter; 3 Title I Eligible; 0 School-wide Title I
Students: 2,571 (50.8% male; 49.1% female)
   Individual Education Program: 260 (10.1%);
   English Language Learner: 4 (0.2%); Migrant: 0 (0.0%)
   Eligible for Free Lunch Program: 495 (19.3%)
   Eligible for Reduced-Price Lunch Program: 153 (6.0%)
Teachers: 159.6 (16.1 to 1)
Librarians/Media Specialists: 4.0 (642.8 to 1)
Guidance Counselors: 6.2 (414.7 to 1)
Current Spending: ($ per student per year):
   Total: $6,451; Instruction: $3,748; Support Services: $2,422
Enrollment, Drop-out Rates and Diploma Recipients by Race/Ethnicity

Category	Total	White	Black	Asian	AIAN	Hisp.
Enrollment (%)	100.0	96.2	1.6	0.7	0.5	1.1
Drop-out Rate (%)	2.3	2.4	0.0	0.0	0.0	0.0
H.S. Diplomas (#)	182	178	0	2	2	0

Pleasant Hill R-III
301 N Mckissock • Pleasant Hill, MO 64080-1445
(816) 540-3161 • http://pleasanthillschools.com/
Grade Span: PK-12; **Agency Type:** 1
Schools: 4
   2 Primary; 1 Middle; 1 High; 0 Other Level
   4 Regular; 0 Special Education; 0 Vocational; 0 Alternative
   0 Magnet; 0 Charter; 1 Title I Eligible; 0 School-wide Title I
Students: 2,088 (53.2% male; 46.7% female)
   Individual Education Program: 309 (14.8%);
   English Language Learner: 0 (0.0%); Migrant: 0 (0.0%)
   Eligible for Free Lunch Program: 256 (12.3%)
   Eligible for Reduced-Price Lunch Program: 108 (5.2%)
Teachers: 124.0 (16.8 to 1)
Librarians/Media Specialists: 5.0 (417.6 to 1)
Guidance Counselors: 5.0 (417.6 to 1)
Current Spending: ($ per student per year):
   Total: $6,057; Instruction: $3,515; Support Services: $2,232
Enrollment, Drop-out Rates and Diploma Recipients by Race/Ethnicity

Category	Total	White	Black	Asian	AIAN	Hisp.
Enrollment (%)	100.0	97.0	0.8	0.3	0.7	1.3
Drop-out Rate (%)	2.6	2.7	0.0	0.0	n/a	0.0
H.S. Diplomas (#)	124	120	0	2	0	2

Raymore-Peculiar R-II
208 W Walnut • Raymore, MO 64083-8800
(816) 331-0050 • http://www.raypec.k12.mo.us/
Grade Span: PK-12; **Agency Type:** 1
Schools: 8

   4 Primary; 3 Middle; 1 High; 0 Other Level
   8 Regular; 0 Special Education; 0 Vocational; 0 Alternative
   0 Magnet; 0 Charter; 3 Title I Eligible; 0 School-wide Title I
Students: 4,885 (50.1% male; 49.8% female)
   Individual Education Program: 393 (8.0%);
   English Language Learner: 0 (0.0%); Migrant: 0 (0.0%)
   Eligible for Free Lunch Program: 627 (12.8%)
   Eligible for Reduced-Price Lunch Program: 230 (4.7%)
Teachers: 308.6 (15.8 to 1)
Librarians/Media Specialists: 8.5 (574.7 to 1)
Guidance Counselors: 11.0 (444.1 to 1)
Current Spending: ($ per student per year):
   Total: $5,779; Instruction: $3,362; Support Services: $2,083
Enrollment, Drop-out Rates and Diploma Recipients by Race/Ethnicity

Category	Total	White	Black	Asian	AIAN	Hisp.
Enrollment (%)	100.0	93.5	4.0	0.7	0.2	1.6
Drop-out Rate (%)	2.8	2.6	3.3	0.0	0.0	25.0
H.S. Diplomas (#)	259	249	5	1	2	2

Christian County

Nixa R-II
205 N St • Nixa, MO 65714-8663
(417) 725-7400 • http://www.nixa.k12.mo.us/
Grade Span: PK-12; **Agency Type:** 1
Schools: 8
   4 Primary; 3 Middle; 1 High; 0 Other Level
   8 Regular; 0 Special Education; 0 Vocational; 0 Alternative
   0 Magnet; 0 Charter; 4 Title I Eligible; 0 School-wide Title I
Students: 4,184 (50.5% male; 49.4% female)
   Individual Education Program: 516 (12.3%);
   English Language Learner: 12 (0.3%); Migrant: 8 (0.2%)
   Eligible for Free Lunch Program: 699 (16.7%)
   Eligible for Reduced-Price Lunch Program: 352 (8.4%)
Teachers: 282.0 (14.8 to 1)
Librarians/Media Specialists: 7.4 (565.4 to 1)
Guidance Counselors: 10.5 (398.5 to 1)
Current Spending: ($ per student per year):
   Total: $5,471; Instruction: $3,528; Support Services: $1,716
Enrollment, Drop-out Rates and Diploma Recipients by Race/Ethnicity

Category	Total	White	Black	Asian	AIAN	Hisp.
Enrollment (%)	100.0	95.5	1.1	0.8	0.4	2.2
Drop-out Rate (%)	2.6	2.6	0.0	0.0	0.0	7.7
H.S. Diplomas (#)	225	219	0	2	1	3

Ozark R-VI
302 N 4th Ave • Ozark, MO 65721-0166
Mailing Address: PO Box 166 • Ozark, MO 65721-0166
(417) 581-7694 • http://ozark.k12.mo.us/
Grade Span: PK-12; **Agency Type:** 1
Schools: 6
   3 Primary; 2 Middle; 1 High; 0 Other Level
   6 Regular; 0 Special Education; 0 Vocational; 0 Alternative
   0 Magnet; 0 Charter; 3 Title I Eligible; 0 School-wide Title I
Students: 4,135 (51.5% male; 48.4% female)
   Individual Education Program: 628 (15.2%);
   English Language Learner: 0 (0.0%); Migrant: 2 (<0.1%)
   Eligible for Free Lunch Program: 690 (16.7%)
   Eligible for Reduced-Price Lunch Program: 235 (5.7%)
Teachers: 252.5 (16.4 to 1)
Librarians/Media Specialists: 6.0 (689.2 to 1)
Guidance Counselors: 7.7 (537.0 to 1)
Current Spending: ($ per student per year):
   Total: $5,101; Instruction: $3,248; Support Services: $1,631
Enrollment, Drop-out Rates and Diploma Recipients by Race/Ethnicity

Category	Total	White	Black	Asian	AIAN	Hisp.
Enrollment (%)	100.0	97.4	0.6	0.5	0.5	1.1
Drop-out Rate (%)	1.4	1.4	0.0	0.0	0.0	0.0
H.S. Diplomas (#)	221	215	0	2	1	3

Clay County

Excelsior Springs 40
100 N Thompson Ave • Excelsior Springs, MO 64024-0248
Mailing Address: PO Box 248 • Excelsior Springs, MO 64024-0248
(816) 630-9200 • http://estigers.k12.mo.us/
Grade Span: PK-12; **Agency Type:** 1
Schools: 7
   3 Primary; 1 Middle; 3 High; 0 Other Level
   6 Regular; 0 Special Education; 1 Vocational; 0 Alternative
   0 Magnet; 0 Charter; 2 Title I Eligible; 0 School-wide Title I
Students: 3,269 (52.7% male; 47.2% female)
   Individual Education Program: 374 (11.4%);
   English Language Learner: 5 (0.2%); Migrant: 0 (0.0%)
   Eligible for Free Lunch Program: 876 (26.8%)

Eligible for Reduced-Price Lunch Program: 209 (6.4%)
Teachers: 206.0 (15.9 to 1)
Librarians/Media Specialists: 3.0 (1,089.7 to 1)
Guidance Counselors: 8.0 (408.6 to 1)
Current Spending: ($ per student per year):
Total: $6,467; Instruction: $3,891; Support Services: $2,367
Enrollment, Drop-out Rates and Diploma Recipients by Race/Ethnicity

Category	Total	White	Black	Asian	AIAN	Hisp.
Enrollment (%)	100.0	90.4	6.7	0.5	0.6	1.8
Drop-out Rate (%)	17.3	11.0	34.1	8.3	20.0	11.5
H.S. Diplomas (#)	316	240	68	3	1	4

Kearney R-I
1002 S Jefferson • Kearney, MO 64060-8520
(816) 628-4116 • http://www.kearney.k12.mo.us/default.htm
Grade Span: PK-12; **Agency Type:** 1
Schools: 7
4 Primary; 1 Middle; 1 High; 1 Other Level
7 Regular; 0 Special Education; 0 Vocational; 0 Alternative
0 Magnet; 0 Charter; 3 Title I Eligible; 0 School-wide Title I
Students: 3,379 (51.4% male; 48.5% female)
Individual Education Program: 379 (11.2%);
English Language Learner: 0 (0.0%); Migrant: 0 (0.0%)
Eligible for Free Lunch Program: 161 (4.8%)
Eligible for Reduced-Price Lunch Program: 58 (1.7%)
Teachers: 205.4 (16.5 to 1)
Librarians/Media Specialists: 4.5 (750.9 to 1)
Guidance Counselors: 7.0 (482.7 to 1)
Current Spending: ($ per student per year):
Total: $5,761; Instruction: $3,722; Support Services: $1,779
Enrollment, Drop-out Rates and Diploma Recipients by Race/Ethnicity

Category	Total	White	Black	Asian	AIAN	Hisp.
Enrollment (%)	100.0	97.7	0.5	0.4	0.2	1.2
Drop-out Rate (%)	2.7	2.7	0.0	0.0	0.0	0.0
H.S. Diplomas (#)	199	195	2	0	0	2

Liberty 53
650 Conistor Ln • Liberty, MO 64068-4202
(816) 415-5300 • http://liberty.k12.mo.us/
Grade Span: PK-12; **Agency Type:** 1
Schools: 14
8 Primary; 2 Middle; 2 High; 2 Other Level
12 Regular; 0 Special Education; 0 Vocational; 2 Alternative
0 Magnet; 0 Charter; 1 Title I Eligible; 0 School-wide Title I
Students: 7,874 (49.5% male; 50.4% female)
Individual Education Program: 927 (11.8%);
English Language Learner: 22 (0.3%); Migrant: 0 (0.0%)
Eligible for Free Lunch Program: 792 (10.1%)
Eligible for Reduced-Price Lunch Program: 227 (2.9%)
Teachers: 481.1 (16.4 to 1)
Librarians/Media Specialists: 12.4 (635.0 to 1)
Guidance Counselors: 19.5 (403.8 to 1)
Current Spending: ($ per student per year):
Total: $7,303; Instruction: $4,192; Support Services: $2,795
Enrollment, Drop-out Rates and Diploma Recipients by Race/Ethnicity

Category	Total	White	Black	Asian	AIAN	Hisp.
Enrollment (%)	100.0	91.0	4.6	1.1	0.6	2.7
Drop-out Rate (%)	2.2	2.2	2.6	0.0	0.0	2.5
H.S. Diplomas (#)	454	424	17	4	1	8

North Kansas City 74
2000 NE 46th St • Kansas City, MO 64116-2099
(816) 413-5000 • http://www.nkcsd.k12.mo.us/
Grade Span: PK-12; **Agency Type:** 1
Schools: 30
21 Primary; 5 Middle; 3 High; 1 Other Level
29 Regular; 0 Special Education; 0 Vocational; 1 Alternative
0 Magnet; 0 Charter; 4 Title I Eligible; 0 School-wide Title I
Students: 17,004 (51.0% male; 48.9% female)
Individual Education Program: 2,491 (14.6%);
English Language Learner: 484 (2.8%); Migrant: 0 (0.0%)
Eligible for Free Lunch Program: 3,382 (19.9%)
Eligible for Reduced-Price Lunch Program: 1,605 (9.4%)
Teachers: 1,213.7 (14.0 to 1)
Librarians/Media Specialists: 27.4 (620.6 to 1)
Guidance Counselors: 46.0 (369.7 to 1)
Current Spending: ($ per student per year):
Total: $7,042; Instruction: $4,545; Support Services: $2,244
Enrollment, Drop-out Rates and Diploma Recipients by Race/Ethnicity

Category	Total	White	Black	Asian	AIAN	Hisp.
Enrollment (%)	100.0	81.0	7.9	3.2	0.9	7.0
Drop-out Rate (%)	2.9	2.9	1.4	1.7	11.1	2.6
H.S. Diplomas (#)	1,137	954	63	47	20	53

Smithville R-II
645 S Commercial • Smithville, MO 64089-9381
(816) 532-0406 • http://www.smithville.k12.mo.us/
Grade Span: PK-12; **Agency Type:** 1
Schools: 4
2 Primary; 1 Middle; 1 High; 0 Other Level
4 Regular; 0 Special Education; 0 Vocational; 0 Alternative
0 Magnet; 0 Charter; 2 Title I Eligible; 0 School-wide Title I
Students: 1,877 (50.7% male; 49.2% female)
Individual Education Program: 209 (11.1%);
English Language Learner: 0 (0.0%); Migrant: 0 (0.0%)
Eligible for Free Lunch Program: 89 (4.7%)
Eligible for Reduced-Price Lunch Program: 59 (3.1%)
Teachers: 120.1 (15.6 to 1)
Librarians/Media Specialists: 5.0 (375.4 to 1)
Guidance Counselors: 5.0 (375.4 to 1)
Current Spending: ($ per student per year):
Total: $5,912; Instruction: $3,834; Support Services: $1,841
Enrollment, Drop-out Rates and Diploma Recipients by Race/Ethnicity

Category	Total	White	Black	Asian	AIAN	Hisp.
Enrollment (%)	100.0	95.5	0.4	1.3	0.9	2.0
Drop-out Rate (%)	2.3	2.4	0.0	0.0	0.0	0.0
H.S. Diplomas (#)	110	101	0	3	2	4

Clinton County

Cameron R-I
105 E Fifth St • Cameron, MO 64429-1714
(816) 632-2170 • http://www.cameron.k12.mo.us/
Grade Span: PK-12; **Agency Type:** 1
Schools: 5
2 Primary; 1 Middle; 2 High; 0 Other Level
5 Regular; 0 Special Education; 0 Vocational; 0 Alternative
0 Magnet; 0 Charter; 3 Title I Eligible; 0 School-wide Title I
Students: 1,705 (54.3% male; 45.6% female)
Individual Education Program: 301 (17.7%);
English Language Learner: 2 (0.1%); Migrant: 0 (0.0%)
Eligible for Free Lunch Program: 372 (21.8%)
Eligible for Reduced-Price Lunch Program: 125 (7.3%)
Teachers: 125.4 (13.6 to 1)
Librarians/Media Specialists: 3.0 (568.3 to 1)
Guidance Counselors: 4.3 (396.5 to 1)
Current Spending: ($ per student per year):
Total: $6,879; Instruction: $4,615; Support Services: $1,929
Enrollment, Drop-out Rates and Diploma Recipients by Race/Ethnicity

Category	Total	White	Black	Asian	AIAN	Hisp.
Enrollment (%)	100.0	96.1	1.6	1.0	0.7	0.6
Drop-out Rate (%)	2.6	2.7	0.0	0.0	0.0	0.0
H.S. Diplomas (#)	106	99	5	2	0	0

Cole County

Jefferson City
315 E Dunklin St • Jefferson City, MO 65101-3197
(573) 659-3000 • http://www.jcps.k12.mo.us/
Grade Span: PK-12; **Agency Type:** 1
Schools: 17
11 Primary; 2 Middle; 3 High; 1 Other Level
15 Regular; 0 Special Education; 1 Vocational; 1 Alternative
0 Magnet; 0 Charter; 7 Title I Eligible; 0 School-wide Title I
Students: 8,228 (50.8% male; 49.1% female)
Individual Education Program: 1,612 (19.6%);
English Language Learner: 266 (3.2%); Migrant: 0 (0.0%)
Eligible for Free Lunch Program: 2,330 (28.3%)
Eligible for Reduced-Price Lunch Program: 475 (5.8%)
Teachers: 570.3 (14.4 to 1)
Librarians/Media Specialists: 16.0 (514.3 to 1)
Guidance Counselors: 30.0 (274.3 to 1)
Current Spending: ($ per student per year):
Total: $6,520; Instruction: $4,317; Support Services: $1,847
Enrollment, Drop-out Rates and Diploma Recipients by Race/Ethnicity

Category	Total	White	Black	Asian	AIAN	Hisp.
Enrollment (%)	100.0	78.9	17.3	1.4	0.3	2.1
Drop-out Rate (%)	4.8	4.2	9.4	5.0	12.5	6.3
H.S. Diplomas (#)	509	453	48	4	2	2

Dallas County

Dallas County R-I
309 W Commercial • Buffalo, MO 65622-7567
(417) 345-2222 • http://www.dallasr1.k12.mo.us/
Grade Span: PK-12; **Agency Type:** 1
Schools: 5
2 Primary; 1 Middle; 2 High; 0 Other Level
4 Regular; 0 Special Education; 1 Vocational; 0 Alternative

0 Magnet; 0 Charter; 3 Title I Eligible; 1 School-wide Title I
Students: 2,018   (52.4% male; 47.5% female)
  Individual Education Program: 281 (13.9%);
  English Language Learner: 9 (0.4%); Migrant: 1 (<0.1%)
  Eligible for Free Lunch Program: 788 (39.0%)
  Eligible for Reduced-Price Lunch Program: 210 (10.4%)
Teachers: 149.6 (13.5 to 1)
Librarians/Media Specialists: 3.2 (630.6 to 1)
Guidance Counselors: 6.4 (315.3 to 1)
Current Spending: ($ per student per year):
  Total: $6,014; Instruction: $3,906; Support Services: $1,848
Enrollment, Drop-out Rates and Diploma Recipients by Race/Ethnicity

Category	Total	White	Black	Asian	AIAN	Hisp.
Enrollment (%)	100.0	96.7	0.2	0.3	0.8	1.9
Drop-out Rate (%)	5.9	5.4	n/a	0.0	37.5	0.0
H.S. Diplomas (#)	134	130	0	0	2	2

Dent County

Salem R-80
1400 W Third St • Salem, MO 65560-2730
(573) 729-6642 • http://www.salem.k12.mo.us/
Grade Span: PK-12; **Agency Type:** 1
Schools: 4
  1 Primary; 2 Middle; 1 High; 0 Other Level
  4 Regular; 0 Special Education; 0 Vocational; 0 Alternative
  0 Magnet; 0 Charter; 2 Title I Eligible; 2 School-wide Title I
Students: 1,501   (52.3% male; 47.6% female)
  Individual Education Program: 187 (12.5%);
  English Language Learner: 0 (0.0%); Migrant: 0 (0.0%)
  Eligible for Free Lunch Program: 488 (32.5%)
  Eligible for Reduced-Price Lunch Program: 90 (6.0%)
Teachers: 99.9 (15.0 to 1)
Librarians/Media Specialists: 3.0 (500.3 to 1)
Guidance Counselors: 5.0 (300.2 to 1)
Current Spending: ($ per student per year):
  Total: $5,951; Instruction: $3,900; Support Services: $1,737
Enrollment, Drop-out Rates and Diploma Recipients by Race/Ethnicity

Category	Total	White	Black	Asian	AIAN	Hisp.
Enrollment (%)	100.0	97.1	1.1	0.4	0.9	0.6
Drop-out Rate (%)	7.9	7.9	0.0	0.0	0.0	100.0
H.S. Diplomas (#)	128	127	1	0	0	0

Douglas County

Ava R-I
507 NE 3rd St • Ava, MO 65608-0338
Mailing Address: PO Box 338 • Ava, MO 65608-0338
(417) 683-4717
Grade Span: PK-12; **Agency Type:** 1
Schools: 3
  1 Primary; 1 Middle; 1 High; 0 Other Level
  3 Regular; 0 Special Education; 0 Vocational; 0 Alternative
  0 Magnet; 0 Charter; 2 Title I Eligible; 2 School-wide Title I
Students: 1,621   (50.5% male; 49.4% female)
  Individual Education Program: 216 (13.3%);
  English Language Learner: 0 (0.0%); Migrant: 5 (0.3%)
  Eligible for Free Lunch Program: 732 (45.2%)
  Eligible for Reduced-Price Lunch Program: 167 (10.3%)
Teachers: 110.9 (14.6 to 1)
Librarians/Media Specialists: 3.0 (540.3 to 1)
Guidance Counselors: 3.9 (415.6 to 1)
Current Spending: ($ per student per year):
  Total: $5,929; Instruction: $3,710; Support Services: $1,888
Enrollment, Drop-out Rates and Diploma Recipients by Race/Ethnicity

Category	Total	White	Black	Asian	AIAN	Hisp.
Enrollment (%)	100.0	98.5	0.5	0.2	0.3	0.5
Drop-out Rate (%)	1.0	1.0	n/a	0.0	n/a	0.0
H.S. Diplomas (#)	99	98	0	0	0	1

Dunklin County

Kennett 39
510 College Ave • Kennett, MO 63857-2006
(573) 717-1100 • http://www.kennett.k12.mo.us/
Grade Span: PK-12; **Agency Type:** 1
Schools: 9
  4 Primary; 1 Middle; 3 High; 1 Other Level
  7 Regular; 1 Special Education; 0 Vocational; 0 Alternative
  0 Magnet; 0 Charter; 4 Title I Eligible; 3 School-wide Title I
Students: 2,322   (50.1% male; 49.8% female)
  Individual Education Program: 341 (14.7%);
  English Language Learner: 22 (0.9%); Migrant: 66 (2.8%)
  Eligible for Free Lunch Program: 1,156 (49.8%)
  Eligible for Reduced-Price Lunch Program: 101 (4.3%)

Teachers: 148.3 (15.7 to 1)
Librarians/Media Specialists: 4.0 (580.5 to 1)
Guidance Counselors: 7.2 (322.5 to 1)
Current Spending: ($ per student per year):
  Total: $6,118; Instruction: $4,177; Support Services: $1,679
Enrollment, Drop-out Rates and Diploma Recipients by Race/Ethnicity

Category	Total	White	Black	Asian	AIAN	Hisp.
Enrollment (%)	100.0	69.5	27.3	0.5	0.1	2.7
Drop-out Rate (%)	4.2	4.4	2.8	n/a	0.0	14.3
H.S. Diplomas (#)	112	94	18	0	0	0

Franklin County

Meramec Valley R-III
126 N Payne St • Pacific, MO 63069-1224
(636) 271-1400 • http://info.csd.org/schools/meramec/
Grade Span: PK-12; **Agency Type:** 1
Schools: 9
  7 Primary; 1 Middle; 1 High; 0 Other Level
  9 Regular; 0 Special Education; 0 Vocational; 0 Alternative
  0 Magnet; 0 Charter; 5 Title I Eligible; 0 School-wide Title I
Students: 3,975   (52.8% male; 47.1% female)
  Individual Education Program: 640 (16.1%);
  English Language Learner: 0 (0.0%); Migrant: 3 (0.1%)
  Eligible for Free Lunch Program: 941 (23.7%)
  Eligible for Reduced-Price Lunch Program: 296 (7.4%)
Teachers: 223.3 (17.8 to 1)
Librarians/Media Specialists: 2.7 (1,472.2 to 1)
Guidance Counselors: 8.7 (456.9 to 1)
Current Spending: ($ per student per year):
  Total: $5,519; Instruction: $3,429; Support Services: $1,852
Enrollment, Drop-out Rates and Diploma Recipients by Race/Ethnicity

Category	Total	White	Black	Asian	AIAN	Hisp.
Enrollment (%)	100.0	95.9	2.5	0.4	0.4	0.8
Drop-out Rate (%)	3.9	3.9	6.9	0.0	0.0	0.0
H.S. Diplomas (#)	242	232	2	4	1	3

St. Clair R-XIII
905 Bardot St • St Clair, MO 63077-1700
(636) 629-3500 • http://stclair.k12.mo.us/
Grade Span: PK-12; **Agency Type:** 1
Schools: 5
  2 Primary; 1 Middle; 1 High; 1 Other Level
  4 Regular; 1 Special Education; 0 Vocational; 0 Alternative
  0 Magnet; 0 Charter; 3 Title I Eligible; 0 School-wide Title I
Students: 2,356   (52.3% male; 47.6% female)
  Individual Education Program: 370 (15.7%);
  English Language Learner: 0 (0.0%); Migrant: 0 (0.0%)
  Eligible for Free Lunch Program: 742 (31.5%)
  Eligible for Reduced-Price Lunch Program: 145 (6.2%)
Teachers: 159.8 (14.7 to 1)
Librarians/Media Specialists: 3.0 (785.3 to 1)
Guidance Counselors: 5.2 (453.1 to 1)
Current Spending: ($ per student per year):
  Total: $5,602; Instruction: $3,580; Support Services: $1,705
Enrollment, Drop-out Rates and Diploma Recipients by Race/Ethnicity

Category	Total	White	Black	Asian	AIAN	Hisp.
Enrollment (%)	100.0	97.4	2.0	0.3	0.1	0.2
Drop-out Rate (%)	3.8	3.9	0.0	0.0	n/a	0.0
H.S. Diplomas (#)	179	178	1	0	0	0

Sullivan
138 Taylor St • Sullivan, MO 63080-1936
(573) 468-5171 • http://eagles.k12.mo.us./
Grade Span: PK-12; **Agency Type:** 1
Schools: 4
  2 Primary; 1 Middle; 1 High; 0 Other Level
  4 Regular; 0 Special Education; 0 Vocational; 0 Alternative
  0 Magnet; 0 Charter; 2 Title I Eligible; 0 School-wide Title I
Students: 2,220   (54.2% male; 45.7% female)
  Individual Education Program: 366 (16.5%);
  English Language Learner: 2 (0.1%); Migrant: 0 (0.0%)
  Eligible for Free Lunch Program: 616 (27.7%)
  Eligible for Reduced-Price Lunch Program: 120 (5.4%)
Teachers: 141.4 (15.7 to 1)
Librarians/Media Specialists: 3.0 (740.0 to 1)
Guidance Counselors: 5.0 (444.0 to 1)
Current Spending: ($ per student per year):
  Total: $6,387; Instruction: $3,923; Support Services: $2,148
Enrollment, Drop-out Rates and Diploma Recipients by Race/Ethnicity

Category	Total	White	Black	Asian	AIAN	Hisp.
Enrollment (%)	100.0	98.4	0.1	0.1	0.2	1.1
Drop-out Rate (%)	4.9	4.9	n/a	0.0	n/a	n/a
H.S. Diplomas (#)	127	126	0	1	0	0

Union R-XI

770 Independence Dr • Union, MO 63084-0440
Mailing Address: PO Box 440 • Union, MO 63084-0440
(636) 583-8626 • http://union.k12.mo.us/
Grade Span: PK-12; Agency Type: 1
Schools: 5
   2 Primary; 2 Middle; 1 High; 0 Other Level
   5 Regular; 0 Special Education; 0 Vocational; 0 Alternative
   0 Magnet; 0 Charter; 3 Title I Eligible; 0 School-wide Title I
Students: 2,938 (51.2% male; 48.7% female)
   Individual Education Program: 406 (13.8%);
   English Language Learner: 5 (0.2%); Migrant: 0 (0.0%)
   Eligible for Free Lunch Program: 628 (21.4%)
   Eligible for Reduced-Price Lunch Program: 237 (8.1%)
Teachers: 194.0 (15.1 to 1)
Librarians/Media Specialists: 5.0 (587.6 to 1)
Guidance Counselors: 8.0 (367.3 to 1)
Current Spending: ($ per student per year):
   Total: $6,089; Instruction: $3,755; Support Services: $1,930
Enrollment, Drop-out Rates and Diploma Recipients by Race/Ethnicity

Category	Total	White	Black	Asian	AIAN	Hisp.
Enrollment (%)	100.0	98.0	1.1	0.3	0.0	0.6
Drop-out Rate (%)	3.6	3.6	0.0	0.0	n/a	12.5
H.S. Diplomas (#)	198	197	0	0	0	1

Washington

220 Locust St • Washington, MO 63090-0357
Mailing Address: PO Box 357 • Washington, MO 63090-0357
(636) 239-2727 • http://www.washington.k12.mo.us/
Grade Span: PK-12; Agency Type: 1
Schools: 12
   9 Primary; 1 Middle; 2 High; 0 Other Level
   11 Regular; 0 Special Education; 1 Vocational; 0 Alternative
   0 Magnet; 0 Charter; 1 Title I Eligible; 0 School-wide Title I
Students: 4,106 (52.1% male; 47.8% female)
   Individual Education Program: 959 (23.4%);
   English Language Learner: 53 (1.3%); Migrant: 2 (<0.1%)
   Eligible for Free Lunch Program: 453 (11.0%)
   Eligible for Reduced-Price Lunch Program: 216 (5.3%)
Teachers: 277.8 (14.8 to 1)
Librarians/Media Specialists: 4.5 (912.4 to 1)
Guidance Counselors: 9.6 (427.7 to 1)
Current Spending: ($ per student per year):
   Total: $6,369; Instruction: $3,918; Support Services: $2,169
Enrollment, Drop-out Rates and Diploma Recipients by Race/Ethnicity

Category	Total	White	Black	Asian	AIAN	Hisp.
Enrollment (%)	100.0	97.9	0.9	0.3	0.1	0.8
Drop-out Rate (%)	0.7	0.7	0.0	0.0	n/a	0.0
H.S. Diplomas (#)	281	278	1	0	0	2

Gasconade County

Gasconade County R-II

402 E Lincoln • Owensville, MO 65066-0536
Mailing Address: PO Box 536 • Owensville, MO 65066-0536
(573) 437-2177 • http://owensville.k12.mo.us/
Grade Span: KG-12; Agency Type: 1
Schools: 5
   3 Primary; 1 Middle; 1 High; 0 Other Level
   5 Regular; 0 Special Education; 0 Vocational; 0 Alternative
   0 Magnet; 0 Charter; 3 Title I Eligible; 0 School-wide Title I
Students: 1,976 (49.2% male; 50.7% female)
   Individual Education Program: 303 (15.3%);
   English Language Learner: 2 (0.1%); Migrant: 0 (0.0%)
   Eligible for Free Lunch Program: 453 (22.9%)
   Eligible for Reduced-Price Lunch Program: 193 (9.8%)
Teachers: 124.8 (15.8 to 1)
Librarians/Media Specialists: 4.9 (403.3 to 1)
Guidance Counselors: 6.0 (329.3 to 1)
Current Spending: ($ per student per year):
   Total: $6,249; Instruction: $4,009; Support Services: $1,942
Enrollment, Drop-out Rates and Diploma Recipients by Race/Ethnicity

Category	Total	White	Black	Asian	AIAN	Hisp.
Enrollment (%)	100.0	99.8	0.0	0.0	0.2	0.1
Drop-out Rate (%)	3.3	3.3	n/a	0.0	0.0	0.0
H.S. Diplomas (#)	147	146	0	0	1	0

Greene County

Logan-Rogersville R-VIII

104 N Beatie St • Rogersville, MO 65742-1001
(417) 753-2891 • http://www.greene-r8.k12.mo.us/index.htm
Grade Span: PK-12; Agency Type: 1
Schools: 4
   2 Primary; 1 Middle; 1 High; 0 Other Level

   4 Regular; 0 Special Education; 0 Vocational; 0 Alternative
   0 Magnet; 0 Charter; 2 Title I Eligible; 0 School-wide Title I
Students: 1,892 (54.1% male; 45.8% female)
   Individual Education Program: 281 (14.9%);
   English Language Learner: 0 (0.0%); Migrant: 0 (0.0%)
   Eligible for Free Lunch Program: 262 (13.8%)
   Eligible for Reduced-Price Lunch Program: 118 (6.2%)
Teachers: 118.5 (16.0 to 1)
Librarians/Media Specialists: 4.0 (473.0 to 1)
Guidance Counselors: 4.2 (450.5 to 1)
Current Spending: ($ per student per year):
   Total: $5,256; Instruction: $3,462; Support Services: $1,589
Enrollment, Drop-out Rates and Diploma Recipients by Race/Ethnicity

Category	Total	White	Black	Asian	AIAN	Hisp.
Enrollment (%)	100.0	97.9	0.7	0.1	0.3	1.0
Drop-out Rate (%)	1.5	1.5	n/a	n/a	0.0	0.0
H.S. Diplomas (#)	132	130	1	0	0	1

Republic R-III

518 N Hampton • Republic, MO 65738-1323
(417) 732-3605 • http://www.republic.k12.mo.us/
Grade Span: PK-12; Agency Type: 1
Schools: 6
   3 Primary; 2 Middle; 1 High; 0 Other Level
   6 Regular; 0 Special Education; 0 Vocational; 0 Alternative
   0 Magnet; 0 Charter; 4 Title I Eligible; 0 School-wide Title I
Students: 3,439 (49.4% male; 50.5% female)
   Individual Education Program: 441 (12.8%);
   English Language Learner: 0 (0.0%); Migrant: 0 (0.0%)
   Eligible for Free Lunch Program: 787 (22.9%)
   Eligible for Reduced-Price Lunch Program: 289 (8.4%)
Teachers: 182.2 (18.9 to 1)
Librarians/Media Specialists: 3.8 (905.0 to 1)
Guidance Counselors: 8.0 (429.9 to 1)
Current Spending: ($ per student per year):
   Total: $4,974; Instruction: $3,103; Support Services: $1,597
Enrollment, Drop-out Rates and Diploma Recipients by Race/Ethnicity

Category	Total	White	Black	Asian	AIAN	Hisp.
Enrollment (%)	100.0	97.3	1.2	0.5	0.2	0.8
Drop-out Rate (%)	3.4	3.4	0.0	0.0	0.0	0.0
H.S. Diplomas (#)	183	178	3	2	0	0

Springfield R-XII

940 N Jefferson • Springfield, MO 65802-3718
(417) 523-0000 • http://sps.k12.mo.us/
Grade Span: PK-12; Agency Type: 1
Schools: 55
   38 Primary; 9 Middle; 6 High; 2 Other Level
   52 Regular; 0 Special Education; 0 Vocational; 3 Alternative
   0 Magnet; 0 Charter; 23 Title I Eligible; 0 School-wide Title I
Students: 24,285 (51.2% male; 48.7% female)
   Individual Education Program: 3,180 (13.1%);
   English Language Learner: 181 (0.7%); Migrant: 133 (0.5%)
   Eligible for Free Lunch Program: 7,450 (30.7%)
   Eligible for Reduced-Price Lunch Program: 1,898 (7.8%)
Teachers: 1,455.5 (16.7 to 1)
Librarians/Media Specialists: 36.5 (665.3 to 1)
Guidance Counselors: 59.4 (408.8 to 1)
Current Spending: ($ per student per year):
   Total: $6,161; Instruction: $3,775; Support Services: $2,061
Enrollment, Drop-out Rates and Diploma Recipients by Race/Ethnicity

Category	Total	White	Black	Asian	AIAN	Hisp.
Enrollment (%)	100.0	88.6	6.1	2.2	0.6	2.4
Drop-out Rate (%)	4.9	4.7	6.8	3.2	15.4	7.6
H.S. Diplomas (#)	1,464	1,353	56	38	4	13

Willard R-II

460 E Kime St • Willard, MO 65781-7233
(417) 742-2584 • http://www.willard.k12.mo.us/
Grade Span: PK-12; Agency Type: 1
Schools: 6
   4 Primary; 1 Middle; 1 High; 0 Other Level
   6 Regular; 0 Special Education; 0 Vocational; 0 Alternative
   0 Magnet; 0 Charter; 4 Title I Eligible; 0 School-wide Title I
Students: 3,441 (50.1% male; 49.8% female)
   Individual Education Program: 615 (17.9%);
   English Language Learner: 16 (0.5%); Migrant: 5 (0.1%)
   Eligible for Free Lunch Program: 727 (21.1%)
   Eligible for Reduced-Price Lunch Program: 323 (9.4%)
Teachers: 235.4 (14.6 to 1)
Librarians/Media Specialists: 4.0 (860.3 to 1)
Guidance Counselors: 7.8 (441.2 to 1)
Current Spending: ($ per student per year):
   Total: $5,637; Instruction: $3,830; Support Services: $1,498

Enrollment, Drop-out Rates and Diploma Recipients by Race/Ethnicity

Category	Total	White	Black	Asian	AIAN	Hisp.
Enrollment (%)	100.0	98.3	0.6	0.2	0.1	0.8
Drop-out Rate (%)	2.7	2.7	16.7	0.0	0.0	0.0
H.S. Diplomas (#)	205	201	1	2	0	1

Henry County

Clinton
701 S 8th St · Clinton, MO 64735-2901
(660) 885-2237 · http://clinton.k12.mo.us/
Grade Span: PK-12; **Agency Type:** 1
Schools: 5
  2 Primary; 1 Middle; 2 High; 0 Other Level
  4 Regular; 0 Special Education; 1 Vocational; 0 Alternative
  0 Magnet; 0 Charter; 3 Title I Eligible; 0 School-wide Title I
Students: 2,081 (52.8% male; 47.1% female)
  Individual Education Program: 293 (14.1%);
  English Language Learner: 1 (<0.1%); Migrant: 0 (0.0%)
  Eligible for Free Lunch Program: 610 (29.3%)
  Eligible for Reduced-Price Lunch Program: 140 (6.7%)
Teachers: 157.5 (13.2 to 1)
Librarians/Media Specialists: 3.0 (693.7 to 1)
Guidance Counselors: 5.5 (378.4 to 1)
Current Spending: ($ per student per year):
  Total: $6,080; Instruction: $4,150; Support Services: $1,656
Enrollment, Drop-out Rates and Diploma Recipients by Race/Ethnicity

Category	Total	White	Black	Asian	AIAN	Hisp.
Enrollment (%)	100.0	95.6	3.2	0.1	0.1	1.0
Drop-out Rate (%)	4.4	4.5	0.0	0.0	n/a	0.0
H.S. Diplomas (#)	133	127	4	1	0	1

Howell County

West Plains R-VII
613 W First St · West Plains, MO 65775-2617
(417) 256-6150 · http://wphs.k12.mo.us/
Grade Span: PK-12; **Agency Type:** 1
Schools: 5
  2 Primary; 1 Middle; 2 High; 0 Other Level
  4 Regular; 0 Special Education; 1 Vocational; 0 Alternative
  0 Magnet; 0 Charter; 3 Title I Eligible; 2 School-wide Title I
Students: 2,504 (52.9% male; 47.0% female)
  Individual Education Program: 295 (11.8%);
  English Language Learner: 2 (0.1%); Migrant: 0 (0.0%)
  Eligible for Free Lunch Program: 993 (39.7%)
  Eligible for Reduced-Price Lunch Program: 169 (6.7%)
Teachers: 172.5 (14.5 to 1)
Librarians/Media Specialists: 3.0 (834.7 to 1)
Guidance Counselors: 8.0 (313.0 to 1)
Current Spending: ($ per student per year):
  Total: $6,945; Instruction: $4,577; Support Services: $2,079
Enrollment, Drop-out Rates and Diploma Recipients by Race/Ethnicity

Category	Total	White	Black	Asian	AIAN	Hisp.
Enrollment (%)	100.0	96.2	1.1	0.7	0.4	1.6
Drop-out Rate (%)	2.8	2.8	0.0	0.0	n/a	10.0
H.S. Diplomas (#)	265	260	1	1	0	3

Jackson County

Blue Springs R-IV
1801 NW Vesper · Blue Springs, MO 64015-3219
(816) 224-1300 ·
http://www.bluesprings-schools.net/bluesprings/gen/blue_springs_gener
ated_ns_pages/Home_Page_m1.html
Grade Span: PK-12; **Agency Type:** 1
Schools: 22
  13 Primary; 4 Middle; 3 High; 2 Other Level
  21 Regular; 1 Special Education; 0 Vocational; 0 Alternative
  0 Magnet; 0 Charter; 8 Title I Eligible; 0 School-wide Title I
Students: 13,297 (51.7% male; 48.2% female)
  Individual Education Program: 1,619 (12.2%);
  English Language Learner: 55 (0.4%); Migrant: 0 (0.0%)
  Eligible for Free Lunch Program: 1,053 (7.9%)
  Eligible for Reduced-Price Lunch Program: 440 (3.3%)
Teachers: 824.1 (16.1 to 1)
Librarians/Media Specialists: 13.0 (1,022.8 to 1)
Guidance Counselors: 35.8 (371.4 to 1)
Current Spending: ($ per student per year):
  Total: $6,604; Instruction: $4,107; Support Services: $2,220

Enrollment, Drop-out Rates and Diploma Recipients by Race/Ethnicity

Category	Total	White	Black	Asian	AIAN	Hisp.
Enrollment (%)	100.0	88.5	6.3	1.6	0.2	3.3
Drop-out Rate (%)	2.1	2.2	0.5	1.3	0.0	0.0
H.S. Diplomas (#)	808	730	33	23	3	19

Center 58
8701 Holmes Rd · Kansas City, MO 64131-2802
(816) 349-3300 · http://www.center.k12.mo.us/
Grade Span: PK-12; **Agency Type:** 1
Schools: 8
  5 Primary; 1 Middle; 2 High; 0 Other Level
  7 Regular; 0 Special Education; 0 Vocational; 1 Alternative
  0 Magnet; 0 Charter; 4 Title I Eligible; 3 School-wide Title I
Students: 2,743 (50.5% male; 49.4% female)
  Individual Education Program: 429 (15.6%);
  English Language Learner: 47 (1.7%); Migrant: 0 (0.0%)
  Eligible for Free Lunch Program: 1,232 (44.9%)
  Eligible for Reduced-Price Lunch Program: 168 (6.1%)
Teachers: 196.4 (14.0 to 1)
Librarians/Media Specialists: 4.0 (685.8 to 1)
Guidance Counselors: 7.3 (375.8 to 1)
Current Spending: ($ per student per year):
  Total: $9,181; Instruction: $5,163; Support Services: $3,743
Enrollment, Drop-out Rates and Diploma Recipients by Race/Ethnicity

Category	Total	White	Black	Asian	AIAN	Hisp.
Enrollment (%)	100.0	30.4	63.0	1.2	0.3	5.1
Drop-out Rate (%)	6.2	5.0	7.2	0.0	n/a	7.7
H.S. Diplomas (#)	155	49	97	0	1	8

Fort Osage R-I
2101 N Twyman Rd · Independence, MO 64058-3200
(816) 650-7000 · http://www.fortosage.k12.mo.us/
Grade Span: PK-12; **Agency Type:** 1
Schools: 10
  5 Primary; 2 Middle; 3 High; 0 Other Level
  9 Regular; 0 Special Education; 1 Vocational; 0 Alternative
  0 Magnet; 0 Charter; 4 Title I Eligible; 0 School-wide Title I
Students: 4,913 (52.9% male; 47.0% female)
  Individual Education Program: 771 (15.7%);
  English Language Learner: 8 (0.2%); Migrant: 0 (0.0%)
  Eligible for Free Lunch Program: 1,328 (27.0%)
  Eligible for Reduced-Price Lunch Program: 503 (10.2%)
Teachers: 331.0 (14.8 to 1)
Librarians/Media Specialists: 5.0 (982.6 to 1)
Guidance Counselors: 13.5 (363.9 to 1)
Current Spending: ($ per student per year):
  Total: $7,362; Instruction: $4,779; Support Services: $2,274
Enrollment, Drop-out Rates and Diploma Recipients by Race/Ethnicity

Category	Total	White	Black	Asian	AIAN	Hisp.
Enrollment (%)	100.0	88.0	5.4	2.6	0.7	3.3
Drop-out Rate (%)	0.3	0.2	0.0	0.0	0.0	3.1
H.S. Diplomas (#)	250	232	6	7	0	5

Grain Valley R-V
503 James Rollo Dr · Grain Valley, MO 64029-0304
Mailing Address: PO Box 304 · Grain Valley, MO 64029-0304
(816) 847-5006 · http://www.grainvalley.k12.mo.us/
Grade Span: PK-12; **Agency Type:** 1
Schools: 4
  2 Primary; 1 Middle; 1 High; 0 Other Level
  4 Regular; 0 Special Education; 0 Vocational; 0 Alternative
  0 Magnet; 0 Charter; 3 Title I Eligible; 0 School-wide Title I
Students: 2,164 (51.9% male; 48.0% female)
  Individual Education Program: 248 (11.5%);
  English Language Learner: 6 (0.3%); Migrant: 0 (0.0%)
  Eligible for Free Lunch Program: 240 (11.1%)
  Eligible for Reduced-Price Lunch Program: 68 (3.1%)
Teachers: 141.3 (15.3 to 1)
Librarians/Media Specialists: 5.0 (432.8 to 1)
Guidance Counselors: 4.4 (491.8 to 1)
Current Spending: ($ per student per year):
  Total: $5,641; Instruction: $3,329; Support Services: $2,041
Enrollment, Drop-out Rates and Diploma Recipients by Race/Ethnicity

Category	Total	White	Black	Asian	AIAN	Hisp.
Enrollment (%)	100.0	95.8	1.5	0.5	0.3	1.9
Drop-out Rate (%)	0.8	0.8	0.0	0.0	0.0	0.0
H.S. Diplomas (#)	90	88	1	0	0	1

Grandview C-4
724 Main St · Grandview, MO 64030-2329
(816) 316-5000 · http://www.csd4.k12.mo.us/
Grade Span: PK-12; **Agency Type:** 1
Schools: 10
  6 Primary; 1 Middle; 1 High; 2 Other Level

9 Regular; 0 Special Education; 0 Vocational; 1 Alternative
0 Magnet; 0 Charter; 5 Title I Eligible; 3 School-wide Title I
Students: 4,229 (51.9% male; 48.0% female)
Individual Education Program: 594 (14.0%);
English Language Learner: 118 (2.8%); Migrant: 0 (0.0%)
Eligible for Free Lunch Program: 1,608 (38.0%)
Eligible for Reduced-Price Lunch Program: 308 (7.3%)
Teachers: 321.9 (13.1 to 1)
Librarians/Media Specialists: 9.5 (445.2 to 1)
Guidance Counselors: 15.4 (274.6 to 1)
Current Spending: ($ per student per year):
Total: $8,360; Instruction: $5,182; Support Services: $2,780

Enrollment, Drop-out Rates and Diploma Recipients by Race/Ethnicity

Category	Total	White	Black	Asian	AIAN	Hisp.
Enrollment (%)	100.0	38.0	53.0	0.9	0.5	7.6
Drop-out Rate (%)	4.0	4.8	3.4	6.7	0.0	2.1
H.S. Diplomas (#)	220	97	112	9	0	2

Hickman Mills C-1
9000 Old Santa Fe Rd • Kansas City, MO 64138-3913
(816) 316-7000 • http://schoolweb.missouri.edu/hickman.k12.mo.us/
Grade Span: PK-12; **Agency Type:** 1
Schools: 16
9 Primary; 2 Middle; 2 High; 3 Other Level
15 Regular; 0 Special Education; 0 Vocational; 1 Alternative
0 Magnet; 0 Charter; 8 Title I Eligible; 0 School-wide Title I
Students: 7,250 (51.7% male; 48.2% female)
Individual Education Program: 1,121 (15.5%);
English Language Learner: 155 (2.1%); Migrant: 0 (0.0%)
Eligible for Free Lunch Program: 3,483 (48.0%)
Eligible for Reduced-Price Lunch Program: 788 (10.9%)
Teachers: 534.6 (13.6 to 1)
Librarians/Media Specialists: 8.0 (906.3 to 1)
Guidance Counselors: 21.5 (337.2 to 1)
Current Spending: ($ per student per year):
Total: $7,674; Instruction: $4,684; Support Services: $2,600

Enrollment, Drop-out Rates and Diploma Recipients by Race/Ethnicity

Category	Total	White	Black	Asian	AIAN	Hisp.
Enrollment (%)	100.0	20.4	74.0	1.2	0.3	4.1
Drop-out Rate (%)	4.2	6.1	3.4	5.3	0.0	7.8
H.S. Diplomas (#)	394	105	275	4	3	7

Independence 30
218 N Pleasant • Independence, MO 64050-2655
(816) 521-2700 • http://www.indep.k12.mo.us/
Grade Span: PK-12; **Agency Type:** 1
Schools: 21
14 Primary; 2 Middle; 3 High; 2 Other Level
21 Regular; 0 Special Education; 0 Vocational; 0 Alternative
0 Magnet; 0 Charter; 10 Title I Eligible; 6 School-wide Title I
Students: 12,193 (50.8% male; 49.1% female)
Individual Education Program: 1,526 (12.5%);
English Language Learner: 145 (1.2%); Migrant: 0 (0.0%)
Eligible for Free Lunch Program: 3,070 (25.2%)
Eligible for Reduced-Price Lunch Program: 1,014 (8.3%)
Teachers: 700.3 (17.4 to 1)
Librarians/Media Specialists: 19.5 (625.3 to 1)
Guidance Counselors: 29.0 (420.4 to 1)
Current Spending: ($ per student per year):
Total: $7,525; Instruction: $4,718; Support Services: $2,456

Enrollment, Drop-out Rates and Diploma Recipients by Race/Ethnicity

Category	Total	White	Black	Asian	AIAN	Hisp.
Enrollment (%)	100.0	83.5	7.3	2.7	0.9	5.6
Drop-out Rate (%)	4.3	4.1	7.0	4.9	6.9	3.6
H.S. Diplomas (#)	666	579	25	21	8	33

Kansas City 33
1211 Mcgee • Kansas City, MO 64106-2416
(816) 418-7000 • http://www.kcmsd.k12.mo.us/
Grade Span: PK-12; **Agency Type:** 1
Schools: 89
59 Primary; 11 Middle; 12 High; 7 Other Level
82 Regular; 1 Special Education; 2 Vocational; 4 Alternative
15 Magnet; 18 Charter; 80 Title I Eligible; 66 School-wide Title I
Students: 38,285 (50.4% male; 49.5% female)
Individual Education Program: 4,227 (11.0%);
English Language Learner: 3,102 (8.1%); Migrant: 238 (0.6%)
Eligible for Free Lunch Program: 23,478 (61.4%)
Eligible for Reduced-Price Lunch Program: 2,787 (7.3%)
Teachers: 2,600.9 (14.7 to 1)
Librarians/Media Specialists: 69.0 (554.2 to 1)
Guidance Counselors: 106.7 (358.4 to 1)
Current Spending: ($ per student per year):
Total: $9,183; Instruction: $4,986; Support Services: $3,811

Enrollment, Drop-out Rates and Diploma Recipients by Race/Ethnicity

Category	Total	White	Black	Asian	AIAN	Hisp.
Enrollment (%)	100.0	13.3	69.8	2.1	0.2	14.5
Drop-out Rate (%)	7.6	11.2	7.1	2.0	10.0	7.8
H.S. Diplomas (#)	1,409	159	1,115	50	2	83

Lee's Summit R-VII
600 SE Miller • Lee's Summit, MO 64063-4297
(816) 986-1000 • http://www.leesummit.k12.mo.us/
Grade Span: PK-12; **Agency Type:** 1
Schools: 22
16 Primary; 3 Middle; 2 High; 1 Other Level
21 Regular; 0 Special Education; 0 Vocational; 1 Alternative
0 Magnet; 0 Charter; 1 Title I Eligible; 0 School-wide Title I
Students: 15,862 (51.4% male; 48.5% female)
Individual Education Program: 1,909 (12.0%);
English Language Learner: 145 (0.9%); Migrant: 4 (<0.1%)
Eligible for Free Lunch Program: 1,102 (6.9%)
Eligible for Reduced-Price Lunch Program: 344 (2.2%)
Teachers: 956.9 (16.6 to 1)
Librarians/Media Specialists: 23.0 (689.7 to 1)
Guidance Counselors: 32.9 (482.1 to 1)
Current Spending: ($ per student per year):
Total: $7,209; Instruction: $4,595; Support Services: $2,323

Enrollment, Drop-out Rates and Diploma Recipients by Race/Ethnicity

Category	Total	White	Black	Asian	AIAN	Hisp.
Enrollment (%)	100.0	87.7	7.6	1.8	0.2	2.7
Drop-out Rate (%)	2.2	2.2	1.7	0.0	0.0	4.1
H.S. Diplomas (#)	956	895	36	8	2	15

Oak Grove R-VI
1305 SE Salem St • Oak Grove, MO 64075-7044
(816) 690-4156 • http://www.oakgrove.k12.mo.us/1024x768.htm
Grade Span: PK-12; **Agency Type:** 1
Schools: 4
2 Primary; 1 Middle; 1 High; 0 Other Level
4 Regular; 0 Special Education; 0 Vocational; 0 Alternative
0 Magnet; 0 Charter; 2 Title I Eligible; 0 School-wide Title I
Students: 1,974 (51.9% male; 48.0% female)
Individual Education Program: 255 (12.9%);
English Language Learner: 0 (0.0%); Migrant: 0 (0.0%)
Eligible for Free Lunch Program: 281 (14.2%)
Eligible for Reduced-Price Lunch Program: 117 (5.9%)
Teachers: 120.0 (16.5 to 1)
Librarians/Media Specialists: 4.0 (493.5 to 1)
Guidance Counselors: 5.0 (394.8 to 1)
Current Spending: ($ per student per year):
Total: $5,584; Instruction: $3,336; Support Services: $1,934

Enrollment, Drop-out Rates and Diploma Recipients by Race/Ethnicity

Category	Total	White	Black	Asian	AIAN	Hisp.
Enrollment (%)	100.0	98.2	0.6	0.4	0.1	0.7
Drop-out Rate (%)	2.3	1.8	0.0	0.0	0.0	150.0
H.S. Diplomas (#)	124	123	0	1	0	0

Raytown C-2
10500 E 60th Terr • Raytown, MO 64133-3999
(816) 268-7000 • http://www.raytown.k12.mo.us/
Grade Span: PK-12; **Agency Type:** 1
Schools: 17
10 Primary; 2 Middle; 3 High; 2 Other Level
14 Regular; 0 Special Education; 1 Vocational; 2 Alternative
0 Magnet; 0 Charter; 6 Title I Eligible; 0 School-wide Title I
Students: 8,902 (52.1% male; 47.8% female)
Individual Education Program: 1,072 (12.0%);
English Language Learner: 97 (1.1%); Migrant: 0 (0.0%)
Eligible for Free Lunch Program: 2,399 (26.9%)
Eligible for Reduced-Price Lunch Program: 790 (8.9%)
Teachers: 543.7 (16.4 to 1)
Librarians/Media Specialists: 7.7 (1,156.1 to 1)
Guidance Counselors: 21.7 (410.2 to 1)
Current Spending: ($ per student per year):
Total: $7,175; Instruction: $4,357; Support Services: $2,414

Enrollment, Drop-out Rates and Diploma Recipients by Race/Ethnicity

Category	Total	White	Black	Asian	AIAN	Hisp.
Enrollment (%)	100.0	59.3	34.7	1.3	0.4	4.3
Drop-out Rate (%)	5.1	5.2	4.3	2.9	9.1	9.2
H.S. Diplomas (#)	520	345	153	11	2	9

Jasper County

Carl Junction R-I
206 S Roney • Carl Junction, MO 64834-0004
Mailing Address: PO Box 4 • Carl Junction, MO 64834-0004
(417) 649-7026 • http://cj.k12.mo.us/
Grade Span: PK-12; **Agency Type:** 1
Schools: 6
    2 Primary; 2 Middle; 1 High; 1 Other Level
    5 Regular; 1 Special Education; 0 Vocational; 0 Alternative
    0 Magnet; 0 Charter; 4 Title I Eligible; 0 School-wide Title I
Students: 2,794 (52.8% male; 47.1% female)
    Individual Education Program: 435 (15.6%);
    English Language Learner: 14 (0.5%); Migrant: 0 (0.0%)
    Eligible for Free Lunch Program: 686 (24.6%)
    Eligible for Reduced-Price Lunch Program: 254 (9.1%)
Teachers: 182.8 (15.3 to 1)
Librarians/Media Specialists: 4.7 (594.5 to 1)
Guidance Counselors: 6.5 (429.8 to 1)
Current Spending: ($ per student per year):
    Total: $5,819; Instruction: $3,725; Support Services: $1,761
Enrollment, Drop-out Rates and Diploma Recipients by Race/Ethnicity

Category	Total	White	Black	Asian	AIAN	Hisp.
Enrollment (%)	100.0	96.9	0.5	0.4	1.3	0.9
Drop-out Rate (%)	3.9	4.0	0.0	0.0	0.0	0.0
H.S. Diplomas (#)	164	158	1	0	3	2

Carthage R-IX
710 Lyon St • Carthage, MO 64836-1700
(417) 359-7000 • http://carthage.k12.mo.us/
Grade Span: PK-12; **Agency Type:** 1
Schools: 8
    5 Primary; 1 Middle; 2 High; 0 Other Level
    7 Regular; 0 Special Education; 1 Vocational; 0 Alternative
    0 Magnet; 0 Charter; 5 Title I Eligible; 3 School-wide Title I
Students: 3,619 (51.6% male; 48.3% female)
    Individual Education Program: 486 (13.4%);
    English Language Learner: 234 (6.5%); Migrant: 208 (5.7%)
    Eligible for Free Lunch Program: 1,335 (36.9%)
    Eligible for Reduced-Price Lunch Program: 303 (8.4%)
Teachers: 245.5 (14.7 to 1)
Librarians/Media Specialists: 6.4 (565.5 to 1)
Guidance Counselors: 10.0 (361.9 to 1)
Current Spending: ($ per student per year):
    Total: $6,101; Instruction: $3,939; Support Services: $1,881
Enrollment, Drop-out Rates and Diploma Recipients by Race/Ethnicity

Category	Total	White	Black	Asian	AIAN	Hisp.
Enrollment (%)	100.0	81.8	2.3	0.3	0.9	14.6
Drop-out Rate (%)	6.2	5.7	9.5	0.0	9.1	14.3
H.S. Diplomas (#)	227	211	3	3	2	8

Joplin R-VIII
1717 E 15th St • Joplin, MO 64802-0128
Mailing Address: PO Box 128 • Joplin, MO 64802-0128
(417) 625-5200 • http://www.joplin.k12.mo.us/
Grade Span: PK-12; **Agency Type:** 1
Schools: 19
    14 Primary; 3 Middle; 2 High; 0 Other Level
    18 Regular; 0 Special Education; 1 Vocational; 0 Alternative
    0 Magnet; 0 Charter; 12 Title I Eligible; 3 School-wide Title I
Students: 7,432 (52.2% male; 47.7% female)
    Individual Education Program: 1,107 (14.9%);
    English Language Learner: 84 (1.1%); Migrant: 41 (0.6%)
    Eligible for Free Lunch Program: 3,128 (42.1%)
    Eligible for Reduced-Price Lunch Program: 575 (7.7%)
Teachers: 494.3 (15.0 to 1)
Librarians/Media Specialists: 11.0 (675.6 to 1)
Guidance Counselors: 17.0 (437.2 to 1)
Current Spending: ($ per student per year):
    Total: $5,864; Instruction: $3,723; Support Services: $1,870
Enrollment, Drop-out Rates and Diploma Recipients by Race/Ethnicity

Category	Total	White	Black	Asian	AIAN	Hisp.
Enrollment (%)	100.0	87.6	4.5	1.0	1.8	5.1
Drop-out Rate (%)	5.6	5.8	7.2	0.0	3.2	1.6
H.S. Diplomas (#)	306	277	13	6	3	7

Webb City R-VII
411 N Madison • Webb City, MO 64870-1238
(417) 673-6000 • http://www.wccards.k12.mo.us/
Grade Span: PK-12; **Agency Type:** 1
Schools: 10
    7 Primary; 2 Middle; 1 High; 0 Other Level
    10 Regular; 0 Special Education; 0 Vocational; 0 Alternative
    0 Magnet; 0 Charter; 8 Title I Eligible; 0 School-wide Title I
Students: 3,853 (50.7% male; 49.2% female)

    Individual Education Program: 478 (12.4%);
    English Language Learner: 15 (0.4%); Migrant: 25 (0.6%)
    Eligible for Free Lunch Program: 1,274 (33.1%)
    Eligible for Reduced-Price Lunch Program: 325 (8.4%)
Teachers: 230.6 (16.7 to 1)
Librarians/Media Specialists: 6.0 (642.2 to 1)
Guidance Counselors: 9.0 (428.1 to 1)
Current Spending: ($ per student per year):
    Total: $5,785; Instruction: $3,698; Support Services: $1,804
Enrollment, Drop-out Rates and Diploma Recipients by Race/Ethnicity

Category	Total	White	Black	Asian	AIAN	Hisp.
Enrollment (%)	100.0	92.5	2.1	0.7	1.6	3.1
Drop-out Rate (%)	5.9	6.1	0.0	0.0	0.0	5.0
H.S. Diplomas (#)	201	191	1	0	5	4

Jefferson County

Desoto 73
221 S Third • Desoto, MO 63020-2081
(636) 586-1000 • http://www.desotoschools.com/
Grade Span: KG-12; **Agency Type:** 1
Schools: 4
    2 Primary; 1 Middle; 1 High; 0 Other Level
    4 Regular; 0 Special Education; 0 Vocational; 0 Alternative
    0 Magnet; 0 Charter; 2 Title I Eligible; 0 School-wide Title I
Students: 2,773 (51.3% male; 48.6% female)
    Individual Education Program: 517 (18.6%);
    English Language Learner: 0 (0.0%); Migrant: 0 (0.0%)
    Eligible for Free Lunch Program: 809 (29.2%)
    Eligible for Reduced-Price Lunch Program: 144 (5.2%)
Teachers: 177.5 (15.6 to 1)
Librarians/Media Specialists: 2.9 (956.2 to 1)
Guidance Counselors: 7.4 (374.7 to 1)
Current Spending: ($ per student per year):
    Total: $6,771; Instruction: $3,863; Support Services: $2,656
Enrollment, Drop-out Rates and Diploma Recipients by Race/Ethnicity

Category	Total	White	Black	Asian	AIAN	Hisp.
Enrollment (%)	100.0	97.2	1.7	0.4	0.1	0.6
Drop-out Rate (%)	5.5	5.6	0.0	0.0	0.0	0.0
H.S. Diplomas (#)	188	186	2	0	0	0

Festus R-VI
1515 Mid-Meadow Ln • Festus, MO 63028-1598
(636) 937-4920 • http://info.csd.org/schools/festus/index.htm
Grade Span: KG-12; **Agency Type:** 1
Schools: 4
    1 Primary; 2 Middle; 1 High; 0 Other Level
    4 Regular; 0 Special Education; 0 Vocational; 0 Alternative
    0 Magnet; 0 Charter; 4 Title I Eligible; 0 School-wide Title I
Students: 2,770 (51.0% male; 48.9% female)
    Individual Education Program: 347 (12.5%);
    English Language Learner: 2 (0.1%); Migrant: 0 (0.0%)
    Eligible for Free Lunch Program: 634 (22.9%)
    Eligible for Reduced-Price Lunch Program: 145 (5.2%)
Teachers: 155.1 (17.9 to 1)
Librarians/Media Specialists: 4.0 (692.5 to 1)
Guidance Counselors: 6.5 (426.2 to 1)
Current Spending: ($ per student per year):
    Total: $5,402; Instruction: $3,612; Support Services: $1,496
Enrollment, Drop-out Rates and Diploma Recipients by Race/Ethnicity

Category	Total	White	Black	Asian	AIAN	Hisp.
Enrollment (%)	100.0	93.5	4.8	0.6	0.1	1.0
Drop-out Rate (%)	1.8	1.7	3.6	0.0	n/a	0.0
H.S. Diplomas (#)	161	152	8	1	0	0

Fox C-6
745 Jeffco Blvd • Arnold, MO 63010-1432
(636) 296-8000 • http://www.fox.k12.mo.us/
Grade Span: PK-12; **Agency Type:** 1
Schools: 17
    12 Primary; 3 Middle; 2 High; 0 Other Level
    17 Regular; 0 Special Education; 0 Vocational; 0 Alternative
    0 Magnet; 0 Charter; 9 Title I Eligible; 0 School-wide Title I
Students: 11,614 (52.1% male; 47.8% female)
    Individual Education Program: 1,988 (17.1%);
    English Language Learner: 69 (0.6%); Migrant: 0 (0.0%)
    Eligible for Free Lunch Program: 1,996 (17.2%)
    Eligible for Reduced-Price Lunch Program: 655 (5.6%)
Teachers: 712.2 (16.3 to 1)
Librarians/Media Specialists: 17.6 (659.9 to 1)
Guidance Counselors: 26.6 (436.6 to 1)
Current Spending: ($ per student per year):
    Total: $6,839; Instruction: $4,503; Support Services: $2,050

Enrollment, Drop-out Rates and Diploma Recipients by Race/Ethnicity

Category	Total	White	Black	Asian	AIAN	Hisp.
Enrollment (%)	100.0	97.6	1.0	0.6	0.1	0.8
Drop-out Rate (%)	3.9	3.9	0.0	0.0	0.0	8.7
H.S. Diplomas (#)	612	612	0	0	0	0

Hillsboro R-III
20 Hawk Dr • Hillsboro, MO 63050-5202
(636) 789-0060 • http://info.csd.org/schools/hills/home/hillsboro.htm
Grade Span: KG-12; **Agency Type:** 1
Schools: 6
  2 Primary; 2 Middle; 1 High; 1 Other Level
  5 Regular; 0 Special Education; 0 Vocational; 1 Alternative
  0 Magnet; 0 Charter; 4 Title I Eligible; 0 School-wide Title I
Students: 3,604 (50.9% male; 49.0% female)
  Individual Education Program: 520 (14.4%);
  English Language Learner: 17 (0.5%); Migrant: 0 (0.0%)
  Eligible for Free Lunch Program: 641 (17.8%)
  Eligible for Reduced-Price Lunch Program: 210 (5.8%)
Teachers: 205.0 (17.6 to 1)
Librarians/Media Specialists: 5.0 (720.8 to 1)
Guidance Counselors: 7.7 (468.1 to 1)
Current Spending: ($ per student per year):
  Total: $5,477; Instruction: $3,303; Support Services: $1,857

Enrollment, Drop-out Rates and Diploma Recipients by Race/Ethnicity

Category	Total	White	Black	Asian	AIAN	Hisp.
Enrollment (%)	100.0	98.8	0.3	0.2	0.2	0.5
Drop-out Rate (%)	2.8	2.8	0.0	0.0	0.0	0.0
H.S. Diplomas (#)	220	217	0	3	0	0

Northwest R-I
2843 Community Ln • House Springs, MO 63051-0500
Mailing Address: PO Box 500 • House Springs, MO 63051-0500
(636) 677-3473 • http://www.nwr1.k12.mo.us/
Grade Span: PK-12; **Agency Type:** 1
Schools: 11
  6 Primary; 4 Middle; 1 High; 0 Other Level
  11 Regular; 0 Special Education; 0 Vocational; 0 Alternative
  0 Magnet; 0 Charter; 6 Title I Eligible; 0 School-wide Title I
Students: 7,385 (51.2% male; 48.7% female)
  Individual Education Program: 1,343 (18.2%);
  English Language Learner: 25 (0.3%); Migrant: 0 (0.0%)
  Eligible for Free Lunch Program: 1,627 (22.0%)
  Eligible for Reduced-Price Lunch Program: 608 (8.2%)
Teachers: 458.8 (16.1 to 1)
Librarians/Media Specialists: 11.8 (625.8 to 1)
Guidance Counselors: 15.1 (489.1 to 1)
Current Spending: ($ per student per year):
  Total: $6,527; Instruction: $4,028; Support Services: $2,228

Enrollment, Drop-out Rates and Diploma Recipients by Race/Ethnicity

Category	Total	White	Black	Asian	AIAN	Hisp.
Enrollment (%)	100.0	98.4	0.5	0.5	0.1	0.5
Drop-out Rate (%)	2.8	2.8	0.0	0.0	0.0	11.1
H.S. Diplomas (#)	415	405	1	4	1	4

Windsor C-1
6208 Hwy 61-67 • Imperial, MO 63052-2311
(636) 464-4400 • http://www.windsor.k12.mo.us/district/
Grade Span: PK-12; **Agency Type:** 1
Schools: 4
  2 Primary; 1 Middle; 1 High; 0 Other Level
  4 Regular; 0 Special Education; 0 Vocational; 0 Alternative
  0 Magnet; 0 Charter; 3 Title I Eligible; 0 School-wide Title I
Students: 2,965 (53.4% male; 46.5% female)
  Individual Education Program: 411 (13.9%);
  English Language Learner: 9 (0.3%); Migrant: 1 (<0.1%)
  Eligible for Free Lunch Program: 472 (15.9%)
  Eligible for Reduced-Price Lunch Program: 225 (7.6%)
Teachers: 227.2 (13.1 to 1)
Librarians/Media Specialists: 5.0 (593.0 to 1)
Guidance Counselors: 7.0 (423.6 to 1)
Current Spending: ($ per student per year):
  Total: $7,189; Instruction: $4,518; Support Services: $2,375

Enrollment, Drop-out Rates and Diploma Recipients by Race/Ethnicity

Category	Total	White	Black	Asian	AIAN	Hisp.
Enrollment (%)	100.0	95.8	2.6	0.7	0.1	0.8
Drop-out Rate (%)	5.0	5.0	0.0	0.0	n/a	11.1
H.S. Diplomas (#)	193	190	0	1	0	2

Knob Noster R-VIII
401 E Wimer • Knob Noster, MO 65336-1444
(660) 563-3186 • http://knobnoster.k12.mo.us/
Grade Span: PK-12; **Agency Type:** 1
Schools: 4
  2 Primary; 1 Middle; 1 High; 0 Other Level
  4 Regular; 0 Special Education; 0 Vocational; 0 Alternative
  0 Magnet; 0 Charter; 2 Title I Eligible; 0 School-wide Title I
Students: 1,710 (51.9% male; 48.0% female)
  Individual Education Program: 270 (15.8%);
  English Language Learner: 47 (2.7%); Migrant: 103 (6.0%)
  Eligible for Free Lunch Program: 334 (19.5%)
  Eligible for Reduced-Price Lunch Program: 291 (17.0%)
Teachers: 129.4 (13.2 to 1)
Librarians/Media Specialists: 3.0 (570.0 to 1)
Guidance Counselors: 6.0 (285.0 to 1)
Current Spending: ($ per student per year):
  Total: $6,862; Instruction: $4,240; Support Services: $2,259

Enrollment, Drop-out Rates and Diploma Recipients by Race/Ethnicity

Category	Total	White	Black	Asian	AIAN	Hisp.
Enrollment (%)	100.0	78.1	12.2	3.6	1.0	5.2
Drop-out Rate (%)	3.9	4.0	1.7	0.0	0.0	9.4
H.S. Diplomas (#)	107	83	12	5	0	7

Warrensburg R-VI
438 E Market • Warrensburg, MO 64093-0638
Mailing Address: PO Box 638 • Warrensburg, MO 64093-0638
(660) 747-7823 • http://warrensburg.k12.mo.us/
Grade Span: PK-12; **Agency Type:** 1
Schools: 9
  3 Primary; 2 Middle; 3 High; 1 Other Level
  7 Regular; 0 Special Education; 1 Vocational; 1 Alternative
  0 Magnet; 0 Charter; 4 Title I Eligible; 0 School-wide Title I
Students: 3,208 (50.6% male; 49.3% female)
  Individual Education Program: 571 (17.8%);
  English Language Learner: 58 (1.8%); Migrant: 12 (0.4%)
  Eligible for Free Lunch Program: 656 (20.4%)
  Eligible for Reduced-Price Lunch Program: 175 (5.5%)
Teachers: 233.8 (13.7 to 1)
Librarians/Media Specialists: 5.0 (641.6 to 1)
Guidance Counselors: 8.0 (401.0 to 1)
Current Spending: ($ per student per year):
  Total: $6,412; Instruction: $4,010; Support Services: $2,177

Enrollment, Drop-out Rates and Diploma Recipients by Race/Ethnicity

Category	Total	White	Black	Asian	AIAN	Hisp.
Enrollment (%)	100.0	86.3	7.7	2.3	0.8	2.8
Drop-out Rate (%)	2.9	2.6	8.5	0.0	0.0	0.0
H.S. Diplomas (#)	217	200	8	1	1	7

Lebanon R-III
321 S Jefferson • Lebanon, MO 65536-3260
(417) 532-9141 • http://www.lebanon.k12.mo.us/
Grade Span: PK-12; **Agency Type:** 1
Schools: 8
  2 Primary; 3 Middle; 3 High; 0 Other Level
  6 Regular; 0 Special Education; 1 Vocational; 1 Alternative
  0 Magnet; 0 Charter; 3 Title I Eligible; 0 School-wide Title I
Students: 4,682 (51.5% male; 48.4% female)
  Individual Education Program: 544 (11.6%);
  English Language Learner: 6 (0.1%); Migrant: 0 (0.0%)
  Eligible for Free Lunch Program: 1,528 (32.6%)
  Eligible for Reduced-Price Lunch Program: 352 (7.5%)
Teachers: 268.9 (17.4 to 1)
Librarians/Media Specialists: 6.0 (780.3 to 1)
Guidance Counselors: 11.0 (425.6 to 1)
Current Spending: ($ per student per year):
  Total: $5,685; Instruction: $3,596; Support Services: $1,843

Enrollment, Drop-out Rates and Diploma Recipients by Race/Ethnicity

Category	Total	White	Black	Asian	AIAN	Hisp.
Enrollment (%)	100.0	96.7	0.7	1.2	0.0	1.4
Drop-out Rate (%)	3.3	3.3	0.0	0.0	0.0	0.0
H.S. Diplomas (#)	297	293	2	2	0	0

Odessa R-VII
701 S Third • Odessa, MO 64076-1453
(816) 633-5316 • http://odessa.k12.mo.us/
Grade Span: PK-12; **Agency Type:** 1
Schools: 4
  2 Primary; 1 Middle; 1 High; 0 Other Level

4 Regular; 0 Special Education; 0 Vocational; 0 Alternative
0 Magnet; 0 Charter; 2 Title I Eligible; 0 School-wide Title I
Students: 2,322   (53.7% male; 46.2% female)
 Individual Education Program: 303 (13.0%);
 English Language Learner: 8 (0.3%); Migrant: 0 (0.0%)
 Eligible for Free Lunch Program: 520 (22.4%)
 Eligible for Reduced-Price Lunch Program: 142 (6.1%)
Teachers: 158.5 (14.6 to 1)
Librarians/Media Specialists: 4.0 (580.5 to 1)
Guidance Counselors: 4.0 (580.5 to 1)
Current Spending: ($ per student per year):
 Total: $6,381; Instruction: $4,307; Support Services: $1,809
Enrollment, Drop-out Rates and Diploma Recipients by Race/Ethnicity

Category	Total	White	Black	Asian	AIAN	Hisp.
Enrollment (%)	100.0	96.7	1.9	0.2	0.3	0.9
Drop-out Rate (%)	2.1	2.0	6.3	0.0	0.0	0.0
H.S. Diplomas (#)	161	149	6	1	0	5

Lawrence County

Aurora R-VIII
409 W Locust St • Aurora, MO 65605-1422
(417) 678-3373 • http://www.hdnet.k12.mo.us/
Grade Span: PK-12; **Agency Type:** 1
Schools: 4
 1 Primary; 2 Middle; 1 High; 0 Other Level
 4 Regular; 0 Special Education; 0 Vocational; 0 Alternative
 0 Magnet; 0 Charter; 2 Title I Eligible; 2 School-wide Title I
Students: 2,127   (51.1% male; 48.8% female)
 Individual Education Program: 270 (12.7%);
 English Language Learner: 27 (1.3%); Migrant: 47 (2.2%)
 Eligible for Free Lunch Program: 779 (36.6%)
 Eligible for Reduced-Price Lunch Program: 167 (7.9%)
Teachers: 145.9 (14.6 to 1)
Librarians/Media Specialists: 3.0 (709.0 to 1)
Guidance Counselors: 5.3 (401.3 to 1)
Current Spending: ($ per student per year):
 Total: $6,239; Instruction: $3,832; Support Services: $2,093
Enrollment, Drop-out Rates and Diploma Recipients by Race/Ethnicity

Category	Total	White	Black	Asian	AIAN	Hisp.
Enrollment (%)	100.0	95.7	0.3	0.4	0.5	3.1
Drop-out Rate (%)	2.3	2.4	0.0	n/a	n/a	0.0
H.S. Diplomas (#)	106	105	1	0	0	0

Lincoln County

Troy R-III
951 W College • Troy, MO 63379-1112
(636) 462-6098 • http://www.troy.k12.mo.us/index.htm
Grade Span: PK-12; **Agency Type:** 1
Schools: 6
 4 Primary; 1 Middle; 1 High; 0 Other Level
 6 Regular; 0 Special Education; 0 Vocational; 0 Alternative
 0 Magnet; 0 Charter; 4 Title I Eligible; 0 School-wide Title I
Students: 5,105   (50.8% male; 49.1% female)
 Individual Education Program: 815 (16.0%);
 English Language Learner: 13 (0.3%); Migrant: 0 (0.0%)
 Eligible for Free Lunch Program: 1,186 (23.2%)
 Eligible for Reduced-Price Lunch Program: 247 (4.8%)
Teachers: 263.6 (19.4 to 1)
Librarians/Media Specialists: 4.0 (1,276.3 to 1)
Guidance Counselors: 9.2 (554.9 to 1)
Current Spending: ($ per student per year):
 Total: $5,250; Instruction: $3,282; Support Services: $1,668
Enrollment, Drop-out Rates and Diploma Recipients by Race/Ethnicity

Category	Total	White	Black	Asian	AIAN	Hisp.
Enrollment (%)	100.0	94.6	3.7	0.5	0.3	1.0
Drop-out Rate (%)	3.2	3.2	5.4	0.0	0.0	0.0
H.S. Diplomas (#)	287	282	3	1	0	1

Winfield R-IV
701 Elm St • Winfield, MO 63389-9511
(636) 668-8188
Grade Span: PK-12; **Agency Type:** 1
Schools: 4
 2 Primary; 1 Middle; 1 High; 0 Other Level
 4 Regular; 0 Special Education; 0 Vocational; 0 Alternative
 0 Magnet; 0 Charter; 2 Title I Eligible; 0 School-wide Title I
Students: 1,603   (51.5% male; 48.4% female)
 Individual Education Program: 264 (16.5%);
 English Language Learner: 0 (0.0%); Migrant: 0 (0.0%)
 Eligible for Free Lunch Program: 517 (32.3%)
 Eligible for Reduced-Price Lunch Program: 92 (5.7%)
Teachers: 101.8 (15.7 to 1)
Librarians/Media Specialists: 2.0 (801.5 to 1)

Guidance Counselors: 4.0 (400.8 to 1)
Current Spending: ($ per student per year):
 Total: $5,368; Instruction: $3,174; Support Services: $1,862
Enrollment, Drop-out Rates and Diploma Recipients by Race/Ethnicity

Category	Total	White	Black	Asian	AIAN	Hisp.
Enrollment (%)	100.0	96.9	1.4	0.3	0.6	0.7
Drop-out Rate (%)	6.5	6.3	50.0	0.0	0.0	0.0
H.S. Diplomas (#)	88	88	0	0	0	0

Livingston County

Chillicothe R-II
1020 Old Hwy 36 W • Chillicothe, MO 64601-0530
Mailing Address: PO Box 530 • Chillicothe, MO 64601-0530
(660) 646-4566 • http://www.chillicothe.k12.mo.us/
Grade Span: PK-12; **Agency Type:** 1
Schools: 7
 3 Primary; 2 Middle; 2 High; 0 Other Level
 6 Regular; 0 Special Education; 1 Vocational; 0 Alternative
 0 Magnet; 0 Charter; 4 Title I Eligible; 0 School-wide Title I
Students: 2,022   (51.2% male; 48.7% female)
 Individual Education Program: 371 (18.3%);
 English Language Learner: 0 (0.0%); Migrant: 0 (0.0%)
 Eligible for Free Lunch Program: 560 (27.7%)
 Eligible for Reduced-Price Lunch Program: 189 (9.3%)
Teachers: 146.3 (13.8 to 1)
Librarians/Media Specialists: 2.0 (1,011.0 to 1)
Guidance Counselors: 7.0 (288.9 to 1)
Current Spending: ($ per student per year):
 Total: $6,769; Instruction: $4,631; Support Services: $1,774
Enrollment, Drop-out Rates and Diploma Recipients by Race/Ethnicity

Category	Total	White	Black	Asian	AIAN	Hisp.
Enrollment (%)	100.0	96.6	2.5	0.5	0.0	0.4
Drop-out Rate (%)	3.3	2.9	30.0	0.0	n/a	0.0
H.S. Diplomas (#)	143	140	1	1	0	1

Madison County

Fredericktown R-I
803 E Hwy 72 • Fredericktown, MO 63645-9620
(573) 783-2570 • http://fredericktown.k12.mo.us/
Grade Span: PK-12; **Agency Type:** 1
Schools: 4
 2 Primary; 1 Middle; 1 High; 0 Other Level
 4 Regular; 0 Special Education; 0 Vocational; 0 Alternative
 0 Magnet; 0 Charter; 2 Title I Eligible; 0 School-wide Title I
Students: 2,005   (53.0% male; 46.9% female)
 Individual Education Program: 221 (11.0%);
 English Language Learner: 9 (0.4%); Migrant: 10 (0.5%)
 Eligible for Free Lunch Program: 637 (31.8%)
 Eligible for Reduced-Price Lunch Program: 206 (10.3%)
Teachers: 120.5 (16.6 to 1)
Librarians/Media Specialists: 3.0 (668.3 to 1)
Guidance Counselors: 5.5 (364.5 to 1)
Current Spending: ($ per student per year):
 Total: $6,036; Instruction: $4,010; Support Services: $1,729
Enrollment, Drop-out Rates and Diploma Recipients by Race/Ethnicity

Category	Total	White	Black	Asian	AIAN	Hisp.
Enrollment (%)	100.0	98.5	0.4	0.1	0.0	1.0
Drop-out Rate (%)	3.1	3.1	0.0	0.0	n/a	n/a
H.S. Diplomas (#)	114	114	0	0	0	0

Marion County

Hannibal 60
4650 Mcmasters Ave • Hannibal, MO 63401-2244
(573) 221-1258 • http://www.hannibal.k12.mo.us/
Grade Span: PK-12; **Agency Type:** 1
Schools: 8
 5 Primary; 1 Middle; 2 High; 0 Other Level
 7 Regular; 0 Special Education; 1 Vocational; 0 Alternative
 0 Magnet; 0 Charter; 5 Title I Eligible; 1 School-wide Title I
Students: 3,630   (50.1% male; 49.8% female)
 Individual Education Program: 614 (16.9%);
 English Language Learner: 4 (0.1%); Migrant: 1 (<0.1%)
 Eligible for Free Lunch Program: 1,494 (41.2%)
 Eligible for Reduced-Price Lunch Program: 319 (8.8%)
Teachers: 274.3 (13.2 to 1)
Librarians/Media Specialists: 4.0 (907.5 to 1)
Guidance Counselors: 14.0 (259.3 to 1)
Current Spending: ($ per student per year):
 Total: $6,069; Instruction: $3,975; Support Services: $1,732

Enrollment, Drop-out Rates and Diploma Recipients by Race/Ethnicity

Category	Total	White	Black	Asian	AIAN	Hisp.
Enrollment (%)	100.0	88.2	10.4	0.6	0.3	0.4
Drop-out Rate (%)	4.6	4.8	2.3	0.0	0.0	0.0
H.S. Diplomas (#)	210	192	16	2	0	0

Mcdonald County

Mcdonald County R-I
100 Mustang Dr • Anderson, MO 64831-7305
(417) 845-3321 • http://mcdonaldco.k12.mo.us/
Grade Span: PK-12; **Agency Type:** 1
Schools: 7
  6 Primary; 0 Middle; 1 High; 0 Other Level
  7 Regular; 0 Special Education; 0 Vocational; 0 Alternative
  0 Magnet; 0 Charter; 6 Title I Eligible; 6 School-wide Title I
Students: 3,554 (51.8% male; 48.1% female)
  Individual Education Program: 426 (12.0%);
  English Language Learner: 396 (11.1%); Migrant: 497 (14.0%)
  Eligible for Free Lunch Program: 1,661 (46.7%)
  Eligible for Reduced-Price Lunch Program: 336 (9.5%)
Teachers: 237.2 (15.0 to 1)
Librarians/Media Specialists: 4.0 (888.5 to 1)
Guidance Counselors: 8.5 (418.1 to 1)
Current Spending: ($ per student per year):
  Total: $5,495; Instruction: $3,632; Support Services: $1,504
Enrollment, Drop-out Rates and Diploma Recipients by Race/Ethnicity

Category	Total	White	Black	Asian	AIAN	Hisp.
Enrollment (%)	100.0	81.7	0.1	0.5	1.8	16.0
Drop-out Rate (%)	5.0	4.8	0.0	0.0	0.0	8.8
H.S. Diplomas (#)	152	143	0	1	0	8

Miller County

Eldon R-I
110 S Oak • Eldon, MO 65026-1576
(573) 392-8000 • http://www.eldon.k12.mo.us/
Grade Span: PK-12; **Agency Type:** 1
Schools: 5
  1 Primary; 2 Middle; 2 High; 0 Other Level
  4 Regular; 0 Special Education; 1 Vocational; 0 Alternative
  0 Magnet; 0 Charter; 3 Title I Eligible; 2 School-wide Title I
Students: 1,996 (51.5% male; 48.4% female)
  Individual Education Program: 265 (13.3%);
  English Language Learner: 0 (0.0%); Migrant: 0 (0.0%)
  Eligible for Free Lunch Program: 764 (38.3%)
  Eligible for Reduced-Price Lunch Program: 198 (9.9%)
Teachers: 150.0 (13.3 to 1)
Librarians/Media Specialists: 4.0 (499.0 to 1)
Guidance Counselors: 5.0 (399.2 to 1)
Current Spending: ($ per student per year):
  Total: $6,338; Instruction: $4,096; Support Services: $1,850
Enrollment, Drop-out Rates and Diploma Recipients by Race/Ethnicity

Category	Total	White	Black	Asian	AIAN	Hisp.
Enrollment (%)	100.0	98.1	0.6	0.2	0.1	1.0
Drop-out Rate (%)	3.9	4.0	0.0	0.0	0.0	0.0
H.S. Diplomas (#)	133	128	0	2	1	2

School of the Osage R-II
1501 School Rd • Lake Ozark, MO 65049-1960
Mailing Address: PO Box 1960 • Lake Ozark, MO 65049-1960
(573) 365-4091 • http://www.osage.k12.mo.us/
Grade Span: PK-12; **Agency Type:** 1
Schools: 4
  2 Primary; 1 Middle; 1 High; 0 Other Level
  4 Regular; 0 Special Education; 0 Vocational; 0 Alternative
  0 Magnet; 0 Charter; 4 Title I Eligible; 2 School-wide Title I
Students: 1,675 (51.9% male; 48.0% female)
  Individual Education Program: 222 (13.3%);
  English Language Learner: 2 (0.1%); Migrant: 0 (0.0%)
  Eligible for Free Lunch Program: 671 (40.1%)
  Eligible for Reduced-Price Lunch Program: 91 (5.4%)
Teachers: 118.5 (14.1 to 1)
Librarians/Media Specialists: 5.0 (335.0 to 1)
Guidance Counselors: 4.8 (349.0 to 1)
Current Spending: ($ per student per year):
  Total: $6,978; Instruction: $4,283; Support Services: $2,333
Enrollment, Drop-out Rates and Diploma Recipients by Race/Ethnicity

Category	Total	White	Black	Asian	AIAN	Hisp.
Enrollment (%)	100.0	96.5	0.7	0.7	0.4	1.8
Drop-out Rate (%)	2.5	2.3	0.0	0.0	0.0	14.3
H.S. Diplomas (#)	108	105	0	0	0	3

Morgan County

Morgan County R-II
913 W Newton • Versailles, MO 65084-1811
(573) 378-4231 • http://schoolweb.missouri.edu/morganr2.k12.mo.us/
Grade Span: PK-12; **Agency Type:** 1
Schools: 4
  2 Primary; 1 Middle; 1 High; 0 Other Level
  4 Regular; 0 Special Education; 0 Vocational; 0 Alternative
  0 Magnet; 0 Charter; 2 Title I Eligible; 2 School-wide Title I
Students: 1,569 (51.0% male; 48.9% female)
  Individual Education Program: 246 (15.7%);
  English Language Learner: 5 (0.3%); Migrant: 3 (0.2%)
  Eligible for Free Lunch Program: 624 (39.8%)
  Eligible for Reduced-Price Lunch Program: 198 (12.6%)
Teachers: 118.1 (13.3 to 1)
Librarians/Media Specialists: 4.6 (341.1 to 1)
Guidance Counselors: 5.0 (313.8 to 1)
Current Spending: ($ per student per year):
  Total: $5,743; Instruction: $3,683; Support Services: $1,755
Enrollment, Drop-out Rates and Diploma Recipients by Race/Ethnicity

Category	Total	White	Black	Asian	AIAN	Hisp.
Enrollment (%)	100.0	98.1	1.1	0.2	0.3	0.4
Drop-out Rate (%)	5.3	5.3	0.0	0.0	0.0	0.0
H.S. Diplomas (#)	109	108	0	1	0	0

New Madrid County

New Madrid County R-I
310 US Hwy 61 • New Madrid, MO 63869-9753
(573) 688-2161 •
http://schoolweb.missouri.edu/newmadridco.k12.mo.us/index-old.html
Grade Span: PK-12; **Agency Type:** 1
Schools: 6
  3 Primary; 1 Middle; 2 High; 0 Other Level
  5 Regular; 0 Special Education; 1 Vocational; 0 Alternative
  0 Magnet; 0 Charter; 4 Title I Eligible; 4 School-wide Title I
Students: 1,911 (52.5% male; 47.4% female)
  Individual Education Program: 348 (18.2%);
  English Language Learner: 0 (0.0%); Migrant: 3 (0.2%)
  Eligible for Free Lunch Program: 1,033 (54.1%)
  Eligible for Reduced-Price Lunch Program: 84 (4.4%)
Teachers: 153.2 (12.5 to 1)
Librarians/Media Specialists: 4.0 (477.8 to 1)
Guidance Counselors: 4.4 (434.3 to 1)
Current Spending: ($ per student per year):
  Total: $6,643; Instruction: $3,926; Support Services: $2,413
Enrollment, Drop-out Rates and Diploma Recipients by Race/Ethnicity

Category	Total	White	Black	Asian	AIAN	Hisp.
Enrollment (%)	100.0	63.5	36.2	0.0	0.1	0.3
Drop-out Rate (%)	4.5	3.0	6.8	n/a	n/a	0.0
H.S. Diplomas (#)	101	64	37	0	0	0

Newton County

East Newton County R-VI
22808 E Hwy 86 • Granby, MO 64844-9998
(417) 472-6231
Grade Span: PK-12; **Agency Type:** 1
Schools: 3
  2 Primary; 0 Middle; 1 High; 0 Other Level
  3 Regular; 0 Special Education; 0 Vocational; 0 Alternative
  0 Magnet; 0 Charter; 2 Title I Eligible; 2 School-wide Title I
Students: 1,550 (50.1% male; 49.8% female)
  Individual Education Program: 223 (14.4%);
  English Language Learner: 4 (0.3%); Migrant: 17 (1.1%)
  Eligible for Free Lunch Program: 606 (39.1%)
  Eligible for Reduced-Price Lunch Program: 159 (10.3%)
Teachers: 107.0 (14.5 to 1)
Librarians/Media Specialists: 3.0 (516.7 to 1)
Guidance Counselors: 3.4 (455.9 to 1)
Current Spending: ($ per student per year):
  Total: $6,055; Instruction: $3,829; Support Services: $1,926
Enrollment, Drop-out Rates and Diploma Recipients by Race/Ethnicity

Category	Total	White	Black	Asian	AIAN	Hisp.
Enrollment (%)	100.0	97.2	0.4	0.6	1.4	0.4
Drop-out Rate (%)	1.8	1.8	n/a	0.0	0.0	0.0
H.S. Diplomas (#)	91	91	0	0	0	0

Neosho R-V
511 Neosho Blvd • Neosho, MO 64850-2098
(417) 451-8600 • http://www.neosho.k12.mo.us/
Grade Span: PK-12; **Agency Type:** 1
Schools: 8
  5 Primary; 1 Middle; 1 High; 1 Other Level

8 Regular; 0 Special Education; 0 Vocational; 0 Alternative
0 Magnet; 0 Charter; 4 Title I Eligible; 4 School-wide Title I
Students: 4,502 (53.3% male; 46.6% female)
 Individual Education Program: 595 (13.2%);
 English Language Learner: 187 (4.2%); Migrant: 206 (4.6%)
 Eligible for Free Lunch Program: 1,632 (36.3%)
 Eligible for Reduced-Price Lunch Program: 457 (10.2%)
Teachers: 246.0 (18.3 to 1)
Librarians/Media Specialists: 5.0 (900.4 to 1)
Guidance Counselors: 7.5 (600.3 to 1)
Current Spending: ($ per student per year):
 Total: $5,265; Instruction: $3,511; Support Services: $1,488
Enrollment, Drop-out Rates and Diploma Recipients by Race/Ethnicity

Category	Total	White	Black	Asian	AIAN	Hisp.
Enrollment (%)	100.0	87.2	1.8	2.4	1.5	7.1
Drop-out Rate (%)	4.3	4.2	0.0	66.7	0.0	5.9
H.S. Diplomas (#)	238	221	6	3	2	6

Seneca R-VII
914 Frisco St • Seneca, MO 64865-0469
Mailing Address: PO Box 469 • Seneca, MO 64865-0469
(417) 776-3426 • http://schoolweb.missouri.edu/seneca.k12.mo.us/
Grade Span: PK-12; **Agency Type:** 1
Schools: 3
 1 Primary; 1 Middle; 1 High; 0 Other Level
 3 Regular; 0 Special Education; 0 Vocational; 0 Alternative
 0 Magnet; 0 Charter; 3 Title I Eligible; 0 School-wide Title I
Students: 1,689 (51.4% male; 48.5% female)
 Individual Education Program: 266 (15.7%);
 English Language Learner: 0 (0.0%); Migrant: 5 (0.3%)
 Eligible for Free Lunch Program: 487 (28.8%)
 Eligible for Reduced-Price Lunch Program: 222 (13.1%)
Teachers: 112.0 (15.1 to 1)
Librarians/Media Specialists: 3.0 (563.0 to 1)
Guidance Counselors: 4.5 (375.3 to 1)
Current Spending: ($ per student per year):
 Total: $6,373; Instruction: $3,518; Support Services: $2,540
Enrollment, Drop-out Rates and Diploma Recipients by Race/Ethnicity

Category	Total	White	Black	Asian	AIAN	Hisp.
Enrollment (%)	100.0	84.9	0.7	0.5	13.6	0.4
Drop-out Rate (%)	3.8	3.4	0.0	0.0	4.3	0.0
H.S. Diplomas (#)	91	81	0	1	9	0

Pemiscot County

Caruthersville 18
1711 Ward Ave • Caruthersville, MO 63830-2555
(573) 333-6100 • http://caruthersville.k12.mo.us/
Grade Span: PK-12; **Agency Type:** 1
Schools: 3
 1 Primary; 1 Middle; 1 High; 0 Other Level
 3 Regular; 0 Special Education; 0 Vocational; 0 Alternative
 0 Magnet; 0 Charter; 2 Title I Eligible; 2 School-wide Title I
Students: 1,722 (51.6% male; 48.3% female)
 Individual Education Program: 244 (14.2%);
 English Language Learner: 7 (0.4%); Migrant: 4 (0.2%)
 Eligible for Free Lunch Program: 1,008 (58.5%)
 Eligible for Reduced-Price Lunch Program: 66 (3.8%)
Teachers: 111.9 (15.4 to 1)
Librarians/Media Specialists: 4.0 (430.5 to 1)
Guidance Counselors: 4.0 (430.5 to 1)
Current Spending: ($ per student per year):
 Total: $5,699; Instruction: $3,945; Support Services: $1,493
Enrollment, Drop-out Rates and Diploma Recipients by Race/Ethnicity

Category	Total	White	Black	Asian	AIAN	Hisp.
Enrollment (%)	100.0	51.1	47.9	0.2	0.1	0.8
Drop-out Rate (%)	5.5	3.8	6.9	0.0	0.0	66.7
H.S. Diplomas (#)	81	46	34	0	0	1

Perry County

Perry County 32
326 College St • Perryville, MO 63775-2699
(573) 547-7500 • http://www.perryville.k12.mo.us/
Grade Span: PK-12; **Agency Type:** 1
Schools: 5
 2 Primary; 1 Middle; 2 High; 0 Other Level
 4 Regular; 0 Special Education; 1 Vocational; 0 Alternative
 0 Magnet; 0 Charter; 2 Title I Eligible; 1 School-wide Title I
Students: 2,300 (52.2% male; 47.7% female)
 Individual Education Program: 444 (19.3%);
 English Language Learner: 20 (0.9%); Migrant: 0 (0.0%)
 Eligible for Free Lunch Program: 645 (28.0%)
 Eligible for Reduced-Price Lunch Program: 184 (8.0%)
Teachers: 174.6 (13.2 to 1)

Librarians/Media Specialists: 3.0 (766.7 to 1)
Guidance Counselors: 8.5 (270.6 to 1)
Current Spending: ($ per student per year):
 Total: $6,347; Instruction: $3,782; Support Services: $2,261
Enrollment, Drop-out Rates and Diploma Recipients by Race/Ethnicity

Category	Total	White	Black	Asian	AIAN	Hisp.
Enrollment (%)	100.0	98.7	0.1	0.8	0.2	0.3
Drop-out Rate (%)	2.2	2.2	n/a	0.0	n/a	n/a
H.S. Diplomas (#)	173	173	0	0	0	0

Pettis County

Sedalia 200
400 W Fourth St • Sedalia, MO 65301-4296
(660) 829-6450 • http://sedalia.k12.mo.us/
Grade Span: PK-12; **Agency Type:** 1
Schools: 9
 6 Primary; 1 Middle; 1 High; 1 Other Level
 8 Regular; 0 Special Education; 0 Vocational; 1 Alternative
 0 Magnet; 0 Charter; 3 Title I Eligible; 0 School-wide Title I
Students: 4,515 (52.1% male; 47.8% female)
 Individual Education Program: 669 (14.8%);
 English Language Learner: 180 (4.0%); Migrant: 378 (8.4%)
 Eligible for Free Lunch Program: 1,559 (34.5%)
 Eligible for Reduced-Price Lunch Program: 363 (8.0%)
Teachers: 281.1 (16.1 to 1)
Librarians/Media Specialists: 6.8 (664.0 to 1)
Guidance Counselors: 12.0 (376.3 to 1)
Current Spending: ($ per student per year):
 Total: $5,456; Instruction: $3,309; Support Services: $1,860
Enrollment, Drop-out Rates and Diploma Recipients by Race/Ethnicity

Category	Total	White	Black	Asian	AIAN	Hisp.
Enrollment (%)	100.0	83.4	6.8	0.7	0.1	9.1
Drop-out Rate (%)	6.9	6.5	12.3	0.0	0.0	10.8
H.S. Diplomas (#)	233	208	13	1	0	11

Phelps County

Rolla 31
708 N Main St • Rolla, MO 65401-3023
(573) 458-0100 • http://rolla.k12.mo.us/index.html
Grade Span: PK-12; **Agency Type:** 1
Schools: 8
 3 Primary; 1 Middle; 3 High; 1 Other Level
 6 Regular; 0 Special Education; 2 Vocational; 0 Alternative
 0 Magnet; 0 Charter; 4 Title I Eligible; 0 School-wide Title I
Students: 4,084 (50.7% male; 49.2% female)
 Individual Education Program: 508 (12.4%);
 English Language Learner: 45 (1.1%); Migrant: 0 (0.0%)
 Eligible for Free Lunch Program: 1,198 (29.3%)
 Eligible for Reduced-Price Lunch Program: 303 (7.4%)
Teachers: 263.2 (15.5 to 1)
Librarians/Media Specialists: 6.0 (680.7 to 1)
Guidance Counselors: 13.8 (295.9 to 1)
Current Spending: ($ per student per year):
 Total: $6,800; Instruction: $4,320; Support Services: $2,113
Enrollment, Drop-out Rates and Diploma Recipients by Race/Ethnicity

Category	Total	White	Black	Asian	AIAN	Hisp.
Enrollment (%)	100.0	91.9	3.3	2.7	0.5	1.6
Drop-out Rate (%)	3.4	3.4	2.7	0.0	0.0	11.1
H.S. Diplomas (#)	297	271	9	13	0	4

St. James R-I
101 E Scioto St • St James, MO 65559-1717
(573) 265-3261 • http://stjames.k12.mo.us/index1024.html
Grade Span: PK-12; **Agency Type:** 1
Schools: 3
 1 Primary; 1 Middle; 1 High; 0 Other Level
 3 Regular; 0 Special Education; 0 Vocational; 0 Alternative
 0 Magnet; 0 Charter; 1 Title I Eligible; 1 School-wide Title I
Students: 1,828 (50.4% male; 49.5% female)
 Individual Education Program: 360 (19.7%);
 English Language Learner: 3 (0.2%); Migrant: 0 (0.0%)
 Eligible for Free Lunch Program: 656 (35.9%)
 Eligible for Reduced-Price Lunch Program: 173 (9.5%)
Teachers: 117.2 (15.6 to 1)
Librarians/Media Specialists: 3.6 (507.8 to 1)
Guidance Counselors: 5.5 (332.4 to 1)
Current Spending: ($ per student per year):
 Total: $6,172; Instruction: $4,022; Support Services: $1,860
Enrollment, Drop-out Rates and Diploma Recipients by Race/Ethnicity

Category	Total	White	Black	Asian	AIAN	Hisp.
Enrollment (%)	100.0	94.6	3.9	0.7	0.3	0.5
Drop-out Rate (%)	5.0	5.3	0.0	0.0	0.0	0.0
H.S. Diplomas (#)	126	122	1	3	0	0

Platte County

Park Hill
7703 NW Barry Rd • Kansas City, MO 64153-1731
(816) 741-1521 • http://www.parkhill.k12.mo.us/
Grade Span: PK-12; **Agency Type:** 1
Schools: 15
  9 Primary; 3 Middle; 2 High; 1 Other Level
  15 Regular; 0 Special Education; 0 Vocational; 0 Alternative
  0 Magnet; 0 Charter; 9 Title I Eligible; 0 School-wide Title I
Students: 9,970 (51.5% male; 48.4% female)
  Individual Education Program: 1,326 (13.3%);
  English Language Learner: 223 (2.2%); Migrant: 0 (0.0%)
  Eligible for Free Lunch Program: 1,091 (10.9%)
  Eligible for Reduced-Price Lunch Program: 453 (4.5%)
Teachers: 636.7 (15.7 to 1)
Librarians/Media Specialists: 15.0 (664.7 to 1)
Guidance Counselors: 23.0 (433.5 to 1)
Current Spending: ($ per student per year):
  Total: $7,827; Instruction: $4,645; Support Services: $2,802
Enrollment, Drop-out Rates and Diploma Recipients by Race/Ethnicity

Category	Total	White	Black	Asian	AIAN	Hisp.
Enrollment (%)	100.0	84.6	7.4	3.2	0.5	4.3
Drop-out Rate (%)	2.5	2.5	2.7	0.0	0.0	2.5
H.S. Diplomas (#)	640	570	34	19	4	13

Platte County R-III
1495 Branch & 92 Hwy • Platte City, MO 64079-1400
Mailing Address: PO Box 1400 • Platte City, MO 64079-1400
(816) 858-5420 • http://www.pcr3pirates.org/
Grade Span: PK-12; **Agency Type:** 1
Schools: 7
  3 Primary; 2 Middle; 2 High; 0 Other Level
  6 Regular; 0 Special Education; 1 Vocational; 0 Alternative
  0 Magnet; 0 Charter; 3 Title I Eligible; 0 School-wide Title I
Students: 2,444 (50.9% male; 49.0% female)
  Individual Education Program: 248 (10.1%);
  English Language Learner: 19 (0.8%); Migrant: 6 (0.2%)
  Eligible for Free Lunch Program: 302 (12.4%)
  Eligible for Reduced-Price Lunch Program: 106 (4.3%)
Teachers: 172.6 (14.2 to 1)
Librarians/Media Specialists: 3.6 (678.9 to 1)
Guidance Counselors: 7.2 (339.4 to 1)
Current Spending: ($ per student per year):
  Total: $7,027; Instruction: $4,667; Support Services: $2,144
Enrollment, Drop-out Rates and Diploma Recipients by Race/Ethnicity

Category	Total	White	Black	Asian	AIAN	Hisp.
Enrollment (%)	100.0	90.9	4.2	1.4	0.3	3.3
Drop-out Rate (%)	3.3	3.2	0.0	0.0	0.0	22.2
H.S. Diplomas (#)	148	140	5	0	0	3

Polk County

Bolivar R-I
524 W Madison • Bolivar, MO 65613-1945
(417) 326-5291 • http://www.bolivar-r1.k12.mo.us/
Grade Span: PK-12; **Agency Type:** 1
Schools: 6
  2 Primary; 1 Middle; 1 High; 2 Other Level
  5 Regular; 1 Special Education; 0 Vocational; 0 Alternative
  0 Magnet; 0 Charter; 2 Title I Eligible; 2 School-wide Title I
Students: 2,493 (52.2% male; 47.7% female)
  Individual Education Program: 392 (15.7%);
  English Language Learner: 9 (0.4%); Migrant: 0 (0.0%)
  Eligible for Free Lunch Program: 816 (32.7%)
  Eligible for Reduced-Price Lunch Program: 244 (9.8%)
Teachers: 183.5 (13.6 to 1)
Librarians/Media Specialists: 4.0 (623.3 to 1)
Guidance Counselors: 5.1 (488.8 to 1)
Current Spending: ($ per student per year):
  Total: $6,720; Instruction: $4,000; Support Services: $2,448
Enrollment, Drop-out Rates and Diploma Recipients by Race/Ethnicity

Category	Total	White	Black	Asian	AIAN	Hisp.
Enrollment (%)	100.0	96.7	1.4	0.3	0.4	1.3
Drop-out Rate (%)	4.0	4.1	0.0	0.0	0.0	0.0
H.S. Diplomas (#)	144	140	0	0	2	2

Pulaski County

Waynesville R-VI
200 Fleetwood Dr • Waynesville, MO 65583-2266
(573) 774-6497 • http://waynesville.k12.mo.us/
Grade Span: PK-12; **Agency Type:** 1
Schools: 12
  7 Primary; 2 Middle; 2 High; 1 Other Level

  11 Regular; 0 Special Education; 1 Vocational; 0 Alternative
  0 Magnet; 0 Charter; 6 Title I Eligible; 0 School-wide Title I
Students: 5,362 (51.1% male; 48.8% female)
  Individual Education Program: 767 (14.3%);
  English Language Learner: 51 (1.0%); Migrant: 0 (0.0%)
  Eligible for Free Lunch Program: 983 (18.3%)
  Eligible for Reduced-Price Lunch Program: 738 (13.8%)
Teachers: 379.0 (14.1 to 1)
Librarians/Media Specialists: 14.0 (383.0 to 1)
Guidance Counselors: 18.0 (297.9 to 1)
Current Spending: ($ per student per year):
  Total: $7,232; Instruction: $4,587; Support Services: $2,330
Enrollment, Drop-out Rates and Diploma Recipients by Race/Ethnicity

Category	Total	White	Black	Asian	AIAN	Hisp.
Enrollment (%)	100.0	63.9	23.8	4.1	1.0	7.2
Drop-out Rate (%)	2.7	2.8	2.0	1.8	0.0	5.1
H.S. Diplomas (#)	271	181	62	11	1	16

Randolph County

Moberly
926 Kwix Rd • Moberly, MO 65270-3813
(660) 269-2600 • http://www.moberly.k12.mo.us/
Grade Span: PK-12; **Agency Type:** 1
Schools: 7
  3 Primary; 1 Middle; 3 High; 0 Other Level
  6 Regular; 0 Special Education; 1 Vocational; 0 Alternative
  0 Magnet; 0 Charter; 3 Title I Eligible; 0 School-wide Title I
Students: 2,327 (51.6% male; 48.3% female)
  Individual Education Program: 435 (18.7%);
  English Language Learner: 8 (0.3%); Migrant: 0 (0.0%)
  Eligible for Free Lunch Program: 982 (42.2%)
  Eligible for Reduced-Price Lunch Program: 207 (8.9%)
Teachers: 175.2 (13.3 to 1)
Librarians/Media Specialists: 4.0 (581.8 to 1)
Guidance Counselors: 7.4 (314.5 to 1)
Current Spending: ($ per student per year):
  Total: $6,955; Instruction: $4,709; Support Services: $1,947
Enrollment, Drop-out Rates and Diploma Recipients by Race/Ethnicity

Category	Total	White	Black	Asian	AIAN	Hisp.
Enrollment (%)	100.0	88.6	10.0	0.8	0.2	0.5
Drop-out Rate (%)	6.3	5.1	13.9	0.0	n/a	33.3
H.S. Diplomas (#)	159	136	20	1	1	1

Ray County

Richmond R-XVI
749 Driskill Dr • Richmond, MO 64085-2202
(816) 776-6912 • http://richmond.k12.mo.us/
Grade Span: PK-12; **Agency Type:** 1
Schools: 4
  2 Primary; 1 Middle; 1 High; 0 Other Level
  4 Regular; 0 Special Education; 0 Vocational; 0 Alternative
  0 Magnet; 0 Charter; 2 Title I Eligible; 0 School-wide Title I
Students: 1,734 (51.7% male; 48.2% female)
  Individual Education Program: 243 (14.0%);
  English Language Learner: 0 (0.0%); Migrant: 2 (0.1%)
  Eligible for Free Lunch Program: 466 (26.9%)
  Eligible for Reduced-Price Lunch Program: 137 (7.9%)
Teachers: 119.4 (14.5 to 1)
Librarians/Media Specialists: 4.0 (433.5 to 1)
Guidance Counselors: 4.0 (433.5 to 1)
Current Spending: ($ per student per year):
  Total: $5,927; Instruction: $3,467; Support Services: $2,177
Enrollment, Drop-out Rates and Diploma Recipients by Race/Ethnicity

Category	Total	White	Black	Asian	AIAN	Hisp.
Enrollment (%)	100.0	94.1	4.3	0.3	0.3	0.9
Drop-out Rate (%)	2.7	2.6	6.3	0.0	0.0	0.0
H.S. Diplomas (#)	103	100	2	0	0	1

Ripley County

Doniphan R-I
309 Pine St • Doniphan, MO 63935-1703
(573) 996-3819 •
http://doniphanr1.k12.mo.us/education/district/district.php?sectionid=1
Grade Span: PK-12; **Agency Type:** 1
Schools: 4
  1 Primary; 1 Middle; 2 High; 0 Other Level
  3 Regular; 0 Special Education; 1 Vocational; 0 Alternative
  0 Magnet; 0 Charter; 3 Title I Eligible; 1 School-wide Title I
Students: 1,646 (47.8% male; 52.1% female)
  Individual Education Program: 271 (16.5%);
  English Language Learner: 0 (0.0%); Migrant: 0 (0.0%)
  Eligible for Free Lunch Program: 821 (49.9%)

Eligible for Reduced-Price Lunch Program: 169 (10.3%)
Teachers: 116.7 (14.1 to 1)
Librarians/Media Specialists: 2.0 (823.0 to 1)
Guidance Counselors: 5.0 (329.2 to 1)
Current Spending: ($ per student per year):
    Total: $5,796; Instruction: $3,966; Support Services: $1,569
Enrollment, Drop-out Rates and Diploma Recipients by Race/Ethnicity

Category	Total	White	Black	Asian	AIAN	Hisp.
Enrollment (%)	100.0	99.3	0.2	0.1	0.1	0.2
Drop-out Rate (%)	3.8	3.9	0.0	0.0	0.0	0.0
H.S. Diplomas (#)	116	116	0	0	0	0

Saline County

Marshall
860 W Vest • Marshall, MO 65340-2139
(660) 886-7414 • http://www.marshallschools.com/
Grade Span: PK-12; **Agency Type:** 1
Schools: 7
    4 Primary; 1 Middle; 2 High; 0 Other Level
    6 Regular; 0 Special Education; 1 Vocational; 0 Alternative
    0 Magnet; 0 Charter; 5 Title I Eligible; 0 School-wide Title I
Students: 2,430   (49.5% male; 50.4% female)
    Individual Education Program: 604 (24.9%);
    English Language Learner: 126 (5.2%); Migrant: 197 (8.1%)
    Eligible for Free Lunch Program: 978 (40.2%)
    Eligible for Reduced-Price Lunch Program: 190 (7.8%)
Teachers: 178.8 (13.6 to 1)
Librarians/Media Specialists: 3.3 (736.4 to 1)
Guidance Counselors: 4.9 (495.9 to 1)
Current Spending: ($ per student per year):
    Total: $6,945; Instruction: $4,993; Support Services: $1,663
Enrollment, Drop-out Rates and Diploma Recipients by Race/Ethnicity

Category	Total	White	Black	Asian	AIAN	Hisp.
Enrollment (%)	100.0	79.8	9.6	1.0	0.1	9.6
Drop-out Rate (%)	4.7	3.4	10.7	0.0	0.0	14.1
H.S. Diplomas (#)	181	161	10	2	0	8

Scott County

Sikeston R-VI
1002 Virginia • Sikeston, MO 63801-3347
(573) 472-2581 • http://www.sikeston.k12.mo.us/
Grade Span: PK-12; **Agency Type:** 1
Schools: 10
    5 Primary; 2 Middle; 2 High; 1 Other Level
    9 Regular; 0 Special Education; 1 Vocational; 0 Alternative
    0 Magnet; 0 Charter; 5 Title I Eligible; 0 School-wide Title I
Students: 3,833   (51.2% male; 48.7% female)
    Individual Education Program: 341 (8.9%);
    English Language Learner: 16 (0.4%); Migrant: 0 (0.0%)
    Eligible for Free Lunch Program: 1,924 (50.2%)
    Eligible for Reduced-Price Lunch Program: 176 (4.6%)
Teachers: 258.9 (14.8 to 1)
Librarians/Media Specialists: 5.5 (696.9 to 1)
Guidance Counselors: 14.0 (273.8 to 1)
Current Spending: ($ per student per year):
    Total: $5,820; Instruction: $3,668; Support Services: $1,866
Enrollment, Drop-out Rates and Diploma Recipients by Race/Ethnicity

Category	Total	White	Black	Asian	AIAN	Hisp.
Enrollment (%)	100.0	64.3	33.8	0.6	0.1	1.1
Drop-out Rate (%)	3.0	3.1	2.3	0.0	25.0	0.0
H.S. Diplomas (#)	210	158	50	1	0	1

St. Charles County

Francis Howell R-III
4545 Central School Rd • St Charles, MO 63304-7113
(636) 851-4000 • http://www.fhsd.k12.mo.us/
Grade Span: PK-12; **Agency Type:** 1
Schools: 23
    13 Primary; 5 Middle; 4 High; 1 Other Level
    21 Regular; 0 Special Education; 0 Vocational; 2 Alternative
    0 Magnet; 0 Charter; 8 Title I Eligible; 0 School-wide Title I
Students: 18,360   (51.8% male; 48.1% female)
    Individual Education Program: 2,890 (15.7%);
    English Language Learner: 160 (0.9%); Migrant: 0 (0.0%)
    Eligible for Free Lunch Program: 1,141 (6.2%)
    Eligible for Reduced-Price Lunch Program: 327 (1.8%)
Teachers: 1,188.1 (15.5 to 1)
Librarians/Media Specialists: 21.0 (874.3 to 1)
Guidance Counselors: 51.5 (356.5 to 1)
Current Spending: ($ per student per year):
    Total: $6,777; Instruction: $4,576; Support Services: $1,940

Enrollment, Drop-out Rates and Diploma Recipients by Race/Ethnicity

Category	Total	White	Black	Asian	AIAN	Hisp.
Enrollment (%)	100.0	92.6	4.4	1.5	0.3	1.3
Drop-out Rate (%)	2.8	2.6	6.8	7.1	0.0	8.1
H.S. Diplomas (#)	1,232	1,184	29	12	1	6

Ft. Zumwalt R-II
110 Virgil St • O'fallon, MO 63366-2637
(636) 240-2072 • http://www.fzschools.org/
Grade Span: PK-12; **Agency Type:** 1
Schools: 23
    15 Primary; 4 Middle; 4 High; 0 Other Level
    22 Regular; 0 Special Education; 0 Vocational; 1 Alternative
    0 Magnet; 0 Charter; 7 Title I Eligible; 0 School-wide Title I
Students: 18,138   (50.7% male; 49.2% female)
    Individual Education Program: 2,877 (15.9%);
    English Language Learner: 54 (0.3%); Migrant: 0 (0.0%)
    Eligible for Free Lunch Program: 1,297 (7.2%)
    Eligible for Reduced-Price Lunch Program: 539 (3.0%)
Teachers: 1,064.9 (17.0 to 1)
Librarians/Media Specialists: 24.5 (740.3 to 1)
Guidance Counselors: 44.3 (409.4 to 1)
Current Spending: ($ per student per year):
    Total: $6,168; Instruction: $3,700; Support Services: $2,233
Enrollment, Drop-out Rates and Diploma Recipients by Race/Ethnicity

Category	Total	White	Black	Asian	AIAN	Hisp.
Enrollment (%)	100.0	93.2	4.1	1.1	0.2	1.5
Drop-out Rate (%)	2.7	2.7	4.7	0.0	0.0	0.0
H.S. Diplomas (#)	1,073	1,030	25	9	1	8

St. Charles R-VI
1025 Country Club Rd • St Charles, MO 63303-3346
(636) 724-5840 • http://www.stcharles.k12.mo.us/
Grade Span: KG-12; **Agency Type:** 1
Schools: 12
    7 Primary; 2 Middle; 3 High; 0 Other Level
    11 Regular; 0 Special Education; 1 Vocational; 0 Alternative
    0 Magnet; 0 Charter; 6 Title I Eligible; 0 School-wide Title I
Students: 5,876   (52.2% male; 47.7% female)
    Individual Education Program: 985 (16.8%);
    English Language Learner: 125 (2.1%); Migrant: 71 (1.2%)
    Eligible for Free Lunch Program: 1,273 (21.7%)
    Eligible for Reduced-Price Lunch Program: 276 (4.7%)
Teachers: 447.3 (13.1 to 1)
Librarians/Media Specialists: 6.8 (864.1 to 1)
Guidance Counselors: 24.0 (244.8 to 1)
Current Spending: ($ per student per year):
    Total: $8,323; Instruction: $5,135; Support Services: $2,797
Enrollment, Drop-out Rates and Diploma Recipients by Race/Ethnicity

Category	Total	White	Black	Asian	AIAN	Hisp.
Enrollment (%)	100.0	85.6	8.5	1.4	0.2	4.4
Drop-out Rate (%)	3.3	3.1	7.1	2.9	n/a	6.9
H.S. Diplomas (#)	416	395	16	5	0	0

Wentzville R-IV
One Campus Dr • Wentzville, MO 63385-3415
(636) 327-3800 • http://wentzville.k12.mo.us/
Grade Span: PK-12; **Agency Type:** 1
Schools: 9
    5 Primary; 2 Middle; 2 High; 0 Other Level
    9 Regular; 0 Special Education; 0 Vocational; 0 Alternative
    0 Magnet; 0 Charter; 5 Title I Eligible; 0 School-wide Title I
Students: 7,788   (51.8% male; 48.1% female)
    Individual Education Program: 1,384 (17.8%);
    English Language Learner: 38 (0.5%); Migrant: 0 (0.0%)
    Eligible for Free Lunch Program: 1,075 (13.8%)
    Eligible for Reduced-Price Lunch Program: 315 (4.0%)
Teachers: 495.2 (15.7 to 1)
Librarians/Media Specialists: 8.1 (961.5 to 1)
Guidance Counselors: 19.7 (395.3 to 1)
Current Spending: ($ per student per year):
    Total: $6,548; Instruction: $3,848; Support Services: $2,326
Enrollment, Drop-out Rates and Diploma Recipients by Race/Ethnicity

Category	Total	White	Black	Asian	AIAN	Hisp.
Enrollment (%)	100.0	90.6	7.5	0.8	0.2	1.0
Drop-out Rate (%)	4.9	4.9	4.9	0.0	0.0	18.8
H.S. Diplomas (#)	342	323	15	0	0	4

St. Francois County

Central R-III
200 High St • Park Hills, MO 63601-2524
(573) 431-2616 • http://www.central-ph.k12.mo.us/
Grade Span: PK-12; **Agency Type:** 1
Schools: 4

2 Primary; 1 Middle; 1 High; 0 Other Level
4 Regular; 0 Special Education; 0 Vocational; 0 Alternative
0 Magnet; 0 Charter; 4 Title I Eligible; 0 School-wide Title I
Students: 1,873   (50.7% male; 49.2% female)
Individual Education Program: 336 (17.9%);
English Language Learner: 0 (0.0%); Migrant: 0 (0.0%)
Eligible for Free Lunch Program: 793 (42.3%)
Eligible for Reduced-Price Lunch Program: 248 (13.2%)
Teachers: 129.2 (14.5 to 1)
Librarians/Media Specialists: 5.0 (374.6 to 1)
Guidance Counselors: 4.5 (416.2 to 1)
Current Spending: ($ per student per year):
Total: $6,935; Instruction: $4,119; Support Services: $2,432
Enrollment, Drop-out Rates and Diploma Recipients by Race/Ethnicity

Category	Total	White	Black	Asian	AIAN	Hisp.
Enrollment (%)	100.0	96.5	2.6	0.5	0.0	0.4
Drop-out Rate (%)	1.9	2.0	0.0	0.0	n/a	n/a
H.S. Diplomas (#)	111	108	2	1	0	0

Farmington R-VII
1022 Ste Genevieve • Farmington, MO 63640-0570
Mailing Address: PO Box 570 • Farmington, MO 63640-0570
(573) 701-1300 • http://www.farmington.k12.mo.us/
Grade Span: PK-12; **Agency Type:** 1
Schools: 10
5 Primary; 2 Middle; 1 High; 2 Other Level
10 Regular; 0 Special Education; 0 Vocational; 0 Alternative
0 Magnet; 0 Charter; 4 Title I Eligible; 0 School-wide Title I
Students: 3,863   (51.8% male; 48.1% female)
Individual Education Program: 654 (16.9%);
English Language Learner: 9 (0.2%); Migrant: 0 (0.0%)
Eligible for Free Lunch Program: 1,175 (30.4%)
Eligible for Reduced-Price Lunch Program: 372 (9.6%)
Teachers: 245.7 (15.7 to 1)
Librarians/Media Specialists: 6.0 (643.8 to 1)
Guidance Counselors: 9.0 (429.2 to 1)
Current Spending: ($ per student per year):
Total: $6,316; Instruction: $3,689; Support Services: $2,308
Enrollment, Drop-out Rates and Diploma Recipients by Race/Ethnicity

Category	Total	White	Black	Asian	AIAN	Hisp.
Enrollment (%)	100.0	96.4	2.1	0.6	0.2	0.7
Drop-out Rate (%)	2.5	2.6	0.0	0.0	n/a	0.0
H.S. Diplomas (#)	244	241	3	0	0	0

North St. Francois Co. R-I
300 Berry Rd • Bonne Terre, MO 63628-4388
(573) 358-2247 • http://ncsd.k12.mo.us/
Grade Span: PK-12; **Agency Type:** 1
Schools: 7
3 Primary; 2 Middle; 2 High; 0 Other Level
6 Regular; 0 Special Education; 1 Vocational; 0 Alternative
0 Magnet; 0 Charter; 2 Title I Eligible; 0 School-wide Title I
Students: 3,231   (53.2% male; 46.7% female)
Individual Education Program: 491 (15.2%);
English Language Learner: 0 (0.0%); Migrant: 0 (0.0%)
Eligible for Free Lunch Program: 1,025 (31.7%)
Eligible for Reduced-Price Lunch Program: 281 (8.7%)
Teachers: 217.1 (14.9 to 1)
Librarians/Media Specialists: 5.0 (646.2 to 1)
Guidance Counselors: 8.3 (389.3 to 1)
Current Spending: ($ per student per year):
Total: $6,092; Instruction: $3,665; Support Services: $2,070
Enrollment, Drop-out Rates and Diploma Recipients by Race/Ethnicity

Category	Total	White	Black	Asian	AIAN	Hisp.
Enrollment (%)	100.0	98.5	0.5	0.3	0.1	0.5
Drop-out Rate (%)	3.2	3.2	0.0	0.0	n/a	0.0
H.S. Diplomas (#)	223	222	1	0	0	0

St. Louis County

Affton 101
8701 Mackenzie Rd • St Louis, MO 63123-3436
(314) 638-8770 • http://info.csd.org/affton.htm
Grade Span: KG-12; **Agency Type:** 1
Schools: 4
2 Primary; 1 Middle; 1 High; 0 Other Level
4 Regular; 0 Special Education; 0 Vocational; 0 Alternative
0 Magnet; 0 Charter; 1 Title I Eligible; 0 School-wide Title I
Students: 2,526   (50.4% male; 49.5% female)
Individual Education Program: 560 (22.2%);
English Language Learner: 127 (5.0%); Migrant: 0 (0.0%)
Eligible for Free Lunch Program: 329 (13.0%)
Eligible for Reduced-Price Lunch Program: 114 (4.5%)
Teachers: 153.5 (16.5 to 1)
Librarians/Media Specialists: 5.0 (505.2 to 1)
Guidance Counselors: 7.9 (319.7 to 1)

Bayless
4530 Weber Rd • St Louis, MO 63123-5798
(314) 631-2244
Grade Span: PK-12; **Agency Type:** 1
Schools: 4
2 Primary; 1 Middle; 1 High; 0 Other Level
4 Regular; 0 Special Education; 0 Vocational; 0 Alternative
0 Magnet; 0 Charter; 4 Title I Eligible; 0 School-wide Title I
Students: 1,616   (49.0% male; 50.9% female)
Individual Education Program: 298 (18.4%);
English Language Learner: 203 (12.6%); Migrant: 0 (0.0%)
Eligible for Free Lunch Program: 355 (22.0%)
Eligible for Reduced-Price Lunch Program: 252 (15.6%)
Teachers: 86.2 (18.7 to 1)
Librarians/Media Specialists: 3.9 (414.4 to 1)
Guidance Counselors: 5.0 (323.2 to 1)
Current Spending: ($ per student per year):
Total: $5,477; Instruction: $3,067; Support Services: $2,113
Enrollment, Drop-out Rates and Diploma Recipients by Race/Ethnicity

Category	Total	White	Black	Asian	AIAN	Hisp.
Enrollment (%)	100.0	79.0	14.0	4.2	0.4	2.4
Drop-out Rate (%)	2.7	3.1	0.0	0.0	n/a	0.0
H.S. Diplomas (#)	94	81	8	1	0	4

Clayton
2 Mark Twain Cir • Clayton, MO 63105-1613
(314) 854-6000 • http://www.clayton.k12.mo.us/
Grade Span: PK-12; **Agency Type:** 1
Schools: 6
4 Primary; 1 Middle; 1 High; 0 Other Level
5 Regular; 0 Special Education; 0 Vocational; 1 Alternative
0 Magnet; 0 Charter; 2 Title I Eligible; 0 School-wide Title I
Students: 2,687   (51.2% male; 48.7% female)
Individual Education Program: 430 (16.0%);
English Language Learner: 114 (4.2%); Migrant: 0 (0.0%)
Eligible for Free Lunch Program: 110 (4.1%)
Eligible for Reduced-Price Lunch Program: 42 (1.6%)
Teachers: 225.0 (11.9 to 1)
Librarians/Media Specialists: 8.4 (319.9 to 1)
Guidance Counselors: 11.0 (244.3 to 1)
Current Spending: ($ per student per year):
Total: $13,872; Instruction: $8,002; Support Services: $5,426
Enrollment, Drop-out Rates and Diploma Recipients by Race/Ethnicity

Category	Total	White	Black	Asian	AIAN	Hisp.
Enrollment (%)	100.0	68.4	21.9	7.7	0.4	1.6
Drop-out Rate (%)	1.3	1.3	1.8	0.0	0.0	0.0
H.S. Diplomas (#)	189	135	35	18	0	1

Ferguson-Florissant R-II
1005 Waterford Dr • Florissant, MO 63033-3694
(314) 506-9000 • http://www.fergflor.k12.mo.us/index.htm
Grade Span: PK-12; **Agency Type:** 1
Schools: 25
18 Primary; 3 Middle; 3 High; 1 Other Level
24 Regular; 0 Special Education; 0 Vocational; 1 Alternative
0 Magnet; 0 Charter; 15 Title I Eligible; 5 School-wide Title I
Students: 13,335   (51.6% male; 48.3% female)
Individual Education Program: 2,415 (18.1%);
English Language Learner: 77 (0.6%); Migrant: 0 (0.0%)
Eligible for Free Lunch Program: 5,448 (40.9%)
Eligible for Reduced-Price Lunch Program: 1,083 (8.1%)
Teachers: 815.4 (16.4 to 1)
Librarians/Media Specialists: 25.0 (533.4 to 1)
Guidance Counselors: 33.2 (401.7 to 1)
Current Spending: ($ per student per year):
Total: $7,888; Instruction: $4,588; Support Services: $3,001
Enrollment, Drop-out Rates and Diploma Recipients by Race/Ethnicity

Category	Total	White	Black	Asian	AIAN	Hisp.
Enrollment (%)	100.0	30.9	66.6	0.8	0.2	1.5
Drop-out Rate (%)	1.3	1.6	1.0	0.0	0.0	0.0
H.S. Diplomas (#)	694	320	361	5	0	8

Hancock Place
9101 S Broadway • St Louis, MO 63125-1516
(314) 544-1300 • http://hancock.k12.mo.us/index.html
Grade Span: PK-12; **Agency Type:** 1
Schools: 3

1 Primary; 1 Middle; 1 High; 0 Other Level
3 Regular; 0 Special Education; 0 Vocational; 0 Alternative
0 Magnet; 0 Charter; 1 Title I Eligible; 0 School-wide Title I
Students: 1,816 (50.6% male; 49.3% female)
Individual Education Program: 337 (18.6%);
English Language Learner: 80 (4.4%); Migrant: 0 (0.0%)
Eligible for Free Lunch Program: 818 (45.0%)
Eligible for Reduced-Price Lunch Program: 213 (11.7%)
Teachers: 117.1 (15.5 to 1)
Librarians/Media Specialists: 2.0 (908.0 to 1)
Guidance Counselors: 5.0 (363.2 to 1)
Current Spending: ($ per student per year):
Total: $6,070; Instruction: $3,896; Support Services: $1,879
Enrollment, Drop-out Rates and Diploma Recipients by Race/Ethnicity

Category	Total	White	Black	Asian	AIAN	Hisp.
Enrollment (%)	100.0	77.9	19.8	0.3	0.2	1.8
Drop-out Rate (%)	4.6	5.1	3.4	0.0	n/a	0.0
H.S. Diplomas (#)	77	62	14	0	0	1

Hazelwood

15955 New Halls Ferry Rd • Florissant, MO 63031-1227
(314) 953-5000 • http://www.hazelwood.k12.mo.us/~mludwig/index.html
Grade Span: PK-12; **Agency Type:** 1
Schools: 25
20 Primary; 2 Middle; 3 High; 0 Other Level
24 Regular; 1 Special Education; 0 Vocational; 0 Alternative
0 Magnet; 0 Charter; 8 Title I Eligible; 0 School-wide Title I
Students: 19,311 (51.1% male; 48.8% female)
Individual Education Program: 3,537 (18.3%);
English Language Learner: 409 (2.1%); Migrant: 0 (0.0%)
Eligible for Free Lunch Program: 5,182 (26.8%)
Eligible for Reduced-Price Lunch Program: 1,179 (6.1%)
Teachers: 1,132.8 (17.0 to 1)
Librarians/Media Specialists: 28.0 (689.7 to 1)
Guidance Counselors: 52.0 (371.4 to 1)
Current Spending: ($ per student per year):
Total: $6,886; Instruction: $4,121; Support Services: $2,535
Enrollment, Drop-out Rates and Diploma Recipients by Race/Ethnicity

Category	Total	White	Black	Asian	AIAN	Hisp.
Enrollment (%)	100.0	40.8	57.1	0.9	0.0	1.1
Drop-out Rate (%)	4.6	4.0	5.3	1.7	0.0	3.2
H.S. Diplomas (#)	1,247	682	544	13	1	7

Jennings

2559 Dorwood • Jennings, MO 63136-4035
(314) 653-8000 • http://www.jenningsk12.net/
Grade Span: PK-12; **Agency Type:** 1
Schools: 7
4 Primary; 2 Middle; 1 High; 0 Other Level
7 Regular; 0 Special Education; 0 Vocational; 0 Alternative
0 Magnet; 0 Charter; 5 Title I Eligible; 4 School-wide Title I
Students: 3,246 (49.4% male; 50.5% female)
Individual Education Program: 682 (21.0%);
English Language Learner: 0 (0.0%); Migrant: 0 (0.0%)
Eligible for Free Lunch Program: 2,259 (69.6%)
Eligible for Reduced-Price Lunch Program: 279 (8.6%)
Teachers: 208.0 (15.6 to 1)
Librarians/Media Specialists: 2.9 (1,119.3 to 1)
Guidance Counselors: 10.0 (324.6 to 1)
Current Spending: ($ per student per year):
Total: $8,266; Instruction: $4,254; Support Services: $3,598
Enrollment, Drop-out Rates and Diploma Recipients by Race/Ethnicity

Category	Total	White	Black	Asian	AIAN	Hisp.
Enrollment (%)	100.0	3.0	96.8	0.0	0.0	0.2
Drop-out Rate (%)	7.5	6.0	7.5	n/a	0.0	16.7
H.S. Diplomas (#)	147	10	134	1	0	2

Kirkwood R-VII

11289 Manchester Rd • Kirkwood, MO 63122-1122
(314) 213-6101 • http://www.kirkwood.k12.mo.us/default.html
Grade Span: PK-12; **Agency Type:** 1
Schools: 9
6 Primary; 2 Middle; 1 High; 0 Other Level
9 Regular; 0 Special Education; 0 Vocational; 0 Alternative
0 Magnet; 0 Charter; 3 Title I Eligible; 0 School-wide Title I
Students: 5,731 (51.0% male; 48.9% female)
Individual Education Program: 1,227 (21.4%);
English Language Learner: 25 (0.4%); Migrant: 0 (0.0%)
Eligible for Free Lunch Program: 378 (6.6%)
Eligible for Reduced-Price Lunch Program: 88 (1.5%)
Teachers: 337.0 (17.0 to 1)
Librarians/Media Specialists: 11.0 (521.0 to 1)
Guidance Counselors: 16.0 (358.2 to 1)
Current Spending: ($ per student per year):
Total: $8,277; Instruction: $4,950; Support Services: $3,113

Enrollment, Drop-out Rates and Diploma Recipients by Race/Ethnicity

Category	Total	White	Black	Asian	AIAN	Hisp.
Enrollment (%)	100.0	75.2	22.2	1.3	0.2	1.1
Drop-out Rate (%)	1.9	1.4	3.5	0.0	0.0	0.0
H.S. Diplomas (#)	409	331	73	2	0	3

Ladue

9703 Conway Rd • St Louis, MO 63124-1646
(314) 994-7080 • http://www.ladue.k12.mo.us/
Grade Span: KG-12; **Agency Type:** 1
Schools: 6
4 Primary; 1 Middle; 1 High; 0 Other Level
6 Regular; 0 Special Education; 0 Vocational; 0 Alternative
0 Magnet; 0 Charter; 2 Title I Eligible; 0 School-wide Title I
Students: 3,204 (49.4% male; 50.5% female)
Individual Education Program: 536 (16.7%);
English Language Learner: 21 (0.7%); Migrant: 0 (0.0%)
Eligible for Free Lunch Program: 183 (5.7%)
Eligible for Reduced-Price Lunch Program: 47 (1.5%)
Teachers: 282.0 (11.4 to 1)
Librarians/Media Specialists: 8.2 (390.7 to 1)
Guidance Counselors: 11.8 (271.5 to 1)
Current Spending: ($ per student per year):
Total: $11,825; Instruction: $7,007; Support Services: $4,562
Enrollment, Drop-out Rates and Diploma Recipients by Race/Ethnicity

Category	Total	White	Black	Asian	AIAN	Hisp.
Enrollment (%)	100.0	74.6	17.5	6.3	0.2	1.3
Drop-out Rate (%)	0.6	0.4	1.2	0.0	n/a	0.0
H.S. Diplomas (#)	217	151	56	8	0	2

Lindbergh R-VIII

4900 S Lindbergh Blvd • St Louis, MO 63126-3235
(314) 729-2480 • http://www.lindbergh.k12.mo.us/
Grade Span: KG-12; **Agency Type:** 1
Schools: 7
5 Primary; 1 Middle; 1 High; 0 Other Level
7 Regular; 0 Special Education; 0 Vocational; 0 Alternative
0 Magnet; 0 Charter; 4 Title I Eligible; 0 School-wide Title I
Students: 5,437 (51.5% male; 48.4% female)
Individual Education Program: 1,103 (20.3%);
English Language Learner: 80 (1.5%); Migrant: 0 (0.0%)
Eligible for Free Lunch Program: 309 (5.7%)
Eligible for Reduced-Price Lunch Program: 126 (2.3%)
Teachers: 353.2 (15.4 to 1)
Librarians/Media Specialists: 7.0 (776.7 to 1)
Guidance Counselors: 15.5 (350.8 to 1)
Current Spending: ($ per student per year):
Total: $7,707; Instruction: $4,636; Support Services: $2,777
Enrollment, Drop-out Rates and Diploma Recipients by Race/Ethnicity

Category	Total	White	Black	Asian	AIAN	Hisp.
Enrollment (%)	100.0	83.8	13.7	1.8	0.0	0.7
Drop-out Rate (%)	3.4	2.6	6.5	0.0	n/a	20.0
H.S. Diplomas (#)	377	306	63	5	0	3

Mehlville R-IX

3120 Lemay Ferry Rd • St Louis, MO 63125-4416
(314) 467-5000 • http://info.csd.org/mehlville/index.html
Grade Span: PK-12; **Agency Type:** 1
Schools: 16
10 Primary; 4 Middle; 2 High; 0 Other Level
16 Regular; 0 Special Education; 0 Vocational; 0 Alternative
0 Magnet; 0 Charter; 4 Title I Eligible; 0 School-wide Title I
Students: 11,727 (51.2% male; 48.7% female)
Individual Education Program: 2,382 (20.3%);
English Language Learner: 303 (2.6%); Migrant: 3 (<0.1%)
Eligible for Free Lunch Program: 1,025 (8.7%)
Eligible for Reduced-Price Lunch Program: 320 (2.7%)
Teachers: 684.4 (17.1 to 1)
Librarians/Media Specialists: 16.0 (732.9 to 1)
Guidance Counselors: 30.6 (383.2 to 1)
Current Spending: ($ per student per year):
Total: $6,271; Instruction: $3,871; Support Services: $2,172
Enrollment, Drop-out Rates and Diploma Recipients by Race/Ethnicity

Category	Total	White	Black	Asian	AIAN	Hisp.
Enrollment (%)	100.0	84.8	12.9	1.7	0.1	0.5
Drop-out Rate (%)	2.7	2.5	4.2	1.7	0.0	0.0
H.S. Diplomas (#)	827	735	82	6	0	4

Normandy

3855 Lucas And Hunt Rd • St Louis, MO 63121-2919
(314) 493-0400 • http://www.normandy.k12.mo.us/
Grade Span: PK-12; **Agency Type:** 1
Schools: 12
8 Primary; 2 Middle; 2 High; 0 Other Level
12 Regular; 0 Special Education; 0 Vocational; 0 Alternative

0 Magnet; 0 Charter; 7 Title I Eligible; 7 School-wide Title I
Students: 5,807 (51.9% male; 48.0% female)
 Individual Education Program: 1,061 (18.3%);
 English Language Learner: 16 (0.3%); Migrant: 2 (<0.1%)
 Eligible for Free Lunch Program: 4,171 (71.8%)
 Eligible for Reduced-Price Lunch Program: 315 (5.4%)
Teachers: 351.0 (16.5 to 1)
Librarians/Media Specialists: 8.0 (725.9 to 1)
Guidance Counselors: 18.0 (322.6 to 1)
Current Spending: ($ per student per year):
 Total: $7,965; Instruction: $4,518; Support Services: $3,075

Enrollment, Drop-out Rates and Diploma Recipients by Race/Ethnicity

Category	Total	White	Black	Asian	AIAN	Hisp.
Enrollment (%)	100.0	1.5	98.2	0.2	0.0	0.1
Drop-out Rate (%)	3.1	0.0	3.2	0.0	n/a	0.0
H.S. Diplomas (#)	312	18	289	1	0	4

Parkway C-2
455 N Woods Mill Rd · Chesterfield, MO 63017-3327
(314) 415-8100 · http://www.pkwy.k12.mo.us/
Grade Span: PK-12; **Agency Type:** 1
Schools: 28
 18 Primary; 5 Middle; 5 High; 0 Other Level
 28 Regular; 0 Special Education; 0 Vocational; 0 Alternative
 0 Magnet; 0 Charter; 12 Title I Eligible; 0 School-wide Title I
Students: 19,578 (50.3% male; 49.6% female)
 Individual Education Program: 4,103 (21.0%);
 English Language Learner: 389 (2.0%); Migrant: 0 (0.0%)
 Eligible for Free Lunch Program: 703 (3.6%)
 Eligible for Reduced-Price Lunch Program: 268 (1.4%)
Teachers: 1,200.1 (16.3 to 1)
Librarians/Media Specialists: 33.0 (593.3 to 1)
Guidance Counselors: 65.7 (298.0 to 1)
Current Spending: ($ per student per year):
 Total: $7,870; Instruction: $4,527; Support Services: $3,094

Enrollment, Drop-out Rates and Diploma Recipients by Race/Ethnicity

Category	Total	White	Black	Asian	AIAN	Hisp.
Enrollment (%)	100.0	71.9	17.3	9.0	0.1	1.7
Drop-out Rate (%)	1.1	1.1	1.5	0.4	0.0	1.4
H.S. Diplomas (#)	1,438	1,077	214	127	2	18

Pattonville R-III
11097 St Charles Rock Rd · St Ann, MO 63074-1509
(314) 213-8500 · http://www.pattonville.k12.mo.us/
Grade Span: PK-12; **Agency Type:** 1
Schools: 11
 8 Primary; 2 Middle; 1 High; 0 Other Level
 11 Regular; 0 Special Education; 0 Vocational; 0 Alternative
 0 Magnet; 0 Charter; 5 Title I Eligible; 2 School-wide Title I
Students: 6,273 (52.5% male; 47.4% female)
 Individual Education Program: 1,162 (18.5%);
 English Language Learner: 224 (3.6%); Migrant: 0 (0.0%)
 Eligible for Free Lunch Program: 1,207 (19.2%)
 Eligible for Reduced-Price Lunch Program: 378 (6.0%)
Teachers: 455.5 (13.8 to 1)
Librarians/Media Specialists: 12.0 (522.8 to 1)
Guidance Counselors: 24.9 (251.9 to 1)
Current Spending: ($ per student per year):
 Total: $10,106; Instruction: $5,758; Support Services: $4,070

Enrollment, Drop-out Rates and Diploma Recipients by Race/Ethnicity

Category	Total	White	Black	Asian	AIAN	Hisp.
Enrollment (%)	100.0	70.2	23.7	2.9	0.1	3.1
Drop-out Rate (%)	2.6	2.5	2.6	0.0	n/a	16.0
H.S. Diplomas (#)	428	322	94	8	0	4

Ritenour
2420 Woodson Rd · St Louis, MO 63114-5423
(314) 493-6010 · http://www.ritenour.k12.mo.us/
Grade Span: PK-12; **Agency Type:** 1
Schools: 9
 6 Primary; 2 Middle; 1 High; 0 Other Level
 9 Regular; 0 Special Education; 0 Vocational; 0 Alternative
 0 Magnet; 0 Charter; 8 Title I Eligible; 0 School-wide Title I
Students: 6,174 (51.4% male; 48.5% female)
 Individual Education Program: 1,221 (19.8%);
 English Language Learner: 233 (3.8%); Migrant: 2 (<0.1%)
 Eligible for Free Lunch Program: 2,527 (40.9%)
 Eligible for Reduced-Price Lunch Program: 562 (9.1%)
Teachers: 360.0 (17.2 to 1)
Librarians/Media Specialists: 10.0 (617.4 to 1)
Guidance Counselors: 15.0 (411.6 to 1)
Current Spending: ($ per student per year):
 Total: $6,893; Instruction: $3,977; Support Services: $2,650

Enrollment, Drop-out Rates and Diploma Recipients by Race/Ethnicity

Category	Total	White	Black	Asian	AIAN	Hisp.
Enrollment (%)	100.0	58.8	33.6	2.1	0.5	5.0
Drop-out Rate (%)	2.9	3.3	2.4	0.0	0.0	0.0
H.S. Diplomas (#)	296	209	75	8	1	3

Riverview Gardens
1370 Northumberland · St Louis, MO 63137-1413
(314) 869-2505 · http://www.rgsd.org/
Grade Span: PK-12; **Agency Type:** 1
Schools: 13
 10 Primary; 2 Middle; 1 High; 0 Other Level
 13 Regular; 0 Special Education; 0 Vocational; 0 Alternative
 0 Magnet; 0 Charter; 12 Title I Eligible; 1 School-wide Title I
Students: 8,003 (51.2% male; 48.7% female)
 Individual Education Program: 1,500 (18.7%);
 English Language Learner: 20 (0.2%); Migrant: 0 (0.0%)
 Eligible for Free Lunch Program: 5,252 (65.6%)
 Eligible for Reduced-Price Lunch Program: 770 (9.6%)
Teachers: 460.5 (17.4 to 1)
Librarians/Media Specialists: 13.0 (615.6 to 1)
Guidance Counselors: 19.0 (421.2 to 1)
Current Spending: ($ per student per year):
 Total: $6,462; Instruction: $3,993; Support Services: $2,186

Enrollment, Drop-out Rates and Diploma Recipients by Race/Ethnicity

Category	Total	White	Black	Asian	AIAN	Hisp.
Enrollment (%)	100.0	4.9	94.6	0.1	0.0	0.3
Drop-out Rate (%)	3.2	2.0	3.3	0.0	n/a	0.0
H.S. Diplomas (#)	306	34	272	0	0	0

Rockwood R-VI
111 E N St · Eureka, MO 63025-1229
(636) 938-2200 · http://www.rockwood.k12.mo.us/
Grade Span: PK-12; **Agency Type:** 1
Schools: 30
 20 Primary; 6 Middle; 4 High; 0 Other Level
 29 Regular; 0 Special Education; 0 Vocational; 1 Alternative
 0 Magnet; 0 Charter; 16 Title I Eligible; 0 School-wide Title I
Students: 22,658 (51.3% male; 48.6% female)
 Individual Education Program: 3,857 (17.0%);
 English Language Learner: 241 (1.1%); Migrant: 4 (<0.1%)
 Eligible for Free Lunch Program: 546 (2.4%)
 Eligible for Reduced-Price Lunch Program: 222 (1.0%)
Teachers: 1,342.7 (16.9 to 1)
Librarians/Media Specialists: 32.6 (695.0 to 1)
Guidance Counselors: 63.4 (357.4 to 1)
Current Spending: ($ per student per year):
 Total: $6,836; Instruction: $3,937; Support Services: $2,661

Enrollment, Drop-out Rates and Diploma Recipients by Race/Ethnicity

Category	Total	White	Black	Asian	AIAN	Hisp.
Enrollment (%)	100.0	83.9	11.7	3.0	0.2	1.2
Drop-out Rate (%)	1.9	1.5	4.6	0.6	0.0	5.5
H.S. Diplomas (#)	1,474	1,263	158	40	1	12

Special School District - St. Louis County
12110 Clayton Rd · Town & Country, MO 63131-2516
(314) 989-8100 · http://ssd.k12.mo.us
Grade Span: PK-12; **Agency Type:** 1
Schools: 11
 3 Primary; 0 Middle; 4 High; 4 Other Level
 0 Regular; 8 Special Education; 3 Vocational; 0 Alternative
 0 Magnet; 0 Charter; 5 Title I Eligible; 0 School-wide Title I
Students: 2,047 (69.0% male; 30.9% female)
 Individual Education Program: n/a;
 English Language Learner: 21 (1.0%); Migrant: 0 (0.0%)
 Eligible for Free Lunch Program: 363 (25.4%)
 Eligible for Reduced-Price Lunch Program: 57 (4.0%)
Teachers: 2,219.2 (0.6 to 1)
Librarians/Media Specialists: 11.9 (120.3 to 1)
Guidance Counselors: 12.7 (112.7 to 1)
Current Spending: ($ per student per year):
 Total: n/a; Instruction: n/a; Support Services: n/a

Enrollment, Drop-out Rates and Diploma Recipients by Race/Ethnicity

Category	Total	White	Black	Asian	AIAN	Hisp.
Enrollment (%)	100.0	45.3	51.9	1.7	0.1	1.0
Drop-out Rate (%)	n/a	n/a	n/a	n/a	n/a	n/a
H.S. Diplomas (#)	253	75	172	3	2	1

University City
8346 Delcrest Dr · University City, MO 63124-2167
(314) 290-4001 · http://ucityschools.org/
Grade Span: PK-12; **Agency Type:** 1
Schools: 10
 7 Primary; 2 Middle; 1 High; 0 Other Level
 10 Regular; 0 Special Education; 0 Vocational; 0 Alternative

0 Magnet; 0 Charter; 6 Title I Eligible; 3 School-wide Title I
Students: 4,120   (50.8% male; 49.1% female)
   Individual Education Program: 792 (19.2%);
   English Language Learner: 46 (1.1%); Migrant: 0 (0.0%)
   Eligible for Free Lunch Program: 1,919 (46.6%)
   Eligible for Reduced-Price Lunch Program: 329 (8.0%)
Teachers: 282.0 (14.6 to 1)
Librarians/Media Specialists: 7.0 (588.6 to 1)
Guidance Counselors: 13.0 (316.9 to 1)
Current Spending: ($ per student per year):
   Total: $7,917; Instruction: $4,305; Support Services: $3,295
Enrollment, Drop-out Rates and Diploma Recipients by Race/Ethnicity

Category	Total	White	Black	Asian	AIAN	Hisp.
Enrollment (%)	100.0	12.3	85.8	1.0	0.1	0.8
Drop-out Rate (%)	7.9	2.9	8.5	0.0	n/a	50.0
H.S. Diplomas (#)	168	19	148	0	0	1

Webster Groves

400 E Lockwood Ave • Webster Groves, MO 63119-3125
(314) 961-1233 • http://www.webster.k12.mo.us/
Grade Span: KG-12; **Agency Type:** 1
Schools: 10
   7 Primary; 2 Middle; 1 High; 0 Other Level
   10 Regular; 0 Special Education; 0 Vocational; 0 Alternative
   0 Magnet; 0 Charter; 7 Title I Eligible; 0 School-wide Title I
Students: 4,186   (52.3% male; 47.6% female)
   Individual Education Program: 845 (20.2%);
   English Language Learner: 19 (0.5%); Migrant: 0 (0.0%)
   Eligible for Free Lunch Program: 411 (9.8%)
   Eligible for Reduced-Price Lunch Program: 80 (1.9%)
Teachers: 281.3 (14.9 to 1)
Librarians/Media Specialists: 8.7 (481.1 to 1)
Guidance Counselors: 14.5 (288.7 to 1)
Current Spending: ($ per student per year):
   Total: $8,017; Instruction: $4,938; Support Services: $2,872
Enrollment, Drop-out Rates and Diploma Recipients by Race/Ethnicity

Category	Total	White	Black	Asian	AIAN	Hisp.
Enrollment (%)	100.0	71.6	25.6	1.8	0.0	0.9
Drop-out Rate (%)	3.6	2.1	7.9	0.0	n/a	10.0
H.S. Diplomas (#)	303	217	75	7	0	4

St. Louis City

801 N 11th St • St Louis, MO 63101-1401
(314) 231-3720 • http://www.slps.org/
Grade Span: PK-12; **Agency Type:** 1
Schools: 108
   64 Primary; 23 Middle; 14 High; 7 Other Level
   105 Regular; 0 Special Education; 1 Vocational; 2 Alternative
   30 Magnet; 8 Charter; 82 Title I Eligible; 68 School-wide Title I
Students: 40,827   (51.1% male; 48.8% female)
   Individual Education Program: 7,415 (18.2%);
   English Language Learner: 2,768 (6.8%); Migrant: 125 (0.3%)
   Eligible for Free Lunch Program: 31,286 (77.6%)
   Eligible for Reduced-Price Lunch Program: 1,802 (4.5%)
Teachers: 3,227.0 (12.5 to 1)
Librarians/Media Specialists: 83.0 (485.8 to 1)
Guidance Counselors: 140.6 (286.8 to 1)
Current Spending: ($ per student per year):
   Total: $10,170; Instruction: $5,296; Support Services: $4,479
Enrollment, Drop-out Rates and Diploma Recipients by Race/Ethnicity

Category	Total	White	Black	Asian	AIAN	Hisp.
Enrollment (%)	100.0	15.5	81.4	1.5	0.1	1.5
Drop-out Rate (%)	8.2	8.0	8.3	4.7	40.0	5.9
H.S. Diplomas (#)	1,424	300	1,057	50	1	16

Ste. Genevieve County

Ste. Genevieve County R-II

375 N Fifth St • Ste Genevieve, MO 63670-1249
(573) 883-4500 • http://www.stegen.k12.mo.us/
Grade Span: PK-12; **Agency Type:** 1
Schools: 4
   2 Primary; 1 Middle; 1 High; 0 Other Level
   4 Regular; 0 Special Education; 0 Vocational; 0 Alternative
   0 Magnet; 0 Charter; 2 Title I Eligible; 0 School-wide Title I
Students: 2,128   (51.6% male; 48.3% female)
   Individual Education Program: 319 (15.0%);
   English Language Learner: 3 (0.1%); Migrant: 0 (0.0%)
   Eligible for Free Lunch Program: 601 (28.2%)
   Eligible for Reduced-Price Lunch Program: 242 (11.4%)
Teachers: 133.5 (15.9 to 1)
Librarians/Media Specialists: 2.0 (1,064.0 to 1)
Guidance Counselors: 5.0 (425.6 to 1)
Current Spending: ($ per student per year):
   Total: $5,936; Instruction: $3,722; Support Services: $1,886

Enrollment, Drop-out Rates and Diploma Recipients by Race/Ethnicity

Category	Total	White	Black	Asian	AIAN	Hisp.
Enrollment (%)	100.0	97.9	1.0	0.1	0.1	0.8
Drop-out Rate (%)	2.6	2.4	0.0	50.0	n/a	n/a
H.S. Diplomas (#)	143	141	1	1	0	0

Stoddard County

Dexter R-XI

1031 Brown Pilot Ln • Dexter, MO 63841-1803
(573) 614-1000 • http://dexter.k12.mo.us/
Grade Span: PK-12; **Agency Type:** 1
Schools: 4
   2 Primary; 1 Middle; 1 High; 0 Other Level
   4 Regular; 0 Special Education; 0 Vocational; 0 Alternative
   0 Magnet; 0 Charter; 2 Title I Eligible; 0 School-wide Title I
Students: 2,062   (49.4% male; 50.5% female)
   Individual Education Program: 339 (16.4%);
   English Language Learner: 0 (0.0%); Migrant: 2 (0.1%)
   Eligible for Free Lunch Program: 693 (33.6%)
   Eligible for Reduced-Price Lunch Program: 221 (10.7%)
Teachers: 138.0 (14.9 to 1)
Librarians/Media Specialists: 3.0 (687.3 to 1)
Guidance Counselors: 6.0 (343.7 to 1)
Current Spending: ($ per student per year):
   Total: $5,433; Instruction: $3,636; Support Services: $1,552
Enrollment, Drop-out Rates and Diploma Recipients by Race/Ethnicity

Category	Total	White	Black	Asian	AIAN	Hisp.
Enrollment (%)	100.0	98.2	0.4	0.3	0.1	1.1
Drop-out Rate (%)	4.5	4.5	n/a	n/a	n/a	0.0
H.S. Diplomas (#)	120	120	0	0	0	0

Stone County

Reeds Spring R-IV

22595 Main St • Reeds Spring, MO 65737-0358
(417) 272-8173 • http://www.wolves.k12.mo.us/
Grade Span: PK-12; **Agency Type:** 1
Schools: 7
   2 Primary; 2 Middle; 2 High; 1 Other Level
   5 Regular; 0 Special Education; 1 Vocational; 1 Alternative
   0 Magnet; 0 Charter; 3 Title I Eligible; 0 School-wide Title I
Students: 2,139   (51.7% male; 48.2% female)
   Individual Education Program: 339 (15.8%);
   English Language Learner: 21 (1.0%); Migrant: 0 (0.0%)
   Eligible for Free Lunch Program: 827 (38.7%)
   Eligible for Reduced-Price Lunch Program: 209 (9.8%)
Teachers: 151.7 (14.1 to 1)
Librarians/Media Specialists: 4.0 (534.8 to 1)
Guidance Counselors: 8.0 (267.4 to 1)
Current Spending: ($ per student per year):
   Total: $6,220; Instruction: $3,812; Support Services: $2,076
Enrollment, Drop-out Rates and Diploma Recipients by Race/Ethnicity

Category	Total	White	Black	Asian	AIAN	Hisp.
Enrollment (%)	100.0	96.1	0.6	0.8	0.7	1.9
Drop-out Rate (%)	3.4	3.6	0.0	0.0	0.0	0.0
H.S. Diplomas (#)	115	110	0	3	1	1

Taney County

Branson R-IV

400 Cedar Ridge Dr • Branson, MO 65616-8143
(417) 334-6541 • http://www.branson.k12.mo.us/
Grade Span: PK-12; **Agency Type:** 1
Schools: 6
   3 Primary; 2 Middle; 1 High; 0 Other Level
   6 Regular; 0 Special Education; 0 Vocational; 0 Alternative
   0 Magnet; 0 Charter; 5 Title I Eligible; 0 School-wide Title I
Students: 3,336   (51.1% male; 48.8% female)
   Individual Education Program: 397 (11.9%);
   English Language Learner: 98 (2.9%); Migrant: 3 (0.1%)
   Eligible for Free Lunch Program: 982 (29.4%)
   Eligible for Reduced-Price Lunch Program: 289 (8.7%)
Teachers: 221.3 (15.1 to 1)
Librarians/Media Specialists: 5.0 (667.2 to 1)
Guidance Counselors: 7.1 (469.9 to 1)
Current Spending: ($ per student per year):
   Total: $6,330; Instruction: $3,945; Support Services: $2,149
Enrollment, Drop-out Rates and Diploma Recipients by Race/Ethnicity

Category	Total	White	Black	Asian	AIAN	Hisp.
Enrollment (%)	100.0	90.4	1.3	1.6	0.9	5.8
Drop-out Rate (%)	1.9	1.6	25.0	0.0	0.0	9.1
H.S. Diplomas (#)	164	159	0	0	1	4

Vernon County

Nevada R-V
800 W Hickory • Nevada, MO 64772-2059
(417) 448-2000 • http://www.nevada.k12.mo.us/
Grade Span: PK-12; **Agency Type:** 1
Schools: 7
  3 Primary; 1 Middle; 2 High; 1 Other Level
  5 Regular; 0 Special Education; 1 Vocational; 1 Alternative
  0 Magnet; 0 Charter; 4 Title I Eligible; 0 School-wide Title I
Students: 2,522 (51.9% male; 48.0% female)
  Individual Education Program: 396 (15.7%);
  English Language Learner: 6 (0.2%); Migrant: 3 (0.1%)
  Eligible for Free Lunch Program: 1,016 (40.3%)
  Eligible for Reduced-Price Lunch Program: 188 (7.5%)
Teachers: 177.7 (14.2 to 1)
Librarians/Media Specialists: 3.0 (840.7 to 1)
Guidance Counselors: 8.0 (315.3 to 1)
Current Spending: ($ per student per year):
  Total: $6,533; Instruction: $4,238; Support Services: $1,962

Enrollment, Drop-out Rates and Diploma Recipients by Race/Ethnicity

Category	Total	White	Black	Asian	AIAN	Hisp.
Enrollment (%)	100.0	96.7	1.7	0.6	0.2	0.8
Drop-out Rate (%)	2.7	2.8	0.0	0.0	0.0	0.0
H.S. Diplomas (#)	170	166	3	1	0	0

Warren County

Warren County R-III
302 Kuhl Ave • Warrenton, MO 63383-2116
(636) 456-6901 • http://www.warrencor3.org/
Grade Span: PK-12; **Agency Type:** 1
Schools: 4
  1 Primary; 2 Middle; 1 High; 0 Other Level
  4 Regular; 0 Special Education; 0 Vocational; 0 Alternative
  0 Magnet; 0 Charter; 2 Title I Eligible; 0 School-wide Title I
Students: 2,693 (51.8% male; 48.1% female)
  Individual Education Program: 397 (14.7%);
  English Language Learner: 9 (0.3%); Migrant: 1 (<0.1%)
  Eligible for Free Lunch Program: 609 (22.6%)
  Eligible for Reduced-Price Lunch Program: 194 (7.2%)
Teachers: 174.9 (15.4 to 1)
Librarians/Media Specialists: 4.0 (673.3 to 1)
Guidance Counselors: 7.1 (379.3 to 1)
Current Spending: ($ per student per year):
  Total: $5,589; Instruction: $3,443; Support Services: $1,842

Enrollment, Drop-out Rates and Diploma Recipients by Race/Ethnicity

Category	Total	White	Black	Asian	AIAN	Hisp.
Enrollment (%)	100.0	94.9	2.4	0.4	0.6	1.6
Drop-out Rate (%)	3.2	3.2	0.0	0.0	0.0	12.5
H.S. Diplomas (#)	175	169	1	0	1	4

Washington County

Potosi R-III
400 N Mine • Potosi, MO 63664-1734
(573) 438-5485 • http://www.potosi.k12.mo.us/
Grade Span: PK-12; **Agency Type:** 1
Schools: 5
  2 Primary; 2 Middle; 1 High; 0 Other Level
  5 Regular; 0 Special Education; 0 Vocational; 0 Alternative
  0 Magnet; 0 Charter; 3 Title I Eligible; 0 School-wide Title I
Students: 2,485 (50.7% male; 49.2% female)
  Individual Education Program: 357 (14.4%);
  English Language Learner: 5 (0.2%); Migrant: 0 (0.0%)
  Eligible for Free Lunch Program: 961 (38.7%)
  Eligible for Reduced-Price Lunch Program: 186 (7.5%)
Teachers: 152.0 (16.3 to 1)
Librarians/Media Specialists: 2.9 (856.9 to 1)
Guidance Counselors: 6.2 (400.8 to 1)
Current Spending: ($ per student per year):
  Total: $5,762; Instruction: $3,445; Support Services: $2,030

Enrollment, Drop-out Rates and Diploma Recipients by Race/Ethnicity

Category	Total	White	Black	Asian	AIAN	Hisp.
Enrollment (%)	100.0	97.9	1.1	0.5	0.0	0.4
Drop-out Rate (%)	4.9	5.0	0.0	0.0	0.0	0.0
H.S. Diplomas (#)	161	157	3	1	0	0

Webster County

Marshfield R-I
114 E Commercial • Marshfield, MO 65706-2104
(417) 859-2120 • http://www.mr1.k12.mo.us/
Grade Span: PK-12; **Agency Type:** 1
Schools: 5

  2 Primary; 2 Middle; 1 High; 0 Other Level
  5 Regular; 0 Special Education; 0 Vocational; 0 Alternative
  0 Magnet; 0 Charter; 3 Title I Eligible; 0 School-wide Title I
Students: 2,985 (50.8% male; 49.1% female)
  Individual Education Program: 467 (15.6%);
  English Language Learner: 0 (0.0%); Migrant: 0 (0.0%)
  Eligible for Free Lunch Program: 831 (27.8%)
  Eligible for Reduced-Price Lunch Program: 314 (10.5%)
Teachers: 194.7 (15.3 to 1)
Librarians/Media Specialists: 5.0 (597.0 to 1)
Guidance Counselors: 7.0 (426.4 to 1)
Current Spending: ($ per student per year):
  Total: $5,660; Instruction: $3,505; Support Services: $1,878

Enrollment, Drop-out Rates and Diploma Recipients by Race/Ethnicity

Category	Total	White	Black	Asian	AIAN	Hisp.
Enrollment (%)	100.0	96.9	0.5	0.8	0.4	1.4
Drop-out Rate (%)	3.9	4.0	0.0	0.0	0.0	0.0
H.S. Diplomas (#)	169	169	0	0	0	0

Wright County

Mountain Grove R-III
207 E Fifth • Mountain Grove, MO 65711-0806
Mailing Address: PO Box 806 • Mountain Grove, MO 65711-0806
(417) 926-3177 • http://www.mgr3.k12.mo.us/
Grade Span: PK-12; **Agency Type:** 1
Schools: 5
  1 Primary; 1 Middle; 3 High; 0 Other Level
  3 Regular; 0 Special Education; 1 Vocational; 1 Alternative
  0 Magnet; 0 Charter; 2 Title I Eligible; 2 School-wide Title I
Students: 1,536 (50.5% male; 49.4% female)
  Individual Education Program: 256 (16.7%);
  English Language Learner: 0 (0.0%); Migrant: 0 (0.0%)
  Eligible for Free Lunch Program: 703 (45.8%)
  Eligible for Reduced-Price Lunch Program: 202 (13.2%)
Teachers: 121.6 (12.6 to 1)
Librarians/Media Specialists: 2.9 (529.7 to 1)
Guidance Counselors: 7.0 (219.4 to 1)
Current Spending: ($ per student per year):
  Total: $7,470; Instruction: $5,175; Support Services: $1,915

Enrollment, Drop-out Rates and Diploma Recipients by Race/Ethnicity

Category	Total	White	Black	Asian	AIAN	Hisp.
Enrollment (%)	100.0	95.4	3.7	0.3	0.3	0.2
Drop-out Rate (%)	6.4	6.5	0.0	0.0	0.0	0.0
H.S. Diplomas (#)	101	101	0	0	0	0

Number of Schools

Rank	Number	District Name	City
1	108	St. Louis City	St Louis
2	89	Kansas City 33	Kansas City
3	55	Springfield R-XII	Springfield
4	31	Columbia 93	Columbia
5	30	North Kansas City 74	Kansas City
5	30	Rockwood R-VI	Eureka
7	29	St. Joseph	St Joseph
8	28	Parkway C-2	Chesterfield
9	25	Ferguson-Florissant R-II	Florissant
9	25	Hazelwood	Florissant
11	23	Francis Howell R-III	St Charles
11	23	Ft. Zumwalt R-II	O'fallon
13	22	Blue Springs R-IV	Blue Springs
13	22	Lee's Summit R-VII	Lee's Summit
15	21	Independence 30	Independence
16	19	Joplin R-VIII	Joplin
17	17	Fox C-6	Arnold
17	17	Jefferson City	Jefferson City
17	17	Raytown C-2	Raytown
20	16	Hickman Mills C-1	Kansas City
20	16	Mehlville R-IX	St Louis
22	15	Park Hill	Kansas City
23	14	Liberty 53	Liberty
24	13	Riverview Gardens	St Louis
25	12	Normandy	St Louis
25	12	St. Charles R-VI	St Charles
25	12	Washington	Washington
25	12	Waynesville R-VI	Waynesville
29	11	Northwest R-I	House Springs
29	11	Pattonville R-III	St Ann
29	11	Poplar Bluff R-I	Poplar Bluff
29	11	Specl. Sch. Dst. St. Louis Co.	Town & Ctry
33	10	Belton 124	Belton
33	10	Farmington R-VII	Farmington
33	10	Fort Osage R-I	Independence
33	10	Grandview C-4	Grandview
33	10	Jackson R-II	Jackson
33	10	Sikeston R-VI	Sikeston
33	10	University City	University City
33	10	Webb City R-VII	Webb City
33	10	Webster Groves	Webster Groves
42	9	Cape Girardeau 63	Cape Girardeau
42	9	Kennett 39	Kennett
42	9	Kirkwood R-VII	Kirkwood
42	9	Meramec Valley R-III	Pacific
42	9	Ritenour	St Louis
42	9	Sedalia 200	Sedalia
42	9	Warrensburg R-VI	Warrensburg
42	9	Wentzville R-IV	Wentzville
50	8	Camdenton R-III	Camdenton
50	8	Carthage R-IX	Carthage
50	8	Center 58	Kansas City
50	8	Hannibal 60	Hannibal
50	8	Lebanon R-III	Lebanon
50	8	Neosho R-V	Neosho
50	8	Nixa R-II	Nixa
50	8	Raymore-Peculiar R-II	Raymore
50	8	Rolla 31	Rolla
59	7	Chillicothe R-II	Chillicothe
59	7	Excelsior Springs 40	Excelsior Spgs
59	7	Harrisonville R-IX	Harrisonville
59	7	Jennings	Jennings
59	7	Kearney R-I	Kearney
59	7	Lindbergh R-VIII	St Louis
59	7	Marshall	Marshall
59	7	Mcdonald County R-I	Anderson
59	7	Moberly	Moberly
59	7	Nevada R-V	Nevada
59	7	North St. Francos Co. R-I	Bonne Terre
59	7	Platte County R-III	Platte City
59	7	Reeds Spring R-IV	Reeds Spring
72	6	Bolivar R-I	Bolivar
72	6	Branson R-IV	Branson
72	6	Carl Junction R-I	Carl Junction
72	6	Clayton	Clayton
72	6	Hillsboro R-III	Hillsboro
72	6	Ladue	St Louis
72	6	Mexico 59	Mexico
72	6	New Madrid County R-I	New Madrid
72	6	Ozark R-VI	Ozark
72	6	Republic R-III	Republic
72	6	Savannah R-III	Savannah
72	6	Troy R-III	Troy
72	6	Willard R-II	Willard
85	5	Cameron R-I	Cameron
85	5	Clinton	Clinton
85	5	Dallas County R-I	Buffalo
85	5	Eldon R-I	Eldon
85	5	Fulton 58	Fulton
85	5	Gasconade County R-II	Owensville
85	5	Kirksville R-III	Kirksville
85	5	Marshfield R-I	Marshfield
85	5	Monett R-I	Monett
85	5	Mountain Grove R-III	Mountain Grove
85	5	Perry County 32	Perryville
85	5	Potosi R-III	Potosi
85	5	St. Clair R-XIII	St Clair
85	5	Union R-XI	Union
85	5	Warsaw R-IX	Warsaw
85	5	West Plains R-VII	West Plains
101	4	Affton 101	St Louis
101	4	Aurora R-VIII	Aurora
101	4	Bayless	St Louis
101	4	Cassville R-IV	Cassville
101	4	Central R-III	Park Hills
101	4	Desoto 73	Desoto
101	4	Dexter R-XI	Dexter
101	4	Doniphan R-I	Doniphan
101	4	Festus R-VI	Festus
101	4	Fredericktown R-I	Fredericktown
101	4	Grain Valley R-V	Grain Valley
101	4	Knob Noster R-VIII	Knob Noster
101	4	Logan-Rogersville R-VIII	Rogersville
101	4	Morgan County R-II	Versailles
101	4	Oak Grove R-VI	Oak Grove
101	4	Odessa R-VII	Odessa
101	4	Pleasant Hill R-III	Pleasant Hill
101	4	Richmond R-XVI	Richmond
101	4	Salem R-80	Salem
101	4	School of the Osage R-II	Lake Ozark
101	4	Smithville R-II	Smithville
101	4	Ste. Genevieve County R-II	Ste Genevieve
101	4	Sullivan	Sullivan
101	4	Warren County R-III	Warrenton
101	4	Windsor C-1	Imperial
101	4	Winfield R-IV	Winfield
127	3	Ava R-I	Ava
127	3	Caruthersville 18	Caruthersville
127	3	East Newton County R-VI	Granby
127	3	Hancock Place	St Louis
127	3	Seneca R-VII	Seneca
127	3	St. James R-I	St James

Number of Teachers

Rank	Number	District Name	City
1	3,227	St. Louis City	St Louis
2	2,600	Kansas City 33	Kansas City
3	2,219	Specl. Dst. St. Louis Co.	Town & Ctry
4	1,455	Springfield R-XII	Springfield
5	1,342	Rockwood R-VI	Eureka
6	1,234	Columbia 93	Columbia
7	1,213	North Kansas City 74	Kansas City
8	1,200	Parkway C-2	Chesterfield
9	1,188	Francis Howell R-III	St Charles
10	1,132	Hazelwood	Florissant
11	1,064	Ft. Zumwalt R-II	O'fallon
12	956	Lee's Summit R-VII	Lee's Summit
13	824	Blue Springs R-IV	Blue Springs
14	815	Ferguson-Florissant R-II	Florissant
15	792	St. Joseph	St Joseph
16	712	Fox C-6	Arnold
17	700	Independence 30	Independence
18	684	Mehlville R-IX	St Louis
19	636	Park Hill	Kansas City
20	570	Jefferson City	Jefferson City
21	543	Raytown C-2	Raytown
22	534	Hickman Mills C-1	Kansas City
23	495	Wentzville R-IV	Wentzville
24	494	Joplin R-VIII	Joplin
25	481	Liberty 53	Liberty
26	460	Riverview Gardens	St Louis
27	458	Northwest R-I	House Springs
28	455	Pattonville R-III	St Ann
29	447	St. Charles R-VI	St Charles
30	379	Waynesville R-VI	Waynesville
31	360	Ritenour	St Louis
32	353	Lindbergh R-VIII	St Louis
33	351	Normandy	St Louis
34	337	Kirkwood R-VII	Kirkwood
35	331	Fort Osage R-I	Independence
36	321	Grandview C-4	Grandview
37	318	Cape Girardeau 63	Cape Girardeau
38	308	Raymore-Peculiar R-II	Raymore
39	295	Belton 124	Belton
40	295	Poplar Bluff R-I	Poplar Bluff
41	286	Camdenton R-III	Camdenton
42	282	Ladue	St Louis
42	282	Nixa R-II	Nixa
42	282	University City	University City
45	281	Webster Groves	Webster Groves
46	281	Sedalia 200	Sedalia
47	277	Washington	Washington
48	274	Hannibal 60	Hannibal
49	270	Jackson R-II	Jackson
50	268	Lebanon R-III	Lebanon
51	263	Troy R-III	Troy
52	263	Rolla 31	Rolla
53	258	Sikeston R-VI	Sikeston
54	252	Ozark R-VI	Ozark
55	246	Neosho R-V	Neosho
56	245	Farmington R-VII	Farmington
57	245	Carthage R-IX	Carthage
58	237	Mcdonald County R-I	Anderson
59	235	Willard R-II	Willard
60	233	Warrensburg R-VI	Warrensburg
61	230	Webb City R-VII	Webb City
62	227	Windsor C-1	Imperial
63	225	Clayton	Clayton
64	223	Meramec Valley R-III	Pacific
65	221	Branson R-IV	Branson
66	217	North St. Francois Co. R-I	Bonne Terre
67	208	Jennings	Jennings
68	206	Excelsior Springs 40	Excelsior Spgs
69	205	Kearney R-I	Kearney
70	205	Hillsboro R-III	Hillsboro
71	196	Center 58	Kansas City
72	194	Marshfield R-I	Marshfield
73	194	Union R-XI	Union
74	190	Kirksville R-III	Kirksville
75	183	Bolivar R-I	Bolivar
76	182	Carl Junction R-I	Carl Junction
77	182	Republic R-III	Republic
78	178	Marshall	Marshall
79	177	Nevada R-V	Nevada
80	177	Desoto 73	Desoto
81	175	Moberly	Moberly
82	174	Warren County R-III	Warrenton
83	174	Perry County 32	Perryville
84	172	Platte County R-III	Platte City
85	172	West Plains R-VII	West Plains
86	171	Mexico 59	Mexico
87	169	Fulton 58	Fulton
88	160	Savannah R-III	Savannah
89	159	St. Clair R-XIII	St Clair
90	159	Harrisonville R-IX	Harrisonville
91	158	Odessa R-VII	Odessa
92	157	Clinton	Clinton
93	155	Festus R-VI	Festus
94	153	Affton 101	St Louis
95	153	New Madrid County R-I	New Madrid
96	152	Potosi R-III	Potosi
97	151	Monett R-I	Monett
98	151	Reeds Spring R-IV	Reeds Spring
99	150	Eldon R-I	Eldon
100	149	Dallas County R-I	Buffalo
101	148	Kennett 39	Kennett
102	146	Chillicothe R-II	Chillicothe
103	145	Aurora R-VIII	Aurora
104	141	Sullivan	Sullivan
105	141	Grain Valley R-V	Grain Valley
106	138	Dexter R-XI	Dexter
107	133	Ste. Genevieve County R-II	Ste Genevieve
108	129	Knob Noster R-VIII	Knob Noster
109	129	Central R-III	Park Hills
110	125	Cameron R-I	Cameron
111	124	Gasconade County R-II	Owensville
112	124	Pleasant Hill R-III	Pleasant Hill
113	123	Cassville R-IV	Cassville
114	121	Mountain Grove R-III	Mountain Grove
115	120	Fredericktown R-I	Fredericktown
116	120	Smithville R-II	Smithville
117	120	Oak Grove R-VI	Oak Grove
118	119	Richmond R-XVI	Richmond
119	118	Logan-Rogersville R-VIII	Rogersville
119	118	School of the Osage R-II	Lake Ozark
121	118	Morgan County R-II	Versailles
122	117	St. James R-I	St James
123	117	Hancock Place	St Louis
124	116	Doniphan R-I	Doniphan
125	112	Seneca R-VII	Seneca
126	111	Caruthersville 18	Caruthersville
127	110	Ava R-I	Ava
128	107	East Newton County R-VI	Granby
129	101	Winfield R-IV	Winfield
130	99	Salem R-80	Salem
131	91	Warsaw R-IX	Warsaw
132	86	Bayless	St Louis

Number of Students

Rank	Number	District Name	City
1	40,827	St. Louis City	St Louis
2	38,285	Kansas City 33	Kansas City
3	24,285	Springfield R-XII	Springfield
4	22,658	Rockwood R-VI	Eureka

Rank	Number	District Name	City
5	19,578	Parkway C-2	Chesterfield
6	19,311	Hazelwood	Florissant
7	18,360	Francis Howell R-III	St Charles
8	18,138	Ft. Zumwalt R-II	O'fallon
9	17,004	North Kansas City 74	Kansas City
10	16,498	Columbia 93	Columbia
11	15,862	Lee's Summit R-VII	Lee's Summit
12	13,335	Ferguson-Florissant R-II	Florissant
13	13,297	Blue Springs R-IV	Blue Springs
14	12,193	Independence 30	Independence
15	12,015	St. Joseph	St Joseph
16	11,727	Mehlville R-IX	St Louis
17	11,614	Fox C-6	Arnold
18	9,970	Park Hill	Kansas City
19	8,902	Raytown C-2	Raytown
20	8,228	Jefferson City	Jefferson City
21	8,003	Riverview Gardens	St Louis
22	7,874	Liberty 53	Liberty
23	7,788	Wentzville R-IV	Wentzville
24	7,432	Joplin R-VIII	Joplin
25	7,385	Northwest R-I	House Springs
26	7,250	Hickman Mills C-1	Kansas City
27	6,273	Pattonville R-III	St Ann
28	6,174	Ritenour	St Louis
29	5,876	St. Charles R-VI	St Charles
30	5,807	Normandy	St Louis
31	5,731	Kirkwood R-VII	Kirkwood
32	5,437	Lindbergh R-VIII	St Louis
33	5,362	Waynesville R-VI	Waynesville
34	5,105	Troy R-III	Troy
35	5,099	Belton 124	Belton
36	4,913	Fort Osage R-I	Independence
37	4,885	Raymore-Peculiar R-II	Raymore
38	4,853	Poplar Bluff R-I	Poplar Bluff
39	4,682	Lebanon R-III	Lebanon
40	4,585	Jackson R-II	Jackson
41	4,515	Sedalia 200	Sedalia
42	4,502	Neosho R-V	Neosho
43	4,229	Grandview C-4	Grandview
44	4,186	Webster Groves	Webster Groves
45	4,184	Nixa R-II	Nixa
46	4,135	Ozark R-VI	Ozark
47	4,120	University City	University City
48	4,106	Washington	Washington
49	4,084	Rolla 31	Rolla
50	4,049	Cape Girardeau 63	Cape Girardeau
51	4,010	Camdenton R-III	Camdenton
52	3,975	Meramec Valley R-III	Pacific
53	3,863	Farmington R-VII	Farmington
54	3,853	Webb City R-VII	Webb City
55	3,833	Sikeston R-VI	Sikeston
56	3,630	Hannibal 60	Hannibal
57	3,619	Carthage R-IX	Carthage
58	3,604	Hillsboro R-III	Hillsboro
59	3,554	Mcdonald County R-I	Anderson
60	3,441	Willard R-II	Willard
61	3,439	Republic R-III	Republic
62	3,379	Kearney R-I	Kearney
63	3,336	Branson R-IV	Branson
64	3,269	Excelsior Springs 40	Excelsior Spgs
65	3,246	Jennings	Jennings
66	3,231	North St. Francois Co. R-I	Bonne Terre
67	3,208	Warrensburg R-VI	Warrensburg
68	3,204	Ladue	St Louis
69	2,985	Marshfield R-I	Marshfield
70	2,965	Windsor C-1	Imperial
71	2,938	Union R-XI	Union
72	2,794	Carl Junction R-I	Carl Junction
73	2,773	Desoto 73	Desoto
74	2,770	Festus R-VI	Festus
75	2,743	Center 58	Kansas City
76	2,693	Warren County R-III	Warrenton
77	2,687	Clayton	Clayton
78	2,571	Harrisonville R-IX	Harrisonville
79	2,526	Affton 101	St Louis
80	2,522	Nevada R-V	Nevada
81	2,504	West Plains R-VII	West Plains
82	2,493	Bolivar R-I	Bolivar
83	2,485	Potosi R-III	Potosi
84	2,471	Kirksville R-III	Kirksville
85	2,444	Platte County R-III	Platte City
86	2,433	Mexico 59	Mexico
87	2,430	Marshall	Marshall
88	2,387	Savannah R-III	Savannah
89	2,356	St. Clair R-XIII	St Clair
90	2,327	Moberly	Moberly
91	2,322	Kennett 39	Kennett
91	2,322	Odessa R-VII	Odessa
93	2,300	Perry County 32	Perryville
94	2,278	Fulton 58	Fulton
95	2,220	Sullivan	Sullivan
96	2,164	Grain Valley R-V	Grain Valley
97	2,139	Reeds Spring R-IV	Reeds Spring
98	2,128	Ste. Genevieve County R-II	Ste Genevieve
99	2,127	Aurora R-VIII	Aurora
100	2,095	Cassville R-IV	Cassville
101	2,088	Pleasant Hill R-III	Pleasant Hill
102	2,081	Clinton	Clinton
103	2,062	Dexter R-XI	Dexter
104	2,047	Specl. Sch. Dst. St. Louis Co.	Town & Ctry
105	2,022	Chillicothe R-II	Chillicothe
106	2,018	Dallas County R-I	Buffalo
107	2,005	Fredericktown R-I	Fredericktown
108	1,996	Eldon R-I	Eldon
109	1,976	Gasconade County R-II	Owensville
110	1,975	Monett R-I	Monett
111	1,974	Oak Grove R-VI	Oak Grove
112	1,911	New Madrid County R-I	New Madrid
113	1,892	Logan-Rogersville R-VIII	Rogersville
114	1,877	Smithville R-II	Smithville
115	1,873	Central R-III	Park Hills
116	1,828	St. James R-I	St James
117	1,816	Hancock Place	St Louis
118	1,734	Richmond R-XVI	Richmond
119	1,722	Caruthersville 18	Caruthersville
120	1,710	Knob Noster R-VIII	Knob Noster
121	1,705	Cameron R-I	Cameron
122	1,689	Seneca R-VII	Seneca
123	1,675	School of the Osage R-II	Lake Ozark
124	1,646	Doniphan R-I	Doniphan
125	1,621	Ava R-I	Ava
126	1,616	Bayless	St Louis
127	1,603	Winfield R-IV	Winfield
128	1,569	Morgan County R-II	Versailles
129	1,550	East Newton County R-VI	Granby
130	1,536	Mountain Grove R-III	Mountain Grove
131	1,530	Warsaw R-IX	Warsaw
132	1,501	Salem R-80	Salem

Male Students

Rank	Percent	District Name	City
1	69.0	Specl. Sch. Dst. St. Louis Co.	Town & Ctry
2	54.3	Cameron R-I	Cameron
3	54.2	Sullivan	Sullivan
4	54.1	Logan-Rogersville R-VIII	Rogersville
5	53.7	Odessa R-VII	Odessa
6	53.4	Windsor C-1	Imperial
7	53.3	Neosho R-V	Neosho
8	53.2	Pleasant Hill R-III	Pleasant Hill
9	53.2	North St. Francois Co. R-I	Bonne Terre
10	53.0	Fredericktown R-I	Fredericktown
11	52.9	Fort Osage R-I	Independence
12	52.9	Camdenton R-III	Camdenton
13	52.9	West Plains R-VII	West Plains
14	52.8	Cassville R-IV	Cassville
15	52.8	Clinton	Clinton
16	52.8	Carl Junction R-I	Carl Junction
17	52.8	Meramec Valley R-III	Pacific
18	52.7	Excelsior Springs 40	Excelsior Spgs
19	52.5	New Madrid County R-I	New Madrid
20	52.5	Pattonville R-III	St Ann
21	52.4	Dallas County R-I	Buffalo
22	52.3	Webster Groves	Webster Groves
23	52.3	St. Clair R-XIII	St Clair
24	52.3	Salem R-80	Salem
25	52.2	Joplin R-VIII	Joplin
26	52.2	St. Charles R-VI	St Charles
27	52.2	Bolivar R-I	Bolivar
28	52.2	Perry County 32	Perryville
29	52.1	Sedalia 200	Sedalia
30	52.1	Washington	Washington
31	52.1	Fox C-6	Arnold
32	52.1	Raytown C-2	Raytown
33	51.9	Belton 124	Belton
34	51.9	Normandy	St Louis
35	51.9	Knob Noster R-VIII	Knob Noster
36	51.9	Grain Valley R-V	Grain Valley
37	51.9	Oak Grove R-VI	Oak Grove
38	51.9	Kirksville R-III	Kirksville
39	51.9	School of the Osage R-II	Lake Ozark
40	51.9	Grandview C-4	Grandview
41	51.9	Nevada R-V	Nevada
42	51.8	Wentzville R-IV	Wentzville
43	51.8	Mexico 59	Mexico
44	51.8	Francis Howell R-III	St Charles
45	51.8	Farmington R-VII	Farmington
46	51.8	Jackson R-II	Jackson
47	51.8	Warren County R-III	Warrenton
48	51.8	Mcdonald County R-I	Anderson
49	51.7	Richmond R-XVI	Richmond
50	51.7	Hickman Mills C-1	Kansas City
51	51.7	Reeds Spring R-IV	Reeds Spring
52	51.7	Blue Springs R-IV	Blue Springs
53	51.6	Caruthersville 18	Caruthersville
54	51.6	Carthage R-IX	Carthage
55	51.6	Ferguson-Florissant R-II	Florissant
56	51.6	Ste. Genevieve County R-II	Ste Genevieve
57	51.6	Savannah R-III	Savannah
58	51.6	Moberly	Moberly
59	51.6	Winfield R-IV	Winfield
60	51.5	Ozark R-VI	Ozark
61	51.5	Lebanon R-III	Lebanon
62	51.5	Poplar Bluff R-I	Poplar Bluff
63	51.5	Park Hill	Kansas City
64	51.5	Lindbergh R-VIII	St Louis
65	51.5	Eldon R-I	Eldon
66	51.4	Seneca R-VII	Seneca
67	51.4	Lee's Summit R-VII	Lee's Summit
68	51.4	Ritenour	St Louis
69	51.4	Kearney R-I	Kearney
70	51.3	Desoto 73	Desoto
71	51.3	Rockwood R-VI	Eureka
72	51.2	Sikeston R-VI	Sikeston
73	51.2	Chillicothe R-II	Chillicothe
74	51.2	Mehlville R-IX	St Louis
75	51.2	Clayton	Clayton
76	51.2	Northwest R-I	House Springs
77	51.2	Union R-XI	Union
78	51.2	Riverview Gardens	St Louis
79	51.2	Springfield R-XII	Springfield
80	51.1	Branson R-IV	Branson
81	51.1	Aurora R-VIII	Aurora
82	51.1	St. Louis City	St Louis
83	51.1	Hazelwood	Florissant
84	51.1	Waynesville R-VI	Waynesville
85	51.0	Fulton 58	Fulton
86	51.0	Festus R-VI	Festus
87	51.0	North Kansas City 74	Kansas City
88	51.0	Kirkwood R-VII	Kirkwood
89	51.0	Morgan County R-II	Versailles
90	51.0	Monett R-I	Monett
91	51.0	St. Joseph	St Joseph
92	50.9	Hillsboro R-III	Hillsboro
93	50.9	Platte County R-III	Platte City
94	50.8	Harrisonville R-IX	Harrisonville
94	50.8	Jefferson City	Jefferson City
96	50.8	Troy R-III	Troy
97	50.8	Columbia 93	Columbia
98	50.8	Independence 30	Independence
99	50.8	University City	University City
100	50.8	Marshfield R-I	Marshfield
101	50.7	Webb City R-VII	Webb City
102	50.7	Ft. Zumwalt R-II	O'fallon
103	50.7	Central R-III	Park Hills
104	50.7	Smithville R-II	Smithville
105	50.7	Potosi R-III	Potosi
106	50.7	Rolla 31	Rolla
107	50.6	Warrensburg R-VI	Warrensburg
108	50.6	Hancock Place	St Louis
109	50.5	Center 58	Kansas City
110	50.5	Ava R-I	Ava
111	50.5	Mountain Grove R-III	Mountain Grove
112	50.5	Nixa R-II	Nixa
113	50.4	St. James R-I	St James
114	50.4	Kansas City 33	Kansas City
115	50.4	Affton 101	St Louis
116	50.3	Parkway C-2	Chesterfield
117	50.3	Cape Girardeau 63	Cape Girardeau
118	50.1	East Newton County R-VI	Granby
119	50.1	Hannibal 60	Hannibal
120	50.1	Raymore-Peculiar R-II	Raymore
121	50.1	Willard R-II	Willard
122	50.1	Kennett 39	Kennett
123	50.0	Warsaw R-IX	Warsaw
124	49.5	Liberty 53	Liberty
125	49.5	Marshall	Marshall
126	49.4	Ladue	St Louis
127	49.4	Dexter R-XI	Dexter
128	49.4	Jennings	Jennings
129	49.4	Republic R-III	Republic
130	49.2	Gasconade County R-II	Owensville
131	49.0	Bayless	St Louis
132	47.8	Doniphan R-I	Doniphan

Female Students

Rank	Percent	District Name	City
1	52.1	Doniphan R-I	Doniphan
2	50.9	Bayless	St Louis
3	50.7	Gasconade County R-II	Owensville
4	50.5	Republic R-III	Republic
5	50.5	Jennings	Jennings
6	50.5	Dexter R-XI	Dexter
7	50.5	Ladue	St Louis
8	50.4	Marshall	Marshall
9	50.4	Liberty 53	Liberty
10	49.9	Warsaw R-IX	Warsaw

11	49.8	Kennett 39	Kennett
12	49.8	Willard R-II	Willard
13	49.8	Raymore-Peculiar R-II	Raymore
14	49.8	Hannibal 60	Hannibal
15	49.8	East Newton County R-VI	Granby
16	49.6	Cape Girardeau 63	Cape Girardeau
17	49.6	Parkway C-2	Chesterfield
18	49.5	Affton 101	St Louis
19	49.5	Kansas City 33	Kansas City
20	49.5	St. James R-I	St James
21	49.4	Nixa R-II	Nixa
22	49.4	Mountain Grove R-III	Mountain Grove
23	49.4	Ava R-I	Ava
24	49.4	Center 58	Kansas City
25	49.3	Hancock Place	St Louis
26	49.3	Warrensburg R-VI	Warrensburg
27	49.2	Rolla 31	Rolla
28	49.2	Potosi R-III	Potosi
29	49.2	Smithville R-II	Smithville
30	49.2	Central R-III	Park Hills
31	49.2	Ft. Zumwalt R-II	O'fallon
32	49.2	Webb City R-VII	Webb City
33	49.1	Marshfield R-I	Marshfield
34	49.1	University City	University City
35	49.1	Independence 30	Independence
36	49.1	Columbia 93	Columbia
37	49.1	Troy R-III	Troy
38	49.1	Harrisonville R-IX	Harrisonville
38	49.1	Jefferson City	Jefferson City
40	49.0	Platte County R-III	Platte City
41	49.0	Hillsboro R-III	Hillsboro
42	48.9	St. Joseph	St Joseph
43	48.9	Monett R-I	Monett
44	48.9	Morgan County R-II	Versailles
45	48.9	Kirkwood R-VII	Kirkwood
46	48.9	North Kansas City 74	Kansas City
47	48.9	Festus R-VI	Festus
48	48.9	Fulton 58	Fulton
49	48.8	Waynesville R-VI	Waynesville
50	48.8	Hazelwood	Florissant
51	48.8	St. Louis City	St Louis
52	48.8	Aurora R-VIII	Aurora
53	48.8	Branson R-IV	Branson
54	48.7	Springfield R-XII	Springfield
55	48.7	Riverview Gardens	St Louis
56	48.7	Union R-XI	Union
57	48.7	Northwest R-I	House Springs
58	48.7	Clayton	Clayton
59	48.7	Mehlville R-IX	St Louis
60	48.7	Chillicothe R-II	Chillicothe
61	48.7	Sikeston R-VI	Sikeston
62	48.6	Rockwood R-VI	Eureka
63	48.6	Desoto 73	Desoto
64	48.5	Kearney R-I	Kearney
65	48.5	Ritenour	St Louis
66	48.5	Lee's Summit R-VII	Lee's Summit
67	48.5	Seneca R-VII	Seneca
68	48.4	Eldon R-I	Eldon
69	48.4	Lindbergh R-VIII	St Louis
70	48.4	Park Hill	Kansas City
71	48.4	Poplar Bluff R-I	Poplar Bluff
72	48.4	Lebanon R-III	Lebanon
73	48.4	Ozark R-VI	Ozark
74	48.4	Winfield R-IV	Winfield
75	48.3	Moberly	Moberly
76	48.3	Savannah R-III	Savannah
77	48.3	Ste. Genevieve County R-II	Ste Genevieve
78	48.3	Ferguson-Florissant R-II	Florissant
79	48.3	Carthage R-IX	Carthage
80	48.3	Caruthersville 18	Caruthersville
81	48.2	Blue Springs R-IV	Blue Springs
82	48.2	Reeds Spring R-IV	Reeds Spring
83	48.2	Hickman Mills C-1	Kansas City
84	48.2	Richmond R-XVI	Richmond
85	48.1	Mcdonald County R-I	Anderson
86	48.1	Warren County R-III	Warrenton
87	48.1	Jackson R-II	Jackson
88	48.1	Farmington R-VII	Farmington
89	48.1	Francis Howell R-III	St Charles
90	48.1	Mexico 59	Mexico
91	48.1	Wentzville R-IV	Wentzville
92	48.0	Nevada R-V	Nevada
93	48.0	Grandview C-4	Grandview
94	48.0	School of the Osage R-II	Lake Ozark
95	48.0	Kirksville R-III	Kirksville
96	48.0	Oak Grove R-VI	Oak Grove
97	48.0	Grain Valley R-V	Grain Valley
98	48.0	Knob Noster R-VIII	Knob Noster
99	48.0	Normandy	St Louis
100	48.0	Belton 124	Belton
101	47.8	Raytown C-2	Raytown
102	47.8	Fox C-6	Arnold

103	47.8	Washington	Washington
104	47.8	Sedalia 200	Sedalia
105	47.7	Perry County 32	Perryville
106	47.7	Bolivar R-I	Bolivar
107	47.7	St. Charles R-VI	St Charles
108	47.7	Joplin R-VIII	Joplin
109	47.6	Salem R-80	Salem
110	47.6	St. Clair R-XIII	St Clair
111	47.6	Webster Groves	Webster Groves
112	47.5	Dallas County R-I	Buffalo
113	47.5	Pattonville R-III	St Ann
114	47.4	New Madrid County R-I	New Madrid
115	47.2	Excelsior Springs 40	Excelsior Spgs
116	47.1	Meramec Valley R-III	Pacific
117	47.1	Carl Junction R-I	Carl Junction
118	47.1	Clinton	Clinton
119	47.1	Cassville R-IV	Cassville
120	47.0	West Plains R-VII	West Plains
121	47.0	Camdenton R-III	Camdenton
122	47.0	Fort Osage R-I	Independence
123	46.9	Fredericktown R-I	Fredericktown
124	46.7	North St. Francois Co. R-I	Bonne Terre
125	46.7	Pleasant Hill R-III	Pleasant Hill
126	46.6	Neosho R-V	Neosho
127	46.5	Windsor C-1	Imperial
128	46.2	Odessa R-VII	Odessa
129	45.8	Logan-Rogersville R-VIII	Rogersville
130	45.7	Sullivan	Sullivan
131	45.6	Cameron R-I	Cameron
132	30.9	Specl. Sch. Dst. St. Louis Co.	Town & Ctry

Individual Education Program Students

Rank	Percent	District Name	City
1	24.9	Marshall	Marshall
2	23.4	Washington	Washington
3	22.2	Affton 101	St Louis
4	21.4	Kirkwood R-VII	Kirkwood
5	21.0	Jennings	Jennings
5	21.0	Parkway C-2	Chesterfield
7	20.3	Lindbergh R-VIII	St Louis
7	20.3	Mehlville R-IX	St Louis
9	20.2	Webster Groves	Webster Groves
10	19.8	Ritenour	St Louis
11	19.7	St. James R-I	St James
12	19.6	Jefferson City	Jefferson City
13	19.3	Perry County 32	Perryville
14	19.2	University City	University City
15	18.7	Moberly	Moberly
15	18.7	Riverview Gardens	St Louis
17	18.6	Desoto 73	Desoto
17	18.6	Hancock Place	St Louis
19	18.5	Pattonville R-III	St Ann
20	18.4	Bayless	St Louis
20	18.4	Cape Girardeau 63	Cape Girardeau
22	18.3	Chillicothe R-II	Chillicothe
22	18.3	Hazelwood	Florissant
22	18.3	Normandy	St Louis
25	18.2	New Madrid County R-I	New Madrid
25	18.2	Northwest R-I	House Springs
25	18.2	St. Louis City	St Louis
28	18.1	Ferguson-Florissant R-II	Florissant
29	17.9	Central R-III	Park Hills
29	17.9	Willard R-II	Willard
31	17.8	Warrensburg R-VI	Warrensburg
31	17.8	Wentzville R-IV	Wentzville
33	17.7	Cameron R-I	Cameron
34	17.5	Kirksville R-III	Kirksville
35	17.1	Fox C-6	Arnold
36	17.0	Rockwood R-VI	Eureka
37	16.9	Farmington R-VII	Farmington
37	16.9	Hannibal 60	Hannibal
39	16.8	St. Charles R-VI	St Charles
40	16.7	Ladue	St Louis
40	16.7	Mountain Grove R-III	Mountain Grove
40	16.7	Warsaw R-IX	Warsaw
43	16.5	Doniphan R-I	Doniphan
43	16.5	Sullivan	Sullivan
43	16.5	Winfield R-IV	Winfield
46	16.4	Dexter R-XI	Dexter
47	16.3	Monett R-I	Monett
48	16.1	Meramec Valley R-III	Pacific
49	16.0	Clayton	Clayton
49	16.0	Troy R-III	Troy
51	15.9	Ft. Zumwalt R-II	O'fallon
52	15.8	Knob Noster R-VIII	Knob Noster
52	15.8	Poplar Bluff R-I	Poplar Bluff
52	15.8	Reeds Spring R-IV	Reeds Spring
55	15.7	Bolivar R-I	Bolivar
55	15.7	Fort Osage R-I	Independence
55	15.7	Francis Howell R-III	St Charles
55	15.7	Morgan County R-II	Versailles
55	15.7	Nevada R-V	Nevada

55	15.7	Seneca R-VII	Seneca
55	15.7	St. Clair R-XIII	St Clair
62	15.6	Carl Junction R-I	Carl Junction
62	15.6	Center 58	Kansas City
62	15.6	Columbia 93	Columbia
62	15.6	Marshfield R-I	Marshfield
66	15.5	Cassville R-IV	Cassville
66	15.5	Hickman Mills C-1	Kansas City
68	15.3	Gasconade County R-II	Owensville
69	15.2	North St. Francois Co. R-I	Bonne Terre
69	15.2	Ozark R-VI	Ozark
71	15.0	Ste. Genevieve County R-II	Ste Genevieve
72	14.9	Joplin R-VIII	Joplin
72	14.9	Logan-Rogersville R-VIII	Rogersville
74	14.8	Pleasant Hill R-III	Pleasant Hill
74	14.8	Sedalia 200	Sedalia
76	14.7	Kennett 39	Kennett
76	14.7	Warren County R-III	Warrenton
78	14.6	North Kansas City 74	Kansas City
79	14.4	East Newton County R-VI	Granby
79	14.4	Hillsboro R-III	Hillsboro
79	14.4	Potosi R-III	Potosi
82	14.3	Waynesville R-VI	Waynesville
83	14.2	Caruthersville 18	Caruthersville
83	14.2	Mexico 59	Mexico
85	14.1	Clinton	Clinton
86	14.0	Grandview C-4	Grandview
86	14.0	Richmond R-XVI	Richmond
88	13.9	Dallas County R-I	Buffalo
88	13.9	Windsor C-1	Imperial
90	13.8	Union R-XI	Union
91	13.4	Carthage R-IX	Carthage
92	13.3	Ava R-I	Ava
92	13.3	Camdenton R-III	Camdenton
92	13.3	Eldon R-I	Eldon
92	13.3	Park Hill	Kansas City
92	13.3	School of the Osage R-II	Lake Ozark
97	13.2	Jackson R-II	Jackson
97	13.2	Neosho R-V	Neosho
99	13.1	Springfield R-XII	Springfield
100	13.0	Odessa R-VII	Odessa
100	13.0	St. Joseph	St Joseph
102	12.9	Oak Grove R-VI	Oak Grove
102	12.9	Savannah R-III	Savannah
104	12.8	Republic R-III	Republic
105	12.7	Aurora R-VIII	Aurora
106	12.5	Festus R-VI	Festus
106	12.5	Independence 30	Independence
106	12.5	Salem R-80	Salem
109	12.4	Rolla 31	Rolla
109	12.4	Webb City R-VII	Webb City
111	12.3	Nixa R-II	Nixa
112	12.2	Blue Springs R-IV	Blue Springs
113	12.0	Fulton 58	Fulton
113	12.0	Lee's Summit R-VII	Lee's Summit
113	12.0	Mcdonald County R-I	Anderson
113	12.0	Raytown C-2	Raytown
117	11.9	Branson R-IV	Branson
118	11.8	Liberty 53	Liberty
118	11.8	West Plains R-VII	West Plains
120	11.6	Belton 124	Belton
120	11.6	Lebanon R-III	Lebanon
122	11.5	Grain Valley R-V	Grain Valley
123	11.4	Excelsior Springs 40	Excelsior Spgs
124	11.2	Kearney R-I	Kearney
125	11.1	Smithville R-II	Smithville
126	11.0	Fredericktown R-I	Fredericktown
126	11.0	Kansas City 33	Kansas City
128	10.1	Harrisonville R-IX	Harrisonville
128	10.1	Platte County R-III	Platte City
130	8.9	Sikeston R-VI	Sikeston
131	8.0	Raymore-Peculiar R-II	Raymore
132	n/a	Specl. Sch. Dst. St. Louis Co.	Town & Ctry

English Language Learner Students

Rank	Percent	District Name	City
1	13.8	Monett R-I	Monett
2	12.6	Bayless	St Louis
3	11.1	Mcdonald County R-I	Anderson
4	8.1	Kansas City 33	Kansas City
5	6.8	St. Louis City	St Louis
6	6.5	Carthage R-IX	Carthage
7	5.2	Marshall	Marshall
8	5.0	Affton 101	St Louis
9	4.4	Hancock Place	St Louis
10	4.2	Clayton	Clayton
10	4.2	Neosho R-V	Neosho
12	4.0	Sedalia 200	Sedalia
13	3.8	Ritenour	St Louis
14	3.6	Pattonville R-III	St Ann
15	3.2	Jefferson City	Jefferson City
16	2.9	Branson R-IV	Branson

Rank	Percent	District Name	City
17	2.8	Grandview C-4	Grandview
17	2.8	North Kansas City 74	Kansas City
19	2.7	Knob Noster R-VIII	Knob Noster
20	2.6	Mehlville R-IX	St Louis
21	2.4	Cassville R-IV	Cassville
22	2.2	Park Hill	Kansas City
23	2.1	Belton 124	Belton
23	2.1	Columbia 93	Columbia
23	2.1	Hazelwood	Florissant
23	2.1	Hickman Mills C-1	Kansas City
23	2.1	St. Charles R-VI	St Charles
28	2.0	Parkway C-2	Chesterfield
29	1.8	Warrensburg R-VI	Warrensburg
30	1.7	Center 58	Kansas City
31	1.5	Lindbergh R-VIII	St Louis
32	1.3	Aurora R-VIII	Aurora
32	1.3	Washington	Washington
34	1.2	Independence 30	Independence
35	1.1	Joplin R-VIII	Joplin
35	1.1	Raytown C-2	Raytown
35	1.1	Rockwood R-VI	Eureka
35	1.1	Rolla 31	Rolla
35	1.1	University City	University City
40	1.0	Reeds Spring R-IV	Reeds Spring
40	1.0	Specl. Sch. Dst. St. Louis Co.	Town & Ctry
40	1.0	Waynesville R-VI	Waynesville
43	0.9	Francis Howell R-III	St Charles
43	0.9	Kennett 39	Kennett
43	0.9	Lee's Summit R-VII	Lee's Summit
43	0.9	Perry County 32	Perryville
47	0.8	Cape Girardeau 63	Cape Girardeau
47	0.8	Platte County R-III	Platte City
49	0.7	Ladue	St Louis
49	0.7	Springfield R-XII	Springfield
51	0.6	Ferguson-Florissant R-II	Florissant
51	0.6	Fox C-6	Arnold
51	0.6	Mexico 59	Mexico
54	0.5	Carl Junction R-I	Carl Junction
54	0.5	Hillsboro R-III	Hillsboro
54	0.5	Webster Groves	Webster Groves
54	0.5	Wentzville R-IV	Wentzville
54	0.5	Willard R-II	Willard
59	0.4	Blue Springs R-IV	Blue Springs
59	0.4	Bolivar R-I	Bolivar
59	0.4	Camdenton R-III	Camdenton
59	0.4	Caruthersville 18	Caruthersville
59	0.4	Dallas County R-I	Buffalo
59	0.4	Fredericktown R-I	Fredericktown
59	0.4	Kirkwood R-VII	Kirkwood
59	0.4	Sikeston R-VI	Sikeston
59	0.4	St. Joseph	St Joseph
59	0.4	Webb City R-VII	Webb City
69	0.3	East Newton County R-VI	Granby
69	0.3	Ft. Zumwalt R-II	O'fallon
69	0.3	Grain Valley R-V	Grain Valley
69	0.3	Liberty 53	Liberty
69	0.3	Moberly	Moberly
69	0.3	Morgan County R-II	Versailles
69	0.3	Nixa R-II	Nixa
69	0.3	Normandy	St Louis
69	0.3	Northwest R-I	House Springs
69	0.3	Odessa R-VII	Odessa
69	0.3	Troy R-III	Troy
69	0.3	Warren County R-III	Warrenton
69	0.3	Windsor C-1	Imperial
82	0.2	Excelsior Springs 40	Excelsior Spgs
82	0.2	Farmington R-VII	Farmington
82	0.2	Fort Osage R-I	Independence
82	0.2	Fulton 58	Fulton
82	0.2	Harrisonville R-IX	Harrisonville
82	0.2	Kirksville R-III	Kirksville
82	0.2	Nevada R-V	Nevada
82	0.2	Potosi R-III	Potosi
82	0.2	Riverview Gardens	St Louis
82	0.2	St. James R-I	St James
82	0.2	Union R-XI	Union
93	0.1	Cameron R-I	Cameron
93	0.1	Festus R-VI	Festus
93	0.1	Gasconade County R-II	Owensville
93	0.1	Hannibal 60	Hannibal
93	0.1	Jackson R-II	Jackson
93	0.1	Lebanon R-III	Lebanon
93	0.1	School of the Osage R-II	Lake Ozark
93	0.1	Ste. Genevieve County R-II	Ste Genevieve
93	0.1	Sullivan	Sullivan
93	0.1	West Plains R-VII	West Plains
103	0.0	Clinton	Clinton
103	0.0	Poplar Bluff R-I	Poplar Bluff
103	0.0	Savannah R-III	Savannah
106	0.0	Ava R-I	Ava
106	0.0	Central R-III	Park Hills
106	0.0	Chillicothe R-II	Chillicothe
106	0.0	Desoto 73	Desoto
106	0.0	Dexter R-XI	Dexter
106	0.0	Doniphan R-I	Doniphan
106	0.0	Eldon R-I	Eldon
106	0.0	Jennings	Jennings
106	0.0	Kearney R-I	Kearney
106	0.0	Logan-Rogersville R-VIII	Rogersville
106	0.0	Marshfield R-I	Marshfield
106	0.0	Meramec Valley R-III	Pacific
106	0.0	Mountain Grove R-III	Mountain Grove
106	0.0	New Madrid County R-I	New Madrid
106	0.0	North St. Francois Co. R-I	Bonne Terre
106	0.0	Oak Grove R-VI	Oak Grove
106	0.0	Ozark R-VI	Ozark
106	0.0	Pleasant Hill R-III	Pleasant Hill
106	0.0	Raymore-Peculiar R-II	Raymore
106	0.0	Republic R-III	Republic
106	0.0	Richmond R-XVI	Richmond
106	0.0	Salem R-80	Salem
106	0.0	Seneca R-V	Seneca
106	0.0	Smithville R-II	Smithville
106	0.0	St. Clair R-XIII	St Clair
106	0.0	Warsaw R-IX	Warsaw
106	0.0	Winfield R-IV	Winfield

Migrant Students

Rank	Percent	District Name	City
1	16.2	Monett R-I	Monett
2	14.0	Mcdonald County R-I	Anderson
3	8.4	Sedalia 200	Sedalia
4	8.1	Marshall	Marshall
5	6.0	Knob Noster R-VIII	Knob Noster
6	5.7	Carthage R-IX	Carthage
7	4.6	Neosho R-V	Neosho
8	3.3	Cassville R-IV	Cassville
9	2.8	Kennett 39	Kennett
10	2.2	Aurora R-VIII	Aurora
11	1.2	St. Charles R-VI	St Charles
12	1.1	East Newton County R-VI	Granby
13	0.7	Mexico 59	Mexico
13	0.7	Warsaw R-IX	Warsaw
15	0.6	Joplin R-VIII	Joplin
15	0.6	Kansas City 33	Kansas City
15	0.6	Webb City R-VII	Webb City
18	0.5	Fredericktown R-I	Fredericktown
18	0.5	Springfield R-XII	Springfield
20	0.4	Warrensburg R-VI	Warrensburg
21	0.3	Ava R-I	Ava
21	0.3	Belton 124	Belton
21	0.3	Seneca R-VII	Seneca
21	0.3	St. Louis City	St Louis
25	0.2	Caruthersville 18	Caruthersville
25	0.2	Morgan County R-II	Versailles
25	0.2	New Madrid County R-I	New Madrid
25	0.2	Nixa R-II	Nixa
25	0.2	Platte County R-III	Platte City
30	0.1	Branson R-IV	Branson
30	0.1	Dexter R-XI	Dexter
30	0.1	Kirksville R-III	Kirksville
30	0.1	Meramec Valley R-III	Pacific
30	0.1	Nevada R-V	Nevada
30	0.1	Richmond R-XVI	Richmond
30	0.1	Willard R-II	Willard
37	0.0	Dallas County R-I	Buffalo
37	0.0	Hannibal 60	Hannibal
37	0.0	Lee's Summit R-VII	Lee's Summit
37	0.0	Mehlville R-IX	St Louis
37	0.0	Normandy	St Louis
37	0.0	Ozark R-VI	Ozark
37	0.0	Ritenour	St Louis
37	0.0	Rockwood R-VI	Eureka
37	0.0	Warren County R-III	Warrenton
37	0.0	Washington	Washington
37	0.0	Windsor C-1	Imperial
48	0.0	Affton 101	St Louis
48	0.0	Bayless	St Louis
48	0.0	Blue Springs R-IV	Blue Springs
48	0.0	Bolivar R-I	Bolivar
48	0.0	Camdenton R-III	Camdenton
48	0.0	Cameron R-I	Cameron
48	0.0	Cape Girardeau 63	Cape Girardeau
48	0.0	Carl Junction R-I	Carl Junction
48	0.0	Center 58	Kansas City
48	0.0	Central R-III	Park Hills
48	0.0	Chillicothe R-II	Chillicothe
48	0.0	Clayton	Clayton
48	0.0	Clinton	Clinton
48	0.0	Columbia 93	Columbia
48	0.0	Desoto 73	Desoto
48	0.0	Doniphan R-I	Doniphan
48	0.0	Eldon R-I	Eldon
48	0.0	Excelsior Springs 40	Excelsior Spgs
48	0.0	Farmington R-VII	Farmington
48	0.0	Ferguson-Florissant R-II	Florissant
48	0.0	Festus R-VI	Festus
48	0.0	Fort Osage R-I	Independence
48	0.0	Fox C-6	Arnold
48	0.0	Francis Howell R-III	St Charles
48	0.0	Ft. Zumwalt R-II	O'fallon
48	0.0	Fulton 58	Fulton
48	0.0	Gasconade County R-II	Owensville
48	0.0	Grain Valley R-V	Grain Valley
48	0.0	Grandview C-4	Grandview
48	0.0	Hancock Place	St Louis
48	0.0	Harrisonville R-IX	Harrisonville
48	0.0	Hazelwood	Florissant
48	0.0	Hickman Mills C-1	Kansas City
48	0.0	Hillsboro R-III	Hillsboro
48	0.0	Independence 30	Independence
48	0.0	Jackson R-II	Jackson
48	0.0	Jefferson City	Jefferson City
48	0.0	Jennings	Jennings
48	0.0	Kearney R-I	Kearney
48	0.0	Kirkwood R-VII	Kirkwood
48	0.0	Ladue	St Louis
48	0.0	Lebanon R-III	Lebanon
48	0.0	Liberty 53	Liberty
48	0.0	Lindbergh R-VIII	St Louis
48	0.0	Logan-Rogersville R-VIII	Rogersville
48	0.0	Marshfield R-I	Marshfield
48	0.0	Moberly	Moberly
48	0.0	Mountain Grove R-III	Mountain Grove
48	0.0	North Kansas City 74	Kansas City
48	0.0	North St. Francois Co. R-I	Bonne Terre
48	0.0	Northwest R-I	House Springs
48	0.0	Oak Grove R-VI	Oak Grove
48	0.0	Odessa R-VII	Odessa
48	0.0	Park Hill	Kansas City
48	0.0	Parkway C-2	Chesterfield
48	0.0	Pattonville R-III	St Ann
48	0.0	Perry County 32	Perryville
48	0.0	Pleasant Hill R-III	Pleasant Hill
48	0.0	Poplar Bluff R-I	Poplar Bluff
48	0.0	Potosi R-III	Potosi
48	0.0	Raymore-Peculiar R-II	Raymore
48	0.0	Raytown C-2	Raytown
48	0.0	Reeds Spring R-IV	Reeds Spring
48	0.0	Republic R-III	Republic
48	0.0	Riverview Gardens	St Louis
48	0.0	Rolla 31	Rolla
48	0.0	Salem R-80	Salem
48	0.0	Savannah R-III	Savannah
48	0.0	School of the Osage R-II	Lake Ozark
48	0.0	Sikeston R-VI	Sikeston
48	0.0	Smithville R-II	Smithville
48	0.0	Specl. Sch. Dst. St. Louis Co.	Town & Ctry
48	0.0	St. Clair R-XIII	St Clair
48	0.0	St. James R-I	St James
48	0.0	St. Joseph	St Joseph
48	0.0	Ste. Genevieve County R-II	Ste Genevieve
48	0.0	Sullivan	Sullivan
48	0.0	Troy R-III	Troy
48	0.0	Union R-XI	Union
48	0.0	University City	University City
48	0.0	Waynesville R-VI	Waynesville
48	0.0	Webster Groves	Webster Groves
48	0.0	Wentzville R-IV	Wentzville
48	0.0	West Plains R-VII	West Plains
48	0.0	Winfield R-IV	Winfield

Students Eligible for Free Lunch

Rank	Percent	District Name	City
1	77.6	St. Louis City	St Louis
2	71.8	Normandy	St Louis
3	69.6	Jennings	Jennings
4	65.6	Riverview Gardens	St Louis
5	61.4	Kansas City 33	Kansas City
6	58.5	Caruthersville 18	Caruthersville
7	54.1	New Madrid County R-I	New Madrid
8	50.2	Sikeston R-VI	Sikeston
9	49.9	Doniphan R-I	Doniphan
10	49.8	Kennett 39	Kennett
11	48.0	Hickman Mills C-1	Kansas City
12	46.7	Mcdonald County R-I	Anderson
13	46.6	University City	University City
14	45.8	Mountain Grove R-III	Mountain Grove
14	45.8	Warsaw R-IX	Warsaw
16	45.2	Ava R-I	Ava
17	45.0	Hancock Place	St Louis
18	44.9	Center 58	Kansas City
19	43.3	Poplar Bluff R-I	Poplar Bluff
20	42.3	Central R-III	Park Hills
21	42.2	Moberly	Moberly
22	42.1	Joplin R-VIII	Joplin

Rank	Value	District Name	City
23	41.2	Hannibal 60	Hannibal
24	40.9	Ferguson-Florissant R-II	Florissant
24	40.9	Ritenour	St Louis
26	40.3	Nevada R-V	Nevada
27	40.2	Marshall	Marshall
28	40.1	School of the Osage R-II	Lake Ozark
29	39.8	Morgan County R-II	Versailles
30	39.7	West Plains R-VII	West Plains
31	39.1	East Newton County R-VI	Granby
32	39.0	Dallas County R-I	Buffalo
33	38.7	Potosi R-III	Potosi
33	38.7	Reeds Spring R-IV	Reeds Spring
35	38.6	St. Joseph	St Joseph
36	38.3	Eldon R-I	Eldon
37	38.0	Grandview C-4	Grandview
38	37.7	Monett R-I	Monett
39	36.9	Cape Girardeau 63	Cape Girardeau
39	36.9	Carthage R-IX	Carthage
41	36.6	Aurora R-VIII	Aurora
42	36.3	Neosho R-V	Neosho
43	35.9	St. James R-I	St James
44	35.7	Cassville R-IV	Cassville
45	34.5	Sedalia 200	Sedalia
46	34.0	Mexico 59	Mexico
47	33.6	Dexter R-XI	Dexter
48	33.1	Webb City R-VII	Webb City
49	32.7	Bolivar R-I	Bolivar
50	32.6	Lebanon R-III	Lebanon
51	32.5	Camdenton R-III	Camdenton
51	32.5	Salem R-80	Salem
53	32.3	Winfield R-IV	Winfield
54	31.8	Fredericktown R-I	Fredericktown
55	31.7	North St. Francois Co. R-I	Bonne Terre
56	31.5	St. Clair R-XIII	St Clair
57	30.7	Springfield R-XII	Springfield
58	30.4	Farmington R-VII	Farmington
58	30.4	Fulton 58	Fulton
60	29.4	Branson R-IV	Branson
61	29.3	Clinton	Clinton
61	29.3	Rolla 31	Rolla
63	29.2	Desoto 73	Desoto
64	28.8	Seneca R-VII	Seneca
65	28.3	Jefferson City	Jefferson City
66	28.2	Ste. Genevieve County R-II	Ste Genevieve
67	28.0	Perry County 32	Perryville
68	27.8	Marshfield R-I	Marshfield
69	27.7	Chillicothe R-II	Chillicothe
69	27.7	Sullivan	Sullivan
71	27.0	Fort Osage R-I	Independence
72	26.9	Raytown C-2	Raytown
72	26.9	Richmond R-XVI	Richmond
74	26.8	Excelsior Springs 40	Excelsior Spgs
74	26.8	Hazelwood	Florissant
76	26.5	Kirksville R-III	Kirksville
77	25.4	Specl. Sch. Dst. St. Louis Co.	Town & Ctry
78	25.2	Independence 30	Independence
79	24.9	Columbia 93	Columbia
80	24.6	Carl Junction R-I	Carl Junction
81	23.7	Meramec Valley R-III	Pacific
82	23.2	Troy R-III	Troy
83	22.9	Festus R-VI	Festus
83	22.9	Gasconade County R-II	Owensville
83	22.9	Republic R-III	Republic
86	22.6	Warren County R-III	Warrenton
87	22.4	Odessa R-VII	Odessa
88	22.0	Bayless	St Louis
88	22.0	Northwest R-I	House Springs
90	21.8	Cameron R-I	Cameron
91	21.7	St. Charles R-VI	St Charles
92	21.4	Union R-XI	Union
93	21.1	Willard R-II	Willard
94	20.9	Savannah R-III	Savannah
95	20.4	Warrensburg R-VI	Warrensburg
96	20.1	Belton 124	Belton
97	19.9	North Kansas City 74	Kansas City
98	19.5	Knob Noster R-VIII	Knob Noster
99	19.3	Harrisonville R-IX	Harrisonville
100	19.2	Pattonville R-III	St Ann
101	18.3	Waynesville R-VI	Waynesville
102	17.8	Hillsboro R-III	Hillsboro
103	17.4	Jackson R-II	Jackson
104	17.2	Fox C-6	Arnold
105	16.7	Nixa R-II	Nixa
105	16.7	Ozark R-VI	Ozark
107	15.9	Windsor C-1	Imperial
108	14.2	Oak Grove R-VI	Oak Grove
109	13.8	Logan-Rogersville R-VIII	Rogersville
109	13.8	Wentzville R-IV	Wentzville
111	13.0	Affton 101	St Louis
112	12.8	Raymore-Peculiar R-II	Raymore
113	12.4	Platte County R-III	Platte City
114	12.3	Pleasant Hill R-III	Pleasant Hill
115	11.1	Grain Valley R-V	Grain Valley
116	11.0	Washington	Washington
117	10.9	Park Hill	Kansas City
118	10.1	Liberty 53	Liberty
119	9.8	Webster Groves	Webster Groves
120	8.7	Mehlville R-IX	St Louis
121	7.9	Blue Springs R-IV	Blue Springs
122	7.2	Ft. Zumwalt R-II	O'fallon
123	6.9	Lee's Summit R-VII	Lee's Summit
124	6.6	Kirkwood R-VII	Kirkwood
125	6.2	Francis Howell R-III	St Charles
126	5.7	Ladue	St Louis
126	5.7	Lindbergh R-VIII	St Louis
128	4.8	Kearney R-I	Kearney
129	4.7	Smithville R-II	Smithville
130	4.1	Clayton	Clayton
131	3.6	Parkway C-2	Chesterfield
132	2.4	Rockwood R-VI	Eureka

Students Eligible for Reduced-Price Lunch

Rank	Percent	District Name	City
1	17.0	Knob Noster R-VIII	Knob Noster
2	15.6	Bayless	St Louis
3	13.8	Waynesville R-VI	Waynesville
4	13.2	Central R-III	Park Hills
4	13.2	Mountain Grove R-III	Mountain Grove
6	13.1	Seneca R-VII	Seneca
7	12.6	Morgan County R-II	Versailles
8	11.7	Hancock Place	St Louis
8	11.7	Warsaw R-IX	Warsaw
10	11.4	Ste. Genevieve County R-II	Ste Genevieve
11	10.9	Hickman Mills C-1	Kansas City
12	10.7	Cassville R-IV	Cassville
12	10.7	Dexter R-XI	Dexter
14	10.5	Marshfield R-I	Marshfield
15	10.4	Dallas County R-I	Buffalo
16	10.3	Ava R-I	Ava
16	10.3	Doniphan R-I	Doniphan
16	10.3	East Newton County R-VI	Granby
16	10.3	Fredericktown R-I	Fredericktown
20	10.2	Fort Osage R-I	Independence
20	10.2	Neosho R-V	Neosho
22	10.1	Mexico 59	Mexico
23	9.9	Eldon R-I	Eldon
23	9.9	St. Joseph	St Joseph
25	9.8	Bolivar R-I	Bolivar
25	9.8	Gasconade County R-II	Owensville
25	9.8	Reeds Spring R-IV	Reeds Spring
28	9.6	Camdenton R-III	Camdenton
28	9.6	Farmington R-VII	Farmington
28	9.6	Riverview Gardens	St Louis
31	9.5	Mcdonald County R-I	Anderson
31	9.5	St. James R-I	St James
33	9.4	North Kansas City 74	Kansas City
33	9.4	Willard R-II	Willard
35	9.3	Chillicothe R-II	Chillicothe
36	9.1	Carl Junction R-I	Carl Junction
36	9.1	Ritenour	St Louis
38	9.0	Monett R-I	Monett
39	8.9	Moberly	Moberly
39	8.9	Raytown C-2	Raytown
41	8.8	Fulton 58	Fulton
41	8.8	Hannibal 60	Hannibal
43	8.7	Branson R-IV	Branson
43	8.7	North St. Francois Co. R-I	Bonne Terre
45	8.6	Jennings	Jennings
46	8.4	Carthage R-IX	Carthage
46	8.4	Nixa R-II	Nixa
46	8.4	Republic R-III	Republic
46	8.4	Webb City R-VII	Webb City
50	8.3	Independence 30	Independence
51	8.2	Northwest R-I	House Springs
52	8.1	Ferguson-Florissant R-II	Florissant
52	8.1	Union R-XI	Union
54	8.0	Perry County 32	Perryville
54	8.0	Sedalia 200	Sedalia
54	8.0	University City	University City
57	7.9	Aurora R-VIII	Aurora
57	7.9	Richmond R-XVI	Richmond
57	7.9	Savannah R-III	Savannah
60	7.8	Marshall	Marshall
60	7.8	Springfield R-XII	Springfield
62	7.7	Joplin R-VIII	Joplin
63	7.6	Windsor C-1	Imperial
64	7.5	Lebanon R-III	Lebanon
64	7.5	Nevada R-V	Nevada
64	7.5	Poplar Bluff R-I	Poplar Bluff
64	7.5	Potosi R-III	Potosi
68	7.4	Meramec Valley R-III	Pacific
68	7.4	Rolla 31	Rolla
70	7.3	Cameron R-I	Cameron
70	7.3	Grandview C-4	Grandview
70	7.3	Kansas City 33	Kansas City
73	7.2	Belton 124	Belton
73	7.2	Warren County R-III	Warrenton
75	6.7	Clinton	Clinton
75	6.7	West Plains R-VII	West Plains
77	6.4	Excelsior Springs 40	Excelsior Spgs
78	6.2	Logan-Rogersville R-VIII	Rogersville
78	6.2	St. Clair R-XIII	St Clair
80	6.1	Center 58	Kansas City
80	6.1	Hazelwood	Florissant
80	6.1	Odessa R-VII	Odessa
83	6.0	Harrisonville R-IX	Harrisonville
83	6.0	Pattonville R-III	St Ann
83	6.0	Salem R-80	Salem
86	5.9	Oak Grove R-VI	Oak Grove
87	5.8	Cape Girardeau 63	Cape Girardeau
87	5.8	Hillsboro R-III	Hillsboro
87	5.8	Jackson R-II	Jackson
87	5.8	Jefferson City	Jefferson City
91	5.7	Ozark R-VI	Ozark
91	5.7	Winfield R-IV	Winfield
93	5.6	Fox C-6	Arnold
94	5.5	Warrensburg R-VI	Warrensburg
95	5.4	Normandy	St Louis
95	5.4	School of the Osage R-II	Lake Ozark
95	5.4	Sullivan	Sullivan
98	5.3	Kirksville R-III	Kirksville
98	5.3	Washington	Washington
100	5.2	Desoto 73	Desoto
100	5.2	Festus R-VI	Festus
100	5.2	Pleasant Hill R-III	Pleasant Hill
103	4.8	Troy R-III	Troy
104	4.7	Raymore-Peculiar R-II	Raymore
104	4.7	St. Charles R-VI	St Charles
106	4.6	Sikeston R-VI	Sikeston
107	4.5	Affton 101	St Louis
107	4.5	Park Hill	Kansas City
107	4.5	St. Louis City	St Louis
110	4.4	New Madrid County R-I	New Madrid
111	4.3	Kennett 39	Kennett
111	4.3	Platte County R-III	Platte City
113	4.2	Columbia 93	Columbia
114	4.0	Specl. Sch. Dst. St. Louis Co.	Town & Ctry
114	4.0	Wentzville R-IV	Wentzville
116	3.8	Caruthersville 18	Caruthersville
117	3.3	Blue Springs R-IV	Blue Springs
118	3.1	Grain Valley R-V	Grain Valley
118	3.1	Smithville R-II	Smithville
120	3.0	Ft. Zumwalt R-II	O'fallon
121	2.9	Liberty 53	Liberty
122	2.7	Mehlville R-IX	St Louis
123	2.3	Lindbergh R-VIII	St Louis
124	2.2	Lee's Summit R-VII	Lee's Summit
125	1.9	Webster Groves	Webster Groves
126	1.8	Francis Howell R-III	St Charles
127	1.7	Kearney R-I	Kearney
128	1.6	Clayton	Clayton
129	1.5	Kirkwood R-VII	Kirkwood
129	1.5	Ladue	St Louis
131	1.4	Parkway C-2	Chesterfield
132	1.0	Rockwood R-VI	Eureka

Student/Teacher Ratio

Rank	Ratio	District Name	City
1	19.4	Troy R-III	Troy
2	18.9	Republic R-III	Republic
3	18.7	Bayless	St Louis
4	18.3	Neosho R-V	Neosho
5	17.9	Festus R-VI	Festus
6	17.8	Meramec Valley R-III	Pacific
7	17.6	Hillsboro R-III	Hillsboro
8	17.4	Independence 30	Independence
8	17.4	Lebanon R-III	Lebanon
8	17.4	Riverview Gardens	St Louis
11	17.3	Belton 124	Belton
12	17.2	Ritenour	St Louis
13	17.1	Mehlville R-IX	St Louis
14	17.0	Cassville R-IV	Cassville
14	17.0	Ft. Zumwalt R-II	O'fallon
14	17.0	Hazelwood	Florissant
14	17.0	Kirkwood R-VII	Kirkwood
18	16.9	Jackson R-II	Jackson
18	16.9	Rockwood R-VI	Eureka
20	16.8	Pleasant Hill R-III	Pleasant Hill
20	16.8	Warsaw R-IX	Warsaw
22	16.7	Springfield R-XII	Springfield
22	16.7	Webb City R-VII	Webb City
24	16.6	Fredericktown R-I	Fredericktown
24	16.6	Lee's Summit R-VII	Lee's Summit
26	16.5	Affton 101	St Louis

26	16.5	Kearney R-I	Kearney
26	16.5	Normandy	St Louis
26	16.5	Oak Grove R-VI	Oak Grove
30	16.4	Ferguson-Florissant R-II	Florissant
30	16.4	Liberty 53	Liberty
30	16.4	Ozark R-VI	Ozark
30	16.4	Poplar Bluff R-I	Poplar Bluff
30	16.4	Raytown C-2	Raytown
35	16.3	Fox C-6	Arnold
35	16.3	Parkway C-2	Chesterfield
35	16.3	Potosi R-III	Potosi
38	16.1	Blue Springs R-IV	Blue Springs
38	16.1	Harrisonville R-IX	Harrisonville
38	16.1	Northwest R-I	House Springs
38	16.1	Sedalia 200	Sedalia
42	16.0	Logan-Rogersville R-VIII	Rogersville
43	15.9	Excelsior Springs 40	Excelsior Spgs
43	15.9	Ste. Genevieve County R-II	Ste Genevieve
45	15.8	Gasconade County R-II	Owensville
45	15.8	Raymore-Peculiar R-II	Raymore
47	15.7	Farmington R-VII	Farmington
47	15.7	Kennett 39	Kennett
47	15.7	Park Hill	Kansas City
47	15.7	Sullivan	Sullivan
47	15.7	Wentzville R-IV	Wentzville
47	15.7	Winfield R-IV	Winfield
53	15.6	Desoto 73	Desoto
53	15.6	Jennings	Jennings
53	15.6	Smithville R-II	Smithville
53	15.6	St. James R-I	St James
57	15.5	Francis Howell R-III	St Charles
57	15.5	Hancock Place	St Louis
57	15.5	Rolla 31	Rolla
60	15.4	Caruthersville 18	Caruthersville
60	15.4	Lindbergh R-VIII	St Louis
60	15.4	Warren County R-III	Warrenton
63	15.3	Carl Junction R-I	Carl Junction
63	15.3	Grain Valley R-V	Grain Valley
63	15.3	Marshfield R-I	Marshfield
66	15.2	St. Joseph	St Joseph
67	15.1	Branson R-IV	Branson
67	15.1	Seneca R-VII	Seneca
67	15.1	Union R-XI	Union
70	15.0	Joplin R-VIII	Joplin
70	15.0	Mcdonald County R-I	Anderson
70	15.0	Salem R-80	Salem
73	14.9	Dexter R-XI	Dexter
73	14.9	North St. Francois Co. R-I	Bonne Terre
73	14.9	Savannah R-III	Savannah
73	14.9	Webster Groves	Webster Groves
77	14.8	Fort Osage R-I	Independence
77	14.8	Nixa R-II	Nixa
77	14.8	Sikeston R-VI	Sikeston
77	14.8	Washington	Washington
81	14.7	Carthage R-IX	Carthage
81	14.7	Kansas City 33	Kansas City
81	14.7	St. Clair R-XIII	St Clair
84	14.6	Aurora R-VIII	Aurora
84	14.6	Ava R-I	Ava
84	14.6	Odessa R-VII	Odessa
84	14.6	University City	University City
84	14.6	Willard R-II	Willard
89	14.5	Central R-III	Park Hills
89	14.5	East Newton County R-VI	Granby
89	14.5	Richmond R-XVI	Richmond
89	14.5	West Plains R-VII	West Plains
93	14.4	Jefferson City	Jefferson City
94	14.2	Mexico 59	Mexico
94	14.2	Nevada R-V	Nevada
94	14.2	Platte County R-III	Platte City
97	14.1	Doniphan R-I	Doniphan
97	14.1	Reeds Spring R-IV	Reeds Spring
97	14.1	School of the Osage R-II	Lake Ozark
97	14.1	Waynesville R-VI	Waynesville
101	14.0	Camdenton R-III	Camdenton
101	14.0	Center 58	Kansas City
101	14.0	North Kansas City 74	Kansas City
104	13.8	Chillicothe R-II	Chillicothe
104	13.8	Pattonville R-III	St Ann
106	13.7	Warrensburg R-VI	Warrensburg
107	13.6	Bolivar R-I	Bolivar
107	13.6	Cameron R-I	Cameron
107	13.6	Hickman Mills C-1	Kansas City
107	13.6	Marshall	Marshall
111	13.5	Dallas County R-I	Buffalo
112	13.4	Columbia 93	Columbia
112	13.4	Fulton 58	Fulton
114	13.3	Eldon R-I	Eldon
114	13.3	Moberly	Moberly
114	13.3	Morgan County R-II	Versailles
117	13.2	Clinton	Clinton
117	13.2	Hannibal 60	Hannibal
117	13.2	Knob Noster R-VIII	Knob Noster
117	13.2	Perry County 32	Perryville
121	13.1	Grandview C-4	Grandview
121	13.1	St. Charles R-VI	St Charles
121	13.1	Windsor C-1	Imperial
124	13.0	Kirksville R-III	Kirksville
124	13.0	Monett R-I	Monett
126	12.7	Cape Girardeau 63	Cape Girardeau
127	12.6	Mountain Grove R-III	Mountain Grove
128	12.5	New Madrid County R-I	New Madrid
128	12.5	St. Louis City	St Louis
130	11.9	Clayton	Clayton
131	11.4	Ladue	St Louis
132	0.6	Specl. Sch. Dst. St. Louis Co.	Town & Ctry

Student/Librarian Ratio

Rank	Ratio	District Name	City
1	1,472.2	Meramec Valley R-III	Pacific
2	1,276.3	Troy R-III	Troy
3	1,251.6	St. Joseph	St Joseph
4	1,156.1	Raytown C-2	Raytown
5	1,119.3	Jennings	Jennings
6	1,089.7	Excelsior Springs 40	Excelsior Spgs
7	1,064.0	Ste. Genevieve County R-II	Ste Genevieve
8	1,022.8	Blue Springs R-IV	Blue Springs
9	1,011.0	Chillicothe R-II	Chillicothe
10	982.6	Fort Osage R-I	Independence
11	961.5	Wentzville R-IV	Wentzville
12	956.2	Desoto 73	Desoto
13	912.4	Washington	Washington
14	908.0	Hancock Place	St Louis
15	907.5	Hannibal 60	Hannibal
16	906.3	Hickman Mills C-1	Kansas City
17	905.0	Republic R-III	Republic
18	900.4	Neosho R-V	Neosho
19	888.5	Mcdonald County R-I	Anderson
20	874.3	Francis Howell R-III	St Charles
21	864.1	St. Charles R-VI	St Charles
22	860.3	Willard R-II	Willard
23	856.9	Potosi R-III	Potosi
24	840.7	Nevada R-V	Nevada
25	834.7	West Plains R-VII	West Plains
26	823.0	Doniphan R-I	Doniphan
27	802.0	Camdenton R-III	Camdenton
28	801.5	Winfield R-IV	Winfield
29	785.3	St. Clair R-XIII	St Clair
30	780.3	Lebanon R-III	Lebanon
31	776.7	Lindbergh R-VIII	St Louis
32	766.7	Perry County 32	Perryville
33	765.0	Warsaw R-IX	Warsaw
34	750.9	Kearney R-I	Kearney
35	745.9	Savannah R-III	Savannah
36	740.3	Ft. Zumwalt R-II	O'fallon
37	740.0	Sullivan	Sullivan
38	736.4	Marshall	Marshall
39	732.9	Mehlville R-IX	St Louis
40	725.9	Normandy	St Louis
41	720.8	Hillsboro R-III	Hillsboro
42	709.0	Aurora R-VIII	Aurora
43	696.9	Sikeston R-VI	Sikeston
44	695.0	Rockwood R-VI	Eureka
45	693.7	Clinton	Clinton
46	693.3	Poplar Bluff R-I	Poplar Bluff
47	692.5	Festus R-VI	Festus
48	689.7	Hazelwood	Florissant
48	689.7	Lee's Summit R-VII	Lee's Summit
50	689.2	Ozark R-VI	Ozark
51	687.3	Dexter R-XI	Dexter
52	685.8	Center 58	Kansas City
53	680.7	Rolla 31	Rolla
54	678.9	Platte County R-III	Platte City
55	675.6	Joplin R-VIII	Joplin
56	673.3	Warren County R-III	Warrenton
57	668.3	Fredericktown R-I	Fredericktown
58	667.2	Branson R-IV	Branson
59	665.3	Springfield R-XII	Springfield
60	664.7	Park Hill	Kansas City
61	664.0	Sedalia 200	Sedalia
62	659.9	Fox C-6	Arnold
63	646.2	North St. Francois Co. R-I	Bonne Terre
64	643.8	Farmington R-VII	Farmington
65	642.8	Harrisonville R-IX	Harrisonville
66	642.2	Webb City R-VII	Webb City
67	641.6	Warrensburg R-VI	Warrensburg
68	635.0	Liberty 53	Liberty
69	630.6	Dallas County R-I	Buffalo
70	625.8	Northwest R-I	House Springs
71	625.3	Independence 30	Independence
72	623.3	Bolivar R-I	Bolivar
73	620.6	North Kansas City 74	Kansas City
74	617.8	Kirksville R-III	Kirksville
75	617.4	Ritenour	St Louis
76	616.2	Cassville R-IV	Cassville
77	615.6	Riverview Gardens	St Louis
78	597.0	Marshfield R-I	Marshfield
79	594.5	Carl Junction R-I	Carl Junction
80	593.3	Parkway C-2	Chesterfield
81	593.0	Windsor C-1	Imperial
82	588.6	University City	University City
83	587.8	Jackson R-II	Jackson
84	587.6	Union R-XI	Union
85	581.8	Moberly	Moberly
86	580.5	Kennett 39	Kennett
86	580.5	Odessa R-VII	Odessa
88	579.4	Belton 124	Belton
89	574.7	Raymore-Peculiar R-II	Raymore
90	570.0	Knob Noster R-VIII	Knob Noster
91	568.3	Cameron R-I	Cameron
92	565.5	Carthage R-IX	Carthage
93	565.4	Nixa R-II	Nixa
94	563.0	Seneca R-VII	Seneca
95	554.2	Kansas City 33	Kansas City
96	540.7	Mexico 59	Mexico
97	540.3	Ava R-I	Ava
98	534.8	Reeds Spring R-IV	Reeds Spring
99	533.4	Ferguson-Florissant R-II	Florissant
100	529.7	Mountain Grove R-III	Mountain Grove
101	528.8	Columbia 93	Columbia
102	522.8	Pattonville R-III	St Ann
103	521.0	Kirkwood R-VII	Kirkwood
104	516.7	East Newton County R-VI	Granby
105	514.3	Jefferson City	Jefferson City
106	507.8	St. James R-I	St James
107	506.1	Cape Girardeau 63	Cape Girardeau
108	505.2	Affton 101	St Louis
109	500.3	Salem R-80	Salem
110	499.0	Eldon R-I	Eldon
111	493.8	Monett R-I	Monett
112	493.5	Oak Grove R-VI	Oak Grove
113	485.8	St. Louis City	St Louis
114	481.1	Webster Groves	Webster Groves
115	477.8	New Madrid County R-I	New Madrid
116	473.0	Logan-Rogersville R-VIII	Rogersville
117	455.6	Fulton 58	Fulton
118	445.2	Grandview C-4	Grandview
119	433.5	Richmond R-XVI	Richmond
120	432.8	Grain Valley R-V	Grain Valley
121	430.5	Caruthersville 18	Caruthersville
122	417.6	Pleasant Hill R-III	Pleasant Hill
123	414.4	Bayless	St Louis
124	403.3	Gasconade County R-II	Owensville
125	390.7	Ladue	St Louis
126	383.0	Waynesville R-VI	Waynesville
127	375.4	Smithville R-II	Smithville
128	374.6	Central R-III	Park Hills
129	341.1	Morgan County R-II	Versailles
130	335.0	School of the Osage R-II	Lake Ozark
131	319.9	Clayton	Clayton
132	120.3	Specl. Sch. Dst. St. Louis Co.	Town & Ctry

Student/Counselor Ratio

Rank	Ratio	District Name	City
1	600.3	Neosho R-V	Neosho
2	582.2	Savannah R-III	Savannah
3	580.5	Odessa R-VII	Odessa
4	554.9	Troy R-III	Troy
5	537.0	Ozark R-VI	Ozark
6	495.9	Marshall	Marshall
7	493.5	Warsaw R-IX	Warsaw
8	491.8	Grain Valley R-V	Grain Valley
9	490.2	Poplar Bluff R-I	Poplar Bluff
10	489.1	Northwest R-I	House Springs
11	488.8	Bolivar R-I	Bolivar
12	482.7	Kearney R-I	Kearney
13	482.1	Lee's Summit R-VII	Lee's Summit
14	469.9	Branson R-IV	Branson
15	468.1	Hillsboro R-III	Hillsboro
16	456.9	Meramec Valley R-III	Pacific
17	455.9	East Newton County R-VI	Granby
18	453.1	St. Clair R-XIII	St Clair
19	450.5	Logan-Rogersville R-VIII	Rogersville
20	444.1	Raymore-Peculiar R-II	Raymore
21	444.0	Sullivan	Sullivan
22	443.4	Belton 124	Belton
23	441.2	Willard R-II	Willard
24	437.2	Joplin R-VIII	Joplin
25	436.6	Fox C-6	Arnold
26	434.3	New Madrid County R-I	New Madrid
27	433.5	Park Hill	Kansas City
27	433.5	Richmond R-XVI	Richmond
29	430.5	Caruthersville 18	Caruthersville
30	429.9	Republic R-III	Republic
31	429.8	Carl Junction R-I	Carl Junction
32	429.2	Farmington R-VII	Farmington
33	428.1	Webb City R-VII	Webb City

34	427.7	Washington	Washington
35	426.4	Marshfield R-I	Marshfield
36	426.2	Festus R-VI	Festus
37	425.6	Lebanon R-III	Lebanon
37	425.6	Ste. Genevieve County R-II	Ste Genevieve
39	423.6	Windsor C-1	Imperial
40	421.2	Riverview Gardens	St Louis
41	420.4	Independence 30	Independence
42	419.0	Cassville R-IV	Cassville
43	418.1	Mcdonald County R-I	Anderson
44	417.6	Pleasant Hill R-III	Pleasant Hill
45	416.8	Jackson R-II	Jackson
46	416.2	Central R-III	Park Hills
47	415.6	Ava R-I	Ava
48	414.7	Harrisonville R-IX	Harrisonville
49	411.6	Ritenour	St Louis
50	410.2	Raytown C-2	Raytown
51	409.4	Ft. Zumwalt R-II	O'fallon
52	408.8	Springfield R-XII	Springfield
53	408.6	Excelsior Springs 40	Excelsior Spgs
54	403.8	Liberty 53	Liberty
55	401.7	Ferguson-Florissant R-II	Florissant
56	401.3	Aurora R-VIII	Aurora
57	401.0	Warrensburg R-VI	Warrensburg
58	400.8	Potosi R-III	Potosi
58	400.8	Winfield R-IV	Winfield
60	399.2	Eldon R-I	Eldon
61	398.5	Nixa R-II	Nixa
62	396.5	Cameron R-I	Cameron
63	395.3	Wentzville R-IV	Wentzville
64	394.8	Oak Grove R-VI	Oak Grove
65	389.3	North St. Francois Co. R-I	Bonne Terre
66	383.2	Mehlville R-IX	St Louis
67	379.3	Warren County R-III	Warrenton
68	378.4	Clinton	Clinton
69	377.8	St. Joseph	St Joseph
70	376.3	Sedalia 200	Sedalia
71	375.8	Center 58	Kansas City
72	375.4	Smithville R-II	Smithville
73	375.3	Seneca R-VII	Seneca
74	374.7	Desoto 73	Desoto
75	371.4	Blue Springs R-IV	Blue Springs
75	371.4	Hazelwood	Florissant
77	369.7	North Kansas City 74	Kansas City
78	367.3	Union R-XI	Union
79	364.5	Fredericktown R-I	Fredericktown
80	363.9	Fort Osage R-I	Independence
81	363.2	Hancock Place	St Louis
82	361.9	Carthage R-IX	Carthage
83	358.4	Kansas City 33	Kansas City
84	358.2	Kirkwood R-VII	Kirkwood
85	357.4	Rockwood R-VI	Eureka
86	356.5	Francis Howell R-III	St Charles
87	353.0	Kirksville R-III	Kirksville
88	350.8	Lindbergh R-VIII	St Louis
89	349.0	School of the Osage R-II	Lake Ozark
90	343.7	Dexter R-XI	Dexter
91	339.4	Platte County R-III	Platte City
92	337.2	Hickman Mills C-1	Kansas City
93	335.0	Fulton 58	Fulton
94	332.4	St. James R-I	St James
95	329.3	Gasconade County R-II	Owensville
96	329.2	Doniphan R-I	Doniphan
97	324.6	Jennings	Jennings
98	324.1	Columbia 93	Columbia
99	323.2	Bayless	St Louis
100	322.6	Normandy	St Louis
101	322.5	Kennett 39	Kennett
102	319.7	Affton 101	St Louis
103	316.9	University City	University City
104	315.3	Dallas County R-I	Buffalo
104	315.3	Nevada R-V	Nevada
106	314.5	Moberly	Moberly
107	313.8	Morgan County R-II	Versailles
108	313.0	West Plains R-VII	West Plains
109	300.2	Salem R-80	Salem
110	298.0	Parkway C-2	Chesterfield
111	297.9	Waynesville R-VI	Waynesville
112	295.9	Rolla 31	Rolla
113	288.9	Chillicothe R-II	Chillicothe
114	288.7	Webster Groves	Webster Groves
115	286.8	St. Louis City	St Louis
116	286.4	Camdenton R-III	Camdenton
117	285.0	Knob Noster R-VIII	Knob Noster
118	274.6	Grandview C-4	Grandview
119	274.3	Jefferson City	Jefferson City
120	273.8	Sikeston R-VI	Sikeston
121	271.5	Ladue	St Louis
122	270.6	Perry County 32	Perryville
123	269.9	Cape Girardeau 63	Cape Girardeau
124	267.4	Mexico 59	Mexico
124	267.4	Reeds Spring R-IV	Reeds Spring
126	259.3	Hannibal 60	Hannibal
127	251.9	Pattonville R-III	St Ann
128	246.9	Monett R-I	Monett
129	244.8	St. Charles R-VI	St Charles
130	244.3	Clayton	Clayton
131	219.4	Mountain Grove R-III	Mountain Grove
132	112.7	Specl. Sch. Dst. St. Louis Co.	Town & Ctry

Current Spending per Student in FY2003

Rank	Dollars	District Name	City
1	13,872	Clayton	Clayton
2	11,825	Ladue	St Louis
3	10,170	St. Louis City	St Louis
4	10,106	Pattonville R-III	St Ann
5	9,183	Kansas City 33	Kansas City
6	9,181	Center 58	Kansas City
7	8,360	Grandview C-4	Grandview
8	8,323	St. Charles R-VI	St Charles
9	8,277	Kirkwood R-VII	Kirkwood
10	8,266	Jennings	Jennings
11	8,017	Webster Groves	Webster Groves
12	7,965	Normandy	St Louis
13	7,917	University City	University City
14	7,888	Ferguson-Florissant R-II	Florissant
15	7,870	Parkway C-2	Chesterfield
16	7,827	Park Hill	Kansas City
17	7,707	Lindbergh R-VIII	St Louis
18	7,674	Hickman Mills C-1	Kansas City
19	7,525	Independence 30	Independence
20	7,470	Mountain Grove R-III	Mountain Grove
21	7,410	Columbia 93	Columbia
22	7,362	Fort Osage R-I	Independence
23	7,303	Liberty 53	Liberty
24	7,232	Waynesville R-VI	Waynesville
25	7,209	Lee's Summit R-VII	Lee's Summit
26	7,189	Windsor C-1	Imperial
27	7,175	Raytown C-2	Raytown
28	7,097	Cape Girardeau 63	Cape Girardeau
29	7,042	North Kansas City 74	Kansas City
30	7,027	Platte County R-III	Platte City
31	6,978	School of the Osage R-II	Lake Ozark
32	6,955	Moberly	Moberly
33	6,945	Marshall	Marshall
33	6,945	West Plains R-VII	West Plains
35	6,935	Central R-III	Park Hills
36	6,893	Ritenour	St Louis
37	6,886	Hazelwood	Florissant
38	6,879	Cameron R-I	Cameron
39	6,862	Knob Noster R-VIII	Knob Noster
40	6,839	Fox C-6	Arnold
41	6,836	Rockwood R-VI	Eureka
42	6,800	Rolla 31	Rolla
43	6,783	Affton 101	St Louis
44	6,777	Francis Howell R-III	St Charles
45	6,771	Desoto 73	Desoto
46	6,769	Chillicothe R-II	Chillicothe
47	6,740	Camdenton R-III	Camdenton
48	6,720	Bolivar R-I	Bolivar
49	6,643	New Madrid County R-I	New Madrid
50	6,629	Fulton 58	Fulton
51	6,604	Blue Springs R-IV	Blue Springs
52	6,549	Monett R-I	Monett
53	6,548	Wentzville R-IV	Wentzville
54	6,533	Nevada R-V	Nevada
55	6,527	Northwest R-I	House Springs
56	6,520	Jefferson City	Jefferson City
57	6,515	St. Joseph	St Joseph
58	6,467	Excelsior Springs 40	Excelsior Spgs
59	6,465	Mexico 59	Mexico
60	6,462	Riverview Gardens	St Louis
61	6,451	Harrisonville R-IX	Harrisonville
62	6,412	Warrensburg R-VI	Warrensburg
63	6,387	Sullivan	Sullivan
64	6,381	Odessa R-VII	Odessa
65	6,373	Seneca R-VII	Seneca
66	6,369	Washington	Washington
67	6,349	Kirksville R-III	Kirksville
68	6,347	Perry County 32	Perryville
69	6,338	Eldon R-I	Eldon
70	6,330	Branson R-IV	Branson
71	6,316	Farmington R-VII	Farmington
72	6,271	Mehlville R-IX	St Louis
73	6,249	Gasconade County R-II	Owensville
74	6,246	Belton 124	Belton
75	6,239	Aurora R-VIII	Aurora
76	6,220	Reeds Spring R-IV	Reeds Spring
77	6,172	St. James R-I	St James
78	6,168	Ft. Zumwalt R-II	O'fallon
79	6,161	Springfield R-XII	Springfield
80	6,118	Kennett 39	Kennett
81	6,101	Carthage R-IX	Carthage
82	6,092	North St. Francois Co. R-I	Bonne Terre
83	6,089	Union R-XI	Union
84	6,080	Clinton	Clinton
85	6,070	Hancock Place	St Louis
86	6,069	Hannibal 60	Hannibal
87	6,057	Pleasant Hill R-III	Pleasant Hill
88	6,055	East Newton County R-VI	Granby
89	6,036	Fredericktown R-I	Fredericktown
90	6,014	Dallas County R-I	Buffalo
91	5,951	Salem R-80	Salem
92	5,936	Ste. Genevieve County R-II	Ste Genevieve
93	5,929	Ava R-I	Ava
94	5,927	Richmond R-XVI	Richmond
95	5,912	Smithville R-II	Smithville
96	5,897	Savannah R-III	Savannah
97	5,864	Joplin R-VIII	Joplin
98	5,820	Sikeston R-VI	Sikeston
99	5,819	Carl Junction R-I	Carl Junction
100	5,796	Doniphan R-I	Doniphan
101	5,785	Webb City R-VII	Webb City
102	5,779	Raymore-Peculiar R-II	Raymore
103	5,762	Potosi R-III	Potosi
104	5,761	Kearney R-I	Kearney
105	5,743	Morgan County R-II	Versailles
106	5,699	Caruthersville 18	Caruthersville
107	5,685	Lebanon R-III	Lebanon
108	5,670	Poplar Bluff R-I	Poplar Bluff
109	5,660	Marshfield R-I	Marshfield
110	5,641	Grain Valley R-V	Grain Valley
111	5,637	Willard R-II	Willard
112	5,602	St. Clair R-XIII	St Clair
113	5,589	Warren County R-III	Warrenton
114	5,584	Oak Grove R-VI	Oak Grove
115	5,533	Warsaw R-IX	Warsaw
116	5,519	Meramec Valley R-III	Pacific
117	5,495	Mcdonald County R-I	Anderson
118	5,477	Bayless	St Louis
118	5,477	Hillsboro R-III	Hillsboro
120	5,471	Nixa R-II	Nixa
121	5,456	Sedalia 200	Sedalia
122	5,433	Dexter R-XI	Dexter
123	5,402	Festus R-VI	Festus
124	5,372	Cassville R-IV	Cassville
125	5,368	Winfield R-IV	Winfield
126	5,265	Neosho R-V	Neosho
127	5,256	Logan-Rogersville R-VIII	Rogersville
128	5,250	Troy R-III	Troy
129	5,230	Jackson R-II	Jackson
130	5,101	Ozark R-VI	Ozark
131	4,974	Republic R-III	Republic
132	n/a	Specl. Sch. Dst. St. Louis Co.	Town & Ctry

Number of Diploma Recipients

Rank	Number	District Name	City
1	1,474	Rockwood R-VI	Eureka
2	1,464	Springfield R-XII	Springfield
3	1,438	Parkway C-2	Chesterfield
4	1,424	St. Louis City	St Louis
5	1,409	Kansas City 33	Kansas City
6	1,247	Hazelwood	Florissant
7	1,232	Francis Howell R-III	St Charles
8	1,137	North Kansas City 74	Kansas City
9	1,073	Ft. Zumwalt R-II	O'fallon
10	1,039	Columbia 93	Columbia
11	956	Lee's Summit R-VII	Lee's Summit
12	827	Mehlville R-IX	St Louis
13	808	Blue Springs R-IV	Blue Springs
14	711	St. Joseph	St Joseph
15	694	Ferguson-Florissant R-II	Florissant
16	666	Independence 30	Independence
17	640	Park Hill	Kansas City
18	612	Fox C-6	Arnold
19	520	Raytown C-2	Raytown
20	509	Jefferson City	Jefferson City
21	454	Liberty 53	Liberty
22	428	Pattonville R-III	St Ann
23	416	St. Charles R-VI	St Charles
24	415	Northwest R-I	House Springs
25	409	Kirkwood R-VII	Kirkwood
26	394	Hickman Mills C-1	Kansas City
27	377	Lindbergh R-VIII	St Louis
28	343	Jackson R-II	Jackson
29	342	Wentzville R-IV	Wentzville
30	316	Excelsior Springs 40	Excelsior Spgs
31	312	Normandy	St Louis
31	312	Poplar Bluff R-I	Poplar Bluff
33	306	Joplin R-VIII	Joplin
33	306	Riverview Gardens	St Louis
35	303	Webster Groves	Webster Groves
36	297	Lebanon R-III	Lebanon
36	297	Rolla 31	Rolla
38	296	Ritenour	St Louis
39	289	Camdenton R-III	Camdenton
40	287	Troy R-III	Troy

41	281	Washington	Washington
42	275	Cape Girardeau 63	Cape Girardeau
43	271	Waynesville R-VI	Waynesville
44	265	West Plains R-VII	West Plains
45	261	Belton 124	Belton
46	259	Raymore-Peculiar R-II	Raymore
47	253	Specl. Sch. Dst. St. Louis Co.	Town & Ctry
48	250	Fort Osage R-I	Independence
49	244	Farmington R-VII	Farmington
50	242	Meramec Valley R-III	Pacific
51	238	Neosho R-V	Neosho
52	233	Sedalia 200	Sedalia
53	227	Carthage R-IX	Carthage
54	225	Nixa R-II	Nixa
55	223	North St. Francois Co. R-I	Bonne Terre
56	221	Ozark R-VI	Ozark
57	220	Grandview C-4	Grandview
57	220	Hillsboro R-III	Hillsboro
59	217	Ladue	St Louis
59	217	Warrensburg R-VI	Warrensburg
61	210	Hannibal 60	Hannibal
61	210	Sikeston R-VI	Sikeston
63	205	Willard R-II	Willard
64	201	Webb City R-VII	Webb City
65	199	Kearney R-I	Kearney
66	198	Union R-XI	Union
67	193	Windsor C-1	Imperial
68	189	Clayton	Clayton
69	188	Desoto 73	Desoto
70	184	Mexico 59	Mexico
71	183	Republic R-III	Republic
72	182	Harrisonville R-IX	Harrisonville
73	181	Affton 101	St Louis
73	181	Marshall	Marshall
75	179	St. Clair R-XIII	St Clair
76	175	Warren County R-III	Warrenton
77	173	Perry County 32	Perryville
78	171	Kirksville R-III	Kirksville
79	170	Nevada R-V	Nevada
80	169	Marshfield R-I	Marshfield
81	168	University City	University City
82	164	Branson R-IV	Branson
82	164	Carl Junction R-I	Carl Junction
82	164	Savannah R-III	Savannah
85	161	Festus R-VI	Festus
85	161	Odessa R-VII	Odessa
85	161	Potosi R-III	Potosi
88	159	Moberly	Moberly
89	155	Center 58	Kansas City
90	152	Mcdonald County R-I	Anderson
91	148	Platte County R-III	Platte City
92	147	Gasconade County R-II	Owensville
92	147	Jennings	Jennings
94	144	Bolivar R-I	Bolivar
95	143	Chillicothe R-II	Chillicothe
95	143	Ste. Genevieve County R-II	Ste Genevieve
97	135	Cassville R-IV	Cassville
98	134	Dallas County R-I	Buffalo
99	133	Clinton	Clinton
99	133	Eldon R-I	Eldon
101	132	Logan-Rogersville R-VIII	Rogersville
102	131	Fulton 58	Fulton
103	128	Salem R-80	Salem
104	127	Sullivan	Sullivan
105	126	St. James R-I	St James
106	124	Oak Grove R-VI	Oak Grove
106	124	Pleasant Hill R-III	Pleasant Hill
108	123	Monett R-I	Monett
109	120	Dexter R-XI	Dexter
110	116	Doniphan R-I	Doniphan
111	115	Reeds Spring R-IV	Reeds Spring
112	114	Fredericktown R-I	Fredericktown
113	112	Kennett 39	Kennett
114	111	Central R-III	Park Hills
115	110	Smithville R-II	Smithville
116	109	Morgan County R-II	Versailles
117	108	School of the Osage R-II	Lake Ozark
118	107	Knob Noster R-VIII	Knob Noster
119	106	Aurora R-VIII	Aurora
119	106	Cameron R-I	Cameron
121	103	Richmond R-XVI	Richmond
122	102	Warsaw R-IX	Warsaw
123	101	Mountain Grove R-III	Mountain Grove
123	101	New Madrid County R-I	New Madrid
125	99	Ava R-I	Ava
126	94	Bayless	St Louis
127	91	East Newton County R-VI	Granby
127	91	Seneca R-VII	Seneca
129	90	Grain Valley R-V	Grain Valley
130	88	Winfield R-IV	Winfield
131	81	Caruthersville 18	Caruthersville
132	77	Hancock Place	St Louis

High School Drop-out Rate

Rank	Percent	District Name	City
1	17.3	Excelsior Springs 40	Excelsior Spgs
2	8.2	St. Louis City	St Louis
3	7.9	Salem R-80	Salem
3	7.9	University City	University City
5	7.6	Kansas City 33	Kansas City
6	7.5	Jennings	Jennings
7	6.9	Sedalia 200	Sedalia
8	6.5	Winfield R-IV	Winfield
9	6.4	Mountain Grove R-III	Mountain Grove
10	6.3	Moberly	Moberly
11	6.2	Carthage R-IX	Carthage
11	6.2	Center 58	Kansas City
13	5.9	Dallas County R-I	Buffalo
13	5.9	Webb City R-VII	Webb City
15	5.8	Fulton 58	Fulton
16	5.6	Joplin R-VIII	Joplin
17	5.5	Caruthersville 18	Caruthersville
17	5.5	Desoto 73	Desoto
19	5.3	Morgan County R-II	Versailles
20	5.2	Poplar Bluff R-I	Poplar Bluff
21	5.1	Raytown C-2	Raytown
22	5.0	Mcdonald County R-I	Anderson
22	5.0	St. James R-I	St James
22	5.0	Windsor C-1	Imperial
25	4.9	Potosi R-III	Potosi
25	4.9	Springfield R-XII	Springfield
25	4.9	Sullivan	Sullivan
25	4.9	Wentzville R-IV	Wentzville
29	4.8	Jefferson City	Jefferson City
30	4.7	Marshall	Marshall
31	4.6	Hancock Place	St Louis
31	4.6	Hannibal 60	Hannibal
31	4.6	Hazelwood	Florissant
34	4.5	Columbia 93	Columbia
34	4.5	Dexter R-XI	Dexter
34	4.5	New Madrid County R-I	New Madrid
37	4.4	Clinton	Clinton
38	4.3	Independence 30	Independence
38	4.3	Neosho R-V	Neosho
40	4.2	Hickman Mills C-1	Kansas City
40	4.2	Kennett 39	Kennett
42	4.0	Bolivar R-I	Bolivar
42	4.0	Grandview C-4	Grandview
44	3.9	Carl Junction R-I	Carl Junction
44	3.9	Eldon R-I	Eldon
44	3.9	Fox C-6	Arnold
44	3.9	Knob Noster R-VIII	Knob Noster
44	3.9	Marshfield R-I	Marshfield
44	3.9	Meramec Valley R-III	Pacific
50	3.8	Affton 101	St Louis
50	3.8	Doniphan R-I	Doniphan
50	3.8	Seneca R-VII	Seneca
50	3.8	St. Clair R-XIII	St Clair
54	3.6	Belton 124	Belton
54	3.6	Union R-XI	Union
54	3.6	Webster Groves	Webster Groves
57	3.5	Cassville R-IV	Cassville
57	3.5	Warsaw R-IX	Warsaw
59	3.4	Lindbergh R-VIII	St Louis
59	3.4	Monett R-I	Monett
59	3.4	Reeds Spring R-IV	Reeds Spring
59	3.4	Republic R-III	Republic
59	3.4	Rolla 31	Rolla
59	3.4	St. Joseph	St Joseph
65	3.3	Chillicothe R-II	Chillicothe
65	3.3	Gasconade County R-II	Owensville
65	3.3	Lebanon R-III	Lebanon
65	3.3	Platte County R-III	Platte City
65	3.3	St. Charles R-VI	St Charles
70	3.2	Mexico 59	Mexico
70	3.2	North St. Francois Co. R-I	Bonne Terre
70	3.2	Riverview Gardens	St Louis
70	3.2	Troy R-III	Troy
70	3.2	Warren County R-III	Warrenton
75	3.1	Fredericktown R-I	Fredericktown
75	3.1	Kirksville R-III	Kirksville
75	3.1	Normandy	St Louis
78	3.0	Sikeston R-VI	Sikeston
79	2.9	North Kansas City 74	Kansas City
79	2.9	Ritenour	St Louis
79	2.9	Warrensburg R-VI	Warrensburg
82	2.8	Francis Howell R-III	St Charles
82	2.8	Hillsboro R-III	Hillsboro
82	2.8	Northwest R-I	House Springs
82	2.8	Raymore-Peculiar R-II	Raymore
82	2.8	West Plains R-VII	West Plains
87	2.7	Bayless	St Louis
87	2.7	Ft. Zumwalt R-II	O'fallon
87	2.7	Kearney R-I	Kearney
87	2.7	Mehlville R-IX	St Louis
87	2.7	Nevada R-V	Nevada
87	2.7	Richmond R-XVI	Richmond
87	2.7	Savannah R-III	Savannah
87	2.7	Waynesville R-VI	Waynesville
87	2.7	Willard R-II	Willard
96	2.6	Cameron R-I	Cameron
96	2.6	Nixa R-II	Nixa
96	2.6	Pattonville R-III	St Ann
96	2.6	Pleasant Hill R-III	Pleasant Hill
96	2.6	Ste. Genevieve County R-II	Ste Genevieve
101	2.5	Farmington R-VII	Farmington
101	2.5	Park Hill	Kansas City
101	2.5	School of the Osage R-II	Lake Ozark
104	2.3	Aurora R-VIII	Aurora
104	2.3	Camdenton R-III	Camdenton
104	2.3	Harrisonville R-IX	Harrisonville
104	2.3	Oak Grove R-VI	Oak Grove
104	2.3	Smithville R-II	Smithville
109	2.2	Jackson R-II	Jackson
109	2.2	Lee's Summit R-VII	Lee's Summit
109	2.2	Liberty 53	Liberty
109	2.2	Perry County 32	Perryville
113	2.1	Blue Springs R-IV	Blue Springs
113	2.1	Odessa R-VII	Odessa
115	1.9	Branson R-IV	Branson
115	1.9	Central R-III	Park Hills
115	1.9	Kirkwood R-VII	Kirkwood
115	1.9	Rockwood R-VI	Eureka
119	1.8	Cape Girardeau 63	Cape Girardeau
119	1.8	East Newton County R-VI	Granby
119	1.8	Festus R-VI	Festus
122	1.5	Logan-Rogersville R-VIII	Rogersville
123	1.4	Ozark R-VI	Ozark
124	1.3	Clayton	Clayton
124	1.3	Ferguson-Florissant R-II	Florissant
126	1.1	Parkway C-2	Chesterfield
127	1.0	Ava R-I	Ava
128	0.8	Grain Valley R-V	Grain Valley
129	0.7	Washington	Washington
130	0.6	Ladue	St Louis
131	0.3	Fort Osage R-I	Independence
132	n/a	Specl. Sch. Dst. St. Louis Co.	Town & Ctry

Montana

Montana Public School Educational Profile

Category	Value	Category	Value
Schools *(2003-2004)*	860	**Diploma Recipients** *(2002-2003)*	10,554
Instructional Level		White, Non-Hispanic	9,537
Primary	441	Black, Non-Hispanic	34
Middle	241	Asian/Pacific Islander	112
High	175	American Indian/Alaskan Native	713
Other Level	2	Hispanic	158
Curriculum		**High School Drop-out Rate** (%) *(2001-2002)*	3.9
Regular	853	White, Non-Hispanic	3.2
Special Education	2	Black, Non-Hispanic	6.7
Vocational	0	Asian/Pacific Islander	2.0
Alternative	4	American Indian/Alaskan Native	10.3
Type		Hispanic	5.2
Magnet	0	**Staff** *(2003-2004)*	
Charter	0	Teachers	10,301.1
Title I Eligible	717	Average Salary ($)	37,184
School-wide Title I	154	Librarians/Media Specialists	355.7
Students *(2003-2004)*	148,356	Guidance Counselors	430.6
Gender (%)		**Ratios** *(2003-2004)*	
Male	51.7	Student/Teacher Ratio	14.4 to 1
Female	48.3	Student/Librarian Ratio	417.1 to 1
Race/Ethnicity (%)		Student/Counselor Ratio	344.5 to 1
White, Non-Hispanic	85.1	**College Entrance Exam Scores** *(2005)*	
Black, Non-Hispanic	0.7	Scholastic Aptitude Test (SAT)	
Asian/Pacific Islander	1.0	Participation Rate (%)	31
American Indian/Alaskan Native	11.0	Mean SAT Reasoning Test Verbal Score	540
Hispanic	2.1	Mean SAT Reasoning Test Math Score	540
Classification (%)		American College Testing Program (ACT)	
Individual Education Program (IEP)	13.0	Participation Rate (%)	57
Migrant *(2002-2003)*	0.0	Average Composite Score	21.8
English Language Learner (ELL)	4.5	Average English Score	21.0
Eligible for Free Lunch Program	25.7	Average Math Score	21.5
Eligible for Reduced-Price Lunch Program	8.1	Average Reading Score	22.4
Current Spending *($ per student in FY 2003)*	7,363	Average Science Score	21.8
Instruction	4,574		
Support Services	2,498		

Note: *For an explanation of data, please refer to the User's Guide in the front of the book*

Montana NAEP 2005 Test Scores

Reading			Mathematics		
Grade/Category	Value	Rank	Grade/Category	Value	Rank
4th Grade			**4th Grade**		
Average Proficiency	224.6 (1.13)	9/51	Average Proficiency	240.6 (0.80)	17/51
Proficiency by Gender/Race/Ethnicity			Proficiency by Gender/Race/Ethnicity		
Male	222.4 (1.34)	6/51	Male	242.7 (0.93)	13/51
Female	226.8 (1.44)	12/51	Female	238.5 (0.96)	21/51
White, Non-Hispanic	227.5 (1.10)	20/51	White, Non-Hispanic	243.1 (0.76)	34/51
Black, Non-Hispanic	n/a	n/a	Black, Non-Hispanic	n/a	n/a
Asian, Non-Hispanic	n/a	n/a	Asian, Non-Hispanic	n/a	n/a
American Indian, Non-Hispanic	200.9 (1.97)	4/7	American Indian, Non-Hispanic	222.6 (2.27)	4/7
Hispanic	226.3 (4.53)	1/40	Hispanic	234.4 (4.54)	3/41
Proficiency by Class Size			Proficiency by Class Size		
Less than 16 Students	216.7 (3.22)	7/34	Less than 16 Students	232.9 (2.67)	10/35
16 to 18 Students	224.4 (2.53)	5/33	16 to 18 Students	240.5 (1.82)	11/31
19 to 20 Students	227.0 (2.10)	6/38	19 to 20 Students	240.8 (1.49)	15/38
21 to 25 Students	227.1 (1.44)	8/51	21 to 25 Students	241.9 (1.11)	20/51
Greater than 25 Students	226.4 (3.14)	3/36	Greater than 25 Students	244.3 (1.91)	2/33
Percent Attaining Achievement Levels			Percent Attaining Achievement Levels		
Below Basic	28.7 (1.20)	44/51	Below Basic	14.6 (1.05)	40/51
Basic or Above	71.3 (1.20)	8/51	Basic or Above	85.4 (1.05)	12/51
Proficient or Above	35.6 (1.44)	10/51	Proficient or Above	38.3 (1.41)	21/51
Advanced or Above	7.6 (0.87)	15/51	Advanced or Above	3.7 (0.45)	36/51
8th Grade			**8th Grade**		
Average Proficiency	269.2 (0.74)	6/51	Average Proficiency	286.4 (0.70)	6/51
Proficiency by Gender/Race/Ethnicity			Proficiency by Gender/Race/Ethnicity		
Male	264.8 (1.08)	4/51	Male	286.0 (1.15)	6/51
Female	273.9 (0.95)	7/51	Female	286.9 (1.05)	5/51
White, Non-Hispanic	272.1 (0.72)	12/51	White, Non-Hispanic	289.9 (0.59)	16/51
Black, Non-Hispanic	n/a	n/a	Black, Non-Hispanic	n/a	n/a
Asian, Non-Hispanic	n/a	n/a	Asian, Non-Hispanic	n/a	n/a
American Indian, Non-Hispanic	248.1 (2.63)	5/9	American Indian, Non-Hispanic	258.9 (2.23)	9/10
Hispanic	n/a	n/a	Hispanic	n/a	n/a
Proficiency by Parents Highest Level of Ed.			Proficiency by Parents Highest Level of Ed.		
Did Not Finish High School	245.4 (3.85)	22/49	Did Not Finish High School	261.8 (3.23)	26/50
Graduated High School	261.5 (1.47)	3/50	Graduated High School	277.2 (1.78)	2/50
Some Education After High School	272.3 (1.34)	1/50	Some Education After High School	287.9 (1.33)	2/50
Graduated College	274.9 (0.88)	15/50	Graduated College	293.3 (0.91)	15/50
Percent Attaining Achievement Levels			Percent Attaining Achievement Levels		
Below Basic	28.7 (1.20)	44/51	Below Basic	20.5 (1.03)	48/51
Basic or Above	71.3 (1.20)	8/51	Basic or Above	79.5 (1.03)	4/51
Proficient or Above	35.6 (1.44)	10/51	Proficient or Above	36.0 (1.13)	5/51
Advanced or Above	7.6 (0.87)	15/51	Advanced or Above	5.5 (0.56)	23/51

Note: *For an explanation of data, please refer to the User's Guide in the front of the book; n/a indicates data not available*

Cascade County

Great Falls Elem
1100 4th St So • Great Falls, MT 59403
Mailing Address: PO Box 2429 • Great Falls, MT 59403
(406) 268-6006 • http://www.gfps.k12.mt.us/
Grade Span: PK-08; **Agency Type:** 1
Schools: 18
  15 Primary; 3 Middle; 0 High; 0 Other Level
  18 Regular; 0 Special Education; 0 Vocational; 0 Alternative
  0 Magnet; 0 Charter; 11 Title I Eligible; 8 School-wide Title I
Students: 7,471 (51.3% male; 48.6% female)
  Individual Education Program: 875 (11.7%);
  English Language Learner: 15 (0.2%); Migrant: n/a
  Eligible for Free Lunch Program: 2,029 (27.2%)
  Eligible for Reduced-Price Lunch Program: 753 (10.1%)
Teachers: 501.1 (14.9 to 1)
Librarians/Media Specialists: 12.5 (597.7 to 1)
Guidance Counselors: 19.0 (393.2 to 1)
Current Spending: ($ per student per year):
  Total: $6,171; Instruction: $3,719; Support Services: $2,137
Enrollment, Drop-out Rates and Diploma Recipients by Race/Ethnicity

Category	Total	White	Black	Asian	AIAN	Hisp.
Enrollment (%)	100.0	85.2	1.9	1.1	9.8	1.9
Drop-out Rate (%)	n/a	n/a	n/a	n/a	n/a	n/a
H.S. Diplomas (#)	n/a	n/a	n/a	n/a	n/a	n/a

Great Falls HS
1100 4th St So • Great Falls, MT 59403
Mailing Address: PO Box 2429 • Great Falls, MT 59403
(406) 268-6051 • http://www.gfps.k12.mt.us/gfhs/index.html
Grade Span: 09-12; **Agency Type:** 1
Schools: 2
  0 Primary; 0 Middle; 2 High; 0 Other Level
  2 Regular; 0 Special Education; 0 Vocational; 0 Alternative
  0 Magnet; 0 Charter; 1 Title I Eligible; 0 School-wide Title I
Students: 3,609 (49.9% male; 50.0% female)
  Individual Education Program: 394 (10.9%);
  English Language Learner: 1 (<0.1%); Migrant: n/a
  Eligible for Free Lunch Program: 456 (12.6%)
  Eligible for Reduced-Price Lunch Program: 159 (4.4%)
Teachers: 226.2 (16.0 to 1)
Librarians/Media Specialists: 5.5 (656.2 to 1)
Guidance Counselors: 13.0 (277.6 to 1)
Current Spending: ($ per student per year):
  Total: $6,467; Instruction: $4,317; Support Services: $2,150
Enrollment, Drop-out Rates and Diploma Recipients by Race/Ethnicity

Category	Total	White	Black	Asian	AIAN	Hisp.
Enrollment (%)	100.0	87.4	1.3	1.4	8.1	1.8
Drop-out Rate (%)	2.8	2.2	2.0	0.0	10.7	0.0
H.S. Diplomas (#)	803	727	9	13	49	5

Flathead County

Columbia Falls Elem
501 6th Ave W • Columbia Falls, MT 59912
Mailing Address: PO Box 1259 • Columbia Falls, MT 59912
(406) 892-6550
Grade Span: PK-08; **Agency Type:** 1
Schools: 5
  3 Primary; 2 Middle; 0 High; 0 Other Level
  5 Regular; 0 Special Education; 0 Vocational; 0 Alternative
  0 Magnet; 0 Charter; 5 Title I Eligible; 3 School-wide Title I
Students: 1,676 (51.7% male; 48.2% female)
  Individual Education Program: 258 (15.4%);
  English Language Learner: 5 (0.3%); Migrant: n/a
  Eligible for Free Lunch Program: 548 (32.7%)
  Eligible for Reduced-Price Lunch Program: 161 (9.6%)
Teachers: 95.2 (17.6 to 1)
Librarians/Media Specialists: 3.0 (558.7 to 1)
Guidance Counselors: 4.4 (380.9 to 1)
Current Spending: ($ per student per year):
  Total: $5,750; Instruction: $3,595; Support Services: $2,156
Enrollment, Drop-out Rates and Diploma Recipients by Race/Ethnicity

Category	Total	White	Black	Asian	AIAN	Hisp.
Enrollment (%)	100.0	94.3	0.8	0.7	2.7	1.6
Drop-out Rate (%)	n/a	n/a	n/a	n/a	n/a	n/a
H.S. Diplomas (#)	n/a	n/a	n/a	n/a	n/a	n/a

Flathead HS
233 First Ave E • Kalispell, MT 59901
(406) 751-3500 • http://www.sd5.k12.mt.us/fhs/index.htm
Grade Span: 09-12; **Agency Type:** 1
Schools: 2
  0 Primary; 0 Middle; 1 High; 1 Other Level

  2 Regular; 0 Special Education; 0 Vocational; 0 Alternative
  0 Magnet; 0 Charter; 2 Title I Eligible; 0 School-wide Title I
Students: 2,495 (51.4% male; 48.5% female)
  Individual Education Program: 177 (7.1%);
  English Language Learner: 16 (0.6%); Migrant: n/a
  Eligible for Free Lunch Program: 434 (17.4%)
  Eligible for Reduced-Price Lunch Program: 136 (5.5%)
Teachers: 136.6 (18.3 to 1)
Librarians/Media Specialists: 4.0 (623.8 to 1)
Guidance Counselors: 7.6 (328.3 to 1)
Current Spending: ($ per student per year):
  Total: $6,711; Instruction: $4,293; Support Services: $2,056
Enrollment, Drop-out Rates and Diploma Recipients by Race/Ethnicity

Category	Total	White	Black	Asian	AIAN	Hisp.
Enrollment (%)	100.0	97.4	0.4	0.6	1.0	0.8
Drop-out Rate (%)	6.1	6.0	12.5	11.1	15.4	11.1
H.S. Diplomas (#)	532	528	0	2	2	0

Kalispell Elem
233 First Ave E • Kalispell, MT 59901
(406) 751-3400 • http://www.sd5.k12.mt.us/
Grade Span: PK-08; **Agency Type:** 1
Schools: 7
  5 Primary; 1 Middle; 0 High; 1 Other Level
  7 Regular; 0 Special Education; 0 Vocational; 0 Alternative
  0 Magnet; 0 Charter; 6 Title I Eligible; 1 School-wide Title I
Students: 2,522 (51.4% male; 48.5% female)
  Individual Education Program: 333 (13.2%);
  English Language Learner: 41 (1.6%); Migrant: n/a
  Eligible for Free Lunch Program: 697 (27.6%)
  Eligible for Reduced-Price Lunch Program: 247 (9.8%)
Teachers: 135.2 (18.7 to 1)
Librarians/Media Specialists: 7.5 (336.3 to 1)
Guidance Counselors: 6.4 (394.1 to 1)
Current Spending: ($ per student per year):
  Total: $5,956; Instruction: $4,106; Support Services: $1,849
Enrollment, Drop-out Rates and Diploma Recipients by Race/Ethnicity

Category	Total	White	Black	Asian	AIAN	Hisp.
Enrollment (%)	100.0	94.7	0.5	0.9	1.8	2.1
Drop-out Rate (%)	n/a	n/a	n/a	n/a	n/a	n/a
H.S. Diplomas (#)	n/a	n/a	n/a	n/a	n/a	n/a

Gallatin County

Belgrade Elem
312 N Weaver • Belgrade, MT 59714
Mailing Address: PO Box 166 • Belgrade, MT 59714
(406) 388-6951
Grade Span: PK-08; **Agency Type:** 1
Schools: 4
  2 Primary; 2 Middle; 0 High; 0 Other Level
  4 Regular; 0 Special Education; 0 Vocational; 0 Alternative
  0 Magnet; 0 Charter; 4 Title I Eligible; 0 School-wide Title I
Students: 1,856 (51.9% male; 48.0% female)
  Individual Education Program: 189 (10.2%);
  English Language Learner: 3 (0.2%); Migrant: n/a
  Eligible for Free Lunch Program: 293 (15.8%)
  Eligible for Reduced-Price Lunch Program: 143 (7.7%)
Teachers: 94.0 (19.7 to 1)
Librarians/Media Specialists: 4.0 (464.0 to 1)
Guidance Counselors: 4.0 (464.0 to 1)
Current Spending: ($ per student per year):
  Total: $5,441; Instruction: $3,268; Support Services: $1,840
Enrollment, Drop-out Rates and Diploma Recipients by Race/Ethnicity

Category	Total	White	Black	Asian	AIAN	Hisp.
Enrollment (%)	100.0	96.3	0.6	0.5	1.6	1.0
Drop-out Rate (%)	n/a	n/a	n/a	n/a	n/a	n/a
H.S. Diplomas (#)	n/a	n/a	n/a	n/a	n/a	n/a

Bozeman Elem
404 W Main • Bozeman, MT 59715
Mailing Address: PO Box 520 • Bozeman, MT 59771
(406) 522-6042 • http://www.bozeman.k12.mt.us/welcome/18.elem.html
Grade Span: PK-08; **Agency Type:** 1
Schools: 8
  6 Primary; 2 Middle; 0 High; 0 Other Level
  8 Regular; 0 Special Education; 0 Vocational; 0 Alternative
  0 Magnet; 0 Charter; 8 Title I Eligible; 1 School-wide Title I
Students: 3,244 (50.2% male; 49.7% female)
  Individual Education Program: 339 (10.5%);
  English Language Learner: 55 (1.7%); Migrant: n/a
  Eligible for Free Lunch Program: 466 (14.4%)
  Eligible for Reduced-Price Lunch Program: 171 (5.3%)
Teachers: 194.6 (16.7 to 1)
Librarians/Media Specialists: 7.5 (432.5 to 1)
Guidance Counselors: 3.8 (853.7 to 1)

Current Spending: ($ per student per year):
   Total: $6,009; Instruction: $3,810; Support Services: $2,188
Enrollment, Drop-out Rates and Diploma Recipients by Race/Ethnicity

Category	Total	White	Black	Asian	AIAN	Hisp.
Enrollment (%)	100.0	93.2	0.6	2.0	2.3	2.0
Drop-out Rate (%)	n/a	n/a	n/a	n/a	n/a	n/a
H.S. Diplomas (#)	n/a	n/a	n/a	n/a	n/a	n/a

Bozeman HS

404 W Main • Bozeman, MT 59715
Mailing Address: PO Box 520 • Bozeman, MT 59771
(406) 522-6042 • http://www.bps.montana.edu/bhs/index.html
Grade Span: 09-12; **Agency Type:** 1
Schools: 1
   0 Primary; 0 Middle; 1 High; 0 Other Level
   1 Regular; 0 Special Education; 0 Vocational; 0 Alternative
   0 Magnet; 0 Charter; 1 Title I Eligible; 0 School-wide Title I
Students: 1,842   (50.9% male; 49.0% female)
   Individual Education Program: 145 (7.9%);
   English Language Learner: 5 (0.3%); Migrant: n/a
   Eligible for Free Lunch Program: 102 (5.5%)
   Eligible for Reduced-Price Lunch Program: 49 (2.7%)
Teachers: 124.0 (14.9 to 1)
Librarians/Media Specialists: 2.7 (682.2 to 1)
Guidance Counselors: 6.0 (307.0 to 1)
Current Spending: ($ per student per year):
   Total: $7,107; Instruction: $4,146; Support Services: $2,372
Enrollment, Drop-out Rates and Diploma Recipients by Race/Ethnicity

Category	Total	White	Black	Asian	AIAN	Hisp.
Enrollment (%)	100.0	95.2	0.5	1.8	1.4	1.1
Drop-out Rate (%)	2.7	2.7	0.0	0.0	5.6	0.0
H.S. Diplomas (#)	448	432	1	5	3	7

Helena Elem

55 S Rodney • Helena, MT 59601-5763
(406) 447-8510 • http://www.is.helena.k12.mt.us/
Grade Span: KG-08; **Agency Type:** 1
Schools: 13
   11 Primary; 2 Middle; 0 High; 0 Other Level
   13 Regular; 0 Special Education; 0 Vocational; 0 Alternative
   0 Magnet; 0 Charter; 8 Title I Eligible; 1 School-wide Title I
Students: 4,987   (51.7% male; 48.2% female)
   Individual Education Program: 676 (13.6%);
   English Language Learner: 5 (0.1%); Migrant: n/a
   Eligible for Free Lunch Program: 1,039 (20.8%)
   Eligible for Reduced-Price Lunch Program: 365 (7.3%)
Teachers: 276.9 (18.0 to 1)
Librarians/Media Specialists: 9.2 (542.1 to 1)
Guidance Counselors: 4.5 (1,108.2 to 1)
Current Spending: ($ per student per year):
   Total: $6,374; Instruction: $3,910; Support Services: $2,100
Enrollment, Drop-out Rates and Diploma Recipients by Race/Ethnicity

Category	Total	White	Black	Asian	AIAN	Hisp.
Enrollment (%)	100.0	90.0	1.0	1.1	6.1	1.8
Drop-out Rate (%)	n/a	n/a	n/a	n/a	n/a	n/a
H.S. Diplomas (#)	n/a	n/a	n/a	n/a	n/a	n/a

Helena HS

55 S Rodney • Helena, MT 59601-5763
(406) 447-8510 • http://www.is.helena.k12.mt.us/
Grade Span: 09-12; **Agency Type:** 1
Schools: 2
   0 Primary; 0 Middle; 2 High; 0 Other Level
   2 Regular; 0 Special Education; 0 Vocational; 0 Alternative
   0 Magnet; 0 Charter; 1 Title I Eligible; 0 School-wide Title I
Students: 3,097   (51.0% male; 48.9% female)
   Individual Education Program: 272 (8.8%);
   English Language Learner: 0 (0.0%); Migrant: n/a
   Eligible for Free Lunch Program: 222 (7.2%)
   Eligible for Reduced-Price Lunch Program: 96 (3.1%)
Teachers: 188.1 (16.5 to 1)
Librarians/Media Specialists: 4.6 (673.3 to 1)
Guidance Counselors: 7.0 (442.4 to 1)
Current Spending: ($ per student per year):
   Total: $6,855; Instruction: $4,688; Support Services: $2,153
Enrollment, Drop-out Rates and Diploma Recipients by Race/Ethnicity

Category	Total	White	Black	Asian	AIAN	Hisp.
Enrollment (%)	100.0	91.9	0.4	1.7	4.3	1.6
Drop-out Rate (%)	4.7	4.3	33.3	0.0	16.3	19.2
H.S. Diplomas (#)	667	639	2	3	18	5

Libby K-12 Schools

724 Louisiana Ave • Libby, MT 59923
(406) 293-8811
Grade Span: PK-12; **Agency Type:** 1
Schools: 3
   1 Primary; 1 Middle; 1 High; 0 Other Level
   3 Regular; 0 Special Education; 0 Vocational; 0 Alternative
   0 Magnet; 0 Charter; 3 Title I Eligible; 0 School-wide Title I
Students: 1,509   (53.0% male; 46.9% female)
   Individual Education Program: 210 (13.9%);
   English Language Learner: 3 (0.2%); Migrant: n/a
   Eligible for Free Lunch Program: 595 (39.4%)
   Eligible for Reduced-Price Lunch Program: 154 (10.2%)
Teachers: 100.8 (15.0 to 1)
Librarians/Media Specialists: 4.0 (377.3 to 1)
Guidance Counselors: 5.0 (301.8 to 1)
Current Spending: ($ per student per year):
   Total: $6,736; Instruction: $4,326; Support Services: $2,246
Enrollment, Drop-out Rates and Diploma Recipients by Race/Ethnicity

Category	Total	White	Black	Asian	AIAN	Hisp.
Enrollment (%)	100.0	94.2	0.8	1.1	2.6	1.3
Drop-out Rate (%)	3.6	3.5	0.0	n/a	20.0	0.0
H.S. Diplomas (#)	140	139	0	0	1	0

Missoula Elem

215 S 6th W • Missoula, MT 59801
(406) 728-2400 • http://www.mcps.k12.mt.us/
Grade Span: PK-08; **Agency Type:** 1
Schools: 14
   9 Primary; 5 Middle; 0 High; 0 Other Level
   14 Regular; 0 Special Education; 0 Vocational; 0 Alternative
   0 Magnet; 0 Charter; 7 Title I Eligible; 3 School-wide Title I
Students: 5,171   (50.8% male; 49.1% female)
   Individual Education Program: 821 (15.9%);
   English Language Learner: 260 (5.0%); Migrant: n/a
   Eligible for Free Lunch Program: 1,465 (28.3%)
   Eligible for Reduced-Price Lunch Program: 344 (6.7%)
Teachers: 307.7 (16.8 to 1)
Librarians/Media Specialists: 14.0 (369.4 to 1)
Guidance Counselors: 8.2 (630.6 to 1)
Current Spending: ($ per student per year):
   Total: $6,920; Instruction: $4,146; Support Services: $2,404
Enrollment, Drop-out Rates and Diploma Recipients by Race/Ethnicity

Category	Total	White	Black	Asian	AIAN	Hisp.
Enrollment (%)	100.0	90.1	1.3	1.9	5.1	1.6
Drop-out Rate (%)	n/a	n/a	n/a	n/a	n/a	n/a
H.S. Diplomas (#)	n/a	n/a	n/a	n/a	n/a	n/a

Missoula HS

215 S 6th W • Missoula, MT 59801
(406) 728-2400 • http://www.mcps.k12.mt.us/
Grade Span: 09-12; **Agency Type:** 1
Schools: 4
   0 Primary; 0 Middle; 4 High; 0 Other Level
   4 Regular; 0 Special Education; 0 Vocational; 0 Alternative
   0 Magnet; 0 Charter; 3 Title I Eligible; 0 School-wide Title I
Students: 3,964   (50.8% male; 49.1% female)
   Individual Education Program: 565 (14.3%);
   English Language Learner: 220 (5.5%); Migrant: n/a
   Eligible for Free Lunch Program: 621 (15.7%)
   Eligible for Reduced-Price Lunch Program: 213 (5.4%)
Teachers: 245.8 (16.1 to 1)
Librarians/Media Specialists: 6.0 (660.7 to 1)
Guidance Counselors: 17.0 (233.2 to 1)
Current Spending: ($ per student per year):
   Total: $7,960; Instruction: $5,198; Support Services: $2,514
Enrollment, Drop-out Rates and Diploma Recipients by Race/Ethnicity

Category	Total	White	Black	Asian	AIAN	Hisp.
Enrollment (%)	100.0	93.4	0.5	1.6	3.3	1.3
Drop-out Rate (%)	3.4	3.1	12.5	1.3	10.9	3.6
H.S. Diplomas (#)	838	785	2	17	22	12

Hamilton K-12 Schools

217 Daly Ave • Hamilton, MT 59840
(406) 363-2280 • http://www.hsd3.org
Grade Span: PK-12; **Agency Type:** 1
Schools: 5
   3 Primary; 1 Middle; 1 High; 0 Other Level
   5 Regular; 0 Special Education; 0 Vocational; 0 Alternative

0 Magnet; 0 Charter; 5 Title I Eligible; 0 School-wide Title I
Students: 1,634   (50.6% male; 49.3% female)
  Individual Education Program: 185 (11.3%);
  English Language Learner: 1 (0.1%); Migrant: n/a
  Eligible for Free Lunch Program: 473 (28.9%)
  Eligible for Reduced-Price Lunch Program: 180 (11.0%)
Teachers: 94.6 (17.3 to 1)
Librarians/Media Specialists: 4.0 (408.5 to 1)
Guidance Counselors: 4.4 (371.4 to 1)
Current Spending: ($ per student per year):
  Total: $5,535; Instruction: $3,346; Support Services: $1,915
Enrollment, Drop-out Rates and Diploma Recipients by Race/Ethnicity

Category	Total	White	Black	Asian	AIAN	Hisp.
Enrollment (%)	100.0	95.8	0.3	1.3	1.1	1.5
Drop-out Rate (%)	2.2	1.9	0.0	0.0	20.0	14.3
H.S. Diplomas (#)	123	119	0	3	0	1

Silver Bow County

Butte Elem
111 N Montana • Butte, MT 59701
(406) 533-2500 • http://www.butte.k12.mt.us/
Grade Span: PK-08; **Agency Type:** 1
Schools: 8
  7 Primary; 1 Middle; 0 High; 0 Other Level
  8 Regular; 0 Special Education; 0 Vocational; 0 Alternative
  0 Magnet; 0 Charter; 6 Title I Eligible; 4 School-wide Title I
Students: 3,298   (50.1% male; 49.8% female)
  Individual Education Program: 448 (13.6%);
  English Language Learner: 0 (0.0%); Migrant: n/a
  Eligible for Free Lunch Program: 1,036 (31.4%)
  Eligible for Reduced-Price Lunch Program: 249 (7.6%)
Teachers: 189.4 (17.4 to 1)
Librarians/Media Specialists: 3.7 (891.4 to 1)
Guidance Counselors: 7.2 (458.1 to 1)
Current Spending: ($ per student per year):
  Total: $5,947; Instruction: $3,288; Support Services: $2,356
Enrollment, Drop-out Rates and Diploma Recipients by Race/Ethnicity

Category	Total	White	Black	Asian	AIAN	Hisp.
Enrollment (%)	100.0	88.9	0.8	1.0	6.1	3.2
Drop-out Rate (%)	n/a	n/a	n/a	n/a	n/a	n/a
H.S. Diplomas (#)	n/a	n/a	n/a	n/a	n/a	n/a

Butte HS
111 N Montana • Butte, MT 59701
(406) 533-2500 • http://www.butte.k12.mt.us/
Grade Span: 09-12; **Agency Type:** 1
Schools: 1
  0 Primary; 0 Middle; 1 High; 0 Other Level
  1 Regular; 0 Special Education; 0 Vocational; 0 Alternative
  0 Magnet; 0 Charter; 1 Title I Eligible; 0 School-wide Title I
Students: 1,554   (50.4% male; 49.5% female)
  Individual Education Program: 189 (12.2%);
  English Language Learner: 0 (0.0%); Migrant: n/a
  Eligible for Free Lunch Program: 249 (16.0%)
  Eligible for Reduced-Price Lunch Program: 58 (3.7%)
Teachers: 95.8 (16.2 to 1)
Librarians/Media Specialists: 2.5 (621.6 to 1)
Guidance Counselors: 4.0 (388.5 to 1)
Current Spending: ($ per student per year):
  Total: $7,786; Instruction: $5,078; Support Services: $2,703
Enrollment, Drop-out Rates and Diploma Recipients by Race/Ethnicity

Category	Total	White	Black	Asian	AIAN	Hisp.
Enrollment (%)	100.0	91.8	0.2	0.6	4.6	2.8
Drop-out Rate (%)	8.5	8.0	25.0	14.3	21.4	0.0
H.S. Diplomas (#)	296	275	1	6	6	8

Yellowstone County

Billings Elem
415 N 30th St • Billings, MT 59101
(406) 247-3745 • http://www.billings.k12.mt.us/
Grade Span: PK-08; **Agency Type:** 1
Schools: 25
  21 Primary; 4 Middle; 0 High; 0 Other Level
  25 Regular; 0 Special Education; 0 Vocational; 0 Alternative
  0 Magnet; 0 Charter; 11 Title I Eligible; 10 School-wide Title I
Students: 10,136   (51.8% male; 48.1% female)
  Individual Education Program: 1,514 (14.9%);
  English Language Learner: 40 (0.4%); Migrant: n/a
  Eligible for Free Lunch Program: 2,518 (24.8%)
  Eligible for Reduced-Price Lunch Program: 1,026 (10.1%)
Teachers: 626.4 (16.2 to 1)
Librarians/Media Specialists: 27.0 (375.4 to 1)
Guidance Counselors: 24.2 (418.8 to 1)

Current Spending: ($ per student per year):
  Total: $6,303; Instruction: $4,233; Support Services: $2,071
Enrollment, Drop-out Rates and Diploma Recipients by Race/Ethnicity

Category	Total	White	Black	Asian	AIAN	Hisp.
Enrollment (%)	100.0	82.5	1.9	1.6	7.9	6.0
Drop-out Rate (%)	n/a	n/a	n/a	n/a	n/a	n/a
H.S. Diplomas (#)	n/a	n/a	n/a	n/a	n/a	n/a

Billings HS
415 N 30th St • Billings, MT 59101
(406) 247-3791 • http://www.billings.k12.mt.us/
Grade Span: 09-12; **Agency Type:** 1
Schools: 3
  0 Primary; 0 Middle; 3 High; 0 Other Level
  3 Regular; 0 Special Education; 0 Vocational; 0 Alternative
  0 Magnet; 0 Charter; 1 Title I Eligible; 0 School-wide Title I
Students: 5,601   (51.8% male; 48.1% female)
  Individual Education Program: 728 (13.0%);
  English Language Learner: 72 (1.3%); Migrant: n/a
  Eligible for Free Lunch Program: 675 (12.1%)
  Eligible for Reduced-Price Lunch Program: 306 (5.5%)
Teachers: 322.8 (17.4 to 1)
Librarians/Media Specialists: 8.0 (700.1 to 1)
Guidance Counselors: 20.8 (269.3 to 1)
Current Spending: ($ per student per year):
  Total: $7,343; Instruction: $4,220; Support Services: $2,501
Enrollment, Drop-out Rates and Diploma Recipients by Race/Ethnicity

Category	Total	White	Black	Asian	AIAN	Hisp.
Enrollment (%)	100.0	87.3	1.0	1.6	5.7	4.4
Drop-out Rate (%)	3.8	3.2	6.0	1.4	11.7	8.4
H.S. Diplomas (#)	1,167	1,072	10	15	36	34

Number of Schools

Rank	Number	District Name	City
1	25	Billings Elem	Billings
2	18	Great Falls Elem	Great Falls
3	14	Missoula Elem	Missoula
4	13	Helena Elem	Helena
5	8	Bozeman Elem	Bozeman
5	8	Butte Elem	Butte
7	7	Kalispell Elem	Kalispell
8	5	Columbia Falls Elem	Columbia Falls
8	5	Hamilton K-12 Schools	Hamilton
10	4	Belgrade Elem	Belgrade
10	4	Missoula HS	Missoula
12	3	Billings HS	Billings
12	3	Libby K-12 Schools	Libby
14	2	Flathead HS	Kalispell
14	2	Great Falls HS	Great Falls
14	2	Helena HS	Helena
17	1	Bozeman HS	Bozeman
17	1	Butte HS	Butte

Number of Teachers

Rank	Number	District Name	City
1	626	Billings Elem	Billings
2	501	Great Falls Elem	Great Falls
3	322	Billings Elem	Billings
4	307	Missoula Elem	Missoula
5	276	Helena Elem	Helena
6	245	Missoula Elem	Missoula
7	226	Great Falls HS	Great Falls
8	194	Bozeman Elem	Bozeman
9	189	Butte Elem	Butte
10	188	Helena Elem	Helena
11	136	Flathead HS	Kalispell
12	135	Kalispell Elem	Kalispell
13	124	Bozeman HS	Bozeman
14	100	Libby K-12 Schools	Libby
15	95	Butte HS	Butte
16	95	Columbia Falls Elem	Columbia Falls
17	94	Hamilton K-12 Schools	Hamilton
18	94	Belgrade Elem	Belgrade

Number of Students

Rank	Number	District Name	City
1	10,136	Billings Elem	Billings
2	7,471	Great Falls Elem	Great Falls
3	5,601	Billings HS	Billings
4	5,171	Missoula Elem	Missoula
5	4,987	Helena Elem	Helena
6	3,964	Missoula HS	Missoula
7	3,609	Great Falls HS	Great Falls
8	3,298	Butte Elem	Butte
9	3,244	Bozeman Elem	Bozeman
10	3,097	Helena HS	Helena
11	2,522	Kalispell Elem	Kalispell
12	2,495	Flathead HS	Kalispell
13	1,856	Belgrade Elem	Belgrade
14	1,842	Bozeman HS	Bozeman
15	1,676	Columbia Falls Elem	Columbia Falls
16	1,634	Hamilton K-12 Schools	Hamilton
17	1,554	Butte HS	Butte
18	1,509	Libby K-12 Schools	Libby

Male Students

Rank	Percent	District Name	City
1	53.0	Libby K-12 Schools	Libby
2	51.9	Belgrade Elem	Belgrade
3	51.8	Billings HS	Billings
4	51.8	Billings Elem	Billings
5	51.7	Columbia Falls Elem	Columbia Falls
6	51.7	Helena Elem	Helena
7	51.4	Kalispell Elem	Kalispell
8	51.4	Flathead HS	Kalispell
9	51.3	Great Falls Elem	Great Falls
10	51.0	Helena HS	Helena
11	50.9	Bozeman HS	Bozeman
12	50.8	Missoula Elem	Missoula
13	50.8	Missoula HS	Missoula
14	50.6	Hamilton K-12 Schools	Hamilton
15	50.4	Butte HS	Butte
16	50.2	Bozeman Elem	Bozeman
17	50.1	Butte Elem	Butte
18	49.9	Great Falls HS	Great Falls

Female Students

Rank	Percent	District Name	City
1	50.0	Great Falls HS	Great Falls
2	49.8	Butte Elem	Butte
3	49.7	Bozeman Elem	Bozeman
4	49.5	Butte HS	Butte
5	49.3	Hamilton K-12 Schools	Hamilton
6	49.1	Missoula HS	Missoula
7	49.1	Missoula Elem	Missoula
8	49.0	Bozeman HS	Bozeman
9	48.9	Helena HS	Helena
10	48.6	Great Falls Elem	Great Falls
11	48.5	Flathead HS	Kalispell
12	48.5	Kalispell Elem	Kalispell
13	48.2	Helena Elem	Helena
14	48.2	Columbia Falls Elem	Columbia Falls
15	48.1	Billings Elem	Billings
16	48.1	Billings HS	Billings
17	48.0	Belgrade Elem	Belgrade
18	46.9	Libby K-12 Schools	Libby

Individual Education Program Students

Rank	Percent	District Name	City
1	15.9	Missoula Elem	Missoula
2	15.4	Columbia Falls Elem	Columbia Falls
3	14.9	Billings Elem	Billings
4	14.3	Missoula HS	Missoula
5	13.9	Libby K-12 Schools	Libby
6	13.6	Butte Elem	Butte
6	13.6	Helena Elem	Helena
8	13.2	Kalispell Elem	Kalispell
9	13.0	Billings HS	Billings
10	12.2	Butte HS	Butte
11	11.7	Great Falls Elem	Great Falls
12	11.3	Hamilton K-12 Schools	Hamilton
13	10.9	Great Falls HS	Great Falls
14	10.5	Bozeman Elem	Bozeman
15	10.2	Belgrade Elem	Belgrade
16	8.8	Helena HS	Helena
17	7.9	Bozeman HS	Bozeman
18	7.1	Flathead HS	Kalispell

English Language Learner Students

Rank	Percent	District Name	City
1	5.5	Missoula HS	Missoula
2	5.0	Missoula Elem	Missoula
3	1.7	Bozeman Elem	Bozeman
4	1.6	Kalispell Elem	Kalispell
5	1.3	Billings HS	Billings
6	0.6	Flathead HS	Kalispell
7	0.4	Billings Elem	Billings
8	0.3	Bozeman HS	Bozeman
8	0.3	Columbia Falls Elem	Columbia Falls
10	0.2	Belgrade Elem	Belgrade
10	0.2	Great Falls Elem	Great Falls
10	0.2	Libby K-12 Schools	Libby
13	0.1	Hamilton K-12 Schools	Hamilton
13	0.1	Helena Elem	Helena
15	0.0	Great Falls HS	Great Falls
16	0.0	Butte Elem	Butte
16	0.0	Butte HS	Butte
16	0.0	Helena HS	Helena

Migrant Students

Rank	Percent	District Name	City
1	n/a	Belgrade Elem	Belgrade
1	n/a	Billings Elem	Billings
1	n/a	Billings HS	Billings
1	n/a	Bozeman Elem	Bozeman
1	n/a	Bozeman HS	Bozeman
1	n/a	Butte Elem	Butte
1	n/a	Butte HS	Butte
1	n/a	Columbia Falls Elem	Columbia Falls
1	n/a	Flathead HS	Kalispell
1	n/a	Great Falls Elem	Great Falls
1	n/a	Great Falls HS	Great Falls
1	n/a	Hamilton K-12 Schools	Hamilton
1	n/a	Helena Elem	Helena
1	n/a	Helena HS	Helena
1	n/a	Kalispell Elem	Kalispell
1	n/a	Libby K-12 Schools	Libby
1	n/a	Missoula Elem	Missoula
1	n/a	Missoula HS	Missoula

Students Eligible for Free Lunch

Rank	Percent	District Name	City
1	39.4	Libby K-12 Schools	Libby
2	32.7	Columbia Falls Elem	Columbia Falls
3	31.4	Butte Elem	Butte
4	28.9	Hamilton K-12 Schools	Hamilton
5	28.3	Missoula Elem	Missoula
6	27.6	Kalispell Elem	Kalispell
7	27.2	Great Falls Elem	Great Falls
8	24.8	Billings Elem	Billings
9	20.8	Helena Elem	Helena
10	17.4	Flathead HS	Kalispell
11	16.0	Butte HS	Butte
12	15.8	Belgrade Elem	Belgrade
13	15.7	Missoula HS	Missoula
14	14.4	Bozeman Elem	Bozeman
15	12.6	Great Falls HS	Great Falls
16	12.1	Billings HS	Billings
17	7.2	Helena HS	Helena
18	5.5	Bozeman HS	Bozeman

Students Eligible for Reduced-Price Lunch

Rank	Percent	District Name	City
1	11.0	Hamilton K-12 Schools	Hamilton
2	10.2	Libby K-12 Schools	Libby
3	10.1	Billings Elem	Billings
3	10.1	Great Falls Elem	Great Falls
5	9.8	Kalispell Elem	Kalispell
6	9.6	Columbia Falls Elem	Columbia Falls
7	7.7	Belgrade Elem	Belgrade
8	7.6	Butte Elem	Butte
9	7.3	Helena Elem	Helena
10	6.7	Missoula Elem	Missoula
11	5.5	Billings HS	Billings
11	5.5	Flathead HS	Kalispell
13	5.4	Missoula HS	Missoula
14	5.3	Bozeman Elem	Bozeman
15	4.4	Great Falls HS	Great Falls
16	3.7	Butte HS	Butte
17	3.1	Helena HS	Helena
18	2.7	Bozeman HS	Bozeman

Student/Teacher Ratio

Rank	Ratio	District Name	City
1	19.7	Belgrade Elem	Belgrade
2	18.7	Kalispell Elem	Kalispell
3	18.3	Flathead HS	Kalispell
4	18.0	Helena Elem	Helena
5	17.6	Columbia Falls Elem	Columbia Falls
6	17.4	Billings HS	Billings
6	17.4	Butte Elem	Butte
8	17.3	Hamilton K-12 Schools	Hamilton
9	16.8	Missoula Elem	Missoula
10	16.7	Bozeman Elem	Bozeman
11	16.5	Helena HS	Helena
12	16.2	Billings Elem	Billings
12	16.2	Butte HS	Butte
14	16.1	Missoula HS	Missoula
15	16.0	Great Falls HS	Great Falls
16	15.0	Libby K-12 Schools	Libby
17	14.9	Bozeman HS	Bozeman
17	14.9	Great Falls Elem	Great Falls

Student/Librarian Ratio

Rank	Ratio	District Name	City
1	891.4	Butte Elem	Butte
2	700.1	Billings HS	Billings
3	682.2	Bozeman HS	Bozeman
4	673.3	Helena Elem	Helena
5	660.7	Missoula HS	Missoula
6	656.2	Great Falls HS	Great Falls
7	623.8	Flathead HS	Kalispell
8	621.6	Butte HS	Butte
9	597.7	Great Falls Elem	Great Falls
10	558.7	Columbia Falls Elem	Columbia Falls
11	542.1	Helena Elem	Helena
12	464.0	Belgrade Elem	Belgrade
13	432.5	Bozeman Elem	Bozeman
14	408.5	Hamilton K-12 Schools	Hamilton
15	377.3	Libby K-12 Schools	Libby
16	375.4	Billings Elem	Billings
17	369.4	Missoula Elem	Missoula
18	336.3	Kalispell Elem	Kalispell

Student/Counselor Ratio

Rank	Ratio	District Name	City
1	1,108.2	Helena Elem	Helena
2	853.7	Bozeman Elem	Bozeman
3	630.6	Missoula Elem	Missoula
4	464.0	Belgrade Elem	Belgrade
5	458.1	Butte Elem	Butte
6	442.4	Helena HS	Helena
7	418.8	Billings Elem	Billings
8	394.1	Kalispell Elem	Kalispell
9	393.2	Great Falls Elem	Great Falls
10	388.5	Butte HS	Butte
11	380.9	Columbia Falls Elem	Columbia Falls

12	371.4	Hamilton K-12 Schools	Hamilton
13	328.3	Flathead HS	Kalispell
14	307.0	Bozeman HS	Bozeman
15	301.8	Libby K-12 Schools	Libby
16	277.6	Great Falls HS	Great Falls
17	269.3	Billings HS	Billings
18	233.2	Missoula HS	Missoula

Current Spending per Student in FY2003

Rank	Dollars	District Name	City
1	7,960	Missoula HS	Missoula
2	7,786	Butte HS	Butte
3	7,343	Billings HS	Billings
4	7,107	Bozeman HS	Bozeman
5	6,920	Missoula Elem	Missoula
6	6,855	Helena HS	Helena
7	6,736	Libby K-12 Schools	Libby
8	6,711	Flathead HS	Kalispell
9	6,467	Great Falls HS	Great Falls
10	6,374	Helena Elem	Helena
11	6,303	Billings Elem	Billings
12	6,171	Great Falls Elem	Great Falls
13	6,009	Bozeman Elem	Bozeman
14	5,956	Kalispell Elem	Kalispell
15	5,947	Butte Elem	Butte
16	5,750	Columbia Falls Elem	Columbia Falls
17	5,535	Hamilton K-12 Schools	Hamilton
18	5,441	Belgrade Elem	Belgrade

Number of Diploma Recipients

Rank	Number	District Name	City
1	1,167	Billings HS	Billings
2	838	Missoula HS	Missoula
3	803	Great Falls HS	Great Falls
4	667	Helena HS	Helena
5	532	Flathead HS	Kalispell
6	448	Bozeman HS	Bozeman
7	296	Butte HS	Butte
8	140	Libby K-12 Schools	Libby
9	123	Hamilton K-12 Schools	Hamilton
10	n/a	Belgrade Elem	Belgrade
10	n/a	Billings Elem	Billings
10	n/a	Bozeman Elem	Bozeman
10	n/a	Butte Elem	Butte
10	n/a	Columbia Falls Elem	Columbia Falls
10	n/a	Great Falls Elem	Great Falls
10	n/a	Helena Elem	Helena
10	n/a	Kalispell Elem	Kalispell
10	n/a	Missoula Elem	Missoula

High School Drop-out Rate

Rank	Percent	District Name	City
1	8.5	Butte HS	Butte
2	6.1	Flathead HS	Kalispell
3	4.7	Helena HS	Helena
4	3.8	Billings HS	Billings
5	3.6	Libby K-12 Schools	Libby
6	3.4	Missoula HS	Missoula
7	2.8	Great Falls HS	Great Falls
8	2.7	Bozeman HS	Bozeman
9	2.2	Hamilton K-12 Schools	Hamilton
10	n/a	Belgrade Elem	Belgrade
10	n/a	Billings Elem	Billings
10	n/a	Bozeman Elem	Bozeman
10	n/a	Butte Elem	Butte
10	n/a	Columbia Falls Elem	Columbia Falls
10	n/a	Great Falls Elem	Great Falls
10	n/a	Helena Elem	Helena
10	n/a	Kalispell Elem	Kalispell
10	n/a	Missoula Elem	Missoula

Nebraska

Nebraska Public School Educational Profile

Category	Value	Category	Value
Schools (2003-2004)	1,248	**Diploma Recipients** (2002-2003)	19,842
Instructional Level		White, Non-Hispanic	17,786
Primary	805	Black, Non-Hispanic	795
Middle	105	Asian/Pacific Islander	355
High	308	American Indian/Alaskan Native	150
Other Level	30	Hispanic	756
Curriculum		**High School Drop-out Rate** (%) (2001-2002)	4.2
Regular	1,202	White, Non-Hispanic	3.1
Special Education	46	Black, Non-Hispanic	11.3
Vocational	0	Asian/Pacific Islander	3.3
Alternative	0	American Indian/Alaskan Native	12.0
Type		Hispanic	11.7
Magnet	0	**Staff** (2003-2004)	
Charter	0	Teachers	20,987.7
Title I Eligible	491	Average Salary ($)	39,635
School-wide Title I	172	Librarians/Media Specialists	560.2
Students (2003-2004)	285,542	Guidance Counselors	762.1
Gender (%)		**Ratios** (2003-2004)	
Male	51.6	Student/Teacher Ratio	13.6 to 1
Female	48.4	Student/Librarian Ratio	509.7 to 1
Race/Ethnicity (%)		Student/Counselor Ratio	374.7 to 1
White, Non-Hispanic	79.5	**College Entrance Exam Scores** (2005)	
Black, Non-Hispanic	7.1	Scholastic Aptitude Test (SAT)	
Asian/Pacific Islander	1.7	Participation Rate (%)	8
American Indian/Alaskan Native	1.6	Mean SAT Reasoning Test Verbal Score	574
Hispanic	10.1	Mean SAT Reasoning Test Math Score	579
Classification (%)		American College Testing Program (ACT)	
Individual Education Program (IEP)	16.0	Participation Rate (%)	76
Migrant (2002-2003)	3.3	Average Composite Score	21.8
English Language Learner (ELL)	5.5	Average English Score	21.4
Eligible for Free Lunch Program	24.9	Average Math Score	21.6
Eligible for Reduced-Price Lunch Program	9.0	Average Reading Score	21.9
Current Spending ($ per student in FY 2003)	7,426	Average Science Score	21.7
Instruction	4,798		
Support Services	2,266		

Note: For an explanation of data, please refer to the User's Guide in the front of the book

Nebraska NAEP 2005 Test Scores

Reading			Mathematics		
Grade/Category	Value	Rank	Grade/Category	Value	Rank
4th Grade			**4th Grade**		
Average Proficiency	221.4 (1.16)	20/51	Average Proficiency	237.7 (0.86)	31/51
Proficiency by Gender/Race/Ethnicity			Proficiency by Gender/Race/Ethnicity		
Male	219.2 (1.25)	16/51	Male	239.3 (0.89)	30/51
Female	223.6 (1.40)	24/51	Female	236.2 (1.08)	31/51
White, Non-Hispanic	227.7 (1.20)	17/51	White, Non-Hispanic	244.3 (0.86)	29/51
Black, Non-Hispanic	193.6 (2.45)	34/42	Black, Non-Hispanic	210.6 (3.26)	39/42
Asian, Non-Hispanic	n/a	n/a	Asian, Non-Hispanic	n/a	n/a
American Indian, Non-Hispanic	n/a	n/a	American Indian, Non-Hispanic	n/a	n/a
Hispanic	201.9 (2.53)	28/40	Hispanic	218.7 (1.37)	36/41
Proficiency by Class Size			Proficiency by Class Size		
Less than 16 Students	218.1 (3.33)	6/34	Less than 16 Students	232.7 (3.29)	11/35
16 to 18 Students	218.1 (2.56)	15/33	16 to 18 Students	237.9 (2.28)	15/31
19 to 20 Students	217.7 (3.22)	24/38	19 to 20 Students	233.7 (3.21)	31/38
21 to 25 Students	226.2 (2.03)	13/51	21 to 25 Students	242.3 (1.90)	19/51
Greater than 25 Students	222.1 (3.77)	16/36	Greater than 25 Students	234.8 (3.67)	24/33
Percent Attaining Achievement Levels			Percent Attaining Achievement Levels		
Below Basic	32.3 (1.39)	31/51	Below Basic	19.7 (1.02)	22/51
Basic or Above	67.7 (1.39)	20/51	Basic or Above	80.3 (1.02)	30/51
Proficient or Above	33.5 (1.41)	18/51	Proficient or Above	36.1 (1.34)	29/51
Advanced or Above	7.3 (0.80)	20/51	Advanced or Above	4.5 (0.59)	26/51
8th Grade			**8th Grade**		
Average Proficiency	267.5 (0.89)	12/51	Average Proficiency	284.0 (1.03)	11/51
Proficiency by Gender/Race/Ethnicity			Proficiency by Gender/Race/Ethnicity		
Male	261.1 (1.04)	18/51	Male	285.4 (1.13)	10/51
Female	274.1 (1.25)	5/51	Female	282.5 (1.36)	13/51
White, Non-Hispanic	271.3 (0.91)	18/51	White, Non-Hispanic	289.2 (1.06)	19/51
Black, Non-Hispanic	243.0 (2.49)	15/40	Black, Non-Hispanic	243.4 (2.28)	38/41
Asian, Non-Hispanic	n/a	n/a	Asian, Non-Hispanic	n/a	n/a
American Indian, Non-Hispanic	n/a	n/a	American Indian, Non-Hispanic	n/a	n/a
Hispanic	245.2 (2.02)	27/38	Hispanic	261.5 (2.21)	22/38
Proficiency by Parents Highest Level of Ed.			Proficiency by Parents Highest Level of Ed.		
Did Not Finish High School	250.8 (2.76)	8/49	Did Not Finish High School	263.1 (3.02)	21/50
Graduated High School	259.6 (1.55)	10/50	Graduated High School	272.8 (1.87)	14/50
Some Education After High School	270.0 (1.54)	8/50	Some Education After High School	284.5 (1.98)	13/50
Graduated College	273.3 (1.22)	22/50	Graduated College	292.9 (1.14)	17/50
Percent Attaining Achievement Levels			Percent Attaining Achievement Levels		
Below Basic	32.3 (1.39)	31/51	Below Basic	25.1 (1.19)	39/51
Basic or Above	67.7 (1.39)	20/51	Basic or Above	74.9 (1.19)	13/51
Proficient or Above	33.5 (1.41)	18/51	Proficient or Above	34.9 (1.55)	9/51
Advanced or Above	7.3 (0.80)	20/51	Advanced or Above	6.0 (0.57)	19/51

Note: *For an explanation of data, please refer to the User's Guide in the front of the book; n/a indicates data not available*

Adams County

Hastings Public Schools
714 W 5th • Hastings, NE 68901-5190
(402) 461-7500 • http://www1.hastings.esu9.k12.ne.us/
Grade Span: PK-12; **Agency Type:** 1
Schools: 8
  6 Primary; 1 Middle; 1 High; 0 Other Level
  8 Regular; 0 Special Education; 0 Vocational; 0 Alternative
  0 Magnet; 0 Charter; 4 Title I Eligible; 2 School-wide Title I
Students: 3,255   (52.0% male; 47.9% female)
  Individual Education Program: 650 (20.0%)
  English Language Learner: 234 (7.2%); Migrant: 247 (7.6%)
  Eligible for Free Lunch Program: 1,016 (31.2%)
  Eligible for Reduced-Price Lunch Program: 323 (9.9%)
Teachers: 226.9 (14.3 to 1)
Librarians/Media Specialists: 4.0 (813.8 to 1)
Guidance Counselors: 10.1 (322.3 to 1)
Current Spending: ($ per student per year):
  Total: $6,880; Instruction: $4,603; Support Services: $2,020
Enrollment, Drop-out Rates and Diploma Recipients by Race/Ethnicity

Category	Total	White	Black	Asian	AIAN	Hisp.
Enrollment (%)	100.0	81.6	1.7	2.5	1.0	13.3
Drop-out Rate (%)	6.1	6.5	20.0	0.0	0.0	4.5
H.S. Diplomas (#)	224	197	0	12	2	13

Box Butte County

Alliance Public Schools
1604 Sweetwater Ave • Alliance, NE 69301
(308) 762-5475 • http://www.aps.k12.ne.us/
Grade Span: PK-12; **Agency Type:** 1
Schools: 5
  3 Primary; 1 Middle; 1 High; 0 Other Level
  4 Regular; 1 Special Education; 0 Vocational; 0 Alternative
  0 Magnet; 0 Charter; 2 Title I Eligible; 1 School-wide Title I
Students: 1,728   (54.9% male; 45.0% female)
  Individual Education Program: 296 (17.1%)
  English Language Learner: 36 (2.1%); Migrant: 146 (8.4%)
  Eligible for Free Lunch Program: 474 (27.4%)
  Eligible for Reduced-Price Lunch Program: 130 (7.5%)
Teachers: 127.1 (13.6 to 1)
Librarians/Media Specialists: 3.0 (576.0 to 1)
Guidance Counselors: 3.0 (576.0 to 1)
Current Spending: ($ per student per year):
  Total: $7,203; Instruction: $4,794; Support Services: $2,177
Enrollment, Drop-out Rates and Diploma Recipients by Race/Ethnicity

Category	Total	White	Black	Asian	AIAN	Hisp.
Enrollment (%)	100.0	76.2	1.0	1.0	7.7	14.1
Drop-out Rate (%)	1.4	1.2	33.3	0.0	7.4	0.0
H.S. Diplomas (#)	169	153	1	0	0	15

Buffalo County

Kearney Public Schools
310 W 24th St • Kearney, NE 68845-5355
(308) 698-8000
Grade Span: PK-12; **Agency Type:** 1
Schools: 13
  10 Primary; 2 Middle; 1 High; 0 Other Level
  12 Regular; 1 Special Education; 0 Vocational; 0 Alternative
  0 Magnet; 0 Charter; 6 Title I Eligible; 1 School-wide Title I
Students: 4,648   (51.4% male; 48.5% female)
  Individual Education Program: 731 (15.7%);
  English Language Learner: 177 (3.8%); Migrant: 147 (3.2%)
  Eligible for Free Lunch Program: 992 (21.3%)
  Eligible for Reduced-Price Lunch Program: 382 (8.2%)
Teachers: 306.0 (15.2 to 1)
Librarians/Media Specialists: 7.5 (619.7 to 1)
Guidance Counselors: 11.2 (415.0 to 1)
Current Spending: ($ per student per year):
  Total: $6,634; Instruction: $4,276; Support Services: $1,976
Enrollment, Drop-out Rates and Diploma Recipients by Race/Ethnicity

Category	Total	White	Black	Asian	AIAN	Hisp.
Enrollment (%)	100.0	88.5	1.9	1.1	0.4	8.0
Drop-out Rate (%)	1.6	1.4	0.0	0.0	0.0	5.1
H.S. Diplomas (#)	317	305	1	2	1	8

Cass County

Plattsmouth Community Schools
1912 E Hwy 34 • Plattsmouth, NE 68048
(402) 296-3361 • http://www.plt.esu3.org
Grade Span: PK-12; **Agency Type:** 1
Schools: 5

  2 Primary; 1 Middle; 2 High; 0 Other Level
  4 Regular; 1 Special Education; 0 Vocational; 0 Alternative
  0 Magnet; 0 Charter; 1 Title I Eligible; 1 School-wide Title I
Students: 1,706   (53.9% male; 46.0% female)
  Individual Education Program: 356 (20.9%)
  English Language Learner: 59 (3.5%); Migrant: 0 (0.0%)
  Eligible for Free Lunch Program: 474 (27.8%)
  Eligible for Reduced-Price Lunch Program: 141 (8.3%)
Teachers: 122.2 (14.0 to 1)
Librarians/Media Specialists: 2.5 (682.4 to 1)
Guidance Counselors: 3.0 (568.7 to 1)
Current Spending: ($ per student per year):
  Total: $7,715; Instruction: $4,993; Support Services: $2,137
Enrollment, Drop-out Rates and Diploma Recipients by Race/Ethnicity

Category	Total	White	Black	Asian	AIAN	Hisp.
Enrollment (%)	100.0	93.7	0.7	1.1	1.4	3.2
Drop-out Rate (%)	4.6	4.8	n/a	0.0	0.0	0.0
H.S. Diplomas (#)	119	110	1	3	2	3

Dakota County

So Sioux City Community Schs
820 E 29th St Box 158 • So Sioux City, NE 68776-0158
(402) 494-2425 • http://www.sioux.esu1.k12.ne.us/
Grade Span: PK-12; **Agency Type:** 1
Schools: 10
  7 Primary; 1 Middle; 1 High; 1 Other Level
  9 Regular; 1 Special Education; 0 Vocational; 0 Alternative
  0 Magnet; 0 Charter; 5 Title I Eligible; 4 School-wide Title I
Students: 3,496   (49.9% male; 50.0% female)
  Individual Education Program: 579 (16.6%);
  English Language Learner: 840 (24.0%); Migrant: 876 (25.1%)
  Eligible for Free Lunch Program: 970 (27.7%)
  Eligible for Reduced-Price Lunch Program: 409 (11.7%)
Teachers: 243.1 (14.4 to 1)
Librarians/Media Specialists: 5.0 (699.2 to 1)
Guidance Counselors: 8.5 (411.3 to 1)
Current Spending: ($ per student per year):
  Total: $6,500; Instruction: $4,197; Support Services: $1,911
Enrollment, Drop-out Rates and Diploma Recipients by Race/Ethnicity

Category	Total	White	Black	Asian	AIAN	Hisp.
Enrollment (%)	100.0	44.1	1.5	3.7	3.9	46.8
Drop-out Rate (%)	5.5	1.7	50.0	6.0	28.6	11.6
H.S. Diplomas (#)	191	137	0	18	2	34

Dawson County

Lexington Public Schools
1610 N Washington Box 890 • Lexington, NE 68850-0890
(308) 324-4681 • http://www.lex.esu10.org/
Grade Span: PK-12; **Agency Type:** 1
Schools: 8
  6 Primary; 1 Middle; 1 High; 0 Other Level
  7 Regular; 1 Special Education; 0 Vocational; 0 Alternative
  0 Magnet; 0 Charter; 4 Title I Eligible; 4 School-wide Title I
Students: 2,809   (52.8% male; 47.1% female)
  Individual Education Program: 365 (13.0%);
  English Language Learner: 938 (33.4%); Migrant: 1,492 (53.1%)
  Eligible for Free Lunch Program: 1,351 (48.1%)
  Eligible for Reduced-Price Lunch Program: 489 (17.4%)
Teachers: 172.8 (16.3 to 1)
Librarians/Media Specialists: 3.0 (936.3 to 1)
Guidance Counselors: 6.0 (468.2 to 1)
Current Spending: ($ per student per year):
  Total: $6,823; Instruction: $4,790; Support Services: $1,693
Enrollment, Drop-out Rates and Diploma Recipients by Race/Ethnicity

Category	Total	White	Black	Asian	AIAN	Hisp.
Enrollment (%)	100.0	26.5	0.7	1.3	0.5	71.0
Drop-out Rate (%)	5.9	1.4	0.0	25.0	0.0	9.9
H.S. Diplomas (#)	126	71	0	2	0	53

Dodge County

Fremont Public Schools
957 N Pierce St • Fremont, NE 68025-3949
(402) 727-3000 • http://www.fpsweb.org/
Grade Span: PK-12; **Agency Type:** 1
Schools: 12
  8 Primary; 1 Middle; 2 High; 1 Other Level
  12 Regular; 0 Special Education; 0 Vocational; 0 Alternative
  0 Magnet; 0 Charter; 3 Title I Eligible; 3 School-wide Title I
Students: 4,535   (50.1% male; 49.8% female)
  Individual Education Program: 872 (19.2%);
  English Language Learner: 227 (5.0%); Migrant: 329 (7.3%)
  Eligible for Free Lunch Program: 1,147 (25.3%)

Eligible for Reduced-Price Lunch Program: 432 (9.5%)
Teachers: 272.7 (16.6 to 1)
Librarians/Media Specialists: 6.0 (755.8 to 1)
Guidance Counselors: 10.8 (419.9 to 1)
Current Spending: ($ per student per year):
  Total: $6,636; Instruction: $4,022; Support Services: $2,260
Enrollment, Drop-out Rates and Diploma Recipients by Race/Ethnicity

Category	Total	White	Black	Asian	AIAN	Hisp.
Enrollment (%)	100.0	85.7	1.2	1.1	0.7	11.2
Drop-out Rate (%)	5.1	4.6	0.0	0.0	0.0	20.4
H.S. Diplomas (#)	287	272	2	3	1	9

Douglas County

Elkhorn Public Schools
502 Glenn St PO Box 439 • Elkhorn, NE 68022-0439
(402) 289-2579 • http://205.202.101.100/
Grade Span: PK-12; **Agency Type:** 1
Schools: 7
  4 Primary; 2 Middle; 1 High; 0 Other Level
  7 Regular; 0 Special Education; 0 Vocational; 0 Alternative
  0 Magnet; 0 Charter; 2 Title I Eligible; 0 School-wide Title I
Students: 3,320 (51.7% male; 48.2% female)
  Individual Education Program: 525 (15.8%);
  English Language Learner: 43 (1.3%); Migrant: 0 (0.0%)
  Eligible for Free Lunch Program: 174 (5.2%)
  Eligible for Reduced-Price Lunch Program: 97 (2.9%)
Teachers: 214.0 (15.5 to 1)
Librarians/Media Specialists: 7.0 (474.3 to 1)
Guidance Counselors: 9.0 (368.9 to 1)
Current Spending: ($ per student per year):
  Total: $6,767; Instruction: $4,492; Support Services: $1,825
Enrollment, Drop-out Rates and Diploma Recipients by Race/Ethnicity

Category	Total	White	Black	Asian	AIAN	Hisp.
Enrollment (%)	100.0	94.9	0.5	1.3	0.2	3.1
Drop-out Rate (%)	2.0	2.1	0.0	0.0	0.0	0.0
H.S. Diplomas (#)	200	193	0	0	2	5

Millard Public Schools
5606 S 147th St • Omaha, NE 68137-2604
(402) 895-8200 • http://www.mpsomaha.org/
Grade Span: PK-12; **Agency Type:** 1
Schools: 34
  22 Primary; 6 Middle; 3 High; 3 Other Level
  31 Regular; 3 Special Education; 0 Vocational; 0 Alternative
  0 Magnet; 0 Charter; 5 Title I Eligible; 1 School-wide Title I
Students: 19,904 (52.0% male; 47.9% female)
  Individual Education Program: 2,851 (14.3%);
  English Language Learner: 136 (0.7%); Migrant: 0 (0.0%)
  Eligible for Free Lunch Program: 1,056 (5.3%)
  Eligible for Reduced-Price Lunch Program: 489 (2.5%)
Teachers: 1,274.5 (15.6 to 1)
Librarians/Media Specialists: 33.7 (590.6 to 1)
Guidance Counselors: 45.6 (436.5 to 1)
Current Spending: ($ per student per year):
  Total: $6,834; Instruction: $4,372; Support Services: $2,088
Enrollment, Drop-out Rates and Diploma Recipients by Race/Ethnicity

Category	Total	White	Black	Asian	AIAN	Hisp.
Enrollment (%)	100.0	92.4	2.2	2.8	0.3	2.3
Drop-out Rate (%)	1.3	1.1	6.8	2.4	8.3	4.4
H.S. Diplomas (#)	1,513	1,433	17	36	5	22

Omaha Public Schools
3215 Cuming St • Omaha, NE 68131-2024
(402) 557-2222 • http://www.ops.org/
Grade Span: PK-12; **Agency Type:** 1
Schools: 84
  61 Primary; 10 Middle; 10 High; 3 Other Level
  81 Regular; 3 Special Education; 0 Vocational; 0 Alternative
  0 Magnet; 0 Charter; 39 Title I Eligible; 39 School-wide Title I
Students: 46,035 (51.3% male; 48.6% female)
  Individual Education Program: 7,056 (15.3%);
  English Language Learner: 5,384 (11.7%); Migrant: 1,288 (2.8%)
  Eligible for Free Lunch Program: 20,878 (45.4%)
  Eligible for Reduced-Price Lunch Program: 4,510 (9.8%)
Teachers: 3,100.9 (14.8 to 1)
Librarians/Media Specialists: 89.4 (514.9 to 1)
Guidance Counselors: 144.0 (319.7 to 1)
Current Spending: ($ per student per year):
  Total: $7,187; Instruction: $4,242; Support Services: $2,637
Enrollment, Drop-out Rates and Diploma Recipients by Race/Ethnicity

Category	Total	White	Black	Asian	AIAN	Hisp.
Enrollment (%)	100.0	47.6	31.1	1.7	1.5	18.1
Drop-out Rate (%)	10.9	8.8	12.4	4.0	28.2	16.9
H.S. Diplomas (#)	2,168	1,385	557	45	14	167

Ralston Public Schools
8545 Park Dr • Ralston, NE 68127-3690
(402) 331-4700 • http://www.ralstonschools.org/
Grade Span: PK-12; **Agency Type:** 1
Schools: 8
  6 Primary; 1 Middle; 1 High; 0 Other Level
  8 Regular; 0 Special Education; 0 Vocational; 0 Alternative
  0 Magnet; 0 Charter; 4 Title I Eligible; 0 School-wide Title I
Students: 3,131 (51.8% male; 48.1% female)
  Individual Education Program: 491 (15.7%);
  English Language Learner: 135 (4.3%); Migrant: 1 (<0.1%)
  Eligible for Free Lunch Program: 632 (20.2%)
  Eligible for Reduced-Price Lunch Program: 274 (8.8%)
Teachers: 200.4 (15.6 to 1)
Librarians/Media Specialists: 4.0 (782.8 to 1)
Guidance Counselors: 5.8 (539.8 to 1)
Current Spending: ($ per student per year):
  Total: $7,012; Instruction: $4,761; Support Services: $1,894
Enrollment, Drop-out Rates and Diploma Recipients by Race/Ethnicity

Category	Total	White	Black	Asian	AIAN	Hisp.
Enrollment (%)	100.0	80.8	4.0	3.3	0.4	11.5
Drop-out Rate (%)	2.3	2.3	4.0	0.0	0.0	5.1
H.S. Diplomas (#)	204	190	6	4	0	4

Westside Community Schools
909 S 76th St • Omaha, NE 68114-4599
(402) 390-2100 • http://www.westside66.org/
Grade Span: PK-12; **Agency Type:** 1
Schools: 14
  11 Primary; 1 Middle; 1 High; 1 Other Level
  13 Regular; 1 Special Education; 0 Vocational; 0 Alternative
  0 Magnet; 0 Charter; 4 Title I Eligible; 0 School-wide Title I
Students: 5,793 (51.0% male; 48.9% female)
  Individual Education Program: 650 (11.2%);
  English Language Learner: 127 (2.2%); Migrant: 0 (0.0%)
  Eligible for Free Lunch Program: 713 (12.3%)
  Eligible for Reduced-Price Lunch Program: 307 (5.3%)
Teachers: 420.9 (13.8 to 1)
Librarians/Media Specialists: 8.6 (673.6 to 1)
Guidance Counselors: 18.5 (313.1 to 1)
Current Spending: ($ per student per year):
  Total: $8,289; Instruction: $5,312; Support Services: $2,560
Enrollment, Drop-out Rates and Diploma Recipients by Race/Ethnicity

Category	Total	White	Black	Asian	AIAN	Hisp.
Enrollment (%)	100.0	86.8	5.9	3.7	0.6	3.0
Drop-out Rate (%)	0.7	0.6	1.9	2.0	0.0	0.0
H.S. Diplomas (#)	338	315	4	11	1	7

Gage County

Beatrice Public Schools
320 N 5th St • Beatrice, NE 68310-2957
(402) 223-1500 • http://www.beatrice.k12.ne.us
Grade Span: PK-12; **Agency Type:** 1
Schools: 6
  4 Primary; 1 Middle; 1 High; 0 Other Level
  6 Regular; 0 Special Education; 0 Vocational; 0 Alternative
  0 Magnet; 0 Charter; 3 Title I Eligible; 0 School-wide Title I
Students: 2,259 (50.9% male; 49.0% female)
  Individual Education Program: 386 (17.1%);
  English Language Learner: 4 (0.2%); Migrant: 0 (0.0%)
  Eligible for Free Lunch Program: 506 (22.4%)
  Eligible for Reduced-Price Lunch Program: 248 (11.0%)
Teachers: 148.4 (15.2 to 1)
Librarians/Media Specialists: 3.0 (753.0 to 1)
Guidance Counselors: 6.0 (376.5 to 1)
Current Spending: ($ per student per year):
  Total: $6,706; Instruction: $4,438; Support Services: $1,846
Enrollment, Drop-out Rates and Diploma Recipients by Race/Ethnicity

Category	Total	White	Black	Asian	AIAN	Hisp.
Enrollment (%)	100.0	95.1	1.6	0.7	0.7	1.9
Drop-out Rate (%)	2.5	2.6	0.0	0.0	n/a	0.0
H.S. Diplomas (#)	180	176	1	1	0	2

Hall County

Grand Island Public Schools
123 S Webb Rd PO Box 4904 • Grand Island, NE 68802-4904
(308) 385-5900 • http://www.gi.esu10.k12.ne.us/SDGI/Buildingweb.html
Grade Span: PK-12; **Agency Type:** 1
Schools: 21
  14 Primary; 4 Middle; 2 High; 1 Other Level
  20 Regular; 1 Special Education; 0 Vocational; 0 Alternative
  0 Magnet; 0 Charter; 9 Title I Eligible; 9 School-wide Title I
Students: 7,925 (51.0% male; 48.9% female)

Individual Education Program: 1,238 (15.6%);
English Language Learner: 1,487 (18.8%); Migrant: 1,011 (12.8%)
Eligible for Free Lunch Program: 2,985 (37.7%)
Eligible for Reduced-Price Lunch Program: 969 (12.2%)
Teachers: 521.0 (15.2 to 1)
Librarians/Media Specialists: 18.0 (440.3 to 1)
Guidance Counselors: 18.2 (435.4 to 1)
Current Spending: ($ per student per year):
Total: $7,373; Instruction: $5,345; Support Services: $1,655
Enrollment, Drop-out Rates and Diploma Recipients by Race/Ethnicity

Category	Total	White	Black	Asian	AIAN	Hisp.
Enrollment (%)	100.0	65.1	1.7	1.9	0.5	30.7
Drop-out Rate (%)	4.5	3.7	18.2	0.0	0.0	7.9
H.S. Diplomas (#)	340	277	3	12	0	48

Lancaster County

Lincoln Public Schools
Box 82889 · Lincoln, NE 68501-2889
(402) 436-1000 · http://www.lps.org/
Grade Span: PK-12; **Agency Type:** 1
Schools: 66
41 Primary; 11 Middle; 13 High; 1 Other Level
64 Regular; 2 Special Education; 0 Vocational; 0 Alternative
0 Magnet; 0 Charter; 12 Title I Eligible; 12 School-wide Title I
Students: 32,120   (51.3% male; 48.6% female)
Individual Education Program: 5,598 (17.4%);
English Language Learner: 2,312 (7.2%); Migrant: 389 (1.2%)
Eligible for Free Lunch Program: 7,595 (23.6%)
Eligible for Reduced-Price Lunch Program: 1,869 (5.8%)
Teachers: 2,341.6 (13.7 to 1)
Librarians/Media Specialists: 50.8 (632.3 to 1)
Guidance Counselors: 69.9 (459.5 to 1)
Current Spending: ($ per student per year):
Total: $7,525; Instruction: $4,962; Support Services: $2,216
Enrollment, Drop-out Rates and Diploma Recipients by Race/Ethnicity

Category	Total	White	Black	Asian	AIAN	Hisp.
Enrollment (%)	100.0	82.1	7.4	3.8	1.4	5.3
Drop-out Rate (%)	6.2	5.4	11.2	3.9	13.1	18.5
H.S. Diplomas (#)	1,896	1,661	77	90	19	49

Norris SD 160
25211 S 68th St · Firth, NE 68358-9732
(402) 791-0000
Grade Span: PK-12; **Agency Type:** 1
Schools: 3
1 Primary; 1 Middle; 1 High; 0 Other Level
3 Regular; 0 Special Education; 0 Vocational; 0 Alternative
0 Magnet; 0 Charter; 1 Title I Eligible; 0 School-wide Title I
Students: 1,690   (53.3% male; 46.6% female)
Individual Education Program: 204 (12.1%);
English Language Learner: 11 (0.7%); Migrant: 0 (0.0%)
Eligible for Free Lunch Program: 114 (6.7%)
Eligible for Reduced-Price Lunch Program: 43 (2.5%)
Teachers: 97.0 (17.4 to 1)
Librarians/Media Specialists: 2.0 (845.0 to 1)
Guidance Counselors: 3.0 (563.3 to 1)
Current Spending: ($ per student per year):
Total: $6,342; Instruction: $3,942; Support Services: $2,101
Enrollment, Drop-out Rates and Diploma Recipients by Race/Ethnicity

Category	Total	White	Black	Asian	AIAN	Hisp.
Enrollment (%)	100.0	95.4	0.9	0.9	0.4	2.3
Drop-out Rate (%)	1.2	1.2	0.0	0.0	0.0	0.0
H.S. Diplomas (#)	120	116	2	0	1	1

Waverly SD 145
14511 Heywood Box 426 · Waverly, NE 68462-0426
(402) 786-2321 · http://www.dist145.esu6.org/whs/
Grade Span: PK-12; **Agency Type:** 1
Schools: 5
3 Primary; 1 Middle; 1 High; 0 Other Level
4 Regular; 1 Special Education; 0 Vocational; 0 Alternative
0 Magnet; 0 Charter; 1 Title I Eligible; 0 School-wide Title I
Students: 1,661   (52.5% male; 47.4% female)
Individual Education Program: 310 (18.7%);
English Language Learner: 41 (2.5%); Migrant: 0 (0.0%)
Eligible for Free Lunch Program: 168 (10.1%)
Eligible for Reduced-Price Lunch Program: 92 (5.5%)
Teachers: 121.1 (13.7 to 1)
Librarians/Media Specialists: 4.0 (415.3 to 1)
Guidance Counselors: 5.0 (332.2 to 1)
Current Spending: ($ per student per year):
Total: $7,805; Instruction: $4,749; Support Services: $2,409

Category	Total	White	Black	Asian	AIAN	Hisp.
Enrollment (%)	100.0	97.4	0.3	0.3	0.6	1.4
Drop-out Rate (%)	0.5	0.5	0.0	n/a	0.0	0.0
H.S. Diplomas (#)	131	130	0	0	0	1

Lincoln County

North Platte Public Schools
301 W F PO Box 1557 · North Platte, NE 69103-1557
(308) 535-7100 · http://www.nppsd.org/
Grade Span: PK-12; **Agency Type:** 1
Schools: 13
8 Primary; 3 Middle; 2 High; 0 Other Level
13 Regular; 0 Special Education; 0 Vocational; 0 Alternative
0 Magnet; 0 Charter; 5 Title I Eligible; 4 School-wide Title I
Students: 3,855   (52.5% male; 47.4% female)
Individual Education Program: 739 (19.2%);
English Language Learner: 21 (0.5%); Migrant: 1 (<0.1%)
Eligible for Free Lunch Program: 1,001 (26.0%)
Eligible for Reduced-Price Lunch Program: 354 (9.2%)
Teachers: 254.0 (15.2 to 1)
Librarians/Media Specialists: 5.0 (771.0 to 1)
Guidance Counselors: 11.0 (350.5 to 1)
Current Spending: ($ per student per year):
Total: $6,648; Instruction: $4,206; Support Services: $2,120
Enrollment, Drop-out Rates and Diploma Recipients by Race/Ethnicity

Category	Total	White	Black	Asian	AIAN	Hisp.
Enrollment (%)	100.0	86.5	1.6	0.7	0.8	10.4
Drop-out Rate (%)	3.4	2.9	7.7	0.0	14.3	7.5
H.S. Diplomas (#)	344	317	4	1	1	21

Madison County

Norfolk Public Schools
512 Philip Ave PO Box 139 · Norfolk, NE 68702-0139
(402) 644-2500 · http://www.norfolkpublicschools.org/
Grade Span: PK-12; **Agency Type:** 1
Schools: 15
10 Primary; 2 Middle; 2 High; 1 Other Level
13 Regular; 2 Special Education; 0 Vocational; 0 Alternative
0 Magnet; 0 Charter; 7 Title I Eligible; 3 School-wide Title I
Students: 4,185   (50.3% male; 49.6% female)
Individual Education Program: 801 (19.1%);
English Language Learner: 314 (7.5%); Migrant: 670 (16.0%)
Eligible for Free Lunch Program: 1,295 (30.9%)
Eligible for Reduced-Price Lunch Program: 480 (11.5%)
Teachers: 292.3 (14.3 to 1)
Librarians/Media Specialists: 5.0 (837.0 to 1)
Guidance Counselors: 11.7 (357.7 to 1)
Current Spending: ($ per student per year):
Total: $6,921; Instruction: $4,640; Support Services: $1,948
Enrollment, Drop-out Rates and Diploma Recipients by Race/Ethnicity

Category	Total	White	Black	Asian	AIAN	Hisp.
Enrollment (%)	100.0	73.2	3.9	0.6	3.2	19.0
Drop-out Rate (%)	2.4	1.9	3.2	0.0	5.4	7.6
H.S. Diplomas (#)	359	322	7	7	5	18

Platte County

Columbus Public Schools
2508 27th St Box 947 · Columbus, NE 68602-0947
(402) 563-7000 · http://www.discoverers.org/
Grade Span: PK-12; **Agency Type:** 1
Schools: 8
6 Primary; 1 Middle; 1 High; 0 Other Level
8 Regular; 0 Special Education; 0 Vocational; 0 Alternative
0 Magnet; 0 Charter; 4 Title I Eligible; 2 School-wide Title I
Students: 3,473   (51.1% male; 48.8% female)
Individual Education Program: 576 (16.6%);
English Language Learner: 526 (15.1%); Migrant: 436 (12.6%)
Eligible for Free Lunch Program: 796 (22.9%)
Eligible for Reduced-Price Lunch Program: 394 (11.3%)
Teachers: 218.6 (15.9 to 1)
Librarians/Media Specialists: 5.5 (631.5 to 1)
Guidance Counselors: 8.0 (434.1 to 1)
Current Spending: ($ per student per year):
Total: $6,698; Instruction: $4,300; Support Services: $1,810
Enrollment, Drop-out Rates and Diploma Recipients by Race/Ethnicity

Category	Total	White	Black	Asian	AIAN	Hisp.
Enrollment (%)	100.0	78.1	1.3	0.9	0.8	18.9
Drop-out Rate (%)	4.3	3.4	7.7	0.0	14.3	14.0
H.S. Diplomas (#)	279	261	2	3	1	12

Saline County

Crete Public Schools
920 Linden Ave • Crete, NE 68333-2292
(402) 471-3464
Grade Span: PK-12; **Agency Type:** 1
Schools: 2
    1 Primary; 0 Middle; 1 High; 0 Other Level
    2 Regular; 0 Special Education; 0 Vocational; 0 Alternative
    0 Magnet; 0 Charter; 2 Title I Eligible; 0 School-wide Title I
Students: 1,523   (51.5% male; 48.4% female)
    Individual Education Program: 180 (11.8%);
    English Language Learner: 420 (27.6%); Migrant: 320 (21.0%)
    Eligible for Free Lunch Program: 359 (23.6%)
    Eligible for Reduced-Price Lunch Program: 180 (11.8%)
Teachers: 102.4 (14.9 to 1)
Librarians/Media Specialists: 1.9 (801.6 to 1)
Guidance Counselors: 3.0 (507.7 to 1)
Current Spending: ($ per student per year):
    Total: $6,299; Instruction: $3,966; Support Services: $2,001
Enrollment, Drop-out Rates and Diploma Recipients by Race/Ethnicity

Category	Total	White	Black	Asian	AIAN	Hisp.
Enrollment (%)	100.0	68.1	1.2	3.5	0.3	26.9
Drop-out Rate (%)	1.9	1.2	0.0	5.9	0.0	6.8
H.S. Diplomas (#)	112	101	1	5	1	4

Sarpy County

Bellevue Public Schools
1600 Hwy 370 • Bellevue, NE 68005-3591
(402) 293-4000 •
http://www.esu3.k12.ne.us/districts/bellevue/bpshome.html
Grade Span: PK-12; **Agency Type:** 1
Schools: 19
    14 Primary; 2 Middle; 2 High; 1 Other Level
    18 Regular; 1 Special Education; 0 Vocational; 0 Alternative
    0 Magnet; 0 Charter; 4 Title I Eligible; 4 School-wide Title I
Students: 8,951   (52.2% male; 47.7% female)
    Individual Education Program: 1,266 (14.1%);
    English Language Learner: 88 (1.0%); Migrant: 0 (0.0%)
    Eligible for Free Lunch Program: 1,056 (11.8%)
    Eligible for Reduced-Price Lunch Program: 818 (9.1%)
Teachers: 591.3 (15.1 to 1)
Librarians/Media Specialists: 15.0 (596.7 to 1)
Guidance Counselors: 22.0 (406.9 to 1)
Current Spending: ($ per student per year):
    Total: $7,122; Instruction: $4,764; Support Services: $2,008
Enrollment, Drop-out Rates and Diploma Recipients by Race/Ethnicity

Category	Total	White	Black	Asian	AIAN	Hisp.
Enrollment (%)	100.0	79.7	9.6	3.6	0.8	6.3
Drop-out Rate (%)	2.8	2.7	3.3	4.1	6.3	2.4
H.S. Diplomas (#)	592	493	61	23	2	13

Gretna Public Schools
801 S St • Gretna, NE 68028-7865
(402) 332-3265
Grade Span: PK-12; **Agency Type:** 1
Schools: 3
    1 Primary; 1 Middle; 1 High; 0 Other Level
    3 Regular; 0 Special Education; 0 Vocational; 0 Alternative
    0 Magnet; 0 Charter; 1 Title I Eligible; 0 School-wide Title I
Students: 1,741   (51.9% male; 48.0% female)
    Individual Education Program: 253 (14.5%);
    English Language Learner: 3 (0.2%); Migrant: 0 (0.0%)
    Eligible for Free Lunch Program: 61 (3.5%)
    Eligible for Reduced-Price Lunch Program: 62 (3.6%)
Teachers: 111.3 (15.6 to 1)
Librarians/Media Specialists: 3.0 (580.3 to 1)
Guidance Counselors: 3.0 (580.3 to 1)
Current Spending: ($ per student per year):
    Total: $6,717; Instruction: $4,355; Support Services: $2,025
Enrollment, Drop-out Rates and Diploma Recipients by Race/Ethnicity

Category	Total	White	Black	Asian	AIAN	Hisp.
Enrollment (%)	100.0	97.6	0.2	1.1	0.2	0.8
Drop-out Rate (%)	0.0	0.0	n/a	0.0	n/a	0.0
H.S. Diplomas (#)	99	99	0	0	0	0

Papillion-La Vista Public Schools
420 S Washington • Papillion, NE 68046-2667
(402) 537-9998 • http://www.paplv.esu3.org/coadm/default2.html
Grade Span: PK-12; **Agency Type:** 1
Schools: 18
    12 Primary; 2 Middle; 3 High; 1 Other Level
    17 Regular; 1 Special Education; 0 Vocational; 0 Alternative
    0 Magnet; 0 Charter; 5 Title I Eligible; 0 School-wide Title I

Students: 8,339   (51.6% male; 48.3% female)
    Individual Education Program: 1,010 (12.1%);
    English Language Learner: 50 (0.6%); Migrant: 0 (0.0%)
    Eligible for Free Lunch Program: 730 (8.8%)
    Eligible for Reduced-Price Lunch Program: 429 (5.1%)
Teachers: 548.5 (15.2 to 1)
Librarians/Media Specialists: 14.8 (563.4 to 1)
Guidance Counselors: 23.3 (357.9 to 1)
Current Spending: ($ per student per year):
    Total: $6,457; Instruction: $4,440; Support Services: $1,750
Enrollment, Drop-out Rates and Diploma Recipients by Race/Ethnicity

Category	Total	White	Black	Asian	AIAN	Hisp.
Enrollment (%)	100.0	89.0	4.8	2.4	0.5	3.3
Drop-out Rate (%)	3.2	3.0	6.1	3.1	0.0	4.5
H.S. Diplomas (#)	534	482	12	22	2	16

Scotts Bluff County

Gering Public Schools
1800 8th St • Gering, NE 69341-2999
(308) 436-3125 • http://www.geringschools.net/
Grade Span: PK-12; **Agency Type:** 1
Schools: 5
    3 Primary; 1 Middle; 1 High; 0 Other Level
    5 Regular; 0 Special Education; 0 Vocational; 0 Alternative
    0 Magnet; 0 Charter; 3 Title I Eligible; 0 School-wide Title I
Students: 1,896   (49.5% male; 50.4% female)
    Individual Education Program: 226 (11.9%);
    English Language Learner: 56 (3.0%); Migrant: 22 (1.2%)
    Eligible for Free Lunch Program: 516 (27.2%)
    Eligible for Reduced-Price Lunch Program: 175 (9.2%)
Teachers: 128.4 (14.8 to 1)
Librarians/Media Specialists: 2.9 (653.8 to 1)
Guidance Counselors: 4.9 (386.9 to 1)
Current Spending: ($ per student per year):
    Total: $6,977; Instruction: $4,813; Support Services: $1,930
Enrollment, Drop-out Rates and Diploma Recipients by Race/Ethnicity

Category	Total	White	Black	Asian	AIAN	Hisp.
Enrollment (%)	100.0	71.1	0.7	0.7	3.1	24.4
Drop-out Rate (%)	2.0	1.5	0.0	0.0	0.0	4.5
H.S. Diplomas (#)	142	124	0	1	1	16

Scottsbluff Public Schools
2601 Broadway • Scottsbluff, NE 69361-1609
(308) 635-6200 • http://www.sbps.net/
Grade Span: PK-12; **Agency Type:** 1
Schools: 6
    4 Primary; 1 Middle; 1 High; 0 Other Level
    6 Regular; 0 Special Education; 0 Vocational; 0 Alternative
    0 Magnet; 0 Charter; 3 Title I Eligible; 1 School-wide Title I
Students: 2,679   (50.2% male; 49.7% female)
    Individual Education Program: 400 (14.9%);
    English Language Learner: 68 (2.5%); Migrant: 54 (2.0%)
    Eligible for Free Lunch Program: 910 (34.0%)
    Eligible for Reduced-Price Lunch Program: 172 (6.4%)
Teachers: 177.1 (15.1 to 1)
Librarians/Media Specialists: 4.0 (669.8 to 1)
Guidance Counselors: 4.0 (669.8 to 1)
Current Spending: ($ per student per year):
    Total: $6,957; Instruction: $4,648; Support Services: $2,021
Enrollment, Drop-out Rates and Diploma Recipients by Race/Ethnicity

Category	Total	White	Black	Asian	AIAN	Hisp.
Enrollment (%)	100.0	59.0	1.2	0.8	6.3	32.7
Drop-out Rate (%)	10.3	6.0	12.5	0.0	38.7	18.9
H.S. Diplomas (#)	195	158	0	1	1	35

Washington County

Blair Community Schools
140 S 16th PO Box 288 • Blair, NE 68008-0288
(402) 426-2610
Grade Span: PK-12; **Agency Type:** 1
Schools: 6
    4 Primary; 1 Middle; 1 High; 0 Other Level
    6 Regular; 0 Special Education; 0 Vocational; 0 Alternative
    0 Magnet; 0 Charter; 3 Title I Eligible; 0 School-wide Title I
Students: 2,272   (51.6% male; 48.3% female)
    Individual Education Program: 374 (16.5%);
    English Language Learner: 14 (0.6%); Migrant: 0 (0.0%)
    Eligible for Free Lunch Program: 219 (9.6%)
    Eligible for Reduced-Price Lunch Program: 114 (5.0%)
Teachers: 137.2 (16.6 to 1)
Librarians/Media Specialists: 4.0 (568.0 to 1)
Guidance Counselors: 7.0 (324.6 to 1)

Current Spending: ($ per student per year):
   Total: $6,511; Instruction: $4,091; Support Services: $1,971

Enrollment, Drop-out Rates and Diploma Recipients by Race/Ethnicity

Category	Total	White	Black	Asian	AIAN	Hisp.
Enrollment (%)	100.0	97.0	0.8	0.5	0.3	1.5
Drop-out Rate (%)	1.4	1.3	33.3	0.0	0.0	0.0
H.S. Diplomas (#)	160	159	0	1	0	0

Number of Schools

Rank	Number	District Name	City
1	84	Omaha Public Schools	Omaha
2	66	Lincoln Public Schools	Lincoln
3	34	Millard Public Schools	Omaha
4	21	Grand Island Public Schools	Grand Island
5	19	Bellevue Public Schools	Bellevue
6	18	Papillion-La Vista Public Schools	Papillion
7	15	Norfolk Public Schools	Norfolk
8	14	Westside Community Schools	Omaha
9	13	Kearney Public Schools	Kearney
9	13	North Platte Public Schools	North Platte
11	12	Fremont Public Schools	Fremont
12	10	So Sioux City Community Schs	So Sioux City
13	8	Columbus Public Schools	Columbus
13	8	Hastings Public Schools	Hastings
13	8	Lexington Public Schools	Lexington
13	8	Ralston Public Schools	Ralston
17	7	Elkhorn Public Schools	Elkhorn
18	6	Beatrice Public Schools	Beatrice
18	6	Blair Community Schools	Blair
18	6	Scottsbluff Public Schools	Scottsbluff
21	5	Alliance Public Schools	Alliance
21	5	Gering Public Schools	Gering
21	5	Plattsmouth Community Schools	Plattsmouth
21	5	Waverly SD 145	Waverly
25	3	Gretna Public Schools	Gretna
25	3	Norris SD 160	Firth
27	2	Crete Public Schools	Crete

Number of Teachers

Rank	Number	District Name	City
1	3,100	Omaha Public Schools	Omaha
2	2,341	Lincoln Public Schools	Lincoln
3	1,274	Millard Public Schools	Omaha
4	591	Bellevue Public Schools	Bellevue
5	548	Papillion-La Vista Public Schools	Papillion
6	521	Grand Island Public Schools	Grand Island
7	420	Westside Community Schools	Omaha
8	306	Kearney Public Schools	Kearney
9	292	Norfolk Public Schools	Norfolk
10	272	Fremont Public Schools	Fremont
11	254	North Platte Public Schools	North Platte
12	243	So Sioux City Community Schs	So Sioux City
13	226	Hastings Public Schools	Hastings
14	218	Columbus Public Schools	Columbus
15	214	Elkhorn Public Schools	Elkhorn
16	200	Ralston Public Schools	Ralston
17	177	Scottsbluff Public Schools	Scottsbluff
18	172	Lexington Public Schools	Lexington
19	148	Beatrice Public Schools	Beatrice
20	137	Blair Community Schools	Blair
21	128	Gering Public Schools	Gering
22	127	Alliance Public Schools	Alliance
23	122	Plattsmouth Community Schools	Plattsmouth
24	121	Waverly SD 145	Waverly
25	111	Gretna Public Schools	Gretna
26	102	Crete Public Schools	Crete
27	97	Norris SD 160	Firth

Number of Students

Rank	Number	District Name	City
1	46,035	Omaha Public Schools	Omaha
2	32,120	Lincoln Public Schools	Lincoln
3	19,904	Millard Public Schools	Omaha
4	8,951	Bellevue Public Schools	Bellevue
5	8,339	Papillion-La Vista Public Schools	Papillion
6	7,925	Grand Island Public Schools	Grand Island
7	5,793	Westside Community Schools	Omaha
8	4,648	Kearney Public Schools	Kearney
9	4,535	Fremont Public Schools	Fremont
10	4,185	Norfolk Public Schools	Norfolk
11	3,855	North Platte Public Schools	North Platte
12	3,496	So Sioux City Community Schs	So Sioux City
13	3,473	Columbus Public Schools	Columbus
14	3,320	Elkhorn Public Schools	Elkhorn
15	3,255	Hastings Public Schools	Hastings
16	3,131	Ralston Public Schools	Ralston
17	2,809	Lexington Public Schools	Lexington
18	2,679	Scottsbluff Public Schools	Scottsbluff
19	2,272	Blair Community Schools	Blair
20	2,259	Beatrice Public Schools	Beatrice
21	1,896	Gering Public Schools	Gering
22	1,741	Gretna Public Schools	Gretna
23	1,728	Alliance Public Schools	Alliance
24	1,706	Plattsmouth Community Schools	Plattsmouth
25	1,690	Norris SD 160	Firth
26	1,661	Waverly SD 145	Waverly
27	1,523	Crete Public Schools	Crete

Male Students

Rank	Percent	District Name	City
1	54.9	Alliance Public Schools	Alliance
2	53.9	Plattsmouth Community Schools	Plattsmouth
3	53.3	Norris SD 160	Firth
4	52.8	Lexington Public Schools	Lexington
5	52.5	Waverly SD 145	Waverly
6	52.5	North Platte Public Schools	North Platte
7	52.2	Bellevue Public Schools	Bellevue
8	52.0	Millard Public Schools	Omaha
9	52.0	Hastings Public Schools	Hastings
10	51.9	Gretna Public Schools	Gretna
11	51.8	Ralston Public Schools	Ralston
12	51.7	Elkhorn Public Schools	Elkhorn
13	51.6	Blair Community Schools	Blair
14	51.6	Papillion-La Vista Public Schools	Papillion
15	51.5	Crete Public Schools	Crete
16	51.4	Kearney Public Schools	Kearney
17	51.3	Lincoln Public Schools	Lincoln
18	51.3	Omaha Public Schools	Omaha
19	51.1	Columbus Public Schools	Columbus
20	51.0	Westside Community Schools	Omaha
21	51.0	Grand Island Public Schools	Grand Island
22	50.9	Beatrice Public Schools	Beatrice
23	50.3	Norfolk Public Schools	Norfolk
24	50.2	Scottsbluff Public Schools	Scottsbluff
25	50.1	Fremont Public Schools	Fremont
26	49.9	So Sioux City Community Schs	So Sioux City
27	49.5	Gering Public Schools	Gering

Female Students

Rank	Percent	District Name	City
1	50.4	Gering Public Schools	Gering
2	50.0	So Sioux City Community Schs	So Sioux City
3	49.8	Fremont Public Schools	Fremont
4	49.7	Scottsbluff Public Schools	Scottsbluff
5	49.6	Norfolk Public Schools	Norfolk
6	49.0	Beatrice Public Schools	Beatrice
7	48.9	Grand Island Public Schools	Grand Island
8	48.9	Westside Community Schools	Omaha
9	48.8	Columbus Public Schools	Columbus
10	48.6	Omaha Public Schools	Omaha
11	48.6	Lincoln Public Schools	Lincoln
12	48.5	Kearney Public Schools	Kearney
13	48.4	Crete Public Schools	Crete
14	48.3	Papillion-La Vista Public Schools	Papillion
15	48.3	Blair Community Schools	Blair
16	48.2	Elkhorn Public Schools	Elkhorn
17	48.1	Ralston Public Schools	Ralston
18	48.0	Gretna Public Schools	Gretna
19	47.9	Hastings Public Schools	Hastings
20	47.9	Millard Public Schools	Omaha
21	47.7	Bellevue Public Schools	Bellevue
22	47.4	North Platte Public Schools	North Platte
23	47.4	Waverly SD 145	Waverly
24	47.1	Lexington Public Schools	Lexington
25	46.6	Norris SD 160	Firth
26	46.0	Plattsmouth Community Schools	Plattsmouth
27	45.0	Alliance Public Schools	Alliance

Individual Education Program Students

Rank	Percent	District Name	City
1	20.9	Plattsmouth Community Schools	Plattsmouth
2	20.0	Hastings Public Schools	Hastings
3	19.2	Fremont Public Schools	Fremont
3	19.2	North Platte Public Schools	North Platte
5	19.1	Norfolk Public Schools	Norfolk
6	18.7	Waverly SD 145	Waverly
7	17.4	Lincoln Public Schools	Lincoln
8	17.1	Alliance Public Schools	Alliance
8	17.1	Beatrice Public Schools	Beatrice
10	16.6	Columbus Public Schools	Columbus
10	16.6	So Sioux City Community Schs	So Sioux City
12	16.5	Blair Community Schools	Blair
13	15.8	Elkhorn Public Schools	Elkhorn
14	15.7	Kearney Public Schools	Kearney
14	15.7	Ralston Public Schools	Ralston
16	15.6	Grand Island Public Schools	Grand Island
17	15.3	Omaha Public Schools	Omaha
18	14.9	Scottsbluff Public Schools	Scottsbluff
19	14.5	Gretna Public Schools	Gretna
20	14.3	Millard Public Schools	Omaha
21	14.1	Bellevue Public Schools	Bellevue
22	13.0	Lexington Public Schools	Lexington
23	12.1	Norris SD 160	Firth
23	12.1	Papillion-La Vista Public Schools	Papillion
25	11.9	Gering Public Schools	Gering
26	11.8	Crete Public Schools	Crete
27	11.2	Westside Community Schools	Omaha

English Language Learner Students

Rank	Percent	District Name	City
1	33.4	Lexington Public Schools	Lexington
2	27.6	Crete Public Schools	Crete
3	24.0	So Sioux City Community Schs	So Sioux City
4	18.8	Grand Island Public Schools	Grand Island
5	15.1	Columbus Public Schools	Columbus
6	11.7	Omaha Public Schools	Omaha
7	7.5	Norfolk Public Schools	Norfolk
8	7.2	Hastings Public Schools	Hastings
8	7.2	Lincoln Public Schools	Lincoln
10	5.0	Fremont Public Schools	Fremont
11	4.3	Ralston Public Schools	Ralston
12	3.8	Kearney Public Schools	Kearney
13	3.5	Plattsmouth Community Schools	Plattsmouth
14	3.0	Gering Public Schools	Gering
15	2.5	Scottsbluff Public Schools	Scottsbluff
15	2.5	Waverly SD 145	Waverly
17	2.2	Westside Community Schools	Omaha
18	2.1	Alliance Public Schools	Alliance
19	1.3	Elkhorn Public Schools	Elkhorn
20	1.0	Bellevue Public Schools	Bellevue
21	0.7	Millard Public Schools	Omaha
21	0.7	Norris SD 160	Firth
23	0.6	Blair Community Schools	Blair
23	0.6	Papillion-La Vista Public Schools	Papillion
25	0.5	North Platte Public Schools	North Platte
26	0.2	Beatrice Public Schools	Beatrice
26	0.2	Gretna Public Schools	Gretna

Migrant Students

Rank	Percent	District Name	City
1	53.1	Lexington Public Schools	Lexington
2	25.1	So Sioux City Community Schs	So Sioux City
3	21.0	Crete Public Schools	Crete
4	16.0	Norfolk Public Schools	Norfolk
5	12.8	Grand Island Public Schools	Grand Island
6	12.6	Columbus Public Schools	Columbus
7	8.4	Alliance Public Schools	Alliance
8	7.6	Hastings Public Schools	Hastings
9	7.3	Fremont Public Schools	Fremont
10	3.2	Kearney Public Schools	Kearney
11	2.8	Omaha Public Schools	Omaha
12	2.0	Scottsbluff Public Schools	Scottsbluff
13	1.2	Gering Public Schools	Gering
13	1.2	Lincoln Public Schools	Lincoln
15	0.0	North Platte Public Schools	North Platte
15	0.0	Ralston Public Schools	Ralston
17	0.0	Beatrice Public Schools	Beatrice
17	0.0	Bellevue Public Schools	Bellevue
17	0.0	Blair Community Schools	Blair
17	0.0	Elkhorn Public Schools	Elkhorn
17	0.0	Gretna Public Schools	Gretna
17	0.0	Millard Public Schools	Omaha
17	0.0	Norris SD 160	Firth
17	0.0	Papillion-La Vista Public Schools	Papillion
17	0.0	Plattsmouth Community Schools	Plattsmouth
17	0.0	Waverly SD 145	Waverly
17	0.0	Westside Community Schools	Omaha

Students Eligible for Free Lunch

Rank	Percent	District Name	City
1	48.1	Lexington Public Schools	Lexington
2	45.4	Omaha Public Schools	Omaha
3	37.7	Grand Island Public Schools	Grand Island
4	34.0	Scottsbluff Public Schools	Scottsbluff
5	31.2	Hastings Public Schools	Hastings
6	30.9	Norfolk Public Schools	Norfolk
7	27.8	Plattsmouth Community Schools	Plattsmouth
8	27.7	So Sioux City Community Schs	So Sioux City
9	27.4	Alliance Public Schools	Alliance
10	27.2	Gering Public Schools	Gering
11	26.0	North Platte Public Schools	North Platte
12	25.3	Fremont Public Schools	Fremont
13	23.6	Crete Public Schools	Crete
13	23.6	Lincoln Public Schools	Lincoln
15	22.9	Columbus Public Schools	Columbus
16	22.4	Beatrice Public Schools	Beatrice
17	21.3	Kearney Public Schools	Kearney
18	20.2	Ralston Public Schools	Ralston
19	12.3	Westside Community Schools	Omaha
20	11.8	Bellevue Public Schools	Bellevue
21	10.1	Waverly SD 145	Waverly
22	9.6	Blair Community Schools	Blair
23	8.8	Papillion-La Vista Public Schools	Papillion
24	6.7	Norris SD 160	Firth
25	5.3	Millard Public Schools	Omaha
26	5.2	Elkhorn Public Schools	Elkhorn
27	3.5	Gretna Public Schools	Gretna

Students Eligible for Reduced-Price Lunch

Rank	Percent	District Name	City
1	17.4	Lexington Public Schools	Lexington
2	12.2	Grand Island Public Schools	Grand Island
3	11.8	Crete Public Schools	Crete
4	11.7	So Sioux City Community Schs	So Sioux City
5	11.5	Norfolk Public Schools	Norfolk
6	11.3	Columbus Public Schools	Columbus
7	11.0	Beatrice Public Schools	Beatrice
8	9.9	Hastings Public Schools	Hastings
9	9.8	Omaha Public Schools	Omaha
10	9.5	Fremont Public Schools	Fremont
11	9.2	Gering Public Schools	Gering
11	9.2	North Platte Public Schools	North Platte
13	9.1	Bellevue Public Schools	Bellevue
14	8.8	Ralston Public Schools	Ralston
15	8.3	Plattsmouth Community Schools	Plattsmouth
16	8.2	Kearney Public Schools	Kearney
17	7.5	Alliance Public Schools	Alliance
18	6.4	Scottsbluff Public Schools	Scottsbluff
19	5.8	Lincoln Public Schools	Lincoln
20	5.5	Waverly SD 145	Waverly
21	5.3	Westside Community Schools	Omaha
22	5.1	Papillion-La Vista Public Schools	Papillion
23	5.0	Blair Community Schools	Blair
24	3.6	Gretna Public Schools	Gretna
25	2.9	Elkhorn Public Schools	Elkhorn
26	2.5	Millard Public Schools	Omaha
26	2.5	Norris SD 160	Firth

Student/Teacher Ratio

Rank	Ratio	District Name	City
1	17.4	Norris SD 160	Firth
2	16.6	Blair Community Schools	Blair
2	16.6	Fremont Public Schools	Fremont
4	16.3	Lexington Public Schools	Lexington
5	15.9	Columbus Public Schools	Columbus
6	15.6	Gretna Public Schools	Gretna
6	15.6	Millard Public Schools	Omaha
6	15.6	Ralston Public Schools	Ralston
9	15.5	Elkhorn Public Schools	Elkhorn
10	15.2	Beatrice Public Schools	Beatrice
10	15.2	Grand Island Public Schools	Grand Island
10	15.2	Kearney Public Schools	Kearney
10	15.2	North Platte Public Schools	North Platte
10	15.2	Papillion-La Vista Public Schools	Papillion
15	15.1	Bellevue Public Schools	Bellevue
15	15.1	Scottsbluff Public Schools	Scottsbluff
17	14.9	Crete Public Schools	Crete
18	14.8	Gering Public Schools	Gering
18	14.8	Omaha Public Schools	Omaha
20	14.4	So Sioux City Community Schs	So Sioux City
21	14.3	Hastings Public Schools	Hastings
21	14.3	Norfolk Public Schools	Norfolk
23	14.0	Plattsmouth Community Schools	Plattsmouth
24	13.8	Westside Community Schools	Omaha
25	13.7	Lincoln Public Schools	Lincoln
25	13.7	Waverly SD 145	Waverly
27	13.6	Alliance Public Schools	Alliance

Student/Librarian Ratio

Rank	Ratio	District Name	City
1	936.3	Lexington Public Schools	Lexington
2	845.0	Norris SD 160	Firth
3	837.0	Norfolk Public Schools	Norfolk
4	813.8	Hastings Public Schools	Hastings
5	801.6	Crete Public Schools	Crete
6	782.8	Ralston Public Schools	Ralston
7	771.0	North Platte Public Schools	North Platte
8	755.8	Fremont Public Schools	Fremont
9	753.0	Beatrice Public Schools	Beatrice
10	699.2	So Sioux City Community Schs	So Sioux City
11	682.4	Plattsmouth Community Schools	Plattsmouth
12	673.6	Westside Community Schools	Omaha
13	669.8	Scottsbluff Public Schools	Scottsbluff
14	653.8	Gering Public Schools	Gering
15	632.3	Lincoln Public Schools	Lincoln
16	631.5	Columbus Public Schools	Columbus
17	619.7	Kearney Public Schools	Kearney
18	596.7	Bellevue Public Schools	Bellevue
19	590.6	Millard Public Schools	Omaha
20	580.3	Gretna Public Schools	Gretna
21	576.0	Alliance Public Schools	Alliance
22	568.0	Blair Community Schools	Blair
23	563.4	Papillion-La Vista Public Schools	Papillion
24	514.9	Omaha Public Schools	Omaha
25	474.3	Elkhorn Public Schools	Elkhorn
26	440.3	Grand Island Public Schools	Grand Island
27	415.3	Waverly SD 145	Waverly

Student/Counselor Ratio

Rank	Ratio	District Name	City
1	669.8	Scottsbluff Public Schools	Scottsbluff
2	580.3	Gretna Public Schools	Gretna
3	576.0	Alliance Public Schools	Alliance
4	568.7	Plattsmouth Community Schools	Plattsmouth
5	563.3	Norris SD 160	Firth
6	539.8	Ralston Public Schools	Ralston
7	507.7	Crete Public Schools	Crete
8	468.2	Lexington Public Schools	Lexington
9	459.5	Lincoln Public Schools	Lincoln
10	436.5	Millard Public Schools	Omaha
11	435.4	Grand Island Public Schools	Grand Island
12	434.1	Columbus Public Schools	Columbus
13	419.9	Fremont Public Schools	Fremont
14	415.0	Kearney Public Schools	Kearney
15	411.3	So Sioux City Community Schs	So Sioux City
16	406.9	Bellevue Public Schools	Bellevue
17	386.9	Gering Public Schools	Gering
18	376.5	Beatrice Public Schools	Beatrice
19	368.9	Elkhorn Public Schools	Elkhorn
20	357.9	Papillion-La Vista Public Schools	Papillion
21	357.7	Norfolk Public Schools	Norfolk
22	350.5	North Platte Public Schools	North Platte
23	332.2	Waverly SD 145	Waverly
24	324.6	Blair Community Schools	Blair
25	322.3	Hastings Public Schools	Hastings
26	319.7	Omaha Public Schools	Omaha
27	313.1	Westside Community Schools	Omaha

Current Spending per Student in FY2003

Rank	Dollars	District Name	City
1	8,289	Westside Community Schools	Omaha
2	7,805	Waverly SD 145	Waverly
3	7,715	Plattsmouth Community Schools	Plattsmouth
4	7,525	Lincoln Public Schools	Lincoln
5	7,373	Grand Island Public Schools	Grand Island
6	7,203	Alliance Public Schools	Alliance
7	7,187	Omaha Public Schools	Omaha
8	7,122	Bellevue Public Schools	Bellevue
9	7,012	Ralston Public Schools	Ralston
10	6,977	Gering Public Schools	Gering
11	6,957	Scottsbluff Public Schools	Scottsbluff
12	6,921	Norfolk Public Schools	Norfolk
13	6,880	Hastings Public Schools	Hastings
14	6,834	Millard Public Schools	Omaha
15	6,823	Lexington Public Schools	Lexington
16	6,767	Elkhorn Public Schools	Elkhorn
17	6,717	Gretna Public Schools	Gretna
18	6,706	Beatrice Public Schools	Beatrice
19	6,698	Columbus Public Schools	Columbus
20	6,648	North Platte Public Schools	North Platte
21	6,636	Fremont Public Schools	Fremont
22	6,634	Kearney Public Schools	Kearney
23	6,511	Blair Community Schools	Blair
24	6,500	So Sioux City Community Schs	So Sioux City
25	6,457	Papillion-La Vista Public Schools	Papillion
26	6,342	Norris SD 160	Firth
27	6,299	Crete Public Schools	Crete

Number of Diploma Recipients

Rank	Number	District Name	City
1	2,168	Omaha Public Schools	Omaha
2	1,896	Lincoln Public Schools	Lincoln
3	1,513	Millard Public Schools	Omaha
4	592	Bellevue Public Schools	Bellevue
5	534	Papillion-La Vista Public Schools	Papillion
6	359	Norfolk Public Schools	Norfolk
7	344	North Platte Public Schools	North Platte
8	340	Grand Island Public Schools	Grand Island
9	338	Westside Community Schools	Omaha
10	317	Kearney Public Schools	Kearney
11	287	Fremont Public Schools	Fremont
12	279	Columbus Public Schools	Columbus
13	224	Hastings Public Schools	Hastings
14	204	Ralston Public Schools	Ralston
15	200	Elkhorn Public Schools	Elkhorn
16	195	Scottsbluff Public Schools	Scottsbluff
17	191	So Sioux City Community Schs	So Sioux City
18	180	Beatrice Public Schools	Beatrice
19	169	Alliance Public Schools	Alliance
20	160	Blair Community Schools	Blair
21	142	Gering Public Schools	Gering
22	131	Waverly SD 145	Waverly
23	126	Lexington Public Schools	Lexington
24	120	Norris SD 160	Firth
25	119	Plattsmouth Community Schools	Plattsmouth
26	112	Crete Public Schools	Crete
27	99	Gretna Public Schools	Gretna

High School Drop-out Rate

Rank	Percent	District Name	City
1	10.9	Omaha Public Schools	Omaha
2	10.3	Scottsbluff Public Schools	Scottsbluff
3	6.2	Lincoln Public Schools	Lincoln
4	6.1	Hastings Public Schools	Hastings
5	5.9	Lexington Public Schools	Lexington
6	5.5	So Sioux City Community Schs	So Sioux City
7	5.1	Fremont Public Schools	Fremont
8	4.6	Plattsmouth Community Schools	Plattsmouth
9	4.5	Grand Island Public Schools	Grand Island
10	4.3	Columbus Public Schools	Columbus
11	3.4	North Platte Public Schools	North Platte
12	3.2	Papillion-La Vista Public Schools	Papillion
13	2.8	Bellevue Public Schools	Bellevue
14	2.5	Beatrice Public Schools	Beatrice
15	2.4	Norfolk Public Schools	Norfolk
16	2.3	Ralston Public Schools	Ralston
17	2.0	Elkhorn Public Schools	Elkhorn
17	2.0	Gering Public Schools	Gering
19	1.9	Crete Public Schools	Crete
20	1.6	Kearney Public Schools	Kearney
21	1.4	Alliance Public Schools	Alliance
21	1.4	Blair Community Schools	Blair
23	1.3	Millard Public Schools	Omaha
24	1.2	Norris SD 160	Firth
25	0.7	Westside Community Schools	Omaha
26	0.5	Waverly SD 145	Waverly
27	0.0	Gretna Public Schools	Gretna

Nevada

Nevada Public School Educational Profile

Category	Value	Category	Value
Schools *(2003-2004)*	558	**Diploma Recipients** *(2002-2003)*	16,122
Instructional Level		White, Non-Hispanic	10,778
Primary	337	Black, Non-Hispanic	1,276
Middle	88	Asian/Pacific Islander	1,117
High	105	American Indian/Alaskan Native	243
Other Level	28	Hispanic	2,708
Curriculum		**High School Drop-out Rate** *(%)* *(2001-2002)*	6.4
Regular	502	White, Non-Hispanic	5.0
Special Education	13	Black, Non-Hispanic	8.9
Vocational	3	Asian/Pacific Islander	5.2
Alternative	40	American Indian/Alaskan Native	5.6
Type		Hispanic	9.3
Magnet	9	**Staff** *(2003-2004)*	
Charter	15	Teachers	20,233.7
Title I Eligible	228	Average Salary ($)	43,211
School-wide Title I	96	Librarians/Media Specialists	323.7
Students *(2003-2004)*	385,414	Guidance Counselors	718.9
Gender (%)		**Ratios** *(2003-2004)*	
Male	51.4	Student/Teacher Ratio	19.0 to 1
Female	48.6	Student/Librarian Ratio	1,190.7 to 1
Race/Ethnicity (%)		Student/Counselor Ratio	536.1 to 1
White, Non-Hispanic	50.8	**College Entrance Exam Scores** *(2005)*	
Black, Non-Hispanic	10.7	Scholastic Aptitude Test (SAT)	
Asian/Pacific Islander	6.7	Participation Rate (%)	39
American Indian/Alaskan Native	1.7	Mean SAT Reasoning Test Verbal Score	508
Hispanic	30.1	Mean SAT Reasoning Test Math Score	513
Classification (%)		American College Testing Program (ACT)	
Individual Education Program (IEP)	11.7	Participation Rate (%)	28
Migrant *(2002-2003)*	0.1	Average Composite Score	21.5
English Language Learner (ELL)	18.1	Average English Score	20.8
Eligible for Free Lunch Program	27.2	Average Math Score	21.3
Eligible for Reduced-Price Lunch Program	6.4	Average Reading Score	22.0
Current Spending *($ per student in FY 2003)*	6,084	Average Science Score	21.3
Instruction	3,807		
Support Services	2,078		

Note: *For an explanation of data, please refer to the User's Guide in the front of the book*

Nevada NAEP 2005 Test Scores

Reading			Mathematics		
Grade/Category	Value	Rank	Grade/Category	Value	Rank
4th Grade			**4th Grade**		
Average Proficiency	207.2 (1.22)	46/51	Average Proficiency	229.9 (0.80)	46/51
Proficiency by Gender/Race/Ethnicity			Proficiency by Gender/Race/Ethnicity		
Male	202.6 (1.57)	49/51	Male	231.1 (1.01)	46/51
Female	211.7 (1.29)	44/51	Female	228.6 (0.93)	46/51
White, Non-Hispanic	218.6 (1.51)	50/51	White, Non-Hispanic	240.0 (0.86)	43/51
Black, Non-Hispanic	191.6 (2.63)	38/42	Black, Non-Hispanic	214.2 (2.02)	32/42
Asian, Non-Hispanic	212.2 (3.37)	25/27	Asian, Non-Hispanic	243.1 (1.94)	17/25
American Indian, Non-Hispanic	n/a	n/a	American Indian, Non-Hispanic	n/a	n/a
Hispanic	194.3 (1.70)	35/40	Hispanic	219.0 (1.18)	33/41
Proficiency by Class Size			Proficiency by Class Size		
Less than 16 Students	n/a	n/a	Less than 16 Students	n/a	n/a
16 to 18 Students	n/a	n/a	16 to 18 Students	n/a	n/a
19 to 20 Students	n/a	n/a	19 to 20 Students	n/a	n/a
21 to 25 Students	205.9 (2.80)	48/51	21 to 25 Students	229.1 (2.36)	46/51
Greater than 25 Students	208.3 (1.56)	33/36	Greater than 25 Students	230.9 (0.89)	28/33
Percent Attaining Achievement Levels			Percent Attaining Achievement Levels		
Below Basic	48.1 (1.46)	5/51	Below Basic	28.3 (1.04)	7/51
Basic or Above	51.9 (1.46)	47/51	Basic or Above	71.7 (1.04)	45/51
Proficient or Above	20.5 (1.26)	47/51	Proficient or Above	26.1 (1.21)	44/51
Advanced or Above	3.6 (0.63)	47/51	Advanced or Above	2.8 (0.43)	42/51
8th Grade			**8th Grade**		
Average Proficiency	252.9 (0.95)	44/51	Average Proficiency	269.9 (0.79)	43/51
Proficiency by Gender/Race/Ethnicity			Proficiency by Gender/Race/Ethnicity		
Male	247.3 (1.26)	44/51	Male	270.5 (0.87)	41/51
Female	258.4 (1.51)	46/51	Female	269.3 (1.16)	44/51
White, Non-Hispanic	260.6 (1.21)	50/51	White, Non-Hispanic	280.2 (0.94)	43/51
Black, Non-Hispanic	239.8 (3.58)	28/40	Black, Non-Hispanic	247.1 (2.50)	35/41
Asian, Non-Hispanic	262.7 (2.96)	19/24	Asian, Non-Hispanic	281.0 (3.13)	19/23
American Indian, Non-Hispanic	n/a	n/a	American Indian, Non-Hispanic	n/a	n/a
Hispanic	241.3 (1.14)	36/38	Hispanic	255.9 (1.32)	32/38
Proficiency by Parents Highest Level of Ed.			Proficiency by Parents Highest Level of Ed.		
Did Not Finish High School	238.2 (2.13)	43/49	Did Not Finish High School	257.2 (2.15)	33/50
Graduated High School	249.5 (1.59)	36/50	Graduated High School	260.8 (1.61)	43/50
Some Education After High School	262.4 (1.71)	38/50	Some Education After High School	277.5 (1.79)	35/50
Graduated College	261.7 (1.56)	44/50	Graduated College	280.7 (1.12)	41/50
Percent Attaining Achievement Levels			Percent Attaining Achievement Levels		
Below Basic	48.1 (1.46)	5/51	Below Basic	39.6 (1.14)	9/51
Basic or Above	51.9 (1.46)	47/51	Basic or Above	60.4 (1.14)	43/51
Proficient or Above	20.5 (1.26)	47/51	Proficient or Above	21.3 (0.93)	42/51
Advanced or Above	3.6 (0.63)	47/51	Advanced or Above	3.1 (0.48)	41/51

Note: *For an explanation of data, please refer to the User's Guide in the front of the book; n/a indicates data not available*

Carson City

Carson City SD
1402 W King • Carson City, NV 89701-4554
Mailing Address: 1402 W King St • Carson City, NV 89701-4554
(702) 885-6300 • http://www.carsoncityschools.com/index2.asp
Grade Span: PK-12; Agency Type: 1
Schools: 11
   7 Primary; 2 Middle; 2 High; 0 Other Level
   9 Regular; 1 Special Education; 0 Vocational; 1 Alternative
   0 Magnet; 0 Charter; 5 Title I Eligible; 3 School-wide Title I
Students: 8,798 (51.1% male; 48.8% female)
   Individual Education Program: 1,257 (14.3%);
   English Language Learner: 1,415 (16.1%); Migrant: 35 (0.4%)
   Eligible for Free Lunch Program: 2,350 (26.7%)
   Eligible for Reduced-Price Lunch Program: 585 (6.6%)
Teachers: 507.7 (17.3 to 1)
Librarians/Media Specialists: 9.0 (977.6 to 1)
Guidance Counselors: 17.0 (517.5 to 1)
Current Spending: ($ per student per year):
   Total: $6,758; Instruction: $4,379; Support Services: $2,164

Enrollment, Drop-out Rates and Diploma Recipients by Race/Ethnicity

Category	Total	White	Black	Asian	AIAN	Hisp.
Enrollment (%)	100.0	68.2	1.2	2.6	3.3	24.7
Drop-out Rate (%)	1.8	1.5	0.0	0.0	1.3	3.9
H.S. Diplomas (#)	543	441	8	13	13	68

Churchill County

Churchill County SD
545 E Richards • Fallon, NV 89406-3430
Mailing Address: 545 E Richards St • Fallon, NV 89406-3430
(702) 423-5184 • http://www.churchill.k12.nv.us/
Grade Span: PK-12; Agency Type: 1
Schools: 10
   6 Primary; 1 Middle; 3 High; 0 Other Level
   8 Regular; 1 Special Education; 0 Vocational; 1 Alternative
   0 Magnet; 1 Charter; 4 Title I Eligible; 0 School-wide Title I
Students: 4,553 (51.3% male; 48.6% female)
   Individual Education Program: 736 (16.2%);
   English Language Learner: 122 (2.7%); Migrant: 86 (1.9%)
   Eligible for Free Lunch Program: 1,124 (24.7%)
   Eligible for Reduced-Price Lunch Program: 412 (9.0%)
Teachers: 264.4 (17.2 to 1)
Librarians/Media Specialists: 4.0 (1,138.3 to 1)
Guidance Counselors: 9.0 (505.9 to 1)
Current Spending: ($ per student per year):
   Total: $7,426; Instruction: $4,552; Support Services: $2,641

Enrollment, Drop-out Rates and Diploma Recipients by Race/Ethnicity

Category	Total	White	Black	Asian	AIAN	Hisp.
Enrollment (%)	100.0	75.3	2.0	4.4	7.0	11.2
Drop-out Rate (%)	1.8	1.6	3.6	0.0	2.1	3.5
H.S. Diplomas (#)	240	195	4	14	9	18

Clark County

Clark County SD
2832 E Flamingo • Las Vegas, NV 89121-5205
Mailing Address: 2832 E Flamingo Rd • Las Vegas, NV 89121-5205
(702) 799-5310 • http://www.ccsd.net/
Grade Span: PK-12; Agency Type: 1
Schools: 298
   183 Primary; 51 Middle; 44 High; 20 Other Level
   267 Regular; 9 Special Education; 2 Vocational; 20 Alternative
   7 Magnet; 5 Charter; 118 Title I Eligible; 43 School-wide Title I
Students: 270,529 (51.3% male; 48.6% female)
   Individual Education Program: 29,617 (10.9%);
   English Language Learner: 57,337 (21.2%); Migrant: 80 (<0.1%)
   Eligible for Free Lunch Program: 77,400 (28.6%)
   Eligible for Reduced-Price Lunch Program: 15,610 (5.8%)
Teachers: 13,483.1 (20.1 to 1)
Librarians/Media Specialists: 244.0 (1,109.0 to 1)
Guidance Counselors: 451.6 (599.2 to 1)
Current Spending: ($ per student per year):
   Total: $5,774; Instruction: $3,583; Support Services: $2,005

Enrollment, Drop-out Rates and Diploma Recipients by Race/Ethnicity

Category	Total	White	Black	Asian	AIAN	Hisp.
Enrollment (%)	100.0	44.0	14.1	7.8	0.9	33.2
Drop-out Rate (%)	8.1	6.9	9.3	6.2	10.4	10.5
H.S. Diplomas (#)	10,215	6,079	1,178	871	82	2,005

Douglas County

Douglas County SD
751 Mono Ave • Minden, NV 89423
(702) 782-5134 • http://dcsd.k12.nv.us/
Grade Span: PK-12; Agency Type: 1
Schools: 15
   7 Primary; 3 Middle; 4 High; 1 Other Level
   12 Regular; 0 Special Education; 0 Vocational; 3 Alternative
   0 Magnet; 0 Charter; 5 Title I Eligible; 4 School-wide Title I
Students: 7,190 (51.7% male; 48.2% female)
   Individual Education Program: 955 (13.3%);
   English Language Learner: 420 (5.8%); Migrant: 0 (0.0%)
   Eligible for Free Lunch Program: 1,029 (14.3%)
   Eligible for Reduced-Price Lunch Program: 530 (7.4%)
Teachers: 388.5 (18.5 to 1)
Librarians/Media Specialists: 4.0 (1,797.5 to 1)
Guidance Counselors: 19.0 (378.4 to 1)
Current Spending: ($ per student per year):
   Total: $7,334; Instruction: $4,480; Support Services: $2,650

Enrollment, Drop-out Rates and Diploma Recipients by Race/Ethnicity

Category	Total	White	Black	Asian	AIAN	Hisp.
Enrollment (%)	100.0	82.6	1.0	2.3	2.9	11.1
Drop-out Rate (%)	0.5	0.4	0.0	0.0	0.0	2.1
H.S. Diplomas (#)	426	394	2	5	4	21

Elko County

Elko County SD
1092 Burns Rd • Elko, NV 89801-3437
(702) 738-5196 • http://www.elko.k12.nv.us/
Grade Span: PK-12; Agency Type: 1
Schools: 25
   16 Primary; 2 Middle; 7 High; 0 Other Level
   25 Regular; 0 Special Education; 0 Vocational; 0 Alternative
   0 Magnet; 0 Charter; 15 Title I Eligible; 6 School-wide Title I
Students: 9,582 (51.7% male; 48.2% female)
   Individual Education Program: 1,144 (11.9%);
   English Language Learner: 755 (7.9%); Migrant: 0 (0.0%)
   Eligible for Free Lunch Program: 2,049 (21.4%)
   Eligible for Reduced-Price Lunch Program: 770 (8.0%)
Teachers: 599.0 (16.0 to 1)
Librarians/Media Specialists: 16.0 (598.9 to 1)
Guidance Counselors: 21.0 (456.3 to 1)
Current Spending: ($ per student per year):
   Total: $7,311; Instruction: $4,814; Support Services: $2,279

Enrollment, Drop-out Rates and Diploma Recipients by Race/Ethnicity

Category	Total	White	Black	Asian	AIAN	Hisp.
Enrollment (%)	100.0	67.1	0.6	1.0	7.1	24.2
Drop-out Rate (%)	3.1	2.9	0.0	2.9	3.4	4.0
H.S. Diplomas (#)	564	424	2	10	28	100

Humboldt County

Humboldt County SD
E 4th And Reinhart • Winnemucca, NV 89445
Mailing Address: E 4th And Reinhart Streets • Winnemucca, NV 89445
(702) 623-8100 • http://www.humboldt.k12.nv.us/
Grade Span: PK-12; Agency Type: 1
Schools: 16
   10 Primary; 3 Middle; 3 High; 0 Other Level
   14 Regular; 1 Special Education; 0 Vocational; 1 Alternative
   0 Magnet; 0 Charter; 6 Title I Eligible; 1 School-wide Title I
Students: 3,523 (51.9% male; 48.0% female)
   Individual Education Program: 487 (13.8%);
   English Language Learner: 349 (9.9%); Migrant: 52 (1.5%)
   Eligible for Free Lunch Program: 782 (22.2%)
   Eligible for Reduced-Price Lunch Program: 278 (7.9%)
Teachers: 211.0 (16.7 to 1)
Librarians/Media Specialists: 1.0 (3,523.0 to 1)
Guidance Counselors: 10.0 (352.3 to 1)
Current Spending: ($ per student per year):
   Total: $7,318; Instruction: $4,813; Support Services: $2,285

Enrollment, Drop-out Rates and Diploma Recipients by Race/Ethnicity

Category	Total	White	Black	Asian	AIAN	Hisp.
Enrollment (%)	100.0	68.1	0.4	0.8	4.8	25.9
Drop-out Rate (%)	5.1	4.4	0.0	0.0	14.6	5.6
H.S. Diplomas (#)	225	182	0	2	4	37

Lyon County

Lyon County SD
25 E Goldfield • Yerington, NV 89447-2315
Mailing Address: 25 E Goldfield Ave • Yerington, NV 89447-2315
(702) 463-2205 • http://www.lyon.k12.nv.us/
Grade Span: PK-12; **Agency Type:** 1
Schools: 17
   7 Primary; 4 Middle; 6 High; 0 Other Level
   16 Regular; 0 Special Education; 0 Vocational; 1 Alternative
   0 Magnet; 0 Charter; 6 Title I Eligible; 4 School-wide Title I
Students: 7,678   (51.9% male; 48.0% female)
   Individual Education Program: 1,167 (15.2%);
   English Language Learner: 307 (4.0%); Migrant: 41 (0.5%)
   Eligible for Free Lunch Program: 2,067 (26.9%)
   Eligible for Reduced-Price Lunch Program: 802 (10.4%)
Teachers: 441.0 (17.4 to 1)
Librarians/Media Specialists: 12.0 (639.8 to 1)
Guidance Counselors: 16.0 (479.9 to 1)
Current Spending: ($ per student per year):
   Total: $7,021; Instruction: $4,101; Support Services: $2,671
Enrollment, Drop-out Rates and Diploma Recipients by Race/Ethnicity

Category	Total	White	Black	Asian	AIAN	Hisp.
Enrollment (%)	100.0	77.5	1.0	1.2	5.2	15.2
Drop-out Rate (%)	1.6	1.4	0.0	0.0	1.5	3.5
H.S. Diplomas (#)	355	293	0	5	18	39

Nye County

Nye County SD
Military Circle • Ton0pah, NV 89049
(702) 482-6258 •
http://www.ezsdk.com/applications/website/outsideView.php?outVOU=52
7&pg=
Grade Span: PK-12; **Agency Type:** 1
Schools: 19
   11 Primary; 2 Middle; 5 High; 1 Other Level
   17 Regular; 0 Special Education; 0 Vocational; 2 Alternative
   0 Magnet; 0 Charter; 7 Title I Eligible; 7 School-wide Title I
Students: 5,471   (51.3% male; 48.6% female)
   Individual Education Program: 1,056 (19.3%);
   English Language Learner: 256 (4.7%); Migrant: 53 (1.0%)
   Eligible for Free Lunch Program: 1,856 (33.9%)
   Eligible for Reduced-Price Lunch Program: 588 (10.7%)
Teachers: 312.0 (17.5 to 1)
Librarians/Media Specialists: 2.0 (2,735.5 to 1)
Guidance Counselors: 13.0 (420.8 to 1)
Current Spending: ($ per student per year):
   Total: $7,810; Instruction: $4,662; Support Services: $2,851
Enrollment, Drop-out Rates and Diploma Recipients by Race/Ethnicity

Category	Total	White	Black	Asian	AIAN	Hisp.
Enrollment (%)	100.0	77.7	2.5	1.9	2.6	15.4
Drop-out Rate (%)	3.6	3.1	2.8	0.0	4.5	7.7
H.S. Diplomas (#)	293	245	4	9	5	30

Washoe County

Washoe County SD
425 E Ninth • Reno, NV 89520-2800
Mailing Address: 425 E Ninth St • Reno, NV 89520-2800
(702) 348-0200 • http://www.washoe.k12.nv.us/
Grade Span: PK-12; **Agency Type:** 1
Schools: 102
   68 Primary; 12 Middle; 16 High; 6 Other Level
   94 Regular; 1 Special Education; 1 Vocational; 6 Alternative
   2 Magnet; 9 Charter; 42 Title I Eligible; 21 School-wide Title I
Students: 62,103   (51.5% male; 48.4% female)
   Individual Education Program: 7,806 (12.6%);
   English Language Learner: 8,779 (14.1%); Migrant: 171 (0.3%)
   Eligible for Free Lunch Program: 14,962 (24.1%)
   Eligible for Reduced-Price Lunch Program: 4,714 (7.6%)
Teachers: 3,614.1 (17.2 to 1)
Librarians/Media Specialists: 25.5 (2,435.4 to 1)
Guidance Counselors: 147.6 (420.8 to 1)
Current Spending: ($ per student per year):
   Total: $6,120; Instruction: $3,973; Support Services: $1,928
Enrollment, Drop-out Rates and Diploma Recipients by Race/Ethnicity

Category	Total	White	Black	Asian	AIAN	Hisp.
Enrollment (%)	100.0	60.6	3.6	6.0	2.8	27.1
Drop-out Rate (%)	3.4	2.6	4.2	2.1	3.4	6.5
H.S. Diplomas (#)	2,851	2,191	73	183	56	348

Number of Schools

Rank	Number	District Name	City
1	298	Clark County SD	Las Vegas
2	102	Washoe County SD	Reno
3	25	Elko County SD	Elko
4	19	Nye County SD	Ton0pah
5	17	Lyon County SD	Yerington
6	16	Humboldt County SD	Winnemucca
7	15	Douglas County SD	Minden
8	11	Carson City SD	Carson City
9	10	Churchill County SD	Fallon

Number of Teachers

Rank	Number	District Name	City
1	13,483	Clark County SD	Las Vegas
2	3,614	Washoe County SD	Reno
3	599	Elko County SD	Elko
4	507	Carson City SD	Carson City
5	441	Lyon County SD	Yerington
6	388	Douglas County SD	Minden
7	312	Nye County SD	Ton0pah
8	264	Churchill County SD	Fallon
9	211	Humboldt County SD	Winnemucca

Number of Students

Rank	Number	District Name	City
1	270,529	Clark County SD	Las Vegas
2	62,103	Washoe County SD	Reno
3	9,582	Elko County SD	Elko
4	8,798	Carson City SD	Carson City
5	7,678	Lyon County SD	Yerington
6	7,190	Douglas County SD	Minden
7	5,471	Nye County SD	Ton0pah
8	4,553	Churchill County SD	Fallon
9	3,523	Humboldt County SD	Winnemucca

Male Students

Rank	Percent	District Name	City
1	51.9	Lyon County SD	Yerington
2	51.9	Humboldt County SD	Winnemucca
3	51.7	Douglas County SD	Minden
4	51.7	Elko County SD	Elko
5	51.5	Washoe County SD	Reno
6	51.3	Nye County SD	Ton0pah
7	51.3	Churchill County SD	Fallon
8	51.3	Clark County SD	Las Vegas
9	51.1	Carson City SD	Carson City

Female Students

Rank	Percent	District Name	City
1	48.8	Carson City SD	Carson City
2	48.6	Clark County SD	Las Vegas
3	48.6	Churchill County SD	Fallon
4	48.6	Nye County SD	Ton0pah
5	48.4	Washoe County SD	Reno
6	48.2	Elko County SD	Elko
7	48.2	Douglas County SD	Minden
8	48.0	Humboldt County SD	Winnemucca
9	48.0	Lyon County SD	Yerington

Individual Education Program Students

Rank	Percent	District Name	City
1	19.3	Nye County SD	Ton0pah
2	16.2	Churchill County SD	Fallon
3	15.2	Lyon County SD	Yerington
4	14.3	Carson City SD	Carson City
5	13.8	Humboldt County SD	Winnemucca
6	13.3	Douglas County SD	Minden
7	12.6	Washoe County SD	Reno
8	11.9	Elko County SD	Elko
9	10.9	Clark County SD	Las Vegas

English Language Learner Students

Rank	Percent	District Name	City
1	21.2	Clark County SD	Las Vegas
2	16.1	Carson City SD	Carson City
3	14.1	Washoe County SD	Reno
4	9.9	Humboldt County SD	Winnemucca
5	7.9	Elko County SD	Elko
6	5.8	Douglas County SD	Minden
7	4.7	Nye County SD	Ton0pah
8	4.0	Lyon County SD	Yerington
9	2.7	Churchill County SD	Fallon

Migrant Students

Rank	Percent	District Name	City
1	1.9	Churchill County SD	Fallon
2	1.5	Humboldt County SD	Winnemucca
3	1.0	Nye County SD	Ton0pah
4	0.5	Lyon County SD	Yerington
5	0.4	Carson City SD	Carson City
6	0.3	Washoe County SD	Reno
7	0.0	Clark County SD	Las Vegas
8	0.0	Douglas County SD	Minden
8	0.0	Elko County SD	Elko

Students Eligible for Free Lunch

Rank	Percent	District Name	City
1	33.9	Nye County SD	Ton0pah
2	28.6	Clark County SD	Las Vegas
3	26.9	Lyon County SD	Yerington
4	26.7	Carson City SD	Carson City
5	24.7	Churchill County SD	Fallon
6	24.1	Washoe County SD	Reno
7	22.2	Humboldt County SD	Winnemucca
8	21.4	Elko County SD	Elko
9	14.3	Douglas County SD	Minden

Students Eligible for Reduced-Price Lunch

Rank	Percent	District Name	City
1	10.7	Nye County SD	Ton0pah
2	10.4	Lyon County SD	Yerington
3	9.0	Churchill County SD	Fallon
4	8.0	Elko County SD	Elko
5	7.9	Humboldt County SD	Winnemucca
6	7.6	Washoe County SD	Reno
7	7.4	Douglas County SD	Minden
8	6.6	Carson City SD	Carson City
9	5.8	Clark County SD	Las Vegas

Student/Teacher Ratio

Rank	Ratio	District Name	City
1	20.1	Clark County SD	Las Vegas
2	18.5	Douglas County SD	Minden
3	17.5	Nye County SD	Ton0pah
4	17.4	Lyon County SD	Yerington
5	17.3	Carson City SD	Carson City
6	17.2	Churchill County SD	Fallon
6	17.2	Washoe County SD	Reno
8	16.7	Humboldt County SD	Winnemucca
9	16.0	Elko County SD	Elko

Student/Librarian Ratio

Rank	Ratio	District Name	City
1	3,523.0	Humboldt County SD	Winnemucca
2	2,735.5	Nye County SD	Ton0pah
3	2,435.4	Washoe County SD	Reno
4	1,797.5	Douglas County SD	Minden
5	1,138.3	Churchill County SD	Fallon
6	1,109.0	Clark County SD	Las Vegas
7	977.6	Carson City SD	Carson City
8	639.8	Lyon County SD	Yerington
9	598.9	Elko County SD	Elko

Student/Counselor Ratio

Rank	Ratio	District Name	City
1	599.2	Clark County SD	Las Vegas
2	517.5	Carson City SD	Carson City
3	505.9	Churchill County SD	Fallon
4	479.9	Lyon County SD	Yerington
5	456.3	Elko County SD	Elko
6	420.8	Nye County SD	Ton0pah
6	420.8	Washoe County SD	Reno
8	378.4	Douglas County SD	Minden
9	352.3	Humboldt County SD	Winnemucca

Current Spending per Student in FY2003

Rank	Dollars	District Name	City
1	7,810	Nye County SD	Ton0pah
2	7,426	Churchill County SD	Fallon
3	7,334	Douglas County SD	Minden
4	7,318	Humboldt County SD	Winnemucca
5	7,311	Elko County SD	Elko
6	7,021	Lyon County SD	Yerington
7	6,758	Carson City SD	Carson City
8	6,120	Washoe County SD	Reno
9	5,774	Clark County SD	Las Vegas

Number of Diploma Recipients

Rank	Number	District Name	City
1	10,215	Clark County SD	Las Vegas
2	2,851	Washoe County SD	Reno
3	564	Elko County SD	Elko
4	543	Carson City SD	Carson City
5	426	Douglas County SD	Minden
6	355	Lyon County SD	Yerington
7	293	Nye County SD	Ton0pah
8	240	Churchill County SD	Fallon
9	225	Humboldt County SD	Winnemucca

High School Drop-out Rate

Rank	Percent	District Name	City
1	8.1	Clark County SD	Las Vegas
2	5.1	Humboldt County SD	Winnemucca
3	3.6	Nye County SD	Ton0pah
4	3.4	Washoe County SD	Reno
5	3.1	Elko County SD	Elko
6	1.8	Carson City SD	Carson City
6	1.8	Churchill County SD	Fallon
8	1.6	Lyon County SD	Yerington
9	0.5	Douglas County SD	Minden

New Hampshire

New Hampshire Public School Educational Profile

Category	Value	Category	Value
Schools *(2003-2004)*	474	**Diploma Recipients** *(2002-2003)*	12,452
Instructional Level		White, Non-Hispanic	n/a
Primary	298	Black, Non-Hispanic	n/a
Middle	96	Asian/Pacific Islander	n/a
High	78	American Indian/Alaskan Native	n/a
Other Level	1	Hispanic	n/a
Curriculum		**High School Drop-out Rate** (%) *(2001-2002)*	4.0
Regular	473	White, Non-Hispanic	3.9
Special Education	0	Black, Non-Hispanic	6.5
Vocational	0	Asian/Pacific Islander	3.2
Alternative	0	American Indian/Alaskan Native	7.5
Type		Hispanic	7.8
Magnet	0	**Staff** *(2003-2004)*	
Charter	0	Teachers	15,110.9
Title I Eligible	248	Average Salary ($)	42,689
School-wide Title I	27	Librarians/Media Specialists	295.9
Students *(2003-2004)*	207,417	Guidance Counselors	771.6
Gender (%)		**Ratios** *(2003-2004)*	
Male	51.5	Student/Teacher Ratio	13.7 to 1
Female	48.5	Student/Librarian Ratio	701.0 to 1
Race/Ethnicity (%)		Student/Counselor Ratio	268.8 to 1
White, Non-Hispanic	94.2	**College Entrance Exam Scores** *(2005)*	
Black, Non-Hispanic	1.4	Scholastic Aptitude Test (SAT)	
Asian/Pacific Islander	1.7	Participation Rate (%)	81
American Indian/Alaskan Native	0.3	Mean SAT Reasoning Test Verbal Score	525
Hispanic	2.4	Mean SAT Reasoning Test Math Score	525
Classification (%)		American College Testing Program (ACT)	
Individual Education Program (IEP)	14.2	Participation Rate (%)	10
Migrant *(2002-2003)*	0.1	Average Composite Score	22.3
English Language Learner (ELL)	1.3	Average English Score	21.9
Eligible for Free Lunch Program	11.3	Average Math Score	22.1
Eligible for Reduced-Price Lunch Program	5.0	Average Reading Score	23.0
Current Spending *($ per student in FY 2003)*	8,557	Average Science Score	21.8
Instruction	5,494		
Support Services	2,794		

Note: *For an explanation of data, please refer to the User's Guide in the front of the book*

New Hampshire NAEP 2005 Test Scores

Reading			Mathematics		
Grade/Category	Value	Rank	Grade/Category	Value	Rank
4th Grade			**4th Grade**		
Average Proficiency	227.4 (0.92)	2/51	Average Proficiency	245.6 (0.85)	4/51
Proficiency by Gender/Race/Ethnicity			Proficiency by Gender/Race/Ethnicity		
Male	224.3 (1.05)	2/51	Male	247.3 (1.05)	2/51
Female	230.9 (1.23)	2/51	Female	243.9 (1.00)	4/51
White, Non-Hispanic	227.7 (0.93)	17/51	White, Non-Hispanic	246.1 (0.79)	20/51
Black, Non-Hispanic	n/a	n/a	Black, Non-Hispanic	n/a	n/a
Asian, Non-Hispanic	n/a	n/a	Asian, Non-Hispanic	n/a	n/a
American Indian, Non-Hispanic	n/a	n/a	American Indian, Non-Hispanic	n/a	n/a
Hispanic	n/a	n/a	Hispanic	225.8 (4.50)	19/41
Proficiency by Class Size			Proficiency by Class Size		
Less than 16 Students	225.2 (3.44)	1/34	Less than 16 Students	245.3 (2.35)	1/35
16 to 18 Students	226.7 (2.01)	2/33	16 to 18 Students	244.4 (1.86)	3/31
19 to 20 Students	227.9 (2.04)	3/38	19 to 20 Students	247.9 (1.59)	3/38
21 to 25 Students	228.7 (1.41)	3/51	21 to 25 Students	245.5 (1.57)	6/51
Greater than 25 Students	n/a	n/a	Greater than 25 Students	n/a	n/a
Percent Attaining Achievement Levels			Percent Attaining Achievement Levels		
Below Basic	25.6 (1.10)	50/51	Below Basic	10.9 (0.91)	50/51
Basic or Above	74.4 (1.10)	2/51	Basic or Above	89.1 (0.91)	2/51
Proficient or Above	38.6 (1.37)	2/51	Proficient or Above	46.9 (1.46)	3/51
Advanced or Above	9.0 (0.78)	6/51	Advanced or Above	6.2 (0.62)	9/51
8th Grade			**8th Grade**		
Average Proficiency	269.7 (1.18)	4/51	Average Proficiency	285.3 (0.81)	7/51
Proficiency by Gender/Race/Ethnicity			Proficiency by Gender/Race/Ethnicity		
Male	264.3 (1.32)	5/51	Male	286.0 (1.10)	6/51
Female	275.3 (1.54)	4/51	Female	284.5 (1.15)	8/51
White, Non-Hispanic	270.2 (1.23)	22/51	White, Non-Hispanic	285.9 (0.86)	31/51
Black, Non-Hispanic	n/a	n/a	Black, Non-Hispanic	n/a	n/a
Asian, Non-Hispanic	n/a	n/a	Asian, Non-Hispanic	n/a	n/a
American Indian, Non-Hispanic	n/a	n/a	American Indian, Non-Hispanic	n/a	n/a
Hispanic	n/a	n/a	Hispanic	n/a	n/a
Proficiency by Parents Highest Level of Ed.			Proficiency by Parents Highest Level of Ed.		
Did Not Finish High School	257.4 (4.51)	2/49	Did Not Finish High School	268.8 (2.75)	4/50
Graduated High School	260.3 (1.90)	7/50	Graduated High School	274.7 (1.42)	6/50
Some Education After High School	268.0 (1.64)	21/50	Some Education After High School	283.0 (1.95)	21/50
Graduated College	277.4 (1.43)	4/50	Graduated College	293.7 (1.01)	11/50
Percent Attaining Achievement Levels			Percent Attaining Achievement Levels		
Below Basic	25.6 (1.10)	50/51	Below Basic	22.7 (0.94)	45/51
Basic or Above	74.4 (1.10)	2/51	Basic or Above	77.3 (0.94)	7/51
Proficient or Above	38.6 (1.37)	2/51	Proficient or Above	34.6 (1.62)	10/51
Advanced or Above	9.0 (0.78)	6/51	Advanced or Above	6.5 (0.71)	14/51

Note: *For an explanation of data, please refer to the User's Guide in the front of the book; n/a indicates data not available*

Belknap County

Laconia SD
PO Box 309 • Laconia, NH 03247-0309
(603) 524-5710 • http://www.laconia.k12.nh.us/
Grade Span: PK-12; **Agency Type:** 2
Schools: 5
   3 Primary; 1 Middle; 1 High; 0 Other Level
   5 Regular; 0 Special Education; 0 Vocational; 0 Alternative
   0 Magnet; 0 Charter; 3 Title I Eligible; 0 School-wide Title I
Students: 2,476 (52.3% male; 47.6% female)
   Individual Education Program: 415 (16.8%);
   English Language Learner: 72 (2.9%); Migrant: 0 (0.0%)
   Eligible for Free Lunch Program: 551 (22.3%)
   Eligible for Reduced-Price Lunch Program: 225 (9.1%)
Teachers: 203.3 (12.2 to 1)
Librarians/Media Specialists: 5.0 (495.2 to 1)
Guidance Counselors: 15.0 (165.1 to 1)
Current Spending: ($ per student per year):
   Total: $8,577; Instruction: $5,796; Support Services: $2,422
Enrollment, Drop-out Rates and Diploma Recipients by Race/Ethnicity

Category	Total	White	Black	Asian	AIAN	Hisp.
Enrollment (%)	100.0	94.6	1.6	2.1	0.3	1.4
Drop-out Rate (%)	3.6	3.5	10.0	9.1	0.0	0.0
H.S. Diplomas (#)	154	n/a	n/a	n/a	n/a	n/a

Shaker Regional SD
58 School St • Belmont, NH 03220-4511
(603) 267-9233
Grade Span: PK-12; **Agency Type:** 2
Schools: 4
   2 Primary; 1 Middle; 1 High; 0 Other Level
   4 Regular; 0 Special Education; 0 Vocational; 0 Alternative
   0 Magnet; 0 Charter; 2 Title I Eligible; 0 School-wide Title I
Students: 1,535 (52.8% male; 47.1% female)
   Individual Education Program: 189 (12.3%);
   English Language Learner: 2 (0.1%); Migrant: 0 (0.0%)
   Eligible for Free Lunch Program: 203 (13.2%)
   Eligible for Reduced-Price Lunch Program: 97 (6.3%)
Teachers: 105.1 (14.6 to 1)
Librarians/Media Specialists: 3.0 (511.7 to 1)
Guidance Counselors: 5.4 (284.3 to 1)
Current Spending: ($ per student per year):
   Total: $8,318; Instruction: $5,184; Support Services: $2,801
Enrollment, Drop-out Rates and Diploma Recipients by Race/Ethnicity

Category	Total	White	Black	Asian	AIAN	Hisp.
Enrollment (%)	100.0	98.6	0.1	0.8	0.1	0.3
Drop-out Rate (%)	3.6	3.7	n/a	0.0	n/a	n/a
H.S. Diplomas (#)	72	n/a	n/a	n/a	n/a	n/a

Winnisquam Regional SD
433 W Main St • Tilton, NH 03276-4021
(603) 286-4416 • http://www.winnisquam.k12.nh.us/
Grade Span: PK-12; **Agency Type:** 2
Schools: 5
   3 Primary; 1 Middle; 1 High; 0 Other Level
   5 Regular; 0 Special Education; 0 Vocational; 0 Alternative
   0 Magnet; 0 Charter; 3 Title I Eligible; 0 School-wide Title I
Students: 1,786 (51.1% male; 48.8% female)
   Individual Education Program: 279 (15.6%);
   English Language Learner: 2 (0.1%); Migrant: 0 (0.0%)
   Eligible for Free Lunch Program: 280 (15.7%)
   Eligible for Reduced-Price Lunch Program: 118 (6.6%)
Teachers: 136.4 (13.1 to 1)
Librarians/Media Specialists: 2.0 (893.0 to 1)
Guidance Counselors: 7.3 (244.7 to 1)
Current Spending: ($ per student per year):
   Total: $8,168; Instruction: $4,705; Support Services: $3,200
Enrollment, Drop-out Rates and Diploma Recipients by Race/Ethnicity

Category	Total	White	Black	Asian	AIAN	Hisp.
Enrollment (%)	100.0	97.5	0.7	0.8	0.1	0.8
Drop-out Rate (%)	5.3	5.4	0.0	0.0	0.0	0.0
H.S. Diplomas (#)	99	n/a	n/a	n/a	n/a	n/a

Carroll County

Conway SD
19 Pine St • North Conway, NH 03860-5556
(603) 356-5534 • http://www.kennett.k12.nh.us/
Grade Span: KG-12; **Agency Type:** 2
Schools: 5
   3 Primary; 1 Middle; 1 High; 0 Other Level
   5 Regular; 0 Special Education; 0 Vocational; 0 Alternative
   0 Magnet; 0 Charter; 3 Title I Eligible; 1 School-wide Title I
Students: 2,168 (51.9% male; 48.0% female)

   Individual Education Program: 298 (13.7%);
   English Language Learner: 7 (0.3%); Migrant: 0 (0.0%)
   Eligible for Free Lunch Program: 358 (16.5%)
   Eligible for Reduced-Price Lunch Program: 133 (6.1%)
Teachers: 169.3 (12.8 to 1)
Librarians/Media Specialists: 1.9 (1,141.1 to 1)
Guidance Counselors: 8.0 (271.0 to 1)
Current Spending: ($ per student per year):
   Total: $9,276; Instruction: $5,900; Support Services: $3,056
Enrollment, Drop-out Rates and Diploma Recipients by Race/Ethnicity

Category	Total	White	Black	Asian	AIAN	Hisp.
Enrollment (%)	100.0	97.7	0.6	1.2	0.2	0.3
Drop-out Rate (%)	5.9	5.6	33.3	0.0	50.0	33.3
H.S. Diplomas (#)	175	n/a	n/a	n/a	n/a	n/a

Governor Wentworth Reg SD
140 Pine Hill Rd • Wolfeboro, NH 03894
Mailing Address: PO Box 190 • Wolfeboro Falls, NH 03896-0190
(603) 569-1658
Grade Span: PK-12; **Agency Type:** 2
Schools: 8
   5 Primary; 2 Middle; 1 High; 0 Other Level
   8 Regular; 0 Special Education; 0 Vocational; 0 Alternative
   0 Magnet; 0 Charter; 4 Title I Eligible; 1 School-wide Title I
Students: 2,904 (51.0% male; 48.9% female)
   Individual Education Program: 371 (12.8%);
   English Language Learner: 7 (0.2%); Migrant: 0 (0.0%)
   Eligible for Free Lunch Program: 419 (14.4%)
   Eligible for Reduced-Price Lunch Program: 293 (10.1%)
Teachers: 203.5 (14.3 to 1)
Librarians/Media Specialists: 4.3 (675.3 to 1)
Guidance Counselors: 9.6 (302.5 to 1)
Current Spending: ($ per student per year):
   Total: $9,108; Instruction: $6,133; Support Services: $2,666
Enrollment, Drop-out Rates and Diploma Recipients by Race/Ethnicity

Category	Total	White	Black	Asian	AIAN	Hisp.
Enrollment (%)	100.0	98.5	0.6	0.6	0.0	0.2
Drop-out Rate (%)	3.1	3.0	0.0	0.0	n/a	n/a
H.S. Diplomas (#)	218	n/a	n/a	n/a	n/a	n/a

Cheshire County

Jaffrey-Rindge Coop SD
10 Main St • Jaffrey, NH 03452-6142
(603) 532-8100 • http://www.sau47.k12.nh.us/
Grade Span: PK-12; **Agency Type:** 2
Schools: 4
   2 Primary; 1 Middle; 1 High; 0 Other Level
   4 Regular; 0 Special Education; 0 Vocational; 0 Alternative
   0 Magnet; 0 Charter; 3 Title I Eligible; 0 School-wide Title I
Students: 1,658 (52.4% male; 47.5% female)
   Individual Education Program: 286 (17.2%);
   English Language Learner: 0 (0.0%); Migrant: 0 (0.0%)
   Eligible for Free Lunch Program: 158 (9.5%)
   Eligible for Reduced-Price Lunch Program: 113 (6.8%)
Teachers: 134.6 (12.3 to 1)
Librarians/Media Specialists: 4.0 (414.5 to 1)
Guidance Counselors: 5.8 (285.9 to 1)
Current Spending: ($ per student per year):
   Total: $9,073; Instruction: $5,765; Support Services: $2,994
Enrollment, Drop-out Rates and Diploma Recipients by Race/Ethnicity

Category	Total	White	Black	Asian	AIAN	Hisp.
Enrollment (%)	100.0	95.3	1.1	1.6	0.7	1.2
Drop-out Rate (%)	1.4	1.4	0.0	0.0	0.0	0.0
H.S. Diplomas (#)	121	n/a	n/a	n/a	n/a	n/a

Keene SD
34 W St • Keene, NH 03431-3392
(603) 357-9002 • http://www.keene.k12.nh.us/
Grade Span: PK-12; **Agency Type:** 2
Schools: 7
   5 Primary; 1 Middle; 1 High; 0 Other Level
   7 Regular; 0 Special Education; 0 Vocational; 0 Alternative
   0 Magnet; 0 Charter; 5 Title I Eligible; 0 School-wide Title I
Students: 3,880 (51.4% male; 48.5% female)
   Individual Education Program: 705 (18.2%);
   English Language Learner: 20 (0.5%); Migrant: 0 (0.0%)
   Eligible for Free Lunch Program: 456 (11.8%)
   Eligible for Reduced-Price Lunch Program: 249 (6.4%)
Teachers: 305.3 (12.7 to 1)
Librarians/Media Specialists: 5.8 (669.0 to 1)
Guidance Counselors: 20.0 (194.0 to 1)
Current Spending: ($ per student per year):
   Total: $10,145; Instruction: $6,208; Support Services: $3,640

Enrollment, Drop-out Rates and Diploma Recipients by Race/Ethnicity

Category	Total	White	Black	Asian	AIAN	Hisp.
Enrollment (%)	100.0	96.7	1.0	1.2	0.2	0.9
Drop-out Rate (%)	2.4	2.5	0.0	0.0	0.0	0.0
H.S. Diplomas (#)	333	n/a	n/a	n/a	n/a	n/a

Monadnock Regional SD
600 Old Homestead Hwy • East Swanzey, NH 03446-2310
(603) 352-6955 • http://www.mrsd.org/LinkM.htm
Grade Span: PK-12; Agency Type: 2
Schools: 9
  6 Primary; 2 Middle; 1 High; 0 Other Level
  9 Regular; 0 Special Education; 0 Vocational; 0 Alternative
  0 Magnet; 0 Charter; 6 Title I Eligible; 0 School-wide Title I
Students: 2,483 (50.5% male; 49.4% female)
  Individual Education Program: 324 (13.0%);
  English Language Learner: 1 (<0.1%); Migrant: 0 (0.0%)
  Eligible for Free Lunch Program: 293 (11.8%)
  Eligible for Reduced-Price Lunch Program: 209 (8.4%)
Teachers: 174.1 (14.3 to 1)
Librarians/Media Specialists: 1.5 (1,655.3 to 1)
Guidance Counselors: 10.0 (248.3 to 1)
Current Spending: ($ per student per year):
  Total: $9,755; Instruction: $6,227; Support Services: $3,195
Enrollment, Drop-out Rates and Diploma Recipients by Race/Ethnicity

Category	Total	White	Black	Asian	AIAN	Hisp.
Enrollment (%)	100.0	97.3	0.6	0.4	0.4	1.2
Drop-out Rate (%)	3.9	3.7	0.0	n/a	n/a	0.0
H.S. Diplomas (#)	170	n/a	n/a	n/a	n/a	n/a

Coos County

Berlin SD
183 Hillside Ave • Berlin, NH 03570-1899
(603) 752-6500 • http://www.sau3.org/
Grade Span: KG-12; Agency Type: 2
Schools: 6
  3 Primary; 2 Middle; 1 High; 0 Other Level
  6 Regular; 0 Special Education; 0 Vocational; 0 Alternative
  0 Magnet; 0 Charter; 4 Title I Eligible; 0 School-wide Title I
Students: 1,615 (55.2% male; 44.7% female)
  Individual Education Program: 116 (7.2%);
  English Language Learner: 0 (0.0%); Migrant: 0 (0.0%)
  Eligible for Free Lunch Program: 426 (26.4%)
  Eligible for Reduced-Price Lunch Program: 116 (7.2%)
Teachers: 112.0 (14.4 to 1)
Librarians/Media Specialists: 3.0 (538.3 to 1)
Guidance Counselors: 5.0 (323.0 to 1)
Current Spending: ($ per student per year):
  Total: $7,011; Instruction: $4,508; Support Services: $2,251
Enrollment, Drop-out Rates and Diploma Recipients by Race/Ethnicity

Category	Total	White	Black	Asian	AIAN	Hisp.
Enrollment (%)	100.0	96.2	0.8	0.6	1.1	1.4
Drop-out Rate (%)	4.3	4.4	0.0	n/a	0.0	0.0
H.S. Diplomas (#)	102	n/a	n/a	n/a	n/a	n/a

Grafton County

Lebanon SD
84 Hanover St • Lebanon, NH 03766-0488
Mailing Address: PO Box 488 • Lebanon, NH 03766-0488
(603) 448-1634 • http://www.lebanon.k12.nh.us/
Grade Span: PK-12; Agency Type: 2
Schools: 7
  4 Primary; 2 Middle; 1 High; 0 Other Level
  7 Regular; 0 Special Education; 0 Vocational; 0 Alternative
  0 Magnet; 0 Charter; 4 Title I Eligible; 0 School-wide Title I
Students: 1,997 (49.8% male; 50.1% female)
  Individual Education Program: 292 (14.6%);
  English Language Learner: 20 (1.0%); Migrant: 0 (0.0%)
  Eligible for Free Lunch Program: 172 (8.6%)
  Eligible for Reduced-Price Lunch Program: 60 (3.0%)
Teachers: 176.4 (11.3 to 1)
Librarians/Media Specialists: 6.9 (289.4 to 1)
Guidance Counselors: 9.5 (210.2 to 1)
Current Spending: ($ per student per year):
  Total: $10,835; Instruction: $7,277; Support Services: $3,328
Enrollment, Drop-out Rates and Diploma Recipients by Race/Ethnicity

Category	Total	White	Black	Asian	AIAN	Hisp.
Enrollment (%)	100.0	92.9	1.1	3.8	0.4	1.8
Drop-out Rate (%)	4.8	5.1	0.0	0.0	0.0	0.0
H.S. Diplomas (#)	168	n/a	n/a	n/a	n/a	n/a

Newfound Area SD
20 N Main St • Bristol, NH 03222-1404
(603) 744-5555 • http://www.newfound.k12.nh.us/
Grade Span: PK-12; Agency Type: 2
Schools: 7
  5 Primary; 1 Middle; 1 High; 0 Other Level
  7 Regular; 0 Special Education; 0 Vocational; 0 Alternative
  0 Magnet; 0 Charter; 5 Title I Eligible; 0 School-wide Title I
Students: 1,532 (53.5% male; 46.4% female)
  Individual Education Program: 235 (15.3%);
  English Language Learner: 4 (0.3%); Migrant: 0 (0.0%)
  Eligible for Free Lunch Program: 250 (16.3%)
  Eligible for Reduced-Price Lunch Program: 138 (9.0%)
Teachers: 128.1 (12.0 to 1)
Librarians/Media Specialists: 3.0 (510.7 to 1)
Guidance Counselors: 7.0 (218.9 to 1)
Current Spending: ($ per student per year):
  Total: $9,227; Instruction: $5,552; Support Services: $3,288
Enrollment, Drop-out Rates and Diploma Recipients by Race/Ethnicity

Category	Total	White	Black	Asian	AIAN	Hisp.
Enrollment (%)	100.0	97.8	0.3	1.0	0.4	0.5
Drop-out Rate (%)	3.8	3.8	n/a	0.0	n/a	n/a
H.S. Diplomas (#)	91	n/a	n/a	n/a	n/a	n/a

Hillsborough County

Amherst SD
1 School St • Amherst, NH 03031-0849
Mailing Address: PO Box 849 • Amherst, NH 03031-0849
(603) 673-2690
Grade Span: KG-08; Agency Type: 2
Schools: 3
  2 Primary; 1 Middle; 0 High; 0 Other Level
  3 Regular; 0 Special Education; 0 Vocational; 0 Alternative
  0 Magnet; 0 Charter; 1 Title I Eligible; 0 School-wide Title I
Students: 1,695 (51.2% male; 48.7% female)
  Individual Education Program: 188 (11.1%);
  English Language Learner: 3 (0.2%); Migrant: 0 (0.0%)
  Eligible for Free Lunch Program: 40 (2.4%)
  Eligible for Reduced-Price Lunch Program: 24 (1.4%)
Teachers: 124.8 (13.6 to 1)
Librarians/Media Specialists: 2.0 (847.5 to 1)
Guidance Counselors: 5.5 (308.2 to 1)
Current Spending: ($ per student per year):
  Total: $9,297; Instruction: $6,734; Support Services: $2,284
Enrollment, Drop-out Rates and Diploma Recipients by Race/Ethnicity

Category	Total	White	Black	Asian	AIAN	Hisp.
Enrollment (%)	100.0	96.2	0.6	1.8	0.6	0.9
Drop-out Rate (%)	n/a	n/a	n/a	n/a	n/a	n/a
H.S. Diplomas (#)	n/a	n/a	n/a	n/a	n/a	n/a

Bedford SD
103 County Rd • Bedford, NH 03110-6202
(603) 472-3755 • http://www.sau25.net/index.ssi
Grade Span: PK-08; Agency Type: 2
Schools: 4
  3 Primary; 1 Middle; 0 High; 0 Other Level
  4 Regular; 0 Special Education; 0 Vocational; 0 Alternative
  0 Magnet; 0 Charter; 3 Title I Eligible; 0 School-wide Title I
Students: 2,863 (52.4% male; 47.5% female)
  Individual Education Program: 321 (11.2%);
  English Language Learner: 7 (0.2%); Migrant: 0 (0.0%)
  Eligible for Free Lunch Program: 28 (1.0%)
  Eligible for Reduced-Price Lunch Program: 23 (0.8%)
Teachers: 184.2 (15.5 to 1)
Librarians/Media Specialists: 4.0 (715.8 to 1)
Guidance Counselors: 8.5 (336.8 to 1)
Current Spending: ($ per student per year):
  Total: $8,843; Instruction: $5,547; Support Services: $3,079
Enrollment, Drop-out Rates and Diploma Recipients by Race/Ethnicity

Category	Total	White	Black	Asian	AIAN	Hisp.
Enrollment (%)	100.0	96.3	0.7	2.0	0.0	0.9
Drop-out Rate (%)	n/a	n/a	n/a	n/a	n/a	n/a
H.S. Diplomas (#)	n/a	n/a	n/a	n/a	n/a	n/a

Contoocook Valley SD
106 Hancock Rd • Peterborough, NH 03458-1197
(603) 924-3336 • http://www.conval.edu/
Grade Span: PK-12; Agency Type: 2
Schools: 12
  9 Primary; 2 Middle; 1 High; 0 Other Level
  12 Regular; 0 Special Education; 0 Vocational; 0 Alternative
  0 Magnet; 0 Charter; 5 Title I Eligible; 0 School-wide Title I
Students: 3,146 (51.8% male; 48.1% female)
  Individual Education Program: 528 (16.8%);

English Language Learner: 3 (0.1%); Migrant: 0 (0.0%)
Eligible for Free Lunch Program: 309 (9.8%)
Eligible for Reduced-Price Lunch Program: 174 (5.5%)
Teachers: 248.2 (12.7 to 1)
Librarians/Media Specialists: 6.5 (484.0 to 1)
Guidance Counselors: 10.3 (305.4 to 1)
Current Spending: ($ per student per year):
Total: $9,484; Instruction: $6,280; Support Services: $2,896
Enrollment, Drop-out Rates and Diploma Recipients by Race/Ethnicity

Category	Total	White	Black	Asian	AIAN	Hisp.
Enrollment (%)	100.0	97.6	0.4	1.2	0.2	0.6
Drop-out Rate (%)	2.7	2.6	50.0	0.0	n/a	0.0
H.S. Diplomas (#)	233	n/a	n/a	n/a	n/a	n/a

Goffstown SD
11 School St · Goffstown, NH 03045-1908
(603) 497-4818 · http://www.goffstown.k12.nh.us/
Grade Span: PK-12; **Agency Type:** 2
Schools: 4
2 Primary; 1 Middle; 1 High; 0 Other Level
4 Regular; 0 Special Education; 0 Vocational; 0 Alternative
0 Magnet; 0 Charter; 2 Title I Eligible; 0 School-wide Title I
Students: 3,085 (49.3% male; 50.6% female)
Individual Education Program: 409 (13.3%);
English Language Learner: 30 (1.0%); Migrant: 0 (0.0%)
Eligible for Free Lunch Program: 132 (4.3%)
Eligible for Reduced-Price Lunch Program: 70 (2.3%)
Teachers: 194.8 (15.8 to 1)
Librarians/Media Specialists: 3.2 (964.1 to 1)
Guidance Counselors: 10.8 (285.6 to 1)
Current Spending: ($ per student per year):
Total: $7,135; Instruction: $4,551; Support Services: $2,347
Enrollment, Drop-out Rates and Diploma Recipients by Race/Ethnicity

Category	Total	White	Black	Asian	AIAN	Hisp.
Enrollment (%)	100.0	98.4	0.4	0.6	0.0	0.6
Drop-out Rate (%)	2.4	2.4	0.0	0.0	n/a	0.0
H.S. Diplomas (#)	180	n/a	n/a	n/a	n/a	n/a

Hudson SD
20 Library St · Hudson, NH 03051-4260
(603) 883-7765 · http://ci.hudson.nh.us/schoolwelcome.html
Grade Span: 01-12; **Agency Type:** 2
Schools: 6
4 Primary; 1 Middle; 1 High; 0 Other Level
6 Regular; 0 Special Education; 0 Vocational; 0 Alternative
0 Magnet; 0 Charter; 0 Title I Eligible; 0 School-wide Title I
Students: 4,144 (51.3% male; 48.6% female)
Individual Education Program: 547 (13.2%);
English Language Learner: 47 (1.1%); Migrant: 0 (0.0%)
Eligible for Free Lunch Program: 195 (4.7%)
Eligible for Reduced-Price Lunch Program: 57 (1.4%)
Teachers: 253.4 (16.4 to 1)
Librarians/Media Specialists: 3.0 (1,381.3 to 1)
Guidance Counselors: 13.0 (318.8 to 1)
Current Spending: ($ per student per year):
Total: $7,491; Instruction: $4,690; Support Services: $2,581
Enrollment, Drop-out Rates and Diploma Recipients by Race/Ethnicity

Category	Total	White	Black	Asian	AIAN	Hisp.
Enrollment (%)	100.0	94.8	1.3	1.2	0.5	2.2
Drop-out Rate (%)	3.3	3.5	0.0	0.0	0.0	0.0
H.S. Diplomas (#)	402	n/a	n/a	n/a	n/a	n/a

Litchfield SD
C/O Campbell High School · Litchfield, NH 03052-8401
(603) 578-3570
Grade Span: 01-12; **Agency Type:** 2
Schools: 3
1 Primary; 1 Middle; 1 High; 0 Other Level
3 Regular; 0 Special Education; 0 Vocational; 0 Alternative
0 Magnet; 0 Charter; 0 Title I Eligible; 0 School-wide Title I
Students: 1,657 (54.4% male; 45.5% female)
Individual Education Program: 239 (14.4%);
English Language Learner: 9 (0.5%); Migrant: 0 (0.0%)
Eligible for Free Lunch Program: 66 (4.0%)
Eligible for Reduced-Price Lunch Program: 24 (1.4%)
Teachers: 109.0 (15.2 to 1)
Librarians/Media Specialists: 3.0 (552.3 to 1)
Guidance Counselors: 5.0 (331.4 to 1)
Current Spending: ($ per student per year):
Total: $7,338; Instruction: $4,403; Support Services: $2,709
Enrollment, Drop-out Rates and Diploma Recipients by Race/Ethnicity

Category	Total	White	Black	Asian	AIAN	Hisp.
Enrollment (%)	100.0	97.1	0.4	0.5	1.0	1.0
Drop-out Rate (%)	0.9	0.9	0.0	0.0	0.0	0.0
H.S. Diplomas (#)	0	0	0	0	0	0

Manchester SD
196 Bridge St · Manchester, NH 03104-4985
(603) 624-6300 · http://www.mansd.org/
Grade Span: PK-12; **Agency Type:** 2
Schools: 22
15 Primary; 4 Middle; 3 High; 0 Other Level
22 Regular; 0 Special Education; 0 Vocational; 0 Alternative
0 Magnet; 0 Charter; 10 Title I Eligible; 5 School-wide Title I
Students: 17,655 (51.3% male; 48.6% female)
Individual Education Program: 2,698 (15.3%);
English Language Learner: 1,296 (7.3%); Migrant: 157 (0.9%)
Eligible for Free Lunch Program: 3,589 (20.3%)
Eligible for Reduced-Price Lunch Program: 1,167 (6.6%)
Teachers: 1,160.0 (15.2 to 1)
Librarians/Media Specialists: 24.1 (732.6 to 1)
Guidance Counselors: 54.2 (325.7 to 1)
Current Spending: ($ per student per year):
Total: $6,973; Instruction: $4,869; Support Services: $1,856
Enrollment, Drop-out Rates and Diploma Recipients by Race/Ethnicity

Category	Total	White	Black	Asian	AIAN	Hisp.
Enrollment (%)	100.0	83.4	4.6	2.3	0.5	9.2
Drop-out Rate (%)	6.8	6.3	10.3	7.2	35.7	14.0
H.S. Diplomas (#)	1,180	n/a	n/a	n/a	n/a	n/a

Merrimack SD
36 Mcelwain St · Merrimack, NH 03054-3693
(603) 424-6200 · http://www.merrimack.k12.nh.us/
Grade Span: 01-12; **Agency Type:** 2
Schools: 5
3 Primary; 1 Middle; 1 High; 0 Other Level
5 Regular; 0 Special Education; 0 Vocational; 0 Alternative
0 Magnet; 0 Charter; 3 Title I Eligible; 0 School-wide Title I
Students: 4,745 (52.0% male; 47.9% female)
Individual Education Program: 746 (15.7%);
English Language Learner: 5 (0.1%); Migrant: 0 (0.0%)
Eligible for Free Lunch Program: 115 (2.4%)
Eligible for Reduced-Price Lunch Program: 88 (1.9%)
Teachers: 342.8 (13.8 to 1)
Librarians/Media Specialists: 6.0 (790.8 to 1)
Guidance Counselors: 19.0 (249.7 to 1)
Current Spending: ($ per student per year):
Total: $8,580; Instruction: $5,650; Support Services: $2,708
Enrollment, Drop-out Rates and Diploma Recipients by Race/Ethnicity

Category	Total	White	Black	Asian	AIAN	Hisp.
Enrollment (%)	100.0	94.8	1.2	1.9	0.5	1.7
Drop-out Rate (%)	1.9	2.0	0.0	0.0	0.0	0.0
H.S. Diplomas (#)	316	n/a	n/a	n/a	n/a	n/a

Milford SD
100 W St · Milford, NH 03055-4871
(603) 673-2202 · http://www.milfordschools.net/district/index.php
Grade Span: PK-12; **Agency Type:** 2
Schools: 4
2 Primary; 1 Middle; 1 High; 0 Other Level
4 Regular; 0 Special Education; 0 Vocational; 0 Alternative
0 Magnet; 0 Charter; 2 Title I Eligible; 0 School-wide Title I
Students: 2,514 (51.7% male; 48.2% female)
Individual Education Program: 402 (16.0%);
English Language Learner: 19 (0.8%); Migrant: 0 (0.0%)
Eligible for Free Lunch Program: 250 (9.9%)
Eligible for Reduced-Price Lunch Program: 155 (6.2%)
Teachers: 181.1 (13.9 to 1)
Librarians/Media Specialists: 5.0 (502.8 to 1)
Guidance Counselors: 8.0 (314.3 to 1)
Current Spending: ($ per student per year):
Total: $8,877; Instruction: $5,567; Support Services: $3,048
Enrollment, Drop-out Rates and Diploma Recipients by Race/Ethnicity

Category	Total	White	Black	Asian	AIAN	Hisp.
Enrollment (%)	100.0	95.1	1.8	1.3	0.2	1.6
Drop-out Rate (%)	3.2	2.8	0.0	0.0	n/a	44.4
H.S. Diplomas (#)	165	n/a	n/a	n/a	n/a	n/a

Nashua SD
141 Ledge St · Nashua, NH 03061-0687
Mailing Address: PO Box 687 · Nashua, NH 03061-0687
(603) 594-4300 · http://district.nashua.edu/
Grade Span: PK-12; **Agency Type:** 2
Schools: 18
12 Primary; 4 Middle; 1 High; 1 Other Level
18 Regular; 0 Special Education; 0 Vocational; 0 Alternative
0 Magnet; 0 Charter; 5 Title I Eligible; 3 School-wide Title I
Students: 13,357 (51.8% male; 48.1% female)
Individual Education Program: 1,935 (14.5%);
English Language Learner: 515 (3.9%); Migrant: 10 (0.1%)
Eligible for Free Lunch Program: 2,460 (18.4%)

Eligible for Reduced-Price Lunch Program: 825 (6.2%)
Teachers: 866.9 (15.4 to 1)
Librarians/Media Specialists: 14.4 (927.6 to 1)
Guidance Counselors: 37.0 (361.0 to 1)
Current Spending: ($ per student per year):
  Total: $7,324; Instruction: $4,648; Support Services: $2,429
Enrollment, Drop-out Rates and Diploma Recipients by Race/Ethnicity

Category	Total	White	Black	Asian	AIAN	Hisp.
Enrollment (%)	100.0	80.3	3.3	4.6	0.3	11.4
Drop-out Rate (%)	4.6	4.4	4.6	2.7	6.3	6.6
H.S. Diplomas (#)	655	n/a	n/a	n/a	n/a	n/a

Pelham SD
19 Haverhill Rd · Windham, NH 03087-0510
Mailing Address: PO Box 510 · Windham, NH 03087-0510
(603) 425-1976 · http://www.windhamsd.org/SAU28/sau28.htm
Grade Span: 01-12; **Agency Type:** 2
Schools: 3
  1 Primary; 1 Middle; 1 High; 0 Other Level
  3 Regular; 0 Special Education; 0 Vocational; 0 Alternative
  0 Magnet; 0 Charter; 1 Title I Eligible; 0 School-wide Title I
Students: 2,047 (49.2% male; 50.7% female)
  Individual Education Program: 331 (16.2%);
  English Language Learner: 13 (0.6%); Migrant: 0 (0.0%)
  Eligible for Free Lunch Program: 80 (3.9%)
  Eligible for Reduced-Price Lunch Program: 61 (3.0%)
Teachers: 135.2 (15.1 to 1)
Librarians/Media Specialists: 3.0 (682.3 to 1)
Guidance Counselors: 7.8 (262.4 to 1)
Current Spending: ($ per student per year):
  Total: $8,040; Instruction: $5,141; Support Services: $2,462
Enrollment, Drop-out Rates and Diploma Recipients by Race/Ethnicity

Category	Total	White	Black	Asian	AIAN	Hisp.
Enrollment (%)	100.0	96.0	0.6	2.0	0.0	1.3
Drop-out Rate (%)	3.4	3.4	0.0	0.0	0.0	12.5
H.S. Diplomas (#)	104	n/a	n/a	n/a	n/a	n/a

Merrimack County

Bow SD
32 White Rock Hill Rd · Bow, NH 03304-4219
(603) 224-4728 · http://www.bow.k12.nh.us/
Grade Span: PK-12; **Agency Type:** 2
Schools: 3
  1 Primary; 1 Middle; 1 High; 0 Other Level
  3 Regular; 0 Special Education; 0 Vocational; 0 Alternative
  0 Magnet; 0 Charter; 0 Title I Eligible; 0 School-wide Title I
Students: 1,811 (52.5% male; 47.4% female)
  Individual Education Program: 112 (6.2%);
  English Language Learner: 4 (0.2%); Migrant: 0 (0.0%)
  Eligible for Free Lunch Program: 30 (1.7%)
  Eligible for Reduced-Price Lunch Program: 9 (0.5%)
Teachers: 128.2 (14.1 to 1)
Librarians/Media Specialists: 3.0 (603.7 to 1)
Guidance Counselors: 5.8 (312.2 to 1)
Current Spending: ($ per student per year):
  Total: $8,246; Instruction: $5,491; Support Services: $2,482
Enrollment, Drop-out Rates and Diploma Recipients by Race/Ethnicity

Category	Total	White	Black	Asian	AIAN	Hisp.
Enrollment (%)	100.0	97.3	0.0	1.7	0.1	0.9
Drop-out Rate (%)	1.9	1.9	n/a	0.0	0.0	0.0
H.S. Diplomas (#)	110	n/a	n/a	n/a	n/a	n/a

Concord SD
16 Rumford St · Concord, NH 03301-3999
(603) 225-0811 ·
http://www.concord.k12.nh.us/comm/dropdownindex.html
Grade Span: PK-12; **Agency Type:** 2
Schools: 11
  9 Primary; 1 Middle; 1 High; 0 Other Level
  11 Regular; 0 Special Education; 0 Vocational; 0 Alternative
  0 Magnet; 0 Charter; 6 Title I Eligible; 2 School-wide Title I
Students: 5,473 (50.9% male; 49.0% female)
  Individual Education Program: 802 (14.7%);
  English Language Learner: 93 (1.7%); Migrant: 0 (0.0%)
  Eligible for Free Lunch Program: 746 (13.6%)
  Eligible for Reduced-Price Lunch Program: 255 (4.7%)
Teachers: 339.9 (16.1 to 1)
Librarians/Media Specialists: 5.3 (1,032.6 to 1)
Guidance Counselors: 17.8 (307.5 to 1)
Current Spending: ($ per student per year):
  Total: $8,990; Instruction: $5,600; Support Services: $3,150

Enrollment, Drop-out Rates and Diploma Recipients by Race/Ethnicity

Category	Total	White	Black	Asian	AIAN	Hisp.
Enrollment (%)	100.0	92.9	2.7	2.9	0.2	1.3
Drop-out Rate (%)	4.5	4.6	6.5	0.0	0.0	14.3
H.S. Diplomas (#)	399	n/a	n/a	n/a	n/a	n/a

Kearsarge Regional SD
169 Main St · New London, NH 03257-4554
(603) 526-2051 · http://www.kearsarge.k12.nh.us/
Grade Span: KG-12; **Agency Type:** 2
Schools: 6
  4 Primary; 1 Middle; 1 High; 0 Other Level
  6 Regular; 0 Special Education; 0 Vocational; 0 Alternative
  0 Magnet; 0 Charter; 2 Title I Eligible; 0 School-wide Title I
Students: 2,099 (53.1% male; 46.8% female)
  Individual Education Program: 320 (15.2%);
  English Language Learner: 7 (0.3%); Migrant: 0 (0.0%)
  Eligible for Free Lunch Program: 143 (6.8%)
  Eligible for Reduced-Price Lunch Program: 88 (4.2%)
Teachers: 163.3 (12.9 to 1)
Librarians/Media Specialists: 4.3 (488.1 to 1)
Guidance Counselors: 8.2 (256.0 to 1)
Current Spending: ($ per student per year):
  Total: $10,201; Instruction: $6,441; Support Services: $3,518
Enrollment, Drop-out Rates and Diploma Recipients by Race/Ethnicity

Category	Total	White	Black	Asian	AIAN	Hisp.
Enrollment (%)	100.0	96.6	0.4	0.8	1.0	1.1
Drop-out Rate (%)	2.5	2.6	0.0	0.0	0.0	0.0
H.S. Diplomas (#)	129	n/a	n/a	n/a	n/a	n/a

Merrimack Valley SD
105 Community Dr · Penacook, NH 03303-1625
(603) 753-6561 · http://www.mv.k12.nh.us/
Grade Span: PK-12; **Agency Type:** 2
Schools: 7
  5 Primary; 1 Middle; 1 High; 0 Other Level
  7 Regular; 0 Special Education; 0 Vocational; 0 Alternative
  0 Magnet; 0 Charter; 5 Title I Eligible; 0 School-wide Title I
Students: 2,771 (51.8% male; 48.1% female)
  Individual Education Program: 394 (14.2%);
  English Language Learner: 9 (0.3%); Migrant: 0 (0.0%)
  Eligible for Free Lunch Program: 239 (8.6%)
  Eligible for Reduced-Price Lunch Program: 160 (5.8%)
Teachers: 190.4 (14.6 to 1)
Librarians/Media Specialists: 1.0 (2,771.0 to 1)
Guidance Counselors: 8.7 (318.5 to 1)
Current Spending: ($ per student per year):
  Total: $7,830; Instruction: $4,825; Support Services: $2,717
Enrollment, Drop-out Rates and Diploma Recipients by Race/Ethnicity

Category	Total	White	Black	Asian	AIAN	Hisp.
Enrollment (%)	100.0	98.1	0.9	0.6	0.0	0.3
Drop-out Rate (%)	5.1	5.2	0.0	0.0	n/a	0.0
H.S. Diplomas (#)	160	n/a	n/a	n/a	n/a	n/a

Pembroke SD
267 Pembroke St · Pembroke, NH 03275-1343
(603) 485-5188 · http://www.sau53.org/sau53/districts/pembroke.htm
Grade Span: KG-12; **Agency Type:** 2
Schools: 4
  2 Primary; 1 Middle; 1 High; 0 Other Level
  4 Regular; 0 Special Education; 0 Vocational; 0 Alternative
  0 Magnet; 0 Charter; 2 Title I Eligible; 0 School-wide Title I
Students: 1,863 (51.5% male; 48.4% female)
  Individual Education Program: 315 (16.9%);
  English Language Learner: 1 (0.1%); Migrant: 0 (0.0%)
  Eligible for Free Lunch Program: 119 (6.4%)
  Eligible for Reduced-Price Lunch Program: 65 (3.5%)
Teachers: 134.1 (13.9 to 1)
Librarians/Media Specialists: 1.0 (1,863.0 to 1)
Guidance Counselors: 7.0 (266.1 to 1)
Current Spending: ($ per student per year):
  Total: $7,934; Instruction: $4,930; Support Services: $2,755
Enrollment, Drop-out Rates and Diploma Recipients by Race/Ethnicity

Category	Total	White	Black	Asian	AIAN	Hisp.
Enrollment (%)	100.0	96.6	0.9	0.5	0.9	1.1
Drop-out Rate (%)	6.0	6.0	0.0	n/a	n/a	50.0
H.S. Diplomas (#)	161	n/a	n/a	n/a	n/a	n/a

Rockingham County

Derry SD
18 S Main St · Derry, NH 03038-2197
(603) 432-1210 · http://www.derry.k12.nh.us/
Grade Span: 01-08; **Agency Type:** 2
Schools: 7

5 Primary; 2 Middle; 0 High; 0 Other Level
7 Regular; 0 Special Education; 0 Vocational; 0 Alternative
0 Magnet; 0 Charter; 3 Title I Eligible; 0 School-wide Title I
Students: 4,228 (51.7% male; 48.2% female)
Individual Education Program: 623 (14.7%);
English Language Learner: 18 (0.4%); Migrant: 0 (0.0%)
Eligible for Free Lunch Program: 401 (9.5%)
Eligible for Reduced-Price Lunch Program: 242 (5.7%)
Teachers: 287.1 (14.7 to 1)
Librarians/Media Specialists: 1.2 (3,523.3 to 1)
Guidance Counselors: 14.3 (295.7 to 1)
Current Spending: ($ per student per year):
Total: $7,753; Instruction: $4,957; Support Services: $2,482
Enrollment, Drop-out Rates and Diploma Recipients by Race/Ethnicity

Category	Total	White	Black	Asian	AIAN	Hisp.
Enrollment (%)	100.0	95.6	1.4	1.1	0.1	1.8
Drop-out Rate (%)	n/a	n/a	n/a	n/a	n/a	n/a
H.S. Diplomas (#)	n/a	n/a	n/a	n/a	n/a	n/a

Exeter Region Cooperative SD
24 Front St • Exeter, NH 03833-2744
(603) 778-7772 • http://www.ercsd.k12.nh.us/
Grade Span: 06-12; **Agency Type:** 2
Schools: 2
0 Primary; 1 Middle; 1 High; 0 Other Level
2 Regular; 0 Special Education; 0 Vocational; 0 Alternative
0 Magnet; 0 Charter; 2 Title I Eligible; 0 School-wide Title I
Students: 2,937 (50.5% male; 49.4% female)
Individual Education Program: 433 (14.7%);
English Language Learner: 2 (0.1%); Migrant: 0 (0.0%)
Eligible for Free Lunch Program: 90 (3.1%)
Eligible for Reduced-Price Lunch Program: 39 (1.3%)
Teachers: 211.2 (13.9 to 1)
Librarians/Media Specialists: 2.0 (1,468.5 to 1)
Guidance Counselors: 14.0 (209.8 to 1)
Current Spending: ($ per student per year):
Total: $9,405; Instruction: $6,286; Support Services: $2,837
Enrollment, Drop-out Rates and Diploma Recipients by Race/Ethnicity

Category	Total	White	Black	Asian	AIAN	Hisp.
Enrollment (%)	100.0	96.7	0.5	1.7	0.1	0.9
Drop-out Rate (%)	2.7	2.5	0.0	5.3	20.0	11.1
H.S. Diplomas (#)	319	n/a	n/a	n/a	n/a	n/a

Londonderry SD
268 Mammoth Rd • Londonderry, NH 03053-3096
(603) 432-6920 • http://www.londonderry.org/page.asp?Page_Id=103
Grade Span: PK-12; **Agency Type:** 2
Schools: 6
4 Primary; 1 Middle; 1 High; 0 Other Level
6 Regular; 0 Special Education; 0 Vocational; 0 Alternative
0 Magnet; 0 Charter; 0 Title I Eligible; 0 School-wide Title I
Students: 5,621 (52.2% male; 47.7% female)
Individual Education Program: 824 (14.7%);
English Language Learner: 5 (0.1%); Migrant: 0 (0.0%)
Eligible for Free Lunch Program: 142 (2.5%)
Eligible for Reduced-Price Lunch Program: 62 (1.1%)
Teachers: 389.8 (14.4 to 1)
Librarians/Media Specialists: 7.7 (730.0 to 1)
Guidance Counselors: 19.5 (288.3 to 1)
Current Spending: ($ per student per year):
Total: $7,961; Instruction: $5,021; Support Services: $2,772
Enrollment, Drop-out Rates and Diploma Recipients by Race/Ethnicity

Category	Total	White	Black	Asian	AIAN	Hisp.
Enrollment (%)	100.0	96.9	0.7	1.3	0.2	0.8
Drop-out Rate (%)	2.6	2.6	16.7	0.0	n/a	0.0
H.S. Diplomas (#)	371	n/a	n/a	n/a	n/a	n/a

Pinkerton Academy SD
5 Pinkerton St • Derry, NH 03038-1515
(603) 432-2588 • http://WWW.PINKERTONACADEMY.NET/
Grade Span: 09-12; **Agency Type:** 2
Schools: 1
0 Primary; 0 Middle; 1 High; 0 Other Level
1 Regular; 0 Special Education; 0 Vocational; 0 Alternative
0 Magnet; 0 Charter; 0 Title I Eligible; 0 School-wide Title I
Students: 3,378 (50.2% male; 49.7% female)
Individual Education Program: 0 (0.0%);
English Language Learner: 0 (0.0%); Migrant: 0 (0.0%)
Eligible for Free Lunch Program: 160 (4.7%)
Eligible for Reduced-Price Lunch Program: 80 (2.4%)
Teachers: 240.0 (14.1 to 1)
Librarians/Media Specialists: 2.0 (1,689.0 to 1)
Guidance Counselors: 15.0 (225.2 to 1)
Current Spending: ($ per student per year):
Total: n/a; Instruction: n/a; Support Services: n/a

Portsmouth SD
50 Clough Dr • Portsmouth, NH 03801-5296
(603) 431-5080 • http://www.ri.net/schools/Portsmouth/Admin/
Grade Span: PK-12; **Agency Type:** 2
Schools: 6
4 Primary; 1 Middle; 1 High; 0 Other Level
6 Regular; 0 Special Education; 0 Vocational; 0 Alternative
0 Magnet; 0 Charter; 3 Title I Eligible; 1 School-wide Title I
Students: 2,696 (49.3% male; 50.6% female)
Individual Education Program: 394 (14.6%);
English Language Learner: 58 (2.2%); Migrant: 0 (0.0%)
Eligible for Free Lunch Program: 354 (13.1%)
Eligible for Reduced-Price Lunch Program: 145 (5.4%)
Teachers: 227.0 (11.9 to 1)
Librarians/Media Specialists: 2.8 (962.9 to 1)
Guidance Counselors: 15.0 (179.7 to 1)
Current Spending: ($ per student per year):
Total: $11,725; Instruction: $7,332; Support Services: $4,128
Enrollment, Drop-out Rates and Diploma Recipients by Race/Ethnicity

Category	Total	White	Black	Asian	AIAN	Hisp.
Enrollment (%)	100.0	90.3	4.2	3.4	0.1	2.0
Drop-out Rate (%)	1.8	1.7	3.2	0.0	n/a	11.1
H.S. Diplomas (#)	229	n/a	n/a	n/a	n/a	n/a

Raymond SD
43 Harriman Hill Rd • Raymond, NH 03077-1509
(603) 895-4299 • http://raymond.k12.nh.us/District_General_Info.htm
Grade Span: 01-12; **Agency Type:** 2
Schools: 3
1 Primary; 1 Middle; 1 High; 0 Other Level
3 Regular; 0 Special Education; 0 Vocational; 0 Alternative
0 Magnet; 0 Charter; 2 Title I Eligible; 0 School-wide Title I
Students: 1,598   (51.3% male; 48.6% female)
Individual Education Program: 244 (15.3%);
English Language Learner: 1 (0.1%); Migrant: 0 (0.0%)
Eligible for Free Lunch Program: 198 (12.4%)
Eligible for Reduced-Price Lunch Program: 126 (7.9%)
Teachers: 128.1 (12.5 to 1)
Librarians/Media Specialists: 2.0 (799.0 to 1)
Guidance Counselors: 6.0 (266.3 to 1)
Current Spending: ($ per student per year):
Total: $9,254; Instruction: $5,791; Support Services: $3,110
Enrollment, Drop-out Rates and Diploma Recipients by Race/Ethnicity

Category	Total	White	Black	Asian	AIAN	Hisp.
Enrollment (%)	100.0	98.2	1.0	0.1	0.4	0.3
Drop-out Rate (%)	5.8	5.9	0.0	0.0	n/a	n/a
H.S. Diplomas (#)	126	n/a	n/a	n/a	n/a	n/a

Salem SD
38 Geremonty Dr • Salem, NH 03079-3313
(603) 893-7040 • http://www.salemschooldistrictnh.com/
Grade Span: 01-12; **Agency Type:** 2
Schools: 8
6 Primary; 1 Middle; 1 High; 0 Other Level
8 Regular; 0 Special Education; 0 Vocational; 0 Alternative
0 Magnet; 0 Charter; 4 Title I Eligible; 0 School-wide Title I
Students: 5,325   (51.6% male; 48.3% female)
Individual Education Program: 689 (12.9%);
English Language Learner: 17 (0.3%); Migrant: 0 (0.0%)
Eligible for Free Lunch Program: 257 (4.8%)
Eligible for Reduced-Price Lunch Program: 132 (2.5%)
Teachers: 313.0 (17.0 to 1)
Librarians/Media Specialists: 5.9 (902.5 to 1)
Guidance Counselors: 35.0 (152.1 to 1)
Current Spending: ($ per student per year):
Total: $7,177; Instruction: $4,748; Support Services: $2,136
Enrollment, Drop-out Rates and Diploma Recipients by Race/Ethnicity

Category	Total	White	Black	Asian	AIAN	Hisp.
Enrollment (%)	100.0	93.4	0.7	3.3	0.1	2.5
Drop-out Rate (%)	1.4	1.5	0.0	0.0	20.0	0.0
H.S. Diplomas (#)	411	n/a	n/a	n/a	n/a	n/a

Sanborn Regional SD
178 Main St • Kingston, NH 03848-3249
(603) 642-3688 • http://sanborn.k12.nh.us/
Grade Span: 01-12; **Agency Type:** 2
Schools: 4
2 Primary; 1 Middle; 1 High; 0 Other Level
4 Regular; 0 Special Education; 0 Vocational;

0 Magnet; 0 Charter; 2 Title I Eligible; 0 School-wide Title I
Students: 1,802   (51.2% male; 48.7% female)
   Individual Education Program: 286 (15.9%);
   English Language Learner: 0 (0.0%); Migrant: 0 (0.0%)
   Eligible for Free Lunch Program: 71 (3.9%)
   Eligible for Reduced-Price Lunch Program: 51 (2.8%)
Teachers: 148.8 (12.1 to 1)
Librarians/Media Specialists: 4.0 (450.5 to 1)
Guidance Counselors: 8.0 (225.3 to 1)
Current Spending: ($ per student per year):
   Total: $9,211; Instruction: $5,962; Support Services: $3,017
Enrollment, Drop-out Rates and Diploma Recipients by Race/Ethnicity

Category	Total	White	Black	Asian	AIAN	Hisp.
Enrollment (%)	100.0	97.8	0.7	0.3	0.3	1.0
Drop-out Rate (%)	2.5	2.5	0.0	0.0	n/a	0.0
H.S. Diplomas (#)	126	n/a	n/a	n/a	n/a	n/a

Timberlane Regional SD
30 Greenough Rd • Plaistow, NH 03865-2762
(603) 382-6119 • http://www.timberlane.net/
Grade Span: 01-12; **Agency Type:** 2
Schools: 7
   4 Primary; 2 Middle; 1 High; 0 Other Level
   7 Regular; 0 Special Education; 0 Vocational; 0 Alternative
   0 Magnet; 0 Charter; 3 Title I Eligible; 0 School-wide Title I
Students: 4,489   (50.6% male; 49.3% female)
   Individual Education Program: 720 (16.0%);
   English Language Learner: 10 (0.2%); Migrant: 0 (0.0%)
   Eligible for Free Lunch Program: 149 (3.3%)
   Eligible for Reduced-Price Lunch Program: 90 (2.0%)
Teachers: 333.3 (13.5 to 1)
Librarians/Media Specialists: 4.6 (975.9 to 1)
Guidance Counselors: 17.0 (264.1 to 1)
Current Spending: ($ per student per year):
   Total: $8,264; Instruction: $5,227; Support Services: $2,832
Enrollment, Drop-out Rates and Diploma Recipients by Race/Ethnicity

Category	Total	White	Black	Asian	AIAN	Hisp.
Enrollment (%)	100.0	98.2	0.6	0.3	0.2	0.7
Drop-out Rate (%)	4.3	4.4	0.0	0.0	0.0	0.0
H.S. Diplomas (#)	241	n/a	n/a	n/a	n/a	n/a

Windham SD
19 Haverhill Rd • Windham, NH 03087-0510
Mailing Address: PO Box 510 • Windham, NH 03087-0510
(603) 425-1976 • http://www.windhamsd.org/
Grade Span: PK-08; **Agency Type:** 2
Schools: 4
   3 Primary; 1 Middle; 0 High; 0 Other Level
   4 Regular; 0 Special Education; 0 Vocational; 0 Alternative
   0 Magnet; 0 Charter; 0 Title I Eligible; 0 School-wide Title I
Students: 1,553   (52.0% male; 47.9% female)
   Individual Education Program: 180 (11.6%);
   English Language Learner: 8 (0.5%); Migrant: 0 (0.0%)
   Eligible for Free Lunch Program: 24 (1.5%)
   Eligible for Reduced-Price Lunch Program: 16 (1.0%)
Teachers: 115.0 (13.5 to 1)
Librarians/Media Specialists: 0.9 (1,725.6 to 1)
Guidance Counselors: 4.0 (388.3 to 1)
Current Spending: ($ per student per year):
   Total: $9,185; Instruction: $6,051; Support Services: $2,963
Enrollment, Drop-out Rates and Diploma Recipients by Race/Ethnicity

Category	Total	White	Black	Asian	AIAN	Hisp.
Enrollment (%)	100.0	96.7	0.8	1.7	0.1	0.7
Drop-out Rate (%)	n/a	n/a	n/a	n/a	n/a	n/a
H.S. Diplomas (#)	n/a	n/a	n/a	n/a	n/a	n/a

Strafford County

Dover SD
288 Central Ave • Dover, NH 03820-4169
(603) 516-6800 • http://www.dover.k12.nh.us/
Grade Span: PK-12; **Agency Type:** 2
Schools: 5
   3 Primary; 1 Middle; 1 High; 0 Other Level
   5 Regular; 0 Special Education; 0 Vocational; 0 Alternative
   0 Magnet; 0 Charter; 3 Title I Eligible; 1 School-wide Title I
Students: 4,090   (51.0% male; 48.9% female)
   Individual Education Program: 547 (13.4%);
   English Language Learner: 57 (1.4%); Migrant: 0 (0.0%)
   Eligible for Free Lunch Program: 591 (14.4%)
   Eligible for Reduced-Price Lunch Program: 232 (5.7%)
Teachers: 266.5 (15.3 to 1)
Librarians/Media Specialists: 5.0 (818.0 to 1)
Guidance Counselors: 14.6 (280.1 to 1)
Current Spending: ($ per student per year):
   Total: $8,295; Instruction: $5,162; Support Services: $2,861

Enrollment, Drop-out Rates and Diploma Recipients by Race/Ethnicity

Category	Total	White	Black	Asian	AIAN	Hisp.
Enrollment (%)	100.0	92.8	2.5	3.3	0.0	1.3
Drop-out Rate (%)	4.9	4.6	15.8	10.0	0.0	0.0
H.S. Diplomas (#)	292	n/a	n/a	n/a	n/a	n/a

Oyster River Coop SD
36 Coe Dr • Durham, NH 03824-2200
(603) 868-5100 • http://www.orcsd.org/
Grade Span: KG-12; **Agency Type:** 2
Schools: 4
   2 Primary; 1 Middle; 1 High; 0 Other Level
   4 Regular; 0 Special Education; 0 Vocational; 0 Alternative
   0 Magnet; 0 Charter; 3 Title I Eligible; 0 School-wide Title I
Students: 2,174   (52.2% male; 47.7% female)
   Individual Education Program: 357 (16.4%);
   English Language Learner: 23 (1.1%); Migrant: 0 (0.0%)
   Eligible for Free Lunch Program: 88 (4.0%)
   Eligible for Reduced-Price Lunch Program: 33 (1.5%)
Teachers: 163.9 (13.3 to 1)
Librarians/Media Specialists: 5.0 (434.8 to 1)
Guidance Counselors: 10.5 (207.0 to 1)
Current Spending: ($ per student per year):
   Total: $10,258; Instruction: $6,540; Support Services: $3,501
Enrollment, Drop-out Rates and Diploma Recipients by Race/Ethnicity

Category	Total	White	Black	Asian	AIAN	Hisp.
Enrollment (%)	100.0	96.0	1.0	2.2	0.0	0.8
Drop-out Rate (%)	0.7	0.7	0.0	0.0	n/a	0.0
H.S. Diplomas (#)	160	n/a	n/a	n/a	n/a	n/a

Rochester SD
150 Wakefield St Ste 8 • Rochester, NH 03867-1348
(603) 332-3678 • http://www.rochesterschools.com/
Grade Span: PK-12; **Agency Type:** 2
Schools: 10
   8 Primary; 1 Middle; 1 High; 0 Other Level
   10 Regular; 0 Special Education; 0 Vocational; 0 Alternative
   0 Magnet; 0 Charter; 5 Title I Eligible; 3 School-wide Title I
Students: 4,809   (52.8% male; 47.1% female)
   Individual Education Program: 1,010 (21.0%);
   English Language Learner: 43 (0.9%); Migrant: 3 (0.1%)
   Eligible for Free Lunch Program: 1,014 (21.1%)
   Eligible for Reduced-Price Lunch Program: 362 (7.5%)
Teachers: 342.9 (14.0 to 1)
Librarians/Media Specialists: 2.9 (1,658.3 to 1)
Guidance Counselors: 18.5 (259.9 to 1)
Current Spending: ($ per student per year):
   Total: $7,759; Instruction: $5,299; Support Services: $2,173
Enrollment, Drop-out Rates and Diploma Recipients by Race/Ethnicity

Category	Total	White	Black	Asian	AIAN	Hisp.
Enrollment (%)	100.0	95.2	1.4	1.6	0.2	1.6
Drop-out Rate (%)	7.7	7.8	4.8	9.5	0.0	5.0
H.S. Diplomas (#)	306	n/a	n/a	n/a	n/a	n/a

Somersworth SD
51 W High St • Somersworth, NH 03878-1099
(603) 692-4450 • http://www.mw.somersworth.k12.nh.us/sau56/
Grade Span: PK-12; **Agency Type:** 2
Schools: 4
   2 Primary; 1 Middle; 1 High; 0 Other Level
   4 Regular; 0 Special Education; 0 Vocational; 0 Alternative
   0 Magnet; 0 Charter; 3 Title I Eligible; 1 School-wide Title I
Students: 1,809   (50.8% male; 49.1% female)
   Individual Education Program: 265 (14.6%);
   English Language Learner: 27 (1.5%); Migrant: 0 (0.0%)
   Eligible for Free Lunch Program: 337 (18.6%)
   Eligible for Reduced-Price Lunch Program: 119 (6.6%)
Teachers: 135.2 (13.4 to 1)
Librarians/Media Specialists: 2.1 (861.4 to 1)
Guidance Counselors: 7.6 (238.0 to 1)
Current Spending: ($ per student per year):
   Total: $7,864; Instruction: $5,063; Support Services: $2,560
Enrollment, Drop-out Rates and Diploma Recipients by Race/Ethnicity

Category	Total	White	Black	Asian	AIAN	Hisp.
Enrollment (%)	100.0	93.3	2.4	2.0	0.4	1.9
Drop-out Rate (%)	4.9	4.7	16.7	11.1	0.0	0.0
H.S. Diplomas (#)	122	n/a	n/a	n/a	n/a	n/a

Sullivan County

Claremont SD
165 Broad St • Claremont, NH 03743-2624
(603) 543-4200 • http://www.sau6.k12.nh.us/claremont/claremont.htm
Grade Span: PK-12; **Agency Type:** 2
Schools: 5

3 Primary; 1 Middle; 1 High; 0 Other Level
5 Regular; 0 Special Education; 0 Vocational; 0 Alternative
0 Magnet; 0 Charter; 3 Title I Eligible; 1 School-wide Title I
Students: 2,062   (49.7% male; 50.2% female)
  Individual Education Program: 330 (16.0%);
  English Language Learner: 14 (0.7%); Migrant: 2 (0.1%)
  Eligible for Free Lunch Program: 365 (17.7%)
  Eligible for Reduced-Price Lunch Program: 167 (8.1%)
Teachers: 161.1 (12.8 to 1)
Librarians/Media Specialists: 2.9 (711.0 to 1)
Guidance Counselors: 9.8 (210.4 to 1)
Current Spending: ($ per student per year):
  Total: $9,853; Instruction: $6,839; Support Services: $2,790
Enrollment, Drop-out Rates and Diploma Recipients by Race/Ethnicity

Category	Total	White	Black	Asian	AIAN	Hisp.
Enrollment (%)	100.0	97.4	1.2	1.1	0.0	0.3
Drop-out Rate (%)	5.8	5.8	n/a	0.0	n/a	n/a
H.S. Diplomas (#)	128	n/a	n/a	n/a	n/a	n/a

Fall Mountain Regional SD

E St • Charlestown, NH 03603-0600
Mailing Address: PO Box 600 • Charlestown, NH 03603-0600
(603) 826-7756 • http://www.fall-mountain.k12.nh.us/
Grade Span: PK-12; **Agency Type:** 2
Schools: 12
  9 Primary; 2 Middle; 1 High; 0 Other Level
  12 Regular; 0 Special Education; 0 Vocational; 0 Alternative
  0 Magnet; 0 Charter; 5 Title I Eligible; 0 School-wide Title I
Students: 2,072   (50.0% male; 49.9% female)
  Individual Education Program: 303 (14.6%);
  English Language Learner: 0 (0.0%); Migrant: 2 (0.1%)
  Eligible for Free Lunch Program: 267 (12.9%)
  Eligible for Reduced-Price Lunch Program: 159 (7.7%)
Teachers: 156.4 (13.2 to 1)
Librarians/Media Specialists: 2.0 (1,036.0 to 1)
Guidance Counselors: 5.9 (351.2 to 1)
Current Spending: ($ per student per year):
  Total: $9,161; Instruction: $6,062; Support Services: $2,794
Enrollment, Drop-out Rates and Diploma Recipients by Race/Ethnicity

Category	Total	White	Black	Asian	AIAN	Hisp.
Enrollment (%)	100.0	99.3	0.4	0.1	0.0	0.1
Drop-out Rate (%)	2.3	2.3	0.0	n/a	n/a	n/a
H.S. Diplomas (#)	133	n/a	n/a	n/a	n/a	n/a

Number of Schools

Rank	Number	District Name	City
1	22	Manchester SD	Manchester
2	18	Nashua SD	Nashua
3	12	Contoocook Valley SD	Peterborough
3	12	Fall Mountain Regional SD	Charlestown
5	11	Concord SD	Concord
6	10	Rochester SD	Rochester
7	9	Monadnock Regional SD	East Swanzey
8	8	Governor Wentworth Reg SD	Wolfeboro
8	8	Salem SD	Salem
10	7	Derry SD	Derry
10	7	Keene SD	Keene
10	7	Lebanon SD	Lebanon
10	7	Merrimack Valley SD	Penacook
10	7	Newfound Area SD	Bristol
10	7	Timberlane Regional SD	Plaistow
16	6	Berlin SD	Berlin
16	6	Hudson SD	Hudson
16	6	Kearsarge Regional SD	New London
16	6	Londonderry SD	Londonderry
16	6	Portsmouth SD	Portsmouth
21	5	Claremont SD	Claremont
21	5	Conway SD	North Conway
21	5	Dover SD	Dover
21	5	Laconia SD	Laconia
21	5	Merrimack SD	Merrimack
21	5	Winnisquam Regional SD	Tilton
27	4	Bedford SD	Bedford
27	4	Goffstown SD	Goffstown
27	4	Jaffrey-Rindge Coop SD	Jaffrey
27	4	Milford SD	Milford
27	4	Oyster River Coop SD	Durham
27	4	Pembroke SD	Pembroke
27	4	Sanborn Regional SD	Kingston
27	4	Shaker Regional SD	Belmont
27	4	Somersworth SD	Somersworth
27	4	Windham SD	Windham
37	3	Amherst SD	Amherst
37	3	Bow SD	Bow
37	3	Litchfield SD	Litchfield
37	3	Pelham SD	Windham
37	3	Raymond SD	Raymond
42	2	Exeter Region Cooperative SD	Exeter
43	1	Pinkerton Academy SD	Derry

Number of Students

Rank	Number	District Name	City
1	17,655	Manchester SD	Manchester
2	13,357	Nashua SD	Nashua
3	5,621	Londonderry SD	Londonderry
4	5,473	Concord SD	Concord
5	5,325	Salem SD	Salem
6	4,809	Rochester SD	Rochester
7	4,745	Merrimack SD	Merrimack
8	4,489	Timberlane Regional SD	Plaistow
9	4,228	Derry SD	Derry
10	4,144	Hudson SD	Hudson
11	4,090	Dover SD	Dover
12	3,880	Keene SD	Keene
13	3,378	Pinkerton Academy SD	Derry
14	3,146	Contoocook Valley SD	Peterborough
15	3,085	Goffstown SD	Goffstown
16	2,937	Exeter Region Cooperative SD	Exeter
17	2,904	Governor Wentworth Reg SD	Wolfeboro
18	2,863	Bedford SD	Bedford
19	2,771	Merrimack Valley SD	Penacook
20	2,696	Portsmouth SD	Portsmouth
21	2,514	Milford SD	Milford
22	2,483	Monadnock Regional SD	East Swanzey
23	2,476	Laconia SD	Laconia
24	2,174	Oyster River Coop SD	Durham
25	2,168	Conway SD	North Conway
26	2,099	Kearsarge Regional SD	New London
27	2,072	Fall Mountain Regional SD	Charlestown
28	2,062	Claremont SD	Claremont
29	2,047	Pelham SD	Windham
30	1,997	Lebanon SD	Lebanon
31	1,863	Pembroke SD	Pembroke
32	1,811	Bow SD	Bow
33	1,809	Somersworth SD	Somersworth
34	1,802	Sanborn Regional SD	Kingston
35	1,786	Winnisquam Regional SD	Tilton
36	1,695	Amherst SD	Amherst
37	1,658	Jaffrey-Rindge Coop SD	Jaffrey
38	1,657	Litchfield SD	Litchfield
39	1,615	Berlin SD	Berlin
40	1,598	Raymond SD	Raymond
41	1,553	Windham SD	Windham
42	1,535	Shaker Regional SD	Belmont
43	1,532	Newfound Area SD	Bristol

Female Students

Rank	Percent	District Name	City
1	50.7	Pelham SD	Windham
2	50.6	Goffstown SD	Goffstown
3	50.6	Portsmouth SD	Portsmouth
4	50.2	Claremont SD	Claremont
5	50.1	Lebanon SD	Lebanon
6	49.9	Fall Mountain Regional SD	Charlestown
7	49.7	Pinkerton Academy SD	Derry
8	49.4	Monadnock Regional SD	East Swanzey
9	49.4	Exeter Region Cooperative SD	Exeter
10	49.3	Timberlane Regional SD	Plaistow
11	49.1	Somersworth SD	Somersworth
12	49.0	Concord SD	Concord
13	48.9	Governor Wentworth Reg SD	Wolfeboro
14	48.9	Dover SD	Dover
15	48.8	Winnisquam Regional SD	Tilton
16	48.7	Amherst SD	Amherst
17	48.7	Sanborn Regional SD	Kingston
18	48.6	Raymond SD	Raymond
19	48.6	Manchester SD	Manchester
20	48.6	Hudson SD	Hudson
21	48.5	Keene SD	Keene
22	48.4	Pembroke SD	Pembroke
23	48.3	Salem SD	Salem
24	48.2	Derry SD	Derry
25	48.2	Milford SD	Milford
26	48.2	Merrimack Valley SD	Penacook
27	48.1	Contoocook Valley SD	Peterborough
28	48.1	Nashua SD	Nashua
29	48.0	Conway SD	North Conway
30	47.9	Merrimack SD	Merrimack
31	47.9	Windham SD	Windham
32	47.7	Oyster River Coop SD	Durham
33	47.7	Londonderry SD	Londonderry
34	47.6	Laconia SD	Laconia
35	47.5	Jaffrey-Rindge Coop SD	Jaffrey
36	47.5	Bedford SD	Bedford
37	47.4	Bow SD	Bow
38	47.1	Rochester SD	Rochester
39	47.1	Shaker Regional SD	Belmont
40	46.8	Kearsarge Regional SD	New London
41	46.4	Newfound Area SD	Bristol
42	45.5	Litchfield SD	Litchfield
43	44.7	Berlin SD	Berlin

Number of Teachers

Rank	Number	District Name	City
1	1,160	Manchester SD	Manchester
2	866	Nashua SD	Nashua
3	389	Londonderry SD	Londonderry
4	342	Rochester SD	Rochester
5	342	Merrimack SD	Merrimack
6	339	Concord SD	Concord
7	333	Timberlane Regional SD	Plaistow
8	313	Salem SD	Salem
9	305	Keene SD	Keene
10	287	Derry SD	Derry
11	266	Dover SD	Dover
12	253	Hudson SD	Hudson
13	248	Contoocook Valley SD	Peterborough
14	240	Pinkerton Academy SD	Derry
15	227	Portsmouth SD	Portsmouth
16	211	Exeter Region Cooperative SD	Exeter
17	203	Governor Wentworth Reg SD	Wolfeboro
18	203	Laconia SD	Laconia
19	194	Goffstown SD	Goffstown
20	190	Merrimack Valley SD	Penacook
21	184	Bedford SD	Bedford
22	181	Milford SD	Milford
23	176	Lebanon SD	Lebanon
24	174	Monadnock Regional SD	East Swanzey
25	169	Conway SD	North Conway
26	163	Oyster River Coop SD	Durham
27	163	Kearsarge Regional SD	New London
28	161	Claremont SD	Claremont
29	156	Fall Mountain Regional SD	Charlestown
30	148	Sanborn Regional SD	Kingston
31	136	Winnisquam Regional SD	Tilton
32	135	Pelham SD	Windham
32	135	Somersworth SD	Somersworth
34	134	Jaffrey-Rindge Coop SD	Jaffrey
35	134	Pembroke SD	Pembroke
36	128	Bow SD	Bow
37	128	Newfound Area SD	Bristol
37	128	Raymond SD	Raymond
39	124	Amherst SD	Amherst
40	115	Windham SD	Windham
41	112	Berlin SD	Berlin
42	109	Litchfield SD	Litchfield
43	105	Shaker Regional SD	Belmont

Male Students

Rank	Percent	District Name	City
1	55.2	Berlin SD	Berlin
2	54.4	Litchfield SD	Litchfield
3	53.5	Newfound Area SD	Bristol
4	53.1	Kearsarge Regional SD	New London
5	52.8	Shaker Regional SD	Belmont
6	52.8	Rochester SD	Rochester
7	52.5	Bow SD	Bow
8	52.4	Bedford SD	Bedford
9	52.4	Jaffrey-Rindge Coop SD	Jaffrey
10	52.3	Laconia SD	Laconia
11	52.2	Londonderry SD	Londonderry
12	52.2	Oyster River Coop SD	Durham
13	52.0	Windham SD	Windham
14	52.0	Merrimack SD	Merrimack
15	51.9	Conway SD	North Conway
16	51.8	Nashua SD	Nashua
17	51.8	Contoocook Valley SD	Peterborough
18	51.8	Merrimack Valley SD	Penacook
19	51.7	Milford SD	Milford
20	51.7	Derry SD	Derry
21	51.6	Salem SD	Salem
22	51.5	Pembroke SD	Pembroke
23	51.4	Keene SD	Keene
24	51.3	Hudson SD	Hudson
25	51.3	Manchester SD	Manchester
26	51.3	Raymond SD	Raymond
27	51.2	Sanborn Regional SD	Kingston
28	51.2	Amherst SD	Amherst
29	51.1	Winnisquam Regional SD	Tilton
30	51.0	Dover SD	Dover
31	51.0	Governor Wentworth Reg SD	Wolfeboro
32	50.9	Concord SD	Concord
33	50.8	Somersworth SD	Somersworth
34	50.6	Timberlane Regional SD	Plaistow
35	50.5	Exeter Region Cooperative SD	Exeter
36	50.5	Monadnock Regional SD	East Swanzey
37	50.2	Pinkerton Academy SD	Derry
38	50.0	Fall Mountain Regional SD	Charlestown
39	49.8	Lebanon SD	Lebanon
40	49.7	Claremont SD	Claremont
41	49.3	Portsmouth SD	Portsmouth
42	49.3	Goffstown SD	Goffstown
43	49.2	Pelham SD	Windham

Individual Education Program Students

Rank	Percent	District Name	City
1	21.0	Rochester SD	Rochester
2	18.2	Keene SD	Keene
3	17.2	Jaffrey-Rindge Coop SD	Jaffrey
4	16.9	Pembroke SD	Pembroke
5	16.8	Contoocook Valley SD	Peterborough
5	16.8	Laconia SD	Laconia
7	16.4	Oyster River Coop SD	Durham
8	16.2	Pelham SD	Windham
9	16.0	Claremont SD	Claremont
9	16.0	Milford SD	Milford
9	16.0	Timberlane Regional SD	Plaistow
12	15.9	Sanborn Regional SD	Kingston
13	15.7	Merrimack SD	Merrimack
14	15.6	Winnisquam Regional SD	Tilton
15	15.3	Manchester SD	Manchester
15	15.3	Newfound Area SD	Bristol
15	15.3	Raymond SD	Raymond
18	15.2	Kearsarge Regional SD	New London
19	14.7	Concord SD	Concord
19	14.7	Derry SD	Derry
19	14.7	Exeter Region Cooperative SD	Exeter
19	14.7	Londonderry SD	Londonderry
23	14.6	Fall Mountain Regional SD	Charlestown
23	14.6	Lebanon SD	Lebanon
23	14.6	Portsmouth SD	Portsmouth
23	14.6	Somersworth SD	Somersworth
27	14.5	Nashua SD	Nashua
28	14.4	Litchfield SD	Litchfield
29	14.2	Merrimack Valley SD	Penacook
30	13.7	Conway SD	North Conway
31	13.4	Dover SD	Dover
32	13.3	Goffstown SD	Goffstown
33	13.2	Hudson SD	Hudson
34	13.0	Monadnock Regional SD	East Swanzey
35	12.9	Salem SD	Salem
36	12.8	Governor Wentworth Reg SD	Wolfeboro
37	12.3	Shaker Regional SD	Belmont
38	11.6	Windham SD	Windham
39	11.2	Bedford SD	Bedford
40	11.1	Amherst SD	Amherst
41	7.2	Berlin SD	Berlin
42	6.2	Bow SD	Bow
43	0.0	Pinkerton Academy SD	Derry

English Language Learner Students

Rank	Percent	District Name	City
1	7.3	Manchester SD	Manchester
2	3.9	Nashua SD	Nashua
3	2.9	Laconia SD	Laconia
4	2.2	Portsmouth SD	Portsmouth
5	1.7	Concord SD	Concord
6	1.5	Somersworth SD	Somersworth
7	1.4	Dover SD	Dover
8	1.1	Hudson SD	Hudson
8	1.1	Oyster River Coop SD	Durham
10	1.0	Goffstown SD	Goffstown
10	1.0	Lebanon SD	Lebanon
12	0.9	Rochester SD	Rochester
13	0.8	Milford SD	Milford
14	0.7	Claremont SD	Claremont
15	0.6	Pelham SD	Windham
16	0.5	Keene SD	Keene
16	0.5	Litchfield SD	Litchfield
16	0.5	Windham SD	Windham
19	0.4	Derry SD	Derry
20	0.3	Conway SD	North Conway
20	0.3	Kearsarge Regional SD	New London
20	0.3	Merrimack Valley SD	Penacook
20	0.3	Newfound Area SD	Bristol
20	0.3	Salem SD	Salem
25	0.2	Amherst SD	Amherst
25	0.2	Bedford SD	Bedford
25	0.2	Bow SD	Bow
25	0.2	Governor Wentworth Reg SD	Wolfeboro
25	0.2	Timberlane Regional SD	Plaistow
30	0.1	Contoocook Valley SD	Peterborough
30	0.1	Exeter Region Cooperative SD	Exeter
30	0.1	Londonderry SD	Londonderry
30	0.1	Merrimack SD	Merrimack
30	0.1	Pembroke SD	Pembroke
30	0.1	Raymond SD	Raymond
30	0.1	Shaker Regional SD	Belmont
30	0.1	Winnisquam Regional SD	Tilton
38	0.0	Monadnock Regional SD	East Swanzey
39	0.0	Berlin SD	Berlin
39	0.0	Fall Mountain Regional SD	Charlestown
39	0.0	Jaffrey-Rindge Coop SD	Jaffrey
39	0.0	Pinkerton Academy SD	Derry
39	0.0	Sanborn Regional SD	Kingston

Migrant Students

Rank	Percent	District Name	City
1	0.9	Manchester SD	Manchester
2	0.1	Claremont SD	Claremont
2	0.1	Fall Mountain Regional SD	Charlestown
2	0.1	Nashua SD	Nashua
2	0.1	Rochester SD	Rochester
6	0.0	Amherst SD	Amherst
6	0.0	Bedford SD	Bedford
6	0.0	Berlin SD	Berlin
6	0.0	Bow SD	Bow
6	0.0	Concord SD	Concord
6	0.0	Contoocook Valley SD	Peterborough
6	0.0	Conway SD	North Conway
6	0.0	Derry SD	Derry
6	0.0	Dover SD	Dover
6	0.0	Exeter Region Cooperative SD	Exeter
6	0.0	Goffstown SD	Goffstown
6	0.0	Governor Wentworth Reg SD	Wolfeboro
6	0.0	Hudson SD	Hudson
6	0.0	Jaffrey-Rindge Coop SD	Jaffrey
6	0.0	Kearsarge Regional SD	New London
6	0.0	Keene SD	Keene
6	0.0	Laconia SD	Laconia
6	0.0	Lebanon SD	Lebanon
6	0.0	Litchfield SD	Litchfield
6	0.0	Londonderry SD	Londonderry
6	0.0	Merrimack SD	Merrimack
6	0.0	Merrimack Valley SD	Penacook
6	0.0	Milford SD	Milford
6	0.0	Monadnock Regional SD	East Swanzey
6	0.0	Newfound Area SD	Bristol
6	0.0	Oyster River Coop SD	Durham
6	0.0	Pelham SD	Windham
6	0.0	Pembroke SD	Pembroke
6	0.0	Pinkerton Academy SD	Derry
6	0.0	Portsmouth SD	Portsmouth
6	0.0	Raymond SD	Raymond
6	0.0	Salem SD	Salem
6	0.0	Sanborn Regional SD	Kingston
6	0.0	Shaker Regional SD	Belmont
6	0.0	Somersworth SD	Somersworth
6	0.0	Timberlane Regional SD	Plaistow
6	0.0	Windham SD	Windham
6	0.0	Winnisquam Regional SD	Tilton

Students Eligible for Free Lunch

Rank	Percent	District Name	City
1	26.4	Berlin SD	Berlin
2	22.3	Laconia SD	Laconia
3	21.1	Rochester SD	Rochester
4	20.3	Manchester SD	Manchester
5	18.6	Somersworth SD	Somersworth
6	18.4	Nashua SD	Nashua
7	17.7	Claremont SD	Claremont
8	16.5	Conway SD	North Conway
9	16.3	Newfound Area SD	Bristol
10	15.7	Winnisquam Regional SD	Tilton
11	14.4	Dover SD	Dover
11	14.4	Governor Wentworth Reg SD	Wolfeboro
13	13.6	Concord SD	Concord
14	13.2	Shaker Regional SD	Belmont
15	13.1	Portsmouth SD	Portsmouth
16	12.9	Fall Mountain Regional SD	Charlestown
17	12.4	Raymond SD	Raymond
18	11.8	Keene SD	Keene
18	11.8	Monadnock Regional SD	East Swanzey
20	9.9	Milford SD	Milford
21	9.8	Contoocook Valley SD	Peterborough
22	9.5	Derry SD	Derry
22	9.5	Jaffrey-Rindge Coop SD	Jaffrey
24	8.6	Lebanon SD	Lebanon
24	8.6	Merrimack Valley SD	Penacook
26	6.8	Kearsarge Regional SD	New London
27	6.4	Pembroke SD	Pembroke
28	4.8	Salem SD	Salem
29	4.7	Hudson SD	Hudson
29	4.7	Pinkerton Academy SD	Derry
31	4.3	Goffstown SD	Goffstown
32	4.0	Litchfield SD	Litchfield
32	4.0	Oyster River Coop SD	Durham
34	3.9	Pelham SD	Windham
34	3.9	Sanborn Regional SD	Kingston
36	3.3	Timberlane Regional SD	Plaistow
37	3.1	Exeter Region Cooperative SD	Exeter
38	2.5	Londonderry SD	Londonderry
39	2.4	Amherst SD	Amherst
39	2.4	Merrimack SD	Merrimack
41	1.7	Bow SD	Bow
42	1.5	Windham SD	Windham
43	1.0	Bedford SD	Bedford

Students Eligible for Reduced-Price Lunch

Rank	Percent	District Name	City
1	10.1	Governor Wentworth Reg SD	Wolfeboro
2	9.1	Laconia SD	Laconia
3	9.0	Newfound Area SD	Bristol
4	8.4	Monadnock Regional SD	East Swanzey
5	8.1	Claremont SD	Claremont
6	7.9	Raymond SD	Raymond
7	7.7	Fall Mountain Regional SD	Charlestown
8	7.5	Rochester SD	Rochester
9	7.2	Berlin SD	Berlin
10	6.8	Jaffrey-Rindge Coop SD	Jaffrey
11	6.6	Manchester SD	Manchester
11	6.6	Somersworth SD	Somersworth
11	6.6	Winnisquam Regional SD	Tilton
14	6.4	Keene SD	Keene
15	6.3	Shaker Regional SD	Belmont
16	6.2	Milford SD	Milford
16	6.2	Nashua SD	Nashua
18	6.1	Conway SD	North Conway
19	5.8	Merrimack Valley SD	Penacook
20	5.7	Derry SD	Derry
20	5.7	Dover SD	Dover
22	5.5	Contoocook Valley SD	Peterborough
23	5.4	Portsmouth SD	Portsmouth
24	4.7	Concord SD	Concord
25	4.2	Kearsarge Regional SD	New London
26	3.5	Pembroke SD	Pembroke
27	3.0	Lebanon SD	Lebanon
27	3.0	Pelham SD	Windham
29	2.8	Sanborn Regional SD	Kingston
30	2.5	Salem SD	Salem
31	2.4	Pinkerton Academy SD	Derry
32	2.3	Goffstown SD	Goffstown
33	2.0	Timberlane Regional SD	Plaistow
34	1.9	Merrimack SD	Merrimack
35	1.5	Oyster River Coop SD	Durham
36	1.4	Amherst SD	Amherst
36	1.4	Hudson SD	Hudson
36	1.4	Litchfield SD	Litchfield
39	1.3	Exeter Region Cooperative SD	Exeter
40	1.1	Londonderry SD	Londonderry
41	1.0	Windham SD	Windham
42	0.8	Bedford SD	Bedford
43	0.5	Bow SD	Bow

Student/Teacher Ratio

Rank	Ratio	District Name	City
1	17.0	Salem SD	Salem
2	16.4	Hudson SD	Hudson
3	16.1	Concord SD	Concord
4	15.8	Goffstown SD	Goffstown
5	15.5	Bedford SD	Bedford
6	15.4	Nashua SD	Nashua
7	15.3	Dover SD	Dover
8	15.2	Litchfield SD	Litchfield
8	15.2	Manchester SD	Manchester
10	15.1	Pelham SD	Windham
11	14.7	Derry SD	Derry
12	14.6	Merrimack Valley SD	Penacook
12	14.6	Shaker Regional SD	Belmont
14	14.4	Berlin SD	Berlin
14	14.4	Londonderry SD	Londonderry
16	14.3	Governor Wentworth Reg SD	Wolfeboro
16	14.3	Monadnock Regional SD	East Swanzey
18	14.1	Bow SD	Bow
18	14.1	Pinkerton Academy SD	Derry
20	14.0	Rochester SD	Rochester
21	13.9	Exeter Region Cooperative SD	Exeter
21	13.9	Milford SD	Milford
21	13.9	Pembroke SD	Pembroke
24	13.8	Merrimack SD	Merrimack
25	13.6	Amherst SD	Amherst
26	13.5	Timberlane Regional SD	Plaistow
26	13.5	Windham SD	Windham
28	13.4	Somersworth SD	Somersworth
29	13.3	Oyster River Coop SD	Durham
30	13.2	Fall Mountain Regional SD	Charlestown
31	13.1	Winnisquam Regional SD	Tilton
32	12.9	Kearsarge Regional SD	New London
33	12.8	Claremont SD	Claremont
33	12.8	Conway SD	North Conway
35	12.7	Contoocook Valley SD	Peterborough
35	12.7	Keene SD	Keene
37	12.5	Raymond SD	Raymond
38	12.3	Jaffrey-Rindge Coop SD	Jaffrey
39	12.2	Laconia SD	Laconia
40	12.1	Sanborn Regional SD	Kingston
41	12.0	Newfound Area SD	Bristol
42	11.9	Portsmouth SD	Portsmouth
43	11.3	Lebanon SD	Lebanon

Student/Librarian Ratio

Rank	Ratio	District Name	City
1	3,523.3	Derry SD	Derry
2	2,771.0	Merrimack Valley SD	Penacook
3	1,863.0	Pembroke SD	Pembroke
4	1,725.6	Windham SD	Windham
5	1,689.0	Pinkerton Academy SD	Derry
6	1,658.3	Rochester SD	Rochester
7	1,655.3	Monadnock Regional SD	East Swanzey
8	1,468.5	Exeter Region Cooperative SD	Exeter
9	1,381.3	Hudson SD	Hudson
10	1,141.1	Conway SD	North Conway
11	1,036.0	Fall Mountain Regional SD	Charlestown
12	1,032.6	Concord SD	Concord
13	975.9	Timberlane Regional SD	Plaistow
14	964.1	Goffstown SD	Goffstown
15	962.9	Portsmouth SD	Portsmouth
16	927.6	Nashua SD	Nashua
17	902.5	Salem SD	Salem
18	893.0	Winnisquam Regional SD	Tilton
19	861.4	Somersworth SD	Somersworth
20	847.5	Amherst SD	Amherst
21	818.0	Dover SD	Dover
22	799.0	Raymond SD	Raymond
23	790.8	Merrimack SD	Merrimack
24	732.6	Manchester SD	Manchester
25	730.0	Londonderry SD	Londonderry
26	715.8	Bedford SD	Bedford
27	711.0	Claremont SD	Claremont
28	682.3	Pelham SD	Windham
29	675.3	Governor Wentworth Reg SD	Wolfeboro
30	669.0	Keene SD	Keene
31	603.7	Bow SD	Bow
32	552.3	Litchfield SD	Litchfield
33	538.3	Berlin SD	Berlin
34	511.7	Shaker Regional SD	Belmont
35	510.7	Newfound Area SD	Bristol
36	502.8	Milford SD	Milford
37	495.2	Laconia SD	Laconia
38	488.1	Kearsarge Regional SD	New London
39	484.0	Contoocook Valley SD	Peterborough
40	450.5	Sanborn Regional SD	Kingston
41	434.8	Oyster River Coop SD	Durham

Additional entry (top of third column, Students Eligible for Free Lunch):

43	0.5	Bow SD	Bow

| 42 | 414.5 | Jaffrey-Rindge Coop SD | Jaffrey |
| 43 | 289.4 | Lebanon SD | Lebanon |

41	7,011	Berlin SD	Berlin
42	6,973	Manchester SD	Manchester
43	n/a	Pinkerton Academy SD	Derry

40	n/a	Amherst SD	Amherst
40	n/a	Bedford SD	Bedford
40	n/a	Derry SD	Derry
40	n/a	Windham SD	Windham

Student/Counselor Ratio

Rank	Ratio	District Name	City
1	388.3	Windham SD	Windham
2	361.0	Nashua SD	Nashua
3	351.2	Fall Mountain Regional SD	Charlestown
4	336.8	Bedford SD	Bedford
5	331.4	Litchfield SD	Litchfield
6	325.7	Manchester SD	Manchester
7	323.0	Berlin SD	Berlin
8	318.8	Hudson SD	Hudson
9	318.5	Merrimack Valley SD	Penacook
10	314.3	Milford SD	Milford
11	312.2	Bow SD	Bow
12	308.2	Amherst SD	Amherst
13	307.5	Concord SD	Concord
14	305.4	Contoocook Valley SD	Peterborough
15	302.5	Governor Wentworth Reg SD	Wolfeboro
16	295.7	Derry SD	Derry
17	288.3	Londonderry SD	Londonderry
18	285.9	Jaffrey-Rindge Coop SD	Jaffrey
19	285.6	Goffstown SD	Goffstown
20	284.3	Shaker Regional SD	Belmont
21	280.1	Dover SD	Dover
22	271.0	Conway SD	North Conway
23	266.3	Raymond SD	Raymond
24	266.1	Pembroke SD	Pembroke
25	264.1	Timberlane Regional SD	Plaistow
26	262.4	Pelham SD	Windham
27	259.9	Rochester SD	Rochester
28	256.0	Kearsarge Regional SD	New London
29	249.7	Merrimack SD	Merrimack
30	248.3	Monadnock Regional SD	East Swanzey
31	244.7	Winnisquam Regional SD	Tilton
32	238.0	Somersworth SD	Somersworth
33	225.3	Sanborn Regional SD	Kingston
34	225.2	Pinkerton Academy SD	Derry
35	218.9	Newfound Area SD	Bristol
36	210.4	Claremont SD	Claremont
37	210.2	Lebanon SD	Lebanon
38	209.8	Exeter Region Cooperative SD	Exeter
39	207.0	Oyster River Coop SD	Durham
40	194.0	Keene SD	Keene
41	179.7	Portsmouth SD	Portsmouth
42	165.1	Laconia SD	Laconia
43	152.1	Salem SD	Salem

Number of Diploma Recipients

Rank	Number	District Name	City
1	1,180	Manchester SD	Manchester
2	655	Nashua SD	Nashua
3	614	Pinkerton Academy SD	Derry
4	411	Salem SD	Salem
5	402	Hudson SD	Hudson
6	399	Concord SD	Concord
7	371	Londonderry SD	Londonderry
8	333	Keene SD	Keene
9	319	Exeter Region Cooperative SD	Exeter
10	316	Merrimack SD	Merrimack
11	306	Rochester SD	Rochester
12	292	Dover SD	Dover
13	241	Timberlane Regional SD	Plaistow
14	233	Contoocook Valley SD	Peterborough
15	229	Portsmouth SD	Portsmouth
16	218	Governor Wentworth Reg SD	Wolfeboro
17	180	Goffstown SD	Goffstown
18	175	Conway SD	North Conway
19	170	Monadnock Regional SD	East Swanzey
20	168	Lebanon SD	Lebanon
21	165	Milford SD	Milford
22	161	Pembroke SD	Pembroke
23	160	Merrimack Valley SD	Penacook
23	160	Oyster River Coop SD	Durham
25	154	Laconia SD	Laconia
26	133	Fall Mountain Regional SD	Charlestown
27	129	Kearsarge Regional SD	New London
28	128	Claremont SD	Claremont
29	126	Raymond SD	Raymond
29	126	Sanborn Regional SD	Kingston
31	122	Somersworth SD	Somersworth
32	121	Jaffrey-Rindge Coop SD	Jaffrey
33	110	Bow SD	Bow
34	104	Pelham SD	Windham
35	102	Berlin SD	Berlin
36	99	Winnisquam Regional SD	Tilton
37	91	Newfound Area SD	Bristol
38	72	Shaker Regional SD	Belmont
39	0	Litchfield SD	Litchfield
40	n/a	Amherst SD	Amherst
40	n/a	Bedford SD	Bedford
40	n/a	Derry SD	Derry
40	n/a	Windham SD	Windham

Current Spending per Student in FY2003

Rank	Dollars	District Name	City
1	11,725	Portsmouth SD	Portsmouth
2	10,835	Lebanon SD	Lebanon
3	10,258	Oyster River Coop SD	Durham
4	10,201	Kearsarge Regional SD	New London
5	10,145	Keene SD	Keene
6	9,853	Claremont SD	Claremont
7	9,755	Monadnock Regional SD	East Swanzey
8	9,484	Contoocook Valley SD	Peterborough
9	9,405	Exeter Region Cooperative SD	Exeter
10	9,297	Amherst SD	Amherst
11	9,276	Conway SD	North Conway
12	9,254	Raymond SD	Raymond
13	9,227	Newfound Area SD	Bristol
14	9,211	Sanborn Regional SD	Kingston
15	9,185	Windham SD	Windham
16	9,161	Fall Mountain Regional SD	Charlestown
17	9,108	Governor Wentworth Reg SD	Wolfeboro
18	9,073	Jaffrey-Rindge Coop SD	Jaffrey
19	8,990	Concord SD	Concord
20	8,877	Milford SD	Milford
21	8,843	Bedford SD	Bedford
22	8,580	Merrimack SD	Merrimack
23	8,577	Laconia SD	Laconia
24	8,318	Shaker Regional SD	Belmont
25	8,295	Dover SD	Dover
26	8,264	Timberlane Regional SD	Plaistow
27	8,246	Bow SD	Bow
28	8,168	Winnisquam Regional SD	Tilton
29	8,040	Pelham SD	Windham
30	7,961	Londonderry SD	Londonderry
31	7,934	Pembroke SD	Pembroke
32	7,864	Somersworth SD	Somersworth
33	7,830	Merrimack Valley SD	Penacook
34	7,759	Rochester SD	Rochester
35	7,753	Derry SD	Derry
36	7,491	Hudson SD	Hudson
37	7,338	Litchfield SD	Litchfield
38	7,324	Nashua SD	Nashua
39	7,177	Salem SD	Salem
40	7,135	Goffstown SD	Goffstown

High School Drop-out Rate

Rank	Percent	District Name	City
1	7.7	Rochester SD	Rochester
2	6.8	Manchester SD	Manchester
3	6.0	Pembroke SD	Pembroke
4	5.9	Conway SD	North Conway
5	5.8	Claremont SD	Claremont
5	5.8	Raymond SD	Raymond
7	5.3	Winnisquam Regional SD	Tilton
8	5.1	Merrimack Valley SD	Penacook
9	4.9	Dover SD	Dover
9	4.9	Somersworth SD	Somersworth
11	4.8	Lebanon SD	Lebanon
12	4.6	Nashua SD	Nashua
13	4.5	Concord SD	Concord
14	4.3	Berlin SD	Berlin
14	4.3	Timberlane Regional SD	Plaistow
16	4.1	Pinkerton Academy SD	Derry
17	3.9	Monadnock Regional SD	East Swanzey
18	3.8	Newfound Area SD	Bristol
19	3.6	Laconia SD	Laconia
19	3.6	Shaker Regional SD	Belmont
21	3.4	Pelham SD	Windham
22	3.3	Hudson SD	Hudson
23	3.2	Milford SD	Milford
24	3.1	Governor Wentworth Reg SD	Wolfeboro
25	2.7	Contoocook Valley SD	Peterborough
25	2.7	Exeter Region Cooperative SD	Exeter
27	2.6	Londonderry SD	Londonderry
28	2.5	Kearsarge Regional SD	New London
28	2.5	Sanborn Regional SD	Kingston
30	2.4	Goffstown SD	Goffstown
30	2.4	Keene SD	Keene
32	2.3	Fall Mountain Regional SD	Charlestown
33	1.9	Bow SD	Bow
33	1.9	Merrimack SD	Merrimack
35	1.8	Portsmouth SD	Portsmouth
36	1.4	Jaffrey-Rindge Coop SD	Jaffrey
36	1.4	Salem SD	Salem
38	0.9	Litchfield SD	Litchfield
39	0.7	Oyster River Coop SD	Durham

New Jersey

New Jersey Public School Educational Profile

Category	Value	Category	Value
Schools (2003-2004)	2,467	**Diploma Recipients** (2002-2003)	77,831
Instructional Level		White, Non-Hispanic	50,429
Primary	1,540	Black, Non-Hispanic	11,944
Middle	437	Asian/Pacific Islander	5,632
High	384	American Indian/Alaskan Native	133
Other Level	106	Hispanic	9,693
Curriculum		**High School Drop-out Rate** (%) (2001-2002)	2.5
Regular	2,311	White, Non-Hispanic	1.5
Special Education	83	Black, Non-Hispanic	4.9
Vocational	55	Asian/Pacific Islander	0.9
Alternative	18	American Indian/Alaskan Native	2.2
Type		Hispanic	4.7
Magnet	3	**Staff** (2003-2004)	
Charter	51	Teachers	109,076.5
Title I Eligible	1,366	Average Salary ($)	53,663
School-wide Title I	256	Librarians/Media Specialists	1,871.2
Students (2003-2004)	1,451,180	Guidance Counselors	3,672.7
Gender (%)		**Ratios** (2003-2004)	
Male	51.4	Student/Teacher Ratio	13.3 to 1
Female	48.6	Student/Librarian Ratio	775.5 to 1
Race/Ethnicity (%)		Student/Counselor Ratio	395.1 to 1
White, Non-Hispanic	57.9	**College Entrance Exam Scores** (2005)	
Black, Non-Hispanic	17.7	Scholastic Aptitude Test (SAT)	
Asian/Pacific Islander	7.0	Participation Rate (%)	86
American Indian/Alaskan Native	0.2	Mean SAT Reasoning Test Verbal Score	503
Hispanic	17.2	Mean SAT Reasoning Test Math Score	517
Classification (%)		American College Testing Program (ACT)	
Individual Education Program (IEP)	15.4	Participation Rate (%)	6
Migrant (2002-2003)	0.1	Average Composite Score	21.3
English Language Learner (ELL)	4.0	Average English Score	20.9
Eligible for Free Lunch Program	20.6	Average Math Score	21.5
Eligible for Reduced-Price Lunch Program	6.3	Average Reading Score	21.7
Current Spending ($ per student in FY 2003)	12,366	Average Science Score	20.8
Instruction	7,421		
Support Services	4,586		

Note: For an explanation of data, please refer to the User's Guide in the front of the book

New Jersey NAEP 2005 Test Scores

Reading			Mathematics		
Grade/Category	Value	Rank	Grade/Category	Value	Rank
4th Grade			**4th Grade**		
Average Proficiency	223.3 (1.28)	13/51	Average Proficiency	244.0 (1.13)	5/51
Proficiency by Gender/Race/Ethnicity			Proficiency by Gender/Race/Ethnicity		
Male	220.6 (1.67)	13/51	Male	245.7 (1.14)	6/51
Female	226.3 (1.50)	16/51	Female	242.2 (1.35)	5/51
White, Non-Hispanic	232.5 (1.14)	6/51	White, Non-Hispanic	250.8 (1.03)	5/51
Black, Non-Hispanic	199.4 (2.40)	21/42	Black, Non-Hispanic	223.8 (1.45)	11/42
Asian, Non-Hispanic	241.3 (2.61)	2/27	Asian, Non-Hispanic	264.4 (2.56)	1/25
American Indian, Non-Hispanic	n/a	n/a	American Indian, Non-Hispanic	n/a	n/a
Hispanic	206.4 (2.28)	16/40	Hispanic	229.7 (1.94)	12/41
Proficiency by Class Size			Proficiency by Class Size		
Less than 16 Students	203.7 (3.64)	19/34	Less than 16 Students	230.7 (3.38)	13/35
16 to 18 Students	224.4 (3.10)	5/33	16 to 18 Students	246.7 (2.40)	1/31
19 to 20 Students	227.7 (2.27)	4/38	19 to 20 Students	248.0 (2.02)	2/38
21 to 25 Students	226.4 (1.90)	11/51	21 to 25 Students	245.1 (1.90)	8/51
Greater than 25 Students	n/a	n/a	Greater than 25 Students	n/a	n/a
Percent Attaining Achievement Levels			Percent Attaining Achievement Levels		
Below Basic	31.7 (1.63)	33/51	Below Basic	14.3 (1.09)	41/51
Basic or Above	68.3 (1.63)	19/51	Basic or Above	85.7 (1.09)	11/51
Proficient or Above	37.2 (1.50)	6/51	Proficient or Above	45.4 (1.69)	5/51
Advanced or Above	9.5 (0.80)	5/51	Advanced or Above	7.6 (0.94)	4/51
8th Grade			**8th Grade**		
Average Proficiency	269.4 (1.20)	5/51	Average Proficiency	283.9 (1.40)	13/51
Proficiency by Gender/Race/Ethnicity			Proficiency by Gender/Race/Ethnicity		
Male	265.7 (1.44)	3/51	Male	285.5 (1.67)	8/51
Female	273.2 (1.34)	9/51	Female	282.2 (1.44)	16/51
White, Non-Hispanic	277.6 (1.27)	3/51	White, Non-Hispanic	294.5 (1.18)	5/51
Black, Non-Hispanic	250.5 (2.77)	6/40	Black, Non-Hispanic	259.6 (2.50)	10/41
Asian, Non-Hispanic	290.9 (3.35)	1/24	Asian, Non-Hispanic	308.5 (2.81)	2/23
American Indian, Non-Hispanic	n/a	n/a	American Indian, Non-Hispanic	n/a	n/a
Hispanic	251.3 (2.11)	10/38	Hispanic	264.2 (2.11)	16/38
Proficiency by Parents Highest Level of Ed.			Proficiency by Parents Highest Level of Ed.		
Did Not Finish High School	252.4 (3.01)	5/49	Did Not Finish High School	266.1 (3.17)	8/50
Graduated High School	255.8 (1.97)	22/50	Graduated High School	272.0 (1.94)	16/50
Some Education After High School	267.0 (1.92)	24/50	Some Education After High School	282.7 (1.84)	22/50
Graduated College	278.0 (1.39)	3/50	Graduated College	293.9 (1.69)	10/50
Percent Attaining Achievement Levels			Percent Attaining Achievement Levels		
Below Basic	31.7 (1.63)	33/51	Below Basic	25.8 (1.40)	36/51
Basic or Above	68.3 (1.63)	19/51	Basic or Above	74.2 (1.40)	16/51
Proficient or Above	37.2 (1.50)	6/51	Proficient or Above	35.9 (1.51)	7/51
Advanced or Above	9.5 (0.80)	5/51	Advanced or Above	8.7 (1.01)	4/51

Note: For an explanation of data, please refer to the User's Guide in the front of the book; n/a indicates data not available

Atlantic County

Atlantic City
1809 Pacific Ave • Atlantic City, NJ 08401-6803
(609) 343-7200 • http://www.acboe.org
Grade Span: PK-12; **Agency Type:** 1
Schools: 11
  8 Primary; 1 Middle; 1 High; 1 Other Level
  11 Regular; 0 Special Education; 0 Vocational; 0 Alternative
  0 Magnet; 0 Charter; 9 Title I Eligible; 5 School-wide Title I
Students: 7,290 (50.5% male; 49.4% female)
  Individual Education Program: 977 (13.4%);
  English Language Learner: 887 (12.2%); Migrant: 1 (<0.1%)
  Eligible for Free Lunch Program: 4,088 (57.6%)
  Eligible for Reduced-Price Lunch Program: 761 (10.7%)
Teachers: 616.8 (11.5 to 1)
Librarians/Media Specialists: 10.0 (709.5 to 1)
Guidance Counselors: 16.0 (443.4 to 1)
Current Spending: ($ per student per year):
  Total: $14,379; Instruction: $8,980; Support Services: $4,825
Enrollment, Drop-out Rates and Diploma Recipients by Race/Ethnicity

Category	Total	White	Black	Asian	AIAN	Hisp.
Enrollment (%)	100.0	10.2	45.0	10.3	0.4	34.1
Drop-out Rate (%)	7.8	3.3	9.0	3.5	7.7	12.4
H.S. Diplomas (#)	416	119	140	57	4	96

Buena Regional
Harding Hwy • Buena, NJ 08310-9701
Mailing Address: PO Box 309 Harding Way • Buena, NJ 08310-9701
(856) 697-0800 • http://www.buena.k12.nj.us
Grade Span: PK-12; **Agency Type:** 1
Schools: 6
  4 Primary; 1 Middle; 1 High; 0 Other Level
  6 Regular; 0 Special Education; 0 Vocational; 0 Alternative
  0 Magnet; 0 Charter; 5 Title I Eligible; 0 School-wide Title I
Students: 2,627 (51.0% male; 48.9% female)
  Individual Education Program: 436 (16.6%);
  English Language Learner: 47 (1.8%); Migrant: 20 (0.8%)
  Eligible for Free Lunch Program: 673 (26.2%)
  Eligible for Reduced-Price Lunch Program: 281 (10.9%)
Teachers: 188.0 (13.7 to 1)
Librarians/Media Specialists: 3.0 (857.3 to 1)
Guidance Counselors: 7.0 (367.4 to 1)
Current Spending: ($ per student per year):
  Total: $11,241; Instruction: $6,773; Support Services: $4,087
Enrollment, Drop-out Rates and Diploma Recipients by Race/Ethnicity

Category	Total	White	Black	Asian	AIAN	Hisp.
Enrollment (%)	100.0	66.0	15.4	0.6	0.0	18.0
Drop-out Rate (%)	1.6	1.6	1.4	0.0	0.0	2.1
H.S. Diplomas (#)	188	146	19	0	0	23

Egg Harbor Twp
202 Naples Ave • West Atlantic City, NJ 08232-2928
Mailing Address: PO Box 31 • West Atlantic City, NJ 08232-2928
(609) 646-7911 • http://www.eht.k12.nj.us
Grade Span: PK-12; **Agency Type:** 1
Schools: 7
  4 Primary; 2 Middle; 1 High; 0 Other Level
  7 Regular; 0 Special Education; 0 Vocational; 0 Alternative
  0 Magnet; 0 Charter; 3 Title I Eligible; 0 School-wide Title I
Students: 6,805 (51.6% male; 48.3% female)
  Individual Education Program: 1,139 (16.7%);
  English Language Learner: 156 (2.3%); Migrant: 0 (0.0%)
  Eligible for Free Lunch Program: 1,049 (15.8%)
  Eligible for Reduced-Price Lunch Program: 622 (9.4%)
Teachers: 486.2 (13.6 to 1)
Librarians/Media Specialists: 7.0 (946.9 to 1)
Guidance Counselors: 19.2 (345.2 to 1)
Current Spending: ($ per student per year):
  Total: $9,542; Instruction: $5,907; Support Services: $3,298
Enrollment, Drop-out Rates and Diploma Recipients by Race/Ethnicity

Category	Total	White	Black	Asian	AIAN	Hisp.
Enrollment (%)	100.0	65.4	13.2	8.5	0.9	12.1
Drop-out Rate (%)	2.5	1.5	4.9	3.1	0.0	5.6
H.S. Diplomas (#)	347	240	52	25	0	30

Galloway Twp
101 S Reeds Rd • Galloway, NJ 08205
(609) 748-1250
Grade Span: PK-08; **Agency Type:** 1
Schools: 9
  8 Primary; 1 Middle; 0 High; 0 Other Level
  9 Regular; 0 Special Education; 0 Vocational; 0 Alternative
  0 Magnet; 0 Charter; 5 Title I Eligible; 0 School-wide Title I
Students: 4,138 (50.6% male; 49.3% female)

  Individual Education Program: 692 (16.7%);
  English Language Learner: 150 (3.6%); Migrant: 1 (<0.1%)
  Eligible for Free Lunch Program: 526 (13.2%)
  Eligible for Reduced-Price Lunch Program: 370 (9.3%)
Teachers: 325.8 (12.2 to 1)
Librarians/Media Specialists: 6.0 (662.5 to 1)
Guidance Counselors: 11.6 (342.7 to 1)
Current Spending: ($ per student per year):
  Total: $10,019; Instruction: $5,799; Support Services: $3,730
Enrollment, Drop-out Rates and Diploma Recipients by Race/Ethnicity

Category	Total	White	Black	Asian	AIAN	Hisp.
Enrollment (%)	100.0	65.8	12.7	12.6	0.1	8.8
Drop-out Rate (%)	n/a	n/a	n/a	n/a	n/a	n/a
H.S. Diplomas (#)	n/a	n/a	n/a	n/a	n/a	n/a

Greater Egg Harbor Reg
1824 Dr Dennis Foreman Dr • Mays Landing, NJ 08330-2640
(609) 625-1456 • http://www.gehrhsd.net/
Grade Span: 09-12; **Agency Type:** 1
Schools: 2
  0 Primary; 0 Middle; 2 High; 0 Other Level
  2 Regular; 0 Special Education; 0 Vocational; 0 Alternative
  0 Magnet; 0 Charter; 2 Title I Eligible; 0 School-wide Title I
Students: 3,844 (50.0% male; 49.9% female)
  Individual Education Program: 662 (17.2%);
  English Language Learner: 51 (1.3%); Migrant: 2 (0.1%)
  Eligible for Free Lunch Program: 553 (14.8%)
  Eligible for Reduced-Price Lunch Program: 287 (7.7%)
Teachers: 260.6 (14.3 to 1)
Librarians/Media Specialists: 3.2 (1,168.4 to 1)
Guidance Counselors: 14.9 (250.9 to 1)
Current Spending: ($ per student per year):
  Total: $11,573; Instruction: $6,296; Support Services: $4,937
Enrollment, Drop-out Rates and Diploma Recipients by Race/Ethnicity

Category	Total	White	Black	Asian	AIAN	Hisp.
Enrollment (%)	100.0	62.6	16.6	8.3	0.6	11.9
Drop-out Rate (%)	4.5	3.6	5.1	4.0	0.0	9.4
H.S. Diplomas (#)	648	426	101	65	1	55

Hamilton Twp
5801 Third St • Mays Landing, NJ 08330-1717
(609) 625-6595 • http://www.hamilton.k12.nj.us/
Grade Span: PK-08; **Agency Type:** 1
Schools: 3
  2 Primary; 1 Middle; 0 High; 0 Other Level
  3 Regular; 0 Special Education; 0 Vocational; 0 Alternative
  0 Magnet; 0 Charter; 3 Title I Eligible; 0 School-wide Title I
Students: 3,065 (51.6% male; 48.3% female)
  Individual Education Program: 495 (16.2%);
  English Language Learner: 62 (2.0%); Migrant: 8 (0.3%)
  Eligible for Free Lunch Program: 638 (21.9%)
  Eligible for Reduced-Price Lunch Program: 313 (10.7%)
Teachers: 230.5 (12.7 to 1)
Librarians/Media Specialists: 4.0 (729.0 to 1)
Guidance Counselors: 6.0 (486.0 to 1)
Current Spending: ($ per student per year):
  Total: $10,222; Instruction: $6,146; Support Services: $3,709
Enrollment, Drop-out Rates and Diploma Recipients by Race/Ethnicity

Category	Total	White	Black	Asian	AIAN	Hisp.
Enrollment (%)	100.0	59.4	24.1	3.8	0.1	12.5
Drop-out Rate (%)	n/a	n/a	n/a	n/a	n/a	n/a
H.S. Diplomas (#)	n/a	n/a	n/a	n/a	n/a	n/a

Hammonton Town
601 N 4th St • Hammonton, NJ 08037-0308
(609) 567-7004
Grade Span: PK-12; **Agency Type:** 1
Schools: 4
  2 Primary; 1 Middle; 1 High; 0 Other Level
  4 Regular; 0 Special Education; 0 Vocational; 0 Alternative
  0 Magnet; 0 Charter; 1 Title I Eligible; 0 School-wide Title I
Students: 3,372 (50.2% male; 49.7% female)
  Individual Education Program: 435 (12.9%);
  English Language Learner: 145 (4.3%); Migrant: 70 (2.2%)
  Eligible for Free Lunch Program: 655 (20.2%)
  Eligible for Reduced-Price Lunch Program: 199 (6.1%)
Teachers: 209.7 (15.5 to 1)
Librarians/Media Specialists: 3.0 (1,081.0 to 1)
Guidance Counselors: 9.0 (360.3 to 1)
Current Spending: ($ per student per year):
  Total: $9,598; Instruction: $6,081; Support Services: $3,199

Enrollment, Drop-out Rates and Diploma Recipients by Race/Ethnicity

Category	Total	White	Black	Asian	AIAN	Hisp.
Enrollment (%)	100.0	80.6	3.5	1.0	0.0	15.0
Drop-out Rate (%)	1.2	1.2	4.8	0.0	n/a	1.0
H.S. Diplomas (#)	137	109	1	4	0	23

Mainland Regional

Oak Ave • Linwood, NJ 08221-1653
(609) 927-2461
Grade Span: 09-12; **Agency Type:** 1
Schools: 1
  0 Primary; 0 Middle; 1 High; 0 Other Level
  1 Regular; 0 Special Education; 0 Vocational; 0 Alternative
  0 Magnet; 0 Charter; 1 Title I Eligible; 0 School-wide Title I
Students: 1,669 (48.0% male; 51.9% female)
  Individual Education Program: 261 (15.6%);
  English Language Learner: 9 (0.5%); Migrant: 0 (0.0%)
  Eligible for Free Lunch Program: 98 (6.0%)
  Eligible for Reduced-Price Lunch Program: 92 (5.6%)
Teachers: 128.5 (12.8 to 1)
Librarians/Media Specialists: 2.0 (823.0 to 1)
Guidance Counselors: 5.0 (329.2 to 1)
Current Spending: ($ per student per year):
  Total: $11,118; Instruction: $6,821; Support Services: $3,467

Enrollment, Drop-out Rates and Diploma Recipients by Race/Ethnicity

Category	Total	White	Black	Asian	AIAN	Hisp.
Enrollment (%)	100.0	83.8	5.5	4.8	0.2	5.7
Drop-out Rate (%)	1.8	1.8	1.5	0.0	0.0	5.6
H.S. Diplomas (#)	302	260	15	15	0	12

Pleasantville City

900 W Leeds Ave • Pleasantville, NJ 08232-0960
Mailing Address: PO Box 960 • Pleasantville, NJ 08232-0960
(609) 383-6800 • http://www.pleasantville.k12.nj.us/
Grade Span: PK-12; **Agency Type:** 1
Schools: 6
  4 Primary; 1 Middle; 1 High; 0 Other Level
  6 Regular; 0 Special Education; 0 Vocational; 0 Alternative
  0 Magnet; 0 Charter; 5 Title I Eligible; 0 School-wide Title I
Students: 4,067 (53.1% male; 46.8% female)
  Individual Education Program: 739 (18.2%);
  English Language Learner: 283 (7.0%); Migrant: 0 (0.0%)
  Eligible for Free Lunch Program: 1,649 (46.6%)
  Eligible for Reduced-Price Lunch Program: 552 (15.6%)
Teachers: 382.0 (9.3 to 1)
Librarians/Media Specialists: 7.0 (505.3 to 1)
Guidance Counselors: 9.0 (393.0 to 1)
Current Spending: ($ per student per year):
  Total: $16,452; Instruction: $9,380; Support Services: $6,487

Enrollment, Drop-out Rates and Diploma Recipients by Race/Ethnicity

Category	Total	White	Black	Asian	AIAN	Hisp.
Enrollment (%)	100.0	2.6	62.8	1.4	0.1	33.1
Drop-out Rate (%)	11.5	5.0	10.0	0.0	0.0	19.2
H.S. Diplomas (#)	204	3	159	6	0	36

Bergen County

Bergen County Special Service

327 E Ridgewood Ave • Paramus, NJ 07652-2915
(201) 343-6000
Grade Span: UG-UG; **Agency Type:** 4
Schools: 7
  0 Primary; 0 Middle; 0 High; 7 Other Level
  0 Regular; 7 Special Education; 0 Vocational; 0 Alternative
  0 Magnet; 0 Charter; 0 Title I Eligible; 0 School-wide Title I
Students: 1,982 (64.4% male; 35.5% female)
  Individual Education Program: 0 (0.0%)
  English Language Learner: 0 (0.0%); Migrant: 0 (0.0%)
  Eligible for Free Lunch Program: 245 (24.7%)
  Eligible for Reduced-Price Lunch Program: 88 (8.9%)
Teachers: 186.0 (5.3 to 1)
Librarians/Media Specialists: 0.0 (n/a to 1)
Guidance Counselors: 1.0 (991.0 to 1)
Current Spending: ($ per student per year):
  Total: $39,428; Instruction: $22,125; Support Services: $16,894

Enrollment, Drop-out Rates and Diploma Recipients by Race/Ethnicity

Category	Total	White	Black	Asian	AIAN	Hisp.
Enrollment (%)	100.0	47.8	21.6	9.2	0.5	20.9
Drop-out Rate (%)	n/a	n/a	n/a	n/a	n/a	n/a
H.S. Diplomas (#)	0	0	0	0	0	0

Bergen County Vocational

327 E Ridgewood Ave • Paramus, NJ 07652-2915
(201) 967-2472 • http://www.bergen.org/
Grade Span: 09-12; **Agency Type:** 1
Schools: 4
  0 Primary; 0 Middle; 3 High; 1 Other Level
  0 Regular; 1 Special Education; 3 Vocational; 0 Alternative
  1 Magnet; 0 Charter; 1 Title I Eligible; 0 School-wide Title I
Students: 2,331 (54.9% male; 45.0% female)
  Individual Education Program: 357 (15.3%);
  English Language Learner: 6 (0.3%); Migrant: 0 (0.0%)
  Eligible for Free Lunch Program: 131 (6.5%)
  Eligible for Reduced-Price Lunch Program: 66 (3.3%)
Teachers: 214.7 (9.4 to 1)
Librarians/Media Specialists: 0.0 (n/a to 1)
Guidance Counselors: 13.0 (155.6 to 1)
Current Spending: ($ per student per year):
  Total: $24,805; Instruction: $16,179; Support Services: $7,811

Enrollment, Drop-out Rates and Diploma Recipients by Race/Ethnicity

Category	Total	White	Black	Asian	AIAN	Hisp.
Enrollment (%)	100.0	53.5	6.3	27.4	0.0	12.8
Drop-out Rate (%)	0.0	0.0	0.0	0.0	0.0	0.0
H.S. Diplomas (#)	285	163	22	72	0	28

Bergenfield Boro

100 So. Prospect Ave • Bergenfield, NJ 07621-1958
(201) 385-8202 • http://www.bergenfield.org
Grade Span: PK-12; **Agency Type:** 1
Schools: 7
  5 Primary; 1 Middle; 1 High; 0 Other Level
  7 Regular; 0 Special Education; 0 Vocational; 0 Alternative
  0 Magnet; 0 Charter; 3 Title I Eligible; 0 School-wide Title I
Students: 3,900 (50.4% male; 49.5% female)
  Individual Education Program: 676 (17.3%);
  English Language Learner: 183 (4.7%); Migrant: 0 (0.0%)
  Eligible for Free Lunch Program: 338 (8.9%)
  Eligible for Reduced-Price Lunch Program: 216 (5.7%)
Teachers: 266.6 (14.3 to 1)
Librarians/Media Specialists: 3.0 (1,267.7 to 1)
Guidance Counselors: 8.3 (458.2 to 1)
Current Spending: ($ per student per year):
  Total: $11,097; Instruction: $6,971; Support Services: $3,841

Enrollment, Drop-out Rates and Diploma Recipients by Race/Ethnicity

Category	Total	White	Black	Asian	AIAN	Hisp.
Enrollment (%)	100.0	32.4	8.3	30.6	0.1	28.6
Drop-out Rate (%)	4.4	1.1	15.9	3.1	n/a	8.6
H.S. Diplomas (#)	222	110	12	56	0	44

Cliffside Park Boro

525 Palisade Ave • Cliffside Park, NJ 07010-2914
(201) 313-2310 • http://www.cliffsidepark.edu
Grade Span: PK-12; **Agency Type:** 1
Schools: 5
  4 Primary; 0 Middle; 1 High; 0 Other Level
  5 Regular; 0 Special Education; 0 Vocational; 0 Alternative
  0 Magnet; 0 Charter; 3 Title I Eligible; 0 School-wide Title I
Students: 2,727 (52.9% male; 47.0% female)
  Individual Education Program: 279 (10.2%);
  English Language Learner: 250 (9.2%); Migrant: 0 (0.0%)
  Eligible for Free Lunch Program: 642 (24.8%)
  Eligible for Reduced-Price Lunch Program: 334 (12.9%)
Teachers: 191.5 (13.5 to 1)
Librarians/Media Specialists: 3.0 (864.3 to 1)
Guidance Counselors: 4.5 (576.2 to 1)
Current Spending: ($ per student per year):
  Total: $10,417; Instruction: $7,225; Support Services: $2,898

Enrollment, Drop-out Rates and Diploma Recipients by Race/Ethnicity

Category	Total	White	Black	Asian	AIAN	Hisp.
Enrollment (%)	100.0	53.8	2.5	7.3	0.5	36.0
Drop-out Rate (%)	1.9	1.2	18.2	0.0	n/a	2.3
H.S. Diplomas (#)	227	119	4	20	0	84

Cresskill Boro

1 Lincoln Dr • Cresskill, NJ 07626
(201) 567-5919
Grade Span: PK-12; **Agency Type:** 1
Schools: 3
  2 Primary; 0 Middle; 1 High; 0 Other Level
  3 Regular; 0 Special Education; 0 Vocational; 0 Alternative
  0 Magnet; 0 Charter; 0 Title I Eligible; 0 School-wide Title I
Students: 1,509 (50.0% male; 50.0% female)
  Individual Education Program: 228 (15.1%);
  English Language Learner: 82 (5.4%); Migrant: 0 (0.0%)
  Eligible for Free Lunch Program: 16 (1.1%)
  Eligible for Reduced-Price Lunch Program: 5 (0.3%)

Teachers: 107.0 (13.9 to 1)
Librarians/Media Specialists: 2.0 (744.0 to 1)
Guidance Counselors: 3.0 (496.0 to 1)
Current Spending: ($ per student per year):
   Total: $11,817; Instruction: $7,539; Support Services: $4,130
Enrollment, Drop-out Rates and Diploma Recipients by Race/Ethnicity

Category	Total	White	Black	Asian	AIAN	Hisp.
Enrollment (%)	100.0	67.0	0.7	28.8	0.0	3.5
Drop-out Rate (%)	0.5	0.8	0.0	0.0	n/a	0.0
H.S. Diplomas (#)	91	63	0	26	0	2

Dumont Boro
25 Depew St • Dumont, NJ 07628-3601
(201) 387-3082 • http://www2.cybernex.net/~dumont/
Grade Span: PK-12; **Agency Type:** 1
Schools: 5
   4 Primary; 0 Middle; 1 High; 0 Other Level
   5 Regular; 0 Special Education; 0 Vocational; 0 Alternative
   0 Magnet; 0 Charter; 5 Title I Eligible; 0 School-wide Title I
Students: 2,717 (49.8% male; 50.1% female)
   Individual Education Program: 395 (14.5%);
   English Language Learner: 118 (4.3%); Migrant: 0 (0.0%)
   Eligible for Free Lunch Program: 79 (3.0%)
   Eligible for Reduced-Price Lunch Program: 46 (1.7%)
Teachers: 185.0 (14.4 to 1)
Librarians/Media Specialists: 3.0 (886.3 to 1)
Guidance Counselors: 6.1 (435.9 to 1)
Current Spending: ($ per student per year):
   Total: $10,951; Instruction: $7,046; Support Services: $3,798
Enrollment, Drop-out Rates and Diploma Recipients by Race/Ethnicity

Category	Total	White	Black	Asian	AIAN	Hisp.
Enrollment (%)	100.0	74.7	1.2	11.8	0.2	12.1
Drop-out Rate (%)	0.8	0.8	0.0	2.6	n/a	0.0
H.S. Diplomas (#)	180	129	4	28	0	19

Elmwood Park
465 Blvd • Elmwood Park, NJ 07407-1622
(201) 794-2979 • http://www.epps.org
Grade Span: PK-12; **Agency Type:** 1
Schools: 5
   3 Primary; 1 Middle; 1 High; 0 Other Level
   5 Regular; 0 Special Education; 0 Vocational; 0 Alternative
   0 Magnet; 0 Charter; 3 Title I Eligible; 0 School-wide Title I
Students: 2,114 (51.1% male; 48.8% female)
   Individual Education Program: 310 (14.7%);
   English Language Learner: 82 (3.9%); Migrant: 0 (0.0%)
   Eligible for Free Lunch Program: 251 (12.1%)
   Eligible for Reduced-Price Lunch Program: 192 (9.3%)
Teachers: 134.9 (15.4 to 1)
Librarians/Media Specialists: 2.0 (1,036.5 to 1)
Guidance Counselors: 5.6 (370.2 to 1)
Current Spending: ($ per student per year):
   Total: $10,846; Instruction: $5,929; Support Services: $4,660
Enrollment, Drop-out Rates and Diploma Recipients by Race/Ethnicity

Category	Total	White	Black	Asian	AIAN	Hisp.
Enrollment (%)	100.0	58.4	3.6	15.0	0.0	23.1
Drop-out Rate (%)	2.7	3.0	8.3	1.5	n/a	2.3
H.S. Diplomas (#)	125	84	6	15	0	20

Englewood City
12 Tenafly Rd • Englewood, NJ 07631-2206
(201) 833-6060 • http://www.epsd.org
Grade Span: PK-12; **Agency Type:** 1
Schools: 5
   3 Primary; 1 Middle; 1 High; 0 Other Level
   4 Regular; 0 Special Education; 0 Vocational; 1 Alternative
   0 Magnet; 0 Charter; 5 Title I Eligible; 0 School-wide Title I
Students: 2,803 (50.1% male; 49.8% female)
   Individual Education Program: 471 (16.8%);
   English Language Learner: 246 (8.8%); Migrant: 0 (0.0%)
   Eligible for Free Lunch Program: 1,146 (42.3%)
   Eligible for Reduced-Price Lunch Program: 357 (13.2%)
Teachers: 237.6 (11.4 to 1)
Librarians/Media Specialists: 1.0 (2,707.0 to 1)
Guidance Counselors: 8.0 (338.4 to 1)
Current Spending: ($ per student per year):
   Total: $17,805; Instruction: $11,429; Support Services: $5,954
Enrollment, Drop-out Rates and Diploma Recipients by Race/Ethnicity

Category	Total	White	Black	Asian	AIAN	Hisp.
Enrollment (%)	100.0	3.7	56.8	4.6	0.1	34.8
Drop-out Rate (%)	5.5	16.7	3.9	0.0	n/a	9.1
H.S. Diplomas (#)	149	2	98	9	1	39

Fair Lawn Boro
37-01 Fair Lawn Ave • Fair Lawn, NJ 07410-4919
(201) 794-5510 • http://www.fairlawnschools.org/
Grade Span: PK-12; **Agency Type:** 1
Schools: 9
   6 Primary; 2 Middle; 1 High; 0 Other Level
   9 Regular; 0 Special Education; 0 Vocational; 0 Alternative
   0 Magnet; 0 Charter; 4 Title I Eligible; 0 School-wide Title I
Students: 4,865 (51.4% male; 48.5% female)
   Individual Education Program: 838 (17.2%);
   English Language Learner: 119 (2.4%); Migrant: 0 (0.0%)
   Eligible for Free Lunch Program: 164 (3.4%)
   Eligible for Reduced-Price Lunch Program: 110 (2.3%)
Teachers: 350.3 (13.6 to 1)
Librarians/Media Specialists: 8.0 (594.3 to 1)
Guidance Counselors: 10.2 (466.1 to 1)
Current Spending: ($ per student per year):
   Total: $12,700; Instruction: $7,724; Support Services: $4,760
Enrollment, Drop-out Rates and Diploma Recipients by Race/Ethnicity

Category	Total	White	Black	Asian	AIAN	Hisp.
Enrollment (%)	100.0	79.7	1.2	9.7	0.1	9.2
Drop-out Rate (%)	0.7	0.7	0.0	0.0	n/a	1.9
H.S. Diplomas (#)	348	318	1	19	0	10

Fort Lee Boro
255 Whiteman St • Fort Lee, NJ 07024-5629
(201) 585-4610 • http://www.fortlee-boe.net/
Grade Span: PK-12; **Agency Type:** 1
Schools: 6
   4 Primary; 1 Middle; 1 High; 0 Other Level
   6 Regular; 0 Special Education; 0 Vocational; 0 Alternative
   0 Magnet; 0 Charter; 3 Title I Eligible; 0 School-wide Title I
Students: 3,461 (51.6% male; 48.3% female)
   Individual Education Program: 434 (12.5%);
   English Language Learner: 318 (9.2%); Migrant: 0 (0.0%)
   Eligible for Free Lunch Program: 185 (5.4%)
   Eligible for Reduced-Price Lunch Program: 155 (4.6%)
Teachers: 249.8 (13.6 to 1)
Librarians/Media Specialists: 7.0 (485.9 to 1)
Guidance Counselors: 10.0 (340.1 to 1)
Current Spending: ($ per student per year):
   Total: $11,668; Instruction: $7,148; Support Services: $4,180
Enrollment, Drop-out Rates and Diploma Recipients by Race/Ethnicity

Category	Total	White	Black	Asian	AIAN	Hisp.
Enrollment (%)	100.0	38.8	2.3	44.6	0.9	13.4
Drop-out Rate (%)	1.1	0.5	6.3	1.1	n/a	2.3
H.S. Diplomas (#)	212	91	2	100	0	19

Franklin Lakes Boro
490 Pulis Ave • Franklin Lakes, NJ 07417-1324
(201) 891-1856
Grade Span: PK-08; **Agency Type:** 1
Schools: 3
   2 Primary; 1 Middle; 0 High; 0 Other Level
   3 Regular; 0 Special Education; 0 Vocational; 0 Alternative
   0 Magnet; 0 Charter; 0 Title I Eligible; 0 School-wide Title I
Students: 1,671 (52.1% male; 47.8% female)
   Individual Education Program: 198 (11.8%);
   English Language Learner: 13 (0.8%); Migrant: 0 (0.0%)
   Eligible for Free Lunch Program: 3 (0.2%)
   Eligible for Reduced-Price Lunch Program: 0 (0.0%)
Teachers: 121.3 (12.2 to 1)
Librarians/Media Specialists: 3.0 (495.0 to 1)
Guidance Counselors: 4.0 (371.3 to 1)
Current Spending: ($ per student per year):
   Total: $11,919; Instruction: $7,253; Support Services: $4,641
Enrollment, Drop-out Rates and Diploma Recipients by Race/Ethnicity

Category	Total	White	Black	Asian	AIAN	Hisp.
Enrollment (%)	100.0	92.1	1.2	4.5	0.2	2.0
Drop-out Rate (%)	n/a	n/a	n/a	n/a	n/a	n/a
H.S. Diplomas (#)	n/a	n/a	n/a	n/a	n/a	n/a

Garfield City
125 Outwater Ln • Garfield, NJ 07026-2637
(973) 340-5000 • http://www.garfield.k12.nj.us
Grade Span: PK-12; **Agency Type:** 1
Schools: 10
   8 Primary; 1 Middle; 1 High; 0 Other Level
   10 Regular; 0 Special Education; 0 Vocational; 0 Alternative
   0 Magnet; 0 Charter; 7 Title I Eligible; 0 School-wide Title I
Students: 4,587 (50.7% male; 49.2% female)
   Individual Education Program: 711 (15.5%);
   English Language Learner: 498 (10.9%); Migrant: 0 (0.0%)
   Eligible for Free Lunch Program: 1,482 (33.6%)
   Eligible for Reduced-Price Lunch Program: 857 (19.4%)

Teachers: 352.7 (12.5 to 1)
Librarians/Media Specialists: 2.0 (2,204.5 to 1)
Guidance Counselors: 8.5 (518.7 to 1)
Current Spending: ($ per student per year):
   Total: $12,539; Instruction: $8,432; Support Services: $3,838
Enrollment, Drop-out Rates and Diploma Recipients by Race/Ethnicity

Category	Total	White	Black	Asian	AIAN	Hisp.
Enrollment (%)	100.0	54.4	5.1	2.5	0.2	37.8
Drop-out Rate (%)	4.3	4.9	0.0	0.0	0.0	4.5
H.S. Diplomas (#)	213	139	14	7	0	53

Glen Rock Boro

620 Harristown Rd • Glen Rock, NJ 07452-2328
(201) 445-7700 • http://www.glenrocknj.org/
Grade Span: PK-12; **Agency Type:** 1
Schools: 6
   4 Primary; 1 Middle; 1 High; 0 Other Level
   6 Regular; 0 Special Education; 0 Vocational; 0 Alternative
   0 Magnet; 0 Charter; 0 Title I Eligible; 0 School-wide Title I
Students: 2,399 (52.6% male; 47.3% female)
   Individual Education Program: 346 (14.4%);
   English Language Learner: 74 (3.1%); Migrant: 0 (0.0%)
   Eligible for Free Lunch Program: 12 (0.5%)
   Eligible for Reduced-Price Lunch Program: 13 (0.5%)
Teachers: 185.1 (12.8 to 1)
Librarians/Media Specialists: 2.0 (1,186.5 to 1)
Guidance Counselors: 6.0 (395.5 to 1)
Current Spending: ($ per student per year):
   Total: $12,217; Instruction: $7,762; Support Services: $4,200
Enrollment, Drop-out Rates and Diploma Recipients by Race/Ethnicity

Category	Total	White	Black	Asian	AIAN	Hisp.
Enrollment (%)	100.0	86.3	1.8	9.7	0.0	2.2
Drop-out Rate (%)	0.0	0.0	0.0	0.0	n/a	0.0
H.S. Diplomas (#)	130	111	1	15	0	3

Hackensack City

355 State St • Hackensack, NJ 07601-5510
(201) 646-7830 • http://www.hackensackelementary.org
Grade Span: PK-12; **Agency Type:** 1
Schools: 7
   4 Primary; 2 Middle; 1 High; 0 Other Level
   7 Regular; 0 Special Education; 0 Vocational; 0 Alternative
   0 Magnet; 0 Charter; 6 Title I Eligible; 1 School-wide Title I
Students: 5,149 (50.6% male; 49.3% female)
   Individual Education Program: 786 (15.3%);
   English Language Learner: 341 (6.6%); Migrant: 0 (0.0%)
   Eligible for Free Lunch Program: 1,528 (30.2%)
   Eligible for Reduced-Price Lunch Program: 591 (11.7%)
Teachers: 379.2 (13.4 to 1)
Librarians/Media Specialists: 6.0 (844.2 to 1)
Guidance Counselors: 9.0 (562.8 to 1)
Current Spending: ($ per student per year):
   Total: $12,506; Instruction: $8,244; Support Services: $4,008
Enrollment, Drop-out Rates and Diploma Recipients by Race/Ethnicity

Category	Total	White	Black	Asian	AIAN	Hisp.
Enrollment (%)	100.0	18.6	34.2	6.1	0.3	40.7
Drop-out Rate (%)	3.8	2.7	2.9	2.1	0.0	5.7
H.S. Diplomas (#)	342	110	82	28	0	122

Hasbrouck Heights Boro

379 Blvd • Hasbrouck Heights, NJ 07604-1421
(201) 393-8145
Grade Span: PK-12; **Agency Type:** 1
Schools: 4
   2 Primary; 1 Middle; 1 High; 0 Other Level
   4 Regular; 0 Special Education; 0 Vocational; 0 Alternative
   0 Magnet; 0 Charter; 0 Title I Eligible; 0 School-wide Title I
Students: 1,558 (50.0% male; 50.0% female)
   Individual Education Program: 221 (14.2%);
   English Language Learner: 21 (1.3%); Migrant: 0 (0.0%)
   Eligible for Free Lunch Program: 31 (2.0%)
   Eligible for Reduced-Price Lunch Program: 4 (0.3%)
Teachers: 117.6 (13.0 to 1)
Librarians/Media Specialists: 3.0 (509.3 to 1)
Guidance Counselors: 3.6 (424.4 to 1)
Current Spending: ($ per student per year):
   Total: $10,688; Instruction: $6,797; Support Services: $3,735
Enrollment, Drop-out Rates and Diploma Recipients by Race/Ethnicity

Category	Total	White	Black	Asian	AIAN	Hisp.
Enrollment (%)	100.0	77.3	2.7	6.7	0.0	13.4
Drop-out Rate (%)	0.5	0.3	14.3	0.0	n/a	0.0
H.S. Diplomas (#)	99	73	3	8	0	15

Leonia Boro

570 Grand Ave • Leonia, NJ 07605-1537
(201) 947-5655 • http://www.bergen.org/edpartners/Leonia/
Grade Span: PK-12; **Agency Type:** 1
Schools: 3
   1 Primary; 1 Middle; 1 High; 0 Other Level
   3 Regular; 0 Special Education; 0 Vocational; 0 Alternative
   0 Magnet; 0 Charter; 3 Title I Eligible; 0 School-wide Title I
Students: 1,809 (49.4% male; 50.5% female)
   Individual Education Program: 221 (12.2%);
   English Language Learner: 158 (8.7%); Migrant: 0 (0.0%)
   Eligible for Free Lunch Program: 92 (5.4%)
   Eligible for Reduced-Price Lunch Program: 64 (3.7%)
Teachers: 171.8 (10.0 to 1)
Librarians/Media Specialists: 2.0 (856.0 to 1)
Guidance Counselors: 6.0 (285.3 to 1)
Current Spending: ($ per student per year):
   Total: $11,222; Instruction: $7,379; Support Services: $3,843
Enrollment, Drop-out Rates and Diploma Recipients by Race/Ethnicity

Category	Total	White	Black	Asian	AIAN	Hisp.
Enrollment (%)	100.0	44.9	3.6	34.1	0.0	17.5
Drop-out Rate (%)	0.5	0.7	0.0	0.0	n/a	1.3
H.S. Diplomas (#)	120	66	4	35	0	15

Lodi Borough

Lincoln School • Lodi, NJ 07644
(973) 778-4620 • http://www.njcommunity.com/sites/lodi
Grade Span: PK-12; **Agency Type:** 1
Schools: 7
   5 Primary; 1 Middle; 1 High; 0 Other Level
   7 Regular; 0 Special Education; 0 Vocational; 0 Alternative
   0 Magnet; 0 Charter; 4 Title I Eligible; 0 School-wide Title I
Students: 3,176 (50.6% male; 49.3% female)
   Individual Education Program: 412 (13.0%);
   English Language Learner: 199 (6.3%); Migrant: 0 (0.0%)
   Eligible for Free Lunch Program: 722 (23.2%)
   Eligible for Reduced-Price Lunch Program: 414 (13.3%)
Teachers: 230.4 (13.5 to 1)
Librarians/Media Specialists: 6.0 (517.7 to 1)
Guidance Counselors: 9.0 (345.1 to 1)
Current Spending: ($ per student per year):
   Total: $10,990; Instruction: $6,823; Support Services: $3,877
Enrollment, Drop-out Rates and Diploma Recipients by Race/Ethnicity

Category	Total	White	Black	Asian	AIAN	Hisp.
Enrollment (%)	100.0	49.2	5.2	14.4	0.0	31.2
Drop-out Rate (%)	4.2	4.1	18.8	0.0	n/a	4.4
H.S. Diplomas (#)	191	111	7	29	0	44

Lyndhurst Twp

Lincoln School • Lyndhurst, NJ 07071-1928
(201) 438-5683 • http://www.lyndhurstschools.org
Grade Span: PK-12; **Agency Type:** 1
Schools: 7
   6 Primary; 0 Middle; 1 High; 0 Other Level
   7 Regular; 0 Special Education; 0 Vocational; 0 Alternative
   0 Magnet; 0 Charter; 6 Title I Eligible; 0 School-wide Title I
Students: 2,192 (51.2% male; 48.7% female)
   Individual Education Program: 441 (20.1%);
   English Language Learner: 42 (1.9%); Migrant: 0 (0.0%)
   Eligible for Free Lunch Program: 179 (8.3%)
   Eligible for Reduced-Price Lunch Program: 129 (6.0%)
Teachers: 149.8 (14.4 to 1)
Librarians/Media Specialists: 1.0 (2,161.0 to 1)
Guidance Counselors: 6.0 (360.2 to 1)
Current Spending: ($ per student per year):
   Total: $11,432; Instruction: $6,990; Support Services: $4,267
Enrollment, Drop-out Rates and Diploma Recipients by Race/Ethnicity

Category	Total	White	Black	Asian	AIAN	Hisp.
Enrollment (%)	100.0	76.3	1.1	5.6	0.1	16.8
Drop-out Rate (%)	1.4	1.4	0.0	0.0	0.0	2.9
H.S. Diplomas (#)	134	108	0	10	0	16

Mahwah Twp

Admin Office 60 Ridge Rd • Mahwah, NJ 07430
(201) 529-6803 • http://www.mahwah.k12.nj.us
Grade Span: PK-12; **Agency Type:** 1
Schools: 7
   4 Primary; 2 Middle; 1 High; 0 Other Level
   7 Regular; 0 Special Education; 0 Vocational; 0 Alternative
   0 Magnet; 0 Charter; 3 Title I Eligible; 0 School-wide Title I
Students: 3,355 (51.3% male; 48.6% female)
   Individual Education Program: 470 (14.0%);
   English Language Learner: 27 (0.8%); Migrant: 0 (0.0%)
   Eligible for Free Lunch Program: 103 (3.2%)
   Eligible for Reduced-Price Lunch Program: 79 (2.4%)

Teachers: 262.1 (12.4 to 1)
Librarians/Media Specialists: 6.0 (542.8 to 1)
Guidance Counselors: 8.0 (407.1 to 1)
Current Spending: ($ per student per year):
 Total: $12,353; Instruction: $7,269; Support Services: $4,855
Enrollment, Drop-out Rates and Diploma Recipients by Race/Ethnicity

Category	Total	White	Black	Asian	AIAN	Hisp.
Enrollment (%)	100.0	81.2	2.4	10.4	2.3	3.7
Drop-out Rate (%)	2.5	1.5	3.2	1.3	26.3	7.1
H.S. Diplomas (#)	174	142	4	14	4	10

New Milford Boro
145 Madison Ave • New Milford, NJ 07646-2707
(201) 261-2952 • http://www.newmilfordschools.org/
Grade Span: PK-12; **Agency Type:** 1
Schools: 4
 2 Primary; 1 Middle; 1 High; 0 Other Level
 4 Regular; 0 Special Education; 0 Vocational; 0 Alternative
 0 Magnet; 0 Charter; 2 Title I Eligible; 0 School-wide Title I
Students: 1,943 (53.6% male; 46.3% female)
 Individual Education Program: 288 (14.8%);
 English Language Learner: 53 (2.7%); Migrant: 0 (0.0%)
 Eligible for Free Lunch Program: 67 (3.5%)
 Eligible for Reduced-Price Lunch Program: 61 (3.2%)
Teachers: 140.2 (13.7 to 1)
Librarians/Media Specialists: 4.2 (457.4 to 1)
Guidance Counselors: 6.0 (320.2 to 1)
Current Spending: ($ per student per year):
 Total: $11,251; Instruction: $6,415; Support Services: $4,454
Enrollment, Drop-out Rates and Diploma Recipients by Race/Ethnicity

Category	Total	White	Black	Asian	AIAN	Hisp.
Enrollment (%)	100.0	61.8	3.1	22.3	0.0	12.8
Drop-out Rate (%)	1.1	1.6	0.0	0.0	n/a	0.0
H.S. Diplomas (#)	113	73	5	12	8	15

North Arlington Boro
222 Ridge Rd • North Arlington, NJ 07031-6036
(201) 955-5200 • http://www.narlington.k12.nj.us/
Grade Span: PK-12; **Agency Type:** 1
Schools: 5
 3 Primary; 1 Middle; 1 High; 0 Other Level
 5 Regular; 0 Special Education; 0 Vocational; 0 Alternative
 0 Magnet; 0 Charter; 2 Title I Eligible; 0 School-wide Title I
Students: 1,624 (53.9% male; 46.0% female)
 Individual Education Program: 304 (18.7%);
 English Language Learner: 76 (4.7%); Migrant: 0 (0.0%)
 Eligible for Free Lunch Program: 78 (4.9%)
 Eligible for Reduced-Price Lunch Program: 54 (3.4%)
Teachers: 113.0 (13.9 to 1)
Librarians/Media Specialists: 1.0 (1,576.0 to 1)
Guidance Counselors: 3.0 (525.3 to 1)
Current Spending: ($ per student per year):
 Total: $10,157; Instruction: $6,316; Support Services: $3,652
Enrollment, Drop-out Rates and Diploma Recipients by Race/Ethnicity

Category	Total	White	Black	Asian	AIAN	Hisp.
Enrollment (%)	100.0	77.9	0.3	5.2	0.2	16.5
Drop-out Rate (%)	0.0	0.0	0.0	0.0	n/a	0.0
H.S. Diplomas (#)	106	93	0	6	0	7

Northern Valley Regional
162 Knickerbocker Rd • Demarest, NJ 07627-1033
(201) 768-2200 • http://www.nvnet.org
Grade Span: 09-12; **Agency Type:** 1
Schools: 2
 0 Primary; 0 Middle; 2 High; 0 Other Level
 2 Regular; 0 Special Education; 0 Vocational; 0 Alternative
 0 Magnet; 0 Charter; 0 Title I Eligible; 0 School-wide Title I
Students: 2,327 (50.1% male; 49.8% female)
 Individual Education Program: 266 (11.4%);
 English Language Learner: 26 (1.1%); Migrant: 0 (0.0%)
 Eligible for Free Lunch Program: 3 (0.1%)
 Eligible for Reduced-Price Lunch Program: 6 (0.3%)
Teachers: 205.5 (11.3 to 1)
Librarians/Media Specialists: 2.0 (1,156.0 to 1)
Guidance Counselors: 12.0 (192.7 to 1)
Current Spending: ($ per student per year):
 Total: $18,756; Instruction: $9,161; Support Services: $5,908
Enrollment, Drop-out Rates and Diploma Recipients by Race/Ethnicity

Category	Total	White	Black	Asian	AIAN	Hisp.
Enrollment (%)	100.0	68.4	1.0	27.2	0.0	3.4
Drop-out Rate (%)	0.0	0.1	0.0	0.0	0.0	0.0
H.S. Diplomas (#)	486	345	9	125	0	7

Oakland Boro
315 Ramapo Valley Rd • Oakland, NJ 07436-1813
(201) 337-6156
Grade Span: PK-08; **Agency Type:** 1
Schools: 4
 3 Primary; 1 Middle; 0 High; 0 Other Level
 4 Regular; 0 Special Education; 0 Vocational; 0 Alternative
 0 Magnet; 0 Charter; 4 Title I Eligible; 0 School-wide Title I
Students: 1,692 (52.3% male; 47.6% female)
 Individual Education Program: 271 (16.0%);
 English Language Learner: 8 (0.5%); Migrant: 0 (0.0%)
 Eligible for Free Lunch Program: 11 (0.7%)
 Eligible for Reduced-Price Lunch Program: 26 (1.6%)
Teachers: 123.5 (13.4 to 1)
Librarians/Media Specialists: 4.0 (414.0 to 1)
Guidance Counselors: 5.0 (331.2 to 1)
Current Spending: ($ per student per year):
 Total: $12,052; Instruction: $7,812; Support Services: $4,031
Enrollment, Drop-out Rates and Diploma Recipients by Race/Ethnicity

Category	Total	White	Black	Asian	AIAN	Hisp.
Enrollment (%)	100.0	92.5	0.7	3.1	0.6	3.1
Drop-out Rate (%)	n/a	n/a	n/a	n/a	n/a	n/a
H.S. Diplomas (#)	n/a	n/a	n/a	n/a	n/a	n/a

Palisades Park
270 First St • Palisades Park, NJ 07650-1502
(201) 947-3560
Grade Span: PK-12; **Agency Type:** 1
Schools: 2
 1 Primary; 0 Middle; 1 High; 0 Other Level
 2 Regular; 0 Special Education; 0 Vocational; 0 Alternative
 0 Magnet; 0 Charter; 2 Title I Eligible; 0 School-wide Title I
Students: 1,514 (52.8% male; 47.1% female)
 Individual Education Program: 172 (11.4%);
 English Language Learner: 246 (16.2%); Migrant: 0 (0.0%)
 Eligible for Free Lunch Program: 157 (10.6%)
 Eligible for Reduced-Price Lunch Program: 124 (8.4%)
Teachers: 111.5 (13.3 to 1)
Librarians/Media Specialists: 2.0 (742.0 to 1)
Guidance Counselors: 3.0 (494.7 to 1)
Current Spending: ($ per student per year):
 Total: $10,906; Instruction: $6,955; Support Services: $3,548
Enrollment, Drop-out Rates and Diploma Recipients by Race/Ethnicity

Category	Total	White	Black	Asian	AIAN	Hisp.
Enrollment (%)	100.0	22.6	2.8	44.5	0.3	29.7
Drop-out Rate (%)	1.8	0.9	8.3	2.0	n/a	1.6
H.S. Diplomas (#)	111	38	0	45	0	28

Paramus Boro
145 Spring Valley Rd • Paramus, NJ 07652-5333
(201) 261-7800 • http://www.paramus.k12.nj.us/
Grade Span: PK-12; **Agency Type:** 1
Schools: 8
 5 Primary; 2 Middle; 1 High; 0 Other Level
 8 Regular; 0 Special Education; 0 Vocational; 0 Alternative
 0 Magnet; 0 Charter; 4 Title I Eligible; 0 School-wide Title I
Students: 4,576 (52.4% male; 47.5% female)
 Individual Education Program: 432 (9.4%);
 English Language Learner: 163 (3.6%); Migrant: 0 (0.0%)
 Eligible for Free Lunch Program: 54 (1.3%)
 Eligible for Reduced-Price Lunch Program: 43 (1.0%)
Teachers: 339.0 (12.5 to 1)
Librarians/Media Specialists: 8.0 (530.9 to 1)
Guidance Counselors: 12.0 (353.9 to 1)
Current Spending: ($ per student per year):
 Total: $12,842; Instruction: $7,426; Support Services: $5,226
Enrollment, Drop-out Rates and Diploma Recipients by Race/Ethnicity

Category	Total	White	Black	Asian	AIAN	Hisp.
Enrollment (%)	100.0	69.0	0.8	24.6	0.0	5.5
Drop-out Rate (%)	0.1	0.0	14.3	0.0	0.0	0.0
H.S. Diplomas (#)	307	205	4	76	0	22

Pascack Valley Regional
46 Akers Ave • Montvale, NJ 07645-2028
(201) 358-7005 • http://www.pascack.k12.nj.us
Grade Span: 09-12; **Agency Type:** 1
Schools: 2
 0 Primary; 0 Middle; 2 High; 0 Other Level
 2 Regular; 0 Special Education; 0 Vocational; 0 Alternative
 0 Magnet; 0 Charter; 1 Title I Eligible; 0 School-wide Title I
Students: 1,614 (50.6% male; 49.3% female)
 Individual Education Program: 217 (13.4%);
 English Language Learner: 9 (0.6%); Migrant: 0 (0.0%)
 Eligible for Free Lunch Program: 16 (1.0%)
 Eligible for Reduced-Price Lunch Program: 0 (0.0%)

Teachers: 133.0 (12.1 to 1)
Librarians/Media Specialists: 2.0 (802.0 to 1)
Guidance Counselors: 8.0 (200.5 to 1)
Current Spending: ($ per student per year):
   Total: $19,083; Instruction: $9,996; Support Services: $6,565
Enrollment, Drop-out Rates and Diploma Recipients by Race/Ethnicity

Category	Total	White	Black	Asian	AIAN	Hisp.
Enrollment (%)	100.0	88.7	0.5	6.4	0.2	4.2
Drop-out Rate (%)	0.1	0.1	0.0	0.0	0.0	1.9
H.S. Diplomas (#)	367	321	1	31	0	14

Ramapo-Indian Hill Reg
331 George St • Franklin Lakes, NJ 07417-3099
(201) 891-1505 • http://www.rih.org
Grade Span: 09-12; **Agency Type:** 1
Schools: 2
   0 Primary; 0 Middle; 2 High; 0 Other Level
   2 Regular; 0 Special Education; 0 Vocational; 0 Alternative
   0 Magnet; 0 Charter; 0 Title I Eligible; 0 School-wide Title I
Students: 2,134 (47.5% male; 52.4% female)
   Individual Education Program: 322 (15.1%);
   English Language Learner: 9 (0.4%); Migrant: 0 (0.0%)
   Eligible for Free Lunch Program: 0 (0.0%)
   Eligible for Reduced-Price Lunch Program: 16 (0.8%)
Teachers: 188.1 (11.3 to 1)
Librarians/Media Specialists: 2.0 (1,061.5 to 1)
Guidance Counselors: 12.0 (176.9 to 1)
Current Spending: ($ per student per year):
   Total: $16,074; Instruction: $9,450; Support Services: $6,254
Enrollment, Drop-out Rates and Diploma Recipients by Race/Ethnicity

Category	Total	White	Black	Asian	AIAN	Hisp.
Enrollment (%)	100.0	91.5	0.6	4.5	0.2	3.2
Drop-out Rate (%)	0.3	0.3	0.0	0.0	0.0	0.0
H.S. Diplomas (#)	439	398	2	29	0	10

Ramsey Boro
266 E Main St • Ramsey, NJ 07446-1927
(201) 785-2300 • http://www.ramsey.k12.nj.us
Grade Span: PK-12; **Agency Type:** 1
Schools: 5
   2 Primary; 2 Middle; 1 High; 0 Other Level
   5 Regular; 0 Special Education; 0 Vocational; 0 Alternative
   0 Magnet; 0 Charter; 0 Title I Eligible; 0 School-wide Title I
Students: 3,038 (52.6% male; 47.3% female)
   Individual Education Program: 470 (15.5%);
   English Language Learner: 22 (0.7%); Migrant: 0 (0.0%)
   Eligible for Free Lunch Program: 39 (1.3%)
   Eligible for Reduced-Price Lunch Program: 24 (0.8%)
Teachers: 224.4 (13.1 to 1)
Librarians/Media Specialists: 4.7 (626.0 to 1)
Guidance Counselors: 7.0 (420.3 to 1)
Current Spending: ($ per student per year):
   Total: $12,446; Instruction: $7,816; Support Services: $4,394
Enrollment, Drop-out Rates and Diploma Recipients by Race/Ethnicity

Category	Total	White	Black	Asian	AIAN	Hisp.
Enrollment (%)	100.0	88.9	0.8	7.2	0.0	3.1
Drop-out Rate (%)	0.0	0.0	0.0	0.0	n/a	0.0
H.S. Diplomas (#)	184	164	1	14	0	5

Ridgefield Boro
555 Chestnut St • Ridgefield, NJ 07657-1825
(201) 945-9236 • http://school.nj.com/school/rmhs
Grade Span: PK-12; **Agency Type:** 1
Schools: 4
   3 Primary; 0 Middle; 1 High; 0 Other Level
   3 Regular; 1 Special Education; 0 Vocational; 0 Alternative
   0 Magnet; 0 Charter; 3 Title I Eligible; 0 School-wide Title I
Students: 2,336 (54.9% male; 45.0% female)
   Individual Education Program: 168 (7.2%)
   English Language Learner: 82 (3.5%); Migrant: 0 (0.0%)
   Eligible for Free Lunch Program: 169 (8.3%)
   Eligible for Reduced-Price Lunch Program: 86 (4.2%)
Teachers: 157.0 (12.9 to 1)
Librarians/Media Specialists: 2.0 (1,014.0 to 1)
Guidance Counselors: 4.0 (507.0 to 1)
Current Spending: ($ per student per year):
   Total: $12,487; Instruction: $8,908; Support Services: $2,974
Enrollment, Drop-out Rates and Diploma Recipients by Race/Ethnicity

Category	Total	White	Black	Asian	AIAN	Hisp.
Enrollment (%)	100.0	48.1	2.9	28.3	0.0	20.7
Drop-out Rate (%)	0.0	0.0	0.0	0.0	n/a	0.0
H.S. Diplomas (#)	127	77	0	26	0	24

Ridgefield Park Twp
712 Lincoln Ave • Ridgefield Park, NJ 07660-1033
(201) 807-2638 • http://www.rpps.net/
Grade Span: PK-12; **Agency Type:** 1
Schools: 4
   3 Primary; 0 Middle; 1 High; 0 Other Level
   4 Regular; 0 Special Education; 0 Vocational; 0 Alternative
   0 Magnet; 0 Charter; 3 Title I Eligible; 0 School-wide Title I
Students: 1,959 (52.0% male; 47.9% female)
   Individual Education Program: 307 (15.7%);
   English Language Learner: 109 (5.6%); Migrant: 0 (0.0%)
   Eligible for Free Lunch Program: 327 (17.3%)
   Eligible for Reduced-Price Lunch Program: 211 (11.2%)
Teachers: 166.4 (11.3 to 1)
Librarians/Media Specialists: 3.2 (589.7 to 1)
Guidance Counselors: 6.0 (314.5 to 1)
Current Spending: ($ per student per year):
   Total: $12,558; Instruction: $7,770; Support Services: $4,514
Enrollment, Drop-out Rates and Diploma Recipients by Race/Ethnicity

Category	Total	White	Black	Asian	AIAN	Hisp.
Enrollment (%)	100.0	45.2	5.6	11.0	0.2	38.0
Drop-out Rate (%)	1.0	0.8	5.3	0.0	n/a	0.9
H.S. Diplomas (#)	158	75	11	28	0	44

Ridgewood Village
49 Cottage Place • Ridgewood, NJ 07451-3813
(201) 670-2700 • http://www.ridgewood.k12.nj.us
Grade Span: PK-12; **Agency Type:** 1
Schools: 10
   6 Primary; 2 Middle; 1 High; 1 Other Level
   10 Regular; 0 Special Education; 0 Vocational; 0 Alternative
   0 Magnet; 0 Charter; 5 Title I Eligible; 0 School-wide Title I
Students: 5,560 (51.0% male; 48.9% female)
   Individual Education Program: 679 (12.2%);
   English Language Learner: 107 (1.9%); Migrant: 0 (0.0%)
   Eligible for Free Lunch Program: 43 (0.8%)
   Eligible for Reduced-Price Lunch Program: 21 (0.4%)
Teachers: 387.4 (14.1 to 1)
Librarians/Media Specialists: 10.0 (546.4 to 1)
Guidance Counselors: 15.4 (354.8 to 1)
Current Spending: ($ per student per year):
   Total: $12,204; Instruction: $7,236; Support Services: $4,622
Enrollment, Drop-out Rates and Diploma Recipients by Race/Ethnicity

Category	Total	White	Black	Asian	AIAN	Hisp.
Enrollment (%)	100.0	80.1	0.9	15.5	0.1	3.4
Drop-out Rate (%)	0.5	0.4	0.0	0.5	n/a	5.4
H.S. Diplomas (#)	332	271	9	43	0	9

Rutherford Boro
176 Park Ave • Rutherford, NJ 07070-2310
(201) 939-1717 • http://www.rutherford.k12.nj.us
Grade Span: PK-12; **Agency Type:** 1
Schools: 6
   5 Primary; 0 Middle; 1 High; 0 Other Level
   6 Regular; 0 Special Education; 0 Vocational; 0 Alternative
   0 Magnet; 0 Charter; 0 Title I Eligible; 0 School-wide Title I
Students: 2,399 (51.0% male; 48.9% female)
   Individual Education Program: 361 (15.0%);
   English Language Learner: 21 (0.9%); Migrant: 0 (0.0%)
   Eligible for Free Lunch Program: 35 (1.5%)
   Eligible for Reduced-Price Lunch Program: 23 (1.0%)
Teachers: 184.8 (12.8 to 1)
Librarians/Media Specialists: 3.0 (790.3 to 1)
Guidance Counselors: 4.0 (592.8 to 1)
Current Spending: ($ per student per year):
   Total: $11,653; Instruction: $7,562; Support Services: $3,866
Enrollment, Drop-out Rates and Diploma Recipients by Race/Ethnicity

Category	Total	White	Black	Asian	AIAN	Hisp.
Enrollment (%)	100.0	69.3	3.4	16.4	0.0	10.8
Drop-out Rate (%)	0.1	0.2	0.0	0.0	n/a	0.0
H.S. Diplomas (#)	149	119	4	17	0	9

Saddle Brook Twp
355 Mayhill St • Saddle Brook, NJ 07663-4628
(201) 843-2133 • http://www.njcommunity.com/
Grade Span: PK-12; **Agency Type:** 1
Schools: 5
   3 Primary; 0 Middle; 1 High; 1 Other Level
   4 Regular; 1 Special Education; 0 Vocational; 0 Alternative
   0 Magnet; 0 Charter; 3 Title I Eligible; 0 School-wide Title I
Students: 1,763 (48.5% male; 51.4% female)
   Individual Education Program: 298 (16.9%);
   English Language Learner: 24 (1.4%); Migrant: 0 (0.0%)
   Eligible for Free Lunch Program: 87 (5.1%)
   Eligible for Reduced-Price Lunch Program: 56 (3.3%)

Teachers: 118.6 (14.4 to 1)
Librarians/Media Specialists: 1.0 (1,705.0 to 1)
Guidance Counselors: 3.0 (568.3 to 1)
Current Spending: ($ per student per year):
    Total: $12,113; Instruction: $7,387; Support Services: $4,148
Enrollment, Drop-out Rates and Diploma Recipients by Race/Ethnicity

Category	Total	White	Black	Asian	AIAN	Hisp.
Enrollment (%)	100.0	78.0	1.8	8.6	0.0	11.6
Drop-out Rate (%)	1.2	1.5	0.0	0.0	0.0	0.0
H.S. Diplomas (#)	111	89	2	9	0	11

Teaneck Twp

One Merrison St • Teaneck, NJ 07666-4616
(201) 833-5510 • http://www.teaneckschools.org/aboutus.asp?mid=27
Grade Span: PK-12; **Agency Type:** 1
Schools: 7
    4 Primary; 2 Middle; 1 High; 0 Other Level
    7 Regular; 0 Special Education; 0 Vocational; 0 Alternative
    0 Magnet; 0 Charter; 6 Title I Eligible; 0 School-wide Title I
Students: 4,512 (50.8% male; 49.1% female)
    Individual Education Program: 690 (15.3%);
    English Language Learner: 101 (2.2%); Migrant: 0 (0.0%)
    Eligible for Free Lunch Program: 433 (9.9%)
    Eligible for Reduced-Price Lunch Program: 314 (7.2%)
Teachers: 348.9 (12.6 to 1)
Librarians/Media Specialists: 5.0 (877.0 to 1)
Guidance Counselors: 14.0 (313.2 to 1)
Current Spending: ($ per student per year):
    Total: $15,208; Instruction: $9,088; Support Services: $5,773
Enrollment, Drop-out Rates and Diploma Recipients by Race/Ethnicity

Category	Total	White	Black	Asian	AIAN	Hisp.
Enrollment (%)	100.0	21.4	48.5	10.7	0.2	19.2
Drop-out Rate (%)	2.4	1.8	2.7	0.0	0.0	3.8
H.S. Diplomas (#)	314	101	144	35	0	34

Tenafly Boro

500 Tenafly Rd • Tenafly, NJ 07670-1727
(201) 816-4501 • http://www.tenafly.k12.nj.us
Grade Span: PK-12; **Agency Type:** 1
Schools: 6
    4 Primary; 1 Middle; 1 High; 0 Other Level
    6 Regular; 0 Special Education; 0 Vocational; 0 Alternative
    0 Magnet; 0 Charter; 0 Title I Eligible; 0 School-wide Title I
Students: 3,128 (52.7% male; 47.2% female)
    Individual Education Program: 435 (13.9%);
    English Language Learner: 213 (6.8%); Migrant: 0 (0.0%)
    Eligible for Free Lunch Program: 9 (0.3%)
    Eligible for Reduced-Price Lunch Program: 2 (0.1%)
Teachers: 259.1 (12.0 to 1)
Librarians/Media Specialists: 6.0 (516.5 to 1)
Guidance Counselors: 7.0 (442.7 to 1)
Current Spending: ($ per student per year):
    Total: $13,101; Instruction: $8,310; Support Services: $4,573
Enrollment, Drop-out Rates and Diploma Recipients by Race/Ethnicity

Category	Total	White	Black	Asian	AIAN	Hisp.
Enrollment (%)	100.0	68.0	0.9	27.5	0.0	3.5
Drop-out Rate (%)	0.1	0.0	0.0	0.4	n/a	0.0
H.S. Diplomas (#)	232	141	6	73	0	12

Waldwick Boro

155 Summit Ave • Waldwick, NJ 07463-2133
(201) 445-3131
Grade Span: PK-12; **Agency Type:** 1
Schools: 3
    2 Primary; 0 Middle; 1 High; 0 Other Level
    3 Regular; 0 Special Education; 0 Vocational; 0 Alternative
    0 Magnet; 0 Charter; 0 Title I Eligible; 0 School-wide Title I
Students: 1,512 (50.2% male; 49.7% female)
    Individual Education Program: 265 (17.5%);
    English Language Learner: 34 (2.2%); Migrant: 0 (0.0%)
    Eligible for Free Lunch Program: 11 (0.7%)
    Eligible for Reduced-Price Lunch Program: 1 (0.1%)
Teachers: 114.8 (13.1 to 1)
Librarians/Media Specialists: 2.0 (752.5 to 1)
Guidance Counselors: 2.0 (752.5 to 1)
Current Spending: ($ per student per year):
    Total: $11,423; Instruction: $7,196; Support Services: $4,035
Enrollment, Drop-out Rates and Diploma Recipients by Race/Ethnicity

Category	Total	White	Black	Asian	AIAN	Hisp.
Enrollment (%)	100.0	84.7	1.2	6.1	0.4	7.6
Drop-out Rate (%)	0.3	0.0	0.0	0.0	0.0	3.0
H.S. Diplomas (#)	84	68	1	9	2	4

Westwood Regional

701 Ridgewood Rd • Westwood, NJ 07675-4811
(201) 664-2765 • http://www.westwood.k12.nj.us
Grade Span: PK-12; **Agency Type:** 1
Schools: 6
    4 Primary; 1 Middle; 1 High; 0 Other Level
    6 Regular; 0 Special Education; 0 Vocational; 0 Alternative
    0 Magnet; 0 Charter; 3 Title I Eligible; 0 School-wide Title I
Students: 2,663 (52.1% male; 47.8% female)
    Individual Education Program: 583 (21.9%);
    English Language Learner: 75 (2.8%); Migrant: 0 (0.0%)
    Eligible for Free Lunch Program: 51 (2.0%)
    Eligible for Reduced-Price Lunch Program: 23 (0.9%)
Teachers: 206.4 (12.6 to 1)
Librarians/Media Specialists: 4.0 (650.3 to 1)
Guidance Counselors: 5.0 (520.2 to 1)
Current Spending: ($ per student per year):
    Total: $13,427; Instruction: $8,059; Support Services: $5,122
Enrollment, Drop-out Rates and Diploma Recipients by Race/Ethnicity

Category	Total	White	Black	Asian	AIAN	Hisp.
Enrollment (%)	100.0	83.6	4.7	6.4	0.0	5.3
Drop-out Rate (%)	1.0	0.9	0.0	0.0	n/a	4.8
H.S. Diplomas (#)	137	116	12	3	0	6

Wyckoff Twp

241 Morse Ave • Wyckoff, NJ 07481-1917
(201) 848-5701 • http://www.wyckoffschools.org
Grade Span: PK-08; **Agency Type:** 1
Schools: 5
    4 Primary; 1 Middle; 0 High; 0 Other Level
    5 Regular; 0 Special Education; 0 Vocational; 0 Alternative
    0 Magnet; 0 Charter; 0 Title I Eligible; 0 School-wide Title I
Students: 2,446 (49.7% male; 50.2% female)
    Individual Education Program: 251 (10.3%);
    English Language Learner: 21 (0.9%); Migrant: 0 (0.0%)
    Eligible for Free Lunch Program: 8 (0.3%)
    Eligible for Reduced-Price Lunch Program: 1 (<0.1%)
Teachers: 165.1 (14.5 to 1)
Librarians/Media Specialists: 5.0 (480.4 to 1)
Guidance Counselors: 6.0 (400.3 to 1)
Current Spending: ($ per student per year):
    Total: $9,768; Instruction: $5,901; Support Services: $3,737
Enrollment, Drop-out Rates and Diploma Recipients by Race/Ethnicity

Category	Total	White	Black	Asian	AIAN	Hisp.
Enrollment (%)	100.0	93.9	0.7	4.2	0.0	1.2
Drop-out Rate (%)	n/a	n/a	n/a	n/a	n/a	n/a
H.S. Diplomas (#)	n/a	n/a	n/a	n/a	n/a	n/a

Burlington County

Bordentown Regional

48 Dunns Mill Rd • Bordentown, NJ 08505-1768
(609) 298-0025 • http://www.bordentown.k12.nj.us
Grade Span: PK-12; **Agency Type:** 1
Schools: 4
    2 Primary; 1 Middle; 1 High; 0 Other Level
    4 Regular; 0 Special Education; 0 Vocational; 0 Alternative
    0 Magnet; 0 Charter; 2 Title I Eligible; 0 School-wide Title I
Students: 2,062 (50.5% male; 49.4% female)
    Individual Education Program: 456 (22.1%);
    English Language Learner: 36 (1.7%); Migrant: 0 (0.0%)
    Eligible for Free Lunch Program: 163 (7.9%)
    Eligible for Reduced-Price Lunch Program: 119 (5.8%)
Teachers: 155.6 (13.3 to 1)
Librarians/Media Specialists: 3.0 (687.3 to 1)
Guidance Counselors: 7.0 (294.6 to 1)
Current Spending: ($ per student per year):
    Total: $11,410; Instruction: $6,454; Support Services: $4,499
Enrollment, Drop-out Rates and Diploma Recipients by Race/Ethnicity

Category	Total	White	Black	Asian	AIAN	Hisp.
Enrollment (%)	100.0	75.5	13.7	6.3	0.0	4.6
Drop-out Rate (%)	1.3	1.6	0.0	0.0	n/a	0.0
H.S. Diplomas (#)	119	98	13	2	1	5

Burlington City

518 Locust Ave • Burlington, NJ 08016-4512
(609) 387-5874 • http://www.burlington-nj.net
Grade Span: PK-12; **Agency Type:** 1
Schools: 5
    3 Primary; 1 Middle; 1 High; 0 Other Level
    5 Regular; 0 Special Education; 0 Vocational; 0 Alternative
    0 Magnet; 0 Charter; 5 Title I Eligible; 4 School-wide Title I
Students: 1,919 (53.5% male; 46.4% female)
    Individual Education Program: 345 (18.0%);
    English Language Learner: 74 (3.9%); Migrant: 0 (0.0%)

Eligible for Free Lunch Program: 566 (30.6%)
Eligible for Reduced-Price Lunch Program: 203 (11.0%)
Teachers: 180.0 (10.3 to 1)
Librarians/Media Specialists: 2.5 (740.0 to 1)
Guidance Counselors: 7.0 (264.3 to 1)
Current Spending: ($ per student per year):
Total: $13,320; Instruction: $8,360; Support Services: $4,532
Enrollment, Drop-out Rates and Diploma Recipients by Race/Ethnicity

Category	Total	White	Black	Asian	AIAN	Hisp.
Enrollment (%)	100.0	43.0	47.9	3.8	0.1	5.1
Drop-out Rate (%)	4.5	4.5	5.3	2.2	n/a	0.0
H.S. Diplomas (#)	112	62	38	11	0	1

Burlington County Spec Serv

20 Pioneer Blvd • Mount Holly, NJ 08060-9614
(609) 261-5600
Grade Span: UG-UG; **Agency Type:** 4
Schools: 3
0 Primary; 0 Middle; 0 High; 3 Other Level
0 Regular; 3 Special Education; 0 Vocational; 0 Alternative
0 Magnet; 0 Charter; 0 Title I Eligible; 0 School-wide Title I
Students: 2,472 (71.6% male; 28.3% female)
Individual Education Program: 0 (0.0%);
English Language Learner: 0 (0.0%); Migrant: 0 (0.0%)
Eligible for Free Lunch Program: 527 (42.6%)
Eligible for Reduced-Price Lunch Program: 125 (10.1%)
Teachers: 152.3 (8.1 to 1)
Librarians/Media Specialists: 0.0 (n/a to 1)
Guidance Counselors: 2.0 (618.0 to 1)
Current Spending: ($ per student per year):
Total: $31,812; Instruction: $13,674; Support Services: $8,593
Enrollment, Drop-out Rates and Diploma Recipients by Race/Ethnicity

Category	Total	White	Black	Asian	AIAN	Hisp.
Enrollment (%)	100.0	55.9	35.7	1.3	0.2	6.9
Drop-out Rate (%)	n/a	n/a	n/a	n/a	n/a	n/a
H.S. Diplomas (#)	0	0	0	0	0	0

Burlington County Vocational

695 Woodlane Rd • Westampton Twp, NJ 08060-9614
Mailing Address: Westampton Camp 695 Woodlane R • Westampton Twp, NJ 08060-9614
(609) 267-4226 • http://www.bcit.tec.nj.us
Grade Span: 09-12; **Agency Type:** 1
Schools: 2
0 Primary; 0 Middle; 2 High; 0 Other Level
0 Regular; 0 Special Education; 2 Vocational; 0 Alternative
0 Magnet; 0 Charter; 2 Title I Eligible; 0 School-wide Title I
Students: 1,803 (52.0% male; 47.9% female)
Individual Education Program: 575 (31.9%);
English Language Learner: 1 (0.1%); Migrant: 0 (0.0%)
Eligible for Free Lunch Program: 317 (17.6%)
Eligible for Reduced-Price Lunch Program: 177 (9.8%)
Teachers: 158.0 (11.4 to 1)
Librarians/Media Specialists: 2.0 (901.5 to 1)
Guidance Counselors: 9.0 (200.3 to 1)
Current Spending: ($ per student per year):
Total: $16,275; Instruction: $9,204; Support Services: $5,703
Enrollment, Drop-out Rates and Diploma Recipients by Race/Ethnicity

Category	Total	White	Black	Asian	AIAN	Hisp.
Enrollment (%)	100.0	55.2	36.2	0.7	0.6	7.3
Drop-out Rate (%)	1.1	1.1	0.8	0.0	0.0	1.7
H.S. Diplomas (#)	929	503	357	3	3	63

Burlington Twp

1508 Mt Holly Rd • Burlington, NJ 08016-0428
Mailing Address: PO Box 428 • Burlington, NJ 08016-0428
(609) 387-3955 • http://www.burltwpsch.org
Grade Span: PK-12; **Agency Type:** 1
Schools: 5
3 Primary; 1 Middle; 1 High; 0 Other Level
5 Regular; 0 Special Education; 0 Vocational; 0 Alternative
0 Magnet; 0 Charter; 4 Title I Eligible; 0 School-wide Title I
Students: 4,098 (50.2% male; 49.7% female)
Individual Education Program: 601 (14.7%);
English Language Learner: 100 (2.4%); Migrant: 0 (0.0%)
Eligible for Free Lunch Program: 331 (8.2%)
Eligible for Reduced-Price Lunch Program: 174 (4.3%)
Teachers: 289.2 (13.9 to 1)
Librarians/Media Specialists: 3.0 (1,342.0 to 1)
Guidance Counselors: 10.4 (387.1 to 1)
Current Spending: ($ per student per year):
Total: $8,921; Instruction: $5,609; Support Services: $3,068

Enrollment, Drop-out Rates and Diploma Recipients by Race/Ethnicity

Category	Total	White	Black	Asian	AIAN	Hisp.
Enrollment (%)	100.0	53.5	34.4	6.9	0.1	5.1
Drop-out Rate (%)	0.7	0.9	0.3	0.0	0.0	2.4
H.S. Diplomas (#)	145	88	40	11	0	6

Cinnaminson Twp

2195 Riverton Rd • Cinnaminson, NJ 08077-2496
Mailing Address: 2195 Riverton Rd PO Box 224 • Cinnaminson, NJ 08077-2496
(856) 829-7600 • http://www.cinnaminson.com
Grade Span: PK-12; **Agency Type:** 1
Schools: 4
2 Primary; 1 Middle; 1 High; 0 Other Level
4 Regular; 0 Special Education; 0 Vocational; 0 Alternative
0 Magnet; 0 Charter; 2 Title I Eligible; 0 School-wide Title I
Students: 2,642 (53.3% male; 46.6% female)
Individual Education Program: 483 (18.3%);
English Language Learner: 10 (0.4%); Migrant: 0 (0.0%)
Eligible for Free Lunch Program: 115 (4.6%)
Eligible for Reduced-Price Lunch Program: 49 (1.9%)
Teachers: 202.3 (12.5 to 1)
Librarians/Media Specialists: 3.0 (841.7 to 1)
Guidance Counselors: 5.5 (459.1 to 1)
Current Spending: ($ per student per year):
Total: $11,214; Instruction: $7,126; Support Services: $3,751
Enrollment, Drop-out Rates and Diploma Recipients by Race/Ethnicity

Category	Total	White	Black	Asian	AIAN	Hisp.
Enrollment (%)	100.0	88.4	6.7	2.7	0.0	2.3
Drop-out Rate (%)	1.0	0.9	5.1	0.0	n/a	0.0
H.S. Diplomas (#)	200	187	7	6	0	0

Delran Twp

52 Hartford Rd • Delran, NJ 08075-1895
(856) 461-6800 • http://www.delran.k12.nj.us
Grade Span: PK-12; **Agency Type:** 1
Schools: 4
2 Primary; 1 Middle; 1 High; 0 Other Level
4 Regular; 0 Special Education; 0 Vocational; 0 Alternative
0 Magnet; 0 Charter; 2 Title I Eligible; 0 School-wide Title I
Students: 2,780 (50.4% male; 49.5% female)
Individual Education Program: 359 (12.9%);
English Language Learner: 65 (2.3%); Migrant: 0 (0.0%)
Eligible for Free Lunch Program: 161 (6.0%)
Eligible for Reduced-Price Lunch Program: 96 (3.6%)
Teachers: 182.3 (14.6 to 1)
Librarians/Media Specialists: 5.0 (532.8 to 1)
Guidance Counselors: 5.8 (459.3 to 1)
Current Spending: ($ per student per year):
Total: $9,824; Instruction: $5,829; Support Services: $3,725
Enrollment, Drop-out Rates and Diploma Recipients by Race/Ethnicity

Category	Total	White	Black	Asian	AIAN	Hisp.
Enrollment (%)	100.0	82.0	9.1	4.0	0.0	4.8
Drop-out Rate (%)	1.8	1.8	0.0	0.0	n/a	6.5
H.S. Diplomas (#)	181	155	17	5	0	4

Evesham Twp

25 S Maple Ave • Marlton, NJ 08053-2001
(856) 983-1800 • http://www.evesham.k12.nj.us
Grade Span: PK-08; **Agency Type:** 1
Schools: 9
7 Primary; 2 Middle; 0 High; 0 Other Level
9 Regular; 0 Special Education; 0 Vocational; 0 Alternative
0 Magnet; 0 Charter; 3 Title I Eligible; 0 School-wide Title I
Students: 5,708 (51.7% male; 48.2% female)
Individual Education Program: 1,096 (19.2%);
English Language Learner: 48 (0.8%); Migrant: 0 (0.0%)
Eligible for Free Lunch Program: 108 (2.0%)
Eligible for Reduced-Price Lunch Program: 121 (2.2%)
Teachers: 406.7 (13.2 to 1)
Librarians/Media Specialists: 9.0 (598.6 to 1)
Guidance Counselors: 12.2 (441.6 to 1)
Current Spending: ($ per student per year):
Total: $9,640; Instruction: $5,676; Support Services: $3,608
Enrollment, Drop-out Rates and Diploma Recipients by Race/Ethnicity

Category	Total	White	Black	Asian	AIAN	Hisp.
Enrollment (%)	100.0	89.0	3.8	5.2	0.4	1.6
Drop-out Rate (%)	n/a	n/a	n/a	n/a	n/a	n/a
H.S. Diplomas (#)	n/a	n/a	n/a	n/a	n/a	n/a

Florence Twp

Admin Bldg 201 Cedar St • Florence, NJ 08518
(609) 499-4600 • http://www.florence.k12.nj.us
Grade Span: PK-12; **Agency Type:** 1
Schools: 4

1 Primary; 2 Middle; 1 High; 0 Other Level
4 Regular; 0 Special Education; 0 Vocational; 0 Alternative
0 Magnet; 0 Charter; 4 Title I Eligible; 0 School-wide Title I
Students: 1,641 (51.0% male; 48.9% female)
Individual Education Program: 307 (18.7%);
English Language Learner: 18 (1.1%); Migrant: 0 (0.0%)
Eligible for Free Lunch Program: 228 (14.5%)
Eligible for Reduced-Price Lunch Program: 101 (6.4%)
Teachers: 129.8 (12.1 to 1)
Librarians/Media Specialists: 3.0 (525.7 to 1)
Guidance Counselors: 5.0 (315.4 to 1)
Current Spending: ($ per student per year):
Total: $11,221; Instruction: $6,606; Support Services: $4,181
Enrollment, Drop-out Rates and Diploma Recipients by Race/Ethnicity

Category	Total	White	Black	Asian	AIAN	Hisp.
Enrollment (%)	100.0	75.0	18.8	3.0	0.3	2.9
Drop-out Rate (%)	1.4	1.3	1.4	0.0	n/a	9.1
H.S. Diplomas (#)	105	88	9	8	0	0

Lenape Regional
93 Willow Grove Rd • Shamong, NJ 08088-8961
(609) 268-2000 • http://www.lr.k12.nj.us
Grade Span: 09-12; **Agency Type:** 1
Schools: 4
0 Primary; 0 Middle; 3 High; 1 Other Level
4 Regular; 0 Special Education; 0 Vocational; 0 Alternative
0 Magnet; 0 Charter; 0 Title I Eligible; 0 School-wide Title I
Students: 7,067 (49.9% male; 50.0% female)
Individual Education Program: 1,071 (15.2%);
English Language Learner: 20 (0.3%); Migrant: 1 (<0.1%)
Eligible for Free Lunch Program: 87 (1.2%)
Eligible for Reduced-Price Lunch Program: 40 (0.6%)
Teachers: 538.9 (13.0 to 1)
Librarians/Media Specialists: 7.5 (934.4 to 1)
Guidance Counselors: 35.0 (200.2 to 1)
Current Spending: ($ per student per year):
Total: $11,924; Instruction: $6,714; Support Services: $4,770
Enrollment, Drop-out Rates and Diploma Recipients by Race/Ethnicity

Category	Total	White	Black	Asian	AIAN	Hisp.
Enrollment (%)	100.0	88.9	4.4	4.0	0.5	2.2
Drop-out Rate (%)	0.4	0.4	1.0	0.4	0.0	0.0
H.S. Diplomas (#)	1,496	1,338	70	58	7	23

Lumberton Twp
30 Dimsdale Dr • Lumberton, NJ 08048
Mailing Address: 30 Dimsdale Dr PO Box 8 • Lumberton, NJ 08048
(609) 265-7709
Grade Span: PK-08; **Agency Type:** 1
Schools: 4
2 Primary; 2 Middle; 0 High; 0 Other Level
4 Regular; 0 Special Education; 0 Vocational; 0 Alternative
0 Magnet; 0 Charter; 2 Title I Eligible; 2 School-wide Title I
Students: 1,844 (51.6% male; 48.3% female)
Individual Education Program: 373 (20.2%);
English Language Learner: 12 (0.7%); Migrant: 0 (0.0%)
Eligible for Free Lunch Program: 98 (5.6%)
Eligible for Reduced-Price Lunch Program: 58 (3.3%)
Teachers: 129.4 (13.5 to 1)
Librarians/Media Specialists: 3.2 (545.3 to 1)
Guidance Counselors: 5.0 (349.0 to 1)
Current Spending: ($ per student per year):
Total: $9,195; Instruction: $5,383; Support Services: $3,336
Enrollment, Drop-out Rates and Diploma Recipients by Race/Ethnicity

Category	Total	White	Black	Asian	AIAN	Hisp.
Enrollment (%)	100.0	71.9	20.3	4.2	0.1	3.5
Drop-out Rate (%)	n/a	n/a	n/a	n/a	n/a	n/a
H.S. Diplomas (#)	n/a	n/a	n/a	n/a	n/a	n/a

Maple Shade Twp
Frederick And Clinton Ave • Maple Shade, NJ 08052-3299
(856) 779-1750 • http://www.mapleshade.org
Grade Span: PK-12; **Agency Type:** 1
Schools: 4
2 Primary; 1 Middle; 1 High; 0 Other Level
4 Regular; 0 Special Education; 0 Vocational; 0 Alternative
0 Magnet; 0 Charter; 4 Title I Eligible; 0 School-wide Title I
Students: 2,404 (51.2% male; 48.7% female)
Individual Education Program: 488 (20.3%);
English Language Learner: 36 (1.5%); Migrant: 0 (0.0%)
Eligible for Free Lunch Program: 261 (12.0%)
Eligible for Reduced-Price Lunch Program: 214 (9.8%)
Teachers: 156.8 (13.9 to 1)
Librarians/Media Specialists: 1.0 (2,181.0 to 1)
Guidance Counselors: 8.0 (272.6 to 1)
Current Spending: ($ per student per year):
Total: $10,878; Instruction: $6,959; Support Services: $3,571

Enrollment, Drop-out Rates and Diploma Recipients by Race/Ethnicity

Category	Total	White	Black	Asian	AIAN	Hisp.
Enrollment (%)	100.0	81.0	7.8	6.1	0.1	5.0
Drop-out Rate (%)	1.5	1.5	3.3	0.0	n/a	0.0
H.S. Diplomas (#)	126	109	5	8	0	4

Medford Twp
128 Route 70 Ste 1 • Medford, NJ 08055
(609) 654-6416 • http://www.medford.k12.nj.us
Grade Span: PK-08; **Agency Type:** 1
Schools: 5
4 Primary; 1 Middle; 0 High; 0 Other Level
5 Regular; 0 Special Education; 0 Vocational; 0 Alternative
0 Magnet; 0 Charter; 2 Title I Eligible; 0 School-wide Title I
Students: 3,028 (50.7% male; 49.2% female)
Individual Education Program: 459 (15.2%);
English Language Learner: 0 (0.0%); Migrant: 0 (0.0%)
Eligible for Free Lunch Program: 48 (1.6%)
Eligible for Reduced-Price Lunch Program: 39 (1.3%)
Teachers: 184.5 (16.1 to 1)
Librarians/Media Specialists: 5.0 (595.8 to 1)
Guidance Counselors: 7.0 (425.6 to 1)
Current Spending: ($ per student per year):
Total: $10,305; Instruction: $6,413; Support Services: $3,690
Enrollment, Drop-out Rates and Diploma Recipients by Race/Ethnicity

Category	Total	White	Black	Asian	AIAN	Hisp.
Enrollment (%)	100.0	96.0	1.4	1.8	0.0	0.9
Drop-out Rate (%)	n/a	n/a	n/a	n/a	n/a	n/a
H.S. Diplomas (#)	n/a	n/a	n/a	n/a	n/a	n/a

Moorestown Twp
803 N Stanwick Rd • Moorestown, NJ 08057-2034
(856) 778-6600 • http://www.mtps.com
Grade Span: PK-12; **Agency Type:** 1
Schools: 6
3 Primary; 2 Middle; 1 High; 0 Other Level
6 Regular; 0 Special Education; 0 Vocational; 0 Alternative
0 Magnet; 0 Charter; 3 Title I Eligible; 0 School-wide Title I
Students: 4,316 (50.3% male; 49.6% female)
Individual Education Program: 733 (17.0%);
English Language Learner: 18 (0.4%); Migrant: 0 (0.0%)
Eligible for Free Lunch Program: 129 (3.1%)
Eligible for Reduced-Price Lunch Program: 72 (1.7%)
Teachers: 296.9 (14.0 to 1)
Librarians/Media Specialists: 7.0 (594.7 to 1)
Guidance Counselors: 10.0 (416.3 to 1)
Current Spending: ($ per student per year):
Total: $10,814; Instruction: $6,525; Support Services: $4,040
Enrollment, Drop-out Rates and Diploma Recipients by Race/Ethnicity

Category	Total	White	Black	Asian	AIAN	Hisp.
Enrollment (%)	100.0	84.7	6.7	6.1	0.1	2.3
Drop-out Rate (%)	1.8	1.4	4.5	3.3	n/a	3.4
H.S. Diplomas (#)	222	190	20	11	0	1

Mount Laurel Twp
330 Moorestown-Mt. Laurel • Mount Laurel, NJ 08054-9521
(856) 235-3387 • http://www.mountlaurel.k12.nj.us
Grade Span: PK-08; **Agency Type:** 1
Schools: 8
6 Primary; 2 Middle; 0 High; 0 Other Level
8 Regular; 0 Special Education; 0 Vocational; 0 Alternative
0 Magnet; 0 Charter; 7 Title I Eligible; 0 School-wide Title I
Students: 4,726 (51.5% male; 48.4% female)
Individual Education Program: 745 (15.8%);
English Language Learner: 31 (0.7%); Migrant: 0 (0.0%)
Eligible for Free Lunch Program: 186 (4.1%)
Eligible for Reduced-Price Lunch Program: 110 (2.4%)
Teachers: 337.9 (13.5 to 1)
Librarians/Media Specialists: 8.0 (571.5 to 1)
Guidance Counselors: 10.0 (457.2 to 1)
Current Spending: ($ per student per year):
Total: $9,910; Instruction: $6,112; Support Services: $3,604
Enrollment, Drop-out Rates and Diploma Recipients by Race/Ethnicity

Category	Total	White	Black	Asian	AIAN	Hisp.
Enrollment (%)	100.0	80.7	10.0	5.7	0.2	3.4
Drop-out Rate (%)	n/a	n/a	n/a	n/a	n/a	n/a
H.S. Diplomas (#)	n/a	n/a	n/a	n/a	n/a	n/a

Northern Burlington Reg
160 Mansfield Rd E • Columbus, NJ 08022-9738
(609) 298-3900 • http://www.nburlington.com
Grade Span: 07-12; **Agency Type:** 1
Schools: 2
0 Primary; 1 Middle; 1 High; 0 Other Level
2 Regular; 0 Special Education; 0 Vocational; 0 Alternative

0 Magnet; 0 Charter; 1 Title I Eligible; 0 School-wide Title I
Students: 1,927 (51.0% male; 48.9% female)
Individual Education Program: 313 (16.2%);
English Language Learner: 4 (0.2%); Migrant: 1 (0.1%)
Eligible for Free Lunch Program: 108 (5.6%)
Eligible for Reduced-Price Lunch Program: 94 (4.9%)
Teachers: 145.2 (13.2 to 1)
Librarians/Media Specialists: 2.0 (957.5 to 1)
Guidance Counselors: 9.0 (212.8 to 1)
Current Spending: ($ per student per year):
Total: $12,140; Instruction: $7,049; Support Services: $4,466
Enrollment, Drop-out Rates and Diploma Recipients by Race/Ethnicity

Category	Total	White	Black	Asian	AIAN	Hisp.
Enrollment (%)	100.0	76.6	13.1	4.7	0.4	5.3
Drop-out Rate (%)	1.5	1.2	2.6	0.0	0.0	7.9
H.S. Diplomas (#)	223	188	17	8	1	9

Pemberton Twp
One Egbert St • Pemberton, NJ 08068
(609) 893-8141 • http://www.pemberton.k12.nj.us/
Grade Span: PK-12; **Agency Type:** 1
Schools: 11
7 Primary; 3 Middle; 1 High; 0 Other Level
11 Regular; 0 Special Education; 0 Vocational; 0 Alternative
0 Magnet; 0 Charter; 9 Title I Eligible; 0 School-wide Title I
Students: 6,210 (50.9% male; 49.0% female)
Individual Education Program: 1,269 (20.4%);
English Language Learner: 39 (0.6%); Migrant: 1 (<0.1%)
Eligible for Free Lunch Program: 1,437 (24.9%)
Eligible for Reduced-Price Lunch Program: 826 (14.3%)
Teachers: 514.0 (11.2 to 1)
Librarians/Media Specialists: 12.0 (481.6 to 1)
Guidance Counselors: 19.0 (304.2 to 1)
Current Spending: ($ per student per year):
Total: $14,669; Instruction: $8,616; Support Services: $5,602
Enrollment, Drop-out Rates and Diploma Recipients by Race/Ethnicity

Category	Total	White	Black	Asian	AIAN	Hisp.
Enrollment (%)	100.0	55.3	30.7	2.6	0.2	11.3
Drop-out Rate (%)	3.4	3.8	2.3	0.0	0.0	5.6
H.S. Diplomas (#)	310	180	88	9	0	33

Rancocas Valley Regional
520 Jacksonville Rd • Mount Holly, NJ 08060-9622
(609) 267-0830 • http://www.rancocasvalley.k12.nj.us
Grade Span: 09-12; **Agency Type:** 1
Schools: 2
0 Primary; 0 Middle; 2 High; 0 Other Level
1 Regular; 0 Special Education; 0 Vocational; 1 Alternative
0 Magnet; 0 Charter; 1 Title I Eligible; 0 School-wide Title I
Students: 2,269 (50.2% male; 49.7% female)
Individual Education Program: 460 (20.3%);
English Language Learner: 8 (0.4%); Migrant: 0 (0.0%)
Eligible for Free Lunch Program: 121 (5.4%)
Eligible for Reduced-Price Lunch Program: 39 (1.8%)
Teachers: 130.6 (17.0 to 1)
Librarians/Media Specialists: 1.8 (1,235.0 to 1)
Guidance Counselors: 8.7 (255.5 to 1)
Current Spending: ($ per student per year):
Total: $10,143; Instruction: $5,589; Support Services: $4,258
Enrollment, Drop-out Rates and Diploma Recipients by Race/Ethnicity

Category	Total	White	Black	Asian	AIAN	Hisp.
Enrollment (%)	100.0	66.7	22.1	3.6	0.5	7.2
Drop-out Rate (%)	2.0	1.8	2.8	0.0	0.0	3.4
H.S. Diplomas (#)	410	280	90	17	0	23

Riverside Twp
Y12 E Washington St • Riverside, NJ 08075-3899
(856) 461-1255
Grade Span: PK-12; **Agency Type:** 1
Schools: 3
1 Primary; 1 Middle; 1 High; 0 Other Level
3 Regular; 0 Special Education; 0 Vocational; 0 Alternative
0 Magnet; 0 Charter; 1 Title I Eligible; 0 School-wide Title I
Students: 1,629 (51.3% male; 48.6% female)
Individual Education Program: 288 (17.7%);
English Language Learner: 24 (1.5%); Migrant: 0 (0.0%)
Eligible for Free Lunch Program: 329 (23.4%)
Eligible for Reduced-Price Lunch Program: 121 (8.6%)
Teachers: 100.0 (14.0 to 1)
Librarians/Media Specialists: 1.0 (1,404.0 to 1)
Guidance Counselors: 4.0 (351.0 to 1)
Current Spending: ($ per student per year):
Total: $9,978; Instruction: $6,680; Support Services: $3,073

Category	Total	White	Black	Asian	AIAN	Hisp.
Enrollment (%)	100.0	80.3	7.7	1.2	0.4	10.4
Drop-out Rate (%)	3.9	4.0	0.0	0.0	n/a	9.1
H.S. Diplomas (#)	96	91	3	0	0	2

Willingboro Twp
Levitt Building • Willingboro, NJ 08046
(609) 835-8600 • http://www.willingboroschools.org/
Grade Span: PK-12; **Agency Type:** 1
Schools: 11
7 Primary; 2 Middle; 1 High; 1 Other Level
10 Regular; 1 Special Education; 0 Vocational; 0 Alternative
0 Magnet; 0 Charter; 6 Title I Eligible; 0 School-wide Title I
Students: 5,875 (51.9% male; 48.0% female)
Individual Education Program: 958 (16.3%);
English Language Learner: 21 (0.4%); Migrant: 0 (0.0%)
Eligible for Free Lunch Program: 1,587 (28.3%)
Eligible for Reduced-Price Lunch Program: 704 (12.5%)
Teachers: 469.0 (12.0 to 1)
Librarians/Media Specialists: 8.0 (701.8 to 1)
Guidance Counselors: 14.0 (401.0 to 1)
Current Spending: ($ per student per year):
Total: $11,703; Instruction: $7,048; Support Services: $4,238
Enrollment, Drop-out Rates and Diploma Recipients by Race/Ethnicity

Category	Total	White	Black	Asian	AIAN	Hisp.
Enrollment (%)	100.0	3.5	88.8	1.3	0.3	6.0
Drop-out Rate (%)	1.5	0.0	1.5	0.0	0.0	1.5
H.S. Diplomas (#)	295	13	262	7	0	13

Camden County

Audubon Boro
350 Edgewood Ave • Audubon, NJ 08106-2299
(856) 547-1325 • http://www.audubon.k12.nj.us/
Grade Span: PK-12; **Agency Type:** 1
Schools: 3
2 Primary; 0 Middle; 1 High; 0 Other Level
3 Regular; 0 Special Education; 0 Vocational; 0 Alternative
0 Magnet; 0 Charter; 3 Title I Eligible; 0 School-wide Title I
Students: 1,755 (51.7% male; 48.2% female)
Individual Education Program: 255 (14.5%);
English Language Learner: 9 (0.5%); Migrant: 0 (0.0%)
Eligible for Free Lunch Program: 113 (6.7%)
Eligible for Reduced-Price Lunch Program: 82 (4.9%)
Teachers: 125.4 (13.4 to 1)
Librarians/Media Specialists: 1.0 (1,686.0 to 1)
Guidance Counselors: 6.5 (259.4 to 1)
Current Spending: ($ per student per year):
Total: $9,936; Instruction: $6,639; Support Services: $2,980
Enrollment, Drop-out Rates and Diploma Recipients by Race/Ethnicity

Category	Total	White	Black	Asian	AIAN	Hisp.
Enrollment (%)	100.0	96.0	0.9	1.2	0.0	1.9
Drop-out Rate (%)	2.0	2.0	0.0	0.0	0.0	0.0
H.S. Diplomas (#)	157	152	1	1	0	3

Black Horse Pike Regional
580 Erial Raod • Blackwood, NJ 08012
(856) 227-4106 • http://www.bhprsd.org/
Grade Span: 09-12; **Agency Type:** 1
Schools: 3
0 Primary; 0 Middle; 3 High; 0 Other Level
3 Regular; 0 Special Education; 0 Vocational; 0 Alternative
0 Magnet; 0 Charter; 3 Title I Eligible; 0 School-wide Title I
Students: 4,438 (51.3% male; 48.6% female)
Individual Education Program: 651 (14.7%);
English Language Learner: 23 (0.5%); Migrant: 0 (0.0%)
Eligible for Free Lunch Program: 286 (7.2%)
Eligible for Reduced-Price Lunch Program: 201 (5.1%)
Teachers: 257.7 (15.3 to 1)
Librarians/Media Specialists: 7.3 (541.2 to 1)
Guidance Counselors: 18.4 (214.7 to 1)
Current Spending: ($ per student per year):
Total: $11,624; Instruction: $6,695; Support Services: $4,596
Enrollment, Drop-out Rates and Diploma Recipients by Race/Ethnicity

Category	Total	White	Black	Asian	AIAN	Hisp.
Enrollment (%)	100.0	78.2	14.5	3.8	0.4	3.1
Drop-out Rate (%)	3.2	2.9	4.2	3.1	0.0	7.3
H.S. Diplomas (#)	730	597	88	30	2	13

Camden City
201 N Front St • Camden, NJ 08102-1935
(856) 966-2040 • http://www.camden.k12.nj.us/
Grade Span: PK-12; **Agency Type:** 1
Schools: 31

21 Primary; 6 Middle; 4 High; 0 Other Level
30 Regular; 0 Special Education; 0 Vocational; 1 Alternative
0 Magnet; 0 Charter; 27 Title I Eligible; 0 School-wide Title I
Students: 18,997 (50.1% male; 49.8% female)
Individual Education Program: 3,231 (17.0%)
English Language Learner: 1,209 (6.4%); Migrant: 2 (<0.1%)
Eligible for Free Lunch Program: 12,676 (74.8%)
Eligible for Reduced-Price Lunch Program: 712 (4.2%)
Teachers: 1,547.0 (11.0 to 1)
Librarians/Media Specialists: 38.0 (446.2 to 1)
Guidance Counselors: 60.0 (282.6 to 1)
Current Spending: ($ per student per year):
Total: $15,122; Instruction: $8,791; Support Services: $5,847
Enrollment, Drop-out Rates and Diploma Recipients by Race/Ethnicity

Category	Total	White	Black	Asian	AIAN	Hisp.
Enrollment (%)	100.0	1.1	54.1	1.7	0.1	42.9
Drop-out Rate (%)	14.1	27.3	13.0	7.9	n/a	16.2
H.S. Diplomas (#)	505	1	316	23	0	165

Camden County Vocational
343 Berlin-Cross Keys Rd • Sicklerville, NJ 08081-0566
(856) 767-7000 • http://www.ccts.tec.nj.us/
Grade Span: 09-12; **Agency Type:** 1
Schools: 2
0 Primary; 0 Middle; 2 High; 0 Other Level
0 Regular; 0 Special Education; 2 Vocational; 0 Alternative
0 Magnet; 0 Charter; 2 Title I Eligible; 0 School-wide Title I
Students: 2,620 (53.7% male; 46.2% female)
Individual Education Program: 624 (23.8%);
English Language Learner: 0 (0.0%); Migrant: 0 (0.0%)
Eligible for Free Lunch Program: 1,025 (51.6%)
Eligible for Reduced-Price Lunch Program: 268 (13.5%)
Teachers: 169.2 (11.7 to 1)
Librarians/Media Specialists: 2.0 (992.5 to 1)
Guidance Counselors: 13.0 (152.7 to 1)
Current Spending: ($ per student per year):
Total: $17,024; Instruction: $9,355; Support Services: $6,918
Enrollment, Drop-out Rates and Diploma Recipients by Race/Ethnicity

Category	Total	White	Black	Asian	AIAN	Hisp.
Enrollment (%)	100.0	26.2	36.1	1.2	0.4	36.2
Drop-out Rate (%)	0.9	1.7	0.5	0.0	100.0	0.5
H.S. Diplomas (#)	314	96	106	3	1	108

Cherry Hill Twp
45 Ranoldo Terrace • Cherry Hill, NJ 08034-0391
(856) 429-5600 • http://www.cherryhill.k12.nj.us/
Grade Span: PK-12; **Agency Type:** 1
Schools: 19
13 Primary; 3 Middle; 2 High; 1 Other Level
17 Regular; 1 Special Education; 0 Vocational; 1 Alternative
0 Magnet; 0 Charter; 8 Title I Eligible; 0 School-wide Title I
Students: 11,911 (52.5% male; 47.4% female)
Individual Education Program: 1,566 (13.1%);
English Language Learner: 146 (1.2%); Migrant: 0 (0.0%)
Eligible for Free Lunch Program: 479 (4.2%)
Eligible for Reduced-Price Lunch Program: 314 (2.7%)
Teachers: 818.6 (14.1 to 1)
Librarians/Media Specialists: 18.4 (627.3 to 1)
Guidance Counselors: 34.6 (333.6 to 1)
Current Spending: ($ per student per year):
Total: $11,303; Instruction: $7,043; Support Services: $3,898
Enrollment, Drop-out Rates and Diploma Recipients by Race/Ethnicity

Category	Total	White	Black	Asian	AIAN	Hisp.
Enrollment (%)	100.0	75.4	7.1	13.6	0.1	3.8
Drop-out Rate (%)	0.7	0.7	1.9	0.7	n/a	0.0
H.S. Diplomas (#)	846	620	49	152	0	25

Collingswood Boro
200 Lees Ave • Collingswood, NJ 08108-3106
(856) 962-5732 • http://collingswood.k12.nj.us
Grade Span: PK-12; **Agency Type:** 1
Schools: 7
5 Primary; 1 Middle; 1 High; 0 Other Level
7 Regular; 0 Special Education; 0 Vocational; 0 Alternative
0 Magnet; 0 Charter; 5 Title I Eligible; 0 School-wide Title I
Students: 2,075 (51.2% male; 48.7% female)
Individual Education Program: 311 (15.0%);
English Language Learner: 43 (2.1%); Migrant: 0 (0.0%)
Eligible for Free Lunch Program: 316 (15.5%)
Eligible for Reduced-Price Lunch Program: 174 (8.5%)
Teachers: 163.4 (12.5 to 1)
Librarians/Media Specialists: 3.0 (680.0 to 1)
Guidance Counselors: 7.0 (291.4 to 1)
Current Spending: ($ per student per year):
Total: $11,578; Instruction: $6,864; Support Services: $4,400

Enrollment, Drop-out Rates and Diploma Recipients by Race/Ethnicity

Category	Total	White	Black	Asian	AIAN	Hisp.
Enrollment (%)	100.0	71.4	13.9	3.7	0.4	10.6
Drop-out Rate (%)	5.4	5.3	0.0	13.9	n/a	9.6
H.S. Diplomas (#)	162	126	17	5	0	14

Eastern Camden County Reg
Laurel Oak Rd • Voorhees, NJ 08043-0995
(856) 346-6740 • http://www.eastern.k12.nj.us
Grade Span: 09-12; **Agency Type:** 1
Schools: 2
0 Primary; 0 Middle; 1 High; 1 Other Level
2 Regular; 0 Special Education; 0 Vocational; 0 Alternative
0 Magnet; 0 Charter; 2 Title I Eligible; 0 School-wide Title I
Students: 2,205 (52.3% male; 47.6% female)
Individual Education Program: 274 (12.4%);
English Language Learner: 15 (0.7%); Migrant: 0 (0.0%)
Eligible for Free Lunch Program: 86 (3.9%)
Eligible for Reduced-Price Lunch Program: 51 (2.3%)
Teachers: 151.6 (14.4 to 1)
Librarians/Media Specialists: 2.0 (1,089.5 to 1)
Guidance Counselors: 11.0 (198.1 to 1)
Current Spending: ($ per student per year):
Total: $11,297; Instruction: $6,608; Support Services: $4,298
Enrollment, Drop-out Rates and Diploma Recipients by Race/Ethnicity

Category	Total	White	Black	Asian	AIAN	Hisp.
Enrollment (%)	100.0	77.1	8.2	12.0	0.2	2.5
Drop-out Rate (%)	1.8	1.9	1.1	0.4	0.0	5.0
H.S. Diplomas (#)	476	361	41	57	1	16

Gloucester City
520 Cumberland St • Gloucester City, NJ 08030-1999
(856) 456-9394 • http://www.gcsd.k12.nj.us/
Grade Span: PK-12; **Agency Type:** 1
Schools: 3
1 Primary; 1 Middle; 1 High; 0 Other Level
3 Regular; 0 Special Education; 0 Vocational; 0 Alternative
0 Magnet; 0 Charter; 3 Title I Eligible; 0 School-wide Title I
Students: 2,273 (49.3% male; 50.6% female)
Individual Education Program: 438 (19.3%);
English Language Learner: 28 (1.2%); Migrant: 0 (0.0%)
Eligible for Free Lunch Program: 724 (33.7%)
Eligible for Reduced-Price Lunch Program: 287 (13.4%)
Teachers: 221.4 (9.7 to 1)
Librarians/Media Specialists: 3.0 (716.0 to 1)
Guidance Counselors: 8.0 (268.5 to 1)
Current Spending: ($ per student per year):
Total: $14,273; Instruction: $9,017; Support Services: $4,867
Enrollment, Drop-out Rates and Diploma Recipients by Race/Ethnicity

Category	Total	White	Black	Asian	AIAN	Hisp.
Enrollment (%)	100.0	94.6	2.0	0.9	0.0	2.5
Drop-out Rate (%)	1.6	1.6	0.0	0.0	n/a	0.0
H.S. Diplomas (#)	150	147	1	2	0	0

Gloucester Twp
17 Erial Rd • Blackwood, NJ 08012-3964
(856) 227-1400 • http://www.jersey.net/~gtps
Grade Span: PK-08; **Agency Type:** 1
Schools: 12
9 Primary; 3 Middle; 0 High; 0 Other Level
12 Regular; 0 Special Education; 0 Vocational; 0 Alternative
0 Magnet; 0 Charter; 7 Title I Eligible; 0 School-wide Title I
Students: 8,090 (52.1% male; 47.8% female)
Individual Education Program: 1,249 (15.4%);
English Language Learner: 55 (0.7%); Migrant: 0 (0.0%)
Eligible for Free Lunch Program: 1,090 (13.7%)
Eligible for Reduced-Price Lunch Program: 635 (8.0%)
Teachers: 544.0 (14.7 to 1)
Librarians/Media Specialists: 10.0 (797.5 to 1)
Guidance Counselors: 17.5 (455.7 to 1)
Current Spending: ($ per student per year):
Total: $9,182; Instruction: $5,755; Support Services: $3,009
Enrollment, Drop-out Rates and Diploma Recipients by Race/Ethnicity

Category	Total	White	Black	Asian	AIAN	Hisp.
Enrollment (%)	100.0	73.5	19.2	3.3	0.1	3.8
Drop-out Rate (%)	n/a	n/a	n/a	n/a	n/a	n/a
H.S. Diplomas (#)	n/a	n/a	n/a	n/a	n/a	n/a

Haddon Twp
Y00 Rhoads Ave • Westmont, NJ 08108
(856) 869-7700 • http://www.haddon.k12.nj.us
Grade Span: PK-12; **Agency Type:** 1
Schools: 7
5 Primary; 1 Middle; 1 High; 0 Other Level
7 Regular; 0 Special Education; 0 Vocational; 0 Alternative

0 Magnet; 0 Charter; 2 Title I Eligible; 0 School-wide Title I
Students: 2,357 (51.0% male; 48.9% female)
Individual Education Program: 331 (14.0%);
English Language Learner: 5 (0.2%); Migrant: 0 (0.0%)
Eligible for Free Lunch Program: 105 (4.7%)
Eligible for Reduced-Price Lunch Program: 72 (3.2%)
Teachers: 151.9 (14.6 to 1)
Librarians/Media Specialists: 1.0 (2,225.0 to 1)
Guidance Counselors: 7.5 (296.7 to 1)
Current Spending: ($ per student per year):
Total: $9,913; Instruction: $6,305; Support Services: $3,327
Enrollment, Drop-out Rates and Diploma Recipients by Race/Ethnicity

Category	Total	White	Black	Asian	AIAN	Hisp.
Enrollment (%)	100.0	92.1	1.3	3.0	1.0	2.6
Drop-out Rate (%)	0.3	0.3	0.0	0.0	0.0	0.0
H.S. Diplomas (#)	160	156	1	2	0	1

Haddonfield Boro
One Lincoln Ave • Haddonfield, NJ 08033-1892
(856) 429-4130 • http://www.haddonfield.k12.nj.us
Grade Span: PK-12; **Agency Type:** 1
Schools: 5
3 Primary; 1 Middle; 1 High; 0 Other Level
5 Regular; 0 Special Education; 0 Vocational; 0 Alternative
0 Magnet; 0 Charter; 0 Title I Eligible; 0 School-wide Title I
Students: 2,317 (50.0% male; 49.9% female)
Individual Education Program: 344 (14.8%);
English Language Learner: 6 (0.3%); Migrant: 0 (0.0%)
Eligible for Free Lunch Program: 20 (0.9%)
Eligible for Reduced-Price Lunch Program: 7 (0.3%)
Teachers: 167.0 (13.7 to 1)
Librarians/Media Specialists: 3.0 (764.7 to 1)
Guidance Counselors: 8.8 (260.7 to 1)
Current Spending: ($ per student per year):
Total: $10,805; Instruction: $6,887; Support Services: $3,704
Enrollment, Drop-out Rates and Diploma Recipients by Race/Ethnicity

Category	Total	White	Black	Asian	AIAN	Hisp.
Enrollment (%)	100.0	95.7	1.2	2.2	0.0	0.9
Drop-out Rate (%)	0.0	0.0	0.0	0.0	0.0	0.0
H.S. Diplomas (#)	175	169	4	1	1	0

Lindenwold Boro
Admin Bldg 1017 E Linden • Lindenwold, NJ 08021-1126
(856) 784-4071
Grade Span: PK-12; **Agency Type:** 1
Schools: 4
2 Primary; 1 Middle; 1 High; 0 Other Level
4 Regular; 0 Special Education; 0 Vocational; 0 Alternative
0 Magnet; 0 Charter; 2 Title I Eligible; 0 School-wide Title I
Students: 2,808 (52.8% male; 47.1% female)
Individual Education Program: 520 (18.5%);
English Language Learner: 110 (3.9%); Migrant: 5 (0.2%)
Eligible for Free Lunch Program: 902 (37.1%)
Eligible for Reduced-Price Lunch Program: 374 (15.4%)
Teachers: 216.9 (11.2 to 1)
Librarians/Media Specialists: 4.0 (607.0 to 1)
Guidance Counselors: 7.0 (346.9 to 1)
Current Spending: ($ per student per year):
Total: $12,139; Instruction: $7,713; Support Services: $4,012
Enrollment, Drop-out Rates and Diploma Recipients by Race/Ethnicity

Category	Total	White	Black	Asian	AIAN	Hisp.
Enrollment (%)	100.0	33.0	48.7	3.4	0.0	14.8
Drop-out Rate (%)	5.5	7.2	3.9	0.0	n/a	5.0
H.S. Diplomas (#)	0	0	0	0	0	0

Pennsauken Twp
1695 Hylton Rd • Pennsauken, NJ 08110-1313
(856) 662-8505 • http://www.pennsauken.net
Grade Span: PK-12; **Agency Type:** 1
Schools: 13
9 Primary; 2 Middle; 1 High; 1 Other Level
12 Regular; 1 Special Education; 0 Vocational; 0 Alternative
1 Magnet; 0 Charter; 7 Title I Eligible; 0 School-wide Title I
Students: 6,646 (52.5% male; 47.4% female)
Individual Education Program: 1,284 (19.3%);
English Language Learner: 149 (2.2%); Migrant: 0 (0.0%)
Eligible for Free Lunch Program: 1,874 (31.1%)
Eligible for Reduced-Price Lunch Program: 841 (14.0%)
Teachers: 427.3 (14.1 to 1)
Librarians/Media Specialists: 4.0 (1,506.8 to 1)
Guidance Counselors: 15.0 (401.8 to 1)
Current Spending: ($ per student per year):
Total: $10,523; Instruction: $6,428; Support Services: $3,781
Enrollment, Drop-out Rates and Diploma Recipients by Race/Ethnicity

Category	Total	White	Black	Asian	AIAN	Hisp.
Enrollment (%)	100.0	27.8	38.4	7.5	0.2	25.9
Drop-out Rate (%)	5.8	3.9	7.8	0.0	0.0	7.9
H.S. Diplomas (#)	385	162	141	19	0	63

Pine Hill Boro
Ctrl. Adm. 1003 Turnervill Rd • Pine Hill, NJ 08021-6339
(856) 783-6900
Grade Span: PK-12; **Agency Type:** 1
Schools: 4
2 Primary; 1 Middle; 1 High; 0 Other Level
4 Regular; 0 Special Education; 0 Vocational; 0 Alternative
0 Magnet; 0 Charter; 3 Title I Eligible; 0 School-wide Title I
Students: 2,431 (51.1% male; 48.8% female)
Individual Education Program: 433 (17.8%);
English Language Learner: 13 (0.5%); Migrant: 0 (0.0%)
Eligible for Free Lunch Program: 547 (24.1%)
Eligible for Reduced-Price Lunch Program: 240 (10.6%)
Teachers: 192.1 (11.8 to 1)
Librarians/Media Specialists: 2.0 (1,135.5 to 1)
Guidance Counselors: 7.0 (324.4 to 1)
Current Spending: ($ per student per year):
Total: $11,656; Instruction: $7,276; Support Services: $4,041
Enrollment, Drop-out Rates and Diploma Recipients by Race/Ethnicity

Category	Total	White	Black	Asian	AIAN	Hisp.
Enrollment (%)	100.0	70.1	22.6	2.3	0.1	4.8
Drop-out Rate (%)	7.3	7.1	8.4	9.1	0.0	4.0
H.S. Diplomas (#)	370	226	122	10	0	12

Voorhees Twp
Admin Bldg 329 Route 73 • Voorhees, NJ 08043
(856) 751-8446 • http://hamilton.voorhees.k12.nj.us
Grade Span: PK-08; **Agency Type:** 1
Schools: 5
4 Primary; 1 Middle; 0 High; 0 Other Level
5 Regular; 0 Special Education; 0 Vocational; 0 Alternative
0 Magnet; 0 Charter; 2 Title I Eligible; 0 School-wide Title I
Students: 3,519 (51.5% male; 48.4% female)
Individual Education Program: 551 (15.7%);
English Language Learner: 46 (1.3%); Migrant: 0 (0.0%)
Eligible for Free Lunch Program: 120 (3.5%)
Eligible for Reduced-Price Lunch Program: 85 (2.5%)
Teachers: 258.2 (13.4 to 1)
Librarians/Media Specialists: 6.0 (577.5 to 1)
Guidance Counselors: 7.0 (495.0 to 1)
Current Spending: ($ per student per year):
Total: $10,723; Instruction: $6,609; Support Services: $3,509
Enrollment, Drop-out Rates and Diploma Recipients by Race/Ethnicity

Category	Total	White	Black	Asian	AIAN	Hisp.
Enrollment (%)	100.0	73.8	10.1	13.8	0.2	2.0
Drop-out Rate (%)	n/a	n/a	n/a	n/a	n/a	n/a
H.S. Diplomas (#)	n/a	n/a	n/a	n/a	n/a	n/a

Winslow Twp
200 Cooper Folly Rd • Atco, NJ 08004-9554
(856) 767-2850
Grade Span: PK-12; **Agency Type:** 1
Schools: 9
6 Primary; 1 Middle; 1 High; 1 Other Level
8 Regular; 1 Special Education; 0 Vocational; 0 Alternative
0 Magnet; 0 Charter; 6 Title I Eligible; 0 School-wide Title I
Students: 6,742 (51.7% male; 48.2% female)
Individual Education Program: 1,251 (18.6%);
English Language Learner: 68 (1.0%); Migrant: 26 (0.4%)
Eligible for Free Lunch Program: 1,592 (25.4%)
Eligible for Reduced-Price Lunch Program: 426 (6.8%)
Teachers: 514.1 (12.2 to 1)
Librarians/Media Specialists: 8.0 (783.9 to 1)
Guidance Counselors: 16.0 (391.9 to 1)
Current Spending: ($ per student per year):
Total: $11,337; Instruction: $6,852; Support Services: $4,117
Enrollment, Drop-out Rates and Diploma Recipients by Race/Ethnicity

Category	Total	White	Black	Asian	AIAN	Hisp.
Enrollment (%)	100.0	42.0	50.4	1.1	0.2	6.2
Drop-out Rate (%)	2.6	3.6	1.2	0.0	0.0	4.8
H.S. Diplomas (#)	328	199	106	10	3	10

Cape May County

Lower Cape May Regional
687 Route 9 • Cape May, NJ 08204-4637
(609) 884-3475 • http://lcmr.capemayschools.com
Grade Span: 07-12; **Agency Type:** 1
Schools: 2

0 Primary; 1 Middle; 1 High; 0 Other Level
2 Regular; 0 Special Education; 0 Vocational; 0 Alternative
0 Magnet; 0 Charter; 1 Title I Eligible; 0 School-wide Title I
Students: 1,845   (52.1% male; 47.8% female)
Individual Education Program: 476 (25.8%);
English Language Learner: 8 (0.4%); Migrant: 0 (0.0%)
Eligible for Free Lunch Program: 427 (23.1%)
Eligible for Reduced-Price Lunch Program: 164 (8.9%)
Teachers: 150.5 (12.3 to 1)
Librarians/Media Specialists: 2.0 (922.5 to 1)
Guidance Counselors: 7.5 (246.0 to 1)
Current Spending: ($ per student per year):
Total: $11,767; Instruction: $7,348; Support Services: $3,926

Enrollment, Drop-out Rates and Diploma Recipients by Race/Ethnicity

Category	Total	White	Black	Asian	AIAN	Hisp.
Enrollment (%)	100.0	93.6	3.0	0.8	0.0	2.7
Drop-out Rate (%)	1.6	1.5	3.1	0.0	0.0	4.8
H.S. Diplomas (#)	256	234	16	0	0	6

Lower Twp

834 Seashore Rd • Cape May, NJ 08204-4650
(609) 884-9400 • http://lowertwp.capemayschools.com
Grade Span: PK-06; **Agency Type:** 1
Schools: 4
3 Primary; 1 Middle; 0 High; 0 Other Level
4 Regular; 0 Special Education; 0 Vocational; 0 Alternative
0 Magnet; 0 Charter; 4 Title I Eligible; 0 School-wide Title I
Students: 2,000   (55.2% male; 44.7% female)
Individual Education Program: 419 (21.0%);
English Language Learner: 12 (0.6%); Migrant: 0 (0.0%)
Eligible for Free Lunch Program: 441 (22.9%)
Eligible for Reduced-Price Lunch Program: 302 (15.7%)
Teachers: 141.2 (13.6 to 1)
Librarians/Media Specialists: 4.0 (481.3 to 1)
Guidance Counselors: 4.0 (481.3 to 1)
Current Spending: ($ per student per year):
Total: $11,473; Instruction: $6,216; Support Services: $4,603

Enrollment, Drop-out Rates and Diploma Recipients by Race/Ethnicity

Category	Total	White	Black	Asian	AIAN	Hisp.
Enrollment (%)	100.0	91.6	3.5	0.9	0.2	3.8
Drop-out Rate (%)	n/a	n/a	n/a	n/a	n/a	n/a
H.S. Diplomas (#)	n/a	n/a	n/a	n/a	n/a	n/a

Middle Twp

216 S Main St • Cape May Court Hou, NJ 08210-2273
(609) 465-1800
Grade Span: PK-12; **Agency Type:** 1
Schools: 4
2 Primary; 1 Middle; 1 High; 0 Other Level
4 Regular; 0 Special Education; 0 Vocational; 0 Alternative
0 Magnet; 0 Charter; 4 Title I Eligible; 0 School-wide Title I
Students: 2,949   (52.2% male; 47.7% female)
Individual Education Program: 566 (19.2%);
English Language Learner: 27 (0.9%); Migrant: 0 (0.0%)
Eligible for Free Lunch Program: 541 (18.6%)
Eligible for Reduced-Price Lunch Program: 236 (8.1%)
Teachers: 231.1 (12.6 to 1)
Librarians/Media Specialists: 2.0 (1,453.0 to 1)
Guidance Counselors: 7.0 (415.1 to 1)
Current Spending: ($ per student per year):
Total: $10,249; Instruction: $6,530; Support Services: $3,431

Enrollment, Drop-out Rates and Diploma Recipients by Race/Ethnicity

Category	Total	White	Black	Asian	AIAN	Hisp.
Enrollment (%)	100.0	75.1	19.5	2.0	0.0	3.5
Drop-out Rate (%)	2.8	2.6	3.5	0.0	n/a	7.4
H.S. Diplomas (#)	232	200	28	2	0	2

Ocean City

801 Asbury Ave • Ocean City, NJ 08226-3625
(609) 399-5150 • http://www.ocean.city.k12.nj.us
Grade Span: PK-12; **Agency Type:** 1
Schools: 3
1 Primary; 1 Middle; 1 High; 0 Other Level
3 Regular; 0 Special Education; 0 Vocational; 0 Alternative
0 Magnet; 0 Charter; 2 Title I Eligible; 0 School-wide Title I
Students: 2,224   (51.2% male; 48.7% female)
Individual Education Program: 239 (10.7%);
English Language Learner: 13 (0.6%); Migrant: 0 (0.0%)
Eligible for Free Lunch Program: 245 (11.3%)
Eligible for Reduced-Price Lunch Program: 77 (3.6%)
Teachers: 211.5 (10.2 to 1)
Librarians/Media Specialists: 4.0 (541.5 to 1)
Guidance Counselors: 9.0 (240.7 to 1)
Current Spending: ($ per student per year):
Total: $14,947; Instruction: $9,754; Support Services: $4,929

Enrollment, Drop-out Rates and Diploma Recipients by Race/Ethnicity

Category	Total	White	Black	Asian	AIAN	Hisp.
Enrollment (%)	100.0	90.0	7.2	0.8	0.0	2.0
Drop-out Rate (%)	0.8	0.9	0.0	0.0	0.0	0.0
H.S. Diplomas (#)	299	279	13	2	1	4

Upper Twp

525 Perry Rd • Petersburg, NJ 08270-9633
(609) 628-3513
Grade Span: PK-08; **Agency Type:** 1
Schools: 3
2 Primary; 1 Middle; 0 High; 0 Other Level
3 Regular; 0 Special Education; 0 Vocational; 0 Alternative
0 Magnet; 0 Charter; 1 Title I Eligible; 0 School-wide Title I
Students: 1,767   (52.0% male; 47.9% female)
Individual Education Program: 413 (23.4%);
English Language Learner: 0 (0.0%); Migrant: 0 (0.0%)
Eligible for Free Lunch Program: 79 (4.5%)
Eligible for Reduced-Price Lunch Program: 54 (3.1%)
Teachers: 131.5 (13.2 to 1)
Librarians/Media Specialists: 3.0 (580.0 to 1)
Guidance Counselors: 2.0 (870.0 to 1)
Current Spending: ($ per student per year):
Total: $9,678; Instruction: $5,852; Support Services: $3,461

Enrollment, Drop-out Rates and Diploma Recipients by Race/Ethnicity

Category	Total	White	Black	Asian	AIAN	Hisp.
Enrollment (%)	100.0	98.0	0.8	0.7	0.0	0.5
Drop-out Rate (%)	n/a	n/a	n/a	n/a	n/a	n/a
H.S. Diplomas (#)	n/a	n/a	n/a	n/a	n/a	n/a

Cumberland County

Bridgeton City

41 Bank St • Bridgeton, NJ 08302-0482
Mailing Address: PO Box 657 • Bridgeton, NJ 08302-0482
(856) 455-8030 • http://www.bridgetonschools.org/
Grade Span: PK-12; **Agency Type:** 1
Schools: 7
6 Primary; 0 Middle; 1 High; 0 Other Level
7 Regular; 0 Special Education; 0 Vocational; 0 Alternative
0 Magnet; 0 Charter; 7 Title I Eligible; 7 School-wide Title I
Students: 4,761   (51.3% male; 48.6% female)
Individual Education Program: 872 (18.3%);
English Language Learner: 398 (8.4%); Migrant: 364 (8.4%)
Eligible for Free Lunch Program: 2,874 (66.1%)
Eligible for Reduced-Price Lunch Program: 495 (11.4%)
Teachers: 400.0 (10.9 to 1)
Librarians/Media Specialists: 8.0 (543.5 to 1)
Guidance Counselors: 12.0 (362.3 to 1)
Current Spending: ($ per student per year):
Total: $13,834; Instruction: $8,417; Support Services: $4,874

Enrollment, Drop-out Rates and Diploma Recipients by Race/Ethnicity

Category	Total	White	Black	Asian	AIAN	Hisp.
Enrollment (%)	100.0	15.1	48.8	0.6	0.2	35.3
Drop-out Rate (%)	3.3	1.6	1.4	8.3	n/a	8.5
H.S. Diplomas (#)	168	53	67	5	2	41

Millville City

110 N Third St • Millville, NJ 08332-3829
Mailing Address: PO Box 5010 • Millville, NJ 08332-3829
(856) 327-7575 • http://www.millville.org
Grade Span: PK-12; **Agency Type:** 1
Schools: 10
7 Primary; 1 Middle; 1 High; 1 Other Level
10 Regular; 0 Special Education; 0 Vocational; 0 Alternative
0 Magnet; 0 Charter; 8 Title I Eligible; 0 School-wide Title I
Students: 6,226   (50.0% male; 50.0% female)
Individual Education Program: 1,154 (18.5%);
English Language Learner: 106 (1.7%); Migrant: 6 (0.1%)
Eligible for Free Lunch Program: 2,228 (36.7%)
Eligible for Reduced-Price Lunch Program: 644 (10.6%)
Teachers: 511.9 (11.9 to 1)
Librarians/Media Specialists: 9.0 (674.7 to 1)
Guidance Counselors: 20.0 (303.6 to 1)
Current Spending: ($ per student per year):
Total: $12,183; Instruction: $7,462; Support Services: $4,303

Enrollment, Drop-out Rates and Diploma Recipients by Race/Ethnicity

Category	Total	White	Black	Asian	AIAN	Hisp.
Enrollment (%)	100.0	57.9	26.0	0.8	0.7	14.6
Drop-out Rate (%)	7.9	6.9	11.3	0.0	0.0	8.9
H.S. Diplomas (#)	451	311	93	0	1	46

Vineland City
625 Plum St • Vineland, NJ 08360-3708
(856) 794-6700 • http://www.vineland.org
Grade Span: PK-12; **Agency Type:** 1
Schools: 19
 11 Primary; 5 Middle; 2 High; 1 Other Level
 19 Regular; 0 Special Education; 0 Vocational; 0 Alternative
 0 Magnet; 0 Charter; 11 Title I Eligible; 0 School-wide Title I
Students: 10,316 (51.8% male; 48.1% female)
 Individual Education Program: 1,990 (19.3%);
 English Language Learner: 403 (3.9%); Migrant: 95 (1.0%)
 Eligible for Free Lunch Program: 4,264 (43.7%)
 Eligible for Reduced-Price Lunch Program: 1,271 (13.0%)
Teachers: 850.8 (11.5 to 1)
Librarians/Media Specialists: 15.0 (650.9 to 1)
Guidance Counselors: 44.0 (221.9 to 1)
Current Spending: ($ per student per year):
 Total: $14,940; Instruction: $9,088; Support Services: $5,404
Enrollment, Drop-out Rates and Diploma Recipients by Race/Ethnicity

Category	Total	White	Black	Asian	AIAN	Hisp.
Enrollment (%)	100.0	33.0	20.9	1.6	0.3	44.2
Drop-out Rate (%)	3.2	2.3	3.3	0.0	0.0	4.4
H.S. Diplomas (#)	562	255	89	10	2	206

Essex County

Belleville Town
102 Passaic Ave • Belleville, NJ 07109-3127
(973) 450-3447 • http://www.belleville.k12.nj.us
Grade Span: PK-12; **Agency Type:** 1
Schools: 9
 7 Primary; 1 Middle; 1 High; 0 Other Level
 9 Regular; 0 Special Education; 0 Vocational; 0 Alternative
 0 Magnet; 0 Charter; 5 Title I Eligible; 0 School-wide Title I
Students: 4,729 (51.7% male; 48.2% female)
 Individual Education Program: 769 (16.3%);
 English Language Learner: 254 (5.4%); Migrant: 0 (0.0%)
 Eligible for Free Lunch Program: 869 (19.0%)
 Eligible for Reduced-Price Lunch Program: 416 (9.1%)
Teachers: 325.7 (14.1 to 1)
Librarians/Media Specialists: 5.0 (915.6 to 1)
Guidance Counselors: 12.0 (381.5 to 1)
Current Spending: ($ per student per year):
 Total: $10,272; Instruction: $6,632; Support Services: $3,329
Enrollment, Drop-out Rates and Diploma Recipients by Race/Ethnicity

Category	Total	White	Black	Asian	AIAN	Hisp.
Enrollment (%)	100.0	33.4	6.6	14.0	0.0	46.0
Drop-out Rate (%)	2.0	2.0	2.3	1.6	n/a	2.2
H.S. Diplomas (#)	325	137	17	48	0	123

Bloomfield Twp
155 Broad St • Bloomfield, NJ 07003-2629
(973) 680-8555 • http://www.bloomfield.k12.nj.us
Grade Span: PK-12; **Agency Type:** 1
Schools: 11
 8 Primary; 0 Middle; 2 High; 1 Other Level
 10 Regular; 1 Special Education; 0 Vocational; 0 Alternative
 0 Magnet; 0 Charter; 4 Title I Eligible; 0 School-wide Title I
Students: 6,354 (51.9% male; 48.0% female)
 Individual Education Program: 948 (14.9%);
 English Language Learner: 258 (4.1%); Migrant: 0 (0.0%)
 Eligible for Free Lunch Program: 1,075 (17.5%)
 Eligible for Reduced-Price Lunch Program: 598 (9.7%)
Teachers: 445.1 (13.8 to 1)
Librarians/Media Specialists: 5.8 (1,057.9 to 1)
Guidance Counselors: 15.0 (409.1 to 1)
Current Spending: ($ per student per year):
 Total: $9,761; Instruction: $5,961; Support Services: $3,580
Enrollment, Drop-out Rates and Diploma Recipients by Race/Ethnicity

Category	Total	White	Black	Asian	AIAN	Hisp.
Enrollment (%)	100.0	42.0	20.6	10.5	0.4	26.5
Drop-out Rate (%)	4.5	2.7	7.5	1.4	0.0	7.5
H.S. Diplomas (#)	344	194	50	48	0	52

Caldwell-West Caldwell
Harrison Bldg Gray St • West Caldwell, NJ 07006-7696
(973) 228-6979 • http://www.cwcboe.org
Grade Span: PK-12; **Agency Type:** 1
Schools: 6
 4 Primary; 1 Middle; 1 High; 0 Other Level
 6 Regular; 0 Special Education; 0 Vocational; 0 Alternative
 0 Magnet; 0 Charter; 0 Title I Eligible; 0 School-wide Title I
Students: 2,627 (50.2% male; 49.7% female)
 Individual Education Program: 371 (14.1%);
 English Language Learner: 22 (0.8%); Migrant: 0 (0.0%)

 Eligible for Free Lunch Program: 12 (0.5%)
 Eligible for Reduced-Price Lunch Program: 12 (0.5%)
Teachers: 185.7 (14.0 to 1)
Librarians/Media Specialists: 5.4 (480.6 to 1)
Guidance Counselors: 5.0 (519.0 to 1)
Current Spending: ($ per student per year):
 Total: $11,660; Instruction: $6,821; Support Services: $4,568
Enrollment, Drop-out Rates and Diploma Recipients by Race/Ethnicity

Category	Total	White	Black	Asian	AIAN	Hisp.
Enrollment (%)	100.0	90.3	1.2	4.5	0.0	4.0
Drop-out Rate (%)	0.8	0.7	0.0	0.0	n/a	4.5
H.S. Diplomas (#)	161	147	2	9	0	3

Cedar Grove Twp
520 Pompton Ave • Cedar Grove, NJ 07009-1147
(973) 239-1550
Grade Span: PK-12; **Agency Type:** 1
Schools: 4
 2 Primary; 1 Middle; 1 High; 0 Other Level
 4 Regular; 0 Special Education; 0 Vocational; 0 Alternative
 0 Magnet; 0 Charter; 0 Title I Eligible; 0 School-wide Title I
Students: 1,511 (51.6% male; 48.3% female)
 Individual Education Program: 276 (18.3%);
 English Language Learner: 6 (0.4%); Migrant: 0 (0.0%)
 Eligible for Free Lunch Program: 13 (0.9%)
 Eligible for Reduced-Price Lunch Program: 2 (0.1%)
Teachers: 113.0 (13.0 to 1)
Librarians/Media Specialists: 4.0 (368.5 to 1)
Guidance Counselors: 4.5 (327.6 to 1)
Current Spending: ($ per student per year):
 Total: $12,416; Instruction: $7,297; Support Services: $4,955
Enrollment, Drop-out Rates and Diploma Recipients by Race/Ethnicity

Category	Total	White	Black	Asian	AIAN	Hisp.
Enrollment (%)	100.0	89.0	1.2	6.5	0.3	3.0
Drop-out Rate (%)	0.3	0.3	0.0	0.0	n/a	0.0
H.S. Diplomas (#)	82	71	1	5	0	5

City of Orange Twp
451 Lincoln Ave • Orange, NJ 07050-2704
(973) 677-4040 • http://www.orange.k12.nj.us
Grade Span: PK-12; **Agency Type:** 1
Schools: 9
 7 Primary; 1 Middle; 1 High; 0 Other Level
 9 Regular; 0 Special Education; 0 Vocational; 0 Alternative
 0 Magnet; 0 Charter; 8 Title I Eligible; 8 School-wide Title I
Students: 4,798 (51.8% male; 48.1% female)
 Individual Education Program: 736 (15.3%);
 English Language Learner: 334 (7.0%); Migrant: 0 (0.0%)
 Eligible for Free Lunch Program: 3,149 (69.0%)
 Eligible for Reduced-Price Lunch Program: 600 (13.1%)
Teachers: 375.3 (12.2 to 1)
Librarians/Media Specialists: 8.0 (570.4 to 1)
Guidance Counselors: 14.0 (325.9 to 1)
Current Spending: ($ per student per year):
 Total: $15,185; Instruction: $8,458; Support Services: $6,377
Enrollment, Drop-out Rates and Diploma Recipients by Race/Ethnicity

Category	Total	White	Black	Asian	AIAN	Hisp.
Enrollment (%)	100.0	0.2	86.6	0.5	0.2	12.4
Drop-out Rate (%)	7.0	0.0	7.0	0.0	n/a	8.3
H.S. Diplomas (#)	209	1	200	1	0	7

East Orange
715 Park Ave • East Orange, NJ 07017-1004
(973) 266-5760 • http://www.eastorange.K12.nj.us
Grade Span: PK-12; **Agency Type:** 1
Schools: 21
 14 Primary; 3 Middle; 2 High; 2 Other Level
 21 Regular; 0 Special Education; 0 Vocational; 0 Alternative
 0 Magnet; 0 Charter; 12 Title I Eligible; 10 School-wide Title I
Students: 12,403 (49.7% male; 50.2% female)
 Individual Education Program: 1,942 (15.7%);
 English Language Learner: 306 (2.5%); Migrant: 0 (0.0%)
 Eligible for Free Lunch Program: 6,899 (59.0%)
 Eligible for Reduced-Price Lunch Program: 1,201 (10.3%)
Teachers: 881.8 (13.3 to 1)
Librarians/Media Specialists: 8.0 (1,462.1 to 1)
Guidance Counselors: 31.0 (377.3 to 1)
Current Spending: ($ per student per year):
 Total: $15,225; Instruction: $8,709; Support Services: $6,031
Enrollment, Drop-out Rates and Diploma Recipients by Race/Ethnicity

Category	Total	White	Black	Asian	AIAN	Hisp.
Enrollment (%)	100.0	0.1	95.5	0.1	0.0	4.3
Drop-out Rate (%)	4.9	0.0	5.1	n/a	n/a	2.6
H.S. Diplomas (#)	462	0	449	2	1	10

Essex County Voc-Tech
61 Main St • West Orange, NJ 07052-1703
(973) 243-2926 • http://www.essextech.org
Grade Span: 09-12; **Agency Type:** 1
Schools: 4
   0 Primary; 0 Middle; 3 High; 1 Other Level
   0 Regular; 0 Special Education; 4 Vocational; 0 Alternative
   0 Magnet; 0 Charter; 3 Title I Eligible; 3 School-wide Title I
Students: 2,368   (43.1% male; 56.8% female)
   Individual Education Program: 287 (12.1%);
   English Language Learner: 142 (6.0%); Migrant: 0 (0.0%)
   Eligible for Free Lunch Program: 1,303 (62.8%)
   Eligible for Reduced-Price Lunch Program: 355 (17.1%)
Teachers: 175.0 (11.9 to 1)
Librarians/Media Specialists: 4.0 (518.8 to 1)
Guidance Counselors: 9.7 (213.9 to 1)
Current Spending: ($ per student per year):
   Total: $16,213; Instruction: $9,398; Support Services: $6,461
Enrollment, Drop-out Rates and Diploma Recipients by Race/Ethnicity

Category	Total	White	Black	Asian	AIAN	Hisp.
Enrollment (%)	100.0	1.4	51.8	1.0	0.0	45.8
Drop-out Rate (%)	0.1	0.0	0.1	0.0	n/a	0.1
H.S. Diplomas (#)	395	16	206	1	0	172

Glen Ridge Boro
12 High St • Glen Ridge, NJ 07028-1424
(973) 429-8302
Grade Span: PK-12; **Agency Type:** 1
Schools: 4
   3 Primary; 0 Middle; 1 High; 0 Other Level
   4 Regular; 0 Special Education; 0 Vocational; 0 Alternative
   0 Magnet; 0 Charter; 0 Title I Eligible; 0 School-wide Title I
Students: 1,797   (51.9% male; 48.0% female)
   Individual Education Program: 195 (10.9%);
   English Language Learner: 1 (0.1%); Migrant: 0 (0.0%)
   Eligible for Free Lunch Program: 0 (0.0%)
   Eligible for Reduced-Price Lunch Program: 0 (0.0%)
Teachers: 126.0 (14.1 to 1)
Librarians/Media Specialists: 3.0 (590.3 to 1)
Guidance Counselors: 5.0 (354.2 to 1)
Current Spending: ($ per student per year):
   Total: $10,264; Instruction: $6,276; Support Services: $3,661
Enrollment, Drop-out Rates and Diploma Recipients by Race/Ethnicity

Category	Total	White	Black	Asian	AIAN	Hisp.
Enrollment (%)	100.0	88.8	5.3	3.5	0.0	2.4
Drop-out Rate (%)	0.3	0.3	0.0	0.0	n/a	0.0
H.S. Diplomas (#)	87	71	7	1	0	8

Irvington Township
1150 Springfield Ave • Irvington, NJ 07111-2441
(973) 399-6801 • http://www.irvington.k12.nj.us
Grade Span: PK-12; **Agency Type:** 1
Schools: 12
   8 Primary; 3 Middle; 1 High; 0 Other Level
   12 Regular; 0 Special Education; 0 Vocational; 0 Alternative
   0 Magnet; 0 Charter; 9 Title I Eligible; 9 School-wide Title I
Students: 8,830   (51.8% male; 48.1% female)
   Individual Education Program: 1,382 (15.7%);
   English Language Learner: 427 (4.8%); Migrant: 0 (0.0%)
   Eligible for Free Lunch Program: 4,797 (58.1%)
   Eligible for Reduced-Price Lunch Program: 937 (11.4%)
Teachers: 567.7 (14.5 to 1)
Librarians/Media Specialists: 13.0 (634.9 to 1)
Guidance Counselors: 20.0 (412.7 to 1)
Current Spending: ($ per student per year):
   Total: $15,257; Instruction: $9,945; Support Services: $4,991
Enrollment, Drop-out Rates and Diploma Recipients by Race/Ethnicity

Category	Total	White	Black	Asian	AIAN	Hisp.
Enrollment (%)	100.0	0.4	93.5	0.2	0.1	5.8
Drop-out Rate (%)	3.4	12.5	3.4	0.0	n/a	4.6
H.S. Diplomas (#)	302	1	278	1	0	22

Livingston Twp
11 Foxcroft Dr • Livingston, NJ 07039-2613
(973) 535-8010 • http://www.livingston.org/
Grade Span: PK-12; **Agency Type:** 1
Schools: 9
   6 Primary; 2 Middle; 1 High; 0 Other Level
   9 Regular; 0 Special Education; 0 Vocational; 0 Alternative
   0 Magnet; 0 Charter; 8 Title I Eligible; 0 School-wide Title I
Students: 5,216   (51.8% male; 48.1% female)
   Individual Education Program: 804 (15.4%);
   English Language Learner: 82 (1.6%); Migrant: 0 (0.0%)
   Eligible for Free Lunch Program: 28 (0.5%)
   Eligible for Reduced-Price Lunch Program: 18 (0.4%)

Teachers: 418.5 (12.3 to 1)
Librarians/Media Specialists: 10.0 (513.0 to 1)
Guidance Counselors: 15.0 (342.0 to 1)
Current Spending: ($ per student per year):
   Total: $13,371; Instruction: $8,573; Support Services: $4,798
Enrollment, Drop-out Rates and Diploma Recipients by Race/Ethnicity

Category	Total	White	Black	Asian	AIAN	Hisp.
Enrollment (%)	100.0	75.4	1.6	20.1	0.1	2.9
Drop-out Rate (%)	0.0	0.0	0.0	0.0	0.0	0.0
H.S. Diplomas (#)	353	249	8	86	0	10

Millburn Twp
434 Millburn Ave • Millburn, NJ 07041-1210
(973) 376-3600 • http://schools.millburn.org/
Grade Span: PK-12; **Agency Type:** 1
Schools: 7
   6 Primary; 0 Middle; 1 High; 0 Other Level
   7 Regular; 0 Special Education; 0 Vocational; 0 Alternative
   0 Magnet; 0 Charter; 0 Title I Eligible; 0 School-wide Title I
Students: 4,365   (50.7% male; 49.2% female)
   Individual Education Program: 584 (13.4%);
   English Language Learner: 55 (1.3%); Migrant: 0 (0.0%)
   Eligible for Free Lunch Program: 20 (0.5%)
   Eligible for Reduced-Price Lunch Program: 6 (0.1%)
Teachers: 344.3 (12.6 to 1)
Librarians/Media Specialists: 9.0 (483.7 to 1)
Guidance Counselors: 9.0 (483.7 to 1)
Current Spending: ($ per student per year):
   Total: $12,493; Instruction: $7,480; Support Services: $4,877
Enrollment, Drop-out Rates and Diploma Recipients by Race/Ethnicity

Category	Total	White	Black	Asian	AIAN	Hisp.
Enrollment (%)	100.0	83.9	1.1	12.7	0.1	2.2
Drop-out Rate (%)	0.0	0.0	0.0	0.0	n/a	0.0
H.S. Diplomas (#)	218	189	2	25	0	2

Montclair Town
22 Valley Rd • Montclair, NJ 07042-2709
(973) 509-4010 • http://www.montclair.k12.nj.us
Grade Span: PK-12; **Agency Type:** 1
Schools: 11
   7 Primary; 3 Middle; 1 High; 0 Other Level
   11 Regular; 0 Special Education; 0 Vocational; 0 Alternative
   0 Magnet; 0 Charter; 5 Title I Eligible; 5 School-wide Title I
Students: 6,617   (50.5% male; 49.4% female)
   Individual Education Program: 1,142 (17.3%);
   English Language Learner: 76 (1.1%); Migrant: 0 (0.0%)
   Eligible for Free Lunch Program: 757 (11.8%)
   Eligible for Reduced-Price Lunch Program: 325 (5.1%)
Teachers: 544.4 (11.8 to 1)
Librarians/Media Specialists: 9.3 (688.0 to 1)
Guidance Counselors: 16.0 (399.9 to 1)
Current Spending: ($ per student per year):
   Total: $12,433; Instruction: $7,785; Support Services: $4,384
Enrollment, Drop-out Rates and Diploma Recipients by Race/Ethnicity

Category	Total	White	Black	Asian	AIAN	Hisp.
Enrollment (%)	100.0	48.3	41.7	4.3	0.3	5.4
Drop-out Rate (%)	1.7	0.7	2.5	1.3	0.0	2.3
H.S. Diplomas (#)	348	151	171	13	0	13

Newark City
2 Cedar St • Newark, NJ 07102-3015
(973) 733-7333 • http://www.nps.k12.nj.us
Grade Span: PK-12; **Agency Type:** 1
Schools: 77
   52 Primary; 7 Middle; 11 High; 7 Other Level
   71 Regular; 5 Special Education; 0 Vocational; 1 Alternative
   0 Magnet; 0 Charter; 50 Title I Eligible; 50 School-wide Title I
Students: 46,825   (51.3% male; 48.6% female)
   Individual Education Program: 6,928 (14.8%);
   English Language Learner: 3,451 (7.4%); Migrant: 0 (0.0%)
   Eligible for Free Lunch Program: 25,887 (60.5%)
   Eligible for Reduced-Price Lunch Program: 3,937 (9.2%)
Teachers: 3,687.0 (11.6 to 1)
Librarians/Media Specialists: 64.0 (668.8 to 1)
Guidance Counselors: 111.0 (385.6 to 1)
Current Spending: ($ per student per year):
   Total: $18,517; Instruction: $10,354; Support Services: $7,597
Enrollment, Drop-out Rates and Diploma Recipients by Race/Ethnicity

Category	Total	White	Black	Asian	AIAN	Hisp.
Enrollment (%)	100.0	8.3	59.4	0.8	0.1	31.3
Drop-out Rate (%)	4.2	0.9	5.2	0.0	0.0	3.0
H.S. Diplomas (#)	1,699	205	1,035	12	0	447

Nutley Town
375 Bloomfield Ave • Nutley, NJ 07110-2252
(973) 661-8798 • http://www.nutleyschools.org
Grade Span: PK-12; **Agency Type:** 1
Schools: 7
   5 Primary; 1 Middle; 1 High; 0 Other Level
   7 Regular; 0 Special Education; 0 Vocational; 0 Alternative
   0 Magnet; 0 Charter; 2 Title I Eligible; 0 School-wide Title I
Students: 4,395 (50.7% male; 49.2% female)
   Individual Education Program: 598 (13.6%);
   English Language Learner: 75 (1.7%); Migrant: 0 (0.0%)
   Eligible for Free Lunch Program: 134 (3.2%)
   Eligible for Reduced-Price Lunch Program: 99 (2.3%)
Teachers: 279.1 (15.1 to 1)
Librarians/Media Specialists: 7.7 (548.1 to 1)
Guidance Counselors: 8.0 (527.5 to 1)
Current Spending: ($ per student per year):
   Total: $10,250; Instruction: $6,412; Support Services: $3,528
Enrollment, Drop-out Rates and Diploma Recipients by Race/Ethnicity

Category	Total	White	Black	Asian	AIAN	Hisp.
Enrollment (%)	100.0	81.4	1.3	8.3	0.0	9.1
Drop-out Rate (%)	0.5	0.4	0.0	1.0	n/a	1.1
H.S. Diplomas (#)	266	226	4	28	0	8

South Orange-Maplewood
525 Academy St • Maplewood, NJ 07040-1311
(973) 378-9630 • http://www.somsd.k12.nj.us
Grade Span: PK-12; **Agency Type:** 1
Schools: 9
   6 Primary; 2 Middle; 1 High; 0 Other Level
   9 Regular; 0 Special Education; 0 Vocational; 0 Alternative
   0 Magnet; 0 Charter; 4 Title I Eligible; 0 School-wide Title I
Students: 6,559 (51.0% male; 48.9% female)
   Individual Education Program: 846 (12.9%);
   English Language Learner: 97 (1.5%); Migrant: 0 (0.0%)
   Eligible for Free Lunch Program: 730 (11.4%)
   Eligible for Reduced-Price Lunch Program: 420 (6.6%)
Teachers: 462.5 (13.8 to 1)
Librarians/Media Specialists: 10.8 (591.7 to 1)
Guidance Counselors: 14.0 (456.4 to 1)
Current Spending: ($ per student per year):
   Total: $11,830; Instruction: $6,671; Support Services: $4,879
Enrollment, Drop-out Rates and Diploma Recipients by Race/Ethnicity

Category	Total	White	Black	Asian	AIAN	Hisp.
Enrollment (%)	100.0	41.3	51.5	3.1	0.2	3.9
Drop-out Rate (%)	1.8	1.0	2.1	0.0	0.0	5.8
H.S. Diplomas (#)	417	157	226	21	0	13

Verona Boro
121 Fairview Ave • Verona, NJ 07044-1320
(973) 239-2100 • http://veronaschools.org
Grade Span: PK-12; **Agency Type:** 1
Schools: 6
   4 Primary; 1 Middle; 1 High; 0 Other Level
   6 Regular; 0 Special Education; 0 Vocational; 0 Alternative
   0 Magnet; 0 Charter; 0 Title I Eligible; 0 School-wide Title I
Students: 2,055 (51.8% male; 48.1% female)
   Individual Education Program: 352 (17.1%);
   English Language Learner: 9 (0.4%); Migrant: 0 (0.0%)
   Eligible for Free Lunch Program: 4 (0.2%)
   Eligible for Reduced-Price Lunch Program: 6 (0.3%)
Teachers: 143.2 (14.0 to 1)
Librarians/Media Specialists: 4.0 (500.5 to 1)
Guidance Counselors: 5.0 (400.4 to 1)
Current Spending: ($ per student per year):
   Total: $10,319; Instruction: $6,503; Support Services: $3,656
Enrollment, Drop-out Rates and Diploma Recipients by Race/Ethnicity

Category	Total	White	Black	Asian	AIAN	Hisp.
Enrollment (%)	100.0	88.4	2.4	5.1	0.0	4.1
Drop-out Rate (%)	0.2	0.0	16.7	0.0	n/a	0.0
H.S. Diplomas (#)	114	95	3	6	2	8

West Orange Town
179 Eagle Rock Ave • West Orange, NJ 07052-5007
(973) 669-5430 • http://www.westorange.k12.nj.us
Grade Span: PK-12; **Agency Type:** 1
Schools: 10
   7 Primary; 2 Middle; 1 High; 0 Other Level
   10 Regular; 0 Special Education; 0 Vocational; 0 Alternative
   0 Magnet; 0 Charter; 3 Title I Eligible; 0 School-wide Title I
Students: 6,588 (50.6% male; 49.3% female)
   Individual Education Program: 883 (13.4%);
   English Language Learner: 330 (5.0%); Migrant: 0 (0.0%)
   Eligible for Free Lunch Program: 924 (14.6%)
   Eligible for Reduced-Price Lunch Program: 485 (7.7%)
Teachers: 515.4 (12.3 to 1)
Librarians/Media Specialists: 9.0 (703.2 to 1)
Guidance Counselors: 19.9 (318.0 to 1)
Current Spending: ($ per student per year):
   Total: $12,708; Instruction: $7,830; Support Services: $4,611
Enrollment, Drop-out Rates and Diploma Recipients by Race/Ethnicity

Category	Total	White	Black	Asian	AIAN	Hisp.
Enrollment (%)	100.0	33.8	38.2	8.6	0.0	19.4
Drop-out Rate (%)	2.7	2.7	2.1	0.6	n/a	5.6
H.S. Diplomas (#)	355	166	108	34	0	47

Gloucester County

Clearview Regional
420 Cedar Rd • Mullica Hill, NJ 08062-9436
(856) 223-2765 • http://www.clearviewregional.edu/
Grade Span: 07-12; **Agency Type:** 1
Schools: 2
   0 Primary; 1 Middle; 1 High; 0 Other Level
   2 Regular; 0 Special Education; 0 Vocational; 0 Alternative
   0 Magnet; 0 Charter; 1 Title I Eligible; 0 School-wide Title I
Students: 2,192 (50.7% male; 49.2% female)
   Individual Education Program: 304 (13.9%);
   English Language Learner: 1 (<0.1%); Migrant: 0 (0.0%)
   Eligible for Free Lunch Program: 75 (3.5%)
   Eligible for Reduced-Price Lunch Program: 40 (1.9%)
Teachers: 153.0 (14.1 to 1)
Librarians/Media Specialists: 2.0 (1,077.5 to 1)
Guidance Counselors: 7.0 (307.9 to 1)
Current Spending: ($ per student per year):
   Total: $10,175; Instruction: $6,247; Support Services: $3,570
Enrollment, Drop-out Rates and Diploma Recipients by Race/Ethnicity

Category	Total	White	Black	Asian	AIAN	Hisp.
Enrollment (%)	100.0	95.6	2.3	0.8	0.2	1.1
Drop-out Rate (%)	2.1	2.2	0.0	0.0	n/a	0.0
H.S. Diplomas (#)	257	245	6	4	0	2

Delsea Regional H.S District
242 Fries Mill Rd • Franklinville, NJ 08322-9139
Mailing Address: PO Box 405 Fries Mill Rd • Franklinville, NJ 08322-9139
(856) 694-0100 • http://www.delsea.k12.nj.us
Grade Span: 07-12; **Agency Type:** 1
Schools: 2
   0 Primary; 1 Middle; 1 High; 0 Other Level
   2 Regular; 0 Special Education; 0 Vocational; 0 Alternative
   0 Magnet; 0 Charter; 2 Title I Eligible; 0 School-wide Title I
Students: 1,989 (51.3% male; 48.6% female)
   Individual Education Program: 337 (16.9%);
   English Language Learner: 6 (0.3%); Migrant: 4 (0.2%)
   Eligible for Free Lunch Program: 237 (12.2%)
   Eligible for Reduced-Price Lunch Program: 154 (7.9%)
Teachers: 138.5 (14.0 to 1)
Librarians/Media Specialists: 3.0 (648.0 to 1)
Guidance Counselors: 7.0 (277.7 to 1)
Current Spending: ($ per student per year):
   Total: $11,069; Instruction: $6,458; Support Services: $4,258
Enrollment, Drop-out Rates and Diploma Recipients by Race/Ethnicity

Category	Total	White	Black	Asian	AIAN	Hisp.
Enrollment (%)	100.0	84.1	12.0	0.6	0.0	3.3
Drop-out Rate (%)	2.2	2.5	0.8	0.0	n/a	0.0
H.S. Diplomas (#)	253	223	21	1	0	8

Deptford Twp
2022 Good Intent Rd • Deptford, NJ 08096-4333
(856) 232-2700 • http://www.deptford.k12.nj.us
Grade Span: PK-12; **Agency Type:** 1
Schools: 10
   7 Primary; 1 Middle; 1 High; 1 Other Level
   9 Regular; 1 Special Education; 0 Vocational; 0 Alternative
   0 Magnet; 0 Charter; 6 Title I Eligible; 0 School-wide Title I
Students: 4,476 (51.3% male; 48.6% female)
   Individual Education Program: 769 (17.2%);
   English Language Learner: 38 (0.8%); Migrant: 0 (0.0%)
   Eligible for Free Lunch Program: 864 (20.3%)
   Eligible for Reduced-Price Lunch Program: 396 (9.3%)
Teachers: 286.0 (14.9 to 1)
Librarians/Media Specialists: 9.0 (472.7 to 1)
Guidance Counselors: 7.0 (607.7 to 1)
Current Spending: ($ per student per year):
   Total: $9,424; Instruction: $5,653; Support Services: $3,463
Enrollment, Drop-out Rates and Diploma Recipients by Race/Ethnicity

Category	Total	White	Black	Asian	AIAN	Hisp.
Enrollment (%)	100.0	73.8	20.4	2.5	0.3	3.0
Drop-out Rate (%)	1.3	0.8	2.9	0.0	0.0	5.9
H.S. Diplomas (#)	197	145	43	2	0	7

Franklin Twp
3228 Coles Mill Rd • Franklinville, NJ 08322-3029
(856) 629-9500
Grade Span: PK-06; **Agency Type:** 1
Schools: 3
  3 Primary; 0 Middle; 0 High; 0 Other Level
  3 Regular; 0 Special Education; 0 Vocational; 0 Alternative
  0 Magnet; 0 Charter; 3 Title I Eligible; 0 School-wide Title I
Students: 1,506 (54.2% male; 45.7% female)
  Individual Education Program: 282 (18.7%);
  English Language Learner: 1 (0.1%); Migrant: 1 (0.1%)
  Eligible for Free Lunch Program: 195 (13.6%)
  Eligible for Reduced-Price Lunch Program: 108 (7.5%)
Teachers: 94.5 (15.1 to 1)
Librarians/Media Specialists: 3.0 (477.0 to 1)
Guidance Counselors: 0.0 (n/a to 1)
Current Spending: ($ per student per year):
  Total: $9,099; Instruction: $5,065; Support Services: $3,738
Enrollment, Drop-out Rates and Diploma Recipients by Race/Ethnicity

Category	Total	White	Black	Asian	AIAN	Hisp.
Enrollment (%)	100.0	88.8	7.5	0.7	0.0	2.9
Drop-out Rate (%)	n/a	n/a	n/a	n/a	n/a	n/a
H.S. Diplomas (#)	n/a	n/a	n/a	n/a	n/a	n/a

Glassboro
George Beach Adm Bldg • Glassboro, NJ 08028
(856) 881-0123 • http://www.glassboro.k12.nj.us
Grade Span: PK-12; **Agency Type:** 1
Schools: 5
  2 Primary; 2 Middle; 1 High; 0 Other Level
  5 Regular; 0 Special Education; 0 Vocational; 0 Alternative
  0 Magnet; 0 Charter; 5 Title I Eligible; 0 School-wide Title I
Students: 2,555 (50.9% male; 49.0% female)
  Individual Education Program: 531 (20.8%);
  English Language Learner: 29 (1.1%); Migrant: 0 (0.0%)
  Eligible for Free Lunch Program: 530 (21.6%)
  Eligible for Reduced-Price Lunch Program: 219 (8.9%)
Teachers: 191.0 (12.8 to 1)
Librarians/Media Specialists: 4.0 (612.5 to 1)
Guidance Counselors: 6.9 (355.1 to 1)
Current Spending: ($ per student per year):
  Total: $11,140; Instruction: $6,732; Support Services: $4,089
Enrollment, Drop-out Rates and Diploma Recipients by Race/Ethnicity

Category	Total	White	Black	Asian	AIAN	Hisp.
Enrollment (%)	100.0	54.8	36.4	3.6	0.1	5.1
Drop-out Rate (%)	3.5	2.6	5.5	0.0	n/a	0.0
H.S. Diplomas (#)	139	75	56	4	0	4

Kingsway Regional
Adm. Off. 213 Kings Hwy • Woolwich Twp, NJ 08085-9608
(856) 467-4600
Grade Span: 07-12; **Agency Type:** 1
Schools: 2
  0 Primary; 1 Middle; 1 High; 0 Other Level
  2 Regular; 0 Special Education; 0 Vocational; 0 Alternative
  0 Magnet; 0 Charter; 1 Title I Eligible; 0 School-wide Title I
Students: 1,751 (51.0% male; 48.9% female)
  Individual Education Program: 200 (11.4%);
  English Language Learner: 6 (0.3%); Migrant: 7 (0.4%)
  Eligible for Free Lunch Program: 97 (5.6%)
  Eligible for Reduced-Price Lunch Program: 52 (3.0%)
Teachers: 123.0 (14.1 to 1)
Librarians/Media Specialists: 2.0 (868.0 to 1)
Guidance Counselors: 8.0 (217.0 to 1)
Current Spending: ($ per student per year):
  Total: $10,788; Instruction: $5,739; Support Services: $3,889
Enrollment, Drop-out Rates and Diploma Recipients by Race/Ethnicity

Category	Total	White	Black	Asian	AIAN	Hisp.
Enrollment (%)	100.0	83.6	11.1	1.8	0.0	3.5
Drop-out Rate (%)	1.0	1.1	0.0	0.0	n/a	3.4
H.S. Diplomas (#)	223	196	22	0	2	3

Mantua Twp
Adm Bldg 684 Main St • Sewell, NJ 08080-9623
(856) 468-2225
Grade Span: PK-06; **Agency Type:** 1
Schools: 3
  3 Primary; 0 Middle; 0 High; 0 Other Level
  3 Regular; 0 Special Education; 0 Vocational; 0 Alternative
  0 Magnet; 0 Charter; 0 Title I Eligible; 0 School-wide Title I
Students: 1,518 (55.2% male; 44.7% female)
  Individual Education Program: 336 (22.1%);
  English Language Learner: 0 (0.0%); Migrant: 0 (0.0%)
  Eligible for Free Lunch Program: 69 (4.8%)
  Eligible for Reduced-Price Lunch Program: 52 (3.6%)

Teachers: 100.6 (14.4 to 1)
Librarians/Media Specialists: 3.0 (481.3 to 1)
Guidance Counselors: 2.0 (722.0 to 1)
Current Spending: ($ per student per year):
  Total: $8,728; Instruction: $5,011; Support Services: $3,361
Enrollment, Drop-out Rates and Diploma Recipients by Race/Ethnicity

Category	Total	White	Black	Asian	AIAN	Hisp.
Enrollment (%)	100.0	96.6	1.4	0.6	0.2	1.2
Drop-out Rate (%)	n/a	n/a	n/a	n/a	n/a	n/a
H.S. Diplomas (#)	n/a	n/a	n/a	n/a	n/a	n/a

Monroe Twp
75 E Academy St • Williamstown, NJ 08094
(856) 629-6400 • http://www.monroetwp.k12.nj.us
Grade Span: PK-12; **Agency Type:** 1
Schools: 6
  4 Primary; 1 Middle; 1 High; 0 Other Level
  6 Regular; 0 Special Education; 0 Vocational; 0 Alternative
  0 Magnet; 0 Charter; 4 Title I Eligible; 0 School-wide Title I
Students: 5,593 (51.3% male; 48.6% female)
  Individual Education Program: 911 (16.3%);
  English Language Learner: 29 (0.5%); Migrant: 1 (<0.1%)
  Eligible for Free Lunch Program: 795 (14.9%)
  Eligible for Reduced-Price Lunch Program: 424 (7.9%)
Teachers: 366.1 (14.6 to 1)
Librarians/Media Specialists: 5.0 (1,070.4 to 1)
Guidance Counselors: 11.5 (465.4 to 1)
Current Spending: ($ per student per year):
  Total: $9,831; Instruction: $5,761; Support Services: $3,782
Enrollment, Drop-out Rates and Diploma Recipients by Race/Ethnicity

Category	Total	White	Black	Asian	AIAN	Hisp.
Enrollment (%)	100.0	77.8	16.8	1.4	0.1	3.9
Drop-out Rate (%)	2.1	1.8	3.7	0.0	0.0	4.5
H.S. Diplomas (#)	264	209	46	4	0	5

Paulsboro Boro
662 N Delaware St • Paulsboro, NJ 08066-1020
(856) 423-5515
Grade Span: PK-12; **Agency Type:** 1
Schools: 3
  2 Primary; 0 Middle; 1 High; 0 Other Level
  3 Regular; 0 Special Education; 0 Vocational; 0 Alternative
  0 Magnet; 0 Charter; 3 Title I Eligible; 0 School-wide Title I
Students: 1,670 (52.5% male; 47.4% female)
  Individual Education Program: 302 (18.1%);
  English Language Learner: 0 (0.0%); Migrant: 0 (0.0%)
  Eligible for Free Lunch Program: 587 (39.8%)
  Eligible for Reduced-Price Lunch Program: 172 (11.7%)
Teachers: 116.0 (12.7 to 1)
Librarians/Media Specialists: 3.0 (491.7 to 1)
Guidance Counselors: 3.0 (491.7 to 1)
Current Spending: ($ per student per year):
  Total: $10,553; Instruction: $6,827; Support Services: $3,362
Enrollment, Drop-out Rates and Diploma Recipients by Race/Ethnicity

Category	Total	White	Black	Asian	AIAN	Hisp.
Enrollment (%)	100.0	49.6	45.2	0.5	0.1	4.7
Drop-out Rate (%)	1.9	1.4	3.3	0.0	n/a	0.0
H.S. Diplomas (#)	111	84	27	0	0	0

Pitman Boro
420 Hudson Ave • Pitman, NJ 08071-0088
(856) 589-2145 • http://pitman.k12.nj.us
Grade Span: PK-12; **Agency Type:** 1
Schools: 5
  3 Primary; 1 Middle; 1 High; 0 Other Level
  5 Regular; 0 Special Education; 0 Vocational; 0 Alternative
  0 Magnet; 0 Charter; 2 Title I Eligible; 0 School-wide Title I
Students: 1,695 (48.1% male; 51.8% female)
  Individual Education Program: 316 (18.6%);
  English Language Learner: 0 (0.0%); Migrant: 0 (0.0%)
  Eligible for Free Lunch Program: 121 (7.5%)
  Eligible for Reduced-Price Lunch Program: 92 (5.7%)
Teachers: 139.2 (11.6 to 1)
Librarians/Media Specialists: 2.0 (805.5 to 1)
Guidance Counselors: 5.0 (322.2 to 1)
Current Spending: ($ per student per year):
  Total: $11,231; Instruction: $7,066; Support Services: $3,922
Enrollment, Drop-out Rates and Diploma Recipients by Race/Ethnicity

Category	Total	White	Black	Asian	AIAN	Hisp.
Enrollment (%)	100.0	96.8	0.9	1.4	0.0	0.9
Drop-out Rate (%)	3.1	3.2	0.0	0.0	n/a	0.0
H.S. Diplomas (#)	112	110	0	1	0	1

Washington Twp

206 E Holly Ave • Sewell, NJ 08080-9231
(856) 589-6644 • http://www.wtps.org
Grade Span: PK-12; **Agency Type:** 1
Schools: 11
   7 Primary; 3 Middle; 1 High; 0 Other Level
   11 Regular; 0 Special Education; 0 Vocational; 0 Alternative
   0 Magnet; 0 Charter; 7 Title I Eligible; 0 School-wide Title I
Students: 9,859 (51.2% male; 48.7% female)
   Individual Education Program: 1,758 (17.8%);
   English Language Learner: 42 (0.4%); Migrant: 0 (0.0%)
   Eligible for Free Lunch Program: 512 (5.3%)
   Eligible for Reduced-Price Lunch Program: 300 (3.1%)
Teachers: 736.0 (13.1 to 1)
Librarians/Media Specialists: 12.0 (802.8 to 1)
Guidance Counselors: 31.0 (310.8 to 1)
Current Spending: ($ per student per year):
   Total: $10,489; Instruction: $6,225; Support Services: $3,874
Enrollment, Drop-out Rates and Diploma Recipients by Race/Ethnicity

Category	Total	White	Black	Asian	AIAN	Hisp.
Enrollment (%)	100.0	88.9	5.0	4.2	0.0	1.9
Drop-out Rate (%)	1.9	1.8	2.2	0.9	n/a	9.1
H.S. Diplomas (#)	675	595	40	33	0	7

West Deptford Twp

675 Grove Rd Ste 804 • West Deptford, NJ 08066-1999
(856) 848-4300 • http://www.wdeptford.k12.nj.us/
Grade Span: PK-12; **Agency Type:** 1
Schools: 5
   3 Primary; 1 Middle; 1 High; 0 Other Level
   5 Regular; 0 Special Education; 0 Vocational; 0 Alternative
   0 Magnet; 0 Charter; 3 Title I Eligible; 0 School-wide Title I
Students: 3,326 (53.2% male; 46.7% female)
   Individual Education Program: 677 (20.4%);
   English Language Learner: 4 (0.1%); Migrant: 0 (0.0%)
   Eligible for Free Lunch Program: 302 (9.5%)
   Eligible for Reduced-Price Lunch Program: 215 (6.8%)
Teachers: 207.1 (15.3 to 1)
Librarians/Media Specialists: 4.0 (791.3 to 1)
Guidance Counselors: 10.0 (316.5 to 1)
Current Spending: ($ per student per year):
   Total: $10,153; Instruction: $5,839; Support Services: $4,002
Enrollment, Drop-out Rates and Diploma Recipients by Race/Ethnicity

Category	Total	White	Black	Asian	AIAN	Hisp.
Enrollment (%)	100.0	90.9	6.6	1.2	0.0	1.2
Drop-out Rate (%)	1.1	1.0	3.5	0.0	n/a	0.0
H.S. Diplomas (#)	227	205	13	4	0	5

Woodbury City

25 N Broad St • Woodbury, NJ 08096-4602
(856) 853-0123 • http://www.woodburysch.com/
Grade Span: PK-12; **Agency Type:** 1
Schools: 4
   3 Primary; 0 Middle; 0 High; 1 Other Level
   4 Regular; 0 Special Education; 0 Vocational; 0 Alternative
   0 Magnet; 0 Charter; 2 Title I Eligible; 0 School-wide Title I
Students: 1,609 (50.9% male; 49.0% female)
   Individual Education Program: 339 (21.1%);
   English Language Learner: 15 (0.9%); Migrant: 0 (0.0%)
   Eligible for Free Lunch Program: 477 (31.0%)
   Eligible for Reduced-Price Lunch Program: 155 (10.1%)
Teachers: 145.5 (10.6 to 1)
Librarians/Media Specialists: 2.0 (769.0 to 1)
Guidance Counselors: 6.0 (256.3 to 1)
Current Spending: ($ per student per year):
   Total: $12,634; Instruction: $7,940; Support Services: $4,381
Enrollment, Drop-out Rates and Diploma Recipients by Race/Ethnicity

Category	Total	White	Black	Asian	AIAN	Hisp.
Enrollment (%)	100.0	50.5	40.1	1.4	0.2	7.7
Drop-out Rate (%)	4.6	4.4	5.8	0.0	n/a	0.0
H.S. Diplomas (#)	103	70	27	3	0	3

Hudson County

Bayonne City

Ave A And 29th St • Bayonne, NJ 07002
(201) 858-5817 • http://www.bhs.bboed.org
Grade Span: PK-12; **Agency Type:** 1
Schools: 12
   10 Primary; 1 Middle; 1 High; 0 Other Level
   12 Regular; 0 Special Education; 0 Vocational; 0 Alternative
   0 Magnet; 0 Charter; 6 Title I Eligible; 0 School-wide Title I
Students: 9,430 (52.1% male; 47.8% female)
   Individual Education Program: 1,480 (15.7%);
   English Language Learner: 227 (2.4%); Migrant: 0 (0.0%)

Eligible for Free Lunch Program: 2,375 (27.4%)
   Eligible for Reduced-Price Lunch Program: 752 (8.7%)
Teachers: 636.0 (13.6 to 1)
Librarians/Media Specialists: 3.0 (2,887.7 to 1)
Guidance Counselors: 22.2 (390.2 to 1)
Current Spending: ($ per student per year):
   Total: $10,586; Instruction: $6,924; Support Services: $3,334
Enrollment, Drop-out Rates and Diploma Recipients by Race/Ethnicity

Category	Total	White	Black	Asian	AIAN	Hisp.
Enrollment (%)	100.0	56.4	8.7	4.9	0.0	30.1
Drop-out Rate (%)	1.7	1.4	1.9	1.7	n/a	2.5
H.S. Diplomas (#)	440	262	41	30	0	107

Harrison Town

430 William St • Harrison, NJ 07029-1430
(973) 483-4627 • http://www.harrison.k12.nj.us
Grade Span: PK-12; **Agency Type:** 1
Schools: 3
   1 Primary; 1 Middle; 1 High; 0 Other Level
   3 Regular; 0 Special Education; 0 Vocational; 0 Alternative
   0 Magnet; 0 Charter; 3 Title I Eligible; 0 School-wide Title I
Students: 2,005 (52.5% male; 47.4% female)
   Individual Education Program: 258 (12.9%);
   English Language Learner: 223 (11.1%); Migrant: 0 (0.0%)
   Eligible for Free Lunch Program: 747 (38.3%)
   Eligible for Reduced-Price Lunch Program: 210 (10.8%)
Teachers: 133.8 (14.6 to 1)
Librarians/Media Specialists: 0.4 (4,880.0 to 1)
Guidance Counselors: 3.6 (542.2 to 1)
Current Spending: ($ per student per year):
   Total: $13,266; Instruction: $8,357; Support Services: $4,745
Enrollment, Drop-out Rates and Diploma Recipients by Race/Ethnicity

Category	Total	White	Black	Asian	AIAN	Hisp.
Enrollment (%)	100.0	36.3	0.8	7.5	0.0	55.3
Drop-out Rate (%)	0.3	0.4	0.0	2.2	n/a	0.0
H.S. Diplomas (#)	148	52	2	9	0	85

Hoboken City

1115 Clinton St • Hoboken, NJ 07030-3201
(201) 420-2151 • http://www.hobokenk12.powertolearn.net/
Grade Span: PK-12; **Agency Type:** 1
Schools: 6
   3 Primary; 2 Middle; 1 High; 0 Other Level
   6 Regular; 0 Special Education; 0 Vocational; 0 Alternative
   0 Magnet; 0 Charter; 5 Title I Eligible; 0 School-wide Title I
Students: 2,218 (52.8% male; 47.1% female)
   Individual Education Program: 410 (18.5%);
   English Language Learner: 33 (1.5%); Migrant: 0 (0.0%)
   Eligible for Free Lunch Program: 1,362 (65.2%)
   Eligible for Reduced-Price Lunch Program: 285 (13.6%)
Teachers: 208.6 (10.0 to 1)
Librarians/Media Specialists: 3.0 (696.0 to 1)
Guidance Counselors: 5.0 (417.6 to 1)
Current Spending: ($ per student per year):
   Total: $20,642; Instruction: $12,574; Support Services: $7,534
Enrollment, Drop-out Rates and Diploma Recipients by Race/Ethnicity

Category	Total	White	Black	Asian	AIAN	Hisp.
Enrollment (%)	100.0	14.8	17.3	2.0	0.0	65.9
Drop-out Rate (%)	3.3	2.2	3.6	0.0	n/a	3.6
H.S. Diplomas (#)	137	19	20	6	0	92

Jersey City

346 Claremont Ave • Jersey City, NJ 07305-1634
(201) 915-6202 • http://www.jerseycity.k12.nj.us
Grade Span: PK-12; **Agency Type:** 1
Schools: 40
   29 Primary; 4 Middle; 6 High; 1 Other Level
   38 Regular; 2 Special Education; 0 Vocational; 0 Alternative
   0 Magnet; 0 Charter; 29 Title I Eligible; 29 School-wide Title I
Students: 35,161 (51.3% male; 48.6% female)
   Individual Education Program: 4,335 (12.3%);
   English Language Learner: 2,736 (7.8%); Migrant: 0 (0.0%)
   Eligible for Free Lunch Program: 17,991 (58.5%)
   Eligible for Reduced-Price Lunch Program: 3,789 (12.3%)
Teachers: 2,701.8 (11.4 to 1)
Librarians/Media Specialists: 42.0 (731.9 to 1)
Guidance Counselors: 126.0 (244.0 to 1)
Current Spending: ($ per student per year):
   Total: $15,888; Instruction: $9,531; Support Services: $5,951
Enrollment, Drop-out Rates and Diploma Recipients by Race/Ethnicity

Category	Total	White	Black	Asian	AIAN	Hisp.
Enrollment (%)	100.0	9.5	35.6	14.3	1.3	39.3
Drop-out Rate (%)	8.6	7.4	10.3	3.6	7.7	9.3
H.S. Diplomas (#)	1,293	100	495	247	1	450

Kearny Town
100 Davis Ave • Kearny, NJ 07032-2612
(201) 955-5021 • http://www.kearnyschools.com/
Grade Span: PK-12; **Agency Type:** 1
Schools: 7
  6 Primary; 0 Middle; 1 High; 0 Other Level
  7 Regular; 0 Special Education; 0 Vocational; 0 Alternative
  0 Magnet; 0 Charter; 3 Title I Eligible; 0 School-wide Title I
Students: 5,888 (52.0% male; 47.9% female)
  Individual Education Program: 709 (12.0%);
  English Language Learner: 416 (7.1%); Migrant: 0 (0.0%)
  Eligible for Free Lunch Program: 1,157 (21.5%)
  Eligible for Reduced-Price Lunch Program: 492 (9.1%)
Teachers: 395.1 (13.6 to 1)
Librarians/Media Specialists: 8.0 (673.0 to 1)
Guidance Counselors: 15.0 (358.9 to 1)
Current Spending: ($ per student per year):
  Total: $10,975; Instruction: $7,362; Support Services: $3,398
Enrollment, Drop-out Rates and Diploma Recipients by Race/Ethnicity

Category	Total	White	Black	Asian	AIAN	Hisp.
Enrollment (%)	100.0	51.7	1.2	4.0	0.2	42.9
Drop-out Rate (%)	3.4	2.3	0.0	0.0	0.0	5.5
H.S. Diplomas (#)	375	250	11	12	3	99

North Bergen Twp
7317 Kennedy Blvd • North Bergen, NJ 07047-4097
(201) 295-3985 • http://www.northbergen.k12.nj.us
Grade Span: PK-12; **Agency Type:** 1
Schools: 7
  6 Primary; 0 Middle; 1 High; 0 Other Level
  7 Regular; 0 Special Education; 0 Vocational; 0 Alternative
  0 Magnet; 0 Charter; 7 Title I Eligible; 0 School-wide Title I
Students: 7,989 (51.8% male; 48.1% female)
  Individual Education Program: 954 (11.9%);
  English Language Learner: 753 (9.4%); Migrant: 0 (0.0%)
  Eligible for Free Lunch Program: 3,061 (40.8%)
  Eligible for Reduced-Price Lunch Program: 981 (13.1%)
Teachers: 482.0 (15.6 to 1)
Librarians/Media Specialists: 5.0 (1,500.2 to 1)
Guidance Counselors: 15.0 (500.1 to 1)
Current Spending: ($ per student per year):
  Total: $9,847; Instruction: $6,137; Support Services: $3,506
Enrollment, Drop-out Rates and Diploma Recipients by Race/Ethnicity

Category	Total	White	Black	Asian	AIAN	Hisp.
Enrollment (%)	100.0	15.4	1.4	5.8	0.0	77.4
Drop-out Rate (%)	3.6	3.1	0.0	0.8	n/a	4.1
H.S. Diplomas (#)	426	97	8	33	0	288

Secaucus Town
20 Centre Ave • Secaucus, NJ 07096-1496
Mailing Address: 20 Centre Ave PO Box 149 • Secaucus, NJ 07096-1496
(201) 974-2004
Grade Span: PK-12; **Agency Type:** 1
Schools: 4
  2 Primary; 1 Middle; 1 High; 0 Other Level
  4 Regular; 0 Special Education; 0 Vocational; 0 Alternative
  0 Magnet; 0 Charter; 3 Title I Eligible; 0 School-wide Title I
Students: 1,892 (51.1% male; 48.8% female)
  Individual Education Program: 257 (13.6%);
  English Language Learner: 30 (1.6%); Migrant: 0 (0.0%)
  Eligible for Free Lunch Program: 214 (11.6%)
  Eligible for Reduced-Price Lunch Program: 118 (6.4%)
Teachers: 143.8 (12.9 to 1)
Librarians/Media Specialists: 1.0 (1,849.0 to 1)
Guidance Counselors: 7.6 (243.3 to 1)
Current Spending: ($ per student per year):
  Total: $12,717; Instruction: $7,252; Support Services: $4,958
Enrollment, Drop-out Rates and Diploma Recipients by Race/Ethnicity

Category	Total	White	Black	Asian	AIAN	Hisp.
Enrollment (%)	100.0	59.8	1.6	19.1	0.0	19.6
Drop-out Rate (%)	1.6	1.3	0.0	1.3	n/a	3.3
H.S. Diplomas (#)	120	72	3	20	0	25

Union City
3912 Bergen Turnpike • Union City, NJ 07087-2507
(201) 348-5851 • http://www.union-city.k12.nj.us
Grade Span: PK-12; **Agency Type:** 1
Schools: 12
  9 Primary; 1 Middle; 2 High; 0 Other Level
  12 Regular; 0 Special Education; 0 Vocational; 0 Alternative
  0 Magnet; 0 Charter; 10 Title I Eligible; 10 School-wide Title I
Students: 10,436 (51.3% male; 48.6% female)
  Individual Education Program: 926 (8.9%);
  English Language Learner: 4,574 (43.8%); Migrant: 0 (0.0%)
  Eligible for Free Lunch Program: 8,745 (87.6%)

Eligible for Reduced-Price Lunch Program: 448 (4.5%)
Teachers: 823.7 (12.1 to 1)
Librarians/Media Specialists: 4.0 (2,495.5 to 1)
Guidance Counselors: 16.0 (623.9 to 1)
Current Spending: ($ per student per year):
  Total: $13,904; Instruction: $8,468; Support Services: $5,131
Enrollment, Drop-out Rates and Diploma Recipients by Race/Ethnicity

Category	Total	White	Black	Asian	AIAN	Hisp.
Enrollment (%)	100.0	3.5	0.8	1.1	0.0	94.6
Drop-out Rate (%)	2.1	1.7	0.0	0.0	0.0	2.1
H.S. Diplomas (#)	560	30	4	18	0	508

West New York Town
6028 Broadway • West New York, NJ 07093-5223
(201) 902-1123 • http://www.wnyschools.net/index2.htm
Grade Span: PK-12; **Agency Type:** 1
Schools: 8
  7 Primary; 0 Middle; 1 High; 0 Other Level
  8 Regular; 0 Special Education; 0 Vocational; 0 Alternative
  0 Magnet; 0 Charter; 6 Title I Eligible; 0 School-wide Title I
Students: 7,153 (50.7% male; 49.2% female)
  Individual Education Program: 1,025 (14.3%);
  English Language Learner: 1,014 (14.2%); Migrant: 0 (0.0%)
  Eligible for Free Lunch Program: 3,919 (59.4%)
  Eligible for Reduced-Price Lunch Program: 1,005 (15.2%)
Teachers: 520.0 (12.7 to 1)
Librarians/Media Specialists: 10.0 (659.8 to 1)
Guidance Counselors: 23.0 (286.9 to 1)
Current Spending: ($ per student per year):
  Total: $12,611; Instruction: $8,039; Support Services: $4,311
Enrollment, Drop-out Rates and Diploma Recipients by Race/Ethnicity

Category	Total	White	Black	Asian	AIAN	Hisp.
Enrollment (%)	100.0	4.1	1.1	0.8	0.1	93.9
Drop-out Rate (%)	0.1	0.0	0.0	0.0	n/a	0.1
H.S. Diplomas (#)	357	16	19	9	0	313

Hunterdon County

Clinton Twp
11 Humphrey Rd • Annandale, NJ 08801-0006
(908) 735-8320 • http://www.ctsd.k12.nj.us
Grade Span: PK-08; **Agency Type:** 1
Schools: 3
  2 Primary; 1 Middle; 0 High; 0 Other Level
  3 Regular; 0 Special Education; 0 Vocational; 0 Alternative
  0 Magnet; 0 Charter; 0 Title I Eligible; 0 School-wide Title I
Students: 1,949 (50.1% male; 49.8% female)
  Individual Education Program: 250 (12.8%);
  English Language Learner: 6 (0.3%); Migrant: 0 (0.0%)
  Eligible for Free Lunch Program: 16 (0.9%)
  Eligible for Reduced-Price Lunch Program: 0 (0.0%)
Teachers: 136.5 (12.9 to 1)
Librarians/Media Specialists: 3.0 (588.0 to 1)
Guidance Counselors: 4.6 (383.5 to 1)
Current Spending: ($ per student per year):
  Total: $10,229; Instruction: $5,791; Support Services: $4,437
Enrollment, Drop-out Rates and Diploma Recipients by Race/Ethnicity

Category	Total	White	Black	Asian	AIAN	Hisp.
Enrollment (%)	100.0	93.6	1.2	3.7	0.1	1.4
Drop-out Rate (%)	n/a	n/a	n/a	n/a	n/a	n/a
H.S. Diplomas (#)	n/a	n/a	n/a	n/a	n/a	n/a

Flemington-Raritan Reg
50 Court St • Flemington, NJ 08822-1325
(908) 284-7561 • http://www.frsd.k12.nj.us
Grade Span: PK-08; **Agency Type:** 1
Schools: 5
  4 Primary; 1 Middle; 0 High; 0 Other Level
  5 Regular; 0 Special Education; 0 Vocational; 0 Alternative
  0 Magnet; 0 Charter; 3 Title I Eligible; 0 School-wide Title I
Students: 3,683 (52.0% male; 47.9% female)
  Individual Education Program: 485 (13.2%);
  English Language Learner: 60 (1.6%); Migrant: 0 (0.0%)
  Eligible for Free Lunch Program: 115 (3.3%)
  Eligible for Reduced-Price Lunch Program: 63 (1.8%)
Teachers: 262.4 (13.5 to 1)
Librarians/Media Specialists: 6.5 (543.5 to 1)
Guidance Counselors: 8.0 (441.6 to 1)
Current Spending: ($ per student per year):
  Total: $10,200; Instruction: $5,914; Support Services: $4,099
Enrollment, Drop-out Rates and Diploma Recipients by Race/Ethnicity

Category	Total	White	Black	Asian	AIAN	Hisp.
Enrollment (%)	100.0	87.4	3.1	4.9	0.1	4.6
Drop-out Rate (%)	n/a	n/a	n/a	n/a	n/a	n/a
H.S. Diplomas (#)	n/a	n/a	n/a	n/a	n/a	n/a

Hunterdon Central Reg

84 Route 31 • Flemington, NJ 08822-1239
(908) 782-5727 • http://www.hcrhs.hunterdon.k12.nj.us/
Grade Span: 09-12; **Agency Type:** 1
Schools: 1
    0 Primary; 0 Middle; 1 High; 0 Other Level
    1 Regular; 0 Special Education; 0 Vocational; 0 Alternative
    0 Magnet; 0 Charter; 1 Title I Eligible; 0 School-wide Title I
Students: 2,839   (50.2% male; 49.7% female)
    Individual Education Program: 414 (14.6%);
    English Language Learner: 18 (0.6%); Migrant: 0 (0.0%)
    Eligible for Free Lunch Program: 50 (1.8%)
    Eligible for Reduced-Price Lunch Program: 21 (0.7%)
Teachers: 219.5 (12.8 to 1)
Librarians/Media Specialists: 3.0 (935.3 to 1)
Guidance Counselors: 15.0 (187.1 to 1)
Current Spending: ($ per student per year):
    Total: $14,863; Instruction: $7,862; Support Services: $5,689
Enrollment, Drop-out Rates and Diploma Recipients by Race/Ethnicity

Category	Total	White	Black	Asian	AIAN	Hisp.
Enrollment (%)	100.0	96.2	0.9	1.0	0.4	1.5
Drop-out Rate (%)	0.6	0.6	0.0	n/a	n/a	0.0
H.S. Diplomas (#)	500	465	7	12	4	12

N Hunt/Voorhees Regional

1445 State Route 31 • Annandale, NJ 08801-3117
(908) 735-2846 • http://www.nhvweb.net
Grade Span: 09-12; **Agency Type:** 1
Schools: 2
    0 Primary; 0 Middle; 2 High; 0 Other Level
    2 Regular; 0 Special Education; 0 Vocational; 0 Alternative
    0 Magnet; 0 Charter; 1 Title I Eligible; 0 School-wide Title I
Students: 2,779   (49.9% male; 50.0% female)
    Individual Education Program: 442 (15.9%);
    English Language Learner: 3 (0.1%); Migrant: 0 (0.0%)
    Eligible for Free Lunch Program: 12 (0.4%)
    Eligible for Reduced-Price Lunch Program: 13 (0.5%)
Teachers: 208.7 (13.0 to 1)
Librarians/Media Specialists: 2.0 (1,360.5 to 1)
Guidance Counselors: 17.4 (156.4 to 1)
Current Spending: ($ per student per year):
    Total: $14,326; Instruction: $8,611; Support Services: $5,421
Enrollment, Drop-out Rates and Diploma Recipients by Race/Ethnicity

Category	Total	White	Black	Asian	AIAN	Hisp.
Enrollment (%)	100.0	96.5	0.6	1.4	0.2	1.2
Drop-out Rate (%)	1.0	0.9	0.0	3.3	0.0	5.0
H.S. Diplomas (#)	521	504	2	10	0	5

Readington Twp

48 Readington Rd • Whitehouse Station, NJ 08889-0807
Mailing Address: PO Box 807 • Whitehouse Station, NJ 08889-0807
(908) 534-2195
Grade Span: PK-08; **Agency Type:** 1
Schools: 4
    3 Primary; 1 Middle; 0 High; 0 Other Level
    4 Regular; 0 Special Education; 0 Vocational; 0 Alternative
    0 Magnet; 0 Charter; 0 Title I Eligible; 0 School-wide Title I
Students: 2,298   (51.2% male; 48.7% female)
    Individual Education Program: 347 (15.1%);
    English Language Learner: 11 (0.5%); Migrant: 0 (0.0%)
    Eligible for Free Lunch Program: 21 (0.9%)
    Eligible for Reduced-Price Lunch Program: 10 (0.4%)
Teachers: 173.9 (12.9 to 1)
Librarians/Media Specialists: 3.0 (748.3 to 1)
Guidance Counselors: 5.0 (449.0 to 1)
Current Spending: ($ per student per year):
    Total: $10,674; Instruction: $6,345; Support Services: $4,104
Enrollment, Drop-out Rates and Diploma Recipients by Race/Ethnicity

Category	Total	White	Black	Asian	AIAN	Hisp.
Enrollment (%)	100.0	92.7	1.2	3.1	0.3	2.9
Drop-out Rate (%)	n/a	n/a	n/a	n/a	n/a	n/a
H.S. Diplomas (#)	n/a	n/a	n/a	n/a	n/a	n/a

Mercer County

East Windsor Regional

384 Stockton St • Hightstown, NJ 08520-4228
(609) 443-7704 • http://eastwindsor.expresspage.net/
Grade Span: PK-12; **Agency Type:** 1
Schools: 6
    4 Primary; 1 Middle; 1 High; 0 Other Level
    6 Regular; 0 Special Education; 0 Vocational; 0 Alternative
    0 Magnet; 0 Charter; 3 Title I Eligible; 0 School-wide Title I
Students: 5,152   (51.2% male; 48.7% female)
    Individual Education Program: 860 (16.7%);

    English Language Learner: 297 (5.8%); Migrant: 0 (0.0%)
    Eligible for Free Lunch Program: 539 (11.1%)
    Eligible for Reduced-Price Lunch Program: 321 (6.6%)
Teachers: 360.4 (13.5 to 1)
Librarians/Media Specialists: 7.0 (693.7 to 1)
Guidance Counselors: 14.0 (346.9 to 1)
Current Spending: ($ per student per year):
    Total: $11,895; Instruction: $6,974; Support Services: $4,620
Enrollment, Drop-out Rates and Diploma Recipients by Race/Ethnicity

Category	Total	White	Black	Asian	AIAN	Hisp.
Enrollment (%)	100.0	55.3	12.0	12.3	0.2	20.1
Drop-out Rate (%)	3.5	1.1	5.7	0.7	0.0	12.4
H.S. Diplomas (#)	225	143	12	44	1	25

Ewing Twp

1331 Lower Ferry Rd • Ewing, NJ 08618-1409
(609) 538-9800 • http://www.ewing.k12.nj.us
Grade Span: PK-12; **Agency Type:** 1
Schools: 5
    3 Primary; 1 Middle; 1 High; 0 Other Level
    5 Regular; 0 Special Education; 0 Vocational; 0 Alternative
    0 Magnet; 0 Charter; 3 Title I Eligible; 0 School-wide Title I
Students: 4,178   (51.3% male; 48.6% female)
    Individual Education Program: 825 (19.7%);
    English Language Learner: 87 (2.1%); Migrant: 0 (0.0%)
    Eligible for Free Lunch Program: 529 (13.6%)
    Eligible for Reduced-Price Lunch Program: 324 (8.3%)
Teachers: 323.9 (12.0 to 1)
Librarians/Media Specialists: 6.0 (648.3 to 1)
Guidance Counselors: 13.0 (299.2 to 1)
Current Spending: ($ per student per year):
    Total: $12,389; Instruction: $7,744; Support Services: $4,229
Enrollment, Drop-out Rates and Diploma Recipients by Race/Ethnicity

Category	Total	White	Black	Asian	AIAN	Hisp.
Enrollment (%)	100.0	45.7	44.0	3.0	0.2	7.1
Drop-out Rate (%)	2.8	4.2	1.8	0.0	0.0	0.0
H.S. Diplomas (#)	230	118	100	3	1	8

Hamilton Twp

90 Park Ave • Hamilton Square, NJ 08690-2024
(609) 890-3723 • http://www.hamilton.k12.nj.us
Grade Span: PK-12; **Agency Type:** 1
Schools: 23
    17 Primary; 3 Middle; 3 High; 0 Other Level
    23 Regular; 0 Special Education; 0 Vocational; 0 Alternative
    0 Magnet; 0 Charter; 21 Title I Eligible; 0 School-wide Title I
Students: 14,074   (51.4% male; 48.5% female)
    Individual Education Program: 3,057 (21.7%);
    English Language Learner: 178 (1.3%); Migrant: 0 (0.0%)
    Eligible for Free Lunch Program: 1,609 (12.1%)
    Eligible for Reduced-Price Lunch Program: 860 (6.5%)
Teachers: 949.8 (14.0 to 1)
Librarians/Media Specialists: 15.0 (888.3 to 1)
Guidance Counselors: 52.5 (253.8 to 1)
Current Spending: ($ per student per year):
    Total: $10,020; Instruction: $6,249; Support Services: $3,509
Enrollment, Drop-out Rates and Diploma Recipients by Race/Ethnicity

Category	Total	White	Black	Asian	AIAN	Hisp.
Enrollment (%)	100.0	72.5	15.1	3.7	0.2	8.5
Drop-out Rate (%)	2.5	2.3	2.9	0.7	0.0	4.5
H.S. Diplomas (#)	899	686	107	42	9	55

Hopewell Valley Regional

425 S Main St • Pennington, NJ 08534-2716
(609) 737-0105 • http://www.hvrsd.k12.nj.us/district/intro.htm
Grade Span: PK-12; **Agency Type:** 1
Schools: 6
    4 Primary; 1 Middle; 1 High; 0 Other Level
    6 Regular; 0 Special Education; 0 Vocational; 0 Alternative
    0 Magnet; 0 Charter; 0 Title I Eligible; 0 School-wide Title I
Students: 3,879   (50.8% male; 49.1% female)
    Individual Education Program: 575 (14.8%);
    English Language Learner: 9 (0.2%); Migrant: 0 (0.0%)
    Eligible for Free Lunch Program: 30 (0.8%)
    Eligible for Reduced-Price Lunch Program: 28 (0.7%)
Teachers: 321.5 (11.9 to 1)
Librarians/Media Specialists: 6.5 (590.6 to 1)
Guidance Counselors: 15.5 (247.7 to 1)
Current Spending: ($ per student per year):
    Total: $12,701; Instruction: $7,902; Support Services: $4,551
Enrollment, Drop-out Rates and Diploma Recipients by Race/Ethnicity

Category	Total	White	Black	Asian	AIAN	Hisp.
Enrollment (%)	100.0	91.3	1.4	5.5	0.1	1.7
Drop-out Rate (%)	0.0	0.0	0.0	0.0	0.0	0.0
H.S. Diplomas (#)	240	217	4	12	1	6

Lawrence Twp

2565 Princeton Pike • Lawrenceville, NJ 08648-3631
(609) 530-8609 • http://www.lawrence.k12.nj.us
Grade Span: PK-12; **Agency Type:** 1
Schools: 7
    4 Primary; 2 Middle; 1 High; 0 Other Level
    7 Regular; 0 Special Education; 0 Vocational; 0 Alternative
    0 Magnet; 0 Charter; 2 Title I Eligible; 0 School-wide Title I
Students: 4,852   (51.7% male; 48.2% female)
    Individual Education Program: 796 (16.4%);
    English Language Learner: 154 (3.2%); Migrant: 0 (0.0%)
    Eligible for Free Lunch Program: 288 (6.8%)
    Eligible for Reduced-Price Lunch Program: 207 (4.9%)
Teachers: 310.7 (13.7 to 1)
Librarians/Media Specialists: 4.0 (1,061.8 to 1)
Guidance Counselors: 13.0 (326.7 to 1)
Current Spending: ($ per student per year):
    Total: $12,065; Instruction: $7,353; Support Services: $4,472
Enrollment, Drop-out Rates and Diploma Recipients by Race/Ethnicity

Category	Total	White	Black	Asian	AIAN	Hisp.
Enrollment (%)	100.0	64.5	16.2	11.8	0.3	7.1
Drop-out Rate (%)	3.2	2.7	4.3	4.6	n/a	3.6
H.S. Diplomas (#)	311	235	35	22	0	19

Mercer County Special Service

1050 Old Trenton Rd • Trenton, NJ 08690-1230
(609) 588-8400
Grade Span: UG-UG; **Agency Type:** 4
Schools: 5
    0 Primary; 0 Middle; 0 High; 5 Other Level
    0 Regular; 5 Special Education; 0 Vocational; 0 Alternative
    0 Magnet; 0 Charter; 0 Title I Eligible; 0 School-wide Title I
Students: 1,752   (71.0% male; 28.9% female)
    Individual Education Program: 0 (0.0%);
    English Language Learner: 0 (0.0%); Migrant: 0 (0.0%)
    Eligible for Free Lunch Program: 331 (37.8%)
    Eligible for Reduced-Price Lunch Program: 82 (9.4%)
Teachers: 137.3 (6.4 to 1)
Librarians/Media Specialists: 1.0 (876.0 to 1)
Guidance Counselors: 1.0 (876.0 to 1)
Current Spending: ($ per student per year):
    Total: $32,907; Instruction: $19,251; Support Services: $13,656
Enrollment, Drop-out Rates and Diploma Recipients by Race/Ethnicity

Category	Total	White	Black	Asian	AIAN	Hisp.
Enrollment (%)	100.0	37.0	43.8	3.1	0.1	16.0
Drop-out Rate (%)	n/a	n/a	n/a	n/a	n/a	n/a
H.S. Diplomas (#)	0	0	0	0	0	0

Princeton Regional

25 Valley Rd • Princeton, NJ 08540-0711
(609) 924-9322 • http://www.prs.k12.nj.us
Grade Span: PK-12; **Agency Type:** 1
Schools: 6
    4 Primary; 1 Middle; 1 High; 0 Other Level
    6 Regular; 0 Special Education; 0 Vocational; 0 Alternative
    0 Magnet; 0 Charter; 4 Title I Eligible; 0 School-wide Title I
Students: 3,304   (51.4% male; 48.5% female)
    Individual Education Program: 514 (15.6%);
    English Language Learner: 109 (3.3%); Migrant: 0 (0.0%)
    Eligible for Free Lunch Program: 203 (6.2%)
    Eligible for Reduced-Price Lunch Program: 89 (2.7%)
Teachers: 278.1 (11.8 to 1)
Librarians/Media Specialists: 7.0 (469.7 to 1)
Guidance Counselors: 11.4 (288.4 to 1)
Current Spending: ($ per student per year):
    Total: $14,582; Instruction: $8,948; Support Services: $5,335
Enrollment, Drop-out Rates and Diploma Recipients by Race/Ethnicity

Category	Total	White	Black	Asian	AIAN	Hisp.
Enrollment (%)	100.0	71.9	9.0	11.4	0.0	7.7
Drop-out Rate (%)	0.9	0.6	0.0	0.0	0.0	6.8
H.S. Diplomas (#)	237	168	22	33	0	14

Trenton City

108 N Clinton Ave • Trenton, NJ 08609-1014
(609) 989-2744 • http://www.trenton.k12.nj.us
Grade Span: PK-12; **Agency Type:** 1
Schools: 24
    18 Primary; 4 Middle; 2 High; 0 Other Level
    24 Regular; 0 Special Education; 0 Vocational; 0 Alternative
    0 Magnet; 0 Charter; 22 Title I Eligible; 22 School-wide Title I
Students: 13,227   (50.3% male; 49.6% female)
    Individual Education Program: 2,631 (19.9%);
    English Language Learner: 1,035 (7.8%); Migrant: 0 (0.0%)
    Eligible for Free Lunch Program: 6,295 (50.6%)
    Eligible for Reduced-Price Lunch Program: 1,233 (9.9%)

Teachers: 1,017.0 (12.2 to 1)
Librarians/Media Specialists: 18.0 (690.7 to 1)
Guidance Counselors: 44.0 (282.6 to 1)
Current Spending: ($ per student per year):
    Total: $17,270; Instruction: $9,521; Support Services: $7,187
Enrollment, Drop-out Rates and Diploma Recipients by Race/Ethnicity

Category	Total	White	Black	Asian	AIAN	Hisp.
Enrollment (%)	100.0	3.8	66.9	0.6	0.0	28.6
Drop-out Rate (%)	14.0	25.5	14.9	0.0	0.0	10.5
H.S. Diplomas (#)	872	10	458	0	0	404

W Windsor-Plainsboro Reg

505 Village Rd W • Princeton Junction, NJ 08550-0248
Mailing Address: PO Box 505 • Princeton Junction, NJ 08550-0248
(609) 716-5040 • http://www.west-windsor-plainsboro.k12.nj.us/
Grade Span: PK-12; **Agency Type:** 1
Schools: 10
    4 Primary; 4 Middle; 2 High; 0 Other Level
    10 Regular; 0 Special Education; 0 Vocational; 0 Alternative
    0 Magnet; 0 Charter; 5 Title I Eligible; 0 School-wide Title I
Students: 9,238   (50.9% male; 49.0% female)
    Individual Education Program: 1,109 (12.0%);
    English Language Learner: 282 (3.1%); Migrant: 0 (0.0%)
    Eligible for Free Lunch Program: 155 (1.7%)
    Eligible for Reduced-Price Lunch Program: 125 (1.4%)
Teachers: 695.9 (13.0 to 1)
Librarians/Media Specialists: 11.0 (822.0 to 1)
Guidance Counselors: 25.1 (360.2 to 1)
Current Spending: ($ per student per year):
    Total: $12,772; Instruction: $7,617; Support Services: $4,645
Enrollment, Drop-out Rates and Diploma Recipients by Race/Ethnicity

Category	Total	White	Black	Asian	AIAN	Hisp.
Enrollment (%)	100.0	52.5	5.1	37.3	0.1	4.9
Drop-out Rate (%)	0.3	0.4	0.0	0.0	n/a	1.2
H.S. Diplomas (#)	554	335	42	149	0	28

Washington Twp

1079 Washington Blvd • Robbinsville, NJ 08691-3037
(609) 448-8254
Grade Span: PK-08; **Agency Type:** 1
Schools: 2
    1 Primary; 1 Middle; 0 High; 0 Other Level
    2 Regular; 0 Special Education; 0 Vocational; 0 Alternative
    0 Magnet; 0 Charter; 1 Title I Eligible; 0 School-wide Title I
Students: 1,544   (49.8% male; 50.1% female)
    Individual Education Program: 309 (20.0%);
    English Language Learner: 8 (0.5%); Migrant: 0 (0.0%)
    Eligible for Free Lunch Program: 15 (1.0%)
    Eligible for Reduced-Price Lunch Program: 21 (1.4%)
Teachers: 123.7 (12.1 to 1)
Librarians/Media Specialists: 3.0 (499.0 to 1)
Guidance Counselors: 3.0 (499.0 to 1)
Current Spending: ($ per student per year):
    Total: $10,322; Instruction: $5,777; Support Services: $4,384
Enrollment, Drop-out Rates and Diploma Recipients by Race/Ethnicity

Category	Total	White	Black	Asian	AIAN	Hisp.
Enrollment (%)	100.0	88.9	3.4	6.5	0.0	1.2
Drop-out Rate (%)	n/a	n/a	n/a	n/a	n/a	n/a
H.S. Diplomas (#)	n/a	n/a	n/a	n/a	n/a	n/a

Middlesex County

Carteret Boro

599 Roosevelt Ave • Carteret, NJ 07008-2912
(732) 541-8961 • http://www.ci.carteret.nj.us
Grade Span: PK-12; **Agency Type:** 1
Schools: 5
    3 Primary; 1 Middle; 1 High; 0 Other Level
    5 Regular; 0 Special Education; 0 Vocational; 0 Alternative
    0 Magnet; 0 Charter; 4 Title I Eligible; 0 School-wide Title I
Students: 3,957   (51.9% male; 48.0% female)
    Individual Education Program: 425 (10.7%);
    English Language Learner: 238 (6.0%); Migrant: 0 (0.0%)
    Eligible for Free Lunch Program: 1,359 (35.2%)
    Eligible for Reduced-Price Lunch Program: 504 (13.1%)
Teachers: 280.5 (13.8 to 1)
Librarians/Media Specialists: 4.0 (965.0 to 1)
Guidance Counselors: 11.0 (350.9 to 1)
Current Spending: ($ per student per year):
    Total: $10,345; Instruction: $6,475; Support Services: $3,651
Enrollment, Drop-out Rates and Diploma Recipients by Race/Ethnicity

Category	Total	White	Black	Asian	AIAN	Hisp.
Enrollment (%)	100.0	27.9	16.7	18.9	0.0	36.6
Drop-out Rate (%)	1.3	0.3	2.1	0.0	n/a	2.8
H.S. Diplomas (#)	200	118	10	23	0	49

East Brunswick Twp
760 Route #18 • East Brunswick, NJ 08816-3068
(732) 613-6705 • http://www.ebruns.k12.nj.us
Grade Span: PK-12; **Agency Type:** 1
Schools: 11
   8 Primary; 1 Middle; 1 High; 1 Other Level
   11 Regular; 0 Special Education; 0 Vocational; 0 Alternative
   0 Magnet; 0 Charter; 6 Title I Eligible; 0 School-wide Title I
Students: 9,141 (51.5% male; 48.4% female)
   Individual Education Program: 1,424 (15.6%);
   English Language Learner: 174 (1.9%); Migrant: 0 (0.0%)
   Eligible for Free Lunch Program: 285 (3.2%)
   Eligible for Reduced-Price Lunch Program: 203 (2.3%)
Teachers: 622.7 (14.4 to 1)
Librarians/Media Specialists: 13.0 (688.5 to 1)
Guidance Counselors: 20.0 (447.5 to 1)
Current Spending: ($ per student per year):
   Total: $11,780; Instruction: $6,967; Support Services: $4,508
Enrollment, Drop-out Rates and Diploma Recipients by Race/Ethnicity

Category	Total	White	Black	Asian	AIAN	Hisp.
Enrollment (%)	100.0	68.8	3.4	23.1	0.1	4.6
Drop-out Rate (%)	0.4	0.5	1.3	0.0	0.0	0.0
H.S. Diplomas (#)	646	462	15	145	0	24

Edison Twp
312 Pierson Ave • Edison, NJ 08837
(732) 452-4900 • http://www.edison.k12.nj.us
Grade Span: PK-12; **Agency Type:** 1
Schools: 17
   11 Primary; 4 Middle; 2 High; 0 Other Level
   17 Regular; 0 Special Education; 0 Vocational; 0 Alternative
   0 Magnet; 0 Charter; 8 Title I Eligible; 0 School-wide Title I
Students: 13,293 (50.3% male; 49.6% female)
   Individual Education Program: 1,709 (12.9%);
   English Language Learner: 313 (2.4%); Migrant: 0 (0.0%)
   Eligible for Free Lunch Program: 844 (6.4%)
   Eligible for Reduced-Price Lunch Program: 458 (3.5%)
Teachers: 1,040.8 (12.7 to 1)
Librarians/Media Specialists: 6.0 (2,199.5 to 1)
Guidance Counselors: 35.0 (377.1 to 1)
Current Spending: ($ per student per year):
   Total: $11,541; Instruction: $7,647; Support Services: $3,675
Enrollment, Drop-out Rates and Diploma Recipients by Race/Ethnicity

Category	Total	White	Black	Asian	AIAN	Hisp.
Enrollment (%)	100.0	41.5	8.4	42.3	0.1	7.7
Drop-out Rate (%)	0.4	0.4	0.0	0.3	0.0	1.2
H.S. Diplomas (#)	926	451	80	343	0	52

Highland Park Boro
435 Mansfield St • Highland Park, NJ 08904-2642
(732) 572-6990
Grade Span: PK-12; **Agency Type:** 1
Schools: 3
   2 Primary; 0 Middle; 1 High; 0 Other Level
   3 Regular; 0 Special Education; 0 Vocational; 0 Alternative
   0 Magnet; 0 Charter; 3 Title I Eligible; 3 School-wide Title I
Students: 1,606 (50.7% male; 49.2% female)
   Individual Education Program: 220 (13.7%);
   English Language Learner: 67 (4.2%); Migrant: 0 (0.0%)
   Eligible for Free Lunch Program: 305 (19.2%)
   Eligible for Reduced-Price Lunch Program: 122 (7.7%)
Teachers: 122.0 (13.0 to 1)
Librarians/Media Specialists: 3.0 (529.7 to 1)
Guidance Counselors: 5.0 (317.8 to 1)
Current Spending: ($ per student per year):
   Total: $13,067; Instruction: $7,323; Support Services: $5,241
Enrollment, Drop-out Rates and Diploma Recipients by Race/Ethnicity

Category	Total	White	Black	Asian	AIAN	Hisp.
Enrollment (%)	100.0	48.9	16.3	20.2	0.0	14.6
Drop-out Rate (%)	0.0	0.0	0.0	0.0	n/a	0.0
H.S. Diplomas (#)	108	62	14	15	0	17

Metuchen Boro
442 Main St • Metuchen, NJ 08840-1886
(732) 321-8714 • http://www.metuchenschools.org/metuchen
Grade Span: PK-12; **Agency Type:** 1
Schools: 4
   2 Primary; 1 Middle; 1 High; 0 Other Level
   4 Regular; 0 Special Education; 0 Vocational; 0 Alternative
   0 Magnet; 0 Charter; 1 Title I Eligible; 0 School-wide Title I
Students: 1,872 (51.5% male; 48.4% female)
   Individual Education Program: 244 (13.0%);
   English Language Learner: 13 (0.7%); Migrant: 0 (0.0%)
   Eligible for Free Lunch Program: 63 (3.4%)
   Eligible for Reduced-Price Lunch Program: 43 (2.3%)
Teachers: 154.2 (12.1 to 1)
Librarians/Media Specialists: 3.0 (619.7 to 1)
Guidance Counselors: 5.0 (371.8 to 1)
Current Spending: ($ per student per year):
   Total: $12,463; Instruction: $7,472; Support Services: $4,647
Enrollment, Drop-out Rates and Diploma Recipients by Race/Ethnicity

Category	Total	White	Black	Asian	AIAN	Hisp.
Enrollment (%)	100.0	76.2	8.1	11.0	0.0	4.7
Drop-out Rate (%)	0.2	0.2	0.0	0.0	n/a	0.0
H.S. Diplomas (#)	136	113	11	6	0	6

Middlesex Boro
H.S Annex • Middlesex, NJ 08846-1489
(732) 317-6000 • http://www.middlesex.k12.nj.us/
Grade Span: PK-12; **Agency Type:** 1
Schools: 5
   3 Primary; 1 Middle; 1 High; 0 Other Level
   5 Regular; 0 Special Education; 0 Vocational; 0 Alternative
   0 Magnet; 0 Charter; 2 Title I Eligible; 0 School-wide Title I
Students: 2,179 (51.2% male; 48.7% female)
   Individual Education Program: 328 (15.1%);
   English Language Learner: 80 (3.7%); Migrant: 0 (0.0%)
   Eligible for Free Lunch Program: 167 (7.8%)
   Eligible for Reduced-Price Lunch Program: 141 (6.6%)
Teachers: 165.0 (12.9 to 1)
Librarians/Media Specialists: 2.0 (1,066.5 to 1)
Guidance Counselors: 5.0 (426.6 to 1)
Current Spending: ($ per student per year):
   Total: $11,041; Instruction: $6,965; Support Services: $3,744
Enrollment, Drop-out Rates and Diploma Recipients by Race/Ethnicity

Category	Total	White	Black	Asian	AIAN	Hisp.
Enrollment (%)	100.0	74.1	4.3	5.1	0.0	16.5
Drop-out Rate (%)	0.9	1.2	0.0	0.0	n/a	0.0
H.S. Diplomas (#)	108	89	5	9	0	5

Middlesex County Vocational
112 Rues Ln • East Brunswick, NJ 08816-0220
Mailing Address: PO Box 1070 • East Brunswick, NJ 08816-0220
(732) 257-3300 • http://www.mc-votech.org
Grade Span: 09-12; **Agency Type:** 1
Schools: 6
   0 Primary; 0 Middle; 5 High; 1 Other Level
   0 Regular; 0 Special Education; 6 Vocational; 0 Alternative
   0 Magnet; 0 Charter; 3 Title I Eligible; 0 School-wide Title I
Students: 2,315 (58.4% male; 41.5% female)
   Individual Education Program: 513 (22.2%);
   English Language Learner: 25 (1.1%); Migrant: 0 (0.0%)
   Eligible for Free Lunch Program: 584 (32.8%)
   Eligible for Reduced-Price Lunch Program: 179 (10.1%)
Teachers: 205.0 (8.7 to 1)
Librarians/Media Specialists: 4.0 (445.0 to 1)
Guidance Counselors: 7.0 (254.3 to 1)
Current Spending: ($ per student per year):
   Total: $20,350; Instruction: $11,418; Support Services: $8,603
Enrollment, Drop-out Rates and Diploma Recipients by Race/Ethnicity

Category	Total	White	Black	Asian	AIAN	Hisp.
Enrollment (%)	100.0	45.3	16.1	3.1	0.0	35.6
Drop-out Rate (%)	0.9	0.9	1.5	0.0	0.0	0.7
H.S. Diplomas (#)	258	121	47	1	0	89

Monroe Twp
423 Buckelew Ave • Monroe Township, NJ 08831-9802
(732) 521-2111
Grade Span: PK-12; **Agency Type:** 1
Schools: 6
   3 Primary; 2 Middle; 1 High; 0 Other Level
   6 Regular; 0 Special Education; 0 Vocational; 0 Alternative
   0 Magnet; 0 Charter; 4 Title I Eligible; 0 School-wide Title I
Students: 4,124 (52.4% male; 47.5% female)
   Individual Education Program: 672 (16.3%);
   English Language Learner: 27 (0.7%); Migrant: 0 (0.0%)
   Eligible for Free Lunch Program: 126 (3.1%)
   Eligible for Reduced-Price Lunch Program: 75 (1.9%)
Teachers: 321.6 (12.6 to 1)
Librarians/Media Specialists: 4.0 (1,010.3 to 1)
Guidance Counselors: 13.0 (310.8 to 1)
Current Spending: ($ per student per year):
   Total: $11,859; Instruction: $6,766; Support Services: $4,821
Enrollment, Drop-out Rates and Diploma Recipients by Race/Ethnicity

Category	Total	White	Black	Asian	AIAN	Hisp.
Enrollment (%)	100.0	83.5	3.9	8.0	0.7	3.9
Drop-out Rate (%)	1.4	1.3	2.5	0.0	n/a	1.8
H.S. Diplomas (#)	179	151	11	5	0	12

New Brunswick City
268 Baldwin St • New Brunswick, NJ 08903-2683
Mailing Address: PO Box 2683 • New Brunswick, NJ 08903-2683
(732) 745-5414 • http://www.nbps.k12.nj.us
Grade Span: PK-12; Agency Type: 1
Schools: 10
   8 Primary; 0 Middle; 2 High; 0 Other Level
   9 Regular; 0 Special Education; 0 Vocational; 1 Alternative
   0 Magnet; 0 Charter; 9 Title I Eligible; 0 School-wide Title I
Students: 6,989 (51.2% male; 48.7% female)
   Individual Education Program: 1,311 (18.8%);
   English Language Learner: 1,630 (23.3%); Migrant: 0 (0.0%)
   Eligible for Free Lunch Program: 4,273 (66.1%)
   Eligible for Reduced-Price Lunch Program: 728 (11.3%)
Teachers: 592.0 (10.9 to 1)
Librarians/Media Specialists: 6.0 (1,076.7 to 1)
Guidance Counselors: 17.0 (380.0 to 1)
Current Spending: ($ per student per year):
   Total: $18,180; Instruction: $11,860; Support Services: $5,853
Enrollment, Drop-out Rates and Diploma Recipients by Race/Ethnicity

Category	Total	White	Black	Asian	AIAN	Hisp.
Enrollment (%)	100.0	2.7	26.6	1.8	0.0	68.9
Drop-out Rate (%)	8.0	20.0	6.4	0.0	n/a	8.6
H.S. Diplomas (#)	158	2	66	4	0	86

North Brunswick Twp
Old Georges Rd • North Brunswick, NJ 08902-0407
Mailing Address: PO Box 6016 • North Brunswick, NJ 08902-0407
(732) 289-3030 • http://www.nbtschools.org
Grade Span: PK-12; Agency Type: 1
Schools: 6
   4 Primary; 1 Middle; 1 High; 0 Other Level
   6 Regular; 0 Special Education; 0 Vocational; 0 Alternative
   0 Magnet; 0 Charter; 3 Title I Eligible; 0 School-wide Title I
Students: 5,519 (50.8% male; 49.1% female)
   Individual Education Program: 691 (12.5%);
   English Language Learner: 233 (4.2%); Migrant: 0 (0.0%)
   Eligible for Free Lunch Program: 708 (13.1%)
   Eligible for Reduced-Price Lunch Program: 374 (6.9%)
Teachers: 395.6 (13.7 to 1)
Librarians/Media Specialists: 6.0 (900.2 to 1)
Guidance Counselors: 12.0 (450.1 to 1)
Current Spending: ($ per student per year):
   Total: $10,729; Instruction: $6,672; Support Services: $3,684
Enrollment, Drop-out Rates and Diploma Recipients by Race/Ethnicity

Category	Total	White	Black	Asian	AIAN	Hisp.
Enrollment (%)	100.0	42.1	21.7	20.1	0.0	16.0
Drop-out Rate (%)	0.8	0.4	1.0	0.0	n/a	3.4
H.S. Diplomas (#)	309	165	57	53	0	34

Old Bridge Twp
Admin Bldg Route 516 • Matawan, NJ 07747-9641
(732) 290-3976 • http://www.oldbridgeschools.org
Grade Span: PK-12; Agency Type: 1
Schools: 15
   12 Primary; 2 Middle; 1 High; 0 Other Level
   15 Regular; 0 Special Education; 0 Vocational; 0 Alternative
   0 Magnet; 0 Charter; 5 Title I Eligible; 0 School-wide Title I
Students: 10,119 (51.3% male; 48.6% female)
   Individual Education Program: 1,230 (12.2%);
   English Language Learner: 274 (2.7%); Migrant: 0 (0.0%)
   Eligible for Free Lunch Program: 743 (7.5%)
   Eligible for Reduced-Price Lunch Program: 517 (5.2%)
Teachers: 670.4 (14.9 to 1)
Librarians/Media Specialists: 13.5 (737.9 to 1)
Guidance Counselors: 18.0 (553.4 to 1)
Current Spending: ($ per student per year):
   Total: $10,861; Instruction: $6,628; Support Services: $3,979
Enrollment, Drop-out Rates and Diploma Recipients by Race/Ethnicity

Category	Total	White	Black	Asian	AIAN	Hisp.
Enrollment (%)	100.0	69.0	6.8	16.0	0.0	8.2
Drop-out Rate (%)	3.3	3.0	4.7	3.9	n/a	3.5
H.S. Diplomas (#)	579	412	40	94	0	33

Perth Amboy City
178 Barracks St • Perth Amboy, NJ 08861-3402
(732) 376-6279 • http://www.perthamboy.k12.nj.us
Grade Span: PK-12; Agency Type: 1
Schools: 11
   8 Primary; 2 Middle; 1 High; 0 Other Level
   11 Regular; 0 Special Education; 0 Vocational; 0 Alternative
   0 Magnet; 0 Charter; 6 Title I Eligible; 4 School-wide Title I
Students: 9,762 (52.4% male; 47.5% female)
   Individual Education Program: 1,062 (10.9%);
   English Language Learner: 1,483 (15.2%); Migrant: 0 (0.0%)

Eligible for Free Lunch Program: 6,183 (66.2%)
   Eligible for Reduced-Price Lunch Program: 1,353 (14.5%)
Teachers: 727.5 (12.8 to 1)
Librarians/Media Specialists: 9.0 (1,037.2 to 1)
Guidance Counselors: 25.0 (373.4 to 1)
Current Spending: ($ per student per year):
   Total: $12,487; Instruction: $8,036; Support Services: $4,082
Enrollment, Drop-out Rates and Diploma Recipients by Race/Ethnicity

Category	Total	White	Black	Asian	AIAN	Hisp.
Enrollment (%)	100.0	3.7	7.3	1.0	0.0	88.0
Drop-out Rate (%)	3.7	2.1	3.8	0.0	0.0	3.8
H.S. Diplomas (#)	322	18	35	0	9	260

Piscataway Twp
1515 Stelton Rd • Piscataway, NJ 08855-1332
Mailing Address: PO Box 1332 • Piscataway, NJ 08855-1332
(732) 572-2289 • http://www.familyeducation.com/nj/piscataway
Grade Span: PK-12; Agency Type: 1
Schools: 10
   4 Primary; 5 Middle; 1 High; 0 Other Level
   10 Regular; 0 Special Education; 0 Vocational; 0 Alternative
   0 Magnet; 0 Charter; 9 Title I Eligible; 0 School-wide Title I
Students: 6,991 (51.2% male; 48.7% female)
   Individual Education Program: 1,002 (14.3%);
   English Language Learner: 276 (3.9%); Migrant: 0 (0.0%)
   Eligible for Free Lunch Program: 738 (10.9%)
   Eligible for Reduced-Price Lunch Program: 416 (6.1%)
Teachers: 504.5 (13.4 to 1)
Librarians/Media Specialists: 10.0 (677.3 to 1)
Guidance Counselors: 17.3 (391.5 to 1)
Current Spending: ($ per student per year):
   Total: $11,820; Instruction: $6,980; Support Services: $4,373
Enrollment, Drop-out Rates and Diploma Recipients by Race/Ethnicity

Category	Total	White	Black	Asian	AIAN	Hisp.
Enrollment (%)	100.0	31.0	32.7	24.5	0.1	11.7
Drop-out Rate (%)	0.5	0.3	0.4	1.1	n/a	0.5
H.S. Diplomas (#)	428	136	142	104	0	46

Sayreville Boro
150 Lincoln St • Sayreville, NJ 08879-0997
Mailing Address: PO Box 997 • Sayreville, NJ 08872-0997
(732) 525-5224 • http://www.sayrevillek12.net
Grade Span: PK-12; Agency Type: 1
Schools: 7
   4 Primary; 1 Middle; 1 High; 1 Other Level
   6 Regular; 1 Special Education; 0 Vocational; 0 Alternative
   0 Magnet; 0 Charter; 4 Title I Eligible; 0 School-wide Title I
Students: 5,924 (52.8% male; 47.1% female)
   Individual Education Program: 961 (16.2%);
   English Language Learner: 94 (1.6%); Migrant: 0 (0.0%)
   Eligible for Free Lunch Program: 564 (9.9%)
   Eligible for Reduced-Price Lunch Program: 362 (6.4%)
Teachers: 387.8 (14.7 to 1)
Librarians/Media Specialists: 6.0 (948.7 to 1)
Guidance Counselors: 14.0 (406.6 to 1)
Current Spending: ($ per student per year):
   Total: $9,873; Instruction: $6,247; Support Services: $3,376
Enrollment, Drop-out Rates and Diploma Recipients by Race/Ethnicity

Category	Total	White	Black	Asian	AIAN	Hisp.
Enrollment (%)	100.0	59.9	12.7	16.1	0.1	11.2
Drop-out Rate (%)	0.6	0.6	0.6	0.5	0.0	0.8
H.S. Diplomas (#)	348	250	37	37	0	24

South Brunswick Twp
PO Box 181 • Monmouth Junction, NJ 08852-0181
(732) 297-7800 • http://www.sbschools.org
Grade Span: PK-12; Agency Type: 1
Schools: 12
   9 Primary; 2 Middle; 1 High; 0 Other Level
   12 Regular; 0 Special Education; 0 Vocational; 0 Alternative
   0 Magnet; 0 Charter; 4 Title I Eligible; 0 School-wide Title I
Students: 8,506 (50.3% male; 49.6% female)
   Individual Education Program: 1,129 (13.3%);
   English Language Learner: 100 (1.2%); Migrant: 0 (0.0%)
   Eligible for Free Lunch Program: 241 (2.9%)
   Eligible for Reduced-Price Lunch Program: 249 (3.0%)
Teachers: 622.5 (13.4 to 1)
Librarians/Media Specialists: 13.0 (640.1 to 1)
Guidance Counselors: 17.7 (470.1 to 1)
Current Spending: ($ per student per year):
   Total: $11,480; Instruction: $6,508; Support Services: $4,439

Enrollment, Drop-out Rates and Diploma Recipients by Race/Ethnicity

Category	Total	White	Black	Asian	AIAN	Hisp.
Enrollment (%)	100.0	57.7	9.4	27.7	0.2	5.1
Drop-out Rate (%)	1.3	1.6	1.7	0.7	n/a	0.0
H.S. Diplomas (#)	427	262	43	102	0	20

South Plainfield Boro
305 Cromwell Place • South Plainfield, NJ 07080-4107
(908) 754-4620 • http://www.spnet.k12.nj.us
Grade Span: PK-12; **Agency Type:** 1
Schools: 8
  5 Primary; 2 Middle; 1 High; 0 Other Level
  8 Regular; 0 Special Education; 0 Vocational; 0 Alternative
  0 Magnet; 0 Charter; 4 Title I Eligible; 0 School-wide Title I
Students: 3,906 (51.6% male; 48.3% female)
  Individual Education Program: 592 (15.2%);
  English Language Learner: 61 (1.6%); Migrant: 0 (0.0%)
  Eligible for Free Lunch Program: 233 (6.0%)
  Eligible for Reduced-Price Lunch Program: 172 (4.5%)
Teachers: 298.1 (12.9 to 1)
Librarians/Media Specialists: 8.0 (481.6 to 1)
Guidance Counselors: 10.0 (385.3 to 1)
Current Spending: ($ per student per year):
  Total: $10,841; Instruction: $6,705; Support Services: $3,777
Enrollment, Drop-out Rates and Diploma Recipients by Race/Ethnicity

Category	Total	White	Black	Asian	AIAN	Hisp.
Enrollment (%)	100.0	64.8	11.4	11.7	0.3	11.8
Drop-out Rate (%)	0.1	0.0	0.0	0.0	0.0	0.9
H.S. Diplomas (#)	236	159	40	20	0	17

South River Boro
Admin Bldg 15 Montgomery Str • South River, NJ 08882
Mailing Address: Admin Bldg 15 Montgomery St • South River, NJ 08882
(732) 613-4000 • http://www.sriver.k12.nj.us
Grade Span: PK-12; **Agency Type:** 1
Schools: 3
  1 Primary; 1 Middle; 1 High; 0 Other Level
  3 Regular; 0 Special Education; 0 Vocational; 0 Alternative
  0 Magnet; 0 Charter; 2 Title I Eligible; 0 School-wide Title I
Students: 2,247 (52.6% male; 47.3% female)
  Individual Education Program: 296 (13.2%);
  English Language Learner: 95 (4.2%); Migrant: 0 (0.0%)
  Eligible for Free Lunch Program: 336 (15.2%)
  Eligible for Reduced-Price Lunch Program: 214 (9.7%)
Teachers: 149.0 (14.8 to 1)
Librarians/Media Specialists: 3.0 (735.7 to 1)
Guidance Counselors: 7.0 (315.3 to 1)
Current Spending: ($ per student per year):
  Total: $8,546; Instruction: $5,414; Support Services: $2,859
Enrollment, Drop-out Rates and Diploma Recipients by Race/Ethnicity

Category	Total	White	Black	Asian	AIAN	Hisp.
Enrollment (%)	100.0	71.2	9.9	3.5	0.0	15.3
Drop-out Rate (%)	4.0	2.8	6.8	10.0	0.0	8.4
H.S. Diplomas (#)	148	111	9	4	0	24

Spotswood Boro
Adm. Off. 105 Summerhill Rd • Spotswood, NJ 08884
(732) 723-2236 • http://www.spotswood.k12.nj.us/
Grade Span: PK-12; **Agency Type:** 1
Schools: 4
  2 Primary; 1 Middle; 1 High; 0 Other Level
  4 Regular; 0 Special Education; 0 Vocational; 0 Alternative
  0 Magnet; 0 Charter; 3 Title I Eligible; 0 School-wide Title I
Students: 1,826 (52.5% male; 47.4% female)
  Individual Education Program: 192 (10.5%);
  English Language Learner: 7 (0.4%); Migrant: 0 (0.0%)
  Eligible for Free Lunch Program: 89 (5.2%)
  Eligible for Reduced-Price Lunch Program: 68 (3.9%)
Teachers: 133.1 (12.9 to 1)
Librarians/Media Specialists: 2.0 (861.5 to 1)
Guidance Counselors: 6.6 (261.1 to 1)
Current Spending: ($ per student per year):
  Total: $10,854; Instruction: $6,511; Support Services: $3,936
Enrollment, Drop-out Rates and Diploma Recipients by Race/Ethnicity

Category	Total	White	Black	Asian	AIAN	Hisp.
Enrollment (%)	100.0	86.8	2.8	4.2	0.1	6.1
Drop-out Rate (%)	0.6	0.3	18.2	0.0	0.0	0.0
H.S. Diplomas (#)	190	166	3	12	0	9

Woodbridge Twp
School St • Woodbridge, NJ 07095-0952
Mailing Address: PO Box 428 • Woodbridge, NJ 07095-0952
(732) 602-8549 • http://www.woodbridge.k12.nj.us
Grade Span: PK-12; **Agency Type:** 1
Schools: 24

  16 Primary; 5 Middle; 3 High; 0 Other Level
  24 Regular; 0 Special Education; 0 Vocational; 0 Alternative
  0 Magnet; 0 Charter; 6 Title I Eligible; 0 School-wide Title I
Students: 14,056 (51.2% male; 48.7% female)
  Individual Education Program: 1,941 (13.8%);
  English Language Learner: 338 (2.4%); Migrant: 0 (0.0%)
  Eligible for Free Lunch Program: 1,655 (12.4%)
  Eligible for Reduced-Price Lunch Program: 830 (6.2%)
Teachers: 996.9 (13.4 to 1)
Librarians/Media Specialists: 19.0 (705.2 to 1)
Guidance Counselors: 31.0 (432.2 to 1)
Current Spending: ($ per student per year):
  Total: $10,638; Instruction: $6,532; Support Services: $3,863
Enrollment, Drop-out Rates and Diploma Recipients by Race/Ethnicity

Category	Total	White	Black	Asian	AIAN	Hisp.
Enrollment (%)	100.0	55.3	12.5	18.5	0.1	13.6
Drop-out Rate (%)	1.3	1.5	0.5	0.8	0.0	1.5
H.S. Diplomas (#)	901	561	120	129	0	91

Monmouth County

Asbury Park City
407 Lake Ave • Asbury Park, NJ 07712-5493
(732) 776-2606 • http://www.asburypark.k12.nj.us/
Grade Span: PK-12; **Agency Type:** 1
Schools: 6
  3 Primary; 1 Middle; 1 High; 1 Other Level
  5 Regular; 1 Special Education; 0 Vocational; 0 Alternative
  0 Magnet; 0 Charter; 4 Title I Eligible; 3 School-wide Title I
Students: 3,181 (49.8% male; 50.1% female)
  Individual Education Program: 685 (21.5%);
  English Language Learner: 161 (5.1%); Migrant: 0 (0.0%)
  Eligible for Free Lunch Program: 2,241 (75.6%)
  Eligible for Reduced-Price Lunch Program: 207 (7.0%)
Teachers: 307.0 (9.7 to 1)
Librarians/Media Specialists: 4.0 (741.5 to 1)
Guidance Counselors: 9.0 (329.6 to 1)
Current Spending: ($ per student per year):
  Total: $22,784; Instruction: $13,687; Support Services: $7,973
Enrollment, Drop-out Rates and Diploma Recipients by Race/Ethnicity

Category	Total	White	Black	Asian	AIAN	Hisp.
Enrollment (%)	100.0	2.4	81.5	0.2	0.0	15.9
Drop-out Rate (%)	9.0	14.3	9.0	0.0	0.0	9.1
H.S. Diplomas (#)	118	1	102	0	0	15

Colts Neck Twp
70 Conover Rd • Colts Neck, NJ 07722-1250
(732) 946-0055
Grade Span: PK-08; **Agency Type:** 1
Schools: 3
  2 Primary; 1 Middle; 0 High; 0 Other Level
  3 Regular; 0 Special Education; 0 Vocational; 0 Alternative
  0 Magnet; 0 Charter; 0 Title I Eligible; 0 School-wide Title I
Students: 1,544 (51.0% male; 48.9% female)
  Individual Education Program: 198 (12.8%);
  English Language Learner: 10 (0.6%); Migrant: 0 (0.0%)
  Eligible for Free Lunch Program: 11 (0.7%)
  Eligible for Reduced-Price Lunch Program: 13 (0.9%)
Teachers: 127.3 (11.9 to 1)
Librarians/Media Specialists: 2.0 (755.5 to 1)
Guidance Counselors: 3.0 (503.7 to 1)
Current Spending: ($ per student per year):
  Total: $10,600; Instruction: $6,508; Support Services: $3,897
Enrollment, Drop-out Rates and Diploma Recipients by Race/Ethnicity

Category	Total	White	Black	Asian	AIAN	Hisp.
Enrollment (%)	100.0	95.0	0.7	3.5	0.0	0.8
Drop-out Rate (%)	n/a	n/a	n/a	n/a	n/a	n/a
H.S. Diplomas (#)	n/a	n/a	n/a	n/a	n/a	n/a

Freehold Regional
11 Pine St • Englishtown, NJ 07726-1595
(732) 792-7300 • http://www.frhsd.com
Grade Span: 09-12; **Agency Type:** 1
Schools: 6
  0 Primary; 0 Middle; 6 High; 0 Other Level
  6 Regular; 0 Special Education; 0 Vocational; 0 Alternative
  0 Magnet; 0 Charter; 4 Title I Eligible; 0 School-wide Title I
Students: 10,935 (49.4% male; 50.5% female)
  Individual Education Program: 1,448 (13.2%);
  English Language Learner: 91 (0.8%); Migrant: 0 (0.0%)
  Eligible for Free Lunch Program: 368 (3.4%)
  Eligible for Reduced-Price Lunch Program: 184 (1.7%)
Teachers: 739.0 (14.7 to 1)
Librarians/Media Specialists: 9.0 (1,203.4 to 1)
Guidance Counselors: 36.0 (300.9 to 1)

Current Spending: ($ per student per year):
Total: $11,216; Instruction: $6,009; Support Services: $4,946
Enrollment, Drop-out Rates and Diploma Recipients by Race/Ethnicity

Category	Total	White	Black	Asian	AIAN	Hisp.
Enrollment (%)	100.0	85.2	3.1	6.9	0.1	4.6
Drop-out Rate (%)	1.1	0.8	2.8	0.6	12.5	5.3
H.S. Diplomas (#)	2,214	1,822	129	142	3	118

Freehold Twp
384 W Main St • Freehold, NJ 07728-3198
(732) 462-8400 • http://www.freeholdtwp.k12.nj.us
Grade Span: PK-08; **Agency Type:** 1
Schools: 7
  5 Primary; 2 Middle; 0 High; 0 Other Level
  7 Regular; 0 Special Education; 0 Vocational; 0 Alternative
  0 Magnet; 0 Charter; 3 Title I Eligible; 0 School-wide Title I
Students: 4,787 (50.3% male; 49.6% female)
  Individual Education Program: 672 (14.0%);
  English Language Learner: 25 (0.5%); Migrant: 0 (0.0%)
  Eligible for Free Lunch Program: 105 (2.3%)
  Eligible for Reduced-Price Lunch Program: 80 (1.8%)
Teachers: 289.3 (15.7 to 1)
Librarians/Media Specialists: 6.5 (696.8 to 1)
Guidance Counselors: 8.0 (566.1 to 1)
Current Spending: ($ per student per year):
Total: $9,623; Instruction: $5,706; Support Services: $3,725
Enrollment, Drop-out Rates and Diploma Recipients by Race/Ethnicity

Category	Total	White	Black	Asian	AIAN	Hisp.
Enrollment (%)	100.0	84.8	3.3	7.2	0.0	4.6
Drop-out Rate (%)	n/a	n/a	n/a	n/a	n/a	n/a
H.S. Diplomas (#)	n/a	n/a	n/a	n/a	n/a	n/a

Hazlet Twp
421 Middle Rd • Hazlet, NJ 07730-2342
(732) 264-8402 • http://www.hazlet.org
Grade Span: PK-12; **Agency Type:** 1
Schools: 8
  6 Primary; 1 Middle; 1 High; 0 Other Level
  8 Regular; 0 Special Education; 0 Vocational; 0 Alternative
  0 Magnet; 0 Charter; 3 Title I Eligible; 0 School-wide Title I
Students: 3,561 (49.1% male; 50.8% female)
  Individual Education Program: 591 (16.6%);
  English Language Learner: 11 (0.3%); Migrant: 0 (0.0%)
  Eligible for Free Lunch Program: 183 (5.3%)
  Eligible for Reduced-Price Lunch Program: 105 (3.1%)
Teachers: 263.6 (13.0 to 1)
Librarians/Media Specialists: 4.0 (855.8 to 1)
Guidance Counselors: 7.0 (489.0 to 1)
Current Spending: ($ per student per year):
Total: $10,882; Instruction: $6,663; Support Services: $4,016
Enrollment, Drop-out Rates and Diploma Recipients by Race/Ethnicity

Category	Total	White	Black	Asian	AIAN	Hisp.
Enrollment (%)	100.0	89.9	1.5	3.0	0.1	5.4
Drop-out Rate (%)	0.4	0.4	0.0	0.0	0.0	0.0
H.S. Diplomas (#)	207	183	8	8	0	8

Holmdel Twp
4 Crawford's Corner Rd • Holmdel, NJ 07733-0407
(732) 946-1800 • http://www.holmdel.k12.nj.us
Grade Span: PK-12; **Agency Type:** 1
Schools: 4
  2 Primary; 1 Middle; 1 High; 0 Other Level
  4 Regular; 0 Special Education; 0 Vocational; 0 Alternative
  0 Magnet; 0 Charter; 0 Title I Eligible; 0 School-wide Title I
Students: 3,617 (51.3% male; 48.6% female)
  Individual Education Program: 394 (10.9%);
  English Language Learner: 20 (0.6%); Migrant: 0 (0.0%)
  Eligible for Free Lunch Program: 11 (0.3%)
  Eligible for Reduced-Price Lunch Program: 2 (0.1%)
Teachers: 241.8 (14.8 to 1)
Librarians/Media Specialists: 3.0 (1,195.3 to 1)
Guidance Counselors: 8.0 (448.3 to 1)
Current Spending: ($ per student per year):
Total: $10,701; Instruction: $6,580; Support Services: $3,793
Enrollment, Drop-out Rates and Diploma Recipients by Race/Ethnicity

Category	Total	White	Black	Asian	AIAN	Hisp.
Enrollment (%)	100.0	76.3	0.5	21.4	0.2	1.6
Drop-out Rate (%)	0.1	0.1	0.0	0.0	0.0	0.0
H.S. Diplomas (#)	218	162	2	51	1	2

Howell Twp
200 Squankum-Yellowbrook • Howell, NJ 07731-0579
(732) 751-2480 • http://www.howell.k12.nj.us
Grade Span: PK-08; **Agency Type:** 1
Schools: 12

  10 Primary; 2 Middle; 0 High; 0 Other Level
  12 Regular; 0 Special Education; 0 Vocational; 0 Alternative
  0 Magnet; 0 Charter; 5 Title I Eligible; 0 School-wide Title I
Students: 7,648 (50.8% male; 49.1% female)
  Individual Education Program: 1,282 (16.8%);
  English Language Learner: 72 (0.9%); Migrant: 0 (0.0%)
  Eligible for Free Lunch Program: 383 (5.2%)
  Eligible for Reduced-Price Lunch Program: 202 (2.7%)
Teachers: 530.3 (13.9 to 1)
Librarians/Media Specialists: 11.0 (668.2 to 1)
Guidance Counselors: 11.0 (668.2 to 1)
Current Spending: ($ per student per year):
Total: $10,330; Instruction: $6,180; Support Services: $3,952
Enrollment, Drop-out Rates and Diploma Recipients by Race/Ethnicity

Category	Total	White	Black	Asian	AIAN	Hisp.
Enrollment (%)	100.0	87.6	4.1	3.8	0.1	4.4
Drop-out Rate (%)	n/a	n/a	n/a	n/a	n/a	n/a
H.S. Diplomas (#)	n/a	n/a	n/a	n/a	n/a	n/a

Keansburg Boro
100 Palmer Place • Keansburg, NJ 07734-2056
(732) 787-7578 • http://titans.khs.keansburg.k12.nj.us
Grade Span: PK-12; **Agency Type:** 1
Schools: 4
  2 Primary; 1 Middle; 1 High; 0 Other Level
  4 Regular; 0 Special Education; 0 Vocational; 0 Alternative
  0 Magnet; 0 Charter; 3 Title I Eligible; 3 School-wide Title I
Students: 2,194 (53.3% male; 46.6% female)
  Individual Education Program: 542 (24.7%);
  English Language Learner: 25 (1.1%); Migrant: 0 (0.0%)
  Eligible for Free Lunch Program: 909 (43.2%)
  Eligible for Reduced-Price Lunch Program: 349 (16.6%)
Teachers: 216.5 (9.7 to 1)
Librarians/Media Specialists: 4.0 (526.3 to 1)
Guidance Counselors: 9.0 (233.9 to 1)
Current Spending: ($ per student per year):
Total: $16,491; Instruction: $9,909; Support Services: $6,204
Enrollment, Drop-out Rates and Diploma Recipients by Race/Ethnicity

Category	Total	White	Black	Asian	AIAN	Hisp.
Enrollment (%)	100.0	79.0	6.5	1.8	0.4	12.3
Drop-out Rate (%)	1.4	1.2	4.2	0.0	n/a	2.1
H.S. Diplomas (#)	85	72	3	3	0	7

Long Branch City
540 Broadway • Long Branch, NJ 07740-5108
(908) 571-2868 • http://www.longbranch.k12.nj.us
Grade Span: PK-12; **Agency Type:** 1
Schools: 9
  7 Primary; 1 Middle; 1 High; 0 Other Level
  9 Regular; 0 Special Education; 0 Vocational; 0 Alternative
  0 Magnet; 0 Charter; 9 Title I Eligible; 0 School-wide Title I
Students: 5,264 (51.2% male; 48.7% female)
  Individual Education Program: 798 (15.2%);
  English Language Learner: 253 (4.8%); Migrant: 0 (0.0%)
  Eligible for Free Lunch Program: 2,452 (50.3%)
  Eligible for Reduced-Price Lunch Program: 748 (15.4%)
Teachers: 489.0 (10.0 to 1)
Librarians/Media Specialists: 5.0 (974.0 to 1)
Guidance Counselors: 16.0 (304.4 to 1)
Current Spending: ($ per student per year):
Total: $15,586; Instruction: $9,811; Support Services: $5,305
Enrollment, Drop-out Rates and Diploma Recipients by Race/Ethnicity

Category	Total	White	Black	Asian	AIAN	Hisp.
Enrollment (%)	100.0	34.3	30.7	1.4	0.2	33.3
Drop-out Rate (%)	3.7	5.3	2.4	0.0	0.0	3.3
H.S. Diplomas (#)	207	79	74	4	1	49

Manalapan-Englishtown Reg
54 Main St • Englishtown, NJ 07726-1599
(732) 446-5506 • http://www.mers.k12.nj.us
Grade Span: PK-08; **Agency Type:** 1
Schools: 7
  3 Primary; 4 Middle; 0 High; 0 Other Level
  7 Regular; 0 Special Education; 0 Vocational; 0 Alternative
  0 Magnet; 0 Charter; 3 Title I Eligible; 0 School-wide Title I
Students: 5,640 (49.9% male; 50.0% female)
  Individual Education Program: 782 (13.9%);
  English Language Learner: 80 (1.4%); Migrant: 0 (0.0%)
  Eligible for Free Lunch Program: 145 (2.6%)
  Eligible for Reduced-Price Lunch Program: 95 (1.7%)
Teachers: 390.0 (14.2 to 1)
Librarians/Media Specialists: 7.0 (790.4 to 1)
Guidance Counselors: 10.5 (527.0 to 1)
Current Spending: ($ per student per year):
Total: $9,581; Instruction: $5,680; Support Services: $3,718

Enrollment, Drop-out Rates and Diploma Recipients by Race/Ethnicity

Category	Total	White	Black	Asian	AIAN	Hisp.
Enrollment (%)	100.0	88.8	2.2	5.8	0.1	3.1
Drop-out Rate (%)	n/a	n/a	n/a	n/a	n/a	n/a
H.S. Diplomas (#)	n/a	n/a	n/a	n/a	n/a	n/a

Manasquan Boro
169 Broad St • Manasquan, NJ 08736-2892
(732) 528-8800 • http://www.manasquanboe.org/public/default.asp
Grade Span: PK-12; Agency Type: 1
Schools: 2
  1 Primary; 0 Middle; 1 High; 0 Other Level
  2 Regular; 0 Special Education; 0 Vocational; 0 Alternative
  0 Magnet; 0 Charter; 2 Title I Eligible; 0 School-wide Title I
Students: 1,804 (50.2% male; 49.7% female)
  Individual Education Program: 122 (6.8%);
  English Language Learner: 18 (1.0%); Migrant: 0 (0.0%)
  Eligible for Free Lunch Program: 103 (5.8%)
  Eligible for Reduced-Price Lunch Program: 38 (2.2%)
Teachers: 122.8 (14.4 to 1)
Librarians/Media Specialists: 2.0 (883.0 to 1)
Guidance Counselors: 6.8 (259.7 to 1)
Current Spending: ($ per student per year):
  Total: $10,074; Instruction: $6,159; Support Services: $3,615

Enrollment, Drop-out Rates and Diploma Recipients by Race/Ethnicity

Category	Total	White	Black	Asian	AIAN	Hisp.
Enrollment (%)	100.0	92.8	2.5	0.9	0.0	3.9
Drop-out Rate (%)	1.5	1.5	0.0	0.0	n/a	3.6
H.S. Diplomas (#)	197	187	5	1	0	4

Marlboro Twp
1980 Township Dr • Marlboro, NJ 07746-2298
(732) 972-2015 • http://www.marlboro.k12.nj.us/
Grade Span: PK-08; Agency Type: 1
Schools: 8
  6 Primary; 2 Middle; 0 High; 0 Other Level
  8 Regular; 0 Special Education; 0 Vocational; 0 Alternative
  0 Magnet; 0 Charter; 4 Title I Eligible; 0 School-wide Title I
Students: 6,084 (51.5% male; 48.4% female)
  Individual Education Program: 748 (12.3%);
  English Language Learner: 91 (1.5%); Migrant: 0 (0.0%)
  Eligible for Free Lunch Program: 54 (0.9%)
  Eligible for Reduced-Price Lunch Program: 54 (0.9%)
Teachers: 399.4 (14.9 to 1)
Librarians/Media Specialists: 7.0 (848.7 to 1)
Guidance Counselors: 10.0 (594.1 to 1)
Current Spending: ($ per student per year):
  Total: $9,158; Instruction: $5,561; Support Services: $3,397

Enrollment, Drop-out Rates and Diploma Recipients by Race/Ethnicity

Category	Total	White	Black	Asian	AIAN	Hisp.
Enrollment (%)	100.0	75.2	2.0	19.6	0.3	2.9
Drop-out Rate (%)	n/a	n/a	n/a	n/a	n/a	n/a
H.S. Diplomas (#)	n/a	n/a	n/a	n/a	n/a	n/a

Matawan-Aberdeen Regional
Cambridge Park School • Aberdeen, NJ 07747-2286
(732) 290-2705 • http://www.marsd.k12.nj.us
Grade Span: PK-12; Agency Type: 1
Schools: 7
  5 Primary; 1 Middle; 1 High; 0 Other Level
  7 Regular; 0 Special Education; 0 Vocational; 0 Alternative
  0 Magnet; 0 Charter; 4 Title I Eligible; 0 School-wide Title I
Students: 3,953 (50.8% male; 49.1% female)
  Individual Education Program: 481 (12.2%);
  English Language Learner: 59 (1.5%); Migrant: 0 (0.0%)
  Eligible for Free Lunch Program: 435 (11.2%)
  Eligible for Reduced-Price Lunch Program: 247 (6.3%)
Teachers: 300.0 (13.0 to 1)
Librarians/Media Specialists: 4.0 (973.5 to 1)
Guidance Counselors: 7.0 (556.3 to 1)
Current Spending: ($ per student per year):
  Total: $11,978; Instruction: $7,523; Support Services: $4,207

Enrollment, Drop-out Rates and Diploma Recipients by Race/Ethnicity

Category	Total	White	Black	Asian	AIAN	Hisp.
Enrollment (%)	100.0	69.8	15.7	6.2	0.0	8.3
Drop-out Rate (%)	1.3	1.1	2.6	0.0	0.0	1.1
H.S. Diplomas (#)	191	132	32	6	0	21

Middletown Twp
59 Tindall Rd • Middletown, NJ 07748-2999
(732) 706-6002 • http://www.middletownk12.org
Grade Span: PK-12; Agency Type: 1
Schools: 17
  12 Primary; 3 Middle; 2 High; 0 Other Level
  17 Regular; 0 Special Education; 0 Vocational; 0 Alternative

0 Magnet; 0 Charter; 8 Title I Eligible; 0 School-wide Title I
Students: 10,777 (52.1% male; 47.8% female)
  Individual Education Program: 1,785 (16.6%);
  English Language Learner: 40 (0.4%); Migrant: 0 (0.0%)
  Eligible for Free Lunch Program: 410 (3.9%)
  Eligible for Reduced-Price Lunch Program: 256 (2.5%)
Teachers: 755.8 (13.8 to 1)
Librarians/Media Specialists: 10.0 (1,041.9 to 1)
Guidance Counselors: 23.0 (453.0 to 1)
Current Spending: ($ per student per year):
  Total: $10,863; Instruction: $6,774; Support Services: $3,910

Enrollment, Drop-out Rates and Diploma Recipients by Race/Ethnicity

Category	Total	White	Black	Asian	AIAN	Hisp.
Enrollment (%)	100.0	91.9	1.7	2.8	0.4	3.2
Drop-out Rate (%)	0.9	0.9	1.9	0.0	0.0	1.4
H.S. Diplomas (#)	696	633	19	20	5	19

Millstone Twp
18 Schoolhouse Ln • Clarksburg, NJ 08510-9701
(732) 446-0890
Grade Span: PK-08; Agency Type: 1
Schools: 2
  1 Primary; 1 Middle; 0 High; 0 Other Level
  2 Regular; 0 Special Education; 0 Vocational; 0 Alternative
  0 Magnet; 0 Charter; 1 Title I Eligible; 0 School-wide Title I
Students: 1,735 (50.3% male; 49.6% female)
  Individual Education Program: 332 (19.1%);
  English Language Learner: 14 (0.8%); Migrant: 0 (0.0%)
  Eligible for Free Lunch Program: 30 (1.8%)
  Eligible for Reduced-Price Lunch Program: 24 (1.4%)
Teachers: 123.5 (13.8 to 1)
Librarians/Media Specialists: 2.0 (851.5 to 1)
Guidance Counselors: 2.0 (851.5 to 1)
Current Spending: ($ per student per year):
  Total: $9,327; Instruction: $5,092; Support Services: $3,969

Enrollment, Drop-out Rates and Diploma Recipients by Race/Ethnicity

Category	Total	White	Black	Asian	AIAN	Hisp.
Enrollment (%)	100.0	90.3	3.3	3.8	0.1	2.6
Drop-out Rate (%)	n/a	n/a	n/a	n/a	n/a	n/a
H.S. Diplomas (#)	n/a	n/a	n/a	n/a	n/a	n/a

Monmouth County Vocational
41 Hwy 34 S • Colts Neck, NJ 07722-1714
(732) 431-7942
Grade Span: 09-12; Agency Type: 1
Schools: 8
  0 Primary; 0 Middle; 6 High; 2 Other Level
  0 Regular; 2 Special Education; 6 Vocational; 0 Alternative
  0 Magnet; 0 Charter; 4 Title I Eligible; 0 School-wide Title I
Students: 1,856 (55.5% male; 44.4% female)
  Individual Education Program: 0 (0.0%);
  English Language Learner: 0 (0.0%); Migrant: 0 (0.0%)
  Eligible for Free Lunch Program: 34 (2.2%)
  Eligible for Reduced-Price Lunch Program: 28 (1.8%)
Teachers: 212.0 (7.2 to 1)
Librarians/Media Specialists: 0.0 (n/a to 1)
Guidance Counselors: 17.0 (89.2 to 1)
Current Spending: ($ per student per year):
  Total: $21,614; Instruction: $13,202; Support Services: $8,352

Enrollment, Drop-out Rates and Diploma Recipients by Race/Ethnicity

Category	Total	White	Black	Asian	AIAN	Hisp.
Enrollment (%)	100.0	77.4	9.3	8.8	0.0	4.5
Drop-out Rate (%)	0.0	0.0	0.0	0.0	0.0	0.0
H.S. Diplomas (#)	271	196	26	32	0	17

Neptune Twp
2106 Bangs Ave • Neptune, NJ 07753-4596
(732) 776-2001 • http://www.neptune.k12.nj.us
Grade Span: PK-12; Agency Type: 1
Schools: 8
  6 Primary; 1 Middle; 1 High; 0 Other Level
  8 Regular; 0 Special Education; 0 Vocational; 0 Alternative
  0 Magnet; 0 Charter; 5 Title I Eligible; 0 School-wide Title I
Students: 4,559 (52.2% male; 47.7% female)
  Individual Education Program: 943 (20.7%);
  English Language Learner: 29 (0.6%); Migrant: 0 (0.0%)
  Eligible for Free Lunch Program: 1,369 (31.7%)
  Eligible for Reduced-Price Lunch Program: 420 (9.7%)
Teachers: 328.5 (13.1 to 1)
Librarians/Media Specialists: 7.0 (616.6 to 1)
Guidance Counselors: 11.5 (375.3 to 1)
Current Spending: ($ per student per year):
  Total: $14,156; Instruction: $9,055; Support Services: $4,756

Enrollment, Drop-out Rates and Diploma Recipients by Race/Ethnicity

Category	Total	White	Black	Asian	AIAN	Hisp.
Enrollment (%)	100.0	27.0	64.5	1.6	0.0	7.0
Drop-out Rate (%)	0.6	0.3	0.8	0.0	n/a	2.1
H.S. Diplomas (#)	233	100	117	5	0	11

Ocean Twp
163 Monmouth Rd • Oakhurst, NJ 07755-1597
(732) 531-5600 • http://www.ocean.k12.nj.us/
Grade Span: PK-12; **Agency Type:** 1
Schools: 5
    3 Primary; 1 Middle; 1 High; 0 Other Level
    5 Regular; 0 Special Education; 0 Vocational; 0 Alternative
    0 Magnet; 0 Charter; 2 Title I Eligible; 0 School-wide Title I
Students: 4,982 (50.7% male; 49.2% female)
    Individual Education Program: 707 (14.2%);
    English Language Learner: 157 (3.2%); Migrant: 0 (0.0%)
    Eligible for Free Lunch Program: 277 (6.2%)
    Eligible for Reduced-Price Lunch Program: 147 (3.3%)
Teachers: 326.4 (13.7 to 1)
Librarians/Media Specialists: 5.0 (896.4 to 1)
Guidance Counselors: 10.1 (443.8 to 1)
Current Spending: ($ per student per year):
    Total: $10,970; Instruction: $6,937; Support Services: $3,809
Enrollment, Drop-out Rates and Diploma Recipients by Race/Ethnicity

Category	Total	White	Black	Asian	AIAN	Hisp.
Enrollment (%)	100.0	78.3	7.3	7.7	0.1	6.6
Drop-out Rate (%)	0.4	0.2	2.7	0.0	0.0	0.0
H.S. Diplomas (#)	286	235	15	27	0	9

Tinton Falls
658 Tinton Ave • Tinton Falls, NJ 07724-3275
(732) 460-2404 • http://tfs.k12.nj.us/
Grade Span: PK-08; **Agency Type:** 1
Schools: 3
    1 Primary; 2 Middle; 0 High; 0 Other Level
    3 Regular; 0 Special Education; 0 Vocational; 0 Alternative
    0 Magnet; 0 Charter; 1 Title I Eligible; 0 School-wide Title I
Students: 1,797 (51.2% male; 48.7% female)
    Individual Education Program: 296 (16.5%);
    English Language Learner: 21 (1.2%); Migrant: 0 (0.0%)
    Eligible for Free Lunch Program: 140 (8.1%)
    Eligible for Reduced-Price Lunch Program: 102 (5.9%)
Teachers: 122.2 (14.2 to 1)
Librarians/Media Specialists: 1.0 (1,731.0 to 1)
Guidance Counselors: 3.0 (577.0 to 1)
Current Spending: ($ per student per year):
    Total: $11,226; Instruction: $6,310; Support Services: $4,555
Enrollment, Drop-out Rates and Diploma Recipients by Race/Ethnicity

Category	Total	White	Black	Asian	AIAN	Hisp.
Enrollment (%)	100.0	71.8	15.0	7.8	0.0	5.4
Drop-out Rate (%)	n/a	n/a	n/a	n/a	n/a	n/a
H.S. Diplomas (#)	n/a	n/a	n/a	n/a	n/a	n/a

Upper Freehold Regional
27 High St • Allentown, NJ 08501-0278
(609) 259-7292 • http://www.ufrsd.net/
Grade Span: PK-12; **Agency Type:** 1
Schools: 2
    1 Primary; 0 Middle; 1 High; 0 Other Level
    2 Regular; 0 Special Education; 0 Vocational; 0 Alternative
    0 Magnet; 0 Charter; 1 Title I Eligible; 0 School-wide Title I
Students: 2,040 (52.5% male; 47.4% female)
    Individual Education Program: 182 (8.9%);
    English Language Learner: 59 (2.9%); Migrant: 0 (0.0%)
    Eligible for Free Lunch Program: 41 (2.0%)
    Eligible for Reduced-Price Lunch Program: 26 (1.3%)
Teachers: 139.4 (14.4 to 1)
Librarians/Media Specialists: 2.0 (1,007.0 to 1)
Guidance Counselors: 5.0 (402.8 to 1)
Current Spending: ($ per student per year):
    Total: $11,059; Instruction: $6,598; Support Services: $4,063
Enrollment, Drop-out Rates and Diploma Recipients by Race/Ethnicity

Category	Total	White	Black	Asian	AIAN	Hisp.
Enrollment (%)	100.0	91.5	2.5	3.4	0.0	2.6
Drop-out Rate (%)	0.2	0.3	0.0	0.0	n/a	0.0
H.S. Diplomas (#)	235	227	5	1	0	2

Wall Twp
18th Ave New Bedford • Wall, NJ 07719-1199
Mailing Address: PO Box 1199 • Wall, NJ 07719-1199
(732) 556-2000 • http://www.wall.k12.nj.us
Grade Span: PK-12; **Agency Type:** 1
Schools: 7
    5 Primary; 1 Middle; 1 High; 0 Other Level

    7 Regular; 0 Special Education; 0 Vocational; 0 Alternative
    0 Magnet; 0 Charter; 0 Title I Eligible; 0 School-wide Title I
Students: 4,360 (52.0% male; 47.9% female)
    Individual Education Program: 733 (16.8%);
    English Language Learner: 42 (1.0%); Migrant: 0 (0.0%)
    Eligible for Free Lunch Program: 199 (4.6%)
    Eligible for Reduced-Price Lunch Program: 97 (2.2%)
Teachers: 326.0 (13.3 to 1)
Librarians/Media Specialists: 2.0 (2,160.5 to 1)
Guidance Counselors: 12.0 (360.1 to 1)
Current Spending: ($ per student per year):
    Total: $10,733; Instruction: $6,230; Support Services: $4,283
Enrollment, Drop-out Rates and Diploma Recipients by Race/Ethnicity

Category	Total	White	Black	Asian	AIAN	Hisp.
Enrollment (%)	100.0	94.1	2.4	1.2	0.2	2.1
Drop-out Rate (%)	2.2	2.2	0.0	0.0	0.0	5.9
H.S. Diplomas (#)	251	249	0	2	0	0

Morris County

Denville Twp
501 Openaki Rd • Denville, NJ 07834-9609
(973) 366-1001 • http://www.denville.org/
Grade Span: PK-08; **Agency Type:** 1
Schools: 3
    2 Primary; 1 Middle; 0 High; 0 Other Level
    3 Regular; 0 Special Education; 0 Vocational; 0 Alternative
    0 Magnet; 0 Charter; 0 Title I Eligible; 0 School-wide Title I
Students: 1,959 (50.5% male; 49.4% female)
    Individual Education Program: 310 (15.8%);
    English Language Learner: 22 (1.1%); Migrant: 0 (0.0%)
    Eligible for Free Lunch Program: 51 (2.7%)
    Eligible for Reduced-Price Lunch Program: 0 (0.0%)
Teachers: 130.0 (14.6 to 1)
Librarians/Media Specialists: 3.0 (633.3 to 1)
Guidance Counselors: 3.0 (633.3 to 1)
Current Spending: ($ per student per year):
    Total: $9,471; Instruction: $5,767; Support Services: $3,687
Enrollment, Drop-out Rates and Diploma Recipients by Race/Ethnicity

Category	Total	White	Black	Asian	AIAN	Hisp.
Enrollment (%)	100.0	86.2	2.4	7.2	0.4	3.8
Drop-out Rate (%)	n/a	n/a	n/a	n/a	n/a	n/a
H.S. Diplomas (#)	n/a	n/a	n/a	n/a	n/a	n/a

Dover Town
100 Grace St • Dover, NJ 07801-2699
(973) 989-2000 • http://www.dover-nj.org
Grade Span: PK-12; **Agency Type:** 1
Schools: 5
    3 Primary; 1 Middle; 1 High; 0 Other Level
    5 Regular; 0 Special Education; 0 Vocational; 0 Alternative
    0 Magnet; 0 Charter; 5 Title I Eligible; 0 School-wide Title I
Students: 3,391 (52.7% male; 47.2% female)
    Individual Education Program: 419 (12.4%);
    English Language Learner: 487 (14.4%); Migrant: 0 (0.0%)
    Eligible for Free Lunch Program: 1,092 (35.5%)
    Eligible for Reduced-Price Lunch Program: 531 (17.3%)
Teachers: 222.5 (13.8 to 1)
Librarians/Media Specialists: 4.0 (769.3 to 1)
Guidance Counselors: 9.0 (341.9 to 1)
Current Spending: ($ per student per year):
    Total: $10,956; Instruction: $6,956; Support Services: $3,432
Enrollment, Drop-out Rates and Diploma Recipients by Race/Ethnicity

Category	Total	White	Black	Asian	AIAN	Hisp.
Enrollment (%)	100.0	15.0	8.3	2.4	0.0	74.3
Drop-out Rate (%)	2.8	2.7	2.0	0.0	n/a	3.2
H.S. Diplomas (#)	171	65	21	6	0	79

Hanover Twp
61 Highland Ave • Whippany, NJ 07981-1364
(973) 515-2404
Grade Span: PK-08; **Agency Type:** 1
Schools: 4
    3 Primary; 1 Middle; 0 High; 0 Other Level
    4 Regular; 0 Special Education; 0 Vocational; 0 Alternative
    0 Magnet; 0 Charter; 0 Title I Eligible; 0 School-wide Title I
Students: 1,504 (53.4% male; 46.5% female)
    Individual Education Program: 206 (13.7%);
    English Language Learner: 35 (2.3%); Migrant: 0 (0.0%)
    Eligible for Free Lunch Program: 7 (0.5%)
    Eligible for Reduced-Price Lunch Program: 0 (0.0%)
Teachers: 117.7 (12.4 to 1)
Librarians/Media Specialists: 3.0 (486.0 to 1)
Guidance Counselors: 2.0 (729.0 to 1)
Current Spending: ($ per student per year):
    Total: $12,393; Instruction: $7,090; Support Services: $5,027

Enrollment, Drop-out Rates and Diploma Recipients by Race/Ethnicity

Category	Total	White	Black	Asian	AIAN	Hisp.
Enrollment (%)	100.0	83.2	1.0	11.9	0.0	3.9
Drop-out Rate (%)	n/a	n/a	n/a	n/a	n/a	n/a
H.S. Diplomas (#)	n/a	n/a	n/a	n/a	n/a	n/a

Jefferson Twp

28 Bowling Green Pkwy • Lake Hopatcong, NJ 07849-2259
(973) 663-5780 • http://www.jefftwp.org/
Grade Span: PK-12; **Agency Type:** 1
Schools: 8
  6 Primary; 1 Middle; 1 High; 0 Other Level
  8 Regular; 0 Special Education; 0 Vocational; 0 Alternative
  0 Magnet; 0 Charter; 4 Title I Eligible; 0 School-wide Title I
Students: 3,694   (51.3% male; 48.6% female)
  Individual Education Program: 532 (14.4%);
  English Language Learner: 16 (0.4%); Migrant: 0 (0.0%)
  Eligible for Free Lunch Program: 159 (4.4%)
  Eligible for Reduced-Price Lunch Program: 112 (3.1%)
Teachers: 262.3 (13.7 to 1)
Librarians/Media Specialists: 4.0 (900.0 to 1)
Guidance Counselors: 9.0 (400.0 to 1)
Current Spending: ($ per student per year):
  Total: $10,855; Instruction: $6,371; Support Services: $4,142

Enrollment, Drop-out Rates and Diploma Recipients by Race/Ethnicity

Category	Total	White	Black	Asian	AIAN	Hisp.
Enrollment (%)	100.0	92.4	1.3	2.4	0.2	3.8
Drop-out Rate (%)	1.8	1.9	0.0	0.0	n/a	0.0
H.S. Diplomas (#)	230	211	4	7	0	8

Kinnelon Boro

109 Kiel Ave • Kinnelon, NJ 07405-1621
(973) 838-1418
Grade Span: PK-12; **Agency Type:** 1
Schools: 4
  2 Primary; 1 Middle; 1 High; 0 Other Level
  4 Regular; 0 Special Education; 0 Vocational; 0 Alternative
  0 Magnet; 0 Charter; 0 Title I Eligible; 0 School-wide Title I
Students: 2,157   (51.6% male; 48.3% female)
  Individual Education Program: 252 (11.7%);
  English Language Learner: 7 (0.3%); Migrant: 0 (0.0%)
  Eligible for Free Lunch Program: 8 (0.4%)
  Eligible for Reduced-Price Lunch Program: 0 (0.0%)
Teachers: 151.5 (14.0 to 1)
Librarians/Media Specialists: 4.5 (470.0 to 1)
Guidance Counselors: 4.0 (528.8 to 1)
Current Spending: ($ per student per year):
  Total: $11,155; Instruction: $6,581; Support Services: $4,246

Enrollment, Drop-out Rates and Diploma Recipients by Race/Ethnicity

Category	Total	White	Black	Asian	AIAN	Hisp.
Enrollment (%)	100.0	96.1	0.6	2.1	0.0	1.2
Drop-out Rate (%)	0.0	0.0	0.0	0.0	n/a	0.0
H.S. Diplomas (#)	113	108	3	2	0	0

Madison Boro

359 Woodland Rd • Madison, NJ 07940-2422
(973) 593-3100 • http://www.mendhamboro.org
Grade Span: PK-12; **Agency Type:** 1
Schools: 5
  3 Primary; 1 Middle; 1 High; 0 Other Level
  5 Regular; 0 Special Education; 0 Vocational; 0 Alternative
  0 Magnet; 0 Charter; 2 Title I Eligible; 0 School-wide Title I
Students: 2,290   (51.9% male; 48.0% female)
  Individual Education Program: 364 (15.9%);
  English Language Learner: 50 (2.2%); Migrant: 0 (0.0%)
  Eligible for Free Lunch Program: 93 (4.2%)
  Eligible for Reduced-Price Lunch Program: 52 (2.3%)
Teachers: 176.4 (12.6 to 1)
Librarians/Media Specialists: 6.3 (352.9 to 1)
Guidance Counselors: 6.0 (370.5 to 1)
Current Spending: ($ per student per year):
  Total: $13,020; Instruction: $8,035; Support Services: $4,741

Enrollment, Drop-out Rates and Diploma Recipients by Race/Ethnicity

Category	Total	White	Black	Asian	AIAN	Hisp.
Enrollment (%)	100.0	82.9	3.0	6.4	0.2	7.5
Drop-out Rate (%)	0.0	0.0	0.0	0.0	n/a	0.0
H.S. Diplomas (#)	139	118	6	9	0	6

Montville Twp

125 Changebridge Rd • Montville, NJ 07045
(973) 331-7117 • http://www.montville.net
Grade Span: PK-12; **Agency Type:** 1
Schools: 7
  5 Primary; 1 Middle; 1 High; 0 Other Level
  7 Regular; 0 Special Education; 0 Vocational

  0 Magnet; 0 Charter; 0 Title I Eligible; 0 School-wide Title I
Students: 4,030   (51.1% male; 48.8% female)
  Individual Education Program: 509 (12.6%);
  English Language Learner: 52 (1.3%); Migrant: 0 (0.0%)
  Eligible for Free Lunch Program: 19 (0.5%)
  Eligible for Reduced-Price Lunch Program: 7 (0.2%)
Teachers: 294.8 (13.4 to 1)
Librarians/Media Specialists: 7.0 (566.3 to 1)
Guidance Counselors: 11.0 (360.4 to 1)
Current Spending: ($ per student per year):
  Total: $11,440; Instruction: $6,880; Support Services: $4,297

Enrollment, Drop-out Rates and Diploma Recipients by Race/Ethnicity

Category	Total	White	Black	Asian	AIAN	Hisp.
Enrollment (%)	100.0	78.3	1.7	17.5	0.0	2.5
Drop-out Rate (%)	0.5	0.6	0.0	0.6	0.0	0.0
H.S. Diplomas (#)	208	163	3	36	0	6

Morris Hills Regional

48 Knoll Dr • Rockaway, NJ 07866-4088
(973) 664-2291 • http://www.mhrd.k12.nj.us
Grade Span: 09-12; **Agency Type:** 1
Schools: 2
  0 Primary; 0 Middle; 2 High; 0 Other Level
  2 Regular; 0 Special Education; 0 Vocational; 0 Alternative
  0 Magnet; 0 Charter; 2 Title I Eligible; 0 School-wide Title I
Students: 2,696   (51.1% male; 48.8% female)
  Individual Education Program: 382 (14.2%);
  English Language Learner: 25 (0.9%); Migrant: 0 (0.0%)
  Eligible for Free Lunch Program: 128 (4.8%)
  Eligible for Reduced-Price Lunch Program: 67 (2.5%)
Teachers: 216.6 (12.2 to 1)
Librarians/Media Specialists: 3.0 (883.7 to 1)
Guidance Counselors: 15.8 (167.8 to 1)
Current Spending: ($ per student per year):
  Total: $15,621; Instruction: $9,130; Support Services: $5,954

Enrollment, Drop-out Rates and Diploma Recipients by Race/Ethnicity

Category	Total	White	Black	Asian	AIAN	Hisp.
Enrollment (%)	100.0	78.2	2.7	7.2	0.2	11.8
Drop-out Rate (%)	1.2	0.8	0.0	0.7	0.0	4.7
H.S. Diplomas (#)	523	424	23	27	1	48

Morris SD

51 Hazel St • Morristown, NJ 07960-3802
(973) 292-2300 • http://www.morrisschooldistrict.org/
Grade Span: PK-12; **Agency Type:** 1
Schools: 10
  7 Primary; 1 Middle; 1 High; 1 Other Level
  9 Regular; 1 Special Education; 0 Vocational; 0 Alternative
  0 Magnet; 0 Charter; 5 Title I Eligible; 0 School-wide Title I
Students: 4,876   (52.7% male; 47.2% female)
  Individual Education Program: 993 (20.4%);
  English Language Learner: 310 (6.4%); Migrant: 0 (0.0%)
  Eligible for Free Lunch Program: 685 (14.7%)
  Eligible for Reduced-Price Lunch Program: 315 (6.8%)
Teachers: 406.0 (11.5 to 1)
Librarians/Media Specialists: 10.0 (466.3 to 1)
Guidance Counselors: 12.0 (388.6 to 1)
Current Spending: ($ per student per year):
  Total: $16,089; Instruction: $9,334; Support Services: $6,211

Enrollment, Drop-out Rates and Diploma Recipients by Race/Ethnicity

Category	Total	White	Black	Asian	AIAN	Hisp.
Enrollment (%)	100.0	55.4	17.7	4.9	0.1	21.9
Drop-out Rate (%)	0.8	0.1	1.2	0.0	n/a	2.6
H.S. Diplomas (#)	316	199	52	16	0	49

Mount Olive Twp

89 Route 46 • Budd Lake, NJ 07828-1793
(973) 691-4008 • http://www.mtoliveboe.org
Grade Span: PK-12; **Agency Type:** 1
Schools: 6
  4 Primary; 1 Middle; 1 High; 0 Other Level
  6 Regular; 0 Special Education; 0 Vocational; 0 Alternative
  0 Magnet; 0 Charter; 5 Title I Eligible; 0 School-wide Title I
Students: 4,961   (51.3% male; 48.6% female)
  Individual Education Program: 769 (15.5%);
  English Language Learner: 92 (1.9%); Migrant: 0 (0.0%)
  Eligible for Free Lunch Program: 168 (3.5%)
  Eligible for Reduced-Price Lunch Program: 192 (4.0%)
Teachers: 352.9 (13.5 to 1)
Librarians/Media Specialists: 6.0 (791.2 to 1)
Guidance Counselors: 9.0 (527.4 to 1)
Current Spending: ($ per student per year):
  Total: $11,593; Instruction: $6,494; Support Services: $4,780

Enrollment, Drop-out Rates and Diploma Recipients by Race/Ethnicity

Category	Total	White	Black	Asian	AIAN	Hisp.
Enrollment (%)	100.0	80.7	4.5	7.0	0.0	7.9
Drop-out Rate (%)	0.7	0.8	0.0	0.0	n/a	0.0
H.S. Diplomas (#)	231	222	3	3	0	3

Mountain Lakes Boro
400 Blvd • Mountain Lakes, NJ 07046-1520
(973) 334-8280 • http://www.mtlakes.org/Schools/
Grade Span: PK-12; **Agency Type:** 1
Schools: 4
 1 Primary; 1 Middle; 1 High; 1 Other Level
 3 Regular; 1 Special Education; 0 Vocational; 0 Alternative
 0 Magnet; 0 Charter; 3 Title I Eligible; 0 School-wide Title I
Students: 1,842 (52.8% male; 47.1% female)
 Individual Education Program: 217 (11.8%);
 English Language Learner: 0 (0.0%); Migrant: 0 (0.0%)
 Eligible for Free Lunch Program: 42 (2.5%)
 Eligible for Reduced-Price Lunch Program: 29 (1.8%)
Teachers: 168.7 (9.8 to 1)
Librarians/Media Specialists: 4.0 (413.8 to 1)
Guidance Counselors: 4.6 (359.8 to 1)
Current Spending: ($ per student per year):
 Total: $15,208; Instruction: $9,659; Support Services: $5,323
Enrollment, Drop-out Rates and Diploma Recipients by Race/Ethnicity

Category	Total	White	Black	Asian	AIAN	Hisp.
Enrollment (%)	100.0	89.7	1.5	5.4	0.0	3.4
Drop-out Rate (%)	0.3	0.3	0.0	0.0	n/a	0.0
H.S. Diplomas (#)	121	114	2	5	0	0

Parsippany-Troy Hills Twp
577 Vail Rd • Parsippany, NJ 07054-0052
Mailing Address: PO Box 52 • Parsippany, NJ 07054-0052
(973) 263-7250 • http://www.pthsd.k12.nj.us
Grade Span: PK-12; **Agency Type:** 1
Schools: 14
 10 Primary; 2 Middle; 2 High; 0 Other Level
 13 Regular; 1 Special Education; 0 Vocational; 0 Alternative
 0 Magnet; 0 Charter; 6 Title I Eligible; 0 School-wide Title I
Students: 7,201 (52.1% male; 47.8% female)
 Individual Education Program: 1,153 (16.0%);
 English Language Learner: 426 (5.9%); Migrant: 0 (0.0%)
 Eligible for Free Lunch Program: 326 (4.7%)
 Eligible for Reduced-Price Lunch Program: 250 (3.6%)
Teachers: 583.1 (11.9 to 1)
Librarians/Media Specialists: 16.0 (433.7 to 1)
Guidance Counselors: 29.0 (239.3 to 1)
Current Spending: ($ per student per year):
 Total: $13,263; Instruction: $8,090; Support Services: $4,899
Enrollment, Drop-out Rates and Diploma Recipients by Race/Ethnicity

Category	Total	White	Black	Asian	AIAN	Hisp.
Enrollment (%)	100.0	58.7	3.5	28.9	0.1	8.8
Drop-out Rate (%)	0.6	0.5	5.6	0.0	0.0	0.6
H.S. Diplomas (#)	526	342	18	128	0	38

Pequannock Twp
85 Sunset Rd • Pompton Plains, NJ 07444
(973) 616-6040 • http://www.morris.k12.nj.us/pequan
Grade Span: PK-12; **Agency Type:** 1
Schools: 5
 3 Primary; 1 Middle; 1 High; 0 Other Level
 5 Regular; 0 Special Education; 0 Vocational; 0 Alternative
 0 Magnet; 0 Charter; 0 Title I Eligible; 0 School-wide Title I
Students: 2,541 (51.9% male; 48.0% female)
 Individual Education Program: 350 (13.8%);
 English Language Learner: 11 (0.4%); Migrant: 0 (0.0%)
 Eligible for Free Lunch Program: 30 (1.2%)
 Eligible for Reduced-Price Lunch Program: 23 (0.9%)
Teachers: 182.9 (13.6 to 1)
Librarians/Media Specialists: 5.0 (498.6 to 1)
Guidance Counselors: 5.0 (498.6 to 1)
Current Spending: ($ per student per year):
 Total: $10,397; Instruction: $6,615; Support Services: $3,590
Enrollment, Drop-out Rates and Diploma Recipients by Race/Ethnicity

Category	Total	White	Black	Asian	AIAN	Hisp.
Enrollment (%)	100.0	94.3	0.4	1.8	0.1	3.4
Drop-out Rate (%)	0.0	0.0	0.0	0.0	0.0	0.0
H.S. Diplomas (#)	151	137	1	6	1	6

Randolph Twp
25 School House Rd • Randolph, NJ 07869-3199
(973) 328-2775 • http://www.rtnj.org
Grade Span: PK-12; **Agency Type:** 1
Schools: 6
 4 Primary; 1 Middle; 1 High; 0 Other Level

 6 Regular; 0 Special Education; 0 Vocational; 0 Alternative
 0 Magnet; 0 Charter; 3 Title I Eligible; 0 School-wide Title I
Students: 5,624 (50.9% male; 49.0% female)
 Individual Education Program: 761 (13.5%);
 English Language Learner: 70 (1.2%); Migrant: 0 (0.0%)
 Eligible for Free Lunch Program: 118 (2.2%)
 Eligible for Reduced-Price Lunch Program: 57 (1.0%)
Teachers: 416.4 (13.2 to 1)
Librarians/Media Specialists: 7.0 (782.3 to 1)
Guidance Counselors: 10.0 (547.6 to 1)
Current Spending: ($ per student per year):
 Total: $10,571; Instruction: $6,332; Support Services: $3,994
Enrollment, Drop-out Rates and Diploma Recipients by Race/Ethnicity

Category	Total	White	Black	Asian	AIAN	Hisp.
Enrollment (%)	100.0	83.6	2.8	8.2	0.0	5.3
Drop-out Rate (%)	0.3	0.3	0.0	0.0	0.0	3.0
H.S. Diplomas (#)	333	264	11	41	0	17

Rockaway Twp
PO Box 500 • Hibernia, NJ 07842
(973) 627-8200 • http://www.morris.k12.nj.us/rocktwp
Grade Span: PK-08; **Agency Type:** 1
Schools: 6
 5 Primary; 1 Middle; 0 High; 0 Other Level
 6 Regular; 0 Special Education; 0 Vocational; 0 Alternative
 0 Magnet; 0 Charter; 1 Title I Eligible; 0 School-wide Title I
Students: 2,985 (53.2% male; 46.7% female)
 Individual Education Program: 498 (16.7%);
 English Language Learner: 32 (1.1%); Migrant: 0 (0.0%)
 Eligible for Free Lunch Program: 94 (3.3%)
 Eligible for Reduced-Price Lunch Program: 79 (2.8%)
Teachers: 250.8 (11.4 to 1)
Librarians/Media Specialists: 5.4 (530.6 to 1)
Guidance Counselors: 2.5 (1,146.0 to 1)
Current Spending: ($ per student per year):
 Total: $12,614; Instruction: $7,194; Support Services: $5,141
Enrollment, Drop-out Rates and Diploma Recipients by Race/Ethnicity

Category	Total	White	Black	Asian	AIAN	Hisp.
Enrollment (%)	100.0	79.9	3.6	7.1	0.1	9.2
Drop-out Rate (%)	n/a	n/a	n/a	n/a	n/a	n/a
H.S. Diplomas (#)	n/a	n/a	n/a	n/a	n/a	n/a

Roxbury Twp
25 Meeker St • Succasunna, NJ 07876-1418
(973) 584-6867 • http://www.roxbury.org
Grade Span: PK-12; **Agency Type:** 1
Schools: 7
 4 Primary; 2 Middle; 1 High; 0 Other Level
 7 Regular; 0 Special Education; 0 Vocational; 0 Alternative
 0 Magnet; 0 Charter; 4 Title I Eligible; 0 School-wide Title I
Students: 4,817 (51.7% male; 48.2% female)
 Individual Education Program: 573 (11.9%);
 English Language Learner: 51 (1.1%); Migrant: 0 (0.0%)
 Eligible for Free Lunch Program: 175 (3.8%)
 Eligible for Reduced-Price Lunch Program: 137 (2.9%)
Teachers: 345.1 (13.5 to 1)
Librarians/Media Specialists: 7.0 (665.7 to 1)
Guidance Counselors: 14.0 (332.9 to 1)
Current Spending: ($ per student per year):
 Total: $11,496; Instruction: $6,782; Support Services: $4,381
Enrollment, Drop-out Rates and Diploma Recipients by Race/Ethnicity

Category	Total	White	Black	Asian	AIAN	Hisp.
Enrollment (%)	100.0	85.8	2.8	5.0	0.0	6.4
Drop-out Rate (%)	1.2	1.3	0.0	0.0	n/a	1.4
H.S. Diplomas (#)	325	287	7	16	0	15

SD of the Chathams
54 Fairmount Ave • Chatham, NJ 07928-2313
(973) 635-5656 • http://www.chatham-nj.org
Grade Span: PK-12; **Agency Type:** 1
Schools: 6
 3 Primary; 2 Middle; 1 High; 0 Other Level
 6 Regular; 0 Special Education; 0 Vocational; 0 Alternative
 0 Magnet; 0 Charter; 0 Title I Eligible; 0 School-wide Title I
Students: 3,199 (51.3% male; 48.6% female)
 Individual Education Program: 531 (16.6%);
 English Language Learner: 20 (0.6%); Migrant: 0 (0.0%)
 Eligible for Free Lunch Program: 9 (0.3%)
 Eligible for Reduced-Price Lunch Program: 3 (0.1%)
Teachers: 233.6 (13.4 to 1)
Librarians/Media Specialists: 6.0 (523.2 to 1)
Guidance Counselors: 8.0 (392.4 to 1)
Current Spending: ($ per student per year):
 Total: $12,097; Instruction: $7,264; Support Services: $4,655

Enrollment, Drop-out Rates and Diploma Recipients by Race/Ethnicity

Category	Total	White	Black	Asian	AIAN	Hisp.
Enrollment (%)	100.0	92.9	0.4	4.3	0.1	2.3
Drop-out Rate (%)	0.5	0.4	0.0	0.0	n/a	4.0
H.S. Diplomas (#)	166	151	0	5	0	10

Washington Twp
53 W Mill Rd • Long Valley, NJ 07853-9205
(908) 876-4172 • http://www.wtschools.org
Grade Span: PK-08; **Agency Type:** 1
Schools: 5
   3 Primary; 2 Middle; 0 High; 0 Other Level
   5 Regular; 0 Special Education; 0 Vocational; 0 Alternative
   0 Magnet; 0 Charter; 0 Title I Eligible; 0 School-wide Title I
Students: 3,073   (49.8% male; 50.1% female)
   Individual Education Program: 487 (15.8%);
   English Language Learner: 9 (0.3%); Migrant: 0 (0.0%)
   Eligible for Free Lunch Program: 14 (0.5%)
   Eligible for Reduced-Price Lunch Program: 23 (0.8%)
Teachers: 192.5 (15.3 to 1)
Librarians/Media Specialists: 5.0 (587.8 to 1)
Guidance Counselors: 3.0 (979.7 to 1)
Current Spending: ($ per student per year):
   Total: $10,809; Instruction: $6,514; Support Services: $4,108

Enrollment, Drop-out Rates and Diploma Recipients by Race/Ethnicity

Category	Total	White	Black	Asian	AIAN	Hisp.
Enrollment (%)	100.0	95.2	0.7	2.6	0.0	1.5
Drop-out Rate (%)	n/a	n/a	n/a	n/a	n/a	n/a
H.S. Diplomas (#)	n/a	n/a	n/a	n/a	n/a	n/a

West Morris Regional
Four Bridges Rd • Chester, NJ 07930
(908) 879-6404 • http://www.wmchs.org
Grade Span: 09-12; **Agency Type:** 1
Schools: 2
   0 Primary; 0 Middle; 2 High; 0 Other Level
   2 Regular; 0 Special Education; 0 Vocational; 0 Alternative
   0 Magnet; 0 Charter; 0 Title I Eligible; 0 School-wide Title I
Students: 2,402   (50.4% male; 49.5% female)
   Individual Education Program: 338 (14.1%);
   English Language Learner: 5 (0.2%); Migrant: 0 (0.0%)
   Eligible for Free Lunch Program: 11 (0.5%)
   Eligible for Reduced-Price Lunch Program: 1 (<0.1%)
Teachers: 193.2 (12.4 to 1)
Librarians/Media Specialists: 2.5 (956.4 to 1)
Guidance Counselors: 13.0 (183.9 to 1)
Current Spending: ($ per student per year):
   Total: $14,125; Instruction: $8,511; Support Services: $5,317

Enrollment, Drop-out Rates and Diploma Recipients by Race/Ethnicity

Category	Total	White	Black	Asian	AIAN	Hisp.
Enrollment (%)	100.0	94.4	1.1	2.0	0.1	2.4
Drop-out Rate (%)	0.6	0.5	5.6	2.0	0.0	0.0
H.S. Diplomas (#)	512	488	1	16	0	7

Ocean County

Barnegat Twp
25 Birdsall St • Barnegat, NJ 08005-2497
(609) 698-5800 • http://barnegatschools.com/main/index.htm
Grade Span: PK-08; **Agency Type:** 1
Schools: 4
   3 Primary; 1 Middle; 0 High; 0 Other Level
   4 Regular; 0 Special Education; 0 Vocational; 0 Alternative
   0 Magnet; 0 Charter; 3 Title I Eligible; 0 School-wide Title I
Students: 2,376   (50.0% male; 50.0% female)
   Individual Education Program: 619 (26.1%);
   English Language Learner: 12 (0.5%); Migrant: 0 (0.0%)
   Eligible for Free Lunch Program: 278 (12.4%)
   Eligible for Reduced-Price Lunch Program: 176 (7.8%)
Teachers: 172.5 (13.0 to 1)
Librarians/Media Specialists: 5.0 (448.8 to 1)
Guidance Counselors: 4.0 (561.0 to 1)
Current Spending: ($ per student per year):
   Total: $10,707; Instruction: $6,259; Support Services: $4,203

Enrollment, Drop-out Rates and Diploma Recipients by Race/Ethnicity

Category	Total	White	Black	Asian	AIAN	Hisp.
Enrollment (%)	100.0	87.8	4.9	1.9	0.0	5.3
Drop-out Rate (%)	n/a	n/a	n/a	n/a	n/a	n/a
H.S. Diplomas (#)	n/a	n/a	n/a	n/a	n/a	n/a

Berkeley Twp
53 Central Pkwy • Bayville, NJ 08721-2414
(732) 269-2233
Grade Span: PK-06; **Agency Type:** 1
Schools: 3

   3 Primary; 0 Middle; 0 High; 0 Other Level
   3 Regular; 0 Special Education; 0 Vocational; 0 Alternative
   0 Magnet; 0 Charter; 2 Title I Eligible; 0 School-wide Title I
Students: 1,983   (52.5% male; 47.4% female)
   Individual Education Program: 272 (13.7%);
   English Language Learner: 28 (1.4%); Migrant: 0 (0.0%)
   Eligible for Free Lunch Program: 201 (10.7%)
   Eligible for Reduced-Price Lunch Program: 115 (6.1%)
Teachers: 133.0 (14.1 to 1)
Librarians/Media Specialists: 3.0 (626.7 to 1)
Guidance Counselors: 3.0 (626.7 to 1)
Current Spending: ($ per student per year):
   Total: $9,418; Instruction: $6,006; Support Services: $3,192

Enrollment, Drop-out Rates and Diploma Recipients by Race/Ethnicity

Category	Total	White	Black	Asian	AIAN	Hisp.
Enrollment (%)	100.0	86.6	5.9	1.2	0.0	6.3
Drop-out Rate (%)	n/a	n/a	n/a	n/a	n/a	n/a
H.S. Diplomas (#)	n/a	n/a	n/a	n/a	n/a	n/a

Brick Twp
101 Hendrickson Ave • Brick, NJ 08724-2599
(732) 785-3002
Grade Span: PK-12; **Agency Type:** 1
Schools: 12
   8 Primary; 2 Middle; 2 High; 0 Other Level
   12 Regular; 0 Special Education; 0 Vocational; 0 Alternative
   0 Magnet; 0 Charter; 7 Title I Eligible; 0 School-wide Title I
Students: 12,065   (52.1% male; 47.8% female)
   Individual Education Program: 2,249 (18.6%);
   English Language Learner: 100 (0.8%); Migrant: 0 (0.0%)
   Eligible for Free Lunch Program: 859 (7.4%)
   Eligible for Reduced-Price Lunch Program: 626 (5.4%)
Teachers: 777.1 (15.0 to 1)
Librarians/Media Specialists: 12.9 (901.2 to 1)
Guidance Counselors: 18.0 (645.9 to 1)
Current Spending: ($ per student per year):
   Total: $9,247; Instruction: $5,911; Support Services: $3,089

Enrollment, Drop-out Rates and Diploma Recipients by Race/Ethnicity

Category	Total	White	Black	Asian	AIAN	Hisp.
Enrollment (%)	100.0	91.7	1.8	1.8	0.0	4.6
Drop-out Rate (%)	1.9	1.9	2.0	2.0	0.0	3.4
H.S. Diplomas (#)	668	625	5	13	3	22

Central Regional
Forest Hills Pkwy • Bayville, NJ 08721-2799
(732) 269-1100 • http://www.centralreg.k12.nj.us
Grade Span: 07-12; **Agency Type:** 1
Schools: 2
   0 Primary; 1 Middle; 1 High; 0 Other Level
   2 Regular; 0 Special Education; 0 Vocational; 0 Alternative
   0 Magnet; 0 Charter; 2 Title I Eligible; 0 School-wide Title I
Students: 2,357   (52.5% male; 47.4% female)
   Individual Education Program: 418 (17.7%);
   English Language Learner: 27 (1.1%); Migrant: 0 (0.0%)
   Eligible for Free Lunch Program: 251 (10.8%)
   Eligible for Reduced-Price Lunch Program: 169 (7.3%)
Teachers: 148.0 (15.7 to 1)
Librarians/Media Specialists: 3.0 (775.7 to 1)
Guidance Counselors: 8.0 (290.9 to 1)
Current Spending: ($ per student per year):
   Total: $10,325; Instruction: $6,054; Support Services: $4,015

Enrollment, Drop-out Rates and Diploma Recipients by Race/Ethnicity

Category	Total	White	Black	Asian	AIAN	Hisp.
Enrollment (%)	100.0	90.6	3.7	0.6	0.0	5.0
Drop-out Rate (%)	4.3	4.3	3.2	0.0	0.0	5.7
H.S. Diplomas (#)	249	237	4	0	3	5

Jackson Twp
151 Don Connor Blvd • Jackson, NJ 08527-3497
(732) 833-4600 • http://www.jacksonsd.k12.nj.us
Grade Span: PK-12; **Agency Type:** 1
Schools: 9
   6 Primary; 2 Middle; 1 High; 0 Other Level
   9 Regular; 0 Special Education; 0 Vocational; 0 Alternative
   0 Magnet; 0 Charter; 4 Title I Eligible; 0 School-wide Title I
Students: 9,762   (51.6% male; 48.3% female)
   Individual Education Program: 1,762 (18.0%);
   English Language Learner: 81 (0.8%); Migrant: 0 (0.0%)
   Eligible for Free Lunch Program: 486 (5.2%)
   Eligible for Reduced-Price Lunch Program: 324 (3.4%)
Teachers: 660.5 (14.3 to 1)
Librarians/Media Specialists: 9.0 (1,046.9 to 1)
Guidance Counselors: 20.0 (471.1 to 1)
Current Spending: ($ per student per year):
   Total: $9,930; Instruction: $6,166; Support Services: $3,421

Enrollment, Drop-out Rates and Diploma Recipients by Race/Ethnicity

Category	Total	White	Black	Asian	AIAN	Hisp.
Enrollment (%)	100.0	86.0	5.8	2.6	0.0	5.5
Drop-out Rate (%)	0.5	0.5	1.5	0.0	0.0	0.0
H.S. Diplomas (#)	435	408	22	3	0	2

Lacey Twp
200 Western Blvd • Lanoka Harbor, NJ 08734-0216
(609) 971-2002 • http://www.lacey.k12.nj.us/
Grade Span: PK-12; Agency Type: 1
Schools: 6
  3 Primary; 2 Middle; 1 High; 0 Other Level
  6 Regular; 0 Special Education; 0 Vocational; 0 Alternative
  0 Magnet; 0 Charter; 4 Title I Eligible; 0 School-wide Title I
Students: 5,323 (51.4% male; 48.5% female)
  Individual Education Program: 899 (16.9%);
  English Language Learner: 19 (0.4%); Migrant: 0 (0.0%)
  Eligible for Free Lunch Program: 405 (7.9%)
  Eligible for Reduced-Price Lunch Program: 278 (5.5%)
Teachers: 344.0 (14.8 to 1)
Librarians/Media Specialists: 6.0 (849.7 to 1)
Guidance Counselors: 11.0 (463.5 to 1)
Current Spending: ($ per student per year):
  Total: $9,249; Instruction: $5,834; Support Services: $3,106
Enrollment, Drop-out Rates and Diploma Recipients by Race/Ethnicity

Category	Total	White	Black	Asian	AIAN	Hisp.
Enrollment (%)	100.0	96.7	0.5	0.8	0.2	1.8
Drop-out Rate (%)	1.0	1.0	0.0	0.0	n/a	0.0
H.S. Diplomas (#)	325	323	0	1	0	1

Lakewood Twp
655 Princeton Ave • Lakewood, NJ 08701-2895
(732) 905-3633 • http://www.lakewood.k12.nj.us/
Grade Span: PK-12; Agency Type: 1
Schools: 6
  4 Primary; 1 Middle; 1 High; 0 Other Level
  6 Regular; 0 Special Education; 0 Vocational; 0 Alternative
  0 Magnet; 0 Charter; 5 Title I Eligible; 0 School-wide Title I
Students: 5,807 (51.8% male; 48.1% female)
  Individual Education Program: 1,018 (17.5%);
  English Language Learner: 484 (8.3%); Migrant: 4 (0.1%)
  Eligible for Free Lunch Program: 2,675 (49.0%)
  Eligible for Reduced-Price Lunch Program: 538 (9.9%)
Teachers: 476.0 (11.5 to 1)
Librarians/Media Specialists: 6.0 (909.8 to 1)
Guidance Counselors: 14.0 (389.9 to 1)
Current Spending: ($ per student per year):
  Total: $15,100; Instruction: $9,261; Support Services: $5,479
Enrollment, Drop-out Rates and Diploma Recipients by Race/Ethnicity

Category	Total	White	Black	Asian	AIAN	Hisp.
Enrollment (%)	100.0	20.9	32.7	1.4	0.7	44.3
Drop-out Rate (%)	3.9	1.2	5.2	0.0	0.0	5.9
H.S. Diplomas (#)	268	122	85	6	4	51

Little Egg Harbor Twp
307 Frog Pond Rd • Little Egg Harbor, NJ 08087-9750
(609) 296-3295 • http://www.lehsd.k12.nj.us
Grade Span: PK-06; Agency Type: 1
Schools: 2
  2 Primary; 0 Middle; 0 High; 0 Other Level
  2 Regular; 0 Special Education; 0 Vocational; 0 Alternative
  0 Magnet; 0 Charter; 2 Title I Eligible; 0 School-wide Title I
Students: 1,844 (51.7% male; 48.2% female)
  Individual Education Program: 325 (17.6%);
  English Language Learner: 16 (0.9%); Migrant: 0 (0.0%)
  Eligible for Free Lunch Program: 327 (18.8%)
  Eligible for Reduced-Price Lunch Program: 184 (10.6%)
Teachers: 137.9 (12.6 to 1)
Librarians/Media Specialists: 2.0 (867.5 to 1)
Guidance Counselors: 0.0 (n/a to 1)
Current Spending: ($ per student per year):
  Total: $10,481; Instruction: $6,390; Support Services: $3,808
Enrollment, Drop-out Rates and Diploma Recipients by Race/Ethnicity

Category	Total	White	Black	Asian	AIAN	Hisp.
Enrollment (%)	100.0	91.1	2.4	0.7	0.1	5.6
Drop-out Rate (%)	n/a	n/a	n/a	n/a	n/a	n/a
H.S. Diplomas (#)	n/a	n/a	n/a	n/a	n/a	n/a

Manchester Twp
121 Route 539 • Whiting, NJ 08759-1237
Mailing Address: 121 Route 539 Box 4100 • Whiting, NJ 08759-1237
(732) 350-5900 • http://www.manchestertwp.org
Grade Span: PK-12; Agency Type: 1
Schools: 6
  3 Primary; 1 Middle; 1 High; 1 Other Level

  5 Regular; 1 Special Education; 0 Vocational; 0 Alternative
  0 Magnet; 0 Charter; 1 Title I Eligible; 0 School-wide Title I
Students: 3,580 (51.8% male; 48.1% female)
  Individual Education Program: 572 (16.0%);
  English Language Learner: 27 (0.8%); Migrant: 0 (0.0%)
  Eligible for Free Lunch Program: 380 (11.3%)
  Eligible for Reduced-Price Lunch Program: 192 (5.7%)
Teachers: 266.2 (12.6 to 1)
Librarians/Media Specialists: 5.0 (671.4 to 1)
Guidance Counselors: 7.0 (479.6 to 1)
Current Spending: ($ per student per year):
  Total: $10,359; Instruction: $5,924; Support Services: $4,160
Enrollment, Drop-out Rates and Diploma Recipients by Race/Ethnicity

Category	Total	White	Black	Asian	AIAN	Hisp.
Enrollment (%)	100.0	78.8	12.0	1.6	0.4	7.1
Drop-out Rate (%)	1.5	0.9	0.8	0.0	0.0	11.1
H.S. Diplomas (#)	182	152	13	6	0	11

Pinelands Regional
520 Nugentown Rd • Tuckerton, NJ 08087-0248
(609) 296-3106 • http://www.pinelandsregional.org/
Grade Span: 07-12; Agency Type: 1
Schools: 2
  0 Primary; 1 Middle; 1 High; 0 Other Level
  2 Regular; 0 Special Education; 0 Vocational; 0 Alternative
  0 Magnet; 0 Charter; 2 Title I Eligible; 0 School-wide Title I
Students: 2,061 (50.2% male; 49.7% female)
  Individual Education Program: 498 (24.2%);
  English Language Learner: 7 (0.3%); Migrant: 0 (0.0%)
  Eligible for Free Lunch Program: 300 (15.2%)
  Eligible for Reduced-Price Lunch Program: 181 (9.2%)
Teachers: 177.8 (11.1 to 1)
Librarians/Media Specialists: 3.0 (656.7 to 1)
Guidance Counselors: 9.0 (218.9 to 1)
Current Spending: ($ per student per year):
  Total: $12,317; Instruction: $7,019; Support Services: $4,979
Enrollment, Drop-out Rates and Diploma Recipients by Race/Ethnicity

Category	Total	White	Black	Asian	AIAN	Hisp.
Enrollment (%)	100.0	97.4	1.0	0.0	0.0	1.7
Drop-out Rate (%)	8.0	7.9	25.0	33.3	n/a	5.9
H.S. Diplomas (#)	194	191	2	1	0	0

Plumsted Twp
117 Evergreen Rd • New Egypt, NJ 08533-1316
(609) 758-6800
Grade Span: PK-12; Agency Type: 1
Schools: 3
  1 Primary; 1 Middle; 1 High; 0 Other Level
  3 Regular; 0 Special Education; 0 Vocational; 0 Alternative
  0 Magnet; 0 Charter; 3 Title I Eligible; 0 School-wide Title I
Students: 1,772 (52.8% male; 47.1% female)
  Individual Education Program: 267 (15.1%);
  English Language Learner: 16 (0.9%); Migrant: 2 (0.1%)
  Eligible for Free Lunch Program: 97 (5.6%)
  Eligible for Reduced-Price Lunch Program: 81 (4.7%)
Teachers: 123.5 (14.0 to 1)
Librarians/Media Specialists: 1.0 (1,732.0 to 1)
Guidance Counselors: 4.5 (384.9 to 1)
Current Spending: ($ per student per year):
  Total: $9,559; Instruction: $5,682; Support Services: $3,545
Enrollment, Drop-out Rates and Diploma Recipients by Race/Ethnicity

Category	Total	White	Black	Asian	AIAN	Hisp.
Enrollment (%)	100.0	94.2	2.5	0.4	0.1	2.7
Drop-out Rate (%)	2.1	2.2	0.0	0.0	n/a	0.0
H.S. Diplomas (#)	0	0	0	0	0	0

Point Pleasant Boro
2100 Panther Path • Point Pleasant, NJ 08742-3770
(732) 701-1900 • http://www.pointpleasant.k12.nj.us
Grade Span: PK-12; Agency Type: 1
Schools: 4
  2 Primary; 1 Middle; 1 High; 0 Other Level
  4 Regular; 0 Special Education; 0 Vocational; 0 Alternative
  0 Magnet; 0 Charter; 2 Title I Eligible; 0 School-wide Title I
Students: 3,238 (52.0% male; 47.9% female)
  Individual Education Program: 411 (12.7%);
  English Language Learner: 24 (0.7%); Migrant: 0 (0.0%)
  Eligible for Free Lunch Program: 121 (3.8%)
  Eligible for Reduced-Price Lunch Program: 92 (2.9%)
Teachers: 226.9 (14.1 to 1)
Librarians/Media Specialists: 4.0 (798.5 to 1)
Guidance Counselors: 7.0 (456.3 to 1)
Current Spending: ($ per student per year):
  Total: $9,127; Instruction: $5,663; Support Services: $3,157

Enrollment, Drop-out Rates and Diploma Recipients by Race/Ethnicity

Category	Total	White	Black	Asian	AIAN	Hisp.
Enrollment (%)	100.0	96.3	0.3	0.7	0.2	2.5
Drop-out Rate (%)	0.4	0.4	0.0	0.0	0.0	0.0
H.S. Diplomas (#)	224	212	0	4	2	6

Southern Regional
105 Cedar Bridge Rd • Manahawkin, NJ 08050-3056
(609) 597-9481 • http://www.srsd.org/
Grade Span: 07-12; Agency Type: 1
Schools: 2
    0 Primary; 1 Middle; 1 High; 0 Other Level
    2 Regular; 0 Special Education; 0 Vocational; 0 Alternative
    0 Magnet; 0 Charter; 2 Title I Eligible; 0 School-wide Title I
Students: 4,163 (50.6% male; 49.3% female)
    Individual Education Program: 456 (11.0%);
    English Language Learner: 29 (0.7%); Migrant: 0 (0.0%)
    Eligible for Free Lunch Program: 243 (6.1%)
    Eligible for Reduced-Price Lunch Program: 224 (5.6%)
Teachers: 282.3 (14.1 to 1)
Librarians/Media Specialists: 1.0 (3,984.0 to 1)
Guidance Counselors: 14.0 (284.6 to 1)
Current Spending: ($ per student per year):
    Total: $9,580; Instruction: $5,730; Support Services: $3,631

Enrollment, Drop-out Rates and Diploma Recipients by Race/Ethnicity

Category	Total	White	Black	Asian	AIAN	Hisp.
Enrollment (%)	100.0	93.1	1.9	1.5	0.1	3.3
Drop-out Rate (%)	1.9	1.9	2.6	0.0	n/a	3.8
H.S. Diplomas (#)	615	597	12	0	0	6

Stafford Twp
775 E Bay Ave • Manahawkin, NJ 08050-2895
(609) 978-5708 • http://www.staffordschools.org
Grade Span: PK-06; Agency Type: 1
Schools: 4
    3 Primary; 1 Middle; 0 High; 0 Other Level
    4 Regular; 0 Special Education; 0 Vocational; 0 Alternative
    0 Magnet; 0 Charter; 4 Title I Eligible; 0 School-wide Title I
Students: 2,727 (52.5% male; 47.4% female)
    Individual Education Program: 428 (15.7%);
    English Language Learner: 6 (0.2%); Migrant: 0 (0.0%)
    Eligible for Free Lunch Program: 174 (7.2%)
    Eligible for Reduced-Price Lunch Program: 152 (6.3%)
Teachers: 173.4 (13.9 to 1)
Librarians/Media Specialists: 4.0 (602.8 to 1)
Guidance Counselors: 3.0 (803.7 to 1)
Current Spending: ($ per student per year):
    Total: $10,092; Instruction: $5,799; Support Services: $3,902

Enrollment, Drop-out Rates and Diploma Recipients by Race/Ethnicity

Category	Total	White	Black	Asian	AIAN	Hisp.
Enrollment (%)	100.0	94.1	2.0	1.2	0.0	2.7
Drop-out Rate (%)	n/a	n/a	n/a	n/a	n/a	n/a
H.S. Diplomas (#)	n/a	n/a	n/a	n/a	n/a	n/a

Toms River Regional
1144 Hooper Ave • Toms River, NJ 08753-7643
(732) 505-5510 • http://www.trschools.com/
Grade Span: PK-12; Agency Type: 1
Schools: 17
    12 Primary; 2 Middle; 3 High; 0 Other Level
    17 Regular; 0 Special Education; 0 Vocational; 0 Alternative
    0 Magnet; 0 Charter; 8 Title I Eligible; 0 School-wide Title I
Students: 19,190 (51.4% male; 48.5% female)
    Individual Education Program: 2,573 (13.4%);
    English Language Learner: 139 (0.7%); Migrant: 0 (0.0%)
    Eligible for Free Lunch Program: 1,629 (8.9%)
    Eligible for Reduced-Price Lunch Program: 695 (3.8%)
Teachers: 1,176.7 (15.6 to 1)
Librarians/Media Specialists: 12.0 (1,531.2 to 1)
Guidance Counselors: 36.0 (510.4 to 1)
Current Spending: ($ per student per year):
    Total: $9,491; Instruction: $5,750; Support Services: $3,492

Enrollment, Drop-out Rates and Diploma Recipients by Race/Ethnicity

Category	Total	White	Black	Asian	AIAN	Hisp.
Enrollment (%)	100.0	88.9	3.6	2.5	0.1	4.9
Drop-out Rate (%)	2.4	2.3	5.7	1.4	0.0	3.3
H.S. Diplomas (#)	1,188	1,095	33	30	0	30

Passaic County

Clifton City
745 Clifton Ave • Clifton, NJ 07015-2209
(973) 470-2260 • http://www.clifton.k12.nj.us
Grade Span: PK-12; Agency Type: 1
Schools: 16

    13 Primary; 2 Middle; 1 High; 0 Other Level
    16 Regular; 0 Special Education; 0 Vocational; 0 Alternative
    0 Magnet; 0 Charter; 7 Title I Eligible; 0 School-wide Title I
Students: 10,984 (52.2% male; 47.7% female)
    Individual Education Program: 1,270 (11.6%);
    English Language Learner: 668 (6.1%); Migrant: 0 (0.0%)
    Eligible for Free Lunch Program: 1,031 (10.0%)
    Eligible for Reduced-Price Lunch Program: 370 (3.6%)
Teachers: 786.3 (13.2 to 1)
Librarians/Media Specialists: 18.0 (575.1 to 1)
Guidance Counselors: 24.0 (431.3 to 1)
Current Spending: ($ per student per year):
    Total: $10,048; Instruction: $6,430; Support Services: $3,358

Enrollment, Drop-out Rates and Diploma Recipients by Race/Ethnicity

Category	Total	White	Black	Asian	AIAN	Hisp.
Enrollment (%)	100.0	49.3	3.6	8.4	0.1	38.6
Drop-out Rate (%)	4.0	3.3	5.7	0.7	n/a	6.0
H.S. Diplomas (#)	703	438	23	65	0	177

Hawthorne Boro
445 Lafayette Ave • Hawthorne, NJ 07507-0002
(973) 423-6401 • http://www.hawthorne.k12.nj.us
Grade Span: PK-12; Agency Type: 1
Schools: 5
    3 Primary; 1 Middle; 1 High; 0 Other Level
    5 Regular; 0 Special Education; 0 Vocational; 0 Alternative
    0 Magnet; 0 Charter; 3 Title I Eligible; 0 School-wide Title I
Students: 2,345 (51.4% male; 48.5% female)
    Individual Education Program: 370 (15.8%);
    English Language Learner: 20 (0.9%); Migrant: 0 (0.0%)
    Eligible for Free Lunch Program: 123 (5.4%)
    Eligible for Reduced-Price Lunch Program: 97 (4.3%)
Teachers: 185.8 (12.2 to 1)
Librarians/Media Specialists: 4.0 (565.5 to 1)
Guidance Counselors: 5.1 (443.5 to 1)
Current Spending: ($ per student per year):
    Total: $11,606; Instruction: $7,101; Support Services: $4,179

Enrollment, Drop-out Rates and Diploma Recipients by Race/Ethnicity

Category	Total	White	Black	Asian	AIAN	Hisp.
Enrollment (%)	100.0	83.8	1.6	2.0	0.1	12.4
Drop-out Rate (%)	0.1	0.2	0.0	0.0	n/a	0.0
H.S. Diplomas (#)	136	129	0	0	0	7

Passaic City
101 Passaic Ave • Passaic, NJ 07055-4828
(973) 470-5201 • http://www.passaic-city.k12.nj.us/
Grade Span: PK-12; Agency Type: 1
Schools: 17
    12 Primary; 3 Middle; 1 High; 1 Other Level
    17 Regular; 0 Special Education; 0 Vocational; 0 Alternative
    0 Magnet; 0 Charter; 12 Title I Eligible; 1 School-wide Title I
Students: 12,162 (49.8% male; 50.1% female)
    Individual Education Program: 2,450 (20.1%);
    English Language Learner: 3,252 (26.7%); Migrant: 0 (0.0%)
    Eligible for Free Lunch Program: 7,385 (63.8%)
    Eligible for Reduced-Price Lunch Program: 1,135 (9.8%)
Teachers: 894.7 (12.9 to 1)
Librarians/Media Specialists: 10.0 (1,158.1 to 1)
Guidance Counselors: 26.4 (438.7 to 1)
Current Spending: ($ per student per year):
    Total: $15,564; Instruction: $10,144; Support Services: $4,974

Enrollment, Drop-out Rates and Diploma Recipients by Race/Ethnicity

Category	Total	White	Black	Asian	AIAN	Hisp.
Enrollment (%)	100.0	1.9	12.0	4.1	0.1	81.9
Drop-out Rate (%)	8.3	19.2	6.7	5.7	0.0	8.7
H.S. Diplomas (#)	0	0	0	0	0	0

Passaic County Vocational
45 Reinhardt Rd • Wayne, NJ 07470-2210
(973) 389-4202 • http://www.pcti.tec.nj.us
Grade Span: 09-12; Agency Type: 1
Schools: 1
    0 Primary; 0 Middle; 1 High; 0 Other Level
    0 Regular; 0 Special Education; 1 Vocational; 0 Alternative
    0 Magnet; 0 Charter; 1 Title I Eligible; 0 School-wide Title I
Students: 2,399 (49.3% male; 50.6% female)
    Individual Education Program: 365 (15.2%);
    English Language Learner: 38 (1.6%); Migrant: 0 (0.0%)
    Eligible for Free Lunch Program: 863 (42.5%)
    Eligible for Reduced-Price Lunch Program: 357 (17.6%)
Teachers: 196.0 (10.4 to 1)
Librarians/Media Specialists: 1.0 (2,031.0 to 1)
Guidance Counselors: 14.0 (145.1 to 1)
Current Spending: ($ per student per year):
    Total: $19,113; Instruction: $10,708; Support Services: $7,543

Enrollment, Drop-out Rates and Diploma Recipients by Race/Ethnicity

Category	Total	White	Black	Asian	AIAN	Hisp.
Enrollment (%)	100.0	15.6	24.1	1.2	0.0	59.1
Drop-out Rate (%)	0.6	0.7	0.4	0.0	n/a	0.7
H.S. Diplomas (#)	451	67	111	1	0	272

Paterson City
33-35 Church St • Paterson, NJ 07505-1306
(973) 321-0980 • http://www.paterson.K12.nj.us
Grade Span: PK-12; **Agency Type:** 1
Schools: 36
   31 Primary; 2 Middle; 3 High; 0 Other Level
   36 Regular; 0 Special Education; 0 Vocational; 0 Alternative
   0 Magnet; 0 Charter; 32 Title I Eligible; 32 School-wide Title I
Students: 27,734 (50.8% male; 49.1% female)
   Individual Education Program: 4,218 (15.2%);
   English Language Learner: 4,954 (17.9%); Migrant: 0 (0.0%)
   Eligible for Free Lunch Program: 13,624 (51.5%)
   Eligible for Reduced-Price Lunch Program: 2,957 (11.2%)
Teachers: 2,419.6 (10.9 to 1)
Librarians/Media Specialists: 38.0 (696.0 to 1)
Guidance Counselors: 82.0 (322.5 to 1)
Current Spending: ($ per student per year):
   Total: $14,966; Instruction: $8,537; Support Services: $6,035
Enrollment, Drop-out Rates and Diploma Recipients by Race/Ethnicity

Category	Total	White	Black	Asian	AIAN	Hisp.
Enrollment (%)	100.0	6.0	37.6	2.5	0.1	53.8
Drop-out Rate (%)	9.3	7.4	10.1	3.0	0.0	9.3
H.S. Diplomas (#)	754	26	327	27	0	374

Pompton Lakes Boro
237 Van Ave • Pompton Lakes, NJ 07442-1343
(973) 835-4334 • http://www.plps.org
Grade Span: PK-12; **Agency Type:** 1
Schools: 4
   2 Primary; 1 Middle; 1 High; 0 Other Level
   4 Regular; 0 Special Education; 0 Vocational; 0 Alternative
   0 Magnet; 0 Charter; 3 Title I Eligible; 0 School-wide Title I
Students: 1,910 (49.4% male; 50.5% female)
   Individual Education Program: 308 (16.1%);
   English Language Learner: 35 (1.8%); Migrant: 0 (0.0%)
   Eligible for Free Lunch Program: 99 (5.3%)
   Eligible for Reduced-Price Lunch Program: 30 (1.6%)
Teachers: 133.5 (14.0 to 1)
Librarians/Media Specialists: 4.0 (468.3 to 1)
Guidance Counselors: 6.0 (312.2 to 1)
Current Spending: ($ per student per year):
   Total: $11,429; Instruction: $7,083; Support Services: $4,149
Enrollment, Drop-out Rates and Diploma Recipients by Race/Ethnicity

Category	Total	White	Black	Asian	AIAN	Hisp.
Enrollment (%)	100.0	87.9	1.0	3.6	0.1	7.4
Drop-out Rate (%)	0.8	0.9	0.0	0.0	n/a	0.0
H.S. Diplomas (#)	140	124	0	6	0	10

Wayne Twp
50 Nellis Dr • Wayne, NJ 07470-3562
(973) 633-3032 • http://wayneschools.com/wboe/dsp_home_page.cfm
Grade Span: PK-12; **Agency Type:** 1
Schools: 13
   9 Primary; 2 Middle; 2 High; 0 Other Level
   13 Regular; 0 Special Education; 0 Vocational; 0 Alternative
   0 Magnet; 0 Charter; 3 Title I Eligible; 0 School-wide Title I
Students: 9,097 (51.3% male; 48.6% female)
   Individual Education Program: 1,103 (12.1%);
   English Language Learner: 94 (1.0%); Migrant: 0 (0.0%)
   Eligible for Free Lunch Program: 254 (2.9%)
   Eligible for Reduced-Price Lunch Program: 149 (1.7%)
Teachers: 625.5 (14.0 to 1)
Librarians/Media Specialists: 14.0 (626.0 to 1)
Guidance Counselors: 21.0 (417.3 to 1)
Current Spending: ($ per student per year):
   Total: $11,364; Instruction: $7,212; Support Services: $3,920
Enrollment, Drop-out Rates and Diploma Recipients by Race/Ethnicity

Category	Total	White	Black	Asian	AIAN	Hisp.
Enrollment (%)	100.0	86.4	1.0	7.9	0.0	4.7
Drop-out Rate (%)	1.7	1.6	7.4	0.0	n/a	6.1
H.S. Diplomas (#)	578	489	17	39	0	33

West Milford Twp
46 Highlander Dr • West Milford, NJ 07480-1511
(973) 697-1700 • http://www.wmtps.org
Grade Span: PK-12; **Agency Type:** 1
Schools: 8
   6 Primary; 1 Middle; 1 High; 0 Other Level
   8 Regular; 0 Special Education; 0 Vocational; 0 Alternative

   0 Magnet; 0 Charter; 8 Title I Eligible; 0 School-wide Title I
Students: 4,878 (52.7% male; 47.2% female)
   Individual Education Program: 842 (17.3%);
   English Language Learner: 14 (0.3%); Migrant: 0 (0.0%)
   Eligible for Free Lunch Program: 184 (3.9%)
   Eligible for Reduced-Price Lunch Program: 111 (2.3%)
Teachers: 332.9 (14.2 to 1)
Librarians/Media Specialists: 8.0 (591.0 to 1)
Guidance Counselors: 10.0 (472.8 to 1)
Current Spending: ($ per student per year):
   Total: $11,563; Instruction: $6,966; Support Services: $4,235
Enrollment, Drop-out Rates and Diploma Recipients by Race/Ethnicity

Category	Total	White	Black	Asian	AIAN	Hisp.
Enrollment (%)	100.0	94.6	1.9	1.0	0.3	2.2
Drop-out Rate (%)	1.9	2.0	0.0	0.0	0.0	0.0
H.S. Diplomas (#)	294	283	5	1	0	5

Salem County

Penns Grv-Carney's Pt Reg
113 W Harmony St • Penns Grove, NJ 08069-1369
(856) 299-4250 • http://www.pennsgrove.k12.nj.us
Grade Span: PK-12; **Agency Type:** 1
Schools: 5
   2 Primary; 2 Middle; 1 High; 0 Other Level
   5 Regular; 0 Special Education; 0 Vocational; 0 Alternative
   0 Magnet; 0 Charter; 5 Title I Eligible; 0 School-wide Title I
Students: 2,371 (50.3% male; 49.6% female)
   Individual Education Program: 409 (17.3%);
   English Language Learner: 62 (2.6%); Migrant: 14 (0.6%)
   Eligible for Free Lunch Program: 1,012 (44.3%)
   Eligible for Reduced-Price Lunch Program: 252 (11.0%)
Teachers: 192.1 (11.9 to 1)
Librarians/Media Specialists: 4.9 (465.7 to 1)
Guidance Counselors: 7.0 (326.0 to 1)
Current Spending: ($ per student per year):
   Total: $11,548; Instruction: $7,262; Support Services: $3,856
Enrollment, Drop-out Rates and Diploma Recipients by Race/Ethnicity

Category	Total	White	Black	Asian	AIAN	Hisp.
Enrollment (%)	100.0	43.9	39.7	1.0	0.2	15.2
Drop-out Rate (%)	3.5	3.4	3.1	0.0	n/a	5.6
H.S. Diplomas (#)	162	94	59	2	0	7

Pennsville
30 Church St • Pennsville, NJ 08070-2123
(856) 540-6210 • http://www.pennsville.k12.nj.us
Grade Span: PK-12; **Agency Type:** 1
Schools: 5
   3 Primary; 1 Middle; 1 High; 0 Other Level
   5 Regular; 0 Special Education; 0 Vocational; 0 Alternative
   0 Magnet; 0 Charter; 3 Title I Eligible; 0 School-wide Title I
Students: 2,105 (50.1% male; 49.8% female)
   Individual Education Program: 392 (18.6%);
   English Language Learner: 12 (0.6%); Migrant: 0 (0.0%)
   Eligible for Free Lunch Program: 175 (8.6%)
   Eligible for Reduced-Price Lunch Program: 83 (4.1%)
Teachers: 159.6 (12.8 to 1)
Librarians/Media Specialists: 5.0 (407.8 to 1)
Guidance Counselors: 6.0 (339.8 to 1)
Current Spending: ($ per student per year):
   Total: $11,555; Instruction: $6,729; Support Services: $4,371
Enrollment, Drop-out Rates and Diploma Recipients by Race/Ethnicity

Category	Total	White	Black	Asian	AIAN	Hisp.
Enrollment (%)	100.0	94.9	0.9	2.3	0.0	2.0
Drop-out Rate (%)	1.9	1.8	14.3	0.0	n/a	0.0
H.S. Diplomas (#)	124	120	0	3	0	1

Pittsgrove Twp
Admin Bldg 1076 Almond Rd • Pittsgrove, NJ 08318-8903
(609) 358-3094 • http://www.pittsgrove.org
Grade Span: PK-12; **Agency Type:** 1
Schools: 4
   2 Primary; 1 Middle; 1 High; 0 Other Level
   4 Regular; 0 Special Education; 0 Vocational; 0 Alternative
   0 Magnet; 0 Charter; 4 Title I Eligible; 0 School-wide Title I
Students: 1,878 (51.5% male; 48.4% female)
   Individual Education Program: 301 (16.0%);
   English Language Learner: 2 (0.1%); Migrant: 4 (0.2%)
   Eligible for Free Lunch Program: 441 (23.6%)
   Eligible for Reduced-Price Lunch Program: 143 (7.7%)
Teachers: 132.8 (14.1 to 1)
Librarians/Media Specialists: 2.0 (933.0 to 1)
Guidance Counselors: 6.5 (287.1 to 1)
Current Spending: ($ per student per year):
   Total: $9,637; Instruction: $5,562; Support Services: $3,649

Enrollment, Drop-out Rates and Diploma Recipients by Race/Ethnicity

Category	Total	White	Black	Asian	AIAN	Hisp.
Enrollment (%)	100.0	85.5	10.0	0.9	0.2	3.4
Drop-out Rate (%)	0.5	0.6	0.0	0.0	n/a	0.0
H.S. Diplomas (#)	125	107	15	2	0	1

Salem City
51 New Market St • Salem, NJ 08079-9048
(856) 935-3800
Grade Span: PK-12; **Agency Type:** 1
Schools: 3
   1 Primary; 1 Middle; 1 High; 0 Other Level
   3 Regular; 0 Special Education; 0 Vocational; 0 Alternative
   0 Magnet; 0 Charter; 3 Title I Eligible; 2 School-wide Title I
Students: 1,518   (47.7% male; 52.2% female)
   Individual Education Program: 255 (16.8%);
   English Language Learner: 4 (0.3%); Migrant: 0 (0.0%)
   Eligible for Free Lunch Program: 910 (62.8%)
   Eligible for Reduced-Price Lunch Program: 128 (8.8%)
Teachers: 126.9 (11.4 to 1)
Librarians/Media Specialists: 2.0 (725.0 to 1)
Guidance Counselors: 6.0 (241.7 to 1)
Current Spending: ($ per student per year):
   Total: $11,704; Instruction: $7,296; Support Services: $3,929
Enrollment, Drop-out Rates and Diploma Recipients by Race/Ethnicity

Category	Total	White	Black	Asian	AIAN	Hisp.
Enrollment (%)	100.0	25.5	69.2	0.4	0.4	4.5
Drop-out Rate (%)	6.4	5.4	7.7	0.0	n/a	7.1
H.S. Diplomas (#)	98	52	41	0	0	5

Woodstown-Pilesgrove Reg
135 E Ave • Woodstown, NJ 08098-1336
(856) 769-1664 • http://www.woodstown.org
Grade Span: PK-12; **Agency Type:** 1
Schools: 3
   1 Primary; 1 Middle; 1 High; 0 Other Level
   3 Regular; 0 Special Education; 0 Vocational; 0 Alternative
   0 Magnet; 0 Charter; 3 Title I Eligible; 0 School-wide Title I
Students: 1,700   (50.9% male; 49.0% female)
   Individual Education Program: 205 (12.1%);
   English Language Learner: 7 (0.4%); Migrant: 8 (0.5%)
   Eligible for Free Lunch Program: 128 (7.6%)
   Eligible for Reduced-Price Lunch Program: 71 (4.2%)
Teachers: 124.0 (13.5 to 1)
Librarians/Media Specialists: 3.0 (560.0 to 1)
Guidance Counselors: 6.0 (280.0 to 1)
Current Spending: ($ per student per year):
   Total: $9,732; Instruction: $5,869; Support Services: $3,609
Enrollment, Drop-out Rates and Diploma Recipients by Race/Ethnicity

Category	Total	White	Black	Asian	AIAN	Hisp.
Enrollment (%)	100.0	86.5	10.5	0.8	0.2	2.0
Drop-out Rate (%)	1.6	1.6	1.6	0.0	n/a	0.0
H.S. Diplomas (#)	166	152	12	0	0	2

Somerset County

Bernards Twp
101 Peachtree Rd • Basking Ridge, NJ 07920
(908) 204-2600 • http://www.bernardsboe.com
Grade Span: PK-12; **Agency Type:** 1
Schools: 6
   4 Primary; 1 Middle; 1 High; 0 Other Level
   6 Regular; 0 Special Education; 0 Vocational; 0 Alternative
   0 Magnet; 0 Charter; 0 Title I Eligible; 0 School-wide Title I
Students: 5,100   (51.0% male; 48.9% female)
   Individual Education Program: 612 (12.0%);
   English Language Learner: 23 (0.5%); Migrant: 0 (0.0%)
   Eligible for Free Lunch Program: 36 (0.7%)
   Eligible for Reduced-Price Lunch Program: 27 (0.5%)
Teachers: 395.2 (12.7 to 1)
Librarians/Media Specialists: 6.0 (833.5 to 1)
Guidance Counselors: 15.0 (333.4 to 1)
Current Spending: ($ per student per year):
   Total: $11,192; Instruction: $6,603; Support Services: $4,327
Enrollment, Drop-out Rates and Diploma Recipients by Race/Ethnicity

Category	Total	White	Black	Asian	AIAN	Hisp.
Enrollment (%)	100.0	84.3	1.2	12.5	0.0	1.9
Drop-out Rate (%)	0.1	0.1	0.0	0.0	n/a	0.0
H.S. Diplomas (#)	231	196	1	28	0	6

Bound Brook Boro
133 W Maple Ave • Bound Brook, NJ 08805-1330
(732) 271-2830
Grade Span: PK-12; **Agency Type:** 1
Schools: 3

   2 Primary; 0 Middle; 1 High; 0 Other Level
   3 Regular; 0 Special Education; 0 Vocational; 0 Alternative
   0 Magnet; 0 Charter; 3 Title I Eligible; 0 School-wide Title I
Students: 1,679   (51.9% male; 48.0% female)
   Individual Education Program: 233 (13.9%);
   English Language Learner: 193 (11.5%); Migrant: 0 (0.0%)
   Eligible for Free Lunch Program: 503 (30.9%)
   Eligible for Reduced-Price Lunch Program: 226 (13.9%)
Teachers: 116.1 (14.0 to 1)
Librarians/Media Specialists: 3.0 (542.3 to 1)
Guidance Counselors: 3.0 (542.3 to 1)
Current Spending: ($ per student per year):
   Total: $10,776; Instruction: $6,812; Support Services: $3,691
Enrollment, Drop-out Rates and Diploma Recipients by Race/Ethnicity

Category	Total	White	Black	Asian	AIAN	Hisp.
Enrollment (%)	100.0	31.5	4.7	3.8	0.0	60.0
Drop-out Rate (%)	0.0	0.0	0.0	0.0	n/a	0.0
H.S. Diplomas (#)	100	52	4	5	0	39

Branchburg Twp
3461 U.S Hwy 22 • Branchburg, NJ 08876-6021
(908) 722-3265 • http://www.branchburg.k12.nj.us
Grade Span: PK-08; **Agency Type:** 1
Schools: 4
   3 Primary; 1 Middle; 0 High; 0 Other Level
   4 Regular; 0 Special Education; 0 Vocational; 0 Alternative
   0 Magnet; 0 Charter; 0 Title I Eligible; 0 School-wide Title I
Students: 1,933   (51.6% male; 48.3% female)
   Individual Education Program: 391 (20.2%);
   English Language Learner: 20 (1.0%); Migrant: 0 (0.0%)
   Eligible for Free Lunch Program: 18 (0.9%)
   Eligible for Reduced-Price Lunch Program: 11 (0.6%)
Teachers: 159.0 (12.2 to 1)
Librarians/Media Specialists: 4.0 (483.3 to 1)
Guidance Counselors: 5.0 (386.6 to 1)
Current Spending: ($ per student per year):
   Total: $12,599; Instruction: $7,059; Support Services: $5,340
Enrollment, Drop-out Rates and Diploma Recipients by Race/Ethnicity

Category	Total	White	Black	Asian	AIAN	Hisp.
Enrollment (%)	100.0	89.3	2.0	6.6	0.2	2.0
Drop-out Rate (%)	n/a	n/a	n/a	n/a	n/a	n/a
H.S. Diplomas (#)	n/a	n/a	n/a	n/a	n/a	n/a

Bridgewater-Raritan Reg
836 Newmans Ln • Bridgewater, NJ 08807-0030
(908) 685-2777 • http://www.brrsd.k12.nj.us
Grade Span: PK-12; **Agency Type:** 1
Schools: 10
   6 Primary; 3 Middle; 1 High; 0 Other Level
   10 Regular; 0 Special Education; 0 Vocational; 0 Alternative
   0 Magnet; 0 Charter; 2 Title I Eligible; 0 School-wide Title I
Students: 8,894   (50.8% male; 49.1% female)
   Individual Education Program: 1,358 (15.3%);
   English Language Learner: 150 (1.7%); Migrant: 0 (0.0%)
   Eligible for Free Lunch Program: 242 (2.8%)
   Eligible for Reduced-Price Lunch Program: 165 (1.9%)
Teachers: 662.9 (13.1 to 1)
Librarians/Media Specialists: 10.8 (806.3 to 1)
Guidance Counselors: 29.0 (300.3 to 1)
Current Spending: ($ per student per year):
   Total: $11,175; Instruction: $6,761; Support Services: $4,175
Enrollment, Drop-out Rates and Diploma Recipients by Race/Ethnicity

Category	Total	White	Black	Asian	AIAN	Hisp.
Enrollment (%)	100.0	74.3	3.0	15.7	0.1	6.9
Drop-out Rate (%)	0.6	0.4	2.5	0.7	n/a	1.9
H.S. Diplomas (#)	455	343	12	69	0	31

Franklin Twp
1755 Amwell Rd • Somerset, NJ 08873-2793
(732) 873-2400 • http://www.franklinboe.org
Grade Span: PK-12; **Agency Type:** 1
Schools: 8
   6 Primary; 1 Middle; 1 High; 0 Other Level
   2 Regular; 0 Special Education; 0 Vocational; 6 Alternative
   0 Magnet; 0 Charter; 5 Title I Eligible; 0 School-wide Title I
Students: 6,840   (51.2% male; 48.7% female)
   Individual Education Program: 1,076 (15.7%);
   English Language Learner: 273 (4.0%); Migrant: 0 (0.0%)
   Eligible for Free Lunch Program: 1,307 (19.8%)
   Eligible for Reduced-Price Lunch Program: 486 (7.4%)
Teachers: 506.1 (13.0 to 1)
Librarians/Media Specialists: 11.5 (573.0 to 1)
Guidance Counselors: 17.0 (387.6 to 1)
Current Spending: ($ per student per year):
   Total: $13,367; Instruction: $7,658; Support Services: $5,328

Enrollment, Drop-out Rates and Diploma Recipients by Race/Ethnicity

Category	Total	White	Black	Asian	AIAN	Hisp.
Enrollment (%)	100.0	28.1	45.5	13.5	0.0	12.9
Drop-out Rate (%)	1.9	2.0	1.5	0.0	0.0	4.8
H.S. Diplomas (#)	287	96	114	47	0	30

Hillsborough Twp
555 Amwell Rd • Neshanic, NJ 08853-3409
(908) 369-0030 • http://www.hillsborough.k12.nj.us
Grade Span: PK-12; Agency Type: 1
Schools: 9
  6 Primary; 2 Middle; 1 High; 0 Other Level
  9 Regular; 0 Special Education; 0 Vocational; 0 Alternative
  0 Magnet; 0 Charter; 0 Title I Eligible; 0 School-wide Title I
Students: 7,782 (52.3% male; 47.6% female)
  Individual Education Program: 1,364 (17.5%);
  English Language Learner: 103 (1.3%); Migrant: 0 (0.0%)
  Eligible for Free Lunch Program: 234 (3.1%)
  Eligible for Reduced-Price Lunch Program: 131 (1.7%)
Teachers: 614.5 (12.4 to 1)
Librarians/Media Specialists: 9.0 (844.6 to 1)
Guidance Counselors: 17.0 (447.1 to 1)
Current Spending: ($ per student per year):
  Total: $10,326; Instruction: $6,343; Support Services: $3,737
Enrollment, Drop-out Rates and Diploma Recipients by Race/Ethnicity

Category	Total	White	Black	Asian	AIAN	Hisp.
Enrollment (%)	100.0	81.6	4.3	8.7	0.1	5.2
Drop-out Rate (%)	0.4	0.4	0.0	0.0	0.0	1.0
H.S. Diplomas (#)	429	359	23	29	0	18

Montgomery Twp
405 Burnt Hill Rd • Skillman, NJ 08558-1705
(908) 874-5201 • http://mtsd.k12.nj.us
Grade Span: PK-12; Agency Type: 1
Schools: 4
  2 Primary; 1 Middle; 1 High; 0 Other Level
  4 Regular; 0 Special Education; 0 Vocational; 0 Alternative
  0 Magnet; 0 Charter; 0 Title I Eligible; 0 School-wide Title I
Students: 4,721 (51.5% male; 48.4% female)
  Individual Education Program: 561 (11.9%);
  English Language Learner: 21 (0.4%); Migrant: 0 (0.0%)
  Eligible for Free Lunch Program: 25 (0.5%)
  Eligible for Reduced-Price Lunch Program: 23 (0.5%)
Teachers: 330.0 (14.2 to 1)
Librarians/Media Specialists: 5.0 (935.4 to 1)
Guidance Counselors: 14.0 (334.1 to 1)
Current Spending: ($ per student per year):
  Total: $9,680; Instruction: $5,574; Support Services: $3,923
Enrollment, Drop-out Rates and Diploma Recipients by Race/Ethnicity

Category	Total	White	Black	Asian	AIAN	Hisp.
Enrollment (%)	100.0	74.5	2.2	20.5	0.1	2.7
Drop-out Rate (%)	0.7	0.5	0.0	0.0	n/a	11.1
H.S. Diplomas (#)	203	163	3	34	0	3

North Plainfield Boro
33 Mountain Ave • North Plainfield, NJ 07060-5336
(908) 769-6060 • http://www.familyeducation.com/NJ/North_Plainfield/
Grade Span: PK-12; Agency Type: 1
Schools: 5
  3 Primary; 1 Middle; 1 High; 0 Other Level
  5 Regular; 0 Special Education; 0 Vocational; 0 Alternative
  0 Magnet; 0 Charter; 3 Title I Eligible; 0 School-wide Title I
Students: 3,352 (50.3% male; 49.6% female)
  Individual Education Program: 522 (15.6%);
  English Language Learner: 252 (7.5%); Migrant: 0 (0.0%)
  Eligible for Free Lunch Program: 766 (23.2%)
  Eligible for Reduced-Price Lunch Program: 370 (11.2%)
Teachers: 286.5 (11.5 to 1)
Librarians/Media Specialists: 5.0 (660.4 to 1)
Guidance Counselors: 10.8 (305.7 to 1)
Current Spending: ($ per student per year):
  Total: $11,142; Instruction: $6,980; Support Services: $4,004
Enrollment, Drop-out Rates and Diploma Recipients by Race/Ethnicity

Category	Total	White	Black	Asian	AIAN	Hisp.
Enrollment (%)	100.0	23.5	20.8	6.8	0.0	48.8
Drop-out Rate (%)	0.6	0.0	1.3	0.0	n/a	1.0
H.S. Diplomas (#)	165	61	29	18	0	57

Somerset Hills Regional
25 Olcott Ave • Bernardsville, NJ 07924-2307
(908) 630-3010 • http://www.shsd.org
Grade Span: PK-12; Agency Type: 1
Schools: 3
  1 Primary; 1 Middle; 1 High; 0 Other Level
  3 Regular; 0 Special Education; 0 Vocational; 0 Alternative

  0 Magnet; 0 Charter; 0 Title I Eligible; 0 School-wide Title I
Students: 1,915 (50.7% male; 49.2% female)
  Individual Education Program: 239 (12.5%);
  English Language Learner: 48 (2.5%); Migrant: 0 (0.0%)
  Eligible for Free Lunch Program: 34 (1.8%)
  Eligible for Reduced-Price Lunch Program: 13 (0.7%)
Teachers: 143.1 (13.2 to 1)
Librarians/Media Specialists: 3.0 (631.0 to 1)
Guidance Counselors: 4.0 (473.3 to 1)
Current Spending: ($ per student per year):
  Total: $13,170; Instruction: $7,642; Support Services: $5,315
Enrollment, Drop-out Rates and Diploma Recipients by Race/Ethnicity

Category	Total	White	Black	Asian	AIAN	Hisp.
Enrollment (%)	100.0	83.7	1.5	4.3	0.1	10.4
Drop-out Rate (%)	1.0	1.2	0.0	0.0	n/a	0.0
H.S. Diplomas (#)	123	112	1	3	0	7

Somerville Boro
51 W Cliff St • Somerville, NJ 08876-1903
(908) 218-4101
Grade Span: PK-12; Agency Type: 1
Schools: 3
  1 Primary; 1 Middle; 1 High; 0 Other Level
  3 Regular; 0 Special Education; 0 Vocational; 0 Alternative
  0 Magnet; 0 Charter; 2 Title I Eligible; 0 School-wide Title I
Students: 2,236 (51.3% male; 48.6% female)
  Individual Education Program: 256 (11.4%);
  English Language Learner: 110 (4.9%); Migrant: 0 (0.0%)
  Eligible for Free Lunch Program: 424 (19.2%)
  Eligible for Reduced-Price Lunch Program: 163 (7.4%)
Teachers: 172.9 (12.8 to 1)
Librarians/Media Specialists: 3.0 (735.7 to 1)
Guidance Counselors: 6.0 (367.8 to 1)
Current Spending: ($ per student per year):
  Total: $12,073; Instruction: $7,806; Support Services: $4,064
Enrollment, Drop-out Rates and Diploma Recipients by Race/Ethnicity

Category	Total	White	Black	Asian	AIAN	Hisp.
Enrollment (%)	100.0	53.6	16.6	8.8	0.0	20.9
Drop-out Rate (%)	0.9	0.3	4.7	0.0	n/a	1.0
H.S. Diplomas (#)	174	133	17	14	0	10

Warren Twp
213 Mt. Horeb Rd • Warren, NJ 07059-5819
(732) 560-8700 • http://www.warrenboe.org
Grade Span: PK-08; Agency Type: 1
Schools: 5
  4 Primary; 1 Middle; 0 High; 0 Other Level
  5 Regular; 0 Special Education; 0 Vocational; 0 Alternative
  0 Magnet; 0 Charter; 0 Title I Eligible; 0 School-wide Title I
Students: 2,229 (49.9% male; 50.0% female)
  Individual Education Program: 364 (16.3%);
  English Language Learner: 32 (1.4%); Migrant: 0 (0.0%)
  Eligible for Free Lunch Program: 10 (0.5%)
  Eligible for Reduced-Price Lunch Program: 0 (0.0%)
Teachers: 209.3 (10.5 to 1)
Librarians/Media Specialists: 5.0 (439.8 to 1)
Guidance Counselors: 6.0 (366.5 to 1)
Current Spending: ($ per student per year):
  Total: $11,820; Instruction: $7,216; Support Services: $4,584
Enrollment, Drop-out Rates and Diploma Recipients by Race/Ethnicity

Category	Total	White	Black	Asian	AIAN	Hisp.
Enrollment (%)	100.0	79.8	1.1	15.4	0.0	3.7
Drop-out Rate (%)	n/a	n/a	n/a	n/a	n/a	n/a
H.S. Diplomas (#)	n/a	n/a	n/a	n/a	n/a	n/a

Watchung Hills Regional
108 Stirling Rd • Warren, NJ 07059
(908) 647-4890
Grade Span: 09-12; Agency Type: 1
Schools: 1
  0 Primary; 0 Middle; 1 High; 0 Other Level
  1 Regular; 0 Special Education; 0 Vocational; 0 Alternative
  0 Magnet; 0 Charter; 0 Title I Eligible; 0 School-wide Title I
Students: 1,735 (51.3% male; 48.6% female)
  Individual Education Program: 221 (12.7%);
  English Language Learner: 12 (0.7%); Migrant: 0 (0.0%)
  Eligible for Free Lunch Program: 6 (0.4%)
  Eligible for Reduced-Price Lunch Program: 7 (0.4%)
Teachers: 132.8 (12.9 to 1)
Librarians/Media Specialists: 2.0 (853.5 to 1)
Guidance Counselors: 8.0 (213.4 to 1)
Current Spending: ($ per student per year):
  Total: $13,657; Instruction: $7,897; Support Services: $5,379

Enrollment, Drop-out Rates and Diploma Recipients by Race/Ethnicity

Category	Total	White	Black	Asian	AIAN	Hisp.
Enrollment (%)	100.0	79.2	1.3	14.4	0.4	4.7
Drop-out Rate (%)	0.3	0.3	0.0	0.5	0.0	0.0
H.S. Diplomas (#)	358	307	3	36	0	12

Sussex County

High Point Regional
299 Pigeon Hill Rd • Sussex, NJ 07461-2732
(973) 875-7204
Grade Span: 09-12; **Agency Type:** 1
Schools: 1
  0 Primary; 0 Middle; 1 High; 0 Other Level
  1 Regular; 0 Special Education; 0 Vocational; 0 Alternative
  0 Magnet; 0 Charter; 1 Title I Eligible; 0 School-wide Title I
Students: 1,540 (49.5% male; 50.4% female)
  Individual Education Program: 201 (13.1%);
  English Language Learner: 0 (0.0%); Migrant: 0 (0.0%)
  Eligible for Free Lunch Program: 46 (3.4%)
  Eligible for Reduced-Price Lunch Program: 31 (2.3%)
Teachers: 107.1 (12.5 to 1)
Librarians/Media Specialists: 1.0 (1,335.0 to 1)
Guidance Counselors: 5.0 (267.0 to 1)
Current Spending: ($ per student per year):
  Total: $15,137; Instruction: $8,640; Support Services: $6,067
Enrollment, Drop-out Rates and Diploma Recipients by Race/Ethnicity

Category	Total	White	Black	Asian	AIAN	Hisp.
Enrollment (%)	100.0	95.6	1.0	1.3	0.1	2.1
Drop-out Rate (%)	0.0	0.0	0.0	0.0	n/a	0.0
H.S. Diplomas (#)	247	237	5	1	1	3

Hopatcong
Windsor Ave • Hopatcong, NJ 07843-0829
Mailing Address: PO Box 1029 • Hopatcong, NJ 07843-0829
(973) 398-8801 • http://www.hopatcongschools.org
Grade Span: PK-12; **Agency Type:** 1
Schools: 5
  2 Primary; 2 Middle; 1 High; 0 Other Level
  5 Regular; 0 Special Education; 0 Vocational; 0 Alternative
  0 Magnet; 0 Charter; 3 Title I Eligible; 0 School-wide Title I
Students: 3,187 (51.9% male; 48.0% female)
  Individual Education Program: 589 (18.5%);
  English Language Learner: 21 (0.7%); Migrant: 0 (0.0%)
  Eligible for Free Lunch Program: 205 (7.1%)
  Eligible for Reduced-Price Lunch Program: 148 (5.2%)
Teachers: 193.2 (14.9 to 1)
Librarians/Media Specialists: 4.0 (717.5 to 1)
Guidance Counselors: 7.2 (398.6 to 1)
Current Spending: ($ per student per year):
  Total: $10,959; Instruction: $6,438; Support Services: $4,273
Enrollment, Drop-out Rates and Diploma Recipients by Race/Ethnicity

Category	Total	White	Black	Asian	AIAN	Hisp.
Enrollment (%)	100.0	84.8	3.6	2.0	0.1	9.5
Drop-out Rate (%)	0.4	0.3	0.0	0.0	n/a	5.0
H.S. Diplomas (#)	160	152	1	2	0	5

Newton Town
57 Trinity St • Newton, NJ 07860-1824
(973) 383-7392 • http://www.newtonnj.org
Grade Span: PK-12; **Agency Type:** 1
Schools: 3
  1 Primary; 1 Middle; 1 High; 0 Other Level
  3 Regular; 0 Special Education; 0 Vocational; 0 Alternative
  0 Magnet; 0 Charter; 2 Title I Eligible; 0 School-wide Title I
Students: 1,779 (53.4% male; 46.5% female)
  Individual Education Program: 205 (11.5%);
  English Language Learner: 20 (1.1%); Migrant: 0 (0.0%)
  Eligible for Free Lunch Program: 246 (14.1%)
  Eligible for Reduced-Price Lunch Program: 107 (6.1%)
Teachers: 137.0 (12.7 to 1)
Librarians/Media Specialists: 3.0 (581.0 to 1)
Guidance Counselors: 4.6 (378.9 to 1)
Current Spending: ($ per student per year):
  Total: $11,760; Instruction: $7,268; Support Services: $4,144
Enrollment, Drop-out Rates and Diploma Recipients by Race/Ethnicity

Category	Total	White	Black	Asian	AIAN	Hisp.
Enrollment (%)	100.0	86.8	5.1	2.8	0.9	4.4
Drop-out Rate (%)	2.7	3.0	0.0	0.0	0.0	0.0
H.S. Diplomas (#)	163	156	3	3	0	1

Sparta Twp
18 Mohawk Ave • Sparta, NJ 07871-1112
(973) 729-7886 • http://www.sparta.org
Grade Span: PK-12; **Agency Type:** 1
Schools: 5
  2 Primary; 2 Middle; 1 High; 0 Other Level
  5 Regular; 0 Special Education; 0 Vocational; 0 Alternative
  0 Magnet; 0 Charter; 0 Title I Eligible; 0 School-wide Title I
Students: 4,025 (51.4% male; 48.5% female)
  Individual Education Program: 563 (14.0%);
  English Language Learner: 12 (0.3%); Migrant: 0 (0.0%)
  Eligible for Free Lunch Program: 45 (1.1%)
  Eligible for Reduced-Price Lunch Program: 28 (0.7%)
Teachers: 261.5 (15.3 to 1)
Librarians/Media Specialists: 4.0 (998.5 to 1)
Guidance Counselors: 11.0 (363.1 to 1)
Current Spending: ($ per student per year):
  Total: $10,268; Instruction: $5,990; Support Services: $4,057
Enrollment, Drop-out Rates and Diploma Recipients by Race/Ethnicity

Category	Total	White	Black	Asian	AIAN	Hisp.
Enrollment (%)	100.0	93.0	0.8	2.9	0.1	3.3
Drop-out Rate (%)	0.1	0.1	0.0	0.0	n/a	0.0
H.S. Diplomas (#)	227	216	1	5	0	5

Sussex-Wantage Regional
31 Ryan Rd • Wantage, NJ 07461-1705
(973) 875-3175
Grade Span: PK-08; **Agency Type:** 1
Schools: 3
  2 Primary; 1 Middle; 0 High; 0 Other Level
  3 Regular; 0 Special Education; 0 Vocational; 0 Alternative
  0 Magnet; 0 Charter; 3 Title I Eligible; 0 School-wide Title I
Students: 1,829 (48.8% male; 51.1% female)
  Individual Education Program: 409 (22.4%);
  English Language Learner: 5 (0.3%); Migrant: 0 (0.0%)
  Eligible for Free Lunch Program: 158 (9.2%)
  Eligible for Reduced-Price Lunch Program: 110 (6.4%)
Teachers: 137.8 (12.5 to 1)
Librarians/Media Specialists: 3.0 (572.7 to 1)
Guidance Counselors: 2.9 (592.4 to 1)
Current Spending: ($ per student per year):
  Total: $11,028; Instruction: $6,681; Support Services: $4,049
Enrollment, Drop-out Rates and Diploma Recipients by Race/Ethnicity

Category	Total	White	Black	Asian	AIAN	Hisp.
Enrollment (%)	100.0	94.0	0.9	0.8	0.0	4.3
Drop-out Rate (%)	n/a	n/a	n/a	n/a	n/a	n/a
H.S. Diplomas (#)	n/a	n/a	n/a	n/a	n/a	n/a

Vernon Twp
Route 515 • Vernon, NJ 07462-0099
Mailing Address: PO Box 99 • Vernon, NJ 07462-0099
(973) 764-2900 • http://www.vtsd.com/
Grade Span: PK-12; **Agency Type:** 1
Schools: 6
  3 Primary; 2 Middle; 1 High; 0 Other Level
  6 Regular; 0 Special Education; 0 Vocational; 0 Alternative
  0 Magnet; 0 Charter; 3 Title I Eligible; 0 School-wide Title I
Students: 5,500 (51.8% male; 48.1% female)
  Individual Education Program: 671 (12.2%);
  English Language Learner: 9 (0.2%); Migrant: 0 (0.0%)
  Eligible for Free Lunch Program: 226 (4.2%)
  Eligible for Reduced-Price Lunch Program: 173 (3.2%)
Teachers: 348.2 (15.3 to 1)
Librarians/Media Specialists: 6.0 (887.3 to 1)
Guidance Counselors: 16.2 (328.6 to 1)
Current Spending: ($ per student per year):
  Total: $10,427; Instruction: $6,218; Support Services: $3,994
Enrollment, Drop-out Rates and Diploma Recipients by Race/Ethnicity

Category	Total	White	Black	Asian	AIAN	Hisp.
Enrollment (%)	100.0	92.8	1.6	0.9	0.0	4.7
Drop-out Rate (%)	1.6	1.5	5.6	0.0	n/a	2.3
H.S. Diplomas (#)	343	341	0	0	0	2

Union County

Berkeley Heights Twp
345 Plainfield Ave • Berkeley Heights, NJ 07922-1436
(908) 464-1718 • http://www.bhs.k12.nj.us
Grade Span: PK-12; **Agency Type:** 1
Schools: 6
  4 Primary; 1 Middle; 1 High; 0 Other Level
  6 Regular; 0 Special Education; 0 Vocational; 0 Alternative
  0 Magnet; 0 Charter; 0 Title I Eligible; 0 School-wide Title I
Students: 2,797 (51.7% male; 48.2% female)
  Individual Education Program: 286 (10.2%);

English Language Learner: 42 (1.5%); Migrant: 0 (0.0%);
Eligible for Free Lunch Program: 18 (0.7%)
Eligible for Reduced-Price Lunch Program: 14 (0.5%)
Teachers: 208.6 (13.2 to 1)
Librarians/Media Specialists: 5.0 (551.8 to 1)
Guidance Counselors: 8.0 (344.9 to 1)
Current Spending: ($ per student per year):
Total: $12,211; Instruction: $7,850; Support Services: $4,088
Enrollment, Drop-out Rates and Diploma Recipients by Race/Ethnicity

Category	Total	White	Black	Asian	AIAN	Hisp.
Enrollment (%)	100.0	86.1	0.7	8.2	0.0	5.1
Drop-out Rate (%)	0.5	0.4	0.0	0.0	0.0	3.1
H.S. Diplomas (#)	171	148	0	17	0	6

Clark Twp
10 Schindler Rd • Clark, NJ 07066-2499
(732) 574-9600 • http://www.clarkschools.org/
Grade Span: PK-12; **Agency Type:** 1
Schools: 4
2 Primary; 1 Middle; 1 High; 0 Other Level
4 Regular; 0 Special Education; 0 Vocational; 0 Alternative
0 Magnet; 0 Charter; 0 Title I Eligible; 0 School-wide Title I
Students: 2,760 (52.9% male; 47.0% female)
Individual Education Program: 282 (10.2%);
English Language Learner: 21 (0.8%); Migrant: 0 (0.0%);
Eligible for Free Lunch Program: 22 (0.9%)
Eligible for Reduced-Price Lunch Program: 28 (1.1%)
Teachers: 175.0 (14.5 to 1)
Librarians/Media Specialists: 4.0 (634.3 to 1)
Guidance Counselors: 8.0 (317.1 to 1)
Current Spending: ($ per student per year):
Total: $10,686; Instruction: $6,383; Support Services: $4,041
Enrollment, Drop-out Rates and Diploma Recipients by Race/Ethnicity

Category	Total	White	Black	Asian	AIAN	Hisp.
Enrollment (%)	100.0	92.9	0.4	2.5	0.0	4.1
Drop-out Rate (%)	0.9	1.0	n/a	0.0	n/a	0.0
H.S. Diplomas (#)	189	169	6	7	0	7

Cranford Twp
132 Thomas St • Cranford, NJ 07016-3134
(908) 709-6202 • http://www.cranfordschools.org
Grade Span: PK-12; **Agency Type:** 1
Schools: 7
6 Primary; 0 Middle; 1 High; 0 Other Level
7 Regular; 0 Special Education; 0 Vocational; 0 Alternative
0 Magnet; 0 Charter; 2 Title I Eligible; 0 School-wide Title I
Students: 3,642 (53.5% male; 46.4% female)
Individual Education Program: 563 (15.5%);
English Language Learner: 2 (0.1%); Migrant: 0 (0.0%);
Eligible for Free Lunch Program: 58 (1.6%)
Eligible for Reduced-Price Lunch Program: 37 (1.1%)
Teachers: 268.2 (13.1 to 1)
Librarians/Media Specialists: 3.0 (1,173.0 to 1)
Guidance Counselors: 5.0 (703.8 to 1)
Current Spending: ($ per student per year):
Total: $11,871; Instruction: $7,421; Support Services: $4,276
Enrollment, Drop-out Rates and Diploma Recipients by Race/Ethnicity

Category	Total	White	Black	Asian	AIAN	Hisp.
Enrollment (%)	100.0	90.5	3.8	2.3	0.0	3.4
Drop-out Rate (%)	0.8	0.8	3.0	0.0	n/a	0.0
H.S. Diplomas (#)	232	221	8	0	0	3

Elizabeth City
Mitchell Building 500 N Broad • Elizabeth, NJ 07207
(908) 436-5010 • http://www.elizabeth.k12.nj.us
Grade Span: PK-12; **Agency Type:** 1
Schools: 26
19 Primary; 6 Middle; 1 High; 0 Other Level
26 Regular; 0 Special Education; 0 Vocational; 0 Alternative
0 Magnet; 0 Charter; 21 Title I Eligible; 21 School-wide Title I
Students: 21,998 (50.4% male; 49.5% female)
Individual Education Program: 2,497 (11.4%);
English Language Learner: 4,161 (18.9%); Migrant: 0 (0.0%);
Eligible for Free Lunch Program: 12,611 (59.8%)
Eligible for Reduced-Price Lunch Program: 2,724 (12.9%)
Teachers: 2,007.8 (10.5 to 1)
Librarians/Media Specialists: 19.0 (1,110.1 to 1)
Guidance Counselors: 51.0 (413.5 to 1)
Current Spending: ($ per student per year):
Total: $13,407; Instruction: $7,329; Support Services: $5,632
Enrollment, Drop-out Rates and Diploma Recipients by Race/Ethnicity

Category	Total	White	Black	Asian	AIAN	Hisp.
Enrollment (%)	100.0	10.7	23.9	2.1	0.0	63.3
Drop-out Rate (%)	5.9	3.9	7.1	3.0	n/a	6.1
H.S. Diplomas (#)	877	161	192	27	0	497

Hillside Twp
195 Virginia St • Hillside, NJ 07205-2742
(908) 352-7664
Grade Span: PK-12; **Agency Type:** 1
Schools: 6
4 Primary; 1 Middle; 1 High; 0 Other Level
6 Regular; 0 Special Education; 0 Vocational; 0 Alternative
0 Magnet; 0 Charter; 4 Title I Eligible; 0 School-wide Title I
Students: 3,626 (50.8% male; 49.1% female)
Individual Education Program: 524 (14.5%);
English Language Learner: 155 (4.3%); Migrant: 0 (0.0%);
Eligible for Free Lunch Program: 1,200 (35.1%)
Eligible for Reduced-Price Lunch Program: 665 (19.5%)
Teachers: 220.4 (15.5 to 1)
Librarians/Media Specialists: 4.5 (758.7 to 1)
Guidance Counselors: 4.0 (853.5 to 1)
Current Spending: ($ per student per year):
Total: $11,277; Instruction: $6,779; Support Services: $4,143
Enrollment, Drop-out Rates and Diploma Recipients by Race/Ethnicity

Category	Total	White	Black	Asian	AIAN	Hisp.
Enrollment (%)	100.0	14.3	66.7	1.9	0.1	17.0
Drop-out Rate (%)	5.5	6.1	5.4	0.0	n/a	6.3
H.S. Diplomas (#)	169	33	105	11	0	20

Linden City
2 E Gibbons St • Linden, NJ 07036-4064
(908) 486-5818 • http://www.geocities.com/lindenschool1/
Grade Span: PK-12; **Agency Type:** 1
Schools: 11
8 Primary; 2 Middle; 1 High; 0 Other Level
11 Regular; 0 Special Education; 0 Vocational; 0 Alternative
0 Magnet; 0 Charter; 6 Title I Eligible; 0 School-wide Title I
Students: 6,508 (50.7% male; 49.2% female)
Individual Education Program: 1,142 (17.5%);
English Language Learner: 334 (5.1%); Migrant: 0 (0.0%);
Eligible for Free Lunch Program: 1,939 (31.2%)
Eligible for Reduced-Price Lunch Program: 901 (14.5%)
Teachers: 460.8 (13.5 to 1)
Librarians/Media Specialists: 7.0 (886.7 to 1)
Guidance Counselors: 9.0 (689.7 to 1)
Current Spending: ($ per student per year):
Total: $10,725; Instruction: $6,435; Support Services: $4,006
Enrollment, Drop-out Rates and Diploma Recipients by Race/Ethnicity

Category	Total	White	Black	Asian	AIAN	Hisp.
Enrollment (%)	100.0	35.4	36.1	3.0	0.0	25.5
Drop-out Rate (%)	3.1	4.4	1.7	0.0	n/a	3.6
H.S. Diplomas (#)	373	159	126	14	0	74

New Providence Boro
356 Elkwood Ave • New Providence, NJ 07974-2322
(908) 464-9050 • http://www.npsd.k12.nj.us
Grade Span: PK-12; **Agency Type:** 1
Schools: 4
2 Primary; 1 Middle; 1 High; 0 Other Level
4 Regular; 0 Special Education; 0 Vocational; 0 Alternative
0 Magnet; 0 Charter; 0 Title I Eligible; 0 School-wide Title I
Students: 2,185 (51.8% male; 48.1% female)
Individual Education Program: 298 (13.6%);
English Language Learner: 18 (0.8%); Migrant: 0 (0.0%);
Eligible for Free Lunch Program: 16 (0.7%)
Eligible for Reduced-Price Lunch Program: 24 (1.1%)
Teachers: 170.8 (12.6 to 1)
Librarians/Media Specialists: 4.0 (540.0 to 1)
Guidance Counselors: 4.0 (540.0 to 1)
Current Spending: ($ per student per year):
Total: $11,112; Instruction: $7,202; Support Services: $3,737
Enrollment, Drop-out Rates and Diploma Recipients by Race/Ethnicity

Category	Total	White	Black	Asian	AIAN	Hisp.
Enrollment (%)	100.0	86.6	0.6	8.4	0.1	4.3
Drop-out Rate (%)	0.0	0.0	0.0	0.0	n/a	0.0
H.S. Diplomas (#)	134	123	0	8	0	3

Plainfield City
504 Madison Ave • Plainfield, NJ 07060-1540
(908) 731-4335 • http://www.plainfieldnjk12.org/
Grade Span: PK-12; **Agency Type:** 1
Schools: 13
10 Primary; 2 Middle; 1 High; 0 Other Level
13 Regular; 0 Special Education; 0 Vocational; 0 Alternative
0 Magnet; 0 Charter; 10 Title I Eligible; 10 School-wide Title I
Students: 8,119 (51.1% male; 48.8% female)
Individual Education Program: 1,024 (12.6%);
English Language Learner: 1,052 (13.0%); Migrant: 0 (0.0%);
Eligible for Free Lunch Program: 4,425 (57.3%)
Eligible for Reduced-Price Lunch Program: 917 (11.9%)

Teachers: 649.5 (11.9 to 1)
Librarians/Media Specialists: 11.0 (702.4 to 1)
Guidance Counselors: 15.0 (515.1 to 1)
Current Spending: ($ per student per year):
   Total: $14,214; Instruction: $8,217; Support Services: $5,577
Enrollment, Drop-out Rates and Diploma Recipients by Race/Ethnicity

Category	Total	White	Black	Asian	AIAN	Hisp.
Enrollment (%)	100.0	0.7	67.9	0.3	0.0	31.1
Drop-out Rate (%)	5.2	0.0	5.0	0.0	n/a	5.7
H.S. Diplomas (#)	276	1	224	1	0	50

Rahway City
Rahway Middle School • Rahway, NJ 07065
(732) 396-1020 • http://www.rahway.net
Grade Span: PK-12; **Agency Type:** 1
Schools: 6
   4 Primary; 1 Middle; 1 High; 0 Other Level
   6 Regular; 0 Special Education; 0 Vocational; 0 Alternative
   0 Magnet; 0 Charter; 1 Title I Eligible; 0 School-wide Title I
Students: 4,155   (52.6% male; 47.3% female)
   Individual Education Program: 758 (18.2%);
   English Language Learner: 102 (2.5%); Migrant: 0 (0.0%)
   Eligible for Free Lunch Program: 1,183 (29.4%)
   Eligible for Reduced-Price Lunch Program: 524 (13.0%)
Teachers: 281.1 (14.3 to 1)
Librarians/Media Specialists: 5.0 (803.4 to 1)
Guidance Counselors: 8.0 (502.1 to 1)
Current Spending: ($ per student per year):
   Total: $12,034; Instruction: $7,536; Support Services: $4,172
Enrollment, Drop-out Rates and Diploma Recipients by Race/Ethnicity

Category	Total	White	Black	Asian	AIAN	Hisp.
Enrollment (%)	100.0	29.0	42.6	3.4	0.4	24.7
Drop-out Rate (%)	3.8	2.9	4.8	1.9	n/a	3.6
H.S. Diplomas (#)	227	99	86	10	0	32

Roselle Boro
710 Locust St • Roselle, NJ 07203-1919
(908) 298-2040 • http://www.roselleschools.com
Grade Span: PK-12; **Agency Type:** 1
Schools: 6
   3 Primary; 2 Middle; 1 High; 0 Other Level
   6 Regular; 0 Special Education; 0 Vocational; 0 Alternative
   0 Magnet; 0 Charter; 5 Title I Eligible; 0 School-wide Title I
Students: 2,899   (50.7% male; 49.2% female)
   Individual Education Program: 579 (20.0%);
   English Language Learner: 253 (8.7%); Migrant: 0 (0.0%)
   Eligible for Free Lunch Program: 962 (34.7%)
   Eligible for Reduced-Price Lunch Program: 340 (12.3%)
Teachers: 201.6 (13.7 to 1)
Librarians/Media Specialists: 1.0 (2,771.0 to 1)
Guidance Counselors: 7.0 (395.9 to 1)
Current Spending: ($ per student per year):
   Total: $12,044; Instruction: $7,773; Support Services: $4,028
Enrollment, Drop-out Rates and Diploma Recipients by Race/Ethnicity

Category	Total	White	Black	Asian	AIAN	Hisp.
Enrollment (%)	100.0	2.3	71.7	1.6	0.0	24.3
Drop-out Rate (%)	2.1	2.3	2.0	0.0	n/a	2.8
H.S. Diplomas (#)	162	10	129	2	0	21

Roselle Park Boro
510 Chestnut St • Roselle Park, NJ 07204-2495
(908) 245-1197 • http://www.roselleschools.com/
Grade Span: PK-12; **Agency Type:** 1
Schools: 5
   3 Primary; 1 Middle; 1 High; 0 Other Level
   5 Regular; 0 Special Education; 0 Vocational; 0 Alternative
   0 Magnet; 0 Charter; 3 Title I Eligible; 0 School-wide Title I
Students: 2,101   (50.5% male; 49.4% female)
   Individual Education Program: 346 (16.5%);
   English Language Learner: 145 (6.9%); Migrant: 0 (0.0%)
   Eligible for Free Lunch Program: 213 (10.4%)
   Eligible for Reduced-Price Lunch Program: 186 (9.1%)
Teachers: 161.0 (12.7 to 1)
Librarians/Media Specialists: 3.0 (680.7 to 1)
Guidance Counselors: 7.0 (291.7 to 1)
Current Spending: ($ per student per year):
   Total: $11,048; Instruction: $6,577; Support Services: $4,043
Enrollment, Drop-out Rates and Diploma Recipients by Race/Ethnicity

Category	Total	White	Black	Asian	AIAN	Hisp.
Enrollment (%)	100.0	59.3	2.7	11.9	0.1	26.1
Drop-out Rate (%)	0.9	0.5	22.2	0.0	n/a	0.9
H.S. Diplomas (#)	104	71	2	6	0	25

Scotch Plains-Fanwood Reg
Evergreen Ave & Cedar • Scotch Plains, NJ 07076-1955
(908) 232-6161 • http://www.njcommunity.org/spfnet/index.htm#Home
Grade Span: PK-12; **Agency Type:** 1
Schools: 8
   5 Primary; 2 Middle; 1 High; 0 Other Level
   8 Regular; 0 Special Education; 0 Vocational; 0 Alternative
   0 Magnet; 0 Charter; 4 Title I Eligible; 0 School-wide Title I
Students: 5,004   (51.2% male; 48.7% female)
   Individual Education Program: 844 (16.9%);
   English Language Learner: 25 (0.5%); Migrant: 0 (0.0%)
   Eligible for Free Lunch Program: 97 (2.0%)
   Eligible for Reduced-Price Lunch Program: 46 (0.9%)
Teachers: 350.2 (14.0 to 1)
Librarians/Media Specialists: 9.0 (546.0 to 1)
Guidance Counselors: 10.5 (468.0 to 1)
Current Spending: ($ per student per year):
   Total: $11,529; Instruction: $6,867; Support Services: $4,475
Enrollment, Drop-out Rates and Diploma Recipients by Race/Ethnicity

Category	Total	White	Black	Asian	AIAN	Hisp.
Enrollment (%)	100.0	77.5	11.4	6.4	0.0	4.7
Drop-out Rate (%)	0.1	0.0	0.6	0.0	n/a	0.0
H.S. Diplomas (#)	254	196	34	19	0	5

Springfield Twp
Springfield Public School • Springfield, NJ 07081-1786
(973) 376-1025 • http://www.springfieldschools.com
Grade Span: PK-12; **Agency Type:** 1
Schools: 5
   3 Primary; 1 Middle; 1 High; 0 Other Level
   5 Regular; 0 Special Education; 0 Vocational; 0 Alternative
   0 Magnet; 0 Charter; 3 Title I Eligible; 0 School-wide Title I
Students: 2,083   (52.0% male; 47.9% female)
   Individual Education Program: 316 (15.2%);
   English Language Learner: 41 (2.0%); Migrant: 0 (0.0%)
   Eligible for Free Lunch Program: 66 (3.3%)
   Eligible for Reduced-Price Lunch Program: 47 (2.3%)
Teachers: 160.1 (12.7 to 1)
Librarians/Media Specialists: 5.0 (405.6 to 1)
Guidance Counselors: 9.0 (225.3 to 1)
Current Spending: ($ per student per year):
   Total: $12,112; Instruction: $7,495; Support Services: $4,498
Enrollment, Drop-out Rates and Diploma Recipients by Race/Ethnicity

Category	Total	White	Black	Asian	AIAN	Hisp.
Enrollment (%)	100.0	78.6	6.4	5.9	0.2	9.0
Drop-out Rate (%)	0.0	0.0	0.0	0.0	0.0	0.0
H.S. Diplomas (#)	110	88	10	6	0	6

Summit City
90 Maple St • Summit, NJ 07901-2545
(908) 273-3023 • http://www.summit.k12.nj.us
Grade Span: PK-12; **Agency Type:** 1
Schools: 7
   5 Primary; 1 Middle; 1 High; 0 Other Level
   7 Regular; 0 Special Education; 0 Vocational; 0 Alternative
   0 Magnet; 0 Charter; 7 Title I Eligible; 0 School-wide Title I
Students: 3,515   (52.0% male; 47.9% female)
   Individual Education Program: 477 (13.6%);
   English Language Learner: 128 (3.6%); Migrant: 0 (0.0%)
   Eligible for Free Lunch Program: 223 (6.4%)
   Eligible for Reduced-Price Lunch Program: 131 (3.7%)
Teachers: 280.6 (12.5 to 1)
Librarians/Media Specialists: 8.6 (407.6 to 1)
Guidance Counselors: 11.6 (302.2 to 1)
Current Spending: ($ per student per year):
   Total: $12,181; Instruction: $7,808; Support Services: $4,067
Enrollment, Drop-out Rates and Diploma Recipients by Race/Ethnicity

Category	Total	White	Black	Asian	AIAN	Hisp.
Enrollment (%)	100.0	75.4	5.3	5.5	0.1	13.6
Drop-out Rate (%)	0.6	0.7	0.0	0.0	0.0	1.0
H.S. Diplomas (#)	171	128	8	15	0	20

Union Twp
2369 Morris Ave • Union, NJ 07083-5703
(908) 851-6420 • http://www.twpunionschools.org
Grade Span: PK-12; **Agency Type:** 1
Schools: 10
   6 Primary; 3 Middle; 1 High; 0 Other Level
   10 Regular; 0 Special Education; 0 Vocational; 0 Alternative
   0 Magnet; 0 Charter; 4 Title I Eligible; 0 School-wide Title I
Students: 8,105   (52.0% male; 47.9% female)
   Individual Education Program: 1,229 (15.2%);
   English Language Learner: 191 (2.4%); Migrant: 0 (0.0%)
   Eligible for Free Lunch Program: 1,066 (13.4%)
   Eligible for Reduced-Price Lunch Program: 682 (8.6%)

Teachers: 544.6 (14.6 to 1)
Librarians/Media Specialists: 6.0 (1,327.7 to 1)
Guidance Counselors: 14.0 (569.0 to 1)
Current Spending: ($ per student per year):
    Total: $10,378; Instruction: $6,294; Support Services: $3,783
Enrollment, Drop-out Rates and Diploma Recipients by Race/Ethnicity

Category	Total	White	Black	Asian	AIAN	Hisp.
Enrollment (%)	100.0	39.4	36.3	11.0	0.0	13.2
Drop-out Rate (%)	1.2	0.9	1.9	0.0	0.0	1.3
H.S. Diplomas (#)	482	241	153	45	0	43

Westfield Town
302 Elm St • Westfield, NJ 07090-3104
(908) 789-4420 • http://westfieldnj.com
Grade Span: PK-12; **Agency Type:** 1
Schools: 9
    6 Primary; 2 Middle; 1 High; 0 Other Level
    9 Regular; 0 Special Education; 0 Vocational; 0 Alternative
    0 Magnet; 0 Charter; 3 Title I Eligible; 0 School-wide Title I
Students: 5,909   (51.5% male; 48.4% female)
    Individual Education Program: 992 (16.8%);
    English Language Learner: 26 (0.4%); Migrant: 0 (0.0%)
    Eligible for Free Lunch Program: 63 (1.1%)
    Eligible for Reduced-Price Lunch Program: 38 (0.7%)
Teachers: 448.1 (13.0 to 1)
Librarians/Media Specialists: 11.0 (528.8 to 1)
Guidance Counselors: 15.0 (387.8 to 1)
Current Spending: ($ per student per year):
    Total: $11,498; Instruction: $7,253; Support Services: $4,071
Enrollment, Drop-out Rates and Diploma Recipients by Race/Ethnicity

Category	Total	White	Black	Asian	AIAN	Hisp.
Enrollment (%)	100.0	87.6	4.0	5.3	0.4	2.6
Drop-out Rate (%)	0.3	0.2	3.3	0.0	n/a	0.0
H.S. Diplomas (#)	327	285	16	15	0	11

Warren County

Hackettstown
315 Washington Ave • Hackettstown, NJ 07840-2235
(908) 850-6500 • http://www.gti.net/hackboe
Grade Span: PK-12; **Agency Type:** 1
Schools: 4
    2 Primary; 1 Middle; 1 High; 0 Other Level
    4 Regular; 0 Special Education; 0 Vocational; 0 Alternative
    0 Magnet; 0 Charter; 3 Title I Eligible; 0 School-wide Title I
Students: 1,980   (51.5% male; 48.4% female)
    Individual Education Program: 233 (11.8%);
    English Language Learner: 47 (2.4%); Migrant: 0 (0.0%)
    Eligible for Free Lunch Program: 147 (7.6%)
    Eligible for Reduced-Price Lunch Program: 99 (5.1%)
Teachers: 149.1 (12.9 to 1)
Librarians/Media Specialists: 3.3 (583.6 to 1)
Guidance Counselors: 6.9 (279.1 to 1)
Current Spending: ($ per student per year):
    Total: $11,645; Instruction: $7,016; Support Services: $4,391
Enrollment, Drop-out Rates and Diploma Recipients by Race/Ethnicity

Category	Total	White	Black	Asian	AIAN	Hisp.
Enrollment (%)	100.0	86.6	1.9	3.2	0.0	8.4
Drop-out Rate (%)	0.2	0.2	0.0	0.0	0.0	0.0
H.S. Diplomas (#)	232	217	3	5	0	7

Phillipsburg Town
445 Marshall St • Phillipsburg, NJ 08865-1656
(908) 454-3400 • http://www.pburg.k12.nj.us
Grade Span: PK-12; **Agency Type:** 1
Schools: 7
    4 Primary; 1 Middle; 2 High; 0 Other Level
    7 Regular; 0 Special Education; 0 Vocational; 0 Alternative
    0 Magnet; 0 Charter; 4 Title I Eligible; 0 School-wide Title I
Students: 3,715   (53.0% male; 46.9% female)
    Individual Education Program: 577 (15.5%);
    English Language Learner: 94 (2.5%); Migrant: 0 (0.0%)
    Eligible for Free Lunch Program: 1,043 (29.0%)
    Eligible for Reduced-Price Lunch Program: 307 (8.5%)
Teachers: 334.2 (10.7 to 1)
Librarians/Media Specialists: 6.0 (598.5 to 1)
Guidance Counselors: 13.0 (276.2 to 1)
Current Spending: ($ per student per year):
    Total: $14,490; Instruction: $8,600; Support Services: $5,585
Enrollment, Drop-out Rates and Diploma Recipients by Race/Ethnicity

Category	Total	White	Black	Asian	AIAN	Hisp.
Enrollment (%)	100.0	82.9	6.8	2.2	0.0	8.0
Drop-out Rate (%)	5.9	6.1	4.9	0.0	n/a	8.5
H.S. Diplomas (#)	280	242	14	6	0	18

Warren Hills Regional
89 Bowerstown Rd • Washington, NJ 07882-4123
(908) 689-3143 • http://www.warrenhills.org
Grade Span: 07-12; **Agency Type:** 1
Schools: 2
    0 Primary; 1 Middle; 1 High; 0 Other Level
    2 Regular; 0 Special Education; 0 Vocational; 0 Alternative
    0 Magnet; 0 Charter; 0 Title I Eligible; 0 School-wide Title I
Students: 2,216   (52.3% male; 47.6% female)
    Individual Education Program: 349 (15.7%);
    English Language Learner: 25 (1.1%); Migrant: 0 (0.0%)
    Eligible for Free Lunch Program: 122 (5.7%)
    Eligible for Reduced-Price Lunch Program: 68 (3.2%)
Teachers: 157.9 (13.5 to 1)
Librarians/Media Specialists: 2.0 (1,066.5 to 1)
Guidance Counselors: 8.0 (266.6 to 1)
Current Spending: ($ per student per year):
    Total: $11,421; Instruction: $6,847; Support Services: $4,345
Enrollment, Drop-out Rates and Diploma Recipients by Race/Ethnicity

Category	Total	White	Black	Asian	AIAN	Hisp.
Enrollment (%)	100.0	88.7	4.3	2.2	0.1	4.6
Drop-out Rate (%)	2.7	2.5	2.6	0.0	33.3	8.9
H.S. Diplomas (#)	288	271	6	4	0	7

Number of Schools

Rank	Number	District Name	City
1	77	Newark City	Newark
2	40	Jersey City	Jersey City
3	36	Paterson City	Paterson
4	31	Camden City	Camden
5	26	Elizabeth City	Elizabeth
6	24	Trenton City	Trenton
6	24	Woodbridge Twp	Woodbridge
8	23	Hamilton Twp	Hamilton Square
9	21	East Orange	East Orange
10	19	Cherry Hill Twp	Cherry Hill
10	19	Vineland City	Vineland
12	17	Edison Twp	Edison
12	17	Middletown Twp	Middletown
12	17	Passaic City	Passaic
12	17	Toms River Regional	Toms River
16	16	Clifton City	Clifton
17	15	Old Bridge Twp	Matawan
18	14	Parsippany-Troy Hills Twp	Parsippany
19	13	Pennsauken Twp	Pennsauken
19	13	Plainfield City	Plainfield
19	13	Wayne Twp	Wayne
22	12	Bayonne City	Bayonne
22	12	Brick Twp	Brick
22	12	Gloucester Twp	Blackwood
22	12	Howell Twp	Howell
22	12	Irvington Township	Irvington
22	12	South Brunswick Twp	Monmouth Jct
22	12	Union City	Union City
29	11	Atlantic City	Atlantic City
29	11	Bloomfield Twp	Bloomfield
29	11	East Brunswick Twp	E Brunswick
29	11	Linden City	Linden
29	11	Montclair Town	Montclair
29	11	Pemberton Twp	Pemberton
29	11	Perth Amboy City	Perth Amboy
29	11	Washington Twp	Sewell
29	11	Willingboro Twp	Willingboro
38	10	Bridgewater-Raritan Reg	Bridgewater
38	10	Deptford Twp	Deptford
38	10	Garfield City	Garfield
38	10	Millville City	Millville
38	10	Morris SD	Morristown
38	10	New Brunswick City	New Brunswick
38	10	Piscataway Twp	Piscataway
38	10	Ridgewood Village	Ridgewood
38	10	Union Twp	Union
38	10	W Windsor-Plainsboro Reg	Princeton Jct
38	10	West Orange Town	West Orange
49	9	Belleville Twp	Belleville
49	9	City of Orange Twp	Orange
49	9	Evesham Twp	Marlton
49	9	Fair Lawn Boro	Fair Lawn
49	9	Galloway Twp	Galloway
49	9	Hillsborough Twp	Neshanic
49	9	Jackson Twp	Jackson
49	9	Livingston Twp	Livingston
49	9	Long Branch City	Long Branch
49	9	South Orange-Maplewood	Maplewood
49	9	Westfield Town	Westfield
49	9	Winslow Twp	Atco
61	8	Franklin Twp	Somerset
61	8	Hazlet Twp	Hazlet
61	8	Jefferson Twp	Lake Hopatcong
61	8	Marlboro Twp	Marlboro
61	8	Monmouth County Vocational	Colts Neck
61	8	Mount Laurel Twp	Mount Laurel
61	8	Neptune Twp	Neptune
61	8	Paramus Boro	Paramus
61	8	Scotch Plains-Fanwood Reg	Scotch Plains
61	8	South Plainfield Boro	S Plainfield
61	8	West Milford Twp	West Milford
61	8	West New York Town	West New York
73	7	Bergen County Special Service	Paramus
73	7	Bergenfield Boro	Bergenfield
73	7	Bridgeton City	Bridgeton
73	7	Collingswood Boro	Collingswood
73	7	Cranford Twp	Cranford
73	7	Egg Harbor Twp	W Atlantic City
73	7	Freehold Twp	Freehold
73	7	Hackensack City	Hackensack
73	7	Haddon Twp	Westmont
73	7	Kearny Town	Kearny
73	7	Lawrence Twp	Lawrenceville
73	7	Lodi Borough	Lodi
73	7	Lyndhurst Twp	Lyndhurst
73	7	Mahwah Twp	Mahwah
73	7	Manalapan-Englishtown Reg	Englishtown
73	7	Matawan-Aberdeen Regional	Aberdeen
73	7	Millburn Twp	Millburn
73	7	Montville Twp	Montville
73	7	North Bergen Twp	North Bergen
73	7	Nutley Town	Nutley
73	7	Phillipsburg Town	Phillipsburg
73	7	Roxbury Twp	Succasunna
73	7	Sayreville Boro	Sayreville
73	7	Summit City	Summit
73	7	Teaneck Twp	Teaneck
73	7	Wall Twp	Wall
99	6	Asbury Park City	Asbury Park
99	6	Berkeley Heights Twp	Berkeley Hgts
99	6	Bernards Twp	Basking Ridge
99	6	Buena Regional	Buena
99	6	Caldwell-West Caldwell	West Caldwell
99	6	East Windsor Regional	Hightstown
99	6	Fort Lee Boro	Fort Lee
99	6	Freehold Regional	Englishtown
99	6	Glen Rock Boro	Glen Rock
99	6	Hillside Twp	Hillside
99	6	Hoboken City	Hoboken
99	6	Hopewell Valley Regional	Pennington
99	6	Lacey Twp	Lanoka Harbor
99	6	Lakewood Twp	Lakewood
99	6	Manchester Twp	Whiting
99	6	Middlesex County Vocational	E Brunswick
99	6	Monroe Twp	Williamstown
99	6	Monroe Twp	Monroe Township
99	6	Moorestown Twp	Moorestown
99	6	Mount Olive Twp	Budd Lake
99	6	North Brunswick Twp	North Brunswick
99	6	Pleasantville City	Pleasantville
99	6	Princeton Regional	Princeton
99	6	Rahway City	Rahway
99	6	Randolph Twp	Randolph
99	6	Rockaway Twp	Hibernia
99	6	Roselle Boro	Roselle
99	6	Rutherford Boro	Rutherford
99	6	SD of the Chathams	Chatham
99	6	Tenafly Boro	Tenafly
99	6	Vernon Twp	Vernon
99	6	Verona Boro	Verona
99	6	Westwood Regional	Westwood
132	5	Burlington City	Burlington
132	5	Burlington Twp	Burlington
132	5	Carteret Boro	Carteret
132	5	Cliffside Park Boro	Cliffside Park
132	5	Dover Town	Dover
132	5	Dumont Boro	Dumont
132	5	Elmwood Park	Elmwood Park
132	5	Englewood City	Englewood
132	5	Ewing Twp	Ewing
132	5	Flemington-Raritan Reg	Flemington
132	5	Glassboro	Glassboro
132	5	Haddonfield Boro	Haddonfield
132	5	Hawthorne Boro	Hawthorne
132	5	Hopatcong	Hopatcong
132	5	Madison Boro	Madison
132	5	Medford Twp	Medford
132	5	Mercer County Special Service	Trenton
132	5	Middlesex Boro	Middlesex
132	5	North Arlington Boro	North Arlington
132	5	North Plainfield Boro	N Plainfield
132	5	Ocean Twp	Oakhurst
132	5	Penns Grv-Carney's Pt Reg	Penns Grove
132	5	Pennsville	Pennsville
132	5	Pequannock Twp	Pompton Plains
132	5	Pitman Boro	Pitman
132	5	Ramsey Boro	Ramsey
132	5	Roselle Park Boro	Roselle Park
132	5	Saddle Brook Twp	Saddle Brook
132	5	Sparta Twp	Sparta
132	5	Springfield Twp	Springfield
132	5	Voorhees Twp	Voorhees
132	5	Warren Twp	Warren
132	5	Washington Twp	Long Valley
132	5	West Deptford Twp	West Deptford
132	5	Wyckoff Twp	Wyckoff
167	4	Barnegat Twp	Barnegat
167	4	Bergen County Vocational	Paramus
167	4	Bordentown Regional	Bordentown
167	4	Branchburg Twp	Branchburg
167	4	Cedar Grove Twp	Cedar Grove
167	4	Cinnaminson Twp	Cinnaminson
167	4	Clark Twp	Clark
167	4	Delran Twp	Delran
167	4	Essex County Voc-Tech	West Orange
167	4	Florence Twp	Florence
167	4	Glen Ridge Boro	Glen Ridge
167	4	Hackettstown	Hackettstown
167	4	Hammonton Town	Hammonton
167	4	Hanover Twp	Whippany
167	4	Hasbrouck Heights Boro	Hasbrouck Hgts
167	4	Holmdel Twp	Holmdel
167	4	Keansburg Boro	Keansburg
167	4	Kinnelon Boro	Kinnelon
167	4	Lenape Regional	Shamong
167	4	Lindenwold Boro	Lindenwold
167	4	Lower Twp	Cape May
167	4	Lumberton Twp	Lumberton
167	4	Maple Shade Twp	Maple Shade
167	4	Metuchen Boro	Metuchen
167	4	Middle Twp	Cape May Ct Hse
167	4	Montgomery Twp	Skillman
167	4	Mountain Lakes Boro	Mountain Lakes
167	4	New Milford Boro	New Milford
167	4	New Providence Boro	New Providence
167	4	Oakland Boro	Oakland
167	4	Pine Hill Boro	Pine Hill
167	4	Pittsgrove Twp	Pittsgrove
167	4	Point Pleasant Boro	Pt Pleasant
167	4	Pompton Lakes Boro	Pompton Lakes
167	4	Readington Twp	Whitehouse Stn
167	4	Ridgefield Boro	Ridgefield
167	4	Ridgefield Park Twp	Ridgefield Park
167	4	Secaucus Town	Secaucus
167	4	Spotswood Boro	Spotswood
167	4	Stafford Twp	Manahawkin
167	4	Woodbury City	Woodbury
208	3	Audubon Boro	Audubon
208	3	Berkeley Twp	Bayville
208	3	Black Horse Pike Regional	Blackwood
208	3	Bound Brook Boro	Bound Brook
208	3	Burlington County Spec Serv	Mount Holly
208	3	Clinton Twp	Annandale
208	3	Colts Neck Twp	Colts Neck
208	3	Cresskill Boro	Cresskill
208	3	Denville Twp	Denville
208	3	Franklin Lakes Boro	Franklin Lakes
208	3	Franklin Twp	Franklinville
208	3	Gloucester City	Gloucester City
208	3	Hamilton Twp	Mays Landing
208	3	Harrison Town	Harrison
208	3	Highland Park Boro	Highland Park
208	3	Leonia Boro	Leonia
208	3	Mantua Twp	Sewell
208	3	Newton Town	Newton
208	3	Ocean City	Ocean City
208	3	Paulsboro Twp	Paulsboro
208	3	Plumsted Twp	New Egypt
208	3	Riverside Twp	Riverside
208	3	Salem City	Salem
208	3	Somerset Hills Regional	Bernardsville
208	3	Somerville Boro	Somerville
208	3	South River Boro	South River
208	3	Sussex-Wantage Regional	Wantage
208	3	Tinton Falls	Tinton Falls
208	3	Upper Twp	Petersburg
208	3	Waldwick Boro	Waldwick
208	3	Woodstown-Pilesgrove Reg	Woodstown
239	2	Burlington County Vocational	Westampton Twp
239	2	Camden County Vocational	Sicklerville
239	2	Central Regional	Bayville
239	2	Clearview Regional	Mullica Hill
239	2	Delsea Regional H.S District	Franklinville
239	2	Eastern Camden County Reg	Voorhees
239	2	Greater Egg Harbor Reg	Mays Landing
239	2	Kingsway Regional	Woolwich Twp
239	2	Little Egg Harbor Twp	Little Egg Hbr
239	2	Lower Cape May Regional	Cape May
239	2	Manasquan Boro	Manasquan
239	2	Millstone Twp	Clarksburg
239	2	Morris Hills Regional	Rockaway
239	2	N Hunt/Voorhees Regional	Annandale
239	2	Northern Burlington Reg	Columbus
239	2	Northern Valley Regional	Demarest
239	2	Palisades Park	Palisades Park
239	2	Pascack Valley Regional	Montvale
239	2	Pinelands Regional	Tuckerton
239	2	Ramapo-Indian Hill Reg	Franklin Lakes
239	2	Rancocas Valley Regional	Mount Holly
239	2	Southern Regional	Manahawkin
239	2	Upper Freehold Regional	Allentown
239	2	Warren Hills Regional	Washington
239	2	Washington Twp	Robbinsville
239	2	West Morris Regional	Chester
265	1	High Point Regional	Sussex
265	1	Hunterdon Central Reg	Flemington
265	1	Mainland Regional	Linwood
265	1	Passaic County Vocational	Wayne
265	1	Watchung Hills Regional	Warren

Number of Teachers

Rank	Number	District Name	City
1	3,687	Newark City	Newark
2	2,701	Jersey City	Jersey City

3	2,419	Paterson City	Paterson
4	2,007	Elizabeth City	Elizabeth
5	1,547	Camden City	Camden
6	1,176	Toms River Regional	Toms River
7	1,040	Edison Twp	Edison
8	1,017	Trenton City	Trenton
9	996	Woodbridge Twp	Woodbridge
10	949	Hamilton Twp	Hamilton Square
11	894	Passaic City	Passaic
12	881	East Orange	East Orange
13	850	Vineland City	Vineland
14	823	Union City	Union City
15	818	Cherry Hill Twp	Cherry Hill
16	786	Clifton City	Clifton
17	777	Brick Twp	Brick
18	755	Middletown Twp	Middletown
19	739	Freehold Regional	Englishtown
20	736	Washington Twp	Sewell
21	727	Perth Amboy City	Perth Amboy
22	695	W Windsor-Plainsboro Reg	Princeton Jct
23	670	Old Bridge Twp	Matawan
24	662	Bridgewater-Raritan Reg	Bridgewater
25	660	Jackson Twp	Jackson
26	649	Plainfield City	Plainfield
27	636	Bayonne City	Bayonne
28	625	Wayne Twp	Wayne
29	622	East Brunswick Twp	E Brunswick
30	622	South Brunswick Twp	Monmouth Jct
31	616	Atlantic City	Atlantic City
32	614	Hillsborough Twp	Neshanic
33	592	New Brunswick City	New Brunswick
34	583	Parsippany-Troy Hills Twp	Parsippany
35	567	Irvington Township	Irvington
36	544	Union Twp	Union
37	544	Montclair Town	Montclair
38	544	Gloucester Twp	Blackwood
39	538	Lenape Regional	Shamong
40	530	Howell Twp	Howell
41	520	West New York Town	West New York
42	515	West Orange Town	West Orange
43	514	Winslow Twp	Atco
44	514	Pemberton Twp	Pemberton
45	511	Millville City	Millville
46	506	Franklin Twp	Somerset
47	504	Piscataway Twp	Piscataway
48	489	Long Branch City	Long Branch
49	486	Egg Harbor Twp	W Atlantic City
50	482	North Bergen Twp	North Bergen
51	476	Lakewood Twp	Lakewood
52	469	Willingboro Twp	Willingboro
53	462	South Orange-Maplewood	Maplewood
54	460	Linden City	Linden
55	448	Westfield Town	Westfield
56	445	Bloomfield Twp	Bloomfield
57	427	Pennsauken Twp	Pennsauken
58	418	Livingston Twp	Livingston
59	416	Randolph Twp	Randolph
60	406	Evesham Twp	Marlton
61	406	Morris SD	Morristown
62	400	Bridgeton City	Bridgeton
63	399	Marlboro Twp	Marlboro
64	395	North Brunswick Twp	North Brunswick
65	395	Bernards Twp	Basking Ridge
66	395	Kearny Town	Kearny
67	390	Manalapan-Englishtown Reg	Englishtown
68	387	Sayreville Boro	Sayreville
69	387	Ridgewood Village	Ridgewood
70	382	Pleasantville City	Pleasantville
71	379	Hackensack City	Hackensack
72	375	City of Orange Twp	Orange
73	366	Monroe Twp	Williamstown
74	360	East Windsor Regional	Hightstown
75	352	Mount Olive Twp	Budd Lake
76	352	Garfield City	Garfield
77	350	Fair Lawn Boro	Fair Lawn
78	350	Scotch Plains-Fanwood Reg	Scotch Plains
79	348	Teaneck Twp	Teaneck
80	348	Vernon Twp	Vernon
81	345	Roxbury Twp	Succasunna
82	344	Millburn Twp	Millburn
83	344	Lacey Twp	Lanoka Harbor
84	339	Paramus Boro	Paramus
85	337	Mount Laurel Twp	Mount Laurel
86	334	Phillipsburg Town	Phillipsburg
87	332	West Milford Twp	West Milford
88	330	Montgomery Twp	Skillman
89	328	Neptune Twp	Neptune
90	326	Ocean Twp	Oakhurst
91	326	Wall Twp	Wall
92	325	Galloway Twp	Galloway
93	325	Belleville Town	Belleville
94	323	Ewing Twp	Ewing
95	321	Monroe Twp	Monroe Township
96	321	Hopewell Valley Regional	Pennington
97	310	Lawrence Twp	Lawrenceville
98	307	Asbury Park City	Asbury Park
99	300	Matawan-Aberdeen Regional	Aberdeen
100	298	South Plainfield Boro	S Plainfield
101	296	Moorestown Twp	Moorestown
102	294	Montville Twp	Montville
103	289	Freehold Twp	Freehold
104	289	Burlington Twp	Burlington
105	286	North Plainfield Boro	N Plainfield
106	286	Deptford Twp	Deptford
107	282	Southern Regional	Manahawkin
108	281	Rahway City	Rahway
109	280	Summit City	Summit
110	280	Carteret Boro	Carteret
111	279	Nutley Town	Nutley
112	278	Princeton Regional	Princeton
113	268	Cranford Twp	Cranford
114	266	Bergenfield Boro	Bergenfield
115	266	Manchester Twp	Whiting
116	263	Hazlet Twp	Hazlet
117	262	Flemington-Raritan Reg	Flemington
118	262	Jefferson Twp	Lake Hopatcong
119	262	Mahwah Twp	Mahwah
120	261	Sparta Twp	Sparta
121	260	Greater Egg Harbor Reg	Mays Landing
122	259	Tenafly Boro	Tenafly
123	258	Voorhees Twp	Voorhees
124	257	Black Horse Pike Regional	Blackwood
125	250	Rockaway Twp	Hibernia
126	249	Fort Lee Boro	Fort Lee
127	241	Holmdel Twp	Holmdel
128	237	Englewood City	Englewood
129	233	SD of the Chathams	Chatham
130	231	Middle Twp	Cape May Ct Hse
131	230	Hamilton Twp	Mays Landing
132	230	Lodi Borough	Lodi
133	226	Point Pleasant Boro	Pt Pleasant
134	224	Ramsey Boro	Ramsey
135	222	Dover Town	Dover
136	221	Gloucester City	Gloucester City
137	220	Hillside Twp	Hillside
138	219	Hunterdon Central Reg	Flemington
139	216	Lindenwold Boro	Lindenwold
140	216	Morris Hills Regional	Rockaway
141	216	Keansburg Boro	Keansburg
142	214	Bergen County Vocational	Paramus
143	212	Monmouth County Vocational	Colts Neck
144	211	Ocean City	Ocean City
145	209	Hammonton Town	Hammonton
146	209	Warren Twp	Warren
147	208	N Hunt/Voorhees Regional	Annandale
148	208	Berkeley Heights Twp	Berkeley Hgts
148	208	Hoboken City	Hoboken
150	207	West Deptford Twp	West Deptford
151	206	Westwood Regional	Westwood
152	205	Northern Valley Regional	Demarest
153	205	Middlesex County Vocational	E Brunswick
154	202	Cinnaminson Twp	Cinnaminson
155	201	Roselle Boro	Roselle
156	196	Passaic County Vocational	Wayne
157	193	Hopatcong	Hopatcong
157	193	West Morris Regional	Chester
159	192	Washington Twp	Long Valley
160	192	Penns Grv-Carney's Pt Reg	Penns Grove
160	192	Pine Hill Boro	Pine Hill
162	191	Cliffside Park Boro	Cliffside Park
163	191	Glassboro	Glassboro
164	188	Ramapo-Indian Hill Reg	Franklin Lakes
165	188	Buena Regional	Buena
166	186	Bergen County Special Service	Paramus
167	185	Hawthorne Boro	Hawthorne
168	185	Caldwell-West Caldwell	West Caldwell
169	185	Glen Rock Boro	Glen Rock
170	185	Dumont Boro	Dumont
171	184	Rutherford Boro	Rutherford
172	184	Medford Twp	Medford
173	182	Pequannock Twp	Pompton Plains
174	182	Delran Twp	Delran
175	180	Burlington City	Burlington
176	177	Pinelands Regional	Tuckerton
177	176	Madison Boro	Madison
178	175	Clark Twp	Clark
178	175	Essex County Voc-Tech	West Orange
180	173	Readington Twp	Whitehouse Stn
181	173	Stafford Twp	Manahawkin
182	172	Somerville Boro	Somerville
183	172	Barnegat Twp	Barnegat
184	171	Leonia Boro	Leonia
185	170	New Providence Boro	New Providence
186	169	Camden County Vocational	Sicklerville
187	168	Mountain Lakes Boro	Mountain Lakes
188	167	Haddonfield Boro	Haddonfield
189	166	Ridgefield Park Twp	Ridgefield Park
190	165	Wyckoff Twp	Wyckoff
191	165	Middlesex Boro	Middlesex
192	163	Collingswood Boro	Collingswood
193	161	Roselle Park Boro	Roselle Park
194	160	Springfield Twp	Springfield
195	159	Pennsville	Pennsville
196	159	Branchburg Twp	Branchburg
197	158	Burlington County Vocational	Westampton Twp
198	157	Warren Hills Regional	Washington
199	157	Ridgefield Boro	Ridgefield
200	156	Maple Shade Twp	Maple Shade
201	155	Bordentown Regional	Bordentown
202	154	Metuchen Boro	Metuchen
203	153	Clearview Regional	Mullica Hill
204	152	Burlington County Spec Serv	Mount Holly
205	151	Haddon Twp	Westmont
206	151	Eastern Camden County Reg	Voorhees
207	151	Kinnelon Boro	Kinnelon
208	150	Lower Cape May Regional	Cape May
209	149	Lyndhurst Twp	Lyndhurst
210	149	Hackettstown	Hackettstown
211	149	South River Boro	South River
212	148	Central Regional	Bayville
213	145	Woodbury City	Woodbury
214	145	Northern Burlington Reg	Columbus
215	143	Secaucus Town	Secaucus
216	143	Verona Boro	Verona
217	143	Somerset Hills Regional	Bernardsville
218	141	Lower Twp	Cape May
219	140	New Milford Boro	New Milford
220	139	Upper Freehold Regional	Allentown
221	139	Pitman Boro	Pitman
222	138	Delsea Regional H.S District	Franklinville
223	137	Little Egg Harbor Twp	Little Egg Hbr
224	137	Sussex-Wantage Regional	Wantage
225	137	Mercer County Special Service	Trenton
226	137	Newton Town	Newton
227	136	Clinton Twp	Annandale
228	134	Elmwood Park	Elmwood Park
229	133	Harrison Town	Harrison
230	133	Pompton Lakes Boro	Pompton Lakes
231	133	Spotswood Boro	Spotswood
232	133	Berkeley Twp	Bayville
232	133	Pascack Valley Regional	Montvale
234	132	Pittsgrove Twp	Pittsgrove
234	132	Watchung Hills Regional	Warren
236	131	Upper Twp	Petersburg
237	130	Rancocas Valley Regional	Mount Holly
238	130	Denville Twp	Denville
239	129	Florence Twp	Florence
240	129	Lumberton Twp	Lumberton
241	128	Mainland Regional	Linwood
242	127	Colts Neck Twp	Colts Neck
243	126	Salem City	Salem
244	126	Glen Ridge Boro	Glen Ridge
245	125	Audubon Boro	Audubon
246	124	Woodstown-Pilesgrove Reg	Woodstown
247	123	Washington Twp	Robbinsville
248	123	Millstone Twp	Clarksburg
248	123	Oakland Boro	Oakland
248	123	Plumsted Twp	New Egypt
251	123	Kingsway Regional	Woolwich Twp
252	122	Manasquan Boro	Manasquan
253	122	Tinton Falls	Tinton Falls
254	122	Highland Park Boro	Highland Park
255	121	Franklin Lakes Boro	Franklin Lakes
256	118	Saddle Brook Twp	Saddle Brook
257	117	Hanover Twp	Whippany
258	117	Hasbrouck Heights Boro	Hasbrouck Hgts
259	116	Bound Brook Boro	Bound Brook
260	116	Paulsboro Boro	Paulsboro
261	114	Waldwick Boro	Waldwick
262	113	Cedar Grove Twp	Cedar Grove
262	113	North Arlington Boro	North Arlington
264	111	Palisades Park	Palisades Park
265	107	High Point Regional	Sussex
266	107	Cresskill Boro	Cresskill
267	100	Mantua Twp	Sewell
268	100	Riverside Twp	Riverside
269	94	Franklin Twp	Franklinville

Number of Students

Rank	Number	District Name	City
1	46,825	Newark City	Newark
2	35,161	Jersey City	Jersey City
3	27,734	Paterson City	Paterson
4	21,998	Elizabeth City	Elizabeth
5	19,190	Toms River Regional	Toms River
6	18,997	Camden City	Camden
7	14,074	Hamilton Twp	Hamilton Square

8	14,056	Woodbridge Twp	Woodbridge
9	13,293	Edison Twp	Edison
10	13,227	Trenton City	Trenton
11	12,403	East Orange	East Orange
12	12,162	Passaic City	Passaic
13	12,065	Brick Twp	Brick
14	11,911	Cherry Hill Twp	Cherry Hill
15	10,984	Clifton City	Clifton
16	10,935	Freehold Regional	Englishtown
17	10,777	Middletown Twp	Middletown
18	10,436	Union City	Union City
19	10,316	Vineland City	Vineland
20	10,119	Old Bridge Twp	Matawan
21	9,859	Washington Twp	Sewell
22	9,762	Jackson Twp	Jackson
22	9,762	Perth Amboy City	Perth Amboy
24	9,430	Bayonne City	Bayonne
25	9,238	W Windsor-Plainsboro Reg	Princeton Jct
26	9,141	East Brunswick Twp	E Brunswick
27	9,097	Wayne Twp	Wayne
28	8,894	Bridgewater-Raritan Reg	Bridgewater
29	8,830	Irvington Township	Irvington
30	8,506	South Brunswick Twp	Monmouth Jct
31	8,119	Plainfield City	Plainfield
32	8,105	Union Twp	Union
33	8,090	Gloucester Twp	Blackwood
34	7,989	North Bergen Twp	North Bergen
35	7,782	Hillsborough Twp	Neshanic
36	7,648	Howell Twp	Howell
37	7,290	Atlantic City	Atlantic City
38	7,201	Parsippany-Troy Hills Twp	Parsippany
39	7,153	West New York Town	West New York
40	7,067	Lenape Regional	Shamong
41	6,991	Piscataway Twp	Piscataway
42	6,989	New Brunswick City	New Brunswick
43	6,840	Franklin Twp	Somerset
44	6,805	Egg Harbor Twp	W Atlantic City
45	6,742	Winslow Twp	Atco
46	6,646	Pennsauken Twp	Pennsauken
47	6,617	Montclair Town	Montclair
48	6,588	West Orange Town	West Orange
49	6,559	South Orange-Maplewood	Maplewood
50	6,508	Linden City	Linden
51	6,354	Bloomfield Twp	Bloomfield
52	6,226	Millville City	Millville
53	6,210	Pemberton Twp	Pemberton
54	6,084	Marlboro Twp	Marlboro
55	5,924	Sayreville Boro	Sayreville
56	5,909	Westfield Town	Westfield
57	5,888	Kearny Town	Kearny
58	5,875	Willingboro Twp	Willingboro
59	5,807	Lakewood Twp	Lakewood
60	5,708	Evesham Twp	Marlton
61	5,640	Manalapan-Englishtown Reg	Englishtown
62	5,624	Randolph Twp	Randolph
63	5,593	Monroe Twp	Williamstown
64	5,560	Ridgewood Village	Ridgewood
65	5,519	North Brunswick Twp	North Brunswick
66	5,500	Vernon Twp	Vernon
67	5,323	Lacey Twp	Lanoka Harbor
68	5,264	Long Branch City	Long Branch
69	5,216	Livingston Twp	Livingston
70	5,152	East Windsor Regional	Hightstown
71	5,149	Hackensack City	Hackensack
72	5,100	Bernards Twp	Basking Ridge
73	5,004	Scotch Plains-Fanwood Reg	Scotch Plains
74	4,982	Ocean Twp	Oakhurst
75	4,961	Mount Olive Twp	Budd Lake
76	4,878	West Milford Twp	West Milford
77	4,876	Morris SD	Morristown
78	4,865	Fair Lawn Boro	Fair Lawn
79	4,852	Lawrence Twp	Lawrenceville
80	4,817	Roxbury Twp	Succasunna
81	4,798	City of Orange Twp	Orange
82	4,787	Freehold Twp	Freehold
83	4,761	Bridgeton City	Bridgeton
84	4,729	Belleville Town	Belleville
85	4,726	Mount Laurel Twp	Mount Laurel
86	4,721	Montgomery Twp	Skillman
87	4,587	Garfield City	Garfield
88	4,576	Paramus Boro	Paramus
89	4,559	Neptune Twp	Neptune
90	4,512	Teaneck Twp	Teaneck
91	4,476	Deptford Twp	Deptford
92	4,438	Black Horse Pike Regional	Blackwood
93	4,395	Nutley Town	Nutley
94	4,365	Millburn Twp	Millburn
95	4,360	Wall Twp	Wall
96	4,316	Moorestown Twp	Moorestown
97	4,178	Ewing Twp	Ewing
98	4,163	Southern Regional	Manahawkin
99	4,155	Rahway City	Rahway
100	4,138	Galloway Twp	Galloway
101	4,124	Monroe Twp	Monroe Township
102	4,098	Burlington Twp	Burlington
103	4,067	Pleasantville City	Pleasantville
104	4,030	Montville Twp	Montville
105	4,025	Sparta Twp	Sparta
106	3,957	Carteret Boro	Carteret
107	3,953	Matawan-Aberdeen Regional	Aberdeen
108	3,906	South Plainfield Boro	S Plainfield
109	3,900	Bergenfield Boro	Bergenfield
110	3,879	Hopewell Valley Regional	Pennington
111	3,844	Greater Egg Harbor Reg	Mays Landing
112	3,715	Phillipsburg Town	Phillipsburg
113	3,694	Jefferson Twp	Lake Hopatcong
114	3,683	Flemington-Raritan Reg	Flemington
115	3,642	Cranford Twp	Cranford
116	3,626	Hillside Twp	Hillside
117	3,617	Holmdel Twp	Holmdel
118	3,580	Manchester Twp	Whiting
119	3,561	Hazlet Twp	Hazlet
120	3,519	Voorhees Twp	Voorhees
121	3,515	Summit City	Summit
122	3,461	Fort Lee Boro	Fort Lee
123	3,391	Dover Town	Dover
124	3,372	Hammonton Town	Hammonton
125	3,355	Mahwah Twp	Mahwah
126	3,352	North Plainfield Boro	N Plainfield
127	3,326	West Deptford Twp	West Deptford
128	3,304	Princeton Regional	Princeton
129	3,238	Point Pleasant Boro	Pt Pleasant
130	3,199	SD of the Chathams	Chatham
131	3,187	Hopatcong	Hopatcong
132	3,181	Asbury Park City	Asbury Park
133	3,176	Lodi Borough	Lodi
134	3,128	Tenafly Boro	Tenafly
135	3,073	Washington Twp	Long Valley
136	3,065	Hamilton Twp	Mays Landing
137	3,038	Ramsey Boro	Ramsey
138	3,028	Medford Twp	Medford
139	2,985	Rockaway Twp	Hibernia
140	2,949	Middle Twp	Cape May Ct Hse
141	2,899	Roselle Boro	Roselle
142	2,839	Hunterdon Central Reg	Flemington
143	2,808	Lindenwold Boro	Lindenwold
144	2,803	Englewood City	Englewood
145	2,797	Berkeley Heights Twp	Berkeley Hgts
146	2,780	Delran Twp	Delran
147	2,779	N Hunt/Voorhees Regional	Annandale
148	2,760	Clark Twp	Clark
149	2,727	Cliffside Park Boro	Cliffside Park
149	2,727	Stafford Twp	Manahawkin
151	2,717	Dumont Boro	Dumont
152	2,696	Morris Hills Regional	Rockaway
153	2,663	Westwood Regional	Westwood
154	2,642	Cinnaminson Twp	Cinnaminson
155	2,627	Buena Regional	Buena
155	2,627	Caldwell-West Caldwell	West Caldwell
157	2,620	Camden County Vocational	Sicklerville
158	2,555	Glassboro	Glassboro
159	2,541	Pequannock Twp	Pompton Plains
160	2,472	Burlington County Spec Serv	Mount Holly
161	2,446	Wyckoff Twp	Wyckoff
162	2,431	Pine Hill Boro	Pine Hill
163	2,404	Maple Shade Twp	Maple Shade
164	2,402	West Morris Regional	Chester
165	2,399	Glen Rock Boro	Glen Rock
165	2,399	Passaic County Vocational	Wayne
165	2,399	Rutherford Boro	Rutherford
168	2,376	Barnegat Twp	Barnegat
169	2,371	Penns Grv-Carney's Pt Reg	Penns Grove
170	2,368	Essex County Voc-Tech	West Orange
171	2,357	Central Regional	Bayville
171	2,357	Haddon Twp	Westmont
173	2,345	Hawthorne Boro	Hawthorne
174	2,336	Ridgefield Boro	Ridgefield
175	2,331	Bergen County Vocational	Paramus
176	2,327	Northern Valley Regional	Demarest
177	2,317	Haddonfield Boro	Haddonfield
178	2,315	Middlesex County Vocational	E Brunswick
179	2,298	Readington Twp	Whitehouse Stn
180	2,290	Madison Boro	Madison
181	2,273	Gloucester City	Gloucester City
182	2,269	Rancocas Valley Regional	Mount Holly
183	2,247	South River Boro	South River
184	2,236	Somerville Boro	Somerville
185	2,229	Warren Twp	Warren
186	2,224	Ocean City	Ocean City
187	2,218	Hoboken City	Hoboken
188	2,216	Warren Hills Regional	Washington
189	2,205	Eastern Camden County Reg	Voorhees
190	2,194	Keansburg Boro	Keansburg
191	2,192	Clearview Regional	Mullica Hill
191	2,192	Lyndhurst Twp	Lyndhurst
193	2,185	New Providence Boro	New Providence
194	2,179	Middlesex Boro	Middlesex
195	2,157	Kinnelon Boro	Kinnelon
196	2,134	Ramapo-Indian Hill Reg	Franklin Lakes
197	2,114	Elmwood Park	Elmwood Park
198	2,105	Pennsville	Pennsville
199	2,101	Roselle Park Boro	Roselle Park
200	2,083	Springfield Twp	Springfield
201	2,075	Collingswood Boro	Collingswood
202	2,062	Bordentown Regional	Bordentown
203	2,061	Pinelands Regional	Tuckerton
204	2,055	Verona Boro	Verona
205	2,040	Upper Freehold Regional	Allentown
206	2,005	Harrison Town	Harrison
207	2,000	Lower Twp	Cape May
208	1,989	Delsea Regional H.S District	Franklinville
209	1,983	Berkeley Twp	Bayville
210	1,982	Bergen County Special Service	Paramus
211	1,980	Hackettstown	Hackettstown
212	1,959	Denville Twp	Denville
212	1,959	Ridgefield Park Twp	Ridgefield Park
214	1,949	Clinton Twp	Annandale
215	1,943	New Milford Boro	New Milford
216	1,933	Branchburg Twp	Branchburg
217	1,927	Northern Burlington Reg	Columbus
218	1,919	Burlington City	Burlington
219	1,915	Somerset Hills Regional	Bernardsville
220	1,910	Pompton Lakes Boro	Pompton Lakes
221	1,892	Secaucus Town	Secaucus
222	1,878	Pittsgrove Twp	Pittsgrove
223	1,872	Metuchen Boro	Metuchen
224	1,856	Monmouth County Vocational	Colts Neck
225	1,845	Lower Cape May Regional	Cape May
226	1,844	Little Egg Harbor Twp	Little Egg Hbr
226	1,844	Lumberton Twp	Lumberton
228	1,842	Mountain Lakes Boro	Mountain Lakes
229	1,829	Sussex-Wantage Regional	Wantage
230	1,826	Spotswood Boro	Spotswood
231	1,809	Leonia Boro	Leonia
232	1,804	Manasquan Boro	Manasquan
233	1,803	Burlington County Vocational	Westampton Twp
234	1,797	Glen Ridge Boro	Glen Ridge
234	1,797	Tinton Falls	Tinton Falls
236	1,779	Newton Town	Newton
237	1,772	Plumsted Twp	New Egypt
238	1,767	Upper Twp	Petersburg
239	1,763	Saddle Brook Twp	Saddle Brook
240	1,755	Audubon Boro	Audubon
241	1,752	Mercer County Special Service	Trenton
242	1,751	Kingsway Regional	Woolwich Twp
243	1,735	Millstone Twp	Clarksburg
243	1,735	Watchung Hills Regional	Warren
245	1,700	Woodstown-Pilesgrove Reg	Woodstown
246	1,695	Pitman Boro	Pitman
247	1,692	Oakland Boro	Oakland
248	1,679	Bound Brook Boro	Bound Brook
249	1,671	Franklin Lakes Boro	Franklin Lakes
250	1,670	Paulsboro Boro	Paulsboro
251	1,669	Mainland Regional	Linwood
252	1,641	Florence Twp	Florence
253	1,629	Riverside Twp	Riverside
254	1,624	North Arlington Boro	North Arlington
255	1,614	Pascack Valley Regional	Montvale
256	1,609	Woodbury City	Woodbury
257	1,606	Highland Park Boro	Highland Park
258	1,558	Hasbrouck Heights Boro	Hasbrouck Hgts
259	1,544	Colts Neck Twp	Colts Neck
259	1,544	Washington Twp	Robbinsville
261	1,540	High Point Regional	Sussex
262	1,518	Mantua Twp	Sewell
262	1,518	Salem City	Salem
264	1,514	Palisades Park	Palisades Park
265	1,512	Waldwick Boro	Waldwick
266	1,511	Cedar Grove Twp	Cedar Grove
267	1,509	Cresskill Boro	Cresskill
268	1,506	Franklin Twp	Franklinville
269	1,504	Hanover Twp	Whippany

Male Students

Rank	Percent	District Name	City
1	71.6	Burlington County Spec Serv	Mount Holly
2	71.0	Mercer County Special Service	Trenton
3	64.4	Bergen County Special Service	Paramus
4	58.4	Middlesex County Vocational	E Brunswick
5	55.5	Monmouth County Vocational	Colts Neck
6	55.2	Mantua Twp	Sewell
7	55.2	Lower Twp	Cape May
8	54.9	Ridgefield Boro	Ridgefield
9	54.9	Bergen County Vocational	Paramus
10	54.2	Franklin Twp	Franklinville
11	53.9	North Arlington Boro	North Arlington
12	53.7	Camden County Vocational	Sicklerville

13	53.6	New Milford Boro	New Milford
14	53.5	Cranford Twp	Cranford
15	53.5	Burlington City	Burlington
16	53.4	Hanover Twp	Whippany
17	53.4	Newton Town	Newton
18	53.3	Cinnaminson Twp	Cinnaminson
19	53.3	Keansburg Boro	Keansburg
20	53.2	Rockaway Twp	Hibernia
21	53.2	West Deptford Twp	West Deptford
22	53.1	Pleasantville City	Pleasantville
23	53.0	Phillipsburg Town	Phillipsburg
24	52.9	Cliffside Park Boro	Cliffside Park
25	52.9	Clark Twp	Clark
26	52.8	Sayreville Boro	Sayreville
27	52.8	Palisades Park	Palisades Park
28	52.8	Hoboken City	Hoboken
29	52.8	Mountain Lakes Boro	Mountain Lakes
30	52.8	Lindenwold Boro	Lindenwold
31	52.8	Plumsted Twp	New Egypt
32	52.7	Morris SD	Morristown
33	52.7	Tenafly Boro	Tenafly
34	52.7	Dover Town	Dover
35	52.7	West Milford Twp	West Milford
36	52.6	Ramsey Boro	Ramsey
37	52.6	South River Boro	South River
38	52.6	Glen Rock Boro	Glen Rock
39	52.6	Rahway City	Rahway
40	52.5	Spotswood Boro	Spotswood
41	52.5	Upper Freehold Regional	Allentown
42	52.5	Pennsauken Twp	Pennsauken
43	52.5	Central Regional	Bayville
44	52.5	Berkeley Twp	Bayville
45	52.5	Stafford Twp	Manahawkin
46	52.5	Paulsboro Boro	Paulsboro
47	52.5	Harrison Town	Harrison
48	52.5	Cherry Hill Twp	Cherry Hill
49	52.4	Perth Amboy City	Perth Amboy
50	52.4	Monroe Twp	Monroe Township
51	52.4	Paramus Boro	Paramus
52	52.3	Warren Hills Regional	Washington
53	52.3	Eastern Camden County Reg	Voorhees
54	52.3	Oakland Boro	Oakland
55	52.3	Hillsborough Twp	Neshanic
56	52.2	Clifton City	Clifton
57	52.2	Neptune Twp	Neptune
58	52.2	Middle Twp	Cape May Ct Hse
59	52.1	Lower Cape May Regional	Cape May
60	52.1	Franklin Lakes Boro	Franklin Lakes
61	52.1	Bayonne City	Bayonne
62	52.1	Gloucester Twp	Blackwood
63	52.1	Brick Twp	Brick
64	52.1	Westwood Regional	Westwood
65	52.1	Parsippany-Troy Hills Twp	Parsippany
66	52.1	Middletown Twp	Middletown
67	52.0	Summit City	Summit
68	52.0	Ridgefield Park Twp	Ridgefield Park
69	52.0	Kearny Town	Kearny
70	52.0	Flemington-Raritan Reg	Flemington
71	52.0	Union Twp	Union
72	52.0	Point Pleasant Boro	Pt Pleasant
73	52.0	Burlington County Vocational	Westampton Twp
74	52.0	Springfield Twp	Springfield
75	52.0	Upper Twp	Petersburg
76	52.0	Wall Twp	Wall
77	51.9	Pequannock Twp	Pompton Plains
78	51.9	Bloomfield Twp	Bloomfield
79	51.9	Hopatcong	Hopatcong
80	51.9	Glen Ridge Boro	Glen Ridge
81	51.9	Bound Brook Boro	Bound Brook
82	51.9	Carteret Boro	Carteret
83	51.9	Madison Boro	Madison
84	51.9	Willingboro Twp	Willingboro
85	51.8	North Bergen Twp	North Bergen
86	51.8	New Providence Boro	New Providence
86	51.8	Verona Boro	Verona
88	51.8	Vernon Twp	Vernon
89	51.8	Vineland City	Vineland
90	51.8	Manchester Twp	Whiting
91	51.8	City of Orange Twp	Orange
92	51.8	Lakewood Twp	Lakewood
93	51.8	Livingston Twp	Livingston
94	51.8	Irvington Township	Irvington
95	51.7	Winslow Twp	Atco
96	51.7	Roxbury Twp	Succasunna
97	51.7	Audubon Boro	Audubon
98	51.7	Evesham Twp	Marlton
99	51.7	Belleville Town	Belleville
100	51.7	Berkeley Heights Twp	Berkeley Hgts
101	51.7	Lawrence Twp	Lawrenceville
102	51.7	Little Egg Harbor Twp	Little Egg Hbr
103	51.6	Egg Harbor Twp	W Atlantic City
104	51.6	Kinnelon Boro	Kinnelon
105	51.6	South Plainfield Boro	S Plainfield
106	51.6	Jackson Twp	Jackson
107	51.6	Lumberton Twp	Lumberton
108	51.6	Branchburg Twp	Branchburg
109	51.6	Cedar Grove Twp	Cedar Grove
110	51.6	Hamilton Twp	Mays Landing
111	51.6	Fort Lee Boro	Fort Lee
112	51.5	Mount Laurel Twp	Mount Laurel
113	51.5	East Brunswick Twp	E Brunswick
114	51.5	Westfield Town	Westfield
115	51.5	Voorhees Twp	Voorhees
116	51.5	Hackettstown	Hackettstown
117	51.5	Pittsgrove Twp	Pittsgrove
118	51.5	Metuchen Boro	Metuchen
119	51.5	Montgomery Twp	Skillman
120	51.5	Marlboro Twp	Marlboro
121	51.4	Hamilton Twp	Hamilton Square
122	51.4	Sparta Twp	Sparta
123	51.4	Lacey Twp	Lanoka Harbor
124	51.4	Hawthorne Boro	Hawthorne
125	51.4	Toms River Regional	Toms River
126	51.4	Fair Lawn Boro	Fair Lawn
127	51.4	Princeton Regional	Princeton
128	51.3	Holmdel Twp	Holmdel
129	51.3	Old Bridge Twp	Matawan
130	51.3	Deptford Twp	Deptford
131	51.3	Union City	Union City
132	51.3	Jefferson Twp	Lake Hopatcong
133	51.3	Wayne Twp	Wayne
134	51.3	Bridgeton City	Bridgeton
135	51.3	SD of the Chathams	Chatham
136	51.3	Riverside Twp	Riverside
137	51.3	Jersey City	Jersey City
138	51.3	Newark City	Newark
139	51.3	Mount Olive Twp	Budd Lake
140	51.3	Delsea Regional H.S District	Franklinville
141	51.3	Ewing Twp	Ewing
142	51.3	Somerville Boro	Somerville
143	51.3	Monroe Twp	Williamstown
144	51.3	Watchung Hills Regional	Warren
145	51.3	Mahwah Twp	Mahwah
146	51.3	Black Horse Pike Regional	Blackwood
147	51.2	Tinton Falls	Tinton Falls
148	51.2	East Windsor Regional	Hightstown
149	51.2	Piscataway Twp	Piscataway
150	51.2	Franklin Twp	Somerset
151	51.2	Middlesex Boro	Middlesex
152	51.2	Readington Twp	Whitehouse Stn
153	51.2	Woodbridge Twp	Woodbridge
154	51.2	Washington Twp	Sewell
155	51.2	Maple Shade Twp	Maple Shade
156	51.2	Scotch Plains-Fanwood Reg	Scotch Plains
157	51.2	New Brunswick City	New Brunswick
158	51.2	Lyndhurst Twp	Lyndhurst
159	51.2	Collingswood Boro	Collingswood
160	51.2	Long Branch City	Long Branch
161	51.2	Ocean City	Ocean City
162	51.1	Elmwood Park	Elmwood Park
163	51.1	Plainfield City	Plainfield
164	51.1	Montville Twp	Montville
165	51.1	Morris Hills Regional	Rockaway
166	51.1	Pine Hill Boro	Pine Hill
167	51.1	Secaucus Town	Secaucus
168	51.0	Colts Neck Twp	Colts Neck
169	51.0	Buena Regional	Buena
170	51.0	Northern Burlington Reg	Columbus
171	51.0	South Orange-Maplewood	Maplewood
172	51.0	Haddon Twp	Westmont
173	51.0	Florence Twp	Florence
174	51.0	Kingsway Regional	Woolwich Twp
175	51.0	Rutherford Boro	Rutherford
176	51.0	Bernards Twp	Basking Ridge
177	51.0	Ridgewood Village	Ridgewood
178	50.9	W Windsor-Plainsboro Reg	Princeton Jct
179	50.9	Pemberton Twp	Pemberton
180	50.9	Glassboro	Glassboro
181	50.9	Woodbury City	Woodbury
182	50.9	Randolph Twp	Randolph
183	50.9	Woodstown-Pilesgrove Reg	Woodstown
184	50.8	North Brunswick Twp	North Brunswick
185	50.8	Hillside Twp	Hillside
186	50.8	Teaneck Twp	Teaneck
187	50.8	Bridgewater-Raritan Reg	Bridgewater
188	50.8	Paterson City	Paterson
189	50.8	Matawan-Aberdeen Regional	Aberdeen
190	50.8	Hopewell Valley Regional	Pennington
191	50.8	Howell Twp	Howell
192	50.7	Millburn Twp	Millburn
193	50.7	Ocean Twp	Oakhurst
194	50.7	West New York Town	West New York
195	50.7	Roselle Boro	Roselle
196	50.7	Highland Park Boro	Highland Park
197	50.7	Medford Twp	Medford
198	50.7	Clearview Regional	Mullica Hill
199	50.7	Garfield City	Garfield
200	50.7	Somerset Hills Regional	Bernardsville
201	50.7	Nutley Town	Nutley
202	50.7	Linden City	Linden
203	50.6	West Orange Town	West Orange
204	50.6	Pascack Valley Regional	Montvale
205	50.6	Hackensack City	Hackensack
206	50.6	Galloway Twp	Galloway
207	50.6	Lodi Borough	Lodi
208	50.6	Southern Regional	Manahawkin
209	50.5	Roselle Park Boro	Roselle Park
210	50.5	Atlantic City	Atlantic City
211	50.5	Bordentown Regional	Bordentown
212	50.5	Montclair Town	Montclair
213	50.5	Denville Twp	Denville
214	50.4	Delran Twp	Delran
215	50.4	West Morris Regional	Chester
216	50.4	Elizabeth City	Elizabeth
217	50.4	Bergenfield Boro	Bergenfield
218	50.3	Moorestown Twp	Moorestown
219	50.3	Penns Grv-Carney's Pt Reg	Penns Grove
220	50.3	Millstone Twp	Clarksburg
221	50.3	North Plainfield Boro	N Plainfield
222	50.3	South Brunswick Twp	Monmouth Jct
223	50.3	Trenton City	Trenton
224	50.3	Edison Twp	Edison
225	50.3	Freehold Twp	Freehold
226	50.2	Waldwick Boro	Waldwick
227	50.2	Hunterdon Central Reg	Flemington
228	50.2	Burlington Twp	Burlington
229	50.2	Caldwell-West Caldwell	West Caldwell
230	50.2	Rancocas Valley Regional	Mount Holly
231	50.2	Manasquan Boro	Manasquan
232	50.2	Pinelands Regional	Tuckerton
233	50.2	Hammonton Town	Hammonton
234	50.1	Northern Valley Regional	Demarest
235	50.1	Clinton Twp	Annandale
236	50.1	Englewood City	Englewood
237	50.1	Pennsville	Pennsville
238	50.1	Camden City	Camden
239	50.0	Greater Egg Harbor Reg	Mays Landing
240	50.0	Haddonfield Boro	Haddonfield
241	50.0	Barnegat Twp	Barnegat
241	50.0	Cresskill Boro	Cresskill
241	50.0	Hasbrouck Heights Boro	Hasbrouck Hgts
241	50.0	Millville City	Millville
245	49.9	Manalapan-Englishtown Reg	Englishtown
246	49.9	N Hunt/Voorhees Regional	Annandale
247	49.9	Warren Twp	Warren
248	49.9	Lenape Regional	Shamong
249	49.8	Asbury Park City	Asbury Park
250	49.8	Washington Twp	Long Valley
251	49.8	Washington Twp	Robbinsville
252	49.8	Dumont Boro	Dumont
253	49.8	Passaic City	Passaic
254	49.7	Wyckoff Twp	Wyckoff
255	49.7	East Orange	East Orange
256	49.5	High Point Regional	Sussex
257	49.4	Freehold Regional	Englishtown
258	49.4	Pompton Lakes Boro	Pompton Lakes
259	49.4	Leonia Boro	Leonia
260	49.3	Passaic County Vocational	Wayne
261	49.3	Gloucester City	Gloucester City
262	49.1	Hazlet Twp	Hazlet
263	48.8	Sussex-Wantage Regional	Wantage
264	48.5	Saddle Brook Twp	Saddle Brook
265	48.1	Pitman Boro	Pitman
266	48.0	Mainland Regional	Linwood
267	47.7	Salem City	Salem
268	47.5	Ramapo-Indian Hill Reg	Franklin Lakes
269	43.1	Essex County Voc-Tech	West Orange

Female Students

Rank	Percent	District Name	City
1	56.8	Essex County Voc-Tech	West Orange
2	52.4	Ramapo-Indian Hill Reg	Franklin Lakes
3	52.2	Salem City	Salem
4	51.9	Mainland Regional	Linwood
5	51.8	Pitman Boro	Pitman
6	51.4	Saddle Brook Twp	Saddle Brook
7	51.1	Sussex-Wantage Regional	Wantage
8	50.8	Hazlet Twp	Hazlet
9	50.6	Gloucester City	Gloucester City
10	50.6	Passaic County Vocational	Wayne
11	50.5	Leonia Boro	Leonia
12	50.5	Pompton Lakes Boro	Pompton Lakes
13	50.5	Freehold Regional	Englishtown
14	50.4	High Point Regional	Sussex
15	50.2	East Orange	East Orange
16	50.2	Wyckoff Twp	Wyckoff
17	50.1	Passaic City	Passaic

18	50.1	Dumont Boro	Dumont
19	50.1	Washington Twp	Robbinsville
20	50.1	Washington Twp	Long Valley
21	50.1	Asbury Park City	Asbury Park
22	50.0	Lenape Regional	Shamong
23	50.0	Warren Twp	Warren
24	50.0	N Hunt/Voorhees Regional	Annandale
25	50.0	Manalapan-Englishtown Reg	Englishtown
26	50.0	Barnegat Twp	Barnegat
26	50.0	Cresskill Boro	Cresskill
26	50.0	Hasbrouck Heights Boro	Hasbrouck Hgts
26	50.0	Millville City	Millville
30	49.9	Haddonfield Boro	Haddonfield
31	49.9	Greater Egg Harbor Reg	Mays Landing
32	49.8	Camden City	Camden
33	49.8	Pennsville	Pennsville
34	49.8	Englewood City	Englewood
35	49.8	Clinton Twp	Annandale
36	49.8	Northern Valley Regional	Demarest
37	49.7	Hammonton Town	Hammonton
38	49.7	Pinelands Regional	Tuckerton
39	49.7	Manasquan Boro	Manasquan
40	49.7	Rancocas Valley Regional	Mount Holly
41	49.7	Caldwell-West Caldwell	West Caldwell
42	49.7	Burlington Twp	Burlington
43	49.7	Hunterdon Central Reg	Flemington
44	49.7	Waldwick Boro	Waldwick
45	49.6	Freehold Twp	Freehold
46	49.6	Edison Twp	Edison
47	49.6	Trenton City	Trenton
48	49.6	South Brunswick Twp	Monmouth Jct
49	49.6	North Plainfield Boro	N Plainfield
50	49.6	Millstone Twp	Clarksburg
51	49.6	Penns Grv-Carney's Pt Reg	Penns Grove
52	49.6	Moorestown Twp	Moorestown
53	49.5	Bergenfield Boro	Bergenfield
54	49.5	Elizabeth City	Elizabeth
55	49.5	West Morris Regional	Chester
56	49.5	Delran Twp	Delran
57	49.4	Denville Twp	Denville
58	49.4	Montclair Town	Montclair
59	49.4	Bordentown Regional	Bordentown
60	49.4	Atlantic City	Atlantic City
61	49.4	Roselle Park Boro	Roselle Park
62	49.3	Southern Regional	Manahawkin
63	49.3	Lodi Borough	Lodi
64	49.3	Galloway Twp	Galloway
65	49.3	Hackensack City	Hackensack
66	49.3	Pascack Valley Regional	Montvale
67	49.3	West Orange Town	West Orange
68	49.2	Linden City	Linden
69	49.2	Nutley Town	Nutley
70	49.2	Somerset Hills Regional	Bernardsville
71	49.2	Garfield City	Garfield
72	49.2	Clearview Regional	Mullica Hill
73	49.2	Medford Twp	Medford
74	49.2	Highland Park Boro	Highland Park
75	49.2	Roselle Boro	Roselle
76	49.2	West New York Town	West New York
77	49.2	Ocean Twp	Oakhurst
78	49.2	Millburn Twp	Millburn
79	49.1	Howell Twp	Howell
80	49.1	Hopewell Valley Regional	Pennington
81	49.1	Matawan-Aberdeen Regional	Aberdeen
82	49.1	Paterson City	Paterson
83	49.1	Bridgewater-Raritan Reg	Bridgewater
84	49.1	Teaneck Twp	Teaneck
85	49.1	Hillside Twp	Hillside
86	49.1	North Brunswick Twp	North Brunswick
87	49.0	Woodstown-Pilesgrove Reg	Woodstown
88	49.0	Randolph Twp	Randolph
89	49.0	Woodbury City	Woodbury
90	49.0	Glassboro	Glassboro
91	49.0	Pemberton Twp	Pemberton
92	49.0	W Windsor-Plainsboro Reg	Princeton Jct
93	48.9	Ridgewood Village	Ridgewood
94	48.9	Bernards Twp	Basking Ridge
95	48.9	Rutherford Boro	Rutherford
96	48.9	Kingsway Regional	Woolwich Twp
97	48.9	Florence Twp	Florence
98	48.9	Haddon Twp	Westmont
99	48.9	South Orange-Maplewood	Maplewood
100	48.9	Northern Burlington Reg	Columbus
101	48.9	Buena Regional	Buena
102	48.9	Colts Neck Twp	Colts Neck
103	48.8	Secaucus Town	Secaucus
104	48.8	Pine Hill Boro	Pine Hill
105	48.8	Morris Hills Regional	Rockaway
106	48.8	Montville Twp	Montville
107	48.8	Plainfield City	Plainfield
108	48.8	Elmwood Park	Elmwood Park
109	48.7	Ocean City	Ocean City
110	48.7	Long Branch City	Long Branch
111	48.7	Collingswood Boro	Collingswood
112	48.7	Lyndhurst Twp	Lyndhurst
113	48.7	New Brunswick City	New Brunswick
114	48.7	Scotch Plains-Fanwood Reg	Scotch Plains
115	48.7	Maple Shade Twp	Maple Shade
116	48.7	Washington Twp	Sewell
117	48.7	Woodbridge Twp	Woodbridge
118	48.7	Readington Twp	Whitehouse Stn
119	48.7	Middlesex Boro	Middlesex
120	48.7	Franklin Twp	Somerset
121	48.7	Piscataway Twp	Piscataway
122	48.7	East Windsor Regional	Hightstown
123	48.7	Tinton Falls	Tinton Falls
124	48.6	Black Horse Pike Regional	Blackwood
125	48.6	Mahwah Twp	Mahwah
126	48.6	Watchung Hills Regional	Warren
127	48.6	Monroe Twp	Williamstown
128	48.6	Somerville Boro	Somerville
129	48.6	Ewing Twp	Ewing
130	48.6	Delsea Regional H.S District	Franklinville
131	48.6	Mount Olive Twp	Budd Lake
132	48.6	Newark City	Newark
133	48.6	Jersey City	Jersey City
134	48.6	Riverside Twp	Riverside
135	48.6	SD of the Chathams	Chatham
136	48.6	Bridgeton City	Bridgeton
137	48.6	Wayne Twp	Wayne
138	48.6	Jefferson Twp	Lake Hopatcong
139	48.6	Union City	Union City
140	48.6	Deptford Twp	Deptford
141	48.6	Old Bridge Twp	Matawan
142	48.6	Holmdel Twp	Holmdel
143	48.5	Princeton Regional	Princeton
144	48.5	Fair Lawn Boro	Fair Lawn
145	48.5	Toms River Regional	Toms River
146	48.5	Hawthorne Boro	Hawthorne
147	48.5	Lacey Twp	Lanoka Harbor
148	48.5	Sparta Twp	Sparta
149	48.5	Hamilton Twp	Hamilton Square
150	48.4	Marlboro Twp	Marlboro
151	48.4	Montgomery Twp	Skillman
152	48.4	Metuchen Boro	Metuchen
153	48.4	Pittsgrove Twp	Pittsgrove
154	48.4	Hackettstown	Hackettstown
155	48.4	Voorhees Twp	Voorhees
156	48.4	Westfield Town	Westfield
157	48.4	East Brunswick Twp	E Brunswick
158	48.4	Mount Laurel Twp	Mount Laurel
159	48.3	Fort Lee Boro	Fort Lee
160	48.3	Hamilton Twp	Mays Landing
161	48.3	Cedar Grove Twp	Cedar Grove
162	48.3	Branchburg Twp	Branchburg
163	48.3	Lumberton Twp	Lumberton
164	48.3	Jackson Twp	Jackson
165	48.3	South Plainfield Boro	S Plainfield
166	48.3	Kinnelon Boro	Kinnelon
167	48.3	Egg Harbor Twp	W Atlantic City
168	48.2	Little Egg Harbor Twp	Little Egg Hbr
169	48.2	Lawrence Twp	Lawrenceville
170	48.2	Berkeley Heights Twp	Berkeley Hgts
171	48.2	Belleville Town	Belleville
172	48.2	Evesham Twp	Marlton
173	48.2	Audubon Boro	Audubon
174	48.2	Roxbury Twp	Succasunna
175	48.2	Winslow Twp	Atco
176	48.1	Irvington Township	Irvington
177	48.1	Livingston Twp	Livingston
178	48.1	Lakewood Twp	Lakewood
179	48.1	City of Orange Twp	Orange
180	48.1	Manchester Twp	Whiting
181	48.1	Vineland City	Vineland
182	48.1	Vernon Twp	Vernon
183	48.1	New Providence Boro	New Providence
183	48.1	Verona Boro	Verona
185	48.1	North Bergen Twp	North Bergen
186	48.0	Willingboro Twp	Willingboro
187	48.0	Madison Boro	Madison
188	48.0	Carteret Boro	Carteret
189	48.0	Bound Brook Boro	Bound Brook
190	48.0	Glen Ridge Boro	Glen Ridge
191	48.0	Hopatcong	Hopatcong
192	48.0	Bloomfield Twp	Bloomfield
193	48.0	Pequannock Twp	Pompton Plains
194	47.9	Wall Twp	Wall
195	47.9	Upper Twp	Petersburg
196	47.9	Springfield Twp	Springfield
197	47.9	Burlington County Vocational	Westampton Twp
198	47.9	Point Pleasant Boro	Pt Pleasant
199	47.9	Union Twp	Union
200	47.9	Flemington-Raritan Reg	Flemington
201	47.9	Kearny Town	Kearny
202	47.9	Ridgefield Park Twp	Ridgefield Park
203	47.9	Summit City	Summit
204	47.8	Middletown Twp	Middletown
205	47.8	Parsippany-Troy Hills Twp	Parsippany
206	47.8	Westwood Regional	Westwood
207	47.8	Brick Twp	Brick
208	47.8	Gloucester Twp	Blackwood
209	47.8	Bayonne City	Bayonne
210	47.8	Franklin Lakes Boro	Franklin Lakes
211	47.8	Lower Cape May Regional	Cape May
212	47.7	Middle Twp	Cape May Ct Hse
213	47.7	Neptune Twp	Neptune
214	47.7	Clifton City	Clifton
215	47.6	Hillsborough Twp	Neshanic
216	47.6	Oakland Boro	Oakland
217	47.6	Eastern Camden County Reg	Voorhees
218	47.6	Warren Hills Regional	Washington
219	47.5	Paramus Boro	Paramus
220	47.5	Monroe Twp	Monroe Township
221	47.5	Perth Amboy City	Perth Amboy
222	47.4	Cherry Hill Twp	Cherry Hill
223	47.4	Harrison Town	Harrison
224	47.4	Paulsboro Boro	Paulsboro
225	47.4	Stafford Twp	Manahawkin
226	47.4	Berkeley Twp	Bayville
227	47.4	Central Regional	Bayville
228	47.4	Pennsauken Twp	Pennsauken
229	47.4	Upper Freehold Regional	Allentown
230	47.4	Spotswood Boro	Spotswood
231	47.3	Rahway City	Rahway
232	47.3	Glen Rock Boro	Glen Rock
233	47.3	South River Boro	South River
234	47.3	Ramsey Boro	Ramsey
235	47.2	West Milford Twp	West Milford
236	47.2	Dover Town	Dover
237	47.2	Tenafly Boro	Tenafly
238	47.2	Morris SD	Morristown
239	47.1	Plumsted Twp	New Egypt
240	47.1	Lindenwold Boro	Lindenwold
241	47.1	Mountain Lakes Boro	Mountain Lakes
242	47.1	Hoboken City	Hoboken
243	47.1	Palisades Park	Palisades Park
244	47.1	Sayreville Boro	Sayreville
245	47.0	Clark Twp	Clark
246	47.0	Cliffside Park Boro	Cliffside Park
247	46.9	Phillipsburg Town	Phillipsburg
248	46.8	Pleasantville City	Pleasantville
249	46.7	West Deptford Twp	West Deptford
250	46.7	Rockaway Twp	Hibernia
251	46.6	Keansburg Boro	Keansburg
252	46.6	Cinnaminson Twp	Cinnaminson
253	46.5	Newton Town	Newton
254	46.5	Hanover Twp	Whippany
255	46.4	Burlington City	Burlington
256	46.4	Cranford Twp	Cranford
257	46.3	New Milford Boro	New Milford
258	46.2	Camden County Vocational	Sicklerville
259	46.0	North Arlington Boro	North Arlington
260	45.7	Franklin Twp	Franklinville
261	45.0	Bergen County Vocational	Paramus
262	45.0	Ridgefield Boro	Ridgefield
263	44.7	Lower Twp	Cape May
264	44.7	Mantua Twp	Sewell
265	44.4	Monmouth County Vocational	Colts Neck
266	41.5	Middlesex County Vocational	E Brunswick
267	35.5	Bergen County Special Service	Paramus
268	28.9	Mercer County Special Service	Trenton
269	28.3	Burlington County Spec Serv	Mount Holly

Individual Education Program Students

Rank	Percent	District Name	City
1	31.9	Burlington County Vocational	Westampton Twp
2	26.1	Barnegat Twp	Barnegat
3	25.8	Lower Cape May Regional	Cape May
4	24.7	Keansburg Boro	Keansburg
5	24.2	Pinelands Regional	Tuckerton
6	23.8	Camden County Vocational	Sicklerville
7	23.4	Upper Twp	Petersburg
8	22.4	Sussex-Wantage Regional	Wantage
9	22.2	Middlesex County Vocational	E Brunswick
10	22.1	Bordentown Regional	Bordentown
10	22.1	Mantua Twp	Sewell
12	21.9	Westwood Regional	Westwood
13	21.7	Hamilton Twp	Hamilton Square
14	21.5	Asbury Park City	Asbury Park
15	21.1	Woodbury City	Woodbury
16	21.0	Lower Twp	Cape May
17	20.8	Glassboro	Glassboro
18	20.7	Neptune Twp	Neptune
19	20.4	Morris SD	Morristown
19	20.4	Pemberton Twp	Pemberton
19	20.4	West Deptford Twp	West Deptford
22	20.3	Maple Shade Twp	Maple Shade

22	20.3	Rancocas Valley Regional	Mount Holly
24	20.2	Branchburg Twp	Branchburg
24	20.2	Lumberton Twp	Lumberton
26	20.1	Lyndhurst Twp	Lyndhurst
26	20.1	Passaic City	Passaic
28	20.0	Roselle Boro	Roselle
28	20.0	Washington Twp	Robbinsville
30	19.9	Trenton City	Trenton
31	19.7	Ewing Twp	Ewing
32	19.3	Gloucester City	Gloucester City
32	19.3	Pennsauken Twp	Pennsauken
32	19.3	Vineland City	Vineland
35	19.2	Evesham Twp	Marlton
35	19.2	Middle Twp	Cape May Ct Hse
37	19.1	Millstone Twp	Clarksburg
38	18.8	New Brunswick City	New Brunswick
39	18.7	Florence Twp	Florence
39	18.7	Franklin Twp	Franklinville
39	18.7	North Arlington Boro	North Arlington
42	18.6	Brick Twp	Brick
42	18.6	Pennsville	Pennsville
42	18.6	Pitman Boro	Pitman
42	18.6	Winslow Twp	Atco
46	18.5	Hoboken City	Hoboken
46	18.5	Hopatcong	Hopatcong
46	18.5	Lindenwold Boro	Lindenwold
46	18.5	Millville City	Millville
50	18.3	Bridgeton City	Bridgeton
50	18.3	Cedar Grove Twp	Cedar Grove
50	18.3	Cinnaminson Twp	Cinnaminson
53	18.2	Pleasantville City	Pleasantville
53	18.2	Rahway City	Rahway
55	18.1	Paulsboro Boro	Paulsboro
56	18.0	Burlington City	Burlington
56	18.0	Jackson Twp	Jackson
58	17.8	Pine Hill Boro	Pine Hill
58	17.8	Washington Twp	Sewell
60	17.7	Central Regional	Bayville
60	17.7	Riverside Twp	Riverside
62	17.6	Little Egg Harbor Twp	Little Egg Hbr
63	17.5	Hillsborough Twp	Neshanic
63	17.5	Lakewood Twp	Lakewood
63	17.5	Linden City	Linden
63	17.5	Waldwick Boro	Waldwick
67	17.3	Bergenfield Boro	Bergenfield
67	17.3	Montclair Town	Montclair
67	17.3	Penns Grv-Carney's Pt Reg	Penns Grove
67	17.3	West Milford Twp	West Milford
71	17.2	Deptford Twp	Deptford
71	17.2	Fair Lawn Boro	Fair Lawn
71	17.2	Greater Egg Harbor Reg	Mays Landing
74	17.1	Verona Boro	Verona
75	17.0	Camden City	Camden
75	17.0	Moorestown Twp	Moorestown
77	16.9	Delsea Regional H.S District	Franklinville
77	16.9	Lacey Twp	Lanoka Harbor
77	16.9	Saddle Brook Twp	Saddle Brook
77	16.9	Scotch Plains-Fanwood Reg	Scotch Plains
81	16.8	Englewood City	Englewood
81	16.8	Howell Twp	Howell
81	16.8	Salem City	Salem
81	16.8	Wall Twp	Wall
81	16.8	Westfield Town	Westfield
86	16.7	East Windsor Regional	Hightstown
86	16.7	Egg Harbor Twp	W Atlantic City
86	16.7	Galloway Twp	Galloway
86	16.7	Rockaway Twp	Hibernia
90	16.6	Buena Regional	Buena
90	16.6	Hazlet Twp	Hazlet
90	16.6	Middletown Twp	Middletown
90	16.6	SD of the Chathams	Chatham
94	16.5	Roselle Park Boro	Roselle Park
94	16.5	Tinton Falls	Tinton Falls
96	16.4	Lawrence Twp	Lawrenceville
97	16.3	Belleville Town	Belleville
97	16.3	Monroe Twp	Williamstown
97	16.3	Monroe Twp	Monroe Township
97	16.3	Warren Twp	Warren
97	16.3	Willingboro Twp	Willingboro
102	16.2	Hamilton Twp	Mays Landing
102	16.2	Northern Burlington Reg	Columbus
102	16.2	Sayreville Boro	Sayreville
105	16.1	Pompton Lakes Boro	Pompton Lakes
106	16.0	Manchester Twp	Whiting
106	16.0	Oakland Boro	Oakland
106	16.0	Parsippany-Troy Hills Twp	Parsippany
106	16.0	Pittsgrove Twp	Pittsgrove
110	15.9	Madison Boro	Madison
110	15.9	N Hunt/Voorhees Regional	Annandale
112	15.8	Denville Twp	Denville
112	15.8	Hawthorne Boro	Hawthorne
112	15.8	Mount Laurel Twp	Mount Laurel
112	15.8	Washington Twp	Long Valley
116	15.7	Bayonne City	Bayonne
116	15.7	East Orange	East Orange
116	15.7	Franklin Twp	Somerset
116	15.7	Irvington Township	Irvington
116	15.7	Ridgefield Park Twp	Ridgefield Park
116	15.7	Stafford Twp	Manahawkin
116	15.7	Voorhees Twp	Voorhees
116	15.7	Warren Hills Regional	Washington
124	15.6	East Brunswick Twp	E Brunswick
124	15.6	Mainland Regional	Linwood
124	15.6	North Plainfield Boro	N Plainfield
124	15.6	Princeton Regional	Princeton
128	15.5	Cranford Twp	Cranford
128	15.5	Garfield City	Garfield
128	15.5	Mount Olive Twp	Budd Lake
128	15.5	Phillipsburg Town	Phillipsburg
128	15.5	Ramsey Boro	Ramsey
133	15.4	Gloucester Twp	Blackwood
133	15.4	Livingston Twp	Livingston
135	15.3	Bergen County Vocational	Paramus
135	15.3	Bridgewater-Raritan Reg	Bridgewater
135	15.3	City of Orange Twp	Orange
135	15.3	Hackensack City	Hackensack
135	15.3	Teaneck Twp	Teaneck
140	15.2	Lenape Regional	Shamong
140	15.2	Long Branch City	Long Branch
140	15.2	Medford Twp	Medford
140	15.2	Passaic County Vocational	Wayne
140	15.2	Paterson City	Paterson
140	15.2	South Plainfield Boro	S Plainfield
140	15.2	Springfield Twp	Springfield
140	15.2	Union Twp	Union
148	15.1	Cresskill Boro	Cresskill
148	15.1	Middlesex Boro	Middlesex
148	15.1	Plumsted Twp	New Egypt
148	15.1	Ramapo-Indian Hill Reg	Franklin Lakes
148	15.1	Readington Twp	Whitehouse Stn
153	15.0	Collingswood Boro	Collingswood
153	15.0	Rutherford Boro	Rutherford
155	14.9	Bloomfield Twp	Bloomfield
156	14.8	Haddonfield Boro	Haddonfield
156	14.8	Hopewell Valley Regional	Pennington
156	14.8	New Milford Boro	New Milford
156	14.8	Newark City	Newark
160	14.7	Black Horse Pike Regional	Blackwood
160	14.7	Burlington Twp	Burlington
160	14.7	Elmwood Park	Elmwood Park
163	14.6	Hunterdon Central Reg	Flemington
164	14.5	Audubon Boro	Audubon
164	14.5	Dumont Boro	Dumont
164	14.5	Hillside Twp	Hillside
167	14.4	Glen Rock Boro	Glen Rock
167	14.4	Jefferson Twp	Lake Hopatcong
169	14.3	Piscataway Twp	Piscataway
169	14.3	West New York Town	West New York
171	14.2	Hasbrouck Heights Boro	Hasbrouck Hgts
171	14.2	Morris Hills Regional	Rockaway
171	14.2	Ocean Twp	Oakhurst
174	14.1	Caldwell-West Caldwell	West Caldwell
174	14.1	West Morris Regional	Chester
176	14.0	Freehold Twp	Freehold
176	14.0	Haddon Twp	Westmont
176	14.0	Mahwah Twp	Mahwah
176	14.0	Sparta Twp	Sparta
180	13.9	Bound Brook Boro	Bound Brook
180	13.9	Clearview Regional	Mullica Hill
180	13.9	Manalapan-Englishtown Reg	Englishtown
180	13.9	Tenafly Boro	Tenafly
184	13.8	Pequannock Twp	Pompton Plains
184	13.8	Woodbridge Twp	Woodbridge
186	13.7	Berkeley Twp	Bayville
186	13.7	Hanover Twp	Whippany
186	13.7	Highland Park Boro	Highland Park
189	13.6	New Providence Boro	New Providence
189	13.6	Nutley Town	Nutley
189	13.6	Secaucus Town	Secaucus
189	13.6	Summit City	Summit
193	13.5	Randolph Twp	Randolph
194	13.4	Atlantic City	Atlantic City
194	13.4	Millburn Twp	Millburn
194	13.4	Pascack Valley Regional	Montvale
194	13.4	Toms River Regional	Toms River
194	13.4	West Orange Town	West Orange
199	13.3	South Brunswick Twp	Monmouth Jct
200	13.2	Flemington-Raritan Reg	Flemington
200	13.2	Freehold Regional	Englishtown
200	13.2	South River Boro	South River
203	13.1	Cherry Hill Twp	Cherry Hill
203	13.1	High Point Regional	Sussex
205	13.0	Lodi Borough	Lodi
205	13.0	Metuchen Boro	Metuchen
207	12.9	Delran Twp	Delran
207	12.9	Edison Twp	Edison
207	12.9	Hammonton Town	Hammonton
207	12.9	Harrison Town	Harrison
207	12.9	South Orange-Maplewood	Maplewood
212	12.8	Clinton Twp	Annandale
212	12.8	Colts Neck Twp	Colts Neck
214	12.7	Point Pleasant Boro	Pt Pleasant
214	12.7	Watchung Hills Regional	Warren
216	12.6	Montville Twp	Montville
216	12.6	Plainfield City	Plainfield
218	12.5	Fort Lee Boro	Fort Lee
218	12.5	North Brunswick Twp	North Brunswick
218	12.5	Somerset Hills Regional	Bernardsville
221	12.4	Dover Town	Dover
221	12.4	Eastern Camden County Reg	Voorhees
223	12.3	Jersey City	Jersey City
223	12.3	Marlboro Twp	Marlboro
225	12.2	Leonia Boro	Leonia
225	12.2	Matawan-Aberdeen Regional	Aberdeen
225	12.2	Old Bridge Twp	Matawan
225	12.2	Ridgewood Village	Ridgewood
225	12.2	Vernon Twp	Vernon
230	12.1	Essex County Voc-Tech	West Orange
230	12.1	Wayne Twp	Wayne
230	12.1	Woodstown-Pilesgrove Reg	Woodstown
233	12.0	Bernards Twp	Basking Ridge
233	12.0	Kearny Town	Kearny
233	12.0	W Windsor-Plainsboro Reg	Princeton Jct
236	11.9	Montgomery Twp	Skillman
236	11.9	North Bergen Twp	North Bergen
236	11.9	Roxbury Twp	Succasunna
239	11.8	Franklin Lakes Boro	Franklin Lakes
239	11.8	Hackettstown	Hackettstown
239	11.8	Mountain Lakes Boro	Mountain Lakes
242	11.7	Kinnelon Boro	Kinnelon
243	11.6	Clifton City	Clifton
244	11.5	Newton Town	Newton
245	11.4	Elizabeth City	Elizabeth
245	11.4	Kingsway Regional	Woolwich Twp
245	11.4	Northern Valley Regional	Demarest
245	11.4	Palisades Park	Palisades Park
245	11.4	Somerville Boro	Somerville
250	11.0	Southern Regional	Manahawkin
251	10.9	Glen Ridge Boro	Glen Ridge
251	10.9	Holmdel Twp	Holmdel
251	10.9	Perth Amboy City	Perth Amboy
254	10.7	Carteret Boro	Carteret
254	10.7	Ocean City	Ocean City
256	10.5	Spotswood Boro	Spotswood
257	10.3	Wyckoff Twp	Wyckoff
258	10.2	Berkeley Heights Twp	Berkeley Hgts
258	10.2	Clark Twp	Clark
258	10.2	Cliffside Park Boro	Cliffside Park
261	9.4	Paramus Boro	Paramus
262	8.9	Union City	Union City
262	8.9	Upper Freehold Regional	Allentown
264	7.2	Ridgefield Boro	Ridgefield
265	6.8	Manasquan Boro	Manasquan
266	0.0	Bergen County Special Service	Paramus
266	0.0	Burlington County Spec Serv	Mount Holly
266	0.0	Mercer County Special Service	Trenton
266	0.0	Monmouth County Vocational	Colts Neck

English Language Learner Students

Rank	Percent	District Name	City
1	43.8	Union City	Union City
2	26.7	Passaic City	Passaic
3	23.3	New Brunswick City	New Brunswick
4	18.9	Elizabeth City	Elizabeth
5	17.9	Paterson City	Paterson
6	16.2	Palisades Park	Palisades Park
7	15.2	Perth Amboy City	Perth Amboy
8	14.4	Dover Town	Dover
9	14.2	West New York Town	West New York
10	13.0	Plainfield City	Plainfield
11	12.2	Atlantic City	Atlantic City
12	11.5	Bound Brook Boro	Bound Brook
13	11.1	Harrison Town	Harrison
14	10.9	Garfield City	Garfield
15	9.4	North Bergen Twp	North Bergen
16	9.2	Cliffside Park Boro	Cliffside Park
16	9.2	Fort Lee Boro	Fort Lee
18	8.8	Englewood City	Englewood
19	8.7	Leonia Boro	Leonia
19	8.7	Roselle Boro	Roselle
21	8.4	Bridgeton City	Bridgeton
22	8.3	Lakewood Twp	Lakewood
23	7.8	Jersey City	Jersey City
23	7.8	Trenton City	Trenton
25	7.5	North Plainfield Boro	N Plainfield
26	7.4	Newark City	Newark

27	7.1	Kearny Town	Kearny
28	7.0	City of Orange Twp	Orange
28	7.0	Pleasantville City	Pleasantville
30	6.9	Roselle Park Boro	Roselle Park
31	6.8	Tenafly Boro	Tenafly
32	6.6	Hackensack City	Hackensack
33	6.4	Camden City	Camden
33	6.4	Morris SD	Morristown
35	6.3	Lodi Borough	Lodi
36	6.1	Clifton City	Clifton
37	6.0	Carteret Boro	Carteret
37	6.0	Essex County Voc-Tech	West Orange
39	5.9	Parsippany-Troy Hills Twp	Parsippany
40	5.8	East Windsor Regional	Hightstown
41	5.6	Ridgefield Park Twp	Ridgefield Park
42	5.4	Belleville Town	Belleville
42	5.4	Cresskill Boro	Cresskill
44	5.1	Asbury Park City	Asbury Park
44	5.1	Linden City	Linden
46	5.0	West Orange Town	West Orange
47	4.9	Somerville Boro	Somerville
48	4.8	Irvington Township	Irvington
48	4.8	Long Branch City	Long Branch
50	4.7	Bergenfield Boro	Bergenfield
50	4.7	North Arlington Boro	North Arlington
52	4.3	Dumont Boro	Dumont
52	4.3	Hammonton Town	Hammonton
52	4.3	Hillside Twp	Hillside
55	4.2	Highland Park Boro	Highland Park
55	4.2	North Brunswick Twp	North Brunswick
55	4.2	South River Boro	South River
58	4.1	Bloomfield Twp	Bloomfield
59	4.0	Franklin Twp	Somerset
60	3.9	Burlington City	Burlington
60	3.9	Elmwood Park	Elmwood Park
60	3.9	Lindenwold Boro	Lindenwold
60	3.9	Piscataway Twp	Piscataway
60	3.9	Vineland City	Vineland
65	3.7	Middlesex Boro	Middlesex
66	3.6	Galloway Twp	Galloway
66	3.6	Paramus Boro	Paramus
66	3.6	Summit City	Summit
69	3.5	Ridgefield Boro	Ridgefield
70	3.3	Princeton Regional	Princeton
71	3.2	Lawrence Twp	Lawrenceville
71	3.2	Ocean Twp	Oakhurst
73	3.1	Glen Rock Boro	Glen Rock
73	3.1	W Windsor-Plainsboro Reg	Princeton Jct
75	2.9	Upper Freehold Regional	Allentown
76	2.8	Westwood Regional	Westwood
77	2.7	New Milford Boro	New Milford
77	2.7	Old Bridge Twp	Matawan
79	2.6	Penns Grv-Carney's Pt Reg	Penns Grove
80	2.5	East Orange	East Orange
80	2.5	Phillipsburg Town	Phillipsburg
80	2.5	Rahway City	Rahway
80	2.5	Somerset Hills Regional	Bernardsville
84	2.4	Bayonne City	Bayonne
84	2.4	Burlington Twp	Burlington
84	2.4	Edison Twp	Edison
84	2.4	Fair Lawn Boro	Fair Lawn
84	2.4	Hackettstown	Hackettstown
84	2.4	Union Twp	Union
84	2.4	Woodbridge Twp	Woodbridge
91	2.3	Delran Twp	Delran
91	2.3	Egg Harbor Twp	W Atlantic City
91	2.3	Hanover Twp	Whippany
94	2.2	Madison Boro	Madison
94	2.2	Pennsauken Twp	Pennsauken
94	2.2	Teaneck Twp	Teaneck
94	2.2	Waldwick Boro	Waldwick
98	2.1	Collingswood Boro	Collingswood
98	2.1	Ewing Twp	Ewing
100	2.0	Hamilton Twp	Mays Landing
100	2.0	Springfield Twp	Springfield
102	1.9	East Brunswick Twp	E Brunswick
102	1.9	Lyndhurst Twp	Lyndhurst
102	1.9	Mount Olive Twp	Budd Lake
102	1.9	Ridgewood Village	Ridgewood
106	1.8	Buena Regional	Buena
106	1.8	Pompton Lakes Boro	Pompton Lakes
108	1.7	Bordentown Regional	Bordentown
108	1.7	Bridgewater-Raritan Reg	Bridgewater
108	1.7	Millville City	Millville
108	1.7	Nutley Town	Nutley
112	1.6	Flemington-Raritan Reg	Flemington
112	1.6	Livingston Twp	Livingston
112	1.6	Passaic County Vocational	Wayne
112	1.6	Sayreville Boro	Sayreville
112	1.6	Secaucus Town	Secaucus
112	1.6	South Plainfield Boro	S Plainfield
118	1.5	Berkeley Heights Twp	Berkeley Hgts
118	1.5	Hoboken City	Hoboken
118	1.5	Maple Shade Twp	Maple Shade
118	1.5	Marlboro Twp	Marlboro
118	1.5	Matawan-Aberdeen Regional	Aberdeen
118	1.5	Riverside Twp	Riverside
118	1.5	South Orange-Maplewood	Maplewood
125	1.4	Berkeley Twp	Bayville
125	1.4	Manalapan-Englishtown Reg	Englishtown
125	1.4	Saddle Brook Twp	Saddle Brook
125	1.4	Warren Twp	Warren
129	1.3	Greater Egg Harbor Reg	Mays Landing
129	1.3	Hamilton Twp	Hamilton Square
129	1.3	Hasbrouck Heights Boro	Hasbrouck Hgts
129	1.3	Hillsborough Twp	Neshanic
129	1.3	Millburn Twp	Millburn
129	1.3	Montville Twp	Montville
129	1.3	Voorhees Twp	Voorhees
136	1.2	Cherry Hill Twp	Cherry Hill
136	1.2	Gloucester City	Gloucester City
136	1.2	Randolph Twp	Randolph
136	1.2	South Brunswick Twp	Monmouth Jct
136	1.2	Tinton Falls	Tinton Falls
141	1.1	Central Regional	Bayville
141	1.1	Denville Twp	Denville
141	1.1	Florence Twp	Florence
141	1.1	Glassboro	Glassboro
141	1.1	Keansburg Boro	Keansburg
141	1.1	Middlesex County Vocational	E Brunswick
141	1.1	Montclair Town	Montclair
141	1.1	Newton Town	Newton
141	1.1	Northern Valley Regional	Demarest
141	1.1	Rockaway Twp	Hibernia
141	1.1	Roxbury Twp	Succasunna
141	1.1	Warren Hills Regional	Washington
153	1.0	Branchburg Twp	Branchburg
153	1.0	Manasquan Boro	Manasquan
153	1.0	Wall Twp	Wall
153	1.0	Wayne Twp	Wayne
153	1.0	Winslow Twp	Atco
158	0.9	Hawthorne Boro	Hawthorne
158	0.9	Howell Twp	Howell
158	0.9	Little Egg Harbor Twp	Little Egg Hbr
158	0.9	Middle Twp	Cape May Ct Hse
158	0.9	Morris Hills Regional	Rockaway
158	0.9	Plumsted Twp	New Egypt
158	0.9	Rutherford Boro	Rutherford
158	0.9	Woodbury City	Woodbury
158	0.9	Wyckoff Twp	Wyckoff
167	0.8	Brick Twp	Brick
167	0.8	Caldwell-West Caldwell	West Caldwell
167	0.8	Clark Twp	Clark
167	0.8	Deptford Twp	Deptford
167	0.8	Evesham Twp	Marlton
167	0.8	Franklin Lakes Boro	Franklin Lakes
167	0.8	Freehold Regional	Englishtown
167	0.8	Jackson Twp	Jackson
167	0.8	Mahwah Twp	Mahwah
167	0.8	Manchester Twp	Whiting
167	0.8	Millstone Twp	Clarksburg
167	0.8	New Providence Boro	New Providence
179	0.7	Eastern Camden County Reg	Voorhees
179	0.7	Gloucester Twp	Blackwood
179	0.7	Hopatcong	Hopatcong
179	0.7	Lumberton Twp	Lumberton
179	0.7	Metuchen Boro	Metuchen
179	0.7	Monroe Twp	Monroe Township
179	0.7	Mount Laurel Twp	Mount Laurel
179	0.7	Point Pleasant Boro	Pt Pleasant
179	0.7	Ramsey Boro	Ramsey
179	0.7	Southern Regional	Manahawkin
179	0.7	Toms River Regional	Toms River
179	0.7	Watchung Hills Regional	Warren
191	0.6	Colts Neck Twp	Colts Neck
191	0.6	Holmdel Twp	Holmdel
191	0.6	Hunterdon Central Reg	Flemington
191	0.6	Lower Twp	Cape May
191	0.6	Neptune Twp	Neptune
191	0.6	Ocean City	Ocean City
191	0.6	Pascack Valley Regional	Montvale
191	0.6	Pemberton Twp	Pemberton
191	0.6	Pennsville	Pennsville
191	0.6	SD of the Chathams	Chatham
201	0.5	Audubon Boro	Audubon
201	0.5	Barnegat Twp	Barnegat
201	0.5	Bernards Twp	Basking Ridge
201	0.5	Black Horse Pike Regional	Blackwood
201	0.5	Freehold Twp	Freehold
201	0.5	Mainland Regional	Linwood
201	0.5	Monroe Twp	Williamstown
201	0.5	Oakland Boro	Oakland
201	0.5	Pine Hill Boro	Pine Hill
201	0.5	Readington Twp	Whitehouse Stn
201	0.5	Scotch Plains-Fanwood Reg	Scotch Plains
201	0.5	Washington Twp	Robbinsville
213	0.4	Cedar Grove Twp	Cedar Grove
213	0.4	Cinnaminson Twp	Cinnaminson
213	0.4	Jefferson Twp	Lake Hopatcong
213	0.4	Lacey Twp	Lanoka Harbor
213	0.4	Lower Cape May Regional	Cape May
213	0.4	Middletown Twp	Middletown
213	0.4	Montgomery Twp	Skillman
213	0.4	Moorestown Twp	Moorestown
213	0.4	Pequannock Twp	Pompton Plains
213	0.4	Ramapo-Indian Hill Reg	Franklin Lakes
213	0.4	Rancocas Valley Regional	Mount Holly
213	0.4	Spotswood Boro	Spotswood
213	0.4	Verona Boro	Verona
213	0.4	Washington Twp	Sewell
213	0.4	Westfield Town	Westfield
213	0.4	Willingboro Twp	Willingboro
213	0.4	Woodstown-Pilesgrove Reg	Woodstown
230	0.3	Bergen County Vocational	Paramus
230	0.3	Clinton Twp	Annandale
230	0.3	Delsea Regional H.S District	Franklinville
230	0.3	Haddonfield Boro	Haddonfield
230	0.3	Hazlet Twp	Hazlet
230	0.3	Kingsway Regional	Woolwich Twp
230	0.3	Kinnelon Boro	Kinnelon
230	0.3	Lenape Regional	Shamong
230	0.3	Pinelands Regional	Tuckerton
230	0.3	Salem City	Salem
230	0.3	Sparta Twp	Sparta
230	0.3	Sussex-Wantage Regional	Wantage
230	0.3	Washington Twp	Long Valley
230	0.3	West Milford Twp	West Milford
244	0.2	Haddon Twp	Westmont
244	0.2	Hopewell Valley Regional	Pennington
244	0.2	Northern Burlington Reg	Columbus
244	0.2	Stafford Twp	Manahawkin
244	0.2	Vernon Twp	Vernon
244	0.2	West Morris Regional	Chester
250	0.1	Burlington County Vocational	Westampton Twp
250	0.1	Cranford Twp	Cranford
250	0.1	Franklin Twp	Franklinville
250	0.1	Glen Ridge Boro	Glen Ridge
250	0.1	N Hunt/Voorhees Regional	Annandale
250	0.1	Pittsgrove Twp	Pittsgrove
250	0.1	West Deptford Twp	West Deptford
257	0.0	Clearview Regional	Mullica Hill
258	0.0	Bergen County Special Service	Paramus
258	0.0	Burlington County Spec Serv	Mount Holly
258	0.0	Camden County Vocational	Sicklerville
258	0.0	High Point Regional	Sussex
258	0.0	Mantua Twp	Sewell
258	0.0	Medford Twp	Medford
258	0.0	Mercer County Special Service	Trenton
258	0.0	Monmouth County Vocational	Colts Neck
258	0.0	Mountain Lakes Boro	Mountain Lakes
258	0.0	Paulsboro Boro	Paulsboro
258	0.0	Pitman Boro	Pitman
258	0.0	Upper Twp	Petersburg

Migrant Students

Rank	Percent	District Name	City
1	8.4	Bridgeton City	Bridgeton
2	2.2	Hammonton Town	Hammonton
3	1.0	Vineland City	Vineland
4	0.8	Buena Regional	Buena
5	0.6	Penns Grv-Carney's Pt Reg	Penns Grove
6	0.5	Woodstown-Pilesgrove Reg	Woodstown
7	0.4	Kingsway Regional	Woolwich Twp
7	0.4	Winslow Twp	Atco
9	0.3	Hamilton Twp	Mays Landing
10	0.2	Delsea Regional H.S District	Franklinville
10	0.2	Lindenwold Boro	Lindenwold
10	0.2	Pittsgrove Twp	Pittsgrove
13	0.1	Franklin Twp	Franklinville
13	0.1	Greater Egg Harbor Reg	Mays Landing
13	0.1	Lakewood Twp	Lakewood
13	0.1	Millville City	Millville
13	0.1	Northern Burlington Reg	Columbus
13	0.1	Plumsted Twp	New Egypt
19	0.0	Atlantic City	Atlantic City
19	0.0	Camden City	Camden
19	0.0	Galloway Twp	Galloway
19	0.0	Lenape Regional	Shamong
19	0.0	Monroe Twp	Williamstown
19	0.0	Pemberton Twp	Pemberton
25	0.0	Asbury Park City	Asbury Park
25	0.0	Audubon Boro	Audubon
25	0.0	Barnegat Twp	Barnegat
25	0.0	Bayonne City	Bayonne
25	0.0	Belleville Town	Belleville
25	0.0	Bergen County Special Service	Paramus
25	0.0	Bergen County Vocational	Paramus

25	0.0	Bergenfield Boro	Bergenfield
25	0.0	Berkeley Heights Twp	Berkeley Hgts
25	0.0	Berkeley Twp	Bayville
25	0.0	Bernards Twp	Basking Ridge
25	0.0	Black Horse Pike Regional	Blackwood
25	0.0	Bloomfield Twp	Bloomfield
25	0.0	Bordentown Regional	Bordentown
25	0.0	Bound Brook Boro	Bound Brook
25	0.0	Branchburg Twp	Branchburg
25	0.0	Brick Twp	Brick
25	0.0	Bridgewater-Raritan Reg	Bridgewater
25	0.0	Burlington City	Burlington
25	0.0	Burlington County Spec Serv	Mount Holly
25	0.0	Burlington County Vocational	Westampton Twp
25	0.0	Burlington Twp	Burlington
25	0.0	Caldwell-West Caldwell	West Caldwell
25	0.0	Camden County Vocational	Sicklerville
25	0.0	Carteret Boro	Carteret
25	0.0	Cedar Grove Twp	Cedar Grove
25	0.0	Central Regional	Bayville
25	0.0	Cherry Hill Twp	Cherry Hill
25	0.0	Cinnaminson Twp	Cinnaminson
25	0.0	City of Orange Twp	Orange
25	0.0	Clark Twp	Clark
25	0.0	Clearview Regional	Mullica Hill
25	0.0	Cliffside Park Boro	Cliffside Park
25	0.0	Clifton City	Clifton
25	0.0	Clinton Twp	Annandale
25	0.0	Collingswood Boro	Collingswood
25	0.0	Colts Neck Twp	Colts Neck
25	0.0	Cranford Twp	Cranford
25	0.0	Cresskill Boro	Cresskill
25	0.0	Delran Twp	Delran
25	0.0	Denville Twp	Denville
25	0.0	Deptford Twp	Deptford
25	0.0	Dover Town	Dover
25	0.0	Dumont Boro	Dumont
25	0.0	East Brunswick Twp	E Brunswick
25	0.0	East Orange	East Orange
25	0.0	East Windsor Regional	Hightstown
25	0.0	Eastern Camden County Reg	Voorhees
25	0.0	Edison Twp	Edison
25	0.0	Egg Harbor Twp	W Atlantic City
25	0.0	Elizabeth City	Elizabeth
25	0.0	Elmwood Park	Elmwood Park
25	0.0	Englewood City	Englewood
25	0.0	Essex County Voc-Tech	West Orange
25	0.0	Evesham Twp	Marlton
25	0.0	Ewing Twp	Ewing
25	0.0	Fair Lawn Boro	Fair Lawn
25	0.0	Flemington-Raritan Reg	Flemington
25	0.0	Florence Twp	Florence
25	0.0	Fort Lee Boro	Fort Lee
25	0.0	Franklin Lakes Boro	Franklin Lakes
25	0.0	Franklin Twp	Somerset
25	0.0	Freehold Regional	Englishtown
25	0.0	Freehold Twp	Freehold
25	0.0	Garfield City	Garfield
25	0.0	Glassboro	Glassboro
25	0.0	Glen Ridge Boro	Glen Ridge
25	0.0	Glen Rock Boro	Glen Rock
25	0.0	Gloucester City	Gloucester City
25	0.0	Gloucester Twp	Blackwood
25	0.0	Hackensack City	Hackensack
25	0.0	Hackettstown	Hackettstown
25	0.0	Haddon Twp	Westmont
25	0.0	Haddonfield Boro	Haddonfield
25	0.0	Hamilton Twp	Hamilton Square
25	0.0	Hanover Twp	Whippany
25	0.0	Harrison Town	Harrison
25	0.0	Hasbrouck Heights Boro	Hasbrouck Hgts
25	0.0	Hawthorne Boro	Hawthorne
25	0.0	Hazlet Twp	Hazlet
25	0.0	High Point Regional	Sussex
25	0.0	Highland Park Boro	Highland Park
25	0.0	Hillsborough Twp	Neshanic
25	0.0	Hillside Twp	Hillside
25	0.0	Hoboken City	Hoboken
25	0.0	Holmdel Twp	Holmdel
25	0.0	Hopatcong	Hopatcong
25	0.0	Hopewell Valley Regional	Pennington
25	0.0	Howell Twp	Howell
25	0.0	Hunterdon Central Reg	Flemington
25	0.0	Irvington Township	Irvington
25	0.0	Jackson Twp	Jackson
25	0.0	Jefferson Twp	Lake Hopatcong
25	0.0	Jersey City	Jersey City
25	0.0	Keansburg Boro	Keansburg
25	0.0	Kearny Town	Kearny
25	0.0	Kinnelon Boro	Kinnelon
25	0.0	Lacey Twp	Lanoka Harbor
25	0.0	Lawrence Twp	Lawrenceville
25	0.0	Leonia Boro	Leonia
25	0.0	Linden City	Linden
25	0.0	Little Egg Harbor Twp	Little Egg Hbr
25	0.0	Livingston Twp	Livingston
25	0.0	Lodi Borough	Lodi
25	0.0	Long Branch City	Long Branch
25	0.0	Lower Cape May Regional	Cape May
25	0.0	Lower Twp	Cape May
25	0.0	Lumberton Twp	Lumberton
25	0.0	Lyndhurst Twp	Lyndhurst
25	0.0	Madison Boro	Madison
25	0.0	Mahwah Twp	Mahwah
25	0.0	Mainland Regional	Linwood
25	0.0	Manalapan-Englishtown Reg	Englishtown
25	0.0	Manasquan Boro	Manasquan
25	0.0	Manchester Twp	Whiting
25	0.0	Mantua Twp	Sewell
25	0.0	Maple Shade Twp	Maple Shade
25	0.0	Marlboro Twp	Marlboro
25	0.0	Matawan-Aberdeen Regional	Aberdeen
25	0.0	Medford Twp	Medford
25	0.0	Mercer County Special Service	Trenton
25	0.0	Metuchen Boro	Metuchen
25	0.0	Middle Twp	Cape May Ct Hse
25	0.0	Middlesex Boro	Middlesex
25	0.0	Middlesex County Vocational	E Brunswick
25	0.0	Middletown Twp	Middletown
25	0.0	Millburn Twp	Millburn
25	0.0	Millstone Twp	Clarksburg
25	0.0	Monmouth County Vocational	Colts Neck
25	0.0	Monroe Twp	Monroe Township
25	0.0	Montclair Town	Montclair
25	0.0	Montgomery Twp	Skillman
25	0.0	Montville Twp	Montville
25	0.0	Moorestown Twp	Moorestown
25	0.0	Morris Hills Regional	Rockaway
25	0.0	Morris SD	Morristown
25	0.0	Mount Laurel Twp	Mount Laurel
25	0.0	Mount Olive Twp	Budd Lake
25	0.0	Mountain Lakes Boro	Mountain Lakes
25	0.0	N Hunt/Voorhees Regional	Annandale
25	0.0	Neptune Twp	Neptune
25	0.0	New Brunswick City	New Brunswick
25	0.0	New Milford Boro	New Milford
25	0.0	New Providence Boro	New Providence
25	0.0	Newark City	Newark
25	0.0	Newton Town	Newton
25	0.0	North Arlington Boro	North Arlington
25	0.0	North Bergen Twp	North Bergen
25	0.0	North Brunswick Twp	North Brunswick
25	0.0	North Plainfield Boro	N Plainfield
25	0.0	Northern Valley Regional	Demarest
25	0.0	Nutley Town	Nutley
25	0.0	Oakland Boro	Oakland
25	0.0	Ocean City	Ocean City
25	0.0	Ocean Twp	Oakhurst
25	0.0	Old Bridge Twp	Matawan
25	0.0	Palisades Park	Palisades Park
25	0.0	Paramus Boro	Paramus
25	0.0	Parsippany-Troy Hills Twp	Parsippany
25	0.0	Pascack Valley Regional	Montvale
25	0.0	Passaic City	Passaic
25	0.0	Passaic County Vocational	Wayne
25	0.0	Paterson City	Paterson
25	0.0	Paulsboro Boro	Paulsboro
25	0.0	Pennsauken Twp	Pennsauken
25	0.0	Pennsville	Pennsville
25	0.0	Pequannock Twp	Pompton Plains
25	0.0	Perth Amboy City	Perth Amboy
25	0.0	Phillipsburg Town	Phillipsburg
25	0.0	Pine Hill Boro	Pine Hill
25	0.0	Pinelands Regional	Tuckerton
25	0.0	Piscataway Twp	Piscataway
25	0.0	Pitman Boro	Pitman
25	0.0	Plainfield City	Plainfield
25	0.0	Pleasantville City	Pleasantville
25	0.0	Point Pleasant Boro	Pt Pleasant
25	0.0	Pompton Lakes Boro	Pompton Lakes
25	0.0	Princeton Regional	Princeton
25	0.0	Rahway City	Rahway
25	0.0	Ramapo-Indian Hill Reg	Franklin Lakes
25	0.0	Ramsey Boro	Ramsey
25	0.0	Rancocas Valley Regional	Mount Holly
25	0.0	Randolph Twp	Randolph
25	0.0	Readington Twp	Whitehouse Stn
25	0.0	Ridgefield Boro	Ridgefield
25	0.0	Ridgefield Park Twp	Ridgefield Park
25	0.0	Ridgewood Village	Ridgewood
25	0.0	Riverside Twp	Riverside
25	0.0	Rockaway Twp	Hibernia
25	0.0	Roselle Boro	Roselle
25	0.0	Roselle Park Boro	Roselle Park
25	0.0	Roxbury Twp	Succasunna
25	0.0	Rutherford Boro	Rutherford
25	0.0	SD of the Chathams	Chatham
25	0.0	Saddle Brook Twp	Saddle Brook
25	0.0	Salem City	Salem
25	0.0	Sayreville Boro	Sayreville
25	0.0	Scotch Plains-Fanwood Reg	Scotch Plains
25	0.0	Secaucus Town	Secaucus
25	0.0	Somerset Hills Regional	Bernardsville
25	0.0	Somerville Boro	Somerville
25	0.0	South Brunswick Twp	Monmouth Jct
25	0.0	South Orange-Maplewood	Maplewood
25	0.0	South Plainfield Boro	S Plainfield
25	0.0	South River Boro	South River
25	0.0	Southern Regional	Manahawkin
25	0.0	Sparta Twp	Sparta
25	0.0	Spotswood Boro	Spotswood
25	0.0	Springfield Twp	Springfield
25	0.0	Stafford Twp	Manahawkin
25	0.0	Summit City	Summit
25	0.0	Sussex-Wantage Regional	Wantage
25	0.0	Teaneck Twp	Teaneck
25	0.0	Tenafly Boro	Tenafly
25	0.0	Tinton Falls	Tinton Falls
25	0.0	Toms River Regional	Toms River
25	0.0	Trenton City	Trenton
25	0.0	Union City	Union City
25	0.0	Union Twp	Union
25	0.0	Upper Freehold Regional	Allentown
25	0.0	Upper Twp	Petersburg
25	0.0	Vernon Twp	Vernon
25	0.0	Verona Boro	Verona
25	0.0	Voorhees Twp	Voorhees
25	0.0	W Windsor-Plainsboro Reg	Princeton Jct
25	0.0	Waldwick Boro	Waldwick
25	0.0	Wall Twp	Wall
25	0.0	Warren Hills Regional	Washington
25	0.0	Warren Twp	Warren
25	0.0	Washington Twp	Robbinsville
25	0.0	Washington Twp	Long Valley
25	0.0	Washington Twp	Sewell
25	0.0	Watchung Hills Regional	Warren
25	0.0	Wayne Twp	Wayne
25	0.0	West Deptford Twp	West Deptford
25	0.0	West Milford Twp	West Milford
25	0.0	West Morris Regional	Chester
25	0.0	West New York Town	West New York
25	0.0	West Orange Town	West Orange
25	0.0	Westfield Town	Westfield
25	0.0	Westwood Regional	Westwood
25	0.0	Willingboro Twp	Willingboro
25	0.0	Woodbridge Twp	Woodbridge
25	0.0	Woodbury City	Woodbury
25	0.0	Wyckoff Twp	Wyckoff

Students Eligible for Free Lunch

Rank	Percent	District Name	City
1	87.6	Union City	Union City
2	75.6	Asbury Park City	Asbury Park
3	74.8	Camden City	Camden
4	69.0	City of Orange Twp	Orange
5	66.2	Perth Amboy City	Perth Amboy
6	66.1	Bridgeton City	Bridgeton
6	66.1	New Brunswick City	New Brunswick
8	65.2	Hoboken City	Hoboken
9	63.8	Passaic City	Passaic
10	62.8	Essex County Voc-Tech	West Orange
10	62.8	Salem City	Salem
12	60.5	Newark City	Newark
13	59.8	Elizabeth City	Elizabeth
14	59.4	West New York Town	West New York
15	59.0	East Orange	East Orange
16	58.5	Jersey City	Jersey City
17	58.1	Irvington Township	Irvington
18	57.6	Atlantic City	Atlantic City
19	57.3	Plainfield City	Plainfield
20	51.6	Camden County Vocational	Sicklerville
21	51.5	Paterson City	Paterson
22	50.6	Trenton City	Trenton
23	50.3	Long Branch City	Long Branch
24	49.0	Lakewood Twp	Lakewood
25	46.6	Pleasantville City	Pleasantville
26	44.3	Penns Grv-Carney's Pt Reg	Penns Grove
27	43.7	Vineland City	Vineland
28	43.2	Keansburg Boro	Keansburg
29	42.6	Burlington County Spec Serv	Mount Holly
30	42.5	Passaic County Vocational	Wayne
31	42.3	Englewood City	Englewood
32	40.8	North Bergen Twp	North Bergen
33	39.8	Paulsboro Boro	Paulsboro
34	38.3	Harrison Town	Harrison
35	37.8	Mercer County Special Service	Trenton
36	37.1	Lindenwold Boro	Lindenwold

37	36.7	Millville City	Millville
38	35.5	Dover Town	Dover
39	35.2	Carteret Boro	Carteret
40	35.1	Hillside Twp	Hillside
41	34.7	Roselle Boro	Roselle
42	33.7	Gloucester City	Gloucester City
43	33.6	Garfield City	Garfield
44	32.8	Middlesex County Vocational	E Brunswick
45	31.7	Neptune Twp	Neptune
46	31.2	Linden City	Linden
47	31.1	Pennsauken Twp	Pennsauken
48	31.0	Woodbury City	Woodbury
49	30.9	Bound Brook Boro	Bound Brook
50	30.6	Burlington City	Burlington
51	30.2	Hackensack City	Hackensack
52	29.4	Rahway City	Rahway
53	29.0	Phillipsburg Town	Phillipsburg
54	28.3	Willingboro Twp	Willingboro
55	27.4	Bayonne City	Bayonne
56	26.2	Buena Regional	Buena
57	25.4	Winslow Twp	Atco
58	24.9	Pemberton Twp	Pemberton
59	24.8	Cliffside Park Boro	Cliffside Park
60	24.7	Bergen County Special Service	Paramus
61	24.1	Pine Hill Boro	Pine Hill
62	23.6	Pittsgrove Twp	Pittsgrove
63	23.4	Riverside Twp	Riverside
64	23.2	Lodi Borough	Lodi
64	23.2	North Plainfield Boro	N Plainfield
66	23.1	Lower Cape May Regional	Cape May
67	22.9	Lower Twp	Cape May
68	21.9	Hamilton Twp	Mays Landing
69	21.6	Glassboro	Glassboro
70	21.5	Kearny Town	Kearny
71	20.3	Deptford Twp	Deptford
72	20.2	Hammonton Town	Hammonton
73	19.8	Franklin Twp	Somerset
74	19.2	Highland Park Boro	Highland Park
74	19.2	Somerville Boro	Somerville
76	19.0	Belleville Town	Belleville
77	18.8	Little Egg Harbor Twp	Little Egg Hbr
78	18.6	Middle Twp	Cape May Ct Hse
79	17.6	Burlington County Vocational	Westampton Twp
80	17.5	Bloomfield Twp	Bloomfield
81	17.3	Ridgefield Park Twp	Ridgefield Park
82	15.8	Egg Harbor Twp	W Atlantic City
83	15.5	Collingswood Boro	Collingswood
84	15.2	Pinelands Regional	Tuckerton
84	15.2	South River Boro	South River
86	14.9	Monroe Twp	Williamstown
87	14.8	Greater Egg Harbor Reg	Mays Landing
88	14.7	Morris SD	Morristown
89	14.6	West Orange Town	West Orange
90	14.5	Florence Twp	Florence
91	14.1	Newton Town	Newton
92	13.7	Gloucester Twp	Blackwood
93	13.6	Ewing Twp	Ewing
93	13.6	Franklin Twp	Franklinville
95	13.4	Union Twp	Union
96	13.2	Galloway Twp	Galloway
97	13.1	North Brunswick Twp	North Brunswick
98	12.4	Barnegat Twp	Barnegat
98	12.4	Woodbridge Twp	Woodbridge
100	12.2	Delsea Regional H.S District	Franklinville
101	12.1	Elmwood Park	Elmwood Park
101	12.1	Hamilton Twp	Hamilton Square
103	12.0	Maple Shade Twp	Maple Shade
104	11.8	Montclair Town	Montclair
105	11.6	Secaucus Town	Secaucus
106	11.4	South Orange-Maplewood	Maplewood
107	11.3	Manchester Twp	Whiting
107	11.3	Ocean City	Ocean City
109	11.2	Matawan-Aberdeen Regional	Aberdeen
110	11.1	East Windsor Regional	Hightstown
111	10.9	Piscataway Twp	Piscataway
112	10.8	Central Regional	Bayville
113	10.7	Berkeley Twp	Bayville
114	10.6	Palisades Park	Palisades Park
115	10.4	Roselle Park Boro	Roselle Park
116	10.0	Clifton City	Clifton
117	9.9	Sayreville Boro	Sayreville
117	9.9	Teaneck Twp	Teaneck
119	9.5	West Deptford Twp	West Deptford
120	9.2	Sussex-Wantage Regional	Wantage
121	8.9	Bergenfield Boro	Bergenfield
121	8.9	Toms River Regional	Toms River
123	8.6	Pennsville	Pennsville
124	8.3	Lyndhurst Twp	Lyndhurst
124	8.3	Ridgefield Boro	Ridgefield
126	8.2	Burlington Twp	Burlington
127	8.1	Tinton Falls	Tinton Falls
128	7.9	Bordentown Regional	Bordentown
128	7.9	Lacey Twp	Lanoka Harbor
130	7.8	Middlesex Boro	Middlesex
131	7.6	Hackettstown	Hackettstown
131	7.6	Woodstown-Pilesgrove Reg	Woodstown
133	7.5	Old Bridge Twp	Matawan
133	7.5	Pitman Boro	Pitman
135	7.4	Brick Twp	Brick
136	7.2	Black Horse Pike Regional	Blackwood
136	7.2	Stafford Twp	Manahawkin
138	7.1	Hopatcong	Hopatcong
139	6.8	Lawrence Twp	Lawrenceville
140	6.7	Audubon Boro	Audubon
141	6.5	Bergen County Vocational	Paramus
142	6.4	Edison Twp	Edison
142	6.4	Summit City	Summit
144	6.2	Ocean Twp	Oakhurst
144	6.2	Princeton Regional	Princeton
146	6.1	Southern Regional	Manahawkin
147	6.0	Delran Twp	Delran
147	6.0	Mainland Regional	Linwood
147	6.0	South Plainfield Boro	S Plainfield
150	5.8	Manasquan Boro	Manasquan
151	5.7	Warren Hills Regional	Washington
152	5.6	Kingsway Regional	Woolwich Twp
152	5.6	Lumberton Twp	Lumberton
152	5.6	Northern Burlington Reg	Columbus
152	5.6	Plumsted Twp	New Egypt
156	5.4	Fort Lee Boro	Fort Lee
156	5.4	Hawthorne Boro	Hawthorne
156	5.4	Leonia Boro	Leonia
156	5.4	Rancocas Valley Regional	Mount Holly
160	5.3	Hazlet Twp	Hazlet
160	5.3	Pompton Lakes Boro	Pompton Lakes
160	5.3	Washington Twp	Sewell
163	5.2	Howell Twp	Howell
163	5.2	Jackson Twp	Jackson
163	5.2	Spotswood Boro	Spotswood
166	5.1	Saddle Brook Twp	Saddle Brook
167	4.9	North Arlington Boro	North Arlington
168	4.8	Mantua Twp	Sewell
168	4.8	Morris Hills Regional	Rockaway
170	4.7	Haddon Twp	Westmont
170	4.7	Parsippany-Troy Hills Twp	Parsippany
172	4.6	Cinnaminson Twp	Cinnaminson
172	4.6	Wall Twp	Wall
174	4.5	Upper Twp	Petersburg
175	4.4	Jefferson Twp	Lake Hopatcong
176	4.2	Cherry Hill Twp	Cherry Hill
176	4.2	Madison Boro	Madison
176	4.2	Vernon Twp	Vernon
179	4.1	Mount Laurel Twp	Mount Laurel
180	3.9	Eastern Camden County Reg	Voorhees
180	3.9	Middletown Twp	Middletown
180	3.9	West Milford Twp	West Milford
183	3.8	Point Pleasant Boro	Pt Pleasant
183	3.8	Roxbury Twp	Succasunna
185	3.5	Clearview Regional	Mullica Hill
185	3.5	Mount Olive Twp	Budd Lake
185	3.5	New Milford Boro	New Milford
185	3.5	Voorhees Twp	Voorhees
189	3.4	Fair Lawn Boro	Fair Lawn
189	3.4	Freehold Regional	Englishtown
189	3.4	High Point Regional	Sussex
189	3.4	Metuchen Boro	Metuchen
193	3.3	Flemington-Raritan Reg	Flemington
193	3.3	Rockaway Twp	Hibernia
193	3.3	Springfield Twp	Springfield
196	3.2	East Brunswick Twp	E Brunswick
196	3.2	Mahwah Twp	Mahwah
196	3.2	Nutley Town	Nutley
199	3.1	Hillsborough Twp	Neshanic
199	3.1	Monroe Twp	Monroe Township
199	3.1	Moorestown Twp	Moorestown
202	3.0	Dumont Boro	Dumont
203	2.9	South Brunswick Twp	Monmouth Jct
203	2.9	Wayne Twp	Wayne
205	2.8	Bridgewater-Raritan Reg	Bridgewater
206	2.7	Denville Twp	Denville
207	2.6	Manalapan-Englishtown Reg	Englishtown
208	2.5	Mountain Lakes Boro	Mountain Lakes
209	2.3	Freehold Twp	Freehold
210	2.2	Monmouth County Vocational	Colts Neck
210	2.2	Randolph Twp	Randolph
212	2.0	Evesham Twp	Marlton
212	2.0	Hasbrouck Heights Boro	Hasbrouck Hgts
212	2.0	Scotch Plains-Fanwood Reg	Scotch Plains
212	2.0	Upper Freehold Regional	Allentown
212	2.0	Westwood Regional	Westwood
217	1.8	Hunterdon Central Reg	Flemington
217	1.8	Millstone Twp	Clarksburg
217	1.8	Somerset Hills Regional	Bernardsville
220	1.7	W Windsor-Plainsboro Reg	Princeton Jct
221	1.6	Cranford Twp	Cranford
221	1.6	Medford Twp	Medford
223	1.5	Rutherford Boro	Rutherford
224	1.3	Paramus Boro	Paramus
224	1.3	Ramsey Boro	Ramsey
226	1.2	Lenape Regional	Shamong
226	1.2	Pequannock Twp	Pompton Plains
228	1.1	Cresskill Boro	Cresskill
228	1.1	Sparta Twp	Sparta
228	1.1	Westfield Town	Westfield
231	1.0	Pascack Valley Regional	Montvale
231	1.0	Washington Twp	Robbinsville
233	0.9	Branchburg Twp	Branchburg
233	0.9	Cedar Grove Twp	Cedar Grove
233	0.9	Clark Twp	Clark
233	0.9	Clinton Twp	Annandale
233	0.9	Haddonfield Boro	Haddonfield
233	0.9	Marlboro Twp	Marlboro
233	0.9	Readington Twp	Whitehouse Stn
240	0.8	Hopewell Valley Regional	Pennington
240	0.8	Ridgewood Village	Ridgewood
242	0.7	Berkeley Heights Twp	Berkeley Hgts
242	0.7	Bernards Twp	Basking Ridge
242	0.7	Colts Neck Twp	Colts Neck
242	0.7	New Providence Boro	New Providence
242	0.7	Oakland Boro	Oakland
242	0.7	Waldwick Boro	Waldwick
248	0.5	Caldwell-West Caldwell	West Caldwell
248	0.5	Glen Rock Boro	Glen Rock
248	0.5	Hanover Twp	Whippany
248	0.5	Livingston Twp	Livingston
248	0.5	Millburn Twp	Millburn
248	0.5	Montgomery Twp	Skillman
248	0.5	Montville Twp	Montville
248	0.5	Warren Twp	Warren
248	0.5	Washington Twp	Long Valley
248	0.5	West Morris Regional	Chester
258	0.4	Kinnelon Boro	Kinnelon
258	0.4	N Hunt/Voorhees Regional	Annandale
258	0.4	Watchung Hills Regional	Warren
261	0.3	Holmdel Twp	Holmdel
261	0.3	SD of the Chathams	Chatham
261	0.3	Tenafly Boro	Tenafly
261	0.3	Wyckoff Twp	Wyckoff
265	0.2	Franklin Lakes Boro	Franklin Lakes
265	0.2	Verona Boro	Verona
267	0.1	Northern Valley Regional	Demarest
268	0.0	Glen Ridge Boro	Glen Ridge
268	0.0	Ramapo-Indian Hill Reg	Franklin Lakes

Students Eligible for Reduced-Price Lunch

Rank	Percent	District Name	City
1	19.5	Hillside Twp	Hillside
2	19.4	Garfield City	Garfield
3	17.6	Passaic County Vocational	Wayne
4	17.3	Dover Town	Dover
5	17.1	Essex County Voc-Tech	West Orange
6	16.6	Keansburg Boro	Keansburg
7	15.7	Lower Twp	Cape May
8	15.6	Pleasantville City	Pleasantville
9	15.4	Lindenwold Boro	Lindenwold
9	15.4	Long Branch City	Long Branch
11	15.2	West New York Town	West New York
12	14.5	Linden City	Linden
12	14.5	Perth Amboy City	Perth Amboy
14	14.3	Pemberton Twp	Pemberton
15	14.0	Pennsauken Twp	Pennsauken
16	13.9	Bound Brook Boro	Bound Brook
17	13.6	Hoboken City	Hoboken
18	13.5	Camden County Vocational	Sicklerville
19	13.4	Gloucester City	Gloucester City
20	13.3	Lodi Borough	Lodi
21	13.2	Englewood City	Englewood
22	13.1	Carteret Boro	Carteret
22	13.1	City of Orange Twp	Orange
22	13.1	North Bergen Twp	North Bergen
25	13.0	Rahway City	Rahway
25	13.0	Vineland City	Vineland
27	12.9	Cliffside Park Boro	Cliffside Park
27	12.9	Elizabeth City	Elizabeth
29	12.5	Willingboro Twp	Willingboro
30	12.3	Jersey City	Jersey City
30	12.3	Roselle Boro	Roselle
32	11.9	Plainfield City	Plainfield
33	11.7	Hackensack City	Hackensack
33	11.7	Paulsboro Boro	Paulsboro
35	11.4	Bridgeton City	Bridgeton
35	11.4	Irvington Township	Irvington
37	11.3	New Brunswick City	New Brunswick
38	11.2	North Plainfield Boro	N Plainfield
38	11.2	Paterson City	Paterson

38	11.2	Ridgefield Park Twp	Ridgefield Park
41	11.0	Burlington City	Burlington
41	11.0	Penns Grv-Carney's Pt Reg	Penns Grove
43	10.9	Buena Regional	Buena
44	10.8	Harrison Town	Harrison
45	10.7	Atlantic City	Atlantic City
45	10.7	Hamilton Twp	Mays Landing
47	10.6	Little Egg Harbor Twp	Little Egg Hbr
47	10.6	Millville City	Millville
47	10.6	Pine Hill Boro	Pine Hill
50	10.3	East Orange	East Orange
51	10.1	Burlington County Spec Serv	Mount Holly
51	10.1	Middlesex County Vocational	E Brunswick
51	10.1	Woodbury City	Woodbury
54	9.9	Lakewood Twp	Lakewood
54	9.9	Trenton City	Trenton
56	9.8	Burlington County Vocational	Westampton Twp
56	9.8	Maple Shade Twp	Maple Shade
56	9.8	Passaic City	Passaic
59	9.7	Bloomfield Twp	Bloomfield
59	9.7	Neptune Twp	Neptune
59	9.7	South River Boro	South River
62	9.4	Egg Harbor Twp	W Atlantic City
62	9.4	Mercer County Special Service	Trenton
64	9.3	Deptford Twp	Deptford
64	9.3	Elmwood Park	Elmwood Park
64	9.3	Galloway Twp	Galloway
67	9.2	Newark City	Newark
67	9.2	Pinelands Regional	Tuckerton
69	9.1	Belleville Town	Belleville
69	9.1	Kearny Town	Kearny
69	9.1	Roselle Park Boro	Roselle Park
72	8.9	Bergen County Special Service	Paramus
72	8.9	Glassboro	Glassboro
72	8.9	Lower Cape May Regional	Cape May
75	8.8	Salem City	Salem
76	8.7	Bayonne City	Bayonne
77	8.6	Riverside Twp	Riverside
77	8.6	Union Twp	Union
79	8.5	Collingswood Boro	Collingswood
79	8.5	Phillipsburg Town	Phillipsburg
81	8.4	Palisades Park	Palisades Park
82	8.3	Ewing Twp	Ewing
83	8.1	Middle Twp	Cape May Ct Hse
84	8.0	Gloucester Twp	Blackwood
85	7.9	Delsea Regional H.S District	Franklinville
85	7.9	Monroe Twp	Williamstown
87	7.8	Barnegat Twp	Barnegat
88	7.7	Greater Egg Harbor Reg	Mays Landing
88	7.7	Highland Park Boro	Highland Park
88	7.7	Pittsgrove Twp	Pittsgrove
88	7.7	West Orange Town	West Orange
92	7.5	Franklin Twp	Franklinville
93	7.4	Franklin Twp	Somerset
93	7.4	Somerville Boro	Somerville
95	7.3	Central Regional	Bayville
96	7.2	Teaneck Twp	Teaneck
97	7.0	Asbury Park City	Asbury Park
98	6.9	North Brunswick Twp	North Brunswick
99	6.8	Morris SD	Morristown
99	6.8	West Deptford Twp	West Deptford
99	6.8	Winslow Twp	Atco
102	6.6	East Windsor Regional	Hightstown
102	6.6	Middlesex Boro	Middlesex
102	6.6	South Orange-Maplewood	Maplewood
105	6.5	Hamilton Twp	Hamilton Square
106	6.4	Florence Twp	Florence
106	6.4	Sayreville Boro	Sayreville
106	6.4	Secaucus Town	Secaucus
106	6.4	Sussex-Wantage Regional	Wantage
110	6.3	Matawan-Aberdeen Regional	Aberdeen
110	6.3	Stafford Twp	Manahawkin
112	6.2	Woodbridge Twp	Woodbridge
113	6.1	Berkeley Twp	Bayville
113	6.1	Hammonton Town	Hammonton
113	6.1	Newton Town	Newton
113	6.1	Piscataway Twp	Piscataway
117	6.0	Lyndhurst Twp	Lyndhurst
118	5.9	Tinton Falls	Tinton Falls
119	5.8	Bordentown Regional	Bordentown
120	5.7	Bergenfield Boro	Bergenfield
120	5.7	Manchester Twp	Whiting
120	5.7	Pitman Boro	Pitman
123	5.6	Mainland Regional	Linwood
123	5.6	Southern Regional	Manahawkin
125	5.5	Lacey Twp	Lanoka Harbor
126	5.4	Brick Twp	Brick
127	5.2	Hopatcong	Hopatcong
127	5.2	Old Bridge Twp	Matawan
129	5.1	Black Horse Pike Regional	Blackwood
129	5.1	Hackettstown	Hackettstown
129	5.1	Montclair Town	Montclair
132	4.9	Audubon Boro	Audubon
132	4.9	Lawrence Twp	Lawrenceville
132	4.9	Northern Burlington Reg	Columbus
135	4.7	Plumsted Twp	New Egypt
136	4.6	Fort Lee Boro	Fort Lee
137	4.5	South Plainfield Boro	S Plainfield
137	4.5	Union City	Union City
139	4.3	Burlington Twp	Burlington
139	4.3	Hawthorne Boro	Hawthorne
141	4.2	Camden City	Camden
141	4.2	Ridgefield Boro	Ridgefield
141	4.2	Woodstown-Pilesgrove Reg	Woodstown
144	4.1	Pennsville	Pennsville
145	4.0	Mount Olive Twp	Budd Lake
146	3.9	Spotswood Boro	Spotswood
147	3.8	Toms River Regional	Toms River
148	3.7	Leonia Boro	Leonia
148	3.7	Summit City	Summit
150	3.6	Clifton City	Clifton
150	3.6	Delran Twp	Delran
150	3.6	Mantua Twp	Sewell
150	3.6	Ocean City	Ocean City
150	3.6	Parsippany-Troy Hills Twp	Parsippany
155	3.5	Edison Twp	Edison
156	3.4	Jackson Twp	Jackson
156	3.4	North Arlington Boro	North Arlington
158	3.3	Bergen County Vocational	Paramus
158	3.3	Lumberton Twp	Lumberton
158	3.3	Ocean Twp	Oakhurst
158	3.3	Saddle Brook Twp	Saddle Brook
162	3.2	Haddon Twp	Westmont
162	3.2	New Milford Boro	New Milford
162	3.2	Vernon Twp	Vernon
162	3.2	Warren Hills Regional	Washington
166	3.1	Hazlet Twp	Hazlet
166	3.1	Jefferson Twp	Lake Hopatcong
166	3.1	Upper Twp	Petersburg
166	3.1	Washington Twp	Sewell
170	3.0	Kingsway Regional	Woolwich Twp
170	3.0	South Brunswick Twp	Monmouth Jct
172	2.9	Point Pleasant Boro	Pt Pleasant
172	2.9	Roxbury Twp	Succasunna
174	2.8	Rockaway Twp	Hibernia
175	2.7	Cherry Hill Twp	Cherry Hill
175	2.7	Howell Twp	Howell
175	2.7	Princeton Regional	Princeton
178	2.5	Middletown Twp	Middletown
178	2.5	Morris Hills Regional	Rockaway
178	2.5	Voorhees Twp	Voorhees
181	2.4	Mahwah Twp	Mahwah
181	2.4	Mount Laurel Twp	Mount Laurel
183	2.3	East Brunswick Twp	E Brunswick
183	2.3	Eastern Camden County Reg	Voorhees
183	2.3	Fair Lawn Boro	Fair Lawn
183	2.3	High Point Regional	Sussex
183	2.3	Madison Boro	Madison
183	2.3	Metuchen Boro	Metuchen
183	2.3	Nutley Town	Nutley
183	2.3	Springfield Twp	Springfield
183	2.3	West Milford Twp	West Milford
192	2.2	Evesham Twp	Marlton
192	2.2	Manasquan Boro	Manasquan
192	2.2	Wall Twp	Wall
195	1.9	Bridgewater-Raritan Reg	Bridgewater
195	1.9	Cinnaminson Twp	Cinnaminson
195	1.9	Clearview Regional	Mullica Hill
195	1.9	Monroe Twp	Monroe Township
199	1.8	Flemington-Raritan Reg	Flemington
199	1.8	Freehold Twp	Freehold
199	1.8	Monmouth County Vocational	Colts Neck
199	1.8	Mountain Lakes Boro	Mountain Lakes
199	1.8	Rancocas Valley Regional	Mount Holly
204	1.7	Dumont Boro	Dumont
204	1.7	Freehold Regional	Englishtown
204	1.7	Hillsborough Twp	Neshanic
204	1.7	Manalapan-Englishtown Reg	Englishtown
204	1.7	Moorestown Twp	Moorestown
204	1.7	Wayne Twp	Wayne
210	1.6	Oakland Boro	Oakland
210	1.6	Pompton Lakes Boro	Pompton Lakes
212	1.4	Millstone Twp	Clarksburg
212	1.4	W Windsor-Plainsboro Reg	Princeton Jct
212	1.4	Washington Twp	Robbinsville
215	1.3	Medford Twp	Medford
215	1.3	Upper Freehold Regional	Allentown
217	1.1	Clark Twp	Clark
217	1.1	Cranford Twp	Cranford
217	1.1	New Providence Boro	New Providence
220	1.0	Paramus Boro	Paramus
220	1.0	Randolph Twp	Randolph
220	1.0	Rutherford Boro	Rutherford
223	0.9	Colts Neck Twp	Colts Neck
223	0.9	Marlboro Twp	Marlboro
223	0.9	Pequannock Twp	Pompton Plains
223	0.9	Scotch Plains-Fanwood Reg	Scotch Plains
223	0.9	Westwood Regional	Westwood
228	0.8	Ramapo-Indian Hill Reg	Franklin Lakes
228	0.8	Ramsey Boro	Ramsey
228	0.8	Washington Twp	Long Valley
231	0.7	Hopewell Valley Regional	Pennington
231	0.7	Hunterdon Central Reg	Flemington
231	0.7	Somerset Hills Regional	Bernardsville
231	0.7	Sparta Twp	Sparta
231	0.7	Westfield Town	Westfield
236	0.6	Branchburg Twp	Branchburg
236	0.6	Lenape Regional	Shamong
238	0.5	Berkeley Heights Twp	Berkeley Hgts
238	0.5	Bernards Twp	Basking Ridge
238	0.5	Caldwell-West Caldwell	West Caldwell
238	0.5	Glen Rock Boro	Glen Rock
238	0.5	Montgomery Twp	Skillman
238	0.5	N Hunt/Voorhees Regional	Annandale
244	0.4	Livingston Twp	Livingston
244	0.4	Readington Twp	Whitehouse Stn
244	0.4	Ridgewood Village	Ridgewood
244	0.4	Watchung Hills Regional	Warren
248	0.3	Cresskill Boro	Cresskill
248	0.3	Haddonfield Boro	Haddonfield
248	0.3	Hasbrouck Heights Boro	Hasbrouck Hgts
248	0.3	Northern Valley Regional	Demarest
248	0.3	Verona Boro	Verona
253	0.2	Montville Twp	Montville
254	0.1	Cedar Grove Twp	Cedar Grove
254	0.1	Holmdel Twp	Holmdel
254	0.1	Millburn Twp	Millburn
254	0.1	SD of the Chathams	Chatham
254	0.1	Tenafly Boro	Tenafly
254	0.1	Waldwick Boro	Waldwick
260	0.0	West Morris Regional	Chester
260	0.0	Wyckoff Twp	Wyckoff
262	0.0	Clinton Twp	Annandale
262	0.0	Denville Twp	Denville
262	0.0	Franklin Lakes Boro	Franklin Lakes
262	0.0	Glen Ridge Boro	Glen Ridge
262	0.0	Hanover Twp	Whippany
262	0.0	Kinnelon Boro	Kinnelon
262	0.0	Pascack Valley Regional	Montvale
262	0.0	Warren Twp	Warren

Student/Teacher Ratio

Rank	Ratio	District Name	City
1	17.0	Rancocas Valley Regional	Mount Holly
2	16.1	Medford Twp	Medford
3	15.7	Central Regional	Bayville
3	15.7	Freehold Twp	Freehold
5	15.6	North Bergen Twp	North Bergen
5	15.6	Toms River Regional	Toms River
7	15.5	Hammonton Town	Hammonton
7	15.5	Hillside Twp	Hillside
9	15.4	Elmwood Park	Elmwood Park
10	15.3	Black Horse Pike Regional	Blackwood
10	15.3	Sparta Twp	Sparta
10	15.3	Vernon Twp	Vernon
10	15.3	Washington Twp	Long Valley
10	15.3	West Deptford Twp	West Deptford
15	15.1	Franklin Twp	Franklinville
15	15.1	Nutley Town	Nutley
17	15.0	Brick Twp	Brick
18	14.9	Deptford Twp	Deptford
18	14.9	Hopatcong	Hopatcong
18	14.9	Marlboro Twp	Marlboro
18	14.9	Old Bridge Twp	Matawan
22	14.8	Holmdel Twp	Holmdel
22	14.8	Lacey Twp	Lanoka Harbor
22	14.8	South River Boro	South River
25	14.7	Freehold Regional	Englishtown
25	14.7	Gloucester Twp	Blackwood
25	14.7	Sayreville Boro	Sayreville
28	14.6	Delran Twp	Delran
28	14.6	Denville Twp	Denville
28	14.6	Haddon Twp	Westmont
28	14.6	Harrison Town	Harrison
28	14.6	Monroe Twp	Williamstown
28	14.6	Union Twp	Union
34	14.5	Clark Twp	Clark
34	14.5	Irvington Township	Irvington
34	14.5	Wyckoff Twp	Wyckoff
37	14.4	Dumont Boro	Dumont
37	14.4	East Brunswick Twp	E Brunswick
37	14.4	Eastern Camden County Reg	Voorhees
37	14.4	Lyndhurst Twp	Lyndhurst
37	14.4	Manasquan Boro	Manasquan
37	14.4	Mantua Twp	Sewell
37	14.4	Saddle Brook Twp	Saddle Brook
37	14.4	Upper Freehold Regional	Allentown

45	14.3	Bergenfield Boro	Bergenfield
45	14.3	Greater Egg Harbor Reg	Mays Landing
45	14.3	Jackson Twp	Jackson
45	14.3	Rahway City	Rahway
49	14.2	Manalapan-Englishtown Reg	Englishtown
49	14.2	Montgomery Twp	Skillman
49	14.2	Tinton Falls	Tinton Falls
49	14.2	West Milford Twp	West Milford
53	14.1	Belleville Town	Belleville
53	14.1	Berkeley Twp	Bayville
53	14.1	Cherry Hill Twp	Cherry Hill
53	14.1	Clearview Regional	Mullica Hill
53	14.1	Glen Ridge Boro	Glen Ridge
53	14.1	Kingsway Regional	Woolwich Twp
53	14.1	Pennsauken Twp	Pennsauken
53	14.1	Pittsgrove Twp	Pittsgrove
53	14.1	Point Pleasant Boro	Pt Pleasant
53	14.1	Ridgewood Village	Ridgewood
53	14.1	Southern Regional	Manahawkin
64	14.0	Bound Brook Boro	Bound Brook
64	14.0	Caldwell-West Caldwell	West Caldwell
64	14.0	Delsea Regional H.S District	Franklinville
64	14.0	Hamilton Twp	Hamilton Square
64	14.0	Kinnelon Boro	Kinnelon
64	14.0	Moorestown Twp	Moorestown
64	14.0	Plumsted Twp	New Egypt
64	14.0	Pompton Lakes Boro	Pompton Lakes
64	14.0	Riverside Twp	Riverside
64	14.0	Scotch Plains-Fanwood Reg	Scotch Plains
64	14.0	Verona Boro	Verona
64	14.0	Wayne Twp	Wayne
76	13.9	Burlington Twp	Burlington
76	13.9	Cresskill Boro	Cresskill
76	13.9	Howell Twp	Howell
76	13.9	Maple Shade Twp	Maple Shade
76	13.9	North Arlington Boro	North Arlington
76	13.9	Stafford Twp	Manahawkin
82	13.8	Bloomfield Twp	Bloomfield
82	13.8	Carteret Boro	Carteret
82	13.8	Dover Town	Dover
82	13.8	Middletown Twp	Middletown
82	13.8	Millstone Twp	Clarksburg
82	13.8	South Orange-Maplewood	Maplewood
88	13.7	Buena Regional	Buena
88	13.7	Haddonfield Boro	Haddonfield
88	13.7	Jefferson Twp	Lake Hopatcong
88	13.7	Lawrence Twp	Lawrenceville
88	13.7	New Milford Boro	New Milford
88	13.7	North Brunswick Twp	North Brunswick
88	13.7	Ocean Twp	Oakhurst
88	13.7	Roselle Boro	Roselle
96	13.6	Bayonne City	Bayonne
96	13.6	Egg Harbor Twp	W Atlantic City
96	13.6	Fair Lawn Boro	Fair Lawn
96	13.6	Fort Lee Boro	Fort Lee
96	13.6	Kearny Town	Kearny
96	13.6	Lower Twp	Cape May
96	13.6	Pequannock Twp	Pompton Plains
103	13.5	Cliffside Park Boro	Cliffside Park
103	13.5	East Windsor Regional	Hightstown
103	13.5	Flemington-Raritan Reg	Flemington
103	13.5	Linden City	Linden
103	13.5	Lodi Borough	Lodi
103	13.5	Lumberton Twp	Lumberton
103	13.5	Mount Laurel Twp	Mount Laurel
103	13.5	Mount Olive Twp	Budd Lake
103	13.5	Roxbury Twp	Succasunna
103	13.5	Warren Hills Regional	Washington
103	13.5	Woodstown-Pilesgrove Reg	Woodstown
114	13.4	Audubon Boro	Audubon
114	13.4	Hackensack City	Hackensack
114	13.4	Montville Twp	Montville
114	13.4	Oakland Boro	Oakland
114	13.4	Piscataway Twp	Piscataway
114	13.4	SD of the Chathams	Chatham
114	13.4	South Brunswick Twp	Monmouth Jct
114	13.4	Voorhees Twp	Voorhees
114	13.4	Woodbridge Twp	Woodbridge
123	13.3	Bordentown Regional	Bordentown
123	13.3	East Orange	East Orange
123	13.3	Palisades Park	Palisades Park
123	13.3	Wall Twp	Wall
127	13.2	Berkeley Heights Twp	Berkeley Hgts
127	13.2	Clifton City	Clifton
127	13.2	Evesham Twp	Marlton
127	13.2	Northern Burlington Reg	Columbus
127	13.2	Randolph Twp	Randolph
127	13.2	Somerset Hills Regional	Bernardsville
127	13.2	Upper Twp	Petersburg
134	13.1	Bridgewater-Raritan Reg	Bridgewater
134	13.1	Cranford Twp	Cranford
134	13.1	Neptune Twp	Neptune
134	13.1	Ramsey Boro	Ramsey
134	13.1	Waldwick Boro	Waldwick
134	13.1	Washington Twp	Sewell
140	13.0	Barnegat Twp	Barnegat
140	13.0	Cedar Grove Twp	Cedar Grove
140	13.0	Franklin Twp	Somerset
140	13.0	Hasbrouck Heights Boro	Hasbrouck Hgts
140	13.0	Hazlet Twp	Hazlet
140	13.0	Highland Park Boro	Highland Park
140	13.0	Lenape Regional	Shamong
140	13.0	Matawan-Aberdeen Regional	Aberdeen
140	13.0	N Hunt/Voorhees Regional	Annandale
140	13.0	W Windsor-Plainsboro Reg	Princeton Jct
140	13.0	Westfield Town	Westfield
151	12.9	Clinton Twp	Annandale
151	12.9	Hackettstown	Hackettstown
151	12.9	Middlesex Boro	Middlesex
151	12.9	Passaic City	Passaic
151	12.9	Readington Twp	Whitehouse Stn
151	12.9	Ridgefield Boro	Ridgefield
151	12.9	Secaucus Town	Secaucus
151	12.9	South Plainfield Boro	S Plainfield
151	12.9	Spotswood Boro	Spotswood
151	12.9	Watchung Hills Regional	Warren
161	12.8	Glassboro	Glassboro
161	12.8	Glen Rock Boro	Glen Rock
161	12.8	Hunterdon Central Reg	Flemington
161	12.8	Mainland Regional	Linwood
161	12.8	Pennsville	Pennsville
161	12.8	Perth Amboy City	Perth Amboy
161	12.8	Rutherford Boro	Rutherford
161	12.8	Somerville Boro	Somerville
169	12.7	Bernards Twp	Basking Ridge
169	12.7	Edison Twp	Edison
169	12.7	Hamilton Twp	Mays Landing
169	12.7	Newton Town	Newton
169	12.7	Paulsboro Boro	Paulsboro
169	12.7	Roselle Park Boro	Roselle Park
169	12.7	Springfield Twp	Springfield
169	12.7	West New York Town	West New York
177	12.6	Little Egg Harbor Twp	Little Egg Hbr
177	12.6	Madison Boro	Madison
177	12.6	Manchester Twp	Whiting
177	12.6	Middle Twp	Cape May Ct Hse
177	12.6	Millburn Twp	Millburn
177	12.6	Monroe Twp	Monroe Township
177	12.6	New Providence Boro	New Providence
177	12.6	Teaneck Twp	Teaneck
177	12.6	Westwood Regional	Westwood
186	12.5	Cinnaminson Twp	Cinnaminson
186	12.5	Collingswood Boro	Collingswood
186	12.5	Garfield City	Garfield
186	12.5	High Point Regional	Sussex
186	12.5	Paramus Boro	Paramus
186	12.5	Summit City	Summit
186	12.5	Sussex-Wantage Regional	Wantage
193	12.4	Hanover Twp	Whippany
193	12.4	Hillsborough Twp	Neshanic
193	12.4	Mahwah Twp	Mahwah
193	12.4	West Morris Regional	Chester
197	12.3	Livingston Twp	Livingston
197	12.3	Lower Cape May Regional	Cape May
197	12.3	West Orange Town	West Orange
200	12.2	Branchburg Twp	Branchburg
200	12.2	City of Orange Twp	Orange
200	12.2	Franklin Lakes Boro	Franklin Lakes
200	12.2	Galloway Twp	Galloway
200	12.2	Hawthorne Boro	Hawthorne
200	12.2	Morris Hills Regional	Rockaway
200	12.2	Trenton City	Trenton
200	12.2	Winslow Twp	Atco
208	12.1	Florence Twp	Florence
208	12.1	Metuchen Boro	Metuchen
208	12.1	Pascack Valley Regional	Montvale
208	12.1	Union City	Union City
208	12.1	Washington Twp	Robbinsville
213	12.0	Ewing Twp	Ewing
213	12.0	Tenafly Boro	Tenafly
213	12.0	Willingboro Twp	Willingboro
216	11.9	Colts Neck Twp	Colts Neck
216	11.9	Essex County Voc-Tech	West Orange
216	11.9	Hopewell Valley Regional	Pennington
216	11.9	Millville City	Millville
216	11.9	Parsippany-Troy Hills Twp	Parsippany
216	11.9	Penns Grv-Carney's Pt Reg	Penns Grove
216	11.9	Plainfield City	Plainfield
223	11.8	Montclair Town	Montclair
223	11.8	Pine Hill Boro	Pine Hill
223	11.8	Princeton Regional	Princeton
226	11.7	Camden County Vocational	Sicklerville
227	11.6	Newark City	Newark
227	11.6	Pitman Boro	Pitman
229	11.5	Atlantic City	Atlantic City
229	11.5	Lakewood Twp	Lakewood
229	11.5	Morris SD	Morristown
229	11.5	North Plainfield Boro	N Plainfield
229	11.5	Vineland City	Vineland
234	11.4	Burlington County Vocational	Westampton Twp
234	11.4	Englewood City	Englewood
234	11.4	Jersey City	Jersey City
234	11.4	Rockaway Twp	Hibernia
234	11.4	Salem City	Salem
239	11.3	Northern Valley Regional	Demarest
239	11.3	Ramapo-Indian Hill Reg	Franklin Lakes
239	11.3	Ridgefield Park Twp	Ridgefield Park
242	11.2	Lindenwold Boro	Lindenwold
242	11.2	Pemberton Twp	Pemberton
244	11.1	Pinelands Regional	Tuckerton
245	11.0	Camden City	Camden
246	10.9	Bridgeton City	Bridgeton
246	10.9	New Brunswick City	New Brunswick
246	10.9	Paterson City	Paterson
249	10.7	Phillipsburg Town	Phillipsburg
250	10.6	Woodbury City	Woodbury
251	10.5	Elizabeth City	Elizabeth
251	10.5	Warren Twp	Warren
253	10.4	Passaic County Vocational	Wayne
254	10.3	Burlington City	Burlington
255	10.2	Ocean City	Ocean City
256	10.0	Hoboken City	Hoboken
256	10.0	Leonia Boro	Leonia
256	10.0	Long Branch City	Long Branch
259	9.8	Mountain Lakes Boro	Mountain Lakes
260	9.7	Asbury Park City	Asbury Park
260	9.7	Gloucester City	Gloucester City
260	9.7	Keansburg Boro	Keansburg
263	9.4	Bergen County Vocational	Paramus
264	9.3	Pleasantville City	Pleasantville
265	8.7	Middlesex County Vocational	E Brunswick
266	8.1	Burlington County Spec Serv	Mount Holly
267	7.2	Monmouth County Vocational	Colts Neck
268	6.4	Mercer County Special Service	Trenton
269	5.3	Bergen County Special Service	Paramus

Student/Librarian Ratio

Rank	Ratio	District Name	City
1	4,880.0	Harrison Town	Harrison
2	3,984.0	Southern Regional	Manahawkin
3	2,887.7	Bayonne City	Bayonne
4	2,771.0	Roselle Boro	Roselle
5	2,707.0	Englewood City	Englewood
6	2,495.5	Union City	Union City
7	2,225.0	Haddon Twp	Westmont
8	2,204.5	Garfield City	Garfield
9	2,199.5	Edison Twp	Edison
10	2,181.0	Maple Shade Twp	Maple Shade
11	2,161.0	Lyndhurst Twp	Lyndhurst
12	2,160.5	Wall Twp	Wall
13	2,031.0	Passaic County Vocational	Wayne
14	1,849.0	Secaucus Town	Secaucus
15	1,732.0	Plumsted Twp	New Egypt
16	1,731.0	Tinton Falls	Tinton Falls
17	1,705.0	Saddle Brook Twp	Saddle Brook
18	1,686.0	Audubon Boro	Audubon
19	1,576.0	North Arlington Boro	North Arlington
20	1,531.2	Toms River Regional	Toms River
21	1,506.8	Pennsauken Twp	Pennsauken
22	1,500.2	North Bergen Twp	North Bergen
23	1,462.1	East Orange	East Orange
24	1,453.0	Middle Twp	Cape May Ct Hse
25	1,404.0	Riverside Twp	Riverside
26	1,360.5	N Hunt/Voorhees Regional	Annandale
27	1,342.0	Burlington Twp	Burlington
28	1,335.0	High Point Regional	Sussex
29	1,327.7	Union Twp	Union
30	1,267.7	Bergenfield Boro	Bergenfield
31	1,235.0	Rancocas Valley Regional	Mount Holly
32	1,203.4	Freehold Regional	Englishtown
33	1,195.3	Holmdel Twp	Holmdel
34	1,186.5	Glen Rock Boro	Glen Rock
35	1,173.0	Cranford Twp	Cranford
36	1,168.4	Greater Egg Harbor Reg	Mays Landing
37	1,158.1	Passaic City	Passaic
38	1,156.0	Northern Valley Regional	Demarest
39	1,135.5	Pine Hill Boro	Pine Hill
40	1,110.1	Elizabeth City	Elizabeth
41	1,089.5	Eastern Camden County Reg	Voorhees
42	1,081.0	Hammonton Town	Hammonton
43	1,077.5	Clearview Regional	Mullica Hill
44	1,076.7	New Brunswick City	New Brunswick
45	1,070.4	Monroe Twp	Williamstown
46	1,066.5	Middlesex Boro	Middlesex
46	1,066.5	Warren Hills Regional	Washington
48	1,061.8	Lawrence Twp	Lawrenceville
49	1,061.5	Ramapo-Indian Hill Reg	Franklin Lakes

50	1,057.9	Bloomfield Twp	Bloomfield
51	1,046.9	Jackson Twp	Jackson
52	1,041.9	Middletown Twp	Middletown
53	1,037.2	Perth Amboy City	Perth Amboy
54	1,036.5	Elmwood Park	Elmwood Park
55	1,014.0	Ridgefield Boro	Ridgefield
56	1,010.3	Monroe Twp	Monroe Township
57	1,007.0	Upper Freehold Regional	Allentown
58	998.5	Sparta Twp	Sparta
59	992.5	Camden County Vocational	Sicklerville
60	974.0	Long Branch City	Long Branch
61	973.5	Matawan-Aberdeen Regional	Aberdeen
62	965.0	Carteret Boro	Carteret
63	957.5	Northern Burlington Reg	Columbus
64	956.4	West Morris Regional	Chester
65	948.7	Sayreville Boro	Sayreville
66	946.9	Egg Harbor Twp	W Atlantic City
67	935.4	Montgomery Twp	Skillman
68	935.3	Hunterdon Central Reg	Flemington
69	934.4	Lenape Regional	Shamong
70	933.0	Pittsgrove Twp	Pittsgrove
71	922.5	Lower Cape May Regional	Cape May
72	915.6	Belleville Town	Belleville
73	909.8	Lakewood Twp	Lakewood
74	901.5	Burlington County Vocational	Westampton Twp
75	901.2	Brick Twp	Brick
76	900.2	North Brunswick Twp	North Brunswick
77	900.0	Jefferson Twp	Lake Hopatcong
78	896.4	Ocean Twp	Oakhurst
79	888.3	Hamilton Twp	Hamilton Square
80	887.3	Vernon Twp	Vernon
81	886.7	Linden City	Linden
82	886.3	Dumont Boro	Dumont
83	883.7	Morris Hills Regional	Rockaway
84	883.0	Manasquan Boro	Manasquan
85	877.0	Teaneck Twp	Teaneck
86	876.0	Mercer County Special Service	Trenton
87	868.0	Kingsway Regional	Woolwich Twp
88	867.5	Little Egg Harbor Twp	Little Egg Hbr
89	864.3	Cliffside Park Boro	Cliffside Park
90	861.5	Spotswood Boro	Spotswood
91	857.3	Buena Regional	Buena
92	856.0	Leonia Boro	Leonia
93	855.8	Hazlet Twp	Hazlet
94	853.5	Watchung Hills Regional	Warren
95	851.5	Millstone Twp	Clarksburg
96	849.7	Lacey Twp	Lanoka Harbor
97	848.7	Marlboro Twp	Marlboro
98	844.6	Hillsborough Twp	Neshanic
99	844.2	Hackensack City	Hackensack
100	841.7	Cinnaminson Twp	Cinnaminson
101	833.5	Bernards Twp	Basking Ridge
102	823.0	Mainland Regional	Linwood
103	822.0	W Windsor-Plainsboro Reg	Princeton Jct
104	806.3	Bridgewater-Raritan Reg	Bridgewater
105	805.5	Pitman Boro	Pitman
106	803.4	Rahway City	Rahway
107	802.8	Washington Twp	Sewell
108	802.0	Pascack Valley Regional	Montvale
109	798.5	Point Pleasant Boro	Pt Pleasant
110	797.5	Gloucester Twp	Blackwood
111	791.3	West Deptford Twp	West Deptford
112	791.2	Mount Olive Twp	Budd Lake
113	790.4	Manalapan-Englishtown Reg	Englishtown
114	790.3	Rutherford Boro	Rutherford
115	783.9	Winslow Twp	Atco
116	782.3	Randolph Twp	Randolph
117	775.7	Central Regional	Bayville
118	769.3	Dover Town	Dover
119	769.0	Woodbury City	Woodbury
120	764.7	Haddonfield Boro	Haddonfield
121	758.7	Hillside Twp	Hillside
122	755.5	Colts Neck Twp	Colts Neck
123	752.5	Waldwick Boro	Waldwick
124	748.3	Readington Twp	Whitehouse Stn
125	744.0	Cresskill Boro	Cresskill
126	742.0	Palisades Park	Palisades Park
127	741.5	Asbury Park City	Asbury Park
128	740.0	Burlington City	Burlington
129	737.9	Old Bridge Twp	Matawan
130	735.7	Somerville Boro	Somerville
130	735.7	South River Boro	South River
132	731.9	Jersey City	Jersey City
133	729.0	Hamilton Twp	Mays Landing
134	725.0	Salem City	Salem
135	717.5	Hopatcong	Hopatcong
136	716.0	Gloucester City	Gloucester City
137	709.5	Atlantic City	Atlantic City
138	705.2	Woodbridge Twp	Woodbridge
139	703.2	West Orange Town	West Orange
140	702.4	Plainfield City	Plainfield
141	701.8	Willingboro Twp	Willingboro
142	696.8	Freehold Twp	Freehold
143	696.0	Hoboken City	Hoboken
143	696.0	Paterson City	Paterson
145	693.7	East Windsor Regional	Hightstown
146	690.7	Trenton City	Trenton
147	688.5	East Brunswick Twp	E Brunswick
148	688.0	Montclair Town	Montclair
149	687.3	Bordentown Regional	Bordentown
150	680.7	Roselle Park Boro	Roselle Park
151	680.0	Collingswood Boro	Collingswood
152	677.3	Piscataway Twp	Piscataway
153	674.7	Millville City	Millville
154	673.0	Kearny Town	Kearny
155	671.4	Manchester Twp	Whiting
156	668.8	Newark City	Newark
157	668.2	Howell Twp	Howell
158	665.7	Roxbury Twp	Succasunna
159	662.5	Galloway Twp	Galloway
160	660.4	North Plainfield Boro	N Plainfield
161	659.8	West New York Town	West New York
162	656.7	Pinelands Regional	Tuckerton
163	650.9	Vineland City	Vineland
164	650.3	Westwood Regional	Westwood
165	648.3	Ewing Twp	Ewing
166	648.0	Delsea Regional H.S District	Franklinville
167	640.1	South Brunswick Twp	Monmouth Jct
168	634.9	Irvington Township	Irvington
169	634.3	Clark Twp	Clark
170	633.3	Denville Twp	Denville
171	631.0	Somerset Hills Regional	Bernardsville
172	627.3	Cherry Hill Twp	Cherry Hill
173	626.7	Berkeley Twp	Bayville
174	626.0	Ramsey Boro	Ramsey
174	626.0	Wayne Twp	Wayne
176	619.7	Metuchen Boro	Metuchen
177	616.6	Neptune Twp	Neptune
178	612.5	Glassboro	Glassboro
179	607.0	Lindenwold Boro	Lindenwold
180	602.8	Stafford Twp	Manahawkin
181	598.6	Evesham Twp	Marlton
182	598.5	Phillipsburg Town	Phillipsburg
183	595.8	Medford Twp	Medford
184	594.7	Moorestown Twp	Moorestown
185	594.3	Fair Lawn Boro	Fair Lawn
186	591.7	South Orange-Maplewood	Maplewood
187	591.0	West Milford Twp	West Milford
188	590.6	Hopewell Valley Regional	Pennington
189	590.3	Glen Ridge Boro	Glen Ridge
190	589.7	Ridgefield Park Twp	Ridgefield Park
191	588.0	Clinton Twp	Annandale
192	587.8	Washington Twp	Long Valley
193	583.6	Hackettstown	Hackettstown
194	581.0	Newton Town	Newton
195	580.0	Upper Twp	Petersburg
196	577.5	Voorhees Twp	Voorhees
197	575.1	Clifton City	Clifton
198	573.0	Franklin Twp	Somerset
199	572.7	Sussex-Wantage Regional	Wantage
200	571.5	Mount Laurel Twp	Mount Laurel
201	570.4	City of Orange Twp	Orange
202	566.3	Montville Twp	Montville
203	565.5	Hawthorne Boro	Hawthorne
204	560.0	Woodstown-Pilesgrove Reg	Woodstown
205	551.8	Berkeley Heights Twp	Berkeley Hgts
206	548.1	Nutley Town	Nutley
207	546.4	Ridgewood Village	Ridgewood
208	546.0	Scotch Plains-Fanwood Reg	Scotch Plains
209	545.3	Lumberton Twp	Lumberton
210	543.5	Bridgeton City	Bridgeton
210	543.5	Flemington-Raritan Reg	Flemington
212	542.8	Mahwah Twp	Mahwah
213	542.3	Bound Brook Boro	Bound Brook
214	541.5	Ocean City	Ocean City
215	541.2	Black Horse Pike Regional	Blackwood
216	540.0	New Providence Boro	New Providence
217	532.8	Delran Twp	Delran
218	530.9	Paramus Boro	Paramus
219	530.6	Rockaway Twp	Hibernia
220	529.7	Highland Park Boro	Highland Park
221	528.8	Westfield Town	Westfield
222	526.3	Keansburg Boro	Keansburg
223	525.7	Florence Twp	Florence
224	523.2	SD of the Chathams	Chatham
225	518.8	Essex County Voc-Tech	West Orange
226	517.7	Lodi Borough	Lodi
227	516.5	Tenafly Boro	Tenafly
228	513.0	Livingston Twp	Livingston
229	509.3	Hasbrouck Heights Boro	Hasbrouck Hgts
230	505.3	Pleasantville City	Pleasantville
231	500.5	Verona Boro	Verona
232	499.0	Washington Twp	Robbinsville
233	498.6	Pequannock Twp	Pompton Plains
234	495.0	Franklin Lakes Boro	Franklin Lakes
235	491.7	Paulsboro Boro	Paulsboro
236	486.0	Hanover Twp	Whippany
237	485.9	Fort Lee Boro	Fort Lee
238	483.7	Millburn Twp	Millburn
239	483.3	Branchburg Twp	Branchburg
240	481.6	Pemberton Twp	Pemberton
240	481.6	South Plainfield Boro	S Plainfield
242	481.3	Lower Twp	Cape May
242	481.3	Mantua Twp	Sewell
244	480.6	Caldwell-West Caldwell	West Caldwell
245	480.4	Wyckoff Twp	Wyckoff
246	477.0	Franklin Twp	Franklinville
247	472.7	Deptford Twp	Deptford
248	470.0	Kinnelon Boro	Kinnelon
249	469.7	Princeton Regional	Princeton
250	468.3	Pompton Lakes Boro	Pompton Lakes
251	466.3	Morris SD	Morristown
252	465.7	Penns Grv-Carney's Pt Reg	Penns Grove
253	457.4	New Milford Boro	New Milford
254	448.8	Barnegat Twp	Barnegat
255	446.2	Camden City	Camden
256	445.0	Middlesex County Vocational	E Brunswick
257	439.8	Warren Twp	Warren
258	433.7	Parsippany-Troy Hills Twp	Parsippany
259	414.0	Oakland Boro	Oakland
260	413.8	Mountain Lakes Boro	Mountain Lakes
261	407.8	Pennsville	Pennsville
262	407.6	Summit City	Summit
263	405.6	Springfield Twp	Springfield
264	368.5	Cedar Grove Twp	Cedar Grove
265	352.9	Madison Boro	Madison
266	n/a	Bergen County Special Service	Paramus
266	n/a	Bergen County Vocational	Paramus
266	n/a	Burlington County Spec Serv	Mount Holly
266	n/a	Monmouth County Vocational	Colts Neck

Student/Counselor Ratio

Rank	Ratio	District Name	City
1	1,146.0	Rockaway Twp	Hibernia
2	991.0	Bergen County Special Service	Paramus
3	979.7	Washington Twp	Long Valley
4	876.0	Mercer County Special Service	Trenton
5	870.0	Upper Twp	Petersburg
6	853.5	Hillside Twp	Hillside
7	851.5	Millstone Twp	Clarksburg
8	803.7	Stafford Twp	Manahawkin
9	752.5	Waldwick Boro	Waldwick
10	729.0	Hanover Twp	Whippany
11	722.0	Mantua Twp	Sewell
12	703.8	Cranford Twp	Cranford
13	689.7	Linden City	Linden
14	668.2	Howell Twp	Howell
15	645.9	Brick Twp	Brick
16	633.3	Denville Twp	Denville
17	626.7	Berkeley Twp	Bayville
18	623.9	Union City	Union City
19	618.0	Burlington County Spec Serv	Mount Holly
20	607.7	Deptford Twp	Deptford
21	594.1	Marlboro Twp	Marlboro
22	592.8	Rutherford Boro	Rutherford
23	592.4	Sussex-Wantage Regional	Wantage
24	577.0	Tinton Falls	Tinton Falls
25	576.2	Cliffside Park Boro	Cliffside Park
26	569.0	Union Twp	Union
27	568.3	Saddle Brook Twp	Saddle Brook
28	566.1	Freehold Twp	Freehold
29	562.8	Hackensack City	Hackensack
30	561.0	Barnegat Twp	Barnegat
31	556.3	Matawan-Aberdeen Regional	Aberdeen
32	553.4	Old Bridge Twp	Matawan
33	547.6	Randolph Twp	Randolph
34	542.3	Bound Brook Boro	Bound Brook
35	542.2	Harrison Town	Harrison
36	540.0	New Providence Boro	New Providence
37	528.8	Kinnelon Boro	Kinnelon
38	527.5	Nutley Town	Nutley
39	527.4	Mount Olive Twp	Budd Lake
40	527.0	Manalapan-Englishtown Reg	Englishtown
41	525.3	North Arlington Boro	North Arlington
42	520.2	Westwood Regional	Westwood
43	519.0	Caldwell-West Caldwell	West Caldwell
44	518.7	Garfield City	Garfield
45	515.1	Plainfield City	Plainfield
46	510.4	Toms River Regional	Toms River
47	507.0	Ridgefield Boro	Ridgefield
48	503.7	Colts Neck Twp	Colts Neck
49	502.1	Rahway City	Rahway
50	500.1	North Bergen Twp	North Bergen
51	499.0	Washington Twp	Robbinsville
52	498.6	Pequannock Twp	Pompton Plains
53	496.0	Cresskill Boro	Cresskill
54	495.0	Voorhees Twp	Voorhees

55	494.7	Palisades Park	Palisades Park
56	491.7	Paulsboro Boro	Paulsboro
57	489.0	Hazlet Twp	Hazlet
58	486.0	Hamilton Twp	Mays Landing
59	483.7	Millburn Twp	Millburn
60	481.3	Lower Twp	Cape May
61	479.6	Manchester Twp	Whiting
62	473.3	Somerset Hills Regional	Bernardsville
63	472.8	West Milford Twp	West Milford
64	471.1	Jackson Twp	Jackson
65	470.1	South Brunswick Twp	Monmouth Jct
66	468.0	Scotch Plains-Fanwood Reg	Scotch Plains
67	466.1	Fair Lawn Boro	Fair Lawn
68	465.4	Monroe Twp	Williamstown
69	463.5	Lacey Twp	Lanoka Harbor
70	459.3	Delran Twp	Delran
71	459.1	Cinnaminson Twp	Cinnaminson
72	458.2	Bergenfield Boro	Bergenfield
73	457.2	Mount Laurel Twp	Mount Laurel
74	456.4	South Orange-Maplewood	Maplewood
75	456.3	Point Pleasant Boro	Pt Pleasant
76	455.7	Gloucester Twp	Blackwood
77	453.0	Middletown Twp	Middletown
78	450.1	North Brunswick Twp	North Brunswick
79	449.0	Readington Twp	Whitehouse Stn
80	448.3	Holmdel Twp	Holmdel
81	447.5	East Brunswick Twp	E Brunswick
82	447.1	Hillsborough Twp	Neshanic
83	443.8	Ocean Twp	Oakhurst
84	443.5	Hawthorne Boro	Hawthorne
85	443.4	Atlantic City	Atlantic City
86	442.7	Tenafly Boro	Tenafly
87	441.6	Evesham Twp	Marlton
87	441.6	Flemington-Raritan Reg	Flemington
89	438.7	Passaic City	Passaic
90	435.9	Dumont Boro	Dumont
91	432.2	Woodbridge Twp	Woodbridge
92	431.3	Clifton City	Clifton
93	426.6	Middlesex Boro	Middlesex
94	425.6	Medford Twp	Medford
95	424.4	Hasbrouck Heights Boro	Hasbrouck Hgts
96	420.3	Ramsey Boro	Ramsey
97	417.6	Hoboken City	Hoboken
98	417.3	Wayne Twp	Wayne
99	416.3	Moorestown Twp	Moorestown
100	415.1	Middle Twp	Cape May Ct Hse
101	413.5	Elizabeth City	Elizabeth
102	412.7	Irvington Township	Irvington
103	409.1	Bloomfield Twp	Bloomfield
104	407.1	Mahwah Twp	Mahwah
105	406.6	Sayreville Boro	Sayreville
106	402.8	Upper Freehold Regional	Allentown
107	401.8	Pennsauken Twp	Pennsauken
108	401.0	Willingboro Twp	Willingboro
109	400.4	Verona Boro	Verona
110	400.3	Wyckoff Twp	Wyckoff
111	400.0	Jefferson Twp	Lake Hopatcong
112	399.9	Montclair Town	Montclair
113	398.6	Hopatcong	Hopatcong
114	395.9	Roselle Boro	Roselle
115	395.5	Glen Rock Boro	Glen Rock
116	393.0	Pleasantville City	Pleasantville
117	392.4	SD of the Chathams	Chatham
118	391.9	Winslow Twp	Atco
119	391.5	Piscataway Twp	Piscataway
120	390.2	Bayonne City	Bayonne
121	389.9	Lakewood Twp	Lakewood
122	388.6	Morris SD	Morristown
123	387.8	Westfield Town	Westfield
124	387.6	Franklin Twp	Somerset
125	387.1	Burlington Twp	Burlington
126	386.6	Branchburg Twp	Branchburg
127	385.6	Newark City	Newark
128	385.3	South Plainfield Boro	S Plainfield
129	384.9	Plumsted Twp	New Egypt
130	383.5	Clinton Twp	Annandale
131	381.5	Belleville Town	Belleville
132	380.0	New Brunswick City	New Brunswick
133	378.9	Newton Town	Newton
134	377.3	East Orange	East Orange
135	377.1	Edison Twp	Edison
136	375.3	Neptune Twp	Neptune
137	373.4	Perth Amboy City	Perth Amboy
138	371.8	Metuchen Boro	Metuchen
139	371.3	Franklin Lakes Boro	Franklin Lakes
140	370.5	Madison Boro	Madison
141	370.2	Elmwood Park	Elmwood Park
142	367.8	Somerville Boro	Somerville
143	367.4	Buena Regional	Buena
144	366.5	Warren Twp	Warren
145	363.1	Sparta Twp	Sparta
146	362.3	Bridgeton City	Bridgeton
147	360.4	Montville Twp	Montville
148	360.3	Hammonton Town	Hammonton
149	360.2	Lyndhurst Twp	Lyndhurst
149	360.2	W Windsor-Plainsboro Reg	Princeton Jct
151	360.1	Wall Twp	Wall
152	359.8	Mountain Lakes Boro	Mountain Lakes
153	358.9	Kearny Town	Kearny
154	355.1	Glassboro	Glassboro
155	354.8	Ridgewood Village	Ridgewood
156	354.2	Glen Ridge Boro	Glen Ridge
157	353.9	Paramus Boro	Paramus
158	351.0	Riverside Twp	Riverside
159	350.9	Carteret Boro	Carteret
160	349.0	Lumberton Twp	Lumberton
161	346.9	East Windsor Regional	Hightstown
161	346.9	Lindenwold Boro	Lindenwold
163	345.2	Egg Harbor Twp	W Atlantic City
164	345.1	Lodi Borough	Lodi
165	344.9	Berkeley Heights Twp	Berkeley Hgts
166	342.7	Galloway Twp	Galloway
167	342.0	Livingston Twp	Livingston
168	341.9	Dover Town	Dover
169	340.1	Fort Lee Boro	Fort Lee
170	339.8	Pennsville	Pennsville
171	338.4	Englewood City	Englewood
172	334.1	Montgomery Twp	Skillman
173	333.6	Cherry Hill Twp	Cherry Hill
174	333.4	Bernards Twp	Basking Ridge
175	332.9	Roxbury Twp	Succasunna
176	331.2	Oakland Boro	Oakland
177	329.6	Asbury Park City	Asbury Park
178	329.2	Mainland Regional	Linwood
179	328.6	Vernon Twp	Vernon
180	327.6	Cedar Grove Twp	Cedar Grove
181	326.7	Lawrence Twp	Lawrenceville
182	326.0	Penns Grv-Carney's Pt Reg	Penns Grove
183	325.9	City of Orange Twp	Orange
184	324.4	Pine Hill Boro	Pine Hill
185	322.5	Paterson City	Paterson
186	322.2	Pitman Boro	Pitman
187	320.2	New Milford Boro	New Milford
188	318.0	West Orange Town	West Orange
189	317.8	Highland Park Boro	Highland Park
190	317.1	Clark Twp	Clark
191	316.5	West Deptford Twp	West Deptford
192	315.4	Florence Twp	Florence
193	315.3	South River Boro	South River
194	314.5	Ridgefield Park Twp	Ridgefield Park
195	313.2	Teaneck Twp	Teaneck
196	312.2	Pompton Lakes Boro	Pompton Lakes
197	310.8	Monroe Twp	Monroe Township
197	310.8	Washington Twp	Sewell
199	307.9	Clearview Regional	Mullica Hill
200	305.7	North Plainfield Boro	N Plainfield
201	304.4	Long Branch City	Long Branch
202	304.2	Pemberton Twp	Pemberton
203	303.6	Millville City	Millville
204	302.2	Summit City	Summit
205	300.9	Freehold Regional	Englishtown
206	300.3	Bridgewater-Raritan Reg	Bridgewater
207	299.2	Ewing Twp	Ewing
208	296.7	Haddon Twp	Westmont
209	294.6	Bordentown Regional	Bordentown
210	291.7	Roselle Park Boro	Roselle Park
211	291.4	Collingswood Boro	Collingswood
212	290.9	Central Regional	Bayville
213	288.4	Princeton Regional	Princeton
214	287.1	Pittsgrove Twp	Pittsgrove
215	286.9	West New York Town	West New York
216	285.3	Leonia Boro	Leonia
217	284.6	Southern Regional	Manahawkin
218	282.6	Camden City	Camden
218	282.6	Trenton City	Trenton
220	280.0	Woodstown-Pilesgrove Reg	Woodstown
221	279.1	Hackettstown	Hackettstown
222	277.7	Delsea Regional H.S District	Franklinville
223	276.2	Phillipsburg Town	Phillipsburg
224	272.6	Maple Shade Twp	Maple Shade
225	268.5	Gloucester City	Gloucester City
226	267.0	High Point Regional	Sussex
227	266.6	Warren Hills Regional	Washington
228	264.3	Burlington City	Burlington
229	261.1	Spotswood Boro	Spotswood
230	260.7	Haddonfield Boro	Haddonfield
231	259.7	Manasquan Boro	Manasquan
232	259.4	Audubon Boro	Audubon
233	256.3	Woodbury City	Woodbury
234	255.5	Rancocas Valley Regional	Mount Holly
235	254.3	Middlesex County Vocational	E Brunswick
236	253.8	Hamilton Twp	Hamilton Square
237	250.9	Greater Egg Harbor Reg	Mays Landing
238	247.7	Hopewell Valley Regional	Pennington
239	246.0	Lower Cape May Regional	Cape May
240	244.0	Jersey City	Jersey City
241	243.3	Secaucus Town	Secaucus
242	241.7	Salem City	Salem
243	240.7	Ocean City	Ocean City
244	239.3	Parsippany-Troy Hills Twp	Parsippany
245	233.9	Keansburg Boro	Keansburg
246	225.3	Springfield Twp	Springfield
247	221.9	Vineland City	Vineland
248	218.9	Pinelands Regional	Tuckerton
249	217.0	Kingsway Regional	Woolwich Twp
250	214.7	Black Horse Pike Regional	Blackwood
251	213.9	Essex County Voc-Tech	West Orange
252	213.4	Watchung Hills Regional	Warren
253	212.8	Northern Burlington Reg	Columbus
254	200.5	Pascack Valley Regional	Montvale
255	200.3	Burlington County Vocational	Westampton Twp
256	200.2	Lenape Regional	Shamong
257	198.1	Eastern Camden County Reg	Voorhees
258	192.7	Northern Valley Regional	Demarest
259	187.1	Hunterdon Central Reg	Flemington
260	183.9	West Morris Regional	Chester
261	176.9	Ramapo-Indian Hill Reg	Franklin Lakes
262	167.8	Morris Hills Regional	Rockaway
263	156.4	N Hunt/Voorhees Regional	Annandale
264	155.6	Bergen County Vocational	Paramus
265	152.7	Camden County Vocational	Sicklerville
266	145.1	Passaic County Vocational	Wayne
267	89.2	Monmouth County Vocational	Colts Neck
268	n/a	Franklin Twp	Franklinville
268	n/a	Little Egg Harbor Twp	Little Egg Hbr

Current Spending per Student in FY2003

Rank	Dollars	District Name	City
1	39,428	Bergen County Special Service	Paramus
2	32,907	Mercer County Special Service	Trenton
3	31,812	Burlington County Spec Serv	Mount Holly
4	24,805	Bergen County Vocational	Paramus
5	22,784	Asbury Park City	Asbury Park
6	21,614	Monmouth County Vocational	Colts Neck
7	20,642	Hoboken City	Hoboken
8	20,350	Middlesex County Vocational	E Brunswick
9	19,113	Passaic County Vocational	Wayne
10	19,083	Pascack Valley Regional	Montvale
11	18,756	Northern Valley Regional	Demarest
12	18,517	Newark City	Newark
13	18,180	New Brunswick City	New Brunswick
14	17,805	Englewood City	Englewood
15	17,270	Trenton City	Trenton
16	17,024	Camden County Vocational	Sicklerville
17	16,491	Keansburg Boro	Keansburg
18	16,452	Pleasantville City	Pleasantville
19	16,275	Burlington County Vocational	Westampton Twp
20	16,213	Essex County Voc-Tech	West Orange
21	16,089	Morris SD	Morristown
22	16,074	Ramapo-Indian Hill Reg	Franklin Lakes
23	15,888	Jersey City	Jersey City
24	15,621	Morris Hills Regional	Rockaway
25	15,586	Long Branch City	Long Branch
26	15,564	Passaic City	Passaic
27	15,257	Irvington Township	Irvington
28	15,225	East Orange	East Orange
29	15,208	Mountain Lakes Boro	Mountain Lakes
29	15,208	Teaneck Twp	Teaneck
31	15,185	City of Orange Twp	Orange
32	15,137	High Point Regional	Sussex
33	15,122	Camden City	Camden
34	15,100	Lakewood Twp	Lakewood
35	14,966	Paterson City	Paterson
36	14,947	Ocean City	Ocean City
37	14,940	Vineland City	Vineland
38	14,863	Hunterdon Central Reg	Flemington
39	14,669	Pemberton Twp	Pemberton
40	14,582	Princeton Regional	Princeton
41	14,490	Phillipsburg Town	Phillipsburg
42	14,379	Atlantic City	Atlantic City
43	14,326	N Hunt/Voorhees Regional	Annandale
44	14,273	Gloucester City	Gloucester City
45	14,214	Plainfield City	Plainfield
46	14,156	Neptune Twp	Neptune
47	14,125	West Morris Regional	Chester
48	13,904	Union City	Union City
49	13,834	Bridgeton City	Bridgeton
50	13,657	Watchung Hills Regional	Warren
51	13,427	Westwood Regional	Westwood
52	13,407	Elizabeth City	Elizabeth
53	13,371	Livingston Twp	Livingston
54	13,367	Franklin Twp	Somerset
55	13,320	Burlington City	Burlington
56	13,266	Harrison Town	Harrison
57	13,263	Parsippany-Troy Hills Twp	Parsippany
58	13,170	Somerset Hills Regional	Bernardsville
59	13,101	Tenafly Boro	Tenafly

60	13,067	Highland Park Boro	Highland Park
61	13,020	Madison Boro	Madison
62	12,842	Paramus Boro	Paramus
63	12,772	W Windsor-Plainsboro Reg	Princeton Jct
64	12,717	Secaucus Town	Secaucus
65	12,708	West Orange Town	West Orange
66	12,701	Hopewell Valley Regional	Pennington
67	12,700	Fair Lawn Boro	Fair Lawn
68	12,634	Woodbury City	Woodbury
69	12,614	Rockaway Twp	Hibernia
70	12,611	West New York Town	West New York
71	12,599	Branchburg Twp	Branchburg
72	12,558	Ridgefield Park Twp	Ridgefield Park
73	12,539	Garfield City	Garfield
74	12,506	Hackensack City	Hackensack
75	12,493	Millburn Twp	Millburn
76	12,487	Perth Amboy City	Perth Amboy
76	12,487	Ridgefield Boro	Ridgefield
78	12,463	Metuchen Boro	Metuchen
79	12,446	Ramsey Boro	Ramsey
80	12,433	Montclair Town	Montclair
81	12,416	Cedar Grove Twp	Cedar Grove
82	12,393	Hanover Twp	Whippany
83	12,389	Ewing Twp	Ewing
84	12,353	Mahwah Twp	Mahwah
85	12,317	Pinelands Regional	Tuckerton
86	12,217	Glen Rock Boro	Glen Rock
87	12,211	Berkeley Heights Twp	Berkeley Hgts
88	12,204	Ridgewood Village	Ridgewood
89	12,183	Millville City	Millville
90	12,181	Summit City	Summit
91	12,140	Northern Burlington Reg	Columbus
92	12,139	Lindenwold Boro	Lindenwold
93	12,113	Saddle Brook Twp	Saddle Brook
94	12,112	Springfield Twp	Springfield
95	12,097	SD of the Chathams	Chatham
96	12,073	Somerville Boro	Somerville
97	12,065	Lawrence Twp	Lawrenceville
98	12,052	Oakland Boro	Oakland
99	12,044	Roselle Boro	Roselle
100	12,034	Rahway City	Rahway
101	11,978	Matawan-Aberdeen Regional	Aberdeen
102	11,924	Lenape Regional	Shamong
103	11,919	Franklin Lakes Boro	Franklin Lakes
104	11,895	East Windsor Regional	Hightstown
105	11,871	Cranford Twp	Cranford
106	11,859	Monroe Twp	Monroe Township
107	11,830	South Orange-Maplewood	Maplewood
108	11,820	Piscataway Twp	Piscataway
108	11,820	Warren Twp	Warren
110	11,817	Cresskill Boro	Cresskill
111	11,780	East Brunswick Twp	E Brunswick
112	11,767	Lower Cape May Regional	Cape May
113	11,760	Newton Town	Newton
114	11,704	Salem City	Salem
115	11,703	Willingboro Twp	Willingboro
116	11,668	Fort Lee Boro	Fort Lee
117	11,660	Caldwell-West Caldwell	West Caldwell
118	11,656	Pine Hill Boro	Pine Hill
119	11,653	Rutherford Boro	Rutherford
120	11,645	Hackettstown	Hackettstown
121	11,624	Black Horse Pike Regional	Blackwood
122	11,606	Hawthorne Boro	Hawthorne
123	11,593	Mount Olive Twp	Budd Lake
124	11,578	Collingswood Boro	Collingswood
125	11,573	Greater Egg Harbor Reg	Mays Landing
126	11,563	West Milford Twp	West Milford
127	11,555	Pennsville	Pennsville
128	11,548	Penns Grv-Carney's Pt Reg	Penns Grove
129	11,541	Edison Twp	Edison
130	11,529	Scotch Plains-Fanwood Reg	Scotch Plains
131	11,498	Westfield Town	Westfield
132	11,496	Roxbury Twp	Succasunna
133	11,480	South Brunswick Twp	Monmouth Jct
134	11,473	Lower Twp	Cape May
135	11,440	Montville Twp	Montville
136	11,432	Lyndhurst Twp	Lyndhurst
137	11,429	Pompton Lakes Boro	Pompton Lakes
138	11,423	Waldwick Boro	Waldwick
139	11,421	Warren Hills Regional	Washington
140	11,410	Bordentown Regional	Bordentown
141	11,364	Wayne Twp	Wayne
142	11,337	Winslow Twp	Atco
143	11,303	Cherry Hill Twp	Cherry Hill
144	11,297	Eastern Camden County Reg	Voorhees
145	11,277	Hillside Twp	Hillside
146	11,251	New Milford Boro	New Milford
147	11,241	Buena Regional	Buena
148	11,231	Pitman Boro	Pitman
149	11,226	Tinton Falls	Tinton Falls
150	11,222	Leonia Boro	Leonia
151	11,221	Florence Twp	Florence
152	11,216	Freehold Regional	Englishtown
153	11,214	Cinnaminson Twp	Cinnaminson
154	11,192	Bernards Twp	Basking Ridge
155	11,175	Bridgewater-Raritan Reg	Bridgewater
156	11,155	Kinnelon Boro	Kinnelon
157	11,142	North Plainfield Boro	N Plainfield
158	11,140	Glassboro	Glassboro
159	11,118	Mainland Regional	Linwood
160	11,112	New Providence Boro	New Providence
161	11,097	Bergenfield Boro	Bergenfield
162	11,069	Delsea Regional H.S District	Franklinville
163	11,059	Upper Freehold Regional	Allentown
164	11,048	Roselle Park Boro	Roselle Park
165	11,041	Middlesex Boro	Middlesex
166	11,028	Sussex-Wantage Regional	Wantage
167	10,990	Lodi Borough	Lodi
168	10,975	Kearny Town	Kearny
169	10,970	Ocean Twp	Oakhurst
170	10,959	Hopatcong	Hopatcong
171	10,951	Dumont Boro	Dumont
172	10,906	Palisades Park	Palisades Park
173	10,882	Hazlet Twp	Hazlet
174	10,878	Maple Shade Twp	Maple Shade
175	10,863	Middletown Twp	Middletown
176	10,861	Old Bridge Twp	Matawan
177	10,855	Jefferson Twp	Lake Hopatcong
178	10,854	Spotswood Boro	Spotswood
179	10,846	Elmwood Park	Elmwood Park
180	10,841	South Plainfield Boro	S Plainfield
181	10,814	Moorestown Twp	Moorestown
182	10,809	Washington Twp	Long Valley
183	10,805	Haddonfield Boro	Haddonfield
184	10,788	Kingsway Regional	Woolwich Twp
185	10,776	Bound Brook Boro	Bound Brook
186	10,733	Wall Twp	Wall
187	10,729	North Brunswick Twp	North Brunswick
188	10,725	Linden City	Linden
189	10,723	Voorhees Twp	Voorhees
190	10,707	Barnegat Twp	Barnegat
191	10,701	Holmdel Twp	Holmdel
192	10,695	Dover Town	Dover
193	10,688	Hasbrouck Heights Boro	Hasbrouck Hgts
194	10,686	Clark Twp	Clark
195	10,674	Readington Twp	Whitehouse Stn
196	10,638	Woodbridge Twp	Woodbridge
197	10,600	Colts Neck Twp	Colts Neck
198	10,586	Bayonne City	Bayonne
199	10,571	Randolph Twp	Randolph
200	10,553	Paulsboro Boro	Paulsboro
201	10,523	Pennsauken Twp	Pennsauken
202	10,489	Washington Twp	Sewell
203	10,481	Little Egg Harbor Twp	Little Egg Hbr
204	10,427	Vernon Twp	Vernon
205	10,417	Cliffside Park Boro	Cliffside Park
206	10,397	Pequannock Twp	Pompton Plains
207	10,378	Union Twp	Union
208	10,359	Manchester Twp	Whiting
209	10,345	Carteret Boro	Carteret
210	10,330	Howell Twp	Howell
211	10,326	Hillsborough Twp	Neshanic
212	10,325	Central Regional	Bayville
213	10,322	Washington Twp	Robbinsville
214	10,319	Verona Boro	Verona
215	10,305	Medford Twp	Medford
216	10,272	Belleville Town	Belleville
217	10,268	Sparta Twp	Sparta
218	10,264	Glen Ridge Boro	Glen Ridge
219	10,250	Nutley Town	Nutley
220	10,249	Middle Twp	Cape May Ct Hse
221	10,229	Clinton Twp	Annandale
222	10,222	Hamilton Twp	Mays Landing
223	10,200	Flemington-Raritan Reg	Flemington
224	10,175	Clearview Regional	Mullica Hill
225	10,157	North Arlington Boro	North Arlington
226	10,153	West Deptford Twp	West Deptford
227	10,143	Rancocas Valley Regional	Mount Holly
228	10,092	Stafford Twp	Manahawkin
229	10,074	Manasquan Boro	Manasquan
230	10,048	Clifton City	Clifton
231	10,020	Hamilton Twp	Hamilton Square
232	10,019	Galloway Twp	Galloway
233	9,978	Riverside Twp	Riverside
234	9,936	Audubon Boro	Audubon
235	9,930	Jackson Twp	Jackson
236	9,913	Haddon Twp	Westmont
237	9,910	Mount Laurel Twp	Mount Laurel
238	9,873	Sayreville Boro	Sayreville
239	9,847	North Bergen Twp	North Bergen
240	9,831	Monroe Twp	Williamstown
241	9,824	Delran Twp	Delran
242	9,768	Wyckoff Twp	Wyckoff
243	9,761	Bloomfield Twp	Bloomfield
244	9,732	Woodstown-Pilesgrove Reg	Woodstown
245	9,680	Montgomery Twp	Skillman
246	9,678	Upper Twp	Petersburg
247	9,640	Evesham Twp	Marlton
248	9,637	Pittsgrove Twp	Pittsgrove
249	9,623	Freehold Twp	Freehold
250	9,598	Hammonton Town	Hammonton
251	9,581	Manalapan-Englishtown Reg	Englishtown
252	9,580	Southern Regional	Manahawkin
253	9,559	Plumsted Twp	New Egypt
254	9,542	Egg Harbor Twp	W Atlantic City
255	9,491	Toms River Regional	Toms River
256	9,471	Denville Twp	Denville
257	9,424	Deptford Twp	Deptford
258	9,418	Berkeley Twp	Bayville
259	9,327	Millstone Twp	Clarksburg
260	9,249	Lacey Twp	Lanoka Harbor
261	9,247	Brick Twp	Brick
262	9,195	Lumberton Twp	Lumberton
263	9,182	Gloucester Twp	Blackwood
264	9,158	Marlboro Twp	Marlboro
265	9,127	Point Pleasant Boro	Pt Pleasant
266	9,099	Franklin Twp	Franklinville
267	8,921	Burlington Twp	Burlington
268	8,728	Mantua Twp	Sewell
269	8,546	South River Boro	South River

Number of Diploma Recipients

Rank	Number	District Name	City
1	2,214	Freehold Regional	Englishtown
2	1,699	Newark City	Newark
3	1,496	Lenape Regional	Shamong
4	1,293	Jersey City	Jersey City
5	1,188	Toms River Regional	Toms River
6	929	Burlington County Vocational	Westampton Twp
7	926	Edison Twp	Edison
8	901	Woodbridge Twp	Woodbridge
9	899	Hamilton Twp	Hamilton Square
10	877	Elizabeth City	Elizabeth
11	872	Trenton City	Trenton
12	846	Cherry Hill Twp	Cherry Hill
13	754	Paterson City	Paterson
14	730	Black Horse Pike Regional	Blackwood
15	703	Clifton City	Clifton
16	696	Middletown Twp	Middletown
17	675	Washington Twp	Sewell
18	668	Brick Twp	Brick
19	648	Greater Egg Harbor Reg	Mays Landing
20	646	East Brunswick Twp	E Brunswick
21	615	Southern Regional	Manahawkin
22	579	Old Bridge Twp	Matawan
23	578	Wayne Twp	Wayne
24	562	Vineland City	Vineland
25	560	Union City	Union City
26	554	W Windsor-Plainsboro Reg	Princeton Jct
27	526	Parsippany-Troy Hills Twp	Parsippany
28	523	Morris Hills Regional	Rockaway
29	521	N Hunt/Voorhees Regional	Annandale
30	512	West Morris Regional	Chester
31	505	Camden City	Camden
32	500	Hunterdon Central Reg	Flemington
33	486	Northern Valley Regional	Demarest
34	482	Union Twp	Union
35	476	Eastern Camden County Reg	Voorhees
36	462	East Orange	East Orange
37	455	Bridgewater-Raritan Reg	Bridgewater
38	451	Millville City	Millville
38	451	Passaic County Vocational	Wayne
40	440	Bayonne City	Bayonne
41	439	Ramapo-Indian Hill Reg	Franklin Lakes
42	435	Jackson Twp	Jackson
43	429	Hillsborough Twp	Neshanic
44	428	Piscataway Twp	Piscataway
45	427	South Brunswick Twp	Monmouth Jct
46	426	North Bergen Twp	North Bergen
47	417	South Orange-Maplewood	Maplewood
48	416	Atlantic City	Atlantic City
49	410	Rancocas Valley Regional	Mount Holly
50	395	Essex County Voc-Tech	West Orange
51	385	Pennsauken Twp	Pennsauken
52	375	Kearny Town	Kearny
53	373	Linden City	Linden
54	370	Pine Hill Boro	Pine Hill
55	367	Pascack Valley Regional	Montvale
56	358	Watchung Hills Regional	Warren
57	357	West New York Town	West New York
58	355	West Orange Town	West Orange
59	353	Livingston Twp	Livingston
60	348	Fair Lawn Boro	Fair Lawn
60	348	Montclair Town	Montclair
60	348	Sayreville Boro	Sayreville
63	347	Egg Harbor Twp	W Atlantic City
64	344	Bloomfield Twp	Bloomfield

65	343	Vernon Twp	Vernon
66	342	Hackensack City	Hackensack
67	333	Randolph Twp	Randolph
68	332	Ridgewood Village	Ridgewood
69	328	Winslow Twp	Atco
70	327	Westfield Town	Westfield
71	325	Belleville Town	Belleville
71	325	Lacey Twp	Lanoka Harbor
71	325	Roxbury Twp	Succasunna
74	322	Perth Amboy City	Perth Amboy
75	316	Morris SD	Morristown
76	314	Camden County Vocational	Sicklerville
76	314	Teaneck Twp	Teaneck
78	311	Lawrence Twp	Lawrenceville
79	310	Pemberton Twp	Pemberton
80	309	North Brunswick Twp	North Brunswick
81	307	Paramus Boro	Paramus
82	302	Irvington Township	Irvington
82	302	Mainland Regional	Linwood
84	299	Ocean City	Ocean City
85	295	Willingboro Twp	Willingboro
86	294	West Milford Twp	West Milford
87	288	Warren Hills Regional	Washington
88	287	Franklin Twp	Somerset
89	286	Ocean Twp	Oakhurst
90	285	Bergen County Vocational	Paramus
91	280	Phillipsburg Town	Phillipsburg
92	276	Plainfield City	Plainfield
93	271	Monmouth County Vocational	Colts Neck
94	268	Lakewood Twp	Lakewood
95	266	Nutley Town	Nutley
96	264	Monroe Twp	Williamstown
97	258	Middlesex County Vocational	E Brunswick
98	257	Clearview Regional	Mullica Hill
99	256	Lower Cape May Regional	Cape May
100	254	Scotch Plains-Fanwood Reg	Scotch Plains
101	253	Delsea Regional H.S District	Franklinville
102	251	Wall Twp	Wall
103	249	Central Regional	Bayville
104	247	High Point Regional	Sussex
105	240	Hopewell Valley Regional	Pennington
106	237	Princeton Regional	Princeton
107	236	South Plainfield Boro	S Plainfield
108	235	Upper Freehold Regional	Allentown
109	233	Neptune Twp	Neptune
110	232	Cranford Twp	Cranford
110	232	Hackettstown	Hackettstown
110	232	Middle Twp	Cape May Ct Hse
110	232	Tenafly Boro	Tenafly
114	231	Bernards Twp	Basking Ridge
114	231	Mount Olive Twp	Budd Lake
116	230	Ewing Twp	Ewing
116	230	Jefferson Twp	Lake Hopatcong
118	227	Cliffside Park Boro	Cliffside Park
118	227	Rahway City	Rahway
118	227	Sparta Twp	Sparta
118	227	West Deptford Twp	West Deptford
122	225	East Windsor Regional	Hightstown
123	224	Point Pleasant Boro	Pt Pleasant
124	223	Kingsway Regional	Woolwich Twp
124	223	Northern Burlington Reg	Columbus
126	222	Bergenfield Boro	Bergenfield
126	222	Moorestown Twp	Moorestown
128	218	Holmdel Twp	Holmdel
128	218	Millburn Twp	Millburn
130	213	Garfield City	Garfield
131	212	Fort Lee Boro	Fort Lee
132	209	City of Orange Twp	Orange
133	208	Montville Twp	Montville
134	207	Hazlet Twp	Hazlet
134	207	Long Branch City	Long Branch
136	204	Pleasantville City	Pleasantville
137	203	Montgomery Twp	Skillman
138	200	Carteret Boro	Carteret
138	200	Cinnaminson Twp	Cinnaminson
140	197	Deptford Twp	Deptford
140	197	Manasquan Boro	Manasquan
142	194	Pinelands Regional	Tuckerton
143	191	Lodi Borough	Lodi
143	191	Matawan-Aberdeen Regional	Aberdeen
145	190	Spotswood Boro	Spotswood
146	189	Clark Twp	Clark
147	188	Buena Regional	Buena
148	184	Ramsey Boro	Ramsey
149	182	Manchester Twp	Whiting
150	181	Delran Twp	Delran
151	180	Dumont Boro	Dumont
152	179	Monroe Twp	Monroe Township
153	175	Haddonfield Boro	Haddonfield
154	174	Mahwah Twp	Mahwah
154	174	Somerville Boro	Somerville
156	171	Berkeley Heights Twp	Berkeley Hgts
156	171	Dover Town	Dover
156	171	Summit City	Summit
159	169	Hillside Twp	Hillside
160	168	Bridgeton City	Bridgeton
161	166	SD of the Chathams	Chatham
161	166	Woodstown-Pilesgrove Reg	Woodstown
163	165	North Plainfield Boro	N Plainfield
164	163	Newton Town	Newton
165	162	Collingswood Boro	Collingswood
165	162	Penns Grv-Carney's Pt Reg	Penns Grove
165	162	Roselle Boro	Roselle
168	161	Caldwell-West Caldwell	West Caldwell
169	160	Haddon Twp	Westmont
169	160	Hopatcong	Hopatcong
171	158	New Brunswick City	New Brunswick
171	158	Ridgefield Park Twp	Ridgefield Park
173	157	Audubon Boro	Audubon
174	151	Pequannock Twp	Pompton Plains
175	150	Gloucester City	Gloucester City
176	149	Englewood City	Englewood
176	149	Rutherford Boro	Rutherford
178	148	Harrison Town	Harrison
178	148	South River Boro	South River
180	145	Burlington Twp	Burlington
181	140	Pompton Lakes Boro	Pompton Lakes
182	139	Glassboro	Glassboro
182	139	Madison Boro	Madison
184	137	Hammonton Town	Hammonton
184	137	Hoboken City	Hoboken
184	137	Westwood Regional	Westwood
187	136	Hawthorne Boro	Hawthorne
187	136	Metuchen Boro	Metuchen
189	134	Lyndhurst Twp	Lyndhurst
189	134	New Providence Boro	New Providence
191	130	Glen Rock Boro	Glen Rock
192	127	Ridgefield Boro	Ridgefield
193	126	Maple Shade Twp	Maple Shade
194	125	Elmwood Park	Elmwood Park
194	125	Pittsgrove Twp	Pittsgrove
196	124	Pennsville	Pennsville
197	123	Somerset Hills Regional	Bernardsville
198	121	Mountain Lakes Boro	Mountain Lakes
199	120	Leonia Boro	Leonia
199	120	Secaucus Town	Secaucus
201	119	Bordentown Regional	Bordentown
202	118	Asbury Park City	Asbury Park
203	114	Verona Boro	Verona
204	113	Kinnelon Boro	Kinnelon
204	113	New Milford Boro	New Milford
206	112	Burlington City	Burlington
206	112	Pitman Boro	Pitman
208	111	Palisades Park	Palisades Park
208	111	Paulsboro Boro	Paulsboro
208	111	Saddle Brook Twp	Saddle Brook
211	110	Springfield Twp	Springfield
212	108	Highland Park Boro	Highland Park
212	108	Middlesex Boro	Middlesex
214	106	North Arlington Boro	North Arlington
215	105	Florence Twp	Florence
216	104	Roselle Park Boro	Roselle Park
217	103	Woodbury City	Woodbury
218	100	Bound Brook Boro	Bound Brook
219	99	Hasbrouck Heights Boro	Hasbrouck Hgts
220	98	Salem City	Salem
221	96	Riverside Twp	Riverside
222	91	Cresskill Boro	Cresskill
223	87	Glen Ridge Boro	Glen Ridge
224	85	Keansburg Boro	Keansburg
225	84	Waldwick Boro	Waldwick
226	82	Cedar Grove Twp	Cedar Grove
227	0	Bergen County Special Service	Paramus
227	0	Burlington County Spec Serv	Mount Holly
227	0	Lindenwold Boro	Lindenwold
227	0	Mercer County Special Service	Trenton
227	0	Passaic City	Passaic
227	0	Plumsted Twp	New Egypt
233	n/a	Barnegat Twp	Barnegat
233	n/a	Berkeley Twp	Bayville
233	n/a	Branchburg Twp	Branchburg
233	n/a	Clinton Twp	Annandale
233	n/a	Colts Neck Twp	Colts Neck
233	n/a	Denville Twp	Denville
233	n/a	Evesham Twp	Marlton
233	n/a	Flemington-Raritan Reg	Flemington
233	n/a	Franklin Lakes Boro	Franklin Lakes
233	n/a	Franklin Twp	Franklinville
233	n/a	Freehold Twp	Freehold
233	n/a	Galloway Twp	Galloway
233	n/a	Gloucester Twp	Blackwood
233	n/a	Hamilton Twp	Mays Landing
233	n/a	Hanover Twp	Whippany
233	n/a	Howell Twp	Howell
233	n/a	Little Egg Harbor Twp	Little Egg Hbr
233	n/a	Lower Twp	Cape May
233	n/a	Lumberton Twp	Lumberton
233	n/a	Manalapan-Englishtown Reg	Englishtown
233	n/a	Mantua Twp	Sewell
233	n/a	Marlboro Twp	Marlboro
233	n/a	Medford Twp	Medford
233	n/a	Millstone Twp	Clarksburg
233	n/a	Mount Laurel Twp	Mount Laurel
233	n/a	Oakland Boro	Oakland
233	n/a	Readington Twp	Whitehouse Stn
233	n/a	Rockaway Twp	Hibernia
233	n/a	Stafford Twp	Manahawkin
233	n/a	Sussex-Wantage Regional	Wantage
233	n/a	Tinton Falls	Tinton Falls
233	n/a	Upper Twp	Petersburg
233	n/a	Voorhees Twp	Voorhees
233	n/a	Warren Twp	Warren
233	n/a	Washington Twp	Robbinsville
233	n/a	Washington Twp	Long Valley
233	n/a	Wyckoff Twp	Wyckoff

High School Drop-out Rate

Rank	Percent	District Name	City
1	14.1	Camden City	Camden
2	14.0	Trenton City	Trenton
3	11.5	Pleasantville City	Pleasantville
4	9.3	Paterson City	Paterson
5	9.0	Asbury Park City	Asbury Park
6	8.6	Jersey City	Jersey City
7	8.3	Passaic City	Passaic
8	8.0	New Brunswick City	New Brunswick
8	8.0	Pinelands Regional	Tuckerton
10	7.9	Millville City	Millville
11	7.8	Atlantic City	Atlantic City
12	7.3	Pine Hill Boro	Pine Hill
13	7.0	City of Orange Twp	Orange
14	6.4	Salem City	Salem
15	5.9	Elizabeth City	Elizabeth
15	5.9	Phillipsburg Town	Phillipsburg
17	5.8	Pennsauken Twp	Pennsauken
18	5.5	Englewood City	Englewood
18	5.5	Hillside Twp	Hillside
18	5.5	Lindenwold Boro	Lindenwold
21	5.4	Collingswood Boro	Collingswood
22	5.2	Plainfield City	Plainfield
23	4.9	East Orange	East Orange
24	4.6	Woodbury City	Woodbury
25	4.5	Bloomfield Twp	Bloomfield
25	4.5	Burlington City	Burlington
25	4.5	Greater Egg Harbor Reg	Mays Landing
28	4.4	Bergenfield Boro	Bergenfield
29	4.3	Central Regional	Bayville
29	4.3	Garfield City	Garfield
31	4.2	Lodi Borough	Lodi
31	4.2	Newark City	Newark
33	4.0	Clifton City	Clifton
33	4.0	South River Boro	South River
35	3.9	Lakewood Twp	Lakewood
35	3.9	Riverside Twp	Riverside
37	3.8	Hackensack City	Hackensack
37	3.8	Rahway City	Rahway
39	3.7	Long Branch City	Long Branch
39	3.7	Perth Amboy City	Perth Amboy
41	3.6	North Bergen Twp	North Bergen
42	3.5	East Windsor Regional	Hightstown
42	3.5	Glassboro	Glassboro
42	3.5	Penns Grv-Carney's Pt Reg	Penns Grove
45	3.4	Irvington Township	Irvington
45	3.4	Kearny Town	Kearny
45	3.4	Pemberton Twp	Pemberton
48	3.3	Bridgeton City	Bridgeton
48	3.3	Hoboken City	Hoboken
48	3.3	Old Bridge Twp	Matawan
51	3.2	Black Horse Pike Regional	Blackwood
51	3.2	Lawrence Twp	Lawrenceville
51	3.2	Vineland City	Vineland
54	3.1	Linden City	Linden
54	3.1	Pitman Boro	Pitman
56	2.8	Dover Town	Dover
56	2.8	Ewing Twp	Ewing
56	2.8	Middle Twp	Cape May Ct Hse
59	2.7	Elmwood Park	Elmwood Park
59	2.7	Newton Town	Newton
59	2.7	Warren Hills Regional	Washington
59	2.7	West Orange Town	West Orange
63	2.6	Winslow Twp	Atco
64	2.5	Egg Harbor Twp	W Atlantic City
64	2.5	Hamilton Twp	Hamilton Square
64	2.5	Mahwah Twp	Mahwah
67	2.4	Teaneck Twp	Teaneck
67	2.4	Toms River Regional	Toms River

Rank	Value	District	Location
69	2.2	Delsea Regional H.S District	Franklinville
69	2.2	Wall Twp	Wall
71	2.1	Clearview Regional	Mullica Hill
71	2.1	Monroe Twp	Williamstown
71	2.1	Plumsted Twp	New Egypt
71	2.1	Roselle Boro	Roselle
71	2.1	Union City	Union City
76	2.0	Audubon Boro	Audubon
76	2.0	Belleville Town	Belleville
76	2.0	Rancocas Valley Regional	Mount Holly
79	1.9	Brick Twp	Brick
79	1.9	Cliffside Park Boro	Cliffside Park
79	1.9	Franklin Twp	Somerset
79	1.9	Paulsboro Boro	Paulsboro
79	1.9	Pennsville	Pennsville
79	1.9	Southern Regional	Manahawkin
79	1.9	Washington Twp	Sewell
79	1.9	West Milford Twp	West Milford
87	1.8	Delran Twp	Delran
87	1.8	Eastern Camden County Reg	Voorhees
87	1.8	Jefferson Twp	Lake Hopatcong
87	1.8	Mainland Regional	Linwood
87	1.8	Moorestown Twp	Moorestown
87	1.8	Palisades Park	Palisades Park
87	1.8	South Orange-Maplewood	Maplewood
94	1.7	Bayonne City	Bayonne
94	1.7	Montclair Town	Montclair
94	1.7	Wayne Twp	Wayne
97	1.6	Buena Regional	Buena
97	1.6	Gloucester City	Gloucester City
97	1.6	Lower Cape May Regional	Cape May
97	1.6	Secaucus Town	Secaucus
97	1.6	Vernon Twp	Vernon
97	1.6	Woodstown-Pilesgrove Reg	Woodstown
103	1.5	Manasquan Boro	Manasquan
103	1.5	Manchester Twp	Whiting
103	1.5	Maple Shade Twp	Maple Shade
103	1.5	Northern Burlington Reg	Columbus
103	1.5	Willingboro Twp	Willingboro
108	1.4	Florence Twp	Florence
108	1.4	Keansburg Boro	Keansburg
108	1.4	Lyndhurst Twp	Lyndhurst
108	1.4	Monroe Twp	Monroe Township
112	1.3	Bordentown Regional	Bordentown
112	1.3	Carteret Boro	Carteret
112	1.3	Deptford Twp	Deptford
112	1.3	Matawan-Aberdeen Regional	Aberdeen
112	1.3	South Brunswick Twp	Monmouth Jct
112	1.3	Woodbridge Twp	Woodbridge
118	1.2	Hammonton Town	Hammonton
118	1.2	Morris Hills Regional	Rockaway
118	1.2	Roxbury Twp	Succasunna
118	1.2	Saddle Brook Twp	Saddle Brook
118	1.2	Union Twp	Union
123	1.1	Burlington County Vocational	Westampton Twp
123	1.1	Fort Lee Boro	Fort Lee
123	1.1	Freehold Regional	Englishtown
123	1.1	New Milford Boro	New Milford
123	1.1	West Deptford Twp	West Deptford
128	1.0	Cinnaminson Twp	Cinnaminson
128	1.0	Kingsway Regional	Woolwich Twp
128	1.0	Lacey Twp	Lanoka Harbor
128	1.0	N Hunt/Voorhees Regional	Annandale
128	1.0	Ridgefield Park Twp	Ridgefield Park
128	1.0	Somerset Hills Regional	Bernardsville
128	1.0	Westwood Regional	Westwood
135	0.9	Camden County Vocational	Sicklerville
135	0.9	Clark Twp	Clark
135	0.9	Middlesex Boro	Middlesex
135	0.9	Middlesex County Vocational	E Brunswick
135	0.9	Middletown Twp	Middletown
135	0.9	Princeton Regional	Princeton
135	0.9	Roselle Park Boro	Roselle Park
135	0.9	Somerville Boro	Somerville
143	0.8	Caldwell-West Caldwell	West Caldwell
143	0.8	Cranford Twp	Cranford
143	0.8	Dumont Boro	Dumont
143	0.8	Morris SD	Morristown
143	0.8	North Brunswick Twp	North Brunswick
143	0.8	Ocean City	Ocean City
143	0.8	Pompton Lakes Boro	Pompton Lakes
150	0.7	Burlington Twp	Burlington
150	0.7	Cherry Hill Twp	Cherry Hill
150	0.7	Fair Lawn Boro	Fair Lawn
150	0.7	Montgomery Twp	Skillman
150	0.7	Mount Olive Twp	Budd Lake
155	0.6	Bridgewater-Raritan Reg	Bridgewater
155	0.6	Hunterdon Central Reg	Flemington
155	0.6	Neptune Twp	Neptune
155	0.6	North Plainfield Boro	N Plainfield
155	0.6	Parsippany-Troy Hills Twp	Parsippany
155	0.6	Passaic County Vocational	Wayne
155	0.6	Sayreville Boro	Sayreville
155	0.6	Spotswood Boro	Spotswood
155	0.6	Summit City	Summit
155	0.6	West Morris Regional	Chester
165	0.5	Berkeley Heights Twp	Berkeley Hgts
165	0.5	Cresskill Boro	Cresskill
165	0.5	Hasbrouck Heights Boro	Hasbrouck Hgts
165	0.5	Jackson Twp	Jackson
165	0.5	Leonia Boro	Leonia
165	0.5	Montville Twp	Montville
165	0.5	Nutley Town	Nutley
165	0.5	Piscataway Twp	Piscataway
165	0.5	Pittsgrove Twp	Pittsgrove
165	0.5	Ridgewood Village	Ridgewood
165	0.5	SD of the Chathams	Chatham
176	0.4	East Brunswick Twp	E Brunswick
176	0.4	Edison Twp	Edison
176	0.4	Hazlet Twp	Hazlet
176	0.4	Hillsborough Twp	Neshanic
176	0.4	Hopatcong	Hopatcong
176	0.4	Lenape Regional	Shamong
176	0.4	Ocean Twp	Oakhurst
176	0.4	Point Pleasant Boro	Pt Pleasant
184	0.3	Cedar Grove Twp	Cedar Grove
184	0.3	Glen Ridge Boro	Glen Ridge
184	0.3	Haddon Twp	Westmont
184	0.3	Harrison Town	Harrison
184	0.3	Mountain Lakes Boro	Mountain Lakes
184	0.3	Ramapo-Indian Hill Reg	Franklin Lakes
184	0.3	Randolph Twp	Randolph
184	0.3	W Windsor-Plainsboro Reg	Princeton Jct
184	0.3	Waldwick Boro	Waldwick
184	0.3	Watchung Hills Regional	Warren
184	0.3	Westfield Town	Westfield
195	0.2	Hackettstown	Hackettstown
195	0.2	Metuchen Boro	Metuchen
195	0.2	Upper Freehold Regional	Allentown
195	0.2	Verona Boro	Verona
199	0.1	Bernards Twp	Basking Ridge
199	0.1	Essex County Voc-Tech	West Orange
199	0.1	Hawthorne Boro	Hawthorne
199	0.1	Holmdel Twp	Holmdel
199	0.1	Paramus Boro	Paramus
199	0.1	Pascack Valley Regional	Montvale
199	0.1	Rutherford Boro	Rutherford
199	0.1	Scotch Plains-Fanwood Reg	Scotch Plains
199	0.1	South Plainfield Boro	S Plainfield
199	0.1	Sparta Twp	Sparta
199	0.1	Tenafly Boro	Tenafly
199	0.1	West New York Town	West New York
211	0.0	Bergen County Vocational	Paramus
211	0.0	Bound Brook Boro	Bound Brook
211	0.0	Glen Rock Boro	Glen Rock
211	0.0	Haddonfield Boro	Haddonfield
211	0.0	High Point Regional	Sussex
211	0.0	Highland Park Boro	Highland Park
211	0.0	Hopewell Valley Regional	Pennington
211	0.0	Kinnelon Boro	Kinnelon
211	0.0	Livingston Twp	Livingston
211	0.0	Madison Boro	Madison
211	0.0	Millburn Twp	Millburn
211	0.0	Monmouth County Vocational	Colts Neck
211	0.0	New Providence Boro	New Providence
211	0.0	North Arlington Boro	North Arlington
211	0.0	Northern Valley Regional	Demarest
211	0.0	Pequannock Twp	Pompton Plains
211	0.0	Ramsey Boro	Ramsey
211	0.0	Ridgefield Boro	Ridgefield
211	0.0	Springfield Twp	Springfield
230	n/a	Barnegat Twp	Barnegat
230	n/a	Bergen County Special Service	Paramus
230	n/a	Berkeley Twp	Bayville
230	n/a	Branchburg Twp	Branchburg
230	n/a	Burlington County Spec Serv	Mount Holly
230	n/a	Clinton Twp	Annandale
230	n/a	Colts Neck Twp	Colts Neck
230	n/a	Denville Twp	Denville
230	n/a	Evesham Twp	Marlton
230	n/a	Flemington-Raritan Reg	Flemington
230	n/a	Franklin Lakes Boro	Franklin Lakes
230	n/a	Franklin Twp	Franklinville
230	n/a	Freehold Twp	Freehold
230	n/a	Galloway Twp	Galloway
230	n/a	Gloucester Twp	Blackwood
230	n/a	Hamilton Twp	Mays Landing
230	n/a	Hanover Twp	Whippany
230	n/a	Howell Twp	Howell
230	n/a	Little Egg Harbor Twp	Little Egg Hbr
230	n/a	Lower Twp	Cape May
230	n/a	Lumberton Twp	Lumberton
230	n/a	Manalapan-Englishtown Reg	Englishtown
230	n/a	Mantua Twp	Sewell
230	n/a	Marlboro Twp	Marlboro
230	n/a	Medford Twp	Medford
230	n/a	Mercer County Special Service	Trenton
230	n/a	Millstone Twp	Clarksburg
230	n/a	Mount Laurel Twp	Mount Laurel
230	n/a	Oakland Boro	Oakland
230	n/a	Readington Twp	Whitehouse Stn
230	n/a	Rockaway Twp	Hibernia
230	n/a	Stafford Twp	Manahawkin
230	n/a	Sussex-Wantage Regional	Wantage
230	n/a	Tinton Falls	Tinton Falls
230	n/a	Upper Twp	Petersburg
230	n/a	Voorhees Twp	Voorhees
230	n/a	Warren Twp	Warren
230	n/a	Washington Twp	Long Valley
230	n/a	Washington Twp	Robbinsville
230	n/a	Wyckoff Twp	Wyckoff

New Mexico

New Mexico Public School Educational Profile

Category	Value	Category	Value
Schools *(2003-2004)*	824	**Diploma Recipients** *(2002-2003)*	18,094
Instructional Level		White, Non-Hispanic	5,174
Primary	445	Black, Non-Hispanic	238
Middle	164	Asian/Pacific Islander	105
High	162	American Indian/Alaskan Native	1,775
Other Level	43	Hispanic	6,094
Curriculum		**High School Drop-out Rate** (%) *(2001-2002)*	5.2
Regular	741	White, Non-Hispanic	3.5
Special Education	16	Black, Non-Hispanic	2.6
Vocational	1	Asian/Pacific Islander	3.4
Alternative	56	American Indian/Alaskan Native	5.8
Type		Hispanic	6.4
Magnet	1	**Staff** *(2003-2004)*	
Charter	34	Teachers	21,568.6
Title I Eligible	518	Average Salary ($)	38,469
School-wide Title I	369	Librarians/Media Specialists	298.1
Students *(2003-2004)*	323,066	Guidance Counselors	768.4
Gender (%)		**Ratios** *(2003-2004)*	
Male	51.5	Student/Teacher Ratio	15.0 to 1
Female	48.5	Student/Librarian Ratio	1,083.8 to 1
Race/Ethnicity (%)		Student/Counselor Ratio	420.4 to 1
White, Non-Hispanic	32.8	**College Entrance Exam Scores** *(2005)*	
Black, Non-Hispanic	2.4	Scholastic Aptitude Test (SAT)	
Asian/Pacific Islander	1.2	Participation Rate (%)	13
American Indian/Alaskan Native	11.2	Mean SAT Reasoning Test Verbal Score	558
Hispanic	52.5	Mean SAT Reasoning Test Math Score	547
Classification (%)		American College Testing Program (ACT)	
Individual Education Program (IEP)	19.7	Participation Rate (%)	61
Migrant *(2002-2003)*	0.7	Average Composite Score	20.0
English Language Learner (ELL)	16.9	Average English Score	19.4
Eligible for Free Lunch Program	48.4	Average Math Score	19.4
Eligible for Reduced-Price Lunch Program	9.8	Average Reading Score	20.6
Current Spending *($ per student in FY 2003)*	6,870	Average Science Score	20.1
Instruction	3,870		
Support Services	2,659		

Note: For an explanation of data, please refer to the User's Guide in the front of the book

New Mexico NAEP 2005 Test Scores

Reading			Mathematics		
Grade/Category	Value	Rank	Grade/Category	Value	Rank
4th Grade			**4th Grade**		
Average Proficiency	206.8 (1.27)	48/51	Average Proficiency	224.0 (0.84)	50/51
Proficiency by Gender/Race/Ethnicity			Proficiency by Gender/Race/Ethnicity		
Male	202.8 (1.47)	48/51	Male	224.9 (0.98)	50/51
Female	211.0 (1.62)	46/51	Female	223.1 (1.07)	50/51
White, Non-Hispanic	224.8 (1.54)	34/51	White, Non-Hispanic	237.8 (1.29)	48/51
Black, Non-Hispanic	206.3 (5.33)	8/42	Black, Non-Hispanic	212.5 (4.62)	35/42
Asian, Non-Hispanic	n/a	n/a	Asian, Non-Hispanic	n/a	n/a
American Indian, Non-Hispanic	190.1 (2.57)	6/7	American Indian, Non-Hispanic	216.7 (1.53)	7/7
Hispanic	199.4 (1.57)	30/40	Hispanic	218.2 (1.01)	37/41
Proficiency by Class Size			Proficiency by Class Size		
Less than 16 Students	200.6 (4.33)	20/34	Less than 16 Students	219.2 (2.04)	28/35
16 to 18 Students	205.3 (3.62)	30/33	16 to 18 Students	222.1 (2.17)	30/31
19 to 20 Students	205.4 (2.63)	36/38	19 to 20 Students	223.6 (2.13)	36/38
21 to 25 Students	209.3 (1.74)	45/51	21 to 25 Students	226.2 (1.34)	48/51
Greater than 25 Students	n/a	n/a	Greater than 25 Students	n/a	n/a
Percent Attaining Achievement Levels			Percent Attaining Achievement Levels		
Below Basic	48.7 (1.47)	4/51	Below Basic	35.2 (1.47)	2/51
Basic or Above	51.3 (1.47)	48/51	Basic or Above	64.8 (1.47)	50/51
Proficient or Above	20.5 (1.36)	47/51	Proficient or Above	19.0 (1.14)	50/51
Advanced or Above	3.6 (0.48)	47/51	Advanced or Above	1.7 (0.37)	47/51
8th Grade			**8th Grade**		
Average Proficiency	251.0 (1.00)	47/51	Average Proficiency	263.3 (0.94)	48/51
Proficiency by Gender/Race/Ethnicity			Proficiency by Gender/Race/Ethnicity		
Male	247.2 (1.26)	45/51	Male	264.2 (1.32)	48/51
Female	255.0 (1.10)	49/51	Female	262.3 (1.11)	49/51
White, Non-Hispanic	264.1 (1.49)	45/51	White, Non-Hispanic	279.1 (1.40)	44/51
Black, Non-Hispanic	n/a	n/a	Black, Non-Hispanic	256.7 (5.62)	15/41
Asian, Non-Hispanic	n/a	n/a	Asian, Non-Hispanic	n/a	n/a
American Indian, Non-Hispanic	239.8 (2.47)	7/9	American Indian, Non-Hispanic	252.9 (2.42)	10/10
Hispanic	244.7 (1.14)	29/38	Hispanic	255.4 (1.28)	33/38
Proficiency by Parents Highest Level of Ed.			Proficiency by Parents Highest Level of Ed.		
Did Not Finish High School	242.3 (2.28)	35/49	Did Not Finish High School	248.8 (1.84)	48/50
Graduated High School	247.1 (1.73)	42/50	Graduated High School	254.1 (1.32)	47/50
Some Education After High School	255.7 (1.71)	47/50	Some Education After High School	270.0 (1.69)	47/50
Graduated College	261.4 (1.64)	45/50	Graduated College	276.4 (1.37)	45/50
Percent Attaining Achievement Levels			Percent Attaining Achievement Levels		
Below Basic	48.7 (1.47)	4/51	Below Basic	47.3 (1.46)	3/51
Basic or Above	51.3 (1.47)	48/51	Basic or Above	52.7 (1.46)	49/51
Proficient or Above	20.5 (1.36)	47/51	Proficient or Above	14.0 (1.13)	49/51
Advanced or Above	3.6 (0.48)	47/51	Advanced or Above	1.4 (0.33)	49/51

Note: For an explanation of data, please refer to the User's Guide in the front of the book; n/a indicates data not available

Bernalillo County

Albuquerque Public Schools
725 University Blvd SE • Albuquerque, NM 87125-0704
Mailing Address: PO Box 25704 • Albuquerque, NM 87125-0704
(505) 842-8211 • http://ww2.aps.edu/
Grade Span: PK-12; **Agency Type:** 1
Schools: 148
  85 Primary; 29 Middle; 26 High; 8 Other Level
  134 Regular; 1 Special Education; 1 Vocational; 12 Alternative
  1 Magnet; 17 Charter; 64 Title I Eligible; 56 School-wide Title I
Students: 90,537 (51.4% male; 48.5% female)
  Individual Education Program: 18,061 (19.9%);
  English Language Learner: 10,783 (11.9%); Migrant: 0 (0.0%)
  Eligible for Free Lunch Program: 36,000 (39.8%)
  Eligible for Reduced-Price Lunch Program: 6,960 (7.7%)
Teachers: 6,191.0 (14.6 to 1)
Librarians/Media Specialists: 93.5 (968.3 to 1)
Guidance Counselors: 206.2 (439.1 to 1)
Current Spending: ($ per student per year):
  Total: $6,414; Instruction: $3,780; Support Services: $2,373
Enrollment, Drop-out Rates and Diploma Recipients by Race/Ethnicity

Category	Total	White	Black	Asian	AIAN	Hisp.
Enrollment (%)	100.0	36.4	3.9	2.3	4.8	52.6
Drop-out Rate (%)	7.1	4.3	3.0	4.6	11.3	9.7
H.S. Diplomas (#)	4,708	n/a	n/a	n/a	n/a	n/a

Chaves County

Roswell Independent Schools
200 W Chisum • Roswell, NM 88202-1437
Mailing Address: PO Box 1437 • Roswell, NM 88202-1437
(505) 627-2511 • http://www.risd.k12.nm.us
Grade Span: PK-12; **Agency Type:** 1
Schools: 24
  15 Primary; 5 Middle; 4 High; 0 Other Level
  22 Regular; 0 Special Education; 0 Vocational; 2 Alternative
  0 Magnet; 1 Charter; 18 Title I Eligible; 16 School-wide Title I
Students: 9,419 (50.8% male; 49.1% female)
  Individual Education Program: 2,375 (25.2%);
  English Language Learner: 548 (5.8%); Migrant: 248 (2.6%)
  Eligible for Free Lunch Program: 5,005 (53.1%)
  Eligible for Reduced-Price Lunch Program: 1,004 (10.7%)
Teachers: 596.5 (15.8 to 1)
Librarians/Media Specialists: 6.0 (1,569.8 to 1)
Guidance Counselors: 20.0 (471.0 to 1)
Current Spending: ($ per student per year):
  Total: $6,630; Instruction: $3,926; Support Services: $2,386
Enrollment, Drop-out Rates and Diploma Recipients by Race/Ethnicity

Category	Total	White	Black	Asian	AIAN	Hisp.
Enrollment (%)	100.0	36.9	2.9	0.6	0.4	59.2
Drop-out Rate (%)	9.4	7.3	2.5	0.0	0.0	11.6
H.S. Diplomas (#)	527	273	16	2	2	234

Cibola County

Grants-Cibola County Schools
401 N Second St • Grants, NM 87020-0008
Mailing Address: PO Box 8 • Grants, NM 87020-0008
(505) 285-2603
Grade Span: PK-12; **Agency Type:** 1
Schools: 12
  7 Primary; 2 Middle; 2 High; 1 Other Level
  11 Regular; 0 Special Education; 0 Vocational; 1 Alternative
  0 Magnet; 0 Charter; 12 Title I Eligible; 12 School-wide Title I
Students: 3,710 (51.5% male; 48.4% female)
  Individual Education Program: 558 (15.0%);
  English Language Learner: 673 (18.1%); Migrant: 0 (0.0%)
  Eligible for Free Lunch Program: 2,379 (64.1%)
  Eligible for Reduced-Price Lunch Program: 353 (9.5%)
Teachers: 251.3 (14.8 to 1)
Librarians/Media Specialists: 3.0 (1,236.7 to 1)
Guidance Counselors: 11.5 (322.6 to 1)
Current Spending: ($ per student per year):
  Total: $7,112; Instruction: $4,203; Support Services: $2,574
Enrollment, Drop-out Rates and Diploma Recipients by Race/Ethnicity

Category	Total	White	Black	Asian	AIAN	Hisp.
Enrollment (%)	100.0	20.9	1.0	0.3	36.8	41.0
Drop-out Rate (%)	8.0	5.4	33.3	0.0	7.2	10.0
H.S. Diplomas (#)	202	39	1	1	90	71

Curry County

Clovis Municipal Schools
1009 Main St • Clovis, NM 88102-9000
Mailing Address: PO Box 19000 • Clovis, NM 88102-9000
(505) 769-4300 • http://www.cms.k12.nm.us
Grade Span: PK-12; **Agency Type:** 1
Schools: 19
  14 Primary; 3 Middle; 1 High; 0 Other Level
  17 Regular; 1 Special Education; 0 Vocational; 0 Alternative
  0 Magnet; 0 Charter; 11 Title I Eligible; 11 School-wide Title I
Students: 8,237 (52.1% male; 47.8% female)
  Individual Education Program: 1,609 (19.5%);
  English Language Learner: 556 (6.8%); Migrant: 144 (1.7%)
  Eligible for Free Lunch Program: 4,112 (49.9%)
  Eligible for Reduced-Price Lunch Program: 1,153 (14.0%)
Teachers: 523.1 (15.7 to 1)
Librarians/Media Specialists: 7.0 (1,176.7 to 1)
Guidance Counselors: 12.7 (648.6 to 1)
Current Spending: ($ per student per year):
  Total: $6,058; Instruction: $3,481; Support Services: $2,170
Enrollment, Drop-out Rates and Diploma Recipients by Race/Ethnicity

Category	Total	White	Black	Asian	AIAN	Hisp.
Enrollment (%)	100.0	44.5	10.0	1.9	0.9	42.7
Drop-out Rate (%)	6.4	3.2	2.9	0.0	0.0	12.4
H.S. Diplomas (#)	400	240	38	10	0	112

Dona Ana County

Gadsden Independent Schools
1325 W Washington • Anthony, NM 88021-0070
Mailing Address: PO Box 70 • Anthony, NM 88021-0070
(505) 882-6203 • http://www.gisd.k12.nm.us/
Grade Span: PK-12; **Agency Type:** 1
Schools: 20
  12 Primary; 4 Middle; 3 High; 1 Other Level
  19 Regular; 0 Special Education; 0 Vocational; 1 Alternative
  0 Magnet; 0 Charter; 18 Title I Eligible; 16 School-wide Title I
Students: 13,796 (51.2% male; 48.7% female)
  Individual Education Program: 2,111 (15.3%);
  English Language Learner: 6,463 (46.8%); Migrant: 274 (2.0%)
  Eligible for Free Lunch Program: 11,970 (86.8%)
  Eligible for Reduced-Price Lunch Program: 658 (4.8%)
Teachers: 853.3 (16.2 to 1)
Librarians/Media Specialists: 6.0 (2,299.3 to 1)
Guidance Counselors: 31.0 (445.0 to 1)
Current Spending: ($ per student per year):
  Total: $6,696; Instruction: $3,585; Support Services: $2,646
Enrollment, Drop-out Rates and Diploma Recipients by Race/Ethnicity

Category	Total	White	Black	Asian	AIAN	Hisp.
Enrollment (%)	100.0	4.8	0.3	0.1	0.1	94.6
Drop-out Rate (%)	4.0	0.4	9.1	0.0	0.0	4.2
H.S. Diplomas (#)	634	34	2	0	0	598

Hatch Valley Public Schools
400 Main And Reed • Hatch, NM 87937-0790
Mailing Address: PO Box 790 • Hatch, NM 87937-0790
(505) 267-8200
Grade Span: PK-12; **Agency Type:** 1
Schools: 6
  3 Primary; 1 Middle; 2 High; 0 Other Level
  5 Regular; 0 Special Education; 0 Vocational; 1 Alternative
  0 Magnet; 0 Charter; 6 Title I Eligible; 6 School-wide Title I
Students: 1,545 (50.3% male; 49.6% female)
  Individual Education Program: 170 (11.0%);
  English Language Learner: 1,058 (68.5%); Migrant: 118 (7.6%)
  Eligible for Free Lunch Program: 1,217 (78.8%)
  Eligible for Reduced-Price Lunch Program: 152 (9.8%)
Teachers: 102.3 (15.1 to 1)
Librarians/Media Specialists: 1.0 (1,545.0 to 1)
Guidance Counselors: 4.0 (386.3 to 1)
Current Spending: ($ per student per year):
  Total: $7,406; Instruction: $4,183; Support Services: $2,806
Enrollment, Drop-out Rates and Diploma Recipients by Race/Ethnicity

Category	Total	White	Black	Asian	AIAN	Hisp.
Enrollment (%)	100.0	10.7	0.0	0.0	0.1	89.3
Drop-out Rate (%)	1.1	1.9	n/a	n/a	0.0	1.0
H.S. Diplomas (#)	62	8	0	0	0	54

Las Cruces Public Schools
505 S Main Ste 249 • Las Cruces, NM 88001-1243
(505) 527-5807 • http://lcps.k12.nm.us/
Grade Span: PK-12; **Agency Type:** 1
Schools: 38
  23 Primary; 7 Middle; 4 High; 3 Other Level

32 Regular; 3 Special Education; 0 Vocational; 2 Alternative
0 Magnet; 0 Charter; 22 Title I Eligible; 17 School-wide Title I
Students: 23,101   (51.0% male; 48.9% female)
Individual Education Program: 5,772 (25.0%);
English Language Learner: 2,092 (9.1%); Migrant: 405 (1.8%)
Eligible for Free Lunch Program: 11,770 (51.0%)
Eligible for Reduced-Price Lunch Program: 2,145 (9.3%)
Teachers: 1,544.7 (15.0 to 1)
Librarians/Media Specialists: 14.5 (1,593.2 to 1)
Guidance Counselors: 43.0 (537.2 to 1)
Current Spending: ($ per student per year):
Total: $6,495; Instruction: $3,753; Support Services: $2,411
Enrollment, Drop-out Rates and Diploma Recipients by Race/Ethnicity

Category	Total	White	Black	Asian	AIAN	Hisp.
Enrollment (%)	100.0	27.5	2.3	1.0	0.9	68.3
Drop-out Rate (%)	5.5	3.9	2.1	2.2	5.3	6.5
H.S. Diplomas (#)	1,417	519	24	17	7	850

Eddy County

Artesia Public Schools
1105 W Quay • Artesia, NM 88210-1826
Mailing Address: 1106 W Quay Ave • Artesia, NM 88210-1826
(505) 746-3585 • http://www.bulldogs.org
Grade Span: PK-12; **Agency Type:** 1
Schools: 11
7 Primary; 1 Middle; 1 High; 1 Other Level
10 Regular; 0 Special Education; 0 Vocational; 0 Alternative
0 Magnet; 0 Charter; 7 Title I Eligible; 0 School-wide Title I
Students: 3,531   (51.6% male; 48.3% female)
Individual Education Program: 728 (20.6%);
English Language Learner: 199 (5.6%); Migrant: 49 (1.4%)
Eligible for Free Lunch Program: 1,389 (39.3%)
Eligible for Reduced-Price Lunch Program: 315 (8.9%)
Teachers: 238.6 (14.8 to 1)
Librarians/Media Specialists: 3.0 (1,177.0 to 1)
Guidance Counselors: 7.0 (504.4 to 1)
Current Spending: ($ per student per year):
Total: $7,110; Instruction: $4,054; Support Services: $2,382
Enrollment, Drop-out Rates and Diploma Recipients by Race/Ethnicity

Category	Total	White	Black	Asian	AIAN	Hisp.
Enrollment (%)	100.0	45.3	1.2	0.1	0.3	53.1
Drop-out Rate (%)	1.7	1.4	0.0	0.0	0.0	2.1
H.S. Diplomas (#)	237	134	2	0	1	100

Carlsbad Municipal Schools
498 N Canyon St • Carlsbad, NM 88220-5812
Mailing Address: 408 N Canyon St • Carlsbad, NM 88220-5812
(505) 234-3300 • http://www.carlsbad.k12.nm.us
Grade Span: PK-12; **Agency Type:** 1
Schools: 15
11 Primary; 2 Middle; 1 High; 1 Other Level
15 Regular; 0 Special Education; 0 Vocational; 0 Alternative
0 Magnet; 1 Charter; 11 Title I Eligible; 10 School-wide Title I
Students: 6,212   (51.6% male; 48.3% female)
Individual Education Program: 1,643 (26.4%);
English Language Learner: 174 (2.8%); Migrant: 0 (0.0%)
Eligible for Free Lunch Program: 2,984 (48.0%)
Eligible for Reduced-Price Lunch Program: 775 (12.5%)
Teachers: 378.4 (16.4 to 1)
Librarians/Media Specialists: 3.0 (2,070.7 to 1)
Guidance Counselors: 8.6 (722.3 to 1)
Current Spending: ($ per student per year):
Total: $7,248; Instruction: $4,288; Support Services: $2,475
Enrollment, Drop-out Rates and Diploma Recipients by Race/Ethnicity

Category	Total	White	Black	Asian	AIAN	Hisp.
Enrollment (%)	100.0	50.0	1.6	0.5	0.7	47.2
Drop-out Rate (%)	1.3	1.3	0.0	0.0	0.0	1.5
H.S. Diplomas (#)	360	218	11	2	1	128

Grant County

Cobre Consolidated Schools
207 N Central Ave • Bayard, NM 88023-1000
Mailing Address: PO Box 1000 • Bayard, NM 88023-1000
(505) 537-4514 • http://www.Cobre-High-School.homepagehere.com/
Grade Span: PK-12; **Agency Type:** 1
Schools: 6
4 Primary; 1 Middle; 1 High; 0 Other Level
6 Regular; 0 Special Education; 0 Vocational; 0 Alternative
0 Magnet; 0 Charter; 5 Title I Eligible; 5 School-wide Title I
Students: 1,540   (51.8% male; 48.1% female)
Individual Education Program: 346 (22.5%);
English Language Learner: 519 (33.7%); Migrant: 1 (0.1%)
Eligible for Free Lunch Program: 944 (61.3%)

Eligible for Reduced-Price Lunch Program: 298 (19.4%)
Teachers: 127.4 (12.1 to 1)
Librarians/Media Specialists: 2.0 (770.0 to 1)
Guidance Counselors: 5.0 (308.0 to 1)
Current Spending: ($ per student per year):
Total: $8,436; Instruction: $4,436; Support Services: $3,572
Enrollment, Drop-out Rates and Diploma Recipients by Race/Ethnicity

Category	Total	White	Black	Asian	AIAN	Hisp.
Enrollment (%)	100.0	12.8	0.7	0.1	1.2	85.2
Drop-out Rate (%)	1.6	1.0	0.0	n/a	0.0	1.7
H.S. Diplomas (#)	110	15	0	0	2	93

Silver City Consolidated Schl
2810 N Swan St • Silver City, NM 88061-5853
(505) 956-2000 • http://silverhigh.com/
Grade Span: PK-12; **Agency Type:** 1
Schools: 10
5 Primary; 1 Middle; 3 High; 0 Other Level
8 Regular; 0 Special Education; 0 Vocational; 1 Alternative
0 Magnet; 0 Charter; 5 Title I Eligible; 1 School-wide Title I
Students: 3,286   (53.6% male; 46.3% female)
Individual Education Program: 642 (19.5%);
English Language Learner: 284 (8.6%); Migrant: 0 (0.0%)
Eligible for Free Lunch Program: 1,430 (43.5%)
Eligible for Reduced-Price Lunch Program: 317 (9.6%)
Teachers: 216.1 (15.2 to 1)
Librarians/Media Specialists: 3.0 (1,095.3 to 1)
Guidance Counselors: 10.0 (328.6 to 1)
Current Spending: ($ per student per year):
Total: $7,417; Instruction: $4,211; Support Services: $2,891
Enrollment, Drop-out Rates and Diploma Recipients by Race/Ethnicity

Category	Total	White	Black	Asian	AIAN	Hisp.
Enrollment (%)	100.0	45.1	1.2	0.8	0.7	52.2
Drop-out Rate (%)	4.8	3.1	0.0	0.0	0.0	6.9
H.S. Diplomas (#)	231	131	5	0	0	95

Lea County

Hobbs Municipal Schools
1515 East.Sanger • Hobbs, NM 88241-1040
Mailing Address: PO Box 1030 • Hobbs, NM 88241-1040
(505) 433-0100 • http://www.hobbsschools.net/
Grade Span: PK-12; **Agency Type:** 1
Schools: 19
13 Primary; 2 Middle; 2 High; 2 Other Level
16 Regular; 1 Special Education; 0 Vocational; 2 Alternative
0 Magnet; 0 Charter; 8 Title I Eligible; 8 School-wide Title I
Students: 7,575   (51.5% male; 48.4% female)
Individual Education Program: 1,295 (17.1%);
English Language Learner: 1,057 (14.0%); Migrant: 0 (0.0%)
Eligible for Free Lunch Program: 3,802 (50.2%)
Eligible for Reduced-Price Lunch Program: 603 (8.0%)
Teachers: 450.2 (16.8 to 1)
Librarians/Media Specialists: 4.0 (1,893.8 to 1)
Guidance Counselors: 10.0 (757.5 to 1)
Current Spending: ($ per student per year):
Total: $5,884; Instruction: $3,371; Support Services: $2,105
Enrollment, Drop-out Rates and Diploma Recipients by Race/Ethnicity

Category	Total	White	Black	Asian	AIAN	Hisp.
Enrollment (%)	100.0	39.0	6.5	0.6	0.3	53.7
Drop-out Rate (%)	2.3	2.0	0.7	0.0	0.0	2.8
H.S. Diplomas (#)	433	191	27	0	3	212

Lovington Public Schools
1310 N 5th St • Lovington, NM 88260-1537
Mailing Address: PO Box 1537 • Lovington, NM 88260-1537
(505) 739-2200 • http://lovschools.leaco.net/
Grade Span: PK-12; **Agency Type:** 1
Schools: 10
4 Primary; 2 Middle; 3 High; 1 Other Level
8 Regular; 0 Special Education; 0 Vocational; 2 Alternative
0 Magnet; 0 Charter; 6 Title I Eligible; 5 School-wide Title I
Students: 2,863   (50.8% male; 49.1% female)
Individual Education Program: 703 (24.6%);
English Language Learner: 5 (0.2%); Migrant: 80 (2.8%)
Eligible for Free Lunch Program: 1,496 (52.3%)
Eligible for Reduced-Price Lunch Program: 406 (14.2%)
Teachers: 177.1 (16.2 to 1)
Librarians/Media Specialists: 1.0 (2,863.0 to 1)
Guidance Counselors: 5.5 (520.5 to 1)
Current Spending: ($ per student per year):
Total: $6,655; Instruction: $3,882; Support Services: $2,462

Enrollment, Drop-out Rates and Diploma Recipients by Race/Ethnicity

Category	Total	White	Black	Asian	AIAN	Hisp.
Enrollment (%)	100.0	35.7	3.4	0.3	0.2	60.3
Drop-out Rate (%)	6.0	4.6	11.8	0.0	0.0	7.0
H.S. Diplomas (#)	203	90	1	2	0	110

Lincoln County

Ruidoso Municipal Schools
200 Horton Circle • Ruidoso, NM 88345-6032
(505) 257-4051 • http://www.ruidoso.k12.nm.us
Grade Span: PK-12; Agency Type: 1
Schools: 7
  3 Primary; 2 Middle; 1 High; 1 Other Level
  6 Regular; 1 Special Education; 0 Vocational; 0 Alternative
  0 Magnet; 0 Charter; 3 Title I Eligible; 3 School-wide Title I
Students: 2,380 (51.9% male; 48.0% female)
  Individual Education Program: 465 (19.5%);
  English Language Learner: 373 (15.7%); Migrant: 0 (0.0%)
  Eligible for Free Lunch Program: 1,146 (48.2%)
  Eligible for Reduced-Price Lunch Program: 341 (14.3%)
Teachers: 150.3 (15.8 to 1)
Librarians/Media Specialists: 3.0 (793.3 to 1)
Guidance Counselors: 2.8 (850.0 to 1)
Current Spending: ($ per student per year):
  Total: $7,834; Instruction: $4,670; Support Services: $2,756

Enrollment, Drop-out Rates and Diploma Recipients by Race/Ethnicity

Category	Total	White	Black	Asian	AIAN	Hisp.
Enrollment (%)	100.0	47.9	1.0	0.4	16.1	34.7
Drop-out Rate (%)	4.1	1.6	0.0	0.0	14.7	3.0
H.S. Diplomas (#)	120	65	0	1	21	33

Los Alamos County

Los Alamos Public Schools
751 Trinity Dr • Los Alamos, NM 87544-0090
Mailing Address: PO Box 90 • Los Alamos, NM 87544-0090
(505) 663-2230 • http://losalamos.k12.nm.us/
Grade Span: PK-12; Agency Type: 1
Schools: 7
  5 Primary; 1 Middle; 1 High; 0 Other Level
  7 Regular; 0 Special Education; 0 Vocational; 0 Alternative
  0 Magnet; 0 Charter; 0 Title I Eligible; 0 School-wide Title I
Students: 3,647 (50.7% male; 49.2% female)
  Individual Education Program: 1,149 (31.5%);
  English Language Learner: 57 (1.6%); Migrant: 0 (0.0%)
  Eligible for Free Lunch Program: 0 (0.0%)
  Eligible for Reduced-Price Lunch Program: 0 (0.0%)
Teachers: 249.7 (14.6 to 1)
Librarians/Media Specialists: 7.5 (486.3 to 1)
Guidance Counselors: 10.0 (364.7 to 1)
Current Spending: ($ per student per year):
  Total: $8,575; Instruction: $4,986; Support Services: $3,443

Enrollment, Drop-out Rates and Diploma Recipients by Race/Ethnicity

Category	Total	White	Black	Asian	AIAN	Hisp.
Enrollment (%)	100.0	75.7	0.5	4.8	0.8	18.1
Drop-out Rate (%)	2.5	2.3	0.0	0.0	0.0	4.0
H.S. Diplomas (#)	258	209	0	9	1	39

Luna County

Deming Public Schools
501 W Florida St • Deming, NM 88030-6302
(505) 546-8841 • http://www.demingps.org/
Grade Span: PK-12; Agency Type: 1
Schools: 14
  8 Primary; 1 Middle; 3 High; 2 Other Level
  10 Regular; 1 Special Education; 0 Vocational; 3 Alternative
  0 Magnet; 0 Charter; 9 Title I Eligible; 8 School-wide Title I
Students: 5,471 (50.5% male; 49.4% female)
  Individual Education Program: 595 (10.9%);
  English Language Learner: 1,458 (26.6%); Migrant: 323 (5.9%)
  Eligible for Free Lunch Program: 3,944 (72.1%)
  Eligible for Reduced-Price Lunch Program: 480 (8.8%)
Teachers: 306.3 (17.9 to 1)
Librarians/Media Specialists: 3.0 (1,823.7 to 1)
Guidance Counselors: 13.0 (420.8 to 1)
Current Spending: ($ per student per year):
  Total: $5,908; Instruction: $3,480; Support Services: $2,036

Enrollment, Drop-out Rates and Diploma Recipients by Race/Ethnicity

Category	Total	White	Black	Asian	AIAN	Hisp.
Enrollment (%)	100.0	19.6	1.0	0.2	0.3	78.9
Drop-out Rate (%)	1.4	1.2	0.0	0.0	0.0	1.6
H.S. Diplomas (#)	236	66	2	2	0	166

Mckinley County

Gallup-Mckinley County School
700 S Boardman • Gallup, NM 87305-1318
Mailing Address: PO Box 1318 • Gallup, NM 87305-1318
(505) 722-7711 • http://www.gmcs.k12.nm.us/
Grade Span: PK-12; Agency Type: 1
Schools: 37
  20 Primary; 6 Middle; 8 High; 3 Other Level
  34 Regular; 1 Special Education; 0 Vocational; 2 Alternative
  0 Magnet; 1 Charter; 34 Title I Eligible; 21 School-wide Title I
Students: 13,620 (50.7% male; 49.2% female)
  Individual Education Program: 2,104 (15.4%);
  English Language Learner: 4,922 (36.1%); Migrant: 17 (0.1%)
  Eligible for Free Lunch Program: 8,888 (65.3%)
  Eligible for Reduced-Price Lunch Program: 1,439 (10.6%)
Teachers: 886.6 (15.4 to 1)
Librarians/Media Specialists: 15.0 (908.0 to 1)
Guidance Counselors: 50.0 (272.4 to 1)
Current Spending: ($ per student per year):
  Total: $7,210; Instruction: $3,803; Support Services: $3,076

Enrollment, Drop-out Rates and Diploma Recipients by Race/Ethnicity

Category	Total	White	Black	Asian	AIAN	Hisp.
Enrollment (%)	100.0	7.6	0.3	0.4	80.7	11.0
Drop-out Rate (%)	3.4	2.0	14.3	15.4	3.2	5.1
H.S. Diplomas (#)	966	107	2	0	715	142

Zuni Public Schools
22 St Anthony Dr • Zuni, NM 87327-0166
Mailing Address: PO Box A • Zuni, NM 87327-0166
(505) 782-5511 • http://www.zuni.k12.nm.us/
Grade Span: PK-12; Agency Type: 1
Schools: 6
  2 Primary; 2 Middle; 2 High; 0 Other Level
  5 Regular; 0 Special Education; 0 Vocational; 1 Alternative
  0 Magnet; 0 Charter; 6 Title I Eligible; 6 School-wide Title I
Students: 1,712 (50.5% male; 49.4% female)
  Individual Education Program: 325 (19.0%);
  English Language Learner: 1,401 (81.8%); Migrant: 0 (0.0%)
  Eligible for Free Lunch Program: 1,094 (63.9%)
  Eligible for Reduced-Price Lunch Program: 139 (8.1%)
Teachers: 120.9 (14.2 to 1)
Librarians/Media Specialists: 4.0 (428.0 to 1)
Guidance Counselors: 7.0 (244.6 to 1)
Current Spending: ($ per student per year):
  Total: $10,049; Instruction: $5,003; Support Services: $4,341

Enrollment, Drop-out Rates and Diploma Recipients by Race/Ethnicity

Category	Total	White	Black	Asian	AIAN	Hisp.
Enrollment (%)	100.0	0.4	0.0	0.0	99.5	0.1
Drop-out Rate (%)	4.4	0.0	n/a	n/a	4.4	n/a
H.S. Diplomas (#)	55	0	0	0	55	0

Otero County

Alamogordo Public Schools
1222 Indiana Ave • Alamogordo, NM 88311-0617
Mailing Address: PO Box 650 • Alamogordo, NM 88311-0617
(505) 439-3270 • http://www.zianet.com/aps4jobs/main.html
Grade Span: PK-12; Agency Type: 1
Schools: 17
  11 Primary; 4 Middle; 2 High; 0 Other Level
  16 Regular; 0 Special Education; 0 Vocational; 1 Alternative
  0 Magnet; 1 Charter; 9 Title I Eligible; 6 School-wide Title I
Students: 6,933 (51.2% male; 48.7% female)
  Individual Education Program: 1,334 (19.2%);
  English Language Learner: 245 (3.5%); Migrant: 0 (0.0%)
  Eligible for Free Lunch Program: 2,220 (32.0%)
  Eligible for Reduced-Price Lunch Program: 862 (12.4%)
Teachers: 422.5 (16.4 to 1)
Librarians/Media Specialists: 5.0 (1,386.6 to 1)
Guidance Counselors: 18.0 (385.2 to 1)
Current Spending: ($ per student per year):
  Total: $5,938; Instruction: $3,332; Support Services: $2,316

Enrollment, Drop-out Rates and Diploma Recipients by Race/Ethnicity

Category	Total	White	Black	Asian	AIAN	Hisp.
Enrollment (%)	100.0	56.3	7.3	2.4	1.4	32.6
Drop-out Rate (%)	0.9	0.8	0.7	1.4	0.0	1.1
H.S. Diplomas (#)	482	305	39	14	0	124

Rio Arriba County

Espanola Municipal Schools
714 Calle Don Diego • Espanola, NM 87532-3414
(505) 753-2254 • http://www.k12espanola.org/
Grade Span: PK-12; **Agency Type:** 1
Schools: 16
  12 Primary; 1 Middle; 1 High; 2 Other Level
  15 Regular; 0 Special Education; 0 Vocational; 1 Alternative
  0 Magnet; 0 Charter; 13 Title I Eligible; 0 School-wide Title I
Students: 4,946 (49.6% male; 50.3% female)
  Individual Education Program: 587 (11.9%);
  English Language Learner: 2,076 (42.0%); Migrant: 120 (2.4%)
  Eligible for Free Lunch Program: 2,918 (59.0%)
  Eligible for Reduced-Price Lunch Program: 640 (12.9%)
Teachers: 300.8 (16.4 to 1)
Librarians/Media Specialists: 6.0 (824.3 to 1)
Guidance Counselors: 13.5 (366.4 to 1)
Current Spending: ($ per student per year):
  Total: $7,304; Instruction: $3,711; Support Services: $3,260
Enrollment, Drop-out Rates and Diploma Recipients by Race/Ethnicity

Category	Total	White	Black	Asian	AIAN	Hisp.
Enrollment (%)	100.0	2.9	0.4	0.1	6.8	89.8
Drop-out Rate (%)	13.8	10.0	n/a	n/a	27.4	13.2
H.S. Diplomas (#)	153	10	0	0	6	137

Roosevelt County

Portales Municipal Schools
501 S Abilene Ave • Portales, NM 88130-6380
(505) 356-6641 • http://www.portalesschools.com
Grade Span: PK-12; **Agency Type:** 1
Schools: 8
  3 Primary; 3 Middle; 2 High; 0 Other Level
  7 Regular; 0 Special Education; 0 Vocational; 1 Alternative
  0 Magnet; 0 Charter; 7 Title I Eligible; 5 School-wide Title I
Students: 2,871 (51.1% male; 48.8% female)
  Individual Education Program: 491 (17.1%);
  English Language Learner: 136 (4.7%); Migrant: 121 (4.2%)
  Eligible for Free Lunch Program: 1,539 (53.6%)
  Eligible for Reduced-Price Lunch Program: 242 (8.4%)
Teachers: 176.4 (16.3 to 1)
Librarians/Media Specialists: 2.0 (1,435.5 to 1)
Guidance Counselors: 6.0 (478.5 to 1)
Current Spending: ($ per student per year):
  Total: $6,794; Instruction: $3,614; Support Services: $2,631
Enrollment, Drop-out Rates and Diploma Recipients by Race/Ethnicity

Category	Total	White	Black	Asian	AIAN	Hisp.
Enrollment (%)	100.0	47.3	2.0	0.4	0.7	49.7
Drop-out Rate (%)	2.4	0.9	0.0	0.0	0.0	4.5
H.S. Diplomas (#)	145	98	5	0	0	42

San Juan County

Aztec Municipal Schools
1118 W Aztec Blvd • Aztec, NM 87410-1818
(505) 334-9474 • http://www.aztecschools.com
Grade Span: PK-12; **Agency Type:** 1
Schools: 7
  2 Primary; 2 Middle; 2 High; 0 Other Level
  5 Regular; 0 Special Education; 0 Vocational; 1 Alternative
  0 Magnet; 0 Charter; 3 Title I Eligible; 0 School-wide Title I
Students: 3,229 (52.5% male; 47.4% female)
  Individual Education Program: 730 (22.6%);
  English Language Learner: 116 (3.6%); Migrant: 0 (0.0%)
  Eligible for Free Lunch Program: 1,099 (34.0%)
  Eligible for Reduced-Price Lunch Program: 330 (10.2%)
Teachers: 214.9 (15.0 to 1)
Librarians/Media Specialists: 3.0 (1,076.3 to 1)
Guidance Counselors: 7.4 (436.4 to 1)
Current Spending: ($ per student per year):
  Total: $6,130; Instruction: $3,558; Support Services: $2,288
Enrollment, Drop-out Rates and Diploma Recipients by Race/Ethnicity

Category	Total	White	Black	Asian	AIAN	Hisp.
Enrollment (%)	100.0	64.4	0.3	0.7	12.0	22.6
Drop-out Rate (%)	7.6	5.8	0.0	0.0	8.5	15.1
H.S. Diplomas (#)	203	127	1	0	35	40

Bloomfield Municipal Schools
325 N Bergin Ln • Bloomfield, NM 87413-6729
(505) 632-4316 • http://www.bsin.k12.nm.us/
Grade Span: PK-12; **Agency Type:** 1
Schools: 8
  4 Primary; 0 Middle; 2 High; 2 Other Level
  7 Regular; 0 Special Education; 0 Vocational; 1 Alternative

---

  0 Magnet; 0 Charter; 4 Title I Eligible; 4 School-wide Title I
Students: 3,178 (50.8% male; 49.1% female)
  Individual Education Program: 735 (23.1%);
  English Language Learner: 462 (14.5%); Migrant: 1 (<0.1%)
  Eligible for Free Lunch Program: 1,642 (51.7%)
  Eligible for Reduced-Price Lunch Program: 386 (12.1%)
Teachers: 202.1 (15.7 to 1)
Librarians/Media Specialists: 6.0 (529.7 to 1)
Guidance Counselors: 6.0 (529.7 to 1)
Current Spending: ($ per student per year):
  Total: $6,581; Instruction: $3,620; Support Services: $2,550
Enrollment, Drop-out Rates and Diploma Recipients by Race/Ethnicity

Category	Total	White	Black	Asian	AIAN	Hisp.
Enrollment (%)	100.0	35.1	0.3	0.2	35.0	29.4
Drop-out Rate (%)	6.3	6.5	n/a	25.0	7.6	3.7
H.S. Diplomas (#)	166	67	0	2	48	49

Central Consolidated Schools
Hwys 64 & Old High School • Shiprock, NM 87420-1179
Mailing Address: PO Box 1199 • Shiprock, NM 87420-1179
(505) 368-4984 • http://bird.kchs.k12.nm.us/
Grade Span: PK-12; **Agency Type:** 1
Schools: 18
  7 Primary; 4 Middle; 4 High; 3 Other Level
  16 Regular; 0 Special Education; 0 Vocational; 2 Alternative
  0 Magnet; 0 Charter; 18 Title I Eligible; 18 School-wide Title I
Students: 6,948 (51.3% male; 48.6% female)
  Individual Education Program: 1,286 (18.5%);
  English Language Learner: 3,318 (47.8%); Migrant: 35 (0.5%)
  Eligible for Free Lunch Program: 4,474 (64.4%)
  Eligible for Reduced-Price Lunch Program: 793 (11.4%)
Teachers: 494.2 (14.1 to 1)
Librarians/Media Specialists: 5.0 (1,389.6 to 1)
Guidance Counselors: 23.0 (302.1 to 1)
Current Spending: ($ per student per year):
  Total: $8,253; Instruction: $4,581; Support Services: $3,302
Enrollment, Drop-out Rates and Diploma Recipients by Race/Ethnicity

Category	Total	White	Black	Asian	AIAN	Hisp.
Enrollment (%)	100.0	9.2	0.2	0.1	88.6	1.9
Drop-out Rate (%)	6.2	6.8	0.0	0.0	5.9	16.3
H.S. Diplomas (#)	433	42	1	0	382	8

Farmington Municipal Schools
2001 N Dustin • Farmington, NM 87499-5850
Mailing Address: PO Box 5850 • Farmington, NM 87499-5850
(505) 324-9840 • http://www.fms.k12.nm.us
Grade Span: PK-12; **Agency Type:** 1
Schools: 23
  13 Primary; 4 Middle; 4 High; 2 Other Level
  16 Regular; 2 Special Education; 0 Vocational; 5 Alternative
  0 Magnet; 0 Charter; 9 Title I Eligible; 7 School-wide Title I
Students: 10,055 (51.5% male; 48.4% female)
  Individual Education Program: 1,659 (16.5%);
  English Language Learner: 2,463 (24.5%); Migrant: 0 (0.0%)
  Eligible for Free Lunch Program: 3,847 (38.3%)
  Eligible for Reduced-Price Lunch Program: 1,079 (10.7%)
Teachers: 635.4 (15.8 to 1)
Librarians/Media Specialists: 5.0 (2,011.0 to 1)
Guidance Counselors: 27.0 (372.4 to 1)
Current Spending: ($ per student per year):
  Total: $5,886; Instruction: $3,603; Support Services: $2,047
Enrollment, Drop-out Rates and Diploma Recipients by Race/Ethnicity

Category	Total	White	Black	Asian	AIAN	Hisp.
Enrollment (%)	100.0	47.3	1.1	0.8	29.0	21.9
Drop-out Rate (%)	5.1	3.6	2.6	0.0	8.0	6.5
H.S. Diplomas (#)	558	333	8	9	107	101

San Miguel County

Las Vegas City Public Schools
901 Douglas Ave • Las Vegas, NM 87701-3928
(505) 454-5700 • http://cybercardinal.com/
Grade Span: PK-12; **Agency Type:** 1
Schools: 9
  6 Primary; 1 Middle; 2 High; 0 Other Level
  8 Regular; 1 Special Education; 0 Vocational; 0 Alternative
  0 Magnet; 1 Charter; 7 Title I Eligible; 0 School-wide Title I
Students: 2,200 (48.3% male; 51.6% female)
  Individual Education Program: 428 (19.5%);
  English Language Learner: 408 (18.5%); Migrant: 0 (0.0%)
  Eligible for Free Lunch Program: 1,018 (46.3%)
  Eligible for Reduced-Price Lunch Program: 305 (13.9%)
Teachers: 159.2 (13.8 to 1)
Librarians/Media Specialists: 2.8 (785.7 to 1)
Guidance Counselors: 6.5 (338.5 to 1)

Current Spending: ($ per student per year):
Total: $7,458; Instruction: $3,793; Support Services: $3,441

Enrollment, Drop-out Rates and Diploma Recipients by Race/Ethnicity

Category	Total	White	Black	Asian	AIAN	Hisp.
Enrollment (%)	100.0	9.8	0.8	0.9	0.5	87.9
Drop-out Rate (%)	0.7	0.0	0.0	0.0	0.0	0.8
H.S. Diplomas (#)	174	19	1	0	0	154

West Las Vegas Public Schools
179 Bridge St • Las Vegas, NM 87701-3426
(505) 426-2333
Grade Span: PK-12; **Agency Type:** 1
Schools: 11
6 Primary; 2 Middle; 1 High; 1 Other Level
9 Regular; 0 Special Education; 0 Vocational; 1 Alternative
0 Magnet; 0 Charter; 7 Title I Eligible; 6 School-wide Title I
Students: 2,011 (51.5% male; 48.4% female)
Individual Education Program: 290 (14.4%);
English Language Learner: 1,341 (66.7%); Migrant: 0 (0.0%)
Eligible for Free Lunch Program: 1,323 (65.8%)
Eligible for Reduced-Price Lunch Program: 278 (13.8%)
Teachers: 150.8 (13.3 to 1)
Librarians/Media Specialists: 3.0 (670.3 to 1)
Guidance Counselors: 6.9 (291.4 to 1)
Current Spending: ($ per student per year):
Total: $9,592; Instruction: $4,977; Support Services: $4,054

Enrollment, Drop-out Rates and Diploma Recipients by Race/Ethnicity

Category	Total	White	Black	Asian	AIAN	Hisp.
Enrollment (%)	100.0	5.0	0.5	0.0	0.4	94.0
Drop-out Rate (%)	3.2	4.8	n/a	n/a	0.0	3.2
H.S. Diplomas (#)	112	4	0	0	2	106

Sandoval County

Bernalillo Public Schools
224 N Camino Del Pueblo • Bernalillo, NM 87004-0640
(505) 867-2317 •
http://www.bernalillo.bps.k12.nm.us/education/district/district.php?sectionid=1
Grade Span: PK-12; **Agency Type:** 1
Schools: 11
6 Primary; 3 Middle; 1 High; 0 Other Level
10 Regular; 0 Special Education; 0 Vocational; 0 Alternative
0 Magnet; 0 Charter; 7 Title I Eligible; 7 School-wide Title I
Students: 3,377 (52.4% male; 47.5% female)
Individual Education Program: 584 (17.3%);
English Language Learner: 1,479 (43.8%); Migrant: 0 (0.0%)
Eligible for Free Lunch Program: 1,957 (58.0%)
Eligible for Reduced-Price Lunch Program: 445 (13.2%)
Teachers: 252.1 (13.4 to 1)
Librarians/Media Specialists: 5.0 (675.4 to 1)
Guidance Counselors: 11.0 (307.0 to 1)
Current Spending: ($ per student per year):
Total: $8,574; Instruction: $4,896; Support Services: $3,351

Enrollment, Drop-out Rates and Diploma Recipients by Race/Ethnicity

Category	Total	White	Black	Asian	AIAN	Hisp.
Enrollment (%)	100.0	9.6	0.4	0.1	42.5	47.4
Drop-out Rate (%)	3.5	0.0	0.0	0.0	5.8	1.8
H.S. Diplomas (#)	141	9	0	0	62	70

Rio Rancho Public Schools
500 Laser Rd NE • Rio Rancho, NM 87124-3765
(505) 896-0667 • http://www.rrps.net/
Grade Span: PK-12; **Agency Type:** 1
Schools: 13
7 Primary; 3 Middle; 2 High; 1 Other Level
12 Regular; 0 Special Education; 0 Vocational; 1 Alternative
0 Magnet; 0 Charter; 2 Title I Eligible; 1 School-wide Title I
Students: 11,776 (51.6% male; 48.3% female)
Individual Education Program: 2,105 (17.9%);
English Language Learner: 585 (5.0%); Migrant: 0 (0.0%)
Eligible for Free Lunch Program: 2,130 (18.1%)
Eligible for Reduced-Price Lunch Program: 1,013 (8.6%)
Teachers: 724.1 (16.3 to 1)
Librarians/Media Specialists: 10.0 (1,177.6 to 1)
Guidance Counselors: 20.0 (588.8 to 1)
Current Spending: ($ per student per year):
Total: $5,677; Instruction: $3,277; Support Services: $2,152

Enrollment, Drop-out Rates and Diploma Recipients by Race/Ethnicity

Category	Total	White	Black	Asian	AIAN	Hisp.
Enrollment (%)	100.0	55.2	3.6	1.9	4.2	35.1
Drop-out Rate (%)	4.2	3.7	2.0	4.3	13.2	4.6
H.S. Diplomas (#)	638	400	22	17	14	185

Santa Fe County

Pojoaque Valley Public Schools
1574 State Rd 502 • Santa Fe, NM 87501-0468
Mailing Address: PO Box 3468 Pojoaque Stat • Santa Fe, NM 87501-0468
(505) 455-2282 • http://pvs.k12.nm.us/
Grade Span: PK-12; **Agency Type:** 1
Schools: 4
1 Primary; 2 Middle; 1 High; 0 Other Level
4 Regular; 0 Special Education; 0 Vocational; 0 Alternative
0 Magnet; 0 Charter; 1 Title I Eligible; 1 School-wide Title I
Students: 1,910 (48.2% male; 51.7% female)
Individual Education Program: 360 (18.8%);
English Language Learner: 917 (48.0%); Migrant: 0 (0.0%)
Eligible for Free Lunch Program: 650 (34.0%)
Eligible for Reduced-Price Lunch Program: 275 (14.4%)
Teachers: 127.1 (15.0 to 1)
Librarians/Media Specialists: 3.0 (636.7 to 1)
Guidance Counselors: 8.0 (238.8 to 1)
Current Spending: ($ per student per year):
Total: $7,572; Instruction: $3,674; Support Services: $3,367

Enrollment, Drop-out Rates and Diploma Recipients by Race/Ethnicity

Category	Total	White	Black	Asian	AIAN	Hisp.
Enrollment (%)	100.0	8.2	0.5	0.3	19.3	71.8
Drop-out Rate (%)	7.2	18.0	0.0	0.0	7.3	6.1
H.S. Diplomas (#)	142	16	0	0	28	98

Santa Fe Public Schools
610 Alta Vista St • Santa Fe, NM 87505-4149
(505) 954-2003 • http://www.sfps.k12.nm.us/
Grade Span: PK-12; **Agency Type:** 1
Schools: 35
22 Primary; 4 Middle; 5 High; 3 Other Level
29 Regular; 2 Special Education; 0 Vocational; 3 Alternative
0 Magnet; 3 Charter; 21 Title I Eligible; 18 School-wide Title I
Students: 13,660 (51.3% male; 48.6% female)
Individual Education Program: 2,321 (17.0%);
English Language Learner: 2,583 (18.9%); Migrant: 0 (0.0%)
Eligible for Free Lunch Program: 5,628 (41.2%)
Eligible for Reduced-Price Lunch Program: 1,422 (10.4%)
Teachers: 882.9 (15.5 to 1)
Librarians/Media Specialists: 11.6 (1,177.6 to 1)
Guidance Counselors: 34.6 (394.8 to 1)
Current Spending: ($ per student per year):
Total: $6,208; Instruction: $3,521; Support Services: $2,439

Enrollment, Drop-out Rates and Diploma Recipients by Race/Ethnicity

Category	Total	White	Black	Asian	AIAN	Hisp.
Enrollment (%)	100.0	24.6	0.6	1.0	2.8	71.0
Drop-out Rate (%)	6.4	4.7	7.7	4.0	7.1	7.2
H.S. Diplomas (#)	661	237	7	10	16	391

Sierra County

Truth Or Consequences Schools
180 N Date St • Truth Or Conseq, NM 87901-0952
(505) 894-8150
Grade Span: PK-12; **Agency Type:** 1
Schools: 6
2 Primary; 2 Middle; 2 High; 0 Other Level
5 Regular; 0 Special Education; 0 Vocational; 1 Alternative
0 Magnet; 0 Charter; 4 Title I Eligible; 4 School-wide Title I
Students: 1,637 (52.5% male; 47.4% female)
Individual Education Program: 370 (22.6%);
English Language Learner: 350 (21.4%); Migrant: 0 (0.0%)
Eligible for Free Lunch Program: 998 (61.0%)
Eligible for Reduced-Price Lunch Program: 168 (10.3%)
Teachers: 106.6 (15.4 to 1)
Librarians/Media Specialists: 1.0 (1,637.0 to 1)
Guidance Counselors: 3.0 (545.7 to 1)
Current Spending: ($ per student per year):
Total: $6,834; Instruction: $3,785; Support Services: $2,715

Enrollment, Drop-out Rates and Diploma Recipients by Race/Ethnicity

Category	Total	White	Black	Asian	AIAN	Hisp.
Enrollment (%)	100.0	54.7	0.6	0.1	1.2	43.3
Drop-out Rate (%)	2.6	1.9	0.0	0.0	0.0	3.7
H.S. Diplomas (#)	74	47	1	0	1	25

Socorro County

Socorro Consolidated Schools
700 Franklin • Socorro, NM 87801-1157
Mailing Address: PO Box 1157 • Socorro, NM 87801-1157
(505) 835-0300 • http://www.nmt.edu/mainpage/socorro/pubsch.html
Grade Span: PK-12; **Agency Type:** 1
Schools: 8

5 Primary; 2 Middle; 1 High; 0 Other Level
8 Regular; 0 Special Education; 0 Vocational; 0 Alternative
0 Magnet; 1 Charter; 6 Title I Eligible; 4 School-wide Title I
Students: 2,079 (50.3% male; 49.6% female)
Individual Education Program: 424 (20.4%);
English Language Learner: 24 (1.2%); Migrant: 0 (0.0%)
Eligible for Free Lunch Program: 1,013 (48.7%)
Eligible for Reduced-Price Lunch Program: 137 (6.6%)
Teachers: 134.4 (15.5 to 1)
Librarians/Media Specialists: 4.0 (519.8 to 1)
Guidance Counselors: 6.0 (346.5 to 1)
Current Spending: ($ per student per year):
Total: $7,652; Instruction: $3,899; Support Services: $3,346
Enrollment, Drop-out Rates and Diploma Recipients by Race/Ethnicity

Category	Total	White	Black	Asian	AIAN	Hisp.
Enrollment (%)	100.0	29.5	1.3	1.6	2.5	65.1
Drop-out Rate (%)	2.0	2.2	0.0	0.0	0.0	2.1
H.S. Diplomas (#)	113	33	2	1	2	75

Taos County

Taos Municipal Schools
213 Paseo Del Canon • Taos, NM 87571-6239
(505) 758-5202 • http://www.taosschools.org/
Grade Span: PK-12; **Agency Type:** 1
Schools: 10
5 Primary; 2 Middle; 1 High; 1 Other Level
8 Regular; 1 Special Education; 0 Vocational; 0 Alternative
0 Magnet; 2 Charter; 8 Title I Eligible; 2 School-wide Title I
Students: 3,299 (66.9% male; 33.0% female)
Individual Education Program: 720 (21.8%);
English Language Learner: 182 (5.5%); Migrant: 0 (0.0%)
Eligible for Free Lunch Program: 2,709 (82.1%)
Eligible for Reduced-Price Lunch Program: 126 (3.8%)
Teachers: 227.2 (14.5 to 1)
Librarians/Media Specialists: 2.0 (1,649.5 to 1)
Guidance Counselors: 9.0 (366.6 to 1)
Current Spending: ($ per student per year):
Total: $7,658; Instruction: $4,182; Support Services: $2,879
Enrollment, Drop-out Rates and Diploma Recipients by Race/Ethnicity

Category	Total	White	Black	Asian	AIAN	Hisp.
Enrollment (%)	100.0	21.4	0.5	0.7	6.6	70.7
Drop-out Rate (%)	5.4	1.5	16.7	0.0	11.5	5.9
H.S. Diplomas (#)	207	58	2	2	5	140

Torrance County

Moriarty Muncipal Schools
200 Center St • Moriarty, NM 87035-0020
Mailing Address: PO Box 2000 • Moriarty, NM 87035-0020
(505) 832-4471 • http://www.moriarty.k12.nm.us/
Grade Span: PK-12; **Agency Type:** 1
Schools: 8
5 Primary; 2 Middle; 1 High; 0 Other Level
8 Regular; 0 Special Education; 0 Vocational; 0 Alternative
0 Magnet; 0 Charter; 5 Title I Eligible; 0 School-wide Title I
Students: 4,218 (52.3% male; 47.6% female)
Individual Education Program: 920 (21.8%);
English Language Learner: 279 (6.6%); Migrant: 14 (0.3%)
Eligible for Free Lunch Program: 1,745 (41.4%)
Eligible for Reduced-Price Lunch Program: 613 (14.5%)
Teachers: 276.5 (15.3 to 1)
Librarians/Media Specialists: 1.9 (2,220.0 to 1)
Guidance Counselors: 7.0 (602.6 to 1)
Current Spending: ($ per student per year):
Total: $6,653; Instruction: $3,506; Support Services: $2,863
Enrollment, Drop-out Rates and Diploma Recipients by Race/Ethnicity

Category	Total	White	Black	Asian	AIAN	Hisp.
Enrollment (%)	100.0	64.2	1.1	0.4	1.6	32.7
Drop-out Rate (%)	0.9	1.1	0.0	n/a	0.0	0.5
H.S. Diplomas (#)	241	181	0	0	3	57

Valencia County

Belen Consolidated Schools
520 N Main St • Belen, NM 87002-3720
(505) 966-1003 • http://www.belen.k12.nm.us/
Grade Span: PK-12; **Agency Type:** 1
Schools: 12
7 Primary; 2 Middle; 2 High; 0 Other Level
9 Regular; 0 Special Education; 0 Vocational; 2 Alternative
0 Magnet; 0 Charter; 9 Title I Eligible; 9 School-wide Title I
Students: 4,873 (50.9% male; 49.0% female)
Individual Education Program: 1,112 (22.8%);
English Language Learner: 81 (1.7%); Migrant: 0 (0.0%)

Eligible for Free Lunch Program: 2,794 (57.3%)
Eligible for Reduced-Price Lunch Program: 679 (13.9%)
Teachers: 315.8 (15.4 to 1)
Librarians/Media Specialists: 1.0 (4,873.0 to 1)
Guidance Counselors: 13.2 (369.2 to 1)
Current Spending: ($ per student per year):
Total: $6,531; Instruction: $3,453; Support Services: $2,733
Enrollment, Drop-out Rates and Diploma Recipients by Race/Ethnicity

Category	Total	White	Black	Asian	AIAN	Hisp.
Enrollment (%)	100.0	29.1	1.9	0.6	1.5	67.0
Drop-out Rate (%)	8.7	7.7	0.0	9.1	16.0	9.2
H.S. Diplomas (#)	239	64	3	0	1	171

Los Lunas Public Schools
343 Main St • Los Lunas, NM 87031-1300
Mailing Address: PO Box 1300 • Los Lunas, NM 87031-1300
(505) 866-8231 • http://llmain.loslunas.k12.nm.us/
Grade Span: PK-12; **Agency Type:** 1
Schools: 18
9 Primary; 5 Middle; 2 High; 2 Other Level
13 Regular; 0 Special Education; 0 Vocational; 5 Alternative
0 Magnet; 0 Charter; 13 Title I Eligible; 12 School-wide Title I
Students: 8,590 (51.5% male; 48.4% female)
Individual Education Program: 1,980 (23.1%);
English Language Learner: 900 (10.5%); Migrant: 0 (0.0%)
Eligible for Free Lunch Program: 4,357 (50.7%)
Eligible for Reduced-Price Lunch Program: 1,113 (13.0%)
Teachers: 534.0 (16.1 to 1)
Librarians/Media Specialists: 11.0 (780.9 to 1)
Guidance Counselors: 19.0 (452.1 to 1)
Current Spending: ($ per student per year):
Total: $6,751; Instruction: $3,564; Support Services: $2,804
Enrollment, Drop-out Rates and Diploma Recipients by Race/Ethnicity

Category	Total	White	Black	Asian	AIAN	Hisp.
Enrollment (%)	100.0	29.7	1.1	0.5	7.2	61.5
Drop-out Rate (%)	2.3	2.0	0.0	0.0	2.4	2.4
H.S. Diplomas (#)	390	135	5	0	32	218

Number of Schools

Rank	Number	District Name	City
1	148	Albuquerque Public Schools	Albuquerque
2	38	Las Cruces Public Schools	Las Cruces
3	37	Gallup-Mckinley County School	Gallup
4	35	Santa Fe Public Schools	Santa Fe
5	24	Roswell Independent Schools	Roswell
6	23	Farmington Municipal Schools	Farmington
7	20	Gadsden Independent Schools	Anthony
8	19	Clovis Municipal Schools	Clovis
8	19	Hobbs Municipal Schools	Hobbs
10	18	Central Consolidated Schools	Shiprock
10	18	Los Lunas Public Schools	Los Lunas
12	17	Alamogordo Public Schools	Alamogordo
13	16	Espanola Municipal Schools	Espanola
14	15	Carlsbad Municipal Schools	Carlsbad
15	14	Deming Public Schools	Deming
16	13	Rio Rancho Public Schools	Rio Rancho
17	12	Belen Consolidated Schools	Belen
17	12	Grants-Cibola County Schools	Grants
19	11	Artesia Public Schools	Artesia
19	11	Bernalillo Public Schools	Bernalillo
19	11	West Las Vegas Public Schools	Las Vegas
22	10	Lovington Public Schools	Lovington
22	10	Silver City Consolidated Schl	Silver City
22	10	Taos Municipal Schools	Taos
25	9	Las Vegas City Public Schools	Las Vegas
26	8	Bloomfield Municipal Schools	Bloomfield
26	8	Moriarty Muncipal Schools	Moriarty
26	8	Portales Municipal Schools	Portales
26	8	Socorro Consolidated Schools	Socorro
30	7	Aztec Municipal Schools	Aztec
30	7	Los Alamos Public Schools	Los Alamos
30	7	Ruidoso Municipal Schools	Ruidoso
33	6	Cobre Consolidated Schools	Bayard
33	6	Hatch Valley Public Schools	Hatch
33	6	Truth Or Consequences Schools	Truth or Conseq
33	6	Zuni Public Schools	Zuni
37	4	Pojoaque Valley Public Schools	Santa Fe

Number of Teachers

Rank	Number	District Name	City
1	6,191	Albuquerque Public Schools	Albuquerque
2	1,544	Las Cruces Public Schools	Las Cruces
3	886	Gallup-Mckinley County School	Gallup
4	882	Santa Fe Public Schools	Santa Fe
5	853	Gadsden Independent Schools	Anthony
6	724	Rio Rancho Public Schools	Rio Rancho
7	635	Farmington Municipal Schools	Farmington
8	596	Roswell Independent Schools	Roswell
9	534	Los Lunas Public Schools	Los Lunas
10	523	Clovis Municipal Schools	Clovis
11	494	Central Consolidated Schools	Shiprock
12	450	Hobbs Municipal Schools	Hobbs
13	422	Alamogordo Public Schools	Alamogordo
14	378	Carlsbad Municipal Schools	Carlsbad
15	315	Belen Consolidated Schools	Belen
16	306	Deming Public Schools	Deming
17	300	Espanola Municipal Schools	Espanola
18	276	Moriarty Muncipal Schools	Moriarty
19	252	Bernalillo Public Schools	Bernalillo
20	251	Grants-Cibola County Schools	Grants
21	249	Los Alamos Public Schools	Los Alamos
22	238	Artesia Public Schools	Artesia
23	227	Taos Municipal Schools	Taos
24	216	Silver City Consolidated Schl	Silver City
25	214	Aztec Municipal Schools	Aztec
26	202	Bloomfield Municipal Schools	Bloomfield
27	177	Lovington Public Schools	Lovington
28	176	Portales Municipal Schools	Portales
29	159	Las Vegas City Public Schools	Las Vegas
30	150	West Las Vegas Public Schools	Las Vegas
31	150	Ruidoso Municipal Schools	Ruidoso
32	134	Socorro Consolidated Schools	Socorro
33	127	Cobre Consolidated Schools	Bayard
34	127	Pojoaque Valley Public Schools	Santa Fe
35	120	Zuni Public Schools	Zuni
36	106	Truth Or Consequences Schools	Truth or Conseq
37	102	Hatch Valley Public Schools	Hatch

Number of Students

Rank	Number	District Name	City
1	90,537	Albuquerque Public Schools	Albuquerque
2	23,101	Las Cruces Public Schools	Las Cruces
3	13,796	Gadsden Independent Schools	Anthony
4	13,660	Santa Fe Public Schools	Santa Fe
5	13,620	Gallup-Mckinley County School	Gallup
6	11,776	Rio Rancho Public Schools	Rio Rancho
7	10,055	Farmington Municipal Schools	Farmington
8	9,419	Roswell Independent Schools	Roswell
9	8,590	Los Lunas Public Schools	Los Lunas
10	8,237	Clovis Municipal Schools	Clovis
11	7,575	Hobbs Municipal Schools	Hobbs
12	6,948	Central Consolidated Schools	Shiprock
13	6,933	Alamogordo Public Schools	Alamogordo
14	6,212	Carlsbad Municipal Schools	Carlsbad
15	5,471	Deming Public Schools	Deming
16	4,946	Espanola Municipal Schools	Espanola
17	4,873	Belen Consolidated Schools	Belen
18	4,218	Moriarty Muncipal Schools	Moriarty
19	3,710	Grants-Cibola County Schools	Grants
20	3,647	Los Alamos Public Schools	Los Alamos
21	3,531	Artesia Public Schools	Artesia
22	3,377	Bernalillo Public Schools	Bernalillo
23	3,299	Taos Municipal Schools	Taos
24	3,286	Silver City Consolidated Schl	Silver City
25	3,229	Aztec Municipal Schools	Aztec
26	3,178	Bloomfield Municipal Schools	Bloomfield
27	2,871	Portales Municipal Schools	Portales
28	2,863	Lovington Public Schools	Lovington
29	2,380	Ruidoso Municipal Schools	Ruidoso
30	2,200	Las Vegas City Public Schools	Las Vegas
31	2,079	Socorro Consolidated Schools	Socorro
32	2,011	West Las Vegas Public Schools	Las Vegas
33	1,910	Pojoaque Valley Public Schools	Santa Fe
34	1,712	Zuni Public Schools	Zuni
35	1,637	Truth Or Consequences Schools	Truth or Conseq
36	1,545	Hatch Valley Public Schools	Hatch
37	1,540	Cobre Consolidated Schools	Bayard

Male Students

Rank	Percent	District Name	City
1	66.9	Taos Municipal Schools	Taos
2	53.6	Silver City Consolidated Schl	Silver City
3	52.5	Truth Or Consequences Schools	Truth or Conseq
4	52.5	Aztec Municipal Schools	Aztec
5	52.4	Bernalillo Public Schools	Bernalillo
6	52.3	Moriarty Muncipal Schools	Moriarty
7	52.1	Clovis Municipal Schools	Clovis
8	51.9	Ruidoso Municipal Schools	Ruidoso
9	51.8	Cobre Consolidated Schools	Bayard
10	51.6	Rio Rancho Public Schools	Rio Rancho
11	51.6	Carlsbad Municipal Schools	Carlsbad
12	51.6	Artesia Public Schools	Artesia
13	51.5	Grants-Cibola County Schools	Grants
14	51.5	Hobbs Municipal Schools	Hobbs
15	51.5	Los Lunas Public Schools	Los Lunas
16	51.5	Farmington Municipal Schools	Farmington
16	51.5	West Las Vegas Public Schools	Las Vegas
18	51.4	Albuquerque Public Schools	Albuquerque
19	51.3	Central Consolidated Schools	Shiprock
20	51.3	Santa Fe Public Schools	Santa Fe
21	51.2	Alamogordo Public Schools	Alamogordo
22	51.2	Gadsden Independent Schools	Anthony
23	51.1	Portales Municipal Schools	Portales
24	51.0	Las Cruces Public Schools	Las Cruces
25	50.9	Belen Consolidated Schools	Belen
26	50.8	Roswell Independent Schools	Roswell
27	50.8	Lovington Public Schools	Lovington
28	50.8	Bloomfield Municipal Schools	Bloomfield
29	50.7	Gallup-Mckinley County School	Gallup
30	50.7	Los Alamos Public Schools	Los Alamos
31	50.5	Zuni Public Schools	Zuni
32	50.5	Deming Public Schools	Deming
33	50.3	Hatch Valley Public Schools	Hatch
34	50.3	Socorro Consolidated Schools	Socorro
35	49.6	Espanola Municipal Schools	Espanola
36	48.3	Las Vegas City Public Schools	Las Vegas
37	48.2	Pojoaque Valley Public Schools	Santa Fe

Female Students

Rank	Percent	District Name	City
1	51.7	Pojoaque Valley Public Schools	Santa Fe
2	51.6	Las Vegas City Public Schools	Las Vegas
3	50.3	Espanola Municipal Schools	Espanola
4	49.6	Socorro Consolidated Schools	Socorro
5	49.6	Hatch Valley Public Schools	Hatch
6	49.4	Deming Public Schools	Deming
7	49.4	Zuni Public Schools	Zuni
8	49.2	Los Alamos Public Schools	Los Alamos
9	49.2	Gallup-Mckinley County School	Gallup
10	49.1	Bloomfield Municipal Schools	Bloomfield
11	49.1	Lovington Public Schools	Lovington
12	49.1	Roswell Independent Schools	Roswell
13	49.0	Belen Consolidated Schools	Belen
14	48.9	Las Cruces Public Schools	Las Cruces
15	48.8	Portales Municipal Schools	Portales
16	48.7	Gadsden Independent Schools	Anthony
17	48.7	Alamogordo Public Schools	Alamogordo
18	48.6	Santa Fe Public Schools	Santa Fe
19	48.6	Central Consolidated Schools	Shiprock
20	48.5	Albuquerque Public Schools	Albuquerque
21	48.4	Farmington Municipal Schools	Farmington
21	48.4	West Las Vegas Public Schools	Las Vegas
23	48.4	Los Lunas Public Schools	Los Lunas
24	48.4	Hobbs Municipal Schools	Hobbs
25	48.4	Grants-Cibola County Schools	Grants
26	48.3	Artesia Public Schools	Artesia
27	48.3	Carlsbad Municipal Schools	Carlsbad
28	48.3	Rio Rancho Public Schools	Rio Rancho
29	48.1	Cobre Consolidated Schools	Bayard
30	48.0	Ruidoso Municipal Schools	Ruidoso
31	47.8	Clovis Municipal Schools	Clovis
32	47.6	Moriarty Muncipal Schools	Moriarty
33	47.5	Bernalillo Public Schools	Bernalillo
34	47.4	Aztec Municipal Schools	Aztec
35	47.4	Truth Or Consequences Schools	Truth or Conseq
36	46.3	Silver City Consolidated Schl	Silver City
37	33.0	Taos Municipal Schools	Taos

Individual Education Program Students

Rank	Percent	District Name	City
1	31.5	Los Alamos Public Schools	Los Alamos
2	26.4	Carlsbad Municipal Schools	Carlsbad
3	25.2	Roswell Independent Schools	Roswell
4	25.0	Las Cruces Public Schools	Las Cruces
5	24.6	Lovington Public Schools	Lovington
6	23.1	Bloomfield Municipal Schools	Bloomfield
6	23.1	Los Lunas Public Schools	Los Lunas
8	22.8	Belen Consolidated Schools	Belen
9	22.6	Aztec Municipal Schools	Aztec
9	22.6	Truth Or Consequences Schools	Truth or Conseq
11	22.5	Cobre Consolidated Schools	Bayard
12	21.8	Moriarty Muncipal Schools	Moriarty
12	21.8	Taos Municipal Schools	Taos
14	20.6	Artesia Public Schools	Artesia
15	20.4	Socorro Consolidated Schools	Socorro
16	19.9	Albuquerque Public Schools	Albuquerque
17	19.5	Clovis Municipal Schools	Clovis
17	19.5	Las Vegas City Public Schools	Las Vegas
17	19.5	Ruidoso Municipal Schools	Ruidoso
17	19.5	Silver City Consolidated Schl	Silver City
21	19.2	Alamogordo Public Schools	Alamogordo
22	19.0	Zuni Public Schools	Zuni
23	18.8	Pojoaque Valley Public Schools	Santa Fe
24	18.5	Central Consolidated Schools	Shiprock
25	17.9	Rio Rancho Public Schools	Rio Rancho
26	17.3	Bernalillo Public Schools	Bernalillo
27	17.1	Hobbs Municipal Schools	Hobbs
27	17.1	Portales Municipal Schools	Portales
29	17.0	Santa Fe Public Schools	Santa Fe
30	16.5	Farmington Municipal Schools	Farmington
31	15.4	Gallup-Mckinley County School	Gallup
32	15.3	Gadsden Independent Schools	Anthony
33	15.0	Grants-Cibola County Schools	Grants
34	14.4	West Las Vegas Public Schools	Las Vegas
35	11.9	Espanola Municipal Schools	Espanola
36	11.0	Hatch Valley Public Schools	Hatch
37	10.9	Deming Public Schools	Deming

English Language Learner Students

Rank	Percent	District Name	City
1	81.8	Zuni Public Schools	Zuni
2	68.5	Hatch Valley Public Schools	Hatch
3	66.7	West Las Vegas Public Schools	Las Vegas
4	48.0	Pojoaque Valley Public Schools	Santa Fe
5	47.8	Central Consolidated Schools	Shiprock
6	46.8	Gadsden Independent Schools	Anthony
7	43.8	Bernalillo Public Schools	Bernalillo
8	42.0	Espanola Municipal Schools	Espanola
9	36.1	Gallup-Mckinley County School	Gallup
10	33.7	Cobre Consolidated Schools	Bayard
11	26.6	Deming Public Schools	Deming
12	24.5	Farmington Municipal Schools	Farmington
13	21.4	Truth Or Consequences Schools	Truth or Conseq
14	18.9	Santa Fe Public Schools	Santa Fe
15	18.5	Las Vegas City Public Schools	Las Vegas
16	18.1	Grants-Cibola County Schools	Grants
17	15.7	Ruidoso Municipal Schools	Ruidoso
18	14.5	Bloomfield Municipal Schools	Bloomfield
19	14.0	Hobbs Municipal Schools	Hobbs
20	11.9	Albuquerque Public Schools	Albuquerque
21	10.5	Los Lunas Public Schools	Los Lunas
22	9.1	Las Cruces Public Schools	Las Cruces
23	8.6	Silver City Consolidated Schl	Silver City
24	6.8	Clovis Municipal Schools	Clovis
25	6.6	Moriarty Muncipal Schools	Moriarty
26	5.8	Roswell Independent Schools	Roswell
27	5.6	Artesia Public Schools	Artesia
28	5.5	Taos Municipal Schools	Taos
29	5.0	Rio Rancho Public Schools	Rio Rancho
30	4.7	Portales Municipal Schools	Portales

31	3.6	Aztec Municipal Schools	Aztec
32	3.5	Alamogordo Public Schools	Alamogordo
33	2.8	Carlsbad Municipal Schools	Carlsbad
34	1.7	Belen Consolidated Schools	Belen
35	1.6	Los Alamos Public Schools	Los Alamos
36	1.2	Socorro Consolidated Schools	Socorro
37	0.2	Lovington Public Schools	Lovington

Migrant Students

Rank	Percent	District Name	City
1	7.6	Hatch Valley Public Schools	Hatch
2	5.9	Deming Public Schools	Deming
3	4.2	Portales Municipal Schools	Portales
4	2.8	Lovington Public Schools	Lovington
5	2.6	Roswell Independent Schools	Roswell
6	2.4	Espanola Municipal Schools	Espanola
7	2.0	Gadsden Independent Schools	Anthony
8	1.8	Las Cruces Public Schools	Las Cruces
9	1.7	Clovis Municipal Schools	Clovis
10	1.4	Artesia Public Schools	Artesia
11	0.5	Central Consolidated Schools	Shiprock
12	0.3	Moriarty Muncipal Schools	Moriarty
13	0.1	Cobre Consolidated Schools	Bayard
13	0.1	Gallup-Mckinley County School	Gallup
15	0.0	Bloomfield Municipal Schools	Bloomfield
16	0.0	Alamogordo Public Schools	Alamogordo
16	0.0	Albuquerque Public Schools	Albuquerque
16	0.0	Aztec Municipal Schools	Aztec
16	0.0	Belen Consolidated Schools	Belen
16	0.0	Bernalillo Public Schools	Bernalillo
16	0.0	Carlsbad Municipal Schools	Carlsbad
16	0.0	Farmington Municipal Schools	Farmington
16	0.0	Grants-Cibola County Schools	Grants
16	0.0	Hobbs Municipal Schools	Hobbs
16	0.0	Las Vegas City Public Schools	Las Vegas
16	0.0	Los Alamos Public Schools	Los Alamos
16	0.0	Los Lunas Public Schools	Los Lunas
16	0.0	Pojoaque Valley Public Schools	Santa Fe
16	0.0	Rio Rancho Public Schools	Rio Rancho
16	0.0	Ruidoso Municipal Schools	Ruidoso
16	0.0	Santa Fe Public Schools	Santa Fe
16	0.0	Silver City Consolidated Schl	Silver City
16	0.0	Socorro Consolidated Schools	Socorro
16	0.0	Taos Municipal Schools	Taos
16	0.0	Truth Or Consequences Schools	Truth or Conseq
16	0.0	West Las Vegas Public Schools	Las Vegas
16	0.0	Zuni Public Schools	Zuni

Students Eligible for Free Lunch

Rank	Percent	District Name	City
1	86.8	Gadsden Independent Schools	Anthony
2	82.1	Taos Municipal Schools	Taos
3	78.8	Hatch Valley Public Schools	Hatch
4	72.1	Deming Public Schools	Deming
5	65.8	West Las Vegas Public Schools	Las Vegas
6	65.3	Gallup-Mckinley County School	Gallup
7	64.4	Central Consolidated Schools	Shiprock
8	64.1	Grants-Cibola County Schools	Grants
9	63.9	Zuni Public Schools	Zuni
10	61.3	Cobre Consolidated Schools	Bayard
11	61.0	Truth Or Consequences Schools	Truth or Conseq
12	59.0	Espanola Municipal Schools	Espanola
13	58.0	Bernalillo Public Schools	Bernalillo
14	57.3	Belen Consolidated Schools	Belen
15	53.6	Portales Municipal Schools	Portales
16	53.1	Roswell Independent Schools	Roswell
17	52.3	Lovington Public Schools	Lovington
18	51.7	Bloomfield Municipal Schools	Bloomfield
19	51.0	Las Cruces Public Schools	Las Cruces
20	50.7	Los Lunas Public Schools	Los Lunas
21	50.2	Hobbs Municipal Schools	Hobbs
22	49.9	Clovis Municipal Schools	Clovis
23	48.7	Socorro Consolidated Schools	Socorro
24	48.2	Ruidoso Municipal Schools	Ruidoso
25	48.0	Carlsbad Municipal Schools	Carlsbad
26	46.3	Las Vegas City Public Schools	Las Vegas
27	43.5	Silver City Consolidated Schl	Silver City
28	41.4	Moriarty Muncipal Schools	Moriarty
29	41.2	Santa Fe Public Schools	Santa Fe
30	39.8	Albuquerque Public Schools	Albuquerque
31	39.3	Artesia Public Schools	Artesia
32	38.3	Farmington Municipal Schools	Farmington
33	34.0	Aztec Municipal Schools	Aztec
33	34.0	Pojoaque Valley Public Schools	Santa Fe
35	32.0	Alamogordo Public Schools	Alamogordo
36	18.1	Rio Rancho Public Schools	Rio Rancho
37	0.0	Los Alamos Public Schools	Los Alamos

Students Eligible for Reduced-Price Lunch

Rank	Percent	District Name	City
1	19.4	Cobre Consolidated Schools	Bayard
2	14.5	Moriarty Muncipal Schools	Moriarty
3	14.4	Pojoaque Valley Public Schools	Santa Fe
4	14.3	Ruidoso Municipal Schools	Ruidoso
5	14.2	Lovington Public Schools	Lovington
6	14.0	Clovis Municipal Schools	Clovis
7	13.9	Belen Consolidated Schools	Belen
7	13.9	Las Vegas City Public Schools	Las Vegas
9	13.8	West Las Vegas Public Schools	Las Vegas
10	13.2	Bernalillo Public Schools	Bernalillo
11	13.0	Los Lunas Public Schools	Los Lunas
12	12.9	Espanola Municipal Schools	Espanola
13	12.5	Carlsbad Municipal Schools	Carlsbad
14	12.4	Alamogordo Public Schools	Alamogordo
15	12.1	Bloomfield Municipal Schools	Bloomfield
16	11.4	Central Consolidated Schools	Shiprock
17	10.7	Farmington Municipal Schools	Farmington
17	10.7	Roswell Independent Schools	Roswell
19	10.6	Gallup-Mckinley County School	Gallup
20	10.4	Santa Fe Public Schools	Santa Fe
21	10.3	Truth Or Consequences Schools	Truth or Conseq
22	10.2	Aztec Municipal Schools	Aztec
23	9.8	Hatch Valley Public Schools	Hatch
24	9.6	Silver City Consolidated Schl	Silver City
25	9.5	Grants-Cibola County Schools	Grants
26	9.3	Las Cruces Public Schools	Las Cruces
27	8.9	Artesia Public Schools	Artesia
28	8.8	Deming Public Schools	Deming
29	8.6	Rio Rancho Public Schools	Rio Rancho
30	8.4	Portales Municipal Schools	Portales
31	8.1	Zuni Public Schools	Zuni
32	8.0	Hobbs Municipal Schools	Hobbs
33	7.7	Albuquerque Public Schools	Albuquerque
34	6.6	Socorro Consolidated Schools	Socorro
35	4.8	Gadsden Independent Schools	Anthony
36	3.8	Taos Municipal Schools	Taos
37	0.0	Los Alamos Public Schools	Los Alamos

Student/Teacher Ratio

Rank	Ratio	District Name	City
1	17.9	Deming Public Schools	Deming
2	16.8	Hobbs Municipal Schools	Hobbs
3	16.4	Alamogordo Public Schools	Alamogordo
3	16.4	Carlsbad Municipal Schools	Carlsbad
3	16.4	Espanola Municipal Schools	Espanola
6	16.3	Portales Municipal Schools	Portales
6	16.3	Rio Rancho Public Schools	Rio Rancho
8	16.2	Gadsden Independent Schools	Anthony
8	16.2	Lovington Public Schools	Lovington
10	16.1	Los Lunas Public Schools	Los Lunas
11	15.8	Farmington Municipal Schools	Farmington
11	15.8	Roswell Independent Schools	Roswell
11	15.8	Ruidoso Municipal Schools	Ruidoso
14	15.7	Bloomfield Municipal Schools	Bloomfield
14	15.7	Clovis Municipal Schools	Clovis
16	15.5	Santa Fe Public Schools	Santa Fe
16	15.5	Socorro Consolidated Schools	Socorro
18	15.4	Belen Consolidated Schools	Belen
18	15.4	Gallup-Mckinley County School	Gallup
18	15.4	Truth Or Consequences Schools	Truth or Conseq
21	15.3	Moriarty Muncipal Schools	Moriarty
22	15.2	Silver City Consolidated Schl	Silver City
23	15.1	Hatch Valley Public Schools	Hatch
24	15.0	Aztec Municipal Schools	Aztec
24	15.0	Las Cruces Public Schools	Las Cruces
24	15.0	Pojoaque Valley Public Schools	Santa Fe
27	14.8	Artesia Public Schools	Artesia
27	14.8	Grants-Cibola County Schools	Grants
29	14.6	Albuquerque Public Schools	Albuquerque
29	14.6	Los Alamos Public Schools	Los Alamos
31	14.5	Taos Municipal Schools	Taos
32	14.2	Zuni Public Schools	Zuni
33	14.1	Central Consolidated Schools	Shiprock
34	13.8	Las Vegas City Public Schools	Las Vegas
35	13.4	Bernalillo Public Schools	Bernalillo
36	13.3	West Las Vegas Public Schools	Las Vegas
37	12.1	Cobre Consolidated Schools	Bayard

Student/Librarian Ratio

Rank	Ratio	District Name	City
1	4,873.0	Belen Consolidated Schools	Belen
2	2,863.0	Lovington Public Schools	Lovington
3	2,299.3	Gadsden Independent Schools	Anthony
4	2,220.0	Moriarty Muncipal Schools	Moriarty
5	2,070.7	Carlsbad Municipal Schools	Carlsbad
6	2,011.0	Farmington Municipal Schools	Farmington
7	1,893.8	Hobbs Municipal Schools	Hobbs
8	1,823.7	Deming Public Schools	Deming
9	1,649.5	Taos Municipal Schools	Taos
10	1,637.0	Truth Or Consequences Schools	Truth or Conseq
11	1,593.2	Las Cruces Public Schools	Las Cruces
12	1,569.8	Roswell Independent Schools	Roswell
13	1,545.0	Hatch Valley Public Schools	Hatch
14	1,435.5	Portales Municipal Schools	Portales
15	1,389.6	Central Consolidated Schools	Shiprock
16	1,386.6	Alamogordo Public Schools	Alamogordo
17	1,236.7	Grants-Cibola County Schools	Grants
18	1,177.6	Rio Rancho Public Schools	Rio Rancho
18	1,177.6	Santa Fe Public Schools	Santa Fe
20	1,177.0	Artesia Public Schools	Artesia
21	1,176.7	Clovis Municipal Schools	Clovis
22	1,095.3	Silver City Consolidated Schl	Silver City
23	1,076.3	Aztec Municipal Schools	Aztec
24	968.3	Albuquerque Public Schools	Albuquerque
25	908.0	Gallup-Mckinley County School	Gallup
26	824.3	Espanola Municipal Schools	Espanola
27	793.3	Ruidoso Municipal Schools	Ruidoso
28	785.7	Las Vegas City Public Schools	Las Vegas
29	780.9	Los Lunas Public Schools	Los Lunas
30	770.0	Cobre Consolidated Schools	Bayard
31	675.4	Bernalillo Public Schools	Bernalillo
32	670.3	West Las Vegas Public Schools	Las Vegas
33	636.7	Pojoaque Valley Public Schools	Santa Fe
34	529.7	Bloomfield Municipal Schools	Bloomfield
35	519.8	Socorro Consolidated Schools	Socorro
36	486.3	Los Alamos Public Schools	Los Alamos
37	428.0	Zuni Public Schools	Zuni

Student/Counselor Ratio

Rank	Ratio	District Name	City
1	850.0	Ruidoso Municipal Schools	Ruidoso
2	757.5	Hobbs Municipal Schools	Hobbs
3	722.3	Carlsbad Municipal Schools	Carlsbad
4	648.6	Clovis Municipal Schools	Clovis
5	602.6	Moriarty Muncipal Schools	Moriarty
6	588.8	Rio Rancho Public Schools	Rio Rancho
7	545.7	Truth Or Consequences Schools	Truth or Conseq
8	537.2	Las Cruces Public Schools	Las Cruces
9	529.7	Bloomfield Municipal Schools	Bloomfield
10	520.5	Lovington Public Schools	Lovington
11	504.4	Artesia Public Schools	Artesia
12	478.5	Portales Municipal Schools	Portales
13	471.0	Roswell Independent Schools	Roswell
14	452.1	Los Lunas Public Schools	Los Lunas
15	445.0	Gadsden Independent Schools	Anthony
16	439.1	Albuquerque Public Schools	Albuquerque
17	436.4	Aztec Municipal Schools	Aztec
18	420.8	Deming Public Schools	Deming
19	394.8	Santa Fe Public Schools	Santa Fe
20	386.3	Hatch Valley Public Schools	Hatch
21	385.2	Alamogordo Public Schools	Alamogordo
22	372.4	Farmington Municipal Schools	Farmington
23	369.2	Belen Consolidated Schools	Belen
24	366.6	Taos Municipal Schools	Taos
25	366.4	Espanola Municipal Schools	Espanola
26	364.7	Los Alamos Public Schools	Los Alamos
27	346.5	Socorro Consolidated Schools	Socorro
28	338.5	Las Vegas City Public Schools	Las Vegas
29	328.6	Silver City Consolidated Schl	Silver City
30	322.6	Grants-Cibola County Schools	Grants
31	308.0	Cobre Consolidated Schools	Bayard
32	307.0	Bernalillo Public Schools	Bernalillo
33	302.1	Central Consolidated Schools	Shiprock
34	291.4	West Las Vegas Public Schools	Las Vegas
35	272.4	Gallup-Mckinley County School	Gallup
36	244.6	Zuni Public Schools	Zuni
37	238.8	Pojoaque Valley Public Schools	Santa Fe

Current Spending per Student in FY2003

Rank	Dollars	District Name	City
1	10,049	Zuni Public Schools	Zuni
2	9,592	West Las Vegas Public Schools	Las Vegas
3	8,575	Los Alamos Public Schools	Los Alamos
4	8,574	Bernalillo Public Schools	Bernalillo
5	8,431	Cobre Consolidated Schools	Bayard
6	8,253	Central Consolidated Schools	Shiprock
7	7,834	Ruidoso Municipal Schools	Ruidoso
8	7,658	Taos Municipal Schools	Taos
9	7,652	Socorro Consolidated Schools	Socorro
10	7,572	Pojoaque Valley Public Schools	Santa Fe
11	7,458	Las Vegas City Public Schools	Las Vegas
12	7,417	Silver City Consolidated Schl	Silver City
13	7,406	Hatch Valley Public Schools	Hatch
14	7,304	Espanola Municipal Schools	Espanola
15	7,248	Carlsbad Municipal Schools	Carlsbad
16	7,210	Gallup-Mckinley County School	Gallup
17	7,112	Grants-Cibola County Schools	Grants
18	7,110	Artesia Public Schools	Artesia

Rank	Number	District Name	City
19	6,834	Truth Or Consequences Schools	Truth or Conseq
20	6,794	Portales Municipal Schools	Portales
21	6,751	Los Lunas Public Schools	Los Lunas
22	6,696	Gadsden Independent Schools	Anthony
23	6,655	Lovington Public Schools	Lovington
24	6,653	Moriarty Muncipal Schools	Moriarty
25	6,630	Roswell Independent Schools	Roswell
26	6,581	Bloomfield Municipal Schools	Bloomfield
27	6,531	Belen Consolidated Schools	Belen
28	6,495	Las Cruces Public Schools	Las Cruces
29	6,414	Albuquerque Public Schools	Albuquerque
30	6,208	Santa Fe Public Schools	Santa Fe
31	6,130	Aztec Municipal Schools	Aztec
32	6,058	Clovis Municipal Schools	Clovis
33	5,938	Alamogordo Public Schools	Alamogordo
34	5,908	Deming Public Schools	Deming
35	5,886	Farmington Municipal Schools	Farmington
36	5,884	Hobbs Municipal Schools	Hobbs
37	5,677	Rio Rancho Public Schools	Rio Rancho

30	1.7	Artesia Public Schools	Artesia
31	1.6	Cobre Consolidated Schools	Bayard
32	1.4	Deming Public Schools	Deming
33	1.3	Carlsbad Municipal Schools	Carlsbad
34	1.1	Hatch Valley Public Schools	Hatch
35	0.9	Alamogordo Public Schools	Alamogordo
35	0.9	Moriarty Muncipal Schools	Moriarty
37	0.7	Las Vegas City Public Schools	Las Vegas

Number of Diploma Recipients

Rank	Number	District Name	City
1	4,708	Albuquerque Public Schools	Albuquerque
2	1,417	Las Cruces Public Schools	Las Cruces
3	966	Gallup-Mckinley County School	Gallup
4	661	Santa Fe Public Schools	Santa Fe
5	638	Rio Rancho Public Schools	Rio Rancho
6	634	Gadsden Independent Schools	Anthony
7	558	Farmington Municipal Schools	Farmington
8	527	Roswell Independent Schools	Roswell
9	482	Alamogordo Public Schools	Alamogordo
10	433	Central Consolidated Schools	Shiprock
10	433	Hobbs Municipal Schools	Hobbs
12	400	Clovis Municipal Schools	Clovis
13	390	Los Lunas Public Schools	Los Lunas
14	360	Carlsbad Municipal Schools	Carlsbad
15	258	Los Alamos Public Schools	Los Alamos
16	241	Moriarty Muncipal Schools	Moriarty
17	239	Belen Consolidated Schools	Belen
18	237	Artesia Public Schools	Artesia
19	236	Deming Public Schools	Deming
20	231	Silver City Consolidated Schl	Silver City
21	207	Taos Municipal Schools	Taos
22	203	Aztec Municipal Schools	Aztec
22	203	Lovington Public Schools	Lovington
24	202	Grants-Cibola County Schools	Grants
25	174	Las Vegas City Public Schools	Las Vegas
26	166	Bloomfield Municipal Schools	Bloomfield
27	153	Espanola Municipal Schools	Espanola
28	145	Portales Municipal Schools	Portales
29	142	Pojoaque Valley Public Schools	Santa Fe
30	141	Bernalillo Public Schools	Bernalillo
31	120	Ruidoso Municipal Schools	Ruidoso
32	113	Socorro Consolidated Schools	Socorro
33	112	West Las Vegas Public Schools	Las Vegas
34	110	Cobre Consolidated Schools	Bayard
35	74	Truth Or Consequences Schools	Truth or Conseq
36	62	Hatch Valley Public Schools	Hatch
37	55	Zuni Public Schools	Zuni

High School Drop-out Rate

Rank	Percent	District Name	City
1	13.8	Espanola Municipal Schools	Espanola
2	9.4	Roswell Independent Schools	Roswell
3	8.7	Belen Consolidated Schools	Belen
4	8.0	Grants-Cibola County Schools	Grants
5	7.6	Aztec Municipal Schools	Aztec
6	7.2	Pojoaque Valley Public Schools	Santa Fe
7	7.1	Albuquerque Public Schools	Albuquerque
8	6.4	Clovis Municipal Schools	Clovis
8	6.4	Santa Fe Public Schools	Santa Fe
10	6.3	Bloomfield Municipal Schools	Bloomfield
11	6.2	Central Consolidated Schools	Shiprock
12	6.0	Lovington Public Schools	Lovington
13	5.5	Las Cruces Public Schools	Las Cruces
14	5.4	Taos Municipal Schools	Taos
15	5.1	Farmington Municipal Schools	Farmington
16	4.8	Silver City Consolidated Schl	Silver City
17	4.4	Zuni Public Schools	Zuni
18	4.2	Rio Rancho Public Schools	Rio Rancho
19	4.1	Ruidoso Municipal Schools	Ruidoso
20	4.0	Gadsden Independent Schools	Anthony
21	3.5	Bernalillo Public Schools	Bernalillo
22	3.4	Gallup-Mckinley County School	Gallup
23	3.2	West Las Vegas Public Schools	Las Vegas
24	2.6	Truth Or Consequences Schools	Truth or Conseq
25	2.5	Los Alamos Public Schools	Los Alamos
26	2.4	Portales Municipal Schools	Portales
27	2.3	Hobbs Municipal Schools	Hobbs
27	2.3	Los Lunas Public Schools	Los Lunas
29	2.0	Socorro Consolidated Schools	Socorro

New York

New York Public School Educational Profile

Category	Value	Category	Value
Schools (2003-2004)	4,531	**Diploma Recipients** (2002-2003)	140,096
Instructional Level		White, Non-Hispanic	94,527
Primary	2,524	Black, Non-Hispanic	19,673
Middle	780	Asian/Pacific Islander	9,940
High	804	American Indian/Alaskan Native	455
Other Level	423	Hispanic	15,501
Curriculum		**High School Drop-out Rate** (%) (2001-2002)	7.1
Regular	4,238	White, Non-Hispanic	3.3
Special Education	73	Black, Non-Hispanic	12.9
Vocational	25	Asian/Pacific Islander	5.9
Alternative	195	American Indian/Alaskan Native	9.4
Type		Hispanic	14.2
Magnet	31	**Staff** (2003-2004)	
Charter	50	Teachers	216,114.6
Title I Eligible	2,820	Average Salary[1] ($)	55,181
School-wide Title I	947	Librarians/Media Specialists	3,317.3
Students (2003-2004)	2,882,218	Guidance Counselors	6,440.7
Gender (%)		**Ratios** (2003-2004)	
Male	51.4	Student/Teacher Ratio	13.3 to 1
Female	48.6	Student/Librarian Ratio	868.8 to 1
Race/Ethnicity (%)		Student/Counselor Ratio	447.5 to 1
White, Non-Hispanic	53.6	**College Entrance Exam Scores** (2005)	
Black, Non-Hispanic	20.0	Scholastic Aptitude Test (SAT)	
Asian/Pacific Islander	6.5	Participation Rate (%)	92
American Indian/Alaskan Native	0.5	Mean SAT Reasoning Test Verbal Score	497
Hispanic	19.4	Mean SAT Reasoning Test Math Score	511
Classification (%)		American College Testing Program (ACT)	
Individual Education Program (IEP)	0.0	Participation Rate (%)	17
Migrant (2002-2003)	0.0	Average Composite Score	22.4
English Language Learner (ELL)	0.0	Average English Score	21.3
Eligible for Free Lunch Program	0.0	Average Math Score	22.5
Eligible for Reduced-Price Lunch Program	0.0	Average Reading Score	23.0
Current Spending ($ per student in FY 2003)	12,398	Average Science Score	22.3
Instruction	8,623		
Support Services	3,483		

Note: For an explanation of data, please refer to the User's Guide in the front of the book; (1) Median

New York NAEP 2005 Test Scores

Reading			Mathematics		
Grade/Category	Value	Rank	Grade/Category	Value	Rank
4th Grade			**4th Grade**		
Average Proficiency	222.7 (1.05)	16/51	Average Proficiency	238.2 (0.85)	30/51
Proficiency by Gender/Race/Ethnicity			Proficiency by Gender/Race/Ethnicity		
Male	220.2 (1.14)	14/51	Male	239.6 (0.96)	29/51
Female	225.2 (1.31)	20/51	Female	236.7 (0.89)	30/51
White, Non-Hispanic	231.8 (0.92)	9/51	White, Non-Hispanic	247.0 (0.78)	16/51
Black, Non-Hispanic	207.4 (1.76)	5/42	Black, Non-Hispanic	221.9 (1.27)	16/42
Asian, Non-Hispanic	236.9 (2.86)	7/27	Asian, Non-Hispanic	254.5 (1.93)	12/25
American Indian, Non-Hispanic	n/a	n/a	American Indian, Non-Hispanic	n/a	n/a
Hispanic	207.9 (1.85)	14/40	Hispanic	225.8 (1.35)	19/41
Proficiency by Class Size			Proficiency by Class Size		
Less than 16 Students	210.1 (5.41)	16/34	Less than 16 Students	224.4 (3.60)	19/35
16 to 18 Students	218.1 (3.68)	15/33	16 to 18 Students	237.9 (2.44)	15/31
19 to 20 Students	227.6 (2.23)	5/38	19 to 20 Students	241.9 (1.90)	12/38
21 to 25 Students	226.3 (1.62)	12/51	21 to 25 Students	240.8 (1.26)	25/51
Greater than 25 Students	220.6 (1.93)	19/36	Greater than 25 Students	236.5 (2.36)	22/33
Percent Attaining Achievement Levels			Percent Attaining Achievement Levels		
Below Basic	31.1 (1.48)	36/51	Below Basic	18.7 (1.04)	25/51
Basic or Above	68.9 (1.48)	16/51	Basic or Above	81.3 (1.04)	27/51
Proficient or Above	33.3 (1.16)	19/51	Proficient or Above	36.1 (1.32)	29/51
Advanced or Above	7.6 (0.64)	15/51	Advanced or Above	4.5 (0.53)	26/51
8th Grade			**8th Grade**		
Average Proficiency	265.1 (0.96)	19/51	Average Proficiency	279.7 (0.90)	28/51
Proficiency by Gender/Race/Ethnicity			Proficiency by Gender/Race/Ethnicity		
Male	260.0 (1.25)	20/51	Male	279.9 (1.01)	30/51
Female	270.2 (1.05)	20/51	Female	279.5 (1.09)	25/51
White, Non-Hispanic	276.2 (0.96)	4/51	White, Non-Hispanic	290.4 (1.23)	15/51
Black, Non-Hispanic	242.5 (2.05)	19/40	Black, Non-Hispanic	258.7 (1.85)	11/41
Asian, Non-Hispanic	273.7 (2.76)	12/24	Asian, Non-Hispanic	297.9 (3.19)	12/23
American Indian, Non-Hispanic	n/a	n/a	American Indian, Non-Hispanic	n/a	n/a
Hispanic	250.5 (1.76)	11/38	Hispanic	262.0 (1.76)	21/38
Proficiency by Parents Highest Level of Ed.			Proficiency by Parents Highest Level of Ed.		
Did Not Finish High School	249.0 (1.88)	13/49	Did Not Finish High School	262.5 (1.92)	24/50
Graduated High School	256.8 (1.52)	17/50	Graduated High School	270.7 (1.36)	20/50
Some Education After High School	267.3 (1.24)	23/50	Some Education After High School	280.1 (1.39)	29/50
Graduated College	274.2 (1.08)	18/50	Graduated College	289.2 (1.25)	29/50
Percent Attaining Achievement Levels			Percent Attaining Achievement Levels		
Below Basic	31.1 (1.48)	36/51	Below Basic	30.0 (1.14)	24/51
Basic or Above	68.9 (1.48)	16/51	Basic or Above	70.0 (1.14)	28/51
Proficient or Above	33.3 (1.16)	19/51	Proficient or Above	30.8 (1.27)	21/51
Advanced or Above	7.6 (0.64)	15/51	Advanced or Above	6.3 (0.51)	16/51

Note: *For an explanation of data, please refer to the User's Guide in the front of the book; n/a indicates data not available*

Albany County

Albany City SD
Academy Park • Albany, NY 12207-1099
(518) 462-7200 • http://www.albany.k12.ny.us/
Grade Span: PK-12; Agency Type: 1
Schools: 15
    11 Primary; 2 Middle; 1 High; 1 Other Level
    14 Regular; 0 Special Education; 0 Vocational; 1 Alternative
    2 Magnet; 0 Charter; 13 Title I Eligible; 10 School-wide Title I
Students: 9,919 (51.0% male; 48.9% female)
    Individual Education Program: n/a;
    English Language Learner: n/a; Migrant: n/a
    Eligible for Free Lunch Program: n/a
    Eligible for Reduced-Price Lunch Program: n/a
Teachers: 787.4 (12.6 to 1)
Librarians/Media Specialists: 14.6 (679.4 to 1)
Guidance Counselors: 14.5 (684.1 to 1)
Current Spending: ($ per student per year):
    Total: $14,121; Instruction: $9,819; Support Services: $3,951
Enrollment, Drop-out Rates and Diploma Recipients by Race/Ethnicity

Category	Total	White	Black	Asian	AIAN	Hisp.
Enrollment (%)	100.0	22.7	65.1	2.8	0.2	9.3
Drop-out Rate (%)	4.7	3.7	5.3	3.6	0.0	4.9
H.S. Diplomas (#)	382	167	172	18	0	25

Bethlehem Central SD
90 Adams Pl • Delmar, NY 12054-3297
(518) 439-7098 • http://bcsd.k12.ny.us/
Grade Span: KG-12; Agency Type: 1
Schools: 7
    5 Primary; 1 Middle; 1 High; 0 Other Level
    7 Regular; 0 Special Education; 0 Vocational; 0 Alternative
    0 Magnet; 0 Charter; 5 Title I Eligible; 0 School-wide Title I
Students: 5,022 (52.9% male; 47.0% female)
    Individual Education Program: n/a;
    English Language Learner: n/a; Migrant: n/a
    Eligible for Free Lunch Program: n/a
    Eligible for Reduced-Price Lunch Program: n/a
Teachers: 342.3 (14.7 to 1)
Librarians/Media Specialists: 7.6 (660.8 to 1)
Guidance Counselors: 13.3 (377.6 to 1)
Current Spending: ($ per student per year):
    Total: $9,938; Instruction: $6,162; Support Services: $3,661
Enrollment, Drop-out Rates and Diploma Recipients by Race/Ethnicity

Category	Total	White	Black	Asian	AIAN	Hisp.
Enrollment (%)	100.0	92.6	2.0	3.9	0.1	1.4
Drop-out Rate (%)	1.5	1.4	3.3	2.2	n/a	9.1
H.S. Diplomas (#)	357	335	6	11	0	5

Cohoes City SD
7 Bevan St • Cohoes, NY 12047-3299
(518) 237-0100 • http://cohoes.neric.org/
Grade Span: KG-12; Agency Type: 1
Schools: 5
    3 Primary; 1 Middle; 1 High; 0 Other Level
    5 Regular; 0 Special Education; 0 Vocational; 0 Alternative
    0 Magnet; 0 Charter; 4 Title I Eligible; 4 School-wide Title I
Students: 2,202 (50.2% male; 49.7% female)
    Individual Education Program: n/a;
    English Language Learner: n/a; Migrant: n/a
    Eligible for Free Lunch Program: n/a
    Eligible for Reduced-Price Lunch Program: n/a
Teachers: 180.1 (12.2 to 1)
Librarians/Media Specialists: 3.0 (734.0 to 1)
Guidance Counselors: 5.0 (440.4 to 1)
Current Spending: ($ per student per year):
    Total: $12,164; Instruction: $7,647; Support Services: $4,060
Enrollment, Drop-out Rates and Diploma Recipients by Race/Ethnicity

Category	Total	White	Black	Asian	AIAN	Hisp.
Enrollment (%)	100.0	88.0	7.3	0.8	0.1	3.8
Drop-out Rate (%)	4.0	4.2	0.0	0.0	0.0	0.0
H.S. Diplomas (#)	107	107	0	0	0	0

Guilderland Central SD
6076 State Farm Rd • Guilderland, NY 12084-9533
(518) 456-6200 • http://www.gcsd.k12.ny.us/gcsddo/
Grade Span: KG-12; Agency Type: 1
Schools: 7
    5 Primary; 1 Middle; 1 High; 0 Other Level
    7 Regular; 0 Special Education; 0 Vocational; 0 Alternative
    0 Magnet; 0 Charter; 4 Title I Eligible; 4 School-wide Title I
Students: 5,664 (51.1% male; 48.8% female)
    Individual Education Program: n/a;
    English Language Learner: n/a; Migrant: n/a

Eligible for Free Lunch Program: n/a
Eligible for Reduced-Price Lunch Program: n/a
Teachers: 426.1 (13.3 to 1)
Librarians/Media Specialists: 9.0 (629.3 to 1)
Guidance Counselors: 11.0 (514.9 to 1)
Current Spending: ($ per student per year):
    Total: $10,536; Instruction: $6,827; Support Services: $3,499
Enrollment, Drop-out Rates and Diploma Recipients by Race/Ethnicity

Category	Total	White	Black	Asian	AIAN	Hisp.
Enrollment (%)	100.0	90.8	3.4	4.5	0.1	1.3
Drop-out Rate (%)	0.2	0.2	0.0	0.0	0.0	0.0
H.S. Diplomas (#)	374	345	10	4	8	7

North Colonie Central SD
91 Fiddler's Ln • Latham, NY 12110-5349
(518) 785-8591 • http://www.northcolonie.org/
Grade Span: KG-12; Agency Type: 1
Schools: 8
    6 Primary; 1 Middle; 1 High; 0 Other Level
    8 Regular; 0 Special Education; 0 Vocational; 0 Alternative
    0 Magnet; 0 Charter; 6 Title I Eligible; 0 School-wide Title I
Students: 5,631 (50.7% male; 49.2% female)
    Individual Education Program: n/a;
    English Language Learner: n/a; Migrant: n/a
    Eligible for Free Lunch Program: n/a
    Eligible for Reduced-Price Lunch Program: n/a
Teachers: 398.7 (14.1 to 1)
Librarians/Media Specialists: 10.5 (536.3 to 1)
Guidance Counselors: 16.5 (341.3 to 1)
Current Spending: ($ per student per year):
    Total: $9,665; Instruction: $6,125; Support Services: $3,296
Enrollment, Drop-out Rates and Diploma Recipients by Race/Ethnicity

Category	Total	White	Black	Asian	AIAN	Hisp.
Enrollment (%)	100.0	88.2	3.7	6.4	0.0	1.6
Drop-out Rate (%)	1.6	1.8	0.0	0.0	n/a	6.1
H.S. Diplomas (#)	454	410	8	33	0	3

Ravena-Coeymans-Selkirk Central SD
26 Thatcher St • Selkirk, NY 12158-0097
(518) 756-5201 • http://www.rcscsd.org/default_40.asp
Grade Span: PK-12; Agency Type: 1
Schools: 4
    2 Primary; 1 Middle; 1 High; 0 Other Level
    4 Regular; 0 Special Education; 0 Vocational; 0 Alternative
    0 Magnet; 0 Charter; 3 Title I Eligible; 0 School-wide Title I
Students: 2,385 (50.6% male; 49.3% female)
    Individual Education Program: n/a;
    English Language Learner: n/a; Migrant: n/a
    Eligible for Free Lunch Program: n/a
    Eligible for Reduced-Price Lunch Program: n/a
Teachers: 192.1 (12.4 to 1)
Librarians/Media Specialists: 4.0 (596.3 to 1)
Guidance Counselors: 7.0 (340.7 to 1)
Current Spending: ($ per student per year):
    Total: $12,585; Instruction: $7,985; Support Services: $4,325
Enrollment, Drop-out Rates and Diploma Recipients by Race/Ethnicity

Category	Total	White	Black	Asian	AIAN	Hisp.
Enrollment (%)	100.0	89.8	4.8	0.8	0.2	4.4
Drop-out Rate (%)	2.0	2.1	0.0	0.0	n/a	0.0
H.S. Diplomas (#)	167	156	2	2	0	7

South Colonie Central SD
102 Loralee Dr • Albany, NY 12205-2298
(518) 869-3576 • http://family.knick.net/scolonie/
Grade Span: PK-12; Agency Type: 1
Schools: 9
    5 Primary; 2 Middle; 1 High; 1 Other Level
    8 Regular; 0 Special Education; 0 Vocational; 1 Alternative
    0 Magnet; 0 Charter; 5 Title I Eligible; 0 School-wide Title I
Students: 5,745 (51.1% male; 48.8% female)
    Individual Education Program: n/a;
    English Language Learner: n/a; Migrant: n/a
    Eligible for Free Lunch Program: n/a
    Eligible for Reduced-Price Lunch Program: n/a
Teachers: 445.8 (12.9 to 1)
Librarians/Media Specialists: 9.0 (638.3 to 1)
Guidance Counselors: 10.8 (531.9 to 1)
Current Spending: ($ per student per year):
    Total: $10,885; Instruction: $7,436; Support Services: $3,198
Enrollment, Drop-out Rates and Diploma Recipients by Race/Ethnicity

Category	Total	White	Black	Asian	AIAN	Hisp.
Enrollment (%)	100.0	88.1	6.0	3.6	0.6	1.8
Drop-out Rate (%)	1.5	1.5	2.0	0.0	0.0	4.0
H.S. Diplomas (#)	389	351	18	17	2	1

Bronx County

New York City Geographic District # 9
1 Fordham Plz - Rm 81 • Bronx, NY 10458
(718) 741-7030
Grade Span: KG-10; **Agency Type:** 1
Schools: 3
   2 Primary; 0 Middle; 0 High; 1 Other Level
   3 Regular; 0 Special Education; 0 Vocational; 0 Alternative
   0 Magnet; 0 Charter; 0 Title I Eligible; 0 School-wide Title I
Students: 1,839 (50.3% male; 49.6% female)
   Individual Education Program: n/a;
   English Language Learner: n/a; Migrant: n/a
   Eligible for Free Lunch Program: n/a
   Eligible for Reduced-Price Lunch Program: n/a
Teachers: n/a
Librarians/Media Specialists: n/a
Guidance Counselors: n/a
Current Spending: ($ per student per year):
   Total: n/a; Instruction: n/a; Support Services: n/a
Enrollment, Drop-out Rates and Diploma Recipients by Race/Ethnicity

Category	Total	White	Black	Asian	AIAN	Hisp.
Enrollment (%)	100.0	0.5	27.5	0.9	0.4	70.8
Drop-out Rate (%)	n/a	n/a	n/a	n/a	n/a	n/a
H.S. Diplomas (#)	n/a	n/a	n/a	n/a	n/a	n/a

Broome County

Binghamton City SD
164 Hawley St • Binghamton, NY 13901-2126
(607) 762-8100 • http://www.bcsd.stier.org/welcome.html
Grade Span: PK-12; **Agency Type:** 1
Schools: 11
   7 Primary; 2 Middle; 0 High; 2 Other Level
   10 Regular; 0 Special Education; 0 Vocational; 1 Alternative
   0 Magnet; 0 Charter; 10 Title I Eligible; 8 School-wide Title I
Students: 6,249 (50.6% male; 49.3% female)
   Individual Education Program: n/a;
   English Language Learner: n/a; Migrant: n/a
   Eligible for Free Lunch Program: n/a
   Eligible for Reduced-Price Lunch Program: n/a
Teachers: 536.5 (11.6 to 1)
Librarians/Media Specialists: 11.0 (568.1 to 1)
Guidance Counselors: 13.0 (480.7 to 1)
Current Spending: ($ per student per year):
   Total: $10,492; Instruction: $7,133; Support Services: $2,933
Enrollment, Drop-out Rates and Diploma Recipients by Race/Ethnicity

Category	Total	White	Black	Asian	AIAN	Hisp.
Enrollment (%)	100.0	67.7	21.6	4.2	0.2	6.4
Drop-out Rate (%)	0.9	0.6	1.8	1.6	0.0	1.3
H.S. Diplomas (#)	253	214	26	9	0	4

Chenango Forks Central SD
One Gordon Dr • Binghamton, NY 13901-5614
(607) 648-7543
Grade Span: PK-12; **Agency Type:** 1
Schools: 4
   2 Primary; 1 Middle; 1 High; 0 Other Level
   4 Regular; 0 Special Education; 0 Vocational; 0 Alternative
   0 Magnet; 0 Charter; 3 Title I Eligible; 0 School-wide Title I
Students: 1,874 (51.6% male; 48.3% female)
   Individual Education Program: n/a;
   English Language Learner: n/a; Migrant: n/a
   Eligible for Free Lunch Program: n/a
   Eligible for Reduced-Price Lunch Program: n/a
Teachers: 142.0 (13.2 to 1)
Librarians/Media Specialists: 3.0 (624.7 to 1)
Guidance Counselors: 4.0 (468.5 to 1)
Current Spending: ($ per student per year):
   Total: $10,766; Instruction: $6,701; Support Services: $3,761
Enrollment, Drop-out Rates and Diploma Recipients by Race/Ethnicity

Category	Total	White	Black	Asian	AIAN	Hisp.
Enrollment (%)	100.0	97.9	0.7	0.3	0.2	0.9
Drop-out Rate (%)	1.9	1.9	0.0	n/a	n/a	0.0
H.S. Diplomas (#)	128	128	0	0	0	0

Chenango Valley Central SD
1160 Chenango St • Binghamton, NY 13901-1653
(607) 779-4710 • http://www.cvcsd.stier.org/
Grade Span: PK-12; **Agency Type:** 1
Schools: 4
   1 Primary; 2 Middle; 1 High; 0 Other Level
   4 Regular; 0 Special Education; 0 Vocational; 0 Alternative
   0 Magnet; 0 Charter; 2 Title I Eligible; 0 School-wide Title I
Students: 2,032 (52.3% male; 47.6% female)

   Individual Education Program: n/a;
   English Language Learner: n/a; Migrant: n/a
   Eligible for Free Lunch Program: n/a
   Eligible for Reduced-Price Lunch Program: n/a
Teachers: 148.8 (13.7 to 1)
Librarians/Media Specialists: 3.0 (677.3 to 1)
Guidance Counselors: 4.0 (508.0 to 1)
Current Spending: ($ per student per year):
   Total: $10,867; Instruction: $7,170; Support Services: $3,429
Enrollment, Drop-out Rates and Diploma Recipients by Race/Ethnicity

Category	Total	White	Black	Asian	AIAN	Hisp.
Enrollment (%)	100.0	95.8	2.2	0.7	0.3	0.9
Drop-out Rate (%)	1.8	1.8	0.0	0.0	n/a	0.0
H.S. Diplomas (#)	130	129	1	0	0	0

Johnson City Central SD
666 Reynolds Rd • Johnson City, NY 13790-1398
(607) 763-1230 • http://www.tier.net/jcschools/
Grade Span: KG-12; **Agency Type:** 1
Schools: 5
   2 Primary; 1 Middle; 1 High; 1 Other Level
   4 Regular; 0 Special Education; 0 Vocational; 1 Alternative
   0 Magnet; 0 Charter; 2 Title I Eligible; 0 School-wide Title I
Students: 2,597 (49.8% male; 50.1% female)
   Individual Education Program: n/a;
   English Language Learner: n/a; Migrant: n/a
   Eligible for Free Lunch Program: n/a
   Eligible for Reduced-Price Lunch Program: n/a
Teachers: 208.9 (12.4 to 1)
Librarians/Media Specialists: 3.0 (865.7 to 1)
Guidance Counselors: 7.0 (371.0 to 1)
Current Spending: ($ per student per year):
   Total: $12,643; Instruction: $8,446; Support Services: $3,869
Enrollment, Drop-out Rates and Diploma Recipients by Race/Ethnicity

Category	Total	White	Black	Asian	AIAN	Hisp.
Enrollment (%)	100.0	80.9	8.6	6.3	0.7	3.4
Drop-out Rate (%)	3.9	3.8	7.3	3.8	0.0	0.0
H.S. Diplomas (#)	156	144	4	6	0	2

Maine-Endwell Central SD
712 Farm-To-Market Rd • Endwell, NY 13760-1199
(607) 754-1400
Grade Span: KG-12; **Agency Type:** 1
Schools: 4
   2 Primary; 1 Middle; 1 High; 0 Other Level
   4 Regular; 0 Special Education; 0 Vocational; 0 Alternative
   0 Magnet; 0 Charter; 3 Title I Eligible; 0 School-wide Title I
Students: 2,675 (50.2% male; 49.7% female)
   Individual Education Program: n/a;
   English Language Learner: n/a; Migrant: n/a
   Eligible for Free Lunch Program: n/a
   Eligible for Reduced-Price Lunch Program: n/a
Teachers: 205.7 (13.0 to 1)
Librarians/Media Specialists: 4.0 (668.8 to 1)
Guidance Counselors: 5.0 (535.0 to 1)
Current Spending: ($ per student per year):
   Total: $10,919; Instruction: $6,760; Support Services: $3,902
Enrollment, Drop-out Rates and Diploma Recipients by Race/Ethnicity

Category	Total	White	Black	Asian	AIAN	Hisp.
Enrollment (%)	100.0	96.4	1.6	1.2	0.1	0.6
Drop-out Rate (%)	1.6	1.5	11.1	0.0	n/a	0.0
H.S. Diplomas (#)	139	134	0	4	0	1

Susquehanna Valley Central SD
1040 Conklin Rd • Conklin, NY 13748-0200
(607) 775-9100 • http://www.sv.stier.org/
Grade Span: KG-12; **Agency Type:** 1
Schools: 5
   3 Primary; 1 Middle; 1 High; 0 Other Level
   5 Regular; 0 Special Education; 0 Vocational; 0 Alternative
   0 Magnet; 0 Charter; 3 Title I Eligible; 0 School-wide Title I
Students: 2,135 (52.0% male; 47.9% female)
   Individual Education Program: n/a;
   English Language Learner: n/a; Migrant: n/a
   Eligible for Free Lunch Program: n/a
   Eligible for Reduced-Price Lunch Program: n/a
Teachers: 182.7 (11.7 to 1)
Librarians/Media Specialists: 3.0 (711.7 to 1)
Guidance Counselors: 5.0 (427.0 to 1)
Current Spending: ($ per student per year):
   Total: $10,505; Instruction: $6,737; Support Services: $3,480

Enrollment, Drop-out Rates and Diploma Recipients by Race/Ethnicity

Category	Total	White	Black	Asian	AIAN	Hisp.
Enrollment (%)	100.0	96.0	2.2	0.6	0.3	1.0
Drop-out Rate (%)	2.1	2.0	7.7	n/a	0.0	0.0
H.S. Diplomas (#)	141	139	1	0	0	1

Union-Endicott Central SD
1100 E Main St • Endicott, NY 13760-5271
(607) 757-2112 • http://www.uetigers.stier.org/
Grade Span: KG-12; **Agency Type:** 1
Schools: 7
    4 Primary; 2 Middle; 1 High; 0 Other Level
    7 Regular; 0 Special Education; 0 Vocational; 0 Alternative
    0 Magnet; 0 Charter; 5 Title I Eligible; 0 School-wide Title I
Students: 4,536   (51.6% male; 48.3% female)
    Individual Education Program: n/a;
    English Language Learner: n/a; Migrant: n/a
    Eligible for Free Lunch Program: n/a
    Eligible for Reduced-Price Lunch Program: n/a
Teachers: 348.1 (13.0 to 1)
Librarians/Media Specialists: 7.5 (604.8 to 1)
Guidance Counselors: 9.0 (504.0 to 1)
Current Spending: ($ per student per year):
    Total: $10,812; Instruction: $6,900; Support Services: $3,638
Enrollment, Drop-out Rates and Diploma Recipients by Race/Ethnicity

Category	Total	White	Black	Asian	AIAN	Hisp.
Enrollment (%)	100.0	89.5	5.8	2.4	0.6	1.7
Drop-out Rate (%)	2.4	2.5	0.0	0.0	0.0	10.0
H.S. Diplomas (#)	279	260	10	8	1	0

Vestal Central SD
201 Main St • Vestal, NY 13850-1599
(607) 757-2241 • http://www.vestal.stier.org/
Grade Span: KG-12; **Agency Type:** 1
Schools: 7
    5 Primary; 1 Middle; 1 High; 0 Other Level
    7 Regular; 0 Special Education; 0 Vocational; 0 Alternative
    0 Magnet; 0 Charter; 6 Title I Eligible; 0 School-wide Title I
Students: 4,266   (52.2% male; 47.7% female)
    Individual Education Program: n/a;
    English Language Learner: n/a; Migrant: n/a
    Eligible for Free Lunch Program: n/a
    Eligible for Reduced-Price Lunch Program: n/a
Teachers: 322.6 (13.2 to 1)
Librarians/Media Specialists: 8.0 (533.3 to 1)
Guidance Counselors: 12.7 (335.9 to 1)
Current Spending: ($ per student per year):
    Total: $9,960; Instruction: $6,819; Support Services: $2,976
Enrollment, Drop-out Rates and Diploma Recipients by Race/Ethnicity

Category	Total	White	Black	Asian	AIAN	Hisp.
Enrollment (%)	100.0	90.6	2.9	5.1	0.3	1.1
Drop-out Rate (%)	0.5	0.5	0.0	1.6	0.0	0.0
H.S. Diplomas (#)	296	267	7	15	1	6

Whitney Point Central SD
10 Keibel Rd • Whitney Point, NY 13862-0249
(607) 692-8202 • http://www.tier.net/whitneypoint/
Grade Span: PK-12; **Agency Type:** 1
Schools: 4
    2 Primary; 1 Middle; 1 High; 0 Other Level
    4 Regular; 0 Special Education; 0 Vocational; 0 Alternative
    0 Magnet; 0 Charter; 3 Title I Eligible; 0 School-wide Title I
Students: 1,858   (50.5% male; 49.4% female)
    Individual Education Program: n/a;
    English Language Learner: n/a; Migrant: n/a
    Eligible for Free Lunch Program: n/a
    Eligible for Reduced-Price Lunch Program: n/a
Teachers: 152.1 (12.2 to 1)
Librarians/Media Specialists: 3.0 (619.3 to 1)
Guidance Counselors: 6.0 (309.7 to 1)
Current Spending: ($ per student per year):
    Total: $9,967; Instruction: $6,721; Support Services: $2,939
Enrollment, Drop-out Rates and Diploma Recipients by Race/Ethnicity

Category	Total	White	Black	Asian	AIAN	Hisp.
Enrollment (%)	100.0	98.1	1.2	0.2	0.1	0.4
Drop-out Rate (%)	2.1	2.1	0.0	n/a	n/a	n/a
H.S. Diplomas (#)	98	97	0	1	0	0

Windsor Central SD
215 Main St • Windsor, NY 13865-4134
(607) 655-8216 • http://www.windsor-csd.org/
Grade Span: KG-12; **Agency Type:** 1
Schools: 4
    3 Primary; 0 Middle; 1 High; 0 Other Level
    4 Regular; 0 Special Education; 0 Vocational; 0 Alternative

---

    0 Magnet; 0 Charter; 3 Title I Eligible; 0 School-wide Title I
Students: 2,045   (49.9% male; 50.0% female)
    Individual Education Program: n/a;
    English Language Learner: n/a; Migrant: n/a
    Eligible for Free Lunch Program: n/a
    Eligible for Reduced-Price Lunch Program: n/a
Teachers: 154.0 (13.3 to 1)
Librarians/Media Specialists: 3.0 (681.7 to 1)
Guidance Counselors: 7.0 (292.1 to 1)
Current Spending: ($ per student per year):
    Total: $10,250; Instruction: $6,629; Support Services: $3,333
Enrollment, Drop-out Rates and Diploma Recipients by Race/Ethnicity

Category	Total	White	Black	Asian	AIAN	Hisp.
Enrollment (%)	100.0	97.9	1.0	0.8	0.0	0.2
Drop-out Rate (%)	3.5	3.6	0.0	0.0	0.0	n/a
H.S. Diplomas (#)	111	108	0	3	0	0

Cattaraugus County

Gowanda Central SD
10674 Prospect St • Gowanda, NY 14070-1384
(716) 532-3325
Grade Span: KG-12; **Agency Type:** 1
Schools: 5
    1 Primary; 1 Middle; 1 High; 2 Other Level
    3 Regular; 0 Special Education; 0 Vocational; 2 Alternative
    0 Magnet; 0 Charter; 2 Title I Eligible; 0 School-wide Title I
Students: 1,532   (51.8% male; 48.1% female)
    Individual Education Program: n/a;
    English Language Learner: n/a; Migrant: n/a
    Eligible for Free Lunch Program: n/a
    Eligible for Reduced-Price Lunch Program: n/a
Teachers: 122.0 (12.6 to 1)
Librarians/Media Specialists: 2.0 (766.0 to 1)
Guidance Counselors: 6.0 (255.3 to 1)
Current Spending: ($ per student per year):
    Total: $12,219; Instruction: $8,313; Support Services: $3,517
Enrollment, Drop-out Rates and Diploma Recipients by Race/Ethnicity

Category	Total	White	Black	Asian	AIAN	Hisp.
Enrollment (%)	100.0	70.6	1.3	0.5	27.2	0.5
Drop-out Rate (%)	5.7	4.5	0.0	0.0	9.0	n/a
H.S. Diplomas (#)	105	79	0	0	26	0

Olean City SD
410 W Sullivan St • Olean, NY 14760-2596
(716) 375-8018 • http://www.oleanschools.org/
Grade Span: PK-12; **Agency Type:** 1
Schools: 7
    5 Primary; 1 Middle; 1 High; 0 Other Level
    7 Regular; 0 Special Education; 0 Vocational; 0 Alternative
    0 Magnet; 0 Charter; 5 Title I Eligible; 0 School-wide Title I
Students: 2,541   (49.5% male; 50.4% female)
    Individual Education Program: n/a;
    English Language Learner: n/a; Migrant: n/a
    Eligible for Free Lunch Program: n/a
    Eligible for Reduced-Price Lunch Program: n/a
Teachers: 193.3 (13.1 to 1)
Librarians/Media Specialists: 3.0 (847.0 to 1)
Guidance Counselors: 10.0 (254.1 to 1)
Current Spending: ($ per student per year):
    Total: $9,745; Instruction: $6,719; Support Services: $2,745
Enrollment, Drop-out Rates and Diploma Recipients by Race/Ethnicity

Category	Total	White	Black	Asian	AIAN	Hisp.
Enrollment (%)	100.0	89.0	6.9	1.6	0.8	1.7
Drop-out Rate (%)	6.3	6.3	9.1	0.0	33.3	0.0
H.S. Diplomas (#)	141	134	3	3	0	1

Salamanca City SD
50 Iroquois Dr • Salamanca, NY 14779-1398
(716) 945-2403 •
http://rin.buffalo.edu/c_catt/educ/scho_publ/scho_sala.html
Grade Span: PK-12; **Agency Type:** 1
Schools: 5
    2 Primary; 1 Middle; 2 High; 0 Other Level
    4 Regular; 0 Special Education; 0 Vocational; 1 Alternative
    0 Magnet; 0 Charter; 4 Title I Eligible; 4 School-wide Title I
Students: 1,513   (50.8% male; 49.1% female)
    Individual Education Program: n/a;
    English Language Learner: n/a; Migrant: n/a
    Eligible for Free Lunch Program: n/a
    Eligible for Reduced-Price Lunch Program: n/a
Teachers: 128.5 (11.8 to 1)
Librarians/Media Specialists: 3.0 (504.3 to 1)
Guidance Counselors: 8.0 (189.1 to 1)
Current Spending: ($ per student per year):
    Total: $10,593; Instruction: $6,906; Support Services: $3,349

Enrollment, Drop-out Rates and Diploma Recipients by Race/Ethnicity

Category	Total	White	Black	Asian	AIAN	Hisp.
Enrollment (%)	100.0	68.1	1.4	0.1	28.6	1.8
Drop-out Rate (%)	4.0	3.7	0.0	0.0	5.5	0.0
H.S. Diplomas (#)	71	58	0	1	10	2

Yorkshire-Pioneer Central SD
County Line Rd • Yorkshire, NY 14173-0579
(716) 492-9304
Grade Span: KG-12; **Agency Type:** 1
Schools: 4
   2 Primary; 1 Middle; 1 High; 0 Other Level
   4 Regular; 0 Special Education; 0 Vocational; 0 Alternative
   0 Magnet; 0 Charter; 3 Title I Eligible; 1 School-wide Title I
Students: 2,928 (51.6% male; 48.3% female)
   Individual Education Program: n/a;
   English Language Learner: n/a; Migrant: n/a
   Eligible for Free Lunch Program: n/a
   Eligible for Reduced-Price Lunch Program: n/a
Teachers: 225.7 (13.0 to 1)
Librarians/Media Specialists: 3.3 (887.3 to 1)
Guidance Counselors: 6.9 (424.3 to 1)
Current Spending: ($ per student per year):
   Total: $11,563; Instruction: $7,628; Support Services: $3,607
Enrollment, Drop-out Rates and Diploma Recipients by Race/Ethnicity

Category	Total	White	Black	Asian	AIAN	Hisp.
Enrollment (%)	100.0	97.5	0.5	0.5	0.9	0.6
Drop-out Rate (%)	6.8	6.4	50.0	28.6	25.0	0.0
H.S. Diplomas (#)	214	212	0	1	1	0

Cayuga County

Auburn City SD
78 Thornton Ave • Auburn, NY 13021-4698
(315) 255-8835 • http://www.auburn.cnyric.org/
Grade Span: KG-12; **Agency Type:** 1
Schools: 11
   5 Primary; 2 Middle; 2 High; 2 Other Level
   8 Regular; 0 Special Education; 0 Vocational; 3 Alternative
   0 Magnet; 0 Charter; 5 Title I Eligible; 2 School-wide Title I
Students: 4,993 (50.7% male; 49.2% female)
   Individual Education Program: n/a;
   English Language Learner: n/a; Migrant: n/a
   Eligible for Free Lunch Program: n/a
   Eligible for Reduced-Price Lunch Program: n/a
Teachers: 378.5 (13.2 to 1)
Librarians/Media Specialists: 5.0 (998.6 to 1)
Guidance Counselors: 10.0 (499.3 to 1)
Current Spending: ($ per student per year):
   Total: $9,897; Instruction: $7,043; Support Services: $2,630
Enrollment, Drop-out Rates and Diploma Recipients by Race/Ethnicity

Category	Total	White	Black	Asian	AIAN	Hisp.
Enrollment (%)	100.0	88.1	9.2	0.7	0.6	1.4
Drop-out Rate (%)	8.1	7.2	19.8	15.4	0.0	8.7
H.S. Diplomas (#)	278	264	12	2	0	0

Chautauqua County

Dunkirk City SD
620 Marauder Dr • Dunkirk, NY 14048-1396
(716) 366-9300
Grade Span: KG-12; **Agency Type:** 1
Schools: 6
   4 Primary; 1 Middle; 1 High; 0 Other Level
   6 Regular; 0 Special Education; 0 Vocational; 0 Alternative
   0 Magnet; 0 Charter; 5 Title I Eligible; 5 School-wide Title I
Students: 2,101 (51.1% male; 48.8% female)
   Individual Education Program: n/a;
   English Language Learner: n/a; Migrant: n/a
   Eligible for Free Lunch Program: n/a
   Eligible for Reduced-Price Lunch Program: n/a
Teachers: 208.5 (10.1 to 1)
Librarians/Media Specialists: 2.0 (1,050.5 to 1)
Guidance Counselors: 8.0 (262.6 to 1)
Current Spending: ($ per student per year):
   Total: $13,689; Instruction: $9,785; Support Services: $3,590
Enrollment, Drop-out Rates and Diploma Recipients by Race/Ethnicity

Category	Total	White	Black	Asian	AIAN	Hisp.
Enrollment (%)	100.0	56.9	8.6	0.4	0.7	33.4
Drop-out Rate (%)	6.2	3.3	18.4	n/a	0.0	10.6
H.S. Diplomas (#)	110	92	6	0	0	12

Fredonia Central SD
425 E Main St • Fredonia, NY 14063-1496
(716) 679-1581 • http://www.fredonia.wnyric.org/
Grade Span: PK-12; **Agency Type:** 1
Schools: 4
   2 Primary; 1 Middle; 1 High; 0 Other Level
   4 Regular; 0 Special Education; 0 Vocational; 0 Alternative
   0 Magnet; 0 Charter; 4 Title I Eligible; 0 School-wide Title I
Students: 1,857 (49.8% male; 50.1% female)
   Individual Education Program: n/a;
   English Language Learner: n/a; Migrant: n/a
   Eligible for Free Lunch Program: n/a
   Eligible for Reduced-Price Lunch Program: n/a
Teachers: 167.0 (11.1 to 1)
Librarians/Media Specialists: 2.5 (742.8 to 1)
Guidance Counselors: 5.0 (371.4 to 1)
Current Spending: ($ per student per year):
   Total: $10,401; Instruction: $7,047; Support Services: $3,082
Enrollment, Drop-out Rates and Diploma Recipients by Race/Ethnicity

Category	Total	White	Black	Asian	AIAN	Hisp.
Enrollment (%)	100.0	92.9	1.3	1.8	0.1	3.9
Drop-out Rate (%)	2.3	2.3	0.0	0.0	100.0	0.0
H.S. Diplomas (#)	152	146	2	2	0	2

Jamestown City SD
201 E Fourth St • Jamestown, NY 14701-5397
(716) 483-4420 • http://www.jamestown.wnyric.org/
Grade Span: PK-12; **Agency Type:** 1
Schools: 10
   6 Primary; 3 Middle; 1 High; 0 Other Level
   10 Regular; 0 Special Education; 0 Vocational; 0 Alternative
   0 Magnet; 0 Charter; 9 Title I Eligible; 4 School-wide Title I
Students: 5,289 (51.0% male; 48.9% female)
   Individual Education Program: n/a;
   English Language Learner: n/a; Migrant: n/a
   Eligible for Free Lunch Program: n/a
   Eligible for Reduced-Price Lunch Program: n/a
Teachers: 461.2 (11.5 to 1)
Librarians/Media Specialists: 12.3 (430.0 to 1)
Guidance Counselors: 19.2 (275.5 to 1)
Current Spending: ($ per student per year):
   Total: $11,426; Instruction: $8,216; Support Services: $2,786
Enrollment, Drop-out Rates and Diploma Recipients by Race/Ethnicity

Category	Total	White	Black	Asian	AIAN	Hisp.
Enrollment (%)	100.0	81.7	7.6	0.7	1.0	9.0
Drop-out Rate (%)	7.8	6.1	22.8	0.0	33.3	16.7
H.S. Diplomas (#)	278	256	5	4	0	13

Southwestern Central SD At Jamestown
600 Hunt Rd W E • Jamestown, NY 14701-5799
(716) 484-1136 • http://swcs.wnyric.org/
Grade Span: KG-12; **Agency Type:** 1
Schools: 3
   1 Primary; 1 Middle; 1 High; 0 Other Level
   3 Regular; 0 Special Education; 0 Vocational; 0 Alternative
   0 Magnet; 0 Charter; 3 Title I Eligible; 0 School-wide Title I
Students: 1,752 (52.9% male; 47.0% female)
   Individual Education Program: n/a;
   English Language Learner: n/a; Migrant: n/a
   Eligible for Free Lunch Program: n/a
   Eligible for Reduced-Price Lunch Program: n/a
Teachers: 128.4 (13.6 to 1)
Librarians/Media Specialists: 2.0 (876.0 to 1)
Guidance Counselors: 4.9 (357.6 to 1)
Current Spending: ($ per student per year):
   Total: $10,077; Instruction: $6,662; Support Services: $3,163
Enrollment, Drop-out Rates and Diploma Recipients by Race/Ethnicity

Category	Total	White	Black	Asian	AIAN	Hisp.
Enrollment (%)	100.0	96.0	1.1	1.9	0.3	0.7
Drop-out Rate (%)	4.9	4.9	33.3	0.0	0.0	0.0
H.S. Diplomas (#)	132	130	0	1	0	1

Chemung County

Elmira City SD
951 Hoffman St • Elmira, NY 14905-1715
(607) 735-3010 • http://www.elmiracityschools.com/index800.html
Grade Span: PK-12; **Agency Type:** 1
Schools: 15
   8 Primary; 2 Middle; 2 High; 3 Other Level
   12 Regular; 0 Special Education; 0 Vocational; 3 Alternative
   0 Magnet; 0 Charter; 10 Title I Eligible; 10 School-wide Title I
Students: 7,613 (51.7% male; 48.2% female)
   Individual Education Program: n/a;
   English Language Learner: n/a; Migrant: n/a

Eligible for Free Lunch Program: n/a
Eligible for Reduced-Price Lunch Program: n/a
Teachers: 566.1 (13.4 to 1)
Librarians/Media Specialists: 7.0 (1,087.6 to 1)
Guidance Counselors: 16.0 (475.8 to 1)
Current Spending: ($ per student per year):
Total: $11,062; Instruction: $7,137; Support Services: $3,622
Enrollment, Drop-out Rates and Diploma Recipients by Race/Ethnicity

Category	Total	White	Black	Asian	AIAN	Hisp.
Enrollment (%)	100.0	81.0	16.0	0.7	0.2	2.0
Drop-out Rate (%)	7.5	7.1	10.5	11.1	50.0	3.3
H.S. Diplomas (#)	324	301	18	2	0	3

Horseheads Central SD

One Raider Ln • Horseheads, NY 14845-2398
(607) 739-5601 • http://www.horseheadsdistrict.com/
Grade Span: KG-12; **Agency Type:** 1
Schools: 7
4 Primary; 2 Middle; 1 High; 0 Other Level
7 Regular; 0 Special Education; 0 Vocational; 0 Alternative
0 Magnet; 0 Charter; 4 Title I Eligible; 0 School-wide Title I
Students: 4,378 (50.1% male; 49.8% female)
Individual Education Program: n/a;
English Language Learner: n/a; Migrant: n/a
Eligible for Free Lunch Program: n/a
Eligible for Reduced-Price Lunch Program: n/a
Teachers: 302.4 (14.5 to 1)
Librarians/Media Specialists: 8.0 (547.3 to 1)
Guidance Counselors: 9.0 (486.4 to 1)
Current Spending: ($ per student per year):
Total: $11,816; Instruction: $6,754; Support Services: $4,788
Enrollment, Drop-out Rates and Diploma Recipients by Race/Ethnicity

Category	Total	White	Black	Asian	AIAN	Hisp.
Enrollment (%)	100.0	94.8	2.2	1.9	0.1	1.0
Drop-out Rate (%)	2.3	2.4	0.0	0.0	0.0	0.0
H.S. Diplomas (#)	320	306	2	9	0	3

Chenango County

Norwich City SD

19 Eaton Ave • Norwich, NY 13815-9964
(607) 334-1600 • http://www.ncs.stier.org/
Grade Span: PK-12; **Agency Type:** 1
Schools: 5
1 Primary; 2 Middle; 1 High; 1 Other Level
4 Regular; 0 Special Education; 0 Vocational; 1 Alternative
0 Magnet; 0 Charter; 4 Title I Eligible; 0 School-wide Title I
Students: 2,247 (49.0% male; 50.9% female)
Individual Education Program: n/a;
English Language Learner: n/a; Migrant: n/a
Eligible for Free Lunch Program: n/a
Eligible for Reduced-Price Lunch Program: n/a
Teachers: 191.1 (11.8 to 1)
Librarians/Media Specialists: 4.0 (561.8 to 1)
Guidance Counselors: 9.0 (249.7 to 1)
Current Spending: ($ per student per year):
Total: $10,674; Instruction: $6,667; Support Services: $3,673
Enrollment, Drop-out Rates and Diploma Recipients by Race/Ethnicity

Category	Total	White	Black	Asian	AIAN	Hisp.
Enrollment (%)	100.0	96.3	1.6	0.8	0.1	1.1
Drop-out Rate (%)	1.0	0.7	22.2	0.0	n/a	0.0
H.S. Diplomas (#)	133	129	1	3	0	0

Sherburne-Earlville Central SD

15 School St • Sherburne, NY 13460-0725
(607) 674-7300
Grade Span: KG-12; **Agency Type:** 2
Schools: 3
1 Primary; 1 Middle; 1 High; 0 Other Level
3 Regular; 0 Special Education; 0 Vocational; 0 Alternative
0 Magnet; 0 Charter; 2 Title I Eligible; 0 School-wide Title I
Students: 1,758 (49.2% male; 50.7% female)
Individual Education Program: n/a;
English Language Learner: n/a; Migrant: n/a
Eligible for Free Lunch Program: n/a
Eligible for Reduced-Price Lunch Program: n/a
Teachers: 165.6 (10.6 to 1)
Librarians/Media Specialists: 3.0 (586.0 to 1)
Guidance Counselors: 5.0 (351.6 to 1)
Current Spending: ($ per student per year):
Total: $11,013; Instruction: $6,814; Support Services: $3,801

Category	Total	White	Black	Asian	AIAN	Hisp.
Enrollment (%)	100.0	99.4	0.5	0.0	0.0	0.1
Drop-out Rate (%)	4.2	4.1	50.0	n/a	n/a	n/a
H.S. Diplomas (#)	100	100	0	0	0	0

Clinton County

Beekmantown Central SD

37 Eagle Way • West Chazy, NY 12992-2577
(518) 563-8250 • http://bcs.neric.org/
Grade Span: PK-12; **Agency Type:** 1
Schools: 4
2 Primary; 1 Middle; 1 High; 0 Other Level
4 Regular; 0 Special Education; 0 Vocational; 0 Alternative
0 Magnet; 0 Charter; 3 Title I Eligible; 2 School-wide Title I
Students: 2,179 (50.3% male; 49.6% female)
Individual Education Program: n/a;
English Language Learner: n/a; Migrant: n/a
Eligible for Free Lunch Program: n/a
Eligible for Reduced-Price Lunch Program: n/a
Teachers: 190.2 (11.5 to 1)
Librarians/Media Specialists: 4.0 (544.8 to 1)
Guidance Counselors: 6.0 (363.2 to 1)
Current Spending: ($ per student per year):
Total: $11,085; Instruction: $7,562; Support Services: $3,224
Enrollment, Drop-out Rates and Diploma Recipients by Race/Ethnicity

Category	Total	White	Black	Asian	AIAN	Hisp.
Enrollment (%)	100.0	96.7	1.5	0.8	0.4	0.6
Drop-out Rate (%)	5.5	4.7	18.2	50.0	50.0	16.7
H.S. Diplomas (#)	113	110	2	0	0	1

Northeastern Clinton Central SD

103 Route 276 • Champlain, NY 12919-0339
(518) 298-8242 • http://www.nccscougars.org/
Grade Span: KG-12; **Agency Type:** 2
Schools: 4
2 Primary; 1 Middle; 1 High; 0 Other Level
4 Regular; 0 Special Education; 0 Vocational; 0 Alternative
0 Magnet; 0 Charter; 3 Title I Eligible; 0 School-wide Title I
Students: 1,657 (50.4% male; 49.5% female)
Individual Education Program: n/a;
English Language Learner: n/a; Migrant: n/a
Eligible for Free Lunch Program: n/a
Eligible for Reduced-Price Lunch Program: n/a
Teachers: 124.5 (13.3 to 1)
Librarians/Media Specialists: 1.0 (1,657.0 to 1)
Guidance Counselors: 5.0 (331.4 to 1)
Current Spending: ($ per student per year):
Total: $11,040; Instruction: $7,563; Support Services: $3,130
Enrollment, Drop-out Rates and Diploma Recipients by Race/Ethnicity

Category	Total	White	Black	Asian	AIAN	Hisp.
Enrollment (%)	100.0	97.5	0.6	0.4	0.7	0.8
Drop-out Rate (%)	0.7	0.8	0.0	0.0	0.0	0.0
H.S. Diplomas (#)	103	103	0	0	0	0

Peru Central SD

17 School St • Peru, NY 12972-0068
(518) 643-6000 • http://www.perucsd.org/
Grade Span: KG-12; **Agency Type:** 1
Schools: 6
2 Primary; 1 Middle; 1 High; 2 Other Level
4 Regular; 0 Special Education; 0 Vocational; 2 Alternative
0 Magnet; 0 Charter; 4 Title I Eligible; 0 School-wide Title I
Students: 2,303 (52.5% male; 47.4% female)
Individual Education Program: n/a;
English Language Learner: n/a; Migrant: n/a
Eligible for Free Lunch Program: n/a
Eligible for Reduced-Price Lunch Program: n/a
Teachers: 185.6 (12.4 to 1)
Librarians/Media Specialists: 4.0 (575.8 to 1)
Guidance Counselors: 8.0 (287.9 to 1)
Current Spending: ($ per student per year):
Total: $11,438; Instruction: $7,810; Support Services: $3,350
Enrollment, Drop-out Rates and Diploma Recipients by Race/Ethnicity

Category	Total	White	Black	Asian	AIAN	Hisp.
Enrollment (%)	100.0	95.0	3.0	1.0	0.4	0.6
Drop-out Rate (%)	4.6	4.7	0.0	0.0	0.0	0.0
H.S. Diplomas (#)	149	143	1	3	0	2

Plattsburgh City SD

49 Broad St • Plattsburgh, NY 12901-3396
(518) 957-6002 • http://plattsburgh.neric.org/
Grade Span: PK-12; **Agency Type:** 1
Schools: 5

3 Primary; 1 Middle; 1 High; 0 Other Level
5 Regular; 0 Special Education; 0 Vocational; 0 Alternative
0 Magnet; 0 Charter; 4 Title I Eligible; 0 School-wide Title I
Students: 2,055 (51.5% male; 48.4% female)
  Individual Education Program: n/a;
  English Language Learner: n/a; Migrant: n/a
  Eligible for Free Lunch Program: n/a
  Eligible for Reduced-Price Lunch Program: n/a
Teachers: 198.6 (10.3 to 1)
Librarians/Media Specialists: 4.0 (513.8 to 1)
Guidance Counselors: 7.0 (293.6 to 1)
Current Spending: ($ per student per year):
  Total: $12,753; Instruction: $8,626; Support Services: $3,820
Enrollment, Drop-out Rates and Diploma Recipients by Race/Ethnicity

Category	Total	White	Black	Asian	AIAN	Hisp.
Enrollment (%)	100.0	90.0	5.8	2.2	0.4	1.6
Drop-out Rate (%)	6.2	6.1	8.7	0.0	0.0	9.1
H.S. Diplomas (#)	155	141	3	4	3	4

Saranac Central SD
32 Emmons St · Dannemora, NY 12929
(518) 565-5600
Grade Span: KG-12; **Agency Type:** 1
Schools: 7
  4 Primary; 1 Middle; 1 High; 1 Other Level
  6 Regular; 0 Special Education; 0 Vocational; 1 Alternative
  0 Magnet; 0 Charter; 4 Title I Eligible; 0 School-wide Title I
Students: 1,968 (51.6% male; 48.3% female)
  Individual Education Program: n/a;
  English Language Learner: n/a; Migrant: n/a
  Eligible for Free Lunch Program: n/a
  Eligible for Reduced-Price Lunch Program: n/a
Teachers: 149.3 (13.2 to 1)
Librarians/Media Specialists: 3.0 (656.0 to 1)
Guidance Counselors: 5.0 (393.6 to 1)
Current Spending: ($ per student per year):
  Total: $11,023; Instruction: $7,313; Support Services: $3,382
Enrollment, Drop-out Rates and Diploma Recipients by Race/Ethnicity

Category	Total	White	Black	Asian	AIAN	Hisp.
Enrollment (%)	100.0	95.2	3.4	0.4	0.1	1.0
Drop-out Rate (%)	1.4	1.4	0.0	0.0	n/a	0.0
H.S. Diplomas (#)	133	128	1	1	0	3

Columbia County

Chatham Central SD
50 Woodbridge Ave · Chatham, NY 12037-1397
(518) 392-1501 · http://www.chathamcentralschools.com/
Grade Span: KG-12; **Agency Type:** 2
Schools: 3
  1 Primary; 1 Middle; 1 High; 0 Other Level
  3 Regular; 0 Special Education; 0 Vocational; 0 Alternative
  0 Magnet; 0 Charter; 2 Title I Eligible; 0 School-wide Title I
Students: 1,501 (51.2% male; 48.7% female)
  Individual Education Program: n/a;
  English Language Learner: n/a; Migrant: n/a
  Eligible for Free Lunch Program: n/a
  Eligible for Reduced-Price Lunch Program: n/a
Teachers: 108.8 (13.8 to 1)
Librarians/Media Specialists: 3.0 (500.3 to 1)
Guidance Counselors: 4.0 (375.3 to 1)
Current Spending: ($ per student per year):
  Total: $10,993; Instruction: $6,988; Support Services: $3,734
Enrollment, Drop-out Rates and Diploma Recipients by Race/Ethnicity

Category	Total	White	Black	Asian	AIAN	Hisp.
Enrollment (%)	100.0	93.2	4.3	0.9	0.1	1.5
Drop-out Rate (%)	0.0	0.0	0.0	0.0	n/a	0.0
H.S. Diplomas (#)	99	98	1	0	0	0

Hudson City SD
621 State Rt 23b · Hudson, NY 12534-4011
(518) 828-4360 · http://www.hudson.edu/
Grade Span: KG-12; **Agency Type:** 1
Schools: 7
  2 Primary; 1 Middle; 3 High; 1 Other Level
  4 Regular; 0 Special Education; 0 Vocational; 3 Alternative
  0 Magnet; 0 Charter; 4 Title I Eligible; 1 School-wide Title I
Students: 2,417 (56.1% male; 43.8% female)
  Individual Education Program: n/a;
  English Language Learner: n/a; Migrant: n/a
  Eligible for Free Lunch Program: n/a
  Eligible for Reduced-Price Lunch Program: n/a
Teachers: 201.7 (12.0 to 1)
Librarians/Media Specialists: 3.0 (805.7 to 1)
Guidance Counselors: 3.0 (805.7 to 1)

Current Spending: ($ per student per year):
  Total: $13,141; Instruction: $8,810; Support Services: $3,908
Enrollment, Drop-out Rates and Diploma Recipients by Race/Ethnicity

Category	Total	White	Black	Asian	AIAN	Hisp.
Enrollment (%)	100.0	58.0	28.8	4.1	0.2	8.9
Drop-out Rate (%)	2.5	2.2	3.6	0.0	n/a	5.3
H.S. Diplomas (#)	90	79	5	1	0	5

Kinderhook Central SD
2910 Rt 9 · Valatie, NY 12184-0137
(518) 758-7575
Grade Span: KG-12; **Agency Type:** 2
Schools: 5
  3 Primary; 1 Middle; 1 High; 0 Other Level
  5 Regular; 0 Special Education; 0 Vocational; 0 Alternative
  0 Magnet; 0 Charter; 4 Title I Eligible; 0 School-wide Title I
Students: 2,285 (52.1% male; 47.8% female)
  Individual Education Program: n/a;
  English Language Learner: n/a; Migrant: n/a
  Eligible for Free Lunch Program: n/a
  Eligible for Reduced-Price Lunch Program: n/a
Teachers: 170.2 (13.4 to 1)
Librarians/Media Specialists: 4.0 (571.3 to 1)
Guidance Counselors: 5.0 (457.0 to 1)
Current Spending: ($ per student per year):
  Total: $9,961; Instruction: $6,505; Support Services: $3,197
Enrollment, Drop-out Rates and Diploma Recipients by Race/Ethnicity

Category	Total	White	Black	Asian	AIAN	Hisp.
Enrollment (%)	100.0	95.4	1.8	0.9	0.1	1.7
Drop-out Rate (%)	2.2	2.3	0.0	0.0	0.0	0.0
H.S. Diplomas (#)	143	142	0	0	0	1

Taconic Hills Central SD
73 County Rt 11a · Craryville, NY 12521-5510
(518) 325-0313 · http://www.taconichills.k12.ny.us/
Grade Span: KG-12; **Agency Type:** 2
Schools: 4
  2 Primary; 1 Middle; 1 High; 0 Other Level
  4 Regular; 0 Special Education; 0 Vocational; 0 Alternative
  0 Magnet; 0 Charter; 4 Title I Eligible; 0 School-wide Title I
Students: 1,871 (51.4% male; 48.5% female)
  Individual Education Program: n/a;
  English Language Learner: n/a; Migrant: n/a
  Eligible for Free Lunch Program: n/a
  Eligible for Reduced-Price Lunch Program: n/a
Teachers: 143.6 (13.0 to 1)
Librarians/Media Specialists: 3.0 (623.7 to 1)
Guidance Counselors: 5.0 (374.2 to 1)
Current Spending: ($ per student per year):
  Total: $12,088; Instruction: $7,425; Support Services: $4,354
Enrollment, Drop-out Rates and Diploma Recipients by Race/Ethnicity

Category	Total	White	Black	Asian	AIAN	Hisp.
Enrollment (%)	100.0	94.8	2.4	0.7	0.1	2.0
Drop-out Rate (%)	5.7	5.8	0.0	0.0	n/a	20.0
H.S. Diplomas (#)	86	80	4	2	0	0

Cortland County

Cortland City SD
1 Valley View Dr · Cortland, NY 13045-3297
(607) 758-4100 · http://www.cortlandschools.org/hslt/
Grade Span: KG-12; **Agency Type:** 1
Schools: 6
  5 Primary; 0 Middle; 1 High; 0 Other Level
  6 Regular; 0 Special Education; 0 Vocational; 0 Alternative
  0 Magnet; 0 Charter; 4 Title I Eligible; 0 School-wide Title I
Students: 2,847 (50.7% male; 49.2% female)
  Individual Education Program: n/a;
  English Language Learner: n/a; Migrant: n/a
  Eligible for Free Lunch Program: n/a
  Eligible for Reduced-Price Lunch Program: n/a
Teachers: 230.0 (12.4 to 1)
Librarians/Media Specialists: 6.0 (474.5 to 1)
Guidance Counselors: 6.0 (474.5 to 1)
Current Spending: ($ per student per year):
  Total: $11,018; Instruction: $7,132; Support Services: $3,487
Enrollment, Drop-out Rates and Diploma Recipients by Race/Ethnicity

Category	Total	White	Black	Asian	AIAN	Hisp.
Enrollment (%)	100.0	93.4	3.9	0.8	0.1	1.7
Drop-out Rate (%)	4.3	4.4	0.0	14.3	0.0	0.0
H.S. Diplomas (#)	180	175	1	2	0	0

Homer Central SD

80 S W St • Homer, NY 13077-0500
(607) 749-7241 • http://www.homer.cnyric.org/
Grade Span: KG-12; **Agency Type:** 1
Schools: 5
    3 Primary; 1 Middle; 1 High; 0 Other Level
    5 Regular; 0 Special Education; 0 Vocational; 0 Alternative
    0 Magnet; 0 Charter; 2 Title I Eligible; 0 School-wide Title I
Students: 2,367   (52.4% male; 47.5% female)
    Individual Education Program: n/a;
    English Language Learner: n/a; Migrant: n/a
    Eligible for Free Lunch Program: n/a
    Eligible for Reduced-Price Lunch Program: n/a
Teachers: 190.1 (12.5 to 1)
Librarians/Media Specialists: 4.0 (591.8 to 1)
Guidance Counselors: 4.0 (591.8 to 1)
Current Spending: ($ per student per year):
    Total: $9,872; Instruction: $6,683; Support Services: $2,931
Enrollment, Drop-out Rates and Diploma Recipients by Race/Ethnicity

Category	Total	White	Black	Asian	AIAN	Hisp.
Enrollment (%)	100.0	97.3	1.2	0.5	0.1	0.9
Drop-out Rate (%)	2.5	2.6	0.0	0.0	n/a	0.0
H.S. Diplomas (#)	176	173	2	1	0	0

Dutchess County

Arlington Central SD

696 Dutchess Tpke • Poughkeepsie, NY 12603
(845) 486-4460 • http://arlingtonschools.org/
Grade Span: KG-12; **Agency Type:** 1
Schools: 11
    8 Primary; 2 Middle; 1 High; 0 Other Level
    11 Regular; 0 Special Education; 0 Vocational; 0 Alternative
    0 Magnet; 0 Charter; 6 Title I Eligible; 0 School-wide Title I
Students: 10,102   (50.9% male; 49.0% female)
    Individual Education Program: n/a;
    English Language Learner: n/a; Migrant: n/a
    Eligible for Free Lunch Program: n/a
    Eligible for Reduced-Price Lunch Program: n/a
Teachers: 631.6 (16.0 to 1)
Librarians/Media Specialists: 12.0 (841.8 to 1)
Guidance Counselors: 19.0 (531.7 to 1)
Current Spending: ($ per student per year):
    Total: $9,594; Instruction: $6,432; Support Services: $2,929
Enrollment, Drop-out Rates and Diploma Recipients by Race/Ethnicity

Category	Total	White	Black	Asian	AIAN	Hisp.
Enrollment (%)	100.0	85.5	5.9	3.6	0.0	5.0
Drop-out Rate (%)	3.2	3.1	3.7	1.2	0.0	6.7
H.S. Diplomas (#)	501	426	27	25	0	23

Beacon City SD

10 Education Dr • Beacon, NY 12508-3994
(845) 838-6900 • http://www.dcboces.org/bcsd/
Grade Span: PK-12; **Agency Type:** 1
Schools: 8
    4 Primary; 1 Middle; 1 High; 2 Other Level
    6 Regular; 0 Special Education; 0 Vocational; 2 Alternative
    0 Magnet; 0 Charter; 4 Title I Eligible; 0 School-wide Title I
Students: 3,613   (51.4% male; 48.5% female)
    Individual Education Program: n/a;
    English Language Learner: n/a; Migrant: n/a
    Eligible for Free Lunch Program: n/a
    Eligible for Reduced-Price Lunch Program: n/a
Teachers: 246.7 (14.6 to 1)
Librarians/Media Specialists: 3.0 (1,204.3 to 1)
Guidance Counselors: 6.0 (602.2 to 1)
Current Spending: ($ per student per year):
    Total: $9,874; Instruction: $6,649; Support Services: $2,967
Enrollment, Drop-out Rates and Diploma Recipients by Race/Ethnicity

Category	Total	White	Black	Asian	AIAN	Hisp.
Enrollment (%)	100.0	54.7	24.3	2.7	0.1	18.3
Drop-out Rate (%)	4.5	3.6	5.3	0.0	0.0	6.5
H.S. Diplomas (#)	144	86	33	1	0	24

Dover Union Free SD

2368 Rt 22 • Dover Plains, NY 12522-6311
(845) 832-4500 • http://www.doverplains.org/
Grade Span: KG-12; **Agency Type:** 2
Schools: 4
    2 Primary; 1 Middle; 1 High; 0 Other Level
    4 Regular; 0 Special Education; 0 Vocational; 0 Alternative
    0 Magnet; 0 Charter; 4 Title I Eligible; 0 School-wide Title I
Students: 1,757   (51.9% male; 48.0% female)
    Individual Education Program: n/a;
    English Language Learner: n/a; Migrant: n/a

Eligible for Free Lunch Program: n/a
Eligible for Reduced-Price Lunch Program: n/a
Teachers: 115.6 (15.2 to 1)
Librarians/Media Specialists: 1.7 (1,033.5 to 1)
Guidance Counselors: 3.0 (585.7 to 1)
Current Spending: ($ per student per year):
    Total: $10,041; Instruction: $6,382; Support Services: $3,468
Enrollment, Drop-out Rates and Diploma Recipients by Race/Ethnicity

Category	Total	White	Black	Asian	AIAN	Hisp.
Enrollment (%)	100.0	87.8	4.5	2.0	0.0	5.6
Drop-out Rate (%)	3.5	3.6	0.0	25.0	n/a	0.0
H.S. Diplomas (#)	104	93	3	2	0	6

Hyde Park Central SD

386 Violet Ave • Poughkeepsie, NY 12601
(845) 483-3600
Grade Span: KG-12; **Agency Type:** 1
Schools: 7
    5 Primary; 1 Middle; 1 High; 0 Other Level
    7 Regular; 0 Special Education; 0 Vocational; 0 Alternative
    0 Magnet; 0 Charter; 3 Title I Eligible; 3 School-wide Title I
Students: 4,682   (50.6% male; 49.3% female)
    Individual Education Program: n/a;
    English Language Learner: n/a; Migrant: n/a
    Eligible for Free Lunch Program: n/a
    Eligible for Reduced-Price Lunch Program: n/a
Teachers: 329.2 (14.2 to 1)
Librarians/Media Specialists: 7.0 (668.9 to 1)
Guidance Counselors: 8.0 (585.3 to 1)
Current Spending: ($ per student per year):
    Total: $10,897; Instruction: $7,116; Support Services: $3,529
Enrollment, Drop-out Rates and Diploma Recipients by Race/Ethnicity

Category	Total	White	Black	Asian	AIAN	Hisp.
Enrollment (%)	100.0	82.7	11.1	1.7	0.0	4.4
Drop-out Rate (%)	4.5	3.9	11.3	0.0	0.0	2.9
H.S. Diplomas (#)	253	221	24	5	1	2

Poughkeepsie City SD

11 College Ave • Poughkeepsie, NY 12603-3313
(845) 451-4950 • http://www.pcsd.k12.ny.us/
Grade Span: PK-12; **Agency Type:** 1
Schools: 10
    7 Primary; 1 Middle; 1 High; 1 Other Level
    9 Regular; 0 Special Education; 0 Vocational; 1 Alternative
    2 Magnet; 0 Charter; 8 Title I Eligible; 2 School-wide Title I
Students: 4,880   (51.6% male; 48.3% female)
    Individual Education Program: n/a;
    English Language Learner: n/a; Migrant: n/a
    Eligible for Free Lunch Program: n/a
    Eligible for Reduced-Price Lunch Program: n/a
Teachers: 356.9 (13.7 to 1)
Librarians/Media Specialists: 8.0 (610.0 to 1)
Guidance Counselors: 9.0 (542.2 to 1)
Current Spending: ($ per student per year):
    Total: $13,001; Instruction: $9,492; Support Services: $3,167
Enrollment, Drop-out Rates and Diploma Recipients by Race/Ethnicity

Category	Total	White	Black	Asian	AIAN	Hisp.
Enrollment (%)	100.0	19.8	62.6	1.3	0.1	16.1
Drop-out Rate (%)	10.7	9.3	11.2	9.1	0.0	11.6
H.S. Diplomas (#)	153	35	102	1	0	15

Red Hook Central SD

7401 S Broadway • Red Hook, NY 12571-9446
(845) 758-2241 • http://www.northerndutchess.com/redhookschool.htm
Grade Span: KG-12; **Agency Type:** 1
Schools: 5
    2 Primary; 1 Middle; 1 High; 1 Other Level
    4 Regular; 0 Special Education; 0 Vocational; 1 Alternative
    0 Magnet; 0 Charter; 4 Title I Eligible; 0 School-wide Title I
Students: 2,381   (52.6% male; 47.3% female)
    Individual Education Program: n/a;
    English Language Learner: n/a; Migrant: n/a
    Eligible for Free Lunch Program: n/a
    Eligible for Reduced-Price Lunch Program: n/a
Teachers: 175.1 (13.6 to 1)
Librarians/Media Specialists: 4.0 (595.3 to 1)
Guidance Counselors: 4.0 (595.3 to 1)
Current Spending: ($ per student per year):
    Total: $11,269; Instruction: $7,690; Support Services: $3,384
Enrollment, Drop-out Rates and Diploma Recipients by Race/Ethnicity

Category	Total	White	Black	Asian	AIAN	Hisp.
Enrollment (%)	100.0	91.9	1.8	3.5	0.1	2.7
Drop-out Rate (%)	3.3	3.5	0.0	0.0	n/a	0.0
H.S. Diplomas (#)	126	116	2	3	0	5

Spackenkill Union Free SD
15 Croft Rd • Poughkeepsie, NY 12603-5028
(845) 463-7800 • http://www.dcboces.org/sufsd/
Grade Span: KG-12; **Agency Type:** 2
Schools: 4
  2 Primary; 1 Middle; 1 High; 0 Other Level
  4 Regular; 0 Special Education; 0 Vocational; 0 Alternative
  0 Magnet; 0 Charter; 1 Title I Eligible; 0 School-wide Title I
Students: 1,835 (50.9% male; 49.0% female)
  Individual Education Program: n/a;
  English Language Learner: n/a; Migrant: n/a
  Eligible for Free Lunch Program: n/a
  Eligible for Reduced-Price Lunch Program: n/a
Teachers: 150.0 (12.2 to 1)
Librarians/Media Specialists: 3.0 (611.7 to 1)
Guidance Counselors: 4.8 (382.3 to 1)
Current Spending: ($ per student per year):
  Total: $12,738; Instruction: $8,262; Support Services: $4,200
Enrollment, Drop-out Rates and Diploma Recipients by Race/Ethnicity

Category	Total	White	Black	Asian	AIAN	Hisp.
Enrollment (%)	100.0	74.4	9.6	9.6	0.3	6.0
Drop-out Rate (%)	5.2	5.1	5.2	2.2	n/a	13.6
H.S. Diplomas (#)	111	85	11	10	0	5

Wappingers Central SD
29 Marshall Rd • Wappingers Falls, NY 12590-3296
(845) 298-5000 • http://wappingersschools.org/
Grade Span: KG-12; **Agency Type:** 1
Schools: 15
  9 Primary; 3 Middle; 2 High; 1 Other Level
  14 Regular; 0 Special Education; 0 Vocational; 1 Alternative
  0 Magnet; 0 Charter; 2 Title I Eligible; 2 School-wide Title I
Students: 12,146 (51.7% male; 48.2% female)
  Individual Education Program: n/a;
  English Language Learner: n/a; Migrant: n/a
  Eligible for Free Lunch Program: n/a
  Eligible for Reduced-Price Lunch Program: n/a
Teachers: 779.5 (15.6 to 1)
Librarians/Media Specialists: 15.0 (809.7 to 1)
Guidance Counselors: 20.0 (607.3 to 1)
Current Spending: ($ per student per year):
  Total: $10,080; Instruction: $6,316; Support Services: $3,544
Enrollment, Drop-out Rates and Diploma Recipients by Race/Ethnicity

Category	Total	White	Black	Asian	AIAN	Hisp.
Enrollment (%)	100.0	82.3	5.1	5.0	0.1	7.5
Drop-out Rate (%)	3.2	3.0	3.9	1.1	0.0	6.6
H.S. Diplomas (#)	761	748	6	1	0	6

Erie County

Akron Central SD
47 Bloomingdale Ave • Akron, NY 14001-1197
(716) 542-5101 • http://www.akronschools.org/
Grade Span: PK-12; **Agency Type:** 2
Schools: 3
  1 Primary; 1 Middle; 1 High; 0 Other Level
  3 Regular; 0 Special Education; 0 Vocational; 0 Alternative
  0 Magnet; 0 Charter; 2 Title I Eligible; 0 School-wide Title I
Students: 1,699 (48.7% male; 51.2% female)
  Individual Education Program: n/a;
  English Language Learner: n/a; Migrant: n/a
  Eligible for Free Lunch Program: n/a
  Eligible for Reduced-Price Lunch Program: n/a
Teachers: 116.2 (14.6 to 1)
Librarians/Media Specialists: 2.0 (849.5 to 1)
Guidance Counselors: 3.6 (471.9 to 1)
Current Spending: ($ per student per year):
  Total: $10,508; Instruction: $6,920; Support Services: $3,282
Enrollment, Drop-out Rates and Diploma Recipients by Race/Ethnicity

Category	Total	White	Black	Asian	AIAN	Hisp.
Enrollment (%)	100.0	89.5	0.9	0.1	9.1	0.4
Drop-out Rate (%)	3.8	4.0	0.0	n/a	0.0	n/a
H.S. Diplomas (#)	98	94	0	0	4	0

Alden Central SD
13190 Park St • Alden, NY 14004-1099
(716) 937-9116 • http://www.alden.wnyric.org/
Grade Span: KG-12; **Agency Type:** 1
Schools: 5
  2 Primary; 1 Middle; 1 High; 1 Other Level
  4 Regular; 0 Special Education; 0 Vocational; 1 Alternative
  0 Magnet; 0 Charter; 3 Title I Eligible; 0 School-wide Title I
Students: 2,072 (53.0% male; 46.9% female)
  Individual Education Program: n/a;
  English Language Learner: n/a; Migrant: n/a

Eligible for Free Lunch Program: n/a
Eligible for Reduced-Price Lunch Program: n/a
Teachers: 153.1 (13.5 to 1)
Librarians/Media Specialists: 4.0 (518.0 to 1)
Guidance Counselors: 4.0 (518.0 to 1)
Current Spending: ($ per student per year):
  Total: $10,009; Instruction: $6,055; Support Services: $3,678
Enrollment, Drop-out Rates and Diploma Recipients by Race/Ethnicity

Category	Total	White	Black	Asian	AIAN	Hisp.
Enrollment (%)	100.0	97.2	1.6	0.4	0.2	0.5
Drop-out Rate (%)	3.3	3.3	0.0	0.0	0.0	0.0
H.S. Diplomas (#)	150	147	1	2	0	0

Amherst Central SD
55 Kings Hwy • Amherst, NY 14226-4330
(716) 362-3051 • http://www.amherst.k12.ny.us/
Grade Span: KG-12; **Agency Type:** 1
Schools: 4
  2 Primary; 1 Middle; 1 High; 0 Other Level
  4 Regular; 0 Special Education; 0 Vocational; 0 Alternative
  0 Magnet; 0 Charter; 1 Title I Eligible; 0 School-wide Title I
Students: 3,125 (50.7% male; 49.2% female)
  Individual Education Program: n/a;
  English Language Learner: n/a; Migrant: n/a
  Eligible for Free Lunch Program: n/a
  Eligible for Reduced-Price Lunch Program: n/a
Teachers: 249.2 (12.5 to 1)
Librarians/Media Specialists: 4.0 (781.3 to 1)
Guidance Counselors: 5.7 (548.2 to 1)
Current Spending: ($ per student per year):
  Total: $10,012; Instruction: $6,209; Support Services: $3,590
Enrollment, Drop-out Rates and Diploma Recipients by Race/Ethnicity

Category	Total	White	Black	Asian	AIAN	Hisp.
Enrollment (%)	100.0	81.3	14.3	2.9	0.1	1.4
Drop-out Rate (%)	2.9	2.7	4.3	6.3	n/a	10.0
H.S. Diplomas (#)	212	189	10	8	1	4

Buffalo City SD
712 City Hall • Buffalo, NY 14202-3375
(716) 851-3575 • http://www.buffaloschools.org/
Grade Span: PK-12; **Agency Type:** 1
Schools: 68
  44 Primary; 8 Middle; 11 High; 5 Other Level
  62 Regular; 1 Special Education; 5 Vocational; 0 Alternative
  1 Magnet; 0 Charter; 54 Title I Eligible; 48 School-wide Title I
Students: 41,089 (51.0% male; 48.9% female)
  Individual Education Program: n/a;
  English Language Learner: n/a; Migrant: n/a
  Eligible for Free Lunch Program: n/a
  Eligible for Reduced-Price Lunch Program: n/a
Teachers: 3,022.7 (13.6 to 1)
Librarians/Media Specialists: 45.3 (907.0 to 1)
Guidance Counselors: 66.3 (619.7 to 1)
Current Spending: ($ per student per year):
  Total: $12,879; Instruction: $8,795; Support Services: $3,664
Enrollment, Drop-out Rates and Diploma Recipients by Race/Ethnicity

Category	Total	White	Black	Asian	AIAN	Hisp.
Enrollment (%)	100.0	25.9	58.5	1.3	1.5	12.8
Drop-out Rate (%)	7.6	7.1	7.8	5.6	8.9	8.2
H.S. Diplomas (#)	1,638	656	794	40	22	126

Cheektowaga Central SD
3600 Union Rd • Cheektowaga, NY 14225-5170
(716) 686-3606 • http://www.ccsd.wnyric.org/
Grade Span: KG-12; **Agency Type:** 1
Schools: 4
  2 Primary; 1 Middle; 1 High; 0 Other Level
  4 Regular; 0 Special Education; 0 Vocational; 0 Alternative
  0 Magnet; 0 Charter; 2 Title I Eligible; 0 School-wide Title I
Students: 2,416 (51.6% male; 48.3% female)
  Individual Education Program: n/a;
  English Language Learner: n/a; Migrant: n/a
  Eligible for Free Lunch Program: n/a
  Eligible for Reduced-Price Lunch Program: n/a
Teachers: 177.5 (13.6 to 1)
Librarians/Media Specialists: 2.5 (966.4 to 1)
Guidance Counselors: 5.0 (483.2 to 1)
Current Spending: ($ per student per year):
  Total: $10,044; Instruction: $6,391; Support Services: $3,418
Enrollment, Drop-out Rates and Diploma Recipients by Race/Ethnicity

Category	Total	White	Black	Asian	AIAN	Hisp.
Enrollment (%)	100.0	76.7	17.8	2.6	0.6	2.3
Drop-out Rate (%)	1.0	0.9	3.1	0.0	0.0	0.0
H.S. Diplomas (#)	165	156	6	2	0	1

Cheektowaga-Maryvale Union Free SD
1050 Maryvale Dr • Cheektowaga, NY 14225-2386
(716) 631-7407 • http://www.maryvale.wnyric.org/
Grade Span: PK-12; **Agency Type:** 1
Schools: 4
   2 Primary; 1 Middle; 1 High; 0 Other Level
   4 Regular; 0 Special Education; 0 Vocational; 0 Alternative
   0 Magnet; 0 Charter; 3 Title I Eligible; 0 School-wide Title I
Students: 2,478   (49.1% male; 50.8% female)
   Individual Education Program: n/a;
   English Language Learner: n/a; Migrant: n/a
   Eligible for Free Lunch Program: n/a
   Eligible for Reduced-Price Lunch Program: n/a
Teachers: 185.7 (13.3 to 1)
Librarians/Media Specialists: 3.8 (652.1 to 1)
Guidance Counselors: 5.8 (427.2 to 1)
Current Spending: ($ per student per year):
   Total: $11,085; Instruction: $7,308; Support Services: $3,586
Enrollment, Drop-out Rates and Diploma Recipients by Race/Ethnicity

Category	Total	White	Black	Asian	AIAN	Hisp.
Enrollment (%)	100.0	92.7	4.2	2.0	0.2	0.9
Drop-out Rate (%)	3.8	3.6	6.7	12.5	n/a	0.0
H.S. Diplomas (#)	160	156	1	2	0	1

Cheektowaga-Sloan Union Free SD
166 Halstead Ave • Sloan, NY 14212-2295
(716) 891-6402 • http://www.sloan.wnyric.org/
Grade Span: PK-12; **Agency Type:** 1
Schools: 4
   2 Primary; 1 Middle; 1 High; 0 Other Level
   4 Regular; 0 Special Education; 0 Vocational; 0 Alternative
   0 Magnet; 0 Charter; 3 Title I Eligible; 0 School-wide Title I
Students: 1,531   (50.8% male; 49.1% female)
   Individual Education Program: n/a;
   English Language Learner: n/a; Migrant: n/a
   Eligible for Free Lunch Program: n/a
   Eligible for Reduced-Price Lunch Program: n/a
Teachers: 114.4 (13.4 to 1)
Librarians/Media Specialists: 1.0 (1,531.0 to 1)
Guidance Counselors: 2.0 (765.5 to 1)
Current Spending: ($ per student per year):
   Total: $11,529; Instruction: $7,460; Support Services: $3,784
Enrollment, Drop-out Rates and Diploma Recipients by Race/Ethnicity

Category	Total	White	Black	Asian	AIAN	Hisp.
Enrollment (%)	100.0	97.2	1.3	0.2	0.5	0.8
Drop-out Rate (%)	2.3	1.9	20.0	n/a	0.0	33.3
H.S. Diplomas (#)	104	101	2	0	1	0

Clarence Central SD
9625 Main St • Clarence, NY 14031-2083
(716) 407-9102 • http://www.clarence.wnyric.org/
Grade Span: KG-12; **Agency Type:** 1
Schools: 6
   4 Primary; 1 Middle; 1 High; 0 Other Level
   6 Regular; 0 Special Education; 0 Vocational; 0 Alternative
   0 Magnet; 0 Charter; 0 Title I Eligible; 0 School-wide Title I
Students: 4,920   (51.9% male; 48.0% female)
   Individual Education Program: n/a;
   English Language Learner: n/a; Migrant: n/a
   Eligible for Free Lunch Program: n/a
   Eligible for Reduced-Price Lunch Program: n/a
Teachers: 353.9 (13.9 to 1)
Librarians/Media Specialists: 6.0 (820.0 to 1)
Guidance Counselors: 9.5 (517.9 to 1)
Current Spending: ($ per student per year):
   Total: $9,155; Instruction: $6,204; Support Services: $2,759
Enrollment, Drop-out Rates and Diploma Recipients by Race/Ethnicity

Category	Total	White	Black	Asian	AIAN	Hisp.
Enrollment (%)	100.0	95.9	0.8	1.7	0.4	1.2
Drop-out Rate (%)	0.9	0.9	0.0	0.0	0.0	0.0
H.S. Diplomas (#)	339	330	2	4	0	3

Cleveland Hill Union Free SD
105 Mapleview Rd • Cheektowaga, NY 14225-1599
(716) 836-7200 • http://www.clevehill.wnyric.org/
Grade Span: KG-12; **Agency Type:** 2
Schools: 3
   1 Primary; 1 Middle; 1 High; 0 Other Level
   3 Regular; 0 Special Education; 0 Vocational; 0 Alternative
   0 Magnet; 0 Charter; 2 Title I Eligible; 0 School-wide Title I
Students: 1,587   (53.7% male; 46.2% female)
   Individual Education Program: n/a;
   English Language Learner: n/a; Migrant: n/a
   Eligible for Free Lunch Program: n/a
   Eligible for Reduced-Price Lunch Program: n/a

Teachers: 122.0 (13.0 to 1)
Librarians/Media Specialists: 2.0 (793.5 to 1)
Guidance Counselors: 4.0 (396.8 to 1)
Current Spending: ($ per student per year):
   Total: $10,310; Instruction: $6,687; Support Services: $3,357
Enrollment, Drop-out Rates and Diploma Recipients by Race/Ethnicity

Category	Total	White	Black	Asian	AIAN	Hisp.
Enrollment (%)	100.0	69.9	21.9	1.3	3.3	3.6
Drop-out Rate (%)	5.5	4.7	11.0	0.0	0.0	0.0
H.S. Diplomas (#)	78	64	10	0	1	3

Depew Union Free SD
591 Terrace Blvd • Depew, NY 14043-4535
(716) 686-2251
Grade Span: KG-12; **Agency Type:** 1
Schools: 3
   1 Primary; 1 Middle; 1 High; 0 Other Level
   3 Regular; 0 Special Education; 0 Vocational; 0 Alternative
   0 Magnet; 0 Charter; 1 Title I Eligible; 0 School-wide Title I
Students: 2,378   (50.5% male; 49.4% female)
   Individual Education Program: n/a;
   English Language Learner: n/a; Migrant: n/a
   Eligible for Free Lunch Program: n/a
   Eligible for Reduced-Price Lunch Program: n/a
Teachers: 187.8 (12.7 to 1)
Librarians/Media Specialists: 3.0 (792.7 to 1)
Guidance Counselors: 9.0 (264.2 to 1)
Current Spending: ($ per student per year):
   Total: $13,052; Instruction: $8,366; Support Services: $4,346
Enrollment, Drop-out Rates and Diploma Recipients by Race/Ethnicity

Category	Total	White	Black	Asian	AIAN	Hisp.
Enrollment (%)	100.0	97.1	1.3	0.9	0.3	0.5
Drop-out Rate (%)	4.5	4.4	0.0	100.0	0.0	0.0
H.S. Diplomas (#)	151	149	0	0	1	1

East Aurora Union Free SD
430 Main St • East Aurora, NY 14052-1786
(716) 687-2302 • http://www.eaur.wnyric.org/
Grade Span: KG-12; **Agency Type:** 1
Schools: 4
   2 Primary; 1 Middle; 1 High; 0 Other Level
   4 Regular; 0 Special Education; 0 Vocational; 0 Alternative
   0 Magnet; 0 Charter; 2 Title I Eligible; 0 School-wide Title I
Students: 2,091   (50.5% male; 49.4% female)
   Individual Education Program: n/a;
   English Language Learner: n/a; Migrant: n/a
   Eligible for Free Lunch Program: n/a
   Eligible for Reduced-Price Lunch Program: n/a
Teachers: 147.4 (14.2 to 1)
Librarians/Media Specialists: 3.0 (697.0 to 1)
Guidance Counselors: 4.6 (454.6 to 1)
Current Spending: ($ per student per year):
   Total: $9,078; Instruction: $5,796; Support Services: $3,121
Enrollment, Drop-out Rates and Diploma Recipients by Race/Ethnicity

Category	Total	White	Black	Asian	AIAN	Hisp.
Enrollment (%)	100.0	98.0	0.6	0.5	0.1	0.8
Drop-out Rate (%)	2.2	2.3	0.0	0.0	0.0	0.0
H.S. Diplomas (#)	150	149	0	1	0	0

Eden Central SD
3150 Schoolview Rd • Eden, NY 14057-0267
(716) 992-3629 • http://www.edencentral.org/
Grade Span: PK-12; **Agency Type:** 1
Schools: 3
   2 Primary; 0 Middle; 1 High; 0 Other Level
   3 Regular; 0 Special Education; 0 Vocational; 0 Alternative
   0 Magnet; 0 Charter; 2 Title I Eligible; 0 School-wide Title I
Students: 1,844   (52.5% male; 47.4% female)
   Individual Education Program: n/a;
   English Language Learner: n/a; Migrant: n/a
   Eligible for Free Lunch Program: n/a
   Eligible for Reduced-Price Lunch Program: n/a
Teachers: 127.7 (14.4 to 1)
Librarians/Media Specialists: 2.0 (922.0 to 1)
Guidance Counselors: 4.0 (461.0 to 1)
Current Spending: ($ per student per year):
   Total: $8,746; Instruction: $5,553; Support Services: $3,017
Enrollment, Drop-out Rates and Diploma Recipients by Race/Ethnicity

Category	Total	White	Black	Asian	AIAN	Hisp.
Enrollment (%)	100.0	98.2	0.7	0.5	0.1	0.6
Drop-out Rate (%)	2.7	2.8	0.0	0.0	n/a	0.0
H.S. Diplomas (#)	111	111	0	0	0	0

Evans-Brant Central SD (Lake Shore)
959 Beach Rd • Angola, NY 14006-9690
(716) 926-2201 • http://www.lakeshore.wnyric.org/
Grade Span: PK-12; **Agency Type:** 1
Schools: 7
    5 Primary; 1 Middle; 1 High; 0 Other Level
    7 Regular; 0 Special Education; 0 Vocational; 0 Alternative
    0 Magnet; 0 Charter; 4 Title I Eligible; 0 School-wide Title I
Students: 3,230 (50.3% male; 49.6% female)
    Individual Education Program: n/a;
    English Language Learner: n/a; Migrant: n/a
    Eligible for Free Lunch Program: n/a
    Eligible for Reduced-Price Lunch Program: n/a
Teachers: 268.5 (12.0 to 1)
Librarians/Media Specialists: 4.0 (807.5 to 1)
Guidance Counselors: 9.7 (333.0 to 1)
Current Spending: ($ per student per year):
    Total: $11,135; Instruction: $7,195; Support Services: $3,717
Enrollment, Drop-out Rates and Diploma Recipients by Race/Ethnicity

Category	Total	White	Black	Asian	AIAN	Hisp.
Enrollment (%)	100.0	89.7	1.1	0.6	7.1	1.5
Drop-out Rate (%)	5.2	4.8	0.0	0.0	18.2	0.0
H.S. Diplomas (#)	188	185	0	0	2	1

Frontier Central SD
S 5120 Orchard Ave • Hamburg, NY 14075-5657
(716) 926-1711 • http://www.frontier.wnyric.org/
Grade Span: KG-12; **Agency Type:** 1
Schools: 6
    4 Primary; 1 Middle; 1 High; 0 Other Level
    6 Regular; 0 Special Education; 0 Vocational; 0 Alternative
    0 Magnet; 0 Charter; 4 Title I Eligible; 0 School-wide Title I
Students: 5,622 (50.5% male; 49.4% female)
    Individual Education Program: n/a;
    English Language Learner: n/a; Migrant: n/a
    Eligible for Free Lunch Program: n/a
    Eligible for Reduced-Price Lunch Program: n/a
Teachers: 429.4 (13.1 to 1)
Librarians/Media Specialists: 6.8 (826.8 to 1)
Guidance Counselors: 11.0 (511.1 to 1)
Current Spending: ($ per student per year):
    Total: $9,457; Instruction: $6,207; Support Services: $3,004
Enrollment, Drop-out Rates and Diploma Recipients by Race/Ethnicity

Category	Total	White	Black	Asian	AIAN	Hisp.
Enrollment (%)	100.0	96.4	1.2	0.6	0.2	1.5
Drop-out Rate (%)	4.1	4.1	0.0	28.6	0.0	4.8
H.S. Diplomas (#)	340	332	0	4	2	2

Grand Island Central SD
1100 Ransom Rd • Grand Island, NY 14072-1460
(716) 773-8801 • http://www.grandisland-cs.k12.ny.us/
Grade Span: KG-12; **Agency Type:** 1
Schools: 5
    3 Primary; 1 Middle; 1 High; 0 Other Level
    5 Regular; 0 Special Education; 0 Vocational; 0 Alternative
    0 Magnet; 0 Charter; 1 Title I Eligible; 0 School-wide Title I
Students: 3,190 (51.6% male; 48.3% female)
    Individual Education Program: n/a;
    English Language Learner: n/a; Migrant: n/a
    Eligible for Free Lunch Program: n/a
    Eligible for Reduced-Price Lunch Program: n/a
Teachers: 228.7 (13.9 to 1)
Librarians/Media Specialists: 5.0 (638.0 to 1)
Guidance Counselors: 6.0 (531.7 to 1)
Current Spending: ($ per student per year):
    Total: $10,213; Instruction: $6,681; Support Services: $3,294
Enrollment, Drop-out Rates and Diploma Recipients by Race/Ethnicity

Category	Total	White	Black	Asian	AIAN	Hisp.
Enrollment (%)	100.0	95.2	2.0	1.5	0.3	1.0
Drop-out Rate (%)	2.5	2.4	15.4	0.0	0.0	0.0
H.S. Diplomas (#)	195	189	1	5	0	0

Hamburg Central SD
5305 Abbott Rd • Hamburg, NY 14075-1699
(716) 646-3220 • http://www.hamburg.wnyric.org/
Grade Span: PK-12; **Agency Type:** 1
Schools: 6
    4 Primary; 1 Middle; 1 High; 0 Other Level
    6 Regular; 0 Special Education; 0 Vocational; 0 Alternative
    0 Magnet; 0 Charter; 5 Title I Eligible; 0 School-wide Title I
Students: 4,153 (50.8% male; 49.1% female)
    Individual Education Program: n/a;
    English Language Learner: n/a; Migrant: n/a
    Eligible for Free Lunch Program: n/a
    Eligible for Reduced-Price Lunch Program: n/a

Teachers: 334.7 (12.4 to 1)
Librarians/Media Specialists: 5.5 (755.1 to 1)
Guidance Counselors: 11.5 (361.1 to 1)
Current Spending: ($ per student per year):
    Total: $10,107; Instruction: $6,576; Support Services: $3,318
Enrollment, Drop-out Rates and Diploma Recipients by Race/Ethnicity

Category	Total	White	Black	Asian	AIAN	Hisp.
Enrollment (%)	100.0	97.5	0.7	0.7	0.3	0.7
Drop-out Rate (%)	2.8	2.8	0.0	9.1	0.0	0.0
H.S. Diplomas (#)	319	309	2	3	1	4

Iroquois Central SD
2111 Girdle Rd • Elma, NY 14059-0032
(716) 652-3000 • http://www.iroquois.wnyric.org/
Grade Span: KG-12; **Agency Type:** 1
Schools: 6
    3 Primary; 2 Middle; 1 High; 0 Other Level
    6 Regular; 0 Special Education; 0 Vocational; 0 Alternative
    0 Magnet; 0 Charter; 5 Title I Eligible; 0 School-wide Title I
Students: 2,905 (51.1% male; 48.8% female)
    Individual Education Program: n/a;
    English Language Learner: n/a; Migrant: n/a
    Eligible for Free Lunch Program: n/a
    Eligible for Reduced-Price Lunch Program: n/a
Teachers: 193.5 (15.0 to 1)
Librarians/Media Specialists: 6.0 (484.2 to 1)
Guidance Counselors: 6.0 (484.2 to 1)
Current Spending: ($ per student per year):
    Total: $9,213; Instruction: $5,824; Support Services: $3,228
Enrollment, Drop-out Rates and Diploma Recipients by Race/Ethnicity

Category	Total	White	Black	Asian	AIAN	Hisp.
Enrollment (%)	100.0	98.3	0.7	0.7	0.0	0.3
Drop-out Rate (%)	1.7	1.7	0.0	0.0	n/a	0.0
H.S. Diplomas (#)	222	221	0	0	0	1

Kenmore-Tonawanda Union Free SD
1500 Colvin Blvd • Buffalo, NY 14223-1196
(716) 874-8400 • http://www.kenton.k12.ny.us/
Grade Span: PK-12; **Agency Type:** 1
Schools: 14
    9 Primary; 3 Middle; 2 High; 0 Other Level
    14 Regular; 0 Special Education; 0 Vocational; 0 Alternative
    0 Magnet; 0 Charter; 3 Title I Eligible; 1 School-wide Title I
Students: 9,033 (51.3% male; 48.6% female)
    Individual Education Program: n/a;
    English Language Learner: n/a; Migrant: n/a
    Eligible for Free Lunch Program: n/a
    Eligible for Reduced-Price Lunch Program: n/a
Teachers: 682.9 (13.2 to 1)
Librarians/Media Specialists: 15.0 (602.2 to 1)
Guidance Counselors: 24.0 (376.4 to 1)
Current Spending: ($ per student per year):
    Total: $11,909; Instruction: $7,378; Support Services: $4,288
Enrollment, Drop-out Rates and Diploma Recipients by Race/Ethnicity

Category	Total	White	Black	Asian	AIAN	Hisp.
Enrollment (%)	100.0	93.5	3.7	1.0	0.3	1.5
Drop-out Rate (%)	2.7	2.6	4.3	4.3	9.1	4.3
H.S. Diplomas (#)	624	618	2	3	0	1

Lackawanna City SD
30 Johnson St • Lackawanna, NY 14218-3595
(716) 827-6767
Grade Span: PK-12; **Agency Type:** 1
Schools: 4
    2 Primary; 1 Middle; 1 High; 0 Other Level
    4 Regular; 0 Special Education; 0 Vocational; 0 Alternative
    0 Magnet; 0 Charter; 4 Title I Eligible; 3 School-wide Title I
Students: 2,041 (53.1% male; 46.8% female)
    Individual Education Program: n/a;
    English Language Learner: n/a; Migrant: n/a
    Eligible for Free Lunch Program: n/a
    Eligible for Reduced-Price Lunch Program: n/a
Teachers: 177.7 (11.5 to 1)
Librarians/Media Specialists: 3.0 (680.3 to 1)
Guidance Counselors: 4.0 (510.3 to 1)
Current Spending: ($ per student per year):
    Total: $14,818; Instruction: $10,170; Support Services: $4,295
Enrollment, Drop-out Rates and Diploma Recipients by Race/Ethnicity

Category	Total	White	Black	Asian	AIAN	Hisp.
Enrollment (%)	100.0	70.3	23.0	0.4	0.2	6.0
Drop-out Rate (%)	11.8	13.0	6.6	0.0	0.0	16.7
H.S. Diplomas (#)	109	91	14	0	0	4

Lancaster Central SD
177 Central Ave • Lancaster, NY 14086-1897
(716) 686-3200 • http://www.lancasterschools.org/
Grade Span: KG-12; **Agency Type:** 1
Schools: 8
  5 Primary; 2 Middle; 1 High; 0 Other Level
  8 Regular; 0 Special Education; 0 Vocational; 0 Alternative
  0 Magnet; 0 Charter; 4 Title I Eligible; 0 School-wide Title I
Students: 6,204 (50.5% male; 49.4% female)
  Individual Education Program: n/a;
  English Language Learner: n/a; Migrant: n/a
  Eligible for Free Lunch Program: n/a
  Eligible for Reduced-Price Lunch Program: n/a
Teachers: 406.4 (15.3 to 1)
Librarians/Media Specialists: 7.8 (795.4 to 1)
Guidance Counselors: 9.0 (689.3 to 1)
Current Spending: ($ per student per year):
  Total: $8,939; Instruction: $5,286; Support Services: $3,417
Enrollment, Drop-out Rates and Diploma Recipients by Race/Ethnicity

Category	Total	White	Black	Asian	AIAN	Hisp.
Enrollment (%)	100.0	97.0	1.1	0.8	0.3	0.8
Drop-out Rate (%)	2.4	2.4	6.7	0.0	0.0	0.0
H.S. Diplomas (#)	412	409	1	1	0	1

Orchard Park Central SD
3330 Baker Rd • Orchard Park, NY 14127-1472
(716) 209-6280 • http://www.opcsd.wnyric.org/
Grade Span: KG-12; **Agency Type:** 1
Schools: 6
  4 Primary; 1 Middle; 1 High; 0 Other Level
  6 Regular; 0 Special Education; 0 Vocational; 0 Alternative
  0 Magnet; 0 Charter; 1 Title I Eligible; 0 School-wide Title I
Students: 5,186 (51.3% male; 48.6% female)
  Individual Education Program: n/a;
  English Language Learner: n/a; Migrant: n/a
  Eligible for Free Lunch Program: n/a
  Eligible for Reduced-Price Lunch Program: n/a
Teachers: 396.4 (13.1 to 1)
Librarians/Media Specialists: 8.3 (624.8 to 1)
Guidance Counselors: 13.0 (398.9 to 1)
Current Spending: ($ per student per year):
  Total: $10,967; Instruction: $7,438; Support Services: $3,374
Enrollment, Drop-out Rates and Diploma Recipients by Race/Ethnicity

Category	Total	White	Black	Asian	AIAN	Hisp.
Enrollment (%)	100.0	97.8	0.7	0.6	0.1	0.8
Drop-out Rate (%)	1.9	1.8	n/a	0.0	n/a	16.7
H.S. Diplomas (#)	406	406	0	0	0	0

Springville-Griffith Institute Central SD
307 Newman St • Springville, NY 14141-1599
(716) 592-3230 • http://www.springvillegi.wnyric.org/
Grade Span: KG-12; **Agency Type:** 1
Schools: 4
  2 Primary; 1 Middle; 1 High; 0 Other Level
  4 Regular; 0 Special Education; 0 Vocational; 0 Alternative
  0 Magnet; 0 Charter; 2 Title I Eligible; 0 School-wide Title I
Students: 2,385 (51.9% male; 48.0% female)
  Individual Education Program: n/a;
  English Language Learner: n/a; Migrant: n/a
  Eligible for Free Lunch Program: n/a
  Eligible for Reduced-Price Lunch Program: n/a
Teachers: 171.7 (13.9 to 1)
Librarians/Media Specialists: 3.0 (795.0 to 1)
Guidance Counselors: 6.0 (397.5 to 1)
Current Spending: ($ per student per year):
  Total: $10,603; Instruction: $6,707; Support Services: $3,696
Enrollment, Drop-out Rates and Diploma Recipients by Race/Ethnicity

Category	Total	White	Black	Asian	AIAN	Hisp.
Enrollment (%)	100.0	97.4	1.0	0.7	0.7	0.3
Drop-out Rate (%)	4.2	4.1	0.0	25.0	0.0	0.0
H.S. Diplomas (#)	156	153	1	0	1	1

Sweet Home Central SD
1901 Sweet Home Rd • Amherst, NY 14228-3399
(716) 250-1402 • http://www.sweethomeschools.com/
Grade Span: PK-12; **Agency Type:** 1
Schools: 6
  4 Primary; 1 Middle; 1 High; 0 Other Level
  6 Regular; 0 Special Education; 0 Vocational; 0 Alternative
  0 Magnet; 0 Charter; 4 Title I Eligible; 0 School-wide Title I
Students: 3,867 (50.9% male; 49.0% female)
  Individual Education Program: n/a;
  English Language Learner: n/a; Migrant: n/a
  Eligible for Free Lunch Program: n/a
  Eligible for Reduced-Price Lunch Program: n/a

Teachers: 305.9 (12.6 to 1)
Librarians/Media Specialists: 4.8 (805.6 to 1)
Guidance Counselors: 12.0 (322.3 to 1)
Current Spending: ($ per student per year):
  Total: $11,510; Instruction: $7,687; Support Services: $3,526
Enrollment, Drop-out Rates and Diploma Recipients by Race/Ethnicity

Category	Total	White	Black	Asian	AIAN	Hisp.
Enrollment (%)	100.0	82.3	10.8	5.4	0.1	1.4
Drop-out Rate (%)	3.6	3.7	1.2	2.1	0.0	18.2
H.S. Diplomas (#)	245	222	13	10	0	0

Tonawanda City SD
202 Broad St • Tonawanda, NY 14150-2098
(716) 694-7784 • http://www.tona.wnyric.org/default.htm
Grade Span: PK-12; **Agency Type:** 1
Schools: 6
  4 Primary; 1 Middle; 1 High; 0 Other Level
  6 Regular; 0 Special Education; 0 Vocational; 0 Alternative
  0 Magnet; 0 Charter; 4 Title I Eligible; 2 School-wide Title I
Students: 2,343 (51.2% male; 48.7% female)
  Individual Education Program: n/a;
  English Language Learner: n/a; Migrant: n/a
  Eligible for Free Lunch Program: n/a
  Eligible for Reduced-Price Lunch Program: n/a
Teachers: 190.5 (12.3 to 1)
Librarians/Media Specialists: 6.0 (390.5 to 1)
Guidance Counselors: 6.0 (390.5 to 1)
Current Spending: ($ per student per year):
  Total: $9,912; Instruction: $6,393; Support Services: $3,268
Enrollment, Drop-out Rates and Diploma Recipients by Race/Ethnicity

Category	Total	White	Black	Asian	AIAN	Hisp.
Enrollment (%)	100.0	96.3	1.1	1.0	0.3	1.3
Drop-out Rate (%)	5.5	5.1	0.0	100.0	n/a	22.2
H.S. Diplomas (#)	174	171	1	1	0	1

West Seneca Central SD
1397 Orchard Park Rd • West Seneca, NY 14224-4098
(716) 677-3101 • http://www.westseneca.wnyric.org/
Grade Span: KG-12; **Agency Type:** 1
Schools: 14
  7 Primary; 2 Middle; 3 High; 2 Other Level
  12 Regular; 0 Special Education; 0 Vocational; 2 Alternative
  0 Magnet; 0 Charter; 5 Title I Eligible; 0 School-wide Title I
Students: 7,697 (51.0% male; 48.9% female)
  Individual Education Program: n/a;
  English Language Learner: n/a; Migrant: n/a
  Eligible for Free Lunch Program: n/a
  Eligible for Reduced-Price Lunch Program: n/a
Teachers: 557.6 (13.8 to 1)
Librarians/Media Specialists: 12.0 (641.4 to 1)
Guidance Counselors: 13.0 (592.1 to 1)
Current Spending: ($ per student per year):
  Total: $9,971; Instruction: $6,471; Support Services: $3,288
Enrollment, Drop-out Rates and Diploma Recipients by Race/Ethnicity

Category	Total	White	Black	Asian	AIAN	Hisp.
Enrollment (%)	100.0	96.5	1.4	0.7	0.4	1.1
Drop-out Rate (%)	4.1	4.1	6.3	0.0	0.0	11.1
H.S. Diplomas (#)	552	535	5	9	2	1

Williamsville Central SD
105 Casey Rd • East Amherst, NY 14051-5000
(716) 626-8005 • http://www.wmsvcsd.wnyric.org/
Grade Span: KG-12; **Agency Type:** 1
Schools: 13
  6 Primary; 4 Middle; 3 High; 0 Other Level
  13 Regular; 0 Special Education; 0 Vocational; 0 Alternative
  0 Magnet; 0 Charter; 3 Title I Eligible; 0 School-wide Title I
Students: 10,760 (50.6% male; 49.3% female)
  Individual Education Program: n/a;
  English Language Learner: n/a; Migrant: n/a
  Eligible for Free Lunch Program: n/a
  Eligible for Reduced-Price Lunch Program: n/a
Teachers: 788.7 (13.6 to 1)
Librarians/Media Specialists: 13.3 (809.0 to 1)
Guidance Counselors: 27.0 (398.5 to 1)
Current Spending: ($ per student per year):
  Total: $9,962; Instruction: $6,608; Support Services: $3,172
Enrollment, Drop-out Rates and Diploma Recipients by Race/Ethnicity

Category	Total	White	Black	Asian	AIAN	Hisp.
Enrollment (%)	100.0	88.4	3.4	6.7	0.3	1.1
Drop-out Rate (%)	1.5	1.5	2.0	0.0	0.0	7.1
H.S. Diplomas (#)	773	700	22	43	0	8

Franklin County

Malone Central SD
64 W St • Malone, NY 12953-1118
(518) 483-7800 • http://www.fehb.org/malone.htm
Grade Span: PK-12; **Agency Type:** 1
Schools: 8
　3 Primary; 1 Middle; 1 High; 3 Other Level
　5 Regular; 0 Special Education; 0 Vocational; 3 Alternative
　0 Magnet; 0 Charter; 3 Title I Eligible; 0 School-wide Title I
Students: 2,499　(51.0% male; 48.9% female)
　Individual Education Program: n/a;
　English Language Learner: n/a; Migrant: n/a
　Eligible for Free Lunch Program: n/a
　Eligible for Reduced-Price Lunch Program: n/a
Teachers: 213.4 (11.7 to 1)
Librarians/Media Specialists: 4.0 (624.8 to 1)
Guidance Counselors: 8.0 (312.4 to 1)
Current Spending: ($ per student per year):
　Total: $11,270; Instruction: $7,762; Support Services: $3,169
Enrollment, Drop-out Rates and Diploma Recipients by Race/Ethnicity

Category	Total	White	Black	Asian	AIAN	Hisp.
Enrollment (%)	100.0	95.4	2.4	0.5	0.5	1.2
Drop-out Rate (%)	2.0	2.1	0.0	0.0	0.0	0.0
H.S. Diplomas (#)	188	181	2	3	0	2

Salmon River Central SD
637 Co. Rt. 1 • Fort Covington, NY 12937-9722
(518) 358-6610 • http://srk12.neric.org/
Grade Span: PK-12; **Agency Type:** 2
Schools: 3
　2 Primary; 0 Middle; 1 High; 0 Other Level
　3 Regular; 0 Special Education; 0 Vocational; 0 Alternative
　0 Magnet; 0 Charter; 3 Title I Eligible; 3 School-wide Title I
Students: 1,604　(50.9% male; 49.0% female)
　Individual Education Program: n/a;
　English Language Learner: n/a; Migrant: n/a
　Eligible for Free Lunch Program: n/a
　Eligible for Reduced-Price Lunch Program: n/a
Teachers: 139.4 (11.5 to 1)
Librarians/Media Specialists: 3.0 (534.7 to 1)
Guidance Counselors: 5.0 (320.8 to 1)
Current Spending: ($ per student per year):
　Total: $14,404; Instruction: $9,661; Support Services: $4,226
Enrollment, Drop-out Rates and Diploma Recipients by Race/Ethnicity

Category	Total	White	Black	Asian	AIAN	Hisp.
Enrollment (%)	100.0	40.9	0.5	0.3	57.9	0.4
Drop-out Rate (%)	3.3	1.9	0.0	0.0	5.3	0.0
H.S. Diplomas (#)	88	42	2	1	42	1

Saranac Lake Central SD
79 Canaras Ave • Saranac Lake, NY 12983-1500
(518) 891-5460 • http://www.slcs.org/
Grade Span: KG-12; **Agency Type:** 1
Schools: 8
　4 Primary; 1 Middle; 1 High; 2 Other Level
　6 Regular; 0 Special Education; 0 Vocational; 2 Alternative
　0 Magnet; 0 Charter; 4 Title I Eligible; 0 School-wide Title I
Students: 1,625　(51.3% male; 48.6% female)
　Individual Education Program: n/a;
　English Language Learner: n/a; Migrant: n/a
　Eligible for Free Lunch Program: n/a
　Eligible for Reduced-Price Lunch Program: n/a
Teachers: 138.7 (11.7 to 1)
Librarians/Media Specialists: 4.0 (406.3 to 1)
Guidance Counselors: 3.0 (541.7 to 1)
Current Spending: ($ per student per year):
　Total: $12,096; Instruction: $7,864; Support Services: $3,963
Enrollment, Drop-out Rates and Diploma Recipients by Race/Ethnicity

Category	Total	White	Black	Asian	AIAN	Hisp.
Enrollment (%)	100.0	97.2	1.3	0.8	0.2	0.5
Drop-out Rate (%)	1.8	1.7	0.0	0.0	n/a	50.0
H.S. Diplomas (#)	112	111	0	1	0	0

Fulton County

Broadalbin-Perth Central SD
14 School St • Broadalbin, NY 12025-9997
(518) 954-2500 • http://www.bpcsd.org/
Grade Span: PK-12; **Agency Type:** 2
Schools: 5
　1 Primary; 2 Middle; 1 High; 1 Other Level
　4 Regular; 0 Special Education; 0 Vocational; 1 Alternative
　0 Magnet; 0 Charter; 3 Title I Eligible; 0 School-wide Title I
Students: 2,208　(56.3% male; 43.6% female)

　Individual Education Program: n/a;
　English Language Learner: n/a; Migrant: n/a
　Eligible for Free Lunch Program: n/a
　Eligible for Reduced-Price Lunch Program: n/a
Teachers: 134.6 (16.4 to 1)
Librarians/Media Specialists: 4.0 (552.0 to 1)
Guidance Counselors: 2.0 (1,104.0 to 1)
Current Spending: ($ per student per year):
　Total: $7,940; Instruction: $5,513; Support Services: $2,175
Enrollment, Drop-out Rates and Diploma Recipients by Race/Ethnicity

Category	Total	White	Black	Asian	AIAN	Hisp.
Enrollment (%)	100.0	89.4	6.9	0.4	0.1	3.1
Drop-out Rate (%)	2.5	2.6	0.0	n/a	n/a	0.0
H.S. Diplomas (#)	128	122	4	0	0	2

Gloversville City SD
243 Lincoln St • Gloversville, NY 12078-0005
(518) 775-5600
Grade Span: PK-12; **Agency Type:** 1
Schools: 7
　5 Primary; 1 Middle; 1 High; 0 Other Level
　7 Regular; 0 Special Education; 0 Vocational; 0 Alternative
　0 Magnet; 0 Charter; 7 Title I Eligible; 0 School-wide Title I
Students: 3,226　(51.7% male; 48.2% female)
　Individual Education Program: n/a;
　English Language Learner: n/a; Migrant: n/a
　Eligible for Free Lunch Program: n/a
　Eligible for Reduced-Price Lunch Program: n/a
Teachers: 259.2 (12.4 to 1)
Librarians/Media Specialists: 6.0 (537.7 to 1)
Guidance Counselors: 10.0 (322.6 to 1)
Current Spending: ($ per student per year):
　Total: $10,587; Instruction: $7,363; Support Services: $2,877
Enrollment, Drop-out Rates and Diploma Recipients by Race/Ethnicity

Category	Total	White	Black	Asian	AIAN	Hisp.
Enrollment (%)	100.0	94.0	3.5	1.1	0.1	1.3
Drop-out Rate (%)	0.2	0.2	0.0	0.0	n/a	0.0
H.S. Diplomas (#)	166	157	1	3	0	5

Johnstown City SD
2 Wright Dr Ste 101 • Johnstown, NY 12095-3099
(518) 762-4611
Grade Span: PK-12; **Agency Type:** 1
Schools: 8
　4 Primary; 1 Middle; 2 High; 1 Other Level
　6 Regular; 0 Special Education; 0 Vocational; 2 Alternative
　0 Magnet; 0 Charter; 4 Title I Eligible; 0 School-wide Title I
Students: 2,168　(47.6% male; 52.3% female)
　Individual Education Program: n/a;
　English Language Learner: n/a; Migrant: n/a
　Eligible for Free Lunch Program: n/a
　Eligible for Reduced-Price Lunch Program: n/a
Teachers: 146.0 (14.8 to 1)
Librarians/Media Specialists: 2.0 (1,084.0 to 1)
Guidance Counselors: 3.0 (722.7 to 1)
Current Spending: ($ per student per year):
　Total: $9,065; Instruction: $6,048; Support Services: $2,655
Enrollment, Drop-out Rates and Diploma Recipients by Race/Ethnicity

Category	Total	White	Black	Asian	AIAN	Hisp.
Enrollment (%)	100.0	94.6	2.9	1.1	0.3	1.2
Drop-out Rate (%)	4.6	4.4	33.3	0.0	n/a	25.0
H.S. Diplomas (#)	140	135	0	4	0	1

Genesee County

Batavia City SD
39 Washington Ave • Batavia, NY 14021-0677
(585) 343-2480 • http://www.bataviacsd.org/
Grade Span: KG-12; **Agency Type:** 1
Schools: 6
　3 Primary; 1 Middle; 1 High; 1 Other Level
　5 Regular; 0 Special Education; 0 Vocational; 1 Alternative
　0 Magnet; 0 Charter; 4 Title I Eligible; 0 School-wide Title I
Students: 2,682　(49.1% male; 50.8% female)
　Individual Education Program: n/a;
　English Language Learner: n/a; Migrant: n/a
　Eligible for Free Lunch Program: n/a
　Eligible for Reduced-Price Lunch Program: n/a
Teachers: 228.1 (11.8 to 1)
Librarians/Media Specialists: 5.0 (536.4 to 1)
Guidance Counselors: 11.0 (243.8 to 1)
Current Spending: ($ per student per year):
　Total: $12,749; Instruction: $8,811; Support Services: $3,604

Enrollment, Drop-out Rates and Diploma Recipients by Race/Ethnicity

Category	Total	White	Black	Asian	AIAN	Hisp.
Enrollment (%)	100.0	84.5	11.3	1.3	0.5	2.3
Drop-out Rate (%)	10.2	9.1	24.2	0.0	0.0	22.2
H.S. Diplomas (#)	152	143	7	1	1	0

Greene County

Cairo-Durham Central SD
424 Main St • Cairo, NY 12413-0780
(518) 622-8534 • http://www.cairodurham.org/
Grade Span: KG-12; **Agency Type:** 2
Schools: 4
    2 Primary; 1 Middle; 1 High; 0 Other Level
    4 Regular; 0 Special Education; 0 Vocational; 0 Alternative
    0 Magnet; 0 Charter; 3 Title I Eligible; 0 School-wide Title I
Students: 1,813   (50.8% male; 49.1% female)
    Individual Education Program: n/a;
    English Language Learner: n/a; Migrant: n/a
    Eligible for Free Lunch Program: n/a
    Eligible for Reduced-Price Lunch Program: n/a
Teachers: 131.6 (13.8 to 1)
Librarians/Media Specialists: 2.0 (906.5 to 1)
Guidance Counselors: 3.0 (604.3 to 1)
Current Spending: ($ per student per year):
    Total: $9,073; Instruction: $5,711; Support Services: $3,104

Enrollment, Drop-out Rates and Diploma Recipients by Race/Ethnicity

Category	Total	White	Black	Asian	AIAN	Hisp.
Enrollment (%)	100.0	94.5	1.4	1.0	0.3	2.9
Drop-out Rate (%)	3.8	3.7	0.0	0.0	n/a	9.1
H.S. Diplomas (#)	74	73	0	0	0	1

Catskill Central SD
343 W Main St • Catskill, NY 12414-1699
(518) 943-4696
Grade Span: KG-12; **Agency Type:** 1
Schools: 3
    1 Primary; 1 Middle; 1 High; 0 Other Level
    3 Regular; 0 Special Education; 0 Vocational; 0 Alternative
    0 Magnet; 0 Charter; 3 Title I Eligible; 0 School-wide Title I
Students: 1,817   (49.9% male; 50.0% female)
    Individual Education Program: n/a;
    English Language Learner: n/a; Migrant: n/a
    Eligible for Free Lunch Program: n/a
    Eligible for Reduced-Price Lunch Program: n/a
Teachers: 147.5 (12.3 to 1)
Librarians/Media Specialists: 3.0 (605.7 to 1)
Guidance Counselors: 3.0 (605.7 to 1)
Current Spending: ($ per student per year):
    Total: $11,760; Instruction: $7,965; Support Services: $3,488

Enrollment, Drop-out Rates and Diploma Recipients by Race/Ethnicity

Category	Total	White	Black	Asian	AIAN	Hisp.
Enrollment (%)	100.0	79.5	13.2	0.9	0.0	6.4
Drop-out Rate (%)	6.3	5.5	5.1	0.0	0.0	21.4
H.S. Diplomas (#)	79	68	4	2	1	4

Coxsackie-Athens Central SD
24 Sunset Blvd • Coxsackie, NY 12051-1132
(518) 731-1710 • http://www.coxsackie-athens.org/
Grade Span: KG-12; **Agency Type:** 2
Schools: 6
    2 Primary; 1 Middle; 1 High; 2 Other Level
    4 Regular; 0 Special Education; 0 Vocational; 2 Alternative
    0 Magnet; 0 Charter; 2 Title I Eligible; 0 School-wide Title I
Students: 2,506   (68.6% male; 31.3% female)
    Individual Education Program: n/a;
    English Language Learner: n/a; Migrant: n/a
    Eligible for Free Lunch Program: n/a
    Eligible for Reduced-Price Lunch Program: n/a
Teachers: 129.8 (19.3 to 1)
Librarians/Media Specialists: 3.0 (835.3 to 1)
Guidance Counselors: 3.0 (835.3 to 1)
Current Spending: ($ per student per year):
    Total: $9,528; Instruction: $5,843; Support Services: $3,358

Enrollment, Drop-out Rates and Diploma Recipients by Race/Ethnicity

Category	Total	White	Black	Asian	AIAN	Hisp.
Enrollment (%)	100.0	66.3	21.3	0.5	0.1	11.8
Drop-out Rate (%)	7.3	7.5	6.7	0.0	n/a	0.0
H.S. Diplomas (#)	98	94	2	0	0	2

Herkimer County

Ilion Central SD
1 Golden Bomber Dr • Ilion, NY 13357-0480
(315) 894-9934 • http://www.moric.org/ilion/
Grade Span: PK-12; **Agency Type:** 1
Schools: 3
    2 Primary; 0 Middle; 1 High; 0 Other Level
    3 Regular; 0 Special Education; 0 Vocational; 0 Alternative
    0 Magnet; 0 Charter; 2 Title I Eligible; 0 School-wide Title I
Students: 1,794   (49.8% male; 50.1% female)
    Individual Education Program: n/a;
    English Language Learner: n/a; Migrant: n/a
    Eligible for Free Lunch Program: n/a
    Eligible for Reduced-Price Lunch Program: n/a
Teachers: 132.0 (13.6 to 1)
Librarians/Media Specialists: 1.0 (1,794.0 to 1)
Guidance Counselors: 2.8 (640.7 to 1)
Current Spending: ($ per student per year):
    Total: $8,473; Instruction: $6,285; Support Services: $1,899

Enrollment, Drop-out Rates and Diploma Recipients by Race/Ethnicity

Category	Total	White	Black	Asian	AIAN	Hisp.
Enrollment (%)	100.0	94.8	2.0	1.0	0.2	2.1
Drop-out Rate (%)	3.6	3.2	20.0	0.0	0.0	12.5
H.S. Diplomas (#)	114	108	1	0	2	3

Jefferson County

Carthage Central SD
25059 County Rt 197 • Carthage, NY 13619-9527
(315) 493-5000 • http://www.carthagecsd.org/
Grade Span: KG-12; **Agency Type:** 1
Schools: 5
    3 Primary; 1 Middle; 1 High; 0 Other Level
    5 Regular; 0 Special Education; 0 Vocational; 0 Alternative
    0 Magnet; 0 Charter; 4 Title I Eligible; 3 School-wide Title I
Students: 2,937   (50.1% male; 49.8% female)
    Individual Education Program: n/a;
    English Language Learner: n/a; Migrant: n/a
    Eligible for Free Lunch Program: n/a
    Eligible for Reduced-Price Lunch Program: n/a
Teachers: 211.9 (13.9 to 1)
Librarians/Media Specialists: 4.0 (734.3 to 1)
Guidance Counselors: 5.0 (587.4 to 1)
Current Spending: ($ per student per year):
    Total: $10,390; Instruction: $6,649; Support Services: $3,384

Enrollment, Drop-out Rates and Diploma Recipients by Race/Ethnicity

Category	Total	White	Black	Asian	AIAN	Hisp.
Enrollment (%)	100.0	88.5	5.6	2.5	0.3	3.1
Drop-out Rate (%)	2.2	2.2	4.1	0.0	0.0	0.0
H.S. Diplomas (#)	193	177	9	4	2	1

General Brown Central SD
17643 Cemetery Rd • Dexter, NY 13634-9731
(315) 639-4711 • http://www.moric.org/genbrown/gb_do.htm
Grade Span: PK-12; **Agency Type:** 2
Schools: 3
    2 Primary; 0 Middle; 1 High; 0 Other Level
    3 Regular; 0 Special Education; 0 Vocational; 0 Alternative
    0 Magnet; 0 Charter; 3 Title I Eligible; 0 School-wide Title I
Students: 1,572   (51.2% male; 48.7% female)
    Individual Education Program: n/a;
    English Language Learner: n/a; Migrant: n/a
    Eligible for Free Lunch Program: n/a
    Eligible for Reduced-Price Lunch Program: n/a
Teachers: 107.4 (14.6 to 1)
Librarians/Media Specialists: 2.0 (786.0 to 1)
Guidance Counselors: 3.0 (524.0 to 1)
Current Spending: ($ per student per year):
    Total: $9,300; Instruction: $6,192; Support Services: $2,796

Enrollment, Drop-out Rates and Diploma Recipients by Race/Ethnicity

Category	Total	White	Black	Asian	AIAN	Hisp.
Enrollment (%)	100.0	96.2	1.7	1.0	0.4	0.8
Drop-out Rate (%)	1.6	1.5	0.0	0.0	0.0	50.0
H.S. Diplomas (#)	121	118	1	2	0	0

Indian River Central SD
32735-B Cnty Rte. 29 • Philadelphia, NY 13673-0308
(315) 642-3481 • http://www.ircsd.org/
Grade Span: KG-12; **Agency Type:** 1
Schools: 8
    5 Primary; 2 Middle; 1 High; 0 Other Level
    8 Regular; 0 Special Education; 0 Vocational; 0 Alternative
    0 Magnet; 0 Charter; 7 Title I Eligible; 5 School-wide Title I
Students: 3,377   (52.2% male; 47.7% female)

Individual Education Program: n/a;
English Language Learner: n/a; Migrant: n/a
Eligible for Free Lunch Program: n/a
Eligible for Reduced-Price Lunch Program: n/a
Teachers: 295.1 (11.4 to 1)
Librarians/Media Specialists: 5.8 (582.2 to 1)
Guidance Counselors: 10.0 (337.7 to 1)
Current Spending: ($ per student per year):
Total: $13,154; Instruction: $7,730; Support Services: $5,076
Enrollment, Drop-out Rates and Diploma Recipients by Race/Ethnicity

Category	Total	White	Black	Asian	AIAN	Hisp.
Enrollment (%)	100.0	77.0	12.9	1.7	0.7	7.8
Drop-out Rate (%)	4.0	4.1	4.1	0.0	n/a	4.5
H.S. Diplomas (#)	155	132	13	1	0	9

South Jefferson Central SD
13180 U S Rt 11 • Adams Center, NY 13606-0010
(315) 583-6104 • http://www.spartanpride.org/
Grade Span: KG-12; **Agency Type:** 2
Schools: 4
3 Primary; 0 Middle; 1 High; 0 Other Level
4 Regular; 0 Special Education; 0 Vocational; 0 Alternative
0 Magnet; 0 Charter; 3 Title I Eligible; 0 School-wide Title I
Students: 2,044 (51.6% male; 48.3% female)
Individual Education Program: n/a;
English Language Learner: n/a; Migrant: n/a
Eligible for Free Lunch Program: n/a
Eligible for Reduced-Price Lunch Program: n/a
Teachers: 143.1 (14.3 to 1)
Librarians/Media Specialists: 2.0 (1,022.0 to 1)
Guidance Counselors: 5.0 (408.8 to 1)
Current Spending: ($ per student per year):
Total: $9,289; Instruction: $6,118; Support Services: $2,833
Enrollment, Drop-out Rates and Diploma Recipients by Race/Ethnicity

Category	Total	White	Black	Asian	AIAN	Hisp.
Enrollment (%)	100.0	98.2	0.9	0.3	0.3	0.3
Drop-out Rate (%)	3.8	3.9	0.0	0.0	0.0	0.0
H.S. Diplomas (#)	123	122	0	0	0	1

Watertown City SD
376 Butterfield Ave • Watertown, NY 13601-4593
(315) 785-3700 • http://watertown.k12.sd.us/
Grade Span: PK-12; **Agency Type:** 1
Schools: 8
4 Primary; 2 Middle; 1 High; 1 Other Level
7 Regular; 0 Special Education; 0 Vocational; 1 Alternative
0 Magnet; 0 Charter; 7 Title I Eligible; 4 School-wide Title I
Students: 4,334 (50.8% male; 49.1% female)
Individual Education Program: n/a;
English Language Learner: n/a; Migrant: n/a
Eligible for Free Lunch Program: n/a
Eligible for Reduced-Price Lunch Program: n/a
Teachers: 301.8 (14.4 to 1)
Librarians/Media Specialists: 5.0 (866.8 to 1)
Guidance Counselors: 7.0 (619.1 to 1)
Current Spending: ($ per student per year):
Total: $10,362; Instruction: $6,983; Support Services: $3,050
Enrollment, Drop-out Rates and Diploma Recipients by Race/Ethnicity

Category	Total	White	Black	Asian	AIAN	Hisp.
Enrollment (%)	100.0	81.9	10.7	2.0	1.0	4.4
Drop-out Rate (%)	5.4	5.8	1.1	5.9	0.0	5.4
H.S. Diplomas (#)	173	156	11	2	0	4

Kings County

New York City Geographic District #15
110 Livingston St Rm • Brooklyn, NY 11201
(718) 330-9300
Grade Span: 06-11; **Agency Type:** 1
Schools: 7
0 Primary; 3 Middle; 0 High; 4 Other Level
7 Regular; 0 Special Education; 0 Vocational; 0 Alternative
0 Magnet; 0 Charter; 3 Title I Eligible; 0 School-wide Title I
Students: 2,011 (49.2% male; 50.7% female)
Individual Education Program: n/a;
English Language Learner: n/a; Migrant: n/a
Eligible for Free Lunch Program: n/a
Eligible for Reduced-Price Lunch Program: n/a
Teachers: n/a
Librarians/Media Specialists: n/a
Guidance Counselors: n/a
Current Spending: ($ per student per year):
Total: n/a; Instruction: n/a; Support Services: n/a

Enrollment, Drop-out Rates and Diploma Recipients by Race/Ethnicity

Category	Total	White	Black	Asian	AIAN	Hisp.
Enrollment (%)	100.0	8.4	18.0	5.7	0.4	67.5
Drop-out Rate (%)	n/a	n/a	n/a	n/a	n/a	n/a
H.S. Diplomas (#)	n/a	n/a	n/a	n/a	n/a	n/a

New York City Public Schools
110 Livingston St • Brooklyn, NY 11201
(718) 935-2794 • http://www.nycenet.edu/
Grade Span: PK-12; **Agency Type:** 1
Schools: 1,225
705 Primary; 207 Middle; 195 High; 118 Other Level
1,072 Regular; 54 Special Education; 18 Vocational; 81 Alternative
8 Magnet; 0 Charter; 704 Title I Eligible; 424 School-wide Title I
Students: 1,023,674 (51.2% male; 48.7% female)
Individual Education Program: n/a;
English Language Learner: n/a; Migrant: n/a
Eligible for Free Lunch Program: n/a
Eligible for Reduced-Price Lunch Program: n/a
Teachers: 70,171.4 (14.6 to 1)
Librarians/Media Specialists: 693.8 (1,475.5 to 1)
Guidance Counselors: 2,000.8 (511.6 to 1)
Current Spending: ($ per student per year):
Total: $12,309; Instruction: $9,349; Support Services: $2,628
Enrollment, Drop-out Rates and Diploma Recipients by Race/Ethnicity

Category	Total	White	Black	Asian	AIAN	Hisp.
Enrollment (%)	100.0	14.8	33.7	12.7	0.4	38.4
Drop-out Rate (%)	14.2	9.6	16.2	7.6	16.6	16.9
H.S. Diplomas (#)	37,915	8,110	12,208	6,698	87	10,812

Note: The New York City Public School System is now organized into 10 Regions across the city, each of which includes approximately 120 schools. Each Region contains 2, 3 or 4 Community School Districts, as well as the high schools located within their geographic boundaries. The National Center for Education Statistics summarizes all the districts' data under this main entry plus 32 other Geographic District entries.

Livingston County

Dansville Central SD
284 Main St • Dansville, NY 14437-1199
(585) 335-4000 • http://www.dansville.k12.ny.us/
Grade Span: PK-12; **Agency Type:** 1
Schools: 4
2 Primary; 1 Middle; 1 High; 0 Other Level
4 Regular; 0 Special Education; 0 Vocational; 0 Alternative
0 Magnet; 0 Charter; 2 Title I Eligible; 0 School-wide Title I
Students: 1,750 (52.1% male; 47.8% female)
Individual Education Program: n/a;
English Language Learner: n/a; Migrant: n/a
Eligible for Free Lunch Program: n/a
Eligible for Reduced-Price Lunch Program: n/a
Teachers: 144.1 (12.1 to 1)
Librarians/Media Specialists: 4.0 (437.5 to 1)
Guidance Counselors: 8.0 (218.8 to 1)
Current Spending: ($ per student per year):
Total: $10,714; Instruction: $7,098; Support Services: $3,375
Enrollment, Drop-out Rates and Diploma Recipients by Race/Ethnicity

Category	Total	White	Black	Asian	AIAN	Hisp.
Enrollment (%)	100.0	96.9	0.9	0.6	0.3	1.3
Drop-out Rate (%)	4.1	4.1	0.0	0.0	n/a	16.7
H.S. Diplomas (#)	107	100	4	2	0	1

Livonia Central SD
6 Puppy Ln • Livonia, NY 14487-0489
(585) 346-4000 • http://www.livonia-csd.k12.ny.us/
Grade Span: KG-12; **Agency Type:** 1
Schools: 4
1 Primary; 2 Middle; 1 High; 0 Other Level
4 Regular; 0 Special Education; 0 Vocational; 0 Alternative
0 Magnet; 0 Charter; 1 Title I Eligible; 0 School-wide Title I
Students: 2,132 (50.4% male; 49.5% female)
Individual Education Program: n/a;
English Language Learner: n/a; Migrant: n/a
Eligible for Free Lunch Program: n/a
Eligible for Reduced-Price Lunch Program: n/a
Teachers: 175.8 (12.1 to 1)
Librarians/Media Specialists: 4.0 (533.0 to 1)
Guidance Counselors: 5.0 (426.4 to 1)
Current Spending: ($ per student per year):
Total: $9,842; Instruction: $6,354; Support Services: $3,252
Enrollment, Drop-out Rates and Diploma Recipients by Race/Ethnicity

Category	Total	White	Black	Asian	AIAN	Hisp.
Enrollment (%)	100.0	97.4	1.1	0.7	0.3	0.5
Drop-out Rate (%)	3.8	3.9	0.0	0.0	n/a	0.0
H.S. Diplomas (#)	146	146	0	0	0	0

Madison County

Canastota Central SD
120 Roberts St • Canastota, NY 13032-1198
(315) 697-2025
Grade Span: KG-12; **Agency Type:** 1
Schools: 4
  2 Primary; 1 Middle; 1 High; 0 Other Level
  4 Regular; 0 Special Education; 0 Vocational; 0 Alternative
  0 Magnet; 0 Charter; 4 Title I Eligible; 0 School-wide Title I
Students: 1,547 (48.6% male; 51.3% female)
  Individual Education Program: n/a;
  English Language Learner: n/a; Migrant: n/a
  Eligible for Free Lunch Program: n/a
  Eligible for Reduced-Price Lunch Program: n/a
Teachers: 111.5 (13.9 to 1)
Librarians/Media Specialists: 2.0 (773.5 to 1)
Guidance Counselors: 3.0 (515.7 to 1)
Current Spending: ($ per student per year):
  Total: $9,710; Instruction: $6,530; Support Services: $2,906
Enrollment, Drop-out Rates and Diploma Recipients by Race/Ethnicity

Category	Total	White	Black	Asian	AIAN	Hisp.
Enrollment (%)	100.0	96.1	2.3	0.6	0.6	0.5
Drop-out Rate (%)	1.5	1.5	n/a	0.0	n/a	0.0
H.S. Diplomas (#)	105	105	0	0	0	0

Cazenovia Central SD
31 Emory Ave • Cazenovia, NY 13035-1098
(315) 655-1317 • http://www.caz.cnyric.org/
Grade Span: KG-12; **Agency Type:** 1
Schools: 3
  1 Primary; 1 Middle; 1 High; 0 Other Level
  3 Regular; 0 Special Education; 0 Vocational; 0 Alternative
  0 Magnet; 0 Charter; 1 Title I Eligible; 0 School-wide Title I
Students: 1,804 (51.3% male; 48.6% female)
  Individual Education Program: n/a;
  English Language Learner: n/a; Migrant: n/a
  Eligible for Free Lunch Program: n/a
  Eligible for Reduced-Price Lunch Program: n/a
Teachers: 138.0 (13.1 to 1)
Librarians/Media Specialists: 3.0 (601.3 to 1)
Guidance Counselors: 5.0 (360.8 to 1)
Current Spending: ($ per student per year):
  Total: $9,733; Instruction: $6,202; Support Services: $3,342
Enrollment, Drop-out Rates and Diploma Recipients by Race/Ethnicity

Category	Total	White	Black	Asian	AIAN	Hisp.
Enrollment (%)	100.0	97.8	0.6	0.8	0.1	0.8
Drop-out Rate (%)	1.9	1.9	0.0	0.0	n/a	0.0
H.S. Diplomas (#)	108	108	0	0	0	0

Chittenango Central SD
1732 Fyler Rd • Chittenango, NY 13037-9520
(315) 687-2669
Grade Span: KG-12; **Agency Type:** 1
Schools: 5
  3 Primary; 1 Middle; 1 High; 0 Other Level
  5 Regular; 0 Special Education; 0 Vocational; 0 Alternative
  0 Magnet; 0 Charter; 4 Title I Eligible; 0 School-wide Title I
Students: 2,565 (49.4% male; 50.5% female)
  Individual Education Program: n/a;
  English Language Learner: n/a; Migrant: n/a
  Eligible for Free Lunch Program: n/a
  Eligible for Reduced-Price Lunch Program: n/a
Teachers: 190.4 (13.5 to 1)
Librarians/Media Specialists: 5.0 (513.0 to 1)
Guidance Counselors: 7.5 (342.0 to 1)
Current Spending: ($ per student per year):
  Total: $9,499; Instruction: $5,832; Support Services: $3,362
Enrollment, Drop-out Rates and Diploma Recipients by Race/Ethnicity

Category	Total	White	Black	Asian	AIAN	Hisp.
Enrollment (%)	100.0	98.2	0.9	0.4	0.3	0.2
Drop-out Rate (%)	3.6	3.5	0.0	0.0	33.3	0.0
H.S. Diplomas (#)	165	163	0	0	1	1

Oneida City SD
565 Sayles St • Oneida, NY 13421-0327
(315) 363-2550 • http://www.oneidany.org/
Grade Span: KG-12; **Agency Type:** 1
Schools: 8
  6 Primary; 1 Middle; 1 High; 0 Other Level
  8 Regular; 0 Special Education; 0 Vocational; 0 Alternative
  0 Magnet; 0 Charter; 5 Title I Eligible; 1 School-wide Title I
Students: 2,550 (50.6% male; 49.3% female)
  Individual Education Program: n/a;
  English Language Learner: n/a; Migrant: n/a

  Eligible for Free Lunch Program: n/a
  Eligible for Reduced-Price Lunch Program: n/a
Teachers: 190.6 (13.4 to 1)
Librarians/Media Specialists: 7.0 (364.3 to 1)
Guidance Counselors: 4.0 (637.5 to 1)
Current Spending: ($ per student per year):
  Total: $10,420; Instruction: $6,950; Support Services: $3,178
Enrollment, Drop-out Rates and Diploma Recipients by Race/Ethnicity

Category	Total	White	Black	Asian	AIAN	Hisp.
Enrollment (%)	100.0	96.6	0.7	0.6	1.3	0.7
Drop-out Rate (%)	6.6	6.3	200.0	0.0	33.3	0.0
H.S. Diplomas (#)	159	155	0	0	1	3

Monroe County

Brighton Central SD
2035 Monroe Ave • Rochester, NY 14618-2027
(585) 242-5080 • http://www.bcsd.org/index_noflash.cfm
Grade Span: KG-12; **Agency Type:** 1
Schools: 5
  2 Primary; 1 Middle; 2 High; 0 Other Level
  4 Regular; 0 Special Education; 0 Vocational; 1 Alternative
  0 Magnet; 0 Charter; 1 Title I Eligible; 0 School-wide Title I
Students: 3,582 (51.2% male; 48.7% female)
  Individual Education Program: n/a;
  English Language Learner: n/a; Migrant: n/a
  Eligible for Free Lunch Program: n/a
  Eligible for Reduced-Price Lunch Program: n/a
Teachers: 280.5 (12.8 to 1)
Librarians/Media Specialists: 4.0 (895.5 to 1)
Guidance Counselors: 12.0 (298.5 to 1)
Current Spending: ($ per student per year):
  Total: $11,722; Instruction: $7,395; Support Services: $4,077
Enrollment, Drop-out Rates and Diploma Recipients by Race/Ethnicity

Category	Total	White	Black	Asian	AIAN	Hisp.
Enrollment (%)	100.0	76.7	6.1	13.8	0.3	3.0
Drop-out Rate (%)	0.5	0.6	0.0	0.0	0.0	0.0
H.S. Diplomas (#)	259	215	8	29	0	7

Brockport Central SD
40 Allen St • Brockport, NY 14420-2296
(585) 637-1810 • http://www.brockport.k12.ny.us/
Grade Span: KG-12; **Agency Type:** 1
Schools: 5
  2 Primary; 2 Middle; 1 High; 0 Other Level
  5 Regular; 0 Special Education; 0 Vocational; 0 Alternative
  0 Magnet; 0 Charter; 4 Title I Eligible; 0 School-wide Title I
Students: 4,480 (49.9% male; 50.0% female)
  Individual Education Program: n/a;
  English Language Learner: n/a; Migrant: n/a
  Eligible for Free Lunch Program: n/a
  Eligible for Reduced-Price Lunch Program: n/a
Teachers: 323.7 (13.8 to 1)
Librarians/Media Specialists: 5.3 (845.3 to 1)
Guidance Counselors: 12.0 (373.3 to 1)
Current Spending: ($ per student per year):
  Total: $10,885; Instruction: $6,756; Support Services: $3,801
Enrollment, Drop-out Rates and Diploma Recipients by Race/Ethnicity

Category	Total	White	Black	Asian	AIAN	Hisp.
Enrollment (%)	100.0	91.1	4.0	1.0	0.5	3.5
Drop-out Rate (%)	1.0	0.9	0.0	0.0	0.0	5.7
H.S. Diplomas (#)	290	264	20	1	0	5

Churchville-Chili Central SD
139 Fairbanks Rd • Churchville, NY 14428-9797
(585) 293-1800 • http://www.cccsd.org/
Grade Span: KG-12; **Agency Type:** 1
Schools: 6
  3 Primary; 2 Middle; 1 High; 0 Other Level
  6 Regular; 0 Special Education; 0 Vocational; 0 Alternative
  0 Magnet; 0 Charter; 5 Title I Eligible; 0 School-wide Title I
Students: 4,482 (53.1% male; 46.8% female)
  Individual Education Program: n/a;
  English Language Learner: n/a; Migrant: n/a
  Eligible for Free Lunch Program: n/a
  Eligible for Reduced-Price Lunch Program: n/a
Teachers: 331.7 (13.5 to 1)
Librarians/Media Specialists: 6.0 (747.0 to 1)
Guidance Counselors: 11.0 (407.5 to 1)
Current Spending: ($ per student per year):
  Total: $10,297; Instruction: $6,580; Support Services: $3,522

Enrollment, Drop-out Rates and Diploma Recipients by Race/Ethnicity

Category	Total	White	Black	Asian	AIAN	Hisp.
Enrollment (%)	100.0	90.1	6.2	1.9	0.1	1.7
Drop-out Rate (%)	1.5	1.6	1.3	0.0	n/a	0.0
H.S. Diplomas (#)	298	297	1	0	0	0

East Irondequoit Central SD
600 Pardee Rd • Rochester, NY 14609-2898
(585) 339-1210 • http://www.eicsd.k12.ny.us/
Grade Span: KG-12; **Agency Type:** 1
Schools: 6
4 Primary; 1 Middle; 1 High; 0 Other Level
6 Regular; 0 Special Education; 0 Vocational; 0 Alternative
0 Magnet; 0 Charter; 2 Title I Eligible; 0 School-wide Title I
Students: 3,514 (50.8% male; 49.1% female)
Individual Education Program: n/a;
English Language Learner: n/a; Migrant: n/a
Eligible for Free Lunch Program: n/a
Eligible for Reduced-Price Lunch Program: n/a
Teachers: 257.8 (13.6 to 1)
Librarians/Media Specialists: 6.0 (585.7 to 1)
Guidance Counselors: 9.1 (386.2 to 1)
Current Spending: ($ per student per year):
Total: $11,766; Instruction: $6,713; Support Services: $4,787
Enrollment, Drop-out Rates and Diploma Recipients by Race/Ethnicity

Category	Total	White	Black	Asian	AIAN	Hisp.
Enrollment (%)	100.0	77.9	12.0	1.9	0.3	7.9
Drop-out Rate (%)	1.7	1.5	1.3	0.0	0.0	6.3
H.S. Diplomas (#)	203	177	9	1	0	16

Fairport Central SD
38 W Church St • Fairport, NY 14450-2130
(585) 421-2004 • http://www.fairport.org/
Grade Span: KG-12; **Agency Type:** 1
Schools: 8
4 Primary; 2 Middle; 1 High; 1 Other Level
8 Regular; 0 Special Education; 0 Vocational; 0 Alternative
0 Magnet; 0 Charter; 3 Title I Eligible; 0 School-wide Title I
Students: 7,115 (51.1% male; 48.8% female)
Individual Education Program: n/a;
English Language Learner: n/a; Migrant: n/a
Eligible for Free Lunch Program: n/a
Eligible for Reduced-Price Lunch Program: n/a
Teachers: 504.9 (14.1 to 1)
Librarians/Media Specialists: 10.5 (677.6 to 1)
Guidance Counselors: 14.5 (490.7 to 1)
Current Spending: ($ per student per year):
Total: $10,539; Instruction: $6,855; Support Services: $3,448
Enrollment, Drop-out Rates and Diploma Recipients by Race/Ethnicity

Category	Total	White	Black	Asian	AIAN	Hisp.
Enrollment (%)	100.0	92.2	2.4	3.9	0.1	1.4
Drop-out Rate (%)	1.4	1.4	0.0	1.1	0.0	0.0
H.S. Diplomas (#)	489	455	12	17	0	5

Gates-Chili Central SD
910 Wegman Rd • Rochester, NY 14624-1440
(585) 247-5050 • http://www.gateschili.org/
Grade Span: KG-12; **Agency Type:** 1
Schools: 7
5 Primary; 1 Middle; 1 High; 0 Other Level
7 Regular; 0 Special Education; 0 Vocational; 0 Alternative
0 Magnet; 0 Charter; 3 Title I Eligible; 0 School-wide Title I
Students: 5,057 (50.3% male; 49.6% female)
Individual Education Program: n/a;
English Language Learner: n/a; Migrant: n/a
Eligible for Free Lunch Program: n/a
Eligible for Reduced-Price Lunch Program: n/a
Teachers: 386.6 (13.1 to 1)
Librarians/Media Specialists: 9.0 (561.9 to 1)
Guidance Counselors: 12.4 (407.8 to 1)
Current Spending: ($ per student per year):
Total: $11,700; Instruction: $7,792; Support Services: $3,600
Enrollment, Drop-out Rates and Diploma Recipients by Race/Ethnicity

Category	Total	White	Black	Asian	AIAN	Hisp.
Enrollment (%)	100.0	83.1	11.0	2.8	0.1	3.0
Drop-out Rate (%)	2.8	2.5	5.1	0.0	0.0	6.4
H.S. Diplomas (#)	379	326	34	8	3	8

Greece Central SD
750 Maiden Ln • Rochester, NY 14615-1296
(585) 621-1000 • http://web001.greece.k12.ny.us/
Grade Span: PK-12; **Agency Type:** 1
Schools: 20
13 Primary; 3 Middle; 3 High; 1 Other Level
20 Regular; 0 Special Education; 0 Vocational; 0 Alternative
0 Magnet; 0 Charter; 9 Title I Eligible; 0 School-wide Title I
Students: 13,799 (51.5% male; 48.4% female)
Individual Education Program: n/a;
English Language Learner: n/a; Migrant: n/a
Eligible for Free Lunch Program: n/a
Eligible for Reduced-Price Lunch Program: n/a
Teachers: 978.5 (14.1 to 1)
Librarians/Media Specialists: 21.0 (657.1 to 1)
Guidance Counselors: 36.0 (383.3 to 1)
Current Spending: ($ per student per year):
Total: $10,942; Instruction: $6,915; Support Services: $3,706
Enrollment, Drop-out Rates and Diploma Recipients by Race/Ethnicity

Category	Total	White	Black	Asian	AIAN	Hisp.
Enrollment (%)	100.0	87.6	6.0	1.9	0.5	3.9
Drop-out Rate (%)	1.7	1.5	6.0	0.8	4.5	1.9
H.S. Diplomas (#)	901	826	25	23	0	27

Hilton Central SD
225 W Ave • Hilton, NY 14468-1283
(585) 392-1000 • http://www.hilton.k12.ny.us/
Grade Span: KG-12; **Agency Type:** 1
Schools: 5
3 Primary; 1 Middle; 1 High; 0 Other Level
5 Regular; 0 Special Education; 0 Vocational; 0 Alternative
0 Magnet; 0 Charter; 1 Title I Eligible; 0 School-wide Title I
Students: 4,441 (50.7% male; 49.2% female)
Individual Education Program: n/a;
English Language Learner: n/a; Migrant: n/a
Eligible for Free Lunch Program: n/a
Eligible for Reduced-Price Lunch Program: n/a
Teachers: 346.8 (12.8 to 1)
Librarians/Media Specialists: 4.0 (1,110.3 to 1)
Guidance Counselors: 12.5 (355.3 to 1)
Current Spending: ($ per student per year):
Total: $10,405; Instruction: $6,986; Support Services: $3,193
Enrollment, Drop-out Rates and Diploma Recipients by Race/Ethnicity

Category	Total	White	Black	Asian	AIAN	Hisp.
Enrollment (%)	100.0	95.9	1.8	0.8	0.4	1.1
Drop-out Rate (%)	1.0	1.1	0.0	0.0	0.0	0.0
H.S. Diplomas (#)	330	315	4	8	1	2

Honeoye Falls-Lima Central SD
20 Church St • Honeoye Falls, NY 14472-1294
(585) 624-7010 • http://www.hfl.monroe.edu/
Grade Span: KG-12; **Agency Type:** 1
Schools: 4
2 Primary; 1 Middle; 1 High; 0 Other Level
4 Regular; 0 Special Education; 0 Vocational; 0 Alternative
0 Magnet; 0 Charter; 4 Title I Eligible; 0 School-wide Title I
Students: 2,601 (51.0% male; 48.9% female)
Individual Education Program: n/a;
English Language Learner: n/a; Migrant: n/a
Eligible for Free Lunch Program: n/a
Eligible for Reduced-Price Lunch Program: n/a
Teachers: 190.2 (13.7 to 1)
Librarians/Media Specialists: 3.0 (867.0 to 1)
Guidance Counselors: 6.0 (433.5 to 1)
Current Spending: ($ per student per year):
Total: $10,660; Instruction: $6,945; Support Services: $3,429
Enrollment, Drop-out Rates and Diploma Recipients by Race/Ethnicity

Category	Total	White	Black	Asian	AIAN	Hisp.
Enrollment (%)	100.0	97.3	0.6	0.8	0.2	1.1
Drop-out Rate (%)	3.6	3.4	20.0	0.0	n/a	20.0
H.S. Diplomas (#)	164	161	1	1	0	1

Penfield Central SD
2590 Atlantic Ave • Penfield, NY 14526-0900
(585) 249-5700 • http://penfield.edu/
Grade Span: KG-12; **Agency Type:** 1
Schools: 6
4 Primary; 1 Middle; 1 High; 0 Other Level
6 Regular; 0 Special Education; 0 Vocational; 0 Alternative
0 Magnet; 0 Charter; 3 Title I Eligible; 0 School-wide Title I
Students: 4,960 (50.5% male; 49.4% female)
Individual Education Program: n/a;
English Language Learner: n/a; Migrant: n/a
Eligible for Free Lunch Program: n/a
Eligible for Reduced-Price Lunch Program: n/a
Teachers: 410.4 (12.1 to 1)
Librarians/Media Specialists: 8.0 (620.0 to 1)
Guidance Counselors: 20.0 (248.0 to 1)
Current Spending: ($ per student per year):
Total: $11,336; Instruction: $7,453; Support Services: $3,651

Enrollment, Drop-out Rates and Diploma Recipients by Race/Ethnicity

Category	Total	White	Black	Asian	AIAN	Hisp.
Enrollment (%)	100.0	90.0	3.6	3.9	0.3	2.2
Drop-out Rate (%)	1.7	1.7	0.0	0.0	0.0	10.0
H.S. Diplomas (#)	302	277	13	8	0	4

Pittsford Central SD

42 W Jefferson Rd • Pittsford, NY 14534-1978
(585) 218-1004 • http://www.pittsfordschools.org/
Grade Span: KG-12; **Agency Type:** 1
Schools: 8
　5 Primary; 1 Middle; 2 High; 0 Other Level
　8 Regular; 0 Special Education; 0 Vocational; 0 Alternative
　0 Magnet; 0 Charter; 0 Title I Eligible; 0 School-wide Title I
Students: 6,022　(49.7% male; 50.2% female)
　Individual Education Program: n/a;
　English Language Learner: n/a; Migrant: n/a
　Eligible for Free Lunch Program: n/a
　Eligible for Reduced-Price Lunch Program: n/a
Teachers: 458.9 (13.1 to 1)
Librarians/Media Specialists: 8.6 (700.2 to 1)
Guidance Counselors: 18.0 (334.6 to 1)
Current Spending: ($ per student per year):
　Total: $11,526; Instruction: $8,046; Support Services: $3,272

Enrollment, Drop-out Rates and Diploma Recipients by Race/Ethnicity

Category	Total	White	Black	Asian	AIAN	Hisp.
Enrollment (%)	100.0	91.4	2.5	5.3	0.1	0.7
Drop-out Rate (%)	3.6	3.5	6.1	2.7	50.0	6.3
H.S. Diplomas (#)	443	410	21	8	0	4

Rochester City SD

131 W Broad St • Rochester, NY 14614-1187
(585) 262-8378 • http://www.rcsd-k12.org/
Grade Span: PK-12; **Agency Type:** 1
Schools: 62
　40 Primary; 6 Middle; 8 High; 8 Other Level
　60 Regular; 0 Special Education; 1 Vocational; 1 Alternative
　1 Magnet; 0 Charter; 54 Title I Eligible; 54 School-wide Title I
Students: 34,598　(51.0% male; 48.9% female)
　Individual Education Program: n/a;
　English Language Learner: n/a; Migrant: n/a
　Eligible for Free Lunch Program: n/a
　Eligible for Reduced-Price Lunch Program: n/a
Teachers: 2,833.0 (12.2 to 1)
Librarians/Media Specialists: 40.9 (845.9 to 1)
Guidance Counselors: 60.0 (576.6 to 1)
Current Spending: ($ per student per year):
　Total: $12,711; Instruction: $7,975; Support Services: $4,321

Enrollment, Drop-out Rates and Diploma Recipients by Race/Ethnicity

Category	Total	White	Black	Asian	AIAN	Hisp.
Enrollment (%)	100.0	13.7	64.4	1.8	0.4	19.8
Drop-out Rate (%)	13.0	9.8	13.1	8.1	10.0	16.4
H.S. Diplomas (#)	1,021	234	617	32	5	133

Rush-Henrietta Central SD

2034 Lehigh Sta Rd • Henrietta, NY 14467-9692
(585) 359-5012 • http://www.rhnet.org/
Grade Span: KG-12; **Agency Type:** 1
Schools: 10
　5 Primary; 2 Middle; 1 High; 2 Other Level
　9 Regular; 0 Special Education; 0 Vocational; 1 Alternative
　0 Magnet; 0 Charter; 6 Title I Eligible; 0 School-wide Title I
Students: 5,859　(50.6% male; 49.3% female)
　Individual Education Program: n/a;
　English Language Learner: n/a; Migrant: n/a
　Eligible for Free Lunch Program: n/a
　Eligible for Reduced-Price Lunch Program: n/a
Teachers: 498.2 (11.8 to 1)
Librarians/Media Specialists: 11.2 (523.1 to 1)
Guidance Counselors: 15.0 (390.6 to 1)
Current Spending: ($ per student per year):
　Total: $12,420; Instruction: $7,759; Support Services: $4,368

Enrollment, Drop-out Rates and Diploma Recipients by Race/Ethnicity

Category	Total	White	Black	Asian	AIAN	Hisp.
Enrollment (%)	100.0	75.9	13.5	6.7	0.7	3.2
Drop-out Rate (%)	2.2	1.9	2.4	0.0	21.1	6.3
H.S. Diplomas (#)	349	271	45	24	3	6

Spencerport Central SD

71 Lyell Ave • Spencerport, NY 14559-1899
(585) 349-5102 • http://www.spencerportschools.org/
Grade Span: KG-12; **Agency Type:** 1
Schools: 6
　4 Primary; 1 Middle; 1 High; 0 Other Level
　6 Regular; 0 Special Education; 0 Vocational; 0 Alternative

　0 Magnet; 0 Charter; 5 Title I Eligible; 0 School-wide Title I
Students: 4,350　(52.2% male; 47.7% female)
　Individual Education Program: n/a;
　English Language Learner: n/a; Migrant: n/a
　Eligible for Free Lunch Program: n/a
　Eligible for Reduced-Price Lunch Program: n/a
Teachers: 331.1 (13.1 to 1)
Librarians/Media Specialists: 6.0 (725.0 to 1)
Guidance Counselors: 14.0 (310.7 to 1)
Current Spending: ($ per student per year):
　Total: $10,139; Instruction: $6,959; Support Services: $2,919

Enrollment, Drop-out Rates and Diploma Recipients by Race/Ethnicity

Category	Total	White	Black	Asian	AIAN	Hisp.
Enrollment (%)	100.0	91.1	4.1	2.5	0.2	2.1
Drop-out Rate (%)	1.7	1.7	3.6	0.0	n/a	0.0
H.S. Diplomas (#)	292	268	12	9	0	3

Webster Central SD

119 S Ave • Webster, NY 14580-3594
(585) 265-3600 • http://www.websterschools.org/
Grade Span: KG-12; **Agency Type:** 1
Schools: 11
　7 Primary; 2 Middle; 2 High; 0 Other Level
　11 Regular; 0 Special Education; 0 Vocational; 0 Alternative
　0 Magnet; 0 Charter; 5 Title I Eligible; 0 School-wide Title I
Students: 8,736　(52.6% male; 47.3% female)
　Individual Education Program: n/a;
　English Language Learner: n/a; Migrant: n/a
　Eligible for Free Lunch Program: n/a
　Eligible for Reduced-Price Lunch Program: n/a
Teachers: 654.2 (13.4 to 1)
Librarians/Media Specialists: 11.0 (794.2 to 1)
Guidance Counselors: 22.5 (388.3 to 1)
Current Spending: ($ per student per year):
　Total: $10,982; Instruction: $7,325; Support Services: $3,469

Enrollment, Drop-out Rates and Diploma Recipients by Race/Ethnicity

Category	Total	White	Black	Asian	AIAN	Hisp.
Enrollment (%)	100.0	94.4	2.1	2.3	0.1	1.0
Drop-out Rate (%)	1.4	1.5	0.0	0.0	0.0	0.0
H.S. Diplomas (#)	600	578	8	12	1	1

West Irondequoit Central SD

95 Stanton Ln • Rochester, NY 14617-3093
(585) 342-5500 • http://www.westirondequoit.org/
Grade Span: KG-12; **Agency Type:** 1
Schools: 10
　6 Primary; 3 Middle; 1 High; 0 Other Level
　10 Regular; 0 Special Education; 0 Vocational; 0 Alternative
　0 Magnet; 0 Charter; 7 Title I Eligible; 0 School-wide Title I
Students: 3,949　(49.9% male; 50.0% female)
　Individual Education Program: n/a;
　English Language Learner: n/a; Migrant: n/a
　Eligible for Free Lunch Program: n/a
　Eligible for Reduced-Price Lunch Program: n/a
Teachers: 260.6 (15.2 to 1)
Librarians/Media Specialists: 6.0 (658.2 to 1)
Guidance Counselors: 14.0 (282.1 to 1)
Current Spending: ($ per student per year):
　Total: $10,006; Instruction: $5,849; Support Services: $3,937

Enrollment, Drop-out Rates and Diploma Recipients by Race/Ethnicity

Category	Total	White	Black	Asian	AIAN	Hisp.
Enrollment (%)	100.0	88.8	5.1	2.3	0.2	3.5
Drop-out Rate (%)	0.6	0.5	0.0	3.0	0.0	0.0
H.S. Diplomas (#)	315	286	12	9	0	8

Montgomery County

Amsterdam City SD

11 Liberty St • Amsterdam, NY 12010-0670
(518) 843-5217
Grade Span: KG-12; **Agency Type:** 1
Schools: 7
　5 Primary; 1 Middle; 1 High; 0 Other Level
　7 Regular; 0 Special Education; 0 Vocational; 0 Alternative
　0 Magnet; 0 Charter; 4 Title I Eligible; 0 School-wide Title I
Students: 3,782　(51.3% male; 48.6% female)
　Individual Education Program: n/a;
　English Language Learner: n/a; Migrant: n/a
　Eligible for Free Lunch Program: n/a
　Eligible for Reduced-Price Lunch Program: n/a
Teachers: 297.1 (12.7 to 1)
Librarians/Media Specialists: 6.3 (600.3 to 1)
Guidance Counselors: 10.0 (378.2 to 1)
Current Spending: ($ per student per year):
　Total: $9,577; Instruction: $6,544; Support Services: $2,798

Enrollment, Drop-out Rates and Diploma Recipients by Race/Ethnicity

Category	Total	White	Black	Asian	AIAN	Hisp.
Enrollment (%)	100.0	69.0	3.3	0.6	0.0	27.0
Drop-out Rate (%)	5.9	5.1	13.6	0.0	n/a	8.1
H.S. Diplomas (#)	0	0	0	0	0	0

Fonda-Fultonville Central SD
112 Old Johnstown Rd • Fonda, NY 12068-1501
(518) 853-4415 • http://ffcs.neric.org/
Grade Span: KG-12; **Agency Type:** 2
Schools: 3
    1 Primary; 1 Middle; 1 High; 0 Other Level
    3 Regular; 0 Special Education; 0 Vocational; 0 Alternative
    0 Magnet; 0 Charter; 3 Title I Eligible; 0 School-wide Title I
Students: 1,606   (55.2% male; 44.7% female)
    Individual Education Program: n/a;
    English Language Learner: n/a; Migrant: n/a
    Eligible for Free Lunch Program: n/a
    Eligible for Reduced-Price Lunch Program: n/a
Teachers: 121.0 (13.3 to 1)
Librarians/Media Specialists: 2.0 (803.0 to 1)
Guidance Counselors: 2.0 (803.0 to 1)
Current Spending: ($ per student per year):
    Total: $11,569; Instruction: $7,737; Support Services: $3,510
Enrollment, Drop-out Rates and Diploma Recipients by Race/Ethnicity

Category	Total	White	Black	Asian	AIAN	Hisp.
Enrollment (%)	100.0	96.8	0.4	1.3	0.1	1.4
Drop-out Rate (%)	1.2	1.0	0.0	n/a	0.0	33.3
H.S. Diplomas (#)	121	120	1	0	0	0

Nassau County

Baldwin Union Free SD
960 Hastings St • Baldwin, NY 11510-4798
(516) 377-9271 • http://www.baldwin.k12.ny.us/
Grade Span: KG-12; **Agency Type:** 1
Schools: 9
    7 Primary; 1 Middle; 1 High; 0 Other Level
    9 Regular; 0 Special Education; 0 Vocational; 0 Alternative
    0 Magnet; 0 Charter; 6 Title I Eligible; 0 School-wide Title I
Students: 5,408   (51.4% male; 48.5% female)
    Individual Education Program: n/a;
    English Language Learner: n/a; Migrant: n/a
    Eligible for Free Lunch Program: n/a
    Eligible for Reduced-Price Lunch Program: n/a
Teachers: 430.2 (12.6 to 1)
Librarians/Media Specialists: 3.3 (1,638.8 to 1)
Guidance Counselors: 10.5 (515.0 to 1)
Current Spending: ($ per student per year):
    Total: $13,546; Instruction: $8,983; Support Services: $4,384
Enrollment, Drop-out Rates and Diploma Recipients by Race/Ethnicity

Category	Total	White	Black	Asian	AIAN	Hisp.
Enrollment (%)	100.0	45.7	35.0	4.8	0.2	14.3
Drop-out Rate (%)	3.1	3.1	3.5	0.0	0.0	3.2
H.S. Diplomas (#)	346	218	95	9	0	24

Bellmore-Merrick Central High SD
1260 Meadowbrook Rd • North Merrick, NY 11566-9998
(516) 992-1001 • http://www.bellmore-merrick.k12.ny.us/
Grade Span: 07-12; **Agency Type:** 2
Schools: 5
    0 Primary; 2 Middle; 3 High; 0 Other Level
    5 Regular; 0 Special Education; 0 Vocational; 0 Alternative
    0 Magnet; 0 Charter; 2 Title I Eligible; 0 School-wide Title I
Students: 5,832   (51.3% male; 48.6% female)
    Individual Education Program: n/a;
    English Language Learner: n/a; Migrant: n/a
    Eligible for Free Lunch Program: n/a
    Eligible for Reduced-Price Lunch Program: n/a
Teachers: 374.3 (15.6 to 1)
Librarians/Media Specialists: 5.0 (1,166.4 to 1)
Guidance Counselors: 22.7 (256.9 to 1)
Current Spending: ($ per student per year):
    Total: $13,482; Instruction: $8,614; Support Services: $4,600
Enrollment, Drop-out Rates and Diploma Recipients by Race/Ethnicity

Category	Total	White	Black	Asian	AIAN	Hisp.
Enrollment (%)	100.0	91.6	1.4	4.2	0.0	2.8
Drop-out Rate (%)	4.8	4.3	7.8	8.2	n/a	16.7
H.S. Diplomas (#)	812	754	12	22	0	24

Bethpage Union Free SD
10 Cherry Ave • Bethpage, NY 11714-1596
(516) 644-4001 • http://www.bethpagecommunity.com/Schools/
Grade Span: KG-12; **Agency Type:** 1
Schools: 5

    3 Primary; 1 Middle; 1 High; 0 Other Level
    5 Regular; 0 Special Education; 0 Vocational; 0 Alternative
    0 Magnet; 0 Charter; 3 Title I Eligible; 0 School-wide Title I
Students: 3,006   (51.8% male; 48.1% female)
    Individual Education Program: n/a;
    English Language Learner: n/a; Migrant: n/a
    Eligible for Free Lunch Program: n/a
    Eligible for Reduced-Price Lunch Program: n/a
Teachers: 242.6 (12.4 to 1)
Librarians/Media Specialists: 5.2 (578.1 to 1)
Guidance Counselors: 7.0 (429.4 to 1)
Current Spending: ($ per student per year):
    Total: $14,885; Instruction: $9,383; Support Services: $5,273
Enrollment, Drop-out Rates and Diploma Recipients by Race/Ethnicity

Category	Total	White	Black	Asian	AIAN	Hisp.
Enrollment (%)	100.0	88.0	0.1	6.4	0.0	5.5
Drop-out Rate (%)	0.9	1.0	0.0	0.0	n/a	0.0
H.S. Diplomas (#)	180	159	1	15	0	5

Boces Nassau
71 Clinton Rd • Garden City, NY 11530-4757
(516) 396-2200
Grade Span: PK-PK; **Agency Type:** 4
Schools: 1
    1 Primary; 0 Middle; 0 High; 0 Other Level
    1 Regular; 0 Special Education; 0 Vocational; 0 Alternative
    0 Magnet; 0 Charter; 0 Title I Eligible; 0 School-wide Title I
Students: 2,039   (75.8% male; 24.1% female)
    Individual Education Program: n/a;
    English Language Learner: n/a; Migrant: n/a
    Eligible for Free Lunch Program: n/a
    Eligible for Reduced-Price Lunch Program: n/a
Teachers: 536.5 (3.8 to 1)
Librarians/Media Specialists: 4.0 (509.8 to 1)
Guidance Counselors: 8.0 (254.9 to 1)
Current Spending: ($ per student per year):
    Total: n/a; Instruction: n/a; Support Services: n/a
Enrollment, Drop-out Rates and Diploma Recipients by Race/Ethnicity

Category	Total	White	Black	Asian	AIAN	Hisp.
Enrollment (%)	100.0	54.2	25.7	4.9	0.0	15.2
Drop-out Rate (%)	n/a	n/a	n/a	n/a	n/a	n/a
H.S. Diplomas (#)	n/a	n/a	n/a	n/a	n/a	n/a

Carle Place Union Free SD
168 Cherry Ln • Carle Place, NY 11514-1788
(516) 622-6442
Grade Span: KG-12; **Agency Type:** 1
Schools: 3
    2 Primary; 0 Middle; 1 High; 0 Other Level
    3 Regular; 0 Special Education; 0 Vocational; 0 Alternative
    0 Magnet; 0 Charter; 2 Title I Eligible; 0 School-wide Title I
Students: 1,500   (50.0% male; 50.0% female)
    Individual Education Program: n/a;
    English Language Learner: n/a; Migrant: n/a
    Eligible for Free Lunch Program: n/a
    Eligible for Reduced-Price Lunch Program: n/a
Teachers: 144.0 (10.4 to 1)
Librarians/Media Specialists: 3.0 (500.0 to 1)
Guidance Counselors: 5.0 (300.0 to 1)
Current Spending: ($ per student per year):
    Total: $18,577; Instruction: $11,551; Support Services: $6,809
Enrollment, Drop-out Rates and Diploma Recipients by Race/Ethnicity

Category	Total	White	Black	Asian	AIAN	Hisp.
Enrollment (%)	100.0	83.2	1.1	6.4	0.1	9.2
Drop-out Rate (%)	1.0	1.0	0.0	0.0	n/a	1.9
H.S. Diplomas (#)	103	89	0	8	0	6

East Meadow Union Free SD
718 The Plain Rd • Westbury, NY 11590
(516) 478-5776 • http://www.eastmeadow.k12.ny.us/
Grade Span: KG-12; **Agency Type:** 1
Schools: 9
    5 Primary; 2 Middle; 2 High; 0 Other Level
    9 Regular; 0 Special Education; 0 Vocational; 0 Alternative
    0 Magnet; 0 Charter; 6 Title I Eligible; 0 School-wide Title I
Students: 8,094   (50.0% male; 49.9% female)
    Individual Education Program: n/a;
    English Language Learner: n/a; Migrant: n/a
    Eligible for Free Lunch Program: n/a
    Eligible for Reduced-Price Lunch Program: n/a
Teachers: 609.9 (13.3 to 1)
Librarians/Media Specialists: 13.0 (622.6 to 1)
Guidance Counselors: 20.0 (404.7 to 1)
Current Spending: ($ per student per year):
    Total: $13,601; Instruction: $9,054; Support Services: $4,338

Enrollment, Drop-out Rates and Diploma Recipients by Race/Ethnicity

Category	Total	White	Black	Asian	AIAN	Hisp.
Enrollment (%)	100.0	74.9	2.3	12.7	0.0	10.1
Drop-out Rate (%)	0.6	0.4	1.8	0.0	n/a	3.0
H.S. Diplomas (#)	507	434	3	44	0	26

East Williston Union Free SD
11 Bacon Rd • Old Westbury, NY 11568-1599
(516) 333-3758 • http://www.ewsdonline.org/
Grade Span: KG-12; **Agency Type:** 1
Schools: 3
 1 Primary; 1 Middle; 1 High; 0 Other Level
 3 Regular; 0 Special Education; 0 Vocational; 0 Alternative
 0 Magnet; 0 Charter; 2 Title I Eligible; 0 School-wide Title I
Students: 1,812   (52.4% male; 47.5% female)
 Individual Education Program: n/a;
 English Language Learner: n/a; Migrant: n/a
 Eligible for Free Lunch Program: n/a
 Eligible for Reduced-Price Lunch Program: n/a
Teachers: 155.0 (11.7 to 1)
Librarians/Media Specialists: 3.0 (604.0 to 1)
Guidance Counselors: 7.0 (258.9 to 1)
Current Spending: ($ per student per year):
 Total: $18,841; Instruction: $12,285; Support Services: $6,374
Enrollment, Drop-out Rates and Diploma Recipients by Race/Ethnicity

Category	Total	White	Black	Asian	AIAN	Hisp.
Enrollment (%)	100.0	88.1	0.4	8.9	0.0	2.6
Drop-out Rate (%)	0.0	0.0	0.0	0.0	n/a	0.0
H.S. Diplomas (#)	127	107	1	15	0	4

Elmont Union Free SD
135 Elmont Rd • Elmont, NY 11003-1609
(516) 326-5500
Grade Span: PK-06; **Agency Type:** 2
Schools: 6
 6 Primary; 0 Middle; 0 High; 0 Other Level
 6 Regular; 0 Special Education; 0 Vocational; 0 Alternative
 0 Magnet; 0 Charter; 3 Title I Eligible; 0 School-wide Title I
Students: 4,248   (51.4% male; 48.5% female)
 Individual Education Program: n/a;
 English Language Learner: n/a; Migrant: n/a
 Eligible for Free Lunch Program: n/a
 Eligible for Reduced-Price Lunch Program: n/a
Teachers: 275.6 (15.4 to 1)
Librarians/Media Specialists: 6.8 (624.7 to 1)
Guidance Counselors: 1.0 (4,248.0 to 1)
Current Spending: ($ per student per year):
 Total: $10,217; Instruction: $6,681; Support Services: $3,241
Enrollment, Drop-out Rates and Diploma Recipients by Race/Ethnicity

Category	Total	White	Black	Asian	AIAN	Hisp.
Enrollment (%)	100.0	17.4	51.0	14.1	0.0	17.5
Drop-out Rate (%)	n/a	n/a	n/a	n/a	n/a	n/a
H.S. Diplomas (#)	n/a	n/a	n/a	n/a	n/a	n/a

Farmingdale Union Free SD
50 Van Cott Ave • Farmingdale, NY 11735-3742
(516) 752-6510 • http://farmingdaleschools.org/fps/
Grade Span: KG-12; **Agency Type:** 1
Schools: 6
 4 Primary; 1 Middle; 1 High; 0 Other Level
 6 Regular; 0 Special Education; 0 Vocational; 0 Alternative
 0 Magnet; 0 Charter; 2 Title I Eligible; 0 School-wide Title I
Students: 6,472   (53.0% male; 46.9% female)
 Individual Education Program: n/a;
 English Language Learner: n/a; Migrant: n/a
 Eligible for Free Lunch Program: n/a
 Eligible for Reduced-Price Lunch Program: n/a
Teachers: 532.4 (12.2 to 1)
Librarians/Media Specialists: 10.0 (647.2 to 1)
Guidance Counselors: 15.0 (431.5 to 1)
Current Spending: ($ per student per year):
 Total: $14,758; Instruction: $9,295; Support Services: $5,243
Enrollment, Drop-out Rates and Diploma Recipients by Race/Ethnicity

Category	Total	White	Black	Asian	AIAN	Hisp.
Enrollment (%)	100.0	79.2	6.8	3.5	0.3	10.2
Drop-out Rate (%)	0.3	0.2	0.7	1.1	0.0	0.6
H.S. Diplomas (#)	367	299	22	18	0	28

Floral Park-Bellerose Union Free SD
One Poppy Pl • Floral Park, NY 11001-2398
(516) 327-9300 • http://www.floralpark.k12.ny.us/
Grade Span: PK-06; **Agency Type:** 2
Schools: 2
 2 Primary; 0 Middle; 0 High; 0 Other Level
 2 Regular; 0 Special Education; 0 Vocational; 0 Alternative

 0 Magnet; 0 Charter; 0 Title I Eligible; 0 School-wide Title I
Students: 1,668   (51.6% male; 48.3% female)
 Individual Education Program: n/a;
 English Language Learner: n/a; Migrant: n/a
 Eligible for Free Lunch Program: n/a
 Eligible for Reduced-Price Lunch Program: n/a
Teachers: 104.9 (15.9 to 1)
Librarians/Media Specialists: 2.0 (834.0 to 1)
Guidance Counselors: 0.0 (n/a to 1)
Current Spending: ($ per student per year):
 Total: $10,233; Instruction: $7,622; Support Services: $2,508
Enrollment, Drop-out Rates and Diploma Recipients by Race/Ethnicity

Category	Total	White	Black	Asian	AIAN	Hisp.
Enrollment (%)	100.0	76.7	2.4	10.3	0.0	10.6
Drop-out Rate (%)	n/a	n/a	n/a	n/a	n/a	n/a
H.S. Diplomas (#)	n/a	n/a	n/a	n/a	n/a	n/a

Franklin Square Union Free SD
760 Washington St • Franklin Square, NY 11010-3898
(516) 505-6975
Grade Span: KG-06; **Agency Type:** 2
Schools: 3
 3 Primary; 0 Middle; 0 High; 0 Other Level
 3 Regular; 0 Special Education; 0 Vocational; 0 Alternative
 0 Magnet; 0 Charter; 3 Title I Eligible; 0 School-wide Title I
Students: 1,942   (50.3% male; 49.6% female)
 Individual Education Program: n/a;
 English Language Learner: n/a; Migrant: n/a
 Eligible for Free Lunch Program: n/a
 Eligible for Reduced-Price Lunch Program: n/a
Teachers: 133.5 (14.5 to 1)
Librarians/Media Specialists: 1.0 (1,942.0 to 1)
Guidance Counselors: 0.0 (n/a to 1)
Current Spending: ($ per student per year):
 Total: $11,128; Instruction: $7,579; Support Services: $3,323
Enrollment, Drop-out Rates and Diploma Recipients by Race/Ethnicity

Category	Total	White	Black	Asian	AIAN	Hisp.
Enrollment (%)	100.0	89.8	0.8	3.0	0.0	6.5
Drop-out Rate (%)	n/a	n/a	n/a	n/a	n/a	n/a
H.S. Diplomas (#)	n/a	n/a	n/a	n/a	n/a	n/a

Freeport Union Free SD
235 N Ocean Ave • Freeport, NY 11520-0801
(516) 867-5205 • http://www.freeportschools.org/
Grade Span: PK-12; **Agency Type:** 1
Schools: 8
 5 Primary; 2 Middle; 1 High; 0 Other Level
 8 Regular; 0 Special Education; 0 Vocational; 0 Alternative
 0 Magnet; 0 Charter; 6 Title I Eligible; 0 School-wide Title I
Students: 7,146   (50.8% male; 49.1% female)
 Individual Education Program: n/a;
 English Language Learner: n/a; Migrant: n/a
 Eligible for Free Lunch Program: n/a
 Eligible for Reduced-Price Lunch Program: n/a
Teachers: 527.1 (13.6 to 1)
Librarians/Media Specialists: 8.0 (893.3 to 1)
Guidance Counselors: 19.0 (376.1 to 1)
Current Spending: ($ per student per year):
 Total: $13,745; Instruction: $9,292; Support Services: $4,208
Enrollment, Drop-out Rates and Diploma Recipients by Race/Ethnicity

Category	Total	White	Black	Asian	AIAN	Hisp.
Enrollment (%)	100.0	11.3	40.1	1.3	0.1	47.2
Drop-out Rate (%)	6.4	3.8	6.2	0.0	n/a	7.9
H.S. Diplomas (#)	281	63	124	7	0	87

Garden City Union Free SD
56 Cathedral Ave • Garden City, NY 11530-0216
(516) 478-1010
Grade Span: KG-12; **Agency Type:** 1
Schools: 7
 5 Primary; 1 Middle; 1 High; 0 Other Level
 7 Regular; 0 Special Education; 0 Vocational; 0 Alternative
 0 Magnet; 0 Charter; 2 Title I Eligible; 0 School-wide Title I
Students: 4,150   (51.8% male; 48.1% female)
 Individual Education Program: n/a;
 English Language Learner: n/a; Migrant: n/a
 Eligible for Free Lunch Program: n/a
 Eligible for Reduced-Price Lunch Program: n/a
Teachers: 314.1 (13.2 to 1)
Librarians/Media Specialists: 4.0 (1,037.5 to 1)
Guidance Counselors: 9.0 (461.1 to 1)
Current Spending: ($ per student per year):
 Total: $14,642; Instruction: $9,669; Support Services: $4,832

Enrollment, Drop-out Rates and Diploma Recipients by Race/Ethnicity

Category	Total	White	Black	Asian	AIAN	Hisp.
Enrollment (%)	100.0	95.4	0.7	2.8	0.1	1.0
Drop-out Rate (%)	0.2	0.2	0.0	0.0	0.0	0.0
H.S. Diplomas (#)	214	197	2	9	3	3

Glen Cove City SD

Dosoris Ln • Glen Cove, NY 11542-1237
(516) 759-7217 • http://www.glencove.k12.ny.us/
Grade Span: PK-12; **Agency Type:** 1
Schools: 6
    4 Primary; 1 Middle; 1 High; 0 Other Level
    6 Regular; 0 Special Education; 0 Vocational; 0 Alternative
    0 Magnet; 0 Charter; 4 Title I Eligible; 0 School-wide Title I
Students: 3,188 (52.4% male; 47.5% female)
    Individual Education Program: n/a;
    English Language Learner: n/a; Migrant: n/a
    Eligible for Free Lunch Program: n/a
    Eligible for Reduced-Price Lunch Program: n/a
Teachers: 254.9 (12.5 to 1)
Librarians/Media Specialists: 4.0 (797.0 to 1)
Guidance Counselors: 10.0 (318.8 to 1)
Current Spending: ($ per student per year):
    Total: $15,125; Instruction: $9,482; Support Services: $5,346

Enrollment, Drop-out Rates and Diploma Recipients by Race/Ethnicity

Category	Total	White	Black	Asian	AIAN	Hisp.
Enrollment (%)	100.0	48.6	12.8	4.1	0.1	34.4
Drop-out Rate (%)	4.6	2.9	6.3	0.0	n/a	7.8
H.S. Diplomas (#)	192	110	20	13	0	49

Great Neck Union Free SD

345 Lakeville Rd • Great Neck, NY 11020-1606
(516) 773-1405 • http://www.greatneck.k12.ny.us/
Grade Span: PK-12; **Agency Type:** 1
Schools: 10
    5 Primary; 2 Middle; 3 High; 0 Other Level
    10 Regular; 0 Special Education; 0 Vocational; 0 Alternative
    0 Magnet; 0 Charter; 4 Title I Eligible; 0 School-wide Title I
Students: 6,113 (52.2% male; 47.7% female)
    Individual Education Program: n/a;
    English Language Learner: n/a; Migrant: n/a
    Eligible for Free Lunch Program: n/a
    Eligible for Reduced-Price Lunch Program: n/a
Teachers: 568.7 (10.7 to 1)
Librarians/Media Specialists: 12.0 (509.4 to 1)
Guidance Counselors: 17.0 (359.6 to 1)
Current Spending: ($ per student per year):
    Total: $19,799; Instruction: $12,956; Support Services: $6,534

Enrollment, Drop-out Rates and Diploma Recipients by Race/Ethnicity

Category	Total	White	Black	Asian	AIAN	Hisp.
Enrollment (%)	100.0	71.8	2.7	17.5	0.0	7.9
Drop-out Rate (%)	0.6	0.2	0.0	0.9	n/a	4.0
H.S. Diplomas (#)	516	402	10	75	0	29

Hempstead Union Free SD

185 Peninsula Blvd • Hempstead, NY 11550
(516) 292-7001 • http://www.hempsteadschools.org/
Grade Span: PK-12; **Agency Type:** 1
Schools: 9
    7 Primary; 1 Middle; 1 High; 0 Other Level
    9 Regular; 0 Special Education; 0 Vocational; 0 Alternative
    0 Magnet; 0 Charter; 9 Title I Eligible; 9 School-wide Title I
Students: 7,128 (51.2% male; 48.7% female)
    Individual Education Program: n/a;
    English Language Learner: n/a; Migrant: n/a
    Eligible for Free Lunch Program: n/a
    Eligible for Reduced-Price Lunch Program: n/a
Teachers: 454.5 (15.7 to 1)
Librarians/Media Specialists: 10.3 (692.0 to 1)
Guidance Counselors: 9.0 (792.0 to 1)
Current Spending: ($ per student per year):
    Total: $15,829; Instruction: $10,473; Support Services: $4,999

Enrollment, Drop-out Rates and Diploma Recipients by Race/Ethnicity

Category	Total	White	Black	Asian	AIAN	Hisp.
Enrollment (%)	100.0	0.4	53.9	0.5	0.2	45.1
Drop-out Rate (%)	9.6	8.3	10.9	0.0	0.0	7.1
H.S. Diplomas (#)	154	0	105	4	0	45

Herricks Union Free SD

999 B Herricks Rd • New Hyde Park, NY 11040-1355
(516) 248-3105 • http://www.herricks.org/
Grade Span: KG-12; **Agency Type:** 1
Schools: 5
    3 Primary; 1 Middle; 1 High; 0 Other Level
    5 Regular; 0 Special Education; 0 Vocational; 0 Alternative

    0 Magnet; 0 Charter; 3 Title I Eligible; 0 School-wide Title I
Students: 3,939 (51.4% male; 48.5% female)
    Individual Education Program: n/a;
    English Language Learner: n/a; Migrant: n/a
    Eligible for Free Lunch Program: n/a
    Eligible for Reduced-Price Lunch Program: n/a
Teachers: 351.3 (11.2 to 1)
Librarians/Media Specialists: 6.0 (656.5 to 1)
Guidance Counselors: 7.6 (518.3 to 1)
Current Spending: ($ per student per year):
    Total: $15,505; Instruction: $10,114; Support Services: $5,177

Enrollment, Drop-out Rates and Diploma Recipients by Race/Ethnicity

Category	Total	White	Black	Asian	AIAN	Hisp.
Enrollment (%)	100.0	55.8	0.4	39.2	0.1	4.5
Drop-out Rate (%)	0.2	0.3	0.0	0.2	0.0	0.0
H.S. Diplomas (#)	276	154	0	114	0	8

Hewlett-Woodmere Union Free SD

1 Johnson Pl • Woodmere, NY 11598-1312
(516) 374-8100
Grade Span: PK-12; **Agency Type:** 1
Schools: 5
    3 Primary; 1 Middle; 1 High; 0 Other Level
    5 Regular; 0 Special Education; 0 Vocational; 0 Alternative
    0 Magnet; 0 Charter; 3 Title I Eligible; 0 School-wide Title I
Students: 3,327 (51.3% male; 48.6% female)
    Individual Education Program: n/a;
    English Language Learner: n/a; Migrant: n/a
    Eligible for Free Lunch Program: n/a
    Eligible for Reduced-Price Lunch Program: n/a
Teachers: 280.9 (11.8 to 1)
Librarians/Media Specialists: 4.8 (693.1 to 1)
Guidance Counselors: 9.0 (369.7 to 1)
Current Spending: ($ per student per year):
    Total: $17,527; Instruction: $10,898; Support Services: $6,426

Enrollment, Drop-out Rates and Diploma Recipients by Race/Ethnicity

Category	Total	White	Black	Asian	AIAN	Hisp.
Enrollment (%)	100.0	84.3	1.8	7.7	0.0	6.2
Drop-out Rate (%)	1.0	0.6	0.0	2.4	n/a	4.8
H.S. Diplomas (#)	267	228	5	22	0	12

Hicksville Union Free SD

200 Division Ave-Adm • Hicksville, NY 11801-4800
(516) 733-6600 • http://www.hicksvillepublicschools.org/
Grade Span: PK-12; **Agency Type:** 1
Schools: 9
    7 Primary; 1 Middle; 1 High; 0 Other Level
    9 Regular; 0 Special Education; 0 Vocational; 0 Alternative
    0 Magnet; 0 Charter; 7 Title I Eligible; 0 School-wide Title I
Students: 5,266 (51.3% male; 48.6% female)
    Individual Education Program: n/a;
    English Language Learner: n/a; Migrant: n/a
    Eligible for Free Lunch Program: n/a
    Eligible for Reduced-Price Lunch Program: n/a
Teachers: 388.2 (13.6 to 1)
Librarians/Media Specialists: 9.0 (585.1 to 1)
Guidance Counselors: 9.0 (585.1 to 1)
Current Spending: ($ per student per year):
    Total: $13,916; Instruction: $8,634; Support Services: $5,008

Enrollment, Drop-out Rates and Diploma Recipients by Race/Ethnicity

Category	Total	White	Black	Asian	AIAN	Hisp.
Enrollment (%)	100.0	64.6	2.3	17.5	0.1	15.6
Drop-out Rate (%)	3.1	2.0	0.0	0.8	n/a	11.9
H.S. Diplomas (#)	310	218	2	60	0	30

Island Trees Union Free SD

74 Farmedge Rd • Levittown, NY 11756-5205
(516) 520-2100
Grade Span: KG-12; **Agency Type:** 1
Schools: 4
    2 Primary; 1 Middle; 1 High; 0 Other Level
    4 Regular; 0 Special Education; 0 Vocational; 0 Alternative
    0 Magnet; 0 Charter; 2 Title I Eligible; 0 School-wide Title I
Students: 2,795 (51.7% male; 48.2% female)
    Individual Education Program: n/a;
    English Language Learner: n/a; Migrant: n/a
    Eligible for Free Lunch Program: n/a
    Eligible for Reduced-Price Lunch Program: n/a
Teachers: 216.3 (12.9 to 1)
Librarians/Media Specialists: 3.8 (735.5 to 1)
Guidance Counselors: 9.0 (310.6 to 1)
Current Spending: ($ per student per year):
    Total: $12,782; Instruction: $8,439; Support Services: $4,132

Enrollment, Drop-out Rates and Diploma Recipients by Race/Ethnicity

Category	Total	White	Black	Asian	AIAN	Hisp.
Enrollment (%)	100.0	87.2	0.4	3.8	0.0	8.6
Drop-out Rate (%)	1.5	1.4	0.0	0.0	n/a	3.1
H.S. Diplomas (#)	140	127	0	4	0	9

Jericho Union Free SD
99 Cedar Swamp Rd • Jericho, NY 11753-1202
(516) 681-4100 • http://www.bestschools.org/
Grade Span: KG-12; **Agency Type:** 1
Schools: 5
   3 Primary; 1 Middle; 1 High; 0 Other Level
   5 Regular; 0 Special Education; 0 Vocational; 0 Alternative
   0 Magnet; 0 Charter; 3 Title I Eligible; 0 School-wide Title I
Students: 3,210 (51.2% male; 48.7% female)
   Individual Education Program: n/a;
   English Language Learner: n/a; Migrant: n/a
   Eligible for Free Lunch Program: n/a
   Eligible for Reduced-Price Lunch Program: n/a
Teachers: 316.5 (10.1 to 1)
Librarians/Media Specialists: 6.0 (535.0 to 1)
Guidance Counselors: 9.0 (356.7 to 1)
Current Spending: ($ per student per year):
   Total: $19,771; Instruction: $12,864; Support Services: $6,625
Enrollment, Drop-out Rates and Diploma Recipients by Race/Ethnicity

Category	Total	White	Black	Asian	AIAN	Hisp.
Enrollment (%)	100.0	80.4	1.8	16.8	0.0	0.9
Drop-out Rate (%)	0.1	0.1	0.0	0.0	n/a	0.0
H.S. Diplomas (#)	191	161	2	26	0	2

Lawrence Union Free SD
195 Broadway • Lawrence, NY 11559-0477
(516) 295-7030 • http://www.lawrence.org/
Grade Span: PK-12; **Agency Type:** 1
Schools: 7
   5 Primary; 1 Middle; 1 High; 0 Other Level
   7 Regular; 0 Special Education; 0 Vocational; 0 Alternative
   0 Magnet; 0 Charter; 3 Title I Eligible; 0 School-wide Title I
Students: 3,692 (51.0% male; 48.9% female)
   Individual Education Program: n/a;
   English Language Learner: n/a; Migrant: n/a
   Eligible for Free Lunch Program: n/a
   Eligible for Reduced-Price Lunch Program: n/a
Teachers: 366.6 (10.1 to 1)
Librarians/Media Specialists: 7.0 (527.4 to 1)
Guidance Counselors: 11.0 (335.6 to 1)
Current Spending: ($ per student per year):
   Total: $20,216; Instruction: $12,734; Support Services: $7,223
Enrollment, Drop-out Rates and Diploma Recipients by Race/Ethnicity

Category	Total	White	Black	Asian	AIAN	Hisp.
Enrollment (%)	100.0	52.9	16.1	5.4	0.1	25.5
Drop-out Rate (%)	0.8	0.9	0.0	0.0	0.0	1.3
H.S. Diplomas (#)	241	153	34	9	0	45

Levittown Union Free SD
150 Abbey Ln • Levittown, NY 11756-4042
(516) 520-8300 • http://www.lawrence.org/
Grade Span: KG-12; **Agency Type:** 1
Schools: 11
   6 Primary; 2 Middle; 2 High; 1 Other Level
   10 Regular; 1 Special Education; 0 Vocational; 0 Alternative
   0 Magnet; 0 Charter; 6 Title I Eligible; 0 School-wide Title I
Students: 8,027 (51.0% male; 48.9% female)
   Individual Education Program: n/a;
   English Language Learner: n/a; Migrant: n/a
   Eligible for Free Lunch Program: n/a
   Eligible for Reduced-Price Lunch Program: n/a
Teachers: 617.1 (13.0 to 1)
Librarians/Media Specialists: 10.8 (743.2 to 1)
Guidance Counselors: 17.0 (472.2 to 1)
Current Spending: ($ per student per year):
   Total: $14,364; Instruction: $9,908; Support Services: $4,249
Enrollment, Drop-out Rates and Diploma Recipients by Race/Ethnicity

Category	Total	White	Black	Asian	AIAN	Hisp.
Enrollment (%)	100.0	88.5	0.9	4.0	0.0	6.6
Drop-out Rate (%)	0.1	0.1	0.0	0.0	n/a	0.0
H.S. Diplomas (#)	455	416	2	19	1	17

Locust Valley Central SD
Horse Hollow Rd • Locust Valley, NY 11560-1118
(516) 674-6310 • http://www.lvcsd.k12.ny.us/
Grade Span: KG-12; **Agency Type:** 1
Schools: 4
   2 Primary; 1 Middle; 1 High; 0 Other Level
   4 Regular; 0 Special Education; 0 Vocational; 0 Alternative

   0 Magnet; 0 Charter; 1 Title I Eligible; 0 School-wide Title I
Students: 2,275 (49.1% male; 50.8% female)
   Individual Education Program: n/a;
   English Language Learner: n/a; Migrant: n/a
   Eligible for Free Lunch Program: n/a
   Eligible for Reduced-Price Lunch Program: n/a
Teachers: 201.4 (11.3 to 1)
Librarians/Media Specialists: 6.0 (379.2 to 1)
Guidance Counselors: 5.5 (413.6 to 1)
Current Spending: ($ per student per year):
   Total: $19,455; Instruction: $11,377; Support Services: $7,793
Enrollment, Drop-out Rates and Diploma Recipients by Race/Ethnicity

Category	Total	White	Black	Asian	AIAN	Hisp.
Enrollment (%)	100.0	88.0	1.8	2.5	0.0	7.7
Drop-out Rate (%)	0.7	0.6	0.0	0.0	n/a	2.6
H.S. Diplomas (#)	131	120	0	2	0	9

Long Beach City SD
235 Lido Blvd • Long Beach, NY 11561-5093
(516) 897-2104 • http://www.lbeach.org/
Grade Span: PK-12; **Agency Type:** 1
Schools: 7
   5 Primary; 1 Middle; 1 High; 0 Other Level
   7 Regular; 0 Special Education; 0 Vocational; 0 Alternative
   0 Magnet; 0 Charter; 4 Title I Eligible; 0 School-wide Title I
Students: 4,458 (51.3% male; 48.6% female)
   Individual Education Program: n/a;
   English Language Learner: n/a; Migrant: n/a
   Eligible for Free Lunch Program: n/a
   Eligible for Reduced-Price Lunch Program: n/a
Teachers: 349.0 (12.8 to 1)
Librarians/Media Specialists: 5.8 (768.6 to 1)
Guidance Counselors: 14.0 (318.4 to 1)
Current Spending: ($ per student per year):
   Total: $17,088; Instruction: $11,227; Support Services: $5,588
Enrollment, Drop-out Rates and Diploma Recipients by Race/Ethnicity

Category	Total	White	Black	Asian	AIAN	Hisp.
Enrollment (%)	100.0	63.6	11.8	4.3	0.0	20.3
Drop-out Rate (%)	2.3	2.0	4.0	0.0	n/a	2.3
H.S. Diplomas (#)	234	169	25	8	0	32

Lynbrook Union Free SD
111 Atlantic Ave • Lynbrook, NY 11563-3437
(516) 887-0253
Grade Span: KG-12; **Agency Type:** 1
Schools: 7
   4 Primary; 2 Middle; 1 High; 0 Other Level
   7 Regular; 0 Special Education; 0 Vocational; 0 Alternative
   0 Magnet; 0 Charter; 3 Title I Eligible; 0 School-wide Title I
Students: 3,141 (51.3% male; 48.6% female)
   Individual Education Program: n/a;
   English Language Learner: n/a; Migrant: n/a
   Eligible for Free Lunch Program: n/a
   Eligible for Reduced-Price Lunch Program: n/a
Teachers: 255.9 (12.3 to 1)
Librarians/Media Specialists: 6.0 (523.5 to 1)
Guidance Counselors: 7.0 (448.7 to 1)
Current Spending: ($ per student per year):
   Total: $13,935; Instruction: $9,033; Support Services: $4,814
Enrollment, Drop-out Rates and Diploma Recipients by Race/Ethnicity

Category	Total	White	Black	Asian	AIAN	Hisp.
Enrollment (%)	100.0	87.8	1.1	3.2	0.1	7.7
Drop-out Rate (%)	1.0	1.0	16.7	0.0	n/a	0.0
H.S. Diplomas (#)	188	161	0	11	1	15

Malverne Union Free SD
301 Wicks Ln • Malverne, NY 11565-2244
(516) 887-6405 • http://www.malverne.k12.ny.us/
Grade Span: KG-12; **Agency Type:** 1
Schools: 4
   2 Primary; 1 Middle; 1 High; 0 Other Level
   4 Regular; 0 Special Education; 0 Vocational; 0 Alternative
   0 Magnet; 0 Charter; 3 Title I Eligible; 0 School-wide Title I
Students: 1,826 (52.0% male; 47.9% female)
   Individual Education Program: n/a;
   English Language Learner: n/a; Migrant: n/a
   Eligible for Free Lunch Program: n/a
   Eligible for Reduced-Price Lunch Program: n/a
Teachers: 160.3 (11.4 to 1)
Librarians/Media Specialists: 4.0 (456.5 to 1)
Guidance Counselors: 4.0 (456.5 to 1)
Current Spending: ($ per student per year):
   Total: $16,643; Instruction: $10,605; Support Services: $5,761

Enrollment, Drop-out Rates and Diploma Recipients by Race/Ethnicity

Category	Total	White	Black	Asian	AIAN	Hisp.
Enrollment (%)	100.0	24.3	62.5	2.6	0.3	10.4
Drop-out Rate (%)	0.2	0.0	0.3	0.0	0.0	0.0
H.S. Diplomas (#)	107	28	61	4	1	13

Manhasset Union Free SD
200 Memorial Pl • Manhasset, NY 11030-2300
(516) 627-4400
Grade Span: KG-12; Agency Type: 1
Schools: 4
  2 Primary; 1 Middle; 1 High; 0 Other Level
  4 Regular; 0 Special Education; 0 Vocational; 0 Alternative
  0 Magnet; 0 Charter; 3 Title I Eligible; 0 School-wide Title I
Students: 2,700 (51.3% male; 48.6% female)
  Individual Education Program: n/a;
  English Language Learner: n/a; Migrant: n/a
  Eligible for Free Lunch Program: n/a
  Eligible for Reduced-Price Lunch Program: n/a
Teachers: 239.7 (11.3 to 1)
Librarians/Media Specialists: 4.0 (675.0 to 1)
Guidance Counselors: 7.0 (385.7 to 1)
Current Spending: ($ per student per year):
  Total: $20,639; Instruction: $13,007; Support Services: $7,447
Enrollment, Drop-out Rates and Diploma Recipients by Race/Ethnicity

Category	Total	White	Black	Asian	AIAN	Hisp.
Enrollment (%)	100.0	80.8	5.1	11.1	0.0	3.0
Drop-out Rate (%)	1.1	1.4	0.0	0.0	n/a	0.0
H.S. Diplomas (#)	170	131	8	25	0	6

Massapequa Union Free SD
4925 Merrick Rd • Massapequa, NY 11758-6298
(516) 797-6160 • http://www.msd.k12.ny.us/
Grade Span: KG-12; Agency Type: 1
Schools: 9
  6 Primary; 1 Middle; 1 High; 1 Other Level
  9 Regular; 0 Special Education; 0 Vocational; 0 Alternative
  0 Magnet; 0 Charter; 5 Title I Eligible; 0 School-wide Title I
Students: 8,248 (50.8% male; 49.1% female)
  Individual Education Program: n/a;
  English Language Learner: n/a; Migrant: n/a
  Eligible for Free Lunch Program: n/a
  Eligible for Reduced-Price Lunch Program: n/a
Teachers: 611.9 (13.5 to 1)
Librarians/Media Specialists: 15.0 (549.9 to 1)
Guidance Counselors: 15.0 (549.9 to 1)
Current Spending: ($ per student per year):
  Total: $12,913; Instruction: $8,705; Support Services: $4,033
Enrollment, Drop-out Rates and Diploma Recipients by Race/Ethnicity

Category	Total	White	Black	Asian	AIAN	Hisp.
Enrollment (%)	100.0	97.5	0.2	1.2	0.0	1.1
Drop-out Rate (%)	0.6	0.6	0.0	0.0	n/a	0.0
H.S. Diplomas (#)	496	496	0	0	0	0

Merrick Union Free SD
21 Babylon Rd • Merrick, NY 11566-4547
(516) 992-7240 • http://www.merrick.k12.ny.us/
Grade Span: KG-06; Agency Type: 2
Schools: 3
  3 Primary; 0 Middle; 0 High; 0 Other Level
  3 Regular; 0 Special Education; 0 Vocational; 0 Alternative
  0 Magnet; 0 Charter; 2 Title I Eligible; 0 School-wide Title I
Students: 1,970 (50.4% male; 49.5% female)
  Individual Education Program: n/a;
  English Language Learner: n/a; Migrant: n/a
  Eligible for Free Lunch Program: n/a
  Eligible for Reduced-Price Lunch Program: n/a
Teachers: 150.9 (13.1 to 1)
Librarians/Media Specialists: 3.0 (656.7 to 1)
Guidance Counselors: 0.0 (n/a to 1)
Current Spending: ($ per student per year):
  Total: $12,235; Instruction: $8,287; Support Services: $3,945
Enrollment, Drop-out Rates and Diploma Recipients by Race/Ethnicity

Category	Total	White	Black	Asian	AIAN	Hisp.
Enrollment (%)	100.0	94.6	0.6	1.9	0.0	2.9
Drop-out Rate (%)	n/a	n/a	n/a	n/a	n/a	n/a
H.S. Diplomas (#)	n/a	n/a	n/a	n/a	n/a	n/a

Mineola Union Free SD
200 Emory Rd • Mineola, NY 11501-2361
(516) 741-5036 • http://mineola.ny.schoolwebpages.com/education/
Grade Span: PK-12; Agency Type: 1
Schools: 7
  5 Primary; 1 Middle; 1 High; 0 Other Level
  7 Regular; 0 Special Education; 0 Vocational; 0 Alternative

---

  0 Magnet; 0 Charter; 3 Title I Eligible; 0 School-wide Title I
Students: 2,903 (51.1% male; 48.8% female)
  Individual Education Program: n/a;
  English Language Learner: n/a; Migrant: n/a
  Eligible for Free Lunch Program: n/a
  Eligible for Reduced-Price Lunch Program: n/a
Teachers: 268.1 (10.8 to 1)
Librarians/Media Specialists: 7.0 (414.7 to 1)
Guidance Counselors: 9.4 (308.8 to 1)
Current Spending: ($ per student per year):
  Total: $20,305; Instruction: $12,397; Support Services: $7,689
Enrollment, Drop-out Rates and Diploma Recipients by Race/Ethnicity

Category	Total	White	Black	Asian	AIAN	Hisp.
Enrollment (%)	100.0	72.8	2.3	7.7	0.0	17.3
Drop-out Rate (%)	1.2	1.4	0.0	0.0	n/a	1.2
H.S. Diplomas (#)	201	158	6	17	0	20

New Hyde Park-Garden City Park Union Free SD
1950 Hillside Ave • New Hyde Park, NY 11040-2607
(516) 352-6257 • http://www.nhp-gcp.org/
Grade Span: PK-06; Agency Type: 2
Schools: 4
  4 Primary; 0 Middle; 0 High; 0 Other Level
  4 Regular; 0 Special Education; 0 Vocational; 0 Alternative
  0 Magnet; 0 Charter; 2 Title I Eligible; 0 School-wide Title I
Students: 1,823 (51.8% male; 48.1% female)
  Individual Education Program: n/a;
  English Language Learner: n/a; Migrant: n/a
  Eligible for Free Lunch Program: n/a
  Eligible for Reduced-Price Lunch Program: n/a
Teachers: 123.0 (14.8 to 1)
Librarians/Media Specialists: 3.4 (536.2 to 1)
Guidance Counselors: 0.0 (n/a to 1)
Current Spending: ($ per student per year):
  Total: $10,242; Instruction: $6,739; Support Services: $3,491
Enrollment, Drop-out Rates and Diploma Recipients by Race/Ethnicity

Category	Total	White	Black	Asian	AIAN	Hisp.
Enrollment (%)	100.0	55.3	0.4	33.9	0.0	10.4
Drop-out Rate (%)	n/a	n/a	n/a	n/a	n/a	n/a
H.S. Diplomas (#)	n/a	n/a	n/a	n/a	n/a	n/a

North Bellmore Union Free SD
2616 Martin Ave • Bellmore, NY 11710-3199
(516) 992-3000
Grade Span: KG-06; Agency Type: 2
Schools: 6
  6 Primary; 0 Middle; 0 High; 0 Other Level
  6 Regular; 0 Special Education; 0 Vocational; 0 Alternative
  0 Magnet; 0 Charter; 3 Title I Eligible; 0 School-wide Title I
Students: 2,528 (52.2% male; 47.7% female)
  Individual Education Program: n/a;
  English Language Learner: n/a; Migrant: n/a
  Eligible for Free Lunch Program: n/a
  Eligible for Reduced-Price Lunch Program: n/a
Teachers: 181.5 (13.9 to 1)
Librarians/Media Specialists: 5.0 (505.6 to 1)
Guidance Counselors: 0.0 (n/a to 1)
Current Spending: ($ per student per year):
  Total: $11,723; Instruction: $7,707; Support Services: $3,788
Enrollment, Drop-out Rates and Diploma Recipients by Race/Ethnicity

Category	Total	White	Black	Asian	AIAN	Hisp.
Enrollment (%)	100.0	90.4	1.9	4.2	0.1	3.4
Drop-out Rate (%)	n/a	n/a	n/a	n/a	n/a	n/a
H.S. Diplomas (#)	n/a	n/a	n/a	n/a	n/a	n/a

North Shore Central SD
112 Franklin Ave • Sea Cliff, NY 11579-1706
(516) 705-0350 • http://www.northshore.k12.ny.us/
Grade Span: KG-12; Agency Type: 1
Schools: 5
  3 Primary; 1 Middle; 1 High; 0 Other Level
  5 Regular; 0 Special Education; 0 Vocational; 0 Alternative
  0 Magnet; 0 Charter; 1 Title I Eligible; 0 School-wide Title I
Students: 2,652 (49.5% male; 50.4% female)
  Individual Education Program: n/a;
  English Language Learner: n/a; Migrant: n/a
  Eligible for Free Lunch Program: n/a
  Eligible for Reduced-Price Lunch Program: n/a
Teachers: 238.2 (11.1 to 1)
Librarians/Media Specialists: 6.0 (442.0 to 1)
Guidance Counselors: 6.5 (408.0 to 1)
Current Spending: ($ per student per year):
  Total: $19,392; Instruction: $13,203; Support Services: $5,914

Enrollment, Drop-out Rates and Diploma Recipients by Race/Ethnicity

Category	Total	White	Black	Asian	AIAN	Hisp.
Enrollment (%)	100.0	90.3	0.9	5.0	0.0	3.7
Drop-out Rate (%)	0.6	0.5	0.0	4.3	0.0	0.0
H.S. Diplomas (#)	132	116	1	7	0	8

Oceanside Union Free SD
145 Merle Ave • Oceanside, NY 11572-2206
(516) 678-1215 • http://www.oceanside.k12.ny.us/
Grade Span: KG-12; **Agency Type:** 1
Schools: 9
  7 Primary; 1 Middle; 1 High; 0 Other Level
  9 Regular; 0 Special Education; 0 Vocational; 0 Alternative
  0 Magnet; 0 Charter; 3 Title I Eligible; 0 School-wide Title I
Students: 6,369 (50.6% male; 49.3% female)
  Individual Education Program: n/a;
  English Language Learner: n/a; Migrant: n/a
  Eligible for Free Lunch Program: n/a
  Eligible for Reduced-Price Lunch Program: n/a
Teachers: 471.2 (13.5 to 1)
Librarians/Media Specialists: 8.4 (758.2 to 1)
Guidance Counselors: 14.9 (427.4 to 1)
Current Spending: ($ per student per year):
  Total: $13,337; Instruction: $9,252; Support Services: $3,941

Enrollment, Drop-out Rates and Diploma Recipients by Race/Ethnicity

Category	Total	White	Black	Asian	AIAN	Hisp.
Enrollment (%)	100.0	91.1	0.9	1.8	0.0	6.2
Drop-out Rate (%)	0.5	0.5	0.0	3.6	n/a	0.0
H.S. Diplomas (#)	380	351	1	6	0	22

Oyster Bay-East Norwich Central SD
1 Mccouns Ln • Oyster Bay, NY 11771-3105
(516) 624-6504 • http://oben.powertolearn.com/
Grade Span: PK-12; **Agency Type:** 1
Schools: 3
  2 Primary; 0 Middle; 1 High; 0 Other Level
  3 Regular; 0 Special Education; 0 Vocational; 0 Alternative
  0 Magnet; 0 Charter; 3 Title I Eligible; 0 School-wide Title I
Students: 1,569 (50.6% male; 49.3% female)
  Individual Education Program: n/a;
  English Language Learner: n/a; Migrant: n/a
  Eligible for Free Lunch Program: n/a
  Eligible for Reduced-Price Lunch Program: n/a
Teachers: 145.0 (10.8 to 1)
Librarians/Media Specialists: 3.3 (475.5 to 1)
Guidance Counselors: 4.0 (392.3 to 1)
Current Spending: ($ per student per year):
  Total: $21,067; Instruction: $12,625; Support Services: $8,216

Enrollment, Drop-out Rates and Diploma Recipients by Race/Ethnicity

Category	Total	White	Black	Asian	AIAN	Hisp.
Enrollment (%)	100.0	78.4	4.4	4.5	0.1	12.6
Drop-out Rate (%)	2.5	1.4	0.0	0.0	n/a	13.6
H.S. Diplomas (#)	108	88	4	4	0	12

Plainedge Union Free SD
241 Wyngate Dr • North Massapequa, NY 11758-0912
(516) 992-7455
Grade Span: PK-12; **Agency Type:** 1
Schools: 5
  3 Primary; 1 Middle; 1 High; 0 Other Level
  5 Regular; 0 Special Education; 0 Vocational; 0 Alternative
  0 Magnet; 0 Charter; 2 Title I Eligible; 0 School-wide Title I
Students: 3,606 (50.1% male; 49.8% female)
  Individual Education Program: n/a;
  English Language Learner: n/a; Migrant: n/a
  Eligible for Free Lunch Program: n/a
  Eligible for Reduced-Price Lunch Program: n/a
Teachers: 248.7 (14.5 to 1)
Librarians/Media Specialists: 5.0 (721.2 to 1)
Guidance Counselors: 8.0 (450.8 to 1)
Current Spending: ($ per student per year):
  Total: $12,505; Instruction: $8,064; Support Services: $4,243

Enrollment, Drop-out Rates and Diploma Recipients by Race/Ethnicity

Category	Total	White	Black	Asian	AIAN	Hisp.
Enrollment (%)	100.0	96.0	0.1	1.8	0.0	2.0
Drop-out Rate (%)	0.4	0.5	0.0	0.0	0.0	0.0
H.S. Diplomas (#)	203	188	2	6	0	7

Plainview-Old Bethpage Central SD
106 Washington Ave • Plainview, NY 11803-3612
(516) 937-6301 • http://www.pob.k12.ny.us/
Grade Span: KG-12; **Agency Type:** 1
Schools: 8
  5 Primary; 2 Middle; 1 High; 0 Other Level
  8 Regular; 0 Special Education; 0 Vocational; 0 Alternative

  0 Magnet; 0 Charter; 3 Title I Eligible; 0 School-wide Title I
Students: 4,970 (51.3% male; 48.6% female)
  Individual Education Program: n/a;
  English Language Learner: n/a; Migrant: n/a
  Eligible for Free Lunch Program: n/a
  Eligible for Reduced-Price Lunch Program: n/a
Teachers: 438.6 (11.3 to 1)
Librarians/Media Specialists: 9.0 (552.2 to 1)
Guidance Counselors: 15.0 (331.3 to 1)
Current Spending: ($ per student per year):
  Total: $16,487; Instruction: $10,369; Support Services: $5,924

Enrollment, Drop-out Rates and Diploma Recipients by Race/Ethnicity

Category	Total	White	Black	Asian	AIAN	Hisp.
Enrollment (%)	100.0	89.8	0.3	8.2	0.0	1.6
Drop-out Rate (%)	1.6	1.4	0.0	6.0	n/a	4.8
H.S. Diplomas (#)	341	308	0	26	0	7

Port Washington Union Free SD
100 Campus Dr • Port Washington, NY 11050-3719
(516) 767-5005 • http://www.portnet.k12.ny.us/
Grade Span: KG-12; **Agency Type:** 1
Schools: 6
  4 Primary; 1 Middle; 1 High; 0 Other Level
  6 Regular; 0 Special Education; 0 Vocational; 0 Alternative
  0 Magnet; 0 Charter; 5 Title I Eligible; 0 School-wide Title I
Students: 4,740 (50.8% male; 49.1% female)
  Individual Education Program: n/a;
  English Language Learner: n/a; Migrant: n/a
  Eligible for Free Lunch Program: n/a
  Eligible for Reduced-Price Lunch Program: n/a
Teachers: 417.2 (11.4 to 1)
Librarians/Media Specialists: 7.0 (677.1 to 1)
Guidance Counselors: 15.2 (311.8 to 1)
Current Spending: ($ per student per year):
  Total: $17,511; Instruction: $11,796; Support Services: $5,520

Enrollment, Drop-out Rates and Diploma Recipients by Race/Ethnicity

Category	Total	White	Black	Asian	AIAN	Hisp.
Enrollment (%)	100.0	70.5	2.4	13.1	0.0	14.1
Drop-out Rate (%)	1.3	0.6	0.0	1.1	n/a	4.3
H.S. Diplomas (#)	282	192	5	36	1	48

Rockville Centre Union Free SD
128 Shepherd St • Rockville Centre, NY 11570-2298
(516) 255-8920
Grade Span: KG-12; **Agency Type:** 1
Schools: 7
  5 Primary; 1 Middle; 1 High; 0 Other Level
  7 Regular; 0 Special Education; 0 Vocational; 0 Alternative
  0 Magnet; 0 Charter; 4 Title I Eligible; 0 School-wide Title I
Students: 3,606 (51.3% male; 48.6% female)
  Individual Education Program: n/a;
  English Language Learner: n/a; Migrant: n/a
  Eligible for Free Lunch Program: n/a
  Eligible for Reduced-Price Lunch Program: n/a
Teachers: 334.6 (10.8 to 1)
Librarians/Media Specialists: 2.0 (1,803.0 to 1)
Guidance Counselors: 8.6 (419.3 to 1)
Current Spending: ($ per student per year):
  Total: $16,093; Instruction: $10,785; Support Services: $5,185

Enrollment, Drop-out Rates and Diploma Recipients by Race/Ethnicity

Category	Total	White	Black	Asian	AIAN	Hisp.
Enrollment (%)	100.0	80.0	7.1	2.9	0.1	9.9
Drop-out Rate (%)	0.1	0.1	0.0	0.0	n/a	0.0
H.S. Diplomas (#)	258	212	20	8	0	18

Roosevelt Union Free SD
240 Denton Pl • Roosevelt, NY 11575-1539
(516) 867-8616 • http://roughridersedu.net/
Grade Span: PK-12; **Agency Type:** 1
Schools: 6
  5 Primary; 0 Middle; 1 High; 0 Other Level
  6 Regular; 0 Special Education; 0 Vocational; 0 Alternative
  0 Magnet; 0 Charter; 5 Title I Eligible; 5 School-wide Title I
Students: 2,882 (50.9% male; 49.0% female)
  Individual Education Program: n/a;
  English Language Learner: n/a; Migrant: n/a
  Eligible for Free Lunch Program: n/a
  Eligible for Reduced-Price Lunch Program: n/a
Teachers: 248.0 (11.6 to 1)
Librarians/Media Specialists: 3.0 (960.7 to 1)
Guidance Counselors: 5.0 (576.4 to 1)
Current Spending: ($ per student per year):
  Total: $16,421; Instruction: $11,372; Support Services: $4,619

Enrollment, Drop-out Rates and Diploma Recipients by Race/Ethnicity

Category	Total	White	Black	Asian	AIAN	Hisp.
Enrollment (%)	100.0	0.4	81.4	0.0	0.0	18.1
Drop-out Rate (%)	17.5	n/a	15.0	n/a	n/a	67.7
H.S. Diplomas (#)	86	0	80	0	0	6

Roslyn Union Free SD
300 Harbor Hill Rd • Roslyn, NY 11576-1531
(516) 625-6303
Grade Span: PK-12; Agency Type: 1
Schools: 5
    3 Primary; 1 Middle; 1 High; 0 Other Level
    5 Regular; 0 Special Education; 0 Vocational; 0 Alternative
    0 Magnet; 0 Charter; 4 Title I Eligible; 0 School-wide Title I
Students: 3,237 (52.3% male; 47.6% female)
    Individual Education Program: n/a;
    English Language Learner: n/a; Migrant: n/a
    Eligible for Free Lunch Program: n/a
    Eligible for Reduced-Price Lunch Program: n/a
Teachers: 263.7 (12.3 to 1)
Librarians/Media Specialists: 5.2 (622.5 to 1)
Guidance Counselors: 9.0 (359.7 to 1)
Current Spending: ($ per student per year):
    Total: $19,936; Instruction: $12,013; Support Services: $7,553
Enrollment, Drop-out Rates and Diploma Recipients by Race/Ethnicity

Category	Total	White	Black	Asian	AIAN	Hisp.
Enrollment (%)	100.0	82.8	4.8	7.8	0.1	4.6
Drop-out Rate (%)	0.1	0.2	0.0	0.0	n/a	0.0
H.S. Diplomas (#)	209	161	16	24	0	8

Seaford Union Free SD
1600 Washington Ave • Seaford, NY 11783-1998
(516) 592-4001 • http://seaford.k12.ny.us/
Grade Span: KG-12; Agency Type: 1
Schools: 4
    2 Primary; 1 Middle; 1 High; 0 Other Level
    4 Regular; 0 Special Education; 0 Vocational; 0 Alternative
    0 Magnet; 0 Charter; 2 Title I Eligible; 0 School-wide Title I
Students: 2,706 (51.4% male; 48.5% female)
    Individual Education Program: n/a;
    English Language Learner: n/a; Migrant: n/a
    Eligible for Free Lunch Program: n/a
    Eligible for Reduced-Price Lunch Program: n/a
Teachers: 204.2 (13.3 to 1)
Librarians/Media Specialists: 3.0 (902.0 to 1)
Guidance Counselors: 7.0 (386.6 to 1)
Current Spending: ($ per student per year):
    Total: $13,236; Instruction: $8,592; Support Services: $4,453
Enrollment, Drop-out Rates and Diploma Recipients by Race/Ethnicity

Category	Total	White	Black	Asian	AIAN	Hisp.
Enrollment (%)	100.0	93.3	0.6	2.5	0.0	3.5
Drop-out Rate (%)	0.6	0.4	0.0	0.0	n/a	9.1
H.S. Diplomas (#)	166	156	1	2	1	6

Sewanhaka Central High SD
77 Landau Ave • Floral Park, NY 11001-3603
(516) 488-9800
Grade Span: 07-12; Agency Type: 2
Schools: 5
    0 Primary; 0 Middle; 5 High; 0 Other Level
    5 Regular; 0 Special Education; 0 Vocational; 0 Alternative
    0 Magnet; 0 Charter; 2 Title I Eligible; 0 School-wide Title I
Students: 8,435 (50.9% male; 49.0% female)
    Individual Education Program: n/a;
    English Language Learner: n/a; Migrant: n/a
    Eligible for Free Lunch Program: n/a
    Eligible for Reduced-Price Lunch Program: n/a
Teachers: 520.4 (16.2 to 1)
Librarians/Media Specialists: 10.6 (795.8 to 1)
Guidance Counselors: 38.0 (222.0 to 1)
Current Spending: ($ per student per year):
    Total: $11,788; Instruction: $7,509; Support Services: $4,066
Enrollment, Drop-out Rates and Diploma Recipients by Race/Ethnicity

Category	Total	White	Black	Asian	AIAN	Hisp.
Enrollment (%)	100.0	49.7	24.9	12.8	0.0	12.6
Drop-out Rate (%)	1.0	1.0	0.6	1.5	0.0	1.6
H.S. Diplomas (#)	1,135	608	247	163	1	116

Syosset Central SD
Po Bx 9029-99 Pell Ln • Syosset, NY 11791-9029
(516) 364-5605 • http://www.syosset.k12.ny.us/
Grade Span: KG-12; Agency Type: 1
Schools: 10
    7 Primary; 2 Middle; 1 High; 0 Other Level
    10 Regular; 0 Special Education; 0 Vocational; 0 Alternative

    0 Magnet; 0 Charter; 3 Title I Eligible; 0 School-wide Title I
Students: 6,623 (51.6% male; 48.3% female)
    Individual Education Program: n/a;
    English Language Learner: n/a; Migrant: n/a
    Eligible for Free Lunch Program: n/a
    Eligible for Reduced-Price Lunch Program: n/a
Teachers: 604.6 (11.0 to 1)
Librarians/Media Specialists: 11.5 (575.9 to 1)
Guidance Counselors: 17.0 (389.6 to 1)
Current Spending: ($ per student per year):
    Total: $17,371; Instruction: $11,532; Support Services: $5,668
Enrollment, Drop-out Rates and Diploma Recipients by Race/Ethnicity

Category	Total	White	Black	Asian	AIAN	Hisp.
Enrollment (%)	100.0	79.8	0.4	18.4	0.0	1.5
Drop-out Rate (%)	0.2	0.2	0.0	0.0	n/a	0.0
H.S. Diplomas (#)	445	345	2	96	0	2

Uniondale Union Free SD
933 Goodrich St • Uniondale, NY 11553-2499
(516) 560-8824 • http://www.uniondale.k12.ny.us/
Grade Span: KG-12; Agency Type: 1
Schools: 8
    5 Primary; 2 Middle; 1 High; 0 Other Level
    8 Regular; 0 Special Education; 0 Vocational; 0 Alternative
    0 Magnet; 0 Charter; 7 Title I Eligible; 0 School-wide Title I
Students: 6,411 (50.7% male; 49.2% female)
    Individual Education Program: n/a;
    English Language Learner: n/a; Migrant: n/a
    Eligible for Free Lunch Program: n/a
    Eligible for Reduced-Price Lunch Program: n/a
Teachers: 537.3 (11.9 to 1)
Librarians/Media Specialists: 12.0 (534.3 to 1)
Guidance Counselors: 14.0 (457.9 to 1)
Current Spending: ($ per student per year):
    Total: $16,026; Instruction: $9,796; Support Services: $5,974
Enrollment, Drop-out Rates and Diploma Recipients by Race/Ethnicity

Category	Total	White	Black	Asian	AIAN	Hisp.
Enrollment (%)	100.0	1.3	67.9	1.2	0.1	29.4
Drop-out Rate (%)	1.4	2.9	1.2	0.0	n/a	2.1
H.S. Diplomas (#)	307	10	235	5	5	52

Valley Stream 13 Union Free SD
585 N Corona Ave • Valley Stream, NY 11580-2099
(516) 568-6100 • http://www.valleystream13.com/
Grade Span: PK-06; Agency Type: 2
Schools: 4
    4 Primary; 0 Middle; 0 High; 0 Other Level
    4 Regular; 0 Special Education; 0 Vocational; 0 Alternative
    0 Magnet; 0 Charter; 1 Title I Eligible; 0 School-wide Title I
Students: 2,103 (52.5% male; 47.4% female)
    Individual Education Program: n/a;
    English Language Learner: n/a; Migrant: n/a
    Eligible for Free Lunch Program: n/a
    Eligible for Reduced-Price Lunch Program: n/a
Teachers: 171.8 (12.2 to 1)
Librarians/Media Specialists: 4.0 (525.8 to 1)
Guidance Counselors: 0.0 (n/a to 1)
Current Spending: ($ per student per year):
    Total: $11,722; Instruction: $8,225; Support Services: $3,496
Enrollment, Drop-out Rates and Diploma Recipients by Race/Ethnicity

Category	Total	White	Black	Asian	AIAN	Hisp.
Enrollment (%)	100.0	60.1	15.1	10.9	0.0	13.8
Drop-out Rate (%)	n/a	n/a	n/a	n/a	n/a	n/a
H.S. Diplomas (#)	n/a	n/a	n/a	n/a	n/a	n/a

Valley Stream 30 Union Free SD
175 N Central Ave • Valley Stream, NY 11580-3801
(516) 285-9881
Grade Span: KG-06; Agency Type: 2
Schools: 3
    3 Primary; 0 Middle; 0 High; 0 Other Level
    3 Regular; 0 Special Education; 0 Vocational; 0 Alternative
    0 Magnet; 0 Charter; 2 Title I Eligible; 0 School-wide Title I
Students: 1,502 (49.7% male; 50.2% female)
    Individual Education Program: n/a;
    English Language Learner: n/a; Migrant: n/a
    Eligible for Free Lunch Program: n/a
    Eligible for Reduced-Price Lunch Program: n/a
Teachers: 117.9 (12.7 to 1)
Librarians/Media Specialists: 3.0 (500.7 to 1)
Guidance Counselors: 0.0 (n/a to 1)
Current Spending: ($ per student per year):
    Total: $12,068; Instruction: $8,230; Support Services: $3,837

Enrollment, Drop-out Rates and Diploma Recipients by Race/Ethnicity

Category	Total	White	Black	Asian	AIAN	Hisp.
Enrollment (%)	100.0	17.4	38.1	20.4	0.4	23.7
Drop-out Rate (%)	n/a	n/a	n/a	n/a	n/a	n/a
H.S. Diplomas (#)	n/a	n/a	n/a	n/a	n/a	n/a

Valley Stream Central High SD
One Kent Rd • Valley Stream, NY 11580-3398
(516) 872-5601 • http://www.valleystream30.com/
Grade Span: 07-12; **Agency Type:** 2
Schools: 4
  0 Primary; 1 Middle; 3 High; 0 Other Level
  4 Regular; 0 Special Education; 0 Vocational; 0 Alternative
  0 Magnet; 0 Charter; 1 Title I Eligible; 0 School-wide Title I
Students: 4,566   (51.5% male; 48.4% female)
  Individual Education Program: n/a;
  English Language Learner: n/a; Migrant: n/a
  Eligible for Free Lunch Program: n/a
  Eligible for Reduced-Price Lunch Program: n/a
Teachers: 343.7 (13.3 to 1)
Librarians/Media Specialists: 4.0 (1,141.5 to 1)
Guidance Counselors: 19.5 (234.2 to 1)
Current Spending: ($ per student per year):
  Total: $13,427; Instruction: $8,475; Support Services: $4,652
Enrollment, Drop-out Rates and Diploma Recipients by Race/Ethnicity

Category	Total	White	Black	Asian	AIAN	Hisp.
Enrollment (%)	100.0	55.5	16.3	11.9	0.1	16.3
Drop-out Rate (%)	2.1	1.7	1.5	2.2	0.0	4.5
H.S. Diplomas (#)	629	401	93	57	0	78

Wantagh Union Free SD
3301 Beltagh Ave • Wantagh, NY 11793-3395
(516) 679-6300 • http://www.wms.wantaghufsd.k12.ny.us/
Grade Span: KG-12; **Agency Type:** 1
Schools: 5
  3 Primary; 1 Middle; 1 High; 0 Other Level
  5 Regular; 0 Special Education; 0 Vocational; 0 Alternative
  0 Magnet; 0 Charter; 0 Title I Eligible; 0 School-wide Title I
Students: 3,578   (50.7% male; 49.2% female)
  Individual Education Program: n/a;
  English Language Learner: n/a; Migrant: n/a
  Eligible for Free Lunch Program: n/a
  Eligible for Reduced-Price Lunch Program: n/a
Teachers: 259.7 (13.8 to 1)
Librarians/Media Specialists: 6.0 (596.3 to 1)
Guidance Counselors: 8.0 (447.3 to 1)
Current Spending: ($ per student per year):
  Total: $12,203; Instruction: $8,037; Support Services: $3,995
Enrollment, Drop-out Rates and Diploma Recipients by Race/Ethnicity

Category	Total	White	Black	Asian	AIAN	Hisp.
Enrollment (%)	100.0	95.5	0.2	2.3	0.1	1.9
Drop-out Rate (%)	1.2	1.1	n/a	5.6	n/a	0.0
H.S. Diplomas (#)	191	183	0	7	0	1

West Hempstead Union Free SD
252 Chestnut St • West Hempstead, NY 11552-2455
(516) 390-3107 • http://www.westhempstead.k12.ny.us/
Grade Span: KG-12; **Agency Type:** 1
Schools: 5
  3 Primary; 1 Middle; 1 High; 0 Other Level
  5 Regular; 0 Special Education; 0 Vocational; 0 Alternative
  0 Magnet; 0 Charter; 3 Title I Eligible; 0 School-wide Title I
Students: 2,349   (50.8% male; 49.1% female)
  Individual Education Program: n/a;
  English Language Learner: n/a; Migrant: n/a
  Eligible for Free Lunch Program: n/a
  Eligible for Reduced-Price Lunch Program: n/a
Teachers: 180.8 (13.0 to 1)
Librarians/Media Specialists: 4.0 (587.3 to 1)
Guidance Counselors: 8.0 (293.6 to 1)
Current Spending: ($ per student per year):
  Total: $14,973; Instruction: $9,771; Support Services: $4,999
Enrollment, Drop-out Rates and Diploma Recipients by Race/Ethnicity

Category	Total	White	Black	Asian	AIAN	Hisp.
Enrollment (%)	100.0	62.1	14.8	3.6	0.0	19.5
Drop-out Rate (%)	4.0	2.7	12.1	0.0	n/a	6.2
H.S. Diplomas (#)	194	142	8	16	0	28

Westbury Union Free SD
2 Hitchcock Ln • Old Westbury, NY 11568-1624
(516) 876-5016
Grade Span: PK-12; **Agency Type:** 1
Schools: 6
  4 Primary; 1 Middle; 1 High; 0 Other Level
  6 Regular; 0 Special Education; 0 Vocational; 0 Alternative

  0 Magnet; 0 Charter; 6 Title I Eligible; 1 School-wide Title I
Students: 4,036   (49.1% male; 50.8% female)
  Individual Education Program: n/a;
  English Language Learner: n/a; Migrant: n/a
  Eligible for Free Lunch Program: n/a
  Eligible for Reduced-Price Lunch Program: n/a
Teachers: 295.0 (13.7 to 1)
Librarians/Media Specialists: 5.0 (807.2 to 1)
Guidance Counselors: 10.0 (403.6 to 1)
Current Spending: ($ per student per year):
  Total: $15,316; Instruction: $10,025; Support Services: $4,946
Enrollment, Drop-out Rates and Diploma Recipients by Race/Ethnicity

Category	Total	White	Black	Asian	AIAN	Hisp.
Enrollment (%)	100.0	1.7	46.3	1.7	0.0	50.3
Drop-out Rate (%)	6.6	0.0	4.3	0.0	n/a	11.2
H.S. Diplomas (#)	157	6	114	2	0	35

New York County

NYC Alternative HS District
52 Chambers St - Rm 3 • New York, NY 10007
(212) 374-5082
Grade Span: n/a; **Agency Type:** 1
Schools: 4
  0 Primary; 0 Middle; 1 High; 3 Other Level
  0 Regular; 0 Special Education; 0 Vocational; 4 Alternative
  0 Magnet; 0 Charter; 2 Title I Eligible; 0 School-wide Title I
Students: 1,828   (47.0% male; 52.9% female)
  Individual Education Program: n/a;
  English Language Learner: n/a; Migrant: n/a
  Eligible for Free Lunch Program: n/a
  Eligible for Reduced-Price Lunch Program: n/a
Teachers: n/a
Librarians/Media Specialists: n/a
Guidance Counselors: n/a
Current Spending: ($ per student per year):
  Total: n/a; Instruction: n/a; Support Services: n/a
Enrollment, Drop-out Rates and Diploma Recipients by Race/Ethnicity

Category	Total	White	Black	Asian	AIAN	Hisp.
Enrollment (%)	100.0	4.0	52.8	4.0	0.1	39.0
Drop-out Rate (%)	n/a	n/a	n/a	n/a	n/a	n/a
H.S. Diplomas (#)	n/a	n/a	n/a	n/a	n/a	n/a

Niagara County

Lewiston-Porter Central SD
4061 Creek Rd • Youngstown, NY 14174-9799
(716) 286-7266 • http://www.lewport.wnyric.org/
Grade Span: PK-12; **Agency Type:** 1
Schools: 4
  2 Primary; 1 Middle; 1 High; 0 Other Level
  4 Regular; 0 Special Education; 0 Vocational; 0 Alternative
  0 Magnet; 0 Charter; 4 Title I Eligible; 0 School-wide Title I
Students: 2,402   (51.5% male; 48.4% female)
  Individual Education Program: n/a;
  English Language Learner: n/a; Migrant: n/a
  Eligible for Free Lunch Program: n/a
  Eligible for Reduced-Price Lunch Program: n/a
Teachers: 182.8 (13.1 to 1)
Librarians/Media Specialists: 4.0 (600.5 to 1)
Guidance Counselors: 5.5 (436.7 to 1)
Current Spending: ($ per student per year):
  Total: $12,166; Instruction: $8,066; Support Services: $3,947
Enrollment, Drop-out Rates and Diploma Recipients by Race/Ethnicity

Category	Total	White	Black	Asian	AIAN	Hisp.
Enrollment (%)	100.0	97.2	0.9	0.8	0.7	0.4
Drop-out Rate (%)	3.9	3.8	50.0	0.0	0.0	0.0
H.S. Diplomas (#)	186	184	0	1	1	0

Lockport City SD
130 Beattie Ave • Lockport, NY 14094-5099
(716) 478-4835 • http://www.lockport.k12.ny.us/education/district/
Grade Span: PK-12; **Agency Type:** 1
Schools: 10
  7 Primary; 2 Middle; 1 High; 0 Other Level
  10 Regular; 0 Special Education; 0 Vocational; 0 Alternative
  0 Magnet; 0 Charter; 7 Title I Eligible; 0 School-wide Title I
Students: 5,703   (50.9% male; 49.0% female)
  Individual Education Program: n/a;
  English Language Learner: n/a; Migrant: n/a
  Eligible for Free Lunch Program: n/a
  Eligible for Reduced-Price Lunch Program: n/a
Teachers: 448.3 (12.7 to 1)
Librarians/Media Specialists: 10.0 (570.3 to 1)
Guidance Counselors: 12.4 (459.9 to 1)

Current Spending: ($ per student per year):
  Total: $10,164; Instruction: $7,217; Support Services: $2,717
Enrollment, Drop-out Rates and Diploma Recipients by Race/Ethnicity

Category	Total	White	Black	Asian	AIAN	Hisp.
Enrollment (%)	100.0	85.5	10.8	0.7	0.5	2.6
Drop-out Rate (%)	3.6	3.3	7.1	0.0	50.0	0.0
H.S. Diplomas (#)	302	280	16	1	1	4

Newfane Central SD
6273 Charlotteville Rd • Newfane, NY 14108-9709
(716) 778-6850 • http://www.newfane.wnyric.org/
Grade Span: PK-12; **Agency Type:** 1
Schools: 5
  2 Primary; 2 Middle; 1 High; 0 Other Level
  5 Regular; 0 Special Education; 0 Vocational; 0 Alternative
  0 Magnet; 0 Charter; 5 Title I Eligible; 0 School-wide Title I
Students: 2,174 (51.8% male; 48.1% female)
  Individual Education Program: n/a;
  English Language Learner: n/a; Migrant: n/a
  Eligible for Free Lunch Program: n/a
  Eligible for Reduced-Price Lunch Program: n/a
Teachers: 150.5 (14.4 to 1)
Librarians/Media Specialists: 2.0 (1,087.0 to 1)
Guidance Counselors: 5.5 (395.3 to 1)
Current Spending: ($ per student per year):
  Total: $10,225; Instruction: $6,625; Support Services: $3,358
Enrollment, Drop-out Rates and Diploma Recipients by Race/Ethnicity

Category	Total	White	Black	Asian	AIAN	Hisp.
Enrollment (%)	100.0	96.8	1.5	0.6	0.4	0.7
Drop-out Rate (%)	3.9	3.9	10.0	0.0	0.0	0.0
H.S. Diplomas (#)	156	152	1	1	1	1

Niagara Falls City SD
607 Walnut Ave • Niagara Falls, NY 14302-0399
(716) 286-4205 • http://www.nfschools.net/wsmgr.nsf
Grade Span: PK-12; **Agency Type:** 1
Schools: 13
  9 Primary; 3 Middle; 1 High; 0 Other Level
  13 Regular; 0 Special Education; 0 Vocational; 0 Alternative
  1 Magnet; 0 Charter; 13 Title I Eligible; 13 School-wide Title I
Students: 8,736 (51.0% male; 48.9% female)
  Individual Education Program: n/a;
  English Language Learner: n/a; Migrant: n/a
  Eligible for Free Lunch Program: n/a
  Eligible for Reduced-Price Lunch Program: n/a
Teachers: 562.9 (15.5 to 1)
Librarians/Media Specialists: 5.0 (1,747.2 to 1)
Guidance Counselors: 26.0 (336.0 to 1)
Current Spending: ($ per student per year):
  Total: $12,044; Instruction: $7,906; Support Services: $3,818
Enrollment, Drop-out Rates and Diploma Recipients by Race/Ethnicity

Category	Total	White	Black	Asian	AIAN	Hisp.
Enrollment (%)	100.0	57.6	35.6	1.2	3.4	2.1
Drop-out Rate (%)	9.5	7.8	14.3	0.0	8.2	14.9
H.S. Diplomas (#)	362	280	61	9	9	3

Niagara-Wheatfield Central SD
6700 Schultz St • Niagara Falls, NY 14304
(716) 215-3003 • http://www.nwcsd.wnyric.org/
Grade Span: PK-12; **Agency Type:** 1
Schools: 6
  4 Primary; 1 Middle; 1 High; 0 Other Level
  6 Regular; 0 Special Education; 0 Vocational; 0 Alternative
  0 Magnet; 0 Charter; 3 Title I Eligible; 0 School-wide Title I
Students: 4,060 (52.8% male; 47.1% female)
  Individual Education Program: n/a;
  English Language Learner: n/a; Migrant: n/a
  Eligible for Free Lunch Program: n/a
  Eligible for Reduced-Price Lunch Program: n/a
Teachers: 300.3 (13.5 to 1)
Librarians/Media Specialists: 6.4 (634.4 to 1)
Guidance Counselors: 9.0 (451.1 to 1)
Current Spending: ($ per student per year):
  Total: $11,607; Instruction: $7,579; Support Services: $3,797
Enrollment, Drop-out Rates and Diploma Recipients by Race/Ethnicity

Category	Total	White	Black	Asian	AIAN	Hisp.
Enrollment (%)	100.0	88.1	2.7	1.1	7.3	0.8
Drop-out Rate (%)	5.1	4.3	0.0	10.0	20.3	0.0
H.S. Diplomas (#)	272	252	8	0	11	1

North Tonawanda City SD
175 Humphrey St • North Tonawanda, NY 14120-4097
(716) 807-3500
Grade Span: PK-12; **Agency Type:** 1
Schools: 9

  6 Primary; 2 Middle; 1 High; 0 Other Level
  9 Regular; 0 Special Education; 0 Vocational; 0 Alternative
  0 Magnet; 0 Charter; 3 Title I Eligible; 0 School-wide Title I
Students: 4,643 (52.2% male; 47.7% female)
  Individual Education Program: n/a;
  English Language Learner: n/a; Migrant: n/a
  Eligible for Free Lunch Program: n/a
  Eligible for Reduced-Price Lunch Program: n/a
Teachers: 340.0 (13.7 to 1)
Librarians/Media Specialists: 6.0 (773.8 to 1)
Guidance Counselors: 9.0 (515.9 to 1)
Current Spending: ($ per student per year):
  Total: $10,105; Instruction: $6,912; Support Services: $2,991
Enrollment, Drop-out Rates and Diploma Recipients by Race/Ethnicity

Category	Total	White	Black	Asian	AIAN	Hisp.
Enrollment (%)	100.0	96.8	0.8	0.4	0.9	1.1
Drop-out Rate (%)	3.3	3.4	0.0	0.0	0.0	0.0
H.S. Diplomas (#)	335	333	0	0	2	0

Royalton-Hartland Central SD
54 State St • Middleport, NY 14105-1199
(716) 735-3031 • http://www.royhart.wnyric.org/
Grade Span: KG-12; **Agency Type:** 1
Schools: 3
  2 Primary; 0 Middle; 1 High; 0 Other Level
  3 Regular; 0 Special Education; 0 Vocational; 0 Alternative
  0 Magnet; 0 Charter; 1 Title I Eligible; 0 School-wide Title I
Students: 1,682 (50.8% male; 49.1% female)
  Individual Education Program: n/a;
  English Language Learner: n/a; Migrant: n/a
  Eligible for Free Lunch Program: n/a
  Eligible for Reduced-Price Lunch Program: n/a
Teachers: 133.6 (12.6 to 1)
Librarians/Media Specialists: 2.0 (841.0 to 1)
Guidance Counselors: 4.0 (420.5 to 1)
Current Spending: ($ per student per year):
  Total: $10,171; Instruction: $6,385; Support Services: $3,529
Enrollment, Drop-out Rates and Diploma Recipients by Race/Ethnicity

Category	Total	White	Black	Asian	AIAN	Hisp.
Enrollment (%)	100.0	98.4	1.0	0.1	0.2	0.4
Drop-out Rate (%)	9.6	9.5	0.0	0.0	0.0	n/a
H.S. Diplomas (#)	117	117	0	0	0	0

Starpoint Central SD
4363 Mapleton Rd • Lockport, NY 14094-9623
(716) 210-2352 • http://www.starpoint.wnyric.org/
Grade Span: KG-12; **Agency Type:** 1
Schools: 4
  2 Primary; 1 Middle; 1 High; 0 Other Level
  4 Regular; 0 Special Education; 0 Vocational; 0 Alternative
  0 Magnet; 0 Charter; 4 Title I Eligible; 0 School-wide Title I
Students: 2,848 (51.3% male; 48.6% female)
  Individual Education Program: n/a;
  English Language Learner: n/a; Migrant: n/a
  Eligible for Free Lunch Program: n/a
  Eligible for Reduced-Price Lunch Program: n/a
Teachers: 177.3 (16.1 to 1)
Librarians/Media Specialists: 3.0 (949.3 to 1)
Guidance Counselors: 6.0 (474.7 to 1)
Current Spending: ($ per student per year):
  Total: $8,966; Instruction: $6,009; Support Services: $2,776
Enrollment, Drop-out Rates and Diploma Recipients by Race/Ethnicity

Category	Total	White	Black	Asian	AIAN	Hisp.
Enrollment (%)	100.0	98.1	0.8	0.3	0.2	0.5
Drop-out Rate (%)	3.1	3.0	25.0	0.0	0.0	0.0
H.S. Diplomas (#)	154	152	1	0	0	1

Wilson Central SD
412 Lake St • Wilson, NY 14172-9799
(716) 751-9341 • http://www.wilson.wnyric.org/
Grade Span: PK-12; **Agency Type:** 1
Schools: 3
  2 Primary; 0 Middle; 0 High; 1 Other Level
  3 Regular; 0 Special Education; 0 Vocational; 0 Alternative
  0 Magnet; 0 Charter; 2 Title I Eligible; 2 School-wide Title I
Students: 1,504 (51.6% male; 48.3% female)
  Individual Education Program: n/a;
  English Language Learner: n/a; Migrant: n/a
  Eligible for Free Lunch Program: n/a
  Eligible for Reduced-Price Lunch Program: n/a
Teachers: 120.6 (12.5 to 1)
Librarians/Media Specialists: 1.0 (1,504.0 to 1)
Guidance Counselors: 5.5 (273.5 to 1)
Current Spending: ($ per student per year):
  Total: $11,645; Instruction: $7,093; Support Services: $4,233

Enrollment, Drop-out Rates and Diploma Recipients by Race/Ethnicity

Category	Total	White	Black	Asian	AIAN	Hisp.
Enrollment (%)	100.0	96.9	0.9	0.5	1.1	0.6
Drop-out Rate (%)	2.9	3.0	0.0	0.0	0.0	0.0
H.S. Diplomas (#)	114	112	0	0	1	1

Oneida County

Adirondack Central SD
110 Ford St • Boonville, NY 13309-1200
(315) 942-9200 • http://www.pikeco.com/compulink/adirondack/
Grade Span: KG-12; **Agency Type:** 1
Schools: 5
　3 Primary; 1 Middle; 1 High; 0 Other Level
　5 Regular; 0 Special Education; 0 Vocational; 0 Alternative
　0 Magnet; 0 Charter; 4 Title I Eligible; 1 School-wide Title I
Students: 1,548　(51.2% male; 48.7% female)
　Individual Education Program: n/a;
　English Language Learner: n/a; Migrant: n/a
　Eligible for Free Lunch Program: n/a
　Eligible for Reduced-Price Lunch Program: n/a
Teachers: 137.3 (11.3 to 1)
Librarians/Media Specialists: 1.0 (1,548.0 to 1)
Guidance Counselors: 3.0 (516.0 to 1)
Current Spending: ($ per student per year):
　Total: $11,020; Instruction: $7,338; Support Services: $3,354
Enrollment, Drop-out Rates and Diploma Recipients by Race/Ethnicity

Category	Total	White	Black	Asian	AIAN	Hisp.
Enrollment (%)	100.0	98.3	0.5	0.6	0.1	0.6
Drop-out Rate (%)	3.7	3.7	n/a	0.0	0.0	n/a
H.S. Diplomas (#)	111	109	0	1	1	0

Camden Central SD
51 Third St • Camden, NY 13316-1114
(315) 245-4075 • http://www.camdenschools.org/
Grade Span: KG-12; **Agency Type:** 2
Schools: 8
　4 Primary; 1 Middle; 1 High; 2 Other Level
　6 Regular; 0 Special Education; 0 Vocational; 2 Alternative
　0 Magnet; 0 Charter; 5 Title I Eligible; 5 School-wide Title I
Students: 2,845　(50.8% male; 49.1% female)
　Individual Education Program: n/a;
　English Language Learner: n/a; Migrant: n/a
　Eligible for Free Lunch Program: n/a
　Eligible for Reduced-Price Lunch Program: n/a
Teachers: 211.9 (13.4 to 1)
Librarians/Media Specialists: 5.0 (569.0 to 1)
Guidance Counselors: 7.0 (406.4 to 1)
Current Spending: ($ per student per year):
　Total: $9,802; Instruction: $6,507; Support Services: $2,966
Enrollment, Drop-out Rates and Diploma Recipients by Race/Ethnicity

Category	Total	White	Black	Asian	AIAN	Hisp.
Enrollment (%)	100.0	96.9	1.8	0.3	0.4	0.7
Drop-out Rate (%)	5.8	5.6	16.7	0.0	n/a	n/a
H.S. Diplomas (#)	159	158	1	0	0	0

Clinton Central SD
75 Chenango Ave • Clinton, NY 13323-1395
(315) 853-5574 • http://www.clintoncsd.org/
Grade Span: KG-12; **Agency Type:** 1
Schools: 3
　1 Primary; 1 Middle; 1 High; 0 Other Level
　3 Regular; 0 Special Education; 0 Vocational; 0 Alternative
　0 Magnet; 0 Charter; 1 Title I Eligible; 0 School-wide Title I
Students: 1,634　(51.8% male; 48.1% female)
　Individual Education Program: n/a;
　English Language Learner: n/a; Migrant: n/a
　Eligible for Free Lunch Program: n/a
　Eligible for Reduced-Price Lunch Program: n/a
Teachers: 125.3 (13.0 to 1)
Librarians/Media Specialists: 2.0 (817.0 to 1)
Guidance Counselors: 3.8 (430.0 to 1)
Current Spending: ($ per student per year):
　Total: $10,002; Instruction: $6,748; Support Services: $3,235
Enrollment, Drop-out Rates and Diploma Recipients by Race/Ethnicity

Category	Total	White	Black	Asian	AIAN	Hisp.
Enrollment (%)	100.0	95.5	1.3	1.3	0.0	1.9
Drop-out Rate (%)	1.6	1.7	0.0	0.0	n/a	0.0
H.S. Diplomas (#)	148	143	2	1	0	2

Holland Patent Central SD
9601 Main St • Holland Patent, NY 13354-4610
(315) 865-7221 • http://www.moric.org/hpknight/home.htm
Grade Span: KG-12; **Agency Type:** 1
Schools: 4

---

　2 Primary; 1 Middle; 1 High; 0 Other Level
　4 Regular; 0 Special Education; 0 Vocational; 0 Alternative
　0 Magnet; 0 Charter; 3 Title I Eligible; 0 School-wide Title I
Students: 1,853　(49.9% male; 50.0% female)
　Individual Education Program: n/a;
　English Language Learner: n/a; Migrant: n/a
　Eligible for Free Lunch Program: n/a
　Eligible for Reduced-Price Lunch Program: n/a
Teachers: 138.2 (13.4 to 1)
Librarians/Media Specialists: 3.0 (617.7 to 1)
Guidance Counselors: 5.0 (370.6 to 1)
Current Spending: ($ per student per year):
　Total: $10,451; Instruction: $6,713; Support Services: $3,482
Enrollment, Drop-out Rates and Diploma Recipients by Race/Ethnicity

Category	Total	White	Black	Asian	AIAN	Hisp.
Enrollment (%)	100.0	97.8	0.4	1.2	0.1	0.4
Drop-out Rate (%)	2.9	2.9	n/a	0.0	n/a	0.0
H.S. Diplomas (#)	129	126	0	1	0	2

New Hartford Central SD
33 Oxford Rd • New Hartford, NY 13413-2699
(315) 624-1218 • http://www.myschoolonline.com/
Grade Span: KG-12; **Agency Type:** 1
Schools: 5
　3 Primary; 1 Middle; 1 High; 0 Other Level
　5 Regular; 0 Special Education; 0 Vocational; 0 Alternative
　0 Magnet; 0 Charter; 3 Title I Eligible; 0 School-wide Title I
Students: 2,670　(51.9% male; 48.0% female)
　Individual Education Program: n/a;
　English Language Learner: n/a; Migrant: n/a
　Eligible for Free Lunch Program: n/a
　Eligible for Reduced-Price Lunch Program: n/a
Teachers: 206.9 (12.9 to 1)
Librarians/Media Specialists: 5.0 (534.0 to 1)
Guidance Counselors: 7.0 (381.4 to 1)
Current Spending: ($ per student per year):
　Total: $10,905; Instruction: $7,567; Support Services: $3,322
Enrollment, Drop-out Rates and Diploma Recipients by Race/Ethnicity

Category	Total	White	Black	Asian	AIAN	Hisp.
Enrollment (%)	100.0	91.9	2.0	4.8	0.3	0.9
Drop-out Rate (%)	1.6	1.7	0.0	0.0	n/a	0.0
H.S. Diplomas (#)	222	209	2	9	0	2

Rome City SD
112 E Thomas St • Rome, NY 13440-5298
(315) 338-6500 • http://www.romecsd.org/
Grade Span: PK-12; **Agency Type:** 1
Schools: 15
　9 Primary; 2 Middle; 1 High; 3 Other Level
　12 Regular; 0 Special Education; 0 Vocational; 3 Alternative
　0 Magnet; 0 Charter; 5 Title I Eligible; 5 School-wide Title I
Students: 6,199　(51.5% male; 48.4% female)
　Individual Education Program: n/a;
　English Language Learner: n/a; Migrant: n/a
　Eligible for Free Lunch Program: n/a
　Eligible for Reduced-Price Lunch Program: n/a
Teachers: 481.7 (12.9 to 1)
Librarians/Media Specialists: 11.5 (539.0 to 1)
Guidance Counselors: 19.6 (316.3 to 1)
Current Spending: ($ per student per year):
　Total: $11,233; Instruction: $7,429; Support Services: $3,524
Enrollment, Drop-out Rates and Diploma Recipients by Race/Ethnicity

Category	Total	White	Black	Asian	AIAN	Hisp.
Enrollment (%)	100.0	87.5	7.1	1.5	0.7	3.3
Drop-out Rate (%)	4.7	4.4	7.6	0.0	75.0	4.0
H.S. Diplomas (#)	276	254	13	2	0	7

Sherrill City SD
5275 State Rt 31 • Verona, NY 13478-0128
(315) 829-2520
Grade Span: PK-12; **Agency Type:** 1
Schools: 5
　3 Primary; 1 Middle; 1 High; 0 Other Level
　5 Regular; 0 Special Education; 0 Vocational; 0 Alternative
　0 Magnet; 0 Charter; 4 Title I Eligible; 0 School-wide Title I
Students: 2,425　(50.3% male; 49.6% female)
　Individual Education Program: n/a;
　English Language Learner: n/a; Migrant: n/a
　Eligible for Free Lunch Program: n/a
　Eligible for Reduced-Price Lunch Program: n/a
Teachers: 174.4 (13.9 to 1)
Librarians/Media Specialists: 5.0 (485.0 to 1)
Guidance Counselors: 4.0 (606.3 to 1)
Current Spending: ($ per student per year):
　Total: $9,656; Instruction: $6,344; Support Services: $3,006

Enrollment, Drop-out Rates and Diploma Recipients by Race/Ethnicity

Category	Total	White	Black	Asian	AIAN	Hisp.
Enrollment (%)	100.0	97.3	1.0	0.9	0.5	0.2
Drop-out Rate (%)	1.0	1.0	0.0	0.0	0.0	0.0
H.S. Diplomas (#)	175	173	0	1	0	1

Utica City SD
1115 Mohawk St • Utica, NY 13501-3709
(315) 792-2222 • http://www.uticaschools.org/
Grade Span: KG-12; **Agency Type:** 1
Schools: 13
    9 Primary; 2 Middle; 1 High; 1 Other Level
    12 Regular; 0 Special Education; 0 Vocational; 1 Alternative
    0 Magnet; 0 Charter; 12 Title I Eligible; 6 School-wide Title I
Students: 9,070 (51.0% male; 48.9% female)
    Individual Education Program: n/a;
    English Language Learner: n/a; Migrant: n/a
    Eligible for Free Lunch Program: n/a
    Eligible for Reduced-Price Lunch Program: n/a
Teachers: 604.8 (15.0 to 1)
Librarians/Media Specialists: 9.1 (996.7 to 1)
Guidance Counselors: 11.0 (824.5 to 1)
Current Spending: ($ per student per year):
    Total: $10,882; Instruction: $7,152; Support Services: $3,408
Enrollment, Drop-out Rates and Diploma Recipients by Race/Ethnicity

Category	Total	White	Black	Asian	AIAN	Hisp.
Enrollment (%)	100.0	56.0	26.7	5.3	0.2	11.8
Drop-out Rate (%)	4.6	3.5	7.0	4.9	0.0	8.2
H.S. Diplomas (#)	341	250	59	10	1	21

Whitesboro Central SD
67 Whtsbro St-Bx 304 • Yorkville, NY 13495-0304
(315) 266-3303 •
http://www.wboro.org/education/district/district.php?sectionid=1
Grade Span: KG-12; **Agency Type:** 1
Schools: 10
    4 Primary; 2 Middle; 1 High; 3 Other Level
    7 Regular; 0 Special Education; 0 Vocational; 3 Alternative
    0 Magnet; 0 Charter; 6 Title I Eligible; 0 School-wide Title I
Students: 3,863 (52.0% male; 47.9% female)
    Individual Education Program: n/a;
    English Language Learner: n/a; Migrant: n/a
    Eligible for Free Lunch Program: n/a
    Eligible for Reduced-Price Lunch Program: n/a
Teachers: 293.1 (13.2 to 1)
Librarians/Media Specialists: 5.6 (689.8 to 1)
Guidance Counselors: 7.0 (551.9 to 1)
Current Spending: ($ per student per year):
    Total: $9,582; Instruction: $6,297; Support Services: $3,076
Enrollment, Drop-out Rates and Diploma Recipients by Race/Ethnicity

Category	Total	White	Black	Asian	AIAN	Hisp.
Enrollment (%)	100.0	95.8	2.0	0.9	0.0	1.2
Drop-out Rate (%)	3.8	3.9	0.0	0.0	0.0	0.0
H.S. Diplomas (#)	257	250	2	3	2	0

Onondaga County

Baldwinsville Central SD
29 E Oneida St • Baldwinsville, NY 13027-2480
(315) 638-6043 • http://www.ocmboces.org/bville/
Grade Span: KG-12; **Agency Type:** 1
Schools: 8
    5 Primary; 1 Middle; 1 High; 1 Other Level
    8 Regular; 0 Special Education; 0 Vocational; 0 Alternative
    0 Magnet; 0 Charter; 4 Title I Eligible; 0 School-wide Title I
Students: 5,960 (51.4% male; 48.5% female)
    Individual Education Program: n/a;
    English Language Learner: n/a; Migrant: n/a
    Eligible for Free Lunch Program: n/a
    Eligible for Reduced-Price Lunch Program: n/a
Teachers: 406.8 (14.7 to 1)
Librarians/Media Specialists: 8.0 (745.0 to 1)
Guidance Counselors: 12.0 (496.7 to 1)
Current Spending: ($ per student per year):
    Total: $9,788; Instruction: $6,549; Support Services: $3,056
Enrollment, Drop-out Rates and Diploma Recipients by Race/Ethnicity

Category	Total	White	Black	Asian	AIAN	Hisp.
Enrollment (%)	100.0	96.8	1.3	0.7	0.4	0.8
Drop-out Rate (%)	1.8	1.8	0.0	0.0	16.7	0.0
H.S. Diplomas (#)	320	313	1	5	1	0

East Syracuse-Minoa Central SD
407 Fremont Rd • East Syracuse, NY 13057-2631
(315) 656-7205 • http://www.esmschools.org/
Grade Span: PK-12; **Agency Type:** 1
Schools: 7
    5 Primary; 1 Middle; 1 High; 0 Other Level
    7 Regular; 0 Special Education; 0 Vocational; 0 Alternative
    0 Magnet; 0 Charter; 4 Title I Eligible; 0 School-wide Title I
Students: 3,824 (50.9% male; 49.0% female)
    Individual Education Program: n/a;
    English Language Learner: n/a; Migrant: n/a
    Eligible for Free Lunch Program: n/a
    Eligible for Reduced-Price Lunch Program: n/a
Teachers: 320.1 (11.9 to 1)
Librarians/Media Specialists: 6.5 (588.3 to 1)
Guidance Counselors: 11.0 (347.6 to 1)
Current Spending: ($ per student per year):
    Total: $12,219; Instruction: $8,224; Support Services: $3,783
Enrollment, Drop-out Rates and Diploma Recipients by Race/Ethnicity

Category	Total	White	Black	Asian	AIAN	Hisp.
Enrollment (%)	100.0	93.4	2.4	1.4	1.5	1.3
Drop-out Rate (%)	2.5	2.6	0.0	0.0	0.0	0.0
H.S. Diplomas (#)	274	265	2	5	1	1

Fayetteville-Manlius Central SD
8199 E Seneca Tpke • Manlius, NY 13104-2140
(315) 682-1200 • http://www.fm.cnyric.org/
Grade Span: KG-12; **Agency Type:** 1
Schools: 6
    3 Primary; 2 Middle; 1 High; 0 Other Level
    6 Regular; 0 Special Education; 0 Vocational; 0 Alternative
    0 Magnet; 0 Charter; 5 Title I Eligible; 0 School-wide Title I
Students: 4,619 (50.9% male; 49.0% female)
    Individual Education Program: n/a;
    English Language Learner: n/a; Migrant: n/a
    Eligible for Free Lunch Program: n/a
    Eligible for Reduced-Price Lunch Program: n/a
Teachers: 326.0 (14.2 to 1)
Librarians/Media Specialists: 7.0 (659.9 to 1)
Guidance Counselors: 14.0 (329.9 to 1)
Current Spending: ($ per student per year):
    Total: $9,658; Instruction: $6,185; Support Services: $3,272
Enrollment, Drop-out Rates and Diploma Recipients by Race/Ethnicity

Category	Total	White	Black	Asian	AIAN	Hisp.
Enrollment (%)	100.0	91.9	1.7	5.3	0.1	0.9
Drop-out Rate (%)	1.2	1.3	0.0	0.0	n/a	0.0
H.S. Diplomas (#)	311	288	7	13	0	3

Jamesville-Dewitt Central SD
6845 Edinger Dr • Dewitt, NY 13214-0606
(315) 445-8304 • http://www.jamesvilledewitt.org/index.tpl
Grade Span: KG-12; **Agency Type:** 1
Schools: 5
    3 Primary; 1 Middle; 1 High; 0 Other Level
    5 Regular; 0 Special Education; 0 Vocational; 0 Alternative
    0 Magnet; 0 Charter; 4 Title I Eligible; 0 School-wide Title I
Students: 2,717 (49.2% male; 50.7% female)
    Individual Education Program: n/a;
    English Language Learner: n/a; Migrant: n/a
    Eligible for Free Lunch Program: n/a
    Eligible for Reduced-Price Lunch Program: n/a
Teachers: 227.0 (12.0 to 1)
Librarians/Media Specialists: 5.0 (543.4 to 1)
Guidance Counselors: 8.0 (339.6 to 1)
Current Spending: ($ per student per year):
    Total: $10,880; Instruction: $7,206; Support Services: $3,406
Enrollment, Drop-out Rates and Diploma Recipients by Race/Ethnicity

Category	Total	White	Black	Asian	AIAN	Hisp.
Enrollment (%)	100.0	85.0	8.6	4.2	0.6	1.6
Drop-out Rate (%)	1.1	1.1	0.0	0.0	0.0	20.0
H.S. Diplomas (#)	179	149	15	12	2	1

Jordan-Elbridge Central SD
9 Chappell St • Jordan, NY 13080-0902
(315) 689-3978
Grade Span: KG-12; **Agency Type:** 1
Schools: 4
    2 Primary; 1 Middle; 1 High; 0 Other Level
    4 Regular; 0 Special Education; 0 Vocational; 0 Alternative
    0 Magnet; 0 Charter; 2 Title I Eligible; 0 School-wide Title I
Students: 1,703 (51.4% male; 48.5% female)
    Individual Education Program: n/a;
    English Language Learner: n/a; Migrant: n/a
    Eligible for Free Lunch Program: n/a
    Eligible for Reduced-Price Lunch Program: n/a

Teachers: 137.4 (12.4 to 1)
Librarians/Media Specialists: 4.0 (425.8 to 1)
Guidance Counselors: 4.0 (425.8 to 1)
Current Spending: ($ per student per year):
    Total: $10,064; Instruction: $6,734; Support Services: $3,049
Enrollment, Drop-out Rates and Diploma Recipients by Race/Ethnicity

Category	Total	White	Black	Asian	AIAN	Hisp.
Enrollment (%)	100.0	97.6	0.7	0.7	0.7	0.3
Drop-out Rate (%)	3.0	3.0	0.0	0.0	0.0	0.0
H.S. Diplomas (#)	116	115	0	0	0	1

Liverpool Central SD
800 Fourth St • Liverpool, NY 13088-4455
(315) 453-0225 • http://www.liverpool.k12.ny.us/
Grade Span: PK-12; **Agency Type:** 1
Schools: 14
    10 Primary; 3 Middle; 1 High; 0 Other Level
    14 Regular; 0 Special Education; 0 Vocational; 0 Alternative
    0 Magnet; 0 Charter; 8 Title I Eligible; 0 School-wide Title I
Students: 8,629 (51.1% male; 48.8% female)
    Individual Education Program: n/a;
    English Language Learner: n/a; Migrant: n/a
    Eligible for Free Lunch Program: n/a
    Eligible for Reduced-Price Lunch Program: n/a
Teachers: 597.7 (14.4 to 1)
Librarians/Media Specialists: 16.0 (539.3 to 1)
Guidance Counselors: 24.1 (358.0 to 1)
Current Spending: ($ per student per year):
    Total: $10,987; Instruction: $7,110; Support Services: $3,624
Enrollment, Drop-out Rates and Diploma Recipients by Race/Ethnicity

Category	Total	White	Black	Asian	AIAN	Hisp.
Enrollment (%)	100.0	87.8	7.2	2.7	0.6	1.7
Drop-out Rate (%)	3.6	3.4	3.8	8.0	0.0	14.3
H.S. Diplomas (#)	512	480	17	10	2	3

Marcellus Central SD
2 Reed Pky • Marcellus, NY 13108-1199
(315) 673-0201 • http://mcs.rway.com/
Grade Span: KG-12; **Agency Type:** 1
Schools: 3
    1 Primary; 1 Middle; 1 High; 0 Other Level
    3 Regular; 0 Special Education; 0 Vocational; 0 Alternative
    0 Magnet; 0 Charter; 3 Title I Eligible; 0 School-wide Title I
Students: 2,147 (51.7% male; 48.2% female)
    Individual Education Program: n/a;
    English Language Learner: n/a; Migrant: n/a
    Eligible for Free Lunch Program: n/a
    Eligible for Reduced-Price Lunch Program: n/a
Teachers: 141.9 (15.1 to 1)
Librarians/Media Specialists: 3.0 (715.7 to 1)
Guidance Counselors: 5.0 (429.4 to 1)
Current Spending: ($ per student per year):
    Total: $8,697; Instruction: $5,818; Support Services: $2,639
Enrollment, Drop-out Rates and Diploma Recipients by Race/Ethnicity

Category	Total	White	Black	Asian	AIAN	Hisp.
Enrollment (%)	100.0	97.9	0.2	0.5	0.5	0.9
Drop-out Rate (%)	3.1	3.1	0.0	0.0	0.0	0.0
H.S. Diplomas (#)	132	128	0	4	0	0

North Syracuse Central SD
5355 W Taft Rd • North Syracuse, NY 13212-2796
(315) 452-3128 • http://www.nscsd.k12.ny.us/
Grade Span: PK-12; **Agency Type:** 1
Schools: 11
    7 Primary; 2 Middle; 1 High; 1 Other Level
    11 Regular; 0 Special Education; 0 Vocational; 0 Alternative
    0 Magnet; 0 Charter; 5 Title I Eligible; 1 School-wide Title I
Students: 10,188 (51.3% male; 48.6% female)
    Individual Education Program: n/a;
    English Language Learner: n/a; Migrant: n/a
    Eligible for Free Lunch Program: n/a
    Eligible for Reduced-Price Lunch Program: n/a
Teachers: 673.7 (15.1 to 1)
Librarians/Media Specialists: 12.0 (849.0 to 1)
Guidance Counselors: 16.8 (606.4 to 1)
Current Spending: ($ per student per year):
    Total: $9,409; Instruction: $6,022; Support Services: $3,151
Enrollment, Drop-out Rates and Diploma Recipients by Race/Ethnicity

Category	Total	White	Black	Asian	AIAN	Hisp.
Enrollment (%)	100.0	93.3	3.2	1.6	1.0	0.8
Drop-out Rate (%)	7.4	7.3	8.3	4.0	9.7	18.2
H.S. Diplomas (#)	582	553	14	7	7	1

Skaneateles Central SD
49 E Elizabeth St • Skaneateles, NY 13152-1398
(315) 291-2221 • http://www.scs.cnyric.org/
Grade Span: KG-12; **Agency Type:** 1
Schools: 4
    2 Primary; 1 Middle; 1 High; 0 Other Level
    4 Regular; 0 Special Education; 0 Vocational; 0 Alternative
    0 Magnet; 0 Charter; 2 Title I Eligible; 0 School-wide Title I
Students: 1,848 (52.2% male; 47.7% female)
    Individual Education Program: n/a;
    English Language Learner: n/a; Migrant: n/a
    Eligible for Free Lunch Program: n/a
    Eligible for Reduced-Price Lunch Program: n/a
Teachers: 142.5 (13.0 to 1)
Librarians/Media Specialists: 4.0 (462.0 to 1)
Guidance Counselors: 5.0 (369.6 to 1)
Current Spending: ($ per student per year):
    Total: $9,573; Instruction: $6,004; Support Services: $3,401
Enrollment, Drop-out Rates and Diploma Recipients by Race/Ethnicity

Category	Total	White	Black	Asian	AIAN	Hisp.
Enrollment (%)	100.0	98.3	0.2	0.8	0.1	0.6
Drop-out Rate (%)	0.9	0.9	n/a	0.0	0.0	0.0
H.S. Diplomas (#)	154	153	0	1	0	0

Solvay Union Free SD
103 3rd St • Solvay, NY 13209-1532
(315) 468-1111
Grade Span: KG-12; **Agency Type:** 1
Schools: 4
    1 Primary; 2 Middle; 1 High; 0 Other Level
    4 Regular; 0 Special Education; 0 Vocational; 0 Alternative
    0 Magnet; 0 Charter; 3 Title I Eligible; 0 School-wide Title I
Students: 1,747 (51.1% male; 48.8% female)
    Individual Education Program: n/a;
    English Language Learner: n/a; Migrant: n/a
    Eligible for Free Lunch Program: n/a
    Eligible for Reduced-Price Lunch Program: n/a
Teachers: 136.5 (12.8 to 1)
Librarians/Media Specialists: 4.0 (436.8 to 1)
Guidance Counselors: 5.0 (349.4 to 1)
Current Spending: ($ per student per year):
    Total: $9,471; Instruction: $6,282; Support Services: $2,955
Enrollment, Drop-out Rates and Diploma Recipients by Race/Ethnicity

Category	Total	White	Black	Asian	AIAN	Hisp.
Enrollment (%)	100.0	94.9	1.9	0.4	0.6	2.1
Drop-out Rate (%)	2.1	2.2	0.0	0.0	0.0	0.0
H.S. Diplomas (#)	116	114	0	1	1	0

Syracuse City SD
725 Harrison St • Syracuse, NY 13210-2325
(315) 435-4161 • http://www.syracusecityschools.com/
Grade Span: PK-12; **Agency Type:** 1
Schools: 35
    24 Primary; 5 Middle; 4 High; 2 Other Level
    33 Regular; 0 Special Education; 0 Vocational; 2 Alternative
    7 Magnet; 0 Charter; 28 Title I Eligible; 28 School-wide Title I
Students: 22,405 (50.1% male; 49.8% female)
    Individual Education Program: n/a;
    English Language Learner: n/a; Migrant: n/a
    Eligible for Free Lunch Program: n/a
    Eligible for Reduced-Price Lunch Program: n/a
Teachers: 1,804.4 (12.4 to 1)
Librarians/Media Specialists: 33.5 (668.8 to 1)
Guidance Counselors: 40.0 (560.1 to 1)
Current Spending: ($ per student per year):
    Total: $11,848; Instruction: $7,985; Support Services: $3,487
Enrollment, Drop-out Rates and Diploma Recipients by Race/Ethnicity

Category	Total	White	Black	Asian	AIAN	Hisp.
Enrollment (%)	100.0	36.2	51.4	2.6	1.2	8.6
Drop-out Rate (%)	3.8	3.8	3.8	1.6	2.1	3.9
H.S. Diplomas (#)	627	387	221	2	1	16

West Genesee Central SD
300 Sanderson Dr • Camillus, NY 13031-1655
(315) 487-4562 • http://www.westgenesee.org/
Grade Span: KG-12; **Agency Type:** 1
Schools: 7
    4 Primary; 2 Middle; 1 High; 0 Other Level
    7 Regular; 0 Special Education; 0 Vocational; 0 Alternative
    0 Magnet; 0 Charter; 4 Title I Eligible; 0 School-wide Title I
Students: 5,153 (51.5% male; 48.4% female)
    Individual Education Program: n/a;
    English Language Learner: n/a; Migrant: n/a
    Eligible for Free Lunch Program: n/a
    Eligible for Reduced-Price Lunch Program: n/a

Teachers: 346.0 (14.9 to 1)
Librarians/Media Specialists: 8.0 (644.1 to 1)
Guidance Counselors: 10.0 (515.3 to 1)
Current Spending: ($ per student per year):
    Total: $8,847; Instruction: $5,900; Support Services: $2,747
Enrollment, Drop-out Rates and Diploma Recipients by Race/Ethnicity

Category	Total	White	Black	Asian	AIAN	Hisp.
Enrollment (%)	100.0	95.8	1.7	1.2	0.5	0.8
Drop-out Rate (%)	2.4	2.4	0.0	0.0	0.0	20.0
H.S. Diplomas (#)	390	384	4	0	1	1

Westhill Central SD
400 Walberta Rd • Syracuse, NY 13219-2297
(315) 488-6322 • http://www.westhillschools.com/
Grade Span: KG-12; **Agency Type:** 1
Schools: 4
    2 Primary; 1 Middle; 1 High; 0 Other Level
    4 Regular; 0 Special Education; 0 Vocational; 0 Alternative
    0 Magnet; 0 Charter; 3 Title I Eligible; 0 School-wide Title I
Students: 2,049   (52.7% male; 47.2% female)
    Individual Education Program: n/a;
    English Language Learner: n/a; Migrant: n/a
    Eligible for Free Lunch Program: n/a
    Eligible for Reduced-Price Lunch Program: n/a
Teachers: 146.3 (14.0 to 1)
Librarians/Media Specialists: 4.0 (512.3 to 1)
Guidance Counselors: 5.0 (409.8 to 1)
Current Spending: ($ per student per year):
    Total: $9,736; Instruction: $6,263; Support Services: $3,269
Enrollment, Drop-out Rates and Diploma Recipients by Race/Ethnicity

Category	Total	White	Black	Asian	AIAN	Hisp.
Enrollment (%)	100.0	95.0	1.9	2.0	0.2	1.0
Drop-out Rate (%)	0.1	0.1	0.0	0.0	n/a	0.0
H.S. Diplomas (#)	167	157	2	5	0	3

Ontario County

Canandaigua City SD
143 N Pearl St • Canandaigua, NY 14424-1496
(585) 396-3700 • http://www.canandaigua.k12.ny.us/
Grade Span: PK-12; **Agency Type:** 1
Schools: 4
    2 Primary; 1 Middle; 1 High; 0 Other Level
    4 Regular; 0 Special Education; 0 Vocational; 0 Alternative
    0 Magnet; 0 Charter; 2 Title I Eligible; 0 School-wide Title I
Students: 4,186   (51.1% male; 48.8% female)
    Individual Education Program: n/a;
    English Language Learner: n/a; Migrant: n/a
    Eligible for Free Lunch Program: n/a
    Eligible for Reduced-Price Lunch Program: n/a
Teachers: 322.6 (13.0 to 1)
Librarians/Media Specialists: 5.0 (837.2 to 1)
Guidance Counselors: 12.0 (348.8 to 1)
Current Spending: ($ per student per year):
    Total: $10,433; Instruction: $7,201; Support Services: $2,984
Enrollment, Drop-out Rates and Diploma Recipients by Race/Ethnicity

Category	Total	White	Black	Asian	AIAN	Hisp.
Enrollment (%)	100.0	95.6	2.2	1.0	0.2	1.0
Drop-out Rate (%)	3.4	3.4	4.0	0.0	0.0	0.0
H.S. Diplomas (#)	244	237	4	2	0	1

Geneva City SD
649 S Exchange St • Geneva, NY 14456-3492
(315) 781-0276 • http://www.genevacsd.org/
Grade Span: KG-12; **Agency Type:** 1
Schools: 4
    2 Primary; 1 Middle; 1 High; 0 Other Level
    4 Regular; 0 Special Education; 0 Vocational; 0 Alternative
    0 Magnet; 0 Charter; 3 Title I Eligible; 0 School-wide Title I
Students: 2,534   (49.2% male; 50.7% female)
    Individual Education Program: n/a;
    English Language Learner: n/a; Migrant: n/a
    Eligible for Free Lunch Program: n/a
    Eligible for Reduced-Price Lunch Program: n/a
Teachers: 222.3 (11.4 to 1)
Librarians/Media Specialists: 4.0 (633.5 to 1)
Guidance Counselors: 5.0 (506.8 to 1)
Current Spending: ($ per student per year):
    Total: $11,012; Instruction: $7,720; Support Services: $2,966
Enrollment, Drop-out Rates and Diploma Recipients by Race/Ethnicity

Category	Total	White	Black	Asian	AIAN	Hisp.
Enrollment (%)	100.0	68.4	19.4	1.6	0.1	10.5
Drop-out Rate (%)	4.7	3.7	5.1	10.0	0.0	14.5
H.S. Diplomas (#)	149	122	14	3	1	9

Gorham-Middlesex Central SD (Marcus Whitman)
4100 Baldwin Rd • Rushville, NY 14544-9799
(585) 554-4848
Grade Span: KG-12; **Agency Type:** 1
Schools: 4
    2 Primary; 1 Middle; 1 High; 0 Other Level
    4 Regular; 0 Special Education; 0 Vocational; 0 Alternative
    0 Magnet; 0 Charter; 3 Title I Eligible; 0 School-wide Title I
Students: 1,597   (49.9% male; 50.0% female)
    Individual Education Program: n/a;
    English Language Learner: n/a; Migrant: n/a
    Eligible for Free Lunch Program: n/a
    Eligible for Reduced-Price Lunch Program: n/a
Teachers: 126.9 (12.6 to 1)
Librarians/Media Specialists: 2.0 (798.5 to 1)
Guidance Counselors: 3.0 (532.3 to 1)
Current Spending: ($ per student per year):
    Total: $11,829; Instruction: $7,812; Support Services: $3,651
Enrollment, Drop-out Rates and Diploma Recipients by Race/Ethnicity

Category	Total	White	Black	Asian	AIAN	Hisp.
Enrollment (%)	100.0	95.9	0.9	0.9	0.6	1.7
Drop-out Rate (%)	3.8	3.9	0.0	0.0	0.0	0.0
H.S. Diplomas (#)	99	96	0	1	0	2

Phelps-Clifton Springs Central SD
1490 Rt 488 • Clifton Springs, NY 14432-9318
(315) 548-6420 • http://www.midlakes.org/
Grade Span: KG-12; **Agency Type:** 1
Schools: 4
    2 Primary; 1 Middle; 1 High; 0 Other Level
    4 Regular; 0 Special Education; 0 Vocational; 0 Alternative
    0 Magnet; 0 Charter; 3 Title I Eligible; 0 School-wide Title I
Students: 2,044   (51.5% male; 48.4% female)
    Individual Education Program: n/a;
    English Language Learner: n/a; Migrant: n/a
    Eligible for Free Lunch Program: n/a
    Eligible for Reduced-Price Lunch Program: n/a
Teachers: 159.7 (12.8 to 1)
Librarians/Media Specialists: 3.0 (681.3 to 1)
Guidance Counselors: 5.0 (408.8 to 1)
Current Spending: ($ per student per year):
    Total: $10,192; Instruction: $6,591; Support Services: $3,323
Enrollment, Drop-out Rates and Diploma Recipients by Race/Ethnicity

Category	Total	White	Black	Asian	AIAN	Hisp.
Enrollment (%)	100.0	96.9	0.7	0.6	0.3	1.5
Drop-out Rate (%)	0.6	0.6	0.0	0.0	0.0	0.0
H.S. Diplomas (#)	135	133	0	1	0	1

Victor Central SD
953 High St • Victor, NY 14564-1167
(585) 924-3252 • http://www.victorschools.org/homeflash.cfm
Grade Span: PK-12; **Agency Type:** 1
Schools: 5
    2 Primary; 2 Middle; 1 High; 0 Other Level
    5 Regular; 0 Special Education; 0 Vocational; 0 Alternative
    0 Magnet; 0 Charter; 4 Title I Eligible; 0 School-wide Title I
Students: 3,556   (52.5% male; 47.4% female)
    Individual Education Program: n/a;
    English Language Learner: n/a; Migrant: n/a
    Eligible for Free Lunch Program: n/a
    Eligible for Reduced-Price Lunch Program: n/a
Teachers: 250.1 (14.2 to 1)
Librarians/Media Specialists: 4.0 (889.0 to 1)
Guidance Counselors: 8.0 (444.5 to 1)
Current Spending: ($ per student per year):
    Total: $10,049; Instruction: $6,650; Support Services: $3,147
Enrollment, Drop-out Rates and Diploma Recipients by Race/Ethnicity

Category	Total	White	Black	Asian	AIAN	Hisp.
Enrollment (%)	100.0	95.5	1.2	2.0	0.3	1.1
Drop-out Rate (%)	2.9	2.9	0.0	0.0	0.0	12.5
H.S. Diplomas (#)	199	190	1	6	1	1

Orange County

Cornwall Central SD
24 Idlewild Ave • Cornwall On Hudson, NY 12520
(845) 534-8009
Grade Span: KG-12; **Agency Type:** 1
Schools: 5
    3 Primary; 1 Middle; 1 High; 0 Other Level
    5 Regular; 0 Special Education; 0 Vocational; 0 Alternative
    0 Magnet; 0 Charter; 4 Title I Eligible; 0 School-wide Title I
Students: 3,093   (51.0% male; 48.9% female)
    Individual Education Program: n/a;
    English Language Learner: n/a; Migrant: n/a

Eligible for Free Lunch Program: n/a
Eligible for Reduced-Price Lunch Program: n/a
Teachers: 203.6 (15.2 to 1)
Librarians/Media Specialists: 5.0 (618.6 to 1)
Guidance Counselors: 8.0 (386.6 to 1)
Current Spending: ($ per student per year):
   Total: $10,469; Instruction: $7,004; Support Services: $3,246

Enrollment, Drop-out Rates and Diploma Recipients by Race/Ethnicity

Category	Total	White	Black	Asian	AIAN	Hisp.
Enrollment (%)	100.0	87.9	3.0	2.3	0.1	6.7
Drop-out Rate (%)	1.7	1.5	15.0	0.0	0.0	0.0
H.S. Diplomas (#)	198	180	4	2	3	9

Goshen Central SD
227 Main St • Goshen, NY 10924-2158
(845) 294-2410 • http://www.gcsny.org/
Grade Span: KG-12; **Agency Type:** 2
Schools: 6
   2 Primary; 1 Middle; 2 High; 1 Other Level
   4 Regular; 0 Special Education; 0 Vocational; 2 Alternative
   0 Magnet; 0 Charter; 4 Title I Eligible; 0 School-wide Title I
Students: 2,921   (50.8% male; 49.1% female)
   Individual Education Program: n/a;
   English Language Learner: n/a; Migrant: n/a
   Eligible for Free Lunch Program: n/a
   Eligible for Reduced-Price Lunch Program: n/a
Teachers: 210.3 (13.9 to 1)
Librarians/Media Specialists: 3.0 (973.7 to 1)
Guidance Counselors: 6.0 (486.8 to 1)
Current Spending: ($ per student per year):
   Total: $11,416; Instruction: $7,339; Support Services: $3,796

Enrollment, Drop-out Rates and Diploma Recipients by Race/Ethnicity

Category	Total	White	Black	Asian	AIAN	Hisp.
Enrollment (%)	100.0	83.7	5.8	1.8	0.2	8.5
Drop-out Rate (%)	1.1	0.9	0.0	0.0	n/a	4.7
H.S. Diplomas (#)	176	160	7	4	0	5

Middletown City SD
223 Wisner Ave Ext • Middletown, NY 10940-3240
(845) 341-5691 • http://www.middletown.k12.ny.us/
Grade Span: PK-12; **Agency Type:** 1
Schools: 10
   5 Primary; 2 Middle; 1 High; 2 Other Level
   8 Regular; 0 Special Education; 0 Vocational; 2 Alternative
   0 Magnet; 0 Charter; 7 Title I Eligible; 7 School-wide Title I
Students: 6,577   (50.5% male; 49.4% female)
   Individual Education Program: n/a;
   English Language Learner: n/a; Migrant: n/a
   Eligible for Free Lunch Program: n/a
   Eligible for Reduced-Price Lunch Program: n/a
Teachers: 447.7 (14.7 to 1)
Librarians/Media Specialists: 7.0 (939.6 to 1)
Guidance Counselors: 15.0 (438.5 to 1)
Current Spending: ($ per student per year):
   Total: $12,077; Instruction: $8,034; Support Services: $3,705

Enrollment, Drop-out Rates and Diploma Recipients by Race/Ethnicity

Category	Total	White	Black	Asian	AIAN	Hisp.
Enrollment (%)	100.0	36.3	24.9	2.5	0.2	36.1
Drop-out Rate (%)	1.0	0.9	1.5	0.0	0.0	0.9
H.S. Diplomas (#)	264	155	62	10	1	36

Minisink Valley Central SD
Rt 6-PO Box 217 • Slate Hill, NY 10973-0217
(845) 355-5110 • http://www.minisink.com/
Grade Span: KG-12; **Agency Type:** 2
Schools: 6
   3 Primary; 1 Middle; 1 High; 1 Other Level
   5 Regular; 0 Special Education; 0 Vocational; 1 Alternative
   0 Magnet; 0 Charter; 3 Title I Eligible; 0 School-wide Title I
Students: 4,543   (52.1% male; 47.8% female)
   Individual Education Program: n/a;
   English Language Learner: n/a; Migrant: n/a
   Eligible for Free Lunch Program: n/a
   Eligible for Reduced-Price Lunch Program: n/a
Teachers: 298.8 (15.2 to 1)
Librarians/Media Specialists: 4.0 (1,135.8 to 1)
Guidance Counselors: 8.0 (567.9 to 1)
Current Spending: ($ per student per year):
   Total: $10,378; Instruction: $7,264; Support Services: $2,879

Enrollment, Drop-out Rates and Diploma Recipients by Race/Ethnicity

Category	Total	White	Black	Asian	AIAN	Hisp.
Enrollment (%)	100.0	88.6	3.3	1.0	0.3	6.7
Drop-out Rate (%)	3.4	3.3	5.3	0.0	0.0	3.3
H.S. Diplomas (#)	246	228	8	3	2	5

Monroe-Woodbury Central SD
278 Rte 32-Educ Ctr • Central Valley, NY 10917-1001
(845) 928-2321 • http://mw.k12.ny.us/
Grade Span: KG-12; **Agency Type:** 1
Schools: 7
   5 Primary; 1 Middle; 1 High; 0 Other Level
   7 Regular; 0 Special Education; 0 Vocational; 0 Alternative
   0 Magnet; 0 Charter; 3 Title I Eligible; 0 School-wide Title I
Students: 7,255   (51.3% male; 48.6% female)
   Individual Education Program: n/a;
   English Language Learner: n/a; Migrant: n/a
   Eligible for Free Lunch Program: n/a
   Eligible for Reduced-Price Lunch Program: n/a
Teachers: 499.1 (14.5 to 1)
Librarians/Media Specialists: 10.2 (711.3 to 1)
Guidance Counselors: 12.5 (580.4 to 1)
Current Spending: ($ per student per year):
   Total: $12,270; Instruction: $7,564; Support Services: $4,474

Enrollment, Drop-out Rates and Diploma Recipients by Race/Ethnicity

Category	Total	White	Black	Asian	AIAN	Hisp.
Enrollment (%)	100.0	80.4	3.8	4.0	0.3	11.5
Drop-out Rate (%)	1.2	1.0	1.7	2.3	20.0	1.5
H.S. Diplomas (#)	411	350	8	19	1	33

Newburgh City SD
124 Grand St • Newburgh, NY 12550-4600
(845) 563-3500 • http://www.newburgh.k12.ny.us/
Grade Span: PK-12; **Agency Type:** 1
Schools: 15
   11 Primary; 3 Middle; 1 High; 0 Other Level
   15 Regular; 0 Special Education; 0 Vocational; 0 Alternative
   6 Magnet; 0 Charter; 13 Title I Eligible; 13 School-wide Title I
Students: 13,108   (51.4% male; 48.5% female)
   Individual Education Program: n/a;
   English Language Learner: n/a; Migrant: n/a
   Eligible for Free Lunch Program: n/a
   Eligible for Reduced-Price Lunch Program: n/a
Teachers: 900.7 (14.6 to 1)
Librarians/Media Specialists: 14.5 (904.0 to 1)
Guidance Counselors: 23.0 (569.9 to 1)
Current Spending: ($ per student per year):
   Total: $11,507; Instruction: $7,593; Support Services: $3,605

Enrollment, Drop-out Rates and Diploma Recipients by Race/Ethnicity

Category	Total	White	Black	Asian	AIAN	Hisp.
Enrollment (%)	100.0	35.1	30.6	1.4	0.2	32.7
Drop-out Rate (%)	2.3	1.4	3.7	1.2	n/a	2.6
H.S. Diplomas (#)	482	279	91	12	0	100

Pine Bush Central SD
Po Bx 700 156 St Rte • Pine Bush, NY 12566-0700
(845) 744-2031 • http://www.pinebushschools.org/
Grade Span: PK-12; **Agency Type:** 1
Schools: 7
   4 Primary; 2 Middle; 1 High; 0 Other Level
   7 Regular; 0 Special Education; 0 Vocational; 0 Alternative
   0 Magnet; 0 Charter; 6 Title I Eligible; 0 School-wide Title I
Students: 6,118   (50.7% male; 49.2% female)
   Individual Education Program: n/a;
   English Language Learner: n/a; Migrant: n/a
   Eligible for Free Lunch Program: n/a
   Eligible for Reduced-Price Lunch Program: n/a
Teachers: 422.4 (14.5 to 1)
Librarians/Media Specialists: 7.5 (815.7 to 1)
Guidance Counselors: 10.0 (611.8 to 1)
Current Spending: ($ per student per year):
   Total: $10,838; Instruction: $7,215; Support Services: $3,340

Enrollment, Drop-out Rates and Diploma Recipients by Race/Ethnicity

Category	Total	White	Black	Asian	AIAN	Hisp.
Enrollment (%)	100.0	81.5	7.8	2.0	0.2	8.5
Drop-out Rate (%)	4.0	3.9	3.7	0.0	0.0	6.1
H.S. Diplomas (#)	306	262	20	3	1	20

Port Jervis City SD
9 Thompson St • Port Jervis, NY 12771-3058
(845) 858-3175 • http://www.portjerviscsd.k12.ny.us/
Grade Span: KG-12; **Agency Type:** 1
Schools: 5
   3 Primary; 1 Middle; 1 High; 0 Other Level
   5 Regular; 0 Special Education; 0 Vocational; 0 Alternative
   0 Magnet; 0 Charter; 5 Title I Eligible; 0 School-wide Title I
Students: 3,444   (51.0% male; 48.9% female)
   Individual Education Program: n/a;
   English Language Learner: n/a; Migrant: n/a
   Eligible for Free Lunch Program: n/a
   Eligible for Reduced-Price Lunch Program: n/a

Teachers: 222.8 (15.5 to 1)
Librarians/Media Specialists: 4.8 (717.5 to 1)
Guidance Counselors: 6.0 (574.0 to 1)
Current Spending: ($ per student per year):
    Total: $11,881; Instruction: $7,886; Support Services: $3,650
Enrollment, Drop-out Rates and Diploma Recipients by Race/Ethnicity

Category	Total	White	Black	Asian	AIAN	Hisp.
Enrollment (%)	100.0	88.7	5.1	0.5	0.3	5.4
Drop-out Rate (%)	6.9	7.1	3.6	0.0	0.0	8.9
H.S. Diplomas (#)	192	171	11	1	0	9

Valley Central SD (Montgomery)
944 State Rt 17k • Montgomery, NY 12549-2240
(845) 457-2400 • http://www.vcsd.k12.ny.us/
Grade Span: KG-12; **Agency Type:** 1
Schools: 7
    5 Primary; 1 Middle; 1 High; 0 Other Level
    7 Regular; 0 Special Education; 0 Vocational; 0 Alternative
    0 Magnet; 0 Charter; 5 Title I Eligible; 0 School-wide Title I
Students: 5,236 (51.4% male; 48.5% female)
    Individual Education Program: n/a;
    English Language Learner: n/a; Migrant: n/a
    Eligible for Free Lunch Program: n/a
    Eligible for Reduced-Price Lunch Program: n/a
Teachers: 376.1 (13.9 to 1)
Librarians/Media Specialists: 7.5 (698.1 to 1)
Guidance Counselors: 11.0 (476.0 to 1)
Current Spending: ($ per student per year):
    Total: $9,703; Instruction: $6,374; Support Services: $3,064
Enrollment, Drop-out Rates and Diploma Recipients by Race/Ethnicity

Category	Total	White	Black	Asian	AIAN	Hisp.
Enrollment (%)	100.0	82.5	6.4	1.6	0.2	9.3
Drop-out Rate (%)	2.4	2.2	5.1	0.0	0.0	3.0
H.S. Diplomas (#)	308	263	17	5	2	21

Warwick Valley Central SD
225 W St Ext • Warwick, NY 10990-0595
(845) 987-3010 • http://www.warwickvalleyschools.com/
Grade Span: KG-12; **Agency Type:** 1
Schools: 7
    4 Primary; 1 Middle; 1 High; 1 Other Level
    6 Regular; 0 Special Education; 0 Vocational; 1 Alternative
    0 Magnet; 0 Charter; 5 Title I Eligible; 0 School-wide Title I
Students: 4,682 (52.2% male; 47.7% female)
    Individual Education Program: n/a;
    English Language Learner: n/a; Migrant: n/a
    Eligible for Free Lunch Program: n/a
    Eligible for Reduced-Price Lunch Program: n/a
Teachers: 310.6 (15.1 to 1)
Librarians/Media Specialists: 6.0 (780.3 to 1)
Guidance Counselors: 10.0 (468.2 to 1)
Current Spending: ($ per student per year):
    Total: $10,637; Instruction: $6,914; Support Services: $3,486
Enrollment, Drop-out Rates and Diploma Recipients by Race/Ethnicity

Category	Total	White	Black	Asian	AIAN	Hisp.
Enrollment (%)	100.0	87.0	5.7	1.4	0.5	5.4
Drop-out Rate (%)	1.0	1.0	0.0	0.0	n/a	1.6
H.S. Diplomas (#)	257	241	6	3	0	7

Washingtonville Central SD
52 W Main St • Washingtonville, NY 10992-1492
(845) 497-2200 • http://www.ws.k12.ny.us/
Grade Span: PK-12; **Agency Type:** 1
Schools: 5
    3 Primary; 1 Middle; 1 High; 0 Other Level
    5 Regular; 0 Special Education; 0 Vocational; 0 Alternative
    0 Magnet; 0 Charter; 3 Title I Eligible; 0 School-wide Title I
Students: 5,106 (52.2% male; 47.7% female)
    Individual Education Program: n/a;
    English Language Learner: n/a; Migrant: n/a
    Eligible for Free Lunch Program: n/a
    Eligible for Reduced-Price Lunch Program: n/a
Teachers: 341.3 (15.0 to 1)
Librarians/Media Specialists: 5.0 (1,021.2 to 1)
Guidance Counselors: 13.0 (392.8 to 1)
Current Spending: ($ per student per year):
    Total: $10,168; Instruction: $6,656; Support Services: $3,283
Enrollment, Drop-out Rates and Diploma Recipients by Race/Ethnicity

Category	Total	White	Black	Asian	AIAN	Hisp.
Enrollment (%)	100.0	81.2	5.7	1.7	0.3	11.0
Drop-out Rate (%)	1.3	1.2	1.2	0.0	0.0	2.4
H.S. Diplomas (#)	312	276	9	2	2	23

Albion Central SD
324 E Ave • Albion, NY 14411-1697
(585) 589-2056 • http://www.albion.wnyric.org/
Grade Span: PK-12; **Agency Type:** 1
Schools: 5
    1 Primary; 1 Middle; 1 High; 2 Other Level
    3 Regular; 0 Special Education; 0 Vocational; 2 Alternative
    0 Magnet; 0 Charter; 2 Title I Eligible; 0 School-wide Title I
Students: 2,797 (50.6% male; 49.3% female)
    Individual Education Program: n/a;
    English Language Learner: n/a; Migrant: n/a
    Eligible for Free Lunch Program: n/a
    Eligible for Reduced-Price Lunch Program: n/a
Teachers: 191.4 (14.6 to 1)
Librarians/Media Specialists: 3.0 (932.3 to 1)
Guidance Counselors: 8.0 (349.6 to 1)
Current Spending: ($ per student per year):
    Total: $8,907; Instruction: $6,201; Support Services: $2,478
Enrollment, Drop-out Rates and Diploma Recipients by Race/Ethnicity

Category	Total	White	Black	Asian	AIAN	Hisp.
Enrollment (%)	100.0	82.2	9.3	1.1	1.0	6.4
Drop-out Rate (%)	4.6	4.2	11.8	0.0	0.0	4.5
H.S. Diplomas (#)	152	139	8	1	1	3

Medina Central SD
One Mustang Dr • Medina, NY 14103-1845
(585) 798-2700 • http://www.medina.wnyric.org/
Grade Span: KG-12; **Agency Type:** 1
Schools: 4
    2 Primary; 1 Middle; 1 High; 0 Other Level
    4 Regular; 0 Special Education; 0 Vocational; 0 Alternative
    0 Magnet; 0 Charter; 4 Title I Eligible; 0 School-wide Title I
Students: 1,954 (51.1% male; 48.8% female)
    Individual Education Program: n/a;
    English Language Learner: n/a; Migrant: n/a
    Eligible for Free Lunch Program: n/a
    Eligible for Reduced-Price Lunch Program: n/a
Teachers: 164.4 (11.9 to 1)
Librarians/Media Specialists: 4.2 (465.2 to 1)
Guidance Counselors: 4.0 (488.5 to 1)
Current Spending: ($ per student per year):
    Total: $10,819; Instruction: $7,422; Support Services: $3,130
Enrollment, Drop-out Rates and Diploma Recipients by Race/Ethnicity

Category	Total	White	Black	Asian	AIAN	Hisp.
Enrollment (%)	100.0	88.5	7.6	0.6	0.4	2.9
Drop-out Rate (%)	8.8	8.3	18.8	0.0	n/a	25.0
H.S. Diplomas (#)	122	115	6	1	0	0

Altmar-Parish-Williamstown Central SD
639 County Rt 22 • Parish, NY 13131-0097
(315) 625-5251 • http://www.apw.cnyric.org/
Grade Span: KG-12; **Agency Type:** 2
Schools: 5
    3 Primary; 1 Middle; 1 High; 0 Other Level
    5 Regular; 0 Special Education; 0 Vocational; 0 Alternative
    0 Magnet; 0 Charter; 5 Title I Eligible; 4 School-wide Title I
Students: 1,647 (48.2% male; 51.7% female)
    Individual Education Program: n/a;
    English Language Learner: n/a; Migrant: n/a
    Eligible for Free Lunch Program: n/a
    Eligible for Reduced-Price Lunch Program: n/a
Teachers: 138.3 (11.9 to 1)
Librarians/Media Specialists: 2.0 (823.5 to 1)
Guidance Counselors: 4.0 (411.8 to 1)
Current Spending: ($ per student per year):
    Total: $11,022; Instruction: $7,088; Support Services: $3,599
Enrollment, Drop-out Rates and Diploma Recipients by Race/Ethnicity

Category	Total	White	Black	Asian	AIAN	Hisp.
Enrollment (%)	100.0	99.1	0.5	0.1	0.1	0.2
Drop-out Rate (%)	4.2	4.3	0.0	0.0	n/a	0.0
H.S. Diplomas (#)	91	89	0	2	0	0

Central Square Central SD
642 S Main St • Central Square, NY 13036-3511
(315) 668-4220 • http://www.centralsquareschools.org/
Grade Span: PK-12; **Agency Type:** 1
Schools: 8
    6 Primary; 1 Middle; 1 High; 0 Other Level
    8 Regular; 0 Special Education; 0 Vocational; 0 Alternative
    0 Magnet; 0 Charter; 6 Title I Eligible; 0 School-wide Title I
Students: 5,013 (52.0% male; 47.9% female)

Individual Education Program: n/a;
English Language Learner: n/a; Migrant: n/a
Eligible for Free Lunch Program: n/a
Eligible for Reduced-Price Lunch Program: n/a
Teachers: 342.8 (14.6 to 1)
Librarians/Media Specialists: 8.0 (626.6 to 1)
Guidance Counselors: 10.0 (501.3 to 1)
Current Spending: ($ per student per year):
Total: $9,121; Instruction: $5,536; Support Services: $3,290

Enrollment, Drop-out Rates and Diploma Recipients by Race/Ethnicity

Category	Total	White	Black	Asian	AIAN	Hisp.
Enrollment (%)	100.0	98.9	0.4	0.2	0.4	0.2
Drop-out Rate (%)	6.6	6.6	28.6	0.0	0.0	10.0
H.S. Diplomas (#)	249	245	0	2	1	1

Fulton City SD

167 S Fourth St • Fulton, NY 13069-1859
(315) 593-5510
Grade Span: KG-12; **Agency Type:** 1
Schools: 6
4 Primary; 1 Middle; 1 High; 0 Other Level
6 Regular; 0 Special Education; 0 Vocational; 0 Alternative
0 Magnet; 0 Charter; 6 Title I Eligible; 2 School-wide Title I
Students: 3,875 (50.2% male; 49.7% female)
Individual Education Program: n/a;
English Language Learner: n/a; Migrant: n/a
Eligible for Free Lunch Program: n/a
Eligible for Reduced-Price Lunch Program: n/a
Teachers: 290.0 (13.4 to 1)
Librarians/Media Specialists: 6.0 (645.8 to 1)
Guidance Counselors: 6.0 (645.8 to 1)
Current Spending: ($ per student per year):
Total: $11,687; Instruction: $8,004; Support Services: $3,353

Enrollment, Drop-out Rates and Diploma Recipients by Race/Ethnicity

Category	Total	White	Black	Asian	AIAN	Hisp.
Enrollment (%)	100.0	95.7	1.4	0.5	0.1	2.3
Drop-out Rate (%)	7.0	6.9	15.4	0.0	33.3	9.1
H.S. Diplomas (#)	213	210	0	1	0	2

Hannibal Central SD

1051 Auburn St • Hannibal, NY 13074-0066
(315) 564-7902 • http://www.hannibal.cnyric.org/
Grade Span: KG-12; **Agency Type:** 2
Schools: 3
1 Primary; 1 Middle; 1 High; 0 Other Level
3 Regular; 0 Special Education; 0 Vocational; 0 Alternative
0 Magnet; 0 Charter; 3 Title I Eligible; 2 School-wide Title I
Students: 1,756 (49.4% male; 50.5% female)
Individual Education Program: n/a;
English Language Learner: n/a; Migrant: n/a
Eligible for Free Lunch Program: n/a
Eligible for Reduced-Price Lunch Program: n/a
Teachers: 128.6 (13.7 to 1)
Librarians/Media Specialists: 3.0 (585.3 to 1)
Guidance Counselors: 2.8 (627.1 to 1)
Current Spending: ($ per student per year):
Total: $10,032; Instruction: $6,684; Support Services: $3,003

Enrollment, Drop-out Rates and Diploma Recipients by Race/Ethnicity

Category	Total	White	Black	Asian	AIAN	Hisp.
Enrollment (%)	100.0	96.6	0.7	0.3	0.3	2.1
Drop-out Rate (%)	9.2	8.5	n/a	0.0	n/a	100.0
H.S. Diplomas (#)	94	93	0	0	0	1

Mexico Central SD

40 Academy St • Mexico, NY 13114-3432
(315) 963-8400 • http://www.mexico.cnyric.org/
Grade Span: KG-12; **Agency Type:** 1
Schools: 5
3 Primary; 1 Middle; 1 High; 0 Other Level
5 Regular; 0 Special Education; 0 Vocational; 0 Alternative
0 Magnet; 0 Charter; 4 Title I Eligible; 0 School-wide Title I
Students: 2,682 (49.9% male; 50.0% female)
Individual Education Program: n/a;
English Language Learner: n/a; Migrant: n/a
Eligible for Free Lunch Program: n/a
Eligible for Reduced-Price Lunch Program: n/a
Teachers: 191.0 (14.0 to 1)
Librarians/Media Specialists: 2.0 (1,341.0 to 1)
Guidance Counselors: 5.0 (536.4 to 1)
Current Spending: ($ per student per year):
Total: $10,525; Instruction: $6,756; Support Services: $3,459

Enrollment, Drop-out Rates and Diploma Recipients by Race/Ethnicity

Category	Total	White	Black	Asian	AIAN	Hisp.
Enrollment (%)	100.0	97.8	0.6	0.1	0.9	0.5
Drop-out Rate (%)	5.2	5.2	0.0	0.0	0.0	33.3
H.S. Diplomas (#)	162	159	1	1	1	0

Oswego City SD

120 E 1st St • Oswego, NY 13126-2114
(315) 341-5885 • http://oswego.org/
Grade Span: KG-12; **Agency Type:** 1
Schools: 7
5 Primary; 1 Middle; 1 High; 0 Other Level
7 Regular; 0 Special Education; 0 Vocational; 0 Alternative
0 Magnet; 0 Charter; 5 Title I Eligible; 1 School-wide Title I
Students: 4,809 (52.6% male; 47.3% female)
Individual Education Program: n/a;
English Language Learner: n/a; Migrant: n/a
Eligible for Free Lunch Program: n/a
Eligible for Reduced-Price Lunch Program: n/a
Teachers: 356.6 (13.5 to 1)
Librarians/Media Specialists: 6.0 (801.5 to 1)
Guidance Counselors: 8.0 (601.1 to 1)
Current Spending: ($ per student per year):
Total: $11,098; Instruction: $7,455; Support Services: $3,436

Enrollment, Drop-out Rates and Diploma Recipients by Race/Ethnicity

Category	Total	White	Black	Asian	AIAN	Hisp.
Enrollment (%)	100.0	93.4	1.4	1.0	0.3	3.9
Drop-out Rate (%)	3.0	3.2	0.0	3.7	0.0	0.0
H.S. Diplomas (#)	253	244	1	3	0	5

Phoenix Central SD

116 Volney St • Phoenix, NY 13135-9778
(315) 695-1555 • http://www.phoenix.k12.ny.us/
Grade Span: KG-12; **Agency Type:** 1
Schools: 3
1 Primary; 1 Middle; 1 High; 0 Other Level
3 Regular; 0 Special Education; 0 Vocational; 0 Alternative
0 Magnet; 0 Charter; 1 Title I Eligible; 1 School-wide Title I
Students: 2,417 (52.8% male; 47.1% female)
Individual Education Program: n/a;
English Language Learner: n/a; Migrant: n/a
Eligible for Free Lunch Program: n/a
Eligible for Reduced-Price Lunch Program: n/a
Teachers: 202.5 (11.9 to 1)
Librarians/Media Specialists: 4.0 (604.3 to 1)
Guidance Counselors: 6.0 (402.8 to 1)
Current Spending: ($ per student per year):
Total: $11,758; Instruction: $8,069; Support Services: $3,429

Enrollment, Drop-out Rates and Diploma Recipients by Race/Ethnicity

Category	Total	White	Black	Asian	AIAN	Hisp.
Enrollment (%)	100.0	97.6	0.5	0.3	0.8	0.7
Drop-out Rate (%)	3.0	3.1	0.0	0.0	0.0	0.0
H.S. Diplomas (#)	174	173	0	1	0	0

Otsego County

Oneonta City SD

189 Main St-Ste 302 • Oneonta, NY 13820-1142
(607) 433-8232 • http://oneonta.k12.ny.us/districtwebpage.htm
Grade Span: PK-12; **Agency Type:** 1
Schools: 6
4 Primary; 1 Middle; 1 High; 0 Other Level
6 Regular; 0 Special Education; 0 Vocational; 0 Alternative
0 Magnet; 0 Charter; 4 Title I Eligible; 0 School-wide Title I
Students: 2,142 (49.3% male; 50.6% female)
Individual Education Program: n/a;
English Language Learner: n/a; Migrant: n/a
Eligible for Free Lunch Program: n/a
Eligible for Reduced-Price Lunch Program: n/a
Teachers: 174.1 (12.3 to 1)
Librarians/Media Specialists: 6.0 (357.0 to 1)
Guidance Counselors: 9.3 (230.3 to 1)
Current Spending: ($ per student per year):
Total: $11,313; Instruction: $7,666; Support Services: $3,429

Enrollment, Drop-out Rates and Diploma Recipients by Race/Ethnicity

Category	Total	White	Black	Asian	AIAN	Hisp.
Enrollment (%)	100.0	89.2	4.8	2.8	0.5	2.7
Drop-out Rate (%)	1.3	1.1	2.9	0.0	0.0	5.9
H.S. Diplomas (#)	148	141	4	0	1	2

Putnam County

Brewster Central SD
30 Farm-To-Market Rd • Brewster, NY 10509-9956
(845) 279-8000 • http://www.brewsterschools.org/
Grade Span: KG-12; Agency Type: 1
Schools: 5
  2 Primary; 2 Middle; 1 High; 0 Other Level
  5 Regular; 0 Special Education; 0 Vocational; 0 Alternative
  0 Magnet; 0 Charter; 1 Title I Eligible; 0 School-wide Title I
Students: 3,726   (52.6% male; 47.3% female)
  Individual Education Program: n/a;
  English Language Learner: n/a; Migrant: n/a
  Eligible for Free Lunch Program: n/a
  Eligible for Reduced-Price Lunch Program: n/a
Teachers: 277.4 (13.4 to 1)
Librarians/Media Specialists: 5.0 (745.2 to 1)
Guidance Counselors: 9.0 (414.0 to 1)
Current Spending: ($ per student per year):
  Total: $14,214; Instruction: $9,485; Support Services: $4,463
Enrollment, Drop-out Rates and Diploma Recipients by Race/Ethnicity

Category	Total	White	Black	Asian	AIAN	Hisp.
Enrollment (%)	100.0	85.5	3.4	2.5	0.2	8.3
Drop-out Rate (%)	0.6	0.6	0.0	0.0	0.0	1.8
H.S. Diplomas (#)	203	184	4	5	1	9

Carmel Central SD
81 S St • Patterson, NY 12563-0296
(845) 878-2094 • http://ccsd.k12.ny.us/
Grade Span: KG-12; Agency Type: 1
Schools: 5
  3 Primary; 1 Middle; 1 High; 0 Other Level
  5 Regular; 0 Special Education; 0 Vocational; 0 Alternative
  0 Magnet; 0 Charter; 4 Title I Eligible; 0 School-wide Title I
Students: 4,857   (50.8% male; 49.1% female)
  Individual Education Program: n/a;
  English Language Learner: n/a; Migrant: n/a
  Eligible for Free Lunch Program: n/a
  Eligible for Reduced-Price Lunch Program: n/a
Teachers: 334.5 (14.5 to 1)
Librarians/Media Specialists: 4.2 (1,156.4 to 1)
Guidance Counselors: 10.6 (458.2 to 1)
Current Spending: ($ per student per year):
  Total: $13,163; Instruction: $9,360; Support Services: $3,599
Enrollment, Drop-out Rates and Diploma Recipients by Race/Ethnicity

Category	Total	White	Black	Asian	AIAN	Hisp.
Enrollment (%)	100.0	88.2	2.4	1.3	0.0	8.1
Drop-out Rate (%)	2.5	2.3	9.4	4.3	n/a	2.0
H.S. Diplomas (#)	288	262	4	4	0	18

Mahopac Central SD
179 E Lake Bouleva • Mahopac, NY 10541-1666
(845) 628-3415 • http://www.mahopac.k12.ny.us/
Grade Span: KG-12; Agency Type: 1
Schools: 6
  4 Primary; 1 Middle; 1 High; 0 Other Level
  6 Regular; 0 Special Education; 0 Vocational; 0 Alternative
  0 Magnet; 0 Charter; 3 Title I Eligible; 0 School-wide Title I
Students: 5,289   (51.7% male; 48.2% female)
  Individual Education Program: n/a;
  English Language Learner: n/a; Migrant: n/a
  Eligible for Free Lunch Program: n/a
  Eligible for Reduced-Price Lunch Program: n/a
Teachers: 402.2 (13.2 to 1)
Librarians/Media Specialists: 2.0 (2,644.5 to 1)
Guidance Counselors: 11.0 (480.8 to 1)
Current Spending: ($ per student per year):
  Total: $13,029; Instruction: $8,822; Support Services: $4,016
Enrollment, Drop-out Rates and Diploma Recipients by Race/Ethnicity

Category	Total	White	Black	Asian	AIAN	Hisp.
Enrollment (%)	100.0	92.5	1.2	1.4	0.2	4.7
Drop-out Rate (%)	1.0	1.0	5.6	0.0	0.0	1.6
H.S. Diplomas (#)	348	335	0	1	0	12

Putnam Valley Central SD
146 Peekskll Hollw Rd • Putnam Valley, NY 10579-3238
(845) 528-8143
Grade Span: KG-11; Agency Type: 2
Schools: 3
  1 Primary; 1 Middle; 1 High; 0 Other Level
  3 Regular; 0 Special Education; 0 Vocational; 0 Alternative
  0 Magnet; 0 Charter; 3 Title I Eligible; 0 School-wide Title I
Students: 1,934   (50.4% male; 49.5% female)
  Individual Education Program: n/a;
  English Language Learner: n/a; Migrant: n/a

Eligible for Free Lunch Program: n/a
  Eligible for Reduced-Price Lunch Program: n/a
Teachers: 142.2 (13.6 to 1)
Librarians/Media Specialists: 1.0 (1,934.0 to 1)
Guidance Counselors: 4.0 (483.5 to 1)
Current Spending: ($ per student per year):
  Total: $14,133; Instruction: $9,279; Support Services: $4,634
Enrollment, Drop-out Rates and Diploma Recipients by Race/Ethnicity

Category	Total	White	Black	Asian	AIAN	Hisp.
Enrollment (%)	100.0	84.2	3.9	1.4	0.1	10.4
Drop-out Rate (%)	0.0	0.0	0.0	0.0	n/a	0.0
H.S. Diplomas (#)	n/a	n/a	n/a	n/a	n/a	n/a

Rensselaer County

Averill Park Central SD
8439 Miller Hill Rd • Averill Park, NY 12018-9798
(518) 674-7055 • http://www.averillpark.k12.ny.us/
Grade Span: KG-12; Agency Type: 1
Schools: 6
  4 Primary; 1 Middle; 1 High; 0 Other Level
  6 Regular; 0 Special Education; 0 Vocational; 0 Alternative
  0 Magnet; 0 Charter; 4 Title I Eligible; 0 School-wide Title I
Students: 3,546   (50.8% male; 49.1% female)
  Individual Education Program: n/a;
  English Language Learner: n/a; Migrant: n/a
  Eligible for Free Lunch Program: n/a
  Eligible for Reduced-Price Lunch Program: n/a
Teachers: 273.7 (13.0 to 1)
Librarians/Media Specialists: 5.0 (709.2 to 1)
Guidance Counselors: 8.0 (443.3 to 1)
Current Spending: ($ per student per year):
  Total: $10,492; Instruction: $6,899; Support Services: $3,332
Enrollment, Drop-out Rates and Diploma Recipients by Race/Ethnicity

Category	Total	White	Black	Asian	AIAN	Hisp.
Enrollment (%)	100.0	97.1	1.2	1.0	0.0	0.7
Drop-out Rate (%)	3.5	3.5	0.0	0.0	0.0	0.0
H.S. Diplomas (#)	219	216	0	3	0	0

East Greenbush Central SD
29 Englewood Ave • East Greenbush, NY 12061-2213
(518) 477-2755 • http://www.egcsd.org/
Grade Span: KG-12; Agency Type: 1
Schools: 7
  5 Primary; 1 Middle; 1 High; 0 Other Level
  7 Regular; 0 Special Education; 0 Vocational; 0 Alternative
  0 Magnet; 0 Charter; 3 Title I Eligible; 0 School-wide Title I
Students: 4,572   (49.8% male; 50.1% female)
  Individual Education Program: n/a;
  English Language Learner: n/a; Migrant: n/a
  Eligible for Free Lunch Program: n/a
  Eligible for Reduced-Price Lunch Program: n/a
Teachers: 338.8 (13.5 to 1)
Librarians/Media Specialists: 6.4 (714.4 to 1)
Guidance Counselors: 8.0 (571.5 to 1)
Current Spending: ($ per student per year):
  Total: $10,800; Instruction: $6,722; Support Services: $3,863
Enrollment, Drop-out Rates and Diploma Recipients by Race/Ethnicity

Category	Total	White	Black	Asian	AIAN	Hisp.
Enrollment (%)	100.0	94.6	2.6	1.8	0.2	0.7
Drop-out Rate (%)	3.9	3.9	3.7	3.7	n/a	0.0
H.S. Diplomas (#)	281	268	7	5	0	1

Lansingburgh Central SD
576 Fifth Ave • Troy, NY 12182-3295
(518) 233-6850
Grade Span: KG-12; Agency Type: 1
Schools: 4
  2 Primary; 1 Middle; 1 High; 0 Other Level
  4 Regular; 0 Special Education; 0 Vocational; 0 Alternative
  0 Magnet; 0 Charter; 4 Title I Eligible; 0 School-wide Title I
Students: 2,428   (52.1% male; 47.8% female)
  Individual Education Program: n/a;
  English Language Learner: n/a; Migrant: n/a
  Eligible for Free Lunch Program: n/a
  Eligible for Reduced-Price Lunch Program: n/a
Teachers: 179.0 (13.6 to 1)
Librarians/Media Specialists: 3.0 (809.3 to 1)
Guidance Counselors: 5.0 (485.6 to 1)
Current Spending: ($ per student per year):
  Total: $10,569; Instruction: $6,986; Support Services: $3,323

Enrollment, Drop-out Rates and Diploma Recipients by Race/Ethnicity

Category	Total	White	Black	Asian	AIAN	Hisp.
Enrollment (%)	100.0	79.3	16.0	0.8	0.1	3.8
Drop-out Rate (%)	7.0	8.0	1.5	0.0	n/a	0.0
H.S. Diplomas (#)	104	102	2	0	0	0

Troy City SD
1728 Tibbits Ave • Troy, NY 12180-7013
(518) 271-5210 • http://www.troy.k12.ny.us/
Grade Span: PK-12; Agency Type: 1
Schools: 8
6 Primary; 1 Middle; 1 High; 0 Other Level
8 Regular; 0 Special Education; 0 Vocational; 0 Alternative
0 Magnet; 0 Charter; 5 Title I Eligible; 5 School-wide Title I
Students: 4,857 (52.0% male; 47.9% female)
Individual Education Program: n/a;
English Language Learner: n/a; Migrant: n/a
Eligible for Free Lunch Program: n/a
Eligible for Reduced-Price Lunch Program: n/a
Teachers: 355.3 (13.7 to 1)
Librarians/Media Specialists: 3.1 (1,566.8 to 1)
Guidance Counselors: 7.0 (693.9 to 1)
Current Spending: ($ per student per year):
Total: $12,641; Instruction: $8,506; Support Services: $3,828
Enrollment, Drop-out Rates and Diploma Recipients by Race/Ethnicity

Category	Total	White	Black	Asian	AIAN	Hisp.
Enrollment (%)	100.0	60.7	28.7	1.9	0.2	8.5
Drop-out Rate (%)	1.3	1.1	1.8	0.0	0.0	2.1
H.S. Diplomas (#)	97	69	22	2	0	4

Rockland County

Clarkstown Central SD
62 Old Middletown Rd • New City, NY 10956
(845) 639-6419 • http://www.ccsd.edu/
Grade Span: KG-12; Agency Type: 1
Schools: 14
10 Primary; 1 Middle; 2 High; 1 Other Level
13 Regular; 1 Special Education; 0 Vocational; 0 Alternative
0 Magnet; 0 Charter; 7 Title I Eligible; 7 School-wide Title I
Students: 9,350 (52.0% male; 47.9% female)
Individual Education Program: n/a;
English Language Learner: n/a; Migrant: n/a
Eligible for Free Lunch Program: n/a
Eligible for Reduced-Price Lunch Program: n/a
Teachers: 689.2 (13.6 to 1)
Librarians/Media Specialists: 15.0 (623.3 to 1)
Guidance Counselors: 17.7 (528.2 to 1)
Current Spending: ($ per student per year):
Total: $12,592; Instruction: $8,444; Support Services: $3,881
Enrollment, Drop-out Rates and Diploma Recipients by Race/Ethnicity

Category	Total	White	Black	Asian	AIAN	Hisp.
Enrollment (%)	100.0	79.8	3.1	10.8	0.1	6.2
Drop-out Rate (%)	0.7	0.6	2.5	0.0	n/a	2.2
H.S. Diplomas (#)	681	573	17	55	0	36

East Ramapo Central SD (Spring Valley)
105 S Madison Ave • Spring Valley, NY 10977-5400
(845) 577-6011 • http://www.j51.com/eastramapo/
Grade Span: PK-12; Agency Type: 1
Schools: 14
6 Primary; 6 Middle; 2 High; 0 Other Level
14 Regular; 0 Special Education; 0 Vocational; 0 Alternative
0 Magnet; 0 Charter; 10 Title I Eligible; 2 School-wide Title I
Students: 9,170 (51.9% male; 48.0% female)
Individual Education Program: n/a;
English Language Learner: n/a; Migrant: n/a
Eligible for Free Lunch Program: n/a
Eligible for Reduced-Price Lunch Program: n/a
Teachers: 720.7 (12.7 to 1)
Librarians/Media Specialists: 13.0 (705.4 to 1)
Guidance Counselors: 21.0 (436.7 to 1)
Current Spending: ($ per student per year):
Total: $16,829; Instruction: $10,601; Support Services: $5,948
Enrollment, Drop-out Rates and Diploma Recipients by Race/Ethnicity

Category	Total	White	Black	Asian	AIAN	Hisp.
Enrollment (%)	100.0	14.0	60.7	9.6	0.2	15.5
Drop-out Rate (%)	8.2	6.1	8.5	5.9	20.0	13.9
H.S. Diplomas (#)	526	162	242	69	0	53

Haverstraw-Stony Point Central SD (North Rockla
65 Chapel St • Garnerville, NY 10923-1280
(845) 942-3000
Grade Span: PK-12; Agency Type: 1
Schools: 9

5 Primary; 3 Middle; 1 High; 0 Other Level
9 Regular; 0 Special Education; 0 Vocational; 0 Alternative
0 Magnet; 0 Charter; 3 Title I Eligible; 2 School-wide Title I
Students: 8,366 (51.2% male; 48.7% female)
Individual Education Program: n/a;
English Language Learner: n/a; Migrant: n/a
Eligible for Free Lunch Program: n/a
Eligible for Reduced-Price Lunch Program: n/a
Teachers: 635.2 (13.2 to 1)
Librarians/Media Specialists: 9.4 (890.0 to 1)
Guidance Counselors: 16.6 (504.0 to 1)
Current Spending: ($ per student per year):
Total: $15,830; Instruction: $10,456; Support Services: $5,095
Enrollment, Drop-out Rates and Diploma Recipients by Race/Ethnicity

Category	Total	White	Black	Asian	AIAN	Hisp.
Enrollment (%)	100.0	50.8	11.4	3.6	0.3	34.0
Drop-out Rate (%)	3.1	2.6	4.0	1.4	0.0	4.0
H.S. Diplomas (#)	442	270	37	16	0	119

Nanuet Union Free SD
101 Church St • Nanuet, NY 10954-3000
(845) 627-9888 • http://nanuet.lhric.org/
Grade Span: KG-12; Agency Type: 1
Schools: 4
1 Primary; 2 Middle; 1 High; 0 Other Level
4 Regular; 0 Special Education; 0 Vocational; 0 Alternative
0 Magnet; 0 Charter; 3 Title I Eligible; 0 School-wide Title I
Students: 2,192 (51.6% male; 48.3% female)
Individual Education Program: n/a;
English Language Learner: n/a; Migrant: n/a
Eligible for Free Lunch Program: n/a
Eligible for Reduced-Price Lunch Program: n/a
Teachers: 183.1 (12.0 to 1)
Librarians/Media Specialists: 4.0 (548.0 to 1)
Guidance Counselors: 6.0 (365.3 to 1)
Current Spending: ($ per student per year):
Total: $16,514; Instruction: $10,441; Support Services: $5,831
Enrollment, Drop-out Rates and Diploma Recipients by Race/Ethnicity

Category	Total	White	Black	Asian	AIAN	Hisp.
Enrollment (%)	100.0	76.7	4.2	11.3	0.0	7.7
Drop-out Rate (%)	0.2	0.2	0.0	0.0	n/a	0.0
H.S. Diplomas (#)	120	79	6	27	0	8

Nyack Union Free SD
13a Dickinson Ave • Nyack, NY 10960-2914
(845) 353-7010
Grade Span: KG-12; Agency Type: 1
Schools: 5
3 Primary; 1 Middle; 1 High; 0 Other Level
5 Regular; 0 Special Education; 0 Vocational; 0 Alternative
0 Magnet; 0 Charter; 4 Title I Eligible; 0 School-wide Title I
Students: 2,858 (51.1% male; 48.8% female)
Individual Education Program: n/a;
English Language Learner: n/a; Migrant: n/a
Eligible for Free Lunch Program: n/a
Eligible for Reduced-Price Lunch Program: n/a
Teachers: 246.0 (11.6 to 1)
Librarians/Media Specialists: 4.0 (714.5 to 1)
Guidance Counselors: 8.0 (357.3 to 1)
Current Spending: ($ per student per year):
Total: $16,303; Instruction: $11,528; Support Services: $4,555
Enrollment, Drop-out Rates and Diploma Recipients by Race/Ethnicity

Category	Total	White	Black	Asian	AIAN	Hisp.
Enrollment (%)	100.0	53.9	28.2	8.4	0.0	9.5
Drop-out Rate (%)	2.1	1.2	2.9	2.7	n/a	6.5
H.S. Diplomas (#)	166	105	40	9	0	12

Pearl River Union Free SD
275 E Central Ave • Pearl River, NY 10965-2799
(845) 620-3900 • http://www.pearlriver.k12.ny.us/
Grade Span: KG-12; Agency Type: 1
Schools: 7
3 Primary; 1 Middle; 1 High; 2 Other Level
5 Regular; 0 Special Education; 0 Vocational; 2 Alternative
0 Magnet; 0 Charter; 5 Title I Eligible; 0 School-wide Title I
Students: 2,544 (49.0% male; 50.9% female)
Individual Education Program: n/a;
English Language Learner: n/a; Migrant: n/a
Eligible for Free Lunch Program: n/a
Eligible for Reduced-Price Lunch Program: n/a
Teachers: 184.1 (13.8 to 1)
Librarians/Media Specialists: 3.2 (795.0 to 1)
Guidance Counselors: 6.0 (424.0 to 1)
Current Spending: ($ per student per year):
Total: $13,840; Instruction: $9,004; Support Services: $4,669

Enrollment, Drop-out Rates and Diploma Recipients by Race/Ethnicity

Category	Total	White	Black	Asian	AIAN	Hisp.
Enrollment (%)	100.0	89.8	1.0	4.8	0.1	4.2
Drop-out Rate (%)	0.6	0.7	0.0	0.0	n/a	0.0
H.S. Diplomas (#)	177	155	0	9	0	13

Ramapo Central SD (Suffern)
45 Mountain Ave • Hillburn, NY 10931-0935
(845) 357-7783 • http://www.ramapocentral.org/
Grade Span: KG-12; **Agency Type:** 1
Schools: 7
  5 Primary; 1 Middle; 1 High; 0 Other Level
  7 Regular; 0 Special Education; 0 Vocational; 0 Alternative
  0 Magnet; 0 Charter; 2 Title I Eligible; 0 School-wide Title I
Students: 4,596   (51.3% male; 48.6% female)
  Individual Education Program: n/a;
  English Language Learner: n/a; Migrant: n/a
  Eligible for Free Lunch Program: n/a
  Eligible for Reduced-Price Lunch Program: n/a
Teachers: 367.9 (12.5 to 1)
Librarians/Media Specialists: 6.0 (766.0 to 1)
Guidance Counselors: 9.0 (510.7 to 1)
Current Spending: ($ per student per year):
  Total: $14,891; Instruction: $10,408; Support Services: $4,308

Enrollment, Drop-out Rates and Diploma Recipients by Race/Ethnicity

Category	Total	White	Black	Asian	AIAN	Hisp.
Enrollment (%)	100.0	81.9	5.0	4.4	0.5	8.2
Drop-out Rate (%)	2.2	1.6	2.7	4.5	11.1	5.3
H.S. Diplomas (#)	277	223	15	18	2	19

South Orangetown Central SD
160 Van Wyck Rd • Blauvelt, NY 10913-1299
(845) 680-1050 • http://www.socsd.k12.ny.us/
Grade Span: KG-12; **Agency Type:** 1
Schools: 5
  2 Primary; 2 Middle; 1 High; 0 Other Level
  5 Regular; 0 Special Education; 0 Vocational; 0 Alternative
  0 Magnet; 0 Charter; 5 Title I Eligible; 0 School-wide Title I
Students: 3,347   (50.1% male; 49.8% female)
  Individual Education Program: n/a;
  English Language Learner: n/a; Migrant: n/a
  Eligible for Free Lunch Program: n/a
  Eligible for Reduced-Price Lunch Program: n/a
Teachers: 267.1 (12.5 to 1)
Librarians/Media Specialists: 4.5 (743.8 to 1)
Guidance Counselors: 7.3 (458.5 to 1)
Current Spending: ($ per student per year):
  Total: $15,344; Instruction: $10,304; Support Services: $4,804

Enrollment, Drop-out Rates and Diploma Recipients by Race/Ethnicity

Category	Total	White	Black	Asian	AIAN	Hisp.
Enrollment (%)	100.0	78.4	3.0	11.7	0.1	6.8
Drop-out Rate (%)	3.2	3.9	2.5	0.6	n/a	2.0
H.S. Diplomas (#)	165	129	3	28	0	5

Saratoga County

Ballston Spa Central SD
70 Malta Ave • Ballston Spa, NY 12020-1599
(518) 884-7195 • http://www.ballstonspa.k12.ny.us/
Grade Span: KG-12; **Agency Type:** 1
Schools: 5
  3 Primary; 1 Middle; 1 High; 0 Other Level
  5 Regular; 0 Special Education; 0 Vocational; 0 Alternative
  0 Magnet; 0 Charter; 4 Title I Eligible; 0 School-wide Title I
Students: 4,521   (50.9% male; 49.0% female)
  Individual Education Program: n/a;
  English Language Learner: n/a; Migrant: n/a
  Eligible for Free Lunch Program: n/a
  Eligible for Reduced-Price Lunch Program: n/a
Teachers: 314.0 (14.4 to 1)
Librarians/Media Specialists: 5.0 (904.2 to 1)
Guidance Counselors: 8.8 (513.8 to 1)
Current Spending: ($ per student per year):
  Total: $11,087; Instruction: $7,684; Support Services: $3,183

Enrollment, Drop-out Rates and Diploma Recipients by Race/Ethnicity

Category	Total	White	Black	Asian	AIAN	Hisp.
Enrollment (%)	100.0	95.9	1.4	1.1	0.1	1.5
Drop-out Rate (%)	3.6	3.7	0.0	0.0	0.0	0.0
H.S. Diplomas (#)	215	209	2	1	0	3

Burnt Hills-Ballston Lake Central SD
50 Cypress Dr • Scotia, NY 12302-4398
(518) 399-6407 • http://www.bhbl.org/
Grade Span: KG-12; **Agency Type:** 1
Schools: 5

  3 Primary; 1 Middle; 1 High; 0 Other Level
  5 Regular; 0 Special Education; 0 Vocational; 0 Alternative
  0 Magnet; 0 Charter; 0 Title I Eligible; 0 School-wide Title I
Students: 3,447   (49.7% male; 50.2% female)
  Individual Education Program: n/a;
  English Language Learner: n/a; Migrant: n/a
  Eligible for Free Lunch Program: n/a
  Eligible for Reduced-Price Lunch Program: n/a
Teachers: 243.3 (14.2 to 1)
Librarians/Media Specialists: 6.2 (556.0 to 1)
Guidance Counselors: 6.3 (547.1 to 1)
Current Spending: ($ per student per year):
  Total: $10,262; Instruction: $7,048; Support Services: $3,016

Enrollment, Drop-out Rates and Diploma Recipients by Race/Ethnicity

Category	Total	White	Black	Asian	AIAN	Hisp.
Enrollment (%)	100.0	97.7	1.0	0.9	0.1	0.3
Drop-out Rate (%)	0.3	0.3	0.0	0.0	n/a	0.0
H.S. Diplomas (#)	213	207	0	3	0	3

Saratoga Springs City SD
5 Wells St • Saratoga Springs, NY 12866-1232
(518) 583-4708 • http://www.saratogaschools.org/
Grade Span: KG-12; **Agency Type:** 1
Schools: 9
  6 Primary; 1 Middle; 1 High; 1 Other Level
  8 Regular; 0 Special Education; 0 Vocational; 1 Alternative
  0 Magnet; 0 Charter; 6 Title I Eligible; 0 School-wide Title I
Students: 6,922   (50.3% male; 49.6% female)
  Individual Education Program: n/a;
  English Language Learner: n/a; Migrant: n/a
  Eligible for Free Lunch Program: n/a
  Eligible for Reduced-Price Lunch Program: n/a
Teachers: 512.9 (13.5 to 1)
Librarians/Media Specialists: 9.0 (769.1 to 1)
Guidance Counselors: 12.0 (576.8 to 1)
Current Spending: ($ per student per year):
  Total: $10,213; Instruction: $7,047; Support Services: $2,921

Enrollment, Drop-out Rates and Diploma Recipients by Race/Ethnicity

Category	Total	White	Black	Asian	AIAN	Hisp.
Enrollment (%)	100.0	94.8	3.3	0.9	0.0	1.0
Drop-out Rate (%)	0.6	0.6	1.5	0.0	0.0	0.0
H.S. Diplomas (#)	461	458	1	1	0	1

Schuylerville Central SD
14 Spring St • Schuylerville, NY 12871-1098
(518) 695-3255 • http://www.schuylervilleschools.org/default_IE4.asp
Grade Span: KG-12; **Agency Type:** 2
Schools: 2
  1 Primary; 0 Middle; 1 High; 0 Other Level
  2 Regular; 0 Special Education; 0 Vocational; 0 Alternative
  0 Magnet; 0 Charter; 2 Title I Eligible; 0 School-wide Title I
Students: 1,693   (50.4% male; 49.5% female)
  Individual Education Program: n/a;
  English Language Learner: n/a; Migrant: n/a
  Eligible for Free Lunch Program: n/a
  Eligible for Reduced-Price Lunch Program: n/a
Teachers: 132.3 (12.8 to 1)
Librarians/Media Specialists: 2.0 (846.5 to 1)
Guidance Counselors: 4.0 (423.3 to 1)
Current Spending: ($ per student per year):
  Total: $12,193; Instruction: $8,418; Support Services: $3,459

Enrollment, Drop-out Rates and Diploma Recipients by Race/Ethnicity

Category	Total	White	Black	Asian	AIAN	Hisp.
Enrollment (%)	100.0	97.3	0.8	0.6	0.0	1.2
Drop-out Rate (%)	0.4	0.5	0.0	0.0	n/a	0.0
H.S. Diplomas (#)	114	114	0	0	0	0

Shenendehowa Central SD
5 Chelsea Pl • Clifton Park, NY 12065-3240
(518) 881-0610 • http://www.shenet.org/
Grade Span: KG-12; **Agency Type:** 1
Schools: 11
  7 Primary; 3 Middle; 1 High; 0 Other Level
  11 Regular; 0 Special Education; 0 Vocational; 0 Alternative
  0 Magnet; 0 Charter; 7 Title I Eligible; 0 School-wide Title I
Students: 9,313   (51.7% male; 48.2% female)
  Individual Education Program: n/a;
  English Language Learner: n/a; Migrant: n/a
  Eligible for Free Lunch Program: n/a
  Eligible for Reduced-Price Lunch Program: n/a
Teachers: 635.6 (14.7 to 1)
Librarians/Media Specialists: 12.5 (745.0 to 1)
Guidance Counselors: 29.0 (321.1 to 1)
Current Spending: ($ per student per year):
  Total: $10,375; Instruction: $6,485; Support Services: $3,616

Enrollment, Drop-out Rates and Diploma Recipients by Race/Ethnicity

Category	Total	White	Black	Asian	AIAN	Hisp.
Enrollment (%)	100.0	92.1	2.3	3.6	0.2	1.9
Drop-out Rate (%)	0.0	0.0	0.0	0.0	0.0	0.0
H.S. Diplomas (#)	580	547	9	14	3	7

South Glens Falls Central SD
6 Bluebird Rd • South Glens Falls, NY 12803-5704
(518) 793-9617 • http://www.sgfallssd.org/
Grade Span: KG-12; **Agency Type:** 2
Schools: 7
　4 Primary; 1 Middle; 1 High; 1 Other Level
　6 Regular; 0 Special Education; 0 Vocational; 1 Alternative
　0 Magnet; 0 Charter; 4 Title I Eligible; 0 School-wide Title I
Students: 3,292　(50.9% male; 49.0% female)
　Individual Education Program: n/a;
　English Language Learner: n/a; Migrant: n/a
　Eligible for Free Lunch Program: n/a
　Eligible for Reduced-Price Lunch Program: n/a
Teachers: 245.2 (13.4 to 1)
Librarians/Media Specialists: 3.0 (1,097.3 to 1)
Guidance Counselors: 5.0 (658.4 to 1)
Current Spending: ($ per student per year):
　Total: $9,830; Instruction: $6,839; Support Services: $2,699

Enrollment, Drop-out Rates and Diploma Recipients by Race/Ethnicity

Category	Total	White	Black	Asian	AIAN	Hisp.
Enrollment (%)	100.0	98.5	0.8	0.3	0.1	0.3
Drop-out Rate (%)	2.2	2.2	0.0	n/a	n/a	0.0
H.S. Diplomas (#)	161	160	0	0	1	0

Schenectady County

Niskayuna Central SD
1239 Van Antwerp Rd • Schenectady, NY 12309-5317
(518) 377-4666 • http://www.nisk.k12.ny.us/
Grade Span: KG-12; **Agency Type:** 1
Schools: 8
　5 Primary; 2 Middle; 1 High; 0 Other Level
　8 Regular; 0 Special Education; 0 Vocational; 0 Alternative
　0 Magnet; 0 Charter; 3 Title I Eligible; 0 School-wide Title I
Students: 4,258　(51.2% male; 48.7% female)
　Individual Education Program: n/a;
　English Language Learner: n/a; Migrant: n/a
　Eligible for Free Lunch Program: n/a
　Eligible for Reduced-Price Lunch Program: n/a
Teachers: 300.0 (14.2 to 1)
Librarians/Media Specialists: 9.3 (457.8 to 1)
Guidance Counselors: 11.6 (367.1 to 1)
Current Spending: ($ per student per year):
　Total: $10,246; Instruction: $6,319; Support Services: $3,709

Enrollment, Drop-out Rates and Diploma Recipients by Race/Ethnicity

Category	Total	White	Black	Asian	AIAN	Hisp.
Enrollment (%)	100.0	90.1	2.2	6.6	0.1	0.9
Drop-out Rate (%)	1.4	1.5	0.0	0.0	0.0	0.0
H.S. Diplomas (#)	280	256	5	17	0	2

Rotterdam-Mohonasen Central SD
2072 Curry Rd • Schenectady, NY 12303-4400
(518) 356-8200
Grade Span: KG-12; **Agency Type:** 1
Schools: 4
　2 Primary; 1 Middle; 1 High; 0 Other Level
　4 Regular; 0 Special Education; 0 Vocational; 0 Alternative
　0 Magnet; 0 Charter; 4 Title I Eligible; 0 School-wide Title I
Students: 3,340　(51.4% male; 48.5% female)
　Individual Education Program: n/a;
　English Language Learner: n/a; Migrant: n/a
　Eligible for Free Lunch Program: n/a
　Eligible for Reduced-Price Lunch Program: n/a
Teachers: 217.8 (15.3 to 1)
Librarians/Media Specialists: 4.0 (835.0 to 1)
Guidance Counselors: 7.0 (477.1 to 1)
Current Spending: ($ per student per year):
　Total: $8,820; Instruction: $5,844; Support Services: $2,704

Enrollment, Drop-out Rates and Diploma Recipients by Race/Ethnicity

Category	Total	White	Black	Asian	AIAN	Hisp.
Enrollment (%)	100.0	95.0	2.5	1.4	0.3	0.8
Drop-out Rate (%)	0.9	0.9	0.0	0.0	0.0	0.0
H.S. Diplomas (#)	201	195	2	4	0	0

Schalmont Central SD
401 Duanesburg Rd • Schenectady, NY 12306-1981
(518) 355-9200 • http://www.schalmont.org/
Grade Span: KG-12; **Agency Type:** 1
Schools: 5

　3 Primary; 1 Middle; 1 High; 0 Other Level
　5 Regular; 0 Special Education; 0 Vocational; 0 Alternative
　0 Magnet; 0 Charter; 1 Title I Eligible; 0 School-wide Title I
Students: 2,228　(49.8% male; 50.1% female)
　Individual Education Program: n/a;
　English Language Learner: n/a; Migrant: n/a
　Eligible for Free Lunch Program: n/a
　Eligible for Reduced-Price Lunch Program: n/a
Teachers: 168.4 (13.2 to 1)
Librarians/Media Specialists: 4.3 (518.1 to 1)
Guidance Counselors: 4.7 (474.0 to 1)
Current Spending: ($ per student per year):
　Total: $17,415; Instruction: $8,085; Support Services: $9,078

Enrollment, Drop-out Rates and Diploma Recipients by Race/Ethnicity

Category	Total	White	Black	Asian	AIAN	Hisp.
Enrollment (%)	100.0	97.4	1.4	0.8	0.0	0.4
Drop-out Rate (%)	1.1	1.2	0.0	0.0	n/a	0.0
H.S. Diplomas (#)	161	158	2	1	0	0

Schenectady City SD
108 Education Dr • Schenectady, NY 12303-3442
(518) 370-8100 • http://www.schenectady.k12.ny.us/
Grade Span: PK-12; **Agency Type:** 1
Schools: 15
　11 Primary; 3 Middle; 1 High; 0 Other Level
　15 Regular; 0 Special Education; 0 Vocational; 0 Alternative
　1 Magnet; 0 Charter; 13 Title I Eligible; 12 School-wide Title I
Students: 9,090　(50.5% male; 49.4% female)
　Individual Education Program: n/a;
　English Language Learner: n/a; Migrant: n/a
　Eligible for Free Lunch Program: n/a
　Eligible for Reduced-Price Lunch Program: n/a
Teachers: 658.4 (13.8 to 1)
Librarians/Media Specialists: 10.5 (865.7 to 1)
Guidance Counselors: 18.0 (505.0 to 1)
Current Spending: ($ per student per year):
　Total: $11,487; Instruction: $8,330; Support Services: $2,870

Enrollment, Drop-out Rates and Diploma Recipients by Race/Ethnicity

Category	Total	White	Black	Asian	AIAN	Hisp.
Enrollment (%)	100.0	47.7	31.4	7.6	0.6	12.6
Drop-out Rate (%)	18.4	12.6	30.2	15.4	0.0	33.8
H.S. Diplomas (#)	358	224	92	20	0	22

Scotia-Glenville Central SD
900 Preddice Pky • Scotia, NY 12302-1049
(518) 382-1215 • http://www.sgcsd.neric.org/
Grade Span: KG-12; **Agency Type:** 1
Schools: 6
　4 Primary; 1 Middle; 1 High; 0 Other Level
　6 Regular; 0 Special Education; 0 Vocational; 0 Alternative
　0 Magnet; 0 Charter; 3 Title I Eligible; 0 School-wide Title I
Students: 2,952　(51.3% male; 48.6% female)
　Individual Education Program: n/a;
　English Language Learner: n/a; Migrant: n/a
　Eligible for Free Lunch Program: n/a
　Eligible for Reduced-Price Lunch Program: n/a
Teachers: 209.3 (14.1 to 1)
Librarians/Media Specialists: 6.0 (492.0 to 1)
Guidance Counselors: 7.0 (421.7 to 1)
Current Spending: ($ per student per year):
　Total: $10,517; Instruction: $6,944; Support Services: $3,403

Enrollment, Drop-out Rates and Diploma Recipients by Race/Ethnicity

Category	Total	White	Black	Asian	AIAN	Hisp.
Enrollment (%)	100.0	96.0	1.2	1.2	0.1	1.5
Drop-out Rate (%)	0.1	0.1	0.0	0.0	0.0	0.0
H.S. Diplomas (#)	218	218	0	0	0	0

Schoharie County

Cobleskill-Richmondville Central SD
155 Washington Ave • Cobleskill, NY 12043-1099
(518) 234-4032 • http://www.crcs.k12.ny.us/
Grade Span: KG-12; **Agency Type:** 1
Schools: 6
　2 Primary; 2 Middle; 1 High; 1 Other Level
　5 Regular; 0 Special Education; 0 Vocational; 1 Alternative
　0 Magnet; 0 Charter; 3 Title I Eligible; 0 School-wide Title I
Students: 2,208　(51.2% male; 48.7% female)
　Individual Education Program: n/a;
　English Language Learner: n/a; Migrant: n/a
　Eligible for Free Lunch Program: n/a
　Eligible for Reduced-Price Lunch Program: n/a
Teachers: 181.7 (12.2 to 1)
Librarians/Media Specialists: 4.0 (552.0 to 1)
Guidance Counselors: 7.0 (315.4 to 1)

Current Spending: ($ per student per year):
Total: $11,794; Instruction: $7,762; Support Services: $3,710

Enrollment, Drop-out Rates and Diploma Recipients by Race/Ethnicity

Category	Total	White	Black	Asian	AIAN	Hisp.
Enrollment (%)	100.0	94.8	1.7	0.6	0.3	2.5
Drop-out Rate (%)	3.1	2.9	16.7	n/a	0.0	0.0
H.S. Diplomas (#)	140	136	0	3	0	1

Schuyler County

Watkins Glen Central SD
303 12th St • Watkins Glen, NY 14891-1699
(607) 535-3219
Grade Span: PK-12; **Agency Type:** 1
Schools: 4
1 Primary; 1 Middle; 1 High; 1 Other Level
3 Regular; 0 Special Education; 0 Vocational; 1 Alternative
0 Magnet; 0 Charter; 3 Title I Eligible; 0 School-wide Title I
Students: 1,524 (55.2% male; 44.7% female)
Individual Education Program: n/a;
English Language Learner: n/a; Migrant: n/a
Eligible for Free Lunch Program: n/a
Eligible for Reduced-Price Lunch Program: n/a
Teachers: 113.0 (13.5 to 1)
Librarians/Media Specialists: 2.5 (609.6 to 1)
Guidance Counselors: 3.0 (508.0 to 1)
Current Spending: ($ per student per year):
Total: $11,695; Instruction: $7,555; Support Services: $3,911

Enrollment, Drop-out Rates and Diploma Recipients by Race/Ethnicity

Category	Total	White	Black	Asian	AIAN	Hisp.
Enrollment (%)	100.0	90.1	5.4	0.9	0.2	3.5
Drop-out Rate (%)	5.5	5.7	0.0	0.0	n/a	0.0
H.S. Diplomas (#)	99	95	1	1	0	2

Seneca County

Waterloo Central SD
109 Washington St • Waterloo, NY 13165-1397
(315) 539-1500 • http://www.flare.net/wcs/
Grade Span: PK-12; **Agency Type:** 1
Schools: 5
3 Primary; 1 Middle; 1 High; 0 Other Level
5 Regular; 0 Special Education; 0 Vocational; 0 Alternative
0 Magnet; 0 Charter; 5 Title I Eligible; 0 School-wide Title I
Students: 2,062 (50.5% male; 49.4% female)
Individual Education Program: n/a;
English Language Learner: n/a; Migrant: n/a
Eligible for Free Lunch Program: n/a
Eligible for Reduced-Price Lunch Program: n/a
Teachers: 154.8 (13.3 to 1)
Librarians/Media Specialists: 2.3 (896.5 to 1)
Guidance Counselors: 7.0 (294.6 to 1)
Current Spending: ($ per student per year):
Total: $10,287; Instruction: $6,482; Support Services: $3,513

Enrollment, Drop-out Rates and Diploma Recipients by Race/Ethnicity

Category	Total	White	Black	Asian	AIAN	Hisp.
Enrollment (%)	100.0	94.0	2.7	0.7	0.2	2.3
Drop-out Rate (%)	4.0	3.8	20.0	n/a	n/a	n/a
H.S. Diplomas (#)	100	100	0	0	0	0

St. Lawrence County

Canton Central SD
99 State St • Canton, NY 13617-1099
(315) 386-8561
Grade Span: PK-12; **Agency Type:** 1
Schools: 3
1 Primary; 1 Middle; 1 High; 0 Other Level
3 Regular; 0 Special Education; 0 Vocational; 0 Alternative
0 Magnet; 0 Charter; 2 Title I Eligible; 2 School-wide Title I
Students: 1,513 (51.2% male; 48.7% female)
Individual Education Program: n/a;
English Language Learner: n/a; Migrant: n/a
Eligible for Free Lunch Program: n/a
Eligible for Reduced-Price Lunch Program: n/a
Teachers: 120.0 (12.6 to 1)
Librarians/Media Specialists: 2.0 (756.5 to 1)
Guidance Counselors: 5.0 (302.6 to 1)
Current Spending: ($ per student per year):
Total: $11,077; Instruction: $7,427; Support Services: $3,341

Enrollment, Drop-out Rates and Diploma Recipients by Race/Ethnicity

Category	Total	White	Black	Asian	AIAN	Hisp.
Enrollment (%)	100.0	97.9	1.1	0.5	0.1	0.4
Drop-out Rate (%)	2.8	2.7	0.0	0.0	50.0	0.0
H.S. Diplomas (#)	97	93	2	0	0	2

Gouverneur Central SD
133 E Barney St • Gouverneur, NY 13642-1100
(315) 287-4870 • http://gcs.neric.org/
Grade Span: KG-12; **Agency Type:** 1
Schools: 5
3 Primary; 0 Middle; 0 High; 2 Other Level
4 Regular; 0 Special Education; 0 Vocational; 1 Alternative
0 Magnet; 0 Charter; 3 Title I Eligible; 3 School-wide Title I
Students: 1,743 (51.5% male; 48.4% female)
Individual Education Program: n/a;
English Language Learner: n/a; Migrant: n/a
Eligible for Free Lunch Program: n/a
Eligible for Reduced-Price Lunch Program: n/a
Teachers: 119.8 (14.5 to 1)
Librarians/Media Specialists: 2.0 (871.5 to 1)
Guidance Counselors: 7.0 (249.0 to 1)
Current Spending: ($ per student per year):
Total: $11,989; Instruction: $7,847; Support Services: $3,810

Enrollment, Drop-out Rates and Diploma Recipients by Race/Ethnicity

Category	Total	White	Black	Asian	AIAN	Hisp.
Enrollment (%)	100.0	96.4	2.0	0.4	0.2	1.0
Drop-out Rate (%)	8.4	8.5	0.0	0.0	n/a	0.0
H.S. Diplomas (#)	119	118	0	0	0	1

Massena Central SD
84 Nightengale Ave • Massena, NY 13662-1999
(315) 764-3700 • http://www.mcs.k12.ny.us/
Grade Span: KG-12; **Agency Type:** 1
Schools: 5
3 Primary; 1 Middle; 1 High; 0 Other Level
5 Regular; 0 Special Education; 0 Vocational; 0 Alternative
0 Magnet; 0 Charter; 5 Title I Eligible; 0 School-wide Title I
Students: 2,861 (50.6% male; 49.3% female)
Individual Education Program: n/a;
English Language Learner: n/a; Migrant: n/a
Eligible for Free Lunch Program: n/a
Eligible for Reduced-Price Lunch Program: n/a
Teachers: 202.0 (14.2 to 1)
Librarians/Media Specialists: 3.9 (733.6 to 1)
Guidance Counselors: 9.0 (317.9 to 1)
Current Spending: ($ per student per year):
Total: $10,016; Instruction: $6,949; Support Services: $2,727

Enrollment, Drop-out Rates and Diploma Recipients by Race/Ethnicity

Category	Total	White	Black	Asian	AIAN	Hisp.
Enrollment (%)	100.0	86.3	0.7	0.8	11.4	0.8
Drop-out Rate (%)	5.4	4.9	0.0	0.0	11.4	0.0
H.S. Diplomas (#)	167	164	0	0	3	0

Ogdensburg City SD
1100 State St • Ogdensburg, NY 13669-3398
(315) 393-0900 • http://www.ogdensburg.neric.org/
Grade Span: PK-12; **Agency Type:** 1
Schools: 8
4 Primary; 0 Middle; 1 High; 3 Other Level
5 Regular; 0 Special Education; 0 Vocational; 3 Alternative
0 Magnet; 0 Charter; 5 Title I Eligible; 5 School-wide Title I
Students: 2,018 (52.4% male; 47.5% female)
Individual Education Program: n/a;
English Language Learner: n/a; Migrant: n/a
Eligible for Free Lunch Program: n/a
Eligible for Reduced-Price Lunch Program: n/a
Teachers: 167.8 (12.0 to 1)
Librarians/Media Specialists: 4.0 (504.5 to 1)
Guidance Counselors: 6.0 (336.3 to 1)
Current Spending: ($ per student per year):
Total: $12,173; Instruction: $8,838; Support Services: $2,942

Enrollment, Drop-out Rates and Diploma Recipients by Race/Ethnicity

Category	Total	White	Black	Asian	AIAN	Hisp.
Enrollment (%)	100.0	97.5	1.6	0.7	0.1	0.0
Drop-out Rate (%)	2.3	2.3	0.0	0.0	n/a	n/a
H.S. Diplomas (#)	127	124	1	2	0	0

Steuben County

Bath Central SD
25 Ellas Ave • Bath, NY 14810-1107
(607) 776-3301
Grade Span: PK-12; **Agency Type:** 1
Schools: 4

1 Primary; 2 Middle; 1 High; 0 Other Level
4 Regular; 0 Special Education; 0 Vocational; 0 Alternative
0 Magnet; 0 Charter; 4 Title I Eligible; 0 School-wide Title I
Students: 2,054   (53.3% male; 46.6% female)
    Individual Education Program: n/a;
    English Language Learner: n/a; Migrant: n/a
    Eligible for Free Lunch Program: n/a
    Eligible for Reduced-Price Lunch Program: n/a
Teachers: 156.4 (13.1 to 1)
Librarians/Media Specialists: 2.0 (1,027.0 to 1)
Guidance Counselors: 4.0 (513.5 to 1)
Current Spending: ($ per student per year):
    Total: $10,052; Instruction: $6,514; Support Services: $3,266
Enrollment, Drop-out Rates and Diploma Recipients by Race/Ethnicity

Category	Total	White	Black	Asian	AIAN	Hisp.
Enrollment (%)	100.0	96.7	1.4	1.1	0.3	0.5
Drop-out Rate (%)	1.7	1.8	0.0	0.0	n/a	0.0
H.S. Diplomas (#)	134	130	2	0	0	2

Corning City SD
165 Charles St • Painted Post, NY 14870-1199
(607) 936-3704 • http://www.corningareaschools.com/
Grade Span: PK-12; **Agency Type:** 1
Schools: 14
    9 Primary; 2 Middle; 3 High; 0 Other Level
    14 Regular; 0 Special Education; 0 Vocational; 0 Alternative
    0 Magnet; 0 Charter; 7 Title I Eligible; 0 School-wide Title I
Students: 5,833   (50.8% male; 49.1% female)
    Individual Education Program: n/a;
    English Language Learner: n/a; Migrant: n/a
    Eligible for Free Lunch Program: n/a
    Eligible for Reduced-Price Lunch Program: n/a
Teachers: 417.3 (14.0 to 1)
Librarians/Media Specialists: 10.1 (577.5 to 1)
Guidance Counselors: 16.0 (364.6 to 1)
Current Spending: ($ per student per year):
    Total: $10,510; Instruction: $6,621; Support Services: $3,666
Enrollment, Drop-out Rates and Diploma Recipients by Race/Ethnicity

Category	Total	White	Black	Asian	AIAN	Hisp.
Enrollment (%)	100.0	93.3	3.4	2.3	0.3	0.7
Drop-out Rate (%)	3.3	3.4	0.0	0.0	0.0	0.0
H.S. Diplomas (#)	358	342	7	5	1	3

Hornell City SD
25 Pearl St • Hornell, NY 14843-1504
(607) 324-1302 • http://www.hornell.wnyric.org/
Grade Span: KG-12; **Agency Type:** 1
Schools: 4
    3 Primary; 0 Middle; 1 High; 0 Other Level
    4 Regular; 0 Special Education; 0 Vocational; 0 Alternative
    0 Magnet; 0 Charter; 4 Title I Eligible; 4 School-wide Title I
Students: 1,884   (53.7% male; 46.2% female)
    Individual Education Program: n/a;
    English Language Learner: n/a; Migrant: n/a
    Eligible for Free Lunch Program: n/a
    Eligible for Reduced-Price Lunch Program: n/a
Teachers: 163.2 (11.5 to 1)
Librarians/Media Specialists: 2.3 (819.1 to 1)
Guidance Counselors: 7.8 (241.5 to 1)
Current Spending: ($ per student per year):
    Total: $10,612; Instruction: $7,187; Support Services: $3,002
Enrollment, Drop-out Rates and Diploma Recipients by Race/Ethnicity

Category	Total	White	Black	Asian	AIAN	Hisp.
Enrollment (%)	100.0	93.8	4.6	0.4	0.2	1.0
Drop-out Rate (%)	7.6	7.4	8.7	0.0	n/a	50.0
H.S. Diplomas (#)	104	102	0	2	0	0

Wayland-Cohocton Central SD
2350 Rt 63 • Wayland, NY 14572-9404
(585) 728-2211 • http://www.wayland-cohocton.k12.ny.us/
Grade Span: PK-12; **Agency Type:** 2
Schools: 4
    2 Primary; 1 Middle; 1 High; 0 Other Level
    4 Regular; 0 Special Education; 0 Vocational; 0 Alternative
    0 Magnet; 0 Charter; 3 Title I Eligible; 0 School-wide Title I
Students: 1,827   (50.4% male; 49.5% female)
    Individual Education Program: n/a;
    English Language Learner: n/a; Migrant: n/a
    Eligible for Free Lunch Program: n/a
    Eligible for Reduced-Price Lunch Program: n/a
Teachers: 152.3 (12.0 to 1)
Librarians/Media Specialists: 2.0 (913.5 to 1)
Guidance Counselors: 5.0 (365.4 to 1)
Current Spending: ($ per student per year):
    Total: $10,924; Instruction: $7,173; Support Services: $3,465

Enrollment, Drop-out Rates and Diploma Recipients by Race/Ethnicity

Category	Total	White	Black	Asian	AIAN	Hisp.
Enrollment (%)	100.0	97.1	1.5	0.5	0.4	0.5
Drop-out Rate (%)	3.4	3.4	0.0	0.0	n/a	0.0
H.S. Diplomas (#)	141	139	1	1	0	0

Suffolk County

Amityville Union Free SD
150 Park Ave • Amityville, NY 11701-3195
(631) 598-6507
Grade Span: PK-12; **Agency Type:** 1
Schools: 5
    2 Primary; 2 Middle; 1 High; 0 Other Level
    5 Regular; 0 Special Education; 0 Vocational; 0 Alternative
    0 Magnet; 0 Charter; 5 Title I Eligible; 0 School-wide Title I
Students: 3,083   (52.1% male; 47.8% female)
    Individual Education Program: n/a;
    English Language Learner: n/a; Migrant: n/a
    Eligible for Free Lunch Program: n/a
    Eligible for Reduced-Price Lunch Program: n/a
Teachers: 257.1 (12.0 to 1)
Librarians/Media Specialists: 5.0 (616.6 to 1)
Guidance Counselors: 7.0 (440.4 to 1)
Current Spending: ($ per student per year):
    Total: $15,744; Instruction: $10,505; Support Services: $4,961
Enrollment, Drop-out Rates and Diploma Recipients by Race/Ethnicity

Category	Total	White	Black	Asian	AIAN	Hisp.
Enrollment (%)	100.0	13.0	63.9	1.4	0.1	21.7
Drop-out Rate (%)	31.3	20.3	32.5	n/a	16.7	39.8
H.S. Diplomas (#)	146	31	97	2	0	16

Babylon Union Free SD
50 Railroad Ave • Babylon, NY 11702-2221
(631) 893-7925
Grade Span: KG-12; **Agency Type:** 1
Schools: 3
    2 Primary; 0 Middle; 1 High; 0 Other Level
    3 Regular; 0 Special Education; 0 Vocational; 0 Alternative
    0 Magnet; 0 Charter; 2 Title I Eligible; 0 School-wide Title I
Students: 2,009   (50.8% male; 49.1% female)
    Individual Education Program: n/a;
    English Language Learner: n/a; Migrant: n/a
    Eligible for Free Lunch Program: n/a
    Eligible for Reduced-Price Lunch Program: n/a
Teachers: 156.4 (12.8 to 1)
Librarians/Media Specialists: 3.0 (669.7 to 1)
Guidance Counselors: 5.0 (401.8 to 1)
Current Spending: ($ per student per year):
    Total: $13,595; Instruction: $9,152; Support Services: $4,213
Enrollment, Drop-out Rates and Diploma Recipients by Race/Ethnicity

Category	Total	White	Black	Asian	AIAN	Hisp.
Enrollment (%)	100.0	85.7	5.0	3.1	0.2	6.0
Drop-out Rate (%)	0.2	0.0	2.6	0.0	0.0	0.0
H.S. Diplomas (#)	141	121	8	5	0	7

Bay Shore Union Free SD
75 W Perkal St • Bay Shore, NY 11706-6696
(631) 968-1117 • http://bayshore.k12.ny.us/
Grade Span: KG-12; **Agency Type:** 1
Schools: 7
    5 Primary; 1 Middle; 1 High; 0 Other Level
    7 Regular; 0 Special Education; 0 Vocational; 0 Alternative
    0 Magnet; 0 Charter; 5 Title I Eligible; 0 School-wide Title I
Students: 5,698   (51.5% male; 48.4% female)
    Individual Education Program: n/a;
    English Language Learner: n/a; Migrant: n/a
    Eligible for Free Lunch Program: n/a
    Eligible for Reduced-Price Lunch Program: n/a
Teachers: 429.4 (13.3 to 1)
Librarians/Media Specialists: 7.0 (814.0 to 1)
Guidance Counselors: 11.5 (495.5 to 1)
Current Spending: ($ per student per year):
    Total: $14,567; Instruction: $9,824; Support Services: $4,479
Enrollment, Drop-out Rates and Diploma Recipients by Race/Ethnicity

Category	Total	White	Black	Asian	AIAN	Hisp.
Enrollment (%)	100.0	51.8	20.9	2.8	0.1	24.4
Drop-out Rate (%)	3.0	1.9	4.7	3.0	0.0	4.4
H.S. Diplomas (#)	287	177	52	10	0	48

Bayport-Blue Point Union Free SD
189 Academy St • Bayport, NY 11705-1799
(631) 472-7860 • http://www.b-bp.k12.ny.us/district.htm
Grade Span: KG-12; **Agency Type:** 2
Schools: 5

3 Primary; 1 Middle; 1 High; 0 Other Level
5 Regular; 0 Special Education; 0 Vocational; 0 Alternative
0 Magnet; 0 Charter; 0 Title I Eligible; 0 School-wide Title I
Students: 2,490 (50.4% male; 49.5% female)
   Individual Education Program: n/a;
   English Language Learner: n/a; Migrant: n/a
   Eligible for Free Lunch Program: n/a
   Eligible for Reduced-Price Lunch Program: n/a
Teachers: 205.7 (12.1 to 1)
Librarians/Media Specialists: 5.0 (498.0 to 1)
Guidance Counselors: 6.0 (415.0 to 1)
Current Spending: ($ per student per year):
   Total: $14,668; Instruction: $9,801; Support Services: $4,720
Enrollment, Drop-out Rates and Diploma Recipients by Race/Ethnicity

Category	Total	White	Black	Asian	AIAN	Hisp.
Enrollment (%)	100.0	94.1	1.3	1.6	0.3	2.7
Drop-out Rate (%)	1.4	1.3	0.0	0.0	0.0	11.1
H.S. Diplomas (#)	138	133	2	2	0	1

Boces Eastern Suffolk (Suffolk I)
201 Sunrise Hwy • Patchogue, NY 11772
(631) 289-2200 • http://www.sricboces.org/
Grade Span: UG-UG; **Agency Type:** 4
Schools: 1
   0 Primary; 0 Middle; 0 High; 1 Other Level
   1 Regular; 0 Special Education; 0 Vocational; 0 Alternative
   0 Magnet; 0 Charter; 0 Title I Eligible; 0 School-wide Title I
Students: 1,908 (74.0% male; 25.9% female)
   Individual Education Program: n/a;
   English Language Learner: n/a; Migrant: n/a
   Eligible for Free Lunch Program: n/a
   Eligible for Reduced-Price Lunch Program: n/a
Teachers: 593.4 (3.2 to 1)
Librarians/Media Specialists: 3.0 (636.0 to 1)
Guidance Counselors: 12.0 (159.0 to 1)
Current Spending: ($ per student per year):
   Total: n/a; Instruction: n/a; Support Services: n/a
Enrollment, Drop-out Rates and Diploma Recipients by Race/Ethnicity

Category	Total	White	Black	Asian	AIAN	Hisp.
Enrollment (%)	100.0	65.7	18.8	1.8	0.3	13.4
Drop-out Rate (%)	n/a	n/a	n/a	n/a	n/a	n/a
H.S. Diplomas (#)	n/a	n/a	n/a	n/a	n/a	n/a

Brentwood Union Free SD
52 Third Ave • Brentwood, NY 11717-6198
(631) 434-2325 • http://www.brentwood.k12.ny.us/
Grade Span: PK-12; **Agency Type:** 1
Schools: 18
   11 Primary; 4 Middle; 1 High; 2 Other Level
   17 Regular; 0 Special Education; 0 Vocational; 1 Alternative
   0 Magnet; 0 Charter; 17 Title I Eligible; 1 School-wide Title I
Students: 16,607 (52.5% male; 47.4% female)
   Individual Education Program: n/a;
   English Language Learner: n/a; Migrant: n/a
   Eligible for Free Lunch Program: n/a
   Eligible for Reduced-Price Lunch Program: n/a
Teachers: 1,072.6 (15.5 to 1)
Librarians/Media Specialists: 15.0 (1,107.1 to 1)
Guidance Counselors: 30.0 (553.6 to 1)
Current Spending: ($ per student per year):
   Total: $12,427; Instruction: $8,323; Support Services: $3,798
Enrollment, Drop-out Rates and Diploma Recipients by Race/Ethnicity

Category	Total	White	Black	Asian	AIAN	Hisp.
Enrollment (%)	100.0	15.0	20.7	1.7	0.1	62.5
Drop-out Rate (%)	3.7	2.5	4.2	0.0	0.0	4.1
H.S. Diplomas (#)	641	140	134	20	0	347

Brookhaven-Comsewogue Union Free SD
290 Norwood Ave • Port Jefferson Sta, NY 11776-2999
(631) 474-8105
Grade Span: KG-12; **Agency Type:** 2
Schools: 6
   4 Primary; 1 Middle; 1 High; 0 Other Level
   6 Regular; 0 Special Education; 0 Vocational; 0 Alternative
   0 Magnet; 0 Charter; 4 Title I Eligible; 0 School-wide Title I
Students: 3,930 (50.4% male; 49.5% female)
   Individual Education Program: n/a;
   English Language Learner: n/a; Migrant: n/a
   Eligible for Free Lunch Program: n/a
   Eligible for Reduced-Price Lunch Program: n/a
Teachers: 272.1 (14.4 to 1)
Librarians/Media Specialists: 6.0 (655.0 to 1)
Guidance Counselors: 7.5 (524.0 to 1)
Current Spending: ($ per student per year):
   Total: $12,986; Instruction: $8,657; Support Services: $4,107

Enrollment, Drop-out Rates and Diploma Recipients by Race/Ethnicity

Category	Total	White	Black	Asian	AIAN	Hisp.
Enrollment (%)	100.0	83.0	1.9	4.0	0.1	11.0
Drop-out Rate (%)	3.8	3.2	0.0	0.0	n/a	9.0
H.S. Diplomas (#)	189	159	7	2	0	21

Central Islip Union Free SD
50 Wheeler Rd • Central Islip, NY 11722-9027
(631) 348-5001 • http://www.centralislip.k12.ny.us/
Grade Span: PK-12; **Agency Type:** 1
Schools: 8
   6 Primary; 1 Middle; 1 High; 0 Other Level
   8 Regular; 0 Special Education; 0 Vocational; 0 Alternative
   0 Magnet; 0 Charter; 8 Title I Eligible; 0 School-wide Title I
Students: 6,741 (51.0% male; 48.9% female)
   Individual Education Program: n/a;
   English Language Learner: n/a; Migrant: n/a
   Eligible for Free Lunch Program: n/a
   Eligible for Reduced-Price Lunch Program: n/a
Teachers: 503.6 (13.4 to 1)
Librarians/Media Specialists: 7.0 (963.0 to 1)
Guidance Counselors: 9.5 (709.6 to 1)
Current Spending: ($ per student per year):
   Total: $16,413; Instruction: $11,353; Support Services: $4,731
Enrollment, Drop-out Rates and Diploma Recipients by Race/Ethnicity

Category	Total	White	Black	Asian	AIAN	Hisp.
Enrollment (%)	100.0	13.4	34.1	3.9	0.5	48.0
Drop-out Rate (%)	1.7	0.3	2.0	2.9	0.0	1.9
H.S. Diplomas (#)	278	58	119	8	1	92

Cold Spring Harbor Central SD
75 Goose Hill Rd • Cold Spring Harbor, NY 11724-9813
(631) 692-8036 • http://www.csh.k12.ny.us/
Grade Span: KG-12; **Agency Type:** 1
Schools: 4
   3 Primary; 0 Middle; 1 High; 0 Other Level
   4 Regular; 0 Special Education; 0 Vocational; 0 Alternative
   0 Magnet; 0 Charter; 0 Title I Eligible; 0 School-wide Title I
Students: 2,092 (50.4% male; 49.5% female)
   Individual Education Program: n/a;
   English Language Learner: n/a; Migrant: n/a
   Eligible for Free Lunch Program: n/a
   Eligible for Reduced-Price Lunch Program: n/a
Teachers: 158.8 (13.2 to 1)
Librarians/Media Specialists: 3.5 (597.7 to 1)
Guidance Counselors: 5.0 (418.4 to 1)
Current Spending: ($ per student per year):
   Total: $14,919; Instruction: $9,444; Support Services: $5,191
Enrollment, Drop-out Rates and Diploma Recipients by Race/Ethnicity

Category	Total	White	Black	Asian	AIAN	Hisp.
Enrollment (%)	100.0	96.8	0.5	1.9	0.0	0.8
Drop-out Rate (%)	0.0	0.0	0.0	0.0	n/a	0.0
H.S. Diplomas (#)	121	120	0	0	0	1

Commack Union Free SD
480 Clay Pitts Rd • East Northport, NY 11731-3828
(631) 912-2010 • http://www.commack.k12.ny.us/
Grade Span: KG-12; **Agency Type:** 1
Schools: 8
   6 Primary; 1 Middle; 1 High; 0 Other Level
   8 Regular; 0 Special Education; 0 Vocational; 0 Alternative
   0 Magnet; 0 Charter; 5 Title I Eligible; 0 School-wide Title I
Students: 7,511 (51.1% male; 48.8% female)
   Individual Education Program: n/a;
   English Language Learner: n/a; Migrant: n/a
   Eligible for Free Lunch Program: n/a
   Eligible for Reduced-Price Lunch Program: n/a
Teachers: 569.3 (13.2 to 1)
Librarians/Media Specialists: 12.0 (625.9 to 1)
Guidance Counselors: 16.0 (469.4 to 1)
Current Spending: ($ per student per year):
   Total: $12,899; Instruction: $8,312; Support Services: $4,412
Enrollment, Drop-out Rates and Diploma Recipients by Race/Ethnicity

Category	Total	White	Black	Asian	AIAN	Hisp.
Enrollment (%)	100.0	90.1	0.9	6.5	0.0	2.4
Drop-out Rate (%)	0.8	0.6	0.0	1.6	0.0	5.9
H.S. Diplomas (#)	408	361	3	32	0	12

Connetquot Central SD
780 Ocean Ave • Bohemia, NY 11716-3629
(631) 244-2211 • http://www.connetquot.k12.ny.us/
Grade Span: KG-12; **Agency Type:** 1
Schools: 10
   7 Primary; 2 Middle; 1 High; 0 Other Level
   10 Regular; 0 Special Education; 0 Vocational; 0 Alternative

0 Magnet; 0 Charter; 6 Title I Eligible; 0 School-wide Title I
Students: 7,160   (52.5% male; 47.4% female)
  Individual Education Program: n/a;
  English Language Learner: n/a; Migrant: n/a
  Eligible for Free Lunch Program: n/a
  Eligible for Reduced-Price Lunch Program: n/a
Teachers: 518.7 (13.8 to 1)
Librarians/Media Specialists: 10.0 (716.0 to 1)
Guidance Counselors: 12.0 (596.7 to 1)
Current Spending: ($ per student per year):
  Total: $14,471; Instruction: $9,617; Support Services: $4,601
Enrollment, Drop-out Rates and Diploma Recipients by Race/Ethnicity

Category	Total	White	Black	Asian	AIAN	Hisp.
Enrollment (%)	100.0	85.5	1.0	3.1	6.0	4.3
Drop-out Rate (%)	2.6	2.2	7.1	6.5	50.0	8.0
H.S. Diplomas (#)	374	343	1	2	14	14

Copiague Union Free SD
2650 Great Neck Rd • Copiague, NY 11726-1699
(631) 842-4015 •
http://www.edutalk.com/leveltwo/sites/copiague/index.asp
Grade Span: KG-12; **Agency Type:** 1
Schools: 5
  3 Primary; 1 Middle; 1 High; 0 Other Level
  5 Regular; 0 Special Education; 0 Vocational; 0 Alternative
  0 Magnet; 0 Charter; 3 Title I Eligible; 3 School-wide Title I
Students: 4,821   (51.2% male; 48.7% female)
  Individual Education Program: n/a;
  English Language Learner: n/a; Migrant: n/a
  Eligible for Free Lunch Program: n/a
  Eligible for Reduced-Price Lunch Program: n/a
Teachers: 306.4 (15.7 to 1)
Librarians/Media Specialists: 5.4 (892.8 to 1)
Guidance Counselors: 11.0 (438.3 to 1)
Current Spending: ($ per student per year):
  Total: $13,846; Instruction: $9,424; Support Services: $4,091
Enrollment, Drop-out Rates and Diploma Recipients by Race/Ethnicity

Category	Total	White	Black	Asian	AIAN	Hisp.
Enrollment (%)	100.0	32.4	35.1	2.2	0.0	30.3
Drop-out Rate (%)	0.3	0.2	0.2	0.0	n/a	0.4
H.S. Diplomas (#)	205	101	60	1	0	43

Deer Park Union Free SD
1881 Deer Park Ave • Deer Park, NY 11729-4326
(631) 274-4010
Grade Span: PK-12; **Agency Type:** 1
Schools: 6
  4 Primary; 1 Middle; 1 High; 0 Other Level
  6 Regular; 0 Special Education; 0 Vocational; 0 Alternative
  0 Magnet; 0 Charter; 4 Title I Eligible; 0 School-wide Title I
Students: 4,461   (52.6% male; 47.3% female)
  Individual Education Program: n/a;
  English Language Learner: n/a; Migrant: n/a
  Eligible for Free Lunch Program: n/a
  Eligible for Reduced-Price Lunch Program: n/a
Teachers: 387.1 (11.5 to 1)
Librarians/Media Specialists: 7.4 (602.8 to 1)
Guidance Counselors: 8.0 (557.6 to 1)
Current Spending: ($ per student per year):
  Total: $14,238; Instruction: $9,429; Support Services: $4,598
Enrollment, Drop-out Rates and Diploma Recipients by Race/Ethnicity

Category	Total	White	Black	Asian	AIAN	Hisp.
Enrollment (%)	100.0	71.0	14.3	6.1	0.0	8.7
Drop-out Rate (%)	0.3	0.4	0.0	0.0	n/a	0.0
H.S. Diplomas (#)	198	150	32	8	0	8

East Hampton Union Free SD
4 Long Ln • East Hampton, NY 11937-2409
(631) 329-4104 • http://www.easthampton.k12.ny.us/
Grade Span: KG-12; **Agency Type:** 2
Schools: 3
  1 Primary; 1 Middle; 1 High; 0 Other Level
  3 Regular; 0 Special Education; 0 Vocational; 0 Alternative
  0 Magnet; 0 Charter; 1 Title I Eligible; 0 School-wide Title I
Students: 1,971   (51.4% male; 48.5% female)
  Individual Education Program: n/a;
  English Language Learner: n/a; Migrant: n/a
  Eligible for Free Lunch Program: n/a
  Eligible for Reduced-Price Lunch Program: n/a
Teachers: 167.6 (11.8 to 1)
Librarians/Media Specialists: 2.6 (758.1 to 1)
Guidance Counselors: 7.4 (266.4 to 1)
Current Spending: ($ per student per year):
  Total: $16,562; Instruction: $10,606; Support Services: $5,643

Category	Total	White	Black	Asian	AIAN	Hisp.
Enrollment (%)	100.0	69.0	5.7	1.3	0.0	24.0
Drop-out Rate (%)	0.5	0.7	0.0	0.0	n/a	0.0
H.S. Diplomas (#)	184	143	6	2	0	33

East Islip Union Free SD
1 C B Gariepy Ave • Islip Terrace, NY 11752-2820
(631) 224-2000 • http://www.eastislip.k12.ny.us/
Grade Span: PK-12; **Agency Type:** 1
Schools: 7
  5 Primary; 1 Middle; 1 High; 0 Other Level
  7 Regular; 0 Special Education; 0 Vocational; 0 Alternative
  0 Magnet; 0 Charter; 5 Title I Eligible; 0 School-wide Title I
Students: 5,432   (53.0% male; 46.9% female)
  Individual Education Program: n/a;
  English Language Learner: n/a; Migrant: n/a
  Eligible for Free Lunch Program: n/a
  Eligible for Reduced-Price Lunch Program: n/a
Teachers: 377.7 (14.4 to 1)
Librarians/Media Specialists: 6.0 (905.3 to 1)
Guidance Counselors: 8.0 (679.0 to 1)
Current Spending: ($ per student per year):
  Total: $12,836; Instruction: $9,230; Support Services: $3,439
Enrollment, Drop-out Rates and Diploma Recipients by Race/Ethnicity

Category	Total	White	Black	Asian	AIAN	Hisp.
Enrollment (%)	100.0	92.8	0.8	2.1	0.1	4.2
Drop-out Rate (%)	3.0	2.6	0.0	4.0	n/a	10.7
H.S. Diplomas (#)	300	288	0	7	0	5

Elwood Union Free SD
100 Kenneth Ave • Greenlawn, NY 11740-2900
(631) 266-5402 • http://www.elwood.k12.ny.us/
Grade Span: KG-12; **Agency Type:** 2
Schools: 4
  2 Primary; 1 Middle; 1 High; 0 Other Level
  4 Regular; 0 Special Education; 0 Vocational; 0 Alternative
  0 Magnet; 0 Charter; 3 Title I Eligible; 0 School-wide Title I
Students: 2,512   (50.9% male; 49.0% female)
  Individual Education Program: n/a;
  English Language Learner: n/a; Migrant: n/a
  Eligible for Free Lunch Program: n/a
  Eligible for Reduced-Price Lunch Program: n/a
Teachers: 167.3 (15.0 to 1)
Librarians/Media Specialists: 3.9 (644.1 to 1)
Guidance Counselors: 5.0 (502.4 to 1)
Current Spending: ($ per student per year):
  Total: $12,785; Instruction: $8,005; Support Services: $4,506
Enrollment, Drop-out Rates and Diploma Recipients by Race/Ethnicity

Category	Total	White	Black	Asian	AIAN	Hisp.
Enrollment (%)	100.0	75.3	9.7	7.2	0.1	7.8
Drop-out Rate (%)	0.7	0.2	3.3	0.0	n/a	0.0
H.S. Diplomas (#)	131	93	20	15	0	3

Half Hollow Hills Central SD
525 Half Hollow Rd • Dix Hills, NY 11746-5899
(631) 592-3008 • http://www.halfhollowhills.k12.ny.us/
Grade Span: KG-12; **Agency Type:** 1
Schools: 13
  7 Primary; 2 Middle; 2 High; 2 Other Level
  11 Regular; 0 Special Education; 0 Vocational; 2 Alternative
  0 Magnet; 0 Charter; 6 Title I Eligible; 0 School-wide Title I
Students: 9,661   (51.8% male; 48.1% female)
  Individual Education Program: n/a;
  English Language Learner: n/a; Migrant: n/a
  Eligible for Free Lunch Program: n/a
  Eligible for Reduced-Price Lunch Program: n/a
Teachers: 706.9 (13.7 to 1)
Librarians/Media Specialists: 11.0 (878.3 to 1)
Guidance Counselors: 28.0 (345.0 to 1)
Current Spending: ($ per student per year):
  Total: $13,881; Instruction: $9,411; Support Services: $4,259
Enrollment, Drop-out Rates and Diploma Recipients by Race/Ethnicity

Category	Total	White	Black	Asian	AIAN	Hisp.
Enrollment (%)	100.0	74.2	11.6	9.9	0.1	4.2
Drop-out Rate (%)	0.5	0.4	0.4	0.4	0.0	2.5
H.S. Diplomas (#)	543	406	56	64	0	17

Hampton Bays Union Free SD
86 E Argonne Rd • Hampton Bays, NY 11946-1739
(631) 723-2100
Grade Span: KG-12; **Agency Type:** 2
Schools: 2
  1 Primary; 0 Middle; 1 High; 0 Other Level
  2 Regular; 0 Special Education; 0 Vocational; 0 Alternative

0 Magnet; 0 Charter; 1 Title I Eligible; 0 School-wide Title I
Students: 1,769   (52.6% male; 47.3% female)
   Individual Education Program: n/a;
   English Language Learner: n/a; Migrant: n/a
   Eligible for Free Lunch Program: n/a
   Eligible for Reduced-Price Lunch Program: n/a
Teachers: 142.1 (12.4 to 1)
Librarians/Media Specialists: 2.0 (884.5 to 1)
Guidance Counselors: 3.0 (589.7 to 1)
Current Spending: ($ per student per year):
   Total: $12,591; Instruction: $8,420; Support Services: $3,942
Enrollment, Drop-out Rates and Diploma Recipients by Race/Ethnicity

Category	Total	White	Black	Asian	AIAN	Hisp.
Enrollment (%)	100.0	71.4	1.4	0.4	0.1	26.8
Drop-out Rate (%)	0.0	0.0	0.0	0.0	n/a	0.0
H.S. Diplomas (#)	0	0	0	0	0	0

Harborfields Central SD
2 Oldfield Rd • Greenlawn, NY 11740-1200
(631) 754-5320 • http://www.harborfields.k12.ny.us/
Grade Span: KG-12; **Agency Type:** 1
Schools: 4
   2 Primary; 1 Middle; 1 High; 0 Other Level
   4 Regular; 0 Special Education; 0 Vocational; 0 Alternative
   0 Magnet; 0 Charter; 2 Title I Eligible; 0 School-wide Title I
Students: 3,560   (51.6% male; 48.3% female)
   Individual Education Program: n/a;
   English Language Learner: n/a; Migrant: n/a
   Eligible for Free Lunch Program: n/a
   Eligible for Reduced-Price Lunch Program: n/a
Teachers: 247.5 (14.4 to 1)
Librarians/Media Specialists: 4.0 (890.0 to 1)
Guidance Counselors: 8.5 (418.8 to 1)
Current Spending: ($ per student per year):
   Total: $12,034; Instruction: $7,852; Support Services: $3,944
Enrollment, Drop-out Rates and Diploma Recipients by Race/Ethnicity

Category	Total	White	Black	Asian	AIAN	Hisp.
Enrollment (%)	100.0	86.6	6.6	3.3	0.0	3.5
Drop-out Rate (%)	1.0	0.8	3.6	0.0	n/a	0.0
H.S. Diplomas (#)	189	152	18	18	0	1

Hauppauge Union Free SD
495 Hoffman Ln • Hauppauge, NY 11788-3103
(631) 265-3630 • http://www.hauppauge.k12.ny.us/
Grade Span: KG-12; **Agency Type:** 1
Schools: 5
   3 Primary; 1 Middle; 1 High; 0 Other Level
   5 Regular; 0 Special Education; 0 Vocational; 0 Alternative
   0 Magnet; 0 Charter; 1 Title I Eligible; 0 School-wide Title I
Students: 4,155   (51.2% male; 48.7% female)
   Individual Education Program: n/a;
   English Language Learner: n/a; Migrant: n/a
   Eligible for Free Lunch Program: n/a
   Eligible for Reduced-Price Lunch Program: n/a
Teachers: 325.5 (12.8 to 1)
Librarians/Media Specialists: 7.0 (593.6 to 1)
Guidance Counselors: 10.0 (415.5 to 1)
Current Spending: ($ per student per year):
   Total: $14,698; Instruction: $8,690; Support Services: $5,808
Enrollment, Drop-out Rates and Diploma Recipients by Race/Ethnicity

Category	Total	White	Black	Asian	AIAN	Hisp.
Enrollment (%)	100.0	89.5	1.7	4.7	0.0	4.1
Drop-out Rate (%)	1.3	1.0	0.0	3.6	n/a	8.1
H.S. Diplomas (#)	259	253	0	5	0	1

Huntington Union Free SD
50 Tower St • Huntington Station, NY 11746
(631) 673-2038
Grade Span: KG-12; **Agency Type:** 1
Schools: 8
   4 Primary; 3 Middle; 1 High; 0 Other Level
   8 Regular; 0 Special Education; 0 Vocational; 0 Alternative
   0 Magnet; 0 Charter; 6 Title I Eligible; 0 School-wide Title I
Students: 4,131   (51.4% male; 48.5% female)
   Individual Education Program: n/a;
   English Language Learner: n/a; Migrant: n/a
   Eligible for Free Lunch Program: n/a
   Eligible for Reduced-Price Lunch Program: n/a
Teachers: 363.5 (11.4 to 1)
Librarians/Media Specialists: 8.0 (516.4 to 1)
Guidance Counselors: 9.0 (459.0 to 1)
Current Spending: ($ per student per year):
   Total: $17,705; Instruction: $11,609; Support Services: $5,764

Enrollment, Drop-out Rates and Diploma Recipients by Race/Ethnicity

Category	Total	White	Black	Asian	AIAN	Hisp.
Enrollment (%)	100.0	62.8	12.9	1.3	0.0	22.9
Drop-out Rate (%)	4.6	1.2	6.5	0.0	n/a	13.0
H.S. Diplomas (#)	205	155	22	6	0	22

Islip Union Free SD
215 Main St • Islip, NY 11751-3435
(631) 859-2209
Grade Span: KG-12; **Agency Type:** 2
Schools: 5
   3 Primary; 1 Middle; 1 High; 0 Other Level
   5 Regular; 0 Special Education; 0 Vocational; 0 Alternative
   0 Magnet; 0 Charter; 3 Title I Eligible; 0 School-wide Title I
Students: 3,636   (50.1% male; 49.8% female)
   Individual Education Program: n/a;
   English Language Learner: n/a; Migrant: n/a
   Eligible for Free Lunch Program: n/a
   Eligible for Reduced-Price Lunch Program: n/a
Teachers: 239.2 (15.2 to 1)
Librarians/Media Specialists: 2.0 (1,818.0 to 1)
Guidance Counselors: 8.0 (454.5 to 1)
Current Spending: ($ per student per year):
   Total: $12,349; Instruction: $8,083; Support Services: $4,016
Enrollment, Drop-out Rates and Diploma Recipients by Race/Ethnicity

Category	Total	White	Black	Asian	AIAN	Hisp.
Enrollment (%)	100.0	85.6	4.1	1.9	0.1	8.2
Drop-out Rate (%)	3.3	2.8	7.5	0.0	0.0	9.2
H.S. Diplomas (#)	203	178	10	5	0	10

Kings Park Central SD
101 Church St • Kings Park, NY 11754-1769
(631) 269-3210 • http://kpcsd.k12.ny.us/
Grade Span: KG-12; **Agency Type:** 1
Schools: 5
   2 Primary; 2 Middle; 1 High; 0 Other Level
   5 Regular; 0 Special Education; 0 Vocational; 0 Alternative
   0 Magnet; 0 Charter; 5 Title I Eligible; 5 School-wide Title I
Students: 4,007   (50.1% male; 49.8% female)
   Individual Education Program: n/a;
   English Language Learner: n/a; Migrant: n/a
   Eligible for Free Lunch Program: n/a
   Eligible for Reduced-Price Lunch Program: n/a
Teachers: 288.1 (13.9 to 1)
Librarians/Media Specialists: 5.0 (801.4 to 1)
Guidance Counselors: 8.2 (488.7 to 1)
Current Spending: ($ per student per year):
   Total: $12,586; Instruction: $8,298; Support Services: $4,093
Enrollment, Drop-out Rates and Diploma Recipients by Race/Ethnicity

Category	Total	White	Black	Asian	AIAN	Hisp.
Enrollment (%)	100.0	94.9	0.6	2.3	0.1	2.1
Drop-out Rate (%)	0.4	0.4	0.0	0.0	0.0	0.0
H.S. Diplomas (#)	247	227	2	11	0	7

Lindenhurst Union Free SD
350 Daniel St • Lindenhurst, NY 11757-0621
(631) 226-6511 • http://lhs.lindy.k12.ny.us/
Grade Span: KG-12; **Agency Type:** 1
Schools: 9
   7 Primary; 1 Middle; 1 High; 0 Other Level
   9 Regular; 0 Special Education; 0 Vocational; 0 Alternative
   0 Magnet; 0 Charter; 5 Title I Eligible; 0 School-wide Title I
Students: 7,689   (51.8% male; 48.1% female)
   Individual Education Program: n/a;
   English Language Learner: n/a; Migrant: n/a
   Eligible for Free Lunch Program: n/a
   Eligible for Reduced-Price Lunch Program: n/a
Teachers: 541.7 (14.2 to 1)
Librarians/Media Specialists: 9.0 (854.3 to 1)
Guidance Counselors: 12.0 (640.8 to 1)
Current Spending: ($ per student per year):
   Total: $12,422; Instruction: $8,321; Support Services: $3,821
Enrollment, Drop-out Rates and Diploma Recipients by Race/Ethnicity

Category	Total	White	Black	Asian	AIAN	Hisp.
Enrollment (%)	100.0	88.0	1.8	1.9	0.2	8.0
Drop-out Rate (%)	0.1	0.2	0.0	0.0	n/a	0.0
H.S. Diplomas (#)	419	385	3	7	0	24

Longwood Central SD
35 Yaphnk-Mid Isl Rd • Middle Island, NY 11953-2369
(631) 345-2172 • http://www.longwood.k12.ny.us/
Grade Span: KG-12; **Agency Type:** 1
Schools: 7
   4 Primary; 2 Middle; 1 High; 0 Other Level
   7 Regular; 0 Special Education; 0 Vocational; 0 Alternative

0 Magnet; 0 Charter; 5 Title I Eligible; 0 School-wide Title I
Students: 9,794 (52.4% male; 47.5% female)
  Individual Education Program: n/a;
  English Language Learner: n/a; Migrant: n/a
  Eligible for Free Lunch Program: n/a
  Eligible for Reduced-Price Lunch Program: n/a
Teachers: 658.1 (14.9 to 1)
Librarians/Media Specialists: 13.0 (753.4 to 1)
Guidance Counselors: 22.7 (431.5 to 1)
Current Spending: ($ per student per year):
  Total: $13,794; Instruction: $9,674; Support Services: $3,927
Enrollment, Drop-out Rates and Diploma Recipients by Race/Ethnicity

Category	Total	White	Black	Asian	AIAN	Hisp.
Enrollment (%)	100.0	64.1	20.6	3.4	0.5	11.4
Drop-out Rate (%)	2.6	1.8	4.3	3.3	4.5	3.8
H.S. Diplomas (#)	516	388	69	9	1	49

Mattituck-Cutchogue Union Free SD
385 Depot Ln • Cutchogue, NY 11935
(631) 298-4242
Grade Span: KG-12; **Agency Type:** 1
Schools: 2
  1 Primary; 0 Middle; 1 High; 0 Other Level
  2 Regular; 0 Special Education; 0 Vocational; 0 Alternative
  0 Magnet; 0 Charter; 1 Title I Eligible; 0 School-wide Title I
Students: 1,563 (50.7% male; 49.2% female)
  Individual Education Program: n/a;
  English Language Learner: n/a; Migrant: n/a
  Eligible for Free Lunch Program: n/a
  Eligible for Reduced-Price Lunch Program: n/a
Teachers: 138.3 (11.3 to 1)
Librarians/Media Specialists: 3.0 (521.0 to 1)
Guidance Counselors: 5.0 (312.6 to 1)
Current Spending: ($ per student per year):
  Total: $14,015; Instruction: $9,859; Support Services: $3,943
Enrollment, Drop-out Rates and Diploma Recipients by Race/Ethnicity

Category	Total	White	Black	Asian	AIAN	Hisp.
Enrollment (%)	100.0	95.6	2.1	0.4	0.2	1.6
Drop-out Rate (%)	1.1	1.1	0.0	0.0	n/a	0.0
H.S. Diplomas (#)	112	110	0	1	0	1

Middle Country Central SD
8 43rd St - Adm Off • Centereach, NY 11720-2325
(631) 285-8005 • http://www.middlecountry.k12.ny.us/
Grade Span: PK-12; **Agency Type:** 1
Schools: 14
  10 Primary; 2 Middle; 2 High; 0 Other Level
  14 Regular; 0 Special Education; 0 Vocational; 0 Alternative
  0 Magnet; 0 Charter; 6 Title I Eligible; 0 School-wide Title I
Students: 11,630 (51.7% male; 48.2% female)
  Individual Education Program: n/a;
  English Language Learner: n/a; Migrant: n/a
  Eligible for Free Lunch Program: n/a
  Eligible for Reduced-Price Lunch Program: n/a
Teachers: 746.6 (15.6 to 1)
Librarians/Media Specialists: 11.0 (1,057.3 to 1)
Guidance Counselors: 19.0 (612.1 to 1)
Current Spending: ($ per student per year):
  Total: $11,143; Instruction: $7,360; Support Services: $3,577
Enrollment, Drop-out Rates and Diploma Recipients by Race/Ethnicity

Category	Total	White	Black	Asian	AIAN	Hisp.
Enrollment (%)	100.0	85.9	2.8	3.4	0.1	7.8
Drop-out Rate (%)	0.7	0.5	2.8	0.0	n/a	2.1
H.S. Diplomas (#)	670	586	19	21	1	43

Miller Place Union Free SD
275 Route 25a • Miller Place, NY 11764-2036
(631) 474-2733 • http://www.millerplace.k12.ny.us/
Grade Span: KG-12; **Agency Type:** 2
Schools: 4
  2 Primary; 1 Middle; 1 High; 0 Other Level
  4 Regular; 0 Special Education; 0 Vocational; 0 Alternative
  0 Magnet; 0 Charter; 4 Title I Eligible; 0 School-wide Title I
Students: 3,030 (51.2% male; 48.7% female)
  Individual Education Program: n/a;
  English Language Learner: n/a; Migrant: n/a
  Eligible for Free Lunch Program: n/a
  Eligible for Reduced-Price Lunch Program: n/a
Teachers: 205.6 (14.7 to 1)
Librarians/Media Specialists: 3.0 (1,010.0 to 1)
Guidance Counselors: 6.0 (505.0 to 1)
Current Spending: ($ per student per year):
  Total: $12,786; Instruction: $8,288; Support Services: $4,291

Category	Total	White	Black	Asian	AIAN	Hisp.
Enrollment (%)	100.0	95.8	0.8	1.5	0.2	1.7
Drop-out Rate (%)	1.6	1.6	0.0	0.0	0.0	0.0
H.S. Diplomas (#)	213	209	1	1	1	1

Mount Sinai Union Free SD
150 N Country Rd • Mount Sinai, NY 11766-0397
(631) 473-1991 • http://www.mtsinai.k12.ny.us/
Grade Span: KG-12; **Agency Type:** 2
Schools: 3
  1 Primary; 1 Middle; 1 High; 0 Other Level
  3 Regular; 0 Special Education; 0 Vocational; 0 Alternative
  0 Magnet; 0 Charter; 3 Title I Eligible; 0 School-wide Title I
Students: 2,417 (48.8% male; 51.1% female)
  Individual Education Program: n/a;
  English Language Learner: n/a; Migrant: n/a
  Eligible for Free Lunch Program: n/a
  Eligible for Reduced-Price Lunch Program: n/a
Teachers: 168.2 (14.4 to 1)
Librarians/Media Specialists: 2.6 (929.6 to 1)
Guidance Counselors: 6.0 (402.8 to 1)
Current Spending: ($ per student per year):
  Total: $13,366; Instruction: $8,572; Support Services: $4,607
Enrollment, Drop-out Rates and Diploma Recipients by Race/Ethnicity

Category	Total	White	Black	Asian	AIAN	Hisp.
Enrollment (%)	100.0	95.0	1.1	1.9	0.0	2.0
Drop-out Rate (%)	0.7	0.8	0.0	0.0	n/a	0.0
H.S. Diplomas (#)	143	133	3	3	0	4

North Babylon Union Free SD
5 Jardine Pl • North Babylon, NY 11703-4203
(631) 321-3226 • http://nbsd.org/
Grade Span: KG-12; **Agency Type:** 1
Schools: 7
  5 Primary; 1 Middle; 1 High; 0 Other Level
  7 Regular; 0 Special Education; 0 Vocational; 0 Alternative
  0 Magnet; 0 Charter; 6 Title I Eligible; 0 School-wide Title I
Students: 5,220 (50.5% male; 49.4% female)
  Individual Education Program: n/a;
  English Language Learner: n/a; Migrant: n/a
  Eligible for Free Lunch Program: n/a
  Eligible for Reduced-Price Lunch Program: n/a
Teachers: 370.9 (14.1 to 1)
Librarians/Media Specialists: 7.0 (745.7 to 1)
Guidance Counselors: 9.0 (580.0 to 1)
Current Spending: ($ per student per year):
  Total: $13,351; Instruction: $8,973; Support Services: $4,159
Enrollment, Drop-out Rates and Diploma Recipients by Race/Ethnicity

Category	Total	White	Black	Asian	AIAN	Hisp.
Enrollment (%)	100.0	66.6	20.4	2.9	0.1	10.0
Drop-out Rate (%)	0.0	0.0	0.0	0.0	n/a	0.0
H.S. Diplomas (#)	385	255	86	7	0	37

Northport-East Northport Union Free SD
158 Laurel Ave • Northport, NY 11768-3455
(631) 262-6604 • http://northport.k12.ny.us/
Grade Span: PK-12; **Agency Type:** 1
Schools: 9
  6 Primary; 2 Middle; 1 High; 0 Other Level
  9 Regular; 0 Special Education; 0 Vocational; 0 Alternative
  0 Magnet; 0 Charter; 4 Title I Eligible; 0 School-wide Title I
Students: 6,392 (50.2% male; 49.7% female)
  Individual Education Program: n/a;
  English Language Learner: n/a; Migrant: n/a
  Eligible for Free Lunch Program: n/a
  Eligible for Reduced-Price Lunch Program: n/a
Teachers: 551.9 (11.6 to 1)
Librarians/Media Specialists: 10.0 (639.2 to 1)
Guidance Counselors: 26.0 (245.8 to 1)
Current Spending: ($ per student per year):
  Total: $14,426; Instruction: $9,338; Support Services: $4,870
Enrollment, Drop-out Rates and Diploma Recipients by Race/Ethnicity

Category	Total	White	Black	Asian	AIAN	Hisp.
Enrollment (%)	100.0	93.5	0.7	2.8	0.0	3.1
Drop-out Rate (%)	1.3	1.4	0.0	0.0	0.0	0.0
H.S. Diplomas (#)	329	307	4	14	1	3

Patchogue-Medford Union Free SD
241 S Ocean Ave • Patchogue, NY 11772-3787
(631) 758-1017 • http://www.pat-med.k12.ny.us/
Grade Span: PK-12; **Agency Type:** 1
Schools: 11
  7 Primary; 3 Middle; 1 High; 0 Other Level
  11 Regular; 0 Special Education; 0 Vocational; 0 Alternative

0 Magnet; 0 Charter; 4 Title I Eligible; 0 School-wide Title I
Students: 9,101   (51.1% male; 48.8% female)
  Individual Education Program: n/a;
  English Language Learner: n/a; Migrant: n/a
  Eligible for Free Lunch Program: n/a
  Eligible for Reduced-Price Lunch Program: n/a
Teachers: 605.5 (15.0 to 1)
Librarians/Media Specialists: 11.9 (764.8 to 1)
Guidance Counselors: 14.1 (645.5 to 1)
Current Spending: ($ per student per year):
  Total: $12,283; Instruction: $8,573; Support Services: $3,438
Enrollment, Drop-out Rates and Diploma Recipients by Race/Ethnicity

Category	Total	White	Black	Asian	AIAN	Hisp.
Enrollment (%)	100.0	78.7	4.6	1.4	0.1	15.1
Drop-out Rate (%)	2.0	1.5	1.1	2.4	0.0	5.2
H.S. Diplomas (#)	496	434	16	7	0	39

Riverhead Central SD
700 Osborne Ave • Riverhead, NY 11901-2996
(631) 369-6716
Grade Span: KG-12; **Agency Type:** 2
Schools: 7
  4 Primary; 2 Middle; 1 High; 0 Other Level
  7 Regular; 0 Special Education; 0 Vocational; 0 Alternative
  0 Magnet; 0 Charter; 3 Title I Eligible; 0 School-wide Title I
Students: 4,862   (52.5% male; 47.4% female)
  Individual Education Program: n/a;
  English Language Learner: n/a; Migrant: n/a
  Eligible for Free Lunch Program: n/a
  Eligible for Reduced-Price Lunch Program: n/a
Teachers: 323.5 (15.0 to 1)
Librarians/Media Specialists: 6.0 (810.3 to 1)
Guidance Counselors: 6.0 (810.3 to 1)
Current Spending: ($ per student per year):
  Total: $13,799; Instruction: $9,633; Support Services: $3,906
Enrollment, Drop-out Rates and Diploma Recipients by Race/Ethnicity

Category	Total	White	Black	Asian	AIAN	Hisp.
Enrollment (%)	100.0	62.1	24.9	1.4	0.6	11.0
Drop-out Rate (%)	8.6	6.3	10.8	21.1	23.1	17.9
H.S. Diplomas (#)	238	173	49	2	2	12

Rocky Point Union Free SD
170 Rt 25a • Rocky Point, NY 11778-8401
(631) 744-1600 • http://www.rockypointschools.org/
Grade Span: KG-12; **Agency Type:** 2
Schools: 4
  2 Primary; 1 Middle; 1 High; 0 Other Level
  4 Regular; 0 Special Education; 0 Vocational; 0 Alternative
  0 Magnet; 0 Charter; 2 Title I Eligible; 0 School-wide Title I
Students: 3,594   (52.8% male; 47.1% female)
  Individual Education Program: n/a;
  English Language Learner: n/a; Migrant: n/a
  Eligible for Free Lunch Program: n/a
  Eligible for Reduced-Price Lunch Program: n/a
Teachers: 233.2 (15.4 to 1)
Librarians/Media Specialists: 4.0 (898.5 to 1)
Guidance Counselors: 7.0 (513.4 to 1)
Current Spending: ($ per student per year):
  Total: $11,434; Instruction: $7,597; Support Services: $3,598
Enrollment, Drop-out Rates and Diploma Recipients by Race/Ethnicity

Category	Total	White	Black	Asian	AIAN	Hisp.
Enrollment (%)	100.0	95.2	1.0	0.8	0.0	3.0
Drop-out Rate (%)	3.1	3.2	0.0	0.0	n/a	3.7
H.S. Diplomas (#)	160	158	1	1	0	0

Sachem Central SD
245 Union Ave • Holbrook, NY 11741-1890
(631) 471-1336 • http://www.sachem.k12.ny.us/
Grade Span: KG-12; **Agency Type:** 1
Schools: 15
  12 Primary; 2 Middle; 1 High; 0 Other Level
  15 Regular; 0 Special Education; 0 Vocational; 0 Alternative
  0 Magnet; 0 Charter; 9 Title I Eligible; 0 School-wide Title I
Students: 15,378   (50.5% male; 49.4% female)
  Individual Education Program: n/a;
  English Language Learner: n/a; Migrant: n/a
  Eligible for Free Lunch Program: n/a
  Eligible for Reduced-Price Lunch Program: n/a
Teachers: 1,161.6 (13.2 to 1)
Librarians/Media Specialists: 17.8 (863.9 to 1)
Guidance Counselors: 35.0 (439.4 to 1)
Current Spending: ($ per student per year):
  Total: $13,289; Instruction: $9,291; Support Services: $3,774

Enrollment, Drop-out Rates and Diploma Recipients by Race/Ethnicity

Category	Total	White	Black	Asian	AIAN	Hisp.
Enrollment (%)	100.0	90.3	1.0	3.5	0.2	5.0
Drop-out Rate (%)	1.2	1.2	2.2	0.0	0.0	3.7
H.S. Diplomas (#)	910	843	5	27	1	34

Sayville Union Free SD
99 Greeley Ave • Sayville, NY 11782-2698
(631) 244-6510
Grade Span: KG-12; **Agency Type:** 1
Schools: 5
  3 Primary; 1 Middle; 1 High; 0 Other Level
  5 Regular; 0 Special Education; 0 Vocational; 0 Alternative
  0 Magnet; 0 Charter; 4 Title I Eligible; 0 School-wide Title I
Students: 3,593   (50.7% male; 49.2% female)
  Individual Education Program: n/a;
  English Language Learner: n/a; Migrant: n/a
  Eligible for Free Lunch Program: n/a
  Eligible for Reduced-Price Lunch Program: n/a
Teachers: 260.8 (13.8 to 1)
Librarians/Media Specialists: 2.8 (1,283.2 to 1)
Guidance Counselors: 7.0 (513.3 to 1)
Current Spending: ($ per student per year):
  Total: $14,524; Instruction: $9,606; Support Services: $4,699
Enrollment, Drop-out Rates and Diploma Recipients by Race/Ethnicity

Category	Total	White	Black	Asian	AIAN	Hisp.
Enrollment (%)	100.0	95.2	0.7	2.6	0.1	1.4
Drop-out Rate (%)	0.8	0.9	0.0	0.0	n/a	0.0
H.S. Diplomas (#)	219	204	1	9	0	5

Shoreham-Wading River Central SD
250b Rt 25a • Shoreham, NY 11786-2192
(631) 821-8105
Grade Span: KG-12; **Agency Type:** 2
Schools: 5
  3 Primary; 1 Middle; 1 High; 0 Other Level
  5 Regular; 0 Special Education; 0 Vocational; 0 Alternative
  0 Magnet; 0 Charter; 2 Title I Eligible; 0 School-wide Title I
Students: 2,677   (51.6% male; 48.3% female)
  Individual Education Program: n/a;
  English Language Learner: n/a; Migrant: n/a
  Eligible for Free Lunch Program: n/a
  Eligible for Reduced-Price Lunch Program: n/a
Teachers: 217.6 (12.3 to 1)
Librarians/Media Specialists: 4.6 (582.0 to 1)
Guidance Counselors: 6.0 (446.2 to 1)
Current Spending: ($ per student per year):
  Total: $13,019; Instruction: $7,999; Support Services: $5,008
Enrollment, Drop-out Rates and Diploma Recipients by Race/Ethnicity

Category	Total	White	Black	Asian	AIAN	Hisp.
Enrollment (%)	100.0	95.0	1.3	1.6	0.1	2.1
Drop-out Rate (%)	0.1	0.0	0.0	0.0	0.0	7.7
H.S. Diplomas (#)	169	154	3	7	0	5

Smithtown Central SD
26 New York Ave • Smithtown, NY 11787-3435
(631) 382-2005 • http://www.smithtown.k12.ny.us/
Grade Span: KG-12; **Agency Type:** 1
Schools: 13
  9 Primary; 2 Middle; 1 High; 1 Other Level
  13 Regular; 0 Special Education; 0 Vocational; 0 Alternative
  0 Magnet; 0 Charter; 5 Title I Eligible; 0 School-wide Title I
Students: 10,188   (51.6% male; 48.3% female)
  Individual Education Program: n/a;
  English Language Learner: n/a; Migrant: n/a
  Eligible for Free Lunch Program: n/a
  Eligible for Reduced-Price Lunch Program: n/a
Teachers: 731.0 (13.9 to 1)
Librarians/Media Specialists: 15.0 (679.2 to 1)
Guidance Counselors: 22.0 (463.1 to 1)
Current Spending: ($ per student per year):
  Total: $13,647; Instruction: $8,523; Support Services: $4,956
Enrollment, Drop-out Rates and Diploma Recipients by Race/Ethnicity

Category	Total	White	Black	Asian	AIAN	Hisp.
Enrollment (%)	100.0	94.1	0.8	2.5	0.1	2.4
Drop-out Rate (%)	0.9	1.0	0.0	0.0	n/a	0.0
H.S. Diplomas (#)	556	522	1	22	0	11

South Country Central SD
189 N Dunton Ave • East Patchogue, NY 11772-5598
(631) 286-4310 • http://www.southcountry.org/
Grade Span: PK-12; **Agency Type:** 1
Schools: 7
  3 Primary; 2 Middle; 1 High; 1 Other Level
  6 Regular; 1 Special Education; 0 Vocational; 0 Alternative

0 Magnet; 0 Charter; 5 Title I Eligible; 0 School-wide Title I
Students: 4,758   (50.5% male; 49.4% female)
  Individual Education Program: n/a;
  English Language Learner: n/a; Migrant: n/a
  Eligible for Free Lunch Program: n/a
  Eligible for Reduced-Price Lunch Program: n/a
Teachers: 358.1 (13.3 to 1)
Librarians/Media Specialists: 4.0 (1,189.5 to 1)
Guidance Counselors: 8.0 (594.8 to 1)
Current Spending: ($ per student per year):
  Total: $15,081; Instruction: $10,360; Support Services: $4,435
Enrollment, Drop-out Rates and Diploma Recipients by Race/Ethnicity

Category	Total	White	Black	Asian	AIAN	Hisp.
Enrollment (%)	100.0	55.1	26.9	2.2	0.2	15.5
Drop-out Rate (%)	2.7	1.3	4.9	0.0	0.0	5.5
H.S. Diplomas (#)	283	192	47	7	0	37

South Huntington Union Free SD
60 Weston St • Huntington Station, NY 11746-4098
(631) 425-5300 • http://www.shuntington.k12.ny.us/
Grade Span: KG-12; **Agency Type:** 1
Schools: 6
  4 Primary; 1 Middle; 1 High; 0 Other Level
  6 Regular; 0 Special Education; 0 Vocational; 0 Alternative
  0 Magnet; 0 Charter; 4 Title I Eligible; 0 School-wide Title I
Students: 6,111   (51.9% male; 48.0% female)
  Individual Education Program: n/a;
  English Language Learner: n/a; Migrant: n/a
  Eligible for Free Lunch Program: n/a
  Eligible for Reduced-Price Lunch Program: n/a
Teachers: 455.1 (13.4 to 1)
Librarians/Media Specialists: 7.1 (860.7 to 1)
Guidance Counselors: 14.8 (412.9 to 1)
Current Spending: ($ per student per year):
  Total: $14,065; Instruction: $9,222; Support Services: $4,541
Enrollment, Drop-out Rates and Diploma Recipients by Race/Ethnicity

Category	Total	White	Black	Asian	AIAN	Hisp.
Enrollment (%)	100.0	69.1	11.0	5.7	0.0	14.3
Drop-out Rate (%)	2.6	1.9	3.5	0.0	n/a	9.6
H.S. Diplomas (#)	317	257	30	12	0	18

Southampton Union Free SD
70 Leland Ln • Southampton, NY 11968-5089
(631) 591-4510 • http://www.southampton.k12.ny.us/
Grade Span: PK-12; **Agency Type:** 1
Schools: 3
  1 Primary; 1 Middle; 1 High; 0 Other Level
  3 Regular; 0 Special Education; 0 Vocational; 0 Alternative
  0 Magnet; 0 Charter; 1 Title I Eligible; 0 School-wide Title I
Students: 1,769   (50.8% male; 49.1% female)
  Individual Education Program: n/a;
  English Language Learner: n/a; Migrant: n/a
  Eligible for Free Lunch Program: n/a
  Eligible for Reduced-Price Lunch Program: n/a
Teachers: 173.9 (10.2 to 1)
Librarians/Media Specialists: 3.0 (589.7 to 1)
Guidance Counselors: 8.0 (221.1 to 1)
Current Spending: ($ per student per year):
  Total: $20,689; Instruction: $12,265; Support Services: $8,103
Enrollment, Drop-out Rates and Diploma Recipients by Race/Ethnicity

Category	Total	White	Black	Asian	AIAN	Hisp.
Enrollment (%)	100.0	69.1	7.8	1.1	6.6	15.3
Drop-out Rate (%)	2.4	0.9	0.0	0.0	2.7	11.0
H.S. Diplomas (#)	151	108	12	0	9	22

Three Village Central SD
200 Nicolls Rd • East Setauket, NY 11733-9050
(631) 730-4010 • http://www.3villagecsd.k12.ny.us/
Grade Span: KG-12; **Agency Type:** 1
Schools: 8
  5 Primary; 2 Middle; 1 High; 0 Other Level
  8 Regular; 0 Special Education; 0 Vocational; 0 Alternative
  0 Magnet; 0 Charter; 8 Title I Eligible; 4 School-wide Title I
Students: 7,986   (50.7% male; 49.2% female)
  Individual Education Program: n/a;
  English Language Learner: n/a; Migrant: n/a
  Eligible for Free Lunch Program: n/a
  Eligible for Reduced-Price Lunch Program: n/a
Teachers: 599.5 (13.3 to 1)
Librarians/Media Specialists: 9.0 (887.3 to 1)
Guidance Counselors: 17.6 (453.7 to 1)
Current Spending: ($ per student per year):
  Total: $13,144; Instruction: $8,523; Support Services: $4,418

Enrollment, Drop-out Rates and Diploma Recipients by Race/Ethnicity

Category	Total	White	Black	Asian	AIAN	Hisp.
Enrollment (%)	100.0	89.1	1.6	6.4	0.5	2.4
Drop-out Rate (%)	3.5	3.4	5.6	1.3	100.0	3.7
H.S. Diplomas (#)	472	416	5	39	0	12

West Babylon Union Free SD
10 Farmingdale Rd • West Babylon, NY 11704-6289
(631) 321-3142 • http://www.westbabylon.k12.ny.us/
Grade Span: KG-12; **Agency Type:** 1
Schools: 7
  5 Primary; 1 Middle; 1 High; 0 Other Level
  7 Regular; 0 Special Education; 0 Vocational; 0 Alternative
  0 Magnet; 0 Charter; 4 Title I Eligible; 0 School-wide Title I
Students: 4,940   (50.7% male; 49.2% female)
  Individual Education Program: n/a;
  English Language Learner: n/a; Migrant: n/a
  Eligible for Free Lunch Program: n/a
  Eligible for Reduced-Price Lunch Program: n/a
Teachers: 342.3 (14.4 to 1)
Librarians/Media Specialists: 7.0 (705.7 to 1)
Guidance Counselors: 8.0 (617.5 to 1)
Current Spending: ($ per student per year):
  Total: $12,498; Instruction: $8,540; Support Services: $3,696
Enrollment, Drop-out Rates and Diploma Recipients by Race/Ethnicity

Category	Total	White	Black	Asian	AIAN	Hisp.
Enrollment (%)	100.0	85.7	4.5	2.3	0.0	7.4
Drop-out Rate (%)	4.1	3.9	4.2	5.9	n/a	6.1
H.S. Diplomas (#)	280	238	18	10	0	14

West Islip Union Free SD
100 Sherman Ave • West Islip, NY 11795-3237
(631) 893-3200 • http://www.westislipufsd.k12.ny.us/
Grade Span: KG-12; **Agency Type:** 1
Schools: 9
  6 Primary; 2 Middle; 1 High; 0 Other Level
  9 Regular; 0 Special Education; 0 Vocational; 0 Alternative
  0 Magnet; 0 Charter; 0 Title I Eligible; 0 School-wide Title I
Students: 5,905   (51.2% male; 48.7% female)
  Individual Education Program: n/a;
  English Language Learner: n/a; Migrant: n/a
  Eligible for Free Lunch Program: n/a
  Eligible for Reduced-Price Lunch Program: n/a
Teachers: 426.5 (13.8 to 1)
Librarians/Media Specialists: 9.0 (656.1 to 1)
Guidance Counselors: 11.5 (513.5 to 1)
Current Spending: ($ per student per year):
  Total: $11,657; Instruction: $7,700; Support Services: $3,739
Enrollment, Drop-out Rates and Diploma Recipients by Race/Ethnicity

Category	Total	White	Black	Asian	AIAN	Hisp.
Enrollment (%)	100.0	96.7	0.5	1.0	0.0	1.8
Drop-out Rate (%)	0.4	0.4	0.0	11.1	n/a	0.0
H.S. Diplomas (#)	302	296	0	4	0	2

Westhampton Beach Union Free SD
340 Mill Rd • Westhampton Beach, NY 11978-2045
(631) 288-3800 • http://www.westhamptonbeach.k12.ny.us/
Grade Span: KG-12; **Agency Type:** 2
Schools: 3
  1 Primary; 1 Middle; 1 High; 0 Other Level
  3 Regular; 0 Special Education; 0 Vocational; 0 Alternative
  0 Magnet; 0 Charter; 2 Title I Eligible; 0 School-wide Title I
Students: 1,727   (50.6% male; 49.3% female)
  Individual Education Program: n/a;
  English Language Learner: n/a; Migrant: n/a
  Eligible for Free Lunch Program: n/a
  Eligible for Reduced-Price Lunch Program: n/a
Teachers: 163.7 (10.5 to 1)
Librarians/Media Specialists: 3.0 (575.7 to 1)
Guidance Counselors: 8.0 (215.9 to 1)
Current Spending: ($ per student per year):
  Total: $15,866; Instruction: $10,310; Support Services: $5,294
Enrollment, Drop-out Rates and Diploma Recipients by Race/Ethnicity

Category	Total	White	Black	Asian	AIAN	Hisp.
Enrollment (%)	100.0	85.3	5.3	2.5	0.0	6.9
Drop-out Rate (%)	2.5	2.0	8.3	0.0	n/a	5.4
H.S. Diplomas (#)	211	192	8	5	0	6

William Floyd Union Free SD
240 Mastic Beach Rd • Mastic Beach, NY 11951-1099
(631) 874-1201 • http://www.wfsd.k12.ny.us/
Grade Span: KG-12; **Agency Type:** 1
Schools: 8
  5 Primary; 2 Middle; 1 High; 0 Other Level
  8 Regular; 0 Special Education; 0 Vocational; 0 Alternative

0 Magnet; 0 Charter; 8 Title I Eligible; 0 School-wide Title I
Students: 10,376   (51.8% male; 48.1% female)
   Individual Education Program: n/a;
   English Language Learner: n/a; Migrant: n/a
   Eligible for Free Lunch Program: n/a
   Eligible for Reduced-Price Lunch Program: n/a
Teachers: 636.1 (16.3 to 1)
Librarians/Media Specialists: 8.4 (1,235.2 to 1)
Guidance Counselors: 16.5 (628.8 to 1)
Current Spending: ($ per student per year):
   Total: $12,533; Instruction: $8,524; Support Services: $3,810

Enrollment, Drop-out Rates and Diploma Recipients by Race/Ethnicity

Category	Total	White	Black	Asian	AIAN	Hisp.
Enrollment (%)	100.0	74.5	8.7	1.5	0.2	15.1
Drop-out Rate (%)	0.6	0.5	0.0	2.1	0.0	1.6
H.S. Diplomas (#)	455	382	26	10	0	37

Wyandanch Union Free SD
1445 Straight Path • Wyandanch, NY 11798-3997
(631) 491-1013
Grade Span: PK-12; **Agency Type:** 2
Schools: 3
   1 Primary; 1 Middle; 1 High; 0 Other Level
   3 Regular; 0 Special Education; 0 Vocational; 0 Alternative
   0 Magnet; 0 Charter; 3 Title I Eligible; 3 School-wide Title I
Students: 2,280   (50.3% male; 49.6% female)
   Individual Education Program: n/a;
   English Language Learner: n/a; Migrant: n/a
   Eligible for Free Lunch Program: n/a
   Eligible for Reduced-Price Lunch Program: n/a
Teachers: 153.6 (14.8 to 1)
Librarians/Media Specialists: 3.0 (760.0 to 1)
Guidance Counselors: 5.0 (456.0 to 1)
Current Spending: ($ per student per year):
   Total: $16,955; Instruction: $10,590; Support Services: $5,940

Enrollment, Drop-out Rates and Diploma Recipients by Race/Ethnicity

Category	Total	White	Black	Asian	AIAN	Hisp.
Enrollment (%)	100.0	0.2	83.3	0.0	0.1	16.4
Drop-out Rate (%)	0.2	0.0	0.2	n/a	n/a	0.0
H.S. Diplomas (#)	66	0	58	0	0	8

Sullivan County

Liberty Central SD
115 Buckley St • Liberty, NY 12754-1600
(845) 292-6990 • http://www.libertyk12.org/
Grade Span: PK-12; **Agency Type:** 1
Schools: 3
   1 Primary; 1 Middle; 1 High; 0 Other Level
   3 Regular; 0 Special Education; 0 Vocational; 0 Alternative
   0 Magnet; 0 Charter; 2 Title I Eligible; 0 School-wide Title I
Students: 1,882   (51.2% male; 48.7% female)
   Individual Education Program: n/a;
   English Language Learner: n/a; Migrant: n/a
   Eligible for Free Lunch Program: n/a
   Eligible for Reduced-Price Lunch Program: n/a
Teachers: 145.4 (12.9 to 1)
Librarians/Media Specialists: 2.0 (941.0 to 1)
Guidance Counselors: 6.0 (313.7 to 1)
Current Spending: ($ per student per year):
   Total: $13,511; Instruction: $9,477; Support Services: $3,719

Enrollment, Drop-out Rates and Diploma Recipients by Race/Ethnicity

Category	Total	White	Black	Asian	AIAN	Hisp.
Enrollment (%)	100.0	68.7	13.4	1.8	0.0	16.1
Drop-out Rate (%)	0.0	0.0	0.0	0.0	n/a	0.0
H.S. Diplomas (#)	77	63	7	3	0	4

Monticello Central SD
237 Forestburgh Rd • Monticello, NY 12701
(845) 794-7700 • http://www.catskill.net/monti/welcome.html
Grade Span: KG-12; **Agency Type:** 1
Schools: 6
   4 Primary; 1 Middle; 1 High; 0 Other Level
   6 Regular; 0 Special Education; 0 Vocational; 0 Alternative
   0 Magnet; 0 Charter; 5 Title I Eligible; 3 School-wide Title I
Students: 3,523   (51.8% male; 48.1% female)
   Individual Education Program: n/a;
   English Language Learner: n/a; Migrant: n/a
   Eligible for Free Lunch Program: n/a
   Eligible for Reduced-Price Lunch Program: n/a
Teachers: 303.2 (11.6 to 1)
Librarians/Media Specialists: 2.7 (1,304.8 to 1)
Guidance Counselors: 7.0 (503.3 to 1)
Current Spending: ($ per student per year):
   Total: $12,723; Instruction: $8,768; Support Services: $3,654

Enrollment, Drop-out Rates and Diploma Recipients by Race/Ethnicity

Category	Total	White	Black	Asian	AIAN	Hisp.
Enrollment (%)	100.0	58.0	20.8	1.8	0.2	19.1
Drop-out Rate (%)	7.7	6.8	9.3	0.0	0.0	10.8
H.S. Diplomas (#)	141	112	14	0	0	15

Sullivan West Central SD
10494 Rt 97 • Callicoon, NY 12723
(845) 887-5300
Grade Span: KG-12; **Agency Type:** 2
Schools: 5
   3 Primary; 1 Middle; 1 High; 0 Other Level
   5 Regular; 0 Special Education; 0 Vocational; 0 Alternative
   0 Magnet; 0 Charter; 2 Title I Eligible; 0 School-wide Title I
Students: 1,568   (49.9% male; 50.0% female)
   Individual Education Program: n/a;
   English Language Learner: n/a; Migrant: n/a
   Eligible for Free Lunch Program: n/a
   Eligible for Reduced-Price Lunch Program: n/a
Teachers: 138.8 (11.3 to 1)
Librarians/Media Specialists: 3.0 (522.7 to 1)
Guidance Counselors: 4.0 (392.0 to 1)
Current Spending: ($ per student per year):
   Total: $14,102; Instruction: $9,762; Support Services: $4,039

Enrollment, Drop-out Rates and Diploma Recipients by Race/Ethnicity

Category	Total	White	Black	Asian	AIAN	Hisp.
Enrollment (%)	100.0	92.5	2.6	1.1	0.0	3.8
Drop-out Rate (%)	2.4	2.4	0.0	0.0	n/a	5.6
H.S. Diplomas (#)	119	110	1	3	0	5

Tioga County

Owego-Apalachin Central SD
36 Talcott St • Owego, NY 13827-9965
(607) 687-6224 • http://www.oacsd.org/
Grade Span: PK-12; **Agency Type:** 1
Schools: 4
   2 Primary; 1 Middle; 1 High; 0 Other Level
   4 Regular; 0 Special Education; 0 Vocational; 0 Alternative
   0 Magnet; 0 Charter; 2 Title I Eligible; 0 School-wide Title I
Students: 2,337   (52.2% male; 47.7% female)
   Individual Education Program: n/a;
   English Language Learner: n/a; Migrant: n/a
   Eligible for Free Lunch Program: n/a
   Eligible for Reduced-Price Lunch Program: n/a
Teachers: 179.8 (13.0 to 1)
Librarians/Media Specialists: 3.5 (667.7 to 1)
Guidance Counselors: 5.5 (424.9 to 1)
Current Spending: ($ per student per year):
   Total: $10,914; Instruction: $7,065; Support Services: $3,500

Enrollment, Drop-out Rates and Diploma Recipients by Race/Ethnicity

Category	Total	White	Black	Asian	AIAN	Hisp.
Enrollment (%)	100.0	95.5	2.1	1.3	0.0	1.1
Drop-out Rate (%)	0.1	0.1	0.0	0.0	n/a	0.0
H.S. Diplomas (#)	166	160	2	3	1	0

Waverly Central SD
15 Frederick St • Waverly, NY 14892-1294
(607) 565-2841 • http://www.sctboces.org/waverly/
Grade Span: KG-12; **Agency Type:** 1
Schools: 5
   3 Primary; 1 Middle; 1 High; 0 Other Level
   5 Regular; 0 Special Education; 0 Vocational; 0 Alternative
   0 Magnet; 0 Charter; 4 Title I Eligible; 0 School-wide Title I
Students: 1,786   (52.1% male; 47.8% female)
   Individual Education Program: n/a;
   English Language Learner: n/a; Migrant: n/a
   Eligible for Free Lunch Program: n/a
   Eligible for Reduced-Price Lunch Program: n/a
Teachers: 125.9 (14.2 to 1)
Librarians/Media Specialists: 1.0 (1,786.0 to 1)
Guidance Counselors: 2.0 (893.0 to 1)
Current Spending: ($ per student per year):
   Total: $9,590; Instruction: $6,369; Support Services: $2,927

Enrollment, Drop-out Rates and Diploma Recipients by Race/Ethnicity

Category	Total	White	Black	Asian	AIAN	Hisp.
Enrollment (%)	100.0	97.9	1.0	0.5	0.2	0.4
Drop-out Rate (%)	3.7	3.7	0.0	0.0	n/a	0.0
H.S. Diplomas (#)	95	95	0	0	0	0

Dryden Central SD

2127 Drydn Rd-Po Bx 8 • Dryden, NY 13053-0088
(607) 844-5361 • http://www.drydenschools.org/
Grade Span: KG-12; **Agency Type:** 1
Schools: 5
   3 Primary; 1 Middle; 1 High; 0 Other Level
   5 Regular; 0 Special Education; 0 Vocational; 0 Alternative
   0 Magnet; 0 Charter; 4 Title I Eligible; 0 School-wide Title I
Students: 1,884 (51.4% male; 48.5% female)
   Individual Education Program: n/a;
   English Language Learner: n/a; Migrant: n/a
   Eligible for Free Lunch Program: n/a
   Eligible for Reduced-Price Lunch Program: n/a
Teachers: 176.9 (10.7 to 1)
Librarians/Media Specialists: 1.5 (1,256.0 to 1)
Guidance Counselors: 6.0 (314.0 to 1)
Current Spending: ($ per student per year):
   Total: $11,592; Instruction: $7,273; Support Services: $3,938
Enrollment, Drop-out Rates and Diploma Recipients by Race/Ethnicity

Category	Total	White	Black	Asian	AIAN	Hisp.
Enrollment (%)	100.0	96.0	2.1	1.2	0.1	0.6
Drop-out Rate (%)	0.9	0.9	0.0	0.0	n/a	0.0
H.S. Diplomas (#)	106	105	0	0	0	1

Ithaca City SD

400 Lake St • Ithaca, NY 14851-0549
(607) 274-2101 • http://www.icsd.k12.ny.us/
Grade Span: PK-12; **Agency Type:** 1
Schools: 13
   8 Primary; 2 Middle; 1 High; 2 Other Level
   11 Regular; 0 Special Education; 0 Vocational; 2 Alternative
   0 Magnet; 0 Charter; 5 Title I Eligible; 1 School-wide Title I
Students: 5,751 (52.3% male; 47.6% female)
   Individual Education Program: n/a;
   English Language Learner: n/a; Migrant: n/a
   Eligible for Free Lunch Program: n/a
   Eligible for Reduced-Price Lunch Program: n/a
Teachers: 478.0 (12.0 to 1)
Librarians/Media Specialists: 13.0 (442.4 to 1)
Guidance Counselors: 13.6 (422.9 to 1)
Current Spending: ($ per student per year):
   Total: $12,619; Instruction: $8,218; Support Services: $4,070
Enrollment, Drop-out Rates and Diploma Recipients by Race/Ethnicity

Category	Total	White	Black	Asian	AIAN	Hisp.
Enrollment (%)	100.0	72.5	12.1	10.2	1.0	4.2
Drop-out Rate (%)	1.3	1.1	3.4	0.0	0.0	5.3
H.S. Diplomas (#)	326	282	15	23	1	5

Lansing Central SD

264 Ridge Rd • Lansing, NY 14882-9021
(607) 533-4294
Grade Span: KG-12; **Agency Type:** 2
Schools: 5
   1 Primary; 1 Middle; 2 High; 1 Other Level
   3 Regular; 0 Special Education; 0 Vocational; 2 Alternative
   0 Magnet; 0 Charter; 2 Title I Eligible; 0 School-wide Title I
Students: 1,529 (55.1% male; 44.8% female)
   Individual Education Program: n/a;
   English Language Learner: n/a; Migrant: n/a
   Eligible for Free Lunch Program: n/a
   Eligible for Reduced-Price Lunch Program: n/a
Teachers: 117.3 (13.0 to 1)
Librarians/Media Specialists: 3.0 (509.7 to 1)
Guidance Counselors: 2.0 (764.5 to 1)
Current Spending: ($ per student per year):
   Total: $10,244; Instruction: $6,558; Support Services: $3,368
Enrollment, Drop-out Rates and Diploma Recipients by Race/Ethnicity

Category	Total	White	Black	Asian	AIAN	Hisp.
Enrollment (%)	100.0	83.3	10.3	2.6	0.1	3.7
Drop-out Rate (%)	0.4	0.5	0.0	0.0	n/a	0.0
H.S. Diplomas (#)	110	105	2	2	0	1

Ellenville Central SD

28 Maple Ave • Ellenville, NY 12428-2000
(845) 647-0100 • http://www.ecs.k12.ny.us/
Grade Span: KG-12; **Agency Type:** 1
Schools: 4
   1 Primary; 1 Middle; 1 High; 1 Other Level
   3 Regular; 0 Special Education; 0 Vocational; 1 Alternative
   0 Magnet; 0 Charter; 3 Title I Eligible; 3 School-wide Title I
Students: 1,812 (50.4% male; 49.5% female)

   Individual Education Program: n/a;
   English Language Learner: n/a; Migrant: n/a
   Eligible for Free Lunch Program: n/a
   Eligible for Reduced-Price Lunch Program: n/a
Teachers: 138.9 (13.0 to 1)
Librarians/Media Specialists: 3.0 (604.0 to 1)
Guidance Counselors: 4.0 (453.0 to 1)
Current Spending: ($ per student per year):
   Total: $15,138; Instruction: $9,939; Support Services: $4,938
Enrollment, Drop-out Rates and Diploma Recipients by Race/Ethnicity

Category	Total	White	Black	Asian	AIAN	Hisp.
Enrollment (%)	100.0	62.1	11.8	1.7	0.3	24.1
Drop-out Rate (%)	10.0	6.9	21.1	0.0	n/a	14.9
H.S. Diplomas (#)	78	59	2	2	0	15

Highland Central SD

320 Pancake Hollow Rd • Highland, NY 12528-2317
(845) 691-1012 • http://www.highland-k12.org/
Grade Span: KG-12; **Agency Type:** 2
Schools: 4
   1 Primary; 1 Middle; 2 High; 0 Other Level
   3 Regular; 0 Special Education; 0 Vocational; 1 Alternative
   0 Magnet; 0 Charter; 1 Title I Eligible; 0 School-wide Title I
Students: 2,075 (54.4% male; 45.5% female)
   Individual Education Program: n/a;
   English Language Learner: n/a; Migrant: n/a
   Eligible for Free Lunch Program: n/a
   Eligible for Reduced-Price Lunch Program: n/a
Teachers: 128.3 (16.2 to 1)
Librarians/Media Specialists: 1.0 (2,075.0 to 1)
Guidance Counselors: 3.0 (691.7 to 1)
Current Spending: ($ per student per year):
   Total: $11,603; Instruction: $7,873; Support Services: $3,423
Enrollment, Drop-out Rates and Diploma Recipients by Race/Ethnicity

Category	Total	White	Black	Asian	AIAN	Hisp.
Enrollment (%)	100.0	83.4	8.6	1.6	0.0	6.4
Drop-out Rate (%)	2.4	2.2	5.1	0.0	n/a	5.3
H.S. Diplomas (#)	140	123	12	1	0	4

Kingston City SD

61 Crown St • Kingston, NY 12401-3833
(845) 339-3000 • http://www.kingstoncityschools.org/
Grade Span: PK-12; **Agency Type:** 1
Schools: 14
   11 Primary; 2 Middle; 1 High; 0 Other Level
   14 Regular; 0 Special Education; 0 Vocational; 0 Alternative
   0 Magnet; 0 Charter; 6 Title I Eligible; 4 School-wide Title I
Students: 8,149 (50.3% male; 49.6% female)
   Individual Education Program: n/a;
   English Language Learner: n/a; Migrant: n/a
   Eligible for Free Lunch Program: n/a
   Eligible for Reduced-Price Lunch Program: n/a
Teachers: 588.1 (13.9 to 1)
Librarians/Media Specialists: 12.0 (679.1 to 1)
Guidance Counselors: 14.5 (562.0 to 1)
Current Spending: ($ per student per year):
   Total: $11,690; Instruction: $8,439; Support Services: $3,022
Enrollment, Drop-out Rates and Diploma Recipients by Race/Ethnicity

Category	Total	White	Black	Asian	AIAN	Hisp.
Enrollment (%)	100.0	74.4	16.2	2.2	0.3	6.8
Drop-out Rate (%)	7.8	6.8	13.8	7.3	0.0	9.1
H.S. Diplomas (#)	485	418	44	13	2	8

Marlboro Central SD

50 Cross Rd • Marlboro, NY 12542-6009
(845) 236-5802
Grade Span: KG-12; **Agency Type:** 1
Schools: 5
   3 Primary; 1 Middle; 1 High; 0 Other Level
   5 Regular; 0 Special Education; 0 Vocational; 0 Alternative
   0 Magnet; 0 Charter; 2 Title I Eligible; 0 School-wide Title I
Students: 2,136 (48.7% male; 51.2% female)
   Individual Education Program: n/a;
   English Language Learner: n/a; Migrant: n/a
   Eligible for Free Lunch Program: n/a
   Eligible for Reduced-Price Lunch Program: n/a
Teachers: 161.8 (13.2 to 1)
Librarians/Media Specialists: 3.5 (610.3 to 1)
Guidance Counselors: 4.0 (534.0 to 1)
Current Spending: ($ per student per year):
   Total: $14,307; Instruction: $9,406; Support Services: $4,658

Enrollment, Drop-out Rates and Diploma Recipients by Race/Ethnicity

Category	Total	White	Black	Asian	AIAN	Hisp.
Enrollment (%)	100.0	89.0	5.8	0.5	0.2	4.5
Drop-out Rate (%)	2.8	2.7	11.1	0.0	n/a	0.0
H.S. Diplomas (#)	106	98	2	2	0	4

New Paltz Central SD
196 Main St • New Paltz, NY 12561-1200
(845) 256-4020 • http://www.newpaltz.k12.ny.us/
Grade Span: KG-12; **Agency Type:** 1
Schools: 4
  2 Primary; 1 Middle; 1 High; 0 Other Level
  4 Regular; 0 Special Education; 0 Vocational; 0 Alternative
  0 Magnet; 0 Charter; 4 Title I Eligible; 0 School-wide Title I
Students: 2,376 (51.1% male; 48.8% female)
  Individual Education Program: n/a;
  English Language Learner: n/a; Migrant: n/a
  Eligible for Free Lunch Program: n/a
  Eligible for Reduced-Price Lunch Program: n/a
Teachers: 176.3 (13.5 to 1)
Librarians/Media Specialists: 4.0 (594.0 to 1)
Guidance Counselors: 5.0 (475.2 to 1)
Current Spending: ($ per student per year):
  Total: $12,355; Instruction: $7,738; Support Services: $4,353

Enrollment, Drop-out Rates and Diploma Recipients by Race/Ethnicity

Category	Total	White	Black	Asian	AIAN	Hisp.
Enrollment (%)	100.0	82.2	7.1	3.5	0.5	6.6
Drop-out Rate (%)	3.4	3.0	7.1	4.5	0.0	5.1
H.S. Diplomas (#)	118	96	9	5	2	6

Onteora Central SD
4166 Rt 28 • Boiceville, NY 12412-0300
(845) 657-6383 • http://www.onteora.k12.ny.us/
Grade Span: KG-12; **Agency Type:** 1
Schools: 6
  4 Primary; 1 Middle; 1 High; 0 Other Level
  6 Regular; 0 Special Education; 0 Vocational; 0 Alternative
  0 Magnet; 0 Charter; 4 Title I Eligible; 0 School-wide Title I
Students: 2,172 (50.7% male; 49.2% female)
  Individual Education Program: n/a;
  English Language Learner: n/a; Migrant: n/a
  Eligible for Free Lunch Program: n/a
  Eligible for Reduced-Price Lunch Program: n/a
Teachers: 177.2 (12.3 to 1)
Librarians/Media Specialists: 3.0 (724.0 to 1)
Guidance Counselors: 5.0 (434.4 to 1)
Current Spending: ($ per student per year):
  Total: $16,766; Instruction: $11,539; Support Services: $4,836

Enrollment, Drop-out Rates and Diploma Recipients by Race/Ethnicity

Category	Total	White	Black	Asian	AIAN	Hisp.
Enrollment (%)	100.0	89.8	3.4	2.6	0.1	4.1
Drop-out Rate (%)	3.6	3.6	0.0	25.0	n/a	0.0
H.S. Diplomas (#)	112	104	4	3	0	1

Rondout Valley Central SD
122 Kyserike Rd • Accord, NY 12404-0009
(845) 687-2400 • http://rondout.k12.ny.us/
Grade Span: KG-12; **Agency Type:** 1
Schools: 5
  3 Primary; 1 Middle; 1 High; 0 Other Level
  5 Regular; 0 Special Education; 0 Vocational; 0 Alternative
  0 Magnet; 0 Charter; 4 Title I Eligible; 0 School-wide Title I
Students: 2,797 (53.1% male; 46.8% female)
  Individual Education Program: n/a;
  English Language Learner: n/a; Migrant: n/a
  Eligible for Free Lunch Program: n/a
  Eligible for Reduced-Price Lunch Program: n/a
Teachers: 218.0 (12.8 to 1)
Librarians/Media Specialists: 5.1 (548.4 to 1)
Guidance Counselors: 11.4 (245.4 to 1)
Current Spending: ($ per student per year):
  Total: $13,613; Instruction: $9,147; Support Services: $4,151

Enrollment, Drop-out Rates and Diploma Recipients by Race/Ethnicity

Category	Total	White	Black	Asian	AIAN	Hisp.
Enrollment (%)	100.0	91.1	3.1	1.1	0.4	4.2
Drop-out Rate (%)	4.0	3.9	9.5	0.0	0.0	9.1
H.S. Diplomas (#)	191	179	5	2	0	5

Saugerties Central SD
310 Washington Ave Ex • Saugerties, NY 12477-0577
(845) 246-1043 • http://www.saugerties.k12.ny.us/
Grade Span: KG-12; **Agency Type:** 1
Schools: 6
  4 Primary; 1 Middle; 1 High; 0 Other Level
  6 Regular; 0 Special Education; 0 Vocational; 0 Alternative

0 Magnet; 0 Charter; 3 Title I Eligible; 0 School-wide Title I
Students: 3,336 (51.4% male; 48.5% female)
  Individual Education Program: n/a;
  English Language Learner: n/a; Migrant: n/a
  Eligible for Free Lunch Program: n/a
  Eligible for Reduced-Price Lunch Program: n/a
Teachers: 223.1 (15.0 to 1)
Librarians/Media Specialists: 6.0 (556.0 to 1)
Guidance Counselors: 7.0 (476.6 to 1)
Current Spending: ($ per student per year):
  Total: $10,352; Instruction: $7,041; Support Services: $3,023

Enrollment, Drop-out Rates and Diploma Recipients by Race/Ethnicity

Category	Total	White	Black	Asian	AIAN	Hisp.
Enrollment (%)	100.0	93.6	2.6	1.2	0.1	2.5
Drop-out Rate (%)	3.8	3.7	7.7	0.0	n/a	0.0
H.S. Diplomas (#)	190	183	7	0	0	0

Wallkill Central SD
19 Main St • Wallkill, NY 12589-0310
(845) 895-7101 • http://wallkillcsd.k12.ny.us/
Grade Span: KG-12; **Agency Type:** 1
Schools: 6
  3 Primary; 1 Middle; 1 High; 1 Other Level
  5 Regular; 0 Special Education; 0 Vocational; 1 Alternative
  0 Magnet; 0 Charter; 3 Title I Eligible; 0 School-wide Title I
Students: 3,638 (52.3% male; 47.6% female)
  Individual Education Program: n/a;
  English Language Learner: n/a; Migrant: n/a
  Eligible for Free Lunch Program: n/a
  Eligible for Reduced-Price Lunch Program: n/a
Teachers: 250.0 (14.6 to 1)
Librarians/Media Specialists: 2.0 (1,819.0 to 1)
Guidance Counselors: 7.0 (519.7 to 1)
Current Spending: ($ per student per year):
  Total: $10,946; Instruction: $7,262; Support Services: $3,422

Enrollment, Drop-out Rates and Diploma Recipients by Race/Ethnicity

Category	Total	White	Black	Asian	AIAN	Hisp.
Enrollment (%)	100.0	79.4	5.1	0.7	0.0	14.7
Drop-out Rate (%)	3.0	2.7	2.0	0.0	100.0	5.5
H.S. Diplomas (#)	203	172	10	1	0	20

Warren County

Glens Falls City SD
15 Quade St • Glens Falls, NY 12801-2724
(518) 792-1212 • http://www.gfsd.org/
Grade Span: KG-12; **Agency Type:** 1
Schools: 6
  4 Primary; 1 Middle; 1 High; 0 Other Level
  6 Regular; 0 Special Education; 0 Vocational; 0 Alternative
  0 Magnet; 0 Charter; 3 Title I Eligible; 0 School-wide Title I
Students: 2,522 (51.6% male; 48.3% female)
  Individual Education Program: n/a;
  English Language Learner: n/a; Migrant: n/a
  Eligible for Free Lunch Program: n/a
  Eligible for Reduced-Price Lunch Program: n/a
Teachers: 197.8 (12.8 to 1)
Librarians/Media Specialists: 4.0 (630.5 to 1)
Guidance Counselors: 7.0 (360.3 to 1)
Current Spending: ($ per student per year):
  Total: $10,292; Instruction: $7,524; Support Services: $2,467

Enrollment, Drop-out Rates and Diploma Recipients by Race/Ethnicity

Category	Total	White	Black	Asian	AIAN	Hisp.
Enrollment (%)	100.0	94.1	3.0	1.1	0.0	1.7
Drop-out Rate (%)	2.6	2.7	0.0	0.0	n/a	0.0
H.S. Diplomas (#)	147	140	3	1	0	3

Queensbury Union Free SD
429 Aviation Rd • Queensbury, NY 12804-2914
(518) 742-6000 • http://www.queensburyschool.org/
Grade Span: KG-12; **Agency Type:** 1
Schools: 4
  1 Primary; 2 Middle; 1 High; 0 Other Level
  4 Regular; 0 Special Education; 0 Vocational; 0 Alternative
  0 Magnet; 0 Charter; 3 Title I Eligible; 0 School-wide Title I
Students: 3,906 (50.6% male; 49.3% female)
  Individual Education Program: n/a;
  English Language Learner: n/a; Migrant: n/a
  Eligible for Free Lunch Program: n/a
  Eligible for Reduced-Price Lunch Program: n/a
Teachers: 255.5 (15.3 to 1)
Librarians/Media Specialists: 4.0 (976.5 to 1)
Guidance Counselors: 9.0 (434.0 to 1)
Current Spending: ($ per student per year):
  Total: $8,280; Instruction: $5,599; Support Services: $2,498

Enrollment, Drop-out Rates and Diploma Recipients by Race/Ethnicity

Category	Total	White	Black	Asian	AIAN	Hisp.
Enrollment (%)	100.0	96.1	1.5	1.2	0.2	0.9
Drop-out Rate (%)	3.5	3.6	14.3	0.0	0.0	0.0
H.S. Diplomas (#)	211	201	1	7	0	2

Washington County

Hudson Falls Central SD
1153 Burgoyne Ave • Hudson Falls, NY 12839-0710
(518) 747-2121 • http://www.hudsonfalls.k12.ny.us/
Grade Span: KG-12; **Agency Type:** 1
Schools: 5
  2 Primary; 2 Middle; 1 High; 0 Other Level
  5 Regular; 0 Special Education; 0 Vocational; 0 Alternative
  0 Magnet; 0 Charter; 5 Title I Eligible; 0 School-wide Title I
Students: 2,418 (51.4% male; 48.5% female)
  Individual Education Program: n/a;
  English Language Learner: n/a; Migrant: n/a
  Eligible for Free Lunch Program: n/a
  Eligible for Reduced-Price Lunch Program: n/a
Teachers: 168.6 (14.3 to 1)
Librarians/Media Specialists: 2.0 (1,209.0 to 1)
Guidance Counselors: 4.0 (604.5 to 1)
Current Spending: ($ per student per year):
  Total: $10,654; Instruction: $6,685; Support Services: $3,598
Enrollment, Drop-out Rates and Diploma Recipients by Race/Ethnicity

Category	Total	White	Black	Asian	AIAN	Hisp.
Enrollment (%)	100.0	98.6	1.2	0.2	0.0	0.0
Drop-out Rate (%)	2.7	2.8	0.0	0.0	n/a	0.0
H.S. Diplomas (#)	128	128	0	0	0	0

Wayne County

Newark Central SD
100 E Miller St • Newark, NY 14513-1599
(315) 332-3217 • http://www.newark.k12.ny.us/
Grade Span: PK-12; **Agency Type:** 1
Schools: 5
  3 Primary; 1 Middle; 1 High; 0 Other Level
  5 Regular; 0 Special Education; 0 Vocational; 0 Alternative
  0 Magnet; 0 Charter; 4 Title I Eligible; 0 School-wide Title I
Students: 2,688 (52.1% male; 47.8% female)
  Individual Education Program: n/a;
  English Language Learner: n/a; Migrant: n/a
  Eligible for Free Lunch Program: n/a
  Eligible for Reduced-Price Lunch Program: n/a
Teachers: 213.8 (12.6 to 1)
Librarians/Media Specialists: 4.0 (672.0 to 1)
Guidance Counselors: 7.0 (384.0 to 1)
Current Spending: ($ per student per year):
  Total: $11,298; Instruction: $7,396; Support Services: $3,629
Enrollment, Drop-out Rates and Diploma Recipients by Race/Ethnicity

Category	Total	White	Black	Asian	AIAN	Hisp.
Enrollment (%)	100.0	82.5	9.4	0.9	0.0	7.1
Drop-out Rate (%)	3.2	2.8	4.0	7.7	0.0	9.3
H.S. Diplomas (#)	165	154	5	2	0	4

North Rose-Wolcott Central SD
11669 Saltr-Colvn Rd • Wolcott, NY 14590-9398
(315) 594-3141
Grade Span: KG-12; **Agency Type:** 1
Schools: 4
  2 Primary; 1 Middle; 1 High; 0 Other Level
  4 Regular; 0 Special Education; 0 Vocational; 0 Alternative
  0 Magnet; 0 Charter; 2 Title I Eligible; 2 School-wide Title I
Students: 1,642 (50.6% male; 49.3% female)
  Individual Education Program: n/a;
  English Language Learner: n/a; Migrant: n/a
  Eligible for Free Lunch Program: n/a
  Eligible for Reduced-Price Lunch Program: n/a
Teachers: 147.5 (11.1 to 1)
Librarians/Media Specialists: 2.0 (821.0 to 1)
Guidance Counselors: 5.0 (328.4 to 1)
Current Spending: ($ per student per year):
  Total: $12,072; Instruction: $7,565; Support Services: $4,234
Enrollment, Drop-out Rates and Diploma Recipients by Race/Ethnicity

Category	Total	White	Black	Asian	AIAN	Hisp.
Enrollment (%)	100.0	92.4	3.5	0.5	0.2	3.4
Drop-out Rate (%)	5.8	5.3	15.4	0.0	0.0	20.0
H.S. Diplomas (#)	95	89	2	2	0	2

Palmyra-Macedon Central SD
151 Hyde Pky • Palmyra, NY 14522-1297
(315) 597-3401 • http://www.palmac.k12.ny.us/
Grade Span: KG-12; **Agency Type:** 1
Schools: 4
  2 Primary; 1 Middle; 1 High; 0 Other Level
  4 Regular; 0 Special Education; 0 Vocational; 0 Alternative
  0 Magnet; 0 Charter; 3 Title I Eligible; 0 School-wide Title I
Students: 2,222 (53.0% male; 46.9% female)
  Individual Education Program: n/a;
  English Language Learner: n/a; Migrant: n/a
  Eligible for Free Lunch Program: n/a
  Eligible for Reduced-Price Lunch Program: n/a
Teachers: 185.8 (12.0 to 1)
Librarians/Media Specialists: 3.0 (740.7 to 1)
Guidance Counselors: 5.2 (427.3 to 1)
Current Spending: ($ per student per year):
  Total: $10,973; Instruction: $6,767; Support Services: $3,923
Enrollment, Drop-out Rates and Diploma Recipients by Race/Ethnicity

Category	Total	White	Black	Asian	AIAN	Hisp.
Enrollment (%)	100.0	96.5	1.3	1.2	0.3	0.7
Drop-out Rate (%)	1.8	1.8	0.0	0.0	0.0	0.0
H.S. Diplomas (#)	139	139	0	0	0	0

Wayne Central SD
6076 Ontario Ctr Rd • Ontario Center, NY 14520-0155
(315) 524-0201 • http://wayne.k12.ny.us/default.htm
Grade Span: KG-12; **Agency Type:** 1
Schools: 5
  3 Primary; 1 Middle; 1 High; 0 Other Level
  5 Regular; 0 Special Education; 0 Vocational; 0 Alternative
  0 Magnet; 0 Charter; 3 Title I Eligible; 0 School-wide Title I
Students: 2,774 (52.6% male; 47.3% female)
  Individual Education Program: n/a;
  English Language Learner: n/a; Migrant: n/a
  Eligible for Free Lunch Program: n/a
  Eligible for Reduced-Price Lunch Program: n/a
Teachers: 221.5 (12.5 to 1)
Librarians/Media Specialists: 5.0 (554.8 to 1)
Guidance Counselors: 12.5 (221.9 to 1)
Current Spending: ($ per student per year):
  Total: $9,909; Instruction: $6,390; Support Services: $3,227
Enrollment, Drop-out Rates and Diploma Recipients by Race/Ethnicity

Category	Total	White	Black	Asian	AIAN	Hisp.
Enrollment (%)	100.0	96.4	1.8	0.6	0.1	1.1
Drop-out Rate (%)	1.5	1.3	14.3	0.0	0.0	0.0
H.S. Diplomas (#)	163	158	2	2	0	1

Westchester County

Ardsley Union Free SD
500 Farm Rd • Ardsley, NY 10502-1410
(914) 693-6300 • http://www.ardsleyschools.k12.ny.us/
Grade Span: KG-12; **Agency Type:** 1
Schools: 3
  1 Primary; 1 Middle; 1 High; 0 Other Level
  3 Regular; 0 Special Education; 0 Vocational; 0 Alternative
  0 Magnet; 0 Charter; 1 Title I Eligible; 0 School-wide Title I
Students: 2,343 (52.2% male; 47.7% female)
  Individual Education Program: n/a;
  English Language Learner: n/a; Migrant: n/a
  Eligible for Free Lunch Program: n/a
  Eligible for Reduced-Price Lunch Program: n/a
Teachers: 184.4 (12.7 to 1)
Librarians/Media Specialists: 2.6 (901.2 to 1)
Guidance Counselors: 9.0 (260.3 to 1)
Current Spending: ($ per student per year):
  Total: $14,464; Instruction: $9,662; Support Services: $4,571
Enrollment, Drop-out Rates and Diploma Recipients by Race/Ethnicity

Category	Total	White	Black	Asian	AIAN	Hisp.
Enrollment (%)	100.0	82.5	3.2	10.7	0.0	3.7
Drop-out Rate (%)	0.2	0.2	0.0	0.0	0.0	0.0
H.S. Diplomas (#)	123	102	3	15	0	3

Bedford Central SD
600 Route 172 • Mount Kisco, NY 10549-0180
(914) 241-6010 • http://www.bedford.k12.ny.us/default.html
Grade Span: PK-12; **Agency Type:** 1
Schools: 9
  5 Primary; 1 Middle; 1 High; 2 Other Level
  7 Regular; 0 Special Education; 0 Vocational; 2 Alternative
  0 Magnet; 0 Charter; 1 Title I Eligible; 0 School-wide Title I
Students: 4,268 (52.3% male; 47.6% female)
  Individual Education Program: n/a;
  English Language Learner: n/a; Migrant: n/a

Eligible for Free Lunch Program: n/a
Eligible for Reduced-Price Lunch Program: n/a
Teachers: 352.2 (12.1 to 1)
Librarians/Media Specialists: 7.9 (540.3 to 1)
Guidance Counselors: 9.6 (444.6 to 1)
Current Spending: ($ per student per year):
   Total: $18,010; Instruction: $11,472; Support Services: $6,299
Enrollment, Drop-out Rates and Diploma Recipients by Race/Ethnicity

Category	Total	White	Black	Asian	AIAN	Hisp.
Enrollment (%)	100.0	73.2	6.1	4.1	0.2	16.5
Drop-out Rate (%)	8.4	6.5	13.3	8.2	n/a	14.8
H.S. Diplomas (#)	247	189	15	17	0	26

Briarcliff Manor Union Free SD
45 Ingham Rd • Briarcliff Manor, NY 10510-2221
(914) 941-8880
Grade Span: KG-12; **Agency Type:** 2
Schools: 3
   1 Primary; 1 Middle; 1 High; 0 Other Level
   3 Regular; 0 Special Education; 0 Vocational; 0 Alternative
   0 Magnet; 0 Charter; 0 Title I Eligible; 0 School-wide Title I
Students: 1,717 (52.1% male; 47.8% female)
   Individual Education Program: n/a;
   English Language Learner: n/a; Migrant: n/a
   Eligible for Free Lunch Program: n/a
   Eligible for Reduced-Price Lunch Program: n/a
Teachers: 148.1 (11.6 to 1)
Librarians/Media Specialists: 3.0 (572.3 to 1)
Guidance Counselors: 5.0 (343.4 to 1)
Current Spending: ($ per student per year):
   Total: $17,822; Instruction: $10,970; Support Services: $6,708
Enrollment, Drop-out Rates and Diploma Recipients by Race/Ethnicity

Category	Total	White	Black	Asian	AIAN	Hisp.
Enrollment (%)	100.0	92.0	1.1	6.1	0.0	0.8
Drop-out Rate (%)	0.0	0.0	0.0	0.0	n/a	0.0
H.S. Diplomas (#)	113	93	4	13	0	3

Byram Hills Central SD
10 Tripp Ln • Armonk, NY 10504-2512
(914) 273-4082 • http://www.byramhills.org/
Grade Span: KG-12; **Agency Type:** 1
Schools: 4
   2 Primary; 1 Middle; 1 High; 0 Other Level
   4 Regular; 0 Special Education; 0 Vocational; 0 Alternative
   0 Magnet; 0 Charter; 0 Title I Eligible; 0 School-wide Title I
Students: 2,707 (50.2% male; 49.7% female)
   Individual Education Program: n/a;
   English Language Learner: n/a; Migrant: n/a
   Eligible for Free Lunch Program: n/a
   Eligible for Reduced-Price Lunch Program: n/a
Teachers: 208.0 (13.0 to 1)
Librarians/Media Specialists: 5.5 (492.2 to 1)
Guidance Counselors: 6.0 (451.2 to 1)
Current Spending: ($ per student per year):
   Total: $14,200; Instruction: $8,705; Support Services: $5,288
Enrollment, Drop-out Rates and Diploma Recipients by Race/Ethnicity

Category	Total	White	Black	Asian	AIAN	Hisp.
Enrollment (%)	100.0	94.1	0.4	4.2	0.0	1.3
Drop-out Rate (%)	0.0	0.0	0.0	0.0	n/a	0.0
H.S. Diplomas (#)	166	152	1	11	0	2

Chappaqua Central SD
66 Roaring Brook Rd • Chappaqua, NY 10514-1703
(914) 238-7200 • http://www.chappaqua.k12.ny.us/ccsd/
Grade Span: KG-12; **Agency Type:** 1
Schools: 6
   3 Primary; 2 Middle; 1 High; 0 Other Level
   6 Regular; 0 Special Education; 0 Vocational; 0 Alternative
   0 Magnet; 0 Charter; 6 Title I Eligible; 0 School-wide Title I
Students: 4,096 (51.6% male; 48.3% female)
   Individual Education Program: n/a;
   English Language Learner: n/a; Migrant: n/a
   Eligible for Free Lunch Program: n/a
   Eligible for Reduced-Price Lunch Program: n/a
Teachers: 354.5 (11.6 to 1)
Librarians/Media Specialists: 7.0 (585.1 to 1)
Guidance Counselors: 13.6 (301.2 to 1)
Current Spending: ($ per student per year):
   Total: $15,929; Instruction: $10,218; Support Services: $5,366
Enrollment, Drop-out Rates and Diploma Recipients by Race/Ethnicity

Category	Total	White	Black	Asian	AIAN	Hisp.
Enrollment (%)	100.0	90.9	1.0	6.5	0.0	1.6
Drop-out Rate (%)	0.0	0.0	0.0	0.0	n/a	0.0
H.S. Diplomas (#)	257	224	1	22	0	10

Croton-Harmon Union Free SD
10 Gerstein St • Croton-On-Hudson, NY 10520-2303
(914) 271-4793
Grade Span: KG-12; **Agency Type:** 1
Schools: 3
   1 Primary; 1 Middle; 1 High; 0 Other Level
   3 Regular; 0 Special Education; 0 Vocational; 0 Alternative
   0 Magnet; 0 Charter; 1 Title I Eligible; 0 School-wide Title I
Students: 1,549 (50.0% male; 49.9% female)
   Individual Education Program: n/a;
   English Language Learner: n/a; Migrant: n/a
   Eligible for Free Lunch Program: n/a
   Eligible for Reduced-Price Lunch Program: n/a
Teachers: 116.7 (13.3 to 1)
Librarians/Media Specialists: 1.0 (1,549.0 to 1)
Guidance Counselors: 3.0 (516.3 to 1)
Current Spending: ($ per student per year):
   Total: $14,750; Instruction: $9,322; Support Services: $5,407
Enrollment, Drop-out Rates and Diploma Recipients by Race/Ethnicity

Category	Total	White	Black	Asian	AIAN	Hisp.
Enrollment (%)	100.0	88.8	2.1	2.6	0.1	6.5
Drop-out Rate (%)	6.5	6.3	0.0	14.3	n/a	7.1
H.S. Diplomas (#)	73	67	1	4	0	1

Eastchester Union Free SD
580 White Plains Rd • Eastchester, NY 10709
(914) 793-6130 • http://www.eastchester.k12.ny.us/
Grade Span: KG-12; **Agency Type:** 1
Schools: 5
   3 Primary; 1 Middle; 1 High; 0 Other Level
   5 Regular; 0 Special Education; 0 Vocational; 0 Alternative
   0 Magnet; 0 Charter; 2 Title I Eligible; 0 School-wide Title I
Students: 2,680 (51.4% male; 48.5% female)
   Individual Education Program: n/a;
   English Language Learner: n/a; Migrant: n/a
   Eligible for Free Lunch Program: n/a
   Eligible for Reduced-Price Lunch Program: n/a
Teachers: 213.6 (12.5 to 1)
Librarians/Media Specialists: 3.0 (893.3 to 1)
Guidance Counselors: 7.8 (343.6 to 1)
Current Spending: ($ per student per year):
   Total: $14,946; Instruction: $10,146; Support Services: $4,650
Enrollment, Drop-out Rates and Diploma Recipients by Race/Ethnicity

Category	Total	White	Black	Asian	AIAN	Hisp.
Enrollment (%)	100.0	85.3	0.7	9.9	0.0	4.1
Drop-out Rate (%)	1.1	0.7	0.0	9.1	n/a	33.3
H.S. Diplomas (#)	105	94	0	8	0	3

Edgemont Union Free SD
300 White Oak Ln • Scarsdale, NY 10583-1725
(914) 472-7768 • http://www.edgemont.org/
Grade Span: KG-12; **Agency Type:** 1
Schools: 3
   2 Primary; 0 Middle; 1 High; 0 Other Level
   3 Regular; 0 Special Education; 0 Vocational; 0 Alternative
   0 Magnet; 0 Charter; 0 Title I Eligible; 0 School-wide Title I
Students: 1,834 (53.2% male; 46.7% female)
   Individual Education Program: n/a;
   English Language Learner: n/a; Migrant: n/a
   Eligible for Free Lunch Program: n/a
   Eligible for Reduced-Price Lunch Program: n/a
Teachers: 139.4 (13.2 to 1)
Librarians/Media Specialists: 3.0 (611.3 to 1)
Guidance Counselors: 4.0 (458.5 to 1)
Current Spending: ($ per student per year):
   Total: $14,849; Instruction: $10,095; Support Services: $4,571
Enrollment, Drop-out Rates and Diploma Recipients by Race/Ethnicity

Category	Total	White	Black	Asian	AIAN	Hisp.
Enrollment (%)	100.0	77.8	0.9	19.5	0.1	1.7
Drop-out Rate (%)	0.0	0.0	0.0	0.0	n/a	0.0
H.S. Diplomas (#)	104	76	1	26	0	1

Greenburgh Central SD
475 W Hartsdale Ave • Hartsdale, NY 10530-1398
(914) 761-6000 • http://www.greenburgh.k12.ny.us/
Grade Span: PK-12; **Agency Type:** 1
Schools: 6
   3 Primary; 2 Middle; 1 High; 0 Other Level
   6 Regular; 0 Special Education; 0 Vocational; 0 Alternative
   0 Magnet; 0 Charter; 3 Title I Eligible; 0 School-wide Title I
Students: 1,981 (52.2% male; 47.7% female)
   Individual Education Program: n/a;
   English Language Learner: n/a; Migrant: n/a
   Eligible for Free Lunch Program: n/a
   Eligible for Reduced-Price Lunch Program: n/a

Teachers: 177.4 (11.2 to 1)
Librarians/Media Specialists: 4.0 (495.3 to 1)
Guidance Counselors: 5.0 (396.2 to 1)
Current Spending: ($ per student per year):
    Total: $19,950; Instruction: $11,747; Support Services: $7,977
Enrollment, Drop-out Rates and Diploma Recipients by Race/Ethnicity

Category	Total	White	Black	Asian	AIAN	Hisp.
Enrollment (%)	100.0	13.8	56.2	6.3	0.1	23.6
Drop-out Rate (%)	1.3	0.9	1.6	3.6	n/a	0.0
H.S. Diplomas (#)	117	28	65	7	0	17

Harrison Central SD
50 Union Ave • Harrison, NY 10528-2032
(914) 630-3002 • http://www.harrisoncsd.org/
Grade Span: KG-12; **Agency Type:** 1
Schools: 6
    4 Primary; 1 Middle; 1 High; 0 Other Level
    6 Regular; 0 Special Education; 0 Vocational; 0 Alternative
    0 Magnet; 0 Charter; 2 Title I Eligible; 0 School-wide Title I
Students: 3,382   (51.0% male; 48.9% female)
    Individual Education Program: n/a;
    English Language Learner: n/a; Migrant: n/a
    Eligible for Free Lunch Program: n/a
    Eligible for Reduced-Price Lunch Program: n/a
Teachers: 301.5 (11.2 to 1)
Librarians/Media Specialists: 3.2 (1,056.9 to 1)
Guidance Counselors: 8.0 (422.8 to 1)
Current Spending: ($ per student per year):
    Total: $18,508; Instruction: $11,806; Support Services: $6,450
Enrollment, Drop-out Rates and Diploma Recipients by Race/Ethnicity

Category	Total	White	Black	Asian	AIAN	Hisp.
Enrollment (%)	100.0	79.8	0.6	9.8	0.0	9.9
Drop-out Rate (%)	0.8	0.8	0.0	2.3	n/a	0.0
H.S. Diplomas (#)	163	139	0	9	0	15

Hastings-On-Hudson Union Free SD
27 Farragut Ave • Hastings-On-Hudson, NY 10706-2395
(914) 478-6200
Grade Span: KG-12; **Agency Type:** 1
Schools: 3
    1 Primary; 1 Middle; 1 High; 0 Other Level
    3 Regular; 0 Special Education; 0 Vocational; 0 Alternative
    0 Magnet; 0 Charter; 0 Title I Eligible; 0 School-wide Title I
Students: 1,670   (50.2% male; 49.7% female)
    Individual Education Program: n/a;
    English Language Learner: n/a; Migrant: n/a
    Eligible for Free Lunch Program: n/a
    Eligible for Reduced-Price Lunch Program: n/a
Teachers: 151.3 (11.0 to 1)
Librarians/Media Specialists: 2.4 (695.8 to 1)
Guidance Counselors: 6.0 (278.3 to 1)
Current Spending: ($ per student per year):
    Total: $14,666; Instruction: $9,610; Support Services: $4,855
Enrollment, Drop-out Rates and Diploma Recipients by Race/Ethnicity

Category	Total	White	Black	Asian	AIAN	Hisp.
Enrollment (%)	100.0	84.3	2.8	6.7	0.4	5.9
Drop-out Rate (%)	0.2	0.3	0.0	0.0	n/a	0.0
H.S. Diplomas (#)	74	64	2	6	0	2

Hendrick Hudson Central SD
61 Trolley Rd • Montrose, NY 10548-1199
(914) 736-5200 • http://www2.lhric.org/henhud/
Grade Span: KG-12; **Agency Type:** 1
Schools: 5
    3 Primary; 1 Middle; 1 High; 0 Other Level
    5 Regular; 0 Special Education; 0 Vocational; 0 Alternative
    0 Magnet; 0 Charter; 3 Title I Eligible; 0 School-wide Title I
Students: 2,884   (52.0% male; 47.9% female)
    Individual Education Program: n/a;
    English Language Learner: n/a; Migrant: n/a
    Eligible for Free Lunch Program: n/a
    Eligible for Reduced-Price Lunch Program: n/a
Teachers: 235.3 (12.3 to 1)
Librarians/Media Specialists: 5.0 (576.8 to 1)
Guidance Counselors: 7.0 (412.0 to 1)
Current Spending: ($ per student per year):
    Total: $15,704; Instruction: $10,729; Support Services: $4,772
Enrollment, Drop-out Rates and Diploma Recipients by Race/Ethnicity

Category	Total	White	Black	Asian	AIAN	Hisp.
Enrollment (%)	100.0	85.3	4.0	4.5	0.0	6.1
Drop-out Rate (%)	1.8	1.9	0.0	0.0	n/a	2.2
H.S. Diplomas (#)	176	155	4	10	0	7

Irvington Union Free SD
40 N Broadway • Irvington, NY 10533-1328
(914) 591-8501 • http://www.irvingtonschools.org/
Grade Span: KG-12; **Agency Type:** 2
Schools: 4
    1 Primary; 2 Middle; 1 High; 0 Other Level
    4 Regular; 0 Special Education; 0 Vocational; 0 Alternative
    0 Magnet; 0 Charter; 1 Title I Eligible; 0 School-wide Title I
Students: 1,967   (51.0% male; 48.9% female)
    Individual Education Program: n/a;
    English Language Learner: n/a; Migrant: n/a
    Eligible for Free Lunch Program: n/a
    Eligible for Reduced-Price Lunch Program: n/a
Teachers: 160.1 (12.3 to 1)
Librarians/Media Specialists: 2.0 (983.5 to 1)
Guidance Counselors: 5.0 (393.4 to 1)
Current Spending: ($ per student per year):
    Total: $14,889; Instruction: $10,037; Support Services: $4,780
Enrollment, Drop-out Rates and Diploma Recipients by Race/Ethnicity

Category	Total	White	Black	Asian	AIAN	Hisp.
Enrollment (%)	100.0	82.1	3.9	10.6	0.0	3.4
Drop-out Rate (%)	0.2	0.3	0.0	0.0	n/a	0.0
H.S. Diplomas (#)	92	70	0	18	0	4

Katonah-Lewisboro Union Free SD
One Shady Ln Rt 123 • South Salem, NY 10590-1930
(914) 763-7001 • http://www.klschools.org/public/
Grade Span: KG-12; **Agency Type:** 1
Schools: 6
    4 Primary; 1 Middle; 1 High; 0 Other Level
    6 Regular; 0 Special Education; 0 Vocational; 0 Alternative
    0 Magnet; 0 Charter; 2 Title I Eligible; 0 School-wide Title I
Students: 4,112   (50.8% male; 49.1% female)
    Individual Education Program: n/a;
    English Language Learner: n/a; Migrant: n/a
    Eligible for Free Lunch Program: n/a
    Eligible for Reduced-Price Lunch Program: n/a
Teachers: 309.1 (13.3 to 1)
Librarians/Media Specialists: 6.6 (623.0 to 1)
Guidance Counselors: 13.0 (316.3 to 1)
Current Spending: ($ per student per year):
    Total: $16,299; Instruction: $9,755; Support Services: $6,347
Enrollment, Drop-out Rates and Diploma Recipients by Race/Ethnicity

Category	Total	White	Black	Asian	AIAN	Hisp.
Enrollment (%)	100.0	94.7	1.2	2.1	0.0	2.0
Drop-out Rate (%)	0.4	0.3	0.0	0.0	n/a	6.7
H.S. Diplomas (#)	208	201	7	0	0	0

Lakeland Central SD
1086 Main St • Shrub Oak, NY 10588-1507
(914) 245-1700 • http://www.lakelandschools.org/
Grade Span: KG-12; **Agency Type:** 1
Schools: 9
    5 Primary; 1 Middle; 3 High; 0 Other Level
    8 Regular; 0 Special Education; 0 Vocational; 1 Alternative
    0 Magnet; 0 Charter; 4 Title I Eligible; 0 School-wide Title I
Students: 6,139   (50.7% male; 49.2% female)
    Individual Education Program: n/a;
    English Language Learner: n/a; Migrant: n/a
    Eligible for Free Lunch Program: n/a
    Eligible for Reduced-Price Lunch Program: n/a
Teachers: 454.5 (13.5 to 1)
Librarians/Media Specialists: 8.0 (767.4 to 1)
Guidance Counselors: 15.0 (409.3 to 1)
Current Spending: ($ per student per year):
    Total: $14,329; Instruction: $8,950; Support Services: $5,091
Enrollment, Drop-out Rates and Diploma Recipients by Race/Ethnicity

Category	Total	White	Black	Asian	AIAN	Hisp.
Enrollment (%)	100.0	80.4	6.1	3.7	0.0	9.8
Drop-out Rate (%)	3.5	3.2	2.2	4.4	0.0	5.7
H.S. Diplomas (#)	472	377	32	11	0	52

Mamaroneck Union Free SD
1000 W Boston Post Rd • Mamaroneck, NY 10543-3399
(914) 220-3005 • http://www.mamkschools.org/
Grade Span: PK-12; **Agency Type:** 1
Schools: 6
    4 Primary; 1 Middle; 1 High; 0 Other Level
    6 Regular; 0 Special Education; 0 Vocational; 0 Alternative
    0 Magnet; 0 Charter; 2 Title I Eligible; 0 School-wide Title I
Students: 4,791   (51.3% male; 48.6% female)
    Individual Education Program: n/a;
    English Language Learner: n/a; Migrant: n/a
    Eligible for Free Lunch Program: n/a
    Eligible for Reduced-Price Lunch Program: n/a

Teachers: 371.2 (12.9 to 1)
Librarians/Media Specialists: 6.0 (798.5 to 1)
Guidance Counselors: 12.0 (399.3 to 1)
Current Spending: ($ per student per year):
 Total: $15,491; Instruction: $10,079; Support Services: $5,354
Enrollment, Drop-out Rates and Diploma Recipients by Race/Ethnicity

Category	Total	White	Black	Asian	AIAN	Hisp.
Enrollment (%)	100.0	79.0	3.4	3.3	0.0	14.3
Drop-out Rate (%)	1.3	0.6	7.0	0.0	0.0	3.1
H.S. Diplomas (#)	289	235	13	9	0	32

Mount Pleasant Central SD
825 Westlake Dr • Thornwood, NY 10594-2120
(914) 769-5500 • http://www2.lhric.org/mpcsd/welcome.htm
Grade Span: KG-12; **Agency Type:** 1
Schools: 4
 2 Primary; 1 Middle; 1 High; 0 Other Level
 4 Regular; 0 Special Education; 0 Vocational; 0 Alternative
 0 Magnet; 0 Charter; 4 Title I Eligible; 0 School-wide Title I
Students: 1,847 (51.5% male; 48.4% female)
 Individual Education Program: n/a;
 English Language Learner: n/a; Migrant: n/a
 Eligible for Free Lunch Program: n/a
 Eligible for Reduced-Price Lunch Program: n/a
Teachers: 169.2 (10.9 to 1)
Librarians/Media Specialists: 0.0 (n/a to 1)
Guidance Counselors: 7.0 (263.9 to 1)
Current Spending: ($ per student per year):
 Total: $16,786; Instruction: $11,207; Support Services: $5,420
Enrollment, Drop-out Rates and Diploma Recipients by Race/Ethnicity

Category	Total	White	Black	Asian	AIAN	Hisp.
Enrollment (%)	100.0	91.3	0.5	3.5	0.2	4.4
Drop-out Rate (%)	0.8	0.6	0.0	0.0	n/a	4.3
H.S. Diplomas (#)	118	107	1	5	0	5

Mount Vernon City SD
165 N Columbus Ave • Mount Vernon, NY 10553-1199
(914) 665-5201 • http://www.lhric.org/mtvernon/index.asp
Grade Span: PK-12; **Agency Type:** 1
Schools: 16
 12 Primary; 2 Middle; 2 High; 0 Other Level
 16 Regular; 0 Special Education; 0 Vocational; 0 Alternative
 0 Magnet; 0 Charter; 15 Title I Eligible; 0 School-wide Title I
Students: 10,347 (50.7% male; 49.2% female)
 Individual Education Program: n/a;
 English Language Learner: n/a; Migrant: n/a
 Eligible for Free Lunch Program: n/a
 Eligible for Reduced-Price Lunch Program: n/a
Teachers: 662.0 (15.6 to 1)
Librarians/Media Specialists: 15.0 (689.8 to 1)
Guidance Counselors: 22.0 (470.3 to 1)
Current Spending: ($ per student per year):
 Total: $12,351; Instruction: $8,727; Support Services: $3,354
Enrollment, Drop-out Rates and Diploma Recipients by Race/Ethnicity

Category	Total	White	Black	Asian	AIAN	Hisp.
Enrollment (%)	100.0	7.4	78.1	1.3	0.2	13.1
Drop-out Rate (%)	4.5	3.0	4.4	15.4	0.0	6.3
H.S. Diplomas (#)	337	16	294	0	2	25

New Rochelle City SD
515 N Ave • New Rochelle, NY 10801-3416
(914) 576-4200 • http://www.nred.org/
Grade Span: PK-12; **Agency Type:** 1
Schools: 10
 7 Primary; 2 Middle; 1 High; 0 Other Level
 10 Regular; 0 Special Education; 0 Vocational; 0 Alternative
 0 Magnet; 0 Charter; 5 Title I Eligible; 1 School-wide Title I
Students: 10,464 (51.9% male; 48.0% female)
 Individual Education Program: n/a;
 English Language Learner: n/a; Migrant: n/a
 Eligible for Free Lunch Program: n/a
 Eligible for Reduced-Price Lunch Program: n/a
Teachers: 711.0 (14.7 to 1)
Librarians/Media Specialists: 11.0 (951.3 to 1)
Guidance Counselors: 22.0 (475.6 to 1)
Current Spending: ($ per student per year):
 Total: $13,979; Instruction: $8,809; Support Services: $4,940
Enrollment, Drop-out Rates and Diploma Recipients by Race/Ethnicity

Category	Total	White	Black	Asian	AIAN	Hisp.
Enrollment (%)	100.0	40.2	25.4	3.8	0.1	30.5
Drop-out Rate (%)	1.2	0.8	1.2	0.0	0.0	2.0
H.S. Diplomas (#)	479	260	106	23	13	77

Ossining Union Free SD
190 Croton Ave • Ossining, NY 10562-4599
(914) 941-7700 • http://www.ossining.k12.ny.us/
Grade Span: PK-12; **Agency Type:** 1
Schools: 7
 3 Primary; 2 Middle; 1 High; 1 Other Level
 6 Regular; 0 Special Education; 0 Vocational; 1 Alternative
 0 Magnet; 0 Charter; 2 Title I Eligible; 0 School-wide Title I
Students: 4,252 (53.2% male; 46.7% female)
 Individual Education Program: n/a;
 English Language Learner: n/a; Migrant: n/a
 Eligible for Free Lunch Program: n/a
 Eligible for Reduced-Price Lunch Program: n/a
Teachers: 326.5 (13.0 to 1)
Librarians/Media Specialists: 4.0 (1,063.0 to 1)
Guidance Counselors: 12.0 (354.3 to 1)
Current Spending: ($ per student per year):
 Total: $15,032; Instruction: $9,619; Support Services: $5,205
Enrollment, Drop-out Rates and Diploma Recipients by Race/Ethnicity

Category	Total	White	Black	Asian	AIAN	Hisp.
Enrollment (%)	100.0	43.2	18.5	6.0	0.0	32.4
Drop-out Rate (%)	3.8	1.4	6.0	1.7	n/a	6.8
H.S. Diplomas (#)	203	122	36	14	0	31

Peekskill City SD
1031 Elm St • Peekskill, NY 10566-3499
(914) 737-3300
Grade Span: PK-12; **Agency Type:** 1
Schools: 7
 3 Primary; 2 Middle; 2 High; 0 Other Level
 7 Regular; 0 Special Education; 0 Vocational; 0 Alternative
 0 Magnet; 0 Charter; 4 Title I Eligible; 4 School-wide Title I
Students: 3,055 (50.9% male; 49.0% female)
 Individual Education Program: n/a;
 English Language Learner: n/a; Migrant: n/a
 Eligible for Free Lunch Program: n/a
 Eligible for Reduced-Price Lunch Program: n/a
Teachers: 234.1 (13.0 to 1)
Librarians/Media Specialists: 5.0 (611.0 to 1)
Guidance Counselors: 7.0 (436.4 to 1)
Current Spending: ($ per student per year):
 Total: $16,420; Instruction: $11,253; Support Services: $4,857
Enrollment, Drop-out Rates and Diploma Recipients by Race/Ethnicity

Category	Total	White	Black	Asian	AIAN	Hisp.
Enrollment (%)	100.0	20.1	47.4	1.2	0.0	31.3
Drop-out Rate (%)	0.5	0.4	0.6	0.0	n/a	0.5
H.S. Diplomas (#)	130	49	53	4	0	24

Pelham Union Free SD
661 Hillside Rd • Pelham, NY 10803-2147
(914) 738-3434 • http://www.pelham.k12.ny.us/
Grade Span: KG-12; **Agency Type:** 1
Schools: 6
 4 Primary; 1 Middle; 1 High; 0 Other Level
 6 Regular; 0 Special Education; 0 Vocational; 0 Alternative
 0 Magnet; 0 Charter; 1 Title I Eligible; 0 School-wide Title I
Students: 2,529 (51.9% male; 48.0% female)
 Individual Education Program: n/a;
 English Language Learner: n/a; Migrant: n/a
 Eligible for Free Lunch Program: n/a
 Eligible for Reduced-Price Lunch Program: n/a
Teachers: 198.1 (12.8 to 1)
Librarians/Media Specialists: 2.0 (1,264.5 to 1)
Guidance Counselors: 6.0 (421.5 to 1)
Current Spending: ($ per student per year):
 Total: $13,581; Instruction: $8,670; Support Services: $4,757
Enrollment, Drop-out Rates and Diploma Recipients by Race/Ethnicity

Category	Total	White	Black	Asian	AIAN	Hisp.
Enrollment (%)	100.0	81.8	6.3	5.4	0.0	6.5
Drop-out Rate (%)	0.6	0.4	3.4	0.0	n/a	0.0
H.S. Diplomas (#)	135	110	7	8	0	10

Pleasantville Union Free SD
60 Romer Ave • Pleasantville, NY 10570-3157
(914) 741-1400 • http://www2.lhric.org/pleasantville/
Grade Span: KG-12; **Agency Type:** 1
Schools: 3
 1 Primary; 1 Middle; 1 High; 0 Other Level
 3 Regular; 0 Special Education; 0 Vocational; 0 Alternative
 0 Magnet; 0 Charter; 1 Title I Eligible; 0 School-wide Title I
Students: 1,727 (52.8% male; 47.1% female)
 Individual Education Program: n/a;
 English Language Learner: n/a; Migrant: n/a
 Eligible for Free Lunch Program: n/a
 Eligible for Reduced-Price Lunch Program: n/a

Teachers: 127.6 (13.5 to 1)
Librarians/Media Specialists: 2.0 (863.5 to 1)
Guidance Counselors: 5.0 (345.4 to 1)
Current Spending: ($ per student per year):
　　Total: $13,925; Instruction: $9,577; Support Services: $4,157
Enrollment, Drop-out Rates and Diploma Recipients by Race/Ethnicity

Category	Total	White	Black	Asian	AIAN	Hisp.
Enrollment (%)	100.0	91.1	1.6	2.8	0.0	4.5
Drop-out Rate (%)	0.6	0.5	0.0	5.0	n/a	0.0
H.S. Diplomas (#)	106	90	4	8	0	4

Port Chester-Rye Union Free SD
113 Bowman Ave • Port Chester, NY 10573-2851
(914) 934-7901 • http://www.portchester.k12.ny.us/
Grade Span: KG-12; **Agency Type:** 1
Schools: 6
　　4 Primary; 1 Middle; 1 High; 0 Other Level
　　6 Regular; 0 Special Education; 0 Vocational; 0 Alternative
　　1 Magnet; 0 Charter; 3 Title I Eligible; 0 School-wide Title I
Students: 3,574　(51.8% male; 48.1% female)
　　Individual Education Program: n/a;
　　English Language Learner: n/a; Migrant: n/a
　　Eligible for Free Lunch Program: n/a
　　Eligible for Reduced-Price Lunch Program: n/a
Teachers: 257.8 (13.9 to 1)
Librarians/Media Specialists: 3.5 (1,021.1 to 1)
Guidance Counselors: 8.0 (446.8 to 1)
Current Spending: ($ per student per year):
　　Total: $12,634; Instruction: $8,399; Support Services: $3,967
Enrollment, Drop-out Rates and Diploma Recipients by Race/Ethnicity

Category	Total	White	Black	Asian	AIAN	Hisp.
Enrollment (%)	100.0	23.0	9.8	1.0	0.0	66.2
Drop-out Rate (%)	6.6	2.1	6.1	0.0	n/a	9.4
H.S. Diplomas (#)	190	76	23	3	0	88

Rye City SD
324 Midland Ave • Rye, NY 10580-3899
(914) 967-6108 • http://ryecityschools.lhric.org/
Grade Span: KG-12; **Agency Type:** 1
Schools: 5
　　3 Primary; 1 Middle; 1 High; 0 Other Level
　　5 Regular; 0 Special Education; 0 Vocational; 0 Alternative
　　0 Magnet; 0 Charter; 4 Title I Eligible; 0 School-wide Title I
Students: 2,688　(52.1% male; 47.8% female)
　　Individual Education Program: n/a;
　　English Language Learner: n/a; Migrant: n/a
　　Eligible for Free Lunch Program: n/a
　　Eligible for Reduced-Price Lunch Program: n/a
Teachers: 218.3 (12.3 to 1)
Librarians/Media Specialists: 5.0 (537.6 to 1)
Guidance Counselors: 6.6 (407.3 to 1)
Current Spending: ($ per student per year):
　　Total: $15,760; Instruction: $9,867; Support Services: $5,483
Enrollment, Drop-out Rates and Diploma Recipients by Race/Ethnicity

Category	Total	White	Black	Asian	AIAN	Hisp.
Enrollment (%)	100.0	88.0	1.1	6.5	0.0	4.4
Drop-out Rate (%)	0.7	0.4	0.0	0.0	n/a	5.1
H.S. Diplomas (#)	121	99	2	10	1	9

Scarsdale Union Free SD
2 Brewster Rd • Scarsdale, NY 10583-3049
(914) 721-2410 • http://www.scarsdaleschools.k12.ny.us/
Grade Span: KG-12; **Agency Type:** 1
Schools: 7
　　5 Primary; 1 Middle; 1 High; 0 Other Level
　　7 Regular; 0 Special Education; 0 Vocational; 0 Alternative
　　0 Magnet; 0 Charter; 0 Title I Eligible; 0 School-wide Title I
Students: 4,568　(51.4% male; 48.5% female)
　　Individual Education Program: n/a;
　　English Language Learner: n/a; Migrant: n/a
　　Eligible for Free Lunch Program: n/a
　　Eligible for Reduced-Price Lunch Program: n/a
Teachers: 372.5 (12.3 to 1)
Librarians/Media Specialists: 9.0 (507.6 to 1)
Guidance Counselors: 13.0 (351.4 to 1)
Current Spending: ($ per student per year):
　　Total: $16,867; Instruction: $11,808; Support Services: $4,911
Enrollment, Drop-out Rates and Diploma Recipients by Race/Ethnicity

Category	Total	White	Black	Asian	AIAN	Hisp.
Enrollment (%)	100.0	83.7	1.9	12.3	0.0	2.1
Drop-out Rate (%)	0.2	0.0	7.4	0.0	n/a	0.0
H.S. Diplomas (#)	267	207	9	44	0	7

Somers Central SD
Po Bx 620-110 Prmrse • Lincolndale, NY 10540-0620
(914) 248-7872 • http://www.somers.k12.ny.us/
Grade Span: KG-12; **Agency Type:** 1
Schools: 4
　　2 Primary; 1 Middle; 1 High; 0 Other Level
　　4 Regular; 0 Special Education; 0 Vocational; 0 Alternative
　　0 Magnet; 0 Charter; 0 Title I Eligible; 0 School-wide Title I
Students: 3,140　(50.8% male; 49.1% female)
　　Individual Education Program: n/a;
　　English Language Learner: n/a; Migrant: n/a
　　Eligible for Free Lunch Program: n/a
　　Eligible for Reduced-Price Lunch Program: n/a
Teachers: 242.8 (12.9 to 1)
Librarians/Media Specialists: 4.0 (785.0 to 1)
Guidance Counselors: 8.0 (392.5 to 1)
Current Spending: ($ per student per year):
　　Total: $15,225; Instruction: $9,704; Support Services: $5,277
Enrollment, Drop-out Rates and Diploma Recipients by Race/Ethnicity

Category	Total	White	Black	Asian	AIAN	Hisp.
Enrollment (%)	100.0	93.0	1.2	3.2	0.0	2.6
Drop-out Rate (%)	1.8	1.9	0.0	0.0	n/a	0.0
H.S. Diplomas (#)	171	154	2	7	0	8

Union Free SD of the Tarrytowns
200 N Broadway • Sleepy Hollow, NY 10591-2696
(914) 631-9404 • http://www.tufsd.org/
Grade Span: PK-12; **Agency Type:** 1
Schools: 5
　　3 Primary; 1 Middle; 1 High; 0 Other Level
　　5 Regular; 0 Special Education; 0 Vocational; 0 Alternative
　　0 Magnet; 0 Charter; 5 Title I Eligible; 0 School-wide Title I
Students: 2,499　(50.8% male; 49.1% female)
　　Individual Education Program: n/a;
　　English Language Learner: n/a; Migrant: n/a
　　Eligible for Free Lunch Program: n/a
　　Eligible for Reduced-Price Lunch Program: n/a
Teachers: 195.6 (12.8 to 1)
Librarians/Media Specialists: 2.0 (1,249.5 to 1)
Guidance Counselors: 5.5 (454.4 to 1)
Current Spending: ($ per student per year):
　　Total: $16,116; Instruction: $11,078; Support Services: $4,791
Enrollment, Drop-out Rates and Diploma Recipients by Race/Ethnicity

Category	Total	White	Black	Asian	AIAN	Hisp.
Enrollment (%)	100.0	38.2	7.1	2.8	0.0	51.9
Drop-out Rate (%)	3.3	1.3	3.6	0.0	n/a	4.7
H.S. Diplomas (#)	111	49	5	1	0	56

White Plains City SD
5 Homeside Ln • White Plains, NY 10605-4299
(914) 422-2019 • http://www.wpcsd.k12.ny.us/
Grade Span: PK-12; **Agency Type:** 1
Schools: 8
　　6 Primary; 0 Middle; 1 High; 1 Other Level
　　7 Regular; 1 Special Education; 0 Vocational; 0 Alternative
　　0 Magnet; 0 Charter; 6 Title I Eligible; 6 School-wide Title I
Students: 6,844　(51.7% male; 48.2% female)
　　Individual Education Program: n/a;
　　English Language Learner: n/a; Migrant: n/a
　　Eligible for Free Lunch Program: n/a
　　Eligible for Reduced-Price Lunch Program: n/a
Teachers: 561.4 (12.2 to 1)
Librarians/Media Specialists: 5.5 (1,244.4 to 1)
Guidance Counselors: 18.5 (369.9 to 1)
Current Spending: ($ per student per year):
　　Total: $18,418; Instruction: $12,162; Support Services: $5,908
Enrollment, Drop-out Rates and Diploma Recipients by Race/Ethnicity

Category	Total	White	Black	Asian	AIAN	Hisp.
Enrollment (%)	100.0	35.8	21.7	3.2	0.1	39.2
Drop-out Rate (%)	2.3	0.8	1.8	0.0	0.0	4.6
H.S. Diplomas (#)	360	177	76	12	1	94

Yonkers City SD
1 Larkin Center • Yonkers, NY 10701-2756
(914) 376-8100 • http://www.yonkerspublicschools.org/
Grade Span: PK-12; **Agency Type:** 1
Schools: 39
　　29 Primary; 5 Middle; 5 High; 0 Other Level
　　38 Regular; 0 Special Education; 1 Vocational; 0 Alternative
　　1 Magnet; 0 Charter; 38 Title I Eligible; 29 School-wide Title I
Students: 26,201　(51.5% male; 48.4% female)
　　Individual Education Program: n/a;
　　English Language Learner: n/a; Migrant: n/a
　　Eligible for Free Lunch Program: n/a
　　Eligible for Reduced-Price Lunch Program: n/a

Teachers: 1,883.1 (13.9 to 1)
Librarians/Media Specialists: 24.0 (1,091.7 to 1)
Guidance Counselors: 65.0 (403.1 to 1)
Current Spending: ($ per student per year):
   Total: $14,107; Instruction: $9,343; Support Services: $4,480
Enrollment, Drop-out Rates and Diploma Recipients by Race/Ethnicity

Category	Total	White	Black	Asian	AIAN	Hisp.
Enrollment (%)	100.0	18.5	29.2	5.9	0.2	46.2
Drop-out Rate (%)	7.7	6.4	7.9	2.9	0.0	8.9
H.S. Diplomas (#)	724	223	188	77	1	235

Enrollment, Drop-out Rates and Diploma Recipients by Race/Ethnicity

Category	Total	White	Black	Asian	AIAN	Hisp.
Enrollment (%)	100.0	97.5	0.8	0.4	0.1	1.0
Drop-out Rate (%)	2.5	2.4	50.0	0.0	n/a	0.0
H.S. Diplomas (#)	152	148	0	2	1	1

Yorktown Central SD

46 Triangle Center • Yorktown Heights, NY 10598-4104
(914) 243-8001 • http://www.yorktown.org/
Grade Span: KG-12; **Agency Type:** 1
Schools: 6
   4 Primary; 1 Middle; 1 High; 0 Other Level
   6 Regular; 0 Special Education; 0 Vocational; 0 Alternative
   0 Magnet; 0 Charter; 4 Title I Eligible; 0 School-wide Title I
Students: 4,219 (50.1% male; 49.8% female)
   Individual Education Program: n/a;
   English Language Learner: n/a; Migrant: n/a
   Eligible for Free Lunch Program: n/a
   Eligible for Reduced-Price Lunch Program: n/a
Teachers: 317.4 (13.3 to 1)
Librarians/Media Specialists: 6.0 (703.2 to 1)
Guidance Counselors: 9.6 (439.5 to 1)
Current Spending: ($ per student per year):
   Total: $13,376; Instruction: $8,966; Support Services: $4,247
Enrollment, Drop-out Rates and Diploma Recipients by Race/Ethnicity

Category	Total	White	Black	Asian	AIAN	Hisp.
Enrollment (%)	100.0	89.6	1.3	4.4	0.1	4.6
Drop-out Rate (%)	1.0	1.0	0.0	0.0	n/a	2.6
H.S. Diplomas (#)	260	233	7	6	0	14

Wyoming County

Attica Central SD

3338 E Main St • Attica, NY 14011-9699
(585) 591-0400 • http://www.atticacs.k12.ny.us/
Grade Span: KG-12; **Agency Type:** 1
Schools: 6
   2 Primary; 1 Middle; 1 High; 2 Other Level
   4 Regular; 0 Special Education; 0 Vocational; 2 Alternative
   0 Magnet; 0 Charter; 3 Title I Eligible; 3 School-wide Title I
Students: 1,840 (54.7% male; 45.2% female)
   Individual Education Program: n/a;
   English Language Learner: n/a; Migrant: n/a
   Eligible for Free Lunch Program: n/a
   Eligible for Reduced-Price Lunch Program: n/a
Teachers: 144.7 (12.7 to 1)
Librarians/Media Specialists: 2.0 (920.0 to 1)
Guidance Counselors: 3.0 (613.3 to 1)
Current Spending: ($ per student per year):
   Total: $9,673; Instruction: $6,478; Support Services: $2,956
Enrollment, Drop-out Rates and Diploma Recipients by Race/Ethnicity

Category	Total	White	Black	Asian	AIAN	Hisp.
Enrollment (%)	100.0	95.3	3.0	0.2	0.4	1.0
Drop-out Rate (%)	1.6	1.5	0.0	0.0	0.0	20.0
H.S. Diplomas (#)	145	145	0	0	0	0

Yates County

Penn Yan Central SD

One School Dr • Penn Yan, NY 14527-1099
(315) 536-3371 • http://www.pennyan.k12.ny.us/
Grade Span: PK-12; **Agency Type:** 1
Schools: 3
   1 Primary; 1 Middle; 1 High; 0 Other Level
   3 Regular; 0 Special Education; 0 Vocational; 0 Alternative
   0 Magnet; 0 Charter; 3 Title I Eligible; 0 School-wide Title I
Students: 2,035 (49.2% male; 50.7% female)
   Individual Education Program: n/a;
   English Language Learner: n/a; Migrant: n/a
   Eligible for Free Lunch Program: n/a
   Eligible for Reduced-Price Lunch Program: n/a
Teachers: 170.1 (12.0 to 1)
Librarians/Media Specialists: 3.0 (678.3 to 1)
Guidance Counselors: 6.0 (339.2 to 1)
Current Spending: ($ per student per year):
   Total: $10,831; Instruction: $7,196; Support Services: $3,328

Number of Schools

Rank	Number	District Name	City
1	1,225	New York City Public Schools	Brooklyn
2	68	Buffalo City SD	Buffalo
3	62	Rochester City SD	Rochester
4	39	Yonkers City SD	Yonkers
5	35	Syracuse City SD	Syracuse
6	20	Greece Central SD	Rochester
7	18	Brentwood Union Free SD	Brentwood
8	16	Mount Vernon City SD	Mount Vernon
9	15	Albany City SD	Albany
9	15	Elmira City SD	Elmira
9	15	Newburgh City SD	Newburgh
9	15	Rome City SD	Rome
9	15	Sachem Central SD	Holbrook
9	15	Schenectady City SD	Schenectady
9	15	Wappingers Central SD	Wappingers Fls
16	14	Clarkstown Central SD	New City
16	14	Corning City SD	Painted Post
16	14	E Ramapo Central SD (Sprg Val)	Spring Valley
16	14	Kenmore-Tonawanda Union Free SD	Buffalo
16	14	Kingston City SD	Kingston
16	14	Liverpool Central SD	Liverpool
16	14	Middle Country Central SD	Centereach
16	14	West Seneca Central SD	West Seneca
24	13	Half Hollow Hills Central SD	Dix Hills
24	13	Ithaca City SD	Ithaca
24	13	Niagara Falls City SD	Niagara Falls
24	13	Smithtown Central SD	Smithtown
24	13	Utica City SD	Utica
24	13	Williamsville Central SD	East Amherst
30	11	Arlington Central SD	Poughkeepsie
30	11	Auburn City SD	Auburn
30	11	Binghamton City SD	Binghamton
30	11	Levittown Union Free SD	Levittown
30	11	North Syracuse Central SD	N Syracuse
30	11	Patchogue-Medford Union Free SD	Patchogue
30	11	Shenendehowa Central SD	Clifton Park
30	11	Webster Central SD	Webster
38	10	Connetquot Central SD	Bohemia
38	10	Great Neck Union Free SD	Great Neck
38	10	Jamestown City SD	Jamestown
38	10	Lockport City SD	Lockport
38	10	Middletown City SD	Middletown
38	10	New Rochelle City SD	New Rochelle
38	10	Poughkeepsie City SD	Poughkeepsie
38	10	Rush-Henrietta Central SD	Henrietta
38	10	Syosset Central SD	Syosset
38	10	West Irondequoit Central SD	Rochester
38	10	Whitesboro Central SD	Yorkville
49	9	Baldwin Union Free SD	Baldwin
49	9	Bedford Central SD	Mount Kisco
49	9	East Meadow Union Free SD	Westbury
49	9	Haverstraw-Stony Point Cent SD	Garnerville
49	9	Hempstead Union Free SD	Hempstead
49	9	Hicksville Union Free SD	Hicksville
49	9	Lakeland Central SD	Shrub Oak
49	9	Lindenhurst Union Free SD	Lindenhurst
49	9	Massapequa Union Free SD	Massapequa
49	9	North Tonawanda City SD	N Tonawanda
49	9	Northport-East Northport UFSD	Northport
49	9	Oceanside Union Free SD	Oceanside
49	9	Saratoga Springs City SD	Saratoga Spgs
49	9	South Colonie Central SD	Albany
49	9	West Islip Union Free SD	West Islip
64	8	Baldwinsville Central SD	Baldwinsville
64	8	Beacon City SD	Beacon
64	8	Camden Central SD	Camden
64	8	Central Islip Union Free SD	Central Islip
64	8	Central Square Central SD	Central Square
64	8	Commack Union Free SD	E Northport
64	8	Fairport Central SD	Fairport
64	8	Freeport Union Free SD	Freeport
64	8	Huntington Union Free SD	Huntington Stn
64	8	Indian River Central SD	Philadelphia
64	8	Johnstown City SD	Johnstown
64	8	Lancaster Central SD	Lancaster
64	8	Malone Central SD	Malone
64	8	Niskayuna Central SD	Schenectady
64	8	North Colonie Central SD	Latham
64	8	Ogdensburg City SD	Ogdensburg
64	8	Oneida City SD	Oneida
64	8	Pittsford Central SD	Pittsford
64	8	Plainview-Old Bethpage Cent SD	Plainview
64	8	Saranac Lake Central SD	Saranac Lake
64	8	Three Village Central SD	East Setauket
64	8	Troy City SD	Troy
64	8	Uniondale Union Free SD	Uniondale
64	8	Watertown City SD	Watertown
64	8	White Plains City SD	White Plains
64	8	William Floyd Union Free SD	Mastic Beach
90	7	Amsterdam City SD	Amsterdam
90	7	Bay Shore Union Free SD	Bay Shore
90	7	Bethlehem Central SD	Delmar
90	7	East Greenbush Central SD	E Greenbush
90	7	East Islip Union Free SD	Islip Terrace
90	7	East Syracuse-Minoa Central SD	East Syracuse
90	7	Evans-Brant Cent SD (Lake Shore)	Angola
90	7	Garden City Union Free SD	Garden City
90	7	Gates-Chili Central SD	Rochester
90	7	Gloversville City SD	Gloversville
90	7	Guilderland Central SD	Guilderland
90	7	Horseheads Central SD	Horseheads
90	7	Hudson City SD	Hudson
90	7	Hyde Park Central SD	Poughkeepsie
90	7	Lawrence Union Free SD	Lawrence
90	7	Long Beach City SD	Long Beach
90	7	Longwood Central SD	Middle Island
90	7	Lynbrook Union Free SD	Lynbrook
90	7	Mineola Union Free SD	Mineola
90	7	Monroe-Woodbury Central SD	Central Valley
90	7	New York City Geographic Dist 15	Brooklyn
90	7	North Babylon Union Free SD	North Babylon
90	7	Olean City SD	Olean
90	7	Ossining Union Free SD	Ossining
90	7	Oswego City SD	Oswego
90	7	Pearl River Union Free SD	Pearl River
90	7	Peekskill City SD	Peekskill
90	7	Pine Bush Central SD	Pine Bush
90	7	Ramapo Central SD (Suffern)	Hillburn
90	7	Riverhead Central SD	Riverhead
90	7	Rockville Centre Union Free SD	Rockville Ctre
90	7	Saranac Central SD	Dannemora
90	7	Scarsdale Union Free SD	Scarsdale
90	7	South Country Central SD	E Patchogue
90	7	South Glens Falls Central SD	S Glens Falls
90	7	Union-Endicott Central SD	Endicott
90	7	Valley Central SD (Montgomery)	Montgomery
90	7	Vestal Central SD	Vestal
90	7	Warwick Valley Central SD	Warwick
90	7	West Babylon Union Free SD	West Babylon
90	7	West Genesee Central SD	Camillus
131	6	Attica Central SD	Attica
131	6	Averill Park Central SD	Averill Park
131	6	Batavia City SD	Batavia
131	6	Brookhaven-Comsewogue UFSD	Pt Jefferson Stn
131	6	Chappaqua Central SD	Chappaqua
131	6	Churchville-Chili Central SD	Churchville
131	6	Clarence Central SD	Clarence
131	6	Cobleskill-Richmondville CSD	Cobleskill
131	6	Cortland City SD	Cortland
131	6	Coxsackie-Athens Central SD	Coxsackie
131	6	Deer Park Union Free SD	Deer Park
131	6	Dunkirk City SD	Dunkirk
131	6	East Irondequoit Central SD	Rochester
131	6	Elmont Union Free SD	Elmont
131	6	Farmingdale Union Free SD	Farmingdale
131	6	Fayetteville-Manlius Central SD	Manlius
131	6	Frontier Central SD	Hamburg
131	6	Fulton City SD	Fulton
131	6	Glen Cove City SD	Glen Cove
131	6	Glens Falls City SD	Glens Falls
131	6	Goshen Central SD	Goshen
131	6	Greenburgh Central SD	Hartsdale
131	6	Hamburg Central SD	Hamburg
131	6	Harrison Central SD	Harrison
131	6	Iroquois Central SD	Elma
131	6	Katonah-Lewisboro Union Free SD	South Salem
131	6	Mahopac Central SD	Mahopac
131	6	Mamaroneck Union Free SD	Mamaroneck
131	6	Minisink Valley Central SD	Slate Hill
131	6	Monticello Central SD	Monticello
131	6	Niagara-Wheatfield Central SD	Niagara Falls
131	6	North Bellmore Union Free SD	Bellmore
131	6	Oneonta City SD	Oneonta
131	6	Onteora Central SD	Boiceville
131	6	Orchard Park Central SD	Orchard Park
131	6	Pelham Union Free SD	Pelham
131	6	Penfield Central SD	Penfield
131	6	Peru Central SD	Peru
131	6	Port Chester-Rye Union Free SD	Port Chester
131	6	Port Washington Union Free SD	Pt Washington
131	6	Roosevelt Union Free SD	Roosevelt
131	6	Saugerties Central SD	Saugerties
131	6	Scotia-Glenville Central SD	Scotia
131	6	South Huntington Union Free SD	Huntington Stn
131	6	Spencerport Central SD	Spencerport
131	6	Sweet Home Central SD	Amherst
131	6	Tonawanda City SD	Tonawanda
131	6	Wallkill Central SD	Wallkill
131	6	Westbury Union Free SD	Old Westbury
131	6	Yorktown Central SD	Yorktown Hgts
181	5	Adirondack Central SD	Boonville
181	5	Albion Central SD	Albion
181	5	Alden Central SD	Alden
181	5	Altmar-Parish-Williamstown CSD	Parish
181	5	Amityville Union Free SD	Amityville
181	5	Ballston Spa Central SD	Ballston Spa
181	5	Bayport-Blue Point Union Free SD	Bayport
181	5	Bellmore-Merrick Central High SD	North Merrick
181	5	Bethpage Union Free SD	Bethpage
181	5	Brewster Central SD	Brewster
181	5	Brighton Central SD	Rochester
181	5	Broadalbin-Perth Central SD	Broadalbin
181	5	Brockport Central SD	Brockport
181	5	Burnt Hls-Ballston Lake Cent SD	Scotia
181	5	Carmel Central SD	Patterson
181	5	Carthage Central SD	Carthage
181	5	Chittenango Central SD	Chittenango
181	5	Cohoes City SD	Cohoes
181	5	Copiague Union Free SD	Copiague
181	5	Cornwall Central SD	Cornwall-on-Hud
181	5	Dryden Central SD	Dryden
181	5	Eastchester Union Free SD	Eastchester
181	5	Gouverneur Central SD	Gouverneur
181	5	Gowanda Central SD	Gowanda
181	5	Grand Island Central SD	Grand Island
181	5	Hauppauge Union Free SD	Hauppauge
181	5	Hendrick Hudson Central SD	Montrose
181	5	Herricks Union Free SD	New Hyde Park
181	5	Hewlett-Woodmere Union Free SD	Woodmere
181	5	Hilton Central SD	Hilton
181	5	Homer Central SD	Homer
181	5	Hudson Falls Central SD	Hudson Falls
181	5	Islip Union Free SD	Islip
181	5	Jamesville-Dewitt Central SD	Dewitt
181	5	Jericho Union Free SD	Jericho
181	5	Johnson City Central SD	Johnson City
181	5	Kinderhook Central SD	Valatie
181	5	Kings Park Central SD	Kings Park
181	5	Lansing Central SD	Lansing
181	5	Marlboro Central SD	Marlboro
181	5	Massena Central SD	Massena
181	5	Mexico Central SD	Mexico
181	5	New Hartford Central SD	New Hartford
181	5	Newark Central SD	Newark
181	5	Newfane Central SD	Newfane
181	5	North Shore Central SD	Sea Cliff
181	5	Norwich City SD	Norwich
181	5	Nyack Union Free SD	Nyack
181	5	Plainedge Union Free SD	N Massapequa
181	5	Plattsburgh City SD	Plattsburgh
181	5	Port Jervis City SD	Port Jervis
181	5	Red Hook Central SD	Red Hook
181	5	Rondout Valley Central SD	Accord
181	5	Roslyn Union Free SD	Roslyn
181	5	Rye City SD	Rye
181	5	Salamanca City SD	Salamanca
181	5	Sayville Union Free SD	Sayville
181	5	Schalmont Central SD	Schenectady
181	5	Sewanhaka Central High SD	Floral Park
181	5	Sherrill City SD	Verona
181	5	Shoreham-Wading River Central SD	Shoreham
181	5	South Orangetown Central SD	Blauvelt
181	5	Sullivan West Central SD	Callicoon
181	5	Susquehanna Valley Central SD	Conklin
181	5	Union Free SD of the Tarrytowns	Sleepy Hollow
181	5	Victor Central SD	Victor
181	5	Wantagh Union Free SD	Wantagh
181	5	Washingtonville Central SD	Washingtonville
181	5	Waterloo Central SD	Waterloo
181	5	Waverly Central SD	Waverly
181	5	Wayne Central SD	Ontario Center
181	5	West Hempstead Union Free SD	W Hempstead
253	4	Amherst Central SD	Amherst
253	4	Bath Central SD	Bath
253	4	Beekmantown Central SD	West Chazy
253	4	Byram Hills Central SD	Armonk
253	4	Cairo-Durham Central SD	Cairo
253	4	Canandaigua City SD	Canandaigua
253	4	Canastota Central SD	Canastota
253	4	Cheektowaga Central SD	Cheektowaga
253	4	Cheektowaga-Maryvale UFSD	Cheektowaga
253	4	Cheektowaga-Sloan Union Free SD	Sloan
253	4	Chenango Forks Central SD	Binghamton
253	4	Chenango Valley Central SD	Binghamton
253	4	Cold Spring Harbor Central SD	Cold Sprg Harbor
253	4	Dansville Central SD	Dansville
253	4	Dover Union Free SD	Dover Plains
253	4	East Aurora Union Free SD	East Aurora
253	4	Ellenville Central SD	Ellenville
253	4	Elwood Union Free SD	Greenlawn
253	4	Fredonia Central SD	Fredonia
253	4	Geneva City SD	Geneva
253	4	Gorham-Middlesex CSD (M Whitman)	Rushville
253	4	Harborfields Central SD	Greenlawn
253	4	Highland Central SD	Highland

253	4	Holland Patent Central SD	Holland Patent
253	4	Honeoye Falls-Lima Central SD	Honeoye Falls
253	4	Hornell City SD	Hornell
253	4	Irvington Union Free SD	Irvington
253	4	Island Trees Union Free SD	Levittown
253	4	Jordan-Elbridge Central SD	Jordan
253	4	Lackawanna City SD	Lackawanna
253	4	Lansingburgh Central SD	Troy
253	4	Lewiston-Porter Central SD	Youngstown
253	4	Livonia Central SD	Livonia
253	4	Locust Valley Central SD	Locust Valley
253	4	Maine-Endwell Central SD	Endwell
253	4	Malverne Union Free SD	Malverne
253	4	Manhasset Union Free SD	Manhasset
253	4	Medina Central SD	Medina
253	4	Miller Place Union Free SD	Miller Place
253	4	Mount Pleasant Central SD	Thornwood
253	4	Nanuet Union Free SD	Nanuet
253	4	New Hyde Park-Garden City Park	New Hyde Park
253	4	New Paltz Central SD	New Paltz
253	4	North Rose-Wolcott Central SD	Wolcott
253	4	Northeastern Clinton Central SD	Champlain
253	4	Nyc Alternative HS District	New York
253	4	Owego-Apalachin Central SD	Owego
253	4	Palmyra-Macedon Central SD	Palmyra
253	4	Phelps-Clifton Springs Cent SD	Clifton Spgs
253	4	Queensbury Union Free SD	Queensbury
253	4	Ravena-Coeymans-Selkirk CSD	Selkirk
253	4	Rocky Point Union Free SD	Rocky Point
253	4	Rotterdam-Mohonasen Central SD	Schenectady
253	4	Seaford Union Free SD	Seaford
253	4	Skaneateles Central SD	Skaneateles
253	4	Solvay Union Free SD	Solvay
253	4	Somers Central SD	Lincolndale
253	4	South Jefferson Central SD	Adams Center
253	4	Spackenkill Union Free SD	Poughkeepsie
253	4	Springville-Griffith Inst Cent	Springville
253	4	Starpoint Central SD	Lockport
253	4	Taconic Hills Central SD	Craryville
253	4	Valley Stream 13 Union Free SD	Valley Stream
253	4	Valley Stream Central High SD	Valley Stream
253	4	Watkins Glen Central SD	Watkins Glen
253	4	Wayland-Cohocton Central SD	Wayland
253	4	Westhill Central SD	Syracuse
253	4	Whitney Point Central SD	Whitney Point
253	4	Windsor Central SD	Windsor
253	4	Yorkshire-Pioneer Central SD	Yorkshire
323	3	Akron Central SD	Akron
323	3	Ardsley Union Free SD	Ardsley
323	3	Babylon Union Free SD	Babylon
323	3	Briarcliff Manor Union Free SD	Briarcliff Manor
323	3	Canton Central SD	Canton
323	3	Carle Place Union Free SD	Carle Place
323	3	Catskill Central SD	Catskill
323	3	Cazenovia Central SD	Cazenovia
323	3	Chatham Central SD	Chatham
323	3	Cleveland Hill Union Free SD	Cheektowaga
323	3	Clinton Central SD	Clinton
323	3	Croton-Harmon Union Free SD	Croton-On-Hud
323	3	Depew Union Free SD	Depew
323	3	East Hampton Union Free SD	East Hampton
323	3	East Williston Union Free SD	Old Westbury
323	3	Eden Central SD	Eden
323	3	Edgemont Union Free SD	Scarsdale
323	3	Fonda-Fultonville Central SD	Fonda
323	3	Franklin Square Union Free SD	Franklin Square
323	3	General Brown Central SD	Dexter
323	3	Hannibal Central SD	Hannibal
323	3	Hastings-On-Hudson Union Free SD	Hastings-on-Hud
323	3	Ilion Central SD	Ilion
323	3	Liberty Central SD	Liberty
323	3	Marcellus Central SD	Marcellus
323	3	Merrick Union Free SD	Merrick
323	3	Mount Sinai Union Free SD	Mount Sinai
323	3	New York City Geographic Dist 9	Bronx
323	3	Oyster Bay-East Norwich CSD	Oyster Bay
323	3	Penn Yan Central SD	Penn Yan
323	3	Phoenix Central SD	Phoenix
323	3	Pleasantville Union Free SD	Pleasantville
323	3	Putnam Valley Central SD	Putnam Valley
323	3	Royalton-Hartland Central SD	Middleport
323	3	Salmon River Central SD	Ft Covington
323	3	Sherburne-Earlville Central SD	Sherburne
323	3	Southampton Union Free SD	Southampton
323	3	Southwestern Cent SD Jamestown	Jamestown
323	3	Valley Stream 30 Union Free SD	Valley Stream
323	3	Westhampton Beach Union Free SD	Westhampton Bch
323	3	Wilson Central SD	Wilson
323	3	Wyandanch Union Free SD	Wyandanch
365	2	Floral Park-Bellerose UFSD	Floral Park
365	2	Hampton Bays Union Free SD	Hampton Bays
365	2	Mattituck-Cutchogue UFSD	Cutchogue
365	2	Schuylerville Central SD	Schuylerville
369	1	Boces Eastern Suffolk	Patchogue
369	1	Boces Nassau	Garden City

Number of Teachers

Rank	Number	District Name	City
1	70,171	New York City Public Schools	Brooklyn
2	3,022	Buffalo City SD	Buffalo
3	2,833	Rochester City SD	Rochester
4	1,883	Yonkers City SD	Yonkers
5	1,804	Syracuse City SD	Syracuse
6	1,161	Sachem Central SD	Holbrook
7	1,072	Brentwood Union Free SD	Brentwood
8	978	Greece Central SD	Rochester
9	900	Newburgh City SD	Newburgh
10	788	Williamsville Central SD	East Amherst
11	787	Albany City SD	Albany
12	779	Wappingers Central SD	Wappingers Fls
13	746	Middle Country Central SD	Centereach
14	731	Smithtown Central SD	Smithtown
15	720	E Ramapo Central SD (Sprg Val)	Spring Valley
16	711	New Rochelle City SD	New Rochelle
17	706	Half Hollow Hills Central SD	Dix Hills
18	689	Clarkstown Central SD	New City
19	682	Kenmore-Tonawanda Union Free SD	Buffalo
20	673	North Syracuse Central SD	N Syracuse
21	662	Mount Vernon City SD	Mount Vernon
22	658	Schenectady City SD	Schenectady
23	658	Longwood Central SD	Middle Island
24	654	Webster Central SD	Webster
25	636	William Floyd Union Free SD	Mastic Beach
26	635	Shenendehowa Central SD	Clifton Park
27	635	Haverstraw-Stony Point Cent SD	Garnerville
28	631	Arlington Central SD	Poughkeepsie
29	617	Levittown Union Free SD	Levittown
30	611	Massapequa Union Free SD	Massapequa
31	609	East Meadow Union Free SD	Westbury
32	605	Patchogue-Medford Union Free SD	Patchogue
33	604	Utica City SD	Utica
34	604	Syosset Central SD	Syosset
35	599	Three Village Central SD	East Setauket
36	597	Liverpool Central SD	Liverpool
37	593	Boces Eastern Suffolk	Patchogue
38	588	Kingston City SD	Kingston
39	569	Commack Union Free SD	E Northport
40	568	Great Neck Union Free SD	Great Neck
41	566	Elmira City SD	Elmira
42	562	Niagara Falls City SD	Niagara Falls
43	561	White Plains City SD	White Plains
44	557	West Seneca Central SD	West Seneca
45	551	Northport-East Northport UFSD	Northport
46	541	Lindenhurst Union Free SD	Lindenhurst
47	537	Uniondale Union Free SD	Uniondale
48	536	Binghamton City SD	Binghamton
48	536	Boces Nassau	Garden City
50	532	Farmingdale Union Free SD	Farmingdale
51	527	Freeport Union Free SD	Freeport
52	520	Sewanhaka Central High SD	Floral Park
53	518	Connetquot Central SD	Bohemia
54	512	Saratoga Springs City SD	Saratoga Spgs
55	504	Fairport Central SD	Fairport
56	503	Central Islip Union Free SD	Central Islip
57	499	Monroe-Woodbury Central SD	Central Valley
58	498	Rush-Henrietta Central SD	Henrietta
59	481	Rome City SD	Rome
60	478	Ithaca City SD	Ithaca
61	471	Oceanside Union Free SD	Oceanside
62	461	Jamestown City SD	Jamestown
63	458	Pittsford Central SD	Pittsford
64	455	South Huntington Union Free SD	Huntington Stn
65	454	Hempstead Union Free SD	Hempstead
65	454	Lakeland Central SD	Shrub Oak
67	448	Lockport City SD	Lockport
68	447	Middletown City SD	Middletown
69	445	South Colonie Central SD	Albany
70	438	Plainview-Old Bethpage Cent SD	Plainview
71	430	Baldwin Union Free SD	Baldwin
72	429	Bay Shore Union Free SD	Bay Shore
72	429	Frontier Central SD	Hamburg
74	426	West Islip Union Free SD	West Islip
75	426	Guilderland Central SD	Guilderland
76	422	Pine Bush Central SD	Pine Bush
77	417	Corning City SD	Painted Post
78	417	Port Washington Union Free SD	Pt Washington
79	410	Penfield Central SD	Penfield
80	406	Baldwinsville Central SD	Baldwinsville
81	406	Lancaster Central SD	Lancaster
82	402	Mahopac Central SD	Mahopac
83	398	North Colonie Central SD	Latham
84	396	Orchard Park Central SD	Orchard Park
85	388	Hicksville Union Free SD	Hicksville
86	387	Deer Park Union Free SD	Deer Park
87	386	Gates-Chili Central SD	Rochester
88	378	Auburn City SD	Auburn
89	377	East Islip Union Free SD	Islip Terrace
90	376	Valley Central SD (Montgomery)	Montgomery
91	374	Bellmore-Merrick Central High SD	North Merrick
92	372	Scarsdale Union Free SD	Scarsdale
93	371	Mamaroneck Union Free SD	Mamaroneck
94	370	North Babylon Union Free SD	North Babylon
95	367	Ramapo Central SD (Suffern)	Hillburn
96	366	Lawrence Union Free SD	Lawrence
97	363	Huntington Union Free SD	Huntington Stn
98	358	South Country Central SD	E Patchogue
99	356	Poughkeepsie City SD	Poughkeepsie
100	356	Oswego City SD	Oswego
101	355	Troy City SD	Troy
102	354	Chappaqua Central SD	Chappaqua
103	353	Clarence Central SD	Clarence
104	352	Bedford Central SD	Mount Kisco
105	351	Herricks Union Free SD	New Hyde Park
106	349	Long Beach City SD	Long Beach
107	348	Union-Endicott Central SD	Endicott
108	346	Hilton Central SD	Hilton
109	346	West Genesee Central SD	Camillus
110	343	Valley Stream Central High SD	Valley Stream
111	342	Central Square Central SD	Central Square
112	342	Bethlehem Central SD	Delmar
112	342	West Babylon Union Free SD	West Babylon
114	341	Washingtonville Central SD	Washingtonville
115	340	North Tonawanda City SD	N Tonawanda
116	338	East Greenbush Central SD	E Greenbush
117	334	Hamburg Central SD	Hamburg
118	334	Rockville Centre Union Free SD	Rockville Ctre
119	334	Carmel Central SD	Patterson
120	331	Churchville-Chili Central SD	Churchville
121	331	Spencerport Central SD	Spencerport
122	329	Hyde Park Central SD	Poughkeepsie
123	326	Ossining Union Free SD	Ossining
124	326	Fayetteville-Manlius Central SD	Manlius
125	325	Hauppauge Union Free SD	Hauppauge
126	323	Brockport Central SD	Brockport
127	323	Riverhead Central SD	Riverhead
128	322	Canandaigua City SD	Canandaigua
128	322	Vestal Central SD	Vestal
130	320	East Syracuse-Minoa Central SD	East Syracuse
131	317	Yorktown Central SD	Yorktown Hgts
132	316	Jericho Union Free SD	Jericho
133	316	Garden City Union Free SD	Garden City
134	314	Ballston Spa Central SD	Ballston Spa
135	310	Warwick Valley Central SD	Warwick
136	309	Katonah-Lewisboro Union Free SD	South Salem
137	306	Copiague Union Free SD	Copiague
138	305	Sweet Home Central SD	Amherst
139	303	Monticello Central SD	Monticello
140	302	Horseheads Central SD	Horseheads
141	301	Watertown City SD	Watertown
142	301	Harrison Central SD	Harrison
143	300	Niagara-Wheatfield Central SD	Niagara Falls
144	300	Niskayuna Central SD	Schenectady
145	298	Minisink Valley Central SD	Slate Hill
146	297	Amsterdam City SD	Amsterdam
147	295	Indian River Central SD	Philadelphia
148	295	Westbury Union Free SD	Old Westbury
149	293	Whitesboro Central SD	Yorkville
150	290	Fulton City SD	Fulton
151	288	Kings Park Central SD	Kings Park
152	280	Hewlett-Woodmere Union Free SD	Woodmere
153	280	Brighton Central SD	Rochester
154	277	Brewster Central SD	Brewster
155	275	Elmont Union Free SD	Elmont
156	273	Averill Park Central SD	Averill Park
157	272	Brookhaven-Comsewogue UFSD	Pt Jefferson Stn
158	268	Evans-Brant Cent SD (Lake Shore)	Angola
159	268	Mineola Union Free SD	Mineola
160	267	South Orangetown Central SD	Blauvelt
161	263	Roslyn Union Free SD	Roslyn
162	260	Sayville Union Free SD	Sayville
163	260	West Irondequoit Central SD	Rochester
164	259	Wantagh Union Free SD	Wantagh
165	259	Gloversville City SD	Gloversville
166	257	East Irondequoit Central SD	Rochester
166	257	Port Chester-Rye Union Free SD	Port Chester
168	257	Amityville Union Free SD	Amityville
169	255	Lynbrook Union Free SD	Lynbrook
170	255	Queensbury Union Free SD	Queensbury
171	254	Glen Cove City SD	Glen Cove
172	250	Victor Central SD	Victor
173	250	Wallkill Central SD	Wallkill
174	249	Amherst Central SD	Amherst
175	248	Plainedge Union Free SD	N Massapequa
176	248	Roosevelt Union Free SD	Roosevelt
177	247	Harborfields Central SD	Greenlawn
178	246	Beacon City SD	Beacon
179	246	Nyack Union Free SD	Nyack

180	245	South Glens Falls Central SD	S Glens Falls
181	243	Burnt Hls-Ballston Lake Cent SD	Scotia
182	242	Somers Central SD	Lincolndale
183	242	Bethpage Union Free SD	Bethpage
184	239	Manhasset Union Free SD	Manhasset
185	239	Islip Union Free SD	Islip
186	238	North Shore Central SD	Sea Cliff
187	235	Hendrick Hudson Central SD	Montrose
188	234	Peekskill City SD	Peekskill
189	233	Rocky Point Union Free SD	Rocky Point
190	230	Cortland City SD	Cortland
191	228	Grand Island Central SD	Grand Island
192	228	Batavia City SD	Batavia
193	227	Jamesville-Dewitt Central SD	Dewitt
194	225	Yorkshire-Pioneer Central SD	Yorkshire
195	223	Saugerties Central SD	Saugerties
196	222	Port Jervis City SD	Port Jervis
197	222	Geneva City SD	Geneva
198	221	Wayne Central SD	Ontario Center
199	218	Rye City SD	Rye
200	218	Rondout Valley Central SD	Accord
201	217	Rotterdam-Mohonasen Central SD	Schenectady
202	217	Shoreham-Wading River Central SD	Shoreham
203	216	Island Trees Union Free SD	Levittown
204	213	Newark Central SD	Newark
205	213	Eastchester Union Free SD	Eastchester
206	213	Malone Central SD	Malone
207	211	Camden Central SD	Camden
207	211	Carthage Central SD	Carthage
209	210	Goshen Central SD	Goshen
210	209	Scotia-Glenville Central SD	Scotia
211	208	Johnson City Central SD	Johnson City
212	208	Dunkirk City SD	Dunkirk
213	208	Byram Hills Central SD	Armonk
214	206	New Hartford Central SD	New Hartford
215	205	Bayport-Blue Point Union Free SD	Bayport
215	205	Maine-Endwell Central SD	Endwell
217	205	Miller Place Union Free SD	Miller Place
218	204	Seaford Union Free SD	Seaford
219	203	Cornwall Central SD	Cornwall-on-Hud
220	202	Phoenix Central SD	Phoenix
221	202	Massena Central SD	Massena
222	201	Hudson City SD	Hudson
223	201	Locust Valley Central SD	Locust Valley
224	198	Plattsburgh City SD	Plattsburgh
225	198	Pelham Union Free SD	Pelham
226	197	Glens Falls City SD	Glens Falls
227	195	Union Free SD of the Tarrytowns	Sleepy Hollow
228	193	Iroquois Central SD	Elma
229	193	Olean City SD	Olean
230	192	Ravena-Coeymans-Selkirk CSD	Selkirk
231	191	Albion Central SD	Albion
232	191	Norwich City SD	Norwich
233	191	Mexico Central SD	Mexico
234	190	Oneida City SD	Oneida
235	190	Tonawanda City SD	Tonawanda
236	190	Chittenango Central SD	Chittenango
237	190	Beekmantown Central SD	West Chazy
237	190	Honeoye Falls-Lima Central SD	Honeoye Falls
239	190	Homer Central SD	Homer
240	187	Depew Union Free SD	Depew
241	185	Palmyra-Macedon Central SD	Palmyra
242	185	Cheektowaga-Maryvale UFSD	Cheektowaga
243	185	Peru Central SD	Peru
244	184	Ardsley Union Free SD	Ardsley
245	184	Pearl River Union Free SD	Pearl River
246	183	Nanuet Union Free SD	Nanuet
247	182	Lewiston-Porter Central SD	Youngstown
248	182	Susquehanna Valley Central SD	Conklin
249	181	Cobleskill-Richmondville CSD	Cobleskill
250	181	North Bellmore Union Free SD	Bellmore
251	180	West Hempstead Union Free SD	W Hempstead
252	180	Cohoes City SD	Cohoes
253	179	Owego-Apalachin Central SD	Owego
254	179	Lansingburgh Central SD	Troy
255	177	Lackawanna City SD	Lackawanna
256	177	Cheektowaga Central SD	Cheektowaga
257	177	Greenburgh Central SD	Hartsdale
258	177	Starpoint Central SD	Lockport
259	177	Onteora Central SD	Boiceville
260	176	Dryden Central SD	Dryden
261	176	New Paltz Central SD	New Paltz
262	175	Livonia Central SD	Livonia
263	175	Red Hook Central SD	Red Hook
264	174	Sherrill City SD	Verona
265	174	Oneonta City SD	Oneonta
266	173	Southampton Union Free SD	Southampton
267	171	Valley Stream 13 Union Free SD	Valley Stream
268	171	Springville-Griffith Inst Cent	Springville
269	170	Kinderhook Central SD	Valatie
270	170	Penn Yan Central SD	Penn Yan
271	169	Mount Pleasant Central SD	Thornwood
272	168	Hudson Falls Central SD	Hudson Falls
273	168	Schalmont Central SD	Schenectady
274	168	Mount Sinai Union Free SD	Mount Sinai
275	167	Ogdensburg City SD	Ogdensburg
276	167	East Hampton Union Free SD	East Hampton
277	167	Elwood Union Free SD	Greenlawn
278	167	Fredonia Central SD	Fredonia
279	165	Sherburne-Earlville Central SD	Sherburne
280	164	Medina Central SD	Medina
281	163	Westhampton Beach Union Free SD	Westhampton Bch
282	163	Hornell City SD	Hornell
283	161	Marlboro Central SD	Marlboro
284	160	Malverne Union Free SD	Malverne
285	160	Irvington Union Free SD	Irvington
286	159	Phelps-Clifton Springs Cent SD	Clifton Spgs
287	158	Cold Spring Harbor Central SD	Cold Sprg Harbor
288	156	Babylon Union Free SD	Babylon
288	156	Bath Central SD	Bath
290	155	East Williston Union Free SD	Old Westbury
291	154	Waterloo Central SD	Waterloo
292	154	Windsor Central SD	Windsor
293	153	Wyandanch Union Free SD	Wyandanch
294	153	Alden Central SD	Alden
295	152	Wayland-Cohocton Central SD	Wayland
296	152	Whitney Point Central SD	Whitney Point
297	151	Hastings-On-Hudson Union Free SD	Hastings-on-Hud
298	150	Merrick Union Free SD	Merrick
299	150	Newfane Central SD	Newfane
300	150	Spackenkill Union Free SD	Poughkeepsie
301	149	Saranac Central SD	Dannemora
302	148	Chenango Valley Central SD	Binghamton
303	148	Briarcliff Manor Union Free SD	Briarcliff Manor
304	147	Catskill Central SD	Catskill
304	147	North Rose-Wolcott Central SD	Wolcott
306	147	East Aurora Union Free SD	East Aurora
307	146	Westhill Central SD	Syracuse
308	146	Johnstown City SD	Johnstown
309	145	Liberty Central SD	Liberty
310	145	Oyster Bay-East Norwich CSD	Oyster Bay
311	144	Attica Central SD	Attica
312	144	Dansville Central SD	Dansville
313	144	Carle Place Union Free SD	Carle Place
314	143	Taconic Hills Central SD	Craryville
315	143	South Jefferson Central SD	Adams Center
316	142	Skaneateles Central SD	Skaneateles
317	142	Putnam Valley Central SD	Putnam Valley
318	142	Hampton Bays Union Free SD	Hampton Bays
319	142	Chenango Forks Central SD	Binghamton
320	141	Marcellus Central SD	Marcellus
321	139	Edgemont Union Free SD	Scarsdale
321	139	Salmon River Central SD	Ft Covington
323	138	Ellenville Central SD	Ellenville
324	138	Sullivan West Central SD	Callicoon
325	138	Saranac Lake Central SD	Saranac Lake
326	138	Altmar-Parish-Williamstown CSD	Parish
326	138	Mattituck-Cutchogue UFSD	Cutchogue
328	138	Holland Patent Central SD	Holland Patent
329	138	Cazenovia Central SD	Cazenovia
330	137	Jordan-Elbridge Central SD	Jordan
331	137	Adirondack Central SD	Boonville
332	136	Solvay Union Free SD	Solvay
333	134	Broadalbin-Perth Central SD	Broadalbin
334	133	Royalton-Hartland Central SD	Middleport
335	133	Franklin Square Union Free SD	Franklin Square
336	132	Schuylerville Central SD	Schuylerville
337	132	Ilion Central SD	Ilion
338	131	Cairo-Durham Central SD	Cairo
339	129	Coxsackie-Athens Central SD	Coxsackie
340	128	Hannibal Central SD	Hannibal
341	128	Salamanca City SD	Salamanca
342	128	Southwestern Cent SD Jamestown	Jamestown
343	128	Highland Central SD	Highland
344	127	Eden Central SD	Eden
345	127	Pleasantville Union Free SD	Pleasantville
346	126	Gorham-Middlesex CSD (M Whitman)	Rushville
347	125	Waverly Central SD	Waverly
348	125	Clinton Central SD	Clinton
349	124	Northeastern Clinton Central SD	Champlain
350	123	New Hyde Park-Garden City Park	New Hyde Park
351	122	Cleveland Hill Union Free SD	Cheektowaga
351	122	Gowanda Central SD	Gowanda
353	121	Fonda-Fultonville Central SD	Fonda
354	120	Wilson Central SD	Wilson
355	120	Canton Central SD	Canton
356	119	Gouverneur Central SD	Gouverneur
357	117	Valley Stream 30 Union Free SD	Valley Stream
358	117	Lansing Central SD	Lansing
359	116	Croton-Harmon Union Free SD	Croton-On-Hud
360	116	Akron Central SD	Akron
361	115	Dover Union Free SD	Dover Plains
362	114	Cheektowaga-Sloan Union Free SD	Sloan
363	113	Watkins Glen Central SD	Watkins Glen
364	111	Canastota Central SD	Canastota
365	108	Chatham Central SD	Chatham
366	107	General Brown Central SD	Dexter
367	104	Floral Park-Bellerose UFSD	Floral Park
368	n/a	New York City Geographic Dist 9	Bronx
368	n/a	New York City Geographic Dist 15	Brooklyn
368	n/a	Nyc Alternative HS District	New York

Number of Students

Rank	Number	District Name	City
1	1,023,674	New York City Public Schools	Brooklyn
2	41,089	Buffalo City SD	Buffalo
3	34,598	Rochester City SD	Rochester
4	26,201	Yonkers City SD	Yonkers
5	22,405	Syracuse City SD	Syracuse
6	16,607	Brentwood Union Free SD	Brentwood
7	15,378	Sachem Central SD	Holbrook
8	13,799	Greece Central SD	Rochester
9	13,108	Newburgh City SD	Newburgh
10	12,146	Wappingers Central SD	Wappingers Fls
11	11,630	Middle Country Central SD	Centereach
12	10,760	Williamsville Central SD	East Amherst
13	10,464	New Rochelle City SD	New Rochelle
14	10,376	William Floyd Union Free SD	Mastic Beach
15	10,347	Mount Vernon City SD	Mount Vernon
16	10,188	North Syracuse Central SD	N Syracuse
16	10,188	Smithtown Central SD	Smithtown
18	10,102	Arlington Central SD	Poughkeepsie
19	9,919	Albany City SD	Albany
20	9,794	Longwood Central SD	Middle Island
21	9,661	Half Hollow Hills Central SD	Dix Hills
22	9,350	Clarkstown Central SD	New City
23	9,313	Shenendehowa Central SD	Clifton Park
24	9,170	E Ramapo Central SD (Sprg Val)	Spring Valley
25	9,101	Patchogue-Medford Union Free SD	Patchogue
26	9,090	Schenectady City SD	Schenectady
27	9,070	Utica City SD	Utica
28	9,033	Kenmore-Tonawanda Union Free SD	Buffalo
29	8,736	Niagara Falls City SD	Niagara Falls
29	8,736	Webster Central SD	Webster
31	8,629	Liverpool Central SD	Liverpool
32	8,435	Sewanhaka Central High SD	Floral Park
33	8,366	Haverstraw-Stony Point Cent SD	Garnerville
34	8,248	Massapequa Union Free SD	Massapequa
35	8,149	Kingston City SD	Kingston
36	8,094	East Meadow Union Free SD	Westbury
37	8,027	Levittown Union Free SD	Levittown
38	7,986	Three Village Central SD	East Setauket
39	7,697	West Seneca Central SD	West Seneca
40	7,689	Lindenhurst Union Free SD	Lindenhurst
41	7,613	Elmira City SD	Elmira
42	7,511	Commack Union Free SD	E Northport
43	7,255	Monroe-Woodbury Central SD	Central Valley
44	7,160	Connetquot Central SD	Bohemia
45	7,146	Freeport Union Free SD	Freeport
46	7,128	Hempstead Union Free SD	Hempstead
47	7,115	Fairport Central SD	Fairport
48	6,922	Saratoga Springs City SD	Saratoga Spgs
49	6,844	White Plains City SD	White Plains
50	6,741	Central Islip Union Free SD	Central Islip
51	6,623	Syosset Central SD	Syosset
52	6,577	Middletown City SD	Middletown
53	6,472	Farmingdale Union Free SD	Farmingdale
54	6,411	Uniondale Union Free SD	Uniondale
55	6,392	Northport-East Northport UFSD	Northport
56	6,369	Oceanside Union Free SD	Oceanside
57	6,249	Binghamton City SD	Binghamton
58	6,204	Lancaster Central SD	Lancaster
59	6,199	Rome City SD	Rome
60	6,139	Lakeland Central SD	Shrub Oak
61	6,118	Pine Bush Central SD	Pine Bush
62	6,113	Great Neck Union Free SD	Great Neck
63	6,111	South Huntington Union Free SD	Huntington Stn
64	6,022	Pittsford Central SD	Pittsford
65	5,960	Baldwinsville Central SD	Baldwinsville
66	5,905	West Islip Union Free SD	West Islip
67	5,859	Rush-Henrietta Central SD	Henrietta
68	5,833	Corning City SD	Painted Post
69	5,832	Bellmore-Merrick Central High SD	North Merrick
70	5,751	Ithaca City SD	Ithaca
71	5,745	South Colonie Central SD	Albany
72	5,703	Lockport City SD	Lockport
73	5,698	Bay Shore Union Free SD	Bay Shore
74	5,664	Guilderland Central SD	Guilderland
75	5,631	North Colonie Central SD	Latham
76	5,622	Frontier Central SD	Hamburg
77	5,432	East Islip Union Free SD	Islip Terrace
78	5,408	Baldwin Union Free SD	Baldwin
79	5,289	Jamestown City SD	Jamestown
79	5,289	Mahopac Central SD	Mahopac
81	5,266	Hicksville Union Free SD	Hicksville
82	5,236	Valley Central SD (Montgomery)	Montgomery
83	5,220	North Babylon Union Free SD	North Babylon

84	5,186	Orchard Park Central SD	Orchard Park
85	5,153	West Genesee Central SD	Camillus
86	5,106	Washingtonville Central SD	Washingtonville
87	5,057	Gates-Chili Central SD	Rochester
88	5,022	Bethlehem Central SD	Delmar
89	5,013	Central Square Central SD	Central Square
90	4,993	Auburn City SD	Auburn
91	4,970	Plainview-Old Bethpage Cent SD	Plainview
92	4,960	Penfield Central SD	Penfield
93	4,940	West Babylon Union Free SD	West Babylon
94	4,920	Clarence Central SD	Clarence
95	4,880	Poughkeepsie City SD	Poughkeepsie
96	4,862	Riverhead Central SD	Riverhead
97	4,857	Carmel Central SD	Patterson
97	4,857	Troy City SD	Troy
99	4,821	Copiague Union Free SD	Copiague
100	4,809	Oswego City SD	Oswego
101	4,791	Mamaroneck Union Free SD	Mamaroneck
102	4,758	South Country Central SD	E Patchogue
103	4,740	Port Washington Union Free SD	Pt Washington
104	4,682	Hyde Park Central SD	Poughkeepsie
104	4,682	Warwick Valley Central SD	Warwick
106	4,643	North Tonawanda City SD	N Tonawanda
107	4,619	Fayetteville-Manlius Central SD	Manlius
108	4,596	Ramapo Central SD (Suffern)	Hillburn
109	4,572	East Greenbush Central SD	E Greenbush
110	4,568	Scarsdale Union Free SD	Scarsdale
111	4,566	Valley Stream Central High SD	Valley Stream
112	4,543	Minisink Valley Central SD	Slate Hill
113	4,536	Union-Endicott Central SD	Endicott
114	4,521	Ballston Spa Central SD	Ballston Spa
115	4,482	Churchville-Chili Central SD	Churchville
116	4,480	Brockport Central SD	Brockport
117	4,461	Deer Park Union Free SD	Deer Park
118	4,458	Long Beach City SD	Long Beach
119	4,441	Hilton Central SD	Hilton
120	4,378	Horseheads Central SD	Horseheads
121	4,350	Spencerport Central SD	Spencerport
122	4,334	Watertown City SD	Watertown
123	4,268	Bedford Central SD	Mount Kisco
124	4,266	Vestal Central SD	Vestal
125	4,258	Niskayuna Central SD	Schenectady
126	4,252	Ossining Union Free SD	Ossining
127	4,248	Elmont Union Free SD	Elmont
128	4,219	Yorktown Central SD	Yorktown Hgts
129	4,186	Canandaigua City SD	Canandaigua
130	4,155	Hauppauge Union Free SD	Hauppauge
131	4,153	Hamburg Central SD	Hamburg
132	4,150	Garden City Union Free SD	Garden City
133	4,131	Huntington Union Free SD	Huntington Stn
134	4,112	Katonah-Lewisboro Union Free SD	South Salem
135	4,096	Chappaqua Central SD	Chappaqua
136	4,060	Niagara-Wheatfield Central SD	Niagara Falls
137	4,036	Westbury Union Free SD	Old Westbury
138	4,007	Kings Park Central SD	Kings Park
139	3,949	West Irondequoit Central SD	Rochester
140	3,939	Herricks Union Free SD	New Hyde Park
141	3,930	Brookhaven-Comsewogue UFSD	Pt Jefferson Stn
142	3,906	Queensbury Union Free SD	Queensbury
143	3,875	Fulton City SD	Fulton
144	3,867	Sweet Home Central SD	Amherst
145	3,863	Whitesboro Central SD	Yorkville
146	3,824	East Syracuse-Minoa Central SD	East Syracuse
147	3,782	Amsterdam City SD	Amsterdam
148	3,726	Brewster Central SD	Brewster
149	3,692	Lawrence Union Free SD	Lawrence
150	3,638	Wallkill Central SD	Wallkill
151	3,636	Islip Union Free SD	Islip
152	3,613	Beacon City SD	Beacon
153	3,606	Plainedge Union Free SD	N Massapequa
153	3,606	Rockville Centre Union Free SD	Rockville Ctre
155	3,594	Rocky Point Union Free SD	Rocky Point
156	3,593	Sayville Union Free SD	Sayville
157	3,582	Brighton Central SD	Rochester
158	3,578	Wantagh Union Free SD	Wantagh
159	3,574	Port Chester-Rye Union Free SD	Port Chester
160	3,560	Harborfields Central SD	Greenlawn
161	3,556	Victor Central SD	Victor
162	3,546	Averill Park Central SD	Averill Park
163	3,523	Monticello Central SD	Monticello
164	3,514	East Irondequoit Central SD	Rochester
165	3,447	Burnt Hls-Ballston Lake Cent SD	Scotia
166	3,444	Port Jervis City SD	Port Jervis
167	3,382	Harrison Central SD	Harrison
168	3,377	Indian River Central SD	Philadelphia
169	3,347	South Orangetown Central SD	Blauvelt
170	3,340	Rotterdam-Mohonasen Central SD	Schenectady
171	3,336	Saugerties Central SD	Saugerties
172	3,327	Hewlett-Woodmere Union Free SD	Woodmere
173	3,292	South Glens Falls Central SD	S Glens Falls
174	3,237	Roslyn Union Free SD	Roslyn
175	3,230	Evans-Brant Cent SD (Lake Shore)	Angola
176	3,226	Gloversville City SD	Gloversville
177	3,210	Jericho Union Free SD	Jericho
178	3,190	Grand Island Central SD	Grand Island
179	3,188	Glen Cove City SD	Glen Cove
180	3,141	Lynbrook Union Free SD	Lynbrook
181	3,140	Somers Central SD	Lincolndale
182	3,125	Amherst Central SD	Amherst
183	3,093	Cornwall Central SD	Cornwall-on-Hud
184	3,083	Amityville Union Free SD	Amityville
185	3,055	Peekskill City SD	Peekskill
186	3,030	Miller Place Union Free SD	Miller Place
187	3,006	Bethpage Union Free SD	Bethpage
188	2,952	Scotia-Glenville Central SD	Scotia
189	2,937	Carthage Central SD	Carthage
190	2,928	Yorkshire-Pioneer Central SD	Yorkshire
191	2,921	Goshen Central SD	Goshen
192	2,905	Iroquois Central SD	Elma
193	2,903	Mineola Union Free SD	Mineola
194	2,884	Hendrick Hudson Central SD	Montrose
195	2,882	Roosevelt Union Free SD	Roosevelt
196	2,861	Massena Central SD	Massena
197	2,858	Nyack Union Free SD	Nyack
198	2,848	Starpoint Central SD	Lockport
199	2,847	Cortland City SD	Cortland
200	2,845	Camden Central SD	Camden
201	2,797	Albion Central SD	Albion
201	2,797	Rondout Valley Central SD	Accord
203	2,795	Island Trees Union Free SD	Levittown
204	2,774	Wayne Central SD	Ontario Center
205	2,717	Jamesville-Dewitt Central SD	Dewitt
206	2,707	Byram Hills Central SD	Armonk
207	2,706	Seaford Union Free SD	Seaford
208	2,700	Manhasset Union Free SD	Manhasset
209	2,688	Newark Central SD	Newark
209	2,688	Rye City SD	Rye
211	2,682	Batavia City SD	Batavia
211	2,682	Mexico Central SD	Mexico
213	2,680	Eastchester Union Free SD	Eastchester
214	2,677	Shoreham-Wading River Central SD	Shoreham
215	2,675	Maine-Endwell Central SD	Endwell
216	2,670	New Hartford Central SD	New Hartford
217	2,652	North Shore Central SD	Sea Cliff
218	2,601	Honeoye Falls-Lima Central SD	Honeoye Falls
219	2,597	Johnson City Central SD	Johnson City
220	2,565	Chittenango Central SD	Chittenango
221	2,550	Oneida City SD	Oneida
222	2,544	Pearl River Union Free SD	Pearl River
223	2,541	Olean City SD	Olean
224	2,534	Geneva City SD	Geneva
225	2,529	Pelham Union Free SD	Pelham
226	2,528	North Bellmore Union Free SD	Bellmore
227	2,522	Glens Falls City SD	Glens Falls
228	2,512	Elwood Union Free SD	Greenlawn
229	2,506	Coxsackie-Athens Central SD	Coxsackie
230	2,499	Malone Central SD	Malone
230	2,499	Union Free SD of the Tarrytowns	Sleepy Hollow
232	2,490	Bayport-Blue Point Union Free SD	Bayport
233	2,478	Cheektowaga-Maryvale UFSD	Cheektowaga
234	2,428	Lansingburgh Central SD	Troy
235	2,425	Sherrill City SD	Verona
236	2,418	Hudson Falls Central SD	Hudson Falls
237	2,417	Hudson City SD	Hudson
237	2,417	Mount Sinai Union Free SD	Mount Sinai
237	2,417	Phoenix Central SD	Phoenix
240	2,416	Cheektowaga Central SD	Cheektowaga
241	2,402	Lewiston-Porter Central SD	Youngstown
242	2,385	Ravena-Coeymans-Selkirk CSD	Selkirk
242	2,385	Springville-Griffith Inst Cent	Springville
244	2,381	Red Hook Central SD	Red Hook
245	2,378	Depew Union Free SD	Depew
246	2,376	New Paltz Central SD	New Paltz
247	2,367	Homer Central SD	Homer
248	2,349	West Hempstead Union Free SD	W Hempstead
249	2,343	Ardsley Union Free SD	Ardsley
249	2,343	Tonawanda City SD	Tonawanda
251	2,337	Owego-Apalachin Central SD	Owego
252	2,303	Peru Central SD	Peru
253	2,285	Kinderhook Central SD	Valatie
254	2,280	Wyandanch Union Free SD	Wyandanch
255	2,275	Locust Valley Central SD	Locust Valley
256	2,247	Norwich City SD	Norwich
257	2,228	Schalmont Central SD	Schenectady
258	2,222	Palmyra-Macedon Central SD	Palmyra
259	2,208	Broadalbin-Perth Central SD	Broadalbin
259	2,208	Cobleskill-Richmondville CSD	Cobleskill
261	2,202	Cohoes City SD	Cohoes
262	2,192	Nanuet Union Free SD	Nanuet
263	2,179	Beekmantown Central SD	West Chazy
264	2,174	Newfane Central SD	Newfane
265	2,172	Onteora Central SD	Boiceville
266	2,168	Johnstown City SD	Johnstown
267	2,147	Marcellus Central SD	Marcellus
268	2,142	Oneonta City SD	Oneonta
269	2,136	Marlboro Central SD	Marlboro
270	2,135	Susquehanna Valley Central SD	Conklin
271	2,132	Livonia Central SD	Livonia
272	2,103	Valley Stream 13 Union Free SD	Valley Stream
273	2,101	Dunkirk City SD	Dunkirk
274	2,092	Cold Spring Harbor Central SD	Cold Sprg Harbor
275	2,091	East Aurora Union Free SD	East Aurora
276	2,075	Highland Central SD	Highland
277	2,072	Alden Central SD	Alden
278	2,062	Waterloo Central SD	Waterloo
279	2,055	Plattsburgh City SD	Plattsburgh
280	2,054	Bath Central SD	Bath
281	2,049	Westhill Central SD	Syracuse
282	2,045	Windsor Central SD	Windsor
283	2,044	Phelps-Clifton Springs Cent SD	Clifton Spgs
283	2,044	South Jefferson Central SD	Adams Center
285	2,041	Lackawanna City SD	Lackawanna
286	2,039	Boces Nassau	Garden City
287	2,035	Penn Yan Central SD	Penn Yan
288	2,032	Chenango Valley Central SD	Binghamton
289	2,018	Ogdensburg City SD	Ogdensburg
290	2,011	New York City Geographic Dist 15	Brooklyn
291	2,009	Babylon Union Free SD	Babylon
292	1,981	Greenburgh Central SD	Hartsdale
293	1,971	East Hampton Union Free SD	East Hampton
294	1,970	Merrick Union Free SD	Merrick
295	1,968	Saranac Central SD	Dannemora
296	1,967	Irvington Union Free SD	Irvington
297	1,954	Medina Central SD	Medina
298	1,942	Franklin Square Union Free SD	Franklin Square
299	1,934	Putnam Valley Central SD	Putnam Valley
300	1,908	Boces Eastern Suffolk	Patchogue
301	1,884	Dryden Central SD	Dryden
301	1,884	Hornell City SD	Hornell
303	1,882	Liberty Central SD	Liberty
304	1,874	Chenango Forks Central SD	Binghamton
305	1,871	Taconic Hills Central SD	Craryville
306	1,858	Whitney Point Central SD	Whitney Point
307	1,857	Fredonia Central SD	Fredonia
308	1,853	Holland Patent Central SD	Holland Patent
309	1,848	Skaneateles Central SD	Skaneateles
310	1,847	Mount Pleasant Central SD	Thornwood
311	1,844	Eden Central SD	Eden
312	1,840	Attica Central SD	Attica
313	1,839	New York City Geographic Dist 9	Bronx
314	1,835	Spackenkill Union Free SD	Poughkeepsie
315	1,834	Edgemont Union Free SD	Scarsdale
316	1,828	Nyc Alternative HS District	New York
317	1,827	Wayland-Cohocton Central SD	Wayland
318	1,826	Malverne Union Free SD	Malverne
319	1,823	New Hyde Park-Garden City Park	New Hyde Park
320	1,817	Catskill Central SD	Catskill
321	1,813	Cairo-Durham Central SD	Cairo
322	1,812	East Williston Union Free SD	Old Westbury
322	1,812	Ellenville Central SD	Ellenville
324	1,804	Cazenovia Central SD	Cazenovia
325	1,794	Ilion Central SD	Ilion
326	1,786	Waverly Central SD	Waverly
327	1,769	Hampton Bays Union Free SD	Hampton Bays
327	1,769	Southampton Union Free SD	Southampton
329	1,758	Sherburne-Earlville Central SD	Sherburne
330	1,757	Dover Union Free SD	Dover Plains
331	1,756	Hannibal Central SD	Hannibal
332	1,752	Southwestern Cent SD Jamestown	Jamestown
333	1,750	Dansville Central SD	Dansville
334	1,747	Solvay Union Free SD	Solvay
335	1,743	Gouverneur Central SD	Gouverneur
336	1,727	Pleasantville Union Free SD	Pleasantville
336	1,727	Westhampton Beach Union Free SD	Westhampton Bch
338	1,717	Briarcliff Manor Union Free SD	Briarcliff Manor
339	1,703	Jordan-Elbridge Central SD	Jordan
340	1,699	Akron Central SD	Akron
341	1,693	Schuylerville Central SD	Schuylerville
342	1,682	Royalton-Hartland Central SD	Middleport
343	1,670	Hastings-On-Hudson Union Free SD	Hastings-on-Hud
344	1,668	Floral Park-Bellerose UFSD	Floral Park
345	1,657	Northeastern Clinton Central SD	Champlain
346	1,647	Altmar-Parish-Williamstown CSD	Parish
347	1,642	North Rose-Wolcott Central SD	Wolcott
348	1,634	Clinton Central SD	Clinton
349	1,625	Saranac Lake Central SD	Saranac Lake
350	1,606	Fonda-Fultonville Central SD	Fonda
351	1,604	Salmon River Central SD	Ft Covington
352	1,597	Gorham-Middlesex CSD (M Whitman)	Rushville
353	1,587	Cleveland Hill Union Free SD	Cheektowaga
354	1,572	General Brown Central SD	Dexter
355	1,569	Oyster Bay-East Norwich CSD	Oyster Bay
356	1,568	Sullivan West Central SD	Callicoon
357	1,563	Mattituck-Cutchogue UFSD	Cutchogue
358	1,549	Croton-Harmon Union Free SD	Croton-On-Hud
359	1,548	Adirondack Central SD	Boonville
360	1,547	Canastota Central SD	Canastota

361	1,532	Gowanda Central SD	Gowanda
362	1,531	Cheektowaga-Sloan Union Free SD	Sloan
363	1,529	Lansing Central SD	Lansing
364	1,524	Watkins Glen Central SD	Watkins Glen
365	1,513	Canton Central SD	Canton
365	1,513	Salamanca City SD	Salamanca
367	1,504	Wilson Central SD	Wilson
368	1,502	Valley Stream 30 Union Free SD	Valley Stream
369	1,501	Chatham Central SD	Chatham
370	1,500	Carle Place Union Free SD	Carle Place

Male Students

Rank	Percent	District Name	City
1	75.8	Boces Nassau	Garden City
2	74.0	Boces Eastern Suffolk	Patchogue
3	68.6	Coxsackie-Athens Central SD	Coxsackie
4	56.3	Broadalbin-Perth Central SD	Broadalbin
5	56.1	Hudson City SD	Hudson
6	55.2	Fonda-Fultonville Central SD	Fonda
7	55.2	Watkins Glen Central SD	Watkins Glen
8	55.1	Lansing Central SD	Lansing
9	54.7	Attica Central SD	Attica
10	54.4	Highland Central SD	Highland
11	53.7	Cleveland Hill Union Free SD	Cheektowaga
12	53.7	Hornell City SD	Hornell
13	53.3	Bath Central SD	Bath
14	53.2	Ossining Union Free SD	Ossining
15	53.2	Edgemont Union Free SD	Scarsdale
16	53.1	Churchville-Chili Central SD	Churchville
17	53.1	Rondout Valley Central SD	Accord
18	53.1	Lackawanna City SD	Lackawanna
19	53.0	Alden Central SD	Alden
20	53.0	East Islip Union Free SD	Islip Terrace
21	53.0	Palmyra-Macedon Central SD	Palmyra
22	53.0	Farmingdale Union Free SD	Farmingdale
23	52.9	Bethlehem Central SD	Delmar
24	52.9	Southwestern Cent SD Jamestown	Jamestown
25	52.8	Phoenix Central SD	Phoenix
26	52.8	Rocky Point Union Free SD	Rocky Point
27	52.8	Niagara-Wheatfield Central SD	Niagara Falls
28	52.8	Pleasantville Union Free SD	Pleasantville
29	52.7	Westhill Central SD	Syracuse
30	52.6	Hampton Bays Union Free SD	Hampton Bays
31	52.6	Deer Park Union Free SD	Deer Park
32	52.6	Wayne Central SD	Ontario Center
33	52.6	Red Hook Central SD	Red Hook
34	52.6	Webster Central SD	Webster
35	52.6	Oswego City SD	Oswego
36	52.6	Brewster Central SD	Brewster
37	52.5	Victor Central SD	Victor
38	52.5	Peru Central SD	Peru
39	52.5	Riverhead Central SD	Riverhead
40	52.5	Eden Central SD	Eden
41	52.5	Valley Stream 13 Union Free SD	Valley Stream
42	52.5	Brentwood Union Free SD	Brentwood
42	52.5	Connetquot Central SD	Bohemia
44	52.4	East Williston Union Free SD	Old Westbury
45	52.4	Homer Central SD	Homer
46	52.4	Longwood Central SD	Middle Island
47	52.4	Glen Cove City SD	Glen Cove
48	52.4	Ogdensburg City SD	Ogdensburg
49	52.3	Roslyn Union Free SD	Roslyn
50	52.3	Wallkill Central SD	Wallkill
51	52.3	Bedford Central SD	Mount Kisco
52	52.3	Chenango Valley Central SD	Binghamton
53	52.3	Ithaca City SD	Ithaca
54	52.2	Greenburgh Central SD	Hartsdale
55	52.2	Washingtonville Central SD	Washingtonville
56	52.2	Ardsley Union Free SD	Ardsley
57	52.2	Vestal Central SD	Vestal
58	52.2	Skaneateles Central SD	Skaneateles
59	52.2	Spencerport Central SD	Spencerport
60	52.2	Warwick Valley Central SD	Warwick
61	52.2	Indian River Central SD	Philadelphia
62	52.2	North Tonawanda City SD	N Tonawanda
63	52.2	North Bellmore Union Free SD	Bellmore
64	52.2	Owego-Apalachin Central SD	Owego
65	52.2	Great Neck Union Free SD	Great Neck
66	52.1	Rye City SD	Rye
67	52.1	Lansingburgh Central SD	Troy
68	52.1	Dansville Central SD	Dansville
69	52.1	Minisink Valley Central SD	Slate Hill
70	52.1	Waverly Central SD	Waverly
71	52.1	Briarcliff Manor Union Free SD	Briarcliff Manor
72	52.1	Amityville Union Free SD	Amityville
73	52.1	Kinderhook Central SD	Valatie
74	52.1	Newark Central SD	Newark
75	52.0	Susquehanna Valley Central SD	Conklin
76	52.0	Whitesboro Central SD	Yorkville
77	52.0	Malverne Union Free SD	Malverne
78	52.0	Hendrick Hudson Central SD	Montrose
79	52.0	Central Square Central SD	Central Square
80	52.0	Clarkstown Central SD	New City
81	52.0	Troy City SD	Troy
82	51.9	New Rochelle City SD	New Rochelle
83	51.9	South Huntington Union Free SD	Huntington Stn
84	51.9	Dover Union Free SD	Dover Plains
85	51.9	Pelham Union Free SD	Pelham
86	51.9	E Ramapo Central SD (Sprg Val)	Spring Valley
87	51.9	New Hartford Central SD	New Hartford
88	51.9	Clarence Central SD	Clarence
89	51.9	Springville-Griffith Inst Cent	Springville
90	51.8	Bethpage Union Free SD	Bethpage
91	51.8	New Hyde Park-Garden City Park	New Hyde Park
92	51.8	Monticello Central SD	Monticello
93	51.8	Newfane Central SD	Newfane
94	51.8	Half Hollow Hills Central SD	Dix Hills
95	51.8	Garden City Union Free SD	Garden City
96	51.8	Lindenhurst Union Free SD	Lindenhurst
97	51.8	Clinton Central SD	Clinton
98	51.8	Gowanda Central SD	Gowanda
99	51.8	William Floyd Union Free SD	Mastic Beach
100	51.8	Port Chester-Rye Union Free SD	Port Chester
101	51.7	Marcellus Central SD	Marcellus
102	51.7	Shenendehowa Central SD	Clifton Park
103	51.7	Island Trees Union Free SD	Levittown
104	51.7	Gloversville City SD	Gloversville
105	51.7	Mahopac Central SD	Mahopac
106	51.7	Wappingers Central SD	Wappingers Fls
107	51.7	Middle Country Central SD	Centereach
108	51.7	Elmira City SD	Elmira
109	51.7	White Plains City SD	White Plains
110	51.6	Cheektowaga Central SD	Cheektowaga
111	51.6	Harborfields Central SD	Greenlawn
112	51.6	Floral Park-Bellerose UFSD	Floral Park
113	51.6	Smithtown Central SD	Smithtown
114	51.6	Saranac Central SD	Dannemora
115	51.6	Union-Endicott Central SD	Endicott
116	51.6	Syosset Central SD	Syosset
117	51.6	South Jefferson Central SD	Adams Center
118	51.6	Wilson Central SD	Wilson
119	51.6	Grand Island Central SD	Grand Island
120	51.6	Chappaqua Central SD	Chappaqua
121	51.6	Nanuet Union Free SD	Nanuet
122	51.6	Yorkshire-Pioneer Central SD	Yorkshire
123	51.6	Glens Falls City SD	Glens Falls
124	51.6	Shoreham-Wading River Central SD	Shoreham
125	51.6	Poughkeepsie City SD	Poughkeepsie
126	51.6	Chenango Forks Central SD	Binghamton
127	51.6	Mount Pleasant Central SD	Thornwood
128	51.5	Rome City SD	Rome
129	51.5	Lewiston-Porter Central SD	Youngstown
130	51.5	West Genesee Central SD	Camillus
131	51.5	Plattsburgh City SD	Plattsburgh
132	51.5	Bay Shore Union Free SD	Bay Shore
133	51.5	Gouverneur Central SD	Gouverneur
134	51.5	Valley Stream Central High SD	Valley Stream
135	51.5	Yonkers City SD	Yonkers
136	51.5	Phelps-Clifton Springs Cent SD	Clifton Spgs
137	51.5	Greece Central SD	Rochester
138	51.4	East Hampton Union Free SD	East Hampton
139	51.4	Hudson Falls Central SD	Hudson Falls
140	51.4	Huntington Union Free SD	Huntington Stn
141	51.4	Beacon City SD	Beacon
142	51.4	Baldwin Union Free SD	Baldwin
143	51.4	Seaford Union Free SD	Seaford
144	51.4	Taconic Hills Central SD	Craryville
145	51.4	Rotterdam-Mohonasen Central SD	Schenectady
146	51.4	Newburgh City SD	Newburgh
147	51.4	Herricks Union Free SD	New Hyde Park
148	51.4	Elmont Union Free SD	Elmont
149	51.4	Eastchester Union Free SD	Eastchester
150	51.4	Valley Central SD (Montgomery)	Montgomery
151	51.4	Scarsdale Union Free SD	Scarsdale
152	51.4	Jordan-Elbridge Central SD	Jordan
153	51.4	Dryden Central SD	Dryden
154	51.4	Baldwinsville Central SD	Baldwinsville
155	51.4	Saugerties Central SD	Saugerties
156	51.3	Ramapo Central SD (Suffern)	Hillburn
157	51.3	Mamaroneck Union Free SD	Mamaroneck
158	51.3	Bellmore-Merrick Central High SD	North Merrick
159	51.3	Manhasset Union Free SD	Manhasset
160	51.3	Starpoint Central SD	Lockport
161	51.3	Scotia-Glenville Central SD	Scotia
162	51.3	Lynbrook Union Free SD	Lynbrook
163	51.3	Orchard Park Central SD	Orchard Park
164	51.3	Kenmore-Tonawanda Union Free SD	Buffalo
165	51.3	Monroe-Woodbury Central SD	Central Valley
166	51.3	Cazenovia Central SD	Cazenovia
167	51.3	Plainview-Old Bethpage Cent SD	Plainview
168	51.3	Long Beach City SD	Long Beach
169	51.3	Saranac Lake Central SD	Saranac Lake
170	51.3	Amsterdam City SD	Amsterdam
171	51.3	North Syracuse Central SD	N Syracuse
172	51.3	Hicksville Union Free SD	Hicksville
173	51.3	Hewlett-Woodmere Union Free SD	Woodmere
174	51.3	Rockville Centre Union Free SD	Rockville Ctre
175	51.2	West Islip Union Free SD	West Islip
176	51.2	Adirondack Central SD	Boonville
177	51.2	Canton Central SD	Canton
178	51.2	Brighton Central SD	Rochester
179	51.2	New York City Public Schools	Brooklyn
180	51.2	Jericho Union Free SD	Jericho
181	51.2	Copiague Union Free SD	Copiague
182	51.2	Miller Place Union Free SD	Miller Place
183	51.2	Niskayuna Central SD	Schenectady
184	51.2	Chatham Central SD	Chatham
185	51.2	Cobleskill-Richmondville CSD	Cobleskill
186	51.2	Liberty Central SD	Liberty
187	51.2	Hempstead Union Free SD	Hempstead
188	51.2	Tonawanda City SD	Tonawanda
189	51.2	Hauppauge Union Free SD	Hauppauge
190	51.2	General Brown Central SD	Dexter
191	51.2	Haverstraw-Stony Point Cent SD	Garnerville
192	51.1	Canandaigua City SD	Canandaigua
193	51.1	Commack Union Free SD	E Northport
194	51.1	Nyack Union Free SD	Nyack
195	51.1	New Paltz Central SD	New Paltz
196	51.1	Medina Central SD	Medina
197	51.1	Liverpool Central SD	Liverpool
198	51.1	Mineola Union Free SD	Mineola
199	51.1	South Colonie Central SD	Albany
200	51.1	Fairport Central SD	Fairport
201	51.1	Guilderland Central SD	Guilderland
202	51.1	Patchogue-Medford Union Free SD	Patchogue
203	51.1	Iroquois Central SD	Elma
204	51.1	Dunkirk City SD	Dunkirk
205	51.1	Solvay Union Free SD	Solvay
206	51.0	West Seneca Central SD	West Seneca
207	51.0	Harrison Central SD	Harrison
208	51.0	Irvington Union Free SD	Irvington
209	51.0	Albany City SD	Albany
210	51.0	Port Jervis City SD	Port Jervis
211	51.0	Cornwall Central SD	Cornwall-on-Hud
212	51.0	Utica City SD	Utica
213	51.0	Rochester City SD	Rochester
214	51.0	Malone Central SD	Malone
215	51.0	Honeoye Falls-Lima Central SD	Honeoye Falls
216	51.0	Central Islip Union Free SD	Central Islip
217	51.0	Buffalo City SD	Buffalo
218	51.0	Jamestown City SD	Jamestown
219	51.0	Niagara Falls City SD	Niagara Falls
220	51.0	Levittown Union Free SD	Levittown
221	51.0	Lawrence Union Free SD	Lawrence
222	50.9	Sweet Home Central SD	Amherst
223	50.9	East Syracuse-Minoa Central SD	East Syracuse
224	50.9	Lockport City SD	Lockport
225	50.9	Roosevelt Union Free SD	Roosevelt
226	50.9	Arlington Central SD	Poughkeepsie
227	50.9	Spackenkill Union Free SD	Poughkeepsie
228	50.9	South Glens Falls Central SD	S Glens Falls
229	50.9	Salmon River Central SD	Ft Covington
230	50.9	Sewanhaka Central High SD	Floral Park
231	50.9	Fayetteville-Manlius Central SD	Manlius
232	50.9	Ballston Spa Central SD	Ballston Spa
233	50.9	Elwood Union Free SD	Greenlawn
234	50.9	Peekskill City SD	Peekskill
235	50.8	Watertown City SD	Watertown
236	50.8	Cheektowaga-Sloan Union Free SD	Sloan
237	50.8	Southampton Union Free SD	Southampton
238	50.8	Katonah-Lewisboro Union Free SD	South Salem
239	50.8	Averill Park Central SD	Averill Park
240	50.8	Goshen Central SD	Goshen
241	50.8	Massapequa Union Free SD	Massapequa
242	50.8	West Hempstead Union Free SD	W Hempstead
243	50.8	Union Free SD of the Tarrytowns	Sleepy Hollow
244	50.8	Cairo-Durham Central SD	Cairo
245	50.8	Hamburg Central SD	Hamburg
246	50.8	Carmel Central SD	Patterson
247	50.8	East Irondequoit Central SD	Rochester
248	50.8	Corning City SD	Painted Post
249	50.8	Port Washington Union Free SD	Pt Washington
250	50.8	Freeport Union Free SD	Freeport
251	50.8	Royalton-Hartland Central SD	Middleport
252	50.8	Somers Central SD	Lincolndale
253	50.8	Salamanca City SD	Salamanca
254	50.8	Camden Central SD	Camden
255	50.8	Babylon Union Free SD	Babylon
256	50.7	Hilton Central SD	Hilton
257	50.7	Mount Vernon City SD	Mount Vernon
258	50.7	West Babylon Union Free SD	West Babylon
259	50.7	Uniondale Union Free SD	Uniondale
260	50.7	North Colonie Central SD	Latham
261	50.7	Three Village Central SD	East Setauket
262	50.7	Pine Bush Central SD	Pine Bush
263	50.7	Auburn City SD	Auburn
264	50.7	Lakeland Central SD	Shrub Oak

265	50.7	Sayville Union Free SD	Sayville
266	50.7	Onteora Central SD	Boiceville
267	50.7	Mattituck-Cutchogue UFSD	Cutchogue
268	50.7	Wantagh Union Free SD	Wantagh
269	50.7	Cortland City SD	Cortland
270	50.7	Amherst Central SD	Amherst
271	50.6	Hyde Park Central SD	Poughkeepsie
272	50.6	Massena Central SD	Massena
273	50.6	Williamsville Central SD	East Amherst
274	50.6	Westhampton Beach Union Free SD	Westhampton Bch
275	50.6	Ravena-Coeymans-Selkirk CSD	Selkirk
276	50.6	Queensbury Union Free SD	Queensbury
276	50.6	Rush-Henrietta Central SD	Henrietta
278	50.6	Oneida City SD	Oneida
279	50.6	Albion Central SD	Albion
280	50.6	North Rose-Wolcott Central SD	Wolcott
281	50.6	Oyster Bay-East Norwich CSD	Oyster Bay
282	50.6	Oceanside Union Free SD	Oceanside
283	50.6	Binghamton City SD	Binghamton
284	50.5	East Aurora Union Free SD	East Aurora
285	50.5	Depew Union Free SD	Depew
286	50.5	Middletown City SD	Middletown
287	50.5	Penfield Central SD	Penfield
288	50.5	Sachem Central SD	Holbrook
289	50.5	Schenectady City SD	Schenectady
290	50.5	Whitney Point Central SD	Whitney Point
291	50.5	North Babylon Union Free SD	North Babylon
292	50.5	Waterloo Central SD	Waterloo
293	50.5	Frontier Central SD	Hamburg
293	50.5	Lancaster Central SD	Lancaster
295	50.5	South Country Central SD	E Patchogue
296	50.4	Ellenville Central SD	Ellenville
297	50.4	Livonia Central SD	Livonia
298	50.4	Putnam Valley Central SD	Putnam Valley
299	50.4	Wayland-Cohocton Central SD	Wayland
300	50.4	Merrick Union Free SD	Merrick
301	50.4	Northeastern Clinton Central SD	Champlain
302	50.4	Schuylerville Central SD	Schuylerville
303	50.4	Bayport-Blue Point Union Free SD	Bayport
304	50.4	Cold Spring Harbor Central SD	Cold Sprg Harbor
305	50.4	Brookhaven-Comsewogue UFSD	Pt Jefferson Stn
306	50.3	Wyandanch Union Free SD	Wyandanch
307	50.3	Saratoga Springs City SD	Saratoga Spgs
308	50.3	Evans-Brant Cent SD (Lake Shore)	Angola
309	50.3	Kingston City SD	Kingston
310	50.3	New York City Geographic Dist 9	Bronx
311	50.3	Sherrill City SD	Verona
312	50.3	Beekmantown Central SD	West Chazy
313	50.3	Gates-Chili Central SD	Rochester
314	50.3	Franklin Square Union Free SD	Franklin Square
315	50.2	Hastings-On-Hudson Union Free SD	Hastings-on-Hud
316	50.2	Northport-East Northport UFSD	Northport
317	50.2	Byram Hills Central SD	Armonk
318	50.2	Cohoes City SD	Cohoes
319	50.2	Fulton City SD	Fulton
320	50.2	Maine-Endwell Central SD	Endwell
321	50.1	Yorktown Central SD	Yorktown Hgts
322	50.1	Islip Union Free SD	Islip
323	50.1	Syracuse City SD	Syracuse
324	50.1	Kings Park Central SD	Kings Park
325	50.1	Horseheads Central SD	Horseheads
326	50.1	Carthage Central SD	Carthage
327	50.1	Plainedge Union Free SD	N Massapequa
328	50.1	South Orangetown Central SD	Blauvelt
329	50.0	East Meadow Union Free SD	Westbury
330	50.0	Croton-Harmon Union Free SD	Croton-On-Hud
331	50.0	Carle Place Union Free SD	Carle Place
332	49.9	Catskill Central SD	Catskill
333	49.9	Gorham-Middlesex CSD (M Whitman)	Rushville
334	49.9	Mexico Central SD	Mexico
335	49.9	Sullivan West Central SD	Callicoon
336	49.9	Brockport Central SD	Brockport
337	49.9	Windsor Central SD	Windsor
338	49.9	Holland Patent Central SD	Holland Patent
339	49.9	West Irondequoit Central SD	Rochester
340	49.8	East Greenbush Central SD	E Greenbush
341	49.8	Ilion Central SD	Ilion
342	49.8	Fredonia Central SD	Fredonia
343	49.8	Johnson City Central SD	Johnson City
344	49.8	Schalmont Central SD	Schenectady
345	49.7	Burnt Hls-Ballston Lake Cent SD	Scotia
346	49.7	Pittsford Central SD	Pittsford
347	49.7	Valley Stream 30 Union Free SD	Valley Stream
348	49.5	Olean City SD	Olean
349	49.5	North Shore Central SD	Sea Cliff
350	49.4	Chittenango Central SD	Chittenango
351	49.4	Hannibal Central SD	Hannibal
352	49.3	Oneonta City SD	Oneonta
353	49.2	Penn Yan Central SD	Penn Yan
354	49.2	New York City Geographic Dist 15	Brooklyn
355	49.2	Sherburne-Earlville Central SD	Sherburne
356	49.2	Geneva City SD	Geneva
357	49.2	Jamesville-Dewitt Central SD	Dewitt
358	49.1	Batavia City SD	Batavia
359	49.1	Cheektowaga-Maryvale UFSD	Cheektowaga
360	49.1	Locust Valley Central SD	Locust Valley
361	49.1	Westbury Union Free SD	Old Westbury
362	49.0	Pearl River Union Free SD	Pearl River
363	49.0	Norwich City SD	Norwich
364	48.8	Mount Sinai Union Free SD	Mount Sinai
365	48.7	Akron Central SD	Akron
366	48.7	Marlboro Central SD	Marlboro
367	48.6	Canastota Central SD	Canastota
368	48.2	Altmar-Parish-Williamstown CSD	Parish
369	47.6	Johnstown City SD	Johnstown
370	47.0	Nyc Alternative HS District	New York

Female Students

Rank	Percent	District Name	City
1	52.9	Nyc Alternative HS District	New York
2	52.3	Johnstown City SD	Johnstown
3	51.7	Altmar-Parish-Williamstown CSD	Parish
4	51.3	Canastota Central SD	Canastota
5	51.2	Marlboro Central SD	Marlboro
6	51.2	Akron Central SD	Akron
7	51.1	Mount Sinai Union Free SD	Mount Sinai
8	50.9	Norwich City SD	Norwich
9	50.9	Pearl River Union Free SD	Pearl River
10	50.8	Westbury Union Free SD	Old Westbury
11	50.8	Locust Valley Central SD	Locust Valley
12	50.8	Cheektowaga-Maryvale UFSD	Cheektowaga
13	50.8	Batavia City SD	Batavia
14	50.7	Jamesville-Dewitt Central SD	Dewitt
15	50.7	Geneva City SD	Geneva
16	50.7	Sherburne-Earlville Central SD	Sherburne
17	50.7	New York City Geographic Dist 15	Brooklyn
18	50.7	Penn Yan Central SD	Penn Yan
19	50.6	Oneonta City SD	Oneonta
20	50.5	Hannibal Central SD	Hannibal
21	50.5	Chittenango Central SD	Chittenango
22	50.4	North Shore Central SD	Sea Cliff
23	50.4	Olean City SD	Olean
24	50.2	Valley Stream 30 Union Free SD	Valley Stream
25	50.2	Pittsford Central SD	Pittsford
26	50.2	Burnt Hls-Ballston Lake Cent SD	Scotia
27	50.1	Schalmont Central SD	Schenectady
28	50.1	Johnson City Central SD	Johnson City
29	50.1	Fredonia Central SD	Fredonia
30	50.1	Ilion Central SD	Ilion
31	50.1	East Greenbush Central SD	E Greenbush
32	50.0	West Irondequoit Central SD	Rochester
33	50.0	Holland Patent Central SD	Holland Patent
34	50.0	Windsor Central SD	Windsor
35	50.0	Brockport Central SD	Brockport
36	50.0	Sullivan West Central SD	Callicoon
37	50.0	Mexico Central SD	Mexico
38	50.0	Gorham-Middlesex CSD (M Whitman)	Rushville
39	50.0	Catskill Central SD	Catskill
40	50.0	Carle Place Union Free SD	Carle Place
41	49.9	Croton-Harmon Union Free SD	Croton-On-Hud
42	49.9	East Meadow Union Free SD	Westbury
43	49.8	South Orangetown Central SD	Blauvelt
44	49.8	Plainedge Union Free SD	N Massapequa
45	49.8	Carthage Central SD	Carthage
46	49.8	Horseheads Central SD	Horseheads
47	49.8	Kings Park Central SD	Kings Park
48	49.8	Syracuse City SD	Syracuse
49	49.8	Islip Union Free SD	Islip
50	49.8	Yorktown Central SD	Yorktown Hgts
51	49.7	Maine-Endwell Central SD	Endwell
52	49.7	Fulton City SD	Fulton
53	49.7	Cohoes City SD	Cohoes
54	49.7	Byram Hills Central SD	Armonk
55	49.7	Northport-East Northport UFSD	Northport
56	49.7	Hastings-On-Hudson Union Free SD	Hastings-on-Hud
57	49.6	Franklin Square Union Free SD	Franklin Square
58	49.6	Gates-Chili Central SD	Rochester
59	49.6	Beekmantown Central SD	West Chazy
60	49.6	Sherrill City SD	Verona
61	49.6	New York City Geographic Dist 9	Bronx
62	49.6	Kingston City SD	Kingston
63	49.6	Evans-Brant Cent SD (Lake Shore)	Angola
64	49.6	Saratoga Springs City SD	Saratoga Spgs
65	49.6	Wyandanch Union Free SD	Wyandanch
66	49.5	Brookhaven-Comsewogue UFSD	Pt Jefferson Stn
67	49.5	Cold Spring Harbor Central SD	Cold Sprg Harbor
68	49.5	Bayport-Blue Point Union Free SD	Bayport
69	49.5	Schuylerville Central SD	Schuylerville
70	49.5	Northeastern Clinton Central SD	Champlain
71	49.5	Merrick Union Free SD	Merrick
72	49.5	Wayland-Cohocton Central SD	Wayland
73	49.5	Putnam Valley Central SD	Putnam Valley
74	49.5	Livonia Central SD	Livonia
75	49.5	Ellenville Central SD	Ellenville
76	49.4	South Country Central SD	E Patchogue
77	49.4	Frontier Central SD	Hamburg
77	49.4	Lancaster Central SD	Lancaster
79	49.4	Waterloo Central SD	Waterloo
80	49.4	North Babylon Union Free SD	North Babylon
81	49.4	Whitney Point Central SD	Whitney Point
82	49.4	Schenectady City SD	Schenectady
83	49.4	Sachem Central SD	Holbrook
84	49.4	Penfield Central SD	Penfield
85	49.4	Middletown City SD	Middletown
86	49.4	Depew Union Free SD	Depew
87	49.4	East Aurora Union Free SD	East Aurora
88	49.3	Binghamton City SD	Binghamton
89	49.3	Oceanside Union Free SD	Oceanside
90	49.3	Oyster Bay-East Norwich CSD	Oyster Bay
91	49.3	North Rose-Wolcott Central SD	Wolcott
92	49.3	Albion Central SD	Albion
93	49.3	Oneida City SD	Oneida
94	49.3	Queensbury Union Free SD	Queensbury
94	49.3	Rush-Henrietta Central SD	Henrietta
96	49.3	Ravena-Coeymans-Selkirk CSD	Selkirk
97	49.3	Westhampton Beach Union Free SD	Westhampton Bch
98	49.3	Williamsville Central SD	East Amherst
99	49.3	Massena Central SD	Massena
100	49.3	Hyde Park Central SD	Poughkeepsie
101	49.2	Amherst Central SD	Amherst
102	49.2	Cortland City SD	Cortland
103	49.2	Wantagh Union Free SD	Wantagh
104	49.2	Mattituck-Cutchogue UFSD	Cutchogue
105	49.2	Onteora Central SD	Boiceville
106	49.2	Sayville Union Free SD	Sayville
107	49.2	Lakeland Central SD	Shrub Oak
108	49.2	Auburn City SD	Auburn
109	49.2	Pine Bush Central SD	Pine Bush
110	49.2	Three Village Central SD	East Setauket
111	49.2	North Colonie Central SD	Latham
112	49.2	Uniondale Union Free SD	Uniondale
113	49.2	West Babylon Union Free SD	West Babylon
114	49.2	Mount Vernon City SD	Mount Vernon
115	49.2	Hilton Central SD	Hilton
116	49.1	Babylon Union Free SD	Babylon
117	49.1	Camden Central SD	Camden
118	49.1	Salamanca City SD	Salamanca
119	49.1	Somers Central SD	Lincolndale
120	49.1	Royalton-Hartland Central SD	Middleport
121	49.1	Freeport Union Free SD	Freeport
122	49.1	Port Washington Union Free SD	Pt Washington
123	49.1	Corning City SD	Painted Post
124	49.1	East Irondequoit Central SD	Rochester
125	49.1	Carmel Central SD	Patterson
126	49.1	Hamburg Central SD	Hamburg
127	49.1	Cairo-Durham Central SD	Cairo
128	49.1	Union Free SD of the Tarrytowns	Sleepy Hollow
129	49.1	West Hempstead Union Free SD	W Hempstead
130	49.1	Massapequa Union Free SD	Massapequa
131	49.1	Goshen Central SD	Goshen
132	49.1	Averill Park Central SD	Averill Park
133	49.1	Katonah-Lewisboro Union Free SD	South Salem
134	49.1	Southampton Union Free SD	Southampton
135	49.1	Cheektowaga-Sloan Union Free SD	Sloan
136	49.1	Watertown City SD	Watertown
137	49.0	Peekskill City SD	Peekskill
138	49.0	Elwood Union Free SD	Greenlawn
139	49.0	Ballston Spa Central SD	Ballston Spa
140	49.0	Fayetteville-Manlius Central SD	Manlius
141	49.0	Sewanhaka Central High SD	Floral Park
142	49.0	Salmon River Central SD	Ft Covington
143	49.0	South Glens Falls Central SD	S Glens Falls
144	49.0	Spackenkill Union Free SD	Poughkeepsie
145	49.0	Arlington Central SD	Poughkeepsie
146	49.0	Roosevelt Union Free SD	Roosevelt
147	49.0	Lockport City SD	Lockport
148	49.0	East Syracuse-Minoa Central SD	East Syracuse
149	49.0	Sweet Home Central SD	Amherst
150	48.9	Lawrence Union Free SD	Lawrence
151	48.9	Levittown Union Free SD	Levittown
152	48.9	Niagara Falls City SD	Niagara Falls
153	48.9	Jamestown City SD	Jamestown
154	48.9	Buffalo City SD	Buffalo
155	48.9	Central Islip Union Free SD	Central Islip
156	48.9	Honeoye Falls-Lima Central SD	Honeoye Falls
157	48.9	Malone Central SD	Malone
158	48.9	Rochester City SD	Rochester
159	48.9	Utica City SD	Utica
160	48.9	Cornwall Central SD	Cornwall-on-Hud
161	48.9	Port Jervis City SD	Port Jervis
162	48.9	Albany City SD	Albany
163	48.9	Irvington Union Free SD	Irvington
164	48.9	Harrison Central SD	Harrison
165	48.9	West Seneca Central SD	West Seneca
166	48.8	Solvay Union Free SD	Solvay
167	48.8	Dunkirk City SD	Dunkirk
168	48.8	Iroquois Central SD	Elma

169	48.8	Patchogue-Medford Union Free SD	Patchogue
170	48.8	Guilderland Central SD	Guilderland
171	48.8	Fairport Central SD	Fairport
172	48.8	South Colonie Central SD	Albany
173	48.8	Mineola Union Free SD	Mineola
174	48.8	Liverpool Central SD	Liverpool
175	48.8	Medina Central SD	Medina
176	48.8	New Paltz Central SD	New Paltz
177	48.8	Nyack Union Free SD	Nyack
178	48.8	Commack Union Free SD	E Northport
179	48.8	Canandaigua City SD	Canandaigua
180	48.7	Haverstraw-Stony Point Cent SD	Garnerville
181	48.7	General Brown Central SD	Dexter
182	48.7	Hauppauge Union Free SD	Hauppauge
183	48.7	Tonawanda City SD	Tonawanda
184	48.7	Hempstead Union Free SD	Hempstead
185	48.7	Liberty Central SD	Liberty
186	48.7	Cobleskill-Richmondville CSD	Cobleskill
187	48.7	Chatham Central SD	Chatham
188	48.7	Niskayuna Central SD	Schenectady
189	48.7	Miller Place Union Free SD	Miller Place
190	48.7	Copiague Union Free SD	Copiague
191	48.7	Jericho Union Free SD	Jericho
192	48.7	New York City Public Schools	Brooklyn
193	48.7	Brighton Central SD	Rochester
194	48.7	Canton Central SD	Canton
195	48.7	Adirondack Central SD	Boonville
196	48.7	West Islip Union Free SD	West Islip
197	48.6	Rockville Centre Union Free SD	Rockville Ctre
198	48.6	Hewlett-Woodmere Union Free SD	Woodmere
199	48.6	Hicksville Union Free SD	Hicksville
200	48.6	North Syracuse Central SD	N Syracuse
201	48.6	Amsterdam City SD	Amsterdam
202	48.6	Saranac Lake Central SD	Saranac Lake
203	48.6	Long Beach City SD	Long Beach
204	48.6	Plainview-Old Bethpage Cent SD	Plainview
205	48.6	Cazenovia Central SD	Cazenovia
206	48.6	Monroe-Woodbury Central SD	Central Valley
207	48.6	Kenmore-Tonawanda Union Free SD	Buffalo
208	48.6	Orchard Park Central SD	Orchard Park
209	48.6	Lynbrook Union Free SD	Lynbrook
210	48.6	Scotia-Glenville Central SD	Scotia
211	48.6	Starpoint Central SD	Lockport
212	48.6	Manhasset Union Free SD	Manhasset
213	48.6	Bellmore-Merrick Central High SD	North Merrick
214	48.6	Mamaroneck Union Free SD	Mamaroneck
215	48.6	Ramapo Central SD (Suffern)	Hillburn
216	48.5	Saugerties Central SD	Saugerties
217	48.5	Baldwinsville Central SD	Baldwinsville
218	48.5	Dryden Central SD	Dryden
219	48.5	Jordan-Elbridge Central SD	Jordan
220	48.5	Scarsdale Union Free SD	Scarsdale
221	48.5	Valley Central SD (Montgomery)	Montgomery
222	48.5	Eastchester Union Free SD	Eastchester
223	48.5	Elmont Union Free SD	Elmont
224	48.5	Herricks Union Free SD	New Hyde Park
225	48.5	Newburgh City SD	Newburgh
226	48.5	Rotterdam-Mohonasen Central SD	Schenectady
227	48.5	Taconic Hills Central SD	Craryville
228	48.5	Seaford Union Free SD	Seaford
229	48.5	Baldwin Union Free SD	Baldwin
230	48.5	Beacon City SD	Beacon
231	48.5	Huntington Union Free SD	Huntington Stn
232	48.5	Hudson Falls Central SD	Hudson Falls
233	48.5	East Hampton Union Free SD	East Hampton
234	48.4	Greece Central SD	Rochester
235	48.4	Phelps-Clifton Springs Cent SD	Clifton Spgs
236	48.4	Yonkers City SD	Yonkers
237	48.4	Valley Stream Central High SD	Valley Stream
238	48.4	Gouverneur Central SD	Gouverneur
239	48.4	Bay Shore Union Free SD	Bay Shore
240	48.4	Plattsburgh City SD	Plattsburgh
241	48.4	West Genesee Central SD	Camillus
242	48.4	Lewiston-Porter Central SD	Youngstown
243	48.4	Rome City SD	Rome
244	48.4	Mount Pleasant Central SD	Thornwood
245	48.3	Chenango Forks Central SD	Binghamton
246	48.3	Poughkeepsie City SD	Poughkeepsie
247	48.3	Shoreham-Wading River Central SD	Shoreham
248	48.3	Glens Falls City SD	Glens Falls
249	48.3	Yorkshire-Pioneer Central SD	Yorkshire
250	48.3	Nanuet Union Free SD	Nanuet
251	48.3	Chappaqua Central SD	Chappaqua
252	48.3	Grand Island Central SD	Grand Island
253	48.3	Wilson Central SD	Wilson
254	48.3	South Jefferson Central SD	Adams Center
255	48.3	Syosset Central SD	Syosset
256	48.3	Union-Endicott Central SD	Endicott
257	48.3	Saranac Central SD	Dannemora
258	48.3	Smithtown Central SD	Smithtown
259	48.3	Floral Park-Bellerose UFSD	Floral Park
260	48.3	Harborfields Central SD	Greenlawn
261	48.3	Cheektowaga Central SD	Cheektowaga
262	48.2	White Plains City SD	White Plains
263	48.2	Elmira City SD	Elmira
264	48.2	Middle Country Central SD	Centereach
265	48.2	Wappingers Central SD	Wappingers Fls
266	48.2	Mahopac Central SD	Mahopac
267	48.2	Gloversville City SD	Gloversville
268	48.2	Island Trees Union Free SD	Levittown
269	48.2	Shenendehowa Central SD	Clifton Park
270	48.2	Marcellus Central SD	Marcellus
271	48.1	Port Chester-Rye Union Free SD	Port Chester
272	48.1	William Floyd Union Free SD	Mastic Beach
273	48.1	Gowanda Central SD	Gowanda
274	48.1	Clinton Central SD	Clinton
275	48.1	Lindenhurst Union Free SD	Lindenhurst
276	48.1	Garden City Union Free SD	Garden City
277	48.1	Half Hollow Hills Central SD	Dix Hills
278	48.1	Newfane Central SD	Newfane
279	48.1	Monticello Central SD	Monticello
280	48.1	New Hyde Park-Garden City Park	New Hyde Park
281	48.1	Bethpage Union Free SD	Bethpage
282	48.0	Springville-Griffith Inst Cent	Springville
283	48.0	Clarence Central SD	Clarence
284	48.0	New Hartford Central SD	New Hartford
285	48.0	E Ramapo Central SD (Sprg Val)	Spring Valley
286	48.0	Pelham Union Free SD	Pelham
287	48.0	Dover Union Free SD	Dover Plains
288	48.0	South Huntington Union Free SD	Huntington Stn
289	48.0	New Rochelle City SD	New Rochelle
290	47.9	Troy City SD	Troy
291	47.9	Clarkstown Central SD	New City
292	47.9	Central Square Central SD	Central Square
293	47.9	Hendrick Hudson Central SD	Montrose
294	47.9	Malverne Union Free SD	Malverne
295	47.9	Whitesboro Central SD	Yorkville
296	47.9	Susquehanna Valley Central SD	Conklin
297	47.8	Newark Central SD	Newark
298	47.8	Kinderhook Central SD	Valatie
299	47.8	Amityville Union Free SD	Amityville
300	47.8	Briarcliff Manor Union Free SD	Briarcliff Manor
301	47.8	Waverly Central SD	Waverly
302	47.8	Minisink Valley Central SD	Slate Hill
303	47.8	Dansville Central SD	Dansville
304	47.8	Lansingburgh Central SD	Troy
305	47.8	Rye City SD	Rye
306	47.7	Great Neck Union Free SD	Great Neck
307	47.7	Owego-Apalachin Central SD	Owego
308	47.7	North Bellmore Union Free SD	Bellmore
309	47.7	North Tonawanda City SD	N Tonawanda
310	47.7	Indian River Central SD	Philadelphia
311	47.7	Warwick Valley Central SD	Warwick
312	47.7	Spencerport Central SD	Spencerport
313	47.7	Skaneateles Central SD	Skaneateles
314	47.7	Vestal Central SD	Vestal
315	47.7	Ardsley Union Free SD	Ardsley
316	47.7	Washingtonville Central SD	Washingtonville
317	47.7	Greenburgh Central SD	Hartsdale
318	47.6	Ithaca City SD	Ithaca
319	47.6	Chenango Valley Central SD	Binghamton
320	47.6	Bedford Central SD	Mount Kisco
321	47.6	Wallkill Central SD	Wallkill
322	47.6	Roslyn Union Free SD	Roslyn
323	47.5	Ogdensburg City SD	Ogdensburg
324	47.5	Glen Cove City SD	Glen Cove
325	47.5	Longwood Central SD	Middle Island
326	47.5	Homer Central SD	Homer
327	47.5	East Williston Union Free SD	Old Westbury
328	47.4	Brentwood Union Free SD	Brentwood
328	47.4	Connetquot Central SD	Bohemia
330	47.4	Valley Stream 13 Union Free SD	Valley Stream
331	47.4	Eden Central SD	Eden
332	47.4	Riverhead Central SD	Riverhead
333	47.4	Peru Central SD	Peru
334	47.4	Victor Central SD	Victor
335	47.3	Brewster Central SD	Brewster
336	47.3	Oswego City SD	Oswego
337	47.3	Webster Central SD	Webster
338	47.3	Red Hook Central SD	Red Hook
339	47.3	Wayne Central SD	Ontario Center
340	47.3	Deer Park Union Free SD	Deer Park
341	47.3	Hampton Bays Union Free SD	Hampton Bays
342	47.2	Westhill Central SD	Syracuse
343	47.1	Pleasantville Union Free SD	Pleasantville
344	47.1	Niagara-Wheatfield Central SD	Niagara Falls
345	47.1	Rocky Point Union Free SD	Rocky Point
346	47.1	Phoenix Central SD	Phoenix
347	47.0	Southwestern Cent SD Jamestown	Jamestown
348	47.0	Bethlehem Central SD	Delmar
349	46.9	Farmingdale Union Free SD	Farmingdale
350	46.9	Palmyra-Macedon Central SD	Palmyra
351	46.9	East Islip Union Free SD	Islip Terrace
352	46.9	Alden Central SD	Alden
353	46.8	Lackawanna City SD	Lackawanna
354	46.8	Rondout Valley Central SD	Accord
355	46.8	Churchville-Chili Central SD	Churchville
356	46.7	Edgemont Union Free SD	Scarsdale
357	46.7	Ossining Union Free SD	Ossining
358	46.6	Bath Central SD	Bath
359	46.2	Hornell City SD	Hornell
360	46.2	Cleveland Hill Union Free SD	Cheektowaga
361	45.5	Highland Central SD	Highland
362	45.2	Attica Central SD	Attica
363	44.8	Lansing Central SD	Lansing
364	44.7	Watkins Glen Central SD	Watkins Glen
365	44.7	Fonda-Fultonville Central SD	Fonda
366	43.8	Hudson City SD	Hudson
367	43.6	Broadalbin-Perth Central SD	Broadalbin
368	31.3	Coxsackie-Athens Central SD	Coxsackie
369	25.9	Boces Eastern Suffolk	Patchogue
370	24.1	Boces Nassau	Garden City

Individual Education Program Students

Rank	Percent	District Name	City
1	n/a	Adirondack Central SD	Boonville
1	n/a	Akron Central SD	Akron
1	n/a	Albany City SD	Albany
1	n/a	Albion Central SD	Albion
1	n/a	Alden Central SD	Alden
1	n/a	Altmar-Parish-Williamstown CSD	Parish
1	n/a	Amherst Central SD	Amherst
1	n/a	Amityville Union Free SD	Amityville
1	n/a	Amsterdam City SD	Amsterdam
1	n/a	Ardsley Union Free SD	Ardsley
1	n/a	Arlington Central SD	Poughkeepsie
1	n/a	Attica Central SD	Attica
1	n/a	Auburn City SD	Auburn
1	n/a	Averill Park Central SD	Averill Park
1	n/a	Babylon Union Free SD	Babylon
1	n/a	Baldwin Union Free SD	Baldwin
1	n/a	Baldwinsville Central SD	Baldwinsville
1	n/a	Ballston Spa Central SD	Ballston Spa
1	n/a	Batavia City SD	Batavia
1	n/a	Bath Central SD	Bath
1	n/a	Bay Shore Union Free SD	Bay Shore
1	n/a	Bayport-Blue Point Union Free SD	Bayport
1	n/a	Beacon City SD	Beacon
1	n/a	Bedford Central SD	Mount Kisco
1	n/a	Beekmantown Central SD	West Chazy
1	n/a	Bellmore-Merrick Central High SD	North Merrick
1	n/a	Bethlehem Central SD	Delmar
1	n/a	Bethpage Union Free SD	Bethpage
1	n/a	Binghamton City SD	Binghamton
1	n/a	Boces Eastern Suffolk	Patchogue
1	n/a	Boces Nassau	Garden City
1	n/a	Brentwood Union Free SD	Brentwood
1	n/a	Brewster Central SD	Brewster
1	n/a	Briarcliff Manor Union Free SD	Briarcliff Manor
1	n/a	Brighton Central SD	Rochester
1	n/a	Broadalbin-Perth Central SD	Broadalbin
1	n/a	Brockport Central SD	Brockport
1	n/a	Brookhaven-Comsewogue UFSD	Pt Jefferson Stn
1	n/a	Buffalo City SD	Buffalo
1	n/a	Burnt Hls-Ballston Lake Cent SD	Scotia
1	n/a	Byram Hills Central SD	Armonk
1	n/a	Cairo-Durham Central SD	Cairo
1	n/a	Camden Central SD	Camden
1	n/a	Canandaigua City SD	Canandaigua
1	n/a	Canastota Central SD	Canastota
1	n/a	Canton Central SD	Canton
1	n/a	Carle Place Union Free SD	Carle Place
1	n/a	Carmel Central SD	Patterson
1	n/a	Carthage Central SD	Carthage
1	n/a	Catskill Central SD	Catskill
1	n/a	Cazenovia Central SD	Cazenovia
1	n/a	Central Islip Union Free SD	Central Islip
1	n/a	Central Square Central SD	Central Square
1	n/a	Chappaqua Central SD	Chappaqua
1	n/a	Chatham Central SD	Chatham
1	n/a	Cheektowaga Central SD	Cheektowaga
1	n/a	Cheektowaga-Maryvale UFSD	Cheektowaga
1	n/a	Cheektowaga-Sloan Union Free SD	Sloan
1	n/a	Chenango Forks Central SD	Binghamton
1	n/a	Chenango Valley Central SD	Binghamton
1	n/a	Chittenango Central SD	Chittenango
1	n/a	Churchville-Chili Central SD	Churchville
1	n/a	Clarence Central SD	Clarence
1	n/a	Clarkstown Central SD	New City
1	n/a	Cleveland Hill Union Free SD	Cheektowaga
1	n/a	Clinton Central SD	Clinton
1	n/a	Cobleskill-Richmondville CSD	Cobleskill
1	n/a	Cohoes City SD	Cohoes
1	n/a	Cold Spring Harbor Central SD	Cold Sprg Harbor
1	n/a	Commack Union Free SD	E Northport
1	n/a	Connetquot Central SD	Bohemia
1	n/a	Copiague Union Free SD	Copiague

1	n/a	Corning City SD	Painted Post
1	n/a	Cornwall Central SD	Cornwall-on-Hud
1	n/a	Cortland City SD	Cortland
1	n/a	Coxsackie-Athens Central SD	Coxsackie
1	n/a	Croton-Harmon Union Free SD	Croton-On-Hud
1	n/a	Dansville Central SD	Dansville
1	n/a	Deer Park Union Free SD	Deer Park
1	n/a	Depew Union Free SD	Depew
1	n/a	Dover Union Free SD	Dover Plains
1	n/a	Dryden Central SD	Dryden
1	n/a	Dunkirk City SD	Dunkirk
1	n/a	East Aurora Union Free SD	East Aurora
1	n/a	East Greenbush Central SD	E Greenbush
1	n/a	East Hampton Union Free SD	East Hampton
1	n/a	East Irondequoit Central SD	Rochester
1	n/a	East Islip Union Free SD	Islip Terrace
1	n/a	East Meadow Union Free SD	Westbury
1	n/a	E Ramapo Central SD (Sprg Val)	Spring Valley
1	n/a	East Syracuse-Minoa Central SD	East Syracuse
1	n/a	East Williston Union Free SD	Old Westbury
1	n/a	Eastchester Union Free SD	Eastchester
1	n/a	Eden Central SD	Eden
1	n/a	Edgemont Union Free SD	Scarsdale
1	n/a	Ellenville Central SD	Ellenville
1	n/a	Elmira City SD	Elmira
1	n/a	Elmont Union Free SD	Elmont
1	n/a	Elwood Union Free SD	Greenlawn
1	n/a	Evans-Brant Cent SD (Lake Shore)	Angola
1	n/a	Fairport Central SD	Fairport
1	n/a	Farmingdale Union Free SD	Farmingdale
1	n/a	Fayetteville-Manlius Central SD	Manlius
1	n/a	Floral Park-Bellerose UFSD	Floral Park
1	n/a	Fonda-Fultonville Central SD	Fonda
1	n/a	Franklin Square Union Free SD	Franklin Square
1	n/a	Fredonia Central SD	Fredonia
1	n/a	Freeport Union Free SD	Freeport
1	n/a	Frontier Central SD	Hamburg
1	n/a	Fulton City SD	Fulton
1	n/a	Garden City Union Free SD	Garden City
1	n/a	Gates-Chili Central SD	Rochester
1	n/a	General Brown Central SD	Dexter
1	n/a	Geneva City SD	Geneva
1	n/a	Glen Cove City SD	Glen Cove
1	n/a	Glens Falls City SD	Glens Falls
1	n/a	Gloversville City SD	Gloversville
1	n/a	Gorham-Middlesex CSD (M Whitman)	Rushville
1	n/a	Goshen Central SD	Goshen
1	n/a	Gouverneur Central SD	Gouverneur
1	n/a	Gowanda Central SD	Gowanda
1	n/a	Grand Island Central SD	Grand Island
1	n/a	Great Neck Union Free SD	Great Neck
1	n/a	Greece Central SD	Rochester
1	n/a	Greenburgh Central SD	Hartsdale
1	n/a	Guilderland Central SD	Guilderland
1	n/a	Half Hollow Hills Central SD	Dix Hills
1	n/a	Hamburg Central SD	Hamburg
1	n/a	Hampton Bays Union Free SD	Hampton Bays
1	n/a	Hannibal Central SD	Hannibal
1	n/a	Harborfields Central SD	Greenlawn
1	n/a	Harrison Central SD	Harrison
1	n/a	Hastings-On-Hudson Union Free SD	Hastings-on-Hud
1	n/a	Hauppauge Union Free SD	Hauppauge
1	n/a	Haverstraw-Stony Point Cent SD	Garnerville
1	n/a	Hempstead Union Free SD	Hempstead
1	n/a	Hendrick Hudson Central SD	Montrose
1	n/a	Herricks Union Free SD	New Hyde Park
1	n/a	Hewlett-Woodmere Union Free SD	Woodmere
1	n/a	Hicksville Union Free SD	Hicksville
1	n/a	Highland Central SD	Highland
1	n/a	Hilton Central SD	Hilton
1	n/a	Holland Patent Central SD	Holland Patent
1	n/a	Homer Central SD	Homer
1	n/a	Honeoye Falls-Lima Central SD	Honeoye Falls
1	n/a	Hornell City SD	Hornell
1	n/a	Horseheads Central SD	Horseheads
1	n/a	Hudson City SD	Hudson
1	n/a	Hudson Falls Central SD	Hudson Falls
1	n/a	Huntington Union Free SD	Huntington Stn
1	n/a	Hyde Park Central SD	Poughkeepsie
1	n/a	Ilion Central SD	Ilion
1	n/a	Indian River Central SD	Philadelphia
1	n/a	Iroquois Central SD	Elma
1	n/a	Irvington Union Free SD	Irvington
1	n/a	Island Trees Union Free SD	Levittown
1	n/a	Islip Union Free SD	Islip
1	n/a	Ithaca City SD	Ithaca
1	n/a	Jamestown City SD	Jamestown
1	n/a	Jamesville-Dewitt Central SD	Dewitt
1	n/a	Jericho Union Free SD	Jericho
1	n/a	Johnson City Central SD	Johnson City
1	n/a	Johnstown City SD	Johnstown
1	n/a	Jordan-Elbridge Central SD	Jordan
1	n/a	Katonah-Lewisboro Union Free SD	South Salem
1	n/a	Kenmore-Tonawanda Union Free SD	Buffalo
1	n/a	Kinderhook Central SD	Valatie
1	n/a	Kings Park Central SD	Kings Park
1	n/a	Kingston City SD	Kingston
1	n/a	Lackawanna City SD	Lackawanna
1	n/a	Lakeland Central SD	Shrub Oak
1	n/a	Lancaster Central SD	Lancaster
1	n/a	Lansing Central SD	Lansing
1	n/a	Lansingburgh Central SD	Troy
1	n/a	Lawrence Union Free SD	Lawrence
1	n/a	Levittown Union Free SD	Levittown
1	n/a	Lewiston-Porter Central SD	Youngstown
1	n/a	Liberty Central SD	Liberty
1	n/a	Lindenhurst Union Free SD	Lindenhurst
1	n/a	Liverpool Central SD	Liverpool
1	n/a	Livonia Central SD	Livonia
1	n/a	Lockport City SD	Lockport
1	n/a	Locust Valley Central SD	Locust Valley
1	n/a	Long Beach City SD	Long Beach
1	n/a	Longwood Central SD	Middle Island
1	n/a	Lynbrook Union Free SD	Lynbrook
1	n/a	Mahopac Central SD	Mahopac
1	n/a	Maine-Endwell Central SD	Endwell
1	n/a	Malone Central SD	Malone
1	n/a	Malverne Union Free SD	Malverne
1	n/a	Mamaroneck Union Free SD	Mamaroneck
1	n/a	Manhasset Union Free SD	Manhasset
1	n/a	Marcellus Central SD	Marcellus
1	n/a	Marlboro Central SD	Marlboro
1	n/a	Massapequa Union Free SD	Massapequa
1	n/a	Massena Central SD	Massena
1	n/a	Mattituck-Cutchogue UFSD	Cutchogue
1	n/a	Medina Central SD	Medina
1	n/a	Merrick Union Free SD	Merrick
1	n/a	Mexico Central SD	Mexico
1	n/a	Middle Country Central SD	Centereach
1	n/a	Middletown City SD	Middletown
1	n/a	Miller Place Union Free SD	Miller Place
1	n/a	Mineola Union Free SD	Mineola
1	n/a	Minisink Valley Central SD	Slate Hill
1	n/a	Monroe-Woodbury Central SD	Central Valley
1	n/a	Monticello Central SD	Monticello
1	n/a	Mount Pleasant Central SD	Thornwood
1	n/a	Mount Sinai Union Free SD	Mount Sinai
1	n/a	Mount Vernon City SD	Mount Vernon
1	n/a	Nanuet Union Free SD	Nanuet
1	n/a	New Hartford Central SD	New Hartford
1	n/a	New Hyde Park-Garden City Park	New Hyde Park
1	n/a	New Paltz Central SD	New Paltz
1	n/a	New Rochelle City SD	New Rochelle
1	n/a	New York City Geographic Dist 9	Bronx
1	n/a	New York City Geographic Dist 15	Brooklyn
1	n/a	New York City Public Schools	Brooklyn
1	n/a	Newark Central SD	Newark
1	n/a	Newburgh City SD	Newburgh
1	n/a	Newfane Central SD	Newfane
1	n/a	Niagara Falls City SD	Niagara Falls
1	n/a	Niagara-Wheatfield Central SD	Niagara Falls
1	n/a	Niskayuna Central SD	Schenectady
1	n/a	North Babylon Union Free SD	North Babylon
1	n/a	North Bellmore Union Free SD	Bellmore
1	n/a	North Colonie Central SD	Latham
1	n/a	North Rose-Wolcott Central SD	Wolcott
1	n/a	North Shore Central SD	Sea Cliff
1	n/a	North Syracuse Central SD	N Syracuse
1	n/a	North Tonawanda City SD	N Tonawanda
1	n/a	Northeastern Clinton Central SD	Champlain
1	n/a	Northport-East Northport UFSD	Northport
1	n/a	Norwich City SD	Norwich
1	n/a	Nyack Union Free SD	Nyack
1	n/a	Nyc Alternative HS District	New York
1	n/a	Oceanside Union Free SD	Oceanside
1	n/a	Ogdensburg City SD	Ogdensburg
1	n/a	Olean City SD	Olean
1	n/a	Oneida City SD	Oneida
1	n/a	Oneonta City SD	Oneonta
1	n/a	Onteora Central SD	Boiceville
1	n/a	Orchard Park Central SD	Orchard Park
1	n/a	Ossining Union Free SD	Ossining
1	n/a	Oswego City SD	Oswego
1	n/a	Owego-Apalachin Central SD	Owego
1	n/a	Oyster Bay-East Norwich CSD	Oyster Bay
1	n/a	Palmyra-Macedon Central SD	Palmyra
1	n/a	Patchogue-Medford Union Free SD	Patchogue
1	n/a	Pearl River Union Free SD	Pearl River
1	n/a	Peekskill City SD	Peekskill
1	n/a	Pelham Union Free SD	Pelham
1	n/a	Penfield Central SD	Penfield
1	n/a	Penn Yan Central SD	Penn Yan
1	n/a	Peru Central SD	Peru
1	n/a	Phelps-Clifton Springs Cent SD	Clifton Spgs
1	n/a	Phoenix Central SD	Phoenix
1	n/a	Pine Bush Central SD	Pine Bush
1	n/a	Pittsford Central SD	Pittsford
1	n/a	Plainedge Union Free SD	N Massapequa
1	n/a	Plainview-Old Bethpage Cent SD	Plainview
1	n/a	Plattsburgh City SD	Plattsburgh
1	n/a	Pleasantville Union Free SD	Pleasantville
1	n/a	Port Chester-Rye Union Free SD	Port Chester
1	n/a	Port Jervis City SD	Port Jervis
1	n/a	Port Washington Union Free SD	Pt Washington
1	n/a	Poughkeepsie City SD	Poughkeepsie
1	n/a	Putnam Valley Central SD	Putnam Valley
1	n/a	Queensbury Union Free SD	Queensbury
1	n/a	Ramapo Central SD (Suffern)	Hillburn
1	n/a	Ravena-Coeymans-Selkirk CSD	Selkirk
1	n/a	Red Hook Central SD	Red Hook
1	n/a	Riverhead Central SD	Riverhead
1	n/a	Rochester City SD	Rochester
1	n/a	Rockville Centre Union Free SD	Rockville Ctre
1	n/a	Rocky Point Union Free SD	Rocky Point
1	n/a	Rome City SD	Rome
1	n/a	Rondout Valley Central SD	Accord
1	n/a	Roosevelt Union Free SD	Roosevelt
1	n/a	Roslyn Union Free SD	Roslyn
1	n/a	Rotterdam-Mohonasen Central SD	Schenectady
1	n/a	Royalton-Hartland Central SD	Middleport
1	n/a	Rush-Henrietta Central SD	Henrietta
1	n/a	Rye City SD	Rye
1	n/a	Sachem Central SD	Holbrook
1	n/a	Salamanca City SD	Salamanca
1	n/a	Salmon River Central SD	Ft Covington
1	n/a	Saranac Central SD	Dannemora
1	n/a	Saranac Lake Central SD	Saranac Lake
1	n/a	Saratoga Springs City SD	Saratoga Spgs
1	n/a	Saugerties Central SD	Saugerties
1	n/a	Sayville Union Free SD	Sayville
1	n/a	Scarsdale Union Free SD	Scarsdale
1	n/a	Schalmont Central SD	Schenectady
1	n/a	Schenectady City SD	Schenectady
1	n/a	Schuylerville Central SD	Schuylerville
1	n/a	Scotia-Glenville Central SD	Scotia
1	n/a	Seaford Union Free SD	Seaford
1	n/a	Sewanhaka Central High SD	Floral Park
1	n/a	Shenendehowa Central SD	Clifton Park
1	n/a	Sherburne-Earlville Central SD	Sherburne
1	n/a	Sherrill City SD	Verona
1	n/a	Shoreham-Wading River Central SD	Shoreham
1	n/a	Skaneateles Central SD	Skaneateles
1	n/a	Smithtown Central SD	Smithtown
1	n/a	Solvay Union Free SD	Solvay
1	n/a	Somers Central SD	Lincolndale
1	n/a	South Colonie Central SD	Albany
1	n/a	South Country Central SD	E Patchogue
1	n/a	South Glens Falls Central SD	S Glens Falls
1	n/a	South Huntington Union Free SD	Huntington Stn
1	n/a	South Jefferson Central SD	Adams Center
1	n/a	South Orangetown Central SD	Blauvelt
1	n/a	Southampton Union Free SD	Southampton
1	n/a	Southwestern Cent SD Jamestown	Jamestown
1	n/a	Spackenkill Union Free SD	Poughkeepsie
1	n/a	Spencerport Central SD	Spencerport
1	n/a	Springville-Griffith Inst Cent	Springville
1	n/a	Starpoint Central SD	Lockport
1	n/a	Sullivan West Central SD	Callicoon
1	n/a	Susquehanna Valley Central SD	Conklin
1	n/a	Sweet Home Central SD	Amherst
1	n/a	Syosset Central SD	Syosset
1	n/a	Syracuse City SD	Syracuse
1	n/a	Taconic Hills Central SD	Craryville
1	n/a	Three Village Central SD	East Setauket
1	n/a	Tonawanda City SD	Tonawanda
1	n/a	Troy City SD	Troy
1	n/a	Union Free SD of the Tarrytowns	Sleepy Hollow
1	n/a	Union-Endicott Central SD	Endicott
1	n/a	Uniondale Union Free SD	Uniondale
1	n/a	Utica City SD	Utica
1	n/a	Valley Central SD (Montgomery)	Montgomery
1	n/a	Valley Stream 13 Union Free SD	Valley Stream
1	n/a	Valley Stream 30 Union Free SD	Valley Stream
1	n/a	Valley Stream Central High SD	Valley Stream
1	n/a	Vestal Central SD	Vestal
1	n/a	Victor Central SD	Victor
1	n/a	Wallkill Central SD	Wallkill
1	n/a	Wantagh Union Free SD	Wantagh
1	n/a	Wappingers Central SD	Wappingers Fls
1	n/a	Warwick Valley Central SD	Warwick
1	n/a	Washingtonville Central SD	Washingtonville
1	n/a	Waterloo Central SD	Waterloo
1	n/a	Watertown City SD	Watertown
1	n/a	Watkins Glen Central SD	Watkins Glen
1	n/a	Waverly Central SD	Waverly
1	n/a	Wayland-Cohocton Central SD	Wayland
1	n/a	Wayne Central SD	Ontario Center

1	n/a	Webster Central SD	Webster
1	n/a	West Babylon Union Free SD	West Babylon
1	n/a	West Genesee Central SD	Camillus
1	n/a	West Hempstead Union Free SD	W Hempstead
1	n/a	West Irondequoit Central SD	Rochester
1	n/a	West Islip Union Free SD	West Islip
1	n/a	West Seneca Central SD	West Seneca
1	n/a	Westbury Union Free SD	Old Westbury
1	n/a	Westhampton Beach Union Free SD	Westhampton Bch
1	n/a	Westhill Central SD	Syracuse
1	n/a	White Plains City SD	White Plains
1	n/a	Whitesboro Central SD	Yorkville
1	n/a	Whitney Point Central SD	Whitney Point
1	n/a	William Floyd Union Free SD	Mastic Beach
1	n/a	Williamsville Central SD	East Amherst
1	n/a	Wilson Central SD	Wilson
1	n/a	Windsor Central SD	Windsor
1	n/a	Wyandanch Union Free SD	Wyandanch
1	n/a	Yonkers City SD	Yonkers
1	n/a	Yorkshire-Pioneer Central SD	Yorkshire
1	n/a	Yorktown Central SD	Yorktown Hgts

English Language Learner Students

Rank	Percent	District Name	City
1	n/a	Adirondack Central SD	Boonville
1	n/a	Akron Central SD	Akron
1	n/a	Albany City SD	Albany
1	n/a	Albion Central SD	Albion
1	n/a	Alden Central SD	Alden
1	n/a	Altmar-Parish-Williamstown CSD	Parish
1	n/a	Amherst Central SD	Amherst
1	n/a	Amityville Union Free SD	Amityville
1	n/a	Amsterdam City SD	Amsterdam
1	n/a	Ardsley Union Free SD	Ardsley
1	n/a	Arlington Central SD	Poughkeepsie
1	n/a	Attica Central SD	Attica
1	n/a	Auburn City SD	Auburn
1	n/a	Averill Park Central SD	Averill Park
1	n/a	Babylon Union Free SD	Babylon
1	n/a	Baldwin Union Free SD	Baldwin
1	n/a	Baldwinsville Central SD	Baldwinsville
1	n/a	Ballston Spa Central SD	Ballston Spa
1	n/a	Batavia City SD	Batavia
1	n/a	Bath Central SD	Bath
1	n/a	Bay Shore Union Free SD	Bay Shore
1	n/a	Bayport-Blue Point Union Free SD	Bayport
1	n/a	Beacon City SD	Beacon
1	n/a	Bedford Central SD	Mount Kisco
1	n/a	Beekmantown Central SD	West Chazy
1	n/a	Bellmore-Merrick Central High SD	North Merrick
1	n/a	Bethlehem Central SD	Delmar
1	n/a	Bethpage Union Free SD	Bethpage
1	n/a	Binghamton City SD	Binghamton
1	n/a	Boces Eastern Suffolk	Patchogue
1	n/a	Boces Nassau	Garden City
1	n/a	Brentwood Union Free SD	Brentwood
1	n/a	Brewster Central SD	Brewster
1	n/a	Briarcliff Manor Union Free SD	Briarcliff Manor
1	n/a	Brighton Central SD	Rochester
1	n/a	Broadalbin-Perth Central SD	Broadalbin
1	n/a	Brockport Central SD	Brockport
1	n/a	Brookhaven-Comsewogue UFSD	Pt Jefferson Stn
1	n/a	Buffalo City SD	Buffalo
1	n/a	Burnt Hls-Ballston Lake Cent SD	Scotia
1	n/a	Byram Hills Central SD	Armonk
1	n/a	Cairo-Durham Central SD	Cairo
1	n/a	Camden Central SD	Camden
1	n/a	Canandaigua City SD	Canandaigua
1	n/a	Canastota Central SD	Canastota
1	n/a	Canton Central SD	Canton
1	n/a	Carle Place Union Free SD	Carle Place
1	n/a	Carmel Central SD	Patterson
1	n/a	Carthage Central SD	Carthage
1	n/a	Catskill Central SD	Catskill
1	n/a	Cazenovia Central SD	Cazenovia
1	n/a	Central Islip Union Free SD	Central Islip
1	n/a	Central Square Central SD	Central Square
1	n/a	Chappaqua Central SD	Chappaqua
1	n/a	Chatham Central SD	Chatham
1	n/a	Cheektowaga Central SD	Cheektowaga
1	n/a	Cheektowaga-Maryvale UFSD	Cheektowaga
1	n/a	Cheektowaga-Sloan Union Free SD	Sloan
1	n/a	Chenango Forks Central SD	Binghamton
1	n/a	Chenango Valley Central SD	Binghamton
1	n/a	Chittenango Central SD	Chittenango
1	n/a	Churchville-Chili Central SD	Churchville
1	n/a	Clarence Central SD	Clarence
1	n/a	Clarkstown Central SD	New City
1	n/a	Cleveland Hill Union Free SD	Cheektowaga
1	n/a	Clinton Central SD	Clinton
1	n/a	Cobleskill-Richmondville CSD	Cobleskill
1	n/a	Cohoes City SD	Cohoes
1	n/a	Cold Spring Harbor Central SD	Cold Sprg Harbor
1	n/a	Commack Union Free SD	E Northport
1	n/a	Connetquot Central SD	Bohemia
1	n/a	Copiague Union Free SD	Copiague
1	n/a	Corning City SD	Painted Post
1	n/a	Cornwall Central SD	Cornwall-on-Hud
1	n/a	Cortland City SD	Cortland
1	n/a	Coxsackie-Athens Central SD	Coxsackie
1	n/a	Croton-Harmon Union Free SD	Croton-On-Hud
1	n/a	Dansville Central SD	Dansville
1	n/a	Deer Park Union Free SD	Deer Park
1	n/a	Depew Union Free SD	Depew
1	n/a	Dover Union Free SD	Dover Plains
1	n/a	Dryden Central SD	Dryden
1	n/a	Dunkirk City SD	Dunkirk
1	n/a	East Aurora Union Free SD	East Aurora
1	n/a	East Greenbush Central SD	E Greenbush
1	n/a	East Hampton Union Free SD	East Hampton
1	n/a	East Irondequoit Central SD	Rochester
1	n/a	East Islip Union Free SD	Islip Terrace
1	n/a	East Meadow Union Free SD	Westbury
1	n/a	E Ramapo Central SD (Sprg Val)	Spring Valley
1	n/a	East Syracuse-Minoa Central SD	East Syracuse
1	n/a	East Williston Union Free SD	Old Westbury
1	n/a	Eastchester Union Free SD	Eastchester
1	n/a	Eden Central SD	Eden
1	n/a	Edgemont Union Free SD	Scarsdale
1	n/a	Ellenville Central SD	Ellenville
1	n/a	Elmira City SD	Elmira
1	n/a	Elmont Union Free SD	Elmont
1	n/a	Elwood Union Free SD	Greenlawn
1	n/a	Evans-Brant Cent SD (Lake Shore)	Angola
1	n/a	Fairport Central SD	Fairport
1	n/a	Farmingdale Union Free SD	Farmingdale
1	n/a	Fayetteville-Manlius Central SD	Manlius
1	n/a	Floral Park-Bellerose UFSD	Floral Park
1	n/a	Fonda-Fultonville Central SD	Fonda
1	n/a	Franklin Square Union Free SD	Franklin Square
1	n/a	Fredonia Central SD	Fredonia
1	n/a	Freeport Union Free SD	Freeport
1	n/a	Frontier Central SD	Hamburg
1	n/a	Fulton City SD	Fulton
1	n/a	Garden City Union Free SD	Garden City
1	n/a	Gates-Chili Central SD	Rochester
1	n/a	General Brown Central SD	Dexter
1	n/a	Geneva City SD	Geneva
1	n/a	Glen Cove City SD	Glen Cove
1	n/a	Glens Falls City SD	Glens Falls
1	n/a	Gloversville City SD	Gloversville
1	n/a	Gorham-Middlesex CSD (M Whitman)	Rushville
1	n/a	Goshen Central SD	Goshen
1	n/a	Gouverneur Central SD	Gouverneur
1	n/a	Gowanda Central SD	Gowanda
1	n/a	Grand Island Central SD	Grand Island
1	n/a	Great Neck Union Free SD	Great Neck
1	n/a	Greece Central SD	Rochester
1	n/a	Greenburgh Central SD	Hartsdale
1	n/a	Guilderland Central SD	Guilderland
1	n/a	Half Hollow Hills Central SD	Dix Hills
1	n/a	Hamburg Central SD	Hamburg
1	n/a	Hampton Bays Union Free SD	Hampton Bays
1	n/a	Hannibal Central SD	Hannibal
1	n/a	Harborfields Central SD	Greenlawn
1	n/a	Harrison Central SD	Harrison
1	n/a	Hastings-On-Hudson Union Free SD	Hastings-on-Hud
1	n/a	Hauppauge Union Free SD	Hauppauge
1	n/a	Haverstraw-Stony Point Cent SD	Garnerville
1	n/a	Hempstead Union Free SD	Hempstead
1	n/a	Hendrick Hudson Central SD	Montrose
1	n/a	Herricks Union Free SD	New Hyde Park
1	n/a	Hewlett-Woodmere Union Free SD	Woodmere
1	n/a	Hicksville Union Free SD	Hicksville
1	n/a	Highland Central SD	Highland
1	n/a	Hilton Central SD	Hilton
1	n/a	Holland Patent Central SD	Holland Patent
1	n/a	Homer Central SD	Homer
1	n/a	Honeoye Falls-Lima Central SD	Honeoye Falls
1	n/a	Hornell City SD	Hornell
1	n/a	Horseheads Central SD	Horseheads
1	n/a	Hudson City SD	Hudson
1	n/a	Hudson Falls Central SD	Hudson Falls
1	n/a	Huntington Union Free SD	Huntington Stn
1	n/a	Hyde Park Central SD	Poughkeepsie
1	n/a	Ilion Central SD	Ilion
1	n/a	Indian River Central SD	Philadelphia
1	n/a	Iroquois Central SD	Elma
1	n/a	Irvington Union Free SD	Irvington
1	n/a	Island Trees Union Free SD	Levittown
1	n/a	Islip Union Free SD	Islip
1	n/a	Ithaca City SD	Ithaca
1	n/a	Jamestown City SD	Jamestown
1	n/a	Jamesville-Dewitt Central SD	Dewitt
1	n/a	Jericho Union Free SD	Jericho
1	n/a	Johnson City Central SD	Johnson City
1	n/a	Johnstown City SD	Johnstown
1	n/a	Jordan-Elbridge Central SD	Jordan
1	n/a	Katonah-Lewisboro Union Free SD	South Salem
1	n/a	Kenmore-Tonawanda Union Free SD	Buffalo
1	n/a	Kinderhook Central SD	Valatie
1	n/a	Kings Park Central SD	Kings Park
1	n/a	Kingston City SD	Kingston
1	n/a	Lackawanna City SD	Lackawanna
1	n/a	Lakeland Central SD	Shrub Oak
1	n/a	Lancaster Central SD	Lancaster
1	n/a	Lansing Central SD	Lansing
1	n/a	Lansingburgh Central SD	Troy
1	n/a	Lawrence Union Free SD	Lawrence
1	n/a	Levittown Union Free SD	Levittown
1	n/a	Lewiston-Porter Central SD	Youngstown
1	n/a	Liberty Central SD	Liberty
1	n/a	Lindenhurst Union Free SD	Lindenhurst
1	n/a	Liverpool Central SD	Liverpool
1	n/a	Livonia Central SD	Livonia
1	n/a	Lockport City SD	Lockport
1	n/a	Locust Valley Central SD	Locust Valley
1	n/a	Long Beach City SD	Long Beach
1	n/a	Longwood Central SD	Middle Island
1	n/a	Lynbrook Union Free SD	Lynbrook
1	n/a	Mahopac Central SD	Mahopac
1	n/a	Maine-Endwell Central SD	Endwell
1	n/a	Malone Central SD	Malone
1	n/a	Malverne Union Free SD	Malverne
1	n/a	Mamaroneck Union Free SD	Mamaroneck
1	n/a	Manhasset Union Free SD	Manhasset
1	n/a	Marcellus Central SD	Marcellus
1	n/a	Marlboro Central SD	Marlboro
1	n/a	Massapequa Union Free SD	Massapequa
1	n/a	Massena Central SD	Massena
1	n/a	Mattituck-Cutchogue UFSD	Cutchogue
1	n/a	Medina Central SD	Medina
1	n/a	Merrick Union Free SD	Merrick
1	n/a	Mexico Central SD	Mexico
1	n/a	Middle Country Central SD	Centereach
1	n/a	Middletown City SD	Middletown
1	n/a	Miller Place Union Free SD	Miller Place
1	n/a	Mineola Union Free SD	Mineola
1	n/a	Minisink Valley Central SD	Slate Hill
1	n/a	Monroe-Woodbury Central SD	Central Valley
1	n/a	Monticello Central SD	Monticello
1	n/a	Mount Pleasant Central SD	Thornwood
1	n/a	Mount Sinai Union Free SD	Mount Sinai
1	n/a	Mount Vernon City SD	Mount Vernon
1	n/a	Nanuet Union Free SD	Nanuet
1	n/a	New Hartford Central SD	New Hartford
1	n/a	New Hyde Park-Garden City Park	New Hyde Park
1	n/a	New Paltz Central SD	New Paltz
1	n/a	New Rochelle City SD	New Rochelle
1	n/a	New York City Geographic Dist 9	Bronx
1	n/a	New York City Geographic Dist 15	Brooklyn
1	n/a	New York City Public Schools	Brooklyn
1	n/a	Newark Central SD	Newark
1	n/a	Newburgh City SD	Newburgh
1	n/a	Newfane Central SD	Newfane
1	n/a	Niagara Falls City SD	Niagara Falls
1	n/a	Niagara-Wheatfield Central SD	Niagara Falls
1	n/a	Niskayuna Central SD	Schenectady
1	n/a	North Babylon Union Free SD	North Babylon
1	n/a	North Bellmore Union Free SD	Bellmore
1	n/a	North Colonie Central SD	Latham
1	n/a	North Rose-Wolcott Central SD	Wolcott
1	n/a	North Shore Central SD	Sea Cliff
1	n/a	North Syracuse Central SD	N Syracuse
1	n/a	North Tonawanda City SD	N Tonawanda
1	n/a	Northeastern Clinton Central SD	Champlain
1	n/a	Northport-East Northport UFSD	Northport
1	n/a	Norwich City SD	Norwich
1	n/a	Nyack Union Free SD	Nyack
1	n/a	Nyc Alternative HS District	New York
1	n/a	Oceanside Union Free SD	Oceanside
1	n/a	Ogdensburg City SD	Ogdensburg
1	n/a	Olean City SD	Olean
1	n/a	Oneida City SD	Oneida
1	n/a	Oneonta City SD	Oneonta
1	n/a	Onteora Central SD	Boiceville
1	n/a	Orchard Park Central SD	Orchard Park
1	n/a	Ossining Union Free SD	Ossining
1	n/a	Oswego City SD	Oswego
1	n/a	Owego-Apalachin Central SD	Owego
1	n/a	Oyster Bay-East Norwich CSD	Oyster Bay
1	n/a	Palmyra-Macedon Central SD	Palmyra
1	n/a	Patchogue-Medford Union Free SD	Patchogue
1	n/a	Pearl River Union Free SD	Pearl River
1	n/a	Peekskill City SD	Peekskill
1	n/a	Pelham Union Free SD	Pelham
1	n/a	Penfield Central SD	Penfield

1	n/a	Penn Yan Central SD	Penn Yan
1	n/a	Peru Central SD	Peru
1	n/a	Phelps-Clifton Springs Cent SD	Clifton Spgs
1	n/a	Phoenix Central SD	Phoenix
1	n/a	Pine Bush Central SD	Pine Bush
1	n/a	Pittsford Central SD	Pittsford
1	n/a	Plainedge Union Free SD	N Massapequa
1	n/a	Plainview-Old Bethpage Cent SD	Plainview
1	n/a	Plattsburgh City SD	Plattsburgh
1	n/a	Pleasantville Union Free SD	Pleasantville
1	n/a	Port Chester-Rye Union Free SD	Port Chester
1	n/a	Port Jervis City SD	Port Jervis
1	n/a	Port Washington Union Free SD	Pt Washington
1	n/a	Poughkeepsie City SD	Poughkeepsie
1	n/a	Putnam Valley Central SD	Putnam Valley
1	n/a	Queensbury Union Free SD	Queensbury
1	n/a	Ramapo Central SD (Suffern)	Hillburn
1	n/a	Ravena-Coeymans-Selkirk CSD	Selkirk
1	n/a	Red Hook Central SD	Red Hook
1	n/a	Riverhead Central SD	Riverhead
1	n/a	Rochester City SD	Rochester
1	n/a	Rockville Centre Union Free SD	Rockville Ctre
1	n/a	Rocky Point Union Free SD	Rocky Point
1	n/a	Rome City SD	Rome
1	n/a	Rondout Valley Central SD	Accord
1	n/a	Roosevelt Union Free SD	Roosevelt
1	n/a	Roslyn Union Free SD	Roslyn
1	n/a	Rotterdam-Mohonasen Central SD	Schenectady
1	n/a	Royalton-Hartland Central SD	Middleport
1	n/a	Rush-Henrietta Central SD	Henrietta
1	n/a	Rye City SD	Rye
1	n/a	Sachem Central SD	Holbrook
1	n/a	Salamanca City SD	Salamanca
1	n/a	Salmon River Central SD	Ft Covington
1	n/a	Saranac Central SD	Dannemora
1	n/a	Saranac Lake Central SD	Saranac Lake
1	n/a	Saratoga Springs City SD	Saratoga Spgs
1	n/a	Saugerties Central SD	Saugerties
1	n/a	Sayville Union Free SD	Sayville
1	n/a	Scarsdale Union Free SD	Scarsdale
1	n/a	Schalmont Central SD	Schenectady
1	n/a	Schenectady City SD	Schenectady
1	n/a	Schuylerville Central SD	Schuylerville
1	n/a	Scotia-Glenville Central SD	Scotia
1	n/a	Seaford Union Free SD	Seaford
1	n/a	Sewanhaka Central High SD	Floral Park
1	n/a	Shenendehowa Central SD	Clifton Park
1	n/a	Sherburne-Earlville Central SD	Sherburne
1	n/a	Sherrill City SD	Verona
1	n/a	Shoreham-Wading River Central SD	Shoreham
1	n/a	Skaneateles Central SD	Skaneateles
1	n/a	Smithtown Central SD	Smithtown
1	n/a	Solvay Union Free SD	Solvay
1	n/a	Somers Central SD	Lincolndale
1	n/a	South Colonie Central SD	Albany
1	n/a	South Country Central SD	E Patchogue
1	n/a	South Glens Falls Central SD	S Glens Falls
1	n/a	South Huntington Union Free SD	Huntington Stn
1	n/a	South Jefferson Central SD	Adams Center
1	n/a	South Orangetown Central SD	Blauvelt
1	n/a	Southampton Union Free SD	Southampton
1	n/a	Southwestern Cent SD Jamestown	Jamestown
1	n/a	Spackenkill Union Free SD	Poughkeepsie
1	n/a	Spencerport Central SD	Spencerport
1	n/a	Springville-Griffith Inst Cent	Springville
1	n/a	Starpoint Central SD	Lockport
1	n/a	Sullivan West Central SD	Callicoon
1	n/a	Susquehanna Valley Central SD	Conklin
1	n/a	Sweet Home Central SD	Amherst
1	n/a	Syosset Central SD	Syosset
1	n/a	Syracuse City SD	Syracuse
1	n/a	Taconic Hills Central SD	Craryville
1	n/a	Three Village Central SD	East Setauket
1	n/a	Tonawanda City SD	Tonawanda
1	n/a	Troy City SD	Troy
1	n/a	Union Free SD of the Tarrytowns	Sleepy Hollow
1	n/a	Union-Endicott Central SD	Endicott
1	n/a	Uniondale Union Free SD	Uniondale
1	n/a	Utica City SD	Utica
1	n/a	Valley Central SD (Montgomery)	Montgomery
1	n/a	Valley Stream 13 Union Free SD	Valley Stream
1	n/a	Valley Stream 30 Union Free SD	Valley Stream
1	n/a	Valley Stream Central High SD	Valley Stream
1	n/a	Vestal Central SD	Vestal
1	n/a	Victor Central SD	Victor
1	n/a	Wallkill Central SD	Wallkill
1	n/a	Wantagh Union Free SD	Wantagh
1	n/a	Wappingers Central SD	Wappingers Fls
1	n/a	Warwick Valley Central SD	Warwick
1	n/a	Washingtonville Central SD	Washingtonville
1	n/a	Waterloo Central SD	Waterloo
1	n/a	Watertown City SD	Watertown
1	n/a	Watkins Glen Central SD	Watkins Glen
1	n/a	Waverly Central SD	Waverly
1	n/a	Wayland-Cohocton Central SD	Wayland
1	n/a	Wayne Central SD	Ontario Center
1	n/a	Webster Central SD	Webster
1	n/a	West Babylon Union Free SD	West Babylon
1	n/a	West Genesee Central SD	Camillus
1	n/a	West Hempstead Union Free SD	W Hempstead
1	n/a	West Irondequoit Central SD	Rochester
1	n/a	West Islip Union Free SD	West Islip
1	n/a	West Seneca Central SD	West Seneca
1	n/a	Westbury Union Free SD	Old Westbury
1	n/a	Westhampton Beach Union Free SD	Westhampton Bch
1	n/a	Westhill Central SD	Syracuse
1	n/a	White Plains City SD	White Plains
1	n/a	Whitesboro Central SD	Yorkville
1	n/a	Whitney Point Central SD	Whitney Point
1	n/a	William Floyd Union Free SD	Mastic Beach
1	n/a	Williamsville Central SD	East Amherst
1	n/a	Wilson Central SD	Wilson
1	n/a	Windsor Central SD	Windsor
1	n/a	Wyandanch Union Free SD	Wyandanch
1	n/a	Yonkers City SD	Yonkers
1	n/a	Yorkshire-Pioneer Central SD	Yorkshire
1	n/a	Yorktown Central SD	Yorktown Hgts

Migrant Students

Rank	Percent	District Name	City
1	n/a	Adirondack Central SD	Boonville
1	n/a	Akron Central SD	Akron
1	n/a	Albany City SD	Albany
1	n/a	Albion Central SD	Albion
1	n/a	Alden Central SD	Alden
1	n/a	Altmar-Parish-Williamstown CSD	Parish
1	n/a	Amherst Central SD	Amherst
1	n/a	Amityville Union Free SD	Amityville
1	n/a	Amsterdam City SD	Amsterdam
1	n/a	Ardsley Union Free SD	Ardsley
1	n/a	Arlington Central SD	Poughkeepsie
1	n/a	Attica Central SD	Attica
1	n/a	Auburn City SD	Auburn
1	n/a	Averill Park Central SD	Averill Park
1	n/a	Babylon Union Free SD	Babylon
1	n/a	Baldwin Union Free SD	Baldwin
1	n/a	Baldwinsville Central SD	Baldwinsville
1	n/a	Ballston Spa Central SD	Ballston Spa
1	n/a	Batavia City SD	Batavia
1	n/a	Bath Central SD	Bath
1	n/a	Bay Shore Union Free SD	Bay Shore
1	n/a	Bayport-Blue Point Union Free SD	Bayport
1	n/a	Beacon City SD	Beacon
1	n/a	Bedford Central SD	Mount Kisco
1	n/a	Beekmantown Central SD	West Chazy
1	n/a	Bellmore-Merrick Central High SD	North Merrick
1	n/a	Bethlehem Central SD	Delmar
1	n/a	Bethpage Union Free SD	Bethpage
1	n/a	Binghamton City SD	Binghamton
1	n/a	Boces Eastern Suffolk	Patchogue
1	n/a	Boces Nassau	Garden City
1	n/a	Brentwood Union Free SD	Brentwood
1	n/a	Brewster Central SD	Brewster
1	n/a	Briarcliff Manor Union Free SD	Briarcliff Manor
1	n/a	Brighton Central SD	Rochester
1	n/a	Broadalbin-Perth Central SD	Broadalbin
1	n/a	Brockport Central SD	Brockport
1	n/a	Brookhaven-Comsewogue UFSD	Pt Jefferson Stn
1	n/a	Buffalo City SD	Buffalo
1	n/a	Burnt Hls-Ballston Lake Cent SD	Scotia
1	n/a	Byram Hills Central SD	Armonk
1	n/a	Cairo-Durham Central SD	Cairo
1	n/a	Camden Central SD	Camden
1	n/a	Canandaigua City SD	Canandaigua
1	n/a	Canastota Central SD	Canastota
1	n/a	Canton Central SD	Canton
1	n/a	Carle Place Union Free SD	Carle Place
1	n/a	Carmel Central SD	Patterson
1	n/a	Carthage Central SD	Carthage
1	n/a	Catskill Central SD	Catskill
1	n/a	Cazenovia Central SD	Cazenovia
1	n/a	Central Islip Union Free SD	Central Islip
1	n/a	Central Square Central SD	Central Square
1	n/a	Chappaqua Central SD	Chappaqua
1	n/a	Chatham Central SD	Chatham
1	n/a	Cheektowaga Central SD	Cheektowaga
1	n/a	Cheektowaga-Maryvale UFSD	Cheektowaga
1	n/a	Cheektowaga-Sloan Union Free SD	Sloan
1	n/a	Chenango Forks Central SD	Binghamton
1	n/a	Chenango Valley Central SD	Binghamton
1	n/a	Chittenango Central SD	Chittenango
1	n/a	Churchville-Chili Central SD	Churchville
1	n/a	Clarence Central SD	Clarence
1	n/a	Clarkstown Central SD	New City
1	n/a	Cleveland Hill Union Free SD	Cheektowaga
1	n/a	Clinton Central SD	Clinton
1	n/a	Cobleskill-Richmondville CSD	Cobleskill
1	n/a	Cohoes City SD	Cohoes
1	n/a	Cold Spring Harbor Central SD	Cold Sprg Harbor
1	n/a	Commack Union Free SD	E Northport
1	n/a	Connetquot Central SD	Bohemia
1	n/a	Copiague Union Free SD	Copiague
1	n/a	Corning City SD	Painted Post
1	n/a	Cornwall Central SD	Cornwall-on-Hud
1	n/a	Cortland City SD	Cortland
1	n/a	Coxsackie-Athens Central SD	Coxsackie
1	n/a	Croton-Harmon Union Free SD	Croton-On-Hud
1	n/a	Dansville Central SD	Dansville
1	n/a	Deer Park Union Free SD	Deer Park
1	n/a	Depew Union Free SD	Depew
1	n/a	Dover Union Free SD	Dover Plains
1	n/a	Dryden Central SD	Dryden
1	n/a	Dunkirk City SD	Dunkirk
1	n/a	East Aurora Union Free SD	East Aurora
1	n/a	East Greenbush Central SD	E Greenbush
1	n/a	East Hampton Union Free SD	East Hampton
1	n/a	East Irondequoit Central SD	Rochester
1	n/a	East Islip Union Free SD	Islip Terrace
1	n/a	East Meadow Union Free SD	Westbury
1	n/a	E Ramapo Central SD (Sprg Val)	Spring Valley
1	n/a	East Syracuse-Minoa Central SD	East Syracuse
1	n/a	East Williston Union Free SD	Old Westbury
1	n/a	Eastchester Union Free SD	Eastchester
1	n/a	Eden Central SD	Eden
1	n/a	Edgemont Union Free SD	Scarsdale
1	n/a	Ellenville Central SD	Ellenville
1	n/a	Elmira City SD	Elmira
1	n/a	Elmont Union Free SD	Elmont
1	n/a	Elwood Union Free SD	Greenlawn
1	n/a	Evans-Brant Cent SD (Lake Shore)	Angola
1	n/a	Fairport Central SD	Fairport
1	n/a	Farmingdale Union Free SD	Farmingdale
1	n/a	Fayetteville-Manlius Central SD	Manlius
1	n/a	Floral Park-Bellerose UFSD	Floral Park
1	n/a	Fonda-Fultonville Central SD	Fonda
1	n/a	Franklin Square Union Free SD	Franklin Square
1	n/a	Fredonia Central SD	Fredonia
1	n/a	Freeport Union Free SD	Freeport
1	n/a	Frontier Central SD	Hamburg
1	n/a	Fulton City SD	Fulton
1	n/a	Garden City Union Free SD	Garden City
1	n/a	Gates-Chili Central SD	Rochester
1	n/a	General Brown Central SD	Dexter
1	n/a	Geneva City SD	Geneva
1	n/a	Glen Cove City SD	Glen Cove
1	n/a	Glens Falls City SD	Glens Falls
1	n/a	Gloversville City SD	Gloversville
1	n/a	Gorham-Middlesex CSD (M Whitman)	Rushville
1	n/a	Goshen Central SD	Goshen
1	n/a	Gouverneur Central SD	Gouverneur
1	n/a	Gowanda Central SD	Gowanda
1	n/a	Grand Island Central SD	Grand Island
1	n/a	Great Neck Union Free SD	Great Neck
1	n/a	Greece Central SD	Rochester
1	n/a	Greenburgh Central SD	Hartsdale
1	n/a	Guilderland Central SD	Guilderland
1	n/a	Half Hollow Hills Central SD	Dix Hills
1	n/a	Hamburg Central SD	Hamburg
1	n/a	Hampton Bays Union Free SD	Hampton Bays
1	n/a	Hannibal Central SD	Hannibal
1	n/a	Harborfields Central SD	Greenlawn
1	n/a	Harrison Central SD	Harrison
1	n/a	Hastings-On-Hudson Union Free SD	Hastings-on-Hud
1	n/a	Hauppauge Union Free SD	Hauppauge
1	n/a	Haverstraw-Stony Point Cent SD	Garnerville
1	n/a	Hempstead Union Free SD	Hempstead
1	n/a	Hendrick Hudson Central SD	Montrose
1	n/a	Herricks Union Free SD	New Hyde Park
1	n/a	Hewlett-Woodmere Union Free SD	Woodmere
1	n/a	Hicksville Union Free SD	Hicksville
1	n/a	Highland Central SD	Highland
1	n/a	Hilton Central SD	Hilton
1	n/a	Holland Patent Central SD	Holland Patent
1	n/a	Homer Central SD	Homer
1	n/a	Honeoye Falls-Lima Central SD	Honeoye Falls
1	n/a	Hornell City SD	Hornell
1	n/a	Horseheads Central SD	Horseheads
1	n/a	Hudson City SD	Hudson
1	n/a	Hudson Falls Central SD	Hudson Falls
1	n/a	Huntington Union Free SD	Huntington Stn
1	n/a	Hyde Park Central SD	Poughkeepsie
1	n/a	Ilion Central SD	Ilion
1	n/a	Indian River Central SD	Philadelphia
1	n/a	Iroquois Central SD	Elma
1	n/a	Irvington Union Free SD	Irvington
1	n/a	Island Trees Union Free SD	Levittown
1	n/a	Islip Union Free SD	Islip

1	n/a	Ithaca City SD	Ithaca
1	n/a	Jamestown City SD	Jamestown
1	n/a	Jamesville-Dewitt Central SD	Dewitt
1	n/a	Jericho Union Free SD	Jericho
1	n/a	Johnson City Central SD	Johnson City
1	n/a	Johnstown City SD	Johnstown
1	n/a	Jordan-Elbridge Central SD	Jordan
1	n/a	Katonah-Lewisboro Union Free SD	South Salem
1	n/a	Kenmore-Tonawanda Union Free SD	Buffalo
1	n/a	Kinderhook Central SD	Valatie
1	n/a	Kings Park Central SD	Kings Park
1	n/a	Kingston City SD	Kingston
1	n/a	Lackawanna City SD	Lackawanna
1	n/a	Lakeland Central SD	Shrub Oak
1	n/a	Lancaster Central SD	Lancaster
1	n/a	Lansing Central SD	Lansing
1	n/a	Lansingburgh Central SD	Troy
1	n/a	Lawrence Union Free SD	Lawrence
1	n/a	Levittown Union Free SD	Levittown
1	n/a	Lewiston-Porter Central SD	Youngstown
1	n/a	Liberty Central SD	Liberty
1	n/a	Lindenhurst Union Free SD	Lindenhurst
1	n/a	Liverpool Central SD	Liverpool
1	n/a	Livonia Central SD	Livonia
1	n/a	Lockport City SD	Lockport
1	n/a	Locust Valley Central SD	Locust Valley
1	n/a	Long Beach City SD	Long Beach
1	n/a	Longwood Central SD	Middle Island
1	n/a	Lynbrook Union Free SD	Lynbrook
1	n/a	Mahopac Central SD	Mahopac
1	n/a	Maine-Endwell Central SD	Endwell
1	n/a	Malone Central SD	Malone
1	n/a	Malverne Union Free SD	Malverne
1	n/a	Mamaroneck Union Free SD	Mamaroneck
1	n/a	Manhasset Union Free SD	Manhasset
1	n/a	Marcellus Central SD	Marcellus
1	n/a	Marlboro Central SD	Marlboro
1	n/a	Massapequa Union Free SD	Massapequa
1	n/a	Massena Central SD	Massena
1	n/a	Mattituck-Cutchogue UFSD	Cutchogue
1	n/a	Medina Central SD	Medina
1	n/a	Merrick Union Free SD	Merrick
1	n/a	Mexico Central SD	Mexico
1	n/a	Middle Country Central SD	Centereach
1	n/a	Middletown City SD	Middletown
1	n/a	Miller Place Union Free SD	Miller Place
1	n/a	Mineola Union Free SD	Mineola
1	n/a	Minisink Valley Central SD	Slate Hill
1	n/a	Monroe-Woodbury Central SD	Central Valley
1	n/a	Monticello Central SD	Monticello
1	n/a	Mount Pleasant Central SD	Thornwood
1	n/a	Mount Sinai Union Free SD	Mount Sinai
1	n/a	Mount Vernon City SD	Mount Vernon
1	n/a	Nanuet Union Free SD	Nanuet
1	n/a	New Hartford Central SD	New Hartford
1	n/a	New Hyde Park-Garden City Park	New Hyde Park
1	n/a	New Paltz Central SD	New Paltz
1	n/a	New Rochelle City SD	New Rochelle
1	n/a	New York City Geographic Dist 9	Bronx
1	n/a	New York City Geographic Dist 15	Brooklyn
1	n/a	New York City Public Schools	Brooklyn
1	n/a	Newark Central SD	Newark
1	n/a	Newburgh City SD	Newburgh
1	n/a	Newfane Central SD	Newfane
1	n/a	Niagara Falls City SD	Niagara Falls
1	n/a	Niagara-Wheatfield Central SD	Niagara Falls
1	n/a	Niskayuna Central SD	Schenectady
1	n/a	North Babylon Union Free SD	North Babylon
1	n/a	North Bellmore Union Free SD	Bellmore
1	n/a	North Colonie Central SD	Latham
1	n/a	North Rose-Wolcott Central SD	Wolcott
1	n/a	North Shore Central SD	Sea Cliff
1	n/a	North Syracuse Central SD	N Syracuse
1	n/a	North Tonawanda City SD	N Tonawanda
1	n/a	Northeastern Clinton Central SD	Champlain
1	n/a	Northport-East Northport UFSD	Northport
1	n/a	Norwich City SD	Norwich
1	n/a	Nyack Union Free SD	Nyack
1	n/a	Nyc Alternative HS District	New York
1	n/a	Oceanside Union Free SD	Oceanside
1	n/a	Ogdensburg City SD	Ogdensburg
1	n/a	Olean City SD	Olean
1	n/a	Oneida City SD	Oneida
1	n/a	Oneonta City SD	Oneonta
1	n/a	Onteora Central SD	Boiceville
1	n/a	Orchard Park Central SD	Orchard Park
1	n/a	Ossining Union Free SD	Ossining
1	n/a	Oswego City SD	Oswego
1	n/a	Owego-Apalachin Central SD	Owego
1	n/a	Oyster Bay-East Norwich CSD	Oyster Bay
1	n/a	Palmyra-Macedon Central SD	Palmyra
1	n/a	Patchogue-Medford Union Free SD	Patchogue
1	n/a	Pearl River Union Free SD	Pearl River
1	n/a	Peekskill City SD	Peekskill
1	n/a	Pelham Union Free SD	Pelham
1	n/a	Penfield Central SD	Penfield
1	n/a	Penn Yan Central SD	Penn Yan
1	n/a	Peru Central SD	Peru
1	n/a	Phelps-Clifton Springs Cent SD	Clifton Spgs
1	n/a	Phoenix Central SD	Phoenix
1	n/a	Pine Bush Central SD	Pine Bush
1	n/a	Pittsford Central SD	Pittsford
1	n/a	Plainedge Union Free SD	N Massapequa
1	n/a	Plainview-Old Bethpage Cent SD	Plainview
1	n/a	Plattsburgh City SD	Plattsburgh
1	n/a	Pleasantville Union Free SD	Pleasantville
1	n/a	Port Chester-Rye Union Free SD	Port Chester
1	n/a	Port Jervis City SD	Port Jervis
1	n/a	Port Washington Union Free SD	Pt Washington
1	n/a	Poughkeepsie City SD	Poughkeepsie
1	n/a	Putnam Valley Central SD	Putnam Valley
1	n/a	Queensbury Union Free SD	Queensbury
1	n/a	Ramapo Central SD (Suffern)	Hillburn
1	n/a	Ravena-Coeymans-Selkirk CSD	Selkirk
1	n/a	Red Hook Central SD	Red Hook
1	n/a	Riverhead Central SD	Riverhead
1	n/a	Rochester City SD	Rochester
1	n/a	Rockville Centre Union Free SD	Rockville Ctre
1	n/a	Rocky Point Union Free SD	Rocky Point
1	n/a	Rome City SD	Rome
1	n/a	Rondout Valley Central SD	Accord
1	n/a	Roosevelt Union Free SD	Roosevelt
1	n/a	Roslyn Union Free SD	Roslyn
1	n/a	Rotterdam-Mohonasen Central SD	Schenectady
1	n/a	Royalton-Hartland Central SD	Middleport
1	n/a	Rush-Henrietta Central SD	Henrietta
1	n/a	Rye City SD	Rye
1	n/a	Sachem Central SD	Holbrook
1	n/a	Salamanca City SD	Salamanca
1	n/a	Salmon River Central SD	Ft Covington
1	n/a	Saranac Central SD	Dannemora
1	n/a	Saranac Lake Central SD	Saranac Lake
1	n/a	Saratoga Springs City SD	Saratoga Spgs
1	n/a	Saugerties Central SD	Saugerties
1	n/a	Sayville Union Free SD	Sayville
1	n/a	Scarsdale Union Free SD	Scarsdale
1	n/a	Schalmont Central SD	Schenectady
1	n/a	Schenectady City SD	Schenectady
1	n/a	Schuylerville Central SD	Schuylerville
1	n/a	Scotia-Glenville Central SD	Scotia
1	n/a	Seaford Union Free SD	Seaford
1	n/a	Sewanhaka Central High SD	Floral Park
1	n/a	Shenendehowa Central SD	Clifton Park
1	n/a	Sherburne-Earlville Central SD	Sherburne
1	n/a	Sherrill City SD	Verona
1	n/a	Shoreham-Wading River Central SD	Shoreham
1	n/a	Skaneateles Central SD	Skaneateles
1	n/a	Smithtown Central SD	Smithtown
1	n/a	Solvay Union Free SD	Solvay
1	n/a	Somers Central SD	Lincolndale
1	n/a	South Colonie Central SD	Albany
1	n/a	South Country Central SD	E Patchogue
1	n/a	South Glens Falls Central SD	S Glens Falls
1	n/a	South Huntington Union Free SD	Huntington Stn
1	n/a	South Jefferson Central SD	Adams Center
1	n/a	South Orangetown Central SD	Blauvelt
1	n/a	Southampton Union Free SD	Southampton
1	n/a	Southwestern Cent SD Jamestown	Jamestown
1	n/a	Spackenkill Union Free SD	Poughkeepsie
1	n/a	Spencerport Central SD	Spencerport
1	n/a	Springville-Griffith Inst Cent	Springville
1	n/a	Starpoint Central SD	Lockport
1	n/a	Sullivan West Central SD	Callicoon
1	n/a	Susquehanna Valley Central SD	Conklin
1	n/a	Sweet Home Central SD	Amherst
1	n/a	Syosset Central SD	Syosset
1	n/a	Syracuse City SD	Syracuse
1	n/a	Taconic Hills Central SD	Craryville
1	n/a	Three Village Central SD	East Setauket
1	n/a	Tonawanda City SD	Tonawanda
1	n/a	Troy City SD	Troy
1	n/a	Union Free SD of the Tarrytowns	Sleepy Hollow
1	n/a	Union-Endicott Central SD	Endicott
1	n/a	Uniondale Union Free SD	Uniondale
1	n/a	Utica City SD	Utica
1	n/a	Valley Central SD (Montgomery)	Montgomery
1	n/a	Valley Stream 13 Union Free SD	Valley Stream
1	n/a	Valley Stream 30 Union Free SD	Valley Stream
1	n/a	Valley Stream Central High SD	Valley Stream
1	n/a	Vestal Central SD	Vestal
1	n/a	Victor Central SD	Victor
1	n/a	Wallkill Central SD	Wallkill
1	n/a	Wantagh Union Free SD	Wantagh
1	n/a	Wappingers Central SD	Wappingers Fls
1	n/a	Warwick Valley Central SD	Warwick
1	n/a	Washingtonville Central SD	Washingtonville
1	n/a	Waterloo Central SD	Waterloo
1	n/a	Watertown City SD	Watertown
1	n/a	Watkins Glen Central SD	Watkins Glen
1	n/a	Waverly Central SD	Waverly
1	n/a	Wayland-Cohocton Central SD	Wayland
1	n/a	Wayne Central SD	Ontario Center
1	n/a	Webster Central SD	Webster
1	n/a	West Babylon Union Free SD	West Babylon
1	n/a	West Genesee Central SD	Camillus
1	n/a	West Hempstead Union Free SD	W Hempstead
1	n/a	West Irondequoit Central SD	Rochester
1	n/a	West Islip Union Free SD	West Islip
1	n/a	West Seneca Central SD	West Seneca
1	n/a	Westbury Union Free SD	Old Westbury
1	n/a	Westhampton Beach Union Free SD	Westhampton Bch
1	n/a	Westhill Central SD	Syracuse
1	n/a	White Plains City SD	White Plains
1	n/a	Whitesboro Central SD	Yorkville
1	n/a	Whitney Point Central SD	Whitney Point
1	n/a	William Floyd Union Free SD	Mastic Beach
1	n/a	Williamsville Central SD	East Amherst
1	n/a	Wilson Central SD	Wilson
1	n/a	Windsor Central SD	Windsor
1	n/a	Wyandanch Union Free SD	Wyandanch
1	n/a	Yonkers City SD	Yonkers
1	n/a	Yorkshire-Pioneer Central SD	Yorkshire
1	n/a	Yorktown Central SD	Yorktown Hgts

Students Eligible for Free Lunch

Rank	Percent	District Name	City
1	n/a	Adirondack Central SD	Boonville
1	n/a	Akron Central SD	Akron
1	n/a	Albany City SD	Albany
1	n/a	Albion Central SD	Albion
1	n/a	Alden Central SD	Alden
1	n/a	Altmar-Parish-Williamstown CSD	Parish
1	n/a	Amherst Central SD	Amherst
1	n/a	Amityville Union Free SD	Amityville
1	n/a	Amsterdam City SD	Amsterdam
1	n/a	Ardsley Union Free SD	Ardsley
1	n/a	Arlington Central SD	Poughkeepsie
1	n/a	Attica Central SD	Attica
1	n/a	Auburn City SD	Auburn
1	n/a	Averill Park Central SD	Averill Park
1	n/a	Babylon Union Free SD	Babylon
1	n/a	Baldwin Union Free SD	Baldwin
1	n/a	Baldwinsville Central SD	Baldwinsville
1	n/a	Ballston Spa Central SD	Ballston Spa
1	n/a	Batavia City SD	Batavia
1	n/a	Bath Central SD	Bath
1	n/a	Bay Shore Union Free SD	Bay Shore
1	n/a	Bayport-Blue Point Union Free SD	Bayport
1	n/a	Beacon City SD	Beacon
1	n/a	Bedford Central SD	Mount Kisco
1	n/a	Beekmantown Central SD	West Chazy
1	n/a	Bellmore-Merrick Central High SD	North Merrick
1	n/a	Bethlehem Central SD	Delmar
1	n/a	Bethpage Union Free SD	Bethpage
1	n/a	Binghamton City SD	Binghamton
1	n/a	Boces Eastern Suffolk	Patchogue
1	n/a	Boces Nassau	Garden City
1	n/a	Brentwood Union Free SD	Brentwood
1	n/a	Brewster Central SD	Brewster
1	n/a	Briarcliff Manor Union Free SD	Briarcliff Manor
1	n/a	Brighton Central SD	Rochester
1	n/a	Broadalbin-Perth Central SD	Broadalbin
1	n/a	Brockport Central SD	Brockport
1	n/a	Brookhaven-Comsewogue UFSD	Pt Jefferson Stn
1	n/a	Buffalo City SD	Buffalo
1	n/a	Burnt Hls-Ballston Lake Cent SD	Scotia
1	n/a	Byram Hills Central SD	Armonk
1	n/a	Cairo-Durham Central SD	Cairo
1	n/a	Camden Central SD	Camden
1	n/a	Canandaigua City SD	Canandaigua
1	n/a	Canastota Central SD	Canastota
1	n/a	Canton Central SD	Canton
1	n/a	Carle Place Union Free SD	Carle Place
1	n/a	Carmel Central SD	Patterson
1	n/a	Carthage Central SD	Carthage
1	n/a	Catskill Central SD	Catskill
1	n/a	Cazenovia Central SD	Cazenovia
1	n/a	Central Islip Union Free SD	Central Islip
1	n/a	Central Square Central SD	Central Square
1	n/a	Chappaqua Central SD	Chappaqua
1	n/a	Chatham Central SD	Chatham
1	n/a	Cheektowaga Central SD	Cheektowaga
1	n/a	Cheektowaga-Maryvale UFSD	Cheektowaga
1	n/a	Cheektowaga-Sloan Union Free SD	Sloan
1	n/a	Chenango Forks Central SD	Binghamton
1	n/a	Chenango Valley Central SD	Binghamton
1	n/a	Chittenango Central SD	Chittenango

1	n/a	Churchville-Chili Central SD	Churchville
1	n/a	Clarence Central SD	Clarence
1	n/a	Clarkstown Central SD	New City
1	n/a	Cleveland Hill Union Free SD	Cheektowaga
1	n/a	Clinton Central SD	Clinton
1	n/a	Cobleskill-Richmondville CSD	Cobleskill
1	n/a	Cohoes City SD	Cohoes
1	n/a	Cold Spring Harbor Central SD	Cold Sprg Harbor
1	n/a	Commack Union Free SD	E Northport
1	n/a	Connetquot Central SD	Bohemia
1	n/a	Copiague Union Free SD	Copiague
1	n/a	Corning City SD	Painted Post
1	n/a	Cornwall Central SD	Cornwall-on-Hud
1	n/a	Cortland City SD	Cortland
1	n/a	Coxsackie-Athens Central SD	Coxsackie
1	n/a	Croton-Harmon Union Free SD	Croton-On-Hud
1	n/a	Dansville Central SD	Dansville
1	n/a	Deer Park Union Free SD	Deer Park
1	n/a	Depew Union Free SD	Depew
1	n/a	Dover Union Free SD	Dover Plains
1	n/a	Dryden Central SD	Dryden
1	n/a	Dunkirk City SD	Dunkirk
1	n/a	East Aurora Union Free SD	East Aurora
1	n/a	East Greenbush Central SD	E Greenbush
1	n/a	East Hampton Union Free SD	East Hampton
1	n/a	East Irondequoit Central SD	Rochester
1	n/a	East Islip Union Free SD	Islip Terrace
1	n/a	East Meadow Union Free SD	Westbury
1	n/a	E Ramapo Central SD (Sprg Val)	Spring Valley
1	n/a	East Syracuse-Minoa Central SD	East Syracuse
1	n/a	East Williston Union Free SD	Old Westbury
1	n/a	Eastchester Union Free SD	Eastchester
1	n/a	Eden Central SD	Eden
1	n/a	Edgemont Union Free SD	Scarsdale
1	n/a	Ellenville Central SD	Ellenville
1	n/a	Elmira City SD	Elmira
1	n/a	Elmont Union Free SD	Elmont
1	n/a	Elwood Union Free SD	Greenlawn
1	n/a	Evans-Brant Cent SD (Lake Shore)	Angola
1	n/a	Fairport Central SD	Fairport
1	n/a	Farmingdale Union Free SD	Farmingdale
1	n/a	Fayetteville-Manlius Central SD	Manlius
1	n/a	Floral Park-Bellerose UFSD	Floral Park
1	n/a	Fonda-Fultonville Central SD	Fonda
1	n/a	Franklin Square Union Free SD	Franklin Square
1	n/a	Fredonia Central SD	Fredonia
1	n/a	Freeport Union Free SD	Freeport
1	n/a	Frontier Central SD	Hamburg
1	n/a	Fulton City SD	Fulton
1	n/a	Garden City Union Free SD	Garden City
1	n/a	Gates-Chili Central SD	Rochester
1	n/a	General Brown Central SD	Dexter
1	n/a	Geneva City SD	Geneva
1	n/a	Glen Cove City SD	Glen Cove
1	n/a	Glens Falls City SD	Glens Falls
1	n/a	Gloversville City SD	Gloversville
1	n/a	Gorham-Middlesex CSD (M Whitman)	Rushville
1	n/a	Goshen Central SD	Goshen
1	n/a	Gouverneur Central SD	Gouverneur
1	n/a	Gowanda Central SD	Gowanda
1	n/a	Grand Island Central SD	Grand Island
1	n/a	Great Neck Union Free SD	Great Neck
1	n/a	Greece Central SD	Rochester
1	n/a	Greenburgh Central SD	Hartsdale
1	n/a	Guilderland Central SD	Guilderland
1	n/a	Half Hollow Hills Central SD	Dix Hills
1	n/a	Hamburg Central SD	Hamburg
1	n/a	Hampton Bays Union Free SD	Hampton Bays
1	n/a	Hannibal Central SD	Hannibal
1	n/a	Harborfields Central SD	Greenlawn
1	n/a	Harrison Central SD	Harrison
1	n/a	Hastings-On-Hudson Union Free SD	Hastings-on-Hud
1	n/a	Hauppauge Union Free SD	Hauppauge
1	n/a	Haverstraw-Stony Point Cent SD	Garnerville
1	n/a	Hempstead Union Free SD	Hempstead
1	n/a	Hendrick Hudson Central SD	Montrose
1	n/a	Herricks Union Free SD	New Hyde Park
1	n/a	Hewlett-Woodmere Union Free SD	Woodmere
1	n/a	Hicksville Union Free SD	Hicksville
1	n/a	Highland Central SD	Highland
1	n/a	Hilton Central SD	Hilton
1	n/a	Holland Patent Central SD	Holland Patent
1	n/a	Homer Central SD	Homer
1	n/a	Honeoye Falls-Lima Central SD	Honeoye Falls
1	n/a	Hornell City SD	Hornell
1	n/a	Horseheads Central SD	Horseheads
1	n/a	Hudson City SD	Hudson
1	n/a	Hudson Falls Central SD	Hudson Falls
1	n/a	Huntington Union Free SD	Huntington Stn
1	n/a	Hyde Park Central SD	Poughkeepsie
1	n/a	Ilion Central SD	Ilion
1	n/a	Indian River Central SD	Philadelphia
1	n/a	Iroquois Central SD	Elma
1	n/a	Irvington Union Free SD	Irvington
1	n/a	Island Trees Union Free SD	Levittown
1	n/a	Islip Union Free SD	Islip
1	n/a	Ithaca City SD	Ithaca
1	n/a	Jamestown City SD	Jamestown
1	n/a	Jamesville-Dewitt Central SD	Dewitt
1	n/a	Jericho Union Free SD	Jericho
1	n/a	Johnson City Central SD	Johnson City
1	n/a	Johnstown City SD	Johnstown
1	n/a	Jordan-Elbridge Central SD	Jordan
1	n/a	Katonah-Lewisboro Union Free SD	South Salem
1	n/a	Kenmore-Tonawanda Union Free SD	Buffalo
1	n/a	Kinderhook Central SD	Valatie
1	n/a	Kings Park Central SD	Kings Park
1	n/a	Kingston City SD	Kingston
1	n/a	Lackawanna City SD	Lackawanna
1	n/a	Lakeland Central SD	Shrub Oak
1	n/a	Lancaster Central SD	Lancaster
1	n/a	Lansing Central SD	Lansing
1	n/a	Lansingburgh Central SD	Troy
1	n/a	Lawrence Union Free SD	Lawrence
1	n/a	Levittown Union Free SD	Levittown
1	n/a	Lewiston-Porter Central SD	Youngstown
1	n/a	Liberty Central SD	Liberty
1	n/a	Lindenhurst Union Free SD	Lindenhurst
1	n/a	Liverpool Central SD	Liverpool
1	n/a	Livonia Central SD	Livonia
1	n/a	Lockport City SD	Lockport
1	n/a	Locust Valley Central SD	Locust Valley
1	n/a	Long Beach City SD	Long Beach
1	n/a	Longwood Central SD	Middle Island
1	n/a	Lynbrook Union Free SD	Lynbrook
1	n/a	Mahopac Central SD	Mahopac
1	n/a	Maine-Endwell Central SD	Endwell
1	n/a	Malone Central SD	Malone
1	n/a	Malverne Union Free SD	Malverne
1	n/a	Mamaroneck Union Free SD	Mamaroneck
1	n/a	Manhasset Union Free SD	Manhasset
1	n/a	Marcellus Central SD	Marcellus
1	n/a	Marlboro Central SD	Marlboro
1	n/a	Massapequa Union Free SD	Massapequa
1	n/a	Massena Central SD	Massena
1	n/a	Mattituck-Cutchogue UFSD	Cutchogue
1	n/a	Medina Central SD	Medina
1	n/a	Merrick Union Free SD	Merrick
1	n/a	Mexico Central SD	Mexico
1	n/a	Middle Country Central SD	Centereach
1	n/a	Middletown City SD	Middletown
1	n/a	Miller Place Union Free SD	Miller Place
1	n/a	Mineola Union Free SD	Mineola
1	n/a	Minisink Valley Central SD	Slate Hill
1	n/a	Monroe-Woodbury Central SD	Central Valley
1	n/a	Monticello Central SD	Monticello
1	n/a	Mount Pleasant Central SD	Thornwood
1	n/a	Mount Sinai Union Free SD	Mount Sinai
1	n/a	Mount Vernon City SD	Mount Vernon
1	n/a	Nanuet Union Free SD	Nanuet
1	n/a	New Hartford Central SD	New Hartford
1	n/a	New Hyde Park-Garden City Park	New Hyde Park
1	n/a	New Paltz Central SD	New Paltz
1	n/a	New Rochelle City SD	New Rochelle
1	n/a	New York City Geographic Dist 9	Bronx
1	n/a	New York City Geographic Dist 15	Brooklyn
1	n/a	New York City Public Schools	Brooklyn
1	n/a	Newark Central SD	Newark
1	n/a	Newburgh City SD	Newburgh
1	n/a	Newfane Central SD	Newfane
1	n/a	Niagara Falls City SD	Niagara Falls
1	n/a	Niagara-Wheatfield Central SD	Niagara Falls
1	n/a	Niskayuna Central SD	Schenectady
1	n/a	North Babylon Union Free SD	North Babylon
1	n/a	North Bellmore Union Free SD	Bellmore
1	n/a	North Colonie Central SD	Latham
1	n/a	North Rose-Wolcott Central SD	Wolcott
1	n/a	North Shore Central SD	Sea Cliff
1	n/a	North Syracuse Central SD	N Syracuse
1	n/a	North Tonawanda City SD	N Tonawanda
1	n/a	Northeastern Clinton Central SD	Champlain
1	n/a	Northport-East Northport UFSD	Northport
1	n/a	Norwich City SD	Norwich
1	n/a	Nyack Union Free SD	Nyack
1	n/a	Nyc Alternative HS District	New York
1	n/a	Oceanside Union Free SD	Oceanside
1	n/a	Ogdensburg City SD	Ogdensburg
1	n/a	Olean City SD	Olean
1	n/a	Oneida City SD	Oneida
1	n/a	Oneonta City SD	Oneonta
1	n/a	Onteora Central SD	Boiceville
1	n/a	Orchard Park Central SD	Orchard Park
1	n/a	Ossining Union Free SD	Ossining
1	n/a	Oswego City SD	Oswego
1	n/a	Owego-Apalachin Central SD	Owego
1	n/a	Oyster Bay-East Norwich CSD	Oyster Bay
1	n/a	Palmyra-Macedon Central SD	Palmyra
1	n/a	Patchogue-Medford Union Free SD	Patchogue
1	n/a	Pearl River Union Free SD	Pearl River
1	n/a	Peekskill City SD	Peekskill
1	n/a	Pelham Union Free SD	Pelham
1	n/a	Penfield Central SD	Penfield
1	n/a	Penn Yan Central SD	Penn Yan
1	n/a	Peru Central SD	Peru
1	n/a	Phelps-Clifton Springs Cent SD	Clifton Spgs
1	n/a	Phoenix Central SD	Phoenix
1	n/a	Pine Bush Central SD	Pine Bush
1	n/a	Pittsford Central SD	Pittsford
1	n/a	Plainedge Union Free SD	N Massapequa
1	n/a	Plainview-Old Bethpage Cent SD	Plainview
1	n/a	Plattsburgh City SD	Plattsburgh
1	n/a	Pleasantville Union Free SD	Pleasantville
1	n/a	Port Chester-Rye Union Free SD	Port Chester
1	n/a	Port Jervis City SD	Port Jervis
1	n/a	Port Washington Union Free SD	Pt Washington
1	n/a	Poughkeepsie City SD	Poughkeepsie
1	n/a	Putnam Valley Central SD	Putnam Valley
1	n/a	Queensbury Union Free SD	Queensbury
1	n/a	Ramapo Central SD (Suffern)	Hillburn
1	n/a	Ravena-Coeymans-Selkirk CSD	Selkirk
1	n/a	Red Hook Central SD	Red Hook
1	n/a	Riverhead Central SD	Riverhead
1	n/a	Rochester City SD	Rochester
1	n/a	Rockville Centre Union Free SD	Rockville Ctre
1	n/a	Rocky Point Union Free SD	Rocky Point
1	n/a	Rome City SD	Rome
1	n/a	Rondout Valley Central SD	Accord
1	n/a	Roosevelt Union Free SD	Roosevelt
1	n/a	Roslyn Union Free SD	Roslyn
1	n/a	Rotterdam-Mohonasen Central SD	Schenectady
1	n/a	Royalton-Hartland Central SD	Middleport
1	n/a	Rush-Henrietta Central SD	Henrietta
1	n/a	Rye City SD	Rye
1	n/a	Sachem Central SD	Holbrook
1	n/a	Salamanca City SD	Salamanca
1	n/a	Salmon River Central SD	Ft Covington
1	n/a	Saranac Central SD	Dannemora
1	n/a	Saranac Lake Central SD	Saranac Lake
1	n/a	Saratoga Springs City SD	Saratoga Spgs
1	n/a	Saugerties Central SD	Saugerties
1	n/a	Sayville Union Free SD	Sayville
1	n/a	Scarsdale Union Free SD	Scarsdale
1	n/a	Schalmont Central SD	Schenectady
1	n/a	Schenectady City SD	Schenectady
1	n/a	Schuylerville Central SD	Schuylerville
1	n/a	Scotia-Glenville Central SD	Scotia
1	n/a	Seaford Union Free SD	Seaford
1	n/a	Sewanhaka Central High SD	Floral Park
1	n/a	Shenendehowa Central SD	Clifton Park
1	n/a	Sherburne-Earlville Central SD	Sherburne
1	n/a	Sherrill City SD	Verona
1	n/a	Shoreham-Wading River Central SD	Shoreham
1	n/a	Skaneateles Central SD	Skaneateles
1	n/a	Smithtown Central SD	Smithtown
1	n/a	Solvay Union Free SD	Solvay
1	n/a	Somers Central SD	Lincolndale
1	n/a	South Colonie Central SD	Albany
1	n/a	South Country Central SD	E Patchogue
1	n/a	South Glens Falls Central SD	S Glens Falls
1	n/a	South Huntington Union Free SD	Huntington Stn
1	n/a	South Jefferson Central SD	Adams Center
1	n/a	South Orangetown Central SD	Blauvelt
1	n/a	Southampton Union Free SD	Southampton
1	n/a	Southwestern Cent SD Jamestown	Jamestown
1	n/a	Spackenkill Union Free SD	Poughkeepsie
1	n/a	Spencerport Central SD	Spencerport
1	n/a	Springville-Griffith Inst Cent	Springville
1	n/a	Starpoint Central SD	Lockport
1	n/a	Sullivan West Central SD	Callicoon
1	n/a	Susquehanna Valley Central SD	Conklin
1	n/a	Sweet Home Central SD	Amherst
1	n/a	Syosset Central SD	Syosset
1	n/a	Syracuse City SD	Syracuse
1	n/a	Taconic Hills Central SD	Craryville
1	n/a	Three Village Central SD	East Setauket
1	n/a	Tonawanda City SD	Tonawanda
1	n/a	Troy City SD	Troy
1	n/a	Union Free SD of the Tarrytowns	Sleepy Hollow
1	n/a	Union-Endicott Central SD	Endicott
1	n/a	Uniondale Union Free SD	Uniondale
1	n/a	Utica City SD	Utica
1	n/a	Valley Central SD (Montgomery)	Montgomery
1	n/a	Valley Stream 13 Union Free SD	Valley Stream
1	n/a	Valley Stream 30 Union Free SD	Valley Stream
1	n/a	Valley Stream Central High SD	Valley Stream
1	n/a	Vestal Central SD	Vestal
1	n/a	Victor Central SD	Victor

1	n/a	Wallkill Central SD	Wallkill
1	n/a	Wantagh Union Free SD	Wantagh
1	n/a	Wappingers Central SD	Wappingers Fls
1	n/a	Warwick Valley Central SD	Warwick
1	n/a	Washingtonville Central SD	Washingtonville
1	n/a	Waterloo Central SD	Waterloo
1	n/a	Watertown City SD	Watertown
1	n/a	Watkins Glen Central SD	Watkins Glen
1	n/a	Waverly Central SD	Waverly
1	n/a	Wayland-Cohocton Central SD	Wayland
1	n/a	Wayne Central SD	Ontario Center
1	n/a	Webster Central SD	Webster
1	n/a	West Babylon Union Free SD	West Babylon
1	n/a	West Genesee Central SD	Camillus
1	n/a	West Hempstead Union Free SD	W Hempstead
1	n/a	West Irondequoit Central SD	Rochester
1	n/a	West Islip Union Free SD	West Islip
1	n/a	West Seneca Central SD	West Seneca
1	n/a	Westbury Union Free SD	Old Westbury
1	n/a	Westhampton Beach Union Free SD	Westhampton Bch
1	n/a	Westhill Central SD	Syracuse
1	n/a	White Plains City SD	White Plains
1	n/a	Whitesboro Central SD	Yorkville
1	n/a	Whitney Point Central SD	Whitney Point
1	n/a	William Floyd Union Free SD	Mastic Beach
1	n/a	Williamsville Central SD	East Amherst
1	n/a	Wilson Central SD	Wilson
1	n/a	Windsor Central SD	Windsor
1	n/a	Wyandanch Union Free SD	Wyandanch
1	n/a	Yonkers City SD	Yonkers
1	n/a	Yorkshire-Pioneer Central SD	Yorkshire
1	n/a	Yorktown Central SD	Yorktown Hgts

Students Eligible for Reduced-Price Lunch

Rank	Percent	District Name	City
1	n/a	Adirondack Central SD	Boonville
1	n/a	Akron Central SD	Akron
1	n/a	Albany City SD	Albany
1	n/a	Albion Central SD	Albion
1	n/a	Alden Central SD	Alden
1	n/a	Altmar-Parish-Williamstown CSD	Parish
1	n/a	Amherst Central SD	Amherst
1	n/a	Amityville Union Free SD	Amityville
1	n/a	Amsterdam City SD	Amsterdam
1	n/a	Ardsley Union Free SD	Ardsley
1	n/a	Arlington Central SD	Poughkeepsie
1	n/a	Attica Central SD	Attica
1	n/a	Auburn City SD	Auburn
1	n/a	Averill Park Central SD	Averill Park
1	n/a	Babylon Union Free SD	Babylon
1	n/a	Baldwin Union Free SD	Baldwin
1	n/a	Baldwinsville Central SD	Baldwinsville
1	n/a	Ballston Spa Central SD	Ballston Spa
1	n/a	Batavia City SD	Batavia
1	n/a	Bath Central SD	Bath
1	n/a	Bay Shore Union Free SD	Bay Shore
1	n/a	Bayport-Blue Point Union Free SD	Bayport
1	n/a	Beacon City SD	Beacon
1	n/a	Bedford Central SD	Mount Kisco
1	n/a	Beekmantown Central SD	West Chazy
1	n/a	Bellmore-Merrick Central High SD	North Merrick
1	n/a	Bethlehem Central SD	Delmar
1	n/a	Bethpage Union Free SD	Bethpage
1	n/a	Binghamton City SD	Binghamton
1	n/a	Boces Eastern Suffolk	Patchogue
1	n/a	Boces Nassau	Garden City
1	n/a	Brentwood Union Free SD	Brentwood
1	n/a	Brewster Central SD	Brewster
1	n/a	Briarcliff Manor Union Free SD	Briarcliff Manor
1	n/a	Brighton Central SD	Rochester
1	n/a	Broadalbin-Perth Central SD	Broadalbin
1	n/a	Brockport Central SD	Brockport
1	n/a	Brookhaven-Comsewogue UFSD	Pt Jefferson Stn
1	n/a	Buffalo City SD	Buffalo
1	n/a	Burnt Hls-Ballston Lake Cent SD	Scotia
1	n/a	Byram Hills Central SD	Armonk
1	n/a	Cairo-Durham Central SD	Cairo
1	n/a	Camden Central SD	Camden
1	n/a	Canandaigua City SD	Canandaigua
1	n/a	Canastota Central SD	Canastota
1	n/a	Canton Central SD	Canton
1	n/a	Carle Place Union Free SD	Carle Place
1	n/a	Carmel Central SD	Patterson
1	n/a	Carthage Central SD	Carthage
1	n/a	Catskill Central SD	Catskill
1	n/a	Cazenovia Central SD	Cazenovia
1	n/a	Central Islip Union Free SD	Central Islip
1	n/a	Central Square Central SD	Central Square
1	n/a	Chappaqua Central SD	Chappaqua
1	n/a	Chatham Central SD	Chatham
1	n/a	Cheektowaga Central SD	Cheektowaga
1	n/a	Cheektowaga-Maryvale UFSD	Cheektowaga
1	n/a	Cheektowaga-Sloan Union Free SD	Sloan
1	n/a	Chenango Forks Central SD	Binghamton
1	n/a	Chenango Valley Central SD	Binghamton
1	n/a	Chittenango Central SD	Chittenango
1	n/a	Churchville-Chili Central SD	Churchville
1	n/a	Clarence Central SD	Clarence
1	n/a	Clarkstown Central SD	New City
1	n/a	Cleveland Hill Union Free SD	Cheektowaga
1	n/a	Clinton Central SD	Clinton
1	n/a	Cobleskill-Richmondville CSD	Cobleskill
1	n/a	Cohoes City SD	Cohoes
1	n/a	Cold Spring Harbor Central SD	Cold Sprg Harbor
1	n/a	Commack Union Free SD	E Northport
1	n/a	Connetquot Central SD	Bohemia
1	n/a	Copiague Union Free SD	Copiague
1	n/a	Corning City SD	Painted Post
1	n/a	Cornwall Central SD	Cornwall-on-Hud
1	n/a	Cortland City SD	Cortland
1	n/a	Coxsackie-Athens Central SD	Coxsackie
1	n/a	Croton-Harmon Union Free SD	Croton-On-Hud
1	n/a	Dansville Central SD	Dansville
1	n/a	Deer Park Union Free SD	Deer Park
1	n/a	Depew Union Free SD	Depew
1	n/a	Dover Union Free SD	Dover Plains
1	n/a	Dryden Central SD	Dryden
1	n/a	Dunkirk City SD	Dunkirk
1	n/a	East Aurora Union Free SD	East Aurora
1	n/a	East Greenbush Central SD	E Greenbush
1	n/a	East Hampton Union Free SD	East Hampton
1	n/a	East Irondequoit Central SD	Rochester
1	n/a	East Islip Union Free SD	Islip Terrace
1	n/a	East Meadow Union Free SD	Westbury
1	n/a	E Ramapo Central SD (Sprg Val)	Spring Valley
1	n/a	East Syracuse-Minoa Central SD	East Syracuse
1	n/a	East Williston Union Free SD	Old Westbury
1	n/a	Eastchester Union Free SD	Eastchester
1	n/a	Eden Central SD	Eden
1	n/a	Edgemont Union Free SD	Scarsdale
1	n/a	Ellenville Central SD	Ellenville
1	n/a	Elmira City SD	Elmira
1	n/a	Elmont Union Free SD	Elmont
1	n/a	Elwood Union Free SD	Greenlawn
1	n/a	Evans-Brant Cent SD (Lake Shore)	Angola
1	n/a	Fairport Central SD	Fairport
1	n/a	Farmingdale Union Free SD	Farmingdale
1	n/a	Fayetteville-Manlius Central SD	Manlius
1	n/a	Floral Park-Bellerose UFSD	Floral Park
1	n/a	Fonda-Fultonville Central SD	Fonda
1	n/a	Franklin Square Union Free SD	Franklin Square
1	n/a	Fredonia Central SD	Fredonia
1	n/a	Freeport Union Free SD	Freeport
1	n/a	Frontier Central SD	Hamburg
1	n/a	Fulton City SD	Fulton
1	n/a	Garden City Union Free SD	Garden City
1	n/a	Gates-Chili Central SD	Rochester
1	n/a	General Brown Central SD	Dexter
1	n/a	Geneva City SD	Geneva
1	n/a	Glen Cove City SD	Glen Cove
1	n/a	Glens Falls City SD	Glens Falls
1	n/a	Gloversville City SD	Gloversville
1	n/a	Gorham-Middlesex CSD (M Whitman)	Rushville
1	n/a	Goshen Central SD	Goshen
1	n/a	Gouverneur Central SD	Gouverneur
1	n/a	Gowanda Central SD	Gowanda
1	n/a	Grand Island Central SD	Grand Island
1	n/a	Great Neck Union Free SD	Great Neck
1	n/a	Greece Central SD	Rochester
1	n/a	Greenburgh Central SD	Hartsdale
1	n/a	Guilderland Central SD	Guilderland
1	n/a	Half Hollow Hills Central SD	Dix Hills
1	n/a	Hamburg Central SD	Hamburg
1	n/a	Hampton Bays Union Free SD	Hampton Bays
1	n/a	Hannibal Central SD	Hannibal
1	n/a	Harborfields Central SD	Greenlawn
1	n/a	Harrison Central SD	Harrison
1	n/a	Hastings-On-Hudson Union Free SD	Hastings-on-Hud
1	n/a	Hauppauge Union Free SD	Hauppauge
1	n/a	Haverstraw-Stony Point Cent SD	Garnerville
1	n/a	Hempstead Union Free SD	Hempstead
1	n/a	Hendrick Hudson Central SD	Montrose
1	n/a	Herricks Union Free SD	New Hyde Park
1	n/a	Hewlett-Woodmere Union Free SD	Woodmere
1	n/a	Hicksville Union Free SD	Hicksville
1	n/a	Highland Central SD	Highland
1	n/a	Hilton Central SD	Hilton
1	n/a	Holland Patent Central SD	Holland Patent
1	n/a	Homer Central SD	Homer
1	n/a	Honeoye Falls-Lima Central SD	Honeoye Falls
1	n/a	Hornell City SD	Hornell
1	n/a	Horseheads Central SD	Horseheads
1	n/a	Hudson City SD	Hudson
1	n/a	Hudson Falls Central SD	Hudson Falls
1	n/a	Huntington Union Free SD	Huntington Stn
1	n/a	Hyde Park Central SD	Poughkeepsie
1	n/a	Ilion Central SD	Ilion
1	n/a	Indian River Central SD	Philadelphia
1	n/a	Iroquois Central SD	Elma
1	n/a	Irvington Union Free SD	Irvington
1	n/a	Island Trees Union Free SD	Levittown
1	n/a	Islip Union Free SD	Islip
1	n/a	Ithaca City SD	Ithaca
1	n/a	Jamestown City SD	Jamestown
1	n/a	Jamesville-Dewitt Central SD	Dewitt
1	n/a	Jericho Union Free SD	Jericho
1	n/a	Johnson City Central SD	Johnson City
1	n/a	Johnstown City SD	Johnstown
1	n/a	Jordan-Elbridge Central SD	Jordan
1	n/a	Katonah-Lewisboro Union Free SD	South Salem
1	n/a	Kenmore-Tonawanda Union Free SD	Buffalo
1	n/a	Kinderhook Central SD	Valatie
1	n/a	Kings Park Central SD	Kings Park
1	n/a	Kingston City SD	Kingston
1	n/a	Lackawanna City SD	Lackawanna
1	n/a	Lakeland Central SD	Shrub Oak
1	n/a	Lancaster Central SD	Lancaster
1	n/a	Lansing Central SD	Lansing
1	n/a	Lansingburgh Central SD	Troy
1	n/a	Lawrence Union Free SD	Lawrence
1	n/a	Levittown Union Free SD	Levittown
1	n/a	Lewiston-Porter Central SD	Youngstown
1	n/a	Liberty Central SD	Liberty
1	n/a	Lindenhurst Union Free SD	Lindenhurst
1	n/a	Liverpool Central SD	Liverpool
1	n/a	Livonia Central SD	Livonia
1	n/a	Lockport City SD	Lockport
1	n/a	Locust Valley Central SD	Locust Valley
1	n/a	Long Beach City SD	Long Beach
1	n/a	Longwood Central SD	Middle Island
1	n/a	Lynbrook Union Free SD	Lynbrook
1	n/a	Mahopac Central SD	Mahopac
1	n/a	Maine-Endwell Central SD	Endwell
1	n/a	Malone Central SD	Malone
1	n/a	Malverne Union Free SD	Malverne
1	n/a	Mamaroneck Union Free SD	Mamaroneck
1	n/a	Manhasset Union Free SD	Manhasset
1	n/a	Marcellus Central SD	Marcellus
1	n/a	Marlboro Central SD	Marlboro
1	n/a	Massapequa Union Free SD	Massapequa
1	n/a	Massena Central SD	Massena
1	n/a	Mattituck-Cutchogue UFSD	Cutchogue
1	n/a	Medina Central SD	Medina
1	n/a	Merrick Union Free SD	Merrick
1	n/a	Mexico Central SD	Mexico
1	n/a	Middle Country Central SD	Centereach
1	n/a	Middletown City SD	Middletown
1	n/a	Miller Place Union Free SD	Miller Place
1	n/a	Mineola Union Free SD	Mineola
1	n/a	Minisink Valley Central SD	Slate Hill
1	n/a	Monroe-Woodbury Central SD	Central Valley
1	n/a	Monticello Central SD	Monticello
1	n/a	Mount Pleasant Central SD	Thornwood
1	n/a	Mount Sinai Union Free SD	Mount Sinai
1	n/a	Mount Vernon City SD	Mount Vernon
1	n/a	Nanuet Union Free SD	Nanuet
1	n/a	New Hartford Central SD	New Hartford
1	n/a	New Hyde Park-Garden City Park	New Hyde Park
1	n/a	New Paltz Central SD	New Paltz
1	n/a	New Rochelle City SD	New Rochelle
1	n/a	New York City Geographic Dist 9	Bronx
1	n/a	New York City Geographic Dist 15	Brooklyn
1	n/a	New York City Public Schools	Brooklyn
1	n/a	Newark Central SD	Newark
1	n/a	Newburgh City SD	Newburgh
1	n/a	Newfane Central SD	Newfane
1	n/a	Niagara Falls City SD	Niagara Falls
1	n/a	Niagara-Wheatfield Central SD	Niagara Falls
1	n/a	Niskayuna Central SD	Schenectady
1	n/a	North Babylon Union Free SD	North Babylon
1	n/a	North Bellmore Union Free SD	Bellmore
1	n/a	North Colonie Central SD	Latham
1	n/a	North Rose-Wolcott Central SD	Wolcott
1	n/a	North Shore Central SD	Sea Cliff
1	n/a	North Syracuse Central SD	N Syracuse
1	n/a	North Tonawanda City SD	N Tonawanda
1	n/a	Northeastern Clinton Central SD	Champlain
1	n/a	Northport-East Northport UFSD	Northport
1	n/a	Norwich City SD	Norwich
1	n/a	Nyack Union Free SD	Nyack
1	n/a	Nyc Alternative HS District	New York
1	n/a	Oceanside Union Free SD	Oceanside
1	n/a	Ogdensburg City SD	Ogdensburg
1	n/a	Olean City SD	Olean
1	n/a	Oneida City SD	Oneida

1	n/a	Oneonta City SD	Oneonta
1	n/a	Onteora Central SD	Boiceville
1	n/a	Orchard Park Central SD	Orchard Park
1	n/a	Ossining Union Free SD	Ossining
1	n/a	Oswego City SD	Oswego
1	n/a	Owego-Apalachin Central SD	Owego
1	n/a	Oyster Bay-East Norwich CSD	Oyster Bay
1	n/a	Palmyra-Macedon Central SD	Palmyra
1	n/a	Patchogue-Medford Union Free SD	Patchogue
1	n/a	Pearl River Union Free SD	Pearl River
1	n/a	Peekskill City SD	Peekskill
1	n/a	Pelham Union Free SD	Pelham
1	n/a	Penfield Central SD	Penfield
1	n/a	Penn Yan Central SD	Penn Yan
1	n/a	Peru Central SD	Peru
1	n/a	Phelps-Clifton Springs Cent SD	Clifton Spgs
1	n/a	Phoenix Central SD	Phoenix
1	n/a	Pine Bush Central SD	Pine Bush
1	n/a	Pittsford Central SD	Pittsford
1	n/a	Plainedge Union Free SD	N Massapequa
1	n/a	Plainview-Old Bethpage Cent SD	Plainview
1	n/a	Plattsburgh City SD	Plattsburgh
1	n/a	Pleasantville Union Free SD	Pleasantville
1	n/a	Port Chester-Rye Union Free SD	Port Chester
1	n/a	Port Jervis City SD	Port Jervis
1	n/a	Port Washington Union Free SD	Pt Washington
1	n/a	Poughkeepsie City SD	Poughkeepsie
1	n/a	Putnam Valley Central SD	Putnam Valley
1	n/a	Queensbury Union Free SD	Queensbury
1	n/a	Ramapo Central SD (Suffern)	Hillburn
1	n/a	Ravena-Coeymans-Selkirk CSD	Selkirk
1	n/a	Red Hook Central SD	Red Hook
1	n/a	Riverhead Central SD	Riverhead
1	n/a	Rochester City SD	Rochester
1	n/a	Rockville Centre Union Free SD	Rockville Ctre
1	n/a	Rocky Point Union Free SD	Rocky Point
1	n/a	Rome City SD	Rome
1	n/a	Rondout Valley Central SD	Accord
1	n/a	Roosevelt Union Free SD	Roosevelt
1	n/a	Roslyn Union Free SD	Roslyn
1	n/a	Rotterdam-Mohonasen Central SD	Schenectady
1	n/a	Royalton-Hartland Central SD	Middleport
1	n/a	Rush-Henrietta Central SD	Henrietta
1	n/a	Rye City SD	Rye
1	n/a	Sachem Central SD	Holbrook
1	n/a	Salamanca City SD	Salamanca
1	n/a	Salmon River Central SD	Ft Covington
1	n/a	Saranac Central SD	Dannemora
1	n/a	Saranac Lake Central SD	Saranac Lake
1	n/a	Saratoga Springs City SD	Saratoga Spgs
1	n/a	Saugerties Central SD	Saugerties
1	n/a	Sayville Union Free SD	Sayville
1	n/a	Scarsdale Union Free SD	Scarsdale
1	n/a	Schalmont Central SD	Schenectady
1	n/a	Schenectady City SD	Schenectady
1	n/a	Schuylerville Central SD	Schuylerville
1	n/a	Scotia-Glenville Central SD	Scotia
1	n/a	Seaford Union Free SD	Seaford
1	n/a	Sewanhaka Central High SD	Floral Park
1	n/a	Shenendehowa Central SD	Clifton Park
1	n/a	Sherburne-Earlville Central SD	Sherburne
1	n/a	Sherrill City SD	Verona
1	n/a	Shoreham-Wading River Central SD	Shoreham
1	n/a	Skaneateles Central SD	Skaneateles
1	n/a	Smithtown Central SD	Smithtown
1	n/a	Solvay Union Free SD	Solvay
1	n/a	Somers Central SD	Lincolndale
1	n/a	South Colonie Central SD	Albany
1	n/a	South Country Central SD	E Patchogue
1	n/a	South Glens Falls Central SD	S Glens Falls
1	n/a	South Huntington Union Free SD	Huntington Stn
1	n/a	South Jefferson Central SD	Adams Center
1	n/a	South Orangetown Central SD	Blauvelt
1	n/a	Southampton Union Free SD	Southampton
1	n/a	Southwestern Cent SD Jamestown	Jamestown
1	n/a	Spackenkill Union Free SD	Poughkeepsie
1	n/a	Spencerport Central SD	Spencerport
1	n/a	Springville-Griffith Inst Cent	Springville
1	n/a	Starpoint Central SD	Lockport
1	n/a	Sullivan West Central SD	Callicoon
1	n/a	Susquehanna Valley Central SD	Conklin
1	n/a	Sweet Home Central SD	Amherst
1	n/a	Syosset Central SD	Syosset
1	n/a	Syracuse City SD	Syracuse
1	n/a	Taconic Hills Central SD	Craryville
1	n/a	Three Village Central SD	East Setauket
1	n/a	Tonawanda City SD	Tonawanda
1	n/a	Troy City SD	Troy
1	n/a	Union Free SD of the Tarrytowns	Sleepy Hollow
1	n/a	Union-Endicott Central SD	Endicott
1	n/a	Uniondale Union Free SD	Uniondale
1	n/a	Utica City SD	Utica
1	n/a	Valley Central SD (Montgomery)	Montgomery
1	n/a	Valley Stream 13 Union Free SD	Valley Stream
1	n/a	Valley Stream 30 Union Free SD	Valley Stream
1	n/a	Valley Stream Central High SD	Valley Stream
1	n/a	Vestal Central SD	Vestal
1	n/a	Victor Central SD	Victor
1	n/a	Wallkill Central SD	Wallkill
1	n/a	Wantagh Union Free SD	Wantagh
1	n/a	Wappingers Central SD	Wappingers Fls
1	n/a	Warwick Valley Central SD	Warwick
1	n/a	Washingtonville Central SD	Washingtonville
1	n/a	Waterloo Central SD	Waterloo
1	n/a	Watertown City SD	Watertown
1	n/a	Watkins Glen Central SD	Watkins Glen
1	n/a	Waverly Central SD	Waverly
1	n/a	Wayland-Cohocton Central SD	Wayland
1	n/a	Wayne Central SD	Ontario Center
1	n/a	Webster Central SD	Webster
1	n/a	West Babylon Union Free SD	West Babylon
1	n/a	West Genesee Central SD	Camillus
1	n/a	West Hempstead Union Free SD	W Hempstead
1	n/a	West Irondequoit Central SD	Rochester
1	n/a	West Islip Union Free SD	West Islip
1	n/a	West Seneca Central SD	West Seneca
1	n/a	Westbury Union Free SD	Old Westbury
1	n/a	Westhampton Beach Union Free SD	Westhampton Bch
1	n/a	Westhill Central SD	Syracuse
1	n/a	White Plains City SD	White Plains
1	n/a	Whitesboro Central SD	Yorkville
1	n/a	Whitney Point Central SD	Whitney Point
1	n/a	William Floyd Union Free SD	Mastic Beach
1	n/a	Williamsville Central SD	East Amherst
1	n/a	Wilson Central SD	Wilson
1	n/a	Windsor Central SD	Windsor
1	n/a	Wyandanch Union Free SD	Wyandanch
1	n/a	Yonkers City SD	Yonkers
1	n/a	Yorkshire-Pioneer Central SD	Yorkshire
1	n/a	Yorktown Central SD	Yorktown Hgts

Student/Teacher Ratio

Rank	Ratio	District Name	City
1	19.3	Coxsackie-Athens Central SD	Coxsackie
2	16.4	Broadalbin-Perth Central SD	Broadalbin
3	16.3	William Floyd Union Free SD	Mastic Beach
4	16.2	Highland Central SD	Highland
4	16.2	Sewanhaka Central High SD	Floral Park
6	16.1	Starpoint Central SD	Lockport
7	16.0	Arlington Central SD	Poughkeepsie
8	15.9	Floral Park-Bellerose UFSD	Floral Park
9	15.7	Copiague Union Free SD	Copiague
9	15.7	Hempstead Union Free SD	Hempstead
11	15.6	Bellmore-Merrick Central High SD	North Merrick
11	15.6	Middle Country Central SD	Centereach
11	15.6	Mount Vernon City SD	Mount Vernon
11	15.6	Wappingers Central SD	Wappingers Fls
15	15.5	Brentwood Union Free SD	Brentwood
15	15.5	Niagara Falls City SD	Niagara Falls
15	15.5	Port Jervis City SD	Port Jervis
18	15.4	Elmont Union Free SD	Elmont
18	15.4	Rocky Point Union Free SD	Rocky Point
20	15.3	Lancaster Central SD	Lancaster
20	15.3	Queensbury Union Free SD	Queensbury
20	15.3	Rotterdam-Mohonasen Central SD	Schenectady
23	15.2	Cornwall Central SD	Cornwall-on-Hud
23	15.2	Dover Union Free SD	Dover Plains
23	15.2	Islip Union Free SD	Islip
23	15.2	Minisink Valley Central SD	Slate Hill
23	15.2	West Irondequoit Central SD	Rochester
28	15.1	Marcellus Central SD	Marcellus
28	15.1	North Syracuse Central SD	N Syracuse
28	15.1	Warwick Valley Central SD	Warwick
31	15.0	Elwood Union Free SD	Greenlawn
31	15.0	Iroquois Central SD	Elma
31	15.0	Patchogue-Medford Union Free SD	Patchogue
31	15.0	Riverhead Central SD	Riverhead
31	15.0	Saugerties Central SD	Saugerties
31	15.0	Utica City SD	Utica
31	15.0	Washingtonville Central SD	Washingtonville
38	14.9	Longwood Central SD	Middle Island
38	14.9	West Genesee Central SD	Camillus
40	14.8	Johnstown City SD	Johnstown
40	14.8	New Hyde Park-Garden City Park	New Hyde Park
40	14.8	Wyandanch Union Free SD	Wyandanch
43	14.7	Baldwinsville Central SD	Baldwinsville
43	14.7	Bethlehem Central SD	Delmar
43	14.7	Middletown City SD	Middletown
43	14.7	Miller Place Union Free SD	Miller Place
43	14.7	New Rochelle City SD	New Rochelle
43	14.7	Shenendehowa Central SD	Clifton Park
49	14.6	Akron Central SD	Akron
49	14.6	Albion Central SD	Albion
49	14.6	Beacon City SD	Beacon
49	14.6	Central Square Central SD	Central Square
49	14.6	General Brown Central SD	Dexter
49	14.6	New York City Public Schools	Brooklyn
49	14.6	Newburgh City SD	Newburgh
49	14.6	Wallkill Central SD	Wallkill
57	14.5	Carmel Central SD	Patterson
57	14.5	Franklin Square Union Free SD	Franklin Square
57	14.5	Gouverneur Central SD	Gouverneur
57	14.5	Horseheads Central SD	Horseheads
57	14.5	Monroe-Woodbury Central SD	Central Valley
57	14.5	Pine Bush Central SD	Pine Bush
57	14.5	Plainedge Union Free SD	N Massapequa
64	14.4	Ballston Spa Central SD	Ballston Spa
64	14.4	Brookhaven-Comsewogue UFSD	Pt Jefferson Stn
64	14.4	East Islip Union Free SD	Islip Terrace
64	14.4	Eden Central SD	Eden
64	14.4	Harborfields Central SD	Greenlawn
64	14.4	Liverpool Central SD	Liverpool
64	14.4	Mount Sinai Union Free SD	Mount Sinai
64	14.4	Newfane Central SD	Newfane
64	14.4	Watertown City SD	Watertown
64	14.4	West Babylon Union Free SD	West Babylon
74	14.3	Hudson Falls Central SD	Hudson Falls
74	14.3	South Jefferson Central SD	Adams Center
76	14.2	Burnt Hls-Ballston Lake Cent SD	Scotia
76	14.2	East Aurora Union Free SD	East Aurora
76	14.2	Fayetteville-Manlius Central SD	Manlius
76	14.2	Hyde Park Central SD	Poughkeepsie
76	14.2	Lindenhurst Union Free SD	Lindenhurst
76	14.2	Massena Central SD	Massena
76	14.2	Niskayuna Central SD	Schenectady
76	14.2	Victor Central SD	Victor
76	14.2	Waverly Central SD	Waverly
85	14.1	Fairport Central SD	Fairport
85	14.1	Greece Central SD	Rochester
85	14.1	North Babylon Union Free SD	North Babylon
85	14.1	North Colonie Central SD	Latham
85	14.1	Scotia-Glenville Central SD	Scotia
90	14.0	Corning City SD	Painted Post
90	14.0	Mexico Central SD	Mexico
90	14.0	Westhill Central SD	Syracuse
93	13.9	Canastota Central SD	Canastota
93	13.9	Carthage Central SD	Carthage
93	13.9	Clarence Central SD	Clarence
93	13.9	Goshen Central SD	Goshen
93	13.9	Grand Island Central SD	Grand Island
93	13.9	Kings Park Central SD	Kings Park
93	13.9	Kingston City SD	Kingston
93	13.9	North Bellmore Union Free SD	Bellmore
93	13.9	Port Chester-Rye Union Free SD	Port Chester
93	13.9	Sherrill City SD	Verona
93	13.9	Smithtown Central SD	Smithtown
93	13.9	Springville-Griffith Inst Cent	Springville
93	13.9	Valley Central SD (Montgomery)	Montgomery
93	13.9	Yonkers City SD	Yonkers
107	13.8	Brockport Central SD	Brockport
107	13.8	Cairo-Durham Central SD	Cairo
107	13.8	Chatham Central SD	Chatham
107	13.8	Connetquot Central SD	Bohemia
107	13.8	Pearl River Union Free SD	Pearl River
107	13.8	Sayville Union Free SD	Sayville
107	13.8	Schenectady City SD	Schenectady
107	13.8	Wantagh Union Free SD	Wantagh
107	13.8	West Islip Union Free SD	West Islip
107	13.8	West Seneca Central SD	West Seneca
117	13.7	Chenango Valley Central SD	Binghamton
117	13.7	Half Hollow Hills Central SD	Dix Hills
117	13.7	Hannibal Central SD	Hannibal
117	13.7	Honeoye Falls-Lima Central SD	Honeoye Falls
117	13.7	North Tonawanda City SD	N Tonawanda
117	13.7	Poughkeepsie City SD	Poughkeepsie
117	13.7	Troy City SD	Troy
117	13.7	Westbury Union Free SD	Old Westbury
125	13.6	Buffalo City SD	Buffalo
125	13.6	Cheektowaga Central SD	Cheektowaga
125	13.6	Clarkstown Central SD	New City
125	13.6	East Irondequoit Central SD	Rochester
125	13.6	Freeport Union Free SD	Freeport
125	13.6	Hicksville Union Free SD	Hicksville
125	13.6	Ilion Central SD	Ilion
125	13.6	Lansingburgh Central SD	Troy
125	13.6	Putnam Valley Central SD	Putnam Valley
125	13.6	Red Hook Central SD	Red Hook
125	13.6	Southwestern Cent SD Jamestown	Jamestown
125	13.6	Williamsville Central SD	East Amherst
137	13.5	Alden Central SD	Alden
137	13.5	Chittenango Central SD	Chittenango
137	13.5	Churchville-Chili Central SD	Churchville
137	13.5	East Greenbush Central SD	E Greenbush
137	13.5	Lakeland Central SD	Shrub Oak
137	13.5	Massapequa Union Free SD	Massapequa
137	13.5	New Paltz Central SD	New Paltz
137	13.5	Niagara-Wheatfield Central SD	Niagara Falls

137	13.5	Oceanside Union Free SD	Oceanside
137	13.5	Oswego City SD	Oswego
137	13.5	Pleasantville Union Free SD	Pleasantville
137	13.5	Saratoga Springs City SD	Saratoga Spgs
137	13.5	Watkins Glen Central SD	Watkins Glen
150	13.4	Brewster Central SD	Brewster
150	13.4	Camden Central SD	Camden
150	13.4	Central Islip Union Free SD	Central Islip
150	13.4	Cheektowaga-Sloan Union Free SD	Sloan
150	13.4	Elmira City SD	Elmira
150	13.4	Fulton City SD	Fulton
150	13.4	Holland Patent Central SD	Holland Patent
150	13.4	Kinderhook Central SD	Valatie
150	13.4	Oneida City SD	Oneida
150	13.4	South Glens Falls Central SD	S Glens Falls
150	13.4	South Huntington Union Free SD	Huntington Stn
150	13.4	Webster Central SD	Webster
162	13.3	Bay Shore Union Free SD	Bay Shore
162	13.3	Cheektowaga-Maryvale UFSD	Cheektowaga
162	13.3	Croton-Harmon Union Free SD	Croton-On-Hud
162	13.3	East Meadow Union Free SD	Westbury
162	13.3	Fonda-Fultonville Central SD	Fonda
162	13.3	Guilderland Central SD	Guilderland
162	13.3	Katonah-Lewisboro Union Free SD	South Salem
162	13.3	Northeastern Clinton Central SD	Champlain
162	13.3	Seaford Union Free SD	Seaford
162	13.3	South Country Central SD	E Patchogue
162	13.3	Three Village Central SD	East Setauket
162	13.3	Valley Stream Central High SD	Valley Stream
162	13.3	Waterloo Central SD	Waterloo
162	13.3	Windsor Central SD	Windsor
162	13.3	Yorktown Central SD	Yorktown Hgts
177	13.2	Auburn City SD	Auburn
177	13.2	Chenango Forks Central SD	Binghamton
177	13.2	Cold Spring Harbor Central SD	Cold Sprg Harbor
177	13.2	Commack Union Free SD	E Northport
177	13.2	Edgemont Union Free SD	Scarsdale
177	13.2	Garden City Union Free SD	Garden City
177	13.2	Haverstraw-Stony Point Cent SD	Garnerville
177	13.2	Kenmore-Tonawanda Union Free SD	Buffalo
177	13.2	Mahopac Central SD	Mahopac
177	13.2	Marlboro Central SD	Marlboro
177	13.2	Sachem Central SD	Holbrook
177	13.2	Saranac Central SD	Dannemora
177	13.2	Schalmont Central SD	Schenectady
177	13.2	Vestal Central SD	Vestal
177	13.2	Whitesboro Central SD	Yorkville
192	13.1	Bath Central SD	Bath
192	13.1	Cazenovia Central SD	Cazenovia
192	13.1	Frontier Central SD	Hamburg
192	13.1	Gates-Chili Central SD	Rochester
192	13.1	Lewiston-Porter Central SD	Youngstown
192	13.1	Merrick Union Free SD	Merrick
192	13.1	Olean City SD	Olean
192	13.1	Orchard Park Central SD	Orchard Park
192	13.1	Pittsford Central SD	Pittsford
192	13.1	Spencerport Central SD	Spencerport
202	13.0	Averill Park Central SD	Averill Park
202	13.0	Byram Hills Central SD	Armonk
202	13.0	Canandaigua City SD	Canandaigua
202	13.0	Cleveland Hill Union Free SD	Cheektowaga
202	13.0	Clinton Central SD	Clinton
202	13.0	Ellenville Central SD	Ellenville
202	13.0	Lansing Central SD	Lansing
202	13.0	Levittown Union Free SD	Levittown
202	13.0	Maine-Endwell Central SD	Endwell
202	13.0	Ossining Union Free SD	Ossining
202	13.0	Owego-Apalachin Central SD	Owego
202	13.0	Peekskill City SD	Peekskill
202	13.0	Skaneateles Central SD	Skaneateles
202	13.0	Taconic Hills Central SD	Craryville
202	13.0	Union-Endicott Central SD	Endicott
202	13.0	West Hempstead Union Free SD	W Hempstead
202	13.0	Yorkshire-Pioneer Central SD	Yorkshire
219	12.9	Island Trees Union Free SD	Levittown
219	12.9	Liberty Central SD	Liberty
219	12.9	Mamaroneck Union Free SD	Mamaroneck
219	12.9	New Hartford Central SD	New Hartford
219	12.9	Rome City SD	Rome
219	12.9	Somers Central SD	Lincolndale
219	12.9	South Colonie Central SD	Albany
226	12.8	Babylon Union Free SD	Babylon
226	12.8	Brighton Central SD	Rochester
226	12.8	Glens Falls City SD	Glens Falls
226	12.8	Hauppauge Union Free SD	Hauppauge
226	12.8	Hilton Central SD	Hilton
226	12.8	Long Beach City SD	Long Beach
226	12.8	Pelham Union Free SD	Pelham
226	12.8	Phelps-Clifton Springs Cent SD	Clifton Spgs
226	12.8	Rondout Valley Central SD	Accord
226	12.8	Schuylerville Central SD	Schuylerville
226	12.8	Solvay Union Free SD	Solvay
226	12.8	Union Free SD of the Tarrytowns	Sleepy Hollow
238	12.7	Amsterdam City SD	Amsterdam
238	12.7	Ardsley Union Free SD	Ardsley
238	12.7	Attica Central SD	Attica
238	12.7	Depew Union Free SD	Depew
238	12.7	E Ramapo Central SD (Sprg Val)	Spring Valley
238	12.7	Lockport City SD	Lockport
238	12.7	Valley Stream 30 Union Free SD	Valley Stream
245	12.6	Albany City SD	Albany
245	12.6	Baldwin Union Free SD	Baldwin
245	12.6	Canton Central SD	Canton
245	12.6	Gorham-Middlesex CSD (M Whitman)	Rushville
245	12.6	Gowanda Central SD	Gowanda
245	12.6	Newark Central SD	Newark
245	12.6	Royalton-Hartland Central SD	Middleport
245	12.6	Sweet Home Central SD	Amherst
253	12.5	Amherst Central SD	Amherst
253	12.5	Eastchester Union Free SD	Eastchester
253	12.5	Glen Cove City SD	Glen Cove
253	12.5	Homer Central SD	Homer
253	12.5	Ramapo Central SD (Suffern)	Hillburn
253	12.5	South Orangetown Central SD	Blauvelt
253	12.5	Wayne Central SD	Ontario Center
253	12.5	Wilson Central SD	Wilson
261	12.4	Bethpage Union Free SD	Bethpage
261	12.4	Cortland City SD	Cortland
261	12.4	Gloversville City SD	Gloversville
261	12.4	Hamburg Central SD	Hamburg
261	12.4	Hampton Bays Union Free SD	Hampton Bays
261	12.4	Johnson City Central SD	Johnson City
261	12.4	Jordan-Elbridge Central SD	Jordan
261	12.4	Peru Central SD	Peru
261	12.4	Ravena-Coeymans-Selkirk CSD	Selkirk
261	12.4	Syracuse City SD	Syracuse
271	12.3	Catskill Central SD	Catskill
271	12.3	Hendrick Hudson Central SD	Montrose
271	12.3	Irvington Union Free SD	Irvington
271	12.3	Lynbrook Union Free SD	Lynbrook
271	12.3	Oneonta City SD	Oneonta
271	12.3	Onteora Central SD	Boiceville
271	12.3	Roslyn Union Free SD	Roslyn
271	12.3	Rye City SD	Rye
271	12.3	Scarsdale Union Free SD	Scarsdale
271	12.3	Shoreham-Wading River Central SD	Shoreham
271	12.3	Tonawanda City SD	Tonawanda
282	12.2	Cobleskill-Richmondville CSD	Cobleskill
282	12.2	Cohoes City SD	Cohoes
282	12.2	Farmingdale Union Free SD	Farmingdale
282	12.2	Rochester City SD	Rochester
282	12.2	Spackenkill Union Free SD	Poughkeepsie
282	12.2	Valley Stream 13 Union Free SD	Valley Stream
282	12.2	White Plains City SD	White Plains
282	12.2	Whitney Point Central SD	Whitney Point
290	12.1	Bayport-Blue Point Union Free SD	Bayport
290	12.1	Bedford Central SD	Mount Kisco
290	12.1	Dansville Central SD	Dansville
290	12.1	Livonia Central SD	Livonia
290	12.1	Penfield Central SD	Penfield
295	12.0	Amityville Union Free SD	Amityville
295	12.0	Evans-Brant Cent SD (Lake Shore)	Angola
295	12.0	Hudson City SD	Hudson
295	12.0	Ithaca City SD	Ithaca
295	12.0	Jamesville-Dewitt Central SD	Dewitt
295	12.0	Nanuet Union Free SD	Nanuet
295	12.0	Ogdensburg City SD	Ogdensburg
295	12.0	Palmyra-Macedon Central SD	Palmyra
295	12.0	Penn Yan Central SD	Penn Yan
295	12.0	Wayland-Cohocton Central SD	Wayland
305	11.9	Altmar-Parish-Williamstown CSD	Parish
305	11.9	East Syracuse-Minoa Central SD	East Syracuse
305	11.9	Medina Central SD	Medina
305	11.9	Phoenix Central SD	Phoenix
305	11.9	Uniondale Union Free SD	Uniondale
310	11.8	Batavia City SD	Batavia
310	11.8	East Hampton Union Free SD	East Hampton
310	11.8	Hewlett-Woodmere Union Free SD	Woodmere
310	11.8	Norwich City SD	Norwich
310	11.8	Rush-Henrietta Central SD	Henrietta
310	11.8	Salamanca City SD	Salamanca
316	11.7	East Williston Union Free SD	Old Westbury
316	11.7	Malone Central SD	Malone
316	11.7	Saranac Lake Central SD	Saranac Lake
316	11.7	Susquehanna Valley Central SD	Conklin
320	11.6	Binghamton City SD	Binghamton
320	11.6	Briarcliff Manor Union Free SD	Briarcliff Manor
320	11.6	Chappaqua Central SD	Chappaqua
320	11.6	Monticello Central SD	Monticello
320	11.6	Northport-East Northport UFSD	Northport
320	11.6	Nyack Union Free SD	Nyack
320	11.6	Roosevelt Union Free SD	Roosevelt
327	11.5	Beekmantown Central SD	West Chazy
327	11.5	Deer Park Union Free SD	Deer Park
327	11.5	Hornell City SD	Hornell
327	11.5	Jamestown City SD	Jamestown
327	11.5	Lackawanna City SD	Lackawanna
327	11.5	Salmon River Central SD	Ft Covington
333	11.4	Geneva City SD	Geneva
333	11.4	Huntington Union Free SD	Huntington Stn
333	11.4	Indian River Central SD	Philadelphia
333	11.4	Malverne Union Free SD	Malverne
333	11.4	Port Washington Union Free SD	Pt Washington
338	11.3	Adirondack Central SD	Boonville
338	11.3	Locust Valley Central SD	Locust Valley
338	11.3	Manhasset Union Free SD	Manhasset
338	11.3	Mattituck-Cutchogue UFSD	Cutchogue
338	11.3	Plainview-Old Bethpage Cent SD	Plainview
338	11.3	Sullivan West Central SD	Callicoon
344	11.2	Greenburgh Central SD	Hartsdale
344	11.2	Harrison Central SD	Harrison
344	11.2	Herricks Union Free SD	New Hyde Park
347	11.1	Fredonia Central SD	Fredonia
347	11.1	North Rose-Wolcott Central SD	Wolcott
347	11.1	North Shore Central SD	Sea Cliff
350	11.0	Hastings-On-Hudson Union Free SD	Hastings-on-Hud
350	11.0	Syosset Central SD	Syosset
352	10.9	Mount Pleasant Central SD	Thornwood
353	10.8	Mineola Union Free SD	Mineola
353	10.8	Oyster Bay-East Norwich CSD	Oyster Bay
353	10.8	Rockville Centre Union Free SD	Rockville Ctre
356	10.7	Dryden Central SD	Dryden
356	10.7	Great Neck Union Free SD	Great Neck
358	10.6	Sherburne-Earlville Central SD	Sherburne
359	10.5	Westhampton Beach Union Free SD	Westhampton Bch
360	10.4	Carle Place Union Free SD	Carle Place
361	10.3	Plattsburgh City SD	Plattsburgh
362	10.2	Southampton Union Free SD	Southampton
363	10.1	Dunkirk City SD	Dunkirk
363	10.1	Jericho Union Free SD	Jericho
363	10.1	Lawrence Union Free SD	Lawrence
366	3.8	Boces Nassau	Garden City
367	3.2	Boces Eastern Suffolk	Patchogue
368	n/a	New York City Geographic Dist 9	Bronx
368	n/a	New York City Geographic Dist 15	Brooklyn
368	n/a	Nyc Alternative HS District	New York

Student/Librarian Ratio

Rank	Ratio	District Name	City
1	2,644.5	Mahopac Central SD	Mahopac
2	2,075.0	Highland Central SD	Highland
3	1,942.0	Franklin Square Union Free SD	Franklin Square
4	1,934.0	Putnam Valley Central SD	Putnam Valley
5	1,819.0	Wallkill Central SD	Wallkill
6	1,818.0	Islip Union Free SD	Islip
7	1,803.0	Rockville Centre Union Free SD	Rockville Ctre
8	1,794.0	Ilion Central SD	Ilion
9	1,786.0	Waverly Central SD	Waverly
10	1,747.2	Niagara Falls City SD	Niagara Falls
11	1,657.0	Northeastern Clinton Central SD	Champlain
12	1,638.8	Baldwin Union Free SD	Baldwin
13	1,566.8	Troy City SD	Troy
14	1,549.0	Croton-Harmon Union Free SD	Croton-On-Hud
15	1,548.0	Adirondack Central SD	Boonville
16	1,531.0	Cheektowaga-Sloan Union Free SD	Sloan
17	1,504.0	Wilson Central SD	Wilson
18	1,475.5	New York City Public Schools	Brooklyn
19	1,341.0	Mexico Central SD	Mexico
20	1,304.8	Monticello Central SD	Monticello
21	1,283.2	Sayville Union Free SD	Sayville
22	1,264.5	Pelham Union Free SD	Pelham
23	1,256.0	Dryden Central SD	Dryden
24	1,249.5	Union Free SD of the Tarrytowns	Sleepy Hollow
25	1,244.4	White Plains City SD	White Plains
26	1,235.2	William Floyd Union Free SD	Mastic Beach
27	1,209.0	Hudson Falls Central SD	Hudson Falls
28	1,204.3	Beacon City SD	Beacon
29	1,189.5	South Country Central SD	E Patchogue
30	1,166.4	Bellmore-Merrick Central High SD	North Merrick
31	1,156.4	Carmel Central SD	Patterson
32	1,141.5	Valley Stream Central High SD	Valley Stream
33	1,135.8	Minisink Valley Central SD	Slate Hill
34	1,110.3	Hilton Central SD	Hilton
35	1,107.1	Brentwood Union Free SD	Brentwood
36	1,097.3	South Glens Falls Central SD	S Glens Falls
37	1,091.7	Yonkers City SD	Yonkers
38	1,087.6	Elmira City SD	Elmira
39	1,087.0	Newfane Central SD	Newfane
40	1,084.0	Johnstown City SD	Johnstown
41	1,063.0	Ossining Union Free SD	Ossining
42	1,057.3	Middle Country Central SD	Centereach
43	1,056.9	Harrison Central SD	Harrison
44	1,050.5	Dunkirk City SD	Dunkirk
45	1,037.5	Garden City Union Free SD	Garden City
46	1,033.5	Dover Union Free SD	Dover Plains
47	1,027.0	Bath Central SD	Bath
48	1,022.0	South Jefferson Central SD	Adams Center

49	1,021.2	Washingtonville Central SD	Washingtonville
50	1,021.1	Port Chester-Rye Union Free SD	Port Chester
51	1,010.0	Miller Place Union Free SD	Miller Place
52	998.6	Auburn City SD	Auburn
53	996.7	Utica City SD	Utica
54	983.5	Irvington Union Free SD	Irvington
55	976.5	Queensbury Union Free SD	Queensbury
56	973.7	Goshen Central SD	Goshen
57	966.4	Cheektowaga Central SD	Cheektowaga
58	963.0	Central Islip Union Free SD	Central Islip
59	960.7	Roosevelt Union Free SD	Roosevelt
60	951.3	New Rochelle City SD	New Rochelle
61	949.3	Starpoint Central SD	Lockport
62	941.0	Liberty Central SD	Liberty
63	939.6	Middletown City SD	Middletown
64	932.3	Albion Central SD	Albion
65	929.6	Mount Sinai Union Free SD	Mount Sinai
66	922.0	Eden Central SD	Eden
67	920.0	Attica Central SD	Attica
68	913.5	Wayland-Cohocton Central SD	Wayland
69	907.0	Buffalo City SD	Buffalo
70	906.5	Cairo-Durham Central SD	Cairo
71	905.3	East Islip Union Free SD	Islip Terrace
72	904.2	Ballston Spa Central SD	Ballston Spa
73	904.0	Newburgh City SD	Newburgh
74	902.0	Seaford Union Free SD	Seaford
75	901.2	Ardsley Union Free SD	Ardsley
76	898.5	Rocky Point Union Free SD	Rocky Point
77	896.5	Waterloo Central SD	Waterloo
78	895.5	Brighton Central SD	Rochester
79	893.3	Eastchester Union Free SD	Eastchester
79	893.3	Freeport Union Free SD	Freeport
81	892.8	Copiague Union Free SD	Copiague
82	890.0	Harborfields Central SD	Greenlawn
82	890.0	Haverstraw-Stony Point Cent SD	Garnerville
84	889.0	Victor Central SD	Victor
85	887.3	Three Village Central SD	East Setauket
85	887.3	Yorkshire-Pioneer Central SD	Yorkshire
87	884.5	Hampton Bays Union Free SD	Hampton Bays
88	878.3	Half Hollow Hills Central SD	Dix Hills
89	876.0	Southwestern Cent SD Jamestown	Jamestown
90	871.5	Gouverneur Central SD	Gouverneur
91	867.0	Honeoye Falls-Lima Central SD	Honeoye Falls
92	866.8	Watertown City SD	Watertown
93	865.7	Johnson City Central SD	Johnson City
93	865.7	Schenectady City SD	Schenectady
95	863.9	Sachem Central SD	Holbrook
96	863.5	Pleasantville Union Free SD	Pleasantville
97	860.7	South Huntington Union Free SD	Huntington Stn
98	854.3	Lindenhurst Union Free SD	Lindenhurst
99	849.5	Akron Central SD	Akron
100	849.0	North Syracuse Central SD	N Syracuse
101	847.0	Olean City SD	Olean
102	846.5	Schuylerville Central SD	Schuylerville
103	845.9	Rochester City SD	Rochester
104	845.3	Brockport Central SD	Brockport
105	841.8	Arlington Central SD	Poughkeepsie
106	841.0	Royalton-Hartland Central SD	Middleport
107	837.2	Canandaigua City SD	Canandaigua
108	835.3	Coxsackie-Athens Central SD	Coxsackie
109	835.0	Rotterdam-Mohonasen Central SD	Schenectady
110	834.0	Floral Park-Bellerose UFSD	Floral Park
111	826.8	Frontier Central SD	Hamburg
112	823.5	Altmar-Parish-Williamstown CSD	Parish
113	821.0	North Rose-Wolcott Central SD	Wolcott
114	820.0	Clarence Central SD	Clarence
115	819.1	Hornell City SD	Hornell
116	817.0	Clinton Central SD	Clinton
117	815.7	Pine Bush Central SD	Pine Bush
118	814.0	Bay Shore Union Free SD	Bay Shore
119	810.3	Riverhead Central SD	Riverhead
120	809.7	Wappingers Central SD	Wappingers Fls
121	809.3	Lansingburgh Central SD	Troy
122	809.0	Williamsville Central SD	East Amherst
123	807.5	Evans-Brant Cent SD (Lake Shore)	Angola
124	807.2	Westbury Union Free SD	Old Westbury
125	805.7	Hudson City SD	Hudson
126	805.6	Sweet Home Central SD	Amherst
127	803.0	Fonda-Fultonville Central SD	Fonda
128	801.5	Oswego City SD	Oswego
129	801.4	Kings Park Central SD	Kings Park
130	798.5	Gorham-Middlesex CSD (M Whitman)	Rushville
130	798.5	Mamaroneck Union Free SD	Mamaroneck
132	797.0	Glen Cove City SD	Glen Cove
133	795.8	Sewanhaka Central High SD	Floral Park
134	795.4	Lancaster Central SD	Lancaster
135	795.0	Pearl River Union Free SD	Pearl River
135	795.0	Springville-Griffith Inst Cent	Springville
137	794.2	Webster Central SD	Webster
138	793.5	Cleveland Hill Union Free SD	Cheektowaga
139	792.7	Depew Union Free SD	Depew
140	786.0	General Brown Central SD	Dexter
141	785.0	Somers Central SD	Lincolndale
142	781.3	Amherst Central SD	Amherst
143	780.3	Warwick Valley Central SD	Warwick
144	773.8	North Tonawanda City SD	N Tonawanda
145	773.5	Canastota Central SD	Canastota
146	769.1	Saratoga Springs City SD	Saratoga Spgs
147	768.6	Long Beach City SD	Long Beach
148	767.4	Lakeland Central SD	Shrub Oak
149	766.0	Gowanda Central SD	Gowanda
149	766.0	Ramapo Central SD (Suffern)	Hillburn
151	764.8	Patchogue-Medford Union Free SD	Patchogue
152	760.0	Wyandanch Union Free SD	Wyandanch
153	758.2	Oceanside Union Free SD	Oceanside
154	758.1	East Hampton Union Free SD	East Hampton
155	756.5	Canton Central SD	Canton
156	755.1	Hamburg Central SD	Hamburg
157	753.4	Longwood Central SD	Middle Island
158	747.0	Churchville-Chili Central SD	Churchville
159	745.7	North Babylon Union Free SD	North Babylon
160	745.2	Brewster Central SD	Brewster
161	745.0	Baldwinsville Central SD	Baldwinsville
161	745.0	Shenendehowa Central SD	Clifton Park
163	743.8	South Orangetown Central SD	Blauvelt
164	743.2	Levittown Union Free SD	Levittown
165	742.8	Fredonia Central SD	Fredonia
166	740.7	Palmyra-Macedon Central SD	Palmyra
167	735.5	Island Trees Union Free SD	Levittown
168	734.3	Carthage Central SD	Carthage
169	734.0	Cohoes City SD	Cohoes
170	733.6	Massena Central SD	Massena
171	725.0	Spencerport Central SD	Spencerport
172	724.0	Onteora Central SD	Boiceville
173	721.2	Plainedge Union Free SD	N Massapequa
174	717.5	Port Jervis City SD	Port Jervis
175	716.0	Connetquot Central SD	Bohemia
176	715.7	Marcellus Central SD	Marcellus
177	714.5	Nyack Union Free SD	Nyack
178	714.4	East Greenbush Central SD	E Greenbush
179	711.7	Susquehanna Valley Central SD	Conklin
180	711.3	Monroe-Woodbury Central SD	Central Valley
181	709.2	Averill Park Central SD	Averill Park
182	705.7	West Babylon Union Free SD	West Babylon
183	705.4	E Ramapo Central SD (Sprg Val)	Spring Valley
184	703.2	Yorktown Central SD	Yorktown Hgts
185	700.2	Pittsford Central SD	Pittsford
186	698.1	Valley Central SD (Montgomery)	Montgomery
187	697.0	East Aurora Union Free SD	East Aurora
188	695.8	Hastings-On-Hudson Union Free SD	Hastings-on-Hud
189	693.1	Hewlett-Woodmere Union Free SD	Woodmere
190	692.0	Hempstead Union Free SD	Hempstead
191	689.8	Mount Vernon City SD	Mount Vernon
191	689.8	Whitesboro Central SD	Yorkville
193	681.7	Windsor Central SD	Windsor
194	681.3	Phelps-Clifton Springs Cent SD	Clifton Spgs
195	680.3	Lackawanna City SD	Lackawanna
196	679.4	Albany City SD	Albany
197	679.2	Smithtown Central SD	Smithtown
198	679.1	Kingston City SD	Kingston
199	678.3	Penn Yan Central SD	Penn Yan
200	677.6	Fairport Central SD	Fairport
201	677.3	Chenango Valley Central SD	Binghamton
202	677.1	Port Washington Union Free SD	Pt Washington
203	675.0	Manhasset Union Free SD	Manhasset
204	672.0	Newark Central SD	Newark
205	669.7	Babylon Union Free SD	Babylon
206	668.9	Hyde Park Central SD	Poughkeepsie
207	668.8	Maine-Endwell Central SD	Endwell
207	668.8	Syracuse City SD	Syracuse
209	667.7	Owego-Apalachin Central SD	Owego
210	660.8	Bethlehem Central SD	Delmar
211	659.9	Fayetteville-Manlius Central SD	Manlius
212	658.2	West Irondequoit Central SD	Rochester
213	657.1	Greece Central SD	Rochester
214	656.7	Merrick Union Free SD	Merrick
215	656.5	Herricks Union Free SD	New Hyde Park
216	656.1	West Islip Union Free SD	West Islip
217	656.0	Saranac Central SD	Dannemora
218	655.0	Brookhaven-Comsewogue UFSD	Pt Jefferson Stn
219	652.1	Cheektowaga-Maryvale UFSD	Cheektowaga
220	647.2	Farmingdale Union Free SD	Farmingdale
221	645.8	Fulton City SD	Fulton
222	644.1	Elwood Union Free SD	Greenlawn
222	644.1	West Genesee Central SD	Camillus
224	641.4	West Seneca Central SD	West Seneca
225	639.2	Northport-East Northport UFSD	Northport
226	638.3	South Colonie Central SD	Albany
227	638.0	Grand Island Central SD	Grand Island
228	636.0	Boces Eastern Suffolk	Patchogue
229	634.4	Niagara-Wheatfield Central SD	Niagara Falls
230	633.5	Geneva City SD	Geneva
231	630.5	Glens Falls City SD	Glens Falls
232	629.3	Guilderland Central SD	Guilderland
233	626.6	Central Square Central SD	Central Square
234	625.9	Commack Union Free SD	E Northport
235	624.8	Malone Central SD	Malone
235	624.8	Orchard Park Central SD	Orchard Park
237	624.7	Chenango Forks Central SD	Binghamton
237	624.7	Elmont Union Free SD	Elmont
239	623.7	Taconic Hills Central SD	Craryville
240	623.3	Clarkstown Central SD	New City
241	623.0	Katonah-Lewisboro Union Free SD	South Salem
242	622.6	East Meadow Union Free SD	Westbury
243	622.5	Roslyn Union Free SD	Roslyn
244	620.0	Penfield Central SD	Penfield
245	619.3	Whitney Point Central SD	Whitney Point
246	618.6	Cornwall Central SD	Cornwall-on-Hud
247	617.7	Holland Patent Central SD	Holland Patent
248	616.6	Amityville Union Free SD	Amityville
249	611.7	Spackenkill Union Free SD	Poughkeepsie
250	611.3	Edgemont Union Free SD	Scarsdale
251	611.0	Peekskill City SD	Peekskill
252	610.3	Marlboro Central SD	Marlboro
253	610.0	Poughkeepsie City SD	Poughkeepsie
254	609.6	Watkins Glen Central SD	Watkins Glen
255	605.7	Catskill Central SD	Catskill
256	604.8	Union-Endicott Central SD	Endicott
257	604.3	Phoenix Central SD	Phoenix
258	604.0	East Williston Union Free SD	Old Westbury
258	604.0	Ellenville Central SD	Ellenville
260	602.8	Deer Park Union Free SD	Deer Park
261	602.2	Kenmore-Tonawanda Union Free SD	Buffalo
262	601.3	Cazenovia Central SD	Cazenovia
263	600.5	Lewiston-Porter Central SD	Youngstown
264	600.3	Amsterdam City SD	Amsterdam
265	597.7	Cold Spring Harbor Central SD	Cold Sprg Harbor
266	596.3	Ravena-Coeymans-Selkirk CSD	Selkirk
266	596.3	Wantagh Union Free SD	Wantagh
268	595.3	Red Hook Central SD	Red Hook
269	594.0	New Paltz Central SD	New Paltz
270	593.6	Hauppauge Union Free SD	Hauppauge
271	591.8	Homer Central SD	Homer
272	589.7	Southampton Union Free SD	Southampton
273	588.3	East Syracuse-Minoa Central SD	East Syracuse
274	587.3	West Hempstead Union Free SD	W Hempstead
275	586.0	Sherburne-Earlville Central SD	Sherburne
276	585.7	East Irondequoit Central SD	Rochester
277	585.3	Hannibal Central SD	Hannibal
278	585.1	Chappaqua Central SD	Chappaqua
278	585.1	Hicksville Union Free SD	Hicksville
280	582.2	Indian River Central SD	Philadelphia
281	582.0	Shoreham-Wading River Central SD	Shoreham
282	578.1	Bethpage Union Free SD	Bethpage
283	577.5	Corning City SD	Painted Post
284	576.8	Hendrick Hudson Central SD	Montrose
285	575.9	Syosset Central SD	Syosset
286	575.8	Peru Central SD	Peru
287	575.7	Westhampton Beach Union Free SD	Westhampton Bch
288	572.3	Briarcliff Manor Union Free SD	Briarcliff Manor
289	571.3	Kinderhook Central SD	Valatie
290	570.3	Lockport City SD	Lockport
291	569.0	Camden Central SD	Camden
292	568.1	Binghamton City SD	Binghamton
293	561.9	Gates-Chili Central SD	Rochester
294	561.8	Norwich City SD	Norwich
295	556.0	Burnt Hls-Ballston Lake Cent SD	Scotia
295	556.0	Saugerties Central SD	Saugerties
297	554.8	Wayne Central SD	Ontario Center
298	552.2	Plainview-Old Bethpage Cent SD	Plainview
299	552.0	Broadalbin-Perth Central SD	Broadalbin
299	552.0	Cobleskill-Richmondville CSD	Cobleskill
301	549.9	Massapequa Union Free SD	Massapequa
302	548.4	Rondout Valley Central SD	Accord
303	548.0	Nanuet Union Free SD	Nanuet
304	547.3	Horseheads Central SD	Horseheads
305	544.8	Beekmantown Central SD	West Chazy
306	543.4	Jamesville-Dewitt Central SD	Dewitt
307	540.3	Bedford Central SD	Mount Kisco
308	539.3	Liverpool Central SD	Liverpool
309	539.0	Rome City SD	Rome
310	537.7	Gloversville City SD	Gloversville
311	537.6	Rye City SD	Rye
312	536.4	Batavia City SD	Batavia
313	536.3	North Colonie Central SD	Latham
314	536.2	New Hyde Park-Garden City Park	New Hyde Park
315	535.0	Jericho Union Free SD	Jericho
316	534.7	Salmon River Central SD	Ft Covington
317	534.3	Uniondale Union Free SD	Uniondale
318	534.0	New Hartford Central SD	New Hartford
319	533.3	Vestal Central SD	Vestal
320	533.0	Livonia Central SD	Livonia
321	527.4	Lawrence Union Free SD	Lawrence
322	525.8	Valley Stream 13 Union Free SD	Valley Stream
323	523.5	Lynbrook Union Free SD	Lynbrook
324	523.1	Rush-Henrietta Central SD	Henrietta
325	522.7	Sullivan West Central SD	Callicoon

326	521.0	Mattituck-Cutchogue UFSD	Cutchogue
327	518.1	Schalmont Central SD	Schenectady
328	518.0	Alden Central SD	Alden
329	516.4	Huntington Union Free SD	Huntington Stn
330	513.8	Plattsburgh City SD	Plattsburgh
331	513.0	Chittenango Central SD	Chittenango
332	512.3	Westhill Central SD	Syracuse
333	509.8	Boces Nassau	Garden City
334	509.7	Lansing Central SD	Lansing
335	509.4	Great Neck Union Free SD	Great Neck
336	507.6	Scarsdale Union Free SD	Scarsdale
337	505.6	North Bellmore Union Free SD	Bellmore
338	504.5	Ogdensburg City SD	Ogdensburg
339	504.3	Salamanca City SD	Salamanca
340	500.7	Valley Stream 30 Union Free SD	Valley Stream
341	500.3	Chatham Central SD	Chatham
342	500.0	Carle Place Union Free SD	Carle Place
343	498.0	Bayport-Blue Point Union Free SD	Bayport
344	495.3	Greenburgh Central SD	Hartsdale
345	492.2	Byram Hills Central SD	Armonk
346	492.0	Scotia-Glenville Central SD	Scotia
347	485.0	Sherrill City SD	Verona
348	484.2	Iroquois Central SD	Elma
349	475.5	Oyster Bay-East Norwich CSD	Oyster Bay
350	474.5	Cortland City SD	Cortland
351	465.2	Medina Central SD	Medina
352	462.0	Skaneateles Central SD	Skaneateles
353	457.8	Niskayuna Central SD	Schenectady
354	456.5	Malverne Union Free SD	Malverne
355	442.4	Ithaca City SD	Ithaca
356	442.0	North Shore Central SD	Sea Cliff
357	437.5	Dansville Central SD	Dansville
358	436.8	Solvay Union Free SD	Solvay
359	430.0	Jamestown City SD	Jamestown
360	425.8	Jordan-Elbridge Central SD	Jordan
361	414.7	Mineola Union Free SD	Mineola
362	406.3	Saranac Lake Central SD	Saranac Lake
363	390.5	Tonawanda City SD	Tonawanda
364	379.2	Locust Valley Central SD	Locust Valley
365	364.3	Oneida City SD	Oneida
366	357.0	Oneonta City SD	Oneonta
367	n/a	Mount Pleasant Central SD	Thornwood
367	n/a	New York City Geographic Dist 9	Bronx
367	n/a	New York City Geographic Dist 15	Brooklyn
367	n/a	Nyc Alternative HS District	New York

Student/Counselor Ratio

Rank	Ratio	District Name	City
1	4,248.0	Elmont Union Free SD	Elmont
2	1,104.0	Broadalbin-Perth Central SD	Broadalbin
3	893.0	Waverly Central SD	Waverly
4	835.3	Coxsackie-Athens Central SD	Coxsackie
5	824.5	Utica City SD	Utica
6	810.3	Riverhead Central SD	Riverhead
7	805.7	Hudson City SD	Hudson
8	803.0	Fonda-Fultonville Central SD	Fonda
9	792.0	Hempstead Union Free SD	Hempstead
10	765.5	Cheektowaga-Sloan Union Free SD	Sloan
11	764.5	Lansing Central SD	Lansing
12	722.7	Johnstown City SD	Johnstown
13	709.6	Central Islip Union Free SD	Central Islip
14	693.9	Troy City SD	Troy
15	691.7	Highland Central SD	Highland
16	689.3	Lancaster Central SD	Lancaster
17	684.1	Albany City SD	Albany
18	679.0	East Islip Union Free SD	Islip Terrace
19	658.4	South Glens Falls Central SD	S Glens Falls
20	645.8	Fulton City SD	Fulton
21	645.5	Patchogue-Medford Union Free SD	Patchogue
22	640.8	Lindenhurst Union Free SD	Lindenhurst
23	640.7	Ilion Central SD	Ilion
24	637.5	Oneida City SD	Oneida
25	628.8	William Floyd Union Free SD	Mastic Beach
26	627.1	Hannibal Central SD	Hannibal
27	619.7	Buffalo City SD	Buffalo
28	619.1	Watertown City SD	Watertown
29	617.5	West Babylon Union Free SD	West Babylon
30	613.3	Attica Central SD	Attica
31	612.1	Middle Country Central SD	Centereach
32	611.8	Pine Bush Central SD	Pine Bush
33	607.3	Wappingers Central SD	Wappingers Fls
34	606.4	North Syracuse Central SD	N Syracuse
35	606.3	Sherrill City SD	Verona
36	605.7	Catskill Central SD	Catskill
37	604.5	Hudson Falls Central SD	Hudson Falls
38	604.3	Cairo-Durham Central SD	Cairo
39	602.2	Beacon City SD	Beacon
40	601.1	Oswego City SD	Oswego
41	596.7	Connetquot Central SD	Bohemia
42	595.3	Red Hook Central SD	Red Hook
43	594.8	South Country Central SD	E Patchogue
44	592.1	West Seneca Central SD	West Seneca
45	591.8	Homer Central SD	Homer
46	589.7	Hampton Bays Union Free SD	Hampton Bays
47	587.4	Carthage Central SD	Carthage
48	585.7	Dover Union Free SD	Dover Plains
49	585.3	Hyde Park Central SD	Poughkeepsie
50	585.1	Hicksville Union Free SD	Hicksville
51	580.4	Monroe-Woodbury Central SD	Central Valley
52	580.0	North Babylon Union Free SD	North Babylon
53	576.8	Saratoga Springs City SD	Saratoga Spgs
54	576.6	Rochester City SD	Rochester
55	576.4	Roosevelt Union Free SD	Roosevelt
56	574.0	Port Jervis City SD	Port Jervis
57	571.5	East Greenbush Central SD	E Greenbush
58	569.9	Newburgh City SD	Newburgh
59	567.9	Minisink Valley Central SD	Slate Hill
60	562.0	Kingston City SD	Kingston
61	560.1	Syracuse City SD	Syracuse
62	557.6	Deer Park Union Free SD	Deer Park
63	553.6	Brentwood Union Free SD	Brentwood
64	551.9	Whitesboro Central SD	Yorkville
65	549.9	Massapequa Union Free SD	Massapequa
66	548.2	Amherst Central SD	Amherst
67	547.1	Burnt Hls-Ballston Lake Cent SD	Scotia
68	542.2	Poughkeepsie City SD	Poughkeepsie
69	541.7	Saranac Lake Central SD	Saranac Lake
70	536.4	Mexico Central SD	Mexico
71	535.0	Maine-Endwell Central SD	Endwell
72	534.0	Marlboro Central SD	Marlboro
73	532.3	Gorham-Middlesex CSD (M Whitman)	Rushville
74	531.9	South Colonie Central SD	Albany
75	531.7	Arlington Central SD	Poughkeepsie
75	531.7	Grand Island Central SD	Grand Island
77	528.2	Clarkstown Central SD	New City
78	524.0	Brookhaven-Comsewogue UFSD	Pt Jefferson Stn
78	524.0	General Brown Central SD	Dexter
80	519.7	Wallkill Central SD	Wallkill
81	518.3	Herricks Union Free SD	New Hyde Park
82	518.0	Alden Central SD	Alden
83	517.9	Clarence Central SD	Clarence
84	516.3	Croton-Harmon Union Free SD	Croton-On-Hud
85	516.0	Adirondack Central SD	Boonville
86	515.9	North Tonawanda City SD	N Tonawanda
87	515.7	Canastota Central SD	Canastota
88	515.3	West Genesee Central SD	Camillus
89	515.0	Baldwin Union Free SD	Baldwin
90	514.9	Guilderland Central SD	Guilderland
91	513.8	Ballston Spa Central SD	Ballston Spa
92	513.5	Bath Central SD	Bath
92	513.5	West Islip Union Free SD	West Islip
94	513.4	Rocky Point Union Free SD	Rocky Point
95	513.3	Sayville Union Free SD	Sayville
96	511.6	New York City Public Schools	Brooklyn
97	511.1	Frontier Central SD	Hamburg
98	510.7	Ramapo Central SD (Suffern)	Hillburn
99	510.3	Lackawanna City SD	Lackawanna
100	508.0	Chenango Valley Central SD	Binghamton
100	508.0	Watkins Glen Central SD	Watkins Glen
102	506.8	Geneva City SD	Geneva
103	505.0	Miller Place Union Free SD	Miller Place
103	505.0	Schenectady City SD	Schenectady
105	504.0	Haverstraw-Stony Point Cent SD	Garnerville
105	504.0	Union-Endicott Central SD	Endicott
107	503.3	Monticello Central SD	Monticello
108	502.4	Elwood Union Free SD	Greenlawn
109	501.3	Central Square Central SD	Central Square
110	499.3	Auburn City SD	Auburn
111	496.7	Baldwinsville Central SD	Baldwinsville
112	495.5	Bay Shore Union Free SD	Bay Shore
113	490.7	Fairport Central SD	Fairport
114	488.7	Kings Park Central SD	Kings Park
115	488.5	Medina Central SD	Medina
116	486.8	Goshen Central SD	Goshen
117	486.4	Horseheads Central SD	Horseheads
118	485.6	Lansingburgh Central SD	Troy
119	484.2	Iroquois Central SD	Elma
120	483.5	Putnam Valley Central SD	Putnam Valley
121	483.2	Cheektowaga Central SD	Cheektowaga
122	480.8	Mahopac Central SD	Mahopac
123	480.7	Binghamton City SD	Binghamton
124	477.1	Rotterdam-Mohonasen Central SD	Schenectady
125	476.6	Saugerties Central SD	Saugerties
126	476.0	Valley Central SD (Montgomery)	Montgomery
127	475.8	Elmira City SD	Elmira
128	475.6	New Rochelle City SD	New Rochelle
129	475.2	New Paltz Central SD	New Paltz
130	474.7	Starpoint Central SD	Lockport
131	474.5	Cortland City SD	Cortland
132	474.0	Schalmont Central SD	Schenectady
133	472.2	Levittown Union Free SD	Levittown
134	471.9	Akron Central SD	Akron
135	470.3	Mount Vernon City SD	Mount Vernon
136	469.4	Commack Union Free SD	E Northport
137	468.5	Chenango Forks Central SD	Binghamton
138	468.2	Warwick Valley Central SD	Warwick
139	463.1	Smithtown Central SD	Smithtown
140	461.1	Garden City Union Free SD	Garden City
141	461.0	Eden Central SD	Eden
142	459.9	Lockport City SD	Lockport
143	459.0	Huntington Union Free SD	Huntington Stn
144	458.5	Edgemont Union Free SD	Scarsdale
144	458.5	South Orangetown Central SD	Blauvelt
146	458.2	Carmel Central SD	Patterson
147	457.9	Uniondale Union Free SD	Uniondale
148	457.0	Kinderhook Central SD	Valatie
149	456.5	Malverne Union Free SD	Malverne
150	456.0	Wyandanch Union Free SD	Wyandanch
151	454.6	East Aurora Union Free SD	East Aurora
152	454.5	Islip Union Free SD	Islip
153	454.4	Union Free SD of the Tarrytowns	Sleepy Hollow
154	453.7	Three Village Central SD	East Setauket
155	453.0	Ellenville Central SD	Ellenville
156	451.2	Byram Hills Central SD	Armonk
157	451.1	Niagara-Wheatfield Central SD	Niagara Falls
158	450.8	Plainedge Union Free SD	N Massapequa
159	448.7	Lynbrook Union Free SD	Lynbrook
160	447.3	Wantagh Union Free SD	Wantagh
161	446.8	Port Chester-Rye Union Free SD	Port Chester
162	446.2	Shoreham-Wading River Central SD	Shoreham
163	444.6	Bedford Central SD	Mount Kisco
164	444.5	Victor Central SD	Victor
165	443.3	Averill Park Central SD	Averill Park
166	440.4	Amityville Union Free SD	Amityville
166	440.4	Cohoes City SD	Cohoes
168	439.5	Yorktown Central SD	Yorktown Hgts
169	439.4	Sachem Central SD	Holbrook
170	438.5	Middletown City SD	Middletown
171	438.3	Copiague Union Free SD	Copiague
172	436.7	E Ramapo Central SD (Sprg Val)	Spring Valley
172	436.7	Lewiston-Porter Central SD	Youngstown
174	436.4	Peekskill City SD	Peekskill
175	434.4	Onteora Central SD	Boiceville
176	434.0	Queensbury Union Free SD	Queensbury
177	433.5	Honeoye Falls-Lima Central SD	Honeoye Falls
178	431.5	Farmingdale Union Free SD	Farmingdale
178	431.5	Longwood Central SD	Middle Island
180	430.0	Clinton Central SD	Clinton
181	429.4	Bethpage Union Free SD	Bethpage
181	429.4	Marcellus Central SD	Marcellus
183	427.4	Oceanside Union Free SD	Oceanside
184	427.3	Palmyra-Macedon Central SD	Palmyra
185	427.2	Cheektowaga-Maryvale UFSD	Cheektowaga
186	427.0	Susquehanna Valley Central SD	Conklin
187	426.4	Livonia Central SD	Livonia
188	425.8	Jordan-Elbridge Central SD	Jordan
189	424.9	Owego-Apalachin Central SD	Owego
190	424.3	Yorkshire-Pioneer Central SD	Yorkshire
191	424.0	Pearl River Union Free SD	Pearl River
192	423.3	Schuylerville Central SD	Schuylerville
193	422.9	Ithaca City SD	Ithaca
194	422.8	Harrison Central SD	Harrison
195	421.7	Scotia-Glenville Central SD	Scotia
196	421.5	Pelham Union Free SD	Pelham
197	420.5	Royalton-Hartland Central SD	Middleport
198	419.3	Rockville Centre Union Free SD	Rockville Ctre
199	418.8	Harborfields Central SD	Greenlawn
200	418.4	Cold Spring Harbor Central SD	Cold Sprg Harbor
201	415.5	Hauppauge Union Free SD	Hauppauge
202	415.0	Bayport-Blue Point Union Free SD	Bayport
203	414.0	Brewster Central SD	Brewster
204	413.6	Locust Valley Central SD	Locust Valley
205	412.9	South Huntington Union Free SD	Huntington Stn
206	412.0	Hendrick Hudson Central SD	Montrose
207	411.8	Altmar-Parish-Williamstown CSD	Parish
208	409.8	Westhill Central SD	Syracuse
209	409.3	Lakeland Central SD	Shrub Oak
210	408.8	Phelps-Clifton Springs Cent SD	Clifton Spgs
210	408.8	South Jefferson Central SD	Adams Center
212	408.0	North Shore Central SD	Sea Cliff
213	407.8	Gates-Chili Central SD	Rochester
214	407.5	Churchville-Chili Central SD	Churchville
215	407.3	Rye City SD	Rye
216	406.4	Camden Central SD	Camden
217	404.7	East Meadow Union Free SD	Westbury
218	403.6	Westbury Union Free SD	Old Westbury
219	403.1	Yonkers City SD	Yonkers
220	402.8	Mount Sinai Union Free SD	Mount Sinai
220	402.8	Phoenix Central SD	Phoenix
222	401.8	Babylon Union Free SD	Babylon
223	399.3	Mamaroneck Union Free SD	Mamaroneck
224	398.9	Orchard Park Central SD	Orchard Park
225	398.5	Williamsville Central SD	East Amherst
226	397.5	Springville-Griffith Inst Cent	Springville
227	396.8	Cleveland Hill Union Free SD	Cheektowaga
228	396.2	Greenburgh Central SD	Hartsdale
229	395.3	Newfane Central SD	Newfane

230	393.6	Saranac Central SD	Dannemora
231	393.4	Irvington Union Free SD	Irvington
232	392.8	Washingtonville Central SD	Washingtonville
233	392.5	Somers Central SD	Lincolndale
234	392.3	Oyster Bay-East Norwich CSD	Oyster Bay
235	392.0	Sullivan West Central SD	Callicoon
236	390.6	Rush-Henrietta Central SD	Henrietta
237	390.5	Tonawanda City SD	Tonawanda
238	389.6	Syosset Central SD	Syosset
239	388.3	Webster Central SD	Webster
240	386.6	Cornwall Central SD	Cornwall-on-Hud
240	386.6	Seaford Union Free SD	Seaford
242	386.2	East Irondequoit Central SD	Rochester
243	385.7	Manhasset Union Free SD	Manhasset
244	384.0	Newark Central SD	Newark
245	383.3	Greece Central SD	Rochester
246	382.3	Spackenkill Union Free SD	Poughkeepsie
247	381.4	New Hartford Central SD	New Hartford
248	378.2	Amsterdam City SD	Amsterdam
249	377.6	Bethlehem Central SD	Delmar
250	376.4	Kenmore-Tonawanda Union Free SD	Buffalo
251	376.1	Freeport Union Free SD	Freeport
252	375.3	Chatham Central SD	Chatham
253	374.2	Taconic Hills Central SD	Craryville
254	373.3	Brockport Central SD	Brockport
255	371.4	Fredonia Central SD	Fredonia
256	371.0	Johnson City Central SD	Johnson City
257	370.6	Holland Patent Central SD	Holland Patent
258	369.9	White Plains City SD	White Plains
259	369.7	Hewlett-Woodmere Union Free SD	Woodmere
260	369.6	Skaneateles Central SD	Skaneateles
261	367.1	Niskayuna Central SD	Schenectady
262	365.4	Wayland-Cohocton Central SD	Wayland
263	365.3	Nanuet Union Free SD	Nanuet
264	364.6	Corning City SD	Painted Post
265	363.2	Beekmantown Central SD	West Chazy
266	361.1	Hamburg Central SD	Hamburg
267	360.8	Cazenovia Central SD	Cazenovia
268	360.3	Glens Falls City SD	Glens Falls
269	359.7	Roslyn Union Free SD	Roslyn
270	359.6	Great Neck Union Free SD	Great Neck
271	358.0	Liverpool Central SD	Liverpool
272	357.6	Southwestern Cent SD Jamestown	Jamestown
273	357.3	Nyack Union Free SD	Nyack
274	356.7	Jericho Union Free SD	Jericho
275	355.3	Hilton Central SD	Hilton
276	354.3	Ossining Union Free SD	Ossining
277	351.6	Sherburne-Earlville Central SD	Sherburne
278	351.4	Scarsdale Union Free SD	Scarsdale
279	349.6	Albion Central SD	Albion
280	349.4	Solvay Union Free SD	Solvay
281	348.8	Canandaigua City SD	Canandaigua
282	347.6	East Syracuse-Minoa Central SD	East Syracuse
283	345.4	Pleasantville Union Free SD	Pleasantville
284	345.0	Half Hollow Hills Central SD	Dix Hills
285	343.6	Eastchester Union Free SD	Eastchester
286	343.4	Briarcliff Manor Union Free SD	Briarcliff Manor
287	342.0	Chittenango Central SD	Chittenango
288	341.3	North Colonie Central SD	Latham
289	340.7	Ravena-Coeymans-Selkirk CSD	Selkirk
290	339.6	Jamesville-Dewitt Central SD	Dewitt
291	339.2	Penn Yan Central SD	Penn Yan
292	337.7	Indian River Central SD	Philadelphia
293	336.3	Ogdensburg City SD	Ogdensburg
294	336.0	Niagara Falls City SD	Niagara Falls
295	335.9	Vestal Central SD	Vestal
296	335.6	Lawrence Union Free SD	Lawrence
297	334.6	Pittsford Central SD	Pittsford
298	333.0	Evans-Brant Cent SD (Lake Shore)	Angola
299	331.4	Northeastern Clinton Central SD	Champlain
300	331.3	Plainview-Old Bethpage Cent SD	Plainview
301	329.9	Fayetteville-Manlius Central SD	Manlius
302	328.4	North Rose-Wolcott Central SD	Wolcott
303	322.6	Gloversville City SD	Gloversville
304	322.3	Sweet Home Central SD	Amherst
305	321.1	Shenendehowa Central SD	Clifton Park
306	320.8	Salmon River Central SD	Ft Covington
307	318.8	Glen Cove City SD	Glen Cove
308	318.4	Long Beach City SD	Long Beach
309	317.9	Massena Central SD	Massena
310	316.3	Katonah-Lewisboro Union Free SD	South Salem
310	316.3	Rome City SD	Rome
312	315.4	Cobleskill-Richmondville CSD	Cobleskill
313	314.0	Dryden Central SD	Dryden
314	313.7	Liberty Central SD	Liberty
315	312.6	Mattituck-Cutchogue UFSD	Cutchogue
316	312.4	Malone Central SD	Malone
317	311.8	Port Washington Union Free SD	Pt Washington
318	310.7	Spencerport Central SD	Spencerport
319	310.6	Island Trees Union Free SD	Levittown
320	309.7	Whitney Point Central SD	Whitney Point
321	308.8	Mineola Union Free SD	Mineola
322	302.6	Canton Central SD	Canton
323	301.2	Chappaqua Central SD	Chappaqua
324	300.0	Carle Place Union Free SD	Carle Place
325	298.5	Brighton Central SD	Rochester
326	294.6	Waterloo Central SD	Waterloo
327	293.6	Plattsburgh City SD	Plattsburgh
327	293.6	West Hempstead Union Free SD	W Hempstead
329	292.1	Windsor Central SD	Windsor
330	287.9	Peru Central SD	Peru
331	282.1	West Irondequoit Central SD	Rochester
332	278.3	Hastings-On-Hudson Union Free SD	Hastings-on-Hud
333	275.5	Jamestown City SD	Jamestown
334	273.5	Wilson Central SD	Wilson
335	266.4	East Hampton Union Free SD	East Hampton
336	264.2	Depew Union Free SD	Depew
337	263.9	Mount Pleasant Central SD	Thornwood
338	262.6	Dunkirk City SD	Dunkirk
339	260.3	Ardsley Union Free SD	Ardsley
340	258.9	East Williston Union Free SD	Old Westbury
341	256.9	Bellmore-Merrick Central High SD	North Merrick
342	255.3	Gowanda Central SD	Gowanda
343	254.9	Boces Nassau	Garden City
344	254.1	Olean City SD	Olean
345	249.7	Norwich City SD	Norwich
346	249.0	Gouverneur Central SD	Gouverneur
347	248.0	Penfield Central SD	Penfield
348	245.8	Northport-East Northport UFSD	Northport
349	245.4	Rondout Valley Central SD	Accord
350	243.8	Batavia City SD	Batavia
351	241.5	Hornell City SD	Hornell
352	234.2	Valley Stream Central High SD	Valley Stream
353	230.3	Oneonta City SD	Oneonta
354	222.0	Sewanhaka Central High SD	Floral Park
355	221.9	Wayne Central SD	Ontario Center
356	221.1	Southampton Union Free SD	Southampton
357	218.8	Dansville Central SD	Dansville
358	215.9	Westhampton Beach Union Free SD	Westhampton Bch
359	189.1	Salamanca City SD	Salamanca
360	159.0	Boces Eastern Suffolk	Patchogue
361	n/a	Floral Park-Bellerose UFSD	Floral Park
361	n/a	Franklin Square Union Free SD	Franklin Square
361	n/a	Merrick Union Free SD	Merrick
361	n/a	New Hyde Park-Garden City Park	New Hyde Park
361	n/a	New York City Geographic Dist 9	Bronx
361	n/a	New York City Geographic Dist 15	Brooklyn
361	n/a	North Bellmore Union Free SD	Bellmore
361	n/a	Nyc Alternative HS District	New York
361	n/a	Valley Stream 13 Union Free SD	Valley Stream
361	n/a	Valley Stream 30 Union Free SD	Valley Stream

Current Spending per Student in FY2003

Rank	Dollars	District Name	City
1	21,067	Oyster Bay-East Norwich CSD	Oyster Bay
2	20,689	Southampton Union Free SD	Southampton
3	20,639	Manhasset Union Free SD	Manhasset
4	20,305	Mineola Union Free SD	Mineola
5	20,216	Lawrence Union Free SD	Lawrence
6	19,950	Greenburgh Central SD	Hartsdale
7	19,936	Roslyn Union Free SD	Roslyn
8	19,799	Great Neck Union Free SD	Great Neck
9	19,771	Jericho Union Free SD	Jericho
10	19,455	Locust Valley Central SD	Locust Valley
11	19,392	North Shore Central SD	Sea Cliff
12	18,841	East Williston Union Free SD	Old Westbury
13	18,577	Carle Place Union Free SD	Carle Place
14	18,508	Harrison Central SD	Harrison
15	18,418	White Plains City SD	White Plains
16	18,010	Bedford Central SD	Mount Kisco
17	17,822	Briarcliff Manor Union Free SD	Briarcliff Manor
18	17,705	Huntington Union Free SD	Huntington Stn
19	17,527	Hewlett-Woodmere Union Free SD	Woodmere
20	17,511	Port Washington Union Free SD	Pt Washington
21	17,415	Schalmont Central SD	Schenectady
22	17,371	Syosset Central SD	Syosset
23	17,088	Long Beach City SD	Long Beach
24	16,955	Wyandanch Union Free SD	Wyandanch
25	16,867	Scarsdale Union Free SD	Scarsdale
26	16,829	E Ramapo Central SD (Sprg Val)	Spring Valley
27	16,786	Mount Pleasant Central SD	Thornwood
28	16,766	Onteora Central SD	Boiceville
29	16,643	Malverne Union Free SD	Malverne
30	16,562	East Hampton Union Free SD	East Hampton
31	16,514	Nanuet Union Free SD	Nanuet
32	16,487	Plainview-Old Bethpage Cent SD	Plainview
33	16,421	Roosevelt Union Free SD	Roosevelt
34	16,420	Peekskill City SD	Peekskill
35	16,410	Central Islip Union Free SD	Central Islip
36	16,303	Nyack Union Free SD	Nyack
37	16,299	Katonah-Lewisboro Union Free SD	South Salem
38	16,116	Union Free SD of the Tarrytowns	Sleepy Hollow
39	16,093	Rockville Centre Union Free SD	Rockville Ctre
40	16,026	Uniondale Union Free SD	Uniondale
41	15,929	Chappaqua Central SD	Chappaqua
42	15,866	Westhampton Beach Union Free SD	Westhampton Bch
43	15,830	Haverstraw-Stony Point Cent SD	Garnerville
44	15,829	Hempstead Union Free SD	Hempstead
45	15,760	Rye City SD	Rye
46	15,744	Amityville Union Free SD	Amityville
47	15,704	Hendrick Hudson Central SD	Montrose
48	15,505	Herricks Union Free SD	New Hyde Park
49	15,491	Mamaroneck Union Free SD	Mamaroneck
50	15,344	South Orangetown Central SD	Blauvelt
51	15,316	Westbury Union Free SD	Old Westbury
52	15,225	Somers Central SD	Lincolndale
53	15,138	Ellenville Central SD	Ellenville
54	15,125	Glen Cove City SD	Glen Cove
55	15,081	South Country Central SD	E Patchogue
56	15,032	Ossining Union Free SD	Ossining
57	14,973	West Hempstead Union Free SD	W Hempstead
58	14,946	Eastchester Union Free SD	Eastchester
59	14,919	Cold Spring Harbor Central SD	Cold Sprg Harbor
60	14,891	Ramapo Central SD (Suffern)	Hillburn
61	14,889	Irvington Union Free SD	Irvington
62	14,885	Bethpage Union Free SD	Bethpage
63	14,849	Edgemont Union Free SD	Scarsdale
64	14,818	Lackawanna City SD	Lackawanna
65	14,758	Farmingdale Union Free SD	Farmingdale
66	14,750	Croton-Harmon Union Free SD	Croton-On-Hud
67	14,698	Hauppauge Union Free SD	Hauppauge
68	14,668	Bayport-Blue Point Union Free SD	Bayport
69	14,666	Hastings-On-Hudson Union Free SD	Hastings-on-Hud
70	14,642	Garden City Union Free SD	Garden City
71	14,567	Bay Shore Union Free SD	Bay Shore
72	14,524	Sayville Union Free SD	Sayville
73	14,471	Connetquot Central SD	Bohemia
74	14,464	Ardsley Union Free SD	Ardsley
75	14,430	Northport-East Northport UFSD	Northport
76	14,404	Salmon River Central SD	Ft Covington
77	14,364	Levittown Union Free SD	Levittown
78	14,329	Lakeland Central SD	Shrub Oak
79	14,307	Marlboro Central SD	Marlboro
80	14,238	Deer Park Union Free SD	Deer Park
81	14,214	Brewster Central SD	Brewster
82	14,200	Byram Hills Central SD	Armonk
83	14,133	Putnam Valley Central SD	Putnam Valley
84	14,121	Albany City SD	Albany
85	14,107	Yonkers City SD	Yonkers
86	14,102	Sullivan West Central SD	Callicoon
87	14,065	South Huntington Union Free SD	Huntington Stn
88	14,015	Mattituck-Cutchogue UFSD	Cutchogue
89	13,979	New Rochelle City SD	New Rochelle
90	13,935	Lynbrook Union Free SD	Lynbrook
91	13,925	Pleasantville Union Free SD	Pleasantville
92	13,916	Hicksville Union Free SD	Hicksville
93	13,881	Half Hollow Hills Central SD	Dix Hills
94	13,846	Copiague Union Free SD	Copiague
95	13,840	Pearl River Union Free SD	Pearl River
96	13,799	Riverhead Central SD	Riverhead
97	13,794	Longwood Central SD	Middle Island
98	13,745	Freeport Union Free SD	Freeport
99	13,689	Dunkirk City SD	Dunkirk
100	13,647	Smithtown Central SD	Smithtown
101	13,613	Rondout Valley Central SD	Accord
102	13,601	East Meadow Union Free SD	Westbury
103	13,595	Babylon Union Free SD	Babylon
104	13,581	Pelham Union Free SD	Pelham
105	13,546	Baldwin Union Free SD	Baldwin
106	13,511	Liberty Central SD	Liberty
107	13,482	Bellmore-Merrick Central High SD	North Merrick
108	13,427	Valley Stream Central High SD	Valley Stream
109	13,376	Yorktown Central SD	Yorktown Hgts
110	13,366	Mount Sinai Union Free SD	Mount Sinai
111	13,351	North Babylon Union Free SD	North Babylon
112	13,337	Oceanside Union Free SD	Oceanside
113	13,289	Sachem Central SD	Holbrook
114	13,236	Seaford Union Free SD	Seaford
115	13,163	Carmel Central SD	Patterson
116	13,154	Indian River Central SD	Philadelphia
117	13,144	Three Village Central SD	East Setauket
118	13,141	Hudson City SD	Hudson
119	13,052	Depew Union Free SD	Depew
120	13,029	Mahopac Central SD	Mahopac
121	13,019	Shoreham-Wading River Central SD	Shoreham
122	13,001	Poughkeepsie City SD	Poughkeepsie
123	12,986	Brookhaven-Comsewogue UFSD	Pt Jefferson Stn
124	12,913	Massapequa Union Free SD	Massapequa
125	12,899	Commack Union Free SD	E Northport
126	12,879	Buffalo City SD	Buffalo
127	12,836	East Islip Union Free SD	Islip Terrace
128	12,788	Miller Place Union Free SD	Miller Place
129	12,785	Elwood Union Free SD	Greenlawn
130	12,782	Island Trees Union Free SD	Levittown
131	12,753	Plattsburgh City SD	Plattsburgh
132	12,749	Batavia City SD	Batavia
133	12,738	Spackenkill Union Free SD	Poughkeepsie

134	12,723	Monticello Central SD	Monticello
135	12,711	Rochester City SD	Rochester
136	12,643	Johnson City Central SD	Johnson City
137	12,641	Troy City SD	Troy
138	12,634	Port Chester-Rye Union Free SD	Port Chester
139	12,619	Ithaca City SD	Ithaca
140	12,592	Clarkstown Central SD	New City
141	12,591	Hampton Bays Union Free SD	Hampton Bays
142	12,586	Kings Park Central SD	Kings Park
143	12,585	Ravena-Coeymans-Selkirk CSD	Selkirk
144	12,533	William Floyd Union Free SD	Mastic Beach
145	12,505	Plainedge Union Free SD	N Massapequa
146	12,498	West Babylon Union Free SD	West Babylon
147	12,427	Brentwood Union Free SD	Brentwood
148	12,422	Lindenhurst Union Free SD	Lindenhurst
149	12,420	Rush-Henrietta Central SD	Henrietta
150	12,355	New Paltz Central SD	New Paltz
151	12,351	Mount Vernon City SD	Mount Vernon
152	12,349	Islip Union Free SD	Islip
153	12,309	New York City Public Schools	Brooklyn
154	12,283	Patchogue-Medford Union Free SD	Patchogue
155	12,270	Monroe-Woodbury Central SD	Central Valley
156	12,235	Merrick Union Free SD	Merrick
157	12,219	East Syracuse-Minoa Central SD	East Syracuse
157	12,219	Gowanda Central SD	Gowanda
159	12,203	Wantagh Union Free SD	Wantagh
160	12,193	Schuylerville Central SD	Schuylerville
161	12,173	Ogdensburg City SD	Ogdensburg
162	12,166	Lewiston-Porter Central SD	Youngstown
163	12,164	Cohoes City SD	Cohoes
164	12,096	Saranac Lake Central SD	Saranac Lake
165	12,088	Taconic Hills Central SD	Craryville
166	12,077	Middletown City SD	Middletown
167	12,072	North Rose-Wolcott Central SD	Wolcott
168	12,068	Valley Stream 30 Union Free SD	Valley Stream
169	12,044	Niagara Falls City SD	Niagara Falls
170	12,034	Harborfields Central SD	Greenlawn
171	11,989	Gouverneur Central SD	Gouverneur
172	11,909	Kenmore-Tonawanda Union Free SD	Buffalo
173	11,881	Port Jervis City SD	Port Jervis
174	11,848	Syracuse City SD	Syracuse
175	11,829	Gorham-Middlesex CSD (M Whitman)	Rushville
176	11,816	Horseheads Central SD	Horseheads
177	11,794	Cobleskill-Richmondville CSD	Cobleskill
178	11,788	Sewanhaka Central High SD	Floral Park
179	11,766	East Irondequoit Central SD	Rochester
180	11,760	Catskill Central SD	Catskill
181	11,758	Phoenix Central SD	Phoenix
182	11,723	North Bellmore Union Free SD	Bellmore
183	11,722	Brighton Central SD	Rochester
183	11,722	Valley Stream 13 Union Free SD	Valley Stream
185	11,700	Gates-Chili Central SD	Rochester
186	11,695	Watkins Glen Central SD	Watkins Glen
187	11,690	Kingston City SD	Kingston
188	11,687	Fulton City SD	Fulton
189	11,657	West Islip Union Free SD	West Islip
190	11,645	Wilson Central SD	Wilson
191	11,607	Niagara-Wheatfield Central SD	Niagara Falls
192	11,603	Highland Central SD	Highland
193	11,592	Dryden Central SD	Dryden
194	11,569	Fonda-Fultonville Central SD	Fonda
195	11,563	Yorkshire-Pioneer Central SD	Yorkshire
196	11,529	Cheektowaga-Sloan Union Free SD	Sloan
197	11,526	Pittsford Central SD	Pittsford
198	11,510	Sweet Home Central SD	Amherst
199	11,507	Newburgh City SD	Newburgh
200	11,487	Schenectady City SD	Schenectady
201	11,438	Peru Central SD	Peru
202	11,434	Rocky Point Union Free SD	Rocky Point
203	11,426	Jamestown City SD	Jamestown
204	11,416	Goshen Central SD	Goshen
205	11,336	Penfield Central SD	Penfield
206	11,313	Oneonta City SD	Oneonta
207	11,298	Newark Central SD	Newark
208	11,270	Malone Central SD	Malone
209	11,269	Red Hook Central SD	Red Hook
210	11,233	Rome City SD	Rome
211	11,143	Middle Country Central SD	Centereach
212	11,135	Evans-Brant Cent SD (Lake Shore)	Angola
213	11,128	Franklin Square Union Free SD	Franklin Square
214	11,098	Oswego City SD	Oswego
215	11,087	Ballston Spa Central SD	Ballston Spa
216	11,085	Beekmantown Central SD	West Chazy
216	11,085	Cheektowaga-Maryvale UFSD	Cheektowaga
218	11,077	Canton Central SD	Canton
219	11,062	Elmira City SD	Elmira
220	11,040	Northeastern Clinton Central SD	Champlain
221	11,023	Saranac Central SD	Dannemora
222	11,022	Altmar-Parish-Williamstown CSD	Parish
223	11,020	Adirondack Central SD	Boonville
224	11,018	Cortland City SD	Cortland
225	11,013	Sherburne-Earlville Central SD	Sherburne
226	11,012	Geneva City SD	Geneva
227	10,993	Chatham Central SD	Chatham
228	10,987	Liverpool Central SD	Liverpool
229	10,982	Webster Central SD	Webster
230	10,973	Palmyra-Macedon Central SD	Palmyra
231	10,967	Orchard Park Central SD	Orchard Park
232	10,946	Wallkill Central SD	Wallkill
233	10,942	Greece Central SD	Rochester
234	10,924	Wayland-Cohocton Central SD	Wayland
235	10,919	Maine-Endwell Central SD	Endwell
236	10,914	Owego-Apalachin Central SD	Owego
237	10,905	New Hartford Central SD	New Hartford
238	10,897	Hyde Park Central SD	Poughkeepsie
239	10,885	Brockport Central SD	Brockport
239	10,885	South Colonie Central SD	Albany
241	10,882	Utica City SD	Utica
242	10,880	Jamesville-Dewitt Central SD	Dewitt
243	10,867	Chenango Valley Central SD	Binghamton
244	10,838	Pine Bush Central SD	Pine Bush
245	10,831	Penn Yan Central SD	Penn Yan
246	10,819	Medina Central SD	Medina
247	10,812	Union-Endicott Central SD	Endicott
248	10,800	East Greenbush Central SD	E Greenbush
249	10,766	Chenango Forks Central SD	Binghamton
250	10,714	Dansville Central SD	Dansville
251	10,674	Norwich City SD	Norwich
252	10,660	Honeoye Falls-Lima Central SD	Honeoye Falls
253	10,654	Hudson Falls Central SD	Hudson Falls
254	10,637	Warwick Valley Central SD	Warwick
255	10,612	Hornell City SD	Hornell
256	10,603	Springville-Griffith Inst Cent	Springville
257	10,593	Salamanca City SD	Salamanca
258	10,587	Gloversville City SD	Gloversville
259	10,569	Lansingburgh Central SD	Troy
260	10,539	Fairport Central SD	Fairport
261	10,536	Guilderland Central SD	Guilderland
262	10,525	Mexico Central SD	Mexico
263	10,517	Scotia-Glenville Central SD	Scotia
264	10,510	Corning City SD	Painted Post
265	10,508	Akron Central SD	Akron
266	10,505	Susquehanna Valley Central SD	Conklin
267	10,492	Averill Park Central SD	Averill Park
267	10,492	Binghamton City SD	Binghamton
269	10,469	Cornwall Central SD	Cornwall-on-Hud
270	10,451	Holland Patent Central SD	Holland Patent
271	10,433	Canandaigua City SD	Canandaigua
272	10,420	Oneida City SD	Oneida
273	10,405	Hilton Central SD	Hilton
274	10,401	Fredonia Central SD	Fredonia
275	10,390	Carthage Central SD	Carthage
276	10,378	Minisink Valley Central SD	Slate Hill
277	10,375	Shenendehowa Central SD	Clifton Park
278	10,362	Watertown City SD	Watertown
279	10,352	Saugerties Central SD	Saugerties
280	10,310	Cleveland Hill Union Free SD	Cheektowaga
281	10,297	Churchville-Chili Central SD	Churchville
282	10,292	Glens Falls City SD	Glens Falls
283	10,287	Waterloo Central SD	Waterloo
284	10,262	Burnt Hls-Ballston Lake Cent SD	Scotia
285	10,250	Windsor Central SD	Windsor
286	10,246	Niskayuna Central SD	Schenectady
287	10,244	Lansing Central SD	Lansing
288	10,242	New Hyde Park-Garden City Park	New Hyde Park
289	10,233	Floral Park-Bellerose UFSD	Floral Park
290	10,225	Newfane Central SD	Newfane
291	10,217	Elmont Union Free SD	Elmont
292	10,213	Grand Island Central SD	Grand Island
292	10,213	Saratoga Springs City SD	Saratoga Spgs
294	10,192	Phelps-Clifton Springs Cent SD	Clifton Spgs
295	10,171	Royalton-Hartland Central SD	Middleport
296	10,168	Washingtonville Central SD	Washingtonville
297	10,164	Lockport City SD	Lockport
298	10,139	Spencerport Central SD	Spencerport
299	10,107	Hamburg Central SD	Hamburg
300	10,105	North Tonawanda City SD	N Tonawanda
301	10,080	Wappingers Central SD	Wappingers Fls
302	10,077	Southwestern Cent SD Jamestown	Jamestown
303	10,064	Jordan-Elbridge Central SD	Jordan
304	10,052	Bath Central SD	Bath
305	10,049	Victor Central SD	Victor
306	10,044	Cheektowaga Central SD	Cheektowaga
307	10,041	Dover Union Free SD	Dover Plains
308	10,032	Hannibal Central SD	Hannibal
309	10,016	Massena Central SD	Massena
310	10,012	Amherst Central SD	Amherst
311	10,009	Alden Central SD	Alden
312	10,006	West Irondequoit Central SD	Rochester
313	10,002	Clinton Central SD	Clinton
314	9,971	West Seneca Central SD	West Seneca
315	9,967	Whitney Point Central SD	Whitney Point
316	9,962	Williamsville Central SD	East Amherst
317	9,961	Kinderhook Central SD	Valatie
318	9,960	Vestal Central SD	Vestal
319	9,938	Bethlehem Central SD	Delmar
320	9,912	Tonawanda City SD	Tonawanda
321	9,909	Wayne Central SD	Ontario Center
322	9,897	Auburn City SD	Auburn
323	9,874	Beacon City SD	Beacon
324	9,872	Homer Central SD	Homer
325	9,842	Livonia Central SD	Livonia
326	9,830	South Glens Falls Central SD	S Glens Falls
327	9,802	Camden Central SD	Camden
328	9,788	Baldwinsville Central SD	Baldwinsville
329	9,745	Olean City SD	Olean
330	9,736	Westhill Central SD	Syracuse
331	9,733	Cazenovia Central SD	Cazenovia
332	9,710	Canastota Central SD	Canastota
333	9,703	Valley Central SD (Montgomery)	Montgomery
334	9,673	Attica Central SD	Attica
335	9,665	North Colonie Central SD	Latham
336	9,658	Fayetteville-Manlius Central SD	Manlius
337	9,656	Sherrill City SD	Verona
338	9,594	Arlington Central SD	Poughkeepsie
339	9,590	Waverly Central SD	Waverly
340	9,582	Whitesboro Central SD	Yorkville
341	9,577	Amsterdam City SD	Amsterdam
342	9,573	Skaneateles Central SD	Skaneateles
343	9,528	Coxsackie-Athens Central SD	Coxsackie
344	9,499	Chittenango Central SD	Chittenango
345	9,471	Solvay Union Free SD	Solvay
346	9,457	Frontier Central SD	Hamburg
347	9,409	North Syracuse Central SD	N Syracuse
348	9,300	General Brown Central SD	Dexter
349	9,289	South Jefferson Central SD	Adams Center
350	9,213	Iroquois Central SD	Elma
351	9,155	Clarence Central SD	Clarence
352	9,121	Central Square Central SD	Central Square
353	9,078	East Aurora Union Free SD	East Aurora
354	9,073	Cairo-Durham Central SD	Cairo
355	9,065	Johnstown City SD	Johnstown
356	8,966	Starpoint Central SD	Lockport
357	8,939	Lancaster Central SD	Lancaster
358	8,907	Albion Central SD	Albion
359	8,847	West Genesee Central SD	Camillus
360	8,820	Rotterdam-Mohonasen Central SD	Schenectady
361	8,746	Eden Central SD	Eden
362	8,697	Marcellus Central SD	Marcellus
363	8,473	Ilion Central SD	Ilion
364	8,280	Queensbury Union Free SD	Queensbury
365	7,940	Broadalbin-Perth Central SD	Broadalbin
366	n/a	Boces Eastern Suffolk	Patchogue
366	n/a	Boces Nassau	Garden City
366	n/a	New York City Geographic Dist 9	Bronx
366	n/a	New York City Geographic Dist 15	Brooklyn
366	n/a	Nyc Alternative HS District	New York

Number of Diploma Recipients

Rank	Number	District Name	City
1	37,915	New York City Public Schools	Brooklyn
2	1,638	Buffalo City SD	Buffalo
3	1,135	Sewanhaka Central High SD	Floral Park
4	1,021	Rochester City SD	Rochester
5	910	Sachem Central SD	Holbrook
6	901	Greece Central SD	Rochester
7	812	Bellmore-Merrick Central High SD	North Merrick
8	773	Williamsville Central SD	East Amherst
9	761	Wappingers Central SD	Wappingers Fls
10	724	Yonkers City SD	Yonkers
11	681	Clarkstown Central SD	New City
12	670	Middle Country Central SD	Centereach
13	641	Brentwood Union Free SD	Brentwood
14	629	Valley Stream Central High SD	Valley Stream
15	627	Syracuse City SD	Syracuse
16	624	Kenmore-Tonawanda Union Free SD	Buffalo
17	600	Webster Central SD	Webster
18	582	North Syracuse Central SD	N Syracuse
19	580	Shenendehowa Central SD	Clifton Park
20	556	Smithtown Central SD	Smithtown
21	552	West Seneca Central SD	West Seneca
22	543	Half Hollow Hills Central SD	Dix Hills
23	526	E Ramapo Central SD (Sprg Val)	Spring Valley
24	516	Great Neck Union Free SD	Great Neck
24	516	Longwood Central SD	Middle Island
26	512	Liverpool Central SD	Liverpool
27	507	East Meadow Union Free SD	Westbury
28	501	Arlington Central SD	Poughkeepsie
29	496	Massapequa Union Free SD	Massapequa
29	496	Patchogue-Medford Union Free SD	Patchogue
31	489	Fairport Central SD	Fairport
32	485	Kingston City SD	Kingston
33	482	Newburgh City SD	Newburgh
34	479	New Rochelle City SD	New Rochelle
35	472	Lakeland Central SD	Shrub Oak
35	472	Three Village Central SD	East Setauket
37	461	Saratoga Springs City SD	Saratoga Spgs

38	455	Levittown Union Free SD	Levittown
38	455	William Floyd Union Free SD	Mastic Beach
40	454	North Colonie Central SD	Latham
41	445	Syosset Central SD	Syosset
42	443	Pittsford Central SD	Pittsford
43	442	Haverstraw-Stony Point Cent SD	Garnerville
44	419	Lindenhurst Union Free SD	Lindenhurst
45	412	Lancaster Central SD	Lancaster
46	411	Monroe-Woodbury Central SD	Central Valley
47	408	Commack Union Free SD	E Northport
48	406	Orchard Park Central SD	Orchard Park
49	390	West Genesee Central SD	Camillus
50	389	South Colonie Central SD	Albany
51	385	North Babylon Union Free SD	North Babylon
52	382	Albany City SD	Albany
53	380	Oceanside Union Free SD	Oceanside
54	379	Gates-Chili Central SD	Rochester
55	374	Connetquot Central SD	Bohemia
55	374	Guilderland Central SD	Guilderland
57	367	Farmingdale Union Free SD	Farmingdale
58	362	Niagara Falls City SD	Niagara Falls
59	360	White Plains City SD	White Plains
60	358	Corning City SD	Painted Post
60	358	Schenectady City SD	Schenectady
62	357	Bethlehem Central SD	Delmar
63	349	Rush-Henrietta Central SD	Henrietta
64	348	Mahopac Central SD	Mahopac
65	346	Baldwin Union Free SD	Baldwin
66	341	Plainview-Old Bethpage Cent SD	Plainview
66	341	Utica City SD	Utica
68	340	Frontier Central SD	Hamburg
69	339	Clarence Central SD	Clarence
70	337	Mount Vernon City SD	Mount Vernon
71	335	North Tonawanda City SD	N Tonawanda
72	330	Hilton Central SD	Hilton
73	329	Northport-East Northport UFSD	Northport
74	326	Ithaca City SD	Ithaca
75	324	Elmira City SD	Elmira
76	320	Baldwinsville Central SD	Baldwinsville
76	320	Horseheads Central SD	Horseheads
78	319	Hamburg Central SD	Hamburg
79	317	South Huntington Union Free SD	Huntington Stn
80	315	West Irondequoit Central SD	Rochester
81	312	Washingtonville Central SD	Washingtonville
82	311	Fayetteville-Manlius Central SD	Manlius
83	310	Hicksville Union Free SD	Hicksville
84	308	Valley Central SD (Montgomery)	Montgomery
85	307	Uniondale Union Free SD	Uniondale
86	306	Pine Bush Central SD	Pine Bush
87	302	Lockport City SD	Lockport
87	302	Penfield Central SD	Penfield
87	302	West Islip Union Free SD	West Islip
90	300	East Islip Union Free SD	Islip Terrace
91	298	Churchville-Chili Central SD	Churchville
92	296	Vestal Central SD	Vestal
93	292	Spencerport Central SD	Spencerport
94	290	Brockport Central SD	Brockport
95	289	Mamaroneck Union Free SD	Mamaroneck
96	288	Carmel Central SD	Patterson
97	287	Bay Shore Union Free SD	Bay Shore
98	283	South Country Central SD	E Patchogue
99	282	Port Washington Union Free SD	Pt Washington
100	281	East Greenbush Central SD	E Greenbush
100	281	Freeport Union Free SD	Freeport
102	280	Niskayuna Central SD	Schenectady
102	280	West Babylon Union Free SD	West Babylon
104	279	Union-Endicott Central SD	Endicott
105	278	Auburn City SD	Auburn
105	278	Central Islip Union Free SD	Central Islip
105	278	Jamestown City SD	Jamestown
108	277	Ramapo Central SD (Suffern)	Hillburn
109	276	Herricks Union Free SD	New Hyde Park
109	276	Rome City SD	Rome
111	274	East Syracuse-Minoa Central SD	East Syracuse
112	272	Niagara-Wheatfield Central SD	Niagara Falls
113	267	Hewlett-Woodmere Union Free SD	Woodmere
113	267	Scarsdale Union Free SD	Scarsdale
115	264	Middletown City SD	Middletown
116	260	Yorktown Central SD	Yorktown Hgts
117	259	Brighton Central SD	Rochester
117	259	Hauppauge Union Free SD	Hauppauge
119	258	Rockville Centre Union Free SD	Rockville Ctre
120	257	Chappaqua Central SD	Chappaqua
120	257	Warwick Valley Central SD	Warwick
120	257	Whitesboro Central SD	Yorkville
123	253	Binghamton City SD	Binghamton
123	253	Hyde Park Central SD	Poughkeepsie
123	253	Oswego City SD	Oswego
126	249	Central Square Central SD	Central Square
127	247	Bedford Central SD	Mount Kisco
127	247	Kings Park Central SD	Kings Park
129	246	Minisink Valley Central SD	Slate Hill
130	245	Sweet Home Central SD	Amherst
131	244	Canandaigua City SD	Canandaigua
132	241	Lawrence Union Free SD	Lawrence
133	238	Riverhead Central SD	Riverhead
134	234	Long Beach City SD	Long Beach
135	222	Iroquois Central SD	Elma
135	222	New Hartford Central SD	New Hartford
137	219	Averill Park Central SD	Averill Park
137	219	Sayville Union Free SD	Sayville
139	218	Scotia-Glenville Central SD	Scotia
140	215	Ballston Spa Central SD	Ballston Spa
141	214	Garden City Union Free SD	Garden City
141	214	Yorkshire-Pioneer Central SD	Yorkshire
143	213	Burnt Hls-Ballston Lake Cent SD	Scotia
143	213	Fulton City SD	Fulton
143	213	Miller Place Union Free SD	Miller Place
146	212	Amherst Central SD	Amherst
147	211	Queensbury Union Free SD	Queensbury
147	211	Westhampton Beach Union Free SD	Westhampton Bch
149	209	Roslyn Union Free SD	Roslyn
150	208	Katonah-Lewisboro Union Free SD	South Salem
151	205	Copiague Union Free SD	Copiague
151	205	Huntington Union Free SD	Huntington Stn
153	203	Brewster Central SD	Brewster
153	203	East Irondequoit Central SD	Rochester
153	203	Islip Union Free SD	Islip
153	203	Ossining Union Free SD	Ossining
153	203	Plainedge Union Free SD	N Massapequa
153	203	Wallkill Central SD	Wallkill
159	201	Mineola Union Free SD	Mineola
159	201	Rotterdam-Mohonasen Central SD	Schenectady
161	199	Victor Central SD	Victor
162	198	Cornwall Central SD	Cornwall-on-Hud
162	198	Deer Park Union Free SD	Deer Park
164	195	Grand Island Central SD	Grand Island
165	194	West Hempstead Union Free SD	W Hempstead
166	193	Carthage Central SD	Carthage
167	192	Glen Cove City SD	Glen Cove
167	192	Port Jervis City SD	Port Jervis
169	191	Jericho Union Free SD	Jericho
169	191	Rondout Valley Central SD	Accord
169	191	Wantagh Union Free SD	Wantagh
172	190	Port Chester-Rye Union Free SD	Port Chester
172	190	Saugerties Central SD	Saugerties
174	189	Brookhaven-Comsewogue UFSD	Pt Jefferson Stn
174	189	Harborfields Central SD	Greenlawn
176	188	Evans-Brant Cent SD (Lake Shore)	Angola
176	188	Lynbrook Union Free SD	Lynbrook
176	188	Malone Central SD	Malone
179	186	Lewiston-Porter Central SD	Youngstown
180	184	East Hampton Union Free SD	East Hampton
181	180	Bethpage Union Free SD	Bethpage
181	180	Cortland City SD	Cortland
183	179	Jamesville-Dewitt Central SD	Dewitt
184	177	Pearl River Union Free SD	Pearl River
185	176	Goshen Central SD	Goshen
185	176	Hendrick Hudson Central SD	Montrose
185	176	Homer Central SD	Homer
188	175	Sherrill City SD	Verona
189	174	Phoenix Central SD	Phoenix
189	174	Tonawanda City SD	Tonawanda
191	173	Watertown City SD	Watertown
192	171	Somers Central SD	Lincolndale
193	170	Manhasset Union Free SD	Manhasset
194	169	Shoreham-Wading River Central SD	Shoreham
195	167	Massena Central SD	Massena
195	167	Ravena-Coeymans-Selkirk CSD	Selkirk
195	167	Westhill Central SD	Syracuse
198	166	Byram Hills Central SD	Armonk
198	166	Gloversville City SD	Gloversville
198	166	Nyack Union Free SD	Nyack
198	166	Owego-Apalachin Central SD	Owego
198	166	Seaford Union Free SD	Seaford
203	165	Cheektowaga Central SD	Cheektowaga
203	165	Chittenango Central SD	Chittenango
203	165	Newark Central SD	Newark
203	165	South Orangetown Central SD	Blauvelt
207	164	Honeoye Falls-Lima Central SD	Honeoye Falls
208	163	Harrison Central SD	Harrison
208	163	Wayne Central SD	Ontario Center
210	162	Mexico Central SD	Mexico
211	161	Schalmont Central SD	Schenectady
211	161	South Glens Falls Central SD	S Glens Falls
213	160	Cheektowaga-Maryvale UFSD	Cheektowaga
213	160	Rocky Point Union Free SD	Rocky Point
215	159	Camden Central SD	Camden
215	159	Oneida City SD	Oneida
217	157	Westbury Union Free SD	Old Westbury
218	156	Johnson City Central SD	Johnson City
218	156	Newfane Central SD	Newfane
218	156	Springville-Griffith Inst Cent	Springville
221	155	Indian River Central SD	Philadelphia
221	155	Plattsburgh City SD	Plattsburgh
223	154	Hempstead Union Free SD	Hempstead
223	154	Skaneateles Central SD	Skaneateles
223	154	Starpoint Central SD	Lockport
226	153	Poughkeepsie City SD	Poughkeepsie
227	152	Albion Central SD	Albion
227	152	Batavia City SD	Batavia
227	152	Fredonia Central SD	Fredonia
227	152	Penn Yan Central SD	Penn Yan
231	151	Depew Union Free SD	Depew
231	151	Southampton Union Free SD	Southampton
233	150	Alden Central SD	Alden
233	150	East Aurora Union Free SD	East Aurora
235	149	Geneva City SD	Geneva
235	149	Peru Central SD	Peru
237	148	Clinton Central SD	Clinton
237	148	Oneonta City SD	Oneonta
239	147	Glens Falls City SD	Glens Falls
240	146	Amityville Union Free SD	Amityville
240	146	Livonia Central SD	Livonia
242	145	Attica Central SD	Attica
243	144	Beacon City SD	Beacon
244	143	Kinderhook Central SD	Valatie
244	143	Mount Sinai Union Free SD	Mount Sinai
246	141	Babylon Union Free SD	Babylon
246	141	Monticello Central SD	Monticello
246	141	Olean City SD	Olean
246	141	Susquehanna Valley Central SD	Conklin
246	141	Wayland-Cohocton Central SD	Wayland
251	140	Cobleskill-Richmondville CSD	Cobleskill
251	140	Highland Central SD	Highland
251	140	Island Trees Union Free SD	Levittown
251	140	Johnstown City SD	Johnstown
255	139	Maine-Endwell Central SD	Endwell
255	139	Palmyra-Macedon Central SD	Palmyra
257	138	Bayport-Blue Point Union Free SD	Bayport
258	135	Pelham Union Free SD	Pelham
258	135	Phelps-Clifton Springs Cent SD	Clifton Spgs
260	134	Bath Central SD	Bath
261	133	Norwich City SD	Norwich
261	133	Saranac Central SD	Dannemora
263	132	Marcellus Central SD	Marcellus
263	132	North Shore Central SD	Sea Cliff
263	132	Southwestern Cent SD Jamestown	Jamestown
266	131	Elwood Union Free SD	Greenlawn
266	131	Locust Valley Central SD	Locust Valley
268	130	Chenango Valley Central SD	Binghamton
268	130	Peekskill City SD	Peekskill
270	129	Holland Patent Central SD	Holland Patent
271	128	Broadalbin-Perth Central SD	Broadalbin
271	128	Chenango Forks Central SD	Binghamton
271	128	Hudson Falls Central SD	Hudson Falls
274	127	East Williston Union Free SD	Old Westbury
274	127	Ogdensburg City SD	Ogdensburg
276	126	Red Hook Central SD	Red Hook
277	123	Ardsley Union Free SD	Ardsley
277	123	South Jefferson Central SD	Adams Center
279	122	Medina Central SD	Medina
280	121	Cold Spring Harbor Central SD	Cold Sprg Harbor
280	121	Fonda-Fultonville Central SD	Fonda
280	121	General Brown Central SD	Dexter
280	121	Rye City SD	Rye
284	120	Nanuet Union Free SD	Nanuet
285	119	Gouverneur Central SD	Gouverneur
285	119	Sullivan West Central SD	Callicoon
287	118	Mount Pleasant Central SD	Thornwood
287	118	New Paltz Central SD	New Paltz
289	117	Greenburgh Central SD	Hartsdale
289	117	Royalton-Hartland Central SD	Middleport
291	116	Jordan-Elbridge Central SD	Jordan
291	116	Solvay Union Free SD	Solvay
293	114	Ilion Central SD	Ilion
293	114	Schuylerville Central SD	Schuylerville
293	114	Wilson Central SD	Wilson
296	113	Beekmantown Central SD	West Chazy
296	113	Briarcliff Manor Union Free SD	Briarcliff Manor
298	112	Mattituck-Cutchogue UFSD	Cutchogue
298	112	Onteora Central SD	Boiceville
298	112	Saranac Lake Central SD	Saranac Lake
301	111	Adirondack Central SD	Boonville
301	111	Eden Central SD	Eden
301	111	Spackenkill Union Free SD	Poughkeepsie
301	111	Union Free SD of the Tarrytowns	Sleepy Hollow
301	111	Windsor Central SD	Windsor
306	110	Dunkirk City SD	Dunkirk
306	110	Lansing Central SD	Lansing
308	109	Lackawanna City SD	Lackawanna
309	108	Cazenovia Central SD	Cazenovia
309	108	Oyster Bay-East Norwich CSD	Oyster Bay
311	107	Cohoes City SD	Cohoes
311	107	Dansville Central SD	Dansville
311	107	Malverne Union Free SD	Malverne
314	106	Dryden Central SD	Dryden

314	106	Marlboro Central SD	Marlboro
314	106	Pleasantville Union Free SD	Pleasantville
317	105	Canastota Central SD	Canastota
317	105	Eastchester Union Free SD	Eastchester
317	105	Gowanda Central SD	Gowanda
320	104	Cheektowaga-Sloan Union Free SD	Sloan
320	104	Dover Union Free SD	Dover Plains
320	104	Edgemont Union Free SD	Scarsdale
320	104	Hornell City SD	Hornell
320	104	Lansingburgh Central SD	Troy
325	103	Carle Place Union Free SD	Carle Place
325	103	Northeastern Clinton Central SD	Champlain
327	100	Sherburne-Earlville Central SD	Sherburne
327	100	Waterloo Central SD	Waterloo
329	99	Chatham Central SD	Chatham
329	99	Gorham-Middlesex CSD (M Whitman)	Rushville
329	99	Watkins Glen Central SD	Watkins Glen
332	98	Akron Central SD	Akron
332	98	Coxsackie-Athens Central SD	Coxsackie
332	98	Whitney Point Central SD	Whitney Point
335	97	Canton Central SD	Canton
335	97	Troy City SD	Troy
337	95	North Rose-Wolcott Central SD	Wolcott
337	95	Waverly Central SD	Waverly
339	94	Hannibal Central SD	Hannibal
340	92	Irvington Union Free SD	Irvington
341	91	Altmar-Parish-Williamstown CSD	Parish
342	90	Hudson City SD	Hudson
343	88	Salmon River Central SD	Ft Covington
344	86	Roosevelt Union Free SD	Roosevelt
344	86	Taconic Hills Central SD	Craryville
346	79	Catskill Central SD	Catskill
347	78	Cleveland Hill Union Free SD	Cheektowaga
347	78	Ellenville Central SD	Ellenville
349	77	Liberty Central SD	Liberty
350	74	Cairo-Durham Central SD	Cairo
350	74	Hastings-On-Hudson Union Free SD	Hastings-on-Hud
352	73	Croton-Harmon Union Free SD	Croton-On-Hud
353	71	Salamanca City SD	Salamanca
354	66	Wyandanch Union Free SD	Wyandanch
355	0	Amsterdam City SD	Amsterdam
355	0	Hampton Bays Union Free SD	Hampton Bays
357	n/a	New York City Geographic Dist 9	Bronx
357	n/a	New York City Geographic Dist 15	Brooklyn
357	n/a	Nyc Alternative HS District	New York
360	n/a	Boces Eastern Suffolk	Patchogue
360	n/a	Boces Nassau	Garden City
360	n/a	Elmont Union Free SD	Elmont
360	n/a	Floral Park-Bellerose UFSD	Floral Park
360	n/a	Franklin Square Union Free SD	Franklin Square
360	n/a	Merrick Union Free SD	Merrick
360	n/a	New Hyde Park-Garden City Park	New Hyde Park
360	n/a	North Bellmore Union Free SD	Bellmore
360	n/a	Putnam Valley Central SD	Putnam Valley
360	n/a	Valley Stream 13 Union Free SD	Valley Stream
360	n/a	Valley Stream 30 Union Free SD	Valley Stream

High School Drop-out Rate

Rank	Percent	District Name	City
1	31.3	Amityville Union Free SD	Amityville
2	18.4	Schenectady City SD	Schenectady
3	17.5	Roosevelt Union Free SD	Roosevelt
4	14.2	New York City Public Schools	Brooklyn
5	13.0	Rochester City SD	Rochester
6	11.8	Lackawanna City SD	Lackawanna
7	10.7	Poughkeepsie City SD	Poughkeepsie
8	10.2	Batavia City SD	Batavia
9	10.0	Ellenville Central SD	Ellenville
10	9.6	Hempstead Union Free SD	Hempstead
10	9.6	Royalton-Hartland Central SD	Middleport
12	9.5	Niagara Falls City SD	Niagara Falls
13	9.2	Hannibal Central SD	Hannibal
14	8.8	Medina Central SD	Medina
15	8.6	Riverhead Central SD	Riverhead
16	8.4	Bedford Central SD	Mount Kisco
16	8.4	Gouverneur Central SD	Gouverneur
18	8.2	E Ramapo Central SD (Sprg Val)	Spring Valley
19	8.1	Auburn City SD	Auburn
20	7.8	Jamestown City SD	Jamestown
20	7.8	Kingston City SD	Kingston
22	7.7	Monticello Central SD	Monticello
22	7.7	Yonkers City SD	Yonkers
24	7.6	Buffalo City SD	Buffalo
24	7.6	Hornell City SD	Hornell
26	7.5	Elmira City SD	Elmira
27	7.4	North Syracuse Central SD	N Syracuse
28	7.3	Coxsackie-Athens Central SD	Coxsackie
29	7.0	Fulton City SD	Fulton
29	7.0	Lansingburgh Central SD	Troy
31	6.9	Port Jervis City SD	Port Jervis
32	6.8	Yorkshire-Pioneer Central SD	Yorkshire
33	6.6	Central Square Central SD	Central Square
33	6.6	Oneida City SD	Oneida
33	6.6	Port Chester-Rye Union Free SD	Port Chester
33	6.6	Westbury Union Free SD	Old Westbury
37	6.5	Croton-Harmon Union Free SD	Croton-On-Hud
38	6.4	Freeport Union Free SD	Freeport
39	6.3	Catskill Central SD	Catskill
39	6.3	Olean City SD	Olean
41	6.2	Dunkirk City SD	Dunkirk
41	6.2	Plattsburgh City SD	Plattsburgh
43	5.9	Amsterdam City SD	Amsterdam
44	5.8	Camden Central SD	Camden
44	5.8	North Rose-Wolcott Central SD	Wolcott
46	5.7	Gowanda Central SD	Gowanda
46	5.7	Taconic Hills Central SD	Craryville
48	5.5	Beekmantown Central SD	West Chazy
48	5.5	Cleveland Hill Union Free SD	Cheektowaga
48	5.5	Tonawanda City SD	Tonawanda
48	5.5	Watkins Glen Central SD	Watkins Glen
52	5.4	Massena Central SD	Massena
52	5.4	Watertown City SD	Watertown
54	5.2	Evans-Brant Cent SD (Lake Shore)	Angola
54	5.2	Mexico Central SD	Mexico
54	5.2	Spackenkill Union Free SD	Poughkeepsie
57	5.1	Niagara-Wheatfield Central SD	Niagara Falls
58	4.9	Southwestern Cent SD Jamestown	Jamestown
59	4.8	Bellmore-Merrick Central High SD	North Merrick
60	4.7	Albany City SD	Albany
60	4.7	Geneva City SD	Geneva
60	4.7	Rome City SD	Rome
63	4.6	Albion Central SD	Albion
63	4.6	Glen Cove City SD	Glen Cove
63	4.6	Huntington Union Free SD	Huntington Stn
63	4.6	Johnstown City SD	Johnstown
63	4.6	Peru Central SD	Peru
63	4.6	Utica City SD	Utica
69	4.5	Beacon City SD	Beacon
69	4.5	Depew Union Free SD	Depew
69	4.5	Hyde Park Central SD	Poughkeepsie
69	4.5	Mount Vernon City SD	Mount Vernon
73	4.3	Cortland City SD	Cortland
74	4.2	Altmar-Parish-Williamstown CSD	Parish
74	4.2	Sherburne-Earlville Central SD	Sherburne
74	4.2	Springville-Griffith Inst Cent	Springville
77	4.1	Dansville Central SD	Dansville
77	4.1	Frontier Central SD	Hamburg
77	4.1	West Babylon Union Free SD	West Babylon
77	4.1	West Seneca Central SD	West Seneca
81	4.0	Cohoes City SD	Cohoes
81	4.0	Indian River Central SD	Philadelphia
81	4.0	Pine Bush Central SD	Pine Bush
81	4.0	Rondout Valley Central SD	Accord
81	4.0	Salamanca City SD	Salamanca
81	4.0	Waterloo Central SD	Waterloo
81	4.0	West Hempstead Union Free SD	W Hempstead
88	3.9	East Greenbush Central SD	E Greenbush
88	3.9	Johnson City Central SD	Johnson City
88	3.9	Lewiston-Porter Central SD	Youngstown
88	3.9	Newfane Central SD	Newfane
92	3.8	Akron Central SD	Akron
92	3.8	Brookhaven-Comsewogue UFSD	Pt Jefferson Stn
92	3.8	Cairo-Durham Central SD	Cairo
92	3.8	Cheektowaga-Maryvale UFSD	Cheektowaga
92	3.8	Gorham-Middlesex CSD (M Whitman)	Rushville
92	3.8	Livonia Central SD	Livonia
92	3.8	Ossining Union Free SD	Ossining
92	3.8	Saugerties Central SD	Saugerties
92	3.8	South Jefferson Central SD	Adams Center
92	3.8	Syracuse City SD	Syracuse
92	3.8	Whitesboro Central SD	Yorkville
103	3.7	Adirondack Central SD	Boonville
103	3.7	Brentwood Union Free SD	Brentwood
103	3.7	Waverly Central SD	Waverly
106	3.6	Ballston Spa Central SD	Ballston Spa
106	3.6	Chittenango Central SD	Chittenango
106	3.6	Honeoye Falls-Lima Central SD	Honeoye Falls
106	3.6	Ilion Central SD	Ilion
106	3.6	Liverpool Central SD	Liverpool
106	3.6	Lockport City SD	Lockport
106	3.6	Onteora Central SD	Boiceville
106	3.6	Pittsford Central SD	Pittsford
106	3.6	Sweet Home Central SD	Amherst
115	3.5	Averill Park Central SD	Averill Park
115	3.5	Dover Union Free SD	Dover Plains
115	3.5	Lakeland Central SD	Shrub Oak
115	3.5	Queensbury Union Free SD	Queensbury
115	3.5	Three Village Central SD	East Setauket
115	3.5	Windsor Central SD	Windsor
121	3.4	Canandaigua City SD	Canandaigua
121	3.4	Minisink Valley Central SD	Slate Hill
121	3.4	New Paltz Central SD	New Paltz
121	3.4	Wayland-Cohocton Central SD	Wayland
125	3.3	Alden Central SD	Alden
125	3.3	Corning City SD	Painted Post
125	3.3	Islip Union Free SD	Islip
125	3.3	North Tonawanda City SD	N Tonawanda
125	3.3	Red Hook Central SD	Red Hook
125	3.3	Salmon River Central SD	Ft Covington
125	3.3	Union Free SD of the Tarrytowns	Sleepy Hollow
132	3.2	Arlington Central SD	Poughkeepsie
132	3.2	Newark Central SD	Newark
132	3.2	South Orangetown Central SD	Blauvelt
132	3.2	Wappingers Central SD	Wappingers Fls
136	3.1	Baldwin Union Free SD	Baldwin
136	3.1	Cobleskill-Richmondville CSD	Cobleskill
136	3.1	Haverstraw-Stony Point Cent SD	Garnerville
136	3.1	Hicksville Union Free SD	Hicksville
136	3.1	Marcellus Central SD	Marcellus
136	3.1	Rocky Point Union Free SD	Rocky Point
136	3.1	Starpoint Central SD	Lockport
143	3.0	Bay Shore Union Free SD	Bay Shore
143	3.0	East Islip Union Free SD	Islip Terrace
143	3.0	Jordan-Elbridge Central SD	Jordan
143	3.0	Oswego City SD	Oswego
143	3.0	Phoenix Central SD	Phoenix
143	3.0	Wallkill Central SD	Wallkill
149	2.9	Amherst Central SD	Amherst
149	2.9	Holland Patent Central SD	Holland Patent
149	2.9	Victor Central SD	Victor
149	2.9	Wilson Central SD	Wilson
153	2.8	Canton Central SD	Canton
153	2.8	Gates-Chili Central SD	Rochester
153	2.8	Hamburg Central SD	Hamburg
153	2.8	Marlboro Central SD	Marlboro
157	2.7	Eden Central SD	Eden
157	2.7	Hudson Falls Central SD	Hudson Falls
157	2.7	Kenmore-Tonawanda Union Free SD	Buffalo
157	2.7	South Country Central SD	E Patchogue
161	2.6	Connetquot Central SD	Bohemia
161	2.6	Glens Falls City SD	Glens Falls
161	2.6	Longwood Central SD	Middle Island
161	2.6	South Huntington Union Free SD	Huntington Stn
165	2.5	Broadalbin-Perth Central SD	Broadalbin
165	2.5	Carmel Central SD	Patterson
165	2.5	East Syracuse-Minoa Central SD	East Syracuse
165	2.5	Grand Island Central SD	Grand Island
165	2.5	Homer Central SD	Homer
165	2.5	Hudson City SD	Hudson
165	2.5	Oyster Bay-East Norwich CSD	Oyster Bay
165	2.5	Penn Yan Central SD	Penn Yan
165	2.5	Westhampton Beach Union Free SD	Westhampton Bch
174	2.4	Highland Central SD	Highland
174	2.4	Lancaster Central SD	Lancaster
174	2.4	Southampton Union Free SD	Southampton
174	2.4	Sullivan West Central SD	Callicoon
174	2.4	Union-Endicott Central SD	Endicott
174	2.4	Valley Central SD (Montgomery)	Montgomery
174	2.4	West Genesee Central SD	Camillus
181	2.3	Cheektowaga-Sloan Union Free SD	Sloan
181	2.3	Fredonia Central SD	Fredonia
181	2.3	Horseheads Central SD	Horseheads
181	2.3	Long Beach City SD	Long Beach
181	2.3	Newburgh City SD	Newburgh
181	2.3	Ogdensburg City SD	Ogdensburg
181	2.3	White Plains City SD	White Plains
188	2.2	Carthage Central SD	Carthage
188	2.2	East Aurora Union Free SD	East Aurora
188	2.2	Kinderhook Central SD	Valatie
188	2.2	Ramapo Central SD (Suffern)	Hillburn
188	2.2	Rush-Henrietta Central SD	Henrietta
188	2.2	South Glens Falls Central SD	S Glens Falls
194	2.1	Nyack Union Free SD	Nyack
194	2.1	Solvay Union Free SD	Solvay
194	2.1	Susquehanna Valley Central SD	Conklin
194	2.1	Valley Stream Central High SD	Valley Stream
194	2.1	Whitney Point Central SD	Whitney Point
199	2.0	Malone Central SD	Malone
199	2.0	Patchogue-Medford Union Free SD	Patchogue
199	2.0	Ravena-Coeymans-Selkirk CSD	Selkirk
202	1.9	Cazenovia Central SD	Cazenovia
202	1.9	Chenango Forks Central SD	Binghamton
202	1.9	Orchard Park Central SD	Orchard Park
205	1.8	Baldwinsville Central SD	Baldwinsville
205	1.8	Chenango Valley Central SD	Binghamton
205	1.8	Hendrick Hudson Central SD	Montrose
205	1.8	Palmyra-Macedon Central SD	Palmyra
205	1.8	Saranac Lake Central SD	Saranac Lake
205	1.8	Somers Central SD	Lincolndale
211	1.7	Bath Central SD	Bath
211	1.7	Central Islip Union Free SD	Central Islip
211	1.7	Cornwall Central SD	Cornwall-on-Hud
211	1.7	East Irondequoit Central SD	Rochester
211	1.7	Greece Central SD	Rochester
211	1.7	Iroquois Central SD	Elma
211	1.7	Penfield Central SD	Penfield
211	1.7	Spencerport Central SD	Spencerport

219	1.6	Attica Central SD	Attica
219	1.6	Clinton Central SD	Clinton
219	1.6	General Brown Central SD	Dexter
219	1.6	Maine-Endwell Central SD	Endwell
219	1.6	Miller Place Union Free SD	Miller Place
219	1.6	New Hartford Central SD	New Hartford
219	1.6	North Colonie Central SD	Latham
219	1.6	Plainview-Old Bethpage Cent SD	Plainview
227	1.5	Bethlehem Central SD	Delmar
227	1.5	Canastota Central SD	Canastota
227	1.5	Churchville-Chili Central SD	Churchville
227	1.5	Island Trees Union Free SD	Levittown
227	1.5	South Colonie Central SD	Albany
227	1.5	Wayne Central SD	Ontario Center
227	1.5	Williamsville Central SD	East Amherst
234	1.4	Bayport-Blue Point Union Free SD	Bayport
234	1.4	Fairport Central SD	Fairport
234	1.4	Niskayuna Central SD	Schenectady
234	1.4	Saranac Central SD	Dannemora
234	1.4	Uniondale Union Free SD	Uniondale
234	1.4	Webster Central SD	Webster
240	1.3	Greenburgh Central SD	Hartsdale
240	1.3	Hauppauge Union Free SD	Hauppauge
240	1.3	Ithaca City SD	Ithaca
240	1.3	Mamaroneck Union Free SD	Mamaroneck
240	1.3	Northport-East Northport UFSD	Northport
240	1.3	Oneonta City SD	Oneonta
240	1.3	Port Washington Union Free SD	Pt Washington
240	1.3	Troy City SD	Troy
240	1.3	Washingtonville Central SD	Washingtonville
249	1.2	Fayetteville-Manlius Central SD	Manlius
249	1.2	Fonda-Fultonville Central SD	Fonda
249	1.2	Mineola Union Free SD	Mineola
249	1.2	Monroe-Woodbury Central SD	Central Valley
249	1.2	New Rochelle City SD	New Rochelle
249	1.2	Sachem Central SD	Holbrook
249	1.2	Wantagh Union Free SD	Wantagh
256	1.1	Eastchester Union Free SD	Eastchester
256	1.1	Goshen Central SD	Goshen
256	1.1	Jamesville-Dewitt Central SD	Dewitt
256	1.1	Manhasset Union Free SD	Manhasset
256	1.1	Mattituck-Cutchogue UFSD	Cutchogue
256	1.1	Schalmont Central SD	Schenectady
262	1.0	Brockport Central SD	Brockport
262	1.0	Carle Place Union Free SD	Carle Place
262	1.0	Cheektowaga Central SD	Cheektowaga
262	1.0	Harborfields Central SD	Greenlawn
262	1.0	Hewlett-Woodmere Union Free SD	Woodmere
262	1.0	Hilton Central SD	Hilton
262	1.0	Lynbrook Union Free SD	Lynbrook
262	1.0	Mahopac Central SD	Mahopac
262	1.0	Middletown City SD	Middletown
262	1.0	Norwich City SD	Norwich
262	1.0	Sewanhaka Central High SD	Floral Park
262	1.0	Sherrill City SD	Verona
262	1.0	Warwick Valley Central SD	Warwick
262	1.0	Yorktown Central SD	Yorktown Hgts
276	0.9	Bethpage Union Free SD	Bethpage
276	0.9	Binghamton City SD	Binghamton
276	0.9	Clarence Central SD	Clarence
276	0.9	Dryden Central SD	Dryden
276	0.9	Rotterdam-Mohonasen Central SD	Schenectady
276	0.9	Skaneateles Central SD	Skaneateles
276	0.9	Smithtown Central SD	Smithtown
283	0.8	Commack Union Free SD	E Northport
283	0.8	Harrison Central SD	Harrison
283	0.8	Lawrence Union Free SD	Lawrence
283	0.8	Mount Pleasant Central SD	Thornwood
283	0.8	Sayville Union Free SD	Sayville
288	0.7	Clarkstown Central SD	New City
288	0.7	Elwood Union Free SD	Greenlawn
288	0.7	Locust Valley Central SD	Locust Valley
288	0.7	Middle Country Central SD	Centereach
288	0.7	Mount Sinai Union Free SD	Mount Sinai
288	0.7	Northeastern Clinton Central SD	Champlain
288	0.7	Rye City SD	Rye
295	0.6	Brewster Central SD	Brewster
295	0.6	East Meadow Union Free SD	Westbury
295	0.6	Great Neck Union Free SD	Great Neck
295	0.6	Massapequa Union Free SD	Massapequa
295	0.6	North Shore Central SD	Sea Cliff
295	0.6	Pearl River Union Free SD	Pearl River
295	0.6	Pelham Union Free SD	Pelham
295	0.6	Phelps-Clifton Springs Cent SD	Clifton Spgs
295	0.6	Pleasantville Union Free SD	Pleasantville
295	0.6	Saratoga Springs City SD	Saratoga Spgs
295	0.6	Seaford Union Free SD	Seaford
295	0.6	West Irondequoit Central SD	Rochester
295	0.6	William Floyd Union Free SD	Mastic Beach
308	0.5	Brighton Central SD	Rochester
308	0.5	East Hampton Union Free SD	East Hampton
308	0.5	Half Hollow Hills Central SD	Dix Hills
308	0.5	Oceanside Union Free SD	Oceanside
308	0.5	Peekskill City SD	Peekskill
308	0.5	Vestal Central SD	Vestal
314	0.4	Katonah-Lewisboro Union Free SD	South Salem
314	0.4	Kings Park Central SD	Kings Park
314	0.4	Lansing Central SD	Lansing
314	0.4	Plainedge Union Free SD	N Massapequa
314	0.4	Schuylerville Central SD	Schuylerville
314	0.4	West Islip Union Free SD	West Islip
320	0.3	Burnt Hls-Ballston Lake Cent SD	Scotia
320	0.3	Copiague Union Free SD	Copiague
320	0.3	Deer Park Union Free SD	Deer Park
320	0.3	Farmingdale Union Free SD	Farmingdale
324	0.2	Ardsley Union Free SD	Ardsley
324	0.2	Babylon Union Free SD	Babylon
324	0.2	Garden City Union Free SD	Garden City
324	0.2	Gloversville City SD	Gloversville
324	0.2	Guilderland Central SD	Guilderland
324	0.2	Hastings-On-Hudson Union Free SD	Hastings-on-Hud
324	0.2	Herricks Union Free SD	New Hyde Park
324	0.2	Irvington Union Free SD	Irvington
324	0.2	Malverne Union Free SD	Malverne
324	0.2	Nanuet Union Free SD	Nanuet
324	0.2	Scarsdale Union Free SD	Scarsdale
324	0.2	Syosset Central SD	Syosset
324	0.2	Wyandanch Union Free SD	Wyandanch
337	0.1	Jericho Union Free SD	Jericho
337	0.1	Levittown Union Free SD	Levittown
337	0.1	Lindenhurst Union Free SD	Lindenhurst
337	0.1	Owego-Apalachin Central SD	Owego
337	0.1	Rockville Centre Union Free SD	Rockville Ctre
337	0.1	Roslyn Union Free SD	Roslyn
337	0.1	Scotia-Glenville Central SD	Scotia
337	0.1	Shoreham-Wading River Central SD	Shoreham
337	0.1	Westhill Central SD	Syracuse
346	0.0	Briarcliff Manor Union Free SD	Briarcliff Manor
346	0.0	Byram Hills Central SD	Armonk
346	0.0	Chappaqua Central SD	Chappaqua
346	0.0	Chatham Central SD	Chatham
346	0.0	Cold Spring Harbor Central SD	Cold Sprg Harbor
346	0.0	East Williston Union Free SD	Old Westbury
346	0.0	Edgemont Union Free SD	Scarsdale
346	0.0	Hampton Bays Union Free SD	Hampton Bays
346	0.0	Liberty Central SD	Liberty
346	0.0	North Babylon Union Free SD	North Babylon
346	0.0	Putnam Valley Central SD	Putnam Valley
346	0.0	Shenendehowa Central SD	Clifton Park
358	n/a	New York City Geographic Dist 9	Bronx
358	n/a	New York City Geographic Dist 15	Brooklyn
358	n/a	Nyc Alternative HS District	New York
361	n/a	Boces Eastern Suffolk	Patchogue
361	n/a	Boces Nassau	Garden City
361	n/a	Elmont Union Free SD	Elmont
361	n/a	Floral Park-Bellerose UFSD	Floral Park
361	n/a	Franklin Square Union Free SD	Franklin Square
361	n/a	Merrick Union Free SD	Merrick
361	n/a	New Hyde Park-Garden City Park	New Hyde Park
361	n/a	North Bellmore Union Free SD	Bellmore
361	n/a	Valley Stream 13 Union Free SD	Valley Stream
361	n/a	Valley Stream 30 Union Free SD	Valley Stream

North Carolina

North Carolina Public School Educational Profile

Category	Value	Category	Value
Schools *(2003-2004)*	2,268	**Diploma Recipients** *(2002-2003)*	65,955
Instructional Level		White, Non-Hispanic	44,888
Primary	1,329	Black, Non-Hispanic	17,385
Middle	465	Asian/Pacific Islander	1,410
High	367	American Indian/Alaskan Native	713
Other Level	107	Hispanic	1,559
Curriculum		**High School Drop-out Rate** (%) *(2001-2002)*	5.7
Regular	2,171	White, Non-Hispanic	4.9
Special Education	19	Black, Non-Hispanic	6.9
Vocational	7	Asian/Pacific Islander	3.7
Alternative	71	American Indian/Alaskan Native	9.9
Type		Hispanic	9.4
Magnet	133	**Staff** *(2003-2004)*	
Charter	93	Teachers	90,146.0
Title I Eligible	1,146	Average Salary[1] ($)	43,211
School-wide Title I	888	Librarians/Media Specialists	2,335.0
Students *(2003-2004)*	1,360,209	Guidance Counselors	3,444.0
Gender (%)		**Ratios** *(2003-2004)*	
Male	51.2	Student/Teacher Ratio	15.1 to 1
Female	48.8	Student/Librarian Ratio	582.5 to 1
Race/Ethnicity (%)		Student/Counselor Ratio	395.0 to 1
White, Non-Hispanic	58.3	**College Entrance Exam Scores** *(2005)*	
Black, Non-Hispanic	31.6	Scholastic Aptitude Test (SAT)	
Asian/Pacific Islander	2.0	Participation Rate (%)	74
American Indian/Alaskan Native	1.5	Mean SAT Reasoning Test Verbal Score	499
Hispanic	6.7	Mean SAT Reasoning Test Math Score	511
Classification (%)		American College Testing Program (ACT)	
Individual Education Program (IEP)	14.2	Participation Rate (%)	15
Migrant *(2002-2003)*	1.1	Average Composite Score	20.2
English Language Learner (ELL)	4.5	Average English Score	19.3
Eligible for Free Lunch Program	36.2	Average Math Score	20.4
Eligible for Reduced-Price Lunch Program	8.3	Average Reading Score	20.6
Current Spending *($ per student in FY 2003)*	6,636	Average Science Score	20.0
Instruction	4,189		
Support Services	2,083		

Note: *For an explanation of data, please refer to the User's Guide in the front of the book; (1) Includes extra-duty pay*

North Carolina NAEP 2005 Test Scores

Reading			Mathematics		
Grade/Category	Value	Rank	Grade/Category	Value	Rank
4th Grade			**4th Grade**		
Average Proficiency	217.1 (1.04)	32/51	Average Proficiency	241.2 (0.86)	15/51
Proficiency by Gender/Race/Ethnicity			Proficiency by Gender/Race/Ethnicity		
Male	213.4 (1.22)	33/51	Male	241.8 (1.10)	19/51
Female	221.1 (1.28)	32/51	Female	240.6 (0.87)	12/51
White, Non-Hispanic	227.2 (1.16)	21/51	White, Non-Hispanic	250.1 (0.94)	6/51
Black, Non-Hispanic	200.5 (1.48)	17/42	Black, Non-Hispanic	224.8 (1.09)	8/42
Asian, Non-Hispanic	220.8 (6.15)	20/27	Asian, Non-Hispanic	256.1 (4.02)	8/25
American Indian, Non-Hispanic	n/a	n/a	American Indian, Non-Hispanic	n/a	n/a
Hispanic	204.1 (2.36)	19/40	Hispanic	233.7 (1.50)	6/41
Proficiency by Class Size			Proficiency by Class Size		
Less than 16 Students	n/a	n/a	Less than 16 Students	n/a	n/a
16 to 18 Students	n/a	n/a	16 to 18 Students	n/a	n/a
19 to 20 Students	216.9 (2.93)	26/38	19 to 20 Students	240.1 (2.39)	17/38
21 to 25 Students	218.9 (1.58)	33/51	21 to 25 Students	243.2 (1.25)	13/51
Greater than 25 Students	218.4 (2.81)	24/36	Greater than 25 Students	n/a	n/a
Percent Attaining Achievement Levels			Percent Attaining Achievement Levels		
Below Basic	38.5 (1.52)	16/51	Below Basic	16.7 (1.09)	31/51
Basic or Above	61.5 (1.52)	36/51	Basic or Above	83.3 (1.09)	21/51
Proficient or Above	29.3 (1.37)	35/51	Proficient or Above	39.9 (1.36)	17/51
Advanced or Above	6.7 (0.63)	30/51	Advanced or Above	6.7 (0.76)	6/51
8th Grade			**8th Grade**		
Average Proficiency	258.2 (0.92)	36/51	Average Proficiency	281.8 (0.94)	18/51
Proficiency by Gender/Race/Ethnicity			Proficiency by Gender/Race/Ethnicity		
Male	251.1 (1.17)	39/51	Male	281.4 (1.19)	24/51
Female	265.7 (1.15)	32/51	Female	282.3 (1.03)	14/51
White, Non-Hispanic	267.4 (1.13)	32/51	White, Non-Hispanic	291.6 (1.13)	10/51
Black, Non-Hispanic	239.8 (1.62)	28/40	Black, Non-Hispanic	263.4 (1.22)	5/41
Asian, Non-Hispanic	275.1 (5.97)	10/24	Asian, Non-Hispanic	303.3 (6.61)	6/23
American Indian, Non-Hispanic	n/a	n/a	American Indian, Non-Hispanic	n/a	n/a
Hispanic	247.5 (2.95)	16/38	Hispanic	265.4 (2.74)	9/38
Proficiency by Parents Highest Level of Ed.			Proficiency by Parents Highest Level of Ed.		
Did Not Finish High School	239.4 (2.70)	41/49	Did Not Finish High School	265.0 (3.06)	11/50
Graduated High School	248.5 (1.82)	38/50	Graduated High School	270.3 (1.39)	23/50
Some Education After High School	263.1 (1.52)	36/50	Some Education After High School	282.5 (1.54)	24/50
Graduated College	266.2 (1.30)	37/50	Graduated College	293.5 (1.53)	14/50
Percent Attaining Achievement Levels			Percent Attaining Achievement Levels		
Below Basic	38.5 (1.52)	16/51	Below Basic	27.8 (1.16)	29/51
Basic or Above	61.5 (1.52)	36/51	Basic or Above	72.2 (1.16)	22/51
Proficient or Above	29.3 (1.37)	35/51	Proficient or Above	31.9 (1.12)	19/51
Advanced or Above	6.7 (0.63)	30/51	Advanced or Above	7.1 (0.80)	9/51

Note: *For an explanation of data, please refer to the User's Guide in the front of the book; n/a indicates data not available*

Alamance County

Alamance-Burlington Schools
1712 Vaughn Rd • Burlington, NC 27217-2916
(336) 570-6060 • http://abss.k12.nc.us/
Grade Span: PK-12; **Agency Type:** 1
Schools: 33
   19 Primary; 7 Middle; 6 High; 1 Other Level
   32 Regular; 0 Special Education; 0 Vocational; 1 Alternative
   0 Magnet; 0 Charter; 10 Title I Eligible; 10 School-wide Title I
Students: 21,788   (50.8% male; 49.1% female)
   Individual Education Program: 3,244 (14.9%);
   English Language Learner: 2,108 (9.7%); Migrant: 644 (3.0%)
   Eligible for Free Lunch Program: 7,765 (35.6%)
   Eligible for Reduced-Price Lunch Program: 1,845 (8.5%)
Teachers: 1,457.0 (15.0 to 1)
Librarians/Media Specialists: 33.0 (660.2 to 1)
Guidance Counselors: 52.0 (419.0 to 1)
Current Spending: ($ per student per year):
   Total: $5,960; Instruction: $3,794; Support Services: $1,801
Enrollment, Drop-out Rates and Diploma Recipients by Race/Ethnicity

Category	Total	White	Black	Asian	AIAN	Hisp.
Enrollment (%)	100.0	59.9	26.8	1.4	0.3	11.6
Drop-out Rate (%)	5.5	4.8	5.9	5.3	18.5	10.4
H.S. Diplomas (#)	1,081	768	251	21	3	38

Alexander County

Alexander County Schools
700 Liledoun Rd • Taylorsville, NC 28681-0128
Mailing Address: PO Box 128 • Taylorsville, NC 28681-0128
(828) 632-7001 • http://www.alexander.k12.nc.us/
Grade Span: PK-12; **Agency Type:** 1
Schools: 10
   7 Primary; 2 Middle; 1 High; 0 Other Level
   10 Regular; 0 Special Education; 0 Vocational; 0 Alternative
   0 Magnet; 0 Charter; 7 Title I Eligible; 1 School-wide Title I
Students: 5,598   (51.9% male; 48.0% female)
   Individual Education Program: 767 (13.7%);
   English Language Learner: 402 (7.2%); Migrant: 0 (0.0%)
   Eligible for Free Lunch Program: 1,606 (28.7%)
   Eligible for Reduced-Price Lunch Program: 487 (8.7%)
Teachers: 335.0 (16.7 to 1)
Librarians/Media Specialists: 10.0 (559.8 to 1)
Guidance Counselors: 16.0 (349.9 to 1)
Current Spending: ($ per student per year):
   Total: $6,097; Instruction: $3,839; Support Services: $1,828
Enrollment, Drop-out Rates and Diploma Recipients by Race/Ethnicity

Category	Total	White	Black	Asian	AIAN	Hisp.
Enrollment (%)	100.0	85.4	6.5	3.4	0.1	4.6
Drop-out Rate (%)	8.1	8.2	6.2	6.4	0.0	13.3
H.S. Diplomas (#)	322	298	15	7	0	2

Alleghany County

Alleghany County Schools
85 Peachtree St • Sparta, NC 28675-9210
(336) 372-4345
Grade Span: PK-12; **Agency Type:** 1
Schools: 4
   3 Primary; 0 Middle; 1 High; 0 Other Level
   4 Regular; 0 Special Education; 0 Vocational; 0 Alternative
   0 Magnet; 0 Charter; 3 Title I Eligible; 3 School-wide Title I
Students: 1,541   (49.2% male; 50.7% female)
   Individual Education Program: 309 (20.1%);
   English Language Learner: 96 (6.2%); Migrant: 132 (8.6%)
   Eligible for Free Lunch Program: 611 (39.6%)
   Eligible for Reduced-Price Lunch Program: 230 (14.9%)
Teachers: 125.0 (12.3 to 1)
Librarians/Media Specialists: 4.0 (385.3 to 1)
Guidance Counselors: 5.0 (308.2 to 1)
Current Spending: ($ per student per year):
   Total: $8,316; Instruction: $5,157; Support Services: $2,680
Enrollment, Drop-out Rates and Diploma Recipients by Race/Ethnicity

Category	Total	White	Black	Asian	AIAN	Hisp.
Enrollment (%)	100.0	89.9	2.3	0.0	0.1	7.7
Drop-out Rate (%)	3.6	3.7	0.0	n/a	n/a	0.0
H.S. Diplomas (#)	79	78	1	0	0	0

Anson County

Anson County Schools
320 Camden Rd • Wadesboro, NC 28170-0719
Mailing Address: PO Box 719 • Wadesboro, NC 28170-0719
(704) 694-4417 • http://www.anson.k12.nc.us/
Grade Span: PK-12; **Agency Type:** 1
Schools: 9
   6 Primary; 1 Middle; 2 High; 0 Other Level
   8 Regular; 0 Special Education; 0 Vocational; 1 Alternative
   0 Magnet; 0 Charter; 5 Title I Eligible; 5 School-wide Title I
Students: 4,441   (50.5% male; 49.4% female)
   Individual Education Program: 853 (19.2%);
   English Language Learner: 57 (1.3%); Migrant: 0 (0.0%)
   Eligible for Free Lunch Program: 2,646 (59.6%)
   Eligible for Reduced-Price Lunch Program: 443 (10.0%)
Teachers: 290.0 (15.3 to 1)
Librarians/Media Specialists: 11.0 (403.7 to 1)
Guidance Counselors: 11.0 (403.7 to 1)
Current Spending: ($ per student per year):
   Total: $6,763; Instruction: $4,136; Support Services: $2,179
Enrollment, Drop-out Rates and Diploma Recipients by Race/Ethnicity

Category	Total	White	Black	Asian	AIAN	Hisp.
Enrollment (%)	100.0	34.2	62.7	1.4	0.5	1.1
Drop-out Rate (%)	6.5	6.0	7.0	6.7	0.0	0.0
H.S. Diplomas (#)	207	67	137	2	1	0

Ashe County

Ashe County Schools
320 S St • Jefferson, NC 28640-0604
Mailing Address: PO Box 604 • Jefferson, NC 28640-0604
(336) 246-7175 • http://www.ashe.k12.nc.us/
Grade Span: PK-12; **Agency Type:** 1
Schools: 6
   4 Primary; 1 Middle; 1 High; 0 Other Level
   6 Regular; 0 Special Education; 0 Vocational; 0 Alternative
   0 Magnet; 0 Charter; 4 Title I Eligible; 4 School-wide Title I
Students: 3,251   (51.5% male; 48.4% female)
   Individual Education Program: 505 (15.5%);
   English Language Learner: 86 (2.6%); Migrant: 112 (3.4%)
   Eligible for Free Lunch Program: 1,141 (35.1%)
   Eligible for Reduced-Price Lunch Program: 542 (16.7%)
Teachers: 251.0 (13.0 to 1)
Librarians/Media Specialists: 6.0 (541.8 to 1)
Guidance Counselors: 10.0 (325.1 to 1)
Current Spending: ($ per student per year):
   Total: $7,190; Instruction: $4,425; Support Services: $2,312
Enrollment, Drop-out Rates and Diploma Recipients by Race/Ethnicity

Category	Total	White	Black	Asian	AIAN	Hisp.
Enrollment (%)	100.0	94.9	1.6	0.3	0.3	2.9
Drop-out Rate (%)	6.6	6.8	0.0	0.0	n/a	0.0
H.S. Diplomas (#)	188	185	1	0	0	2

Avery County

Avery County Schools
775 Cranberry St • Newland, NC 28657-1360
Mailing Address: PO Box 1360 • Newland, NC 28657-1360
(828) 733-6006 • http://www.avery.k12.nc.us/
Grade Span: PK-12; **Agency Type:** 1
Schools: 9
   6 Primary; 2 Middle; 1 High; 0 Other Level
   9 Regular; 0 Special Education; 0 Vocational; 0 Alternative
   0 Magnet; 0 Charter; 7 Title I Eligible; 7 School-wide Title I
Students: 2,406   (51.7% male; 48.2% female)
   Individual Education Program: 409 (17.0%);
   English Language Learner: 65 (2.7%); Migrant: 0 (0.0%)
   Eligible for Free Lunch Program: 850 (35.3%)
   Eligible for Reduced-Price Lunch Program: 399 (16.6%)
Teachers: 194.0 (12.4 to 1)
Librarians/Media Specialists: 10.0 (240.6 to 1)
Guidance Counselors: 11.0 (218.7 to 1)
Current Spending: ($ per student per year):
   Total: $7,784; Instruction: $4,717; Support Services: $2,693
Enrollment, Drop-out Rates and Diploma Recipients by Race/Ethnicity

Category	Total	White	Black	Asian	AIAN	Hisp.
Enrollment (%)	100.0	95.6	1.0	0.3	0.2	2.9
Drop-out Rate (%)	3.9	3.9	0.0	0.0	n/a	0.0
H.S. Diplomas (#)	133	131	1	1	0	0

Beaufort County

Beaufort County Schools
321 Smaw Rd • Washington, NC 27889-3937
(252) 946-6593 • http://www.beaufort.k12.nc.us/
Grade Span: PK-12; **Agency Type:** 1
Schools: 14
   6 Primary; 4 Middle; 3 High; 1 Other Level
   13 Regular; 0 Special Education; 0 Vocational; 1 Alternative
   0 Magnet; 0 Charter; 7 Title I Eligible; 7 School-wide Title I
Students: 7,443 (51.4% male; 48.5% female)
   Individual Education Program: 1,243 (16.7%);
   English Language Learner: 274 (3.7%); Migrant: 95 (1.3%)
   Eligible for Free Lunch Program: 4,082 (54.8%)
   Eligible for Reduced-Price Lunch Program: 713 (9.6%)
Teachers: 546.0 (13.6 to 1)
Librarians/Media Specialists: 13.0 (572.5 to 1)
Guidance Counselors: 16.0 (465.2 to 1)
Current Spending: ($ per student per year):
   Total: $6,747; Instruction: $4,305; Support Services: $2,067

Enrollment, Drop-out Rates and Diploma Recipients by Race/Ethnicity

Category	Total	White	Black	Asian	AIAN	Hisp.
Enrollment (%)	100.0	51.9	41.4	0.3	0.1	6.3
Drop-out Rate (%)	6.9	5.6	8.7	0.0	0.0	7.8
H.S. Diplomas (#)	380	247	126	3	0	4

Bertie County

Bertie County Schools
222 County Farm Rd • Windsor, NC 27983-0010
Mailing Address: PO Box 10 • Windsor, NC 27983-0010
(252) 794-3173 • http://www.bertieschools.com/
Grade Span: PK-12; **Agency Type:** 1
Schools: 10
   6 Primary; 2 Middle; 1 High; 1 Other Level
   9 Regular; 0 Special Education; 0 Vocational; 1 Alternative
   0 Magnet; 0 Charter; 7 Title I Eligible; 7 School-wide Title I
Students: 3,474 (51.5% male; 48.4% female)
   Individual Education Program: 515 (14.8%);
   English Language Learner: 10 (0.3%); Migrant: 27 (0.8%)
   Eligible for Free Lunch Program: 2,442 (70.3%)
   Eligible for Reduced-Price Lunch Program: 577 (16.6%)
Teachers: 236.0 (14.7 to 1)
Librarians/Media Specialists: 9.0 (386.0 to 1)
Guidance Counselors: 8.0 (434.3 to 1)
Current Spending: ($ per student per year):
   Total: $7,377; Instruction: $4,066; Support Services: $2,844

Enrollment, Drop-out Rates and Diploma Recipients by Race/Ethnicity

Category	Total	White	Black	Asian	AIAN	Hisp.
Enrollment (%)	100.0	13.7	85.0	0.1	0.3	0.8
Drop-out Rate (%)	5.7	4.9	5.9	0.0	n/a	0.0
H.S. Diplomas (#)	196	44	152	0	0	0

Bladen County

Bladen County Schools
Hwy 701 S • Elizabethtown, NC 28337-0037
Mailing Address: PO Box 37 • Elizabethtown, NC 28337-0037
(910) 862-4136 • http://bladen.schoolwebpages.com/education/district/
Grade Span: PK-12; **Agency Type:** 1
Schools: 14
   7 Primary; 4 Middle; 2 High; 1 Other Level
   13 Regular; 0 Special Education; 0 Vocational; 1 Alternative
   0 Magnet; 0 Charter; 9 Title I Eligible; 9 School-wide Title I
Students: 5,986 (51.9% male; 48.0% female)
   Individual Education Program: 733 (12.2%);
   English Language Learner: 260 (4.3%); Migrant: 376 (6.3%)
   Eligible for Free Lunch Program: 3,498 (58.4%)
   Eligible for Reduced-Price Lunch Program: 631 (10.5%)
Teachers: 391.0 (15.3 to 1)
Librarians/Media Specialists: 13.0 (460.5 to 1)
Guidance Counselors: 15.0 (399.1 to 1)
Current Spending: ($ per student per year):
   Total: $6,771; Instruction: $4,117; Support Services: $2,240

Enrollment, Drop-out Rates and Diploma Recipients by Race/Ethnicity

Category	Total	White	Black	Asian	AIAN	Hisp.
Enrollment (%)	100.0	43.4	50.2	0.1	0.8	5.5
Drop-out Rate (%)	4.1	5.5	2.6	0.0	8.3	3.7
H.S. Diplomas (#)	288	133	155	0	0	0

Brunswick County

Brunswick County Schools
35 Referendum Dr NE • Bolivia, NC 28422-0189
(910) 253-2900 • http://www.brunswickcountyschools.org/
Grade Span: PK-12; **Agency Type:** 1
Schools: 16
   9 Primary; 3 Middle; 3 High; 1 Other Level
   15 Regular; 0 Special Education; 0 Vocational; 1 Alternative
   0 Magnet; 0 Charter; 9 Title I Eligible; 9 School-wide Title I
Students: 10,914 (51.2% male; 48.7% female)
   Individual Education Program: 1,700 (15.6%);
   English Language Learner: 325 (3.0%); Migrant: 240 (2.2%)
   Eligible for Free Lunch Program: 4,904 (44.9%)
   Eligible for Reduced-Price Lunch Program: 1,314 (12.0%)
Teachers: 714.0 (15.3 to 1)
Librarians/Media Specialists: 15.0 (727.6 to 1)
Guidance Counselors: 28.0 (389.8 to 1)
Current Spending: ($ per student per year):
   Total: $6,998; Instruction: $4,156; Support Services: $2,507

Enrollment, Drop-out Rates and Diploma Recipients by Race/Ethnicity

Category	Total	White	Black	Asian	AIAN	Hisp.
Enrollment (%)	100.0	70.8	24.0	0.3	0.8	4.1
Drop-out Rate (%)	9.1	9.2	6.7	0.0	14.3	37.7
H.S. Diplomas (#)	474	325	137	3	0	9

Buncombe County

Asheville City Schools
85 Mountain St • Asheville, NC 28801
Mailing Address: PO Box 7347 • Asheville, NC 28802-7347
(828) 255-5304 • http://www.asheville.k12.nc.us/
Grade Span: KG-12; **Agency Type:** 1
Schools: 8
   5 Primary; 1 Middle; 1 High; 1 Other Level
   7 Regular; 0 Special Education; 0 Vocational; 1 Alternative
   5 Magnet; 0 Charter; 5 Title I Eligible; 5 School-wide Title I
Students: 3,859 (51.0% male; 48.9% female)
   Individual Education Program: 481 (12.5%);
   English Language Learner: 78 (2.0%); Migrant: 0 (0.0%)
   Eligible for Free Lunch Program: 1,653 (42.8%)
   Eligible for Reduced-Price Lunch Program: 215 (5.6%)
Teachers: 333.0 (11.6 to 1)
Librarians/Media Specialists: 10.0 (385.9 to 1)
Guidance Counselors: 15.0 (257.3 to 1)
Current Spending: ($ per student per year):
   Total: $9,326; Instruction: $5,779; Support Services: $3,153

Enrollment, Drop-out Rates and Diploma Recipients by Race/Ethnicity

Category	Total	White	Black	Asian	AIAN	Hisp.
Enrollment (%)	100.0	49.3	45.7	0.9	0.2	3.9
Drop-out Rate (%)	4.8	3.9	6.7	0.0	n/a	2.9
H.S. Diplomas (#)	249	172	71	2	0	4

Buncombe County Schools
175 Bingham Rd • Asheville, NC 28806-3800
(828) 255-5921 • http://www.buncombe.k12.nc.us/public/
Grade Span: PK-12; **Agency Type:** 1
Schools: 41
   23 Primary; 9 Middle; 9 High; 0 Other Level
   38 Regular; 0 Special Education; 1 Vocational; 2 Alternative
   0 Magnet; 0 Charter; 18 Title I Eligible; 13 School-wide Title I
Students: 24,828 (51.2% male; 48.7% female)
   Individual Education Program: 3,404 (13.7%);
   English Language Learner: 961 (3.9%); Migrant: 147 (0.6%)
   Eligible for Free Lunch Program: 6,746 (27.2%)
   Eligible for Reduced-Price Lunch Program: 1,999 (8.1%)
Teachers: 1,626.0 (15.3 to 1)
Librarians/Media Specialists: 50.0 (496.6 to 1)
Guidance Counselors: 59.0 (420.8 to 1)
Current Spending: ($ per student per year):
   Total: $6,541; Instruction: $4,218; Support Services: $1,948

Enrollment, Drop-out Rates and Diploma Recipients by Race/Ethnicity

Category	Total	White	Black	Asian	AIAN	Hisp.
Enrollment (%)	100.0	85.5	8.5	0.9	0.5	4.6
Drop-out Rate (%)	6.4	6.0	11.0	0.0	18.9	7.3
H.S. Diplomas (#)	1,370	1,261	72	13	3	21

Burke County

Burke County Schools
700 E Parker Rd • Morganton, NC 28655
Mailing Address: PO Drawer 989 • Morganton, NC 28680-0989
(828) 439-4312 • http://www.burke.k12.nc.us/
Grade Span: PK-12; **Agency Type:** 1
Schools: 25

16 Primary; 5 Middle; 2 High; 2 Other Level
23 Regular; 0 Special Education; 0 Vocational; 2 Alternative
0 Magnet; 0 Charter; 16 Title I Eligible; 14 School-wide Title I
Students: 14,803 (51.3% male; 48.6% female)
Individual Education Program: 2,386 (16.1%);
English Language Learner: 1,223 (8.3%); Migrant: 0 (0.0%)
Eligible for Free Lunch Program: 4,989 (33.7%)
Eligible for Reduced-Price Lunch Program: 1,686 (11.4%)
Teachers: 1,038.0 (14.3 to 1)
Librarians/Media Specialists: 25.0 (592.1 to 1)
Guidance Counselors: 39.0 (379.6 to 1)
Current Spending: ($ per student per year):
Total: $6,043; Instruction: $3,925; Support Services: $1,734
Enrollment, Drop-out Rates and Diploma Recipients by Race/Ethnicity

Category	Total	White	Black	Asian	AIAN	Hisp.
Enrollment (%)	100.0	77.7	8.7	9.1	0.2	4.3
Drop-out Rate (%)	5.0	5.1	5.8	2.8	0.0	4.9
H.S. Diplomas (#)	682	550	51	64	2	15

Cabarrus County

Cabarrus County Schools
4401 Old Airport Rd • Concord, NC 28025
Mailing Address: PO Box 388 • Concord, NC 28026-0388
(704) 786-6191 • http://www.cabarrus.k12.nc.us/
Grade Span: PK-12; **Agency Type:** 1
Schools: 28
15 Primary; 7 Middle; 5 High; 1 Other Level
27 Regular; 0 Special Education; 0 Vocational; 1 Alternative
1 Magnet; 0 Charter; 7 Title I Eligible; 3 School-wide Title I
Students: 21,860 (50.9% male; 49.0% female)
Individual Education Program: 3,098 (14.2%);
English Language Learner: 1,116 (5.1%); Migrant: 39 (0.2%)
Eligible for Free Lunch Program: 5,134 (23.5%)
Eligible for Reduced-Price Lunch Program: 1,479 (6.8%)
Teachers: 1,423.0 (15.4 to 1)
Librarians/Media Specialists: 29.0 (753.8 to 1)
Guidance Counselors: 61.0 (358.4 to 1)
Current Spending: ($ per student per year):
Total: $6,048; Instruction: $3,812; Support Services: $1,863
Enrollment, Drop-out Rates and Diploma Recipients by Race/Ethnicity

Category	Total	White	Black	Asian	AIAN	Hisp.
Enrollment (%)	100.0	73.8	17.1	1.3	0.4	7.4
Drop-out Rate (%)	5.1	4.4	8.0	1.8	12.5	12.5
H.S. Diplomas (#)	1,097	944	127	13	1	12

Kannapolis City Schools
100 Denver St • Kannapolis, NC 28083-3609
(704) 938-1131 • http://www.kannapolis.k12.nc.us/
Grade Span: PK-12; **Agency Type:** 1
Schools: 7
5 Primary; 1 Middle; 1 High; 0 Other Level
7 Regular; 0 Special Education; 0 Vocational; 0 Alternative
0 Magnet; 0 Charter; 5 Title I Eligible; 5 School-wide Title I
Students: 4,525 (52.2% male; 47.7% female)
Individual Education Program: 730 (16.1%);
English Language Learner: 731 (16.2%); Migrant: 0 (0.0%)
Eligible for Free Lunch Program: 2,226 (49.2%)
Eligible for Reduced-Price Lunch Program: 449 (9.9%)
Teachers: 348.0 (13.0 to 1)
Librarians/Media Specialists: 8.0 (565.6 to 1)
Guidance Counselors: 11.0 (411.4 to 1)
Current Spending: ($ per student per year):
Total: $6,660; Instruction: $4,210; Support Services: $2,003
Enrollment, Drop-out Rates and Diploma Recipients by Race/Ethnicity

Category	Total	White	Black	Asian	AIAN	Hisp.
Enrollment (%)	100.0	52.3	31.6	1.6	0.2	14.2
Drop-out Rate (%)	4.8	4.9	4.8	4.2	0.0	2.9
H.S. Diplomas (#)	231	138	83	2	0	8

Caldwell County

Caldwell County Schools
1914 Hickory Blvd SW • Lenoir, NC 28645-6404
(828) 728-8407 • http://205.152.116.5/CCSMainSite/
Grade Span: PK-12; **Agency Type:** 1
Schools: 25
16 Primary; 4 Middle; 4 High; 1 Other Level
22 Regular; 0 Special Education; 1 Vocational; 2 Alternative
0 Magnet; 0 Charter; 17 Title I Eligible; 15 School-wide Title I
Students: 12,903 (50.9% male; 49.0% female)
Individual Education Program: 1,528 (11.8%);
English Language Learner: 389 (3.0%); Migrant: 0 (0.0%)
Eligible for Free Lunch Program: 4,230 (32.8%)
Eligible for Reduced-Price Lunch Program: 1,244 (9.6%)

Teachers: 848.0 (15.2 to 1)
Librarians/Media Specialists: 24.0 (537.6 to 1)
Guidance Counselors: 35.0 (368.7 to 1)
Current Spending: ($ per student per year):
Total: $6,274; Instruction: $4,026; Support Services: $1,842
Enrollment, Drop-out Rates and Diploma Recipients by Race/Ethnicity

Category	Total	White	Black	Asian	AIAN	Hisp.
Enrollment (%)	100.0	87.1	8.5	0.7	0.1	3.6
Drop-out Rate (%)	5.1	5.0	4.5	0.0	33.3	10.4
H.S. Diplomas (#)	686	622	52	2	2	8

Camden County

Camden County Schools
174 N 343 • Camden, NC 27921-9614
(252) 335-0831
Grade Span: PK-12; **Agency Type:** 1
Schools: 3
1 Primary; 1 Middle; 1 High; 0 Other Level
3 Regular; 0 Special Education; 0 Vocational; 0 Alternative
0 Magnet; 0 Charter; 2 Title I Eligible; 0 School-wide Title I
Students: 1,591 (51.3% male; 48.6% female)
Individual Education Program: 206 (12.9%);
English Language Learner: 2 (0.1%); Migrant: 0 (0.0%)
Eligible for Free Lunch Program: 282 (17.7%)
Eligible for Reduced-Price Lunch Program: 160 (10.1%)
Teachers: 101.0 (15.8 to 1)
Librarians/Media Specialists: 3.0 (530.3 to 1)
Guidance Counselors: 2.0 (795.5 to 1)
Current Spending: ($ per student per year):
Total: $7,141; Instruction: $4,153; Support Services: $2,670
Enrollment, Drop-out Rates and Diploma Recipients by Race/Ethnicity

Category	Total	White	Black	Asian	AIAN	Hisp.
Enrollment (%)	100.0	81.6	16.5	1.1	0.1	0.6
Drop-out Rate (%)	5.6	6.2	3.7	0.0	n/a	0.0
H.S. Diplomas (#)	85	62	23	0	0	0

Carteret County

Carteret County Public Schools
107 Safrit Dr • Beaufort, NC 28516-9017
(252) 728-4583 • http://www.carteretcountyschools.org/
Grade Span: PK-12; **Agency Type:** 1
Schools: 16
8 Primary; 5 Middle; 3 High; 0 Other Level
16 Regular; 0 Special Education; 0 Vocational; 0 Alternative
0 Magnet; 0 Charter; 9 Title I Eligible; 9 School-wide Title I
Students: 8,324 (51.9% male; 48.0% female)
Individual Education Program: 1,455 (17.5%);
English Language Learner: 93 (1.1%); Migrant: 0 (0.0%)
Eligible for Free Lunch Program: 2,464 (29.6%)
Eligible for Reduced-Price Lunch Program: 799 (9.6%)
Teachers: 648.0 (12.8 to 1)
Librarians/Media Specialists: 16.0 (520.3 to 1)
Guidance Counselors: 29.0 (287.0 to 1)
Current Spending: ($ per student per year):
Total: $7,286; Instruction: $4,783; Support Services: $2,130
Enrollment, Drop-out Rates and Diploma Recipients by Race/Ethnicity

Category	Total	White	Black	Asian	AIAN	Hisp.
Enrollment (%)	100.0	85.2	11.6	0.6	0.3	2.2
Drop-out Rate (%)	4.9	4.9	3.9	0.0	12.5	9.8
H.S. Diplomas (#)	543	465	66	5	4	3

Caswell County

Caswell County Schools
353 County Home Rd • Yanceyville, NC 27379-0160
Mailing Address: PO Box 160 • Yanceyville, NC 27379-0160
(336) 694-4116 • http://www.caswellschools.org/
Grade Span: PK-12; **Agency Type:** 1
Schools: 6
4 Primary; 1 Middle; 1 High; 0 Other Level
6 Regular; 0 Special Education; 0 Vocational; 0 Alternative
0 Magnet; 0 Charter; 5 Title I Eligible; 3 School-wide Title I
Students: 3,491 (51.8% male; 48.1% female)
Individual Education Program: 498 (14.3%);
English Language Learner: 51 (1.5%); Migrant: 0 (0.0%)
Eligible for Free Lunch Program: 1,477 (42.3%)
Eligible for Reduced-Price Lunch Program: 331 (9.5%)
Teachers: 236.0 (14.8 to 1)
Librarians/Media Specialists: 6.0 (581.8 to 1)
Guidance Counselors: 10.0 (349.1 to 1)
Current Spending: ($ per student per year):
Total: $6,771; Instruction: $4,323; Support Services: $2,019

Enrollment, Drop-out Rates and Diploma Recipients by Race/Ethnicity

Category	Total	White	Black	Asian	AIAN	Hisp.
Enrollment (%)	100.0	53.1	43.7	0.2	0.1	2.9
Drop-out Rate (%)	4.0	3.8	4.0	0.0	33.3	10.0
H.S. Diplomas (#)	182	109	73	0	0	0

Catawba County

Catawba County Schools
10 E 25th St • Newton, NC 28658-1000
Mailing Address: PO Box 1010 • Newton, NC 28658-1000
(828) 464-8333 • http://www.catawba.k12.nc.us/
Grade Span: PK-12; **Agency Type:** 1
Schools: 25
 14 Primary; 6 Middle; 5 High; 0 Other Level
 25 Regular; 0 Special Education; 0 Vocational; 0 Alternative
 0 Magnet; 0 Charter; 10 Title I Eligible; 1 School-wide Title I
Students: 16,635 (51.2% male; 48.7% female)
 Individual Education Program: 2,424 (14.6%);
 English Language Learner: 1,414 (8.5%); Migrant: 0 (0.0%)
 Eligible for Free Lunch Program: 4,291 (25.8%)
 Eligible for Reduced-Price Lunch Program: 1,405 (8.4%)
Teachers: 1,063.0 (15.6 to 1)
Librarians/Media Specialists: 27.0 (616.1 to 1)
Guidance Counselors: 43.0 (386.9 to 1)
Current Spending: ($ per student per year):
 Total: $5,879; Instruction: $3,957; Support Services: $1,585
Enrollment, Drop-out Rates and Diploma Recipients by Race/Ethnicity

Category	Total	White	Black	Asian	AIAN	Hisp.
Enrollment (%)	100.0	77.5	8.7	7.5	0.2	6.1
Drop-out Rate (%)	4.7	4.3	7.9	3.5	0.0	12.9
H.S. Diplomas (#)	827	711	47	54	1	14

Hickory City Schools
432 4th Ave SW • Hickory, NC 28602-2805
(828) 322-2855 • http://www.hickory.k12.nc.us/
Grade Span: PK-12; **Agency Type:** 1
Schools: 10
 5 Primary; 2 Middle; 1 High; 2 Other Level
 8 Regular; 0 Special Education; 0 Vocational; 2 Alternative
 0 Magnet; 0 Charter; 8 Title I Eligible; 6 School-wide Title I
Students: 4,591 (50.2% male; 49.7% female)
 Individual Education Program: 550 (12.0%);
 English Language Learner: 687 (15.0%); Migrant: 0 (0.0%)
 Eligible for Free Lunch Program: 2,056 (44.8%)
 Eligible for Reduced-Price Lunch Program: 405 (8.8%)
Teachers: 306.0 (15.0 to 1)
Librarians/Media Specialists: 9.0 (510.1 to 1)
Guidance Counselors: 15.0 (306.1 to 1)
Current Spending: ($ per student per year):
 Total: $6,634; Instruction: $4,266; Support Services: $1,933
Enrollment, Drop-out Rates and Diploma Recipients by Race/Ethnicity

Category	Total	White	Black	Asian	AIAN	Hisp.
Enrollment (%)	100.0	51.5	28.7	7.7	0.2	11.9
Drop-out Rate (%)	6.6	6.3	6.9	2.7	0.0	13.2
H.S. Diplomas (#)	237	154	51	26	0	6

Newton Conover City Schools
605 N Ashe Ave • Newton, NC 28658-3120
(828) 464-3191 • http://www.nccs.k12.nc.us/
Grade Span: PK-12; **Agency Type:** 1
Schools: 6
 3 Primary; 1 Middle; 1 High; 1 Other Level
 5 Regular; 1 Special Education; 0 Vocational; 0 Alternative
 0 Magnet; 0 Charter; 2 Title I Eligible; 2 School-wide Title I
Students: 2,918 (51.2% male; 48.7% female)
 Individual Education Program: 394 (13.5%);
 English Language Learner: 319 (10.9%); Migrant: 0 (0.0%)
 Eligible for Free Lunch Program: 1,085 (37.2%)
 Eligible for Reduced-Price Lunch Program: 256 (8.8%)
Teachers: 197.0 (14.8 to 1)
Librarians/Media Specialists: 5.0 (583.6 to 1)
Guidance Counselors: 8.0 (364.8 to 1)
Current Spending: ($ per student per year):
 Total: $6,698; Instruction: $4,395; Support Services: $1,922
Enrollment, Drop-out Rates and Diploma Recipients by Race/Ethnicity

Category	Total	White	Black	Asian	AIAN	Hisp.
Enrollment (%)	100.0	58.2	21.9	7.3	0.3	12.3
Drop-out Rate (%)	3.1	2.7	3.9	0.0	0.0	8.8
H.S. Diplomas (#)	144	115	9	16	0	4

Chatham County

Chatham County Schools
369 W St • Pittsboro, NC 27312-0128
Mailing Address: PO Box 128 • Pittsboro, NC 27312-0128
(919) 542-3626 • http://www.chatham.k12.nc.us/index.nsf?OpenDatabase
Grade Span: PK-12; **Agency Type:** 1
Schools: 15
 9 Primary; 2 Middle; 4 High; 0 Other Level
 14 Regular; 0 Special Education; 0 Vocational; 1 Alternative
 0 Magnet; 0 Charter; 3 Title I Eligible; 3 School-wide Title I
Students: 7,291 (52.5% male; 47.4% female)
 Individual Education Program: 931 (12.8%);
 English Language Learner: 844 (11.6%); Migrant: 631 (8.7%)
 Eligible for Free Lunch Program: 2,231 (30.6%)
 Eligible for Reduced-Price Lunch Program: 570 (7.8%)
Teachers: 501.0 (14.6 to 1)
Librarians/Media Specialists: 14.0 (520.8 to 1)
Guidance Counselors: 26.0 (280.4 to 1)
Current Spending: ($ per student per year):
 Total: $7,215; Instruction: $4,469; Support Services: $2,363
Enrollment, Drop-out Rates and Diploma Recipients by Race/Ethnicity

Category	Total	White	Black	Asian	AIAN	Hisp.
Enrollment (%)	100.0	59.6	22.6	0.5	0.3	17.0
Drop-out Rate (%)	7.4	6.9	6.4	17.6	33.3	12.6
H.S. Diplomas (#)	306	202	87	2	0	15

Cherokee County

Cherokee County Schools
911 Andrews Rd • Murphy, NC 28906-2730
(828) 837-2722
Grade Span: PK-12; **Agency Type:** 1
Schools: 13
 7 Primary; 2 Middle; 3 High; 1 Other Level
 12 Regular; 0 Special Education; 0 Vocational; 1 Alternative
 0 Magnet; 0 Charter; 7 Title I Eligible; 7 School-wide Title I
Students: 3,820 (51.9% male; 48.0% female)
 Individual Education Program: 623 (16.3%);
 English Language Learner: 2 (0.1%); Migrant: 0 (0.0%)
 Eligible for Free Lunch Program: 1,478 (38.7%)
 Eligible for Reduced-Price Lunch Program: 613 (16.0%)
Teachers: 281.0 (13.6 to 1)
Librarians/Media Specialists: 10.0 (382.0 to 1)
Guidance Counselors: 10.0 (382.0 to 1)
Current Spending: ($ per student per year):
 Total: $7,116; Instruction: $4,485; Support Services: $2,132
Enrollment, Drop-out Rates and Diploma Recipients by Race/Ethnicity

Category	Total	White	Black	Asian	AIAN	Hisp.
Enrollment (%)	100.0	94.2	2.7	0.5	1.4	1.2
Drop-out Rate (%)	3.4	3.5	0.0	0.0	5.3	0.0
H.S. Diplomas (#)	236	228	4	0	4	0

Chowan County

Edenton/Chowan Schools
E King St • Edenton, NC 27932-0206
Mailing Address: PO Box 206 • Edenton, NC 27932-0206
(252) 482-4436 • http://www.ecps.k12.nc.us/
Grade Span: PK-12; **Agency Type:** 1
Schools: 4
 2 Primary; 1 Middle; 1 High; 0 Other Level
 4 Regular; 0 Special Education; 0 Vocational; 0 Alternative
 0 Magnet; 0 Charter; 3 Title I Eligible; 3 School-wide Title I
Students: 2,574 (51.5% male; 48.4% female)
 Individual Education Program: 324 (12.6%);
 English Language Learner: 30 (1.2%); Migrant: 0 (0.0%)
 Eligible for Free Lunch Program: 982 (38.2%)
 Eligible for Reduced-Price Lunch Program: 195 (7.6%)
Teachers: 185.0 (13.9 to 1)
Librarians/Media Specialists: 4.0 (643.5 to 1)
Guidance Counselors: 7.0 (367.7 to 1)
Current Spending: ($ per student per year):
 Total: $7,381; Instruction: $4,553; Support Services: $2,473
Enrollment, Drop-out Rates and Diploma Recipients by Race/Ethnicity

Category	Total	White	Black	Asian	AIAN	Hisp.
Enrollment (%)	100.0	49.2	48.5	0.2	0.2	1.9
Drop-out Rate (%)	5.2	5.1	5.3	0.0	0.0	0.0
H.S. Diplomas (#)	138	83	55	0	0	0

Cleveland County

Cleveland County Schools
130 S Post Rd Ste 2 • Shelby, NC 28152-6297
(704) 487-8581 • http://www.ccss.k12.nc.us/
Grade Span: PK-12; **Agency Type:** 1
Schools: 12
　8 Primary; 2 Middle; 2 High; 0 Other Level
　12 Regular; 0 Special Education; 0 Vocational; 0 Alternative
　0 Magnet; 0 Charter; 7 Title I Eligible; 3 School-wide Title I
Students: 9,973　(51.3% male; 48.6% female)
　Individual Education Program: 1,492 (15.0%);
　English Language Learner: 146 (1.5%); Migrant: 0 (0.0%)
　Eligible for Free Lunch Program: 3,408 (34.2%)
　Eligible for Reduced-Price Lunch Program: 653 (6.5%)
Teachers: 670.0 (14.9 to 1)
Librarians/Media Specialists: 15.0 (664.9 to 1)
Guidance Counselors: 24.0 (415.5 to 1)
Current Spending: ($ per student per year):
　Total: $6,320; Instruction: $4,181; Support Services: $1,736
Enrollment, Drop-out Rates and Diploma Recipients by Race/Ethnicity

Category	Total	White	Black	Asian	AIAN	Hisp.
Enrollment (%)	100.0	73.0	24.5	0.2	0.1	2.2
Drop-out Rate (%)	4.7	4.8	4.0	0.0	n/a	16.7
H.S. Diplomas (#)	442	355	83	0	0	4

Kings Mountain District
105 E Ridge St • Kings Mountain, NC 28086-0279
(704) 734-5637 • http://www.kmds.k12.nc.us/
Grade Span: PK-12; **Agency Type:** 1
Schools: 9
　5 Primary; 2 Middle; 1 High; 1 Other Level
　8 Regular; 0 Special Education; 0 Vocational; 1 Alternative
　0 Magnet; 0 Charter; 5 Title I Eligible; 1 School-wide Title I
Students: 4,691　(49.9% male; 50.0% female)
　Individual Education Program: 526 (11.2%);
　English Language Learner: 34 (0.7%); Migrant: 0 (0.0%)
　Eligible for Free Lunch Program: 1,575 (33.6%)
　Eligible for Reduced-Price Lunch Program: 347 (7.4%)
Teachers: 302.0 (15.5 to 1)
Librarians/Media Specialists: 9.0 (521.2 to 1)
Guidance Counselors: 14.0 (335.1 to 1)
Current Spending: ($ per student per year):
　Total: $6,523; Instruction: $4,100; Support Services: $2,032
Enrollment, Drop-out Rates and Diploma Recipients by Race/Ethnicity

Category	Total	White	Black	Asian	AIAN	Hisp.
Enrollment (%)	100.0	72.3	24.0	2.0	0.1	1.6
Drop-out Rate (%)	5.5	5.8	4.4	6.9	0.0	6.3
H.S. Diplomas (#)	184	138	38	7	0	1

Shelby City Schools
315 Patton Dr • Shelby, NC 28150-5499
(704) 487-6367 • http://www.blueridge.net/scs/scs.htm
Grade Span: PK-12; **Agency Type:** 1
Schools: 7
　3 Primary; 2 Middle; 1 High; 1 Other Level
　6 Regular; 1 Special Education; 0 Vocational; 0 Alternative
　0 Magnet; 0 Charter; 3 Title I Eligible; 3 School-wide Title I
Students: 3,172　(51.6% male; 48.3% female)
　Individual Education Program: 522 (16.5%);
　English Language Learner: 30 (0.9%); Migrant: 0 (0.0%)
　Eligible for Free Lunch Program: 1,619 (51.0%)
　Eligible for Reduced-Price Lunch Program: 186 (5.9%)
Teachers: 258.0 (12.3 to 1)
Librarians/Media Specialists: 6.0 (528.7 to 1)
Guidance Counselors: 7.0 (453.1 to 1)
Current Spending: ($ per student per year):
　Total: $7,224; Instruction: $4,652; Support Services: $2,141
Enrollment, Drop-out Rates and Diploma Recipients by Race/Ethnicity

Category	Total	White	Black	Asian	AIAN	Hisp.
Enrollment (%)	100.0	38.7	58.8	0.6	0.1	1.9
Drop-out Rate (%)	6.9	4.0	10.0	0.0	n/a	0.0
H.S. Diplomas (#)	141	77	62	2	0	0

Columbus County

Columbus County Schools
817 Washington St • Whiteville, NC 28472-0729
Mailing Address: PO Box 729 • Whiteville, NC 28472-0729
(910) 642-5168 • http://www.columbus.k12.nc.us/
Grade Span: PK-12; **Agency Type:** 1
Schools: 19
　10 Primary; 5 Middle; 3 High; 1 Other Level
　18 Regular; 0 Special Education; 0 Vocational; 1 Alternative
　0 Magnet; 0 Charter; 16 Title I Eligible; 16 School-wide Title I

Students: 7,125　(50.9% male; 49.0% female)
　Individual Education Program: 976 (13.7%);
　English Language Learner: 166 (2.3%); Migrant: 632 (8.9%)
　Eligible for Free Lunch Program: 4,212 (59.1%)
　Eligible for Reduced-Price Lunch Program: 781 (11.0%)
Teachers: 452.0 (15.8 to 1)
Librarians/Media Specialists: 17.0 (419.1 to 1)
Guidance Counselors: 21.0 (339.3 to 1)
Current Spending: ($ per student per year):
　Total: $6,636; Instruction: $4,067; Support Services: $2,161
Enrollment, Drop-out Rates and Diploma Recipients by Race/Ethnicity

Category	Total	White	Black	Asian	AIAN	Hisp.
Enrollment (%)	100.0	49.9	40.7	0.0	5.7	3.7
Drop-out Rate (%)	7.3	8.0	6.7	0.0	3.5	21.1
H.S. Diplomas (#)	386	198	170	0	17	1

Whiteville City Schools
107 W Walter St • Whiteville, NC 28472-4019
Mailing Address: PO Box 609 • Whiteville, NC 28472-0609
(910) 642-4116 • http://www.whiteville.k12.nc.us/
Grade Span: PK-12; **Agency Type:** 1
Schools: 5
　2 Primary; 1 Middle; 1 High; 1 Other Level
　4 Regular; 0 Special Education; 0 Vocational; 1 Alternative
　0 Magnet; 0 Charter; 4 Title I Eligible; 4 School-wide Title I
Students: 2,711　(50.8% male; 49.1% female)
　Individual Education Program: 394 (14.5%);
　English Language Learner: 40 (1.5%); Migrant: 65 (2.4%)
　Eligible for Free Lunch Program: 1,459 (53.8%)
　Eligible for Reduced-Price Lunch Program: 239 (8.8%)
Teachers: 205.0 (13.2 to 1)
Librarians/Media Specialists: 4.0 (677.8 to 1)
Guidance Counselors: 6.0 (451.8 to 1)
Current Spending: ($ per student per year):
　Total: $6,706; Instruction: $4,295; Support Services: $2,032
Enrollment, Drop-out Rates and Diploma Recipients by Race/Ethnicity

Category	Total	White	Black	Asian	AIAN	Hisp.
Enrollment (%)	100.0	51.1	44.9	0.4	1.2	2.4
Drop-out Rate (%)	5.7	4.8	6.9	0.0	0.0	8.3
H.S. Diplomas (#)	132	77	54	1	0	0

Craven County

Craven County Schools
3600 Trent Rd • New Bern, NC 28562-2224
(252) 514-6300 • http://schools.craven.k12.nc.us/
Grade Span: PK-12; **Agency Type:** 1
Schools: 22
　14 Primary; 5 Middle; 3 High; 0 Other Level
　22 Regular; 0 Special Education; 0 Vocational; 0 Alternative
　0 Magnet; 0 Charter; 18 Title I Eligible; 18 School-wide Title I
Students: 14,597　(50.7% male; 49.2% female)
　Individual Education Program: 1,905 (13.1%);
　English Language Learner: 250 (1.7%); Migrant: 0 (0.0%)
　Eligible for Free Lunch Program: 5,342 (36.6%)
　Eligible for Reduced-Price Lunch Program: 1,923 (13.2%)
Teachers: 1,018.0 (14.3 to 1)
Librarians/Media Specialists: 22.0 (663.5 to 1)
Guidance Counselors: 37.0 (394.5 to 1)
Current Spending: ($ per student per year):
　Total: $6,409; Instruction: $4,057; Support Services: $2,018
Enrollment, Drop-out Rates and Diploma Recipients by Race/Ethnicity

Category	Total	White	Black	Asian	AIAN	Hisp.
Enrollment (%)	100.0	58.5	36.6	1.0	0.3	3.7
Drop-out Rate (%)	6.6	5.2	8.9	4.7	8.3	13.5
H.S. Diplomas (#)	816	521	263	11	0	21

Cumberland County

Cumberland County Schools
2465 Gillespie St • Fayetteville, NC 28306
Mailing Address: PO Box 2357 • Fayetteville, NC 28302-2357
(910) 678-2300 • http://www.ccs.k12.nc.us/
Grade Span: PK-12; **Agency Type:** 1
Schools: 85
　54 Primary; 16 Middle; 13 High; 2 Other Level
　81 Regular; 1 Special Education; 0 Vocational; 3 Alternative
　0 Magnet; 0 Charter; 62 Title I Eligible; 62 School-wide Title I
Students: 53,159　(51.0% male; 48.9% female)
　Individual Education Program: 7,268 (13.7%);
　English Language Learner: 770 (1.4%); Migrant: 0 (0.0%)
　Eligible for Free Lunch Program: 21,728 (40.9%)
　Eligible for Reduced-Price Lunch Program: 5,836 (11.0%)
Teachers: 3,255.0 (16.3 to 1)
Librarians/Media Specialists: 94.0 (565.5 to 1)

Guidance Counselors: 140.0 (379.7 to 1)
Current Spending: ($ per student per year):
  Total: $6,301; Instruction: $3,941; Support Services: $1,983
Enrollment, Drop-out Rates and Diploma Recipients by Race/Ethnicity

Category	Total	White	Black	Asian	AIAN	Hisp.
Enrollment (%)	100.0	40.4	50.4	1.6	1.7	5.9
Drop-out Rate (%)	4.3	4.2	4.5	2.3	9.0	3.9
H.S. Diplomas (#)	2,809	1,211	1,290	80	50	178

Currituck County

Currituck County Schools
2958 Caratoke Hwy • Currituck, NC 27929-0040
Mailing Address: PO Box 40 • Currituck, NC 27929-0040
(252) 232-2223 • http://www.currituck.k12.nc.us
Grade Span: KG-12; **Agency Type:** 1
Schools: 8
  5 Primary; 2 Middle; 1 High; 0 Other Level
  8 Regular; 0 Special Education; 0 Vocational; 0 Alternative
  0 Magnet; 0 Charter; 5 Title I Eligible; 0 School-wide Title I
Students: 3,663 (50.8% male; 49.1% female)
  Individual Education Program: 552 (15.1%);
  English Language Learner: 15 (0.4%); Migrant: 0 (0.0%)
  Eligible for Free Lunch Program: 675 (18.4%)
  Eligible for Reduced-Price Lunch Program: 252 (6.9%)
Teachers: 247.0 (14.8 to 1)
Librarians/Media Specialists: 10.0 (366.3 to 1)
Guidance Counselors: 9.0 (407.0 to 1)
Current Spending: ($ per student per year):
  Total: $7,544; Instruction: $4,456; Support Services: $2,714
Enrollment, Drop-out Rates and Diploma Recipients by Race/Ethnicity

Category	Total	White	Black	Asian	AIAN	Hisp.
Enrollment (%)	100.0	87.6	10.3	0.3	0.2	1.6
Drop-out Rate (%)	6.2	6.3	5.6	0.0	33.3	0.0
H.S. Diplomas (#)	195	170	23	1	0	1

Dare County

Dare County Schools
510 Budleigh St • Manteo, NC 27954-0640
Mailing Address: PO Box 640 • Manteo, NC 27954-0640
(252) 473-1151 • http://www.dare.k12.nc.us/
Grade Span: PK-12; **Agency Type:** 1
Schools: 9
  4 Primary; 2 Middle; 2 High; 1 Other Level
  8 Regular; 0 Special Education; 0 Vocational; 1 Alternative
  0 Magnet; 0 Charter; 3 Title I Eligible; 0 School-wide Title I
Students: 4,804 (51.7% male; 48.2% female)
  Individual Education Program: 550 (11.4%);
  English Language Learner: 106 (2.2%); Migrant: 0 (0.0%)
  Eligible for Free Lunch Program: 695 (14.5%)
  Eligible for Reduced-Price Lunch Program: 245 (5.1%)
Teachers: 342.0 (14.0 to 1)
Librarians/Media Specialists: 9.0 (533.8 to 1)
Guidance Counselors: 16.0 (300.3 to 1)
Current Spending: ($ per student per year):
  Total: $7,792; Instruction: $4,904; Support Services: $2,598
Enrollment, Drop-out Rates and Diploma Recipients by Race/Ethnicity

Category	Total	White	Black	Asian	AIAN	Hisp.
Enrollment (%)	100.0	90.3	5.1	0.5	0.2	3.9
Drop-out Rate (%)	5.7	5.4	10.2	0.0	50.0	10.0
H.S. Diplomas (#)	259	245	10	0	0	4

Davidson County

Davidson County Schools
250 County School Rd • Lexington, NC 27292
Mailing Address: PO Box 2057 • Lexington, NC 27293-2057
(336) 249-8181 • http://www.davidson.k12.nc.us/
Grade Span: PK-12; **Agency Type:** 1
Schools: 29
  15 Primary; 6 Middle; 6 High; 2 Other Level
  27 Regular; 1 Special Education; 0 Vocational; 1 Alternative
  0 Magnet; 0 Charter; 11 Title I Eligible; 0 School-wide Title I
Students: 19,549 (50.8% male; 49.1% female)
  Individual Education Program: 2,408 (12.3%);
  English Language Learner: 107 (0.5%); Migrant: 0 (0.0%)
  Eligible for Free Lunch Program: 4,001 (20.5%)
  Eligible for Reduced-Price Lunch Program: 1,258 (6.4%)
Teachers: 1,178.0 (16.6 to 1)
Librarians/Media Specialists: 28.0 (698.2 to 1)
Guidance Counselors: 44.0 (444.3 to 1)
Current Spending: ($ per student per year):
  Total: $5,573; Instruction: $3,611; Support Services: $1,626

Enrollment, Drop-out Rates and Diploma Recipients by Race/Ethnicity

Category	Total	White	Black	Asian	AIAN	Hisp.
Enrollment (%)	100.0	93.7	3.1	0.8	0.3	2.1
Drop-out Rate (%)	5.9	6.0	6.2	2.6	7.1	4.2
H.S. Diplomas (#)	1,046	1,010	22	5	1	8

Lexington City Schools
1010 Fair St • Lexington, NC 27292-1665
(336) 242-1527 • http://www.lexcs.org/
Grade Span: PK-12; **Agency Type:** 1
Schools: 6
  3 Primary; 2 Middle; 1 High; 0 Other Level
  6 Regular; 0 Special Education; 0 Vocational; 0 Alternative
  0 Magnet; 0 Charter; 5 Title I Eligible; 5 School-wide Title I
Students: 3,262 (51.5% male; 48.4% female)
  Individual Education Program: 509 (15.6%);
  English Language Learner: 416 (12.8%); Migrant: 0 (0.0%)
  Eligible for Free Lunch Program: 2,262 (69.3%)
  Eligible for Reduced-Price Lunch Program: 326 (10.0%)
Teachers: 237.0 (13.8 to 1)
Librarians/Media Specialists: 6.0 (543.7 to 1)
Guidance Counselors: 8.0 (407.8 to 1)
Current Spending: ($ per student per year):
  Total: $7,129; Instruction: $4,441; Support Services: $2,249
Enrollment, Drop-out Rates and Diploma Recipients by Race/Ethnicity

Category	Total	White	Black	Asian	AIAN	Hisp.
Enrollment (%)	100.0	28.3	46.9	5.2	0.4	19.1
Drop-out Rate (%)	9.0	7.3	7.0	18.2	33.3	16.3
H.S. Diplomas (#)	136	47	70	12	1	6

Thomasville City Schools
400 Turner St • Thomasville, NC 27360-3129
(336) 474-4200 • http://www.tcs.k12.nc.us/
Grade Span: PK-12; **Agency Type:** 1
Schools: 4
  2 Primary; 1 Middle; 1 High; 0 Other Level
  4 Regular; 0 Special Education; 0 Vocational; 0 Alternative
  0 Magnet; 0 Charter; 2 Title I Eligible; 2 School-wide Title I
Students: 2,604 (52.3% male; 47.6% female)
  Individual Education Program: 279 (10.7%);
  English Language Learner: 250 (9.6%); Migrant: 0 (0.0%)
  Eligible for Free Lunch Program: 1,877 (72.1%)
  Eligible for Reduced-Price Lunch Program: 257 (9.9%)
Teachers: 217.0 (12.0 to 1)
Librarians/Media Specialists: 4.0 (651.0 to 1)
Guidance Counselors: 5.0 (520.8 to 1)
Current Spending: ($ per student per year):
  Total: $7,344; Instruction: $4,718; Support Services: $2,047
Enrollment, Drop-out Rates and Diploma Recipients by Race/Ethnicity

Category	Total	White	Black	Asian	AIAN	Hisp.
Enrollment (%)	100.0	32.1	50.7	0.7	0.2	16.4
Drop-out Rate (%)	3.8	6.2	2.2	0.0	n/a	2.1
H.S. Diplomas (#)	91	37	48	1	0	5

Davie County

Davie County Schools
220 Cherry St • Mocksville, NC 27028-2206
(336) 751-5921 • http://www.davie.k12.nc.us/
Grade Span: PK-12; **Agency Type:** 1
Schools: 9
  6 Primary; 2 Middle; 1 High; 0 Other Level
  9 Regular; 0 Special Education; 0 Vocational; 0 Alternative
  0 Magnet; 0 Charter; 5 Title I Eligible; 0 School-wide Title I
Students: 6,058 (51.1% male; 48.8% female)
  Individual Education Program: 873 (14.4%);
  English Language Learner: 236 (3.9%); Migrant: 0 (0.0%)
  Eligible for Free Lunch Program: 1,361 (22.5%)
  Eligible for Reduced-Price Lunch Program: 387 (6.4%)
Teachers: 408.0 (14.8 to 1)
Librarians/Media Specialists: 11.0 (550.7 to 1)
Guidance Counselors: 16.0 (378.6 to 1)
Current Spending: ($ per student per year):
  Total: $6,155; Instruction: $3,960; Support Services: $1,833
Enrollment, Drop-out Rates and Diploma Recipients by Race/Ethnicity

Category	Total	White	Black	Asian	AIAN	Hisp.
Enrollment (%)	100.0	83.3	9.7	0.4	0.1	6.6
Drop-out Rate (%)	7.0	6.2	11.9	0.0	n/a	13.4
H.S. Diplomas (#)	327	288	29	3	0	7

Duplin County

Duplin County Schools
Hwy 11 N • Kenansville, NC 28349-0128
Mailing Address: PO Box 128 • Kenansville, NC 28349-0128
(910) 296-1521 • http://www.duplinschools.net/
Grade Span: PK-12; Agency Type: 1
Schools: 15
   8 Primary; 3 Middle; 4 High; 0 Other Level
   15 Regular; 0 Special Education; 0 Vocational; 0 Alternative
   0 Magnet; 0 Charter; 9 Title I Eligible; 9 School-wide Title I
Students: 8,873 (50.8% male; 49.1% female)
   Individual Education Program: 1,005 (11.3%)
   English Language Learner: 1,584 (17.9%); Migrant: 376 (4.2%)
   Eligible for Free Lunch Program: 5,031 (56.7%)
   Eligible for Reduced-Price Lunch Program: 841 (9.5%)
Teachers: 583.0 (15.2 to 1)
Librarians/Media Specialists: 15.0 (591.5 to 1)
Guidance Counselors: 22.0 (403.3 to 1)
Current Spending: ($ per student per year):
   Total: $6,271; Instruction: $4,074; Support Services: $1,817
Enrollment, Drop-out Rates and Diploma Recipients by Race/Ethnicity

Category	Total	White	Black	Asian	AIAN	Hisp.
Enrollment (%)	100.0	44.5	33.8	0.1	0.2	21.5
Drop-out Rate (%)	6.2	4.8	6.3	0.0	0.0	13.1
H.S. Diplomas (#)	442	273	145	0	0	24

Durham County

Durham Public Schools
511 Cleveland St • Durham, NC 27701
Mailing Address: PO Box 30002 • Durham, NC 27702-3002
(919) 560-2000 • http://www.dpsnc.net/
Grade Span: PK-12; Agency Type: 1
Schools: 43
   27 Primary; 8 Middle; 5 High; 3 Other Level
   41 Regular; 0 Special Education; 0 Vocational; 2 Alternative
   7 Magnet; 0 Charter; 19 Title I Eligible; 16 School-wide Title I
Students: 30,889 (51.2% male; 48.7% female)
   Individual Education Program: 3,973 (12.9%);
   English Language Learner: 2,248 (7.3%); Migrant: 0 (0.0%)
   Eligible for Free Lunch Program: 11,897 (38.5%)
   Eligible for Reduced-Price Lunch Program: 1,769 (5.7%)
Teachers: 2,094.0 (14.8 to 1)
Librarians/Media Specialists: 44.0 (702.0 to 1)
Guidance Counselors: 76.0 (406.4 to 1)
Current Spending: ($ per student per year):
   Total: $7,599; Instruction: $4,624; Support Services: $2,657
Enrollment, Drop-out Rates and Diploma Recipients by Race/Ethnicity

Category	Total	White	Black	Asian	AIAN	Hisp.
Enrollment (%)	100.0	27.8	59.7	2.2	0.3	10.0
Drop-out Rate (%)	6.5	3.6	8.0	2.0	0.0	15.6
H.S. Diplomas (#)	1,435	677	663	41	3	51

Edgecombe County

Edgecombe County Schools
412 Pearl St • Tarboro, NC 27886-7128
Mailing Address: PO Box 7128 • Tarboro, NC 27886-7128
(252) 641-2600 •
http://schools.eastnet.ecu.edu/edgecomb/visitschools.htm
Grade Span: PK-12; Agency Type: 1
Schools: 15
   6 Primary; 5 Middle; 3 High; 1 Other Level
   14 Regular; 0 Special Education; 0 Vocational; 1 Alternative
   0 Magnet; 0 Charter; 7 Title I Eligible; 7 School-wide Title I
Students: 7,826 (50.7% male; 49.2% female)
   Individual Education Program: 954 (12.2%);
   English Language Learner: 296 (3.8%); Migrant: 411 (5.3%)
   Eligible for Free Lunch Program: 4,275 (54.6%)
   Eligible for Reduced-Price Lunch Program: 911 (11.6%)
Teachers: 513.0 (15.3 to 1)
Librarians/Media Specialists: 13.0 (602.0 to 1)
Guidance Counselors: 19.0 (411.9 to 1)
Current Spending: ($ per student per year):
   Total: $6,601; Instruction: $4,001; Support Services: $2,258
Enrollment, Drop-out Rates and Diploma Recipients by Race/Ethnicity

Category	Total	White	Black	Asian	AIAN	Hisp.
Enrollment (%)	100.0	37.0	58.0	0.2	0.1	4.8
Drop-out Rate (%)	5.8	4.6	6.4	0.0	n/a	16.7
H.S. Diplomas (#)	391	158	230	0	0	3

Forsyth County

Forsyth County Schools
1605 Miller St • Winston Salem, NC 27103
Mailing Address: PO Box 2513 • Winston Salem, NC 27102-2513
(336) 727-2816 • http://mts.admin.wsfcs.k12.nc.us/
Grade Span: PK-12; Agency Type: 1
Schools: 69
   39 Primary; 15 Middle; 10 High; 5 Other Level
   62 Regular; 3 Special Education; 1 Vocational; 3 Alternative
   6 Magnet; 0 Charter; 29 Title I Eligible; 19 School-wide Title I
Students: 47,788 (51.5% male; 48.4% female)
   Individual Education Program: 6,936 (14.5%);
   English Language Learner: 3,149 (6.6%); Migrant: 0 (0.0%)
   Eligible for Free Lunch Program: 15,981 (33.4%)
   Eligible for Reduced-Price Lunch Program: 2,951 (6.2%)
Teachers: 3,251.0 (14.7 to 1)
Librarians/Media Specialists: 64.0 (746.7 to 1)
Guidance Counselors: 97.0 (492.7 to 1)
Current Spending: ($ per student per year):
   Total: $6,915; Instruction: $4,580; Support Services: $1,976
Enrollment, Drop-out Rates and Diploma Recipients by Race/Ethnicity

Category	Total	White	Black	Asian	AIAN	Hisp.
Enrollment (%)	100.0	49.8	37.6	1.3	0.2	11.1
Drop-out Rate (%)	6.3	4.8	7.9	3.8	13.3	11.7
H.S. Diplomas (#)	2,271	1,441	716	29	4	81

Franklin County

Franklin County Schools
105 S Bickett Blvd • Louisburg, NC 27549-0449
Mailing Address: PO Box 449 • Louisburg, NC 27549-0449
(919) 496-4159 • http://www.franklinco.k12.nc.us/
Grade Span: PK-12; Agency Type: 1
Schools: 14
   8 Primary; 3 Middle; 3 High; 0 Other Level
   14 Regular; 0 Special Education; 0 Vocational; 0 Alternative
   1 Magnet; 0 Charter; 8 Title I Eligible; 8 School-wide Title I
Students: 8,015 (51.8% male; 48.1% female)
   Individual Education Program: 859 (10.7%);
   English Language Learner: 275 (3.4%); Migrant: 146 (1.8%)
   Eligible for Free Lunch Program: 3,495 (43.6%)
   Eligible for Reduced-Price Lunch Program: 804 (10.0%)
Teachers: 536.0 (15.0 to 1)
Librarians/Media Specialists: 14.0 (572.5 to 1)
Guidance Counselors: 17.0 (471.5 to 1)
Current Spending: ($ per student per year):
   Total: $6,299; Instruction: $3,821; Support Services: $2,060
Enrollment, Drop-out Rates and Diploma Recipients by Race/Ethnicity

Category	Total	White	Black	Asian	AIAN	Hisp.
Enrollment (%)	100.0	52.3	39.5	0.5	0.4	7.2
Drop-out Rate (%)	6.6	6.1	6.3	0.0	25.0	18.6
H.S. Diplomas (#)	352	209	135	1	0	7

Gaston County

Gaston County Schools
943 Osceola St • Gastonia, NC 28054-1397
Mailing Address: PO Box 1397 • Gastonia, NC 28053-1397
(704) 866-6100 • http://www.gaston.k12.nc.us/
Grade Span: PK-12; Agency Type: 1
Schools: 52
   30 Primary; 11 Middle; 9 High; 2 Other Level
   50 Regular; 1 Special Education; 0 Vocational; 1 Alternative
   1 Magnet; 0 Charter; 13 Title I Eligible; 12 School-wide Title I
Students: 31,288 (51.5% male; 48.4% female)
   Individual Education Program: 3,930 (12.6%);
   English Language Learner: 1,360 (4.3%); Migrant: 0 (0.0%)
   Eligible for Free Lunch Program: 9,861 (31.5%)
   Eligible for Reduced-Price Lunch Program: 2,509 (8.0%)
Teachers: 1,932.0 (16.2 to 1)
Librarians/Media Specialists: 53.0 (590.3 to 1)
Guidance Counselors: 65.0 (481.4 to 1)
Current Spending: ($ per student per year):
   Total: $5,977; Instruction: $3,930; Support Services: $1,638
Enrollment, Drop-out Rates and Diploma Recipients by Race/Ethnicity

Category	Total	White	Black	Asian	AIAN	Hisp.
Enrollment (%)	100.0	73.0	20.8	1.4	0.2	4.7
Drop-out Rate (%)	6.4	6.8	5.1	4.6	23.1	5.3
H.S. Diplomas (#)	1,466	1,137	286	15	1	27

Gates County

Gates County Schools
205 Main St • Gatesville, NC 27938-0125
Mailing Address: PO Box 125 • Gatesville, NC 27938-0125
(252) 357-1113 • http://coserver.gates.k12.nc.us/
Grade Span: PK-12; Agency Type: 1
Schools: 5
　3 Primary; 1 Middle; 1 High; 0 Other Level
　5 Regular; 0 Special Education; 0 Vocational; 0 Alternative
　0 Magnet; 0 Charter; 3 Title I Eligible; 3 School-wide Title I
Students: 1,968　(50.7% male; 49.2% female)
　Individual Education Program: 406 (20.6%);
　English Language Learner: 16 (0.8%); Migrant: 0 (0.0%)
　Eligible for Free Lunch Program: 739 (37.6%)
　Eligible for Reduced-Price Lunch Program: 264 (13.4%)
Teachers: 157.0 (12.5 to 1)
Librarians/Media Specialists: 5.0 (393.6 to 1)
Guidance Counselors: 7.0 (281.1 to 1)
Current Spending: ($ per student per year):
　Total: $7,858; Instruction: $4,619; Support Services: $2,743

Enrollment, Drop-out Rates and Diploma Recipients by Race/Ethnicity

Category	Total	White	Black	Asian	AIAN	Hisp.
Enrollment (%)	100.0	56.8	41.8	0.4	0.2	0.9
Drop-out Rate (%)	6.9	5.9	8.0	0.0	n/a	0.0
H.S. Diplomas (#)	92	48	44	0	0	0

Granville County

Granville County Schools
101 Delacroix St • Oxford, NC 27565-2516
Mailing Address: PO Box 927 • Oxford, NC 27565-0927
(919) 693-4613 • http://eclipse.gcs.k12.nc.us/public/
Grade Span: PK-12; Agency Type: 1
Schools: 14
　8 Primary; 4 Middle; 2 High; 0 Other Level
　14 Regular; 0 Special Education; 0 Vocational; 0 Alternative
　0 Magnet; 0 Charter; 7 Title I Eligible; 7 School-wide Title I
Students: 8,680　(51.2% male; 48.7% female)
　Individual Education Program: 1,058 (12.2%);
　English Language Learner: 385 (4.4%); Migrant: 138 (1.6%)
　Eligible for Free Lunch Program: 3,310 (38.1%)
　Eligible for Reduced-Price Lunch Program: 789 (9.1%)
Teachers: 554.0 (15.7 to 1)
Librarians/Media Specialists: 16.0 (542.5 to 1)
Guidance Counselors: 24.0 (361.7 to 1)
Current Spending: ($ per student per year):
　Total: $6,150; Instruction: $3,852; Support Services: $1,953

Enrollment, Drop-out Rates and Diploma Recipients by Race/Ethnicity

Category	Total	White	Black	Asian	AIAN	Hisp.
Enrollment (%)	100.0	53.8	40.5	0.4	0.2	5.1
Drop-out Rate (%)	8.5	8.3	9.1	0.0	0.0	8.2
H.S. Diplomas (#)	328	201	117	2	0	8

Greene County

Greene County Schools
301 Kingold Blvd • Snow Hill, NC 28580-1393
(252) 747-3425 • http://www.greene.k12.nc.us/gc/greene.htm
Grade Span: PK-12; Agency Type: 1
Schools: 4
　2 Primary; 1 Middle; 1 High; 0 Other Level
　4 Regular; 0 Special Education; 0 Vocational; 0 Alternative
　0 Magnet; 0 Charter; 2 Title I Eligible; 2 School-wide Title I
Students: 3,250　(52.8% male; 47.1% female)
　Individual Education Program: 491 (15.1%);
　English Language Learner: 313 (9.6%); Migrant: 104 (3.2%)
　Eligible for Free Lunch Program: 1,898 (58.4%)
　Eligible for Reduced-Price Lunch Program: 305 (9.4%)
Teachers: 247.0 (13.2 to 1)
Librarians/Media Specialists: 4.0 (812.5 to 1)
Guidance Counselors: 11.0 (295.5 to 1)
Current Spending: ($ per student per year):
　Total: $6,978; Instruction: $4,274; Support Services: $2,232

Enrollment, Drop-out Rates and Diploma Recipients by Race/Ethnicity

Category	Total	White	Black	Asian	AIAN	Hisp.
Enrollment (%)	100.0	34.0	50.9	0.3	0.0	14.8
Drop-out Rate (%)	6.4	5.1	6.7	0.0	0.0	12.1
H.S. Diplomas (#)	117	53	60	0	0	4

Guilford County

Guilford County Schools
712 N Eugene St • Greensboro, NC 27401
Mailing Address: PO Box 880 • Greensboro, NC 27402-0880
(336) 370-8100 • http://www.guilford.k12.nc.us/
Grade Span: PK-12; Agency Type: 1
Schools: 105
　64 Primary; 18 Middle; 20 High; 3 Other Level
　102 Regular; 2 Special Education; 0 Vocational; 1 Alternative
　16 Magnet; 0 Charter; 52 Title I Eligible; 42 School-wide Title I
Students: 66,971　(50.9% male; 49.0% female)
　Individual Education Program: 10,714 (16.0%);
　English Language Learner: 3,877 (5.8%); Migrant: 0 (0.0%)
　Eligible for Free Lunch Program: 26,505 (39.6%)
　Eligible for Reduced-Price Lunch Program: 4,891 (7.3%)
Teachers: 4,390.0 (15.3 to 1)
Librarians/Media Specialists: 106.0 (631.8 to 1)
Guidance Counselors: 189.0 (354.3 to 1)
Current Spending: ($ per student per year):
　Total: $6,943; Instruction: $4,313; Support Services: $2,269

Enrollment, Drop-out Rates and Diploma Recipients by Race/Ethnicity

Category	Total	White	Black	Asian	AIAN	Hisp.
Enrollment (%)	100.0	45.7	43.9	4.4	0.7	5.4
Drop-out Rate (%)	3.9	2.6	5.6	4.3	5.1	6.8
H.S. Diplomas (#)	3,304	2,020	1,106	122	8	48

Halifax County

Halifax County Schools
9525 Hwy 301s • Halifax, NC 27839-0468
Mailing Address: PO Box 468 • Halifax, NC 27839-0468
(252) 583-5111 • http://www.schoollink.net/hcs/departments/index.html
Grade Span: PK-12; Agency Type: 1
Schools: 15
　9 Primary; 4 Middle; 2 High; 0 Other Level
　15 Regular; 0 Special Education; 0 Vocational; 0 Alternative
　0 Magnet; 0 Charter; 13 Title I Eligible; 13 School-wide Title I
Students: 5,685　(51.6% male; 48.3% female)
　Individual Education Program: 933 (16.4%);
　English Language Learner: 31 (0.5%); Migrant: 165 (2.9%)
　Eligible for Free Lunch Program: 4,255 (74.8%)
　Eligible for Reduced-Price Lunch Program: 564 (9.9%)
Teachers: 357.0 (15.9 to 1)
Librarians/Media Specialists: 12.0 (473.8 to 1)
Guidance Counselors: 16.0 (355.3 to 1)
Current Spending: ($ per student per year):
　Total: $7,565; Instruction: $4,677; Support Services: $2,417

Enrollment, Drop-out Rates and Diploma Recipients by Race/Ethnicity

Category	Total	White	Black	Asian	AIAN	Hisp.
Enrollment (%)	100.0	5.8	87.8	0.1	5.5	0.8
Drop-out Rate (%)	6.9	15.8	6.3	n/a	11.5	0.0
H.S. Diplomas (#)	267	7	249	0	11	0

Roanoke Rapids City Schools
536 Hamilton St • Roanoke Rapids, NC 27870-9990
(252) 535-3111 • http://www.rrgsd.org/
Grade Span: PK-12; Agency Type: 1
Schools: 4
　2 Primary; 1 Middle; 1 High; 0 Other Level
　4 Regular; 0 Special Education; 0 Vocational; 0 Alternative
　0 Magnet; 0 Charter; 1 Title I Eligible; 1 School-wide Title I
Students: 3,008　(50.2% male; 49.7% female)
　Individual Education Program: 381 (12.7%);
　English Language Learner: 25 (0.8%); Migrant: 0 (0.0%)
　Eligible for Free Lunch Program: 1,079 (35.9%)
　Eligible for Reduced-Price Lunch Program: 298 (9.9%)
Teachers: 212.0 (14.2 to 1)
Librarians/Media Specialists: 4.0 (752.0 to 1)
Guidance Counselors: 8.0 (376.0 to 1)
Current Spending: ($ per student per year):
　Total: $6,658; Instruction: $4,155; Support Services: $2,161

Enrollment, Drop-out Rates and Diploma Recipients by Race/Ethnicity

Category	Total	White	Black	Asian	AIAN	Hisp.
Enrollment (%)	100.0	74.6	21.9	1.4	0.4	1.7
Drop-out Rate (%)	6.4	5.6	9.8	5.0	0.0	0.0
H.S. Diplomas (#)	165	134	24	1	1	5

Harnett County

Harnett County Schools

1 W Harnett St • Lillington, NC 27546-1029
Mailing Address: PO Box 1029 • Lillington, NC 27546-1029
(910) 893-8151 • http://www.harnett.k12.nc.us/
Grade Span: PK-12; **Agency Type:** 1
Schools: 25
   14 Primary; 7 Middle; 3 High; 1 Other Level
   24 Regular; 0 Special Education; 0 Vocational; 1 Alternative
   0 Magnet; 0 Charter; 22 Title I Eligible; 21 School-wide Title I
Students: 16,914 (51.1% male; 48.8% female)
   Individual Education Program: 2,546 (15.1%);
   English Language Learner: 820 (4.8%); Migrant: 519 (3.1%)
   Eligible for Free Lunch Program: 6,763 (40.0%)
   Eligible for Reduced-Price Lunch Program: 1,892 (11.2%)
Teachers: 1,064.0 (15.9 to 1)
Librarians/Media Specialists: 27.0 (626.4 to 1)
Guidance Counselors: 39.0 (433.7 to 1)
Current Spending: ($ per student per year):
   Total: $5,854; Instruction: $3,938; Support Services: $1,562

Enrollment, Drop-out Rates and Diploma Recipients by Race/Ethnicity

Category	Total	White	Black	Asian	AIAN	Hisp.
Enrollment (%)	100.0	56.8	32.9	0.4	0.9	8.9
Drop-out Rate (%)	7.9	7.0	9.7	0.0	11.8	9.3
H.S. Diplomas (#)	759	522	191	7	8	31

Haywood County

Haywood County Schools

1230 N Main St • Waynesville, NC 28786-3461
(828) 456-2400 • http://www.haywood.k12.nc.us/
Grade Span: PK-12; **Agency Type:** 1
Schools: 15
   9 Primary; 3 Middle; 3 High; 0 Other Level
   14 Regular; 0 Special Education; 0 Vocational; 1 Alternative
   0 Magnet; 0 Charter; 11 Title I Eligible; 6 School-wide Title I
Students: 7,943 (50.9% male; 49.0% female)
   Individual Education Program: 1,185 (14.9%);
   English Language Learner: 117 (1.5%); Migrant: 134 (1.7%)
   Eligible for Free Lunch Program: 2,341 (29.5%)
   Eligible for Reduced-Price Lunch Program: 776 (9.8%)
Teachers: 540.0 (14.7 to 1)
Librarians/Media Specialists: 15.0 (529.5 to 1)
Guidance Counselors: 22.0 (361.0 to 1)
Current Spending: ($ per student per year):
   Total: $6,853; Instruction: $4,132; Support Services: $2,278

Enrollment, Drop-out Rates and Diploma Recipients by Race/Ethnicity

Category	Total	White	Black	Asian	AIAN	Hisp.
Enrollment (%)	100.0	94.6	2.1	0.4	0.8	2.1
Drop-out Rate (%)	7.5	7.3	17.3	0.0	14.3	8.3
H.S. Diplomas (#)	431	414	7	1	1	8

Henderson County

Henderson County Schools

414 4th Ave W • Hendersonville, NC 28739-4261
(828) 697-4733 • http://www.henderson.k12.nc.us/
Grade Span: PK-12; **Agency Type:** 1
Schools: 21
   12 Primary; 4 Middle; 4 High; 1 Other Level
   20 Regular; 0 Special Education; 0 Vocational; 1 Alternative
   0 Magnet; 0 Charter; 9 Title I Eligible; 9 School-wide Title I
Students: 12,288 (51.8% male; 48.1% female)
   Individual Education Program: 1,646 (13.4%);
   English Language Learner: 981 (8.0%); Migrant: 414 (3.4%)
   Eligible for Free Lunch Program: 3,741 (30.4%)
   Eligible for Reduced-Price Lunch Program: 1,024 (8.3%)
Teachers: 800.0 (15.4 to 1)
Librarians/Media Specialists: 20.0 (614.4 to 1)
Guidance Counselors: 32.0 (384.0 to 1)
Current Spending: ($ per student per year):
   Total: $6,453; Instruction: $4,227; Support Services: $1,881

Enrollment, Drop-out Rates and Diploma Recipients by Race/Ethnicity

Category	Total	White	Black	Asian	AIAN	Hisp.
Enrollment (%)	100.0	80.7	7.3	1.0	0.3	10.7
Drop-out Rate (%)	5.9	5.7	5.4	5.6	25.0	8.4
H.S. Diplomas (#)	650	577	46	7	0	20

Hertford County

Hertford County Schools

701 N Martin St • Winton, NC 27986-0158
Mailing Address: PO Box 158 • Winton, NC 27986-0158
(252) 358-1761
Grade Span: PK-12; **Agency Type:** 1
Schools: 5
   3 Primary; 1 Middle; 1 High; 0 Other Level
   5 Regular; 0 Special Education; 0 Vocational; 0 Alternative
   0 Magnet; 0 Charter; 4 Title I Eligible; 4 School-wide Title I
Students: 3,755 (50.3% male; 49.6% female)
   Individual Education Program: 595 (15.8%);
   English Language Learner: 15 (0.4%); Migrant: 0 (0.0%)
   Eligible for Free Lunch Program: 2,611 (69.5%)
   Eligible for Reduced-Price Lunch Program: 426 (11.3%)
Teachers: 268.0 (14.0 to 1)
Librarians/Media Specialists: 5.0 (751.0 to 1)
Guidance Counselors: 12.0 (312.9 to 1)
Current Spending: ($ per student per year):
   Total: $7,059; Instruction: $4,143; Support Services: $2,506

Enrollment, Drop-out Rates and Diploma Recipients by Race/Ethnicity

Category	Total	White	Black	Asian	AIAN	Hisp.
Enrollment (%)	100.0	17.1	80.8	0.5	1.0	0.6
Drop-out Rate (%)	7.2	5.5	7.8	0.0	0.0	0.0
H.S. Diplomas (#)	215	64	149	0	2	0

Hoke County

Hoke County Schools

310 Wooley St • Raeford, NC 28376-3299
Mailing Address: PO Box 370 • Raeford, NC 28376-0370
(910) 875-4106 • http://www.hcs.k12.nc.us/
Grade Span: PK-12; **Agency Type:** 1
Schools: 11
   7 Primary; 2 Middle; 2 High; 0 Other Level
   10 Regular; 0 Special Education; 0 Vocational; 1 Alternative
   0 Magnet; 0 Charter; 7 Title I Eligible; 7 School-wide Title I
Students: 6,568 (50.8% male; 49.1% female)
   Individual Education Program: 965 (14.7%);
   English Language Learner: 281 (4.3%); Migrant: 256 (3.9%)
   Eligible for Free Lunch Program: 3,215 (48.9%)
   Eligible for Reduced-Price Lunch Program: 903 (13.7%)
Teachers: 395.0 (16.6 to 1)
Librarians/Media Specialists: 10.0 (656.8 to 1)
Guidance Counselors: 14.0 (469.1 to 1)
Current Spending: ($ per student per year):
   Total: $6,185; Instruction: $4,011; Support Services: $1,779

Enrollment, Drop-out Rates and Diploma Recipients by Race/Ethnicity

Category	Total	White	Black	Asian	AIAN	Hisp.
Enrollment (%)	100.0	29.0	47.0	1.2	15.0	7.7
Drop-out Rate (%)	9.1	9.5	8.9	0.0	8.3	15.7
H.S. Diplomas (#)	263	84	138	4	30	7

Iredell County

Iredell-Statesville Schools

549 N Race St • Statesville, NC 28677
Mailing Address: PO Box 911 • Statesville, NC 28687-0911
(704) 872-8931 • http://www.iss.k12.nc.us/
Grade Span: PK-12; **Agency Type:** 1
Schools: 32
   19 Primary; 7 Middle; 5 High; 1 Other Level
   31 Regular; 0 Special Education; 0 Vocational; 1 Alternative
   0 Magnet; 0 Charter; 14 Title I Eligible; 13 School-wide Title I
Students: 19,098 (51.2% male; 48.7% female)
   Individual Education Program: 2,482 (13.0%);
   English Language Learner: 831 (4.4%); Migrant: 0 (0.0%)
   Eligible for Free Lunch Program: 4,782 (25.0%)
   Eligible for Reduced-Price Lunch Program: 1,671 (8.7%)
Teachers: 1,204.0 (15.9 to 1)
Librarians/Media Specialists: 36.0 (530.5 to 1)
Guidance Counselors: 46.0 (415.2 to 1)
Current Spending: ($ per student per year):
   Total: $5,849; Instruction: $3,652; Support Services: $1,844

Enrollment, Drop-out Rates and Diploma Recipients by Race/Ethnicity

Category	Total	White	Black	Asian	AIAN	Hisp.
Enrollment (%)	100.0	72.9	18.1	2.6	0.2	6.2
Drop-out Rate (%)	6.1	5.7	6.4	3.5	0.0	14.1
H.S. Diplomas (#)	821	637	138	23	2	21

Mooresville City Schools

305 N Main • Mooresville, NC 28115-2453
(704) 664-5553 • http://www.mgsd.k12.nc.us/
Grade Span: PK-12; **Agency Type:** 1
Schools: 6
   2 Primary; 2 Middle; 2 High; 0 Other Level
   5 Regular; 0 Special Education; 1 Vocational; 0 Alternative
   0 Magnet; 0 Charter; 1 Title I Eligible; 0 School-wide Title I
Students: 4,283   (50.2% male; 49.7% female)
   Individual Education Program: 553 (12.9%);
   English Language Learner: 63 (1.5%); Migrant: 0 (0.0%)
   Eligible for Free Lunch Program: 958 (22.4%)
   Eligible for Reduced-Price Lunch Program: 328 (7.7%)
Teachers: 279.0 (15.4 to 1)
Librarians/Media Specialists: 5.0 (856.6 to 1)
Guidance Counselors: 11.0 (389.4 to 1)
Current Spending: ($ per student per year):
   Total: $6,381; Instruction: $4,060; Support Services: $1,977
Enrollment, Drop-out Rates and Diploma Recipients by Race/Ethnicity

Category	Total	White	Black	Asian	AIAN	Hisp.
Enrollment (%)	100.0	76.6	18.3	2.1	0.2	2.8
Drop-out Rate (%)	4.9	4.4	6.1	0.0	100.0	60.0
H.S. Diplomas (#)	247	220	24	3	0	0

Jackson County

Jackson County Schools

398 Hospital Rd • Sylva, NC 28779-5196
(828) 586-2311 • http://www.main.nc.us/jackson/jc50educ.html
Grade Span: PK-12; **Agency Type:** 1
Schools: 7
   4 Primary; 0 Middle; 1 High; 2 Other Level
   6 Regular; 0 Special Education; 0 Vocational; 1 Alternative
   0 Magnet; 0 Charter; 5 Title I Eligible; 4 School-wide Title I
Students: 3,722   (51.7% male; 48.2% female)
   Individual Education Program: 602 (16.2%);
   English Language Learner: 64 (1.7%); Migrant: 35 (0.9%)
   Eligible for Free Lunch Program: 1,201 (32.3%)
   Eligible for Reduced-Price Lunch Program: 476 (12.8%)
Teachers: 267.0 (13.9 to 1)
Librarians/Media Specialists: 6.0 (620.3 to 1)
Guidance Counselors: 9.0 (413.6 to 1)
Current Spending: ($ per student per year):
   Total: $7,033; Instruction: $4,446; Support Services: $2,181
Enrollment, Drop-out Rates and Diploma Recipients by Race/Ethnicity

Category	Total	White	Black	Asian	AIAN	Hisp.
Enrollment (%)	100.0	83.6	2.3	0.7	10.6	2.8
Drop-out Rate (%)	5.2	4.7	5.6	0.0	10.3	8.3
H.S. Diplomas (#)	225	203	4	0	17	1

Johnston County

Johnston County Schools

2320 Hwy 70 E Business • Smithfield, NC 27577-1336
Mailing Address: PO Box 1336 • Smithfield, NC 27577-1336
(919) 934-6031 • http://www.johnston.k12.nc.us/
Grade Span: PK-12; **Agency Type:** 1
Schools: 34
   18 Primary; 9 Middle; 5 High; 2 Other Level
   33 Regular; 0 Special Education; 0 Vocational; 1 Alternative
   0 Magnet; 0 Charter; 11 Title I Eligible; 11 School-wide Title I
Students: 24,946   (51.4% male; 48.5% female)
   Individual Education Program: 3,986 (16.0%);
   English Language Learner: 1,756 (7.0%); Migrant: 897 (3.6%)
   Eligible for Free Lunch Program: 7,676 (30.8%)
   Eligible for Reduced-Price Lunch Program: 1,892 (7.6%)
Teachers: 1,785.0 (14.0 to 1)
Librarians/Media Specialists: 38.0 (656.5 to 1)
Guidance Counselors: 66.0 (378.0 to 1)
Current Spending: ($ per student per year):
   Total: $6,309; Instruction: $4,131; Support Services: $1,840
Enrollment, Drop-out Rates and Diploma Recipients by Race/Ethnicity

Category	Total	White	Black	Asian	AIAN	Hisp.
Enrollment (%)	100.0	66.0	22.4	0.4	0.4	10.8
Drop-out Rate (%)	6.5	5.0	9.9	3.7	33.3	10.9
H.S. Diplomas (#)	942	735	157	8	4	38

Lee County

Lee County Schools

106 Gordon St • Sanford, NC 27330
Mailing Address: PO Box 1010 • Sanford, NC 27331-1010
(919) 774-6226 • http://www.lee.k12.nc.us/
Grade Span: PK-12; **Agency Type:** 1
Schools: 12

---

   7 Primary; 2 Middle; 1 High; 2 Other Level
   10 Regular; 1 Special Education; 0 Vocational; 1 Alternative
   0 Magnet; 0 Charter; 7 Title I Eligible; 7 School-wide Title I
Students: 9,139   (51.1% male; 48.8% female)
   Individual Education Program: 1,102 (12.1%);
   English Language Learner: 1,097 (12.0%); Migrant: 480 (5.3%)
   Eligible for Free Lunch Program: 3,780 (41.4%)
   Eligible for Reduced-Price Lunch Program: 827 (9.0%)
Teachers: 571.0 (16.0 to 1)
Librarians/Media Specialists: 11.0 (830.8 to 1)
Guidance Counselors: 17.0 (537.6 to 1)
Current Spending: ($ per student per year):
   Total: $6,370; Instruction: $4,211; Support Services: $1,809
Enrollment, Drop-out Rates and Diploma Recipients by Race/Ethnicity

Category	Total	White	Black	Asian	AIAN	Hisp.
Enrollment (%)	100.0	52.0	27.2	0.8	0.5	19.6
Drop-out Rate (%)	8.2	7.0	10.6	4.8	0.0	9.8
H.S. Diplomas (#)	429	302	96	2	1	28

Lenoir County

Lenoir County Public Schools

2017 W Vernon Ave • Kinston, NC 28504
Mailing Address: PO Box 729 • Kinston, NC 28502-0729
(252) 527-1109 • http://www.lenoir.k12.nc.us/
Grade Span: PK-12; **Agency Type:** 1
Schools: 19
   10 Primary; 4 Middle; 3 High; 2 Other Level
   17 Regular; 0 Special Education; 0 Vocational; 2 Alternative
   0 Magnet; 0 Charter; 15 Title I Eligible; 15 School-wide Title I
Students: 10,354   (51.8% male; 48.1% female)
   Individual Education Program: 1,542 (14.9%);
   English Language Learner: 229 (2.2%); Migrant: 356 (3.4%)
   Eligible for Free Lunch Program: 5,226 (50.5%)
   Eligible for Reduced-Price Lunch Program: 1,041 (10.1%)
Teachers: 721.0 (14.4 to 1)
Librarians/Media Specialists: 18.0 (575.2 to 1)
Guidance Counselors: 26.0 (398.2 to 1)
Current Spending: ($ per student per year):
   Total: $6,556; Instruction: $4,167; Support Services: $2,015
Enrollment, Drop-out Rates and Diploma Recipients by Race/Ethnicity

Category	Total	White	Black	Asian	AIAN	Hisp.
Enrollment (%)	100.0	42.5	51.7	0.5	0.1	5.1
Drop-out Rate (%)	6.9	5.5	8.1	0.0	0.0	10.1
H.S. Diplomas (#)	474	240	217	1	2	14

Lincoln County

Lincoln County Schools

353 N Generals Blvd • Lincolnton, NC 28092
Mailing Address: PO Box 400 • Lincolnton, NC 28093-0400
(704) 732-2261 • http://www.lincoln.k12.nc.us/
Grade Span: PK-12; **Agency Type:** 1
Schools: 21
   11 Primary; 4 Middle; 5 High; 1 Other Level
   19 Regular; 0 Special Education; 1 Vocational; 1 Alternative
   0 Magnet; 0 Charter; 9 Title I Eligible; 7 School-wide Title I
Students: 11,372   (51.3% male; 48.6% female)
   Individual Education Program: 1,710 (15.0%);
   English Language Learner: 700 (6.2%); Migrant: 0 (0.0%)
   Eligible for Free Lunch Program: 3,028 (26.6%)
   Eligible for Reduced-Price Lunch Program: 982 (8.6%)
Teachers: 790.0 (14.4 to 1)
Librarians/Media Specialists: 19.0 (598.5 to 1)
Guidance Counselors: 31.0 (366.8 to 1)
Current Spending: ($ per student per year):
   Total: $6,027; Instruction: $3,946; Support Services: $1,709
Enrollment, Drop-out Rates and Diploma Recipients by Race/Ethnicity

Category	Total	White	Black	Asian	AIAN	Hisp.
Enrollment (%)	100.0	81.8	9.9	0.3	0.3	7.6
Drop-out Rate (%)	5.5	5.0	7.2	5.0	10.0	9.7
H.S. Diplomas (#)	613	521	54	4	0	34

Macon County

Macon County Schools

1202 Old Murphy Rd • Franklin, NC 28734
Mailing Address: PO Box 1029 • Franklin, NC 28744-1029
(828) 524-3314 • http://www.mcsk-12.org/
Grade Span: PK-12; **Agency Type:** 1
Schools: 10
   6 Primary; 1 Middle; 1 High; 2 Other Level
   10 Regular; 0 Special Education; 0 Vocational; 0 Alternative
   0 Magnet; 0 Charter; 8 Title I Eligible; 8 School-wide Title I
Students: 4,139   (50.9% male; 49.0% female)

Individual Education Program: 681 (16.5%);
English Language Learner: 115 (2.8%); Migrant: 0 (0.0%)
Eligible for Free Lunch Program: 1,482 (35.8%)
Eligible for Reduced-Price Lunch Program: 507 (12.2%)
Teachers: 293.0 (14.1 to 1)
Librarians/Media Specialists: 10.0 (413.9 to 1)
Guidance Counselors: 11.0 (376.3 to 1)
Current Spending: ($ per student per year):
Total: $6,730; Instruction: $4,183; Support Services: $2,117
Enrollment, Drop-out Rates and Diploma Recipients by Race/Ethnicity

Category	Total	White	Black	Asian	AIAN	Hisp.
Enrollment (%)	100.0	93.6	1.9	0.7	0.3	3.4
Drop-out Rate (%)	6.1	6.1	0.0	11.1	0.0	12.5
H.S. Diplomas (#)	247	238	4	4	0	1

Madison County

Madison County Schools
5738 US 25-70 Hwy • Marshall, NC 28753-9006
(828) 649-9276
Grade Span: PK-12; **Agency Type:** 1
Schools: 6
4 Primary; 1 Middle; 1 High; 0 Other Level
6 Regular; 0 Special Education; 0 Vocational; 0 Alternative
0 Magnet; 0 Charter; 4 Title I Eligible; 4 School-wide Title I
Students: 2,580   (53.4% male; 46.5% female)
Individual Education Program: 417 (16.2%);
English Language Learner: 40 (1.6%); Migrant: 0 (0.0%)
Eligible for Free Lunch Program: 932 (36.1%)
Eligible for Reduced-Price Lunch Program: 317 (12.3%)
Teachers: 213.0 (12.1 to 1)
Librarians/Media Specialists: 5.0 (516.0 to 1)
Guidance Counselors: 5.0 (516.0 to 1)
Current Spending: ($ per student per year):
Total: $7,475; Instruction: $4,524; Support Services: $2,546
Enrollment, Drop-out Rates and Diploma Recipients by Race/Ethnicity

Category	Total	White	Black	Asian	AIAN	Hisp.
Enrollment (%)	100.0	96.9	0.8	0.2	0.3	1.8
Drop-out Rate (%)	4.1	4.2	0.0	0.0	0.0	0.0
H.S. Diplomas (#)	129	129	0	0	0	0

Martin County

Martin County Schools
300 N Watts St • Williamston, NC 27892-2099
(252) 792-1575 • http://www.schoollink.net/martin/
Grade Span: PK-12; **Agency Type:** 1
Schools: 12
6 Primary; 2 Middle; 4 High; 0 Other Level
12 Regular; 0 Special Education; 0 Vocational; 0 Alternative
0 Magnet; 0 Charter; 8 Title I Eligible; 8 School-wide Title I
Students: 4,573   (51.4% male; 48.5% female)
Individual Education Program: 647 (14.1%);
English Language Learner: 17 (0.4%); Migrant: 0 (0.0%)
Eligible for Free Lunch Program: 2,501 (54.7%)
Eligible for Reduced-Price Lunch Program: 409 (8.9%)
Teachers: 334.0 (13.7 to 1)
Librarians/Media Specialists: 13.0 (351.8 to 1)
Guidance Counselors: 15.0 (304.9 to 1)
Current Spending: ($ per student per year):
Total: $7,104; Instruction: $4,392; Support Services: $2,312
Enrollment, Drop-out Rates and Diploma Recipients by Race/Ethnicity

Category	Total	White	Black	Asian	AIAN	Hisp.
Enrollment (%)	100.0	41.1	56.5	0.2	0.1	2.2
Drop-out Rate (%)	5.3	3.2	7.1	0.0	50.0	5.0
H.S. Diplomas (#)	270	130	137	1	0	2

Mcdowell County

Mcdowell County Schools
334 S Main St • Marion, NC 28752-0130
Mailing Address: PO Box 130 • Marion, NC 28752-0130
(828) 652-4535 • http://www.mcdowell.k12.nc.us/
Grade Span: KG-12; **Agency Type:** 1
Schools: 11
8 Primary; 2 Middle; 1 High; 0 Other Level
11 Regular; 0 Special Education; 0 Vocational; 0 Alternative
0 Magnet; 0 Charter; 8 Title I Eligible; 4 School-wide Title I
Students: 6,472   (51.4% male; 48.5% female)
Individual Education Program: 1,024 (15.8%);
English Language Learner: 360 (5.6%); Migrant: 0 (0.0%)
Eligible for Free Lunch Program: 2,541 (39.3%)
Eligible for Reduced-Price Lunch Program: 804 (12.4%)
Teachers: 409.0 (15.8 to 1)
Librarians/Media Specialists: 11.0 (588.4 to 1)

Guidance Counselors: 14.0 (462.3 to 1)
Current Spending: ($ per student per year):
Total: $6,545; Instruction: $4,399; Support Services: $1,754
Enrollment, Drop-out Rates and Diploma Recipients by Race/Ethnicity

Category	Total	White	Black	Asian	AIAN	Hisp.
Enrollment (%)	100.0	88.2	4.9	1.8	0.3	4.8
Drop-out Rate (%)	4.0	4.3	2.4	0.0	0.0	3.1
H.S. Diplomas (#)	306	279	15	10	0	2

Mecklenburg County

Charlotte-Mecklenburg Schools
701 E 2nd St • Charlotte, NC 28202-2825
Mailing Address: PO Box 30035 • Charlotte, NC 28230-0035
(980) 343-3000 • http://www.cms.k12.nc.us/
Grade Span: PK-12; **Agency Type:** 1
Schools: 137
88 Primary; 28 Middle; 15 High; 6 Other Level
133 Regular; 2 Special Education; 0 Vocational; 2 Alternative
50 Magnet; 0 Charter; 29 Title I Eligible; 29 School-wide Title I
Students: 114,071   (51.0% male; 48.9% female)
Individual Education Program: 13,697 (12.0%);
English Language Learner: 490 (0.4%); Migrant: 0 (0.0%)
Eligible for Free Lunch Program: 41,867 (36.7%)
Eligible for Reduced-Price Lunch Program: 7,378 (6.5%)
Teachers: 7,350.0 (15.5 to 1)
Librarians/Media Specialists: 158.0 (722.0 to 1)
Guidance Counselors: 281.0 (405.9 to 1)
Current Spending: ($ per student per year):
Total: $7,188; Instruction: $4,441; Support Services: $2,371
Enrollment, Drop-out Rates and Diploma Recipients by Race/Ethnicity

Category	Total	White	Black	Asian	AIAN	Hisp.
Enrollment (%)	100.0	41.6	44.5	4.3	0.6	9.0
Drop-out Rate (%)	5.5	3.7	7.0	5.9	11.2	8.6
H.S. Diplomas (#)	5,087	2,773	1,911	238	10	155

Mitchell County

Mitchell County Schools
72 Ledger School Rd • Bakersville, NC 28705-9533
(828) 688-4432 • http://central.mitchell.k12.nc.us/
Grade Span: PK-12; **Agency Type:** 1
Schools: 8
5 Primary; 2 Middle; 1 High; 0 Other Level
8 Regular; 0 Special Education; 0 Vocational; 0 Alternative
0 Magnet; 0 Charter; 7 Title I Eligible; 7 School-wide Title I
Students: 2,335   (52.7% male; 47.2% female)
Individual Education Program: 398 (17.0%);
English Language Learner: 103 (4.4%); Migrant: 36 (1.5%)
Eligible for Free Lunch Program: 905 (38.8%)
Eligible for Reduced-Price Lunch Program: 320 (13.7%)
Teachers: 166.0 (14.1 to 1)
Librarians/Media Specialists: 7.0 (333.6 to 1)
Guidance Counselors: 6.0 (389.2 to 1)
Current Spending: ($ per student per year):
Total: $7,134; Instruction: $4,294; Support Services: $2,474
Enrollment, Drop-out Rates and Diploma Recipients by Race/Ethnicity

Category	Total	White	Black	Asian	AIAN	Hisp.
Enrollment (%)	100.0	94.6	0.6	0.1	0.1	4.6
Drop-out Rate (%)	7.1	7.2	0.0	0.0	n/a	0.0
H.S. Diplomas (#)	150	144	1	1	0	4

Montgomery County

Montgomery County Schools
441 Page St • Troy, NC 27371-0427
Mailing Address: PO Box 427 • Troy, NC 27371-0427
(910) 576-6511 • http://www.montgomerycountyschool.org/
Grade Span: PK-12; **Agency Type:** 1
Schools: 10
5 Primary; 2 Middle; 2 High; 1 Other Level
9 Regular; 0 Special Education; 0 Vocational; 1 Alternative
0 Magnet; 0 Charter; 5 Title I Eligible; 5 School-wide Title I
Students: 4,608   (51.0% male; 48.9% female)
Individual Education Program: 612 (13.3%);
English Language Learner: 877 (19.0%); Migrant: 295 (6.4%)
Eligible for Free Lunch Program: 2,241 (48.6%)
Eligible for Reduced-Price Lunch Program: 464 (10.1%)
Teachers: 339.0 (13.6 to 1)
Librarians/Media Specialists: 9.0 (512.0 to 1)
Guidance Counselors: 11.0 (418.9 to 1)
Current Spending: ($ per student per year):
Total: $7,040; Instruction: $4,504; Support Services: $2,075

Enrollment, Drop-out Rates and Diploma Recipients by Race/Ethnicity

Category	Total	White	Black	Asian	AIAN	Hisp.
Enrollment (%)	100.0	49.9	27.6	2.6	0.1	19.8
Drop-out Rate (%)	6.1	6.0	5.7	1.8	0.0	9.7
H.S. Diplomas (#)	220	139	53	14	1	13

Moore County

Moore County Schools
Hwy 15-501 S · Carthage, NC 28327-1180
Mailing Address: PO Box 1180 · Carthage, NC 28327-1180
(910) 947-2976 · http://www.mcs.k12.nc.us/
Grade Span: KG-12; **Agency Type:** 1
Schools: 22
  14 Primary; 4 Middle; 3 High; 1 Other Level
  21 Regular; 0 Special Education; 0 Vocational; 1 Alternative
  0 Magnet; 0 Charter; 10 Title I Eligible; 8 School-wide Title I
Students: 11,778 (50.7% male; 49.2% female)
  Individual Education Program: 1,577 (13.4%);
  English Language Learner: 450 (3.8%); Migrant: 178 (1.5%)
  Eligible for Free Lunch Program: 3,975 (33.7%)
  Eligible for Reduced-Price Lunch Program: 811 (6.9%)
Teachers: 778.0 (15.1 to 1)
Librarians/Media Specialists: 22.0 (535.4 to 1)
Guidance Counselors: 29.0 (406.1 to 1)
Current Spending: ($ per student per year):
  Total: $6,723; Instruction: $4,160; Support Services: $2,267
Enrollment, Drop-out Rates and Diploma Recipients by Race/Ethnicity

Category	Total	White	Black	Asian	AIAN	Hisp.
Enrollment (%)	100.0	67.9	24.3	0.6	0.9	6.2
Drop-out Rate (%)	3.1	2.5	4.4	0.0	17.9	2.2
H.S. Diplomas (#)	625	479	135	0	4	7

Nash County

Nash-Rocky Mount Schools
930 Eastern Ave · Nashville, NC 27856-1716
(252) 459-5220 · http://www.nrms.k12.nc.us/
Grade Span: PK-12; **Agency Type:** 1
Schools: 29
  18 Primary; 5 Middle; 5 High; 1 Other Level
  28 Regular; 0 Special Education; 0 Vocational; 1 Alternative
  0 Magnet; 0 Charter; 17 Title I Eligible; 17 School-wide Title I
Students: 18,526 (51.2% male; 48.7% female)
  Individual Education Program: 2,702 (14.6%);
  English Language Learner: 750 (4.0%); Migrant: 454 (2.5%)
  Eligible for Free Lunch Program: 8,417 (45.4%)
  Eligible for Reduced-Price Lunch Program: 1,709 (9.2%)
Teachers: 1,226.0 (15.1 to 1)
Librarians/Media Specialists: 31.0 (597.6 to 1)
Guidance Counselors: 64.0 (289.5 to 1)
Current Spending: ($ per student per year):
  Total: $6,515; Instruction: $4,214; Support Services: $1,935
Enrollment, Drop-out Rates and Diploma Recipients by Race/Ethnicity

Category	Total	White	Black	Asian	AIAN	Hisp.
Enrollment (%)	100.0	38.5	54.5	1.3	0.4	5.3
Drop-out Rate (%)	6.2	5.6	6.6	4.3	8.7	9.2
H.S. Diplomas (#)	918	458	430	5	4	21

New Hanover County

New Hanover County Schools
6410 Carolina Beach Rd · Wilmington, NC 28412-6479
(910) 763-5431 · http://www.nhcs.k12.nc.us/
Grade Span: PK-12; **Agency Type:** 1
Schools: 34
  22 Primary; 7 Middle; 4 High; 1 Other Level
  33 Regular; 0 Special Education; 0 Vocational; 1 Alternative
  1 Magnet; 0 Charter; 16 Title I Eligible; 16 School-wide Title I
Students: 22,268 (51.0% male; 48.9% female)
  Individual Education Program: 3,120 (14.0%);
  English Language Learner: 560 (2.5%); Migrant: 0 (0.0%)
  Eligible for Free Lunch Program: 7,513 (33.7%)
  Eligible for Reduced-Price Lunch Program: 1,537 (6.9%)
Teachers: 1,470.0 (15.1 to 1)
Librarians/Media Specialists: 37.0 (601.8 to 1)
Guidance Counselors: 56.0 (397.6 to 1)
Current Spending: ($ per student per year):
  Total: $7,197; Instruction: $4,290; Support Services: $2,529
Enrollment, Drop-out Rates and Diploma Recipients by Race/Ethnicity

Category	Total	White	Black	Asian	AIAN	Hisp.
Enrollment (%)	100.0	65.7	30.1	1.1	0.4	2.7
Drop-out Rate (%)	5.5	4.2	9.1	4.1	8.0	9.6
H.S. Diplomas (#)	1,272	978	256	13	6	19

Northampton County

Northampton County Schools
320 Bagley Dr · Jackson, NC 27845-0158
Mailing Address: PO Box 158 · Jackson, NC 27845-0158
(252) 534-1371 · http://www.northampton.k12.nc.us/
Grade Span: PK-12; **Agency Type:** 1
Schools: 10
  6 Primary; 2 Middle; 2 High; 0 Other Level
  10 Regular; 0 Special Education; 0 Vocational; 0 Alternative
  0 Magnet; 0 Charter; 8 Title I Eligible; 8 School-wide Title I
Students: 3,405 (52.0% male; 47.9% female)
  Individual Education Program: 421 (12.4%);
  English Language Learner: 29 (0.9%); Migrant: 171 (5.0%)
  Eligible for Free Lunch Program: 2,248 (66.0%)
  Eligible for Reduced-Price Lunch Program: 388 (11.4%)
Teachers: 249.0 (13.7 to 1)
Librarians/Media Specialists: 9.0 (378.3 to 1)
Guidance Counselors: 11.0 (309.5 to 1)
Current Spending: ($ per student per year):
  Total: $7,060; Instruction: $4,292; Support Services: $2,342
Enrollment, Drop-out Rates and Diploma Recipients by Race/Ethnicity

Category	Total	White	Black	Asian	AIAN	Hisp.
Enrollment (%)	100.0	18.7	79.9	0.0	0.1	1.2
Drop-out Rate (%)	5.7	4.9	5.8	n/a	100.0	0.0
H.S. Diplomas (#)	181	48	133	0	0	0

Onslow County

Onslow County Schools
200 Broadhurst Rd · Jacksonville, NC 28540-3551
Mailing Address: PO Box 99 · Jacksonville, NC 28541-0099
(910) 455-2211 · http://www.onslow.k12.nc.us/
Grade Span: PK-12; **Agency Type:** 1
Schools: 33
  18 Primary; 8 Middle; 7 High; 0 Other Level
  33 Regular; 0 Special Education; 0 Vocational; 0 Alternative
  0 Magnet; 0 Charter; 17 Title I Eligible; 13 School-wide Title I
Students: 21,745 (50.6% male; 49.3% female)
  Individual Education Program: 3,071 (14.1%);
  English Language Learner: 351 (1.6%); Migrant: 0 (0.0%)
  Eligible for Free Lunch Program: 6,225 (28.6%)
  Eligible for Reduced-Price Lunch Program: 2,640 (12.1%)
Teachers: 1,344.0 (16.2 to 1)
Librarians/Media Specialists: 45.0 (483.2 to 1)
Guidance Counselors: 47.0 (462.7 to 1)
Current Spending: ($ per student per year):
  Total: $5,990; Instruction: $3,767; Support Services: $1,912
Enrollment, Drop-out Rates and Diploma Recipients by Race/Ethnicity

Category	Total	White	Black	Asian	AIAN	Hisp.
Enrollment (%)	100.0	63.5	29.3	1.4	1.0	4.8
Drop-out Rate (%)	6.0	5.8	6.1	7.5	6.6	7.8
H.S. Diplomas (#)	1,161	774	296	30	10	51

Orange County

Chapel Hill-Carrboro Schools
750 S Merritt Mill Rd · Chapel Hill, NC 27516-2878
(919) 967-8211 · http://www.chccs.k12.nc.us/
Grade Span: PK-12; **Agency Type:** 1
Schools: 16
  9 Primary; 4 Middle; 2 High; 1 Other Level
  15 Regular; 0 Special Education; 0 Vocational; 1 Alternative
  0 Magnet; 0 Charter; 7 Title I Eligible; 0 School-wide Title I
Students: 10,644 (51.6% male; 48.3% female)
  Individual Education Program: 1,333 (12.5%);
  English Language Learner: 822 (7.7%); Migrant: 0 (0.0%)
  Eligible for Free Lunch Program: 1,753 (16.5%)
  Eligible for Reduced-Price Lunch Program: 382 (3.6%)
Teachers: 843.0 (12.6 to 1)
Librarians/Media Specialists: 29.0 (367.0 to 1)
Guidance Counselors: 29.0 (367.0 to 1)
Current Spending: ($ per student per year):
  Total: $9,025; Instruction: $5,874; Support Services: $2,860
Enrollment, Drop-out Rates and Diploma Recipients by Race/Ethnicity

Category	Total	White	Black	Asian	AIAN	Hisp.
Enrollment (%)	100.0	62.4	19.3	10.5	0.3	7.4
Drop-out Rate (%)	1.4	0.7	2.7	0.0	0.0	10.4
H.S. Diplomas (#)	599	456	86	44	2	11

Orange County Schools
200 E King St · Hillsborough, NC 27278-2570
(919) 732-8126 · http://www.orange.k12.nc.us/
Grade Span: PK-12; **Agency Type:** 1
Schools: 11

7 Primary; 2 Middle; 2 High; 0 Other Level
11 Regular; 0 Special Education; 0 Vocational; 0 Alternative
0 Magnet; 0 Charter; 5 Title I Eligible; 0 School-wide Title I
Students: 6,557   (51.3% male; 48.6% female)
Individual Education Program: 1,227 (18.7%);
English Language Learner: 190 (2.9%); Migrant: 80 (1.2%)
Eligible for Free Lunch Program: 1,529 (23.3%)
Eligible for Reduced-Price Lunch Program: 486 (7.4%)
Teachers: 472.0 (13.9 to 1)
Librarians/Media Specialists: 11.0 (596.1 to 1)
Guidance Counselors: 18.0 (364.3 to 1)
Current Spending: ($ per student per year):
Total: $7,816; Instruction: $4,894; Support Services: $2,576
Enrollment, Drop-out Rates and Diploma Recipients by Race/Ethnicity

Category	Total	White	Black	Asian	AIAN	Hisp.
Enrollment (%)	100.0	70.3	23.9	0.7	0.4	4.7
Drop-out Rate (%)	4.9	4.2	7.0	0.0	0.0	8.3
H.S. Diplomas (#)	310	228	73	4	0	5

Pamlico County

Pamlico County Schools
507 Anderson Dr • Bayboro, NC 28515-9799
(252) 745-4171 • http://www.pamlico.k12.nc.us/
Grade Span: PK-12; **Agency Type:** 1
Schools: 4
2 Primary; 1 Middle; 1 High; 0 Other Level
4 Regular; 0 Special Education; 0 Vocational; 0 Alternative
0 Magnet; 0 Charter; 2 Title I Eligible; 2 School-wide Title I
Students: 1,775   (52.7% male; 47.2% female)
Individual Education Program: 376 (21.2%);
English Language Learner: 18 (1.0%); Migrant: 0 (0.0%)
Eligible for Free Lunch Program: 769 (43.3%)
Eligible for Reduced-Price Lunch Program: 182 (10.3%)
Teachers: 149.0 (11.9 to 1)
Librarians/Media Specialists: 4.0 (443.8 to 1)
Guidance Counselors: 5.0 (355.0 to 1)
Current Spending: ($ per student per year):
Total: $8,017; Instruction: $5,106; Support Services: $2,529
Enrollment, Drop-out Rates and Diploma Recipients by Race/Ethnicity

Category	Total	White	Black	Asian	AIAN	Hisp.
Enrollment (%)	100.0	63.4	34.2	0.5	0.5	1.5
Drop-out Rate (%)	4.8	6.0	2.6	0.0	0.0	0.0
H.S. Diplomas (#)	132	86	38	3	2	3

Pasquotank County

Pasquotank County Schools
1200 S Halstead Blvd • Elizabeth City, NC 27906-2247
Mailing Address: PO Box 2247 • Elizabeth City, NC 27906-2247
(252) 335-2981 • http://www.ecpps.com/
Grade Span: PK-12; **Agency Type:** 1
Schools: 12
7 Primary; 2 Middle; 2 High; 1 Other Level
11 Regular; 0 Special Education; 0 Vocational; 1 Alternative
0 Magnet; 0 Charter; 7 Title I Eligible; 7 School-wide Title I
Students: 6,012   (51.0% male; 48.9% female)
Individual Education Program: 830 (13.8%);
English Language Learner: 37 (0.6%); Migrant: 0 (0.0%)
Eligible for Free Lunch Program: 2,813 (46.8%)
Eligible for Reduced-Price Lunch Program: 604 (10.0%)
Teachers: 414.0 (14.5 to 1)
Librarians/Media Specialists: 11.0 (546.5 to 1)
Guidance Counselors: 15.0 (400.8 to 1)
Current Spending: ($ per student per year):
Total: $6,677; Instruction: $4,165; Support Services: $2,061
Enrollment, Drop-out Rates and Diploma Recipients by Race/Ethnicity

Category	Total	White	Black	Asian	AIAN	Hisp.
Enrollment (%)	100.0	46.9	51.3	0.4	0.1	1.3
Drop-out Rate (%)	6.8	6.0	7.8	0.0	0.0	0.0
H.S. Diplomas (#)	270	126	138	3	0	3

Pender County

Pender County Schools
925 Penderlea Hwy • Burgaw, NC 28425-4546
(910) 259-2187 • http://www.schoollink.net/pender/
Grade Span: PK-12; **Agency Type:** 1
Schools: 15
7 Primary; 4 Middle; 3 High; 1 Other Level
14 Regular; 0 Special Education; 0 Vocational; 1 Alternative
0 Magnet; 0 Charter; 9 Title I Eligible; 9 School-wide Title I
Students: 6,984   (52.1% male; 47.8% female)
Individual Education Program: 924 (13.2%);
English Language Learner: 372 (5.3%); Migrant: 732 (10.5%)

Eligible for Free Lunch Program: 2,855 (40.9%)
Eligible for Reduced-Price Lunch Program: 837 (12.0%)
Teachers: 487.0 (14.3 to 1)
Librarians/Media Specialists: 14.0 (498.9 to 1)
Guidance Counselors: 18.0 (388.0 to 1)
Current Spending: ($ per student per year):
Total: $6,744; Instruction: $4,097; Support Services: $2,272
Enrollment, Drop-out Rates and Diploma Recipients by Race/Ethnicity

Category	Total	White	Black	Asian	AIAN	Hisp.
Enrollment (%)	100.0	64.5	29.8	0.2	0.2	5.2
Drop-out Rate (%)	7.1	6.7	7.5	0.0	0.0	11.1
H.S. Diplomas (#)	305	199	98	1	3	4

Perquimans County

Perquimans County Schools
411 Edenton Rd St • Hertford, NC 27944-0337
Mailing Address: PO Box 337 • Hertford, NC 27944-0337
(252) 426-5741 • http://www.perquimans.k12.nc.us/
Grade Span: PK-12; **Agency Type:** 1
Schools: 4
2 Primary; 1 Middle; 1 High; 0 Other Level
4 Regular; 0 Special Education; 0 Vocational; 0 Alternative
0 Magnet; 0 Charter; 2 Title I Eligible; 2 School-wide Title I
Students: 1,829   (52.4% male; 47.5% female)
Individual Education Program: 298 (16.3%);
English Language Learner: 0 (0.0%); Migrant: 0 (0.0%)
Eligible for Free Lunch Program: 807 (44.1%)
Eligible for Reduced-Price Lunch Program: 267 (14.6%)
Teachers: 131.0 (14.0 to 1)
Librarians/Media Specialists: 4.0 (457.3 to 1)
Guidance Counselors: 5.0 (365.8 to 1)
Current Spending: ($ per student per year):
Total: $7,802; Instruction: $4,497; Support Services: $2,793
Enrollment, Drop-out Rates and Diploma Recipients by Race/Ethnicity

Category	Total	White	Black	Asian	AIAN	Hisp.
Enrollment (%)	100.0	60.1	38.7	0.4	0.3	0.6
Drop-out Rate (%)	5.7	6.0	5.4	0.0	0.0	0.0
H.S. Diplomas (#)	103	67	34	0	0	2

Person County

Person County Schools
304 S Morgan St Rm 25 • Roxboro, NC 27573-5245
(336) 599-2191 • http://www.person.k12.nc.us/
Grade Span: KG-12; **Agency Type:** 1
Schools: 10
7 Primary; 2 Middle; 1 High; 0 Other Level
10 Regular; 0 Special Education; 0 Vocational; 0 Alternative
0 Magnet; 0 Charter; 6 Title I Eligible; 4 School-wide Title I
Students: 5,779   (50.6% male; 49.3% female)
Individual Education Program: 951 (16.5%);
English Language Learner: 95 (1.6%); Migrant: 0 (0.0%)
Eligible for Free Lunch Program: 1,930 (33.4%)
Eligible for Reduced-Price Lunch Program: 563 (9.7%)
Teachers: 407.0 (14.2 to 1)
Librarians/Media Specialists: 11.0 (525.4 to 1)
Guidance Counselors: 16.0 (361.2 to 1)
Current Spending: ($ per student per year):
Total: $6,334; Instruction: $4,118; Support Services: $1,815
Enrollment, Drop-out Rates and Diploma Recipients by Race/Ethnicity

Category	Total	White	Black	Asian	AIAN	Hisp.
Enrollment (%)	100.0	57.5	38.6	0.2	0.5	3.2
Drop-out Rate (%)	6.2	4.8	8.6	0.0	0.0	20.0
H.S. Diplomas (#)	304	197	97	1	1	8

Pitt County

Pitt County Schools
1717 W 5th St • Greenville, NC 27834-1698
(252) 830-4200 • http://schools.eastnet.ecu.edu/pitt/pitt.htm
Grade Span: PK-12; **Agency Type:** 1
Schools: 33
20 Primary; 6 Middle; 5 High; 2 Other Level
32 Regular; 0 Special Education; 0 Vocational; 1 Alternative
0 Magnet; 0 Charter; 17 Title I Eligible; 2 School-wide Title I
Students: 21,412   (51.2% male; 48.7% female)
Individual Education Program: 3,043 (14.2%);
English Language Learner: 603 (2.8%); Migrant: 428 (2.0%)
Eligible for Free Lunch Program: 9,560 (44.6%)
Eligible for Reduced-Price Lunch Program: 1,596 (7.5%)
Teachers: 1,440.0 (14.9 to 1)
Librarians/Media Specialists: 33.0 (648.8 to 1)
Guidance Counselors: 67.0 (319.6 to 1)

Current Spending: ($ per student per year):
Total: $6,637; Instruction: $4,383; Support Services: $1,883
Enrollment, Drop-out Rates and Diploma Recipients by Race/Ethnicity

Category	Total	White	Black	Asian	AIAN	Hisp.
Enrollment (%)	100.0	42.4	52.0	1.3	0.2	4.2
Drop-out Rate (%)	6.7	4.4	9.3	5.3	11.1	4.7
H.S. Diplomas (#)	994	595	375	14	2	8

Polk County

Polk County Schools
125 E Mills St • Columbus, NC 28722-0638
Mailing Address: PO Box 638 • Columbus, NC 28722-0638
(828) 894-3051 • http://server.sec.polk.k12.nc.us/
Grade Span: PK-12; **Agency Type:** 1
Schools: 6
4 Primary; 1 Middle; 1 High; 0 Other Level
6 Regular; 0 Special Education; 0 Vocational; 0 Alternative
0 Magnet; 0 Charter; 4 Title I Eligible; 0 School-wide Title I
Students: 2,519 (50.6% male; 49.3% female)
Individual Education Program: 417 (16.6%);
English Language Learner: 99 (3.9%); Migrant: 0 (0.0%)
Eligible for Free Lunch Program: 749 (29.7%)
Eligible for Reduced-Price Lunch Program: 282 (11.2%)
Teachers: 192.0 (13.1 to 1)
Librarians/Media Specialists: 6.0 (419.8 to 1)
Guidance Counselors: 9.0 (279.9 to 1)
Current Spending: ($ per student per year):
Total: $7,478; Instruction: $4,864; Support Services: $2,221
Enrollment, Drop-out Rates and Diploma Recipients by Race/Ethnicity

Category	Total	White	Black	Asian	AIAN	Hisp.
Enrollment (%)	100.0	83.0	10.3	0.4	0.1	6.2
Drop-out Rate (%)	4.6	4.8	5.6	0.0	0.0	0.0
H.S. Diplomas (#)	117	105	10	0	0	2

Randolph County

Asheboro City Schools
1126 S Park St • Asheboro, NC 27203
Mailing Address: PO Box 1103 • Asheboro, NC 27204-1103
(336) 625-5104 • http://www.asheboro.k12.nc.us/
Grade Span: KG-12; **Agency Type:** 1
Schools: 8
5 Primary; 2 Middle; 1 High; 0 Other Level
8 Regular; 0 Special Education; 0 Vocational; 0 Alternative
0 Magnet; 0 Charter; 5 Title I Eligible; 5 School-wide Title I
Students: 4,447 (50.1% male; 49.8% female)
Individual Education Program: 590 (13.3%);
English Language Learner: 807 (18.1%); Migrant: 74 (1.7%)
Eligible for Free Lunch Program: 1,969 (44.3%)
Eligible for Reduced-Price Lunch Program: 337 (7.6%)
Teachers: 306.0 (14.5 to 1)
Librarians/Media Specialists: 9.0 (494.1 to 1)
Guidance Counselors: 9.0 (494.1 to 1)
Current Spending: ($ per student per year):
Total: $6,464; Instruction: $4,011; Support Services: $2,040
Enrollment, Drop-out Rates and Diploma Recipients by Race/Ethnicity

Category	Total	White	Black	Asian	AIAN	Hisp.
Enrollment (%)	100.0	55.4	16.6	2.3	0.2	25.5
Drop-out Rate (%)	6.1	5.3	8.3	0.0	0.0	10.3
H.S. Diplomas (#)	180	147	21	5	0	7

Randolph County Schools
2222-C S Fayetteville St • Asheboro, NC 27205-7379
(336) 318-6100 • http://www.randolph.k12.nc.us/
Grade Span: PK-12; **Agency Type:** 1
Schools: 28
17 Primary; 7 Middle; 4 High; 0 Other Level
28 Regular; 0 Special Education; 0 Vocational; 0 Alternative
0 Magnet; 0 Charter; 13 Title I Eligible; 0 School-wide Title I
Students: 18,211 (51.9% male; 48.0% female)
Individual Education Program: 2,343 (12.9%);
English Language Learner: 854 (4.7%); Migrant: 356 (2.0%)
Eligible for Free Lunch Program: 5,366 (29.5%)
Eligible for Reduced-Price Lunch Program: 1,387 (7.6%)
Teachers: 1,140.0 (16.0 to 1)
Librarians/Media Specialists: 30.0 (607.0 to 1)
Guidance Counselors: 40.0 (455.3 to 1)
Current Spending: ($ per student per year):
Total: $5,518; Instruction: $3,570; Support Services: $1,600
Enrollment, Drop-out Rates and Diploma Recipients by Race/Ethnicity

Category	Total	White	Black	Asian	AIAN	Hisp.
Enrollment (%)	100.0	84.9	6.6	0.7	0.4	7.3
Drop-out Rate (%)	6.5	6.0	9.8	9.4	14.3	11.2
H.S. Diplomas (#)	825	759	43	3	2	18

Richmond County

Richmond County Schools
522 W Hamlet Ave • Hamlet, NC 28345-2624
Mailing Address: PO Drawer 1259 • Hamlet, NC 28345-1259
(910) 582-5860 • http://www.richmond.k12.nc.us/
Grade Span: PK-12; **Agency Type:** 1
Schools: 18
8 Primary; 8 Middle; 1 High; 1 Other Level
16 Regular; 1 Special Education; 0 Vocational; 1 Alternative
0 Magnet; 0 Charter; 9 Title I Eligible; 9 School-wide Title I
Students: 8,296 (50.9% male; 49.0% female)
Individual Education Program: 1,083 (13.1%);
English Language Learner: 195 (2.4%); Migrant: 0 (0.0%)
Eligible for Free Lunch Program: 4,296 (51.8%)
Eligible for Reduced-Price Lunch Program: 808 (9.7%)
Teachers: 560.0 (14.8 to 1)
Librarians/Media Specialists: 17.0 (488.0 to 1)
Guidance Counselors: 20.0 (414.8 to 1)
Current Spending: ($ per student per year):
Total: $6,423; Instruction: $4,149; Support Services: $1,867
Enrollment, Drop-out Rates and Diploma Recipients by Race/Ethnicity

Category	Total	White	Black	Asian	AIAN	Hisp.
Enrollment (%)	100.0	52.3	41.0	0.8	2.2	3.7
Drop-out Rate (%)	6.0	6.1	5.8	8.0	10.0	4.7
H.S. Diplomas (#)	394	197	178	6	6	7

Robeson County

Robeson County Schools
410 Caton Rd • Lumberton, NC 28359-9767
Mailing Address: PO Drawer 2909 • Lumberton, NC 28359-2909
(910) 671-6000 • http://www.robeson.k12.nc.us/
Grade Span: PK-12; **Agency Type:** 1
Schools: 41
23 Primary; 11 Middle; 7 High; 0 Other Level
40 Regular; 0 Special Education; 1 Vocational; 0 Alternative
0 Magnet; 0 Charter; 33 Title I Eligible; 33 School-wide Title I
Students: 24,352 (51.2% male; 48.7% female)
Individual Education Program: 4,283 (17.6%);
English Language Learner: 1,058 (4.3%); Migrant: 691 (2.8%)
Eligible for Free Lunch Program: 16,984 (69.7%)
Eligible for Reduced-Price Lunch Program: 2,320 (9.5%)
Teachers: 1,470.0 (16.6 to 1)
Librarians/Media Specialists: 70.0 (347.9 to 1)
Guidance Counselors: 58.0 (419.9 to 1)
Current Spending: ($ per student per year):
Total: $6,288; Instruction: $4,010; Support Services: $1,861
Enrollment, Drop-out Rates and Diploma Recipients by Race/Ethnicity

Category	Total	White	Black	Asian	AIAN	Hisp.
Enrollment (%)	100.0	20.4	30.9	0.4	43.1	5.2
Drop-out Rate (%)	9.1	7.8	8.4	8.3	10.1	13.0
H.S. Diplomas (#)	963	252	308	5	393	5

Rockingham County

Rockingham County Schools
511 Harrington Hwy • Eden, NC 27288-7547
(336) 627-2600 • http://www.rock.k12.nc.us/
Grade Span: PK-12; **Agency Type:** 1
Schools: 25
16 Primary; 4 Middle; 4 High; 1 Other Level
24 Regular; 0 Special Education; 0 Vocational; 1 Alternative
0 Magnet; 0 Charter; 11 Title I Eligible; 10 School-wide Title I
Students: 14,799 (51.7% male; 48.2% female)
Individual Education Program: 2,310 (15.6%);
English Language Learner: 724 (4.9%); Migrant: 553 (3.7%)
Eligible for Free Lunch Program: 5,733 (38.7%)
Eligible for Reduced-Price Lunch Program: 1,276 (8.6%)
Teachers: 948.0 (15.6 to 1)
Librarians/Media Specialists: 31.0 (477.4 to 1)
Guidance Counselors: 32.0 (462.5 to 1)
Current Spending: ($ per student per year):
Total: $6,336; Instruction: $4,005; Support Services: $1,943
Enrollment, Drop-out Rates and Diploma Recipients by Race/Ethnicity

Category	Total	White	Black	Asian	AIAN	Hisp.
Enrollment (%)	100.0	67.3	27.3	0.4	0.3	4.8
Drop-out Rate (%)	6.0	6.0	5.5	0.0	18.2	13.4
H.S. Diplomas (#)	716	545	160	4	1	6

Rowan County

Rowan-Salisbury Schools
314 N Ellis St • Salisbury, NC 28144
Mailing Address: PO Box 2349 • Salisbury, NC 28145-2349
(704) 636-7500 • http://www.rss.k12.nc.us/menu/menu.asp
Grade Span: PK-12; **Agency Type:** 1
Schools: 30
  17 Primary; 7 Middle; 6 High; 0 Other Level
  29 Regular; 0 Special Education; 0 Vocational; 1 Alternative
  0 Magnet; 0 Charter; 14 Title I Eligible; 6 School-wide Title I
Students: 20,907 (51.4% male; 48.5% female)
  Individual Education Program: 2,917 (14.0%);
  English Language Learner: 1,364 (6.5%); Migrant: 637 (3.0%)
  Eligible for Free Lunch Program: 7,217 (34.5%)
  Eligible for Reduced-Price Lunch Program: 1,879 (9.0%)
Teachers: 1,323.0 (15.8 to 1)
Librarians/Media Specialists: 31.0 (674.4 to 1)
Guidance Counselors: 64.0 (326.7 to 1)
Current Spending: ($ per student per year):
  Total: $6,180; Instruction: $4,011; Support Services: $1,775
Enrollment, Drop-out Rates and Diploma Recipients by Race/Ethnicity

Category	Total	White	Black	Asian	AIAN	Hisp.
Enrollment (%)	100.0	69.4	23.2	1.3	0.2	5.8
Drop-out Rate (%)	5.6	5.3	5.8	7.4	5.6	11.4
H.S. Diplomas (#)	1,093	841	205	20	4	23

Rutherford County

Rutherford County Schools
382 W Main St • Forest City, NC 28043
(828) 245-0252 • http://www2.rutherford.k12.nc.us/
Grade Span: PK-12; **Agency Type:** 1
Schools: 18
  11 Primary; 3 Middle; 3 High; 1 Other Level
  17 Regular; 0 Special Education; 0 Vocational; 1 Alternative
  0 Magnet; 0 Charter; 11 Title I Eligible; 11 School-wide Title I
Students: 9,960 (50.9% male; 49.0% female)
  Individual Education Program: 1,467 (14.7%);
  English Language Learner: 174 (1.7%); Migrant: 0 (0.0%)
  Eligible for Free Lunch Program: 4,295 (43.1%)
  Eligible for Reduced-Price Lunch Program: 913 (9.2%)
Teachers: 668.0 (14.9 to 1)
Librarians/Media Specialists: 20.0 (498.0 to 1)
Guidance Counselors: 28.0 (355.7 to 1)
Current Spending: ($ per student per year):
  Total: $6,644; Instruction: $4,360; Support Services: $1,931
Enrollment, Drop-out Rates and Diploma Recipients by Race/Ethnicity

Category	Total	White	Black	Asian	AIAN	Hisp.
Enrollment (%)	100.0	78.8	17.9	0.4	0.1	2.8
Drop-out Rate (%)	8.1	7.9	9.2	0.0	0.0	10.9
H.S. Diplomas (#)	452	383	62	2	0	5

Sampson County

Clinton City Schools
606 College St • Clinton, NC 28328-4118
(910) 592-3132 • http://www.clinton.k12.nc.us/
Grade Span: PK-12; **Agency Type:** 1
Schools: 4
  2 Primary; 1 Middle; 1 High; 0 Other Level
  4 Regular; 0 Special Education; 0 Vocational; 0 Alternative
  0 Magnet; 0 Charter; 3 Title I Eligible; 3 School-wide Title I
Students: 2,847 (49.1% male; 50.8% female)
  Individual Education Program: 307 (10.8%);
  English Language Learner: 141 (5.0%); Migrant: 0 (0.0%)
  Eligible for Free Lunch Program: 1,501 (52.7%)
  Eligible for Reduced-Price Lunch Program: 239 (8.4%)
Teachers: 196.0 (14.5 to 1)
Librarians/Media Specialists: 4.0 (711.8 to 1)
Guidance Counselors: 6.0 (474.5 to 1)
Current Spending: ($ per student per year):
  Total: $6,801; Instruction: $4,340; Support Services: $2,008
Enrollment, Drop-out Rates and Diploma Recipients by Race/Ethnicity

Category	Total	White	Black	Asian	AIAN	Hisp.
Enrollment (%)	100.0	37.6	48.2	1.0	3.8	9.4
Drop-out Rate (%)	6.3	5.7	6.3	0.0	12.9	6.7
H.S. Diplomas (#)	146	79	57	1	5	4

Sampson County Schools
437 Rowan Rd • Clinton, NC 28328
Mailing Address: PO Box 439 • Clinton, NC 28329-0439
(910) 592-1401 • http://www.sampson.k12.nc.us/
Grade Span: PK-12; **Agency Type:** 1
Schools: 16

  8 Primary; 4 Middle; 4 High; 0 Other Level
  16 Regular; 0 Special Education; 0 Vocational; 0 Alternative
  0 Magnet; 0 Charter; 14 Title I Eligible; 14 School-wide Title I
Students: 8,177 (52.0% male; 47.9% female)
  Individual Education Program: 1,148 (14.0%);
  English Language Learner: 889 (10.9%); Migrant: 654 (8.0%)
  Eligible for Free Lunch Program: 4,627 (56.6%)
  Eligible for Reduced-Price Lunch Program: 960 (11.7%)
Teachers: 552.0 (14.8 to 1)
Librarians/Media Specialists: 17.0 (481.0 to 1)
Guidance Counselors: 17.0 (481.0 to 1)
Current Spending: ($ per student per year):
  Total: $6,380; Instruction: $4,158; Support Services: $1,746
Enrollment, Drop-out Rates and Diploma Recipients by Race/Ethnicity

Category	Total	White	Black	Asian	AIAN	Hisp.
Enrollment (%)	100.0	50.0	30.9	0.2	1.4	17.5
Drop-out Rate (%)	5.0	3.8	6.2	0.0	8.0	8.9
H.S. Diplomas (#)	357	231	107	0	4	15

Scotland County

Scotland County Schools
322 S Main St • Laurinburg, NC 28352-3855
(910) 276-1138 • http://www.scsnc.org/
Grade Span: PK-12; **Agency Type:** 1
Schools: 15
  9 Primary; 3 Middle; 1 High; 2 Other Level
  14 Regular; 0 Special Education; 0 Vocational; 1 Alternative
  0 Magnet; 0 Charter; 8 Title I Eligible; 8 School-wide Title I
Students: 7,114 (50.7% male; 49.2% female)
  Individual Education Program: 1,118 (15.7%);
  English Language Learner: 55 (0.8%); Migrant: 0 (0.0%)
  Eligible for Free Lunch Program: 4,237 (59.6%)
  Eligible for Reduced-Price Lunch Program: 696 (9.8%)
Teachers: 554.0 (12.8 to 1)
Librarians/Media Specialists: 12.0 (592.8 to 1)
Guidance Counselors: 20.0 (355.7 to 1)
Current Spending: ($ per student per year):
  Total: $7,488; Instruction: $4,794; Support Services: $2,281
Enrollment, Drop-out Rates and Diploma Recipients by Race/Ethnicity

Category	Total	White	Black	Asian	AIAN	Hisp.
Enrollment (%)	100.0	37.8	48.0	0.7	12.6	0.9
Drop-out Rate (%)	4.7	4.4	4.3	0.0	8.5	0.0
H.S. Diplomas (#)	339	174	137	4	23	1

Stanly County

Stanly County Schools
1000-4 N First St • Albemarle, NC 28001
(704) 983-5151 • http://www.scs.k12.nc.us/
Grade Span: PK-12; **Agency Type:** 1
Schools: 22
  15 Primary; 2 Middle; 4 High; 1 Other Level
  22 Regular; 0 Special Education; 0 Vocational; 0 Alternative
  0 Magnet; 0 Charter; 5 Title I Eligible; 5 School-wide Title I
Students: 9,993 (52.2% male; 47.7% female)
  Individual Education Program: 1,830 (18.3%);
  English Language Learner: 526 (5.3%); Migrant: 0 (0.0%)
  Eligible for Free Lunch Program: 3,044 (30.5%)
  Eligible for Reduced-Price Lunch Program: 951 (9.5%)
Teachers: 672.0 (14.9 to 1)
Librarians/Media Specialists: 22.0 (454.2 to 1)
Guidance Counselors: 40.0 (249.8 to 1)
Current Spending: ($ per student per year):
  Total: $6,115; Instruction: $4,057; Support Services: $1,665
Enrollment, Drop-out Rates and Diploma Recipients by Race/Ethnicity

Category	Total	White	Black	Asian	AIAN	Hisp.
Enrollment (%)	100.0	75.3	16.7	4.2	0.3	3.6
Drop-out Rate (%)	3.4	3.2	4.3	1.9	7.7	12.8
H.S. Diplomas (#)	569	476	68	20	1	4

Stokes County

Stokes County Schools
501 N Main St • Danbury, NC 27016-0050
Mailing Address: PO Box 50 • Danbury, NC 27016-0050
(336) 593-8146 • http://www.stokes.k12.nc.us/
Grade Span: PK-12; **Agency Type:** 1
Schools: 18
  11 Primary; 3 Middle; 3 High; 1 Other Level
  17 Regular; 0 Special Education; 0 Vocational; 1 Alternative
  0 Magnet; 0 Charter; 10 Title I Eligible; 7 School-wide Title I
Students: 7,538 (51.4% male; 48.5% female)
  Individual Education Program: 1,200 (15.9%);
  English Language Learner: 75 (1.0%); Migrant: 0 (0.0%)

Eligible for Free Lunch Program: 1,777 (23.6%)
Eligible for Reduced-Price Lunch Program: 618 (8.2%)
Teachers: 502.0 (15.0 to 1)
Librarians/Media Specialists: 17.0 (443.4 to 1)
Guidance Counselors: 23.0 (327.7 to 1)
Current Spending: ($ per student per year):
Total: $6,531; Instruction: $3,942; Support Services: $2,164
Enrollment, Drop-out Rates and Diploma Recipients by Race/Ethnicity

Category	Total	White	Black	Asian	AIAN	Hisp.
Enrollment (%)	100.0	91.4	6.6	0.1	0.2	1.6
Drop-out Rate (%)	5.6	5.5	4.7	0.0	0.0	15.2
H.S. Diplomas (#)	414	379	28	0	0	7

Surry County

Mount Airy City Schools
130 Rawley Ave • Mount Airy, NC 27030-0710
Mailing Address: PO Drawer 710 • Mount Airy, NC 27030-0710
(336) 786-8355
Grade Span: PK-12; **Agency Type:** 1
Schools: 4
2 Primary; 1 Middle; 1 High; 0 Other Level
4 Regular; 0 Special Education; 0 Vocational; 0 Alternative
0 Magnet; 0 Charter; 2 Title I Eligible; 2 School-wide Title I
Students: 1,904 (49.9% male; 50.0% female)
Individual Education Program: 346 (18.2%);
English Language Learner: 156 (8.2%); Migrant: 0 (0.0%)
Eligible for Free Lunch Program: 776 (40.8%)
Eligible for Reduced-Price Lunch Program: 131 (6.9%)
Teachers: 143.0 (13.3 to 1)
Librarians/Media Specialists: 4.0 (476.0 to 1)
Guidance Counselors: 5.0 (380.8 to 1)
Current Spending: ($ per student per year):
Total: $7,101; Instruction: $4,309; Support Services: $2,291
Enrollment, Drop-out Rates and Diploma Recipients by Race/Ethnicity

Category	Total	White	Black	Asian	AIAN	Hisp.
Enrollment (%)	100.0	75.0	13.2	4.1	0.1	7.6
Drop-out Rate (%)	4.4	4.0	7.7	0.0	0.0	6.3
H.S. Diplomas (#)	87	70	9	5	0	3

Surry County Schools
209 N Crutchfield St • Dobson, NC 27017-0364
Mailing Address: PO Box 364 • Dobson, NC 27017-0364
(336) 386-8211 • http://surry.k12.nc.us/
Grade Span: PK-12; **Agency Type:** 1
Schools: 16
9 Primary; 4 Middle; 3 High; 0 Other Level
16 Regular; 0 Special Education; 0 Vocational; 0 Alternative
0 Magnet; 0 Charter; 8 Title I Eligible; 8 School-wide Title I
Students: 8,688 (51.5% male; 48.4% female)
Individual Education Program: 1,471 (16.9%);
English Language Learner: 690 (7.9%); Migrant: 333 (3.8%)
Eligible for Free Lunch Program: 3,164 (36.4%)
Eligible for Reduced-Price Lunch Program: 1,021 (11.8%)
Teachers: 586.0 (14.8 to 1)
Librarians/Media Specialists: 15.0 (579.2 to 1)
Guidance Counselors: 20.0 (434.4 to 1)
Current Spending: ($ per student per year):
Total: $6,428; Instruction: $4,188; Support Services: $1,832
Enrollment, Drop-out Rates and Diploma Recipients by Race/Ethnicity

Category	Total	White	Black	Asian	AIAN	Hisp.
Enrollment (%)	100.0	83.1	4.6	0.7	0.1	11.5
Drop-out Rate (%)	5.9	5.6	9.7	0.0	33.3	7.7
H.S. Diplomas (#)	476	431	19	3	0	23

Swain County

Swain County Schools
280 School Dr • Bryson City, NC 28713-2340
Mailing Address: PO Box 2340 • Bryson City, NC 28713-2340
(828) 488-3129 • http://www.swaincountyschools.com/
Grade Span: PK-12; **Agency Type:** 1
Schools: 5
2 Primary; 1 Middle; 1 High; 1 Other Level
5 Regular; 0 Special Education; 0 Vocational; 0 Alternative
0 Magnet; 0 Charter; 3 Title I Eligible; 3 School-wide Title I
Students: 1,854 (52.2% male; 47.7% female)
Individual Education Program: 340 (18.3%);
English Language Learner: 18 (1.0%); Migrant: 0 (0.0%)
Eligible for Free Lunch Program: 751 (40.5%)
Eligible for Reduced-Price Lunch Program: 269 (14.5%)
Teachers: 142.0 (13.1 to 1)
Librarians/Media Specialists: 4.0 (463.5 to 1)
Guidance Counselors: 4.0 (463.5 to 1)

Current Spending: ($ per student per year):
Total: $8,468; Instruction: $5,329; Support Services: $2,619
Enrollment, Drop-out Rates and Diploma Recipients by Race/Ethnicity

Category	Total	White	Black	Asian	AIAN	Hisp.
Enrollment (%)	100.0	75.4	1.0	0.3	21.1	2.2
Drop-out Rate (%)	3.1	2.7	0.0	0.0	5.0	0.0
H.S. Diplomas (#)	111	90	1	3	16	1

Transylvania County

Transylvania County Schools
400 Rosenwald Ln • Brevard, NC 28712-3239
(828) 884-6173 • http://www.transylvania.k12.nc.us/
Grade Span: KG-12; **Agency Type:** 1
Schools: 9
4 Primary; 2 Middle; 2 High; 1 Other Level
8 Regular; 0 Special Education; 0 Vocational; 1 Alternative
0 Magnet; 0 Charter; 4 Title I Eligible; 4 School-wide Title I
Students: 3,786 (51.0% male; 48.9% female)
Individual Education Program: 458 (12.1%);
English Language Learner: 56 (1.5%); Migrant: 0 (0.0%)
Eligible for Free Lunch Program: 1,230 (32.5%)
Eligible for Reduced-Price Lunch Program: 378 (10.0%)
Teachers: 267.0 (14.2 to 1)
Librarians/Media Specialists: 7.0 (540.9 to 1)
Guidance Counselors: 9.0 (420.7 to 1)
Current Spending: ($ per student per year):
Total: $6,931; Instruction: $4,447; Support Services: $2,057
Enrollment, Drop-out Rates and Diploma Recipients by Race/Ethnicity

Category	Total	White	Black	Asian	AIAN	Hisp.
Enrollment (%)	100.0	89.6	8.1	0.7	0.2	1.4
Drop-out Rate (%)	5.1	4.8	9.2	0.0	0.0	16.7
H.S. Diplomas (#)	252	234	18	0	0	0

Union County

Union County Public Schools
500 N Main St Ste 700 • Monroe, NC 28112-4730
(704) 283-3733 • http://www.ucps.k12.nc.us/
Grade Span: PK-12; **Agency Type:** 1
Schools: 34
19 Primary; 6 Middle; 7 High; 2 Other Level
32 Regular; 1 Special Education; 0 Vocational; 1 Alternative
0 Magnet; 0 Charter; 6 Title I Eligible; 6 School-wide Title I
Students: 26,993 (51.3% male; 48.6% female)
Individual Education Program: 3,296 (12.2%);
English Language Learner: 852 (3.2%); Migrant: 0 (0.0%)
Eligible for Free Lunch Program: 6,514 (24.1%)
Eligible for Reduced-Price Lunch Program: 1,525 (5.6%)
Teachers: 1,684.0 (16.0 to 1)
Librarians/Media Specialists: 40.0 (674.8 to 1)
Guidance Counselors: 72.0 (374.9 to 1)
Current Spending: ($ per student per year):
Total: $5,905; Instruction: $3,850; Support Services: $1,718
Enrollment, Drop-out Rates and Diploma Recipients by Race/Ethnicity

Category	Total	White	Black	Asian	AIAN	Hisp.
Enrollment (%)	100.0	73.5	17.2	0.9	0.3	8.1
Drop-out Rate (%)	4.7	4.1	6.8	2.0	23.1	7.3
H.S. Diplomas (#)	1,085	893	162	7	1	22

Vance County

Vance County Schools
1724 Graham Ave • Henderson, NC 27536-4295
Mailing Address: PO Box 7001 • Henderson, NC 27536-7001
(252) 492-2127 • http://www.vcs.k12.nc.us/
Grade Span: PK-12; **Agency Type:** 1
Schools: 15
10 Primary; 2 Middle; 3 High; 0 Other Level
14 Regular; 0 Special Education; 0 Vocational; 1 Alternative
0 Magnet; 0 Charter; 10 Title I Eligible; 9 School-wide Title I
Students: 8,587 (51.9% male; 48.0% female)
Individual Education Program: 1,171 (13.6%);
English Language Learner: 312 (3.6%); Migrant: 82 (1.0%)
Eligible for Free Lunch Program: 5,286 (61.6%)
Eligible for Reduced-Price Lunch Program: 785 (9.1%)
Teachers: 608.0 (14.1 to 1)
Librarians/Media Specialists: 16.0 (536.7 to 1)
Guidance Counselors: 21.0 (408.9 to 1)
Current Spending: ($ per student per year):
Total: $6,168; Instruction: $3,982; Support Services: $1,799

Enrollment, Drop-out Rates and Diploma Recipients by Race/Ethnicity

Category	Total	White	Black	Asian	AIAN	Hisp.
Enrollment (%)	100.0	27.4	66.1	0.3	0.1	6.1
Drop-out Rate (%)	8.7	7.7	9.4	7.1	20.0	4.5
H.S. Diplomas (#)	334	146	178	3	0	7

Enrollment, Drop-out Rates and Diploma Recipients by Race/Ethnicity

Category	Total	White	Black	Asian	AIAN	Hisp.
Enrollment (%)	100.0	23.6	74.7	0.3	0.0	1.4
Drop-out Rate (%)	6.7	5.1	7.3	100.0	n/a	0.0
H.S. Diplomas (#)	134	49	84	0	0	1

Wake County

Wake County Schools
3600 Wake Forest Rd · Raleigh, NC 27609-7329
Mailing Address: PO Box 28041 · Raleigh, NC 27611-8041
(919) 850-1600 · http://www.wcpss.net/
Grade Span: PK-12; **Agency Type:** 1
Schools: 126
   81 Primary; 27 Middle; 17 High; 1 Other Level
   123 Regular; 0 Special Education; 0 Vocational; 3 Alternative
   44 Magnet; 0 Charter; 41 Title I Eligible; 0 School-wide Title I
Students: 109,424 (51.0% male; 48.9% female)
   Individual Education Program: 16,421 (15.0%);
   English Language Learner: 7,645 (7.0%); Migrant: 569 (0.5%)
   Eligible for Free Lunch Program: 24,515 (22.4%)
   Eligible for Reduced-Price Lunch Program: 5,033 (4.6%)
Teachers: 7,302.0 (15.0 to 1)
Librarians/Media Specialists: 168.0 (651.3 to 1)
Guidance Counselors: 260.0 (420.9 to 1)
Current Spending: ($ per student per year):
   Total: $6,695; Instruction: $4,148; Support Services: $2,299
Enrollment, Drop-out Rates and Diploma Recipients by Race/Ethnicity

Category	Total	White	Black	Asian	AIAN	Hisp.
Enrollment (%)	100.0	58.3	29.9	4.3	0.3	7.3
Drop-out Rate (%)	3.7	2.3	6.7	1.5	14.3	8.4
H.S. Diplomas (#)	5,411	3,845	1,170	234	10	152

Warren County

Warren County Schools
109 Cousin Lucy's Ln · Warrenton, NC 27589-0110
Mailing Address: PO Box 110 · Warrenton, NC 27589-0110
(252) 257-3184 · http://www.warren-county.k12.nc.us/
Grade Span: KG-12; **Agency Type:** 1
Schools: 6
   4 Primary; 1 Middle; 1 High; 0 Other Level
   6 Regular; 0 Special Education; 0 Vocational; 0 Alternative
   0 Magnet; 0 Charter; 4 Title I Eligible; 4 School-wide Title I
Students: 3,120 (51.7% male; 48.2% female)
   Individual Education Program: 524 (16.8%);
   English Language Learner: 38 (1.2%); Migrant: 0 (0.0%)
   Eligible for Free Lunch Program: 1,767 (56.6%)
   Eligible for Reduced-Price Lunch Program: 414 (13.3%)
Teachers: 226.0 (13.8 to 1)
Librarians/Media Specialists: 6.0 (520.0 to 1)
Guidance Counselors: 10.0 (312.0 to 1)
Current Spending: ($ per student per year):
   Total: $7,099; Instruction: $4,312; Support Services: $2,341
Enrollment, Drop-out Rates and Diploma Recipients by Race/Ethnicity

Category	Total	White	Black	Asian	AIAN	Hisp.
Enrollment (%)	100.0	19.9	73.0	0.0	4.8	2.2
Drop-out Rate (%)	8.1	9.3	7.9	0.0	7.4	0.0
H.S. Diplomas (#)	144	32	106	0	6	0

Washington County

Washington County Schools
802 Washington St · Plymouth, NC 27962-0747
(252) 793-5171 · http://www.washingtonco.k12.nc.us/
Grade Span: PK-12; **Agency Type:** 1
Schools: 5
   2 Primary; 1 Middle; 2 High; 0 Other Level
   5 Regular; 0 Special Education; 0 Vocational; 0 Alternative
   0 Magnet; 0 Charter; 3 Title I Eligible; 3 School-wide Title I
Students: 2,281 (51.9% male; 48.0% female)
   Individual Education Program: 421 (18.5%);
   English Language Learner: 21 (0.9%); Migrant: 21 (0.9%)
   Eligible for Free Lunch Program: 1,644 (72.1%)
   Eligible for Reduced-Price Lunch Program: 220 (9.6%)
Teachers: 192.0 (11.9 to 1)
Librarians/Media Specialists: 4.0 (570.3 to 1)
Guidance Counselors: 5.0 (456.2 to 1)
Current Spending: ($ per student per year):
   Total: $7,855; Instruction: $5,090; Support Services: $2,309

Watauga County

Watauga County Schools
175 Pioneer Dr · Boone, NC 28607-1790
Mailing Address: PO Box 1790 · Boone, NC 28607-1790
(828) 264-7190 · http://nt.watauga.k12.nc.us/co/default.htm
Grade Span: PK-12; **Agency Type:** 1
Schools: 9
   8 Primary; 0 Middle; 1 High; 0 Other Level
   9 Regular; 0 Special Education; 0 Vocational; 0 Alternative
   0 Magnet; 0 Charter; 5 Title I Eligible; 2 School-wide Title I
Students: 4,687 (52.5% male; 47.4% female)
   Individual Education Program: 783 (16.7%);
   English Language Learner: 53 (1.1%); Migrant: 0 (0.0%)
   Eligible for Free Lunch Program: 908 (19.4%)
   Eligible for Reduced-Price Lunch Program: 345 (7.4%)
Teachers: 344.0 (13.6 to 1)
Librarians/Media Specialists: 12.0 (390.6 to 1)
Guidance Counselors: 15.0 (312.5 to 1)
Current Spending: ($ per student per year):
   Total: $7,002; Instruction: $4,621; Support Services: $2,107
Enrollment, Drop-out Rates and Diploma Recipients by Race/Ethnicity

Category	Total	White	Black	Asian	AIAN	Hisp.
Enrollment (%)	100.0	94.9	2.8	0.9	0.0	1.4
Drop-out Rate (%)	5.2	5.0	5.3	10.0	0.0	25.0
H.S. Diplomas (#)	327	323	2	1	0	1

Wayne County

Wayne County Public Schools
2001 E Royall Ave · Goldsboro, NC 27534
Mailing Address: PO Drawer 1797 · Goldsboro, NC 27533-1797
(919) 731-5900 · http://www.waynecountyschools.org/
Grade Span: PK-12; **Agency Type:** 1
Schools: 31
   14 Primary; 8 Middle; 5 High; 4 Other Level
   28 Regular; 1 Special Education; 0 Vocational; 2 Alternative
   0 Magnet; 0 Charter; 18 Title I Eligible; 18 School-wide Title I
Students: 19,424 (51.3% male; 48.6% female)
   Individual Education Program: 2,927 (15.1%);
   English Language Learner: 1,043 (5.4%); Migrant: 0 (0.0%)
   Eligible for Free Lunch Program: 7,508 (38.7%)
   Eligible for Reduced-Price Lunch Program: 2,043 (10.5%)
Teachers: 1,283.0 (15.1 to 1)
Librarians/Media Specialists: 35.0 (555.0 to 1)
Guidance Counselors: 45.0 (431.6 to 1)
Current Spending: ($ per student per year):
   Total: $6,253; Instruction: $4,156; Support Services: $1,748
Enrollment, Drop-out Rates and Diploma Recipients by Race/Ethnicity

Category	Total	White	Black	Asian	AIAN	Hisp.
Enrollment (%)	100.0	47.5	43.7	1.3	0.1	7.2
Drop-out Rate (%)	4.8	4.2	5.3	3.5	0.0	9.4
H.S. Diplomas (#)	996	567	393	12	3	21

Wilkes County

Wilkes County Schools
201 W Main St · Wilkesboro, NC 28697-2424
(336) 667-1121 · http://www.wilkes.k12.nc.us/
Grade Span: PK-12; **Agency Type:** 1
Schools: 24
   15 Primary; 4 Middle; 4 High; 1 Other Level
   23 Regular; 0 Special Education; 1 Vocational; 0 Alternative
   0 Magnet; 0 Charter; 12 Title I Eligible; 9 School-wide Title I
Students: 10,337 (50.7% male; 49.2% female)
   Individual Education Program: 1,569 (15.2%);
   English Language Learner: 537 (5.2%); Migrant: 355 (3.4%)
   Eligible for Free Lunch Program: 3,759 (36.4%)
   Eligible for Reduced-Price Lunch Program: 1,010 (9.8%)
Teachers: 679.0 (15.2 to 1)
Librarians/Media Specialists: 24.0 (430.7 to 1)
Guidance Counselors: 31.0 (333.5 to 1)
Current Spending: ($ per student per year):
   Total: $6,489; Instruction: $4,054; Support Services: $1,975

Enrollment, Drop-out Rates and Diploma Recipients by Race/Ethnicity

Category	Total	White	Black	Asian	AIAN	Hisp.
Enrollment (%)	100.0	87.2	6.4	0.7	0.0	5.7
Drop-out Rate (%)	8.3	8.2	6.4	7.7	0.0	14.3
H.S. Diplomas (#)	536	501	28	3	0	4

Enrollment, Drop-out Rates and Diploma Recipients by Race/Ethnicity

Category	Total	White	Black	Asian	AIAN	Hisp.
Enrollment (%)	100.0	93.8	1.5	0.3	0.3	4.1
Drop-out Rate (%)	6.0	5.5	11.1	0.0	0.0	42.9
H.S. Diplomas (#)	146	142	2	0	0	2

Wilson County

Wilson County Schools
117 NE Tarboro St · Wilson, NC 27893-4016
Mailing Address: PO Box 2048 · Wilson, NC 27894-2048
(252) 399-7700 · http://schools.eastnet.ecu.edu/wilson/
Grade Span: PK-12; **Agency Type:** 1
Schools: 23
   13 Primary; 6 Middle; 3 High; 1 Other Level
   22 Regular; 0 Special Education; 0 Vocational; 1 Alternative
   1 Magnet; 0 Charter; 13 Title I Eligible; 13 School-wide Title I
Students: 12,541 (51.4% male; 48.5% female)
   Individual Education Program: 1,419 (11.3%);
   English Language Learner: 587 (4.7%); Migrant: 250 (2.0%)
   Eligible for Free Lunch Program: 5,979 (47.7%)
   Eligible for Reduced-Price Lunch Program: 1,217 (9.7%)
Teachers: 791.0 (15.9 to 1)
Librarians/Media Specialists: 22.0 (570.0 to 1)
Guidance Counselors: 30.0 (418.0 to 1)
Current Spending: ($ per student per year):
   Total: $6,353; Instruction: $4,054; Support Services: $1,912

Enrollment, Drop-out Rates and Diploma Recipients by Race/Ethnicity

Category	Total	White	Black	Asian	AIAN	Hisp.
Enrollment (%)	100.0	39.1	52.9	0.9	0.1	7.1
Drop-out Rate (%)	6.8	6.4	7.3	12.5	0.0	4.3
H.S. Diplomas (#)	594	295	278	6	0	15

Yadkin County

Yadkin County Schools
121 Washington St · Yadkinville, NC 27055-9806
(336) 679-2051 · http://www.yadkin.k12.nc.us/
Grade Span: PK-12; **Agency Type:** 1
Schools: 11
   8 Primary; 0 Middle; 2 High; 1 Other Level
   10 Regular; 0 Special Education; 0 Vocational; 1 Alternative
   0 Magnet; 0 Charter; 5 Title I Eligible; 1 School-wide Title I
Students: 6,045 (51.0% male; 48.9% female)
   Individual Education Program: 1,009 (16.7%);
   English Language Learner: 379 (6.3%); Migrant: 111 (1.8%)
   Eligible for Free Lunch Program: 1,366 (22.6%)
   Eligible for Reduced-Price Lunch Program: 437 (7.2%)
Teachers: 371.0 (16.3 to 1)
Librarians/Media Specialists: 11.0 (549.5 to 1)
Guidance Counselors: 15.0 (403.0 to 1)
Current Spending: ($ per student per year):
   Total: $6,210; Instruction: $3,790; Support Services: $1,965

Enrollment, Drop-out Rates and Diploma Recipients by Race/Ethnicity

Category	Total	White	Black	Asian	AIAN	Hisp.
Enrollment (%)	100.0	82.9	4.4	0.3	0.2	12.2
Drop-out Rate (%)	6.3	5.8	3.0	0.0	0.0	14.9
H.S. Diplomas (#)	304	281	9	1	1	12

Yancey County

Yancey County Schools
100 School Circle · Burnsville, NC 28714-0190
Mailing Address: PO Box 190 · Burnsville, NC 28714-0190
(828) 682-6101 · http://www.yanceync.net/
Grade Span: KG-12; **Agency Type:** 1
Schools: 9
   6 Primary; 2 Middle; 1 High; 0 Other Level
   9 Regular; 0 Special Education; 0 Vocational; 0 Alternative
   0 Magnet; 0 Charter; 8 Title I Eligible; 6 School-wide Title I
Students: 2,548 (51.2% male; 48.7% female)
   Individual Education Program: 434 (17.0%);
   English Language Learner: 110 (4.3%); Migrant: 104 (4.1%)
   Eligible for Free Lunch Program: 827 (32.5%)
   Eligible for Reduced-Price Lunch Program: 288 (11.3%)
Teachers: 161.0 (15.8 to 1)
Librarians/Media Specialists: 8.0 (318.5 to 1)
Guidance Counselors: 8.0 (318.5 to 1)
Current Spending: ($ per student per year):
   Total: $7,283; Instruction: $4,372; Support Services: $2,489

Number of Schools

Rank	Number	District Name	City
1	137	Charlotte-Mecklenburg Schools	Charlotte
2	126	Wake County Schools	Raleigh
3	105	Guilford County Schools	Greensboro
4	85	Cumberland County Schools	Fayetteville
5	69	Forsyth County Schools	Winston Salem
6	52	Gaston County Schools	Gastonia
7	43	Durham Public Schools	Durham
8	41	Buncombe County Schools	Asheville
8	41	Robeson County Schools	Lumberton
10	34	Johnston County Schools	Smithfield
10	34	New Hanover County Schools	Wilmington
10	34	Union County Public Schools	Monroe
13	33	Alamance-Burlington Schools	Burlington
13	33	Onslow County Schools	Jacksonville
13	33	Pitt County Schools	Greenville
16	32	Iredell-Statesville Schools	Statesville
17	31	Wayne County Public Schools	Goldsboro
18	30	Rowan-Salisbury Schools	Salisbury
19	29	Davidson County Schools	Lexington
19	29	Nash-Rocky Mount Schools	Nashville
21	28	Cabarrus County Schools	Concord
21	28	Randolph County Schools	Asheboro
23	25	Burke County Schools	Morganton
23	25	Caldwell County Schools	Lenoir
23	25	Catawba County Schools	Newton
23	25	Harnett County Schools	Lillington
23	25	Rockingham County Schools	Eden
28	24	Wilkes County Schools	Wilkesboro
29	23	Wilson County Schools	Wilson
30	22	Craven County Schools	New Bern
30	22	Moore County Schools	Carthage
30	22	Stanly County Schools	Albemarle
33	21	Henderson County Schools	Hendersonville
33	21	Lincoln County Schools	Lincolnton
35	19	Columbus County Schools	Whiteville
35	19	Lenoir County Public Schools	Kinston
37	18	Richmond County Schools	Hamlet
37	18	Rutherford County Schools	Forest City
37	18	Stokes County Schools	Danbury
40	16	Brunswick County Schools	Bolivia
40	16	Carteret County Public Schools	Beaufort
40	16	Chapel Hill-Carrboro Schools	Chapel Hill
40	16	Sampson County Schools	Clinton
40	16	Surry County Schools	Dobson
45	15	Chatham County Schools	Pittsboro
45	15	Duplin County Schools	Kenansville
45	15	Edgecombe County Schools	Tarboro
45	15	Halifax County Schools	Halifax
45	15	Haywood County Schools	Waynesville
45	15	Pender County Schools	Burgaw
45	15	Scotland County Schools	Laurinburg
45	15	Vance County Schools	Henderson
53	14	Beaufort County Schools	Washington
53	14	Bladen County Schools	Elizabethtown
53	14	Franklin County Schools	Louisburg
53	14	Granville County Schools	Oxford
57	13	Cherokee County Schools	Murphy
58	12	Cleveland County Schools	Shelby
58	12	Lee County Schools	Sanford
58	12	Martin County Schools	Williamston
58	12	Pasquotank County Schools	Elizabeth City
62	11	Hoke County Schools	Raeford
62	11	Mcdowell County Schools	Marion
62	11	Orange County Schools	Hillsborough
62	11	Yadkin County Schools	Yadkinville
66	10	Alexander County Schools	Taylorsville
66	10	Bertie County Schools	Windsor
66	10	Hickory City Schools	Hickory
66	10	Macon County Schools	Franklin
66	10	Montgomery County Schools	Troy
66	10	Northampton County Schools	Jackson
66	10	Person County Schools	Roxboro
73	9	Anson County Schools	Wadesboro
73	9	Avery County Schools	Newland
73	9	Dare County Schools	Manteo
73	9	Davie County Schools	Mocksville
73	9	Kings Mountain District	Kings Mountain
73	9	Transylvania County Schools	Brevard
73	9	Watauga County Schools	Boone
73	9	Yancey County Schools	Burnsville
81	8	Asheboro City Schools	Asheboro
81	8	Asheville City Schools	Asheville
81	8	Currituck County Schools	Currituck
81	8	Mitchell County Schools	Bakersville
85	7	Jackson County Schools	Sylva
85	7	Kannapolis City Schools	Kannapolis
85	7	Shelby City Schools	Shelby
88	6	Ashe County Schools	Jefferson
88	6	Caswell County Schools	Yanceyville
88	6	Lexington City Schools	Lexington
88	6	Madison County Schools	Marshall
88	6	Mooresville City Schools	Mooresville
88	6	Newton Conover City Schools	Newton
88	6	Polk County Schools	Columbus
88	6	Warren County Schools	Warrenton
96	5	Gates County Schools	Gatesville
96	5	Hertford County Schools	Winton
96	5	Swain County Schools	Bryson City
96	5	Washington County Schools	Plymouth
96	5	Whiteville City Schools	Whiteville
101	4	Alleghany County Schools	Sparta
101	4	Clinton City Schools	Clinton
101	4	Edenton/Chowan Schools	Edenton
101	4	Greene County Schools	Snow Hill
101	4	Mount Airy City Schools	Mount Airy
101	4	Pamlico County Schools	Bayboro
101	4	Perquimans County Schools	Hertford
101	4	Roanoke Rapids City Schools	Roanoke Rapids
101	4	Thomasville City Schools	Thomasville
110	3	Camden County Schools	Camden

Number of Teachers

Rank	Number	District Name	City
1	7,350	Charlotte-Mecklenburg Schools	Charlotte
2	7,302	Wake County Schools	Raleigh
3	4,390	Guilford County Schools	Greensboro
4	3,255	Cumberland County Schools	Fayetteville
5	3,251	Forsyth County Schools	Winston Salem
6	2,094	Durham Public Schools	Durham
7	1,932	Gaston County Schools	Gastonia
8	1,785	Johnston County Schools	Smithfield
9	1,684	Union County Public Schools	Monroe
10	1,626	Buncombe County Schools	Asheville
11	1,470	New Hanover County Schools	Wilmington
11	1,470	Robeson County Schools	Lumberton
13	1,457	Alamance-Burlington Schools	Burlington
14	1,440	Pitt County Schools	Greenville
15	1,423	Cabarrus County Schools	Concord
16	1,344	Onslow County Schools	Jacksonville
17	1,323	Rowan-Salisbury Schools	Salisbury
18	1,283	Wayne County Public Schools	Goldsboro
19	1,226	Nash-Rocky Mount Schools	Nashville
20	1,204	Iredell-Statesville Schools	Statesville
21	1,178	Davidson County Schools	Lexington
22	1,140	Randolph County Schools	Asheboro
23	1,064	Harnett County Schools	Lillington
24	1,063	Catawba County Schools	Newton
25	1,038	Burke County Schools	Morganton
26	1,018	Craven County Schools	New Bern
27	948	Rockingham County Schools	Eden
28	848	Caldwell County Schools	Lenoir
29	843	Chapel Hill-Carrboro Schools	Chapel Hill
30	800	Henderson County Schools	Hendersonville
31	791	Wilson County Schools	Wilson
32	790	Lincoln County Schools	Lincolnton
33	778	Moore County Schools	Carthage
34	721	Lenoir County Public Schools	Kinston
35	714	Brunswick County Schools	Bolivia
36	679	Wilkes County Schools	Wilkesboro
37	672	Stanly County Schools	Albemarle
38	670	Cleveland County Schools	Shelby
39	668	Rutherford County Schools	Forest City
40	648	Carteret County Public Schools	Beaufort
41	608	Vance County Schools	Henderson
42	586	Surry County Schools	Dobson
43	583	Duplin County Schools	Kenansville
44	571	Lee County Schools	Sanford
45	560	Richmond County Schools	Hamlet
46	554	Granville County Schools	Oxford
46	554	Scotland County Schools	Laurinburg
48	552	Sampson County Schools	Clinton
49	546	Beaufort County Schools	Washington
50	540	Haywood County Schools	Waynesville
51	536	Franklin County Schools	Louisburg
52	513	Edgecombe County Schools	Tarboro
53	502	Stokes County Schools	Danbury
54	501	Chatham County Schools	Pittsboro
55	487	Pender County Schools	Burgaw
56	472	Orange County Schools	Hillsborough
57	452	Columbus County Schools	Whiteville
58	414	Pasquotank County Schools	Elizabeth City
59	409	Mcdowell County Schools	Marion
60	408	Davie County Schools	Mocksville
61	407	Person County Schools	Roxboro
62	395	Hoke County Schools	Raeford
63	391	Bladen County Schools	Elizabethtown
64	371	Yadkin County Schools	Yadkinville
65	357	Halifax County Schools	Halifax
66	348	Kannapolis City Schools	Kannapolis
67	344	Watauga County Schools	Boone
68	342	Dare County Schools	Manteo
69	339	Montgomery County Schools	Troy
70	335	Alexander County Schools	Taylorsville
71	334	Martin County Schools	Williamston
72	333	Asheville City Schools	Asheville
73	306	Asheboro City Schools	Asheboro
73	306	Hickory City Schools	Hickory
75	302	Kings Mountain District	Kings Mountain
76	293	Macon County Schools	Franklin
77	290	Anson County Schools	Wadesboro
78	281	Cherokee County Schools	Murphy
79	279	Mooresville City Schools	Mooresville
80	268	Hertford County Schools	Winton
81	267	Jackson County Schools	Sylva
81	267	Transylvania County Schools	Brevard
83	258	Shelby City Schools	Shelby
84	251	Ashe County Schools	Jefferson
85	249	Northampton County Schools	Jackson
86	247	Currituck County Schools	Currituck
86	247	Greene County Schools	Snow Hill
88	237	Lexington City Schools	Lexington
89	236	Bertie County Schools	Windsor
89	236	Caswell County Schools	Yanceyville
91	226	Warren County Schools	Warrenton
92	217	Thomasville City Schools	Thomasville
93	213	Madison County Schools	Marshall
94	212	Roanoke Rapids City Schools	Roanoke Rapids
95	205	Whiteville City Schools	Whiteville
96	197	Newton Conover City Schools	Newton
97	196	Clinton City Schools	Clinton
98	194	Avery County Schools	Newland
99	192	Polk County Schools	Columbus
99	192	Washington County Schools	Plymouth
101	185	Edenton/Chowan Schools	Edenton
102	166	Mitchell County Schools	Bakersville
103	161	Yancey County Schools	Burnsville
104	157	Gates County Schools	Gatesville
105	149	Pamlico County Schools	Bayboro
106	143	Mount Airy City Schools	Mount Airy
107	142	Swain County Schools	Bryson City
108	131	Perquimans County Schools	Hertford
109	125	Alleghany County Schools	Sparta
110	101	Camden County Schools	Camden

Number of Students

Rank	Number	District Name	City
1	114,071	Charlotte-Mecklenburg Schools	Charlotte
2	109,424	Wake County Schools	Raleigh
3	66,971	Guilford County Schools	Greensboro
4	53,159	Cumberland County Schools	Fayetteville
5	47,788	Forsyth County Schools	Winston Salem
6	31,288	Gaston County Schools	Gastonia
7	30,889	Durham Public Schools	Durham
8	26,993	Union County Public Schools	Monroe
9	24,946	Johnston County Schools	Smithfield
10	24,828	Buncombe County Schools	Asheville
11	24,352	Robeson County Schools	Lumberton
12	22,268	New Hanover County Schools	Wilmington
13	21,860	Cabarrus County Schools	Concord
14	21,788	Alamance-Burlington Schools	Burlington
15	21,745	Onslow County Schools	Jacksonville
16	21,412	Pitt County Schools	Greenville
17	20,907	Rowan-Salisbury Schools	Salisbury
18	19,549	Davidson County Schools	Lexington
19	19,424	Wayne County Public Schools	Goldsboro
20	19,098	Iredell-Statesville Schools	Statesville
21	18,526	Nash-Rocky Mount Schools	Nashville
22	18,211	Randolph County Schools	Asheboro
23	16,914	Harnett County Schools	Lillington
24	16,635	Catawba County Schools	Newton
25	14,803	Burke County Schools	Morganton
26	14,799	Rockingham County Schools	Eden
27	14,597	Craven County Schools	New Bern
28	12,903	Caldwell County Schools	Lenoir
29	12,541	Wilson County Schools	Wilson
30	12,288	Henderson County Schools	Hendersonville
31	11,778	Moore County Schools	Carthage
32	11,372	Lincoln County Schools	Lincolnton
33	10,914	Brunswick County Schools	Bolivia
34	10,644	Chapel Hill-Carrboro Schools	Chapel Hill
35	10,354	Lenoir County Public Schools	Kinston
36	10,337	Wilkes County Schools	Wilkesboro
37	9,993	Stanly County Schools	Albemarle
38	9,973	Cleveland County Schools	Shelby
39	9,960	Rutherford County Schools	Forest City
40	9,139	Lee County Schools	Sanford
41	8,873	Duplin County Schools	Kenansville
42	8,688	Surry County Schools	Dobson
43	8,680	Granville County Schools	Oxford
44	8,587	Vance County Schools	Henderson
45	8,324	Carteret County Public Schools	Beaufort
46	8,296	Richmond County Schools	Hamlet
47	8,177	Sampson County Schools	Clinton
48	8,015	Franklin County Schools	Louisburg

49	7,943	Haywood County Schools	Waynesville
50	7,826	Edgecombe County Schools	Tarboro
51	7,538	Stokes County Schools	Danbury
52	7,443	Beaufort County Schools	Washington
53	7,291	Chatham County Schools	Pittsboro
54	7,125	Columbus County Schools	Whiteville
55	7,114	Scotland County Schools	Laurinburg
56	6,984	Pender County Schools	Burgaw
57	6,568	Hoke County Schools	Raeford
58	6,557	Orange County Schools	Hillsborough
59	6,472	Mcdowell County Schools	Marion
60	6,058	Davie County Schools	Mocksville
61	6,045	Yadkin County Schools	Yadkinville
62	6,012	Pasquotank County Schools	Elizabeth City
63	5,986	Bladen County Schools	Elizabethtown
64	5,779	Person County Schools	Roxboro
65	5,685	Halifax County Schools	Halifax
66	5,598	Alexander County Schools	Taylorsville
67	4,804	Dare County Schools	Manteo
68	4,691	Kings Mountain District	Kings Mountain
69	4,687	Watauga County Schools	Boone
70	4,608	Montgomery County Schools	Troy
71	4,591	Hickory City Schools	Hickory
72	4,573	Martin County Schools	Williamston
73	4,525	Kannapolis City Schools	Kannapolis
74	4,447	Asheboro City Schools	Asheboro
75	4,441	Anson County Schools	Wadesboro
76	4,283	Mooresville City Schools	Mooresville
77	4,139	Macon County Schools	Franklin
78	3,859	Asheville City Schools	Asheville
79	3,820	Cherokee County Schools	Murphy
80	3,786	Transylvania County Schools	Brevard
81	3,755	Hertford County Schools	Winton
82	3,722	Jackson County Schools	Sylva
83	3,663	Currituck County Schools	Currituck
84	3,491	Caswell County Schools	Yanceyville
85	3,474	Bertie County Schools	Windsor
86	3,405	Northampton County Schools	Jackson
87	3,262	Lexington City Schools	Lexington
88	3,251	Ashe County Schools	Jefferson
89	3,250	Greene County Schools	Snow Hill
90	3,172	Shelby City Schools	Shelby
91	3,120	Warren County Schools	Warrenton
92	3,008	Roanoke Rapids City Schools	Roanoke Rapids
93	2,918	Newton Conover City Schools	Newton
94	2,847	Clinton City Schools	Clinton
95	2,711	Whiteville City Schools	Whiteville
96	2,604	Thomasville City Schools	Thomasville
97	2,580	Madison County Schools	Marshall
98	2,574	Edenton/Chowan Schools	Edenton
99	2,548	Yancey County Schools	Burnsville
100	2,519	Polk County Schools	Columbus
101	2,406	Avery County Schools	Newland
102	2,335	Mitchell County Schools	Bakersville
103	2,281	Washington County Schools	Plymouth
104	1,968	Gates County Schools	Gatesville
105	1,904	Mount Airy City Schools	Mount Airy
106	1,854	Swain County Schools	Bryson City
107	1,829	Perquimans County Schools	Hertford
108	1,775	Pamlico County Schools	Bayboro
109	1,591	Camden County Schools	Camden
110	1,541	Alleghany County Schools	Sparta

Male Students

Rank	Percent	District Name	City
1	53.4	Madison County Schools	Marshall
2	52.8	Greene County Schools	Snow Hill
3	52.7	Pamlico County Schools	Bayboro
4	52.7	Mitchell County Schools	Bakersville
5	52.5	Watauga County Schools	Boone
6	52.5	Chatham County Schools	Pittsboro
7	52.4	Perquimans County Schools	Hertford
8	52.3	Thomasville City Schools	Thomasville
9	52.2	Stanly County Schools	Albemarle
10	52.2	Swain County Schools	Bryson City
11	52.2	Kannapolis City Schools	Kannapolis
12	52.1	Pender County Schools	Burgaw
13	52.0	Sampson County Schools	Clinton
14	52.0	Northampton County Schools	Jackson
15	51.9	Cherokee County Schools	Murphy
16	51.9	Randolph County Schools	Asheboro
17	51.9	Bladen County Schools	Elizabethtown
18	51.9	Alexander County Schools	Taylorsville
19	51.9	Washington County Schools	Plymouth
20	51.9	Carteret County Public Schools	Beaufort
21	51.9	Vance County Schools	Henderson
22	51.8	Lenoir County Public Schools	Kinston
23	51.8	Franklin County Schools	Louisburg
24	51.8	Henderson County Schools	Hendersonville
25	51.8	Caswell County Schools	Yanceyville
26	51.7	Rockingham County Schools	Eden
27	51.7	Dare County Schools	Manteo
28	51.7	Jackson County Schools	Sylva
29	51.7	Warren County Schools	Warrenton
30	51.7	Avery County Schools	Newland
31	51.6	Halifax County Schools	Halifax
32	51.6	Chapel Hill-Carrboro Schools	Chapel Hill
33	51.6	Shelby City Schools	Shelby
34	51.5	Lexington City Schools	Lexington
35	51.5	Edenton/Chowan Schools	Edenton
36	51.5	Surry County Schools	Dobson
37	51.5	Bertie County Schools	Windsor
38	51.5	Ashe County Schools	Jefferson
39	51.5	Forsyth County Schools	Winston Salem
40	51.5	Gaston County Schools	Gastonia
41	51.4	Johnston County Schools	Smithfield
42	51.4	Mcdowell County Schools	Marion
43	51.4	Rowan-Salisbury Schools	Salisbury
44	51.4	Beaufort County Schools	Washington
45	51.4	Martin County Schools	Williamston
46	51.4	Wilson County Schools	Wilson
47	51.4	Stokes County Schools	Danbury
48	51.3	Lincoln County Schools	Lincolnton
49	51.3	Camden County Schools	Camden
50	51.3	Burke County Schools	Morganton
51	51.3	Union County Public Schools	Monroe
52	51.3	Orange County Schools	Hillsborough
53	51.3	Wayne County Public Schools	Goldsboro
54	51.3	Cleveland County Schools	Shelby
55	51.2	Iredell-Statesville Schools	Statesville
56	51.2	Catawba County Schools	Newton
57	51.2	Newton Conover City Schools	Newton
58	51.2	Durham Public Schools	Durham
59	51.2	Yancey County Schools	Burnsville
60	51.2	Granville County Schools	Oxford
61	51.2	Robeson County Schools	Lumberton
62	51.2	Nash-Rocky Mount Schools	Nashville
63	51.2	Buncombe County Schools	Asheville
64	51.2	Pitt County Schools	Greenville
65	51.2	Brunswick County Schools	Bolivia
66	51.1	Lee County Schools	Sanford
67	51.1	Harnett County Schools	Lillington
68	51.1	Davie County Schools	Mocksville
69	51.0	Yadkin County Schools	Yadkinville
70	51.0	Charlotte-Mecklenburg Schools	Charlotte
71	51.0	Montgomery County Schools	Troy
72	51.0	Transylvania County Schools	Brevard
73	51.0	Wake County Schools	Raleigh
74	51.0	New Hanover County Schools	Wilmington
75	51.0	Pasquotank County Schools	Elizabeth City
76	51.0	Asheville City Schools	Asheville
77	51.0	Cumberland County Schools	Fayetteville
78	50.9	Richmond County Schools	Hamlet
79	50.9	Cabarrus County Schools	Concord
80	50.9	Caldwell County Schools	Lenoir
81	50.9	Rutherford County Schools	Forest City
82	50.9	Columbus County Schools	Whiteville
83	50.9	Macon County Schools	Franklin
84	50.9	Guilford County Schools	Greensboro
85	50.9	Haywood County Schools	Waynesville
86	50.8	Davidson County Schools	Lexington
87	50.8	Duplin County Schools	Kenansville
88	50.8	Whiteville City Schools	Whiteville
89	50.8	Hoke County Schools	Raeford
90	50.8	Currituck County Schools	Currituck
91	50.8	Alamance-Burlington Schools	Burlington
92	50.7	Moore County Schools	Carthage
93	50.7	Craven County Schools	New Bern
94	50.7	Edgecombe County Schools	Tarboro
95	50.7	Wilkes County Schools	Wilkesboro
96	50.7	Scotland County Schools	Laurinburg
97	50.7	Gates County Schools	Gatesville
98	50.6	Polk County Schools	Columbus
99	50.6	Person County Schools	Roxboro
100	50.6	Onslow County Schools	Jacksonville
101	50.5	Anson County Schools	Wadesboro
102	50.3	Hertford County Schools	Winton
103	50.2	Mooresville City Schools	Mooresville
104	50.2	Roanoke Rapids City Schools	Roanoke Rapids
105	50.2	Hickory City Schools	Hickory
106	50.1	Asheboro City Schools	Asheboro
107	49.9	Kings Mountain District	Kings Mountain
108	49.9	Mount Airy City Schools	Mount Airy
109	49.2	Alleghany County Schools	Sparta
110	49.1	Clinton City Schools	Clinton

Female Students

Rank	Percent	District Name	City
1	50.8	Clinton City Schools	Clinton
2	50.7	Alleghany County Schools	Sparta
3	50.0	Mount Airy City Schools	Mount Airy
4	50.0	Kings Mountain District	Kings Mountain
5	49.8	Asheboro City Schools	Asheboro
6	49.7	Hickory City Schools	Hickory
7	49.7	Roanoke Rapids City Schools	Roanoke Rapids
8	49.7	Mooresville City Schools	Mooresville
9	49.6	Hertford County Schools	Winton
10	49.4	Anson County Schools	Wadesboro
11	49.3	Onslow County Schools	Jacksonville
12	49.3	Person County Schools	Roxboro
13	49.3	Polk County Schools	Columbus
14	49.2	Gates County Schools	Gatesville
15	49.2	Scotland County Schools	Laurinburg
16	49.2	Wilkes County Schools	Wilkesboro
17	49.2	Edgecombe County Schools	Tarboro
18	49.2	Craven County Schools	New Bern
19	49.2	Moore County Schools	Carthage
20	49.1	Alamance-Burlington Schools	Burlington
21	49.1	Currituck County Schools	Currituck
22	49.1	Hoke County Schools	Raeford
23	49.1	Whiteville City Schools	Whiteville
24	49.1	Duplin County Schools	Kenansville
25	49.1	Davidson County Schools	Lexington
26	49.0	Haywood County Schools	Waynesville
27	49.0	Guilford County Schools	Greensboro
28	49.0	Macon County Schools	Franklin
29	49.0	Columbus County Schools	Whiteville
30	49.0	Rutherford County Schools	Forest City
31	49.0	Caldwell County Schools	Lenoir
32	49.0	Cabarrus County Schools	Concord
33	49.0	Richmond County Schools	Hamlet
34	48.9	Cumberland County Schools	Fayetteville
35	48.9	Asheville City Schools	Asheville
36	48.9	Pasquotank County Schools	Elizabeth City
37	48.9	New Hanover County Schools	Wilmington
38	48.9	Wake County Schools	Raleigh
39	48.9	Transylvania County Schools	Brevard
40	48.9	Montgomery County Schools	Troy
41	48.9	Charlotte-Mecklenburg Schools	Charlotte
42	48.9	Yadkin County Schools	Yadkinville
43	48.8	Davie County Schools	Mocksville
44	48.8	Harnett County Schools	Lillington
45	48.8	Lee County Schools	Sanford
46	48.7	Brunswick County Schools	Bolivia
47	48.7	Pitt County Schools	Greenville
48	48.7	Buncombe County Schools	Asheville
49	48.7	Nash-Rocky Mount Schools	Nashville
50	48.7	Robeson County Schools	Lumberton
51	48.7	Granville County Schools	Oxford
52	48.7	Yancey County Schools	Burnsville
53	48.7	Durham Public Schools	Durham
54	48.7	Newton Conover City Schools	Newton
55	48.7	Catawba County Schools	Newton
56	48.7	Iredell-Statesville Schools	Statesville
57	48.6	Cleveland County Schools	Shelby
58	48.6	Wayne County Public Schools	Goldsboro
59	48.6	Orange County Schools	Hillsborough
60	48.6	Union County Public Schools	Monroe
61	48.6	Burke County Schools	Morganton
62	48.6	Camden County Schools	Camden
63	48.6	Lincoln County Schools	Lincolnton
64	48.5	Stokes County Schools	Danbury
65	48.5	Wilson County Schools	Wilson
66	48.5	Martin County Schools	Williamston
67	48.5	Beaufort County Schools	Washington
68	48.5	Rowan-Salisbury Schools	Salisbury
69	48.5	Mcdowell County Schools	Marion
70	48.5	Johnston County Schools	Smithfield
71	48.4	Gaston County Schools	Gastonia
72	48.4	Forsyth County Schools	Winston Salem
73	48.4	Ashe County Schools	Jefferson
74	48.4	Bertie County Schools	Windsor
75	48.4	Surry County Schools	Dobson
76	48.4	Edenton/Chowan Schools	Edenton
77	48.4	Lexington City Schools	Lexington
78	48.3	Shelby City Schools	Shelby
79	48.3	Chapel Hill-Carrboro Schools	Chapel Hill
80	48.3	Halifax County Schools	Halifax
81	48.2	Avery County Schools	Newland
82	48.2	Warren County Schools	Warrenton
83	48.2	Jackson County Schools	Sylva
84	48.2	Dare County Schools	Manteo
85	48.2	Rockingham County Schools	Eden
86	48.1	Caswell County Schools	Yanceyville
87	48.1	Henderson County Schools	Hendersonville
88	48.1	Franklin County Schools	Louisburg
89	48.1	Lenoir County Public Schools	Kinston
90	48.0	Vance County Schools	Henderson
91	48.0	Carteret County Public Schools	Beaufort
92	48.0	Washington County Schools	Plymouth
93	48.0	Alexander County Schools	Taylorsville
94	48.0	Bladen County Schools	Elizabethtown
95	48.0	Randolph County Schools	Asheboro
96	48.0	Cherokee County Schools	Murphy
97	47.9	Northampton County Schools	Jackson
98	47.9	Sampson County Schools	Clinton

99	47.8	Pender County Schools	Burgaw
100	47.7	Kannapolis City Schools	Kannapolis
101	47.7	Swain County Schools	Bryson City
102	47.7	Stanly County Schools	Albemarle
103	47.6	Thomasville City Schools	Thomasville
104	47.5	Perquimans County Schools	Hertford
105	47.4	Chatham County Schools	Pittsboro
106	47.4	Watauga County Schools	Boone
107	47.2	Mitchell County Schools	Bakersville
108	47.2	Pamlico County Schools	Bayboro
109	47.1	Greene County Schools	Snow Hill
110	46.5	Madison County Schools	Marshall

Individual Education Program Students

Rank	Percent	District Name	City
1	21.2	Pamlico County Schools	Bayboro
2	20.6	Gates County Schools	Gatesville
3	20.1	Alleghany County Schools	Sparta
4	19.2	Anson County Schools	Wadesboro
5	18.7	Orange County Schools	Hillsborough
6	18.5	Washington County Schools	Plymouth
7	18.3	Stanly County Schools	Albemarle
7	18.3	Swain County Schools	Bryson City
9	18.2	Mount Airy City Schools	Mount Airy
10	17.6	Robeson County Schools	Lumberton
11	17.5	Carteret County Public Schools	Beaufort
12	17.0	Avery County Schools	Newland
12	17.0	Mitchell County Schools	Bakersville
12	17.0	Yancey County Schools	Burnsville
15	16.9	Surry County Schools	Dobson
16	16.8	Warren County Schools	Warrenton
17	16.7	Beaufort County Schools	Washington
17	16.7	Watauga County Schools	Boone
17	16.7	Yadkin County Schools	Yadkinville
20	16.6	Polk County Schools	Columbus
21	16.5	Macon County Schools	Franklin
21	16.5	Person County Schools	Roxboro
21	16.5	Shelby City Schools	Shelby
24	16.4	Halifax County Schools	Halifax
25	16.3	Cherokee County Schools	Murphy
25	16.3	Perquimans County Schools	Hertford
27	16.2	Jackson County Schools	Sylva
27	16.2	Madison County Schools	Marshall
29	16.1	Burke County Schools	Morganton
29	16.1	Kannapolis City Schools	Kannapolis
31	16.0	Guilford County Schools	Greensboro
31	16.0	Johnston County Schools	Smithfield
33	15.9	Stokes County Schools	Danbury
34	15.8	Hertford County Schools	Winton
34	15.8	Mcdowell County Schools	Marion
36	15.7	Scotland County Schools	Laurinburg
37	15.6	Brunswick County Schools	Bolivia
37	15.6	Lexington City Schools	Lexington
37	15.6	Rockingham County Schools	Eden
40	15.5	Ashe County Schools	Jefferson
41	15.2	Wilkes County Schools	Wilkesboro
42	15.1	Currituck County Schools	Currituck
42	15.1	Greene County Schools	Snow Hill
42	15.1	Harnett County Schools	Lillington
42	15.1	Wayne County Public Schools	Goldsboro
46	15.0	Cleveland County Schools	Shelby
46	15.0	Lincoln County Schools	Lincolnton
46	15.0	Wake County Schools	Raleigh
49	14.9	Alamance-Burlington Schools	Burlington
49	14.9	Haywood County Schools	Waynesville
49	14.9	Lenoir County Public Schools	Kinston
52	14.8	Bertie County Schools	Windsor
53	14.7	Hoke County Schools	Raeford
53	14.7	Rutherford County Schools	Forest City
55	14.6	Catawba County Schools	Newton
55	14.6	Nash-Rocky Mount Schools	Nashville
57	14.5	Forsyth County Schools	Winston Salem
57	14.5	Whiteville City Schools	Whiteville
59	14.4	Davie County Schools	Mocksville
60	14.3	Caswell County Schools	Yanceyville
61	14.2	Cabarrus County Schools	Concord
61	14.2	Pitt County Schools	Greenville
63	14.1	Martin County Schools	Williamston
63	14.1	Onslow County Schools	Jacksonville
65	14.0	New Hanover County Schools	Wilmington
65	14.0	Rowan-Salisbury Schools	Salisbury
65	14.0	Sampson County Schools	Clinton
68	13.8	Pasquotank County Schools	Elizabeth City
69	13.7	Alexander County Schools	Taylorsville
69	13.7	Buncombe County Schools	Asheville
69	13.7	Columbus County Schools	Whiteville
69	13.7	Cumberland County Schools	Fayetteville
73	13.6	Vance County Schools	Henderson
74	13.5	Newton Conover City Schools	Newton
75	13.4	Henderson County Schools	Hendersonville
75	13.4	Moore County Schools	Carthage
77	13.3	Asheboro City Schools	Asheboro
77	13.3	Montgomery County Schools	Troy
79	13.2	Pender County Schools	Burgaw
80	13.1	Craven County Schools	New Bern
80	13.1	Richmond County Schools	Hamlet
82	13.0	Iredell-Statesville Schools	Statesville
83	12.9	Camden County Schools	Camden
83	12.9	Durham Public Schools	Durham
83	12.9	Mooresville City Schools	Mooresville
83	12.9	Randolph County Schools	Asheboro
87	12.8	Chatham County Schools	Pittsboro
88	12.7	Roanoke Rapids City Schools	Roanoke Rapids
89	12.6	Edenton/Chowan Schools	Edenton
89	12.6	Gaston County Schools	Gastonia
91	12.5	Asheville City Schools	Asheville
91	12.5	Chapel Hill-Carrboro Schools	Chapel Hill
93	12.4	Northampton County Schools	Jackson
94	12.3	Davidson County Schools	Lexington
95	12.2	Bladen County Schools	Elizabethtown
95	12.2	Edgecombe County Schools	Tarboro
95	12.2	Granville County Schools	Oxford
95	12.2	Union County Public Schools	Monroe
99	12.1	Lee County Schools	Sanford
99	12.1	Transylvania County Schools	Brevard
101	12.0	Charlotte-Mecklenburg Schools	Charlotte
101	12.0	Hickory City Schools	Hickory
103	11.8	Caldwell County Schools	Lenoir
104	11.4	Dare County Schools	Manteo
105	11.3	Duplin County Schools	Kenansville
105	11.3	Wilson County Schools	Wilson
107	11.2	Kings Mountain District	Kings Mountain
108	10.8	Clinton City Schools	Clinton
109	10.7	Franklin County Schools	Louisburg
109	10.7	Thomasville City Schools	Thomasville

English Language Learner Students

Rank	Percent	District Name	City
1	19.0	Montgomery County Schools	Troy
2	18.1	Asheboro City Schools	Asheboro
3	17.9	Duplin County Schools	Kenansville
4	16.2	Kannapolis City Schools	Kannapolis
5	15.0	Hickory City Schools	Hickory
6	12.8	Lexington City Schools	Lexington
7	12.0	Lee County Schools	Sanford
8	11.6	Chatham County Schools	Pittsboro
9	10.9	Newton Conover City Schools	Newton
9	10.9	Sampson County Schools	Clinton
11	9.7	Alamance-Burlington Schools	Burlington
12	9.6	Greene County Schools	Snow Hill
12	9.6	Thomasville City Schools	Thomasville
14	8.5	Catawba County Schools	Newton
15	8.3	Burke County Schools	Morganton
16	8.2	Mount Airy City Schools	Mount Airy
17	8.0	Henderson County Schools	Hendersonville
18	7.9	Surry County Schools	Dobson
19	7.7	Chapel Hill-Carrboro Schools	Chapel Hill
20	7.3	Durham Public Schools	Durham
21	7.2	Alexander County Schools	Taylorsville
22	7.0	Johnston County Schools	Smithfield
22	7.0	Wake County Schools	Raleigh
24	6.6	Forsyth County Schools	Winston Salem
25	6.5	Rowan-Salisbury Schools	Salisbury
26	6.3	Yadkin County Schools	Yadkinville
27	6.2	Alleghany County Schools	Sparta
27	6.2	Lincoln County Schools	Lincolnton
29	5.8	Guilford County Schools	Greensboro
30	5.6	Mcdowell County Schools	Marion
31	5.4	Wayne County Public Schools	Goldsboro
32	5.3	Pender County Schools	Burgaw
32	5.3	Stanly County Schools	Albemarle
34	5.2	Wilkes County Schools	Wilkesboro
35	5.1	Cabarrus County Schools	Concord
36	5.0	Clinton City Schools	Clinton
37	4.9	Rockingham County Schools	Eden
38	4.8	Harnett County Schools	Lillington
39	4.7	Randolph County Schools	Asheboro
39	4.7	Wilson County Schools	Wilson
41	4.4	Granville County Schools	Oxford
41	4.4	Iredell-Statesville Schools	Statesville
41	4.4	Mitchell County Schools	Bakersville
44	4.3	Bladen County Schools	Elizabethtown
44	4.3	Gaston County Schools	Gastonia
44	4.3	Hoke County Schools	Raeford
44	4.3	Robeson County Schools	Lumberton
44	4.3	Yancey County Schools	Burnsville
49	4.0	Nash-Rocky Mount Schools	Nashville
50	3.9	Buncombe County Schools	Asheville
50	3.9	Davie County Schools	Mocksville
50	3.9	Polk County Schools	Columbus
53	3.8	Edgecombe County Schools	Tarboro
53	3.8	Moore County Schools	Carthage
55	3.7	Beaufort County Schools	Washington
56	3.6	Vance County Schools	Henderson
57	3.4	Franklin County Schools	Louisburg
58	3.2	Union County Public Schools	Monroe
59	3.0	Brunswick County Schools	Bolivia
59	3.0	Caldwell County Schools	Lenoir
61	2.9	Orange County Schools	Hillsborough
62	2.8	Macon County Schools	Franklin
62	2.8	Pitt County Schools	Greenville
64	2.7	Avery County Schools	Newland
65	2.6	Ashe County Schools	Jefferson
66	2.5	New Hanover County Schools	Wilmington
67	2.4	Richmond County Schools	Hamlet
68	2.3	Columbus County Schools	Whiteville
69	2.2	Dare County Schools	Manteo
69	2.2	Lenoir County Public Schools	Kinston
71	2.0	Asheville City Schools	Asheville
72	1.7	Craven County Schools	New Bern
72	1.7	Jackson County Schools	Sylva
72	1.7	Rutherford County Schools	Forest City
75	1.6	Madison County Schools	Marshall
75	1.6	Onslow County Schools	Jacksonville
75	1.6	Person County Schools	Roxboro
78	1.5	Caswell County Schools	Yanceyville
78	1.5	Cleveland County Schools	Shelby
78	1.5	Haywood County Schools	Waynesville
78	1.5	Mooresville City Schools	Mooresville
78	1.5	Transylvania County Schools	Brevard
78	1.5	Whiteville City Schools	Whiteville
84	1.4	Cumberland County Schools	Fayetteville
85	1.3	Anson County Schools	Wadesboro
86	1.2	Edenton/Chowan Schools	Edenton
86	1.2	Warren County Schools	Warrenton
88	1.1	Carteret County Public Schools	Beaufort
88	1.1	Watauga County Schools	Boone
90	1.0	Pamlico County Schools	Bayboro
90	1.0	Stokes County Schools	Danbury
90	1.0	Swain County Schools	Bryson City
93	0.9	Northampton County Schools	Jackson
93	0.9	Shelby City Schools	Shelby
93	0.9	Washington County Schools	Plymouth
96	0.8	Gates County Schools	Gatesville
96	0.8	Roanoke Rapids City Schools	Roanoke Rapids
96	0.8	Scotland County Schools	Laurinburg
99	0.7	Kings Mountain District	Kings Mountain
100	0.6	Pasquotank County Schools	Elizabeth City
101	0.5	Davidson County Schools	Lexington
101	0.5	Halifax County Schools	Halifax
103	0.4	Charlotte-Mecklenburg Schools	Charlotte
103	0.4	Currituck County Schools	Currituck
103	0.4	Hertford County Schools	Winton
103	0.4	Martin County Schools	Williamston
107	0.3	Bertie County Schools	Windsor
108	0.1	Camden County Schools	Camden
108	0.1	Cherokee County Schools	Murphy
110	0.0	Perquimans County Schools	Hertford

Migrant Students

Rank	Percent	District Name	City
1	10.5	Pender County Schools	Burgaw
2	8.9	Columbus County Schools	Whiteville
3	8.7	Chatham County Schools	Pittsboro
4	8.6	Alleghany County Schools	Sparta
5	8.0	Sampson County Schools	Clinton
6	6.4	Montgomery County Schools	Troy
7	6.3	Bladen County Schools	Elizabethtown
8	5.3	Edgecombe County Schools	Tarboro
8	5.3	Lee County Schools	Sanford
10	5.0	Northampton County Schools	Jackson
11	4.2	Duplin County Schools	Kenansville
12	4.1	Yancey County Schools	Burnsville
13	3.9	Hoke County Schools	Raeford
14	3.8	Surry County Schools	Dobson
15	3.7	Rockingham County Schools	Eden
16	3.6	Johnston County Schools	Smithfield
17	3.4	Ashe County Schools	Jefferson
17	3.4	Henderson County Schools	Hendersonville
17	3.4	Lenoir County Public Schools	Kinston
17	3.4	Wilkes County Schools	Wilkesboro
21	3.2	Greene County Schools	Snow Hill
22	3.1	Harnett County Schools	Lillington
23	3.0	Alamance-Burlington Schools	Burlington
23	3.0	Rowan-Salisbury Schools	Salisbury
25	2.9	Halifax County Schools	Halifax
26	2.8	Robeson County Schools	Lumberton
27	2.5	Nash-Rocky Mount Schools	Nashville
28	2.4	Whiteville City Schools	Whiteville
29	2.2	Brunswick County Schools	Bolivia
30	2.0	Pitt County Schools	Greenville
30	2.0	Randolph County Schools	Asheboro
30	2.0	Wilson County Schools	Wilson
33	1.8	Franklin County Schools	Louisburg
33	1.8	Yadkin County Schools	Yadkinville
35	1.7	Asheboro City Schools	Asheboro

35	1.7	Haywood County Schools	Waynesville
37	1.6	Granville County Schools	Oxford
38	1.5	Mitchell County Schools	Bakersville
38	1.5	Moore County Schools	Carthage
40	1.3	Beaufort County Schools	Washington
41	1.2	Orange County Schools	Hillsborough
42	1.0	Vance County Schools	Henderson
43	0.9	Jackson County Schools	Sylva
43	0.9	Washington County Schools	Plymouth
45	0.8	Bertie County Schools	Windsor
46	0.6	Buncombe County Schools	Asheville
47	0.5	Wake County Schools	Raleigh
48	0.2	Cabarrus County Schools	Concord
49	0.0	Alexander County Schools	Taylorsville
49	0.0	Anson County Schools	Wadesboro
49	0.0	Asheville City Schools	Asheville
49	0.0	Avery County Schools	Newland
49	0.0	Burke County Schools	Morganton
49	0.0	Caldwell County Schools	Lenoir
49	0.0	Camden County Schools	Camden
49	0.0	Carteret County Public Schools	Beaufort
49	0.0	Caswell County Schools	Yanceyville
49	0.0	Catawba County Schools	Newton
49	0.0	Chapel Hill-Carrboro Schools	Chapel Hill
49	0.0	Charlotte-Mecklenburg Schools	Charlotte
49	0.0	Cherokee County Schools	Murphy
49	0.0	Cleveland County Schools	Shelby
49	0.0	Clinton City Schools	Clinton
49	0.0	Craven County Schools	New Bern
49	0.0	Cumberland County Schools	Fayetteville
49	0.0	Currituck County Schools	Currituck
49	0.0	Dare County Schools	Manteo
49	0.0	Davidson County Schools	Lexington
49	0.0	Davie County Schools	Mocksville
49	0.0	Durham Public Schools	Durham
49	0.0	Edenton/Chowan Schools	Edenton
49	0.0	Forsyth County Schools	Winston Salem
49	0.0	Gaston County Schools	Gastonia
49	0.0	Gates County Schools	Gatesville
49	0.0	Guilford County Schools	Greensboro
49	0.0	Hertford County Schools	Winton
49	0.0	Hickory City Schools	Hickory
49	0.0	Iredell-Statesville Schools	Statesville
49	0.0	Kannapolis City Schools	Kannapolis
49	0.0	Kings Mountain District	Kings Mountain
49	0.0	Lexington City Schools	Lexington
49	0.0	Lincoln County Schools	Lincolnton
49	0.0	Macon County Schools	Franklin
49	0.0	Madison County Schools	Marshall
49	0.0	Martin County Schools	Williamston
49	0.0	Mcdowell County Schools	Marion
49	0.0	Mooresville City Schools	Mooresville
49	0.0	Mount Airy City Schools	Mount Airy
49	0.0	New Hanover County Schools	Wilmington
49	0.0	Newton Conover City Schools	Newton
49	0.0	Onslow County Schools	Jacksonville
49	0.0	Pamlico County Schools	Bayboro
49	0.0	Pasquotank County Schools	Elizabeth City
49	0.0	Perquimans County Schools	Hertford
49	0.0	Person County Schools	Roxboro
49	0.0	Polk County Schools	Columbus
49	0.0	Richmond County Schools	Hamlet
49	0.0	Roanoke Rapids City Schools	Roanoke Rapids
49	0.0	Rutherford County Schools	Forest City
49	0.0	Scotland County Schools	Laurinburg
49	0.0	Shelby City Schools	Shelby
49	0.0	Stanly County Schools	Albemarle
49	0.0	Stokes County Schools	Danbury
49	0.0	Swain County Schools	Bryson City
49	0.0	Thomasville City Schools	Thomasville
49	0.0	Transylvania County Schools	Brevard
49	0.0	Union County Public Schools	Monroe
49	0.0	Warren County Schools	Warrenton
49	0.0	Watauga County Schools	Boone
49	0.0	Wayne County Public Schools	Goldsboro

Students Eligible for Free Lunch

Rank	Percent	District Name	City
1	74.8	Halifax County Schools	Halifax
2	72.1	Thomasville City Schools	Thomasville
2	72.1	Washington County Schools	Plymouth
4	70.3	Bertie County Schools	Windsor
5	69.7	Robeson County Schools	Lumberton
6	69.5	Hertford County Schools	Winton
7	69.3	Lexington City Schools	Lexington
8	66.0	Northampton County Schools	Jackson
9	61.6	Vance County Schools	Henderson
10	59.6	Anson County Schools	Wadesboro
10	59.6	Scotland County Schools	Laurinburg
12	59.1	Columbus County Schools	Whiteville
13	58.4	Bladen County Schools	Elizabethtown
13	58.4	Greene County Schools	Snow Hill
15	56.7	Duplin County Schools	Kenansville
16	56.6	Sampson County Schools	Clinton
16	56.6	Warren County Schools	Warrenton
18	54.8	Beaufort County Schools	Washington
19	54.7	Martin County Schools	Williamston
20	54.6	Edgecombe County Schools	Tarboro
21	53.8	Whiteville City Schools	Whiteville
22	52.7	Clinton City Schools	Clinton
23	51.8	Richmond County Schools	Hamlet
24	51.0	Shelby City Schools	Shelby
25	50.5	Lenoir County Public Schools	Kinston
26	49.2	Kannapolis City Schools	Kannapolis
27	48.9	Hoke County Schools	Raeford
28	48.6	Montgomery County Schools	Troy
29	47.7	Wilson County Schools	Wilson
30	46.8	Pasquotank County Schools	Elizabeth City
31	45.4	Nash-Rocky Mount Schools	Nashville
32	44.9	Brunswick County Schools	Bolivia
33	44.8	Hickory City Schools	Hickory
34	44.6	Pitt County Schools	Greenville
35	44.3	Asheboro City Schools	Asheboro
36	44.1	Perquimans County Schools	Hertford
37	43.6	Franklin County Schools	Louisburg
38	43.3	Pamlico County Schools	Bayboro
39	43.1	Rutherford County Schools	Forest City
40	42.8	Asheville City Schools	Asheville
41	42.3	Caswell County Schools	Yanceyville
42	41.4	Lee County Schools	Sanford
43	40.9	Cumberland County Schools	Fayetteville
43	40.9	Pender County Schools	Burgaw
45	40.8	Mount Airy City Schools	Mount Airy
46	40.5	Swain County Schools	Bryson City
47	40.0	Harnett County Schools	Lillington
48	39.6	Alleghany County Schools	Sparta
48	39.6	Guilford County Schools	Greensboro
50	39.3	Mcdowell County Schools	Marion
51	38.8	Mitchell County Schools	Bakersville
52	38.7	Cherokee County Schools	Murphy
52	38.7	Rockingham County Schools	Eden
52	38.7	Wayne County Public Schools	Goldsboro
55	38.5	Durham Public Schools	Durham
56	38.2	Edenton/Chowan Schools	Edenton
57	38.1	Granville County Schools	Oxford
58	37.6	Gates County Schools	Gatesville
59	37.2	Newton Conover City Schools	Newton
60	36.7	Charlotte-Mecklenburg Schools	Charlotte
61	36.6	Craven County Schools	New Bern
62	36.4	Surry County Schools	Dobson
62	36.4	Wilkes County Schools	Wilkesboro
64	36.1	Madison County Schools	Marshall
65	35.9	Roanoke Rapids City Schools	Roanoke Rapids
66	35.8	Macon County Schools	Franklin
67	35.6	Alamance-Burlington Schools	Burlington
68	35.3	Avery County Schools	Newland
69	35.1	Ashe County Schools	Jefferson
70	34.5	Rowan-Salisbury Schools	Salisbury
71	34.2	Cleveland County Schools	Shelby
72	33.7	Burke County Schools	Morganton
72	33.7	Moore County Schools	Carthage
72	33.7	New Hanover County Schools	Wilmington
75	33.6	Kings Mountain District	Kings Mountain
76	33.4	Forsyth County Schools	Winston Salem
76	33.4	Person County Schools	Roxboro
78	32.8	Caldwell County Schools	Lenoir
79	32.5	Transylvania County Schools	Brevard
79	32.5	Yancey County Schools	Burnsville
81	32.3	Jackson County Schools	Sylva
82	31.5	Gaston County Schools	Gastonia
83	30.8	Johnston County Schools	Smithfield
84	30.6	Chatham County Schools	Pittsboro
85	30.5	Stanly County Schools	Albemarle
86	30.4	Henderson County Schools	Hendersonville
87	29.7	Polk County Schools	Columbus
88	29.6	Carteret County Public Schools	Beaufort
89	29.5	Haywood County Schools	Waynesville
89	29.5	Randolph County Schools	Asheboro
91	28.7	Alexander County Schools	Taylorsville
92	28.6	Onslow County Schools	Jacksonville
93	27.2	Buncombe County Schools	Asheville
94	26.6	Lincoln County Schools	Lincolnton
95	25.8	Catawba County Schools	Newton
96	25.0	Iredell-Statesville Schools	Statesville
97	24.1	Union County Public Schools	Monroe
98	23.6	Stokes County Schools	Danbury
99	23.5	Cabarrus County Schools	Concord
100	23.3	Orange County Schools	Hillsborough
101	22.6	Yadkin County Schools	Yadkinville
102	22.5	Davie County Schools	Mocksville
103	22.4	Mooresville City Schools	Mooresville
103	22.4	Wake County Schools	Raleigh
105	20.5	Davidson County Schools	Lexington
106	19.4	Watauga County Schools	Boone
107	18.4	Currituck County Schools	Currituck
108	17.7	Camden County Schools	Camden
109	16.5	Chapel Hill-Carrboro Schools	Chapel Hill
110	14.5	Dare County Schools	Manteo

Students Eligible for Reduced-Price Lunch

Rank	Percent	District Name	City
1	16.7	Ashe County Schools	Jefferson
2	16.6	Avery County Schools	Newland
2	16.6	Bertie County Schools	Windsor
4	16.0	Cherokee County Schools	Murphy
5	14.9	Alleghany County Schools	Sparta
6	14.6	Perquimans County Schools	Hertford
7	14.5	Swain County Schools	Bryson City
8	13.7	Hoke County Schools	Raeford
8	13.7	Mitchell County Schools	Bakersville
10	13.4	Gates County Schools	Gatesville
11	13.3	Warren County Schools	Warrenton
12	13.2	Craven County Schools	New Bern
13	12.8	Jackson County Schools	Sylva
14	12.4	Mcdowell County Schools	Marion
15	12.3	Madison County Schools	Marshall
16	12.2	Macon County Schools	Franklin
17	12.1	Onslow County Schools	Jacksonville
18	12.0	Brunswick County Schools	Bolivia
18	12.0	Pender County Schools	Burgaw
20	11.8	Surry County Schools	Dobson
21	11.7	Sampson County Schools	Clinton
22	11.6	Edgecombe County Schools	Tarboro
23	11.4	Burke County Schools	Morganton
23	11.4	Northampton County Schools	Jackson
25	11.3	Hertford County Schools	Winton
25	11.3	Yancey County Schools	Burnsville
27	11.2	Harnett County Schools	Lillington
27	11.2	Polk County Schools	Columbus
29	11.0	Columbus County Schools	Whiteville
29	11.0	Cumberland County Schools	Fayetteville
31	10.5	Bladen County Schools	Elizabethtown
31	10.5	Wayne County Public Schools	Goldsboro
33	10.3	Pamlico County Schools	Bayboro
34	10.1	Camden County Schools	Camden
34	10.1	Lenoir County Public Schools	Kinston
34	10.1	Montgomery County Schools	Troy
37	10.0	Anson County Schools	Wadesboro
37	10.0	Franklin County Schools	Louisburg
37	10.0	Lexington City Schools	Lexington
37	10.0	Pasquotank County Schools	Elizabeth City
37	10.0	Transylvania County Schools	Brevard
42	9.9	Halifax County Schools	Halifax
42	9.9	Kannapolis City Schools	Kannapolis
42	9.9	Roanoke Rapids City Schools	Roanoke Rapids
42	9.9	Thomasville City Schools	Thomasville
46	9.8	Haywood County Schools	Waynesville
46	9.8	Scotland County Schools	Laurinburg
46	9.8	Wilkes County Schools	Wilkesboro
49	9.7	Person County Schools	Roxboro
49	9.7	Richmond County Schools	Hamlet
49	9.7	Wilson County Schools	Wilson
52	9.6	Beaufort County Schools	Washington
52	9.6	Caldwell County Schools	Lenoir
52	9.6	Carteret County Public Schools	Beaufort
52	9.6	Washington County Schools	Plymouth
56	9.5	Caswell County Schools	Yanceyville
56	9.5	Duplin County Schools	Kenansville
56	9.5	Robeson County Schools	Lumberton
56	9.5	Stanly County Schools	Albemarle
60	9.4	Greene County Schools	Snow Hill
61	9.2	Nash-Rocky Mount Schools	Nashville
61	9.2	Rutherford County Schools	Forest City
63	9.1	Granville County Schools	Oxford
63	9.1	Vance County Schools	Henderson
65	9.0	Lee County Schools	Sanford
65	9.0	Rowan-Salisbury Schools	Salisbury
67	8.9	Martin County Schools	Williamston
68	8.8	Hickory City Schools	Hickory
68	8.8	Newton Conover City Schools	Newton
68	8.8	Whiteville City Schools	Whiteville
71	8.7	Alexander County Schools	Taylorsville
71	8.7	Iredell-Statesville Schools	Statesville
73	8.6	Lincoln County Schools	Lincolnton
73	8.6	Rockingham County Schools	Eden
75	8.5	Alamance-Burlington Schools	Burlington
76	8.4	Catawba County Schools	Newton
76	8.4	Clinton City Schools	Clinton
78	8.3	Henderson County Schools	Hendersonville
79	8.2	Stokes County Schools	Danbury
80	8.1	Buncombe County Schools	Asheville
81	8.0	Gaston County Schools	Gastonia
82	7.8	Chatham County Schools	Pittsboro
83	7.7	Mooresville City Schools	Mooresville
84	7.6	Asheboro City Schools	Asheboro

84	7.6	Edenton/Chowan Schools	Edenton
84	7.6	Johnston County Schools	Smithfield
84	7.6	Randolph County Schools	Asheboro
88	7.5	Pitt County Schools	Greenville
89	7.4	Kings Mountain District	Kings Mountain
89	7.4	Orange County Schools	Hillsborough
89	7.4	Watauga County Schools	Boone
92	7.3	Guilford County Schools	Greensboro
93	7.2	Yadkin County Schools	Yadkinville
94	6.9	Currituck County Schools	Currituck
94	6.9	Moore County Schools	Carthage
94	6.9	Mount Airy City Schools	Mount Airy
94	6.9	New Hanover County Schools	Wilmington
98	6.8	Cabarrus County Schools	Concord
99	6.5	Charlotte-Mecklenburg Schools	Charlotte
99	6.5	Cleveland County Schools	Shelby
101	6.4	Davidson County Schools	Lexington
101	6.4	Davie County Schools	Mocksville
103	6.2	Forsyth County Schools	Winston Salem
104	5.9	Shelby City Schools	Shelby
105	5.7	Durham Public Schools	Durham
106	5.6	Asheville City Schools	Asheville
106	5.6	Union County Public Schools	Monroe
108	5.1	Dare County Schools	Manteo
109	4.6	Wake County Schools	Raleigh
110	3.6	Chapel Hill-Carrboro Schools	Chapel Hill

Student/Teacher Ratio

Rank	Ratio	District Name	City
1	16.7	Alexander County Schools	Taylorsville
2	16.6	Davidson County Schools	Lexington
2	16.6	Hoke County Schools	Raeford
2	16.6	Robeson County Schools	Lumberton
5	16.3	Cumberland County Schools	Fayetteville
5	16.3	Yadkin County Schools	Yadkinville
7	16.2	Gaston County Schools	Gastonia
7	16.2	Onslow County Schools	Jacksonville
9	16.0	Lee County Schools	Sanford
9	16.0	Randolph County Schools	Asheboro
9	16.0	Union County Public Schools	Monroe
12	15.9	Halifax County Schools	Halifax
12	15.9	Harnett County Schools	Lillington
12	15.9	Iredell-Statesville Schools	Statesville
12	15.9	Wilson County Schools	Wilson
16	15.8	Camden County Schools	Camden
16	15.8	Columbus County Schools	Whiteville
16	15.8	Mcdowell County Schools	Marion
16	15.8	Rowan-Salisbury Schools	Salisbury
16	15.8	Yancey County Schools	Burnsville
21	15.7	Granville County Schools	Oxford
22	15.6	Catawba County Schools	Newton
22	15.6	Rockingham County Schools	Eden
24	15.5	Charlotte-Mecklenburg Schools	Charlotte
24	15.5	Kings Mountain District	Kings Mountain
26	15.4	Cabarrus County Schools	Concord
26	15.4	Henderson County Schools	Hendersonville
26	15.4	Mooresville City Schools	Mooresville
29	15.3	Anson County Schools	Wadesboro
29	15.3	Bladen County Schools	Elizabethtown
29	15.3	Brunswick County Schools	Bolivia
29	15.3	Buncombe County Schools	Asheville
29	15.3	Edgecombe County Schools	Tarboro
29	15.3	Guilford County Schools	Greensboro
35	15.2	Caldwell County Schools	Lenoir
35	15.2	Duplin County Schools	Kenansville
35	15.2	Wilkes County Schools	Wilkesboro
38	15.1	Moore County Schools	Carthage
38	15.1	Nash-Rocky Mount Schools	Nashville
38	15.1	New Hanover County Schools	Wilmington
38	15.1	Wayne County Public Schools	Goldsboro
42	15.0	Alamance-Burlington Schools	Burlington
42	15.0	Franklin County Schools	Louisburg
42	15.0	Hickory City Schools	Hickory
42	15.0	Stokes County Schools	Danbury
42	15.0	Wake County Schools	Raleigh
47	14.9	Cleveland County Schools	Shelby
47	14.9	Pitt County Schools	Greenville
47	14.9	Rutherford County Schools	Forest City
47	14.9	Stanly County Schools	Albemarle
51	14.8	Caswell County Schools	Yanceyville
51	14.8	Currituck County Schools	Currituck
51	14.8	Davie County Schools	Mocksville
51	14.8	Durham Public Schools	Durham
51	14.8	Newton Conover City Schools	Newton
51	14.8	Richmond County Schools	Hamlet
51	14.8	Sampson County Schools	Clinton
51	14.8	Surry County Schools	Dobson
59	14.7	Bertie County Schools	Windsor
59	14.7	Forsyth County Schools	Winston Salem
59	14.7	Haywood County Schools	Waynesville
62	14.6	Chatham County Schools	Pittsboro
63	14.5	Asheboro City Schools	Asheboro
63	14.5	Clinton City Schools	Clinton
63	14.5	Pasquotank County Schools	Elizabeth City
66	14.4	Lenoir County Public Schools	Kinston
66	14.4	Lincoln County Schools	Lincolnton
68	14.3	Burke County Schools	Morganton
68	14.3	Craven County Schools	New Bern
68	14.3	Pender County Schools	Burgaw
71	14.2	Person County Schools	Roxboro
71	14.2	Roanoke Rapids City Schools	Roanoke Rapids
71	14.2	Transylvania County Schools	Brevard
74	14.1	Macon County Schools	Franklin
74	14.1	Mitchell County Schools	Bakersville
74	14.1	Vance County Schools	Henderson
77	14.0	Dare County Schools	Manteo
77	14.0	Hertford County Schools	Winton
77	14.0	Johnston County Schools	Smithfield
77	14.0	Perquimans County Schools	Hertford
81	13.9	Edenton/Chowan Schools	Edenton
81	13.9	Jackson County Schools	Sylva
81	13.9	Orange County Schools	Hillsborough
84	13.8	Lexington City Schools	Lexington
84	13.8	Warren County Schools	Warrenton
86	13.7	Martin County Schools	Williamston
86	13.7	Northampton County Schools	Jackson
88	13.6	Beaufort County Schools	Washington
88	13.6	Cherokee County Schools	Murphy
88	13.6	Montgomery County Schools	Troy
88	13.6	Watauga County Schools	Boone
92	13.3	Mount Airy City Schools	Mount Airy
93	13.2	Greene County Schools	Snow Hill
93	13.2	Whiteville City Schools	Whiteville
95	13.1	Polk County Schools	Columbus
95	13.1	Swain County Schools	Bryson City
97	13.0	Ashe County Schools	Jefferson
97	13.0	Kannapolis City Schools	Kannapolis
99	12.8	Carteret County Public Schools	Beaufort
99	12.8	Scotland County Schools	Laurinburg
101	12.6	Chapel Hill-Carrboro Schools	Chapel Hill
102	12.5	Gates County Schools	Gatesville
103	12.4	Avery County Schools	Newland
104	12.3	Alleghany County Schools	Sparta
104	12.3	Shelby City Schools	Shelby
106	12.1	Madison County Schools	Marshall
107	12.0	Thomasville City Schools	Thomasville
108	11.9	Pamlico County Schools	Bayboro
108	11.9	Washington County Schools	Plymouth
110	11.6	Asheville City Schools	Asheville

Student/Librarian Ratio

Rank	Ratio	District Name	City
1	856.6	Mooresville City Schools	Mooresville
2	830.8	Lee County Schools	Sanford
3	812.5	Greene County Schools	Snow Hill
4	753.8	Cabarrus County Schools	Concord
5	752.0	Roanoke Rapids City Schools	Roanoke Rapids
6	751.0	Hertford County Schools	Winton
7	746.7	Forsyth County Schools	Winston Salem
8	727.6	Brunswick County Schools	Bolivia
9	722.0	Charlotte-Mecklenburg Schools	Charlotte
10	711.8	Clinton City Schools	Clinton
11	702.0	Durham Public Schools	Durham
12	698.2	Davidson County Schools	Lexington
13	677.8	Whiteville City Schools	Whiteville
14	674.8	Union County Public Schools	Monroe
15	674.4	Rowan-Salisbury Schools	Salisbury
16	664.9	Cleveland County Schools	Shelby
17	663.5	Craven County Schools	New Bern
18	660.2	Alamance-Burlington Schools	Burlington
19	656.8	Hoke County Schools	Raeford
20	656.5	Johnston County Schools	Smithfield
21	651.3	Wake County Schools	Raleigh
22	651.0	Thomasville City Schools	Thomasville
23	648.8	Pitt County Schools	Greenville
24	643.5	Edenton/Chowan Schools	Edenton
25	631.8	Guilford County Schools	Greensboro
26	626.4	Harnett County Schools	Lillington
27	620.3	Jackson County Schools	Sylva
28	616.1	Catawba County Schools	Newton
29	614.4	Henderson County Schools	Hendersonville
30	607.0	Randolph County Schools	Asheboro
31	602.0	Edgecombe County Schools	Tarboro
32	601.8	New Hanover County Schools	Wilmington
33	598.5	Lincoln County Schools	Lincolnton
34	597.6	Nash-Rocky Mount Schools	Nashville
35	596.1	Orange County Schools	Hillsborough
36	592.8	Scotland County Schools	Laurinburg
37	592.1	Burke County Schools	Morganton
38	591.5	Duplin County Schools	Kenansville
39	590.3	Gaston County Schools	Gastonia
40	588.4	Mcdowell County Schools	Marion
41	583.6	Newton Conover City Schools	Newton
42	581.8	Caswell County Schools	Yanceyville
43	579.2	Surry County Schools	Dobson
44	575.2	Lenoir County Public Schools	Kinston
45	572.5	Beaufort County Schools	Washington
45	572.5	Franklin County Schools	Louisburg
47	570.3	Washington County Schools	Plymouth
48	570.0	Wilson County Schools	Wilson
49	565.6	Kannapolis City Schools	Kannapolis
50	565.5	Cumberland County Schools	Fayetteville
51	559.8	Alexander County Schools	Taylorsville
52	555.0	Wayne County Public Schools	Goldsboro
53	550.7	Davie County Schools	Mocksville
54	549.5	Yadkin County Schools	Yadkinville
55	546.5	Pasquotank County Schools	Elizabeth City
56	543.7	Lexington City Schools	Lexington
57	542.5	Granville County Schools	Oxford
58	541.8	Ashe County Schools	Jefferson
59	540.9	Transylvania County Schools	Brevard
60	537.6	Caldwell County Schools	Lenoir
61	536.7	Vance County Schools	Henderson
62	535.4	Moore County Schools	Carthage
63	533.8	Dare County Schools	Manteo
64	530.5	Iredell-Statesville Schools	Statesville
65	530.3	Camden County Schools	Camden
66	529.5	Haywood County Schools	Waynesville
67	528.7	Shelby City Schools	Shelby
68	525.4	Person County Schools	Roxboro
69	521.2	Kings Mountain District	Kings Mountain
70	520.8	Chatham County Schools	Pittsboro
71	520.3	Carteret County Public Schools	Beaufort
72	520.0	Warren County Schools	Warrenton
73	516.0	Madison County Schools	Marshall
74	512.0	Montgomery County Schools	Troy
75	510.1	Hickory City Schools	Hickory
76	498.9	Pender County Schools	Burgaw
77	498.0	Rutherford County Schools	Forest City
78	496.6	Buncombe County Schools	Asheville
79	494.1	Asheboro City Schools	Asheboro
80	488.0	Richmond County Schools	Hamlet
81	483.2	Onslow County Schools	Jacksonville
82	481.0	Sampson County Schools	Clinton
83	477.4	Rockingham County Schools	Eden
84	476.0	Mount Airy City Schools	Mount Airy
85	473.8	Halifax County Schools	Halifax
86	463.5	Swain County Schools	Bryson City
87	460.5	Bladen County Schools	Elizabethtown
88	457.3	Perquimans County Schools	Hertford
89	454.2	Stanly County Schools	Albemarle
90	443.8	Pamlico County Schools	Bayboro
91	443.4	Stokes County Schools	Danbury
92	430.7	Wilkes County Schools	Wilkesboro
93	419.8	Polk County Schools	Columbus
94	419.1	Columbus County Schools	Whiteville
95	413.9	Macon County Schools	Franklin
96	403.7	Anson County Schools	Wadesboro
97	393.6	Gates County Schools	Gatesville
98	390.6	Watauga County Schools	Boone
99	386.0	Bertie County Schools	Windsor
100	385.9	Asheville City Schools	Asheville
101	385.3	Alleghany County Schools	Sparta
102	382.0	Cherokee County Schools	Murphy
103	378.3	Northampton County Schools	Jackson
104	367.0	Chapel Hill-Carrboro Schools	Chapel Hill
105	366.3	Currituck County Schools	Currituck
106	351.8	Martin County Schools	Williamston
107	347.9	Robeson County Schools	Lumberton
108	333.6	Mitchell County Schools	Bakersville
109	318.5	Yancey County Schools	Burnsville
110	240.6	Avery County Schools	Newland

Student/Counselor Ratio

Rank	Ratio	District Name	City
1	795.5	Camden County Schools	Camden
2	537.6	Lee County Schools	Sanford
3	520.8	Thomasville City Schools	Thomasville
4	516.0	Madison County Schools	Marshall
5	494.1	Asheboro City Schools	Asheboro
6	492.7	Forsyth County Schools	Winston Salem
7	481.4	Gaston County Schools	Gastonia
8	481.0	Sampson County Schools	Clinton
9	474.5	Clinton City Schools	Clinton
10	471.5	Franklin County Schools	Louisburg
11	469.1	Hoke County Schools	Raeford
12	465.2	Beaufort County Schools	Washington
13	463.5	Swain County Schools	Bryson City
14	462.7	Onslow County Schools	Jacksonville
15	462.5	Rockingham County Schools	Eden
16	462.3	Mcdowell County Schools	Marion
17	456.2	Washington County Schools	Plymouth
18	455.3	Randolph County Schools	Asheboro
19	453.1	Shelby City Schools	Shelby
20	451.8	Whiteville City Schools	Whiteville
21	444.3	Davidson County Schools	Lexington

22	434.4	Surry County Schools	Dobson
23	434.3	Bertie County Schools	Windsor
24	433.7	Harnett County Schools	Lillington
25	431.6	Wayne County Public Schools	Goldsboro
26	420.9	Wake County Schools	Raleigh
27	420.8	Buncombe County Schools	Asheville
28	420.7	Transylvania County Schools	Brevard
29	419.9	Robeson County Schools	Lumberton
30	419.0	Alamance-Burlington Schools	Burlington
31	418.9	Montgomery County Schools	Troy
32	418.0	Wilson County Schools	Wilson
33	415.5	Cleveland County Schools	Shelby
34	415.2	Iredell-Statesville Schools	Statesville
35	414.8	Richmond County Schools	Hamlet
36	413.6	Jackson County Schools	Sylva
37	411.9	Edgecombe County Schools	Tarboro
38	411.4	Kannapolis City Schools	Kannapolis
39	408.9	Vance County Schools	Henderson
40	407.8	Lexington City Schools	Lexington
41	407.0	Currituck County Schools	Currituck
42	406.4	Durham Public Schools	Durham
43	406.1	Moore County Schools	Carthage
44	405.9	Charlotte-Mecklenburg Schools	Charlotte
45	403.7	Anson County Schools	Wadesboro
46	403.3	Duplin County Schools	Kenansville
47	403.0	Yadkin County Schools	Yadkinville
48	400.8	Pasquotank County Schools	Elizabeth City
49	399.1	Bladen County Schools	Elizabethtown
50	398.2	Lenoir County Public Schools	Kinston
51	397.6	New Hanover County Schools	Wilmington
52	394.5	Craven County Schools	New Bern
53	389.8	Brunswick County Schools	Bolivia
54	389.4	Mooresville City Schools	Mooresville
55	389.2	Mitchell County Schools	Bakersville
56	388.0	Pender County Schools	Burgaw
57	386.9	Catawba County Schools	Newton
58	384.0	Henderson County Schools	Hendersonville
59	382.0	Cherokee County Schools	Murphy
60	380.8	Mount Airy City Schools	Mount Airy
61	379.7	Cumberland County Schools	Fayetteville
62	379.6	Burke County Schools	Morganton
63	378.6	Davie County Schools	Mocksville
64	378.0	Johnston County Schools	Smithfield
65	376.3	Macon County Schools	Franklin
66	376.0	Roanoke Rapids City Schools	Roanoke Rapids
67	374.9	Union County Public Schools	Monroe
68	368.7	Caldwell County Schools	Lenoir
69	367.7	Edenton/Chowan Schools	Edenton
70	367.0	Chapel Hill-Carrboro Schools	Chapel Hill
71	366.8	Lincoln County Schools	Lincolnton
72	365.8	Perquimans County Schools	Hertford
73	364.8	Newton Conover City Schools	Newton
74	364.3	Orange County Schools	Hillsborough
75	361.7	Granville County Schools	Oxford
76	361.2	Person County Schools	Roxboro
77	361.0	Haywood County Schools	Waynesville
78	358.4	Cabarrus County Schools	Concord
79	355.7	Rutherford County Schools	Forest City
79	355.7	Scotland County Schools	Laurinburg
81	355.3	Halifax County Schools	Halifax
82	355.0	Pamlico County Schools	Bayboro
83	354.3	Guilford County Schools	Greensboro
84	349.9	Alexander County Schools	Taylorsville
85	349.1	Caswell County Schools	Yanceyville
86	339.3	Columbus County Schools	Whiteville
87	335.1	Kings Mountain District	Kings Mountain
88	333.5	Wilkes County Schools	Wilkesboro
89	327.7	Stokes County Schools	Danbury
90	326.7	Rowan-Salisbury Schools	Salisbury
91	325.1	Ashe County Schools	Jefferson
92	319.6	Pitt County Schools	Greenville
93	318.5	Yancey County Schools	Burnsville
94	312.9	Hertford County Schools	Winton
95	312.5	Watauga County Schools	Boone
96	312.0	Warren County Schools	Warrenton
97	309.5	Northampton County Schools	Jackson
98	308.2	Alleghany County Schools	Sparta
99	306.1	Hickory City Schools	Hickory
100	304.9	Martin County Schools	Williamston
101	300.3	Dare County Schools	Manteo
102	295.5	Greene County Schools	Snow Hill
103	289.5	Nash-Rocky Mount Schools	Nashville
104	287.0	Carteret County Public Schools	Beaufort
105	281.1	Gates County Schools	Gatesville
106	280.4	Chatham County Schools	Pittsboro
107	279.9	Polk County Schools	Columbus
108	257.3	Asheville City Schools	Asheville
109	249.8	Stanly County Schools	Albemarle
110	218.7	Avery County Schools	Newland

Current Spending per Student in FY2003

Rank	Dollars	District Name	City
1	9,326	Asheville City Schools	Asheville
2	9,025	Chapel Hill-Carrboro Schools	Chapel Hill
3	8,468	Swain County Schools	Bryson City
4	8,316	Alleghany County Schools	Sparta
5	8,017	Pamlico County Schools	Bayboro
6	7,858	Gates County Schools	Gatesville
7	7,855	Washington County Schools	Plymouth
8	7,816	Orange County Schools	Hillsborough
9	7,802	Perquimans County Schools	Hertford
10	7,792	Dare County Schools	Manteo
11	7,784	Avery County Schools	Newland
12	7,599	Durham Public Schools	Durham
13	7,565	Halifax County Schools	Halifax
14	7,544	Currituck County Schools	Currituck
15	7,488	Scotland County Schools	Laurinburg
16	7,478	Polk County Schools	Columbus
17	7,475	Madison County Schools	Marshall
18	7,381	Edenton/Chowan Schools	Edenton
19	7,377	Bertie County Schools	Windsor
20	7,344	Thomasville City Schools	Thomasville
21	7,286	Carteret County Public Schools	Beaufort
22	7,283	Yancey County Schools	Burnsville
23	7,224	Shelby City Schools	Shelby
24	7,215	Chatham County Schools	Pittsboro
25	7,197	New Hanover County Schools	Wilmington
26	7,190	Ashe County Schools	Jefferson
27	7,188	Charlotte-Mecklenburg Schools	Charlotte
28	7,141	Camden County Schools	Camden
29	7,134	Mitchell County Schools	Bakersville
30	7,129	Lexington City Schools	Lexington
31	7,116	Cherokee County Schools	Murphy
32	7,104	Martin County Schools	Williamston
33	7,101	Mount Airy City Schools	Mount Airy
34	7,099	Warren County Schools	Warrenton
35	7,060	Northampton County Schools	Jackson
36	7,059	Hertford County Schools	Winton
37	7,040	Montgomery County Schools	Troy
38	7,033	Jackson County Schools	Sylva
39	7,002	Watauga County Schools	Boone
40	6,998	Brunswick County Schools	Bolivia
41	6,978	Greene County Schools	Snow Hill
42	6,943	Guilford County Schools	Greensboro
43	6,931	Transylvania County Schools	Brevard
44	6,915	Forsyth County Schools	Winston Salem
45	6,853	Haywood County Schools	Waynesville
46	6,801	Clinton City Schools	Clinton
47	6,771	Bladen County Schools	Elizabethtown
47	6,771	Caswell County Schools	Yanceyville
49	6,763	Anson County Schools	Wadesboro
50	6,747	Beaufort County Schools	Washington
51	6,744	Pender County Schools	Burgaw
52	6,730	Macon County Schools	Franklin
53	6,723	Moore County Schools	Carthage
54	6,706	Whiteville City Schools	Whiteville
55	6,698	Newton Conover City Schools	Newton
56	6,695	Wake County Schools	Raleigh
57	6,677	Pasquotank County Schools	Elizabeth City
58	6,660	Kannapolis City Schools	Kannapolis
59	6,658	Roanoke Rapids City Schools	Roanoke Rapids
60	6,644	Rutherford County Schools	Forest City
61	6,637	Pitt County Schools	Greenville
62	6,636	Columbus County Schools	Whiteville
63	6,634	Hickory City Schools	Hickory
64	6,601	Edgecombe County Schools	Tarboro
65	6,556	Lenoir County Public Schools	Kinston
66	6,545	Mcdowell County Schools	Marion
67	6,541	Buncombe County Schools	Asheville
68	6,531	Stokes County Schools	Danbury
69	6,523	Kings Mountain District	Kings Mountain
70	6,515	Nash-Rocky Mount Schools	Nashville
71	6,489	Wilkes County Schools	Wilkesboro
72	6,464	Asheboro City Schools	Asheboro
73	6,453	Henderson County Schools	Hendersonville
74	6,428	Surry County Schools	Dobson
75	6,423	Richmond County Schools	Hamlet
76	6,409	Craven County Schools	New Bern
77	6,381	Mooresville City Schools	Mooresville
78	6,380	Sampson County Schools	Clinton
79	6,370	Lee County Schools	Sanford
80	6,353	Wilson County Schools	Wilson
81	6,336	Rockingham County Schools	Eden
82	6,334	Person County Schools	Roxboro
83	6,320	Cleveland County Schools	Shelby
84	6,309	Johnston County Schools	Smithfield
85	6,301	Cumberland County Schools	Fayetteville
86	6,299	Franklin County Schools	Louisburg
87	6,288	Robeson County Schools	Lumberton
88	6,274	Caldwell County Schools	Lenoir
89	6,271	Duplin County Schools	Kenansville
90	6,253	Wayne County Public Schools	Goldsboro
91	6,210	Yadkin County Schools	Yadkinville
92	6,185	Hoke County Schools	Raeford
93	6,180	Rowan-Salisbury Schools	Salisbury
94	6,168	Vance County Schools	Henderson
95	6,155	Davie County Schools	Mocksville
96	6,150	Granville County Schools	Oxford
97	6,115	Stanly County Schools	Albemarle
98	6,097	Alexander County Schools	Taylorsville
99	6,048	Cabarrus County Schools	Concord
100	6,043	Burke County Schools	Morganton
101	6,027	Lincoln County Schools	Lincolnton
102	5,990	Onslow County Schools	Jacksonville
103	5,977	Gaston County Schools	Gastonia
104	5,960	Alamance-Burlington Schools	Burlington
105	5,905	Union County Public Schools	Monroe
106	5,879	Catawba County Schools	Newton
107	5,854	Harnett County Schools	Lillington
108	5,849	Iredell-Statesville Schools	Statesville
109	5,573	Davidson County Schools	Lexington
110	5,518	Randolph County Schools	Asheboro

Number of Diploma Recipients

Rank	Number	District Name	City
1	5,411	Wake County Schools	Raleigh
2	5,087	Charlotte-Mecklenburg Schools	Charlotte
3	3,304	Guilford County Schools	Greensboro
4	2,809	Cumberland County Schools	Fayetteville
5	2,271	Forsyth County Schools	Winston Salem
6	1,466	Gaston County Schools	Gastonia
7	1,435	Durham Public Schools	Durham
8	1,370	Buncombe County Schools	Asheville
9	1,272	New Hanover County Schools	Wilmington
10	1,161	Onslow County Schools	Jacksonville
11	1,097	Cabarrus County Schools	Concord
12	1,093	Rowan-Salisbury Schools	Salisbury
13	1,085	Union County Public Schools	Monroe
14	1,081	Alamance-Burlington Schools	Burlington
15	1,046	Davidson County Schools	Lexington
16	996	Wayne County Public Schools	Goldsboro
17	994	Pitt County Schools	Greenville
18	963	Robeson County Schools	Lumberton
19	942	Johnston County Schools	Smithfield
20	918	Nash-Rocky Mount Schools	Nashville
21	827	Catawba County Schools	Newton
22	825	Randolph County Schools	Asheboro
23	821	Iredell-Statesville Schools	Statesville
24	816	Craven County Schools	New Bern
25	759	Harnett County Schools	Lillington
26	716	Rockingham County Schools	Eden
27	686	Caldwell County Schools	Lenoir
28	682	Burke County Schools	Morganton
29	650	Henderson County Schools	Hendersonville
30	625	Moore County Schools	Carthage
31	613	Lincoln County Schools	Lincolnton
32	599	Chapel Hill-Carrboro Schools	Chapel Hill
33	594	Wilson County Schools	Wilson
34	569	Stanly County Schools	Albemarle
35	543	Carteret County Public Schools	Beaufort
36	536	Wilkes County Schools	Wilkesboro
37	476	Surry County Schools	Dobson
38	474	Brunswick County Schools	Bolivia
38	474	Lenoir County Public Schools	Kinston
40	452	Rutherford County Schools	Forest City
41	442	Cleveland County Schools	Shelby
41	442	Duplin County Schools	Kenansville
43	431	Haywood County Schools	Waynesville
44	429	Lee County Schools	Sanford
45	414	Stokes County Schools	Danbury
46	394	Richmond County Schools	Hamlet
47	391	Edgecombe County Schools	Tarboro
48	386	Columbus County Schools	Whiteville
49	380	Beaufort County Schools	Washington
50	357	Sampson County Schools	Clinton
51	352	Franklin County Schools	Louisburg
52	339	Scotland County Schools	Laurinburg
53	334	Vance County Schools	Henderson
54	328	Granville County Schools	Oxford
55	327	Davie County Schools	Mocksville
55	327	Watauga County Schools	Boone
57	322	Alexander County Schools	Taylorsville
58	310	Orange County Schools	Hillsborough
59	306	Chatham County Schools	Pittsboro
59	306	Mcdowell County Schools	Marion
61	305	Pender County Schools	Burgaw
62	304	Person County Schools	Roxboro
62	304	Yadkin County Schools	Yadkinville
64	288	Bladen County Schools	Elizabethtown
65	270	Martin County Schools	Williamston
65	270	Pasquotank County Schools	Elizabeth City
67	267	Halifax County Schools	Halifax
68	263	Hoke County Schools	Raeford
69	259	Dare County Schools	Manteo
70	252	Transylvania County Schools	Brevard
71	249	Asheville City Schools	Asheville

72	247	Macon County Schools	Franklin
72	247	Mooresville City Schools	Mooresville
74	237	Hickory City Schools	Hickory
75	236	Cherokee County Schools	Murphy
76	231	Kannapolis City Schools	Kannapolis
77	225	Jackson County Schools	Sylva
78	220	Montgomery County Schools	Troy
79	215	Hertford County Schools	Winton
80	207	Anson County Schools	Wadesboro
81	196	Bertie County Schools	Windsor
82	195	Currituck County Schools	Currituck
83	188	Ashe County Schools	Jefferson
84	184	Kings Mountain District	Kings Mountain
85	182	Caswell County Schools	Yanceyville
86	181	Northampton County Schools	Jackson
87	180	Asheboro City Schools	Asheboro
88	165	Roanoke Rapids City Schools	Roanoke Rapids
89	150	Mitchell County Schools	Bakersville
90	146	Clinton City Schools	Clinton
90	146	Yancey County Schools	Burnsville
92	144	Newton Conover City Schools	Newton
92	144	Warren County Schools	Warrenton
94	141	Shelby City Schools	Shelby
95	138	Edenton/Chowan Schools	Edenton
96	136	Lexington City Schools	Lexington
97	134	Washington County Schools	Plymouth
98	133	Avery County Schools	Newland
99	132	Pamlico County Schools	Bayboro
99	132	Whiteville City Schools	Whiteville
101	129	Madison County Schools	Marshall
102	117	Greene County Schools	Snow Hill
102	117	Polk County Schools	Columbus
104	111	Swain County Schools	Bryson City
105	103	Perquimans County Schools	Hertford
106	92	Gates County Schools	Gatesville
107	91	Thomasville City Schools	Thomasville
108	87	Mount Airy City Schools	Mount Airy
109	85	Camden County Schools	Camden
110	79	Alleghany County Schools	Sparta

High School Drop-out Rate

Rank	Percent	District Name	City
1	9.1	Brunswick County Schools	Bolivia
1	9.1	Hoke County Schools	Raeford
1	9.1	Robeson County Schools	Lumberton
4	9.0	Lexington City Schools	Lexington
5	8.7	Vance County Schools	Henderson
6	8.5	Granville County Schools	Oxford
7	8.3	Wilkes County Schools	Wilkesboro
8	8.2	Lee County Schools	Sanford
9	8.1	Alexander County Schools	Taylorsville
9	8.1	Rutherford County Schools	Forest City
9	8.1	Warren County Schools	Warrenton
12	7.9	Harnett County Schools	Lillington
13	7.5	Haywood County Schools	Waynesville
14	7.4	Chatham County Schools	Pittsboro
15	7.3	Columbus County Schools	Whiteville
16	7.2	Hertford County Schools	Winton
17	7.1	Mitchell County Schools	Bakersville
17	7.1	Pender County Schools	Burgaw
19	7.0	Davie County Schools	Mocksville
20	6.9	Beaufort County Schools	Washington
20	6.9	Gates County Schools	Gatesville
20	6.9	Halifax County Schools	Halifax
20	6.9	Lenoir County Public Schools	Kinston
20	6.9	Shelby City Schools	Shelby
25	6.8	Pasquotank County Schools	Elizabeth City
25	6.8	Wilson County Schools	Wilson
27	6.7	Pitt County Schools	Greenville
27	6.7	Washington County Schools	Plymouth
29	6.6	Ashe County Schools	Jefferson
29	6.6	Craven County Schools	New Bern
29	6.6	Franklin County Schools	Louisburg
29	6.6	Hickory City Schools	Hickory
33	6.5	Anson County Schools	Wadesboro
33	6.5	Durham Public Schools	Durham
33	6.5	Johnston County Schools	Smithfield
33	6.5	Randolph County Schools	Asheboro
37	6.4	Buncombe County Schools	Asheville
37	6.4	Gaston County Schools	Gastonia
37	6.4	Greene County Schools	Snow Hill
37	6.4	Roanoke Rapids City Schools	Roanoke Rapids
41	6.3	Clinton City Schools	Clinton
41	6.3	Forsyth County Schools	Winston Salem
41	6.3	Yadkin County Schools	Yadkinville
44	6.2	Currituck County Schools	Currituck
44	6.2	Duplin County Schools	Kenansville
44	6.2	Nash-Rocky Mount Schools	Nashville
44	6.2	Person County Schools	Roxboro
48	6.1	Asheboro City Schools	Asheboro
48	6.1	Iredell-Statesville Schools	Statesville
48	6.1	Macon County Schools	Franklin
48	6.1	Montgomery County Schools	Troy
52	6.0	Onslow County Schools	Jacksonville
52	6.0	Richmond County Schools	Hamlet
52	6.0	Rockingham County Schools	Eden
52	6.0	Yancey County Schools	Burnsville
56	5.9	Davidson County Schools	Lexington
56	5.9	Henderson County Schools	Hendersonville
56	5.9	Surry County Schools	Dobson
59	5.8	Edgecombe County Schools	Tarboro
60	5.7	Bertie County Schools	Windsor
60	5.7	Dare County Schools	Manteo
60	5.7	Northampton County Schools	Jackson
60	5.7	Perquimans County Schools	Hertford
60	5.7	Whiteville City Schools	Whiteville
65	5.6	Camden County Schools	Camden
65	5.6	Rowan-Salisbury Schools	Salisbury
65	5.6	Stokes County Schools	Danbury
68	5.5	Alamance-Burlington Schools	Burlington
68	5.5	Charlotte-Mecklenburg Schools	Charlotte
68	5.5	Kings Mountain District	Kings Mountain
68	5.5	Lincoln County Schools	Lincolnton
68	5.5	New Hanover County Schools	Wilmington
73	5.3	Martin County Schools	Williamston
74	5.2	Edenton/Chowan Schools	Edenton
74	5.2	Jackson County Schools	Sylva
74	5.2	Watauga County Schools	Boone
77	5.1	Cabarrus County Schools	Concord
77	5.1	Caldwell County Schools	Lenoir
77	5.1	Transylvania County Schools	Brevard
80	5.0	Burke County Schools	Morganton
80	5.0	Sampson County Schools	Clinton
82	4.9	Carteret County Public Schools	Beaufort
82	4.9	Mooresville City Schools	Mooresville
82	4.9	Orange County Schools	Hillsborough
85	4.8	Asheville City Schools	Asheville
85	4.8	Kannapolis City Schools	Kannapolis
85	4.8	Pamlico County Schools	Bayboro
85	4.8	Wayne County Public Schools	Goldsboro
89	4.7	Catawba County Schools	Newton
89	4.7	Cleveland County Schools	Shelby
89	4.7	Scotland County Schools	Laurinburg
89	4.7	Union County Public Schools	Monroe
93	4.6	Polk County Schools	Columbus
94	4.4	Mount Airy City Schools	Mount Airy
95	4.3	Cumberland County Schools	Fayetteville
96	4.1	Bladen County Schools	Elizabethtown
96	4.1	Madison County Schools	Marshall
98	4.0	Caswell County Schools	Yanceyville
98	4.0	Mcdowell County Schools	Marion
100	3.9	Avery County Schools	Newland
100	3.9	Guilford County Schools	Greensboro
102	3.8	Thomasville City Schools	Thomasville
103	3.7	Wake County Schools	Raleigh
104	3.6	Alleghany County Schools	Sparta
105	3.4	Cherokee County Schools	Murphy
105	3.4	Stanly County Schools	Albemarle
107	3.1	Moore County Schools	Carthage
107	3.1	Newton Conover City Schools	Newton
107	3.1	Swain County Schools	Bryson City
110	1.4	Chapel Hill-Carrboro Schools	Chapel Hill

North Dakota

North Dakota Public School Educational Profile

Category	Value	Category	Value
Schools *(2003-2004)*	556	**Diploma Recipients** *(2002-2003)*	8,061
Instructional Level		White, Non-Hispanic	7,511
Primary	298	Black, Non-Hispanic	58
Middle	38	Asian/Pacific Islander	62
High	177	American Indian/Alaskan Native	362
Other Level	43	Hispanic	68
Curriculum		**High School Drop-out Rate** (%) *(2001-2002)*	2.0
Regular	519	White, Non-Hispanic	1.5
Special Education	30	Black, Non-Hispanic	2.7
Vocational	7	Asian/Pacific Islander	1.9
Alternative	0	American Indian/Alaskan Native	8.0
Type		Hispanic	3.4
Magnet	0	**Staff** *(2003-2004)*	
Charter	0	Teachers	8,036.5
Title I Eligible	367	Average Salary ($)	35,411
School-wide Title I	63	Librarians/Media Specialists	197.7
Students *(2003-2004)*	102,233	Guidance Counselors	277.6
Gender (%)		**Ratios** *(2003-2004)*	
Male	51.7	Student/Teacher Ratio	12.7 to 1
Female	48.3	Student/Librarian Ratio	517.1 to 1
Race/Ethnicity (%)		Student/Counselor Ratio	368.3 to 1
White, Non-Hispanic	88.0	**College Entrance Exam Scores** *(2005)*	
Black, Non-Hispanic	1.2	Scholastic Aptitude Test (SAT)	
Asian/Pacific Islander	0.8	Participation Rate (%)	4
American Indian/Alaskan Native	8.5	Mean SAT Reasoning Test Verbal Score	590
Hispanic	1.4	Mean SAT Reasoning Test Math Score	605
Classification (%)		American College Testing Program (ACT)	
Individual Education Program (IEP)	13.5	Participation Rate (%)	82
Migrant *(2002-2003)*	0.3	Average Composite Score	21.3
English Language Learner (ELL)	1.6	Average English Score	20.4
Eligible for Free Lunch Program	20.4	Average Math Score	21.2
Eligible for Reduced-Price Lunch Program	7.9	Average Reading Score	21.4
Current Spending *($ per student in FY 2003)*	6,877	Average Science Score	21.5
Instruction	4,188		
Support Services	2,172		

Note: For an explanation of data, please refer to the User's Guide in the front of the book

North Dakota NAEP 2005 Test Scores

Reading			Mathematics		
Grade/Category	**Value**	**Rank**	**Grade/Category**	**Value**	**Rank**
4th Grade			**4th Grade**		
Average Proficiency	224.8 (0.66)	8/51	Average Proficiency	242.7 (0.50)	8/51
Proficiency by Gender/Race/Ethnicity			Proficiency by Gender/Race/Ethnicity		
Male	222.4 (0.92)	6/51	Male	244.1 (0.75)	8/51
Female	227.2 (1.02)	10/51	Female	241.3 (0.72)	7/51
White, Non-Hispanic	227.6 (0.73)	19/51	White, Non-Hispanic	244.9 (0.62)	23/51
Black, Non-Hispanic	n/a	n/a	Black, Non-Hispanic	n/a	n/a
Asian, Non-Hispanic	n/a	n/a	Asian, Non-Hispanic	n/a	n/a
American Indian, Non-Hispanic	198.5 (2.87)	5/7	American Indian, Non-Hispanic	223.1 (2.18)	3/7
Hispanic	n/a	n/a	Hispanic	n/a	n/a
Proficiency by Class Size			Proficiency by Class Size		
Less than 16 Students	220.8 (1.49)	4/34	Less than 16 Students	238.7 (1.09)	5/35
16 to 18 Students	225.5 (1.95)	3/33	16 to 18 Students	242.6 (1.19)	6/31
19 to 20 Students	225.1 (1.34)	14/38	19 to 20 Students	243.7 (0.94)	8/38
21 to 25 Students	228.3 (1.39)	6/51	21 to 25 Students	244.6 (1.21)	10/51
Greater than 25 Students	225.0 (2.82)	5/36	Greater than 25 Students	243.0 (2.22)	5/33
Percent Attaining Achievement Levels			Percent Attaining Achievement Levels		
Below Basic	28.2 (1.06)	46/51	Below Basic	11.2 (0.76)	49/51
Basic or Above	71.8 (1.06)	6/51	Basic or Above	88.8 (0.76)	3/51
Proficient or Above	35.5 (1.13)	11/51	Proficient or Above	40.4 (1.46)	13/51
Advanced or Above	7.2 (0.58)	22/51	Advanced or Above	3.8 (0.55)	34/51
8th Grade			**8th Grade**		
Average Proficiency	270.2 (0.64)	2/51	Average Proficiency	287.0 (0.63)	5/51
Proficiency by Gender/Race/Ethnicity			Proficiency by Gender/Race/Ethnicity		
Male	266.9 (0.98)	2/51	Male	287.4 (0.96)	3/51
Female	273.6 (1.04)	8/51	Female	286.5 (1.06)	6/51
White, Non-Hispanic	271.9 (0.75)	14/51	White, Non-Hispanic	289.9 (0.69)	16/51
Black, Non-Hispanic	n/a	n/a	Black, Non-Hispanic	n/a	n/a
Asian, Non-Hispanic	n/a	n/a	Asian, Non-Hispanic	n/a	n/a
American Indian, Non-Hispanic	250.4 (2.85)	4/9	American Indian, Non-Hispanic	260.7 (2.52)	6/10
Hispanic	n/a	n/a	Hispanic	n/a	n/a
Proficiency by Parents Highest Level of Ed.			Proficiency by Parents Highest Level of Ed.		
Did Not Finish High School	n/a	n/a	Did Not Finish High School	270.5 (3.72)	2/50
Graduated High School	261.4 (1.75)	5/50	Graduated High School	273.9 (1.78)	11/50
Some Education After High School	270.2 (1.86)	7/50	Some Education After High School	286.1 (1.50)	6/50
Graduated College	274.7 (0.68)	16/50	Graduated College	292.3 (0.77)	20/50
Percent Attaining Achievement Levels			Percent Attaining Achievement Levels		
Below Basic	28.2 (1.06)	46/51	Below Basic	19.2 (1.12)	51/51
Basic or Above	71.8 (1.06)	6/51	Basic or Above	80.8 (1.12)	1/51
Proficient or Above	35.5 (1.13)	11/51	Proficient or Above	34.6 (1.16)	10/51
Advanced or Above	7.2 (0.58)	22/51	Advanced or Above	4.7 (0.54)	30/51

Note: For an explanation of data, please refer to the User's Guide in the front of the book; n/a indicates data not available

Burleigh County

Bismarck 1
806 N Washington St • Bismarck, ND 58501-3623
(701) 355-3000 • http://www.bismarck.k12.il.us/
Grade Span: PK-12; **Agency Type:** 1
Schools: 22
  16 Primary; 3 Middle; 3 High; 0 Other Level
  22 Regular; 0 Special Education; 0 Vocational; 0 Alternative
  0 Magnet; 0 Charter; 10 Title I Eligible; 2 School-wide Title I
Students: 10,477 (50.9% male; 49.0% female)
  Individual Education Program: 1,243 (11.9%);
  English Language Learner: 24 (0.2%); Migrant: 0 (0.0%)
  Eligible for Free Lunch Program: 1,316 (12.6%)
  Eligible for Reduced-Price Lunch Program: 584 (5.6%)
Teachers: 662.1 (15.8 to 1)
Librarians/Media Specialists: 12.4 (844.9 to 1)
Guidance Counselors: 25.1 (417.4 to 1)
Current Spending: ($ per student per year):
  Total: $6,247; Instruction: $3,988; Support Services: $1,967
Enrollment, Drop-out Rates and Diploma Recipients by Race/Ethnicity

Category	Total	White	Black	Asian	AIAN	Hisp.
Enrollment (%)	100.0	92.3	0.7	0.6	5.8	0.6
Drop-out Rate (%)	1.3	1.0	6.3	3.4	3.8	7.1
H.S. Diplomas (#)	828	800	2	11	13	2

Cass County

Fargo 1
415 4th St N • Fargo, ND 58102-4514
(701) 446-1000 • http://www.fargo.k12.nd.us/
Grade Span: PK-12; **Agency Type:** 1
Schools: 22
  14 Primary; 3 Middle; 3 High; 2 Other Level
  22 Regular; 0 Special Education; 0 Vocational; 0 Alternative
  0 Magnet; 0 Charter; 9 Title I Eligible; 1 School-wide Title I
Students: 11,214 (50.8% male; 49.1% female)
  Individual Education Program: 1,291 (11.5%);
  English Language Learner: 571 (5.1%); Migrant: 0 (0.0%)
  Eligible for Free Lunch Program: 1,379 (12.3%)
  Eligible for Reduced-Price Lunch Program: 481 (4.3%)
Teachers: 703.3 (15.9 to 1)
Librarians/Media Specialists: 17.0 (659.6 to 1)
Guidance Counselors: 29.2 (384.0 to 1)
Current Spending: ($ per student per year):
  Total: $7,328; Instruction: $4,697; Support Services: $2,291
Enrollment, Drop-out Rates and Diploma Recipients by Race/Ethnicity

Category	Total	White	Black	Asian	AIAN	Hisp.
Enrollment (%)	100.0	91.4	2.5	2.3	2.1	1.8
Drop-out Rate (%)	3.8	3.7	2.5	0.0	8.9	7.1
H.S. Diplomas (#)	781	727	19	22	8	5

West Fargo 6
207 Main Ave W • West Fargo, ND 58078-1793
(701) 356-2000 • http://www.west-fargo.k12.nd.us/
Grade Span: PK-12; **Agency Type:** 1
Schools: 9
  7 Primary; 1 Middle; 1 High; 0 Other Level
  9 Regular; 0 Special Education; 0 Vocational; 0 Alternative
  0 Magnet; 0 Charter; 4 Title I Eligible; 0 School-wide Title I
Students: 5,424 (51.0% male; 48.9% female)
  Individual Education Program: 653 (12.0%);
  English Language Learner: 212 (3.9%); Migrant: 0 (0.0%)
  Eligible for Free Lunch Program: 738 (13.6%)
  Eligible for Reduced-Price Lunch Program: 333 (6.1%)
Teachers: 327.7 (16.6 to 1)
Librarians/Media Specialists: 4.6 (1,179.1 to 1)
Guidance Counselors: 11.2 (484.3 to 1)
Current Spending: ($ per student per year):
  Total: $6,448; Instruction: $3,680; Support Services: $2,254
Enrollment, Drop-out Rates and Diploma Recipients by Race/Ethnicity

Category	Total	White	Black	Asian	AIAN	Hisp.
Enrollment (%)	100.0	91.2	2.8	1.2	2.8	1.9
Drop-out Rate (%)	2.7	2.5	7.7	11.1	7.1	0.0
H.S. Diplomas (#)	337	320	3	3	4	7

Grand Forks County

Grand Forks 1
2400 47th Ave S • Grand Forks, ND 58201-3405
Mailing Address: PO Box 6000 • Grand Forks, ND 58206-6000
(701) 746-2200 • http://www.grand-forks.k12.nd.us/
Grade Span: PK-12; **Agency Type:** 1
Schools: 19
  11 Primary; 5 Middle; 3 High; 0 Other Level

  19 Regular; 0 Special Education; 0 Vocational; 0 Alternative
  0 Magnet; 0 Charter; 11 Title I Eligible; 6 School-wide Title I
Students: 7,932 (51.8% male; 48.1% female)
  Individual Education Program: 1,078 (13.6%);
  English Language Learner: 68 (0.9%); Migrant: 4 (0.1%)
  Eligible for Free Lunch Program: 1,463 (18.4%)
  Eligible for Reduced-Price Lunch Program: 673 (8.5%)
Teachers: 597.1 (13.3 to 1)
Librarians/Media Specialists: 14.6 (543.3 to 1)
Guidance Counselors: 21.0 (377.7 to 1)
Current Spending: ($ per student per year):
  Total: $6,729; Instruction: $4,360; Support Services: $2,037
Enrollment, Drop-out Rates and Diploma Recipients by Race/Ethnicity

Category	Total	White	Black	Asian	AIAN	Hisp.
Enrollment (%)	100.0	87.4	2.5	1.6	6.1	2.4
Drop-out Rate (%)	1.2	0.8	0.0	2.8	6.6	6.1
H.S. Diplomas (#)	540	507	9	7	8	9

Morton County

Mandan 1
309 Collins Ave • Mandan, ND 58554-3000
(701) 663-9531
Grade Span: PK-12; **Agency Type:** 1
Schools: 8
  6 Primary; 1 Middle; 1 High; 0 Other Level
  8 Regular; 0 Special Education; 0 Vocational; 0 Alternative
  0 Magnet; 0 Charter; 4 Title I Eligible; 0 School-wide Title I
Students: 3,309 (51.6% male; 48.3% female)
  Individual Education Program: 515 (15.6%);
  English Language Learner: 0 (0.0%); Migrant: 0 (0.0%)
  Eligible for Free Lunch Program: 594 (18.0%)
  Eligible for Reduced-Price Lunch Program: 230 (7.0%)
Teachers: 211.9 (15.6 to 1)
Librarians/Media Specialists: 4.0 (827.3 to 1)
Guidance Counselors: 7.5 (441.2 to 1)
Current Spending: ($ per student per year):
  Total: $5,393; Instruction: $3,329; Support Services: $1,649
Enrollment, Drop-out Rates and Diploma Recipients by Race/Ethnicity

Category	Total	White	Black	Asian	AIAN	Hisp.
Enrollment (%)	100.0	93.4	0.9	0.0	5.2	0.5
Drop-out Rate (%)	2.5	2.3	0.0	0.0	10.3	0.0
H.S. Diplomas (#)	248	246	0	0	2	0

Ramsey County

Devils Lake 1
1601 College Dr N • Devils Lake, ND 58301-1550
(701) 662-7640
Grade Span: PK-12; **Agency Type:** 1
Schools: 5
  3 Primary; 1 Middle; 1 High; 0 Other Level
  5 Regular; 0 Special Education; 0 Vocational; 0 Alternative
  0 Magnet; 0 Charter; 4 Title I Eligible; 1 School-wide Title I
Students: 1,870 (50.3% male; 49.6% female)
  Individual Education Program: 294 (15.7%);
  English Language Learner: 0 (0.0%); Migrant: 0 (0.0%)
  Eligible for Free Lunch Program: 527 (28.2%)
  Eligible for Reduced-Price Lunch Program: 115 (6.1%)
Teachers: 124.6 (15.0 to 1)
Librarians/Media Specialists: 3.0 (623.3 to 1)
Guidance Counselors: 3.0 (623.3 to 1)
Current Spending: ($ per student per year):
  Total: $6,053; Instruction: $3,512; Support Services: $1,922
Enrollment, Drop-out Rates and Diploma Recipients by Race/Ethnicity

Category	Total	White	Black	Asian	AIAN	Hisp.
Enrollment (%)	100.0	75.6	0.4	0.5	22.7	0.9
Drop-out Rate (%)	3.4	1.9	50.0	n/a	9.6	0.0
H.S. Diplomas (#)	159	140	2	0	16	1

Richland County

Wahpeton 37
1505 11th St N • Wahpeton, ND 58075-3551
(701) 642-6741
Grade Span: PK-12; **Agency Type:** 1
Schools: 4
  2 Primary; 1 Middle; 1 High; 0 Other Level
  4 Regular; 0 Special Education; 0 Vocational; 0 Alternative
  0 Magnet; 0 Charter; 3 Title I Eligible; 0 School-wide Title I
Students: 1,514 (52.9% male; 47.0% female)
  Individual Education Program: 198 (13.1%);
  English Language Learner: 28 (1.8%); Migrant: 36 (2.4%)
  Eligible for Free Lunch Program: 247 (16.3%)
  Eligible for Reduced-Price Lunch Program: 72 (4.8%)

Teachers: 90.7 (16.7 to 1)
Librarians/Media Specialists: 2.0 (757.0 to 1)
Guidance Counselors: 2.0 (757.0 to 1)
Current Spending: ($ per student per year):
Total: $5,410; Instruction: $3,513; Support Services: $1,556
Enrollment, Drop-out Rates and Diploma Recipients by Race/Ethnicity

Category	Total	White	Black	Asian	AIAN	Hisp.
Enrollment (%)	100.0	91.0	0.8	1.0	4.8	2.4
Drop-out Rate (%)	2.8	2.6	n/a	0.0	13.3	0.0
H.S. Diplomas (#)	115	113	0	0	1	1

Rolette County

Belcourt 7
Hwy 5 E • Belcourt, ND 58316-0440
Mailing Address: PO Box 440 • Belcourt, ND 58316-0440
(701) 477-6471
Grade Span: KG-12; **Agency Type:** 1
Schools: 3
1 Primary; 1 Middle; 1 High; 0 Other Level
3 Regular; 0 Special Education; 0 Vocational; 0 Alternative
0 Magnet; 0 Charter; 3 Title I Eligible; 3 School-wide Title I
Students: 1,727 (51.9% male; 48.0% female)
Individual Education Program: 69 (4.0%);
English Language Learner: 0 (0.0%); Migrant: 0 (0.0%)
Eligible for Free Lunch Program: 1,189 (68.8%)
Eligible for Reduced-Price Lunch Program: 51 (3.0%)
Teachers: 176.5 (9.8 to 1)
Librarians/Media Specialists: 3.8 (454.5 to 1)
Guidance Counselors: 7.0 (246.7 to 1)
Current Spending: ($ per student per year):
Total: $7,959; Instruction: $4,619; Support Services: $2,685
Enrollment, Drop-out Rates and Diploma Recipients by Race/Ethnicity

Category	Total	White	Black	Asian	AIAN	Hisp.
Enrollment (%)	100.0	4.3	0.1	0.0	95.5	0.1
Drop-out Rate (%)	15.4	0.0	n/a	n/a	16.5	n/a
H.S. Diplomas (#)	100	0	0	0	100	0

Stark County

Dickinson 1
444 4th St W • Dickinson, ND 58601-4951
Mailing Address: PO Box 1057 • Dickinson, ND 58602-1057
(701) 456-0002
Grade Span: PK-12; **Agency Type:** 1
Schools: 9
6 Primary; 1 Middle; 2 High; 0 Other Level
9 Regular; 0 Special Education; 0 Vocational; 0 Alternative
0 Magnet; 0 Charter; 6 Title I Eligible; 2 School-wide Title I
Students: 2,710 (52.2% male; 47.7% female)
Individual Education Program: 385 (14.2%);
English Language Learner: 0 (0.0%); Migrant: 0 (0.0%)
Eligible for Free Lunch Program: 507 (18.7%)
Eligible for Reduced-Price Lunch Program: 271 (10.0%)
Teachers: 179.5 (15.1 to 1)
Librarians/Media Specialists: 4.0 (677.5 to 1)
Guidance Counselors: 6.0 (451.7 to 1)
Current Spending: ($ per student per year):
Total: $5,944; Instruction: $3,851; Support Services: $1,495
Enrollment, Drop-out Rates and Diploma Recipients by Race/Ethnicity

Category	Total	White	Black	Asian	AIAN	Hisp.
Enrollment (%)	100.0	96.0	0.8	0.6	1.8	0.7
Drop-out Rate (%)	2.3	2.4	n/a	0.0	0.0	0.0
H.S. Diplomas (#)	216	215	0	0	1	0

Stutsman County

Jamestown 1
120 2nd St SE • Jamestown, ND 58401-4260
Mailing Address: PO Box 269 • Jamestown, ND 58402-0269
(701) 252-1950
Grade Span: PK-12; **Agency Type:** 1
Schools: 8
5 Primary; 1 Middle; 1 High; 1 Other Level
8 Regular; 0 Special Education; 0 Vocational; 0 Alternative
0 Magnet; 0 Charter; 5 Title I Eligible; 0 School-wide Title I
Students: 2,487 (50.4% male; 49.5% female)
Individual Education Program: 370 (14.9%);
English Language Learner: 19 (0.8%); Migrant: 16 (0.6%)
Eligible for Free Lunch Program: 431 (17.3%)
Eligible for Reduced-Price Lunch Program: 246 (9.9%)
Teachers: 166.4 (14.9 to 1)
Librarians/Media Specialists: 3.0 (829.0 to 1)
Guidance Counselors: 6.0 (414.5 to 1)

Current Spending: ($ per student per year):
Total: $5,851; Instruction: $3,723; Support Services: $1,698
Enrollment, Drop-out Rates and Diploma Recipients by Race/Ethnicity

Category	Total	White	Black	Asian	AIAN	Hisp.
Enrollment (%)	100.0	94.9	0.9	0.8	2.2	1.2
Drop-out Rate (%)	1.6	1.6	0.0	0.0	0.0	0.0
H.S. Diplomas (#)	214	210	0	3	1	0

Ward County

Minot 1
215 2nd St SE • Minot, ND 58701-3985
(701) 857-4400 • http://www4.minot.k12.nd.us/
Grade Span: PK-12; **Agency Type:** 1
Schools: 18
12 Primary; 3 Middle; 2 High; 1 Other Level
18 Regular; 0 Special Education; 0 Vocational; 0 Alternative
0 Magnet; 0 Charter; 11 Title I Eligible; 1 School-wide Title I
Students: 6,858 (51.9% male; 48.0% female)
Individual Education Program: 1,118 (16.3%);
English Language Learner: 0 (0.0%); Migrant: 0 (0.0%)
Eligible for Free Lunch Program: 1,235 (18.0%)
Eligible for Reduced-Price Lunch Program: 655 (9.6%)
Teachers: 471.9 (14.5 to 1)
Librarians/Media Specialists: 4.5 (1,524.0 to 1)
Guidance Counselors: 20.2 (339.5 to 1)
Current Spending: ($ per student per year):
Total: $6,559; Instruction: $4,344; Support Services: $1,829
Enrollment, Drop-out Rates and Diploma Recipients by Race/Ethnicity

Category	Total	White	Black	Asian	AIAN	Hisp.
Enrollment (%)	100.0	88.8	3.2	1.3	5.2	1.4
Drop-out Rate (%)	2.2	2.1	1.4	4.3	4.6	1.7
H.S. Diplomas (#)	463	427	15	1	7	13

Williams County

Williston 1
1201 9th Ave NW • Williston, ND 58801-3804
Mailing Address: PO Box 1407 • Williston, ND 58802-1407
(701) 572-1580
Grade Span: KG-12; **Agency Type:** 1
Schools: 6
4 Primary; 1 Middle; 1 High; 0 Other Level
6 Regular; 0 Special Education; 0 Vocational; 0 Alternative
0 Magnet; 0 Charter; 5 Title I Eligible; 2 School-wide Title I
Students: 2,204 (51.4% male; 48.5% female)
Individual Education Program: 359 (16.3%);
English Language Learner: 0 (0.0%); Migrant: 0 (0.0%)
Eligible for Free Lunch Program: 475 (21.6%)
Eligible for Reduced-Price Lunch Program: 141 (6.4%)
Teachers: 160.7 (13.7 to 1)
Librarians/Media Specialists: 3.4 (648.2 to 1)
Guidance Counselors: 6.3 (349.8 to 1)
Current Spending: ($ per student per year):
Total: $5,484; Instruction: $3,594; Support Services: $1,432
Enrollment, Drop-out Rates and Diploma Recipients by Race/Ethnicity

Category	Total	White	Black	Asian	AIAN	Hisp.
Enrollment (%)	100.0	90.3	0.3	0.1	8.0	1.3
Drop-out Rate (%)	2.7	2.9	0.0	0.0	0.0	0.0
H.S. Diplomas (#)	235	220	0	1	14	0

Number of Schools

Rank	Number	District Name	City
1	22	Bismarck 1	Bismarck
1	22	Fargo 1	Fargo
3	19	Grand Forks 1	Grand Forks
4	18	Minot 1	Minot
5	9	Dickinson 1	Dickinson
5	9	West Fargo 6	West Fargo
7	8	Jamestown 1	Jamestown
7	8	Mandan 1	Mandan
9	6	Williston 1	Williston
10	5	Devils Lake 1	Devils Lake
11	4	Wahpeton 37	Wahpeton
12	3	Belcourt 7	Belcourt

Number of Teachers

Rank	Number	District Name	City
1	703	Fargo 1	Fargo
2	662	Bismarck 1	Bismarck
3	597	Grand Forks 1	Grand Forks
4	471	Minot 1	Minot
5	327	West Fargo 6	West Fargo
6	211	Mandan 1	Mandan
7	179	Dickinson 1	Dickinson
8	176	Belcourt 7	Belcourt
9	166	Jamestown 1	Jamestown
10	160	Williston 1	Williston
11	124	Devils Lake 1	Devils Lake
12	90	Wahpeton 37	Wahpeton

Number of Students

Rank	Number	District Name	City
1	11,214	Fargo 1	Fargo
2	10,477	Bismarck 1	Bismarck
3	7,932	Grand Forks 1	Grand Forks
4	6,858	Minot 1	Minot
5	5,424	West Fargo 6	West Fargo
6	3,309	Mandan 1	Mandan
7	2,710	Dickinson 1	Dickinson
8	2,487	Jamestown 1	Jamestown
9	2,204	Williston 1	Williston
10	1,870	Devils Lake 1	Devils Lake
11	1,727	Belcourt 7	Belcourt
12	1,514	Wahpeton 37	Wahpeton

Male Students

Rank	Percent	District Name	City
1	52.9	Wahpeton 37	Wahpeton
2	52.2	Dickinson 1	Dickinson
3	51.9	Belcourt 7	Belcourt
4	51.9	Minot 1	Minot
5	51.8	Grand Forks 1	Grand Forks
6	51.6	Mandan 1	Mandan
7	51.4	Williston 1	Williston
8	51.0	West Fargo 6	West Fargo
9	50.9	Bismarck 1	Bismarck
10	50.8	Fargo 1	Fargo
11	50.4	Jamestown 1	Jamestown
12	50.3	Devils Lake 1	Devils Lake

Female Students

Rank	Percent	District Name	City
1	49.6	Devils Lake 1	Devils Lake
2	49.5	Jamestown 1	Jamestown
3	49.1	Fargo 1	Fargo
4	49.0	Bismarck 1	Bismarck
5	48.9	West Fargo 6	West Fargo
6	48.5	Williston 1	Williston
7	48.3	Mandan 1	Mandan
8	48.1	Grand Forks 1	Grand Forks
9	48.0	Minot 1	Minot
10	48.0	Belcourt 7	Belcourt
11	47.7	Dickinson 1	Dickinson
12	47.0	Wahpeton 37	Wahpeton

Individual Education Program Students

Rank	Percent	District Name	City
1	16.3	Minot 1	Minot
1	16.3	Williston 1	Williston
3	15.7	Devils Lake 1	Devils Lake
4	15.6	Mandan 1	Mandan
5	14.9	Jamestown 1	Jamestown
6	14.2	Dickinson 1	Dickinson
7	13.6	Grand Forks 1	Grand Forks
8	13.1	Wahpeton 37	Wahpeton
9	12.0	West Fargo 6	West Fargo
10	11.9	Bismarck 1	Bismarck
11	11.5	Fargo 1	Fargo

| 12 | 4.0 | Belcourt 7 | Belcourt |

English Language Learner Students

Rank	Percent	District Name	City
1	5.1	Fargo 1	Fargo
2	3.9	West Fargo 6	West Fargo
3	1.8	Wahpeton 37	Wahpeton
4	0.9	Grand Forks 1	Grand Forks
5	0.8	Jamestown 1	Jamestown
6	0.2	Bismarck 1	Bismarck
7	0.0	Belcourt 7	Belcourt
7	0.0	Devils Lake 1	Devils Lake
7	0.0	Dickinson 1	Dickinson
7	0.0	Mandan 1	Mandan
7	0.0	Minot 1	Minot
7	0.0	Williston 1	Williston

Migrant Students

Rank	Percent	District Name	City
1	2.4	Wahpeton 37	Wahpeton
2	0.6	Jamestown 1	Jamestown
3	0.1	Grand Forks 1	Grand Forks
4	0.0	Belcourt 7	Belcourt
4	0.0	Bismarck 1	Bismarck
4	0.0	Devils Lake 1	Devils Lake
4	0.0	Dickinson 1	Dickinson
4	0.0	Fargo 1	Fargo
4	0.0	Mandan 1	Mandan
4	0.0	Minot 1	Minot
4	0.0	West Fargo 6	West Fargo
4	0.0	Williston 1	Williston

Students Eligible for Free Lunch

Rank	Percent	District Name	City
1	68.8	Belcourt 7	Belcourt
2	28.2	Devils Lake 1	Devils Lake
3	21.6	Williston 1	Williston
4	18.7	Dickinson 1	Dickinson
5	18.4	Grand Forks 1	Grand Forks
6	18.0	Mandan 1	Mandan
6	18.0	Minot 1	Minot
8	17.3	Jamestown 1	Jamestown
9	16.3	Wahpeton 37	Wahpeton
10	13.6	West Fargo 6	West Fargo
11	12.6	Bismarck 1	Bismarck
12	12.3	Fargo 1	Fargo

Students Eligible for Reduced-Price Lunch

Rank	Percent	District Name	City
1	10.0	Dickinson 1	Dickinson
2	9.9	Jamestown 1	Jamestown
3	9.6	Minot 1	Minot
4	8.5	Grand Forks 1	Grand Forks
5	7.0	Mandan 1	Mandan
6	6.4	Williston 1	Williston
7	6.1	Devils Lake 1	Devils Lake
7	6.1	West Fargo 6	West Fargo
9	5.6	Bismarck 1	Bismarck
10	4.8	Wahpeton 37	Wahpeton
11	4.3	Fargo 1	Fargo
12	3.0	Belcourt 7	Belcourt

Student/Teacher Ratio

Rank	Ratio	District Name	City
1	16.7	Wahpeton 37	Wahpeton
2	16.6	West Fargo 6	West Fargo
3	15.9	Fargo 1	Fargo
4	15.8	Bismarck 1	Bismarck
5	15.6	Mandan 1	Mandan
6	15.1	Dickinson 1	Dickinson
7	15.0	Devils Lake 1	Devils Lake
8	14.9	Jamestown 1	Jamestown
9	14.5	Minot 1	Minot
10	13.7	Williston 1	Williston
11	13.3	Grand Forks 1	Grand Forks
12	9.8	Belcourt 7	Belcourt

Student/Librarian Ratio

Rank	Ratio	District Name	City
1	1,524.0	Minot 1	Minot
2	1,179.1	West Fargo 6	West Fargo
3	844.9	Bismarck 1	Bismarck
4	829.0	Jamestown 1	Jamestown
5	827.3	Mandan 1	Mandan
6	757.0	Wahpeton 37	Wahpeton
7	677.5	Dickinson 1	Dickinson
8	659.6	Fargo 1	Fargo
9	648.2	Williston 1	Williston
10	623.3	Devils Lake 1	Devils Lake
11	543.3	Grand Forks 1	Grand Forks
12	454.5	Belcourt 7	Belcourt

Student/Counselor Ratio

Rank	Ratio	District Name	City
1	757.0	Wahpeton 37	Wahpeton
2	623.3	Devils Lake 1	Devils Lake
3	484.3	West Fargo 6	West Fargo
4	451.7	Dickinson 1	Dickinson
5	441.2	Mandan 1	Mandan
6	417.4	Bismarck 1	Bismarck
7	414.5	Jamestown 1	Jamestown
8	384.0	Fargo 1	Fargo
9	377.7	Grand Forks 1	Grand Forks
10	349.8	Williston 1	Williston
11	339.5	Minot 1	Minot
12	246.7	Belcourt 7	Belcourt

Current Spending per Student in FY2003

Rank	Dollars	District Name	City
1	7,959	Belcourt 7	Belcourt
2	7,328	Fargo 1	Fargo
3	6,729	Grand Forks 1	Grand Forks
4	6,559	Minot 1	Minot
5	6,448	West Fargo 6	West Fargo
6	6,247	Bismarck 1	Bismarck
7	6,053	Devils Lake 1	Devils Lake
8	5,944	Dickinson 1	Dickinson
9	5,851	Jamestown 1	Jamestown
10	5,484	Williston 1	Williston
11	5,410	Wahpeton 37	Wahpeton
12	5,393	Mandan 1	Mandan

Number of Diploma Recipients

Rank	Number	District Name	City
1	828	Bismarck 1	Bismarck
2	781	Fargo 1	Fargo
3	540	Grand Forks 1	Grand Forks
4	463	Minot 1	Minot
5	337	West Fargo 6	West Fargo
6	248	Mandan 1	Mandan
7	235	Williston 1	Williston
8	216	Dickinson 1	Dickinson
9	214	Jamestown 1	Jamestown
10	159	Devils Lake 1	Devils Lake
11	115	Wahpeton 37	Wahpeton
12	100	Belcourt 7	Belcourt

High School Drop-out Rate

Rank	Percent	District Name	City
1	15.4	Belcourt 7	Belcourt
2	3.8	Fargo 1	Fargo
3	3.4	Devils Lake 1	Devils Lake
4	2.8	Wahpeton 37	Wahpeton
5	2.7	West Fargo 6	West Fargo
5	2.7	Williston 1	Williston
7	2.5	Mandan 1	Mandan
8	2.3	Dickinson 1	Dickinson
9	2.2	Minot 1	Minot
10	1.6	Jamestown 1	Jamestown
11	1.3	Bismarck 1	Bismarck
12	1.2	Grand Forks 1	Grand Forks

Ohio

Ohio Public School Educational Profile

Category	Value	Category	Value
Schools (2003-2004)	3,988	**Diploma Recipients** (2002-2003)	110,608
Instructional Level		White, Non-Hispanic	95,036
Primary	2,187	Black, Non-Hispanic	11,945
Middle	744	Asian/Pacific Islander	1,568
High	802	American Indian/Alaskan Native	100
Other Level	209	Hispanic	1,441
Curriculum		**High School Drop-out Rate** (%) (2001-2002)	3.1
Regular	3,797	White, Non-Hispanic	2.4
Special Education	61	Black, Non-Hispanic	7.2
Vocational	75	Asian/Pacific Islander	2.0
Alternative	9	American Indian/Alaskan Native	7.1
Type		Hispanic	6.6
Magnet	0	**Staff** (2003-2004)	
Charter	165	Teachers	121,734.7
Title I Eligible	2,659	Average Salary ($)	47,791
School-wide Title I	1,000	Librarians/Media Specialists	1,669.4
Students (2003-2004)	1,845,428	Guidance Counselors	3,694.1
Gender (%)		**Ratios** (2003-2004)	
Male	51.5	Student/Teacher Ratio	15.2 to 1
Female	48.5	Student/Librarian Ratio	1,105.4 to 1
Race/Ethnicity (%)		Student/Counselor Ratio	499.6 to 1
White, Non-Hispanic	77.8	**College Entrance Exam Scores** (2005)	
Black, Non-Hispanic	16.7	Scholastic Aptitude Test (SAT)	
Asian/Pacific Islander	1.3	Participation Rate (%)	29
American Indian/Alaskan Native	0.1	Mean SAT Reasoning Test Verbal Score	539
Hispanic	2.1	Mean SAT Reasoning Test Math Score	543
Classification (%)		American College Testing Program (ACT)	
Individual Education Program (IEP)	13.9	Participation Rate (%)	66
Migrant (2002-2003)	0.1	Average Composite Score	21.4
English Language Learner (ELL)	1.3	Average English Score	20.7
Eligible for Free Lunch Program	24.0	Average Math Score	21.2
Eligible for Reduced-Price Lunch Program	5.5	Average Reading Score	21.9
Current Spending ($ per student in FY 2003)	8,027	Average Science Score	21.5
Instruction	4,693		
Support Services	3,049		

Note: *For an explanation of data, please refer to the User's Guide in the front of the book*

Ohio NAEP 2005 Test Scores

Reading			Mathematics		
Grade/Category	Value	Rank	Grade/Category	Value	Rank
4th Grade			**4th Grade**		
Average Proficiency	222.5 (1.35)	17/51	Average Proficiency	242.1 (1.00)	9/51
Proficiency by Gender/Race/Ethnicity			Proficiency by Gender/Race/Ethnicity		
Male	219.4 (1.82)	15/51	Male	243.2 (1.13)	12/51
Female	225.7 (1.32)	17/51	Female	241.0 (1.11)	8/51
White, Non-Hispanic	229.5 (1.28)	13/51	White, Non-Hispanic	248.5 (0.98)	12/51
Black, Non-Hispanic	196.5 (1.94)	27/42	Black, Non-Hispanic	220.8 (2.06)	18/42
Asian, Non-Hispanic	n/a	n/a	Asian, Non-Hispanic	n/a	n/a
American Indian, Non-Hispanic	n/a	n/a	American Indian, Non-Hispanic	n/a	n/a
Hispanic	210.6 (5.59)	8/40	Hispanic	230.8 (3.51)	9/41
Proficiency by Class Size			Proficiency by Class Size		
Less than 16 Students	n/a	n/a	Less than 16 Students	n/a	n/a
16 to 18 Students	214.6 (4.89)	23/33	16 to 18 Students	n/a	n/a
19 to 20 Students	223.5 (2.68)	18/38	19 to 20 Students	244.9 (2.77)	6/38
21 to 25 Students	223.8 (2.21)	20/51	21 to 25 Students	242.5 (1.88)	17/51
Greater than 25 Students	225.0 (3.24)	5/36	Greater than 25 Students	242.2 (3.23)	6/33
Percent Attaining Achievement Levels			Percent Attaining Achievement Levels		
Below Basic	31.3 (1.61)	35/51	Below Basic	16.0 (1.16)	34/51
Basic or Above	68.7 (1.61)	17/51	Basic or Above	84.0 (1.16)	17/51
Proficient or Above	34.4 (1.64)	15/51	Proficient or Above	42.5 (1.51)	8/51
Advanced or Above	7.7 (0.88)	13/51	Advanced or Above	6.6 (0.67)	7/51
8th Grade			**8th Grade**		
Average Proficiency	266.8 (1.25)	14/51	Average Proficiency	283.3 (1.10)	15/51
Proficiency by Gender/Race/Ethnicity			Proficiency by Gender/Race/Ethnicity		
Male	261.3 (1.50)	15/51	Male	284.2 (1.22)	14/51
Female	271.9 (1.39)	14/51	Female	282.3 (1.37)	14/51
White, Non-Hispanic	272.0 (1.25)	13/51	White, Non-Hispanic	288.9 (0.99)	21/51
Black, Non-Hispanic	242.7 (2.60)	18/40	Black, Non-Hispanic	255.2 (2.12)	20/41
Asian, Non-Hispanic	n/a	n/a	Asian, Non-Hispanic	n/a	n/a
American Indian, Non-Hispanic	n/a	n/a	American Indian, Non-Hispanic	n/a	n/a
Hispanic	245.2 (4.49)	27/38	Hispanic	259.4 (5.85)	27/38
Proficiency by Parents Highest Level of Ed.			Proficiency by Parents Highest Level of Ed.		
Did Not Finish High School	244.1 (4.98)	29/49	Did Not Finish High School	265.5 (3.78)	10/50
Graduated High School	260.2 (1.38)	8/50	Graduated High School	272.2 (1.62)	15/50
Some Education After High School	270.4 (1.70)	6/50	Some Education After High School	283.4 (1.91)	17/50
Graduated College	275.4 (1.41)	11/50	Graduated College	293.7 (1.32)	11/50
Percent Attaining Achievement Levels			Percent Attaining Achievement Levels		
Below Basic	31.3 (1.61)	35/51	Below Basic	25.7 (1.35)	37/51
Basic or Above	68.7 (1.61)	17/51	Basic or Above	74.3 (1.35)	15/51
Proficient or Above	34.4 (1.64)	15/51	Proficient or Above	33.1 (1.44)	17/51
Advanced or Above	7.7 (0.88)	13/51	Advanced or Above	6.6 (0.59)	13/51

Note: For an explanation of data, please refer to the User's Guide in the front of the book; n/a indicates data not available

Adams County

Adams County/Ohio Valley Local SD
141 Lloyd Rd • West Union, OH 45693-8974
(937) 544-5586 • http://www.ohiovalley.k12.oh.us/
Grade Span: PK-12; **Agency Type:** 2
Schools: 10
  4 Primary; 0 Middle; 5 High; 1 Other Level
  8 Regular; 1 Special Education; 1 Vocational; 0 Alternative
  0 Magnet; 0 Charter; 7 Title I Eligible; 4 School-wide Title I
Students: 5,098 (50.0% male; 49.9% female)
  Individual Education Program: 772 (15.1%);
  English Language Learner: 1 (<0.1%); Migrant: n/a
  Eligible for Free Lunch Program: 2,048 (40.2%)
  Eligible for Reduced-Price Lunch Program: 441 (8.7%)
Teachers: 336.5 (15.2 to 1)
Librarians/Media Specialists: 3.0 (1,699.3 to 1)
Guidance Counselors: 9.0 (566.4 to 1)
Current Spending: ($ per student per year):
  Total: $7,149; Instruction: $4,301; Support Services: $2,470
Enrollment, Drop-out Rates and Diploma Recipients by Race/Ethnicity

Category	Total	White	Black	Asian	AIAN	Hisp.
Enrollment (%)	100.0	98.5	0.3	0.2	0.2	0.4
Drop-out Rate (%)	3.2	3.1	0.0	0.0	25.0	12.5
H.S. Diplomas (#)	306	304	1	0	1	0

Allen County

Bath Local SD
2650 Bible Rd • Lima, OH 45801-2246
(419) 221-0807 • http://www.noacsc.org/allen/ba/
Grade Span: PK-12; **Agency Type:** 2
Schools: 3
  1 Primary; 1 Middle; 1 High; 0 Other Level
  3 Regular; 0 Special Education; 0 Vocational; 0 Alternative
  0 Magnet; 0 Charter; 3 Title I Eligible; 0 School-wide Title I
Students: 2,085 (50.6% male; 49.3% female)
  Individual Education Program: 220 (10.6%);
  English Language Learner: 1 (<0.1%); Migrant: n/a
  Eligible for Free Lunch Program: 347 (16.6%)
  Eligible for Reduced-Price Lunch Program: 167 (8.0%)
Teachers: 102.8 (20.3 to 1)
Librarians/Media Specialists: 2.0 (1,042.5 to 1)
Guidance Counselors: 4.0 (521.3 to 1)
Current Spending: ($ per student per year):
  Total: $6,751; Instruction: $3,900; Support Services: $2,503
Enrollment, Drop-out Rates and Diploma Recipients by Race/Ethnicity

Category	Total	White	Black	Asian	AIAN	Hisp.
Enrollment (%)	100.0	92.9	3.5	1.2	0.0	1.2
Drop-out Rate (%)	1.8	1.7	9.1	0.0	0.0	0.0
H.S. Diplomas (#)	152	145	1	2	1	3

Elida Local SD
4380 Sunnydale St • Elida, OH 45807-9593
(419) 331-4155 • http://www.noacsc.org/allen/el/
Grade Span: PK-12; **Agency Type:** 2
Schools: 4
  1 Primary; 2 Middle; 1 High; 0 Other Level
  4 Regular; 0 Special Education; 0 Vocational; 0 Alternative
  0 Magnet; 0 Charter; 3 Title I Eligible; 1 School-wide Title I
Students: 2,591 (51.7% male; 48.2% female)
  Individual Education Program: 269 (10.4%);
  English Language Learner: 15 (0.6%); Migrant: n/a
  Eligible for Free Lunch Program: 538 (20.8%)
  Eligible for Reduced-Price Lunch Program: 155 (6.0%)
Teachers: 140.0 (18.5 to 1)
Librarians/Media Specialists: 1.0 (2,591.0 to 1)
Guidance Counselors: 5.0 (518.2 to 1)
Current Spending: ($ per student per year):
  Total: $6,552; Instruction: $3,965; Support Services: $2,237
Enrollment, Drop-out Rates and Diploma Recipients by Race/Ethnicity

Category	Total	White	Black	Asian	AIAN	Hisp.
Enrollment (%)	100.0	82.6	10.3	1.8	0.1	1.7
Drop-out Rate (%)	2.1	1.9	1.5	15.4	0.0	0.0
H.S. Diplomas (#)	187	168	14	2	0	1

Lima City SD
515 Calumet Ave • Lima, OH 45804-1405
(419) 996-3400 • http://www.limacityschools.org/
Grade Span: PK-12; **Agency Type:** 1
Schools: 14
  7 Primary; 3 Middle; 2 High; 0 Other Level
  11 Regular; 1 Special Education; 0 Vocational; 0 Alternative
  0 Magnet; 0 Charter; 12 Title I Eligible; 10 School-wide Title I
Students: 4,994 (52.4% male; 47.5% female)

Individual Education Program: 1,021 (20.4%);
English Language Learner: 11 (0.2%); Migrant: n/a
Eligible for Free Lunch Program: 3,135 (62.8%)
Eligible for Reduced-Price Lunch Program: 320 (6.4%)
Teachers: 365.6 (13.7 to 1)
Librarians/Media Specialists: 3.0 (1,664.7 to 1)
Guidance Counselors: 8.6 (580.7 to 1)
Current Spending: ($ per student per year):
  Total: $8,698; Instruction: $4,950; Support Services: $3,342
Enrollment, Drop-out Rates and Diploma Recipients by Race/Ethnicity

Category	Total	White	Black	Asian	AIAN	Hisp.
Enrollment (%)	100.0	48.0	41.5	0.1	0.3	1.5
Drop-out Rate (%)	12.2	10.5	13.3	0.0	n/a	11.1
H.S. Diplomas (#)	244	128	111	0	0	0

Shawnee Local SD
3255 Zurmehly Rd • Lima, OH 45806-1434
(419) 998-8031 • http://shawnee.noacsc.org/
Grade Span: PK-12; **Agency Type:** 2
Schools: 4
  2 Primary; 1 Middle; 1 High; 0 Other Level
  4 Regular; 0 Special Education; 0 Vocational; 0 Alternative
  0 Magnet; 0 Charter; 3 Title I Eligible; 0 School-wide Title I
Students: 2,657 (51.5% male; 48.4% female)
  Individual Education Program: 240 (9.0%);
  English Language Learner: 0 (0.0%); Migrant: n/a
  Eligible for Free Lunch Program: 336 (12.6%)
  Eligible for Reduced-Price Lunch Program: 124 (4.7%)
Teachers: 139.8 (19.0 to 1)
Librarians/Media Specialists: 1.0 (2,657.0 to 1)
Guidance Counselors: 7.0 (379.6 to 1)
Current Spending: ($ per student per year):
  Total: $6,908; Instruction: $3,905; Support Services: $2,709
Enrollment, Drop-out Rates and Diploma Recipients by Race/Ethnicity

Category	Total	White	Black	Asian	AIAN	Hisp.
Enrollment (%)	100.0	85.9	7.6	2.0	0.4	1.6
Drop-out Rate (%)	2.0	1.7	4.0	0.0	0.0	0.0
H.S. Diplomas (#)	171	146	16	5	0	2

Ashland County

Ashland City SD
416 Arthur St • Ashland, OH 44805-3207
Mailing Address: PO Box 160 • Ashland, OH 44805-0160
(419) 289-1117 • http://www.ashland-city.k12.oh.us/index.asp
Grade Span: PK-12; **Agency Type:** 1
Schools: 8
  5 Primary; 1 Middle; 2 High; 0 Other Level
  8 Regular; 0 Special Education; 0 Vocational; 0 Alternative
  0 Magnet; 0 Charter; 4 Title I Eligible; 2 School-wide Title I
Students: 3,817 (53.2% male; 46.7% female)
  Individual Education Program: 584 (15.3%);
  English Language Learner: 7 (0.2%); Migrant: n/a
  Eligible for Free Lunch Program: 792 (20.7%)
  Eligible for Reduced-Price Lunch Program: 271 (7.1%)
Teachers: 225.8 (16.9 to 1)
Librarians/Media Specialists: 3.0 (1,272.3 to 1)
Guidance Counselors: 7.0 (545.3 to 1)
Current Spending: ($ per student per year):
  Total: $7,110; Instruction: $4,381; Support Services: $2,429
Enrollment, Drop-out Rates and Diploma Recipients by Race/Ethnicity

Category	Total	White	Black	Asian	AIAN	Hisp.
Enrollment (%)	100.0	95.7	1.2	0.9	0.2	0.6
Drop-out Rate (%)	2.9	3.0	0.0	0.0	n/a	0.0
H.S. Diplomas (#)	288	278	3	5	0	2

Ashtabula County

Ashtabula Area City SD
401 W 44th St • Ashtabula, OH 44004-6807
Mailing Address: PO Box 290 • Ashtabula, OH 44005-0290
(440) 993-2500 • http://aacs.net/
Grade Span: KG-12; **Agency Type:** 1
Schools: 12
  8 Primary; 2 Middle; 1 High; 1 Other Level
  12 Regular; 0 Special Education; 0 Vocational; 0 Alternative
  0 Magnet; 0 Charter; 10 Title I Eligible; 7 School-wide Title I
Students: 4,661 (52.0% male; 47.9% female)
  Individual Education Program: 872 (18.7%);
  English Language Learner: 139 (3.0%); Migrant: 1 (<0.1%)
  Eligible for Free Lunch Program: 2,081 (45.6%)
  Eligible for Reduced-Price Lunch Program: 355 (7.8%)
Teachers: 282.5 (16.2 to 1)
Librarians/Media Specialists: 1.0 (4,568.0 to 1)
Guidance Counselors: 6.0 (761.3 to 1)

Current Spending: ($ per student per year):
Total: $7,739; Instruction: $5,006; Support Services: $2,430
Enrollment, Drop-out Rates and Diploma Recipients by Race/Ethnicity

Category	Total	White	Black	Asian	AIAN	Hisp.
Enrollment (%)	100.0	76.1	11.2	0.5	0.1	7.2
Drop-out Rate (%)	6.1	5.7	4.0	0.0	n/a	18.0
H.S. Diplomas (#)	240	190	40	1	0	8

Buckeye Local SD
3436 Edgewood Dr • Ashtabula, OH 44004-5967
(440) 998-4411
Grade Span: PK-12; **Agency Type:** 2
Schools: 6
4 Primary; 1 Middle; 1 High; 0 Other Level
6 Regular; 0 Special Education; 0 Vocational; 0 Alternative
0 Magnet; 0 Charter; 3 Title I Eligible; 3 School-wide Title I
Students: 2,287   (49.1% male; 50.8% female)
Individual Education Program: 244 (10.7%);
English Language Learner: 7 (0.3%); Migrant: n/a
Eligible for Free Lunch Program: 548 (24.0%)
Eligible for Reduced-Price Lunch Program: 256 (11.2%)
Teachers: 139.0 (16.5 to 1)
Librarians/Media Specialists: 1.0 (2,287.0 to 1)
Guidance Counselors: 3.0 (762.3 to 1)
Current Spending: ($ per student per year):
Total: $7,653; Instruction: $4,664; Support Services: $2,644
Enrollment, Drop-out Rates and Diploma Recipients by Race/Ethnicity

Category	Total	White	Black	Asian	AIAN	Hisp.
Enrollment (%)	100.0	96.3	1.4	0.5	0.1	0.6
Drop-out Rate (%)	3.0	2.8	14.3	0.0	n/a	33.3
H.S. Diplomas (#)	160	155	2	1	0	1

Conneaut Area City SD
263 Liberty St • Conneaut, OH 44030-2705
(440) 593-7200
Grade Span: PK-12; **Agency Type:** 1
Schools: 8
4 Primary; 1 Middle; 1 High; 0 Other Level
6 Regular; 0 Special Education; 0 Vocational; 0 Alternative
0 Magnet; 0 Charter; 6 Title I Eligible; 4 School-wide Title I
Students: 2,527   (52.4% male; 47.5% female)
Individual Education Program: 370 (14.6%);
English Language Learner: 0 (0.0%); Migrant: n/a
Eligible for Free Lunch Program: 990 (39.2%)
Eligible for Reduced-Price Lunch Program: 242 (9.6%)
Teachers: 156.5 (16.1 to 1)
Librarians/Media Specialists: 1.0 (2,527.0 to 1)
Guidance Counselors: 4.0 (631.8 to 1)
Current Spending: ($ per student per year):
Total: $6,848; Instruction: $4,158; Support Services: $2,459
Enrollment, Drop-out Rates and Diploma Recipients by Race/Ethnicity

Category	Total	White	Black	Asian	AIAN	Hisp.
Enrollment (%)	100.0	96.1	1.6	0.5	0.1	0.3
Drop-out Rate (%)	2.4	2.3	0.0	50.0	n/a	0.0
H.S. Diplomas (#)	162	158	3	0	0	0

Geneva Area City Schools
135 S Eagle St • Geneva, OH 44041-1513
(440) 466-4831
Grade Span: PK-12; **Agency Type:** 1
Schools: 7
4 Primary; 2 Middle; 1 High; 0 Other Level
7 Regular; 0 Special Education; 0 Vocational; 0 Alternative
0 Magnet; 0 Charter; 4 Title I Eligible; 0 School-wide Title I
Students: 3,011   (52.2% male; 47.7% female)
Individual Education Program: 433 (14.4%);
English Language Learner: 24 (0.8%); Migrant: 1 (<0.1%)
Eligible for Free Lunch Program: 807 (26.8%)
Eligible for Reduced-Price Lunch Program: 337 (11.2%)
Teachers: 155.5 (19.4 to 1)
Librarians/Media Specialists: 0.9 (3,345.6 to 1)
Guidance Counselors: 6.0 (501.8 to 1)
Current Spending: ($ per student per year):
Total: $6,567; Instruction: $4,124; Support Services: $2,089
Enrollment, Drop-out Rates and Diploma Recipients by Race/Ethnicity

Category	Total	White	Black	Asian	AIAN	Hisp.
Enrollment (%)	100.0	93.7	0.6	0.3	0.0	4.4
Drop-out Rate (%)	1.9	1.7	7.1	0.0	100.0	2.3
H.S. Diplomas (#)	224	213	3	0	0	8

Jefferson Area Local SD
45 E Satin St • Jefferson, OH 44047-1416
(440) 576-9180 • http://www.west-jefferson.k12.oh.us/
Grade Span: PK-12; **Agency Type:** 2
Schools: 3

2 Primary; 0 Middle; 1 High; 0 Other Level
3 Regular; 0 Special Education; 0 Vocational; 0 Alternative
0 Magnet; 0 Charter; 2 Title I Eligible; 1 School-wide Title I
Students: 2,257   (52.5% male; 47.4% female)
Individual Education Program: 267 (11.8%);
English Language Learner: 3 (0.1%); Migrant: n/a
Eligible for Free Lunch Program: 452 (20.0%)
Eligible for Reduced-Price Lunch Program: 182 (8.1%)
Teachers: 124.6 (18.1 to 1)
Librarians/Media Specialists: 1.0 (2,257.0 to 1)
Guidance Counselors: 3.0 (752.3 to 1)
Current Spending: ($ per student per year):
Total: $6,643; Instruction: $3,856; Support Services: $2,477
Enrollment, Drop-out Rates and Diploma Recipients by Race/Ethnicity

Category	Total	White	Black	Asian	AIAN	Hisp.
Enrollment (%)	100.0	96.1	1.8	0.2	0.1	0.3
Drop-out Rate (%)	1.6	1.5	6.3	0.0	0.0	0.0
H.S. Diplomas (#)	139	138	1	0	0	0

Athens County

Alexander Local SD
6091 Ayers Rd • Albany, OH 45710-9492
(740) 698-8831
Grade Span: PK-12; **Agency Type:** 2
Schools: 4
1 Primary; 2 Middle; 1 High; 0 Other Level
4 Regular; 0 Special Education; 0 Vocational; 0 Alternative
0 Magnet; 0 Charter; 3 Title I Eligible; 2 School-wide Title I
Students: 1,679   (51.2% male; 48.7% female)
Individual Education Program: 327 (19.5%);
English Language Learner: 1 (0.1%); Migrant: n/a
Eligible for Free Lunch Program: 408 (24.3%)
Eligible for Reduced-Price Lunch Program: 77 (4.6%)
Teachers: 116.0 (14.5 to 1)
Librarians/Media Specialists: 0.0 (n/a to 1)
Guidance Counselors: 3.0 (559.7 to 1)
Current Spending: ($ per student per year):
Total: $6,642; Instruction: $4,017; Support Services: $2,381
Enrollment, Drop-out Rates and Diploma Recipients by Race/Ethnicity

Category	Total	White	Black	Asian	AIAN	Hisp.
Enrollment (%)	100.0	98.6	0.7	0.0	0.1	0.2
Drop-out Rate (%)	3.9	4.0	0.0	0.0	0.0	0.0
H.S. Diplomas (#)	120	118	0	1	1	0

Athens City SD
25 S Plains Rd • The Plains, OH 45780-1333
(740) 797-4544
Grade Span: PK-12; **Agency Type:** 1
Schools: 7
5 Primary; 1 Middle; 1 High; 0 Other Level
7 Regular; 0 Special Education; 0 Vocational; 0 Alternative
0 Magnet; 0 Charter; 4 Title I Eligible; 3 School-wide Title I
Students: 2,975   (50.8% male; 49.1% female)
Individual Education Program: 431 (14.5%);
English Language Learner: 91 (3.1%); Migrant: n/a
Eligible for Free Lunch Program: 846 (28.4%)
Eligible for Reduced-Price Lunch Program: 154 (5.2%)
Teachers: 222.9 (13.3 to 1)
Librarians/Media Specialists: 1.0 (2,975.0 to 1)
Guidance Counselors: 5.0 (595.0 to 1)
Current Spending: ($ per student per year):
Total: $8,096; Instruction: $4,734; Support Services: $3,073
Enrollment, Drop-out Rates and Diploma Recipients by Race/Ethnicity

Category	Total	White	Black	Asian	AIAN	Hisp.
Enrollment (%)	100.0	88.9	2.6	4.7	0.2	1.2
Drop-out Rate (%)	2.1	2.0	0.0	0.0	0.0	0.0
H.S. Diplomas (#)	87	81	2	3	0	0

Auglaize County

St Marys City SD
101 W S St • Saint Marys, OH 45885-2523
(419) 394-4312
Grade Span: PK-12; **Agency Type:** 1
Schools: 6
3 Primary; 1 Middle; 1 High; 1 Other Level
6 Regular; 0 Special Education; 0 Vocational; 0 Alternative
0 Magnet; 0 Charter; 3 Title I Eligible; 0 School-wide Title I
Students: 2,591   (54.3% male; 45.6% female)
Individual Education Program: 473 (18.3%);
English Language Learner: 12 (0.5%); Migrant: n/a
Eligible for Free Lunch Program: 398 (15.4%)
Eligible for Reduced-Price Lunch Program: 140 (5.4%)
Teachers: 147.1 (17.6 to 1)

Librarians/Media Specialists: 3.0 (863.7 to 1)
Guidance Counselors: 5.0 (518.2 to 1)
Current Spending: ($ per student per year):
Total: $6,414; Instruction: $3,987; Support Services: $2,204

Enrollment, Drop-out Rates and Diploma Recipients by Race/Ethnicity

Category	Total	White	Black	Asian	AIAN	Hisp.
Enrollment (%)	100.0	96.8	0.5	0.9	0.0	0.4
Drop-out Rate (%)	0.3	0.3	n/a	0.0	n/a	0.0
H.S. Diplomas (#)	193	189	0	2	0	0

Wapakoneta City City SD
1102 Gardenia Dr • Wapakoneta, OH 45895-1063
(419) 739-2900 • http://www.noacsc.org/auglaize/wk/
Grade Span: PK-12; **Agency Type:** 1
Schools: 6
3 Primary; 2 Middle; 1 High; 0 Other Level
6 Regular; 0 Special Education; 0 Vocational; 0 Alternative
0 Magnet; 0 Charter; 4 Title I Eligible; 0 School-wide Title I
Students: 3,160   (51.1% male; 48.8% female)
Individual Education Program: 495 (15.7%);
English Language Learner: 1 (<0.1%); Migrant: n/a
Eligible for Free Lunch Program: 560 (17.7%)
Eligible for Reduced-Price Lunch Program: 191 (6.0%)
Teachers: 161.4 (19.6 to 1)
Librarians/Media Specialists: 1.0 (3,160.0 to 1)
Guidance Counselors: 6.1 (518.0 to 1)
Current Spending: ($ per student per year):
Total: $6,541; Instruction: $3,939; Support Services: $2,291

Enrollment, Drop-out Rates and Diploma Recipients by Race/Ethnicity

Category	Total	White	Black	Asian	AIAN	Hisp.
Enrollment (%)	100.0	97.8	0.2	0.1	0.1	0.7
Drop-out Rate (%)	1.6	1.7	0.0	0.0	n/a	0.0
H.S. Diplomas (#)	231	228	0	2	0	1

Belmont County

Bellaire Local SD
340 34th St • Bellaire, OH 43906-1589
(740) 676-1826
Grade Span: PK-12; **Agency Type:** 2
Schools: 3
1 Primary; 1 Middle; 1 High; 0 Other Level
3 Regular; 0 Special Education; 0 Vocational; 0 Alternative
0 Magnet; 0 Charter; 2 Title I Eligible; 2 School-wide Title I
Students: 1,549   (52.1% male; 47.8% female)
Individual Education Program: 341 (22.0%);
English Language Learner: 0 (0.0%); Migrant: n/a
Eligible for Free Lunch Program: 786 (50.7%)
Eligible for Reduced-Price Lunch Program: 93 (6.0%)
Teachers: 106.6 (14.5 to 1)
Librarians/Media Specialists: 0.0 (n/a to 1)
Guidance Counselors: 3.0 (516.3 to 1)
Current Spending: ($ per student per year):
Total: $8,729; Instruction: $5,092; Support Services: $3,231

Enrollment, Drop-out Rates and Diploma Recipients by Race/Ethnicity

Category	Total	White	Black	Asian	AIAN	Hisp.
Enrollment (%)	100.0	92.1	4.8	0.1	0.1	0.1
Drop-out Rate (%)	3.6	3.6	3.7	n/a	n/a	0.0
H.S. Diplomas (#)	110	105	4	0	0	1

Martins Ferry City SD
633 Hanover St • Martins Ferry, OH 43935-1575
(740) 633-1732
Grade Span: PK-12; **Agency Type:** 1
Schools: 5
3 Primary; 1 Middle; 1 High; 0 Other Level
5 Regular; 0 Special Education; 0 Vocational; 0 Alternative
0 Magnet; 0 Charter; 4 Title I Eligible; 3 School-wide Title I
Students: 1,522   (51.9% male; 48.0% female)
Individual Education Program: 225 (14.8%);
English Language Learner: 0 (0.0%); Migrant: n/a
Eligible for Free Lunch Program: 509 (33.4%)
Eligible for Reduced-Price Lunch Program: 107 (7.0%)
Teachers: 91.0 (16.7 to 1)
Librarians/Media Specialists: 2.0 (761.0 to 1)
Guidance Counselors: 5.0 (304.4 to 1)
Current Spending: ($ per student per year):
Total: $6,603; Instruction: $3,929; Support Services: $2,424

Enrollment, Drop-out Rates and Diploma Recipients by Race/Ethnicity

Category	Total	White	Black	Asian	AIAN	Hisp.
Enrollment (%)	100.0	90.2	8.5	0.3	0.1	0.2
Drop-out Rate (%)	0.4	0.4	0.0	n/a	n/a	n/a
H.S. Diplomas (#)	129	126	3	0	0	0

St Clairsville-Richland City SD
108 Woodrow Ave • Saint Clairsville, OH 43950-1567
(740) 695-1624
Grade Span: PK-12; **Agency Type:** 1
Schools: 3
1 Primary; 1 Middle; 1 High; 0 Other Level
3 Regular; 0 Special Education; 0 Vocational; 0 Alternative
0 Magnet; 0 Charter; 2 Title I Eligible; 0 School-wide Title I
Students: 1,579   (52.1% male; 47.8% female)
Individual Education Program: 195 (12.3%);
English Language Learner: 4 (0.3%); Migrant: n/a
Eligible for Free Lunch Program: 303 (19.2%)
Eligible for Reduced-Price Lunch Program: 88 (5.6%)
Teachers: 105.0 (15.0 to 1)
Librarians/Media Specialists: 1.0 (1,579.0 to 1)
Guidance Counselors: 3.0 (526.3 to 1)
Current Spending: ($ per student per year):
Total: $7,599; Instruction: $4,556; Support Services: $2,811

Enrollment, Drop-out Rates and Diploma Recipients by Race/Ethnicity

Category	Total	White	Black	Asian	AIAN	Hisp.
Enrollment (%)	100.0	96.4	1.8	0.5	0.0	0.4
Drop-out Rate (%)	1.9	1.8	7.7	0.0	n/a	0.0
H.S. Diplomas (#)	120	111	3	3	0	1

Union Local SD
201 W Cross St • Morristown, OH 43759-0300
Mailing Address: PO Box 300 • Morristown, OH 43759-0300
(740) 695-5776
Grade Span: PK-12; **Agency Type:** 2
Schools: 3
1 Primary; 1 Middle; 1 High; 0 Other Level
3 Regular; 0 Special Education; 0 Vocational; 0 Alternative
0 Magnet; 0 Charter; 2 Title I Eligible; 0 School-wide Title I
Students: 1,553   (54.1% male; 45.8% female)
Individual Education Program: 251 (16.2%);
English Language Learner: 0 (0.0%); Migrant: n/a
Eligible for Free Lunch Program: 488 (31.4%)
Eligible for Reduced-Price Lunch Program: 103 (6.6%)
Teachers: 113.6 (13.7 to 1)
Librarians/Media Specialists: 2.0 (776.5 to 1)
Guidance Counselors: 2.0 (776.5 to 1)
Current Spending: ($ per student per year):
Total: $7,295; Instruction: $4,607; Support Services: $2,409

Enrollment, Drop-out Rates and Diploma Recipients by Race/Ethnicity

Category	Total	White	Black	Asian	AIAN	Hisp.
Enrollment (%)	100.0	98.4	0.4	0.2	0.0	0.0
Drop-out Rate (%)	1.9	1.9	n/a	n/a	n/a	n/a
H.S. Diplomas (#)	149	148	0	0	0	0

Brown County

Eastern Local SD
11479 US Rt 62 • Sardinia, OH 45171-0500
Mailing Address: PO Box 500 • Sardinia, OH 45171-0500
(937) 378-3981
Grade Span: PK-12; **Agency Type:** 2
Schools: 4
2 Primary; 1 Middle; 1 High; 0 Other Level
4 Regular; 0 Special Education; 0 Vocational; 0 Alternative
0 Magnet; 0 Charter; 2 Title I Eligible; 2 School-wide Title I
Students: 1,543   (51.6% male; 48.3% female)
Individual Education Program: 162 (10.5%);
English Language Learner: 0 (0.0%); Migrant: n/a
Eligible for Free Lunch Program: 349 (22.6%)
Eligible for Reduced-Price Lunch Program: 137 (8.9%)
Teachers: 90.6 (17.0 to 1)
Librarians/Media Specialists: 1.0 (1,543.0 to 1)
Guidance Counselors: 2.0 (771.5 to 1)
Current Spending: ($ per student per year):
Total: $6,623; Instruction: $3,745; Support Services: $2,619

Enrollment, Drop-out Rates and Diploma Recipients by Race/Ethnicity

Category	Total	White	Black	Asian	AIAN	Hisp.
Enrollment (%)	100.0	98.3	0.5	0.1	0.1	0.2
Drop-out Rate (%)	2.2	2.2	n/a	0.0	n/a	0.0
H.S. Diplomas (#)	95	93	0	1	0	0

Western Brown Local SD
211 S High St • Mount Orab, OH 45154-9039
Mailing Address: PO Box 455 • Mount Orab, OH 45154-0455
(937) 444-2044
Grade Span: PK-12; **Agency Type:** 2
Schools: 4
2 Primary; 1 Middle; 1 High; 0 Other Level
4 Regular; 0 Special Education; 0 Vocational; 0 Alternative
0 Magnet; 0 Charter; 2 Title I Eligible; 0 School-wide Title I

Students: 3,418   (51.3% male; 48.6% female)
  Individual Education Program: 306 (9.0%);
  English Language Learner: 0 (0.0%); Migrant: n/a
  Eligible for Free Lunch Program: 700 (20.5%)
  Eligible for Reduced-Price Lunch Program: 245 (7.2%)
Teachers: 186.3 (18.3 to 1)
Librarians/Media Specialists: 4.1 (833.7 to 1)
Guidance Counselors: 7.4 (461.9 to 1)
Current Spending: ($ per student per year):
  Total: $6,231; Instruction: $3,670; Support Services: $2,286
Enrollment, Drop-out Rates and Diploma Recipients by Race/Ethnicity

Category	Total	White	Black	Asian	AIAN	Hisp.
Enrollment (%)	100.0	99.4	0.3	0.0	0.0	0.1
Drop-out Rate (%)	5.2	5.2	0.0	0.0	n/a	0.0
H.S. Diplomas (#)	143	142	1	0	0	0

Butler County

Edgewood City SD
3500 Busenbark Rd • Trenton, OH 45067-9566
(513) 863-4692
Grade Span: PK-12; **Agency Type:** 1
Schools: 5
  3 Primary; 1 Middle; 1 High; 0 Other Level
  5 Regular; 0 Special Education; 0 Vocational; 0 Alternative
  0 Magnet; 0 Charter; 4 Title I Eligible; 0 School-wide Title I
Students: 3,595   (52.6% male; 47.3% female)
  Individual Education Program: 604 (16.8%);
  English Language Learner: 1 (<0.1%); Migrant: n/a
  Eligible for Free Lunch Program: 405 (11.3%)
  Eligible for Reduced-Price Lunch Program: 201 (5.6%)
Teachers: 203.3 (17.7 to 1)
Librarians/Media Specialists: 6.0 (599.2 to 1)
Guidance Counselors: 8.0 (449.4 to 1)
Current Spending: ($ per student per year):
  Total: $6,840; Instruction: $3,983; Support Services: $2,555
Enrollment, Drop-out Rates and Diploma Recipients by Race/Ethnicity

Category	Total	White	Black	Asian	AIAN	Hisp.
Enrollment (%)	100.0	98.6	0.8	0.1	0.0	0.2
Drop-out Rate (%)	3.4	3.4	0.0	0.0	n/a	0.0
H.S. Diplomas (#)	182	180	0	1	0	0

Fairfield City SD
211 Donald Dr • Fairfield, OH 45014-3006
(513) 829-6300 • http://www.fairfieldcityschools.com
Grade Span: PK-12; **Agency Type:** 1
Schools: 10
  6 Primary; 2 Middle; 2 High; 0 Other Level
  10 Regular; 0 Special Education; 0 Vocational; 0 Alternative
  0 Magnet; 0 Charter; 5 Title I Eligible; 0 School-wide Title I
Students: 9,547   (50.4% male; 49.5% female)
  Individual Education Program: 1,073 (11.2%);
  English Language Learner: 200 (2.1%); Migrant: n/a
  Eligible for Free Lunch Program: 810 (8.5%)
  Eligible for Reduced-Price Lunch Program: 292 (3.1%)
Teachers: 504.3 (18.9 to 1)
Librarians/Media Specialists: 7.0 (1,364.0 to 1)
Guidance Counselors: 12.6 (757.8 to 1)
Current Spending: ($ per student per year):
  Total: $6,991; Instruction: $4,144; Support Services: $2,619
Enrollment, Drop-out Rates and Diploma Recipients by Race/Ethnicity

Category	Total	White	Black	Asian	AIAN	Hisp.
Enrollment (%)	100.0	84.4	8.8	1.7	0.1	2.2
Drop-out Rate (%)	1.2	1.0	2.2	0.0	20.0	8.8
H.S. Diplomas (#)	608	550	33	15	2	6

Hamilton City SD
533 Dayton St • Hamilton, OH 45011-3455
Mailing Address: PO Box 627 • Hamilton, OH 45012-0627
(513) 887-5000 • http://www.hamiltoncityschools.com/
Grade Span: PK-12; **Agency Type:** 1
Schools: 20
  14 Primary; 3 Middle; 1 High; 0 Other Level
  18 Regular; 0 Special Education; 0 Vocational; 0 Alternative
  0 Magnet; 0 Charter; 14 Title I Eligible; 9 School-wide Title I
Students: 9,607   (51.4% male; 48.5% female)
  Individual Education Program: 1,825 (19.0%);
  English Language Learner: 360 (3.7%); Migrant: 2 (<0.1%)
  Eligible for Free Lunch Program: 4,052 (42.2%)
  Eligible for Reduced-Price Lunch Program: 698 (7.3%)
Teachers: 569.4 (16.9 to 1)
Librarians/Media Specialists: 4.0 (2,401.8 to 1)
Guidance Counselors: 24.0 (400.3 to 1)
Current Spending: ($ per student per year):
  Total: $7,349; Instruction: $4,303; Support Services: $2,715

Category	Total	White	Black	Asian	AIAN	Hisp.
Enrollment (%)	100.0	82.5	10.1	0.5	0.1	4.7
Drop-out Rate (%)	6.8	6.6	7.0	5.3	0.0	13.2
H.S. Diplomas (#)	524	459	52	5	0	4

Lakota Local SD
5572 Princeton Rd • Hamilton, OH 45011-9726
(513) 874-5505 • http://www.lakotaonline.com/
Grade Span: PK-12; **Agency Type:** 2
Schools: 19
  12 Primary; 4 Middle; 2 High; 1 Other Level
  19 Regular; 0 Special Education; 0 Vocational; 0 Alternative
  0 Magnet; 0 Charter; 8 Title I Eligible; 0 School-wide Title I
Students: 16,358   (51.9% male; 48.0% female)
  Individual Education Program: 1,365 (8.3%);
  English Language Learner: 212 (1.3%); Migrant: 3 (<0.1%)
  Eligible for Free Lunch Program: 704 (4.3%)
  Eligible for Reduced-Price Lunch Program: 202 (1.2%)
Teachers: 964.8 (16.9 to 1)
Librarians/Media Specialists: 18.0 (907.6 to 1)
Guidance Counselors: 29.9 (546.4 to 1)
Current Spending: ($ per student per year):
  Total: $7,122; Instruction: $4,096; Support Services: $2,809
Enrollment, Drop-out Rates and Diploma Recipients by Race/Ethnicity

Category	Total	White	Black	Asian	AIAN	Hisp.
Enrollment (%)	100.0	85.1	6.2	4.3	0.1	2.1
Drop-out Rate (%)	0.9	0.9	0.4	0.0	0.0	2.9
H.S. Diplomas (#)	963	864	36	54	0	8

Madison Local SD
1324 Middletown Eaton Rd • Middletown, OH 45042-1525
(513) 420-4750
Grade Span: PK-12; **Agency Type:** 2
Schools: 3
  2 Primary; 0 Middle; 1 High; 0 Other Level
  3 Regular; 0 Special Education; 0 Vocational; 0 Alternative
  0 Magnet; 0 Charter; 2 Title I Eligible; 0 School-wide Title I
Students: 1,590   (49.7% male; 50.2% female)
  Individual Education Program: 204 (12.8%);
  English Language Learner: 0 (0.0%); Migrant: n/a
  Eligible for Free Lunch Program: 188 (11.8%)
  Eligible for Reduced-Price Lunch Program: 59 (3.7%)
Teachers: 97.1 (16.4 to 1)
Librarians/Media Specialists: 1.0 (1,590.0 to 1)
Guidance Counselors: 6.0 (265.0 to 1)
Current Spending: ($ per student per year):
  Total: $6,914; Instruction: $3,805; Support Services: $2,808
Enrollment, Drop-out Rates and Diploma Recipients by Race/Ethnicity

Category	Total	White	Black	Asian	AIAN	Hisp.
Enrollment (%)	100.0	97.5	0.4	0.4	0.1	0.3
Drop-out Rate (%)	2.9	2.9	n/a	0.0	n/a	0.0
H.S. Diplomas (#)	95	94	0	0	0	0

Middletown City SD
1515 Girard Ave • Middletown, OH 45044-4364
(513) 423-0781 • http://www.middletowncityschools.com/
Grade Span: PK-12; **Agency Type:** 1
Schools: 14
  8 Primary; 3 Middle; 2 High; 1 Other Level
  13 Regular; 1 Special Education; 0 Vocational; 0 Alternative
  0 Magnet; 0 Charter; 11 Title I Eligible; 6 School-wide Title I
Students: 7,296   (51.5% male; 48.4% female)
  Individual Education Program: 1,298 (17.8%);
  English Language Learner: 113 (1.5%); Migrant: n/a
  Eligible for Free Lunch Program: 2,385 (32.7%)
  Eligible for Reduced-Price Lunch Program: 529 (7.2%)
Teachers: 492.1 (14.8 to 1)
Librarians/Media Specialists: 3.0 (2,433.0 to 1)
Guidance Counselors: 11.0 (663.5 to 1)
Current Spending: ($ per student per year):
  Total: $8,376; Instruction: $4,746; Support Services: $3,267
Enrollment, Drop-out Rates and Diploma Recipients by Race/Ethnicity

Category	Total	White	Black	Asian	AIAN	Hisp.
Enrollment (%)	100.0	77.0	17.3	0.5	0.1	2.1
Drop-out Rate (%)	5.2	5.3	5.5	0.0	0.0	0.0
H.S. Diplomas (#)	360	281	72	4	0	2

Monroe Local SD
30 Overbrook Dr Ste D • Monroe, OH 45050-1168
(513) 539-2536
Grade Span: PK-12; **Agency Type:** 2
Schools: 3
  1 Primary; 1 Middle; 1 High; 0 Other Level
  3 Regular; 0 Special Education; 0 Vocational; 0 Alternative

0 Magnet; 0 Charter; 2 Title I Eligible; 0 School-wide Title I
Students: 1,521 (51.6% male; 48.3% female)
  Individual Education Program: 172 (11.3%);
  English Language Learner: 1 (0.1%); Migrant: n/a
  Eligible for Free Lunch Program: 183 (12.0%)
  Eligible for Reduced-Price Lunch Program: 73 (4.8%)
Teachers: 98.5 (15.4 to 1)
Librarians/Media Specialists: 2.0 (760.5 to 1)
Guidance Counselors: 3.0 (507.0 to 1)
Current Spending: ($ per student per year):
  Total: $8,902; Instruction: $4,711; Support Services: $3,876
Enrollment, Drop-out Rates and Diploma Recipients by Race/Ethnicity

Category	Total	White	Black	Asian	AIAN	Hisp.
Enrollment (%)	100.0	95.0	2.0	0.5	0.3	0.5
Drop-out Rate (%)	2.4	2.5	0.0	0.0	0.0	0.0
H.S. Diplomas (#)	147	144	1	1	0	1

Ross Local SD
3371 Hamilton Cleves Rd • Hamilton, OH 45013-9535
(513) 863-1253 • http://www.rosd.k12.oh.us/
Grade Span: PK-12; **Agency Type:** 2
Schools: 4
  2 Primary; 1 Middle; 1 High; 0 Other Level
  4 Regular; 0 Special Education; 0 Vocational; 0 Alternative
  0 Magnet; 0 Charter; 3 Title I Eligible; 0 School-wide Title I
Students: 2,580 (53.6% male; 46.3% female)
  Individual Education Program: 353 (13.7%);
  English Language Learner: 0 (0.0%); Migrant: n/a
  Eligible for Free Lunch Program: 177 (6.9%)
  Eligible for Reduced-Price Lunch Program: 60 (2.3%)
Teachers: 146.1 (17.7 to 1)
Librarians/Media Specialists: 1.0 (2,580.0 to 1)
Guidance Counselors: 6.0 (430.0 to 1)
Current Spending: ($ per student per year):
  Total: $6,594; Instruction: $4,006; Support Services: $2,297
Enrollment, Drop-out Rates and Diploma Recipients by Race/Ethnicity

Category	Total	White	Black	Asian	AIAN	Hisp.
Enrollment (%)	100.0	98.4	0.2	0.1	0.2	0.3
Drop-out Rate (%)	3.2	3.2	0.0	0.0	0.0	0.0
H.S. Diplomas (#)	169	165	0	1	0	0

Talawanda City SD
131 W Chestnut St • Oxford, OH 45056-2619
(513) 523-4716 • http://www.talawanda.net/
Grade Span: PK-12; **Agency Type:** 1
Schools: 4
  2 Primary; 1 Middle; 1 High; 0 Other Level
  4 Regular; 0 Special Education; 0 Vocational; 0 Alternative
  0 Magnet; 0 Charter; 3 Title I Eligible; 0 School-wide Title I
Students: 3,104 (51.1% male; 48.8% female)
  Individual Education Program: 336 (10.8%);
  English Language Learner: 13 (0.4%); Migrant: n/a
  Eligible for Free Lunch Program: 437 (14.1%)
  Eligible for Reduced-Price Lunch Program: 92 (3.0%)
Teachers: 197.4 (15.7 to 1)
Librarians/Media Specialists: 2.0 (1,552.0 to 1)
Guidance Counselors: 7.0 (443.4 to 1)
Current Spending: ($ per student per year):
  Total: $7,429; Instruction: $4,322; Support Services: $2,848
Enrollment, Drop-out Rates and Diploma Recipients by Race/Ethnicity

Category	Total	White	Black	Asian	AIAN	Hisp.
Enrollment (%)	100.0	93.5	2.9	1.8	0.1	0.3
Drop-out Rate (%)	4.0	4.1	3.2	0.0	0.0	0.0
H.S. Diplomas (#)	260	246	7	5	0	2

Carroll County

Carrollton Ex Vill SD
252 3rd St NE • Carrollton, OH 44615-1236
(330) 627-2181
Grade Span: PK-12; **Agency Type:** 1
Schools: 9
  6 Primary; 2 Middle; 1 High; 0 Other Level
  9 Regular; 0 Special Education; 0 Vocational; 0 Alternative
  0 Magnet; 0 Charter; 8 Title I Eligible; 8 School-wide Title I
Students: 2,932 (50.1% male; 49.8% female)
  Individual Education Program: 403 (13.7%);
  English Language Learner: 0 (0.0%); Migrant: n/a
  Eligible for Free Lunch Program: 750 (25.6%)
  Eligible for Reduced-Price Lunch Program: 326 (11.1%)
Teachers: 168.0 (17.5 to 1)
Librarians/Media Specialists: 1.0 (2,932.0 to 1)
Guidance Counselors: 3.0 (977.3 to 1)
Current Spending: ($ per student per year):
  Total: $6,403; Instruction: $3,682; Support Services: $2,410

Enrollment, Drop-out Rates and Diploma Recipients by Race/Ethnicity

Category	Total	White	Black	Asian	AIAN	Hisp.
Enrollment (%)	100.0	98.4	0.2	0.1	0.3	0.4
Drop-out Rate (%)	1.1	1.2	0.0	0.0	0.0	0.0
H.S. Diplomas (#)	199	197	0	1	0	1

Champaign County

Graham Local SD
370 E Main St • Saint Paris, OH 43072-9200
(937) 663-4123 • http://www.graham.k12.oh.us/
Grade Span: PK-12; **Agency Type:** 2
Schools: 4
  2 Primary; 1 Middle; 1 High; 0 Other Level
  4 Regular; 0 Special Education; 0 Vocational; 0 Alternative
  0 Magnet; 0 Charter; 3 Title I Eligible; 0 School-wide Title I
Students: 2,189 (51.1% male; 48.8% female)
  Individual Education Program: 337 (15.4%);
  English Language Learner: 0 (0.0%); Migrant: n/a
  Eligible for Free Lunch Program: 208 (9.5%)
  Eligible for Reduced-Price Lunch Program: 108 (4.9%)
Teachers: 128.3 (17.1 to 1)
Librarians/Media Specialists: 4.0 (547.3 to 1)
Guidance Counselors: 5.0 (437.8 to 1)
Current Spending: ($ per student per year):
  Total: $6,554; Instruction: $3,948; Support Services: $2,356
Enrollment, Drop-out Rates and Diploma Recipients by Race/Ethnicity

Category	Total	White	Black	Asian	AIAN	Hisp.
Enrollment (%)	100.0	97.5	0.2	0.1	0.2	0.5
Drop-out Rate (%)	1.4	1.3	0.0	n/a	n/a	0.0
H.S. Diplomas (#)	132	131	0	0	0	1

Urbana City SD
711 Wood St • Urbana, OH 43078-1498
(937) 653-1402 • http://www.urbana.k12.oh.us/
Grade Span: PK-12; **Agency Type:** 1
Schools: 6
  3 Primary; 2 Middle; 1 High; 0 Other Level
  6 Regular; 0 Special Education; 0 Vocational; 0 Alternative
  0 Magnet; 0 Charter; 4 Title I Eligible; 0 School-wide Title I
Students: 2,353 (52.2% male; 47.7% female)
  Individual Education Program: 445 (18.9%);
  English Language Learner: 0 (0.0%); Migrant: 7 (0.3%)
  Eligible for Free Lunch Program: 583 (24.7%)
  Eligible for Reduced-Price Lunch Program: 193 (8.2%)
Teachers: 144.8 (16.3 to 1)
Librarians/Media Specialists: 1.0 (2,356.0 to 1)
Guidance Counselors: 5.0 (471.2 to 1)
Current Spending: ($ per student per year):
  Total: $7,335; Instruction: $4,700; Support Services: $2,366
Enrollment, Drop-out Rates and Diploma Recipients by Race/Ethnicity

Category	Total	White	Black	Asian	AIAN	Hisp.
Enrollment (%)	100.0	88.3	5.2	0.5	0.0	1.4
Drop-out Rate (%)	2.8	3.0	1.8	0.0	0.0	0.0
H.S. Diplomas (#)	118	107	7	1	0	3

Clark County

Clark-Shawnee Local SD
3680 Selma Rd • Springfield, OH 45502-6310
(937) 328-5378
Grade Span: PK-12; **Agency Type:** 2
Schools: 5
  4 Primary; 0 Middle; 1 High; 0 Other Level
  5 Regular; 0 Special Education; 0 Vocational; 0 Alternative
  0 Magnet; 0 Charter; 3 Title I Eligible; 0 School-wide Title I
Students: 2,547 (51.1% male; 48.8% female)
  Individual Education Program: 216 (8.5%);
  English Language Learner: 0 (0.0%); Migrant: n/a
  Eligible for Free Lunch Program: 267 (10.5%)
  Eligible for Reduced-Price Lunch Program: 103 (4.0%)
Teachers: 139.2 (18.3 to 1)
Librarians/Media Specialists: 2.0 (1,273.5 to 1)
Guidance Counselors: 5.0 (509.4 to 1)
Current Spending: ($ per student per year):
  Total: $6,491; Instruction: $3,985; Support Services: $2,243
Enrollment, Drop-out Rates and Diploma Recipients by Race/Ethnicity

Category	Total	White	Black	Asian	AIAN	Hisp.
Enrollment (%)	100.0	94.1	2.7	0.4	0.1	0.6
Drop-out Rate (%)	1.8	1.8	5.0	0.0	n/a	0.0
H.S. Diplomas (#)	203	201	1	1	0	0

Greenon Local SD
1215 Old Mill Rd • Springfield, OH 45506-4319
(937) 328-5351
Grade Span: PK-12; **Agency Type:** 2
Schools: 4
  2 Primary; 1 Middle; 1 High; 0 Other Level
  4 Regular; 0 Special Education; 0 Vocational; 0 Alternative
  0 Magnet; 0 Charter; 3 Title I Eligible; 0 School-wide Title I
Students: 1,980   (50.5% male; 49.4% female)
  Individual Education Program: 207 (10.5%);
  English Language Learner: 2 (0.1%); Migrant: n/a
  Eligible for Free Lunch Program: 136 (6.9%)
  Eligible for Reduced-Price Lunch Program: 54 (2.7%)
Teachers: 116.0 (17.1 to 1)
Librarians/Media Specialists: 1.0 (1,980.0 to 1)
Guidance Counselors: 2.0 (990.0 to 1)
Current Spending: ($ per student per year):
  Total: $6,292; Instruction: $3,534; Support Services: $2,526
Enrollment, Drop-out Rates and Diploma Recipients by Race/Ethnicity

Category	Total	White	Black	Asian	AIAN	Hisp.
Enrollment (%)	100.0	97.1	0.7	0.5	0.3	0.5
Drop-out Rate (%)	3.9	4.0	0.0	0.0	0.0	0.0
H.S. Diplomas (#)	146	135	2	4	1	1

Northeastern Local SD
1414 Bowman Rd • Springfield, OH 45502-8826
(937) 325-7615 • http://www.northeastern.k12.oh.us/
Grade Span: PK-12; **Agency Type:** 2
Schools: 7
  3 Primary; 2 Middle; 2 High; 0 Other Level
  7 Regular; 0 Special Education; 0 Vocational; 0 Alternative
  0 Magnet; 0 Charter; 3 Title I Eligible; 0 School-wide Title I
Students: 3,628   (51.8% male; 48.1% female)
  Individual Education Program: 309 (8.5%);
  English Language Learner: 12 (0.3%); Migrant: n/a
  Eligible for Free Lunch Program: 231 (6.4%)
  Eligible for Reduced-Price Lunch Program: 92 (2.5%)
Teachers: 232.4 (15.6 to 1)
Librarians/Media Specialists: 4.0 (907.3 to 1)
Guidance Counselors: 7.6 (477.5 to 1)
Current Spending: ($ per student per year):
  Total: $6,444; Instruction: $3,828; Support Services: $2,387
Enrollment, Drop-out Rates and Diploma Recipients by Race/Ethnicity

Category	Total	White	Black	Asian	AIAN	Hisp.
Enrollment (%)	100.0	95.9	1.0	0.9	0.0	0.6
Drop-out Rate (%)	1.7	1.7	14.3	0.0	0.0	0.0
H.S. Diplomas (#)	198	193	1	2	0	0

Northwestern Local SD
5610 Troy Rd • Springfield, OH 45502-9032
(937) 964-1318
Grade Span: PK-12; **Agency Type:** 2
Schools: 3
  1 Primary; 1 Middle; 1 High; 0 Other Level
  3 Regular; 0 Special Education; 0 Vocational; 0 Alternative
  0 Magnet; 0 Charter; 2 Title I Eligible; 0 School-wide Title I
Students: 1,951   (49.7% male; 50.2% female)
  Individual Education Program: 222 (11.4%);
  English Language Learner: 5 (0.3%); Migrant: n/a
  Eligible for Free Lunch Program: 215 (11.0%)
  Eligible for Reduced-Price Lunch Program: 59 (3.0%)
Teachers: 105.8 (18.4 to 1)
Librarians/Media Specialists: 2.0 (975.5 to 1)
Guidance Counselors: 3.0 (650.3 to 1)
Current Spending: ($ per student per year):
  Total: $6,447; Instruction: $3,938; Support Services: $2,266
Enrollment, Drop-out Rates and Diploma Recipients by Race/Ethnicity

Category	Total	White	Black	Asian	AIAN	Hisp.
Enrollment (%)	100.0	96.7	0.2	1.0	0.2	0.7
Drop-out Rate (%)	1.8	1.9	0.0	0.0	0.0	0.0
H.S. Diplomas (#)	135	134	0	0	0	1

Springfield City SD
49 E College Ave • Springfield, OH 45504-2502
(937) 328-2000 • http://www.spr.k12.oh.us/
Grade Span: PK-12; **Agency Type:** 1
Schools: 19
  10 Primary; 5 Middle; 3 High; 1 Other Level
  18 Regular; 1 Special Education; 0 Vocational; 0 Alternative
  0 Magnet; 0 Charter; 17 Title I Eligible; 6 School-wide Title I
Students: 9,358   (52.3% male; 47.6% female)
  Individual Education Program: 1,457 (15.6%);
  English Language Learner: 17 (0.2%); Migrant: 7 (0.1%)
  Eligible for Free Lunch Program: 4,479 (48.0%)
  Eligible for Reduced-Price Lunch Program: 485 (5.2%)

Teachers: 617.1 (15.1 to 1)
Librarians/Media Specialists: 7.0 (1,333.1 to 1)
Guidance Counselors: 27.8 (335.7 to 1)
Current Spending: ($ per student per year):
  Total: $8,949; Instruction: $4,986; Support Services: $3,646
Enrollment, Drop-out Rates and Diploma Recipients by Race/Ethnicity

Category	Total	White	Black	Asian	AIAN	Hisp.
Enrollment (%)	100.0	66.7	25.9	0.7	0.1	1.1
Drop-out Rate (%)	6.2	5.9	6.8	0.0	0.0	4.2
H.S. Diplomas (#)	411	284	122	2	1	2

Tecumseh Local SD
9760 W National Rd • New Carlisle, OH 45344-9290
(937) 845-3576 • http://www.tecumseh.k12.oh.us/
Grade Span: PK-12; **Agency Type:** 2
Schools: 8
  5 Primary; 2 Middle; 1 High; 0 Other Level
  8 Regular; 0 Special Education; 0 Vocational; 0 Alternative
  0 Magnet; 0 Charter; 5 Title I Eligible; 3 School-wide Title I
Students: 3,578   (51.2% male; 48.7% female)
  Individual Education Program: 412 (11.5%);
  English Language Learner: 161 (4.5%); Migrant: 112 (3.1%)
  Eligible for Free Lunch Program: 736 (20.6%)
  Eligible for Reduced-Price Lunch Program: 264 (7.4%)
Teachers: 218.4 (16.4 to 1)
Librarians/Media Specialists: 2.0 (1,789.0 to 1)
Guidance Counselors: 6.5 (550.5 to 1)
Current Spending: ($ per student per year):
  Total: $7,593; Instruction: $4,163; Support Services: $3,092
Enrollment, Drop-out Rates and Diploma Recipients by Race/Ethnicity

Category	Total	White	Black	Asian	AIAN	Hisp.
Enrollment (%)	100.0	92.2	0.5	0.4	0.2	5.2
Drop-out Rate (%)	4.6	4.4	0.0	50.0	0.0	8.0
H.S. Diplomas (#)	224	216	0	0	1	4

Clermont County

Batavia Local SD
800 Bauer Ave • Batavia, OH 45103-2837
(513) 732-2343 • http://www.bataviaschools.org/
Grade Span: PK-12; **Agency Type:** 2
Schools: 3
  1 Primary; 1 Middle; 1 High; 0 Other Level
  3 Regular; 0 Special Education; 0 Vocational; 0 Alternative
  0 Magnet; 0 Charter; 2 Title I Eligible; 1 School-wide Title I
Students: 1,924   (51.9% male; 48.0% female)
  Individual Education Program: 202 (10.5%);
  English Language Learner: 2 (0.1%); Migrant: n/a
  Eligible for Free Lunch Program: 416 (21.6%)
  Eligible for Reduced-Price Lunch Program: 134 (7.0%)
Teachers: 111.6 (17.2 to 1)
Librarians/Media Specialists: 2.0 (962.0 to 1)
Guidance Counselors: 3.0 (641.3 to 1)
Current Spending: ($ per student per year):
  Total: $7,042; Instruction: $4,075; Support Services: $2,719
Enrollment, Drop-out Rates and Diploma Recipients by Race/Ethnicity

Category	Total	White	Black	Asian	AIAN	Hisp.
Enrollment (%)	100.0	95.2	1.8	0.3	0.1	0.8
Drop-out Rate (%)	3.9	3.7	12.5	n/a	n/a	0.0
H.S. Diplomas (#)	92	86	4	0	0	0

Bethel-Tate Local SD
112 N Union St • Bethel, OH 45106-1122
(513) 734-2238 • http://www.betheltate.org/
Grade Span: PK-12; **Agency Type:** 2
Schools: 4
  2 Primary; 1 Middle; 1 High; 0 Other Level
  4 Regular; 0 Special Education; 0 Vocational; 0 Alternative
  0 Magnet; 0 Charter; 3 Title I Eligible; 0 School-wide Title I
Students: 1,970   (50.9% male; 49.0% female)
  Individual Education Program: 145 (7.4%);
  English Language Learner: 0 (0.0%); Migrant: n/a
  Eligible for Free Lunch Program: 310 (15.7%)
  Eligible for Reduced-Price Lunch Program: 100 (5.1%)
Teachers: 100.6 (19.6 to 1)
Librarians/Media Specialists: 2.0 (985.0 to 1)
Guidance Counselors: 3.0 (656.7 to 1)
Current Spending: ($ per student per year):
  Total: $5,828; Instruction: $3,446; Support Services: $2,173
Enrollment, Drop-out Rates and Diploma Recipients by Race/Ethnicity

Category	Total	White	Black	Asian	AIAN	Hisp.
Enrollment (%)	100.0	98.2	0.3	0.0	0.5	0.4
Drop-out Rate (%)	4.2	4.3	n/a	n/a	0.0	0.0
H.S. Diplomas (#)	138	137	0	0	0	1

Clermont Northeastern Local SD
2792 US Hwy 50 • Batavia, OH 45103-8532
(513) 625-5478
Grade Span: PK-12; **Agency Type:** 2
Schools: 4
   2 Primary; 1 Middle; 1 High; 0 Other Level
   4 Regular; 0 Special Education; 0 Vocational; 0 Alternative
   0 Magnet; 0 Charter; 3 Title I Eligible; 0 School-wide Title I
Students: 1,972 (52.2% male; 47.7% female)
   Individual Education Program: 270 (13.7%);
   English Language Learner: 0 (0.0%); Migrant: n/a
   Eligible for Free Lunch Program: 285 (14.5%)
   Eligible for Reduced-Price Lunch Program: 101 (5.1%)
Teachers: 103.3 (19.1 to 1)
Librarians/Media Specialists: 2.0 (986.0 to 1)
Guidance Counselors: 3.0 (657.3 to 1)
Current Spending: ($ per student per year):
   Total: $5,735; Instruction: $3,352; Support Services: $2,112
Enrollment, Drop-out Rates and Diploma Recipients by Race/Ethnicity

Category	Total	White	Black	Asian	AIAN	Hisp.
Enrollment (%)	100.0	97.9	0.1	0.1	0.2	0.7
Drop-out Rate (%)	4.2	4.2	n/a	0.0	0.0	0.0
H.S. Diplomas (#)	121	117	0	1	1	0

Goshen Local SD
6785 Goshen Rd • Goshen, OH 45122-9317
(513) 722-2222
Grade Span: PK-12; **Agency Type:** 2
Schools: 4
   2 Primary; 1 Middle; 1 High; 0 Other Level
   4 Regular; 0 Special Education; 0 Vocational; 0 Alternative
   0 Magnet; 0 Charter; 2 Title I Eligible; 0 School-wide Title I
Students: 2,525 (50.7% male; 49.2% female)
   Individual Education Program: 422 (16.7%);
   English Language Learner: 0 (0.0%); Migrant: n/a
   Eligible for Free Lunch Program: 488 (19.3%)
   Eligible for Reduced-Price Lunch Program: 187 (7.4%)
Teachers: 138.1 (18.3 to 1)
Librarians/Media Specialists: 2.0 (1,262.5 to 1)
Guidance Counselors: 5.0 (505.0 to 1)
Current Spending: ($ per student per year):
   Total: $7,357; Instruction: $3,800; Support Services: $3,304
Enrollment, Drop-out Rates and Diploma Recipients by Race/Ethnicity

Category	Total	White	Black	Asian	AIAN	Hisp.
Enrollment (%)	100.0	98.3	0.3	0.2	0.0	0.3
Drop-out Rate (%)	4.5	4.5	0.0	n/a	n/a	0.0
H.S. Diplomas (#)	146	146	0	0	0	0

Milford Ex Vill SD
745 Center St Ste 300 • Milford, OH 45150-1300
(513) 831-1314 • http://www.milfordschools.org/
Grade Span: PK-12; **Agency Type:** 1
Schools: 8
   6 Primary; 0 Middle; 1 High; 1 Other Level
   8 Regular; 0 Special Education; 0 Vocational; 0 Alternative
   0 Magnet; 0 Charter; 4 Title I Eligible; 0 School-wide Title I
Students: 6,225 (51.6% male; 48.3% female)
   Individual Education Program: 672 (10.8%);
   English Language Learner: 7 (0.1%); Migrant: n/a
   Eligible for Free Lunch Program: 541 (8.7%)
   Eligible for Reduced-Price Lunch Program: 196 (3.1%)
Teachers: 338.7 (18.4 to 1)
Librarians/Media Specialists: 6.0 (1,037.5 to 1)
Guidance Counselors: 14.0 (444.6 to 1)
Current Spending: ($ per student per year):
   Total: $7,194; Instruction: $3,840; Support Services: $3,122
Enrollment, Drop-out Rates and Diploma Recipients by Race/Ethnicity

Category	Total	White	Black	Asian	AIAN	Hisp.
Enrollment (%)	100.0	96.5	1.7	0.6	0.0	0.5
Drop-out Rate (%)	2.3	2.1	5.3	0.0	0.0	16.7
H.S. Diplomas (#)	417	399	6	1	0	3

New Richmond Ex Vill SD
212 Market St Fl 3rd • New Richmond, OH 45157-1373
(513) 553-2616 • http://www.nrschools.org/
Grade Span: PK-12; **Agency Type:** 1
Schools: 5
   2 Primary; 1 Middle; 1 High; 1 Other Level
   5 Regular; 0 Special Education; 0 Vocational; 0 Alternative
   0 Magnet; 0 Charter; 3 Title I Eligible; 1 School-wide Title I
Students: 2,411 (51.7% male; 48.2% female)
   Individual Education Program: 360 (14.9%);
   English Language Learner: 1 (<0.1%); Migrant: n/a
   Eligible for Free Lunch Program: 665 (27.6%)
   Eligible for Reduced-Price Lunch Program: 162 (6.7%)

Teachers: 156.7 (15.4 to 1)
Librarians/Media Specialists: 1.0 (2,411.0 to 1)
Guidance Counselors: 5.0 (482.2 to 1)
Current Spending: ($ per student per year):
   Total: $9,258; Instruction: $5,020; Support Services: $3,975
Enrollment, Drop-out Rates and Diploma Recipients by Race/Ethnicity

Category	Total	White	Black	Asian	AIAN	Hisp.
Enrollment (%)	100.0	97.1	0.8	0.3	0.3	0.6
Drop-out Rate (%)	5.8	5.5	50.0	n/a	0.0	50.0
H.S. Diplomas (#)	155	155	0	0	0	0

West Clermont Local SD
4578 E Tech Dr Ste 101 • Cincinnati, OH 45245-1054
(513) 943-5000 • http://www.westcler.k12.oh.us
Grade Span: PK-12; **Agency Type:** 2
Schools: 12
   8 Primary; 2 Middle; 2 High; 0 Other Level
   12 Regular; 0 Special Education; 0 Vocational; 0 Alternative
   0 Magnet; 0 Charter; 6 Title I Eligible; 1 School-wide Title I
Students: 9,189 (51.7% male; 48.2% female)
   Individual Education Program: 1,077 (11.7%);
   English Language Learner: 101 (1.1%); Migrant: n/a
   Eligible for Free Lunch Program: 950 (10.4%)
   Eligible for Reduced-Price Lunch Program: 291 (3.2%)
Teachers: 505.8 (18.1 to 1)
Librarians/Media Specialists: 2.0 (4,568.0 to 1)
Guidance Counselors: 11.0 (830.5 to 1)
Current Spending: ($ per student per year):
   Total: $6,743; Instruction: $4,109; Support Services: $2,450
Enrollment, Drop-out Rates and Diploma Recipients by Race/Ethnicity

Category	Total	White	Black	Asian	AIAN	Hisp.
Enrollment (%)	100.0	96.3	0.8	1.0	0.1	0.8
Drop-out Rate (%)	5.6	5.5	10.0	0.0	40.0	13.3
H.S. Diplomas (#)	520	514	1	4	0	0

Clinton County

Blanchester Local SD
3580 State Route 28 • Blanchester, OH 45107-7846
(937) 783-3523 • http://www.blanchester.k12.oh.us/
Grade Span: PK-12; **Agency Type:** 2
Schools: 3
   1 Primary; 1 Middle; 1 High; 0 Other Level
   3 Regular; 0 Special Education; 0 Vocational; 0 Alternative
   0 Magnet; 0 Charter; 2 Title I Eligible; 1 School-wide Title I
Students: 1,771 (50.7% male; 49.2% female)
   Individual Education Program: 258 (14.6%);
   English Language Learner: 0 (0.0%); Migrant: n/a
   Eligible for Free Lunch Program: 339 (19.1%)
   Eligible for Reduced-Price Lunch Program: 154 (8.7%)
Teachers: 114.8 (15.4 to 1)
Librarians/Media Specialists: 1.0 (1,771.0 to 1)
Guidance Counselors: 3.0 (590.3 to 1)
Current Spending: ($ per student per year):
   Total: $6,522; Instruction: $3,645; Support Services: $2,558
Enrollment, Drop-out Rates and Diploma Recipients by Race/Ethnicity

Category	Total	White	Black	Asian	AIAN	Hisp.
Enrollment (%)	100.0	98.6	0.3	0.2	0.0	0.0
Drop-out Rate (%)	1.9	1.9	0.0	n/a	n/a	n/a
H.S. Diplomas (#)	93	92	1	0	0	0

Clinton-Massie Local SD
2556 Lebanon Rd • Clarksville, OH 45113-8201
(937) 289-2471 • http://www.clinton-massie.k12.oh.us/
Grade Span: PK-12; **Agency Type:** 2
Schools: 3
   1 Primary; 1 Middle; 1 High; 0 Other Level
   3 Regular; 0 Special Education; 0 Vocational; 0 Alternative
   0 Magnet; 0 Charter; 2 Title I Eligible; 0 School-wide Title I
Students: 1,774 (51.8% male; 48.1% female)
   Individual Education Program: 192 (10.8%);
   English Language Learner: 0 (0.0%); Migrant: n/a
   Eligible for Free Lunch Program: 155 (8.7%)
   Eligible for Reduced-Price Lunch Program: 69 (3.9%)
Teachers: 91.5 (19.4 to 1)
Librarians/Media Specialists: 1.0 (1,774.0 to 1)
Guidance Counselors: 4.0 (443.5 to 1)
Current Spending: ($ per student per year):
   Total: $5,825; Instruction: $3,335; Support Services: $2,286
Enrollment, Drop-out Rates and Diploma Recipients by Race/Ethnicity

Category	Total	White	Black	Asian	AIAN	Hisp.
Enrollment (%)	100.0	97.6	1.4	0.1	0.1	0.4
Drop-out Rate (%)	2.3	2.3	0.0	0.0	n/a	n/a
H.S. Diplomas (#)	117	116	0	1	0	0

East Clinton Local SD
97 College St • Lees Creek, OH 45138
(937) 584-2461 • http://www.east-clinton.k12.oh.us/
Grade Span: PK-12; **Agency Type:** 2
Schools: 4
  2 Primary; 1 Middle; 1 High; 0 Other Level
  4 Regular; 0 Special Education; 0 Vocational; 0 Alternative
  0 Magnet; 0 Charter; 3 Title I Eligible; 0 School-wide Title I
Students: 1,571 (50.1% male; 49.8% female)
  Individual Education Program: 216 (13.7%);
  English Language Learner: 0 (0.0%); Migrant: n/a
  Eligible for Free Lunch Program: 234 (14.9%)
  Eligible for Reduced-Price Lunch Program: 79 (5.0%)
Teachers: 91.0 (17.3 to 1)
Librarians/Media Specialists: 1.0 (1,571.0 to 1)
Guidance Counselors: 1.0 (1,571.0 to 1)
Current Spending: ($ per student per year):
  Total: $6,323; Instruction: $3,421; Support Services: $2,655
Enrollment, Drop-out Rates and Diploma Recipients by Race/Ethnicity

Category	Total	White	Black	Asian	AIAN	Hisp.
Enrollment (%)	100.0	97.5	0.9	0.6	0.1	0.1
Drop-out Rate (%)	3.3	3.1	0.0	0.0	n/a	50.0
H.S. Diplomas (#)	93	93	0	0	0	0

Wilmington City SD
341 S Nelson Ave • Wilmington, OH 45177-2034
(937) 382-1641
Grade Span: PK-12; **Agency Type:** 1
Schools: 5
  3 Primary; 1 Middle; 1 High; 0 Other Level
  5 Regular; 0 Special Education; 0 Vocational; 0 Alternative
  0 Magnet; 0 Charter; 3 Title I Eligible; 0 School-wide Title I
Students: 3,195 (52.0% male; 47.9% female)
  Individual Education Program: 348 (10.9%);
  English Language Learner: 1 (<0.1%); Migrant: n/a
  Eligible for Free Lunch Program: 632 (19.8%)
  Eligible for Reduced-Price Lunch Program: 195 (6.1%)
Teachers: 183.0 (17.5 to 1)
Librarians/Media Specialists: 2.0 (1,597.5 to 1)
Guidance Counselors: 6.0 (532.5 to 1)
Current Spending: ($ per student per year):
  Total: $6,178; Instruction: $3,847; Support Services: $2,089
Enrollment, Drop-out Rates and Diploma Recipients by Race/Ethnicity

Category	Total	White	Black	Asian	AIAN	Hisp.
Enrollment (%)	100.0	91.5	4.0	0.6	0.2	0.8
Drop-out Rate (%)	1.3	1.0	6.1	0.0	n/a	25.0
H.S. Diplomas (#)	231	213	15	2	0	0

Columbiana County

Beaver Local SD
13093 State Route 7 • Lisbon, OH 44432-9559
(330) 385-6831 • http://www.beaver.k12.oh.us/
Grade Span: PK-12; **Agency Type:** 2
Schools: 5
  3 Primary; 1 Middle; 1 High; 0 Other Level
  5 Regular; 0 Special Education; 0 Vocational; 0 Alternative
  0 Magnet; 0 Charter; 4 Title I Eligible; 3 School-wide Title I
Students: 2,455 (52.0% male; 47.9% female)
  Individual Education Program: 325 (13.2%);
  English Language Learner: 0 (0.0%); Migrant: n/a
  Eligible for Free Lunch Program: 656 (26.7%)
  Eligible for Reduced-Price Lunch Program: 208 (8.5%)
Teachers: 139.0 (17.7 to 1)
Librarians/Media Specialists: 2.0 (1,227.5 to 1)
Guidance Counselors: 4.0 (613.8 to 1)
Current Spending: ($ per student per year):
  Total: $6,129; Instruction: $3,836; Support Services: $1,975
Enrollment, Drop-out Rates and Diploma Recipients by Race/Ethnicity

Category	Total	White	Black	Asian	AIAN	Hisp.
Enrollment (%)	100.0	97.8	0.2	0.3	0.3	0.3
Drop-out Rate (%)	1.9	1.7	100.0	0.0	n/a	0.0
H.S. Diplomas (#)	161	161	0	0	0	0

East Liverpool City SD
500 Maryland St • East Liverpool, OH 43920-2121
(330) 385-7132
Grade Span: PK-12; **Agency Type:** 1
Schools: 6
  4 Primary; 1 Middle; 1 High; 0 Other Level
  6 Regular; 0 Special Education; 0 Vocational; 0 Alternative
  0 Magnet; 0 Charter; 5 Title I Eligible; 5 School-wide Title I
Students: 3,082 (51.5% male; 48.4% female)
  Individual Education Program: 598 (19.4%);
  English Language Learner: 0 (0.0%); Migrant: n/a

  Eligible for Free Lunch Program: 1,349 (43.8%)
  Eligible for Reduced-Price Lunch Program: 171 (5.5%)
Teachers: 221.0 (13.9 to 1)
Librarians/Media Specialists: 4.0 (770.5 to 1)
Guidance Counselors: 7.0 (440.3 to 1)
Current Spending: ($ per student per year):
  Total: $8,528; Instruction: $5,261; Support Services: $2,933
Enrollment, Drop-out Rates and Diploma Recipients by Race/Ethnicity

Category	Total	White	Black	Asian	AIAN	Hisp.
Enrollment (%)	100.0	90.5	6.0	0.1	0.2	0.2
Drop-out Rate (%)	2.2	2.2	2.4	0.0	0.0	0.0
H.S. Diplomas (#)	185	170	15	0	0	0

Salem City SD
1226 E State St • Salem, OH 44460-2222
(330) 332-0316 • http://www.salem.k12.oh.us/
Grade Span: PK-12; **Agency Type:** 1
Schools: 6
  2 Primary; 3 Middle; 1 High; 0 Other Level
  6 Regular; 0 Special Education; 0 Vocational; 0 Alternative
  0 Magnet; 0 Charter; 4 Title I Eligible; 0 School-wide Title I
Students: 2,445 (50.4% male; 49.5% female)
  Individual Education Program: 303 (12.4%);
  English Language Learner: 1 (<0.1%); Migrant: n/a
  Eligible for Free Lunch Program: 527 (21.6%)
  Eligible for Reduced-Price Lunch Program: 107 (4.4%)
Teachers: 158.4 (15.4 to 1)
Librarians/Media Specialists: 2.0 (1,222.5 to 1)
Guidance Counselors: 4.0 (611.3 to 1)
Current Spending: ($ per student per year):
  Total: $8,065; Instruction: $4,864; Support Services: $2,967
Enrollment, Drop-out Rates and Diploma Recipients by Race/Ethnicity

Category	Total	White	Black	Asian	AIAN	Hisp.
Enrollment (%)	100.0	97.1	0.3	0.4	0.3	0.5
Drop-out Rate (%)	2.0	2.0	0.0	0.0	n/a	0.0
H.S. Diplomas (#)	183	182	0	0	0	1

United Local SD
8143 State Route 9 • Hanoverton, OH 44423-8618
(330) 223-1521
Grade Span: KG-12; **Agency Type:** 2
Schools: 2
  0 Primary; 0 Middle; 1 High; 1 Other Level
  2 Regular; 0 Special Education; 0 Vocational; 0 Alternative
  0 Magnet; 0 Charter; 2 Title I Eligible; 0 School-wide Title I
Students: 1,537 (50.5% male; 49.4% female)
  Individual Education Program: 210 (13.7%);
  English Language Learner: 0 (0.0%); Migrant: n/a
  Eligible for Free Lunch Program: 329 (21.4%)
  Eligible for Reduced-Price Lunch Program: 103 (6.7%)
Teachers: 83.0 (18.5 to 1)
Librarians/Media Specialists: 1.5 (1,024.7 to 1)
Guidance Counselors: 3.0 (512.3 to 1)
Current Spending: ($ per student per year):
  Total: $6,478; Instruction: $4,279; Support Services: $1,910
Enrollment, Drop-out Rates and Diploma Recipients by Race/Ethnicity

Category	Total	White	Black	Asian	AIAN	Hisp.
Enrollment (%)	100.0	97.8	0.8	0.1	0.8	0.1
Drop-out Rate (%)	2.4	2.5	0.0	0.0	0.0	0.0
H.S. Diplomas (#)	99	97	0	1	0	1

Coshocton County

Coshocton City SD
1207 Cambridge Rd • Coshocton, OH 43812-2742
(740) 622-1901 • http://www.coshoctonredskins.com/
Grade Span: PK-12; **Agency Type:** 1
Schools: 5
  4 Primary; 0 Middle; 1 High; 0 Other Level
  5 Regular; 0 Special Education; 0 Vocational; 0 Alternative
  0 Magnet; 0 Charter; 3 Title I Eligible; 3 School-wide Title I
Students: 1,978 (51.7% male; 48.2% female)
  Individual Education Program: 437 (22.1%);
  English Language Learner: 0 (0.0%); Migrant: n/a
  Eligible for Free Lunch Program: 704 (35.6%)
  Eligible for Reduced-Price Lunch Program: 159 (8.0%)
Teachers: 123.6 (16.0 to 1)
Librarians/Media Specialists: 2.0 (989.0 to 1)
Guidance Counselors: 3.0 (659.3 to 1)
Current Spending: ($ per student per year):
  Total: $7,410; Instruction: $4,464; Support Services: $2,601

Category	Total	White	Black	Asian	AIAN	Hisp.
Enrollment (%)	100.0	95.3	2.1	0.9	0.0	0.2
Drop-out Rate (%)	0.7	0.7	0.0	0.0	n/a	n/a
H.S. Diplomas (#)	122	112	4	5	0	0

Ridgewood Local SD
301 S Oak St • West Lafayette, OH 43845-1339
(740) 545-5312
Grade Span: PK-12; **Agency Type:** 2
Schools: 5
  3 Primary; 1 Middle; 1 High; 0 Other Level
  5 Regular; 0 Special Education; 0 Vocational; 0 Alternative
  0 Magnet; 0 Charter; 4 Title I Eligible; 1 School-wide Title I
Students: 1,501 (51.2% male; 48.7% female)
  Individual Education Program: 197 (13.1%);
  English Language Learner: 0 (0.0%); Migrant: n/a
  Eligible for Free Lunch Program: 330 (22.0%)
  Eligible for Reduced-Price Lunch Program: 113 (7.5%)
Teachers: 84.6 (17.7 to 1)
Librarians/Media Specialists: 1.0 (1,501.0 to 1)
Guidance Counselors: 2.0 (750.5 to 1)
Current Spending: ($ per student per year):
  Total: $7,273; Instruction: $4,366; Support Services: $2,538
Enrollment, Drop-out Rates and Diploma Recipients by Race/Ethnicity

Category	Total	White	Black	Asian	AIAN	Hisp.
Enrollment (%)	100.0	99.0	0.0	0.2	0.0	0.2
Drop-out Rate (%)	2.2	2.2	n/a	n/a	n/a	0.0
H.S. Diplomas (#)	110	109	0	0	0	1

River View Local SD
26496 State Route 60 • Warsaw, OH 43844-9714
(740) 824-3521
Grade Span: PK-12; **Agency Type:** 2
Schools: 7
  4 Primary; 1 Middle; 1 High; 1 Other Level
  6 Regular; 0 Special Education; 0 Vocational; 1 Alternative
  0 Magnet; 0 Charter; 4 Title I Eligible; 3 School-wide Title I
Students: 2,586 (52.1% male; 47.8% female)
  Individual Education Program: 420 (16.2%);
  English Language Learner: 0 (0.0%); Migrant: n/a
  Eligible for Free Lunch Program: 420 (16.5%)
  Eligible for Reduced-Price Lunch Program: 183 (7.2%)
Teachers: 154.5 (16.4 to 1)
Librarians/Media Specialists: 1.0 (2,541.0 to 1)
Guidance Counselors: 2.0 (1,270.5 to 1)
Current Spending: ($ per student per year):
  Total: $6,823; Instruction: $3,901; Support Services: $2,625
Enrollment, Drop-out Rates and Diploma Recipients by Race/Ethnicity

Category	Total	White	Black	Asian	AIAN	Hisp.
Enrollment (%)	100.0	98.4	1.2	0.0	0.0	0.0
Drop-out Rate (%)	2.6	2.6	0.0	n/a	n/a	n/a
H.S. Diplomas (#)	184	181	3	0	0	0

Crawford County

Bucyrus City SD
630 Jump St • Bucyrus, OH 44820-1525
(419) 562-4045
Grade Span: PK-12; **Agency Type:** 1
Schools: 7
  4 Primary; 2 Middle; 1 High; 0 Other Level
  7 Regular; 0 Special Education; 0 Vocational; 0 Alternative
  0 Magnet; 0 Charter; 6 Title I Eligible; 6 School-wide Title I
Students: 1,891 (51.9% male; 48.0% female)
  Individual Education Program: 369 (19.5%);
  English Language Learner: 14 (0.7%); Migrant: n/a
  Eligible for Free Lunch Program: 642 (34.0%)
  Eligible for Reduced-Price Lunch Program: 246 (13.0%)
Teachers: 114.8 (16.5 to 1)
Librarians/Media Specialists: 2.0 (945.5 to 1)
Guidance Counselors: 1.0 (1,891.0 to 1)
Current Spending: ($ per student per year):
  Total: $7,356; Instruction: $4,117; Support Services: $2,762
Enrollment, Drop-out Rates and Diploma Recipients by Race/Ethnicity

Category	Total	White	Black	Asian	AIAN	Hisp.
Enrollment (%)	100.0	96.2	0.5	1.1	0.2	0.5
Drop-out Rate (%)	4.5	4.5	0.0	0.0	n/a	0.0
H.S. Diplomas (#)	118	117	1	0	0	0

Galion City SD
200 W Church St • Galion, OH 44833-1707
(419) 468-3432 • http://www.galion-city.k12.oh.us/
Grade Span: PK-12; **Agency Type:** 1
Schools: 6

4 Primary; 1 Middle; 1 High; 0 Other Level
  6 Regular; 0 Special Education; 0 Vocational; 0 Alternative
  0 Magnet; 0 Charter; 3 Title I Eligible; 2 School-wide Title I
Students: 2,238 (48.1% male; 51.8% female)
  Individual Education Program: 376 (16.8%);
  English Language Learner: 0 (0.0%); Migrant: n/a
  Eligible for Free Lunch Program: 515 (23.0%)
  Eligible for Reduced-Price Lunch Program: 140 (6.3%)
Teachers: 142.9 (15.7 to 1)
Librarians/Media Specialists: 1.0 (2,238.0 to 1)
Guidance Counselors: 3.0 (746.0 to 1)
Current Spending: ($ per student per year):
  Total: $7,149; Instruction: $4,468; Support Services: $2,424
Enrollment, Drop-out Rates and Diploma Recipients by Race/Ethnicity

Category	Total	White	Black	Asian	AIAN	Hisp.
Enrollment (%)	100.0	98.3	0.4	0.1	0.0	0.4
Drop-out Rate (%)	3.3	3.2	50.0	0.0	0.0	n/a
H.S. Diplomas (#)	170	168	0	1	1	0

Cuyahoga County

Bay Village City SD
377 Dover Center Rd • Bay Village, OH 44140-2304
(440) 617-7300 • http://www.bayvillageschools.com/
Grade Span: KG-12; **Agency Type:** 1
Schools: 4
  2 Primary; 1 Middle; 1 High; 0 Other Level
  4 Regular; 0 Special Education; 0 Vocational; 0 Alternative
  0 Magnet; 0 Charter; 3 Title I Eligible; 0 School-wide Title I
Students: 2,455 (50.1% male; 49.8% female)
  Individual Education Program: 340 (13.8%);
  English Language Learner: 20 (0.8%); Migrant: 1 (<0.1%)
  Eligible for Free Lunch Program: 78 (3.2%)
  Eligible for Reduced-Price Lunch Program: 44 (1.8%)
Teachers: 164.5 (14.9 to 1)
Librarians/Media Specialists: 3.0 (818.3 to 1)
Guidance Counselors: 8.0 (306.9 to 1)
Current Spending: ($ per student per year):
  Total: $9,131; Instruction: $5,106; Support Services: $3,773
Enrollment, Drop-out Rates and Diploma Recipients by Race/Ethnicity

Category	Total	White	Black	Asian	AIAN	Hisp.
Enrollment (%)	100.0	96.6	0.6	1.7	0.1	0.6
Drop-out Rate (%)	1.2	1.2	0.0	0.0	n/a	0.0
H.S. Diplomas (#)	168	163	1	2	0	2

Beachwood City SD
24601 Fairmount Blvd • Beachwood, OH 44122-2239
(216) 464-2600
Grade Span: PK-12; **Agency Type:** 1
Schools: 5
  3 Primary; 0 Middle; 1 High; 1 Other Level
  5 Regular; 0 Special Education; 0 Vocational; 0 Alternative
  0 Magnet; 0 Charter; 3 Title I Eligible; 0 School-wide Title I
Students: 1,596 (53.9% male; 46.0% female)
  Individual Education Program: 165 (10.3%);
  English Language Learner: 5 (0.3%); Migrant: n/a
  Eligible for Free Lunch Program: 50 (3.1%)
  Eligible for Reduced-Price Lunch Program: 21 (1.3%)
Teachers: 151.3 (10.5 to 1)
Librarians/Media Specialists: 4.0 (399.0 to 1)
Guidance Counselors: 6.0 (266.0 to 1)
Current Spending: ($ per student per year):
  Total: $16,952; Instruction: $8,880; Support Services: $7,750
Enrollment, Drop-out Rates and Diploma Recipients by Race/Ethnicity

Category	Total	White	Black	Asian	AIAN	Hisp.
Enrollment (%)	100.0	76.3	15.1	6.0	0.1	0.7
Drop-out Rate (%)	0.6	0.4	2.3	0.0	n/a	0.0
H.S. Diplomas (#)	142	122	14	3	0	1

Bedford City SD
475 Northfield Rd • Bedford, OH 44146-2201
(440) 439-1500 • http://www.bedford.k12.oh.us/
Grade Span: PK-12; **Agency Type:** 1
Schools: 7
  4 Primary; 2 Middle; 1 High; 0 Other Level
  7 Regular; 0 Special Education; 0 Vocational; 0 Alternative
  0 Magnet; 0 Charter; 6 Title I Eligible; 4 School-wide Title I
Students: 3,890 (50.7% male; 49.2% female)
  Individual Education Program: 525 (13.5%);
  English Language Learner: 17 (0.4%); Migrant: n/a
  Eligible for Free Lunch Program: 1,114 (28.6%)
  Eligible for Reduced-Price Lunch Program: 267 (6.9%)
Teachers: 252.4 (15.4 to 1)
Librarians/Media Specialists: 3.0 (1,296.7 to 1)
Guidance Counselors: 10.0 (389.0 to 1)

Current Spending: ($ per student per year):
Total: $10,255; Instruction: $5,403; Support Services: $4,541

Enrollment, Drop-out Rates and Diploma Recipients by Race/Ethnicity

Category	Total	White	Black	Asian	AIAN	Hisp.
Enrollment (%)	100.0	25.0	68.1	0.7	0.1	0.7
Drop-out Rate (%)	7.8	7.8	7.7	6.7	0.0	10.0
H.S. Diplomas (#)	231	86	138	4	0	1

Berea City SD
390 Fair St • Berea, OH 44017-2308
(440) 243-6000 • http://berea.k12.oh.us/webmain/
Grade Span: PK-12; **Agency Type:** 1
Schools: 13
7 Primary; 2 Middle; 2 High; 2 Other Level
11 Regular; 2 Special Education; 0 Vocational; 0 Alternative
0 Magnet; 0 Charter; 7 Title I Eligible; 1 School-wide Title I
Students: 8,027 (52.8% male; 47.1% female)
Individual Education Program: 1,162 (14.5%);
English Language Learner: 115 (1.4%); Migrant: n/a
Eligible for Free Lunch Program: 967 (12.1%)
Eligible for Reduced-Price Lunch Program: 557 (7.0%)
Teachers: 489.0 (16.4 to 1)
Librarians/Media Specialists: 9.0 (889.6 to 1)
Guidance Counselors: 18.2 (439.9 to 1)
Current Spending: ($ per student per year):
Total: $8,737; Instruction: $4,839; Support Services: $3,654

Enrollment, Drop-out Rates and Diploma Recipients by Race/Ethnicity

Category	Total	White	Black	Asian	AIAN	Hisp.
Enrollment (%)	100.0	91.1	3.8	1.5	0.1	1.3
Drop-out Rate (%)	1.6	1.6	1.9	0.0	0.0	0.0
H.S. Diplomas (#)	611	560	20	9	1	12

Brecksville-Broadview Heights City SD
6638 Mill Rd • Brecksville, OH 44141-1512
(440) 740-4010 • http://www.bbhcsd.org/
Grade Span: PK-12; **Agency Type:** 1
Schools: 6
3 Primary; 2 Middle; 1 High; 0 Other Level
6 Regular; 0 Special Education; 0 Vocational; 0 Alternative
0 Magnet; 0 Charter; 3 Title I Eligible; 0 School-wide Title I
Students: 4,666 (50.7% male; 49.2% female)
Individual Education Program: 492 (10.5%);
English Language Learner: 68 (1.5%); Migrant: n/a
Eligible for Free Lunch Program: 162 (3.5%)
Eligible for Reduced-Price Lunch Program: 86 (1.8%)
Teachers: 269.8 (17.3 to 1)
Librarians/Media Specialists: 4.0 (1,166.5 to 1)
Guidance Counselors: 10.0 (466.6 to 1)
Current Spending: ($ per student per year):
Total: $8,325; Instruction: $4,854; Support Services: $3,202

Enrollment, Drop-out Rates and Diploma Recipients by Race/Ethnicity

Category	Total	White	Black	Asian	AIAN	Hisp.
Enrollment (%)	100.0	92.5	1.6	3.7	0.1	0.7
Drop-out Rate (%)	0.7	0.7	0.0	0.0	0.0	12.5
H.S. Diplomas (#)	340	324	2	11	0	3

Chagrin Falls Ex Vill SD
400 E Washington St • Chagrin Falls, OH 44022-2924
(440) 247-5500
Grade Span: PK-12; **Agency Type:** 1
Schools: 4
1 Primary; 1 Middle; 2 High; 0 Other Level
4 Regular; 0 Special Education; 0 Vocational; 0 Alternative
0 Magnet; 0 Charter; 1 Title I Eligible; 0 School-wide Title I
Students: 1,970 (52.3% male; 47.6% female)
Individual Education Program: 227 (11.5%);
English Language Learner: 14 (0.7%); Migrant: n/a
Eligible for Free Lunch Program: 10 (0.5%)
Eligible for Reduced-Price Lunch Program: 2 (0.1%)
Teachers: 136.5 (14.4 to 1)
Librarians/Media Specialists: 2.0 (985.0 to 1)
Guidance Counselors: 5.0 (394.0 to 1)
Current Spending: ($ per student per year):
Total: $9,298; Instruction: $5,292; Support Services: $3,735

Enrollment, Drop-out Rates and Diploma Recipients by Race/Ethnicity

Category	Total	White	Black	Asian	AIAN	Hisp.
Enrollment (%)	100.0	97.7	0.9	0.3	0.0	0.3
Drop-out Rate (%)	0.5	0.5	0.0	0.0	n/a	0.0
H.S. Diplomas (#)	146	141	0	2	0	2

Cleveland Hts-Univ Hts City SD
2155 Miramar Blvd • University Heights, OH 44118-3301
(216) 371-7171
Grade Span: KG-12; **Agency Type:** 1
Schools: 13

8 Primary; 3 Middle; 1 High; 1 Other Level
12 Regular; 1 Special Education; 0 Vocational; 0 Alternative
0 Magnet; 0 Charter; 12 Title I Eligible; 0 School-wide Title I
Students: 6,887 (50.5% male; 49.4% female)
Individual Education Program: 1,049 (15.2%);
English Language Learner: 53 (0.8%); Migrant: n/a
Eligible for Free Lunch Program: 2,226 (32.9%)
Eligible for Reduced-Price Lunch Program: 564 (8.3%)
Teachers: 477.0 (14.2 to 1)
Librarians/Media Specialists: 12.6 (536.7 to 1)
Guidance Counselors: 27.1 (249.5 to 1)
Current Spending: ($ per student per year):
Total: $12,002; Instruction: $6,366; Support Services: $5,294

Enrollment, Drop-out Rates and Diploma Recipients by Race/Ethnicity

Category	Total	White	Black	Asian	AIAN	Hisp.
Enrollment (%)	100.0	18.4	75.7	1.1	0.1	0.9
Drop-out Rate (%)	3.5	2.6	3.6	3.4	0.0	5.6
H.S. Diplomas (#)	346	108	224	8	0	4

Cleveland Municipal City SD
1380 E 6th St • Cleveland, OH 44114-1606
(216) 574-8000 • http://www.cmsdnet.net/
Grade Span: PK-12; **Agency Type:** 1
Schools: 122
84 Primary; 15 Middle; 12 High; 11 Other Level
122 Regular; 0 Special Education; 0 Vocational; 0 Alternative
0 Magnet; 0 Charter; 119 Title I Eligible; 105 School-wide Title I
Students: 69,655 (51.4% male; 48.5% female)
Individual Education Program: 12,711 (18.2%);
English Language Learner: 2,752 (4.0%); Migrant: n/a
Eligible for Free Lunch Program: 50,286 (72.9%)
Eligible for Reduced-Price Lunch Program: 4,892 (7.1%)
Teachers: 5,108.9 (13.5 to 1)
Librarians/Media Specialists: 106.0 (650.8 to 1)
Guidance Counselors: 104.0 (663.3 to 1)
Current Spending: ($ per student per year):
Total: $10,199; Instruction: $5,782; Support Services: $4,007

Enrollment, Drop-out Rates and Diploma Recipients by Race/Ethnicity

Category	Total	White	Black	Asian	AIAN	Hisp.
Enrollment (%)	100.0	17.8	70.6	0.7	0.3	9.5
Drop-out Rate (%)	15.1	16.2	14.7	12.6	15.4	13.8
H.S. Diplomas (#)	2,443	405	1,796	34	7	194

East Cleveland City SD
15305 Terrace Rd • East Cleveland, OH 44112-2933
(216) 268-6570 • http://www.east-cleveland.k12.oh.us/
Grade Span: PK-12; **Agency Type:** 1
Schools: 8
5 Primary; 1 Middle; 1 High; 1 Other Level
8 Regular; 0 Special Education; 0 Vocational; 0 Alternative
0 Magnet; 0 Charter; 8 Title I Eligible; 7 School-wide Title I
Students: 5,092 (48.9% male; 51.0% female)
Individual Education Program: 567 (11.1%);
English Language Learner: 0 (0.0%); Migrant: n/a
Eligible for Free Lunch Program: 3,199 (62.8%)
Eligible for Reduced-Price Lunch Program: 344 (6.8%)
Teachers: 295.0 (17.3 to 1)
Librarians/Media Specialists: 7.0 (727.4 to 1)
Guidance Counselors: 6.0 (848.7 to 1)
Current Spending: ($ per student per year):
Total: $10,734; Instruction: $5,945; Support Services: $4,310

Enrollment, Drop-out Rates and Diploma Recipients by Race/Ethnicity

Category	Total	White	Black	Asian	AIAN	Hisp.
Enrollment (%)	100.0	0.2	99.4	0.0	0.0	0.1
Drop-out Rate (%)	10.7	n/a	10.6	n/a	0.0	n/a
H.S. Diplomas (#)	252	0	252	0	0	0

Euclid City SD
651 E 222nd St • Euclid, OH 44123-2031
(216) 261-2900 • http://www.euclid.k12.oh.us/
Grade Span: PK-12; **Agency Type:** 1
Schools: 10
5 Primary; 1 Middle; 1 High; 1 Other Level
8 Regular; 0 Special Education; 0 Vocational; 0 Alternative
0 Magnet; 0 Charter; 8 Title I Eligible; 5 School-wide Title I
Students: 6,420 (52.9% male; 47.0% female)
Individual Education Program: 1,139 (17.7%);
English Language Learner: 33 (0.5%); Migrant: n/a
Eligible for Free Lunch Program: 2,413 (37.6%)
Eligible for Reduced-Price Lunch Program: 845 (13.2%)
Teachers: 383.0 (16.8 to 1)
Librarians/Media Specialists: 3.0 (2,140.0 to 1)
Guidance Counselors: 12.0 (535.0 to 1)
Current Spending: ($ per student per year):
Total: $9,405; Instruction: $5,208; Support Services: $3,914

Enrollment, Drop-out Rates and Diploma Recipients by Race/Ethnicity

Category	Total	White	Black	Asian	AIAN	Hisp.
Enrollment (%)	100.0	31.1	64.1	0.7	0.1	0.7
Drop-out Rate (%)	0.1	0.0	0.2	0.0	0.0	0.0
H.S. Diplomas (#)	363	192	165	1	0	2

Fairview Park City SD

20770 Lorain Rd • Fairview Park, OH 44126-2019
(440) 331-5500
Grade Span: PK-12; **Agency Type:** 1
Schools: 5
 2 Primary; 2 Middle; 1 High; 0 Other Level
 5 Regular; 0 Special Education; 0 Vocational; 0 Alternative
 0 Magnet; 0 Charter; 3 Title I Eligible; 0 School-wide Title I
Students: 1,831 (52.1% male; 47.8% female)
 Individual Education Program: 278 (15.2%);
 English Language Learner: 69 (3.8%); Migrant: 1 (0.1%)
 Eligible for Free Lunch Program: 246 (13.5%)
 Eligible for Reduced-Price Lunch Program: 98 (5.4%)
Teachers: 131.2 (13.9 to 1)
Librarians/Media Specialists: 3.0 (607.3 to 1)
Guidance Counselors: 4.0 (455.5 to 1)
Current Spending: ($ per student per year):
 Total: $9,880; Instruction: $5,971; Support Services: $3,764

Enrollment, Drop-out Rates and Diploma Recipients by Race/Ethnicity

Category	Total	White	Black	Asian	AIAN	Hisp.
Enrollment (%)	100.0	92.5	1.3	2.5	0.1	2.3
Drop-out Rate (%)	1.3	1.3	0.0	0.0	0.0	0.0
H.S. Diplomas (#)	167	161	1	3	0	2

Garfield Heights City SD

5640 Briarcliff Dr • Garfield Heights, OH 44125-4158
(216) 475-8100
Grade Span: PK-12; **Agency Type:** 1
Schools: 5
 2 Primary; 2 Middle; 1 High; 0 Other Level
 5 Regular; 0 Special Education; 0 Vocational; 0 Alternative
 0 Magnet; 0 Charter; 4 Title I Eligible; 3 School-wide Title I
Students: 3,859 (52.8% male; 47.1% female)
 Individual Education Program: 557 (14.4%);
 English Language Learner: 18 (0.5%); Migrant: n/a
 Eligible for Free Lunch Program: 984 (25.5%)
 Eligible for Reduced-Price Lunch Program: 365 (9.5%)
Teachers: 197.4 (19.5 to 1)
Librarians/Media Specialists: 5.0 (771.8 to 1)
Guidance Counselors: 7.0 (551.3 to 1)
Current Spending: ($ per student per year):
 Total: $7,756; Instruction: $4,191; Support Services: $3,246

Enrollment, Drop-out Rates and Diploma Recipients by Race/Ethnicity

Category	Total	White	Black	Asian	AIAN	Hisp.
Enrollment (%)	100.0	73.9	20.0	1.6	0.0	1.5
Drop-out Rate (%)	3.0	2.9	2.8	0.0	0.0	0.0
H.S. Diplomas (#)	263	223	30	4	0	3

Lakewood City SD

1470 Warren Rd • Lakewood, OH 44107-3918
(216) 529-4092 • http://www.lkwdpl.org/schools/
Grade Span: PK-12; **Agency Type:** 1
Schools: 14
 10 Primary; 3 Middle; 1 High; 0 Other Level
 14 Regular; 0 Special Education; 0 Vocational; 0 Alternative
 0 Magnet; 0 Charter; 10 Title I Eligible; 7 School-wide Title I
Students: 7,083 (52.3% male; 47.6% female)
 Individual Education Program: 997 (14.1%);
 English Language Learner: 577 (8.1%); Migrant: n/a
 Eligible for Free Lunch Program: 1,645 (23.7%)
 Eligible for Reduced-Price Lunch Program: 402 (5.8%)
Teachers: 423.0 (16.4 to 1)
Librarians/Media Specialists: 7.0 (990.0 to 1)
Guidance Counselors: 13.0 (533.1 to 1)
Current Spending: ($ per student per year):
 Total: $9,274; Instruction: $5,755; Support Services: $3,278

Enrollment, Drop-out Rates and Diploma Recipients by Race/Ethnicity

Category	Total	White	Black	Asian	AIAN	Hisp.
Enrollment (%)	100.0	86.9	4.2	1.7	0.4	2.5
Drop-out Rate (%)	3.4	3.3	5.8	5.0	0.0	4.2
H.S. Diplomas (#)	518	488	15	4	0	7

Maple Heights City SD

14605 Granger Rd • Maple Heights, OH 44137-1023
(216) 587-6100
Grade Span: PK-12; **Agency Type:** 1
Schools: 6
 4 Primary; 1 Middle; 1 High; 0 Other Level
 6 Regular; 0 Special Education; 0 Vocational; 0 Alternative

 0 Magnet; 0 Charter; 5 Title I Eligible; 4 School-wide Title I
Students: 3,686 (52.1% male; 47.8% female)
 Individual Education Program: 498 (13.5%);
 English Language Learner: 28 (0.8%); Migrant: n/a
 Eligible for Free Lunch Program: 1,312 (35.8%)
 Eligible for Reduced-Price Lunch Program: 386 (10.5%)
Teachers: 221.7 (16.5 to 1)
Librarians/Media Specialists: 2.0 (1,834.0 to 1)
Guidance Counselors: 6.0 (611.3 to 1)
Current Spending: ($ per student per year):
 Total: $7,279; Instruction: $3,879; Support Services: $3,089

Enrollment, Drop-out Rates and Diploma Recipients by Race/Ethnicity

Category	Total	White	Black	Asian	AIAN	Hisp.
Enrollment (%)	100.0	11.2	84.6	1.3	0.0	0.9
Drop-out Rate (%)	5.9	5.1	5.9	0.0	0.0	33.3
H.S. Diplomas (#)	189	44	141	2	0	1

Mayfield City SD

59 Alpha Park • Highland Heights, OH 44143-2202
(440) 995-6800
Grade Span: PK-12; **Agency Type:** 1
Schools: 7
 5 Primary; 1 Middle; 1 High; 0 Other Level
 6 Regular; 1 Special Education; 0 Vocational; 0 Alternative
 0 Magnet; 0 Charter; 4 Title I Eligible; 0 School-wide Title I
Students: 4,331 (53.8% male; 46.1% female)
 Individual Education Program: 690 (15.9%);
 English Language Learner: 209 (4.8%); Migrant: n/a
 Eligible for Free Lunch Program: 257 (5.9%)
 Eligible for Reduced-Price Lunch Program: 69 (1.6%)
Teachers: 330.6 (13.1 to 1)
Librarians/Media Specialists: 3.0 (1,444.7 to 1)
Guidance Counselors: 10.0 (433.4 to 1)
Current Spending: ($ per student per year):
 Total: $10,019; Instruction: $5,376; Support Services: $4,438

Enrollment, Drop-out Rates and Diploma Recipients by Race/Ethnicity

Category	Total	White	Black	Asian	AIAN	Hisp.
Enrollment (%)	100.0	84.0	7.4	5.3	0.1	0.9
Drop-out Rate (%)	1.0	1.1	0.6	0.0	0.0	0.0
H.S. Diplomas (#)	341	304	8	20	1	5

North Olmsted City Schools

24100 Palm Dr • North Olmsted, OH 44070-2844
(440) 779-3549 • http://www.nocs.leeca.esu.k12.oh.us/
Grade Span: PK-12; **Agency Type:** 1
Schools: 9
 5 Primary; 3 Middle; 1 High; 0 Other Level
 9 Regular; 0 Special Education; 0 Vocational; 0 Alternative
 0 Magnet; 0 Charter; 7 Title I Eligible; 0 School-wide Title I
Students: 4,573 (52.2% male; 47.7% female)
 Individual Education Program: 578 (12.6%);
 English Language Learner: 268 (5.9%); Migrant: 2 (<0.1%)
 Eligible for Free Lunch Program: 470 (10.3%)
 Eligible for Reduced-Price Lunch Program: 240 (5.3%)
Teachers: 313.9 (14.6 to 1)
Librarians/Media Specialists: 2.0 (2,285.0 to 1)
Guidance Counselors: 12.0 (380.8 to 1)
Current Spending: ($ per student per year):
 Total: $8,832; Instruction: $5,613; Support Services: $2,937

Enrollment, Drop-out Rates and Diploma Recipients by Race/Ethnicity

Category	Total	White	Black	Asian	AIAN	Hisp.
Enrollment (%)	100.0	91.8	1.3	3.4	0.1	1.7
Drop-out Rate (%)	1.2	1.2	4.0	0.0	n/a	0.0
H.S. Diplomas (#)	368	345	3	14	0	5

North Royalton City SD

6579 Royalton Rd • North Royalton, OH 44133-4925
(440) 237-8800 • http://www.lnoca.org/~nrcs/
Grade Span: PK-12; **Agency Type:** 1
Schools: 6
 4 Primary; 1 Middle; 1 High; 0 Other Level
 6 Regular; 0 Special Education; 0 Vocational; 0 Alternative
 0 Magnet; 0 Charter; 0 Title I Eligible; 0 School-wide Title I
Students: 4,496 (50.7% male; 49.2% female)
 Individual Education Program: 486 (10.8%);
 English Language Learner: 62 (1.4%); Migrant: 8 (0.2%)
 Eligible for Free Lunch Program: 232 (5.2%)
 Eligible for Reduced-Price Lunch Program: 124 (2.8%)
Teachers: 250.6 (17.9 to 1)
Librarians/Media Specialists: 3.5 (1,284.6 to 1)
Guidance Counselors: 11.0 (408.7 to 1)
Current Spending: ($ per student per year):
 Total: $7,711; Instruction: $4,610; Support Services: $2,829

Enrollment, Drop-out Rates and Diploma Recipients by Race/Ethnicity

Category	Total	White	Black	Asian	AIAN	Hisp.
Enrollment (%)	100.0	94.9	0.3	2.6	0.0	0.5
Drop-out Rate (%)	0.5	0.5	0.0	0.0	0.0	0.0
H.S. Diplomas (#)	335	324	0	10	0	1

Olmsted Falls City SD
26937 Bagley Rd • Olmsted Falls, OH 44138-1161
Mailing Address: PO Box 38010 • Olmsted Falls, OH 44138-0010
(440) 427-6000
Grade Span: PK-12; **Agency Type:** 1
Schools: 4
   1 Primary; 2 Middle; 1 High; 0 Other Level
   4 Regular; 0 Special Education; 0 Vocational; 0 Alternative
   0 Magnet; 0 Charter; 0 Title I Eligible; 0 School-wide Title I
Students: 3,342   (50.6% male; 49.3% female)
   Individual Education Program: 346 (10.4%);
   English Language Learner: 2 (0.1%); Migrant: 1 (<0.1%)
   Eligible for Free Lunch Program: 232 (6.9%)
   Eligible for Reduced-Price Lunch Program: 112 (3.4%)
Teachers: 196.8 (17.0 to 1)
Librarians/Media Specialists: 3.0 (1,113.3 to 1)
Guidance Counselors: 6.2 (538.7 to 1)
Current Spending: ($ per student per year):
   Total: $8,729; Instruction: $5,069; Support Services: $3,390
Enrollment, Drop-out Rates and Diploma Recipients by Race/Ethnicity

Category	Total	White	Black	Asian	AIAN	Hisp.
Enrollment (%)	100.0	95.6	1.1	1.2	0.1	1.3
Drop-out Rate (%)	1.6	1.6	0.0	0.0	n/a	3.8
H.S. Diplomas (#)	219	205	4	5	0	5

Orange City SD
32000 Chagrin Blvd • Cleveland, OH 44124-5922
(216) 831-8600 • http://www.orangeschools.org/
Grade Span: PK-12; **Agency Type:** 1
Schools: 4
   2 Primary; 1 Middle; 1 High; 0 Other Level
   3 Regular; 1 Special Education; 0 Vocational; 0 Alternative
   0 Magnet; 0 Charter; 2 Title I Eligible; 0 School-wide Title I
Students: 2,368   (54.6% male; 45.3% female)
   Individual Education Program: 287 (12.1%);
   English Language Learner: 39 (1.6%); Migrant: n/a
   Eligible for Free Lunch Program: 41 (1.7%)
   Eligible for Reduced-Price Lunch Program: 11 (0.5%)
Teachers: 193.6 (12.2 to 1)
Librarians/Media Specialists: 4.0 (592.0 to 1)
Guidance Counselors: 8.0 (296.0 to 1)
Current Spending: ($ per student per year):
   Total: $14,304; Instruction: $8,043; Support Services: $6,062
Enrollment, Drop-out Rates and Diploma Recipients by Race/Ethnicity

Category	Total	White	Black	Asian	AIAN	Hisp.
Enrollment (%)	100.0	73.1	19.0	4.6	0.3	0.3
Drop-out Rate (%)	1.0	0.6	3.7	0.0	0.0	0.0
H.S. Diplomas (#)	193	144	28	16	1	1

Parma City SD
6726 Ridge Rd • Parma, OH 44129-5703
(440) 842-5300 • http://www.parmacityschools.org/
Grade Span: KG-12; **Agency Type:** 1
Schools: 21
   15 Primary; 3 Middle; 3 High; 0 Other Level
   21 Regular; 0 Special Education; 0 Vocational; 0 Alternative
   0 Magnet; 0 Charter; 13 Title I Eligible; 0 School-wide Title I
Students: 13,427   (50.6% male; 49.3% female)
   Individual Education Program: 2,092 (15.6%);
   English Language Learner: 342 (2.5%); Migrant: n/a
   Eligible for Free Lunch Program: 1,883 (14.3%)
   Eligible for Reduced-Price Lunch Program: 946 (7.2%)
Teachers: 787.7 (16.7 to 1)
Librarians/Media Specialists: 9.0 (1,461.6 to 1)
Guidance Counselors: 20.0 (657.7 to 1)
Current Spending: ($ per student per year):
   Total: $8,964; Instruction: $5,051; Support Services: $3,713
Enrollment, Drop-out Rates and Diploma Recipients by Race/Ethnicity

Category	Total	White	Black	Asian	AIAN	Hisp.
Enrollment (%)	100.0	93.0	1.5	2.3	0.1	1.7
Drop-out Rate (%)	5.0	4.9	9.6	8.3	0.0	4.2
H.S. Diplomas (#)	886	851	8	16	0	7

Rocky River City SD
21600 Center Ridge Rd • Rocky River, OH 44116-3918
(440) 333-6000
Grade Span: PK-12; **Agency Type:** 1
Schools: 4
   2 Primary; 1 Middle; 1 High; 0 Other Level

   4 Regular; 0 Special Education; 0 Vocational; 0 Alternative
   0 Magnet; 0 Charter; 2 Title I Eligible; 0 School-wide Title I
Students: 2,598   (50.3% male; 49.6% female)
   Individual Education Program: 347 (13.4%);
   English Language Learner: 25 (1.0%); Migrant: n/a
   Eligible for Free Lunch Program: 70 (2.7%)
   Eligible for Reduced-Price Lunch Program: 25 (1.0%)
Teachers: 157.5 (16.5 to 1)
Librarians/Media Specialists: 3.0 (866.0 to 1)
Guidance Counselors: 7.0 (371.1 to 1)
Current Spending: ($ per student per year):
   Total: $8,917; Instruction: $5,335; Support Services: $3,417
Enrollment, Drop-out Rates and Diploma Recipients by Race/Ethnicity

Category	Total	White	Black	Asian	AIAN	Hisp.
Enrollment (%)	100.0	94.1	0.7	1.5	0.2	1.6
Drop-out Rate (%)	1.7	1.8	0.0	0.0	0.0	0.0
H.S. Diplomas (#)	145	137	0	4	0	4

Shaker Heights City SD
15600 Parkland Dr • Shaker Heights, OH 44120-2529
(216) 295-4000 • http://www.shaker.org/
Grade Span: PK-12; **Agency Type:** 1
Schools: 9
   6 Primary; 1 Middle; 1 High; 1 Other Level
   9 Regular; 0 Special Education; 0 Vocational; 0 Alternative
   0 Magnet; 0 Charter; 2 Title I Eligible; 0 School-wide Title I
Students: 5,625   (51.8% male; 48.1% female)
   Individual Education Program: 841 (15.0%);
   English Language Learner: 129 (2.3%); Migrant: n/a
   Eligible for Free Lunch Program: 460 (8.2%)
   Eligible for Reduced-Price Lunch Program: 107 (1.9%)
Teachers: 413.1 (13.6 to 1)
Librarians/Media Specialists: 10.0 (562.4 to 1)
Guidance Counselors: 11.0 (511.3 to 1)
Current Spending: ($ per student per year):
   Total: $12,683; Instruction: $6,728; Support Services: $5,805
Enrollment, Drop-out Rates and Diploma Recipients by Race/Ethnicity

Category	Total	White	Black	Asian	AIAN	Hisp.
Enrollment (%)	100.0	39.6	51.4	3.4	0.0	1.2
Drop-out Rate (%)	0.0	0.0	0.0	0.0	n/a	0.0
H.S. Diplomas (#)	362	177	169	7	0	2

Solon City SD
33800 Inwood Dr • Solon, OH 44139-4133
(440) 248-1600 • http://www.solonschools.org/
Grade Span: PK-12; **Agency Type:** 1
Schools: 7
   4 Primary; 1 Middle; 1 High; 1 Other Level
   7 Regular; 0 Special Education; 0 Vocational; 0 Alternative
   0 Magnet; 0 Charter; 5 Title I Eligible; 0 School-wide Title I
Students: 5,180   (51.2% male; 48.7% female)
   Individual Education Program: 612 (11.8%);
   English Language Learner: 94 (1.8%); Migrant: n/a
   Eligible for Free Lunch Program: 91 (1.8%)
   Eligible for Reduced-Price Lunch Program: 74 (1.4%)
Teachers: 333.1 (15.6 to 1)
Librarians/Media Specialists: 7.0 (740.0 to 1)
Guidance Counselors: 13.0 (398.5 to 1)
Current Spending: ($ per student per year):
   Total: $9,917; Instruction: $6,057; Support Services: $3,620
Enrollment, Drop-out Rates and Diploma Recipients by Race/Ethnicity

Category	Total	White	Black	Asian	AIAN	Hisp.
Enrollment (%)	100.0	80.9	8.5	7.7	0.0	0.6
Drop-out Rate (%)	0.7	0.5	2.6	1.0	0.0	0.0
H.S. Diplomas (#)	390	342	27	14	0	1

South Euclid-Lyndhurst City SD
5044 Mayfield Rd • Lyndhurst, OH 44124-2605
(216) 691-2000 •
http://www.sel.k12.oh.us/_vti_bin/owssvr.dll?Using=Default%2ehtm
Grade Span: PK-12; **Agency Type:** 1
Schools: 9
   6 Primary; 2 Middle; 1 High; 0 Other Level
   9 Regular; 0 Special Education; 0 Vocational; 0 Alternative
   0 Magnet; 0 Charter; 5 Title I Eligible; 0 School-wide Title I
Students: 4,583   (52.0% male; 47.9% female)
   Individual Education Program: 703 (15.3%);
   English Language Learner: 12 (0.3%); Migrant: n/a
   Eligible for Free Lunch Program: 659 (14.4%)
   Eligible for Reduced-Price Lunch Program: 251 (5.5%)
Teachers: 303.7 (15.1 to 1)
Librarians/Media Specialists: 6.0 (761.8 to 1)
Guidance Counselors: 8.0 (571.4 to 1)
Current Spending: ($ per student per year):
   Total: $10,439; Instruction: $5,682; Support Services: $4,491

Enrollment, Drop-out Rates and Diploma Recipients by Race/Ethnicity

Category	Total	White	Black	Asian	AIAN	Hisp.
Enrollment (%)	100.0	57.4	36.6	1.5	0.0	0.7
Drop-out Rate (%)	0.6	0.4	1.3	0.0	0.0	0.0
H.S. Diplomas (#)	342	250	76	13	0	2

Strongsville City SD
13200 Pearl Rd • Strongsville, OH 44136-3402
(440) 572-7000 • http://schools.strongnet.org/districthomepage.html
Grade Span: PK-12; **Agency Type:** 1
Schools: 11
  8 Primary; 2 Middle; 1 High; 0 Other Level
  11 Regular; 0 Special Education; 0 Vocational; 0 Alternative
  0 Magnet; 0 Charter; 0 Title I Eligible; 0 School-wide Title I
Students: 7,340 (52.4% male; 47.5% female)
  Individual Education Program: 934 (12.7%);
  English Language Learner: 88 (1.2%); Migrant: 1 (<0.1%)
  Eligible for Free Lunch Program: 325 (4.4%)
  Eligible for Reduced-Price Lunch Program: 151 (2.1%)
Teachers: 409.2 (17.9 to 1)
Librarians/Media Specialists: 6.0 (1,222.8 to 1)
Guidance Counselors: 11.0 (667.0 to 1)
Current Spending: ($ per student per year):
  Total: $8,277; Instruction: $5,310; Support Services: $2,744
Enrollment, Drop-out Rates and Diploma Recipients by Race/Ethnicity

Category	Total	White	Black	Asian	AIAN	Hisp.
Enrollment (%)	100.0	90.4	1.5	4.4	0.0	1.0
Drop-out Rate (%)	1.3	1.3	3.1	0.0	0.0	0.0
H.S. Diplomas (#)	508	482	4	19	0	3

Warrensville Heights City SD
4500 Warrensville Center Rd • Warrensville Heights, OH 44128-4134
(216) 295-7710
Grade Span: PK-12; **Agency Type:** 1
Schools: 6
  2 Primary; 1 Middle; 1 High; 2 Other Level
  6 Regular; 0 Special Education; 0 Vocational; 0 Alternative
  0 Magnet; 0 Charter; 6 Title I Eligible; 5 School-wide Title I
Students: 2,821 (49.1% male; 50.8% female)
  Individual Education Program: 433 (15.3%);
  English Language Learner: 0 (0.0%); Migrant: 2 (0.1%)
  Eligible for Free Lunch Program: 1,570 (55.8%)
  Eligible for Reduced-Price Lunch Program: 325 (11.5%)
Teachers: 192.0 (14.7 to 1)
Librarians/Media Specialists: 4.0 (704.0 to 1)
Guidance Counselors: 7.0 (402.3 to 1)
Current Spending: ($ per student per year):
  Total: $10,821; Instruction: $5,882; Support Services: $4,587
Enrollment, Drop-out Rates and Diploma Recipients by Race/Ethnicity

Category	Total	White	Black	Asian	AIAN	Hisp.
Enrollment (%)	100.0	0.4	98.9	0.1	0.0	0.3
Drop-out Rate (%)	0.1	0.0	0.1	0.0	n/a	n/a
H.S. Diplomas (#)	160	0	159	0	0	0

Westlake City SD
27200 Hilliard Blvd • Westlake, OH 44145-3049
(440) 871-7300 • http://www.westlake.k12.oh.us/
Grade Span: PK-12; **Agency Type:** 1
Schools: 7
  4 Primary; 2 Middle; 1 High; 0 Other Level
  7 Regular; 0 Special Education; 0 Vocational; 0 Alternative
  0 Magnet; 0 Charter; 6 Title I Eligible; 0 School-wide Title I
Students: 3,917 (51.2% male; 48.7% female)
  Individual Education Program: 595 (15.2%);
  English Language Learner: 7 (0.2%); Migrant: n/a
  Eligible for Free Lunch Program: 119 (3.0%)
  Eligible for Reduced-Price Lunch Program: 65 (1.7%)
Teachers: 244.2 (16.0 to 1)
Librarians/Media Specialists: 6.0 (651.5 to 1)
Guidance Counselors: 10.0 (390.9 to 1)
Current Spending: ($ per student per year):
  Total: $9,388; Instruction: $5,622; Support Services: $3,561
Enrollment, Drop-out Rates and Diploma Recipients by Race/Ethnicity

Category	Total	White	Black	Asian	AIAN	Hisp.
Enrollment (%)	100.0	93.6	1.0	3.5	0.1	0.6
Drop-out Rate (%)	1.2	1.3	0.0	0.0	0.0	0.0
H.S. Diplomas (#)	276	258	3	12	0	3

Darke County

Greenville City SD
215 W 4th St • Greenville, OH 45331-1423
(937) 548-3185
Grade Span: PK-12; **Agency Type:** 1
Schools: 7

  4 Primary; 2 Middle; 1 High; 0 Other Level
  7 Regular; 0 Special Education; 0 Vocational; 0 Alternative
  0 Magnet; 0 Charter; 5 Title I Eligible; 1 School-wide Title I
Students: 3,419 (50.9% male; 49.0% female)
  Individual Education Program: 515 (15.1%);
  English Language Learner: 3 (0.1%); Migrant: 1 (<0.1%)
  Eligible for Free Lunch Program: 666 (19.6%)
  Eligible for Reduced-Price Lunch Program: 216 (6.3%)
Teachers: 229.6 (14.8 to 1)
Librarians/Media Specialists: 2.0 (1,701.0 to 1)
Guidance Counselors: 6.0 (567.0 to 1)
Current Spending: ($ per student per year):
  Total: $6,884; Instruction: $4,333; Support Services: $2,363
Enrollment, Drop-out Rates and Diploma Recipients by Race/Ethnicity

Category	Total	White	Black	Asian	AIAN	Hisp.
Enrollment (%)	100.0	96.4	0.5	0.7	0.1	0.6
Drop-out Rate (%)	2.0	2.0	0.0	0.0	50.0	0.0
H.S. Diplomas (#)	267	263	2	2	0	0

Defiance County

Defiance City SD
629 Arabella St • Defiance, OH 43512-2856
(419) 782-0070 • http://www.defiance-city.k12.oh.us/
Grade Span: PK-12; **Agency Type:** 1
Schools: 7
  4 Primary; 2 Middle; 1 High; 0 Other Level
  7 Regular; 0 Special Education; 0 Vocational; 0 Alternative
  0 Magnet; 0 Charter; 6 Title I Eligible; 0 School-wide Title I
Students: 2,541 (51.7% male; 48.2% female)
  Individual Education Program: 441 (17.4%);
  English Language Learner: 7 (0.3%); Migrant: n/a
  Eligible for Free Lunch Program: 452 (17.8%)
  Eligible for Reduced-Price Lunch Program: 141 (5.5%)
Teachers: 165.8 (15.3 to 1)
Librarians/Media Specialists: 2.0 (1,270.5 to 1)
Guidance Counselors: 7.0 (363.0 to 1)
Current Spending: ($ per student per year):
  Total: $6,765; Instruction: $4,167; Support Services: $2,347
Enrollment, Drop-out Rates and Diploma Recipients by Race/Ethnicity

Category	Total	White	Black	Asian	AIAN	Hisp.
Enrollment (%)	100.0	74.9	4.2	0.5	0.1	16.2
Drop-out Rate (%)	4.8	4.0	0.0	0.0	n/a	11.1
H.S. Diplomas (#)	207	180	5	2	0	20

Delaware County

Big Walnut Local SD
70 N Walnut St • Galena, OH 43021-8549
Mailing Address: PO Box 218 • Galena, OH 43021-0218
(740) 965-2706 • http://www.bigwalnut.k12.oh.us/
Grade Span: PK-12; **Agency Type:** 2
Schools: 5
  3 Primary; 1 Middle; 1 High; 0 Other Level
  5 Regular; 0 Special Education; 0 Vocational; 0 Alternative
  0 Magnet; 0 Charter; 3 Title I Eligible; 0 School-wide Title I
Students: 2,633 (51.2% male; 48.7% female)
  Individual Education Program: 359 (13.6%);
  English Language Learner: 4 (0.2%); Migrant: n/a
  Eligible for Free Lunch Program: 206 (7.8%)
  Eligible for Reduced-Price Lunch Program: 85 (3.2%)
Teachers: 169.1 (15.6 to 1)
Librarians/Media Specialists: 1.0 (2,633.0 to 1)
Guidance Counselors: 5.0 (526.6 to 1)
Current Spending: ($ per student per year):
  Total: $7,126; Instruction: $4,234; Support Services: $2,653
Enrollment, Drop-out Rates and Diploma Recipients by Race/Ethnicity

Category	Total	White	Black	Asian	AIAN	Hisp.
Enrollment (%)	100.0	97.7	0.8	0.2	0.0	0.5
Drop-out Rate (%)	2.3	2.3	0.0	0.0	n/a	0.0
H.S. Diplomas (#)	191	189	1	1	0	0

Buckeye Valley Local SD
679 Coover Rd • Delaware, OH 43015-9562
(740) 369-8735 • http://www.buckeyevalley.k12.oh.us/
Grade Span: PK-12; **Agency Type:** 2
Schools: 5
  3 Primary; 1 Middle; 1 High; 0 Other Level
  5 Regular; 0 Special Education; 0 Vocational; 0 Alternative
  0 Magnet; 0 Charter; 1 Title I Eligible; 0 School-wide Title I
Students: 2,237 (53.4% male; 46.5% female)
  Individual Education Program: 315 (14.1%);
  English Language Learner: 0 (0.0%); Migrant: n/a
  Eligible for Free Lunch Program: 149 (6.7%)
  Eligible for Reduced-Price Lunch Program: 47 (2.1%)

Teachers: 130.5 (17.1 to 1)
Librarians/Media Specialists: 2.0 (1,118.5 to 1)
Guidance Counselors: 2.0 (1,118.5 to 1)
Current Spending: ($ per student per year):
  Total: $7,681; Instruction: $4,265; Support Services: $3,125
Enrollment, Drop-out Rates and Diploma Recipients by Race/Ethnicity

Category	Total	White	Black	Asian	AIAN	Hisp.
Enrollment (%)	100.0	97.9	0.9	0.0	0.2	0.4
Drop-out Rate (%)	0.7	0.7	0.0	0.0	0.0	0.0
H.S. Diplomas (#)	157	153	1	0	1	2

Delaware City SD
248 N Washington St • Delaware, OH 43015-1649
(740) 833-1100 • http://www.dcs.k12.oh.us/
Grade Span: PK-12; **Agency Type:** 1
Schools: 9
  5 Primary; 2 Middle; 1 High; 0 Other Level
  8 Regular; 0 Special Education; 0 Vocational; 0 Alternative
  0 Magnet; 0 Charter; 4 Title I Eligible; 1 School-wide Title I
Students: 4,498 (51.6% male; 48.3% female)
  Individual Education Program: 768 (17.1%);
  English Language Learner: 50 (1.1%); Migrant: n/a
  Eligible for Free Lunch Program: 682 (15.2%)
  Eligible for Reduced-Price Lunch Program: 217 (4.8%)
Teachers: 282.2 (15.9 to 1)
Librarians/Media Specialists: 1.0 (4,498.0 to 1)
Guidance Counselors: 10.0 (449.8 to 1)
Current Spending: ($ per student per year):
  Total: $7,881; Instruction: $4,715; Support Services: $2,923
Enrollment, Drop-out Rates and Diploma Recipients by Race/Ethnicity

Category	Total	White	Black	Asian	AIAN	Hisp.
Enrollment (%)	100.0	90.6	4.1	0.9	0.1	1.5
Drop-out Rate (%)	3.9	3.9	3.8	0.0	0.0	9.1
H.S. Diplomas (#)	261	240	14	3	1	2

Olentangy Local SD
814 Shanahan Rd Ste 100 • Lewis Center, OH 43035-9078
(740) 657-4050 • http://www.olentangy.k12.oh.us/
Grade Span: PK-12; **Agency Type:** 2
Schools: 14
  9 Primary; 2 Middle; 2 High; 0 Other Level
  13 Regular; 0 Special Education; 0 Vocational; 0 Alternative
  0 Magnet; 0 Charter; 4 Title I Eligible; 0 School-wide Title I
Students: 8,560 (50.6% male; 49.3% female)
  Individual Education Program: 875 (10.2%);
  English Language Learner: 105 (1.2%); Migrant: n/a
  Eligible for Free Lunch Program: 331 (3.9%)
  Eligible for Reduced-Price Lunch Program: 115 (1.3%)
Teachers: 517.0 (16.6 to 1)
Librarians/Media Specialists: 12.0 (713.3 to 1)
Guidance Counselors: 17.5 (489.1 to 1)
Current Spending: ($ per student per year):
  Total: $7,695; Instruction: $4,503; Support Services: $2,900
Enrollment, Drop-out Rates and Diploma Recipients by Race/Ethnicity

Category	Total	White	Black	Asian	AIAN	Hisp.
Enrollment (%)	100.0	88.8	3.7	3.2	0.0	1.3
Drop-out Rate (%)	0.4	0.5	0.0	0.0	0.0	0.0
H.S. Diplomas (#)	315	301	7	4	0	2

Erie County

Berlin-Milan Local SD
140 Main St S • Milan, OH 44846-9735
(419) 499-4272
Grade Span: PK-12; **Agency Type:** 2
Schools: 4
  2 Primary; 1 Middle; 1 High; 0 Other Level
  4 Regular; 0 Special Education; 0 Vocational; 0 Alternative
  0 Magnet; 0 Charter; 2 Title I Eligible; 0 School-wide Title I
Students: 1,874 (53.8% male; 46.1% female)
  Individual Education Program: 267 (14.2%);
  English Language Learner: 5 (0.3%); Migrant: 13 (0.7%)
  Eligible for Free Lunch Program: 174 (9.3%)
  Eligible for Reduced-Price Lunch Program: 77 (4.1%)
Teachers: 114.6 (16.4 to 1)
Librarians/Media Specialists: 1.0 (1,874.0 to 1)
Guidance Counselors: 2.0 (937.0 to 1)
Current Spending: ($ per student per year):
  Total: $6,997; Instruction: $4,423; Support Services: $2,337
Enrollment, Drop-out Rates and Diploma Recipients by Race/Ethnicity

Category	Total	White	Black	Asian	AIAN	Hisp.
Enrollment (%)	100.0	95.8	0.5	0.5	0.0	1.5
Drop-out Rate (%)	1.3	1.3	0.0	0.0	n/a	0.0
H.S. Diplomas (#)	132	131	1	0	0	0

Huron City Schools
712 Cleveland Rd E • Huron, OH 44839-1871
(419) 433-3911
Grade Span: PK-12; **Agency Type:** 1
Schools: 3
  1 Primary; 1 Middle; 1 High; 0 Other Level
  3 Regular; 0 Special Education; 0 Vocational; 0 Alternative
  0 Magnet; 0 Charter; 2 Title I Eligible; 0 School-wide Title I
Students: 1,664 (51.7% male; 48.2% female)
  Individual Education Program: 214 (12.9%);
  English Language Learner: 3 (0.2%); Migrant: n/a
  Eligible for Free Lunch Program: 182 (10.9%)
  Eligible for Reduced-Price Lunch Program: 47 (2.8%)
Teachers: 95.5 (17.4 to 1)
Librarians/Media Specialists: 1.0 (1,664.0 to 1)
Guidance Counselors: 2.0 (832.0 to 1)
Current Spending: ($ per student per year):
  Total: $7,527; Instruction: $4,469; Support Services: $2,740
Enrollment, Drop-out Rates and Diploma Recipients by Race/Ethnicity

Category	Total	White	Black	Asian	AIAN	Hisp.
Enrollment (%)	100.0	96.9	0.5	1.0	0.0	0.5
Drop-out Rate (%)	0.7	0.8	0.0	0.0	0.0	0.0
H.S. Diplomas (#)	136	135	0	0	0	1

Perkins Local SD
1210 E Bogart Rd • Sandusky, OH 44870-6411
(419) 625-0484 • http://www.perkins.k12.oh.us/
Grade Span: PK-12; **Agency Type:** 2
Schools: 4
  2 Primary; 1 Middle; 1 High; 0 Other Level
  4 Regular; 0 Special Education; 0 Vocational; 0 Alternative
  0 Magnet; 0 Charter; 3 Title I Eligible; 0 School-wide Title I
Students: 2,267 (49.5% male; 50.4% female)
  Individual Education Program: 375 (16.5%);
  English Language Learner: 2 (0.1%); Migrant: n/a
  Eligible for Free Lunch Program: 223 (9.8%)
  Eligible for Reduced-Price Lunch Program: 93 (4.1%)
Teachers: 139.0 (16.3 to 1)
Librarians/Media Specialists: 2.0 (1,133.5 to 1)
Guidance Counselors: 7.0 (323.9 to 1)
Current Spending: ($ per student per year):
  Total: $8,288; Instruction: $4,852; Support Services: $3,146
Enrollment, Drop-out Rates and Diploma Recipients by Race/Ethnicity

Category	Total	White	Black	Asian	AIAN	Hisp.
Enrollment (%)	100.0	89.7	5.7	1.1	0.1	0.6
Drop-out Rate (%)	0.5	0.6	0.0	0.0	n/a	0.0
H.S. Diplomas (#)	150	136	8	3	0	2

Sandusky City SD
407 Decatur St • Sandusky, OH 44870-2442
(419) 626-6940
Grade Span: PK-12; **Agency Type:** 1
Schools: 12
  8 Primary; 1 Middle; 1 High; 2 Other Level
  11 Regular; 1 Special Education; 0 Vocational; 0 Alternative
  0 Magnet; 0 Charter; 12 Title I Eligible; 8 School-wide Title I
Students: 4,227 (50.7% male; 49.2% female)
  Individual Education Program: 845 (20.0%);
  English Language Learner: 1 (<0.1%); Migrant: n/a
  Eligible for Free Lunch Program: 2,312 (54.7%)
  Eligible for Reduced-Price Lunch Program: 429 (10.1%)
Teachers: 297.6 (14.2 to 1)
Librarians/Media Specialists: 3.0 (1,409.0 to 1)
Guidance Counselors: 10.0 (422.7 to 1)
Current Spending: ($ per student per year):
  Total: $8,859; Instruction: $5,507; Support Services: $2,967
Enrollment, Drop-out Rates and Diploma Recipients by Race/Ethnicity

Category	Total	White	Black	Asian	AIAN	Hisp.
Enrollment (%)	100.0	52.6	33.2	0.1	0.0	3.0
Drop-out Rate (%)	3.7	3.0	4.7	0.0	n/a	6.9
H.S. Diplomas (#)	231	149	76	1	0	4

Vermilion Local SD
1230 Beechview Dr • Vermilion, OH 44089-1604
(440) 967-5210 • http://vermilionschools.org/
Grade Span: PK-12; **Agency Type:** 2
Schools: 4
  2 Primary; 1 Middle; 1 High; 0 Other Level
  4 Regular; 0 Special Education; 0 Vocational; 0 Alternative
  0 Magnet; 0 Charter; 3 Title I Eligible; 0 School-wide Title I
Students: 2,525 (51.0% male; 48.9% female)
  Individual Education Program: 375 (14.9%);
  English Language Learner: 0 (0.0%); Migrant: 1 (<0.1%)
  Eligible for Free Lunch Program: 439 (17.6%)
  Eligible for Reduced-Price Lunch Program: 167 (6.7%)

Teachers: 145.7 (17.1 to 1)
Librarians/Media Specialists: 2.0 (1,246.0 to 1)
Guidance Counselors: 5.0 (498.4 to 1)
Current Spending: ($ per student per year):
   Total: $7,298; Instruction: $4,193; Support Services: $2,892
Enrollment, Drop-out Rates and Diploma Recipients by Race/Ethnicity

Category	Total	White	Black	Asian	AIAN	Hisp.
Enrollment (%)	100.0	96.5	0.2	0.2	0.3	1.8
Drop-out Rate (%)	2.0	2.0	0.0	0.0	n/a	0.0
H.S. Diplomas (#)	171	170	0	0	0	1

Fairfield County

Amanda-Clearcreek Local SD
328 E Main St • Amanda, OH 43102-9330
(740) 969-7250
Grade Span: PK-12; **Agency Type:** 2
Schools: 4
   2 Primary; 1 Middle; 1 High; 0 Other Level
   4 Regular; 0 Special Education; 0 Vocational; 0 Alternative
   0 Magnet; 0 Charter; 2 Title I Eligible; 0 School-wide Title I
Students: 1,653 (52.6% male; 47.3% female)
   Individual Education Program: 213 (12.9%);
   English Language Learner: 0 (0.0%); Migrant: n/a
   Eligible for Free Lunch Program: 228 (13.8%)
   Eligible for Reduced-Price Lunch Program: 82 (5.0%)
Teachers: 91.0 (18.2 to 1)
Librarians/Media Specialists: 1.0 (1,653.0 to 1)
Guidance Counselors: 2.0 (826.5 to 1)
Current Spending: ($ per student per year):
   Total: $6,266; Instruction: $4,028; Support Services: $2,009
Enrollment, Drop-out Rates and Diploma Recipients by Race/Ethnicity

Category	Total	White	Black	Asian	AIAN	Hisp.
Enrollment (%)	100.0	98.4	0.8	0.0	0.1	0.4
Drop-out Rate (%)	1.5	1.5	0.0	0.0	n/a	0.0
H.S. Diplomas (#)	87	87	0	0	0	0

Fairfield Union Local SD
7698 Main St • West Rushville, OH 43163-0067
Mailing Address: PO Box 67 • West Rushville, OH 43163-0067
(740) 536-7384 • http://www.fairfield-union.k12.oh.us/
Grade Span: PK-12; **Agency Type:** 2
Schools: 5
   2 Primary; 2 Middle; 1 High; 0 Other Level
   5 Regular; 0 Special Education; 0 Vocational; 0 Alternative
   0 Magnet; 0 Charter; 3 Title I Eligible; 0 School-wide Title I
Students: 1,958 (51.9% male; 48.0% female)
   Individual Education Program: 157 (8.0%);
   English Language Learner: 0 (0.0%); Migrant: n/a
   Eligible for Free Lunch Program: 266 (13.6%)
   Eligible for Reduced-Price Lunch Program: 78 (4.0%)
Teachers: 103.5 (18.9 to 1)
Librarians/Media Specialists: 1.0 (1,958.0 to 1)
Guidance Counselors: 2.6 (753.1 to 1)
Current Spending: ($ per student per year):
   Total: $7,054; Instruction: $4,358; Support Services: $2,458
Enrollment, Drop-out Rates and Diploma Recipients by Race/Ethnicity

Category	Total	White	Black	Asian	AIAN	Hisp.
Enrollment (%)	100.0	98.5	0.3	0.2	0.2	0.1
Drop-out Rate (%)	0.7	0.7	0.0	n/a	n/a	0.0
H.S. Diplomas (#)	142	142	0	0	0	0

Lancaster City SD
111 S Broad St • Lancaster, OH 43130-4398
(740) 687-7300 • http://198.234.204.51/
Grade Span: PK-12; **Agency Type:** 1
Schools: 12
   9 Primary; 2 Middle; 1 High; 0 Other Level
   12 Regular; 0 Special Education; 0 Vocational; 0 Alternative
   0 Magnet; 0 Charter; 9 Title I Eligible; 7 School-wide Title I
Students: 6,104 (52.5% male; 47.4% female)
   Individual Education Program: 775 (12.7%);
   English Language Learner: 2 (<0.1%); Migrant: n/a
   Eligible for Free Lunch Program: 1,744 (28.6%)
   Eligible for Reduced-Price Lunch Program: 496 (8.1%)
Teachers: 346.3 (17.6 to 1)
Librarians/Media Specialists: 5.0 (1,220.8 to 1)
Guidance Counselors: 8.0 (763.0 to 1)
Current Spending: ($ per student per year):
   Total: $7,744; Instruction: $4,510; Support Services: $2,962
Enrollment, Drop-out Rates and Diploma Recipients by Race/Ethnicity

Category	Total	White	Black	Asian	AIAN	Hisp.
Enrollment (%)	100.0	97.3	0.9	0.4	0.1	0.3
Drop-out Rate (%)	4.4	4.4	6.7	0.0	0.0	0.0
H.S. Diplomas (#)	358	349	2	2	1	3

Pickerington Local SD
777 Long Rd • Pickerington, OH 43147-1061
(614) 833-2110 • http://www.pickerington.k12.oh.us/
Grade Span: PK-12; **Agency Type:** 2
Schools: 11
   5 Primary; 4 Middle; 2 High; 0 Other Level
   11 Regular; 0 Special Education; 0 Vocational; 0 Alternative
   0 Magnet; 0 Charter; 4 Title I Eligible; 0 School-wide Title I
Students: 8,917 (52.3% male; 47.6% female)
   Individual Education Program: 837 (9.4%);
   English Language Learner: 54 (0.6%); Migrant: n/a
   Eligible for Free Lunch Program: 480 (5.4%)
   Eligible for Reduced-Price Lunch Program: 218 (2.4%)
Teachers: 499.8 (17.8 to 1)
Librarians/Media Specialists: 7.5 (1,188.9 to 1)
Guidance Counselors: 20.0 (445.9 to 1)
Current Spending: ($ per student per year):
   Total: $7,130; Instruction: $4,376; Support Services: $2,547
Enrollment, Drop-out Rates and Diploma Recipients by Race/Ethnicity

Category	Total	White	Black	Asian	AIAN	Hisp.
Enrollment (%)	100.0	80.3	11.9	2.4	0.1	1.5
Drop-out Rate (%)	0.9	0.8	1.9	2.1	0.0	0.0
H.S. Diplomas (#)	494	449	26	12	0	5

Fayette County

Miami Trace Local SD
1400 US Hwy 22 NW • Washington Court Hou, OH 43160-8604
(740) 335-3010
Grade Span: PK-12; **Agency Type:** 2
Schools: 10
   6 Primary; 3 Middle; 1 High; 0 Other Level
   10 Regular; 0 Special Education; 0 Vocational; 0 Alternative
   0 Magnet; 0 Charter; 8 Title I Eligible; 0 School-wide Title I
Students: 2,719 (52.3% male; 47.6% female)
   Individual Education Program: 359 (13.2%);
   English Language Learner: 0 (0.0%); Migrant: n/a
   Eligible for Free Lunch Program: 469 (17.2%)
   Eligible for Reduced-Price Lunch Program: 157 (5.8%)
Teachers: 160.4 (17.0 to 1)
Librarians/Media Specialists: 1.5 (1,812.7 to 1)
Guidance Counselors: 6.0 (453.2 to 1)
Current Spending: ($ per student per year):
   Total: $7,456; Instruction: $3,931; Support Services: $3,185
Enrollment, Drop-out Rates and Diploma Recipients by Race/Ethnicity

Category	Total	White	Black	Asian	AIAN	Hisp.
Enrollment (%)	100.0	96.5	1.1	0.3	0.5	0.4
Drop-out Rate (%)	3.3	3.4	0.0	0.0	0.0	0.0
H.S. Diplomas (#)	170	168	0	0	0	2

Washington Court House City SD
306 Highland Ave • Washington Court Hou, OH 43160-1819
(740) 335-6620
Grade Span: PK-12; **Agency Type:** 1
Schools: 7
   5 Primary; 1 Middle; 1 High; 0 Other Level
   7 Regular; 0 Special Education; 0 Vocational; 0 Alternative
   0 Magnet; 0 Charter; 6 Title I Eligible; 0 School-wide Title I
Students: 2,315 (52.3% male; 47.6% female)
   Individual Education Program: 322 (13.9%);
   English Language Learner: 3 (0.1%); Migrant: n/a
   Eligible for Free Lunch Program: 582 (25.1%)
   Eligible for Reduced-Price Lunch Program: 135 (5.8%)
Teachers: 154.3 (15.0 to 1)
Librarians/Media Specialists: 2.0 (1,157.5 to 1)
Guidance Counselors: 8.0 (289.4 to 1)
Current Spending: ($ per student per year):
   Total: $6,399; Instruction: $3,986; Support Services: $2,133
Enrollment, Drop-out Rates and Diploma Recipients by Race/Ethnicity

Category	Total	White	Black	Asian	AIAN	Hisp.
Enrollment (%)	100.0	92.8	3.0	1.2	0.0	0.8
Drop-out Rate (%)	3.5	3.7	0.0	0.0	n/a	0.0
H.S. Diplomas (#)	144	139	4	1	0	0

Franklin County

Bexley City SD
348 S Cassingham Rd • Bexley, OH 43209-1897
(614) 231-7611
Grade Span: PK-12; **Agency Type:** 1
Schools: 5
   3 Primary; 1 Middle; 1 High; 0 Other Level
   5 Regular; 0 Special Education; 0 Vocational; 0 Alternative
   0 Magnet; 0 Charter; 3 Title I Eligible; 0 School-wide Title I
Students: 2,211 (52.7% male; 47.2% female)

Individual Education Program: 245 (11.1%);
English Language Learner: 13 (0.6%); Migrant: 1 (<0.1%)
Eligible for Free Lunch Program: 100 (4.5%)
Eligible for Reduced-Price Lunch Program: 49 (2.2%)
Teachers: 159.3 (13.9 to 1)
Librarians/Media Specialists: 5.0 (442.2 to 1)
Guidance Counselors: 8.6 (257.1 to 1)
Current Spending: ($ per student per year):
Total: $10,281; Instruction: $6,697; Support Services: $3,418
Enrollment, Drop-out Rates and Diploma Recipients by Race/Ethnicity

Category	Total	White	Black	Asian	AIAN	Hisp.
Enrollment (%)	100.0	90.1	5.7	1.4	0.0	0.7
Drop-out Rate (%)	0.5	0.4	2.8	0.0	n/a	0.0
H.S. Diplomas (#)	177	164	9	3	0	1

Canal Winchester Local SD
290 Washington St • Canal Winchester, OH 43110-1226
(614) 837-4533
Grade Span: PK-12; **Agency Type:** 2
Schools: 5
2 Primary; 2 Middle; 1 High; 0 Other Level
5 Regular; 0 Special Education; 0 Vocational; 0 Alternative
0 Magnet; 0 Charter; 3 Title I Eligible; 0 School-wide Title I
Students: 2,622 (50.7% male; 49.2% female)
Individual Education Program: 321 (12.2%);
English Language Learner: 13 (0.5%); Migrant: n/a
Eligible for Free Lunch Program: 290 (11.1%)
Eligible for Reduced-Price Lunch Program: 87 (3.3%)
Teachers: 161.5 (16.2 to 1)
Librarians/Media Specialists: 5.0 (524.4 to 1)
Guidance Counselors: 6.0 (437.0 to 1)
Current Spending: ($ per student per year):
Total: $7,996; Instruction: $4,414; Support Services: $3,325
Enrollment, Drop-out Rates and Diploma Recipients by Race/Ethnicity

Category	Total	White	Black	Asian	AIAN	Hisp.
Enrollment (%)	100.0	81.1	13.0	1.0	0.4	0.6
Drop-out Rate (%)	2.6	2.2	3.0	0.0	0.0	0.0
H.S. Diplomas (#)	135	123	10	1	0	1

Columbus Public Schools
270 E State St • Columbus, OH 43215-4312
(614) 365-5000 • http://www.columbus.k12.oh.us/
Grade Span: PK-12; **Agency Type:** 1
Schools: 153
96 Primary; 27 Middle; 25 High; 3 Other Level
136 Regular; 11 Special Education; 4 Vocational; 0 Alternative
0 Magnet; 0 Charter; 133 Title I Eligible; 116 School-wide Title I
Students: 63,098 (50.9% male; 49.0% female)
Individual Education Program: 9,218 (14.6%);
English Language Learner: 4,339 (6.9%); Migrant: 137 (0.2%)
Eligible for Free Lunch Program: 31,663 (50.2%)
Eligible for Reduced-Price Lunch Program: 4,214 (6.7%)
Teachers: 3,838.4 (16.4 to 1)
Librarians/Media Specialists: 70.8 (891.2 to 1)
Guidance Counselors: 126.8 (497.6 to 1)
Current Spending: ($ per student per year):
Total: $10,188; Instruction: $5,472; Support Services: $4,364
Enrollment, Drop-out Rates and Diploma Recipients by Race/Ethnicity

Category	Total	White	Black	Asian	AIAN	Hisp.
Enrollment (%)	100.0	32.0	62.1	2.2	0.2	3.4
Drop-out Rate (%)	8.7	10.6	7.8	6.8	8.8	9.7
H.S. Diplomas (#)	2,600	918	1,546	87	6	43

Dublin City SD
7030 Coffman Rd • Dublin, OH 43017-1068
(614) 764-5913 • http://the.dublinschools.net/
Grade Span: KG-12; **Agency Type:** 1
Schools: 18
11 Primary; 4 Middle; 2 High; 0 Other Level
17 Regular; 0 Special Education; 0 Vocational; 0 Alternative
0 Magnet; 0 Charter; 8 Title I Eligible; 0 School-wide Title I
Students: 12,376 (51.5% male; 48.4% female)
Individual Education Program: 1,221 (9.9%);
English Language Learner: 632 (5.1%); Migrant: n/a
Eligible for Free Lunch Program: 370 (3.0%)
Eligible for Reduced-Price Lunch Program: 125 (1.0%)
Teachers: 792.9 (15.5 to 1)
Librarians/Media Specialists: 18.0 (682.2 to 1)
Guidance Counselors: 31.0 (396.1 to 1)
Current Spending: ($ per student per year):
Total: $8,941; Instruction: $5,427; Support Services: $3,227

Enrollment, Drop-out Rates and Diploma Recipients by Race/Ethnicity

Category	Total	White	Black	Asian	AIAN	Hisp.
Enrollment (%)	100.0	80.8	2.8	11.2	0.1	2.1
Drop-out Rate (%)	1.0	0.9	1.2	1.6	0.0	1.8
H.S. Diplomas (#)	767	654	19	79	0	11

Electronic Classrm of Tomorrow
3700 S High St Ste 95 • Columbus, OH 43207-4083
(614) 492-8884
Grade Span: KG-12; **Agency Type:** 7
Schools: 1
0 Primary; 0 Middle; 0 High; 1 Other Level
1 Regular; 0 Special Education; 0 Vocational; 0 Alternative
0 Magnet; 1 Charter; 1 Title I Eligible; 0 School-wide Title I
Students: 5,213 (45.7% male; 54.2% female)
Individual Education Program: 496 (9.5%);
English Language Learner: 27 (0.5%); Migrant: n/a
Eligible for Free Lunch Program: n/a
Eligible for Reduced-Price Lunch Program: n/a
Teachers: 142.3 (36.6 to 1)
Librarians/Media Specialists: 0.0 (n/a to 1)
Guidance Counselors: 1.0 (5,213.0 to 1)
Current Spending: ($ per student per year):
Total: $4,819; Instruction: $2,550; Support Services: $2,269
Enrollment, Drop-out Rates and Diploma Recipients by Race/Ethnicity

Category	Total	White	Black	Asian	AIAN	Hisp.
Enrollment (%)	100.0	78.0	14.8	0.3	0.6	1.5
Drop-out Rate (%)	0.0	0.0	0.0	0.0	0.0	0.0
H.S. Diplomas (#)	31	23	6	0	0	0

Gahanna-Jefferson City SD
160 S Hamilton Rd • Gahanna, OH 43230-2919
(614) 471-7065 • http://www.gahannaschools.org/
Grade Span: PK-12; **Agency Type:** 1
Schools: 11
7 Primary; 3 Middle; 1 High; 0 Other Level
11 Regular; 0 Special Education; 0 Vocational; 0 Alternative
0 Magnet; 0 Charter; 6 Title I Eligible; 0 School-wide Title I
Students: 6,806 (52.3% male; 47.6% female)
Individual Education Program: 1,006 (14.8%);
English Language Learner: 71 (1.0%); Migrant: 1 (<0.1%)
Eligible for Free Lunch Program: 459 (6.7%)
Eligible for Reduced-Price Lunch Program: 158 (2.3%)
Teachers: 508.6 (13.4 to 1)
Librarians/Media Specialists: 12.0 (567.2 to 1)
Guidance Counselors: 17.8 (382.4 to 1)
Current Spending: ($ per student per year):
Total: $8,032; Instruction: $5,083; Support Services: $2,713
Enrollment, Drop-out Rates and Diploma Recipients by Race/Ethnicity

Category	Total	White	Black	Asian	AIAN	Hisp.
Enrollment (%)	100.0	80.4	12.4	2.7	0.2	1.4
Drop-out Rate (%)	2.7	2.5	3.3	0.0	0.0	3.6
H.S. Diplomas (#)	424	366	44	9	1	2

Groveport Madison Local SD
5055 S Hamilton Rd • Groveport, OH 43125-9336
(614) 836-5371 • http://www.swcs.k12.oh.us/
Grade Span: PK-12; **Agency Type:** 2
Schools: 10
6 Primary; 2 Middle; 1 High; 1 Other Level
10 Regular; 0 Special Education; 0 Vocational; 0 Alternative
0 Magnet; 0 Charter; 6 Title I Eligible; 0 School-wide Title I
Students: 6,440 (51.0% male; 48.9% female)
Individual Education Program: 1,023 (15.9%);
English Language Learner: 81 (1.3%); Migrant: n/a
Eligible for Free Lunch Program: 1,547 (24.0%)
Eligible for Reduced-Price Lunch Program: 475 (7.4%)
Teachers: 364.1 (17.7 to 1)
Librarians/Media Specialists: 10.0 (644.0 to 1)
Guidance Counselors: 11.0 (585.5 to 1)
Current Spending: ($ per student per year):
Total: $8,373; Instruction: $4,762; Support Services: $3,358
Enrollment, Drop-out Rates and Diploma Recipients by Race/Ethnicity

Category	Total	White	Black	Asian	AIAN	Hisp.
Enrollment (%)	100.0	70.0	23.5	1.5	0.2	2.4
Drop-out Rate (%)	4.3	4.4	4.9	0.0	0.0	0.0
H.S. Diplomas (#)	314	254	44	11	0	2

Hamilton Local SD
1055 Rathmell Rd • Columbus, OH 43207-4742
(614) 491-8044 • http://www.hamilton-local.k12.oh.us/
Grade Span: PK-12; **Agency Type:** 2
Schools: 5
2 Primary; 2 Middle; 1 High; 0 Other Level
5 Regular; 0 Special Education; 0 Vocational

0 Magnet; 0 Charter; 3 Title I Eligible; 1 School-wide Title I

Students: 2,989 (50.5% male; 49.4% female)
  Individual Education Program: 354 (11.8%);
  English Language Learner: 2 (0.1%); Migrant: n/a
  Eligible for Free Lunch Program: 603 (20.2%)
  Eligible for Reduced-Price Lunch Program: 208 (7.0%)

Teachers: 183.5 (16.3 to 1)
Librarians/Media Specialists: 2.0 (1,494.5 to 1)
Guidance Counselors: 5.0 (597.8 to 1)
Current Spending: ($ per student per year):
  Total: $7,169; Instruction: $3,917; Support Services: $2,980

Enrollment, Drop-out Rates and Diploma Recipients by Race/Ethnicity

Category	Total	White	Black	Asian	AIAN	Hisp.
Enrollment (%)	100.0	84.8	11.3	1.0	0.3	1.6
Drop-out Rate (%)	3.9	4.0	4.2	0.0	0.0	0.0
H.S. Diplomas (#)	133	113	15	2	0	3

Hilliard City SD
5323 Cemetery Rd • Hilliard, OH 43026-1546
(614) 771-4273 • http://www.hilliard.k12.oh.us/
Grade Span: PK-12; **Agency Type:** 1
Schools: 20
  13 Primary; 5 Middle; 2 High; 0 Other Level
  20 Regular; 0 Special Education; 0 Vocational; 0 Alternative
  0 Magnet; 0 Charter; 11 Title I Eligible; 0 School-wide Title I

Students: 14,219 (51.6% male; 48.3% female)
  Individual Education Program: 1,631 (11.5%);
  English Language Learner: 485 (3.4%); Migrant: n/a
  Eligible for Free Lunch Program: 1,011 (7.1%)
  Eligible for Reduced-Price Lunch Program: 311 (2.2%)

Teachers: 921.8 (15.4 to 1)
Librarians/Media Specialists: 21.3 (667.3 to 1)
Guidance Counselors: 31.6 (449.8 to 1)
Current Spending: ($ per student per year):
  Total: $8,127; Instruction: $4,955; Support Services: $2,952

Enrollment, Drop-out Rates and Diploma Recipients by Race/Ethnicity

Category	Total	White	Black	Asian	AIAN	Hisp.
Enrollment (%)	100.0	85.4	4.8	4.2	0.1	2.8
Drop-out Rate (%)	1.7	1.6	3.3	1.5	0.0	6.3
H.S. Diplomas (#)	785	717	19	36	1	4

Plain Local SD
99 W Main St Fl 2nd • New Albany, OH 43054-9270
(614) 855-2040
Grade Span: PK-12; **Agency Type:** 2
Schools: 4
  2 Primary; 1 Middle; 0 High; 1 Other Level
  4 Regular; 0 Special Education; 0 Vocational; 0 Alternative
  0 Magnet; 0 Charter; 2 Title I Eligible; 0 School-wide Title I

Students: 2,877 (50.6% male; 49.3% female)
  Individual Education Program: 244 (8.5%);
  English Language Learner: 24 (0.8%); Migrant: n/a
  Eligible for Free Lunch Program: 72 (2.5%)
  Eligible for Reduced-Price Lunch Program: 54 (1.9%)

Teachers: 179.6 (16.0 to 1)
Librarians/Media Specialists: 5.0 (575.4 to 1)
Guidance Counselors: 5.0 (575.4 to 1)
Current Spending: ($ per student per year):
  Total: $8,737; Instruction: $4,771; Support Services: $3,532

Enrollment, Drop-out Rates and Diploma Recipients by Race/Ethnicity

Category	Total	White	Black	Asian	AIAN	Hisp.
Enrollment (%)	100.0	84.9	4.8	6.0	0.1	1.5
Drop-out Rate (%)	1.6	1.3	0.0	5.3	n/a	25.0
H.S. Diplomas (#)	108	98	1	5	0	3

Reynoldsburg City SD
7244 E Main St • Reynoldsburg, OH 43068-2014
(614) 501-1020 • http://www.reynoldsburgcityschools.com/
Grade Span: PK-12; **Agency Type:** 1
Schools: 8
  5 Primary; 2 Middle; 1 High; 0 Other Level
  8 Regular; 0 Special Education; 0 Vocational; 0 Alternative
  0 Magnet; 0 Charter; 6 Title I Eligible; 0 School-wide Title I

Students: 6,607 (50.9% male; 49.0% female)
  Individual Education Program: 888 (13.4%);
  English Language Learner: 129 (2.0%); Migrant: 44 (0.7%)
  Eligible for Free Lunch Program: 633 (9.6%)
  Eligible for Reduced-Price Lunch Program: 153 (2.3%)

Teachers: 336.9 (19.6 to 1)
Librarians/Media Specialists: 2.0 (3,303.5 to 1)
Guidance Counselors: 7.0 (943.9 to 1)
Current Spending: ($ per student per year):
  Total: $6,261; Instruction: $3,816; Support Services: $2,248

Category	Total	White	Black	Asian	AIAN	Hisp.
Enrollment (%)	100.0	69.0	22.3	2.0	0.1	1.7
Drop-out Rate (%)	1.6	1.2	2.9	0.0	0.0	12.0
H.S. Diplomas (#)	458	372	62	10	1	6

South-Western City SD
3805 Marlane Dr • Grove City, OH 43123-9224
(614) 801-3000 • http://www.swcs.k12.oh.us/
Grade Span: PK-12; **Agency Type:** 1
Schools: 36
  17 Primary; 5 Middle; 7 High; 6 Other Level
  32 Regular; 2 Special Education; 1 Vocational; 0 Alternative
  0 Magnet; 0 Charter; 16 Title I Eligible; 8 School-wide Title I

Students: 21,230 (51.3% male; 48.6% female)
  Individual Education Program: 2,912 (13.7%);
  English Language Learner: 1,108 (5.2%); Migrant: 348 (1.7%)
  Eligible for Free Lunch Program: 6,073 (28.9%)
  Eligible for Reduced-Price Lunch Program: 1,863 (8.9%)

Teachers: 1,326.8 (15.9 to 1)
Librarians/Media Specialists: 4.0 (5,259.5 to 1)
Guidance Counselors: 24.0 (876.6 to 1)
Current Spending: ($ per student per year):
  Total: $7,883; Instruction: $4,372; Support Services: $3,217

Enrollment, Drop-out Rates and Diploma Recipients by Race/Ethnicity

Category	Total	White	Black	Asian	AIAN	Hisp.
Enrollment (%)	100.0	79.9	11.8	1.7	0.3	5.3
Drop-out Rate (%)	5.9	5.5	8.6	9.7	33.3	8.6
H.S. Diplomas (#)	1,003	921	57	18	0	7

Upper Arlington City SD
1950 N Mallway Dr • Upper Arlington, OH 43221-4326
(614) 487-5000 • http://www.uaschools.org/
Grade Span: KG-12; **Agency Type:** 1
Schools: 8
  5 Primary; 2 Middle; 1 High; 0 Other Level
  8 Regular; 0 Special Education; 0 Vocational; 0 Alternative
  0 Magnet; 0 Charter; 3 Title I Eligible; 0 School-wide Title I

Students: 5,597 (51.0% male; 48.9% female)
  Individual Education Program: 540 (9.6%);
  English Language Learner: 86 (1.5%); Migrant: n/a
  Eligible for Free Lunch Program: 44 (0.8%)
  Eligible for Reduced-Price Lunch Program: 30 (0.5%)

Teachers: 400.4 (13.9 to 1)
Librarians/Media Specialists: 10.0 (557.9 to 1)
Guidance Counselors: 16.1 (346.5 to 1)
Current Spending: ($ per student per year):
  Total: $10,402; Instruction: $6,310; Support Services: $3,909

Enrollment, Drop-out Rates and Diploma Recipients by Race/Ethnicity

Category	Total	White	Black	Asian	AIAN	Hisp.
Enrollment (%)	100.0	92.1	0.7	5.8	0.1	0.7
Drop-out Rate (%)	0.3	0.3	0.0	0.0	n/a	0.0
H.S. Diplomas (#)	421	397	2	18	0	3

Westerville City SD
336 S Otterbein Ave • Westerville, OH 43081-2334
(614) 797-5700 • http://www.westerville.k12.oh.us/
Grade Span: PK-12; **Agency Type:** 1
Schools: 23
  16 Primary; 4 Middle; 2 High; 1 Other Level
  23 Regular; 0 Special Education; 0 Vocational; 0 Alternative
  0 Magnet; 0 Charter; 10 Title I Eligible; 0 School-wide Title I

Students: 14,142 (51.4% male; 48.5% female)
  Individual Education Program: 1,606 (11.4%);
  English Language Learner: 445 (3.1%); Migrant: n/a
  Eligible for Free Lunch Program: 1,201 (8.5%)
  Eligible for Reduced-Price Lunch Program: 323 (2.3%)

Teachers: 784.0 (18.0 to 1)
Librarians/Media Specialists: 16.0 (883.5 to 1)
Guidance Counselors: 27.0 (523.6 to 1)
Current Spending: ($ per student per year):
  Total: $7,701; Instruction: $4,624; Support Services: $2,854

Enrollment, Drop-out Rates and Diploma Recipients by Race/Ethnicity

Category	Total	White	Black	Asian	AIAN	Hisp.
Enrollment (%)	100.0	76.1	15.1	2.3	0.2	1.8
Drop-out Rate (%)	2.2	1.7	4.6	1.7	0.0	4.9
H.S. Diplomas (#)	970	802	112	28	0	9

Whitehall City SD
625 S Yearling Rd • Whitehall, OH 43213-2861
(614) 417-5000
Grade Span: KG-12; **Agency Type:** 1
Schools: 5
  3 Primary; 1 Middle; 1 High; 0 Other Level
  5 Regular; 0 Special Education; 0 Vocational; 0 Alternative

0 Magnet; 0 Charter; 5 Title I Eligible; 3 School-wide Title I
Students: 3,064 (51.0% male; 48.9% female)
Individual Education Program: 484 (15.8%);
English Language Learner: 234 (7.6%); Migrant: n/a
Eligible for Free Lunch Program: 1,218 (40.8%)
Eligible for Reduced-Price Lunch Program: 294 (9.9%)
Teachers: 191.0 (15.6 to 1)
Librarians/Media Specialists: 5.0 (596.4 to 1)
Guidance Counselors: 3.0 (994.0 to 1)
Current Spending: ($ per student per year):
Total: $7,811; Instruction: $4,701; Support Services: $2,821
Enrollment, Drop-out Rates and Diploma Recipients by Race/Ethnicity

Category	Total	White	Black	Asian	AIAN	Hisp.
Enrollment (%)	100.0	61.5	25.3	2.1	0.2	5.8
Drop-out Rate (%)	5.9	5.1	7.2	0.0	0.0	15.8
H.S. Diplomas (#)	192	150	36	3	0	1

Worthington City SD

200 E Wilson Bridge Rd • Worthington, OH 43085-2332
(614) 883-3000 • http://www.worthington.k12.oh.us/
Grade Span: PK-12; **Agency Type:** 1
Schools: 18
12 Primary; 4 Middle; 2 High; 0 Other Level
18 Regular; 0 Special Education; 0 Vocational; 0 Alternative
0 Magnet; 0 Charter; 9 Title I Eligible; 0 School-wide Title I
Students: 9,754 (52.1% male; 47.8% female)
Individual Education Program: 1,006 (10.3%);
English Language Learner: 276 (2.8%); Migrant: n/a
Eligible for Free Lunch Program: 489 (5.0%)
Eligible for Reduced-Price Lunch Program: 250 (2.6%)
Teachers: 657.3 (14.8 to 1)
Librarians/Media Specialists: 18.0 (540.4 to 1)
Guidance Counselors: 20.9 (465.4 to 1)
Current Spending: ($ per student per year):
Total: $10,146; Instruction: $6,065; Support Services: $3,807
Enrollment, Drop-out Rates and Diploma Recipients by Race/Ethnicity

Category	Total	White	Black	Asian	AIAN	Hisp.
Enrollment (%)	100.0	83.2	5.8	7.0	0.2	2.4
Drop-out Rate (%)	0.9	1.0	0.0	0.0	0.0	4.8
H.S. Diplomas (#)	803	699	30	66	0	8

Fulton County

Pike-Delta-York Local SD

504 Fernwood St • Delta, OH 43515-1204
(419) 822-3391
Grade Span: PK-12; **Agency Type:** 2
Schools: 4
1 Primary; 2 Middle; 1 High; 0 Other Level
4 Regular; 0 Special Education; 0 Vocational; 0 Alternative
0 Magnet; 0 Charter; 2 Title I Eligible; 0 School-wide Title I
Students: 1,574 (50.9% male; 49.0% female)
Individual Education Program: 233 (14.8%);
English Language Learner: 7 (0.4%); Migrant: 1 (0.1%)
Eligible for Free Lunch Program: 229 (14.5%)
Eligible for Reduced-Price Lunch Program: 125 (7.9%)
Teachers: 87.2 (18.1 to 1)
Librarians/Media Specialists: 1.0 (1,574.0 to 1)
Guidance Counselors: 3.0 (524.7 to 1)
Current Spending: ($ per student per year):
Total: $7,817; Instruction: $4,833; Support Services: $2,714
Enrollment, Drop-out Rates and Diploma Recipients by Race/Ethnicity

Category	Total	White	Black	Asian	AIAN	Hisp.
Enrollment (%)	100.0	93.8	0.3	0.3	0.0	4.2
Drop-out Rate (%)	1.9	2.0	n/a	0.0	n/a	0.0
H.S. Diplomas (#)	116	111	0	1	0	4

Swanton Local SD

108 N Main St • Swanton, OH 43558-1032
(419) 826-7085 • http://www.swanton.k12.oh.us/
Grade Span: PK-12; **Agency Type:** 2
Schools: 4
2 Primary; 1 Middle; 1 High; 0 Other Level
4 Regular; 0 Special Education; 0 Vocational; 0 Alternative
0 Magnet; 0 Charter; 3 Title I Eligible; 0 School-wide Title I
Students: 1,585 (51.7% male; 48.2% female)
Individual Education Program: 218 (13.8%);
English Language Learner: 0 (0.0%); Migrant: n/a
Eligible for Free Lunch Program: 194 (12.2%)
Eligible for Reduced-Price Lunch Program: 82 (5.2%)
Teachers: 89.6 (17.7 to 1)
Librarians/Media Specialists: 2.0 (792.5 to 1)
Guidance Counselors: 3.0 (528.3 to 1)
Current Spending: ($ per student per year):
Total: $7,245; Instruction: $4,237; Support Services: $2,753

Category	Total	White	Black	Asian	AIAN	Hisp.
Enrollment (%)	100.0	93.2	1.1	0.0	0.7	2.1
Drop-out Rate (%)	1.5	1.5	0.0	0.0	0.0	0.0
H.S. Diplomas (#)	141	137	0	0	1	1

Wauseon Ex Vill SD

120 E Chestnut St • Wauseon, OH 43567-1443
(419) 335-6616
Grade Span: PK-12; **Agency Type:** 1
Schools: 4
2 Primary; 1 Middle; 1 High; 0 Other Level
4 Regular; 0 Special Education; 0 Vocational; 0 Alternative
0 Magnet; 0 Charter; 3 Title I Eligible; 0 School-wide Title I
Students: 2,133 (50.4% male; 49.5% female)
Individual Education Program: 233 (10.9%);
English Language Learner: 62 (2.9%); Migrant: 46 (2.2%)
Eligible for Free Lunch Program: 324 (15.2%)
Eligible for Reduced-Price Lunch Program: 143 (6.7%)
Teachers: 116.8 (18.3 to 1)
Librarians/Media Specialists: 1.0 (2,133.0 to 1)
Guidance Counselors: 4.0 (533.3 to 1)
Current Spending: ($ per student per year):
Total: $6,017; Instruction: $3,685; Support Services: $2,034
Enrollment, Drop-out Rates and Diploma Recipients by Race/Ethnicity

Category	Total	White	Black	Asian	AIAN	Hisp.
Enrollment (%)	100.0	86.1	0.4	1.1	0.1	11.2
Drop-out Rate (%)	1.6	1.4	0.0	0.0	n/a	3.4
H.S. Diplomas (#)	145	132	1	1	0	11

Gallia County

Gallia County Local SD

230 Shawnee Ln • Gallipolis, OH 45631-8594
(740) 446-7917
Grade Span: PK-12; **Agency Type:** 2
Schools: 8
5 Primary; 1 Middle; 2 High; 0 Other Level
8 Regular; 0 Special Education; 0 Vocational; 0 Alternative
0 Magnet; 0 Charter; 6 Title I Eligible; 6 School-wide Title I
Students: 2,544 (51.3% male; 48.6% female)
Individual Education Program: 473 (18.6%);
English Language Learner: 2 (0.1%); Migrant: n/a
Eligible for Free Lunch Program: 946 (37.2%)
Eligible for Reduced-Price Lunch Program: 160 (6.3%)
Teachers: 169.5 (15.0 to 1)
Librarians/Media Specialists: 2.0 (1,272.0 to 1)
Guidance Counselors: 4.0 (636.0 to 1)
Current Spending: ($ per student per year):
Total: $7,123; Instruction: $4,195; Support Services: $2,610
Enrollment, Drop-out Rates and Diploma Recipients by Race/Ethnicity

Category	Total	White	Black	Asian	AIAN	Hisp.
Enrollment (%)	100.0	96.2	2.8	0.4	0.2	0.2
Drop-out Rate (%)	3.7	3.6	8.0	0.0	0.0	0.0
H.S. Diplomas (#)	165	160	3	0	0	1

Gallipolis City SD

61 State St • Gallipolis, OH 45631-1131
(740) 446-3211 • http://gallianet.scoca-k12.org/
Grade Span: PK-12; **Agency Type:** 1
Schools: 5
3 Primary; 0 Middle; 1 High; 1 Other Level
4 Regular; 1 Special Education; 0 Vocational; 0 Alternative
0 Magnet; 0 Charter; 2 Title I Eligible; 2 School-wide Title I
Students: 2,366 (51.2% male; 48.7% female)
Individual Education Program: 513 (21.7%);
English Language Learner: 1 (<0.1%); Migrant: n/a
Eligible for Free Lunch Program: 663 (28.0%)
Eligible for Reduced-Price Lunch Program: 88 (3.7%)
Teachers: 151.4 (15.6 to 1)
Librarians/Media Specialists: 1.0 (2,366.0 to 1)
Guidance Counselors: 2.0 (1,183.0 to 1)
Current Spending: ($ per student per year):
Total: $6,843; Instruction: $4,304; Support Services: $2,324
Enrollment, Drop-out Rates and Diploma Recipients by Race/Ethnicity

Category	Total	White	Black	Asian	AIAN	Hisp.
Enrollment (%)	100.0	93.1	5.1	0.5	0.0	0.5
Drop-out Rate (%)	4.3	4.4	5.9	0.0	0.0	0.0
H.S. Diplomas (#)	149	140	6	1	0	2

Geauga County

Chardon Local SD
428 N St • Chardon, OH 44024-1036
(440) 285-4052
Grade Span: PK-12; **Agency Type:** 2
Schools: 6
   4 Primary; 1 Middle; 1 High; 0 Other Level
   6 Regular; 0 Special Education; 0 Vocational; 0 Alternative
   0 Magnet; 0 Charter; 4 Title I Eligible; 0 School-wide Title I
Students: 3,272 (51.1% male; 48.8% female)
   Individual Education Program: 378 (11.6%);
   English Language Learner: 3 (0.1%); Migrant: n/a
   Eligible for Free Lunch Program: 223 (6.9%)
   Eligible for Reduced-Price Lunch Program: 109 (3.4%)
Teachers: 193.7 (16.8 to 1)
Librarians/Media Specialists: 4.0 (812.0 to 1)
Guidance Counselors: 6.0 (541.3 to 1)
Current Spending: ($ per student per year):
   Total: $7,413; Instruction: $4,176; Support Services: $2,995
Enrollment, Drop-out Rates and Diploma Recipients by Race/Ethnicity

Category	Total	White	Black	Asian	AIAN	Hisp.
Enrollment (%)	100.0	96.9	0.7	1.0	0.1	0.7
Drop-out Rate (%)	1.2	1.1	0.0	0.0	n/a	25.0
H.S. Diplomas (#)	232	229	1	2	0	0

Kenston Local SD
17419 Snyder Rd • Chagrin Falls, OH 44023-2730
(440) 543-9677
Grade Span: KG-12; **Agency Type:** 2
Schools: 5
   3 Primary; 1 Middle; 1 High; 0 Other Level
   5 Regular; 0 Special Education; 0 Vocational; 0 Alternative
   0 Magnet; 0 Charter; 3 Title I Eligible; 0 School-wide Title I
Students: 3,134 (51.4% male; 48.5% female)
   Individual Education Program: 314 (10.0%);
   English Language Learner: 5 (0.2%); Migrant: 1 (<0.1%)
   Eligible for Free Lunch Program: 133 (4.3%)
   Eligible for Reduced-Price Lunch Program: 62 (2.0%)
Teachers: 205.3 (15.1 to 1)
Librarians/Media Specialists: 1.0 (3,093.0 to 1)
Guidance Counselors: 6.8 (454.9 to 1)
Current Spending: ($ per student per year):
   Total: $8,246; Instruction: $4,774; Support Services: $3,256
Enrollment, Drop-out Rates and Diploma Recipients by Race/Ethnicity

Category	Total	White	Black	Asian	AIAN	Hisp.
Enrollment (%)	100.0	92.3	4.9	0.6	0.0	0.4
Drop-out Rate (%)	0.4	0.5	0.0	0.0	n/a	0.0
H.S. Diplomas (#)	214	191	17	1	0	3

West Geauga Local SD
8615 Cedar Rd • Chesterland, OH 44026-3519
(440) 729-5900
Grade Span: KG-12; **Agency Type:** 2
Schools: 4
   2 Primary; 1 Middle; 1 High; 0 Other Level
   4 Regular; 0 Special Education; 0 Vocational; 0 Alternative
   0 Magnet; 0 Charter; 3 Title I Eligible; 0 School-wide Title I
Students: 2,550 (52.1% male; 47.8% female)
   Individual Education Program: 358 (14.0%);
   English Language Learner: 0 (0.0%); Migrant: n/a
   Eligible for Free Lunch Program: 56 (2.2%)
   Eligible for Reduced-Price Lunch Program: 43 (1.7%)
Teachers: 153.5 (16.5 to 1)
Librarians/Media Specialists: 2.0 (1,268.5 to 1)
Guidance Counselors: 8.6 (295.0 to 1)
Current Spending: ($ per student per year):
   Total: $7,395; Instruction: $4,032; Support Services: $3,214
Enrollment, Drop-out Rates and Diploma Recipients by Race/Ethnicity

Category	Total	White	Black	Asian	AIAN	Hisp.
Enrollment (%)	100.0	98.1	0.4	0.6	0.0	0.4
Drop-out Rate (%)	0.4	0.4	0.0	0.0	n/a	0.0
H.S. Diplomas (#)	195	188	5	1	0	0

Greene County

Beavercreek City SD
3040 Kemp Rd • Beavercreek, OH 45431-2644
(937) 426-1522 • http://www.beavercreek.k12.oh.us/
Grade Span: PK-12; **Agency Type:** 1
Schools: 8
   4 Primary; 2 Middle; 1 High; 1 Other Level
   8 Regular; 0 Special Education; 0 Vocational; 0 Alternative
   0 Magnet; 0 Charter; 4 Title I Eligible; 0 School-wide Title I
Students: 7,184 (51.1% male; 48.8% female)

   Individual Education Program: 909 (12.7%);
   English Language Learner: 27 (0.4%); Migrant: n/a
   Eligible for Free Lunch Program: 267 (3.7%)
   Eligible for Reduced-Price Lunch Program: 162 (2.3%)
Teachers: 369.8 (19.3 to 1)
Librarians/Media Specialists: 5.0 (1,425.8 to 1)
Guidance Counselors: 18.0 (396.1 to 1)
Current Spending: ($ per student per year):
   Total: $7,189; Instruction: $4,251; Support Services: $2,718
Enrollment, Drop-out Rates and Diploma Recipients by Race/Ethnicity

Category	Total	White	Black	Asian	AIAN	Hisp.
Enrollment (%)	100.0	89.0	1.7	5.3	0.0	1.5
Drop-out Rate (%)	2.3	2.2	3.4	3.0	0.0	0.0
H.S. Diplomas (#)	495	463	7	14	1	3

Fairborn City Schools
306 E Whittier Ave • Fairborn, OH 45324-5313
(937) 878-3961 • http://www.fairborn.k12.oh.us/
Grade Span: PK-12; **Agency Type:** 1
Schools: 7
   5 Primary; 1 Middle; 1 High; 0 Other Level
   7 Regular; 0 Special Education; 0 Vocational; 0 Alternative
   0 Magnet; 0 Charter; 5 Title I Eligible; 1 School-wide Title I
Students: 5,427 (52.7% male; 47.2% female)
   Individual Education Program: 684 (12.6%);
   English Language Learner: 34 (0.6%); Migrant: 7 (0.1%)
   Eligible for Free Lunch Program: 1,280 (23.6%)
   Eligible for Reduced-Price Lunch Program: 350 (6.4%)
Teachers: 310.8 (17.5 to 1)
Librarians/Media Specialists: 2.0 (2,713.5 to 1)
Guidance Counselors: 8.0 (678.4 to 1)
Current Spending: ($ per student per year):
   Total: $7,665; Instruction: $4,671; Support Services: $2,773
Enrollment, Drop-out Rates and Diploma Recipients by Race/Ethnicity

Category	Total	White	Black	Asian	AIAN	Hisp.
Enrollment (%)	100.0	84.1	7.6	2.2	0.3	1.8
Drop-out Rate (%)	5.5	5.3	7.0	2.4	40.0	10.7
H.S. Diplomas (#)	349	311	19	6	1	5

Greeneview Local SD
4 S Charleston Rd • Jamestown, OH 45335-1557
(937) 675-2728
Grade Span: PK-12; **Agency Type:** 2
Schools: 5
   3 Primary; 1 Middle; 1 High; 0 Other Level
   5 Regular; 0 Special Education; 0 Vocational; 0 Alternative
   0 Magnet; 0 Charter; 3 Title I Eligible; 0 School-wide Title I
Students: 1,645 (51.5% male; 48.4% female)
   Individual Education Program: 194 (11.8%);
   English Language Learner: 3 (0.2%); Migrant: n/a
   Eligible for Free Lunch Program: 171 (10.4%)
   Eligible for Reduced-Price Lunch Program: 48 (2.9%)
Teachers: 90.6 (18.2 to 1)
Librarians/Media Specialists: 1.0 (1,645.0 to 1)
Guidance Counselors: 4.0 (411.3 to 1)
Current Spending: ($ per student per year):
   Total: $6,487; Instruction: $3,443; Support Services: $2,809
Enrollment, Drop-out Rates and Diploma Recipients by Race/Ethnicity

Category	Total	White	Black	Asian	AIAN	Hisp.
Enrollment (%)	100.0	96.5	1.0	0.6	0.0	0.6
Drop-out Rate (%)	2.2	2.0	14.3	0.0	0.0	0.0
H.S. Diplomas (#)	102	95	3	1	1	0

Sugarcreek Local SD
60 E S St • Bellbrook, OH 45305-1944
(937) 848-6251
Grade Span: PK-12; **Agency Type:** 2
Schools: 5
   2 Primary; 2 Middle; 1 High; 0 Other Level
   5 Regular; 0 Special Education; 0 Vocational; 0 Alternative
   0 Magnet; 0 Charter; 4 Title I Eligible; 0 School-wide Title I
Students: 2,761 (51.5% male; 48.4% female)
   Individual Education Program: 279 (10.1%);
   English Language Learner: 15 (0.5%); Migrant: n/a
   Eligible for Free Lunch Program: 130 (4.7%)
   Eligible for Reduced-Price Lunch Program: 34 (1.2%)
Teachers: 138.4 (19.9 to 1)
Librarians/Media Specialists: 0.0 (n/a to 1)
Guidance Counselors: 5.6 (493.0 to 1)
Current Spending: ($ per student per year):
   Total: $6,714; Instruction: $3,684; Support Services: $2,852

Enrollment, Drop-out Rates and Diploma Recipients by Race/Ethnicity

Category	Total	White	Black	Asian	AIAN	Hisp.
Enrollment (%)	100.0	93.5	2.2	1.6	0.1	0.7
Drop-out Rate (%)	1.0	0.9	100.0	0.0	0.0	0.0
H.S. Diplomas (#)	184	183	0	0	0	0

Xenia Community City SD

578 E Market St • Xenia, OH 45385-3145
(937) 376-2961 • http://www.xenia.k12.oh.us/
Grade Span: PK-12; **Agency Type:** 1
Schools: 10
   7 Primary; 2 Middle; 1 High; 0 Other Level
   10 Regular; 0 Special Education; 0 Vocational; 0 Alternative
   0 Magnet; 0 Charter; 7 Title I Eligible; 3 School-wide Title I
Students: 5,202   (51.6% male; 48.3% female)
   Individual Education Program: 761 (14.6%);
   English Language Learner: 9 (0.2%); Migrant: n/a
   Eligible for Free Lunch Program: 1,407 (27.0%)
   Eligible for Reduced-Price Lunch Program: 277 (5.3%)
Teachers: 329.8 (15.8 to 1)
Librarians/Media Specialists: 4.0 (1,300.5 to 1)
Guidance Counselors: 12.4 (419.5 to 1)
Current Spending: ($ per student per year):
   Total: $7,838; Instruction: $4,318; Support Services: $3,216

Enrollment, Drop-out Rates and Diploma Recipients by Race/Ethnicity

Category	Total	White	Black	Asian	AIAN	Hisp.
Enrollment (%)	100.0	79.5	15.3	0.6	0.1	0.8
Drop-out Rate (%)	4.9	4.5	6.9	7.7	0.0	7.1
H.S. Diplomas (#)	314	262	39	3	0	6

Guernsey County

Cambridge City SD

6111 Fairdale Dr • Cambridge, OH 43725-8865
(740) 439-5021 • http://www.cambridge.k12.oh.us/
Grade Span: PK-12; **Agency Type:** 1
Schools: 5
   3 Primary; 1 Middle; 1 High; 0 Other Level
   5 Regular; 0 Special Education; 0 Vocational; 0 Alternative
   0 Magnet; 0 Charter; 5 Title I Eligible; 3 School-wide Title I
Students: 2,739   (52.4% male; 47.5% female)
   Individual Education Program: 451 (16.5%);
   English Language Learner: 0 (0.0%); Migrant: n/a
   Eligible for Free Lunch Program: 992 (36.2%)
   Eligible for Reduced-Price Lunch Program: 200 (7.3%)
Teachers: 179.9 (15.2 to 1)
Librarians/Media Specialists: 2.0 (1,369.5 to 1)
Guidance Counselors: 6.0 (456.5 to 1)
Current Spending: ($ per student per year):
   Total: $7,346; Instruction: $4,525; Support Services: $2,521

Enrollment, Drop-out Rates and Diploma Recipients by Race/Ethnicity

Category	Total	White	Black	Asian	AIAN	Hisp.
Enrollment (%)	100.0	89.9	5.8	0.4	0.2	0.8
Drop-out Rate (%)	3.7	3.5	6.7	0.0	0.0	33.3
H.S. Diplomas (#)	154	138	13	2	0	1

Rolling Hills Local SD

60851 Southgate Rd • Cambridge, OH 43725-9414
Mailing Address: PO Box 38 • Byesville, OH 43723-0038
(740) 432-5370 • http://www.omeresa.net/Schools/Meadowbrook/
Grade Span: PK-12; **Agency Type:** 2
Schools: 5
   3 Primary; 1 Middle; 1 High; 0 Other Level
   5 Regular; 0 Special Education; 0 Vocational; 0 Alternative
   0 Magnet; 0 Charter; 4 Title I Eligible; 3 School-wide Title I
Students: 2,226   (49.3% male; 50.6% female)
   Individual Education Program: 311 (14.0%);
   English Language Learner: 5 (0.2%); Migrant: n/a
   Eligible for Free Lunch Program: 700 (31.4%)
   Eligible for Reduced-Price Lunch Program: 193 (8.7%)
Teachers: 112.0 (19.9 to 1)
Librarians/Media Specialists: 1.0 (2,226.0 to 1)
Guidance Counselors: 4.0 (556.5 to 1)
Current Spending: ($ per student per year):
   Total: $6,684; Instruction: $3,722; Support Services: $2,626

Enrollment, Drop-out Rates and Diploma Recipients by Race/Ethnicity

Category	Total	White	Black	Asian	AIAN	Hisp.
Enrollment (%)	100.0	97.5	0.4	0.2	0.0	0.3
Drop-out Rate (%)	4.2	4.2	0.0	0.0	n/a	0.0
H.S. Diplomas (#)	124	124	0	0	0	0

Hamilton County

Cincinnati City SD

2651 Burnet Ave • Cincinnati, OH 45219-2551
Mailing Address: PO Box 5381 • Cincinnati, OH 45201-5381
(513) 363-0000 • http://www.cpsboe.k12.oh.us/
Grade Span: PK-12; **Agency Type:** 1
Schools: 86
   56 Primary; 2 Middle; 13 High; 13 Other Level
   83 Regular; 0 Special Education; 1 Vocational; 0 Alternative
   0 Magnet; 0 Charter; 72 Title I Eligible; 59 School-wide Title I
Students: 40,374   (49.1% male; 50.8% female)
   Individual Education Program: 7,642 (18.9%);
   English Language Learner: 359 (0.9%); Migrant: 3 (<0.1%)
   Eligible for Free Lunch Program: 22,929 (57.3%)
   Eligible for Reduced-Price Lunch Program: 2,826 (7.1%)
Teachers: 3,132.5 (12.8 to 1)
Librarians/Media Specialists: 47.4 (844.9 to 1)
Guidance Counselors: 20.8 (1,925.3 to 1)
Current Spending: ($ per student per year):
   Total: $10,300; Instruction: $6,443; Support Services: $3,527

Enrollment, Drop-out Rates and Diploma Recipients by Race/Ethnicity

Category	Total	White	Black	Asian	AIAN	Hisp.
Enrollment (%)	100.0	24.6	70.3	0.9	0.1	0.9
Drop-out Rate (%)	8.2	6.3	8.8	7.8	0.0	11.8
H.S. Diplomas (#)	1,305	454	814	13	2	4

Finneytown Local SD

8916 Fontainebleau Ter • Cincinnati, OH 45231-4806
(513) 728-3700 • http://www.finneytown.org/
Grade Span: PK-12; **Agency Type:** 2
Schools: 5
   2 Primary; 2 Middle; 1 High; 0 Other Level
   5 Regular; 0 Special Education; 0 Vocational; 0 Alternative
   0 Magnet; 0 Charter; 4 Title I Eligible; 0 School-wide Title I
Students: 1,787   (53.2% male; 46.7% female)
   Individual Education Program: 210 (11.8%);
   English Language Learner: 12 (0.7%); Migrant: n/a
   Eligible for Free Lunch Program: 233 (13.0%)
   Eligible for Reduced-Price Lunch Program: 59 (3.3%)
Teachers: 117.1 (15.3 to 1)
Librarians/Media Specialists: 1.0 (1,787.0 to 1)
Guidance Counselors: 6.4 (279.2 to 1)
Current Spending: ($ per student per year):
   Total: $8,579; Instruction: $4,947; Support Services: $3,396

Enrollment, Drop-out Rates and Diploma Recipients by Race/Ethnicity

Category	Total	White	Black	Asian	AIAN	Hisp.
Enrollment (%)	100.0	67.2	28.7	1.2	0.0	0.1
Drop-out Rate (%)	2.5	2.4	3.2	0.0	n/a	0.0
H.S. Diplomas (#)	141	114	19	5	0	1

Forest Hills Local SD

7550 Forest Rd • Cincinnati, OH 45255-4307
(513) 231-3600 • http://www.foresthills.edu/
Grade Span: PK-12; **Agency Type:** 2
Schools: 9
   6 Primary; 1 Middle; 2 High; 0 Other Level
   9 Regular; 0 Special Education; 0 Vocational; 0 Alternative
   0 Magnet; 0 Charter; 5 Title I Eligible; 0 School-wide Title I
Students: 7,621   (50.7% male; 49.2% female)
   Individual Education Program: 802 (10.5%);
   English Language Learner: 26 (0.3%); Migrant: n/a
   Eligible for Free Lunch Program: 206 (2.7%)
   Eligible for Reduced-Price Lunch Program: 89 (1.2%)
Teachers: 434.7 (17.5 to 1)
Librarians/Media Specialists: 7.0 (1,088.7 to 1)
Guidance Counselors: 15.9 (479.3 to 1)
Current Spending: ($ per student per year):
   Total: $7,355; Instruction: $4,637; Support Services: $2,521

Enrollment, Drop-out Rates and Diploma Recipients by Race/Ethnicity

Category	Total	White	Black	Asian	AIAN	Hisp.
Enrollment (%)	100.0	94.7	1.1	1.8	0.1	0.9
Drop-out Rate (%)	1.5	1.5	0.0	0.0	n/a	0.0
H.S. Diplomas (#)	585	558	12	11	0	3

Indian Hill Ex Vill SD

6855 Drake Rd • Cincinnati, OH 45243-2737
(513) 272-4500 • http://www.ih.k12.oh.us/
Grade Span: PK-12; **Agency Type:** 1
Schools: 4
   2 Primary; 1 Middle; 1 High; 0 Other Level
   4 Regular; 0 Special Education; 0 Vocational; 0 Alternative
   0 Magnet; 0 Charter; 3 Title I Eligible; 0 School-wide Title I
Students: 2,260   (53.0% male; 46.9% female)
   Individual Education Program: 189 (8.4%);

English Language Learner: 16 (0.7%); Migrant: n/a
Eligible for Free Lunch Program: 17 (0.8%)
Eligible for Reduced-Price Lunch Program: 4 (0.2%)
Teachers: 153.8 (14.7 to 1)
Librarians/Media Specialists: 4.0 (565.0 to 1)
Guidance Counselors: 9.8 (230.6 to 1)
Current Spending: ($ per student per year):
Total: $10,168; Instruction: $5,580; Support Services: $4,217
Enrollment, Drop-out Rates and Diploma Recipients by Race/Ethnicity

Category	Total	White	Black	Asian	AIAN	Hisp.
Enrollment (%)	100.0	87.2	3.0	6.9	0.0	1.0
Drop-out Rate (%)	0.6	0.5	0.0	0.0	n/a	0.0
H.S. Diplomas (#)	151	127	1	18	0	1

Loveland City SD

757 S Lebanon Rd • Loveland, OH 45140-9308
(513) 683-5600 • http://www.lovelandschools.onlinecommunity.com/
Grade Span: PK-12; **Agency Type:** 1
Schools: 6
3 Primary; 2 Middle; 1 High; 0 Other Level
6 Regular; 0 Special Education; 0 Vocational; 0 Alternative
0 Magnet; 0 Charter; 4 Title I Eligible; 0 School-wide Title I
Students: 4,278   (50.5% male; 49.4% female)
Individual Education Program: 377 (8.8%);
English Language Learner: 37 (0.9%); Migrant: n/a
Eligible for Free Lunch Program: 223 (5.2%)
Eligible for Reduced-Price Lunch Program: 87 (2.0%)
Teachers: 231.4 (18.5 to 1)
Librarians/Media Specialists: 3.0 (1,426.0 to 1)
Guidance Counselors: 6.5 (658.2 to 1)
Current Spending: ($ per student per year):
Total: $7,171; Instruction: $4,202; Support Services: $2,738
Enrollment, Drop-out Rates and Diploma Recipients by Race/Ethnicity

Category	Total	White	Black	Asian	AIAN	Hisp.
Enrollment (%)	100.0	94.7	1.4	1.9	0.0	0.7
Drop-out Rate (%)	1.7	1.8	0.0	0.0	n/a	0.0
H.S. Diplomas (#)	285	272	4	4	0	5

Madeira City SD

7465 Loannes Dr • Cincinnati, OH 45243-1851
(513) 985-6070
Grade Span: PK-12; **Agency Type:** 1
Schools: 3
1 Primary; 1 Middle; 1 High; 0 Other Level
3 Regular; 0 Special Education; 0 Vocational; 0 Alternative
0 Magnet; 0 Charter; 2 Title I Eligible; 0 School-wide Title I
Students: 1,508   (52.4% male; 47.5% female)
Individual Education Program: 176 (11.7%);
English Language Learner: 27 (1.8%); Migrant: n/a
Eligible for Free Lunch Program: 36 (2.4%)
Eligible for Reduced-Price Lunch Program: 9 (0.6%)
Teachers: 100.6 (15.0 to 1)
Librarians/Media Specialists: 3.0 (502.7 to 1)
Guidance Counselors: 3.0 (502.7 to 1)
Current Spending: ($ per student per year):
Total: $8,437; Instruction: $5,262; Support Services: $2,958
Enrollment, Drop-out Rates and Diploma Recipients by Race/Ethnicity

Category	Total	White	Black	Asian	AIAN	Hisp.
Enrollment (%)	100.0	92.8	1.3	2.6	0.1	1.5
Drop-out Rate (%)	0.4	0.4	0.0	0.0	0.0	0.0
H.S. Diplomas (#)	109	103	3	1	0	1

Mariemont City SD

6743 Chestnut St • Cincinnati, OH 45227-3600
(513) 272-7500 • http://www.mariemontschools.org/
Grade Span: PK-12; **Agency Type:** 1
Schools: 5
3 Primary; 1 Middle; 1 High; 0 Other Level
5 Regular; 0 Special Education; 0 Vocational; 0 Alternative
0 Magnet; 0 Charter; 2 Title I Eligible; 0 School-wide Title I
Students: 1,708   (52.0% male; 47.9% female)
Individual Education Program: 160 (9.4%);
English Language Learner: 0 (0.0%); Migrant: n/a
Eligible for Free Lunch Program: 73 (4.3%)
Eligible for Reduced-Price Lunch Program: 33 (1.9%)
Teachers: 122.8 (13.9 to 1)
Librarians/Media Specialists: 3.0 (569.3 to 1)
Guidance Counselors: 4.0 (427.0 to 1)
Current Spending: ($ per student per year):
Total: $8,598; Instruction: $5,186; Support Services: $3,239
Enrollment, Drop-out Rates and Diploma Recipients by Race/Ethnicity

Category	Total	White	Black	Asian	AIAN	Hisp.
Enrollment (%)	100.0	94.1	2.6	1.1	0.1	1.0
Drop-out Rate (%)	3.5	3.3	10.0	0.0	n/a	50.0
H.S. Diplomas (#)	113	113	0	0	0	0

Mt Healthy City SD

7615 Harrison Ave • Cincinnati, OH 45231-3107
(513) 729-0077 • http://www.hccanet.org/mhs
Grade Span: KG-12; **Agency Type:** 1
Schools: 9
6 Primary; 2 Middle; 1 High; 0 Other Level
9 Regular; 0 Special Education; 0 Vocational; 0 Alternative
0 Magnet; 0 Charter; 9 Title I Eligible; 6 School-wide Title I
Students: 3,788   (52.8% male; 47.1% female)
Individual Education Program: 655 (17.3%);
English Language Learner: 33 (0.9%); Migrant: n/a
Eligible for Free Lunch Program: 1,583 (41.8%)
Eligible for Reduced-Price Lunch Program: 377 (10.0%)
Teachers: 260.3 (14.6 to 1)
Librarians/Media Specialists: 3.0 (1,262.7 to 1)
Guidance Counselors: 9.0 (420.9 to 1)
Current Spending: ($ per student per year):
Total: $8,299; Instruction: $4,887; Support Services: $3,128
Enrollment, Drop-out Rates and Diploma Recipients by Race/Ethnicity

Category	Total	White	Black	Asian	AIAN	Hisp.
Enrollment (%)	100.0	31.0	63.7	0.7	0.0	1.2
Drop-out Rate (%)	4.4	5.4	3.8	0.0	n/a	0.0
H.S. Diplomas (#)	198	90	104	4	0	0

North College Hill City SD

1498 W Galbraith Rd • Cincinnati, OH 45231-5588
(513) 728-4770 • http://www.nchcityschools.org/
Grade Span: PK-12; **Agency Type:** 1
Schools: 4
3 Primary; 0 Middle; 1 High; 0 Other Level
4 Regular; 0 Special Education; 0 Vocational; 0 Alternative
0 Magnet; 0 Charter; 3 Title I Eligible; 3 School-wide Title I
Students: 1,538   (53.3% male; 46.6% female)
Individual Education Program: 256 (16.6%);
English Language Learner: 0 (0.0%); Migrant: n/a
Eligible for Free Lunch Program: 550 (35.8%)
Eligible for Reduced-Price Lunch Program: 178 (11.6%)
Teachers: 87.0 (17.7 to 1)
Librarians/Media Specialists: 1.0 (1,538.0 to 1)
Guidance Counselors: 3.0 (512.7 to 1)
Current Spending: ($ per student per year):
Total: $7,049; Instruction: $4,174; Support Services: $2,621
Enrollment, Drop-out Rates and Diploma Recipients by Race/Ethnicity

Category	Total	White	Black	Asian	AIAN	Hisp.
Enrollment (%)	100.0	35.5	59.4	0.4	0.1	0.7
Drop-out Rate (%)	2.9	3.2	2.6	0.0	n/a	0.0
H.S. Diplomas (#)	92	49	41	0	0	1

Northwest Local SD

3240 Banning Rd • Cincinnati, OH 45239-5207
(513) 923-1000 • http://www.nwlsd.org/
Grade Span: PK-12; **Agency Type:** 2
Schools: 14
9 Primary; 3 Middle; 2 High; 0 Other Level
14 Regular; 0 Special Education; 0 Vocational; 0 Alternative
0 Magnet; 0 Charter; 9 Title I Eligible; 3 School-wide Title I
Students: 10,657   (52.5% male; 47.4% female)
Individual Education Program: 1,314 (12.3%);
English Language Learner: 84 (0.8%); Migrant: n/a
Eligible for Free Lunch Program: 1,869 (17.5%)
Eligible for Reduced-Price Lunch Program: 781 (7.3%)
Teachers: 615.6 (17.3 to 1)
Librarians/Media Specialists: 5.0 (2,131.4 to 1)
Guidance Counselors: 19.0 (560.9 to 1)
Current Spending: ($ per student per year):
Total: $7,326; Instruction: $4,285; Support Services: $2,774
Enrollment, Drop-out Rates and Diploma Recipients by Race/Ethnicity

Category	Total	White	Black	Asian	AIAN	Hisp.
Enrollment (%)	100.0	76.9	17.4	1.1	0.2	0.9
Drop-out Rate (%)	5.2	4.9	5.9	6.7	0.0	13.6
H.S. Diplomas (#)	656	571	62	6	1	3

Norwood City SD

2132 Williams Ave • Norwood, OH 45212-3806
(513) 924-2500 • http://www.norwoodschools.org/
Grade Span: PK-12; **Agency Type:** 1
Schools: 7
5 Primary; 1 Middle; 1 High; 0 Other Level
7 Regular; 0 Special Education; 0 Vocational; 0 Alternative
0 Magnet; 0 Charter; 6 Title I Eligible; 5 School-wide Title I
Students: 2,659   (52.1% male; 47.8% female)
Individual Education Program: 331 (12.4%);
English Language Learner: 40 (1.5%); Migrant: n/a
Eligible for Free Lunch Program: 1,043 (39.2%)
Eligible for Reduced-Price Lunch Program: 221 (8.3%)

Teachers: 178.5 (14.9 to 1)
Librarians/Media Specialists: 1.0 (2,659.0 to 1)
Guidance Counselors: 4.0 (664.8 to 1)
Current Spending: ($ per student per year):
Total: $8,501; Instruction: $5,177; Support Services: $2,919
Enrollment, Drop-out Rates and Diploma Recipients by Race/Ethnicity

Category	Total	White	Black	Asian	AIAN	Hisp.
Enrollment (%)	100.0	87.9	4.0	1.0	0.5	3.6
Drop-out Rate (%)	8.1	8.0	20.0	0.0	25.0	0.0
H.S. Diplomas (#)	137	131	0	1	0	3

Oak Hills Local SD

6325 Rapid Run Rd • Cincinnati, OH 45233-4555
(513) 574-3200 • http://www.oakhills.k12.oh.us/
Grade Span: PK-12; **Agency Type:** 2
Schools: 9
5 Primary; 3 Middle; 1 High; 0 Other Level
9 Regular; 0 Special Education; 0 Vocational; 0 Alternative
0 Magnet; 0 Charter; 4 Title I Eligible; 0 School-wide Title I
Students: 8,132 (52.5% male; 47.4% female)
Individual Education Program: 1,052 (12.9%);
English Language Learner: 1 (<0.1%); Migrant: n/a
Eligible for Free Lunch Program: 129 (1.6%)
Eligible for Reduced-Price Lunch Program: 51 (0.6%)
Teachers: 445.4 (18.3 to 1)
Librarians/Media Specialists: 6.0 (1,355.3 to 1)
Guidance Counselors: 12.1 (672.1 to 1)
Current Spending: ($ per student per year):
Total: $6,611; Instruction: $4,070; Support Services: $2,275
Enrollment, Drop-out Rates and Diploma Recipients by Race/Ethnicity

Category	Total	White	Black	Asian	AIAN	Hisp.
Enrollment (%)	100.0	95.9	1.1	1.0	0.4	0.4
Drop-out Rate (%)	0.5	0.5	0.0	0.0	0.0	0.0
H.S. Diplomas (#)	633	616	3	8	4	1

Princeton City SD

25 W Sharon Rd • Cincinnati, OH 45246-4322
(513) 771-8560 • http://www.princeton.k12.oh.us/
Grade Span: PK-12; **Agency Type:** 1
Schools: 11
8 Primary; 2 Middle; 0 High; 1 Other Level
11 Regular; 0 Special Education; 0 Vocational; 0 Alternative
0 Magnet; 0 Charter; 6 Title I Eligible; 3 School-wide Title I
Students: 6,105 (51.7% male; 48.2% female)
Individual Education Program: 787 (12.9%);
English Language Learner: 232 (3.8%); Migrant: n/a
Eligible for Free Lunch Program: 2,137 (35.0%)
Eligible for Reduced-Price Lunch Program: 411 (6.7%)
Teachers: 485.4 (12.6 to 1)
Librarians/Media Specialists: 10.0 (610.3 to 1)
Guidance Counselors: 14.0 (435.9 to 1)
Current Spending: ($ per student per year):
Total: $10,866; Instruction: $5,811; Support Services: $4,690
Enrollment, Drop-out Rates and Diploma Recipients by Race/Ethnicity

Category	Total	White	Black	Asian	AIAN	Hisp.
Enrollment (%)	100.0	40.7	49.7	2.7	0.0	4.0
Drop-out Rate (%)	4.0	3.2	4.7	3.8	n/a	5.4
H.S. Diplomas (#)	403	213	170	12	0	7

Southwest Local SD

230 S Elm St • Harrison, OH 45030-1444
(513) 367-4139 • http://www.southwestschools.org/
Grade Span: PK-12; **Agency Type:** 2
Schools: 8
5 Primary; 2 Middle; 1 High; 0 Other Level
8 Regular; 0 Special Education; 0 Vocational; 0 Alternative
0 Magnet; 0 Charter; 5 Title I Eligible; 0 School-wide Title I
Students: 3,971 (52.2% male; 47.7% female)
Individual Education Program: 559 (14.1%);
English Language Learner: 5 (0.1%); Migrant: n/a
Eligible for Free Lunch Program: 529 (13.3%)
Eligible for Reduced-Price Lunch Program: 170 (4.3%)
Teachers: 208.3 (19.1 to 1)
Librarians/Media Specialists: 2.5 (1,588.4 to 1)
Guidance Counselors: 8.5 (467.2 to 1)
Current Spending: ($ per student per year):
Total: $6,972; Instruction: $4,067; Support Services: $2,575
Enrollment, Drop-out Rates and Diploma Recipients by Race/Ethnicity

Category	Total	White	Black	Asian	AIAN	Hisp.
Enrollment (%)	100.0	97.8	0.3	0.2	0.2	0.6
Drop-out Rate (%)	5.0	4.9	100.0	0.0	50.0	0.0
H.S. Diplomas (#)	277	277	0	0	0	0

Sycamore Community City SD

4881 Cooper Rd • Cincinnati, OH 45242-6902
(513) 791-4848 •
http://my.sycamoreschools.org/webapps/portal/frameset.jsp
Grade Span: PK-12; **Agency Type:** 1
Schools: 7
4 Primary; 2 Middle; 1 High; 0 Other Level
7 Regular; 0 Special Education; 0 Vocational; 0 Alternative
0 Magnet; 0 Charter; 4 Title I Eligible; 0 School-wide Title I
Students: 5,759 (51.4% male; 48.5% female)
Individual Education Program: 543 (9.4%);
English Language Learner: 249 (4.3%); Migrant: 60 (1.0%)
Eligible for Free Lunch Program: 304 (5.3%)
Eligible for Reduced-Price Lunch Program: 122 (2.1%)
Teachers: 398.9 (14.4 to 1)
Librarians/Media Specialists: 7.0 (822.7 to 1)
Guidance Counselors: 16.5 (349.0 to 1)
Current Spending: ($ per student per year):
Total: $11,616; Instruction: $6,460; Support Services: $4,895
Enrollment, Drop-out Rates and Diploma Recipients by Race/Ethnicity

Category	Total	White	Black	Asian	AIAN	Hisp.
Enrollment (%)	100.0	79.7	6.7	9.2	0.3	1.6
Drop-out Rate (%)	0.9	1.0	1.7	0.0	0.0	0.0
H.S. Diplomas (#)	425	366	23	33	0	3

Three Rivers Local Schools

92 Cleves Ave • Cleves, OH 45002-1368
(513) 941-6400 • http://www.threeriversschools.org/
Grade Span: PK-12; **Agency Type:** 2
Schools: 5
2 Primary; 1 Middle; 1 High; 1 Other Level
5 Regular; 0 Special Education; 0 Vocational; 0 Alternative
0 Magnet; 0 Charter; 4 Title I Eligible; 0 School-wide Title I
Students: 2,164 (52.1% male; 47.8% female)
Individual Education Program: 309 (14.3%);
English Language Learner: 0 (0.0%); Migrant: n/a
Eligible for Free Lunch Program: 351 (16.2%)
Eligible for Reduced-Price Lunch Program: 107 (4.9%)
Teachers: 126.4 (17.1 to 1)
Librarians/Media Specialists: 2.0 (1,082.0 to 1)
Guidance Counselors: 4.5 (480.9 to 1)
Current Spending: ($ per student per year):
Total: $7,622; Instruction: $4,490; Support Services: $2,867
Enrollment, Drop-out Rates and Diploma Recipients by Race/Ethnicity

Category	Total	White	Black	Asian	AIAN	Hisp.
Enrollment (%)	100.0	96.1	1.6	0.4	0.0	0.5
Drop-out Rate (%)	3.9	3.8	0.0	0.0	n/a	0.0
H.S. Diplomas (#)	136	129	3	1	0	0

Winton Woods City SD

1215 W Kemper Rd • Cincinnati, OH 45240-1617
(513) 619-2300
Grade Span: PK-12; **Agency Type:** 1
Schools: 7
5 Primary; 1 Middle; 1 High; 0 Other Level
7 Regular; 0 Special Education; 0 Vocational; 0 Alternative
0 Magnet; 0 Charter; 3 Title I Eligible; 1 School-wide Title I
Students: 4,156 (52.5% male; 47.4% female)
Individual Education Program: 714 (17.2%);
English Language Learner: 57 (1.4%); Migrant: n/a
Eligible for Free Lunch Program: 886 (21.3%)
Eligible for Reduced-Price Lunch Program: 254 (6.1%)
Teachers: 283.8 (14.6 to 1)
Librarians/Media Specialists: 4.0 (1,039.0 to 1)
Guidance Counselors: 6.6 (629.7 to 1)
Current Spending: ($ per student per year):
Total: $8,458; Instruction: $4,878; Support Services: $3,364
Enrollment, Drop-out Rates and Diploma Recipients by Race/Ethnicity

Category	Total	White	Black	Asian	AIAN	Hisp.
Enrollment (%)	100.0	25.6	63.2	1.7	0.0	2.6
Drop-out Rate (%)	3.2	3.3	3.0	0.0	0.0	5.0
H.S. Diplomas (#)	218	84	125	3	0	1

Wyoming City SD

420 Springfield Pike • Wyoming, OH 45215-4298
(513) 772-2343 • http://www.wyomingcityschools.org/
Grade Span: PK-12; **Agency Type:** 1
Schools: 5
3 Primary; 1 Middle; 1 High; 0 Other Level
5 Regular; 0 Special Education; 0 Vocational; 0 Alternative
0 Magnet; 0 Charter; 1 Title I Eligible; 0 School-wide Title I
Students: 1,984 (52.0% male; 47.9% female)
Individual Education Program: 192 (9.7%);
English Language Learner: 12 (0.6%); Migrant: n/a
Eligible for Free Lunch Program: 47 (2.4%)

Eligible for Reduced-Price Lunch Program: 21 (1.1%)
Teachers: 133.7 (14.8 to 1)
Librarians/Media Specialists: 2.0 (992.0 to 1)
Guidance Counselors: 5.0 (396.8 to 1)
Current Spending: ($ per student per year):
    Total: $8,729; Instruction: $6,048; Support Services: $2,477
Enrollment, Drop-out Rates and Diploma Recipients by Race/Ethnicity

Category	Total	White	Black	Asian	AIAN	Hisp.
Enrollment (%)	100.0	83.9	11.3	1.6	0.0	0.8
Drop-out Rate (%)	0.0	0.0	0.0	0.0	0.0	0.0
H.S. Diplomas (#)	143	115	21	2	1	3

Hancock County

Findlay City SD
227 S W St • Findlay, OH 45840-3324
(419) 425-8212 • http://www.findlaycityschools.org/
Grade Span: PK-12; **Agency Type:** 1
Schools: 16
    9 Primary; 3 Middle; 0 High; 4 Other Level
    13 Regular; 2 Special Education; 1 Vocational; 0 Alternative
    0 Magnet; 0 Charter; 11 Title I Eligible; 2 School-wide Title I
Students: 6,479 (51.4% male; 48.5% female)
    Individual Education Program: 1,152 (17.8%);
    English Language Learner: 38 (0.6%); Migrant: 1 (<0.1%)
    Eligible for Free Lunch Program: 1,275 (19.7%)
    Eligible for Reduced-Price Lunch Program: 374 (5.8%)
Teachers: 437.1 (14.8 to 1)
Librarians/Media Specialists: 2.0 (3,239.5 to 1)
Guidance Counselors: 12.0 (539.9 to 1)
Current Spending: ($ per student per year):
    Total: $7,882; Instruction: $4,830; Support Services: $2,797
Enrollment, Drop-out Rates and Diploma Recipients by Race/Ethnicity

Category	Total	White	Black	Asian	AIAN	Hisp.
Enrollment (%)	100.0	87.8	1.5	2.7	0.1	3.8
Drop-out Rate (%)	2.6	2.4	2.0	0.0	0.0	4.5
H.S. Diplomas (#)	426	391	6	10	1	14

Hardin County

Kenton City SD
400 Decatur St • Kenton, OH 43326-2043
(419) 673-0775 • http://www.kentoncityschools.org/
Grade Span: PK-12; **Agency Type:** 1
Schools: 8
    6 Primary; 1 Middle; 1 High; 0 Other Level
    8 Regular; 0 Special Education; 0 Vocational; 0 Alternative
    0 Magnet; 0 Charter; 4 Title I Eligible; 4 School-wide Title I
Students: 2,145 (52.5% male; 47.4% female)
    Individual Education Program: 348 (16.2%);
    English Language Learner: 2 (0.1%); Migrant: n/a
    Eligible for Free Lunch Program: 473 (22.1%)
    Eligible for Reduced-Price Lunch Program: 167 (7.8%)
Teachers: 136.6 (15.7 to 1)
Librarians/Media Specialists: 1.0 (2,145.0 to 1)
Guidance Counselors: 3.0 (715.0 to 1)
Current Spending: ($ per student per year):
    Total: $7,319; Instruction: $4,581; Support Services: $2,445
Enrollment, Drop-out Rates and Diploma Recipients by Race/Ethnicity

Category	Total	White	Black	Asian	AIAN	Hisp.
Enrollment (%)	100.0	96.6	0.5	0.3	0.3	0.3
Drop-out Rate (%)	3.1	3.0	0.0	0.0	n/a	0.0
H.S. Diplomas (#)	147	140	0	4	0	1

Harrison County

Harrison Hills City SD
422 Normal St • Hopedale, OH 43976-8707
Mailing Address: PO Box 356 • Hopedale, OH 43976-0356
(740) 942-7800
Grade Span: PK-12; **Agency Type:** 1
Schools: 6
    4 Primary; 1 Middle; 1 High; 0 Other Level
    6 Regular; 0 Special Education; 0 Vocational; 0 Alternative
    0 Magnet; 0 Charter; 5 Title I Eligible; 4 School-wide Title I
Students: 2,118 (54.6% male; 45.3% female)
    Individual Education Program: 626 (29.6%);
    English Language Learner: 0 (0.0%); Migrant: n/a
    Eligible for Free Lunch Program: 650 (30.7%)
    Eligible for Reduced-Price Lunch Program: 170 (8.0%)
Teachers: 133.5 (15.9 to 1)
Librarians/Media Specialists: 2.0 (1,059.0 to 1)
Guidance Counselors: 3.0 (706.0 to 1)
Current Spending: ($ per student per year):
    Total: $6,811; Instruction: $4,147; Support Services: $2,346

Enrollment, Drop-out Rates and Diploma Recipients by Race/Ethnicity

Category	Total	White	Black	Asian	AIAN	Hisp.
Enrollment (%)	100.0	93.6	3.5	0.3	0.0	0.1
Drop-out Rate (%)	3.5	3.2	9.1	0.0	n/a	n/a
H.S. Diplomas (#)	138	132	6	0	0	0

Henry County

Napoleon Area City SD
701 Briarheath Ave Ste 108 • Napoleon, OH 43545-1251
(419) 599-7015
Grade Span: PK-12; **Agency Type:** 1
Schools: 5
    3 Primary; 1 Middle; 1 High; 0 Other Level
    5 Regular; 0 Special Education; 0 Vocational; 0 Alternative
    0 Magnet; 0 Charter; 4 Title I Eligible; 0 School-wide Title I
Students: 2,387 (51.2% male; 48.7% female)
    Individual Education Program: 486 (20.4%);
    English Language Learner: 42 (1.8%); Migrant: 38 (1.6%)
    Eligible for Free Lunch Program: 438 (18.3%)
    Eligible for Reduced-Price Lunch Program: 120 (5.0%)
Teachers: 151.0 (15.8 to 1)
Librarians/Media Specialists: 2.0 (1,193.5 to 1)
Guidance Counselors: 6.0 (397.8 to 1)
Current Spending: ($ per student per year):
    Total: $7,051; Instruction: $4,377; Support Services: $2,407
Enrollment, Drop-out Rates and Diploma Recipients by Race/Ethnicity

Category	Total	White	Black	Asian	AIAN	Hisp.
Enrollment (%)	100.0	88.1	0.8	1.3	0.1	9.3
Drop-out Rate (%)	3.6	2.9	0.0	0.0	n/a	14.8
H.S. Diplomas (#)	194	181	4	0	0	9

Highland County

Greenfield Ex Vill SD
200 N 5th St • Greenfield, OH 45123-1373
(937) 981-2152
Grade Span: PK-12; **Agency Type:** 1
Schools: 5
    3 Primary; 1 Middle; 1 High; 0 Other Level
    5 Regular; 0 Special Education; 0 Vocational; 0 Alternative
    0 Magnet; 0 Charter; 4 Title I Eligible; 0 School-wide Title I
Students: 2,319 (53.0% male; 46.9% female)
    Individual Education Program: 278 (12.0%);
    English Language Learner: 0 (0.0%); Migrant: n/a
    Eligible for Free Lunch Program: 525 (22.6%)
    Eligible for Reduced-Price Lunch Program: 179 (7.7%)
Teachers: 147.8 (15.7 to 1)
Librarians/Media Specialists: 1.0 (2,319.0 to 1)
Guidance Counselors: 4.0 (579.8 to 1)
Current Spending: ($ per student per year):
    Total: $7,096; Instruction: $4,289; Support Services: $2,524
Enrollment, Drop-out Rates and Diploma Recipients by Race/Ethnicity

Category	Total	White	Black	Asian	AIAN	Hisp.
Enrollment (%)	100.0	97.2	1.2	0.3	0.0	0.1
Drop-out Rate (%)	3.9	3.9	8.3	0.0	n/a	0.0
H.S. Diplomas (#)	132	128	4	0	0	0

Hillsboro City SD
338 W Main St • Hillsboro, OH 45133-1314
(937) 393-3475 • http://www.Hillsboro.k12.oh.us/
Grade Span: PK-12; **Agency Type:** 1
Schools: 6
    2 Primary; 3 Middle; 1 High; 0 Other Level
    6 Regular; 0 Special Education; 0 Vocational; 0 Alternative
    0 Magnet; 0 Charter; 4 Title I Eligible; 2 School-wide Title I
Students: 2,833 (51.6% male; 48.3% female)
    Individual Education Program: 367 (13.0%);
    English Language Learner: 17 (0.6%); Migrant: n/a
    Eligible for Free Lunch Program: 739 (26.1%)
    Eligible for Reduced-Price Lunch Program: 183 (6.5%)
Teachers: 185.3 (15.3 to 1)
Librarians/Media Specialists: 3.0 (944.3 to 1)
Guidance Counselors: 6.0 (472.2 to 1)
Current Spending: ($ per student per year):
    Total: $6,804; Instruction: $3,923; Support Services: $2,579
Enrollment, Drop-out Rates and Diploma Recipients by Race/Ethnicity

Category	Total	White	Black	Asian	AIAN	Hisp.
Enrollment (%)	100.0	93.4	3.2	0.6	0.2	0.2
Drop-out Rate (%)	1.2	1.3	0.0	0.0	0.0	0.0
H.S. Diplomas (#)	182	178	4	0	0	0

Hocking County

Logan-Hocking Local SD
57 S Walnut St • Logan, OH 43138-1317
(740) 385-8517
Grade Span: PK-12; **Agency Type:** 2
Schools: 14
  8 Primary; 1 Middle; 1 High; 0 Other Level
  10 Regular; 0 Special Education; 0 Vocational; 0 Alternative
  0 Magnet; 0 Charter; 8 Title I Eligible; 7 School-wide Title I
Students: 4,028 (52.1% male; 47.8% female)
  Individual Education Program: 684 (17.0%);
  English Language Learner: 0 (0.0%); Migrant: n/a
  Eligible for Free Lunch Program: 1,109 (27.5%)
  Eligible for Reduced-Price Lunch Program: 320 (7.9%)
Teachers: 227.6 (17.7 to 1)
Librarians/Media Specialists: 2.0 (2,014.0 to 1)
Guidance Counselors: 6.0 (671.3 to 1)
Current Spending: ($ per student per year):
  Total: $6,818; Instruction: $3,627; Support Services: $2,873
Enrollment, Drop-out Rates and Diploma Recipients by Race/Ethnicity

Category	Total	White	Black	Asian	AIAN	Hisp.
Enrollment (%)	100.0	98.6	0.5	0.0	0.1	0.2
Drop-out Rate (%)	6.2	6.0	9.1	n/a	n/a	0.0
H.S. Diplomas (#)	227	225	2	0	0	0

Holmes County

East Holmes Local Schools
6108 Co Rd 77 • Berlin, OH 44610-0182
Mailing Address: PO Box 182 • Berlin, OH 44610-0182
(330) 893-2610
Grade Span: KG-12; **Agency Type:** 2
Schools: 10
  8 Primary; 0 Middle; 1 High; 1 Other Level
  10 Regular; 0 Special Education; 0 Vocational; 0 Alternative
  0 Magnet; 0 Charter; 9 Title I Eligible; 9 School-wide Title I
Students: 1,857 (52.2% male; 47.7% female)
  Individual Education Program: 235 (12.7%);
  English Language Learner: 1,096 (59.0%); Migrant: n/a
  Eligible for Free Lunch Program: 249 (13.4%)
  Eligible for Reduced-Price Lunch Program: 152 (8.2%)
Teachers: 123.6 (15.0 to 1)
Librarians/Media Specialists: 1.0 (1,857.0 to 1)
Guidance Counselors: 2.0 (928.5 to 1)
Current Spending: ($ per student per year):
  Total: $6,979; Instruction: $4,313; Support Services: $2,407
Enrollment, Drop-out Rates and Diploma Recipients by Race/Ethnicity

Category	Total	White	Black	Asian	AIAN	Hisp.
Enrollment (%)	100.0	98.6	0.7	0.3	0.0	0.2
Drop-out Rate (%)	0.0	0.0	n/a	n/a	n/a	n/a
H.S. Diplomas (#)	63	63	0	0	0	0

West Holmes Local SD
28 W Jackson St • Millersburg, OH 44654-1302
(330) 674-3546 • http://www.westholmes.k12.oh.us/
Grade Span: KG-12; **Agency Type:** 2
Schools: 7
  5 Primary; 1 Middle; 1 High; 0 Other Level
  7 Regular; 0 Special Education; 0 Vocational; 0 Alternative
  0 Magnet; 0 Charter; 6 Title I Eligible; 6 School-wide Title I
Students: 2,805 (50.7% male; 49.2% female)
  Individual Education Program: 424 (15.1%);
  English Language Learner: 6 (0.2%); Migrant: n/a
  Eligible for Free Lunch Program: 680 (24.2%)
  Eligible for Reduced-Price Lunch Program: 271 (9.7%)
Teachers: 173.4 (16.2 to 1)
Librarians/Media Specialists: 5.4 (519.4 to 1)
Guidance Counselors: 4.0 (701.3 to 1)
Current Spending: ($ per student per year):
  Total: $6,571; Instruction: $3,839; Support Services: $2,416
Enrollment, Drop-out Rates and Diploma Recipients by Race/Ethnicity

Category	Total	White	Black	Asian	AIAN	Hisp.
Enrollment (%)	100.0	98.1	0.4	0.3	0.0	0.7
Drop-out Rate (%)	2.0	2.0	n/a	n/a	n/a	0.0
H.S. Diplomas (#)	150	147	0	0	0	3

Huron County

Bellevue City SD
125 N St • Bellevue, OH 44811-1423
(419) 484-5000 • http://www.bellevueschools.org/district/mainindex.html
Grade Span: PK-12; **Agency Type:** 1
Schools: 7
  5 Primary; 1 Middle; 1 High; 0 Other Level
  7 Regular; 0 Special Education; 0 Vocational; 0 Alternative
  0 Magnet; 0 Charter; 5 Title I Eligible; 2 School-wide Title I
Students: 2,388 (51.7% male; 48.2% female)
  Individual Education Program: 414 (17.3%);
  English Language Learner: 1 (<0.1%); Migrant: 2 (0.1%)
  Eligible for Free Lunch Program: 344 (14.4%)
  Eligible for Reduced-Price Lunch Program: 205 (8.6%)
Teachers: 144.7 (16.5 to 1)
Librarians/Media Specialists: 2.0 (1,194.0 to 1)
Guidance Counselors: 5.0 (477.6 to 1)
Current Spending: ($ per student per year):
  Total: $6,844; Instruction: $3,953; Support Services: $2,639
Enrollment, Drop-out Rates and Diploma Recipients by Race/Ethnicity

Category	Total	White	Black	Asian	AIAN	Hisp.
Enrollment (%)	100.0	95.6	0.5	0.3	0.1	2.4
Drop-out Rate (%)	1.8	1.6	0.0	0.0	n/a	15.4
H.S. Diplomas (#)	180	175	0	1	0	4

Norwalk City SD
134 Benedict Ave • Norwalk, OH 44857-2349
(419) 668-2779
Grade Span: PK-12; **Agency Type:** 1
Schools: 6
  3 Primary; 1 Middle; 1 High; 0 Other Level
  5 Regular; 0 Special Education; 0 Vocational; 0 Alternative
  0 Magnet; 0 Charter; 4 Title I Eligible; 1 School-wide Title I
Students: 2,952 (51.5% male; 48.4% female)
  Individual Education Program: 469 (15.9%);
  English Language Learner: 0 (0.0%); Migrant: n/a
  Eligible for Free Lunch Program: 655 (22.2%)
  Eligible for Reduced-Price Lunch Program: 220 (7.5%)
Teachers: 145.6 (20.3 to 1)
Librarians/Media Specialists: 3.0 (984.0 to 1)
Guidance Counselors: 5.0 (590.4 to 1)
Current Spending: ($ per student per year):
  Total: $5,770; Instruction: $3,326; Support Services: $2,230
Enrollment, Drop-out Rates and Diploma Recipients by Race/Ethnicity

Category	Total	White	Black	Asian	AIAN	Hisp.
Enrollment (%)	100.0	89.5	2.9	0.2	0.1	4.7
Drop-out Rate (%)	5.2	5.0	4.2	0.0	n/a	10.7
H.S. Diplomas (#)	160	153	3	1	0	3

Willard City SD
955 S Main St • Willard, OH 44890-9598
(419) 935-1541
Grade Span: PK-12; **Agency Type:** 1
Schools: 6
  4 Primary; 1 Middle; 1 High; 0 Other Level
  6 Regular; 0 Special Education; 0 Vocational; 0 Alternative
  0 Magnet; 0 Charter; 4 Title I Eligible; 1 School-wide Title I
Students: 2,362 (50.7% male; 49.2% female)
  Individual Education Program: 331 (14.0%);
  English Language Learner: 41 (1.7%); Migrant: 143 (6.1%)
  Eligible for Free Lunch Program: 659 (27.9%)
  Eligible for Reduced-Price Lunch Program: 142 (6.0%)
Teachers: 136.0 (17.4 to 1)
Librarians/Media Specialists: 1.0 (2,362.0 to 1)
Guidance Counselors: 6.0 (393.7 to 1)
Current Spending: ($ per student per year):
  Total: $6,555; Instruction: $3,935; Support Services: $2,325
Enrollment, Drop-out Rates and Diploma Recipients by Race/Ethnicity

Category	Total	White	Black	Asian	AIAN	Hisp.
Enrollment (%)	100.0	80.8	1.5	0.4	0.0	16.2
Drop-out Rate (%)	3.4	3.5	0.0	0.0	n/a	3.0
H.S. Diplomas (#)	144	129	0	0	0	15

Jackson County

Jackson City SD
450 Vaughn St • Jackson, OH 45640-1944
(740) 286-6442 • http://www.jcs.k12.oh.us/
Grade Span: PK-12; **Agency Type:** 1
Schools: 7
  4 Primary; 1 Middle; 1 High; 0 Other Level
  6 Regular; 0 Special Education; 0 Vocational; 0 Alternative
  0 Magnet; 0 Charter; 4 Title I Eligible; 4 School-wide Title I
Students: 2,745 (52.6% male; 47.3% female)
  Individual Education Program: 421 (15.3%);
  English Language Learner: 1 (<0.1%); Migrant: n/a
  Eligible for Free Lunch Program: 743 (27.1%)
  Eligible for Reduced-Price Lunch Program: 165 (6.0%)
Teachers: 144.0 (19.1 to 1)
Librarians/Media Specialists: 1.0 (2,745.0 to 1)
Guidance Counselors: 4.0 (686.3 to 1)
Current Spending: ($ per student per year):
  Total: $6,519; Instruction: $3,860; Support Services: $2,389

Enrollment, Drop-out Rates and Diploma Recipients by Race/Ethnicity

Category	Total	White	Black	Asian	AIAN	Hisp.
Enrollment (%)	100.0	98.0	0.3	0.3	0.0	0.5
Drop-out Rate (%)	2.5	2.6	0.0	0.0	0.0	0.0
H.S. Diplomas (#)	203	199	0	3	0	0

Wellston City Schools
1 E Broadway St • Wellston, OH 45692-1225
(740) 384-2152
Grade Span: PK-12; **Agency Type:** 1
Schools: 4
  2 Primary; 1 Middle; 1 High; 0 Other Level
  4 Regular; 0 Special Education; 0 Vocational; 0 Alternative
  0 Magnet; 0 Charter; 3 Title I Eligible; 3 School-wide Title I
Students: 1,854   (50.8% male; 49.1% female)
  Individual Education Program: 316 (17.0%);
  English Language Learner: 0 (0.0%); Migrant: n/a
  Eligible for Free Lunch Program: 653 (35.2%)
  Eligible for Reduced-Price Lunch Program: 123 (6.6%)
Teachers: 118.6 (15.6 to 1)
Librarians/Media Specialists: 2.0 (927.0 to 1)
Guidance Counselors: 3.0 (618.0 to 1)
Current Spending: ($ per student per year):
  Total: $7,020; Instruction: $4,314; Support Services: $2,377

Enrollment, Drop-out Rates and Diploma Recipients by Race/Ethnicity

Category	Total	White	Black	Asian	AIAN	Hisp.
Enrollment (%)	100.0	98.8	0.3	0.2	0.3	0.2
Drop-out Rate (%)	2.1	2.1	0.0	0.0	n/a	0.0
H.S. Diplomas (#)	78	77	0	1	0	0

Jefferson County

Buckeye Local SD
198 Main St • Rayland, OH 43943-9741
Mailing Address: PO Box 300 • Rayland, OH 43943-0300
(740) 769-7395
Grade Span: PK-12; **Agency Type:** 2
Schools: 7
  4 Primary; 2 Middle; 1 High; 0 Other Level
  7 Regular; 0 Special Education; 0 Vocational; 0 Alternative
  0 Magnet; 0 Charter; 7 Title I Eligible; 7 School-wide Title I
Students: 2,415   (51.6% male; 48.3% female)
  Individual Education Program: 439 (18.2%);
  English Language Learner: 0 (0.0%); Migrant: n/a
  Eligible for Free Lunch Program: 790 (32.7%)
  Eligible for Reduced-Price Lunch Program: 158 (6.5%)
Teachers: 163.0 (14.8 to 1)
Librarians/Media Specialists: 1.0 (2,415.0 to 1)
Guidance Counselors: 4.0 (603.8 to 1)
Current Spending: ($ per student per year):
  Total: $7,014; Instruction: $4,249; Support Services: $2,451

Enrollment, Drop-out Rates and Diploma Recipients by Race/Ethnicity

Category	Total	White	Black	Asian	AIAN	Hisp.
Enrollment (%)	100.0	98.1	1.2	0.2	0.0	0.0
Drop-out Rate (%)	1.2	1.2	0.0	0.0	0.0	0.0
H.S. Diplomas (#)	183	181	0	0	0	2

Edison Local SD
14890 State Route 213 • Hammondsville, OH 43930-7902
(330) 532-3199
Grade Span: PK-12; **Agency Type:** 2
Schools: 7
  4 Primary; 2 Middle; 1 High; 0 Other Level
  7 Regular; 0 Special Education; 0 Vocational; 0 Alternative
  0 Magnet; 0 Charter; 6 Title I Eligible; 6 School-wide Title I
Students: 2,689   (51.4% male; 48.5% female)
  Individual Education Program: 337 (12.5%);
  English Language Learner: 0 (0.0%); Migrant: n/a
  Eligible for Free Lunch Program: 722 (26.9%)
  Eligible for Reduced-Price Lunch Program: 271 (10.1%)
Teachers: 167.6 (16.0 to 1)
Librarians/Media Specialists: 1.0 (2,689.0 to 1)
Guidance Counselors: 4.0 (672.3 to 1)
Current Spending: ($ per student per year):
  Total: $6,779; Instruction: $4,112; Support Services: $2,428

Enrollment, Drop-out Rates and Diploma Recipients by Race/Ethnicity

Category	Total	White	Black	Asian	AIAN	Hisp.
Enrollment (%)	100.0	98.7	0.3	0.3	0.0	0.2
Drop-out Rate (%)	1.1	1.1	0.0	0.0	0.0	0.0
H.S. Diplomas (#)	177	175	1	0	0	1

Indian Creek Local SD
587 Bantam Ridge Rd • Wintersville, OH 43953-4231
(740) 264-3502 • http://www.indian-creek.k12.oh.us/
Grade Span: PK-12; **Agency Type:** 2
Schools: 6
  4 Primary; 1 Middle; 1 High; 0 Other Level
  6 Regular; 0 Special Education; 0 Vocational; 0 Alternative
  0 Magnet; 0 Charter; 5 Title I Eligible; 2 School-wide Title I
Students: 2,322   (51.8% male; 48.1% female)
  Individual Education Program: 357 (15.4%);
  English Language Learner: 0 (0.0%); Migrant: n/a
  Eligible for Free Lunch Program: 709 (30.5%)
  Eligible for Reduced-Price Lunch Program: 153 (6.6%)
Teachers: 133.0 (17.5 to 1)
Librarians/Media Specialists: 2.0 (1,161.0 to 1)
Guidance Counselors: 4.0 (580.5 to 1)
Current Spending: ($ per student per year):
  Total: $6,651; Instruction: $3,852; Support Services: $2,561

Enrollment, Drop-out Rates and Diploma Recipients by Race/Ethnicity

Category	Total	White	Black	Asian	AIAN	Hisp.
Enrollment (%)	100.0	93.6	4.4	0.6	0.0	0.5
Drop-out Rate (%)	1.1	1.0	3.2	0.0	n/a	0.0
H.S. Diplomas (#)	132	124	7	0	0	1

Steubenville City SD
932 N 5th St • Steubenville, OH 43952-1812
Mailing Address: PO Box 189 • Steubenville, OH 43952-5189
(740) 283-3767
Grade Span: PK-12; **Agency Type:** 1
Schools: 8
  6 Primary; 1 Middle; 0 High; 1 Other Level
  8 Regular; 0 Special Education; 0 Vocational; 0 Alternative
  0 Magnet; 0 Charter; 7 Title I Eligible; 7 School-wide Title I
Students: 2,391   (51.6% male; 48.3% female)
  Individual Education Program: 306 (12.8%);
  English Language Learner: 0 (0.0%); Migrant: n/a
  Eligible for Free Lunch Program: 1,112 (46.5%)
  Eligible for Reduced-Price Lunch Program: 124 (5.2%)
Teachers: 152.0 (15.7 to 1)
Librarians/Media Specialists: 0.0 (n/a to 1)
Guidance Counselors: 4.0 (597.8 to 1)
Current Spending: ($ per student per year):
  Total: $7,257; Instruction: $4,750; Support Services: $2,252

Enrollment, Drop-out Rates and Diploma Recipients by Race/Ethnicity

Category	Total	White	Black	Asian	AIAN	Hisp.
Enrollment (%)	100.0	58.3	32.2	0.7	0.0	0.4
Drop-out Rate (%)	5.2	5.5	4.1	14.3	n/a	0.0
H.S. Diplomas (#)	171	126	39	1	0	2

Knox County

Mount Vernon City SD
302 Martinsburg Rd • Mount Vernon, OH 43050-4252
(740) 397-7422 • http://www.mt-vernon.k12.oh.us/
Grade Span: PK-12; **Agency Type:** 1
Schools: 9
  7 Primary; 1 Middle; 1 High; 0 Other Level
  9 Regular; 0 Special Education; 0 Vocational; 0 Alternative
  0 Magnet; 0 Charter; 6 Title I Eligible; 4 School-wide Title I
Students: 4,301   (51.8% male; 48.1% female)
  Individual Education Program: 893 (20.8%);
  English Language Learner: 8 (0.2%); Migrant: n/a
  Eligible for Free Lunch Program: 1,018 (23.7%)
  Eligible for Reduced-Price Lunch Program: 222 (5.2%)
Teachers: 252.5 (17.0 to 1)
Librarians/Media Specialists: 3.0 (1,433.7 to 1)
Guidance Counselors: 5.0 (860.2 to 1)
Current Spending: ($ per student per year):
  Total: $6,475; Instruction: $3,988; Support Services: $2,276

Enrollment, Drop-out Rates and Diploma Recipients by Race/Ethnicity

Category	Total	White	Black	Asian	AIAN	Hisp.
Enrollment (%)	100.0	95.9	0.8	0.6	0.3	0.7
Drop-out Rate (%)	2.8	2.7	0.0	0.0	50.0	50.0
H.S. Diplomas (#)	284	272	6	4	0	2

Lake County

Madison Local SD
6741 N Ridge Rd • Madison, OH 44057-2656
(440) 428-2166 • http://www.madison-richland.k12.oh.us/
Grade Span: PK-12; **Agency Type:** 2
Schools: 5
  3 Primary; 1 Middle; 1 High; 0 Other Level
  5 Regular; 0 Special Education; 0 Vocational; 0 Alternative
  0 Magnet; 0 Charter; 3 Title I Eligible; 0 School-wide Title I

Students: 3,739 (52.0% male; 47.9% female)
Individual Education Program: 429 (11.5%);
English Language Learner: 0 (0.0%); Migrant: 1 (<0.1%)
Eligible for Free Lunch Program: 657 (17.6%)
Eligible for Reduced-Price Lunch Program: 247 (6.6%)
Teachers: 194.5 (19.2 to 1)
Librarians/Media Specialists: 1.0 (3,739.0 to 1)
Guidance Counselors: 5.0 (747.8 to 1)
Current Spending: ($ per student per year):
Total: $6,503; Instruction: $3,859; Support Services: $2,435
Enrollment, Drop-out Rates and Diploma Recipients by Race/Ethnicity

Category	Total	White	Black	Asian	AIAN	Hisp.
Enrollment (%)	100.0	97.6	0.4	0.3	0.0	1.1
Drop-out Rate (%)	3.4	3.4	0.0	0.0	0.0	16.7
H.S. Diplomas (#)	254	248	1	2	1	2

Mentor Ex Vill SD

6451 Center St • Mentor, OH 44060-4109
(440) 255-4444 • http://www.mentorschools.org/
Grade Span: PK-12; **Agency Type:** 1
Schools: 16
12 Primary; 3 Middle; 1 High; 0 Other Level
16 Regular; 0 Special Education; 0 Vocational; 0 Alternative
0 Magnet; 0 Charter; 7 Title I Eligible; 0 School-wide Title I
Students: 9,777 (50.7% male; 49.2% female)
Individual Education Program: 1,176 (12.0%);
English Language Learner: 65 (0.7%); Migrant: n/a
Eligible for Free Lunch Program: 682 (7.0%)
Eligible for Reduced-Price Lunch Program: 324 (3.3%)
Teachers: 627.0 (15.6 to 1)
Librarians/Media Specialists: 17.0 (573.9 to 1)
Guidance Counselors: 15.0 (650.5 to 1)
Current Spending: ($ per student per year):
Total: $8,617; Instruction: $5,284; Support Services: $3,091
Enrollment, Drop-out Rates and Diploma Recipients by Race/Ethnicity

Category	Total	White	Black	Asian	AIAN	Hisp.
Enrollment (%)	100.0	96.9	0.8	1.0	0.0	0.5
Drop-out Rate (%)	0.9	0.9	0.0	0.0	50.0	4.5
H.S. Diplomas (#)	730	711	8	8	0	3

Painesville City Local SD

58 Jefferson St • Painesville, OH 44077-3114
(440) 392-5060
Grade Span: KG-12; **Agency Type:** 2
Schools: 7
5 Primary; 1 Middle; 1 High; 0 Other Level
7 Regular; 0 Special Education; 0 Vocational; 0 Alternative
0 Magnet; 0 Charter; 7 Title I Eligible; 5 School-wide Title I
Students: 2,845 (52.8% male; 47.1% female)
Individual Education Program: 415 (14.6%);
English Language Learner: 677 (23.8%); Migrant: 385 (14.2%)
Eligible for Free Lunch Program: 1,955 (72.0%)
Eligible for Reduced-Price Lunch Program: 213 (7.8%)
Teachers: 182.6 (14.9 to 1)
Librarians/Media Specialists: 2.0 (1,358.5 to 1)
Guidance Counselors: 6.0 (452.8 to 1)
Current Spending: ($ per student per year):
Total: $8,230; Instruction: $4,473; Support Services: $3,447
Enrollment, Drop-out Rates and Diploma Recipients by Race/Ethnicity

Category	Total	White	Black	Asian	AIAN	Hisp.
Enrollment (%)	100.0	39.3	22.1	0.3	0.2	28.1
Drop-out Rate (%)	5.9	3.7	8.7	16.7	n/a	7.3
H.S. Diplomas (#)	88	53	23	3	0	7

Painesville Township Local SD

585 Riverside Dr • Painesville, OH 44077-5323
(440) 352-0668
Grade Span: PK-12; **Agency Type:** 2
Schools: 8
6 Primary; 1 Middle; 1 High; 0 Other Level
8 Regular; 0 Special Education; 0 Vocational; 0 Alternative
0 Magnet; 0 Charter; 4 Title I Eligible; 0 School-wide Title I
Students: 4,519 (51.4% male; 48.5% female)
Individual Education Program: 477 (10.6%);
English Language Learner: 10 (0.2%); Migrant: 5 (0.1%)
Eligible for Free Lunch Program: 442 (9.8%)
Eligible for Reduced-Price Lunch Program: 158 (3.5%)
Teachers: 233.5 (19.2 to 1)
Librarians/Media Specialists: 2.0 (2,244.0 to 1)
Guidance Counselors: 12.0 (374.0 to 1)
Current Spending: ($ per student per year):
Total: $7,291; Instruction: $3,994; Support Services: $3,038

Category	Total	White	Black	Asian	AIAN	Hisp.
Enrollment (%)	100.0	95.7	1.5	0.5	0.2	1.0
Drop-out Rate (%)	1.9	1.8	0.0	0.0	0.0	33.3
H.S. Diplomas (#)	306	302	3	1	0	0

Perry Local SD

4325 Manchester Ave • Perry, OH 44081-9413
(440) 259-3881 • http://www.perry-lake.k12.oh.us/
Grade Span: KG-12; **Agency Type:** 2
Schools: 3
1 Primary; 1 Middle; 1 High; 0 Other Level
3 Regular; 0 Special Education; 0 Vocational; 0 Alternative
0 Magnet; 0 Charter; 2 Title I Eligible; 0 School-wide Title I
Students: 1,854 (50.3% male; 49.6% female)
Individual Education Program: 141 (7.6%);
English Language Learner: 0 (0.0%); Migrant: n/a
Eligible for Free Lunch Program: 148 (8.0%)
Eligible for Reduced-Price Lunch Program: 107 (5.8%)
Teachers: 118.0 (15.7 to 1)
Librarians/Media Specialists: 3.0 (618.0 to 1)
Guidance Counselors: 4.0 (463.5 to 1)
Current Spending: ($ per student per year):
Total: $13,555; Instruction: $6,898; Support Services: $6,228
Enrollment, Drop-out Rates and Diploma Recipients by Race/Ethnicity

Category	Total	White	Black	Asian	AIAN	Hisp.
Enrollment (%)	100.0	98.2	0.2	0.4	0.0	0.6
Drop-out Rate (%)	0.7	0.7	n/a	n/a	n/a	n/a
H.S. Diplomas (#)	132	132	0	0	0	0

Wickliffe City SD

2221 Rockefeller Rd • Wickliffe, OH 44092-2020
(440) 943-6900 • http://www.wickliffe-city.k12.oh.us/
Grade Span: PK-12; **Agency Type:** 1
Schools: 3
1 Primary; 1 Middle; 1 High; 0 Other Level
3 Regular; 0 Special Education; 0 Vocational; 0 Alternative
0 Magnet; 0 Charter; 2 Title I Eligible; 0 School-wide Title I
Students: 1,570 (53.9% male; 46.0% female)
Individual Education Program: 239 (15.2%);
English Language Learner: 1 (0.1%); Migrant: n/a
Eligible for Free Lunch Program: 159 (10.1%)
Eligible for Reduced-Price Lunch Program: 104 (6.6%)
Teachers: 112.9 (13.9 to 1)
Librarians/Media Specialists: 1.0 (1,570.0 to 1)
Guidance Counselors: 4.0 (392.5 to 1)
Current Spending: ($ per student per year):
Total: $9,198; Instruction: $4,505; Support Services: $4,420
Enrollment, Drop-out Rates and Diploma Recipients by Race/Ethnicity

Category	Total	White	Black	Asian	AIAN	Hisp.
Enrollment (%)	100.0	92.5	4.3	1.7	0.1	0.2
Drop-out Rate (%)	2.8	2.3	18.8	0.0	0.0	n/a
H.S. Diplomas (#)	117	112	4	0	0	1

Willoughby-Eastlake City SD

37047 Ridge Rd • Willoughby, OH 44094-4130
(440) 946-5000 • http://www.willoughby-eastlake.k12.oh.us/
Grade Span: PK-12; **Agency Type:** 1
Schools: 14
8 Primary; 3 Middle; 3 High; 0 Other Level
13 Regular; 0 Special Education; 1 Vocational; 0 Alternative
0 Magnet; 0 Charter; 8 Title I Eligible; 1 School-wide Title I
Students: 8,876 (51.8% male; 48.1% female)
Individual Education Program: 1,281 (14.4%);
English Language Learner: 170 (1.9%); Migrant: 5 (0.1%)
Eligible for Free Lunch Program: 1,258 (14.2%)
Eligible for Reduced-Price Lunch Program: 540 (6.1%)
Teachers: 518.8 (17.1 to 1)
Librarians/Media Specialists: 5.0 (1,775.2 to 1)
Guidance Counselors: 13.0 (682.8 to 1)
Current Spending: ($ per student per year):
Total: $7,918; Instruction: $4,846; Support Services: $2,838
Enrollment, Drop-out Rates and Diploma Recipients by Race/Ethnicity

Category	Total	White	Black	Asian	AIAN	Hisp.
Enrollment (%)	100.0	93.9	2.6	1.2	0.1	0.4
Drop-out Rate (%)	3.0	3.0	3.7	5.3	0.0	0.0
H.S. Diplomas (#)	637	616	7	8	0	4

Lawrence County

Fairland Local SD

228 Private Dr 10010 • Proctorville, OH 45669-8600
(740) 886-3100 • http://fairland.k12.oh.us/
Grade Span: KG-12; **Agency Type:** 2
Schools: 4

2 Primary; 1 Middle; 1 High; 0 Other Level
4 Regular; 0 Special Education; 0 Vocational; 0 Alternative
0 Magnet; 0 Charter; 2 Title I Eligible; 2 School-wide Title I
Students: 1,838   (51.7% male; 48.2% female)
Individual Education Program: 239 (13.0%);
English Language Learner: 0 (0.0%); Migrant: n/a
Eligible for Free Lunch Program: 416 (22.6%)
Eligible for Reduced-Price Lunch Program: 87 (4.7%)
Teachers: 99.5 (18.5 to 1)
Librarians/Media Specialists: 2.3 (799.1 to 1)
Guidance Counselors: 4.5 (408.4 to 1)
Current Spending: ($ per student per year):
Total: $6,353; Instruction: $3,861; Support Services: $2,299

Enrollment, Drop-out Rates and Diploma Recipients by Race/Ethnicity

Category	Total	White	Black	Asian	AIAN	Hisp.
Enrollment (%)	100.0	97.8	0.4	0.6	0.1	0.1
Drop-out Rate (%)	3.8	3.8	0.0	0.0	n/a	n/a
H.S. Diplomas (#)	115	114	0	1	0	0

Ironton City SD
105 S 5th St • **Ironton, OH 45638-1426**
(740) 532-4133 • **http://www.tigertown.com/**
Grade Span: PK-12; **Agency Type:** 1
Schools: 6
3 Primary; 2 Middle; 1 High; 0 Other Level
6 Regular; 0 Special Education; 0 Vocational; 0 Alternative
0 Magnet; 0 Charter; 6 Title I Eligible; 2 School-wide Title I
Students: 1,626   (52.6% male; 47.3% female)
Individual Education Program: 289 (17.8%);
English Language Learner: 0 (0.0%); Migrant: n/a
Eligible for Free Lunch Program: 584 (35.9%)
Eligible for Reduced-Price Lunch Program: 74 (4.6%)
Teachers: 110.6 (14.7 to 1)
Librarians/Media Specialists: 2.0 (813.0 to 1)
Guidance Counselors: 7.0 (232.3 to 1)
Current Spending: ($ per student per year):
Total: $7,358; Instruction: $4,259; Support Services: $2,776

Enrollment, Drop-out Rates and Diploma Recipients by Race/Ethnicity

Category	Total	White	Black	Asian	AIAN	Hisp.
Enrollment (%)	100.0	88.7	7.4	0.2	0.0	0.1
Drop-out Rate (%)	4.7	4.3	6.5	0.0	n/a	0.0
H.S. Diplomas (#)	128	115	12	0	0	0

Rock Hill Local SD
2325a County Rd 26 • **Ironton, OH 45638-8385**
(740) 532-7030 • **http://rockhill.org/**
Grade Span: KG-12; **Agency Type:** 2
Schools: 3
1 Primary; 1 Middle; 1 High; 0 Other Level
3 Regular; 0 Special Education; 0 Vocational; 0 Alternative
0 Magnet; 0 Charter; 3 Title I Eligible; 1 School-wide Title I
Students: 1,926   (52.1% male; 47.8% female)
Individual Education Program: 296 (15.4%);
English Language Learner: 0 (0.0%); Migrant: n/a
Eligible for Free Lunch Program: 893 (46.4%)
Eligible for Reduced-Price Lunch Program: 270 (14.0%)
Teachers: 131.2 (14.7 to 1)
Librarians/Media Specialists: 2.0 (963.0 to 1)
Guidance Counselors: 2.0 (963.0 to 1)
Current Spending: ($ per student per year):
Total: $7,110; Instruction: $4,128; Support Services: $2,629

Enrollment, Drop-out Rates and Diploma Recipients by Race/Ethnicity

Category	Total	White	Black	Asian	AIAN	Hisp.
Enrollment (%)	100.0	99.1	0.5	0.1	0.1	0.1
Drop-out Rate (%)	3.4	3.4	0.0	n/a	n/a	n/a
H.S. Diplomas (#)	100	99	1	0	0	0

South Point Local SD
203 Park Ave • **South Point, OH 45680-9622**
(740) 377-4315
Grade Span: PK-12; **Agency Type:** 2
Schools: 4
2 Primary; 1 Middle; 1 High; 0 Other Level
4 Regular; 0 Special Education; 0 Vocational; 0 Alternative
0 Magnet; 0 Charter; 3 Title I Eligible; 2 School-wide Title I
Students: 1,866   (49.3% male; 50.6% female)
Individual Education Program: 402 (21.5%);
English Language Learner: 0 (0.0%); Migrant: n/a
Eligible for Free Lunch Program: 687 (36.8%)
Eligible for Reduced-Price Lunch Program: 109 (5.8%)
Teachers: 113.6 (16.4 to 1)
Librarians/Media Specialists: 1.0 (1,866.0 to 1)
Guidance Counselors: 2.0 (933.0 to 1)
Current Spending: ($ per student per year):
Total: $6,815; Instruction: $3,893; Support Services: $2,574

Category	Total	White	Black	Asian	AIAN	Hisp.
Enrollment (%)	100.0	92.0	6.0	0.3	0.0	0.2
Drop-out Rate (%)	2.3	2.4	2.1	n/a	n/a	n/a
H.S. Diplomas (#)	105	93	12	0	0	0

Licking County

Granville Ex Vill SD
130 N Granger • **Granville, OH 43023-0417**
Mailing Address: PO Box 417 • **Granville, OH 43023-0417**
(740) 587-0332
Grade Span: PK-12; **Agency Type:** 1
Schools: 4
1 Primary; 2 Middle; 1 High; 0 Other Level
4 Regular; 0 Special Education; 0 Vocational; 0 Alternative
0 Magnet; 0 Charter; 2 Title I Eligible; 0 School-wide Title I
Students: 2,113   (51.4% male; 48.5% female)
Individual Education Program: 224 (10.6%);
English Language Learner: 4 (0.2%); Migrant: n/a
Eligible for Free Lunch Program: 13 (0.6%)
Eligible for Reduced-Price Lunch Program: 12 (0.6%)
Teachers: 114.5 (18.5 to 1)
Librarians/Media Specialists: 3.0 (704.3 to 1)
Guidance Counselors: 6.0 (352.2 to 1)
Current Spending: ($ per student per year):
Total: $7,491; Instruction: $4,465; Support Services: $3,026

Enrollment, Drop-out Rates and Diploma Recipients by Race/Ethnicity

Category	Total	White	Black	Asian	AIAN	Hisp.
Enrollment (%)	100.0	97.2	0.8	1.4	0.0	0.5
Drop-out Rate (%)	0.3	0.3	0.0	0.0	n/a	0.0
H.S. Diplomas (#)	152	150	1	1	0	0

Heath City SD
107 Lancaster Dr • **Heath, OH 43056-1220**
(740) 522-2816
Grade Span: PK-12; **Agency Type:** 1
Schools: 4
2 Primary; 1 Middle; 1 High; 0 Other Level
4 Regular; 0 Special Education; 0 Vocational; 0 Alternative
0 Magnet; 0 Charter; 2 Title I Eligible; 0 School-wide Title I
Students: 1,707   (50.6% male; 49.3% female)
Individual Education Program: 177 (10.4%);
English Language Learner: 0 (0.0%); Migrant: n/a
Eligible for Free Lunch Program: 215 (12.6%)
Eligible for Reduced-Price Lunch Program: 80 (4.7%)
Teachers: 93.7 (18.2 to 1)
Librarians/Media Specialists: 2.0 (853.5 to 1)
Guidance Counselors: 3.0 (569.0 to 1)
Current Spending: ($ per student per year):
Total: $6,642; Instruction: $3,772; Support Services: $2,649

Enrollment, Drop-out Rates and Diploma Recipients by Race/Ethnicity

Category	Total	White	Black	Asian	AIAN	Hisp.
Enrollment (%)	100.0	91.3	2.8	1.3	0.3	0.8
Drop-out Rate (%)	2.7	2.3	9.1	0.0	100.0	0.0
H.S. Diplomas (#)	104	99	1	2	0	1

Lakewood Local SD
525 E Main St • **Hebron, OH 43025-9702**
Mailing Address: PO Box 70 • **Hebron, OH 43025-0070**
(740) 928-5878
Grade Span: PK-12; **Agency Type:** 2
Schools: 5
2 Primary; 2 Middle; 1 High; 0 Other Level
5 Regular; 0 Special Education; 0 Vocational; 0 Alternative
0 Magnet; 0 Charter; 2 Title I Eligible; 1 School-wide Title I
Students: 2,265   (52.7% male; 47.2% female)
Individual Education Program: 296 (13.1%);
English Language Learner: 6 (0.3%); Migrant: n/a
Eligible for Free Lunch Program: 520 (23.0%)
Eligible for Reduced-Price Lunch Program: 105 (4.6%)
Teachers: 153.0 (14.8 to 1)
Librarians/Media Specialists: 3.0 (755.0 to 1)
Guidance Counselors: 4.0 (566.3 to 1)
Current Spending: ($ per student per year):
Total: $7,014; Instruction: $4,097; Support Services: $2,644

Enrollment, Drop-out Rates and Diploma Recipients by Race/Ethnicity

Category	Total	White	Black	Asian	AIAN	Hisp.
Enrollment (%)	100.0	98.1	0.7	0.4	0.1	0.3
Drop-out Rate (%)	0.8	0.7	100.0	n/a	n/a	0.0
H.S. Diplomas (#)	155	155	0	0	0	0

Licking Heights Local SD
6539 Summit Rd SW • Summit Station, OH 43073-0027
(740) 927-6926
Grade Span: PK-12; Agency Type: 2
Schools: 3
   2 Primary; 0 Middle; 1 High; 0 Other Level
   3 Regular; 0 Special Education; 0 Vocational; 0 Alternative
   0 Magnet; 0 Charter; 2 Title I Eligible; 0 School-wide Title I
Students: 2,008   (51.5% male; 48.4% female)
   Individual Education Program: 225 (11.2%);
   English Language Learner: 30 (1.5%); Migrant: n/a
   Eligible for Free Lunch Program: 271 (13.5%)
   Eligible for Reduced-Price Lunch Program: 82 (4.1%)
Teachers: 111.5 (18.0 to 1)
Librarians/Media Specialists: 1.0 (2,008.0 to 1)
Guidance Counselors: 3.5 (573.7 to 1)
Current Spending: ($ per student per year):
   Total: $6,607; Instruction: $3,922; Support Services: $2,419
Enrollment, Drop-out Rates and Diploma Recipients by Race/Ethnicity

Category	Total	White	Black	Asian	AIAN	Hisp.
Enrollment (%)	100.0	77.4	18.5	0.4	0.1	1.2
Drop-out Rate (%)	2.5	1.7	6.8	0.0	n/a	0.0
H.S. Diplomas (#)	92	82	8	2	0	0

Licking Valley Local SD Sd
1379 Licking Valley Rd • Newark, OH 43055-9450
(740) 763-3525 • http://www.lickingvalley.k12.oh.us/
Grade Span: PK-12; Agency Type: 2
Schools: 6
   4 Primary; 1 Middle; 1 High; 0 Other Level
   6 Regular; 0 Special Education; 0 Vocational; 0 Alternative
   0 Magnet; 0 Charter; 5 Title I Eligible; 0 School-wide Title I
Students: 2,166   (51.1% male; 48.8% female)
   Individual Education Program: 276 (12.7%);
   English Language Learner: 0 (0.0%); Migrant: n/a
   Eligible for Free Lunch Program: 315 (14.5%)
   Eligible for Reduced-Price Lunch Program: 111 (5.1%)
Teachers: 130.7 (16.6 to 1)
Librarians/Media Specialists: 3.0 (722.0 to 1)
Guidance Counselors: 4.0 (541.5 to 1)
Current Spending: ($ per student per year):
   Total: $6,986; Instruction: $3,718; Support Services: $3,000
Enrollment, Drop-out Rates and Diploma Recipients by Race/Ethnicity

Category	Total	White	Black	Asian	AIAN	Hisp.
Enrollment (%)	100.0	97.9	0.8	0.1	0.0	0.3
Drop-out Rate (%)	2.7	2.6	0.0	0.0	33.3	0.0
H.S. Diplomas (#)	115	113	0	0	1	0

Newark City SD
85 E Main St • Newark, OH 43055-5605
(740) 345-9891 • http://www.newarkcity.k12.oh.us/
Grade Span: PK-12; Agency Type: 1
Schools: 16
   9 Primary; 6 Middle; 1 High; 0 Other Level
   16 Regular; 0 Special Education; 0 Vocational; 0 Alternative
   0 Magnet; 0 Charter; 11 Title I Eligible; 8 School-wide Title I
Students: 6,969   (50.9% male; 49.0% female)
   Individual Education Program: 929 (13.3%);
   English Language Learner: 22 (0.3%); Migrant: n/a
   Eligible for Free Lunch Program: 1,896 (27.2%)
   Eligible for Reduced-Price Lunch Program: 503 (7.2%)
Teachers: 417.9 (16.7 to 1)
Librarians/Media Specialists: 5.0 (1,393.8 to 1)
Guidance Counselors: 8.6 (810.3 to 1)
Current Spending: ($ per student per year):
   Total: $7,311; Instruction: $4,324; Support Services: $2,692
Enrollment, Drop-out Rates and Diploma Recipients by Race/Ethnicity

Category	Total	White	Black	Asian	AIAN	Hisp.
Enrollment (%)	100.0	91.3	3.8	0.6	0.1	0.4
Drop-out Rate (%)	9.0	8.7	10.1	20.0	0.0	0.0
H.S. Diplomas (#)	389	368	8	5	3	3

North Fork Local SD
312 Maple Ave • Utica, OH 43080-9756
Mailing Address: PO Box 497 • Utica, OH 43080-0497
(740) 892-3666
Grade Span: PK-12; Agency Type: 2
Schools: 4
   2 Primary; 1 Middle; 1 High; 0 Other Level
   4 Regular; 0 Special Education; 0 Vocational; 0 Alternative
   0 Magnet; 0 Charter; 3 Title I Eligible; 0 School-wide Title I
Students: 1,908   (51.9% male; 48.0% female)
   Individual Education Program: 255 (13.4%);
   English Language Learner: 1 (0.1%); Migrant: n/a
   Eligible for Free Lunch Program: 249 (13.1%)

Eligible for Reduced-Price Lunch Program: 151 (7.9%)
Teachers: 105.6 (18.1 to 1)
Librarians/Media Specialists: 2.0 (954.0 to 1)
Guidance Counselors: 4.0 (477.0 to 1)
Current Spending: ($ per student per year):
   Total: $6,451; Instruction: $3,763; Support Services: $2,402
Enrollment, Drop-out Rates and Diploma Recipients by Race/Ethnicity

Category	Total	White	Black	Asian	AIAN	Hisp.
Enrollment (%)	100.0	98.4	0.5	0.1	0.0	0.5
Drop-out Rate (%)	4.1	4.1	n/a	0.0	n/a	0.0
H.S. Diplomas (#)	117	116	0	0	0	0

Southwest Licking Local SD
927 S St • Etna, OH 43018-0180
Mailing Address: PO Box 180 • Etna, OH 43018-0180
(740) 927-3941 • http://www.swl.k12.oh.us/
Grade Span: PK-12; Agency Type: 2
Schools: 6
   4 Primary; 1 Middle; 1 High; 0 Other Level
   6 Regular; 0 Special Education; 0 Vocational; 0 Alternative
   0 Magnet; 0 Charter; 4 Title I Eligible; 0 School-wide Title I
Students: 3,527   (50.7% male; 49.2% female)
   Individual Education Program: 488 (13.8%);
   English Language Learner: 5 (0.1%); Migrant: 1 (<0.1%)
   Eligible for Free Lunch Program: 297 (8.4%)
   Eligible for Reduced-Price Lunch Program: 135 (3.8%)
Teachers: 206.0 (17.1 to 1)
Librarians/Media Specialists: 2.0 (1,763.5 to 1)
Guidance Counselors: 8.2 (430.1 to 1)
Current Spending: ($ per student per year):
   Total: $7,532; Instruction: $4,242; Support Services: $3,053
Enrollment, Drop-out Rates and Diploma Recipients by Race/Ethnicity

Category	Total	White	Black	Asian	AIAN	Hisp.
Enrollment (%)	100.0	94.9	1.7	0.3	0.3	0.9
Drop-out Rate (%)	2.4	2.3	0.0	0.0	33.3	0.0
H.S. Diplomas (#)	233	227	1	0	1	4

Logan County

Bellefontaine City Schools
820 Ludlow Rd • Bellefontaine, OH 43311-1852
(937) 593-9060 • http://www.bellefontaine.k12.oh.us/
Grade Span: KG-12; Agency Type: 1
Schools: 6
   4 Primary; 1 Middle; 1 High; 0 Other Level
   6 Regular; 0 Special Education; 0 Vocational; 0 Alternative
   0 Magnet; 0 Charter; 3 Title I Eligible; 1 School-wide Title I
Students: 2,808   (51.1% male; 48.8% female)
   Individual Education Program: 549 (19.6%);
   English Language Learner: 26 (0.9%); Migrant: n/a
   Eligible for Free Lunch Program: 668 (23.8%)
   Eligible for Reduced-Price Lunch Program: 148 (5.3%)
Teachers: 186.6 (15.0 to 1)
Librarians/Media Specialists: 2.0 (1,400.5 to 1)
Guidance Counselors: 5.8 (482.9 to 1)
Current Spending: ($ per student per year):
   Total: $6,966; Instruction: $4,220; Support Services: $2,441
Enrollment, Drop-out Rates and Diploma Recipients by Race/Ethnicity

Category	Total	White	Black	Asian	AIAN	Hisp.
Enrollment (%)	100.0	87.0	5.0	1.7	0.4	1.2
Drop-out Rate (%)	2.9	2.4	4.8	20.0	0.0	12.5
H.S. Diplomas (#)	199	183	15	0	0	1

Benjamin Logan Local SD
4626 County Rd 26 • Bellefontaine, OH 43311-9532
(937) 593-9211 •
http://www.benlogan.k12.oh.us/education/district/district.php?sectionid=1
Grade Span: KG-12; Agency Type: 2
Schools: 3
   1 Primary; 1 Middle; 1 High; 0 Other Level
   3 Regular; 0 Special Education; 0 Vocational; 0 Alternative
   0 Magnet; 0 Charter; 2 Title I Eligible; 0 School-wide Title I
Students: 1,966   (50.8% male; 49.1% female)
   Individual Education Program: 290 (14.8%);
   English Language Learner: 0 (0.0%); Migrant: n/a
   Eligible for Free Lunch Program: 195 (9.9%)
   Eligible for Reduced-Price Lunch Program: 56 (2.8%)
Teachers: 113.6 (17.3 to 1)
Librarians/Media Specialists: 2.0 (983.0 to 1)
Guidance Counselors: 4.0 (491.5 to 1)
Current Spending: ($ per student per year):
   Total: $6,445; Instruction: $3,727; Support Services: $2,404

Enrollment, Drop-out Rates and Diploma Recipients by Race/Ethnicity

Category	Total	White	Black	Asian	AIAN	Hisp.
Enrollment (%)	100.0	98.4	0.7	0.1	0.3	0.2
Drop-out Rate (%)	2.2	2.2	0.0	n/a	0.0	0.0
H.S. Diplomas (#)	131	128	1	0	0	1

Indian Lake Local SD

6210 State Route 235 N • Lewistown, OH 43333-9704
(937) 686-8601 • http://indianlake.k12.oh.us/
Grade Span: KG-12; **Agency Type:** 2
Schools: 4
  2 Primary; 1 Middle; 1 High; 0 Other Level
  4 Regular; 0 Special Education; 0 Vocational; 0 Alternative
  0 Magnet; 0 Charter; 2 Title I Eligible; 1 School-wide Title I
Students: 1,992 (50.8% male; 49.1% female)
  Individual Education Program: 359 (18.0%)
  English Language Learner: 0 (0.0%); Migrant: n/a
  Eligible for Free Lunch Program: 397 (19.9%)
  Eligible for Reduced-Price Lunch Program: 101 (5.1%)
Teachers: 126.2 (15.8 to 1)
Librarians/Media Specialists: 1.0 (1,992.0 to 1)
Guidance Counselors: 4.0 (498.0 to 1)
Current Spending: ($ per student per year):
  Total: $6,860; Instruction: $4,139; Support Services: $2,382

Enrollment, Drop-out Rates and Diploma Recipients by Race/Ethnicity

Category	Total	White	Black	Asian	AIAN	Hisp.
Enrollment (%)	100.0	98.8	0.3	0.3	0.2	0.3
Drop-out Rate (%)	4.4	4.4	0.0	0.0	n/a	n/a
H.S. Diplomas (#)	130	130	0	0	0	0

Lorain County

Amherst Ex Vill SD

185 Forest St • Amherst, OH 44001-1605
(440) 988-4406 • http://www.amherst.k12.oh.us/index.php
Grade Span: PK-12; **Agency Type:** 1
Schools: 6
  2 Primary; 3 Middle; 1 High; 0 Other Level
  6 Regular; 0 Special Education; 0 Vocational; 0 Alternative
  0 Magnet; 0 Charter; 0 Title I Eligible; 0 School-wide Title I
Students: 4,190 (50.6% male; 49.3% female)
  Individual Education Program: 512 (12.2%);
  English Language Learner: 0 (0.0%); Migrant: 1 (<0.1%)
  Eligible for Free Lunch Program: 268 (6.4%)
  Eligible for Reduced-Price Lunch Program: 162 (3.9%)
Teachers: 219.2 (19.1 to 1)
Librarians/Media Specialists: 0.3 (13,963.3 to 1)
Guidance Counselors: 6.0 (698.2 to 1)
Current Spending: ($ per student per year):
  Total: $6,637; Instruction: $4,060; Support Services: $2,319

Enrollment, Drop-out Rates and Diploma Recipients by Race/Ethnicity

Category	Total	White	Black	Asian	AIAN	Hisp.
Enrollment (%)	100.0	91.0	1.2	0.7	0.4	4.9
Drop-out Rate (%)	0.2	0.2	0.0	0.0	0.0	1.9
H.S. Diplomas (#)	281	249	8	3	1	19

Avon Lake City Schools

175 Avon Belden Rd • Avon Lake, OH 44012-1600
(440) 933-6210
Grade Span: PK-12; **Agency Type:** 1
Schools: 7
  4 Primary; 2 Middle; 1 High; 0 Other Level
  7 Regular; 0 Special Education; 0 Vocational; 0 Alternative
  0 Magnet; 0 Charter; 3 Title I Eligible; 0 School-wide Title I
Students: 3,343 (52.6% male; 47.3% female)
  Individual Education Program: 303 (9.1%);
  English Language Learner: 21 (0.6%); Migrant: 1 (<0.1%)
  Eligible for Free Lunch Program: 102 (3.1%)
  Eligible for Reduced-Price Lunch Program: 67 (2.0%)
Teachers: 209.8 (15.9 to 1)
Librarians/Media Specialists: 4.0 (835.8 to 1)
Guidance Counselors: 8.5 (393.3 to 1)
Current Spending: ($ per student per year):
  Total: $8,166; Instruction: $4,701; Support Services: $3,283

Enrollment, Drop-out Rates and Diploma Recipients by Race/Ethnicity

Category	Total	White	Black	Asian	AIAN	Hisp.
Enrollment (%)	100.0	96.6	0.5	1.1	0.0	0.9
Drop-out Rate (%)	1.7	1.7	0.0	0.0	n/a	0.0
H.S. Diplomas (#)	243	240	1	0	0	2

Avon Local SD

3075 Stoney Ridge Rd • Avon, OH 44011-1821
(440) 937-4680 • http://www.avon.k12.oh.us/
Grade Span: KG-12; **Agency Type:** 2
Schools: 5

  2 Primary; 2 Middle; 1 High; 0 Other Level
  5 Regular; 0 Special Education; 0 Vocational; 0 Alternative
  0 Magnet; 0 Charter; 0 Title I Eligible; 0 School-wide Title I
Students: 2,508 (49.9% male; 50.0% female)
  Individual Education Program: 343 (13.7%)
  English Language Learner: 3 (0.1%); Migrant: n/a
  Eligible for Free Lunch Program: 165 (6.7%)
  Eligible for Reduced-Price Lunch Program: 50 (2.0%)
Teachers: 148.7 (16.6 to 1)
Librarians/Media Specialists: 2.0 (1,235.0 to 1)
Guidance Counselors: 4.0 (617.5 to 1)
Current Spending: ($ per student per year):
  Total: $6,249; Instruction: $3,656; Support Services: $2,366

Enrollment, Drop-out Rates and Diploma Recipients by Race/Ethnicity

Category	Total	White	Black	Asian	AIAN	Hisp.
Enrollment (%)	100.0	91.3	3.1	1.9	0.2	2.3
Drop-out Rate (%)	0.4	0.4	0.0	0.0	0.0	0.0
H.S. Diplomas (#)	117	109	1	2	0	5

Clearview Local SD

4700 Broadway • Lorain, OH 44052-5542
(440) 233-5412
Grade Span: PK-12; **Agency Type:** 2
Schools: 3
  1 Primary; 1 Middle; 0 High; 1 Other Level
  3 Regular; 0 Special Education; 0 Vocational; 0 Alternative
  0 Magnet; 0 Charter; 3 Title I Eligible; 2 School-wide Title I
Students: 1,503 (49.1% male; 50.8% female)
  Individual Education Program: 208 (13.8%);
  English Language Learner: 20 (1.3%); Migrant: 1 (0.1%)
  Eligible for Free Lunch Program: 724 (48.2%)
  Eligible for Reduced-Price Lunch Program: 167 (11.1%)
Teachers: 98.2 (15.3 to 1)
Librarians/Media Specialists: 1.0 (1,503.0 to 1)
Guidance Counselors: 2.2 (683.2 to 1)
Current Spending: ($ per student per year):
  Total: $7,733; Instruction: $4,356; Support Services: $2,976

Enrollment, Drop-out Rates and Diploma Recipients by Race/Ethnicity

Category	Total	White	Black	Asian	AIAN	Hisp.
Enrollment (%)	100.0	59.5	16.8	0.4	0.3	18.2
Drop-out Rate (%)	1.1	0.3	2.6	0.0	0.0	3.2
H.S. Diplomas (#)	97	59	17	0	0	18

Elyria City SD

42101 Griswold Rd • Elyria, OH 44035-2117
(440) 284-8000 • http://www.elyriaschools.k12.oh.us/
Grade Span: KG-12; **Agency Type:** 1
Schools: 17
  12 Primary; 3 Middle; 1 High; 1 Other Level
  17 Regular; 0 Special Education; 0 Vocational; 0 Alternative
  0 Magnet; 0 Charter; 14 Title I Eligible; 9 School-wide Title I
Students: 8,127 (50.9% male; 49.0% female)
  Individual Education Program: 1,214 (14.9%);
  English Language Learner: 21 (0.3%); Migrant: 5 (0.1%)
  Eligible for Free Lunch Program: 2,914 (36.7%)
  Eligible for Reduced-Price Lunch Program: 737 (9.3%)
Teachers: 549.0 (14.4 to 1)
Librarians/Media Specialists: 9.0 (881.2 to 1)
Guidance Counselors: 21.0 (377.7 to 1)
Current Spending: ($ per student per year):
  Total: $8,236; Instruction: $4,752; Support Services: $3,180

Enrollment, Drop-out Rates and Diploma Recipients by Race/Ethnicity

Category	Total	White	Black	Asian	AIAN	Hisp.
Enrollment (%)	100.0	68.5	20.9	0.8	0.2	3.0
Drop-out Rate (%)	6.0	5.1	9.5	0.0	100.0	0.0
H.S. Diplomas (#)	362	288	55	4	1	7

Firelands Local SD

11970 Vermilion Rd • Oberlin, OH 44074-9495
(440) 965-5821 • http://www.firelandsschools.org/district/
Grade Span: PK-12; **Agency Type:** 2
Schools: 3
  1 Primary; 1 Middle; 1 High; 0 Other Level
  3 Regular; 0 Special Education; 0 Vocational; 0 Alternative
  0 Magnet; 0 Charter; 2 Title I Eligible; 0 School-wide Title I
Students: 2,239 (51.9% male; 48.0% female)
  Individual Education Program: 256 (11.4%);
  English Language Learner: 0 (0.0%); Migrant: 2 (0.1%)
  Eligible for Free Lunch Program: 221 (9.9%)
  Eligible for Reduced-Price Lunch Program: 84 (3.8%)
Teachers: 120.5 (18.4 to 1)
Librarians/Media Specialists: 1.0 (2,222.0 to 1)
Guidance Counselors: 4.0 (555.5 to 1)
Current Spending: ($ per student per year):
  Total: $6,574; Instruction: $4,011; Support Services: $2,308

Enrollment, Drop-out Rates and Diploma Recipients by Race/Ethnicity

Category	Total	White	Black	Asian	AIAN	Hisp.
Enrollment (%)	100.0	96.3	0.2	0.1	0.2	1.4
Drop-out Rate (%)	1.4	1.5	0.0	n/a	0.0	0.0
H.S. Diplomas (#)	140	138	0	0	2	0

Keystone Local SD

301 Liberty St • Lagrange, OH 44050-9496
Mailing Address: PO Box 65 • Lagrange, OH 44050-0065
(440) 355-5131
Grade Span: KG-12; **Agency Type:** 2
Schools: 4
  2 Primary; 1 Middle; 1 High; 0 Other Level
  4 Regular; 0 Special Education; 0 Vocational; 0 Alternative
  0 Magnet; 0 Charter; 3 Title I Eligible; 0 School-wide Title I
Students: 1,843 (50.2% male; 49.7% female)
  Individual Education Program: 183 (9.9%);
  English Language Learner: 0 (0.0%); Migrant: 1 (0.1%)
  Eligible for Free Lunch Program: 131 (7.2%)
  Eligible for Reduced-Price Lunch Program: 91 (5.0%)
Teachers: 96.6 (19.0 to 1)
Librarians/Media Specialists: 1.0 (1,831.0 to 1)
Guidance Counselors: 5.0 (366.2 to 1)
Current Spending: ($ per student per year):
  Total: $6,373; Instruction: $3,750; Support Services: $2,426
Enrollment, Drop-out Rates and Diploma Recipients by Race/Ethnicity

Category	Total	White	Black	Asian	AIAN	Hisp.
Enrollment (%)	100.0	98.1	0.4	0.1	0.0	0.4
Drop-out Rate (%)	1.1	1.1	0.0	0.0	n/a	0.0
H.S. Diplomas (#)	113	109	0	0	0	2

Lorain City SD

2350 Pole Ave • Lorain, OH 44052-4301
(440) 233-2271 • http://www.lorainschools.org/
Grade Span: PK-12; **Agency Type:** 1
Schools: 16
  11 Primary; 3 Middle; 2 High; 0 Other Level
  16 Regular; 0 Special Education; 0 Vocational; 0 Alternative
  0 Magnet; 0 Charter; 15 Title I Eligible; 11 School-wide Title I
Students: 10,320 (51.6% male; 48.3% female)
  Individual Education Program: 1,488 (14.4%);
  English Language Learner: 229 (2.2%); Migrant: 8 (0.1%)
  Eligible for Free Lunch Program: 5,522 (53.5%)
  Eligible for Reduced-Price Lunch Program: 971 (9.4%)
Teachers: 628.9 (16.4 to 1)
Librarians/Media Specialists: 5.0 (2,064.0 to 1)
Guidance Counselors: 16.0 (645.0 to 1)
Current Spending: ($ per student per year):
  Total: $8,391; Instruction: $5,604; Support Services: $2,402
Enrollment, Drop-out Rates and Diploma Recipients by Race/Ethnicity

Category	Total	White	Black	Asian	AIAN	Hisp.
Enrollment (%)	100.0	36.7	26.5	0.3	0.3	27.7
Drop-out Rate (%)	6.8	7.1	6.6	8.3	7.1	6.1
H.S. Diplomas (#)	476	203	113	1	4	148

Midview Local SD

1010 Vivian Dr • Grafton, OH 44044-1250
(440) 926-3737
Grade Span: KG-12; **Agency Type:** 2
Schools: 5
  2 Primary; 2 Middle; 1 High; 0 Other Level
  5 Regular; 0 Special Education; 0 Vocational; 0 Alternative
  0 Magnet; 0 Charter; 4 Title I Eligible; 0 School-wide Title I
Students: 3,464 (51.6% male; 48.3% female)
  Individual Education Program: 388 (11.2%);
  English Language Learner: 15 (0.4%); Migrant: n/a
  Eligible for Free Lunch Program: 423 (12.3%)
  Eligible for Reduced-Price Lunch Program: 164 (4.8%)
Teachers: 175.1 (19.6 to 1)
Librarians/Media Specialists: 2.0 (1,717.5 to 1)
Guidance Counselors: 6.0 (572.5 to 1)
Current Spending: ($ per student per year):
  Total: $6,574; Instruction: $3,648; Support Services: $2,737
Enrollment, Drop-out Rates and Diploma Recipients by Race/Ethnicity

Category	Total	White	Black	Asian	AIAN	Hisp.
Enrollment (%)	100.0	93.2	2.8	0.4	0.3	1.0
Drop-out Rate (%)	2.8	2.8	4.3	0.0	0.0	0.0
H.S. Diplomas (#)	208	200	6	0	0	1

North Ridgeville City SD

5490 Mills Creek Ln • North Ridgeville, OH 44039-2339
(440) 327-4444
Grade Span: KG-12; **Agency Type:** 1
Schools: 6
  4 Primary; 1 Middle; 1 High; 0 Other Level

  6 Regular; 0 Special Education; 0 Vocational; 0 Alternative
  0 Magnet; 0 Charter; 4 Title I Eligible; 0 School-wide Title I
Students: 3,550 (52.2% male; 47.7% female)
  Individual Education Program: 546 (15.4%);
  English Language Learner: 0 (0.0%); Migrant: 3 (0.1%)
  Eligible for Free Lunch Program: 355 (10.1%)
  Eligible for Reduced-Price Lunch Program: 112 (3.2%)
Teachers: 223.3 (15.7 to 1)
Librarians/Media Specialists: 4.0 (874.8 to 1)
Guidance Counselors: 11.0 (318.1 to 1)
Current Spending: ($ per student per year):
  Total: $7,061; Instruction: $4,246; Support Services: $2,584
Enrollment, Drop-out Rates and Diploma Recipients by Race/Ethnicity

Category	Total	White	Black	Asian	AIAN	Hisp.
Enrollment (%)	100.0	94.4	0.9	0.8	0.2	1.7
Drop-out Rate (%)	1.6	1.6	0.0	0.0	0.0	0.0
H.S. Diplomas (#)	198	191	1	3	0	3

Sheffield-Sheffield Lake City SD

1824 Harris Rd • Sheffield Village, OH 44054-2628
(440) 949-6181
Grade Span: PK-12; **Agency Type:** 1
Schools: 6
  3 Primary; 2 Middle; 1 High; 0 Other Level
  6 Regular; 0 Special Education; 0 Vocational; 0 Alternative
  0 Magnet; 0 Charter; 4 Title I Eligible; 0 School-wide Title I
Students: 2,084 (48.0% male; 51.9% female)
  Individual Education Program: 262 (12.6%);
  English Language Learner: 0 (0.0%); Migrant: n/a
  Eligible for Free Lunch Program: 330 (15.9%)
  Eligible for Reduced-Price Lunch Program: 159 (7.6%)
Teachers: 121.5 (17.1 to 1)
Librarians/Media Specialists: 0.0 (n/a to 1)
Guidance Counselors: 4.0 (520.0 to 1)
Current Spending: ($ per student per year):
  Total: $7,719; Instruction: $4,679; Support Services: $2,851
Enrollment, Drop-out Rates and Diploma Recipients by Race/Ethnicity

Category	Total	White	Black	Asian	AIAN	Hisp.
Enrollment (%)	100.0	91.2	1.3	0.6	0.5	4.0
Drop-out Rate (%)	1.6	1.6	0.0	0.0	0.0	5.0
H.S. Diplomas (#)	130	123	2	0	0	3

Wellington Ex Vill SD

201 S Main St • Wellington, OH 44090-1345
(440) 647-4286 • http://www.wellington.k12.oh.us/
Grade Span: KG-12; **Agency Type:** 1
Schools: 3
  1 Primary; 1 Middle; 1 High; 0 Other Level
  3 Regular; 0 Special Education; 0 Vocational; 0 Alternative
  0 Magnet; 0 Charter; 2 Title I Eligible; 0 School-wide Title I
Students: 1,648 (51.2% male; 48.7% female)
  Individual Education Program: 164 (10.0%);
  English Language Learner: 2 (0.1%); Migrant: 3 (0.2%)
  Eligible for Free Lunch Program: 260 (15.9%)
  Eligible for Reduced-Price Lunch Program: 161 (9.9%)
Teachers: 94.9 (17.2 to 1)
Librarians/Media Specialists: 2.0 (815.5 to 1)
Guidance Counselors: 4.0 (407.8 to 1)
Current Spending: ($ per student per year):
  Total: $7,020; Instruction: $4,184; Support Services: $2,564
Enrollment, Drop-out Rates and Diploma Recipients by Race/Ethnicity

Category	Total	White	Black	Asian	AIAN	Hisp.
Enrollment (%)	100.0	94.1	0.8	0.9	0.7	0.8
Drop-out Rate (%)	1.9	1.9	0.0	0.0	n/a	0.0
H.S. Diplomas (#)	109	107	1	0	0	1

Lucas County

Anthony Wayne Local SD

11012 Shepler St • Whitehouse, OH 43571-9612
Mailing Address: PO Box 2487 • Whitehouse, OH 43571-0487
(419) 877-5377 • http://198.234.116.31/
Grade Span: PK-12; **Agency Type:** 2
Schools: 6
  3 Primary; 2 Middle; 1 High; 0 Other Level
  6 Regular; 0 Special Education; 0 Vocational; 0 Alternative
  0 Magnet; 0 Charter; 4 Title I Eligible; 0 School-wide Title I
Students: 3,879 (49.8% male; 50.1% female)
  Individual Education Program: 266 (6.9%);
  English Language Learner: 0 (0.0%); Migrant: n/a
  Eligible for Free Lunch Program: 161 (4.2%)
  Eligible for Reduced-Price Lunch Program: 44 (1.1%)
Teachers: 214.6 (18.1 to 1)
Librarians/Media Specialists: 2.0 (1,939.5 to 1)
Guidance Counselors: 9.1 (426.3 to 1)

Current Spending: ($ per student per year):
    Total: $7,011; Instruction: $4,124; Support Services: $2,668
Enrollment, Drop-out Rates and Diploma Recipients by Race/Ethnicity

Category	Total	White	Black	Asian	AIAN	Hisp.
Enrollment (%)	100.0	96.1	0.9	0.7	0.1	1.6
Drop-out Rate (%)	2.0	2.0	33.3	0.0	0.0	0.0
H.S. Diplomas (#)	233	227	1	0	0	5

Maumee City SD
2345 Detroit Ave • Maumee, OH 43537-3712
(419) 893-3200 • http://www.maumee.k12.oh.us/
Grade Span: PK-12; **Agency Type:** 1
Schools: 6
    4 Primary; 1 Middle; 1 High; 0 Other Level
    6 Regular; 0 Special Education; 0 Vocational; 0 Alternative
    0 Magnet; 0 Charter; 5 Title I Eligible; 0 School-wide Title I
Students: 2,847   (53.7% male; 46.2% female)
    Individual Education Program: 424 (14.9%);
    English Language Learner: 9 (0.3%); Migrant: n/a
    Eligible for Free Lunch Program: 209 (7.3%)
    Eligible for Reduced-Price Lunch Program: 116 (4.1%)
Teachers: 197.2 (14.4 to 1)
Librarians/Media Specialists: 3.0 (949.0 to 1)
Guidance Counselors: 9.0 (316.3 to 1)
Current Spending: ($ per student per year):
    Total: $8,957; Instruction: $5,833; Support Services: $2,826
Enrollment, Drop-out Rates and Diploma Recipients by Race/Ethnicity

Category	Total	White	Black	Asian	AIAN	Hisp.
Enrollment (%)	100.0	90.9	4.2	1.2	0.3	2.6
Drop-out Rate (%)	1.4	1.2	4.3	0.0	n/a	5.3
H.S. Diplomas (#)	242	230	3	2	0	6

Ohio Virtual Academy
1657 Holland Rd Ste B • Maumee, OH 43537-1661
(419) 482-0948
Grade Span: KG-05; **Agency Type:** 7
Schools: 1
    0 Primary; 0 Middle; 0 High; 1 Other Level
    1 Regular; 0 Special Education; 0 Vocational; 0 Alternative
    0 Magnet; 1 Charter; 1 Title I Eligible; 0 School-wide Title I
Students: 2,135   (52.0% male; 47.9% female)
    Individual Education Program: 116 (5.4%);
    English Language Learner: 0 (0.0%); Migrant: n/a
    Eligible for Free Lunch Program: n/a
    Eligible for Reduced-Price Lunch Program: n/a
Teachers: 53.9 (39.6 to 1)
Librarians/Media Specialists: 0.0 (n/a to 1)
Guidance Counselors: 0.0 (n/a to 1)
Current Spending: ($ per student per year):
    Total: $4,285; Instruction: $3,073; Support Services: $1,212
Enrollment, Drop-out Rates and Diploma Recipients by Race/Ethnicity

Category	Total	White	Black	Asian	AIAN	Hisp.
Enrollment (%)	100.0	88.4	4.6	0.3	0.3	1.5
Drop-out Rate (%)	n/a	n/a	n/a	n/a	n/a	n/a
H.S. Diplomas (#)	n/a	n/a	n/a	n/a	n/a	n/a

Oregon City SD
5721 Seaman St • Oregon, OH 43616-2631
(419) 693-0661
Grade Span: PK-12; **Agency Type:** 1
Schools: 7
    4 Primary; 2 Middle; 1 High; 0 Other Level
    7 Regular; 0 Special Education; 0 Vocational; 0 Alternative
    0 Magnet; 0 Charter; 4 Title I Eligible; 0 School-wide Title I
Students: 3,862   (52.6% male; 47.3% female)
    Individual Education Program: 429 (11.1%);
    English Language Learner: 30 (0.8%); Migrant: n/a
    Eligible for Free Lunch Program: 503 (13.0%)
    Eligible for Reduced-Price Lunch Program: 235 (6.1%)
Teachers: 256.0 (15.1 to 1)
Librarians/Media Specialists: 4.0 (965.5 to 1)
Guidance Counselors: 8.0 (482.8 to 1)
Current Spending: ($ per student per year):
    Total: $8,406; Instruction: $5,092; Support Services: $3,032
Enrollment, Drop-out Rates and Diploma Recipients by Race/Ethnicity

Category	Total	White	Black	Asian	AIAN	Hisp.
Enrollment (%)	100.0	89.6	0.6	1.2	0.0	5.4
Drop-out Rate (%)	3.0	2.8	0.0	0.0	n/a	6.1
H.S. Diplomas (#)	225	204	1	4	0	12

Springfield Local Schools
6900 Hall St • Holland, OH 43528-9485
(419) 867-5600 • http://www.springfield.k12.oh.us/
Grade Span: PK-12; **Agency Type:** 2
Schools: 6

    4 Primary; 1 Middle; 1 High; 0 Other Level
    6 Regular; 0 Special Education; 0 Vocational; 0 Alternative
    0 Magnet; 0 Charter; 5 Title I Eligible; 0 School-wide Title I
Students: 3,779   (52.6% male; 47.3% female)
    Individual Education Program: 716 (18.9%);
    English Language Learner: 35 (0.9%); Migrant: n/a
    Eligible for Free Lunch Program: 783 (20.7%)
    Eligible for Reduced-Price Lunch Program: 244 (6.5%)
Teachers: 229.4 (16.5 to 1)
Librarians/Media Specialists: 2.8 (1,349.6 to 1)
Guidance Counselors: 7.0 (539.9 to 1)
Current Spending: ($ per student per year):
    Total: $8,316; Instruction: $5,300; Support Services: $2,723
Enrollment, Drop-out Rates and Diploma Recipients by Race/Ethnicity

Category	Total	White	Black	Asian	AIAN	Hisp.
Enrollment (%)	100.0	78.4	10.8	2.2	0.3	3.1
Drop-out Rate (%)	2.8	2.9	2.9	0.0	0.0	0.0
H.S. Diplomas (#)	236	208	15	6	0	4

Sylvania City SD
6850 Monroe St • Sylvania, OH 43560-1922
Mailing Address: PO Box 608 • Sylvania, OH 43560-0608
(419) 824-8501 • http://www.sylvania.k12.oh.us/
Grade Span: PK-12; **Agency Type:** 1
Schools: 12
    7 Primary; 3 Middle; 2 High; 0 Other Level
    12 Regular; 0 Special Education; 0 Vocational; 0 Alternative
    0 Magnet; 0 Charter; 7 Title I Eligible; 0 School-wide Title I
Students: 7,832   (51.1% male; 48.8% female)
    Individual Education Program: 1,024 (13.1%);
    English Language Learner: 25 (0.3%); Migrant: 5 (0.1%)
    Eligible for Free Lunch Program: 481 (6.1%)
    Eligible for Reduced-Price Lunch Program: 143 (1.8%)
Teachers: 499.7 (15.7 to 1)
Librarians/Media Specialists: 5.0 (1,566.4 to 1)
Guidance Counselors: 19.0 (412.2 to 1)
Current Spending: ($ per student per year):
    Total: $8,614; Instruction: $4,948; Support Services: $3,431
Enrollment, Drop-out Rates and Diploma Recipients by Race/Ethnicity

Category	Total	White	Black	Asian	AIAN	Hisp.
Enrollment (%)	100.0	89.9	3.1	3.3	0.0	1.6
Drop-out Rate (%)	1.8	1.7	1.5	0.0	50.0	2.9
H.S. Diplomas (#)	599	567	13	12	0	6

Toledo City SD
420 E Manhattan Blvd • Toledo, OH 43608-1200
(419) 729-8200 • http://www.tps.org/
Grade Span: PK-12; **Agency Type:** 1
Schools: 67
    46 Primary; 7 Middle; 8 High; 5 Other Level
    62 Regular; 1 Special Education; 2 Vocational; 1 Alternative
    0 Magnet; 0 Charter; 49 Title I Eligible; 19 School-wide Title I
Students: 34,486   (51.8% male; 48.1% female)
    Individual Education Program: 5,917 (17.2%);
    English Language Learner: 493 (1.4%); Migrant: n/a
    Eligible for Free Lunch Program: 17,885 (51.9%)
    Eligible for Reduced-Price Lunch Program: 1,676 (4.9%)
Teachers: 2,538.7 (13.6 to 1)
Librarians/Media Specialists: 24.0 (1,436.9 to 1)
Guidance Counselors: 67.0 (514.7 to 1)
Current Spending: ($ per student per year):
    Total: $10,156; Instruction: $5,940; Support Services: $3,732
Enrollment, Drop-out Rates and Diploma Recipients by Race/Ethnicity

Category	Total	White	Black	Asian	AIAN	Hisp.
Enrollment (%)	100.0	43.4	46.3	0.6	0.1	7.3
Drop-out Rate (%)	6.7	6.4	6.6	2.9	0.0	10.2
H.S. Diplomas (#)	1,478	784	602	16	0	74

Washington Local Schools
3505 W Lincolnshire Blvd • Toledo, OH 43606-1231
(419) 473-8220 • http://www.washloc.k12.oh.us/
Grade Span: PK-12; **Agency Type:** 2
Schools: 12
    9 Primary; 1 Middle; 1 High; 1 Other Level
    12 Regular; 0 Special Education; 0 Vocational; 0 Alternative
    0 Magnet; 0 Charter; 10 Title I Eligible; 2 School-wide Title I
Students: 6,942   (52.2% male; 47.7% female)
    Individual Education Program: 948 (13.7%);
    English Language Learner: 80 (1.2%); Migrant: n/a
    Eligible for Free Lunch Program: 1,359 (19.7%)
    Eligible for Reduced-Price Lunch Program: 400 (5.8%)
Teachers: 455.0 (15.2 to 1)
Librarians/Media Specialists: 3.5 (1,970.3 to 1)
Guidance Counselors: 15.0 (459.7 to 1)
Current Spending: ($ per student per year):
    Total: $8,392; Instruction: $5,083; Support Services: $3,064

Enrollment, Drop-out Rates and Diploma Recipients by Race/Ethnicity

Category	Total	White	Black	Asian	AIAN	Hisp.
Enrollment (%)	100.0	85.0	7.5	0.6	0.4	3.8
Drop-out Rate (%)	6.1	5.8	6.5	5.9	25.0	13.5
H.S. Diplomas (#)	448	404	22	5	1	14

Madison County

Jonathan Alder Local SD
6440 Kilbury Huber Rd • Plain City, OH 43064-9573
(614) 873-5621 • http://www.alder.k12.oh.us/metadot/index.pl
Grade Span: PK-12; **Agency Type:** 2
Schools: 4
  2 Primary; 1 Middle; 1 High; 0 Other Level
  4 Regular; 0 Special Education; 0 Vocational; 0 Alternative
  0 Magnet; 0 Charter; 1 Title I Eligible; 0 School-wide Title I
Students: 1,809   (50.9% male; 49.0% female)
  Individual Education Program: 197 (10.9%);
  English Language Learner: 0 (0.0%); Migrant: n/a
  Eligible for Free Lunch Program: 172 (9.5%)
  Eligible for Reduced-Price Lunch Program: 75 (4.1%)
Teachers: 90.6 (20.0 to 1)
Librarians/Media Specialists: 1.0 (1,809.0 to 1)
Guidance Counselors: 4.0 (452.3 to 1)
Current Spending: ($ per student per year):
  Total: $6,311; Instruction: $3,508; Support Services: $2,561
Enrollment, Drop-out Rates and Diploma Recipients by Race/Ethnicity

Category	Total	White	Black	Asian	AIAN	Hisp.
Enrollment (%)	100.0	97.9	1.2	0.3	0.0	0.5
Drop-out Rate (%)	2.2	2.2	0.0	0.0	n/a	0.0
H.S. Diplomas (#)	109	107	2	0	0	0

London City SD
60 S Walnut St • London, OH 43140-1246
(740) 852-5700 • http://www.london.k12.oh.us/
Grade Span: PK-12; **Agency Type:** 1
Schools: 6
  4 Primary; 1 Middle; 1 High; 0 Other Level
  6 Regular; 0 Special Education; 0 Vocational; 0 Alternative
  0 Magnet; 0 Charter; 3 Title I Eligible; 2 School-wide Title I
Students: 2,081   (51.1% male; 48.8% female)
  Individual Education Program: 324 (15.6%);
  English Language Learner: 31 (1.5%); Migrant: n/a
  Eligible for Free Lunch Program: 354 (17.0%)
  Eligible for Reduced-Price Lunch Program: 92 (4.4%)
Teachers: 134.0 (15.5 to 1)
Librarians/Media Specialists: 2.0 (1,040.5 to 1)
Guidance Counselors: 3.0 (693.7 to 1)
Current Spending: ($ per student per year):
  Total: $7,041; Instruction: $4,384; Support Services: $2,439
Enrollment, Drop-out Rates and Diploma Recipients by Race/Ethnicity

Category	Total	White	Black	Asian	AIAN	Hisp.
Enrollment (%)	100.0	86.1	8.9	1.5	0.0	1.3
Drop-out Rate (%)	4.5	4.5	5.7	0.0	n/a	0.0
H.S. Diplomas (#)	134	122	10	2	0	0

Madison-Plains Local SD
55 Linson Rd • London, OH 43140-9751
(740) 852-0290
Grade Span: KG-12; **Agency Type:** 2
Schools: 6
  5 Primary; 0 Middle; 1 High; 0 Other Level
  6 Regular; 0 Special Education; 0 Vocational; 0 Alternative
  0 Magnet; 0 Charter; 3 Title I Eligible; 0 School-wide Title I
Students: 1,627   (51.2% male; 48.7% female)
  Individual Education Program: 188 (11.6%);
  English Language Learner: 8 (0.5%); Migrant: n/a
  Eligible for Free Lunch Program: 184 (11.3%)
  Eligible for Reduced-Price Lunch Program: 91 (5.6%)
Teachers: 95.0 (17.1 to 1)
Librarians/Media Specialists: 1.0 (1,627.0 to 1)
Guidance Counselors: 2.0 (813.5 to 1)
Current Spending: ($ per student per year):
  Total: $7,094; Instruction: $4,143; Support Services: $2,684
Enrollment, Drop-out Rates and Diploma Recipients by Race/Ethnicity

Category	Total	White	Black	Asian	AIAN	Hisp.
Enrollment (%)	100.0	99.1	0.1	0.4	0.0	0.3
Drop-out Rate (%)	2.4	2.4	n/a	0.0	n/a	0.0
H.S. Diplomas (#)	127	127	0	0	0	0

Mahoning County

Austintown Local SD
225 Idaho Rd • Youngstown, OH 44515-3703
(330) 797-3900 • http://www.austintown.k12.oh.us/
Grade Span: PK-12; **Agency Type:** 2
Schools: 8
  5 Primary; 2 Middle; 1 High; 0 Other Level
  8 Regular; 0 Special Education; 0 Vocational; 0 Alternative
  0 Magnet; 0 Charter; 5 Title I Eligible; 0 School-wide Title I
Students: 5,046   (51.4% male; 48.5% female)
  Individual Education Program: 866 (17.2%);
  English Language Learner: 7 (0.1%); Migrant: n/a
  Eligible for Free Lunch Program: 971 (19.2%)
  Eligible for Reduced-Price Lunch Program: 361 (7.2%)
Teachers: 291.5 (17.3 to 1)
Librarians/Media Specialists: 3.0 (1,682.0 to 1)
Guidance Counselors: 12.0 (420.5 to 1)
Current Spending: ($ per student per year):
  Total: $7,632; Instruction: $4,755; Support Services: $2,593
Enrollment, Drop-out Rates and Diploma Recipients by Race/Ethnicity

Category	Total	White	Black	Asian	AIAN	Hisp.
Enrollment (%)	100.0	89.3	6.9	0.7	0.2	1.5
Drop-out Rate (%)	0.3	0.2	2.0	0.0	n/a	0.0
H.S. Diplomas (#)	351	318	21	5	0	6

Boardman Local SD
7410 Market St • Youngstown, OH 44512-5612
(330) 726-3404 • http://www.boardman.k12.oh.us/
Grade Span: PK-12; **Agency Type:** 2
Schools: 7
  4 Primary; 2 Middle; 1 High; 0 Other Level
  7 Regular; 0 Special Education; 0 Vocational; 0 Alternative
  0 Magnet; 0 Charter; 5 Title I Eligible; 0 School-wide Title I
Students: 4,897   (51.8% male; 48.1% female)
  Individual Education Program: 451 (9.2%);
  English Language Learner: 56 (1.1%); Migrant: n/a
  Eligible for Free Lunch Program: 606 (12.4%)
  Eligible for Reduced-Price Lunch Program: 259 (5.3%)
Teachers: 298.8 (16.4 to 1)
Librarians/Media Specialists: 3.0 (1,632.3 to 1)
Guidance Counselors: 11.0 (445.2 to 1)
Current Spending: ($ per student per year):
  Total: $7,614; Instruction: $4,572; Support Services: $2,784
Enrollment, Drop-out Rates and Diploma Recipients by Race/Ethnicity

Category	Total	White	Black	Asian	AIAN	Hisp.
Enrollment (%)	100.0	88.6	5.5	2.2	0.1	1.4
Drop-out Rate (%)	1.2	1.1	4.0	0.0	0.0	0.0
H.S. Diplomas (#)	380	357	7	8	0	8

Campbell City SD
280 6th St • Campbell, OH 44405-1325
(330) 799-8777
Grade Span: PK-12; **Agency Type:** 1
Schools: 3
  1 Primary; 1 Middle; 1 High; 0 Other Level
  3 Regular; 0 Special Education; 0 Vocational; 0 Alternative
  0 Magnet; 0 Charter; 3 Title I Eligible; 3 School-wide Title I
Students: 1,579   (52.2% male; 47.7% female)
  Individual Education Program: 239 (15.1%);
  English Language Learner: 29 (1.8%); Migrant: n/a
  Eligible for Free Lunch Program: 678 (42.9%)
  Eligible for Reduced-Price Lunch Program: 108 (6.8%)
Teachers: 100.0 (15.8 to 1)
Librarians/Media Specialists: 2.0 (789.5 to 1)
Guidance Counselors: 2.0 (789.5 to 1)
Current Spending: ($ per student per year):
  Total: $7,882; Instruction: $4,872; Support Services: $2,700
Enrollment, Drop-out Rates and Diploma Recipients by Race/Ethnicity

Category	Total	White	Black	Asian	AIAN	Hisp.
Enrollment (%)	100.0	50.2	28.4	0.1	0.0	14.8
Drop-out Rate (%)	0.2	0.3	0.0	n/a	n/a	0.0
H.S. Diplomas (#)	100	65	23	0	0	12

Canfield Local SD
100 Wadsworth St • Canfield, OH 44406-1451
(330) 533-3303 • http://canfield.access-k12.org/
Grade Span: PK-12; **Agency Type:** 2
Schools: 4
  2 Primary; 1 Middle; 1 High; 0 Other Level
  4 Regular; 0 Special Education; 0 Vocational; 0 Alternative
  0 Magnet; 0 Charter; 3 Title I Eligible; 0 School-wide Title I
Students: 3,097   (51.2% male; 48.7% female)
  Individual Education Program: 315 (10.2%);
  English Language Learner: 7 (0.2%); Migrant: 1 (<0.1%)

Eligible for Free Lunch Program: 92 (3.0%)
Eligible for Reduced-Price Lunch Program: 61 (2.0%)
Teachers: 181.0 (17.1 to 1)
Librarians/Media Specialists: 2.0 (1,548.5 to 1)
Guidance Counselors: 4.0 (774.3 to 1)
Current Spending: ($ per student per year):
Total: $6,695; Instruction: $4,058; Support Services: $2,440
Enrollment, Drop-out Rates and Diploma Recipients by Race/Ethnicity

Category	Total	White	Black	Asian	AIAN	Hisp.
Enrollment (%)	100.0	95.9	0.7	2.2		0.5
Drop-out Rate (%)	0.3	0.3	0.0	0.0	n/a	0.0
H.S. Diplomas (#)	225	212	1	7	0	5

Poland Local SD
30 Riverside Dr • Poland, OH 44514-2049
(330) 757-7000 • http://www.polandbulldogs.com/
Grade Span: PK-12; **Agency Type:** 2
Schools: 6
3 Primary; 2 Middle; 1 High; 0 Other Level
6 Regular; 0 Special Education; 0 Vocational; 0 Alternative
0 Magnet; 0 Charter; 3 Title I Eligible; 0 School-wide Title I
Students: 2,514 (51.6% male; 48.3% female)
Individual Education Program: 286 (11.4%);
English Language Learner: 0 (0.0%); Migrant: n/a
Eligible for Free Lunch Program: 88 (3.5%)
Eligible for Reduced-Price Lunch Program: 50 (2.0%)
Teachers: 122.8 (20.5 to 1)
Librarians/Media Specialists: 2.0 (1,257.0 to 1)
Guidance Counselors: 4.0 (628.5 to 1)
Current Spending: ($ per student per year):
Total: $6,784; Instruction: $4,326; Support Services: $2,166
Enrollment, Drop-out Rates and Diploma Recipients by Race/Ethnicity

Category	Total	White	Black	Asian	AIAN	Hisp.
Enrollment (%)	100.0	96.5	0.4	0.5	0.3	1.2
Drop-out Rate (%)	0.2	0.2	0.0	0.0	0.0	0.0
H.S. Diplomas (#)	198	193	0	1	1	3

Struthers City SD
99 Euclid Ave • Struthers, OH 44471-1831
(330) 750-1061
Grade Span: PK-12; **Agency Type:** 1
Schools: 3
1 Primary; 1 Middle; 1 High; 0 Other Level
3 Regular; 0 Special Education; 0 Vocational; 0 Alternative
0 Magnet; 0 Charter; 3 Title I Eligible; 2 School-wide Title I
Students: 2,004 (50.7% male; 49.2% female)
Individual Education Program: 244 (12.2%);
English Language Learner: 0 (0.0%); Migrant: n/a
Eligible for Free Lunch Program: 788 (39.3%)
Eligible for Reduced-Price Lunch Program: 282 (14.1%)
Teachers: 117.8 (17.0 to 1)
Librarians/Media Specialists: 1.0 (2,004.0 to 1)
Guidance Counselors: 4.0 (501.0 to 1)
Current Spending: ($ per student per year):
Total: $7,543; Instruction: $4,910; Support Services: $2,349
Enrollment, Drop-out Rates and Diploma Recipients by Race/Ethnicity

Category	Total	White	Black	Asian	AIAN	Hisp.
Enrollment (%)	100.0	94.8	1.9	0.0	0.4	1.7
Drop-out Rate (%)	2.5	2.5	10.0	0.0	0.0	0.0
H.S. Diplomas (#)	123	121	0	0	0	1

West Branch Local SD
14277 S Main St • Beloit, OH 44609-9504
(330) 938-9324
Grade Span: PK-12; **Agency Type:** 2
Schools: 6
4 Primary; 1 Middle; 1 High; 0 Other Level
6 Regular; 0 Special Education; 0 Vocational; 0 Alternative
0 Magnet; 0 Charter; 5 Title I Eligible; 0 School-wide Title I
Students: 2,443 (52.0% male; 47.9% female)
Individual Education Program: 263 (10.8%);
English Language Learner: 2 (0.1%); Migrant: n/a
Eligible for Free Lunch Program: 470 (19.2%)
Eligible for Reduced-Price Lunch Program: 162 (6.6%)
Teachers: 131.6 (18.6 to 1)
Librarians/Media Specialists: 1.0 (2,443.0 to 1)
Guidance Counselors: 5.0 (488.6 to 1)
Current Spending: ($ per student per year):
Total: $6,485; Instruction: $3,776; Support Services: $2,415
Enrollment, Drop-out Rates and Diploma Recipients by Race/Ethnicity

Category	Total	White	Black	Asian	AIAN	Hisp.
Enrollment (%)	100.0	99.0	0.2	0.1	0.4	0.1
Drop-out Rate (%)	0.4	0.4	0.0	0.0	0.0	n/a
H.S. Diplomas (#)	187	185	1	0	1	0

Youngstown City SD
20 W Wood St • Youngstown, OH 44503-1028
Mailing Address: PO Box 550 • Youngstown, OH 44501-0550
(330) 744-6900 • http://www.youngstown.k12.oh.us/
Grade Span: KG-12; **Agency Type:** 1
Schools: 26
13 Primary; 4 Middle; 6 High; 2 Other Level
23 Regular; 0 Special Education; 1 Vocational; 1 Alternative
0 Magnet; 0 Charter; 21 Title I Eligible; 18 School-wide Title I
Students: 9,748 (51.2% male; 48.7% female)
Individual Education Program: 1,976 (20.3%);
English Language Learner: 31 (0.3%); Migrant: n/a
Eligible for Free Lunch Program: 6,378 (66.8%)
Eligible for Reduced-Price Lunch Program: 496 (5.2%)
Teachers: 717.7 (13.3 to 1)
Librarians/Media Specialists: 6.0 (1,592.3 to 1)
Guidance Counselors: 26.0 (367.5 to 1)
Current Spending: ($ per student per year):
Total: $11,064; Instruction: $6,201; Support Services: $4,526
Enrollment, Drop-out Rates and Diploma Recipients by Race/Ethnicity

Category	Total	White	Black	Asian	AIAN	Hisp.
Enrollment (%)	100.0	24.2	66.4	0.2	0.0	6.2
Drop-out Rate (%)	8.7	7.8	9.3	0.0	0.0	6.4
H.S. Diplomas (#)	421	134	262	1	0	22

Marion County

Elgin Local SD
4616 Larue Prospect Rd W • Marion, OH 43302-8859
(740) 382-1101 • http://www.treca.org/schools/elgin/
Grade Span: PK-12; **Agency Type:** 2
Schools: 4
2 Primary; 1 Middle; 1 High; 0 Other Level
4 Regular; 0 Special Education; 0 Vocational; 0 Alternative
0 Magnet; 0 Charter; 1 Title I Eligible; 0 School-wide Title I
Students: 1,627 (50.8% male; 49.1% female)
Individual Education Program: 194 (11.9%);
English Language Learner: 6 (0.4%); Migrant: n/a
Eligible for Free Lunch Program: 306 (18.8%)
Eligible for Reduced-Price Lunch Program: 116 (7.1%)
Teachers: 108.8 (15.0 to 1)
Librarians/Media Specialists: 2.0 (813.5 to 1)
Guidance Counselors: 7.0 (232.4 to 1)
Current Spending: ($ per student per year):
Total: $6,601; Instruction: $3,979; Support Services: $2,350
Enrollment, Drop-out Rates and Diploma Recipients by Race/Ethnicity

Category	Total	White	Black	Asian	AIAN	Hisp.
Enrollment (%)	100.0	98.0	0.2	0.1	0.2	0.9
Drop-out Rate (%)	1.4	1.4	n/a	0.0	n/a	n/a
H.S. Diplomas (#)	125	124	0	1	0	0

Marion City SD
910 E Church St • Marion, OH 43302-4317
(740) 387-3300 • http://www.marioncity.k12.oh.us/
Grade Span: PK-12; **Agency Type:** 1
Schools: 19
10 Primary; 4 Middle; 1 High; 0 Other Level
15 Regular; 0 Special Education; 0 Vocational; 0 Alternative
0 Magnet; 0 Charter; 11 Title I Eligible; 7 School-wide Title I
Students: 5,592 (51.9% male; 48.0% female)
Individual Education Program: 1,071 (19.2%);
English Language Learner: 10 (0.2%); Migrant: 4 (0.1%)
Eligible for Free Lunch Program: 1,767 (31.6%)
Eligible for Reduced-Price Lunch Program: 472 (8.4%)
Teachers: 351.5 (15.9 to 1)
Librarians/Media Specialists: 4.0 (1,398.0 to 1)
Guidance Counselors: 9.6 (582.5 to 1)
Current Spending: ($ per student per year):
Total: $7,439; Instruction: $4,821; Support Services: $2,282
Enrollment, Drop-out Rates and Diploma Recipients by Race/Ethnicity

Category	Total	White	Black	Asian	AIAN	Hisp.
Enrollment (%)	100.0	88.3	7.2	0.5	0.0	2.3
Drop-out Rate (%)	6.8	6.9	3.7	15.4	n/a	8.7
H.S. Diplomas (#)	280	251	22	0	0	4

River Valley Local SD
197 Brockelsby Rd • Caledonia, OH 43314
(740) 725-5400
Grade Span: PK-12; **Agency Type:** 2
Schools: 4
2 Primary; 1 Middle; 1 High; 0 Other Level
4 Regular; 0 Special Education; 0 Vocational; 0 Alternative
0 Magnet; 0 Charter; 2 Title I Eligible; 0 School-wide Title I
Students: 1,831 (53.0% male; 46.9% female)
Individual Education Program: 213 (11.6%);

English Language Learner: 0 (0.0%); Migrant: n/a
Eligible for Free Lunch Program: 262 (14.3%)
Eligible for Reduced-Price Lunch Program: 124 (6.8%)
Teachers: 105.3 (17.4 to 1)
Librarians/Media Specialists: 1.0 (1,831.0 to 1)
Guidance Counselors: 3.0 (610.3 to 1)
Current Spending: ($ per student per year):
Total: $6,999; Instruction: $4,119; Support Services: $2,618
Enrollment, Drop-out Rates and Diploma Recipients by Race/Ethnicity

Category	Total	White	Black	Asian	AIAN	Hisp.
Enrollment (%)	100.0	97.4	0.5	0.5	0.0	0.8
Drop-out Rate (%)	1.3	1.3	0.0	0.0	n/a	0.0
H.S. Diplomas (#)	139	137	0	1	0	1

Medina County

Black River Local SD
257 County Rd 40 - A • Sullivan, OH 44880-9731
(419) 736-3300 • http://www.leeca.esu.k12.oh.us/black_river/index.html
Grade Span: PK-12; **Agency Type:** 2
Schools: 3
1 Primary; 1 Middle; 1 High; 0 Other Level
3 Regular; 0 Special Education; 0 Vocational; 0 Alternative
0 Magnet; 0 Charter; 2 Title I Eligible; 0 School-wide Title I
Students: 1,669 (53.1% male; 46.8% female)
Individual Education Program: 177 (10.6%);
English Language Learner: 0 (0.0%); Migrant: 2 (0.1%)
Eligible for Free Lunch Program: 248 (14.9%)
Eligible for Reduced-Price Lunch Program: 92 (5.5%)
Teachers: 95.0 (17.6 to 1)
Librarians/Media Specialists: 2.0 (834.5 to 1)
Guidance Counselors: 7.0 (238.4 to 1)
Current Spending: ($ per student per year):
Total: $6,302; Instruction: $3,879; Support Services: $2,201
Enrollment, Drop-out Rates and Diploma Recipients by Race/Ethnicity

Category	Total	White	Black	Asian	AIAN	Hisp.
Enrollment (%)	100.0	96.5	1.4	0.6	0.1	0.6
Drop-out Rate (%)	0.8	0.8	0.0	0.0	0.0	0.0
H.S. Diplomas (#)	98	97	0	0	1	0

Brunswick City SD
3643 Center Rd • Brunswick, OH 44212-3619
(330) 225-7731 • http://www.bcsoh.org/
Grade Span: PK-12; **Agency Type:** 1
Schools: 11
7 Primary; 3 Middle; 1 High; 0 Other Level
11 Regular; 0 Special Education; 0 Vocational; 0 Alternative
0 Magnet; 0 Charter; 6 Title I Eligible; 1 School-wide Title I
Students: 7,254 (50.5% male; 49.4% female)
Individual Education Program: 790 (10.9%);
English Language Learner: 28 (0.4%); Migrant: n/a
Eligible for Free Lunch Program: 577 (8.0%)
Eligible for Reduced-Price Lunch Program: 310 (4.3%)
Teachers: 404.5 (17.9 to 1)
Librarians/Media Specialists: 4.0 (1,813.5 to 1)
Guidance Counselors: 12.1 (599.5 to 1)
Current Spending: ($ per student per year):
Total: $7,376; Instruction: $4,470; Support Services: $2,679
Enrollment, Drop-out Rates and Diploma Recipients by Race/Ethnicity

Category	Total	White	Black	Asian	AIAN	Hisp.
Enrollment (%)	100.0	96.1	0.7	0.8	0.2	0.9
Drop-out Rate (%)	1.1	1.1	7.7	0.0	0.0	0.0
H.S. Diplomas (#)	475	466	1	4	0	2

Buckeye Local SD
3044 Columbia Rd • Medina, OH 44256-9411
(330) 722-8257 • http://www.buckeye.k12.oh.us/
Grade Span: PK-12; **Agency Type:** 2
Schools: 5
3 Primary; 1 Middle; 1 High; 0 Other Level
5 Regular; 0 Special Education; 0 Vocational; 0 Alternative
0 Magnet; 0 Charter; 2 Title I Eligible; 0 School-wide Title I
Students: 2,456 (50.7% male; 49.2% female)
Individual Education Program: 285 (11.6%);
English Language Learner: 0 (0.0%); Migrant: n/a
Eligible for Free Lunch Program: 270 (11.0%)
Eligible for Reduced-Price Lunch Program: 41 (1.7%)
Teachers: 143.8 (17.1 to 1)
Librarians/Media Specialists: 1.0 (2,453.0 to 1)
Guidance Counselors: 5.0 (490.6 to 1)
Current Spending: ($ per student per year):
Total: $7,713; Instruction: $4,606; Support Services: $2,904

Enrollment, Drop-out Rates and Diploma Recipients by Race/Ethnicity

Category	Total	White	Black	Asian	AIAN	Hisp.
Enrollment (%)	100.0	95.6	1.8	0.6	0.2	0.4
Drop-out Rate (%)	1.5	1.4	0.0	11.1	0.0	n/a
H.S. Diplomas (#)	182	177	1	2	1	0

Cloverleaf Local SD
8525 Friendsville Rd • Lodi, OH 44254-9706
(330) 948-2500 • http://www.cls.k12.oh.us/
Grade Span: PK-12; **Agency Type:** 2
Schools: 7
5 Primary; 1 Middle; 1 High; 0 Other Level
7 Regular; 0 Special Education; 0 Vocational; 0 Alternative
0 Magnet; 0 Charter; 3 Title I Eligible; 0 School-wide Title I
Students: 3,568 (51.5% male; 48.4% female)
Individual Education Program: 427 (12.0%);
English Language Learner: 0 (0.0%); Migrant: 4 (0.1%)
Eligible for Free Lunch Program: 441 (12.4%)
Eligible for Reduced-Price Lunch Program: 256 (7.2%)
Teachers: 196.9 (18.1 to 1)
Librarians/Media Specialists: 2.0 (1,782.5 to 1)
Guidance Counselors: 7.0 (509.3 to 1)
Current Spending: ($ per student per year):
Total: $6,599; Instruction: $3,918; Support Services: $2,433
Enrollment, Drop-out Rates and Diploma Recipients by Race/Ethnicity

Category	Total	White	Black	Asian	AIAN	Hisp.
Enrollment (%)	100.0	97.9	0.2	0.3	0.2	0.8
Drop-out Rate (%)	1.6	1.6	0.0	0.0	n/a	0.0
H.S. Diplomas (#)	273	272	0	0	0	1

Highland Local SD
3880 Ridge Rd • Medina, OH 44256-7920
(330) 239-1901 • http://www.highlandschools.org/
Grade Span: PK-12; **Agency Type:** 2
Schools: 5
2 Primary; 1 Middle; 1 High; 0 Other Level
4 Regular; 0 Special Education; 0 Vocational; 0 Alternative
0 Magnet; 0 Charter; 3 Title I Eligible; 0 School-wide Title I
Students: 2,780 (51.3% male; 48.6% female)
Individual Education Program: 273 (9.8%);
English Language Learner: 1 (<0.1%); Migrant: 2 (0.1%)
Eligible for Free Lunch Program: 90 (3.2%)
Eligible for Reduced-Price Lunch Program: 59 (2.1%)
Teachers: 155.1 (17.9 to 1)
Librarians/Media Specialists: 3.0 (926.3 to 1)
Guidance Counselors: 5.0 (555.8 to 1)
Current Spending: ($ per student per year):
Total: $6,649; Instruction: $3,928; Support Services: $2,490
Enrollment, Drop-out Rates and Diploma Recipients by Race/Ethnicity

Category	Total	White	Black	Asian	AIAN	Hisp.
Enrollment (%)	100.0	98.7	0.2	0.6	0.0	0.3
Drop-out Rate (%)	1.6	1.6	0.0	0.0	n/a	0.0
H.S. Diplomas (#)	196	195	0	1	0	0

Medina City SD
120 W Washington St • Medina, OH 44256-2260
(330) 636-3000 • http://www.mcsoh.org/
Grade Span: PK-12; **Agency Type:** 1
Schools: 9
6 Primary; 2 Middle; 1 High; 0 Other Level
9 Regular; 0 Special Education; 0 Vocational; 0 Alternative
0 Magnet; 0 Charter; 3 Title I Eligible; 0 School-wide Title I
Students: 7,323 (50.9% male; 49.0% female)
Individual Education Program: 1,094 (14.9%);
English Language Learner: 13 (0.2%); Migrant: 2 (<0.1%)
Eligible for Free Lunch Program: 383 (5.2%)
Eligible for Reduced-Price Lunch Program: 151 (2.1%)
Teachers: 470.2 (15.6 to 1)
Librarians/Media Specialists: 7.0 (1,046.1 to 1)
Guidance Counselors: 12.0 (610.3 to 1)
Current Spending: ($ per student per year):
Total: $8,914; Instruction: $5,358; Support Services: $3,372
Enrollment, Drop-out Rates and Diploma Recipients by Race/Ethnicity

Category	Total	White	Black	Asian	AIAN	Hisp.
Enrollment (%)	100.0	93.6	2.5	0.9	0.2	0.6
Drop-out Rate (%)	0.3	0.3	0.0	0.0	n/a	0.0
H.S. Diplomas (#)	501	470	16	6	0	4

Wadsworth City SD
360 College St • Wadsworth, OH 44281-1146
(330) 336-3571 • http://www.wadsworth.k12.oh.us/
Grade Span: PK-12; **Agency Type:** 1
Schools: 8
5 Primary; 1 Middle; 1 High; 1 Other Level
8 Regular; 0 Special Education; 0 Vocational; 0 Alternative

0 Magnet; 0 Charter; 4 Title I Eligible; 0 School-wide Title I
Students: 4,695   (52.7% male; 47.2% female)
   Individual Education Program: 462 (9.8%);
   English Language Learner: 4 (0.1%); Migrant: n/a
   Eligible for Free Lunch Program: 331 (7.1%)
   Eligible for Reduced-Price Lunch Program: 148 (3.2%)
Teachers: 237.0 (19.8 to 1)
Librarians/Media Specialists: 2.0 (2,347.5 to 1)
Guidance Counselors: 8.0 (586.9 to 1)
Current Spending: ($ per student per year):
   Total: $6,669; Instruction: $3,773; Support Services: $2,667
Enrollment, Drop-out Rates and Diploma Recipients by Race/Ethnicity

Category	Total	White	Black	Asian	AIAN	Hisp.
Enrollment (%)	100.0	97.3	0.4	0.7	0.2	0.6
Drop-out Rate (%)	1.9	1.9	0.0	0.0	0.0	0.0
H.S. Diplomas (#)	327	319	3	3	0	1

Meigs County

Meigs Local SD
320 E Main St • Pomeroy, OH 45769-1096
Mailing Address: PO Box 272 • Pomeroy, OH 45769-0272
(740) 992-2153
Grade Span: PK-12; **Agency Type:** 2
Schools: 4
   2 Primary; 1 Middle; 1 High; 0 Other Level
   4 Regular; 0 Special Education; 0 Vocational; 0 Alternative
   0 Magnet; 0 Charter; 4 Title I Eligible; 0 School-wide Title I
Students: 2,092   (50.7% male; 49.2% female)
   Individual Education Program: 411 (19.6%);
   English Language Learner: 0 (0.0%); Migrant: n/a
   Eligible for Free Lunch Program: 895 (42.8%)
   Eligible for Reduced-Price Lunch Program: 184 (8.8%)
Teachers: 158.0 (13.2 to 1)
Librarians/Media Specialists: 4.0 (523.0 to 1)
Guidance Counselors: 5.0 (418.4 to 1)
Current Spending: ($ per student per year):
   Total: $7,785; Instruction: $4,504; Support Services: $2,880
Enrollment, Drop-out Rates and Diploma Recipients by Race/Ethnicity

Category	Total	White	Black	Asian	AIAN	Hisp.
Enrollment (%)	100.0	97.6	1.6	0.0	0.0	0.1
Drop-out Rate (%)	0.9	0.9	0.0	n/a	0.0	n/a
H.S. Diplomas (#)	125	121	4	0	0	0

Mercer County

Celina City SD
585 E Livingston St • Celina, OH 45822-1742
(419) 586-8300 • http://www.noacsc.org/mercer/ce/
Grade Span: KG-12; **Agency Type:** 1
Schools: 5
   2 Primary; 2 Middle; 1 High; 0 Other Level
   5 Regular; 0 Special Education; 0 Vocational; 0 Alternative
   0 Magnet; 0 Charter; 4 Title I Eligible; 0 School-wide Title I
Students: 3,199   (52.6% male; 47.3% female)
   Individual Education Program: 592 (18.5%);
   English Language Learner: 0 (0.0%); Migrant: n/a
   Eligible for Free Lunch Program: 577 (18.5%)
   Eligible for Reduced-Price Lunch Program: 173 (5.6%)
Teachers: 191.9 (16.2 to 1)
Librarians/Media Specialists: 1.0 (3,116.0 to 1)
Guidance Counselors: 5.0 (623.2 to 1)
Current Spending: ($ per student per year):
   Total: $7,787; Instruction: $4,756; Support Services: $2,705
Enrollment, Drop-out Rates and Diploma Recipients by Race/Ethnicity

Category	Total	White	Black	Asian	AIAN	Hisp.
Enrollment (%)	100.0	97.9	0.2	0.4	0.1	0.8
Drop-out Rate (%)	1.8	1.7	0.0	0.0	33.3	8.3
H.S. Diplomas (#)	282	274	1	3	0	4

Coldwater Ex Vill SD
310 N 2nd St • Coldwater, OH 45828-1242
(419) 678-2611 • http://cw.noacsc.org/
Grade Span: PK-12; **Agency Type:** 1
Schools: 3
   1 Primary; 1 Middle; 1 High; 0 Other Level
   3 Regular; 0 Special Education; 0 Vocational; 0 Alternative
   0 Magnet; 0 Charter; 2 Title I Eligible; 0 School-wide Title I
Students: 1,623   (53.4% male; 46.5% female)
   Individual Education Program: 209 (12.9%);
   English Language Learner: 0 (0.0%); Migrant: n/a
   Eligible for Free Lunch Program: 115 (7.1%)
   Eligible for Reduced-Price Lunch Program: 62 (3.8%)
Teachers: 95.8 (16.9 to 1)
Librarians/Media Specialists: 1.0 (1,623.0 to 1)

Guidance Counselors: 2.0 (811.5 to 1)
Current Spending: ($ per student per year):
   Total: $6,785; Instruction: $4,748; Support Services: $1,794
Enrollment, Drop-out Rates and Diploma Recipients by Race/Ethnicity

Category	Total	White	Black	Asian	AIAN	Hisp.
Enrollment (%)	100.0	98.2	0.0	0.1	0.0	0.6
Drop-out Rate (%)	0.9	0.9	n/a	0.0	n/a	0.0
H.S. Diplomas (#)	124	123	0	0	0	1

Miami County

Milton-Union Exempted Village Schools
112 S Spring St • West Milton, OH 45383-1609
(937) 884-7910
Grade Span: PK-12; **Agency Type:** 1
Schools: 3
   1 Primary; 1 Middle; 1 High; 0 Other Level
   3 Regular; 0 Special Education; 0 Vocational; 0 Alternative
   0 Magnet; 0 Charter; 2 Title I Eligible; 0 School-wide Title I
Students: 1,806   (52.6% male; 47.3% female)
   Individual Education Program: 201 (11.1%);
   English Language Learner: 0 (0.0%); Migrant: n/a
   Eligible for Free Lunch Program: 306 (16.9%)
   Eligible for Reduced-Price Lunch Program: 89 (4.9%)
Teachers: 106.4 (17.0 to 1)
Librarians/Media Specialists: 2.0 (903.0 to 1)
Guidance Counselors: 3.0 (602.0 to 1)
Current Spending: ($ per student per year):
   Total: $6,874; Instruction: $4,012; Support Services: $2,610
Enrollment, Drop-out Rates and Diploma Recipients by Race/Ethnicity

Category	Total	White	Black	Asian	AIAN	Hisp.
Enrollment (%)	100.0	97.7	0.2	0.2	0.1	0.6
Drop-out Rate (%)	2.5	2.5	0.0	0.0	0.0	0.0
H.S. Diplomas (#)	116	115	1	0	0	0

Piqua City SD
719 E Ash St • Piqua, OH 45356-2411
(937) 773-4321 • http://www.piqua.org/
Grade Span: PK-12; **Agency Type:** 1
Schools: 9
   4 Primary; 4 Middle; 1 High; 0 Other Level
   9 Regular; 0 Special Education; 0 Vocational; 0 Alternative
   0 Magnet; 0 Charter; 6 Title I Eligible; 3 School-wide Title I
Students: 3,954   (53.2% male; 46.7% female)
   Individual Education Program: 665 (16.8%);
   English Language Learner: 13 (0.3%); Migrant: n/a
   Eligible for Free Lunch Program: 1,130 (28.6%)
   Eligible for Reduced-Price Lunch Program: 377 (9.5%)
Teachers: 182.9 (21.6 to 1)
Librarians/Media Specialists: 2.0 (1,977.5 to 1)
Guidance Counselors: 8.0 (494.4 to 1)
Current Spending: ($ per student per year):
   Total: $6,751; Instruction: $4,075; Support Services: $2,360
Enrollment, Drop-out Rates and Diploma Recipients by Race/Ethnicity

Category	Total	White	Black	Asian	AIAN	Hisp.
Enrollment (%)	100.0	91.2	5.1	0.6	0.3	0.9
Drop-out Rate (%)	3.3	3.5	1.4	0.0	0.0	0.0
H.S. Diplomas (#)	228	211	16	0	1	0

Tipp City Ex Vill SD
90 S Tippecanoe Dr • Tipp City, OH 45371-1139
(937) 667-8444
Grade Span: KG-12; **Agency Type:** 1
Schools: 5
   2 Primary; 2 Middle; 1 High; 0 Other Level
   5 Regular; 0 Special Education; 0 Vocational; 0 Alternative
   0 Magnet; 0 Charter; 3 Title I Eligible; 0 School-wide Title I
Students: 2,638   (51.4% male; 48.5% female)
   Individual Education Program: 230 (8.7%);
   English Language Learner: 45 (1.7%); Migrant: 24 (0.9%)
   Eligible for Free Lunch Program: 130 (5.0%)
   Eligible for Reduced-Price Lunch Program: 50 (1.9%)
Teachers: 147.6 (17.7 to 1)
Librarians/Media Specialists: 2.0 (1,304.5 to 1)
Guidance Counselors: 6.0 (434.8 to 1)
Current Spending: ($ per student per year):
   Total: $6,409; Instruction: $4,202; Support Services: $1,987
Enrollment, Drop-out Rates and Diploma Recipients by Race/Ethnicity

Category	Total	White	Black	Asian	AIAN	Hisp.
Enrollment (%)	100.0	96.4	0.4	1.1	0.0	1.8
Drop-out Rate (%)	0.4	0.4	0.0	0.0	0.0	0.0
H.S. Diplomas (#)	175	173	1	1	0	0

Troy City SD
500 N Market St • Troy, OH 45373-1418
(937) 332-6700
Grade Span: KG-12; **Agency Type:** 1
Schools: 9
  6 Primary; 1 Middle; 1 High; 1 Other Level
  8 Regular; 1 Special Education; 0 Vocational; 0 Alternative
  0 Magnet; 0 Charter; 5 Title I Eligible; 2 School-wide Title I
Students: 4,538   (51.7% male; 48.2% female)
  Individual Education Program: 532 (11.7%);
  English Language Learner: 59 (1.3%); Migrant: n/a
  Eligible for Free Lunch Program: 660 (14.8%)
  Eligible for Reduced-Price Lunch Program: 216 (4.8%)
Teachers: 234.2 (19.0 to 1)
Librarians/Media Specialists: 2.0 (2,230.5 to 1)
Guidance Counselors: 8.5 (524.8 to 1)
Current Spending: ($ per student per year):
  Total: $7,010; Instruction: $4,517; Support Services: $2,172
Enrollment, Drop-out Rates and Diploma Recipients by Race/Ethnicity

Category	Total	White	Black	Asian	AIAN	Hisp.
Enrollment (%)	100.0	86.7	4.6	2.5	0.2	0.8
Drop-out Rate (%)	3.1	3.1	1.2	0.0	n/a	0.0
H.S. Diplomas (#)	294	263	17	9	0	3

Monroe County

Switzerland of Ohio Local SD
304 Mill St • Woodsfield, OH 43793-1256
(740) 472-5801
Grade Span: PK-12; **Agency Type:** 2
Schools: 10
  6 Primary; 0 Middle; 4 High; 0 Other Level
  9 Regular; 0 Special Education; 1 Vocational; 0 Alternative
  0 Magnet; 0 Charter; 8 Title I Eligible; 0 School-wide Title I
Students: 2,764   (52.1% male; 47.8% female)
  Individual Education Program: 462 (16.7%);
  English Language Learner: 0 (0.0%); Migrant: n/a
  Eligible for Free Lunch Program: 821 (29.7%)
  Eligible for Reduced-Price Lunch Program: 272 (9.8%)
Teachers: 196.7 (14.1 to 1)
Librarians/Media Specialists: 3.0 (921.3 to 1)
Guidance Counselors: 4.0 (691.0 to 1)
Current Spending: ($ per student per year):
  Total: $7,576; Instruction: $4,596; Support Services: $2,697
Enrollment, Drop-out Rates and Diploma Recipients by Race/Ethnicity

Category	Total	White	Black	Asian	AIAN	Hisp.
Enrollment (%)	100.0	98.2	0.4	0.0	0.0	0.1
Drop-out Rate (%)	2.7	2.7	0.0	n/a	n/a	n/a
H.S. Diplomas (#)	202	199	1	0	0	0

Montgomery County

Brookville Local SD
325 Simmons Ave • Brookville, OH 45309-1636
(937) 833-2181
Grade Span: PK-12; **Agency Type:** 2
Schools: 3
  1 Primary; 1 Middle; 1 High; 0 Other Level
  3 Regular; 0 Special Education; 0 Vocational; 0 Alternative
  0 Magnet; 0 Charter; 1 Title I Eligible; 0 School-wide Title I
Students: 1,631   (53.5% male; 46.4% female)
  Individual Education Program: 242 (14.8%);
  English Language Learner: 4 (0.2%); Migrant: n/a
  Eligible for Free Lunch Program: 174 (10.7%)
  Eligible for Reduced-Price Lunch Program: 67 (4.1%)
Teachers: 85.6 (19.1 to 1)
Librarians/Media Specialists: 3.0 (543.7 to 1)
Guidance Counselors: 3.0 (543.7 to 1)
Current Spending: ($ per student per year):
  Total: $6,760; Instruction: $3,773; Support Services: $2,711
Enrollment, Drop-out Rates and Diploma Recipients by Race/Ethnicity

Category	Total	White	Black	Asian	AIAN	Hisp.
Enrollment (%)	100.0	98.5	0.2	0.7	0.0	0.2
Drop-out Rate (%)	2.5	2.5	n/a	0.0	n/a	0.0
H.S. Diplomas (#)	104	102	0	2	0	0

Centerville City SD
111 Virginia Ave • Centerville, OH 45458-2249
(937) 433-8841 • http://www.centerville.k12.oh.us/
Grade Span: KG-12; **Agency Type:** 1
Schools: 11
  7 Primary; 3 Middle; 1 High; 0 Other Level
  11 Regular; 0 Special Education; 0 Vocational; 0 Alternative
  0 Magnet; 0 Charter; 5 Title I Eligible; 0 School-wide Title I
Students: 8,120   (51.7% male; 48.2% female)

  Individual Education Program: 1,003 (12.4%);
  English Language Learner: 194 (2.4%); Migrant: 1 (<0.1%)
  Eligible for Free Lunch Program: 342 (4.3%)
  Eligible for Reduced-Price Lunch Program: 80 (1.0%)
Teachers: 535.7 (15.0 to 1)
Librarians/Media Specialists: 13.0 (618.9 to 1)
Guidance Counselors: 19.2 (419.1 to 1)
Current Spending: ($ per student per year):
  Total: $7,944; Instruction: $4,925; Support Services: $2,793
Enrollment, Drop-out Rates and Diploma Recipients by Race/Ethnicity

Category	Total	White	Black	Asian	AIAN	Hisp.
Enrollment (%)	100.0	86.4	4.0	6.0	0.1	1.2
Drop-out Rate (%)	0.9	0.8	2.7	0.8	0.0	0.0
H.S. Diplomas (#)	590	539	15	27	1	7

Dayton City SD
115 S Ludlow St • Dayton, OH 45402-1812
(937) 542-3000 • http://www.dps.k12.oh.us/
Grade Span: PK-12; **Agency Type:** 1
Schools: 39
  25 Primary; 5 Middle; 7 High; 2 Other Level
  37 Regular; 1 Special Education; 1 Vocational; 0 Alternative
  0 Magnet; 0 Charter; 36 Title I Eligible; 23 School-wide Title I
Students: 18,491   (51.3% male; 48.6% female)
  Individual Education Program: 4,353 (23.5%);
  English Language Learner: 184 (1.0%); Migrant: n/a
  Eligible for Free Lunch Program: 12,243 (66.2%)
  Eligible for Reduced-Price Lunch Program: 1,865 (10.1%)
Teachers: 1,417.8 (13.0 to 1)
Librarians/Media Specialists: 12.0 (1,541.0 to 1)
Guidance Counselors: 18.0 (1,027.3 to 1)
Current Spending: ($ per student per year):
  Total: $10,491; Instruction: $5,113; Support Services: $4,874
Enrollment, Drop-out Rates and Diploma Recipients by Race/Ethnicity

Category	Total	White	Black	Asian	AIAN	Hisp.
Enrollment (%)	100.0	26.6	69.0	0.3	0.0	1.6
Drop-out Rate (%)	8.4	11.0	7.5	0.0	0.0	5.7
H.S. Diplomas (#)	858	166	674	8	0	4

Huber Heights City SD
5954 Longford Rd • Huber Heights, OH 45424-2943
(937) 237-6300 • http://www.huberheights.k12.oh.us/
Grade Span: PK-12; **Agency Type:** 1
Schools: 10
  7 Primary; 2 Middle; 1 High; 0 Other Level
  10 Regular; 0 Special Education; 0 Vocational; 0 Alternative
  0 Magnet; 0 Charter; 7 Title I Eligible; 0 School-wide Title I
Students: 6,821   (52.1% male; 47.8% female)
  Individual Education Program: 819 (12.0%);
  English Language Learner: 169 (2.5%); Migrant: n/a
  Eligible for Free Lunch Program: 945 (13.9%)
  Eligible for Reduced-Price Lunch Program: 428 (6.3%)
Teachers: 626.9 (10.8 to 1)
Librarians/Media Specialists: 3.0 (2,266.7 to 1)
Guidance Counselors: 14.0 (485.7 to 1)
Current Spending: ($ per student per year):
  Total: $7,353; Instruction: $4,511; Support Services: $2,555
Enrollment, Drop-out Rates and Diploma Recipients by Race/Ethnicity

Category	Total	White	Black	Asian	AIAN	Hisp.
Enrollment (%)	100.0	75.9	14.8	3.1	0.2	1.9
Drop-out Rate (%)	5.3	5.4	5.1	1.6	0.0	7.7
H.S. Diplomas (#)	437	337	75	18	0	5

Kettering City SD
3750 Far Hills Ave • Kettering, OH 45429-2506
(937) 499-1400 • http://www.kettering.k12.oh.us/
Grade Span: KG-12; **Agency Type:** 1
Schools: 12
  9 Primary; 2 Middle; 1 High; 0 Other Level
  12 Regular; 0 Special Education; 0 Vocational; 0 Alternative
  0 Magnet; 0 Charter; 6 Title I Eligible; 2 School-wide Title I
Students: 7,747   (52.4% male; 47.5% female)
  Individual Education Program: 1,143 (14.8%);
  English Language Learner: 48 (0.6%); Migrant: n/a
  Eligible for Free Lunch Program: 1,125 (14.8%)
  Eligible for Reduced-Price Lunch Program: 508 (6.7%)
Teachers: 494.0 (15.4 to 1)
Librarians/Media Specialists: 3.0 (2,529.0 to 1)
Guidance Counselors: 26.2 (289.6 to 1)
Current Spending: ($ per student per year):
  Total: $7,943; Instruction: $4,472; Support Services: $3,227

Enrollment, Drop-out Rates and Diploma Recipients by Race/Ethnicity

Category	Total	White	Black	Asian	AIAN	Hisp.
Enrollment (%)	100.0	93.0	2.5	1.4	0.3	1.0
Drop-out Rate (%)	0.5	0.5	0.0	0.0	n/a	0.0
H.S. Diplomas (#)	534	509	8	10	0	3

Mad River Local SD
801 Harshman Rd • Dayton, OH 45431-1238
(937) 259-6606
Grade Span: KG-12; **Agency Type:** 2
Schools: 7
4 Primary; 2 Middle; 1 High; 0 Other Level
7 Regular; 0 Special Education; 0 Vocational; 0 Alternative
0 Magnet; 0 Charter; 6 Title I Eligible; 2 School-wide Title I
Students: 3,619 (50.3% male; 49.6% female)
Individual Education Program: 547 (15.1%);
English Language Learner: 31 (0.9%); Migrant: 1 (<0.1%)
Eligible for Free Lunch Program: 918 (25.7%)
Eligible for Reduced-Price Lunch Program: 471 (13.2%)
Teachers: 238.4 (15.0 to 1)
Librarians/Media Specialists: 2.0 (1,785.5 to 1)
Guidance Counselors: 10.4 (343.4 to 1)
Current Spending: ($ per student per year):
Total: $7,942; Instruction: $5,030; Support Services: $2,563
Enrollment, Drop-out Rates and Diploma Recipients by Race/Ethnicity

Category	Total	White	Black	Asian	AIAN	Hisp.
Enrollment (%)	100.0	85.9	7.2	1.6	0.2	1.8
Drop-out Rate (%)	7.2	7.7	2.3	0.0	100.0	5.0
H.S. Diplomas (#)	182	159	14	6	0	2

Miamisburg City SD
540 E Park Ave • Miamisburg, OH 45342-2854
(937) 866-3381 • http://www.miamisburgcityschools.org/
Grade Span: PK-12; **Agency Type:** 1
Schools: 9
6 Primary; 2 Middle; 1 High; 0 Other Level
9 Regular; 0 Special Education; 0 Vocational; 0 Alternative
0 Magnet; 0 Charter; 7 Title I Eligible; 1 School-wide Title I
Students: 5,306 (52.0% male; 47.9% female)
Individual Education Program: 659 (12.4%);
English Language Learner: 17 (0.3%); Migrant: n/a
Eligible for Free Lunch Program: 783 (14.8%)
Eligible for Reduced-Price Lunch Program: 267 (5.0%)
Teachers: 306.5 (17.3 to 1)
Librarians/Media Specialists: 2.0 (2,647.5 to 1)
Guidance Counselors: 10.5 (504.3 to 1)
Current Spending: ($ per student per year):
Total: $7,273; Instruction: $4,245; Support Services: $2,745
Enrollment, Drop-out Rates and Diploma Recipients by Race/Ethnicity

Category	Total	White	Black	Asian	AIAN	Hisp.
Enrollment (%)	100.0	89.4	4.7	2.3	0.2	1.3
Drop-out Rate (%)	1.6	1.5	1.9	0.0	0.0	5.3
H.S. Diplomas (#)	330	303	5	12	2	4

Northmont City SD
4001 Old Salem Rd • Englewood, OH 45322-2681
(937) 832-5000 • http://www.northmont.k12.oh.us/
Grade Span: KG-12; **Agency Type:** 1
Schools: 9
7 Primary; 1 Middle; 1 High; 0 Other Level
9 Regular; 0 Special Education; 0 Vocational; 0 Alternative
0 Magnet; 0 Charter; 6 Title I Eligible; 0 School-wide Title I
Students: 5,933 (51.0% male; 48.9% female)
Individual Education Program: 671 (11.3%);
English Language Learner: 77 (1.3%); Migrant: n/a
Eligible for Free Lunch Program: 520 (8.8%)
Eligible for Reduced-Price Lunch Program: 369 (6.3%)
Teachers: 316.4 (18.7 to 1)
Librarians/Media Specialists: 1.0 (5,903.0 to 1)
Guidance Counselors: 13.0 (454.1 to 1)
Current Spending: ($ per student per year):
Total: $7,011; Instruction: $4,306; Support Services: $2,327
Enrollment, Drop-out Rates and Diploma Recipients by Race/Ethnicity

Category	Total	White	Black	Asian	AIAN	Hisp.
Enrollment (%)	100.0	83.3	10.6	1.3	0.2	0.6
Drop-out Rate (%)	0.7	0.7	1.0	0.0	0.0	0.0
H.S. Diplomas (#)	393	367	19	3	0	1

Northridge Local SD
2011 Timber Ln • Dayton, OH 45414-4528
(937) 278-5885 • http://northridge.k12.oh.us/
Grade Span: KG-12; **Agency Type:** 2
Schools: 5
3 Primary; 1 Middle; 1 High; 0 Other Level
5 Regular; 0 Special Education; 0 Vocational; 0 Alternative

0 Magnet; 0 Charter; 5 Title I Eligible; 4 School-wide Title I
Students: 1,990 (49.6% male; 50.3% female)
Individual Education Program: 261 (13.1%);
English Language Learner: 5 (0.3%); Migrant: n/a
Eligible for Free Lunch Program: 760 (41.9%)
Eligible for Reduced-Price Lunch Program: 135 (7.4%)
Teachers: 126.2 (14.4 to 1)
Librarians/Media Specialists: 1.0 (1,814.0 to 1)
Guidance Counselors: 3.0 (604.7 to 1)
Current Spending: ($ per student per year):
Total: $9,059; Instruction: $5,422; Support Services: $3,280
Enrollment, Drop-out Rates and Diploma Recipients by Race/Ethnicity

Category	Total	White	Black	Asian	AIAN	Hisp.
Enrollment (%)	100.0	78.2	18.5	0.5	0.2	0.7
Drop-out Rate (%)	5.7	5.0	16.2	0.0	0.0	0.0
H.S. Diplomas (#)	93	90	3	0	0	0

Oakwood City SD
20 Rubicon Rd • Dayton, OH 45409-2239
(937) 297-5332 • http://www.oakwood.k12.oh.us
Grade Span: KG-12; **Agency Type:** 1
Schools: 5
3 Primary; 1 Middle; 1 High; 0 Other Level
5 Regular; 0 Special Education; 0 Vocational; 0 Alternative
0 Magnet; 0 Charter; 1 Title I Eligible; 0 School-wide Title I
Students: 2,042 (49.2% male; 50.7% female)
Individual Education Program: 158 (7.7%);
English Language Learner: 10 (0.5%); Migrant: n/a
Eligible for Free Lunch Program: 13 (0.6%)
Eligible for Reduced-Price Lunch Program: 9 (0.4%)
Teachers: 146.6 (13.9 to 1)
Librarians/Media Specialists: 3.0 (680.7 to 1)
Guidance Counselors: 4.0 (510.5 to 1)
Current Spending: ($ per student per year):
Total: $8,494; Instruction: $5,521; Support Services: $2,864
Enrollment, Drop-out Rates and Diploma Recipients by Race/Ethnicity

Category	Total	White	Black	Asian	AIAN	Hisp.
Enrollment (%)	100.0	95.4	0.8	1.7	0.0	1.4
Drop-out Rate (%)	1.1	1.1	0.0	0.0	n/a	0.0
H.S. Diplomas (#)	140	137	1	1	0	1

Trotwood-Madison City Schools
444 S Broadway St • Trotwood, OH 45426-3327
(937) 854-3050
Grade Span: PK-12; **Agency Type:** 1
Schools: 7
5 Primary; 1 Middle; 1 High; 0 Other Level
7 Regular; 0 Special Education; 0 Vocational; 0 Alternative
0 Magnet; 0 Charter; 7 Title I Eligible; 5 School-wide Title I
Students: 3,470 (51.8% male; 48.1% female)
Individual Education Program: 442 (12.7%);
English Language Learner: 0 (0.0%); Migrant: n/a
Eligible for Free Lunch Program: 1,681 (48.9%)
Eligible for Reduced-Price Lunch Program: 263 (7.7%)
Teachers: 203.0 (16.9 to 1)
Librarians/Media Specialists: 2.0 (1,718.0 to 1)
Guidance Counselors: 3.0 (1,145.3 to 1)
Current Spending: ($ per student per year):
Total: $8,474; Instruction: $4,800; Support Services: $3,267
Enrollment, Drop-out Rates and Diploma Recipients by Race/Ethnicity

Category	Total	White	Black	Asian	AIAN	Hisp.
Enrollment (%)	100.0	13.0	83.1	0.1	0.0	0.7
Drop-out Rate (%)	6.9	10.5	6.1	0.0	n/a	0.0
H.S. Diplomas (#)	192	27	158	1	0	0

Valley View Local SD
64 Comstock St • Germantown, OH 45327-1004
(937) 855-6581
Grade Span: PK-12; **Agency Type:** 2
Schools: 4
2 Primary; 1 Middle; 1 High; 0 Other Level
4 Regular; 0 Special Education; 0 Vocational; 0 Alternative
0 Magnet; 0 Charter; 3 Title I Eligible; 0 School-wide Title I
Students: 2,056 (52.2% male; 47.7% female)
Individual Education Program: 226 (11.0%);
English Language Learner: 0 (0.0%); Migrant: n/a
Eligible for Free Lunch Program: 97 (4.7%)
Eligible for Reduced-Price Lunch Program: 49 (2.4%)
Teachers: 117.9 (17.4 to 1)
Librarians/Media Specialists: 2.0 (1,028.0 to 1)
Guidance Counselors: 3.0 (685.3 to 1)
Current Spending: ($ per student per year):
Total: $7,380; Instruction: $4,352; Support Services: $2,716

Category	Total	White	Black	Asian	AIAN	Hisp.
Enrollment (%)	100.0	98.8	0.6	0.2	0.0	0.0
Drop-out Rate (%)	2.9	2.9	0.0	0.0	n/a	n/a
H.S. Diplomas (#)	138	137	0	1	0	0

Vandalia-Butler City SD

306 S Dixie Dr • Vandalia, OH 45377-2128
(937) 415-6400
Grade Span: PK-12; **Agency Type:** 1
Schools: 6
  2 Primary; 2 Middle; 1 High; 1 Other Level
  6 Regular; 0 Special Education; 0 Vocational; 0 Alternative
  0 Magnet; 0 Charter; 5 Title I Eligible; 0 School-wide Title I
Students: 3,518   (53.0% male; 46.9% female)
  Individual Education Program: 454 (12.9%);
  English Language Learner: 14 (0.4%); Migrant: 1 (<0.1%)
  Eligible for Free Lunch Program: 263 (7.5%)
  Eligible for Reduced-Price Lunch Program: 151 (4.3%)
Teachers: 234.0 (15.0 to 1)
Librarians/Media Specialists: 1.0 (3,518.0 to 1)
Guidance Counselors: 5.0 (703.6 to 1)
Current Spending: ($ per student per year):
  Total: $7,857; Instruction: $4,843; Support Services: $2,789
Enrollment, Drop-out Rates and Diploma Recipients by Race/Ethnicity

Category	Total	White	Black	Asian	AIAN	Hisp.
Enrollment (%)	100.0	92.5	2.7	1.7	0.4	0.4
Drop-out Rate (%)	0.9	0.7	15.4	0.0	0.0	0.0
H.S. Diplomas (#)	244	234	0	4	2	3

West Carrollton City SD

430 E Pease Ave • West Carrollton, OH 45449-1357
(937) 859-5121
Grade Span: PK-12; **Agency Type:** 1
Schools: 7
  5 Primary; 0 Middle; 1 High; 1 Other Level
  7 Regular; 0 Special Education; 0 Vocational; 0 Alternative
  0 Magnet; 0 Charter; 5 Title I Eligible; 1 School-wide Title I
Students: 3,898   (53.5% male; 46.4% female)
  Individual Education Program: 465 (11.9%);
  English Language Learner: 145 (3.7%); Migrant: n/a
  Eligible for Free Lunch Program: 592 (15.2%)
  Eligible for Reduced-Price Lunch Program: 211 (5.4%)
Teachers: 251.2 (15.5 to 1)
Librarians/Media Specialists: 2.0 (1,943.0 to 1)
Guidance Counselors: 5.0 (777.2 to 1)
Current Spending: ($ per student per year):
  Total: $7,852; Instruction: $4,795; Support Services: $2,843
Enrollment, Drop-out Rates and Diploma Recipients by Race/Ethnicity

Category	Total	White	Black	Asian	AIAN	Hisp.
Enrollment (%)	100.0	84.4	7.4	3.2	0.3	2.0
Drop-out Rate (%)	1.5	1.5	1.8	0.0	0.0	0.0
H.S. Diplomas (#)	254	224	12	11	0	5

Morgan County

Morgan Local SD

65 W Union Ave • Mc Connelsville, OH 43756-1218
Mailing Address: PO Box 509 • Mc Connelsville, OH 43756-0509
(740) 962-2782
Grade Span: PK-12; **Agency Type:** 2
Schools: 5
  3 Primary; 1 Middle; 1 High; 0 Other Level
  5 Regular; 0 Special Education; 0 Vocational; 0 Alternative
  0 Magnet; 0 Charter; 4 Title I Eligible; 3 School-wide Title I
Students: 2,265   (51.1% male; 48.8% female)
  Individual Education Program: 299 (13.2%);
  English Language Learner: 0 (0.0%); Migrant: n/a
  Eligible for Free Lunch Program: 802 (35.4%)
  Eligible for Reduced-Price Lunch Program: 171 (7.5%)
Teachers: 152.7 (14.8 to 1)
Librarians/Media Specialists: 5.0 (453.0 to 1)
Guidance Counselors: 3.0 (755.0 to 1)
Current Spending: ($ per student per year):
  Total: $7,943; Instruction: $4,736; Support Services: $2,895
Enrollment, Drop-out Rates and Diploma Recipients by Race/Ethnicity

Category	Total	White	Black	Asian	AIAN	Hisp.
Enrollment (%)	100.0	91.7	4.4	0.1	0.3	0.1
Drop-out Rate (%)	5.0	5.2	0.0	n/a	0.0	0.0
H.S. Diplomas (#)	157	154	1	0	1	1

Morrow County

Highland Local SD

6506 State Route 229 • Sparta, OH 43350-0098
Mailing Address: PO Box 98 • Sparta, OH 43350-0098
(419) 768-2206
Grade Span: PK-12; **Agency Type:** 2
Schools: 5
  3 Primary; 0 Middle; 1 High; 1 Other Level
  5 Regular; 0 Special Education; 0 Vocational; 0 Alternative
  0 Magnet; 0 Charter; 4 Title I Eligible; 1 School-wide Title I
Students: 1,781   (52.8% male; 47.1% female)
  Individual Education Program: 261 (14.7%);
  English Language Learner: 0 (0.0%); Migrant: n/a
  Eligible for Free Lunch Program: 332 (18.6%)
  Eligible for Reduced-Price Lunch Program: 91 (5.1%)
Teachers: 101.6 (17.5 to 1)
Librarians/Media Specialists: 1.0 (1,781.0 to 1)
Guidance Counselors: 2.0 (890.5 to 1)
Current Spending: ($ per student per year):
  Total: $6,845; Instruction: $3,743; Support Services: $2,821
Enrollment, Drop-out Rates and Diploma Recipients by Race/Ethnicity

Category	Total	White	Black	Asian	AIAN	Hisp.
Enrollment (%)	100.0	98.5	0.3	0.1	0.4	0.1
Drop-out Rate (%)	1.5	1.5	n/a	n/a	0.0	n/a
H.S. Diplomas (#)	106	104	0	0	2	0

Muskingum County

East Muskingum Local SD

13505 John Glenn School Rd • New Concord, OH 43762-9702
(740) 826-7655 •
http://www.east-muskingum.k12.oh.us/emsd/site/default.asp
Grade Span: PK-12; **Agency Type:** 2
Schools: 6
  4 Primary; 1 Middle; 1 High; 0 Other Level
  6 Regular; 0 Special Education; 0 Vocational; 0 Alternative
  0 Magnet; 0 Charter; 4 Title I Eligible; 0 School-wide Title I
Students: 2,121   (53.4% male; 46.5% female)
  Individual Education Program: 277 (13.1%);
  English Language Learner: 0 (0.0%); Migrant: n/a
  Eligible for Free Lunch Program: 326 (15.4%)
  Eligible for Reduced-Price Lunch Program: 111 (5.2%)
Teachers: 122.2 (17.4 to 1)
Librarians/Media Specialists: 2.0 (1,060.5 to 1)
Guidance Counselors: 3.0 (707.0 to 1)
Current Spending: ($ per student per year):
  Total: $6,640; Instruction: $4,059; Support Services: $2,294
Enrollment, Drop-out Rates and Diploma Recipients by Race/Ethnicity

Category	Total	White	Black	Asian	AIAN	Hisp.
Enrollment (%)	100.0	97.4	0.7	0.3	0.2	0.2
Drop-out Rate (%)	1.9	1.9	0.0	0.0	0.0	0.0
H.S. Diplomas (#)	177	171	2	2	0	0

Franklin Local SD

360 Cedar St • Duncan Falls, OH 43734-9710
Mailing Address: PO Box 428 • Duncan Falls, OH 43734-0428
(740) 674-5203
Grade Span: PK-12; **Agency Type:** 2
Schools: 5
  2 Primary; 2 Middle; 1 High; 0 Other Level
  5 Regular; 0 Special Education; 0 Vocational; 0 Alternative
  0 Magnet; 0 Charter; 3 Title I Eligible; 3 School-wide Title I
Students: 2,418   (51.7% male; 48.2% female)
  Individual Education Program: 337 (13.9%);
  English Language Learner: 0 (0.0%); Migrant: n/a
  Eligible for Free Lunch Program: 730 (30.2%)
  Eligible for Reduced-Price Lunch Program: 194 (8.0%)
Teachers: 142.5 (17.0 to 1)
Librarians/Media Specialists: 1.0 (2,418.0 to 1)
Guidance Counselors: 3.1 (780.0 to 1)
Current Spending: ($ per student per year):
  Total: $6,554; Instruction: $3,801; Support Services: $2,422
Enrollment, Drop-out Rates and Diploma Recipients by Race/Ethnicity

Category	Total	White	Black	Asian	AIAN	Hisp.
Enrollment (%)	100.0	98.3	0.5	0.2	0.2	0.1
Drop-out Rate (%)	3.0	3.0	0.0	0.0	n/a	n/a
H.S. Diplomas (#)	165	164	0	0	0	1

Maysville Local SD

2739 Pinkerton Ln • Zanesville, OH 43701-8592
Mailing Address: PO Box 1818 • Zanesville, OH 43702-1818
(740) 453-0754
Grade Span: PK-12; **Agency Type:** 2
Schools: 3

1 Primary; 1 Middle; 1 High; 0 Other Level
3 Regular; 0 Special Education; 0 Vocational; 0 Alternative
0 Magnet; 0 Charter; 2 Title I Eligible; 1 School-wide Title I
Students: 2,265 (50.1% male; 49.8% female)
Individual Education Program: 291 (12.8%);
English Language Learner: 1 (<0.1%); Migrant: n/a
Eligible for Free Lunch Program: 724 (32.0%)
Eligible for Reduced-Price Lunch Program: 178 (7.9%)
Teachers: 119.8 (18.9 to 1)
Librarians/Media Specialists: 2.0 (1,132.5 to 1)
Guidance Counselors: 4.0 (566.3 to 1)
Current Spending: ($ per student per year):
Total: $6,386; Instruction: $3,585; Support Services: $2,520
Enrollment, Drop-out Rates and Diploma Recipients by Race/Ethnicity

Category	Total	White	Black	Asian	AIAN	Hisp.
Enrollment (%)	100.0	97.8	1.1	0.3	0.0	0.1
Drop-out Rate (%)	1.4	1.4	0.0	n/a	n/a	0.0
H.S. Diplomas (#)	160	159	1	0	0	0

Tri-Valley Local Schools
36 E Muskingum Ave • Dresden, OH 43821-9701
Mailing Address: PO Box 125 • Dresden, OH 43821-0125
(740) 754-1572
Grade Span: PK-12; **Agency Type:** 2
Schools: 7
4 Primary; 2 Middle; 1 High; 0 Other Level
7 Regular; 0 Special Education; 0 Vocational; 0 Alternative
0 Magnet; 0 Charter; 4 Title I Eligible; 0 School-wide Title I
Students: 3,150 (51.2% male; 48.7% female)
Individual Education Program: 347 (11.0%);
English Language Learner: 0 (0.0%); Migrant: n/a
Eligible for Free Lunch Program: 485 (15.4%)
Eligible for Reduced-Price Lunch Program: 142 (4.5%)
Teachers: 164.9 (19.1 to 1)
Librarians/Media Specialists: 2.0 (1,575.0 to 1)
Guidance Counselors: 4.0 (787.5 to 1)
Current Spending: ($ per student per year):
Total: $6,020; Instruction: $3,648; Support Services: $2,109
Enrollment, Drop-out Rates and Diploma Recipients by Race/Ethnicity

Category	Total	White	Black	Asian	AIAN	Hisp.
Enrollment (%)	100.0	97.5	1.1	0.1	0.0	0.4
Drop-out Rate (%)	2.2	2.2	0.0	n/a	n/a	0.0
H.S. Diplomas (#)	194	194	0	0	0	0

West Muskingum Local SD
4880 W Pike • Zanesville, OH 43701-9390
(740) 455-4052
Grade Span: PK-12; **Agency Type:** 2
Schools: 5
3 Primary; 1 Middle; 1 High; 0 Other Level
5 Regular; 0 Special Education; 0 Vocational; 0 Alternative
0 Magnet; 0 Charter; 4 Title I Eligible; 0 School-wide Title I
Students: 1,816 (51.3% male; 48.6% female)
Individual Education Program: 281 (15.5%);
English Language Learner: 3 (0.2%); Migrant: n/a
Eligible for Free Lunch Program: 350 (19.3%)
Eligible for Reduced-Price Lunch Program: 56 (3.1%)
Teachers: 104.6 (17.4 to 1)
Librarians/Media Specialists: 1.5 (1,210.7 to 1)
Guidance Counselors: 2.0 (908.0 to 1)
Current Spending: ($ per student per year):
Total: $6,458; Instruction: $3,671; Support Services: $2,531
Enrollment, Drop-out Rates and Diploma Recipients by Race/Ethnicity

Category	Total	White	Black	Asian	AIAN	Hisp.
Enrollment (%)	100.0	95.4	3.0	0.6	0.0	0.4
Drop-out Rate (%)	0.2	0.0	5.9	0.0	0.0	0.0
H.S. Diplomas (#)	142	134	6	1	1	0

Zanesville City SD
160 N 4th St • Zanesville, OH 43701-3518
(740) 454-9751 • http://www.zanesville.k12.oh.us/
Grade Span: PK-12; **Agency Type:** 1
Schools: 12
9 Primary; 2 Middle; 1 High; 0 Other Level
12 Regular; 0 Special Education; 0 Vocational; 0 Alternative
0 Magnet; 0 Charter; 10 Title I Eligible; 6 School-wide Title I
Students: 4,251 (49.3% male; 50.6% female)
Individual Education Program: 968 (22.8%);
English Language Learner: 0 (0.0%); Migrant: n/a
Eligible for Free Lunch Program: 2,276 (53.5%)
Eligible for Reduced-Price Lunch Program: 243 (5.7%)
Teachers: 290.6 (14.6 to 1)
Librarians/Media Specialists: 3.0 (1,417.0 to 1)
Guidance Counselors: 7.8 (545.0 to 1)
Current Spending: ($ per student per year):
Total: $8,491; Instruction: $5,242; Support Services: $2,870

Enrollment, Drop-out Rates and Diploma Recipients by Race/Ethnicity

Category	Total	White	Black	Asian	AIAN	Hisp.
Enrollment (%)	100.0	77.9	16.0	0.3	0.1	0.4
Drop-out Rate (%)	8.5	7.1	12.7	0.0	n/a	75.0
H.S. Diplomas (#)	181	146	29	2	0	2

Ottawa County

Benton Carroll Salem Local SD
11685 W State Route 163 • Oak Harbor, OH 43449-1278
(419) 898-6210 • http://www.bcs.k12.oh.us/
Grade Span: PK-12; **Agency Type:** 2
Schools: 6
4 Primary; 1 Middle; 1 High; 0 Other Level
6 Regular; 0 Special Education; 0 Vocational; 0 Alternative
0 Magnet; 0 Charter; 5 Title I Eligible; 0 School-wide Title I
Students: 2,024 (51.2% male; 48.7% female)
Individual Education Program: 308 (15.2%);
English Language Learner: 0 (0.0%); Migrant: 21 (1.0%)
Eligible for Free Lunch Program: 260 (12.8%)
Eligible for Reduced-Price Lunch Program: 168 (8.3%)
Teachers: 112.1 (18.1 to 1)
Librarians/Media Specialists: 2.0 (1,012.0 to 1)
Guidance Counselors: 5.0 (404.8 to 1)
Current Spending: ($ per student per year):
Total: $8,403; Instruction: $4,951; Support Services: $3,128
Enrollment, Drop-out Rates and Diploma Recipients by Race/Ethnicity

Category	Total	White	Black	Asian	AIAN	Hisp.
Enrollment (%)	100.0	94.0	0.1	0.2	0.0	1.9
Drop-out Rate (%)	0.7	0.7	0.0	n/a	0.0	0.0
H.S. Diplomas (#)	152	147	0	0	0	2

Genoa Area Local SD
2810 N Genoa Clay Center Rd • Genoa, OH 43430-9730
(419) 855-7741
Grade Span: PK-12; **Agency Type:** 2
Schools: 4
2 Primary; 1 Middle; 1 High; 0 Other Level
4 Regular; 0 Special Education; 0 Vocational; 0 Alternative
0 Magnet; 0 Charter; 2 Title I Eligible; 0 School-wide Title I
Students: 1,737 (54.2% male; 45.7% female)
Individual Education Program: 183 (10.5%);
English Language Learner: 0 (0.0%); Migrant: n/a
Eligible for Free Lunch Program: 199 (11.5%)
Eligible for Reduced-Price Lunch Program: 58 (3.3%)
Teachers: 89.4 (19.4 to 1)
Librarians/Media Specialists: 1.0 (1,737.0 to 1)
Guidance Counselors: 3.0 (579.0 to 1)
Current Spending: ($ per student per year):
Total: $6,842; Instruction: $4,238; Support Services: $2,346
Enrollment, Drop-out Rates and Diploma Recipients by Race/Ethnicity

Category	Total	White	Black	Asian	AIAN	Hisp.
Enrollment (%)	100.0	92.3	0.2	0.2	0.1	6.0
Drop-out Rate (%)	1.8	1.7	n/a	n/a	0.0	3.4
H.S. Diplomas (#)	127	122	0	0	0	5

Port Clinton City SD
431 Portage Dr • Port Clinton, OH 43452-1724
(419) 732-2102 • http://www.port-clinton.k12.oh.us/
Grade Span: PK-12; **Agency Type:** 1
Schools: 6
4 Primary; 1 Middle; 1 High; 0 Other Level
6 Regular; 0 Special Education; 0 Vocational; 0 Alternative
0 Magnet; 0 Charter; 4 Title I Eligible; 1 School-wide Title I
Students: 1,971 (52.2% male; 47.7% female)
Individual Education Program: 346 (17.6%);
English Language Learner: 0 (0.0%); Migrant: n/a
Eligible for Free Lunch Program: 471 (23.9%)
Eligible for Reduced-Price Lunch Program: 88 (4.5%)
Teachers: 127.0 (15.5 to 1)
Librarians/Media Specialists: 1.0 (1,971.0 to 1)
Guidance Counselors: 2.0 (985.5 to 1)
Current Spending: ($ per student per year):
Total: $8,869; Instruction: $5,367; Support Services: $3,243
Enrollment, Drop-out Rates and Diploma Recipients by Race/Ethnicity

Category	Total	White	Black	Asian	AIAN	Hisp.
Enrollment (%)	100.0	89.3	1.8	0.3	0.1	4.3
Drop-out Rate (%)	3.2	2.8	14.3	0.0	0.0	7.0
H.S. Diplomas (#)	169	153	1	1	0	12

Paulding County

Paulding Ex Vill SD
405 N Water St • Paulding, OH 45879-1251
(419) 399-4656
Grade Span: PK-12; **Agency Type:** 1
Schools: 4
  2 Primary; 1 Middle; 1 High; 0 Other Level
  4 Regular; 0 Special Education; 0 Vocational; 0 Alternative
  0 Magnet; 0 Charter; 2 Title I Eligible; 0 School-wide Title I
Students: 1,809 (51.2% male; 48.7% female)
  Individual Education Program: 330 (18.2%);
  English Language Learner: 0 (0.0%); Migrant: n/a
  Eligible for Free Lunch Program: 256 (14.2%)
  Eligible for Reduced-Price Lunch Program: 86 (4.8%)
Teachers: 124.0 (14.6 to 1)
Librarians/Media Specialists: 1.0 (1,809.0 to 1)
Guidance Counselors: 3.0 (603.0 to 1)
Current Spending: ($ per student per year):
  Total: $7,470; Instruction: $4,577; Support Services: $2,602
Enrollment, Drop-out Rates and Diploma Recipients by Race/Ethnicity

Category	Total	White	Black	Asian	AIAN	Hisp.
Enrollment (%)	100.0	92.5	1.1	0.3	0.0	3.8
Drop-out Rate (%)	1.2	1.1	0.0	n/a	n/a	0.0
H.S. Diplomas (#)	134	121	2	0	1	10

Perry County

New Lexington City SD
101 3rd Ave • New Lexington, OH 43764-1407
(740) 342-4133 • http://www.nlcs.k12.oh.us/
Grade Span: PK-12; **Agency Type:** 1
Schools: 4
  2 Primary; 1 Middle; 1 High; 0 Other Level
  4 Regular; 0 Special Education; 0 Vocational; 0 Alternative
  0 Magnet; 0 Charter; 4 Title I Eligible; 2 School-wide Title I
Students: 1,966 (52.7% male; 47.2% female)
  Individual Education Program: 268 (13.6%);
  English Language Learner: 0 (0.0%); Migrant: n/a
  Eligible for Free Lunch Program: 852 (43.3%)
  Eligible for Reduced-Price Lunch Program: 197 (10.0%)
Teachers: 111.4 (17.6 to 1)
Librarians/Media Specialists: 3.0 (655.3 to 1)
Guidance Counselors: 1.2 (1,638.3 to 1)
Current Spending: ($ per student per year):
  Total: $6,694; Instruction: $3,837; Support Services: $2,478
Enrollment, Drop-out Rates and Diploma Recipients by Race/Ethnicity

Category	Total	White	Black	Asian	AIAN	Hisp.
Enrollment (%)	100.0	99.1	0.3	0.2	0.0	0.2
Drop-out Rate (%)	6.8	6.8	n/a	n/a	n/a	n/a
H.S. Diplomas (#)	100	100	0	0	0	0

Northern Local SD
8700 Sheridan Dr • Thornville, OH 43076-9757
(740) 743-1303 • http://nlsd.k12.oh.us/
Grade Span: PK-12; **Agency Type:** 2
Schools: 5
  3 Primary; 1 Middle; 1 High; 0 Other Level
  5 Regular; 0 Special Education; 0 Vocational; 0 Alternative
  0 Magnet; 0 Charter; 4 Title I Eligible; 2 School-wide Title I
Students: 2,360 (51.3% male; 48.6% female)
  Individual Education Program: 323 (13.7%);
  English Language Learner: 0 (0.0%); Migrant: n/a
  Eligible for Free Lunch Program: 422 (18.0%)
  Eligible for Reduced-Price Lunch Program: 145 (6.2%)
Teachers: 135.5 (17.3 to 1)
Librarians/Media Specialists: 2.0 (1,169.5 to 1)
Guidance Counselors: 3.0 (779.7 to 1)
Current Spending: ($ per student per year):
  Total: $6,168; Instruction: $3,575; Support Services: $2,353
Enrollment, Drop-out Rates and Diploma Recipients by Race/Ethnicity

Category	Total	White	Black	Asian	AIAN	Hisp.
Enrollment (%)	100.0	99.2	0.2	0.1	0.0	0.1
Drop-out Rate (%)	1.3	1.3	n/a	0.0	n/a	n/a
H.S. Diplomas (#)	151	150	0	1	0	0

Pickaway County

Circleville City SD
388 Clark Dr • Circleville, OH 43113-1517
(740) 474-4340
Grade Span: PK-12; **Agency Type:** 1
Schools: 6
  4 Primary; 1 Middle; 1 High; 0 Other Level
  6 Regular; 0 Special Education; 0 Vocational; 0 Alternative

0 Magnet; 0 Charter; 2 Title I Eligible; 1 School-wide Title I
Students: 2,490 (50.5% male; 49.4% female)
  Individual Education Program: 380 (15.3%);
  English Language Learner: 1 (<0.1%); Migrant: n/a
  Eligible for Free Lunch Program: 597 (24.0%)
  Eligible for Reduced-Price Lunch Program: 124 (5.0%)
Teachers: 145.7 (17.1 to 1)
Librarians/Media Specialists: 3.0 (830.0 to 1)
Guidance Counselors: 4.0 (622.5 to 1)
Current Spending: ($ per student per year):
  Total: $7,581; Instruction: $4,593; Support Services: $2,712
Enrollment, Drop-out Rates and Diploma Recipients by Race/Ethnicity

Category	Total	White	Black	Asian	AIAN	Hisp.
Enrollment (%)	100.0	93.9	2.1	0.6	0.3	1.0
Drop-out Rate (%)	4.0	4.0	0.0	0.0	n/a	0.0
H.S. Diplomas (#)	142	135	2	0	0	1

Logan Elm Local SD
9579 Tarlton Rd • Circleville, OH 43113-9448
(740) 474-7501
Grade Span: PK-12; **Agency Type:** 2
Schools: 6
  4 Primary; 1 Middle; 1 High; 0 Other Level
  6 Regular; 0 Special Education; 0 Vocational; 0 Alternative
  0 Magnet; 0 Charter; 2 Title I Eligible; 1 School-wide Title I
Students: 2,323 (52.4% male; 47.5% female)
  Individual Education Program: 319 (13.7%);
  English Language Learner: 0 (0.0%); Migrant: n/a
  Eligible for Free Lunch Program: 339 (14.6%)
  Eligible for Reduced-Price Lunch Program: 120 (5.2%)
Teachers: 140.2 (16.6 to 1)
Librarians/Media Specialists: 1.0 (2,323.0 to 1)
Guidance Counselors: 4.0 (580.8 to 1)
Current Spending: ($ per student per year):
  Total: $7,348; Instruction: $4,215; Support Services: $2,825
Enrollment, Drop-out Rates and Diploma Recipients by Race/Ethnicity

Category	Total	White	Black	Asian	AIAN	Hisp.
Enrollment (%)	100.0	98.6	0.7	0.1	0.0	0.2
Drop-out Rate (%)	1.4	1.4	0.0	0.0	n/a	n/a
H.S. Diplomas (#)	167	165	2	0	0	0

Teays Valley Local SD
385 Circleville Ave • Ashville, OH 43103-9417
(740) 983-4111
Grade Span: PK-12; **Agency Type:** 2
Schools: 5
  3 Primary; 0 Middle; 1 High; 1 Other Level
  5 Regular; 0 Special Education; 0 Vocational; 0 Alternative
  0 Magnet; 0 Charter; 4 Title I Eligible; 0 School-wide Title I
Students: 3,233 (52.2% male; 47.7% female)
  Individual Education Program: 432 (13.4%);
  English Language Learner: 1 (<0.1%); Migrant: n/a
  Eligible for Free Lunch Program: 412 (12.7%)
  Eligible for Reduced-Price Lunch Program: 132 (4.1%)
Teachers: 197.0 (16.4 to 1)
Librarians/Media Specialists: 2.0 (1,616.5 to 1)
Guidance Counselors: 4.0 (808.3 to 1)
Current Spending: ($ per student per year):
  Total: $6,807; Instruction: $4,084; Support Services: $2,511
Enrollment, Drop-out Rates and Diploma Recipients by Race/Ethnicity

Category	Total	White	Black	Asian	AIAN	Hisp.
Enrollment (%)	100.0	98.4	0.3	0.1	0.1	0.2
Drop-out Rate (%)	3.9	3.9	0.0	0.0	n/a	n/a
H.S. Diplomas (#)	168	168	0	0	0	0

Westfall Local SD
19463 Pherson Pike • Williamsport, OH 43164-9745
(740) 986-3671
Grade Span: PK-12; **Agency Type:** 2
Schools: 3
  1 Primary; 1 Middle; 1 High; 0 Other Level
  3 Regular; 0 Special Education; 0 Vocational; 0 Alternative
  0 Magnet; 0 Charter; 1 Title I Eligible; 1 School-wide Title I
Students: 1,655 (51.1% male; 48.8% female)
  Individual Education Program: 192 (11.6%);
  English Language Learner: 0 (0.0%); Migrant: n/a
  Eligible for Free Lunch Program: 335 (20.2%)
  Eligible for Reduced-Price Lunch Program: 124 (7.5%)
Teachers: 99.0 (16.7 to 1)
Librarians/Media Specialists: 1.0 (1,655.0 to 1)
Guidance Counselors: 3.0 (551.7 to 1)
Current Spending: ($ per student per year):
  Total: $6,811; Instruction: $3,921; Support Services: $2,609

Enrollment, Drop-out Rates and Diploma Recipients by Race/Ethnicity

Category	Total	White	Black	Asian	AIAN	Hisp.
Enrollment (%)	100.0	99.5	0.4	0.0	0.0	0.0
Drop-out Rate (%)	1.8	1.8	0.0	0.0	n/a	0.0
H.S. Diplomas (#)	97	95	1	1	0	0

Pike County

Scioto Valley Local SD
1414 Piketon Rd • Piketon, OH 45661-9801
Mailing Address: PO Box 600 • Piketon, OH 45661-0600
(740) 289-4456
Grade Span: PK-12; **Agency Type:** 2
Schools: 3
　3 Primary; 0 Middle; 1 High; 0 Other Level
　3 Regular; 0 Special Education; 0 Vocational; 0 Alternative
　0 Magnet; 0 Charter; 3 Title I Eligible; 2 School-wide Title I
Students: 1,679　(51.7% male; 48.2% female)
　Individual Education Program: 246 (14.7%);
　English Language Learner: 0 (0.0%); Migrant: n/a
　Eligible for Free Lunch Program: 627 (37.3%)
　Eligible for Reduced-Price Lunch Program: 105 (6.3%)
Teachers: 91.0 (18.5 to 1)
Librarians/Media Specialists: 1.0 (1,679.0 to 1)
Guidance Counselors: 3.0 (559.7 to 1)
Current Spending: ($ per student per year):
　Total: $7,167; Instruction: $3,681; Support Services: $3,195
Enrollment, Drop-out Rates and Diploma Recipients by Race/Ethnicity

Category	Total	White	Black	Asian	AIAN	Hisp.
Enrollment (%)	100.0	99.2	0.4	0.1	0.0	0.2
Drop-out Rate (%)	5.2	5.0	33.3	0.0	n/a	0.0
H.S. Diplomas (#)	89	86	2	1	0	0

Waverly City SD
500 E 2nd St • Waverly, OH 45690-1286
(740) 947-4770
Grade Span: PK-12; **Agency Type:** 1
Schools: 4
　2 Primary; 1 Middle; 0 High; 1 Other Level
　4 Regular; 0 Special Education; 0 Vocational; 0 Alternative
　0 Magnet; 0 Charter; 3 Title I Eligible; 2 School-wide Title I
Students: 2,174　(51.9% male; 48.0% female)
　Individual Education Program: 324 (14.9%);
　English Language Learner: 0 (0.0%); Migrant: n/a
　Eligible for Free Lunch Program: 672 (30.9%)
　Eligible for Reduced-Price Lunch Program: 100 (4.6%)
Teachers: 122.0 (17.8 to 1)
Librarians/Media Specialists: 1.0 (2,174.0 to 1)
Guidance Counselors: 4.0 (543.5 to 1)
Current Spending: ($ per student per year):
　Total: $6,254; Instruction: $3,670; Support Services: $2,300
Enrollment, Drop-out Rates and Diploma Recipients by Race/Ethnicity

Category	Total	White	Black	Asian	AIAN	Hisp.
Enrollment (%)	100.0	96.4	2.6	0.2	0.0	0.6
Drop-out Rate (%)	3.9	3.8	7.1	0.0	n/a	0.0
H.S. Diplomas (#)	114	108	5	1	0	0

Portage County

Aurora City SD
102 E Garfield Rd • Aurora, OH 44202-8854
(330) 562-6106 • http://aurora.portage.k12.oh.us/
Grade Span: PK-12; **Agency Type:** 1
Schools: 4
　2 Primary; 1 Middle; 1 High; 0 Other Level
　4 Regular; 0 Special Education; 0 Vocational; 0 Alternative
　0 Magnet; 0 Charter; 2 Title I Eligible; 0 School-wide Title I
Students: 2,851　(50.8% male; 49.1% female)
　Individual Education Program: 249 (8.7%);
　English Language Learner: 5 (0.2%); Migrant: n/a
　Eligible for Free Lunch Program: 96 (3.4%)
　Eligible for Reduced-Price Lunch Program: 40 (1.4%)
Teachers: 163.0 (17.5 to 1)
Librarians/Media Specialists: 3.0 (950.3 to 1)
Guidance Counselors: 6.5 (438.6 to 1)
Current Spending: ($ per student per year):
　Total: $7,962; Instruction: $4,461; Support Services: $3,279
Enrollment, Drop-out Rates and Diploma Recipients by Race/Ethnicity

Category	Total	White	Black	Asian	AIAN	Hisp.
Enrollment (%)	100.0	95.1	2.8	1.4	0.1	0.3
Drop-out Rate (%)	1.0	1.0	0.0	0.0	n/a	0.0
H.S. Diplomas (#)	149	144	4	0	0	1

Crestwood Local SD
4565 W Prospect St • Mantua, OH 44255-9103
(330) 274-8511
Grade Span: PK-12; **Agency Type:** 2
Schools: 9
　4 Primary; 1 Middle; 1 High; 1 Other Level
　6 Regular; 1 Special Education; 0 Vocational; 0 Alternative
　0 Magnet; 0 Charter; 5 Title I Eligible; 0 School-wide Title I
Students: 2,725　(52.4% male; 47.5% female)
　Individual Education Program: 362 (13.3%);
　English Language Learner: 1 (<0.1%); Migrant: n/a
　Eligible for Free Lunch Program: 285 (10.5%)
　Eligible for Reduced-Price Lunch Program: 99 (3.6%)
Teachers: 156.7 (17.4 to 1)
Librarians/Media Specialists: 3.0 (908.3 to 1)
Guidance Counselors: 4.0 (681.3 to 1)
Current Spending: ($ per student per year):
　Total: $7,116; Instruction: $4,074; Support Services: $2,833
Enrollment, Drop-out Rates and Diploma Recipients by Race/Ethnicity

Category	Total	White	Black	Asian	AIAN	Hisp.
Enrollment (%)	100.0	98.0	1.0	0.3	0.0	0.3
Drop-out Rate (%)	1.3	1.3	0.0	0.0	0.0	0.0
H.S. Diplomas (#)	196	193	0	2	0	1

Field Local SD
1473 Saxe Rd • Mogadore, OH 44260-9790
(330) 673-2659 • http://156.63.123.52/fieldweb/index.html
Grade Span: PK-12; **Agency Type:** 2
Schools: 5
　3 Primary; 1 Middle; 1 High; 0 Other Level
　5 Regular; 0 Special Education; 0 Vocational; 0 Alternative
　0 Magnet; 0 Charter; 2 Title I Eligible; 0 School-wide Title I
Students: 2,310　(52.9% male; 47.0% female)
　Individual Education Program: 342 (14.8%);
　English Language Learner: 12 (0.5%); Migrant: 2 (0.1%)
　Eligible for Free Lunch Program: 334 (14.5%)
　Eligible for Reduced-Price Lunch Program: 114 (4.9%)
Teachers: 132.6 (17.4 to 1)
Librarians/Media Specialists: 3.0 (770.0 to 1)
Guidance Counselors: 4.0 (577.5 to 1)
Current Spending: ($ per student per year):
　Total: $7,138; Instruction: $4,239; Support Services: $2,692
Enrollment, Drop-out Rates and Diploma Recipients by Race/Ethnicity

Category	Total	White	Black	Asian	AIAN	Hisp.
Enrollment (%)	100.0	97.1	1.3	0.3	0.1	0.3
Drop-out Rate (%)	1.7	1.7	0.0	0.0	n/a	0.0
H.S. Diplomas (#)	175	167	5	2	0	1

James A Garfield Local SD
10235 State Route 88 • Garrettsville, OH 44231-9205
(330) 527-4336
Grade Span: PK-12; **Agency Type:** 2
Schools: 4
　1 Primary; 2 Middle; 1 High; 0 Other Level
　4 Regular; 0 Special Education; 0 Vocational; 0 Alternative
　0 Magnet; 0 Charter; 2 Title I Eligible; 0 School-wide Title I
Students: 1,570　(50.3% male; 49.6% female)
　Individual Education Program: 185 (11.8%);
　English Language Learner: 0 (0.0%); Migrant: n/a
　Eligible for Free Lunch Program: 220 (14.0%)
　Eligible for Reduced-Price Lunch Program: 112 (7.1%)
Teachers: 94.0 (16.7 to 1)
Librarians/Media Specialists: 2.0 (785.0 to 1)
Guidance Counselors: 3.1 (506.5 to 1)
Current Spending: ($ per student per year):
　Total: $6,830; Instruction: $3,746; Support Services: $2,789
Enrollment, Drop-out Rates and Diploma Recipients by Race/Ethnicity

Category	Total	White	Black	Asian	AIAN	Hisp.
Enrollment (%)	100.0	98.6	0.3	0.3	0.1	0.1
Drop-out Rate (%)	3.3	3.1	0.0	0.0	n/a	33.3
H.S. Diplomas (#)	101	99	2	0	0	0

Kent City SD
321 N Depeyster St • Kent, OH 44240-2514
(330) 673-6515
Grade Span: PK-12; **Agency Type:** 1
Schools: 7
　5 Primary; 1 Middle; 1 High; 0 Other Level
　7 Regular; 0 Special Education; 0 Vocational; 0 Alternative
　0 Magnet; 0 Charter; 5 Title I Eligible; 0 School-wide Title I
Students: 3,796　(52.1% male; 47.8% female)
　Individual Education Program: 458 (12.1%);
　English Language Learner: 31 (0.8%); Migrant: n/a
　Eligible for Free Lunch Program: 813 (21.4%)
　Eligible for Reduced-Price Lunch Program: 186 (4.9%)

Teachers: 298.1 (12.7 to 1)
Librarians/Media Specialists: 6.0 (632.7 to 1)
Guidance Counselors: 8.0 (474.5 to 1)
Current Spending: ($ per student per year):
    Total: $9,901; Instruction: $6,131; Support Services: $3,516
Enrollment, Drop-out Rates and Diploma Recipients by Race/Ethnicity

Category	Total	White	Black	Asian	AIAN	Hisp.
Enrollment (%)	100.0	80.6	11.1	2.7	0.3	0.7
Drop-out Rate (%)	2.2	2.2	2.5	0.0	n/a	0.0
H.S. Diplomas (#)	308	261	30	9	0	5

Ravenna City SD
507 E Main St • Ravenna, OH 44266-3257
(330) 296-9679 • http://www.ravenna.portage.k12.oh.us/
Grade Span: PK-12; **Agency Type:** 1
Schools: 8
    5 Primary; 1 Middle; 1 High; 1 Other Level
    8 Regular; 0 Special Education; 0 Vocational; 0 Alternative
    0 Magnet; 0 Charter; 7 Title I Eligible; 7 School-wide Title I
Students: 3,386   (51.5% male; 48.4% female)
    Individual Education Program: 561 (16.6%);
    English Language Learner: 0 (0.0%); Migrant: n/a
    Eligible for Free Lunch Program: 919 (28.4%)
    Eligible for Reduced-Price Lunch Program: 313 (9.7%)
Teachers: 212.5 (15.2 to 1)
Librarians/Media Specialists: 2.0 (1,617.5 to 1)
Guidance Counselors: 7.0 (462.1 to 1)
Current Spending: ($ per student per year):
    Total: $7,933; Instruction: $4,781; Support Services: $2,855
Enrollment, Drop-out Rates and Diploma Recipients by Race/Ethnicity

Category	Total	White	Black	Asian	AIAN	Hisp.
Enrollment (%)	100.0	89.1	7.3	0.3	0.0	2.1
Drop-out Rate (%)	4.9	4.8	4.1	0.0	n/a	33.3
H.S. Diplomas (#)	174	161	12	1	0	0

Southeast Local SD
8245 Tallmadge Rd • Ravenna, OH 44266-8547
(330) 654-5841 • http://pirate.portage.k12.oh.us/Main.html
Grade Span: PK-12; **Agency Type:** 2
Schools: 5
    3 Primary; 1 Middle; 1 High; 0 Other Level
    5 Regular; 0 Special Education; 0 Vocational; 0 Alternative
    0 Magnet; 0 Charter; 3 Title I Eligible; 0 School-wide Title I
Students: 2,210   (52.0% male; 47.9% female)
    Individual Education Program: 300 (13.6%);
    English Language Learner: 6 (0.3%); Migrant: n/a
    Eligible for Free Lunch Program: 320 (14.5%)
    Eligible for Reduced-Price Lunch Program: 147 (6.7%)
Teachers: 126.0 (17.5 to 1)
Librarians/Media Specialists: 2.0 (1,105.0 to 1)
Guidance Counselors: 3.0 (736.7 to 1)
Current Spending: ($ per student per year):
    Total: $7,070; Instruction: $3,713; Support Services: $3,119
Enrollment, Drop-out Rates and Diploma Recipients by Race/Ethnicity

Category	Total	White	Black	Asian	AIAN	Hisp.
Enrollment (%)	100.0	99.1	0.3	0.0	0.0	0.1
Drop-out Rate (%)	2.3	2.3	0.0	0.0	n/a	0.0
H.S. Diplomas (#)	171	167	2	1	0	1

Streetsboro City Schools
9000 Kirby Ln • Streetsboro, OH 44241-1725
(330) 626-4900 • http://www.rockets.sparcc.org/
Grade Span: PK-12; **Agency Type:** 1
Schools: 5
    2 Primary; 2 Middle; 1 High; 0 Other Level
    5 Regular; 0 Special Education; 0 Vocational; 0 Alternative
    0 Magnet; 0 Charter; 4 Title I Eligible; 0 School-wide Title I
Students: 2,087   (51.4% male; 48.5% female)
    Individual Education Program: 288 (13.8%);
    English Language Learner: 5 (0.2%); Migrant: n/a
    Eligible for Free Lunch Program: 323 (15.5%)
    Eligible for Reduced-Price Lunch Program: 152 (7.3%)
Teachers: 150.0 (13.9 to 1)
Librarians/Media Specialists: 1.0 (2,087.0 to 1)
Guidance Counselors: 3.0 (695.7 to 1)
Current Spending: ($ per student per year):
    Total: $7,781; Instruction: $4,412; Support Services: $3,063
Enrollment, Drop-out Rates and Diploma Recipients by Race/Ethnicity

Category	Total	White	Black	Asian	AIAN	Hisp.
Enrollment (%)	100.0	90.5	5.9	1.8	0.2	0.4
Drop-out Rate (%)	0.9	0.8	5.9	0.0	n/a	0.0
H.S. Diplomas (#)	119	111	5	3	0	0

Eaton Community Schools
307 N Cherry St • Eaton, OH 45320-1855
(937) 456-1107
Grade Span: PK-12; **Agency Type:** 1
Schools: 4
    2 Primary; 1 Middle; 1 High; 0 Other Level
    4 Regular; 0 Special Education; 0 Vocational; 0 Alternative
    0 Magnet; 0 Charter; 3 Title I Eligible; 1 School-wide Title I
Students: 2,334   (51.7% male; 48.2% female)
    Individual Education Program: 256 (11.0%);
    English Language Learner: 9 (0.4%); Migrant: n/a
    Eligible for Free Lunch Program: 290 (12.4%)
    Eligible for Reduced-Price Lunch Program: 105 (4.5%)
Teachers: 130.0 (18.0 to 1)
Librarians/Media Specialists: 1.0 (2,334.0 to 1)
Guidance Counselors: 5.0 (466.8 to 1)
Current Spending: ($ per student per year):
    Total: $6,474; Instruction: $3,925; Support Services: $2,299
Enrollment, Drop-out Rates and Diploma Recipients by Race/Ethnicity

Category	Total	White	Black	Asian	AIAN	Hisp.
Enrollment (%)	100.0	97.5	0.9	0.6	0.0	0.3
Drop-out Rate (%)	4.5	4.5	0.0	0.0	n/a	0.0
H.S. Diplomas (#)	135	135	0	0	0	0

Preble Shawnee Local SD
124 Bloomfield St • Camden, OH 45311-1154
(937) 452-3323
Grade Span: KG-12; **Agency Type:** 2
Schools: 4
    2 Primary; 1 Middle; 1 High; 0 Other Level
    4 Regular; 0 Special Education; 0 Vocational; 0 Alternative
    0 Magnet; 0 Charter; 2 Title I Eligible; 0 School-wide Title I
Students: 1,667   (53.2% male; 46.7% female)
    Individual Education Program: 200 (12.0%);
    English Language Learner: 0 (0.0%); Migrant: n/a
    Eligible for Free Lunch Program: 246 (14.8%)
    Eligible for Reduced-Price Lunch Program: 121 (7.3%)
Teachers: 115.0 (14.5 to 1)
Librarians/Media Specialists: 2.0 (833.5 to 1)
Guidance Counselors: 4.0 (416.8 to 1)
Current Spending: ($ per student per year):
    Total: $7,003; Instruction: $4,127; Support Services: $2,582
Enrollment, Drop-out Rates and Diploma Recipients by Race/Ethnicity

Category	Total	White	Black	Asian	AIAN	Hisp.
Enrollment (%)	100.0	99.7	0.1	0.1	0.0	0.0
Drop-out Rate (%)	2.4	2.4	0.0	0.0	n/a	n/a
H.S. Diplomas (#)	116	115	0	1	0	0

Ottawa-Glandorf Local SD
630 Glendale Ave • Ottawa, OH 45875-1162
(419) 523-5261
Grade Span: PK-12; **Agency Type:** 2
Schools: 4
    3 Primary; 0 Middle; 1 High; 0 Other Level
    4 Regular; 0 Special Education; 0 Vocational; 0 Alternative
    0 Magnet; 0 Charter; 1 Title I Eligible; 0 School-wide Title I
Students: 1,731   (49.5% male; 50.4% female)
    Individual Education Program: 217 (12.5%);
    English Language Learner: 2 (0.1%); Migrant: 10 (0.6%)
    Eligible for Free Lunch Program: 110 (6.4%)
    Eligible for Reduced-Price Lunch Program: 43 (2.5%)
Teachers: 95.5 (18.1 to 1)
Librarians/Media Specialists: 0.0 (n/a to 1)
Guidance Counselors: 4.0 (432.8 to 1)
Current Spending: ($ per student per year):
    Total: $6,378; Instruction: $4,168; Support Services: $1,969
Enrollment, Drop-out Rates and Diploma Recipients by Race/Ethnicity

Category	Total	White	Black	Asian	AIAN	Hisp.
Enrollment (%)	100.0	92.0	0.3	0.3	0.0	4.6
Drop-out Rate (%)	1.2	0.9	n/a	0.0	n/a	10.0
H.S. Diplomas (#)	164	160	0	0	0	3

Clear Fork Valley Local SD
92 Hines Ave • Bellville, OH 44813-1232
(419) 886-3855
Grade Span: PK-12; **Agency Type:** 2
Schools: 4
    2 Primary; 1 Middle; 1 High; 0 Other Level
    4 Regular; 0 Special Education; 0 Vocational; 0 Alternative

0 Magnet; 0 Charter; 3 Title I Eligible; 0 School-wide Title I
Students: 1,843 (50.9% male; 49.0% female)
Individual Education Program: 242 (13.1%);
English Language Learner: 0 (0.0%); Migrant: n/a
Eligible for Free Lunch Program: 288 (15.6%)
Eligible for Reduced-Price Lunch Program: 100 (5.4%)
Teachers: 105.6 (17.5 to 1)
Librarians/Media Specialists: 1.0 (1,843.0 to 1)
Guidance Counselors: 4.0 (460.8 to 1)
Current Spending: ($ per student per year):
Total: $6,430; Instruction: $3,479; Support Services: $2,655
Enrollment, Drop-out Rates and Diploma Recipients by Race/Ethnicity

Category	Total	White	Black	Asian	AIAN	Hisp.
Enrollment (%)	100.0	98.0	0.8	0.5	0.1	0.1
Drop-out Rate (%)	1.7	1.8	0.0	0.0	n/a	n/a
H.S. Diplomas (#)	139	139	0	0	0	0

Lexington Local SD
103 Clever Ln • Lexington, OH 44904-1209
(419) 884-2132 • http://www.lexington.k12.oh.us/
Grade Span: PK-12; **Agency Type:** 2
Schools: 5
2 Primary; 2 Middle; 1 High; 0 Other Level
5 Regular; 0 Special Education; 0 Vocational; 0 Alternative
0 Magnet; 0 Charter; 3 Title I Eligible; 0 School-wide Title I
Students: 2,819 (52.2% male; 47.7% female)
Individual Education Program: 346 (12.3%);
English Language Learner: 0 (0.0%); Migrant: n/a
Eligible for Free Lunch Program: 210 (7.4%)
Eligible for Reduced-Price Lunch Program: 128 (4.5%)
Teachers: 156.6 (18.0 to 1)
Librarians/Media Specialists: 3.0 (939.7 to 1)
Guidance Counselors: 3.0 (939.7 to 1)
Current Spending: ($ per student per year):
Total: $6,483; Instruction: $3,909; Support Services: $2,318
Enrollment, Drop-out Rates and Diploma Recipients by Race/Ethnicity

Category	Total	White	Black	Asian	AIAN	Hisp.
Enrollment (%)	100.0	94.1	2.8	1.9	0.0	0.4
Drop-out Rate (%)	0.8	0.8	0.0	0.0	0.0	0.0
H.S. Diplomas (#)	215	201	1	6	0	3

Madison Local SD
1379 Grace St • Mansfield, OH 44905-2742
(419) 589-2600
Grade Span: KG-12; **Agency Type:** 2
Schools: 6
4 Primary; 1 Middle; 1 High; 0 Other Level
6 Regular; 0 Special Education; 0 Vocational; 0 Alternative
0 Magnet; 0 Charter; 4 Title I Eligible; 0 School-wide Title I
Students: 3,601 (53.2% male; 46.7% female)
Individual Education Program: 515 (14.3%);
English Language Learner: 0 (0.0%); Migrant: n/a
Eligible for Free Lunch Program: 833 (23.6%)
Eligible for Reduced-Price Lunch Program: 287 (8.1%)
Teachers: 249.5 (14.2 to 1)
Librarians/Media Specialists: 2.0 (1,766.5 to 1)
Guidance Counselors: 8.0 (441.6 to 1)
Current Spending: ($ per student per year):
Total: $8,364; Instruction: $5,145; Support Services: $2,894
Enrollment, Drop-out Rates and Diploma Recipients by Race/Ethnicity

Category	Total	White	Black	Asian	AIAN	Hisp.
Enrollment (%)	100.0	93.0	3.7	0.1	0.1	1.0
Drop-out Rate (%)	5.4	5.2	9.4	14.3	n/a	0.0
H.S. Diplomas (#)	224	206	15	2	0	0

Mansfield City SD
53 W 4th St • Mansfield, OH 44902-1205
Mailing Address: PO Box 1448 • Mansfield, OH 44901-1448
(419) 525-6400 • http://www.mansfieldschools.org/
Grade Span: PK-12; **Agency Type:** 1
Schools: 14
9 Primary; 2 Middle; 2 High; 1 Other Level
14 Regular; 0 Special Education; 0 Vocational; 0 Alternative
0 Magnet; 0 Charter; 14 Title I Eligible; 9 School-wide Title I
Students: 5,802 (51.8% male; 48.1% female)
Individual Education Program: 1,149 (19.8%);
English Language Learner: 0 (0.0%); Migrant: n/a
Eligible for Free Lunch Program: 3,579 (61.7%)
Eligible for Reduced-Price Lunch Program: 511 (8.8%)
Teachers: 428.3 (13.5 to 1)
Librarians/Media Specialists: 5.0 (1,160.4 to 1)
Guidance Counselors: 14.0 (414.4 to 1)
Current Spending: ($ per student per year):
Total: $9,760; Instruction: $5,501; Support Services: $3,882

Enrollment, Drop-out Rates and Diploma Recipients by Race/Ethnicity

Category	Total	White	Black	Asian	AIAN	Hisp.
Enrollment (%)	100.0	60.0	34.4	0.2	0.1	0.7
Drop-out Rate (%)	5.8	6.0	5.6	n/a	n/a	0.0
H.S. Diplomas (#)	258	172	86	0	0	0

Ontario Local SD
457 Shelby Ontario Rd • Mansfield, OH 44906-1029
(419) 747-4311
Grade Span: PK-12; **Agency Type:** 2
Schools: 4
2 Primary; 1 Middle; 1 High; 0 Other Level
4 Regular; 0 Special Education; 0 Vocational; 0 Alternative
0 Magnet; 0 Charter; 2 Title I Eligible; 0 School-wide Title I
Students: 1,781 (52.1% male; 47.8% female)
Individual Education Program: 144 (8.1%);
English Language Learner: 2 (0.1%); Migrant: n/a
Eligible for Free Lunch Program: 122 (6.9%)
Eligible for Reduced-Price Lunch Program: 50 (2.8%)
Teachers: 92.5 (19.3 to 1)
Librarians/Media Specialists: 2.0 (890.5 to 1)
Guidance Counselors: 3.0 (593.7 to 1)
Current Spending: ($ per student per year):
Total: $6,971; Instruction: $3,868; Support Services: $2,821
Enrollment, Drop-out Rates and Diploma Recipients by Race/Ethnicity

Category	Total	White	Black	Asian	AIAN	Hisp.
Enrollment (%)	100.0	92.9	3.5	1.5	0.1	0.3
Drop-out Rate (%)	1.2	1.3	0.0	0.0	n/a	0.0
H.S. Diplomas (#)	119	112	3	3	0	1

Shelby City SD
25 High School Ave • Shelby, OH 44875-1576
(419) 342-3520 • http://www.shelby-city.k12.oh.us/
Grade Span: KG-12; **Agency Type:** 1
Schools: 6
4 Primary; 1 Middle; 1 High; 0 Other Level
6 Regular; 0 Special Education; 0 Vocational; 0 Alternative
0 Magnet; 0 Charter; 3 Title I Eligible; 3 School-wide Title I
Students: 2,254 (51.9% male; 48.0% female)
Individual Education Program: 338 (15.0%);
English Language Learner: 0 (0.0%); Migrant: n/a
Eligible for Free Lunch Program: 419 (18.6%)
Eligible for Reduced-Price Lunch Program: 175 (7.8%)
Teachers: 140.7 (16.0 to 1)
Librarians/Media Specialists: 2.0 (1,127.0 to 1)
Guidance Counselors: 5.0 (450.8 to 1)
Current Spending: ($ per student per year):
Total: $7,468; Instruction: $4,513; Support Services: $2,612
Enrollment, Drop-out Rates and Diploma Recipients by Race/Ethnicity

Category	Total	White	Black	Asian	AIAN	Hisp.
Enrollment (%)	100.0	97.6	0.2	0.3	0.0	0.4
Drop-out Rate (%)	3.2	3.2	0.0	0.0	n/a	0.0
H.S. Diplomas (#)	171	166	0	2	0	2

Ross County

Chillicothe City SD
235 Cherry St • Chillicothe, OH 45601-2350
(740) 775-4250
Grade Span: PK-12; **Agency Type:** 1
Schools: 6
4 Primary; 1 Middle; 1 High; 0 Other Level
6 Regular; 0 Special Education; 0 Vocational; 0 Alternative
0 Magnet; 0 Charter; 3 Title I Eligible; 2 School-wide Title I
Students: 3,520 (51.0% male; 48.9% female)
Individual Education Program: 463 (13.2%);
English Language Learner: 0 (0.0%); Migrant: n/a
Eligible for Free Lunch Program: 956 (28.3%)
Eligible for Reduced-Price Lunch Program: 186 (5.5%)
Teachers: 181.4 (18.6 to 1)
Librarians/Media Specialists: 3.0 (1,125.3 to 1)
Guidance Counselors: 6.0 (562.7 to 1)
Current Spending: ($ per student per year):
Total: $6,983; Instruction: $3,982; Support Services: $2,676
Enrollment, Drop-out Rates and Diploma Recipients by Race/Ethnicity

Category	Total	White	Black	Asian	AIAN	Hisp.
Enrollment (%)	100.0	84.0	9.1	0.9	0.1	0.9
Drop-out Rate (%)	3.3	3.1	5.0	0.0	0.0	0.0
H.S. Diplomas (#)	285	251	18	4	0	5

Union-Scioto Local SD
1432 Egypt Pike • Chillicothe, OH 45601-3905
(740) 773-4102
Grade Span: PK-12; **Agency Type:** 2
Schools: 3

1 Primary; 1 Middle; 1 High; 0 Other Level
3 Regular; 0 Special Education; 0 Vocational; 0 Alternative
0 Magnet; 0 Charter; 0 Title I Eligible; 0 School-wide Title I
Students: 1,954   (49.9% male; 50.0% female)
Individual Education Program: 201 (10.3%);
English Language Learner: 0 (0.0%); Migrant: n/a
Eligible for Free Lunch Program: 120 (6.1%)
Eligible for Reduced-Price Lunch Program: 32 (1.6%)
Teachers: 106.6 (18.3 to 1)
Librarians/Media Specialists: 1.0 (1,954.0 to 1)
Guidance Counselors: 3.0 (651.3 to 1)
Current Spending: ($ per student per year):
Total: $6,548; Instruction: $3,914; Support Services: $2,380
Enrollment, Drop-out Rates and Diploma Recipients by Race/Ethnicity

Category	Total	White	Black	Asian	AIAN	Hisp.
Enrollment (%)	100.0	94.4	2.1	0.6	0.5	0.2
Drop-out Rate (%)	3.2	3.1	7.7	0.0	n/a	0.0
H.S. Diplomas (#)	133	130	2	1	0	0

Zane Trace Local SD

946 State Route 180 • Chillicothe, OH 45601-8141
(740) 775-1355 • http://gsn.k12.oh.us/zanetrace/index.html
Grade Span: PK-12; **Agency Type:** 2
Schools: 3
1 Primary; 1 Middle; 1 High; 0 Other Level
3 Regular; 0 Special Education; 0 Vocational; 0 Alternative
0 Magnet; 0 Charter; 1 Title I Eligible; 0 School-wide Title I
Students: 1,589   (48.6% male; 51.3% female)
Individual Education Program: 192 (12.1%);
English Language Learner: 0 (0.0%); Migrant: n/a
Eligible for Free Lunch Program: 192 (12.1%)
Eligible for Reduced-Price Lunch Program: 98 (6.2%)
Teachers: 84.0 (18.9 to 1)
Librarians/Media Specialists: 1.0 (1,589.0 to 1)
Guidance Counselors: 3.0 (529.7 to 1)
Current Spending: ($ per student per year):
Total: $5,890; Instruction: $3,298; Support Services: $2,345
Enrollment, Drop-out Rates and Diploma Recipients by Race/Ethnicity

Category	Total	White	Black	Asian	AIAN	Hisp.
Enrollment (%)	100.0	99.0	0.6	0.2	0.0	0.1
Drop-out Rate (%)	2.1	2.1	n/a	0.0	n/a	0.0
H.S. Diplomas (#)	95	95	0	0	0	0

Sandusky County

Clyde-Green Springs Ex Vill SD

106 S Main St • Clyde, OH 43410-1633
(419) 547-0588 • http://www.clyde.k12.oh.us/
Grade Span: PK-12; **Agency Type:** 1
Schools: 5
3 Primary; 1 Middle; 1 High; 0 Other Level
5 Regular; 0 Special Education; 0 Vocational; 0 Alternative
0 Magnet; 0 Charter; 4 Title I Eligible; 0 School-wide Title I
Students: 2,297   (50.9% male; 49.0% female)
Individual Education Program: 343 (14.9%);
English Language Learner: 2 (0.1%); Migrant: 2 (0.1%)
Eligible for Free Lunch Program: 359 (15.6%)
Eligible for Reduced-Price Lunch Program: 218 (9.5%)
Teachers: 130.2 (17.6 to 1)
Librarians/Media Specialists: 1.0 (2,297.0 to 1)
Guidance Counselors: 4.0 (574.3 to 1)
Current Spending: ($ per student per year):
Total: $6,881; Instruction: $4,185; Support Services: $2,430
Enrollment, Drop-out Rates and Diploma Recipients by Race/Ethnicity

Category	Total	White	Black	Asian	AIAN	Hisp.
Enrollment (%)	100.0	92.9	0.4	0.5	0.0	4.1
Drop-out Rate (%)	2.1	2.1	n/a	0.0	n/a	2.5
H.S. Diplomas (#)	171	165	0	2	0	4

Fremont City SD

1220 Cedar St Ste A • Fremont, OH 43420-5118
(419) 332-6454
Grade Span: PK-12; **Agency Type:** 1
Schools: 9
7 Primary; 1 Middle; 1 High; 0 Other Level
9 Regular; 0 Special Education; 0 Vocational; 0 Alternative
0 Magnet; 0 Charter; 7 Title I Eligible; 3 School-wide Title I
Students: 4,598   (51.5% male; 48.4% female)
Individual Education Program: 685 (14.9%);
English Language Learner: 264 (5.7%); Migrant: 75 (1.6%)
Eligible for Free Lunch Program: 1,390 (30.2%)
Eligible for Reduced-Price Lunch Program: 436 (9.5%)
Teachers: 249.7 (18.4 to 1)
Librarians/Media Specialists: 3.0 (1,532.3 to 1)
Guidance Counselors: 8.0 (574.6 to 1)

Current Spending: ($ per student per year):
Total: $7,047; Instruction: $4,351; Support Services: $2,404
Enrollment, Drop-out Rates and Diploma Recipients by Race/Ethnicity

Category	Total	White	Black	Asian	AIAN	Hisp.
Enrollment (%)	100.0	68.9	9.1	0.5	0.1	14.3
Drop-out Rate (%)	4.6	3.4	8.5	0.0	0.0	9.9
H.S. Diplomas (#)	325	254	22	2	1	37

Scioto County

Minford Local SD

491 Bond Rd • Minford, OH 45653-0204
Mailing Address: PO Box 204 • Minford, OH 45653-0204
(740) 820-3896 • http://www.minford.k12.oh.us/
Grade Span: PK-12; **Agency Type:** 2
Schools: 3
1 Primary; 1 Middle; 1 High; 0 Other Level
3 Regular; 0 Special Education; 0 Vocational; 0 Alternative
0 Magnet; 0 Charter; 2 Title I Eligible; 0 School-wide Title I
Students: 1,652   (50.7% male; 49.2% female)
Individual Education Program: 185 (11.2%);
English Language Learner: 0 (0.0%); Migrant: n/a
Eligible for Free Lunch Program: 519 (31.4%)
Eligible for Reduced-Price Lunch Program: 152 (9.2%)
Teachers: 93.2 (17.7 to 1)
Librarians/Media Specialists: 3.0 (550.7 to 1)
Guidance Counselors: 3.0 (550.7 to 1)
Current Spending: ($ per student per year):
Total: $6,935; Instruction: $4,074; Support Services: $2,549
Enrollment, Drop-out Rates and Diploma Recipients by Race/Ethnicity

Category	Total	White	Black	Asian	AIAN	Hisp.
Enrollment (%)	100.0	97.8	0.3	0.1	0.4	0.5
Drop-out Rate (%)	1.2	1.2	n/a	0.0	n/a	n/a
H.S. Diplomas (#)	113	113	0	0	0	0

Northwest Local SD

800 Mohawk Dr • Mc Dermott, OH 45652-9000
(740) 259-5558
Grade Span: PK-12; **Agency Type:** 2
Schools: 3
1 Primary; 1 Middle; 1 High; 0 Other Level
3 Regular; 0 Special Education; 0 Vocational; 0 Alternative
0 Magnet; 0 Charter; 2 Title I Eligible; 1 School-wide Title I
Students: 1,780   (53.1% male; 46.8% female)
Individual Education Program: 251 (14.1%);
English Language Learner: 0 (0.0%); Migrant: n/a
Eligible for Free Lunch Program: 819 (46.0%)
Eligible for Reduced-Price Lunch Program: 183 (10.3%)
Teachers: 106.0 (16.8 to 1)
Librarians/Media Specialists: 2.0 (890.0 to 1)
Guidance Counselors: 4.0 (445.0 to 1)
Current Spending: ($ per student per year):
Total: $7,401; Instruction: $4,129; Support Services: $2,952
Enrollment, Drop-out Rates and Diploma Recipients by Race/Ethnicity

Category	Total	White	Black	Asian	AIAN	Hisp.
Enrollment (%)	100.0	99.5	0.0	0.1	0.0	0.0
Drop-out Rate (%)	2.5	2.6	n/a	0.0	n/a	0.0
H.S. Diplomas (#)	118	118	0	0	0	0

Portsmouth City SD

1149 Gallia St • Portsmouth, OH 45662-4159
(740) 354-4727
Grade Span: KG-12; **Agency Type:** 1
Schools: 6
3 Primary; 2 Middle; 1 High; 0 Other Level
6 Regular; 0 Special Education; 0 Vocational; 0 Alternative
0 Magnet; 0 Charter; 6 Title I Eligible; 5 School-wide Title I
Students: 2,166   (53.4% male; 46.5% female)
Individual Education Program: 251 (11.6%);
English Language Learner: 0 (0.0%); Migrant: n/a
Eligible for Free Lunch Program: 1,004 (46.4%)
Eligible for Reduced-Price Lunch Program: 126 (5.8%)
Teachers: 143.9 (15.1 to 1)
Librarians/Media Specialists: 2.0 (1,083.0 to 1)
Guidance Counselors: 6.0 (361.0 to 1)
Current Spending: ($ per student per year):
Total: $9,469; Instruction: $5,621; Support Services: $3,417
Enrollment, Drop-out Rates and Diploma Recipients by Race/Ethnicity

Category	Total	White	Black	Asian	AIAN	Hisp.
Enrollment (%)	100.0	86.9	7.9	0.4	0.2	0.4
Drop-out Rate (%)	7.6	7.6	8.3	0.0	n/a	0.0
H.S. Diplomas (#)	102	86	12	1	0	1

Washington-Nile Local SD
15332 US Hwy 52 • West Portsmouth, OH 45663-9093
(740) 858-1111
Grade Span: PK-12; **Agency Type:** 2
Schools: 3
    1 Primary; 0 Middle; 1 High; 1 Other Level
    3 Regular; 0 Special Education; 0 Vocational; 0 Alternative
    0 Magnet; 0 Charter; 2 Title I Eligible; 2 School-wide Title I
Students: 1,699 (51.4% male; 48.5% female)
    Individual Education Program: 170 (10.0%);
    English Language Learner: 1 (0.1%); Migrant: n/a
    Eligible for Free Lunch Program: 639 (37.6%)
    Eligible for Reduced-Price Lunch Program: 135 (7.9%)
Teachers: 106.6 (15.9 to 1)
Librarians/Media Specialists: 3.0 (566.3 to 1)
Guidance Counselors: 5.0 (339.8 to 1)
Current Spending: ($ per student per year):
    Total: $7,137; Instruction: $4,177; Support Services: $2,635
Enrollment, Drop-out Rates and Diploma Recipients by Race/Ethnicity

Category	Total	White	Black	Asian	AIAN	Hisp.
Enrollment (%)	100.0	98.6	0.1	0.1	0.1	0.4
Drop-out Rate (%)	3.6	3.6	0.0	n/a	0.0	n/a
H.S. Diplomas (#)	113	112	0	0	1	0

Seneca County

Fostoria City SD
500 Pkwy Dr • Fostoria, OH 44830-1513
(419) 288-8400
Grade Span: PK-12; **Agency Type:** 1
Schools: 5
    3 Primary; 1 Middle; 1 High; 0 Other Level
    5 Regular; 0 Special Education; 0 Vocational; 0 Alternative
    0 Magnet; 0 Charter; 4 Title I Eligible; 4 School-wide Title I
Students: 2,339 (51.8% male; 48.1% female)
    Individual Education Program: 434 (18.6%);
    English Language Learner: 78 (3.3%); Migrant: n/a
    Eligible for Free Lunch Program: 970 (41.5%)
    Eligible for Reduced-Price Lunch Program: 250 (10.7%)
Teachers: 123.5 (18.9 to 1)
Librarians/Media Specialists: 1.0 (2,339.0 to 1)
Guidance Counselors: 5.8 (403.3 to 1)
Current Spending: ($ per student per year):
    Total: $7,598; Instruction: $4,282; Support Services: $2,992
Enrollment, Drop-out Rates and Diploma Recipients by Race/Ethnicity

Category	Total	White	Black	Asian	AIAN	Hisp.
Enrollment (%)	100.0	69.0	7.4	0.5	0.0	9.1
Drop-out Rate (%)	5.3	4.8	6.8	0.0	0.0	3.1
H.S. Diplomas (#)	115	96	9	0	0	6

Tiffin City SD
244 S Monroe St • Tiffin, OH 44883-2906
(419) 447-2515 • http://www.tiffin.k12.oh.us/
Grade Span: PK-12; **Agency Type:** 1
Schools: 7
    5 Primary; 1 Middle; 1 High; 0 Other Level
    7 Regular; 0 Special Education; 0 Vocational; 0 Alternative
    0 Magnet; 0 Charter; 4 Title I Eligible; 3 School-wide Title I
Students: 3,022 (52.2% male; 47.7% female)
    Individual Education Program: 525 (17.4%);
    English Language Learner: 3 (0.1%); Migrant: 2 (0.1%)
    Eligible for Free Lunch Program: 503 (16.6%)
    Eligible for Reduced-Price Lunch Program: 247 (8.2%)
Teachers: 177.5 (17.0 to 1)
Librarians/Media Specialists: 2.0 (1,512.0 to 1)
Guidance Counselors: 8.0 (378.0 to 1)
Current Spending: ($ per student per year):
    Total: $6,586; Instruction: $3,982; Support Services: $2,405
Enrollment, Drop-out Rates and Diploma Recipients by Race/Ethnicity

Category	Total	White	Black	Asian	AIAN	Hisp.
Enrollment (%)	100.0	93.5	1.4	0.7	0.1	2.1
Drop-out Rate (%)	4.9	4.8	25.0	11.1	n/a	0.0
H.S. Diplomas (#)	247	237	1	3	0	2

Shelby County

Sidney City SD
232 N Miami Ave • Sidney, OH 45365-2708
(937) 497-2200 • http://www.sidney.k12.oh.us/
Grade Span: KG-12; **Agency Type:** 1
Schools: 9
    5 Primary; 1 Middle; 1 High; 2 Other Level
    9 Regular; 0 Special Education; 0 Vocational; 0 Alternative
    0 Magnet; 0 Charter; 6 Title I Eligible; 3 School-wide Title I
Students: 3,897 (51.6% male; 48.3% female)

    Individual Education Program: 731 (18.8%);
    English Language Learner: 62 (1.6%); Migrant: n/a
    Eligible for Free Lunch Program: 1,079 (27.9%)
    Eligible for Reduced-Price Lunch Program: 286 (7.4%)
Teachers: 219.8 (17.6 to 1)
Librarians/Media Specialists: 3.0 (1,287.3 to 1)
Guidance Counselors: 12.0 (321.8 to 1)
Current Spending: ($ per student per year):
    Total: $6,617; Instruction: $3,737; Support Services: $2,566
Enrollment, Drop-out Rates and Diploma Recipients by Race/Ethnicity

Category	Total	White	Black	Asian	AIAN	Hisp.
Enrollment (%)	100.0	87.4	4.1	2.3	0.1	1.1
Drop-out Rate (%)	2.9	3.0	0.0	0.0	0.0	0.0
H.S. Diplomas (#)	233	210	12	9	0	1

Stark County

Alliance City SD
200 Glamorgan St • Alliance, OH 44601-2946
(330) 821-2100 • http://www.aviators.stark.k12.oh.us/
Grade Span: PK-12; **Agency Type:** 1
Schools: 6
    4 Primary; 1 Middle; 1 High; 0 Other Level
    6 Regular; 0 Special Education; 0 Vocational; 0 Alternative
    0 Magnet; 0 Charter; 6 Title I Eligible; 5 School-wide Title I
Students: 3,323 (51.1% male; 48.8% female)
    Individual Education Program: 574 (17.3%);
    English Language Learner: 8 (0.2%); Migrant: 7 (0.2%)
    Eligible for Free Lunch Program: 1,675 (50.4%)
    Eligible for Reduced-Price Lunch Program: 314 (9.4%)
Teachers: 223.2 (14.9 to 1)
Librarians/Media Specialists: 2.5 (1,329.6 to 1)
Guidance Counselors: 6.0 (554.0 to 1)
Current Spending: ($ per student per year):
    Total: $7,913; Instruction: $5,069; Support Services: $2,523
Enrollment, Drop-out Rates and Diploma Recipients by Race/Ethnicity

Category	Total	White	Black	Asian	AIAN	Hisp.
Enrollment (%)	100.0	78.8	16.3	0.5	0.1	1.2
Drop-out Rate (%)	5.9	4.8	9.5	33.3	n/a	18.2
H.S. Diplomas (#)	213	185	25	0	0	3

Canton City SD
617 Mckinley Ave SW • Canton, OH 44707-4727
(330) 438-2500 • http://www.ccsdistrict.org/
Grade Span: PK-12; **Agency Type:** 1
Schools: 30
    20 Primary; 4 Middle; 5 High; 0 Other Level
    26 Regular; 2 Special Education; 0 Vocational; 1 Alternative
    0 Magnet; 0 Charter; 23 Title I Eligible; 13 School-wide Title I
Students: 11,798 (51.1% male; 48.8% female)
    Individual Education Program: 1,997 (16.9%);
    English Language Learner: 29 (0.2%); Migrant: n/a
    Eligible for Free Lunch Program: 6,440 (55.1%)
    Eligible for Reduced-Price Lunch Program: 1,208 (10.3%)
Teachers: 755.0 (15.5 to 1)
Librarians/Media Specialists: 4.0 (2,924.0 to 1)
Guidance Counselors: 25.0 (467.8 to 1)
Current Spending: ($ per student per year):
    Total: $9,505; Instruction: $5,601; Support Services: $3,603
Enrollment, Drop-out Rates and Diploma Recipients by Race/Ethnicity

Category	Total	White	Black	Asian	AIAN	Hisp.
Enrollment (%)	100.0	55.5	34.5	0.3	0.4	0.8
Drop-out Rate (%)	16.0	14.8	16.2	50.0	18.8	29.4
H.S. Diplomas (#)	495	324	162	2	1	1

Canton Local SD
4526 Ridge Ave SE • Canton, OH 44707-1118
(330) 484-8010 • http://www.cantonlocal.org/
Grade Span: PK-12; **Agency Type:** 2
Schools: 5
    3 Primary; 1 Middle; 1 High; 0 Other Level
    5 Regular; 0 Special Education; 0 Vocational; 0 Alternative
    0 Magnet; 0 Charter; 3 Title I Eligible; 0 School-wide Title I
Students: 2,538 (53.9% male; 46.0% female)
    Individual Education Program: 367 (14.5%);
    English Language Learner: 1 (<0.1%); Migrant: n/a
    Eligible for Free Lunch Program: 610 (24.0%)
    Eligible for Reduced-Price Lunch Program: 231 (9.1%)
Teachers: 169.2 (15.0 to 1)
Librarians/Media Specialists: 1.0 (2,538.0 to 1)
Guidance Counselors: 4.6 (551.7 to 1)
Current Spending: ($ per student per year):
    Total: $7,838; Instruction: $4,651; Support Services: $2,899

Enrollment, Drop-out Rates and Diploma Recipients by Race/Ethnicity

Category	Total	White	Black	Asian	AIAN	Hisp.
Enrollment (%)	100.0	88.9	8.8	0.2	0.1	0.5
Drop-out Rate (%)	0.2	0.2	0.0	0.0	n/a	0.0
H.S. Diplomas (#)	162	153	8	0	0	1

Fairless Local SD

11885 Navarre Rd SW • Navarre, OH 44662-9485
(330) 767-3577 • http://falcon.stark.k12.oh.us/FLocal/index.html
Grade Span: PK-12; **Agency Type:** 2
Schools: 5
    3 Primary; 1 Middle; 1 High; 0 Other Level
    5 Regular; 0 Special Education; 0 Vocational; 0 Alternative
    0 Magnet; 0 Charter; 3 Title I Eligible; 2 School-wide Title I
Students: 1,883 (50.8% male; 49.1% female)
    Individual Education Program: 293 (15.6%);
    English Language Learner: 3 (0.2%); Migrant: n/a
    Eligible for Free Lunch Program: 419 (22.3%)
    Eligible for Reduced-Price Lunch Program: 156 (8.3%)
Teachers: 123.5 (15.2 to 1)
Librarians/Media Specialists: 1.0 (1,883.0 to 1)
Guidance Counselors: 1.0 (1,883.0 to 1)
Current Spending: ($ per student per year):
    Total: $6,821; Instruction: $4,085; Support Services: $2,440

Enrollment, Drop-out Rates and Diploma Recipients by Race/Ethnicity

Category	Total	White	Black	Asian	AIAN	Hisp.
Enrollment (%)	100.0	98.2	0.4	0.5	0.1	0.4
Drop-out Rate (%)	1.6	1.6	0.0	0.0	n/a	0.0
H.S. Diplomas (#)	119	118	0	0	0	0

Jackson Local SD

7984 Fulton Dr NW • Massillon, OH 44646-9393
(330) 830-8000 • http://jackson.stark.k12.oh.us/
Grade Span: PK-12; **Agency Type:** 2
Schools: 6
    4 Primary; 1 Middle; 1 High; 0 Other Level
    6 Regular; 0 Special Education; 0 Vocational; 0 Alternative
    0 Magnet; 0 Charter; 3 Title I Eligible; 0 School-wide Title I
Students: 5,561 (50.3% male; 49.6% female)
    Individual Education Program: 423 (7.6%);
    English Language Learner: 69 (1.2%); Migrant: n/a
    Eligible for Free Lunch Program: 265 (4.8%)
    Eligible for Reduced-Price Lunch Program: 135 (2.4%)
Teachers: 311.5 (17.9 to 1)
Librarians/Media Specialists: 3.0 (1,853.7 to 1)
Guidance Counselors: 12.0 (463.4 to 1)
Current Spending: ($ per student per year):
    Total: $7,401; Instruction: $3,996; Support Services: $3,170

Enrollment, Drop-out Rates and Diploma Recipients by Race/Ethnicity

Category	Total	White	Black	Asian	AIAN	Hisp.
Enrollment (%)	100.0	93.9	2.2	2.6	0.0	0.7
Drop-out Rate (%)	0.6	0.6	3.2	0.0	n/a	0.0
H.S. Diplomas (#)	422	406	5	8	0	3

Lake Local SD

225 Lincoln St SW • Hartville, OH 44632-9382
Mailing Address: 12077 Lisa St NW • Hartville, OH 44632-9670
(330) 877-9383 •
http://lakelocal.oh.schoolwebpages.com/education/district/district.php?sectionid=1
Grade Span: PK-12; **Agency Type:** 2
Schools: 5
    2 Primary; 2 Middle; 1 High; 0 Other Level
    5 Regular; 0 Special Education; 0 Vocational; 0 Alternative
    0 Magnet; 0 Charter; 3 Title I Eligible; 0 School-wide Title I
Students: 3,359 (52.3% male; 47.6% female)
    Individual Education Program: 365 (10.9%);
    English Language Learner: 58 (1.7%); Migrant: n/a
    Eligible for Free Lunch Program: 195 (5.8%)
    Eligible for Reduced-Price Lunch Program: 100 (3.0%)
Teachers: 190.9 (17.6 to 1)
Librarians/Media Specialists: 2.0 (1,679.5 to 1)
Guidance Counselors: 8.0 (419.9 to 1)
Current Spending: ($ per student per year):
    Total: $6,177; Instruction: $3,721; Support Services: $2,267

Enrollment, Drop-out Rates and Diploma Recipients by Race/Ethnicity

Category	Total	White	Black	Asian	AIAN	Hisp.
Enrollment (%)	100.0	98.7	0.1	0.4	0.0	0.6
Drop-out Rate (%)	0.8	0.8	0.0	0.0	n/a	0.0
H.S. Diplomas (#)	248	244	1	2	0	1

Louisville City SD

418 E Main St • Louisville, OH 44641-1420
(330) 875-1666 • http://leopard.stark.k12.oh.us/
Grade Span: PK-12; **Agency Type:** 1
Schools: 6
    4 Primary; 1 Middle; 1 High; 0 Other Level
    6 Regular; 0 Special Education; 0 Vocational; 0 Alternative
    0 Magnet; 0 Charter; 3 Title I Eligible; 2 School-wide Title I
Students: 3,274 (49.3% male; 50.6% female)
    Individual Education Program: 354 (10.8%);
    English Language Learner: 8 (0.2%); Migrant: n/a
    Eligible for Free Lunch Program: 437 (13.3%)
    Eligible for Reduced-Price Lunch Program: 244 (7.5%)
Teachers: 193.0 (17.0 to 1)
Librarians/Media Specialists: 2.0 (1,637.0 to 1)
Guidance Counselors: 8.4 (389.8 to 1)
Current Spending: ($ per student per year):
    Total: $6,319; Instruction: $4,135; Support Services: $1,891

Enrollment, Drop-out Rates and Diploma Recipients by Race/Ethnicity

Category	Total	White	Black	Asian	AIAN	Hisp.
Enrollment (%)	100.0	99.5	0.2	0.2	0.0	0.2
Drop-out Rate (%)	1.1	1.1	n/a	0.0	n/a	0.0
H.S. Diplomas (#)	199	198	0	1	0	0

Marlington Local SD

10320 Moulin Ave NE • Alliance, OH 44601-5906
(330) 823-7458 • http://dukes.stark.k12.oh.us/
Grade Span: PK-12; **Agency Type:** 2
Schools: 5
    3 Primary; 1 Middle; 1 High; 0 Other Level
    5 Regular; 0 Special Education; 0 Vocational; 0 Alternative
    0 Magnet; 0 Charter; 2 Title I Eligible; 0 School-wide Title I
Students: 2,738 (49.4% male; 50.5% female)
    Individual Education Program: 420 (15.3%);
    English Language Learner: 37 (1.4%); Migrant: 27 (1.0%)
    Eligible for Free Lunch Program: 360 (13.1%)
    Eligible for Reduced-Price Lunch Program: 153 (5.6%)
Teachers: 159.4 (17.2 to 1)
Librarians/Media Specialists: 1.0 (2,738.0 to 1)
Guidance Counselors: 4.4 (622.3 to 1)
Current Spending: ($ per student per year):
    Total: $6,543; Instruction: $4,043; Support Services: $2,266

Enrollment, Drop-out Rates and Diploma Recipients by Race/Ethnicity

Category	Total	White	Black	Asian	AIAN	Hisp.
Enrollment (%)	100.0	95.5	1.6	0.5	0.0	1.4
Drop-out Rate (%)	0.3	0.4	0.0	0.0	n/a	0.0
H.S. Diplomas (#)	171	168	2	0	0	1

Massillon City SD

207 Oak Ave SE • Massillon, OH 44646-6790
(330) 830-1810
Grade Span: PK-12; **Agency Type:** 1
Schools: 10
    7 Primary; 2 Middle; 1 High; 0 Other Level
    10 Regular; 0 Special Education; 0 Vocational; 0 Alternative
    0 Magnet; 0 Charter; 9 Title I Eligible; 4 School-wide Title I
Students: 4,547 (52.9% male; 47.0% female)
    Individual Education Program: 679 (14.9%);
    English Language Learner: 11 (0.2%); Migrant: n/a
    Eligible for Free Lunch Program: 1,679 (36.9%)
    Eligible for Reduced-Price Lunch Program: 408 (9.0%)
Teachers: 326.7 (13.9 to 1)
Librarians/Media Specialists: 3.0 (1,515.7 to 1)
Guidance Counselors: 8.4 (541.3 to 1)
Current Spending: ($ per student per year):
    Total: $8,349; Instruction: $4,777; Support Services: $3,286

Enrollment, Drop-out Rates and Diploma Recipients by Race/Ethnicity

Category	Total	White	Black	Asian	AIAN	Hisp.
Enrollment (%)	100.0	83.2	13.5	0.4	0.1	0.5
Drop-out Rate (%)	5.1	5.1	5.5	0.0	n/a	0.0
H.S. Diplomas (#)	255	227	28	0	0	0

Minerva Local SD

303 Latzer Ave • Minerva, OH 44657-1434
(330) 868-4332 • http://lion.stark.k12.oh.us/
Grade Span: KG-12; **Agency Type:** 2
Schools: 4
    2 Primary; 1 Middle; 1 High; 0 Other Level
    4 Regular; 0 Special Education; 0 Vocational; 0 Alternative
    0 Magnet; 0 Charter; 2 Title I Eligible; 0 School-wide Title I
Students: 2,202 (53.7% male; 46.2% female)
    Individual Education Program: 300 (13.6%);
    English Language Learner: 3 (0.1%); Migrant: n/a
    Eligible for Free Lunch Program: 533 (24.2%)
    Eligible for Reduced-Price Lunch Program: 195 (8.9%)

Teachers: 129.5 (17.0 to 1)
Librarians/Media Specialists: 1.0 (2,202.0 to 1)
Guidance Counselors: 4.0 (550.5 to 1)
Current Spending: ($ per student per year):
   Total: $7,076; Instruction: $4,437; Support Services: $2,389
Enrollment, Drop-out Rates and Diploma Recipients by Race/Ethnicity

Category	Total	White	Black	Asian	AIAN	Hisp.
Enrollment (%)	100.0	99.5	0.1	0.3	0.0	0.0
Drop-out Rate (%)	3.6	3.6	0.0	0.0	n/a	0.0
H.S. Diplomas (#)	145	144	0	0	0	1

North Canton City SD
525 7th St NE • North Canton, OH 44720-2012
(330) 497-5600
Grade Span: PK-12; **Agency Type:** 1
Schools: 7
   5 Primary; 1 Middle; 1 High; 0 Other Level
   7 Regular; 0 Special Education; 0 Vocational; 0 Alternative
   0 Magnet; 0 Charter; 4 Title I Eligible; 0 School-wide Title I
Students: 4,924   (50.7% male; 49.2% female)
   Individual Education Program: 534 (10.8%);
   English Language Learner: 23 (0.5%); Migrant: n/a
   Eligible for Free Lunch Program: 268 (5.4%)
   Eligible for Reduced-Price Lunch Program: 165 (3.4%)
Teachers: 292.5 (16.8 to 1)
Librarians/Media Specialists: 2.0 (2,462.0 to 1)
Guidance Counselors: 10.8 (455.9 to 1)
Current Spending: ($ per student per year):
   Total: $7,005; Instruction: $4,180; Support Services: $2,576
Enrollment, Drop-out Rates and Diploma Recipients by Race/Ethnicity

Category	Total	White	Black	Asian	AIAN	Hisp.
Enrollment (%)	100.0	94.8	1.4	1.5	0.2	0.9
Drop-out Rate (%)	0.6	0.6	0.0	4.8	0.0	0.0
H.S. Diplomas (#)	319	304	5	6	0	3

Northwest Local SD
104 Market St W • Canal Fulton, OH 44614-1050
(330) 854-2291
Grade Span: PK-12; **Agency Type:** 2
Schools: 5
   2 Primary; 2 Middle; 1 High; 0 Other Level
   5 Regular; 0 Special Education; 0 Vocational; 0 Alternative
   0 Magnet; 0 Charter; 3 Title I Eligible; 0 School-wide Title I
Students: 2,447   (51.5% male; 48.4% female)
   Individual Education Program: 339 (13.9%);
   English Language Learner: 0 (0.0%); Migrant: n/a
   Eligible for Free Lunch Program: 255 (10.4%)
   Eligible for Reduced-Price Lunch Program: 136 (5.6%)
Teachers: 148.9 (16.4 to 1)
Librarians/Media Specialists: 2.0 (1,223.5 to 1)
Guidance Counselors: 4.6 (532.0 to 1)
Current Spending: ($ per student per year):
   Total: $6,702; Instruction: $4,364; Support Services: $2,138
Enrollment, Drop-out Rates and Diploma Recipients by Race/Ethnicity

Category	Total	White	Black	Asian	AIAN	Hisp.
Enrollment (%)	100.0	98.4	1.0	0.4	0.0	0.2
Drop-out Rate (%)	0.7	0.7	0.0	0.0	n/a	0.0
H.S. Diplomas (#)	151	149	2	0	0	0

Perry Local SD
4201 13th St SW • Massillon, OH 44646-3447
(330) 477-8121
Grade Span: PK-12; **Agency Type:** 2
Schools: 9
   6 Primary; 1 Middle; 1 High; 1 Other Level
   9 Regular; 0 Special Education; 0 Vocational; 0 Alternative
   0 Magnet; 0 Charter; 6 Title I Eligible; 1 School-wide Title I
Students: 4,854   (52.5% male; 47.4% female)
   Individual Education Program: 714 (14.7%);
   English Language Learner: 32 (0.7%); Migrant: n/a
   Eligible for Free Lunch Program: 703 (14.5%)
   Eligible for Reduced-Price Lunch Program: 308 (6.3%)
Teachers: 256.9 (18.9 to 1)
Librarians/Media Specialists: 3.0 (1,618.0 to 1)
Guidance Counselors: 15.0 (323.6 to 1)
Current Spending: ($ per student per year):
   Total: $6,807; Instruction: $4,104; Support Services: $2,436
Enrollment, Drop-out Rates and Diploma Recipients by Race/Ethnicity

Category	Total	White	Black	Asian	AIAN	Hisp.
Enrollment (%)	100.0	93.5	3.6	0.4	0.1	0.7
Drop-out Rate (%)	0.4	0.4	0.0	0.0	0.0	0.0
H.S. Diplomas (#)	342	324	16	0	0	1

Plain Local SD
901 44th St NW • Canton, OH 44709-1611
(330) 492-3500 • http://eagle.stark.k12.oh.us/
Grade Span: PK-12; **Agency Type:** 2
Schools: 10
   6 Primary; 3 Middle; 1 High; 0 Other Level
   10 Regular; 0 Special Education; 0 Vocational; 0 Alternative
   0 Magnet; 0 Charter; 5 Title I Eligible; 3 School-wide Title I
Students: 6,122   (50.8% male; 49.1% female)
   Individual Education Program: 813 (13.3%);
   English Language Learner: 18 (0.3%); Migrant: n/a
   Eligible for Free Lunch Program: 1,124 (18.4%)
   Eligible for Reduced-Price Lunch Program: 339 (5.5%)
Teachers: 387.8 (15.8 to 1)
Librarians/Media Specialists: 4.0 (1,530.5 to 1)
Guidance Counselors: 16.8 (364.4 to 1)
Current Spending: ($ per student per year):
   Total: $6,984; Instruction: $4,224; Support Services: $2,512
Enrollment, Drop-out Rates and Diploma Recipients by Race/Ethnicity

Category	Total	White	Black	Asian	AIAN	Hisp.
Enrollment (%)	100.0	85.9	11.4	1.0	0.0	0.6
Drop-out Rate (%)	2.6	2.2	6.1	0.0	n/a	0.0
H.S. Diplomas (#)	390	358	27	3	0	2

Sandy Valley Local SD
5362 State Route 183 NE • Magnolia, OH 44643-8481
(330) 866-3339 • http://cardweb.stark.k12.oh.us/
Grade Span: PK-12; **Agency Type:** 2
Schools: 4
   2 Primary; 1 Middle; 1 High; 0 Other Level
   4 Regular; 0 Special Education; 0 Vocational; 0 Alternative
   0 Magnet; 0 Charter; 4 Title I Eligible; 3 School-wide Title I
Students: 1,568   (52.2% male; 47.7% female)
   Individual Education Program: 212 (13.5%);
   English Language Learner: 0 (0.0%); Migrant: n/a
   Eligible for Free Lunch Program: 286 (18.2%)
   Eligible for Reduced-Price Lunch Program: 147 (9.4%)
Teachers: 104.0 (15.1 to 1)
Librarians/Media Specialists: 1.0 (1,568.0 to 1)
Guidance Counselors: 2.0 (784.0 to 1)
Current Spending: ($ per student per year):
   Total: $6,731; Instruction: $4,054; Support Services: $2,386
Enrollment, Drop-out Rates and Diploma Recipients by Race/Ethnicity

Category	Total	White	Black	Asian	AIAN	Hisp.
Enrollment (%)	100.0	99.0	0.4	0.3	0.0	0.2
Drop-out Rate (%)	2.0	2.0	0.0	n/a	n/a	0.0
H.S. Diplomas (#)	113	108	3	0	0	2

Summit County

Akron Public Schools
70 N Broadway St • Akron, OH 44308-1911
(330) 761-1661 • http://www.akronschools.com/
Grade Span: KG-12; **Agency Type:** 1
Schools: 63
   40 Primary; 10 Middle; 9 High; 4 Other Level
   61 Regular; 0 Special Education; 0 Vocational; 2 Alternative
   0 Magnet; 0 Charter; 50 Title I Eligible; 36 School-wide Title I
Students: 28,816   (51.3% male; 48.6% female)
   Individual Education Program: 4,754 (16.5%);
   English Language Learner: 369 (1.3%); Migrant: n/a
   Eligible for Free Lunch Program: 7,115 (24.7%)
   Eligible for Reduced-Price Lunch Program: 909 (3.2%)
Teachers: 3,133.6 (9.2 to 1)
Librarians/Media Specialists: 17.0 (1,694.5 to 1)
Guidance Counselors: 56.5 (509.9 to 1)
Current Spending: ($ per student per year):
   Total: $9,498; Instruction: $5,756; Support Services: $3,435
Enrollment, Drop-out Rates and Diploma Recipients by Race/Ethnicity

Category	Total	White	Black	Asian	AIAN	Hisp.
Enrollment (%)	100.0	45.7	48.6	1.8	0.1	1.0
Drop-out Rate (%)	5.0	5.4	4.8	2.6	0.0	3.1
H.S. Diplomas (#)	1,526	805	651	49	2	16

Barberton City SD
479 Norton Ave • Barberton, OH 44203-1737
(330) 753-1025 • http://www.barberton.summit.k12.oh.us/
Grade Span: PK-12; **Agency Type:** 1
Schools: 10
   6 Primary; 2 Middle; 1 High; 1 Other Level
   9 Regular; 1 Special Education; 0 Vocational; 0 Alternative
   0 Magnet; 0 Charter; 8 Title I Eligible; 8 School-wide Title I
Students: 4,596   (51.7% male; 48.2% female)
   Individual Education Program: 700 (15.2%);
   English Language Learner: 29 (0.6%); Migrant: n/a

Eligible for Free Lunch Program: 1,592 (37.2%)
Eligible for Reduced-Price Lunch Program: 430 (10.1%)
Teachers: 291.8 (14.6 to 1)
Librarians/Media Specialists: 3.0 (1,424.7 to 1)
Guidance Counselors: 10.0 (427.4 to 1)
Current Spending: ($ per student per year):
Total: $8,221; Instruction: $5,138; Support Services: $2,702
Enrollment, Drop-out Rates and Diploma Recipients by Race/Ethnicity

Category	Total	White	Black	Asian	AIAN	Hisp.
Enrollment (%)	100.0	85.0	12.4	0.5	0.1	0.5
Drop-out Rate (%)	4.8	4.8	4.7	0.0	0.0	0.0
H.S. Diplomas (#)	264	244	18	0	2	0

Copley-Fairlawn City SD

3797 Ridgewood Rd • Copley, OH 44321-1665
(330) 664-4800 • http://www.copley.summit.k12.oh.us/
Grade Span: PK-12; **Agency Type:** 1
Schools: 5
3 Primary; 1 Middle; 1 High; 0 Other Level
5 Regular; 0 Special Education; 0 Vocational; 0 Alternative
0 Magnet; 0 Charter; 3 Title I Eligible; 0 School-wide Title I
Students: 3,254 (51.2% male; 48.7% female)
Individual Education Program: 332 (10.2%);
English Language Learner: 184 (5.7%); Migrant: n/a
Eligible for Free Lunch Program: 180 (5.5%)
Eligible for Reduced-Price Lunch Program: 98 (3.0%)
Teachers: 200.6 (16.2 to 1)
Librarians/Media Specialists: 1.0 (3,254.0 to 1)
Guidance Counselors: 6.6 (493.0 to 1)
Current Spending: ($ per student per year):
Total: $8,188; Instruction: $5,083; Support Services: $2,879
Enrollment, Drop-out Rates and Diploma Recipients by Race/Ethnicity

Category	Total	White	Black	Asian	AIAN	Hisp.
Enrollment (%)	100.0	78.2	11.7	5.9	0.4	1.2
Drop-out Rate (%)	0.6	0.6	0.0	0.0	0.0	0.0
H.S. Diplomas (#)	211	167	32	5	0	2

Coventry Local SD

3257 Cormany Rd • Akron, OH 44319-1425
(330) 644-8489
Grade Span: PK-12; **Agency Type:** 2
Schools: 6
3 Primary; 1 Middle; 1 High; 1 Other Level
6 Regular; 0 Special Education; 0 Vocational; 0 Alternative
0 Magnet; 0 Charter; 5 Title I Eligible; 0 School-wide Title I
Students: 2,334 (49.7% male; 50.2% female)
Individual Education Program: 240 (10.3%);
English Language Learner: 0 (0.0%); Migrant: n/a
Eligible for Free Lunch Program: n/a
Eligible for Reduced-Price Lunch Program: n/a
Teachers: 126.8 (18.4 to 1)
Librarians/Media Specialists: 2.0 (1,167.0 to 1)
Guidance Counselors: 3.0 (778.0 to 1)
Current Spending: ($ per student per year):
Total: $6,543; Instruction: $3,852; Support Services: $2,426
Enrollment, Drop-out Rates and Diploma Recipients by Race/Ethnicity

Category	Total	White	Black	Asian	AIAN	Hisp.
Enrollment (%)	100.0	95.6	2.3	0.6	0.3	0.2
Drop-out Rate (%)	1.4	1.5	0.0	0.0	n/a	n/a
H.S. Diplomas (#)	178	175	2	1	0	0

Cuyahoga Falls City SD

431 Stow Ave • Cuyahoga Falls, OH 44221-2521
Mailing Address: PO Box 396 • Cuyahoga Falls, OH 44222-0396
(330) 926-3800 • http://www.cfalls.summit.k12.oh.us/
Grade Span: PK-12; **Agency Type:** 1
Schools: 12
7 Primary; 3 Middle; 1 High; 0 Other Level
11 Regular; 0 Special Education; 0 Vocational; 0 Alternative
0 Magnet; 0 Charter; 7 Title I Eligible; 0 School-wide Title I
Students: 5,399 (50.9% male; 49.0% female)
Individual Education Program: 746 (13.8%);
English Language Learner: 66 (1.2%); Migrant: n/a
Eligible for Free Lunch Program: 700 (13.0%)
Eligible for Reduced-Price Lunch Program: 377 (7.0%)
Teachers: 359.4 (15.0 to 1)
Librarians/Media Specialists: 4.0 (1,349.8 to 1)
Guidance Counselors: 10.0 (539.9 to 1)
Current Spending: ($ per student per year):
Total: $7,573; Instruction: $4,744; Support Services: $2,578
Enrollment, Drop-out Rates and Diploma Recipients by Race/Ethnicity

Category	Total	White	Black	Asian	AIAN	Hisp.
Enrollment (%)	100.0	95.5	2.2	1.1	0.2	0.7
Drop-out Rate (%)	2.0	1.9	10.0	7.7	0.0	0.0
H.S. Diplomas (#)	360	353	2	3	1	1

Green Local SD

1900 Greensburg Rd • Green, OH 44232-0218
Mailing Address: PO Box 218 • Green, OH 44232-0218
(330) 896-7500 • http://green.summit.k12.oh.us/
Grade Span: PK-12; **Agency Type:** 2
Schools: 5
3 Primary; 1 Middle; 1 High; 0 Other Level
5 Regular; 0 Special Education; 0 Vocational; 0 Alternative
0 Magnet; 0 Charter; 4 Title I Eligible; 0 School-wide Title I
Students: 4,165 (52.5% male; 47.4% female)
Individual Education Program: 499 (12.0%);
English Language Learner: 33 (0.8%); Migrant: n/a
Eligible for Free Lunch Program: 339 (8.1%)
Eligible for Reduced-Price Lunch Program: 120 (2.9%)
Teachers: 232.6 (17.9 to 1)
Librarians/Media Specialists: 3.0 (1,388.3 to 1)
Guidance Counselors: 9.2 (452.7 to 1)
Current Spending: ($ per student per year):
Total: $6,920; Instruction: $4,254; Support Services: $2,414
Enrollment, Drop-out Rates and Diploma Recipients by Race/Ethnicity

Category	Total	White	Black	Asian	AIAN	Hisp.
Enrollment (%)	100.0	95.8	0.9	1.7	0.1	0.4
Drop-out Rate (%)	0.4	0.4	0.0	0.0	n/a	0.0
H.S. Diplomas (#)	247	243	0	4	0	0

Hudson City SD

2400 Hudson Aurora Rd • Hudson, OH 44236-2322
(330) 653-1200 • http://www.hudson.edu/hcsd/
Grade Span: PK-12; **Agency Type:** 1
Schools: 6
3 Primary; 2 Middle; 1 High; 0 Other Level
6 Regular; 0 Special Education; 0 Vocational; 0 Alternative
0 Magnet; 0 Charter; 4 Title I Eligible; 0 School-wide Title I
Students: 5,566 (53.2% male; 46.7% female)
Individual Education Program: 620 (11.1%);
English Language Learner: 27 (0.5%); Migrant: 2 (<0.1%)
Eligible for Free Lunch Program: 72 (1.3%)
Eligible for Reduced-Price Lunch Program: 28 (0.5%)
Teachers: 357.3 (15.6 to 1)
Librarians/Media Specialists: 8.0 (695.8 to 1)
Guidance Counselors: 13.5 (412.3 to 1)
Current Spending: ($ per student per year):
Total: $8,989; Instruction: $5,253; Support Services: $3,482
Enrollment, Drop-out Rates and Diploma Recipients by Race/Ethnicity

Category	Total	White	Black	Asian	AIAN	Hisp.
Enrollment (%)	100.0	94.2	1.0	3.2	0.0	0.6
Drop-out Rate (%)	0.7	0.7	0.0	0.0	0.0	0.0
H.S. Diplomas (#)	381	364	2	14	1	0

Manchester Local SD

6075 Manchester Rd • Akron, OH 44319-4654
(330) 882-6926
Grade Span: PK-12; **Agency Type:** 2
Schools: 3
1 Primary; 1 Middle; 1 High; 0 Other Level
3 Regular; 0 Special Education; 0 Vocational; 0 Alternative
0 Magnet; 0 Charter; 2 Title I Eligible; 0 School-wide Title I
Students: 1,520 (49.3% male; 50.6% female)
Individual Education Program: 130 (8.6%);
English Language Learner: 0 (0.0%); Migrant: n/a
Eligible for Free Lunch Program: 109 (7.2%)
Eligible for Reduced-Price Lunch Program: 47 (3.1%)
Teachers: 80.0 (19.0 to 1)
Librarians/Media Specialists: 1.0 (1,520.0 to 1)
Guidance Counselors: 3.0 (506.7 to 1)
Current Spending: ($ per student per year):
Total: $6,845; Instruction: $3,760; Support Services: $2,891
Enrollment, Drop-out Rates and Diploma Recipients by Race/Ethnicity

Category	Total	White	Black	Asian	AIAN	Hisp.
Enrollment (%)	100.0	98.2	0.5	0.5	0.1	0.6
Drop-out Rate (%)	1.3	1.4	0.0	0.0	n/a	0.0
H.S. Diplomas (#)	133	131	1	1	0	0

Nordonia Hills City SD

9370 Olde Eight Rd • Northfield, OH 44067-2097
(330) 467-0580
Grade Span: PK-12; **Agency Type:** 1
Schools: 6
3 Primary; 2 Middle; 1 High; 0 Other Level
6 Regular; 0 Special Education; 0 Vocational; 0 Alternative
0 Magnet; 0 Charter; 3 Title I Eligible; 0 School-wide Title I
Students: 3,887 (51.5% male; 48.4% female)
Individual Education Program: 447 (11.5%);
English Language Learner: 81 (2.1%); Migrant: 1 (<0.1%)
Eligible for Free Lunch Program: 235 (6.0%)

Eligible for Reduced-Price Lunch Program: 164 (4.2%)
Teachers: 200.3 (19.4 to 1)
Librarians/Media Specialists: 2.0 (1,943.5 to 1)
Guidance Counselors: 8.5 (457.3 to 1)
Current Spending: ($ per student per year):
    Total: $8,241; Instruction: $4,641; Support Services: $3,344
Enrollment, Drop-out Rates and Diploma Recipients by Race/Ethnicity

Category	Total	White	Black	Asian	AIAN	Hisp.
Enrollment (%)	100.0	89.1	6.5	2.4	0.2	0.6
Drop-out Rate (%)	2.1	2.0	3.3	0.0	0.0	0.0
H.S. Diplomas (#)	309	281	15	11	0	1

Norton City Schools
4128 Cleveland Massillon Rd • Norton, OH 44203-5633
(330) 825-0863
Grade Span: PK-12; **Agency Type:** 1
Schools: 6
    4 Primary; 1 Middle; 1 High; 0 Other Level
    6 Regular; 0 Special Education; 0 Vocational; 0 Alternative
    0 Magnet; 0 Charter; 3 Title I Eligible; 0 School-wide Title I
Students: 2,558 (50.0% male; 49.9% female)
    Individual Education Program: 210 (8.2%);
    English Language Learner: 12 (0.5%); Migrant: n/a
    Eligible for Free Lunch Program: 317 (12.4%)
    Eligible for Reduced-Price Lunch Program: 132 (5.2%)
Teachers: 149.5 (17.1 to 1)
Librarians/Media Specialists: 1.0 (2,558.0 to 1)
Guidance Counselors: 3.0 (852.7 to 1)
Current Spending: ($ per student per year):
    Total: $7,227; Instruction: $4,450; Support Services: $2,527
Enrollment, Drop-out Rates and Diploma Recipients by Race/Ethnicity

Category	Total	White	Black	Asian	AIAN	Hisp.
Enrollment (%)	100.0	96.4	1.2	0.5	0.2	0.6
Drop-out Rate (%)	0.5	0.5	0.0	0.0	n/a	0.0
H.S. Diplomas (#)	183	178	0	2	0	3

Revere Local SD
3496 Everett Rd • Bath, OH 44210-0340
Mailing Address: PO Box 340 • Bath, OH 44210-0340
(330) 666-4155 • http://www.edline.net/InterstitialLogin.page
Grade Span: KG-12; **Agency Type:** 2
Schools: 4
    1 Primary; 2 Middle; 1 High; 0 Other Level
    4 Regular; 0 Special Education; 0 Vocational; 0 Alternative
    0 Magnet; 0 Charter; 3 Title I Eligible; 0 School-wide Title I
Students: 2,835 (51.6% male; 48.3% female)
    Individual Education Program: 233 (8.2%);
    English Language Learner: 8 (0.3%); Migrant: n/a
    Eligible for Free Lunch Program: 57 (2.0%)
    Eligible for Reduced-Price Lunch Program: 17 (0.6%)
Teachers: 177.6 (15.8 to 1)
Librarians/Media Specialists: 2.0 (1,403.5 to 1)
Guidance Counselors: 7.0 (401.0 to 1)
Current Spending: ($ per student per year):
    Total: $8,268; Instruction: $4,936; Support Services: $3,132
Enrollment, Drop-out Rates and Diploma Recipients by Race/Ethnicity

Category	Total	White	Black	Asian	AIAN	Hisp.
Enrollment (%)	100.0	95.5	0.6	2.6	0.1	0.5
Drop-out Rate (%)	0.8	0.5	0.0	0.0	n/a	25.0
H.S. Diplomas (#)	225	218	1	4	0	1

Springfield Local SD
2960 Sanitarium Rd • Akron, OH 44312-4467
(330) 798-1111
Grade Span: PK-12; **Agency Type:** 2
Schools: 7
    4 Primary; 2 Middle; 1 High; 0 Other Level
    7 Regular; 0 Special Education; 0 Vocational; 0 Alternative
    0 Magnet; 0 Charter; 5 Title I Eligible; 0 School-wide Title I
Students: 3,076 (51.0% male; 48.9% female)
    Individual Education Program: 541 (17.6%);
    English Language Learner: 0 (0.0%); Migrant: n/a
    Eligible for Free Lunch Program: 700 (22.8%)
    Eligible for Reduced-Price Lunch Program: 246 (8.0%)
Teachers: 200.8 (15.3 to 1)
Librarians/Media Specialists: 2.0 (1,538.0 to 1)
Guidance Counselors: 8.0 (384.5 to 1)
Current Spending: ($ per student per year):
    Total: $7,461; Instruction: $4,527; Support Services: $2,694
Enrollment, Drop-out Rates and Diploma Recipients by Race/Ethnicity

Category	Total	White	Black	Asian	AIAN	Hisp.
Enrollment (%)	100.0	95.9	1.5	1.1	0.3	0.7
Drop-out Rate (%)	2.0	2.0	0.0	0.0	0.0	0.0
H.S. Diplomas (#)	191	188	2	1	0	0

Stow-Munroe Falls City SD
4350 Allen Rd • Stow, OH 44224-1032
(330) 689-5445 • http://www.stow.summit.k12.oh.us/
Grade Span: PK-12; **Agency Type:** 1
Schools: 9
    6 Primary; 1 Middle; 1 High; 1 Other Level
    9 Regular; 0 Special Education; 0 Vocational; 0 Alternative
    0 Magnet; 0 Charter; 6 Title I Eligible; 0 School-wide Title I
Students: 6,080 (51.8% male; 48.1% female)
    Individual Education Program: 653 (10.7%);
    English Language Learner: 48 (0.8%); Migrant: n/a
    Eligible for Free Lunch Program: 216 (3.6%)
    Eligible for Reduced-Price Lunch Program: 121 (2.0%)
Teachers: 335.8 (18.1 to 1)
Librarians/Media Specialists: 5.0 (1,216.0 to 1)
Guidance Counselors: 10.2 (596.1 to 1)
Current Spending: ($ per student per year):
    Total: $7,110; Instruction: $4,333; Support Services: $2,581
Enrollment, Drop-out Rates and Diploma Recipients by Race/Ethnicity

Category	Total	White	Black	Asian	AIAN	Hisp.
Enrollment (%)	100.0	94.1	2.1	2.2	0.0	0.5
Drop-out Rate (%)	1.1	1.1	3.8	0.0	n/a	0.0
H.S. Diplomas (#)	420	408	3	6	0	0

Tallmadge City Schools
486 E Ave • Tallmadge, OH 44278-2000
(330) 633-3291
Grade Span: PK-12; **Agency Type:** 1
Schools: 5
    2 Primary; 2 Middle; 1 High; 0 Other Level
    5 Regular; 0 Special Education; 0 Vocational; 0 Alternative
    0 Magnet; 0 Charter; 4 Title I Eligible; 0 School-wide Title I
Students: 2,760 (54.3% male; 45.6% female)
    Individual Education Program: 309 (11.2%);
    English Language Learner: 3 (0.1%); Migrant: n/a
    Eligible for Free Lunch Program: 236 (8.6%)
    Eligible for Reduced-Price Lunch Program: 77 (2.8%)
Teachers: 178.4 (15.5 to 1)
Librarians/Media Specialists: 2.0 (1,380.0 to 1)
Guidance Counselors: 6.0 (460.0 to 1)
Current Spending: ($ per student per year):
    Total: $7,471; Instruction: $4,701; Support Services: $2,591
Enrollment, Drop-out Rates and Diploma Recipients by Race/Ethnicity

Category	Total	White	Black	Asian	AIAN	Hisp.
Enrollment (%)	100.0	94.5	2.6	0.7	0.2	0.5
Drop-out Rate (%)	0.7	0.7	0.0	0.0	n/a	0.0
H.S. Diplomas (#)	185	178	3	4	0	0

Twinsburg City SD
11136 Ravenna Rd • Twinsburg, OH 44087-1022
(330) 486-2000
Grade Span: PK-12; **Agency Type:** 1
Schools: 5
    2 Primary; 2 Middle; 1 High; 0 Other Level
    5 Regular; 0 Special Education; 0 Vocational; 0 Alternative
    0 Magnet; 0 Charter; 4 Title I Eligible; 0 School-wide Title I
Students: 3,953 (51.8% male; 48.1% female)
    Individual Education Program: 417 (10.5%);
    English Language Learner: 40 (1.0%); Migrant: n/a
    Eligible for Free Lunch Program: 325 (8.2%)
    Eligible for Reduced-Price Lunch Program: 118 (3.0%)
Teachers: 229.1 (17.3 to 1)
Librarians/Media Specialists: 5.0 (790.6 to 1)
Guidance Counselors: 8.6 (459.7 to 1)
Current Spending: ($ per student per year):
    Total: $8,594; Instruction: $5,495; Support Services: $2,840
Enrollment, Drop-out Rates and Diploma Recipients by Race/Ethnicity

Category	Total	White	Black	Asian	AIAN	Hisp.
Enrollment (%)	100.0	72.2	21.9	3.2	0.0	0.6
Drop-out Rate (%)	1.6	1.4	2.5	0.0	n/a	0.0
H.S. Diplomas (#)	206	162	36	4	0	2

Woodridge Local SD
4411 Quick Rd • Peninsula, OH 44264-9706
(330) 928-9074
Grade Span: PK-12; **Agency Type:** 2
Schools: 4
    2 Primary; 1 Middle; 1 High; 0 Other Level
    4 Regular; 0 Special Education; 0 Vocational; 0 Alternative
    0 Magnet; 0 Charter; 3 Title I Eligible; 0 School-wide Title I
Students: 1,786 (51.8% male; 48.1% female)
    Individual Education Program: 251 (14.1%);
    English Language Learner: 32 (1.8%); Migrant: 59 (3.3%)
    Eligible for Free Lunch Program: 376 (21.1%)
    Eligible for Reduced-Price Lunch Program: 88 (4.9%)

Teachers: 127.9 (14.0 to 1)
Librarians/Media Specialists: 4.0 (446.5 to 1)
Guidance Counselors: 5.0 (357.2 to 1)
Current Spending: ($ per student per year):
    Total: $8,548; Instruction: $4,921; Support Services: $3,349
Enrollment, Drop-out Rates and Diploma Recipients by Race/Ethnicity

Category	Total	White	Black	Asian	AIAN	Hisp.
Enrollment (%)	100.0	78.4	15.0	1.9	0.3	1.6
Drop-out Rate (%)	2.4	1.9	6.3	0.0	0.0	0.0
H.S. Diplomas (#)	96	87	7	1	1	0

Trumbull County

Champion Local SD
5759 Mahoning Ave NW • Warren, OH 44483-1139
(330) 847-2330 • http://www.champion.k12.oh.us/
Grade Span: PK-12; **Agency Type:** 2
Schools: 3
    1 Primary; 1 Middle; 0 High; 1 Other Level
    3 Regular; 0 Special Education; 0 Vocational; 0 Alternative
    0 Magnet; 0 Charter; 2 Title I Eligible; 0 School-wide Title I
Students: 1,722 (52.2% male; 47.7% female)
    Individual Education Program: 76 (4.4%);
    English Language Learner: 0 (0.0%); Migrant: n/a
    Eligible for Free Lunch Program: 180 (10.5%)
    Eligible for Reduced-Price Lunch Program: 86 (5.0%)
Teachers: 108.8 (15.8 to 1)
Librarians/Media Specialists: 4.0 (430.5 to 1)
Guidance Counselors: 4.0 (430.5 to 1)
Current Spending: ($ per student per year):
    Total: $7,633; Instruction: $4,738; Support Services: $2,679
Enrollment, Drop-out Rates and Diploma Recipients by Race/Ethnicity

Category	Total	White	Black	Asian	AIAN	Hisp.
Enrollment (%)	100.0	99.0	0.6	0.1	0.0	0.1
Drop-out Rate (%)	1.2	1.2	0.0	0.0	n/a	n/a
H.S. Diplomas (#)	148	143	5	0	0	0

Girard City SD
31 N Ward Ave • Girard, OH 44420-2722
(330) 545-2596
Grade Span: PK-12; **Agency Type:** 1
Schools: 4
    1 Primary; 2 Middle; 1 High; 0 Other Level
    4 Regular; 0 Special Education; 0 Vocational; 0 Alternative
    0 Magnet; 0 Charter; 3 Title I Eligible; 1 School-wide Title I
Students: 1,769 (51.5% male; 48.4% female)
    Individual Education Program: 260 (14.7%);
    English Language Learner: 10 (0.6%); Migrant: n/a
    Eligible for Free Lunch Program: 493 (27.9%)
    Eligible for Reduced-Price Lunch Program: 165 (9.3%)
Teachers: 100.0 (17.7 to 1)
Librarians/Media Specialists: 1.0 (1,769.0 to 1)
Guidance Counselors: 3.0 (589.7 to 1)
Current Spending: ($ per student per year):
    Total: $7,127; Instruction: $4,673; Support Services: $2,161
Enrollment, Drop-out Rates and Diploma Recipients by Race/Ethnicity

Category	Total	White	Black	Asian	AIAN	Hisp.
Enrollment (%)	100.0	94.8	4.0	0.2	0.1	0.2
Drop-out Rate (%)	1.5	1.5	0.0	0.0	n/a	0.0
H.S. Diplomas (#)	119	114	4	1	0	0

Howland Local SD
8200 S St SE • Warren, OH 44484-2447
(330) 856-8200 • http://www.howlandschools.com/
Grade Span: PK-12; **Agency Type:** 2
Schools: 6
    4 Primary; 1 Middle; 1 High; 0 Other Level
    6 Regular; 0 Special Education; 0 Vocational; 0 Alternative
    0 Magnet; 0 Charter; 4 Title I Eligible; 0 School-wide Title I
Students: 3,228 (50.8% male; 49.1% female)
    Individual Education Program: 426 (13.2%);
    English Language Learner: 15 (0.5%); Migrant: n/a
    Eligible for Free Lunch Program: 326 (10.1%)
    Eligible for Reduced-Price Lunch Program: 165 (5.1%)
Teachers: 193.9 (16.7 to 1)
Librarians/Media Specialists: 3.0 (1,076.3 to 1)
Guidance Counselors: 7.0 (461.3 to 1)
Current Spending: ($ per student per year):
    Total: $7,438; Instruction: $4,487; Support Services: $2,715
Enrollment, Drop-out Rates and Diploma Recipients by Race/Ethnicity

Category	Total	White	Black	Asian	AIAN	Hisp.
Enrollment (%)	100.0	90.9	4.6	1.7	0.1	0.9
Drop-out Rate (%)	0.5	0.5	0.0	0.0	0.0	0.0
H.S. Diplomas (#)	230	215	6	5	1	1

Hubbard Ex Vill SD
150 Hall Ave • Hubbard, OH 44425-2065
(330) 534-1921
Grade Span: PK-12; **Agency Type:** 1
Schools: 3
    1 Primary; 1 Middle; 1 High; 0 Other Level
    3 Regular; 0 Special Education; 0 Vocational; 0 Alternative
    0 Magnet; 0 Charter; 2 Title I Eligible; 0 School-wide Title I
Students: 2,305 (50.6% male; 49.3% female)
    Individual Education Program: 248 (10.8%);
    English Language Learner: 3 (0.1%); Migrant: n/a
    Eligible for Free Lunch Program: 495 (21.5%)
    Eligible for Reduced-Price Lunch Program: 236 (10.2%)
Teachers: 130.0 (17.7 to 1)
Librarians/Media Specialists: 3.0 (768.3 to 1)
Guidance Counselors: 4.0 (576.3 to 1)
Current Spending: ($ per student per year):
    Total: $6,874; Instruction: $4,000; Support Services: $2,635
Enrollment, Drop-out Rates and Diploma Recipients by Race/Ethnicity

Category	Total	White	Black	Asian	AIAN	Hisp.
Enrollment (%)	100.0	94.4	3.4	0.4	0.1	0.6
Drop-out Rate (%)	1.4	1.4	0.0	0.0	0.0	0.0
H.S. Diplomas (#)	199	191	7	0	0	0

Lakeview Local SD
300 Hillman Dr • Cortland, OH 44410-1562
(330) 637-8741 • http://www.cboss.com/lakeview/
Grade Span: PK-12; **Agency Type:** 2
Schools: 4
    2 Primary; 1 Middle; 1 High; 0 Other Level
    4 Regular; 0 Special Education; 0 Vocational; 0 Alternative
    0 Magnet; 0 Charter; 3 Title I Eligible; 0 School-wide Title I
Students: 2,234 (50.0% male; 50.0% female)
    Individual Education Program: 260 (11.6%);
    English Language Learner: 1 (<0.1%); Migrant: n/a
    Eligible for Free Lunch Program: 189 (8.5%)
    Eligible for Reduced-Price Lunch Program: 55 (2.5%)
Teachers: 116.3 (19.2 to 1)
Librarians/Media Specialists: 3.0 (744.7 to 1)
Guidance Counselors: 5.0 (446.8 to 1)
Current Spending: ($ per student per year):
    Total: $6,855; Instruction: $4,189; Support Services: $2,446
Enrollment, Drop-out Rates and Diploma Recipients by Race/Ethnicity

Category	Total	White	Black	Asian	AIAN	Hisp.
Enrollment (%)	100.0	96.7	1.2	0.4	0.0	0.6
Drop-out Rate (%)	0.3	0.3	0.0	0.0	0.0	0.0
H.S. Diplomas (#)	175	174	0	1	0	0

Liberty Local SD
4115 Shady Rd • Youngstown, OH 44505-1353
(330) 759-0807 • http://www.liberty.k12.oh.us/
Grade Span: PK-12; **Agency Type:** 2
Schools: 3
    1 Primary; 1 Middle; 1 High; 0 Other Level
    3 Regular; 0 Special Education; 0 Vocational; 0 Alternative
    0 Magnet; 0 Charter; 2 Title I Eligible; 0 School-wide Title I
Students: 1,819 (52.7% male; 47.2% female)
    Individual Education Program: 145 (8.0%);
    English Language Learner: 0 (0.0%); Migrant: n/a
    Eligible for Free Lunch Program: 385 (21.2%)
    Eligible for Reduced-Price Lunch Program: 129 (7.1%)
Teachers: 101.7 (17.9 to 1)
Librarians/Media Specialists: 1.0 (1,819.0 to 1)
Guidance Counselors: 4.0 (454.8 to 1)
Current Spending: ($ per student per year):
    Total: $7,795; Instruction: $4,710; Support Services: $2,850
Enrollment, Drop-out Rates and Diploma Recipients by Race/Ethnicity

Category	Total	White	Black	Asian	AIAN	Hisp.
Enrollment (%)	100.0	74.2	22.4	1.2	0.1	0.9
Drop-out Rate (%)	0.9	1.0	0.8	0.0	n/a	0.0
H.S. Diplomas (#)	150	120	22	6	0	2

Newton Falls Ex Vill SD
909 1/2 Milton Blvd • Newton Falls, OH 44444-9707
(330) 872-5445
Grade Span: PK-12; **Agency Type:** 1
Schools: 4
    2 Primary; 1 Middle; 1 High; 0 Other Level
    4 Regular; 0 Special Education; 0 Vocational; 0 Alternative
    0 Magnet; 0 Charter; 2 Title I Eligible; 0 School-wide Title I
Students: 1,520 (51.2% male; 48.7% female)
    Individual Education Program: 193 (12.7%);
    English Language Learner: 0 (0.0%); Migrant: n/a
    Eligible for Free Lunch Program: 299 (19.7%)
    Eligible for Reduced-Price Lunch Program: 136 (8.9%)

Teachers: 91.0 (16.7 to 1)
Librarians/Media Specialists: 1.0 (1,520.0 to 1)
Guidance Counselors: 3.0 (506.7 to 1)
Current Spending: ($ per student per year):
    Total: $7,087; Instruction: $4,453; Support Services: $2,355
Enrollment, Drop-out Rates and Diploma Recipients by Race/Ethnicity

Category	Total	White	Black	Asian	AIAN	Hisp.
Enrollment (%)	100.0	97.3	1.3	0.1	0.1	0.4
Drop-out Rate (%)	1.1	1.1	0.0	0.0	n/a	0.0
H.S. Diplomas (#)	89	89	0	0	0	0

Niles City SD

100 W St • Niles, OH 44446-2644
(330) 652-2509
Grade Span: PK-12; **Agency Type:** 1
Schools: 6
    4 Primary; 0 Middle; 1 High; 1 Other Level
    6 Regular; 0 Special Education; 0 Vocational; 0 Alternative
    0 Magnet; 0 Charter; 5 Title I Eligible; 0 School-wide Title I
Students: 2,861 (51.0% male; 48.9% female)
    Individual Education Program: 369 (12.9%);
    English Language Learner: 0 (0.0%); Migrant: n/a
    Eligible for Free Lunch Program: 874 (30.5%)
    Eligible for Reduced-Price Lunch Program: 240 (8.4%)
Teachers: 168.0 (17.0 to 1)
Librarians/Media Specialists: 2.0 (1,430.5 to 1)
Guidance Counselors: 5.0 (572.2 to 1)
Current Spending: ($ per student per year):
    Total: $7,396; Instruction: $4,637; Support Services: $2,416
Enrollment, Drop-out Rates and Diploma Recipients by Race/Ethnicity

Category	Total	White	Black	Asian	AIAN	Hisp.
Enrollment (%)	100.0	94.2	4.6	0.4	0.1	0.4
Drop-out Rate (%)	3.2	3.2	0.0	n/a	n/a	n/a
H.S. Diplomas (#)	210	207	2	0	0	0

Warren City SD

261 Monroe St NW • Warren, OH 44483-4810
(330) 841-2321 • http://www.warrenschools.k12.oh.us/
Grade Span: KG-12; **Agency Type:** 1
Schools: 15
    10 Primary; 2 Middle; 0 High; 3 Other Level
    15 Regular; 0 Special Education; 0 Vocational; 0 Alternative
    0 Magnet; 0 Charter; 15 Title I Eligible; 5 School-wide Title I
Students: 6,901 (50.3% male; 49.6% female)
    Individual Education Program: 1,307 (18.9%);
    English Language Learner: 2 (<0.1%); Migrant: n/a
    Eligible for Free Lunch Program: 3,366 (48.9%)
    Eligible for Reduced-Price Lunch Program: 544 (7.9%)
Teachers: 487.2 (14.1 to 1)
Librarians/Media Specialists: 4.0 (1,721.3 to 1)
Guidance Counselors: 11.0 (625.9 to 1)
Current Spending: ($ per student per year):
    Total: $9,008; Instruction: $5,217; Support Services: $3,517
Enrollment, Drop-out Rates and Diploma Recipients by Race/Ethnicity

Category	Total	White	Black	Asian	AIAN	Hisp.
Enrollment (%)	100.0	50.3	43.8	0.2	0.1	0.5
Drop-out Rate (%)	5.3	4.9	5.6	0.0	0.0	12.5
H.S. Diplomas (#)	352	211	138	1	0	1

Tuscarawas County

Claymont City SD

201 N 3rd St • Dennison, OH 44621-1237
(740) 922-5478 • http://www.claymont.k12.oh.us/
Grade Span: PK-12; **Agency Type:** 1
Schools: 6
    3 Primary; 1 Middle; 1 High; 1 Other Level
    6 Regular; 0 Special Education; 0 Vocational; 0 Alternative
    0 Magnet; 0 Charter; 4 Title I Eligible; 4 School-wide Title I
Students: 2,346 (53.4% male; 46.5% female)
    Individual Education Program: 512 (21.8%);
    English Language Learner: 0 (0.0%); Migrant: n/a
    Eligible for Free Lunch Program: 639 (27.2%)
    Eligible for Reduced-Price Lunch Program: 166 (7.1%)
Teachers: 139.8 (16.8 to 1)
Librarians/Media Specialists: 2.0 (1,173.0 to 1)
Guidance Counselors: 5.0 (469.2 to 1)
Current Spending: ($ per student per year):
    Total: $6,500; Instruction: $3,798; Support Services: $2,426
Enrollment, Drop-out Rates and Diploma Recipients by Race/Ethnicity

Category	Total	White	Black	Asian	AIAN	Hisp.
Enrollment (%)	100.0	97.4	1.2	0.2	0.0	0.0
Drop-out Rate (%)	0.5	0.6	0.0	0.0	n/a	0.0
H.S. Diplomas (#)	145	142	2	0	0	1

Dover City SD

219 W 6th St • Dover, OH 44622-2803
(330) 364-1906 • http://www.dover.k12.oh.us/
Grade Span: PK-12; **Agency Type:** 1
Schools: 5
    3 Primary; 1 Middle; 1 High; 0 Other Level
    5 Regular; 0 Special Education; 0 Vocational; 0 Alternative
    0 Magnet; 0 Charter; 4 Title I Eligible; 0 School-wide Title I
Students: 2,598 (51.7% male; 48.2% female)
    Individual Education Program: 392 (15.1%);
    English Language Learner: 10 (0.4%); Migrant: n/a
    Eligible for Free Lunch Program: 234 (9.0%)
    Eligible for Reduced-Price Lunch Program: 67 (2.6%)
Teachers: 164.0 (15.8 to 1)
Librarians/Media Specialists: 1.0 (2,598.0 to 1)
Guidance Counselors: 4.0 (649.5 to 1)
Current Spending: ($ per student per year):
    Total: $7,033; Instruction: $4,340; Support Services: $2,468
Enrollment, Drop-out Rates and Diploma Recipients by Race/Ethnicity

Category	Total	White	Black	Asian	AIAN	Hisp.
Enrollment (%)	100.0	96.8	1.1	0.4	0.0	0.5
Drop-out Rate (%)	1.3	1.3	0.0	0.0	0.0	0.0
H.S. Diplomas (#)	240	235	2	2	0	0

Indian Valley Local SD

100 N Walnut St • Gnadenhutten, OH 44629-0171
Mailing Address: PO Box 171 • Gnadenhutten, OH 44629-0171
(740) 254-4334
Grade Span: PK-12; **Agency Type:** 2
Schools: 4
    2 Primary; 1 Middle; 1 High; 0 Other Level
    4 Regular; 0 Special Education; 0 Vocational; 0 Alternative
    0 Magnet; 0 Charter; 3 Title I Eligible; 2 School-wide Title I
Students: 1,916 (50.7% male; 49.2% female)
    Individual Education Program: 294 (15.3%);
    English Language Learner: 0 (0.0%); Migrant: n/a
    Eligible for Free Lunch Program: 463 (24.2%)
    Eligible for Reduced-Price Lunch Program: 180 (9.4%)
Teachers: 130.0 (14.7 to 1)
Librarians/Media Specialists: 0.2 (9,580.0 to 1)
Guidance Counselors: 3.6 (532.2 to 1)
Current Spending: ($ per student per year):
    Total: $6,419; Instruction: $3,816; Support Services: $2,306
Enrollment, Drop-out Rates and Diploma Recipients by Race/Ethnicity

Category	Total	White	Black	Asian	AIAN	Hisp.
Enrollment (%)	100.0	98.9	0.0	0.0	0.0	0.3
Drop-out Rate (%)	0.5	0.5	n/a	n/a	n/a	n/a
H.S. Diplomas (#)	122	122	0	0	0	0

New Philadelphia City SD

248 Front Ave SW • New Philadelphia, OH 44663-2150
(330) 364-0600 • http://www.new-phila.k12.oh.us/
Grade Span: PK-12; **Agency Type:** 1
Schools: 8
    6 Primary; 1 Middle; 1 High; 0 Other Level
    8 Regular; 0 Special Education; 0 Vocational; 0 Alternative
    0 Magnet; 0 Charter; 5 Title I Eligible; 0 School-wide Title I
Students: 3,307 (51.4% male; 48.5% female)
    Individual Education Program: 557 (16.8%);
    English Language Learner: 13 (0.4%); Migrant: n/a
    Eligible for Free Lunch Program: 435 (13.2%)
    Eligible for Reduced-Price Lunch Program: 121 (3.7%)
Teachers: 212.2 (15.6 to 1)
Librarians/Media Specialists: 1.0 (3,307.0 to 1)
Guidance Counselors: 2.8 (1,181.1 to 1)
Current Spending: ($ per student per year):
    Total: $6,426; Instruction: $4,051; Support Services: $2,172
Enrollment, Drop-out Rates and Diploma Recipients by Race/Ethnicity

Category	Total	White	Black	Asian	AIAN	Hisp.
Enrollment (%)	100.0	94.6	1.0	0.2	0.2	1.2
Drop-out Rate (%)	2.1	2.1	0.0	0.0	n/a	0.0
H.S. Diplomas (#)	238	236	2	0	0	0

Tuscarawas Valley Local SD

2637 Tuscarawas Valley Rd NE • Zoarville, OH 44656-9692
(330) 859-2213
Grade Span: PK-12; **Agency Type:** 2
Schools: 5
    3 Primary; 1 Middle; 1 High; 0 Other Level
    5 Regular; 0 Special Education; 0 Vocational; 0 Alternative
    0 Magnet; 0 Charter; 2 Title I Eligible; 0 School-wide Title I
Students: 1,744 (53.8% male; 46.1% female)
    Individual Education Program: 224 (12.8%);
    English Language Learner: 0 (0.0%); Migrant: n/a
    Eligible for Free Lunch Program: 252 (14.4%)

Eligible for Reduced-Price Lunch Program: 109 (6.3%)
Teachers: 101.2 (17.2 to 1)
Librarians/Media Specialists: 1.0 (1,744.0 to 1)
Guidance Counselors: 3.0 (581.3 to 1)
Current Spending: ($ per student per year):
   Total: $6,342; Support Services: $3,701; Support Services: $2,373
Enrollment, Drop-out Rates and Diploma Recipients by Race/Ethnicity

Category	Total	White	Black	Asian	AIAN	Hisp.
Enrollment (%)	100.0	99.0	0.3	0.1	0.1	0.0
Drop-out Rate (%)	4.6	4.6	0.0	n/a	0.0	0.0
H.S. Diplomas (#)	108	105	1	0	2	0

Union County

Marysville Exempted Village SD
1000 Edgewood Dr • Marysville, OH 43040-2105
(937) 644-8105 • http://www.marysville.k12.oh.us/site/
Grade Span: KG-12; **Agency Type:** 1
Schools: 8
   5 Primary; 2 Middle; 1 High; 0 Other Level
   8 Regular; 0 Special Education; 0 Vocational; 0 Alternative
   0 Magnet; 0 Charter; 4 Title I Eligible; 0 School-wide Title I
Students: 4,721 (52.1% male; 47.8% female)
   Individual Education Program: 731 (15.5%);
   English Language Learner: 9 (0.2%); Migrant: n/a
   Eligible for Free Lunch Program: 399 (8.5%)
   Eligible for Reduced-Price Lunch Program: 214 (4.5%)
Teachers: 298.4 (15.8 to 1)
Librarians/Media Specialists: 2.0 (2,360.5 to 1)
Guidance Counselors: 11.0 (429.2 to 1)
Current Spending: ($ per student per year):
   Total: $8,350; Instruction: $4,748; Support Services: $3,286
Enrollment, Drop-out Rates and Diploma Recipients by Race/Ethnicity

Category	Total	White	Black	Asian	AIAN	Hisp.
Enrollment (%)	100.0	96.9	1.0	0.5	0.0	0.3
Drop-out Rate (%)	0.7	0.6	7.7	12.5	0.0	0.0
H.S. Diplomas (#)	257	253	2	1	0	0

Van Wert County

Van Wert City SD
641 N Jefferson St • Van Wert, OH 45891-1167
(419) 238-0648
Grade Span: PK-12; **Agency Type:** 1
Schools: 7
   5 Primary; 1 Middle; 1 High; 0 Other Level
   7 Regular; 0 Special Education; 0 Vocational; 0 Alternative
   0 Magnet; 0 Charter; 4 Title I Eligible; 0 School-wide Title I
Students: 2,290 (50.8% male; 49.1% female)
   Individual Education Program: 357 (15.6%);
   English Language Learner: 0 (0.0%); Migrant: n/a
   Eligible for Free Lunch Program: 410 (17.9%)
   Eligible for Reduced-Price Lunch Program: 181 (7.9%)
Teachers: 147.9 (15.5 to 1)
Librarians/Media Specialists: 1.0 (2,290.0 to 1)
Guidance Counselors: 4.0 (572.5 to 1)
Current Spending: ($ per student per year):
   Total: $6,818; Instruction: $4,392; Support Services: $2,186
Enrollment, Drop-out Rates and Diploma Recipients by Race/Ethnicity

Category	Total	White	Black	Asian	AIAN	Hisp.
Enrollment (%)	100.0	92.0	1.5	1.1	0.3	2.2
Drop-out Rate (%)	2.9	2.9	5.6	0.0	0.0	0.0
H.S. Diplomas (#)	153	145	1	2	0	3

Vinton County

Vinton County Local SD
307 W High St • Mc Arthur, OH 45651-1093
(740) 596-5218
Grade Span: PK-12; **Agency Type:** 2
Schools: 7
   5 Primary; 1 Middle; 1 High; 0 Other Level
   7 Regular; 0 Special Education; 0 Vocational; 0 Alternative
   0 Magnet; 0 Charter; 7 Title I Eligible; 5 School-wide Title I
Students: 2,633 (52.5% male; 47.4% female)
   Individual Education Program: 455 (17.3%);
   English Language Learner: 0 (0.0%); Migrant: n/a
   Eligible for Free Lunch Program: 1,168 (44.4%)
   Eligible for Reduced-Price Lunch Program: 244 (9.3%)
Teachers: 167.1 (15.8 to 1)
Librarians/Media Specialists: 1.0 (2,633.0 to 1)
Guidance Counselors: 2.0 (1,316.5 to 1)
Current Spending: ($ per student per year):
   Total: $7,307; Instruction: $4,058; Support Services: $2,925

Enrollment, Drop-out Rates and Diploma Recipients by Race/Ethnicity

Category	Total	White	Black	Asian	AIAN	Hisp.
Enrollment (%)	100.0	99.5	0.0	0.0	0.0	0.0
Drop-out Rate (%)	5.0	5.0	0.0	0.0	n/a	n/a
H.S. Diplomas (#)	144	143	1	0	0	0

Warren County

Carlisle Local SD
724 Fairview Dr • Carlisle, OH 45005-3148
(937) 746-0710 • http://www.carlisle-local.k12.oh.us/
Grade Span: KG-12; **Agency Type:** 2
Schools: 4
   2 Primary; 1 Middle; 1 High; 0 Other Level
   4 Regular; 0 Special Education; 0 Vocational; 0 Alternative
   0 Magnet; 0 Charter; 3 Title I Eligible; 0 School-wide Title I
Students: 1,775 (52.4% male; 47.5% female)
   Individual Education Program: 203 (11.4%);
   English Language Learner: 2 (0.1%); Migrant: n/a
   Eligible for Free Lunch Program: 191 (10.8%)
   Eligible for Reduced-Price Lunch Program: 58 (3.3%)
Teachers: 104.7 (17.0 to 1)
Librarians/Media Specialists: 2.0 (887.5 to 1)
Guidance Counselors: 4.1 (432.9 to 1)
Current Spending: ($ per student per year):
   Total: $7,766; Instruction: $4,633; Support Services: $2,856
Enrollment, Drop-out Rates and Diploma Recipients by Race/Ethnicity

Category	Total	White	Black	Asian	AIAN	Hisp.
Enrollment (%)	100.0	97.7	0.6	0.1	0.1	0.3
Drop-out Rate (%)	1.9	2.0	0.0	0.0	n/a	0.0
H.S. Diplomas (#)	111	111	0	0	0	0

Franklin City SD
150 E 6th St • Franklin, OH 45005-2559
(937) 746-1699 • http://www.franklin-city.k12.oh.us/
Grade Span: KG-12; **Agency Type:** 1
Schools: 8
   6 Primary; 1 Middle; 1 High; 0 Other Level
   8 Regular; 0 Special Education; 0 Vocational; 0 Alternative
   0 Magnet; 0 Charter; 5 Title I Eligible; 3 School-wide Title I
Students: 3,094 (51.2% male; 48.7% female)
   Individual Education Program: 465 (15.0%);
   English Language Learner: 3 (0.1%); Migrant: n/a
   Eligible for Free Lunch Program: 511 (16.5%)
   Eligible for Reduced-Price Lunch Program: 135 (4.4%)
Teachers: 177.6 (17.4 to 1)
Librarians/Media Specialists: 3.0 (1,031.3 to 1)
Guidance Counselors: 5.0 (618.8 to 1)
Current Spending: ($ per student per year):
   Total: $7,139; Instruction: $4,371; Support Services: $2,485
Enrollment, Drop-out Rates and Diploma Recipients by Race/Ethnicity

Category	Total	White	Black	Asian	AIAN	Hisp.
Enrollment (%)	100.0	97.7	0.7	0.2	0.0	0.8
Drop-out Rate (%)	5.3	5.1	0.0	16.7	n/a	33.3
H.S. Diplomas (#)	190	184	2	3	0	1

Kings Local SD
1797 King Ave • Kings Mills, OH 45034
(513) 398-8050
Grade Span: PK-12; **Agency Type:** 2
Schools: 6
   3 Primary; 2 Middle; 1 High; 0 Other Level
   6 Regular; 0 Special Education; 0 Vocational; 0 Alternative
   0 Magnet; 0 Charter; 2 Title I Eligible; 1 School-wide Title I
Students: 3,849 (52.2% male; 47.7% female)
   Individual Education Program: 523 (13.6%);
   English Language Learner: 27 (0.7%); Migrant: n/a
   Eligible for Free Lunch Program: 258 (6.7%)
   Eligible for Reduced-Price Lunch Program: 69 (1.8%)
Teachers: 215.6 (17.9 to 1)
Librarians/Media Specialists: 3.0 (1,283.0 to 1)
Guidance Counselors: 8.6 (447.6 to 1)
Current Spending: ($ per student per year):
   Total: $7,636; Instruction: $4,391; Support Services: $3,014
Enrollment, Drop-out Rates and Diploma Recipients by Race/Ethnicity

Category	Total	White	Black	Asian	AIAN	Hisp.
Enrollment (%)	100.0	94.7	1.4	1.7	0.1	1.0
Drop-out Rate (%)	1.1	1.1	0.0	0.0	n/a	0.0
H.S. Diplomas (#)	223	219	0	4	0	0

Lebanon City SD
645 Oak St • Lebanon, OH 45036-1634
(513) 934-5770
Grade Span: PK-12; **Agency Type:** 1
Schools: 6

3 Primary; 2 Middle; 1 High; 0 Other Level
6 Regular; 0 Special Education; 0 Vocational; 0 Alternative
0 Magnet; 0 Charter; 5 Title I Eligible; 0 School-wide Title I
Students: 4,780   (50.8% male; 49.1% female)
   Individual Education Program: 428 (9.0%);
   English Language Learner: 40 (0.8%); Migrant: n/a
   Eligible for Free Lunch Program: 478 (10.0%)
   Eligible for Reduced-Price Lunch Program: 158 (3.3%)
Teachers: 239.0 (20.0 to 1)
Librarians/Media Specialists: 4.0 (1,195.0 to 1)
Guidance Counselors: 9.0 (531.1 to 1)
Current Spending: ($ per student per year):
   Total: $6,499; Instruction: $3,672; Support Services: $2,598
Enrollment, Drop-out Rates and Diploma Recipients by Race/Ethnicity

Category	Total	White	Black	Asian	AIAN	Hisp.
Enrollment (%)	100.0	94.6	2.5	0.6	0.2	0.8
Drop-out Rate (%)	1.7	1.7	0.0	0.0	n/a	20.0
H.S. Diplomas (#)	279	275	3	0	0	1

Little Miami Local SD
5819 Morrow Rossburg Rd • Morrow, OH 45152-9426
(513) 899-2264
Grade Span: PK-12; **Agency Type:** 2
Schools: 6
3 Primary; 2 Middle; 1 High; 0 Other Level
6 Regular; 0 Special Education; 0 Vocational; 0 Alternative
0 Magnet; 0 Charter; 3 Title I Eligible; 0 School-wide Title I
Students: 3,201   (49.8% male; 50.1% female)
   Individual Education Program: 338 (10.6%);
   English Language Learner: 9 (0.3%); Migrant: n/a
   Eligible for Free Lunch Program: 212 (6.6%)
   Eligible for Reduced-Price Lunch Program: 56 (1.7%)
Teachers: 179.8 (17.8 to 1)
Librarians/Media Specialists: 2.0 (1,600.5 to 1)
Guidance Counselors: 5.0 (640.2 to 1)
Current Spending: ($ per student per year):
   Total: $6,499; Instruction: $3,834; Support Services: $2,417
Enrollment, Drop-out Rates and Diploma Recipients by Race/Ethnicity

Category	Total	White	Black	Asian	AIAN	Hisp.
Enrollment (%)	100.0	97.5	0.5	0.5	0.1	0.9
Drop-out Rate (%)	1.9	1.8	n/a	n/a	n/a	0.0
H.S. Diplomas (#)	169	169	0	0	0	0

Mason City SD
211 N E St • Mason, OH 45040-1760
(513) 398-0474 • http://www.masonohioschools.com/
Grade Span: PK-12; **Agency Type:** 1
Schools: 6
3 Primary; 2 Middle; 1 High; 0 Other Level
6 Regular; 0 Special Education; 0 Vocational; 0 Alternative
0 Magnet; 0 Charter; 2 Title I Eligible; 0 School-wide Title I
Students: 8,635   (51.4% male; 48.5% female)
   Individual Education Program: 750 (8.7%);
   English Language Learner: 104 (1.2%); Migrant: n/a
   Eligible for Free Lunch Program: 141 (1.6%)
   Eligible for Reduced-Price Lunch Program: 113 (1.3%)
Teachers: 482.9 (17.9 to 1)
Librarians/Media Specialists: 3.0 (2,878.3 to 1)
Guidance Counselors: 16.6 (520.2 to 1)
Current Spending: ($ per student per year):
   Total: $7,383; Instruction: $3,747; Support Services: $3,344
Enrollment, Drop-out Rates and Diploma Recipients by Race/Ethnicity

Category	Total	White	Black	Asian	AIAN	Hisp.
Enrollment (%)	100.0	87.2	3.0	6.3	0.2	1.8
Drop-out Rate (%)	1.5	1.6	1.7	0.0	0.0	0.0
H.S. Diplomas (#)	367	342	11	8	0	4

Springboro Community City SD
1685 S Main St • Springboro, OH 45066-1524
(937) 748-3960
Grade Span: PK-12; **Agency Type:** 1
Schools: 5
2 Primary; 2 Middle; 1 High; 0 Other Level
5 Regular; 0 Special Education; 0 Vocational; 0 Alternative
0 Magnet; 0 Charter; 3 Title I Eligible; 0 School-wide Title I
Students: 4,320   (50.8% male; 49.1% female)
   Individual Education Program: 466 (10.8%);
   English Language Learner: 11 (0.3%); Migrant: n/a
   Eligible for Free Lunch Program: 120 (2.8%)
   Eligible for Reduced-Price Lunch Program: 49 (1.1%)
Teachers: 225.6 (19.1 to 1)
Librarians/Media Specialists: 2.0 (2,160.0 to 1)
Guidance Counselors: 8.0 (540.0 to 1)
Current Spending: ($ per student per year):
   Total: $6,428; Instruction: $3,754; Support Services: $2,476

Enrollment, Drop-out Rates and Diploma Recipients by Race/Ethnicity

Category	Total	White	Black	Asian	AIAN	Hisp.
Enrollment (%)	100.0	94.8	0.9	1.7	0.2	0.8
Drop-out Rate (%)	1.1	1.1	0.0	0.0	33.3	0.0
H.S. Diplomas (#)	231	221	4	3	1	1

Washington County

Marietta City Schools
701 3rd St • Marietta, OH 45750-1801
(740) 374-6500
Grade Span: PK-12; **Agency Type:** 1
Schools: 6
4 Primary; 1 Middle; 1 High; 0 Other Level
6 Regular; 0 Special Education; 0 Vocational; 0 Alternative
0 Magnet; 0 Charter; 4 Title I Eligible; 0 School-wide Title I
Students: 3,202   (51.5% male; 48.4% female)
   Individual Education Program: 560 (17.5%);
   English Language Learner: 1 (<0.1%); Migrant: n/a
   Eligible for Free Lunch Program: 643 (20.1%)
   Eligible for Reduced-Price Lunch Program: 126 (3.9%)
Teachers: 178.4 (17.9 to 1)
Librarians/Media Specialists: 2.0 (1,601.0 to 1)
Guidance Counselors: 5.0 (640.4 to 1)
Current Spending: ($ per student per year):
   Total: $6,934; Instruction: $4,072; Support Services: $2,664
Enrollment, Drop-out Rates and Diploma Recipients by Race/Ethnicity

Category	Total	White	Black	Asian	AIAN	Hisp.
Enrollment (%)	100.0	97.7	1.3	0.2	0.2	0.5
Drop-out Rate (%)	1.6	1.7	0.0	0.0	n/a	0.0
H.S. Diplomas (#)	216	213	2	0	0	0

Warren Local SD
220 Sweetapple Rd • Vincent, OH 45784-5005
(740) 678-2366
Grade Span: PK-12; **Agency Type:** 2
Schools: 6
4 Primary; 1 Middle; 1 High; 0 Other Level
6 Regular; 0 Special Education; 0 Vocational; 0 Alternative
0 Magnet; 0 Charter; 5 Title I Eligible; 2 School-wide Title I
Students: 2,692   (52.4% male; 47.5% female)
   Individual Education Program: 363 (13.5%);
   English Language Learner: 0 (0.0%); Migrant: n/a
   Eligible for Free Lunch Program: 401 (14.9%)
   Eligible for Reduced-Price Lunch Program: 170 (6.3%)
Teachers: 163.6 (16.5 to 1)
Librarians/Media Specialists: 2.0 (1,346.0 to 1)
Guidance Counselors: 9.0 (299.1 to 1)
Current Spending: ($ per student per year):
   Total: $6,608; Instruction: $4,020; Support Services: $2,354
Enrollment, Drop-out Rates and Diploma Recipients by Race/Ethnicity

Category	Total	White	Black	Asian	AIAN	Hisp.
Enrollment (%)	100.0	96.7	1.1	0.2	0.0	0.1
Drop-out Rate (%)	2.5	2.5	7.7	0.0	0.0	0.0
H.S. Diplomas (#)	190	180	4	2	0	2

Wayne County

Orrville City SD
815 N Ella St • Orrville, OH 44667-1154
(330) 682-4651
Grade Span: PK-12; **Agency Type:** 1
Schools: 5
3 Primary; 1 Middle; 1 High; 0 Other Level
5 Regular; 0 Special Education; 0 Vocational; 0 Alternative
0 Magnet; 0 Charter; 4 Title I Eligible; 0 School-wide Title I
Students: 1,863   (54.3% male; 45.6% female)
   Individual Education Program: 237 (12.7%);
   English Language Learner: 0 (0.0%); Migrant: n/a
   Eligible for Free Lunch Program: 358 (19.2%)
   Eligible for Reduced-Price Lunch Program: 180 (9.7%)
Teachers: 117.4 (15.9 to 1)
Librarians/Media Specialists: 2.0 (931.5 to 1)
Guidance Counselors: 4.0 (465.8 to 1)
Current Spending: ($ per student per year):
   Total: $7,423; Instruction: $4,623; Support Services: $2,515
Enrollment, Drop-out Rates and Diploma Recipients by Race/Ethnicity

Category	Total	White	Black	Asian	AIAN	Hisp.
Enrollment (%)	100.0	88.6	5.7	1.4	0.2	0.8
Drop-out Rate (%)	2.9	2.8	4.7	0.0	n/a	n/a
H.S. Diplomas (#)	127	118	5	4	0	0

Southeast Local SD

9048 Dover Rd • Apple Creek, OH 44606-9408
(330) 698-3001
Grade Span: PK-12; **Agency Type:** 2
Schools: 6
    4 Primary; 0 Middle; 1 High; 1 Other Level
    6 Regular; 0 Special Education; 0 Vocational; 0 Alternative
    0 Magnet; 0 Charter; 6 Title I Eligible; 6 School-wide Title I
Students: 1,718 (54.4% male; 45.5% female)
    Individual Education Program: 243 (14.1%);
    English Language Learner: 7 (0.4%); Migrant: n/a
    Eligible for Free Lunch Program: 329 (19.2%)
    Eligible for Reduced-Price Lunch Program: 245 (14.3%)
Teachers: 114.6 (15.0 to 1)
Librarians/Media Specialists: 0.0 (n/a to 1)
Guidance Counselors: 4.0 (429.5 to 1)
Current Spending: ($ per student per year):
    Total: $7,973; Instruction: $4,858; Support Services: $2,810
Enrollment, Drop-out Rates and Diploma Recipients by Race/Ethnicity

Category	Total	White	Black	Asian	AIAN	Hisp.
Enrollment (%)	100.0	98.4	0.2	0.3	0.2	0.7
Drop-out Rate (%)	1.7	1.7	n/a	n/a	n/a	n/a
H.S. Diplomas (#)	96	96	0	0	0	0

Triway Local SD

3205 Shreve Rd • Wooster, OH 44691-4439
(330) 264-9491
Grade Span: PK-12; **Agency Type:** 2
Schools: 5
    2 Primary; 1 Middle; 1 High; 1 Other Level
    5 Regular; 0 Special Education; 0 Vocational; 0 Alternative
    0 Magnet; 0 Charter; 2 Title I Eligible; 0 School-wide Title I
Students: 2,150 (50.4% male; 49.5% female)
    Individual Education Program: 291 (13.5%);
    English Language Learner: 2 (0.1%); Migrant: n/a
    Eligible for Free Lunch Program: 313 (14.6%)
    Eligible for Reduced-Price Lunch Program: 113 (5.3%)
Teachers: 126.6 (17.0 to 1)
Librarians/Media Specialists: 1.0 (2,150.0 to 1)
Guidance Counselors: 4.0 (537.5 to 1)
Current Spending: ($ per student per year):
    Total: $7,036; Instruction: $4,308; Support Services: $2,448
Enrollment, Drop-out Rates and Diploma Recipients by Race/Ethnicity

Category	Total	White	Black	Asian	AIAN	Hisp.
Enrollment (%)	100.0	96.2	1.0	0.9	0.5	0.6
Drop-out Rate (%)	2.0	1.9	0.0	0.0	33.3	0.0
H.S. Diplomas (#)	146	144	0	2	0	0

Wooster City SD

144 N Market St • Wooster, OH 44691-4810
(330) 264-0869 • http://www.wooster.k12.oh.us/
Grade Span: PK-12; **Agency Type:** 1
Schools: 11
    7 Primary; 1 Middle; 1 High; 2 Other Level
    9 Regular; 2 Special Education; 0 Vocational; 0 Alternative
    0 Magnet; 0 Charter; 4 Title I Eligible; 2 School-wide Title I
Students: 4,144 (53.0% male; 46.9% female)
    Individual Education Program: 586 (14.1%);
    English Language Learner: 2 (<0.1%); Migrant: n/a
    Eligible for Free Lunch Program: 1,059 (25.6%)
    Eligible for Reduced-Price Lunch Program: 283 (6.8%)
Teachers: 293.2 (14.1 to 1)
Librarians/Media Specialists: 3.0 (1,381.3 to 1)
Guidance Counselors: 8.6 (481.9 to 1)
Current Spending: ($ per student per year):
    Total: $9,150; Instruction: $5,449; Support Services: $3,363
Enrollment, Drop-out Rates and Diploma Recipients by Race/Ethnicity

Category	Total	White	Black	Asian	AIAN	Hisp.
Enrollment (%)	100.0	89.2	5.7	1.1	0.1	0.9
Drop-out Rate (%)	0.8	0.8	1.1	0.0	0.0	0.0
H.S. Diplomas (#)	281	259	9	7	1	3

Bryan City SD

1350 Fountain Grove Dr • Bryan, OH 43506-8733
(419) 636-6973 • http://www.bryan.k12.oh.us/
Grade Span: PK-12; **Agency Type:** 1
Schools: 4
    2 Primary; 0 Middle; 1 High; 1 Other Level
    4 Regular; 0 Special Education; 0 Vocational; 0 Alternative
    0 Magnet; 0 Charter; 3 Title I Eligible; 0 School-wide Title I
Students: 2,288 (52.4% male; 47.5% female)
    Individual Education Program: 268 (11.7%);
    English Language Learner: 5 (0.2%); Migrant: n/a

    Eligible for Free Lunch Program: 272 (11.9%)
    Eligible for Reduced-Price Lunch Program: 129 (5.6%)
Teachers: 143.5 (15.9 to 1)
Librarians/Media Specialists: 2.0 (1,144.0 to 1)
Guidance Counselors: 6.0 (381.3 to 1)
Current Spending: ($ per student per year):
    Total: $6,577; Instruction: $4,294; Support Services: $2,061
Enrollment, Drop-out Rates and Diploma Recipients by Race/Ethnicity

Category	Total	White	Black	Asian	AIAN	Hisp.
Enrollment (%)	100.0	94.6	0.2	0.9	0.0	4.0
Drop-out Rate (%)	2.7	2.7	0.0	0.0	0.0	4.5
H.S. Diplomas (#)	149	139	0	6	0	4

Bowling Green City SD

140 S Grove St • Bowling Green, OH 43402-2819
(419) 352-3576 • http://www.bgcs.k12.oh.us/
Grade Span: PK-12; **Agency Type:** 1
Schools: 8
    6 Primary; 1 Middle; 1 High; 0 Other Level
    8 Regular; 0 Special Education; 0 Vocational; 0 Alternative
    0 Magnet; 0 Charter; 6 Title I Eligible; 0 School-wide Title I
Students: 3,203 (51.4% male; 48.5% female)
    Individual Education Program: 424 (13.2%);
    English Language Learner: 16 (0.5%); Migrant: 5 (0.2%)
    Eligible for Free Lunch Program: 403 (12.6%)
    Eligible for Reduced-Price Lunch Program: 97 (3.0%)
Teachers: 206.3 (15.5 to 1)
Librarians/Media Specialists: 4.0 (800.8 to 1)
Guidance Counselors: 8.0 (400.4 to 1)
Current Spending: ($ per student per year):
    Total: $8,090; Instruction: $5,111; Support Services: $2,712
Enrollment, Drop-out Rates and Diploma Recipients by Race/Ethnicity

Category	Total	White	Black	Asian	AIAN	Hisp.
Enrollment (%)	100.0	86.8	1.7	1.3	0.2	5.2
Drop-out Rate (%)	1.0	0.8	8.3	0.0	0.0	1.6
H.S. Diplomas (#)	256	229	1	8	1	12

Eastwood Local SD

4800 Sugar Ridge Rd • Pemberville, OH 43450-9626
(419) 833-6411
Grade Span: PK-12; **Agency Type:** 2
Schools: 6
    4 Primary; 1 Middle; 1 High; 0 Other Level
    6 Regular; 0 Special Education; 0 Vocational; 0 Alternative
    0 Magnet; 0 Charter; 4 Title I Eligible; 0 School-wide Title I
Students: 1,978 (51.2% male; 48.7% female)
    Individual Education Program: 174 (8.8%);
    English Language Learner: 0 (0.0%); Migrant: 2 (0.1%)
    Eligible for Free Lunch Program: 164 (8.3%)
    Eligible for Reduced-Price Lunch Program: 119 (6.0%)
Teachers: 94.1 (21.0 to 1)
Librarians/Media Specialists: 1.0 (1,978.0 to 1)
Guidance Counselors: 4.0 (494.5 to 1)
Current Spending: ($ per student per year):
    Total: $8,028; Instruction: $4,404; Support Services: $3,323
Enrollment, Drop-out Rates and Diploma Recipients by Race/Ethnicity

Category	Total	White	Black	Asian	AIAN	Hisp.
Enrollment (%)	100.0	92.9	0.4	0.4	0.1	3.5
Drop-out Rate (%)	0.5	0.5	0.0	0.0	n/a	0.0
H.S. Diplomas (#)	140	135	0	2	0	3

Lake Local SD

28025 Main St • Millbury, OH 43447-9602
Mailing Address: PO Box 151 • Millbury, OH 43447-0151
(419) 836-2552 • http://www.lakelocal.k12.oh.us/
Grade Span: KG-12; **Agency Type:** 2
Schools: 4
    2 Primary; 1 Middle; 1 High; 0 Other Level
    4 Regular; 0 Special Education; 0 Vocational; 0 Alternative
    0 Magnet; 0 Charter; 2 Title I Eligible; 0 School-wide Title I
Students: 1,795 (51.2% male; 48.7% female)
    Individual Education Program: 195 (10.9%);
    English Language Learner: 9 (0.5%); Migrant: n/a
    Eligible for Free Lunch Program: 257 (15.0%)
    Eligible for Reduced-Price Lunch Program: 134 (7.8%)
Teachers: 79.5 (21.6 to 1)
Librarians/Media Specialists: 1.0 (1,716.0 to 1)
Guidance Counselors: 4.0 (429.0 to 1)
Current Spending: ($ per student per year):
    Total: $6,161; Instruction: $3,457; Support Services: $2,440

Enrollment, Drop-out Rates and Diploma Recipients by Race/Ethnicity

Category	Total	White	Black	Asian	AIAN	Hisp.
Enrollment (%)	100.0	91.9	1.5	0.1	0.3	5.1
Drop-out Rate (%)	1.2	0.9	0.0	0.0	0.0	7.4
H.S. Diplomas (#)	137	131	1	0	0	5

Otsego Local SD

18505 Tontogany Creek • Tontogany, OH 43565-0290
Mailing Address: PO Box 290 • Tontogany, OH 43565-0290
(419) 823-4381
Grade Span: PK-12; **Agency Type:** 2
Schools: 5
    3 Primary; 1 Middle; 1 High; 0 Other Level
    5 Regular; 0 Special Education; 0 Vocational; 0 Alternative
    0 Magnet; 0 Charter; 2 Title I Eligible; 0 School-wide Title I
Students: 1,689 (50.7% male; 49.2% female)
    Individual Education Program: 243 (14.4%);
    English Language Learner: 0 (0.0%); Migrant: n/a
    Eligible for Free Lunch Program: 150 (8.9%)
    Eligible for Reduced-Price Lunch Program: 42 (2.5%)
Teachers: 94.2 (17.9 to 1)
Librarians/Media Specialists: 2.0 (844.5 to 1)
Guidance Counselors: 3.0 (563.0 to 1)
Current Spending: ($ per student per year):
    Total: $6,843; Instruction: $4,237; Support Services: $2,364

Enrollment, Drop-out Rates and Diploma Recipients by Race/Ethnicity

Category	Total	White	Black	Asian	AIAN	Hisp.
Enrollment (%)	100.0	93.3	0.1	0.3	0.2	3.0
Drop-out Rate (%)	2.1	2.2	n/a	0.0	0.0	0.0
H.S. Diplomas (#)	117	113	0	0	0	4

Perrysburg Exempted Village

140 E Indiana Ave • Perrysburg, OH 43551-2261
(419) 874-9131
Grade Span: PK-12; **Agency Type:** 1
Schools: 6
    4 Primary; 1 Middle; 1 High; 0 Other Level
    6 Regular; 0 Special Education; 0 Vocational; 0 Alternative
    0 Magnet; 0 Charter; 4 Title I Eligible; 0 School-wide Title I
Students: 4,348 (52.4% male; 47.5% female)
    Individual Education Program: 352 (8.1%);
    English Language Learner: 17 (0.4%); Migrant: 14 (0.3%)
    Eligible for Free Lunch Program: 161 (3.7%)
    Eligible for Reduced-Price Lunch Program: 92 (2.1%)
Teachers: 275.3 (15.8 to 1)
Librarians/Media Specialists: 2.0 (2,174.0 to 1)
Guidance Counselors: 10.0 (434.8 to 1)
Current Spending: ($ per student per year):
    Total: $7,293; Instruction: $4,647; Support Services: $2,383

Enrollment, Drop-out Rates and Diploma Recipients by Race/Ethnicity

Category	Total	White	Black	Asian	AIAN	Hisp.
Enrollment (%)	100.0	90.0	1.2	3.0	0.1	3.3
Drop-out Rate (%)	1.0	0.8	0.0	0.0	0.0	8.5
H.S. Diplomas (#)	328	310	3	5	0	9

Rossford Ex Vill SD

601 Superior St • Rossford, OH 43460-1247
(419) 666-2010 • http://www.rossford.k12.oh.us/
Grade Span: PK-12; **Agency Type:** 1
Schools: 5
    3 Primary; 1 Middle; 1 High; 0 Other Level
    5 Regular; 0 Special Education; 0 Vocational; 0 Alternative
    0 Magnet; 0 Charter; 2 Title I Eligible; 1 School-wide Title I
Students: 2,020 (52.1% male; 47.8% female)
    Individual Education Program: 301 (14.9%);
    English Language Learner: 1 (<0.1%); Migrant: n/a
    Eligible for Free Lunch Program: 285 (14.1%)
    Eligible for Reduced-Price Lunch Program: 140 (6.9%)
Teachers: 131.7 (15.3 to 1)
Librarians/Media Specialists: 1.0 (2,020.0 to 1)
Guidance Counselors: 5.0 (404.0 to 1)
Current Spending: ($ per student per year):
    Total: $8,183; Instruction: $4,947; Support Services: $3,011

Enrollment, Drop-out Rates and Diploma Recipients by Race/Ethnicity

Category	Total	White	Black	Asian	AIAN	Hisp.
Enrollment (%)	100.0	92.8	1.2	0.6	0.0	2.2
Drop-out Rate (%)	2.6	2.4	0.0	0.0	0.0	0.0
H.S. Diplomas (#)	137	131	1	1	0	2

Wyandot County

Upper Sandusky Ex Vill SD

390 W Walker St • Upper Sandusky, OH 43351-1364
(419) 294-2307 • http://www.uppersandusky.k12.oh.us/
Grade Span: PK-12; **Agency Type:** 1
Schools: 5
    4 Primary; 0 Middle; 1 High; 0 Other Level
    5 Regular; 0 Special Education; 0 Vocational; 0 Alternative
    0 Magnet; 0 Charter; 3 Title I Eligible; 0 School-wide Title I
Students: 1,807 (51.0% male; 48.9% female)
    Individual Education Program: 300 (16.6%);
    English Language Learner: 0 (0.0%); Migrant: n/a
    Eligible for Free Lunch Program: 270 (14.9%)
    Eligible for Reduced-Price Lunch Program: 84 (4.6%)
Teachers: 119.0 (15.2 to 1)
Librarians/Media Specialists: 2.0 (903.5 to 1)
Guidance Counselors: 4.0 (451.8 to 1)
Current Spending: ($ per student per year):
    Total: $6,691; Instruction: $3,862; Support Services: $2,546

Enrollment, Drop-out Rates and Diploma Recipients by Race/Ethnicity

Category	Total	White	Black	Asian	AIAN	Hisp.
Enrollment (%)	100.0	96.3	0.1	0.3	0.2	1.9
Drop-out Rate (%)	2.3	2.0	50.0	0.0	100.0	12.5
H.S. Diplomas (#)	153	148	1	1	0	3

Number of Schools

Rank	Number	District Name	City
1	153	Columbus Public Schools	Columbus
2	122	Cleveland Municipal City SD	Cleveland
3	86	Cincinnati City SD	Cincinnati
4	67	Toledo City SD	Toledo
5	63	Akron Public Schools	Akron
6	39	Dayton City SD	Dayton
7	36	South-Western City SD	Grove City
8	30	Canton City SD	Canton
9	26	Youngstown City SD	Youngstown
10	23	Westerville City SD	Westerville
11	21	Parma City SD	Parma
12	20	Hamilton City SD	Hamilton
12	20	Hilliard City SD	Hilliard
14	19	Lakota Local SD	Liberty Twp
14	19	Marion City SD	Marion
14	19	Springfield City SD	Springfield
17	18	Dublin City SD	Dublin
17	18	Worthington City SD	Worthington
19	17	Elyria City SD	Elyria
20	16	Findlay City SD	Findlay
20	16	Lorain City SD	Lorain
20	16	Mentor Ex Vill SD	Mentor
20	16	Newark City SD	Newark
24	15	Warren City SD	Warren
25	14	Lakewood City SD	Lakewood
25	14	Lima City SD	Lima
25	14	Logan-Hocking Local SD	Logan
25	14	Mansfield City SD	Mansfield
25	14	Middletown City SD	Middletown
25	14	Northwest Local SD	Cincinnati
25	14	Olentangy Local SD	Lewis Center
25	14	Willoughby-Eastlake City SD	Willoughby
33	13	Berea City SD	Berea
33	13	Cleveland Hts-Univ Hts City SD	University Hgts
35	12	Ashtabula Area City SD	Ashtabula
35	12	Cuyahoga Falls City SD	Cuyahoga Falls
35	12	Kettering City SD	Kettering
35	12	Lancaster City SD	Lancaster
35	12	Sandusky City SD	Sandusky
35	12	Sylvania City SD	Sylvania
35	12	Washington Local Schools	Toledo
35	12	West Clermont Local SD	Cincinnati
35	12	Zanesville City SD	Zanesville
44	11	Brunswick City SD	Brunswick
44	11	Centerville City SD	Centerville
44	11	Gahanna-Jefferson City SD	Gahanna
44	11	Pickerington Local SD	Pickerington
44	11	Princeton City SD	Cincinnati
44	11	Strongsville City SD	Strongsville
44	11	Wooster City SD	Wooster
51	10	Adams County/Ohio Valley LSD	West Union
51	10	Barberton City SD	Barberton
51	10	East Holmes Local Schools	Berlin
51	10	Euclid City SD	Euclid
51	10	Fairfield City SD	Fairfield
51	10	Groveport Madison Local SD	Groveport
51	10	Huber Heights City SD	Huber Heights
51	10	Massillon City SD	Massillon
51	10	Miami Trace Local SD	Wash Ct House
51	10	Plain Local SD	Canton
51	10	Switzerland of Ohio Local SD	Woodsfield
51	10	Xenia Community City SD	Xenia
63	9	Carrollton Ex Vill SD	Carrollton
63	9	Crestwood Local SD	Mantua
63	9	Delaware City SD	Delaware
63	9	Forest Hills Local SD	Cincinnati
63	9	Fremont City SD	Fremont
63	9	Medina City SD	Medina
63	9	Miamisburg City SD	Miamisburg
63	9	Mount Vernon City SD	Mount Vernon
63	9	Mt Healthy City SD	Cincinnati
63	9	North Olmsted City Schools	North Olmsted
63	9	Northmont City SD	Englewood
63	9	Oak Hills Local SD	Cincinnati
63	9	Perry Local SD	Massillon
63	9	Piqua City SD	Piqua
63	9	Shaker Heights City SD	Shaker Heights
63	9	Sidney City SD	Sidney
63	9	South Euclid-Lyndhurst City SD	Lyndhurst
63	9	Stow-Munroe Falls City SD	Stow
63	9	Troy City SD	Troy
82	8	Ashland City SD	Ashland
82	8	Austintown Local SD	Youngstown
82	8	Beavercreek City SD	Beavercreek
82	8	Bowling Green City SD	Bowling Green
82	8	Conneaut Area City SD	Conneaut
82	8	East Cleveland City SD	East Cleveland
82	8	Franklin City SD	Franklin
82	8	Gallia County Local SD	Gallipolis
82	8	Kenton City SD	Kenton
82	8	Marysville Exempted Village SD	Marysville
82	8	Milford Ex Vill SD	Milford
82	8	New Philadelphia City SD	New Philadelphia
82	8	Painesville Township Local SD	Painesville
82	8	Ravenna City SD	Ravenna
82	8	Reynoldsburg City SD	Reynoldsburg
82	8	Southwest Local SD	Harrison
82	8	Steubenville City SD	Steubenville
82	8	Tecumseh Local SD	New Carlisle
82	8	Upper Arlington City SD	Upper Arlington
82	8	Wadsworth City SD	Wadsworth
102	7	Athens City SD	The Plains
102	7	Avon Lake City Schools	Avon Lake
102	7	Bedford City SD	Bedford
102	7	Bellevue City SD	Bellevue
102	7	Boardman Local SD	Youngstown
102	7	Buckeye Local SD	Rayland
102	7	Bucyrus City SD	Bucyrus
102	7	Cloverleaf Local SD	Lodi
102	7	Defiance City SD	Defiance
102	7	Edison Local SD	Hammondsville
102	7	Fairborn City Schools	Fairborn
102	7	Geneva Area City Schools	Geneva
102	7	Greenville City SD	Greenville
102	7	Jackson City SD	Jackson
102	7	Kent City SD	Kent
102	7	Mad River Local SD	Dayton
102	7	Mayfield City SD	Highland Hgts
102	7	North Canton City SD	North Canton
102	7	Northeastern Local SD	Springfield
102	7	Norwood City SD	Norwood
102	7	Oregon City SD	Oregon
102	7	Painesville City Local SD	Painesville
102	7	River View Local SD	Warsaw
102	7	Solon City SD	Solon
102	7	Springfield Local SD	Akron
102	7	Sycamore Community City SD	Cincinnati
102	7	Tiffin City SD	Tiffin
102	7	Tri-Valley Local Schools	Dresden
102	7	Trotwood-Madison City Schools	Trotwood
102	7	Van Wert City SD	Van Wert
102	7	Vinton County Local SD	Mc Arthur
102	7	Washington Court House City SD	Wash Ct House
102	7	West Carrollton City SD	West Carrollton
102	7	West Holmes Local SD	Millersburg
102	7	Westlake City SD	Westlake
102	7	Winton Woods City SD	Cincinnati
138	6	Alliance City SD	Alliance
138	6	Amherst Ex Vill SD	Amherst
138	6	Anthony Wayne Local SD	Whitehouse
138	6	Bellefontaine City Schools	Bellefontaine
138	6	Benton Carroll Salem Local SD	Oak Harbor
138	6	Brecksville-Broadview Hgts City	Brecksville
138	6	Buckeye Local SD	Ashtabula
138	6	Chardon Local SD	Chardon
138	6	Chillicothe City SD	Chillicothe
138	6	Circleville City SD	Circleville
138	6	Claymont City SD	Dennison
138	6	Coventry Local SD	Akron
138	6	East Liverpool City SD	East Liverpool
138	6	East Muskingum Local SD	New Concord
138	6	Eastwood Local SD	Pemberville
138	6	Galion City SD	Galion
138	6	Harrison Hills City SD	Hopedale
138	6	Hillsboro City SD	Hillsboro
138	6	Howland Local SD	Warren
138	6	Hudson City SD	Hudson
138	6	Indian Creek Local SD	Wintersville
138	6	Ironton City SD	Ironton
138	6	Jackson Local SD	Massillon
138	6	Kings Local SD	Kings Mills
138	6	Lebanon City SD	Lebanon
138	6	Licking Valley Local SD Sd	Newark
138	6	Little Miami Local SD	Morrow
138	6	Logan Elm Local SD	Circleville
138	6	London City SD	London
138	6	Louisville City SD	Louisville
138	6	Loveland City SD	Loveland
138	6	Madison Local SD	Mansfield
138	6	Madison-Plains Local SD	London
138	6	Maple Heights City SD	Maple Heights
138	6	Marietta City Schools	Marietta
138	6	Mason City SD	Mason
138	6	Maumee City SD	Maumee
138	6	Niles City SD	Niles
138	6	Nordonia Hills City SD	Northfield
138	6	North Ridgeville City SD	N Ridgeville
138	6	North Royalton City SD	N Royalton
138	6	Norton City Schools	Norton
138	6	Norwalk City SD	Norwalk
138	6	Perrysburg Exempted Village	Perrysburg
138	6	Poland Local SD	Poland
138	6	Port Clinton City SD	Port Clinton
138	6	Portsmouth City SD	Portsmouth
138	6	Salem City SD	Salem
138	6	Sheffield-Sheffield Lake City SD	Sheffield Vlg
138	6	Shelby City SD	Shelby
138	6	Southeast Local SD	Apple Creek
138	6	Southwest Licking Local SD	Etna
138	6	Springfield Local Schools	Holland
138	6	St Marys City SD	Saint Marys
138	6	Urbana City SD	Urbana
138	6	Vandalia-Butler City SD	Vandalia
138	6	Wapakoneta City City SD	Wapakoneta
138	6	Warren Local SD	Vincent
138	6	Warrensville Heights City SD	Warrensville Hgts
138	6	West Branch Local SD	Beloit
138	6	Willard City SD	Willard
199	5	Avon Local SD	Avon
199	5	Beachwood City SD	Beachwood
199	5	Beaver Local SD	Lisbon
199	5	Bexley City SD	Bexley
199	5	Big Walnut Local SD	Galena
199	5	Buckeye Local SD	Medina
199	5	Buckeye Valley Local SD	Delaware
199	5	Cambridge City SD	Cambridge
199	5	Canal Winchester Local SD	Canal Winchester
199	5	Canton Local SD	Canton
199	5	Celina City SD	Celina
199	5	Clark-Shawnee Local SD	Springfield
199	5	Clyde-Green Springs Ex Vill SD	Clyde
199	5	Copley-Fairlawn City SD	Copley
199	5	Coshocton City SD	Coshocton
199	5	Dover City SD	Dover
199	5	Edgewood City SD	Trenton
199	5	Fairfield Union Local SD	W Rushville
199	5	Fairless Local SD	Navarre
199	5	Fairview Park City SD	Fairview Park
199	5	Field Local SD	Mogadore
199	5	Finneytown Local SD	Cincinnati
199	5	Fostoria City SD	Fostoria
199	5	Franklin Local SD	Duncan Falls
199	5	Gallipolis City SD	Gallipolis
199	5	Garfield Heights City SD	Garfield Hgts
199	5	Green Local SD	Green
199	5	Greeneview Local SD	Jamestown
199	5	Greenfield Ex Vill SD	Greenfield
199	5	Hamilton Local SD	Columbus
199	5	Highland Local SD	Sparta
199	5	Highland Local SD	Medina
199	5	Kenston Local SD	Chagrin Falls
199	5	Lake Local SD	Hartville
199	5	Lakewood Local SD	Hebron
199	5	Lexington Local SD	Lexington
199	5	Madison Local SD	Madison
199	5	Mariemont City SD	Cincinnati
199	5	Marlington Local SD	Alliance
199	5	Martins Ferry City SD	Martins Ferry
199	5	Midview Local SD	Grafton
199	5	Morgan Local SD	McConnelsville
199	5	Napoleon Area City SD	Napoleon
199	5	New Richmond Ex Vill SD	New Richmond
199	5	Northern Local SD	Thornville
199	5	Northridge Local SD	Dayton
199	5	Northwest Local SD	Canal Fulton
199	5	Oakwood City SD	Dayton
199	5	Orrville City SD	Orrville
199	5	Otsego Local SD	Tontogany
199	5	Ridgewood Local SD	West Lafayette
199	5	Rolling Hills Local SD	Cambridge
199	5	Rossford Ex Vill SD	Rossford
199	5	Southeast Local SD	Ravenna
199	5	Springboro Community City SD	Springboro
199	5	Streetsboro City Schools	Streetsboro
199	5	Sugarcreek Local SD	Bellbrook
199	5	Tallmadge City Schools	Tallmadge
199	5	Teays Valley Local SD	Ashville
199	5	Three Rivers Local Schools	Cleves
199	5	Tipp City Ex Vill SD	Tipp City
199	5	Triway Local SD	Wooster
199	5	Tuscarawas Valley Local SD	Zoarville
199	5	Twinsburg City SD	Twinsburg
199	5	Upper Sandusky Ex Vill SD	Upper Sandusky
199	5	West Muskingum Local SD	Zanesville
199	5	Whitehall City SD	Whitehall
199	5	Wilmington City SD	Wilmington
199	5	Wyoming City SD	Wyoming
268	4	Alexander Local SD	Albany
268	4	Amanda-Clearcreek Local SD	Amanda
268	4	Aurora City SD	Aurora
268	4	Bay Village City SD	Bay Village
268	4	Berlin-Milan Local SD	Milan
268	4	Bethel-Tate Local SD	Bethel
268	4	Bryan City SD	Bryan
268	4	Canfield Local SD	Canfield

268	4	Carlisle Local SD	Carlisle
268	4	Chagrin Falls Ex Vill SD	Chagrin Falls
268	4	Clear Fork Valley Local SD	Bellville
268	4	Clermont Northeastern Local SD	Batavia
268	4	East Clinton Local SD	Lees Creek
268	4	Eastern Local SD	Sardinia
268	4	Eaton Community Schools	Eaton
268	4	Elgin Local SD	Marion
268	4	Elida Local SD	Elida
268	4	Fairland Local SD	Proctorville
268	4	Genoa Area Local SD	Genoa
268	4	Girard City SD	Girard
268	4	Goshen Local SD	Goshen
268	4	Graham Local SD	Saint Paris
268	4	Granville Ex Vill SD	Granville
268	4	Greenon Local SD	Springfield
268	4	Heath City SD	Heath
268	4	Indian Hill Ex Vill SD	Cincinnati
268	4	Indian Lake Local SD	Lewistown
268	4	Indian Valley Local SD	Gnadenhutten
268	4	James A Garfield Local SD	Garrettsville
268	4	Jonathan Alder Local SD	Plain City
268	4	Keystone Local SD	Lagrange
268	4	Lake Local SD	Millbury
268	4	Lakeview Local SD	Cortland
268	4	Meigs Local SD	Pomeroy
268	4	Minerva Local SD	Minerva
268	4	New Lexington City SD	New Lexington
268	4	Newton Falls Ex Vill SD	Newton Falls
268	4	North College Hill City SD	Cincinnati
268	4	North Fork Local SD	Utica
268	4	Olmsted Falls City SD	Olmsted Falls
268	4	Ontario Local SD	Mansfield
268	4	Orange City SD	Cleveland
268	4	Ottawa-Glandorf Local SD	Ottawa
268	4	Paulding Ex Vill SD	Paulding
268	4	Perkins Local SD	Sandusky
268	4	Pike-Delta-York Local SD	Delta
268	4	Plain Local SD	New Albany
268	4	Preble Shawnee Local SD	Camden
268	4	Revere Local SD	Bath
268	4	River Valley Local SD	Caledonia
268	4	Rocky River City SD	Rocky River
268	4	Ross Local SD	Hamilton
268	4	Sandy Valley Local SD	Magnolia
268	4	Shawnee Local SD	Lima
268	4	South Point Local SD	South Point
268	4	Swanton Local SD	Swanton
268	4	Talawanda City SD	Oxford
268	4	Valley View Local SD	Germantown
268	4	Vermilion Local SD	Vermilion
268	4	Wauseon Ex Vill SD	Wauseon
268	4	Waverly City SD	Waverly
268	4	Wellston City Schools	Wellston
268	4	West Geauga Local SD	Chesterland
268	4	Western Brown Local SD	Mount Orab
268	4	Woodridge Local SD	Peninsula
333	3	Batavia Local SD	Batavia
333	3	Bath Local SD	Lima
333	3	Bellaire Local SD	Bellaire
333	3	Benjamin Logan Local SD	Bellefontaine
333	3	Black River Local SD	Sullivan
333	3	Blanchester Local SD	Blanchester
333	3	Brookville Local SD	Brookville
333	3	Campbell City SD	Campbell
333	3	Champion Local SD	Warren
333	3	Clearview Local SD	Lorain
333	3	Clinton-Massie Local SD	Clarksville
333	3	Coldwater Ex Vill SD	Coldwater
333	3	Firelands Local SD	Oberlin
333	3	Hubbard Ex Vill SD	Hubbard
333	3	Huron City Schools	Huron
333	3	Jefferson Area Local SD	Jefferson
333	3	Liberty Local SD	Youngstown
333	3	Licking Heights Local SD	Summit Station
333	3	Madeira City SD	Cincinnati
333	3	Madison Local SD	Middletown
333	3	Manchester Local SD	Akron
333	3	Maysville Local SD	Zanesville
333	3	Milton-Union Exempted Vill Schls	West Milton
333	3	Minford Local SD	Minford
333	3	Monroe Local SD	Monroe
333	3	Northwest Local SD	Mc Dermott
333	3	Northwestern Local SD	Springfield
333	3	Perry Local SD	Perry
333	3	Rock Hill Local SD	Ironton
333	3	Scioto Valley Local SD	Piketon
333	3	St Clairsville-Richland City SD	St Clairsville
333	3	Struthers City SD	Struthers
333	3	Union Local SD	Morristown
333	3	Union-Scioto Local SD	Chillicothe
333	3	Washington-Nile Local SD	West Portsmouth
333	3	Wellington Ex Vill SD	Wellington
333	3	Westfall Local SD	Williamsport
333	3	Wickliffe City SD	Wickliffe
333	3	Zane Trace Local SD	Chillicothe
372	2	United Local SD	Hanoverton
373	1	Electronic Classrm of Tomorrow	Columbus
373	1	Ohio Virtual Academy	Maumee

Number of Teachers

Rank	Number	District Name	City
1	5,108	Cleveland Municipal City SD	Cleveland
2	3,838	Columbus Public Schools	Columbus
3	3,133	Akron Public Schools	Akron
4	3,132	Cincinnati City SD	Cincinnati
5	2,538	Toledo City SD	Toledo
6	1,417	Dayton City SD	Dayton
7	1,326	South-Western City SD	Grove City
8	964	Lakota Local SD	Liberty Twp
9	921	Hilliard City SD	Hilliard
10	792	Dublin City SD	Dublin
11	787	Parma City SD	Parma
12	784	Westerville City SD	Westerville
13	755	Canton City SD	Canton
14	717	Youngstown City SD	Youngstown
15	657	Worthington City SD	Worthington
16	628	Lorain City SD	Lorain
17	627	Mentor Ex Vill SD	Mentor
18	626	Huber Heights City SD	Huber Heights
19	617	Springfield City SD	Springfield
20	615	Northwest Local SD	Cincinnati
21	569	Hamilton City SD	Hamilton
22	549	Elyria City SD	Elyria
23	535	Centerville City SD	Centerville
24	518	Willoughby-Eastlake City SD	Willoughby
25	517	Olentangy Local SD	Lewis Center
26	508	Gahanna-Jefferson City SD	Gahanna
27	505	West Clermont Local SD	Cincinnati
28	504	Fairfield City SD	Fairfield
29	499	Pickerington Local SD	Pickerington
30	499	Sylvania City SD	Sylvania
31	494	Kettering City SD	Kettering
32	492	Middletown City SD	Middletown
33	489	Berea City SD	Berea
34	487	Warren City SD	Warren
35	485	Princeton City SD	Cincinnati
36	482	Mason City SD	Mason
37	477	Cleveland Hts-Univ Hts City SD	University Hgts
38	470	Medina City SD	Medina
39	455	Washington Local Schools	Toledo
40	445	Oak Hills Local SD	Cincinnati
41	437	Findlay City SD	Findlay
42	434	Forest Hills Local SD	Cincinnati
43	428	Mansfield City SD	Mansfield
44	423	Lakewood City SD	Lakewood
45	417	Newark City SD	Newark
46	413	Shaker Heights City SD	Shaker Heights
47	409	Strongsville City SD	Strongsville
48	404	Brunswick City SD	Brunswick
49	400	Upper Arlington City SD	Upper Arlington
50	398	Sycamore Community City SD	Cincinnati
51	387	Plain Local SD	Canton
52	383	Euclid City SD	Euclid
53	369	Beavercreek City SD	Beavercreek
54	365	Lima City SD	Lima
55	364	Groveport Madison Local SD	Groveport
56	359	Cuyahoga Falls City SD	Cuyahoga Falls
57	357	Hudson City SD	Hudson
58	351	Marion City SD	Marion
59	346	Lancaster City SD	Lancaster
60	338	Milford Ex Vill SD	Milford
61	336	Reynoldsburg City SD	Reynoldsburg
62	336	Adams County/Ohio Valley LSD	West Union
63	335	Stow-Munroe Falls City SD	Stow
64	333	Solon City SD	Solon
65	330	Mayfield City SD	Highland Hgts
66	329	Xenia Community City SD	Xenia
67	326	Massillon City SD	Massillon
68	316	Northmont City SD	Englewood
69	313	North Olmsted City Schools	North Olmsted
70	311	Jackson Local SD	Massillon
71	310	Fairborn City Schools	Fairborn
72	306	Miamisburg City SD	Miamisburg
73	303	South Euclid-Lyndhurst City SD	Lyndhurst
74	298	Boardman Local SD	Youngstown
75	298	Marysville Exempted Village SD	Marysville
76	298	Kent City SD	Kent
77	297	Sandusky City SD	Sandusky
78	295	East Cleveland City SD	East Cleveland
79	293	Wooster City SD	Wooster
80	292	North Canton City SD	North Canton
81	291	Barberton City SD	Barberton
82	291	Austintown Local SD	Youngstown
83	290	Zanesville City SD	Zanesville
84	283	Winton Woods City SD	Cincinnati
85	282	Ashtabula Area City SD	Ashtabula
86	282	Delaware City SD	Delaware
87	275	Perrysburg Exempted Village	Perrysburg
88	269	Brecksville-Broadview Hgts City	Brecksville
89	260	Mt Healthy City SD	Cincinnati
90	256	Perry Local SD	Massillon
91	256	Oregon City SD	Oregon
92	252	Mount Vernon City SD	Mount Vernon
93	252	Bedford City SD	Bedford
94	251	West Carrollton City SD	West Carrollton
95	250	North Royalton City SD	N Royalton
96	249	Fremont City SD	Fremont
97	249	Madison Local SD	Mansfield
98	244	Westlake City SD	Westlake
99	239	Lebanon City SD	Lebanon
100	238	Mad River Local SD	Dayton
101	237	Wadsworth City SD	Wadsworth
102	234	Troy City SD	Troy
103	234	Vandalia-Butler City SD	Vandalia
104	233	Painesville Township Local SD	Painesville
105	232	Green Local SD	Green
106	232	Northeastern Local SD	Springfield
107	231	Loveland City SD	Loveland
108	229	Greenville City SD	Greenville
109	229	Springfield Local Schools	Holland
110	229	Twinsburg City SD	Twinsburg
111	227	Logan-Hocking Local SD	Logan
112	225	Ashland City SD	Ashland
113	225	Springboro Community City SD	Springboro
114	223	North Ridgeville City SD	N Ridgeville
115	223	Alliance City SD	Alliance
116	222	Athens City SD	The Plains
117	221	Maple Heights City SD	Maple Heights
118	221	East Liverpool City SD	East Liverpool
119	219	Sidney City SD	Sidney
120	219	Amherst Ex Vill SD	Amherst
121	218	Tecumseh Local SD	New Carlisle
122	215	Kings Local SD	Kings Mills
123	214	Anthony Wayne Local SD	Whitehouse
124	212	Ravenna City SD	Ravenna
125	212	New Philadelphia City SD	New Philadelphia
126	209	Avon Lake City Schools	Avon Lake
127	208	Southwest Local SD	Harrison
128	206	Bowling Green City SD	Bowling Green
129	206	Southwest Licking Local SD	Etna
130	205	Kenston Local SD	Chagrin Falls
131	203	Edgewood City SD	Trenton
132	203	Trotwood-Madison City Schools	Trotwood
133	200	Springfield Local SD	Akron
134	200	Copley-Fairlawn City SD	Copley
135	200	Nordonia Hills City SD	Northfield
136	197	Garfield Heights City SD	Garfield Hgts
136	197	Talawanda City SD	Oxford
138	197	Maumee City SD	Maumee
139	197	Teays Valley Local SD	Ashville
140	196	Cloverleaf Local SD	Lodi
141	196	Olmsted Falls City SD	Olmsted Falls
142	196	Switzerland of Ohio Local SD	Woodsfield
143	194	Madison Local SD	Madison
144	193	Howland Local SD	Warren
145	193	Chardon Local SD	Chardon
146	193	Orange City SD	Cleveland
147	193	Louisville City SD	Louisville
148	192	Warrensville Heights City SD	Warrensville Hgts
149	191	Celina City SD	Celina
150	191	Whitehall City SD	Whitehall
151	190	Lake Local SD	Hartville
152	186	Bellefontaine City Schools	Bellefontaine
153	186	Western Brown Local SD	Mount Orab
154	185	Hillsboro City SD	Hillsboro
155	183	Hamilton Local SD	Columbus
156	183	Wilmington City SD	Wilmington
157	182	Piqua City SD	Piqua
158	182	Painesville City Local SD	Painesville
159	181	Chillicothe City SD	Chillicothe
160	181	Canfield Local SD	Canfield
161	179	Cambridge City SD	Cambridge
162	179	Little Miami Local SD	Morrow
163	179	Plain Local SD	New Albany
164	178	Norwood City SD	Norwood
165	178	Marietta City Schools	Marietta
165	178	Tallmadge City Schools	Tallmadge
167	177	Franklin City SD	Franklin
167	177	Revere Local SD	Bath
169	177	Tiffin City SD	Tiffin
170	175	Midview Local SD	Grafton
171	173	West Holmes Local SD	Millersburg
172	169	Gallia County Local SD	Gallipolis
173	169	Canton Local SD	Canton
174	169	Big Walnut Local SD	Galena

175	168	Carrollton Ex Vill SD	Carrollton
175	168	Niles City SD	Niles
177	167	Edison Local SD	Hammondsville
178	167	Vinton County Local SD	Mc Arthur
179	165	Defiance City SD	Defiance
180	164	Tri-Valley Local Schools	Dresden
181	164	Bay Village City SD	Bay Village
182	164	Dover City SD	Dover
183	163	Warren Local SD	Vincent
184	163	Aurora City SD	Aurora
184	163	Buckeye Local SD	Rayland
186	161	Canal Winchester Local SD	Canal Winchester
187	161	Wapakoneta City City SD	Wapakoneta
188	160	Miami Trace Local SD	Wash Ct House
189	159	Marlington Local SD	Alliance
190	159	Bexley City SD	Bexley
191	158	Salem City SD	Salem
192	158	Meigs Local SD	Pomeroy
193	157	Rocky River City SD	Rocky River
194	156	Crestwood Local SD	Mantua
194	156	New Richmond Ex Vill SD	New Richmond
196	156	Lexington Local SD	Lexington
197	156	Conneaut Area City SD	Conneaut
198	155	Geneva Area City Schools	Geneva
199	155	Highland Local SD	Medina
200	154	River View Local SD	Warsaw
201	154	Washington Court House City SD	Wash Ct House
202	153	Indian Hill Ex Vill SD	Cincinnati
203	153	West Geauga Local SD	Chesterland
204	153	Lakewood Local SD	Hebron
205	152	Morgan Local SD	McConnelsville
206	152	Steubenville City SD	Steubenville
207	151	Gallipolis City SD	Gallipolis
208	151	Beachwood City SD	Beachwood
209	151	Napoleon Area City SD	Napoleon
210	150	Streetsboro City Schools	Streetsboro
211	149	Norton City Schools	Norton
212	148	Northwest Local SD	Canal Fulton
213	148	Avon Local SD	Avon
214	147	Van Wert City SD	Van Wert
215	147	Greenfield Ex Vill SD	Greenfield
216	147	Tipp City Ex Vill SD	Tipp City
217	147	St Marys City SD	Saint Marys
218	146	Oakwood City SD	Dayton
219	146	Ross Local SD	Hamilton
220	145	Circleville City SD	Circleville
220	145	Vermilion Local SD	Vermilion
222	145	Norwalk City SD	Norwalk
223	144	Urbana City SD	Urbana
224	144	Bellevue City SD	Bellevue
225	144	Jackson City SD	Jackson
226	143	Portsmouth City SD	Portsmouth
227	143	Buckeye Local SD	Medina
228	143	Bryan City SD	Bryan
229	142	Galion City SD	Galion
230	142	Franklin Local SD	Duncan Falls
231	142	Electronic Classrm of Tomorrow	Columbus
232	140	Shelby City SD	Shelby
233	140	Logan Elm Local SD	Circleville
234	140	Elida Local SD	Elida
235	139	Claymont City SD	Dennison
235	139	Shawnee Local SD	Lima
237	139	Clark-Shawnee Local SD	Springfield
238	139	Beaver Local SD	Lisbon
238	139	Buckeye Local SD	Ashtabula
238	139	Perkins Local SD	Sandusky
241	138	Sugarcreek Local SD	Bellbrook
242	138	Goshen Local SD	Goshen
243	136	Kenton City SD	Kenton
244	136	Chagrin Falls Ex Vill SD	Chagrin Falls
245	136	Willard City SD	Willard
246	135	Northern Local SD	Thornville
247	134	London City SD	London
248	133	Wyoming City SD	Wyoming
249	133	Harrison Hills City SD	Hopedale
250	133	Indian Creek Local SD	Wintersville
251	132	Field Local SD	Mogadore
252	131	Rossford Ex Vill SD	Rossford
253	131	West Branch Local SD	Beloit
254	131	Fairview Park City SD	Fairview Park
254	131	Rock Hill Local SD	Ironton
256	130	Licking Valley Local SD Sd	Newark
257	130	Buckeye Valley Local SD	Delaware
258	130	Clyde-Green Springs Ex Vill SD	Clyde
259	130	Eaton Community Schools	Eaton
259	130	Hubbard Ex Vill SD	Hubbard
259	130	Indian Valley Local SD	Gnadenhutten
262	129	Minerva Local SD	Minerva
263	128	Graham Local SD	Saint Paris
264	127	Woodridge Local SD	Peninsula
265	127	Port Clinton City SD	Port Clinton
266	126	Coventry Local SD	Akron
267	126	Triway Local SD	Wooster
268	126	Three Rivers Local Schools	Cleves
269	126	Indian Lake Local SD	Lewistown
269	126	Northridge Local SD	Dayton
271	126	Southeast Local SD	Ravenna
272	124	Jefferson Area Local SD	Jefferson
273	124	Paulding Ex Vill SD	Paulding
274	123	Coshocton City SD	Coshocton
274	123	East Holmes Local Schools	Berlin
276	123	Fairless Local SD	Navarre
276	123	Fostoria City SD	Fostoria
278	122	Mariemont City SD	Cincinnati
278	122	Poland Local SD	Poland
280	122	East Muskingum Local SD	New Concord
281	122	Waverly City SD	Waverly
282	121	Sheffield-Sheffield Lake City SD	Sheffield Vlg
283	120	Firelands Local SD	Oberlin
284	119	Maysville Local SD	Zanesville
285	119	Upper Sandusky Ex Vill SD	Upper Sandusky
286	118	Wellston City Schools	Wellston
287	118	Perry Local SD	Perry
288	117	Valley View Local SD	Germantown
289	117	Struthers City SD	Struthers
290	117	Orrville City SD	Orrville
291	117	Finneytown Local SD	Cincinnati
292	116	Wauseon Ex Vill SD	Wauseon
293	116	Lakeview Local SD	Cortland
294	116	Alexander Local SD	Albany
294	116	Greenon Local SD	Springfield
296	115	Preble Shawnee Local SD	Camden
297	114	Blanchester Local SD	Blanchester
297	114	Bucyrus City SD	Bucyrus
299	114	Berlin-Milan Local SD	Milan
299	114	Southeast Local SD	Apple Creek
301	114	Granville Ex Vill SD	Granville
302	113	Benjamin Logan Local SD	Bellefontaine
302	113	South Point Local SD	South Point
302	113	Union Local SD	Morristown
305	112	Wickliffe City SD	Wickliffe
306	112	Benton Carroll Salem Local SD	Oak Harbor
307	112	Rolling Hills Local SD	Cambridge
308	111	Batavia Local SD	Batavia
309	111	Licking Heights Local SD	Summit Station
310	111	New Lexington City SD	New Lexington
311	110	Ironton City SD	Ironton
312	108	Champion Local SD	Warren
312	108	Elgin Local SD	Marion
314	106	Bellaire Local SD	Bellaire
314	106	Union-Scioto Local SD	Chillicothe
314	106	Washington-Nile Local SD	West Portsmouth
317	106	Milton-Union Exempted Vill Schls	West Milton
318	106	Northwest Local SD	Mc Dermott
319	105	Northwestern Local SD	Springfield
320	105	Clear Fork Valley Local SD	Bellville
320	105	North Fork Local SD	Utica
322	105	River Valley Local SD	Caledonia
323	105	St Clairsville-Richland City SD	St Clairsville
324	104	Carlisle Local SD	Carlisle
325	104	West Muskingum Local SD	Zanesville
326	104	Sandy Valley Local SD	Magnolia
327	103	Fairfield Union Local SD	W Rushville
328	103	Clermont Northeastern Local SD	Batavia
329	102	Bath Local SD	Lima
330	101	Liberty Local SD	Youngstown
331	101	Highland Local SD	Sparta
332	101	Tuscarawas Valley Local SD	Zoarville
333	100	Bethel-Tate Local SD	Bethel
333	100	Madeira City SD	Cincinnati
335	100	Campbell City SD	Campbell
335	100	Girard City SD	Girard
337	99	Fairland Local SD	Proctorville
338	99	Westfall Local SD	Williamsport
339	98	Monroe Local SD	Monroe
340	98	Clearview Local SD	Lorain
341	97	Madison Local SD	Middletown
342	96	Keystone Local SD	Lagrange
343	95	Coldwater Ex Vill SD	Coldwater
344	95	Huron City Schools	Huron
344	95	Ottawa-Glandorf Local SD	Ottawa
346	95	Black River Local SD	Sullivan
346	95	Madison-Plains Local SD	London
348	94	Wellington Ex Vill SD	Wellington
349	94	Otsego Local SD	Tontogany
350	94	Eastwood Local SD	Pemberville
351	94	James A Garfield Local SD	Garrettsville
352	93	Heath City SD	Heath
353	93	Minford Local SD	Minford
354	92	Ontario Local SD	Mansfield
355	91	Clinton-Massie Local SD	Clarksville
356	91	Amanda-Clearcreek Local SD	Amanda
356	91	East Clinton Local SD	Lees Creek
356	91	Martins Ferry City SD	Martins Ferry
356	91	Newton Falls Ex Vill SD	Newton Falls
356	91	Scioto Valley Local SD	Piketon
361	90	Eastern Local SD	Sardinia
361	90	Greeneview Local SD	Jamestown
361	90	Jonathan Alder Local SD	Plain City
364	89	Swanton Local SD	Swanton
365	89	Genoa Area Local SD	Genoa
366	87	Pike-Delta-York Local SD	Delta
367	87	North College Hill City SD	Cincinnati
368	85	Brookville Local SD	Brookville
369	84	Ridgewood Local SD	West Lafayette
370	84	Zane Trace Local SD	Chillicothe
371	83	United Local SD	Hanoverton
372	80	Manchester Local SD	Akron
373	79	Lake Local SD	Millbury
374	53	Ohio Virtual Academy	Maumee

Number of Students

Rank	Number	District Name	City
1	69,655	Cleveland Municipal City SD	Cleveland
2	63,098	Columbus Public Schools	Columbus
3	40,374	Cincinnati City SD	Cincinnati
4	34,486	Toledo City SD	Toledo
5	28,816	Akron Public Schools	Akron
6	21,230	South-Western City SD	Grove City
7	18,491	Dayton City SD	Dayton
8	16,358	Lakota Local SD	Liberty Twp
9	14,219	Hilliard City SD	Hilliard
10	14,142	Westerville City SD	Westerville
11	13,427	Parma City SD	Parma
12	12,376	Dublin City SD	Dublin
13	11,798	Canton City SD	Canton
14	10,657	Northwest Local SD	Cincinnati
15	10,320	Lorain City SD	Lorain
16	9,777	Mentor Ex Vill SD	Mentor
17	9,754	Worthington City SD	Worthington
18	9,748	Youngstown City SD	Youngstown
19	9,607	Hamilton City SD	Hamilton
20	9,547	Fairfield City SD	Fairfield
21	9,358	Springfield City SD	Springfield
22	9,189	West Clermont Local SD	Cincinnati
23	8,917	Pickerington Local SD	Pickerington
24	8,876	Willoughby-Eastlake City SD	Willoughby
25	8,635	Mason City SD	Mason
26	8,560	Olentangy Local SD	Lewis Center
27	8,132	Oak Hills Local SD	Cincinnati
28	8,127	Elyria City SD	Elyria
29	8,120	Centerville City SD	Centerville
30	8,027	Berea City SD	Berea
31	7,832	Sylvania City SD	Sylvania
32	7,747	Kettering City SD	Kettering
33	7,621	Forest Hills Local SD	Cincinnati
34	7,340	Strongsville City SD	Strongsville
35	7,323	Medina City SD	Medina
36	7,296	Middletown City SD	Middletown
37	7,254	Brunswick City SD	Brunswick
38	7,184	Beavercreek City SD	Beavercreek
39	7,083	Lakewood City SD	Lakewood
40	6,969	Newark City SD	Newark
41	6,942	Washington Local Schools	Toledo
42	6,901	Warren City SD	Warren
43	6,887	Cleveland Hts-Univ Hts City SD	University Hgts
44	6,821	Huber Heights City SD	Huber Heights
45	6,806	Gahanna-Jefferson City SD	Gahanna
46	6,607	Reynoldsburg City SD	Reynoldsburg
47	6,479	Findlay City SD	Findlay
48	6,440	Groveport Madison Local SD	Groveport
49	6,420	Euclid City SD	Euclid
50	6,225	Milford Ex Vill SD	Milford
51	6,122	Plain Local SD	Canton
52	6,105	Princeton City SD	Cincinnati
53	6,104	Lancaster City SD	Lancaster
54	6,080	Stow-Munroe Falls City SD	Stow
55	5,933	Northmont City SD	Englewood
56	5,802	Mansfield City SD	Mansfield
57	5,759	Sycamore Community City SD	Cincinnati
58	5,625	Shaker Heights City SD	Shaker Heights
59	5,597	Upper Arlington City SD	Upper Arlington
60	5,592	Marion City SD	Marion
61	5,566	Hudson City SD	Hudson
62	5,561	Jackson Local SD	Massillon
63	5,427	Fairborn City Schools	Fairborn
64	5,399	Cuyahoga Falls City SD	Cuyahoga Falls
65	5,306	Miamisburg City SD	Miamisburg
66	5,213	Electronic Classrm of Tomorrow	Columbus
67	5,202	Xenia Community City SD	Xenia
68	5,180	Solon City SD	Solon
69	5,098	Adams County/Ohio Valley LSD	West Union
70	5,092	East Cleveland City SD	East Cleveland
71	5,046	Austintown Local SD	Youngstown
72	4,994	Lima City SD	Lima
73	4,924	North Canton City SD	North Canton
74	4,897	Boardman Local SD	Youngstown

75	4,854	Perry Local SD	Massillon
76	4,780	Lebanon City SD	Lebanon
77	4,721	Marysville Exempted Village SD	Marysville
78	4,695	Wadsworth City SD	Wadsworth
79	4,666	Brecksville-Broadview Hgts City	Brecksville
80	4,661	Ashtabula Area City SD	Ashtabula
81	4,598	Fremont City SD	Fremont
82	4,596	Barberton City SD	Barberton
83	4,583	South Euclid-Lyndhurst City SD	Lyndhurst
84	4,573	North Olmsted City Schools	North Olmsted
85	4,547	Massillon City SD	Massillon
86	4,538	Troy City SD	Troy
87	4,519	Painesville Township Local SD	Painesville
88	4,498	Delaware City SD	Delaware
89	4,496	North Royalton City SD	N Royalton
90	4,348	Perrysburg Exempted Village	Perrysburg
91	4,331	Mayfield City SD	Highland Hgts
92	4,320	Springboro Community City SD	Springboro
93	4,301	Mount Vernon City SD	Mount Vernon
94	4,278	Loveland City SD	Loveland
95	4,251	Zanesville City SD	Zanesville
96	4,227	Sandusky City SD	Sandusky
97	4,190	Amherst Ex Vill SD	Amherst
98	4,165	Green Local SD	Green
99	4,156	Winton Woods City SD	Cincinnati
100	4,144	Wooster City SD	Wooster
101	4,028	Logan-Hocking Local SD	Logan
102	3,971	Southwest Local SD	Harrison
103	3,954	Piqua City SD	Piqua
104	3,953	Twinsburg City SD	Twinsburg
105	3,917	Westlake City SD	Westlake
106	3,898	West Carrollton City SD	West Carrollton
107	3,897	Sidney City SD	Sidney
108	3,890	Bedford City SD	Bedford
109	3,887	Nordonia Hills City SD	Northfield
110	3,879	Anthony Wayne Local SD	Whitehouse
111	3,862	Oregon City SD	Oregon
112	3,859	Garfield Heights City SD	Garfield Hgts
113	3,849	Kings Local SD	Kings Mills
114	3,817	Ashland City SD	Ashland
115	3,796	Kent City SD	Kent
116	3,788	Mt Healthy City SD	Cincinnati
117	3,779	Springfield Local Schools	Holland
118	3,739	Madison Local SD	Madison
119	3,686	Maple Heights City SD	Maple Heights
120	3,628	Northeastern Local SD	Springfield
121	3,619	Mad River Local SD	Dayton
122	3,601	Madison Local SD	Mansfield
123	3,595	Edgewood City SD	Trenton
124	3,578	Tecumseh Local SD	New Carlisle
125	3,568	Cloverleaf Local SD	Lodi
126	3,550	North Ridgeville City SD	N Ridgeville
127	3,527	Southwest Licking Local SD	Etna
128	3,520	Chillicothe City SD	Chillicothe
129	3,518	Vandalia-Butler City SD	Vandalia
130	3,470	Trotwood-Madison City Schools	Trotwood
131	3,464	Midview Local SD	Grafton
132	3,419	Greenville City SD	Greenville
133	3,418	Western Brown Local SD	Mount Orab
134	3,386	Ravenna City SD	Ravenna
135	3,359	Lake Local SD	Hartville
136	3,343	Avon Lake City Schools	Avon Lake
137	3,342	Olmsted Falls City SD	Olmsted Falls
138	3,323	Alliance City SD	Alliance
139	3,307	New Philadelphia City SD	New Philadelphia
140	3,274	Louisville City SD	Louisville
141	3,272	Chardon Local SD	Chardon
142	3,254	Copley-Fairlawn City SD	Copley
143	3,233	Teays Valley Local SD	Ashville
144	3,228	Howland Local SD	Warren
145	3,203	Bowling Green City SD	Bowling Green
146	3,202	Marietta City Schools	Marietta
147	3,201	Little Miami Local SD	Morrow
148	3,199	Celina City SD	Celina
149	3,195	Wilmington City SD	Wilmington
150	3,160	Wapakoneta City City SD	Wapakoneta
151	3,150	Tri-Valley Local Schools	Dresden
152	3,134	Kenston Local SD	Chagrin Falls
153	3,104	Talawanda City SD	Oxford
154	3,097	Canfield Local SD	Canfield
155	3,094	Franklin City SD	Franklin
156	3,082	East Liverpool City SD	East Liverpool
157	3,076	Springfield Local SD	Akron
158	3,064	Whitehall City SD	Whitehall
159	3,022	Tiffin City SD	Tiffin
160	3,011	Geneva Area City Schools	Geneva
161	2,989	Hamilton Local SD	Columbus
162	2,975	Athens City SD	The Plains
163	2,952	Norwalk City SD	Norwalk
164	2,932	Carrollton Ex Vill SD	Carrollton
165	2,877	Plain Local SD	New Albany
166	2,861	Niles City SD	Niles
167	2,851	Aurora City SD	Aurora
168	2,847	Maumee City SD	Maumee
169	2,845	Painesville City Local SD	Painesville
170	2,835	Revere Local SD	Bath
171	2,833	Hillsboro City SD	Hillsboro
172	2,821	Warrensville Heights City SD	Warrensville Hgts
173	2,819	Lexington Local SD	Lexington
174	2,808	Bellefontaine City Schools	Bellefontaine
175	2,805	West Holmes Local SD	Millersburg
176	2,780	Highland Local SD	Medina
177	2,764	Switzerland of Ohio Local SD	Woodsfield
178	2,761	Sugarcreek Local SD	Bellbrook
179	2,760	Tallmadge City Schools	Tallmadge
180	2,745	Jackson City SD	Jackson
181	2,739	Cambridge City SD	Cambridge
182	2,738	Marlington Local SD	Alliance
183	2,725	Crestwood Local SD	Mantua
184	2,719	Miami Trace Local SD	Wash Ct House
185	2,692	Warren Local SD	Vincent
186	2,689	Edison Local SD	Hammondsville
187	2,659	Norwood City SD	Norwood
188	2,657	Shawnee Local SD	Lima
189	2,638	Tipp City Ex Vill SD	Tipp City
190	2,633	Big Walnut Local SD	Galena
190	2,633	Vinton County Local SD	Mc Arthur
192	2,622	Canal Winchester Local SD	Canal Winchester
193	2,598	Dover City SD	Dover
193	2,598	Rocky River City SD	Rocky River
195	2,591	Elida Local SD	Elida
195	2,591	St Marys City SD	Saint Marys
197	2,586	River View Local SD	Warsaw
198	2,580	Ross Local SD	Hamilton
199	2,558	Norton City Schools	Norton
200	2,550	West Geauga Local SD	Chesterland
201	2,547	Clark-Shawnee Local SD	Springfield
202	2,544	Gallia County Local SD	Gallipolis
203	2,541	Defiance City SD	Defiance
204	2,538	Canton Local SD	Canton
205	2,527	Conneaut Area City SD	Conneaut
206	2,525	Goshen Local SD	Goshen
206	2,525	Vermilion Local SD	Vermilion
208	2,514	Poland Local SD	Poland
209	2,508	Avon Local SD	Avon
210	2,490	Circleville City SD	Circleville
211	2,456	Buckeye Local SD	Medina
212	2,455	Bay Village City SD	Bay Village
212	2,455	Beaver Local SD	Lisbon
214	2,447	Northwest Local SD	Canal Fulton
215	2,445	Salem City SD	Salem
216	2,443	West Branch Local SD	Beloit
217	2,418	Franklin Local SD	Duncan Falls
218	2,415	Buckeye Local SD	Rayland
219	2,411	New Richmond Ex Vill SD	New Richmond
220	2,391	Steubenville City SD	Steubenville
221	2,388	Bellevue City SD	Bellevue
222	2,387	Napoleon Area City SD	Napoleon
223	2,368	Orange City SD	Cleveland
224	2,366	Gallipolis City SD	Gallipolis
225	2,362	Willard City SD	Willard
226	2,360	Northern Local SD	Thornville
227	2,353	Urbana City SD	Urbana
228	2,346	Claymont City SD	Dennison
229	2,339	Fostoria City SD	Fostoria
230	2,334	Coventry Local SD	Akron
230	2,334	Eaton Community Schools	Eaton
232	2,323	Logan Elm Local SD	Circleville
233	2,322	Indian Creek Local SD	Wintersville
234	2,319	Greenfield Ex Vill SD	Greenfield
235	2,315	Washington Court House City SD	Wash Ct House
236	2,310	Field Local SD	Mogadore
237	2,305	Hubbard Ex Vill SD	Hubbard
238	2,297	Clyde-Green Springs Ex Vill SD	Clyde
239	2,290	Van Wert City SD	Van Wert
240	2,288	Bryan City SD	Bryan
241	2,287	Buckeye Local SD	Ashtabula
242	2,267	Perkins Local SD	Sandusky
243	2,265	Lakewood Local SD	Hebron
243	2,265	Maysville Local SD	Zanesville
243	2,265	Morgan Local SD	McConnelsville
246	2,260	Indian Hill Ex Vill SD	Cincinnati
247	2,257	Jefferson Area Local SD	Jefferson
248	2,254	Shelby City SD	Shelby
249	2,239	Firelands Local SD	Oberlin
250	2,238	Galion City SD	Galion
251	2,237	Buckeye Valley Local SD	Delaware
252	2,234	Lakeview Local SD	Cortland
253	2,226	Rolling Hills Local SD	Cambridge
254	2,211	Bexley City SD	Bexley
255	2,210	Southeast Local SD	Ravenna
256	2,202	Minerva Local SD	Minerva
257	2,189	Graham Local SD	Saint Paris
258	2,174	Waverly City SD	Waverly
259	2,166	Licking Valley Local SD Sd	Newark
259	2,166	Portsmouth City SD	Portsmouth
261	2,164	Three Rivers Local Schools	Cleves
262	2,150	Triway Local SD	Wooster
263	2,145	Kenton City SD	Kenton
264	2,135	Ohio Virtual Academy	Maumee
265	2,133	Wauseon Ex Vill SD	Wauseon
266	2,121	East Muskingum Local SD	New Concord
267	2,118	Harrison Hills City SD	Hopedale
268	2,113	Granville Ex Vill SD	Granville
269	2,092	Meigs Local SD	Pomeroy
270	2,087	Streetsboro City Schools	Streetsboro
271	2,085	Bath Local SD	Lima
272	2,084	Sheffield-Sheffield Lake City SD	Sheffield Vlg
273	2,081	London City SD	London
274	2,056	Valley View Local SD	Germantown
275	2,042	Oakwood City SD	Dayton
276	2,024	Benton Carroll Salem Local SD	Oak Harbor
277	2,020	Rossford Ex Vill SD	Rossford
278	2,008	Licking Heights Local SD	Summit Station
279	2,004	Struthers City SD	Struthers
280	1,992	Indian Lake Local SD	Lewistown
281	1,990	Northridge Local SD	Dayton
282	1,984	Wyoming City SD	Wyoming
283	1,980	Greenon Local SD	Springfield
284	1,978	Coshocton City SD	Coshocton
284	1,978	Eastwood Local SD	Pemberville
286	1,972	Clermont Northeastern Local SD	Batavia
287	1,971	Port Clinton City SD	Port Clinton
288	1,970	Bethel-Tate Local SD	Bethel
288	1,970	Chagrin Falls Ex Vill SD	Chagrin Falls
290	1,966	Benjamin Logan Local SD	Bellefontaine
290	1,966	New Lexington City SD	New Lexington
292	1,958	Fairfield Union Local SD	W Rushville
293	1,954	Union-Scioto Local SD	Chillicothe
294	1,951	Northwestern Local SD	Springfield
295	1,926	Rock Hill Local SD	Ironton
296	1,924	Batavia Local SD	Batavia
297	1,916	Indian Valley Local SD	Gnadenhutten
298	1,908	North Fork Local SD	Utica
299	1,891	Bucyrus City SD	Bucyrus
300	1,883	Fairless Local SD	Navarre
301	1,874	Berlin-Milan Local SD	Milan
302	1,866	South Point Local SD	South Point
303	1,863	Orrville City SD	Orrville
304	1,857	East Holmes Local Schools	Berlin
305	1,854	Perry Local SD	Perry
305	1,854	Wellston City Schools	Wellston
307	1,843	Clear Fork Valley Local SD	Bellville
307	1,843	Keystone Local SD	Lagrange
309	1,838	Fairland Local SD	Proctorville
310	1,831	Fairview Park City SD	Fairview Park
310	1,831	River Valley Local SD	Caledonia
312	1,819	Liberty Local SD	Youngstown
313	1,816	West Muskingum Local SD	Zanesville
314	1,809	Jonathan Alder Local SD	Plain City
314	1,809	Paulding Ex Vill SD	Paulding
316	1,807	Upper Sandusky Ex Vill SD	Upper Sandusky
317	1,806	Milton-Union Exempted Vill Schls	West Milton
318	1,795	Lake Local SD	Millbury
319	1,787	Finneytown Local SD	Cincinnati
320	1,786	Woodridge Local SD	Peninsula
321	1,781	Highland Local SD	Sparta
321	1,781	Ontario Local SD	Mansfield
323	1,780	Northwest Local SD	Mc Dermott
324	1,775	Carlisle Local SD	Carlisle
325	1,774	Clinton-Massie Local SD	Clarksville
326	1,771	Blanchester Local SD	Blanchester
327	1,769	Girard City SD	Girard
328	1,744	Tuscarawas Valley Local SD	Zoarville
329	1,737	Genoa Area Local SD	Genoa
330	1,731	Ottawa-Glandorf Local SD	Ottawa
331	1,722	Champion Local SD	Warren
332	1,718	Southeast Local SD	Apple Creek
333	1,708	Mariemont City SD	Cincinnati
334	1,707	Heath City SD	Heath
335	1,699	Washington-Nile Local SD	West Portsmouth
336	1,689	Otsego Local SD	Tontogany
337	1,679	Alexander Local SD	Albany
337	1,679	Scioto Valley Local SD	Piketon
339	1,669	Black River Local SD	Sullivan
340	1,667	Preble Shawnee Local SD	Camden
341	1,664	Huron City Schools	Huron
342	1,655	Westfall Local SD	Williamsport
343	1,653	Amanda-Clearcreek Local SD	Amanda
344	1,652	Minford Local SD	Minford
345	1,648	Wellington Ex Vill SD	Wellington
346	1,645	Greeneview Local SD	Jamestown
347	1,631	Brookville Local SD	Brookville
348	1,627	Elgin Local SD	Marion
348	1,627	Madison-Plains Local SD	London
350	1,626	Ironton City SD	Ironton
351	1,623	Coldwater Ex Vill SD	Coldwater
352	1,596	Beachwood City SD	Beachwood

353	1,590	Madison Local SD	Middletown
354	1,589	Zane Trace Local SD	Chillicothe
355	1,585	Swanton Local SD	Swanton
356	1,579	Campbell City SD	Campbell
356	1,579	St Clairsville-Richland City SD	St Clairsville
358	1,574	Pike-Delta-York Local SD	Delta
359	1,571	East Clinton Local SD	Lees Creek
360	1,570	James A Garfield Local SD	Garrettsville
360	1,570	Wickliffe City SD	Wickliffe
362	1,568	Sandy Valley Local SD	Magnolia
363	1,553	Union Local SD	Morristown
364	1,549	Bellaire Local SD	Bellaire
365	1,543	Eastern Local SD	Sardinia
366	1,538	North College Hill City SD	Cincinnati
367	1,537	United Local SD	Hanoverton
368	1,522	Martins Ferry City SD	Martins Ferry
369	1,521	Monroe Local SD	Monroe
370	1,520	Manchester Local SD	Akron
370	1,520	Newton Falls Ex Vill SD	Newton Falls
372	1,508	Madeira City SD	Cincinnati
373	1,503	Clearview Local SD	Lorain
374	1,501	Ridgewood Local SD	West Lafayette

Male Students

Rank	Percent	District Name	City
1	54.6	Harrison Hills City SD	Hopedale
2	54.6	Orange City SD	Cleveland
3	54.4	Southeast Local SD	Apple Creek
4	54.3	St Marys City SD	Saint Marys
5	54.3	Orrville City SD	Orrville
6	54.3	Tallmadge City Schools	Tallmadge
7	54.2	Genoa Area Local SD	Genoa
8	54.1	Union Local SD	Morristown
9	53.9	Beachwood City SD	Beachwood
10	53.9	Canton Local SD	Canton
11	53.9	Wickliffe City SD	Wickliffe
12	53.8	Tuscarawas Valley Local SD	Zoarville
13	53.8	Mayfield City SD	Highland Hgts
14	53.8	Berlin-Milan Local SD	Milan
15	53.7	Minerva Local SD	Minerva
16	53.7	Maumee City SD	Maumee
17	53.6	Ross Local SD	Hamilton
18	53.5	Brookville Local SD	Brookville
19	53.5	West Carrollton City SD	West Carrollton
20	53.4	Portsmouth City SD	Portsmouth
21	53.4	Buckeye Valley Local SD	Delaware
22	53.4	East Muskingum Local SD	New Concord
23	53.4	Claymont City SD	Dennison
24	53.4	Coldwater Ex Vill SD	Coldwater
25	53.3	North College Hill City SD	Cincinnati
26	53.2	Finneytown Local SD	Cincinnati
27	53.2	Madison Local SD	Mansfield
28	53.2	Hudson City SD	Hudson
29	53.2	Preble Shawnee Local SD	Camden
30	53.2	Piqua City SD	Piqua
31	53.2	Ashland City SD	Ashland
32	53.1	Black River Local SD	Sullivan
33	53.1	Northwest Local SD	Mc Dermott
34	53.0	Wooster City SD	Wooster
35	53.0	River Valley Local SD	Caledonia
36	53.0	Greenfield Ex Vill SD	Greenfield
37	53.0	Vandalia-Butler City SD	Vandalia
38	53.0	Indian Hill Ex Vill SD	Cincinnati
39	52.9	Euclid City SD	Euclid
40	52.9	Field Local SD	Mogadore
41	52.9	Massillon City SD	Massillon
42	52.8	Mt Healthy City SD	Cincinnati
43	52.8	Painesville City Local SD	Painesville
44	52.8	Berea City SD	Berea
45	52.8	Highland Local SD	Sparta
46	52.8	Garfield Heights City SD	Garfield Hgts
47	52.7	Lakewood Local SD	Hebron
48	52.7	Liberty Local SD	Youngstown
49	52.7	New Lexington City SD	New Lexington
50	52.7	Fairborn City Schools	Fairborn
51	52.7	Wadsworth City SD	Wadsworth
52	52.7	Bexley City SD	Bexley
53	52.6	Avon Lake City Schools	Avon Lake
54	52.6	Milton-Union Exempted Vill Schls	West Milton
55	52.6	Edgewood City SD	Trenton
56	52.6	Ironton City SD	Ironton
57	52.6	Jackson City SD	Jackson
58	52.6	Springfield Local Schools	Holland
59	52.6	Celina City SD	Celina
60	52.6	Amanda-Clearcreek Local SD	Amanda
61	52.6	Oregon City SD	Oregon
62	52.5	Vinton County Local SD	Mc Arthur
63	52.5	Oak Hills Local SD	Cincinnati
64	52.5	Green Local SD	Green
65	52.5	Kenton City SD	Kenton
66	52.5	Northwest Local SD	Cincinnati
67	52.5	Lancaster City SD	Lancaster
68	52.5	Perry Local SD	Massillon
69	52.5	Winton Woods City SD	Cincinnati
70	52.5	Jefferson Area Local SD	Jefferson
71	52.4	Carlisle Local SD	Carlisle
72	52.4	Lima City SD	Lima
73	52.4	Madeira City SD	Cincinnati
74	52.4	Warren Local SD	Vincent
75	52.4	Crestwood Local SD	Mantua
76	52.4	Logan Elm Local SD	Circleville
77	52.4	Perrysburg Exempted Village	Perrysburg
78	52.4	Bryan City SD	Bryan
79	52.4	Conneaut Area City SD	Conneaut
80	52.4	Cambridge City SD	Cambridge
81	52.4	Strongsville City SD	Strongsville
82	52.4	Kettering City SD	Kettering
83	52.3	Lake Local SD	Hartville
84	52.3	Lakewood City SD	Lakewood
85	52.3	Washington Court House City SD	Wash Ct House
86	52.3	Pickerington Local SD	Pickerington
87	52.3	Miami Trace Local SD	Wash Ct House
88	52.3	Gahanna-Jefferson City SD	Gahanna
89	52.3	Springfield City SD	Springfield
90	52.3	Chagrin Falls Ex Vill SD	Chagrin Falls
91	52.2	Washington Local Schools	Toledo
92	52.2	Geneva Area City Schools	Geneva
93	52.2	Southwest Local SD	Harrison
94	52.2	Tiffin City SD	Tiffin
95	52.2	Campbell City SD	Campbell
96	52.2	East Holmes Local Schools	Berlin
97	52.2	Port Clinton City SD	Port Clinton
98	52.2	North Olmsted City Schools	North Olmsted
99	52.2	Valley View Local SD	Germantown
100	52.2	Champion Local SD	Warren
101	52.2	Urbana City SD	Urbana
102	52.2	Lexington Local SD	Lexington
103	52.2	Teays Valley Local SD	Ashville
104	52.2	Kings Local SD	Kings Mills
105	52.2	Clermont Northeastern Local SD	Batavia
106	52.2	Sandy Valley Local SD	Magnolia
107	52.2	North Ridgeville City SD	N Ridgeville
108	52.1	Ontario Local SD	Mansfield
109	52.1	Worthington City SD	Worthington
110	52.1	Norwood City SD	Norwood
111	52.1	Maple Heights City SD	Maple Heights
112	52.1	Rossford Ex Vill SD	Rossford
113	52.1	Logan-Hocking Local SD	Logan
114	52.1	Bellaire Local SD	Bellaire
115	52.1	Marysville Exempted Village SD	Marysville
116	52.1	Switzerland of Ohio Local SD	Woodsfield
117	52.1	St Clairsville-Richland City SD	St Clairsville
118	52.1	River View Local SD	Warsaw
119	52.1	Kent City SD	Kent
120	52.1	Fairview Park City SD	Fairview Park
121	52.1	Three Rivers Local Schools	Cleves
122	52.1	Rock Hill Local SD	Ironton
123	52.1	Huber Heights City SD	Huber Heights
124	52.1	West Geauga Local SD	Chesterland
125	52.0	Madison Local SD	Madison
126	52.0	Wyoming City SD	Wyoming
127	52.0	Miamisburg City SD	Miamisburg
128	52.0	Beaver Local SD	Lisbon
129	52.0	Ohio Virtual Academy	Maumee
130	52.0	Ashtabula Area City SD	Ashtabula
131	52.0	Southeast Local SD	Ravenna
132	52.0	South Euclid-Lyndhurst City SD	Lyndhurst
133	52.0	Mariemont City SD	Cincinnati
134	52.0	Wilmington City SD	Wilmington
135	52.0	West Branch Local SD	Beloit
136	51.9	Marion City SD	Marion
137	51.9	Batavia Local SD	Batavia
138	51.9	Shelby City SD	Shelby
139	51.9	Waverly City SD	Waverly
140	51.9	North Fork Local SD	Utica
141	51.9	Bucyrus City SD	Bucyrus
142	51.9	Martins Ferry City SD	Martins Ferry
143	51.9	Lakota Local SD	Liberty Twp
144	51.9	Fairfield Union Local SD	W Rushville
145	51.9	Firelands Local SD	Oberlin
146	51.8	Twinsburg City SD	Twinsburg
147	51.8	Clinton-Massie Local SD	Clarksville
148	51.8	Willoughby-Eastlake City SD	Willoughby
149	51.8	Northeastern Local SD	Springfield
150	51.8	Boardman Local SD	Youngstown
151	51.8	Mount Vernon City SD	Mount Vernon
152	51.8	Shaker Heights City SD	Shaker Heights
153	51.8	Woodridge Local SD	Peninsula
154	51.8	Fostoria City SD	Fostoria
155	51.8	Stow-Munroe Falls City SD	Stow
156	51.8	Indian Creek Local SD	Wintersville
157	51.8	Toledo City SD	Toledo
158	51.8	Trotwood-Madison City Schools	Trotwood
159	51.8	Mansfield City SD	Mansfield
160	51.7	Barberton City SD	Barberton
161	51.7	Centerville City SD	Centerville
162	51.7	Swanton Local SD	Swanton
163	51.7	Bellevue City SD	Bellevue
164	51.7	Dover City SD	Dover
165	51.7	Franklin Local SD	Duncan Falls
166	51.7	Huron City Schools	Huron
167	51.7	Scioto Valley Local SD	Piketon
168	51.7	Fairland Local SD	Proctorville
169	51.7	New Richmond Ex Vill SD	New Richmond
170	51.7	Princeton City SD	Cincinnati
171	51.7	Eaton Community Schools	Eaton
172	51.7	Coshocton City SD	Coshocton
173	51.7	West Clermont Local SD	Cincinnati
174	51.7	Troy City SD	Troy
175	51.7	Elida Local SD	Elida
176	51.7	Defiance City SD	Defiance
177	51.6	Delaware City SD	Delaware
178	51.6	Poland Local SD	Poland
178	51.6	Steubenville City SD	Steubenville
180	51.6	Xenia Community City SD	Xenia
181	51.6	Lorain City SD	Lorain
182	51.6	Monroe Local SD	Monroe
183	51.6	Milford Ex Vill SD	Milford
184	51.6	Sidney City SD	Sidney
185	51.6	Hilliard City SD	Hilliard
186	51.6	Midview Local SD	Grafton
187	51.6	Buckeye Local SD	Rayland
188	51.6	Revere Local SD	Bath
189	51.6	Hillsboro City SD	Hillsboro
190	51.6	Eastern Local SD	Sardinia
191	51.5	Fremont City SD	Fremont
192	51.5	Licking Heights Local SD	Summit Station
193	51.5	Cloverleaf Local SD	Lodi
194	51.5	Nordonia Hills City SD	Northfield
195	51.5	East Liverpool City SD	East Liverpool
196	51.5	Greeneview Local SD	Jamestown
197	51.5	Girard City SD	Girard
198	51.5	Shawnee Local SD	Lima
199	51.5	Dublin City SD	Dublin
200	51.5	Middletown City SD	Middletown
201	51.5	Ravenna City SD	Ravenna
202	51.5	Norwalk City SD	Norwalk
203	51.5	Sugarcreek Local SD	Bellbrook
204	51.5	Northwest Local SD	Canal Fulton
205	51.5	Marietta City Schools	Marietta
206	51.4	New Philadelphia City SD	New Philadelphia
207	51.4	Bowling Green City SD	Bowling Green
208	51.4	Austintown Local SD	Youngstown
209	51.4	Washington-Nile Local SD	West Portsmouth
210	51.4	Streetsboro City Schools	Streetsboro
211	51.4	Mason City SD	Mason
212	51.4	Hamilton City SD	Hamilton
213	51.4	Tipp City Ex Vill SD	Tipp City
214	51.4	Painesville Township Local SD	Painesville
215	51.4	Findlay City SD	Findlay
216	51.4	Edison Local SD	Hammondsville
217	51.4	Sycamore Community City SD	Cincinnati
218	51.4	Kenston Local SD	Chagrin Falls
219	51.4	Granville Ex Vill SD	Granville
220	51.4	Cleveland Municipal City SD	Cleveland
221	51.4	Westerville City SD	Westerville
222	51.3	South-Western City SD	Grove City
223	51.3	Dayton City SD	Dayton
224	51.3	Highland Local SD	Medina
225	51.3	West Muskingum Local SD	Zanesville
226	51.3	Akron Public Schools	Akron
227	51.3	Northern Local SD	Thornville
228	51.3	Western Brown Local SD	Mount Orab
229	51.3	Gallia County Local SD	Gallipolis
230	51.2	Canfield Local SD	Canfield
231	51.2	Alexander Local SD	Albany
232	51.2	Gallipolis City SD	Gallipolis
233	51.2	Eastwood Local SD	Pemberville
234	51.2	Ridgewood Local SD	West Lafayette
235	51.2	Youngstown City SD	Youngstown
236	51.2	Westlake City SD	Westlake
237	51.2	Lake Local SD	Millbury
238	51.2	Big Walnut Local SD	Galena
239	51.2	Newton Falls Ex Vill SD	Newton Falls
240	51.2	Madison-Plains Local SD	London
241	51.2	Tecumseh Local SD	New Carlisle
242	51.2	Paulding Ex Vill SD	Paulding
243	51.2	Benton Carroll Salem Local SD	Oak Harbor
244	51.2	Wellington Ex Vill SD	Wellington
245	51.2	Napoleon Area City SD	Napoleon
246	51.2	Franklin City SD	Franklin
247	51.2	Tri-Valley Local Schools	Dresden
248	51.2	Copley-Fairlawn City SD	Copley
249	51.2	Solon City SD	Solon
250	51.1	Wapakoneta City City SD	Wapakoneta
251	51.1	Clark-Shawnee Local SD	Springfield
252	51.1	London City SD	London

253	51.1	Canton City SD	Canton
254	51.1	Morgan Local SD	McConnelsville
255	51.1	Talawanda City SD	Oxford
256	51.1	Chardon Local SD	Chardon
257	51.1	Licking Valley Local SD Sd	Newark
258	51.1	Graham Local SD	Saint Paris
259	51.1	Sylvania City SD	Sylvania
260	51.1	Beavercreek City SD	Beavercreek
261	51.1	Bellefontaine City Schools	Bellefontaine
262	51.1	Westfall Local SD	Williamsport
263	51.1	Alliance City SD	Alliance
264	51.0	Northmont City SD	Englewood
265	51.0	Vermilion Local SD	Vermilion
266	51.0	Springfield Local SD	Akron
267	51.0	Whitehall City SD	Whitehall
268	51.0	Niles City SD	Niles
269	51.0	Groveport Madison Local SD	Groveport
270	51.0	Chillicothe City SD	Chillicothe
271	51.0	Upper Arlington City SD	Upper Arlington
272	51.0	Upper Sandusky Ex Vill SD	Upper Sandusky
273	50.9	Medina City SD	Medina
274	50.9	Jonathan Alder Local SD	Plain City
275	50.9	Clyde-Green Springs Ex Vill SD	Clyde
276	50.9	Bethel-Tate Local SD	Bethel
277	50.9	Cuyahoga Falls City SD	Cuyahoga Falls
278	50.9	Clear Fork Valley Local SD	Bellville
279	50.9	Columbus Public Schools	Columbus
280	50.9	Elyria City SD	Elyria
281	50.9	Greenville City SD	Greenville
282	50.9	Reynoldsburg City SD	Reynoldsburg
283	50.9	Pike-Delta-York Local SD	Delta
284	50.9	Newark City SD	Newark
285	50.8	Springboro Community City SD	Springboro
286	50.8	Benjamin Logan Local SD	Bellefontaine
287	50.8	Elgin Local SD	Marion
288	50.8	Indian Lake Local SD	Lewistown
289	50.8	Lebanon City SD	Lebanon
290	50.8	Aurora City SD	Aurora
291	50.8	Athens City SD	The Plains
292	50.8	Howland Local SD	Warren
293	50.8	Wellston City Schools	Wellston
294	50.8	Van Wert City SD	Van Wert
295	50.8	Plain Local SD	Canton
296	50.8	Fairless Local SD	Navarre
297	50.7	Blanchester Local SD	Blanchester
298	50.7	Forest Hills Local SD	Cincinnati
299	50.7	Sandusky City SD	Sandusky
300	50.7	Otsego Local SD	Tontogany
301	50.7	Indian Valley Local SD	Gnadenhutten
302	50.7	Struthers City SD	Struthers
303	50.7	Canal Winchester Local SD	Canal Winchester
304	50.7	Mentor Ex Vill SD	Mentor
305	50.7	Brecksville-Broadview Hgts City	Brecksville
306	50.7	Bedford City SD	Bedford
307	50.7	Meigs Local SD	Pomeroy
308	50.7	West Holmes Local SD	Millersburg
309	50.7	North Canton City SD	North Canton
310	50.7	Buckeye Local SD	Medina
311	50.7	Goshen Local SD	Goshen
312	50.7	North Royalton City SD	N Royalton
313	50.7	Southwest Licking Local SD	Etna
314	50.7	Willard City SD	Willard
315	50.7	Minford Local SD	Minford
316	50.6	Bath Local SD	Lima
317	50.6	Hubbard Ex Vill SD	Hubbard
318	50.6	Olmsted Falls City SD	Olmsted Falls
319	50.6	Amherst Ex Vill SD	Amherst
320	50.6	Olentangy Local SD	Lewis Center
321	50.6	Parma City SD	Parma
322	50.6	Plain Local SD	New Albany
323	50.6	Heath City SD	Heath
324	50.5	Hamilton Local SD	Columbus
325	50.5	United Local SD	Hanoverton
326	50.5	Circleville City SD	Circleville
327	50.5	Loveland City SD	Loveland
328	50.5	Cleveland Hts-Univ Hts City SD	University Hgts
329	50.5	Brunswick City SD	Brunswick
330	50.5	Greenon Local SD	Springfield
331	50.4	Salem City SD	Salem
332	50.4	Wauseon Ex Vill SD	Wauseon
333	50.4	Fairfield City SD	Fairfield
334	50.4	Triway Local SD	Wooster
335	50.3	Mad River Local SD	Dayton
336	50.3	Jackson Local SD	Massillon
337	50.3	Warren City SD	Warren
338	50.3	Perry Local SD	Perry
339	50.3	James A Garfield Local SD	Garrettsville
340	50.3	Rocky River City SD	Rocky River
341	50.2	Keystone Local SD	Lagrange
342	50.1	Bay Village City SD	Bay Village
343	50.1	Maysville Local SD	Zanesville
344	50.1	East Clinton Local SD	Lees Creek
345	50.1	Carrollton Ex Vill SD	Carrollton
346	50.0	Norton City Schools	Norton
347	50.0	Adams County/Ohio Valley LSD	West Union
348	50.0	Lakeview Local SD	Cortland
349	49.9	Avon Local SD	Avon
350	49.9	Union-Scioto Local SD	Chillicothe
351	49.8	Little Miami Local SD	Morrow
352	49.8	Anthony Wayne Local SD	Whitehouse
353	49.7	Madison Local SD	Middletown
354	49.7	Northwestern Local SD	Springfield
355	49.7	Coventry Local SD	Akron
356	49.6	Northridge Local SD	Dayton
357	49.5	Perkins Local SD	Sandusky
358	49.5	Ottawa-Glandorf Local SD	Ottawa
359	49.4	Marlington Local SD	Alliance
360	49.3	Louisville City SD	Louisville
361	49.3	South Point Local SD	South Point
362	49.3	Manchester Local SD	Akron
363	49.3	Rolling Hills Local SD	Cambridge
364	49.3	Zanesville City SD	Zanesville
365	49.2	Oakwood City SD	Dayton
366	49.1	Cincinnati City SD	Cincinnati
367	49.1	Clearview Local SD	Lorain
368	49.1	Buckeye Local SD	Ashtabula
369	49.1	Warrensville Heights City SD	Warrensville Hgts
370	48.9	East Cleveland City SD	East Cleveland
371	48.6	Zane Trace Local SD	Chillicothe
372	48.1	Galion City SD	Galion
373	48.0	Sheffield-Sheffield Lake City SD	Sheffield Vlg
374	45.7	Electronic Classrm of Tomorrow	Columbus

Female Students

Rank	Percent	District Name	City
1	54.2	Electronic Classrm of Tomorrow	Columbus
2	51.9	Sheffield-Sheffield Lake City SD	Sheffield Vlg
3	51.8	Galion City SD	Galion
4	51.3	Zane Trace Local SD	Chillicothe
5	51.0	East Cleveland City SD	East Cleveland
6	50.8	Warrensville Heights City SD	Warrensville Hgts
7	50.8	Buckeye Local SD	Ashtabula
8	50.8	Clearview Local SD	Lorain
9	50.8	Cincinnati City SD	Cincinnati
10	50.7	Oakwood City SD	Dayton
11	50.6	Zanesville City SD	Zanesville
12	50.6	Rolling Hills Local SD	Cambridge
13	50.6	Manchester Local SD	Akron
14	50.6	South Point Local SD	South Point
15	50.6	Louisville City SD	Louisville
16	50.5	Marlington Local SD	Alliance
17	50.4	Ottawa-Glandorf Local SD	Ottawa
18	50.4	Perkins Local SD	Sandusky
19	50.3	Northridge Local SD	Dayton
20	50.2	Coventry Local SD	Akron
21	50.2	Northwestern Local SD	Springfield
22	50.2	Madison Local SD	Middletown
23	50.1	Anthony Wayne Local SD	Whitehouse
24	50.1	Little Miami Local SD	Morrow
25	50.0	Union-Scioto Local SD	Chillicothe
26	50.0	Avon Local SD	Avon
27	50.0	Lakeview Local SD	Cortland
28	49.9	Adams County/Ohio Valley LSD	West Union
29	49.9	Norton City Schools	Norton
30	49.8	Carrollton Ex Vill SD	Carrollton
31	49.8	East Clinton Local SD	Lees Creek
32	49.8	Maysville Local SD	Zanesville
33	49.8	Bay Village City SD	Bay Village
34	49.7	Keystone Local SD	Lagrange
35	49.6	Rocky River City SD	Rocky River
36	49.6	James A Garfield Local SD	Garrettsville
37	49.6	Perry Local SD	Perry
38	49.6	Warren City SD	Warren
39	49.6	Jackson Local SD	Massillon
40	49.6	Mad River Local SD	Dayton
41	49.5	Triway Local SD	Wooster
42	49.5	Fairfield City SD	Fairfield
43	49.5	Wauseon Ex Vill SD	Wauseon
44	49.5	Salem City SD	Salem
45	49.4	Greenon Local SD	Springfield
46	49.4	Brunswick City SD	Brunswick
47	49.4	Cleveland Hts-Univ Hts City SD	University Hgts
48	49.4	Loveland City SD	Loveland
49	49.4	Circleville City SD	Circleville
50	49.4	United Local SD	Hanoverton
51	49.4	Hamilton Local SD	Columbus
52	49.3	Heath City SD	Heath
53	49.3	Plain Local SD	New Albany
54	49.3	Parma City SD	Parma
55	49.3	Olentangy Local SD	Lewis Center
56	49.3	Amherst Ex Vill SD	Amherst
57	49.3	Olmsted Falls City SD	Olmsted Falls
58	49.3	Hubbard Ex Vill SD	Hubbard
59	49.3	Bath Local SD	Lima
60	49.2	Minford Local SD	Minford
61	49.2	Willard City SD	Willard
62	49.2	Southwest Licking Local SD	Etna
63	49.2	North Royalton City SD	N Royalton
64	49.2	Goshen Local SD	Goshen
65	49.2	Buckeye Local SD	Medina
66	49.2	North Canton City SD	North Canton
67	49.2	West Holmes Local SD	Millersburg
68	49.2	Meigs Local SD	Pomeroy
69	49.2	Bedford City SD	Bedford
70	49.2	Brecksville-Broadview Hgts City	Brecksville
71	49.2	Mentor Ex Vill SD	Mentor
72	49.2	Canal Winchester Local SD	Canal Winchester
73	49.2	Struthers City SD	Struthers
74	49.2	Indian Valley Local SD	Gnadenhutten
75	49.2	Otsego Local SD	Tontogany
76	49.2	Sandusky City SD	Sandusky
77	49.2	Forest Hills Local SD	Cincinnati
78	49.2	Blanchester Local SD	Blanchester
79	49.1	Fairless Local SD	Navarre
80	49.1	Plain Local SD	Canton
81	49.1	Van Wert City SD	Van Wert
82	49.1	Wellston City Schools	Wellston
83	49.1	Howland Local SD	Warren
84	49.1	Athens City SD	The Plains
85	49.1	Aurora City SD	Aurora
86	49.1	Lebanon City SD	Lebanon
87	49.1	Indian Lake Local SD	Lewistown
88	49.1	Elgin Local SD	Marion
89	49.1	Benjamin Logan Local SD	Bellefontaine
90	49.1	Springboro Community City SD	Springboro
91	49.0	Newark City SD	Newark
92	49.0	Pike-Delta-York Local SD	Delta
93	49.0	Reynoldsburg City SD	Reynoldsburg
94	49.0	Greenville City SD	Greenville
95	49.0	Elyria City SD	Elyria
96	49.0	Columbus Public Schools	Columbus
97	49.0	Clear Fork Valley Local SD	Bellville
98	49.0	Cuyahoga Falls City SD	Cuyahoga Falls
99	49.0	Bethel-Tate Local SD	Bethel
100	49.0	Clyde-Green Springs Ex Vill SD	Clyde
101	49.0	Jonathan Alder Local SD	Plain City
102	49.0	Medina City SD	Medina
103	48.9	Upper Sandusky Ex Vill SD	Upper Sandusky
104	48.9	Upper Arlington City SD	Upper Arlington
105	48.9	Chillicothe City SD	Chillicothe
106	48.9	Groveport Madison Local SD	Groveport
107	48.9	Niles City SD	Niles
108	48.9	Whitehall City SD	Whitehall
109	48.9	Springfield Local SD	Akron
110	48.9	Vermilion Local SD	Vermilion
111	48.9	Northmont City SD	Englewood
112	48.8	Alliance City SD	Alliance
113	48.8	Westfall Local SD	Williamsport
114	48.8	Bellefontaine City Schools	Bellefontaine
115	48.8	Beavercreek City SD	Beavercreek
116	48.8	Sylvania City SD	Sylvania
117	48.8	Graham Local SD	Saint Paris
118	48.8	Licking Valley Local SD Sd	Newark
119	48.8	Chardon Local SD	Chardon
120	48.8	Talawanda City SD	Oxford
121	48.8	Morgan Local SD	McConnelsville
122	48.8	Canton City SD	Canton
123	48.8	London City SD	London
124	48.8	Clark-Shawnee Local SD	Springfield
125	48.8	Wapakoneta City City SD	Wapakoneta
126	48.7	Solon City SD	Solon
127	48.7	Copley-Fairlawn City SD	Copley
128	48.7	Tri-Valley Local Schools	Dresden
129	48.7	Franklin City SD	Franklin
130	48.7	Napoleon Area City SD	Napoleon
131	48.7	Wellington Ex Vill SD	Wellington
132	48.7	Benton Carroll Salem Local SD	Oak Harbor
133	48.7	Paulding Ex Vill SD	Paulding
134	48.7	Tecumseh Local SD	New Carlisle
135	48.7	Madison-Plains Local SD	London
136	48.7	Newton Falls Ex Vill SD	Newton Falls
137	48.7	Big Walnut Local SD	Galena
138	48.7	Lake Local SD	Millbury
139	48.7	Westlake City SD	Westlake
140	48.7	Youngstown City SD	Youngstown
141	48.7	Ridgewood Local SD	West Lafayette
142	48.7	Eastwood Local SD	Pemberville
143	48.7	Gallipolis City SD	Gallipolis
144	48.7	Alexander Local SD	Albany
145	48.7	Canfield Local SD	Canfield
146	48.6	Gallia County Local SD	Gallipolis
147	48.6	Western Brown Local SD	Mount Orab
148	48.6	Northern Local SD	Thornville
149	48.6	Akron Public Schools	Akron
150	48.6	West Muskingum Local SD	Zanesville
151	48.6	Highland Local SD	Medina

152	48.6	Dayton City SD	Dayton
153	48.6	South-Western City SD	Grove City
154	48.5	Westerville City SD	Westerville
155	48.5	Cleveland Municipal City SD	Cleveland
156	48.5	Granville Ex Vill SD	Granville
157	48.5	Kenston Local SD	Chagrin Falls
158	48.5	Sycamore Community City SD	Cincinnati
159	48.5	Edison Local SD	Hammondsville
160	48.5	Findlay City SD	Findlay
161	48.5	Painesville Township Local SD	Painesville
162	48.5	Tipp City Ex Vill SD	Tipp City
163	48.5	Hamilton City SD	Hamilton
164	48.5	Mason City SD	Mason
165	48.5	Streetsboro City Schools	Streetsboro
166	48.5	Washington-Nile Local SD	West Portsmouth
167	48.5	Austintown Local SD	Youngstown
168	48.5	Bowling Green City SD	Bowling Green
169	48.5	New Philadelphia City SD	New Philadelphia
170	48.4	Marietta City Schools	Marietta
171	48.4	Northwest Local SD	Canal Fulton
172	48.4	Sugarcreek Local SD	Bellbrook
173	48.4	Norwalk City SD	Norwalk
174	48.4	Ravenna City SD	Ravenna
175	48.4	Middletown City SD	Middletown
176	48.4	Dublin City SD	Dublin
177	48.4	Shawnee Local SD	Lima
178	48.4	Girard City SD	Girard
179	48.4	Greeneview Local SD	Jamestown
180	48.4	East Liverpool City SD	East Liverpool
181	48.4	Nordonia Hills City SD	Northfield
182	48.4	Cloverleaf Local SD	Lodi
183	48.4	Licking Heights Local SD	Summit Station
184	48.4	Fremont City SD	Fremont
185	48.3	Eastern Local SD	Sardinia
186	48.3	Hillsboro City SD	Hillsboro
187	48.3	Revere Local SD	Bath
188	48.3	Buckeye Local SD	Rayland
189	48.3	Midview Local SD	Grafton
190	48.3	Hilliard City SD	Hilliard
191	48.3	Sidney City SD	Sidney
192	48.3	Milford Ex Vill SD	Milford
193	48.3	Monroe Local SD	Monroe
194	48.3	Lorain City SD	Lorain
195	48.3	Xenia Community City SD	Xenia
196	48.3	Poland Local SD	Poland
196	48.3	Steubenville City SD	Steubenville
198	48.3	Delaware City SD	Delaware
199	48.2	Defiance City SD	Defiance
200	48.2	Elida Local SD	Elida
201	48.2	Troy City SD	Troy
202	48.2	West Clermont Local SD	Cincinnati
203	48.2	Coshocton City SD	Coshocton
204	48.2	Eaton Community Schools	Eaton
205	48.2	Princeton City SD	Cincinnati
206	48.2	New Richmond Ex Vill SD	New Richmond
207	48.2	Fairland Local SD	Proctorville
208	48.2	Scioto Valley Local SD	Piketon
209	48.2	Huron City Schools	Huron
210	48.2	Franklin Local SD	Duncan Falls
211	48.2	Dover City SD	Dover
212	48.2	Bellevue City SD	Bellevue
213	48.2	Swanton Local SD	Swanton
214	48.2	Centerville City SD	Centerville
215	48.2	Barberton City SD	Barberton
216	48.1	Mansfield City SD	Mansfield
217	48.1	Trotwood-Madison City Schools	Trotwood
218	48.1	Toledo City SD	Toledo
219	48.1	Indian Creek Local SD	Wintersville
220	48.1	Stow-Munroe Falls City SD	Stow
221	48.1	Fostoria City SD	Fostoria
222	48.1	Woodridge Local SD	Peninsula
223	48.1	Shaker Heights City SD	Shaker Heights
224	48.1	Mount Vernon City SD	Mount Vernon
225	48.1	Boardman Local SD	Youngstown
226	48.1	Northeastern Local SD	Springfield
227	48.1	Willoughby-Eastlake City SD	Willoughby
228	48.1	Clinton-Massie Local SD	Clarksville
229	48.1	Twinsburg City SD	Twinsburg
230	48.0	Firelands Local SD	Oberlin
231	48.0	Fairfield Union Local SD	W Rushville
232	48.0	Lakota Local SD	Liberty Twp
233	48.0	Martins Ferry City SD	Martins Ferry
234	48.0	Bucyrus City SD	Bucyrus
235	48.0	North Fork Local SD	Utica
236	48.0	Waverly City SD	Waverly
237	48.0	Shelby City SD	Shelby
238	48.0	Batavia Local SD	Batavia
239	48.0	Marion City SD	Marion
240	47.9	West Branch Local SD	Beloit
241	47.9	Wilmington City SD	Wilmington
242	47.9	Mariemont City SD	Cincinnati
243	47.9	South Euclid-Lyndhurst City SD	Lyndhurst
244	47.9	Southeast Local SD	Ravenna
245	47.9	Ashtabula Area City SD	Ashtabula
246	47.9	Ohio Virtual Academy	Maumee
247	47.9	Beaver Local SD	Lisbon
248	47.9	Miamisburg City SD	Miamisburg
249	47.9	Wyoming City SD	Wyoming
250	47.9	Madison Local SD	Madison
251	47.8	West Geauga Local SD	Chesterland
252	47.8	Huber Heights City SD	Huber Heights
253	47.8	Rock Hill Local SD	Ironton
254	47.8	Three Rivers Local Schools	Cleves
255	47.8	Fairview Park City SD	Fairview Park
256	47.8	Kent City SD	Kent
257	47.8	River View Local SD	Warsaw
258	47.8	St Clairsville-Richland City SD	St Clairsville
259	47.8	Switzerland of Ohio Local SD	Woodsfield
260	47.8	Marysville Exempted Village SD	Marysville
261	47.8	Bellaire Local SD	Bellaire
262	47.8	Logan-Hocking Local SD	Logan
263	47.8	Rossford Ex Vill SD	Rossford
264	47.8	Maple Heights City SD	Maple Heights
265	47.8	Norwood City SD	Norwood
266	47.8	Worthington City SD	Worthington
267	47.8	Ontario Local SD	Mansfield
268	47.7	North Ridgeville City SD	N Ridgeville
269	47.7	Sandy Valley Local SD	Magnolia
270	47.7	Clermont Northeastern Local SD	Batavia
271	47.7	Kings Local SD	Kings Mills
272	47.7	Teays Valley Local SD	Ashville
273	47.7	Lexington Local SD	Lexington
274	47.7	Urbana City SD	Urbana
275	47.7	Champion Local SD	Warren
276	47.7	Valley View Local SD	Germantown
277	47.7	North Olmsted City Schools	North Olmsted
278	47.7	Port Clinton City SD	Port Clinton
279	47.7	East Holmes Local Schools	Berlin
280	47.7	Campbell City SD	Campbell
281	47.7	Tiffin City SD	Tiffin
282	47.7	Southwest Local SD	Harrison
283	47.7	Geneva Area City Schools	Geneva
284	47.7	Washington Local Schools	Toledo
285	47.6	Chagrin Falls Ex Vill SD	Chagrin Falls
286	47.6	Springfield City SD	Springfield
287	47.6	Gahanna-Jefferson City SD	Gahanna
288	47.6	Miami Trace Local SD	Wash Ct House
289	47.6	Pickerington Local SD	Pickerington
290	47.6	Washington Court House City SD	Wash Ct House
291	47.6	Lakewood City SD	Lakewood
292	47.6	Lake Local SD	Hartville
293	47.5	Kettering City SD	Kettering
294	47.5	Strongsville City SD	Strongsville
295	47.5	Cambridge City SD	Cambridge
296	47.5	Conneaut Area City SD	Conneaut
297	47.5	Bryan City SD	Bryan
298	47.5	Perrysburg Exempted Village	Perrysburg
299	47.5	Logan Elm Local SD	Circleville
300	47.5	Crestwood Local SD	Mantua
301	47.5	Warren Local SD	Vincent
302	47.5	Madeira City SD	Cincinnati
303	47.5	Lima City SD	Lima
304	47.5	Carlisle Local SD	Carlisle
305	47.4	Jefferson Area Local SD	Jefferson
306	47.4	Winton Woods City SD	Cincinnati
307	47.4	Perry Local SD	Massillon
308	47.4	Lancaster City SD	Lancaster
309	47.4	Northwest Local SD	Cincinnati
310	47.4	Kenton City SD	Kenton
311	47.4	Green Local SD	Green
312	47.4	Oak Hills Local SD	Cincinnati
313	47.4	Vinton County Local SD	Mc Arthur
314	47.3	Oregon City SD	Oregon
315	47.3	Amanda-Clearcreek Local SD	Amanda
316	47.3	Celina City SD	Celina
317	47.3	Springfield Local Schools	Holland
318	47.3	Jackson City SD	Jackson
319	47.3	Ironton City SD	Ironton
320	47.3	Edgewood City SD	Trenton
321	47.3	Milton-Union Exempted Vill Schls	West Milton
322	47.3	Avon Lake City Schools	Avon Lake
323	47.2	Bexley City SD	Bexley
324	47.2	Wadsworth City SD	Wadsworth
325	47.2	Fairborn City Schools	Fairborn
326	47.2	New Lexington City SD	New Lexington
327	47.2	Liberty Local SD	Youngstown
328	47.2	Lakewood Local SD	Hebron
329	47.1	Garfield Heights City SD	Garfield Hgts
330	47.1	Highland Local SD	Sparta
331	47.1	Berea City SD	Berea
332	47.1	Painesville City Local SD	Painesville
333	47.1	Mt Healthy City SD	Cincinnati
334	47.0	Massillon City SD	Massillon
335	47.0	Field Local SD	Mogadore
336	47.0	Euclid City SD	Euclid
337	46.9	Indian Hill Ex Vill SD	Cincinnati
338	46.9	Vandalia-Butler City SD	Vandalia
339	46.9	Greenfield Ex Vill SD	Greenfield
340	46.9	River Valley Local SD	Caledonia
341	46.9	Wooster City SD	Wooster
342	46.8	Northwest Local SD	Mc Dermott
343	46.8	Black River Local SD	Sullivan
344	46.7	Ashland City SD	Ashland
345	46.7	Piqua City SD	Piqua
346	46.7	Preble Shawnee Local SD	Camden
347	46.7	Hudson City SD	Hudson
348	46.7	Madison Local SD	Mansfield
349	46.7	Finneytown Local SD	Cincinnati
350	46.6	North College Hill City SD	Cincinnati
351	46.5	Coldwater Ex Vill SD	Coldwater
352	46.5	Claymont City SD	Dennison
353	46.5	East Muskingum Local SD	New Concord
354	46.5	Buckeye Valley Local SD	Delaware
355	46.5	Portsmouth City SD	Portsmouth
356	46.4	West Carrollton City SD	West Carrollton
357	46.4	Brookville Local SD	Brookville
358	46.3	Ross Local SD	Hamilton
359	46.2	Maumee City SD	Maumee
360	46.2	Minerva Local SD	Minerva
361	46.1	Berlin-Milan Local SD	Milan
362	46.1	Mayfield City SD	Highland Hgts
363	46.1	Tuscarawas Valley Local SD	Zoarville
364	46.0	Wickliffe City SD	Wickliffe
365	46.0	Canton Local SD	Canton
366	46.0	Beachwood City SD	Beachwood
367	45.8	Union Local SD	Morristown
368	45.7	Genoa Area Local SD	Genoa
369	45.6	Tallmadge City Schools	Tallmadge
370	45.6	Orrville City SD	Orrville
371	45.6	St Marys City SD	Saint Marys
372	45.5	Southeast Local SD	Apple Creek
373	45.3	Orange City SD	Cleveland
374	45.3	Harrison Hills City SD	Hopedale

Individual Education Program Students

Rank	Percent	District Name	City
1	29.6	Harrison Hills City SD	Hopedale
2	23.5	Dayton City SD	Dayton
3	22.8	Zanesville City SD	Zanesville
4	22.1	Coshocton City SD	Coshocton
5	22.0	Bellaire Local SD	Bellaire
6	21.8	Claymont City SD	Dennison
7	21.7	Gallipolis City SD	Gallipolis
8	21.5	South Point Local SD	South Point
9	20.8	Mount Vernon City SD	Mount Vernon
10	20.4	Lima City SD	Lima
10	20.4	Napoleon Area City SD	Napoleon
12	20.3	Youngstown City SD	Youngstown
13	20.0	Sandusky City SD	Sandusky
14	19.8	Mansfield City SD	Mansfield
15	19.6	Bellefontaine City Schools	Bellefontaine
15	19.6	Meigs Local SD	Pomeroy
17	19.5	Alexander Local SD	Albany
17	19.5	Bucyrus City SD	Bucyrus
19	19.4	East Liverpool City SD	East Liverpool
20	19.2	Marion City SD	Marion
21	19.0	Hamilton City SD	Hamilton
22	18.9	Cincinnati City SD	Cincinnati
22	18.9	Springfield Local Schools	Holland
22	18.9	Urbana City SD	Urbana
22	18.9	Warren City SD	Warren
26	18.8	Sidney City SD	Sidney
27	18.7	Ashtabula Area City SD	Ashtabula
28	18.6	Fostoria City SD	Fostoria
28	18.6	Gallia County Local SD	Gallipolis
30	18.5	Celina City SD	Celina
31	18.3	St Marys City SD	Saint Marys
32	18.2	Buckeye Local SD	Rayland
32	18.2	Cleveland Municipal City SD	Cleveland
32	18.2	Paulding Ex Vill SD	Paulding
35	18.0	Indian Lake Local SD	Lewistown
36	17.8	Findlay City SD	Findlay
36	17.8	Ironton City SD	Ironton
36	17.8	Middletown City SD	Middletown
39	17.7	Euclid City SD	Euclid
40	17.6	Port Clinton City SD	Port Clinton
40	17.6	Springfield Local SD	Akron
42	17.5	Marietta City Schools	Marietta
43	17.4	Defiance City SD	Defiance
43	17.4	Tiffin City SD	Tiffin
45	17.3	Alliance City SD	Alliance
45	17.3	Bellevue City SD	Bellevue
45	17.3	Mt Healthy City SD	Cincinnati
45	17.3	Vinton County Local SD	Mc Arthur
49	17.2	Austintown Local SD	Youngstown
49	17.2	Toledo City SD	Toledo
49	17.2	Winton Woods City SD	Cincinnati

52	17.1	Delaware City SD	Delaware
53	17.0	Logan-Hocking Local SD	Logan
53	17.0	Wellston City Schools	Wellston
55	16.9	Canton City SD	Canton
56	16.8	Edgewood City SD	Trenton
56	16.8	Galion City SD	Galion
56	16.8	New Philadelphia City SD	New Philadelphia
56	16.8	Piqua City SD	Piqua
60	16.7	Goshen Local SD	Goshen
60	16.7	Switzerland of Ohio Local SD	Woodsfield
62	16.6	North College Hill City SD	Cincinnati
62	16.6	Ravenna City SD	Ravenna
62	16.6	Upper Sandusky Ex Vill SD	Upper Sandusky
65	16.5	Akron Public Schools	Akron
65	16.5	Cambridge City SD	Cambridge
65	16.5	Perkins Local SD	Sandusky
68	16.2	Kenton City SD	Kenton
68	16.2	River View Local SD	Warsaw
68	16.2	Union Local SD	Morristown
71	15.9	Groveport Madison Local SD	Groveport
71	15.9	Mayfield City SD	Highland Hgts
71	15.9	Norwalk City SD	Norwalk
74	15.8	Whitehall City SD	Whitehall
75	15.7	Wapakoneta City City SD	Wapakoneta
76	15.6	Fairless Local SD	Navarre
76	15.6	London City SD	London
76	15.6	Parma City SD	Parma
76	15.6	Springfield City SD	Springfield
76	15.6	Van Wert City SD	Van Wert
81	15.5	Marysville Exempted Village SD	Marysville
81	15.5	West Muskingum Local SD	Zanesville
83	15.4	Graham Local SD	Saint Paris
83	15.4	Indian Creek Local SD	Wintersville
83	15.4	North Ridgeville City SD	N Ridgeville
83	15.4	Rock Hill Local SD	Ironton
87	15.3	Ashland City SD	Ashland
87	15.3	Circleville City SD	Circleville
87	15.3	Indian Valley Local SD	Gnadenhutten
87	15.3	Jackson City SD	Jackson
87	15.3	Marlington Local SD	Alliance
87	15.3	South Euclid-Lyndhurst City SD	Lyndhurst
87	15.3	Warrensville Heights City SD	Warrensville Hgts
94	15.2	Barberton City SD	Barberton
94	15.2	Benton Carroll Salem Local SD	Oak Harbor
94	15.2	Cleveland Hts-Univ Hts City SD	University Hgts
94	15.2	Fairview Park City SD	Fairview Park
94	15.2	Westlake City SD	Westlake
94	15.2	Wickliffe City SD	Wickliffe
100	15.1	Adams County/Ohio Valley LSD	West Union
100	15.1	Campbell City SD	Campbell
100	15.1	Dover City SD	Dover
100	15.1	Greenville City SD	Greenville
100	15.1	Mad River Local SD	Dayton
100	15.1	West Holmes Local SD	Millersburg
106	15.0	Franklin City SD	Franklin
106	15.0	Shaker Heights City SD	Shaker Heights
106	15.0	Shelby City SD	Shelby
109	14.9	Clyde-Green Springs Ex Vill SD	Clyde
109	14.9	Elyria City SD	Elyria
109	14.9	Fremont City SD	Fremont
109	14.9	Massillon City SD	Massillon
109	14.9	Maumee City SD	Maumee
109	14.9	Medina City SD	Medina
109	14.9	New Richmond Ex Vill SD	New Richmond
109	14.9	Rossford Ex Vill SD	Rossford
109	14.9	Vermilion Local SD	Vermilion
109	14.9	Waverly City SD	Waverly
119	14.8	Benjamin Logan Local SD	Bellefontaine
119	14.8	Brookville Local SD	Brookville
119	14.8	Field Local SD	Mogadore
119	14.8	Gahanna-Jefferson City SD	Gahanna
119	14.8	Kettering City SD	Kettering
119	14.8	Martins Ferry City SD	Martins Ferry
119	14.8	Pike-Delta-York Local SD	Delta
126	14.7	Girard City SD	Girard
126	14.7	Highland Local SD	Sparta
126	14.7	Perry Local SD	Massillon
126	14.7	Scioto Valley Local SD	Piketon
130	14.6	Blanchester Local SD	Blanchester
130	14.6	Columbus Public Schools	Columbus
130	14.6	Conneaut Area City SD	Conneaut
130	14.6	Painesville City Local SD	Painesville
130	14.6	Xenia Community City SD	Xenia
135	14.5	Athens City SD	The Plains
135	14.5	Berea City SD	Berea
135	14.5	Canton Local SD	Canton
138	14.4	Garfield Heights City SD	Garfield Hgts
138	14.4	Geneva Area City Schools	Geneva
138	14.4	Lorain City SD	Lorain
138	14.4	Otsego Local SD	Tontogany
138	14.4	Willoughby-Eastlake City SD	Willoughby
143	14.3	Madison Local SD	Mansfield
143	14.3	Three Rivers Local Schools	Cleves
145	14.2	Berlin-Milan Local SD	Milan
146	14.1	Buckeye Valley Local SD	Delaware
146	14.1	Lakewood City SD	Lakewood
146	14.1	Northwest Local SD	Mc Dermott
146	14.1	Southeast Local SD	Apple Creek
146	14.1	Southwest Local SD	Harrison
146	14.1	Woodridge Local SD	Peninsula
146	14.1	Wooster City SD	Wooster
153	14.0	Rolling Hills Local SD	Cambridge
153	14.0	West Geauga Local SD	Chesterland
153	14.0	Willard City SD	Willard
156	13.9	Franklin Local SD	Duncan Falls
156	13.9	Northwest Local SD	Canal Fulton
156	13.9	Washington Court House City SD	Wash Ct House
159	13.8	Bay Village City SD	Bay Village
159	13.8	Clearview Local SD	Lorain
159	13.8	Cuyahoga Falls City SD	Cuyahoga Falls
159	13.8	Southwest Licking Local SD	Etna
159	13.8	Streetsboro City Schools	Streetsboro
159	13.8	Swanton Local SD	Swanton
165	13.7	Avon Local SD	Avon
165	13.7	Carrollton Ex Vill SD	Carrollton
165	13.7	Clermont Northeastern Local SD	Batavia
165	13.7	East Clinton Local SD	Lees Creek
165	13.7	Logan Elm Local SD	Circleville
165	13.7	Northern Local SD	Thornville
165	13.7	Ross Local SD	Hamilton
165	13.7	South-Western City SD	Grove City
165	13.7	United Local SD	Hanoverton
165	13.7	Washington Local Schools	Toledo
175	13.6	Big Walnut Local SD	Galena
175	13.6	Kings Local SD	Kings Mills
175	13.6	Minerva Local SD	Minerva
175	13.6	New Lexington City SD	New Lexington
175	13.6	Southeast Local SD	Ravenna
180	13.5	Bedford City SD	Bedford
180	13.5	Maple Heights City SD	Maple Heights
180	13.5	Sandy Valley Local SD	Magnolia
180	13.5	Triway Local SD	Wooster
180	13.5	Warren Local SD	Vincent
185	13.4	North Fork Local SD	Utica
185	13.4	Reynoldsburg City SD	Reynoldsburg
185	13.4	Rocky River City SD	Rocky River
185	13.4	Teays Valley Local SD	Ashville
189	13.3	Crestwood Local SD	Mantua
189	13.3	Newark City SD	Newark
189	13.3	Plain Local SD	Canton
192	13.2	Beaver Local SD	Lisbon
192	13.2	Bowling Green City SD	Bowling Green
192	13.2	Chillicothe City SD	Chillicothe
192	13.2	Howland Local SD	Warren
192	13.2	Miami Trace Local SD	Wash Ct House
192	13.2	Morgan Local SD	McConnelsville
198	13.1	Clear Fork Valley Local SD	Bellville
198	13.1	East Muskingum Local SD	New Concord
198	13.1	Lakewood Local SD	Hebron
198	13.1	Northridge Local SD	Dayton
198	13.1	Ridgewood Local SD	West Lafayette
198	13.1	Sylvania City SD	Sylvania
204	13.0	Fairland Local SD	Proctorville
204	13.0	Hillsboro City SD	Hillsboro
206	12.9	Amanda-Clearcreek Local SD	Amanda
206	12.9	Coldwater Ex Vill SD	Coldwater
206	12.9	Huron City Schools	Huron
206	12.9	Niles City SD	Niles
206	12.9	Oak Hills Local SD	Cincinnati
206	12.9	Princeton City SD	Cincinnati
206	12.9	Vandalia-Butler City SD	Vandalia
213	12.8	Madison Local SD	Middletown
213	12.8	Maysville Local SD	Zanesville
213	12.8	Steubenville City SD	Steubenville
213	12.8	Tuscarawas Valley Local SD	Zoarville
217	12.7	Beavercreek City SD	Beavercreek
217	12.7	East Holmes Local Schools	Berlin
217	12.7	Lancaster City SD	Lancaster
217	12.7	Licking Valley Local SD Sd	Newark
217	12.7	Newton Falls Ex Vill SD	Newton Falls
217	12.7	Orrville City SD	Orrville
217	12.7	Strongsville City SD	Strongsville
217	12.7	Trotwood-Madison City Schools	Trotwood
225	12.6	Fairborn City Schools	Fairborn
225	12.6	North Olmsted City Schools	North Olmsted
225	12.6	Sheffield-Sheffield Lake City SD	Sheffield Vlg
228	12.5	Edison Local SD	Hammondsville
228	12.5	Ottawa-Glandorf Local SD	Ottawa
230	12.4	Centerville City SD	Centerville
230	12.4	Miamisburg City SD	Miamisburg
230	12.4	Norwood City SD	Norwood
230	12.4	Salem City SD	Salem
234	12.3	Lexington Local SD	Lexington
234	12.3	Northwest Local SD	Cincinnati
234	12.3	St Clairsville-Richland City SD	St Clairsville
237	12.2	Amherst Ex Vill SD	Amherst
237	12.2	Canal Winchester Local SD	Canal Winchester
237	12.2	Struthers City SD	Struthers
240	12.1	Kent City SD	Kent
240	12.1	Orange City SD	Cleveland
240	12.1	Zane Trace Local SD	Chillicothe
243	12.0	Cloverleaf Local SD	Lodi
243	12.0	Green Local SD	Green
243	12.0	Greenfield Ex Vill SD	Greenfield
243	12.0	Huber Heights City SD	Huber Heights
243	12.0	Mentor Ex Vill SD	Mentor
243	12.0	Preble Shawnee Local SD	Camden
249	11.9	Elgin Local SD	Marion
249	11.9	West Carrollton City SD	West Carrollton
251	11.8	Finneytown Local SD	Cincinnati
251	11.8	Greeneview Local SD	Jamestown
251	11.8	Hamilton Local SD	Columbus
251	11.8	James A Garfield Local SD	Garrettsville
251	11.8	Jefferson Area Local SD	Jefferson
251	11.8	Solon City SD	Solon
257	11.7	Bryan City SD	Bryan
257	11.7	Madeira City SD	Cincinnati
257	11.7	Troy City SD	Troy
257	11.7	West Clermont Local SD	Cincinnati
261	11.6	Buckeye Local SD	Medina
261	11.6	Chardon Local SD	Chardon
261	11.6	Lakeview Local SD	Cortland
261	11.6	Madison-Plains Local SD	London
261	11.6	Portsmouth City SD	Portsmouth
261	11.6	River Valley Local SD	Caledonia
261	11.6	Westfall Local SD	Williamsport
268	11.5	Chagrin Falls Ex Vill SD	Chagrin Falls
268	11.5	Hilliard City SD	Hilliard
268	11.5	Madison Local SD	Madison
268	11.5	Nordonia Hills City SD	Northfield
268	11.5	Tecumseh Local SD	New Carlisle
273	11.4	Carlisle Local SD	Carlisle
273	11.4	Firelands Local SD	Oberlin
273	11.4	Northwestern Local SD	Springfield
273	11.4	Poland Local SD	Poland
273	11.4	Westerville City SD	Westerville
278	11.3	Monroe Local SD	Monroe
278	11.3	Northmont City SD	Englewood
280	11.2	Fairfield City SD	Fairfield
280	11.2	Licking Heights Local SD	Summit Station
280	11.2	Midview Local SD	Grafton
280	11.2	Minford Local SD	Minford
280	11.2	Tallmadge City Schools	Tallmadge
285	11.1	Bexley City SD	Bexley
285	11.1	East Cleveland City SD	East Cleveland
285	11.1	Hudson City SD	Hudson
285	11.1	Milton-Union Exempted Vill Schls	West Milton
285	11.1	Oregon City SD	Oregon
290	11.0	Eaton Community Schools	Eaton
290	11.0	Tri-Valley Local Schools	Dresden
290	11.0	Valley View Local SD	Germantown
293	10.9	Brunswick City SD	Brunswick
293	10.9	Jonathan Alder Local SD	Plain City
293	10.9	Lake Local SD	Millbury
293	10.9	Lake Local SD	Hartville
293	10.9	Wauseon Ex Vill SD	Wauseon
293	10.9	Wilmington City SD	Wilmington
299	10.8	Clinton-Massie Local SD	Clarksville
299	10.8	Hubbard Ex Vill SD	Hubbard
299	10.8	Louisville City SD	Louisville
299	10.8	Milford Ex Vill SD	Milford
299	10.8	North Canton City SD	North Canton
299	10.8	North Royalton City SD	N Royalton
299	10.8	Springboro Community City SD	Springboro
299	10.8	Talawanda City SD	Oxford
299	10.8	West Branch Local SD	Beloit
308	10.7	Buckeye Local SD	Ashtabula
308	10.7	Stow-Munroe Falls City SD	Stow
310	10.6	Bath Local SD	Lima
310	10.6	Black River Local SD	Sullivan
310	10.6	Granville Ex Vill SD	Granville
310	10.6	Little Miami Local SD	Morrow
310	10.6	Painesville Township Local SD	Painesville
315	10.5	Batavia Local SD	Batavia
315	10.5	Brecksville-Broadview Hgts City	Brecksville
315	10.5	Eastern Local SD	Sardinia
315	10.5	Forest Hills Local SD	Cincinnati
315	10.5	Genoa Area Local SD	Genoa
315	10.5	Greenon Local SD	Springfield
315	10.5	Twinsburg City SD	Twinsburg
322	10.4	Elida Local SD	Elida
322	10.4	Heath City SD	Heath
322	10.4	Olmsted Falls City SD	Olmsted Falls
325	10.3	Beachwood City SD	Beachwood
325	10.3	Coventry Local SD	Akron
325	10.3	Union-Scioto Local SD	Chillicothe
325	10.3	Worthington City SD	Worthington
329	10.2	Canfield Local SD	Canfield

329	10.2	Copley-Fairlawn City SD	Copley
329	10.2	Olentangy Local SD	Lewis Center
332	10.1	Sugarcreek Local SD	Bellbrook
333	10.0	Kenston Local SD	Chagrin Falls
333	10.0	Washington-Nile Local SD	West Portsmouth
333	10.0	Wellington Ex Vill SD	Wellington
336	9.9	Dublin City SD	Dublin
336	9.9	Keystone Local SD	Lagrange
338	9.8	Highland Local SD	Medina
338	9.8	Wadsworth City SD	Wadsworth
340	9.7	Wyoming City SD	Wyoming
341	9.6	Upper Arlington City SD	Upper Arlington
342	9.5	Electronic Classrm of Tomorrow	Columbus
343	9.4	Mariemont City SD	Cincinnati
343	9.4	Pickerington Local SD	Pickerington
343	9.4	Sycamore Community City SD	Cincinnati
346	9.2	Boardman Local SD	Youngstown
347	9.1	Avon Lake City Schools	Avon Lake
348	9.0	Lebanon City SD	Lebanon
348	9.0	Shawnee Local SD	Lima
348	9.0	Western Brown Local SD	Mount Orab
351	8.8	Eastwood Local SD	Pemberville
351	8.8	Loveland City SD	Loveland
353	8.7	Aurora City SD	Aurora
353	8.7	Mason City SD	Mason
353	8.7	Tipp City Ex Vill SD	Tipp City
356	8.6	Manchester Local SD	Akron
357	8.5	Clark-Shawnee Local SD	Springfield
357	8.5	Northeastern Local SD	Springfield
357	8.5	Plain Local SD	New Albany
360	8.4	Indian Hill Ex Vill SD	Cincinnati
361	8.3	Lakota Local SD	Liberty Twp
362	8.2	Norton City Schools	Norton
362	8.2	Revere Local SD	Bath
364	8.1	Ontario Local SD	Mansfield
364	8.1	Perrysburg Exempted Village	Perrysburg
366	8.0	Fairfield Union Local SD	W Rushville
366	8.0	Liberty Local SD	Youngstown
368	7.7	Oakwood City SD	Dayton
369	7.6	Jackson Local SD	Massillon
369	7.6	Perry Local SD	Perry
371	7.4	Bethel-Tate Local SD	Bethel
372	6.9	Anthony Wayne Local SD	Whitehouse
373	5.4	Ohio Virtual Academy	Maumee
374	4.4	Champion Local SD	Warren

English Language Learner Students

Rank	Percent	District Name	City
1	59.0	East Holmes Local Schools	Berlin
2	23.8	Painesville City Local SD	Painesville
3	8.1	Lakewood City SD	Lakewood
4	7.6	Whitehall City SD	Whitehall
5	6.9	Columbus Public Schools	Columbus
6	5.9	North Olmsted City Schools	North Olmsted
7	5.7	Copley-Fairlawn City SD	Copley
7	5.7	Fremont City SD	Fremont
9	5.2	South-Western City SD	Grove City
10	5.1	Dublin City SD	Dublin
11	4.8	Mayfield City SD	Highland Hgts
12	4.5	Tecumseh Local SD	New Carlisle
13	4.3	Sycamore Community City SD	Cincinnati
14	4.0	Cleveland Municipal City SD	Cleveland
15	3.8	Fairview Park City SD	Fairview Park
15	3.8	Princeton City SD	Cincinnati
17	3.7	Hamilton City SD	Hamilton
17	3.7	West Carrollton City SD	West Carrollton
19	3.4	Hilliard City SD	Hilliard
20	3.3	Fostoria City SD	Fostoria
21	3.1	Athens City SD	The Plains
21	3.1	Westerville City SD	Westerville
23	3.0	Ashtabula Area City SD	Ashtabula
24	2.9	Wauseon Ex Vill SD	Wauseon
25	2.8	Worthington City SD	Worthington
26	2.5	Huber Heights City SD	Huber Heights
26	2.5	Parma City SD	Parma
28	2.4	Centerville City SD	Centerville
29	2.3	Shaker Heights City SD	Shaker Heights
30	2.2	Lorain City SD	Lorain
31	2.1	Fairfield City SD	Fairfield
31	2.1	Nordonia Hills City SD	Northfield
33	2.0	Reynoldsburg City SD	Reynoldsburg
34	1.9	Willoughby-Eastlake City SD	Willoughby
35	1.8	Campbell City SD	Campbell
35	1.8	Madeira City SD	Cincinnati
35	1.8	Napoleon Area City SD	Napoleon
35	1.8	Solon City SD	Solon
35	1.8	Woodridge Local SD	Peninsula
40	1.7	Lake Local SD	Hartville
40	1.7	Tipp City Ex Vill SD	Tipp City
40	1.7	Willard City SD	Willard
43	1.6	Orange City SD	Cleveland
43	1.6	Sidney City SD	Sidney
45	1.5	Brecksville-Broadview Hgts City	Brecksville
45	1.5	Licking Heights Local SD	Summit Station
45	1.5	London City SD	London
45	1.5	Middletown City SD	Middletown
45	1.5	Norwood City SD	Norwood
45	1.5	Upper Arlington City SD	Upper Arlington
51	1.4	Berea City SD	Berea
51	1.4	Marlington Local SD	Alliance
51	1.4	North Royalton City SD	N Royalton
51	1.4	Toledo City SD	Toledo
51	1.4	Winton Woods City SD	Cincinnati
56	1.3	Akron Public Schools	Akron
56	1.3	Clearview Local SD	Lorain
56	1.3	Groveport Madison Local SD	Groveport
56	1.3	Lakota Local SD	Liberty Twp
56	1.3	Northmont City SD	Englewood
56	1.3	Troy City SD	Troy
62	1.2	Cuyahoga Falls City SD	Cuyahoga Falls
62	1.2	Jackson Local SD	Massillon
62	1.2	Mason City SD	Mason
62	1.2	Olentangy Local SD	Lewis Center
62	1.2	Strongsville City SD	Strongsville
62	1.2	Washington Local Schools	Toledo
68	1.1	Boardman Local SD	Youngstown
68	1.1	Delaware City SD	Delaware
68	1.1	West Clermont Local SD	Cincinnati
71	1.0	Dayton City SD	Dayton
71	1.0	Gahanna-Jefferson City SD	Gahanna
71	1.0	Rocky River City SD	Rocky River
71	1.0	Twinsburg City SD	Twinsburg
75	0.9	Bellefontaine City Schools	Bellefontaine
75	0.9	Cincinnati City SD	Cincinnati
75	0.9	Loveland City SD	Loveland
75	0.9	Mad River Local SD	Dayton
75	0.9	Mt Healthy City SD	Cincinnati
75	0.9	Springfield Local Schools	Holland
81	0.8	Bay Village City SD	Bay Village
81	0.8	Cleveland Hts-Univ Hts City SD	University Hgts
81	0.8	Geneva Area City Schools	Geneva
81	0.8	Green Local SD	Green
81	0.8	Kent City SD	Kent
81	0.8	Lebanon City SD	Lebanon
81	0.8	Maple Heights City SD	Maple Heights
81	0.8	Northwest Local SD	Cincinnati
81	0.8	Oregon City SD	Oregon
81	0.8	Plain Local SD	New Albany
81	0.8	Stow-Munroe Falls City SD	Stow
92	0.7	Bucyrus City SD	Bucyrus
92	0.7	Chagrin Falls Ex Vill SD	Chagrin Falls
92	0.7	Finneytown Local SD	Cincinnati
92	0.7	Indian Hill Ex Vill SD	Cincinnati
92	0.7	Kings Local SD	Kings Mills
92	0.7	Mentor Ex Vill SD	Mentor
92	0.7	Perry Local SD	Massillon
99	0.6	Avon Lake City Schools	Avon Lake
99	0.6	Barberton City SD	Barberton
99	0.6	Bexley City SD	Bexley
99	0.6	Elida Local SD	Elida
99	0.6	Fairborn City Schools	Fairborn
99	0.6	Findlay City SD	Findlay
99	0.6	Girard City SD	Girard
99	0.6	Hillsboro City SD	Hillsboro
99	0.6	Kettering City SD	Kettering
99	0.6	Pickerington Local SD	Pickerington
99	0.6	Wyoming City SD	Wyoming
110	0.5	Bowling Green City SD	Bowling Green
110	0.5	Canal Winchester Local SD	Canal Winchester
110	0.5	Electronic Classrm of Tomorrow	Columbus
110	0.5	Euclid City SD	Euclid
110	0.5	Field Local SD	Mogadore
110	0.5	Garfield Heights City SD	Garfield Hgts
110	0.5	Howland Local SD	Warren
110	0.5	Hudson City SD	Hudson
110	0.5	Lake Local SD	Millbury
110	0.5	Madison-Plains Local SD	London
110	0.5	North Canton City SD	North Canton
110	0.5	Norton City Schools	Norton
110	0.5	Oakwood City SD	Dayton
110	0.5	St Marys City SD	Saint Marys
110	0.5	Sugarcreek Local SD	Bellbrook
125	0.4	Beavercreek City SD	Beavercreek
125	0.4	Bedford City SD	Bedford
125	0.4	Brunswick City SD	Brunswick
125	0.4	Dover City SD	Dover
125	0.4	Eaton Community Schools	Eaton
125	0.4	Elgin Local SD	Marion
125	0.4	Midview Local SD	Grafton
125	0.4	New Philadelphia City SD	New Philadelphia
125	0.4	Perrysburg Exempted Village	Perrysburg
125	0.4	Pike-Delta-York Local SD	Delta
125	0.4	Southeast Local SD	Apple Creek
125	0.4	Talawanda City SD	Oxford
125	0.4	Vandalia-Butler City SD	Vandalia
138	0.3	Beachwood City SD	Beachwood
138	0.3	Berlin-Milan Local SD	Milan
138	0.3	Buckeye Local SD	Ashtabula
138	0.3	Defiance City SD	Defiance
138	0.3	Elyria City SD	Elyria
138	0.3	Forest Hills Local SD	Cincinnati
138	0.3	Lakewood Local SD	Hebron
138	0.3	Little Miami Local SD	Morrow
138	0.3	Maumee City SD	Maumee
138	0.3	Miamisburg City SD	Miamisburg
138	0.3	Newark City SD	Newark
138	0.3	Northeastern Local SD	Springfield
138	0.3	Northridge Local SD	Dayton
138	0.3	Northwestern Local SD	Springfield
138	0.3	Piqua City SD	Piqua
138	0.3	Plain Local SD	Canton
138	0.3	Revere Local SD	Bath
138	0.3	South Euclid-Lyndhurst City SD	Lyndhurst
138	0.3	Southeast Local SD	Ravenna
138	0.3	Springboro Community City SD	Springboro
138	0.3	St Clairsville-Richland City SD	St Clairsville
138	0.3	Sylvania City SD	Sylvania
138	0.3	Youngstown City SD	Youngstown
161	0.2	Alliance City SD	Alliance
161	0.2	Ashland City SD	Ashland
161	0.2	Aurora City SD	Aurora
161	0.2	Big Walnut Local SD	Galena
161	0.2	Brookville Local SD	Brookville
161	0.2	Bryan City SD	Bryan
161	0.2	Canfield Local SD	Canfield
161	0.2	Canton City SD	Canton
161	0.2	Fairless Local SD	Navarre
161	0.2	Granville Ex Vill SD	Granville
161	0.2	Greeneview Local SD	Jamestown
161	0.2	Huron City Schools	Huron
161	0.2	Kenston Local SD	Chagrin Falls
161	0.2	Lima City SD	Lima
161	0.2	Louisville City SD	Louisville
161	0.2	Marion City SD	Marion
161	0.2	Marysville Exempted Village SD	Marysville
161	0.2	Massillon City SD	Massillon
161	0.2	Medina City SD	Medina
161	0.2	Mount Vernon City SD	Mount Vernon
161	0.2	Painesville Township Local SD	Painesville
161	0.2	Rolling Hills Local SD	Cambridge
161	0.2	Springfield City SD	Springfield
161	0.2	Streetsboro City Schools	Streetsboro
161	0.2	West Holmes Local SD	Millersburg
161	0.2	West Muskingum Local SD	Zanesville
161	0.2	Westlake City SD	Westlake
161	0.2	Xenia Community City SD	Xenia
189	0.1	Alexander Local SD	Albany
189	0.1	Austintown Local SD	Youngstown
189	0.1	Avon Local SD	Avon
189	0.1	Batavia Local SD	Batavia
189	0.1	Carlisle Local SD	Carlisle
189	0.1	Chardon Local SD	Chardon
189	0.1	Clyde-Green Springs Ex Vill SD	Clyde
189	0.1	Franklin City SD	Franklin
189	0.1	Gallia County Local SD	Gallipolis
189	0.1	Greenon Local SD	Springfield
189	0.1	Greenville City SD	Greenville
189	0.1	Hamilton Local SD	Columbus
189	0.1	Hubbard Ex Vill SD	Hubbard
189	0.1	Jefferson Area Local SD	Jefferson
189	0.1	Kenton City SD	Kenton
189	0.1	Milford Ex Vill SD	Milford
189	0.1	Minerva Local SD	Minerva
189	0.1	Monroe Local SD	Monroe
189	0.1	North Fork Local SD	Utica
189	0.1	Olmsted Falls City SD	Olmsted Falls
189	0.1	Ontario Local SD	Mansfield
189	0.1	Ottawa-Glandorf Local SD	Ottawa
189	0.1	Perkins Local SD	Sandusky
189	0.1	Southwest Licking Local SD	Etna
189	0.1	Southwest Local SD	Harrison
189	0.1	Tallmadge City Schools	Tallmadge
189	0.1	Tiffin City SD	Tiffin
189	0.1	Triway Local SD	Wooster
189	0.1	Wadsworth City SD	Wadsworth
189	0.1	Washington Court House City SD	Wash Ct House
189	0.1	Washington-Nile Local SD	West Portsmouth
189	0.1	Wellington Ex Vill SD	Wellington
189	0.1	West Branch Local SD	Beloit
189	0.1	Wickliffe City SD	Wickliffe
223	0.0	Adams County/Ohio Valley LSD	West Union
223	0.0	Bath Local SD	Lima
223	0.0	Bellevue City SD	Bellevue
223	0.0	Canton Local SD	Canton
223	0.0	Circleville City SD	Circleville
223	0.0	Crestwood Local SD	Mantua
223	0.0	Edgewood City SD	Trenton

223	0.0	Gallipolis City SD	Gallipolis
223	0.0	Highland Local SD	Medina
223	0.0	Jackson City SD	Jackson
223	0.0	Lakeview Local SD	Cortland
223	0.0	Lancaster City SD	Lancaster
223	0.0	Marietta City Schools	Marietta
223	0.0	Maysville Local SD	Zanesville
223	0.0	New Richmond Ex Vill SD	New Richmond
223	0.0	Oak Hills Local SD	Cincinnati
223	0.0	Rossford Ex Vill SD	Rossford
223	0.0	Salem City SD	Salem
223	0.0	Sandusky City SD	Sandusky
223	0.0	Teays Valley Local SD	Ashville
223	0.0	Wapakoneta City City SD	Wapakoneta
223	0.0	Warren City SD	Warren
223	0.0	Wilmington City SD	Wilmington
223	0.0	Wooster City SD	Wooster
247	0.0	Amanda-Clearcreek Local SD	Amanda
247	0.0	Amherst Ex Vill SD	Amherst
247	0.0	Anthony Wayne Local SD	Whitehouse
247	0.0	Beaver Local SD	Lisbon
247	0.0	Bellaire Local SD	Bellaire
247	0.0	Benjamin Logan Local SD	Bellefontaine
247	0.0	Benton Carroll Salem Local SD	Oak Harbor
247	0.0	Bethel-Tate Local SD	Bethel
247	0.0	Black River Local SD	Sullivan
247	0.0	Blanchester Local SD	Blanchester
247	0.0	Buckeye Local SD	Medina
247	0.0	Buckeye Local SD	Rayland
247	0.0	Buckeye Valley Local SD	Delaware
247	0.0	Cambridge City SD	Cambridge
247	0.0	Carrollton Ex Vill SD	Carrollton
247	0.0	Celina City SD	Celina
247	0.0	Champion Local SD	Warren
247	0.0	Chillicothe City SD	Chillicothe
247	0.0	Clark-Shawnee Local SD	Springfield
247	0.0	Claymont City SD	Dennison
247	0.0	Clear Fork Valley Local SD	Bellville
247	0.0	Clermont Northeastern Local SD	Batavia
247	0.0	Clinton-Massie Local SD	Clarksville
247	0.0	Cloverleaf Local SD	Lodi
247	0.0	Coldwater Ex Vill SD	Coldwater
247	0.0	Conneaut Area City SD	Conneaut
247	0.0	Coshocton City SD	Coshocton
247	0.0	Coventry Local SD	Akron
247	0.0	East Cleveland City SD	East Cleveland
247	0.0	East Clinton Local SD	Lees Creek
247	0.0	East Liverpool City SD	East Liverpool
247	0.0	East Muskingum Local SD	New Concord
247	0.0	Eastern Local SD	Sardinia
247	0.0	Eastwood Local SD	Pemberville
247	0.0	Edison Local SD	Hammondsville
247	0.0	Fairfield Union Local SD	W Rushville
247	0.0	Fairland Local SD	Proctorville
247	0.0	Firelands Local SD	Oberlin
247	0.0	Franklin Local SD	Duncan Falls
247	0.0	Galion City SD	Galion
247	0.0	Genoa Area Local SD	Genoa
247	0.0	Goshen Local SD	Goshen
247	0.0	Graham Local SD	Saint Paris
247	0.0	Greenfield Ex Vill SD	Greenfield
247	0.0	Harrison Hills City SD	Hopedale
247	0.0	Heath City SD	Heath
247	0.0	Highland Local SD	Sparta
247	0.0	Indian Creek Local SD	Wintersville
247	0.0	Indian Lake Local SD	Lewistown
247	0.0	Indian Valley Local SD	Gnadenhutten
247	0.0	Ironton City SD	Ironton
247	0.0	James A Garfield Local SD	Garrettsville
247	0.0	Jonathan Alder Local SD	Plain City
247	0.0	Keystone Local SD	Lagrange
247	0.0	Lexington Local SD	Lexington
247	0.0	Liberty Local SD	Youngstown
247	0.0	Licking Valley Local SD Sd	Newark
247	0.0	Logan Elm Local SD	Circleville
247	0.0	Logan-Hocking Local SD	Logan
247	0.0	Madison Local SD	Mansfield
247	0.0	Madison Local SD	Middletown
247	0.0	Madison Local SD	Madison
247	0.0	Manchester Local SD	Akron
247	0.0	Mansfield City SD	Mansfield
247	0.0	Mariemont City SD	Cincinnati
247	0.0	Martins Ferry City SD	Martins Ferry
247	0.0	Meigs Local SD	Pomeroy
247	0.0	Miami Trace Local SD	Wash Ct House
247	0.0	Milton-Union Exempted Vill Schls	West Milton
247	0.0	Minford Local SD	Minford
247	0.0	Morgan Local SD	McConnelsville
247	0.0	New Lexington City SD	New Lexington
247	0.0	Newton Falls Ex Vill SD	Newton Falls
247	0.0	Niles City SD	Niles
247	0.0	North College Hill City SD	Cincinnati
247	0.0	North Ridgeville City SD	N Ridgeville
247	0.0	Northern Local SD	Thornville
247	0.0	Northwest Local SD	Mc Dermott
247	0.0	Northwest Local SD	Canal Fulton
247	0.0	Norwalk City SD	Norwalk
247	0.0	Ohio Virtual Academy	Maumee
247	0.0	Orrville City SD	Orrville
247	0.0	Otsego Local SD	Tontogany
247	0.0	Paulding Ex Vill SD	Paulding
247	0.0	Perry Local SD	Perry
247	0.0	Poland Local SD	Poland
247	0.0	Port Clinton City SD	Port Clinton
247	0.0	Portsmouth City SD	Portsmouth
247	0.0	Preble Shawnee Local SD	Camden
247	0.0	Ravenna City SD	Ravenna
247	0.0	Ridgewood Local SD	West Lafayette
247	0.0	River Valley Local SD	Caledonia
247	0.0	River View Local SD	Warsaw
247	0.0	Rock Hill Local SD	Ironton
247	0.0	Ross Local SD	Hamilton
247	0.0	Sandy Valley Local SD	Magnolia
247	0.0	Scioto Valley Local SD	Piketon
247	0.0	Shawnee Local SD	Lima
247	0.0	Sheffield-Sheffield Lake City SD	Sheffield Vlg
247	0.0	Shelby City SD	Shelby
247	0.0	South Point Local SD	South Point
247	0.0	Springfield Local SD	Akron
247	0.0	Steubenville City SD	Steubenville
247	0.0	Struthers City SD	Struthers
247	0.0	Swanton Local SD	Swanton
247	0.0	Switzerland of Ohio Local SD	Woodsfield
247	0.0	Three Rivers Local Schools	Cleves
247	0.0	Tri-Valley Local Schools	Dresden
247	0.0	Trotwood-Madison City Schools	Trotwood
247	0.0	Tuscarawas Valley Local SD	Zoarville
247	0.0	Union Local SD	Morristown
247	0.0	Union-Scioto Local SD	Chillicothe
247	0.0	United Local SD	Hanoverton
247	0.0	Upper Sandusky Ex Vill SD	Upper Sandusky
247	0.0	Urbana City SD	Urbana
247	0.0	Valley View Local SD	Germantown
247	0.0	Van Wert City SD	Van Wert
247	0.0	Vermilion Local SD	Vermilion
247	0.0	Vinton County Local SD	Mc Arthur
247	0.0	Warren Local SD	Vincent
247	0.0	Warrensville Heights City SD	Warrensville Hgts
247	0.0	Waverly City SD	Waverly
247	0.0	Wellston City Schools	Wellston
247	0.0	West Geauga Local SD	Chesterland
247	0.0	Western Brown Local SD	Mount Orab
247	0.0	Westfall Local SD	Williamsport
247	0.0	Zane Trace Local SD	Chillicothe
247	0.0	Zanesville City SD	Zanesville

Migrant Students

Rank	Percent	District Name	City
1	14.2	Painesville City Local SD	Painesville
2	6.1	Willard City SD	Willard
3	3.3	Woodridge Local SD	Peninsula
4	3.1	Tecumseh Local SD	New Carlisle
5	2.2	Wauseon Ex Vill SD	Wauseon
6	1.7	South-Western City SD	Grove City
7	1.6	Fremont City SD	Fremont
7	1.6	Napoleon Area City SD	Napoleon
9	1.0	Benton Carroll Salem Local SD	Oak Harbor
9	1.0	Marlington Local SD	Alliance
9	1.0	Sycamore Community City SD	Cincinnati
12	0.9	Tipp City Ex Vill SD	Tipp City
13	0.7	Berlin-Milan Local SD	Milan
13	0.7	Reynoldsburg City SD	Reynoldsburg
15	0.6	Ottawa-Glandorf Local SD	Ottawa
16	0.3	Perrysburg Exempted Village	Perrysburg
16	0.3	Urbana City SD	Urbana
18	0.2	Alliance City SD	Alliance
18	0.2	Bowling Green City SD	Bowling Green
18	0.2	Columbus Public Schools	Columbus
18	0.2	North Royalton City SD	N Royalton
18	0.2	Wellington Ex Vill SD	Wellington
23	0.1	Bellevue City SD	Bellevue
23	0.1	Black River Local SD	Sullivan
23	0.1	Clearview Local SD	Lorain
23	0.1	Cloverleaf Local SD	Lodi
23	0.1	Clyde-Green Springs Ex Vill SD	Clyde
23	0.1	Eastwood Local SD	Pemberville
23	0.1	Elyria City SD	Elyria
23	0.1	Fairborn City Schools	Fairborn
23	0.1	Fairview Park City SD	Fairview Park
23	0.1	Field Local SD	Mogadore
23	0.1	Firelands Local SD	Oberlin
23	0.1	Highland Local SD	Medina
23	0.1	Keystone Local SD	Lagrange
23	0.1	Lorain City SD	Lorain
23	0.1	Marion City SD	Marion
23	0.1	North Ridgeville City SD	N Ridgeville
23	0.1	Painesville Township Local SD	Painesville
23	0.1	Pike-Delta-York Local SD	Delta
23	0.1	Springfield City SD	Springfield
23	0.1	Sylvania City SD	Sylvania
23	0.1	Tiffin City SD	Tiffin
23	0.1	Warrensville Heights City SD	Warrensville Hgts
23	0.1	Willoughby-Eastlake City SD	Willoughby
46	0.0	Amherst Ex Vill SD	Amherst
46	0.0	Ashtabula Area City SD	Ashtabula
46	0.0	Avon Lake City Schools	Avon Lake
46	0.0	Bay Village City SD	Bay Village
46	0.0	Bexley City SD	Bexley
46	0.0	Canfield Local SD	Canfield
46	0.0	Centerville City SD	Centerville
46	0.0	Cincinnati City SD	Cincinnati
46	0.0	Findlay City SD	Findlay
46	0.0	Gahanna-Jefferson City SD	Gahanna
46	0.0	Geneva Area City Schools	Geneva
46	0.0	Greenville City SD	Greenville
46	0.0	Hamilton City SD	Hamilton
46	0.0	Hudson City SD	Hudson
46	0.0	Kenston Local SD	Chagrin Falls
46	0.0	Lakota Local SD	Liberty Twp
46	0.0	Mad River Local SD	Dayton
46	0.0	Madison Local SD	Madison
46	0.0	Medina City SD	Medina
46	0.0	Nordonia Hills City SD	Northfield
46	0.0	North Olmsted City Schools	North Olmsted
46	0.0	Olmsted Falls City SD	Olmsted Falls
46	0.0	Southwest Licking Local SD	Etna
46	0.0	Strongsville City SD	Strongsville
46	0.0	Vandalia-Butler City SD	Vandalia
46	0.0	Vermilion Local SD	Vermilion
72	n/a	Adams County/Ohio Valley LSD	West Union
72	n/a	Akron Public Schools	Akron
72	n/a	Alexander Local SD	Albany
72	n/a	Amanda-Clearcreek Local SD	Amanda
72	n/a	Anthony Wayne Local SD	Whitehouse
72	n/a	Ashland City SD	Ashland
72	n/a	Athens City SD	The Plains
72	n/a	Aurora City SD	Aurora
72	n/a	Austintown Local SD	Youngstown
72	n/a	Avon Local SD	Avon
72	n/a	Barberton City SD	Barberton
72	n/a	Batavia Local SD	Batavia
72	n/a	Bath Local SD	Lima
72	n/a	Beachwood City SD	Beachwood
72	n/a	Beaver Local SD	Lisbon
72	n/a	Beavercreek City SD	Beavercreek
72	n/a	Bedford City SD	Bedford
72	n/a	Bellaire Local SD	Bellaire
72	n/a	Bellefontaine City Schools	Bellefontaine
72	n/a	Benjamin Logan Local SD	Bellefontaine
72	n/a	Berea City SD	Berea
72	n/a	Bethel-Tate Local SD	Bethel
72	n/a	Big Walnut Local SD	Galena
72	n/a	Blanchester Local SD	Blanchester
72	n/a	Boardman Local SD	Youngstown
72	n/a	Brecksville-Broadview Hgts City	Brecksville
72	n/a	Brookville Local SD	Brookville
72	n/a	Brunswick City SD	Brunswick
72	n/a	Bryan City SD	Bryan
72	n/a	Buckeye Local SD	Rayland
72	n/a	Buckeye Local SD	Ashtabula
72	n/a	Buckeye Local SD	Medina
72	n/a	Buckeye Valley Local SD	Delaware
72	n/a	Bucyrus City SD	Bucyrus
72	n/a	Cambridge City SD	Cambridge
72	n/a	Campbell City SD	Campbell
72	n/a	Canal Winchester Local SD	Canal Winchester
72	n/a	Canton City SD	Canton
72	n/a	Canton Local SD	Canton
72	n/a	Carlisle Local SD	Carlisle
72	n/a	Carrollton Ex Vill SD	Carrollton
72	n/a	Celina City SD	Celina
72	n/a	Chagrin Falls Ex Vill SD	Chagrin Falls
72	n/a	Champion Local SD	Warren
72	n/a	Chardon Local SD	Chardon
72	n/a	Chillicothe City SD	Chillicothe
72	n/a	Circleville City SD	Circleville
72	n/a	Clark-Shawnee Local SD	Springfield
72	n/a	Claymont City SD	Dennison
72	n/a	Clear Fork Valley Local SD	Bellville
72	n/a	Clermont Northeastern Local SD	Batavia
72	n/a	Cleveland Hts-Univ Hts City SD	University Hgts
72	n/a	Cleveland Municipal City SD	Cleveland
72	n/a	Clinton-Massie Local SD	Clarksville
72	n/a	Coldwater Ex Vill SD	Coldwater
72	n/a	Conneaut Area City SD	Conneaut
72	n/a	Copley-Fairlawn City SD	Copley
72	n/a	Coshocton City SD	Coshocton
72	n/a	Coventry Local SD	Akron

72	n/a	Crestwood Local SD	Mantua
72	n/a	Cuyahoga Falls City SD	Cuyahoga Falls
72	n/a	Dayton City SD	Dayton
72	n/a	Defiance City SD	Defiance
72	n/a	Delaware City SD	Delaware
72	n/a	Dover City SD	Dover
72	n/a	Dublin City SD	Dublin
72	n/a	East Cleveland City SD	East Cleveland
72	n/a	East Clinton Local SD	Lees Creek
72	n/a	East Holmes Local Schools	Berlin
72	n/a	East Liverpool City SD	East Liverpool
72	n/a	East Muskingum Local SD	New Concord
72	n/a	Eastern Local SD	Sardinia
72	n/a	Eaton Community Schools	Eaton
72	n/a	Edgewood City SD	Trenton
72	n/a	Edison Local SD	Hammondsville
72	n/a	Electronic Classrm of Tomorrow	Columbus
72	n/a	Elgin Local SD	Marion
72	n/a	Elida Local SD	Elida
72	n/a	Euclid City SD	Euclid
72	n/a	Fairfield City SD	Fairfield
72	n/a	Fairfield Union Local SD	W Rushville
72	n/a	Fairland Local SD	Proctorville
72	n/a	Fairless Local SD	Navarre
72	n/a	Finneytown Local SD	Cincinnati
72	n/a	Forest Hills Local SD	Cincinnati
72	n/a	Fostoria City SD	Fostoria
72	n/a	Franklin City SD	Franklin
72	n/a	Franklin Local SD	Duncan Falls
72	n/a	Galion City SD	Galion
72	n/a	Gallia County Local SD	Gallipolis
72	n/a	Gallipolis City SD	Gallipolis
72	n/a	Garfield Heights City SD	Garfield Hgts
72	n/a	Genoa Area Local SD	Genoa
72	n/a	Girard City SD	Girard
72	n/a	Goshen Local SD	Goshen
72	n/a	Graham Local SD	Saint Paris
72	n/a	Granville Ex Vill SD	Granville
72	n/a	Green Local SD	Green
72	n/a	Greeneview Local SD	Jamestown
72	n/a	Greenfield Ex Vill SD	Greenfield
72	n/a	Greenon Local SD	Springfield
72	n/a	Groveport Madison Local SD	Groveport
72	n/a	Hamilton Local SD	Columbus
72	n/a	Harrison Hills City SD	Hopedale
72	n/a	Heath City SD	Heath
72	n/a	Highland Local SD	Sparta
72	n/a	Hilliard City SD	Hilliard
72	n/a	Hillsboro City SD	Hillsboro
72	n/a	Howland Local SD	Warren
72	n/a	Hubbard Ex Vill SD	Hubbard
72	n/a	Huber Heights City SD	Huber Heights
72	n/a	Huron City Schools	Huron
72	n/a	Indian Creek Local SD	Wintersville
72	n/a	Indian Hill Ex Vill SD	Cincinnati
72	n/a	Indian Lake Local SD	Lewistown
72	n/a	Indian Valley Local SD	Gnadenhutten
72	n/a	Ironton City SD	Ironton
72	n/a	Jackson City SD	Jackson
72	n/a	Jackson Local SD	Massillon
72	n/a	James A Garfield Local SD	Garrettsville
72	n/a	Jefferson Area Local SD	Jefferson
72	n/a	Jonathan Alder Local SD	Plain City
72	n/a	Kent City SD	Kent
72	n/a	Kenton City SD	Kenton
72	n/a	Kettering City SD	Kettering
72	n/a	Kings Local SD	Kings Mills
72	n/a	Lake Local SD	Millbury
72	n/a	Lake Local SD	Hartville
72	n/a	Lakeview Local SD	Cortland
72	n/a	Lakewood City SD	Lakewood
72	n/a	Lakewood Local SD	Hebron
72	n/a	Lancaster City SD	Lancaster
72	n/a	Lebanon City SD	Lebanon
72	n/a	Lexington Local SD	Lexington
72	n/a	Liberty Local SD	Youngstown
72	n/a	Licking Heights Local SD	Summit Station
72	n/a	Licking Valley Local SD Sd	Newark
72	n/a	Lima City SD	Lima
72	n/a	Little Miami Local SD	Morrow
72	n/a	Logan Elm Local SD	Circleville
72	n/a	Logan-Hocking Local SD	Logan
72	n/a	London City SD	London
72	n/a	Louisville City SD	Louisville
72	n/a	Loveland City SD	Loveland
72	n/a	Madeira City SD	Cincinnati
72	n/a	Madison Local SD	Middletown
72	n/a	Madison Local SD	Mansfield
72	n/a	Madison-Plains Local SD	London
72	n/a	Manchester Local SD	Akron
72	n/a	Mansfield City SD	Mansfield
72	n/a	Maple Heights City SD	Maple Heights
72	n/a	Mariemont City SD	Cincinnati
72	n/a	Marietta City Schools	Marietta
72	n/a	Martins Ferry City SD	Martins Ferry
72	n/a	Marysville Exempted Village SD	Marysville
72	n/a	Mason City SD	Mason
72	n/a	Massillon City SD	Massillon
72	n/a	Maumee City SD	Maumee
72	n/a	Mayfield City SD	Highland Hgts
72	n/a	Maysville Local SD	Zanesville
72	n/a	Meigs Local SD	Pomeroy
72	n/a	Mentor Ex Vill SD	Mentor
72	n/a	Miami Trace Local SD	Wash Ct House
72	n/a	Miamisburg City SD	Miamisburg
72	n/a	Middletown City SD	Middletown
72	n/a	Midview Local SD	Grafton
72	n/a	Milford Ex Vill SD	Milford
72	n/a	Milton-Union Exempted Vill Schls	West Milton
72	n/a	Minerva Local SD	Minerva
72	n/a	Minford Local SD	Minford
72	n/a	Monroe Local SD	Monroe
72	n/a	Morgan Local SD	McConnelsville
72	n/a	Mount Vernon City SD	Mount Vernon
72	n/a	Mt Healthy City SD	Cincinnati
72	n/a	New Lexington City SD	New Lexington
72	n/a	New Philadelphia City SD	New Philadelphia
72	n/a	New Richmond Ex Vill SD	New Richmond
72	n/a	Newark City SD	Newark
72	n/a	Newton Falls Ex Vill SD	Newton Falls
72	n/a	Niles City SD	Niles
72	n/a	North Canton City SD	North Canton
72	n/a	North College Hill City SD	Cincinnati
72	n/a	North Fork Local SD	Utica
72	n/a	Northeastern Local SD	Springfield
72	n/a	Northern Local SD	Thornville
72	n/a	Northmont City SD	Englewood
72	n/a	Northridge Local SD	Dayton
72	n/a	Northwest Local SD	Cincinnati
72	n/a	Northwest Local SD	Mc Dermott
72	n/a	Northwest Local SD	Canal Fulton
72	n/a	Northwestern Local SD	Springfield
72	n/a	Norton City Schools	Norton
72	n/a	Norwalk City SD	Norwalk
72	n/a	Norwood City SD	Norwood
72	n/a	Oak Hills Local SD	Cincinnati
72	n/a	Oakwood City SD	Dayton
72	n/a	Ohio Virtual Academy	Maumee
72	n/a	Olentangy Local SD	Lewis Center
72	n/a	Ontario Local SD	Mansfield
72	n/a	Orange City SD	Cleveland
72	n/a	Oregon City SD	Oregon
72	n/a	Orrville City SD	Orrville
72	n/a	Otsego Local SD	Tontogany
72	n/a	Parma City SD	Parma
72	n/a	Paulding Ex Vill SD	Paulding
72	n/a	Perkins Local SD	Sandusky
72	n/a	Perry Local SD	Perry
72	n/a	Perry Local SD	Massillon
72	n/a	Pickerington Local SD	Pickerington
72	n/a	Piqua City SD	Piqua
72	n/a	Plain Local SD	New Albany
72	n/a	Plain Local SD	Canton
72	n/a	Poland Local SD	Poland
72	n/a	Port Clinton City SD	Port Clinton
72	n/a	Portsmouth City SD	Portsmouth
72	n/a	Preble Shawnee Local SD	Camden
72	n/a	Princeton City SD	Cincinnati
72	n/a	Ravenna City SD	Ravenna
72	n/a	Revere Local SD	Bath
72	n/a	Ridgewood Local SD	West Lafayette
72	n/a	River Valley Local SD	Caledonia
72	n/a	River View Local SD	Warsaw
72	n/a	Rock Hill Local SD	Ironton
72	n/a	Rocky River City SD	Rocky River
72	n/a	Rolling Hills Local SD	Cambridge
72	n/a	Ross Local SD	Hamilton
72	n/a	Rossford Ex Vill SD	Rossford
72	n/a	Salem City SD	Salem
72	n/a	Sandusky City SD	Sandusky
72	n/a	Sandy Valley Local SD	Magnolia
72	n/a	Scioto Valley Local SD	Piketon
72	n/a	Shaker Heights City SD	Shaker Heights
72	n/a	Shawnee Local SD	Lima
72	n/a	Sheffield-Sheffield Lake City SD	Sheffield Vlg
72	n/a	Shelby City SD	Shelby
72	n/a	Sidney City SD	Sidney
72	n/a	Solon City SD	Solon
72	n/a	South Euclid-Lyndhurst City SD	Lyndhurst
72	n/a	South Point Local SD	South Point
72	n/a	Southeast Local SD	Ravenna
72	n/a	Southeast Local SD	Apple Creek
72	n/a	Southwest Local SD	Harrison
72	n/a	Springboro Community City SD	Springboro
72	n/a	Springfield Local SD	Akron
72	n/a	Springfield Local Schools	Holland
72	n/a	St Clairsville-Richland City SD	St Clairsville
72	n/a	St Marys City SD	Saint Marys
72	n/a	Steubenville City SD	Steubenville
72	n/a	Stow-Munroe Falls City SD	Stow
72	n/a	Streetsboro City Schools	Streetsboro
72	n/a	Struthers City SD	Struthers
72	n/a	Sugarcreek Local SD	Bellbrook
72	n/a	Swanton Local SD	Swanton
72	n/a	Switzerland of Ohio Local SD	Woodsfield
72	n/a	Talawanda City SD	Oxford
72	n/a	Tallmadge City Schools	Tallmadge
72	n/a	Teays Valley Local SD	Ashville
72	n/a	Three Rivers Local Schools	Cleves
72	n/a	Toledo City SD	Toledo
72	n/a	Tri-Valley Local Schools	Dresden
72	n/a	Triway Local SD	Wooster
72	n/a	Trotwood-Madison City Schools	Trotwood
72	n/a	Troy City SD	Troy
72	n/a	Tuscarawas Valley Local SD	Zoarville
72	n/a	Twinsburg City SD	Twinsburg
72	n/a	Union Local SD	Morristown
72	n/a	Union-Scioto Local SD	Chillicothe
72	n/a	United Local SD	Hanoverton
72	n/a	Upper Arlington City SD	Upper Arlington
72	n/a	Upper Sandusky Ex Vill SD	Upper Sandusky
72	n/a	Valley View Local SD	Germantown
72	n/a	Van Wert City SD	Van Wert
72	n/a	Vinton County Local SD	Mc Arthur
72	n/a	Wadsworth City SD	Wadsworth
72	n/a	Wapakoneta City City SD	Wapakoneta
72	n/a	Warren City SD	Warren
72	n/a	Warren Local SD	Vincent
72	n/a	Washington Court House City SD	Wash Ct House
72	n/a	Washington Local Schools	Toledo
72	n/a	Washington-Nile Local SD	West Portsmouth
72	n/a	Waverly City SD	Waverly
72	n/a	Wellston City Schools	Wellston
72	n/a	West Branch Local SD	Beloit
72	n/a	West Carrollton City SD	West Carrollton
72	n/a	West Clermont Local SD	Cincinnati
72	n/a	West Geauga Local SD	Chesterland
72	n/a	West Holmes Local SD	Millersburg
72	n/a	West Muskingum Local SD	Zanesville
72	n/a	Western Brown Local SD	Mount Orab
72	n/a	Westerville City SD	Westerville
72	n/a	Westfall Local SD	Williamsport
72	n/a	Westlake City SD	Westlake
72	n/a	Whitehall City SD	Whitehall
72	n/a	Wickliffe City SD	Wickliffe
72	n/a	Wilmington City SD	Wilmington
72	n/a	Winton Woods City SD	Cincinnati
72	n/a	Wooster City SD	Wooster
72	n/a	Worthington City SD	Worthington
72	n/a	Wyoming City SD	Wyoming
72	n/a	Xenia Community City SD	Xenia
72	n/a	Youngstown City SD	Youngstown
72	n/a	Zane Trace Local SD	Chillicothe
72	n/a	Zanesville City SD	Zanesville

Students Eligible for Free Lunch

Rank	Percent	District Name	City
1	72.9	Cleveland Municipal City SD	Cleveland
2	72.0	Painesville City Local SD	Painesville
3	66.8	Youngstown City SD	Youngstown
4	66.2	Dayton City SD	Dayton
5	62.8	East Cleveland City SD	East Cleveland
5	62.8	Lima City SD	Lima
7	61.7	Mansfield City SD	Mansfield
8	57.3	Cincinnati City SD	Cincinnati
9	55.8	Warrensville Heights City SD	Warrensville Hgts
10	55.1	Canton City SD	Canton
11	54.7	Sandusky City SD	Sandusky
12	53.5	Lorain City SD	Lorain
12	53.5	Zanesville City SD	Zanesville
14	51.9	Toledo City SD	Toledo
15	50.7	Bellaire Local SD	Bellaire
16	50.4	Alliance City SD	Alliance
17	50.2	Columbus Public Schools	Columbus
18	48.9	Trotwood-Madison City Schools	Trotwood
18	48.9	Warren City SD	Warren
20	48.2	Clearview Local SD	Lorain
21	48.0	Springfield City SD	Springfield
22	46.5	Steubenville City SD	Steubenville
23	46.4	Portsmouth City SD	Portsmouth
23	46.4	Rock Hill Local SD	Ironton
25	46.0	Northwest Local SD	Mc Dermott
26	45.6	Ashtabula Area City SD	Ashtabula
27	44.4	Vinton County Local SD	Mc Arthur
28	43.8	East Liverpool City SD	East Liverpool
29	43.3	New Lexington City SD	New Lexington

30	42.9	Campbell City SD	Campbell
31	42.8	Meigs Local SD	Pomeroy
32	42.2	Hamilton City SD	Hamilton
33	41.9	Northridge Local SD	Dayton
34	41.8	Mt Healthy City SD	Cincinnati
35	41.5	Fostoria City SD	Fostoria
36	40.8	Whitehall City SD	Whitehall
37	40.2	Adams County/Ohio Valley LSD	West Union
38	39.3	Struthers City SD	Struthers
39	39.2	Conneaut Area City SD	Conneaut
39	39.2	Norwood City SD	Norwood
41	37.6	Euclid City SD	Euclid
41	37.6	Washington-Nile Local SD	West Portsmouth
43	37.3	Scioto Valley Local SD	Piketon
44	37.2	Barberton City SD	Barberton
44	37.2	Gallia County Local SD	Gallipolis
46	36.9	Massillon City SD	Massillon
47	36.8	South Point Local SD	South Point
48	36.7	Elyria City SD	Elyria
49	36.2	Cambridge City SD	Cambridge
50	35.9	Ironton City SD	Ironton
51	35.8	Maple Heights City SD	Maple Heights
51	35.8	North College Hill City SD	Cincinnati
53	35.6	Coshocton City SD	Coshocton
54	35.4	Morgan Local SD	McConnelsville
55	35.2	Wellston City Schools	Wellston
56	35.0	Princeton City SD	Cincinnati
57	34.0	Bucyrus City SD	Bucyrus
58	33.4	Martins Ferry City SD	Martins Ferry
59	32.9	Cleveland Hts-Univ Hts City SD	University Hgts
60	32.7	Buckeye Local SD	Rayland
60	32.7	Middletown City SD	Middletown
62	32.0	Maysville Local SD	Zanesville
63	31.6	Marion City SD	Marion
64	31.4	Minford Local SD	Minford
64	31.4	Rolling Hills Local SD	Cambridge
64	31.4	Union Local SD	Morristown
67	30.9	Waverly City SD	Waverly
68	30.7	Harrison Hills City SD	Hopedale
69	30.5	Indian Creek Local SD	Wintersville
69	30.5	Niles City SD	Niles
71	30.2	Franklin Local SD	Duncan Falls
71	30.2	Fremont City SD	Fremont
73	29.7	Switzerland of Ohio Local SD	Woodsfield
74	28.9	South-Western City SD	Grove City
75	28.6	Bedford City SD	Bedford
75	28.6	Lancaster City SD	Lancaster
75	28.6	Piqua City SD	Piqua
78	28.4	Athens City SD	The Plains
78	28.4	Ravenna City SD	Ravenna
80	28.3	Chillicothe City SD	Chillicothe
81	28.0	Gallipolis City SD	Gallipolis
82	27.9	Girard City SD	Girard
82	27.9	Sidney City SD	Sidney
82	27.9	Willard City SD	Willard
85	27.6	New Richmond Ex Vill SD	New Richmond
86	27.5	Logan-Hocking Local SD	Logan
87	27.2	Claymont City SD	Dennison
87	27.2	Newark City SD	Newark
89	27.1	Jackson City SD	Jackson
90	27.0	Xenia Community City SD	Xenia
91	26.9	Edison Local SD	Hammondsville
92	26.8	Geneva Area City Schools	Geneva
93	26.7	Beaver Local SD	Lisbon
94	26.1	Hillsboro City SD	Hillsboro
95	25.7	Mad River Local SD	Dayton
96	25.6	Carrollton Ex Vill SD	Carrollton
96	25.6	Wooster City SD	Wooster
98	25.5	Garfield Heights City SD	Garfield Hgts
99	25.1	Washington Court House City SD	Wash Ct House
100	24.7	Akron Public Schools	Akron
100	24.7	Urbana City SD	Urbana
102	24.3	Alexander Local SD	Albany
103	24.2	Indian Valley Local SD	Gnadenhutten
103	24.2	Minerva Local SD	Minerva
103	24.2	West Holmes Local SD	Millersburg
106	24.0	Buckeye Local SD	Ashtabula
106	24.0	Canton Local SD	Canton
106	24.0	Circleville City SD	Circleville
106	24.0	Groveport Madison Local SD	Groveport
110	23.9	Port Clinton City SD	Port Clinton
111	23.8	Bellefontaine City Schools	Bellefontaine
112	23.7	Lakewood City SD	Lakewood
112	23.7	Mount Vernon City SD	Mount Vernon
114	23.6	Fairborn City Schools	Fairborn
114	23.6	Madison Local SD	Mansfield
116	23.0	Galion City SD	Galion
116	23.0	Lakewood Local SD	Hebron
118	22.8	Springfield Local SD	Akron
119	22.6	Eastern Local SD	Sardinia
119	22.6	Fairland Local SD	Proctorville
119	22.6	Greenfield Ex Vill SD	Greenfield
122	22.3	Fairless Local SD	Navarre
123	22.2	Norwalk City SD	Norwalk
124	22.1	Kenton City SD	Kenton
125	22.0	Ridgewood Local SD	West Lafayette
126	21.6	Batavia Local SD	Batavia
126	21.6	Salem City SD	Salem
128	21.5	Hubbard Ex Vill SD	Hubbard
129	21.4	Kent City SD	Kent
129	21.4	United Local SD	Hanoverton
131	21.3	Winton Woods City SD	Cincinnati
132	21.2	Liberty Local SD	Youngstown
133	21.1	Woodridge Local SD	Peninsula
134	20.8	Elida Local SD	Elida
135	20.7	Ashland City SD	Ashland
135	20.7	Springfield Local Schools	Holland
137	20.6	Tecumseh Local SD	New Carlisle
138	20.5	Western Brown Local SD	Mount Orab
139	20.2	Hamilton Local SD	Columbus
139	20.2	Westfall Local SD	Williamsport
141	20.1	Marietta City Schools	Marietta
142	20.0	Jefferson Area Local SD	Jefferson
143	19.9	Indian Lake Local SD	Lewistown
144	19.8	Wilmington City SD	Wilmington
145	19.7	Findlay City SD	Findlay
145	19.7	Newton Falls Ex Vill SD	Newton Falls
145	19.7	Washington Local Schools	Toledo
148	19.6	Greenville City SD	Greenville
149	19.3	Goshen Local SD	Goshen
149	19.3	West Muskingum Local SD	Zanesville
151	19.2	Austintown Local SD	Youngstown
151	19.2	Orrville City SD	Orrville
151	19.2	Southeast Local SD	Apple Creek
151	19.2	St Clairsville-Richland City SD	St Clairsville
151	19.2	West Branch Local SD	Beloit
156	19.1	Blanchester Local SD	Blanchester
157	18.8	Elgin Local SD	Marion
158	18.6	Highland Local SD	Sparta
158	18.6	Shelby City SD	Shelby
160	18.5	Celina City SD	Celina
161	18.4	Plain Local SD	Canton
162	18.3	Napoleon Area City SD	Napoleon
163	18.2	Sandy Valley Local SD	Magnolia
164	18.0	Northern Local SD	Thornville
165	17.9	Van Wert City SD	Van Wert
166	17.8	Defiance City SD	Defiance
167	17.7	Wapakoneta City City SD	Wapakoneta
168	17.6	Madison Local SD	Madison
168	17.6	Vermilion Local SD	Vermilion
170	17.5	Northwest Local SD	Cincinnati
171	17.2	Miami Trace Local SD	Wash Ct House
172	17.0	London City SD	London
173	16.9	Milton-Union Exempted Vill Schls	West Milton
174	16.6	Bath Local SD	Lima
174	16.6	Tiffin City SD	Tiffin
176	16.5	Franklin City SD	Franklin
176	16.5	River View Local SD	Warsaw
178	16.2	Three Rivers Local Schools	Cleves
179	15.9	Sheffield-Sheffield Lake City SD	Sheffield Vlg
179	15.9	Wellington Ex Vill SD	Wellington
181	15.7	Bethel-Tate Local SD	Bethel
182	15.6	Clear Fork Valley Local SD	Bellville
182	15.6	Clyde-Green Springs Ex Vill SD	Clyde
184	15.5	Streetsboro City Schools	Streetsboro
185	15.4	East Muskingum Local SD	New Concord
185	15.4	St Marys City SD	Saint Marys
185	15.4	Tri-Valley Local Schools	Dresden
188	15.2	Delaware City SD	Delaware
188	15.2	Wauseon Ex Vill SD	Wauseon
188	15.2	West Carrollton City SD	West Carrollton
191	15.0	Lake Local SD	Millbury
192	14.9	Black River Local SD	Sullivan
192	14.9	East Clinton Local SD	Lees Creek
192	14.9	Upper Sandusky Ex Vill SD	Upper Sandusky
192	14.9	Warren Local SD	Vincent
196	14.8	Kettering City SD	Kettering
196	14.8	Miamisburg City SD	Miamisburg
196	14.8	Preble Shawnee Local SD	Camden
196	14.8	Troy City SD	Troy
200	14.6	Logan Elm Local SD	Circleville
200	14.6	Triway Local SD	Wooster
202	14.5	Clermont Northeastern Local SD	Batavia
202	14.5	Field Local SD	Mogadore
202	14.5	Licking Valley Local SD Sd	Newark
202	14.5	Perry Local SD	Massillon
202	14.5	Pike-Delta-York Local SD	Delta
202	14.5	Southeast Local SD	Ravenna
208	14.4	Bellevue City SD	Bellevue
208	14.4	South Euclid-Lyndhurst City SD	Lyndhurst
208	14.4	Tuscarawas Valley Local SD	Zoarville
211	14.3	Parma City SD	Parma
211	14.3	River Valley Local SD	Caledonia
213	14.2	Paulding Ex Vill SD	Paulding
213	14.2	Willoughby-Eastlake City SD	Willoughby
215	14.1	Rossford Ex Vill SD	Rossford
215	14.1	Talawanda City SD	Oxford
217	14.0	James A Garfield Local SD	Garrettsville
218	13.9	Huber Heights City SD	Huber Heights
219	13.8	Amanda-Clearcreek Local SD	Amanda
220	13.6	Fairfield Union Local SD	W Rushville
221	13.5	Fairview Park City SD	Fairview Park
221	13.5	Licking Heights Local SD	Summit Station
223	13.4	East Holmes Local Schools	Berlin
224	13.3	Louisville City SD	Louisville
224	13.3	Southwest Local SD	Harrison
226	13.2	New Philadelphia City SD	New Philadelphia
227	13.1	Marlington Local SD	Alliance
227	13.1	North Fork Local SD	Utica
229	13.0	Cuyahoga Falls City SD	Cuyahoga Falls
229	13.0	Finneytown Local SD	Cincinnati
229	13.0	Oregon City SD	Oregon
232	12.8	Benton Carroll Salem Local SD	Oak Harbor
233	12.7	Teays Valley Local SD	Ashville
234	12.6	Bowling Green City SD	Bowling Green
234	12.6	Heath City SD	Heath
234	12.6	Shawnee Local SD	Lima
237	12.4	Boardman Local SD	Youngstown
237	12.4	Cloverleaf Local SD	Lodi
237	12.4	Eaton Community Schools	Eaton
237	12.4	Norton City Schools	Norton
241	12.3	Midview Local SD	Grafton
242	12.2	Swanton Local SD	Swanton
243	12.1	Berea City SD	Berea
243	12.1	Zane Trace Local SD	Chillicothe
245	12.0	Monroe Local SD	Monroe
246	11.9	Bryan City SD	Bryan
247	11.8	Madison Local SD	Middletown
248	11.5	Genoa Area Local SD	Genoa
249	11.3	Edgewood City SD	Trenton
249	11.3	Madison-Plains Local SD	London
251	11.1	Canal Winchester Local SD	Canal Winchester
252	11.0	Buckeye Local SD	Medina
252	11.0	Northwestern Local SD	Springfield
254	10.9	Huron City Schools	Huron
255	10.8	Carlisle Local SD	Carlisle
256	10.7	Brookville Local SD	Brookville
257	10.5	Champion Local SD	Warren
257	10.5	Clark-Shawnee Local SD	Springfield
257	10.5	Crestwood Local SD	Mantua
260	10.4	Greeneview Local SD	Jamestown
260	10.4	Northwest Local SD	Canal Fulton
260	10.4	West Clermont Local SD	Cincinnati
263	10.3	North Olmsted City Schools	North Olmsted
264	10.1	Howland Local SD	Warren
264	10.1	North Ridgeville City SD	N Ridgeville
264	10.1	Wickliffe City SD	Wickliffe
267	10.0	Lebanon City SD	Lebanon
268	9.9	Benjamin Logan Local SD	Bellefontaine
268	9.9	Firelands Local SD	Oberlin
270	9.8	Painesville Township Local SD	Painesville
270	9.8	Perkins Local SD	Sandusky
272	9.6	Reynoldsburg City SD	Reynoldsburg
273	9.5	Graham Local SD	Saint Paris
273	9.5	Jonathan Alder Local SD	Plain City
275	9.3	Berlin-Milan Local SD	Milan
276	9.0	Dover City SD	Dover
277	8.9	Otsego Local SD	Tontogany
278	8.8	Northmont City SD	Englewood
279	8.7	Clinton-Massie Local SD	Clarksville
279	8.7	Milford Ex Vill SD	Milford
281	8.6	Tallmadge City Schools	Tallmadge
282	8.5	Fairfield City SD	Fairfield
282	8.5	Lakeview Local SD	Cortland
282	8.5	Marysville Exempted Village SD	Marysville
282	8.5	Westerville City SD	Westerville
286	8.4	Southwest Licking Local SD	Etna
287	8.3	Eastwood Local SD	Pemberville
288	8.2	Shaker Heights City SD	Shaker Heights
288	8.2	Twinsburg City SD	Twinsburg
290	8.1	Green Local SD	Green
291	8.0	Brunswick City SD	Brunswick
291	8.0	Perry Local SD	Perry
293	7.8	Big Walnut Local SD	Galena
294	7.5	Vandalia-Butler City SD	Vandalia
295	7.4	Lexington Local SD	Lexington
296	7.3	Maumee City SD	Maumee
297	7.2	Keystone Local SD	Lagrange
297	7.2	Manchester Local SD	Akron
299	7.1	Coldwater Ex Vill SD	Coldwater
299	7.1	Hilliard City SD	Hilliard
299	7.1	Wadsworth City SD	Wadsworth
302	7.0	Mentor Ex Vill SD	Mentor
303	6.9	Chardon Local SD	Chardon
303	6.9	Greenon Local SD	Springfield
303	6.9	Olmsted Falls City SD	Olmsted Falls
303	6.9	Ontario Local SD	Mansfield

303	6.9	Ross Local SD	Hamilton
308	6.7	Avon Local SD	Avon
308	6.7	Buckeye Valley Local SD	Delaware
308	6.7	Gahanna-Jefferson City SD	Gahanna
308	6.7	Kings Local SD	Kings Mills
312	6.6	Little Miami Local SD	Morrow
313	6.4	Amherst Ex Vill SD	Amherst
313	6.4	Northeastern Local SD	Springfield
313	6.4	Ottawa-Glandorf Local SD	Ottawa
316	6.1	Sylvania City SD	Sylvania
316	6.1	Union-Scioto Local SD	Chillicothe
318	6.0	Nordonia Hills City SD	Northfield
319	5.9	Mayfield City SD	Highland Hgts
320	5.8	Lake Local SD	Hartville
321	5.5	Copley-Fairlawn City SD	Copley
322	5.4	North Canton City SD	North Canton
322	5.4	Pickerington Local SD	Pickerington
324	5.3	Sycamore Community City SD	Cincinnati
325	5.2	Loveland City SD	Loveland
325	5.2	Medina City SD	Medina
325	5.2	North Royalton City SD	N Royalton
328	5.0	Tipp City Ex Vill SD	Tipp City
328	5.0	Worthington City SD	Worthington
330	4.8	Jackson Local SD	Massillon
331	4.7	Sugarcreek Local SD	Bellbrook
331	4.7	Valley View Local SD	Germantown
333	4.5	Bexley City SD	Bexley
334	4.4	Strongsville City SD	Strongsville
335	4.3	Centerville City SD	Centerville
335	4.3	Kenston Local SD	Chagrin Falls
335	4.3	Lakota Local SD	Liberty Twp
335	4.3	Mariemont City SD	Cincinnati
339	4.2	Anthony Wayne Local SD	Whitehouse
340	3.9	Olentangy Local SD	Lewis Center
341	3.7	Beavercreek City SD	Beavercreek
341	3.7	Perrysburg Exempted Village	Perrysburg
343	3.6	Stow-Munroe Falls City SD	Stow
344	3.5	Brecksville-Broadview Hgts City	Brecksville
344	3.5	Poland Local SD	Poland
346	3.4	Aurora City SD	Aurora
347	3.2	Bay Village City SD	Bay Village
347	3.2	Highland Local SD	Medina
349	3.1	Avon Lake City Schools	Avon Lake
349	3.1	Beachwood City SD	Beachwood
351	3.0	Canfield Local SD	Canfield
351	3.0	Dublin City SD	Dublin
351	3.0	Westlake City SD	Westlake
354	2.8	Springboro Community City SD	Springboro
355	2.7	Forest Hills Local SD	Cincinnati
355	2.7	Rocky River City SD	Rocky River
357	2.5	Plain Local SD	New Albany
358	2.4	Madeira City SD	Cincinnati
358	2.4	Wyoming City SD	Wyoming
360	2.2	West Geauga Local SD	Chesterland
361	2.0	Revere Local SD	Bath
362	1.8	Solon City SD	Solon
363	1.7	Orange City SD	Cleveland
364	1.6	Mason City SD	Mason
364	1.6	Oak Hills Local SD	Cincinnati
366	1.3	Hudson City SD	Hudson
367	0.8	Indian Hill Ex Vill SD	Cincinnati
367	0.8	Upper Arlington City SD	Upper Arlington
369	0.6	Granville Ex Vill SD	Granville
369	0.6	Oakwood City SD	Dayton
371	0.5	Chagrin Falls Ex Vill SD	Chagrin Falls
372	n/a	Coventry Local SD	Akron
372	n/a	Electronic Classrm of Tomorrow	Columbus
372	n/a	Ohio Virtual Academy	Maumee

Students Eligible for Reduced-Price Lunch

Rank	Percent	District Name	City
1	14.3	Southeast Local SD	Apple Creek
2	14.1	Struthers City SD	Struthers
3	14.0	Rock Hill Local SD	Ironton
4	13.2	Euclid City SD	Euclid
4	13.2	Mad River Local SD	Dayton
6	13.0	Bucyrus City SD	Bucyrus
7	11.6	North College Hill City SD	Cincinnati
8	11.5	Warrensville Heights City SD	Warrensville Hgts
9	11.2	Buckeye Local SD	Ashtabula
9	11.2	Geneva Area City Schools	Geneva
11	11.1	Carrollton Ex Vill SD	Carrollton
11	11.1	Clearview Local SD	Lorain
13	10.7	Fostoria City SD	Fostoria
14	10.5	Maple Heights City SD	Maple Heights
15	10.3	Canton City SD	Canton
15	10.3	Northwest Local SD	Mc Dermott
17	10.2	Hubbard Ex Vill SD	Hubbard
18	10.1	Barberton City SD	Barberton
18	10.1	Dayton City SD	Dayton
18	10.1	Edison Local SD	Hammondsville
18	10.1	Sandusky City SD	Sandusky
22	10.0	Mt Healthy City SD	Cincinnati
22	10.0	New Lexington City SD	New Lexington
24	9.9	Wellington Ex Vill SD	Wellington
24	9.9	Whitehall City SD	Whitehall
26	9.8	Switzerland of Ohio Local SD	Woodsfield
27	9.7	Orrville City SD	Orrville
27	9.7	Ravenna City SD	Ravenna
27	9.7	West Holmes Local SD	Millersburg
30	9.6	Conneaut Area City SD	Conneaut
31	9.5	Clyde-Green Springs Ex Vill SD	Clyde
31	9.5	Fremont City SD	Fremont
31	9.5	Garfield Heights City SD	Garfield Hgts
31	9.5	Piqua City SD	Piqua
35	9.4	Alliance City SD	Alliance
35	9.4	Indian Valley Local SD	Gnadenhutten
35	9.4	Lorain City SD	Lorain
35	9.4	Sandy Valley Local SD	Magnolia
39	9.3	Elyria City SD	Elyria
39	9.3	Girard City SD	Girard
39	9.3	Vinton County Local SD	Mc Arthur
42	9.2	Minford Local SD	Minford
43	9.1	Canton Local SD	Canton
44	9.0	Massillon City SD	Massillon
45	8.9	Eastern Local SD	Sardinia
45	8.9	Minerva Local SD	Minerva
45	8.9	Newton Falls Ex Vill SD	Newton Falls
45	8.9	South-Western City SD	Grove City
49	8.8	Mansfield City SD	Mansfield
49	8.8	Meigs Local SD	Pomeroy
51	8.7	Adams County/Ohio Valley LSD	West Union
51	8.7	Blanchester Local SD	Blanchester
51	8.7	Rolling Hills Local SD	Cambridge
54	8.6	Bellevue City SD	Bellevue
55	8.5	Beaver Local SD	Lisbon
56	8.4	Marion City SD	Marion
56	8.4	Niles City SD	Niles
58	8.3	Benton Carroll Salem Local SD	Oak Harbor
58	8.3	Cleveland Hts-Univ Hts City SD	University Hgts
58	8.3	Fairless Local SD	Navarre
58	8.3	Norwood City SD	Norwood
62	8.2	East Holmes Local Schools	Berlin
62	8.2	Tiffin City SD	Tiffin
62	8.2	Urbana City SD	Urbana
65	8.1	Jefferson Area Local SD	Jefferson
65	8.1	Lancaster City SD	Lancaster
65	8.1	Madison Local SD	Mansfield
68	8.0	Bath Local SD	Lima
68	8.0	Coshocton City SD	Coshocton
68	8.0	Franklin Local SD	Duncan Falls
68	8.0	Harrison Hills City SD	Hopedale
68	8.0	Springfield Local SD	Akron
73	7.9	Logan-Hocking Local SD	Logan
73	7.9	Maysville Local SD	Zanesville
73	7.9	North Fork Local SD	Utica
73	7.9	Pike-Delta-York Local SD	Delta
73	7.9	Van Wert City SD	Van Wert
73	7.9	Warren City SD	Warren
73	7.9	Washington-Nile Local SD	West Portsmouth
80	7.8	Ashtabula Area City SD	Ashtabula
80	7.8	Kenton City SD	Kenton
80	7.8	Lake Local SD	Millbury
80	7.8	Painesville City Local SD	Painesville
80	7.8	Shelby City SD	Shelby
85	7.7	Greenfield Ex Vill SD	Greenfield
85	7.7	Trotwood-Madison City Schools	Trotwood
87	7.6	Sheffield-Sheffield Lake City SD	Sheffield Vlg
88	7.5	Louisville City SD	Louisville
88	7.5	Morgan Local SD	McConnelsville
88	7.5	Norwalk City SD	Norwalk
88	7.5	Ridgewood Local SD	West Lafayette
88	7.5	Westfall Local SD	Williamsport
93	7.4	Goshen Local SD	Goshen
93	7.4	Groveport Madison Local SD	Groveport
93	7.4	Northridge Local SD	Dayton
93	7.4	Sidney City SD	Sidney
93	7.4	Tecumseh Local SD	New Carlisle
98	7.3	Cambridge City SD	Cambridge
98	7.3	Hamilton City SD	Hamilton
98	7.3	Northwest Local SD	Cincinnati
98	7.3	Preble Shawnee Local SD	Camden
98	7.3	Streetsboro City Schools	Streetsboro
103	7.2	Austintown Local SD	Youngstown
103	7.2	Cloverleaf Local SD	Lodi
103	7.2	Middletown City SD	Middletown
103	7.2	Newark City SD	Newark
103	7.2	Parma City SD	Parma
103	7.2	River View Local SD	Warsaw
103	7.2	Western Brown Local SD	Mount Orab
110	7.1	Ashland City SD	Ashland
110	7.1	Cincinnati City SD	Cincinnati
110	7.1	Claymont City SD	Dennison
110	7.1	Cleveland Municipal City SD	Cleveland
110	7.1	Elgin Local SD	Marion
110	7.1	James A Garfield Local SD	Garrettsville
110	7.1	Liberty Local SD	Youngstown
117	7.0	Batavia Local SD	Batavia
117	7.0	Berea City SD	Berea
117	7.0	Cuyahoga Falls City SD	Cuyahoga Falls
117	7.0	Hamilton Local SD	Columbus
117	7.0	Martins Ferry City SD	Martins Ferry
122	6.9	Bedford City SD	Bedford
122	6.9	Rossford Ex Vill SD	Rossford
124	6.8	Campbell City SD	Campbell
124	6.8	East Cleveland City SD	East Cleveland
124	6.8	River Valley Local SD	Caledonia
124	6.8	Wooster City SD	Wooster
128	6.7	Columbus Public Schools	Columbus
128	6.7	Kettering City SD	Kettering
128	6.7	New Richmond Ex Vill SD	New Richmond
128	6.7	Princeton City SD	Cincinnati
128	6.7	Southeast Local SD	Ravenna
128	6.7	United Local SD	Hanoverton
128	6.7	Vermilion Local SD	Vermilion
128	6.7	Wauseon Ex Vill SD	Wauseon
136	6.6	Indian Creek Local SD	Wintersville
136	6.6	Madison Local SD	Madison
136	6.6	Union Local SD	Morristown
136	6.6	Wellston City Schools	Wellston
136	6.6	West Branch Local SD	Beloit
136	6.6	Wickliffe City SD	Wickliffe
142	6.5	Buckeye Local SD	Rayland
142	6.5	Hillsboro City SD	Hillsboro
142	6.5	Springfield Local Schools	Holland
145	6.4	Fairborn City Schools	Fairborn
145	6.4	Lima City SD	Lima
147	6.3	Galion City SD	Galion
147	6.3	Gallia County Local SD	Gallipolis
147	6.3	Greenville City SD	Greenville
147	6.3	Huber Heights City SD	Huber Heights
147	6.3	Northmont City SD	Englewood
147	6.3	Perry Local SD	Massillon
147	6.3	Scioto Valley Local SD	Piketon
147	6.3	Tuscarawas Valley Local SD	Zoarville
147	6.3	Warren Local SD	Vincent
156	6.2	Northern Local SD	Thornville
156	6.2	Zane Trace Local SD	Chillicothe
158	6.1	Oregon City SD	Oregon
158	6.1	Willoughby-Eastlake City SD	Willoughby
158	6.1	Wilmington City SD	Wilmington
158	6.1	Winton Woods City SD	Cincinnati
162	6.0	Bellaire Local SD	Bellaire
162	6.0	Eastwood Local SD	Pemberville
162	6.0	Elida Local SD	Elida
162	6.0	Jackson City SD	Jackson
162	6.0	Wapakoneta City City SD	Wapakoneta
162	6.0	Willard City SD	Willard
168	5.8	Findlay City SD	Findlay
168	5.8	Lakewood City SD	Lakewood
168	5.8	Miami Trace Local SD	Wash Ct House
168	5.8	Perry Local SD	Perry
168	5.8	Portsmouth City SD	Portsmouth
168	5.8	South Point Local SD	South Point
168	5.8	Washington Court House City SD	Wash Ct House
168	5.8	Washington Local Schools	Toledo
176	5.7	Zanesville City SD	Zanesville
177	5.6	Bryan City SD	Bryan
177	5.6	Celina City SD	Celina
177	5.6	Edgewood City SD	Trenton
177	5.6	Madison-Plains Local SD	London
177	5.6	Marlington Local SD	Alliance
177	5.6	Northwest Local SD	Canal Fulton
177	5.6	St Clairsville-Richland City SD	St Clairsville
184	5.5	Black River Local SD	Sullivan
184	5.5	Chillicothe City SD	Chillicothe
184	5.5	Defiance City SD	Defiance
184	5.5	East Liverpool City SD	East Liverpool
184	5.5	Plain Local SD	Canton
184	5.5	South Euclid-Lyndhurst City SD	Lyndhurst
190	5.4	Clear Fork Valley Local SD	Bellville
190	5.4	Fairview Park City SD	Fairview Park
190	5.4	St Marys City SD	Saint Marys
190	5.4	West Carrollton City SD	West Carrollton
194	5.3	Bellefontaine City Schools	Bellefontaine
194	5.3	Boardman Local SD	Youngstown
194	5.3	North Olmsted City Schools	North Olmsted
194	5.3	Triway Local SD	Wooster
194	5.3	Xenia Community City SD	Xenia
199	5.2	Athens City SD	The Plains
199	5.2	East Muskingum Local SD	New Concord
199	5.2	Logan Elm Local SD	Circleville
199	5.2	Mount Vernon City SD	Mount Vernon
199	5.2	Norton City Schools	Norton
199	5.2	Springfield City SD	Springfield

199	5.2	Steubenville City SD	Steubenville
199	5.2	Swanton Local SD	Swanton
199	5.2	Youngstown City SD	Youngstown
208	5.1	Bethel-Tate Local SD	Bethel
208	5.1	Clermont Northeastern Local SD	Batavia
208	5.1	Highland Local SD	Sparta
208	5.1	Howland Local SD	Warren
208	5.1	Indian Lake Local SD	Lewistown
208	5.1	Licking Valley Local SD Sd	Newark
214	5.0	Amanda-Clearcreek Local SD	Amanda
214	5.0	Champion Local SD	Warren
214	5.0	Circleville City SD	Circleville
214	5.0	East Clinton Local SD	Lees Creek
214	5.0	Keystone Local SD	Lagrange
214	5.0	Miamisburg City SD	Miamisburg
214	5.0	Napoleon Area City SD	Napoleon
221	4.9	Field Local SD	Mogadore
221	4.9	Graham Local SD	Saint Paris
221	4.9	Kent City SD	Kent
221	4.9	Milton-Union Exempted Vill Schls	West Milton
221	4.9	Three Rivers Local Schools	Cleves
221	4.9	Toledo City SD	Toledo
221	4.9	Woodridge Local SD	Peninsula
228	4.8	Delaware City SD	Delaware
228	4.8	Midview Local SD	Grafton
228	4.8	Monroe Local SD	Monroe
228	4.8	Paulding Ex Vill SD	Paulding
228	4.8	Troy City SD	Troy
233	4.7	Fairland Local SD	Proctorville
233	4.7	Heath City SD	Heath
233	4.7	Shawnee Local SD	Lima
236	4.6	Alexander Local SD	Albany
236	4.6	Ironton City SD	Ironton
236	4.6	Lakewood Local SD	Hebron
236	4.6	Upper Sandusky Ex Vill SD	Upper Sandusky
236	4.6	Waverly City SD	Waverly
241	4.5	Eaton Community Schools	Eaton
241	4.5	Lexington Local SD	Lexington
241	4.5	Marysville Exempted Village SD	Marysville
241	4.5	Port Clinton City SD	Port Clinton
241	4.5	Tri-Valley Local Schools	Dresden
246	4.4	Franklin City SD	Franklin
246	4.4	London City SD	London
246	4.4	Salem City SD	Salem
249	4.3	Brunswick City SD	Brunswick
249	4.3	Southwest Local SD	Harrison
249	4.3	Vandalia-Butler City SD	Vandalia
252	4.2	Nordonia Hills City SD	Northfield
253	4.1	Berlin-Milan Local SD	Milan
253	4.1	Brookville Local SD	Brookville
253	4.1	Jonathan Alder Local SD	Plain City
253	4.1	Licking Heights Local SD	Summit Station
253	4.1	Maumee City SD	Maumee
253	4.1	Perkins Local SD	Sandusky
253	4.1	Teays Valley Local SD	Ashville
260	4.0	Clark-Shawnee Local SD	Springfield
260	4.0	Fairfield Union Local SD	W Rushville
262	3.9	Amherst Ex Vill SD	Amherst
262	3.9	Clinton-Massie Local SD	Clarksville
262	3.9	Marietta City Schools	Marietta
265	3.8	Coldwater Ex Vill SD	Coldwater
265	3.8	Firelands Local SD	Oberlin
265	3.8	Southwest Licking Local SD	Etna
268	3.7	Gallipolis City SD	Gallipolis
268	3.7	Madison Local SD	Middletown
268	3.7	New Philadelphia City SD	New Philadelphia
271	3.6	Crestwood Local SD	Mantua
272	3.5	Painesville Township Local SD	Painesville
273	3.4	Chardon Local SD	Chardon
273	3.4	North Canton City SD	North Canton
273	3.4	Olmsted Falls City SD	Olmsted Falls
276	3.3	Canal Winchester Local SD	Canal Winchester
276	3.3	Carlisle Local SD	Carlisle
276	3.3	Finneytown Local SD	Cincinnati
276	3.3	Genoa Area Local SD	Genoa
276	3.3	Lebanon City SD	Lebanon
276	3.3	Mentor Ex Vill SD	Mentor
282	3.2	Akron Public Schools	Akron
282	3.2	Big Walnut Local SD	Galena
282	3.2	North Ridgeville City SD	N Ridgeville
282	3.2	Wadsworth City SD	Wadsworth
282	3.2	West Clermont Local SD	Cincinnati
287	3.1	Fairfield City SD	Fairfield
287	3.1	Manchester Local SD	Akron
287	3.1	Milford Ex Vill SD	Milford
287	3.1	West Muskingum Local SD	Zanesville
291	3.0	Bowling Green City SD	Bowling Green
291	3.0	Copley-Fairlawn City SD	Copley
291	3.0	Lake Local SD	Hartville
291	3.0	Northwestern Local SD	Springfield
291	3.0	Talawanda City SD	Oxford
291	3.0	Twinsburg City SD	Twinsburg
297	2.9	Green Local SD	Green
297	2.9	Greeneview Local SD	Jamestown
299	2.8	Benjamin Logan Local SD	Bellefontaine
299	2.8	Huron City Schools	Huron
299	2.8	North Royalton City SD	N Royalton
299	2.8	Ontario Local SD	Mansfield
299	2.8	Tallmadge City Schools	Tallmadge
304	2.7	Greenon Local SD	Springfield
305	2.6	Dover City SD	Dover
305	2.6	Worthington City SD	Worthington
307	2.5	Lakeview Local SD	Cortland
307	2.5	Northeastern Local SD	Springfield
307	2.5	Otsego Local SD	Tontogany
307	2.5	Ottawa-Glandorf Local SD	Ottawa
311	2.4	Jackson Local SD	Massillon
311	2.4	Pickerington Local SD	Pickerington
311	2.4	Valley View Local SD	Germantown
314	2.3	Beavercreek City SD	Beavercreek
314	2.3	Gahanna-Jefferson City SD	Gahanna
314	2.3	Reynoldsburg City SD	Reynoldsburg
314	2.3	Ross Local SD	Hamilton
314	2.3	Westerville City SD	Westerville
319	2.2	Bexley City SD	Bexley
319	2.2	Hilliard City SD	Hilliard
321	2.1	Buckeye Valley Local SD	Delaware
321	2.1	Highland Local SD	Medina
321	2.1	Medina City SD	Medina
321	2.1	Perrysburg Exempted Village	Perrysburg
321	2.1	Strongsville City SD	Strongsville
321	2.1	Sycamore Community City SD	Cincinnati
327	2.0	Avon Lake City Schools	Avon Lake
327	2.0	Avon Local SD	Avon
327	2.0	Canfield Local SD	Canfield
327	2.0	Kenston Local SD	Chagrin Falls
327	2.0	Loveland City SD	Loveland
327	2.0	Poland Local SD	Poland
327	2.0	Stow-Munroe Falls City SD	Stow
334	1.9	Mariemont City SD	Cincinnati
334	1.9	Plain Local SD	New Albany
334	1.9	Shaker Heights City SD	Shaker Heights
334	1.9	Tipp City Ex Vill SD	Tipp City
338	1.8	Bay Village City SD	Bay Village
338	1.8	Brecksville-Broadview Hgts City	Brecksville
338	1.8	Kings Local SD	Kings Mills
338	1.8	Sylvania City SD	Sylvania
342	1.7	Buckeye Local SD	Medina
342	1.7	Little Miami Local SD	Morrow
342	1.7	West Geauga Local SD	Chesterland
342	1.7	Westlake City SD	Westlake
346	1.6	Mayfield City SD	Highland Hgts
346	1.6	Union-Scioto Local SD	Chillicothe
348	1.4	Aurora City SD	Aurora
348	1.4	Solon City SD	Solon
350	1.3	Beachwood City SD	Beachwood
350	1.3	Mason City SD	Mason
350	1.3	Olentangy Local SD	Lewis Center
353	1.2	Forest Hills Local SD	Cincinnati
353	1.2	Lakota Local SD	Liberty Twp
353	1.2	Sugarcreek Local SD	Bellbrook
356	1.1	Anthony Wayne Local SD	Whitehouse
356	1.1	Springboro Community City SD	Springboro
356	1.1	Wyoming City SD	Wyoming
359	1.0	Centerville City SD	Centerville
359	1.0	Dublin City SD	Dublin
359	1.0	Rocky River City SD	Rocky River
362	0.6	Granville Ex Vill SD	Granville
362	0.6	Madeira City SD	Cincinnati
362	0.6	Oak Hills Local SD	Cincinnati
362	0.6	Revere Local SD	Bath
366	0.5	Hudson City SD	Hudson
366	0.5	Orange City SD	Cleveland
366	0.5	Upper Arlington City SD	Upper Arlington
369	0.4	Oakwood City SD	Dayton
370	0.2	Indian Hill Ex Vill SD	Cincinnati
371	0.1	Chagrin Falls Ex Vill SD	Chagrin Falls
372	n/a	Coventry Local SD	Akron
372	n/a	Electronic Classrm of Tomorrow	Columbus
372	n/a	Ohio Virtual Academy	Maumee

Student/Teacher Ratio

Rank	Ratio	District Name	City
1	39.6	Ohio Virtual Academy	Maumee
2	36.6	Electronic Classrm of Tomorrow	Columbus
3	21.6	Lake Local SD	Millbury
3	21.6	Piqua City SD	Piqua
5	21.0	Eastwood Local SD	Pemberville
6	20.5	Poland Local SD	Poland
7	20.3	Bath Local SD	Lima
7	20.3	Norwalk City SD	Norwalk
9	20.0	Jonathan Alder Local SD	Plain City
9	20.0	Lebanon City SD	Lebanon
11	19.9	Rolling Hills Local SD	Cambridge
11	19.9	Sugarcreek Local SD	Bellbrook
13	19.8	Wadsworth City SD	Wadsworth
14	19.6	Bethel-Tate Local SD	Bethel
14	19.6	Midview Local SD	Grafton
14	19.6	Reynoldsburg City SD	Reynoldsburg
14	19.6	Wapakoneta City City SD	Wapakoneta
18	19.5	Garfield Heights City SD	Garfield Hgts
19	19.4	Clinton-Massie Local SD	Clarksville
19	19.4	Geneva Area City Schools	Geneva
19	19.4	Genoa Area Local SD	Genoa
19	19.4	Nordonia Hills City SD	Northfield
23	19.3	Beavercreek City SD	Beavercreek
23	19.3	Ontario Local SD	Mansfield
25	19.2	Lakeview Local SD	Cortland
25	19.2	Madison Local SD	Madison
25	19.2	Painesville Township Local SD	Painesville
28	19.1	Amherst Ex Vill SD	Amherst
28	19.1	Brookville Local SD	Brookville
28	19.1	Clermont Northeastern Local SD	Batavia
28	19.1	Jackson City SD	Jackson
28	19.1	Southwest Local SD	Harrison
28	19.1	Springboro Community City SD	Springboro
28	19.1	Tri-Valley Local Schools	Dresden
35	19.0	Keystone Local SD	Lagrange
35	19.0	Manchester Local SD	Akron
35	19.0	Shawnee Local SD	Lima
35	19.0	Troy City SD	Troy
39	18.9	Fairfield City SD	Fairfield
39	18.9	Fairfield Union Local SD	W Rushville
39	18.9	Fostoria City SD	Fostoria
39	18.9	Maysville Local SD	Zanesville
39	18.9	Perry Local SD	Massillon
39	18.9	Zane Trace Local SD	Chillicothe
45	18.7	Northmont City SD	Englewood
46	18.6	Chillicothe City SD	Chillicothe
46	18.6	West Branch Local SD	Beloit
48	18.5	Elida Local SD	Elida
48	18.5	Fairland Local SD	Proctorville
48	18.5	Granville Ex Vill SD	Granville
48	18.5	Loveland City SD	Loveland
48	18.5	Scioto Valley Local SD	Piketon
48	18.5	United Local SD	Hanoverton
54	18.4	Coventry Local SD	Akron
54	18.4	Firelands Local SD	Oberlin
54	18.4	Fremont City SD	Fremont
54	18.4	Milford Ex Vill SD	Milford
54	18.4	Northwestern Local SD	Springfield
59	18.3	Clark-Shawnee Local SD	Springfield
59	18.3	Goshen Local SD	Goshen
59	18.3	Oak Hills Local SD	Cincinnati
59	18.3	Union-Scioto Local SD	Chillicothe
59	18.3	Wauseon Ex Vill SD	Wauseon
59	18.3	Western Brown Local SD	Mount Orab
65	18.2	Amanda-Clearcreek Local SD	Amanda
65	18.2	Greeneview Local SD	Jamestown
65	18.2	Heath City SD	Heath
68	18.1	Anthony Wayne Local SD	Whitehouse
68	18.1	Benton Carroll Salem Local SD	Oak Harbor
68	18.1	Cloverleaf Local SD	Lodi
68	18.1	Jefferson Area Local SD	Jefferson
68	18.1	North Fork Local SD	Utica
68	18.1	Ottawa-Glandorf Local SD	Ottawa
68	18.1	Pike-Delta-York Local SD	Delta
68	18.1	Stow-Munroe Falls City SD	Stow
68	18.1	West Clermont Local SD	Cincinnati
77	18.0	Eaton Community Schools	Eaton
77	18.0	Lexington Local SD	Lexington
77	18.0	Licking Heights Local SD	Summit Station
77	18.0	Westerville City SD	Westerville
81	17.9	Brunswick City SD	Brunswick
81	17.9	Green Local SD	Green
81	17.9	Highland Local SD	Medina
81	17.9	Jackson Local SD	Massillon
81	17.9	Kings Local SD	Kings Mills
81	17.9	Liberty Local SD	Youngstown
81	17.9	Marietta City Schools	Marietta
81	17.9	Mason City SD	Mason
81	17.9	North Royalton City SD	N Royalton
81	17.9	Otsego Local SD	Tontogany
81	17.9	Strongsville City SD	Strongsville
92	17.8	Little Miami Local SD	Morrow
92	17.8	Pickerington Local SD	Pickerington
92	17.8	Waverly City SD	Waverly
95	17.7	Beaver Local SD	Lisbon
95	17.7	Edgewood City SD	Trenton
95	17.7	Girard City SD	Girard
95	17.7	Groveport Madison Local SD	Groveport
95	17.7	Hubbard Ex Vill SD	Hubbard
95	17.7	Logan-Hocking Local SD	Logan
95	17.7	Minford Local SD	Minford
95	17.7	North College Hill City SD	Cincinnati
95	17.7	Ridgewood Local SD	West Lafayette

95	17.7	Ross Local SD	Hamilton
95	17.7	Swanton Local SD	Swanton
95	17.7	Tipp City Ex Vill SD	Tipp City
107	17.6	Black River Local SD	Sullivan
107	17.6	Clyde-Green Springs Ex Vill SD	Clyde
107	17.6	Lake Local SD	Hartville
107	17.6	Lancaster City SD	Lancaster
107	17.6	New Lexington City SD	New Lexington
107	17.6	Sidney City SD	Sidney
107	17.6	St Marys City SD	Saint Marys
114	17.5	Aurora City SD	Aurora
114	17.5	Carrollton Ex Vill SD	Carrollton
114	17.5	Clear Fork Valley Local SD	Bellville
114	17.5	Fairborn City Schools	Fairborn
114	17.5	Forest Hills Local SD	Cincinnati
114	17.5	Highland Local SD	Sparta
114	17.5	Indian Creek Local SD	Wintersville
114	17.5	Southeast Local SD	Ravenna
114	17.5	Wilmington City SD	Wilmington
123	17.4	Crestwood Local SD	Mantua
123	17.4	East Muskingum Local SD	New Concord
123	17.4	Field Local SD	Mogadore
123	17.4	Franklin City SD	Franklin
123	17.4	Huron City Schools	Huron
123	17.4	River Valley Local SD	Caledonia
123	17.4	Valley View Local SD	Germantown
123	17.4	West Muskingum Local SD	Zanesville
123	17.4	Willard City SD	Willard
132	17.3	Austintown Local SD	Youngstown
132	17.3	Benjamin Logan Local SD	Bellefontaine
132	17.3	Brecksville-Broadview Hgts City	Brecksville
132	17.3	East Cleveland City SD	East Cleveland
132	17.3	East Clinton Local SD	Lees Creek
132	17.3	Miamisburg City SD	Miamisburg
132	17.3	Northern Local SD	Thornville
132	17.3	Northwest Local SD	Cincinnati
132	17.3	Twinsburg City SD	Twinsburg
141	17.2	Batavia Local SD	Batavia
141	17.2	Marlington Local SD	Alliance
141	17.2	Tuscarawas Valley Local SD	Zoarville
141	17.2	Wellington Ex Vill SD	Wellington
145	17.1	Buckeye Local SD	Medina
145	17.1	Buckeye Valley Local SD	Delaware
145	17.1	Canfield Local SD	Canfield
145	17.1	Circleville City SD	Circleville
145	17.1	Graham Local SD	Saint Paris
145	17.1	Greenon Local SD	Springfield
145	17.1	Madison-Plains Local SD	London
145	17.1	Norton City Schools	Norton
145	17.1	Sheffield-Sheffield Lake City SD	Sheffield Vlg
145	17.1	Southwest Licking Local SD	Etna
145	17.1	Three Rivers Local Schools	Cleves
145	17.1	Vermilion Local SD	Vermilion
145	17.1	Willoughby-Eastlake City SD	Willoughby
158	17.0	Carlisle Local SD	Carlisle
158	17.0	Eastern Local SD	Sardinia
158	17.0	Franklin Local SD	Duncan Falls
158	17.0	Louisville City SD	Louisville
158	17.0	Miami Trace Local SD	Wash Ct House
158	17.0	Milton-Union Exempted Vill Schls	West Milton
158	17.0	Minerva Local SD	Minerva
158	17.0	Mount Vernon City SD	Mount Vernon
158	17.0	Niles City SD	Niles
158	17.0	Olmsted Falls City SD	Olmsted Falls
158	17.0	Struthers City SD	Struthers
158	17.0	Tiffin City SD	Tiffin
158	17.0	Triway Local SD	Wooster
171	16.9	Ashland City SD	Ashland
171	16.9	Coldwater Ex Vill SD	Coldwater
171	16.9	Hamilton City SD	Hamilton
171	16.9	Lakota Local SD	Liberty Twp
171	16.9	Trotwood-Madison City Schools	Trotwood
176	16.8	Chardon Local SD	Chardon
176	16.8	Claymont City SD	Dennison
176	16.8	Euclid City SD	Euclid
176	16.8	North Canton City SD	North Canton
176	16.8	Northwest Local SD	Mc Dermott
181	16.7	Howland Local SD	Warren
181	16.7	James A Garfield Local SD	Garrettsville
181	16.7	Martins Ferry City SD	Martins Ferry
181	16.7	Newark City SD	Newark
181	16.7	Newton Falls Ex Vill SD	Newton Falls
181	16.7	Parma City SD	Parma
181	16.7	Westfall Local SD	Williamsport
188	16.6	Avon Local SD	Avon
188	16.6	Licking Valley Local SD Sd	Newark
188	16.6	Logan Elm Local SD	Circleville
188	16.6	Olentangy Local SD	Lewis Center
192	16.5	Bellevue City SD	Bellevue
192	16.5	Buckeye Local SD	Ashtabula
192	16.5	Bucyrus City SD	Bucyrus
192	16.5	Maple Heights City SD	Maple Heights
192	16.5	Rocky River City SD	Rocky River
192	16.5	Springfield Local Schools	Holland
192	16.5	Warren Local SD	Vincent
192	16.5	West Geauga Local SD	Chesterland
200	16.4	Berea City SD	Berea
200	16.4	Berlin-Milan Local SD	Milan
200	16.4	Boardman Local SD	Youngstown
200	16.4	Columbus Public Schools	Columbus
200	16.4	Lakewood City SD	Lakewood
200	16.4	Lorain City SD	Lorain
200	16.4	Madison Local SD	Middletown
200	16.4	Northwest Local SD	Canal Fulton
200	16.4	River View Local SD	Warsaw
200	16.4	South Point Local SD	South Point
200	16.4	Teays Valley Local SD	Ashville
200	16.4	Tecumseh Local SD	New Carlisle
212	16.3	Hamilton Local SD	Columbus
212	16.3	Perkins Local SD	Sandusky
212	16.3	Urbana City SD	Urbana
215	16.2	Ashtabula Area City SD	Ashtabula
215	16.2	Canal Winchester Local SD	Canal Winchester
215	16.2	Celina City SD	Celina
215	16.2	Copley-Fairlawn City SD	Copley
215	16.2	West Holmes Local SD	Millersburg
220	16.1	Conneaut Area City SD	Conneaut
221	16.0	Coshocton City SD	Coshocton
221	16.0	Edison Local SD	Hammondsville
221	16.0	Plain Local SD	New Albany
221	16.0	Shelby City SD	Shelby
221	16.0	Westlake City SD	Westlake
226	15.9	Avon Lake City Schools	Avon Lake
226	15.9	Bryan City SD	Bryan
226	15.9	Delaware City SD	Delaware
226	15.9	Harrison Hills City SD	Hopedale
226	15.9	Marion City SD	Marion
226	15.9	Orrville City SD	Orrville
226	15.9	South-Western City SD	Grove City
226	15.9	Washington-Nile Local SD	West Portsmouth
234	15.8	Campbell City SD	Campbell
234	15.8	Champion Local SD	Warren
234	15.8	Dover City SD	Dover
234	15.8	Indian Lake Local SD	Lewistown
234	15.8	Marysville Exempted Village SD	Marysville
234	15.8	Napoleon Area City SD	Napoleon
234	15.8	Perrysburg Exempted Village	Perrysburg
234	15.8	Plain Local SD	Canton
234	15.8	Revere Local SD	Bath
234	15.8	Vinton County Local SD	Mc Arthur
234	15.8	Xenia Community City SD	Xenia
245	15.7	Galion City SD	Galion
245	15.7	Greenfield Ex Vill SD	Greenfield
245	15.7	Kenton City SD	Kenton
245	15.7	North Ridgeville City SD	N Ridgeville
245	15.7	Perry Local SD	Perry
245	15.7	Steubenville City SD	Steubenville
245	15.7	Sylvania City SD	Sylvania
245	15.7	Talawanda City SD	Oxford
253	15.6	Big Walnut Local SD	Galena
253	15.6	Gallipolis City SD	Gallipolis
253	15.6	Hudson City SD	Hudson
253	15.6	Medina City SD	Medina
253	15.6	Mentor Ex Vill SD	Mentor
253	15.6	New Philadelphia City SD	New Philadelphia
253	15.6	Northeastern Local SD	Springfield
253	15.6	Solon City SD	Solon
253	15.6	Wellston City Schools	Wellston
253	15.6	Whitehall City SD	Whitehall
263	15.5	Bowling Green City SD	Bowling Green
263	15.5	Canton City SD	Canton
263	15.5	Dublin City SD	Dublin
263	15.5	London City SD	London
263	15.5	Port Clinton City SD	Port Clinton
263	15.5	Tallmadge City Schools	Tallmadge
263	15.5	Van Wert City SD	Van Wert
263	15.5	West Carrollton City SD	West Carrollton
271	15.4	Bedford City SD	Bedford
271	15.4	Blanchester Local SD	Blanchester
271	15.4	Hilliard City SD	Hilliard
271	15.4	Kettering City SD	Kettering
271	15.4	Monroe Local SD	Monroe
271	15.4	New Richmond Ex Vill SD	New Richmond
271	15.4	Salem City SD	Salem
278	15.3	Clearview Local SD	Lorain
278	15.3	Defiance City SD	Defiance
278	15.3	Finneytown Local SD	Cincinnati
278	15.3	Hillsboro City SD	Hillsboro
278	15.3	Rossford Ex Vill SD	Rossford
278	15.3	Springfield Local SD	Akron
284	15.2	Adams County/Ohio Valley LSD	West Union
284	15.2	Cambridge City SD	Cambridge
284	15.2	Fairless Local SD	Navarre
284	15.2	Ravenna City SD	Ravenna
284	15.2	Upper Sandusky Ex Vill SD	Upper Sandusky
284	15.2	Washington Local Schools	Toledo
290	15.1	Kenston Local SD	Chagrin Falls
290	15.1	Oregon City SD	Oregon
290	15.1	Portsmouth City SD	Portsmouth
290	15.1	Sandy Valley Local SD	Magnolia
290	15.1	South Euclid-Lyndhurst City SD	Lyndhurst
290	15.1	Springfield City SD	Springfield
296	15.0	Bellefontaine City Schools	Bellefontaine
296	15.0	Canton Local SD	Canton
296	15.0	Centerville City SD	Centerville
296	15.0	Cuyahoga Falls City SD	Cuyahoga Falls
296	15.0	East Holmes Local Schools	Berlin
296	15.0	Elgin Local SD	Marion
296	15.0	Gallia County Local SD	Gallipolis
296	15.0	Mad River Local SD	Dayton
296	15.0	Madeira City SD	Cincinnati
296	15.0	Southeast Local SD	Apple Creek
296	15.0	St Clairsville-Richland City SD	St Clairsville
296	15.0	Vandalia-Butler City SD	Vandalia
296	15.0	Washington Court House City SD	Wash Ct House
309	14.9	Alliance City SD	Alliance
309	14.9	Bay Village City SD	Bay Village
309	14.9	Norwood City SD	Norwood
309	14.9	Painesville City Local SD	Painesville
313	14.8	Buckeye Local SD	Rayland
313	14.8	Findlay City SD	Findlay
313	14.8	Greenville City SD	Greenville
313	14.8	Lakewood Local SD	Hebron
313	14.8	Middletown City SD	Middletown
313	14.8	Morgan Local SD	McConnelsville
313	14.8	Worthington City SD	Worthington
313	14.8	Wyoming City SD	Wyoming
321	14.7	Indian Hill Ex Vill SD	Cincinnati
321	14.7	Indian Valley Local SD	Gnadenhutten
321	14.7	Ironton City SD	Ironton
321	14.7	Rock Hill Local SD	Ironton
321	14.7	Warrensville Heights City SD	Warrensville Hgts
326	14.6	Barberton City SD	Barberton
326	14.6	Mt Healthy City SD	Cincinnati
326	14.6	North Olmsted City Schools	North Olmsted
326	14.6	Paulding Ex Vill SD	Paulding
326	14.6	Winton Woods City SD	Cincinnati
326	14.6	Zanesville City SD	Zanesville
332	14.5	Alexander Local SD	Albany
332	14.5	Bellaire Local SD	Bellaire
332	14.5	Preble Shawnee Local SD	Camden
335	14.4	Chagrin Falls Ex Vill SD	Chagrin Falls
335	14.4	Elyria City SD	Elyria
335	14.4	Maumee City SD	Maumee
335	14.4	Northridge Local SD	Dayton
335	14.4	Sycamore Community City SD	Cincinnati
340	14.2	Cleveland Hts-Univ Hts City SD	University Hgts
340	14.2	Madison Local SD	Mansfield
340	14.2	Sandusky City SD	Sandusky
343	14.1	Switzerland of Ohio Local SD	Woodsfield
343	14.1	Warren City SD	Warren
343	14.1	Wooster City SD	Wooster
346	14.0	Woodridge Local SD	Peninsula
347	13.9	Bexley City SD	Bexley
347	13.9	East Liverpool City SD	East Liverpool
347	13.9	Fairview Park City SD	Fairview Park
347	13.9	Mariemont City SD	Cincinnati
347	13.9	Massillon City SD	Massillon
347	13.9	Oakwood City SD	Dayton
347	13.9	Streetsboro City Schools	Streetsboro
347	13.9	Upper Arlington City SD	Upper Arlington
347	13.9	Wickliffe City SD	Wickliffe
356	13.7	Lima City SD	Lima
356	13.7	Union Local SD	Morristown
358	13.6	Shaker Heights City SD	Shaker Heights
358	13.6	Toledo City SD	Toledo
360	13.5	Cleveland Municipal City SD	Cleveland
360	13.5	Mansfield City SD	Mansfield
362	13.4	Gahanna-Jefferson City SD	Gahanna
363	13.3	Athens City SD	The Plains
363	13.3	Youngstown City SD	Youngstown
365	13.2	Meigs Local SD	Pomeroy
366	13.1	Mayfield City SD	Highland Hgts
367	13.0	Dayton City SD	Dayton
368	12.8	Cincinnati City SD	Cincinnati
369	12.7	Kent City SD	Kent
370	12.6	Princeton City SD	Cincinnati
371	12.2	Orange City SD	Cleveland
372	10.8	Huber Heights City SD	Huber Heights
373	10.5	Beachwood City SD	Beachwood
374	9.2	Akron Public Schools	Akron

Student/Librarian Ratio

Rank	Ratio	District Name	City
1	13,963.3	Amherst Ex Vill SD	Amherst
2	9,580.0	Indian Valley Local SD	Gnadenhutten
3	5,903.0	Northmont City SD	Englewood

4	5,259.5	South-Western City SD	Grove City
5	4,568.0	Ashtabula Area City SD	Ashtabula
5	4,568.0	West Clermont Local SD	Cincinnati
7	4,498.0	Delaware City SD	Delaware
8	3,739.0	Madison Local SD	Madison
9	3,518.0	Vandalia-Butler City SD	Vandalia
10	3,345.6	Geneva Area City Schools	Geneva
11	3,307.0	New Philadelphia City SD	New Philadelphia
12	3,303.5	Reynoldsburg City SD	Reynoldsburg
13	3,254.0	Copley-Fairlawn City SD	Copley
14	3,239.5	Findlay City SD	Findlay
15	3,160.0	Wapakoneta City City SD	Wapakoneta
16	3,116.0	Celina City SD	Celina
17	3,093.0	Kenston Local SD	Chagrin Falls
18	2,975.0	Athens City SD	The Plains
19	2,932.0	Carrollton Ex Vill SD	Carrollton
20	2,924.0	Canton City SD	Canton
21	2,878.3	Mason City SD	Mason
22	2,745.0	Jackson City SD	Jackson
23	2,738.0	Marlington Local SD	Alliance
24	2,713.5	Fairborn City Schools	Fairborn
25	2,689.0	Edison Local SD	Hammondsville
26	2,659.0	Norwood City SD	Norwood
27	2,657.0	Shawnee Local SD	Lima
28	2,647.5	Miamisburg City SD	Miamisburg
29	2,633.0	Big Walnut Local SD	Galena
29	2,633.0	Vinton County Local SD	Mc Arthur
31	2,598.0	Dover City SD	Dover
32	2,591.0	Elida Local SD	Elida
33	2,580.0	Ross Local SD	Hamilton
34	2,558.0	Norton City Schools	Norton
35	2,541.0	River View Local SD	Warsaw
36	2,538.0	Canton Local SD	Canton
37	2,529.0	Kettering City SD	Kettering
38	2,527.0	Conneaut Area City SD	Conneaut
39	2,462.0	North Canton City SD	North Canton
40	2,453.0	Buckeye Local SD	Medina
41	2,443.0	West Branch Local SD	Beloit
42	2,433.0	Middletown City SD	Middletown
43	2,418.0	Franklin Local SD	Duncan Falls
44	2,415.0	Buckeye Local SD	Rayland
45	2,411.0	New Richmond Ex Vill SD	New Richmond
46	2,401.8	Hamilton City SD	Hamilton
47	2,366.0	Gallipolis City SD	Gallipolis
48	2,362.0	Willard City SD	Willard
49	2,360.5	Marysville Exempted Village SD	Marysville
50	2,356.0	Urbana City SD	Urbana
51	2,347.5	Wadsworth City SD	Wadsworth
52	2,339.0	Fostoria City SD	Fostoria
53	2,334.0	Eaton Community Schools	Eaton
54	2,323.0	Logan Elm Local SD	Circleville
55	2,319.0	Greenfield Ex Vill SD	Greenfield
56	2,297.0	Clyde-Green Springs Ex Vill SD	Clyde
57	2,290.0	Van Wert City SD	Van Wert
58	2,287.0	Buckeye Local SD	Ashtabula
59	2,285.0	North Olmsted City Schools	North Olmsted
60	2,266.7	Huber Heights City SD	Huber Heights
61	2,257.0	Jefferson Area Local SD	Jefferson
62	2,244.0	Painesville Township Local SD	Painesville
63	2,238.0	Galion City SD	Galion
64	2,230.5	Troy City SD	Troy
65	2,226.0	Rolling Hills Local SD	Cambridge
66	2,222.0	Firelands Local SD	Oberlin
67	2,202.0	Minerva Local SD	Minerva
68	2,174.0	Perrysburg Exempted Village	Perrysburg
68	2,174.0	Waverly City SD	Waverly
70	2,160.0	Springboro Community City SD	Springboro
71	2,150.0	Triway Local SD	Wooster
72	2,145.0	Kenton City SD	Kenton
73	2,140.0	Euclid City SD	Euclid
74	2,133.0	Wauseon Ex Vill SD	Wauseon
75	2,131.4	Northwest Local SD	Cincinnati
76	2,087.0	Streetsboro City Schools	Streetsboro
77	2,064.0	Lorain City SD	Lorain
78	2,020.0	Rossford Ex Vill SD	Rossford
79	2,014.0	Logan-Hocking Local SD	Logan
80	2,008.0	Licking Heights Local SD	Summit Station
81	2,004.0	Struthers City SD	Struthers
82	1,992.0	Indian Lake Local SD	Lewistown
83	1,980.0	Greenon Local SD	Springfield
84	1,978.0	Eastwood Local SD	Pemberville
85	1,977.5	Piqua City SD	Piqua
86	1,971.0	Port Clinton City SD	Port Clinton
87	1,970.3	Washington Local Schools	Toledo
88	1,958.0	Fairfield Union Local SD	W Rushville
89	1,954.0	Union-Scioto Local SD	Chillicothe
90	1,943.5	Nordonia Hills City SD	Northfield
91	1,943.0	West Carrollton City SD	West Carrollton
92	1,939.5	Anthony Wayne Local SD	Whitehouse
93	1,883.0	Fairless Local SD	Navarre
94	1,874.0	Berlin-Milan Local SD	Milan
95	1,866.0	South Point Local SD	South Point
96	1,857.0	East Holmes Local Schools	Berlin
97	1,853.7	Jackson Local SD	Massillon
98	1,843.0	Clear Fork Valley Local SD	Bellville
99	1,834.0	Maple Heights City SD	Maple Heights
100	1,831.0	Keystone Local SD	Lagrange
100	1,831.0	River Valley Local SD	Caledonia
102	1,819.0	Liberty Local SD	Youngstown
103	1,814.0	Northridge Local SD	Dayton
104	1,813.5	Brunswick City SD	Brunswick
105	1,812.7	Miami Trace Local SD	Wash Ct House
106	1,809.0	Jonathan Alder Local SD	Plain City
106	1,809.0	Paulding Ex Vill SD	Paulding
108	1,789.0	Tecumseh Local SD	New Carlisle
109	1,787.0	Finneytown Local SD	Cincinnati
110	1,785.5	Mad River Local SD	Dayton
111	1,782.5	Cloverleaf Local SD	Lodi
112	1,781.0	Highland Local SD	Sparta
113	1,775.2	Willoughby-Eastlake City SD	Willoughby
114	1,774.0	Clinton-Massie Local SD	Clarksville
115	1,771.0	Blanchester Local SD	Blanchester
116	1,769.0	Girard City SD	Girard
117	1,766.5	Madison Local SD	Mansfield
118	1,763.5	Southwest Licking Local SD	Etna
119	1,744.0	Tuscarawas Valley Local SD	Zoarville
120	1,737.0	Genoa Area Local SD	Genoa
121	1,721.3	Warren City SD	Warren
122	1,718.0	Trotwood-Madison City Schools	Trotwood
123	1,717.5	Midview Local SD	Grafton
124	1,716.0	Lake Local SD	Millbury
125	1,701.0	Greenville City SD	Greenville
126	1,699.3	Adams County/Ohio Valley LSD	West Union
127	1,694.5	Akron Public Schools	Akron
128	1,682.0	Austintown Local SD	Youngstown
129	1,679.5	Lake Local SD	Hartville
130	1,679.0	Scioto Valley Local SD	Piketon
131	1,664.7	Lima City SD	Lima
132	1,664.0	Huron City Schools	Huron
133	1,655.0	Westfall Local SD	Williamsport
134	1,653.0	Amanda-Clearcreek Local SD	Amanda
135	1,645.0	Greeneview Local SD	Jamestown
136	1,637.0	Louisville City SD	Louisville
137	1,632.3	Boardman Local SD	Youngstown
138	1,627.0	Madison-Plains Local SD	London
139	1,623.0	Coldwater Ex Vill SD	Coldwater
140	1,618.0	Perry Local SD	Massillon
141	1,617.5	Ravenna City SD	Ravenna
142	1,616.5	Teays Valley Local SD	Ashville
143	1,601.0	Marietta City Schools	Marietta
144	1,600.5	Little Miami Local SD	Morrow
145	1,597.5	Wilmington City SD	Wilmington
146	1,592.3	Youngstown City SD	Youngstown
147	1,590.0	Madison Local SD	Middletown
148	1,589.0	Zane Trace Local SD	Chillicothe
149	1,588.4	Southwest Local SD	Harrison
150	1,579.0	St Clairsville-Richland City SD	St Clairsville
151	1,575.0	Tri-Valley Local Schools	Dresden
152	1,574.0	Pike-Delta-York Local SD	Delta
153	1,571.0	East Clinton Local SD	Lees Creek
154	1,570.0	Wickliffe City SD	Wickliffe
155	1,568.0	Sandy Valley Local SD	Magnolia
156	1,566.4	Sylvania City SD	Sylvania
157	1,552.0	Talawanda City SD	Oxford
158	1,548.5	Canfield Local SD	Canfield
159	1,543.0	Eastern Local SD	Sardinia
160	1,541.0	Dayton City SD	Dayton
161	1,538.0	North College Hill City SD	Cincinnati
161	1,538.0	Springfield Local SD	Akron
163	1,532.3	Fremont City SD	Fremont
164	1,530.5	Plain Local SD	Canton
165	1,520.0	Manchester Local SD	Akron
165	1,520.0	Newton Falls Ex Vill SD	Newton Falls
167	1,515.7	Massillon City SD	Massillon
168	1,512.0	Tiffin City SD	Tiffin
169	1,503.0	Clearview Local SD	Lorain
170	1,501.0	Ridgewood Local SD	West Lafayette
171	1,494.5	Hamilton Local SD	Columbus
172	1,461.6	Parma City SD	Parma
173	1,444.7	Mayfield City SD	Highland Hgts
174	1,436.9	Toledo City SD	Toledo
175	1,433.7	Mount Vernon City SD	Mount Vernon
176	1,430.5	Niles City SD	Niles
177	1,426.0	Loveland City SD	Loveland
178	1,425.8	Beavercreek City SD	Beavercreek
179	1,424.7	Barberton City SD	Barberton
180	1,417.0	Zanesville City SD	Zanesville
181	1,409.0	Sandusky City SD	Sandusky
182	1,403.5	Revere Local SD	Bath
183	1,400.5	Bellefontaine City Schools	Bellefontaine
184	1,398.0	Marion City SD	Marion
185	1,393.8	Newark City SD	Newark
186	1,388.3	Green Local SD	Green
187	1,381.3	Wooster City SD	Wooster
188	1,380.0	Tallmadge City Schools	Tallmadge
189	1,369.5	Cambridge City SD	Cambridge
190	1,364.0	Fairfield City SD	Fairfield
191	1,358.5	Painesville City Local SD	Painesville
192	1,355.3	Oak Hills Local SD	Cincinnati
193	1,349.8	Cuyahoga Falls City SD	Cuyahoga Falls
194	1,349.6	Springfield Local Schools	Holland
195	1,346.0	Warren Local SD	Vincent
196	1,333.1	Springfield City SD	Springfield
197	1,329.6	Alliance City SD	Alliance
198	1,304.5	Tipp City Ex Vill SD	Tipp City
199	1,300.5	Xenia Community City SD	Xenia
200	1,296.7	Bedford City SD	Bedford
201	1,287.3	Sidney City SD	Sidney
202	1,284.6	North Royalton City SD	N Royalton
203	1,283.0	Kings Local SD	Kings Mills
204	1,273.5	Clark-Shawnee Local SD	Springfield
205	1,272.3	Ashland City SD	Ashland
206	1,272.0	Gallia County Local SD	Gallipolis
207	1,270.5	Defiance City SD	Defiance
208	1,268.5	West Geauga Local SD	Chesterland
209	1,262.7	Mt Healthy City SD	Cincinnati
210	1,262.5	Goshen Local SD	Goshen
211	1,257.0	Poland Local SD	Poland
212	1,246.0	Vermilion Local SD	Vermilion
213	1,235.0	Avon Local SD	Avon
214	1,227.5	Beaver Local SD	Lisbon
215	1,223.5	Northwest Local SD	Canal Fulton
216	1,222.8	Strongsville City SD	Strongsville
217	1,222.5	Salem City SD	Salem
218	1,220.8	Lancaster City SD	Lancaster
219	1,216.0	Stow-Munroe Falls City SD	Stow
220	1,210.7	West Muskingum Local SD	Zanesville
221	1,195.0	Lebanon City SD	Lebanon
222	1,194.0	Bellevue City SD	Bellevue
223	1,193.5	Napoleon Area City SD	Napoleon
224	1,188.9	Pickerington Local SD	Pickerington
225	1,173.0	Claymont City SD	Dennison
226	1,169.5	Northern Local SD	Thornville
227	1,167.0	Coventry Local SD	Akron
228	1,166.5	Brecksville-Broadview Hgts City	Brecksville
229	1,161.0	Indian Creek Local SD	Wintersville
230	1,160.4	Mansfield City SD	Mansfield
231	1,157.5	Washington Court House City SD	Wash Ct House
232	1,144.0	Bryan City SD	Bryan
233	1,133.5	Perkins Local SD	Sandusky
234	1,132.5	Maysville Local SD	Zanesville
235	1,127.0	Shelby City SD	Shelby
236	1,125.3	Chillicothe City SD	Chillicothe
237	1,118.5	Buckeye Valley Local SD	Delaware
238	1,113.3	Olmsted Falls City SD	Olmsted Falls
239	1,105.0	Southeast Local SD	Ravenna
240	1,088.7	Forest Hills Local SD	Cincinnati
241	1,083.0	Portsmouth City SD	Portsmouth
242	1,082.0	Three Rivers Local Schools	Cleves
243	1,076.3	Howland Local SD	Warren
244	1,060.5	East Muskingum Local SD	New Concord
245	1,059.0	Harrison Hills City SD	Hopedale
246	1,046.1	Medina City SD	Medina
247	1,042.5	Bath Local SD	Lima
248	1,040.5	London City SD	London
249	1,039.0	Winton Woods City SD	Cincinnati
250	1,037.5	Milford Ex Vill SD	Milford
251	1,031.3	Franklin City SD	Franklin
252	1,028.0	Valley View Local SD	Germantown
253	1,024.7	United Local SD	Hanoverton
254	1,012.0	Benton Carroll Salem Local SD	Oak Harbor
255	992.0	Wyoming City SD	Wyoming
256	990.0	Lakewood City SD	Lakewood
257	989.0	Coshocton City SD	Coshocton
258	986.0	Clermont Northeastern Local SD	Batavia
259	985.0	Bethel-Tate Local SD	Bethel
259	985.0	Chagrin Falls Ex Vill SD	Chagrin Falls
261	984.0	Norwalk City SD	Norwalk
262	983.0	Benjamin Logan Local SD	Bellefontaine
263	975.5	Northwestern Local SD	Springfield
264	965.5	Oregon City SD	Oregon
265	963.0	Rock Hill Local SD	Ironton
266	962.0	Batavia Local SD	Batavia
267	954.0	North Fork Local SD	Utica
268	950.3	Aurora City SD	Aurora
269	949.0	Maumee City SD	Maumee
270	945.5	Bucyrus City SD	Bucyrus
271	944.3	Hillsboro City SD	Hillsboro
272	939.7	Lexington Local SD	Lexington
273	931.5	Orrville City SD	Orrville
274	927.0	Wellston City Schools	Wellston
275	926.3	Highland Local SD	Medina
276	921.3	Switzerland of Ohio Local SD	Woodsfield
277	908.3	Crestwood Local SD	Mantua
278	907.6	Lakota Local SD	Liberty Twp
279	907.3	Northeastern Local SD	Springfield
280	903.5	Upper Sandusky Ex Vill SD	Upper Sandusky
281	903.0	Milton-Union Exempted Vill Schls	West Milton

282	891.2	Columbus Public Schools	Columbus
283	890.5	Ontario Local SD	Mansfield
284	890.0	Northwest Local SD	Mc Dermott
285	889.6	Berea City SD	Berea
286	887.5	Carlisle Local SD	Carlisle
287	883.5	Westerville City SD	Westerville
288	881.2	Elyria City SD	Elyria
289	874.8	North Ridgeville City SD	N Ridgeville
290	866.0	Rocky River City SD	Rocky River
291	863.7	St Marys City SD	Saint Marys
292	853.5	Heath City SD	Heath
293	844.9	Cincinnati City SD	Cincinnati
294	844.5	Otsego Local SD	Tontogany
295	835.8	Avon Lake City Schools	Avon Lake
296	834.5	Black River Local SD	Sullivan
297	833.7	Western Brown Local SD	Mount Orab
298	833.5	Preble Shawnee Local SD	Camden
299	830.0	Circleville City SD	Circleville
300	822.7	Sycamore Community City SD	Cincinnati
301	818.3	Bay Village City SD	Bay Village
302	815.5	Wellington Ex Vill SD	Wellington
303	813.5	Elgin Local SD	Marion
304	813.0	Ironton City SD	Ironton
305	812.0	Chardon Local SD	Chardon
306	800.8	Bowling Green City SD	Bowling Green
307	799.1	Fairland Local SD	Proctorville
308	792.5	Swanton Local SD	Swanton
309	790.6	Twinsburg City SD	Twinsburg
310	789.5	Campbell City SD	Campbell
311	785.0	James A Garfield Local SD	Garrettsville
312	776.5	Union Local SD	Morristown
313	771.8	Garfield Heights City SD	Garfield Hgts
314	770.5	East Liverpool City SD	East Liverpool
315	770.0	Field Local SD	Mogadore
316	768.3	Hubbard Ex Vill SD	Hubbard
317	761.8	South Euclid-Lyndhurst City SD	Lyndhurst
318	761.0	Martins Ferry City SD	Martins Ferry
319	760.5	Monroe Local SD	Monroe
320	755.0	Lakewood Local SD	Hebron
321	744.7	Lakeview Local SD	Cortland
322	740.0	Solon City SD	Solon
323	727.4	East Cleveland City SD	East Cleveland
324	722.0	Licking Valley Local SD Sd	Newark
325	713.3	Olentangy Local SD	Lewis Center
326	704.3	Granville Ex Vill SD	Granville
327	704.0	Warrensville Heights City SD	Warrensville Hgts
328	695.8	Hudson City SD	Hudson
329	682.2	Dublin City SD	Dublin
330	680.7	Oakwood City SD	Dayton
331	667.3	Hilliard City SD	Hilliard
332	655.3	New Lexington City SD	New Lexington
333	651.5	Westlake City SD	Westlake
334	650.8	Cleveland Municipal City SD	Cleveland
335	644.0	Groveport Madison Local SD	Groveport
336	632.7	Kent City SD	Kent
337	618.9	Centerville City SD	Centerville
338	618.0	Perry Local SD	Perry
339	610.3	Princeton City SD	Cincinnati
340	607.3	Fairview Park City SD	Fairview Park
341	599.2	Edgewood City SD	Trenton
342	596.4	Whitehall City SD	Whitehall
343	592.0	Orange City SD	Cleveland
344	575.4	Plain Local SD	New Albany
345	573.9	Mentor Ex Vill SD	Mentor
346	569.3	Mariemont City SD	Cincinnati
347	567.2	Gahanna-Jefferson City SD	Gahanna
348	566.3	Washington-Nile Local SD	West Portsmouth
349	565.0	Indian Hill Ex Vill SD	Cincinnati
350	562.4	Shaker Heights City SD	Shaker Heights
351	557.9	Upper Arlington City SD	Upper Arlington
352	550.7	Minford Local SD	Minford
353	547.3	Graham Local SD	Saint Paris
354	543.7	Brookville Local SD	Brookville
355	540.4	Worthington City SD	Worthington
356	536.7	Cleveland Hts-Univ Hts City SD	University Hgts
357	524.4	Canal Winchester Local SD	Canal Winchester
358	523.0	Meigs Local SD	Pomeroy
359	519.4	West Holmes Local SD	Millersburg
360	502.7	Madeira City SD	Cincinnati
361	453.0	Morgan Local SD	McConnelsville
362	446.5	Woodridge Local SD	Peninsula
363	442.2	Bexley City SD	Bexley
364	430.5	Champion Local SD	Warren
365	399.0	Beachwood City SD	Beachwood
366	n/a	Alexander Local SD	Albany
366	n/a	Bellaire Local SD	Bellaire
366	n/a	Electronic Classrm of Tomorrow	Columbus
366	n/a	Ohio Virtual Academy	Maumee
366	n/a	Ottawa-Glandorf Local SD	Ottawa
366	n/a	Sheffield-Sheffield Lake City SD	Sheffield Vlg
366	n/a	Southeast Local SD	Apple Creek
366	n/a	Steubenville City SD	Steubenville
366	n/a	Sugarcreek Local SD	Bellbrook

Student/Counselor Ratio

Rank	Ratio	District Name	City
1	5,213.0	Electronic Classrm of Tomorrow	Columbus
2	1,925.3	Cincinnati City SD	Cincinnati
3	1,891.0	Bucyrus City SD	Bucyrus
4	1,883.0	Fairless Local SD	Navarre
5	1,638.3	New Lexington City SD	New Lexington
6	1,571.0	East Clinton Local SD	Lees Creek
7	1,316.5	Vinton County Local SD	Mc Arthur
8	1,270.5	River View Local SD	Warsaw
9	1,183.0	Gallipolis City SD	Gallipolis
10	1,181.1	New Philadelphia City SD	New Philadelphia
11	1,145.3	Trotwood-Madison City Schools	Trotwood
12	1,118.5	Buckeye Valley Local SD	Delaware
13	1,027.3	Dayton City SD	Dayton
14	994.0	Whitehall City SD	Whitehall
15	990.0	Greenon Local SD	Springfield
16	985.5	Port Clinton City SD	Port Clinton
17	977.3	Carrollton Ex Vill SD	Carrollton
18	963.0	Rock Hill Local SD	Ironton
19	943.9	Reynoldsburg City SD	Reynoldsburg
20	939.7	Lexington Local SD	Lexington
21	937.0	Berlin-Milan Local SD	Milan
22	933.0	South Point Local SD	South Point
23	928.5	East Holmes Local Schools	Berlin
24	908.0	West Muskingum Local SD	Zanesville
25	890.5	Highland Local SD	Sparta
26	876.6	South-Western City SD	Grove City
27	860.2	Mount Vernon City SD	Mount Vernon
28	852.7	Norton City Schools	Norton
29	848.7	East Cleveland City SD	East Cleveland
30	832.0	Huron City Schools	Huron
31	830.5	West Clermont Local SD	Cincinnati
32	826.5	Amanda-Clearcreek Local SD	Amanda
33	813.5	Madison-Plains Local SD	London
34	811.5	Coldwater Ex Vill SD	Coldwater
35	810.3	Newark City SD	Newark
36	808.3	Teays Valley Local SD	Ashville
37	789.5	Campbell City SD	Campbell
38	787.5	Tri-Valley Local Schools	Dresden
39	784.0	Sandy Valley Local SD	Magnolia
40	780.0	Franklin Local SD	Duncan Falls
41	779.7	Northern Local SD	Thornville
42	778.0	Coventry Local SD	Akron
43	777.2	West Carrollton City SD	West Carrollton
44	776.5	Union Local SD	Morristown
45	774.3	Canfield Local SD	Canfield
46	771.5	Eastern Local SD	Sardinia
47	763.0	Lancaster City SD	Lancaster
48	762.3	Buckeye Local SD	Ashtabula
49	761.3	Ashtabula Area City SD	Ashtabula
50	757.8	Fairfield City SD	Fairfield
51	755.0	Morgan Local SD	McConnelsville
52	753.1	Fairfield Union Local SD	W Rushville
53	752.3	Jefferson Area Local SD	Jefferson
54	750.5	Ridgewood Local SD	West Lafayette
55	747.8	Madison Local SD	Madison
56	746.0	Galion City SD	Galion
57	736.7	Southeast Local SD	Ravenna
58	715.0	Kenton City SD	Kenton
59	707.0	East Muskingum Local SD	New Concord
60	706.0	Harrison Hills City SD	Hopedale
61	703.6	Vandalia-Butler City SD	Vandalia
62	701.3	West Holmes Local SD	Millersburg
63	698.2	Amherst Ex Vill SD	Amherst
64	695.7	Streetsboro City Schools	Streetsboro
65	693.7	London City SD	London
66	691.0	Switzerland of Ohio Local SD	Woodsfield
67	686.3	Jackson City SD	Jackson
68	685.3	Valley View Local SD	Germantown
69	683.2	Clearview Local SD	Lorain
70	682.8	Willoughby-Eastlake City SD	Willoughby
71	681.3	Crestwood Local SD	Mantua
72	678.4	Fairborn City Schools	Fairborn
73	672.3	Edison Local SD	Hammondsville
74	672.1	Oak Hills Local SD	Cincinnati
75	671.3	Logan-Hocking Local SD	Logan
76	667.0	Strongsville City SD	Strongsville
77	664.8	Norwood City SD	Norwood
78	663.5	Middletown City SD	Middletown
79	663.3	Cleveland Municipal City SD	Cleveland
80	659.3	Coshocton City SD	Coshocton
81	658.2	Loveland City SD	Loveland
82	657.7	Parma City SD	Parma
83	657.3	Clermont Northeastern Local SD	Batavia
84	656.7	Bethel-Tate Local SD	Bethel
85	651.3	Union-Scioto Local SD	Chillicothe
86	650.5	Mentor Ex Vill SD	Mentor
87	650.3	Northwestern Local SD	Springfield
88	649.5	Dover City SD	Dover
89	645.0	Lorain City SD	Lorain
90	641.3	Batavia Local SD	Batavia
91	640.4	Marietta City Schools	Marietta
92	640.2	Little Miami Local SD	Morrow
93	636.0	Gallia County Local SD	Gallipolis
94	631.8	Conneaut Area City SD	Conneaut
95	629.7	Winton Woods City SD	Cincinnati
96	628.5	Poland Local SD	Poland
97	625.9	Warren City SD	Warren
98	623.2	Celina City SD	Celina
99	622.5	Circleville City SD	Circleville
100	622.3	Marlington Local SD	Alliance
101	618.8	Franklin City SD	Franklin
102	618.0	Wellston City Schools	Wellston
103	617.5	Avon Local SD	Avon
104	613.8	Beaver Local SD	Lisbon
105	611.3	Maple Heights City SD	Maple Heights
105	611.3	Salem City SD	Salem
107	610.3	Medina City SD	Medina
107	610.3	River Valley Local SD	Caledonia
109	604.7	Northridge Local SD	Dayton
110	603.8	Buckeye Local SD	Rayland
111	603.0	Paulding Ex Vill SD	Paulding
112	602.0	Milton-Union Exempted Vill Schls	West Milton
113	599.5	Brunswick City SD	Brunswick
114	597.8	Hamilton Local SD	Columbus
114	597.8	Steubenville City SD	Steubenville
116	596.1	Stow-Munroe Falls City SD	Stow
117	595.0	Athens City SD	The Plains
118	593.7	Ontario Local SD	Mansfield
119	590.4	Norwalk City SD	Norwalk
120	590.3	Blanchester Local SD	Blanchester
121	589.7	Girard City SD	Girard
122	586.9	Wadsworth City SD	Wadsworth
123	585.5	Groveport Madison Local SD	Groveport
124	582.5	Marion City SD	Marion
125	581.3	Tuscarawas Valley Local SD	Zoarville
126	580.8	Logan Elm Local SD	Circleville
127	580.7	Lima City SD	Lima
128	580.5	Indian Creek Local SD	Wintersville
129	579.8	Greenfield Ex Vill SD	Greenfield
130	579.0	Genoa Area Local SD	Genoa
131	577.5	Field Local SD	Mogadore
132	576.3	Hubbard Ex Vill SD	Hubbard
133	575.4	Plain Local SD	New Albany
134	574.6	Fremont City SD	Fremont
135	574.3	Clyde-Green Springs Ex Vill SD	Clyde
136	573.7	Licking Heights Local SD	Summit Station
137	572.5	Midview Local SD	Grafton
137	572.5	Van Wert City SD	Van Wert
139	572.2	Niles City SD	Niles
140	571.4	South Euclid-Lyndhurst City SD	Lyndhurst
141	569.0	Heath City SD	Heath
142	567.0	Greenville City SD	Greenville
143	566.4	Adams County/Ohio Valley LSD	West Union
144	566.3	Lakewood Local SD	Hebron
144	566.3	Maysville Local SD	Zanesville
146	563.0	Otsego Local SD	Tontogany
147	562.7	Chillicothe City SD	Chillicothe
148	560.9	Northwest Local SD	Cincinnati
149	559.7	Alexander Local SD	Albany
149	559.7	Scioto Valley Local SD	Piketon
151	556.5	Rolling Hills Local SD	Cambridge
152	555.8	Highland Local SD	Medina
153	555.5	Firelands Local SD	Oberlin
154	554.0	Alliance City SD	Alliance
155	551.7	Canton Local SD	Canton
155	551.7	Westfall Local SD	Williamsport
157	551.3	Garfield Heights City SD	Garfield Hgts
158	550.7	Minford Local SD	Minford
159	550.5	Minerva Local SD	Minerva
159	550.5	Tecumseh Local SD	New Carlisle
161	546.4	Lakota Local SD	Liberty Twp
162	545.3	Ashland City SD	Ashland
163	545.0	Zanesville City SD	Zanesville
164	543.7	Brookville Local SD	Brookville
165	543.5	Waverly City SD	Waverly
166	541.5	Licking Valley Local SD Sd	Newark
167	541.3	Chardon Local SD	Chardon
167	541.3	Massillon City SD	Massillon
169	540.0	Springboro Community City SD	Springboro
170	539.9	Cuyahoga Falls City SD	Cuyahoga Falls
170	539.9	Findlay City SD	Findlay
170	539.9	Springfield Local Schools	Holland
173	538.7	Olmsted Falls City SD	Olmsted Falls
174	537.5	Triway Local SD	Wooster
175	535.0	Euclid City SD	Euclid
176	533.3	Wauseon Ex Vill SD	Wauseon
177	533.1	Lakewood City SD	Lakewood
178	532.5	Wilmington City SD	Wilmington
179	532.2	Indian Valley Local SD	Gnadenhutten
180	532.0	Northwest Local SD	Canal Fulton

181	531.1	Lebanon City SD	Lebanon
182	529.7	Zane Trace Local SD	Chillicothe
183	528.3	Swanton Local SD	Swanton
184	526.6	Big Walnut Local SD	Galena
185	526.3	St Clairsville-Richland City SD	St Clairsville
186	524.8	Troy City SD	Troy
187	524.7	Pike-Delta-York Local SD	Delta
188	523.6	Westerville City SD	Westerville
189	521.3	Bath Local SD	Lima
190	520.2	Mason City SD	Mason
191	520.0	Sheffield-Sheffield Lake City SD	Sheffield Vlg
192	518.2	Elida Local SD	Elida
192	518.2	St Marys City SD	Saint Marys
194	518.0	Wapakoneta City City SD	Wapakoneta
195	516.3	Bellaire Local SD	Bellaire
196	514.7	Toledo City SD	Toledo
197	512.7	North College Hill City SD	Cincinnati
198	512.3	United Local SD	Hanoverton
199	511.3	Shaker Heights City SD	Shaker Heights
200	510.5	Oakwood City SD	Dayton
201	509.9	Akron Public Schools	Akron
202	509.4	Clark-Shawnee Local SD	Springfield
203	509.3	Cloverleaf Local SD	Lodi
204	507.0	Monroe Local SD	Monroe
205	506.7	Manchester Local SD	Akron
205	506.7	Newton Falls Ex Vill SD	Newton Falls
207	506.5	James A Garfield Local SD	Garrettsville
208	505.0	Goshen Local SD	Goshen
209	504.3	Miamisburg City SD	Miamisburg
210	502.7	Madeira City SD	Cincinnati
211	501.8	Geneva Area City Schools	Geneva
212	501.0	Struthers City SD	Struthers
213	498.4	Vermilion Local SD	Vermilion
214	498.0	Indian Lake Local SD	Lewistown
215	497.6	Columbus Public Schools	Columbus
216	494.5	Eastwood Local SD	Pemberville
217	494.4	Piqua City SD	Piqua
218	493.0	Copley-Fairlawn City SD	Copley
218	493.0	Sugarcreek Local SD	Bellbrook
220	491.5	Benjamin Logan Local SD	Bellefontaine
221	490.6	Buckeye Local SD	Medina
222	489.1	Olentangy Local SD	Lewis Center
223	488.6	West Branch Local SD	Beloit
224	485.7	Huber Heights City SD	Huber Heights
225	482.9	Bellefontaine City Schools	Bellefontaine
226	482.8	Oregon City SD	Oregon
227	482.2	New Richmond Ex Vill SD	New Richmond
228	481.9	Wooster City SD	Wooster
229	480.9	Three Rivers Local Schools	Cleves
230	479.3	Forest Hills Local SD	Cincinnati
231	477.6	Bellevue City SD	Bellevue
232	477.5	Northeastern Local SD	Springfield
233	477.0	North Fork Local SD	Utica
234	474.5	Kent City SD	Kent
235	472.2	Hillsboro City SD	Hillsboro
236	471.2	Urbana City SD	Urbana
237	469.2	Claymont City SD	Dennison
238	467.8	Canton City SD	Canton
239	467.2	Southwest Local SD	Harrison
240	466.8	Eaton Community Schools	Eaton
241	466.6	Brecksville-Broadview Hgts City	Brecksville
242	465.8	Orrville City SD	Orrville
243	465.4	Worthington City SD	Worthington
244	463.5	Perry Local SD	Perry
245	463.4	Jackson Local SD	Massillon
246	462.1	Ravenna City SD	Ravenna
247	461.9	Western Brown Local SD	Mount Orab
248	461.3	Howland Local SD	Warren
249	460.8	Clear Fork Valley Local SD	Bellville
250	460.0	Tallmadge City Schools	Tallmadge
251	459.7	Twinsburg City SD	Twinsburg
251	459.7	Washington Local Schools	Toledo
253	457.3	Nordonia Hills City SD	Northfield
254	456.5	Cambridge City SD	Cambridge
255	455.9	North Canton City SD	North Canton
256	455.5	Fairview Park City SD	Fairview Park
257	454.9	Kenston Local SD	Chagrin Falls
258	454.8	Liberty Local SD	Youngstown
259	454.1	Northmont City SD	Englewood
260	453.2	Miami Trace Local SD	Wash Ct House
261	452.8	Painesville City Local SD	Painesville
262	452.7	Green Local SD	Green
263	452.3	Jonathan Alder Local SD	Plain City
264	451.8	Upper Sandusky Ex Vill SD	Upper Sandusky
265	450.8	Shelby City SD	Shelby
266	449.8	Delaware City SD	Delaware
266	449.8	Hilliard City SD	Hilliard
268	449.4	Edgewood City SD	Trenton
269	447.6	Kings Local SD	Kings Mills
270	446.8	Lakeview Local SD	Cortland
271	445.9	Pickerington Local SD	Pickerington
272	445.2	Boardman Local SD	Youngstown
273	445.0	Northwest Local SD	Mc Dermott
274	444.6	Milford Ex Vill SD	Milford
275	443.5	Clinton-Massie Local SD	Clarksville
276	443.4	Talawanda City SD	Oxford
277	441.6	Madison Local SD	Mansfield
278	440.3	East Liverpool City SD	East Liverpool
279	439.9	Berea City SD	Berea
280	438.6	Aurora City SD	Aurora
281	437.8	Graham Local SD	Saint Paris
282	437.0	Canal Winchester Local SD	Canal Winchester
283	435.9	Princeton City SD	Cincinnati
284	434.8	Perrysburg Exempted Village	Perrysburg
284	434.8	Tipp City Ex Vill SD	Tipp City
286	433.4	Mayfield City SD	Highland Hgts
287	432.9	Carlisle Local SD	Carlisle
288	432.8	Ottawa-Glandorf Local SD	Ottawa
289	430.5	Champion Local SD	Warren
290	430.1	Southwest Licking Local SD	Etna
291	430.0	Ross Local SD	Hamilton
292	429.5	Southeast Local SD	Apple Creek
293	429.2	Marysville Exempted Village SD	Marysville
294	429.0	Lake Local SD	Millbury
295	427.4	Barberton City SD	Barberton
296	427.0	Mariemont City SD	Cincinnati
297	426.3	Anthony Wayne Local SD	Whitehouse
298	422.7	Sandusky City SD	Sandusky
299	420.9	Mt Healthy City SD	Cincinnati
300	420.5	Austintown Local SD	Youngstown
301	419.9	Lake Local SD	Hartville
302	419.5	Xenia Community City SD	Xenia
303	419.1	Centerville City SD	Centerville
304	418.4	Meigs Local SD	Pomeroy
305	416.8	Preble Shawnee Local SD	Camden
306	414.4	Mansfield City SD	Mansfield
307	412.3	Hudson City SD	Hudson
308	412.2	Sylvania City SD	Sylvania
309	411.3	Greeneview Local SD	Jamestown
310	408.7	North Royalton City SD	N Royalton
311	408.4	Fairland Local SD	Proctorville
312	407.8	Wellington Ex Vill SD	Wellington
313	404.8	Benton Carroll Salem Local SD	Oak Harbor
314	404.0	Rossford Ex Vill SD	Rossford
315	403.3	Fostoria City SD	Fostoria
316	402.3	Warrensville Heights City SD	Warrensville Hgts
317	401.0	Revere Local SD	Bath
318	400.4	Bowling Green City SD	Bowling Green
319	400.3	Hamilton City SD	Hamilton
320	398.5	Solon City SD	Solon
321	397.8	Napoleon Area City SD	Napoleon
322	396.8	Wyoming City SD	Wyoming
323	396.1	Beavercreek City SD	Beavercreek
323	396.1	Dublin City SD	Dublin
325	394.0	Chagrin Falls Ex Vill SD	Chagrin Falls
326	393.7	Willard City SD	Willard
327	393.3	Avon Lake City Schools	Avon Lake
328	392.5	Wickliffe City SD	Wickliffe
329	390.9	Westlake City SD	Westlake
330	389.8	Louisville City SD	Louisville
331	389.0	Bedford City SD	Bedford
332	384.5	Springfield Local SD	Akron
333	382.4	Gahanna-Jefferson City SD	Gahanna
334	381.3	Bryan City SD	Bryan
335	380.8	North Olmsted City Schools	North Olmsted
336	379.6	Shawnee Local SD	Lima
337	378.0	Tiffin City SD	Tiffin
338	377.7	Elyria City SD	Elyria
339	374.0	Painesville Township Local SD	Painesville
340	371.1	Rocky River City SD	Rocky River
341	367.5	Youngstown City SD	Youngstown
342	366.2	Keystone Local SD	Lagrange
343	364.4	Plain Local SD	Canton
344	363.0	Defiance City SD	Defiance
345	361.0	Portsmouth City SD	Portsmouth
346	357.2	Woodridge Local SD	Peninsula
347	352.2	Granville Ex Vill SD	Granville
348	349.0	Sycamore Community City SD	Cincinnati
349	346.5	Upper Arlington City SD	Upper Arlington
350	343.4	Mad River Local SD	Dayton
351	339.8	Washington-Nile Local SD	West Portsmouth
352	335.7	Springfield City SD	Springfield
353	323.9	Perkins Local SD	Sandusky
354	323.6	Perry Local SD	Massillon
355	321.8	Sidney City SD	Sidney
356	318.1	North Ridgeville City SD	N Ridgeville
357	316.3	Maumee City SD	Maumee
358	306.9	Bay Village City SD	Bay Village
359	304.4	Martins Ferry City SD	Martins Ferry
360	299.1	Warren Local SD	Vincent
361	296.0	Orange City SD	Cleveland
362	295.0	West Geauga Local SD	Chesterland
363	289.6	Kettering City SD	Kettering
364	289.4	Washington Court House City SD	Wash Ct House
365	279.2	Finneytown Local SD	Cincinnati
366	266.0	Beachwood City SD	Beachwood
367	265.0	Madison Local SD	Middletown
368	257.1	Bexley City SD	Bexley
369	249.5	Cleveland Hts-Univ Hts City SD	University Hgts
370	238.4	Black River Local SD	Sullivan
371	232.4	Elgin Local SD	Marion
372	232.3	Ironton City SD	Ironton
373	230.6	Indian Hill Ex Vill SD	Cincinnati
374	n/a	Ohio Virtual Academy	Maumee

Current Spending per Student in FY2003

Rank	Dollars	District Name	City
1	16,952	Beachwood City SD	Beachwood
2	14,304	Orange City SD	Cleveland
3	13,555	Perry Local SD	Perry
4	12,683	Shaker Heights City SD	Shaker Heights
5	12,002	Cleveland Hts-Univ Hts City SD	University Hgts
6	11,616	Sycamore Community City SD	Cincinnati
7	11,064	Youngstown City SD	Youngstown
8	10,866	Princeton City SD	Cincinnati
9	10,821	Warrensville Heights City SD	Warrensville Hgts
10	10,734	East Cleveland City SD	East Cleveland
11	10,491	Dayton City SD	Dayton
12	10,439	South Euclid-Lyndhurst City SD	Lyndhurst
13	10,402	Upper Arlington City SD	Upper Arlington
14	10,300	Cincinnati City SD	Cincinnati
15	10,281	Bexley City SD	Bexley
16	10,255	Bedford City SD	Bedford
17	10,199	Cleveland Municipal City SD	Cleveland
18	10,188	Columbus Public Schools	Columbus
19	10,168	Indian Hill Ex Vill SD	Cincinnati
20	10,156	Toledo City SD	Toledo
21	10,146	Worthington City SD	Worthington
22	10,019	Mayfield City SD	Highland Hgts
23	9,917	Solon City SD	Solon
24	9,901	Kent City SD	Kent
25	9,880	Fairview Park City SD	Fairview Park
26	9,760	Mansfield City SD	Mansfield
27	9,505	Canton City SD	Canton
28	9,498	Akron Public Schools	Akron
29	9,469	Portsmouth City SD	Portsmouth
30	9,405	Euclid City SD	Euclid
31	9,388	Westlake City SD	Westlake
32	9,298	Chagrin Falls Ex Vill SD	Chagrin Falls
33	9,274	Lakewood City SD	Lakewood
34	9,258	New Richmond Ex Vill SD	New Richmond
35	9,198	Wickliffe City SD	Wickliffe
36	9,150	Wooster City SD	Wooster
37	9,131	Bay Village City SD	Bay Village
38	9,059	Northridge Local SD	Dayton
39	9,008	Warren City SD	Warren
40	8,989	Hudson City SD	Hudson
41	8,964	Parma City SD	Parma
42	8,957	Maumee City SD	Maumee
43	8,949	Springfield City SD	Springfield
44	8,941	Dublin City SD	Dublin
45	8,917	Rocky River City SD	Rocky River
46	8,914	Medina City SD	Medina
47	8,902	Monroe Local SD	Monroe
48	8,869	Port Clinton City SD	Port Clinton
49	8,859	Sandusky City SD	Sandusky
50	8,832	North Olmsted City Schools	North Olmsted
51	8,737	Berea City SD	Berea
51	8,737	Plain Local SD	New Albany
53	8,729	Bellaire Local SD	Bellaire
53	8,729	Olmsted Falls City SD	Olmsted Falls
53	8,729	Wyoming City SD	Wyoming
56	8,698	Lima City SD	Lima
57	8,617	Mentor Ex Vill SD	Mentor
58	8,614	Sylvania City SD	Sylvania
59	8,598	Mariemont City SD	Cincinnati
60	8,594	Twinsburg City SD	Twinsburg
61	8,579	Finneytown Local SD	Cincinnati
62	8,548	Woodridge Local SD	Peninsula
63	8,528	East Liverpool City SD	East Liverpool
64	8,501	Norwood City SD	Norwood
65	8,494	Oakwood City SD	Dayton
66	8,491	Zanesville City SD	Zanesville
67	8,474	Trotwood-Madison City Schools	Trotwood
68	8,458	Winton Woods City SD	Cincinnati
69	8,437	Madeira City SD	Cincinnati
70	8,406	Oregon City SD	Oregon
71	8,403	Benton Carroll Salem Local SD	Oak Harbor
72	8,392	Washington Local Schools	Toledo
73	8,391	Lorain City SD	Lorain
74	8,376	Middletown City SD	Middletown
75	8,373	Groveport Madison Local SD	Groveport
76	8,364	Madison Local SD	Mansfield
77	8,350	Marysville Exempted Village SD	Marysville
78	8,349	Massillon City SD	Massillon
79	8,325	Brecksville-Broadview Hgts City	Brecksville
80	8,316	Springfield Local Schools	Holland

81	8,299	Mt Healthy City SD	Cincinnati
82	8,288	Perkins Local SD	Sandusky
83	8,277	Strongsville City SD	Strongsville
84	8,268	Revere Local SD	Bath
85	8,246	Kenston Local SD	Chagrin Falls
86	8,241	Nordonia Hills City SD	Northfield
87	8,236	Elyria City SD	Elyria
88	8,230	Painesville City Local SD	Painesville
89	8,221	Barberton City SD	Barberton
90	8,188	Copley-Fairlawn City SD	Copley
91	8,183	Rossford Ex Vill SD	Rossford
92	8,166	Avon Lake City Schools	Avon Lake
93	8,127	Hilliard City SD	Hilliard
94	8,096	Athens City SD	The Plains
95	8,090	Bowling Green City SD	Bowling Green
96	8,065	Salem City SD	Salem
97	8,032	Gahanna-Jefferson City SD	Gahanna
98	8,028	Eastwood Local SD	Pemberville
99	7,996	Canal Winchester Local SD	Canal Winchester
100	7,973	Southeast Local SD	Apple Creek
101	7,962	Aurora City SD	Aurora
102	7,944	Centerville City SD	Centerville
103	7,943	Kettering City SD	Kettering
103	7,943	Morgan Local SD	McConnelsville
105	7,942	Mad River Local SD	Dayton
106	7,933	Ravenna City SD	Ravenna
107	7,918	Willoughby-Eastlake City SD	Willoughby
108	7,913	Alliance City SD	Alliance
109	7,883	South-Western City SD	Grove City
110	7,882	Campbell City SD	Campbell
110	7,882	Findlay City SD	Findlay
112	7,881	Delaware City SD	Delaware
113	7,857	Vandalia-Butler City SD	Vandalia
114	7,852	West Carrollton City SD	West Carrollton
115	7,838	Canton Local SD	Canton
115	7,838	Xenia Community City SD	Xenia
117	7,817	Pike-Delta-York Local SD	Delta
118	7,811	Whitehall City SD	Whitehall
119	7,795	Liberty Local SD	Youngstown
120	7,787	Celina City SD	Celina
121	7,785	Meigs Local SD	Pomeroy
122	7,781	Streetsboro City Schools	Streetsboro
123	7,766	Carlisle Local SD	Carlisle
124	7,756	Garfield Heights City SD	Garfield Hgts
125	7,744	Lancaster City SD	Lancaster
126	7,739	Ashtabula Area City SD	Ashtabula
127	7,733	Clearview Local SD	Lorain
128	7,719	Sheffield-Sheffield Lake City SD	Sheffield Vlg
129	7,713	Buckeye Local SD	Medina
130	7,711	North Royalton City SD	N Royalton
131	7,701	Westerville City SD	Westerville
132	7,695	Olentangy Local SD	Lewis Center
133	7,681	Buckeye Valley Local SD	Delaware
134	7,665	Fairborn City Schools	Fairborn
135	7,653	Buckeye Local SD	Ashtabula
136	7,636	Kings Local SD	Kings Mills
137	7,633	Champion Local SD	Warren
138	7,632	Austintown Local SD	Youngstown
139	7,622	Three Rivers Local Schools	Cleves
140	7,614	Boardman Local SD	Youngstown
141	7,599	St Clairsville-Richland City SD	St Clairsville
142	7,598	Fostoria City SD	Fostoria
143	7,593	Tecumseh Local SD	New Carlisle
144	7,581	Circleville City SD	Circleville
145	7,576	Switzerland of Ohio Local SD	Woodsfield
146	7,573	Cuyahoga Falls City SD	Cuyahoga Falls
147	7,543	Struthers City SD	Struthers
148	7,532	Southwest Licking Local SD	Etna
149	7,527	Huron City Schools	Huron
150	7,491	Granville Ex Vill SD	Granville
151	7,471	Tallmadge City Schools	Tallmadge
152	7,470	Paulding Ex Vill SD	Paulding
153	7,468	Shelby City SD	Shelby
154	7,461	Springfield Local SD	Akron
155	7,456	Miami Trace Local SD	Wash Ct House
156	7,439	Marion City SD	Marion
157	7,438	Howland Local SD	Warren
158	7,429	Talawanda City SD	Oxford
159	7,423	Orrville City SD	Orrville
160	7,413	Chardon Local SD	Chardon
161	7,410	Coshocton City SD	Coshocton
162	7,401	Jackson Local SD	Massillon
162	7,401	Northwest Local SD	Mc Dermott
164	7,396	Niles City SD	Niles
165	7,395	West Geauga Local SD	Chesterland
166	7,383	Mason City SD	Mason
167	7,380	Valley View Local SD	Germantown
168	7,376	Brunswick City SD	Brunswick
169	7,358	Ironton City SD	Ironton
170	7,357	Goshen Local SD	Goshen
171	7,356	Bucyrus City SD	Bucyrus
172	7,355	Forest Hills Local SD	Cincinnati
173	7,353	Huber Heights City SD	Huber Heights
174	7,349	Hamilton City SD	Hamilton
175	7,348	Logan Elm Local SD	Circleville
176	7,346	Cambridge City SD	Cambridge
177	7,335	Urbana City SD	Urbana
178	7,326	Northwest Local SD	Cincinnati
179	7,319	Kenton City SD	Kenton
180	7,311	Newark City SD	Newark
181	7,307	Vinton County Local SD	Mc Arthur
182	7,298	Vermilion Local SD	Vermilion
183	7,295	Union Local SD	Morristown
184	7,293	Perrysburg Exempted Village	Perrysburg
185	7,291	Painesville Township Local SD	Painesville
186	7,279	Maple Heights City SD	Maple Heights
187	7,273	Miamisburg City SD	Miamisburg
187	7,273	Ridgewood Local SD	West Lafayette
189	7,257	Steubenville City SD	Steubenville
190	7,245	Swanton Local SD	Swanton
191	7,227	Norton City Schools	Norton
192	7,194	Milford Ex Vill SD	Milford
193	7,189	Beavercreek City SD	Beavercreek
194	7,171	Loveland City SD	Loveland
195	7,169	Hamilton Local SD	Columbus
196	7,167	Scioto Valley Local SD	Piketon
197	7,149	Adams County/Ohio Valley LSD	West Union
197	7,149	Galion City SD	Galion
199	7,139	Franklin City SD	Franklin
200	7,138	Field Local SD	Mogadore
201	7,137	Washington-Nile Local SD	West Portsmouth
202	7,130	Pickerington Local SD	Pickerington
203	7,127	Girard City SD	Girard
204	7,126	Big Walnut Local SD	Galena
205	7,123	Gallia County Local SD	Gallipolis
206	7,122	Lakota Local SD	Liberty Twp
207	7,116	Crestwood Local SD	Mantua
208	7,110	Ashland City SD	Ashland
208	7,110	Rock Hill Local SD	Ironton
208	7,110	Stow-Munroe Falls City SD	Stow
211	7,096	Greenfield Ex Vill SD	Greenfield
212	7,094	Madison-Plains Local SD	London
213	7,087	Newton Falls Ex Vill SD	Newton Falls
214	7,076	Minerva Local SD	Minerva
215	7,070	Southeast Local SD	Ravenna
216	7,061	North Ridgeville City SD	N Ridgeville
217	7,054	Fairfield Union Local SD	W Rushville
218	7,051	Napoleon Area City SD	Napoleon
219	7,049	North College Hill City SD	Cincinnati
220	7,047	Fremont City SD	Fremont
221	7,042	Batavia Local SD	Batavia
222	7,041	London City SD	London
223	7,036	Triway Local SD	Wooster
224	7,033	Dover City SD	Dover
225	7,020	Wellington Ex Vill SD	Wellington
225	7,020	Wellston City Schools	Wellston
227	7,014	Buckeye Local SD	Rayland
227	7,014	Lakewood Local SD	Hebron
229	7,011	Anthony Wayne Local SD	Whitehouse
229	7,011	Northmont City SD	Englewood
231	7,010	Troy City SD	Troy
232	7,005	North Canton City SD	North Canton
233	7,003	Preble Shawnee Local SD	Camden
234	6,999	River Valley Local SD	Caledonia
235	6,997	Berlin-Milan Local SD	Milan
236	6,991	Fairfield City SD	Fairfield
237	6,986	Licking Valley Local SD Sd	Newark
238	6,984	Plain Local SD	Canton
239	6,983	Chillicothe City SD	Chillicothe
240	6,979	East Holmes Local Schools	Berlin
241	6,972	Southwest Local SD	Harrison
242	6,971	Ontario Local SD	Mansfield
243	6,966	Bellefontaine City Schools	Bellefontaine
244	6,935	Minford Local SD	Minford
245	6,934	Marietta City Schools	Marietta
246	6,920	Green Local SD	Green
247	6,914	Madison Local SD	Middletown
248	6,908	Shawnee Local SD	Lima
249	6,884	Greenville City SD	Greenville
250	6,881	Clyde-Green Springs Ex Vill SD	Clyde
251	6,874	Hubbard Ex Vill SD	Hubbard
251	6,874	Milton-Union Exempted Vill Schls	West Milton
253	6,860	Indian Lake Local SD	Lewistown
254	6,855	Lakeview Local SD	Cortland
255	6,848	Conneaut Area City SD	Conneaut
256	6,845	Highland Local SD	Sparta
256	6,845	Manchester Local SD	Akron
258	6,844	Bellevue City SD	Bellevue
259	6,843	Gallipolis City SD	Gallipolis
259	6,843	Otsego Local SD	Tontogany
261	6,842	Genoa Area Local SD	Genoa
262	6,840	Edgewood City SD	Trenton
263	6,830	James A Garfield Local SD	Garrettsville
264	6,823	River View Local SD	Warsaw
265	6,821	Fairless Local SD	Navarre
266	6,818	Logan-Hocking Local SD	Logan
266	6,818	Van Wert City SD	Van Wert
268	6,815	South Point Local SD	South Point
269	6,811	Harrison Hills City SD	Hopedale
269	6,811	Westfall Local SD	Williamsport
271	6,807	Perry Local SD	Massillon
271	6,807	Teays Valley Local SD	Ashville
273	6,804	Hillsboro City SD	Hillsboro
274	6,785	Coldwater Ex Vill SD	Coldwater
275	6,784	Poland Local SD	Poland
276	6,779	Edison Local SD	Hammondsville
277	6,765	Defiance City SD	Defiance
278	6,760	Brookville Local SD	Brookville
279	6,751	Bath Local SD	Lima
279	6,751	Piqua City SD	Piqua
281	6,743	West Clermont Local SD	Cincinnati
282	6,731	Sandy Valley Local SD	Magnolia
283	6,714	Sugarcreek Local SD	Bellbrook
284	6,702	Northwest Local SD	Canal Fulton
285	6,695	Canfield Local SD	Canfield
286	6,694	New Lexington City SD	New Lexington
287	6,691	Upper Sandusky Ex Vill SD	Upper Sandusky
288	6,684	Rolling Hills Local SD	Cambridge
289	6,669	Wadsworth City SD	Wadsworth
290	6,651	Indian Creek Local SD	Wintersville
291	6,649	Highland Local SD	Medina
292	6,643	Jefferson Area Local SD	Jefferson
293	6,642	Alexander Local SD	Albany
293	6,642	Heath City SD	Heath
295	6,640	East Muskingum Local SD	New Concord
296	6,637	Amherst Ex Vill SD	Amherst
297	6,623	Eastern Local SD	Sardinia
298	6,617	Sidney City SD	Sidney
299	6,611	Oak Hills Local SD	Cincinnati
300	6,608	Warren Local SD	Vincent
301	6,607	Licking Heights Local SD	Summit Station
302	6,603	Martins Ferry City SD	Martins Ferry
303	6,601	Elgin Local SD	Marion
304	6,599	Cloverleaf Local SD	Lodi
305	6,594	Ross Local SD	Hamilton
306	6,586	Tiffin City SD	Tiffin
307	6,577	Bryan City SD	Bryan
308	6,574	Firelands Local SD	Oberlin
308	6,574	Midview Local SD	Grafton
310	6,571	West Holmes Local SD	Millersburg
311	6,567	Geneva Area City Schools	Geneva
312	6,555	Willard City SD	Willard
313	6,554	Franklin Local SD	Duncan Falls
313	6,554	Graham Local SD	Saint Paris
315	6,552	Elida Local SD	Elida
316	6,548	Union-Scioto Local SD	Chillicothe
317	6,543	Coventry Local SD	Akron
317	6,543	Marlington Local SD	Alliance
319	6,541	Wapakoneta City City SD	Wapakoneta
320	6,522	Blanchester Local SD	Blanchester
321	6,519	Jackson City SD	Jackson
322	6,503	Madison Local SD	Madison
323	6,500	Claymont City SD	Dennison
324	6,499	Lebanon City SD	Lebanon
324	6,499	Little Miami Local SD	Morrow
326	6,491	Clark-Shawnee Local SD	Springfield
327	6,487	Greeneview Local SD	Jamestown
328	6,485	West Branch Local SD	Beloit
329	6,483	Lexington Local SD	Lexington
330	6,478	United Local SD	Hanoverton
331	6,475	Mount Vernon City SD	Mount Vernon
332	6,474	Eaton Community Schools	Eaton
333	6,458	West Muskingum Local SD	Zanesville
334	6,451	North Fork Local SD	Utica
335	6,447	Northwestern Local SD	Springfield
336	6,445	Benjamin Logan Local SD	Bellefontaine
337	6,444	Northeastern Local SD	Springfield
338	6,430	Clear Fork Valley Local SD	Bellville
339	6,428	Springboro Community City SD	Springboro
340	6,426	New Philadelphia City SD	New Philadelphia
341	6,419	Indian Valley Local SD	Gnadenhutten
342	6,414	St Marys City SD	Saint Marys
343	6,409	Tipp City Ex Vill SD	Tipp City
344	6,403	Carrollton Ex Vill SD	Carrollton
345	6,399	Washington Court House City SD	Wash Ct House
346	6,386	Maysville Local SD	Zanesville
347	6,378	Ottawa-Glandorf Local SD	Ottawa
348	6,373	Keystone Local SD	Lagrange
349	6,353	Fairland Local SD	Proctorville
350	6,342	Tuscarawas Valley Local SD	Zoarville
351	6,323	East Clinton Local SD	Lees Creek
352	6,319	Louisville City SD	Louisville
353	6,311	Jonathan Alder Local SD	Plain City
354	6,302	Black River Local SD	Sullivan
355	6,292	Greenon Local SD	Springfield
356	6,266	Amanda-Clearcreek Local SD	Amanda
357	6,261	Reynoldsburg City SD	Reynoldsburg
358	6,254	Waverly City SD	Waverly

359	6,249	Avon Local SD	Avon
360	6,231	Western Brown Local SD	Mount Orab
361	6,178	Wilmington City SD	Wilmington
362	6,177	Lake Local SD	Hartville
363	6,168	Northern Local SD	Thornville
364	6,161	Lake Local SD	Millbury
365	6,129	Beaver Local SD	Lisbon
366	6,020	Tri-Valley Local Schools	Dresden
367	6,017	Wauseon Ex Vill SD	Wauseon
368	5,890	Zane Trace Local SD	Chillicothe
369	5,828	Bethel-Tate Local SD	Bethel
370	5,825	Clinton-Massie Local SD	Clarksville
371	5,770	Norwalk City SD	Norwalk
372	5,735	Clermont Northeastern Local SD	Batavia
373	4,819	Electronic Classrm of Tomorrow	Columbus
374	4,285	Ohio Virtual Academy	Maumee

Number of Diploma Recipients

Rank	Number	District Name	City
1	2,600	Columbus Public Schools	Columbus
2	2,443	Cleveland Municipal City SD	Cleveland
3	1,526	Akron Public Schools	Akron
4	1,478	Toledo City SD	Toledo
5	1,305	Cincinnati City SD	Cincinnati
6	1,003	South-Western City SD	Grove City
7	970	Westerville City SD	Westerville
8	963	Lakota Local SD	Liberty Twp
9	886	Parma City SD	Parma
10	858	Dayton City SD	Dayton
11	803	Worthington City SD	Worthington
12	785	Hilliard City SD	Hilliard
13	767	Dublin City SD	Dublin
14	730	Mentor Ex Vill SD	Mentor
15	656	Northwest Local SD	Cincinnati
16	637	Willoughby-Eastlake City SD	Willoughby
17	633	Oak Hills Local SD	Cincinnati
18	611	Berea City SD	Berea
19	608	Fairfield City SD	Fairfield
20	599	Sylvania City SD	Sylvania
21	590	Centerville City SD	Centerville
22	585	Forest Hills Local SD	Cincinnati
23	534	Kettering City SD	Kettering
24	524	Hamilton City SD	Hamilton
25	520	West Clermont Local SD	Cincinnati
26	518	Lakewood City SD	Lakewood
27	508	Strongsville City SD	Strongsville
28	501	Medina City SD	Medina
29	495	Beavercreek City SD	Beavercreek
29	495	Canton City SD	Canton
31	494	Pickerington Local SD	Pickerington
32	476	Lorain City SD	Lorain
33	475	Brunswick City SD	Brunswick
34	458	Reynoldsburg City SD	Reynoldsburg
35	448	Washington Local Schools	Toledo
36	437	Huber Heights City SD	Huber Heights
37	426	Findlay City SD	Findlay
38	425	Sycamore Community City SD	Cincinnati
39	424	Gahanna-Jefferson City SD	Gahanna
40	422	Jackson Local SD	Massillon
41	421	Upper Arlington City SD	Upper Arlington
41	421	Youngstown City SD	Youngstown
43	420	Stow-Munroe Falls City SD	Stow
44	417	Milford Ex Vill SD	Milford
45	411	Springfield City SD	Springfield
46	403	Princeton City SD	Cincinnati
47	393	Northmont City SD	Englewood
48	390	Plain Local SD	Canton
48	390	Solon City SD	Solon
50	389	Newark City SD	Newark
51	381	Hudson City SD	Hudson
52	380	Boardman Local SD	Youngstown
53	368	North Olmsted City Schools	North Olmsted
54	367	Mason City SD	Mason
55	363	Euclid City SD	Euclid
56	362	Elyria City SD	Elyria
56	362	Shaker Heights City SD	Shaker Heights
58	360	Cuyahoga Falls City SD	Cuyahoga Falls
58	360	Middletown City SD	Middletown
60	358	Lancaster City SD	Lancaster
61	352	Warren City SD	Warren
62	351	Austintown Local SD	Youngstown
63	349	Fairborn City Schools	Fairborn
64	346	Cleveland Hts-Univ Hts City SD	University Hgts
65	342	Perry Local SD	Massillon
65	342	South Euclid-Lyndhurst City SD	Lyndhurst
67	341	Mayfield City SD	Highland Hgts
68	340	Brecksville-Broadview Hgts City	Brecksville
69	335	North Royalton City SD	N Royalton
70	330	Miamisburg City SD	Miamisburg
71	328	Perrysburg Exempted Village	Perrysburg
72	327	Wadsworth City SD	Wadsworth
73	325	Fremont City SD	Fremont
74	319	North Canton City SD	North Canton
75	315	Olentangy Local SD	Lewis Center
76	314	Groveport Madison Local SD	Groveport
76	314	Xenia Community City SD	Xenia
78	309	Nordonia Hills City SD	Northfield
79	308	Kent City SD	Kent
80	306	Adams County/Ohio Valley LSD	West Union
80	306	Painesville Township Local SD	Painesville
82	294	Troy City SD	Troy
83	288	Ashland City SD	Ashland
84	285	Chillicothe City SD	Chillicothe
84	285	Loveland City SD	Loveland
86	284	Mount Vernon City SD	Mount Vernon
87	282	Celina City SD	Celina
88	281	Amherst Ex Vill SD	Amherst
88	281	Wooster City SD	Wooster
90	280	Marion City SD	Marion
91	279	Lebanon City SD	Lebanon
92	277	Southwest Local SD	Harrison
93	276	Westlake City SD	Westlake
94	273	Cloverleaf Local SD	Lodi
95	267	Greenville City SD	Greenville
96	264	Barberton City SD	Barberton
97	263	Garfield Heights City SD	Garfield Hgts
98	261	Delaware City SD	Delaware
99	260	Talawanda City SD	Oxford
100	258	Mansfield City SD	Mansfield
101	257	Marysville Exempted Village SD	Marysville
102	256	Bowling Green City SD	Bowling Green
103	255	Massillon City SD	Massillon
104	254	Madison Local SD	Madison
104	254	West Carrollton City SD	West Carrollton
106	252	East Cleveland City SD	East Cleveland
107	248	Lake Local SD	Hartville
108	247	Green Local SD	Green
108	247	Tiffin City SD	Tiffin
110	244	Lima City SD	Lima
110	244	Vandalia-Butler City SD	Vandalia
112	243	Avon Lake City Schools	Avon Lake
113	242	Maumee City SD	Maumee
114	240	Ashtabula Area City SD	Ashtabula
114	240	Dover City SD	Dover
116	238	New Philadelphia City SD	New Philadelphia
117	236	Springfield Local Schools	Holland
118	233	Anthony Wayne Local SD	Whitehouse
118	233	Sidney City SD	Sidney
118	233	Southwest Licking Local SD	Etna
121	232	Chardon Local SD	Chardon
122	231	Bedford City SD	Bedford
122	231	Sandusky City SD	Sandusky
122	231	Springboro Community City SD	Springboro
122	231	Wapakoneta City SD	Wapakoneta
122	231	Wilmington City SD	Wilmington
127	230	Howland Local SD	Warren
128	228	Piqua City SD	Piqua
129	227	Logan-Hocking Local SD	Logan
130	225	Canfield Local SD	Canfield
130	225	Oregon City SD	Oregon
130	225	Revere Local SD	Bath
133	224	Geneva Area City Schools	Geneva
133	224	Madison Local SD	Mansfield
133	224	Tecumseh Local SD	New Carlisle
136	223	Kings Local SD	Kings Mills
137	219	Olmsted Falls City SD	Olmsted Falls
138	218	Winton Woods City SD	Cincinnati
139	216	Marietta City Schools	Marietta
140	215	Lexington Local SD	Lexington
141	214	Kenston Local SD	Chagrin Falls
142	213	Alliance City SD	Alliance
143	211	Copley-Fairlawn City SD	Copley
144	210	Niles City SD	Niles
145	208	Midview Local SD	Grafton
146	207	Defiance City SD	Defiance
147	206	Twinsburg City SD	Twinsburg
148	203	Clark-Shawnee Local SD	Springfield
148	203	Jackson City SD	Jackson
150	202	Switzerland of Ohio Local SD	Woodsfield
151	199	Bellefontaine City Schools	Bellefontaine
151	199	Carrollton Ex Vill SD	Carrollton
151	199	Hubbard Ex Vill SD	Hubbard
151	199	Louisville City SD	Louisville
155	198	Mt Healthy City SD	Cincinnati
155	198	North Ridgeville City SD	N Ridgeville
155	198	Northeastern Local SD	Springfield
155	198	Poland Local SD	Poland
159	196	Crestwood Local SD	Mantua
159	196	Highland Local SD	Medina
161	195	West Geauga Local SD	Chesterland
162	194	Napoleon Area City SD	Napoleon
162	194	Tri-Valley Local Schools	Dresden
164	193	Orange City SD	Cleveland
164	193	St Marys City SD	Saint Marys
166	192	Trotwood-Madison City Schools	Trotwood
166	192	Whitehall City SD	Whitehall
168	191	Big Walnut Local SD	Galena
168	191	Springfield Local SD	Akron
170	190	Franklin City SD	Franklin
170	190	Warren Local SD	Vincent
172	189	Maple Heights City SD	Maple Heights
173	187	Elida Local SD	Elida
173	187	West Branch Local SD	Beloit
175	185	East Liverpool City SD	East Liverpool
175	185	Tallmadge City Schools	Tallmadge
177	184	River View Local SD	Warsaw
177	184	Sugarcreek Local SD	Bellbrook
179	183	Buckeye Local SD	Rayland
179	183	Norton City Schools	Norton
179	183	Salem City SD	Salem
182	182	Buckeye Local SD	Medina
182	182	Edgewood City SD	Trenton
182	182	Hillsboro City SD	Hillsboro
182	182	Mad River Local SD	Dayton
186	181	Zanesville City SD	Zanesville
187	180	Bellevue City SD	Bellevue
188	178	Coventry Local SD	Akron
189	177	Bexley City SD	Bexley
189	177	East Muskingum Local SD	New Concord
189	177	Edison Local SD	Hammondsville
192	175	Field Local SD	Mogadore
192	175	Lakeview Local SD	Cortland
192	175	Tipp City Ex Vill SD	Tipp City
195	174	Ravenna City SD	Ravenna
196	171	Clyde-Green Springs Ex Vill SD	Clyde
196	171	Marlington Local SD	Alliance
196	171	Shawnee Local SD	Lima
196	171	Shelby City SD	Shelby
196	171	Southeast Local SD	Ravenna
196	171	Steubenville City SD	Steubenville
196	171	Vermilion Local SD	Vermilion
203	170	Galion City SD	Galion
203	170	Miami Trace Local SD	Wash Ct House
205	169	Little Miami Local SD	Morrow
205	169	Port Clinton City SD	Port Clinton
205	169	Ross Local SD	Hamilton
208	168	Bay Village City SD	Bay Village
208	168	Teays Valley Local SD	Ashville
210	167	Fairview Park City SD	Fairview Park
210	167	Logan Elm Local SD	Circleville
212	165	Franklin Local SD	Duncan Falls
212	165	Gallia County Local SD	Gallipolis
214	164	Ottawa-Glandorf Local SD	Ottawa
215	162	Canton Local SD	Canton
215	162	Conneaut Area City SD	Conneaut
217	161	Beaver Local SD	Lisbon
218	160	Buckeye Local SD	Ashtabula
218	160	Maysville Local SD	Zanesville
218	160	Norwalk City SD	Norwalk
218	160	Warrensville Heights City SD	Warrensville Hgts
222	157	Buckeye Valley Local SD	Delaware
222	157	Morgan Local SD	McConnelsville
224	155	Lakewood Local SD	Hebron
224	155	New Richmond Ex Vill SD	New Richmond
226	154	Cambridge City SD	Cambridge
227	153	Upper Sandusky Ex Vill SD	Upper Sandusky
227	153	Van Wert City SD	Van Wert
229	152	Bath Local SD	Lima
229	152	Benton Carroll Salem Local SD	Oak Harbor
229	152	Granville Ex Vill SD	Granville
232	151	Indian Hill Ex Vill SD	Cincinnati
232	151	Northern Local SD	Thornville
232	151	Northwest Local SD	Canal Fulton
235	150	Liberty Local SD	Youngstown
235	150	Perkins Local SD	Sandusky
235	150	West Holmes Local SD	Millersburg
238	149	Aurora City SD	Aurora
238	149	Bryan City SD	Bryan
238	149	Gallipolis City SD	Gallipolis
238	149	Union Local SD	Morristown
242	148	Champion Local SD	Warren
243	147	Kenton City SD	Kenton
243	147	Monroe Local SD	Monroe
245	146	Chagrin Falls Ex Vill SD	Chagrin Falls
245	146	Goshen Local SD	Goshen
245	146	Greenon Local SD	Springfield
245	146	Triway Local SD	Wooster
249	145	Claymont City SD	Dennison
249	145	Minerva Local SD	Minerva
249	145	Rocky River City SD	Rocky River
249	145	Wauseon Ex Vill SD	Wauseon
253	144	Vinton County Local SD	Mc Arthur
253	144	Washington Court House City SD	Wash Ct House
253	144	Willard City SD	Willard
256	143	Western Brown Local SD	Mount Orab
256	143	Wyoming City SD	Wyoming
258	142	Beachwood City SD	Beachwood

258	142	Circleville City SD	Circleville
258	142	Fairfield Union Local SD	W Rushville
258	142	West Muskingum Local SD	Zanesville
262	141	Finneytown Local SD	Cincinnati
262	141	Swanton Local SD	Swanton
264	140	Eastwood Local SD	Pemberville
264	140	Firelands Local SD	Oberlin
264	140	Oakwood City SD	Dayton
267	139	Clear Fork Valley Local SD	Bellville
267	139	Jefferson Area Local SD	Jefferson
267	139	River Valley Local SD	Caledonia
270	138	Bethel-Tate Local SD	Bethel
270	138	Harrison Hills City SD	Hopedale
270	138	Valley View Local SD	Germantown
273	137	Lake Local SD	Millbury
273	137	Norwood City SD	Norwood
273	137	Rossford Ex Vill SD	Rossford
276	136	Huron City Schools	Huron
276	136	Three Rivers Local Schools	Cleves
278	135	Canal Winchester Local SD	Canal Winchester
278	135	Eaton Community Schools	Eaton
278	135	Northwestern Local SD	Springfield
281	134	London City SD	London
281	134	Paulding Ex Vill SD	Paulding
283	133	Hamilton Local SD	Columbus
283	133	Manchester Local SD	Akron
283	133	Union-Scioto Local SD	Chillicothe
286	132	Berlin-Milan Local SD	Milan
286	132	Graham Local SD	Saint Paris
286	132	Greenfield Ex Vill SD	Greenfield
286	132	Indian Creek Local SD	Wintersville
286	132	Perry Local SD	Perry
291	131	Benjamin Logan Local SD	Bellefontaine
292	130	Indian Lake Local SD	Lewistown
292	130	Sheffield-Sheffield Lake City SD	Sheffield Vlg
294	129	Martins Ferry City SD	Martins Ferry
295	128	Ironton City SD	Ironton
296	127	Genoa Area Local SD	Genoa
296	127	Madison-Plains Local SD	London
296	127	Orrville City SD	Orrville
299	125	Elgin Local SD	Marion
299	125	Meigs Local SD	Pomeroy
301	124	Coldwater Ex Vill SD	Coldwater
301	124	Rolling Hills Local SD	Cambridge
303	123	Struthers City SD	Struthers
304	122	Coshocton City SD	Coshocton
304	122	Indian Valley Local SD	Gnadenhutten
306	121	Clermont Northeastern Local SD	Batavia
307	120	Alexander Local SD	Albany
307	120	St Clairsville-Richland City SD	St Clairsville
309	119	Fairless Local SD	Navarre
309	119	Girard City SD	Girard
309	119	Ontario Local SD	Mansfield
309	119	Streetsboro City Schools	Streetsboro
313	118	Bucyrus City SD	Bucyrus
313	118	Northwest Local SD	Mc Dermott
313	118	Urbana City SD	Urbana
316	117	Avon Local SD	Avon
316	117	Clinton-Massie Local SD	Clarksville
316	117	North Fork Local SD	Utica
316	117	Otsego Local SD	Tontogany
316	117	Wickliffe City SD	Wickliffe
321	116	Milton-Union Exempted Vill Schls	West Milton
321	116	Pike-Delta-York Local SD	Delta
321	116	Preble Shawnee Local SD	Camden
324	115	Fairland Local SD	Proctorville
324	115	Fostoria City SD	Fostoria
324	115	Licking Valley Local SD Sd	Newark
327	114	Waverly City SD	Waverly
328	113	Keystone Local SD	Lagrange
328	113	Mariemont City SD	Cincinnati
328	113	Minford Local SD	Minford
328	113	Sandy Valley Local SD	Magnolia
328	113	Washington-Nile Local SD	West Portsmouth
333	111	Carlisle Local SD	Carlisle
334	110	Bellaire Local SD	Bellaire
334	110	Ridgewood Local SD	West Lafayette
336	109	Jonathan Alder Local SD	Plain City
336	109	Madeira City SD	Cincinnati
336	109	Wellington Ex Vill SD	Wellington
339	108	Plain Local SD	New Albany
339	108	Tuscarawas Valley Local SD	Zoarville
341	106	Highland Local SD	Sparta
342	105	South Point Local SD	South Point
343	104	Brookville Local SD	Brookville
343	104	Heath City SD	Heath
345	102	Greeneview Local SD	Jamestown
345	102	Portsmouth City SD	Portsmouth
347	101	James A Garfield Local SD	Garrettsville
348	100	Campbell City SD	Campbell
348	100	New Lexington City SD	New Lexington
348	100	Rock Hill Local SD	Ironton
351	99	United Local SD	Hanoverton
352	98	Black River Local SD	Sullivan
353	97	Clearview Local SD	Lorain
353	97	Westfall Local SD	Williamsport
355	96	Southeast Local SD	Apple Creek
355	96	Woodridge Local SD	Peninsula
357	95	Eastern Local SD	Sardinia
357	95	Madison Local SD	Middletown
357	95	Zane Trace Local SD	Chillicothe
360	93	Blanchester Local SD	Blanchester
360	93	East Clinton Local SD	Lees Creek
360	93	Northridge Local SD	Dayton
363	92	Batavia Local SD	Batavia
363	92	Licking Heights Local SD	Summit Station
363	92	North College Hill City SD	Cincinnati
366	89	Newton Falls Ex Vill SD	Newton Falls
366	89	Scioto Valley Local SD	Piketon
368	88	Painesville City Local SD	Painesville
369	87	Amanda-Clearcreek Local SD	Amanda
369	87	Athens City SD	The Plains
371	78	Wellston City Schools	Wellston
372	63	East Holmes Local Schools	Berlin
373	31	Electronic Classrm of Tomorrow	Columbus
374	n/a	Ohio Virtual Academy	Maumee

High School Drop-out Rate

Rank	Percent	District Name	City
1	16.0	Canton City SD	Canton
2	15.1	Cleveland Municipal City SD	Cleveland
3	12.2	Lima City SD	Lima
4	10.7	East Cleveland City SD	East Cleveland
5	9.0	Newark City SD	Newark
6	8.7	Columbus Public Schools	Columbus
6	8.7	Youngstown City SD	Youngstown
8	8.5	Zanesville City SD	Zanesville
9	8.4	Dayton City SD	Dayton
10	8.2	Cincinnati City SD	Cincinnati
11	8.1	Norwood City SD	Norwood
12	7.8	Bedford City SD	Bedford
13	7.6	Portsmouth City SD	Portsmouth
14	7.2	Mad River Local SD	Dayton
15	6.9	Trotwood-Madison City Schools	Trotwood
16	6.8	Hamilton City SD	Hamilton
16	6.8	Lorain City SD	Lorain
16	6.8	Marion City SD	Marion
16	6.8	New Lexington City SD	New Lexington
20	6.7	Toledo City SD	Toledo
21	6.2	Logan-Hocking Local SD	Logan
21	6.2	Springfield City SD	Springfield
23	6.1	Ashtabula Area City SD	Ashtabula
23	6.1	Washington Local Schools	Toledo
25	6.0	Elyria City SD	Elyria
26	5.9	Alliance City SD	Alliance
26	5.9	Maple Heights City SD	Maple Heights
26	5.9	Painesville City Local SD	Painesville
26	5.9	South-Western City SD	Grove City
26	5.9	Whitehall City SD	Whitehall
31	5.8	Mansfield City SD	Mansfield
31	5.8	New Richmond Ex Vill SD	New Richmond
33	5.7	Northridge Local SD	Dayton
34	5.6	West Clermont Local SD	Cincinnati
35	5.5	Fairborn City Schools	Fairborn
36	5.4	Madison Local SD	Mansfield
37	5.3	Fostoria City SD	Fostoria
37	5.3	Franklin City SD	Franklin
37	5.3	Huber Heights City SD	Huber Heights
37	5.3	Warren City SD	Warren
41	5.2	Middletown City SD	Middletown
41	5.2	Northwest Local SD	Cincinnati
41	5.2	Norwalk City SD	Norwalk
41	5.2	Scioto Valley Local SD	Piketon
41	5.2	Steubenville City SD	Steubenville
41	5.2	Western Brown Local SD	Mount Orab
47	5.1	Massillon City SD	Massillon
48	5.0	Akron Public Schools	Akron
48	5.0	Morgan Local SD	McConnelsville
48	5.0	Parma City SD	Parma
48	5.0	Southwest Local SD	Harrison
48	5.0	Vinton County Local SD	Mc Arthur
53	4.9	Ravenna City SD	Ravenna
53	4.9	Tiffin City SD	Tiffin
53	4.9	Xenia Community City SD	Xenia
56	4.8	Barberton City SD	Barberton
56	4.8	Defiance City SD	Defiance
58	4.7	Ironton City SD	Ironton
59	4.6	Fremont City SD	Fremont
59	4.6	Tecumseh Local SD	New Carlisle
59	4.6	Tuscarawas Valley Local SD	Zoarville
62	4.5	Bucyrus City SD	Bucyrus
62	4.5	Eaton Community Schools	Eaton
62	4.5	Goshen Local SD	Goshen
62	4.5	London City SD	London
66	4.4	Indian Lake Local SD	Lewistown
66	4.4	Lancaster City SD	Lancaster
66	4.4	Mt Healthy City SD	Cincinnati
69	4.3	Gallipolis City SD	Gallipolis
69	4.3	Groveport Madison Local SD	Groveport
71	4.2	Bethel-Tate Local SD	Bethel
71	4.2	Clermont Northeastern Local SD	Batavia
71	4.2	Rolling Hills Local SD	Cambridge
74	4.1	North Fork Local SD	Utica
75	4.0	Circleville City SD	Circleville
75	4.0	Princeton City SD	Cincinnati
75	4.0	Talawanda City SD	Oxford
78	3.9	Alexander Local SD	Albany
78	3.9	Batavia Local SD	Batavia
78	3.9	Delaware City SD	Delaware
78	3.9	Greenfield Ex Vill SD	Greenfield
78	3.9	Greenon Local SD	Springfield
78	3.9	Hamilton Local SD	Columbus
78	3.9	Teays Valley Local SD	Ashville
78	3.9	Three Rivers Local Schools	Cleves
78	3.9	Waverly City SD	Waverly
87	3.8	Fairland Local SD	Proctorville
88	3.7	Cambridge City SD	Cambridge
88	3.7	Gallia County Local SD	Gallipolis
88	3.7	Sandusky City SD	Sandusky
91	3.6	Bellaire Local SD	Bellaire
91	3.6	Minerva Local SD	Minerva
91	3.6	Napoleon Area City SD	Napoleon
91	3.6	Washington-Nile Local SD	West Portsmouth
95	3.5	Cleveland Hts-Univ Hts City SD	University Hgts
95	3.5	Harrison Hills City SD	Hopedale
95	3.5	Mariemont City SD	Cincinnati
95	3.5	Washington Court House City SD	Wash Ct House
99	3.4	Edgewood City SD	Trenton
99	3.4	Lakewood City SD	Lakewood
99	3.4	Madison Local SD	Madison
99	3.4	Rock Hill Local SD	Ironton
99	3.4	Willard City SD	Willard
104	3.3	Chillicothe City SD	Chillicothe
104	3.3	East Clinton Local SD	Lees Creek
104	3.3	Galion City SD	Galion
104	3.3	James A Garfield Local SD	Garrettsville
104	3.3	Miami Trace Local SD	Wash Ct House
104	3.3	Piqua City SD	Piqua
110	3.2	Adams County/Ohio Valley LSD	West Union
110	3.2	Niles City SD	Niles
110	3.2	Port Clinton City SD	Port Clinton
110	3.2	Ross Local SD	Hamilton
110	3.2	Shelby City SD	Shelby
110	3.2	Union-Scioto Local SD	Chillicothe
110	3.2	Winton Woods City SD	Cincinnati
117	3.1	Kenton City SD	Kenton
117	3.1	Troy City SD	Troy
119	3.0	Buckeye Local SD	Ashtabula
119	3.0	Franklin Local SD	Duncan Falls
119	3.0	Garfield Heights City SD	Garfield Hgts
119	3.0	Oregon City SD	Oregon
119	3.0	Willoughby-Eastlake City SD	Willoughby
124	2.9	Ashland City SD	Ashland
124	2.9	Bellefontaine City Schools	Bellefontaine
124	2.9	Madison Local SD	Middletown
124	2.9	North College Hill City SD	Cincinnati
124	2.9	Orrville City SD	Orrville
124	2.9	Sidney City SD	Sidney
124	2.9	Valley View Local SD	Germantown
124	2.9	Van Wert City SD	Van Wert
132	2.8	Midview Local SD	Grafton
132	2.8	Mount Vernon City SD	Mount Vernon
132	2.8	Springfield Local Schools	Holland
132	2.8	Urbana City SD	Urbana
132	2.8	Wickliffe City SD	Wickliffe
137	2.7	Bryan City SD	Bryan
137	2.7	Gahanna-Jefferson City SD	Gahanna
137	2.7	Heath City SD	Heath
137	2.7	Licking Valley Local SD Sd	Newark
137	2.7	Switzerland of Ohio Local SD	Woodsfield
142	2.6	Canal Winchester Local SD	Canal Winchester
142	2.6	Findlay City SD	Findlay
142	2.6	Plain Local SD	Canton
142	2.6	River View Local SD	Warsaw
142	2.6	Rossford Ex Vill SD	Rossford
147	2.5	Brookville Local SD	Brookville
147	2.5	Finneytown Local SD	Cincinnati
147	2.5	Jackson City SD	Jackson
147	2.5	Licking Heights Local SD	Summit Station
147	2.5	Milton-Union Exempted Vill Schls	West Milton
147	2.5	Northwest Local SD	Mc Dermott
147	2.5	Struthers City SD	Struthers
147	2.5	Warren Local SD	Vincent
155	2.4	Conneaut Area City SD	Conneaut
155	2.4	Madison-Plains Local SD	London
155	2.4	Monroe Local SD	Monroe

155	2.4	Preble Shawnee Local SD	Camden	248	1.4	Graham Local SD	Saint Paris	334	0.5	Oak Hills Local SD	Cincinnati
155	2.4	Southwest Licking Local SD	Etna	248	1.4	Hubbard Ex Vill SD	Hubbard	334	0.5	Perkins Local SD	Sandusky
155	2.4	United Local SD	Hanoverton	248	1.4	Logan Elm Local SD	Circleville	345	0.4	Avon Local SD	Avon
155	2.4	Woodridge Local SD	Peninsula	248	1.4	Maumee City SD	Maumee	345	0.4	Green Local SD	Green
162	2.3	Beavercreek City SD	Beavercreek	248	1.4	Maysville Local SD	Zanesville	345	0.4	Kenston Local SD	Chagrin Falls
162	2.3	Big Walnut Local SD	Galena	256	1.3	Berlin-Milan Local SD	Milan	345	0.4	Madeira City SD	Cincinnati
162	2.3	Clinton-Massie Local SD	Clarksville	256	1.3	Crestwood Local SD	Mantua	345	0.4	Martins Ferry City SD	Martins Ferry
162	2.3	Milford Ex Vill SD	Milford	256	1.3	Dover City SD	Dover	345	0.4	Olentangy Local SD	Lewis Center
162	2.3	South Point Local SD	South Point	256	1.3	Fairview Park City SD	Fairview Park	345	0.4	Perry Local SD	Massillon
162	2.3	Southeast Local SD	Ravenna	256	1.3	Manchester Local SD	Akron	345	0.4	Tipp City Ex Vill SD	Tipp City
162	2.3	Upper Sandusky Ex Vill SD	Upper Sandusky	256	1.3	Northern Local SD	Thornville	345	0.4	West Branch Local SD	Beloit
169	2.2	Benjamin Logan Local SD	Bellefontaine	256	1.3	River Valley Local SD	Caledonia	345	0.4	West Geauga Local SD	Chesterland
169	2.2	East Liverpool City SD	East Liverpool	256	1.3	Strongsville City SD	Strongsville	355	0.3	Austintown Local SD	Youngstown
169	2.2	Eastern Local SD	Sardinia	256	1.3	Wilmington City SD	Wilmington	355	0.3	Canfield Local SD	Canfield
169	2.2	Greeneview Local SD	Jamestown	265	1.2	Bay Village City SD	Bay Village	355	0.3	Granville Ex Vill SD	Granville
169	2.2	Jonathan Alder Local SD	Plain City	265	1.2	Boardman Local SD	Youngstown	355	0.3	Lakeview Local SD	Cortland
169	2.2	Kent City SD	Kent	265	1.2	Buckeye Local SD	Rayland	355	0.3	Marlington Local SD	Alliance
169	2.2	Ridgewood Local SD	West Lafayette	265	1.2	Champion Local SD	Warren	355	0.3	Medina City SD	Medina
169	2.2	Tri-Valley Local Schools	Dresden	265	1.2	Chardon Local SD	Chardon	355	0.3	St Marys City SD	Saint Marys
169	2.2	Westerville City SD	Westerville	265	1.2	Fairfield City SD	Fairfield	355	0.3	Upper Arlington City SD	Upper Arlington
178	2.1	Athens City SD	The Plains	265	1.2	Hillsboro City SD	Hillsboro	363	0.2	Amherst Ex Vill SD	Amherst
178	2.1	Clyde-Green Springs Ex Vill SD	Clyde	265	1.2	Lake Local SD	Millbury	363	0.2	Campbell City SD	Campbell
178	2.1	Elida Local SD	Elida	265	1.2	Minford Local SD	Minford	363	0.2	Canton Local SD	Canton
178	2.1	New Philadelphia City SD	New Philadelphia	265	1.2	North Olmsted City Schools	North Olmsted	363	0.2	Poland Local SD	Poland
178	2.1	Nordonia Hills City SD	Northfield	265	1.2	Ontario Local SD	Mansfield	363	0.2	West Muskingum Local SD	Zanesville
178	2.1	Otsego Local SD	Tontogany	265	1.2	Ottawa-Glandorf Local SD	Ottawa	368	0.1	Euclid City SD	Euclid
178	2.1	Wellston City Schools	Wellston	265	1.2	Paulding Ex Vill SD	Paulding	368	0.1	Warrensville Heights City SD	Warrensville Hgts
178	2.1	Zane Trace Local SD	Chillicothe	265	1.2	Westlake City SD	Westlake	370	0.0	East Holmes Local Schools	Berlin
186	2.0	Anthony Wayne Local SD	Whitehouse	279	1.1	Brunswick City SD	Brunswick	370	0.0	Electronic Classrm of Tomorrow	Columbus
186	2.0	Cuyahoga Falls City SD	Cuyahoga Falls	279	1.1	Carrollton Ex Vill SD	Carrollton	370	0.0	Shaker Heights City SD	Shaker Heights
186	2.0	Greenville City SD	Greenville	279	1.1	Clearview Local SD	Lorain	370	0.0	Wyoming City SD	Wyoming
186	2.0	Salem City SD	Salem	279	1.1	Edison Local SD	Hammondsville	374	n/a	Ohio Virtual Academy	Maumee
186	2.0	Sandy Valley Local SD	Magnolia	279	1.1	Indian Creek Local SD	Wintersville				
186	2.0	Shawnee Local SD	Lima	279	1.1	Keystone Local SD	Lagrange				
186	2.0	Springfield Local SD	Akron	279	1.1	Kings Local SD	Kings Mills				
186	2.0	Triway Local SD	Wooster	279	1.1	Louisville City SD	Louisville				
186	2.0	Vermilion Local SD	Vermilion	279	1.1	Newton Falls Ex Vill SD	Newton Falls				
186	2.0	West Holmes Local SD	Millersburg	279	1.1	Oakwood City SD	Dayton				
196	1.9	Beaver Local SD	Lisbon	279	1.1	Springboro Community City SD	Springboro				
196	1.9	Blanchester Local SD	Blanchester	279	1.1	Stow-Munroe Falls City SD	Stow				
196	1.9	Carlisle Local SD	Carlisle	291	1.0	Aurora City SD	Aurora				
196	1.9	East Muskingum Local SD	New Concord	291	1.0	Bowling Green City SD	Bowling Green				
196	1.9	Geneva Area City Schools	Geneva	291	1.0	Dublin City SD	Dublin				
196	1.9	Little Miami Local SD	Morrow	291	1.0	Mayfield City SD	Highland Hgts				
196	1.9	Painesville Township Local SD	Painesville	291	1.0	Orange City SD	Cleveland				
196	1.9	Pike-Delta-York Local SD	Delta	291	1.0	Perrysburg Exempted Village	Perrysburg				
196	1.9	St Clairsville-Richland City SD	St Clairsville	291	1.0	Sugarcreek Local SD	Bellbrook				
196	1.9	Union Local SD	Morristown	298	0.9	Centerville City SD	Centerville				
196	1.9	Wadsworth City SD	Wadsworth	298	0.9	Coldwater Ex Vill SD	Coldwater				
196	1.9	Wellington Ex Vill SD	Wellington	298	0.9	Lakota Local SD	Liberty Twp				
208	1.8	Bath Local SD	Lima	298	0.9	Liberty Local SD	Youngstown				
208	1.8	Bellevue City SD	Bellevue	298	0.9	Meigs Local SD	Pomeroy				
208	1.8	Celina City SD	Celina	298	0.9	Mentor Ex Vill SD	Mentor				
208	1.8	Clark-Shawnee Local SD	Springfield	298	0.9	Pickerington Local SD	Pickerington				
208	1.8	Genoa Area Local SD	Genoa	298	0.9	Streetsboro City Schools	Streetsboro				
208	1.8	Northwestern Local SD	Springfield	298	0.9	Sycamore Community City SD	Cincinnati				
208	1.8	Sylvania City SD	Sylvania	298	0.9	Vandalia-Butler City SD	Vandalia				
208	1.8	Westfall Local SD	Williamsport	298	0.9	Worthington City SD	Worthington				
216	1.7	Avon Lake City Schools	Avon Lake	309	0.8	Black River Local SD	Sullivan				
216	1.7	Clear Fork Valley Local SD	Bellville	309	0.8	Lake Local SD	Hartville				
216	1.7	Field Local SD	Mogadore	309	0.8	Lakewood Local SD	Hebron				
216	1.7	Hilliard City SD	Hilliard	309	0.8	Lexington Local SD	Lexington				
216	1.7	Lebanon City SD	Lebanon	309	0.8	Revere Local SD	Bath				
216	1.7	Loveland City SD	Loveland	309	0.8	Wooster City SD	Wooster				
216	1.7	Northeastern Local SD	Springfield	315	0.7	Benton Carroll Salem Local SD	Oak Harbor				
216	1.7	Rocky River City SD	Rocky River	315	0.7	Brecksville-Broadview Hgts City	Brecksville				
216	1.7	Southeast Local SD	Apple Creek	315	0.7	Buckeye Valley Local SD	Delaware				
225	1.6	Berea City SD	Berea	315	0.7	Coshocton City SD	Coshocton				
225	1.6	Cloverleaf Local SD	Lodi	315	0.7	Fairfield Union Local SD	W Rushville				
225	1.6	Fairless Local SD	Navarre	315	0.7	Hudson City SD	Hudson				
225	1.6	Highland Local SD	Medina	315	0.7	Huron City Schools	Huron				
225	1.6	Jefferson Area Local SD	Jefferson	315	0.7	Marysville Exempted Village SD	Marysville				
225	1.6	Marietta City Schools	Marietta	315	0.7	Northmont City SD	Englewood				
225	1.6	Miamisburg City SD	Miamisburg	315	0.7	Northwest Local SD	Canal Fulton				
225	1.6	North Ridgeville City SD	N Ridgeville	315	0.7	Perry Local SD	Perry				
225	1.6	Olmsted Falls City SD	Olmsted Falls	315	0.7	Solon City SD	Solon				
225	1.6	Plain Local SD	New Albany	315	0.7	Tallmadge City Schools	Tallmadge				
225	1.6	Reynoldsburg City SD	Reynoldsburg	328	0.6	Beachwood City SD	Beachwood				
225	1.6	Sheffield-Sheffield Lake City SD	Sheffield Vlg	328	0.6	Copley-Fairlawn City SD	Copley				
225	1.6	Twinsburg City SD	Twinsburg	328	0.6	Indian Hill Ex Vill SD	Cincinnati				
225	1.6	Wapakoneta City SD	Wapakoneta	328	0.6	Jackson Local SD	Massillon				
225	1.6	Wauseon Ex Vill SD	Wauseon	328	0.6	North Canton City SD	North Canton				
240	1.5	Amanda-Clearcreek Local SD	Amanda	328	0.6	South Euclid-Lyndhurst City SD	Lyndhurst				
240	1.5	Buckeye Local SD	Medina	334	0.5	Bexley City SD	Bexley				
240	1.5	Forest Hills Local SD	Cincinnati	334	0.5	Chagrin Falls Ex Vill SD	Chagrin Falls				
240	1.5	Girard City SD	Girard	334	0.5	Claymont City SD	Dennison				
240	1.5	Highland Local SD	Sparta	334	0.5	Eastwood Local SD	Pemberville				
240	1.5	Mason City SD	Mason	334	0.5	Howland Local SD	Warren				
240	1.5	Swanton Local SD	Swanton	334	0.5	Indian Valley Local SD	Gnadenhutten				
240	1.5	West Carrollton City SD	West Carrollton	334	0.5	Kettering City SD	Kettering				
248	1.4	Coventry Local SD	Akron	334	0.5	North Royalton City SD	N Royalton				
248	1.4	Elgin Local SD	Marion	334	0.5	Norton City Schools	Norton				
248	1.4	Firelands Local SD	Oberlin								

Oklahoma

Oklahoma Public School Educational Profile

Category	Value	Category	Value
Schools *(2003-2004)*	1,786	**Diploma Recipients** *(2002-2003)*	36,853
Instructional Level		White, Non-Hispanic	25,383
Primary	967	Black, Non-Hispanic	3,301
Middle	329	Asian/Pacific Islander	650
High	465	American Indian/Alaskan Native	5,957
Other Level	25	Hispanic	1,562
Curriculum		**High School Drop-out Rate** (%) *(2001-2002)*	4.4
Regular	1,786	White, Non-Hispanic	3.8
Special Education	0	Black, Non-Hispanic	6.7
Vocational	0	Asian/Pacific Islander	3.2
Alternative	0	American Indian/Alaskan Native	3.8
Type		Hispanic	9.4
Magnet	0	**Staff** *(2003-2004)*	
Charter	12	Teachers	39,250.6
Title I Eligible	1,236	Average Salary[1] ($)	35,061
School-wide Title I	881	Librarians/Media Specialists	996.5
Students *(2003-2004)*	626,160	Guidance Counselors	1,494.2
Gender (%)		**Ratios** *(2003-2004)*	
Male	51.5	Student/Teacher Ratio	16.0 to 1
Female	48.5	Student/Librarian Ratio	628.4 to 1
Race/Ethnicity (%)		Student/Counselor Ratio	419.1 to 1
White, Non-Hispanic	61.5	**College Entrance Exam Scores** *(2005)*	
Black, Non-Hispanic	10.9	Scholastic Aptitude Test (SAT)	
Asian/Pacific Islander	1.5	Participation Rate (%)	7
American Indian/Alaskan Native	18.5	Mean SAT Reasoning Test Verbal Score	570
Hispanic	7.6	Mean SAT Reasoning Test Math Score	563
Classification (%)		American College Testing Program (ACT)	
Individual Education Program (IEP)	14.9	Participation Rate (%)	69
Migrant *(2002-2003)*	0.9	Average Composite Score	20.4
English Language Learner (ELL)	6.4	Average English Score	20.3
Eligible for Free Lunch Program	42.5	Average Math Score	19.6
Eligible for Reduced-Price Lunch Program	10.5	Average Reading Score	21.0
Current Spending *($ per student in FY 2003)*	5,961	Average Science Score	20.4
Instruction	3,401		
Support Services	2,164		

Note: For an explanation of data, please refer to the User's Guide in the front of the book; (1) Includes fringe benefits such as healthcare and employer pick-up of employee pension contributions where applicable

Oklahoma NAEP 2005 Test Scores

Reading			Mathematics		
Grade/Category	Value	Rank	Grade/Category	Value	Rank
4th Grade			**4th Grade**		
Average Proficiency	213.9 (1.09)	40/51	Average Proficiency	234.0 (0.97)	36/51
Proficiency by Gender/Race/Ethnicity			Proficiency by Gender/Race/Ethnicity		
Male	210.7 (1.32)	38/51	Male	235.3 (1.11)	36/51
Female	217.0 (1.17)	40/51	Female	232.5 (1.02)	38/51
White, Non-Hispanic	218.9 (1.28)	49/51	White, Non-Hispanic	239.6 (1.02)	45/51
Black, Non-Hispanic	196.6 (2.85)	25/42	Black, Non-Hispanic	216.8 (1.83)	28/42
Asian, Non-Hispanic	n/a	n/a	Asian, Non-Hispanic	n/a	n/a
American Indian, Non-Hispanic	210.6 (1.82)	2/7	American Indian, Non-Hispanic	229.0 (1.44)	1/7
Hispanic	203.5 (3.17)	21/40	Hispanic	226.2 (1.54)	18/41
Proficiency by Class Size			Proficiency by Class Size		
Less than 16 Students	193.4 (4.26)	28/34	Less than 16 Students	222.8 (2.59)	21/35
16 to 18 Students	209.7 (2.35)	26/33	16 to 18 Students	230.6 (2.32)	24/31
19 to 20 Students	212.9 (2.57)	32/38	19 to 20 Students	232.4 (1.51)	32/38
21 to 25 Students	219.4 (1.67)	32/51	21 to 25 Students	238.4 (1.52)	35/51
Greater than 25 Students	n/a	n/a	Greater than 25 Students	n/a	n/a
Percent Attaining Achievement Levels			Percent Attaining Achievement Levels		
Below Basic	39.7 (1.56)	14/51	Below Basic	21.0 (1.18)	20/51
Basic or Above	60.3 (1.56)	38/51	Basic or Above	79.0 (1.18)	32/51
Proficient or Above	25.1 (1.54)	42/51	Proficient or Above	28.6 (1.53)	39/51
Advanced or Above	4.6 (0.65)	45/51	Advanced or Above	2.4 (0.43)	45/51
8th Grade			**8th Grade**		
Average Proficiency	259.6 (1.06)	33/51	Average Proficiency	271.4 (1.03)	41/51
Proficiency by Gender/Race/Ethnicity			Proficiency by Gender/Race/Ethnicity		
Male	254.4 (1.27)	34/51	Male	271.5 (1.27)	40/51
Female	265.0 (1.24)	34/51	Female	271.2 (1.13)	41/51
White, Non-Hispanic	265.4 (1.18)	39/51	White, Non-Hispanic	277.7 (1.10)	47/51
Black, Non-Hispanic	243.0 (2.71)	15/40	Black, Non-Hispanic	248.7 (2.30)	30/41
Asian, Non-Hispanic	n/a	n/a	Asian, Non-Hispanic	n/a	n/a
American Indian, Non-Hispanic	254.0 (1.57)	2/9	American Indian, Non-Hispanic	267.1 (1.86)	3/10
Hispanic	246.9 (2.44)	20/38	Hispanic	257.0 (3.69)	30/38
Proficiency by Parents Highest Level of Ed.			Proficiency by Parents Highest Level of Ed.		
Did Not Finish High School	248.8 (2.52)	15/49	Did Not Finish High School	252.1 (2.13)	43/50
Graduated High School	251.6 (1.78)	29/50	Graduated High School	262.3 (1.96)	40/50
Some Education After High School	265.6 (1.60)	27/50	Some Education After High School	275.1 (1.49)	40/50
Graduated College	266.4 (1.41)	36/50	Graduated College	280.9 (1.30)	40/50
Percent Attaining Achievement Levels			Percent Attaining Achievement Levels		
Below Basic	39.7 (1.56)	14/51	Below Basic	36.5 (1.22)	12/51
Basic or Above	60.3 (1.56)	38/51	Basic or Above	63.5 (1.22)	39/51
Proficient or Above	25.1 (1.54)	42/51	Proficient or Above	20.6 (1.33)	43/51
Advanced or Above	4.6 (0.65)	45/51	Advanced or Above	2.4 (0.40)	45/51

Note: *For an explanation of data, please refer to the User's Guide in the front of the book; n/a indicates data not available*

Beckham County

Elk City
222 W Broadway Ave • Elk City, OK 73644-4742
(580) 225-0175 • http://www.elkcityschools.com/
Grade Span: PK-12; **Agency Type:** 1
Schools: 6
  3 Primary; 2 Middle; 1 High; 0 Other Level
  6 Regular; 0 Special Education; 0 Vocational; 0 Alternative
  0 Magnet; 0 Charter; 6 Title I Eligible; 5 School-wide Title I
Students: 2,156   (50.1% male; 49.8% female)
  Individual Education Program: 246 (11.4%);
  English Language Learner: 91 (4.2%); Migrant: 0 (0.0%)
  Eligible for Free Lunch Program: 810 (37.6%)
  Eligible for Reduced-Price Lunch Program: 233 (10.8%)
Teachers: 148.8 (14.5 to 1)
Librarians/Media Specialists: 3.0 (718.7 to 1)
Guidance Counselors: 7.4 (291.4 to 1)
Current Spending: ($ per student per year):
  Total: $5,601; Instruction: $3,543; Support Services: $1,706
Enrollment, Drop-out Rates and Diploma Recipients by Race/Ethnicity

Category	Total	White	Black	Asian	AIAN	Hisp.
Enrollment (%)	100.0	74.4	3.8	0.5	11.6	9.7
Drop-out Rate (%)	3.4	2.9	4.5	0.0	5.4	6.8
H.S. Diplomas (#)	123	111	3	1	4	4

Bryan County

Durant
PO Box 1160 • Durant, OK 74702-1160
(580) 924-1276 • http://www.durantisd.org/
Grade Span: PK-12; **Agency Type:** 1
Schools: 6
  3 Primary; 2 Middle; 1 High; 0 Other Level
  6 Regular; 0 Special Education; 0 Vocational; 0 Alternative
  0 Magnet; 0 Charter; 3 Title I Eligible; 3 School-wide Title I
Students: 3,173   (50.7% male; 49.2% female)
  Individual Education Program: 451 (14.2%);
  English Language Learner: 76 (2.4%); Migrant: 0 (0.0%)
  Eligible for Free Lunch Program: 1,615 (50.9%)
  Eligible for Reduced-Price Lunch Program: 325 (10.2%)
Teachers: 182.8 (17.4 to 1)
Librarians/Media Specialists: 6.0 (528.8 to 1)
Guidance Counselors: 10.1 (314.2 to 1)
Current Spending: ($ per student per year):
  Total: $6,160; Instruction: $3,651; Support Services: $1,989
Enrollment, Drop-out Rates and Diploma Recipients by Race/Ethnicity

Category	Total	White	Black	Asian	AIAN	Hisp.
Enrollment (%)	100.0	64.9	2.0	1.1	28.3	3.8
Drop-out Rate (%)	9.9	10.0	25.0	0.0	9.4	9.4
H.S. Diplomas (#)	152	104	1	2	40	5

Caddo County

Anadarko
1400 S Mission St • Anadarko, OK 73005-5813
(405) 247-6605
Grade Span: PK-12; **Agency Type:** 1
Schools: 5
  3 Primary; 1 Middle; 1 High; 0 Other Level
  5 Regular; 0 Special Education; 0 Vocational; 0 Alternative
  0 Magnet; 0 Charter; 5 Title I Eligible; 5 School-wide Title I
Students: 2,127   (50.1% male; 49.8% female)
  Individual Education Program: 425 (20.0%);
  English Language Learner: 183 (8.6%); Migrant: 0 (0.0%)
  Eligible for Free Lunch Program: 1,401 (65.9%)
  Eligible for Reduced-Price Lunch Program: 229 (10.8%)
Teachers: 148.2 (14.4 to 1)
Librarians/Media Specialists: 5.0 (425.4 to 1)
Guidance Counselors: 6.0 (354.5 to 1)
Current Spending: ($ per student per year):
  Total: $6,767; Instruction: $4,006; Support Services: $2,309
Enrollment, Drop-out Rates and Diploma Recipients by Race/Ethnicity

Category	Total	White	Black	Asian	AIAN	Hisp.
Enrollment (%)	100.0	26.3	5.6	0.1	61.2	6.7
Drop-out Rate (%)	3.4	3.8	4.3	0.0	0.6	22.5
H.S. Diplomas (#)	115	48	4	0	56	7

Canadian County

El Reno
PO Box 580 • El Reno, OK 73036-0580
(405) 262-1703 • http://www.elreno.k12.ok.us/
Grade Span: PK-12; **Agency Type:** 1
Schools: 7

4 Primary; 1 Middle; 1 High; 1 Other Level
7 Regular; 0 Special Education; 0 Vocational; 0 Alternative
0 Magnet; 0 Charter; 6 Title I Eligible; 5 School-wide Title I
Students: 2,562   (52.1% male; 47.8% female)
  Individual Education Program: 375 (14.6%);
  English Language Learner: 200 (7.8%); Migrant: 0 (0.0%)
  Eligible for Free Lunch Program: 1,326 (51.8%)
  Eligible for Reduced-Price Lunch Program: 341 (13.3%)
Teachers: 167.3 (15.3 to 1)
Librarians/Media Specialists: 4.0 (640.5 to 1)
Guidance Counselors: 7.6 (337.1 to 1)
Current Spending: ($ per student per year):
  Total: $5,702; Instruction: $3,299; Support Services: $2,065
Enrollment, Drop-out Rates and Diploma Recipients by Race/Ethnicity

Category	Total	White	Black	Asian	AIAN	Hisp.
Enrollment (%)	100.0	69.2	6.0	0.5	13.8	10.5
Drop-out Rate (%)	9.8	6.3	21.5	18.2	21.1	7.8
H.S. Diplomas (#)	173	128	12	3	21	9

Mustang
906 S Heights Dr • Mustang, OK 73064-3542
(405) 376-2461 • http://www.mustangps.org/
Grade Span: KG-12; **Agency Type:** 1
Schools: 9
  5 Primary; 2 Middle; 1 High; 1 Other Level
  9 Regular; 0 Special Education; 0 Vocational; 0 Alternative
  0 Magnet; 0 Charter; 6 Title I Eligible; 0 School-wide Title I
Students: 7,193   (51.8% male; 48.1% female)
  Individual Education Program: 725 (10.1%);
  English Language Learner: 277 (3.9%); Migrant: 0 (0.0%)
  Eligible for Free Lunch Program: 828 (11.5%)
  Eligible for Reduced-Price Lunch Program: 719 (10.0%)
Teachers: 407.1 (17.7 to 1)
Librarians/Media Specialists: 9.0 (799.2 to 1)
Guidance Counselors: 19.0 (378.6 to 1)
Current Spending: ($ per student per year):
  Total: $4,974; Instruction: $2,809; Support Services: $1,818
Enrollment, Drop-out Rates and Diploma Recipients by Race/Ethnicity

Category	Total	White	Black	Asian	AIAN	Hisp.
Enrollment (%)	100.0	82.0	1.6	5.6	7.0	3.7
Drop-out Rate (%)	2.6	2.6	0.0	0.8	4.4	5.6
H.S. Diplomas (#)	456	375	7	32	28	14

Piedmont
713 Piedmont Rd N • Piedmont, OK 73078-9248
(405) 373-2311
Grade Span: KG-12; **Agency Type:** 1
Schools: 4
  2 Primary; 1 Middle; 1 High; 0 Other Level
  4 Regular; 0 Special Education; 0 Vocational; 0 Alternative
  0 Magnet; 0 Charter; 1 Title I Eligible; 0 School-wide Title I
Students: 1,599   (51.3% male; 48.6% female)
  Individual Education Program: 180 (11.3%);
  English Language Learner: 17 (1.1%); Migrant: 0 (0.0%)
  Eligible for Free Lunch Program: 95 (5.9%)
  Eligible for Reduced-Price Lunch Program: 49 (3.1%)
Teachers: 90.9 (17.6 to 1)
Librarians/Media Specialists: 2.0 (799.5 to 1)
Guidance Counselors: 4.0 (399.8 to 1)
Current Spending: ($ per student per year):
  Total: $4,805; Instruction: $3,073; Support Services: $1,420
Enrollment, Drop-out Rates and Diploma Recipients by Race/Ethnicity

Category	Total	White	Black	Asian	AIAN	Hisp.
Enrollment (%)	100.0	76.5	3.7	1.4	16.2	2.2
Drop-out Rate (%)	1.3	1.1	3.7	0.0	0.0	12.5
H.S. Diplomas (#)	94	67	9	1	14	3

Yukon
600 Maple St • Yukon, OK 73099-2533
(405) 354-2587 • http://www.yukonps.com/
Grade Span: PK-12; **Agency Type:** 1
Schools: 10
  7 Primary; 2 Middle; 1 High; 0 Other Level
  10 Regular; 0 Special Education; 0 Vocational; 0 Alternative
  0 Magnet; 0 Charter; 4 Title I Eligible; 0 School-wide Title I
Students: 6,162   (50.2% male; 49.7% female)
  Individual Education Program: 654 (10.6%);
  English Language Learner: 162 (2.6%); Migrant: 0 (0.0%)
  Eligible for Free Lunch Program: 1,149 (18.6%)
  Eligible for Reduced-Price Lunch Program: 487 (7.9%)
Teachers: 348.4 (17.7 to 1)
Librarians/Media Specialists: 8.0 (770.3 to 1)
Guidance Counselors: 17.0 (362.5 to 1)
Current Spending: ($ per student per year):
  Total: $5,427; Instruction: $3,076; Support Services: $2,027

Enrollment, Drop-out Rates and Diploma Recipients by Race/Ethnicity

Category	Total	White	Black	Asian	AIAN	Hisp.
Enrollment (%)	100.0	87.2	1.4	2.1	5.3	4.0
Drop-out Rate (%)	3.3	3.3	14.3	4.3	1.2	1.9
H.S. Diplomas (#)	467	423	3	10	18 ·	13

Carter County

Ardmore
PO Box 1709 • Ardmore, OK 73402-1709
(580) 226-7650 • http://www.ardmore.k12.ok.us/
Grade Span: PK-12; **Agency Type:** 1
Schools: 7
    5 Primary; 1 Middle; 1 High; 0 Other Level
    7 Regular; 0 Special Education; 0 Vocational; 0 Alternative
    0 Magnet; 0 Charter; 6 Title I Eligible; 4 School-wide Title I
Students: 3,102 (50.5% male; 49.4% female)
    Individual Education Program: 578 (18.6%);
    English Language Learner: 81 (2.6%); Migrant: 0 (0.0%)
    Eligible for Free Lunch Program: 1,759 (56.7%)
    Eligible for Reduced-Price Lunch Program: 390 (12.6%)
Teachers: 194.9 (15.9 to 1)
Librarians/Media Specialists: 5.0 (620.4 to 1)
Guidance Counselors: 10.0 (310.2 to 1)
Current Spending: ($ per student per year):
    Total: $6,145; Instruction: $3,273; Support Services: $2,406

Enrollment, Drop-out Rates and Diploma Recipients by Race/Ethnicity

Category	Total	White	Black	Asian	AIAN	Hisp.
Enrollment (%)	100.0	51.2	23.3	1.1	17.2	7.2
Drop-out Rate (%)	3.1	4.3	1.5	0.0	1.7	2.4
H.S. Diplomas (#)	183	106	42	3	21	11

Cherokee County

Tahlequah
PO Box 517 • Tahlequah, OK 74465-0517
(918) 458-4100 • http://www.tahlequah.k12.ok.us/
Grade Span: PK-12; **Agency Type:** 1
Schools: 6
    3 Primary; 2 Middle; 1 High; 0 Other Level
    6 Regular; 0 Special Education; 0 Vocational; 0 Alternative
    0 Magnet; 0 Charter; 6 Title I Eligible; 4 School-wide Title I
Students: 3,607 (52.2% male; 47.7% female)
    Individual Education Program: 585 (16.2%);
    English Language Learner: 300 (8.3%); Migrant: 20 (0.6%)
    Eligible for Free Lunch Program: 1,930 (53.5%)
    Eligible for Reduced-Price Lunch Program: 576 (16.0%)
Teachers: 224.8 (16.0 to 1)
Librarians/Media Specialists: 5.0 (721.2 to 1)
Guidance Counselors: 11.9 (303.0 to 1)
Current Spending: ($ per student per year):
    Total: $6,662; Instruction: $3,750; Support Services: $2,491

Enrollment, Drop-out Rates and Diploma Recipients by Race/Ethnicity

Category	Total	White	Black	Asian	AIAN	Hisp.
Enrollment (%)	100.0	33.6	1.6	0.4	56.8	7.6
Drop-out Rate (%)	3.8	3.6	25.0	0.0	3.1	10.8
H.S. Diplomas (#)	318	119	5	1	189	4

Cleveland County

Moore
1500 SE 4th St • Moore, OK 73160-8232
(405) 793-3188 • http://moore.k12.ok.us/
Grade Span: PK-12; **Agency Type:** 1
Schools: 27
    20 Primary; 5 Middle; 2 High; 0 Other Level
    27 Regular; 0 Special Education; 0 Vocational; 0 Alternative
    0 Magnet; 0 Charter; 12 Title I Eligible; 4 School-wide Title I
Students: 18,946 (51.5% male; 48.4% female)
    Individual Education Program: 2,299 (12.1%);
    English Language Learner: 679 (3.6%); Migrant: 0 (0.0%)
    Eligible for Free Lunch Program: 3,777 (19.9%)
    Eligible for Reduced-Price Lunch Program: 1,593 (8.4%)
Teachers: 1,068.8 (17.7 to 1)
Librarians/Media Specialists: 28.5 (664.8 to 1)
Guidance Counselors: 36.9 (513.4 to 1)
Current Spending: ($ per student per year):
    Total: $5,240; Instruction: $3,174; Support Services: $1,765

Enrollment, Drop-out Rates and Diploma Recipients by Race/Ethnicity

Category	Total	White	Black	Asian	AIAN	Hisp.
Enrollment (%)	100.0	66.7	5.6	4.3	17.6	5.7
Drop-out Rate (%)	3.9	4.5	4.3	0.4	2.4	3.8
H.S. Diplomas (#)	1,137	835	46	56	159	41

Noble
PO Box 499 • Noble, OK 73068-0499
(405) 872-3452 • http://www.nobleps.com/
Grade Span: PK-12; **Agency Type:** 1
Schools: 5
    2 Primary; 2 Middle; 1 High; 0 Other Level
    5 Regular; 0 Special Education; 0 Vocational; 0 Alternative
    0 Magnet; 0 Charter; 5 Title I Eligible; 4 School-wide Title I
Students: 2,783 (51.1% male; 48.8% female)
    Individual Education Program: 364 (13.1%);
    English Language Learner: 0 (0.0%); Migrant: 0 (0.0%)
    Eligible for Free Lunch Program: 926 (33.3%)
    Eligible for Reduced-Price Lunch Program: 429 (15.4%)
Teachers: 155.8 (17.9 to 1)
Librarians/Media Specialists: 4.0 (695.8 to 1)
Guidance Counselors: 4.4 (632.5 to 1)
Current Spending: ($ per student per year):
    Total: $5,025; Instruction: $3,065; Support Services: $1,655

Enrollment, Drop-out Rates and Diploma Recipients by Race/Ethnicity

Category	Total	White	Black	Asian	AIAN	Hisp.
Enrollment (%)	100.0	89.1	0.8	0.3	7.0	2.9
Drop-out Rate (%)	5.3	5.2	100.0	50.0	1.9	9.1
H.S. Diplomas (#)	165	152	0	1	11	1

Norman
131 S Flood Ave • Norman, OK 73069-5463
(405) 364-1339 • http://www.norman.k12.ok.us/
Grade Span: PK-12; **Agency Type:** 1
Schools: 23
    16 Primary; 4 Middle; 2 High; 1 Other Level
    23 Regular; 0 Special Education; 0 Vocational; 0 Alternative
    0 Magnet; 0 Charter; 9 Title I Eligible; 5 School-wide Title I
Students: 12,810 (52.2% male; 47.7% female)
    Individual Education Program: 1,884 (14.7%);
    English Language Learner: 468 (3.7%); Migrant: 0 (0.0%)
    Eligible for Free Lunch Program: 3,581 (28.0%)
    Eligible for Reduced-Price Lunch Program: 973 (7.6%)
Teachers: 774.1 (16.5 to 1)
Librarians/Media Specialists: 24.0 (533.8 to 1)
Guidance Counselors: 39.0 (328.5 to 1)
Current Spending: ($ per student per year):
    Total: $5,527; Instruction: $3,174; Support Services: $2,137

Enrollment, Drop-out Rates and Diploma Recipients by Race/Ethnicity

Category	Total	White	Black	Asian	AIAN	Hisp.
Enrollment (%)	100.0	77.4	6.6	3.2	7.6	5.1
Drop-out Rate (%)	4.7	4.6	6.2	4.1	5.1	4.8
H.S. Diplomas (#)	867	713	43	28	51	32

Comanche County

Lawton
PO Box 1009 • Lawton, OK 73502-1009
(580) 357-6900 • http://www.lawtonps.org/
Grade Span: PK-12; **Agency Type:** 1
Schools: 35
    28 Primary; 4 Middle; 3 High; 0 Other Level
    35 Regular; 0 Special Education; 0 Vocational; 0 Alternative
    0 Magnet; 0 Charter; 13 Title I Eligible; 13 School-wide Title I
Students: 17,069 (51.4% male; 48.5% female)
    Individual Education Program: 2,721 (15.9%);
    English Language Learner: 1,675 (9.8%); Migrant: 0 (0.0%)
    Eligible for Free Lunch Program: 6,156 (36.1%)
    Eligible for Reduced-Price Lunch Program: 2,004 (11.7%)
Teachers: 1,025.2 (16.6 to 1)
Librarians/Media Specialists: 15.0 (1,137.9 to 1)
Guidance Counselors: 48.5 (351.9 to 1)
Current Spending: ($ per student per year):
    Total: $5,692; Instruction: $3,162; Support Services: $2,180

Enrollment, Drop-out Rates and Diploma Recipients by Race/Ethnicity

Category	Total	White	Black	Asian	AIAN	Hisp.
Enrollment (%)	100.0	50.2	31.9	2.2	6.5	9.2
Drop-out Rate (%)	4.8	4.6	3.2	2.9	15.3	5.7
H.S. Diplomas (#)	894	476	257	40	28	93

Craig County

Vinita
PO Box 408 • Vinita, OK 74301-0408
(918) 256-6778 • http://www.vinita.k12.ok.us/
Grade Span: PK-12; **Agency Type:** 1
Schools: 4
    2 Primary; 1 Middle; 1 High; 0 Other Level
    4 Regular; 0 Special Education; 0 Vocational; 0 Alternative
    0 Magnet; 0 Charter; 2 Title I Eligible; 2 School-wide Title I
Students: 1,732 (53.1% male; 46.8% female)

Individual Education Program: 349 (20.2%);
English Language Learner: 0 (0.0%); Migrant: 0 (0.0%)
Eligible for Free Lunch Program: 667 (38.5%)
Eligible for Reduced-Price Lunch Program: 268 (15.5%)
Teachers: 105.6 (16.4 to 1)
Librarians/Media Specialists: 4.0 (433.0 to 1)
Guidance Counselors: 4.0 (433.0 to 1)
Current Spending: ($ per student per year):
Total: $6,143; Instruction: $3,658; Support Services: $2,067
Enrollment, Drop-out Rates and Diploma Recipients by Race/Ethnicity

Category	Total	White	Black	Asian	AIAN	Hisp.
Enrollment (%)	100.0	46.1	2.4	0.7	49.7	1.2
Drop-out Rate (%)	3.0	2.6	7.1	0.0	3.2	0.0
H.S. Diplomas (#)	88	38	4	0	46	0

Creek County

Bristow
134 W 9th Ave • Bristow, OK 74010-2499
(918) 367-5555 • http://www.bristow.k12.ok.us/
Grade Span: PK-12; **Agency Type:** 1
Schools: 4
1 Primary; 2 Middle; 1 High; 0 Other Level
4 Regular; 0 Special Education; 0 Vocational; 0 Alternative
0 Magnet; 0 Charter; 3 Title I Eligible; 3 School-wide Title I
Students: 1,730 (51.3% male; 48.6% female)
Individual Education Program: 236 (13.6%);
English Language Learner: 9 (0.5%); Migrant: 0 (0.0%)
Eligible for Free Lunch Program: 1,015 (58.7%)
Eligible for Reduced-Price Lunch Program: 274 (15.8%)
Teachers: 106.6 (16.2 to 1)
Librarians/Media Specialists: 3.5 (494.3 to 1)
Guidance Counselors: 3.0 (576.7 to 1)
Current Spending: ($ per student per year):
Total: $5,867; Instruction: $3,351; Support Services: $2,025
Enrollment, Drop-out Rates and Diploma Recipients by Race/Ethnicity

Category	Total	White	Black	Asian	AIAN	Hisp.
Enrollment (%)	100.0	59.5	10.4	0.1	28.4	1.7
Drop-out Rate (%)	4.7	5.2	5.0	0.0	1.8	50.0
H.S. Diplomas (#)	90	60	6	0	24	0

Mannford
PO Box 100 • Mannford, OK 74044-0100
(918) 865-4062
Grade Span: PK-12; **Agency Type:** 1
Schools: 4
1 Primary; 2 Middle; 1 High; 0 Other Level
4 Regular; 0 Special Education; 0 Vocational; 0 Alternative
0 Magnet; 0 Charter; 3 Title I Eligible; 0 School-wide Title I
Students: 1,668 (52.6% male; 47.3% female)
Individual Education Program: 180 (10.8%);
English Language Learner: 0 (0.0%); Migrant: 0 (0.0%)
Eligible for Free Lunch Program: 565 (33.9%)
Eligible for Reduced-Price Lunch Program: 237 (14.2%)
Teachers: 96.7 (17.2 to 1)
Librarians/Media Specialists: 3.0 (556.0 to 1)
Guidance Counselors: 3.0 (556.0 to 1)
Current Spending: ($ per student per year):
Total: $4,786; Instruction: $2,799; Support Services: $1,713
Enrollment, Drop-out Rates and Diploma Recipients by Race/Ethnicity

Category	Total	White	Black	Asian	AIAN	Hisp.
Enrollment (%)	100.0	71.2	0.7	0.7	26.1	1.4
Drop-out Rate (%)	5.8	5.7	n/a	0.0	5.6	20.0
H.S. Diplomas (#)	94	73	0	0	21	0

Sapulpa
1 S Mission St • Sapulpa, OK 74066-4633
(918) 224-3400 • http://www.sapulpa.k12.ok.us/
Grade Span: PK-12; **Agency Type:** 1
Schools: 9
6 Primary; 1 Middle; 1 High; 1 Other Level
9 Regular; 0 Special Education; 0 Vocational; 0 Alternative
0 Magnet; 0 Charter; 5 Title I Eligible; 5 School-wide Title I
Students: 4,231 (50.6% male; 49.3% female)
Individual Education Program: 575 (13.6%);
English Language Learner: 90 (2.1%); Migrant: 0 (0.0%)
Eligible for Free Lunch Program: 1,660 (39.2%)
Eligible for Reduced-Price Lunch Program: 534 (12.6%)
Teachers: 245.3 (17.2 to 1)
Librarians/Media Specialists: 6.0 (705.2 to 1)
Guidance Counselors: 11.6 (364.7 to 1)
Current Spending: ($ per student per year):
Total: $5,505; Instruction: $3,198; Support Services: $1,918

Enrollment, Drop-out Rates and Diploma Recipients by Race/Ethnicity

Category	Total	White	Black	Asian	AIAN	Hisp.
Enrollment (%)	100.0	73.0	5.1	0.6	18.3	3.1
Drop-out Rate (%)	3.0	2.9	5.3	10.0	3.7	0.0
H.S. Diplomas (#)	275	232	4	3	33	3

Custer County

Clinton
PO Box 729 • Clinton, OK 73601-0729
(580) 323-1800 • http://www.clinton.k12.ok.us/
Grade Span: PK-12; **Agency Type:** 1
Schools: 5
2 Primary; 2 Middle; 1 High; 0 Other Level
5 Regular; 0 Special Education; 0 Vocational; 0 Alternative
0 Magnet; 0 Charter; 4 Title I Eligible; 4 School-wide Title I
Students: 1,816 (51.2% male; 48.7% female)
Individual Education Program: 220 (12.1%);
English Language Learner: 415 (22.9%); Migrant: 857 (47.2%)
Eligible for Free Lunch Program: 1,140 (62.8%)
Eligible for Reduced-Price Lunch Program: 246 (13.5%)
Teachers: 134.2 (13.5 to 1)
Librarians/Media Specialists: 5.0 (363.2 to 1)
Guidance Counselors: 6.0 (302.7 to 1)
Current Spending: ($ per student per year):
Total: $6,423; Instruction: $3,787; Support Services: $2,206
Enrollment, Drop-out Rates and Diploma Recipients by Race/Ethnicity

Category	Total	White	Black	Asian	AIAN	Hisp.
Enrollment (%)	100.0	49.9	10.7	0.8	9.2	29.4
Drop-out Rate (%)	2.6	1.2	2.1	0.0	8.1	4.0
H.S. Diplomas (#)	112	87	4	1	7	13

Weatherford
516 N Broadway St • Weatherford, OK 73096-4910
(580) 772-3327
Grade Span: PK-12; **Agency Type:** 1
Schools: 5
2 Primary; 2 Middle; 1 High; 0 Other Level
5 Regular; 0 Special Education; 0 Vocational; 0 Alternative
0 Magnet; 0 Charter; 4 Title I Eligible; 0 School-wide Title I
Students: 1,734 (50.1% male; 49.8% female)
Individual Education Program: 251 (14.5%);
English Language Learner: 64 (3.7%); Migrant: 0 (0.0%)
Eligible for Free Lunch Program: 556 (32.1%)
Eligible for Reduced-Price Lunch Program: 181 (10.4%)
Teachers: 112.0 (15.5 to 1)
Librarians/Media Specialists: 3.1 (559.4 to 1)
Guidance Counselors: 4.0 (433.5 to 1)
Current Spending: ($ per student per year):
Total: $6,083; Instruction: $3,374; Support Services: $2,253
Enrollment, Drop-out Rates and Diploma Recipients by Race/Ethnicity

Category	Total	White	Black	Asian	AIAN	Hisp.
Enrollment (%)	100.0	80.3	1.6	1.3	9.2	7.6
Drop-out Rate (%)	5.5	4.1	0.0	0.0	17.5	15.6
H.S. Diplomas (#)	162	146	2	1	10	3

Delaware County

Grove
PO Box 450789 • Grove, OK 74345-0789
(918) 786-3003
Grade Span: PK-12; **Agency Type:** 1
Schools: 4
1 Primary; 2 Middle; 1 High; 0 Other Level
4 Regular; 0 Special Education; 0 Vocational; 0 Alternative
0 Magnet; 0 Charter; 1 Title I Eligible; 1 School-wide Title I
Students: 2,353 (50.9% male; 49.0% female)
Individual Education Program: 373 (15.9%);
English Language Learner: 34 (1.4%); Migrant: 0 (0.0%)
Eligible for Free Lunch Program: 923 (39.2%)
Eligible for Reduced-Price Lunch Program: 361 (15.3%)
Teachers: 144.0 (16.3 to 1)
Librarians/Media Specialists: 3.0 (784.3 to 1)
Guidance Counselors: 8.0 (294.1 to 1)
Current Spending: ($ per student per year):
Total: $5,429; Instruction: $3,197; Support Services: $1,884
Enrollment, Drop-out Rates and Diploma Recipients by Race/Ethnicity

Category	Total	White	Black	Asian	AIAN	Hisp.
Enrollment (%)	100.0	65.5	0.8	0.5	31.9	1.3
Drop-out Rate (%)	7.8	9.4	n/a	0.0	5.0	0.0
H.S. Diplomas (#)	138	88	0	2	45	3

Jay

PO Box 630 • Jay, OK 74346-0630
(918) 253-4293 • http://www.brightok.net/~jayschl
Grade Span: PK-12; **Agency Type:** 1
Schools: 3
  1 Primary; 1 Middle; 1 High; 0 Other Level
  3 Regular; 0 Special Education; 0 Vocational; 0 Alternative
  0 Magnet; 0 Charter; 2 Title I Eligible; 2 School-wide Title I
Students: 1,750   (50.5% male; 49.4% female)
  Individual Education Program: 312 (17.8%);
  English Language Learner: 134 (7.7%); Migrant: 0 (0.0%)
  Eligible for Free Lunch Program: 1,029 (58.8%)
  Eligible for Reduced-Price Lunch Program: 280 (16.0%)
Teachers: 111.7 (15.7 to 1)
Librarians/Media Specialists: 3.0 (583.3 to 1)
Guidance Counselors: 5.0 (350.0 to 1)
Current Spending: ($ per student per year):
  Total: $5,852; Instruction: $3,454; Support Services: $1,987
Enrollment, Drop-out Rates and Diploma Recipients by Race/Ethnicity

Category	Total	White	Black	Asian	AIAN	Hisp.
Enrollment (%)	100.0	36.6	0.6	0.8	58.8	3.2
Drop-out Rate (%)	5.5	3.8	0.0	0.0	6.7	5.9
H.S. Diplomas (#)	96	27	0	1	65	3

Garfield County

Enid

500 S Independence St • Enid, OK 73701-5693
(580) 234-5270 • http://www.enidpublicschools.org/
Grade Span: PK-12; **Agency Type:** 1
Schools: 14
  10 Primary; 3 Middle; 1 High; 0 Other Level
  14 Regular; 0 Special Education; 0 Vocational; 0 Alternative
  0 Magnet; 0 Charter; 9 Title I Eligible; 3 School-wide Title I
Students: 6,485   (51.2% male; 48.7% female)
  Individual Education Program: 969 (14.9%);
  English Language Learner: 578 (8.9%); Migrant: 0 (0.0%)
  Eligible for Free Lunch Program: 2,731 (42.1%)
  Eligible for Reduced-Price Lunch Program: 513 (7.9%)
Teachers: 425.4 (15.2 to 1)
Librarians/Media Specialists: 13.0 (498.8 to 1)
Guidance Counselors: 19.6 (330.9 to 1)
Current Spending: ($ per student per year):
  Total: $5,870; Instruction: $3,584; Support Services: $1,979
Enrollment, Drop-out Rates and Diploma Recipients by Race/Ethnicity

Category	Total	White	Black	Asian	AIAN	Hisp.
Enrollment (%)	100.0	71.1	7.4	3.7	7.0	10.8
Drop-out Rate (%)	6.3	5.6	8.1	13.8	6.1	8.6
H.S. Diplomas (#)	406	314	23	15	35	19

Grady County

Chickasha

900 W Choctaw Ave • Chickasha, OK 73018-2213
(405) 222-6500
Grade Span: PK-12; **Agency Type:** 1
Schools: 7
  5 Primary; 1 Middle; 1 High; 0 Other Level
  7 Regular; 0 Special Education; 0 Vocational; 0 Alternative
  0 Magnet; 0 Charter; 6 Title I Eligible; 6 School-wide Title I
Students: 2,784   (50.4% male; 49.5% female)
  Individual Education Program: 431 (15.5%);
  English Language Learner: 40 (1.4%); Migrant: 0 (0.0%)
  Eligible for Free Lunch Program: 1,176 (42.2%)
  Eligible for Reduced-Price Lunch Program: 264 (9.5%)
Teachers: 184.1 (15.1 to 1)
Librarians/Media Specialists: 5.5 (506.2 to 1)
Guidance Counselors: 8.0 (348.0 to 1)
Current Spending: ($ per student per year):
  Total: $5,478; Instruction: $3,282; Support Services: $1,863
Enrollment, Drop-out Rates and Diploma Recipients by Race/Ethnicity

Category	Total	White	Black	Asian	AIAN	Hisp.
Enrollment (%)	100.0	74.1	11.9	0.6	7.9	5.4
Drop-out Rate (%)	5.5	5.5	5.3	0.0	4.0	11.1
H.S. Diplomas (#)	190	153	20	4	5	8

Jackson County

Altus

PO Box 558 • Altus, OK 73522-0558
(580) 481-2100 • http://www.altusschools.k12.ok.us/
Grade Span: PK-12; **Agency Type:** 1
Schools: 8
  5 Primary; 1 Middle; 1 High; 1 Other Level
  8 Regular; 0 Special Education; 0 Vocational; 0 Alternative

---

  0 Magnet; 0 Charter; 6 Title I Eligible; 0 School-wide Title I
Students: 4,279   (52.6% male; 47.3% female)
  Individual Education Program: 441 (10.3%);
  English Language Learner: 716 (16.7%); Migrant: 522 (12.2%)
  Eligible for Free Lunch Program: 1,692 (39.5%)
  Eligible for Reduced-Price Lunch Program: 395 (9.2%)
Teachers: 267.2 (16.0 to 1)
Librarians/Media Specialists: 5.0 (855.8 to 1)
Guidance Counselors: 10.0 (427.9 to 1)
Current Spending: ($ per student per year):
  Total: $5,835; Instruction: $3,608; Support Services: $1,867
Enrollment, Drop-out Rates and Diploma Recipients by Race/Ethnicity

Category	Total	White	Black	Asian	AIAN	Hisp.
Enrollment (%)	100.0	57.8	13.5	2.5	2.1	24.1
Drop-out Rate (%)	5.5	4.7	3.5	0.0	0.0	10.9
H.S. Diplomas (#)	295	196	44	6	3	46

Kay County

Blackwell

201 E Blackwell Ave • Blackwell, OK 74631-2909
(580) 363-2570 • http://www.blackwell.k12.ok.us/
Grade Span: PK-12; **Agency Type:** 1
Schools: 5
  2 Primary; 2 Middle; 1 High; 0 Other Level
  5 Regular; 0 Special Education; 0 Vocational; 0 Alternative
  0 Magnet; 0 Charter; 3 Title I Eligible; 2 School-wide Title I
Students: 1,544   (51.4% male; 48.5% female)
  Individual Education Program: 262 (17.0%);
  English Language Learner: 77 (5.0%); Migrant: 0 (0.0%)
  Eligible for Free Lunch Program: 763 (49.4%)
  Eligible for Reduced-Price Lunch Program: 191 (12.4%)
Teachers: 94.2 (16.4 to 1)
Librarians/Media Specialists: 2.0 (772.0 to 1)
Guidance Counselors: 4.0 (386.0 to 1)
Current Spending: ($ per student per year):
  Total: $5,495; Instruction: $3,310; Support Services: $1,912
Enrollment, Drop-out Rates and Diploma Recipients by Race/Ethnicity

Category	Total	White	Black	Asian	AIAN	Hisp.
Enrollment (%)	100.0	54.6	0.3	0.5	36.9	7.6
Drop-out Rate (%)	8.1	7.8	100.0	0.0	4.3	22.2
H.S. Diplomas (#)	101	91	0	0	7	3

Ponca City

111 W Grand Ave • Ponca City, OK 74601-5211
(580) 767-8000 • http://www.poncacity.k12.ok.us/
Grade Span: PK-12; **Agency Type:** 1
Schools: 10
  7 Primary; 1 Middle; 1 High; 1 Other Level
  10 Regular; 0 Special Education; 0 Vocational; 0 Alternative
  0 Magnet; 0 Charter; 7 Title I Eligible; 6 School-wide Title I
Students: 5,588   (51.4% male; 48.5% female)
  Individual Education Program: 830 (14.9%);
  English Language Learner: 188 (3.4%); Migrant: 69 (1.2%)
  Eligible for Free Lunch Program: 2,415 (43.2%)
  Eligible for Reduced-Price Lunch Program: 683 (12.2%)
Teachers: 348.0 (16.1 to 1)
Librarians/Media Specialists: 9.0 (620.9 to 1)
Guidance Counselors: 13.2 (423.3 to 1)
Current Spending: ($ per student per year):
  Total: $5,771; Instruction: $3,260; Support Services: $2,054
Enrollment, Drop-out Rates and Diploma Recipients by Race/Ethnicity

Category	Total	White	Black	Asian	AIAN	Hisp.
Enrollment (%)	100.0	71.3	4.9	1.1	16.6	6.1
Drop-out Rate (%)	6.2	4.9	14.8	0.0	9.6	14.1
H.S. Diplomas (#)	387	300	12	5	52	18

Le Flore County

Poteau

100 Mockingbird Ln • Poteau, OK 74953-2602
(918) 647-7700 • http://www.poteau.k12.ok.us/
Grade Span: PK-12; **Agency Type:** 1
Schools: 4
  2 Primary; 1 Middle; 1 High; 0 Other Level
  4 Regular; 0 Special Education; 0 Vocational; 0 Alternative
  0 Magnet; 0 Charter; 3 Title I Eligible; 3 School-wide Title I
Students: 2,055   (50.4% male; 49.5% female)
  Individual Education Program: 324 (15.8%);
  English Language Learner: 87 (4.2%); Migrant: 0 (0.0%)
  Eligible for Free Lunch Program: 988 (48.1%)
  Eligible for Reduced-Price Lunch Program: 313 (15.2%)
Teachers: 132.1 (15.6 to 1)
Librarians/Media Specialists: 4.0 (513.8 to 1)
Guidance Counselors: 5.0 (411.0 to 1)

Current Spending: ($ per student per year):
Total: $5,950; Instruction: $3,883; Support Services: $1,716
Enrollment, Drop-out Rates and Diploma Recipients by Race/Ethnicity

Category	Total	White	Black	Asian	AIAN	Hisp.
Enrollment (%)	100.0	69.1	1.6	0.7	24.3	4.3
Drop-out Rate (%)	4.8	5.1	0.0	33.3	1.3	8.3
H.S. Diplomas (#)	119	100	0	0	18	1

Logan County

Guthrie
802 E Vilas Ave • Guthrie, OK 73044-5228
(405) 282-8900 • http://www.guthrie.k12.ok.us/
Grade Span: PK-12; **Agency Type:** 1
Schools: 5
2 Primary; 2 Middle; 1 High; 0 Other Level
5 Regular; 0 Special Education; 0 Vocational; 0 Alternative
0 Magnet; 0 Charter; 4 Title I Eligible; 4 School-wide Title I
Students: 3,181   (52.4% male; 47.5% female)
Individual Education Program: 453 (14.2%);
English Language Learner: 23 (0.7%); Migrant: 0 (0.0%)
Eligible for Free Lunch Program: 1,430 (45.0%)
Eligible for Reduced-Price Lunch Program: 386 (12.1%)
Teachers: 203.4 (15.6 to 1)
Librarians/Media Specialists: 4.0 (795.3 to 1)
Guidance Counselors: 6.0 (530.2 to 1)
Current Spending: ($ per student per year):
Total: $5,677; Instruction: $3,273; Support Services: $1,903
Enrollment, Drop-out Rates and Diploma Recipients by Race/Ethnicity

Category	Total	White	Black	Asian	AIAN	Hisp.
Enrollment (%)	100.0	77.1	11.3	0.5	7.3	3.7
Drop-out Rate (%)	2.9	2.8	4.2	0.0	4.1	0.0
H.S. Diplomas (#)	181	138	25	1	14	3

Marshall County

Madill
601 W Mcarthur St • Madill, OK 73446-2846
(580) 795-3303
Grade Span: PK-12; **Agency Type:** 1
Schools: 3
1 Primary; 1 Middle; 1 High; 0 Other Level
3 Regular; 0 Special Education; 0 Vocational; 0 Alternative
0 Magnet; 0 Charter; 3 Title I Eligible; 3 School-wide Title I
Students: 1,617   (52.3% male; 47.6% female)
Individual Education Program: 132 (8.2%);
English Language Learner: 407 (25.2%); Migrant: 143 (8.8%)
Eligible for Free Lunch Program: 874 (54.1%)
Eligible for Reduced-Price Lunch Program: 171 (10.6%)
Teachers: 91.7 (17.6 to 1)
Librarians/Media Specialists: 3.0 (539.0 to 1)
Guidance Counselors: 5.0 (323.4 to 1)
Current Spending: ($ per student per year):
Total: $5,964; Instruction: $3,725; Support Services: $1,824
Enrollment, Drop-out Rates and Diploma Recipients by Race/Ethnicity

Category	Total	White	Black	Asian	AIAN	Hisp.
Enrollment (%)	100.0	49.3	3.6	0.1	20.8	26.2
Drop-out Rate (%)	1.3	0.0	0.0	0.0	0.0	6.8
H.S. Diplomas (#)	76	46	4	1	18	7

Mayes County

Locust Grove
PO Box 399 • Locust Grove, OK 74352-0399
(918) 479-5243
Grade Span: PK-12; **Agency Type:** 1
Schools: 4
2 Primary; 1 Middle; 1 High; 0 Other Level
4 Regular; 0 Special Education; 0 Vocational; 0 Alternative
0 Magnet; 0 Charter; 4 Title I Eligible; 4 School-wide Title I
Students: 1,517   (51.8% male; 48.1% female)
Individual Education Program: 332 (21.9%);
English Language Learner: 65 (4.3%); Migrant: 0 (0.0%)
Eligible for Free Lunch Program: 829 (54.6%)
Eligible for Reduced-Price Lunch Program: 290 (19.1%)
Teachers: 101.6 (14.9 to 1)
Librarians/Media Specialists: 3.0 (505.7 to 1)
Guidance Counselors: 4.9 (309.6 to 1)
Current Spending: ($ per student per year):
Total: $6,852; Instruction: $3,795; Support Services: $2,617

Category	Total	White	Black	Asian	AIAN	Hisp.
Enrollment (%)	100.0	29.6	0.3	0.1	69.0	1.0
Drop-out Rate (%)	4.9	3.6	n/a	n/a	6.3	0.0
H.S. Diplomas (#)	97	48	0	0	43	6

Pryor
PO Box 548 • Pryor, OK 74362-0548
(918) 825-1255 • http://www.pryor.k12.ok.us/
Grade Span: PK-12; **Agency Type:** 1
Schools: 6
4 Primary; 1 Middle; 1 High; 0 Other Level
6 Regular; 0 Special Education; 0 Vocational; 0 Alternative
0 Magnet; 0 Charter; 5 Title I Eligible; 0 School-wide Title I
Students: 2,372   (50.9% male; 49.0% female)
Individual Education Program: 250 (10.5%);
English Language Learner: 51 (2.2%); Migrant: 0 (0.0%)
Eligible for Free Lunch Program: 930 (39.2%)
Eligible for Reduced-Price Lunch Program: 207 (8.7%)
Teachers: 138.4 (17.1 to 1)
Librarians/Media Specialists: 6.0 (395.3 to 1)
Guidance Counselors: 8.0 (296.5 to 1)
Current Spending: ($ per student per year):
Total: $5,168; Instruction: $3,109; Support Services: $1,827
Enrollment, Drop-out Rates and Diploma Recipients by Race/Ethnicity

Category	Total	White	Black	Asian	AIAN	Hisp.
Enrollment (%)	100.0	57.1	0.6	0.6	38.6	3.1
Drop-out Rate (%)	3.0	2.8	0.0	0.0	2.8	9.5
H.S. Diplomas (#)	147	104	1	1	38	3

McCurtain County

Broken Bow
108 W 5th St • Broken Bow, OK 74728-2912
(580) 584-3306 • http://www.bbisd.org/
Grade Span: PK-12; **Agency Type:** 1
Schools: 4
2 Primary; 1 Middle; 1 High; 0 Other Level
4 Regular; 0 Special Education; 0 Vocational; 0 Alternative
0 Magnet; 0 Charter; 4 Title I Eligible; 4 School-wide Title I
Students: 1,758   (53.5% male; 46.4% female)
Individual Education Program: 235 (13.4%);
English Language Learner: 118 (6.7%); Migrant: 117 (6.7%)
Eligible for Free Lunch Program: 1,123 (63.9%)
Eligible for Reduced-Price Lunch Program: 218 (12.4%)
Teachers: 116.5 (15.1 to 1)
Librarians/Media Specialists: 3.0 (586.0 to 1)
Guidance Counselors: 6.0 (293.0 to 1)
Current Spending: ($ per student per year):
Total: $6,109; Instruction: $3,580; Support Services: $2,078
Enrollment, Drop-out Rates and Diploma Recipients by Race/Ethnicity

Category	Total	White	Black	Asian	AIAN	Hisp.
Enrollment (%)	100.0	54.8	10.2	0.5	29.4	5.2
Drop-out Rate (%)	1.7	1.9	0.0	0.0	1.5	4.3
H.S. Diplomas (#)	125	90	8	1	23	3

Idabel
200 NE Ave C • Idabel, OK 74745-0029
(580) 286-7639
Grade Span: PK-12; **Agency Type:** 1
Schools: 5
3 Primary; 1 Middle; 1 High; 0 Other Level
5 Regular; 0 Special Education; 0 Vocational; 0 Alternative
0 Magnet; 0 Charter; 4 Title I Eligible; 4 School-wide Title I
Students: 1,590   (50.8% male; 49.1% female)
Individual Education Program: 234 (14.7%);
English Language Learner: 77 (4.8%); Migrant: 0 (0.0%)
Eligible for Free Lunch Program: 1,132 (71.2%)
Eligible for Reduced-Price Lunch Program: 109 (6.9%)
Teachers: 116.2 (13.7 to 1)
Librarians/Media Specialists: 2.0 (795.0 to 1)
Guidance Counselors: 4.0 (397.5 to 1)
Current Spending: ($ per student per year):
Total: $6,619; Instruction: $3,864; Support Services: $2,338
Enrollment, Drop-out Rates and Diploma Recipients by Race/Ethnicity

Category	Total	White	Black	Asian	AIAN	Hisp.
Enrollment (%)	100.0	37.2	33.5	0.2	21.0	8.1
Drop-out Rate (%)	2.2	0.8	3.3	0.0	4.7	0.0
H.S. Diplomas (#)	94	53	29	1	11	0

Mcintosh County

Checotah

PO Box 289 • Checotah, OK 74426-0289
(918) 473-5610 • http://www.checotah.k12.ok.us/
Grade Span: PK-12; **Agency Type:** 1
Schools: 4
  1 Primary; 2 Middle; 1 High; 0 Other Level
  4 Regular; 0 Special Education; 0 Vocational; 0 Alternative
  0 Magnet; 0 Charter; 4 Title I Eligible; 4 School-wide Title I
Students: 1,534 (49.7% male; 50.2% female)
  Individual Education Program: 240 (15.6%);
  English Language Learner: 27 (1.8%); Migrant: 0 (0.0%)
  Eligible for Free Lunch Program: 933 (60.8%)
  Eligible for Reduced-Price Lunch Program: 243 (15.8%)
Teachers: 100.0 (15.3 to 1)
Librarians/Media Specialists: 3.0 (511.3 to 1)
Guidance Counselors: 5.0 (306.8 to 1)
Current Spending: ($ per student per year):
  Total: $6,046; Instruction: $3,193; Support Services: $2,416
Enrollment, Drop-out Rates and Diploma Recipients by Race/Ethnicity

Category	Total	White	Black	Asian	AIAN	Hisp.
Enrollment (%)	100.0	58.0	6.5	0.4	34.0	1.2
Drop-out Rate (%)	3.3	3.9	0.0	100.0	1.9	14.3
H.S. Diplomas (#)	88	49	3	0	36	0

Muskogee County

Fort Gibson

500 S Ross Ave • Fort Gibson, OK 74434-8422
(918) 478-2474
Grade Span: PK-12; **Agency Type:** 1
Schools: 4
  2 Primary; 1 Middle; 1 High; 0 Other Level
  4 Regular; 0 Special Education; 0 Vocational; 0 Alternative
  0 Magnet; 0 Charter; 2 Title I Eligible; 0 School-wide Title I
Students: 1,835 (53.2% male; 46.7% female)
  Individual Education Program: 232 (12.6%);
  English Language Learner: 53 (2.9%); Migrant: 0 (0.0%)
  Eligible for Free Lunch Program: 569 (31.0%)
  Eligible for Reduced-Price Lunch Program: 192 (10.5%)
Teachers: 111.8 (16.4 to 1)
Librarians/Media Specialists: 3.0 (611.7 to 1)
Guidance Counselors: 4.0 (458.8 to 1)
Current Spending: ($ per student per year):
  Total: $6,106; Instruction: $3,517; Support Services: $2,179
Enrollment, Drop-out Rates and Diploma Recipients by Race/Ethnicity

Category	Total	White	Black	Asian	AIAN	Hisp.
Enrollment (%)	100.0	49.6	1.0	0.4	44.9	4.0
Drop-out Rate (%)	3.5	3.0	6.7	0.0	4.2	0.0
H.S. Diplomas (#)	135	76	4	0	52	3

Hilldale

500 E Smith Ferry Rd • Muskogee, OK 74403-8639
(918) 683-0273 • http://www.hilldale.k12.ok.us/
Grade Span: PK-12; **Agency Type:** 1
Schools: 4
  2 Primary; 1 Middle; 1 High; 0 Other Level
  4 Regular; 0 Special Education; 0 Vocational; 0 Alternative
  0 Magnet; 0 Charter; 3 Title I Eligible; 0 School-wide Title I
Students: 1,781 (52.2% male; 47.7% female)
  Individual Education Program: 236 (13.3%);
  English Language Learner: 173 (9.7%); Migrant: 0 (0.0%)
  Eligible for Free Lunch Program: 438 (24.6%)
  Eligible for Reduced-Price Lunch Program: 210 (11.8%)
Teachers: 105.9 (16.8 to 1)
Librarians/Media Specialists: 2.0 (890.5 to 1)
Guidance Counselors: 3.0 (593.7 to 1)
Current Spending: ($ per student per year):
  Total: $4,950; Instruction: $2,899; Support Services: $1,739
Enrollment, Drop-out Rates and Diploma Recipients by Race/Ethnicity

Category	Total	White	Black	Asian	AIAN	Hisp.
Enrollment (%)	100.0	50.1	2.4	2.0	43.9	1.6
Drop-out Rate (%)	1.6	2.4	0.0	0.0	0.0	14.3
H.S. Diplomas (#)	107	68	6	2	31	0

Muskogee

202 W Broadway St • Muskogee, OK 74401-6651
(918) 684-3700 • http://www.mpsi20.org/
Grade Span: PK-12; **Agency Type:** 1
Schools: 13
  11 Primary; 1 Middle; 1 High; 0 Other Level
  13 Regular; 0 Special Education; 0 Vocational; 0 Alternative
  0 Magnet; 0 Charter; 12 Title I Eligible; 12 School-wide Title I
Students: 6,289 (51.0% male; 48.9% female)
  Individual Education Program: 795 (12.6%);
  English Language Learner: 301 (4.8%); Migrant: 0 (0.0%)
  Eligible for Free Lunch Program: 3,719 (59.1%)
  Eligible for Reduced-Price Lunch Program: 683 (10.9%)
Teachers: 373.3 (16.8 to 1)
Librarians/Media Specialists: 9.0 (698.8 to 1)
Guidance Counselors: 13.3 (472.9 to 1)
Current Spending: ($ per student per year):
  Total: $5,924; Instruction: $3,235; Support Services: $2,265
Enrollment, Drop-out Rates and Diploma Recipients by Race/Ethnicity

Category	Total	White	Black	Asian	AIAN	Hisp.
Enrollment (%)	100.0	37.6	27.6	0.7	29.0	5.2
Drop-out Rate (%)	3.1	4.4	3.1	0.0	0.9	3.6
H.S. Diplomas (#)	319	151	74	5	79	10

Oklahoma County

Choctaw/Nicoma Park

12880 NE 10th St • Choctaw, OK 73020-8129
(405) 769-4859 • http://www.cnpschools.org/
Grade Span: KG-12; **Agency Type:** 1
Schools: 9
  5 Primary; 3 Middle; 1 High; 0 Other Level
  9 Regular; 0 Special Education; 0 Vocational; 0 Alternative
  0 Magnet; 0 Charter; 6 Title I Eligible; 0 School-wide Title I
Students: 4,493 (52.7% male; 47.2% female)
  Individual Education Program: 650 (14.5%);
  English Language Learner: 17 (0.4%); Migrant: 0 (0.0%)
  Eligible for Free Lunch Program: 961 (21.4%)
  Eligible for Reduced-Price Lunch Program: 372 (8.3%)
Teachers: 262.2 (17.1 to 1)
Librarians/Media Specialists: 9.0 (499.2 to 1)
Guidance Counselors: 11.0 (408.5 to 1)
Current Spending: ($ per student per year):
  Total: $5,122; Instruction: $2,936; Support Services: $1,901
Enrollment, Drop-out Rates and Diploma Recipients by Race/Ethnicity

Category	Total	White	Black	Asian	AIAN	Hisp.
Enrollment (%)	100.0	78.1	4.2	1.1	13.2	3.5
Drop-out Rate (%)	3.0	3.0	3.4	5.0	3.5	0.0
H.S. Diplomas (#)	308	248	8	4	35	13

Deer Creek

20825 N Macarthur Blvd • Edmond, OK 73003-9342
(405) 348-6100 • http://www.deercreek.k12.ok.us/
Grade Span: KG-12; **Agency Type:** 1
Schools: 4
  2 Primary; 1 Middle; 1 High; 0 Other Level
  4 Regular; 0 Special Education; 0 Vocational; 0 Alternative
  0 Magnet; 0 Charter; 2 Title I Eligible; 0 School-wide Title I
Students: 2,044 (52.8% male; 47.1% female)
  Individual Education Program: 268 (13.1%);
  English Language Learner: 28 (1.4%); Migrant: 0 (0.0%)
  Eligible for Free Lunch Program: 63 (3.1%)
  Eligible for Reduced-Price Lunch Program: 27 (1.3%)
Teachers: 122.1 (16.7 to 1)
Librarians/Media Specialists: 4.0 (511.0 to 1)
Guidance Counselors: 5.0 (408.8 to 1)
Current Spending: ($ per student per year):
  Total: $5,226; Instruction: $2,886; Support Services: $1,902
Enrollment, Drop-out Rates and Diploma Recipients by Race/Ethnicity

Category	Total	White	Black	Asian	AIAN	Hisp.
Enrollment (%)	100.0	86.3	3.2	1.9	6.0	2.6
Drop-out Rate (%)	2.0	1.6	0.0	12.5	4.3	5.6
H.S. Diplomas (#)	98	85	2	3	6	2

Edmond

1001 W Danforth Rd • Edmond, OK 73003-4801
(405) 340-2828 • http://www.edmond.k12.ok.us/
Grade Span: PK-12; **Agency Type:** 1
Schools: 21
  13 Primary; 5 Middle; 3 High; 0 Other Level
  21 Regular; 0 Special Education; 0 Vocational; 0 Alternative
  0 Magnet; 0 Charter; 7 Title I Eligible; 0 School-wide Title I
Students: 18,158 (51.5% male; 48.4% female)
  Individual Education Program: 2,413 (13.3%);
  English Language Learner: 499 (2.7%); Migrant: 0 (0.0%)
  Eligible for Free Lunch Program: 2,210 (12.2%)
  Eligible for Reduced-Price Lunch Program: 727 (4.0%)
Teachers: 1,030.6 (17.6 to 1)
Librarians/Media Specialists: 24.1 (753.4 to 1)
Guidance Counselors: 45.0 (403.5 to 1)
Current Spending: ($ per student per year):
  Total: $5,638; Instruction: $3,012; Support Services: $2,311

Enrollment, Drop-out Rates and Diploma Recipients by Race/Ethnicity

Category	Total	White	Black	Asian	AIAN	Hisp.
Enrollment (%)	100.0	81.6	8.1	3.2	3.7	3.4
Drop-out Rate (%)	2.5	2.4	3.1	4.8	4.1	1.8
H.S. Diplomas (#)	1,267	1,104	80	17	47	19

Harrah
20670 Walker St • Harrah, OK 73045-9782
(405) 454-6244
Grade Span: KG-12; **Agency Type:** 1
Schools: 6
  2 Primary; 2 Middle; 1 High; 1 Other Level
  6 Regular; 0 Special Education; 0 Vocational; 0 Alternative
  0 Magnet; 0 Charter; 4 Title I Eligible; 0 School-wide Title I
Students: 2,213   (50.5% male; 49.4% female)
  Individual Education Program: 403 (18.2%);
  English Language Learner: 7 (0.3%); Migrant: 0 (0.0%)
  Eligible for Free Lunch Program: 609 (27.5%)
  Eligible for Reduced-Price Lunch Program: 274 (12.4%)
Teachers: 124.7 (17.7 to 1)
Librarians/Media Specialists: 3.0 (737.7 to 1)
Guidance Counselors: 4.0 (553.3 to 1)
Current Spending: ($ per student per year):
  Total: $5,222; Instruction: $2,981; Support Services: $1,898

Enrollment, Drop-out Rates and Diploma Recipients by Race/Ethnicity

Category	Total	White	Black	Asian	AIAN	Hisp.
Enrollment (%)	100.0	75.0	0.7	0.6	18.7	5.0
Drop-out Rate (%)	3.2	3.0	0.0	0.0	4.3	0.0
H.S. Diplomas (#)	163	122	1	1	38	1

Midwest City-Del City
PO Box 10630 • Midwest City, OK 73140-1630
(405) 737-4461
Grade Span: PK-12; **Agency Type:** 1
Schools: 25
  17 Primary; 5 Middle; 3 High; 0 Other Level
  25 Regular; 0 Special Education; 0 Vocational; 0 Alternative
  0 Magnet; 0 Charter; 15 Title I Eligible; 13 School-wide Title I
Students: 14,251   (51.5% male; 48.4% female)
  Individual Education Program: 2,028 (14.2%);
  English Language Learner: 424 (3.0%); Migrant: 0 (0.0%)
  Eligible for Free Lunch Program: 5,509 (38.7%)
  Eligible for Reduced-Price Lunch Program: 1,587 (11.1%)
Teachers: 846.1 (16.8 to 1)
Librarians/Media Specialists: 26.6 (535.8 to 1)
Guidance Counselors: 24.0 (593.8 to 1)
Current Spending: ($ per student per year):
  Total: $5,625; Instruction: $3,218; Support Services: $2,028

Enrollment, Drop-out Rates and Diploma Recipients by Race/Ethnicity

Category	Total	White	Black	Asian	AIAN	Hisp.
Enrollment (%)	100.0	57.0	28.0	2.0	8.7	4.2
Drop-out Rate (%)	2.3	2.4	1.2	2.9	4.2	5.9
H.S. Diplomas (#)	1,076	633	295	33	73	42

Oklahoma City
900 N Klein Ave • Oklahoma City, OK 73106-7036
(405) 587-0448 • http://www.okcps.k12.ok.us/
Grade Span: PK-12; **Agency Type:** 1
Schools: 89
  61 Primary; 12 Middle; 12 High; 4 Other Level
  89 Regular; 0 Special Education; 0 Vocational; 0 Alternative
  0 Magnet; 9 Charter; 62 Title I Eligible; 47 School-wide Title I
Students: 40,599   (50.8% male; 49.1% female)
  Individual Education Program: 6,192 (15.3%);
  English Language Learner: 9,505 (23.4%); Migrant: 0 (0.0%)
  Eligible for Free Lunch Program: 30,921 (76.2%)
  Eligible for Reduced-Price Lunch Program: 2,819 (6.9%)
Teachers: 2,344.9 (17.3 to 1)
Librarians/Media Specialists: 49.0 (828.6 to 1)
Guidance Counselors: 70.4 (576.7 to 1)
Current Spending: ($ per student per year):
  Total: $6,538; Instruction: $3,538; Support Services: $2,555

Enrollment, Drop-out Rates and Diploma Recipients by Race/Ethnicity

Category	Total	White	Black	Asian	AIAN	Hisp.
Enrollment (%)	100.0	27.3	34.8	2.6	5.6	29.6
Drop-out Rate (%)	12.1	11.9	11.9	4.8	15.7	13.2
H.S. Diplomas (#)	1,441	382	733	53	51	222

Putnam City
5401 NW 40th St • Warr Acres, OK 73122-3302
(405) 495-5200 • http://www.putnamcityschools.org/
Grade Span: PK-12; **Agency Type:** 1
Schools: 26
  18 Primary; 5 Middle; 3 High; 0 Other Level
  26 Regular; 0 Special Education; 0 Vocational; 0 Alternative

  0 Magnet; 0 Charter; 8 Title I Eligible; 8 School-wide Title I
Students: 19,365   (51.1% male; 48.8% female)
  Individual Education Program: 2,378 (12.3%);
  English Language Learner: 1,269 (6.6%); Migrant: 0 (0.0%)
  Eligible for Free Lunch Program: 7,397 (38.2%)
  Eligible for Reduced-Price Lunch Program: 1,737 (9.0%)
Teachers: 1,144.5 (16.9 to 1)
Librarians/Media Specialists: 28.0 (691.6 to 1)
Guidance Counselors: 38.9 (497.8 to 1)
Current Spending: ($ per student per year):
  Total: $5,493; Instruction: $3,160; Support Services: $2,023

Enrollment, Drop-out Rates and Diploma Recipients by Race/Ethnicity

Category	Total	White	Black	Asian	AIAN	Hisp.
Enrollment (%)	100.0	61.3	21.6	4.3	3.9	8.9
Drop-out Rate (%)	5.9	4.7	10.2	2.2	5.3	13.8
H.S. Diplomas (#)	1,185	882	129	66	41	67

Western Heights
8401 SW 44th St • Oklahoma City, OK 73179-4010
(405) 350-3410 • http://westernheights.k12.ok.us/
Grade Span: PK-12; **Agency Type:** 1
Schools: 6
  4 Primary; 1 Middle; 1 High; 0 Other Level
  6 Regular; 0 Special Education; 0 Vocational; 0 Alternative
  0 Magnet; 0 Charter; 6 Title I Eligible; 2 School-wide Title I
Students: 3,082   (51.4% male; 48.5% female)
  Individual Education Program: 470 (15.2%);
  English Language Learner: 433 (14.0%); Migrant: 0 (0.0%)
  Eligible for Free Lunch Program: 1,835 (59.5%)
  Eligible for Reduced-Price Lunch Program: 347 (11.3%)
Teachers: 204.2 (15.1 to 1)
Librarians/Media Specialists: 3.0 (1,027.3 to 1)
Guidance Counselors: 6.5 (474.2 to 1)
Current Spending: ($ per student per year):
  Total: $6,369; Instruction: $3,166; Support Services: $2,823

Enrollment, Drop-out Rates and Diploma Recipients by Race/Ethnicity

Category	Total	White	Black	Asian	AIAN	Hisp.
Enrollment (%)	100.0	52.6	19.2	5.2	9.2	13.8
Drop-out Rate (%)	7.9	7.1	8.5	0.0	10.0	14.5
H.S. Diplomas (#)	164	100	20	14	15	15

Okmulgee County

Okmulgee
PO Box 1346 • Okmulgee, OK 74447-1346
(918) 758-2000
Grade Span: PK-12; **Agency Type:** 1
Schools: 4
  2 Primary; 1 Middle; 1 High; 0 Other Level
  4 Regular; 0 Special Education; 0 Vocational; 0 Alternative
  0 Magnet; 0 Charter; 4 Title I Eligible; 4 School-wide Title I
Students: 2,039   (52.8% male; 47.1% female)
  Individual Education Program: 344 (16.9%);
  English Language Learner: 58 (2.8%); Migrant: 0 (0.0%)
  Eligible for Free Lunch Program: 1,293 (63.4%)
  Eligible for Reduced-Price Lunch Program: 285 (14.0%)
Teachers: 122.7 (16.6 to 1)
Librarians/Media Specialists: 4.0 (509.8 to 1)
Guidance Counselors: 5.0 (407.8 to 1)
Current Spending: ($ per student per year):
  Total: $6,648; Instruction: $3,483; Support Services: $2,741

Enrollment, Drop-out Rates and Diploma Recipients by Race/Ethnicity

Category	Total	White	Black	Asian	AIAN	Hisp.
Enrollment (%)	100.0	40.7	33.4	0.4	24.0	1.4
Drop-out Rate (%)	6.9	7.8	1.6	0.0	5.1	83.3
H.S. Diplomas (#)	94	41	39	0	10	4

Ottawa County

Miami
418 G St SE • Miami, OK 74354-8218
(918) 542-8455
Grade Span: PK-12; **Agency Type:** 1
Schools: 8
  6 Primary; 1 Middle; 1 High; 0 Other Level
  8 Regular; 0 Special Education; 0 Vocational; 0 Alternative
  0 Magnet; 0 Charter; 6 Title I Eligible; 6 School-wide Title I
Students: 2,463   (51.6% male; 48.3% female)
  Individual Education Program: 285 (11.6%);
  English Language Learner: 38 (1.5%); Migrant: 0 (0.0%)
  Eligible for Free Lunch Program: 1,229 (49.9%)
  Eligible for Reduced-Price Lunch Program: 312 (12.7%)
Teachers: 142.6 (17.3 to 1)
Librarians/Media Specialists: 5.0 (492.6 to 1)
Guidance Counselors: 7.0 (351.9 to 1)

Current Spending: ($ per student per year):
Total: $5,607; Instruction: $3,475; Support Services: $1,726
Enrollment, Drop-out Rates and Diploma Recipients by Race/Ethnicity

Category	Total	White	Black	Asian	AIAN	Hisp.
Enrollment (%)	100.0	51.2	1.6	1.0	43.4	2.8
Drop-out Rate (%)	4.6	3.2	0.0	0.0	6.3	16.7
H.S. Diplomas (#)	112	57	1	1	50	3

Pawnee County

Cleveland
600 N Gilbert St • Cleveland, OK 74020-1023
(918) 358-2210 • http://www.cleveland.k12.ok.us/
Grade Span: PK-12; **Agency Type:** 1
Schools: 4
   2 Primary; 1 Middle; 1 High; 0 Other Level
   4 Regular; 0 Special Education; 0 Vocational; 0 Alternative
   0 Magnet; 0 Charter; 4 Title I Eligible; 4 School-wide Title I
Students: 1,729   (49.9% male; 50.0% female)
   Individual Education Program: 269 (15.6%);
   English Language Learner: 2 (0.1%); Migrant: 0 (0.0%)
   Eligible for Free Lunch Program: 650 (37.6%)
   Eligible for Reduced-Price Lunch Program: 253 (14.6%)
Teachers: 103.9 (16.6 to 1)
Librarians/Media Specialists: 3.0 (576.3 to 1)
Guidance Counselors: 4.0 (432.3 to 1)
Current Spending: ($ per student per year):
Total: $4,955; Instruction: $2,880; Support Services: $1,695
Enrollment, Drop-out Rates and Diploma Recipients by Race/Ethnicity

Category	Total	White	Black	Asian	AIAN	Hisp.
Enrollment (%)	100.0	83.1	0.3	0.5	14.3	1.8
Drop-out Rate (%)	8.0	8.7	0.0	0.0	4.9	0.0
H.S. Diplomas (#)	69	57	0	0	12	0

Payne County

Cushing
PO Box 1609 • Cushing, OK 74023-1609
(918) 225-3425
Grade Span: PK-12; **Agency Type:** 1
Schools: 7
   5 Primary; 1 Middle; 1 High; 0 Other Level
   7 Regular; 0 Special Education; 0 Vocational; 0 Alternative
   0 Magnet; 0 Charter; 5 Title I Eligible; 0 School-wide Title I
Students: 1,788   (50.2% male; 49.7% female)
   Individual Education Program: 300 (16.8%);
   English Language Learner: 0 (0.0%); Migrant: 0 (0.0%)
   Eligible for Free Lunch Program: 745 (41.7%)
   Eligible for Reduced-Price Lunch Program: 252 (14.1%)
Teachers: 122.6 (14.6 to 1)
Librarians/Media Specialists: 5.0 (357.6 to 1)
Guidance Counselors: 5.0 (357.6 to 1)
Current Spending: ($ per student per year):
Total: $6,605; Instruction: $3,400; Support Services: $2,865
Enrollment, Drop-out Rates and Diploma Recipients by Race/Ethnicity

Category	Total	White	Black	Asian	AIAN	Hisp.
Enrollment (%)	100.0	77.2	3.6	0.4	16.2	2.5
Drop-out Rate (%)	7.1	7.5	0.0	0.0	4.8	15.4
H.S. Diplomas (#)	133	117	3	0	11	2

Stillwater
PO Box 879 • Stillwater, OK 74076-0879
(405) 533-6300 • http://www.stillwater.k12.ok.us/
Grade Span: PK-12; **Agency Type:** 1
Schools: 9
   6 Primary; 1 Middle; 1 High; 1 Other Level
   9 Regular; 0 Special Education; 0 Vocational; 0 Alternative
   0 Magnet; 0 Charter; 4 Title I Eligible; 3 School-wide Title I
Students: 5,291   (51.3% male; 48.6% female)
   Individual Education Program: 904 (17.1%);
   English Language Learner: 272 (5.1%); Migrant: 0 (0.0%)
   Eligible for Free Lunch Program: 1,203 (22.7%)
   Eligible for Reduced-Price Lunch Program: 314 (5.9%)
Teachers: 319.0 (16.6 to 1)
Librarians/Media Specialists: 9.0 (587.9 to 1)
Guidance Counselors: 14.0 (377.9 to 1)
Current Spending: ($ per student per year):
Total: $5,504; Instruction: $3,015; Support Services: $2,172
Enrollment, Drop-out Rates and Diploma Recipients by Race/Ethnicity

Category	Total	White	Black	Asian	AIAN	Hisp.
Enrollment (%)	100.0	78.9	7.4	3.7	7.5	2.5
Drop-out Rate (%)	4.3	3.8	8.2	0.0	6.6	9.8
H.S. Diplomas (#)	380	332	10	11	19	8

Pittsburg County

Mc Alester
PO Box 1027 • Mcalester, OK 74502-1027
(918) 423-4771
Grade Span: PK-12; **Agency Type:** 1
Schools: 10
   7 Primary; 1 Middle; 1 High; 1 Other Level
   10 Regular; 0 Special Education; 0 Vocational; 0 Alternative
   0 Magnet; 0 Charter; 8 Title I Eligible; 8 School-wide Title I
Students: 2,787   (52.0% male; 47.9% female)
   Individual Education Program: 567 (20.3%);
   English Language Learner: 59 (2.1%); Migrant: 28 (1.0%)
   Eligible for Free Lunch Program: 1,295 (46.5%)
   Eligible for Reduced-Price Lunch Program: 267 (9.6%)
Teachers: 172.7 (16.1 to 1)
Librarians/Media Specialists: 3.0 (929.0 to 1)
Guidance Counselors: 7.5 (371.6 to 1)
Current Spending: ($ per student per year):
Total: $6,612; Instruction: $3,760; Support Services: $2,323
Enrollment, Drop-out Rates and Diploma Recipients by Race/Ethnicity

Category	Total	White	Black	Asian	AIAN	Hisp.
Enrollment (%)	100.0	65.3	9.5	0.5	21.1	3.5
Drop-out Rate (%)	7.4	6.9	5.4	0.0	8.8	19.4
H.S. Diplomas (#)	167	113	20	5	26	3

Pontotoc County

Ada
PO Box 1359 • Ada, OK 74821-1359
(580) 310-7200 • http://www.adapss.com/
Grade Span: PK-12; **Agency Type:** 1
Schools: 6
   3 Primary; 2 Middle; 1 High; 0 Other Level
   6 Regular; 0 Special Education; 0 Vocational; 0 Alternative
   0 Magnet; 0 Charter; 4 Title I Eligible; 4 School-wide Title I
Students: 2,582   (50.6% male; 49.3% female)
   Individual Education Program: 374 (14.5%);
   English Language Learner: 61 (2.4%); Migrant: 0 (0.0%)
   Eligible for Free Lunch Program: 1,228 (47.6%)
   Eligible for Reduced-Price Lunch Program: 279 (10.8%)
Teachers: 176.8 (14.6 to 1)
Librarians/Media Specialists: 2.0 (1,291.0 to 1)
Guidance Counselors: 6.0 (430.3 to 1)
Current Spending: ($ per student per year):
Total: $5,972; Instruction: $3,544; Support Services: $2,001
Enrollment, Drop-out Rates and Diploma Recipients by Race/Ethnicity

Category	Total	White	Black	Asian	AIAN	Hisp.
Enrollment (%)	100.0	61.5	4.2	0.3	30.7	3.3
Drop-out Rate (%)	3.1	2.9	8.7	0.0	0.9	31.3
H.S. Diplomas (#)	159	107	5	0	46	1

Byng
500 S Bethel Blvd • Ada, OK 74820-1177
(580) 310-6751 • http://www.byngschools.com/
Grade Span: PK-12; **Agency Type:** 1
Schools: 5
   2 Primary; 2 Middle; 1 High; 0 Other Level
   5 Regular; 0 Special Education; 0 Vocational; 0 Alternative
   0 Magnet; 0 Charter; 5 Title I Eligible; 5 School-wide Title I
Students: 1,675   (48.1% male; 51.8% female)
   Individual Education Program: 290 (17.3%);
   English Language Learner: 27 (1.6%); Migrant: 0 (0.0%)
   Eligible for Free Lunch Program: 844 (50.4%)
   Eligible for Reduced-Price Lunch Program: 214 (12.8%)
Teachers: 116.5 (14.4 to 1)
Librarians/Media Specialists: 3.5 (478.6 to 1)
Guidance Counselors: 5.0 (335.0 to 1)
Current Spending: ($ per student per year):
Total: $6,317; Instruction: $3,475; Support Services: $2,334
Enrollment, Drop-out Rates and Diploma Recipients by Race/Ethnicity

Category	Total	White	Black	Asian	AIAN	Hisp.
Enrollment (%)	100.0	57.0	2.9	0.1	37.8	2.2
Drop-out Rate (%)	2.5	2.5	0.0	0.0	0.0	40.0
H.S. Diplomas (#)	103	61	1	1	36	4

Pottawatomie County

Mc Loud
PO Box 240 • Mcloud, OK 74851-0240
(405) 964-3314
Grade Span: PK-12; **Agency Type:** 1
Schools: 3
   1 Primary; 1 Middle; 1 High; 0 Other Level
   3 Regular; 0 Special Education; 0 Vocational; 0 Alternative

0 Magnet; 0 Charter; 3 Title I Eligible; 3 School-wide Title I
Students: 1,700   (51.5% male; 48.4% female)
  Individual Education Program: 241 (14.2%);
  English Language Learner: 43 (2.5%); Migrant: 0 (0.0%)
  Eligible for Free Lunch Program: 604 (35.5%)
  Eligible for Reduced-Price Lunch Program: 203 (11.9%)
Teachers: 111.9 (15.2 to 1)
Librarians/Media Specialists: 2.0 (850.0 to 1)
Guidance Counselors: 5.0 (340.0 to 1)
Current Spending: ($ per student per year):
  Total: $5,253; Instruction: $3,218; Support Services: $1,732
Enrollment, Drop-out Rates and Diploma Recipients by Race/Ethnicity

Category	Total	White	Black	Asian	AIAN	Hisp.
Enrollment (%)	100.0	74.9	1.6	0.9	19.3	3.3
Drop-out Rate (%)	2.9	1.6	0.0	0.0	8.5	6.7
H.S. Diplomas (#)	133	110	3	0	16	4

Shawnee
326 N Union St • Shawnee, OK 74801-7053
(405) 273-0653 • http://www.shawnee.k12.ok.us/
Grade Span: PK-12; **Agency Type:** 1
Schools: 7
  5 Primary; 1 Middle; 1 High; 0 Other Level
  7 Regular; 0 Special Education; 0 Vocational; 0 Alternative
  0 Magnet; 0 Charter; 7 Title I Eligible; 5 School-wide Title I
Students: 3,777   (51.6% male; 48.3% female)
  Individual Education Program: 576 (15.3%);
  English Language Learner: 194 (5.1%); Migrant: 0 (0.0%)
  Eligible for Free Lunch Program: 1,908 (50.5%)
  Eligible for Reduced-Price Lunch Program: 300 (7.9%)
Teachers: 238.4 (15.8 to 1)
Librarians/Media Specialists: 6.0 (629.5 to 1)
Guidance Counselors: 12.0 (314.8 to 1)
Current Spending: ($ per student per year):
  Total: $6,005; Instruction: $3,518; Support Services: $2,144
Enrollment, Drop-out Rates and Diploma Recipients by Race/Ethnicity

Category	Total	White	Black	Asian	AIAN	Hisp.
Enrollment (%)	100.0	60.0	8.3	0.8	27.5	3.4
Drop-out Rate (%)	8.3	5.8	8.8	0.0	14.5	9.5
H.S. Diplomas (#)	239	185	7	1	44	2

Tecumseh
302 S 9th St • Tecumseh, OK 74873-4021
(405) 598-3739
Grade Span: PK-12; **Agency Type:** 1
Schools: 6
  3 Primary; 1 Middle; 2 High; 0 Other Level
  6 Regular; 0 Special Education; 0 Vocational; 0 Alternative
  0 Magnet; 0 Charter; 3 Title I Eligible; 3 School-wide Title I
Students: 2,245   (53.9% male; 46.0% female)
  Individual Education Program: 324 (14.4%);
  English Language Learner: 42 (1.9%); Migrant: 0 (0.0%)
  Eligible for Free Lunch Program: 1,065 (47.4%)
  Eligible for Reduced-Price Lunch Program: 310 (13.8%)
Teachers: 138.8 (16.2 to 1)
Librarians/Media Specialists: 4.0 (561.3 to 1)
Guidance Counselors: 4.8 (467.7 to 1)
Current Spending: ($ per student per year):
  Total: $5,503; Instruction: $3,292; Support Services: $1,784
Enrollment, Drop-out Rates and Diploma Recipients by Race/Ethnicity

Category	Total	White	Black	Asian	AIAN	Hisp.
Enrollment (%)	100.0	63.4	3.9	0.4	29.9	2.3
Drop-out Rate (%)	4.7	4.0	2.2	0.0	8.6	0.0
H.S. Diplomas (#)	137	98	4	0	31	4

Rogers County

Catoosa
2000 S Cherokee St • Catoosa, OK 74015-3232
(918) 266-8603
Grade Span: PK-12; **Agency Type:** 1
Schools: 5
  2 Primary; 2 Middle; 1 High; 0 Other Level
  5 Regular; 0 Special Education; 0 Vocational; 0 Alternative
  0 Magnet; 0 Charter; 4 Title I Eligible; 0 School-wide Title I
Students: 2,260   (49.9% male; 50.0% female)
  Individual Education Program: 395 (17.5%);
  English Language Learner: 24 (1.1%); Migrant: 0 (0.0%)
  Eligible for Free Lunch Program: 713 (31.5%)
  Eligible for Reduced-Price Lunch Program: 292 (12.9%)
Teachers: 140.7 (16.1 to 1)
Librarians/Media Specialists: 3.0 (753.3 to 1)
Guidance Counselors: 7.0 (322.9 to 1)
Current Spending: ($ per student per year):
  Total: $5,526; Instruction: $2,965; Support Services: $2,189

Category	Total	White	Black	Asian	AIAN	Hisp.
Enrollment (%)	100.0	61.3	0.5	0.5	34.9	2.8
Drop-out Rate (%)	3.0	3.0	33.3	0.0	2.7	3.6
H.S. Diplomas (#)	139	81	1	1	56	0

Claremore
310 N Weenonah Ave • Claremore, OK 74017-7007
(918) 699-7300 • http://www.claremore.k12.ok.us/
Grade Span: PK-12; **Agency Type:** 1
Schools: 6
  3 Primary; 2 Middle; 1 High; 0 Other Level
  6 Regular; 0 Special Education; 0 Vocational; 0 Alternative
  0 Magnet; 0 Charter; 3 Title I Eligible; 1 School-wide Title I
Students: 4,111   (51.1% male; 48.8% female)
  Individual Education Program: 616 (15.0%);
  English Language Learner: 144 (3.5%); Migrant: 0 (0.0%)
  Eligible for Free Lunch Program: 1,296 (31.5%)
  Eligible for Reduced-Price Lunch Program: 385 (9.4%)
Teachers: 263.8 (15.6 to 1)
Librarians/Media Specialists: 6.0 (685.2 to 1)
Guidance Counselors: 11.0 (373.7 to 1)
Current Spending: ($ per student per year):
  Total: $4,996; Instruction: $3,048; Support Services: $1,722
Enrollment, Drop-out Rates and Diploma Recipients by Race/Ethnicity

Category	Total	White	Black	Asian	AIAN	Hisp.
Enrollment (%)	100.0	65.2	2.0	0.7	27.5	4.6
Drop-out Rate (%)	2.8	2.9	0.0	0.0	3.1	0.0
H.S. Diplomas (#)	270	207	6	2	49	6

Oologah-Talala
PO Box 189 • Oologah, OK 74053-0189
(918) 443-6079 • http://www.oologah.k12.ok.us/
Grade Span: KG-12; **Agency Type:** 1
Schools: 4
  2 Primary; 1 Middle; 1 High; 0 Other Level
  4 Regular; 0 Special Education; 0 Vocational; 0 Alternative
  0 Magnet; 0 Charter; 3 Title I Eligible; 0 School-wide Title I
Students: 1,656   (51.0% male; 48.9% female)
  Individual Education Program: 218 (13.2%);
  English Language Learner: 0 (0.0%); Migrant: 0 (0.0%)
  Eligible for Free Lunch Program: 313 (18.9%)
  Eligible for Reduced-Price Lunch Program: 157 (9.5%)
Teachers: 97.3 (17.0 to 1)
Librarians/Media Specialists: 3.0 (552.0 to 1)
Guidance Counselors: 3.0 (552.0 to 1)
Current Spending: ($ per student per year):
  Total: $5,830; Instruction: $3,081; Support Services: $2,374
Enrollment, Drop-out Rates and Diploma Recipients by Race/Ethnicity

Category	Total	White	Black	Asian	AIAN	Hisp.
Enrollment (%)	100.0	63.7	0.7	0.8	34.1	0.7
Drop-out Rate (%)	0.8	1.3	0.0	0.0	0.0	0.0
H.S. Diplomas (#)	103	62	1	0	40	0

Seminole County

Seminole
PO Box 1031 • Seminole, OK 74818-1031
(405) 382-5085
Grade Span: PK-12; **Agency Type:** 1
Schools: 4
  2 Primary; 1 Middle; 1 High; 0 Other Level
  4 Regular; 0 Special Education; 0 Vocational; 0 Alternative
  0 Magnet; 0 Charter; 4 Title I Eligible; 4 School-wide Title I
Students: 1,551   (50.2% male; 49.7% female)
  Individual Education Program: 196 (12.6%);
  English Language Learner: 32 (2.1%); Migrant: 0 (0.0%)
  Eligible for Free Lunch Program: 892 (57.5%)
  Eligible for Reduced-Price Lunch Program: 147 (9.5%)
Teachers: 93.3 (16.6 to 1)
Librarians/Media Specialists: 4.0 (387.8 to 1)
Guidance Counselors: 5.0 (310.2 to 1)
Current Spending: ($ per student per year):
  Total: $5,830; Instruction: $3,467; Support Services: $1,993
Enrollment, Drop-out Rates and Diploma Recipients by Race/Ethnicity

Category	Total	White	Black	Asian	AIAN	Hisp.
Enrollment (%)	100.0	60.9	6.6	0.6	29.2	2.6
Drop-out Rate (%)	7.7	5.3	0.0	0.0	18.3	0.0
H.S. Diplomas (#)	94	65	5	1	20	3

Sequoyah County

Muldrow

PO Box 660 • Muldrow, OK 74948-0660
(918) 427-7406
Grade Span: PK-12; **Agency Type:** 1
Schools: 3
  1 Primary; 1 Middle; 1 High; 0 Other Level
  3 Regular; 0 Special Education; 0 Vocational; 0 Alternative
  0 Magnet; 0 Charter; 3 Title I Eligible; 3 School-wide Title I
Students: 1,599 (53.0% male; 46.9% female)
  Individual Education Program: 226 (14.1%);
  English Language Learner: 144 (9.0%); Migrant: 49 (3.1%)
  Eligible for Free Lunch Program: 806 (50.4%)
  Eligible for Reduced-Price Lunch Program: 209 (13.1%)
Teachers: 104.0 (15.4 to 1)
Librarians/Media Specialists: 2.0 (799.5 to 1)
Guidance Counselors: 3.0 (533.0 to 1)
Current Spending: ($ per student per year):
  Total: $5,483; Instruction: $3,382; Support Services: $1,676
Enrollment, Drop-out Rates and Diploma Recipients by Race/Ethnicity

Category	Total	White	Black	Asian	AIAN	Hisp.
Enrollment (%)	100.0	58.8	1.8	1.4	33.1	4.9
Drop-out Rate (%)	4.4	4.8	0.0	0.0	3.2	15.4
H.S. Diplomas (#)	114	55	2	1	55	1

Sallisaw

701 J T Stites Blvd • Sallisaw, OK 74955-9304
(918) 775-5544
Grade Span: KG-12; **Agency Type:** 1
Schools: 4
  2 Primary; 1 Middle; 1 High; 0 Other Level
  4 Regular; 0 Special Education; 0 Vocational; 0 Alternative
  0 Magnet; 0 Charter; 4 Title I Eligible; 2 School-wide Title I
Students: 2,031 (53.6% male; 46.3% female)
  Individual Education Program: 327 (16.1%);
  English Language Learner: 68 (3.3%); Migrant: 0 (0.0%)
  Eligible for Free Lunch Program: 1,058 (52.1%)
  Eligible for Reduced-Price Lunch Program: 188 (9.3%)
Teachers: 128.8 (15.8 to 1)
Librarians/Media Specialists: 2.0 (1,015.5 to 1)
Guidance Counselors: 4.0 (507.8 to 1)
Current Spending: ($ per student per year):
  Total: $5,608; Instruction: $3,256; Support Services: $2,023
Enrollment, Drop-out Rates and Diploma Recipients by Race/Ethnicity

Category	Total	White	Black	Asian	AIAN	Hisp.
Enrollment (%)	100.0	53.1	2.1	0.5	41.3	3.0
Drop-out Rate (%)	2.8	3.1	0.0	0.0	2.5	0.0
H.S. Diplomas (#)	108	65	1	0	41	1

Stephens County

Duncan

PO Box 1548 • Duncan, OK 73534-1548
(580) 255-0686
Grade Span: PK-12; **Agency Type:** 1
Schools: 9
  7 Primary; 1 Middle; 1 High; 0 Other Level
  9 Regular; 0 Special Education; 0 Vocational; 0 Alternative
  0 Magnet; 0 Charter; 5 Title I Eligible; 5 School-wide Title I
Students: 3,694 (51.6% male; 48.3% female)
  Individual Education Program: 375 (10.2%);
  English Language Learner: 244 (6.6%); Migrant: 0 (0.0%)
  Eligible for Free Lunch Program: 1,512 (40.9%)
  Eligible for Reduced-Price Lunch Program: 291 (7.9%)
Teachers: 206.9 (17.9 to 1)
Librarians/Media Specialists: 4.5 (820.9 to 1)
Guidance Counselors: 9.0 (410.4 to 1)
Current Spending: ($ per student per year):
  Total: $5,410; Instruction: $2,999; Support Services: $2,064
Enrollment, Drop-out Rates and Diploma Recipients by Race/Ethnicity

Category	Total	White	Black	Asian	AIAN	Hisp.
Enrollment (%)	100.0	74.5	6.4	0.8	7.2	11.1
Drop-out Rate (%)	6.0	5.6	5.1	0.0	10.5	8.2
H.S. Diplomas (#)	245	197	15	0	6	27

Texas County

Guymon

PO Box 1307 • Guymon, OK 73942-1307
(580) 338-4340 • http://www.ptsi.net/user/guymonhs/
Grade Span: PK-12; **Agency Type:** 1
Schools: 8
  5 Primary; 2 Middle; 1 High; 0 Other Level
  8 Regular; 0 Special Education; 0 Vocational; 0 Alternative

---

  0 Magnet; 0 Charter; 7 Title I Eligible; 5 School-wide Title I
Students: 2,373 (50.8% male; 49.1% female)
  Individual Education Program: 254 (10.7%);
  English Language Learner: 960 (40.5%); Migrant: 1,013 (42.7%)
  Eligible for Free Lunch Program: 1,156 (48.7%)
  Eligible for Reduced-Price Lunch Program: 304 (12.8%)
Teachers: 168.3 (14.1 to 1)
Librarians/Media Specialists: 3.9 (608.5 to 1)
Guidance Counselors: 5.9 (402.2 to 1)
Current Spending: ($ per student per year):
  Total: $6,283; Instruction: $3,740; Support Services: $2,080
Enrollment, Drop-out Rates and Diploma Recipients by Race/Ethnicity

Category	Total	White	Black	Asian	AIAN	Hisp.
Enrollment (%)	100.0	44.2	0.7	0.9	0.9	53.4
Drop-out Rate (%)	6.6	2.0	0.0	0.0	0.0	14.5
H.S. Diplomas (#)	150	94	2	0	0	54

Tulsa County

Bixby

109 N Armstrong St • Bixby, OK 74008-4449
(918) 366-2200 • http://www.bixby.k12.ok.us/
Grade Span: PK-12; **Agency Type:** 1
Schools: 5
  2 Primary; 2 Middle; 1 High; 0 Other Level
  5 Regular; 0 Special Education; 0 Vocational; 0 Alternative
  0 Magnet; 0 Charter; 3 Title I Eligible; 0 School-wide Title I
Students: 3,847 (51.4% male; 48.5% female)
  Individual Education Program: 490 (12.7%);
  English Language Learner: 99 (2.6%); Migrant: 150 (3.9%)
  Eligible for Free Lunch Program: 599 (15.6%)
  Eligible for Reduced-Price Lunch Program: 272 (7.1%)
Teachers: 192.8 (20.0 to 1)
Librarians/Media Specialists: 5.0 (769.4 to 1)
Guidance Counselors: 10.0 (384.7 to 1)
Current Spending: ($ per student per year):
  Total: $4,997; Instruction: $2,678; Support Services: $1,982
Enrollment, Drop-out Rates and Diploma Recipients by Race/Ethnicity

Category	Total	White	Black	Asian	AIAN	Hisp.
Enrollment (%)	100.0	81.6	1.8	0.4	11.9	4.3
Drop-out Rate (%)	1.2	1.2	0.0	0.0	1.2	3.0
H.S. Diplomas (#)	286	248	2	2	22	12

Broken Arrow

601 S Main St • Broken Arrow, OK 74012-4334
(918) 259-4300 • http://www.ba.k12.ok.us/
Grade Span: PK-12; **Agency Type:** 1
Schools: 21
  13 Primary; 5 Middle; 1 High; 2 Other Level
  21 Regular; 0 Special Education; 0 Vocational; 0 Alternative
  0 Magnet; 0 Charter; 7 Title I Eligible; 0 School-wide Title I
Students: 14,746 (51.3% male; 48.6% female)
  Individual Education Program: 2,144 (14.5%);
  English Language Learner: 299 (2.0%); Migrant: 0 (0.0%)
  Eligible for Free Lunch Program: 2,740 (18.6%)
  Eligible for Reduced-Price Lunch Program: 1,273 (8.6%)
Teachers: 835.6 (17.6 to 1)
Librarians/Media Specialists: 22.0 (670.3 to 1)
Guidance Counselors: 39.9 (369.6 to 1)
Current Spending: ($ per student per year):
  Total: $5,583; Instruction: $2,927; Support Services: $2,265
Enrollment, Drop-out Rates and Diploma Recipients by Race/Ethnicity

Category	Total	White	Black	Asian	AIAN	Hisp.
Enrollment (%)	100.0	80.8	4.9	1.7	8.7	3.9
Drop-out Rate (%)	3.9	3.5	5.2	6.3	5.5	8.2
H.S. Diplomas (#)	885	781	29	9	56	10

Collinsville

1119 W Broadway St • Collinsville, OK 74021-2339
(918) 371-2326 • http://www.collinsville.k12.ok.us/
Grade Span: PK-12; **Agency Type:** 1
Schools: 4
  2 Primary; 1 Middle; 1 High; 0 Other Level
  4 Regular; 0 Special Education; 0 Vocational; 0 Alternative
  0 Magnet; 0 Charter; 3 Title I Eligible; 0 School-wide Title I
Students: 2,137 (50.9% male; 49.0% female)
  Individual Education Program: 260 (12.2%);
  English Language Learner: 0 (0.0%); Migrant: 0 (0.0%)
  Eligible for Free Lunch Program: 479 (22.4%)
  Eligible for Reduced-Price Lunch Program: 159 (7.4%)
Teachers: 110.2 (19.4 to 1)
Librarians/Media Specialists: 4.0 (534.3 to 1)
Guidance Counselors: 4.0 (534.3 to 1)
Current Spending: ($ per student per year):
  Total: $4,822; Instruction: $2,875; Support Services: $1,652

Enrollment, Drop-out Rates and Diploma Recipients by Race/Ethnicity

Category	Total	White	Black	Asian	AIAN	Hisp.
Enrollment (%)	100.0	62.0	0.2	0.0	37.1	0.7
Drop-out Rate (%)	2.5	3.1	0.0	n/a	1.3	0.0
H.S. Diplomas (#)	128	73	0	0	51	4

Glenpool
PO Box 1149 • Glenpool, OK 74033-1149
(918) 322-9500 • http://www.glenpool.k12.ok.us/
Grade Span: PK-12; **Agency Type:** 1
Schools: 3
  1 Primary; 1 Middle; 1 High; 0 Other Level
  3 Regular; 0 Special Education; 0 Vocational; 0 Alternative
  0 Magnet; 0 Charter; 1 Title I Eligible; 0 School-wide Title I
Students: 2,150   (52.0% male; 47.9% female)
  Individual Education Program: 291 (13.5%);
  English Language Learner: 54 (2.5%); Migrant: 0 (0.0%)
  Eligible for Free Lunch Program: 594 (27.6%)
  Eligible for Reduced-Price Lunch Program: 269 (12.5%)
Teachers: 130.0 (16.5 to 1)
Librarians/Media Specialists: 3.0 (716.7 to 1)
Guidance Counselors: 5.0 (430.0 to 1)
Current Spending: ($ per student per year):
  Total: $5,106; Instruction: $3,076; Support Services: $1,681
Enrollment, Drop-out Rates and Diploma Recipients by Race/Ethnicity

Category	Total	White	Black	Asian	AIAN	Hisp.
Enrollment (%)	100.0	62.5	3.1	0.8	28.9	4.7
Drop-out Rate (%)	3.4	2.3	5.0	0.0	3.0	33.3
H.S. Diplomas (#)	130	89	4	0	36	1

Jenks
205 E B St • Jenks, OK 74037-3906
(918) 299-4411 • http://www.jenksps.org/
Grade Span: PK-12; **Agency Type:** 1
Schools: 9
  4 Primary; 3 Middle; 1 High; 1 Other Level
  9 Regular; 0 Special Education; 0 Vocational; 0 Alternative
  0 Magnet; 0 Charter; 5 Title I Eligible; 0 School-wide Title I
Students: 9,331   (51.2% male; 48.7% female)
  Individual Education Program: 1,481 (15.9%);
  English Language Learner: 596 (6.4%); Migrant: 0 (0.0%)
  Eligible for Free Lunch Program: 1,402 (15.0%)
  Eligible for Reduced-Price Lunch Program: 360 (3.9%)
Teachers: 491.5 (19.0 to 1)
Librarians/Media Specialists: 11.0 (848.3 to 1)
Guidance Counselors: 18.5 (504.4 to 1)
Current Spending: ($ per student per year):
  Total: $5,608; Instruction: $2,895; Support Services: $2,396
Enrollment, Drop-out Rates and Diploma Recipients by Race/Ethnicity

Category	Total	White	Black	Asian	AIAN	Hisp.
Enrollment (%)	100.0	76.7	6.2	3.1	8.0	6.1
Drop-out Rate (%)	1.7	1.4	2.9	1.4	3.2	3.0
H.S. Diplomas (#)	625	522	28	19	30	26

Owasso
1501 N Ash St • Owasso, OK 74055-4920
(918) 272-5367 • http://www.owasso.k12.ok.us/
Grade Span: PK-12; **Agency Type:** 1
Schools: 12
  7 Primary; 2 Middle; 1 High; 2 Other Level
  12 Regular; 0 Special Education; 0 Vocational; 0 Alternative
  0 Magnet; 0 Charter; 4 Title I Eligible; 0 School-wide Title I
Students: 7,495   (51.0% male; 48.9% female)
  Individual Education Program: 746 (10.0%);
  English Language Learner: 241 (3.2%); Migrant: 43 (0.6%)
  Eligible for Free Lunch Program: 828 (11.0%)
  Eligible for Reduced-Price Lunch Program: 353 (4.7%)
Teachers: 417.3 (18.0 to 1)
Librarians/Media Specialists: 13.1 (572.1 to 1)
Guidance Counselors: 15.0 (499.7 to 1)
Current Spending: ($ per student per year):
  Total: $5,112; Instruction: $3,042; Support Services: $1,752
Enrollment, Drop-out Rates and Diploma Recipients by Race/Ethnicity

Category	Total	White	Black	Asian	AIAN	Hisp.
Enrollment (%)	100.0	84.3	1.8	1.1	9.0	3.8
Drop-out Rate (%)	2.1	1.9	2.7	2.6	1.4	7.6
H.S. Diplomas (#)	408	347	10	5	31	15

Sand Springs
PO Box 970 • Sand Springs, OK 74063-0970
(918) 246-1400 • http://www.sandsprings.k12.ok.us/
Grade Span: PK-12; **Agency Type:** 1
Schools: 10
  6 Primary; 1 Middle; 2 High; 1 Other Level
  10 Regular; 0 Special Education; 0 Vocational; 0 Alternative

0 Magnet; 0 Charter; 9 Title I Eligible; 2 School-wide Title I
Students: 5,176   (52.9% male; 47.0% female)
  Individual Education Program: 902 (17.4%);
  English Language Learner: 37 (0.7%); Migrant: 0 (0.0%)
  Eligible for Free Lunch Program: 2,092 (40.4%)
  Eligible for Reduced-Price Lunch Program: 714 (13.8%)
Teachers: 311.9 (16.6 to 1)
Librarians/Media Specialists: 5.5 (941.1 to 1)
Guidance Counselors: 13.5 (383.4 to 1)
Current Spending: ($ per student per year):
  Total: $5,922; Instruction: $3,404; Support Services: $2,178
Enrollment, Drop-out Rates and Diploma Recipients by Race/Ethnicity

Category	Total	White	Black	Asian	AIAN	Hisp.
Enrollment (%)	100.0	74.0	4.8	0.3	18.1	2.7
Drop-out Rate (%)	1.2	1.1	0.0	0.0	1.9	2.1
H.S. Diplomas (#)	349	255	18	0	69	7

Skiatook
355 S Osage St • Skiatook, OK 74070-2015
(918) 396-5702
Grade Span: PK-12; **Agency Type:** 1
Schools: 4
  2 Primary; 1 Middle; 1 High; 0 Other Level
  4 Regular; 0 Special Education; 0 Vocational; 0 Alternative
  0 Magnet; 0 Charter; 2 Title I Eligible; 0 School-wide Title I
Students: 2,310   (51.3% male; 48.6% female)
  Individual Education Program: 289 (12.5%);
  English Language Learner: 0 (0.0%); Migrant: 0 (0.0%)
  Eligible for Free Lunch Program: 626 (27.1%)
  Eligible for Reduced-Price Lunch Program: 199 (8.6%)
Teachers: 135.5 (17.0 to 1)
Librarians/Media Specialists: 3.0 (770.0 to 1)
Guidance Counselors: 5.0 (462.0 to 1)
Current Spending: ($ per student per year):
  Total: $5,097; Instruction: $3,012; Support Services: $1,767
Enrollment, Drop-out Rates and Diploma Recipients by Race/Ethnicity

Category	Total	White	Black	Asian	AIAN	Hisp.
Enrollment (%)	100.0	65.2	0.3	0.2	32.5	1.8
Drop-out Rate (%)	7.0	6.7	0.0	n/a	7.8	0.0
H.S. Diplomas (#)	158	105	1	0	51	1

Tulsa
PO Box 470208 • Tulsa, OK 74147-0208
(918) 746-6303 • http://www.tulsaschools.org/
Grade Span: PK-12; **Agency Type:** 1
Schools: 86
  60 Primary; 15 Middle; 10 High; 1 Other Level
  86 Regular; 0 Special Education; 0 Vocational; 0 Alternative
  0 Magnet; 3 Charter; 45 Title I Eligible; 45 School-wide Title I
Students: 42,280   (50.9% male; 49.0% female)
  Individual Education Program: 7,301 (17.3%);
  English Language Learner: 4,181 (9.9%); Migrant: 0 (0.0%)
  Eligible for Free Lunch Program: 26,560 (62.8%)
  Eligible for Reduced-Price Lunch Program: 5,287 (12.5%)
Teachers: 2,566.7 (16.5 to 1)
Librarians/Media Specialists: 77.1 (548.4 to 1)
Guidance Counselors: 148.6 (284.5 to 1)
Current Spending: ($ per student per year):
  Total: $6,129; Instruction: $3,189; Support Services: $2,555
Enrollment, Drop-out Rates and Diploma Recipients by Race/Ethnicity

Category	Total	White	Black	Asian	AIAN	Hisp.
Enrollment (%)	100.0	39.7	35.9	1.2	8.8	14.3
Drop-out Rate (%)	7.7	6.4	8.2	4.8	10.2	11.4
H.S. Diplomas (#)	1,758	900	596	33	115	114

Union
5656 S 129th E Ave • Tulsa, OK 74134-6715
(918) 459-5432 • http://www.unionps.org/
Grade Span: PK-12; **Agency Type:** 1
Schools: 15
  11 Primary; 1 Middle; 1 High; 2 Other Level
  15 Regular; 0 Special Education; 0 Vocational; 0 Alternative
  0 Magnet; 0 Charter; 5 Title I Eligible; 1 School-wide Title I
Students: 13,819   (50.6% male; 49.3% female)
  Individual Education Program: 1,175 (8.5%);
  English Language Learner: 1,802 (13.0%); Migrant: 0 (0.0%)
  Eligible for Free Lunch Program: 2,831 (20.5%)
  Eligible for Reduced-Price Lunch Program: 697 (5.0%)
Teachers: 668.8 (20.7 to 1)
Librarians/Media Specialists: 16.0 (863.7 to 1)
Guidance Counselors: 27.0 (511.8 to 1)
Current Spending: ($ per student per year):
  Total: $5,150; Instruction: $2,955; Support Services: $1,960

Enrollment, Drop-out Rates and Diploma Recipients by Race/Ethnicity

Category	Total	White	Black	Asian	AIAN	Hisp.
Enrollment (%)	100.0	62.2	10.8	5.4	10.7	10.9
Drop-out Rate (%)	3.5	2.7	5.2	4.5	3.1	9.3
H.S. Diplomas (#)	768	553	57	52	63	43

Wagoner County

Coweta
PO Box 550 • Coweta, OK 74429-0550
(918) 486-6506
Grade Span: KG-12; **Agency Type:** 1
Schools: 6
  3 Primary; 2 Middle; 1 High; 0 Other Level
  6 Regular; 0 Special Education; 0 Vocational; 0 Alternative
  0 Magnet; 0 Charter; 3 Title I Eligible; 1 School-wide Title I
Students: 2,713 (51.3% male; 48.6% female)
  Individual Education Program: 482 (17.8%);
  English Language Learner: 57 (2.1%); Migrant: 0 (0.0%)
  Eligible for Free Lunch Program: 722 (26.6%)
  Eligible for Reduced-Price Lunch Program: 324 (11.9%)
Teachers: 162.8 (16.7 to 1)
Librarians/Media Specialists: 5.0 (542.6 to 1)
Guidance Counselors: 8.0 (339.1 to 1)
Current Spending: ($ per student per year):
  Total: $5,090; Instruction: $3,061; Support Services: $1,619
Enrollment, Drop-out Rates and Diploma Recipients by Race/Ethnicity

Category	Total	White	Black	Asian	AIAN	Hisp.
Enrollment (%)	100.0	63.4	4.1	0.3	30.0	2.3
Drop-out Rate (%)	4.3	3.9	3.7	0.0	5.1	0.0
H.S. Diplomas (#)	154	95	9	0	50	0

Wagoner
PO Box 707 • Wagoner, OK 74477-0707
(918) 485-4046 • http://www.wagoner.k12.ok.us/
Grade Span: PK-12; **Agency Type:** 1
Schools: 6
  3 Primary; 2 Middle; 1 High; 0 Other Level
  6 Regular; 0 Special Education; 0 Vocational; 0 Alternative
  0 Magnet; 0 Charter; 5 Title I Eligible; 5 School-wide Title I
Students: 2,422 (51.3% male; 48.6% female)
  Individual Education Program: 455 (18.8%);
  English Language Learner: 15 (0.6%); Migrant: 0 (0.0%)
  Eligible for Free Lunch Program: 1,469 (60.7%)
  Eligible for Reduced-Price Lunch Program: 242 (10.0%)
Teachers: 165.8 (14.6 to 1)
Librarians/Media Specialists: 1.5 (1,614.7 to 1)
Guidance Counselors: 6.7 (361.5 to 1)
Current Spending: ($ per student per year):
  Total: $5,817; Instruction: $3,512; Support Services: $1,860
Enrollment, Drop-out Rates and Diploma Recipients by Race/Ethnicity

Category	Total	White	Black	Asian	AIAN	Hisp.
Enrollment (%)	100.0	58.5	11.1	0.7	27.8	1.9
Drop-out Rate (%)	6.1	5.4	5.6	0.0	6.7	40.0
H.S. Diplomas (#)	133	97	17	1	17	1

Washington County

Bartlesville
PO Box 1357 • Bartlesville, OK 74005-1357
(918) 336-8600 • http://www.bartlesville.k12.ok.us/
Grade Span: PK-12; **Agency Type:** 1
Schools: 11
  7 Primary; 2 Middle; 1 High; 1 Other Level
  11 Regular; 0 Special Education; 0 Vocational; 0 Alternative
  0 Magnet; 0 Charter; 4 Title I Eligible; 3 School-wide Title I
Students: 5,978 (52.7% male; 47.2% female)
  Individual Education Program: 719 (12.0%);
  English Language Learner: 118 (2.0%); Migrant: 0 (0.0%)
  Eligible for Free Lunch Program: 1,815 (30.4%)
  Eligible for Reduced-Price Lunch Program: 482 (8.1%)
Teachers: 393.1 (15.2 to 1)
Librarians/Media Specialists: 11.0 (543.5 to 1)
Guidance Counselors: 18.7 (319.7 to 1)
Current Spending: ($ per student per year):
  Total: $5,902; Instruction: $3,499; Support Services: $2,105
Enrollment, Drop-out Rates and Diploma Recipients by Race/Ethnicity

Category	Total	White	Black	Asian	AIAN	Hisp.
Enrollment (%)	100.0	77.8	5.3	1.0	11.6	4.3
Drop-out Rate (%)	3.3	3.7	3.0	0.0	0.7	1.6
H.S. Diplomas (#)	421	346	22	8	37	8

Woodward County

Woodward
PO Box 668 • Woodward, OK 73802-0668
(580) 256-6063 • http://www.woodward.k12.ok.us/
Grade Span: PK-12; **Agency Type:** 1
Schools: 7
  4 Primary; 2 Middle; 1 High; 0 Other Level
  7 Regular; 0 Special Education; 0 Vocational; 0 Alternative
  0 Magnet; 0 Charter; 6 Title I Eligible; 3 School-wide Title I
Students: 2,501 (51.2% male; 48.7% female)
  Individual Education Program: 321 (12.8%);
  English Language Learner: 129 (5.2%); Migrant: 0 (0.0%)
  Eligible for Free Lunch Program: 702 (28.1%)
  Eligible for Reduced-Price Lunch Program: 234 (9.4%)
Teachers: 161.7 (15.5 to 1)
Librarians/Media Specialists: 4.0 (625.3 to 1)
Guidance Counselors: 7.0 (357.3 to 1)
Current Spending: ($ per student per year):
  Total: $5,456; Instruction: $3,230; Support Services: $1,891
Enrollment, Drop-out Rates and Diploma Recipients by Race/Ethnicity

Category	Total	White	Black	Asian	AIAN	Hisp.
Enrollment (%)	100.0	85.8	1.1	1.0	2.6	9.5
Drop-out Rate (%)	6.5	6.0	100.0	0.0	18.8	9.1
H.S. Diplomas (#)	160	150	0	3	1	6

Number of Schools

Rank	Number	District Name	City
1	89	Oklahoma City	Oklahoma City
2	86	Tulsa	Tulsa
3	35	Lawton	Lawton
4	27	Moore	Moore
5	26	Putnam City	Warr Acres
6	25	Midwest City-Del City	Midwest City
7	23	Norman	Norman
8	21	Broken Arrow	Broken Arrow
8	21	Edmond	Edmond
10	15	Union	Tulsa
11	14	Enid	Enid
12	13	Muskogee	Muskogee
13	12	Owasso	Owasso
14	11	Bartlesville	Bartlesville
15	10	Mc Alester	Mcalester
15	10	Ponca City	Ponca City
15	10	Sand Springs	Sand Springs
15	10	Yukon	Yukon
19	9	Choctaw/Nicoma Park	Choctaw
19	9	Duncan	Duncan
19	9	Jenks	Jenks
19	9	Mustang	Mustang
19	9	Sapulpa	Sapulpa
19	9	Stillwater	Stillwater
25	8	Altus	Altus
25	8	Guymon	Guymon
25	8	Miami	Miami
28	7	Ardmore	Ardmore
28	7	Chickasha	Chickasha
28	7	Cushing	Cushing
28	7	El Reno	El Reno
28	7	Shawnee	Shawnee
28	7	Woodward	Woodward
34	6	Ada	Ada
34	6	Claremore	Claremore
34	6	Coweta	Coweta
34	6	Durant	Durant
34	6	Elk City	Elk City
34	6	Harrah	Harrah
34	6	Pryor	Pryor
34	6	Tahlequah	Tahlequah
34	6	Tecumseh	Tecumseh
34	6	Wagoner	Wagoner
34	6	Western Heights	Oklahoma City
45	5	Anadarko	Anadarko
45	5	Bixby	Bixby
45	5	Blackwell	Blackwell
45	5	Byng	Ada
45	5	Catoosa	Catoosa
45	5	Clinton	Clinton
45	5	Guthrie	Guthrie
45	5	Idabel	Idabel
45	5	Noble	Noble
45	5	Weatherford	Weatherford
55	4	Bristow	Bristow
55	4	Broken Bow	Broken Bow
55	4	Checotah	Checotah
55	4	Cleveland	Cleveland
55	4	Collinsville	Collinsville
55	4	Deer Creek	Edmond
55	4	Fort Gibson	Fort Gibson
55	4	Grove	Grove
55	4	Hilldale	Muskogee
55	4	Locust Grove	Locust Grove
55	4	Mannford	Mannford
55	4	Okmulgee	Okmulgee
55	4	Oologah-Talala	Oologah
55	4	Piedmont	Piedmont
55	4	Poteau	Poteau
55	4	Sallisaw	Sallisaw
55	4	Seminole	Seminole
55	4	Skiatook	Skiatook
55	4	Vinita	Vinita
74	3	Glenpool	Glenpool
74	3	Jay	Jay
74	3	Madill	Madill
74	3	Mc Loud	Mcloud
74	3	Muldrow	Muldrow

Number of Teachers

Rank	Number	District Name	City
1	2,566	Tulsa	Tulsa
2	2,344	Oklahoma City	Oklahoma City
3	1,144	Putnam City	Warr Acres
4	1,068	Moore	Moore
5	1,030	Edmond	Edmond
6	1,025	Lawton	Lawton
7	846	Midwest City-Del City	Midwest City
8	835	Broken Arrow	Broken Arrow
9	774	Norman	Norman
10	668	Union	Tulsa
11	491	Jenks	Jenks
12	425	Enid	Enid
13	417	Owasso	Owasso
14	407	Mustang	Mustang
15	393	Bartlesville	Bartlesville
16	373	Muskogee	Muskogee
17	348	Yukon	Yukon
18	348	Ponca City	Ponca City
19	319	Stillwater	Stillwater
20	311	Sand Springs	Sand Springs
21	267	Altus	Altus
22	263	Claremore	Claremore
23	262	Choctaw/Nicoma Park	Choctaw
24	245	Sapulpa	Sapulpa
25	238	Shawnee	Shawnee
26	224	Tahlequah	Tahlequah
27	206	Duncan	Duncan
28	204	Western Heights	Oklahoma City
29	203	Guthrie	Guthrie
30	194	Ardmore	Ardmore
31	192	Bixby	Bixby
32	184	Chickasha	Chickasha
33	182	Durant	Durant
34	176	Ada	Ada
35	172	Mc Alester	Mcalester
36	168	Guymon	Guymon
37	167	El Reno	El Reno
38	165	Wagoner	Wagoner
39	162	Coweta	Coweta
40	161	Woodward	Woodward
41	155	Noble	Noble
42	148	Elk City	Elk City
43	148	Anadarko	Anadarko
44	144	Grove	Grove
45	142	Miami	Miami
46	140	Catoosa	Catoosa
47	138	Tecumseh	Tecumseh
48	138	Pryor	Pryor
49	135	Skiatook	Skiatook
50	134	Clinton	Clinton
51	132	Poteau	Poteau
52	130	Glenpool	Glenpool
53	128	Sallisaw	Sallisaw
54	124	Harrah	Harrah
55	122	Okmulgee	Okmulgee
56	122	Cushing	Cushing
57	122	Deer Creek	Edmond
58	116	Broken Bow	Broken Bow
58	116	Byng	Ada
60	116	Idabel	Idabel
61	112	Weatherford	Weatherford
62	111	Mc Loud	Mcloud
63	111	Fort Gibson	Fort Gibson
64	111	Jay	Jay
65	110	Collinsville	Collinsville
66	106	Bristow	Bristow
67	105	Hilldale	Muskogee
68	105	Vinita	Vinita
69	104	Muldrow	Muldrow
70	103	Cleveland	Cleveland
71	101	Locust Grove	Locust Grove
72	100	Checotah	Checotah
73	97	Oologah-Talala	Oologah
74	96	Mannford	Mannford
75	94	Blackwell	Blackwell
76	93	Seminole	Seminole
77	91	Madill	Madill
78	90	Piedmont	Piedmont

Number of Students

Rank	Number	District Name	City
1	42,280	Tulsa	Tulsa
2	40,599	Oklahoma City	Oklahoma City
3	19,365	Putnam City	Warr Acres
4	18,946	Moore	Moore
5	18,158	Edmond	Edmond
6	17,069	Lawton	Lawton
7	14,746	Broken Arrow	Broken Arrow
8	14,251	Midwest City-Del City	Midwest City
9	13,819	Union	Tulsa
10	12,810	Norman	Norman
11	9,331	Jenks	Jenks
12	7,495	Owasso	Owasso
13	7,193	Mustang	Mustang
14	6,485	Enid	Enid
15	6,289	Muskogee	Muskogee
16	6,162	Yukon	Yukon
17	5,978	Bartlesville	Bartlesville
18	5,588	Ponca City	Ponca City
19	5,291	Stillwater	Stillwater
20	5,176	Sand Springs	Sand Springs
21	4,493	Choctaw/Nicoma Park	Choctaw
22	4,279	Altus	Altus
23	4,231	Sapulpa	Sapulpa
24	4,111	Claremore	Claremore
25	3,847	Bixby	Bixby
26	3,777	Shawnee	Shawnee
27	3,694	Duncan	Duncan
28	3,607	Tahlequah	Tahlequah
29	3,181	Guthrie	Guthrie
30	3,173	Durant	Durant
31	3,102	Ardmore	Ardmore
32	3,082	Western Heights	Oklahoma City
33	2,787	Mc Alester	Mcalester
34	2,784	Chickasha	Chickasha
35	2,783	Noble	Noble
36	2,713	Coweta	Coweta
37	2,582	Ada	Ada
38	2,562	El Reno	El Reno
39	2,501	Woodward	Woodward
40	2,463	Miami	Miami
41	2,422	Wagoner	Wagoner
42	2,373	Guymon	Guymon
43	2,372	Pryor	Pryor
44	2,353	Grove	Grove
45	2,310	Skiatook	Skiatook
46	2,260	Catoosa	Catoosa
47	2,245	Tecumseh	Tecumseh
48	2,213	Harrah	Harrah
49	2,156	Elk City	Elk City
50	2,150	Glenpool	Glenpool
51	2,137	Collinsville	Collinsville
52	2,127	Anadarko	Anadarko
53	2,055	Poteau	Poteau
54	2,044	Deer Creek	Edmond
55	2,039	Okmulgee	Okmulgee
56	2,031	Sallisaw	Sallisaw
57	1,835	Fort Gibson	Fort Gibson
58	1,816	Clinton	Clinton
59	1,788	Cushing	Cushing
60	1,781	Hilldale	Muskogee
61	1,758	Broken Bow	Broken Bow
62	1,750	Jay	Jay
63	1,734	Weatherford	Weatherford
64	1,732	Vinita	Vinita
65	1,730	Bristow	Bristow
66	1,729	Cleveland	Cleveland
67	1,700	Mc Loud	Mcloud
68	1,675	Byng	Ada
69	1,668	Mannford	Mannford
70	1,656	Oologah-Talala	Oologah
71	1,617	Madill	Madill
72	1,599	Muldrow	Muldrow
72	1,599	Piedmont	Piedmont
74	1,590	Idabel	Idabel
75	1,551	Seminole	Seminole
76	1,544	Blackwell	Blackwell
77	1,534	Checotah	Checotah
78	1,517	Locust Grove	Locust Grove

Male Students

Rank	Percent	District Name	City
1	53.9	Tecumseh	Tecumseh
2	53.6	Sallisaw	Sallisaw
3	53.5	Broken Bow	Broken Bow
4	53.2	Fort Gibson	Fort Gibson
5	53.1	Vinita	Vinita
6	53.0	Muldrow	Muldrow
7	52.9	Sand Springs	Sand Springs
8	52.8	Okmulgee	Okmulgee
9	52.8	Deer Creek	Edmond
10	52.7	Choctaw/Nicoma Park	Choctaw
11	52.7	Bartlesville	Bartlesville
12	52.6	Mannford	Mannford
13	52.6	Altus	Altus
14	52.4	Guthrie	Guthrie
15	52.3	Madill	Madill
16	52.2	Norman	Norman
17	52.2	Tahlequah	Tahlequah
18	52.2	Hilldale	Muskogee
19	52.1	El Reno	El Reno
20	52.0	Mc Alester	Mcalester
21	52.0	Glenpool	Glenpool
22	51.8	Mustang	Mustang
23	51.8	Locust Grove	Locust Grove
24	51.6	Miami	Miami
25	51.6	Duncan	Duncan
26	51.6	Shawnee	Shawnee
27	51.5	Midwest City-Del City	Midwest City
28	51.5	Edmond	Edmond
29	51.5	Moore	Moore
30	51.5	Mc Loud	Mcloud

31	51.4	Lawton	Lawton
32	51.4	Bixby	Bixby
33	51.4	Western Heights	Oklahoma City
34	51.4	Blackwell	Blackwell
35	51.4	Ponca City	Ponca City
36	51.3	Stillwater	Stillwater
37	51.3	Skiatook	Skiatook
38	51.3	Broken Arrow	Broken Arrow
39	51.3	Piedmont	Piedmont
40	51.3	Bristow	Bristow
41	51.3	Wagoner	Wagoner
42	51.3	Coweta	Coweta
43	51.2	Enid	Enid
44	51.2	Jenks	Jenks
45	51.2	Woodward	Woodward
46	51.2	Clinton	Clinton
47	51.1	Putnam City	Warr Acres
48	51.1	Claremore	Claremore
49	51.1	Noble	Noble
50	51.0	Oologah-Talala	Oologah
51	51.0	Owasso	Owasso
52	51.0	Muskogee	Muskogee
53	50.9	Grove	Grove
54	50.9	Tulsa	Tulsa
55	50.9	Pryor	Pryor
56	50.9	Collinsville	Collinsville
57	50.8	Guymon	Guymon
58	50.8	Oklahoma City	Oklahoma City
59	50.8	Idabel	Idabel
60	50.7	Durant	Durant
61	50.6	Ada	Ada
62	50.6	Union	Tulsa
63	50.6	Sapulpa	Sapulpa
64	50.5	Jay	Jay
65	50.5	Ardmore	Ardmore
66	50.5	Harrah	Harrah
67	50.4	Chickasha	Chickasha
68	50.4	Poteau	Poteau
69	50.2	Yukon	Yukon
70	50.2	Seminole	Seminole
71	50.2	Cushing	Cushing
72	50.1	Anadarko	Anadarko
73	50.1	Elk City	Elk City
74	50.1	Weatherford	Weatherford
75	49.9	Catoosa	Catoosa
76	49.9	Cleveland	Cleveland
77	49.7	Checotah	Checotah
78	48.1	Byng	Ada

Female Students

Rank	Percent	District Name	City
1	51.8	Byng	Ada
2	50.2	Checotah	Checotah
3	50.0	Cleveland	Cleveland
4	50.0	Catoosa	Catoosa
5	49.8	Weatherford	Weatherford
6	49.8	Elk City	Elk City
7	49.8	Anadarko	Anadarko
8	49.7	Cushing	Cushing
9	49.7	Seminole	Seminole
10	49.7	Yukon	Yukon
11	49.5	Poteau	Poteau
12	49.5	Chickasha	Chickasha
13	49.4	Harrah	Harrah
14	49.4	Ardmore	Ardmore
15	49.4	Jay	Jay
16	49.3	Sapulpa	Sapulpa
17	49.3	Union	Tulsa
18	49.3	Ada	Ada
19	49.2	Durant	Durant
20	49.1	Idabel	Idabel
21	49.1	Oklahoma City	Oklahoma City
22	49.1	Guymon	Guymon
23	49.0	Collinsville	Collinsville
24	49.0	Pryor	Pryor
25	49.0	Tulsa	Tulsa
26	49.0	Grove	Grove
27	48.9	Muskogee	Muskogee
28	48.9	Owasso	Owasso
29	48.9	Oologah-Talala	Oologah
30	48.8	Noble	Noble
31	48.8	Claremore	Claremore
32	48.8	Putnam City	Warr Acres
33	48.7	Clinton	Clinton
34	48.7	Woodward	Woodward
35	48.7	Jenks	Jenks
36	48.7	Enid	Enid
37	48.6	Coweta	Coweta
38	48.6	Wagoner	Wagoner
39	48.6	Bristow	Bristow
40	48.6	Piedmont	Piedmont
41	48.6	Broken Arrow	Broken Arrow

42	48.6	Skiatook	Skiatook
43	48.6	Stillwater	Stillwater
44	48.5	Ponca City	Ponca City
45	48.5	Blackwell	Blackwell
46	48.5	Western Heights	Oklahoma City
47	48.5	Bixby	Bixby
48	48.5	Lawton	Lawton
49	48.4	Mc Loud	Mcloud
50	48.4	Moore	Moore
51	48.4	Edmond	Edmond
52	48.4	Midwest City-Del City	Midwest City
53	48.3	Shawnee	Shawnee
54	48.3	Duncan	Duncan
55	48.3	Miami	Miami
56	48.1	Locust Grove	Locust Grove
57	48.1	Mustang	Mustang
58	47.9	Glenpool	Glenpool
59	47.9	Mc Alester	Mcalester
60	47.8	El Reno	El Reno
61	47.7	Hilldale	Muskogee
62	47.7	Tahlequah	Tahlequah
63	47.7	Norman	Norman
64	47.6	Madill	Madill
65	47.5	Guthrie	Guthrie
66	47.3	Altus	Altus
67	47.3	Mannford	Mannford
68	47.2	Bartlesville	Bartlesville
69	47.2	Choctaw/Nicoma Park	Choctaw
70	47.1	Deer Creek	Edmond
71	47.1	Okmulgee	Okmulgee
72	47.0	Sand Springs	Sand Springs
73	46.9	Muldrow	Muldrow
74	46.8	Vinita	Vinita
75	46.7	Fort Gibson	Fort Gibson
76	46.4	Broken Bow	Broken Bow
77	46.3	Sallisaw	Sallisaw
78	46.0	Tecumseh	Tecumseh

Individual Education Program Students

Rank	Percent	District Name	City
1	21.9	Locust Grove	Locust Grove
2	20.3	Mc Alester	Mcalester
3	20.2	Vinita	Vinita
4	20.0	Anadarko	Anadarko
5	18.8	Wagoner	Wagoner
6	18.6	Ardmore	Ardmore
7	18.2	Harrah	Harrah
8	17.8	Coweta	Coweta
8	17.8	Jay	Jay
10	17.5	Catoosa	Catoosa
11	17.4	Sand Springs	Sand Springs
12	17.3	Byng	Ada
12	17.3	Tulsa	Tulsa
14	17.1	Stillwater	Stillwater
15	17.0	Blackwell	Blackwell
16	16.9	Okmulgee	Okmulgee
17	16.8	Cushing	Cushing
18	16.2	Tahlequah	Tahlequah
19	16.1	Sallisaw	Sallisaw
20	15.9	Grove	Grove
20	15.9	Jenks	Jenks
20	15.9	Lawton	Lawton
23	15.8	Poteau	Poteau
24	15.6	Checotah	Checotah
24	15.6	Cleveland	Cleveland
26	15.5	Chickasha	Chickasha
27	15.3	Oklahoma City	Oklahoma City
27	15.3	Shawnee	Shawnee
29	15.2	Western Heights	Oklahoma City
30	15.0	Claremore	Claremore
31	14.9	Enid	Enid
31	14.9	Ponca City	Ponca City
33	14.7	Idabel	Idabel
33	14.7	Norman	Norman
35	14.6	El Reno	El Reno
36	14.5	Ada	Ada
36	14.5	Broken Arrow	Broken Arrow
36	14.5	Choctaw/Nicoma Park	Choctaw
36	14.5	Weatherford	Weatherford
40	14.4	Tecumseh	Tecumseh
41	14.2	Durant	Durant
41	14.2	Guthrie	Guthrie
41	14.2	Mc Loud	Mcloud
41	14.2	Midwest City-Del City	Midwest City
45	14.1	Muldrow	Muldrow
46	13.6	Bristow	Bristow
46	13.6	Sapulpa	Sapulpa
48	13.5	Glenpool	Glenpool
49	13.4	Broken Bow	Broken Bow
50	13.3	Edmond	Edmond
50	13.3	Hilldale	Muskogee
52	13.2	Oologah-Talala	Oologah

53	13.1	Deer Creek	Edmond
53	13.1	Noble	Noble
55	12.8	Woodward	Woodward
56	12.7	Bixby	Bixby
57	12.6	Fort Gibson	Fort Gibson
57	12.6	Muskogee	Muskogee
57	12.6	Seminole	Seminole
60	12.5	Skiatook	Skiatook
61	12.3	Putnam City	Warr Acres
62	12.2	Collinsville	Collinsville
63	12.1	Clinton	Clinton
63	12.1	Moore	Moore
65	12.0	Bartlesville	Bartlesville
66	11.6	Miami	Miami
67	11.4	Elk City	Elk City
68	11.3	Piedmont	Piedmont
69	10.8	Mannford	Mannford
70	10.7	Guymon	Guymon
71	10.6	Yukon	Yukon
72	10.5	Pryor	Pryor
73	10.3	Altus	Altus
74	10.2	Duncan	Duncan
75	10.1	Mustang	Mustang
76	10.0	Owasso	Owasso
77	8.5	Union	Tulsa
78	8.2	Madill	Madill

English Language Learner Students

Rank	Percent	District Name	City
1	40.5	Guymon	Guymon
2	25.2	Madill	Madill
3	23.4	Oklahoma City	Oklahoma City
4	22.9	Clinton	Clinton
5	16.7	Altus	Altus
6	14.0	Western Heights	Oklahoma City
7	13.0	Union	Tulsa
8	9.9	Tulsa	Tulsa
9	9.8	Lawton	Lawton
10	9.7	Hilldale	Muskogee
11	9.0	Muldrow	Muldrow
12	8.9	Enid	Enid
13	8.6	Anadarko	Anadarko
14	8.3	Tahlequah	Tahlequah
15	7.8	El Reno	El Reno
16	7.7	Jay	Jay
17	6.7	Broken Bow	Broken Bow
18	6.6	Duncan	Duncan
18	6.6	Putnam City	Warr Acres
20	6.4	Jenks	Jenks
21	5.2	Woodward	Woodward
22	5.1	Shawnee	Shawnee
22	5.1	Stillwater	Stillwater
24	5.0	Blackwell	Blackwell
25	4.8	Idabel	Idabel
25	4.8	Muskogee	Muskogee
27	4.3	Locust Grove	Locust Grove
28	4.2	Elk City	Elk City
28	4.2	Poteau	Poteau
30	3.9	Mustang	Mustang
31	3.7	Norman	Norman
31	3.7	Weatherford	Weatherford
33	3.6	Moore	Moore
34	3.5	Claremore	Claremore
35	3.4	Ponca City	Ponca City
36	3.3	Sallisaw	Sallisaw
37	3.2	Owasso	Owasso
38	3.0	Midwest City-Del City	Midwest City
39	2.9	Fort Gibson	Fort Gibson
40	2.8	Okmulgee	Okmulgee
41	2.7	Edmond	Edmond
42	2.6	Ardmore	Ardmore
42	2.6	Bixby	Bixby
42	2.6	Yukon	Yukon
45	2.5	Glenpool	Glenpool
45	2.5	Mc Loud	Mcloud
47	2.4	Ada	Ada
47	2.4	Durant	Durant
49	2.2	Pryor	Pryor
50	2.1	Coweta	Coweta
50	2.1	Mc Alester	Mcalester
50	2.1	Sapulpa	Sapulpa
50	2.1	Seminole	Seminole
54	2.0	Bartlesville	Bartlesville
54	2.0	Broken Arrow	Broken Arrow
56	1.9	Tecumseh	Tecumseh
57	1.8	Checotah	Checotah
58	1.6	Byng	Ada
59	1.5	Miami	Miami
60	1.4	Chickasha	Chickasha
60	1.4	Deer Creek	Edmond
60	1.4	Grove	Grove
63	1.1	Catoosa	Catoosa

Rank	Percent	District Name	City
63	1.1	Piedmont	Piedmont
65	0.7	Guthrie	Guthrie
65	0.7	Sand Springs	Sand Springs
67	0.6	Wagoner	Wagoner
68	0.5	Bristow	Bristow
69	0.4	Choctaw/Nicoma Park	Choctaw
70	0.3	Harrah	Harrah
71	0.1	Cleveland	Cleveland
72	0.0	Collinsville	Collinsville
72	0.0	Cushing	Cushing
72	0.0	Mannford	Mannford
72	0.0	Noble	Noble
72	0.0	Oologah-Talala	Oologah
72	0.0	Skiatook	Skiatook
72	0.0	Vinita	Vinita

Migrant Students

Rank	Percent	District Name	City
1	47.2	Clinton	Clinton
2	42.7	Guymon	Guymon
3	12.2	Altus	Altus
4	8.8	Madill	Madill
5	6.7	Broken Bow	Broken Bow
6	3.9	Bixby	Bixby
7	3.1	Muldrow	Muldrow
8	1.2	Ponca City	Ponca City
9	1.0	Mc Alester	Mcalester
10	0.6	Owasso	Owasso
10	0.6	Tahlequah	Tahlequah
12	0.0	Ada	Ada
12	0.0	Anadarko	Anadarko
12	0.0	Ardmore	Ardmore
12	0.0	Bartlesville	Bartlesville
12	0.0	Blackwell	Blackwell
12	0.0	Bristow	Bristow
12	0.0	Broken Arrow	Broken Arrow
12	0.0	Byng	Ada
12	0.0	Catoosa	Catoosa
12	0.0	Checotah	Checotah
12	0.0	Chickasha	Chickasha
12	0.0	Choctaw/Nicoma Park	Choctaw
12	0.0	Claremore	Claremore
12	0.0	Cleveland	Cleveland
12	0.0	Collinsville	Collinsville
12	0.0	Coweta	Coweta
12	0.0	Cushing	Cushing
12	0.0	Deer Creek	Edmond
12	0.0	Duncan	Duncan
12	0.0	Durant	Durant
12	0.0	Edmond	Edmond
12	0.0	El Reno	El Reno
12	0.0	Elk City	Elk City
12	0.0	Enid	Enid
12	0.0	Fort Gibson	Fort Gibson
12	0.0	Glenpool	Glenpool
12	0.0	Grove	Grove
12	0.0	Guthrie	Guthrie
12	0.0	Harrah	Harrah
12	0.0	Hilldale	Muskogee
12	0.0	Idabel	Idabel
12	0.0	Jay	Jay
12	0.0	Jenks	Jenks
12	0.0	Lawton	Lawton
12	0.0	Locust Grove	Locust Grove
12	0.0	Mannford	Mannford
12	0.0	Mc Loud	Mcloud
12	0.0	Miami	Miami
12	0.0	Midwest City-Del City	Midwest City
12	0.0	Moore	Moore
12	0.0	Muskogee	Muskogee
12	0.0	Mustang	Mustang
12	0.0	Noble	Noble
12	0.0	Norman	Norman
12	0.0	Oklahoma City	Oklahoma City
12	0.0	Okmulgee	Okmulgee
12	0.0	Oologah-Talala	Oologah
12	0.0	Piedmont	Piedmont
12	0.0	Poteau	Poteau
12	0.0	Pryor	Pryor
12	0.0	Putnam City	Warr Acres
12	0.0	Sallisaw	Sallisaw
12	0.0	Sand Springs	Sand Springs
12	0.0	Sapulpa	Sapulpa
12	0.0	Seminole	Seminole
12	0.0	Shawnee	Shawnee
12	0.0	Skiatook	Skiatook
12	0.0	Stillwater	Stillwater
12	0.0	Tecumseh	Tecumseh
12	0.0	Tulsa	Tulsa
12	0.0	Union	Tulsa
12	0.0	Vinita	Vinita
12	0.0	Wagoner	Wagoner

Rank	Percent	District Name	City
12	0.0	Weatherford	Weatherford
12	0.0	Western Heights	Oklahoma City
12	0.0	Woodward	Woodward
12	0.0	Yukon	Yukon

Students Eligible for Free Lunch

Rank	Percent	District Name	City
1	76.2	Oklahoma City	Oklahoma City
2	71.2	Idabel	Idabel
3	65.9	Anadarko	Anadarko
4	63.9	Broken Bow	Broken Bow
5	63.4	Okmulgee	Okmulgee
6	62.8	Clinton	Clinton
6	62.8	Tulsa	Tulsa
8	60.8	Checotah	Checotah
9	60.7	Wagoner	Wagoner
10	59.5	Western Heights	Oklahoma City
11	59.1	Muskogee	Muskogee
12	58.8	Jay	Jay
13	58.7	Bristow	Bristow
14	57.5	Seminole	Seminole
15	56.7	Ardmore	Ardmore
16	54.6	Locust Grove	Locust Grove
17	54.1	Madill	Madill
18	53.5	Tahlequah	Tahlequah
19	52.1	Sallisaw	Sallisaw
20	51.8	El Reno	El Reno
21	50.9	Durant	Durant
22	50.5	Shawnee	Shawnee
23	50.4	Byng	Ada
23	50.4	Muldrow	Muldrow
25	49.9	Miami	Miami
26	49.4	Blackwell	Blackwell
27	48.7	Guymon	Guymon
28	48.1	Poteau	Poteau
29	47.6	Ada	Ada
30	47.4	Tecumseh	Tecumseh
31	46.5	Mc Alester	Mcalester
32	45.0	Guthrie	Guthrie
33	43.2	Ponca City	Ponca City
34	42.2	Chickasha	Chickasha
35	42.1	Enid	Enid
36	41.7	Cushing	Cushing
37	40.9	Duncan	Duncan
38	40.4	Sand Springs	Sand Springs
39	39.5	Altus	Altus
40	39.2	Grove	Grove
40	39.2	Pryor	Pryor
40	39.2	Sapulpa	Sapulpa
43	38.7	Midwest City-Del City	Midwest City
44	38.5	Vinita	Vinita
45	38.2	Putnam City	Warr Acres
46	37.6	Cleveland	Cleveland
46	37.6	Elk City	Elk City
48	36.1	Lawton	Lawton
49	35.5	Mc Loud	Mcloud
50	33.9	Mannford	Mannford
51	33.3	Noble	Noble
52	32.1	Weatherford	Weatherford
53	31.5	Catoosa	Catoosa
53	31.5	Claremore	Claremore
55	31.0	Fort Gibson	Fort Gibson
56	30.4	Bartlesville	Bartlesville
57	28.1	Woodward	Woodward
58	28.0	Norman	Norman
59	27.6	Glenpool	Glenpool
60	27.5	Harrah	Harrah
61	27.1	Skiatook	Skiatook
62	26.6	Coweta	Coweta
63	24.6	Hilldale	Muskogee
64	22.7	Stillwater	Stillwater
65	22.4	Collinsville	Collinsville
66	21.4	Choctaw/Nicoma Park	Choctaw
67	20.5	Union	Tulsa
68	19.9	Moore	Moore
69	18.9	Oologah-Talala	Oologah
70	18.6	Broken Arrow	Broken Arrow
70	18.6	Yukon	Yukon
72	15.6	Bixby	Bixby
73	15.0	Jenks	Jenks
74	12.2	Edmond	Edmond
75	11.5	Mustang	Mustang
76	11.0	Owasso	Owasso
77	5.9	Piedmont	Piedmont
78	3.1	Deer Creek	Edmond

Students Eligible for Reduced-Price Lunch

Rank	Percent	District Name	City
1	19.1	Locust Grove	Locust Grove
2	16.0	Jay	Jay

Rank	Percent	District Name	City
2	16.0	Tahlequah	Tahlequah
4	15.8	Bristow	Bristow
4	15.8	Checotah	Checotah
6	15.5	Vinita	Vinita
7	15.4	Noble	Noble
8	15.3	Grove	Grove
9	15.2	Poteau	Poteau
10	14.6	Cleveland	Cleveland
11	14.2	Mannford	Mannford
12	14.1	Cushing	Cushing
13	14.0	Okmulgee	Okmulgee
14	13.8	Sand Springs	Sand Springs
14	13.8	Tecumseh	Tecumseh
16	13.5	Clinton	Clinton
17	13.3	El Reno	El Reno
18	13.1	Muldrow	Muldrow
19	12.9	Catoosa	Catoosa
20	12.8	Byng	Ada
20	12.8	Guymon	Guymon
22	12.7	Miami	Miami
23	12.6	Ardmore	Ardmore
23	12.6	Sapulpa	Sapulpa
25	12.5	Glenpool	Glenpool
25	12.5	Tulsa	Tulsa
27	12.4	Blackwell	Blackwell
27	12.4	Broken Bow	Broken Bow
27	12.4	Harrah	Harrah
30	12.2	Ponca City	Ponca City
31	12.1	Guthrie	Guthrie
32	11.9	Coweta	Coweta
32	11.9	Mc Loud	Mcloud
34	11.8	Hilldale	Muskogee
35	11.7	Lawton	Lawton
36	11.3	Western Heights	Oklahoma City
37	11.1	Midwest City-Del City	Midwest City
38	10.9	Muskogee	Muskogee
39	10.8	Ada	Ada
39	10.8	Anadarko	Anadarko
39	10.8	Elk City	Elk City
42	10.6	Madill	Madill
43	10.5	Fort Gibson	Fort Gibson
44	10.4	Weatherford	Weatherford
45	10.2	Durant	Durant
46	10.0	Mustang	Mustang
46	10.0	Wagoner	Wagoner
48	9.6	Mc Alester	Mcalester
49	9.5	Chickasha	Chickasha
49	9.5	Oologah-Talala	Oologah
49	9.5	Seminole	Seminole
52	9.4	Claremore	Claremore
52	9.4	Woodward	Woodward
54	9.3	Sallisaw	Sallisaw
55	9.2	Altus	Altus
56	9.0	Putnam City	Warr Acres
57	8.7	Pryor	Pryor
58	8.6	Broken Arrow	Broken Arrow
58	8.6	Skiatook	Skiatook
60	8.4	Moore	Moore
61	8.3	Choctaw/Nicoma Park	Choctaw
62	8.1	Bartlesville	Bartlesville
63	7.9	Duncan	Duncan
63	7.9	Enid	Enid
63	7.9	Shawnee	Shawnee
63	7.9	Yukon	Yukon
67	7.6	Norman	Norman
68	7.4	Collinsville	Collinsville
69	7.1	Bixby	Bixby
70	6.9	Idabel	Idabel
70	6.9	Oklahoma City	Oklahoma City
72	5.9	Stillwater	Stillwater
73	5.0	Union	Tulsa
74	4.7	Owasso	Owasso
75	4.0	Edmond	Edmond
76	3.9	Jenks	Jenks
77	3.1	Piedmont	Piedmont
78	1.3	Deer Creek	Edmond

Student/Teacher Ratio

Rank	Ratio	District Name	City
1	20.7	Union	Tulsa
2	20.0	Bixby	Bixby
3	19.4	Collinsville	Collinsville
4	19.0	Jenks	Jenks
5	18.0	Owasso	Owasso
6	17.9	Duncan	Duncan
6	17.9	Noble	Noble
8	17.7	Harrah	Harrah
8	17.7	Moore	Moore
8	17.7	Mustang	Mustang
8	17.7	Yukon	Yukon
12	17.6	Broken Arrow	Broken Arrow
12	17.6	Edmond	Edmond

Rank	Ratio	District Name	City
12	17.6	Madill	Madill
12	17.6	Piedmont	Piedmont
16	17.4	Durant	Durant
17	17.3	Miami	Miami
17	17.3	Oklahoma City	Oklahoma City
19	17.2	Mannford	Mannford
19	17.2	Sapulpa	Sapulpa
21	17.1	Choctaw/Nicoma Park	Choctaw
21	17.1	Pryor	Pryor
23	17.0	Oologah-Talala	Oologah
23	17.0	Skiatook	Skiatook
25	16.9	Putnam City	Warr Acres
26	16.8	Hilldale	Muskogee
26	16.8	Midwest City-Del City	Midwest City
26	16.8	Muskogee	Muskogee
29	16.7	Coweta	Coweta
29	16.7	Deer Creek	Edmond
31	16.6	Cleveland	Cleveland
31	16.6	Lawton	Lawton
31	16.6	Okmulgee	Okmulgee
31	16.6	Sand Springs	Sand Springs
31	16.6	Seminole	Seminole
31	16.6	Stillwater	Stillwater
37	16.5	Glenpool	Glenpool
37	16.5	Norman	Norman
37	16.5	Tulsa	Tulsa
40	16.4	Blackwell	Blackwell
40	16.4	Fort Gibson	Fort Gibson
40	16.4	Vinita	Vinita
43	16.3	Grove	Grove
44	16.2	Bristow	Bristow
44	16.2	Tecumseh	Tecumseh
46	16.1	Catoosa	Catoosa
46	16.1	Mc Alester	Mcalester
46	16.1	Ponca City	Ponca City
49	16.0	Altus	Altus
49	16.0	Tahlequah	Tahlequah
51	15.9	Ardmore	Ardmore
52	15.8	Sallisaw	Sallisaw
52	15.8	Shawnee	Shawnee
54	15.7	Jay	Jay
55	15.6	Claremore	Claremore
55	15.6	Guthrie	Guthrie
55	15.6	Poteau	Poteau
58	15.5	Weatherford	Weatherford
58	15.5	Woodward	Woodward
60	15.4	Muldrow	Muldrow
61	15.3	Checotah	Checotah
61	15.3	El Reno	El Reno
63	15.2	Bartlesville	Bartlesville
63	15.2	Enid	Enid
63	15.2	Mc Loud	Mcloud
66	15.1	Broken Bow	Broken Bow
66	15.1	Chickasha	Chickasha
66	15.1	Western Heights	Oklahoma City
69	14.9	Locust Grove	Locust Grove
70	14.6	Ada	Ada
70	14.6	Cushing	Cushing
70	14.6	Wagoner	Wagoner
73	14.5	Elk City	Elk City
74	14.4	Anadarko	Anadarko
74	14.4	Byng	Ada
76	14.1	Guymon	Guymon
77	13.7	Idabel	Idabel
78	13.5	Clinton	Clinton

Student/Librarian Ratio

Rank	Ratio	District Name	City
1	1,614.7	Wagoner	Wagoner
2	1,291.0	Ada	Ada
3	1,137.9	Lawton	Lawton
4	1,027.3	Western Heights	Oklahoma City
5	1,015.5	Sallisaw	Sallisaw
6	941.1	Sand Springs	Sand Springs
7	929.0	Mc Alester	Mcalester
8	890.5	Hilldale	Muskogee
9	863.7	Union	Tulsa
10	855.8	Altus	Altus
11	850.0	Mc Loud	Mcloud
12	848.3	Jenks	Jenks
13	828.6	Oklahoma City	Oklahoma City
14	820.9	Duncan	Duncan
15	799.5	Muldrow	Muldrow
15	799.5	Piedmont	Piedmont
17	799.2	Mustang	Mustang
18	795.3	Guthrie	Guthrie
19	795.0	Idabel	Idabel
20	784.3	Grove	Grove
21	772.0	Blackwell	Blackwell
22	770.3	Yukon	Yukon
23	770.0	Skiatook	Skiatook
24	769.4	Bixby	Bixby
25	753.4	Edmond	Edmond
26	753.3	Catoosa	Catoosa
27	737.7	Harrah	Harrah
28	721.2	Tahlequah	Tahlequah
29	718.7	Elk City	Elk City
30	716.7	Glenpool	Glenpool
31	705.2	Sapulpa	Sapulpa
32	698.8	Muskogee	Muskogee
33	695.8	Noble	Noble
34	691.6	Putnam City	Warr Acres
35	685.2	Claremore	Claremore
36	670.3	Broken Arrow	Broken Arrow
37	664.8	Moore	Moore
38	640.5	El Reno	El Reno
39	629.5	Shawnee	Shawnee
40	625.3	Woodward	Woodward
41	620.9	Ponca City	Ponca City
42	620.4	Ardmore	Ardmore
43	611.7	Fort Gibson	Fort Gibson
44	608.5	Guymon	Guymon
45	587.9	Stillwater	Stillwater
46	586.0	Broken Bow	Broken Bow
47	583.3	Jay	Jay
48	576.3	Cleveland	Cleveland
49	572.1	Owasso	Owasso
50	561.3	Tecumseh	Tecumseh
51	559.4	Weatherford	Weatherford
52	556.0	Mannford	Mannford
53	552.0	Oologah-Talala	Oologah
54	548.4	Tulsa	Tulsa
55	543.5	Bartlesville	Bartlesville
56	542.6	Coweta	Coweta
57	539.0	Madill	Madill
58	535.8	Midwest City-Del City	Midwest City
59	534.3	Collinsville	Collinsville
60	533.8	Norman	Norman
61	528.8	Durant	Durant
62	513.8	Poteau	Poteau
63	511.3	Checotah	Checotah
64	511.0	Deer Creek	Edmond
65	509.8	Okmulgee	Okmulgee
66	506.2	Chickasha	Chickasha
67	505.7	Locust Grove	Locust Grove
68	499.2	Choctaw/Nicoma Park	Choctaw
69	498.8	Enid	Enid
70	494.3	Bristow	Bristow
71	492.6	Miami	Miami
72	478.6	Byng	Ada
73	433.0	Vinita	Vinita
74	425.4	Anadarko	Anadarko
75	395.3	Pryor	Pryor
76	387.8	Seminole	Seminole
77	363.2	Clinton	Clinton
78	357.6	Cushing	Cushing

Student/Counselor Ratio

Rank	Ratio	District Name	City
1	632.5	Noble	Noble
2	593.8	Midwest City-Del City	Midwest City
3	593.7	Hilldale	Muskogee
4	576.7	Bristow	Bristow
4	576.7	Oklahoma City	Oklahoma City
6	556.0	Mannford	Mannford
7	553.3	Harrah	Harrah
8	552.0	Oologah-Talala	Oologah
9	534.3	Collinsville	Collinsville
10	533.0	Muldrow	Muldrow
11	530.2	Guthrie	Guthrie
12	513.4	Moore	Moore
13	511.8	Union	Tulsa
14	507.8	Sallisaw	Sallisaw
15	504.4	Jenks	Jenks
16	499.7	Owasso	Owasso
17	497.8	Putnam City	Warr Acres
18	474.2	Western Heights	Oklahoma City
19	472.9	Muskogee	Muskogee
20	467.7	Tecumseh	Tecumseh
21	462.0	Skiatook	Skiatook
22	458.8	Fort Gibson	Fort Gibson
23	433.5	Weatherford	Weatherford
24	433.0	Vinita	Vinita
25	432.3	Cleveland	Cleveland
26	430.3	Ada	Ada
27	430.0	Glenpool	Glenpool
28	427.9	Altus	Altus
29	423.3	Ponca City	Ponca City
30	411.0	Poteau	Poteau
31	410.4	Duncan	Duncan
32	408.8	Deer Creek	Edmond
33	408.5	Choctaw/Nicoma Park	Choctaw
34	407.8	Okmulgee	Okmulgee
35	403.5	Edmond	Edmond
36	402.2	Guymon	Guymon
37	399.8	Piedmont	Piedmont
38	397.5	Idabel	Idabel
39	386.0	Blackwell	Blackwell
40	384.7	Bixby	Bixby
41	383.4	Sand Springs	Sand Springs
42	378.6	Mustang	Mustang
43	377.9	Stillwater	Stillwater
44	373.7	Claremore	Claremore
45	371.6	Mc Alester	Mcalester
46	369.6	Broken Arrow	Broken Arrow
47	364.7	Sapulpa	Sapulpa
48	362.5	Yukon	Yukon
49	361.5	Wagoner	Wagoner
50	357.6	Cushing	Cushing
51	357.3	Woodward	Woodward
52	354.5	Anadarko	Anadarko
53	351.9	Lawton	Lawton
53	351.7	Miami	Miami
55	350.0	Jay	Jay
56	348.0	Chickasha	Chickasha
57	340.0	Mc Loud	Mcloud
58	339.1	Coweta	Coweta
59	337.1	El Reno	El Reno
60	335.0	Byng	Ada
61	330.9	Enid	Enid
62	328.5	Norman	Norman
63	323.4	Madill	Madill
64	322.9	Catoosa	Catoosa
65	319.7	Bartlesville	Bartlesville
66	314.8	Shawnee	Shawnee
67	314.2	Durant	Durant
68	310.2	Ardmore	Ardmore
68	310.2	Seminole	Seminole
70	309.6	Locust Grove	Locust Grove
71	306.8	Checotah	Checotah
72	303.0	Tahlequah	Tahlequah
73	302.7	Clinton	Clinton
74	296.5	Pryor	Pryor
75	294.1	Grove	Grove
76	293.0	Broken Bow	Broken Bow
77	291.4	Elk City	Elk City
78	284.5	Tulsa	Tulsa

Current Spending per Student in FY2003

Rank	Dollars	District Name	City
1	6,852	Locust Grove	Locust Grove
2	6,767	Anadarko	Anadarko
3	6,662	Tahlequah	Tahlequah
4	6,648	Okmulgee	Okmulgee
5	6,619	Idabel	Idabel
6	6,612	Mc Alester	Mcalester
7	6,605	Cushing	Cushing
8	6,538	Oklahoma City	Oklahoma City
9	6,423	Clinton	Clinton
10	6,369	Western Heights	Oklahoma City
11	6,317	Byng	Ada
12	6,283	Guymon	Guymon
13	6,160	Durant	Durant
14	6,145	Ardmore	Ardmore
15	6,143	Vinita	Vinita
16	6,129	Tulsa	Tulsa
17	6,109	Broken Bow	Broken Bow
18	6,106	Fort Gibson	Fort Gibson
19	6,083	Weatherford	Weatherford
20	6,046	Checotah	Checotah
21	6,005	Shawnee	Shawnee
22	5,972	Ada	Ada
23	5,964	Madill	Madill
24	5,950	Poteau	Poteau
25	5,924	Muskogee	Muskogee
26	5,922	Sand Springs	Sand Springs
27	5,902	Bartlesville	Bartlesville
28	5,870	Enid	Enid
29	5,867	Bristow	Bristow
30	5,852	Jay	Jay
31	5,835	Altus	Altus
32	5,830	Oologah-Talala	Oologah
32	5,830	Seminole	Seminole
34	5,817	Wagoner	Wagoner
35	5,771	Ponca City	Ponca City
36	5,702	El Reno	El Reno
37	5,692	Lawton	Lawton
38	5,677	Guthrie	Guthrie
39	5,638	Edmond	Edmond
40	5,625	Midwest City-Del City	Midwest City
41	5,608	Jenks	Jenks
41	5,608	Sallisaw	Sallisaw
43	5,607	Miami	Miami
44	5,601	Elk City	Elk City
45	5,583	Broken Arrow	Broken Arrow
46	5,527	Norman	Norman

Rank		District Name	City
47	5,526	Catoosa	Catoosa
48	5,505	Sapulpa	Sapulpa
49	5,504	Stillwater	Stillwater
50	5,503	Tecumseh	Tecumseh
51	5,495	Blackwell	Blackwell
52	5,493	Putnam City	Warr Acres
53	5,483	Muldrow	Muldrow
54	5,478	Chickasha	Chickasha
55	5,456	Woodward	Woodward
56	5,429	Grove	Grove
57	5,427	Yukon	Yukon
58	5,410	Duncan	Duncan
59	5,253	Mc Loud	Mcloud
60	5,240	Moore	Moore
61	5,226	Deer Creek	Edmond
62	5,222	Harrah	Harrah
63	5,168	Pryor	Pryor
64	5,150	Union	Tulsa
65	5,122	Choctaw/Nicoma Park	Choctaw
66	5,112	Owasso	Owasso
67	5,106	Glenpool	Glenpool
68	5,097	Skiatook	Skiatook
69	5,090	Coweta	Coweta
70	5,025	Noble	Noble
71	4,997	Bixby	Bixby
72	4,996	Claremore	Claremore
73	4,974	Mustang	Mustang
74	4,955	Cleveland	Cleveland
75	4,950	Hilldale	Muskogee
76	4,822	Collinsville	Collinsville
77	4,805	Piedmont	Piedmont
78	4,786	Mannford	Mannford

Number of Diploma Recipients

Rank	Number	District Name	City
1	1,758	Tulsa	Tulsa
2	1,441	Oklahoma City	Oklahoma City
3	1,267	Edmond	Edmond
4	1,185	Putnam City	Warr Acres
5	1,137	Moore	Moore
6	1,076	Midwest City-Del City	Midwest City
7	894	Lawton	Lawton
8	885	Broken Arrow	Broken Arrow
9	867	Norman	Norman
10	768	Union	Tulsa
11	625	Jenks	Jenks
12	467	Yukon	Yukon
13	456	Mustang	Mustang
14	421	Bartlesville	Bartlesville
15	408	Owasso	Owasso
16	406	Enid	Enid
17	387	Ponca City	Ponca City
18	380	Stillwater	Stillwater
19	349	Sand Springs	Sand Springs
20	319	Muskogee	Muskogee
21	318	Tahlequah	Tahlequah
22	308	Choctaw/Nicoma Park	Choctaw
23	295	Altus	Altus
24	286	Bixby	Bixby
25	275	Sapulpa	Sapulpa
26	270	Claremore	Claremore
27	245	Duncan	Duncan
28	239	Shawnee	Shawnee
29	190	Chickasha	Chickasha
30	183	Ardmore	Ardmore
31	181	Guthrie	Guthrie
32	173	El Reno	El Reno
33	167	Mc Alester	Mcalester
34	165	Noble	Noble
35	164	Western Heights	Oklahoma City
36	163	Harrah	Harrah
37	162	Weatherford	Weatherford
38	160	Woodward	Woodward
39	159	Ada	Ada
40	158	Skiatook	Skiatook
41	154	Coweta	Coweta
42	152	Durant	Durant
43	150	Guymon	Guymon
44	147	Pryor	Pryor
45	139	Catoosa	Catoosa
46	138	Grove	Grove
47	137	Tecumseh	Tecumseh
48	135	Fort Gibson	Fort Gibson
49	133	Cushing	Cushing
49	133	Mc Loud	Mcloud
49	133	Wagoner	Wagoner
52	130	Glenpool	Glenpool
53	128	Collinsville	Collinsville
54	125	Broken Bow	Broken Bow
55	123	Elk City	Elk City
56	119	Poteau	Poteau
57	115	Anadarko	Anadarko

Rank		District Name	City
58	114	Muldrow	Muldrow
59	112	Clinton	Clinton
59	112	Miami	Miami
61	108	Sallisaw	Sallisaw
62	107	Hilldale	Muskogee
63	103	Byng	Ada
63	103	Oologah-Talala	Oologah
65	101	Blackwell	Blackwell
66	98	Deer Creek	Edmond
67	97	Locust Grove	Locust Grove
68	96	Jay	Jay
69	94	Idabel	Idabel
69	94	Mannford	Mannford
69	94	Okmulgee	Okmulgee
69	94	Piedmont	Piedmont
69	94	Seminole	Seminole
74	90	Bristow	Bristow
75	88	Checotah	Checotah
75	88	Vinita	Vinita
77	76	Madill	Madill
78	69	Cleveland	Cleveland

High School Drop-out Rate

Rank	Percent	District Name	City
1	12.1	Oklahoma City	Oklahoma City
2	9.9	Durant	Durant
3	9.8	El Reno	El Reno
4	8.3	Shawnee	Shawnee
5	8.1	Blackwell	Blackwell
6	8.0	Cleveland	Cleveland
7	7.9	Western Heights	Oklahoma City
8	7.8	Grove	Grove
9	7.7	Seminole	Seminole
9	7.7	Tulsa	Tulsa
11	7.4	Mc Alester	Mcalester
12	7.1	Cushing	Cushing
13	7.0	Skiatook	Skiatook
14	6.9	Okmulgee	Okmulgee
15	6.6	Guymon	Guymon
16	6.5	Woodward	Woodward
17	6.3	Enid	Enid
18	6.2	Ponca City	Ponca City
19	6.1	Wagoner	Wagoner
20	6.0	Duncan	Duncan
21	5.9	Putnam City	Warr Acres
22	5.8	Mannford	Mannford
23	5.5	Altus	Altus
23	5.5	Chickasha	Chickasha
23	5.5	Jay	Jay
23	5.5	Weatherford	Weatherford
27	5.3	Noble	Noble
28	4.9	Locust Grove	Locust Grove
29	4.8	Lawton	Lawton
29	4.8	Poteau	Poteau
31	4.7	Bristow	Bristow
31	4.7	Norman	Norman
31	4.7	Tecumseh	Tecumseh
34	4.6	Miami	Miami
35	4.4	Muldrow	Muldrow
36	4.3	Coweta	Coweta
36	4.3	Stillwater	Stillwater
38	3.9	Broken Arrow	Broken Arrow
38	3.9	Moore	Moore
40	3.8	Tahlequah	Tahlequah
41	3.5	Fort Gibson	Fort Gibson
41	3.5	Union	Tulsa
43	3.4	Anadarko	Anadarko
43	3.4	Elk City	Elk City
43	3.4	Glenpool	Glenpool
46	3.3	Bartlesville	Bartlesville
46	3.3	Checotah	Checotah
46	3.3	Yukon	Yukon
49	3.2	Harrah	Harrah
50	3.1	Ada	Ada
50	3.1	Ardmore	Ardmore
50	3.1	Muskogee	Muskogee
53	3.0	Catoosa	Catoosa
53	3.0	Choctaw/Nicoma Park	Choctaw
53	3.0	Pryor	Pryor
53	3.0	Sapulpa	Sapulpa
53	3.0	Vinita	Vinita
58	2.9	Guthrie	Guthrie
58	2.9	Mc Loud	Mcloud
60	2.8	Claremore	Claremore
60	2.8	Sallisaw	Sallisaw
62	2.6	Clinton	Clinton
62	2.6	Mustang	Mustang
64	2.5	Byng	Ada
64	2.5	Collinsville	Collinsville
64	2.5	Edmond	Edmond
67	2.3	Midwest City-Del City	Midwest City
68	2.2	Idabel	Idabel

Rank		District Name	City
69	2.1	Owasso	Owasso
70	2.0	Deer Creek	Edmond
71	1.7	Broken Bow	Broken Bow
71	1.7	Jenks	Jenks
73	1.6	Hilldale	Muskogee
74	1.3	Madill	Madill
74	1.3	Piedmont	Piedmont
76	1.2	Bixby	Bixby
76	1.2	Sand Springs	Sand Springs
78	0.8	Oologah-Talala	Oologah

Oregon

Oregon Public School Educational Profile

Category	Value	Category	Value
Schools *(2003-2004)*	1,239	**Diploma Recipients** *(2002-2003)*	31,153
Instructional Level		White, Non-Hispanic	26,464
Primary	727	Black, Non-Hispanic	594
Middle	225	Asian/Pacific Islander	1,283
High	235	American Indian/Alaskan Native	490
Other Level	51	Hispanic	1,990
Curriculum		**High School Drop-out Rate** (%) *(2001-2002)*	4.9
Regular	1,178	White, Non-Hispanic	4.0
Special Education	2	Black, Non-Hispanic	9.9
Vocational	0	Asian/Pacific Islander	3.6
Alternative	58	American Indian/Alaskan Native	n/a
Type		Hispanic	10.5
Magnet	6	**Staff** *(2003-2004)*	
Charter	24	Teachers	26,810.1
Title I Eligible	586	Average Salary ($)	47,829
School-wide Title I	317	Librarians/Media Specialists	460.6
Students *(2003-2004)*	550,762	Guidance Counselors	1,118.1
Gender (%)		**Ratios** *(2003-2004)*	
Male	***.*	Student/Teacher Ratio	20.5 to 1
Female	***.*	Student/Librarian Ratio	1,195.7 to 1
Race/Ethnicity (%)		Student/Counselor Ratio	492.6 to 1
White, Non-Hispanic	75.3	**College Entrance Exam Scores** *(2005)*	
Black, Non-Hispanic	2.8	Scholastic Aptitude Test (SAT)	
Asian/Pacific Islander	4.3	Participation Rate (%)	59
American Indian/Alaskan Native	2.3	Mean SAT Reasoning Test Verbal Score	526
Hispanic	13.3	Mean SAT Reasoning Test Math Score	528
Classification (%)		American College Testing Program (ACT)	
Individual Education Program (IEP)	12.8	Participation Rate (%)	12
Migrant *(2002-2003)*	3.9	Average Composite Score	22.6
English Language Learner (ELL)	0.0	Average English Score	21.8
Eligible for Free Lunch Program	32.1	Average Math Score	22.4
Eligible for Reduced-Price Lunch Program	8.6	Average Reading Score	23.4
Current Spending *($ per student in FY 2003)*	7,010	Average Science Score	22.2
Instruction	4,218		
Support Services	2,536		

Note: *For an explanation of data, please refer to the User's Guide in the front of the book*

Oregon NAEP 2005 Test Scores

Reading			Mathematics		
Grade/Category	Value	Rank	Grade/Category	Value	Rank
4th Grade			**4th Grade**		
Average Proficiency	216.9 (1.38)	34/51	Average Proficiency	238.3 (0.79)	28/51
Proficiency by Gender/Race/Ethnicity			Proficiency by Gender/Race/Ethnicity		
Male	213.3 (1.56)	34/51	Male	238.7 (0.92)	31/51
Female	220.4 (1.59)	35/51	Female	238.0 (1.03)	24/51
White, Non-Hispanic	223.1 (1.22)	43/51	White, Non-Hispanic	243.2 (0.80)	33/51
Black, Non-Hispanic	200.2 (4.84)	19/42	Black, Non-Hispanic	222.0 (3.15)	15/42
Asian, Non-Hispanic	220.5 (4.21)	21/27	Asian, Non-Hispanic	248.2 (3.97)	15/25
American Indian, Non-Hispanic	n/a	n/a	American Indian, Non-Hispanic	n/a	n/a
Hispanic	194.0 (2.22)	36/40	Hispanic	218.0 (1.71)	39/41
Proficiency by Class Size			Proficiency by Class Size		
Less than 16 Students	n/a	n/a	Less than 16 Students	n/a	n/a
16 to 18 Students	n/a	n/a	16 to 18 Students	n/a	n/a
19 to 20 Students	211.1 (4.13)	33/38	19 to 20 Students	233.9 (2.55)	30/38
21 to 25 Students	215.9 (2.41)	41/51	21 to 25 Students	237.5 (1.92)	36/51
Greater than 25 Students	219.3 (1.92)	23/36	Greater than 25 Students	240.4 (1.30)	11/33
Percent Attaining Achievement Levels			Percent Attaining Achievement Levels		
Below Basic	37.6 (1.68)	19/51	Below Basic	19.6 (0.91)	23/51
Basic or Above	62.4 (1.68)	33/51	Basic or Above	80.4 (0.91)	29/51
Proficient or Above	29.4 (1.47)	33/51	Proficient or Above	37.0 (1.30)	26/51
Advanced or Above	6.7 (0.71)	30/51	Advanced or Above	5.6 (0.63)	14/51
8th Grade			**8th Grade**		
Average Proficiency	263.2 (1.14)	27/51	Average Proficiency	282.2 (1.04)	16/51
Proficiency by Gender/Race/Ethnicity			Proficiency by Gender/Race/Ethnicity		
Male	258.2 (1.51)	24/51	Male	283.5 (1.22)	15/51
Female	268.2 (1.39)	28/51	Female	280.8 (1.30)	20/51
White, Non-Hispanic	267.3 (1.26)	33/51	White, Non-Hispanic	286.7 (1.21)	27/51
Black, Non-Hispanic	244.9 (3.80)	12/40	Black, Non-Hispanic	257.5 (5.05)	13/41
Asian, Non-Hispanic	267.0 (3.87)	16/24	Asian, Non-Hispanic	298.5 (4.68)	11/23
American Indian, Non-Hispanic	n/a	n/a	American Indian, Non-Hispanic	274.1 (3.94)	1/10
Hispanic	244.7 (3.09)	29/38	Hispanic	256.6 (2.36)	31/38
Proficiency by Parents Highest Level of Ed.			Proficiency by Parents Highest Level of Ed.		
Did Not Finish High School	245.4 (2.69)	22/49	Did Not Finish High School	261.9 (3.20)	25/50
Graduated High School	255.8 (2.13)	22/50	Graduated High School	269.7 (1.84)	24/50
Some Education After High School	268.2 (1.58)	20/50	Some Education After High School	283.2 (2.00)	20/50
Graduated College	275.1 (1.32)	13/50	Graduated College	295.2 (1.32)	5/50
Percent Attaining Achievement Levels			Percent Attaining Achievement Levels		
Below Basic	37.6 (1.68)	19/51	Below Basic	27.7 (1.10)	31/51
Basic or Above	62.4 (1.68)	33/51	Basic or Above	72.3 (1.10)	20/51
Proficient or Above	29.4 (1.47)	33/51	Proficient or Above	33.7 (1.26)	14/51
Advanced or Above	6.7 (0.71)	30/51	Advanced or Above	7.3 (0.79)	8/51

Note: *For an explanation of data, please refer to the User's Guide in the front of the book; n/a indicates data not available*

Baker County

Baker SD 5J
2090 Fourth St • Baker City, OR 97814-3391
(541) 524-2260 • http://www.baker.k12.or.us
Grade Span: KG-12; **Agency Type:** 1
Schools: 7
   5 Primary; 1 Middle; 1 High; 0 Other Level
   7 Regular; 0 Special Education; 0 Vocational; 0 Alternative
   0 Magnet; 0 Charter; 6 Title I Eligible; 3 School-wide Title I
Students: 2,115 (n/a% male; n/a% female)
   Individual Education Program: 347 (16.4%);
   English Language Learner: n/a; Migrant: 0 (0.0%)
   Eligible for Free Lunch Program: 770 (36.7%)
   Eligible for Reduced-Price Lunch Program: 193 (9.2%)
Teachers: 104.3 (20.1 to 1)
Librarians/Media Specialists: 5.1 (411.8 to 1)
Guidance Counselors: 6.0 (350.0 to 1)
Current Spending: ($ per student per year):
   Total: $6,991; Instruction: $4,054; Support Services: $2,706
Enrollment, Drop-out Rates and Diploma Recipients by Race/Ethnicity

Category	Total	White	Black	Asian	AIAN	Hisp.
Enrollment (%)	100.0	91.8	0.4	1.1	2.3	3.6
Drop-out Rate (%)	0.6	0.6	0.0	0.0	0.0	0.0
H.S. Diplomas (#)	137	133	0	0	0	3

Benton County

Corvallis SD 509J
1555 SW 35th St • Corvallis, OR 97333-1198
Mailing Address: PO Box 3509j • Corvallis, OR 97339-1198
(541) 757-5811 • http://www.corvallis.k12.or.us/
Grade Span: KG-12; **Agency Type:** 1
Schools: 13
   9 Primary; 2 Middle; 2 High; 0 Other Level
   13 Regular; 0 Special Education; 0 Vocational; 0 Alternative
   0 Magnet; 0 Charter; 5 Title I Eligible; 2 School-wide Title I
Students: 7,063 (n/a% male; n/a% female)
   Individual Education Program: 755 (10.7%);
   English Language Learner: n/a; Migrant: 93 (1.3%)
   Eligible for Free Lunch Program: 1,532 (22.1%)
   Eligible for Reduced-Price Lunch Program: 357 (5.1%)
Teachers: 288.1 (24.1 to 1)
Librarians/Media Specialists: 3.0 (2,311.0 to 1)
Guidance Counselors: 16.3 (425.3 to 1)
Current Spending: ($ per student per year):
   Total: $7,114; Instruction: $3,956; Support Services: $2,838
Enrollment, Drop-out Rates and Diploma Recipients by Race/Ethnicity

Category	Total	White	Black	Asian	AIAN	Hisp.
Enrollment (%)	100.0	78.9	2.0	6.9	0.8	7.6
Drop-out Rate (%)	2.8	2.0	4.3	1.5	0.0	6.9
H.S. Diplomas (#)	491	446	7	20	2	16

Philomath SD 17J
1620 Applegate • Philomath, OR 97370-9328
(541) 929-3169 • http://www.philomath.k12.or.us/
Grade Span: KG-12; **Agency Type:** 1
Schools: 6
   4 Primary; 1 Middle; 1 High; 0 Other Level
   6 Regular; 0 Special Education; 0 Vocational; 0 Alternative
   0 Magnet; 1 Charter; 4 Title I Eligible; 0 School-wide Title I
Students: 1,848 (n/a% male; n/a% female)
   Individual Education Program: 222 (12.0%);
   English Language Learner: n/a; Migrant: 1 (0.1%)
   Eligible for Free Lunch Program: 392 (21.2%)
   Eligible for Reduced-Price Lunch Program: 94 (5.1%)
Teachers: 89.2 (20.7 to 1)
Librarians/Media Specialists: 1.5 (1,232.0 to 1)
Guidance Counselors: 3.8 (486.3 to 1)
Current Spending: ($ per student per year):
   Total: $6,305; Instruction: $3,756; Support Services: $2,473
Enrollment, Drop-out Rates and Diploma Recipients by Race/Ethnicity

Category	Total	White	Black	Asian	AIAN	Hisp.
Enrollment (%)	100.0	89.9	0.7	2.3	1.4	3.6
Drop-out Rate (%)	3.4	3.0	0.0	0.0	0.0	23.5
H.S. Diplomas (#)	135	117	0	4	2	5

Clackamas County

Canby SD 86
1110 S Ivy • Canby, OR 97013-4298
(503) 266-7861 • http://www.canby.k12.or.us/
Grade Span: KG-12; **Agency Type:** 1
Schools: 7
   5 Primary; 1 Middle; 1 High; 0 Other Level
   7 Regular; 0 Special Education; 0 Vocational; 0 Alternative
   0 Magnet; 0 Charter; 5 Title I Eligible; 0 School-wide Title I
Students: 5,254 (n/a% male; n/a% female)
   Individual Education Program: 527 (10.0%);
   English Language Learner: n/a; Migrant: 430 (8.2%)
   Eligible for Free Lunch Program: 1,294 (24.7%)
   Eligible for Reduced-Price Lunch Program: 390 (7.4%)
Teachers: 241.7 (21.7 to 1)
Librarians/Media Specialists: 1.5 (3,490.0 to 1)
Guidance Counselors: 13.5 (387.8 to 1)
Current Spending: ($ per student per year):
   Total: $6,698; Instruction: $4,000; Support Services: $2,469
Enrollment, Drop-out Rates and Diploma Recipients by Race/Ethnicity

Category	Total	White	Black	Asian	AIAN	Hisp.
Enrollment (%)	100.0	78.8	0.6	1.5	1.0	17.3
Drop-out Rate (%)	3.4	2.5	50.0	5.3	0.0	11.4
H.S. Diplomas (#)	352	322	0	4	0	26

Estacada SD 108
255 NE 6th Ave • Estacada, OR 97023-9719
(503) 630-6871 • http://www.estacada.k12.or.us/
Grade Span: KG-12; **Agency Type:** 1
Schools: 5
   3 Primary; 1 Middle; 1 High; 0 Other Level
   5 Regular; 0 Special Education; 0 Vocational; 0 Alternative
   0 Magnet; 0 Charter; 3 Title I Eligible; 0 School-wide Title I
Students: 2,326 (n/a% male; n/a% female)
   Individual Education Program: 388 (16.7%);
   English Language Learner: n/a; Migrant: 79 (3.4%)
   Eligible for Free Lunch Program: 1,080 (46.4%)
   Eligible for Reduced-Price Lunch Program: 327 (14.1%)
Teachers: 110.4 (21.1 to 1)
Librarians/Media Specialists: 0.0 (n/a to 1)
Guidance Counselors: 5.0 (465.2 to 1)
Current Spending: ($ per student per year):
   Total: $6,555; Instruction: $3,722; Support Services: $2,617
Enrollment, Drop-out Rates and Diploma Recipients by Race/Ethnicity

Category	Total	White	Black	Asian	AIAN	Hisp.
Enrollment (%)	100.0	78.8	0.3	1.0	0.0	6.1
Drop-out Rate (%)	4.7	4.5	0.0	16.7	0.0	6.9
H.S. Diplomas (#)	149	143	1	1	2	2

Gladstone SD 115
17789 Webster Rd • Gladstone, OR 97027-1498
(503) 655-2777 • http://www.gladstone.k12.or.us/
Grade Span: KG-12; **Agency Type:** 1
Schools: 3
   1 Primary; 1 Middle; 1 High; 0 Other Level
   3 Regular; 0 Special Education; 0 Vocational; 0 Alternative
   0 Magnet; 0 Charter; 1 Title I Eligible; 0 School-wide Title I
Students: 2,212 (n/a% male; n/a% female)
   Individual Education Program: 255 (11.5%);
   English Language Learner: n/a; Migrant: 12 (0.5%)
   Eligible for Free Lunch Program: 453 (20.5%)
   Eligible for Reduced-Price Lunch Program: 167 (7.5%)
Teachers: 95.7 (23.1 to 1)
Librarians/Media Specialists: 1.2 (1,843.3 to 1)
Guidance Counselors: 4.0 (553.0 to 1)
Current Spending: ($ per student per year):
   Total: $6,025; Instruction: $3,508; Support Services: $2,304
Enrollment, Drop-out Rates and Diploma Recipients by Race/Ethnicity

Category	Total	White	Black	Asian	AIAN	Hisp.
Enrollment (%)	100.0	84.6	1.8	3.1	1.5	7.7
Drop-out Rate (%)	0.8	0.8	0.0	3.8	0.0	0.0
H.S. Diplomas (#)	178	178	0	0	0	0

Lake Oswego SD 7J
2455 SW Country Club Rd • Lake Oswego, OR 97034-0070
Mailing Address: PO Box 70 • Lake Oswego, OR 97034-0070
(503) 534-2000 • http://www.loswego.k12.or.us/
Grade Span: KG-12; **Agency Type:** 1
Schools: 13
   9 Primary; 2 Middle; 2 High; 0 Other Level
   13 Regular; 0 Special Education; 0 Vocational; 0 Alternative
   0 Magnet; 0 Charter; 1 Title I Eligible; 0 School-wide Title I
Students: 6,956 (n/a% male; n/a% female)
   Individual Education Program: 613 (8.8%);
   English Language Learner: n/a; Migrant: 2 (<0.1%)
   Eligible for Free Lunch Program: 273 (3.9%)
   Eligible for Reduced-Price Lunch Program: 144 (2.1%)
Teachers: 341.2 (20.4 to 1)
Librarians/Media Specialists: 2.7 (2,576.3 to 1)
Guidance Counselors: 13.5 (515.3 to 1)
Current Spending: ($ per student per year):
   Total: $6,970; Instruction: $4,155; Support Services: $2,450

Enrollment, Drop-out Rates and Diploma Recipients by Race/Ethnicity

Category	Total	White	Black	Asian	AIAN	Hisp.
Enrollment (%)	100.0	88.8	0.9	6.7	0.4	2.7
Drop-out Rate (%)	1.7	1.8	18.2	1.2	0.0	0.0
H.S. Diplomas (#)	489	445	1	31	1	7

Molalla River SD 35
412 Sweigle • Molalla, OR 97038-0188
Mailing Address: PO Box 188 • Molalla, OR 97038-0188
(503) 829-2359 • http://www.molallariv.k12.or.us/
Grade Span: KG-12; **Agency Type:** 1
Schools: 8
　6 Primary; 1 Middle; 1 High; 0 Other Level
　8 Regular; 0 Special Education; 0 Vocational; 0 Alternative
　0 Magnet; 0 Charter; 4 Title I Eligible; 1 School-wide Title I
Students: 2,801　(n/a% male; n/a% female)
　Individual Education Program: 389 (13.9%);
　English Language Learner: n/a; Migrant: 191 (6.8%)
　Eligible for Free Lunch Program: 661 (23.6%)
　Eligible for Reduced-Price Lunch Program: 356 (12.7%)
Teachers: 132.5 (21.1 to 1)
Librarians/Media Specialists: 1.0 (2,801.0 to 1)
Guidance Counselors: 3.0 (933.7 to 1)
Current Spending: ($ per student per year):
　Total: $6,262; Instruction: $3,508; Support Services: $2,530
Enrollment, Drop-out Rates and Diploma Recipients by Race/Ethnicity

Category	Total	White	Black	Asian	AIAN	Hisp.
Enrollment (%)	100.0	85.8	0.4	1.1	1.2	10.7
Drop-out Rate (%)	3.5	3.3	0.0	0.0	0.0	7.5
H.S. Diplomas (#)	111	101	0	2	0	8

North Clackamas SD 12
4444 SE Lake Rd • Milwaukie, OR 97222-4799
(503) 653-3600 • http://www.nclack.k12.or.us/
Grade Span: KG-12; **Agency Type:** 1
Schools: 27
　20 Primary; 3 Middle; 4 High; 0 Other Level
　24 Regular; 0 Special Education; 0 Vocational; 3 Alternative
　0 Magnet; 0 Charter; 9 Title I Eligible; 7 School-wide Title I
Students: 16,170　(n/a% male; n/a% female)
　Individual Education Program: 1,747 (10.8%);
　English Language Learner: n/a; Migrant: 56 (0.3%)
　Eligible for Free Lunch Program: 3,741 (23.1%)
　Eligible for Reduced-Price Lunch Program: 1,184 (7.3%)
Teachers: 788.1 (20.5 to 1)
Librarians/Media Specialists: 22.5 (718.7 to 1)
Guidance Counselors: 36.5 (443.0 to 1)
Current Spending: ($ per student per year):
　Total: $6,314; Instruction: $3,538; Support Services: $2,524
Enrollment, Drop-out Rates and Diploma Recipients by Race/Ethnicity

Category	Total	White	Black	Asian	AIAN	Hisp.
Enrollment (%)	100.0	77.9	1.9	5.7	0.9	8.7
Drop-out Rate (%)	4.0	3.8	5.1	1.2	0.0	6.9
H.S. Diplomas (#)	789	682	7	0	7	27

Oregon City SD 62
PO Box 2110 • Oregon City, OR 97045-5010
(503) 785-8000 • http://www.orecity.k12.or.us/
Grade Span: KG-12; **Agency Type:** 1
Schools: 13
　10 Primary; 2 Middle; 1 High; 0 Other Level
　13 Regular; 0 Special Education; 0 Vocational; 0 Alternative
　0 Magnet; 0 Charter; 7 Title I Eligible; 0 School-wide Title I
Students: 7,984　(n/a% male; n/a% female)
　Individual Education Program: 1,242 (15.6%);
　English Language Learner: n/a; Migrant: 75 (0.9%)
　Eligible for Free Lunch Program: 1,620 (20.3%)
　Eligible for Reduced-Price Lunch Program: 613 (7.7%)
Teachers: 341.5 (23.4 to 1)
Librarians/Media Specialists: 2.0 (3,992.0 to 1)
Guidance Counselors: 16.5 (483.9 to 1)
Current Spending: ($ per student per year):
　Total: $6,729; Instruction: $4,111; Support Services: $2,388
Enrollment, Drop-out Rates and Diploma Recipients by Race/Ethnicity

Category	Total	White	Black	Asian	AIAN	Hisp.
Enrollment (%)	100.0	89.0	1.2	1.8	0.9	5.8
Drop-out Rate (%)	1.3	1.3	20.0	0.0	0.0	0.0
H.S. Diplomas (#)	344	310	3	6	12	12

Oregon Trail SD 46
PO Box 547 • Sandy, OR 97055-0547
(503) 668-5541 • http://www.ortrail.k12.or.us/
Grade Span: KG-12; **Agency Type:** 1
Schools: 10
　6 Primary; 3 Middle; 1 High; 0 Other Level

　10 Regular; 0 Special Education; 0 Vocational; 0 Alternative
　0 Magnet; 0 Charter; 5 Title I Eligible; 2 School-wide Title I
Students: 4,201　(n/a% male; n/a% female)
　Individual Education Program: 561 (13.4%);
　English Language Learner: n/a; Migrant: 28 (0.7%)
　Eligible for Free Lunch Program: 1,005 (23.9%)
　Eligible for Reduced-Price Lunch Program: 310 (7.4%)
Teachers: 176.0 (23.9 to 1)
Librarians/Media Specialists: 1.0 (4,201.0 to 1)
Guidance Counselors: 8.5 (494.2 to 1)
Current Spending: ($ per student per year):
　Total: $6,368; Instruction: $3,604; Support Services: $2,513
Enrollment, Drop-out Rates and Diploma Recipients by Race/Ethnicity

Category	Total	White	Black	Asian	AIAN	Hisp.
Enrollment (%)	100.0	88.0	0.7	1.7	2.2	7.2
Drop-out Rate (%)	3.1	2.8	0.0	0.0	0.0	8.8
H.S. Diplomas (#)	297	278	0	3	4	12

West Linn-Wilsonville SD 3J
PO Box 35 • West Linn, OR 97068-0035
(503) 673-7000 • http://www.wlwv.k12.or.us/
Grade Span: PK-12; **Agency Type:** 1
Schools: 13
　7 Primary; 4 Middle; 2 High; 0 Other Level
　13 Regular; 0 Special Education; 0 Vocational; 0 Alternative
　0 Magnet; 1 Charter; 3 Title I Eligible; 0 School-wide Title I
Students: 7,934　(n/a% male; n/a% female)
　Individual Education Program: 869 (11.0%);
　English Language Learner: n/a; Migrant: 8 (0.1%)
　Eligible for Free Lunch Program: 599 (7.6%)
　Eligible for Reduced-Price Lunch Program: 232 (2.9%)
Teachers: 381.7 (20.8 to 1)
Librarians/Media Specialists: 9.7 (816.7 to 1)
Guidance Counselors: 14.8 (535.3 to 1)
Current Spending: ($ per student per year):
　Total: $6,455; Instruction: $3,991; Support Services: $2,310
Enrollment, Drop-out Rates and Diploma Recipients by Race/Ethnicity

Category	Total	White	Black	Asian	AIAN	Hisp.
Enrollment (%)	100.0	88.3	1.0	3.9	0.5	5.4
Drop-out Rate (%)	2.5	2.3	0.0	0.0	0.0	11.3
H.S. Diplomas (#)	476	452	2	11	0	8

Clatsop County

Astoria SD 1
3196 Marine Dr • Astoria, OR 97103-2798
(503) 325-6441 • http://www.astoriaschools.org/
Grade Span: KG-12; **Agency Type:** 1
Schools: 5
　3 Primary; 1 Middle; 1 High; 0 Other Level
　5 Regular; 0 Special Education; 0 Vocational; 0 Alternative
　0 Magnet; 0 Charter; 4 Title I Eligible; 1 School-wide Title I
Students: 2,167　(n/a% male; n/a% female)
　Individual Education Program: 314 (14.5%);
　English Language Learner: n/a; Migrant: 0 (0.0%)
　Eligible for Free Lunch Program: 628 (29.0%)
　Eligible for Reduced-Price Lunch Program: 158 (7.3%)
Teachers: 113.0 (19.2 to 1)
Librarians/Media Specialists: 3.5 (619.1 to 1)
Guidance Counselors: 6.5 (333.4 to 1)
Current Spending: ($ per student per year):
　Total: $7,227; Instruction: $4,542; Support Services: $2,406
Enrollment, Drop-out Rates and Diploma Recipients by Race/Ethnicity

Category	Total	White	Black	Asian	AIAN	Hisp.
Enrollment (%)	100.0	87.2	0.8	2.2	0.6	8.9
Drop-out Rate (%)	2.5	1.6	200.0	0.0	0.0	33.3
H.S. Diplomas (#)	146	141	0	3	0	1

Seaside SD 10
1801 S Franklin St • Seaside, OR 97138-5299
(503) 738-5591 • http://www.seaside.k12.or.us/
Grade Span: KG-12; **Agency Type:** 1
Schools: 5
　3 Primary; 1 Middle; 1 High; 0 Other Level
　5 Regular; 0 Special Education; 0 Vocational; 0 Alternative
　0 Magnet; 0 Charter; 3 Title I Eligible; 0 School-wide Title I
Students: 1,703　(n/a% male; n/a% female)
　Individual Education Program: 241 (14.2%);
　English Language Learner: n/a; Migrant: 0 (0.0%)
　Eligible for Free Lunch Program: 517 (30.4%)
　Eligible for Reduced-Price Lunch Program: 163 (9.6%)
Teachers: 89.4 (19.0 to 1)
Librarians/Media Specialists: 0.8 (2,128.8 to 1)
Guidance Counselors: 5.0 (340.6 to 1)
Current Spending: ($ per student per year):
　Total: $7,286; Instruction: $4,521; Support Services: $2,520

Enrollment, Drop-out Rates and Diploma Recipients by Race/Ethnicity

Category	Total	White	Black	Asian	AIAN	Hisp.
Enrollment (%)	100.0	85.3	0.8	1.7	1.0	10.0
Drop-out Rate (%)	6.2	6.0	0.0	0.0	0.0	14.8
H.S. Diplomas (#)	88	86	0	0	0	2

Columbia County

Scappoose SD 1J
33589 High School Way • Scappoose, OR 97056-3326
(503) 543-6374 • http://www.scappoose.k12.or.us/
Grade Span: KG-12; **Agency Type:** 1
Schools: 6
   3 Primary; 2 Middle; 1 High; 0 Other Level
   6 Regular; 0 Special Education; 0 Vocational; 0 Alternative
   0 Magnet; 0 Charter; 3 Title I Eligible; 0 School-wide Title I
Students: 2,156   (n/a% male; n/a% female)
   Individual Education Program: 272 (12.6%);
   English Language Learner: n/a; Migrant: 0 (0.0%)
   Eligible for Free Lunch Program: 243 (11.3%)
   Eligible for Reduced-Price Lunch Program: 182 (8.4%)
Teachers: 107.0 (20.1 to 1)
Librarians/Media Specialists: 0.0 (n/a to 1)
Guidance Counselors: 5.5 (392.0 to 1)
Current Spending: ($ per student per year):
   Total: $6,528; Instruction: $3,802; Support Services: $2,507
Enrollment, Drop-out Rates and Diploma Recipients by Race/Ethnicity

Category	Total	White	Black	Asian	AIAN	Hisp.
Enrollment (%)	100.0	91.1	0.4	1.3	3.3	3.4
Drop-out Rate (%)	1.4	1.3	25.0	0.0	0.0	0.0
H.S. Diplomas (#)	142	136	0	1	2	3

St Helens SD 502
474 N 16th St • St Helens, OR 97051-1340
(503) 397-3085 • http://www.sthelens.k12.or.us/sthelens/
Grade Span: KG-12; **Agency Type:** 1
Schools: 6
   2 Primary; 2 Middle; 1 High; 1 Other Level
   6 Regular; 0 Special Education; 0 Vocational; 0 Alternative
   0 Magnet; 0 Charter; 2 Title I Eligible; 1 School-wide Title I
Students: 3,504   (n/a% male; n/a% female)
   Individual Education Program: 547 (15.6%);
   English Language Learner: n/a; Migrant: 0 (0.0%)
   Eligible for Free Lunch Program: 862 (25.2%)
   Eligible for Reduced-Price Lunch Program: 257 (7.5%)
Teachers: 157.4 (21.8 to 1)
Librarians/Media Specialists: 2.2 (1,557.7 to 1)
Guidance Counselors: 12.5 (274.2 to 1)
Current Spending: ($ per student per year):
   Total: $6,409; Instruction: $3,971; Support Services: $2,206
Enrollment, Drop-out Rates and Diploma Recipients by Race/Ethnicity

Category	Total	White	Black	Asian	AIAN	Hisp.
Enrollment (%)	100.0	89.0	0.9	2.6	2.4	5.0
Drop-out Rate (%)	3.0	0.0	0.0	0.0	0.0	8.1
H.S. Diplomas (#)	176	159	2	6	4	5

Coos County

Coos Bay SD 9
PO Box 509 • Coos Bay, OR 97420-0102
(541) 267-3104 • http://www.coos-bay.k12.or.us/
Grade Span: KG-12; **Agency Type:** 1
Schools: 8
   3 Primary; 2 Middle; 2 High; 0 Other Level
   7 Regular; 0 Special Education; 0 Vocational; 0 Alternative
   0 Magnet; 1 Charter; 4 Title I Eligible; 4 School-wide Title I
Students: 3,730   (n/a% male; n/a% female)
   Individual Education Program: 607 (16.3%);
   English Language Learner: n/a; Migrant: 0 (0.0%)
   Eligible for Free Lunch Program: 1,571 (42.1%)
   Eligible for Reduced-Price Lunch Program: 332 (8.9%)
Teachers: 166.4 (22.4 to 1)
Librarians/Media Specialists: 2.0 (1,865.0 to 1)
Guidance Counselors: 6.0 (621.7 to 1)
Current Spending: ($ per student per year):
   Total: $7,550; Instruction: $4,181; Support Services: $3,081
Enrollment, Drop-out Rates and Diploma Recipients by Race/Ethnicity

Category	Total	White	Black	Asian	AIAN	Hisp.
Enrollment (%)	100.0	75.3	0.6	2.0	15.9	6.2
Drop-out Rate (%)	4.9	4.9	0.0	3.2	0.0	7.8
H.S. Diplomas (#)	239	195	0	3	33	8

North Bend SD 13
1913 Meade St • North Bend, OR 97459-3432
(541) 756-2521 • http://www.nbend.k12.or.us/
Grade Span: KG-12; **Agency Type:** 1
Schools: 6
   3 Primary; 1 Middle; 1 High; 1 Other Level
   5 Regular; 0 Special Education; 0 Vocational; 1 Alternative
   0 Magnet; 2 Charter; 3 Title I Eligible; 2 School-wide Title I
Students: 2,258   (n/a% male; n/a% female)
   Individual Education Program: 298 (13.2%);
   English Language Learner: n/a; Migrant: 0 (0.0%)
   Eligible for Free Lunch Program: 779 (34.6%)
   Eligible for Reduced-Price Lunch Program: 180 (8.0%)
Teachers: 109.9 (20.5 to 1)
Librarians/Media Specialists: 2.0 (1,126.0 to 1)
Guidance Counselors: 3.0 (750.7 to 1)
Current Spending: ($ per student per year):
   Total: $7,199; Instruction: $3,903; Support Services: $2,949
Enrollment, Drop-out Rates and Diploma Recipients by Race/Ethnicity

Category	Total	White	Black	Asian	AIAN	Hisp.
Enrollment (%)	100.0	86.4	1.2	2.4	6.2	3.6
Drop-out Rate (%)	3.2	2.7	33.3	0.0	0.0	6.7
H.S. Diplomas (#)	166	156	1	5	3	1

Crook County

Crook County Unit SD
1390 SE 2nd St • Prineville, OR 97754-2498
(541) 447-5664 • http://www.crookcounty.k12.or.us/
Grade Span: KG-12; **Agency Type:** 1
Schools: 7
   5 Primary; 1 Middle; 1 High; 0 Other Level
   7 Regular; 0 Special Education; 0 Vocational; 0 Alternative
   0 Magnet; 0 Charter; 5 Title I Eligible; 1 School-wide Title I
Students: 3,207   (n/a% male; n/a% female)
   Individual Education Program: 393 (12.3%);
   English Language Learner: n/a; Migrant: 165 (5.1%)
   Eligible for Free Lunch Program: 1,133 (35.3%)
   Eligible for Reduced-Price Lunch Program: 371 (11.6%)
Teachers: 156.4 (20.5 to 1)
Librarians/Media Specialists: 1.5 (2,138.0 to 1)
Guidance Counselors: 8.0 (400.9 to 1)
Current Spending: ($ per student per year):
   Total: $6,738; Instruction: $4,152; Support Services: $2,297
Enrollment, Drop-out Rates and Diploma Recipients by Race/Ethnicity

Category	Total	White	Black	Asian	AIAN	Hisp.
Enrollment (%)	100.0	88.6	0.5	0.6	0.8	9.5
Drop-out Rate (%)	5.2	5.3	0.0	0.0	0.0	3.2
H.S. Diplomas (#)	179	164	0	0	0	15

Curry County

Brookings-Harbor SD 17c
564 Fern St • Brookings, OR 97415-9657
(541) 469-7443 • http://www.brookings.k12.or.us/
Grade Span: KG-12; **Agency Type:** 1
Schools: 3
   1 Primary; 1 Middle; 1 High; 0 Other Level
   3 Regular; 0 Special Education; 0 Vocational; 0 Alternative
   0 Magnet; 0 Charter; 1 Title I Eligible; 1 School-wide Title I
Students: 1,810   (n/a% male; n/a% female)
   Individual Education Program: 269 (14.9%);
   English Language Learner: n/a; Migrant: 0 (0.0%)
   Eligible for Free Lunch Program: 621 (34.3%)
   Eligible for Reduced-Price Lunch Program: 336 (18.6%)
Teachers: 93.0 (19.5 to 1)
Librarians/Media Specialists: 0.0 (n/a to 1)
Guidance Counselors: 4.0 (452.5 to 1)
Current Spending: ($ per student per year):
   Total: $6,842; Instruction: $4,312; Support Services: $2,285
Enrollment, Drop-out Rates and Diploma Recipients by Race/Ethnicity

Category	Total	White	Black	Asian	AIAN	Hisp.
Enrollment (%)	100.0	83.3	0.1	1.9	4.8	6.8
Drop-out Rate (%)	3.4	2.8	0.0	12.5	0.0	6.7
H.S. Diplomas (#)	121	102	1	1	13	4

Deschutes County

Bend-Lapine Administrative SD 1
520 NW Wall St • Bend, OR 97701-2699
(541) 383-6000 • http://www.bend.k12.or.us/
Grade Span: KG-12; **Agency Type:** 1
Schools: 25
   13 Primary; 6 Middle; 5 High; 1 Other Level
   24 Regular; 0 Special Education; 0 Vocational; 1 Alternative

2 Magnet; 1 Charter; 8 Title I Eligible; 3 School-wide Title I
Students: 13,940 (n/a% male; n/a% female)
  Individual Education Program: 1,977 (14.2%);
  English Language Learner: n/a; Migrant: 94 (0.7%)
  Eligible for Free Lunch Program: 3,675 (26.7%)
  Eligible for Reduced-Price Lunch Program: 1,144 (8.3%)
Teachers: 651.0 (21.1 to 1)
Librarians/Media Specialists: 10.4 (1,322.3 to 1)
Guidance Counselors: 26.1 (526.9 to 1)
Current Spending: ($ per student per year):
  Total: $6,288; Instruction: $3,937; Support Services: $2,127
Enrollment, Drop-out Rates and Diploma Recipients by Race/Ethnicity

Category	Total	White	Black	Asian	AIAN	Hisp.
Enrollment (%)	100.0	90.7	0.8	1.5	1.1	5.7
Drop-out Rate (%)	3.8	3.3	15.8	0.0	0.0	17.1
H.S. Diplomas (#)	805	766	2	5	0	32

Redmond SD 2J
145 SE Salmon Ave • Redmond, OR 97756-8422
(541) 923-5437 • http://www.redmond.k12.or.us/
Grade Span: KG-12; **Agency Type:** 1
Schools: 10
  6 Primary; 2 Middle; 2 High; 0 Other Level
  9 Regular; 0 Special Education; 0 Vocational; 1 Alternative
  0 Magnet; 0 Charter; 5 Title I Eligible; 0 School-wide Title I
Students: 6,159 (n/a% male; n/a% female)
  Individual Education Program: 777 (12.6%);
  English Language Learner: n/a; Migrant: 60 (1.0%)
  Eligible for Free Lunch Program: 1,903 (30.9%)
  Eligible for Reduced-Price Lunch Program: 533 (8.7%)
Teachers: 274.5 (22.4 to 1)
Librarians/Media Specialists: 1.0 (6,159.0 to 1)
Guidance Counselors: 17.0 (362.3 to 1)
Current Spending: ($ per student per year):
  Total: $6,298; Instruction: $3,719; Support Services: $2,333
Enrollment, Drop-out Rates and Diploma Recipients by Race/Ethnicity

Category	Total	White	Black	Asian	AIAN	Hisp.
Enrollment (%)	100.0	90.6	0.7	1.1	1.2	6.2
Drop-out Rate (%)	1.6	1.6	0.0	0.0	0.0	2.9
H.S. Diplomas (#)	304	286	2	2	3	11

Douglas County

Douglas County SD 4
1419 NW Valley View Dr • Roseburg, OR 97470-1767
(541) 440-4015 • http://www.roseburg.k12.or.us/
Grade Span: KG-12; **Agency Type:** 1
Schools: 12
  8 Primary; 3 Middle; 1 High; 0 Other Level
  12 Regular; 0 Special Education; 0 Vocational; 0 Alternative
  0 Magnet; 0 Charter; 7 Title I Eligible; 4 School-wide Title I
Students: 6,691 (n/a% male; n/a% female)
  Individual Education Program: 861 (12.9%);
  English Language Learner: n/a; Migrant: 0 (0.0%)
  Eligible for Free Lunch Program: 2,334 (34.9%)
  Eligible for Reduced-Price Lunch Program: 620 (9.3%)
Teachers: 300.2 (22.3 to 1)
Librarians/Media Specialists: 3.0 (2,230.3 to 1)
Guidance Counselors: 14.0 (477.9 to 1)
Current Spending: ($ per student per year):
  Total: $6,463; Instruction: $4,016; Support Services: $2,210
Enrollment, Drop-out Rates and Diploma Recipients by Race/Ethnicity

Category	Total	White	Black	Asian	AIAN	Hisp.
Enrollment (%)	100.0	89.2	0.6	1.8	2.3	4.7
Drop-out Rate (%)	5.5	5.7	0.0	0.0	0.0	3.6
H.S. Diplomas (#)	399	366	0	3	12	18

South Umpqua SD 19
558 SW Chadwick Ln • Myrtle Creek, OR 97457-9798
(541) 863-3115
Grade Span: KG-12; **Agency Type:** 1
Schools: 5
  3 Primary; 1 Middle; 1 High; 0 Other Level
  5 Regular; 0 Special Education; 0 Vocational; 0 Alternative
  0 Magnet; 0 Charter; 3 Title I Eligible; 0 School-wide Title I
Students: 1,905 (n/a% male; n/a% female)
  Individual Education Program: 286 (15.0%);
  English Language Learner: n/a; Migrant: 0 (0.0%)
  Eligible for Free Lunch Program: 764 (40.1%)
  Eligible for Reduced-Price Lunch Program: 200 (10.5%)
Teachers: 98.6 (19.3 to 1)
Librarians/Media Specialists: 0.9 (2,116.7 to 1)
Guidance Counselors: 4.4 (433.0 to 1)
Current Spending: ($ per student per year):
  Total: $6,488; Instruction: $3,581; Support Services: $2,566

Enrollment, Drop-out Rates and Diploma Recipients by Race/Ethnicity

Category	Total	White	Black	Asian	AIAN	Hisp.
Enrollment (%)	100.0	87.2	1.0	1.7	5.8	4.1
Drop-out Rate (%)	3.9	3.7	0.0	0.0	0.0	4.5
H.S. Diplomas (#)	116	108	0	2	1	5

Sutherlin SD 130
531 E Central Ave • Sutherlin, OR 97479-9532
(541) 459-2228
Grade Span: KG-12; **Agency Type:** 1
Schools: 4
  1 Primary; 2 Middle; 1 High; 0 Other Level
  4 Regular; 0 Special Education; 0 Vocational; 0 Alternative
  0 Magnet; 0 Charter; 2 Title I Eligible; 2 School-wide Title I
Students: 1,550 (n/a% male; n/a% female)
  Individual Education Program: 198 (12.8%);
  English Language Learner: n/a; Migrant: 0 (0.0%)
  Eligible for Free Lunch Program: 625 (40.3%)
  Eligible for Reduced-Price Lunch Program: 141 (9.1%)
Teachers: 73.2 (21.2 to 1)
Librarians/Media Specialists: 0.0 (n/a to 1)
Guidance Counselors: 3.0 (516.7 to 1)
Current Spending: ($ per student per year):
  Total: $6,363; Instruction: $3,890; Support Services: $2,278
Enrollment, Drop-out Rates and Diploma Recipients by Race/Ethnicity

Category	Total	White	Black	Asian	AIAN	Hisp.
Enrollment (%)	100.0	90.3	0.5	1.0	2.4	5.4
Drop-out Rate (%)	4.7	4.8	0.0	0.0	0.0	9.4
H.S. Diplomas (#)	68	61	0	0	6	1

Winston-Dillard SD 116
620 NW Elwood • Winston, OR 97496-8568
(541) 679-3000 • http://www.wdsd.org/
Grade Span: PK-12; **Agency Type:** 1
Schools: 6
  3 Primary; 2 Middle; 1 High; 0 Other Level
  6 Regular; 0 Special Education; 0 Vocational; 0 Alternative
  0 Magnet; 0 Charter; 5 Title I Eligible; 1 School-wide Title I
Students: 1,663 (n/a% male; n/a% female)
  Individual Education Program: 258 (15.5%);
  English Language Learner: n/a; Migrant: 0 (0.0%)
  Eligible for Free Lunch Program: 711 (43.7%)
  Eligible for Reduced-Price Lunch Program: 181 (11.1%)
Teachers: 87.5 (18.6 to 1)
Librarians/Media Specialists: 1.0 (1,626.0 to 1)
Guidance Counselors: 2.0 (813.0 to 1)
Current Spending: ($ per student per year):
  Total: $7,411; Instruction: $4,377; Support Services: $2,720
Enrollment, Drop-out Rates and Diploma Recipients by Race/Ethnicity

Category	Total	White	Black	Asian	AIAN	Hisp.
Enrollment (%)	100.0	93.7	0.6	0.2	1.0	3.8
Drop-out Rate (%)	5.4	5.6	0.0	0.0	0.0	0.0
H.S. Diplomas (#)	81	79	0	0	0	2

Hood River County

Hood River County SD
PO Box 920 • Hood River, OR 97031-0030
(541) 386-2511 • http://www.hoodriver.k12.or.us/index.htm
Grade Span: KG-12; **Agency Type:** 1
Schools: 9
  5 Primary; 2 Middle; 1 High; 1 Other Level
  9 Regular; 0 Special Education; 0 Vocational; 0 Alternative
  0 Magnet; 0 Charter; 5 Title I Eligible; 3 School-wide Title I
Students: 3,945 (n/a% male; n/a% female)
  Individual Education Program: 484 (12.3%);
  English Language Learner: n/a; Migrant: 765 (19.4%)
  Eligible for Free Lunch Program: 1,716 (43.6%)
  Eligible for Reduced-Price Lunch Program: 430 (10.9%)
Teachers: 218.6 (18.0 to 1)
Librarians/Media Specialists: 1.3 (3,030.0 to 1)
Guidance Counselors: 5.5 (716.2 to 1)
Current Spending: ($ per student per year):
  Total: $7,657; Instruction: $4,847; Support Services: $2,509
Enrollment, Drop-out Rates and Diploma Recipients by Race/Ethnicity

Category	Total	White	Black	Asian	AIAN	Hisp.
Enrollment (%)	100.0	57.2	0.8	1.5	0.8	39.6
Drop-out Rate (%)	2.0	1.5	0.0	0.0	0.0	3.3
H.S. Diplomas (#)	231	172	1	8	3	47

Jackson County

Ashland SD 5
885 Siskiyou Blvd • Ashland, OR 97520-2197
(541) 482-2811 • http://www.ashland.k12.or.us/splash/
Grade Span: KG-12; **Agency Type:** 1
Schools: 6
   4 Primary; 1 Middle; 1 High; 0 Other Level
   6 Regular; 0 Special Education; 0 Vocational; 0 Alternative
   0 Magnet; 0 Charter; 3 Title I Eligible; 3 School-wide Title I
Students: 3,040   (n/a% male; n/a% female)
   Individual Education Program: 336 (11.1%);
   English Language Learner: n/a; Migrant: 26 (0.9%)
   Eligible for Free Lunch Program: 637 (21.2%)
   Eligible for Reduced-Price Lunch Program: 130 (4.3%)
Teachers: 150.8 (19.9 to 1)
Librarians/Media Specialists: 3.0 (1,001.0 to 1)
Guidance Counselors: 9.0 (333.7 to 1)
Current Spending: ($ per student per year):
   Total: $7,099; Instruction: $4,551; Support Services: $2,410
Enrollment, Drop-out Rates and Diploma Recipients by Race/Ethnicity

Category	Total	White	Black	Asian	AIAN	Hisp.
Enrollment (%)	100.0	87.9	1.5	3.1	2.0	4.8
Drop-out Rate (%)	3.2	2.9	15.4	3.2	0.0	6.5
H.S. Diplomas (#)	255	244	1	2	3	5

Central Point SD 6
300 Ash St • Central Point, OR 97502-2279
(541) 494-6200 • http://www.district6.org/
Grade Span: KG-12; **Agency Type:** 1
Schools: 8
   5 Primary; 2 Middle; 1 High; 0 Other Level
   8 Regular; 0 Special Education; 0 Vocational; 0 Alternative
   0 Magnet; 0 Charter; 5 Title I Eligible; 0 School-wide Title I
Students: 4,738   (n/a% male; n/a% female)
   Individual Education Program: 589 (12.4%);
   English Language Learner: n/a; Migrant: 15 (0.3%)
   Eligible for Free Lunch Program: 1,311 (27.8%)
   Eligible for Reduced-Price Lunch Program: 426 (9.0%)
Teachers: 191.9 (24.6 to 1)
Librarians/Media Specialists: 1.2 (3,935.8 to 1)
Guidance Counselors: 11.3 (418.0 to 1)
Current Spending: ($ per student per year):
   Total: $6,143; Instruction: $3,806; Support Services: $2,118
Enrollment, Drop-out Rates and Diploma Recipients by Race/Ethnicity

Category	Total	White	Black	Asian	AIAN	Hisp.
Enrollment (%)	100.0	84.2	0.4	1.8	1.7	6.4
Drop-out Rate (%)	6.1	5.2	0.0	4.0	0.0	4.5
H.S. Diplomas (#)	273	242	1	4	7	15

Eagle Point SD 9
11 N Royal Ave • Eagle Point, OR 97524-0548
Mailing Address: PO Box 548 • Eagle Point, OR 97524-0548
(541) 830-1200 • http://www.eaglepnt.k12.or.us/
Grade Span: KG-12; **Agency Type:** 1
Schools: 10
   7 Primary; 2 Middle; 1 High; 0 Other Level
   8 Regular; 0 Special Education; 0 Vocational; 2 Alternative
   0 Magnet; 0 Charter; 8 Title I Eligible; 8 School-wide Title I
Students: 4,077   (n/a% male; n/a% female)
   Individual Education Program: 479 (11.7%);
   English Language Learner: n/a; Migrant: 131 (3.2%)
   Eligible for Free Lunch Program: 1,690 (41.5%)
   Eligible for Reduced-Price Lunch Program: 548 (13.4%)
Teachers: 163.1 (25.0 to 1)
Librarians/Media Specialists: 1.0 (4,077.0 to 1)
Guidance Counselors: 5.5 (741.3 to 1)
Current Spending: ($ per student per year):
   Total: $6,867; Instruction: $3,988; Support Services: $2,631
Enrollment, Drop-out Rates and Diploma Recipients by Race/Ethnicity

Category	Total	White	Black	Asian	AIAN	Hisp.
Enrollment (%)	100.0	75.9	0.8	0.9	2.1	15.4
Drop-out Rate (%)	7.2	5.7	0.0	0.0	0.0	8.8
H.S. Diplomas (#)	241	216	0	2	0	23

Medford SD 549c
500 Monroe St • Medford, OR 97501-3522
(541) 842-3636 • http://www.medford.k12.or.us/
Grade Span: KG-12; **Agency Type:** 1
Schools: 19
   14 Primary; 2 Middle; 3 High; 0 Other Level
   18 Regular; 0 Special Education; 0 Vocational; 1 Alternative
   0 Magnet; 0 Charter; 7 Title I Eligible; 7 School-wide Title I
Students: 12,853   (n/a% male; n/a% female)
   Individual Education Program: 1,402 (10.9%);

   English Language Learner: n/a; Migrant: 371 (2.9%)
   Eligible for Free Lunch Program: 4,032 (31.4%)
   Eligible for Reduced-Price Lunch Program: 1,011 (7.9%)
Teachers: 560.5 (22.9 to 1)
Librarians/Media Specialists: 16.4 (783.7 to 1)
Guidance Counselors: 19.7 (652.4 to 1)
Current Spending: ($ per student per year):
   Total: $6,419; Instruction: $4,032; Support Services: $2,186
Enrollment, Drop-out Rates and Diploma Recipients by Race/Ethnicity

Category	Total	White	Black	Asian	AIAN	Hisp.
Enrollment (%)	100.0	81.2	1.5	2.0	1.6	13.7
Drop-out Rate (%)	7.9	7.3	14.8	8.1	0.0	12.1
H.S. Diplomas (#)	660	568	1	23	5	63

Phoenix-Talent SD 4
PO Box 698 • Phoenix, OR 97535-0698
(541) 535-1517 • http://www.phoenix.k12.or.us/
Grade Span: KG-12; **Agency Type:** 1
Schools: 6
   3 Primary; 1 Middle; 1 High; 1 Other Level
   5 Regular; 0 Special Education; 0 Vocational; 1 Alternative
   0 Magnet; 1 Charter; 3 Title I Eligible; 3 School-wide Title I
Students: 2,899   (n/a% male; n/a% female)
   Individual Education Program: 296 (10.2%);
   English Language Learner: n/a; Migrant: 177 (6.2%)
   Eligible for Free Lunch Program: 1,116 (39.1%)
   Eligible for Reduced-Price Lunch Program: 242 (8.5%)
Teachers: 139.9 (20.4 to 1)
Librarians/Media Specialists: 4.7 (606.6 to 1)
Guidance Counselors: 4.9 (581.8 to 1)
Current Spending: ($ per student per year):
   Total: $6,605; Instruction: $3,945; Support Services: $2,433
Enrollment, Drop-out Rates and Diploma Recipients by Race/Ethnicity

Category	Total	White	Black	Asian	AIAN	Hisp.
Enrollment (%)	100.0	73.7	1.4	1.2	1.4	21.8
Drop-out Rate (%)	9.4	9.6	0.0	0.0	0.0	10.0
H.S. Diplomas (#)	127	112	2	1	1	11

Jefferson County

Jefferson County SD 509J
445 SE Buff St • Madras, OR 97741-1595
(541) 475-6192 • http://www.whitebuffalos.net/
Grade Span: KG-12; **Agency Type:** 1
Schools: 8
   5 Primary; 1 Middle; 1 High; 1 Other Level
   8 Regular; 0 Special Education; 0 Vocational; 0 Alternative
   0 Magnet; 0 Charter; 5 Title I Eligible; 4 School-wide Title I
Students: 3,099   (n/a% male; n/a% female)
   Individual Education Program: 395 (12.7%);
   English Language Learner: n/a; Migrant: 627 (20.2%)
   Eligible for Free Lunch Program: 1,840 (59.4%)
   Eligible for Reduced-Price Lunch Program: 344 (11.1%)
Teachers: 154.3 (20.1 to 1)
Librarians/Media Specialists: 2.0 (1,549.5 to 1)
Guidance Counselors: 6.5 (476.8 to 1)
Current Spending: ($ per student per year):
   Total: $8,503; Instruction: $4,730; Support Services: $3,372
Enrollment, Drop-out Rates and Diploma Recipients by Race/Ethnicity

Category	Total	White	Black	Asian	AIAN	Hisp.
Enrollment (%)	100.0	37.6	0.6	0.6	33.0	27.9
Drop-out Rate (%)	3.8	0.8	0.0	0.0	0.0	7.7
H.S. Diplomas (#)	127	67	1	0	35	24

Josephine County

Grants Pass SD 7
725 NE Dean Dr • Grants Pass, OR 97526-1649
(541) 474-5700 • http://www.grantspass.k12.or.us/
Grade Span: PK-12; **Agency Type:** 1
Schools: 9
   6 Primary; 2 Middle; 1 High; 0 Other Level
   9 Regular; 0 Special Education; 0 Vocational; 0 Alternative
   0 Magnet; 0 Charter; 6 Title I Eligible; 6 School-wide Title I
Students: 5,726   (n/a% male; n/a% female)
   Individual Education Program: 536 (9.4%);
   English Language Learner: n/a; Migrant: 1 (<0.1%)
   Eligible for Free Lunch Program: 2,088 (36.5%)
   Eligible for Reduced-Price Lunch Program: 718 (12.6%)
Teachers: 272.1 (21.0 to 1)
Librarians/Media Specialists: 2.0 (2,856.5 to 1)
Guidance Counselors: 11.0 (519.4 to 1)
Current Spending: ($ per student per year):
   Total: $6,857; Instruction: $4,447; Support Services: $2,139

Category	Total	White	Black	Asian	AIAN	Hisp.
Enrollment (%)	100.0	88.7	0.8	1.6	2.0	6.9
Drop-out Rate (%)	5.9	5.9	50.0	0.0	0.0	3.6
H.S. Diplomas (#)	287	268	0	6	1	12

Three Rivers/Josephine County SD

PO Box 160 • Murphy, OR 97533-0160
(541) 862-3111 •
http://www.threerivers.k12.or.us/public2003/district/index.htm
Grade Span: KG-12; Agency Type: 1
Schools: 15
   9 Primary; 3 Middle; 3 High; 0 Other Level
   15 Regular; 0 Special Education; 0 Vocational; 0 Alternative
   0 Magnet; 0 Charter; 10 Title I Eligible; 10 School-wide Title I
Students: 5,887 (n/a% male; n/a% female)
   Individual Education Program: 677 (11.5%);
   English Language Learner: n/a; Migrant: 8 (0.1%)
   Eligible for Free Lunch Program: 2,476 (42.1%)
   Eligible for Reduced-Price Lunch Program: 785 (13.3%)
Teachers: 263.5 (22.3 to 1)
Librarians/Media Specialists: 0.0 (n/a to 1)
Guidance Counselors: 6.0 (981.2 to 1)
Current Spending: ($ per student per year):
   Total: $7,271; Instruction: $4,303; Support Services: $2,677

Enrollment, Drop-out Rates and Diploma Recipients by Race/Ethnicity

Category	Total	White	Black	Asian	AIAN	Hisp.
Enrollment (%)	100.0	88.8	0.7	1.4	3.0	6.1
Drop-out Rate (%)	4.5	4.4	10.5	6.1	0.0	7.0
H.S. Diplomas (#)	358	331	1	7	9	10

Klamath County

Klamath County SD

10501 Washburn Way • Klamath Falls, OR 97603-8626
(541) 883-5000 • http://www.kcsd.k12.or.us/
Grade Span: KG-12; Agency Type: 1
Schools: 19
   12 Primary; 2 Middle; 3 High; 2 Other Level
   19 Regular; 0 Special Education; 0 Vocational; 0 Alternative
   0 Magnet; 0 Charter; 15 Title I Eligible; 8 School-wide Title I
Students: 6,565 (n/a% male; n/a% female)
   Individual Education Program: 932 (14.2%);
   English Language Learner: n/a; Migrant: 325 (5.0%)
   Eligible for Free Lunch Program: 2,685 (41.4%)
   Eligible for Reduced-Price Lunch Program: 742 (11.4%)
Teachers: 338.7 (19.1 to 1)
Librarians/Media Specialists: 1.0 (6,486.0 to 1)
Guidance Counselors: 14.2 (456.8 to 1)
Current Spending: ($ per student per year):
   Total: $7,443; Instruction: $4,406; Support Services: $2,707

Enrollment, Drop-out Rates and Diploma Recipients by Race/Ethnicity

Category	Total	White	Black	Asian	AIAN	Hisp.
Enrollment (%)	100.0	77.3	1.0	1.0	8.4	12.2
Drop-out Rate (%)	2.2	1.9	0.0	0.0	0.0	6.7
H.S. Diplomas (#)	223	185	2	7	13	16

Klamath Falls City Schools

1336 Avalon • Klamath Falls, OR 97603-4423
(541) 883-4700 • http://www.kfalls.k12.or.us/
Grade Span: KG-12; Agency Type: 1
Schools: 8
   5 Primary; 1 Middle; 2 High; 0 Other Level
   8 Regular; 0 Special Education; 0 Vocational; 0 Alternative
   0 Magnet; 0 Charter; 7 Title I Eligible; 7 School-wide Title I
Students: 3,978 (n/a% male; n/a% female)
   Individual Education Program: 601 (15.1%);
   English Language Learner: n/a; Migrant: 187 (4.7%)
   Eligible for Free Lunch Program: 1,764 (44.5%)
   Eligible for Reduced-Price Lunch Program: 609 (15.4%)
Teachers: 199.8 (19.8 to 1)
Librarians/Media Specialists: 5.5 (720.0 to 1)
Guidance Counselors: 11.6 (341.4 to 1)
Current Spending: ($ per student per year):
   Total: $8,629; Instruction: $5,419; Support Services: $2,956

Enrollment, Drop-out Rates and Diploma Recipients by Race/Ethnicity

Category	Total	White	Black	Asian	AIAN	Hisp.
Enrollment (%)	100.0	75.5	1.9	2.0	7.4	13.0
Drop-out Rate (%)	4.1	3.6	2.8	3.7	0.0	8.0
H.S. Diplomas (#)	306	254	4	4	10	33

Lane County

Bethel SD 52

4640 Barger Dr • Eugene, OR 97402-1297
(541) 689-3280 • http://www.bethel.k12.or.us/
Grade Span: KG-12; Agency Type: 1
Schools: 11
   7 Primary; 2 Middle; 2 High; 0 Other Level
   10 Regular; 0 Special Education; 0 Vocational; 1 Alternative
   0 Magnet; 0 Charter; 6 Title I Eligible; 1 School-wide Title I
Students: 5,679 (n/a% male; n/a% female)
   Individual Education Program: 847 (14.9%);
   English Language Learner: n/a; Migrant: 47 (0.8%)
   Eligible for Free Lunch Program: 1,990 (35.0%)
   Eligible for Reduced-Price Lunch Program: 560 (9.9%)
Teachers: 253.1 (22.4 to 1)
Librarians/Media Specialists: 1.0 (5,679.0 to 1)
Guidance Counselors: 11.9 (477.2 to 1)
Current Spending: ($ per student per year):
   Total: $7,495; Instruction: $4,571; Support Services: $2,681

Enrollment, Drop-out Rates and Diploma Recipients by Race/Ethnicity

Category	Total	White	Black	Asian	AIAN	Hisp.
Enrollment (%)	100.0	83.2	2.4	2.3	2.1	9.0
Drop-out Rate (%)	4.2	4.3	3.2	5.1	0.0	3.5
H.S. Diplomas (#)	224	208	1	3	2	10

Eugene SD 4J

200 N Monroe St • Eugene, OR 97402-4295
(541) 687-3123 • http://www.4j.lane.edu/
Grade Span: KG-12; Agency Type: 1
Schools: 48
   30 Primary; 8 Middle; 7 High; 3 Other Level
   39 Regular; 0 Special Education; 0 Vocational; 9 Alternative
   0 Magnet; 2 Charter; 11 Title I Eligible; 3 School-wide Title I
Students: 18,476 (n/a% male; n/a% female)
   Individual Education Program: 2,469 (13.4%);
   English Language Learner: n/a; Migrant: 90 (0.5%)
   Eligible for Free Lunch Program: 4,013 (22.0%)
   Eligible for Reduced-Price Lunch Program: 853 (4.7%)
Teachers: 813.9 (22.4 to 1)
Librarians/Media Specialists: 16.4 (1,110.2 to 1)
Guidance Counselors: 26.7 (681.9 to 1)
Current Spending: ($ per student per year):
   Total: $7,401; Instruction: $4,373; Support Services: $2,808

Enrollment, Drop-out Rates and Diploma Recipients by Race/Ethnicity

Category	Total	White	Black	Asian	AIAN	Hisp.
Enrollment (%)	100.0	73.2	2.9	5.3	4.9	6.5
Drop-out Rate (%)	3.1	2.8	2.9	3.5	0.0	8.0
H.S. Diplomas (#)	1,378	1,176	26	45	25	51

Fern Ridge SD 28J

88834 Territorial Rd • Elmira, OR 97437-9756
(541) 935-2253 • http://www.fernridge.k12.or.us/
Grade Span: KG-12; Agency Type: 1
Schools: 6
   2 Primary; 1 Middle; 2 High; 1 Other Level
   4 Regular; 0 Special Education; 0 Vocational; 2 Alternative
   0 Magnet; 0 Charter; 3 Title I Eligible; 0 School-wide Title I
Students: 1,653 (n/a% male; n/a% female)
   Individual Education Program: 281 (17.0%);
   English Language Learner: n/a; Migrant: 0 (0.0%)
   Eligible for Free Lunch Program: 534 (32.3%)
   Eligible for Reduced-Price Lunch Program: 166 (10.0%)
Teachers: 60.8 (27.2 to 1)
Librarians/Media Specialists: 1.0 (1,653.0 to 1)
Guidance Counselors: 2.3 (718.7 to 1)
Current Spending: ($ per student per year):
   Total: $6,764; Instruction: $3,661; Support Services: $2,797

Enrollment, Drop-out Rates and Diploma Recipients by Race/Ethnicity

Category	Total	White	Black	Asian	AIAN	Hisp.
Enrollment (%)	100.0	84.0	0.4	2.1	9.1	3.7
Drop-out Rate (%)	3.8	4.0	0.0	0.0	0.0	0.0
H.S. Diplomas (#)	112	108	0	2	1	1

Junction City SD 69

325 Maple St • Junction City, OR 97448-1359
(541) 998-6311 • http://www.junctioncity.k12.or.us/
Grade Span: KG-12; Agency Type: 1
Schools: 4
   2 Primary; 1 Middle; 1 High; 0 Other Level
   4 Regular; 0 Special Education; 0 Vocational; 0 Alternative
   0 Magnet; 0 Charter; 2 Title I Eligible; 0 School-wide Title I
Students: 1,864 (n/a% male; n/a% female)
   Individual Education Program: 290 (15.6%);
   English Language Learner: n/a; Migrant: 37 (2.0%)

Eligible for Free Lunch Program: 551 (29.6%)
Eligible for Reduced-Price Lunch Program: 175 (9.4%)
Teachers: 78.8 (23.7 to 1)
Librarians/Media Specialists: 1.5 (1,242.7 to 1)
Guidance Counselors: 3.0 (621.3 to 1)
Current Spending: ($ per student per year):
Total: $6,927; Instruction: $4,193; Support Services: $2,452
Enrollment, Drop-out Rates and Diploma Recipients by Race/Ethnicity

Category	Total	White	Black	Asian	AIAN	Hisp.
Enrollment (%)	100.0	88.9	0.8	1.0	2.4	6.3
Drop-out Rate (%)	3.6	3.1	14.3	10.0	0.0	9.1
H.S. Diplomas (#)	146	136	1	1	0	5

Siuslaw SD 97J

2111 Oak St · Florence, OR 97439-9618
(541) 997-2651 · http://www.siuslaw.k12.or.us/
Grade Span: KG-12; **Agency Type:** 1
Schools: 4
1 Primary; 2 Middle; 1 High; 0 Other Level
4 Regular; 0 Special Education; 0 Vocational; 0 Alternative
0 Magnet; 0 Charter; 2 Title I Eligible; 0 School-wide Title I
Students: 1,582 (n/a% male; n/a% female)
Individual Education Program: 221 (14.0%);
English Language Learner: n/a; Migrant: 0 (0.0%)
Eligible for Free Lunch Program: 537 (33.9%)
Eligible for Reduced-Price Lunch Program: 107 (6.8%)
Teachers: 82.9 (19.1 to 1)
Librarians/Media Specialists: 1.0 (1,582.0 to 1)
Guidance Counselors: 5.0 (316.4 to 1)
Current Spending: ($ per student per year):
Total: $7,515; Instruction: $4,585; Support Services: $2,741
Enrollment, Drop-out Rates and Diploma Recipients by Race/Ethnicity

Category	Total	White	Black	Asian	AIAN	Hisp.
Enrollment (%)	100.0	86.5	0.8	1.8	7.6	3.1
Drop-out Rate (%)	5.3	5.1	0.0	16.7	0.0	0.0
H.S. Diplomas (#)	83	72	1	4	6	0

South Lane SD 45j3

455 Adams · Cottage Grove, OR 97424-0218
Mailing Address: PO Box 218 · Cottage Grove, OR 97424-0218
(541) 942-3381 · http://www.slane.k12.or.us/dsc/index.html
Grade Span: KG-12; **Agency Type:** 1
Schools: 9
6 Primary; 1 Middle; 1 High; 1 Other Level
8 Regular; 0 Special Education; 0 Vocational; 1 Alternative
0 Magnet; 0 Charter; 6 Title I Eligible; 6 School-wide Title I
Students: 2,897 (n/a% male; n/a% female)
Individual Education Program: 507 (17.5%);
English Language Learner: n/a; Migrant: 53 (1.8%)
Eligible for Free Lunch Program: 1,202 (41.5%)
Eligible for Reduced-Price Lunch Program: 354 (12.2%)
Teachers: 140.3 (20.6 to 1)
Librarians/Media Specialists: 2.0 (1,448.5 to 1)
Guidance Counselors: 3.3 (877.9 to 1)
Current Spending: ($ per student per year):
Total: $7,378; Instruction: $4,073; Support Services: $2,978
Enrollment, Drop-out Rates and Diploma Recipients by Race/Ethnicity

Category	Total	White	Black	Asian	AIAN	Hisp.
Enrollment (%)	100.0	90.2	0.6	1.0	1.9	5.8
Drop-out Rate (%)	6.9	7.3	0.0	8.3	0.0	2.5
H.S. Diplomas (#)	163	151	1	2	3	5

Springfield SD 19

525 Mill St · Springfield, OR 97477-4598
(541) 747-3331 · http://www.sps.lane.edu/index.html
Grade Span: PK-12; **Agency Type:** 1
Schools: 24
16 Primary; 5 Middle; 3 High; 0 Other Level
23 Regular; 0 Special Education; 0 Vocational; 1 Alternative
0 Magnet; 0 Charter; 9 Title I Eligible; 9 School-wide Title I
Students: 11,038 (n/a% male; n/a% female)
Individual Education Program: 1,768 (16.0%);
English Language Learner: n/a; Migrant: 132 (1.2%)
Eligible for Free Lunch Program: 4,456 (40.5%)
Eligible for Reduced-Price Lunch Program: 883 (8.0%)
Teachers: 503.1 (21.9 to 1)
Librarians/Media Specialists: 15.1 (728.7 to 1)
Guidance Counselors: 22.4 (491.3 to 1)
Current Spending: ($ per student per year):
Total: $7,234; Instruction: $4,167; Support Services: $2,856
Enrollment, Drop-out Rates and Diploma Recipients by Race/Ethnicity

Category	Total	White	Black	Asian	AIAN	Hisp.
Enrollment (%)	100.0	82.4	1.7	2.1	2.2	10.1
Drop-out Rate (%)	4.7	4.4	8.3	0.0	0.0	11.5
H.S. Diplomas (#)	586	499	4	15	16	29

Lincoln County SD

PO Box 1110 · Newport, OR 97365-0088
(541) 265-9211 · http://www.lincoln.k12.or.us/
Grade Span: KG-12; **Agency Type:** 1
Schools: 20
9 Primary; 5 Middle; 5 High; 1 Other Level
18 Regular; 0 Special Education; 0 Vocational; 2 Alternative
1 Magnet; 2 Charter; 8 Title I Eligible; 4 School-wide Title I
Students: 5,964 (n/a% male; n/a% female)
Individual Education Program: 951 (15.9%);
English Language Learner: n/a; Migrant: 170 (2.9%)
Eligible for Free Lunch Program: 2,553 (42.9%)
Eligible for Reduced-Price Lunch Program: 496 (8.3%)
Teachers: 248.7 (23.9 to 1)
Librarians/Media Specialists: 2.0 (2,977.0 to 1)
Guidance Counselors: 5.5 (1,082.5 to 1)
Current Spending: ($ per student per year):
Total: $7,763; Instruction: $4,486; Support Services: $3,016
Enrollment, Drop-out Rates and Diploma Recipients by Race/Ethnicity

Category	Total	White	Black	Asian	AIAN	Hisp.
Enrollment (%)	100.0	73.3	0.8	1.6	8.0	8.2
Drop-out Rate (%)	5.9	5.5	9.1	2.1	0.0	13.3
H.S. Diplomas (#)	406	337	0	12	24	13

Greater Albany Public SD 8J

718 SW 7th St · Albany, OR 97321-2320
(541) 967-4501 · http://www.8j.net/
Grade Span: KG-12; **Agency Type:** 1
Schools: 20
14 Primary; 3 Middle; 3 High; 0 Other Level
19 Regular; 0 Special Education; 0 Vocational; 1 Alternative
0 Magnet; 0 Charter; 3 Title I Eligible; 3 School-wide Title I
Students: 8,446 (n/a% male; n/a% female)
Individual Education Program: 1,109 (13.1%);
English Language Learner: n/a; Migrant: 122 (1.4%)
Eligible for Free Lunch Program: 2,539 (30.1%)
Eligible for Reduced-Price Lunch Program: 661 (7.8%)
Teachers: 370.2 (22.8 to 1)
Librarians/Media Specialists: 8.5 (993.6 to 1)
Guidance Counselors: 13.3 (635.0 to 1)
Current Spending: ($ per student per year):
Total: $6,525; Instruction: $4,031; Support Services: $2,252
Enrollment, Drop-out Rates and Diploma Recipients by Race/Ethnicity

Category	Total	White	Black	Asian	AIAN	Hisp.
Enrollment (%)	100.0	84.7	1.1	1.9	1.2	9.6
Drop-out Rate (%)	5.8	5.5	18.8	1.6	0.0	11.2
H.S. Diplomas (#)	417	383	2	10	6	16

Lebanon Community SD 9

485 S 5th St · Lebanon, OR 97355-2602
(541) 451-8511 · http://www.lebanon.k12.or.us/
Grade Span: KG-12; **Agency Type:** 1
Schools: 9
6 Primary; 1 Middle; 1 High; 1 Other Level
9 Regular; 0 Special Education; 0 Vocational; 0 Alternative
0 Magnet; 1 Charter; 6 Title I Eligible; 4 School-wide Title I
Students: 4,499 (n/a% male; n/a% female)
Individual Education Program: 471 (10.5%);
English Language Learner: n/a; Migrant: 20 (0.4%)
Eligible for Free Lunch Program: 1,948 (43.3%)
Eligible for Reduced-Price Lunch Program: 569 (12.6%)
Teachers: 175.1 (25.7 to 1)
Librarians/Media Specialists: 1.5 (2,999.3 to 1)
Guidance Counselors: 6.5 (692.2 to 1)
Current Spending: ($ per student per year):
Total: $6,614; Instruction: $3,875; Support Services: $2,497
Enrollment, Drop-out Rates and Diploma Recipients by Race/Ethnicity

Category	Total	White	Black	Asian	AIAN	Hisp.
Enrollment (%)	100.0	91.2	0.9	1.4	1.8	4.2
Drop-out Rate (%)	9.6	9.8	25.0	10.0	0.0	0.0
H.S. Diplomas (#)	236	225	1	5	2	3

Sweet Home SD 55

1920 Long St · Sweet Home, OR 97386-2395
(541) 367-7126 · http://www.sweethome.k12.or.us/
Grade Span: KG-12; **Agency Type:** 1
Schools: 7
5 Primary; 1 Middle; 1 High; 0 Other Level
7 Regular; 0 Special Education; 0 Vocational; 0 Alternative
0 Magnet; 0 Charter; 5 Title I Eligible; 0 School-wide Title I
Students: 2,359 (n/a% male; n/a% female)

Individual Education Program: 401 (17.0%);
English Language Learner: n/a; Migrant: 1 (<0.1%)
Eligible for Free Lunch Program: 1,023 (43.4%)
Eligible for Reduced-Price Lunch Program: 260 (11.0%)
Teachers: 111.2 (21.2 to 1)
Librarians/Media Specialists: 0.0 (n/a to 1)
Guidance Counselors: 6.5 (362.9 to 1)
Current Spending: ($ per student per year):
Total: $6,810; Instruction: $3,733; Support Services: $2,799
Enrollment, Drop-out Rates and Diploma Recipients by Race/Ethnicity

Category	Total	White	Black	Asian	AIAN	Hisp.
Enrollment (%)	100.0	91.9	0.3	0.7	1.4	3.3
Drop-out Rate (%)	5.1	5.1	0.0	5.6	0.0	6.7
H.S. Diplomas (#)	152	145	1	2	1	3

Malheur County

Ontario SD 8c
195 SW 3rd Ave • Ontario, OR 97914-2786
(541) 889-5374 • http://www.ontario.k12.or.us/
Grade Span: KG-12; **Agency Type:** 1
Schools: 7
5 Primary; 1 Middle; 1 High; 0 Other Level
7 Regular; 0 Special Education; 0 Vocational; 0 Alternative
0 Magnet; 0 Charter; 5 Title I Eligible; 4 School-wide Title I
Students: 2,756   (n/a% male; n/a% female)
Individual Education Program: 317 (11.5%);
English Language Learner: n/a; Migrant: 1,004 (36.4%)
Eligible for Free Lunch Program: 1,575 (57.1%)
Eligible for Reduced-Price Lunch Program: 238 (8.6%)
Teachers: 163.3 (16.9 to 1)
Librarians/Media Specialists: 4.0 (689.0 to 1)
Guidance Counselors: 4.0 (689.0 to 1)
Current Spending: ($ per student per year):
Total: $7,225; Instruction: $4,265; Support Services: $2,649
Enrollment, Drop-out Rates and Diploma Recipients by Race/Ethnicity

Category	Total	White	Black	Asian	AIAN	Hisp.
Enrollment (%)	100.0	47.6	1.1	2.4	1.1	47.9
Drop-out Rate (%)	4.2	2.0	16.7	0.0	0.0	7.8
H.S. Diplomas (#)	123	89	0	6	0	28

Marion County

Cascade SD 5
10226 Marion Rd SE • Turner, OR 97392-9721
(503) 749-8488 • http://www.cascade.k12.or.us/
Grade Span: KG-12; **Agency Type:** 1
Schools: 6
4 Primary; 1 Middle; 1 High; 0 Other Level
6 Regular; 0 Special Education; 0 Vocational; 0 Alternative
0 Magnet; 0 Charter; 3 Title I Eligible; 0 School-wide Title I
Students: 2,263   (n/a% male; n/a% female)
Individual Education Program: 289 (12.8%);
English Language Learner: n/a; Migrant: 98 (4.5%)
Eligible for Free Lunch Program: 789 (36.0%)
Eligible for Reduced-Price Lunch Program: 191 (8.7%)
Teachers: 111.6 (19.6 to 1)
Librarians/Media Specialists: 3.0 (730.7 to 1)
Guidance Counselors: 6.3 (347.9 to 1)
Current Spending: ($ per student per year):
Total: $6,414; Instruction: $3,840; Support Services: $2,289
Enrollment, Drop-out Rates and Diploma Recipients by Race/Ethnicity

Category	Total	White	Black	Asian	AIAN	Hisp.
Enrollment (%)	100.0	77.0	0.5	1.3	2.6	9.7
Drop-out Rate (%)	3.3	3.4	0.0	0.0	0.0	1.6
H.S. Diplomas (#)	118	100	0	4	0	14

North Marion SD 15
20256 Grim Rd NE • Aurora, OR 97002-9499
(503) 678-5835 • http://www.nmarion.k12.or.us/
Grade Span: KG-12; **Agency Type:** 1
Schools: 4
2 Primary; 1 Middle; 1 High; 0 Other Level
4 Regular; 0 Special Education; 0 Vocational; 0 Alternative
0 Magnet; 0 Charter; 3 Title I Eligible; 2 School-wide Title I
Students: 1,801   (n/a% male; n/a% female)
Individual Education Program: 231 (12.8%);
English Language Learner: n/a; Migrant: 308 (17.1%)
Eligible for Free Lunch Program: 737 (40.9%)
Eligible for Reduced-Price Lunch Program: 165 (9.2%)
Teachers: 87.5 (20.6 to 1)
Librarians/Media Specialists: 1.0 (1,801.0 to 1)
Guidance Counselors: 6.0 (300.2 to 1)
Current Spending: ($ per student per year):
Total: $6,404; Instruction: $3,734; Support Services: $2,355

Enrollment, Drop-out Rates and Diploma Recipients by Race/Ethnicity

Category	Total	White	Black	Asian	AIAN	Hisp.
Enrollment (%)	100.0	67.2	0.8	1.3	1.8	28.0
Drop-out Rate (%)	2.4	1.8	0.0	0.0	0.0	4.9
H.S. Diplomas (#)	113	83	0	0	1	29

North Santiam SD 29J
1155 N 3rd Ave • Stayton, OR 97383-1801
(503) 769-6924 • http://www.northsantiamsd.com/
Grade Span: KG-12; **Agency Type:** 1
Schools: 5
3 Primary; 1 Middle; 1 High; 0 Other Level
5 Regular; 0 Special Education; 0 Vocational; 0 Alternative
0 Magnet; 0 Charter; 2 Title I Eligible; 2 School-wide Title I
Students: 2,456   (n/a% male; n/a% female)
Individual Education Program: 364 (14.8%);
English Language Learner: n/a; Migrant: 123 (5.0%)
Eligible for Free Lunch Program: 838 (34.1%)
Eligible for Reduced-Price Lunch Program: 329 (13.4%)
Teachers: 116.0 (21.2 to 1)
Librarians/Media Specialists: 1.7 (1,444.7 to 1)
Guidance Counselors: 4.9 (501.2 to 1)
Current Spending: ($ per student per year):
Total: $6,435; Instruction: $3,755; Support Services: $2,397
Enrollment, Drop-out Rates and Diploma Recipients by Race/Ethnicity

Category	Total	White	Black	Asian	AIAN	Hisp.
Enrollment (%)	100.0	83.6	0.5	1.7	2.6	10.8
Drop-out Rate (%)	4.4	3.6	0.0	8.3	0.0	11.5
H.S. Diplomas (#)	130	123	2	3	0	2

Salem-Keizer SD 24J
PO Box 12024 • Salem, OR 97309-0024
(503) 399-3000 • http://www.salkeiz.k12.or.us/
Grade Span: KG-12; **Agency Type:** 1
Schools: 67
47 Primary; 12 Middle; 8 High; 0 Other Level
62 Regular; 0 Special Education; 0 Vocational; 5 Alternative
0 Magnet; 4 Charter; 27 Title I Eligible; 21 School-wide Title I
Students: 37,785   (n/a% male; n/a% female)
Individual Education Program: 4,582 (12.1%);
English Language Learner: n/a; Migrant: 2,960 (7.9%)
Eligible for Free Lunch Program: 13,945 (37.4%)
Eligible for Reduced-Price Lunch Program: 2,907 (7.8%)
Teachers: 1,772.5 (21.1 to 1)
Librarians/Media Specialists: 49.9 (747.8 to 1)
Guidance Counselors: 90.7 (411.4 to 1)
Current Spending: ($ per student per year):
Total: $6,889; Instruction: $4,416; Support Services: $2,226
Enrollment, Drop-out Rates and Diploma Recipients by Race/Ethnicity

Category	Total	White	Black	Asian	AIAN	Hisp.
Enrollment (%)	100.0	61.1	1.4	3.2	1.6	22.1
Drop-out Rate (%)	7.4	6.0	7.9	4.7	0.0	13.8
H.S. Diplomas (#)	1,810	1,465	14	57	16	185

Silver Falls SD 4J
210 E C St • Silverton, OR 97381-1444
(503) 873-5303 • http://www.silverfalls.k12.or.us/
Grade Span: KG-12; **Agency Type:** 1
Schools: 13
10 Primary; 2 Middle; 1 High; 0 Other Level
13 Regular; 0 Special Education; 0 Vocational; 0 Alternative
0 Magnet; 0 Charter; 6 Title I Eligible; 2 School-wide Title I
Students: 3,554   (n/a% male; n/a% female)
Individual Education Program: 408 (11.5%);
English Language Learner: n/a; Migrant: 220 (6.2%)
Eligible for Free Lunch Program: 1,004 (28.2%)
Eligible for Reduced-Price Lunch Program: 266 (7.5%)
Teachers: 176.5 (20.1 to 1)
Librarians/Media Specialists: 3.1 (1,146.5 to 1)
Guidance Counselors: 6.5 (546.8 to 1)
Current Spending: ($ per student per year):
Total: $6,726; Instruction: $4,157; Support Services: $2,374
Enrollment, Drop-out Rates and Diploma Recipients by Race/Ethnicity

Category	Total	White	Black	Asian	AIAN	Hisp.
Enrollment (%)	100.0	85.1	0.2	1.4	1.2	12.0
Drop-out Rate (%)	4.0	3.6	33.3	0.0	0.0	6.4
H.S. Diplomas (#)	214	195	1	5	3	10

Woodburn SD 103
965 N Boones Ferry Rd • Woodburn, OR 97071-9602
(503) 981-9555 • http://www.woodburn.k12.or.us/
Grade Span: KG-12; **Agency Type:** 1
Schools: 7
4 Primary; 2 Middle; 1 High; 0 Other Level
7 Regular; 0 Special Education; 0 Vocational; 0 Alternative

0 Magnet; 0 Charter; 7 Title I Eligible; 7 School-wide Title I
Students: 4,710   (n/a% male; n/a% female)
    Individual Education Program: 574 (12.2%);
    English Language Learner: n/a; Migrant: 1,407 (29.9%)
    Eligible for Free Lunch Program: 3,593 (76.3%)
    Eligible for Reduced-Price Lunch Program: 456 (9.7%)
Teachers: 274.9 (17.1 to 1)
Librarians/Media Specialists: 7.0 (672.9 to 1)
Guidance Counselors: 9.0 (523.3 to 1)
Current Spending: ($ per student per year):
    Total: $8,495; Instruction: $5,373; Support Services: $2,768
Enrollment, Drop-out Rates and Diploma Recipients by Race/Ethnicity

Category	Total	White	Black	Asian	AIAN	Hisp.
Enrollment (%)	100.0	25.0	0.4	0.2	0.2	70.6
Drop-out Rate (%)	7.0	5.8	0.0	0.0	0.0	7.8
H.S. Diplomas (#)	207	99	2	1	0	105

Morrow County

Morrow SD 1
270 W Main • Lexington, OR 97839-0368
Mailing Address: PO Box 368 • Lexington, OR 97839-0368
(541) 989-8202 • http://www.morrow.k12.or.us/
Grade Span: KG-12; **Agency Type:** 1
Schools: 9
    3 Primary; 3 Middle; 2 High; 1 Other Level
    7 Regular; 0 Special Education; 0 Vocational; 2 Alternative
    0 Magnet; 0 Charter; 5 Title I Eligible; 5 School-wide Title I
Students: 2,195   (n/a% male; n/a% female)
    Individual Education Program: 274 (12.5%);
    English Language Learner: n/a; Migrant: 657 (28.0%)
    Eligible for Free Lunch Program: 1,153 (49.2%)
    Eligible for Reduced-Price Lunch Program: 276 (11.8%)
Teachers: 122.4 (19.2 to 1)
Librarians/Media Specialists: 5.5 (426.4 to 1)
Guidance Counselors: 3.5 (670.0 to 1)
Current Spending: ($ per student per year):
    Total: $7,429; Instruction: $4,706; Support Services: $2,440
Enrollment, Drop-out Rates and Diploma Recipients by Race/Ethnicity

Category	Total	White	Black	Asian	AIAN	Hisp.
Enrollment (%)	100.0	61.0	0.5	0.4	0.7	36.9
Drop-out Rate (%)	2.6	1.4	0.0	0.0	0.0	5.4
H.S. Diplomas (#)	119	87	0	2	2	28

Multnomah County

Centennial SD 28J
18135 SE Brooklyn St • Portland, OR 97236-1099
(503) 760-7990 • http://www.centennial.k12.or.us/home.htm
Grade Span: KG-12; **Agency Type:** 1
Schools: 10
    6 Primary; 2 Middle; 2 High; 0 Other Level
    9 Regular; 0 Special Education; 0 Vocational; 1 Alternative
    0 Magnet; 0 Charter; 6 Title I Eligible; 5 School-wide Title I
Students: 6,324   (n/a% male; n/a% female)
    Individual Education Program: 758 (12.0%);
    English Language Learner: n/a; Migrant: 67 (1.1%)
    Eligible for Free Lunch Program: 2,301 (36.4%)
    Eligible for Reduced-Price Lunch Program: 699 (11.1%)
Teachers: 320.0 (19.8 to 1)
Librarians/Media Specialists: 9.0 (702.7 to 1)
Guidance Counselors: 15.0 (421.6 to 1)
Current Spending: ($ per student per year):
    Total: $6,394; Instruction: $3,803; Support Services: $2,295
Enrollment, Drop-out Rates and Diploma Recipients by Race/Ethnicity

Category	Total	White	Black	Asian	AIAN	Hisp.
Enrollment (%)	100.0	75.0	4.0	9.4	0.9	10.5
Drop-out Rate (%)	4.5	3.8	13.7	4.0	0.0	10.1
H.S. Diplomas (#)	326	262	9	43	4	8

David Douglas SD 40
1500 SE 130th Ave • Portland, OR 97233-1799
(503) 252-2900 • http://www.ddouglas.k12.or.us/
Grade Span: KG-12; **Agency Type:** 1
Schools: 13
    10 Primary; 2 Middle; 1 High; 0 Other Level
    13 Regular; 0 Special Education; 0 Vocational; 0 Alternative
    0 Magnet; 1 Charter; 9 Title I Eligible; 6 School-wide Title I
Students: 9,256   (n/a% male; n/a% female)
    Individual Education Program: 1,094 (11.8%);
    English Language Learner: n/a; Migrant: 64 (0.7%)
    Eligible for Free Lunch Program: 4,302 (47.6%)
    Eligible for Reduced-Price Lunch Program: 1,028 (11.4%)
Teachers: 442.4 (20.4 to 1)
Librarians/Media Specialists: 12.0 (753.1 to 1)

Guidance Counselors: 18.6 (485.9 to 1)
Current Spending: ($ per student per year):
    Total: $6,803; Instruction: $4,114; Support Services: $2,383
Enrollment, Drop-out Rates and Diploma Recipients by Race/Ethnicity

Category	Total	White	Black	Asian	AIAN	Hisp.
Enrollment (%)	100.0	67.4	6.2	11.1	1.4	13.9
Drop-out Rate (%)	4.0	4.0	6.9	1.2	0.0	7.8
H.S. Diplomas (#)	360	293	6	44	1	16

Gresham-Barlow SD 10J
1331 NW Eastman Pkwy • Gresham, OR 97030-3825
(503) 618-2450 • http://district.gresham.k12.or.us/
Grade Span: KG-12; **Agency Type:** 1
Schools: 20
    11 Primary; 5 Middle; 4 High; 0 Other Level
    20 Regular; 0 Special Education; 0 Vocational; 0 Alternative
    0 Magnet; 0 Charter; 7 Title I Eligible; 2 School-wide Title I
Students: 11,845   (n/a% male; n/a% female)
    Individual Education Program: 1,379 (11.6%);
    English Language Learner: n/a; Migrant: 161 (1.4%)
    Eligible for Free Lunch Program: 3,223 (27.3%)
    Eligible for Reduced-Price Lunch Program: 909 (7.7%)
Teachers: 569.4 (20.8 to 1)
Librarians/Media Specialists: 3.7 (3,195.4 to 1)
Guidance Counselors: 32.8 (360.5 to 1)
Current Spending: ($ per student per year):
    Total: $6,652; Instruction: $3,979; Support Services: $2,451
Enrollment, Drop-out Rates and Diploma Recipients by Race/Ethnicity

Category	Total	White	Black	Asian	AIAN	Hisp.
Enrollment (%)	100.0	80.8	2.4	3.4	0.9	11.6
Drop-out Rate (%)	4.2	3.9	5.8	2.5	0.0	8.8
H.S. Diplomas (#)	721	641	9	30	9	32

Parkrose SD 3
10636 NE Prescott St • Portland, OR 97220-2699
(503) 408-2100 • http://www.parkrose.k12.or.us/
Grade Span: KG-12; **Agency Type:** 1
Schools: 6
    4 Primary; 1 Middle; 1 High; 0 Other Level
    6 Regular; 0 Special Education; 0 Vocational; 0 Alternative
    0 Magnet; 0 Charter; 4 Title I Eligible; 2 School-wide Title I
Students: 3,664   (n/a% male; n/a% female)
    Individual Education Program: 421 (11.5%);
    English Language Learner: n/a; Migrant: 26 (0.7%)
    Eligible for Free Lunch Program: 1,542 (42.1%)
    Eligible for Reduced-Price Lunch Program: 428 (11.7%)
Teachers: 176.7 (20.7 to 1)
Librarians/Media Specialists: 1.5 (2,441.3 to 1)
Guidance Counselors: 9.0 (406.9 to 1)
Current Spending: ($ per student per year):
    Total: $6,262; Instruction: $3,626; Support Services: $2,373
Enrollment, Drop-out Rates and Diploma Recipients by Race/Ethnicity

Category	Total	White	Black	Asian	AIAN	Hisp.
Enrollment (%)	100.0	58.6	11.2	17.0	1.6	11.6
Drop-out Rate (%)	8.0	6.6	8.8	5.3	0.0	26.2
H.S. Diplomas (#)	190	157	6	21	2	4

Portland SD 1J
PO Box 3107 • Portland, OR 97208-3107
(503) 916-2000 • http://www.pps.k12.or.us/
Grade Span: PK-12; **Agency Type:** 1
Schools: 97
    62 Primary; 20 Middle; 9 High; 6 Other Level
    92 Regular; 0 Special Education; 0 Vocational; 5 Alternative
    0 Magnet; 3 Charter; 48 Title I Eligible; 47 School-wide Title I
Students: 48,344   (n/a% male; n/a% female)
    Individual Education Program: 6,155 (12.7%);
    English Language Learner: n/a; Migrant: 592 (1.3%)
    Eligible for Free Lunch Program: 14,889 (33.7%)
    Eligible for Reduced-Price Lunch Program: 3,402 (7.7%)
Teachers: 2,684.9 (16.5 to 1)
Librarians/Media Specialists: 31.3 (1,411.2 to 1)
Guidance Counselors: 66.8 (661.2 to 1)
Current Spending: ($ per student per year):
    Total: $8,076; Instruction: $4,891; Support Services: $2,926
Enrollment, Drop-out Rates and Diploma Recipients by Race/Ethnicity

Category	Total	White	Black	Asian	AIAN	Hisp.
Enrollment (%)	100.0	60.7	15.8	10.2	2.1	10.9
Drop-out Rate (%)	10.8	8.3	13.2	7.7	0.0	26.3
H.S. Diplomas (#)	2,592	1,789	347	284	43	129

Reynolds SD 7

1204 NE 201st Ave • Fairview, OR 97024-9642
(503) 661-7200 • http://www.reynolds.k12.or.us/
Grade Span: KG-12; **Agency Type:** 1
Schools: 16
   12 Primary; 3 Middle; 1 High; 0 Other Level
   16 Regular; 0 Special Education; 0 Vocational; 0 Alternative
   0 Magnet; 1 Charter; 7 Title I Eligible; 2 School-wide Title I
Students: 10,447 (n/a% male; n/a% female)
   Individual Education Program: 1,525 (14.6%)
   English Language Learner: n/a; Migrant: 312 (3.0%)
   Eligible for Free Lunch Program: 4,759 (46.5%)
   Eligible for Reduced-Price Lunch Program: 960 (9.4%)
Teachers: 532.9 (19.2 to 1)
Librarians/Media Specialists: 14.6 (701.7 to 1)
Guidance Counselors: 27.5 (372.5 to 1)
Current Spending: ($ per student per year):
   Total: $6,544; Instruction: $4,058; Support Services: $2,227
Enrollment, Drop-out Rates and Diploma Recipients by Race/Ethnicity

Category	Total	White	Black	Asian	AIAN	Hisp.
Enrollment (%)	100.0	63.1	5.8	6.2	1.1	23.6
Drop-out Rate (%)	4.7	4.0	4.6	3.0	0.0	10.1
H.S. Diplomas (#)	358	310	6	19	3	20

Polk County

Central SD 13J

1610 Monmouth St • Independence, OR 97351-1096
(503) 838-0030 • http://www.central.k12.or.us/
Grade Span: KG-12; **Agency Type:** 1
Schools: 6
   3 Primary; 2 Middle; 1 High; 0 Other Level
   6 Regular; 0 Special Education; 0 Vocational; 0 Alternative
   0 Magnet; 0 Charter; 4 Title I Eligible; 2 School-wide Title I
Students: 2,649 (n/a% male; n/a% female)
   Individual Education Program: 337 (12.7%);
   English Language Learner: n/a; Migrant: 326 (12.4%)
   Eligible for Free Lunch Program: 1,279 (48.6%)
   Eligible for Reduced-Price Lunch Program: 274 (10.4%)
Teachers: 119.6 (22.0 to 1)
Librarians/Media Specialists: 0.0 (n/a to 1)
Guidance Counselors: 2.0 (1,317.0 to 1)
Current Spending: ($ per student per year):
   Total: $7,235; Instruction: $4,383; Support Services: $2,575
Enrollment, Drop-out Rates and Diploma Recipients by Race/Ethnicity

Category	Total	White	Black	Asian	AIAN	Hisp.
Enrollment (%)	100.0	60.8	1.1	1.8	1.3	34.1
Drop-out Rate (%)	5.7	4.5	0.0	0.0	0.0	8.3
H.S. Diplomas (#)	143	97	4	4	3	32

Dallas SD 2

111 SW Ash St • Dallas, OR 97338-2299
(503) 623-5594 • http://www.dallas.k12.or.us/
Grade Span: KG-12; **Agency Type:** 1
Schools: 7
   3 Primary; 2 Middle; 2 High; 0 Other Level
   6 Regular; 0 Special Education; 0 Vocational; 1 Alternative
   0 Magnet; 1 Charter; 3 Title I Eligible; 0 School-wide Title I
Students: 3,202 (n/a% male; n/a% female)
   Individual Education Program: 385 (12.0%);
   English Language Learner: n/a; Migrant: 21 (0.7%)
   Eligible for Free Lunch Program: 807 (25.3%)
   Eligible for Reduced-Price Lunch Program: 226 (7.1%)
Teachers: 140.1 (22.8 to 1)
Librarians/Media Specialists: 2.9 (1,099.3 to 1)
Guidance Counselors: 7.4 (430.8 to 1)
Current Spending: ($ per student per year):
   Total: $7,585; Instruction: $5,042; Support Services: $2,340
Enrollment, Drop-out Rates and Diploma Recipients by Race/Ethnicity

Category	Total	White	Black	Asian	AIAN	Hisp.
Enrollment (%)	100.0	86.0	1.0	1.4	2.9	6.1
Drop-out Rate (%)	4.0	3.9	12.5	5.6	0.0	6.7
H.S. Diplomas (#)	202	188	3	2	3	5

Tillamook County

Tillamook SD 9

6825 Officers' Row • Tillamook, OR 97141-9699
(503) 842-4414 • http://www.tillamook.k12.or.us/
Grade Span: KG-12; **Agency Type:** 1
Schools: 5
   2 Primary; 2 Middle; 1 High; 0 Other Level
   5 Regular; 0 Special Education; 0 Vocational; 0 Alternative
   0 Magnet; 0 Charter; 3 Title I Eligible; 3 School-wide Title I
Students: 2,064 (n/a% male; n/a% female)

   Individual Education Program: 293 (14.2%);
   English Language Learner: n/a; Migrant: 0 (0.0%)
   Eligible for Free Lunch Program: 794 (38.5%)
   Eligible for Reduced-Price Lunch Program: 223 (10.8%)
Teachers: 101.2 (20.4 to 1)
Librarians/Media Specialists: 2.0 (1,032.0 to 1)
Guidance Counselors: 4.3 (480.0 to 1)
Current Spending: ($ per student per year):
   Total: $6,552; Instruction: $3,787; Support Services: $2,483
Enrollment, Drop-out Rates and Diploma Recipients by Race/Ethnicity

Category	Total	White	Black	Asian	AIAN	Hisp.
Enrollment (%)	100.0	77.5	0.6	1.6	2.0	18.1
Drop-out Rate (%)	4.5	4.1	0.0	0.0	0.0	13.0
H.S. Diplomas (#)	162	144	1	4	8	5

Umatilla County

Hermiston SD 8

341 NE 3rd St • Hermiston, OR 97838-1890
(541) 667-6000 • http://www.hermiston.k12.or.us/
Grade Span: KG-12; **Agency Type:** 1
Schools: 8
   5 Primary; 2 Middle; 1 High; 0 Other Level
   8 Regular; 0 Special Education; 0 Vocational; 0 Alternative
   0 Magnet; 0 Charter; 4 Title I Eligible; 4 School-wide Title I
Students: 4,413 (n/a% male; n/a% female)
   Individual Education Program: 581 (13.2%);
   English Language Learner: n/a; Migrant: 896 (20.3%)
   Eligible for Free Lunch Program: 1,746 (39.6%)
   Eligible for Reduced-Price Lunch Program: 477 (10.8%)
Teachers: 235.6 (18.7 to 1)
Librarians/Media Specialists: 5.5 (802.4 to 1)
Guidance Counselors: 13.0 (339.5 to 1)
Current Spending: ($ per student per year):
   Total: $7,370; Instruction: $4,810; Support Services: $2,263
Enrollment, Drop-out Rates and Diploma Recipients by Race/Ethnicity

Category	Total	White	Black	Asian	AIAN	Hisp.
Enrollment (%)	100.0	62.1	1.2	1.6	0.8	34.1
Drop-out Rate (%)	4.4	2.1	11.1	0.0	0.0	8.5
H.S. Diplomas (#)	183	146	1	3	1	32

Milton-Freewater Unified SD 7

138 S Main St • Milton-Freewater, OR 97862-1343
(541) 938-3551
Grade Span: KG-12; **Agency Type:** 1
Schools: 5
   3 Primary; 1 Middle; 1 High; 0 Other Level
   5 Regular; 0 Special Education; 0 Vocational; 0 Alternative
   0 Magnet; 0 Charter; 3 Title I Eligible; 3 School-wide Title I
Students: 1,901 (n/a% male; n/a% female)
   Individual Education Program: 245 (12.9%);
   English Language Learner: n/a; Migrant: 273 (14.4%)
   Eligible for Free Lunch Program: 955 (50.2%)
   Eligible for Reduced-Price Lunch Program: 213 (11.2%)
Teachers: 101.8 (18.7 to 1)
Librarians/Media Specialists: 2.6 (731.2 to 1)
Guidance Counselors: 4.3 (442.1 to 1)
Current Spending: ($ per student per year):
   Total: $6,896; Instruction: $4,351; Support Services: $2,238
Enrollment, Drop-out Rates and Diploma Recipients by Race/Ethnicity

Category	Total	White	Black	Asian	AIAN	Hisp.
Enrollment (%)	100.0	51.5	0.5	0.4	0.4	46.8
Drop-out Rate (%)	6.4	4.0	0.0	0.0	0.0	10.3
H.S. Diplomas (#)	91	70	0	0	0	21

Pendleton SD 16

1207 SW Frazer Ave • Pendleton, OR 97801-2899
(541) 276-6711 • http://www.pendleton.k12.or.us/
Grade Span: KG-12; **Agency Type:** 1
Schools: 7
   5 Primary; 1 Middle; 1 High; 0 Other Level
   7 Regular; 0 Special Education; 0 Vocational; 0 Alternative
   0 Magnet; 0 Charter; 4 Title I Eligible; 1 School-wide Title I
Students: 3,419 (n/a% male; n/a% female)
   Individual Education Program: 434 (12.7%);
   English Language Learner: n/a; Migrant: 6 (0.2%)
   Eligible for Free Lunch Program: 983 (29.1%)
   Eligible for Reduced-Price Lunch Program: 336 (9.9%)
Teachers: 162.2 (20.8 to 1)
Librarians/Media Specialists: 3.5 (965.4 to 1)
Guidance Counselors: 8.4 (402.3 to 1)
Current Spending: ($ per student per year):
   Total: $6,273; Instruction: $3,656; Support Services: $2,332

Enrollment, Drop-out Rates and Diploma Recipients by Race/Ethnicity

Category	Total	White	Black	Asian	AIAN	Hisp.
Enrollment (%)	100.0	78.6	0.9	1.5	11.9	6.3
Drop-out Rate (%)	4.2	3.7	0.0	0.0	0.0	3.6
H.S. Diplomas (#)	173	153	1	3	8	8

Union County

La Grande SD 1

2802 Adams Ave • La Grande, OR 97850-2179
(541) 663-3202 • http://www.lagrande.k12.or.us/
Grade Span: KG-12; **Agency Type:** 1
Schools: 6
    4 Primary; 1 Middle; 1 High; 0 Other Level
    6 Regular; 0 Special Education; 0 Vocational; 0 Alternative
    0 Magnet; 0 Charter; 3 Title I Eligible; 2 School-wide Title I
Students: 2,264   (n/a% male; n/a% female)
    Individual Education Program: 385 (17.0%);
    English Language Learner: n/a; Migrant: 0 (0.0%)
    Eligible for Free Lunch Program: 617 (27.3%)
    Eligible for Reduced-Price Lunch Program: 194 (8.6%)
Teachers: 114.7 (19.7 to 1)
Librarians/Media Specialists: 5.0 (452.8 to 1)
Guidance Counselors: 6.0 (377.3 to 1)
Current Spending: ($ per student per year):
    Total: $7,258; Instruction: $4,424; Support Services: $2,624

Enrollment, Drop-out Rates and Diploma Recipients by Race/Ethnicity

Category	Total	White	Black	Asian	AIAN	Hisp.
Enrollment (%)	100.0	92.0	1.2	1.9	2.0	2.8
Drop-out Rate (%)	3.8	3.4	0.0	6.3	0.0	11.1
H.S. Diplomas (#)	152	140	0	0	1	11

Wasco County

The Dalles SD 12

1413 E 12th St • The Dalles, OR 97058-4096
(541) 298-6134 • http://www.thedalles.k12.or.us/
Grade Span: KG-12; **Agency Type:** 1
Schools: 4
    2 Primary; 1 Middle; 1 High; 0 Other Level
    4 Regular; 0 Special Education; 0 Vocational; 0 Alternative
    0 Magnet; 0 Charter; 3 Title I Eligible; 3 School-wide Title I
Students: 2,027   (n/a% male; n/a% female)
    Individual Education Program: 256 (12.6%);
    English Language Learner: n/a; Migrant: 270 (13.3%)
    Eligible for Free Lunch Program: 882 (43.5%)
    Eligible for Reduced-Price Lunch Program: 177 (8.7%)
Teachers: 102.2 (19.8 to 1)
Librarians/Media Specialists: 1.0 (2,027.0 to 1)
Guidance Counselors: 6.0 (337.8 to 1)
Current Spending: ($ per student per year):
    Total: $6,799; Instruction: $4,089; Support Services: $2,504

Enrollment, Drop-out Rates and Diploma Recipients by Race/Ethnicity

Category	Total	White	Black	Asian	AIAN	Hisp.
Enrollment (%)	100.0	74.1	2.3	3.1	1.9	18.5
Drop-out Rate (%)	2.8	3.2	0.0	0.0	0.0	1.1
H.S. Diplomas (#)	142	115	2	5	3	17

Washington County

Beaverton SD 48J

16550 SW Merlo Rd • Beaverton, OR 97006-5152
(503) 591-8000 • http://www.beaverton.k12.or.us/
Grade Span: KG-12; **Agency Type:** 1
Schools: 49
    31 Primary; 9 Middle; 9 High; 0 Other Level
    47 Regular; 0 Special Education; 0 Vocational; 2 Alternative
    3 Magnet; 0 Charter; 10 Title I Eligible; 9 School-wide Title I
Students: 35,333   (n/a% male; n/a% female)
    Individual Education Program: 4,154 (11.8%);
    English Language Learner: n/a; Migrant: 804 (2.3%)
    Eligible for Free Lunch Program: 7,386 (20.9%)
    Eligible for Reduced-Price Lunch Program: 2,500 (7.1%)
Teachers: 1,699.1 (20.8 to 1)
Librarians/Media Specialists: 44.8 (788.7 to 1)
Guidance Counselors: 83.6 (422.6 to 1)
Current Spending: ($ per student per year):
    Total: $6,233; Instruction: $3,749; Support Services: $2,227

Enrollment, Drop-out Rates and Diploma Recipients by Race/Ethnicity

Category	Total	White	Black	Asian	AIAN	Hisp.
Enrollment (%)	100.0	68.0	3.3	13.1	0.8	13.8
Drop-out Rate (%)	4.1	3.2	5.9	1.8	0.0	12.6
H.S. Diplomas (#)	1,957	1,495	32	270	11	96

Forest Grove SD 15

1728 Main St • Forest Grove, OR 97116-2737
(503) 357-6171 • http://www.fgsd.k12.or.us/
Grade Span: KG-12; **Agency Type:** 1
Schools: 10
    7 Primary; 2 Middle; 1 High; 0 Other Level
    10 Regular; 0 Special Education; 0 Vocational; 0 Alternative
    0 Magnet; 0 Charter; 5 Title I Eligible; 2 School-wide Title I
Students: 5,798   (n/a% male; n/a% female)
    Individual Education Program: 716 (12.3%);
    English Language Learner: n/a; Migrant: 750 (13.2%)
    Eligible for Free Lunch Program: 2,579 (45.4%)
    Eligible for Reduced-Price Lunch Program: 533 (9.4%)
Teachers: 281.0 (20.2 to 1)
Librarians/Media Specialists: 1.0 (5,676.0 to 1)
Guidance Counselors: 14.8 (383.5 to 1)
Current Spending: ($ per student per year):
    Total: $6,850; Instruction: $4,302; Support Services: $2,264

Enrollment, Drop-out Rates and Diploma Recipients by Race/Ethnicity

Category	Total	White	Black	Asian	AIAN	Hisp.
Enrollment (%)	100.0	59.5	0.7	1.3	0.5	37.6
Drop-out Rate (%)	8.1	6.1	13.3	6.3	0.0	14.3
H.S. Diplomas (#)	260	202	3	5	2	48

Hillsboro SD 1J

3083 NE 49th Pl • Hillsboro, OR 97124-6009
(503) 844-1500 • http://www.hsd.k12.or.us/default.asp
Grade Span: KG-12; **Agency Type:** 1
Schools: 31
    23 Primary; 4 Middle; 3 High; 1 Other Level
    30 Regular; 0 Special Education; 0 Vocational; 1 Alternative
    0 Magnet; 0 Charter; 8 Title I Eligible; 2 School-wide Title I
Students: 18,951   (n/a% male; n/a% female)
    Individual Education Program: 2,294 (12.1%);
    English Language Learner: n/a; Migrant: 1,714 (9.1%)
    Eligible for Free Lunch Program: 5,024 (26.6%)
    Eligible for Reduced-Price Lunch Program: 1,537 (8.1%)
Teachers: 792.8 (23.8 to 1)
Librarians/Media Specialists: 0.0 (n/a to 1)
Guidance Counselors: 31.2 (604.8 to 1)
Current Spending: ($ per student per year):
    Total: $6,569; Instruction: $3,869; Support Services: $2,480

Enrollment, Drop-out Rates and Diploma Recipients by Race/Ethnicity

Category	Total	White	Black	Asian	AIAN	Hisp.
Enrollment (%)	100.0	65.5	2.0	6.8	0.6	24.4
Drop-out Rate (%)	3.1	1.6	2.7	1.8	0.0	10.1
H.S. Diplomas (#)	888	701	13	68	9	97

Sherwood SD 88J

23295 S Sherwood Blvd • Sherwood, OR 97140-9104
(503) 625-8100 • http://www.sherwood.k12.or.us/
Grade Span: KG-12; **Agency Type:** 1
Schools: 5
    3 Primary; 1 Middle; 1 High; 0 Other Level
    5 Regular; 0 Special Education; 0 Vocational; 0 Alternative
    0 Magnet; 0 Charter; 1 Title I Eligible; 0 School-wide Title I
Students: 3,386   (n/a% male; n/a% female)
    Individual Education Program: 355 (10.5%);
    English Language Learner: n/a; Migrant: 0 (0.0%)
    Eligible for Free Lunch Program: 270 (8.0%)
    Eligible for Reduced-Price Lunch Program: 95 (2.8%)
Teachers: 152.5 (22.2 to 1)
Librarians/Media Specialists: 3.5 (967.1 to 1)
Guidance Counselors: 6.0 (564.2 to 1)
Current Spending: ($ per student per year):
    Total: $5,760; Instruction: $3,358; Support Services: $2,194

Enrollment, Drop-out Rates and Diploma Recipients by Race/Ethnicity

Category	Total	White	Black	Asian	AIAN	Hisp.
Enrollment (%)	100.0	90.3	0.9	3.1	0.4	5.3
Drop-out Rate (%)	2.0	1.6	0.0	9.1	0.0	9.1
H.S. Diplomas (#)	137	130	1	1	0	5

Tigard-Tualatin SD 23J

6960 SW Sandburg St • Tigard, OR 97223-8039
(503) 431-4000 • http://www.ttsd.k12.or.us/ttsdwebsite/
Grade Span: KG-12; **Agency Type:** 1
Schools: 15
    10 Primary; 3 Middle; 2 High; 0 Other Level
    15 Regular; 0 Special Education; 0 Vocational; 0 Alternative
    0 Magnet; 1 Charter; 6 Title I Eligible; 0 School-wide Title I
Students: 11,909   (n/a% male; n/a% female)
    Individual Education Program: 1,139 (9.6%);
    English Language Learner: n/a; Migrant: 0 (0.0%)
    Eligible for Free Lunch Program: 2,310 (19.4%)
    Eligible for Reduced-Price Lunch Program: 563 (4.7%)

Teachers: 574.5 (20.7 to 1)
Librarians/Media Specialists: 11.5 (1,035.6 to 1)
Guidance Counselors: 24.5 (486.1 to 1)
Current Spending: ($ per student per year):
    Total: $6,546; Instruction: $4,024; Support Services: $2,313
Enrollment, Drop-out Rates and Diploma Recipients by Race/Ethnicity

Category	Total	White	Black	Asian	AIAN	Hisp.
Enrollment (%)	100.0	75.9	2.5	7.0	0.9	13.7
Drop-out Rate (%)	4.5	3.5	6.3	3.1	0.0	16.1
H.S. Diplomas (#)	743	646	6	48	3	40

Yamhill County

Mcminnville SD 40
1500 NE Baker St • Mcminnville, OR 97128-3004
(503) 565-4000 • http://www.msd.k12.or.us/
Grade Span: KG-12; **Agency Type:** 1
Schools: 9
    6 Primary; 2 Middle; 1 High; 0 Other Level
    9 Regular; 0 Special Education; 0 Vocational; 0 Alternative
    0 Magnet; 0 Charter; 5 Title I Eligible; 5 School-wide Title I
Students: 5,741   (n/a% male; n/a% female)
    Individual Education Program: 746 (13.0%);
    English Language Learner: n/a; Migrant: 460 (8.0%)
    Eligible for Free Lunch Program: 2,081 (36.2%)
    Eligible for Reduced-Price Lunch Program: 506 (8.8%)
Teachers: 270.6 (21.2 to 1)
Librarians/Media Specialists: 6.0 (956.8 to 1)
Guidance Counselors: 12.5 (459.3 to 1)
Current Spending: ($ per student per year):
    Total: $6,077; Instruction: $3,713; Support Services: $2,112
Enrollment, Drop-out Rates and Diploma Recipients by Race/Ethnicity

Category	Total	White	Black	Asian	AIAN	Hisp.
Enrollment (%)	100.0	72.5	0.9	1.6	1.0	22.5
Drop-out Rate (%)	6.3	6.2	11.1	10.3	0.0	6.5
H.S. Diplomas (#)	314	268	1	4	3	38

Newberg SD 29J
714 E 6th St • Newberg, OR 97132-3498
(503) 554-5000 • http://www.newberg.k12.or.us/
Grade Span: KG-12; **Agency Type:** 1
Schools: 8
    5 Primary; 2 Middle; 1 High; 0 Other Level
    8 Regular; 0 Special Education; 0 Vocational; 0 Alternative
    0 Magnet; 0 Charter; 3 Title I Eligible; 1 School-wide Title I
Students: 5,012   (n/a% male; n/a% female)
    Individual Education Program: 589 (11.8%);
    English Language Learner: n/a; Migrant: 252 (5.1%)
    Eligible for Free Lunch Program: 1,222 (24.5%)
    Eligible for Reduced-Price Lunch Program: 342 (6.9%)
Teachers: 227.8 (21.9 to 1)
Librarians/Media Specialists: 2.8 (1,780.7 to 1)
Guidance Counselors: 11.5 (433.6 to 1)
Current Spending: ($ per student per year):
    Total: $6,428; Instruction: $3,852; Support Services: $2,312
Enrollment, Drop-out Rates and Diploma Recipients by Race/Ethnicity

Category	Total	White	Black	Asian	AIAN	Hisp.
Enrollment (%)	100.0	84.3	1.4	1.7	0.6	12.0
Drop-out Rate (%)	4.3	3.9	0.0	0.0	0.0	9.1
H.S. Diplomas (#)	318	290	1	3	1	23

Number of Schools

Rank	Number	District Name	City
1	97	Portland SD 1J	Portland
2	67	Salem-Keizer SD 24J	Salem
3	49	Beaverton SD 48J	Beaverton
4	48	Eugene SD 4J	Eugene
5	31	Hillsboro SD 1J	Hillsboro
6	27	North Clackamas SD 12	Milwaukie
7	25	Bend-Lapine Administrative SD 1	Bend
8	24	Springfield SD 19	Springfield
9	20	Greater Albany Public SD 8J	Albany
9	20	Gresham-Barlow SD 10J	Gresham
9	20	Lincoln County SD	Newport
12	19	Klamath County SD	Klamath Falls
12	19	Medford SD 549c	Medford
14	16	Reynolds SD 7	Fairview
15	15	Three Rivers/Josephine County SD	Murphy
15	15	Tigard-Tualatin SD 23J	Tigard
17	13	Corvallis SD 509J	Corvallis
17	13	David Douglas SD 40	Portland
17	13	Lake Oswego SD 7J	Lake Oswego
17	13	Oregon City SD 62	Oregon City
17	13	Silver Falls SD 4J	Silverton
17	13	West Linn-Wilsonville SD 3J	West Linn
23	12	Douglas County SD 4	Roseburg
24	11	Bethel SD 52	Eugene
25	10	Centennial SD 28J	Portland
25	10	Eagle Point SD 9	Eagle Point
25	10	Forest Grove SD 15	Forest Grove
25	10	Oregon Trail SD 46	Sandy
25	10	Redmond SD 2J	Redmond
30	9	Grants Pass SD 7	Grants Pass
30	9	Hood River County SD	Hood River
30	9	Lebanon Community SD 9	Lebanon
30	9	Mcminnville SD 40	Mcminnville
30	9	Morrow SD 1	Lexington
30	9	South Lane SD 45j3	Cottage Grove
36	8	Central Point SD 6	Central Point
36	8	Coos Bay SD 9	Coos Bay
36	8	Hermiston SD 8	Hermiston
36	8	Jefferson County SD 509J	Madras
36	8	Klamath Falls City Schools	Klamath Falls
36	8	Molalla River SD 35	Molalla
36	8	Newberg SD 29J	Newberg
43	7	Baker SD 5J	Baker City
43	7	Canby SD 86	Canby
43	7	Crook County Unit SD	Prineville
43	7	Dallas SD 2	Dallas
43	7	Ontario SD 8c	Ontario
43	7	Pendleton SD 16	Pendleton
43	7	Sweet Home SD 55	Sweet Home
43	7	Woodburn SD 103	Woodburn
51	6	Ashland SD 5	Ashland
51	6	Cascade SD 5	Turner
51	6	Central SD 13J	Independence
51	6	Fern Ridge SD 28J	Elmira
51	6	La Grande SD 1	La Grande
51	6	North Bend SD 13	North Bend
51	6	Parkrose SD 3	Portland
51	6	Philomath SD 17J	Philomath
51	6	Phoenix-Talent SD 4	Phoenix
51	6	Scappoose SD 1J	Scappoose
51	6	St Helens SD 502	St Helens
51	6	Winston-Dillard SD 116	Winston
63	5	Astoria SD 1	Astoria
63	5	Estacada SD 108	Estacada
63	5	Milton-Freewater Unified SD 7	Milton-Freewater
63	5	North Santiam SD 29J	Stayton
63	5	Seaside SD 10	Seaside
63	5	Sherwood SD 88J	Sherwood
63	5	South Umpqua SD 19	Myrtle Creek
63	5	Tillamook SD 9	Tillamook
71	4	Junction City SD 69	Junction City
71	4	North Marion SD 15	Aurora
71	4	Siuslaw SD 97J	Florence
71	4	Sutherlin SD 130	Sutherlin
71	4	The Dalles SD 12	The Dalles
76	3	Brookings-Harbor SD 17c	Brookings
76	3	Gladstone SD 115	Gladstone

Number of Teachers

Rank	Number	District Name	City
1	2,684	Portland SD 1J	Portland
2	1,772	Salem-Keizer SD 24J	Salem
3	1,699	Beaverton SD 48J	Beaverton
4	813	Eugene SD 4J	Eugene
5	792	Hillsboro SD 1J	Hillsboro
6	788	North Clackamas SD 12	Milwaukie
7	651	Bend-Lapine Administrative SD 1	Bend
8	574	Tigard-Tualatin SD 23J	Tigard
9	569	Gresham-Barlow SD 10J	Gresham
10	560	Medford SD 549c	Medford
11	532	Reynolds SD 7	Fairview
12	503	Springfield SD 19	Springfield
13	442	David Douglas SD 40	Portland
14	381	West Linn-Wilsonville SD 3J	West Linn
15	370	Greater Albany Public SD 8J	Albany
16	341	Oregon City SD 62	Oregon City
17	341	Lake Oswego SD 7J	Lake Oswego
18	338	Klamath County SD	Klamath Falls
19	320	Centennial SD 28J	Portland
20	300	Douglas County SD 4	Roseburg
21	288	Corvallis SD 509J	Corvallis
22	281	Forest Grove SD 15	Forest Grove
23	274	Woodburn SD 103	Woodburn
24	274	Redmond SD 2J	Redmond
25	272	Grants Pass SD 7	Grants Pass
26	270	Mcminnville SD 40	Mcminnville
27	263	Three Rivers/Josephine County SD	Murphy
28	253	Bethel SD 52	Eugene
29	248	Lincoln County SD	Newport
30	241	Canby SD 86	Canby
31	235	Hermiston SD 8	Hermiston
32	227	Newberg SD 29J	Newberg
33	218	Hood River County SD	Hood River
34	199	Klamath Falls City Schools	Klamath Falls
35	191	Central Point SD 6	Central Point
36	176	Parkrose SD 3	Portland
37	176	Silver Falls SD 4J	Silverton
38	176	Oregon Trail SD 46	Sandy
39	175	Lebanon Community SD 9	Lebanon
40	166	Coos Bay SD 9	Coos Bay
41	163	Ontario SD 8c	Ontario
42	163	Eagle Point SD 9	Eagle Point
43	162	Pendleton SD 16	Pendleton
44	157	St Helens SD 502	St Helens
45	156	Crook County Unit SD	Prineville
46	154	Jefferson County SD 509J	Madras
47	152	Sherwood SD 88J	Sherwood
48	150	Ashland SD 5	Ashland
49	140	South Lane SD 45j3	Cottage Grove
50	140	Dallas SD 2	Dallas
51	139	Phoenix-Talent SD 4	Phoenix
52	132	Molalla River SD 35	Molalla
53	122	Morrow SD 1	Lexington
54	119	Central SD 13J	Independence
55	116	North Santiam SD 29J	Stayton
56	114	La Grande SD 1	La Grande
57	113	Astoria SD 1	Astoria
58	111	Cascade SD 5	Turner
59	111	Sweet Home SD 55	Sweet Home
60	110	Estacada SD 108	Estacada
61	109	North Bend SD 13	North Bend
62	107	Scappoose SD 1J	Scappoose
63	104	Baker SD 5J	Baker City
64	102	The Dalles SD 12	The Dalles
65	101	Milton-Freewater Unified SD 7	Milton-Freewater
66	101	Tillamook SD 9	Tillamook
67	98	South Umpqua SD 19	Myrtle Creek
68	95	Gladstone SD 115	Gladstone
69	93	Brookings-Harbor SD 17c	Brookings
70	89	Seaside SD 10	Seaside
71	89	Philomath SD 17J	Philomath
72	87	North Marion SD 15	Aurora
72	87	Winston-Dillard SD 116	Winston
74	82	Siuslaw SD 97J	Florence
75	78	Junction City SD 69	Junction City
76	73	Sutherlin SD 130	Sutherlin
77	60	Fern Ridge SD 28J	Elmira

Number of Students

Rank	Number	District Name	City
1	48,344	Portland SD 1J	Portland
2	37,785	Salem-Keizer SD 24J	Salem
3	35,333	Beaverton SD 48J	Beaverton
4	18,951	Hillsboro SD 1J	Hillsboro
5	18,476	Eugene SD 4J	Eugene
6	16,170	North Clackamas SD 12	Milwaukie
7	13,940	Bend-Lapine Administrative SD 1	Bend
8	12,853	Medford SD 549c	Medford
9	11,909	Tigard-Tualatin SD 23J	Tigard
10	11,845	Gresham-Barlow SD 10J	Gresham
11	11,038	Springfield SD 19	Springfield
12	10,447	Reynolds SD 7	Fairview
13	9,256	David Douglas SD 40	Portland
14	8,446	Greater Albany Public SD 8J	Albany
15	7,984	Oregon City SD 62	Oregon City
16	7,934	West Linn-Wilsonville SD 3J	West Linn
17	7,063	Corvallis SD 509J	Corvallis
18	6,956	Lake Oswego SD 7J	Lake Oswego
19	6,691	Douglas County SD 4	Roseburg
20	6,565	Klamath County SD	Klamath Falls
21	6,324	Centennial SD 28J	Portland
22	6,159	Redmond SD 2J	Redmond
23	5,964	Lincoln County SD	Newport
24	5,887	Three Rivers/Josephine County SD	Murphy
25	5,798	Forest Grove SD 15	Forest Grove
26	5,741	Mcminnville SD 40	Mcminnville
27	5,726	Grants Pass SD 7	Grants Pass
28	5,679	Bethel SD 52	Eugene
29	5,254	Canby SD 86	Canby
30	5,012	Newberg SD 29J	Newberg
31	4,738	Central Point SD 6	Central Point
32	4,710	Woodburn SD 103	Woodburn
33	4,499	Lebanon Community SD 9	Lebanon
34	4,413	Hermiston SD 8	Hermiston
35	4,201	Oregon Trail SD 46	Sandy
36	4,077	Eagle Point SD 9	Eagle Point
37	3,978	Klamath Falls City Schools	Klamath Falls
38	3,945	Hood River County SD	Hood River
39	3,730	Coos Bay SD 9	Coos Bay
40	3,664	Parkrose SD 3	Portland
41	3,554	Silver Falls SD 4J	Silverton
42	3,504	St Helens SD 502	St Helens
43	3,419	Pendleton SD 16	Pendleton
44	3,386	Sherwood SD 88J	Sherwood
45	3,207	Crook County Unit SD	Prineville
46	3,202	Dallas SD 2	Dallas
47	3,099	Jefferson County SD 509J	Madras
48	3,040	Ashland SD 5	Ashland
49	2,899	Phoenix-Talent SD 4	Phoenix
50	2,897	South Lane SD 45j3	Cottage Grove
51	2,801	Molalla River SD 35	Molalla
52	2,756	Ontario SD 8c	Ontario
53	2,649	Central SD 13J	Independence
54	2,456	North Santiam SD 29J	Stayton
55	2,359	Sweet Home SD 55	Sweet Home
56	2,326	Estacada SD 108	Estacada
57	2,264	La Grande SD 1	La Grande
58	2,263	Cascade SD 5	Turner
59	2,258	North Bend SD 13	North Bend
60	2,212	Gladstone SD 115	Gladstone
61	2,195	Morrow SD 1	Lexington
62	2,167	Astoria SD 1	Astoria
63	2,156	Scappoose SD 1J	Scappoose
64	2,115	Baker SD 5J	Baker City
65	2,064	Tillamook SD 9	Tillamook
66	2,027	The Dalles SD 12	The Dalles
67	1,905	South Umpqua SD 19	Myrtle Creek
68	1,901	Milton-Freewater Unified SD 7	Milton-Freewater
69	1,864	Junction City SD 69	Junction City
70	1,848	Philomath SD 17J	Philomath
71	1,810	Brookings-Harbor SD 17c	Brookings
72	1,801	North Marion SD 15	Aurora
73	1,703	Seaside SD 10	Seaside
74	1,663	Winston-Dillard SD 116	Winston
75	1,653	Fern Ridge SD 28J	Elmira
76	1,582	Siuslaw SD 97J	Florence
77	1,550	Sutherlin SD 130	Sutherlin

Male Students

Rank	Percent	District Name	City
1	n/a	Ashland SD 5	Ashland
1	n/a	Astoria SD 1	Astoria
1	n/a	Baker SD 5J	Baker City
1	n/a	Beaverton SD 48J	Beaverton
1	n/a	Bend-Lapine Administrative SD 1	Bend
1	n/a	Bethel SD 52	Eugene
1	n/a	Brookings-Harbor SD 17c	Brookings
1	n/a	Canby SD 86	Canby
1	n/a	Cascade SD 5	Turner
1	n/a	Centennial SD 28J	Portland
1	n/a	Central Point SD 6	Central Point
1	n/a	Central SD 13J	Independence
1	n/a	Coos Bay SD 9	Coos Bay
1	n/a	Corvallis SD 509J	Corvallis
1	n/a	Crook County Unit SD	Prineville
1	n/a	Dallas SD 2	Dallas
1	n/a	David Douglas SD 40	Portland
1	n/a	Douglas County SD 4	Roseburg
1	n/a	Eagle Point SD 9	Eagle Point
1	n/a	Estacada SD 108	Estacada
1	n/a	Eugene SD 4J	Eugene
1	n/a	Fern Ridge SD 28J	Elmira
1	n/a	Forest Grove SD 15	Forest Grove
1	n/a	Gladstone SD 115	Gladstone
1	n/a	Grants Pass SD 7	Grants Pass
1	n/a	Greater Albany Public SD 8J	Albany
1	n/a	Gresham-Barlow SD 10J	Gresham
1	n/a	Hermiston SD 8	Hermiston
1	n/a	Hillsboro SD 1J	Hillsboro
1	n/a	Hood River County SD	Hood River
1	n/a	Jefferson County SD 509J	Madras
1	n/a	Junction City SD 69	Junction City
1	n/a	Klamath County SD	Klamath Falls

1	n/a	Klamath Falls City Schools	Klamath Falls
1	n/a	La Grande SD 1	La Grande
1	n/a	Lake Oswego SD 7J	Lake Oswego
1	n/a	Lebanon Community SD 9	Lebanon
1	n/a	Lincoln County SD	Newport
1	n/a	Mcminnville SD 40	Mcminnville
1	n/a	Medford SD 549c	Medford
1	n/a	Milton-Freewater Unified SD 7	Milton-Freewater
1	n/a	Molalla River SD 35	Molalla
1	n/a	Morrow SD 1	Lexington
1	n/a	Newberg SD 29J	Newberg
1	n/a	North Bend SD 13	North Bend
1	n/a	North Clackamas SD 12	Milwaukie
1	n/a	North Marion SD 15	Aurora
1	n/a	North Santiam SD 29J	Stayton
1	n/a	Ontario SD 8c	Ontario
1	n/a	Oregon City SD 62	Oregon City
1	n/a	Oregon Trail SD 46	Sandy
1	n/a	Parkrose SD 3	Portland
1	n/a	Pendleton SD 16	Pendleton
1	n/a	Philomath SD 17J	Philomath
1	n/a	Phoenix-Talent SD 4	Phoenix
1	n/a	Portland SD 1J	Portland
1	n/a	Redmond SD 2J	Redmond
1	n/a	Reynolds SD 7	Fairview
1	n/a	Salem-Keizer SD 24J	Salem
1	n/a	Scappoose SD 1J	Scappoose
1	n/a	Seaside SD 10	Seaside
1	n/a	Sherwood SD 88J	Sherwood
1	n/a	Silver Falls SD 4J	Silverton
1	n/a	Siuslaw SD 97J	Florence
1	n/a	South Lane SD 45j3	Cottage Grove
1	n/a	South Umpqua SD 19	Myrtle Creek
1	n/a	Springfield SD 19	Springfield
1	n/a	St Helens SD 502	St Helens
1	n/a	Sutherlin SD 130	Sutherlin
1	n/a	Sweet Home SD 55	Sweet Home
1	n/a	The Dalles SD 12	The Dalles
1	n/a	Three Rivers/Josephine County SD	Murphy
1	n/a	Tigard-Tualatin SD 23J	Tigard
1	n/a	Tillamook SD 9	Tillamook
1	n/a	West Linn-Wilsonville SD 3J	West Linn
1	n/a	Winston-Dillard SD 116	Winston
1	n/a	Woodburn SD 103	Woodburn

Female Students

Rank	Percent	District Name	City
1	n/a	Ashland SD 5	Ashland
1	n/a	Astoria SD 1	Astoria
1	n/a	Baker SD 5J	Baker City
1	n/a	Beaverton SD 48J	Beaverton
1	n/a	Bend-Lapine Administrative SD 1	Bend
1	n/a	Bethel SD 52	Eugene
1	n/a	Brookings-Harbor SD 17c	Brookings
1	n/a	Canby SD 86	Canby
1	n/a	Cascade SD 5	Turner
1	n/a	Centennial SD 28J	Portland
1	n/a	Central Point SD 6	Central Point
1	n/a	Central SD 13J	Independence
1	n/a	Coos Bay SD 9	Coos Bay
1	n/a	Corvallis SD 509J	Corvallis
1	n/a	Crook County Unit SD	Prineville
1	n/a	Dallas SD 2	Dallas
1	n/a	David Douglas SD 40	Portland
1	n/a	Douglas County SD 4	Roseburg
1	n/a	Eagle Point SD 9	Eagle Point
1	n/a	Estacada SD 108	Estacada
1	n/a	Eugene SD 4J	Eugene
1	n/a	Fern Ridge SD 28J	Elmira
1	n/a	Forest Grove SD 15	Forest Grove
1	n/a	Gladstone SD 115	Gladstone
1	n/a	Grants Pass SD 7	Grants Pass
1	n/a	Greater Albany Public SD 8J	Albany
1	n/a	Gresham-Barlow SD 10J	Gresham
1	n/a	Hermiston SD 8	Hermiston
1	n/a	Hillsboro SD 1J	Hillsboro
1	n/a	Hood River County SD	Hood River
1	n/a	Jefferson County SD 509J	Madras
1	n/a	Junction City SD 69	Junction City
1	n/a	Klamath County SD	Klamath Falls
1	n/a	Klamath Falls City Schools	Klamath Falls
1	n/a	La Grande SD 1	La Grande
1	n/a	Lake Oswego SD 7J	Lake Oswego
1	n/a	Lebanon Community SD 9	Lebanon
1	n/a	Lincoln County SD	Newport
1	n/a	Mcminnville SD 40	Mcminnville
1	n/a	Medford SD 549c	Medford
1	n/a	Milton-Freewater Unified SD 7	Milton-Freewater
1	n/a	Molalla River SD 35	Molalla
1	n/a	Morrow SD 1	Lexington
1	n/a	Newberg SD 29J	Newberg
1	n/a	North Bend SD 13	North Bend
1	n/a	North Clackamas SD 12	Milwaukie
1	n/a	North Marion SD 15	Aurora
1	n/a	North Santiam SD 29J	Stayton
1	n/a	Ontario SD 8c	Ontario
1	n/a	Oregon City SD 62	Oregon City
1	n/a	Oregon Trail SD 46	Sandy
1	n/a	Parkrose SD 3	Portland
1	n/a	Pendleton SD 16	Pendleton
1	n/a	Philomath SD 17J	Philomath
1	n/a	Phoenix-Talent SD 4	Phoenix
1	n/a	Portland SD 1J	Portland
1	n/a	Redmond SD 2J	Redmond
1	n/a	Reynolds SD 7	Fairview
1	n/a	Salem-Keizer SD 24J	Salem
1	n/a	Scappoose SD 1J	Scappoose
1	n/a	Seaside SD 10	Seaside
1	n/a	Sherwood SD 88J	Sherwood
1	n/a	Silver Falls SD 4J	Silverton
1	n/a	Siuslaw SD 97J	Florence
1	n/a	South Lane SD 45j3	Cottage Grove
1	n/a	South Umpqua SD 19	Myrtle Creek
1	n/a	Springfield SD 19	Springfield
1	n/a	St Helens SD 502	St Helens
1	n/a	Sutherlin SD 130	Sutherlin
1	n/a	Sweet Home SD 55	Sweet Home
1	n/a	The Dalles SD 12	The Dalles
1	n/a	Three Rivers/Josephine County SD	Murphy
1	n/a	Tigard-Tualatin SD 23J	Tigard
1	n/a	Tillamook SD 9	Tillamook
1	n/a	West Linn-Wilsonville SD 3J	West Linn
1	n/a	Winston-Dillard SD 116	Winston
1	n/a	Woodburn SD 103	Woodburn

Individual Education Program Students

Rank	Percent	District Name	City
1	17.5	South Lane SD 45j3	Cottage Grove
2	17.0	Fern Ridge SD 28J	Elmira
2	17.0	La Grande SD 1	La Grande
2	17.0	Sweet Home SD 55	Sweet Home
5	16.7	Estacada SD 108	Estacada
6	16.4	Baker SD 5J	Baker City
7	16.3	Coos Bay SD 9	Coos Bay
8	16.0	Springfield SD 19	Springfield
9	15.9	Lincoln County SD	Newport
10	15.6	Junction City SD 69	Junction City
10	15.6	Oregon City SD 62	Oregon City
10	15.6	St Helens SD 502	St Helens
13	15.5	Winston-Dillard SD 116	Winston
14	15.1	Klamath Falls City Schools	Klamath Falls
15	15.0	South Umpqua SD 19	Myrtle Creek
16	14.9	Bethel SD 52	Eugene
16	14.9	Brookings-Harbor SD 17c	Brookings
18	14.8	North Santiam SD 29J	Stayton
19	14.6	Reynolds SD 7	Fairview
20	14.5	Astoria SD 1	Astoria
21	14.2	Bend-Lapine Administrative SD 1	Bend
21	14.2	Klamath County SD	Klamath Falls
21	14.2	Seaside SD 10	Seaside
21	14.2	Tillamook SD 9	Tillamook
25	14.0	Siuslaw SD 97J	Florence
26	13.9	Molalla River SD 35	Molalla
27	13.4	Eugene SD 4J	Eugene
27	13.4	Oregon Trail SD 46	Sandy
29	13.2	Hermiston SD 8	Hermiston
29	13.2	North Bend SD 13	North Bend
31	13.1	Greater Albany Public SD 8J	Albany
32	13.0	Mcminnville SD 40	Mcminnville
33	12.9	Douglas County SD 4	Roseburg
33	12.9	Milton-Freewater Unified SD 7	Milton-Freewater
35	12.8	Cascade SD 5	Turner
35	12.8	North Marion SD 15	Aurora
35	12.8	Sutherlin SD 130	Sutherlin
38	12.7	Central SD 13J	Independence
38	12.7	Jefferson County SD 509J	Madras
38	12.7	Pendleton SD 16	Pendleton
38	12.7	Portland SD 1J	Portland
42	12.6	Redmond SD 2J	Redmond
42	12.6	Scappoose SD 1J	Scappoose
42	12.6	The Dalles SD 12	The Dalles
45	12.5	Morrow SD 1	Lexington
46	12.4	Central Point SD 6	Central Point
47	12.3	Crook County Unit SD	Prineville
47	12.3	Forest Grove SD 15	Forest Grove
47	12.3	Hood River County SD	Hood River
50	12.2	Woodburn SD 103	Woodburn
51	12.1	Hillsboro SD 1J	Hillsboro
51	12.1	Salem-Keizer SD 24J	Salem
53	12.0	Centennial SD 28J	Portland
53	12.0	Dallas SD 2	Dallas
53	12.0	Philomath SD 17J	Philomath
56	11.8	Beaverton SD 48J	Beaverton
56	11.8	David Douglas SD 40	Portland
56	11.8	Newberg SD 29J	Newberg
59	11.7	Eagle Point SD 9	Eagle Point
60	11.6	Gresham-Barlow SD 10J	Gresham
61	11.5	Gladstone SD 115	Gladstone
61	11.5	Ontario SD 8c	Ontario
61	11.5	Parkrose SD 3	Portland
61	11.5	Silver Falls SD 4J	Silverton
61	11.5	Three Rivers/Josephine County SD	Murphy
66	11.1	Ashland SD 5	Ashland
67	11.0	West Linn-Wilsonville SD 3J	West Linn
68	10.9	Medford SD 549c	Medford
69	10.8	North Clackamas SD 12	Milwaukie
70	10.7	Corvallis SD 509J	Corvallis
71	10.5	Lebanon Community SD 9	Lebanon
71	10.5	Sherwood SD 88J	Sherwood
73	10.2	Phoenix-Talent SD 4	Phoenix
74	10.0	Canby SD 86	Canby
75	9.6	Tigard-Tualatin SD 23J	Tigard
76	9.4	Grants Pass SD 7	Grants Pass
77	8.8	Lake Oswego SD 7J	Lake Oswego

English Language Learner Students

Rank	Percent	District Name	City
1	n/a	Ashland SD 5	Ashland
1	n/a	Astoria SD 1	Astoria
1	n/a	Baker SD 5J	Baker City
1	n/a	Beaverton SD 48J	Beaverton
1	n/a	Bend-Lapine Administrative SD 1	Bend
1	n/a	Bethel SD 52	Eugene
1	n/a	Brookings-Harbor SD 17c	Brookings
1	n/a	Canby SD 86	Canby
1	n/a	Cascade SD 5	Turner
1	n/a	Centennial SD 28J	Portland
1	n/a	Central Point SD 6	Central Point
1	n/a	Central SD 13J	Independence
1	n/a	Coos Bay SD 9	Coos Bay
1	n/a	Corvallis SD 509J	Corvallis
1	n/a	Crook County Unit SD	Prineville
1	n/a	Dallas SD 2	Dallas
1	n/a	David Douglas SD 40	Portland
1	n/a	Douglas County SD 4	Roseburg
1	n/a	Eagle Point SD 9	Eagle Point
1	n/a	Estacada SD 108	Estacada
1	n/a	Eugene SD 4J	Eugene
1	n/a	Fern Ridge SD 28J	Elmira
1	n/a	Forest Grove SD 15	Forest Grove
1	n/a	Gladstone SD 115	Gladstone
1	n/a	Grants Pass SD 7	Grants Pass
1	n/a	Greater Albany Public SD 8J	Albany
1	n/a	Gresham-Barlow SD 10J	Gresham
1	n/a	Hermiston SD 8	Hermiston
1	n/a	Hillsboro SD 1J	Hillsboro
1	n/a	Hood River County SD	Hood River
1	n/a	Jefferson County SD 509J	Madras
1	n/a	Junction City SD 69	Junction City
1	n/a	Klamath County SD	Klamath Falls
1	n/a	Klamath Falls City Schools	Klamath Falls
1	n/a	La Grande SD 1	La Grande
1	n/a	Lake Oswego SD 7J	Lake Oswego
1	n/a	Lebanon Community SD 9	Lebanon
1	n/a	Lincoln County SD	Newport
1	n/a	Mcminnville SD 40	Mcminnville
1	n/a	Medford SD 549c	Medford
1	n/a	Milton-Freewater Unified SD 7	Milton-Freewater
1	n/a	Molalla River SD 35	Molalla
1	n/a	Morrow SD 1	Lexington
1	n/a	Newberg SD 29J	Newberg
1	n/a	North Bend SD 13	North Bend
1	n/a	North Clackamas SD 12	Milwaukie
1	n/a	North Marion SD 15	Aurora
1	n/a	North Santiam SD 29J	Stayton
1	n/a	Ontario SD 8c	Ontario
1	n/a	Oregon City SD 62	Oregon City
1	n/a	Oregon Trail SD 46	Sandy
1	n/a	Parkrose SD 3	Portland
1	n/a	Pendleton SD 16	Pendleton
1	n/a	Philomath SD 17J	Philomath
1	n/a	Phoenix-Talent SD 4	Phoenix
1	n/a	Portland SD 1J	Portland
1	n/a	Redmond SD 2J	Redmond
1	n/a	Reynolds SD 7	Fairview
1	n/a	Salem-Keizer SD 24J	Salem
1	n/a	Scappoose SD 1J	Scappoose
1	n/a	Seaside SD 10	Seaside
1	n/a	Sherwood SD 88J	Sherwood
1	n/a	Silver Falls SD 4J	Silverton
1	n/a	Siuslaw SD 97J	Florence
1	n/a	South Lane SD 45j3	Cottage Grove
1	n/a	South Umpqua SD 19	Myrtle Creek
1	n/a	Springfield SD 19	Springfield
1	n/a	St Helens SD 502	St Helens
1	n/a	Sutherlin SD 130	Sutherlin

1	n/a	Sweet Home SD 55	Sweet Home
1	n/a	The Dalles SD 12	The Dalles
1	n/a	Three Rivers/Josephine County SD	Murphy
1	n/a	Tigard-Tualatin SD 23J	Tigard
1	n/a	Tillamook SD 9	Tillamook
1	n/a	West Linn-Wilsonville SD 3J	West Linn
1	n/a	Winston-Dillard SD 116	Winston
1	n/a	Woodburn SD 103	Woodburn

Migrant Students

Rank	Percent	District Name	City
1	36.4	Ontario SD 8c	Ontario
2	29.9	Woodburn SD 103	Woodburn
3	28.0	Morrow SD 1	Lexington
4	20.3	Hermiston SD 8	Hermiston
5	20.2	Jefferson County SD 509J	Madras
6	19.4	Hood River County SD	Hood River
7	17.1	North Marion SD 15	Aurora
8	14.4	Milton-Freewater Unified SD 7	Milton-Freewater
9	13.3	The Dalles SD 12	The Dalles
10	13.2	Forest Grove SD 15	Forest Grove
11	12.4	Central SD 13J	Independence
12	9.1	Hillsboro SD 1J	Hillsboro
13	8.2	Canby SD 86	Canby
14	8.0	Mcminnville SD 40	Mcminnville
15	7.9	Salem-Keizer SD 24J	Salem
16	6.8	Molalla River SD 35	Molalla
17	6.2	Phoenix-Talent SD 4	Phoenix
17	6.2	Silver Falls SD 4J	Silverton
19	5.1	Crook County Unit SD	Prineville
19	5.1	Newberg SD 29J	Newberg
21	5.0	Klamath County SD	Klamath Falls
21	5.0	North Santiam SD 29J	Stayton
23	4.7	Klamath Falls City Schools	Klamath Falls
24	4.5	Cascade SD 5	Turner
25	3.4	Estacada SD 108	Estacada
26	3.2	Eagle Point SD 9	Eagle Point
27	3.0	Reynolds SD 7	Fairview
28	2.9	Lincoln County SD	Newport
28	2.9	Medford SD 549c	Medford
30	2.3	Beaverton SD 48J	Beaverton
31	2.0	Junction City SD 69	Junction City
32	1.8	South Lane SD 45j3	Cottage Grove
33	1.4	Greater Albany Public SD 8J	Albany
33	1.4	Gresham-Barlow SD 10J	Gresham
35	1.3	Corvallis SD 509J	Corvallis
35	1.3	Portland SD 1J	Portland
37	1.2	Springfield SD 19	Springfield
38	1.1	Centennial SD 28J	Portland
39	1.0	Redmond SD 2J	Redmond
40	0.9	Ashland SD 5	Ashland
40	0.9	Oregon City SD 62	Oregon City
42	0.8	Bethel SD 52	Eugene
43	0.7	Bend-Lapine Administrative SD 1	Bend
43	0.7	Dallas SD 2	Dallas
43	0.7	David Douglas SD 40	Portland
43	0.7	Oregon Trail SD 46	Sandy
43	0.7	Parkrose SD 3	Portland
48	0.5	Eugene SD 4J	Eugene
48	0.5	Gladstone SD 115	Gladstone
50	0.4	Lebanon Community SD 9	Lebanon
51	0.3	Central Point SD 6	Central Point
51	0.3	North Clackamas SD 12	Milwaukie
53	0.2	Pendleton SD 16	Pendleton
54	0.1	Philomath SD 17J	Philomath
54	0.1	Three Rivers/Josephine County SD	Murphy
54	0.1	West Linn-Wilsonville SD 3J	West Linn
57	0.0	Grants Pass SD 7	Grants Pass
57	0.0	Lake Oswego SD 7J	Lake Oswego
57	0.0	Sweet Home SD 55	Sweet Home
60	0.0	Astoria SD 1	Astoria
60	0.0	Baker SD 5J	Baker City
60	0.0	Brookings-Harbor SD 17c	Brookings
60	0.0	Coos Bay SD 9	Coos Bay
60	0.0	Douglas County SD 4	Roseburg
60	0.0	Fern Ridge SD 28J	Elmira
60	0.0	La Grande SD 1	La Grande
60	0.0	North Bend SD 13	North Bend
60	0.0	Scappoose SD 1J	Scappoose
60	0.0	Seaside SD 10	Seaside
60	0.0	Sherwood SD 88J	Sherwood
60	0.0	Siuslaw SD 97J	Florence
60	0.0	South Umpqua SD 19	Myrtle Creek
60	0.0	St Helens SD 502	St Helens
60	0.0	Sutherlin SD 130	Sutherlin
60	0.0	Tigard-Tualatin SD 23J	Tigard
60	0.0	Tillamook SD 9	Tillamook
60	0.0	Winston-Dillard SD 116	Winston

Students Eligible for Free Lunch

Rank	Percent	District Name	City
1	76.3	Woodburn SD 103	Woodburn
2	59.4	Jefferson County SD 509J	Madras
3	57.1	Ontario SD 8c	Ontario
4	50.2	Milton-Freewater Unified SD 7	Milton-Freewater
5	49.2	Morrow SD 1	Lexington
6	48.6	Central SD 13J	Independence
7	47.6	David Douglas SD 40	Portland
8	46.5	Reynolds SD 7	Fairview
9	46.4	Estacada SD 108	Estacada
10	45.4	Forest Grove SD 15	Forest Grove
11	44.5	Klamath Falls City Schools	Klamath Falls
12	43.7	Winston-Dillard SD 116	Winston
13	43.6	Hood River County SD	Hood River
14	43.5	The Dalles SD 12	The Dalles
15	43.4	Sweet Home SD 55	Sweet Home
16	43.3	Lebanon Community SD 9	Lebanon
17	42.9	Lincoln County SD	Newport
18	42.1	Coos Bay SD 9	Coos Bay
18	42.1	Parkrose SD 3	Portland
18	42.1	Three Rivers/Josephine County SD	Murphy
21	41.5	Eagle Point SD 9	Eagle Point
21	41.5	South Lane SD 45j3	Cottage Grove
23	41.4	Klamath County SD	Klamath Falls
24	40.9	North Marion SD 15	Aurora
25	40.5	Springfield SD 19	Springfield
26	40.3	Sutherlin SD 130	Sutherlin
27	40.1	South Umpqua SD 19	Myrtle Creek
28	39.6	Hermiston SD 8	Hermiston
29	39.1	Phoenix-Talent SD 4	Phoenix
30	38.5	Tillamook SD 9	Tillamook
31	37.4	Salem-Keizer SD 24J	Salem
32	36.7	Baker SD 5J	Baker City
33	36.5	Grants Pass SD 7	Grants Pass
34	36.4	Centennial SD 28J	Portland
35	36.2	Mcminnville SD 40	Mcminnville
36	36.0	Cascade SD 5	Turner
37	35.3	Crook County Unit SD	Prineville
38	35.0	Bethel SD 52	Eugene
39	34.9	Douglas County SD 4	Roseburg
40	34.6	North Bend SD 13	North Bend
41	34.3	Brookings-Harbor SD 17c	Brookings
42	34.1	North Santiam SD 29J	Stayton
43	33.9	Siuslaw SD 97J	Florence
44	33.7	Portland SD 1J	Portland
45	32.3	Fern Ridge SD 28J	Elmira
46	31.4	Medford SD 549c	Medford
47	30.9	Redmond SD 2J	Redmond
48	30.4	Seaside SD 10	Seaside
49	30.1	Greater Albany Public SD 8J	Albany
50	29.6	Junction City SD 69	Junction City
51	29.1	Pendleton SD 16	Pendleton
52	29.0	Astoria SD 1	Astoria
53	28.2	Silver Falls SD 4J	Silverton
54	27.8	Central Point SD 6	Central Point
55	27.3	Gresham-Barlow SD 10J	Gresham
55	27.3	La Grande SD 1	La Grande
57	26.7	Bend-Lapine Administrative SD 1	Bend
58	26.6	Hillsboro SD 1J	Hillsboro
59	25.3	Dallas SD 2	Dallas
60	25.2	St Helens SD 502	St Helens
61	24.7	Canby SD 86	Canby
62	24.5	Newberg SD 29J	Newberg
63	23.9	Oregon Trail SD 46	Sandy
64	23.6	Molalla River SD 35	Molalla
65	23.1	North Clackamas SD 12	Milwaukie
66	22.1	Corvallis SD 509J	Corvallis
67	22.0	Eugene SD 4J	Eugene
68	21.2	Ashland SD 5	Ashland
68	21.2	Philomath SD 17J	Philomath
70	20.9	Beaverton SD 48J	Beaverton
71	20.5	Gladstone SD 115	Gladstone
72	20.3	Oregon City SD 62	Oregon City
73	19.4	Tigard-Tualatin SD 23J	Tigard
74	11.3	Scappoose SD 1J	Scappoose
75	8.0	Sherwood SD 88J	Sherwood
76	7.6	West Linn-Wilsonville SD 3J	West Linn
77	3.9	Lake Oswego SD 7J	Lake Oswego

Students Eligible for Reduced-Price Lunch

Rank	Percent	District Name	City
1	18.6	Brookings-Harbor SD 17c	Brookings
2	15.4	Klamath Falls City Schools	Klamath Falls
3	14.1	Estacada SD 108	Estacada
4	13.4	Eagle Point SD 9	Eagle Point
4	13.4	North Santiam SD 29J	Stayton
6	13.3	Three Rivers/Josephine County SD	Murphy
7	12.7	Molalla River SD 35	Molalla
8	12.6	Grants Pass SD 7	Grants Pass
8	12.6	Lebanon Community SD 9	Lebanon
10	12.2	South Lane SD 45j3	Cottage Grove
11	11.8	Morrow SD 1	Lexington
12	11.7	Parkrose SD 3	Portland
13	11.6	Crook County Unit SD	Prineville
14	11.4	David Douglas SD 40	Portland
14	11.4	Klamath County SD	Klamath Falls
16	11.2	Milton-Freewater Unified SD 7	Milton-Freewater
17	11.1	Centennial SD 28J	Portland
17	11.1	Jefferson County SD 509J	Madras
17	11.1	Winston-Dillard SD 116	Winston
20	11.0	Sweet Home SD 55	Sweet Home
21	10.9	Hood River County SD	Hood River
22	10.8	Hermiston SD 8	Hermiston
22	10.8	Tillamook SD 9	Tillamook
24	10.5	South Umpqua SD 19	Myrtle Creek
25	10.4	Central SD 13J	Independence
26	10.0	Fern Ridge SD 28J	Elmira
27	9.9	Bethel SD 52	Eugene
27	9.9	Pendleton SD 16	Pendleton
29	9.7	Woodburn SD 103	Woodburn
30	9.6	Seaside SD 10	Seaside
31	9.4	Forest Grove SD 15	Forest Grove
31	9.4	Junction City SD 69	Junction City
31	9.4	Reynolds SD 7	Fairview
34	9.3	Douglas County SD 4	Roseburg
35	9.2	Baker SD 5J	Baker City
35	9.2	North Marion SD 15	Aurora
37	9.1	Sutherlin SD 130	Sutherlin
38	9.0	Central Point SD 6	Central Point
39	8.9	Coos Bay SD 9	Coos Bay
40	8.8	Mcminnville SD 40	Mcminnville
41	8.7	Cascade SD 5	Turner
41	8.7	Redmond SD 2J	Redmond
41	8.7	The Dalles SD 12	The Dalles
44	8.6	La Grande SD 1	La Grande
44	8.6	Ontario SD 8c	Ontario
46	8.5	Phoenix-Talent SD 4	Phoenix
47	8.4	Scappoose SD 1J	Scappoose
48	8.3	Bend-Lapine Administrative SD 1	Bend
48	8.3	Lincoln County SD	Newport
50	8.1	Hillsboro SD 1J	Hillsboro
51	8.0	North Bend SD 13	North Bend
51	8.0	Springfield SD 19	Springfield
53	7.9	Medford SD 549c	Medford
54	7.8	Greater Albany Public SD 8J	Albany
54	7.8	Salem-Keizer SD 24J	Salem
56	7.7	Gresham-Barlow SD 10J	Gresham
56	7.7	Oregon City SD 62	Oregon City
56	7.7	Portland SD 1J	Portland
59	7.5	Gladstone SD 115	Gladstone
59	7.5	Silver Falls SD 4J	Silverton
59	7.5	St Helens SD 502	St Helens
62	7.4	Canby SD 86	Canby
62	7.4	Oregon Trail SD 46	Sandy
64	7.3	Astoria SD 1	Astoria
64	7.3	North Clackamas SD 12	Milwaukie
66	7.1	Beaverton SD 48J	Beaverton
66	7.1	Dallas SD 2	Dallas
68	6.9	Newberg SD 29J	Newberg
69	6.8	Siuslaw SD 97J	Florence
70	5.1	Corvallis SD 509J	Corvallis
70	5.1	Philomath SD 17J	Philomath
72	4.7	Eugene SD 4J	Eugene
72	4.7	Tigard-Tualatin SD 23J	Tigard
74	4.3	Ashland SD 5	Ashland
75	2.9	West Linn-Wilsonville SD 3J	West Linn
76	2.8	Sherwood SD 88J	Sherwood
77	2.1	Lake Oswego SD 7J	Lake Oswego

Student/Teacher Ratio

Rank	Ratio	District Name	City
1	27.2	Fern Ridge SD 28J	Elmira
2	25.7	Lebanon Community SD 9	Lebanon
3	25.0	Eagle Point SD 9	Eagle Point
4	24.6	Central Point SD 6	Central Point
5	24.1	Corvallis SD 509J	Corvallis
6	23.9	Lincoln County SD	Newport
6	23.9	Oregon Trail SD 46	Sandy
8	23.8	Hillsboro SD 1J	Hillsboro
9	23.7	Junction City SD 69	Junction City
10	23.4	Oregon City SD 62	Oregon City
11	23.1	Gladstone SD 115	Gladstone
12	22.9	Medford SD 549c	Medford
13	22.8	Dallas SD 2	Dallas
13	22.8	Greater Albany Public SD 8J	Albany
15	22.4	Bethel SD 52	Eugene
15	22.4	Coos Bay SD 9	Coos Bay
15	22.4	Eugene SD 4J	Eugene
15	22.4	Redmond SD 2J	Redmond
19	22.3	Douglas County SD 4	Roseburg
19	22.3	Three Rivers/Josephine County SD	Murphy
21	22.2	Sherwood SD 88J	Sherwood
22	22.0	Central SD 13J	Independence

23	21.9	Newberg SD 29J	Newberg
23	21.9	Springfield SD 19	Springfield
25	21.8	St Helens SD 502	St Helens
26	21.7	Canby SD 86	Canby
27	21.2	Mcminnville SD 40	Mcminnville
27	21.2	North Santiam SD 29J	Stayton
27	21.2	Sutherlin SD 130	Sutherlin
27	21.2	Sweet Home SD 55	Sweet Home
31	21.1	Bend-Lapine Administrative SD 1	Bend
31	21.1	Estacada SD 108	Estacada
31	21.1	Molalla River SD 35	Molalla
31	21.1	Salem-Keizer SD 24J	Salem
35	21.0	Grants Pass SD 7	Grants Pass
36	20.8	Beaverton SD 48J	Beaverton
36	20.8	Gresham-Barlow SD 10J	Gresham
36	20.8	Pendleton SD 16	Pendleton
36	20.8	West Linn-Wilsonville SD 3J	West Linn
40	20.7	Parkrose SD 3	Portland
40	20.7	Philomath SD 17J	Philomath
40	20.7	Tigard-Tualatin SD 23J	Tigard
43	20.6	North Marion SD 15	Aurora
43	20.6	South Lane SD 45j3	Cottage Grove
45	20.5	Crook County Unit SD	Prineville
45	20.5	North Bend SD 13	North Bend
45	20.5	North Clackamas SD 12	Milwaukie
48	20.4	David Douglas SD 40	Portland
48	20.4	Lake Oswego SD 7J	Lake Oswego
48	20.4	Phoenix-Talent SD 4	Phoenix
48	20.4	Tillamook SD 9	Tillamook
52	20.2	Forest Grove SD 15	Forest Grove
53	20.1	Baker SD 5J	Baker City
53	20.1	Jefferson County SD 509J	Madras
53	20.1	Scappoose SD 1J	Scappoose
53	20.1	Silver Falls SD 4J	Silverton
57	19.9	Ashland SD 5	Ashland
58	19.8	Centennial SD 28J	Portland
58	19.8	Klamath Falls City Schools	Klamath Falls
58	19.8	The Dalles SD 12	The Dalles
61	19.7	La Grande SD 1	La Grande
62	19.6	Cascade SD 5	Turner
63	19.5	Brookings-Harbor SD 17c	Brookings
64	19.3	South Umpqua SD 19	Myrtle Creek
65	19.2	Astoria SD 1	Astoria
65	19.2	Morrow SD 1	Lexington
65	19.2	Reynolds SD 7	Fairview
68	19.1	Klamath County SD	Klamath Falls
68	19.1	Siuslaw SD 97J	Florence
70	19.0	Seaside SD 10	Seaside
71	18.7	Hermiston SD 8	Hermiston
71	18.7	Milton-Freewater Unified SD 7	Milton-Freewater
73	18.6	Winston-Dillard SD 116	Winston
74	18.0	Hood River County SD	Hood River
75	17.1	Woodburn SD 103	Woodburn
76	16.9	Ontario SD 8c	Ontario
77	16.5	Portland SD 1J	Portland

Student/Librarian Ratio

Rank	Ratio	District Name	City
1	6,486.0	Klamath County SD	Klamath Falls
2	6,159.0	Redmond SD 2J	Redmond
3	5,679.0	Bethel SD 52	Eugene
4	5,676.0	Forest Grove SD 15	Forest Grove
5	4,201.0	Oregon Trail SD 46	Sandy
6	4,077.0	Eagle Point SD 9	Eagle Point
7	3,992.0	Oregon City SD 62	Oregon City
8	3,935.8	Central Point SD 6	Central Point
9	3,490.0	Canby SD 86	Canby
10	3,195.4	Gresham-Barlow SD 10J	Gresham
11	3,030.0	Hood River County SD	Hood River
12	2,999.3	Lebanon Community SD 9	Lebanon
13	2,977.0	Lincoln County SD	Newport
14	2,856.5	Grants Pass SD 7	Grants Pass
15	2,801.0	Molalla River SD 35	Molalla
16	2,576.3	Lake Oswego SD 7J	Lake Oswego
17	2,441.3	Parkrose SD 3	Portland
18	2,311.0	Corvallis SD 509J	Corvallis
19	2,230.3	Douglas County SD 4	Roseburg
20	2,138.0	Crook County Unit SD	Prineville
21	2,128.8	Seaside SD 10	Seaside
22	2,116.7	South Umpqua SD 19	Myrtle Creek
23	2,027.0	The Dalles SD 12	The Dalles
24	1,865.0	Coos Bay SD 9	Coos Bay
25	1,843.3	Gladstone SD 115	Gladstone
26	1,801.0	North Marion SD 15	Aurora
27	1,780.7	Newberg SD 29J	Newberg
28	1,653.0	Fern Ridge SD 28J	Elmira
29	1,626.0	Winston-Dillard SD 116	Winston
30	1,582.0	Siuslaw SD 97J	Florence
31	1,557.7	St Helens SD 502	St Helens
32	1,549.5	Jefferson County SD 509J	Madras
33	1,448.5	South Lane SD 45j3	Cottage Grove
34	1,444.7	North Santiam SD 29J	Stayton
35	1,411.2	Portland SD 1J	Portland
36	1,322.3	Bend-Lapine Administrative SD 1	Bend
37	1,242.7	Junction City SD 69	Junction City
38	1,232.0	Philomath SD 17J	Philomath
39	1,146.5	Silver Falls SD 4J	Silverton
40	1,126.0	North Bend SD 13	North Bend
41	1,110.2	Eugene SD 4J	Eugene
42	1,099.3	Dallas SD 2	Dallas
43	1,035.6	Tigard-Tualatin SD 23J	Tigard
44	1,032.0	Tillamook SD 9	Tillamook
45	1,001.0	Ashland SD 5	Ashland
46	993.6	Greater Albany Public SD 8J	Albany
47	967.1	Sherwood SD 88J	Sherwood
48	965.4	Pendleton SD 16	Pendleton
49	956.8	Mcminnville SD 40	Mcminnville
50	816.7	West Linn-Wilsonville SD 3J	West Linn
51	802.4	Hermiston SD 8	Hermiston
52	788.7	Beaverton SD 48J	Beaverton
53	783.7	Medford SD 549c	Medford
54	753.1	David Douglas SD 40	Portland
55	747.8	Salem-Keizer SD 24J	Salem
56	731.2	Milton-Freewater Unified SD 7	Milton-Freewater
57	730.7	Cascade SD 5	Turner
58	728.7	Springfield SD 19	Springfield
59	720.0	Klamath Falls City Schools	Klamath Falls
60	718.7	North Clackamas SD 12	Milwaukie
61	702.7	Centennial SD 28J	Portland
62	701.7	Reynolds SD 7	Fairview
63	689.0	Ontario SD 8c	Ontario
64	672.9	Woodburn SD 103	Woodburn
65	619.1	Astoria SD 1	Astoria
66	606.6	Phoenix-Talent SD 4	Phoenix
67	452.8	La Grande SD 1	La Grande
68	426.4	Morrow SD 1	Lexington
69	411.8	Baker SD 5J	Baker City
70	n/a	Brookings-Harbor SD 17c	Brookings
70	n/a	Central SD 13J	Independence
70	n/a	Estacada SD 108	Estacada
70	n/a	Hillsboro SD 1J	Hillsboro
70	n/a	Scappoose SD 1J	Scappoose
70	n/a	Sutherlin SD 130	Sutherlin
70	n/a	Sweet Home SD 55	Sweet Home
70	n/a	Three Rivers/Josephine County SD	Murphy

Student/Counselor Ratio

Rank	Ratio	District Name	City
1	1,317.0	Central SD 13J	Independence
2	1,082.5	Lincoln County SD	Newport
3	981.2	Three Rivers/Josephine County SD	Murphy
4	933.7	Molalla River SD 35	Molalla
5	877.9	South Lane SD 45j3	Cottage Grove
6	813.0	Winston-Dillard SD 116	Winston
7	750.7	North Bend SD 13	North Bend
8	741.3	Eagle Point SD 9	Eagle Point
9	718.7	Fern Ridge SD 28J	Elmira
10	716.2	Hood River County SD	Hood River
11	692.2	Lebanon Community SD 9	Lebanon
12	689.0	Ontario SD 8c	Ontario
13	681.9	Eugene SD 4J	Eugene
14	670.0	Morrow SD 1	Lexington
15	661.2	Portland SD 1J	Portland
16	652.4	Medford SD 549c	Medford
17	635.0	Greater Albany Public SD 8J	Albany
18	621.7	Coos Bay SD 9	Coos Bay
19	621.3	Junction City SD 69	Junction City
20	604.8	Hillsboro SD 1J	Hillsboro
21	581.8	Phoenix-Talent SD 4	Phoenix
22	564.2	Sherwood SD 88J	Sherwood
23	553.0	Gladstone SD 115	Gladstone
24	546.8	Silver Falls SD 4J	Silverton
25	535.3	West Linn-Wilsonville SD 3J	West Linn
26	526.9	Bend-Lapine Administrative SD 1	Bend
27	523.3	Woodburn SD 103	Woodburn
28	519.4	Grants Pass SD 7	Grants Pass
29	516.7	Sutherlin SD 130	Sutherlin
30	515.3	Lake Oswego SD 7J	Lake Oswego
31	501.2	North Santiam SD 29J	Stayton
32	494.2	Oregon Trail SD 46	Sandy
33	491.3	Springfield SD 19	Springfield
34	486.3	Philomath SD 17J	Philomath
35	486.1	Tigard-Tualatin SD 23J	Tigard
36	485.9	David Douglas SD 40	Portland
37	483.9	Oregon City SD 62	Oregon City
38	480.0	Tillamook SD 9	Tillamook
39	477.9	Douglas County SD 4	Roseburg
40	477.2	Bethel SD 52	Eugene
41	476.8	Jefferson County SD 509J	Madras
42	465.2	Estacada SD 108	Estacada
43	459.3	Mcminnville SD 40	Mcminnville
44	456.8	Klamath County SD	Klamath Falls
45	452.5	Brookings-Harbor SD 17c	Brookings
46	443.0	North Clackamas SD 12	Milwaukie
47	442.1	Milton-Freewater Unified SD 7	Milton-Freewater
48	433.6	Newberg SD 29J	Newberg
49	433.0	South Umpqua SD 19	Myrtle Creek
50	430.8	Dallas SD 2	Dallas
51	425.3	Corvallis SD 509J	Corvallis
52	422.6	Beaverton SD 48J	Beaverton
53	421.6	Centennial SD 28J	Portland
54	418.0	Central Point SD 6	Central Point
55	411.4	Salem-Keizer SD 24J	Salem
56	406.9	Parkrose SD 3	Portland
57	402.3	Pendleton SD 16	Pendleton
58	400.9	Crook County Unit SD	Prineville
59	392.0	Scappoose SD 1J	Scappoose
60	387.8	Canby SD 86	Canby
61	383.5	Forest Grove SD 15	Forest Grove
62	377.3	La Grande SD 1	La Grande
63	372.5	Reynolds SD 7	Fairview
64	362.9	Sweet Home SD 55	Sweet Home
65	362.3	Redmond SD 2J	Redmond
66	360.5	Gresham-Barlow SD 10J	Gresham
67	350.0	Baker SD 5J	Baker City
68	347.9	Cascade SD 5	Turner
69	341.4	Klamath Falls City Schools	Klamath Falls
70	340.6	Seaside SD 10	Seaside
71	339.5	Hermiston SD 8	Hermiston
72	337.8	The Dalles SD 12	The Dalles
73	333.7	Ashland SD 5	Ashland
74	333.4	Astoria SD 1	Astoria
75	316.4	Siuslaw SD 97J	Florence
76	300.2	North Marion SD 15	Aurora
77	274.2	St Helens SD 502	St Helens

Current Spending per Student in FY2003

Rank	Dollars	District Name	City
1	8,629	Klamath Falls City Schools	Klamath Falls
2	8,503	Jefferson County SD 509J	Madras
3	8,495	Woodburn SD 103	Woodburn
4	8,076	Portland SD 1J	Portland
5	7,763	Lincoln County SD	Newport
6	7,657	Hood River County SD	Hood River
7	7,585	Dallas SD 2	Dallas
8	7,550	Coos Bay SD 9	Coos Bay
9	7,515	Siuslaw SD 97J	Florence
10	7,495	Bethel SD 52	Eugene
11	7,443	Klamath County SD	Klamath Falls
12	7,429	Morrow SD 1	Lexington
13	7,411	Winston-Dillard SD 116	Winston
14	7,401	Eugene SD 4J	Eugene
15	7,378	South Lane SD 45j3	Cottage Grove
16	7,370	Hermiston SD 8	Hermiston
17	7,286	Seaside SD 10	Seaside
18	7,271	Three Rivers/Josephine County SD	Murphy
19	7,258	La Grande SD 1	La Grande
20	7,235	Central SD 13J	Independence
21	7,234	Springfield SD 19	Springfield
22	7,227	Astoria SD 1	Astoria
23	7,225	Ontario SD 8c	Ontario
24	7,199	North Bend SD 13	North Bend
25	7,114	Corvallis SD 509J	Corvallis
26	7,099	Ashland SD 5	Ashland
27	6,991	Baker SD 5J	Baker City
28	6,970	Lake Oswego SD 7J	Lake Oswego
29	6,927	Junction City SD 69	Junction City
30	6,896	Milton-Freewater Unified SD 7	Milton-Freewater
31	6,889	Salem-Keizer SD 24J	Salem
32	6,867	Eagle Point SD 9	Eagle Point
33	6,857	Grants Pass SD 7	Grants Pass
34	6,850	Forest Grove SD 15	Forest Grove
35	6,842	Brookings-Harbor SD 17c	Brookings
36	6,810	Sweet Home SD 55	Sweet Home
37	6,803	David Douglas SD 40	Portland
38	6,799	The Dalles SD 12	The Dalles
39	6,764	Fern Ridge SD 28J	Elmira
40	6,738	Crook County Unit SD	Prineville
41	6,729	Oregon City SD 62	Oregon City
42	6,726	Silver Falls SD 4J	Silverton
43	6,698	Canby SD 86	Canby
44	6,652	Gresham-Barlow SD 10J	Gresham
45	6,614	Lebanon Community SD 9	Lebanon
46	6,605	Phoenix-Talent SD 4	Phoenix
47	6,569	Hillsboro SD 1J	Hillsboro
48	6,555	Estacada SD 108	Estacada
49	6,552	Tillamook SD 9	Tillamook
50	6,546	Tigard-Tualatin SD 23J	Tigard
51	6,544	Reynolds SD 7	Fairview
52	6,528	Scappoose SD 1J	Scappoose
53	6,525	Greater Albany Public SD 8J	Albany
54	6,488	South Umpqua SD 19	Myrtle Creek
55	6,463	Douglas County SD 4	Roseburg
56	6,455	West Linn-Wilsonville SD 3J	West Linn
57	6,435	North Santiam SD 29J	Stayton
58	6,428	Newberg SD 29J	Newberg

59	6,419	Medford SD 549c	Medford
60	6,414	Cascade SD 5	Turner
61	6,409	St Helens SD 502	St Helens
62	6,404	North Marion SD 15	Aurora
63	6,394	Centennial SD 28J	Portland
64	6,368	Oregon Trail SD 46	Sandy
65	6,363	Sutherlin SD 130	Sutherlin
66	6,314	North Clackamas SD 12	Milwaukie
67	6,305	Philomath SD 17J	Philomath
68	6,298	Redmond SD 2J	Redmond
69	6,288	Bend-Lapine Administrative SD 1	Bend
70	6,273	Pendleton SD 16	Pendleton
71	6,262	Molalla River SD 35	Molalla
71	6,262	Parkrose SD 3	Portland
73	6,233	Beaverton SD 48J	Beaverton
74	6,143	Central Point SD 6	Central Point
75	6,077	Mcminnville SD 40	Mcminnville
76	6,025	Gladstone SD 115	Gladstone
77	5,760	Sherwood SD 88J	Sherwood

Number of Diploma Recipients

Rank	Number	District Name	City
1	2,592	Portland SD 1J	Portland
2	1,957	Beaverton SD 48J	Beaverton
3	1,810	Salem-Keizer SD 24J	Salem
4	1,378	Eugene SD 4J	Eugene
5	888	Hillsboro SD 1J	Hillsboro
6	805	Bend-Lapine Administrative SD 1	Bend
7	789	North Clackamas SD 12	Milwaukie
8	743	Tigard-Tualatin SD 23J	Tigard
9	721	Gresham-Barlow SD 10J	Gresham
10	660	Medford SD 549c	Medford
11	586	Springfield SD 19	Springfield
12	491	Corvallis SD 509J	Corvallis
13	489	Lake Oswego SD 7J	Lake Oswego
14	476	West Linn-Wilsonville SD 3J	West Linn
15	417	Greater Albany Public SD 8J	Albany
16	406	Lincoln County SD	Newport
17	399	Douglas County SD 4	Roseburg
18	360	David Douglas SD 40	Portland
19	358	Reynolds SD 7	Fairview
19	358	Three Rivers/Josephine County SD	Murphy
21	352	Canby SD 86	Canby
22	344	Oregon City SD 62	Oregon City
23	326	Centennial SD 28J	Portland
24	318	Newberg SD 29J	Newberg
25	314	Mcminnville SD 40	Mcminnville
26	306	Klamath Falls City Schools	Klamath Falls
27	304	Redmond SD 2J	Redmond
28	297	Oregon Trail SD 46	Sandy
29	287	Grants Pass SD 7	Grants Pass
30	273	Central Point SD 6	Central Point
31	260	Forest Grove SD 15	Forest Grove
32	255	Ashland SD 5	Ashland
33	241	Eagle Point SD 9	Eagle Point
34	239	Coos Bay SD 9	Coos Bay
35	236	Lebanon Community SD 9	Lebanon
36	231	Hood River County SD	Hood River
37	224	Bethel SD 52	Eugene
38	223	Klamath County SD	Klamath Falls
39	214	Silver Falls SD 4J	Silverton
40	207	Woodburn SD 103	Woodburn
41	202	Dallas SD 2	Dallas
42	190	Parkrose SD 3	Portland
43	183	Hermiston SD 8	Hermiston
44	179	Crook County Unit SD	Prineville
45	178	Gladstone SD 115	Gladstone
46	176	St Helens SD 502	St Helens
47	173	Pendleton SD 16	Pendleton
48	166	North Bend SD 13	North Bend
49	163	South Lane SD 45j3	Cottage Grove
50	162	Tillamook SD 9	Tillamook
51	152	La Grande SD 1	La Grande
51	152	Sweet Home SD 55	Sweet Home
53	149	Estacada SD 108	Estacada
54	146	Astoria SD 1	Astoria
54	146	Junction City SD 69	Junction City
56	143	Central SD 13J	Independence
57	142	Scappoose SD 1J	Scappoose
57	142	The Dalles SD 12	The Dalles
59	137	Baker SD 5J	Baker City
59	137	Sherwood SD 88J	Sherwood
61	135	Philomath SD 17J	Philomath
62	130	North Santiam SD 29J	Stayton
63	127	Jefferson County SD 509J	Madras
63	127	Phoenix-Talent SD 4	Phoenix
65	123	Ontario SD 8c	Ontario
66	121	Brookings-Harbor SD 17c	Brookings
67	119	Morrow SD 1	Lexington
68	118	Cascade SD 5	Turner
69	116	South Umpqua SD 19	Myrtle Creek
70	113	North Marion SD 15	Aurora

71	112	Fern Ridge SD 28J	Elmira
72	111	Molalla River SD 35	Molalla
73	91	Milton-Freewater Unified SD 7	Milton-Freewater
74	88	Seaside SD 10	Seaside
75	83	Siuslaw SD 97J	Florence
76	81	Winston-Dillard SD 116	Winston
77	68	Sutherlin SD 130	Sutherlin

High School Drop-out Rate

Rank	Percent	District Name	City
1	10.8	Portland SD 1J	Portland
2	9.6	Lebanon Community SD 9	Lebanon
3	9.4	Phoenix-Talent SD 4	Phoenix
4	8.1	Forest Grove SD 15	Forest Grove
5	8.0	Parkrose SD 3	Portland
6	7.9	Medford SD 549c	Medford
7	7.4	Salem-Keizer SD 24J	Salem
8	7.2	Eagle Point SD 9	Eagle Point
9	7.0	Woodburn SD 103	Woodburn
10	6.9	South Lane SD 45j3	Cottage Grove
11	6.4	Milton-Freewater Unified SD 7	Milton-Freewater
12	6.3	Mcminnville SD 40	Mcminnville
13	6.2	Seaside SD 10	Seaside
14	6.1	Central Point SD 6	Central Point
15	5.9	Grants Pass SD 7	Grants Pass
15	5.9	Lincoln County SD	Newport
17	5.8	Greater Albany Public SD 8J	Albany
18	5.7	Central SD 13J	Independence
19	5.5	Douglas County SD 4	Roseburg
20	5.4	Winston-Dillard SD 116	Winston
21	5.3	Siuslaw SD 97J	Florence
22	5.2	Crook County Unit SD	Prineville
23	5.1	Sweet Home SD 55	Sweet Home
24	4.9	Coos Bay SD 9	Coos Bay
25	4.7	Estacada SD 108	Estacada
25	4.7	Reynolds SD 7	Fairview
25	4.7	Springfield SD 19	Springfield
25	4.7	Sutherlin SD 130	Sutherlin
29	4.5	Centennial SD 28J	Portland
29	4.5	Three Rivers/Josephine County SD	Murphy
29	4.5	Tigard-Tualatin SD 23J	Tigard
29	4.5	Tillamook SD 9	Tillamook
33	4.4	Hermiston SD 8	Hermiston
33	4.4	North Santiam SD 29J	Stayton
35	4.3	Newberg SD 29J	Newberg
36	4.2	Bethel SD 52	Eugene
36	4.2	Gresham-Barlow SD 10J	Gresham
36	4.2	Ontario SD 8c	Ontario
36	4.2	Pendleton SD 16	Pendleton
40	4.1	Beaverton SD 48J	Beaverton
40	4.1	Klamath Falls City Schools	Klamath Falls
42	4.0	Dallas SD 2	Dallas
42	4.0	David Douglas SD 40	Portland
42	4.0	North Clackamas SD 12	Milwaukie
42	4.0	Silver Falls SD 4J	Silverton
46	3.9	South Umpqua SD 19	Myrtle Creek
47	3.8	Bend-Lapine Administrative SD 1	Bend
47	3.8	Fern Ridge SD 28J	Elmira
47	3.8	Jefferson County SD 509J	Madras
47	3.8	La Grande SD 1	La Grande
51	3.6	Junction City SD 69	Junction City
52	3.5	Molalla River SD 35	Molalla
53	3.4	Brookings-Harbor SD 17c	Brookings
53	3.4	Canby SD 86	Canby
53	3.4	Philomath SD 17J	Philomath
56	3.3	Cascade SD 5	Turner
57	3.2	Ashland SD 5	Ashland
57	3.2	North Bend SD 13	North Bend
59	3.1	Eugene SD 4J	Eugene
59	3.1	Hillsboro SD 1J	Hillsboro
59	3.1	Oregon Trail SD 46	Sandy
62	3.0	St Helens SD 502	St Helens
63	2.8	Corvallis SD 509J	Corvallis
63	2.8	The Dalles SD 12	The Dalles
65	2.6	Morrow SD 1	Lexington
66	2.5	Astoria SD 1	Astoria
66	2.5	West Linn-Wilsonville SD 3J	West Linn
68	2.4	North Marion SD 15	Aurora
69	2.2	Klamath County SD	Klamath Falls
70	2.0	Hood River County SD	Hood River
70	2.0	Sherwood SD 88J	Sherwood
72	1.7	Lake Oswego SD 7J	Lake Oswego
73	1.6	Redmond SD 2J	Redmond
74	1.4	Scappoose SD 1J	Scappoose
75	1.3	Oregon City SD 62	Oregon City
76	0.8	Gladstone SD 115	Gladstone
77	0.6	Baker SD 5J	Baker City

Pennsylvania

Pennsylvania Public School Educational Profile

Category	Value	Category	Value
Schools *(2003-2004)*	3,267	**Diploma Recipients** *(2002-2003)*	114,897
Instructional Level		White, Non-Hispanic	97,378
Primary	1,917	Black, Non-Hispanic	11,628
Middle	572	Asian/Pacific Islander	2,696
High	619	American Indian/Alaskan Native	102
Other Level	151	Hispanic	3,093
Curriculum		**High School Drop-out Rate** *(%)* *(2001-2002)*	3.3
Regular	3,153	White, Non-Hispanic	2.4
Special Education	12	Black, Non-Hispanic	7.1
Vocational	81	Asian/Pacific Islander	2.9
Alternative	13	American Indian/Alaskan Native	3.3
Type		Hispanic	8.9
Magnet	35	**Staff** *(2003-2004)*	
Charter	102	Teachers	119,894.0
Title I Eligible	2,135	Average Salary ($)	52,640
School-wide Title I	497	Librarians/Media Specialists	2,217.2
Students *(2003-2004)*	1,821,146	Guidance Counselors	4,343.4
Gender (%)		**Ratios** *(2003-2004)*	
Male	***.*	Student/Teacher Ratio	15.2 to 1
Female	***.*	Student/Librarian Ratio	821.4 to 1
Race/Ethnicity (%)		Student/Counselor Ratio	419.3 to 1
White, Non-Hispanic	76.3	**College Entrance Exam Scores** *(2005)*	
Black, Non-Hispanic	15.8	Scholastic Aptitude Test (SAT)	
Asian/Pacific Islander	2.3	Participation Rate (%)	75
American Indian/Alaskan Native	0.1	Mean SAT Reasoning Test Verbal Score	501
Hispanic	5.5	Mean SAT Reasoning Test Math Score	503
Classification (%)		American College Testing Program (ACT)	
Individual Education Program (IEP)	13.9	Participation Rate (%)	9
Migrant *(2002-2003)*	0.5	Average Composite Score	21.7
English Language Learner (ELL)	0.0	Average English Score	21.2
Eligible for Free Lunch Program	22.3	Average Math Score	21.5
Eligible for Reduced-Price Lunch Program	5.8	Average Reading Score	22.3
Current Spending *($ per student in FY 2003)*	8,285	Average Science Score	21.4
Instruction	5,148		
Support Services	2,808		

Note: *For an explanation of data, please refer to the User's Guide in the front of the book*

Pennsylvania NAEP 2005 Test Scores

Reading			Mathematics		
Grade/Category	**Value**	**Rank**	**Grade/Category**	**Value**	**Rank**
4th Grade			**4th Grade**		
Average Proficiency	222.8 (1.31)	15/51	Average Proficiency	240.6 (1.17)	17/51
Proficiency by Gender/Race/Ethnicity			Proficiency by Gender/Race/Ethnicity		
Male	218.7 (1.52)	18/51	Male	241.3 (1.48)	21/51
Female	226.9 (1.42)	11/51	Female	239.8 (1.16)	16/51
White, Non-Hispanic	229.1 (1.28)	14/51	White, Non-Hispanic	246.9 (1.10)	17/51
Black, Non-Hispanic	200.0 (2.48)	20/42	Black, Non-Hispanic	219.4 (2.06)	22/42
Asian, Non-Hispanic	233.5 (5.37)	11/27	Asian, Non-Hispanic	n/a	n/a
American Indian, Non-Hispanic	n/a	n/a	American Indian, Non-Hispanic	n/a	n/a
Hispanic	202.5 (4.27)	26/40	Hispanic	220.4 (2.74)	30/41
Proficiency by Class Size			Proficiency by Class Size		
Less than 16 Students	195.5 (5.21)	26/34	Less than 16 Students	217.9 (5.45)	30/35
16 to 18 Students	221.8 (3.34)	9/33	16 to 18 Students	241.8 (3.54)	7/31
19 to 20 Students	224.9 (3.78)	15/38	19 to 20 Students	242.0 (3.46)	11/38
21 to 25 Students	228.3 (1.65)	6/51	21 to 25 Students	245.1 (1.80)	8/51
Greater than 25 Students	221.2 (3.77)	18/36	Greater than 25 Students	238.5 (3.32)	19/33
Percent Attaining Achievement Levels			Percent Attaining Achievement Levels		
Below Basic	31.4 (1.56)	34/51	Below Basic	17.8 (1.21)	27/51
Basic or Above	68.6 (1.56)	18/51	Basic or Above	82.2 (1.21)	24/51
Proficient or Above	35.9 (1.54)	9/51	Proficient or Above	41.5 (1.61)	11/51
Advanced or Above	8.7 (0.82)	7/51	Advanced or Above	6.1 (0.77)	11/51
8th Grade			**8th Grade**		
Average Proficiency	266.8 (1.32)	14/51	Average Proficiency	280.7 (1.47)	27/51
Proficiency by Gender/Race/Ethnicity			Proficiency by Gender/Race/Ethnicity		
Male	262.2 (1.66)	12/51	Male	282.7 (1.77)	20/51
Female	271.4 (1.59)	16/51	Female	278.6 (1.52)	28/51
White, Non-Hispanic	273.1 (0.93)	7/51	White, Non-Hispanic	286.9 (1.18)	26/51
Black, Non-Hispanic	239.4 (3.90)	31/40	Black, Non-Hispanic	250.0 (3.37)	26/41
Asian, Non-Hispanic	275.4 (8.58)	9/24	Asian, Non-Hispanic	297.0 (5.31)	13/23
American Indian, Non-Hispanic	n/a	n/a	American Indian, Non-Hispanic	n/a	n/a
Hispanic	246.1 (6.79)	25/38	Hispanic	267.0 (2.88)	6/38
Proficiency by Parents Highest Level of Ed.			Proficiency by Parents Highest Level of Ed.		
Did Not Finish High School	251.2 (2.60)	7/49	Did Not Finish High School	263.2 (2.90)	20/50
Graduated High School	259.4 (1.76)	12/50	Graduated High School	268.5 (1.90)	27/50
Some Education After High School	268.9 (1.92)	14/50	Some Education After High School	282.7 (1.98)	22/50
Graduated College	275.9 (1.42)	8/50	Graduated College	291.5 (1.50)	21/50
Percent Attaining Achievement Levels			Percent Attaining Achievement Levels		
Below Basic	31.4 (1.56)	34/51	Below Basic	27.8 (1.59)	29/51
Basic or Above	68.6 (1.56)	18/51	Basic or Above	72.2 (1.59)	22/51
Proficient or Above	35.9 (1.54)	9/51	Proficient or Above	30.9 (1.61)	20/51
Advanced or Above	8.7 (0.82)	7/51	Advanced or Above	5.7 (0.79)	21/51

Note: For an explanation of data, please refer to the User's Guide in the front of the book; n/a indicates data not available

Adams County

Bermudian Springs SD
PO Box 501 • York Springs, PA 17372-0501
(717) 528-4113 • http://www.bermudian.k12.pa.us
Grade Span: KG-12; Agency Type: 1
Schools: 3
  1 Primary; 1 Middle; 1 High; 0 Other Level
  3 Regular; 0 Special Education; 0 Vocational; 0 Alternative
  0 Magnet; 0 Charter; 2 Title I Eligible; 0 School-wide Title I
Students: 2,160 (n/a% male; n/a% female)
  Individual Education Program: 191 (8.8%);
  English Language Learner: n/a; Migrant: 108 (5.0%)
  Eligible for Free Lunch Program: 248 (11.5%)
  Eligible for Reduced-Price Lunch Program: 122 (5.6%)
Teachers: 128.4 (16.8 to 1)
Librarians/Media Specialists: 3.0 (720.0 to 1)
Guidance Counselors: 4.0 (540.0 to 1)
Current Spending: ($ per student per year):
  Total: $6,141; Instruction: $3,842; Support Services: $2,018
Enrollment, Drop-out Rates and Diploma Recipients by Race/Ethnicity

Category	Total	White	Black	Asian	AIAN	Hisp.
Enrollment (%)	100.0	91.2	0.6	1.1	0.0	7.1
Drop-out Rate (%)	2.4	2.5	0.0	0.0	0.0	0.0
H.S. Diplomas (#)	140	137	1	0	1	1

Conewago Valley SD
130 Berlin Rd • New Oxford, PA 17350-1206
(717) 624-2157 • http://www.conewago.k12.pa.us
Grade Span: KG-12; Agency Type: 1
Schools: 4
  2 Primary; 1 Middle; 1 High; 0 Other Level
  4 Regular; 0 Special Education; 0 Vocational; 0 Alternative
  0 Magnet; 0 Charter; 3 Title I Eligible; 0 School-wide Title I
Students: 3,686 (n/a% male; n/a% female)
  Individual Education Program: 505 (13.7%);
  English Language Learner: n/a; Migrant: 136 (3.7%)
  Eligible for Free Lunch Program: 557 (15.1%)
  Eligible for Reduced-Price Lunch Program: 259 (7.0%)
Teachers: 201.9 (18.3 to 1)
Librarians/Media Specialists: 4.0 (921.5 to 1)
Guidance Counselors: 6.0 (614.3 to 1)
Current Spending: ($ per student per year):
  Total: $6,211; Instruction: $4,119; Support Services: $1,785
Enrollment, Drop-out Rates and Diploma Recipients by Race/Ethnicity

Category	Total	White	Black	Asian	AIAN	Hisp.
Enrollment (%)	100.0	91.0	0.9	0.4	0.0	7.7
Drop-out Rate (%)	1.1	1.1	0.0	0.0	n/a	0.0
H.S. Diplomas (#)	217	195	1	2	0	19

Gettysburg Area SD
900 Biglerville Rd • Gettysburg, PA 17325-8007
(717) 334-6254 • http://www.gettysburg.k12.pa.us
Grade Span: KG-12; Agency Type: 1
Schools: 6
  3 Primary; 2 Middle; 1 High; 0 Other Level
  6 Regular; 0 Special Education; 0 Vocational; 0 Alternative
  0 Magnet; 0 Charter; 5 Title I Eligible; 0 School-wide Title I
Students: 3,396 (n/a% male; n/a% female)
  Individual Education Program: 503 (14.8%);
  English Language Learner: n/a; Migrant: 168 (4.9%)
  Eligible for Free Lunch Program: 572 (16.8%)
  Eligible for Reduced-Price Lunch Program: 239 (7.0%)
Teachers: 228.8 (14.8 to 1)
Librarians/Media Specialists: 5.0 (679.2 to 1)
Guidance Counselors: 11.0 (308.7 to 1)
Current Spending: ($ per student per year):
  Total: $9,082; Instruction: $5,628; Support Services: $3,140
Enrollment, Drop-out Rates and Diploma Recipients by Race/Ethnicity

Category	Total	White	Black	Asian	AIAN	Hisp.
Enrollment (%)	100.0	82.8	7.1	1.4	0.3	8.5
Drop-out Rate (%)	2.6	2.2	4.9	0.0	0.0	7.9
H.S. Diplomas (#)	256	225	14	8	0	9

Littlestown Area SD
75 Maple Ave • Littlestown, PA 17340-1343
(717) 359-4146 • http://www.lasd.k12.pa.us
Grade Span: KG-12; Agency Type: 1
Schools: 4
  1 Primary; 1 Middle; 1 High; 1 Other Level
  4 Regular; 0 Special Education; 0 Vocational; 0 Alternative
  0 Magnet; 0 Charter; 3 Title I Eligible; 0 School-wide Title I
Students: 2,378 (n/a% male; n/a% female)
  Individual Education Program: 311 (13.1%);
  English Language Learner: n/a; Migrant: 6 (0.3%)

  Eligible for Free Lunch Program: 260 (10.9%)
  Eligible for Reduced-Price Lunch Program: 151 (6.3%)
Teachers: 137.0 (17.4 to 1)
Librarians/Media Specialists: 3.0 (792.7 to 1)
Guidance Counselors: 4.0 (594.5 to 1)
Current Spending: ($ per student per year):
  Total: $6,325; Instruction: $4,144; Support Services: $1,879
Enrollment, Drop-out Rates and Diploma Recipients by Race/Ethnicity

Category	Total	White	Black	Asian	AIAN	Hisp.
Enrollment (%)	100.0	96.6	1.3	0.8	0.0	1.2
Drop-out Rate (%)	3.4	3.1	0.0	0.0	n/a	22.2
H.S. Diplomas (#)	146	140	0	5	0	1

Upper Adams SD
161 N Main St PO Box 847 • Biglerville, PA 17307-0847
(717) 677-7191 • http://www.uasd.k12.pa.us
Grade Span: KG-12; Agency Type: 1
Schools: 5
  3 Primary; 1 Middle; 1 High; 0 Other Level
  5 Regular; 0 Special Education; 0 Vocational; 0 Alternative
  0 Magnet; 0 Charter; 4 Title I Eligible; 0 School-wide Title I
Students: 1,774 (n/a% male; n/a% female)
  Individual Education Program: 308 (17.4%);
  English Language Learner: n/a; Migrant: 195 (11.0%)
  Eligible for Free Lunch Program: 421 (23.7%)
  Eligible for Reduced-Price Lunch Program: 182 (10.3%)
Teachers: 112.0 (15.8 to 1)
Librarians/Media Specialists: 2.0 (887.0 to 1)
Guidance Counselors: 4.0 (443.5 to 1)
Current Spending: ($ per student per year):
  Total: $7,572; Instruction: $4,569; Support Services: $2,614
Enrollment, Drop-out Rates and Diploma Recipients by Race/Ethnicity

Category	Total	White	Black	Asian	AIAN	Hisp.
Enrollment (%)	100.0	82.0	0.8	0.2	0.2	16.8
Drop-out Rate (%)	4.2	3.3	0.0	n/a	n/a	12.3
H.S. Diplomas (#)	114	107	2	0	0	5

Allegheny County

Baldwin-Whitehall SD
4900 Curry Rd • Pittsburgh, PA 15236-1817
(412) 885-7810 • http://www.baldwin.k12.pa.us
Grade Span: KG-12; Agency Type: 1
Schools: 5
  3 Primary; 1 Middle; 1 High; 0 Other Level
  5 Regular; 0 Special Education; 0 Vocational; 0 Alternative
  0 Magnet; 0 Charter; 3 Title I Eligible; 0 School-wide Title I
Students: 4,613 (n/a% male; n/a% female)
  Individual Education Program: 558 (12.1%);
  English Language Learner: n/a; Migrant: 0 (0.0%)
  Eligible for Free Lunch Program: 573 (12.4%)
  Eligible for Reduced-Price Lunch Program: 248 (5.4%)
Teachers: 278.5 (16.6 to 1)
Librarians/Media Specialists: 5.5 (838.7 to 1)
Guidance Counselors: 8.0 (576.6 to 1)
Current Spending: ($ per student per year):
  Total: $8,810; Instruction: $5,223; Support Services: $3,243
Enrollment, Drop-out Rates and Diploma Recipients by Race/Ethnicity

Category	Total	White	Black	Asian	AIAN	Hisp.
Enrollment (%)	100.0	90.3	8.1	0.9	0.1	0.6
Drop-out Rate (%)	1.2	1.0	5.3	0.0	0.0	0.0
H.S. Diplomas (#)	395	385	8	2	0	0

Bethel Park SD
301 Church Rd • Bethel Park, PA 15102-1607
(412) 833-5000 • http://www.bpsd.k12.pa.us
Grade Span: KG-12; Agency Type: 1
Schools: 8
  5 Primary; 2 Middle; 1 High; 0 Other Level
  8 Regular; 0 Special Education; 0 Vocational; 0 Alternative
  0 Magnet; 0 Charter; 5 Title I Eligible; 0 School-wide Title I
Students: 5,212 (n/a% male; n/a% female)
  Individual Education Program: 594 (11.4%);
  English Language Learner: n/a; Migrant: 0 (0.0%)
  Eligible for Free Lunch Program: 199 (3.8%)
  Eligible for Reduced-Price Lunch Program: 164 (3.1%)
Teachers: 355.0 (14.7 to 1)
Librarians/Media Specialists: 9.0 (579.1 to 1)
Guidance Counselors: 10.0 (521.2 to 1)
Current Spending: ($ per student per year):
  Total: $8,887; Instruction: $5,805; Support Services: $2,817

Enrollment, Drop-out Rates and Diploma Recipients by Race/Ethnicity

Category	Total	White	Black	Asian	AIAN	Hisp.
Enrollment (%)	100.0	96.8	1.6	1.2	0.1	0.4
Drop-out Rate (%)	0.5	0.4	0.0	8.7	0.0	0.0
H.S. Diplomas (#)	402	387	4	8	0	3

Carlynton SD
435 Kings Hwy • Carnegie, PA 15106-1043
(412) 429-8400 • http://www.carlynton.k12.pa.us
Grade Span: KG-12; **Agency Type:** 1
Schools: 3
    2 Primary; 0 Middle; 1 High; 0 Other Level
    3 Regular; 0 Special Education; 0 Vocational; 0 Alternative
    0 Magnet; 0 Charter; 2 Title I Eligible; 0 School-wide Title I
Students: 1,623 (n/a% male; n/a% female)
    Individual Education Program: 189 (11.6%);
    English Language Learner: n/a; Migrant: 0 (0.0%)
    Eligible for Free Lunch Program: 0 (0.0%)
    Eligible for Reduced-Price Lunch Program: 0 (0.0%)
Teachers: 103.0 (15.8 to 1)
Librarians/Media Specialists: 2.0 (811.5 to 1)
Guidance Counselors: 3.0 (541.0 to 1)
Current Spending: ($ per student per year):
    Total: $10,002; Instruction: $6,257; Support Services: $3,439
Enrollment, Drop-out Rates and Diploma Recipients by Race/Ethnicity

Category	Total	White	Black	Asian	AIAN	Hisp.
Enrollment (%)	100.0	87.6	10.8	0.8	0.0	0.9
Drop-out Rate (%)	2.2	2.2	2.4	0.0	n/a	0.0
H.S. Diplomas (#)	120	105	12	3	0	0

Chartiers Valley SD
2030 Swallow Hill Rd • Pittsburgh, PA 15220-1699
(412) 429-2201 • http://www.chartiersvalley.k12.pa.us
Grade Span: KG-12; **Agency Type:** 1
Schools: 4
    2 Primary; 1 Middle; 1 High; 0 Other Level
    4 Regular; 0 Special Education; 0 Vocational; 0 Alternative
    0 Magnet; 0 Charter; 4 Title I Eligible; 0 School-wide Title I
Students: 3,455 (n/a% male; n/a% female)
    Individual Education Program: 366 (10.6%);
    English Language Learner: n/a; Migrant: 0 (0.0%)
    Eligible for Free Lunch Program: 457 (13.2%)
    Eligible for Reduced-Price Lunch Program: 145 (4.2%)
Teachers: 233.5 (14.8 to 1)
Librarians/Media Specialists: 4.0 (863.8 to 1)
Guidance Counselors: 8.0 (431.9 to 1)
Current Spending: ($ per student per year):
    Total: $8,721; Instruction: $4,907; Support Services: $3,485
Enrollment, Drop-out Rates and Diploma Recipients by Race/Ethnicity

Category	Total	White	Black	Asian	AIAN	Hisp.
Enrollment (%)	100.0	91.3	4.3	4.0	0.0	0.4
Drop-out Rate (%)	1.1	1.0	3.3	0.0	n/a	0.0
H.S. Diplomas (#)	234	221	6	6	0	1

Deer Lakes SD
PO Box 10 • Russellton, PA 15076-0010
(724) 265-5300 • http://www.dlsd.k12.pa.us
Grade Span: KG-12; **Agency Type:** 1
Schools: 4
    2 Primary; 1 Middle; 1 High; 0 Other Level
    4 Regular; 0 Special Education; 0 Vocational; 0 Alternative
    0 Magnet; 0 Charter; 4 Title I Eligible; 0 School-wide Title I
Students: 2,098 (n/a% male; n/a% female)
    Individual Education Program: 302 (14.4%);
    English Language Learner: n/a; Migrant: 0 (0.0%)
    Eligible for Free Lunch Program: 144 (6.9%)
    Eligible for Reduced-Price Lunch Program: 81 (3.9%)
Teachers: 137.5 (15.3 to 1)
Librarians/Media Specialists: 4.0 (524.5 to 1)
Guidance Counselors: 3.0 (699.3 to 1)
Current Spending: ($ per student per year):
    Total: $9,151; Instruction: $5,401; Support Services: $3,383
Enrollment, Drop-out Rates and Diploma Recipients by Race/Ethnicity

Category	Total	White	Black	Asian	AIAN	Hisp.
Enrollment (%)	100.0	98.8	0.6	0.1	0.0	0.4
Drop-out Rate (%)	0.5	0.6	0.0	n/a	n/a	0.0
H.S. Diplomas (#)	170	170	0	0	0	0

East Allegheny SD
1150 Jacks Run Rd • North Versailles, PA 15137-2797
(412) 824-8012
Grade Span: KG-12; **Agency Type:** 1
Schools: 3
    2 Primary; 0 Middle; 1 High; 0 Other Level
    3 Regular; 0 Special Education; 0 Vocational; 0 Alternative

0 Magnet; 0 Charter; 3 Title I Eligible; 0 School-wide Title I
Students: 1,994 (n/a% male; n/a% female)
    Individual Education Program: 326 (16.3%);
    English Language Learner: n/a; Migrant: 0 (0.0%)
    Eligible for Free Lunch Program: 616 (30.9%)
    Eligible for Reduced-Price Lunch Program: 138 (6.9%)
Teachers: 108.8 (18.3 to 1)
Librarians/Media Specialists: 2.0 (997.0 to 1)
Guidance Counselors: 3.5 (569.7 to 1)
Current Spending: ($ per student per year):
    Total: $8,094; Instruction: $4,660; Support Services: $3,086
Enrollment, Drop-out Rates and Diploma Recipients by Race/Ethnicity

Category	Total	White	Black	Asian	AIAN	Hisp.
Enrollment (%)	100.0	82.6	16.3	0.6	0.1	0.4
Drop-out Rate (%)	3.7	3.5	6.7	0.0	0.0	0.0
H.S. Diplomas (#)	119	105	13	1	0	0

Elizabeth Forward SD
401 Rock Run Rd • Elizabeth, PA 15037-2416
(412) 896-2300 • http://www.efsd.net
Grade Span: KG-12; **Agency Type:** 1
Schools: 7
    5 Primary; 1 Middle; 1 High; 0 Other Level
    7 Regular; 0 Special Education; 0 Vocational; 0 Alternative
    0 Magnet; 0 Charter; 5 Title I Eligible; 0 School-wide Title I
Students: 2,959 (n/a% male; n/a% female)
    Individual Education Program: 416 (14.1%);
    English Language Learner: n/a; Migrant: 0 (0.0%)
    Eligible for Free Lunch Program: 364 (12.3%)
    Eligible for Reduced-Price Lunch Program: 216 (7.3%)
Teachers: 186.5 (15.9 to 1)
Librarians/Media Specialists: 3.0 (986.3 to 1)
Guidance Counselors: 3.0 (986.3 to 1)
Current Spending: ($ per student per year):
    Total: $8,016; Instruction: $5,035; Support Services: $2,691
Enrollment, Drop-out Rates and Diploma Recipients by Race/Ethnicity

Category	Total	White	Black	Asian	AIAN	Hisp.
Enrollment (%)	100.0	97.2	2.2	0.2	0.2	0.1
Drop-out Rate (%)	1.9	1.8	5.9	0.0	0.0	0.0
H.S. Diplomas (#)	197	191	5	1	0	0

Fox Chapel Area SD
611 Field Club Rd • Pittsburgh, PA 15238-2406
(412) 963-9600 • http://www.fcasd.edu
Grade Span: KG-12; **Agency Type:** 1
Schools: 6
    4 Primary; 1 Middle; 1 High; 0 Other Level
    6 Regular; 0 Special Education; 0 Vocational; 0 Alternative
    0 Magnet; 0 Charter; 3 Title I Eligible; 0 School-wide Title I
Students: 4,644 (n/a% male; n/a% female)
    Individual Education Program: 534 (11.5%);
    English Language Learner: n/a; Migrant: 0 (0.0%)
    Eligible for Free Lunch Program: 324 (7.0%)
    Eligible for Reduced-Price Lunch Program: 128 (2.8%)
Teachers: 375.0 (12.4 to 1)
Librarians/Media Specialists: 6.0 (774.0 to 1)
Guidance Counselors: 13.0 (357.2 to 1)
Current Spending: ($ per student per year):
    Total: $10,652; Instruction: $6,886; Support Services: $3,545
Enrollment, Drop-out Rates and Diploma Recipients by Race/Ethnicity

Category	Total	White	Black	Asian	AIAN	Hisp.
Enrollment (%)	100.0	93.4	1.2	4.4	0.1	0.9
Drop-out Rate (%)	0.7	0.6	4.0	0.0	n/a	0.0
H.S. Diplomas (#)	318	298	2	15	0	3

Gateway SD
9000 Gateway Campus Blvd • Monroeville, PA 15146-3378
(412) 372-5300 • http://gator.gasd.k12.pa.us/
Grade Span: KG-12; **Agency Type:** 1
Schools: 8
    5 Primary; 2 Middle; 1 High; 0 Other Level
    8 Regular; 0 Special Education; 0 Vocational; 0 Alternative
    0 Magnet; 0 Charter; 4 Title I Eligible; 0 School-wide Title I
Students: 4,432 (n/a% male; n/a% female)
    Individual Education Program: 646 (14.6%);
    English Language Learner: n/a; Migrant: 0 (0.0%)
    Eligible for Free Lunch Program: 659 (14.9%)
    Eligible for Reduced-Price Lunch Program: 233 (5.3%)
Teachers: 305.0 (14.5 to 1)
Librarians/Media Specialists: 5.0 (886.4 to 1)
Guidance Counselors: 10.0 (443.2 to 1)
Current Spending: ($ per student per year):
    Total: $10,578; Instruction: $6,840; Support Services: $3,340

Enrollment, Drop-out Rates and Diploma Recipients by Race/Ethnicity

Category	Total	White	Black	Asian	AIAN	Hisp.
Enrollment (%)	100.0	79.9	13.4	5.6	0.0	1.1
Drop-out Rate (%)	1.8	1.9	1.8	1.4	0.0	0.0
H.S. Diplomas (#)	340	282	36	22	0	0

Hampton Township SD
4591 School Dr • Allison Park, PA 15101
(412) 486-6000 • http://www.htsd.k12.pa.us
Grade Span: KG-12; **Agency Type:** 1
Schools: 5
  3 Primary; 1 Middle; 1 High; 0 Other Level
  5 Regular; 0 Special Education; 0 Vocational; 0 Alternative
  0 Magnet; 0 Charter; 2 Title I Eligible; 0 School-wide Title I
Students: 3,219   (n/a% male; n/a% female)
  Individual Education Program: 359 (11.2%);
  English Language Learner: n/a; Migrant: 0 (0.0%)
  Eligible for Free Lunch Program: 119 (3.7%)
  Eligible for Reduced-Price Lunch Program: 61 (1.9%)
Teachers: 200.9 (16.0 to 1)
Librarians/Media Specialists: 5.0 (643.8 to 1)
Guidance Counselors: 6.0 (536.5 to 1)
Current Spending: ($ per student per year):
  Total: $8,421; Instruction: $5,477; Support Services: $2,635
Enrollment, Drop-out Rates and Diploma Recipients by Race/Ethnicity

Category	Total	White	Black	Asian	AIAN	Hisp.
Enrollment (%)	100.0	97.5	0.9	1.2	0.0	0.3
Drop-out Rate (%)	0.7	0.6	20.0	0.0	n/a	0.0
H.S. Diplomas (#)	252	245	1	5	0	1

Highlands SD
PO Box 288 • Natrona Heights, PA 15065-0288
(724) 226-2400
Grade Span: KG-12; **Agency Type:** 1
Schools: 6
  4 Primary; 1 Middle; 1 High; 0 Other Level
  6 Regular; 0 Special Education; 0 Vocational; 0 Alternative
  0 Magnet; 0 Charter; 5 Title I Eligible; 1 School-wide Title I
Students: 2,748   (n/a% male; n/a% female)
  Individual Education Program: 485 (17.6%);
  English Language Learner: n/a; Migrant: 0 (0.0%)
  Eligible for Free Lunch Program: 828 (30.1%)
  Eligible for Reduced-Price Lunch Program: 290 (10.6%)
Teachers: 207.0 (13.3 to 1)
Librarians/Media Specialists: 3.0 (916.0 to 1)
Guidance Counselors: 6.0 (458.0 to 1)
Current Spending: ($ per student per year):
  Total: $9,233; Instruction: $5,551; Support Services: $3,341
Enrollment, Drop-out Rates and Diploma Recipients by Race/Ethnicity

Category	Total	White	Black	Asian	AIAN	Hisp.
Enrollment (%)	100.0	91.7	7.0	0.7	0.2	0.5
Drop-out Rate (%)	2.4	2.3	2.2	20.0	0.0	0.0
H.S. Diplomas (#)	209	197	8	2	1	1

Keystone Oaks SD
1000 Kelton Ave • Pittsburgh, PA 15216-2421
(412) 571-6000 • http://www.kosd.org
Grade Span: KG-12; **Agency Type:** 1
Schools: 5
  3 Primary; 1 Middle; 1 High; 0 Other Level
  5 Regular; 0 Special Education; 0 Vocational; 0 Alternative
  0 Magnet; 0 Charter; 3 Title I Eligible; 0 School-wide Title I
Students: 2,537   (n/a% male; n/a% female)
  Individual Education Program: 319 (12.6%);
  English Language Learner: n/a; Migrant: 0 (0.0%)
  Eligible for Free Lunch Program: 338 (13.3%)
  Eligible for Reduced-Price Lunch Program: 213 (8.4%)
Teachers: 168.2 (15.1 to 1)
Librarians/Media Specialists: 4.0 (634.3 to 1)
Guidance Counselors: 5.0 (507.4 to 1)
Current Spending: ($ per student per year):
  Total: $9,833; Instruction: $6,039; Support Services: $3,494
Enrollment, Drop-out Rates and Diploma Recipients by Race/Ethnicity

Category	Total	White	Black	Asian	AIAN	Hisp.
Enrollment (%)	100.0	95.7	2.1	1.7	0.0	0.5
Drop-out Rate (%)	2.9	2.8	0.0	40.0	0.0	0.0
H.S. Diplomas (#)	198	190	3	3	1	1

Mckeesport Area SD
2225 5th Ave • Mc Keesport, PA 15132-1145
(412) 664-3610
Grade Span: KG-12; **Agency Type:** 1
Schools: 7
  3 Primary; 3 Middle; 1 High; 0 Other Level
  7 Regular; 0 Special Education; 0 Vocational; 0 Alternative

0 Magnet; 0 Charter; 6 Title I Eligible; 2 School-wide Title I
Students: 4,704   (n/a% male; n/a% female)
  Individual Education Program: 784 (16.7%);
  English Language Learner: n/a; Migrant: 0 (0.0%)
  Eligible for Free Lunch Program: 2,278 (48.4%)
  Eligible for Reduced-Price Lunch Program: 350 (7.4%)
Teachers: 290.0 (16.2 to 1)
Librarians/Media Specialists: 7.0 (672.0 to 1)
Guidance Counselors: 9.0 (522.7 to 1)
Current Spending: ($ per student per year):
  Total: $8,408; Instruction: $5,496; Support Services: $2,628
Enrollment, Drop-out Rates and Diploma Recipients by Race/Ethnicity

Category	Total	White	Black	Asian	AIAN	Hisp.
Enrollment (%)	100.0	59.4	39.2	0.2	0.4	0.8
Drop-out Rate (%)	3.4	3.6	2.8	0.0	0.0	7.1
H.S. Diplomas (#)	292	220	69	1	1	1

Montour SD
223 Clever Rd • Mc Kees Rocks, PA 15136-4012
(412) 490-6500
Grade Span: KG-12; **Agency Type:** 1
Schools: 5
  3 Primary; 1 Middle; 1 High; 0 Other Level
  5 Regular; 0 Special Education; 0 Vocational; 0 Alternative
  0 Magnet; 0 Charter; 0 Title I Eligible; 0 School-wide Title I
Students: 3,332   (n/a% male; n/a% female)
  Individual Education Program: 429 (12.9%);
  English Language Learner: n/a; Migrant: 0 (0.0%)
  Eligible for Free Lunch Program: 140 (4.2%)
  Eligible for Reduced-Price Lunch Program: 41 (1.2%)
Teachers: 213.0 (15.6 to 1)
Librarians/Media Specialists: 5.0 (666.4 to 1)
Guidance Counselors: 11.0 (302.9 to 1)
Current Spending: ($ per student per year):
  Total: $8,980; Instruction: $5,582; Support Services: $3,171
Enrollment, Drop-out Rates and Diploma Recipients by Race/Ethnicity

Category	Total	White	Black	Asian	AIAN	Hisp.
Enrollment (%)	100.0	95.2	3.0	1.2	0.3	0.3
Drop-out Rate (%)	1.9	1.9	0.0	0.0	0.0	0.0
H.S. Diplomas (#)	256	250	3	3	0	0

Moon Area SD
8353 University Blvd • Moon Township, PA 15108-2509
(412) 264-9440 • http://www.masd.k12.pa.us
Grade Span: KG-12; **Agency Type:** 1
Schools: 6
  4 Primary; 1 Middle; 1 High; 0 Other Level
  6 Regular; 0 Special Education; 0 Vocational; 0 Alternative
  0 Magnet; 0 Charter; 6 Title I Eligible; 0 School-wide Title I
Students: 3,751   (n/a% male; n/a% female)
  Individual Education Program: 532 (14.2%);
  English Language Learner: n/a; Migrant: 0 (0.0%)
  Eligible for Free Lunch Program: 220 (5.9%)
  Eligible for Reduced-Price Lunch Program: 83 (2.2%)
Teachers: 260.9 (14.4 to 1)
Librarians/Media Specialists: 5.0 (750.2 to 1)
Guidance Counselors: 6.0 (625.2 to 1)
Current Spending: ($ per student per year):
  Total: $10,252; Instruction: $7,015; Support Services: $2,985
Enrollment, Drop-out Rates and Diploma Recipients by Race/Ethnicity

Category	Total	White	Black	Asian	AIAN	Hisp.
Enrollment (%)	100.0	92.2	5.0	1.9	0.0	0.9
Drop-out Rate (%)	0.8	0.6	6.5	0.0	n/a	0.0
H.S. Diplomas (#)	220	202	7	7	0	4

Mt Lebanon SD
7 Horsman Dr • Pittsburgh, PA 15228-1107
(412) 344-2077 • http://www.mtlebanon.k12.pa.us
Grade Span: KG-12; **Agency Type:** 1
Schools: 10
  7 Primary; 2 Middle; 1 High; 0 Other Level
  10 Regular; 0 Special Education; 0 Vocational; 0 Alternative
  0 Magnet; 0 Charter; 5 Title I Eligible; 0 School-wide Title I
Students: 5,551   (n/a% male; n/a% female)
  Individual Education Program: 599 (10.8%);
  English Language Learner: n/a; Migrant: 0 (0.0%)
  Eligible for Free Lunch Program: 20 (0.4%)
  Eligible for Reduced-Price Lunch Program: 19 (0.3%)
Teachers: 373.8 (14.9 to 1)
Librarians/Media Specialists: 10.0 (555.1 to 1)
Guidance Counselors: 12.0 (462.6 to 1)
Current Spending: ($ per student per year):
  Total: $9,327; Instruction: $5,982; Support Services: $3,139

Enrollment, Drop-out Rates and Diploma Recipients by Race/Ethnicity

Category	Total	White	Black	Asian	AIAN	Hisp.
Enrollment (%)	100.0	94.1	1.5	3.5	0.1	0.9
Drop-out Rate (%)	0.7	0.8	0.0	0.0	0.0	0.0
H.S. Diplomas (#)	452	426	5	19	0	2

North Allegheny SD
200 Hillvue Ln • Pittsburgh, PA 15237-5344
(412) 366-2100 • http://NAllegheny.k12.pa.us
Grade Span: KG-12; **Agency Type:** 1
Schools: 12
   7 Primary; 3 Middle; 1 High; 1 Other Level
   12 Regular; 0 Special Education; 0 Vocational; 0 Alternative
   0 Magnet; 0 Charter; 0 Title I Eligible; 0 School-wide Title I
Students: 8,185 (n/a% male; n/a% female)
   Individual Education Program: 800 (9.8%);
   English Language Learner: n/a; Migrant: 0 (0.0%)
   Eligible for Free Lunch Program: 103 (1.3%)
   Eligible for Reduced-Price Lunch Program: 78 (1.0%)
Teachers: 553.2 (14.8 to 1)
Librarians/Media Specialists: 14.0 (584.6 to 1)
Guidance Counselors: 22.0 (372.0 to 1)
Current Spending: ($ per student per year):
   Total: $9,515; Instruction: $6,262; Support Services: $3,031

Enrollment, Drop-out Rates and Diploma Recipients by Race/Ethnicity

Category	Total	White	Black	Asian	AIAN	Hisp.
Enrollment (%)	100.0	92.7	1.1	5.6	0.1	0.5
Drop-out Rate (%)	0.5	0.4	2.3	1.2	0.0	0.0
H.S. Diplomas (#)	685	661	8	15	0	1

North Hills SD
135 6th Ave • Pittsburgh, PA 15229-1291
(412) 318-1000 • http://www.nhsd.k12.pa.us
Grade Span: KG-12; **Agency Type:** 1
Schools: 9
   7 Primary; 1 Middle; 1 High; 0 Other Level
   9 Regular; 0 Special Education; 0 Vocational; 0 Alternative
   0 Magnet; 0 Charter; 3 Title I Eligible; 0 School-wide Title I
Students: 4,859 (n/a% male; n/a% female)
   Individual Education Program: 588 (12.1%);
   English Language Learner: n/a; Migrant: 0 (0.0%)
   Eligible for Free Lunch Program: 338 (7.0%)
   Eligible for Reduced-Price Lunch Program: 273 (5.6%)
Teachers: 333.9 (14.6 to 1)
Librarians/Media Specialists: 5.0 (971.8 to 1)
Guidance Counselors: 12.5 (388.7 to 1)
Current Spending: ($ per student per year):
   Total: $9,716; Instruction: $6,255; Support Services: $3,145

Enrollment, Drop-out Rates and Diploma Recipients by Race/Ethnicity

Category	Total	White	Black	Asian	AIAN	Hisp.
Enrollment (%)	100.0	95.4	2.3	1.6	0.1	0.6
Drop-out Rate (%)	1.2	1.0	5.4	8.3	n/a	0.0
H.S. Diplomas (#)	385	368	10	2	0	5

Northgate SD
591 Union Ave • Pittsburgh, PA 15202-2958
(412) 734-8001 • http://www.northgate.k12.pa.us
Grade Span: KG-12; **Agency Type:** 1
Schools: 3
   2 Primary; 0 Middle; 1 High; 0 Other Level
   3 Regular; 0 Special Education; 0 Vocational; 0 Alternative
   0 Magnet; 0 Charter; 3 Title I Eligible; 0 School-wide Title I
Students: 1,526 (n/a% male; n/a% female)
   Individual Education Program: 204 (13.4%);
   English Language Learner: n/a; Migrant: 0 (0.0%)
   Eligible for Free Lunch Program: 393 (25.8%)
   Eligible for Reduced-Price Lunch Program: 131 (8.6%)
Teachers: 107.5 (14.2 to 1)
Librarians/Media Specialists: 2.0 (763.0 to 1)
Guidance Counselors: 4.0 (381.5 to 1)
Current Spending: ($ per student per year):
   Total: $8,214; Instruction: $5,351; Support Services: $2,559

Enrollment, Drop-out Rates and Diploma Recipients by Race/Ethnicity

Category	Total	White	Black	Asian	AIAN	Hisp.
Enrollment (%)	100.0	87.7	10.9	1.0	0.0	0.3
Drop-out Rate (%)	2.3	2.5	0.0	0.0	n/a	0.0
H.S. Diplomas (#)	99	86	12	1	0	0

Penn Hills SD
309 Collins Dr • Pittsburgh, PA 15235-3839
(412) 793-7000 • http://www.phsd.k12.pa.us
Grade Span: KG-12; **Agency Type:** 1
Schools: 8
   6 Primary; 1 Middle; 1 High; 0 Other Level
   8 Regular; 0 Special Education; 0 Vocational; 0 Alternative

   0 Magnet; 0 Charter; 7 Title I Eligible; 0 School-wide Title I
Students: 5,891 (n/a% male; n/a% female)
   Individual Education Program: 846 (14.4%);
   English Language Learner: n/a; Migrant: 0 (0.0%)
   Eligible for Free Lunch Program: 1,424 (24.2%)
   Eligible for Reduced-Price Lunch Program: 562 (9.5%)
Teachers: 436.5 (13.5 to 1)
Librarians/Media Specialists: 7.0 (841.6 to 1)
Guidance Counselors: 13.0 (453.2 to 1)
Current Spending: ($ per student per year):
   Total: $8,265; Instruction: $5,114; Support Services: $2,830

Enrollment, Drop-out Rates and Diploma Recipients by Race/Ethnicity

Category	Total	White	Black	Asian	AIAN	Hisp.
Enrollment (%)	100.0	50.3	48.6	0.6	0.0	0.5
Drop-out Rate (%)	2.4	1.9	3.2	0.0	n/a	0.0
H.S. Diplomas (#)	411	261	149	1	0	0

Pine-Richland SD
702 Warrendale Rd • Gibsonia, PA 15044-9534
(724) 625-7773 • http://www.prsd.k12.pa.us
Grade Span: KG-12; **Agency Type:** 1
Schools: 5
   3 Primary; 1 Middle; 1 High; 0 Other Level
   5 Regular; 0 Special Education; 0 Vocational; 0 Alternative
   0 Magnet; 0 Charter; 1 Title I Eligible; 0 School-wide Title I
Students: 3,715 (n/a% male; n/a% female)
   Individual Education Program: 417 (11.2%);
   English Language Learner: n/a; Migrant: 0 (0.0%)
   Eligible for Free Lunch Program: 73 (2.0%)
   Eligible for Reduced-Price Lunch Program: 50 (1.3%)
Teachers: 262.7 (14.1 to 1)
Librarians/Media Specialists: 5.0 (743.0 to 1)
Guidance Counselors: 8.0 (464.4 to 1)
Current Spending: ($ per student per year):
   Total: $8,342; Instruction: $5,420; Support Services: $2,641

Enrollment, Drop-out Rates and Diploma Recipients by Race/Ethnicity

Category	Total	White	Black	Asian	AIAN	Hisp.
Enrollment (%)	100.0	97.4	1.0	1.0	0.1	0.4
Drop-out Rate (%)	0.5	0.5	0.0	0.0	n/a	n/a
H.S. Diplomas (#)	261	258	1	2	0	0

Pittsburgh SD
341 S Bellefield Ave • Pittsburgh, PA 15213-3552
(412) 622-3500 • http://www.pps.pgh.pa.us
Grade Span: KG-12; **Agency Type:** 1
Schools: 92
   57 Primary; 19 Middle; 12 High; 4 Other Level
   88 Regular; 4 Special Education; 0 Vocational; 0 Alternative
   17 Magnet; 0 Charter; 79 Title I Eligible; 57 School-wide Title I
Students: 34,658 (n/a% male; n/a% female)
   Individual Education Program: 6,230 (18.0%);
   English Language Learner: n/a; Migrant: 0 (0.0%)
   Eligible for Free Lunch Program: 19,463 (56.2%)
   Eligible for Reduced-Price Lunch Program: 1,636 (4.7%)
Teachers: 2,686.5 (12.9 to 1)
Librarians/Media Specialists: 57.8 (599.6 to 1)
Guidance Counselors: 69.0 (502.3 to 1)
Current Spending: ($ per student per year):
   Total: $10,902; Instruction: $6,043; Support Services: $4,446

Enrollment, Drop-out Rates and Diploma Recipients by Race/Ethnicity

Category	Total	White	Black	Asian	AIAN	Hisp.
Enrollment (%)	100.0	38.6	59.0	1.6	0.1	0.7
Drop-out Rate (%)	5.4	4.7	6.0	4.8	18.2	2.0
H.S. Diplomas (#)	1,899	1,031	828	26	3	11

Plum Borough SD
200 School Rd • Plum, PA 15239-1453
(412) 795-0100 • http://www.pbsd.k12.pa.us
Grade Span: KG-12; **Agency Type:** 1
Schools: 7
   5 Primary; 1 Middle; 1 High; 0 Other Level
   7 Regular; 0 Special Education; 0 Vocational; 0 Alternative
   0 Magnet; 0 Charter; 5 Title I Eligible; 0 School-wide Title I
Students: 4,397 (n/a% male; n/a% female)
   Individual Education Program: 373 (8.5%);
   English Language Learner: n/a; Migrant: 0 (0.0%)
   Eligible for Free Lunch Program: 312 (7.1%)
   Eligible for Reduced-Price Lunch Program: 127 (2.9%)
Teachers: 260.0 (16.9 to 1)
Librarians/Media Specialists: 4.0 (1,099.3 to 1)
Guidance Counselors: 9.0 (488.6 to 1)
Current Spending: ($ per student per year):
   Total: $7,375; Instruction: $4,817; Support Services: $2,269

Enrollment, Drop-out Rates and Diploma Recipients by Race/Ethnicity

Category	Total	White	Black	Asian	AIAN	Hisp.
Enrollment (%)	100.0	95.0	3.5	0.9	0.1	0.4
Drop-out Rate (%)	0.9	0.9	0.0	0.0	0.0	0.0
H.S. Diplomas (#)	324	306	8	5	3	2

Quaker Valley SD
203 Graham St · Sewickley, PA 15143-1813
(412) 749-3600 · http://www.qvsd.org
Grade Span: KG-12; **Agency Type:** 1
Schools: 4
  2 Primary; 1 Middle; 1 High; 0 Other Level
  4 Regular; 0 Special Education; 0 Vocational; 0 Alternative
  0 Magnet; 0 Charter; 2 Title I Eligible; 0 School-wide Title I
Students: 1,962   (n/a% male; n/a% female)
  Individual Education Program: 248 (12.6%);
  English Language Learner: n/a; Migrant: 0 (0.0%)
  Eligible for Free Lunch Program: 165 (8.4%)
  Eligible for Reduced-Price Lunch Program: 46 (2.3%)
Teachers: 135.8 (14.4 to 1)
Librarians/Media Specialists: 4.0 (490.5 to 1)
Guidance Counselors: 6.0 (327.0 to 1)
Current Spending: ($ per student per year):
  Total: $10,564; Instruction: $6,417; Support Services: $3,874

Enrollment, Drop-out Rates and Diploma Recipients by Race/Ethnicity

Category	Total	White	Black	Asian	AIAN	Hisp.
Enrollment (%)	100.0	89.6	7.6	1.5	0.3	1.0
Drop-out Rate (%)	0.9	0.8	2.4	0.0	n/a	0.0
H.S. Diplomas (#)	146	137	8	1	0	0

Shaler Area SD
1800 Mount Royal Blvd · Glenshaw, PA 15116-2117
(412) 492-1200 · http://sasd.k12.pa.us
Grade Span: KG-12; **Agency Type:** 1
Schools: 8
  5 Primary; 1 Middle; 1 High; 1 Other Level
  8 Regular; 0 Special Education; 0 Vocational; 0 Alternative
  0 Magnet; 0 Charter; 5 Title I Eligible; 0 School-wide Title I
Students: 5,595   (n/a% male; n/a% female)
  Individual Education Program: 1,008 (18.0%);
  English Language Learner: n/a; Migrant: 0 (0.0%)
  Eligible for Free Lunch Program: 634 (11.3%)
  Eligible for Reduced-Price Lunch Program: 252 (4.5%)
Teachers: 380.8 (14.7 to 1)
Librarians/Media Specialists: 8.0 (699.4 to 1)
Guidance Counselors: 9.0 (621.7 to 1)
Current Spending: ($ per student per year):
  Total: $8,467; Instruction: $5,408; Support Services: $2,810

Enrollment, Drop-out Rates and Diploma Recipients by Race/Ethnicity

Category	Total	White	Black	Asian	AIAN	Hisp.
Enrollment (%)	100.0	97.9	1.0	0.6	0.4	0.2
Drop-out Rate (%)	1.3	1.3	0.0	0.0	0.0	0.0
H.S. Diplomas (#)	418	417	0	0	1	0

South Allegheny SD
2743 Washington Blvd · Mc Keesport, PA 15133-2017
(412) 675-3070
Grade Span: KG-12; **Agency Type:** 1
Schools: 3
  2 Primary; 0 Middle; 1 High; 0 Other Level
  3 Regular; 0 Special Education; 0 Vocational; 0 Alternative
  0 Magnet; 0 Charter; 1 Title I Eligible; 0 School-wide Title I
Students: 1,834   (n/a% male; n/a% female)
  Individual Education Program: 252 (13.7%);
  English Language Learner: n/a; Migrant: 0 (0.0%)
  Eligible for Free Lunch Program: 239 (13.0%)
  Eligible for Reduced-Price Lunch Program: 133 (7.3%)
Teachers: 114.0 (16.1 to 1)
Librarians/Media Specialists: 2.0 (917.0 to 1)
Guidance Counselors: 5.0 (366.8 to 1)
Current Spending: ($ per student per year):
  Total: $7,302; Instruction: $4,402; Support Services: $2,617

Enrollment, Drop-out Rates and Diploma Recipients by Race/Ethnicity

Category	Total	White	Black	Asian	AIAN	Hisp.
Enrollment (%)	100.0	97.9	1.3	0.2	0.1	0.4
Drop-out Rate (%)	0.8	0.9	0.0	0.0	0.0	0.0
H.S. Diplomas (#)	123	123	0	0	0	0

South Fayette Township SD
2250 Old Oakdale Rd · Mc Donald, PA 15057-2580
(412) 221-4542
Grade Span: KG-12; **Agency Type:** 1
Schools: 3
  1 Primary; 1 Middle; 1 High; 0 Other Level
  3 Regular; 0 Special Education; 0 Vocational; 0 Alternative

---

  0 Magnet; 0 Charter; 2 Title I Eligible; 0 School-wide Title I
Students: 1,868   (n/a% male; n/a% female)
  Individual Education Program: 173 (9.3%);
  English Language Learner: n/a; Migrant: 0 (0.0%)
  Eligible for Free Lunch Program: 79 (4.2%)
  Eligible for Reduced-Price Lunch Program: 55 (2.9%)
Teachers: 121.0 (15.4 to 1)
Librarians/Media Specialists: 3.0 (622.7 to 1)
Guidance Counselors: 4.0 (467.0 to 1)
Current Spending: ($ per student per year):
  Total: $9,661; Instruction: $5,905; Support Services: $3,395

Enrollment, Drop-out Rates and Diploma Recipients by Race/Ethnicity

Category	Total	White	Black	Asian	AIAN	Hisp.
Enrollment (%)	100.0	92.8	4.5	2.0	0.1	0.6
Drop-out Rate (%)	0.6	0.4	5.0	0.0	n/a	0.0
H.S. Diplomas (#)	94	90	3	1	0	0

South Park SD
2178 Ridge Rd · South Park, PA 15129-8885
(412) 655-3111
Grade Span: KG-12; **Agency Type:** 1
Schools: 3
  1 Primary; 1 Middle; 1 High; 0 Other Level
  3 Regular; 0 Special Education; 0 Vocational; 0 Alternative
  0 Magnet; 0 Charter; 2 Title I Eligible; 0 School-wide Title I
Students: 2,238   (n/a% male; n/a% female)
  Individual Education Program: 225 (10.1%);
  English Language Learner: n/a; Migrant: 0 (0.0%)
  Eligible for Free Lunch Program: 88 (3.9%)
  Eligible for Reduced-Price Lunch Program: 55 (2.5%)
Teachers: 118.5 (18.9 to 1)
Librarians/Media Specialists: 3.0 (746.0 to 1)
Guidance Counselors: 5.0 (447.6 to 1)
Current Spending: ($ per student per year):
  Total: $7,398; Instruction: $4,475; Support Services: $2,678

Enrollment, Drop-out Rates and Diploma Recipients by Race/Ethnicity

Category	Total	White	Black	Asian	AIAN	Hisp.
Enrollment (%)	100.0	94.7	4.2	0.8	0.1	0.1
Drop-out Rate (%)	1.3	1.1	5.9	0.0	n/a	n/a
H.S. Diplomas (#)	168	164	4	0	0	0

Steel Valley SD
220 E Oliver Rd · Munhall, PA 15120-2759
(412) 464-3650
Grade Span: KG-12; **Agency Type:** 1
Schools: 5
  3 Primary; 1 Middle; 1 High; 0 Other Level
  5 Regular; 0 Special Education; 0 Vocational; 0 Alternative
  0 Magnet; 0 Charter; 3 Title I Eligible; 1 School-wide Title I
Students: 2,116   (n/a% male; n/a% female)
  Individual Education Program: 281 (13.3%);
  English Language Learner: n/a; Migrant: 0 (0.0%)
  Eligible for Free Lunch Program: 703 (33.2%)
  Eligible for Reduced-Price Lunch Program: 153 (7.2%)
Teachers: 139.0 (15.2 to 1)
Librarians/Media Specialists: 3.0 (705.3 to 1)
Guidance Counselors: 5.0 (423.2 to 1)
Current Spending: ($ per student per year):
  Total: $7,780; Instruction: $5,180; Support Services: $2,329

Enrollment, Drop-out Rates and Diploma Recipients by Race/Ethnicity

Category	Total	White	Black	Asian	AIAN	Hisp.
Enrollment (%)	100.0	71.0	26.5	2.2	0.1	0.2
Drop-out Rate (%)	1.7	0.9	5.3	0.0	n/a	0.0
H.S. Diplomas (#)	160	124	26	8	0	2

Sto-Rox SD
19 May Ave Ste 205 · Mckees Rocks, PA 15136-3615
(412) 778-8871
Grade Span: KG-12; **Agency Type:** 1
Schools: 4
  2 Primary; 1 Middle; 1 High; 0 Other Level
  4 Regular; 0 Special Education; 0 Vocational; 0 Alternative
  0 Magnet; 0 Charter; 4 Title I Eligible; 1 School-wide Title I
Students: 1,528   (n/a% male; n/a% female)
  Individual Education Program: 358 (23.4%);
  English Language Learner: n/a; Migrant: 0 (0.0%)
  Eligible for Free Lunch Program: 884 (57.9%)
  Eligible for Reduced-Price Lunch Program: 165 (10.8%)
Teachers: 109.0 (14.0 to 1)
Librarians/Media Specialists: 3.0 (509.3 to 1)
Guidance Counselors: 4.0 (382.0 to 1)
Current Spending: ($ per student per year):
  Total: $10,950; Instruction: $6,703; Support Services: $3,779

Enrollment, Drop-out Rates and Diploma Recipients by Race/Ethnicity

Category	Total	White	Black	Asian	AIAN	Hisp.
Enrollment (%)	100.0	64.2	34.8	0.5	0.1	0.5
Drop-out Rate (%)	2.7	2.9	2.2	0.0	n/a	0.0
H.S. Diplomas (#)	74	59	14	0	0	1

Upper Saint Clair SD
1820 Mclughln Rn Rd Upr St Clr • Pittsburgh, PA 15241-2396
(412) 833-1600 • http://www.uscsd.k12.pa.us
Grade Span: KG-12; Agency Type: 1
Schools: 6
 3 Primary; 2 Middle; 1 High; 0 Other Level
 6 Regular; 0 Special Education; 0 Vocational; 0 Alternative
 0 Magnet; 0 Charter; 2 Title I Eligible; 0 School-wide Title I
Students: 4,127 (n/a% male; n/a% female)
 Individual Education Program: 428 (10.4%);
 English Language Learner: n/a; Migrant: 0 (0.0%)
 Eligible for Free Lunch Program: 38 (0.9%)
 Eligible for Reduced-Price Lunch Program: 17 (0.4%)
Teachers: 261.3 (15.8 to 1)
Librarians/Media Specialists: 6.0 (687.8 to 1)
Guidance Counselors: 13.0 (317.5 to 1)
Current Spending: ($ per student per year):
 Total: $9,370; Instruction: $5,840; Support Services: $3,195

Enrollment, Drop-out Rates and Diploma Recipients by Race/Ethnicity

Category	Total	White	Black	Asian	AIAN	Hisp.
Enrollment (%)	100.0	93.5	0.8	5.2	0.0	0.5
Drop-out Rate (%)	0.0	0.0	0.0	0.0	n/a	0.0
H.S. Diplomas (#)	308	284	5	17	0	2

West Allegheny SD
PO Box 55 • Imperial, PA 15126-0055
(724) 695-3422 • http://www.westallegheny.k12.pa.us
Grade Span: KG-12; Agency Type: 1
Schools: 5
 3 Primary; 1 Middle; 1 High; 0 Other Level
 5 Regular; 0 Special Education; 0 Vocational; 0 Alternative
 0 Magnet; 0 Charter; 3 Title I Eligible; 0 School-wide Title I
Students: 3,204 (n/a% male; n/a% female)
 Individual Education Program: 414 (12.9%);
 English Language Learner: n/a; Migrant: 0 (0.0%)
 Eligible for Free Lunch Program: 320 (10.0%)
 Eligible for Reduced-Price Lunch Program: 181 (5.6%)
Teachers: 217.0 (14.8 to 1)
Librarians/Media Specialists: 5.0 (640.8 to 1)
Guidance Counselors: 7.0 (457.7 to 1)
Current Spending: ($ per student per year):
 Total: $9,100; Instruction: $5,445; Support Services: $3,367

Enrollment, Drop-out Rates and Diploma Recipients by Race/Ethnicity

Category	Total	White	Black	Asian	AIAN	Hisp.
Enrollment (%)	100.0	95.1	3.1	1.4	0.1	0.4
Drop-out Rate (%)	2.2	2.2	0.0	0.0	n/a	0.0
H.S. Diplomas (#)	206	195	10	1	0	0

West Jefferson Hills SD
835 Old Clairton Rd • Jefferson Hills, PA 15025-3131
(412) 655-8452
Grade Span: KG-12; Agency Type: 1
Schools: 5
 3 Primary; 1 Middle; 1 High; 0 Other Level
 5 Regular; 0 Special Education; 0 Vocational; 0 Alternative
 0 Magnet; 0 Charter; 2 Title I Eligible; 0 School-wide Title I
Students: 2,911 (n/a% male; n/a% female)
 Individual Education Program: 319 (11.0%);
 English Language Learner: n/a; Migrant: 0 (0.0%)
 Eligible for Free Lunch Program: 139 (4.8%)
 Eligible for Reduced-Price Lunch Program: 88 (3.0%)
Teachers: 159.5 (18.3 to 1)
Librarians/Media Specialists: 4.0 (727.8 to 1)
Guidance Counselors: 4.0 (727.8 to 1)
Current Spending: ($ per student per year):
 Total: $7,762; Instruction: $4,700; Support Services: $2,810

Enrollment, Drop-out Rates and Diploma Recipients by Race/Ethnicity

Category	Total	White	Black	Asian	AIAN	Hisp.
Enrollment (%)	100.0	96.5	2.4	0.8	0.2	0.2
Drop-out Rate (%)	1.3	1.3	0.0	0.0	0.0	0.0
H.S. Diplomas (#)	212	208	2	2	0	0

West Mifflin Area SD
515 Camp Hollow Rd • West Mifflin, PA 15122-2697
(412) 466-9131 • http://www.wmasd.org
Grade Span: KG-12; Agency Type: 1
Schools: 6
 4 Primary; 1 Middle; 1 High; 0 Other Level
 6 Regular; 0 Special Education; 0 Vocational; 0 Alternative

---

 0 Magnet; 0 Charter; 4 Title I Eligible; 0 School-wide Title I
Students: 3,301 (n/a% male; n/a% female)
 Individual Education Program: 431 (13.1%);
 English Language Learner: n/a; Migrant: 0 (0.0%)
 Eligible for Free Lunch Program: 679 (20.6%)
 Eligible for Reduced-Price Lunch Program: 175 (5.3%)
Teachers: 180.0 (18.3 to 1)
Librarians/Media Specialists: 5.0 (660.2 to 1)
Guidance Counselors: 3.0 (1,100.3 to 1)
Current Spending: ($ per student per year):
 Total: $8,030; Instruction: $4,734; Support Services: $3,012

Enrollment, Drop-out Rates and Diploma Recipients by Race/Ethnicity

Category	Total	White	Black	Asian	AIAN	Hisp.
Enrollment (%)	100.0	80.6	18.7	0.2	0.0	0.5
Drop-out Rate (%)	0.8	0.6	1.6	0.0	n/a	0.0
H.S. Diplomas (#)	208	185	22	1	0	0

Wilkinsburg Borough SD
718 Wallace Ave • Wilkinsburg, PA 15221-2215
(412) 371-9667
Grade Span: PK-12; Agency Type: 1
Schools: 5
 3 Primary; 1 Middle; 1 High; 0 Other Level
 5 Regular; 0 Special Education; 0 Vocational; 0 Alternative
 0 Magnet; 0 Charter; 3 Title I Eligible; 3 School-wide Title I
Students: 1,661 (n/a% male; n/a% female)
 Individual Education Program: 422 (25.4%);
 English Language Learner: n/a; Migrant: 0 (0.0%)
 Eligible for Free Lunch Program: 1,187 (71.5%)
 Eligible for Reduced-Price Lunch Program: 139 (8.4%)
Teachers: 152.0 (10.9 to 1)
Librarians/Media Specialists: 1.0 (1,661.0 to 1)
Guidance Counselors: 4.0 (415.3 to 1)
Current Spending: ($ per student per year):
 Total: $10,987; Instruction: $6,918; Support Services: $3,663

Enrollment, Drop-out Rates and Diploma Recipients by Race/Ethnicity

Category	Total	White	Black	Asian	AIAN	Hisp.
Enrollment (%)	100.0	1.9	97.9	0.1	0.0	0.2
Drop-out Rate (%)	11.2	10.0	11.2	n/a	n/a	n/a
H.S. Diplomas (#)	74	5	69	0	0	0

Woodland Hills SD
2430 Greensburg Pike • Pittsburgh, PA 15221-3611
(412) 731-1300 • http://www.whsd.k12.pa.us
Grade Span: KG-12; Agency Type: 1
Schools: 9
 3 Primary; 5 Middle; 1 High; 0 Other Level
 9 Regular; 0 Special Education; 0 Vocational; 0 Alternative
 0 Magnet; 0 Charter; 8 Title I Eligible; 6 School-wide Title I
Students: 5,797 (n/a% male; n/a% female)
 Individual Education Program: 942 (16.2%);
 English Language Learner: n/a; Migrant: 0 (0.0%)
 Eligible for Free Lunch Program: 2,377 (41.0%)
 Eligible for Reduced-Price Lunch Program: 481 (8.3%)
Teachers: 363.8 (15.9 to 1)
Librarians/Media Specialists: 9.5 (610.2 to 1)
Guidance Counselors: 15.0 (386.5 to 1)
Current Spending: ($ per student per year):
 Total: $9,549; Instruction: $5,907; Support Services: $3,300

Enrollment, Drop-out Rates and Diploma Recipients by Race/Ethnicity

Category	Total	White	Black	Asian	AIAN	Hisp.
Enrollment (%)	100.0	43.1	55.5	0.8	0.1	0.5
Drop-out Rate (%)	4.2	2.9	6.0	0.0	0.0	0.0
H.S. Diplomas (#)	359	247	108	4	0	0

Armstrong County

Apollo-Ridge SD
PO Box 219 • Spring Church, PA 15686-0219
(724) 478-1141
Grade Span: KG-12; Agency Type: 1
Schools: 7
 4 Primary; 1 Middle; 1 High; 1 Other Level
 7 Regular; 0 Special Education; 0 Vocational; 0 Alternative
 0 Magnet; 0 Charter; 6 Title I Eligible; 0 School-wide Title I
Students: 1,638 (n/a% male; n/a% female)
 Individual Education Program: 240 (14.7%);
 English Language Learner: n/a; Migrant: 0 (0.0%)
 Eligible for Free Lunch Program: 518 (31.6%)
 Eligible for Reduced-Price Lunch Program: 158 (9.6%)
Teachers: 99.0 (16.5 to 1)
Librarians/Media Specialists: 3.0 (546.0 to 1)
Guidance Counselors: 4.0 (409.5 to 1)
Current Spending: ($ per student per year):
 Total: $8,024; Instruction: $4,962; Support Services: $2,652

Enrollment, Drop-out Rates and Diploma Recipients by Race/Ethnicity

Category	Total	White	Black	Asian	AIAN	Hisp.
Enrollment (%)	100.0	97.5	2.0	0.3	0.1	0.1
Drop-out Rate (%)	3.4	3.3	10.0	0.0	n/a	0.0
H.S. Diplomas (#)	89	88	1	0	0	0

Armstrong SD
410 Main St • Ford City, PA 16226-1613
(724) 763-7151 • http://www.asd.k12.pa.us
Grade Span: KG-12; **Agency Type:** 1
Schools: 13
  8 Primary; 1 Middle; 4 High; 0 Other Level
  13 Regular; 0 Special Education; 0 Vocational; 0 Alternative
  0 Magnet; 0 Charter; 8 Title I Eligible; 0 School-wide Title I
Students: 6,425 (n/a% male; n/a% female)
  Individual Education Program: 1,023 (15.9%);
  English Language Learner: n/a; Migrant: 0 (0.0%)
  Eligible for Free Lunch Program: 1,344 (20.9%)
  Eligible for Reduced-Price Lunch Program: 599 (9.3%)
Teachers: 442.0 (14.5 to 1)
Librarians/Media Specialists: 10.0 (642.5 to 1)
Guidance Counselors: 9.0 (713.9 to 1)
Current Spending: ($ per student per year):
  Total: $9,313; Instruction: $5,763; Support Services: $3,213

Enrollment, Drop-out Rates and Diploma Recipients by Race/Ethnicity

Category	Total	White	Black	Asian	AIAN	Hisp.
Enrollment (%)	100.0	98.8	0.9	0.1	0.0	0.2
Drop-out Rate (%)	2.6	2.6	0.0	0.0	0.0	0.0
H.S. Diplomas (#)	388	380	7	0	1	0

Freeport Area SD
PO Box C • Freeport, PA 16229-0303
(724) 295-5141 • http://www.freeport.k12.pa.us
Grade Span: KG-12; **Agency Type:** 1
Schools: 5
  3 Primary; 1 Middle; 1 High; 0 Other Level
  5 Regular; 0 Special Education; 0 Vocational; 0 Alternative
  0 Magnet; 0 Charter; 3 Title I Eligible; 0 School-wide Title I
Students: 1,950 (n/a% male; n/a% female)
  Individual Education Program: 207 (10.6%);
  English Language Learner: n/a; Migrant: 0 (0.0%)
  Eligible for Free Lunch Program: 216 (11.1%)
  Eligible for Reduced-Price Lunch Program: 155 (7.9%)
Teachers: 127.0 (15.4 to 1)
Librarians/Media Specialists: 4.0 (487.5 to 1)
Guidance Counselors: 4.0 (487.5 to 1)
Current Spending: ($ per student per year):
  Total: $8,877; Instruction: $5,765; Support Services: $2,684

Enrollment, Drop-out Rates and Diploma Recipients by Race/Ethnicity

Category	Total	White	Black	Asian	AIAN	Hisp.
Enrollment (%)	100.0	98.8	1.0	0.2	0.1	0.1
Drop-out Rate (%)	0.5	0.5	0.0	0.0	n/a	n/a
H.S. Diplomas (#)	117	117	0	0	0	0

Beaver County

Ambridge Area SD
740 Park Rd • Ambridge, PA 15003-2474
(724) 266-8870 • http://www.ambridge.k12.pa.us
Grade Span: KG-12; **Agency Type:** 1
Schools: 5
  3 Primary; 1 Middle; 1 High; 0 Other Level
  5 Regular; 0 Special Education; 0 Vocational; 0 Alternative
  0 Magnet; 0 Charter; 2 Title I Eligible; 0 School-wide Title I
Students: 3,043 (n/a% male; n/a% female)
  Individual Education Program: 601 (19.8%);
  English Language Learner: n/a; Migrant: 0 (0.0%)
  Eligible for Free Lunch Program: 493 (16.2%)
  Eligible for Reduced-Price Lunch Program: 175 (5.8%)
Teachers: 191.5 (15.9 to 1)
Librarians/Media Specialists: 4.0 (760.8 to 1)
Guidance Counselors: 4.0 (760.8 to 1)
Current Spending: ($ per student per year):
  Total: $8,083; Instruction: $5,001; Support Services: $2,779

Enrollment, Drop-out Rates and Diploma Recipients by Race/Ethnicity

Category	Total	White	Black	Asian	AIAN	Hisp.
Enrollment (%)	100.0	90.0	8.9	0.5	0.1	0.5
Drop-out Rate (%)	1.2	0.9	4.3	16.7	0.0	0.0
H.S. Diplomas (#)	234	221	13	0	0	0

Beaver Area SD
855 2nd St • Beaver, PA 15009-2600
(724) 774-4010 • http://www.basd.k12.pa.us
Grade Span: KG-12; **Agency Type:** 1
Schools: 4

  2 Primary; 1 Middle; 1 High; 0 Other Level
  4 Regular; 0 Special Education; 0 Vocational; 0 Alternative
  0 Magnet; 0 Charter; 3 Title I Eligible; 0 School-wide Title I
Students: 2,073 (n/a% male; n/a% female)
  Individual Education Program: 196 (9.5%);
  English Language Learner: n/a; Migrant: 0 (0.0%)
  Eligible for Free Lunch Program: 101 (4.9%)
  Eligible for Reduced-Price Lunch Program: 35 (1.7%)
Teachers: 125.0 (16.6 to 1)
Librarians/Media Specialists: 2.0 (1,036.5 to 1)
Guidance Counselors: 7.0 (296.1 to 1)
Current Spending: ($ per student per year):
  Total: $7,257; Instruction: $4,457; Support Services: $2,620

Enrollment, Drop-out Rates and Diploma Recipients by Race/Ethnicity

Category	Total	White	Black	Asian	AIAN	Hisp.
Enrollment (%)	100.0	97.3	1.7	0.3	0.0	0.5
Drop-out Rate (%)	0.4	0.5	0.0	0.0	n/a	0.0
H.S. Diplomas (#)	153	152	1	0	0	0

Big Beaver Falls Area SD
820 16th St • Beaver Falls, PA 15010-4065
(724) 843-3470 • http://www.tigerweb.org
Grade Span: KG-12; **Agency Type:** 1
Schools: 5
  3 Primary; 1 Middle; 1 High; 0 Other Level
  5 Regular; 0 Special Education; 0 Vocational; 0 Alternative
  0 Magnet; 0 Charter; 5 Title I Eligible; 0 School-wide Title I
Students: 1,929 (n/a% male; n/a% female)
  Individual Education Program: 237 (12.3%);
  English Language Learner: n/a; Migrant: 0 (0.0%)
  Eligible for Free Lunch Program: 853 (44.2%)
  Eligible for Reduced-Price Lunch Program: 228 (11.8%)
Teachers: 144.0 (13.4 to 1)
Librarians/Media Specialists: 3.0 (643.0 to 1)
Guidance Counselors: 7.0 (275.6 to 1)
Current Spending: ($ per student per year):
  Total: $8,757; Instruction: $5,176; Support Services: $3,168

Enrollment, Drop-out Rates and Diploma Recipients by Race/Ethnicity

Category	Total	White	Black	Asian	AIAN	Hisp.
Enrollment (%)	100.0	70.5	28.4	0.5	0.1	0.6
Drop-out Rate (%)	7.2	7.4	6.7	n/a	n/a	0.0
H.S. Diplomas (#)	119	84	35	0	0	0

Blackhawk SD
500 Blackhawk Rd • Beaver Falls, PA 15010-1410
(724) 846-6600 • http://www.ccia.com/~bhhs2/bhs1.html
Grade Span: KG-12; **Agency Type:** 1
Schools: 5
  3 Primary; 1 Middle; 1 High; 0 Other Level
  5 Regular; 0 Special Education; 0 Vocational; 0 Alternative
  0 Magnet; 0 Charter; 3 Title I Eligible; 0 School-wide Title I
Students: 2,777 (n/a% male; n/a% female)
  Individual Education Program: 240 (8.6%);
  English Language Learner: n/a; Migrant: 0 (0.0%)
  Eligible for Free Lunch Program: 259 (9.3%)
  Eligible for Reduced-Price Lunch Program: 113 (4.1%)
Teachers: 165.5 (16.8 to 1)
Librarians/Media Specialists: 3.0 (925.7 to 1)
Guidance Counselors: 6.0 (462.8 to 1)
Current Spending: ($ per student per year):
  Total: $7,573; Instruction: $4,785; Support Services: $2,484

Enrollment, Drop-out Rates and Diploma Recipients by Race/Ethnicity

Category	Total	White	Black	Asian	AIAN	Hisp.
Enrollment (%)	100.0	97.5	1.6	0.7	0.1	0.1
Drop-out Rate (%)	1.6	1.6	0.0	0.0	n/a	0.0
H.S. Diplomas (#)	221	216	3	2	0	0

Center Area SD
160 Baker Rd Ext • Monaca, PA 15061-2571
(724) 775-5600
Grade Span: KG-12; **Agency Type:** 1
Schools: 3
  1 Primary; 1 Middle; 1 High; 0 Other Level
  3 Regular; 0 Special Education; 0 Vocational; 0 Alternative
  0 Magnet; 0 Charter; 3 Title I Eligible; 0 School-wide Title I
Students: 2,015 (n/a% male; n/a% female)
  Individual Education Program: 180 (8.9%);
  English Language Learner: n/a; Migrant: 0 (0.0%)
  Eligible for Free Lunch Program: 105 (5.2%)
  Eligible for Reduced-Price Lunch Program: 61 (3.0%)
Teachers: 128.4 (15.7 to 1)
Librarians/Media Specialists: 3.0 (671.7 to 1)
Guidance Counselors: 4.0 (503.8 to 1)
Current Spending: ($ per student per year):
  Total: $7,505; Instruction: $4,950; Support Services: $2,274

Enrollment, Drop-out Rates and Diploma Recipients by Race/Ethnicity

Category	Total	White	Black	Asian	AIAN	Hisp.
Enrollment (%)	100.0	94.5	4.4	0.8	0.0	0.2
Drop-out Rate (%)	0.5	0.5	0.0	0.0	n/a	0.0
H.S. Diplomas (#)	137	130	6	0	0	1

Freedom Area SD
1701 8th Ave • Freedom, PA 15042-2000
(724) 775-7644 • http://www.freedom.k12.pa.us
Grade Span: KG-12; **Agency Type:** 1
Schools: 4
  2 Primary; 1 Middle; 1 High; 0 Other Level
  4 Regular; 0 Special Education; 0 Vocational; 0 Alternative
  0 Magnet; 0 Charter; 3 Title I Eligible; 0 School-wide Title I
Students: 1,785 (n/a% male; n/a% female)
  Individual Education Program: 224 (12.5%);
  English Language Learner: n/a; Migrant: 0 (0.0%)
  Eligible for Free Lunch Program: 361 (20.2%)
  Eligible for Reduced-Price Lunch Program: 135 (7.6%)
Teachers: 103.0 (17.3 to 1)
Librarians/Media Specialists: 3.0 (595.0 to 1)
Guidance Counselors: 3.0 (595.0 to 1)
Current Spending: ($ per student per year):
  Total: $7,280; Instruction: $4,527; Support Services: $2,403

Enrollment, Drop-out Rates and Diploma Recipients by Race/Ethnicity

Category	Total	White	Black	Asian	AIAN	Hisp.
Enrollment (%)	100.0	96.9	2.4	0.4	0.0	0.3
Drop-out Rate (%)	1.6	1.4	7.7	0.0	0.0	n/a
H.S. Diplomas (#)	129	126	3	0	0	0

Hopewell Area SD
2354 Brodhead Rd • Aliquippa, PA 15001-4501
(724) 375-6691 • http://www.hopewell.k12.pa.us
Grade Span: KG-12; **Agency Type:** 1
Schools: 6
  4 Primary; 1 Middle; 1 High; 0 Other Level
  6 Regular; 0 Special Education; 0 Vocational; 0 Alternative
  0 Magnet; 0 Charter; 5 Title I Eligible; 0 School-wide Title I
Students: 2,868 (n/a% male; n/a% female)
  Individual Education Program: 357 (12.4%);
  English Language Learner: n/a; Migrant: 0 (0.0%)
  Eligible for Free Lunch Program: 331 (11.5%)
  Eligible for Reduced-Price Lunch Program: 120 (4.2%)
Teachers: 183.9 (15.6 to 1)
Librarians/Media Specialists: 4.0 (717.0 to 1)
Guidance Counselors: 7.0 (409.7 to 1)
Current Spending: ($ per student per year):
  Total: $7,416; Instruction: $4,609; Support Services: $2,518

Enrollment, Drop-out Rates and Diploma Recipients by Race/Ethnicity

Category	Total	White	Black	Asian	AIAN	Hisp.
Enrollment (%)	100.0	96.5	2.8	0.3	0.1	0.3
Drop-out Rate (%)	1.3	1.3	0.0	0.0	0.0	0.0
H.S. Diplomas (#)	228	218	4	2	3	1

New Brighton Area SD
3225 43rd St • New Brighton, PA 15066-2655
(724) 843-1795 • http://nbsd.k12.pa.us
Grade Span: KG-12; **Agency Type:** 1
Schools: 3
  1 Primary; 1 Middle; 1 High; 0 Other Level
  3 Regular; 0 Special Education; 0 Vocational; 0 Alternative
  0 Magnet; 0 Charter; 3 Title I Eligible; 0 School-wide Title I
Students: 1,965 (n/a% male; n/a% female)
  Individual Education Program: 196 (10.0%);
  English Language Learner: n/a; Migrant: 0 (0.0%)
  Eligible for Free Lunch Program: 785 (39.9%)
  Eligible for Reduced-Price Lunch Program: 293 (14.9%)
Teachers: 119.5 (16.4 to 1)
Librarians/Media Specialists: 2.0 (982.5 to 1)
Guidance Counselors: 4.0 (491.3 to 1)
Current Spending: ($ per student per year):
  Total: $7,366; Instruction: $4,555; Support Services: $2,422

Enrollment, Drop-out Rates and Diploma Recipients by Race/Ethnicity

Category	Total	White	Black	Asian	AIAN	Hisp.
Enrollment (%)	100.0	86.1	12.9	0.3	0.2	0.6
Drop-out Rate (%)	0.7	0.6	1.9	0.0	n/a	n/a
H.S. Diplomas (#)	123	111	11	1	0	0

Riverside Beaver County SD
318 Country Club Dr • Ellwood City, PA 16117-4910
(724) 758-7512 • http://www.riverside.k12.pa.us
Grade Span: KG-12; **Agency Type:** 1
Schools: 4
  2 Primary; 1 Middle; 1 High; 0 Other Level
  4 Regular; 0 Special Education; 0 Vocational; 0 Alternative

  0 Magnet; 0 Charter; 4 Title I Eligible; 0 School-wide Title I
Students: 1,929 (n/a% male; n/a% female)
  Individual Education Program: 246 (12.8%);
  English Language Learner: n/a; Migrant: 0 (0.0%)
  Eligible for Free Lunch Program: 391 (20.3%)
  Eligible for Reduced-Price Lunch Program: 168 (8.7%)
Teachers: 119.0 (16.2 to 1)
Librarians/Media Specialists: 3.0 (643.0 to 1)
Guidance Counselors: 3.5 (551.1 to 1)
Current Spending: ($ per student per year):
  Total: $7,439; Instruction: $4,508; Support Services: $2,592

Enrollment, Drop-out Rates and Diploma Recipients by Race/Ethnicity

Category	Total	White	Black	Asian	AIAN	Hisp.
Enrollment (%)	100.0	98.9	0.7	0.1	0.1	0.3
Drop-out Rate (%)	2.8	2.9	0.0	n/a	n/a	0.0
H.S. Diplomas (#)	133	132	0	0	0	1

Western Pennsylvania Cyber CS
900 Midland Ave • Midland, PA 15059
(724) 643-1180
Grade Span: KG-12; **Agency Type:** 7
Schools: 1
  0 Primary; 0 Middle; 0 High; 1 Other Level
  1 Regular; 0 Special Education; 0 Vocational; 0 Alternative
  0 Magnet; 1 Charter; 0 Title I Eligible; 0 School-wide Title I
Students: 2,087 (n/a% male; n/a% female)
  Individual Education Program: 129 (6.2%);
  English Language Learner: n/a; Migrant: 0 (0.0%)
  Eligible for Free Lunch Program: 0 (0.0%)
  Eligible for Reduced-Price Lunch Program: 0 (0.0%)
Teachers: 39.2 (53.2 to 1)
Librarians/Media Specialists: 0.0 (n/a to 1)
Guidance Counselors: 1.0 (2,087.0 to 1)
Current Spending: ($ per student per year):
  Total: $4,781; Instruction: $2,835; Support Services: $1,946

Enrollment, Drop-out Rates and Diploma Recipients by Race/Ethnicity

Category	Total	White	Black	Asian	AIAN	Hisp.
Enrollment (%)	100.0	92.2	4.9	0.4	0.7	1.7
Drop-out Rate (%)	25.8	25.8	8.3	0.0	n/a	300.0
H.S. Diplomas (#)	57	56	1	0	0	0

Bedford County

Bedford Area SD
330 E John St • Bedford, PA 15522-1427
(814) 623-4290 • http://www.bedford.k12.pa.us
Grade Span: KG-12; **Agency Type:** 1
Schools: 5
  2 Primary; 1 Middle; 1 High; 1 Other Level
  5 Regular; 0 Special Education; 0 Vocational; 0 Alternative
  0 Magnet; 0 Charter; 4 Title I Eligible; 0 School-wide Title I
Students: 2,342 (n/a% male; n/a% female)
  Individual Education Program: 370 (15.8%);
  English Language Learner: n/a; Migrant: 1 (<0.1%)
  Eligible for Free Lunch Program: 317 (13.5%)
  Eligible for Reduced-Price Lunch Program: 156 (6.7%)
Teachers: 142.5 (16.4 to 1)
Librarians/Media Specialists: 4.0 (585.5 to 1)
Guidance Counselors: 5.0 (468.4 to 1)
Current Spending: ($ per student per year):
  Total: $7,645; Instruction: $4,855; Support Services: $2,423

Enrollment, Drop-out Rates and Diploma Recipients by Race/Ethnicity

Category	Total	White	Black	Asian	AIAN	Hisp.
Enrollment (%)	100.0	98.4	0.7	0.6	0.0	0.3
Drop-out Rate (%)	2.8	2.9	0.0	0.0	n/a	0.0
H.S. Diplomas (#)	136	136	0	0	0	0

Chestnut Ridge SD
3281 Valley Rd • Fishertown, PA 15539-9843
(814) 839-4195 • http://lion.crsd.k12.pa.us
Grade Span: KG-12; **Agency Type:** 1
Schools: 4
  2 Primary; 1 Middle; 1 High; 0 Other Level
  4 Regular; 0 Special Education; 0 Vocational; 0 Alternative
  0 Magnet; 0 Charter; 3 Title I Eligible; 0 School-wide Title I
Students: 1,828 (n/a% male; n/a% female)
  Individual Education Program: 285 (15.6%);
  English Language Learner: n/a; Migrant: 1 (0.1%)
  Eligible for Free Lunch Program: 420 (23.0%)
  Eligible for Reduced-Price Lunch Program: 232 (12.7%)
Teachers: 108.5 (16.8 to 1)
Librarians/Media Specialists: 3.0 (609.3 to 1)
Guidance Counselors: 4.0 (457.0 to 1)
Current Spending: ($ per student per year):
  Total: $7,126; Instruction: $4,310; Support Services: $2,447

Enrollment, Drop-out Rates and Diploma Recipients by Race/Ethnicity

Category	Total	White	Black	Asian	AIAN	Hisp.
Enrollment (%)	100.0	98.8	0.6	0.4	0.0	0.2
Drop-out Rate (%)	2.2	2.2	0.0	0.0	0.0	0.0
H.S. Diplomas (#)	138	135	0	3	0	0

Everett Area SD
427 E S St • Everett, PA 15537-1295
(814) 652-9114 • http://www.everett.k12.pa.us/
Grade Span: KG-12; **Agency Type:** 1
Schools: 5
    4 Primary; 0 Middle; 1 High; 0 Other Level
    5 Regular; 0 Special Education; 0 Vocational; 0 Alternative
    0 Magnet; 0 Charter; 4 Title I Eligible; 0 School-wide Title I
Students: 1,565   (n/a% male; n/a% female)
    Individual Education Program: 265 (16.9%);
    English Language Learner: n/a; Migrant: 0 (0.0%)
    Eligible for Free Lunch Program: 406 (25.9%)
    Eligible for Reduced-Price Lunch Program: 235 (15.0%)
Teachers: 94.0 (16.6 to 1)
Librarians/Media Specialists: 2.0 (782.5 to 1)
Guidance Counselors: 3.0 (521.7 to 1)
Current Spending: ($ per student per year):
    Total: $8,000; Instruction: $4,963; Support Services: $2,631

Enrollment, Drop-out Rates and Diploma Recipients by Race/Ethnicity

Category	Total	White	Black	Asian	AIAN	Hisp.
Enrollment (%)	100.0	98.8	0.8	0.2	0.1	0.1
Drop-out Rate (%)	3.6	3.7	0.0	0.0	n/a	0.0
H.S. Diplomas (#)	114	112	1	0	0	1

Berks County

Boyertown Area SD
911 Montgomery Ave • Boyertown, PA 19512-9607
(610) 367-6031 • http://www.netjunction.com/basd/index.html
Grade Span: KG-12; **Agency Type:** 1
Schools: 10
    7 Primary; 2 Middle; 1 High; 0 Other Level
    10 Regular; 0 Special Education; 0 Vocational; 0 Alternative
    0 Magnet; 0 Charter; 6 Title I Eligible; 0 School-wide Title I
Students: 6,934   (n/a% male; n/a% female)
    Individual Education Program: 887 (12.8%);
    English Language Learner: n/a; Migrant: 0 (0.0%)
    Eligible for Free Lunch Program: 386 (5.6%)
    Eligible for Reduced-Price Lunch Program: 251 (3.6%)
Teachers: 407.7 (17.0 to 1)
Librarians/Media Specialists: 9.5 (729.9 to 1)
Guidance Counselors: 13.0 (533.4 to 1)
Current Spending: ($ per student per year):
    Total: $7,298; Instruction: $4,569; Support Services: $2,448

Enrollment, Drop-out Rates and Diploma Recipients by Race/Ethnicity

Category	Total	White	Black	Asian	AIAN	Hisp.
Enrollment (%)	100.0	97.6	1.1	0.5	0.1	0.7
Drop-out Rate (%)	1.5	1.5	0.0	0.0	0.0	20.0
H.S. Diplomas (#)	464	458	1	4	0	1

Brandywine Heights Area SD
200 W Weis St • Topton, PA 19562-1532
(610) 682-5100 • http://www.bhasd.k12.pa.us
Grade Span: KG-12; **Agency Type:** 1
Schools: 5
    3 Primary; 1 Middle; 1 High; 0 Other Level
    5 Regular; 0 Special Education; 0 Vocational; 0 Alternative
    0 Magnet; 0 Charter; 4 Title I Eligible; 0 School-wide Title I
Students: 1,983   (n/a% male; n/a% female)
    Individual Education Program: 333 (16.8%);
    English Language Learner: n/a; Migrant: 1 (0.1%)
    Eligible for Free Lunch Program: 120 (6.1%)
    Eligible for Reduced-Price Lunch Program: 44 (2.2%)
Teachers: 134.5 (14.7 to 1)
Librarians/Media Specialists: 3.6 (550.8 to 1)
Guidance Counselors: 6.0 (330.5 to 1)
Current Spending: ($ per student per year):
    Total: $8,451; Instruction: $5,240; Support Services: $2,941

Enrollment, Drop-out Rates and Diploma Recipients by Race/Ethnicity

Category	Total	White	Black	Asian	AIAN	Hisp.
Enrollment (%)	100.0	98.5	0.4	0.4	0.3	0.6
Drop-out Rate (%)	2.1	2.1	n/a	n/a	0.0	0.0
H.S. Diplomas (#)	135	134	0	0	0	1

Conrad Weiser Area SD
44 Big Spring Rd • Robesonia, PA 19551-8948
(610) 693-8545
Grade Span: KG-12; **Agency Type:** 1
Schools: 4

    2 Primary; 1 Middle; 1 High; 0 Other Level
    4 Regular; 0 Special Education; 0 Vocational; 0 Alternative
    0 Magnet; 0 Charter; 2 Title I Eligible; 0 School-wide Title I
Students: 2,804   (n/a% male; n/a% female)
    Individual Education Program: 425 (15.2%);
    English Language Learner: n/a; Migrant: 4 (0.1%)
    Eligible for Free Lunch Program: 158 (5.6%)
    Eligible for Reduced-Price Lunch Program: 64 (2.3%)
Teachers: 184.5 (15.2 to 1)
Librarians/Media Specialists: 4.0 (701.0 to 1)
Guidance Counselors: 9.0 (311.6 to 1)
Current Spending: ($ per student per year):
    Total: $8,248; Instruction: $5,550; Support Services: $2,352

Enrollment, Drop-out Rates and Diploma Recipients by Race/Ethnicity

Category	Total	White	Black	Asian	AIAN	Hisp.
Enrollment (%)	100.0	93.7	3.0	0.6	0.1	2.7
Drop-out Rate (%)	2.1	2.0	3.6	0.0	n/a	5.3
H.S. Diplomas (#)	175	166	4	0	0	5

Daniel Boone Area SD
321 Furnace St PO Box 490 • Birdsboro, PA 19508
(610) 582-6140 • http://www.dboone.k12.pa.us
Grade Span: KG-12; **Agency Type:** 1
Schools: 6
    4 Primary; 1 Middle; 1 High; 0 Other Level
    6 Regular; 0 Special Education; 0 Vocational; 0 Alternative
    0 Magnet; 0 Charter; 0 Title I Eligible; 0 School-wide Title I
Students: 3,489   (n/a% male; n/a% female)
    Individual Education Program: 461 (13.2%);
    English Language Learner: n/a; Migrant: 0 (0.0%)
    Eligible for Free Lunch Program: 214 (6.1%)
    Eligible for Reduced-Price Lunch Program: 143 (4.1%)
Teachers: 215.8 (16.2 to 1)
Librarians/Media Specialists: 4.0 (872.3 to 1)
Guidance Counselors: 8.0 (436.1 to 1)
Current Spending: ($ per student per year):
    Total: $7,095; Instruction: $4,280; Support Services: $2,482

Enrollment, Drop-out Rates and Diploma Recipients by Race/Ethnicity

Category	Total	White	Black	Asian	AIAN	Hisp.
Enrollment (%)	100.0	93.6	3.0	1.1	0.2	2.1
Drop-out Rate (%)	4.0	4.2	0.0	0.0	0.0	0.0
H.S. Diplomas (#)	166	166	0	0	0	0

Exeter Township SD
3650 Perkiomen Ave • Reading, PA 19606-2798
(610) 779-0700 • http://www.exeter.k12.pa.us
Grade Span: KG-12; **Agency Type:** 1
Schools: 6
    3 Primary; 2 Middle; 1 High; 0 Other Level
    6 Regular; 0 Special Education; 0 Vocational; 0 Alternative
    0 Magnet; 0 Charter; 3 Title I Eligible; 0 School-wide Title I
Students: 4,082   (n/a% male; n/a% female)
    Individual Education Program: 554 (13.6%);
    English Language Learner: n/a; Migrant: 3 (0.1%)
    Eligible for Free Lunch Program: 276 (6.8%)
    Eligible for Reduced-Price Lunch Program: 133 (3.3%)
Teachers: 241.5 (16.9 to 1)
Librarians/Media Specialists: 6.0 (680.3 to 1)
Guidance Counselors: 10.0 (408.2 to 1)
Current Spending: ($ per student per year):
    Total: $7,114; Instruction: $4,662; Support Services: $2,158

Enrollment, Drop-out Rates and Diploma Recipients by Race/Ethnicity

Category	Total	White	Black	Asian	AIAN	Hisp.
Enrollment (%)	100.0	92.7	3.3	1.5	0.0	2.4
Drop-out Rate (%)	1.6	1.6	0.0	0.0	0.0	4.2
H.S. Diplomas (#)	268	249	3	12	0	4

Fleetwood Area SD
801 N Richmond St • Fleetwood, PA 19522-1031
(610) 944-9598
Grade Span: KG-12; **Agency Type:** 1
Schools: 5
    3 Primary; 1 Middle; 1 High; 0 Other Level
    5 Regular; 0 Special Education; 0 Vocational; 0 Alternative
    0 Magnet; 0 Charter; 4 Title I Eligible; 0 School-wide Title I
Students: 2,644   (n/a% male; n/a% female)
    Individual Education Program: 300 (11.3%);
    English Language Learner: n/a; Migrant: 8 (0.3%)
    Eligible for Free Lunch Program: 137 (5.2%)
    Eligible for Reduced-Price Lunch Program: 114 (4.3%)
Teachers: 168.1 (15.7 to 1)
Librarians/Media Specialists: 3.0 (881.3 to 1)
Guidance Counselors: 6.0 (440.7 to 1)
Current Spending: ($ per student per year):
    Total: $7,711; Instruction: $4,548; Support Services: $2,831

Enrollment, Drop-out Rates and Diploma Recipients by Race/Ethnicity

Category	Total	White	Black	Asian	AIAN	Hisp.
Enrollment (%)	100.0	95.0	1.2	1.0	0.1	2.6
Drop-out Rate (%)	2.0	1.9	16.7	0.0	n/a	0.0
H.S. Diplomas (#)	158	151	2	2	0	3

Governor Mifflin SD
10 S Waverly St • Shillington, PA 19607-2642
(610) 775-1461 • http://www.gmsd.k12.pa.us
Grade Span: KG-12; **Agency Type:** 1
Schools: 5
   2 Primary; 2 Middle; 1 High; 0 Other Level
   5 Regular; 0 Special Education; 0 Vocational; 0 Alternative
   0 Magnet; 0 Charter; 3 Title I Eligible; 0 School-wide Title I
Students: 4,157   (n/a% male; n/a% female)
   Individual Education Program: 503 (12.1%);
   English Language Learner: n/a; Migrant: 1 (<0.1%)
   Eligible for Free Lunch Program: 240 (5.8%)
   Eligible for Reduced-Price Lunch Program: 118 (2.8%)
Teachers: 261.0 (15.9 to 1)
Librarians/Media Specialists: 5.0 (831.4 to 1)
Guidance Counselors: 11.0 (377.9 to 1)
Current Spending: ($ per student per year):
   Total: $7,648; Instruction: $4,795; Support Services: $2,512

Enrollment, Drop-out Rates and Diploma Recipients by Race/Ethnicity

Category	Total	White	Black	Asian	AIAN	Hisp.
Enrollment (%)	100.0	90.4	3.5	1.9	0.0	4.2
Drop-out Rate (%)	1.4	1.1	5.9	0.0	n/a	12.1
H.S. Diplomas (#)	316	298	3	8	0	7

Hamburg Area SD
Windsor St • Hamburg, PA 19526-0401
(610) 562-2241
Grade Span: KG-12; **Agency Type:** 1
Schools: 7
   5 Primary; 1 Middle; 1 High; 0 Other Level
   7 Regular; 0 Special Education; 0 Vocational; 0 Alternative
   0 Magnet; 0 Charter; 4 Title I Eligible; 0 School-wide Title I
Students: 2,748   (n/a% male; n/a% female)
   Individual Education Program: 344 (12.5%);
   English Language Learner: n/a; Migrant: 0 (0.0%)
   Eligible for Free Lunch Program: 188 (6.8%)
   Eligible for Reduced-Price Lunch Program: 52 (1.9%)
Teachers: 159.0 (17.3 to 1)
Librarians/Media Specialists: 4.0 (687.0 to 1)
Guidance Counselors: 6.0 (458.0 to 1)
Current Spending: ($ per student per year):
   Total: $7,446; Instruction: $4,994; Support Services: $2,145

Enrollment, Drop-out Rates and Diploma Recipients by Race/Ethnicity

Category	Total	White	Black	Asian	AIAN	Hisp.
Enrollment (%)	100.0	97.5	0.5	0.4	0.0	1.6
Drop-out Rate (%)	2.3	2.3	0.0	0.0	n/a	10.0
H.S. Diplomas (#)	180	176	1	2	0	1

Kutztown Area SD
50 Trexler Ave • Kutztown, PA 19530-9722
(610) 683-7361 • http://www.kasd.org
Grade Span: KG-12; **Agency Type:** 1
Schools: 6
   4 Primary; 1 Middle; 1 High; 0 Other Level
   6 Regular; 0 Special Education; 0 Vocational; 0 Alternative
   0 Magnet; 0 Charter; 5 Title I Eligible; 0 School-wide Title I
Students: 1,812   (n/a% male; n/a% female)
   Individual Education Program: 322 (17.8%);
   English Language Learner: n/a; Migrant: 0 (0.0%)
   Eligible for Free Lunch Program: 114 (6.3%)
   Eligible for Reduced-Price Lunch Program: 66 (3.6%)
Teachers: 134.2 (13.5 to 1)
Librarians/Media Specialists: 4.0 (453.0 to 1)
Guidance Counselors: 5.0 (362.4 to 1)
Current Spending: ($ per student per year):
   Total: $9,158; Instruction: $5,733; Support Services: $3,045

Enrollment, Drop-out Rates and Diploma Recipients by Race/Ethnicity

Category	Total	White	Black	Asian	AIAN	Hisp.
Enrollment (%)	100.0	98.3	0.4	0.5	0.0	0.7
Drop-out Rate (%)	1.3	1.4	0.0	0.0	n/a	0.0
H.S. Diplomas (#)	133	132	0	1	0	0

Muhlenberg SD
801 Bellevue Ave Laureldale • Reading, PA 19605-1799
(610) 921-8070 • http://www.muhlsd.berksiu.k12.pa.us
Grade Span: KG-12; **Agency Type:** 1
Schools: 3
   1 Primary; 1 Middle; 1 High; 0 Other Level
   3 Regular; 0 Special Education; 0 Vocational; 0 Alternative

   0 Magnet; 0 Charter; 3 Title I Eligible; 0 School-wide Title I
Students: 3,029   (n/a% male; n/a% female)
   Individual Education Program: 370 (12.2%);
   English Language Learner: n/a; Migrant: 8 (0.3%)
   Eligible for Free Lunch Program: 265 (8.7%)
   Eligible for Reduced-Price Lunch Program: 157 (5.2%)
Teachers: 196.5 (15.4 to 1)
Librarians/Media Specialists: 3.0 (1,009.7 to 1)
Guidance Counselors: 11.0 (275.4 to 1)
Current Spending: ($ per student per year):
   Total: $8,241; Instruction: $5,233; Support Services: $2,694

Enrollment, Drop-out Rates and Diploma Recipients by Race/Ethnicity

Category	Total	White	Black	Asian	AIAN	Hisp.
Enrollment (%)	100.0	88.0	2.1	1.2	0.0	8.7
Drop-out Rate (%)	3.2	2.9	9.1	7.7	0.0	5.0
H.S. Diplomas (#)	199	181	1	4	0	13

Oley Valley SD
17 Jefferson St • Oley, PA 19547-8774
(610) 987-4100 • http://www.oleysd.k12.pa.us
Grade Span: KG-12; **Agency Type:** 1
Schools: 3
   1 Primary; 1 Middle; 1 High; 0 Other Level
   3 Regular; 0 Special Education; 0 Vocational; 0 Alternative
   0 Magnet; 0 Charter; 2 Title I Eligible; 0 School-wide Title I
Students: 2,121   (n/a% male; n/a% female)
   Individual Education Program: 268 (12.6%);
   English Language Learner: n/a; Migrant: 0 (0.0%)
   Eligible for Free Lunch Program: 48 (2.3%)
   Eligible for Reduced-Price Lunch Program: 26 (1.2%)
Teachers: 139.0 (15.3 to 1)
Librarians/Media Specialists: 3.0 (707.0 to 1)
Guidance Counselors: 6.0 (353.5 to 1)
Current Spending: ($ per student per year):
   Total: $7,447; Instruction: $4,670; Support Services: $2,496

Enrollment, Drop-out Rates and Diploma Recipients by Race/Ethnicity

Category	Total	White	Black	Asian	AIAN	Hisp.
Enrollment (%)	100.0	98.5	0.4	0.6	0.0	0.5
Drop-out Rate (%)	1.1	1.1	0.0	0.0	n/a	0.0
H.S. Diplomas (#)	127	123	2	0	0	2

Reading SD
800 Washington St • Reading, PA 19601-3616
(610) 371-5611 • http://www.readingsd.org/
Grade Span: PK-12; **Agency Type:** 1
Schools: 19
   14 Primary; 4 Middle; 1 High; 0 Other Level
   19 Regular; 0 Special Education; 0 Vocational; 0 Alternative
   0 Magnet; 0 Charter; 11 Title I Eligible; 9 School-wide Title I
Students: 16,515   (n/a% male; n/a% female)
   Individual Education Program: 1,978 (12.0%);
   English Language Learner: n/a; Migrant: 1,241 (7.5%)
   Eligible for Free Lunch Program: 9,127 (55.3%)
   Eligible for Reduced-Price Lunch Program: 1,294 (7.8%)
Teachers: 931.0 (17.7 to 1)
Librarians/Media Specialists: 18.0 (917.5 to 1)
Guidance Counselors: 37.0 (446.4 to 1)
Current Spending: ($ per student per year):
   Total: $6,639; Instruction: $4,309; Support Services: $1,931

Enrollment, Drop-out Rates and Diploma Recipients by Race/Ethnicity

Category	Total	White	Black	Asian	AIAN	Hisp.
Enrollment (%)	100.0	19.3	14.8	1.1	0.1	64.7
Drop-out Rate (%)	8.7	7.5	8.5	3.6	0.0	9.6
H.S. Diplomas (#)	570	195	115	11	0	249

Schuylkill Valley SD
929 Lakeshore Dr • Leesport, PA 19533-8631
(610) 916-0957
Grade Span: KG-12; **Agency Type:** 1
Schools: 3
   1 Primary; 1 Middle; 1 High; 0 Other Level
   3 Regular; 0 Special Education; 0 Vocational; 0 Alternative
   0 Magnet; 0 Charter; 3 Title I Eligible; 0 School-wide Title I
Students: 1,908   (n/a% male; n/a% female)
   Individual Education Program: 228 (11.9%);
   English Language Learner: n/a; Migrant: 0 (0.0%)
   Eligible for Free Lunch Program: 109 (5.7%)
   Eligible for Reduced-Price Lunch Program: 83 (4.4%)
Teachers: 125.0 (15.3 to 1)
Librarians/Media Specialists: 3.0 (636.0 to 1)
Guidance Counselors: 5.0 (381.6 to 1)
Current Spending: ($ per student per year):
   Total: $9,106; Instruction: $6,221; Support Services: $2,557

Enrollment, Drop-out Rates and Diploma Recipients by Race/Ethnicity

Category	Total	White	Black	Asian	AIAN	Hisp.
Enrollment (%)	100.0	95.2	1.3	0.4	0.0	3.1
Drop-out Rate (%)	0.8	0.9	0.0	0.0	n/a	0.0
H.S. Diplomas (#)	141	138	2	0	0	1

Tulpehocken Area SD
428 New Schaefferstown Rd • Bernville, PA 19506-8939
(610) 488-6286
Grade Span: KG-12; **Agency Type:** 1
Schools: 3
   2 Primary; 0 Middle; 1 High; 0 Other Level
   3 Regular; 0 Special Education; 0 Vocational; 0 Alternative
   0 Magnet; 0 Charter; 2 Title I Eligible; 0 School-wide Title I
Students: 1,695 (n/a% male; n/a% female)
   Individual Education Program: 310 (18.3%);
   English Language Learner: n/a; Migrant: 18 (1.1%)
   Eligible for Free Lunch Program: 183 (10.8%)
   Eligible for Reduced-Price Lunch Program: 82 (4.8%)
Teachers: 116.8 (14.5 to 1)
Librarians/Media Specialists: 3.0 (565.0 to 1)
Guidance Counselors: 5.4 (313.9 to 1)
Current Spending: ($ per student per year):
   Total: $8,739; Instruction: $5,343; Support Services: $3,053

Enrollment, Drop-out Rates and Diploma Recipients by Race/Ethnicity

Category	Total	White	Black	Asian	AIAN	Hisp.
Enrollment (%)	100.0	94.1	1.2	0.2	0.2	4.2
Drop-out Rate (%)	3.0	2.7	0.0	0.0	n/a	22.2
H.S. Diplomas (#)	119	113	0	4	0	2

Twin Valley SD
4851 N Twin Valley Rd • Elverson, PA 19520-8995
(610) 286-8600
Grade Span: KG-12; **Agency Type:** 1
Schools: 5
   3 Primary; 1 Middle; 1 High; 0 Other Level
   5 Regular; 0 Special Education; 0 Vocational; 0 Alternative
   0 Magnet; 0 Charter; 4 Title I Eligible; 0 School-wide Title I
Students: 3,222 (n/a% male; n/a% female)
   Individual Education Program: 451 (14.0%);
   English Language Learner: n/a; Migrant: 0 (0.0%)
   Eligible for Free Lunch Program: 206 (6.4%)
   Eligible for Reduced-Price Lunch Program: 169 (5.2%)
Teachers: 202.9 (15.9 to 1)
Librarians/Media Specialists: 5.0 (644.4 to 1)
Guidance Counselors: 9.0 (358.0 to 1)
Current Spending: ($ per student per year):
   Total: $8,615; Instruction: $5,521; Support Services: $2,809

Enrollment, Drop-out Rates and Diploma Recipients by Race/Ethnicity

Category	Total	White	Black	Asian	AIAN	Hisp.
Enrollment (%)	100.0	97.0	1.5	0.5	0.0	1.0
Drop-out Rate (%)	2.3	2.2	6.3	16.7	0.0	0.0
H.S. Diplomas (#)	190	186	0	3	0	1

Wilson SD
2601 Grandview Blvd • West Lawn, PA 19609-1324
(610) 670-0180 • http://www.wilson.k12.pa.us
Grade Span: KG-12; **Agency Type:** 1
Schools: 10
   7 Primary; 2 Middle; 1 High; 0 Other Level
   10 Regular; 0 Special Education; 0 Vocational; 0 Alternative
   0 Magnet; 0 Charter; 4 Title I Eligible; 0 School-wide Title I
Students: 5,314 (n/a% male; n/a% female)
   Individual Education Program: 656 (12.3%);
   English Language Learner: n/a; Migrant: 5 (0.1%)
   Eligible for Free Lunch Program: 319 (6.0%)
   Eligible for Reduced-Price Lunch Program: 171 (3.2%)
Teachers: 317.1 (16.8 to 1)
Librarians/Media Specialists: 8.0 (664.3 to 1)
Guidance Counselors: 14.0 (379.6 to 1)
Current Spending: ($ per student per year):
   Total: $8,213; Instruction: $5,225; Support Services: $2,515

Enrollment, Drop-out Rates and Diploma Recipients by Race/Ethnicity

Category	Total	White	Black	Asian	AIAN	Hisp.
Enrollment (%)	100.0	85.0	6.2	2.8	0.3	5.7
Drop-out Rate (%)	1.8	1.7	4.5	2.1	0.0	2.7
H.S. Diplomas (#)	362	344	10	5	0	3

Wyomissing Area SD
630 Evans Ave • Wyomissing, PA 19610-2636
(610) 374-4031 • http://www.wyoarea.k12.pa.us
Grade Span: KG-12; **Agency Type:** 1
Schools: 3
   1 Primary; 1 Middle; 1 High; 0 Other Level
   3 Regular; 0 Special Education; 0 Vocational; 0 Alternative

   0 Magnet; 0 Charter; 0 Title I Eligible; 0 School-wide Title I
Students: 1,858 (n/a% male; n/a% female)
   Individual Education Program: 175 (9.4%);
   English Language Learner: n/a; Migrant: 4 (0.2%)
   Eligible for Free Lunch Program: 116 (6.2%)
   Eligible for Reduced-Price Lunch Program: 71 (3.8%)
Teachers: 131.2 (14.2 to 1)
Librarians/Media Specialists: 3.0 (619.3 to 1)
Guidance Counselors: 7.0 (265.4 to 1)
Current Spending: ($ per student per year):
   Total: $8,847; Instruction: $5,647; Support Services: $2,861

Enrollment, Drop-out Rates and Diploma Recipients by Race/Ethnicity

Category	Total	White	Black	Asian	AIAN	Hisp.
Enrollment (%)	100.0	88.6	2.4	2.4	0.1	6.6
Drop-out Rate (%)	1.0	0.5	6.3	0.0	n/a	8.0
H.S. Diplomas (#)	123	116	0	0	0	7

Blair County

Altoona Area SD
1415 6th Ave • Altoona, PA 16602-2427
(814) 946-8211 • http://www.aasdcat.com/aasd
Grade Span: KG-12; **Agency Type:** 1
Schools: 14
   10 Primary; 2 Middle; 2 High; 0 Other Level
   14 Regular; 0 Special Education; 0 Vocational; 0 Alternative
   1 Magnet; 0 Charter; 11 Title I Eligible; 5 School-wide Title I
Students: 8,390 (n/a% male; n/a% female)
   Individual Education Program: 1,490 (17.8%);
   English Language Learner: n/a; Migrant: 0 (0.0%)
   Eligible for Free Lunch Program: 3,059 (36.5%)
   Eligible for Reduced-Price Lunch Program: 799 (9.5%)
Teachers: 497.0 (16.9 to 1)
Librarians/Media Specialists: 6.0 (1,398.3 to 1)
Guidance Counselors: 17.0 (493.5 to 1)
Current Spending: ($ per student per year):
   Total: $7,682; Instruction: $5,005; Support Services: $2,352

Enrollment, Drop-out Rates and Diploma Recipients by Race/Ethnicity

Category	Total	White	Black	Asian	AIAN	Hisp.
Enrollment (%)	100.0	94.0	5.2	0.4	0.0	0.4
Drop-out Rate (%)	4.3	4.3	4.8	0.0	n/a	16.7
H.S. Diplomas (#)	567	549	13	4	0	1

Hollidaysburg Area SD
201 Jackson St • Hollidaysburg, PA 16648-1615
(814) 695-8702 • http://www.tigerwires.com
Grade Span: KG-12; **Agency Type:** 1
Schools: 6
   4 Primary; 1 Middle; 1 High; 0 Other Level
   6 Regular; 0 Special Education; 0 Vocational; 0 Alternative
   0 Magnet; 0 Charter; 4 Title I Eligible; 0 School-wide Title I
Students: 3,793 (n/a% male; n/a% female)
   Individual Education Program: 479 (12.6%);
   English Language Learner: n/a; Migrant: 0 (0.0%)
   Eligible for Free Lunch Program: 593 (15.6%)
   Eligible for Reduced-Price Lunch Program: 268 (7.1%)
Teachers: 247.0 (15.4 to 1)
Librarians/Media Specialists: 4.0 (948.3 to 1)
Guidance Counselors: 10.0 (379.3 to 1)
Current Spending: ($ per student per year):
   Total: $7,725; Instruction: $4,954; Support Services: $2,424

Enrollment, Drop-out Rates and Diploma Recipients by Race/Ethnicity

Category	Total	White	Black	Asian	AIAN	Hisp.
Enrollment (%)	100.0	97.9	0.6	1.2	0.1	0.3
Drop-out Rate (%)	2.0	2.0	16.7	0.0	0.0	n/a
H.S. Diplomas (#)	326	319	4	2	1	0

Spring Cove SD
1100 E Main St • Roaring Spring, PA 16673-1633
(814) 224-5124
Grade Span: KG-12; **Agency Type:** 1
Schools: 5
   3 Primary; 1 Middle; 1 High; 0 Other Level
   5 Regular; 0 Special Education; 0 Vocational; 0 Alternative
   0 Magnet; 0 Charter; 4 Title I Eligible; 0 School-wide Title I
Students: 1,939 (n/a% male; n/a% female)
   Individual Education Program: 313 (16.1%);
   English Language Learner: n/a; Migrant: 7 (0.4%)
   Eligible for Free Lunch Program: 397 (20.5%)
   Eligible for Reduced-Price Lunch Program: 200 (10.3%)
Teachers: 135.5 (14.3 to 1)
Librarians/Media Specialists: 3.0 (646.3 to 1)
Guidance Counselors: 5.0 (387.8 to 1)
Current Spending: ($ per student per year):
   Total: $7,064; Instruction: $4,316; Support Services: $2,395

Enrollment, Drop-out Rates and Diploma Recipients by Race/Ethnicity

Category	Total	White	Black	Asian	AIAN	Hisp.
Enrollment (%)	100.0	99.1	0.4	0.4	0.0	0.1
Drop-out Rate (%)	1.8	1.8	0.0	0.0	n/a	0.0
H.S. Diplomas (#)	159	158	0	1	0	0

Tyrone Area SD

701 Clay Ave • Tyrone, PA 16686-1415
(814) 684-0710 • http://www.tyrone.k12.pa.us
Grade Span: KG-12; **Agency Type:** 1
Schools: 3
 1 Primary; 1 Middle; 1 High; 0 Other Level
 3 Regular; 0 Special Education; 0 Vocational; 0 Alternative
 0 Magnet; 0 Charter; 1 Title I Eligible; 0 School-wide Title I
Students: 1,953   (n/a% male; n/a% female)
 Individual Education Program: 378 (19.4%);
 English Language Learner: n/a; Migrant: 1 (0.1%)
 Eligible for Free Lunch Program: 483 (24.7%)
 Eligible for Reduced-Price Lunch Program: 217 (11.1%)
Teachers: 127.5 (15.3 to 1)
Librarians/Media Specialists: 2.0 (976.5 to 1)
Guidance Counselors: 5.5 (355.1 to 1)
Current Spending: ($ per student per year):
 Total: $7,664; Instruction: $4,496; Support Services: $2,803

Enrollment, Drop-out Rates and Diploma Recipients by Race/Ethnicity

Category	Total	White	Black	Asian	AIAN	Hisp.
Enrollment (%)	100.0	98.4	0.9	0.3	0.0	0.5
Drop-out Rate (%)	2.4	2.4	0.0	0.0	n/a	0.0
H.S. Diplomas (#)	122	120	1	1	0	0

Bradford County

Athens Area SD

204 Willow St • Athens, PA 18810-1213
(570) 888-7766 • http://www.athensasd.k12.pa.us
Grade Span: KG-12; **Agency Type:** 1
Schools: 7
 4 Primary; 1 Middle; 1 High; 1 Other Level
 7 Regular; 0 Special Education; 0 Vocational; 0 Alternative
 0 Magnet; 0 Charter; 3 Title I Eligible; 1 School-wide Title I
Students: 2,439   (n/a% male; n/a% female)
 Individual Education Program: 449 (18.4%);
 English Language Learner: n/a; Migrant: 21 (0.9%)
 Eligible for Free Lunch Program: 335 (13.7%)
 Eligible for Reduced-Price Lunch Program: 161 (6.6%)
Teachers: 182.5 (13.4 to 1)
Librarians/Media Specialists: 5.0 (487.8 to 1)
Guidance Counselors: 4.0 (609.8 to 1)
Current Spending: ($ per student per year):
 Total: $8,714; Instruction: $5,586; Support Services: $2,737

Enrollment, Drop-out Rates and Diploma Recipients by Race/Ethnicity

Category	Total	White	Black	Asian	AIAN	Hisp.
Enrollment (%)	100.0	97.5	1.4	0.7	0.0	0.4
Drop-out Rate (%)	4.9	5.0	0.0	0.0	n/a	0.0
H.S. Diplomas (#)	162	155	0	5	1	1

Towanda Area SD

PO Box 231 • Towanda, PA 18848-0231
(570) 265-9894 • http://www.tsd.k12.pa.us
Grade Span: PK-12; **Agency Type:** 1
Schools: 6
 4 Primary; 1 Middle; 1 High; 0 Other Level
 6 Regular; 0 Special Education; 0 Vocational; 0 Alternative
 0 Magnet; 0 Charter; 5 Title I Eligible; 0 School-wide Title I
Students: 1,853   (n/a% male; n/a% female)
 Individual Education Program: 267 (14.4%);
 English Language Learner: n/a; Migrant: 1 (0.1%)
 Eligible for Free Lunch Program: 495 (26.7%)
 Eligible for Reduced-Price Lunch Program: 251 (13.5%)
Teachers: 119.1 (15.6 to 1)
Librarians/Media Specialists: 3.0 (617.7 to 1)
Guidance Counselors: 4.0 (463.3 to 1)
Current Spending: ($ per student per year):
 Total: $8,408; Instruction: $5,075; Support Services: $2,882

Enrollment, Drop-out Rates and Diploma Recipients by Race/Ethnicity

Category	Total	White	Black	Asian	AIAN	Hisp.
Enrollment (%)	100.0	98.9	0.6	0.1	0.1	0.4
Drop-out Rate (%)	2.2	2.2	0.0	0.0	0.0	0.0
H.S. Diplomas (#)	126	121	1	1	0	3

Troy Area SD

PO Box 67 • Troy, PA 16947-0067
(570) 297-2750 • http://www.troyschoolspa.org
Grade Span: KG-12; **Agency Type:** 1
Schools: 5

 3 Primary; 1 Middle; 1 High; 0 Other Level
 5 Regular; 0 Special Education; 0 Vocational; 0 Alternative
 0 Magnet; 0 Charter; 4 Title I Eligible; 0 School-wide Title I
Students: 1,890   (n/a% male; n/a% female)
 Individual Education Program: 280 (14.8%);
 English Language Learner: n/a; Migrant: 40 (2.1%)
 Eligible for Free Lunch Program: 483 (25.6%)
 Eligible for Reduced-Price Lunch Program: 139 (7.4%)
Teachers: 116.0 (16.3 to 1)
Librarians/Media Specialists: 4.0 (472.5 to 1)
Guidance Counselors: 4.0 (472.5 to 1)
Current Spending: ($ per student per year):
 Total: $7,568; Instruction: $4,793; Support Services: $2,462

Enrollment, Drop-out Rates and Diploma Recipients by Race/Ethnicity

Category	Total	White	Black	Asian	AIAN	Hisp.
Enrollment (%)	100.0	96.9	1.4	0.5	0.3	0.8
Drop-out Rate (%)	2.4	2.4	0.0	n/a	0.0	0.0
H.S. Diplomas (#)	119	119	0	0	0	0

Wyalusing Area SD

PO Box 157 • Wyalusing, PA 18853-0157
(570) 746-1605
Grade Span: KG-12; **Agency Type:** 1
Schools: 5
 4 Primary; 0 Middle; 1 High; 0 Other Level
 5 Regular; 0 Special Education; 0 Vocational; 0 Alternative
 0 Magnet; 0 Charter; 5 Title I Eligible; 0 School-wide Title I
Students: 1,504   (n/a% male; n/a% female)
 Individual Education Program: 163 (10.8%);
 English Language Learner: n/a; Migrant: 24 (1.6%)
 Eligible for Free Lunch Program: 319 (21.2%)
 Eligible for Reduced-Price Lunch Program: 152 (10.1%)
Teachers: 96.0 (15.7 to 1)
Librarians/Media Specialists: 2.0 (752.0 to 1)
Guidance Counselors: 3.0 (501.3 to 1)
Current Spending: ($ per student per year):
 Total: $8,097; Instruction: $4,957; Support Services: $2,789

Enrollment, Drop-out Rates and Diploma Recipients by Race/Ethnicity

Category	Total	White	Black	Asian	AIAN	Hisp.
Enrollment (%)	100.0	95.9	1.5	0.6	0.2	1.8
Drop-out Rate (%)	3.5	3.5	0.0	0.0	50.0	0.0
H.S. Diplomas (#)	99	95	1	2	0	1

Bucks County

Bensalem Township SD

3000 Donallen Dr • Bensalem, PA 19020-1898
(215) 750-2800 • http://www.bensalemschools.org
Grade Span: KG-12; **Agency Type:** 1
Schools: 10
 6 Primary; 3 Middle; 1 High; 0 Other Level
 10 Regular; 0 Special Education; 0 Vocational; 0 Alternative
 0 Magnet; 0 Charter; 5 Title I Eligible; 1 School-wide Title I
Students: 6,360   (n/a% male; n/a% female)
 Individual Education Program: 1,043 (16.4%);
 English Language Learner: n/a; Migrant: 0 (0.0%)
 Eligible for Free Lunch Program: 1,371 (21.6%)
 Eligible for Reduced-Price Lunch Program: 421 (6.6%)
Teachers: 393.6 (16.2 to 1)
Librarians/Media Specialists: 9.0 (706.7 to 1)
Guidance Counselors: 18.0 (353.3 to 1)
Current Spending: ($ per student per year):
 Total: $10,347; Instruction: $6,176; Support Services: $3,836

Enrollment, Drop-out Rates and Diploma Recipients by Race/Ethnicity

Category	Total	White	Black	Asian	AIAN	Hisp.
Enrollment (%)	100.0	71.8	11.9	9.9	0.0	6.4
Drop-out Rate (%)	2.9	2.8	2.9	1.8	n/a	7.1
H.S. Diplomas (#)	500	394	37	48	0	21

Bristol Township SD

6401 Mill Creek Rd • Levittown, PA 19057-4014
(215) 943-3200 • http://www.bciu.k12.pa.us/btsd
Grade Span: KG-12; **Agency Type:** 1
Schools: 13
 9 Primary; 3 Middle; 1 High; 0 Other Level
 13 Regular; 0 Special Education; 0 Vocational; 0 Alternative
 0 Magnet; 0 Charter; 9 Title I Eligible; 0 School-wide Title I
Students: 6,890   (n/a% male; n/a% female)
 Individual Education Program: 1,324 (19.2%);
 English Language Learner: n/a; Migrant: 0 (0.0%)
 Eligible for Free Lunch Program: 1,850 (26.9%)
 Eligible for Reduced-Price Lunch Program: 549 (8.0%)
Teachers: 457.0 (15.1 to 1)
Librarians/Media Specialists: 13.0 (530.0 to 1)
Guidance Counselors: 11.0 (626.4 to 1)

Current Spending: ($ per student per year):
  Total: $10,735; Instruction: $6,914; Support Services: $3,508
Enrollment, Drop-out Rates and Diploma Recipients by Race/Ethnicity

Category	Total	White	Black	Asian	AIAN	Hisp.
Enrollment (%)	100.0	73.9	17.3	2.8	0.6	5.4
Drop-out Rate (%)	2.3	2.3	2.6	2.5	0.0	2.1
H.S. Diplomas (#)	426	319	59	28	3	17

Centennial SD
433 Centennial Rd • Warminster, PA 18974-5448
(215) 441-6000 • http://www.centennialsd.org
Grade Span: KG-12; **Agency Type:** 1
Schools: 9
  6 Primary; 2 Middle; 1 High; 0 Other Level
  9 Regular; 0 Special Education; 0 Vocational; 0 Alternative
  0 Magnet; 0 Charter; 6 Title I Eligible; 0 School-wide Title I
Students: 6,327   (n/a% male; n/a% female)
  Individual Education Program: 1,102 (17.4%);
  English Language Learner: n/a; Migrant: 0 (0.0%)
  Eligible for Free Lunch Program: 593 (9.4%)
  Eligible for Reduced-Price Lunch Program: 341 (5.4%)
Teachers: 381.5 (16.6 to 1)
Librarians/Media Specialists: 10.0 (632.7 to 1)
Guidance Counselors: 16.0 (395.4 to 1)
Current Spending: ($ per student per year):
  Total: $8,928; Instruction: $5,517; Support Services: $3,148
Enrollment, Drop-out Rates and Diploma Recipients by Race/Ethnicity

Category	Total	White	Black	Asian	AIAN	Hisp.
Enrollment (%)	100.0	86.5	4.9	2.6	0.3	5.8
Drop-out Rate (%)	1.6	1.2	11.5	0.0	0.0	5.4
H.S. Diplomas (#)	456	417	9	15	0	15

Central Bucks SD
16 Welden Dr • Doylestown, PA 18901-2359
(267) 893-2000 • http://www.cbsd.org
Grade Span: KG-12; **Agency Type:** 1
Schools: 23
  14 Primary; 5 Middle; 2 High; 0 Other Level
  21 Regular; 0 Special Education; 0 Vocational; 0 Alternative
  0 Magnet; 0 Charter; 9 Title I Eligible; 0 School-wide Title I
Students: 19,089   (n/a% male; n/a% female)
  Individual Education Program: 2,039 (10.7%);
  English Language Learner: n/a; Migrant: 2 (<0.1%)
  Eligible for Free Lunch Program: 356 (1.9%)
  Eligible for Reduced-Price Lunch Program: 163 (0.9%)
Teachers: 983.5 (19.4 to 1)
Librarians/Media Specialists: 22.6 (844.6 to 1)
Guidance Counselors: 37.0 (515.9 to 1)
Current Spending: ($ per student per year):
  Total: $8,078; Instruction: $5,198; Support Services: $2,675
Enrollment, Drop-out Rates and Diploma Recipients by Race/Ethnicity

Category	Total	White	Black	Asian	AIAN	Hisp.
Enrollment (%)	100.0	94.4	1.6	2.7	0.0	1.2
Drop-out Rate (%)	1.2	1.2	3.8	1.0	n/a	0.0
H.S. Diplomas (#)	1,082	1,023	23	27	0	9

Council Rock SD
30 N Chancellor St • Newtown, PA 18940
(215) 944-1000 • http://www.crsd.org
Grade Span: KG-12; **Agency Type:** 1
Schools: 15
  10 Primary; 3 Middle; 2 High; 0 Other Level
  15 Regular; 0 Special Education; 0 Vocational; 0 Alternative
  0 Magnet; 0 Charter; 7 Title I Eligible; 0 School-wide Title I
Students: 12,482   (n/a% male; n/a% female)
  Individual Education Program: 1,749 (14.0%);
  English Language Learner: n/a; Migrant: 0 (0.0%)
  Eligible for Free Lunch Program: 95 (0.8%)
  Eligible for Reduced-Price Lunch Program: 58 (0.5%)
Teachers: 793.8 (15.7 to 1)
Librarians/Media Specialists: 18.1 (689.6 to 1)
Guidance Counselors: 22.5 (554.8 to 1)
Current Spending: ($ per student per year):
  Total: $10,260; Instruction: $7,053; Support Services: $2,942
Enrollment, Drop-out Rates and Diploma Recipients by Race/Ethnicity

Category	Total	White	Black	Asian	AIAN	Hisp.
Enrollment (%)	100.0	95.5	0.8	3.4	0.0	0.3
Drop-out Rate (%)	0.3	0.3	0.0	0.0	0.0	0.0
H.S. Diplomas (#)	912	872	6	28	0	6

Neshaminy SD
2001 Old Lincoln Hwy • Langhorne, PA 19047-3295
(215) 752-6300 • http://www.neshaminy.k12.pa.us
Grade Span: KG-12; **Agency Type:** 1
Schools: 14

  8 Primary; 4 Middle; 2 High; 0 Other Level
  14 Regular; 0 Special Education; 0 Vocational; 0 Alternative
  0 Magnet; 0 Charter; 8 Title I Eligible; 0 School-wide Title I
Students: 9,419   (n/a% male; n/a% female)
  Individual Education Program: 1,700 (18.0%);
  English Language Learner: n/a; Migrant: 0 (0.0%)
  Eligible for Free Lunch Program: 536 (5.7%)
  Eligible for Reduced-Price Lunch Program: 251 (2.7%)
Teachers: 616.3 (15.3 to 1)
Librarians/Media Specialists: 13.0 (724.5 to 1)
Guidance Counselors: 26.5 (355.4 to 1)
Current Spending: ($ per student per year):
  Total: $11,277; Instruction: $7,620; Support Services: $3,367
Enrollment, Drop-out Rates and Diploma Recipients by Race/Ethnicity

Category	Total	White	Black	Asian	AIAN	Hisp.
Enrollment (%)	100.0	93.3	3.2	2.2	0.1	1.2
Drop-out Rate (%)	1.6	1.6	1.1	1.3	33.3	3.0
H.S. Diplomas (#)	796	755	20	20	0	1

Palisades SD
39 Thomas Free Dr • Kintnersville, PA 18930-9657
(610) 847-5131 • http://www.palisadessd.org
Grade Span: KG-12; **Agency Type:** 1
Schools: 5
  3 Primary; 1 Middle; 1 High; 0 Other Level
  5 Regular; 0 Special Education; 0 Vocational; 0 Alternative
  0 Magnet; 0 Charter; 3 Title I Eligible; 0 School-wide Title I
Students: 2,123   (n/a% male; n/a% female)
  Individual Education Program: 374 (17.6%);
  English Language Learner: n/a; Migrant: 0 (0.0%)
  Eligible for Free Lunch Program: 86 (4.1%)
  Eligible for Reduced-Price Lunch Program: 50 (2.4%)
Teachers: 144.5 (14.7 to 1)
Librarians/Media Specialists: 3.0 (707.7 to 1)
Guidance Counselors: 6.0 (353.8 to 1)
Current Spending: ($ per student per year):
  Total: $10,352; Instruction: $6,024; Support Services: $4,048
Enrollment, Drop-out Rates and Diploma Recipients by Race/Ethnicity

Category	Total	White	Black	Asian	AIAN	Hisp.
Enrollment (%)	100.0	98.1	0.7	0.7	0.0	0.6
Drop-out Rate (%)	2.3	2.3	0.0	0.0	n/a	0.0
H.S. Diplomas (#)	161	160	0	1	0	0

Pennridge SD
1506 N 5th St • Perkasie, PA 18944-2207
(215) 257-5011 • http://www.bciu.k12.pa.us/pennridge/psd/psd.htm
Grade Span: KG-12; **Agency Type:** 1
Schools: 10
  7 Primary; 2 Middle; 1 High; 0 Other Level
  10 Regular; 0 Special Education; 0 Vocational; 0 Alternative
  0 Magnet; 0 Charter; 7 Title I Eligible; 0 School-wide Title I
Students: 7,085   (n/a% male; n/a% female)
  Individual Education Program: 936 (13.2%);
  English Language Learner: n/a; Migrant: 4 (0.1%)
  Eligible for Free Lunch Program: 388 (5.5%)
  Eligible for Reduced-Price Lunch Program: 265 (3.7%)
Teachers: 409.2 (17.3 to 1)
Librarians/Media Specialists: 10.0 (708.5 to 1)
Guidance Counselors: 15.0 (472.3 to 1)
Current Spending: ($ per student per year):
  Total: $8,693; Instruction: $5,358; Support Services: $3,044
Enrollment, Drop-out Rates and Diploma Recipients by Race/Ethnicity

Category	Total	White	Black	Asian	AIAN	Hisp.
Enrollment (%)	100.0	96.2	1.3	0.9	0.1	1.5
Drop-out Rate (%)	1.3	1.3	3.8	0.0	0.0	2.9
H.S. Diplomas (#)	477	451	6	6	4	10

Pennsbury SD
134 Yardley Ave • Fallsington, PA 19058-0338
(215) 428-4100 • http://www.pennsbury.k12.pa.us
Grade Span: KG-12; **Agency Type:** 1
Schools: 16
  11 Primary; 3 Middle; 1 High; 1 Other Level
  16 Regular; 0 Special Education; 0 Vocational; 0 Alternative
  0 Magnet; 0 Charter; 8 Title I Eligible; 0 School-wide Title I
Students: 11,207   (n/a% male; n/a% female)
  Individual Education Program: 1,510 (13.5%);
  English Language Learner: n/a; Migrant: 0 (0.0%)
  Eligible for Free Lunch Program: 566 (5.1%)
  Eligible for Reduced-Price Lunch Program: 247 (2.2%)
Teachers: 690.2 (16.2 to 1)
Librarians/Media Specialists: 15.0 (747.1 to 1)
Guidance Counselors: 30.0 (373.6 to 1)
Current Spending: ($ per student per year):
  Total: $10,001; Instruction: $6,711; Support Services: $3,048

Enrollment, Drop-out Rates and Diploma Recipients by Race/Ethnicity

Category	Total	White	Black	Asian	AIAN	Hisp.
Enrollment (%)	100.0	87.9	4.8	4.8	0.3	2.1
Drop-out Rate (%)	0.7	0.7	1.4	0.0	0.0	0.0
H.S. Diplomas (#)	737	681	21	22	4	9

Quakertown Community SD

600 Park Ave • Quakertown, PA 18951-1588
(215) 529-2000 • http://www.qcsd.org
Grade Span: KG-12; Agency Type: 1
Schools: 9
   6 Primary; 2 Middle; 1 High; 0 Other Level
   9 Regular; 0 Special Education; 0 Vocational; 0 Alternative
   0 Magnet; 0 Charter; 4 Title I Eligible; 0 School-wide Title I
Students: 5,270   (n/a% male; n/a% female)
   Individual Education Program: 696 (13.2%);
   English Language Learner: n/a; Migrant: 0 (0.0%)
   Eligible for Free Lunch Program: 411 (7.8%)
   Eligible for Reduced-Price Lunch Program: 329 (6.2%)
Teachers: 280.0 (18.8 to 1)
Librarians/Media Specialists: 8.0 (658.8 to 1)
Guidance Counselors: 11.6 (454.3 to 1)
Current Spending: ($ per student per year):
   Total: $8,861; Instruction: $5,527; Support Services: $3,052
Enrollment, Drop-out Rates and Diploma Recipients by Race/Ethnicity

Category	Total	White	Black	Asian	AIAN	Hisp.
Enrollment (%)	100.0	95.5	1.3	1.0	0.2	2.0
Drop-out Rate (%)	2.7	2.6	3.7	0.0	n/a	13.3
H.S. Diplomas (#)	334	326	4	1	0	3

Butler County

Butler Area SD

110 Campus Ln • Butler, PA 16001-2662
(724) 287-8721 • http://www.butler.k12.pa.us
Grade Span: KG-12; Agency Type: 1
Schools: 14
   11 Primary; 1 Middle; 1 High; 1 Other Level
   14 Regular; 0 Special Education; 0 Vocational; 0 Alternative
   0 Magnet; 0 Charter; 9 Title I Eligible; 2 School-wide Title I
Students: 8,384   (n/a% male; n/a% female)
   Individual Education Program: 1,316 (15.7%);
   English Language Learner: n/a; Migrant: 2 (<0.1%)
   Eligible for Free Lunch Program: 1,426 (17.0%)
   Eligible for Reduced-Price Lunch Program: 446 (5.3%)
Teachers: 496.6 (16.9 to 1)
Librarians/Media Specialists: 8.6 (974.9 to 1)
Guidance Counselors: 13.0 (644.9 to 1)
Current Spending: ($ per student per year):
   Total: $7,279; Instruction: $4,738; Support Services: $2,269
Enrollment, Drop-out Rates and Diploma Recipients by Race/Ethnicity

Category	Total	White	Black	Asian	AIAN	Hisp.
Enrollment (%)	100.0	96.0	2.2	0.7	0.2	1.0
Drop-out Rate (%)	3.5	3.5	3.2	0.0	0.0	5.6
H.S. Diplomas (#)	558	546	3	2	1	6

Karns City Area SD

1446 Kittanning Pike • Karns City, PA 16041-1818
(724) 756-2030 • http://www.karnscity.k12.pa.us
Grade Span: KG-12; Agency Type: 1
Schools: 4
   3 Primary; 0 Middle; 1 High; 0 Other Level
   4 Regular; 0 Special Education; 0 Vocational; 0 Alternative
   0 Magnet; 0 Charter; 0 Title I Eligible; 0 School-wide Title I
Students: 1,832   (n/a% male; n/a% female)
   Individual Education Program: 210 (11.5%);
   English Language Learner: n/a; Migrant: 0 (0.0%)
   Eligible for Free Lunch Program: 406 (22.2%)
   Eligible for Reduced-Price Lunch Program: 165 (9.0%)
Teachers: 118.0 (15.5 to 1)
Librarians/Media Specialists: 2.0 (916.0 to 1)
Guidance Counselors: 4.0 (458.0 to 1)
Current Spending: ($ per student per year):
   Total: $7,959; Instruction: $4,973; Support Services: $2,597
Enrollment, Drop-out Rates and Diploma Recipients by Race/Ethnicity

Category	Total	White	Black	Asian	AIAN	Hisp.
Enrollment (%)	100.0	99.4	0.5	0.0	0.0	0.1
Drop-out Rate (%)	1.4	1.4	0.0	n/a	n/a	0.0
H.S. Diplomas (#)	130	129	1	0	0	0

Mars Area SD

545 Route 228 • Mars, PA 16046-3123
(724) 625-1518
Grade Span: KG-12; Agency Type: 1
Schools: 5

   2 Primary; 2 Middle; 1 High; 0 Other Level
   5 Regular; 0 Special Education; 0 Vocational; 0 Alternative
   0 Magnet; 0 Charter; 0 Title I Eligible; 0 School-wide Title I
Students: 2,751   (n/a% male; n/a% female)
   Individual Education Program: 134 (4.9%);
   English Language Learner: n/a; Migrant: 0 (0.0%)
   Eligible for Free Lunch Program: 144 (5.2%)
   Eligible for Reduced-Price Lunch Program: 110 (4.0%)
Teachers: 173.0 (15.9 to 1)
Librarians/Media Specialists: 4.0 (687.8 to 1)
Guidance Counselors: 6.0 (458.5 to 1)
Current Spending: ($ per student per year):
   Total: $7,270; Instruction: $4,535; Support Services: $2,531
Enrollment, Drop-out Rates and Diploma Recipients by Race/Ethnicity

Category	Total	White	Black	Asian	AIAN	Hisp.
Enrollment (%)	100.0	99.1	0.3	0.3	0.1	0.3
Drop-out Rate (%)	1.1	1.1	0.0	0.0	n/a	0.0
H.S. Diplomas (#)	207	202	2	2	0	1

Moniteau SD

1810 W Sunbury Rd • West Sunbury, PA 16061-1220
(724) 637-2117 • http://www.moniteau.k12.pa.us
Grade Span: KG-12; Agency Type: 1
Schools: 3
   2 Primary; 0 Middle; 1 High; 0 Other Level
   3 Regular; 0 Special Education; 0 Vocational; 0 Alternative
   0 Magnet; 0 Charter; 0 Title I Eligible; 0 School-wide Title I
Students: 1,705   (n/a% male; n/a% female)
   Individual Education Program: 254 (14.9%);
   English Language Learner: n/a; Migrant: 0 (0.0%)
   Eligible for Free Lunch Program: 416 (24.4%)
   Eligible for Reduced-Price Lunch Program: 152 (8.9%)
Teachers: 93.0 (18.3 to 1)
Librarians/Media Specialists: 2.0 (852.5 to 1)
Guidance Counselors: 3.0 (568.3 to 1)
Current Spending: ($ per student per year):
   Total: $7,650; Instruction: $4,644; Support Services: $2,588
Enrollment, Drop-out Rates and Diploma Recipients by Race/Ethnicity

Category	Total	White	Black	Asian	AIAN	Hisp.
Enrollment (%)	100.0	98.8	0.6	0.1	0.0	0.6
Drop-out Rate (%)	2.5	2.5	0.0	0.0	0.0	0.0
H.S. Diplomas (#)	103	102	0	1	0	0

Seneca Valley SD

124 Seneca School Rd • Harmony, PA 16037-9101
(724) 452-6040 • http://www.seneca.k12.pa.us
Grade Span: KG-12; Agency Type: 1
Schools: 9
   4 Primary; 3 Middle; 1 High; 1 Other Level
   9 Regular; 0 Special Education; 0 Vocational; 0 Alternative
   0 Magnet; 0 Charter; 6 Title I Eligible; 0 School-wide Title I
Students: 7,646   (n/a% male; n/a% female)
   Individual Education Program: 1,034 (13.5%);
   English Language Learner: n/a; Migrant: 0 (0.0%)
   Eligible for Free Lunch Program: 445 (5.8%)
   Eligible for Reduced-Price Lunch Program: 186 (2.4%)
Teachers: 511.6 (14.9 to 1)
Librarians/Media Specialists: 8.0 (955.8 to 1)
Guidance Counselors: 16.5 (463.4 to 1)
Current Spending: ($ per student per year):
   Total: $7,204; Instruction: $4,829; Support Services: $2,096
Enrollment, Drop-out Rates and Diploma Recipients by Race/Ethnicity

Category	Total	White	Black	Asian	AIAN	Hisp.
Enrollment (%)	100.0	96.7	1.4	1.3	0.0	0.6
Drop-out Rate (%)	2.0	2.0	6.3	0.0	0.0	0.0
H.S. Diplomas (#)	497	485	3	6	0	3

Slippery Rock Area SD

201 Kiester Rd • Slippery Rock, PA 16057-1601
(724) 794-2960
Grade Span: KG-12; Agency Type: 1
Schools: 5
   3 Primary; 1 Middle; 1 High; 0 Other Level
   5 Regular; 0 Special Education; 0 Vocational; 0 Alternative
   0 Magnet; 0 Charter; 0 Title I Eligible; 0 School-wide Title I
Students: 2,568   (n/a% male; n/a% female)
   Individual Education Program: 369 (14.4%);
   English Language Learner: n/a; Migrant: 0 (0.0%)
   Eligible for Free Lunch Program: 406 (15.8%)
   Eligible for Reduced-Price Lunch Program: 225 (8.8%)
Teachers: 148.4 (17.3 to 1)
Librarians/Media Specialists: 3.0 (856.0 to 1)
Guidance Counselors: 5.0 (513.6 to 1)
Current Spending: ($ per student per year):
   Total: $6,924; Instruction: $4,354; Support Services: $2,288

Enrollment, Drop-out Rates and Diploma Recipients by Race/Ethnicity

Category	Total	White	Black	Asian	AIAN	Hisp.
Enrollment (%)	100.0	97.7	0.9	0.9	0.4	0.2
Drop-out Rate (%)	1.7	1.7	0.0	0.0	n/a	n/a
H.S. Diplomas (#)	151	151	0	0	0	0

South Butler County SD
328 Knoch Rd · Saxonburg, PA 16056-0657
(724) 352-1700 · http://southbutler.k12.pa.us
Grade Span: KG-12; **Agency Type:** 1
Schools: 4
    1 Primary; 2 Middle; 1 High; 0 Other Level
    4 Regular; 0 Special Education; 0 Vocational; 0 Alternative
    0 Magnet; 0 Charter; 0 Title I Eligible; 0 School-wide Title I
Students: 2,917   (n/a% male; n/a% female)
    Individual Education Program: 266 (9.1%);
    English Language Learner: n/a; Migrant: 0 (0.0%)
    Eligible for Free Lunch Program: 140 (4.8%)
    Eligible for Reduced-Price Lunch Program: 79 (2.7%)
Teachers: 167.5 (17.4 to 1)
Librarians/Media Specialists: 4.0 (729.3 to 1)
Guidance Counselors: 5.0 (583.4 to 1)
Current Spending: ($ per student per year):
    Total: $6,898; Instruction: $4,092; Support Services: $2,575
Enrollment, Drop-out Rates and Diploma Recipients by Race/Ethnicity

Category	Total	White	Black	Asian	AIAN	Hisp.
Enrollment (%)	100.0	99.2	0.4	0.1	0.1	0.1
Drop-out Rate (%)	1.7	1.6	33.3	n/a	n/a	0.0
H.S. Diplomas (#)	220	220	0	0	0	0

Cambria County

Cambria Heights SD
PO Box 66 · Patton, PA 16668-0066
(814) 674-3626 · http://www.chsd.k12.pa.us
Grade Span: KG-12; **Agency Type:** 1
Schools: 3
    1 Primary; 1 Middle; 1 High; 0 Other Level
    3 Regular; 0 Special Education; 0 Vocational; 0 Alternative
    0 Magnet; 0 Charter; 3 Title I Eligible; 0 School-wide Title I
Students: 1,549   (n/a% male; n/a% female)
    Individual Education Program: 222 (14.3%);
    English Language Learner: n/a; Migrant: 0 (0.0%)
    Eligible for Free Lunch Program: 387 (25.0%)
    Eligible for Reduced-Price Lunch Program: 135 (8.7%)
Teachers: 115.2 (13.4 to 1)
Librarians/Media Specialists: 3.0 (516.3 to 1)
Guidance Counselors: 5.0 (309.8 to 1)
Current Spending: ($ per student per year):
    Total: $8,700; Instruction: $5,600; Support Services: $2,769
Enrollment, Drop-out Rates and Diploma Recipients by Race/Ethnicity

Category	Total	White	Black	Asian	AIAN	Hisp.
Enrollment (%)	100.0	99.3	0.4	0.1	0.0	0.3
Drop-out Rate (%)	1.3	1.3	n/a	n/a	n/a	0.0
H.S. Diplomas (#)	147	147	0	0	0	0

Central Cambria SD
208 Schoolhouse Rd · Ebensburg, PA 15931-7617
(814) 472-8870 · http://www.cchs.k12.pa.us
Grade Span: KG-12; **Agency Type:** 1
Schools: 4
    2 Primary; 1 Middle; 1 High; 0 Other Level
    4 Regular; 0 Special Education; 0 Vocational; 0 Alternative
    0 Magnet; 0 Charter; 2 Title I Eligible; 0 School-wide Title I
Students: 1,912   (n/a% male; n/a% female)
    Individual Education Program: 287 (15.0%);
    English Language Learner: n/a; Migrant: 0 (0.0%)
    Eligible for Free Lunch Program: 369 (19.3%)
    Eligible for Reduced-Price Lunch Program: 195 (10.2%)
Teachers: 123.0 (15.5 to 1)
Librarians/Media Specialists: 3.0 (637.3 to 1)
Guidance Counselors: 5.0 (382.4 to 1)
Current Spending: ($ per student per year):
    Total: $7,999; Instruction: $4,911; Support Services: $2,705
Enrollment, Drop-out Rates and Diploma Recipients by Race/Ethnicity

Category	Total	White	Black	Asian	AIAN	Hisp.
Enrollment (%)	100.0	98.3	0.7	0.8	0.0	0.2
Drop-out Rate (%)	1.0	1.0	0.0	0.0	n/a	0.0
H.S. Diplomas (#)	180	179	0	1	0	0

Forest Hills SD
PO Box 158 · Sidman, PA 15955-0158
(814) 487-7613 · http://www.fhsd.k12.pa.us
Grade Span: KG-12; **Agency Type:** 1
Schools: 3

    1 Primary; 1 Middle; 1 High; 0 Other Level
    3 Regular; 0 Special Education; 0 Vocational; 0 Alternative
    0 Magnet; 0 Charter; 2 Title I Eligible; 0 School-wide Title I
Students: 2,334   (n/a% male; n/a% female)
    Individual Education Program: 244 (10.5%);
    English Language Learner: n/a; Migrant: 0 (0.0%)
    Eligible for Free Lunch Program: 533 (22.8%)
    Eligible for Reduced-Price Lunch Program: 287 (12.3%)
Teachers: 143.5 (16.3 to 1)
Librarians/Media Specialists: 4.0 (583.5 to 1)
Guidance Counselors: 5.0 (466.8 to 1)
Current Spending: ($ per student per year):
    Total: $6,863; Instruction: $4,321; Support Services: $2,207
Enrollment, Drop-out Rates and Diploma Recipients by Race/Ethnicity

Category	Total	White	Black	Asian	AIAN	Hisp.
Enrollment (%)	100.0	99.1	0.7	0.0	0.0	0.2
Drop-out Rate (%)	1.1	1.1	n/a	n/a	n/a	0.0
H.S. Diplomas (#)	157	157	0	0	0	0

Greater Johnstown SD
1091 Broad St · Johnstown, PA 15906-2437
(814) 533-5651 · http://trojan.gjsd.k12.pa.us
Grade Span: PK-12; **Agency Type:** 1
Schools: 4
    3 Primary; 0 Middle; 1 High; 0 Other Level
    4 Regular; 0 Special Education; 0 Vocational; 0 Alternative
    0 Magnet; 0 Charter; 4 Title I Eligible; 2 School-wide Title I
Students: 3,578   (n/a% male; n/a% female)
    Individual Education Program: 561 (15.7%);
    English Language Learner: n/a; Migrant: 0 (0.0%)
    Eligible for Free Lunch Program: 2,152 (60.1%)
    Eligible for Reduced-Price Lunch Program: 419 (11.7%)
Teachers: 239.0 (15.0 to 1)
Librarians/Media Specialists: 4.0 (894.5 to 1)
Guidance Counselors: 6.0 (596.3 to 1)
Current Spending: ($ per student per year):
    Total: $8,689; Instruction: $5,591; Support Services: $2,675
Enrollment, Drop-out Rates and Diploma Recipients by Race/Ethnicity

Category	Total	White	Black	Asian	AIAN	Hisp.
Enrollment (%)	100.0	71.6	26.6	0.3	0.1	1.4
Drop-out Rate (%)	3.0	3.7	1.0	0.0	0.0	0.0
H.S. Diplomas (#)	177	135	36	2	0	4

Penn Cambria SD
201 6th St · Cresson, PA 16630-1363
(814) 886-8121
Grade Span: KG-12; **Agency Type:** 1
Schools: 5
    2 Primary; 2 Middle; 1 High; 0 Other Level
    5 Regular; 0 Special Education; 0 Vocational; 0 Alternative
    0 Magnet; 0 Charter; 5 Title I Eligible; 0 School-wide Title I
Students: 1,867   (n/a% male; n/a% female)
    Individual Education Program: 275 (14.7%);
    English Language Learner: n/a; Migrant: 0 (0.0%)
    Eligible for Free Lunch Program: 576 (30.9%)
    Eligible for Reduced-Price Lunch Program: 271 (14.5%)
Teachers: 125.0 (14.9 to 1)
Librarians/Media Specialists: 4.0 (466.8 to 1)
Guidance Counselors: 6.0 (311.2 to 1)
Current Spending: ($ per student per year):
    Total: $8,626; Instruction: $5,378; Support Services: $2,774
Enrollment, Drop-out Rates and Diploma Recipients by Race/Ethnicity

Category	Total	White	Black	Asian	AIAN	Hisp.
Enrollment (%)	100.0	99.0	0.4	0.1	0.4	0.2
Drop-out Rate (%)	1.9	1.7	16.7	n/a	0.0	50.0
H.S. Diplomas (#)	173	171	2	0	0	0

Richland SD
PO Box 5370 · Johnstown, PA 15904-5370
(814) 266-6063
Grade Span: KG-12; **Agency Type:** 1
Schools: 3
    1 Primary; 1 Middle; 1 High; 0 Other Level
    3 Regular; 0 Special Education; 0 Vocational; 0 Alternative
    0 Magnet; 0 Charter; 2 Title I Eligible; 0 School-wide Title I
Students: 1,593   (n/a% male; n/a% female)
    Individual Education Program: 152 (9.5%);
    English Language Learner: n/a; Migrant: 0 (0.0%)
    Eligible for Free Lunch Program: 124 (7.8%)
    Eligible for Reduced-Price Lunch Program: 59 (3.7%)
Teachers: 93.5 (17.0 to 1)
Librarians/Media Specialists: 3.0 (531.0 to 1)
Guidance Counselors: 3.0 (531.0 to 1)
Current Spending: ($ per student per year):
    Total: $7,721; Instruction: $4,641; Support Services: $2,772

Enrollment, Drop-out Rates and Diploma Recipients by Race/Ethnicity

Category	Total	White	Black	Asian	AIAN	Hisp.
Enrollment (%)	100.0	96.7	1.1	1.6	0.0	0.6
Drop-out Rate (%)	1.7	1.8	0.0	0.0	n/a	0.0
H.S. Diplomas (#)	136	133	1	2	0	0

Westmont Hilltop SD

827 Diamond Blvd • Johnstown, PA 15905-2348
(814) 255-6751 • http://westy.jtwn.k12.pa.us
Grade Span: KG-12; **Agency Type:** 1
Schools: 3
   1 Primary; 1 Middle; 1 High; 0 Other Level
   3 Regular; 0 Special Education; 0 Vocational; 0 Alternative
   0 Magnet; 0 Charter; 3 Title I Eligible; 0 School-wide Title I
Students: 1,720 (n/a% male; n/a% female)
   Individual Education Program: 166 (9.7%);
   English Language Learner: n/a; Migrant: 0 (0.0%)
   Eligible for Free Lunch Program: 143 (8.3%)
   Eligible for Reduced-Price Lunch Program: 96 (5.6%)
Teachers: 103.5 (16.6 to 1)
Librarians/Media Specialists: 2.0 (860.0 to 1)
Guidance Counselors: 5.0 (344.0 to 1)
Current Spending: ($ per student per year):
   Total: $7,510; Instruction: $4,553; Support Services: $2,651

Enrollment, Drop-out Rates and Diploma Recipients by Race/Ethnicity

Category	Total	White	Black	Asian	AIAN	Hisp.
Enrollment (%)	100.0	96.9	0.9	1.0	0.2	0.9
Drop-out Rate (%)	0.0	0.0	0.0	0.0	0.0	0.0
H.S. Diplomas (#)	139	134	2	1	0	2

Carbon County

Jim Thorpe Area SD

140 W 10th St • Jim Thorpe, PA 18229-1702
(570) 325-3691 • http://www.jtasd.k12.pa.us/index.html
Grade Span: KG-12; **Agency Type:** 1
Schools: 4
   1 Primary; 1 Middle; 1 High; 1 Other Level
   4 Regular; 0 Special Education; 0 Vocational; 0 Alternative
   0 Magnet; 0 Charter; 3 Title I Eligible; 0 School-wide Title I
Students: 1,822 (n/a% male; n/a% female)
   Individual Education Program: 301 (16.5%);
   English Language Learner: n/a; Migrant: 0 (0.0%)
   Eligible for Free Lunch Program: 320 (17.6%)
   Eligible for Reduced-Price Lunch Program: 138 (7.6%)
Teachers: 114.0 (16.0 to 1)
Librarians/Media Specialists: 3.0 (607.3 to 1)
Guidance Counselors: 3.0 (607.3 to 1)
Current Spending: ($ per student per year):
   Total: $8,040; Instruction: $4,671; Support Services: $3,060

Enrollment, Drop-out Rates and Diploma Recipients by Race/Ethnicity

Category	Total	White	Black	Asian	AIAN	Hisp.
Enrollment (%)	100.0	89.7	4.8	0.9	0.1	4.4
Drop-out Rate (%)	1.7	1.6	0.0	0.0	0.0	6.3
H.S. Diplomas (#)	96	81	10	2	0	3

Lehighton Area SD

1000 Union St • Lehighton, PA 18235-1700
(610) 377-4490
Grade Span: KG-12; **Agency Type:** 1
Schools: 6
   4 Primary; 1 Middle; 1 High; 0 Other Level
   6 Regular; 0 Special Education; 0 Vocational; 0 Alternative
   0 Magnet; 0 Charter; 4 Title I Eligible; 0 School-wide Title I
Students: 2,451 (n/a% male; n/a% female)
   Individual Education Program: 306 (12.5%);
   English Language Learner: n/a; Migrant: 0 (0.0%)
   Eligible for Free Lunch Program: 360 (14.7%)
   Eligible for Reduced-Price Lunch Program: 182 (7.4%)
Teachers: 174.0 (14.1 to 1)
Librarians/Media Specialists: 4.0 (612.8 to 1)
Guidance Counselors: 6.0 (408.5 to 1)
Current Spending: ($ per student per year):
   Total: $8,084; Instruction: $5,291; Support Services: $2,466

Enrollment, Drop-out Rates and Diploma Recipients by Race/Ethnicity

Category	Total	White	Black	Asian	AIAN	Hisp.
Enrollment (%)	100.0	97.3	0.8	0.8	0.0	1.0
Drop-out Rate (%)	1.3	1.4	0.0	0.0	0.0	0.0
H.S. Diplomas (#)	172	169	1	1	0	1

Palmerton Area SD

PO Box 350 • Palmerton, PA 18071-0350
(610) 826-2364 • http://www.palmerton.k12.pa.us/
Grade Span: KG-12; **Agency Type:** 1
Schools: 4

   2 Primary; 1 Middle; 1 High; 0 Other Level
   4 Regular; 0 Special Education; 0 Vocational; 0 Alternative
   0 Magnet; 0 Charter; 3 Title I Eligible; 0 School-wide Title I
Students: 1,995 (n/a% male; n/a% female)
   Individual Education Program: 293 (14.7%);
   English Language Learner: n/a; Migrant: 0 (0.0%)
   Eligible for Free Lunch Program: 265 (13.3%)
   Eligible for Reduced-Price Lunch Program: 117 (5.9%)
Teachers: 113.0 (17.7 to 1)
Librarians/Media Specialists: 2.0 (997.5 to 1)
Guidance Counselors: 6.0 (332.5 to 1)
Current Spending: ($ per student per year):
   Total: $7,287; Instruction: $4,690; Support Services: $2,286

Enrollment, Drop-out Rates and Diploma Recipients by Race/Ethnicity

Category	Total	White	Black	Asian	AIAN	Hisp.
Enrollment (%)	100.0	97.5	0.4	0.6	0.2	1.3
Drop-out Rate (%)	0.9	0.9	0.0	0.0	n/a	0.0
H.S. Diplomas (#)	129	128	0	0	0	1

Centre County

Bald Eagle Area SD

751 S Eaglevalley Rd • Wingate, PA 16823-4740
(814) 355-4860 • http://www.beasd.k12.pa.us
Grade Span: KG-12; **Agency Type:** 1
Schools: 5
   4 Primary; 0 Middle; 1 High; 0 Other Level
   5 Regular; 0 Special Education; 0 Vocational; 0 Alternative
   0 Magnet; 0 Charter; 3 Title I Eligible; 0 School-wide Title I
Students: 2,054 (n/a% male; n/a% female)
   Individual Education Program: 279 (13.6%);
   English Language Learner: n/a; Migrant: 0 (0.0%)
   Eligible for Free Lunch Program: 437 (21.3%)
   Eligible for Reduced-Price Lunch Program: 247 (12.0%)
Teachers: 137.0 (15.0 to 1)
Librarians/Media Specialists: 2.0 (1,027.0 to 1)
Guidance Counselors: 5.0 (410.8 to 1)
Current Spending: ($ per student per year):
   Total: $7,910; Instruction: $4,744; Support Services: $2,763

Enrollment, Drop-out Rates and Diploma Recipients by Race/Ethnicity

Category	Total	White	Black	Asian	AIAN	Hisp.
Enrollment (%)	100.0	99.2	0.3	0.1	0.0	0.3
Drop-out Rate (%)	2.4	2.4	0.0	0.0	n/a	n/a
H.S. Diplomas (#)	186	184	0	2	0	0

Bellefonte Area SD

318 N Allegheny St • Bellefonte, PA 16823-1613
(814) 355-4814 • http://www.basd.net
Grade Span: KG-12; **Agency Type:** 1
Schools: 6
   4 Primary; 1 Middle; 1 High; 0 Other Level
   6 Regular; 0 Special Education; 0 Vocational; 0 Alternative
   0 Magnet; 0 Charter; 4 Title I Eligible; 0 School-wide Title I
Students: 3,006 (n/a% male; n/a% female)
   Individual Education Program: 485 (16.1%);
   English Language Learner: n/a; Migrant: 1 (<0.1%)
   Eligible for Free Lunch Program: 459 (15.3%)
   Eligible for Reduced-Price Lunch Program: 262 (8.7%)
Teachers: 200.5 (15.0 to 1)
Librarians/Media Specialists: 4.0 (751.5 to 1)
Guidance Counselors: 8.0 (375.8 to 1)
Current Spending: ($ per student per year):
   Total: $7,858; Instruction: $4,702; Support Services: $2,815

Enrollment, Drop-out Rates and Diploma Recipients by Race/Ethnicity

Category	Total	White	Black	Asian	AIAN	Hisp.
Enrollment (%)	100.0	97.6	1.4	0.3	0.0	0.6
Drop-out Rate (%)	2.9	2.8	14.3	0.0	n/a	n/a
H.S. Diplomas (#)	218	216	2	0	0	0

Penns Valley Area SD

4528 Penns Valley Rd • Spring Mills, PA 16875-9403
(814) 422-8814 • http://www.pennsvalley.org
Grade Span: KG-12; **Agency Type:** 1
Schools: 5
   4 Primary; 0 Middle; 1 High; 0 Other Level
   5 Regular; 0 Special Education; 0 Vocational; 0 Alternative
   0 Magnet; 0 Charter; 4 Title I Eligible; 0 School-wide Title I
Students: 1,615 (n/a% male; n/a% female)
   Individual Education Program: 260 (16.1%);
   English Language Learner: n/a; Migrant: 1 (0.1%)
   Eligible for Free Lunch Program: 209 (12.9%)
   Eligible for Reduced-Price Lunch Program: 120 (7.4%)
Teachers: 109.5 (14.7 to 1)
Librarians/Media Specialists: 2.0 (807.5 to 1)
Guidance Counselors: 4.0 (403.8 to 1)

Current Spending: ($ per student per year):
    Total: $8,175; Instruction: $4,900; Support Services: $2,958
Enrollment, Drop-out Rates and Diploma Recipients by Race/Ethnicity

Category	Total	White	Black	Asian	AIAN	Hisp.
Enrollment (%)	100.0	98.3	0.3	0.7	0.1	0.6
Drop-out Rate (%)	0.6	0.6	n/a	0.0	0.0	0.0
H.S. Diplomas (#)	103	103	0	0	0	0

State College Area SD
131 W Nittany Ave • State College, PA 16801-4812
(814) 231-1011 • http://www.scasd.k12.pa.us
Grade Span: KG-12; **Agency Type:** 1
Schools: 11
    8 Primary; 2 Middle; 1 High; 0 Other Level
    11 Regular; 0 Special Education; 0 Vocational; 0 Alternative
    0 Magnet; 0 Charter; 5 Title I Eligible; 0 School-wide Title I
Students: 7,343   (n/a% male; n/a% female)
    Individual Education Program: 856 (11.7%);
    English Language Learner: n/a; Migrant: 1 (<0.1%)
    Eligible for Free Lunch Program: 577 (7.9%)
    Eligible for Reduced-Price Lunch Program: 274 (3.7%)
Teachers: 514.2 (14.3 to 1)
Librarians/Media Specialists: 12.0 (611.9 to 1)
Guidance Counselors: 22.0 (333.8 to 1)
Current Spending: ($ per student per year):
    Total: $9,071; Instruction: $5,659; Support Services: $3,052
Enrollment, Drop-out Rates and Diploma Recipients by Race/Ethnicity

Category	Total	White	Black	Asian	AIAN	Hisp.
Enrollment (%)	100.0	87.3	3.0	6.6	0.4	2.7
Drop-out Rate (%)	0.9	1.0	0.0	0.0	0.0	0.0
H.S. Diplomas (#)	610	592	9	6	0	3

Chester County

Avon Grove SD
375 S Jennersville Rd • West Grove, PA 19390-8401
(610) 869-2441 • http://www.avongrove.org
Grade Span: KG-12; **Agency Type:** 1
Schools: 4
    2 Primary; 1 Middle; 1 High; 0 Other Level
    4 Regular; 0 Special Education; 0 Vocational; 0 Alternative
    0 Magnet; 0 Charter; 2 Title I Eligible; 0 School-wide Title I
Students: 4,854   (n/a% male; n/a% female)
    Individual Education Program: 620 (12.8%);
    English Language Learner: n/a; Migrant: 253 (5.2%)
    Eligible for Free Lunch Program: 294 (6.1%)
    Eligible for Reduced-Price Lunch Program: 173 (3.6%)
Teachers: 276.6 (17.5 to 1)
Librarians/Media Specialists: 5.0 (970.8 to 1)
Guidance Counselors: 15.0 (323.6 to 1)
Current Spending: ($ per student per year):
    Total: $7,914; Instruction: $4,401; Support Services: $3,249
Enrollment, Drop-out Rates and Diploma Recipients by Race/Ethnicity

Category	Total	White	Black	Asian	AIAN	Hisp.
Enrollment (%)	100.0	83.6	3.5	0.7	0.0	12.3
Drop-out Rate (%)	1.8	1.1	0.0	0.0	n/a	8.7
H.S. Diplomas (#)	272	245	6	1	0	20

Coatesville Area SD
1515 E Lincoln Hwy • Coatesville, PA 19320-2447
(610) 383-7900 • http://www.coatesville.k12.pa.us
Grade Span: KG-12; **Agency Type:** 1
Schools: 12
    7 Primary; 3 Middle; 1 High; 1 Other Level
    12 Regular; 0 Special Education; 0 Vocational; 0 Alternative
    0 Magnet; 0 Charter; 7 Title I Eligible; 0 School-wide Title I
Students: 7,319   (n/a% male; n/a% female)
    Individual Education Program: 1,081 (14.8%);
    English Language Learner: n/a; Migrant: 47 (0.6%)
    Eligible for Free Lunch Program: 1,892 (25.9%)
    Eligible for Reduced-Price Lunch Program: 486 (6.6%)
Teachers: 442.5 (16.5 to 1)
Librarians/Media Specialists: 11.0 (665.4 to 1)
Guidance Counselors: 24.0 (305.0 to 1)
Current Spending: ($ per student per year):
    Total: $8,895; Instruction: $5,507; Support Services: $3,135
Enrollment, Drop-out Rates and Diploma Recipients by Race/Ethnicity

Category	Total	White	Black	Asian	AIAN	Hisp.
Enrollment (%)	100.0	59.4	31.7	1.0	0.1	7.7
Drop-out Rate (%)	2.0	1.7	2.6	0.0	n/a	2.9
H.S. Diplomas (#)	526	353	146	9	0	18

Downingtown Area SD
126 Wallace Ave • Downingtown, PA 19335-2643
(610) 269-8460 • http://www.dasd-adm.org/
Grade Span: KG-12; **Agency Type:** 1
Schools: 13
    9 Primary; 2 Middle; 2 High; 0 Other Level
    13 Regular; 0 Special Education; 0 Vocational; 0 Alternative
    0 Magnet; 0 Charter; 5 Title I Eligible; 0 School-wide Title I
Students: 10,700   (n/a% male; n/a% female)
    Individual Education Program: 1,526 (14.3%);
    English Language Learner: n/a; Migrant: 0 (0.0%)
    Eligible for Free Lunch Program: 157 (1.5%)
    Eligible for Reduced-Price Lunch Program: 104 (1.0%)
Teachers: 683.7 (15.7 to 1)
Librarians/Media Specialists: 13.4 (798.5 to 1)
Guidance Counselors: 25.0 (428.0 to 1)
Current Spending: ($ per student per year):
    Total: $8,678; Instruction: $5,454; Support Services: $3,020
Enrollment, Drop-out Rates and Diploma Recipients by Race/Ethnicity

Category	Total	White	Black	Asian	AIAN	Hisp.
Enrollment (%)	100.0	92.1	3.9	2.7	0.0	1.2
Drop-out Rate (%)	0.5	0.4	1.9	0.0	0.0	0.0
H.S. Diplomas (#)	610	570	21	17	0	2

Great Valley SD
47 Church Rd • Malvern, PA 19355-1539
(610) 889-2100 • http://www.great-valley.k12.pa.us
Grade Span: KG-12; **Agency Type:** 1
Schools: 5
    3 Primary; 1 Middle; 1 High; 0 Other Level
    5 Regular; 0 Special Education; 0 Vocational; 0 Alternative
    0 Magnet; 0 Charter; 4 Title I Eligible; 0 School-wide Title I
Students: 3,807   (n/a% male; n/a% female)
    Individual Education Program: 623 (16.4%);
    English Language Learner: n/a; Migrant: 0 (0.0%)
    Eligible for Free Lunch Program: 47 (1.2%)
    Eligible for Reduced-Price Lunch Program: 33 (0.9%)
Teachers: 250.3 (15.2 to 1)
Librarians/Media Specialists: 5.0 (761.4 to 1)
Guidance Counselors: 11.0 (346.1 to 1)
Current Spending: ($ per student per year):
    Total: $11,616; Instruction: $7,252; Support Services: $4,005
Enrollment, Drop-out Rates and Diploma Recipients by Race/Ethnicity

Category	Total	White	Black	Asian	AIAN	Hisp.
Enrollment (%)	100.0	89.7	3.1	5.7	0.1	1.5
Drop-out Rate (%)	0.4	0.4	0.0	0.0	0.0	0.0
H.S. Diplomas (#)	232	207	10	12	1	2

Kennett Consolidated SD
300 E S St • Kennett Square, PA 19348-3655
(610) 444-6600 • http://www.kennett.k12.pa.us
Grade Span: KG-12; **Agency Type:** 1
Schools: 5
    3 Primary; 1 Middle; 1 High; 0 Other Level
    5 Regular; 0 Special Education; 0 Vocational; 0 Alternative
    0 Magnet; 0 Charter; 2 Title I Eligible; 0 School-wide Title I
Students: 4,038   (n/a% male; n/a% female)
    Individual Education Program: 490 (12.1%);
    English Language Learner: n/a; Migrant: 634 (15.7%)
    Eligible for Free Lunch Program: 700 (17.3%)
    Eligible for Reduced-Price Lunch Program: 212 (5.3%)
Teachers: 241.1 (16.7 to 1)
Librarians/Media Specialists: 5.0 (807.6 to 1)
Guidance Counselors: 10.5 (384.6 to 1)
Current Spending: ($ per student per year):
    Total: $9,062; Instruction: $5,395; Support Services: $3,369
Enrollment, Drop-out Rates and Diploma Recipients by Race/Ethnicity

Category	Total	White	Black	Asian	AIAN	Hisp.
Enrollment (%)	100.0	62.1	4.4	1.9	0.0	31.6
Drop-out Rate (%)	1.6	0.8	2.1	0.0	n/a	4.1
H.S. Diplomas (#)	189	137	19	5	0	28

Octorara Area SD
PO Box 500 • Atglen, PA 19310-0500
(610) 593-8213 • http://www.octorara.k12.pa.us/
Grade Span: KG-12; **Agency Type:** 1
Schools: 4
    2 Primary; 1 Middle; 1 High; 0 Other Level
    4 Regular; 0 Special Education; 0 Vocational; 0 Alternative
    0 Magnet; 0 Charter; 4 Title I Eligible; 0 School-wide Title I
Students: 2,669   (n/a% male; n/a% female)
    Individual Education Program: 381 (14.3%);
    English Language Learner: n/a; Migrant: 30 (1.1%)
    Eligible for Free Lunch Program: 275 (10.3%)
    Eligible for Reduced-Price Lunch Program: 95 (3.6%)

Teachers: 159.5 (16.7 to 1)
Librarians/Media Specialists: 3.0 (889.7 to 1)
Guidance Counselors: 8.0 (333.6 to 1)
Current Spending: ($ per student per year):
    Total: $8,569; Instruction: $5,415; Support Services: $2,916
Enrollment, Drop-out Rates and Diploma Recipients by Race/Ethnicity

Category	Total	White	Black	Asian	AIAN	Hisp.
Enrollment (%)	100.0	90.6	5.2	0.1	0.0	4.0
Drop-out Rate (%)	1.9	1.3	11.1	0.0	n/a	11.1
H.S. Diplomas (#)	141	127	8	2	0	4

Owen J Roberts SD

901 Ridge Rd • Pottstown, PA 19465-8402
(610) 469-5100 • http://www.ojr.k12.pa.us
Grade Span: KG-12; **Agency Type:** 1
Schools: 6
    4 Primary; 1 Middle; 1 High; 0 Other Level
    6 Regular; 0 Special Education; 0 Vocational; 0 Alternative
    0 Magnet; 0 Charter; 2 Title I Eligible; 0 School-wide Title I
Students: 4,253 (n/a% male; n/a% female)
    Individual Education Program: 575 (13.5%);
    English Language Learner: n/a; Migrant: 0 (0.0%)
    Eligible for Free Lunch Program: 233 (5.5%)
    Eligible for Reduced-Price Lunch Program: 111 (2.6%)
Teachers: 273.4 (15.6 to 1)
Librarians/Media Specialists: 4.0 (1,063.3 to 1)
Guidance Counselors: 11.0 (386.6 to 1)
Current Spending: ($ per student per year):
    Total: $10,804; Instruction: $6,325; Support Services: $4,174
Enrollment, Drop-out Rates and Diploma Recipients by Race/Ethnicity

Category	Total	White	Black	Asian	AIAN	Hisp.
Enrollment (%)	100.0	96.2	2.7	0.6	0.2	0.4
Drop-out Rate (%)	1.4	1.3	0.0	0.0	100.0	0.0
H.S. Diplomas (#)	261	258	2	0	0	1

Oxford Area SD

119 S 5th St • Oxford, PA 19363-1770
(610) 932-6600 • http://www.oxford.k12.pa.us
Grade Span: KG-12; **Agency Type:** 1
Schools: 5
    2 Primary; 2 Middle; 1 High; 0 Other Level
    5 Regular; 0 Special Education; 0 Vocational; 0 Alternative
    0 Magnet; 0 Charter; 5 Title I Eligible; 0 School-wide Title I
Students: 3,336 (n/a% male; n/a% female)
    Individual Education Program: 324 (9.7%);
    English Language Learner: n/a; Migrant: 111 (3.3%)
    Eligible for Free Lunch Program: 609 (18.3%)
    Eligible for Reduced-Price Lunch Program: 178 (5.3%)
Teachers: 218.3 (15.3 to 1)
Librarians/Media Specialists: 5.0 (667.2 to 1)
Guidance Counselors: 6.5 (513.2 to 1)
Current Spending: ($ per student per year):
    Total: $7,728; Instruction: $4,846; Support Services: $2,579
Enrollment, Drop-out Rates and Diploma Recipients by Race/Ethnicity

Category	Total	White	Black	Asian	AIAN	Hisp.
Enrollment (%)	100.0	78.5	6.5	0.7	0.0	14.3
Drop-out Rate (%)	6.2	5.9	2.7	0.0	n/a	12.0
H.S. Diplomas (#)	162	136	16	3	0	7

Phoenixville Area SD

1120 Gay St • Phoenixville, PA 19460-4417
(484) 527-5000 • http://www.pasd.com
Grade Span: KG-12; **Agency Type:** 1
Schools: 6
    4 Primary; 1 Middle; 1 High; 0 Other Level
    6 Regular; 0 Special Education; 0 Vocational; 0 Alternative
    0 Magnet; 0 Charter; 2 Title I Eligible; 0 School-wide Title I
Students: 3,169 (n/a% male; n/a% female)
    Individual Education Program: 505 (15.9%);
    English Language Learner: n/a; Migrant: 0 (0.0%)
    Eligible for Free Lunch Program: 271 (8.6%)
    Eligible for Reduced-Price Lunch Program: 152 (4.8%)
Teachers: 235.0 (13.5 to 1)
Librarians/Media Specialists: 5.6 (565.9 to 1)
Guidance Counselors: 10.6 (299.0 to 1)
Current Spending: ($ per student per year):
    Total: n/a; Instruction: n/a; Support Services: n/a
Enrollment, Drop-out Rates and Diploma Recipients by Race/Ethnicity

Category	Total	White	Black	Asian	AIAN	Hisp.
Enrollment (%)	100.0	83.7	10.0	2.9	0.1	3.3
Drop-out Rate (%)	1.0	1.1	0.0	0.0	0.0	4.8
H.S. Diplomas (#)	184	165	14	3	0	2

Tredyffrin-Easttown SD

738 First Ave • Berwyn, PA 19312-1779
(610) 240-1900 • http://www.tesd.k12.pa.us
Grade Span: KG-12; **Agency Type:** 1
Schools: 8
    5 Primary; 2 Middle; 1 High; 0 Other Level
    8 Regular; 0 Special Education; 0 Vocational; 0 Alternative
    0 Magnet; 0 Charter; 0 Title I Eligible; 0 School-wide Title I
Students: 5,726 (n/a% male; n/a% female)
    Individual Education Program: 726 (12.7%);
    English Language Learner: n/a; Migrant: 0 (0.0%)
    Eligible for Free Lunch Program: 85 (1.5%)
    Eligible for Reduced-Price Lunch Program: 40 (0.7%)
Teachers: 396.6 (14.4 to 1)
Librarians/Media Specialists: 9.0 (636.2 to 1)
Guidance Counselors: 21.0 (272.7 to 1)
Current Spending: ($ per student per year):
    Total: $11,061; Instruction: $6,730; Support Services: $4,045
Enrollment, Drop-out Rates and Diploma Recipients by Race/Ethnicity

Category	Total	White	Black	Asian	AIAN	Hisp.
Enrollment (%)	100.0	88.1	3.3	7.5	0.1	1.0
Drop-out Rate (%)	0.1	0.0	2.6	0.0	0.0	0.0
H.S. Diplomas (#)	372	331	9	29	0	3

Unionville-Chadds Ford SD

740 Unionville Rd • Kennett Square, PA 19348-1531
(610) 347-0970 • http://www.ucf.k12.pa.us
Grade Span: KG-12; **Agency Type:** 1
Schools: 6
    4 Primary; 1 Middle; 1 High; 0 Other Level
    6 Regular; 0 Special Education; 0 Vocational; 0 Alternative
    0 Magnet; 0 Charter; 0 Title I Eligible; 0 School-wide Title I
Students: 3,879 (n/a% male; n/a% female)
    Individual Education Program: 498 (12.8%);
    English Language Learner: n/a; Migrant: 5 (0.1%)
    Eligible for Free Lunch Program: 40 (1.0%)
    Eligible for Reduced-Price Lunch Program: 21 (0.5%)
Teachers: 260.6 (14.9 to 1)
Librarians/Media Specialists: 5.7 (680.5 to 1)
Guidance Counselors: 12.0 (323.3 to 1)
Current Spending: ($ per student per year):
    Total: $10,087; Instruction: $6,046; Support Services: $3,743
Enrollment, Drop-out Rates and Diploma Recipients by Race/Ethnicity

Category	Total	White	Black	Asian	AIAN	Hisp.
Enrollment (%)	100.0	94.4	0.6	3.4	0.1	1.5
Drop-out Rate (%)	0.2	0.2	0.0	0.0	0.0	0.0
H.S. Diplomas (#)	279	264	0	11	1	3

West Chester Area SD

829 Paoli Pike • West Chester, PA 19380-4551
(610) 436-7000 • http://www.wcasd.k12.pa.us
Grade Span: KG-12; **Agency Type:** 1
Schools: 15
    10 Primary; 3 Middle; 2 High; 0 Other Level
    15 Regular; 0 Special Education; 0 Vocational; 0 Alternative
    0 Magnet; 0 Charter; 12 Title I Eligible; 0 School-wide Title I
Students: 11,646 (n/a% male; n/a% female)
    Individual Education Program: 1,450 (12.5%);
    English Language Learner: n/a; Migrant: 14 (0.1%)
    Eligible for Free Lunch Program: 573 (4.9%)
    Eligible for Reduced-Price Lunch Program: 168 (1.4%)
Teachers: 722.3 (16.1 to 1)
Librarians/Media Specialists: 15.0 (776.4 to 1)
Guidance Counselors: 35.3 (329.9 to 1)
Current Spending: ($ per student per year):
    Total: $9,839; Instruction: $6,190; Support Services: $3,453
Enrollment, Drop-out Rates and Diploma Recipients by Race/Ethnicity

Category	Total	White	Black	Asian	AIAN	Hisp.
Enrollment (%)	100.0	84.6	7.4	4.6	0.1	3.4
Drop-out Rate (%)	1.4	1.2	2.1	0.0	50.0	5.3
H.S. Diplomas (#)	876	744	76	34	0	22

Clearfield County

Clearfield Area SD

PO Box 710 • Clearfield, PA 16830-0710
(814) 765-5511 • http://www.clearfield.org
Grade Span: KG-12; **Agency Type:** 1
Schools: 6
    4 Primary; 1 Middle; 1 High; 0 Other Level
    6 Regular; 0 Special Education; 0 Vocational; 0 Alternative
    0 Magnet; 0 Charter; 5 Title I Eligible; 0 School-wide Title I
Students: 2,992 (n/a% male; n/a% female)
    Individual Education Program: 425 (14.2%);
    English Language Learner: n/a; Migrant: 0 (0.0%)

Eligible for Free Lunch Program: 1,067 (35.7%)
Eligible for Reduced-Price Lunch Program: 297 (9.9%)
Teachers: 191.5 (15.6 to 1)
Librarians/Media Specialists: 4.0 (748.0 to 1)
Guidance Counselors: 6.0 (498.7 to 1)
Current Spending: ($ per student per year):
  Total: $7,299; Instruction: $4,600; Support Services: $2,341
Enrollment, Drop-out Rates and Diploma Recipients by Race/Ethnicity

Category	Total	White	Black	Asian	AIAN	Hisp.
Enrollment (%)	100.0	98.2	1.0	0.5	0.0	0.2
Drop-out Rate (%)	2.2	2.2	0.0	0.0	n/a	0.0
H.S. Diplomas (#)	193	187	1	4	0	1

Dubois Area SD
500 Liberty Blvd • Du Bois, PA 15801-2437
(814) 371-2700 • http://www.dasd.k12.pa.us
Grade Span: KG-12; **Agency Type:** 1
Schools: 10
  8 Primary; 1 Middle; 1 High; 0 Other Level
  10 Regular; 0 Special Education; 0 Vocational; 0 Alternative
  0 Magnet; 0 Charter; 9 Title I Eligible; 0 School-wide Title I
Students: 4,528 (n/a% male; n/a% female)
  Individual Education Program: 649 (14.3%);
  English Language Learner: n/a; Migrant: 0 (0.0%)
  Eligible for Free Lunch Program: 1,219 (26.9%)
  Eligible for Reduced-Price Lunch Program: 398 (8.8%)
Teachers: 295.1 (15.3 to 1)
Librarians/Media Specialists: 3.0 (1,509.3 to 1)
Guidance Counselors: 11.0 (411.6 to 1)
Current Spending: ($ per student per year):
  Total: $7,354; Instruction: $4,788; Support Services: $2,273
Enrollment, Drop-out Rates and Diploma Recipients by Race/Ethnicity

Category	Total	White	Black	Asian	AIAN	Hisp.
Enrollment (%)	100.0	98.8	0.4	0.4	0.1	0.3
Drop-out Rate (%)	1.6	1.5	0.0	0.0	50.0	33.3
H.S. Diplomas (#)	246	243	1	0	0	2

Philipsburg-Osceola Area SD
200 Short St • Philipsburg, PA 16866-2640
(814) 342-1050 • http://www.poasd.org
Grade Span: KG-12; **Agency Type:** 1
Schools: 6
  4 Primary; 1 Middle; 1 High; 0 Other Level
  6 Regular; 0 Special Education; 0 Vocational; 0 Alternative
  0 Magnet; 0 Charter; 5 Title I Eligible; 0 School-wide Title I
Students: 2,136 (n/a% male; n/a% female)
  Individual Education Program: 294 (13.8%);
  English Language Learner: n/a; Migrant: 0 (0.0%)
  Eligible for Free Lunch Program: 526 (24.6%)
  Eligible for Reduced-Price Lunch Program: 206 (9.6%)
Teachers: 157.5 (13.6 to 1)
Librarians/Media Specialists: 5.0 (427.2 to 1)
Guidance Counselors: 6.0 (356.0 to 1)
Current Spending: ($ per student per year):
  Total: $7,735; Instruction: $4,737; Support Services: $2,623
Enrollment, Drop-out Rates and Diploma Recipients by Race/Ethnicity

Category	Total	White	Black	Asian	AIAN	Hisp.
Enrollment (%)	100.0	98.4	0.6	0.4	0.0	0.6
Drop-out Rate (%)	2.1	2.1	0.0	0.0	n/a	0.0
H.S. Diplomas (#)	148	147	1	0	0	0

Clinton County

Keystone Central SD
95 W 4th St • Lock Haven, PA 17745-1100
(570) 893-4900 • http://oak.kcsd.k12.pa.us
Grade Span: KG-12; **Agency Type:** 1
Schools: 13
  9 Primary; 1 Middle; 1 High; 1 Other Level
  12 Regular; 0 Special Education; 0 Vocational; 0 Alternative
  0 Magnet; 0 Charter; 10 Title I Eligible; 5 School-wide Title I
Students: 4,727 (n/a% male; n/a% female)
  Individual Education Program: 815 (17.2%);
  English Language Learner: n/a; Migrant: 2 (<0.1%)
  Eligible for Free Lunch Program: 1,345 (28.5%)
  Eligible for Reduced-Price Lunch Program: 528 (11.2%)
Teachers: 356.5 (13.3 to 1)
Librarians/Media Specialists: 5.0 (945.4 to 1)
Guidance Counselors: 12.0 (393.9 to 1)
Current Spending: ($ per student per year):
  Total: $9,666; Instruction: $6,376; Support Services: $2,976

Category	Total	White	Black	Asian	AIAN	Hisp.
Enrollment (%)	100.0	98.0	0.8	0.5	0.3	0.3
Drop-out Rate (%)	2.5	2.5	0.0	0.0	0.0	0.0
H.S. Diplomas (#)	369	365	2	0	1	1

Columbia County

Berwick Area SD
500 Line St • Berwick, PA 18603-3300
(570) 759-6400 • http://www.berwicksd.org
Grade Span: KG-12; **Agency Type:** 1
Schools: 7
  5 Primary; 1 Middle; 1 High; 0 Other Level
  7 Regular; 0 Special Education; 0 Vocational; 0 Alternative
  0 Magnet; 0 Charter; 0 Title I Eligible; 0 School-wide Title I
Students: 3,396 (n/a% male; n/a% female)
  Individual Education Program: 619 (18.2%);
  English Language Learner: n/a; Migrant: 0 (0.0%)
  Eligible for Free Lunch Program: 931 (27.4%)
  Eligible for Reduced-Price Lunch Program: 343 (10.1%)
Teachers: 240.0 (14.2 to 1)
Librarians/Media Specialists: 3.0 (1,132.0 to 1)
Guidance Counselors: 5.0 (679.2 to 1)
Current Spending: ($ per student per year):
  Total: $7,905; Instruction: $5,376; Support Services: $2,189
Enrollment, Drop-out Rates and Diploma Recipients by Race/Ethnicity

Category	Total	White	Black	Asian	AIAN	Hisp.
Enrollment (%)	100.0	96.2	1.2	0.4	0.0	2.1
Drop-out Rate (%)	4.9	4.7	8.3	20.0	n/a	11.8
H.S. Diplomas (#)	208	205	1	1	0	1

Bloomsburg Area SD
728 E 5th St • Bloomsburg, PA 17815-2305
(570) 784-5000
Grade Span: KG-12; **Agency Type:** 1
Schools: 5
  3 Primary; 1 Middle; 1 High; 0 Other Level
  5 Regular; 0 Special Education; 0 Vocational; 0 Alternative
  0 Magnet; 0 Charter; 3 Title I Eligible; 0 School-wide Title I
Students: 1,780 (n/a% male; n/a% female)
  Individual Education Program: 276 (15.5%);
  English Language Learner: n/a; Migrant: 0 (0.0%)
  Eligible for Free Lunch Program: 430 (24.2%)
  Eligible for Reduced-Price Lunch Program: 199 (11.2%)
Teachers: 125.7 (14.2 to 1)
Librarians/Media Specialists: 3.0 (593.3 to 1)
Guidance Counselors: 4.0 (445.0 to 1)
Current Spending: ($ per student per year):
  Total: $7,776; Instruction: $4,890; Support Services: $2,577
Enrollment, Drop-out Rates and Diploma Recipients by Race/Ethnicity

Category	Total	White	Black	Asian	AIAN	Hisp.
Enrollment (%)	100.0	92.4	3.8	1.6	0.0	2.2
Drop-out Rate (%)	6.3	5.4	23.1	0.0	n/a	25.0
H.S. Diplomas (#)	100	97	1	1	0	1

Central Columbia SD
4777 Old Berwick Rd • Bloomsburg, PA 17815-3515
(570) 784-2850 • http://www.centralcolumbia.k12.pa.us
Grade Span: KG-12; **Agency Type:** 1
Schools: 3
  1 Primary; 1 Middle; 1 High; 0 Other Level
  3 Regular; 0 Special Education; 0 Vocational; 0 Alternative
  0 Magnet; 0 Charter; 2 Title I Eligible; 0 School-wide Title I
Students: 2,219 (n/a% male; n/a% female)
  Individual Education Program: 239 (10.8%);
  English Language Learner: n/a; Migrant: 0 (0.0%)
  Eligible for Free Lunch Program: 212 (9.6%)
  Eligible for Reduced-Price Lunch Program: 125 (5.6%)
Teachers: 137.0 (16.2 to 1)
Librarians/Media Specialists: 3.0 (739.7 to 1)
Guidance Counselors: 4.0 (554.8 to 1)
Current Spending: ($ per student per year):
  Total: $6,998; Instruction: $4,294; Support Services: $2,451
Enrollment, Drop-out Rates and Diploma Recipients by Race/Ethnicity

Category	Total	White	Black	Asian	AIAN	Hisp.
Enrollment (%)	100.0	96.0	1.1	2.1	0.0	0.7
Drop-out Rate (%)	1.2	1.3	0.0	0.0	0.0	0.0
H.S. Diplomas (#)	146	139	1	6	0	0

Crawford County

Conneaut SD
219 W School Dr • Linesville, PA 16424-8609
(814) 683-5900 • http://connwww.iu5.org
Grade Span: KG-12; **Agency Type:** 1
Schools: 6
  3 Primary; 0 Middle; 3 High; 0 Other Level
  6 Regular; 0 Special Education; 0 Vocational; 0 Alternative
  0 Magnet; 0 Charter; 0 Title I Eligible; 0 School-wide Title I
Students: 2,800   (n/a% male; n/a% female)
  Individual Education Program: 432 (15.4%);
  English Language Learner: n/a; Migrant: 6 (0.2%)
  Eligible for Free Lunch Program: 800 (28.6%)
  Eligible for Reduced-Price Lunch Program: 303 (10.8%)
Teachers: 184.0 (15.2 to 1)
Librarians/Media Specialists: 6.0 (466.7 to 1)
Guidance Counselors: 6.0 (466.7 to 1)
Current Spending: ($ per student per year):
  Total: $7,088; Instruction: $4,240; Support Services: $2,546
Enrollment, Drop-out Rates and Diploma Recipients by Race/Ethnicity

Category	Total	White	Black	Asian	AIAN	Hisp.
Enrollment (%)	100.0	98.4	0.9	0.3	0.0	0.4
Drop-out Rate (%)	3.5	3.3	0.0	0.0	n/a	66.7
H.S. Diplomas (#)	223	219	1	1	0	2

Crawford Central SD
11280 Mercer Pike • Meadville, PA 16335-9504
(814) 724-3960 • http://craw.org
Grade Span: KG-12; **Agency Type:** 1
Schools: 9
  6 Primary; 1 Middle; 2 High; 0 Other Level
  9 Regular; 0 Special Education; 0 Vocational; 0 Alternative
  0 Magnet; 0 Charter; 7 Title I Eligible; 1 School-wide Title I
Students: 4,236   (n/a% male; n/a% female)
  Individual Education Program: 730 (17.2%);
  English Language Learner: n/a; Migrant: 0 (0.0%)
  Eligible for Free Lunch Program: 1,049 (24.8%)
  Eligible for Reduced-Price Lunch Program: 269 (6.4%)
Teachers: 292.1 (14.5 to 1)
Librarians/Media Specialists: 6.0 (706.0 to 1)
Guidance Counselors: 13.0 (325.8 to 1)
Current Spending: ($ per student per year):
  Total: $8,658; Instruction: $4,936; Support Services: $3,456
Enrollment, Drop-out Rates and Diploma Recipients by Race/Ethnicity

Category	Total	White	Black	Asian	AIAN	Hisp.
Enrollment (%)	100.0	89.3	7.8	1.0	0.8	1.1
Drop-out Rate (%)	3.5	3.2	5.6	6.3	0.0	18.2
H.S. Diplomas (#)	343	327	10	1	0	5

Penncrest SD
PO Box 808 • Saegertown, PA 16433-0808
(814) 763-2323 • http://penncrest.iu5.org
Grade Span: KG-12; **Agency Type:** 1
Schools: 7
  4 Primary; 0 Middle; 3 High; 0 Other Level
  7 Regular; 0 Special Education; 0 Vocational; 0 Alternative
  0 Magnet; 0 Charter; 0 Title I Eligible; 0 School-wide Title I
Students: 3,945   (n/a% male; n/a% female)
  Individual Education Program: 549 (13.9%);
  English Language Learner: n/a; Migrant: 1 (<0.1%)
  Eligible for Free Lunch Program: 789 (20.0%)
  Eligible for Reduced-Price Lunch Program: 339 (8.6%)
Teachers: 247.5 (15.9 to 1)
Librarians/Media Specialists: 6.5 (606.9 to 1)
Guidance Counselors: 9.0 (438.3 to 1)
Current Spending: ($ per student per year):
  Total: $8,726; Instruction: $5,297; Support Services: $2,868
Enrollment, Drop-out Rates and Diploma Recipients by Race/Ethnicity

Category	Total	White	Black	Asian	AIAN	Hisp.
Enrollment (%)	100.0	99.1	0.5	0.1	0.0	0.3
Drop-out Rate (%)	1.4	1.4	0.0	n/a	n/a	0.0
H.S. Diplomas (#)	299	295	4	0	0	0

Cumberland County

Big Spring SD
45 Mount Rock Rd • Newville, PA 17241-9412
(717) 776-2000 • http://www.bigspring.k12.pa.us/
Grade Span: KG-12; **Agency Type:** 1
Schools: 7
  5 Primary; 1 Middle; 1 High; 0 Other Level
  7 Regular; 0 Special Education; 0 Vocational; 0 Alternative
  0 Magnet; 0 Charter; 5 Title I Eligible; 0 School-wide Title I
Students: 3,191   (n/a% male; n/a% female)

  Individual Education Program: 569 (17.8%);
  English Language Learner: n/a; Migrant: 6 (0.2%)
  Eligible for Free Lunch Program: 310 (9.7%)
  Eligible for Reduced-Price Lunch Program: 217 (6.8%)
Teachers: 224.9 (14.2 to 1)
Librarians/Media Specialists: 4.0 (797.8 to 1)
Guidance Counselors: 7.5 (425.5 to 1)
Current Spending: ($ per student per year):
  Total: $7,263; Instruction: $4,499; Support Services: $2,439
Enrollment, Drop-out Rates and Diploma Recipients by Race/Ethnicity

Category	Total	White	Black	Asian	AIAN	Hisp.
Enrollment (%)	100.0	97.9	0.9	0.3	0.2	0.7
Drop-out Rate (%)	4.1	4.0	11.1	0.0	0.0	50.0
H.S. Diplomas (#)	209	204	3	2	0	0

Carlisle Area SD
623 W Penn St • Carlisle, PA 17013-2239
(717) 240-6800 • http://www.carlisleschools.org
Grade Span: KG-12; **Agency Type:** 1
Schools: 10
  7 Primary; 2 Middle; 1 High; 0 Other Level
  10 Regular; 0 Special Education; 0 Vocational; 0 Alternative
  0 Magnet; 0 Charter; 5 Title I Eligible; 0 School-wide Title I
Students: 4,820   (n/a% male; n/a% female)
  Individual Education Program: 699 (14.5%);
  English Language Learner: n/a; Migrant: 44 (0.9%)
  Eligible for Free Lunch Program: 579 (12.0%)
  Eligible for Reduced-Price Lunch Program: 204 (4.2%)
Teachers: 331.5 (14.5 to 1)
Librarians/Media Specialists: 5.2 (926.9 to 1)
Guidance Counselors: 15.5 (311.0 to 1)
Current Spending: ($ per student per year):
  Total: $7,916; Instruction: $4,971; Support Services: $2,598
Enrollment, Drop-out Rates and Diploma Recipients by Race/Ethnicity

Category	Total	White	Black	Asian	AIAN	Hisp.
Enrollment (%)	100.0	85.4	8.8	1.8	1.3	2.7
Drop-out Rate (%)	3.1	3.0	5.0	0.0	50.0	0.0
H.S. Diplomas (#)	319	272	22	12	2	11

Cumberland Valley SD
6746 Carlisle Pike • Mechanicsburg, PA 17050-1711
(717) 697-8261 • http://www.cvschools.org/
Grade Span: KG-12; **Agency Type:** 1
Schools: 10
  7 Primary; 2 Middle; 1 High; 0 Other Level
  10 Regular; 0 Special Education; 0 Vocational; 0 Alternative
  0 Magnet; 0 Charter; 6 Title I Eligible; 0 School-wide Title I
Students: 7,708   (n/a% male; n/a% female)
  Individual Education Program: 963 (12.5%);
  English Language Learner: n/a; Migrant: 8 (0.1%)
  Eligible for Free Lunch Program: 239 (3.1%)
  Eligible for Reduced-Price Lunch Program: 179 (2.3%)
Teachers: 485.8 (15.9 to 1)
Librarians/Media Specialists: 4.0 (1,927.0 to 1)
Guidance Counselors: 21.0 (367.0 to 1)
Current Spending: ($ per student per year):
  Total: $7,185; Instruction: $4,410; Support Services: $2,499
Enrollment, Drop-out Rates and Diploma Recipients by Race/Ethnicity

Category	Total	White	Black	Asian	AIAN	Hisp.
Enrollment (%)	100.0	92.7	1.5	4.8	0.2	0.8
Drop-out Rate (%)	1.6	1.5	7.7	1.8	0.0	3.8
H.S. Diplomas (#)	545	512	4	20	1	8

East Pennsboro Area SD
890 Valley St • Enola, PA 17025-1541
(717) 732-3601 • http://www.epasd.k12.pa.us
Grade Span: KG-12; **Agency Type:** 1
Schools: 4
  2 Primary; 1 Middle; 1 High; 0 Other Level
  4 Regular; 0 Special Education; 0 Vocational; 0 Alternative
  0 Magnet; 0 Charter; 3 Title I Eligible; 0 School-wide Title I
Students: 2,821   (n/a% male; n/a% female)
  Individual Education Program: 383 (13.6%);
  English Language Learner: n/a; Migrant: 15 (0.5%)
  Eligible for Free Lunch Program: 230 (8.2%)
  Eligible for Reduced-Price Lunch Program: 125 (4.4%)
Teachers: 188.2 (15.0 to 1)
Librarians/Media Specialists: 4.0 (705.3 to 1)
Guidance Counselors: 7.0 (403.0 to 1)
Current Spending: ($ per student per year):
  Total: $7,391; Instruction: $4,766; Support Services: $2,306

Enrollment, Drop-out Rates and Diploma Recipients by Race/Ethnicity

Category	Total	White	Black	Asian	AIAN	Hisp.
Enrollment (%)	100.0	91.8	2.6	3.5	0.2	1.9
Drop-out Rate (%)	2.7	2.5	6.7	0.0	0.0	22.2
H.S. Diplomas (#)	149	139	2	5	0	3

Mechanicsburg Area SD
500 S Broad St • Mechanicsburg, PA 17050
(717) 691-4500 • http://www.mbgsd.k12.pa.us/
Grade Span: KG-12; **Agency Type:** 1
Schools: 8
   6 Primary; 1 Middle; 1 High; 0 Other Level
   8 Regular; 0 Special Education; 0 Vocational; 0 Alternative
   0 Magnet; 0 Charter; 4 Title I Eligible; 0 School-wide Title I
Students: 3,558   (n/a% male; n/a% female)
   Individual Education Program: 421 (11.8%);
   English Language Learner: n/a; Migrant: 16 (0.4%)
   Eligible for Free Lunch Program: 263 (7.4%)
   Eligible for Reduced-Price Lunch Program: 183 (5.1%)
Teachers: 242.3 (14.7 to 1)
Librarians/Media Specialists: 4.0 (889.5 to 1)
Guidance Counselors: 10.0 (355.8 to 1)
Current Spending: ($ per student per year):
   Total: $8,226; Instruction: $5,233; Support Services: $2,638

Enrollment, Drop-out Rates and Diploma Recipients by Race/Ethnicity

Category	Total	White	Black	Asian	AIAN	Hisp.
Enrollment (%)	100.0	91.7	3.9	2.1	0.0	2.2
Drop-out Rate (%)	1.5	1.4	0.0	0.0	0.0	9.1
H.S. Diplomas (#)	230	219	4	5	0	2

Shippensburg Area SD
317 N Morris St • Shippensburg, PA 17257-1654
(717) 530-2700 • http://www.ship.k12.pa.us
Grade Span: KG-12; **Agency Type:** 1
Schools: 5
   3 Primary; 1 Middle; 1 High; 0 Other Level
   5 Regular; 0 Special Education; 0 Vocational; 0 Alternative
   0 Magnet; 0 Charter; 3 Title I Eligible; 0 School-wide Title I
Students: 3,304   (n/a% male; n/a% female)
   Individual Education Program: 516 (15.6%);
   English Language Learner: n/a; Migrant: 1 (<0.1%)
   Eligible for Free Lunch Program: 414 (12.5%)
   Eligible for Reduced-Price Lunch Program: 195 (5.9%)
Teachers: 190.4 (17.4 to 1)
Librarians/Media Specialists: 4.0 (826.0 to 1)
Guidance Counselors: 7.0 (472.0 to 1)
Current Spending: ($ per student per year):
   Total: $6,558; Instruction: $4,236; Support Services: $2,043

Enrollment, Drop-out Rates and Diploma Recipients by Race/Ethnicity

Category	Total	White	Black	Asian	AIAN	Hisp.
Enrollment (%)	100.0	94.8	3.4	1.0	0.0	0.8
Drop-out Rate (%)	1.5	1.6	0.0	0.0	n/a	0.0
H.S. Diplomas (#)	208	199	4	1	0	4

South Middleton SD
4 Forge Rd • Boiling Springs, PA 17007-9523
(717) 258-6484 • http://www.bubblers.k12.pa.us
Grade Span: KG-12; **Agency Type:** 1
Schools: 4
   1 Primary; 2 Middle; 1 High; 0 Other Level
   4 Regular; 0 Special Education; 0 Vocational; 0 Alternative
   0 Magnet; 0 Charter; 0 Title I Eligible; 0 School-wide Title I
Students: 2,120   (n/a% male; n/a% female)
   Individual Education Program: 268 (12.6%);
   English Language Learner: n/a; Migrant: 2 (0.1%)
   Eligible for Free Lunch Program: 98 (4.6%)
   Eligible for Reduced-Price Lunch Program: 37 (1.7%)
Teachers: 152.3 (13.9 to 1)
Librarians/Media Specialists: 4.0 (530.0 to 1)
Guidance Counselors: 7.0 (302.9 to 1)
Current Spending: ($ per student per year):
   Total: $7,597; Instruction: $4,674; Support Services: $2,639

Enrollment, Drop-out Rates and Diploma Recipients by Race/Ethnicity

Category	Total	White	Black	Asian	AIAN	Hisp.
Enrollment (%)	100.0	96.5	1.0	1.4	0.3	0.9
Drop-out Rate (%)	2.0	2.0	0.0	0.0	0.0	0.0
H.S. Diplomas (#)	154	152	0	1	1	0

Dauphin County

Central Dauphin SD
600 Rutherford Rd • Harrisburg, PA 17109-5227
(717) 545-4703 • http://www.cdsd.k12.pa.us/
Grade Span: KG-12; **Agency Type:** 1
Schools: 18

   13 Primary; 3 Middle; 2 High; 0 Other Level
   18 Regular; 0 Special Education; 0 Vocational; 0 Alternative
   0 Magnet; 0 Charter; 9 Title I Eligible; 0 School-wide Title I
Students: 11,104   (n/a% male; n/a% female)
   Individual Education Program: 1,471 (13.2%);
   English Language Learner: n/a; Migrant: 115 (1.0%)
   Eligible for Free Lunch Program: 1,220 (11.0%)
   Eligible for Reduced-Price Lunch Program: 567 (5.1%)
Teachers: 719.1 (15.4 to 1)
Librarians/Media Specialists: 17.0 (653.2 to 1)
Guidance Counselors: 27.5 (403.8 to 1)
Current Spending: ($ per student per year):
   Total: $8,510; Instruction: $5,643; Support Services: $2,567

Enrollment, Drop-out Rates and Diploma Recipients by Race/Ethnicity

Category	Total	White	Black	Asian	AIAN	Hisp.
Enrollment (%)	100.0	71.6	19.2	3.6	0.1	5.5
Drop-out Rate (%)	1.9	1.7	3.5	0.9	14.3	1.9
H.S. Diplomas (#)	706	569	82	28	1	26

Derry Township SD
PO Box 898 • Hershey, PA 17033-0898
(717) 534-2501 • http://www.hershey.k12.pa.us
Grade Span: KG-12; **Agency Type:** 1
Schools: 5
   2 Primary; 2 Middle; 1 High; 0 Other Level
   5 Regular; 0 Special Education; 0 Vocational; 0 Alternative
   0 Magnet; 0 Charter; 0 Title I Eligible; 0 School-wide Title I
Students: 3,448   (n/a% male; n/a% female)
   Individual Education Program: 359 (10.4%);
   English Language Learner: n/a; Migrant: 3 (0.1%)
   Eligible for Free Lunch Program: 122 (3.5%)
   Eligible for Reduced-Price Lunch Program: 79 (2.3%)
Teachers: 214.2 (16.1 to 1)
Librarians/Media Specialists: 5.0 (689.6 to 1)
Guidance Counselors: 9.0 (383.1 to 1)
Current Spending: ($ per student per year):
   Total: $8,194; Instruction: $4,858; Support Services: $2,974

Enrollment, Drop-out Rates and Diploma Recipients by Race/Ethnicity

Category	Total	White	Black	Asian	AIAN	Hisp.
Enrollment (%)	100.0	90.8	1.9	4.8	0.1	2.3
Drop-out Rate (%)	3.9	3.7	0.0	7.3	0.0	20.0
H.S. Diplomas (#)	247	239	1	3	2	2

Harrisburg City SD
2101 N Front St Bldg 2 • Harrisburg, PA 17110-1081
(717) 703-4000 • http://www.hbgsd.k12.pa.us
Grade Span: KG-12; **Agency Type:** 1
Schools: 15
   11 Primary; 0 Middle; 1 High; 3 Other Level
   15 Regular; 0 Special Education; 0 Vocational; 0 Alternative
   0 Magnet; 0 Charter; 14 Title I Eligible; 13 School-wide Title I
Students: 7,883   (n/a% male; n/a% female)
   Individual Education Program: 1,573 (20.0%);
   English Language Learner: n/a; Migrant: 244 (3.1%)
   Eligible for Free Lunch Program: 4,361 (55.3%)
   Eligible for Reduced-Price Lunch Program: 409 (5.2%)
Teachers: 587.0 (13.4 to 1)
Librarians/Media Specialists: 6.0 (1,313.8 to 1)
Guidance Counselors: 24.0 (328.5 to 1)
Current Spending: ($ per student per year):
   Total: $12,111; Instruction: $7,423; Support Services: $4,191

Enrollment, Drop-out Rates and Diploma Recipients by Race/Ethnicity

Category	Total	White	Black	Asian	AIAN	Hisp.
Enrollment (%)	100.0	6.3	76.2	2.0	0.0	15.5
Drop-out Rate (%)	5.8	9.6	5.3	0.0	0.0	9.4
H.S. Diplomas (#)	199	20	153	14	0	12

Lower Dauphin SD
291 E Main St • Hummelstown, PA 17036-1799
(717) 566-5300 • http://www.ldsd.org
Grade Span: KG-12; **Agency Type:** 1
Schools: 7
   5 Primary; 1 Middle; 1 High; 0 Other Level
   7 Regular; 0 Special Education; 0 Vocational; 0 Alternative
   0 Magnet; 0 Charter; 4 Title I Eligible; 0 School-wide Title I
Students: 3,900   (n/a% male; n/a% female)
   Individual Education Program: 653 (16.7%);
   English Language Learner: n/a; Migrant: 3 (0.1%)
   Eligible for Free Lunch Program: 295 (7.6%)
   Eligible for Reduced-Price Lunch Program: 157 (4.0%)
Teachers: 266.3 (14.6 to 1)
Librarians/Media Specialists: 3.0 (1,300.0 to 1)
Guidance Counselors: 11.0 (354.5 to 1)
Current Spending: ($ per student per year):
   Total: $7,705; Instruction: $4,874; Support Services: $2,514

Enrollment, Drop-out Rates and Diploma Recipients by Race/Ethnicity

Category	Total	White	Black	Asian	AIAN	Hisp.
Enrollment (%)	100.0	95.6	1.8	0.8	0.3	1.5
Drop-out Rate (%)	0.9	0.9	0.0	0.0	n/a	11.1
H.S. Diplomas (#)	254	248	1	0	0	5

Middletown Area SD
55 W Water St • Middletown, PA 17057-1448
(717) 948-3300 • http://www.middletownschools.com/
Grade Span: KG-12; **Agency Type:** 1
Schools: 5
   2 Primary; 2 Middle; 1 High; 0 Other Level
   5 Regular; 0 Special Education; 0 Vocational; 0 Alternative
   0 Magnet; 0 Charter; 4 Title I Eligible; 0 School-wide Title I
Students: 2,546   (n/a% male; n/a% female)
   Individual Education Program: 444 (17.4%);
   English Language Learner: n/a; Migrant: 0 (0.0%)
   Eligible for Free Lunch Program: 268 (10.5%)
   Eligible for Reduced-Price Lunch Program: 179 (7.0%)
Teachers: 192.0 (13.3 to 1)
Librarians/Media Specialists: 4.5 (565.8 to 1)
Guidance Counselors: 9.0 (282.9 to 1)
Current Spending: ($ per student per year):
   Total: $8,359; Instruction: $5,289; Support Services: $2,792

Enrollment, Drop-out Rates and Diploma Recipients by Race/Ethnicity

Category	Total	White	Black	Asian	AIAN	Hisp.
Enrollment (%)	100.0	82.9	10.9	1.1	0.4	4.7
Drop-out Rate (%)	2.8	3.1	1.4	0.0	0.0	0.0
H.S. Diplomas (#)	173	153	9	3	0	8

Pde Division of Data Services
333market St 14th Floor • Harrisburg, PA 17126-0333
(717) 778-2644
Grade Span: KG-12; **Agency Type:** 5
Schools: 2
   0 Primary; 0 Middle; 0 High; 2 Other Level
   0 Regular; 2 Special Education; 0 Vocational; 0 Alternative
   0 Magnet; 0 Charter; 0 Title I Eligible; 0 School-wide Title I
Students: 15,792   (n/a% male; n/a% female)
   Individual Education Program: n/a;
   English Language Learner: n/a; Migrant: n/a
   Eligible for Free Lunch Program: n/a
   Eligible for Reduced-Price Lunch Program: n/a
Teachers: n/a
Librarians/Media Specialists: n/a
Guidance Counselors: n/a
Current Spending: ($ per student per year):
   Total: n/a; Instruction: n/a; Support Services: n/a

Enrollment, Drop-out Rates and Diploma Recipients by Race/Ethnicity

Category	Total	White	Black	Asian	AIAN	Hisp.
Enrollment (%)	100.0	76.9	17.1	0.9	0.2	4.9
Drop-out Rate (%)	n/a	n/a	n/a	n/a	n/a	n/a
H.S. Diplomas (#)	0	0	0	0	0	0

Susquehanna Township SD
3550 Elmerton Ave • Harrisburg, PA 17109-1131
(717) 657-5100 • http://www.hannasd.org
Grade Span: KG-12; **Agency Type:** 1
Schools: 5
   3 Primary; 1 Middle; 1 High; 0 Other Level
   5 Regular; 0 Special Education; 0 Vocational; 0 Alternative
   0 Magnet; 0 Charter; 5 Title I Eligible; 0 School-wide Title I
Students: 3,121   (n/a% male; n/a% female)
   Individual Education Program: 518 (16.6%);
   English Language Learner: n/a; Migrant: 12 (0.4%)
   Eligible for Free Lunch Program: 352 (11.3%)
   Eligible for Reduced-Price Lunch Program: 224 (7.2%)
Teachers: 198.4 (15.7 to 1)
Librarians/Media Specialists: 4.0 (780.3 to 1)
Guidance Counselors: 8.0 (390.1 to 1)
Current Spending: ($ per student per year):
   Total: $7,427; Instruction: $4,858; Support Services: $2,228

Enrollment, Drop-out Rates and Diploma Recipients by Race/Ethnicity

Category	Total	White	Black	Asian	AIAN	Hisp.
Enrollment (%)	100.0	52.9	39.9	3.6	0.4	3.3
Drop-out Rate (%)	1.3	0.7	2.5	0.0	0.0	0.0
H.S. Diplomas (#)	190	116	59	9	0	6

Delaware County

Chester-Upland SD
1720 Melrose Ave • Chester, PA 19013-5837
(610) 447-3600 • http://www.chesteruplandsd.org/
Grade Span: KG-12; **Agency Type:** 1
Schools: 9

   5 Primary; 3 Middle; 1 High; 0 Other Level
   9 Regular; 0 Special Education; 0 Vocational; 0 Alternative
   0 Magnet; 0 Charter; 9 Title I Eligible; 5 School-wide Title I
Students: 5,048   (n/a% male; n/a% female)
   Individual Education Program: 1,142 (22.6%);
   English Language Learner: n/a; Migrant: 31 (0.6%)
   Eligible for Free Lunch Program: 3,374 (66.8%)
   Eligible for Reduced-Price Lunch Program: 186 (3.7%)
Teachers: 295.0 (17.1 to 1)
Librarians/Media Specialists: 1.0 (5,048.0 to 1)
Guidance Counselors: 11.0 (458.9 to 1)
Current Spending: ($ per student per year):
   Total: $11,290; Instruction: $6,583; Support Services: $4,321

Enrollment, Drop-out Rates and Diploma Recipients by Race/Ethnicity

Category	Total	White	Black	Asian	AIAN	Hisp.
Enrollment (%)	100.0	2.9	89.5	0.0	0.0	7.5
Drop-out Rate (%)	0.8	0.0	0.8	n/a	n/a	2.0
H.S. Diplomas (#)	267	3	255	0	0	9

Chichester SD
PO Box 2100 • Boothwyn, PA 19061-2499
(610) 485-6881 • http://www.chichesterschools.net
Grade Span: PK-12; **Agency Type:** 1
Schools: 6
   4 Primary; 1 Middle; 1 High; 0 Other Level
   6 Regular; 0 Special Education; 0 Vocational; 0 Alternative
   0 Magnet; 0 Charter; 2 Title I Eligible; 0 School-wide Title I
Students: 3,646   (n/a% male; n/a% female)
   Individual Education Program: 648 (17.8%);
   English Language Learner: n/a; Migrant: 0 (0.0%)
   Eligible for Free Lunch Program: 764 (21.0%)
   Eligible for Reduced-Price Lunch Program: 247 (6.8%)
Teachers: 236.0 (15.4 to 1)
Librarians/Media Specialists: 3.0 (1,215.3 to 1)
Guidance Counselors: 12.0 (303.8 to 1)
Current Spending: ($ per student per year):
   Total: $8,983; Instruction: $5,467; Support Services: $3,223

Enrollment, Drop-out Rates and Diploma Recipients by Race/Ethnicity

Category	Total	White	Black	Asian	AIAN	Hisp.
Enrollment (%)	100.0	85.0	12.5	1.2	0.1	1.2
Drop-out Rate (%)	3.4	3.6	1.7	0.0	n/a	0.0
H.S. Diplomas (#)	285	242	31	6	0	6

Garnet Valley SD
80 Station Rd • Glen Mills, PA 19342-1558
(610) 579-7300
Grade Span: KG-12; **Agency Type:** 1
Schools: 5
   3 Primary; 1 Middle; 1 High; 0 Other Level
   5 Regular; 0 Special Education; 0 Vocational; 0 Alternative
   0 Magnet; 0 Charter; 4 Title I Eligible; 0 School-wide Title I
Students: 3,980   (n/a% male; n/a% female)
   Individual Education Program: 728 (18.3%);
   English Language Learner: n/a; Migrant: 0 (0.0%)
   Eligible for Free Lunch Program: 34 (0.9%)
   Eligible for Reduced-Price Lunch Program: 15 (0.4%)
Teachers: 298.6 (13.3 to 1)
Librarians/Media Specialists: 5.0 (796.0 to 1)
Guidance Counselors: 10.6 (375.5 to 1)
Current Spending: ($ per student per year):
   Total: $9,766; Instruction: $6,245; Support Services: $3,162

Enrollment, Drop-out Rates and Diploma Recipients by Race/Ethnicity

Category	Total	White	Black	Asian	AIAN	Hisp.
Enrollment (%)	100.0	93.7	1.3	4.5	0.1	0.5
Drop-out Rate (%)	0.6	0.6	0.0	0.0	n/a	0.0
H.S. Diplomas (#)	198	190	2	3	0	3

Haverford Township SD
1801 Darby Rd • Havertown, PA 19083-3729
(610) 853-5900 • http://www.haverford.k12.pa.us
Grade Span: KG-12; **Agency Type:** 1
Schools: 7
   5 Primary; 1 Middle; 1 High; 0 Other Level
   7 Regular; 0 Special Education; 0 Vocational; 0 Alternative
   0 Magnet; 0 Charter; 6 Title I Eligible; 0 School-wide Title I
Students: 5,512   (n/a% male; n/a% female)
   Individual Education Program: 904 (16.4%);
   English Language Learner: n/a; Migrant: 0 (0.0%)
   Eligible for Free Lunch Program: 113 (2.1%)
   Eligible for Reduced-Price Lunch Program: 48 (0.9%)
Teachers: 337.6 (16.3 to 1)
Librarians/Media Specialists: 7.0 (787.4 to 1)
Guidance Counselors: 13.0 (424.0 to 1)
Current Spending: ($ per student per year):
   Total: $9,147; Instruction: $5,750; Support Services: $3,168

Enrollment, Drop-out Rates and Diploma Recipients by Race/Ethnicity

Category	Total	White	Black	Asian	AIAN	Hisp.
Enrollment (%)	100.0	90.4	3.7	5.1	0.1	0.7
Drop-out Rate (%)	1.1	1.1	4.4	0.0	0.0	0.0
H.S. Diplomas (#)	420	379	13	23	0	5

Interboro SD
900 Washington Ave • Prospect Park, PA 19076-1412
(610) 461-6700 • http://www.interboro.k12.pa.us
Grade Span: KG-12; **Agency Type:** 1
Schools: 6
   5 Primary; 0 Middle; 1 High; 0 Other Level
   6 Regular; 0 Special Education; 0 Vocational; 0 Alternative
   0 Magnet; 0 Charter; 4 Title I Eligible; 0 School-wide Title I
Students: 3,982   (n/a% male; n/a% female)
   Individual Education Program: 607 (15.2%);
   English Language Learner: n/a; Migrant: 0 (0.0%)
   Eligible for Free Lunch Program: 458 (11.5%)
   Eligible for Reduced-Price Lunch Program: 183 (4.6%)
Teachers: 249.4 (16.0 to 1)
Librarians/Media Specialists: 4.0 (995.5 to 1)
Guidance Counselors: 7.0 (568.9 to 1)
Current Spending: ($ per student per year):
   Total: $9,462; Instruction: $6,199; Support Services: $3,020

Enrollment, Drop-out Rates and Diploma Recipients by Race/Ethnicity

Category	Total	White	Black	Asian	AIAN	Hisp.
Enrollment (%)	100.0	95.1	2.6	1.3	0.2	1.0
Drop-out Rate (%)	1.5	1.6	0.0	0.0	0.0	0.0
H.S. Diplomas (#)	283	280	1	2	0	0

Marple Newtown SD
40 Media Line Rd Ste 206 • Newtown Square, PA 19073-4614
(610) 359-4200 • http://www.marple.net/schools
Grade Span: KG-12; **Agency Type:** 1
Schools: 6
   4 Primary; 1 Middle; 1 High; 0 Other Level
   6 Regular; 0 Special Education; 0 Vocational; 0 Alternative
   0 Magnet; 0 Charter; 4 Title I Eligible; 0 School-wide Title I
Students: 3,406   (n/a% male; n/a% female)
   Individual Education Program: 603 (17.7%);
   English Language Learner: n/a; Migrant: 0 (0.0%)
   Eligible for Free Lunch Program: 96 (2.8%)
   Eligible for Reduced-Price Lunch Program: 28 (0.8%)
Teachers: 243.2 (14.0 to 1)
Librarians/Media Specialists: 6.0 (567.7 to 1)
Guidance Counselors: 10.0 (340.6 to 1)
Current Spending: ($ per student per year):
   Total: $10,990; Instruction: $6,961; Support Services: $3,747

Enrollment, Drop-out Rates and Diploma Recipients by Race/Ethnicity

Category	Total	White	Black	Asian	AIAN	Hisp.
Enrollment (%)	100.0	89.8	1.0	8.5	0.0	0.6
Drop-out Rate (%)	1.6	1.3	0.0	4.5	n/a	0.0
H.S. Diplomas (#)	277	254	3	19	0	1

Penn-Delco SD
2821 Concord Rd • Aston, PA 19014-2907
(610) 497-6300 • http://www.pdsd.org
Grade Span: KG-12; **Agency Type:** 1
Schools: 6
   4 Primary; 1 Middle; 1 High; 0 Other Level
   6 Regular; 0 Special Education; 0 Vocational; 0 Alternative
   0 Magnet; 0 Charter; 5 Title I Eligible; 0 School-wide Title I
Students: 3,315   (n/a% male; n/a% female)
   Individual Education Program: 556 (16.8%);
   English Language Learner: n/a; Migrant: 0 (0.0%)
   Eligible for Free Lunch Program: 113 (3.4%)
   Eligible for Reduced-Price Lunch Program: 58 (1.7%)
Teachers: 214.5 (15.5 to 1)
Librarians/Media Specialists: 4.0 (828.8 to 1)
Guidance Counselors: 10.0 (331.5 to 1)
Current Spending: ($ per student per year):
   Total: $8,977; Instruction: $5,451; Support Services: $3,254

Enrollment, Drop-out Rates and Diploma Recipients by Race/Ethnicity

Category	Total	White	Black	Asian	AIAN	Hisp.
Enrollment (%)	100.0	95.4	2.7	1.1	0.2	0.6
Drop-out Rate (%)	2.3	2.2	4.3	0.0	0.0	0.0
H.S. Diplomas (#)	222	213	0	7	0	2

Radnor Township SD
135 S Wayne Ave • Wayne, PA 19087-4194
(610) 688-8100 • http://www.radnor.com/schools/schools.html
Grade Span: KG-12; **Agency Type:** 1
Schools: 5
   3 Primary; 1 Middle; 1 High; 0 Other Level
   5 Regular; 0 Special Education; 0 Vocational; 0 Alternative

   0 Magnet; 0 Charter; 2 Title I Eligible; 0 School-wide Title I
Students: 3,315   (n/a% male; n/a% female)
   Individual Education Program: 554 (16.7%);
   English Language Learner: n/a; Migrant: 0 (0.0%)
   Eligible for Free Lunch Program: 46 (1.4%)
   Eligible for Reduced-Price Lunch Program: 29 (0.9%)
Teachers: 252.9 (13.1 to 1)
Librarians/Media Specialists: 6.0 (552.5 to 1)
Guidance Counselors: 11.0 (301.4 to 1)
Current Spending: ($ per student per year):
   Total: $13,744; Instruction: $8,286; Support Services: $5,150

Enrollment, Drop-out Rates and Diploma Recipients by Race/Ethnicity

Category	Total	White	Black	Asian	AIAN	Hisp.
Enrollment (%)	100.0	82.9	4.1	11.1	0.2	1.7
Drop-out Rate (%)	0.6	0.7	0.0	0.0	n/a	0.0
H.S. Diplomas (#)	229	200	6	19	0	4

Ridley SD
901 Morton Ave Ste 100 • Folsom, PA 19033-2934
(610) 534-1900 • http://www.ridleysd.k12.pa.us
Grade Span: KG-12; **Agency Type:** 1
Schools: 9
   7 Primary; 1 Middle; 1 High; 0 Other Level
   9 Regular; 0 Special Education; 0 Vocational; 0 Alternative
   0 Magnet; 0 Charter; 3 Title I Eligible; 0 School-wide Title I
Students: 5,743   (n/a% male; n/a% female)
   Individual Education Program: 1,080 (18.8%);
   English Language Learner: n/a; Migrant: 0 (0.0%)
   Eligible for Free Lunch Program: 718 (12.5%)
   Eligible for Reduced-Price Lunch Program: 295 (5.1%)
Teachers: 396.3 (14.5 to 1)
Librarians/Media Specialists: 2.0 (2,871.5 to 1)
Guidance Counselors: 10.0 (574.3 to 1)
Current Spending: ($ per student per year):
   Total: $9,227; Instruction: $6,317; Support Services: $2,624

Enrollment, Drop-out Rates and Diploma Recipients by Race/Ethnicity

Category	Total	White	Black	Asian	AIAN	Hisp.
Enrollment (%)	100.0	90.8	6.3	1.8	0.4	0.8
Drop-out Rate (%)	2.0	1.9	3.1	0.0	n/a	0.0
H.S. Diplomas (#)	421	394	22	5	0	0

Rose Tree Media SD
308 N Olive St • Media, PA 19063-2403
(610) 627-6000 • http://www.rosetree.k12.pa.us/
Grade Span: KG-12; **Agency Type:** 1
Schools: 6
   4 Primary; 1 Middle; 1 High; 0 Other Level
   6 Regular; 0 Special Education; 0 Vocational; 0 Alternative
   0 Magnet; 0 Charter; 3 Title I Eligible; 0 School-wide Title I
Students: 4,037   (n/a% male; n/a% female)
   Individual Education Program: 651 (16.1%);
   English Language Learner: n/a; Migrant: 0 (0.0%)
   Eligible for Free Lunch Program: 125 (3.1%)
   Eligible for Reduced-Price Lunch Program: 52 (1.3%)
Teachers: 289.4 (13.9 to 1)
Librarians/Media Specialists: 4.0 (1,009.3 to 1)
Guidance Counselors: 12.0 (336.4 to 1)
Current Spending: ($ per student per year):
   Total: $10,979; Instruction: $6,560; Support Services: $4,093

Enrollment, Drop-out Rates and Diploma Recipients by Race/Ethnicity

Category	Total	White	Black	Asian	AIAN	Hisp.
Enrollment (%)	100.0	88.9	6.9	3.2	0.1	0.9
Drop-out Rate (%)	0.6	0.7	0.0	0.0	0.0	0.0
H.S. Diplomas (#)	294	256	23	9	1	5

Southeast Delco SD
1560 Delmar Dr • Folcroft, PA 19032-0328
(610) 522-4300
Grade Span: KG-12; **Agency Type:** 1
Schools: 7
   4 Primary; 1 Middle; 2 High; 0 Other Level
   7 Regular; 0 Special Education; 0 Vocational; 0 Alternative
   0 Magnet; 0 Charter; 6 Title I Eligible; 0 School-wide Title I
Students: 4,069   (n/a% male; n/a% female)
   Individual Education Program: 868 (21.3%);
   English Language Learner: n/a; Migrant: 0 (0.0%)
   Eligible for Free Lunch Program: 1,362 (33.5%)
   Eligible for Reduced-Price Lunch Program: 360 (8.8%)
Teachers: 266.0 (15.3 to 1)
Librarians/Media Specialists: 5.0 (813.8 to 1)
Guidance Counselors: 10.0 (406.9 to 1)
Current Spending: ($ per student per year):
   Total: $8,580; Instruction: $5,728; Support Services: $2,530

Enrollment, Drop-out Rates and Diploma Recipients by Race/Ethnicity

Category	Total	White	Black	Asian	AIAN	Hisp.
Enrollment (%)	100.0	52.6	44.4	1.3	0.1	1.5
Drop-out Rate (%)	5.2	6.5	3.2	16.7	n/a	0.0
H.S. Diplomas (#)	205	126	73	4	0	2

Springfield SD
111 W Leamy Ave • Springfield, PA 19064-2396
(610) 938-6004 • http://www.springfieldsd-delco.org
Grade Span: KG-12; **Agency Type:** 1
Schools: 4
  2 Primary; 1 Middle; 1 High; 0 Other Level
  4 Regular; 0 Special Education; 0 Vocational; 0 Alternative
  0 Magnet; 0 Charter; 3 Title I Eligible; 0 School-wide Title I
Students: 3,357   (n/a% male; n/a% female)
  Individual Education Program: 473 (14.1%);
  English Language Learner: n/a; Migrant: 0 (0.0%)
  Eligible for Free Lunch Program: 98 (2.9%)
  Eligible for Reduced-Price Lunch Program: 29 (0.9%)
Teachers: 219.5 (15.3 to 1)
Librarians/Media Specialists: 4.0 (839.3 to 1)
Guidance Counselors: 9.0 (373.0 to 1)
Current Spending: ($ per student per year):
  Total: $9,997; Instruction: $6,146; Support Services: $3,599

Enrollment, Drop-out Rates and Diploma Recipients by Race/Ethnicity

Category	Total	White	Black	Asian	AIAN	Hisp.
Enrollment (%)	100.0	90.2	5.9	3.4	0.0	0.6
Drop-out Rate (%)	0.8	0.8	0.0	0.0	0.0	0.0
H.S. Diplomas (#)	281	251	18	11	0	1

Upper Darby SD
4611 Bond Ave • Drexel Hill, PA 19026-4592
(610) 789-7200 • http://www.udsd.k12.pa.us
Grade Span: KG-12; **Agency Type:** 1
Schools: 12
  9 Primary; 2 Middle; 1 High; 0 Other Level
  12 Regular; 0 Special Education; 0 Vocational; 0 Alternative
  0 Magnet; 0 Charter; 5 Title I Eligible; 0 School-wide Title I
Students: 12,263   (n/a% male; n/a% female)
  Individual Education Program: 1,713 (14.0%);
  English Language Learner: n/a; Migrant: 0 (0.0%)
  Eligible for Free Lunch Program: 2,030 (16.6%)
  Eligible for Reduced-Price Lunch Program: 551 (4.5%)
Teachers: 742.0 (16.5 to 1)
Librarians/Media Specialists: 12.5 (981.0 to 1)
Guidance Counselors: 21.0 (584.0 to 1)
Current Spending: ($ per student per year):
  Total: $7,530; Instruction: $5,138; Support Services: $2,182

Enrollment, Drop-out Rates and Diploma Recipients by Race/Ethnicity

Category	Total	White	Black	Asian	AIAN	Hisp.
Enrollment (%)	100.0	57.0	29.7	11.8	0.0	1.5
Drop-out Rate (%)	3.8	3.9	4.1	2.6	n/a	7.3
H.S. Diplomas (#)	694	513	75	103	1	2

Wallingford-Swarthmore SD
200 S Providence Rd • Wallingford, PA 19086-6334
(610) 892-3470
Grade Span: KG-12; **Agency Type:** 1
Schools: 6
  4 Primary; 1 Middle; 1 High; 0 Other Level
  6 Regular; 0 Special Education; 0 Vocational; 0 Alternative
  0 Magnet; 0 Charter; 2 Title I Eligible; 0 School-wide Title I
Students: 3,578   (n/a% male; n/a% female)
  Individual Education Program: 606 (16.9%);
  English Language Learner: n/a; Migrant: 0 (0.0%)
  Eligible for Free Lunch Program: 109 (3.0%)
  Eligible for Reduced-Price Lunch Program: 38 (1.1%)
Teachers: 256.8 (13.9 to 1)
Librarians/Media Specialists: 5.0 (715.6 to 1)
Guidance Counselors: 8.8 (406.6 to 1)
Current Spending: ($ per student per year):
  Total: $10,369; Instruction: $6,733; Support Services: $3,375

Enrollment, Drop-out Rates and Diploma Recipients by Race/Ethnicity

Category	Total	White	Black	Asian	AIAN	Hisp.
Enrollment (%)	100.0	86.3	7.5	5.3	0.1	0.7
Drop-out Rate (%)	0.5	0.6	0.0	0.0	0.0	0.0
H.S. Diplomas (#)	289	253	20	9	0	7

William Penn SD
100 Green Ave Annex • Lansdowne, PA 19050-2095
(610) 284-8000 • http://www.wpsd.k12.pa.us
Grade Span: KG-12; **Agency Type:** 1
Schools: 11
  8 Primary; 2 Middle; 1 High; 0 Other Level
  11 Regular; 0 Special Education; 0 Vocational; 0 Alternative

  3 Magnet; 0 Charter; 7 Title I Eligible; 3 School-wide Title I
Students: 5,611   (n/a% male; n/a% female)
  Individual Education Program: 1,102 (19.6%);
  English Language Learner: n/a; Migrant: 0 (0.0%)
  Eligible for Free Lunch Program: 2,054 (36.6%)
  Eligible for Reduced-Price Lunch Program: 384 (6.8%)
Teachers: 346.7 (16.2 to 1)
Librarians/Media Specialists: 7.7 (728.7 to 1)
Guidance Counselors: 12.0 (467.6 to 1)
Current Spending: ($ per student per year):
  Total: $9,518; Instruction: $6,182; Support Services: $3,006

Enrollment, Drop-out Rates and Diploma Recipients by Race/Ethnicity

Category	Total	White	Black	Asian	AIAN	Hisp.
Enrollment (%)	100.0	11.4	85.4	1.5	0.5	1.1
Drop-out Rate (%)	4.0	2.2	4.4	5.9	0.0	4.8
H.S. Diplomas (#)	306	52	250	2	0	2

Elk County

Saint Marys Area SD
977 S Saint Marys Rd • Saint Marys, PA 15857-2832
(814) 834-7831 • http://www.smasd.org
Grade Span: KG-12; **Agency Type:** 1
Schools: 5
  3 Primary; 1 Middle; 1 High; 0 Other Level
  5 Regular; 0 Special Education; 0 Vocational; 0 Alternative
  0 Magnet; 0 Charter; 0 Title I Eligible; 0 School-wide Title I
Students: 2,555   (n/a% male; n/a% female)
  Individual Education Program: 317 (12.4%);
  English Language Learner: n/a; Migrant: 0 (0.0%)
  Eligible for Free Lunch Program: 376 (14.7%)
  Eligible for Reduced-Price Lunch Program: 215 (8.4%)
Teachers: 153.0 (16.7 to 1)
Librarians/Media Specialists: 3.0 (851.7 to 1)
Guidance Counselors: 6.0 (425.8 to 1)
Current Spending: ($ per student per year):
  Total: $7,165; Instruction: $4,464; Support Services: $2,383

Enrollment, Drop-out Rates and Diploma Recipients by Race/Ethnicity

Category	Total	White	Black	Asian	AIAN	Hisp.
Enrollment (%)	100.0	98.6	0.5	0.5	0.1	0.3
Drop-out Rate (%)	3.5	3.5	0.0	0.0	0.0	0.0
H.S. Diplomas (#)	207	205	0	2	0	0

Erie County

Corry Area SD
800 E S St • Corry, PA 16407-2054
(814) 664-4677 • http://corry.iu5.org
Grade Span: KG-12; **Agency Type:** 1
Schools: 7
  5 Primary; 0 Middle; 1 High; 0 Other Level
  6 Regular; 0 Special Education; 0 Vocational; 0 Alternative
  0 Magnet; 0 Charter; 0 Title I Eligible; 0 School-wide Title I
Students: 2,485   (n/a% male; n/a% female)
  Individual Education Program: 483 (19.4%);
  English Language Learner: n/a; Migrant: 0 (0.0%)
  Eligible for Free Lunch Program: 830 (33.4%)
  Eligible for Reduced-Price Lunch Program: 252 (10.1%)
Teachers: 178.0 (14.0 to 1)
Librarians/Media Specialists: 3.0 (828.3 to 1)
Guidance Counselors: 5.0 (497.0 to 1)
Current Spending: ($ per student per year):
  Total: $7,673; Instruction: $4,596; Support Services: $2,747

Enrollment, Drop-out Rates and Diploma Recipients by Race/Ethnicity

Category	Total	White	Black	Asian	AIAN	Hisp.
Enrollment (%)	100.0	98.9	0.6	0.1	0.1	0.2
Drop-out Rate (%)	3.2	3.2	0.0	0.0	n/a	0.0
H.S. Diplomas (#)	178	174	0	2	0	2

Erie City SD
148 W 21st St • Erie, PA 16502
(814) 874-6001 • http://esd.iu5.org
Grade Span: KG-12; **Agency Type:** 1
Schools: 21
  14 Primary; 3 Middle; 4 High; 0 Other Level
  21 Regular; 0 Special Education; 0 Vocational; 0 Alternative
  0 Magnet; 0 Charter; 20 Title I Eligible; 0 School-wide Title I
Students: 12,690   (n/a% male; n/a% female)
  Individual Education Program: 2,544 (20.0%);
  English Language Learner: n/a; Migrant: 1,060 (8.4%)
  Eligible for Free Lunch Program: 7,630 (60.1%)
  Eligible for Reduced-Price Lunch Program: 1,201 (9.5%)
Teachers: 827.0 (15.3 to 1)
Librarians/Media Specialists: 8.0 (1,586.3 to 1)
Guidance Counselors: 29.0 (437.6 to 1)

Current Spending: ($ per student per year):
Total: $8,465; Instruction: $4,988; Support Services: $3,093
Enrollment, Drop-out Rates and Diploma Recipients by Race/Ethnicity

Category	Total	White	Black	Asian	AIAN	Hisp.
Enrollment (%)	100.0	54.1	34.4	1.8	0.1	9.7
Drop-out Rate (%)	3.8	3.2	4.6	5.2	0.0	5.6
H.S. Diplomas (#)	630	435	151	15	0	29

Fairview SD
7460 Mccray Rd · Fairview, PA 16415-2401
(814) 474-2600 · http://www.iu5.org/fsd/
Grade Span: KG-12; **Agency Type:** 1
Schools: 3
1 Primary; 1 Middle; 1 High; 0 Other Level
3 Regular; 0 Special Education; 0 Vocational; 0 Alternative
0 Magnet; 0 Charter; 0 Title I Eligible; 0 School-wide Title I
Students: 1,591   (n/a% male; n/a% female)
Individual Education Program: 163 (10.2%);
English Language Learner: n/a; Migrant: 0 (0.0%)
Eligible for Free Lunch Program: 122 (7.7%)
Eligible for Reduced-Price Lunch Program: 52 (3.3%)
Teachers: 99.5 (16.0 to 1)
Librarians/Media Specialists: 3.0 (530.3 to 1)
Guidance Counselors: 3.0 (530.3 to 1)
Current Spending: ($ per student per year):
Total: $8,559; Instruction: $5,216; Support Services: $3,076
Enrollment, Drop-out Rates and Diploma Recipients by Race/Ethnicity

Category	Total	White	Black	Asian	AIAN	Hisp.
Enrollment (%)	100.0	95.5	1.4	1.1	0.4	1.6
Drop-out Rate (%)	1.6	1.7	0.0	0.0	0.0	0.0
H.S. Diplomas (#)	114	111	2	1	0	0

Fort Leboeuf SD
PO Box 810 · Waterford, PA 16441-0810
(814) 796-2638
Grade Span: KG-12; **Agency Type:** 1
Schools: 5
3 Primary; 1 Middle; 1 High; 0 Other Level
5 Regular; 0 Special Education; 0 Vocational; 0 Alternative
0 Magnet; 0 Charter; 4 Title I Eligible; 0 School-wide Title I
Students: 2,351   (n/a% male; n/a% female)
Individual Education Program: 381 (16.2%);
English Language Learner: n/a; Migrant: 1 (<0.1%)
Eligible for Free Lunch Program: 423 (18.0%)
Eligible for Reduced-Price Lunch Program: 236 (10.0%)
Teachers: 138.0 (17.0 to 1)
Librarians/Media Specialists: 3.0 (783.7 to 1)
Guidance Counselors: 6.0 (391.8 to 1)
Current Spending: ($ per student per year):
Total: $6,577; Instruction: $4,002; Support Services: $2,295
Enrollment, Drop-out Rates and Diploma Recipients by Race/Ethnicity

Category	Total	White	Black	Asian	AIAN	Hisp.
Enrollment (%)	100.0	98.6	0.7	0.4	0.0	0.2
Drop-out Rate (%)	1.1	1.0	10.0	0.0	n/a	0.0
H.S. Diplomas (#)	174	173	1	0	0	0

General Mclane SD
11771 Edinboro Rd · Edinboro, PA 16412-1025
(814) 734-1033
Grade Span: KG-12; **Agency Type:** 1
Schools: 4
2 Primary; 1 Middle; 1 High; 0 Other Level
4 Regular; 0 Special Education; 0 Vocational; 0 Alternative
0 Magnet; 0 Charter; 3 Title I Eligible; 0 School-wide Title I
Students: 2,485   (n/a% male; n/a% female)
Individual Education Program: 304 (12.2%);
English Language Learner: n/a; Migrant: 0 (0.0%)
Eligible for Free Lunch Program: 275 (11.1%)
Eligible for Reduced-Price Lunch Program: 185 (7.4%)
Teachers: 157.5 (15.8 to 1)
Librarians/Media Specialists: 4.0 (621.3 to 1)
Guidance Counselors: 7.0 (355.0 to 1)
Current Spending: ($ per student per year):
Total: $7,194; Instruction: $4,670; Support Services: $2,313
Enrollment, Drop-out Rates and Diploma Recipients by Race/Ethnicity

Category	Total	White	Black	Asian	AIAN	Hisp.
Enrollment (%)	100.0	97.1	1.6	0.6	0.4	0.2
Drop-out Rate (%)	2.0	2.1	0.0	0.0	n/a	0.0
H.S. Diplomas (#)	258	253	3	1	0	1

Girard SD
1100 Rice Ave · Girard, PA 16417-1143
(814) 774-5666 · http://www.gsd.k12.pa.us
Grade Span: KG-12; **Agency Type:** 1
Schools: 3

1 Primary; 1 Middle; 1 High; 0 Other Level
3 Regular; 0 Special Education; 0 Vocational; 0 Alternative
0 Magnet; 0 Charter; 2 Title I Eligible; 0 School-wide Title I
Students: 1,991   (n/a% male; n/a% female)
Individual Education Program: 294 (14.8%);
English Language Learner: n/a; Migrant: 0 (0.0%)
Eligible for Free Lunch Program: 472 (23.7%)
Eligible for Reduced-Price Lunch Program: 269 (13.5%)
Teachers: 127.5 (15.6 to 1)
Librarians/Media Specialists: 2.0 (995.5 to 1)
Guidance Counselors: 4.0 (497.8 to 1)
Current Spending: ($ per student per year):
Total: $6,767; Instruction: $4,345; Support Services: $2,091
Enrollment, Drop-out Rates and Diploma Recipients by Race/Ethnicity

Category	Total	White	Black	Asian	AIAN	Hisp.
Enrollment (%)	100.0	98.0	1.2	0.1	0.1	0.7
Drop-out Rate (%)	3.1	3.1	0.0	0.0	n/a	0.0
H.S. Diplomas (#)	127	123	3	1	0	0

Harbor Creek SD
6375 Buffalo Rd · Harborcreek, PA 16421-1632
(814) 897-2100 · http://hcsd.iu5.org
Grade Span: KG-12; **Agency Type:** 1
Schools: 4
3 Primary; 0 Middle; 1 High; 0 Other Level
4 Regular; 0 Special Education; 0 Vocational; 0 Alternative
0 Magnet; 0 Charter; 3 Title I Eligible; 0 School-wide Title I
Students: 2,095   (n/a% male; n/a% female)
Individual Education Program: 262 (12.5%);
English Language Learner: n/a; Migrant: 0 (0.0%)
Eligible for Free Lunch Program: 241 (11.5%)
Eligible for Reduced-Price Lunch Program: 93 (4.4%)
Teachers: 146.0 (14.3 to 1)
Librarians/Media Specialists: 2.0 (1,047.5 to 1)
Guidance Counselors: 5.0 (419.0 to 1)
Current Spending: ($ per student per year):
Total: $8,197; Instruction: $5,373; Support Services: $2,477
Enrollment, Drop-out Rates and Diploma Recipients by Race/Ethnicity

Category	Total	White	Black	Asian	AIAN	Hisp.
Enrollment (%)	100.0	97.8	1.2	0.5	0.0	0.5
Drop-out Rate (%)	2.7	2.6	11.1	0.0	n/a	n/a
H.S. Diplomas (#)	219	217	2	0	0	0

Millcreek Township SD
3740 W 26th St · Erie, PA 16506-2039
(814) 835-5300 · http://www.mtsd.org/main/index.html
Grade Span: KG-12; **Agency Type:** 1
Schools: 13
7 Primary; 3 Middle; 2 High; 1 Other Level
13 Regular; 0 Special Education; 0 Vocational; 0 Alternative
0 Magnet; 0 Charter; 0 Title I Eligible; 0 School-wide Title I
Students: 7,107   (n/a% male; n/a% female)
Individual Education Program: 843 (11.9%);
English Language Learner: n/a; Migrant: 39 (0.5%)
Eligible for Free Lunch Program: 842 (11.8%)
Eligible for Reduced-Price Lunch Program: 502 (7.1%)
Teachers: 439.5 (16.2 to 1)
Librarians/Media Specialists: 5.5 (1,292.2 to 1)
Guidance Counselors: 9.0 (789.7 to 1)
Current Spending: ($ per student per year):
Total: $7,834; Instruction: $4,829; Support Services: $2,702
Enrollment, Drop-out Rates and Diploma Recipients by Race/Ethnicity

Category	Total	White	Black	Asian	AIAN	Hisp.
Enrollment (%)	100.0	94.3	2.1	1.8	0.2	1.6
Drop-out Rate (%)	2.7	2.7	5.1	0.0	0.0	2.9
H.S. Diplomas (#)	504	483	4	11	0	6

North East SD
50 E Division St · North East, PA 16428-1351
(814) 725-8671 · http://www.nesd1.k12.pa.us
Grade Span: KG-12; **Agency Type:** 1
Schools: 4
2 Primary; 1 Middle; 1 High; 0 Other Level
4 Regular; 0 Special Education; 0 Vocational; 0 Alternative
0 Magnet; 0 Charter; 3 Title I Eligible; 0 School-wide Title I
Students: 1,924   (n/a% male; n/a% female)
Individual Education Program: 206 (10.7%);
English Language Learner: n/a; Migrant: 3 (0.2%)
Eligible for Free Lunch Program: 405 (21.0%)
Eligible for Reduced-Price Lunch Program: 203 (10.6%)
Teachers: 107.5 (17.9 to 1)
Librarians/Media Specialists: 3.0 (641.3 to 1)
Guidance Counselors: 5.0 (384.8 to 1)
Current Spending: ($ per student per year):
Total: $6,691; Instruction: $4,116; Support Services: $2,316

Enrollment, Drop-out Rates and Diploma Recipients by Race/Ethnicity

Category	Total	White	Black	Asian	AIAN	Hisp.
Enrollment (%)	100.0	98.4	0.6	0.3	0.1	0.7
Drop-out Rate (%)	1.9	1.9	0.0	n/a	n/a	0.0
H.S. Diplomas (#)	157	155	2	0	0	0

Northwestern SD
100 Harthan Way · Albion, PA 16401-1368
(814) 756-4116
Grade Span: KG-12; **Agency Type:** 1
Schools: 4
  2 Primary; 1 Middle; 1 High; 0 Other Level
  4 Regular; 0 Special Education; 0 Vocational; 0 Alternative
  0 Magnet; 0 Charter; 3 Title I Eligible; 0 School-wide Title I
Students: 1,854 (n/a% male; n/a% female)
  Individual Education Program: 303 (16.3%);
  English Language Learner: n/a; Migrant: 2 (0.1%)
  Eligible for Free Lunch Program: 479 (25.8%)
  Eligible for Reduced-Price Lunch Program: 154 (8.3%)
Teachers: 106.6 (17.4 to 1)
Librarians/Media Specialists: 3.0 (618.0 to 1)
Guidance Counselors: 4.0 (463.5 to 1)
Current Spending: ($ per student per year):
  Total: $5,804; Instruction: $3,860; Support Services: $1,944

Enrollment, Drop-out Rates and Diploma Recipients by Race/Ethnicity

Category	Total	White	Black	Asian	AIAN	Hisp.
Enrollment (%)	100.0	98.7	0.8	0.1	0.1	0.4
Drop-out Rate (%)	2.6	2.3	0.0	0.0	0.0	50.0
H.S. Diplomas (#)	125	125	0	0	0	0

Wattsburg Area SD
10782 Wattsburg Rd · Erie, PA 16509
(814) 824-3400
Grade Span: KG-12; **Agency Type:** 1
Schools: 3
  1 Primary; 1 Middle; 1 High; 0 Other Level
  3 Regular; 0 Special Education; 0 Vocational; 0 Alternative
  0 Magnet; 0 Charter; 0 Title I Eligible; 0 School-wide Title I
Students: 1,680 (n/a% male; n/a% female)
  Individual Education Program: 222 (13.2%);
  English Language Learner: n/a; Migrant: 0 (0.0%)
  Eligible for Free Lunch Program: 249 (14.8%)
  Eligible for Reduced-Price Lunch Program: 153 (9.1%)
Teachers: 88.0 (19.1 to 1)
Librarians/Media Specialists: 3.0 (560.0 to 1)
Guidance Counselors: 5.0 (336.0 to 1)
Current Spending: ($ per student per year):
  Total: $6,664; Instruction: $3,763; Support Services: $2,640

Enrollment, Drop-out Rates and Diploma Recipients by Race/Ethnicity

Category	Total	White	Black	Asian	AIAN	Hisp.
Enrollment (%)	100.0	99.5	0.3	0.2	0.0	0.1
Drop-out Rate (%)	1.2	1.0	n/a	0.0	100.0	n/a
H.S. Diplomas (#)	147	147	0	0	0	0

Fayette County

Albert Gallatin Area SD
2625 Morgantown Rd · Uniontown, PA 15401-6703
(724) 564-7190
Grade Span: KG-12; **Agency Type:** 1
Schools: 9
  6 Primary; 2 Middle; 1 High; 0 Other Level
  9 Regular; 0 Special Education; 0 Vocational; 0 Alternative
  0 Magnet; 0 Charter; 9 Title I Eligible; 7 School-wide Title I
Students: 4,081 (n/a% male; n/a% female)
  Individual Education Program: 764 (18.7%);
  English Language Learner: n/a; Migrant: 0 (0.0%)
  Eligible for Free Lunch Program: 1,405 (34.4%)
  Eligible for Reduced-Price Lunch Program: 301 (7.4%)
Teachers: 255.0 (16.0 to 1)
Librarians/Media Specialists: 4.0 (1,020.3 to 1)
Guidance Counselors: 8.0 (510.1 to 1)
Current Spending: ($ per student per year):
  Total: $7,808; Instruction: $4,838; Support Services: $2,593

Enrollment, Drop-out Rates and Diploma Recipients by Race/Ethnicity

Category	Total	White	Black	Asian	AIAN	Hisp.
Enrollment (%)	100.0	94.2	5.2	0.1	0.2	0.3
Drop-out Rate (%)	3.4	3.6	0.0	0.0	0.0	n/a
H.S. Diplomas (#)	289	277	11	1	0	0

Brownsville Area SD
1025 Lewis St · Brownsville, PA 15417
(724) 785-2021
Grade Span: KG-12; **Agency Type:** 1
Schools: 5

---

  3 Primary; 1 Middle; 1 High; 0 Other Level
  5 Regular; 0 Special Education; 0 Vocational; 0 Alternative
  0 Magnet; 0 Charter; 5 Title I Eligible; 3 School-wide Title I
Students: 1,974 (n/a% male; n/a% female)
  Individual Education Program: 343 (17.4%);
  English Language Learner: n/a; Migrant: 0 (0.0%)
  Eligible for Free Lunch Program: 1,052 (53.3%)
  Eligible for Reduced-Price Lunch Program: 198 (10.0%)
Teachers: 131.0 (15.1 to 1)
Librarians/Media Specialists: 4.0 (493.5 to 1)
Guidance Counselors: 5.0 (394.8 to 1)
Current Spending: ($ per student per year):
  Total: $8,082; Instruction: $5,020; Support Services: $2,701

Enrollment, Drop-out Rates and Diploma Recipients by Race/Ethnicity

Category	Total	White	Black	Asian	AIAN	Hisp.
Enrollment (%)	100.0	85.7	13.9	0.3	0.0	0.1
Drop-out Rate (%)	6.4	5.7	12.7	0.0	n/a	0.0
H.S. Diplomas (#)	139	124	15	0	0	0

Connellsville Area SD
125 N 7th St · Connellsville, PA 15425-2556
(724) 628-3300 · http://www.casdfalcons.org/
Grade Span: KG-12; **Agency Type:** 1
Schools: 11
  8 Primary; 2 Middle; 1 High; 0 Other Level
  11 Regular; 0 Special Education; 0 Vocational; 0 Alternative
  0 Magnet; 0 Charter; 11 Title I Eligible; 10 School-wide Title I
Students: 5,766 (n/a% male; n/a% female)
  Individual Education Program: 1,104 (19.1%);
  English Language Learner: n/a; Migrant: 0 (0.0%)
  Eligible for Free Lunch Program: 2,290 (39.7%)
  Eligible for Reduced-Price Lunch Program: 664 (11.5%)
Teachers: 350.5 (16.5 to 1)
Librarians/Media Specialists: 7.0 (823.7 to 1)
Guidance Counselors: 11.0 (524.2 to 1)
Current Spending: ($ per student per year):
  Total: $7,722; Instruction: $4,629; Support Services: $2,695

Enrollment, Drop-out Rates and Diploma Recipients by Race/Ethnicity

Category	Total	White	Black	Asian	AIAN	Hisp.
Enrollment (%)	100.0	96.8	2.7	0.2	0.0	0.2
Drop-out Rate (%)	5.2	5.2	6.8	0.0	n/a	0.0
H.S. Diplomas (#)	375	368	7	0	0	0

Laurel Highlands SD
304 Bailey Ave · Uniontown, PA 15401-2461
(724) 437-2821 · http://www.hhs.net/lhsd/
Grade Span: KG-12; **Agency Type:** 1
Schools: 7
  5 Primary; 1 Middle; 1 High; 0 Other Level
  7 Regular; 0 Special Education; 0 Vocational; 0 Alternative
  0 Magnet; 0 Charter; 6 Title I Eligible; 4 School-wide Title I
Students: 3,675 (n/a% male; n/a% female)
  Individual Education Program: 427 (11.6%);
  English Language Learner: n/a; Migrant: 0 (0.0%)
  Eligible for Free Lunch Program: 1,321 (35.9%)
  Eligible for Reduced-Price Lunch Program: 270 (7.3%)
Teachers: 195.0 (18.8 to 1)
Librarians/Media Specialists: 5.0 (735.0 to 1)
Guidance Counselors: 4.0 (918.8 to 1)
Current Spending: ($ per student per year):
  Total: $7,458; Instruction: $4,737; Support Services: $2,392

Enrollment, Drop-out Rates and Diploma Recipients by Race/Ethnicity

Category	Total	White	Black	Asian	AIAN	Hisp.
Enrollment (%)	100.0	92.8	6.1	0.5	0.0	0.6
Drop-out Rate (%)	4.9	4.8	7.9	0.0	0.0	0.0
H.S. Diplomas (#)	244	236	6	1	1	0

Uniontown Area SD
23 E Church St · Uniontown, PA 15401-3510
(724) 438-4501
Grade Span: KG-12; **Agency Type:** 1
Schools: 8
  6 Primary; 1 Middle; 1 High; 0 Other Level
  8 Regular; 0 Special Education; 0 Vocational; 0 Alternative
  0 Magnet; 0 Charter; 8 Title I Eligible; 2 School-wide Title I
Students: 3,543 (n/a% male; n/a% female)
  Individual Education Program: 528 (14.9%);
  English Language Learner: n/a; Migrant: 0 (0.0%)
  Eligible for Free Lunch Program: 1,548 (43.7%)
  Eligible for Reduced-Price Lunch Program: 289 (8.2%)
Teachers: 227.0 (15.6 to 1)
Librarians/Media Specialists: 6.0 (590.5 to 1)
Guidance Counselors: 10.0 (354.3 to 1)
Current Spending: ($ per student per year):
  Total: $8,141; Instruction: $4,726; Support Services: $3,092

Enrollment, Drop-out Rates and Diploma Recipients by Race/Ethnicity

Category	Total	White	Black	Asian	AIAN	Hisp.
Enrollment (%)	100.0	81.1	18.5	0.1	0.0	0.3
Drop-out Rate (%)	1.6	1.4	2.6	0.0	n/a	0.0
H.S. Diplomas (#)	216	195	21	0	0	0

Franklin County

Chambersburg Area SD
435 Stanley Ave • Chambersburg, PA 17201-3405
(717) 263-9281 • http://www.chambersburg.k12.pa.us
Grade Span: KG-12; **Agency Type:** 1
Schools: 21
  18 Primary; 1 Middle; 1 High; 1 Other Level
  21 Regular; 0 Special Education; 0 Vocational; 0 Alternative
  0 Magnet; 0 Charter; 10 Title I Eligible; 2 School-wide Title I
Students: 8,022   (n/a% male; n/a% female)
  Individual Education Program: 1,323 (16.5%);
  English Language Learner: n/a; Migrant: 225 (2.8%)
  Eligible for Free Lunch Program: 1,292 (16.1%)
  Eligible for Reduced-Price Lunch Program: 404 (5.0%)
Teachers: 460.5 (17.4 to 1)
Librarians/Media Specialists: 12.0 (668.5 to 1)
Guidance Counselors: 19.0 (422.2 to 1)
Current Spending: ($ per student per year):
  Total: $6,632; Instruction: $4,263; Support Services: $2,057
Enrollment, Drop-out Rates and Diploma Recipients by Race/Ethnicity

Category	Total	White	Black	Asian	AIAN	Hisp.
Enrollment (%)	100.0	83.4	8.7	1.2	0.2	6.6
Drop-out Rate (%)	2.7	2.3	7.1	0.0	0.0	3.3
H.S. Diplomas (#)	502	451	25	10	0	16

Greencastle-Antrim SD
500 E Leitersburg St • Greencastle, PA 17225-1138
(717) 597-2187 • http://www.greencastle.k12.pa.us
Grade Span: KG-12; **Agency Type:** 1
Schools: 4
  2 Primary; 1 Middle; 1 High; 0 Other Level
  4 Regular; 0 Special Education; 0 Vocational; 0 Alternative
  0 Magnet; 0 Charter; 4 Title I Eligible; 0 School-wide Title I
Students: 2,700   (n/a% male; n/a% female)
  Individual Education Program: 322 (11.9%);
  English Language Learner: n/a; Migrant: 0 (0.0%)
  Eligible for Free Lunch Program: 133 (4.9%)
  Eligible for Reduced-Price Lunch Program: 106 (3.9%)
Teachers: 144.6 (18.7 to 1)
Librarians/Media Specialists: 3.0 (900.0 to 1)
Guidance Counselors: 5.0 (540.0 to 1)
Current Spending: ($ per student per year):
  Total: $6,547; Instruction: $4,153; Support Services: $2,098
Enrollment, Drop-out Rates and Diploma Recipients by Race/Ethnicity

Category	Total	White	Black	Asian	AIAN	Hisp.
Enrollment (%)	100.0	95.6	2.3	0.8	0.0	1.4
Drop-out Rate (%)	3.1	3.2	0.0	0.0	0.0	0.0
H.S. Diplomas (#)	169	168	0	1	0	0

Tuscarora SD
118 E Seminary St • Mercersburg, PA 17236-1606
(717) 328-3127
Grade Span: KG-12; **Agency Type:** 1
Schools: 6
  4 Primary; 1 Middle; 1 High; 0 Other Level
  6 Regular; 0 Special Education; 0 Vocational; 0 Alternative
  0 Magnet; 0 Charter; 5 Title I Eligible; 0 School-wide Title I
Students: 2,601   (n/a% male; n/a% female)
  Individual Education Program: 461 (17.7%);
  English Language Learner: n/a; Migrant: 16 (0.6%)
  Eligible for Free Lunch Program: 424 (16.3%)
  Eligible for Reduced-Price Lunch Program: 270 (10.4%)
Teachers: 167.2 (15.6 to 1)
Librarians/Media Specialists: 3.0 (867.0 to 1)
Guidance Counselors: 5.0 (520.2 to 1)
Current Spending: ($ per student per year):
  Total: $7,656; Instruction: $4,626; Support Services: $2,622
Enrollment, Drop-out Rates and Diploma Recipients by Race/Ethnicity

Category	Total	White	Black	Asian	AIAN	Hisp.
Enrollment (%)	100.0	95.9	2.4	0.4	0.1	1.2
Drop-out Rate (%)	1.3	1.4	0.0	0.0	0.0	0.0
H.S. Diplomas (#)	157	155	1	0	0	1

Waynesboro Area SD
210 Clayton Ave • Waynesboro, PA 17268-2066
(717) 762-1191
Grade Span: KG-12; **Agency Type:** 1
Schools: 6

  4 Primary; 1 Middle; 1 High; 0 Other Level
  6 Regular; 0 Special Education; 0 Vocational; 0 Alternative
  0 Magnet; 0 Charter; 3 Title I Eligible; 0 School-wide Title I
Students: 4,092   (n/a% male; n/a% female)
  Individual Education Program: 565 (13.8%);
  English Language Learner: n/a; Migrant: 2 (<0.1%)
  Eligible for Free Lunch Program: 748 (18.3%)
  Eligible for Reduced-Price Lunch Program: 332 (8.1%)
Teachers: 254.0 (16.1 to 1)
Librarians/Media Specialists: 6.0 (682.0 to 1)
Guidance Counselors: 7.0 (584.6 to 1)
Current Spending: ($ per student per year):
  Total: $7,129; Instruction: $4,588; Support Services: $2,209
Enrollment, Drop-out Rates and Diploma Recipients by Race/Ethnicity

Category	Total	White	Black	Asian	AIAN	Hisp.
Enrollment (%)	100.0	94.8	3.1	0.7	0.2	1.1
Drop-out Rate (%)	2.9	2.7	10.0	0.0	0.0	0.0
H.S. Diplomas (#)	293	274	10	6	1	2

Greene County

Central Greene SD
PO Box 472 • Waynesburg, PA 15370-0472
(724) 627-8151 • http://gctc.grvt.org/~cg/
Grade Span: KG-12; **Agency Type:** 1
Schools: 4
  2 Primary; 1 Middle; 1 High; 0 Other Level
  4 Regular; 0 Special Education; 0 Vocational; 0 Alternative
  0 Magnet; 0 Charter; 2 Title I Eligible; 2 School-wide Title I
Students: 2,310   (n/a% male; n/a% female)
  Individual Education Program: 513 (22.2%);
  English Language Learner: n/a; Migrant: 0 (0.0%)
  Eligible for Free Lunch Program: 860 (37.2%)
  Eligible for Reduced-Price Lunch Program: 187 (8.1%)
Teachers: 161.9 (14.3 to 1)
Librarians/Media Specialists: 3.0 (770.0 to 1)
Guidance Counselors: 5.0 (462.0 to 1)
Current Spending: ($ per student per year):
  Total: $8,852; Instruction: $5,493; Support Services: $2,967
Enrollment, Drop-out Rates and Diploma Recipients by Race/Ethnicity

Category	Total	White	Black	Asian	AIAN	Hisp.
Enrollment (%)	100.0	97.7	1.1	0.6	0.1	0.4
Drop-out Rate (%)	3.6	3.7	0.0	0.0	n/a	n/a
H.S. Diplomas (#)	145	141	1	3	0	0

Huntingdon County

Huntingdon Area SD
2400 Cassady Ave Ste 2 • Huntingdon, PA 16652-2618
(814) 643-4140
Grade Span: KG-12; **Agency Type:** 1
Schools: 6
  4 Primary; 1 Middle; 1 High; 0 Other Level
  6 Regular; 0 Special Education; 0 Vocational; 0 Alternative
  0 Magnet; 0 Charter; 5 Title I Eligible; 0 School-wide Title I
Students: 2,395   (n/a% male; n/a% female)
  Individual Education Program: 397 (16.6%);
  English Language Learner: n/a; Migrant: 1 (<0.1%)
  Eligible for Free Lunch Program: 518 (21.6%)
  Eligible for Reduced-Price Lunch Program: 293 (12.2%)
Teachers: 171.5 (14.0 to 1)
Librarians/Media Specialists: 4.0 (598.8 to 1)
Guidance Counselors: 3.0 (798.3 to 1)
Current Spending: ($ per student per year):
  Total: $7,026; Instruction: $4,264; Support Services: $2,419
Enrollment, Drop-out Rates and Diploma Recipients by Race/Ethnicity

Category	Total	White	Black	Asian	AIAN	Hisp.
Enrollment (%)	100.0	96.2	2.3	0.8	0.1	0.6
Drop-out Rate (%)	3.2	2.9	25.0	0.0	n/a	0.0
H.S. Diplomas (#)	156	154	0	0	0	2

Mount Union Area SD
28 W Market St • Mount Union, PA 17066-1232
(814) 542-8631
Grade Span: KG-12; **Agency Type:** 1
Schools: 4
  3 Primary; 0 Middle; 1 High; 0 Other Level
  4 Regular; 0 Special Education; 0 Vocational; 0 Alternative
  0 Magnet; 0 Charter; 2 Title I Eligible; 0 School-wide Title I
Students: 1,545   (n/a% male; n/a% female)
  Individual Education Program: 277 (17.9%);
  English Language Learner: n/a; Migrant: 0 (0.0%)
  Eligible for Free Lunch Program: 350 (22.7%)
  Eligible for Reduced-Price Lunch Program: 139 (9.0%)
Teachers: 121.5 (12.7 to 1)

Librarians/Media Specialists: 2.0 (772.5 to 1)
Guidance Counselors: 3.0 (515.0 to 1)
Current Spending: ($ per student per year):
Total: $7,513; Instruction: $4,796; Support Services: $2,342
Enrollment, Drop-out Rates and Diploma Recipients by Race/Ethnicity

Category	Total	White	Black	Asian	AIAN	Hisp.
Enrollment (%)	100.0	92.6	6.0	0.2	0.2	1.0
Drop-out Rate (%)	3.2	3.2	3.8	0.0	0.0	0.0
H.S. Diplomas (#)	95	90	4	1	0	0

Indiana County

Blairsville-Saltsburg SD
102 School Ln • Blairsville, PA 15717-8709
(724) 459-5500 • http://www.ARIN.k12.pa.us/blarsalt.html
Grade Span: KG-12; **Agency Type:** 1
Schools: 5
2 Primary; 1 Middle; 2 High; 0 Other Level
5 Regular; 0 Special Education; 0 Vocational; 0 Alternative
0 Magnet; 0 Charter; 3 Title I Eligible; 0 School-wide Title I
Students: 2,220 (n/a% male; n/a% female)
Individual Education Program: 373 (16.8%);
English Language Learner: n/a; Migrant: 0 (0.0%)
Eligible for Free Lunch Program: 587 (26.4%)
Eligible for Reduced-Price Lunch Program: 211 (9.5%)
Teachers: 134.0 (16.6 to 1)
Librarians/Media Specialists: 4.0 (555.0 to 1)
Guidance Counselors: 6.0 (370.0 to 1)
Current Spending: ($ per student per year):
Total: $7,990; Instruction: $4,880; Support Services: $2,769
Enrollment, Drop-out Rates and Diploma Recipients by Race/Ethnicity

Category	Total	White	Black	Asian	AIAN	Hisp.
Enrollment (%)	100.0	97.1	2.7	0.0	0.0	0.1
Drop-out Rate (%)	2.9	2.9	5.9	n/a	n/a	0.0
H.S. Diplomas (#)	139	138	0	0	0	1

Indiana Area SD
501 E Pike • Indiana, PA 15701-2234
(724) 463-8713 • http://www.iasd.cc
Grade Span: KG-12; **Agency Type:** 1
Schools: 6
4 Primary; 1 Middle; 1 High; 0 Other Level
6 Regular; 0 Special Education; 0 Vocational; 0 Alternative
0 Magnet; 0 Charter; 5 Title I Eligible; 0 School-wide Title I
Students: 3,233 (n/a% male; n/a% female)
Individual Education Program: 392 (12.1%);
English Language Learner: n/a; Migrant: 0 (0.0%)
Eligible for Free Lunch Program: 595 (18.4%)
Eligible for Reduced-Price Lunch Program: 173 (5.4%)
Teachers: 232.3 (13.9 to 1)
Librarians/Media Specialists: 6.0 (538.8 to 1)
Guidance Counselors: 9.0 (359.2 to 1)
Current Spending: ($ per student per year):
Total: $9,348; Instruction: $6,287; Support Services: $2,777
Enrollment, Drop-out Rates and Diploma Recipients by Race/Ethnicity

Category	Total	White	Black	Asian	AIAN	Hisp.
Enrollment (%)	100.0	92.5	3.7	3.2	0.2	0.4
Drop-out Rate (%)	2.0	2.1	0.0	0.0	0.0	0.0
H.S. Diplomas (#)	264	248	9	6	0	1

Marion Center Area SD
PO Box 156 • Marion Center, PA 15759-0156
(724) 397-4911 • http://www.arin.k12.pa.us/marion/
Grade Span: PK-12; **Agency Type:** 1
Schools: 3
1 Primary; 1 Middle; 1 High; 0 Other Level
3 Regular; 0 Special Education; 0 Vocational; 0 Alternative
0 Magnet; 0 Charter; 2 Title I Eligible; 0 School-wide Title I
Students: 1,706 (n/a% male; n/a% female)
Individual Education Program: 222 (13.0%);
English Language Learner: n/a; Migrant: 1 (0.1%)
Eligible for Free Lunch Program: 504 (29.5%)
Eligible for Reduced-Price Lunch Program: 218 (12.8%)
Teachers: 123.0 (13.9 to 1)
Librarians/Media Specialists: 3.0 (568.7 to 1)
Guidance Counselors: 6.0 (284.3 to 1)
Current Spending: ($ per student per year):
Total: $8,467; Instruction: $5,035; Support Services: $3,049
Enrollment, Drop-out Rates and Diploma Recipients by Race/Ethnicity

Category	Total	White	Black	Asian	AIAN	Hisp.
Enrollment (%)	100.0	98.7	0.7	0.1	0.1	0.4
Drop-out Rate (%)	1.3	1.4	0.0	n/a	n/a	0.0
H.S. Diplomas (#)	159	158	1	0	0	0

Jefferson County

Brookville Area SD
PO Box 479 • Brookville, PA 15825-0479
(814) 849-8372 • http://www.brookville.k12.pa.us
Grade Span: KG-12; **Agency Type:** 1
Schools: 4
3 Primary; 0 Middle; 1 High; 0 Other Level
4 Regular; 0 Special Education; 0 Vocational; 0 Alternative
0 Magnet; 0 Charter; 4 Title I Eligible; 0 School-wide Title I
Students: 1,885 (n/a% male; n/a% female)
Individual Education Program: 300 (15.9%);
English Language Learner: n/a; Migrant: 1 (0.1%)
Eligible for Free Lunch Program: 424 (22.5%)
Eligible for Reduced-Price Lunch Program: 164 (8.7%)
Teachers: 124.5 (15.1 to 1)
Librarians/Media Specialists: 2.5 (754.0 to 1)
Guidance Counselors: 5.0 (377.0 to 1)
Current Spending: ($ per student per year):
Total: $8,140; Instruction: $5,041; Support Services: $2,800
Enrollment, Drop-out Rates and Diploma Recipients by Race/Ethnicity

Category	Total	White	Black	Asian	AIAN	Hisp.
Enrollment (%)	100.0	97.9	0.7	0.7	0.2	0.5
Drop-out Rate (%)	2.2	2.2	0.0	0.0	n/a	0.0
H.S. Diplomas (#)	122	121	0	1	0	0

Punxsutawney Area SD
475 Beyer Ave • Punxsutawney, PA 15767-1467
(814) 938-5151 • http://www.punxsy.k12.pa.us
Grade Span: KG-12; **Agency Type:** 1
Schools: 9
7 Primary; 1 Middle; 1 High; 0 Other Level
9 Regular; 0 Special Education; 0 Vocational; 0 Alternative
0 Magnet; 0 Charter; 8 Title I Eligible; 2 School-wide Title I
Students: 2,768 (n/a% male; n/a% female)
Individual Education Program: 486 (17.6%);
English Language Learner: n/a; Migrant: 2 (0.1%)
Eligible for Free Lunch Program: 539 (19.5%)
Eligible for Reduced-Price Lunch Program: 220 (7.9%)
Teachers: 196.8 (14.1 to 1)
Librarians/Media Specialists: 4.0 (692.0 to 1)
Guidance Counselors: 8.0 (346.0 to 1)
Current Spending: ($ per student per year):
Total: $9,287; Instruction: $5,870; Support Services: $2,992
Enrollment, Drop-out Rates and Diploma Recipients by Race/Ethnicity

Category	Total	White	Black	Asian	AIAN	Hisp.
Enrollment (%)	100.0	98.5	0.6	0.3	0.1	0.5
Drop-out Rate (%)	1.1	1.1	0.0	0.0	n/a	0.0
H.S. Diplomas (#)	202	200	1	1	0	0

Juniata County

Juniata County SD
Hcr-63 Box 7d S 7th Street • Mifflintown, PA 17059-9806
(717) 436-2111
Grade Span: KG-12; **Agency Type:** 1
Schools: 12
9 Primary; 1 Middle; 2 High; 0 Other Level
12 Regular; 0 Special Education; 0 Vocational; 0 Alternative
0 Magnet; 0 Charter; 7 Title I Eligible; 0 School-wide Title I
Students: 3,176 (n/a% male; n/a% female)
Individual Education Program: 367 (11.6%);
English Language Learner: n/a; Migrant: 37 (1.2%)
Eligible for Free Lunch Program: 516 (16.2%)
Eligible for Reduced-Price Lunch Program: 336 (10.6%)
Teachers: 209.0 (15.2 to 1)
Librarians/Media Specialists: 5.0 (635.2 to 1)
Guidance Counselors: 7.0 (453.7 to 1)
Current Spending: ($ per student per year):
Total: $6,566; Instruction: $3,947; Support Services: $2,303
Enrollment, Drop-out Rates and Diploma Recipients by Race/Ethnicity

Category	Total	White	Black	Asian	AIAN	Hisp.
Enrollment (%)	100.0	96.0	0.5	0.7	0.1	2.7
Drop-out Rate (%)	2.0	1.9	0.0	0.0	0.0	9.1
H.S. Diplomas (#)	233	228	0	0	0	5

Lackawanna County

Abington Heights SD
200 E Grove St • Clarks Summit, PA 18411-1776
(570) 586-2511 • http://www.ahsd.org
Grade Span: KG-12; **Agency Type:** 1
Schools: 6
4 Primary; 1 Middle; 1 High; 0 Other Level
6 Regular; 0 Special Education; 0 Vocational; 0 Alternative

0 Magnet; 0 Charter; 3 Title I Eligible; 0 School-wide Title I
Students: 3,699   (n/a% male; n/a% female)
   Individual Education Program: 486 (13.1%);
   English Language Learner: n/a; Migrant: 6 (0.2%)
   Eligible for Free Lunch Program: 164 (4.4%)
   Eligible for Reduced-Price Lunch Program: 71 (1.9%)
Teachers: 224.6 (16.5 to 1)
Librarians/Media Specialists: 4.0 (924.8 to 1)
Guidance Counselors: 9.5 (389.4 to 1)
Current Spending: ($ per student per year):
   Total: $8,081; Instruction: $5,191; Support Services: $2,647
Enrollment, Drop-out Rates and Diploma Recipients by Race/Ethnicity

Category	Total	White	Black	Asian	AIAN	Hisp.
Enrollment (%)	100.0	95.5	1.4	2.1	0.0	0.9
Drop-out Rate (%)	0.5	0.5	0.0	0.0	n/a	0.0
H.S. Diplomas (#)	278	276	1	1	0	0

Dunmore SD
300 W Warren St • Dunmore, PA 18512-1992
(570) 343-2110 • http://ns.neiu.k12.pa.us/WWW/DUN/dunmore.htm
Grade Span: KG-12; **Agency Type:** 1
Schools: 3
   1 Primary; 1 Middle; 1 High; 0 Other Level
   3 Regular; 0 Special Education; 0 Vocational; 0 Alternative
   0 Magnet; 0 Charter; 1 Title I Eligible; 0 School-wide Title I
Students: 1,724   (n/a% male; n/a% female)
   Individual Education Program: 223 (12.9%);
   English Language Learner: n/a; Migrant: 0 (0.0%)
   Eligible for Free Lunch Program: 277 (16.1%)
   Eligible for Reduced-Price Lunch Program: 50 (2.9%)
Teachers: 94.0 (18.3 to 1)
Librarians/Media Specialists: 2.0 (862.0 to 1)
Guidance Counselors: 4.0 (431.0 to 1)
Current Spending: ($ per student per year):
   Total: $7,442; Instruction: $4,916; Support Services: $2,222
Enrollment, Drop-out Rates and Diploma Recipients by Race/Ethnicity

Category	Total	White	Black	Asian	AIAN	Hisp.
Enrollment (%)	100.0	96.4	1.7	0.4	0.0	1.5
Drop-out Rate (%)	1.7	1.7	0.0	0.0	n/a	0.0
H.S. Diplomas (#)	122	121	1	0	0	0

Lakeland SD
1593 Lakeland Dr • Jermyn, PA 18433-9801
(570) 254-9485 • http://ns.neiu.k12.pa.us/WWW/LAKELAND/index.html
Grade Span: KG-12; **Agency Type:** 1
Schools: 3
   2 Primary; 0 Middle; 1 High; 0 Other Level
   3 Regular; 0 Special Education; 0 Vocational; 0 Alternative
   0 Magnet; 0 Charter; 2 Title I Eligible; 0 School-wide Title I
Students: 1,649   (n/a% male; n/a% female)
   Individual Education Program: 207 (12.6%);
   English Language Learner: n/a; Migrant: 0 (0.0%)
   Eligible for Free Lunch Program: 280 (17.0%)
   Eligible for Reduced-Price Lunch Program: 95 (5.8%)
Teachers: 90.5 (18.2 to 1)
Librarians/Media Specialists: 2.0 (824.5 to 1)
Guidance Counselors: 4.0 (412.3 to 1)
Current Spending: ($ per student per year):
   Total: $6,630; Instruction: $4,171; Support Services: $2,207
Enrollment, Drop-out Rates and Diploma Recipients by Race/Ethnicity

Category	Total	White	Black	Asian	AIAN	Hisp.
Enrollment (%)	100.0	97.6	0.8	0.9	0.1	0.6
Drop-out Rate (%)	1.4	1.4	0.0	0.0	0.0	0.0
H.S. Diplomas (#)	118	117	0	0	1	0

Mid Valley SD
52 Underwood Rd • Throop, PA 18512-1196
(570) 307-1119 • http://mvsd.neiu.k12.pa.us
Grade Span: KG-12; **Agency Type:** 1
Schools: 2
   1 Primary; 0 Middle; 1 High; 0 Other Level
   2 Regular; 0 Special Education; 0 Vocational; 0 Alternative
   0 Magnet; 0 Charter; 1 Title I Eligible; 0 School-wide Title I
Students: 1,538   (n/a% male; n/a% female)
   Individual Education Program: 275 (17.9%);
   English Language Learner: n/a; Migrant: 3 (0.2%)
   Eligible for Free Lunch Program: 291 (18.9%)
   Eligible for Reduced-Price Lunch Program: 129 (8.4%)
Teachers: 99.6 (15.4 to 1)
Librarians/Media Specialists: 2.0 (769.0 to 1)
Guidance Counselors: 4.0 (384.5 to 1)
Current Spending: ($ per student per year):
   Total: $7,251; Instruction: $4,704; Support Services: $2,309

Enrollment, Drop-out Rates and Diploma Recipients by Race/Ethnicity

Category	Total	White	Black	Asian	AIAN	Hisp.
Enrollment (%)	100.0	95.5	2.0	0.3	0.1	2.1
Drop-out Rate (%)	1.6	1.6	0.0	n/a	n/a	n/a
H.S. Diplomas (#)	118	118	0	0	0	0

North Pocono SD
701 Church St • Moscow, PA 18444-9391
(570) 842-7659 • http://ns.neiu.k12.pa.us./WWW/NP/
Grade Span: KG-12; **Agency Type:** 1
Schools: 5
   3 Primary; 1 Middle; 1 High; 0 Other Level
   5 Regular; 0 Special Education; 0 Vocational; 0 Alternative
   0 Magnet; 0 Charter; 4 Title I Eligible; 0 School-wide Title I
Students: 3,248   (n/a% male; n/a% female)
   Individual Education Program: 388 (11.9%);
   English Language Learner: n/a; Migrant: 0 (0.0%)
   Eligible for Free Lunch Program: 485 (14.9%)
   Eligible for Reduced-Price Lunch Program: 166 (5.1%)
Teachers: 196.0 (16.6 to 1)
Librarians/Media Specialists: 3.0 (1,082.7 to 1)
Guidance Counselors: 8.0 (406.0 to 1)
Current Spending: ($ per student per year):
   Total: $7,498; Instruction: $4,684; Support Services: $2,547
Enrollment, Drop-out Rates and Diploma Recipients by Race/Ethnicity

Category	Total	White	Black	Asian	AIAN	Hisp.
Enrollment (%)	100.0	96.8	1.4	0.6	0.2	1.0
Drop-out Rate (%)	1.0	1.1	0.0	0.0	0.0	0.0
H.S. Diplomas (#)	260	255	2	1	0	2

Scranton SD
425 N Washington Ave • Scranton, PA 18503-1305
(570) 348-3400 • http://www.scrsd.org/
Grade Span: KG-12; **Agency Type:** 1
Schools: 18
   13 Primary; 3 Middle; 2 High; 0 Other Level
   18 Regular; 0 Special Education; 0 Vocational; 0 Alternative
   0 Magnet; 0 Charter; 17 Title I Eligible; 0 School-wide Title I
Students: 8,940   (n/a% male; n/a% female)
   Individual Education Program: 1,617 (18.1%);
   English Language Learner: n/a; Migrant: 302 (3.4%)
   Eligible for Free Lunch Program: 2,905 (32.5%)
   Eligible for Reduced-Price Lunch Program: 516 (5.8%)
Teachers: 629.6 (14.2 to 1)
Librarians/Media Specialists: 14.0 (638.6 to 1)
Guidance Counselors: 21.0 (425.7 to 1)
Current Spending: ($ per student per year):
   Total: $9,277; Instruction: $6,388; Support Services: $2,628
Enrollment, Drop-out Rates and Diploma Recipients by Race/Ethnicity

Category	Total	White	Black	Asian	AIAN	Hisp.
Enrollment (%)	100.0	80.7	8.8	1.2	0.1	9.2
Drop-out Rate (%)	3.3	3.4	2.9	5.1	0.0	1.6
H.S. Diplomas (#)	525	477	24	9	1	14

Valley View SD
1 Columbus Dr • Archbald, PA 18403-1538
(570) 876-5080 • http://vvsd.neiu.k12.pa.us/vvsd/dist/vvsd.html
Grade Span: KG-12; **Agency Type:** 1
Schools: 4
   2 Primary; 1 Middle; 1 High; 0 Other Level
   4 Regular; 0 Special Education; 0 Vocational; 0 Alternative
   0 Magnet; 0 Charter; 2 Title I Eligible; 0 School-wide Title I
Students: 2,587   (n/a% male; n/a% female)
   Individual Education Program: 343 (13.3%);
   English Language Learner: n/a; Migrant: 0 (0.0%)
   Eligible for Free Lunch Program: 405 (15.7%)
   Eligible for Reduced-Price Lunch Program: 223 (8.6%)
Teachers: 157.0 (16.5 to 1)
Librarians/Media Specialists: 3.0 (862.3 to 1)
Guidance Counselors: 7.0 (369.6 to 1)
Current Spending: ($ per student per year):
   Total: $6,490; Instruction: $3,923; Support Services: $2,315
Enrollment, Drop-out Rates and Diploma Recipients by Race/Ethnicity

Category	Total	White	Black	Asian	AIAN	Hisp.
Enrollment (%)	100.0	97.4	0.8	0.6	0.2	1.0
Drop-out Rate (%)	2.0	2.1	0.0	0.0	n/a	0.0
H.S. Diplomas (#)	183	181	1	0	1	0

Lancaster County

Cocalico SD
PO Box 800 • Denver, PA 17517-1139
(717) 336-1413 • http://www.cocalico.k12.pa.us
Grade Span: KG-12; **Agency Type:** 1
Schools: 6

4 Primary; 1 Middle; 1 High; 0 Other Level
6 Regular; 0 Special Education; 0 Vocational; 0 Alternative
0 Magnet; 0 Charter; 4 Title I Eligible; 0 School-wide Title I
Students: 3,542　(n/a% male; n/a% female)
　Individual Education Program: 543 (15.3%)
　English Language Learner: n/a; Migrant: 11 (0.3%)
　Eligible for Free Lunch Program: 271 (7.7%)
　Eligible for Reduced-Price Lunch Program: 188 (5.3%)
Teachers: 210.0 (16.9 to 1)
Librarians/Media Specialists: 5.0 (708.4 to 1)
Guidance Counselors: 8.0 (442.8 to 1)
Current Spending: ($ per student per year):
　Total: $6,830; Instruction: $4,308; Support Services: $2,174
Enrollment, Drop-out Rates and Diploma Recipients by Race/Ethnicity

Category	Total	White	Black	Asian	AIAN	Hisp.
Enrollment (%)	100.0	93.9	1.5	2.6	0.2	1.9
Drop-out Rate (%)	1.0	1.0	16.7	0.0	0.0	0.0
H.S. Diplomas (#)	203	196	1	3	0	3

Conestoga Valley SD
2110 Horseshoe Rd • Lancaster, PA 17601-6099
(717) 397-2421 • http://www.cvsd.k12.pa.us
Grade Span: KG-12; **Agency Type:** 1
Schools: 7
　5 Primary; 1 Middle; 1 High; 0 Other Level
　7 Regular; 0 Special Education; 0 Vocational; 0 Alternative
　0 Magnet; 0 Charter; 5 Title I Eligible; 0 School-wide Title I
Students: 3,884　(n/a% male; n/a% female)
　Individual Education Program: 500 (12.9%);
　English Language Learner: n/a; Migrant: 13 (0.3%)
　Eligible for Free Lunch Program: 278 (7.2%)
　Eligible for Reduced-Price Lunch Program: 270 (7.0%)
Teachers: 234.1 (16.6 to 1)
Librarians/Media Specialists: 6.0 (647.3 to 1)
Guidance Counselors: 10.5 (369.9 to 1)
Current Spending: ($ per student per year):
　Total: $9,245; Instruction: $6,001; Support Services: $2,304
Enrollment, Drop-out Rates and Diploma Recipients by Race/Ethnicity

Category	Total	White	Black	Asian	AIAN	Hisp.
Enrollment (%)	100.0	84.3	3.3	5.4	0.0	7.0
Drop-out Rate (%)	2.8	2.6	2.6	0.0	n/a	8.8
H.S. Diplomas (#)	254	231	4	7	0	12

Donegal SD
1051 Koser Rd • Mount Joy, PA 17552-2700
(717) 653-1447 • http://www.donegal.k12.pa.us
Grade Span: KG-12; **Agency Type:** 1
Schools: 7
　4 Primary; 1 Middle; 1 High; 1 Other Level
　7 Regular; 0 Special Education; 0 Vocational; 0 Alternative
　0 Magnet; 0 Charter; 4 Title I Eligible; 0 School-wide Title I
Students: 2,540　(n/a% male; n/a% female)
　Individual Education Program: 424 (16.7%);
　English Language Learner: n/a; Migrant: 14 (0.6%)
　Eligible for Free Lunch Program: 283 (11.1%)
　Eligible for Reduced-Price Lunch Program: 133 (5.2%)
Teachers: 163.2 (15.6 to 1)
Librarians/Media Specialists: 4.0 (635.0 to 1)
Guidance Counselors: 7.0 (362.9 to 1)
Current Spending: ($ per student per year):
　Total: $7,660; Instruction: $4,927; Support Services: $2,445
Enrollment, Drop-out Rates and Diploma Recipients by Race/Ethnicity

Category	Total	White	Black	Asian	AIAN	Hisp.
Enrollment (%)	100.0	93.4	1.9	0.9	0.3	3.5
Drop-out Rate (%)	2.9	2.6	9.1	0.0	0.0	8.3
H.S. Diplomas (#)	152	146	3	3	0	0

Eastern Lancaster County SD
PO Box 609 • New Holland, PA 17557-0609
(717) 354-1500 • http://www.elanco.k12.pa.us
Grade Span: KG-12; **Agency Type:** 1
Schools: 6
　4 Primary; 1 Middle; 1 High; 0 Other Level
　6 Regular; 0 Special Education; 0 Vocational; 0 Alternative
　0 Magnet; 0 Charter; 4 Title I Eligible; 0 School-wide Title I
Students: 3,467　(n/a% male; n/a% female)
　Individual Education Program: 430 (12.4%);
　English Language Learner: n/a; Migrant: 14 (0.4%)
　Eligible for Free Lunch Program: 343 (9.9%)
　Eligible for Reduced-Price Lunch Program: 171 (4.9%)
Teachers: 212.8 (16.3 to 1)
Librarians/Media Specialists: 5.0 (693.4 to 1)
Guidance Counselors: 8.0 (433.4 to 1)
Current Spending: ($ per student per year):
　Total: $7,839; Instruction: $4,692; Support Services: $2,846

Category	Total	White	Black	Asian	AIAN	Hisp.
Enrollment (%)	100.0	92.1	1.7	2.5	0.0	3.7
Drop-out Rate (%)	1.3	1.4	0.0	0.0	n/a	0.0
H.S. Diplomas (#)	234	224	2	7	0	1

Elizabethtown Area SD
600 E High St • Elizabethtown, PA 17022-1713
(717) 367-1521 • http://www.etown.k12.pa.us
Grade Span: KG-12; **Agency Type:** 1
Schools: 7
　5 Primary; 1 Middle; 1 High; 0 Other Level
　7 Regular; 0 Special Education; 0 Vocational; 0 Alternative
　0 Magnet; 0 Charter; 4 Title I Eligible; 0 School-wide Title I
Students: 3,902　(n/a% male; n/a% female)
　Individual Education Program: 607 (15.6%)
　English Language Learner: n/a; Migrant: 11 (0.3%)
　Eligible for Free Lunch Program: 209 (5.4%)
　Eligible for Reduced-Price Lunch Program: 141 (3.6%)
Teachers: 230.6 (16.9 to 1)
Librarians/Media Specialists: 5.0 (780.4 to 1)
Guidance Counselors: 9.0 (433.6 to 1)
Current Spending: ($ per student per year):
　Total: $6,581; Instruction: $4,143; Support Services: $2,160
Enrollment, Drop-out Rates and Diploma Recipients by Race/Ethnicity

Category	Total	White	Black	Asian	AIAN	Hisp.
Enrollment (%)	100.0	94.7	1.3	1.4	0.2	2.4
Drop-out Rate (%)	1.8	1.6	9.1	0.0	0.0	11.1
H.S. Diplomas (#)	244	232	1	8	0	3

Ephrata Area SD
803 Oak Blvd • Ephrata, PA 17522-1960
(717) 733-1513 • http://www.easd.k12.pa.us
Grade Span: PK-12; **Agency Type:** 1
Schools: 7
　5 Primary; 1 Middle; 1 High; 0 Other Level
　7 Regular; 0 Special Education; 0 Vocational; 0 Alternative
　0 Magnet; 0 Charter; 5 Title I Eligible; 0 School-wide Title I
Students: 4,079　(n/a% male; n/a% female)
　Individual Education Program: 594 (14.6%);
　English Language Learner: n/a; Migrant: 14 (0.3%)
　Eligible for Free Lunch Program: 492 (12.1%)
　Eligible for Reduced-Price Lunch Program: 257 (6.3%)
Teachers: 247.1 (16.5 to 1)
Librarians/Media Specialists: 7.5 (543.9 to 1)
Guidance Counselors: 10.0 (407.9 to 1)
Current Spending: ($ per student per year):
　Total: $7,103; Instruction: $4,488; Support Services: $2,251
Enrollment, Drop-out Rates and Diploma Recipients by Race/Ethnicity

Category	Total	White	Black	Asian	AIAN	Hisp.
Enrollment (%)	100.0	95.0	0.6	1.8	0.1	2.5
Drop-out Rate (%)	1.3	1.3	0.0	0.0	0.0	3.3
H.S. Diplomas (#)	269	262	1	5	0	1

Hempfield SD
200 Church St • Landisville, PA 17538-1300
(717) 898-5560 • http://www.hempfield.k12.pa.us
Grade Span: KG-12; **Agency Type:** 1
Schools: 10
　6 Primary; 3 Middle; 1 High; 0 Other Level
　10 Regular; 0 Special Education; 0 Vocational; 0 Alternative
　0 Magnet; 0 Charter; 7 Title I Eligible; 0 School-wide Title I
Students: 7,229　(n/a% male; n/a% female)
　Individual Education Program: 1,090 (15.1%);
　English Language Learner: n/a; Migrant: 69 (1.0%)
　Eligible for Free Lunch Program: 505 (7.0%)
　Eligible for Reduced-Price Lunch Program: 253 (3.5%)
Teachers: 416.5 (17.4 to 1)
Librarians/Media Specialists: 11.0 (657.2 to 1)
Guidance Counselors: 15.0 (481.9 to 1)
Current Spending: ($ per student per year):
　Total: $7,569; Instruction: $4,932; Support Services: $2,245
Enrollment, Drop-out Rates and Diploma Recipients by Race/Ethnicity

Category	Total	White	Black	Asian	AIAN	Hisp.
Enrollment (%)	100.0	87.0	3.0	3.1	0.3	6.7
Drop-out Rate (%)	2.2	2.0	9.8	3.7	0.0	2.2
H.S. Diplomas (#)	546	499	10	19	1	17

Lampeter-Strasburg SD
PO Box 428 • Lampeter, PA 17537-0428
(717) 464-3311 • http://www.lampstras.k12.pa.us
Grade Span: KG-12; **Agency Type:** 1
Schools: 5
　3 Primary; 1 Middle; 1 High; 0 Other Level
　5 Regular; 0 Special Education; 0 Vocational

0 Magnet; 0 Charter; 4 Title I Eligible; 0 School-wide Title I
Students: 3,201   (n/a% male; n/a% female)
  Individual Education Program: 434 (13.6%);
  English Language Learner: n/a; Migrant: 0 (0.0%)
  Eligible for Free Lunch Program: 125 (3.9%)
  Eligible for Reduced-Price Lunch Program: 76 (2.4%)
Teachers: 200.7 (15.9 to 1)
Librarians/Media Specialists: 3.0 (1,067.0 to 1)
Guidance Counselors: 7.0 (457.3 to 1)
Current Spending: ($ per student per year):
  Total: $7,103; Instruction: $4,482; Support Services: $2,182
Enrollment, Drop-out Rates and Diploma Recipients by Race/Ethnicity

Category	Total	White	Black	Asian	AIAN	Hisp.
Enrollment (%)	100.0	94.9	1.4	1.2	0.1	2.3
Drop-out Rate (%)	1.5	1.6	0.0	0.0	n/a	0.0
H.S. Diplomas (#)	183	173	1	2	0	7

Lancaster SD
1020 Lehigh Ave • Lancaster, PA 17602-2452
(717) 291-6121 • http://www.lancaster.k12.pa.us/
Grade Span: PK-12; **Agency Type:** 1
Schools: 19
  13 Primary; 4 Middle; 1 High; 1 Other Level
  19 Regular; 0 Special Education; 0 Vocational; 0 Alternative
  0 Magnet; 0 Charter; 12 Title I Eligible; 11 School-wide Title I
Students: 11,045   (n/a% male; n/a% female)
  Individual Education Program: 2,741 (24.8%);
  English Language Learner: n/a; Migrant: 1,040 (9.4%)
  Eligible for Free Lunch Program: 5,683 (51.5%)
  Eligible for Reduced-Price Lunch Program: 1,190 (10.8%)
Teachers: 706.0 (15.6 to 1)
Librarians/Media Specialists: 19.0 (581.3 to 1)
Guidance Counselors: 25.9 (426.4 to 1)
Current Spending: ($ per student per year):
  Total: $9,079; Instruction: $5,291; Support Services: $2,540
Enrollment, Drop-out Rates and Diploma Recipients by Race/Ethnicity

Category	Total	White	Black	Asian	AIAN	Hisp.
Enrollment (%)	100.0	24.5	23.3	2.6	0.2	49.5
Drop-out Rate (%)	10.7	7.5	10.4	6.3	20.0	13.4
H.S. Diplomas (#)	461	172	110	28	0	151

Manheim Central SD
71 N Hazel St • Manheim, PA 17545-1511
(717) 665-3422 • http://www.mcsd.k12.pa.us
Grade Span: KG-12; **Agency Type:** 1
Schools: 8
  6 Primary; 1 Middle; 1 High; 0 Other Level
  8 Regular; 0 Special Education; 0 Vocational; 0 Alternative
  0 Magnet; 0 Charter; 5 Title I Eligible; 0 School-wide Title I
Students: 3,087   (n/a% male; n/a% female)
  Individual Education Program: 512 (16.6%);
  English Language Learner: n/a; Migrant: 15 (0.5%)
  Eligible for Free Lunch Program: 304 (9.8%)
  Eligible for Reduced-Price Lunch Program: 190 (6.2%)
Teachers: 193.0 (16.0 to 1)
Librarians/Media Specialists: 4.6 (671.1 to 1)
Guidance Counselors: 8.0 (385.9 to 1)
Current Spending: ($ per student per year):
  Total: $7,699; Instruction: $5,055; Support Services: $2,273
Enrollment, Drop-out Rates and Diploma Recipients by Race/Ethnicity

Category	Total	White	Black	Asian	AIAN	Hisp.
Enrollment (%)	100.0	95.2	1.6	1.1	0.2	2.0
Drop-out Rate (%)	2.2	2.3	0.0	0.0	0.0	0.0
H.S. Diplomas (#)	221	205	3	10	0	3

Manheim Township SD
PO Box 5134 • Lancaster, PA 17606-5134
(717) 569-8231 • http://www.mtwp.k12.pa.us
Grade Span: KG-12; **Agency Type:** 1
Schools: 9
  6 Primary; 2 Middle; 1 High; 0 Other Level
  9 Regular; 0 Special Education; 0 Vocational; 0 Alternative
  0 Magnet; 0 Charter; 4 Title I Eligible; 0 School-wide Title I
Students: 5,369   (n/a% male; n/a% female)
  Individual Education Program: 616 (11.5%);
  English Language Learner: n/a; Migrant: 19 (0.4%)
  Eligible for Free Lunch Program: 245 (4.6%)
  Eligible for Reduced-Price Lunch Program: 199 (3.7%)
Teachers: 349.2 (15.4 to 1)
Librarians/Media Specialists: 9.5 (565.2 to 1)
Guidance Counselors: 14.0 (383.5 to 1)
Current Spending: ($ per student per year):
  Total: $7,965; Instruction: $4,884; Support Services: $2,821

Enrollment, Drop-out Rates and Diploma Recipients by Race/Ethnicity

Category	Total	White	Black	Asian	AIAN	Hisp.
Enrollment (%)	100.0	84.1	3.4	5.6	0.2	6.7
Drop-out Rate (%)	1.3	0.9	3.8	0.0	0.0	7.2
H.S. Diplomas (#)	356	325	8	14	0	9

Penn Manor SD
PO Box 1001 • Millersville, PA 17551-0301
(717) 872-9500 • http://www.pmsd.k12.pa.us
Grade Span: KG-12; **Agency Type:** 1
Schools: 10
  7 Primary; 2 Middle; 1 High; 0 Other Level
  10 Regular; 0 Special Education; 0 Vocational; 0 Alternative
  0 Magnet; 0 Charter; 7 Title I Eligible; 0 School-wide Title I
Students: 5,342   (n/a% male; n/a% female)
  Individual Education Program: 816 (15.3%);
  English Language Learner: n/a; Migrant: 7 (0.1%)
  Eligible for Free Lunch Program: 370 (6.9%)
  Eligible for Reduced-Price Lunch Program: 288 (5.4%)
Teachers: 316.0 (16.9 to 1)
Librarians/Media Specialists: 6.0 (890.3 to 1)
Guidance Counselors: 13.5 (395.7 to 1)
Current Spending: ($ per student per year):
  Total: $7,186; Instruction: $4,755; Support Services: $2,081
Enrollment, Drop-out Rates and Diploma Recipients by Race/Ethnicity

Category	Total	White	Black	Asian	AIAN	Hisp.
Enrollment (%)	100.0	92.7	2.3	1.2	0.1	3.7
Drop-out Rate (%)	1.5	1.5	0.0	0.0	0.0	2.0
H.S. Diplomas (#)	350	332	7	4	1	6

Pequea Valley SD
PO Box 130 • Kinzers, PA 17535-0130
(717) 768-5530 • http://www.pvsd.k12.pa.us
Grade Span: KG-12; **Agency Type:** 1
Schools: 5
  3 Primary; 1 Middle; 1 High; 0 Other Level
  5 Regular; 0 Special Education; 0 Vocational; 0 Alternative
  0 Magnet; 0 Charter; 2 Title I Eligible; 0 School-wide Title I
Students: 1,959   (n/a% male; n/a% female)
  Individual Education Program: 265 (13.5%);
  English Language Learner: n/a; Migrant: 1 (0.1%)
  Eligible for Free Lunch Program: 236 (12.0%)
  Eligible for Reduced-Price Lunch Program: 104 (5.3%)
Teachers: 127.0 (15.4 to 1)
Librarians/Media Specialists: 4.0 (489.8 to 1)
Guidance Counselors: 5.0 (391.8 to 1)
Current Spending: ($ per student per year):
  Total: $8,568; Instruction: $4,655; Support Services: $2,981
Enrollment, Drop-out Rates and Diploma Recipients by Race/Ethnicity

Category	Total	White	Black	Asian	AIAN	Hisp.
Enrollment (%)	100.0	96.4	1.8	0.8	0.0	1.0
Drop-out Rate (%)	2.3	2.2	0.0	12.5	n/a	0.0
H.S. Diplomas (#)	108	100	2	3	0	3

Solanco SD
121 S Hess St • Quarryville, PA 17566-1225
(717) 786-8401 • http://www.solanco.k12.pa.us
Grade Span: KG-12; **Agency Type:** 1
Schools: 7
  4 Primary; 2 Middle; 1 High; 0 Other Level
  7 Regular; 0 Special Education; 0 Vocational; 0 Alternative
  0 Magnet; 0 Charter; 6 Title I Eligible; 0 School-wide Title I
Students: 3,939   (n/a% male; n/a% female)
  Individual Education Program: 377 (9.6%);
  English Language Learner: n/a; Migrant: 9 (0.2%)
  Eligible for Free Lunch Program: 426 (10.8%)
  Eligible for Reduced-Price Lunch Program: 163 (4.1%)
Teachers: 211.6 (18.6 to 1)
Librarians/Media Specialists: 6.0 (656.5 to 1)
Guidance Counselors: 9.0 (437.7 to 1)
Current Spending: ($ per student per year):
  Total: $6,825; Instruction: $4,165; Support Services: $2,356
Enrollment, Drop-out Rates and Diploma Recipients by Race/Ethnicity

Category	Total	White	Black	Asian	AIAN	Hisp.
Enrollment (%)	100.0	95.4	1.4	0.6	0.2	2.5
Drop-out Rate (%)	2.6	2.6	0.0	0.0	n/a	8.0
H.S. Diplomas (#)	305	302	2	0	0	1

Warwick SD
301 W Orange St • Lititz, PA 17543-1814
(717) 626-3734 • http://www.warwick.k12.pa.us
Grade Span: KG-12; **Agency Type:** 1
Schools: 6
  4 Primary; 1 Middle; 1 High; 0 Other Level
  6 Regular; 0 Special Education; 0 Vocational; 0 Alternative

0 Magnet; 0 Charter; 6 Title I Eligible; 0 School-wide Title I
Students: 4,644   (n/a% male; n/a% female)
Individual Education Program: 748 (16.1%);
English Language Learner: n/a; Migrant: 15 (0.3%)
Eligible for Free Lunch Program: 282 (6.1%)
Eligible for Reduced-Price Lunch Program: 176 (3.8%)
Teachers: 289.3 (16.1 to 1)
Librarians/Media Specialists: 6.0 (774.0 to 1)
Guidance Counselors: 6.8 (682.9 to 1)
Current Spending: ($ per student per year):
Total: $6,977; Instruction: $4,601; Support Services: $2,061
Enrollment, Drop-out Rates and Diploma Recipients by Race/Ethnicity

Category	Total	White	Black	Asian	AIAN	Hisp.
Enrollment (%)	100.0	94.9	1.4	1.3	0.0	2.4
Drop-out Rate (%)	2.5	2.5	6.3	3.8	0.0	0.0
H.S. Diplomas (#)	305	289	0	4	2	10

Lawrence County

Ellwood City Area SD
501 Crescent Ave • Ellwood City, PA 16117-1957
(724) 752-1591 • http://www.ellwood.k12.pa.us
Grade Span: KG-12; **Agency Type:** 1
Schools: 5
4 Primary; 0 Middle; 1 High; 0 Other Level
5 Regular; 0 Special Education; 0 Vocational; 0 Alternative
0 Magnet; 0 Charter; 0 Title I Eligible; 0 School-wide Title I
Students: 2,206   (n/a% male; n/a% female)
Individual Education Program: 315 (14.3%);
English Language Learner: n/a; Migrant: 0 (0.0%)
Eligible for Free Lunch Program: 610 (27.7%)
Eligible for Reduced-Price Lunch Program: 183 (8.3%)
Teachers: 133.5 (16.5 to 1)
Librarians/Media Specialists: 2.0 (1,103.0 to 1)
Guidance Counselors: 3.0 (735.3 to 1)
Current Spending: ($ per student per year):
Total: $7,468; Instruction: $4,866; Support Services: $2,305
Enrollment, Drop-out Rates and Diploma Recipients by Race/Ethnicity

Category	Total	White	Black	Asian	AIAN	Hisp.
Enrollment (%)	100.0	96.6	2.8	0.3	0.0	0.2
Drop-out Rate (%)	2.2	2.1	10.0	0.0	n/a	0.0
H.S. Diplomas (#)	155	151	2	1	0	1

Mohawk Area SD
PO Box 25 • Bessemer, PA 16112-0025
(724) 667-7723 • http://www.mohawk.k12.pa.us
Grade Span: KG-12; **Agency Type:** 1
Schools: 2
1 Primary; 0 Middle; 1 High; 0 Other Level
2 Regular; 0 Special Education; 0 Vocational; 0 Alternative
0 Magnet; 0 Charter; 0 Title I Eligible; 0 School-wide Title I
Students: 1,992   (n/a% male; n/a% female)
Individual Education Program: 211 (10.6%);
English Language Learner: n/a; Migrant: 0 (0.0%)
Eligible for Free Lunch Program: 382 (19.2%)
Eligible for Reduced-Price Lunch Program: 139 (7.0%)
Teachers: 125.0 (15.9 to 1)
Librarians/Media Specialists: 2.0 (996.0 to 1)
Guidance Counselors: 3.0 (664.0 to 1)
Current Spending: ($ per student per year):
Total: $6,575; Instruction: $4,507; Support Services: $1,777
Enrollment, Drop-out Rates and Diploma Recipients by Race/Ethnicity

Category	Total	White	Black	Asian	AIAN	Hisp.
Enrollment (%)	100.0	99.0	0.6	0.4	0.0	0.0
Drop-out Rate (%)	1.2	1.2	0.0	0.0	0.0	n/a
H.S. Diplomas (#)	109	109	0	0	0	0

New Castle Area SD
420 Fern St • New Castle, PA 16101-2596
(724) 656-4756 • http://www.newcastle.k12.pa.us
Grade Span: KG-12; **Agency Type:** 1
Schools: 8
5 Primary; 2 Middle; 1 High; 0 Other Level
8 Regular; 0 Special Education; 0 Vocational; 0 Alternative
0 Magnet; 0 Charter; 6 Title I Eligible; 5 School-wide Title I
Students: 3,839   (n/a% male; n/a% female)
Individual Education Program: 679 (17.7%);
English Language Learner: n/a; Migrant: 0 (0.0%)
Eligible for Free Lunch Program: 1,689 (44.0%)
Eligible for Reduced-Price Lunch Program: 164 (4.3%)
Teachers: 237.0 (16.2 to 1)
Librarians/Media Specialists: 6.0 (639.8 to 1)
Guidance Counselors: 3.0 (1,279.7 to 1)
Current Spending: ($ per student per year):
Total: $7,771; Instruction: $5,241; Support Services: $2,211

Category	Total	White	Black	Asian	AIAN	Hisp.
Enrollment	100.0	72.9	25.9	0.4	0.1	0.7
Drop-out Rate (%)	4.3	3.6	8.0	0.4	0.1	0.7
H.S. Diplomas (#)	163	146	17	0	0	0

Wilmington Area SD
300 Wood St • New Wilmington, PA 16142-1016
(724) 656-8866
Grade Span: KG-12; **Agency Type:** 1
Schools: 5
3 Primary; 1 Middle; 1 High; 0 Other Level
5 Regular; 0 Special Education; 0 Vocational; 0 Alternative
0 Magnet; 0 Charter; 0 Title I Eligible; 0 School-wide Title I
Students: 1,576   (n/a% male; n/a% female)
Individual Education Program: 285 (18.1%);
English Language Learner: n/a; Migrant: 0 (0.0%)
Eligible for Free Lunch Program: 265 (16.8%)
Eligible for Reduced-Price Lunch Program: 104 (6.6%)
Teachers: 105.4 (15.0 to 1)
Librarians/Media Specialists: 1.0 (1,576.0 to 1)
Guidance Counselors: 3.0 (525.3 to 1)
Current Spending: ($ per student per year):
Total: $7,193; Instruction: $4,478; Support Services: $2,475
Enrollment, Drop-out Rates and Diploma Recipients by Race/Ethnicity

Category	Total	White	Black	Asian	AIAN	Hisp.
Enrollment (%)	100.0	98.1	1.0	0.3	0.0	0.6
Drop-out Rate (%)	0.9	0.8	20.0	0.0	n/a	0.0
H.S. Diplomas (#)	129	128	0	0	0	1

Lebanon County

Annville-Cleona SD
520 S White Oak St • Annville, PA 17003-2200
(717) 867-7600 • http://www.acsd.k12.pa.us
Grade Span: KG-12; **Agency Type:** 1
Schools: 4
2 Primary; 1 Middle; 1 High; 0 Other Level
4 Regular; 0 Special Education; 0 Vocational; 0 Alternative
0 Magnet; 0 Charter; 4 Title I Eligible; 0 School-wide Title I
Students: 1,686   (n/a% male; n/a% female)
Individual Education Program: 234 (13.9%);
English Language Learner: n/a; Migrant: 0 (0.0%)
Eligible for Free Lunch Program: 95 (5.6%)
Eligible for Reduced-Price Lunch Program: 57 (3.4%)
Teachers: 106.3 (15.9 to 1)
Librarians/Media Specialists: 3.0 (562.0 to 1)
Guidance Counselors: 5.0 (337.2 to 1)
Current Spending: ($ per student per year):
Total: $7,093; Instruction: $4,364; Support Services: $2,416
Enrollment, Drop-out Rates and Diploma Recipients by Race/Ethnicity

Category	Total	White	Black	Asian	AIAN	Hisp.
Enrollment (%)	100.0	95.0	1.1	1.5	0.0	2.4
Drop-out Rate (%)	2.1	2.2	0.0	0.0	n/a	0.0
H.S. Diplomas (#)	119	116	0	2	0	1

Cornwall-Lebanon SD
105 E Evergreen Rd • Lebanon, PA 17042-7595
(717) 272-2031 • http://www.clsd.k12.pa.us
Grade Span: KG-12; **Agency Type:** 1
Schools: 6
4 Primary; 1 Middle; 1 High; 0 Other Level
6 Regular; 0 Special Education; 0 Vocational; 0 Alternative
0 Magnet; 0 Charter; 4 Title I Eligible; 0 School-wide Title I
Students: 4,714   (n/a% male; n/a% female)
Individual Education Program: 530 (11.2%);
English Language Learner: n/a; Migrant: 96 (2.0%)
Eligible for Free Lunch Program: 655 (13.9%)
Eligible for Reduced-Price Lunch Program: 273 (5.8%)
Teachers: 294.5 (16.0 to 1)
Librarians/Media Specialists: 6.0 (785.7 to 1)
Guidance Counselors: 5.0 (942.8 to 1)
Current Spending: ($ per student per year):
Total: $7,446; Instruction: $4,718; Support Services: $2,413
Enrollment, Drop-out Rates and Diploma Recipients by Race/Ethnicity

Category	Total	White	Black	Asian	AIAN	Hisp.
Enrollment (%)	100.0	86.2	2.4	2.1	0.2	9.1
Drop-out Rate (%)	2.1	1.9	0.0	3.6	0.0	4.3
H.S. Diplomas (#)	322	292	3	4	0	23

Eastern Lebanon County SD
180 Elco Dr • Myerstown, PA 17067-2604
(717) 866-7117 • http://www.elco.k12.pa.us
Grade Span: KG-12; **Agency Type:** 1
Schools: 6

4 Primary; 1 Middle; 1 High; 0 Other Level
6 Regular; 0 Special Education; 0 Vocational; 0 Alternative
0 Magnet; 0 Charter; 5 Title I Eligible; 0 School-wide Title I
Students: 2,425 (n/a% male; n/a% female)
    Individual Education Program: 324 (13.4%);
    English Language Learner: n/a; Migrant: 4 (0.2%)
    Eligible for Free Lunch Program: 171 (7.1%)
    Eligible for Reduced-Price Lunch Program: 111 (4.6%)
Teachers: 146.5 (16.6 to 1)
Librarians/Media Specialists: 3.0 (808.3 to 1)
Guidance Counselors: 5.0 (485.0 to 1)
Current Spending: ($ per student per year):
    Total: $7,589; Instruction: $4,618; Support Services: $2,595
Enrollment, Drop-out Rates and Diploma Recipients by Race/Ethnicity

Category	Total	White	Black	Asian	AIAN	Hisp.
Enrollment (%)	100.0	97.1	1.4	0.5	0.1	0.9
Drop-out Rate (%)	1.5	1.2	0.0	12.5	n/a	16.7
H.S. Diplomas (#)	164	162	0	1	0	1

Lebanon SD
1000 S 8th St • Lebanon, PA 17042-6726
(717) 273-9391 • http://www.lebanon.k12.pa.us
Grade Span: PK-12; **Agency Type:** 1
Schools: 7
5 Primary; 1 Middle; 1 High; 0 Other Level
7 Regular; 0 Special Education; 0 Vocational; 0 Alternative
0 Magnet; 0 Charter; 7 Title I Eligible; 1 School-wide Title I
Students: 4,243 (n/a% male; n/a% female)
    Individual Education Program: 720 (17.0%);
    English Language Learner: n/a; Migrant: 477 (11.2%)
    Eligible for Free Lunch Program: 1,483 (35.0%)
    Eligible for Reduced-Price Lunch Program: 351 (8.3%)
Teachers: 244.5 (17.4 to 1)
Librarians/Media Specialists: 4.0 (1,060.8 to 1)
Guidance Counselors: 11.0 (385.7 to 1)
Current Spending: ($ per student per year):
    Total: $6,511; Instruction: $4,350; Support Services: $1,833
Enrollment, Drop-out Rates and Diploma Recipients by Race/Ethnicity

Category	Total	White	Black	Asian	AIAN	Hisp.
Enrollment (%)	100.0	55.8	5.3	1.4	0.1	37.4
Drop-out Rate (%)	6.4	6.2	5.1	8.3	n/a	7.1
H.S. Diplomas (#)	192	141	5	4	0	42

Northern Lebanon SD
PO Box 100 • Fredericksburg, PA 17026-0100
(717) 865-2117 • http://www.norleb.k12.pa.us
Grade Span: KG-12; **Agency Type:** 1
Schools: 6
4 Primary; 1 Middle; 1 High; 0 Other Level
6 Regular; 0 Special Education; 0 Vocational; 0 Alternative
0 Magnet; 0 Charter; 4 Title I Eligible; 0 School-wide Title I
Students: 2,454 (n/a% male; n/a% female)
    Individual Education Program: 323 (13.2%);
    English Language Learner: n/a; Migrant: 3 (0.1%)
    Eligible for Free Lunch Program: 194 (7.9%)
    Eligible for Reduced-Price Lunch Program: 136 (5.5%)
Teachers: 159.0 (15.4 to 1)
Librarians/Media Specialists: 2.0 (1,227.0 to 1)
Guidance Counselors: 6.0 (409.0 to 1)
Current Spending: ($ per student per year):
    Total: $7,546; Instruction: $4,386; Support Services: $2,705
Enrollment, Drop-out Rates and Diploma Recipients by Race/Ethnicity

Category	Total	White	Black	Asian	AIAN	Hisp.
Enrollment (%)	100.0	97.0	0.5	0.4	0.0	2.0
Drop-out Rate (%)	5.4	5.6	0.0	0.0	n/a	0.0
H.S. Diplomas (#)	161	159	0	0	0	2

Palmyra Area SD
1125 Park Dr • Palmyra, PA 17078-3447
(717) 838-3144 • http://www.palmyra.k12.pa.us
Grade Span: KG-12; **Agency Type:** 1
Schools: 5
3 Primary; 1 Middle; 1 High; 0 Other Level
5 Regular; 0 Special Education; 0 Vocational; 0 Alternative
0 Magnet; 0 Charter; 2 Title I Eligible; 0 School-wide Title I
Students: 2,911 (n/a% male; n/a% female)
    Individual Education Program: 292 (10.0%);
    English Language Learner: n/a; Migrant: 2 (0.1%)
    Eligible for Free Lunch Program: 122 (4.2%)
    Eligible for Reduced-Price Lunch Program: 104 (3.6%)
Teachers: 175.3 (16.6 to 1)
Librarians/Media Specialists: 3.0 (970.3 to 1)
Guidance Counselors: 7.0 (415.9 to 1)
Current Spending: ($ per student per year):
    Total: $6,441; Instruction: $4,165; Support Services: $1,962

Category	Total	White	Black	Asian	AIAN	Hisp.
Enrollment (%)	100.0	95.5	1.2	2.2	0.1	1.0
Drop-out Rate (%)	0.6	0.7	0.0	0.0	0.0	0.0
H.S. Diplomas (#)	191	186	1	1	0	3

Lehigh County

Allentown City SD
PO Box 328 • Allentown, PA 18105-0328
(484) 765-4000 • http://www.allentownsd.org/
Grade Span: KG-12; **Agency Type:** 1
Schools: 23
17 Primary; 4 Middle; 2 High; 0 Other Level
23 Regular; 0 Special Education; 0 Vocational; 0 Alternative
0 Magnet; 0 Charter; 15 Title I Eligible; 14 School-wide Title I
Students: 16,964 (n/a% male; n/a% female)
    Individual Education Program: 2,263 (13.3%);
    English Language Learner: n/a; Migrant: 425 (2.5%)
    Eligible for Free Lunch Program: 7,560 (44.6%)
    Eligible for Reduced-Price Lunch Program: 1,618 (9.5%)
Teachers: 883.4 (19.2 to 1)
Librarians/Media Specialists: 16.0 (1,060.3 to 1)
Guidance Counselors: 39.0 (435.0 to 1)
Current Spending: ($ per student per year):
    Total: $6,941; Instruction: $4,677; Support Services: $1,997
Enrollment, Drop-out Rates and Diploma Recipients by Race/Ethnicity

Category	Total	White	Black	Asian	AIAN	Hisp.
Enrollment (%)	100.0	29.8	16.1	1.9	0.1	52.0
Drop-out Rate (%)	9.3	5.7	8.2	6.1	33.3	13.1
H.S. Diplomas (#)	686	371	74	20	0	221

Catasauqua Area SD
201 N 14th St • Catasauqua, PA 18032-1107
(610) 264-5571 • http://www.cattysd.org
Grade Span: KG-12; **Agency Type:** 1
Schools: 3
1 Primary; 1 Middle; 1 High; 0 Other Level
3 Regular; 0 Special Education; 0 Vocational; 0 Alternative
0 Magnet; 0 Charter; 2 Title I Eligible; 0 School-wide Title I
Students: 1,717 (n/a% male; n/a% female)
    Individual Education Program: 270 (15.7%);
    English Language Learner: n/a; Migrant: 0 (0.0%)
    Eligible for Free Lunch Program: 221 (12.9%)
    Eligible for Reduced-Price Lunch Program: 70 (4.1%)
Teachers: 118.0 (14.6 to 1)
Librarians/Media Specialists: 3.0 (572.3 to 1)
Guidance Counselors: 5.0 (343.4 to 1)
Current Spending: ($ per student per year):
    Total: $8,096; Instruction: $5,286; Support Services: $2,508
Enrollment, Drop-out Rates and Diploma Recipients by Race/Ethnicity

Category	Total	White	Black	Asian	AIAN	Hisp.
Enrollment (%)	100.0	86.9	5.0	1.0	0.3	6.8
Drop-out Rate (%)	4.0	3.8	7.1	0.0	0.0	8.0
H.S. Diplomas (#)	96	84	4	2	0	6

East Penn SD
800 Pine St • Emmaus, PA 18049
(610) 966-8300 • http://www.eastpenn.k12.pa.us
Grade Span: KG-12; **Agency Type:** 1
Schools: 11
8 Primary; 2 Middle; 1 High; 0 Other Level
11 Regular; 0 Special Education; 0 Vocational; 0 Alternative
0 Magnet; 0 Charter; 8 Title I Eligible; 0 School-wide Title I
Students: 7,116 (n/a% male; n/a% female)
    Individual Education Program: 662 (9.3%);
    English Language Learner: n/a; Migrant: 1 (<0.1%)
    Eligible for Free Lunch Program: 244 (3.4%)
    Eligible for Reduced-Price Lunch Program: 81 (1.1%)
Teachers: 412.5 (17.3 to 1)
Librarians/Media Specialists: 8.0 (889.5 to 1)
Guidance Counselors: 18.6 (382.6 to 1)
Current Spending: ($ per student per year):
    Total: $8,135; Instruction: $5,010; Support Services: $2,857
Enrollment, Drop-out Rates and Diploma Recipients by Race/Ethnicity

Category	Total	White	Black	Asian	AIAN	Hisp.
Enrollment (%)	100.0	92.2	1.7	4.1	0.0	2.0
Drop-out Rate (%)	2.3	2.4	0.0	0.0	0.0	4.3
H.S. Diplomas (#)	490	455	3	27	0	5

Northern Lehigh SD
1201 Shadow Oaks Ln • Slatington, PA 18080-1237
(610) 767-9800 • http://www.nlsd.k12.pa.us
Grade Span: KG-12; **Agency Type:** 1
Schools: 4

2 Primary; 1 Middle; 1 High; 0 Other Level
4 Regular; 0 Special Education; 0 Vocational; 0 Alternative
0 Magnet; 0 Charter; 3 Title I Eligible; 0 School-wide Title I
Students: 2,132 (n/a% male; n/a% female)
   Individual Education Program: 281 (13.2%);
   English Language Learner: n/a; Migrant: 0 (0.0%)
   Eligible for Free Lunch Program: 417 (19.6%)
   Eligible for Reduced-Price Lunch Program: 105 (4.9%)
Teachers: 126.5 (16.9 to 1)
Librarians/Media Specialists: 3.0 (710.7 to 1)
Guidance Counselors: 6.0 (355.3 to 1)
Current Spending: ($ per student per year):
   Total: $7,681; Instruction: $4,719; Support Services: $2,632
Enrollment, Drop-out Rates and Diploma Recipients by Race/Ethnicity

Category	Total	White	Black	Asian	AIAN	Hisp.
Enrollment (%)	100.0	94.8	1.7	0.3	0.0	3.1
Drop-out Rate (%)	1.3	1.4	0.0	0.0	n/a	0.0
H.S. Diplomas (#)	145	142	1	1	0	1

Northwestern Lehigh SD
6493 Route 309 • New Tripoli, PA 18066-2038
(610) 298-8661 • http://www.nwlehighsd.org
Grade Span: KG-12; **Agency Type:** 1
Schools: 4
   2 Primary; 1 Middle; 1 High; 0 Other Level
   4 Regular; 0 Special Education; 0 Vocational; 0 Alternative
   0 Magnet; 0 Charter; 0 Title I Eligible; 0 School-wide Title I
Students: 2,355 (n/a% male; n/a% female)
   Individual Education Program: 349 (14.8%);
   English Language Learner: n/a; Migrant: 0 (0.0%)
   Eligible for Free Lunch Program: 88 (3.7%)
   Eligible for Reduced-Price Lunch Program: 77 (3.3%)
Teachers: 154.3 (15.3 to 1)
Librarians/Media Specialists: 3.8 (619.7 to 1)
Guidance Counselors: 6.0 (392.5 to 1)
Current Spending: ($ per student per year):
   Total: $8,408; Instruction: $5,057; Support Services: $3,006
Enrollment, Drop-out Rates and Diploma Recipients by Race/Ethnicity

Category	Total	White	Black	Asian	AIAN	Hisp.
Enrollment (%)	100.0	96.1	0.7	1.1	0.1	2.0
Drop-out Rate (%)	0.8	0.7	0.0	0.0	n/a	9.1
H.S. Diplomas (#)	160	156	0	1	0	3

Parkland SD
1210 Springhouse Rd • Allentown, PA 18104-2119
(610) 351-5503 • http://www.parklandsd.org/
Grade Span: KG-12; **Agency Type:** 1
Schools: 10
   7 Primary; 2 Middle; 1 High; 0 Other Level
   10 Regular; 0 Special Education; 0 Vocational; 0 Alternative
   0 Magnet; 0 Charter; 6 Title I Eligible; 0 School-wide Title I
Students: 8,695 (n/a% male; n/a% female)
   Individual Education Program: 1,026 (11.8%);
   English Language Learner: n/a; Migrant: 0 (0.0%)
   Eligible for Free Lunch Program: 223 (2.6%)
   Eligible for Reduced-Price Lunch Program: 167 (1.9%)
Teachers: 498.2 (17.5 to 1)
Librarians/Media Specialists: 10.3 (844.2 to 1)
Guidance Counselors: 23.0 (378.0 to 1)
Current Spending: ($ per student per year):
   Total: $8,009; Instruction: $4,840; Support Services: $2,914
Enrollment, Drop-out Rates and Diploma Recipients by Race/Ethnicity

Category	Total	White	Black	Asian	AIAN	Hisp.
Enrollment (%)	100.0	89.5	1.9	5.7	0.2	2.7
Drop-out Rate (%)	0.7	0.7	0.0	0.0	0.0	4.0
H.S. Diplomas (#)	600	563	9	17	1	10

Salisbury Township SD
1140 Salisbury Rd • Allentown, PA 18103-4299
(610) 797-2062 • http://www.salisbury.k12.pa.us
Grade Span: KG-12; **Agency Type:** 1
Schools: 4
   2 Primary; 1 Middle; 1 High; 0 Other Level
   4 Regular; 0 Special Education; 0 Vocational; 0 Alternative
   0 Magnet; 0 Charter; 2 Title I Eligible; 0 School-wide Title I
Students: 1,837 (n/a% male; n/a% female)
   Individual Education Program: 289 (15.7%);
   English Language Learner: n/a; Migrant: 0 (0.0%)
   Eligible for Free Lunch Program: 135 (7.3%)
   Eligible for Reduced-Price Lunch Program: 51 (2.8%)
Teachers: 118.5 (15.5 to 1)
Librarians/Media Specialists: 4.0 (459.3 to 1)
Guidance Counselors: 4.0 (459.3 to 1)
Current Spending: ($ per student per year):
   Total: $10,851; Instruction: $5,329; Support Services: $5,231

Enrollment, Drop-out Rates and Diploma Recipients by Race/Ethnicity

Category	Total	White	Black	Asian	AIAN	Hisp.
Enrollment (%)	100.0	87.7	4.8	2.6	0.2	4.6
Drop-out Rate (%)	0.5	0.4	5.6	0.0	n/a	0.0
H.S. Diplomas (#)	131	118	4	4	0	5

Southern Lehigh SD
5775 Main St • Center Valley, PA 18034-9703
(610) 282-3121 • http://www.solehi.k12.pa.us
Grade Span: KG-12; **Agency Type:** 1
Schools: 5
   3 Primary; 1 Middle; 1 High; 0 Other Level
   5 Regular; 0 Special Education; 0 Vocational; 0 Alternative
   0 Magnet; 0 Charter; 3 Title I Eligible; 0 School-wide Title I
Students: 2,961 (n/a% male; n/a% female)
   Individual Education Program: 365 (12.3%);
   English Language Learner: n/a; Migrant: 0 (0.0%)
   Eligible for Free Lunch Program: 87 (2.9%)
   Eligible for Reduced-Price Lunch Program: 49 (1.7%)
Teachers: 174.1 (17.0 to 1)
Librarians/Media Specialists: 4.8 (616.9 to 1)
Guidance Counselors: 5.0 (592.2 to 1)
Current Spending: ($ per student per year):
   Total: $8,281; Instruction: $4,583; Support Services: $3,410
Enrollment, Drop-out Rates and Diploma Recipients by Race/Ethnicity

Category	Total	White	Black	Asian	AIAN	Hisp.
Enrollment (%)	100.0	93.8	1.2	2.8	0.1	2.2
Drop-out Rate (%)	1.1	1.1	0.0	0.0	n/a	0.0
H.S. Diplomas (#)	198	192	0	4	0	2

Whitehall-Coplay SD
2940 Macarthur Rd • Whitehall, PA 18052-3408
(610) 439-1431 • http://www.whitehallcoplay.org/
Grade Span: KG-12; **Agency Type:** 1
Schools: 4
   2 Primary; 1 Middle; 1 High; 0 Other Level
   4 Regular; 0 Special Education; 0 Vocational; 0 Alternative
   0 Magnet; 0 Charter; 3 Title I Eligible; 0 School-wide Title I
Students: 3,969 (n/a% male; n/a% female)
   Individual Education Program: 442 (11.1%);
   English Language Learner: n/a; Migrant: 8 (0.2%)
   Eligible for Free Lunch Program: 435 (11.0%)
   Eligible for Reduced-Price Lunch Program: 250 (6.3%)
Teachers: 222.0 (17.9 to 1)
Librarians/Media Specialists: 4.0 (992.3 to 1)
Guidance Counselors: 9.0 (441.0 to 1)
Current Spending: ($ per student per year):
   Total: $6,891; Instruction: $4,279; Support Services: $2,339
Enrollment, Drop-out Rates and Diploma Recipients by Race/Ethnicity

Category	Total	White	Black	Asian	AIAN	Hisp.
Enrollment (%)	100.0	79.8	7.4	3.8	0.2	8.8
Drop-out Rate (%)	1.7	1.7	0.0	0.0	0.0	4.7
H.S. Diplomas (#)	276	246	17	6	0	7

Luzerne County

Crestwood SD
281 S Mountain Blvd • Mountain Top, PA 18707-1913
(570) 474-6888 • http://www.crestwoodhigh.org
Grade Span: KG-12; **Agency Type:** 1
Schools: 4
   2 Primary; 1 Middle; 1 High; 0 Other Level
   4 Regular; 0 Special Education; 0 Vocational; 0 Alternative
   0 Magnet; 0 Charter; 3 Title I Eligible; 0 School-wide Title I
Students: 2,986 (n/a% male; n/a% female)
   Individual Education Program: 350 (11.7%);
   English Language Learner: n/a; Migrant: 0 (0.0%)
   Eligible for Free Lunch Program: 297 (9.9%)
   Eligible for Reduced-Price Lunch Program: 124 (4.2%)
Teachers: 148.9 (20.1 to 1)
Librarians/Media Specialists: 3.0 (995.3 to 1)
Guidance Counselors: 5.0 (597.2 to 1)
Current Spending: ($ per student per year):
   Total: $6,856; Instruction: $4,213; Support Services: $2,363
Enrollment, Drop-out Rates and Diploma Recipients by Race/Ethnicity

Category	Total	White	Black	Asian	AIAN	Hisp.
Enrollment (%)	100.0	96.2	1.0	1.8	0.3	0.7
Drop-out Rate (%)	1.2	1.3	0.0	0.0	0.0	0.0
H.S. Diplomas (#)	235	230	0	2	1	2

Dallas SD
PO Box 2000 • Dallas, PA 18612-0720
(570) 675-5201 • http://www.dallassd.com
Grade Span: KG-12; **Agency Type:** 1
Schools: 4

2 Primary; 1 Middle; 1 High; 0 Other Level
4 Regular; 0 Special Education; 0 Vocational; 0 Alternative
0 Magnet; 0 Charter; 4 Title I Eligible; 0 School-wide Title I
Students: 2,559   (n/a% male; n/a% female)
Individual Education Program: 306 (12.0%)
English Language Learner: n/a; Migrant: 0 (0.0%)
Eligible for Free Lunch Program: 107 (4.2%)
Eligible for Reduced-Price Lunch Program: 56 (2.2%)
Teachers: 145.5 (17.6 to 1)
Librarians/Media Specialists: 3.0 (853.0 to 1)
Guidance Counselors: 6.0 (426.5 to 1)
Current Spending: ($ per student per year):
Total: $7,318; Instruction: $4,421; Support Services: $2,684
Enrollment, Drop-out Rates and Diploma Recipients by Race/Ethnicity

Category	Total	White	Black	Asian	AIAN	Hisp.
Enrollment (%)	100.0	98.0	0.6	0.7	0.2	0.5
Drop-out Rate (%)	0.9	1.0	0.0	0.0	n/a	0.0
H.S. Diplomas (#)	176	173	1	2	0	0

Greater Nanticoke Area SD
427 Kosciuszko St • Nanticoke, PA 18634-2690
(570) 735-1270 • http://www.gnasd.com
Grade Span: KG-12; Agency Type: 1
Schools: 5
3 Primary; 1 Middle; 1 High; 0 Other Level
5 Regular; 0 Special Education; 0 Vocational; 0 Alternative
0 Magnet; 0 Charter; 3 Title I Eligible; 0 School-wide Title I
Students: 2,131   (n/a% male; n/a% female)
Individual Education Program: 349 (16.4%)
English Language Learner: n/a; Migrant: 0 (0.0%)
Eligible for Free Lunch Program: 238 (11.2%)
Eligible for Reduced-Price Lunch Program: 100 (4.7%)
Teachers: 108.8 (19.6 to 1)
Librarians/Media Specialists: 2.0 (1,065.5 to 1)
Guidance Counselors: 4.0 (532.8 to 1)
Current Spending: ($ per student per year):
Total: $7,212; Instruction: $4,673; Support Services: $2,341
Enrollment, Drop-out Rates and Diploma Recipients by Race/Ethnicity

Category	Total	White	Black	Asian	AIAN	Hisp.
Enrollment (%)	100.0	95.7	2.6	0.6	0.0	1.2
Drop-out Rate (%)	2.4	2.5	0.0	n/a	n/a	0.0
H.S. Diplomas (#)	139	137	2	0	0	0

Hanover Area SD
1600 Sans Souci Pkwy • Wilkes Barre, PA 18706
(570) 831-2313 • http://www.hanoverarea.org
Grade Span: KG-12; Agency Type: 1
Schools: 5
3 Primary; 1 Middle; 1 High; 0 Other Level
5 Regular; 0 Special Education; 0 Vocational; 0 Alternative
0 Magnet; 0 Charter; 4 Title I Eligible; 0 School-wide Title I
Students: 2,076   (n/a% male; n/a% female)
Individual Education Program: 380 (18.3%);
English Language Learner: n/a; Migrant: 0 (0.0%)
Eligible for Free Lunch Program: 673 (32.4%)
Eligible for Reduced-Price Lunch Program: 267 (12.9%)
Teachers: 118.0 (17.6 to 1)
Librarians/Media Specialists: 3.0 (692.0 to 1)
Guidance Counselors: 6.0 (346.0 to 1)
Current Spending: ($ per student per year):
Total: $8,429; Instruction: $5,242; Support Services: $2,858
Enrollment, Drop-out Rates and Diploma Recipients by Race/Ethnicity

Category	Total	White	Black	Asian	AIAN	Hisp.
Enrollment (%)	100.0	95.2	3.2	0.4	0.0	1.3
Drop-out Rate (%)	2.1	2.1	0.0	0.0	n/a	0.0
H.S. Diplomas (#)	145	145	0	0	0	0

Hazleton Area SD
1515 W 23rd St • Hazleton, PA 18202-1647
(570) 459-3111 • http://www.hasd.k12.pa.us/
Grade Span: KG-12; Agency Type: 1
Schools: 9
8 Primary; 0 Middle; 1 High; 0 Other Level
9 Regular; 0 Special Education; 0 Vocational; 0 Alternative
0 Magnet; 0 Charter; 6 Title I Eligible; 0 School-wide Title I
Students: 9,300   (n/a% male; n/a% female)
Individual Education Program: 910 (9.8%)
English Language Learner: n/a; Migrant: 209 (2.2%)
Eligible for Free Lunch Program: 1,697 (18.2%)
Eligible for Reduced-Price Lunch Program: 760 (8.2%)
Teachers: 471.5 (19.7 to 1)
Librarians/Media Specialists: 4.5 (2,066.7 to 1)
Guidance Counselors: 13.0 (715.4 to 1)
Current Spending: ($ per student per year):
Total: $7,303; Instruction: $4,885; Support Services: $2,102

Enrollment, Drop-out Rates and Diploma Recipients by Race/Ethnicity

Category	Total	White	Black	Asian	AIAN	Hisp.
Enrollment (%)	100.0	86.6	1.6	0.8	0.1	10.8
Drop-out Rate (%)	3.1	3.1	0.0	0.0	0.0	2.9
H.S. Diplomas (#)	535	513	2	3	0	17

Lake-Lehman SD
PO Box 38 • Lehman, PA 18627-0038
(570) 675-2165
Grade Span: KG-12; Agency Type: 1
Schools: 4
3 Primary; 0 Middle; 1 High; 0 Other Level
4 Regular; 0 Special Education; 0 Vocational; 0 Alternative
0 Magnet; 0 Charter; 4 Title I Eligible; 0 School-wide Title I
Students: 2,176   (n/a% male; n/a% female)
Individual Education Program: 271 (12.5%);
English Language Learner: n/a; Migrant: 4 (0.2%)
Eligible for Free Lunch Program: 378 (17.4%)
Eligible for Reduced-Price Lunch Program: 128 (5.9%)
Teachers: 132.0 (16.5 to 1)
Librarians/Media Specialists: 2.0 (1,088.0 to 1)
Guidance Counselors: 5.0 (435.2 to 1)
Current Spending: ($ per student per year):
Total: $7,796; Instruction: $4,688; Support Services: $2,818
Enrollment, Drop-out Rates and Diploma Recipients by Race/Ethnicity

Category	Total	White	Black	Asian	AIAN	Hisp.
Enrollment (%)	100.0	98.1	0.7	0.3	0.3	0.6
Drop-out Rate (%)	2.5	2.5	0.0	0.0	0.0	0.0
H.S. Diplomas (#)	145	144	0	1	0	0

Pittston Area SD
5 Stout St • Pittston, PA 18640-3391
(570) 654-2271 • http://www.pittstonarea.com
Grade Span: KG-12; Agency Type: 1
Schools: 5
3 Primary; 1 Middle; 1 High; 0 Other Level
5 Regular; 0 Special Education; 0 Vocational; 0 Alternative
0 Magnet; 0 Charter; 3 Title I Eligible; 0 School-wide Title I
Students: 3,157   (n/a% male; n/a% female)
Individual Education Program: 361 (11.4%);
English Language Learner: n/a; Migrant: 0 (0.0%)
Eligible for Free Lunch Program: 613 (19.4%)
Eligible for Reduced-Price Lunch Program: 232 (7.3%)
Teachers: 181.0 (17.4 to 1)
Librarians/Media Specialists: 4.0 (789.3 to 1)
Guidance Counselors: 3.0 (1,052.3 to 1)
Current Spending: ($ per student per year):
Total: $8,375; Instruction: $5,299; Support Services: $2,729
Enrollment, Drop-out Rates and Diploma Recipients by Race/Ethnicity

Category	Total	White	Black	Asian	AIAN	Hisp.
Enrollment (%)	100.0	97.9	0.8	0.8	0.1	0.4
Drop-out Rate (%)	2.7	2.6	0.0	33.3	0.0	100.0
H.S. Diplomas (#)	245	240	1	4	0	0

Wilkes-Barre Area SD
730 S Main St • Wilkes Barre, PA 18711-0376
(570) 826-7182 • http://www.wbasd.k12.pa.us
Grade Span: KG-12; Agency Type: 1
Schools: 9
5 Primary; 1 Middle; 3 High; 0 Other Level
9 Regular; 0 Special Education; 0 Vocational; 0 Alternative
0 Magnet; 0 Charter; 6 Title I Eligible; 0 School-wide Title I
Students: 6,952   (n/a% male; n/a% female)
Individual Education Program: 1,074 (15.4%);
English Language Learner: n/a; Migrant: 0 (0.0%)
Eligible for Free Lunch Program: 1,623 (23.3%)
Eligible for Reduced-Price Lunch Program: 439 (6.3%)
Teachers: 444.0 (15.7 to 1)
Librarians/Media Specialists: 7.0 (993.1 to 1)
Guidance Counselors: 12.0 (579.3 to 1)
Current Spending: ($ per student per year):
Total: $8,797; Instruction: $5,709; Support Services: $2,837
Enrollment, Drop-out Rates and Diploma Recipients by Race/Ethnicity

Category	Total	White	Black	Asian	AIAN	Hisp.
Enrollment (%)	100.0	80.7	12.0	1.2	0.2	5.9
Drop-out Rate (%)	3.3	3.1	5.3	0.0	0.0	11.1
H.S. Diplomas (#)	525	494	20	6	0	5

Wyoming Area SD
20 Memorial St • Exeter, PA 18643-2659
(570) 655-3733 • http://www.wyoarea.com
Grade Span: KG-12; Agency Type: 1
Schools: 5
4 Primary; 0 Middle; 1 High; 0 Other Level
5 Regular; 0 Special Education; 0 Vocational; 0 Alternative

0 Magnet; 0 Charter; 4 Title I Eligible; 0 School-wide Title I
Students: 2,607 (n/a% male; n/a% female)
  Individual Education Program: 345 (13.2%);
  English Language Learner: n/a; Migrant: 0 (0.0%)
  Eligible for Free Lunch Program: 469 (18.0%)
  Eligible for Reduced-Price Lunch Program: 212 (8.1%)
Teachers: 145.0 (18.0 to 1)
Librarians/Media Specialists: 2.0 (1,303.5 to 1)
Guidance Counselors: 4.0 (651.8 to 1)
Current Spending: ($ per student per year):
  Total: $7,137; Instruction: $4,641; Support Services: $2,276
Enrollment, Drop-out Rates and Diploma Recipients by Race/Ethnicity

Category	Total	White	Black	Asian	AIAN	Hisp.
Enrollment (%)	100.0	97.9	1.5	0.1	0.0	0.5
Drop-out Rate (%)	3.0	2.9	0.0	0.0	100.0	0.0
H.S. Diplomas (#)	180	179	1	0	0	0

Wyoming Valley West SD
450 N Maple Ave • Kingston, PA 18704-3630
(570) 288-6551 • http://www.wvw.liu18.k12.pa.us
Grade Span: KG-12; **Agency Type:** 1
Schools: 9
  7 Primary; 1 Middle; 1 High; 0 Other Level
  9 Regular; 0 Special Education; 0 Vocational; 0 Alternative
  0 Magnet; 0 Charter; 7 Title I Eligible; 0 School-wide Title I
Students: 5,152 (n/a% male; n/a% female)
  Individual Education Program: 784 (15.2%);
  English Language Learner: n/a; Migrant: 0 (0.0%)
  Eligible for Free Lunch Program: 1,370 (26.6%)
  Eligible for Reduced-Price Lunch Program: 407 (7.9%)
Teachers: 300.5 (17.1 to 1)
Librarians/Media Specialists: 5.0 (1,030.4 to 1)
Guidance Counselors: 10.0 (515.2 to 1)
Current Spending: ($ per student per year):
  Total: $7,721; Instruction: $5,375; Support Services: $1,929
Enrollment, Drop-out Rates and Diploma Recipients by Race/Ethnicity

Category	Total	White	Black	Asian	AIAN	Hisp.
Enrollment (%)	100.0	93.1	3.7	1.0	0.3	1.8
Drop-out Rate (%)	1.2	1.2	0.0	0.0	0.0	0.0
H.S. Diplomas (#)	321	314	1	3	1	2

Lycoming County

East Lycoming SD
349 Cemetery St • Hughesville, PA 17737-1028
(570) 584-2131 • http://www.eastlycoming.net
Grade Span: KG-12; **Agency Type:** 1
Schools: 4
  3 Primary; 0 Middle; 1 High; 0 Other Level
  4 Regular; 0 Special Education; 0 Vocational; 0 Alternative
  0 Magnet; 0 Charter; 4 Title I Eligible; 0 School-wide Title I
Students: 1,781 (n/a% male; n/a% female)
  Individual Education Program: 223 (12.5%);
  English Language Learner: n/a; Migrant: 0 (0.0%)
  Eligible for Free Lunch Program: 361 (20.3%)
  Eligible for Reduced-Price Lunch Program: 135 (7.6%)
Teachers: 123.0 (14.5 to 1)
Librarians/Media Specialists: 0.0 (n/a to 1)
Guidance Counselors: 3.0 (593.7 to 1)
Current Spending: ($ per student per year):
  Total: $8,040; Instruction: $5,240; Support Services: $2,421
Enrollment, Drop-out Rates and Diploma Recipients by Race/Ethnicity

Category	Total	White	Black	Asian	AIAN	Hisp.
Enrollment (%)	100.0	98.9	0.8	0.2	0.1	0.1
Drop-out Rate (%)	2.7	2.7	0.0	0.0	n/a	0.0
H.S. Diplomas (#)	141	141	0	0	0	0

Jersey Shore Area SD
175 A & P Dr • Jersey Shore, PA 17740-9268
(570) 398-1561 • http://www.jsasd.k12.pa.us
Grade Span: KG-12; **Agency Type:** 1
Schools: 6
  4 Primary; 1 Middle; 1 High; 0 Other Level
  6 Regular; 0 Special Education; 0 Vocational; 0 Alternative
  0 Magnet; 0 Charter; 4 Title I Eligible; 0 School-wide Title I
Students: 3,022 (n/a% male; n/a% female)
  Individual Education Program: 506 (16.7%);
  English Language Learner: n/a; Migrant: 0 (0.0%)
  Eligible for Free Lunch Program: 539 (17.8%)
  Eligible for Reduced-Price Lunch Program: 319 (10.6%)
Teachers: 201.5 (15.0 to 1)
Librarians/Media Specialists: 5.0 (604.4 to 1)
Guidance Counselors: 6.0 (503.7 to 1)
Current Spending: ($ per student per year):
  Total: $8,205; Instruction: $5,190; Support Services: $2,650

Enrollment, Drop-out Rates and Diploma Recipients by Race/Ethnicity

Category	Total	White	Black	Asian	AIAN	Hisp.
Enrollment (%)	100.0	98.1	0.7	0.9	0.1	0.2
Drop-out Rate (%)	4.7	4.7	50.0	0.0	n/a	0.0
H.S. Diplomas (#)	197	195	0	2	0	0

Montoursville Area SD
50 N Arch St • Montoursville, PA 17754-1902
(570) 368-2491 • http://www.montoursville.k12.pa.us
Grade Span: KG-12; **Agency Type:** 1
Schools: 4
  2 Primary; 1 Middle; 1 High; 0 Other Level
  4 Regular; 0 Special Education; 0 Vocational; 0 Alternative
  0 Magnet; 0 Charter; 3 Title I Eligible; 0 School-wide Title I
Students: 2,139 (n/a% male; n/a% female)
  Individual Education Program: 204 (9.5%);
  English Language Learner: n/a; Migrant: 0 (0.0%)
  Eligible for Free Lunch Program: 145 (6.8%)
  Eligible for Reduced-Price Lunch Program: 92 (4.3%)
Teachers: 136.0 (15.7 to 1)
Librarians/Media Specialists: 2.0 (1,069.5 to 1)
Guidance Counselors: 6.0 (356.5 to 1)
Current Spending: ($ per student per year):
  Total: $7,350; Instruction: $4,638; Support Services: $2,436
Enrollment, Drop-out Rates and Diploma Recipients by Race/Ethnicity

Category	Total	White	Black	Asian	AIAN	Hisp.
Enrollment (%)	100.0	98.6	0.4	0.5	0.2	0.3
Drop-out Rate (%)	1.8	1.8	0.0	n/a	0.0	0.0
H.S. Diplomas (#)	168	165	1	2	0	0

Williamsport Area SD
201 W 3rd St • Williamsport, PA 17701-6409
(570) 327-5500 • http://www.wasd.org
Grade Span: KG-12; **Agency Type:** 1
Schools: 11
  6 Primary; 3 Middle; 1 High; 1 Other Level
  11 Regular; 0 Special Education; 0 Vocational; 0 Alternative
  0 Magnet; 0 Charter; 6 Title I Eligible; 5 School-wide Title I
Students: 5,985 (n/a% male; n/a% female)
  Individual Education Program: 1,293 (21.6%);
  English Language Learner: n/a; Migrant: 0 (0.0%)
  Eligible for Free Lunch Program: 2,089 (34.9%)
  Eligible for Reduced-Price Lunch Program: 510 (8.5%)
Teachers: 423.5 (14.1 to 1)
Librarians/Media Specialists: 5.0 (1,197.0 to 1)
Guidance Counselors: 19.0 (315.0 to 1)
Current Spending: ($ per student per year):
  Total: $8,843; Instruction: $5,830; Support Services: $2,591
Enrollment, Drop-out Rates and Diploma Recipients by Race/Ethnicity

Category	Total	White	Black	Asian	AIAN	Hisp.
Enrollment (%)	100.0	76.4	21.8	0.9	0.1	0.8
Drop-out Rate (%)	5.9	5.5	7.3	4.3	n/a	20.0
H.S. Diplomas (#)	372	321	47	2	0	2

Mckean County

Bradford Area SD
PO Box 375 • Bradford, PA 16701-1831
(814) 362-3841 • http://www.bradfordareaschools.org
Grade Span: KG-12; **Agency Type:** 1
Schools: 4
  2 Primary; 1 Middle; 1 High; 0 Other Level
  4 Regular; 0 Special Education; 0 Vocational; 0 Alternative
  0 Magnet; 0 Charter; 3 Title I Eligible; 0 School-wide Title I
Students: 2,965 (n/a% male; n/a% female)
  Individual Education Program: 415 (14.0%);
  English Language Learner: n/a; Migrant: 0 (0.0%)
  Eligible for Free Lunch Program: 878 (29.6%)
  Eligible for Reduced-Price Lunch Program: 151 (5.1%)
Teachers: 197.0 (15.1 to 1)
Librarians/Media Specialists: 7.0 (423.6 to 1)
Guidance Counselors: 6.0 (494.2 to 1)
Current Spending: ($ per student per year):
  Total: $8,626; Instruction: $5,615; Support Services: $2,740
Enrollment, Drop-out Rates and Diploma Recipients by Race/Ethnicity

Category	Total	White	Black	Asian	AIAN	Hisp.
Enrollment (%)	100.0	96.1	1.2	0.8	0.7	1.2
Drop-out Rate (%)	5.2	5.2	0.0	6.7	8.3	0.0
H.S. Diplomas (#)	177	169	0	5	0	3

Mercer County

Greenville Area SD
9 Donation Rd · Greenville, PA 16125-1789
(724) 588-2500 · http://www.greenville.k12.pa.us
Grade Span: KG-12; **Agency Type:** 1
Schools: 3
   1 Primary; 1 Middle; 1 High; 0 Other Level
   3 Regular; 0 Special Education; 0 Vocational; 0 Alternative
   0 Magnet; 0 Charter; 0 Title I Eligible; 0 School-wide Title I
Students: 1,602   (n/a% male; n/a% female)
   Individual Education Program: 234 (14.6%);
   English Language Learner: n/a; Migrant: 0 (0.0%)
   Eligible for Free Lunch Program: 394 (24.6%)
   Eligible for Reduced-Price Lunch Program: 70 (4.4%)
Teachers: 104.5 (15.3 to 1)
Librarians/Media Specialists: 1.0 (1,602.0 to 1)
Guidance Counselors: 3.0 (534.0 to 1)
Current Spending: ($ per student per year):
   Total: $7,188; Instruction: $4,648; Support Services: $2,212
Enrollment, Drop-out Rates and Diploma Recipients by Race/Ethnicity

Category	Total	White	Black	Asian	AIAN	Hisp.
Enrollment (%)	100.0	98.1	0.9	0.6	0.2	0.2
Drop-out Rate (%)	2.4	2.4	0.0	0.0	n/a	0.0
H.S. Diplomas (#)	116	114	1	1	0	0

Grove City Area SD
511 Highland Ave · Grove City, PA 16127-1107
(724) 458-6733 · http://www.grovecity.k12.pa.us
Grade Span: KG-12; **Agency Type:** 1
Schools: 7
   4 Primary; 1 Middle; 2 High; 0 Other Level
   7 Regular; 0 Special Education; 0 Vocational; 0 Alternative
   0 Magnet; 0 Charter; 0 Title I Eligible; 0 School-wide Title I
Students: 2,788   (n/a% male; n/a% female)
   Individual Education Program: 316 (11.3%);
   English Language Learner: n/a; Migrant: 0 (0.0%)
   Eligible for Free Lunch Program: 285 (10.2%)
   Eligible for Reduced-Price Lunch Program: 123 (4.4%)
Teachers: 168.1 (16.6 to 1)
Librarians/Media Specialists: 4.0 (697.0 to 1)
Guidance Counselors: 6.0 (464.7 to 1)
Current Spending: ($ per student per year):
   Total: $7,263; Instruction: $4,939; Support Services: $2,092
Enrollment, Drop-out Rates and Diploma Recipients by Race/Ethnicity

Category	Total	White	Black	Asian	AIAN	Hisp.
Enrollment (%)	100.0	87.9	9.3	0.9	0.0	1.9
Drop-out Rate (%)	0.9	1.2	0.0	0.0	0.0	0.0
H.S. Diplomas (#)	187	161	18	4	0	4

Hermitage SD
411 N Hermitage Rd · Hermitage, PA 16148-3316
(724) 981-8750 · http://www.hermitage.k12.pa.us
Grade Span: KG-12; **Agency Type:** 1
Schools: 5
   2 Primary; 2 Middle; 1 High; 0 Other Level
   5 Regular; 0 Special Education; 0 Vocational; 0 Alternative
   0 Magnet; 0 Charter; 0 Title I Eligible; 0 School-wide Title I
Students: 2,297   (n/a% male; n/a% female)
   Individual Education Program: 267 (11.6%);
   English Language Learner: n/a; Migrant: 0 (0.0%)
   Eligible for Free Lunch Program: 406 (17.7%)
   Eligible for Reduced-Price Lunch Program: 124 (5.4%)
Teachers: 137.6 (16.7 to 1)
Librarians/Media Specialists: 4.0 (574.3 to 1)
Guidance Counselors: 4.0 (574.3 to 1)
Current Spending: ($ per student per year):
   Total: $7,914; Instruction: $5,138; Support Services: $2,468
Enrollment, Drop-out Rates and Diploma Recipients by Race/Ethnicity

Category	Total	White	Black	Asian	AIAN	Hisp.
Enrollment (%)	100.0	90.8	7.6	0.9	0.1	0.7
Drop-out Rate (%)	1.3	1.2	3.0	0.0	n/a	0.0
H.S. Diplomas (#)	164	158	4	2	0	0

Mercer Area SD
545 W Butler St · Mercer, PA 16137-0032
(724) 662-5100 · http://www.mercer.k12.pa.us
Grade Span: KG-12; **Agency Type:** 1
Schools: 3
   1 Primary; 0 Middle; 1 High; 0 Other Level
   2 Regular; 0 Special Education; 0 Vocational; 0 Alternative
   0 Magnet; 0 Charter; 0 Title I Eligible; 0 School-wide Title I
Students: 1,529   (n/a% male; n/a% female)
   Individual Education Program: 230 (15.0%);
   English Language Learner: n/a; Migrant: 0 (0.0%)

   Eligible for Free Lunch Program: 271 (17.7%)
   Eligible for Reduced-Price Lunch Program: 97 (6.3%)
Teachers: 93.7 (16.3 to 1)
Librarians/Media Specialists: 2.0 (764.5 to 1)
Guidance Counselors: 3.0 (509.7 to 1)
Current Spending: ($ per student per year):
   Total: $6,515; Instruction: $4,044; Support Services: $2,197
Enrollment, Drop-out Rates and Diploma Recipients by Race/Ethnicity

Category	Total	White	Black	Asian	AIAN	Hisp.
Enrollment (%)	100.0	96.5	1.5	1.2	0.1	0.7
Drop-out Rate (%)	3.0	3.1	0.0	0.0	n/a	0.0
H.S. Diplomas (#)	106	106	0	0	0	0

Reynolds SD
531 Reynolds Rd · Greenville, PA 16125-8804
(724) 646-3240 · http://www.reynoldssd.com
Grade Span: KG-12; **Agency Type:** 1
Schools: 2
   1 Primary; 0 Middle; 1 High; 0 Other Level
   2 Regular; 0 Special Education; 0 Vocational; 0 Alternative
   0 Magnet; 0 Charter; 0 Title I Eligible; 0 School-wide Title I
Students: 1,538   (n/a% male; n/a% female)
   Individual Education Program: 220 (14.3%);
   English Language Learner: n/a; Migrant: 0 (0.0%)
   Eligible for Free Lunch Program: 446 (29.0%)
   Eligible for Reduced-Price Lunch Program: 157 (10.2%)
Teachers: 82.5 (18.6 to 1)
Librarians/Media Specialists: 2.0 (769.0 to 1)
Guidance Counselors: 3.0 (512.7 to 1)
Current Spending: ($ per student per year):
   Total: $7,775; Instruction: $4,791; Support Services: $2,726
Enrollment, Drop-out Rates and Diploma Recipients by Race/Ethnicity

Category	Total	White	Black	Asian	AIAN	Hisp.
Enrollment (%)	100.0	97.9	1.6	0.1	0.2	0.2
Drop-out Rate (%)	0.8	0.9	0.0	n/a	0.0	n/a
H.S. Diplomas (#)	109	107	0	0	2	0

Sharon City SD
215 Forker Blvd · Sharon, PA 16146-3606
(724) 983-4000 · http://www.sharon.k12.pa.us
Grade Span: KG-12; **Agency Type:** 1
Schools: 4
   3 Primary; 0 Middle; 1 High; 0 Other Level
   4 Regular; 0 Special Education; 0 Vocational; 0 Alternative
   0 Magnet; 0 Charter; 0 Title I Eligible; 0 School-wide Title I
Students: 2,407   (n/a% male; n/a% female)
   Individual Education Program: 403 (16.7%);
   English Language Learner: n/a; Migrant: 0 (0.0%)
   Eligible for Free Lunch Program: 1,154 (47.9%)
   Eligible for Reduced-Price Lunch Program: 206 (8.6%)
Teachers: 153.0 (15.7 to 1)
Librarians/Media Specialists: 2.0 (1,203.5 to 1)
Guidance Counselors: 5.0 (481.4 to 1)
Current Spending: ($ per student per year):
   Total: $9,666; Instruction: $5,773; Support Services: $2,249
Enrollment, Drop-out Rates and Diploma Recipients by Race/Ethnicity

Category	Total	White	Black	Asian	AIAN	Hisp.
Enrollment (%)	100.0	73.3	24.8	0.6	0.1	1.2
Drop-out Rate (%)	4.7	4.9	4.4	0.0	0.0	0.0
H.S. Diplomas (#)	133	116	17	0	0	0

Mifflin County

Mifflin County SD
201 Eighth St - Highland Park · Lewistown, PA 17044-1197
(717) 248-0148 · http://www.mcsdk12.org
Grade Span: KG-12; **Agency Type:** 1
Schools: 15
   9 Primary; 3 Middle; 2 High; 0 Other Level
   14 Regular; 0 Special Education; 0 Vocational; 0 Alternative
   0 Magnet; 0 Charter; 8 Title I Eligible; 0 School-wide Title I
Students: 6,093   (n/a% male; n/a% female)
   Individual Education Program: 922 (15.1%);
   English Language Learner: n/a; Migrant: 27 (0.4%)
   Eligible for Free Lunch Program: 1,364 (22.4%)
   Eligible for Reduced-Price Lunch Program: 559 (9.2%)
Teachers: 428.0 (14.2 to 1)
Librarians/Media Specialists: 6.0 (1,015.5 to 1)
Guidance Counselors: 12.0 (507.8 to 1)
Current Spending: ($ per student per year):
   Total: $7,184; Instruction: $4,601; Support Services: $2,261

Enrollment, Drop-out Rates and Diploma Recipients by Race/Ethnicity

Category	Total	White	Black	Asian	AIAN	Hisp.
Enrollment (%)	100.0	95.4	2.2	0.9	0.2	1.2
Drop-out Rate (%)	4.3	4.4	4.8	0.0	0.0	0.0
H.S. Diplomas (#)	376	371	2	3	0	0

Monroe County

East Stroudsburg Area SD
PO Box 298 • East Stroudsburg, PA 18301-0298
(570) 424-8500 • http://www.cavalier.net/
Grade Span: KG-12; **Agency Type:** 1
Schools: 10
  5 Primary; 3 Middle; 2 High; 0 Other Level
  10 Regular; 0 Special Education; 0 Vocational; 0 Alternative
  0 Magnet; 0 Charter; 5 Title I Eligible; 0 School-wide Title I
Students: 7,598 (n/a% male; n/a% female)
  Individual Education Program: 1,278 (16.8%);
  English Language Learner: n/a; Migrant: 0 (0.0%)
  Eligible for Free Lunch Program: 806 (10.6%)
  Eligible for Reduced-Price Lunch Program: 317 (4.2%)
Teachers: 527.4 (14.4 to 1)
Librarians/Media Specialists: 10.0 (759.8 to 1)
Guidance Counselors: 19.0 (399.9 to 1)
Current Spending: ($ per student per year):
  Total: $9,120; Instruction: $6,324; Support Services: $2,474

Enrollment, Drop-out Rates and Diploma Recipients by Race/Ethnicity

Category	Total	White	Black	Asian	AIAN	Hisp.
Enrollment (%)	100.0	68.7	15.5	2.1	0.1	13.6
Drop-out Rate (%)	2.4	2.5	2.4	0.0	0.0	2.0
H.S. Diplomas (#)	436	324	53	10	2	47

Pleasant Valley SD
Route 115 • Brodheadsville, PA 18322-2002
(570) 402-1000 • http://www.pvbears.org
Grade Span: KG-12; **Agency Type:** 1
Schools: 7
  4 Primary; 2 Middle; 1 High; 0 Other Level
  7 Regular; 0 Special Education; 0 Vocational; 0 Alternative
  0 Magnet; 0 Charter; 3 Title I Eligible; 0 School-wide Title I
Students: 6,905 (n/a% male; n/a% female)
  Individual Education Program: 772 (11.2%);
  English Language Learner: n/a; Migrant: 0 (0.0%)
  Eligible for Free Lunch Program: 417 (6.0%)
  Eligible for Reduced-Price Lunch Program: 149 (2.2%)
Teachers: 382.0 (18.1 to 1)
Librarians/Media Specialists: 7.0 (986.4 to 1)
Guidance Counselors: 14.0 (493.2 to 1)
Current Spending: ($ per student per year):
  Total: $6,591; Instruction: $4,088; Support Services: $2,261

Enrollment, Drop-out Rates and Diploma Recipients by Race/Ethnicity

Category	Total	White	Black	Asian	AIAN	Hisp.
Enrollment (%)	100.0	85.2	6.4	1.1	0.2	7.1
Drop-out Rate (%)	2.9	2.7	5.7	0.0	0.0	2.5
H.S. Diplomas (#)	391	361	13	4	0	13

Pocono Mountain SD
PO Box 200 • Swiftwater, PA 18370-0200
(570) 839-7121 • http://www.pmsd.org/index.html
Grade Span: KG-12; **Agency Type:** 1
Schools: 11
  7 Primary; 1 Middle; 2 High; 1 Other Level
  11 Regular; 0 Special Education; 0 Vocational; 0 Alternative
  0 Magnet; 0 Charter; 4 Title I Eligible; 0 School-wide Title I
Students: 11,190 (n/a% male; n/a% female)
  Individual Education Program: 1,470 (13.1%);
  English Language Learner: n/a; Migrant: 0 (0.0%)
  Eligible for Free Lunch Program: 1,885 (16.8%)
  Eligible for Reduced-Price Lunch Program: 693 (6.2%)
Teachers: 724.2 (15.5 to 1)
Librarians/Media Specialists: 10.0 (1,119.0 to 1)
Guidance Counselors: 33.0 (339.1 to 1)
Current Spending: ($ per student per year):
  Total: $7,761; Instruction: $4,565; Support Services: $2,909

Enrollment, Drop-out Rates and Diploma Recipients by Race/Ethnicity

Category	Total	White	Black	Asian	AIAN	Hisp.
Enrollment (%)	100.0	65.8	17.9	1.4	0.3	14.6
Drop-out Rate (%)	2.3	2.5	2.0	0.0	0.0	1.6
H.S. Diplomas (#)	729	505	118	11	2	93

Stroudsburg Area SD
123 Linden St • Stroudsburg, PA 18360-1315
(570) 421-1990 • http://www.stroudsburg.k12.pa.us
Grade Span: KG-12; **Agency Type:** 1
Schools: 8

---

  5 Primary; 2 Middle; 1 High; 0 Other Level
  8 Regular; 0 Special Education; 0 Vocational; 0 Alternative
  0 Magnet; 0 Charter; 5 Title I Eligible; 0 School-wide Title I
Students: 5,536 (n/a% male; n/a% female)
  Individual Education Program: 677 (12.2%);
  English Language Learner: n/a; Migrant: 0 (0.0%)
  Eligible for Free Lunch Program: 673 (12.2%)
  Eligible for Reduced-Price Lunch Program: 198 (3.6%)
Teachers: 344.9 (16.1 to 1)
Librarians/Media Specialists: 5.7 (971.2 to 1)
Guidance Counselors: 13.0 (425.8 to 1)
Current Spending: ($ per student per year):
  Total: $8,109; Instruction: $5,242; Support Services: $2,592

Enrollment, Drop-out Rates and Diploma Recipients by Race/Ethnicity

Category	Total	White	Black	Asian	AIAN	Hisp.
Enrollment (%)	100.0	73.0	13.8	2.0	0.3	10.9
Drop-out Rate (%)	2.1	1.8	3.8	0.0	0.0	2.9
H.S. Diplomas (#)	298	219	35	13	0	31

Montgomery County

Abington SD
970 Highland Ave • Abington, PA 19001-4535
(215) 884-4700 • http://www.abington.k12.pa.us
Grade Span: KG-12; **Agency Type:** 1
Schools: 9
  7 Primary; 1 Middle; 1 High; 0 Other Level
  9 Regular; 0 Special Education; 0 Vocational; 0 Alternative
  0 Magnet; 0 Charter; 5 Title I Eligible; 0 School-wide Title I
Students: 7,411 (n/a% male; n/a% female)
  Individual Education Program: 856 (11.6%);
  English Language Learner: n/a; Migrant: 0 (0.0%)
  Eligible for Free Lunch Program: 434 (5.9%)
  Eligible for Reduced-Price Lunch Program: 185 (2.5%)
Teachers: 442.5 (16.7 to 1)
Librarians/Media Specialists: 12.0 (617.6 to 1)
Guidance Counselors: 12.0 (617.6 to 1)
Current Spending: ($ per student per year):
  Total: $10,383; Instruction: $6,253; Support Services: $3,900

Enrollment, Drop-out Rates and Diploma Recipients by Race/Ethnicity

Category	Total	White	Black	Asian	AIAN	Hisp.
Enrollment (%)	100.0	72.5	19.0	6.1	0.1	2.3
Drop-out Rate (%)	1.5	1.3	2.3	0.6	0.0	5.0
H.S. Diplomas (#)	556	418	100	30	0	8

Cheltenham Township SD
1000 Ashbourne Rd • Elkins Park, PA 19027-1031
(215) 886-9500 • http://www.cheltenham.org
Grade Span: KG-12; **Agency Type:** 1
Schools: 7
  4 Primary; 2 Middle; 1 High; 0 Other Level
  7 Regular; 0 Special Education; 0 Vocational; 0 Alternative
  0 Magnet; 0 Charter; 6 Title I Eligible; 0 School-wide Title I
Students: 4,734 (n/a% male; n/a% female)
  Individual Education Program: 616 (13.0%);
  English Language Learner: n/a; Migrant: 0 (0.0%)
  Eligible for Free Lunch Program: 153 (3.2%)
  Eligible for Reduced-Price Lunch Program: 60 (1.3%)
Teachers: 338.7 (14.0 to 1)
Librarians/Media Specialists: 8.0 (591.8 to 1)
Guidance Counselors: 14.0 (338.1 to 1)
Current Spending: ($ per student per year):
  Total: $11,943; Instruction: $7,725; Support Services: $3,963

Enrollment, Drop-out Rates and Diploma Recipients by Race/Ethnicity

Category	Total	White	Black	Asian	AIAN	Hisp.
Enrollment (%)	100.0	50.7	38.0	8.6	0.1	2.7
Drop-out Rate (%)	1.6	0.6	2.9	3.6	0.0	0.0
H.S. Diplomas (#)	383	238	110	26	1	8

Colonial SD
2260 Butler Pike Ste 350 • Plymouth Meeting, PA 19462-1252
(610) 834-1670 • http://www.colonialsd.org
Grade Span: KG-12; **Agency Type:** 1
Schools: 7
  4 Primary; 2 Middle; 1 High; 0 Other Level
  7 Regular; 0 Special Education; 0 Vocational; 0 Alternative
  0 Magnet; 0 Charter; 3 Title I Eligible; 1 School-wide Title I
Students: 4,612 (n/a% male; n/a% female)
  Individual Education Program: 677 (14.7%);
  English Language Learner: n/a; Migrant: 0 (0.0%)
  Eligible for Free Lunch Program: 272 (5.9%)
  Eligible for Reduced-Price Lunch Program: 111 (2.4%)
Teachers: 339.4 (13.6 to 1)
Librarians/Media Specialists: 7.4 (623.2 to 1)
Guidance Counselors: 14.0 (329.4 to 1)

Current Spending: ($ per student per year):
Total: $11,780; Instruction: $7,420; Support Services: $4,064

Enrollment, Drop-out Rates and Diploma Recipients by Race/Ethnicity

Category	Total	White	Black	Asian	AIAN	Hisp.
Enrollment (%)	100.0	84.8	9.3	4.5	0.2	1.2
Drop-out Rate (%)	1.2	1.0	3.1	3.1	n/a	0.0
H.S. Diplomas (#)	350	308	19	16	0	7

Hatboro-Horsham SD

229 Meetinghouse Rd • Horsham, PA 19044-2192
(215) 672-5660 • http://www.hatboro-horsham.org
Grade Span: KG-12; **Agency Type:** 1
Schools: 8
  6 Primary; 1 Middle; 1 High; 0 Other Level
  8 Regular; 0 Special Education; 0 Vocational; 0 Alternative
  0 Magnet; 0 Charter; 4 Title I Eligible; 0 School-wide Title I
Students: 5,503   (n/a% male; n/a% female)
  Individual Education Program: 623 (11.3%);
  English Language Learner: n/a; Migrant: 0 (0.0%)
  Eligible for Free Lunch Program: 133 (2.4%)
  Eligible for Reduced-Price Lunch Program: 84 (1.5%)
Teachers: 357.5 (15.4 to 1)
Librarians/Media Specialists: 8.3 (663.0 to 1)
Guidance Counselors: 14.4 (382.2 to 1)
Current Spending: ($ per student per year):
Total: $9,681; Instruction: $6,391; Support Services: $3,037

Enrollment, Drop-out Rates and Diploma Recipients by Race/Ethnicity

Category	Total	White	Black	Asian	AIAN	Hisp.
Enrollment (%)	100.0	89.7	3.2	6.0	0.1	1.1
Drop-out Rate (%)	1.1	1.3	0.0	0.0	0.0	0.0
H.S. Diplomas (#)	355	314	15	18	1	7

Lower Merion SD

301 E Montgomery Ave • Ardmore, PA 19003-3399
(610) 645-1800 • http://www.lmsd.org
Grade Span: KG-12; **Agency Type:** 1
Schools: 10
  6 Primary; 2 Middle; 2 High; 0 Other Level
  10 Regular; 0 Special Education; 0 Vocational; 0 Alternative
  0 Magnet; 0 Charter; 9 Title I Eligible; 0 School-wide Title I
Students: 6,662   (n/a% male; n/a% female)
  Individual Education Program: 1,213 (18.2%);
  English Language Learner: n/a; Migrant: 0 (0.0%)
  Eligible for Free Lunch Program: 200 (3.0%)
  Eligible for Reduced-Price Lunch Program: 105 (1.6%)
Teachers: 522.0 (12.8 to 1)
Librarians/Media Specialists: 10.0 (666.2 to 1)
Guidance Counselors: 23.4 (284.7 to 1)
Current Spending: ($ per student per year):
Total: $16,376; Instruction: $9,961; Support Services: $6,126

Enrollment, Drop-out Rates and Diploma Recipients by Race/Ethnicity

Category	Total	White	Black	Asian	AIAN	Hisp.
Enrollment (%)	100.0	85.7	7.5	5.2	0.2	1.4
Drop-out Rate (%)	0.4	0.3	1.9	0.0	0.0	0.0
H.S. Diplomas (#)	455	399	33	18	0	5

Lower Moreland Township SD

2551 Murray Ave • Huntingdon Valley, PA 19006-6208
(215) 938-0270 • http://www.lmtsd.org
Grade Span: KG-12; **Agency Type:** 1
Schools: 3
  1 Primary; 1 Middle; 1 High; 0 Other Level
  3 Regular; 0 Special Education; 0 Vocational; 0 Alternative
  0 Magnet; 0 Charter; 3 Title I Eligible; 0 School-wide Title I
Students: 1,755   (n/a% male; n/a% female)
  Individual Education Program: 196 (11.2%);
  English Language Learner: n/a; Migrant: 0 (0.0%)
  Eligible for Free Lunch Program: 17 (1.0%)
  Eligible for Reduced-Price Lunch Program: 4 (0.2%)
Teachers: 115.0 (15.3 to 1)
Librarians/Media Specialists: 3.0 (585.0 to 1)
Guidance Counselors: 6.0 (292.5 to 1)
Current Spending: ($ per student per year):
Total: $11,192; Instruction: $6,987; Support Services: $3,959

Enrollment, Drop-out Rates and Diploma Recipients by Race/Ethnicity

Category	Total	White	Black	Asian	AIAN	Hisp.
Enrollment (%)	100.0	92.1	0.6	6.3	0.1	1.0
Drop-out Rate (%)	0.5	0.6	0.0	0.0	n/a	0.0
H.S. Diplomas (#)	126	115	0	10	0	1

Methacton SD

1000 Kriebel Mill Rd • Norristown, PA 19403-1047
(610) 489-5000 • http://www.methacton.org
Grade Span: KG-12; **Agency Type:** 1
Schools: 7

  5 Primary; 1 Middle; 1 High; 0 Other Level
  7 Regular; 0 Special Education; 0 Vocational; 0 Alternative
  0 Magnet; 0 Charter; 4 Title I Eligible; 0 School-wide Title I
Students: 5,231   (n/a% male; n/a% female)
  Individual Education Program: 560 (10.7%);
  English Language Learner: n/a; Migrant: 2 (<0.1%)
  Eligible for Free Lunch Program: 62 (1.2%)
  Eligible for Reduced-Price Lunch Program: 57 (1.1%)
Teachers: 355.7 (14.7 to 1)
Librarians/Media Specialists: 7.0 (747.3 to 1)
Guidance Counselors: 13.5 (387.5 to 1)
Current Spending: ($ per student per year):
Total: $9,716; Instruction: $6,073; Support Services: $3,376

Enrollment, Drop-out Rates and Diploma Recipients by Race/Ethnicity

Category	Total	White	Black	Asian	AIAN	Hisp.
Enrollment (%)	100.0	86.4	3.2	9.0	0.2	1.2
Drop-out Rate (%)	1.3	1.2	2.5	4.3	0.0	0.0
H.S. Diplomas (#)	301	271	10	15	1	4

Norristown Area SD

401 N Whitehall Rd • Norristown, PA 19403-2745
(610) 630-5000 • http://www.nasd.k12.pa.us
Grade Span: KG-12; **Agency Type:** 1
Schools: 11
  6 Primary; 2 Middle; 1 High; 2 Other Level
  11 Regular; 0 Special Education; 0 Vocational; 0 Alternative
  0 Magnet; 0 Charter; 11 Title I Eligible; 3 School-wide Title I
Students: 6,950   (n/a% male; n/a% female)
  Individual Education Program: 1,195 (17.2%);
  English Language Learner: n/a; Migrant: 30 (0.4%)
  Eligible for Free Lunch Program: 2,619 (37.7%)
  Eligible for Reduced-Price Lunch Program: 686 (9.9%)
Teachers: 512.0 (13.6 to 1)
Librarians/Media Specialists: 10.0 (695.0 to 1)
Guidance Counselors: 15.5 (448.4 to 1)
Current Spending: ($ per student per year):
Total: $10,521; Instruction: $6,502; Support Services: $3,670

Enrollment, Drop-out Rates and Diploma Recipients by Race/Ethnicity

Category	Total	White	Black	Asian	AIAN	Hisp.
Enrollment (%)	100.0	34.7	51.6	2.0	0.1	11.7
Drop-out Rate (%)	5.1	4.3	5.7	1.9	0.0	8.5
H.S. Diplomas (#)	396	211	144	14	1	26

North Penn SD

401 E Hancock St • Lansdale, PA 19446-3960
(215) 368-0400 • http://www.northpennschools.k12.pa.us
Grade Span: KG-12; **Agency Type:** 1
Schools: 17
  13 Primary; 3 Middle; 1 High; 0 Other Level
  17 Regular; 0 Special Education; 0 Vocational; 0 Alternative
  0 Magnet; 0 Charter; 9 Title I Eligible; 0 School-wide Title I
Students: 13,521   (n/a% male; n/a% female)
  Individual Education Program: 1,922 (14.2%);
  English Language Learner: n/a; Migrant: 112 (0.8%)
  Eligible for Free Lunch Program: 953 (7.0%)
  Eligible for Reduced-Price Lunch Program: 499 (3.7%)
Teachers: 850.0 (15.9 to 1)
Librarians/Media Specialists: 19.0 (711.6 to 1)
Guidance Counselors: 33.6 (402.4 to 1)
Current Spending: ($ per student per year):
Total: $9,381; Instruction: $6,103; Support Services: $2,815

Enrollment, Drop-out Rates and Diploma Recipients by Race/Ethnicity

Category	Total	White	Black	Asian	AIAN	Hisp.
Enrollment (%)	100.0	79.2	5.2	13.3	0.1	2.3
Drop-out Rate (%)	0.8	0.8	1.0	0.4	0.0	6.3
H.S. Diplomas (#)	1,003	826	39	122	1	15

Pennsylvania Virtual CS

425 Swede St • Norristown, PA 19401
(610) 275-8501
Grade Span: KG-05; **Agency Type:** 7
Schools: 1
  1 Primary; 0 Middle; 0 High; 0 Other Level
  1 Regular; 0 Special Education; 0 Vocational; 0 Alternative
  0 Magnet; 1 Charter; 0 Title I Eligible; 0 School-wide Title I
Students: 3,330   (n/a% male; n/a% female)
  Individual Education Program: 198 (5.9%);
  English Language Learner: n/a; Migrant: 0 (0.0%)
  Eligible for Free Lunch Program: 0 (0.0%)
  Eligible for Reduced-Price Lunch Program: 0 (0.0%)
Teachers: 72.0 (46.3 to 1)
Librarians/Media Specialists: 0.0 (n/a to 1)
Guidance Counselors: 0.0 (n/a to 1)
Current Spending: ($ per student per year):
Total: $6,059; Instruction: $3,932; Support Services: $2,127

Enrollment, Drop-out Rates and Diploma Recipients by Race/Ethnicity

Category	Total	White	Black	Asian	AIAN	Hisp.
Enrollment (%)	100.0	84.9	10.8	0.7	0.9	2.7
Drop-out Rate (%)	n/a	n/a	n/a	n/a	n/a	n/a
H.S. Diplomas (#)	n/a	n/a	n/a	n/a	n/a	n/a

Perkiomen Valley SD
3 Iron Bridge Dr • Collegeville, PA 19426-2042
(610) 489-8506 • http://mciunix.mciu.k12.pa.us:80/~pvweb/
Grade Span: KG-12; **Agency Type:** 1
Schools: 7
    4 Primary; 1 Middle; 1 High; 0 Other Level
    6 Regular; 0 Special Education; 0 Vocational; 0 Alternative
    0 Magnet; 0 Charter; 5 Title I Eligible; 0 School-wide Title I
Students: 4,964   (n/a% male; n/a% female)
    Individual Education Program: 482 (9.7%);
    English Language Learner: n/a; Migrant: 0 (0.0%)
    Eligible for Free Lunch Program: 291 (5.9%)
    Eligible for Reduced-Price Lunch Program: 218 (4.4%)
Teachers: 314.1 (15.8 to 1)
Librarians/Media Specialists: 6.0 (827.3 to 1)
Guidance Counselors: 11.0 (451.3 to 1)
Current Spending: ($ per student per year):
    Total: $8,749; Instruction: $5,201; Support Services: $3,276

Enrollment, Drop-out Rates and Diploma Recipients by Race/Ethnicity

Category	Total	White	Black	Asian	AIAN	Hisp.
Enrollment (%)	100.0	90.9	3.8	3.2	0.3	1.8
Drop-out Rate (%)	1.7	1.8	4.3	0.0	0.0	0.0
H.S. Diplomas (#)	222	212	8	1	1	0

Pottsgrove SD
1301 Kauffman Rd • Pottstown, PA 19464-2303
(610) 327-2277 • http://pgsd.org
Grade Span: KG-12; **Agency Type:** 1
Schools: 5
    3 Primary; 1 Middle; 1 High; 0 Other Level
    5 Regular; 0 Special Education; 0 Vocational; 0 Alternative
    0 Magnet; 0 Charter; 4 Title I Eligible; 0 School-wide Title I
Students: 3,246   (n/a% male; n/a% female)
    Individual Education Program: 437 (13.5%);
    English Language Learner: n/a; Migrant: 0 (0.0%)
    Eligible for Free Lunch Program: 317 (9.8%)
    Eligible for Reduced-Price Lunch Program: 67 (2.1%)
Teachers: 203.5 (16.0 to 1)
Librarians/Media Specialists: 5.0 (649.2 to 1)
Guidance Counselors: 8.5 (381.9 to 1)
Current Spending: ($ per student per year):
    Total: $8,716; Instruction: $5,446; Support Services: $2,983

Enrollment, Drop-out Rates and Diploma Recipients by Race/Ethnicity

Category	Total	White	Black	Asian	AIAN	Hisp.
Enrollment (%)	100.0	81.3	15.3	1.5	0.2	1.7
Drop-out Rate (%)	2.8	2.6	6.0	0.0	0.0	0.0
H.S. Diplomas (#)	220	190	23	1	2	4

Pottstown SD
230 Beech St • Pottstown, PA 19464-5591
(610) 323-8200 • http://www.pottstownschools.com
Grade Span: PK-12; **Agency Type:** 1
Schools: 7
    5 Primary; 1 Middle; 1 High; 0 Other Level
    7 Regular; 0 Special Education; 0 Vocational; 0 Alternative
    0 Magnet; 0 Charter; 7 Title I Eligible; 0 School-wide Title I
Students: 3,317   (n/a% male; n/a% female)
    Individual Education Program: 631 (19.0%);
    English Language Learner: n/a; Migrant: 1 (<0.1%)
    Eligible for Free Lunch Program: 949 (28.6%)
    Eligible for Reduced-Price Lunch Program: 335 (10.1%)
Teachers: 211.8 (15.7 to 1)
Librarians/Media Specialists: 4.6 (721.1 to 1)
Guidance Counselors: 8.0 (414.6 to 1)
Current Spending: ($ per student per year):
    Total: $9,676; Instruction: $5,851; Support Services: $3,415

Enrollment, Drop-out Rates and Diploma Recipients by Race/Ethnicity

Category	Total	White	Black	Asian	AIAN	Hisp.
Enrollment (%)	100.0	55.9	36.2	0.6	0.2	7.0
Drop-out Rate (%)	6.0	4.9	7.4	12.5	n/a	8.5
H.S. Diplomas (#)	143	96	41	0	0	6

Souderton Area SD
760 Lower Rd • Souderton, PA 18964-2311
(215) 723-6061 • http://www.soudertonsd.org
Grade Span: KG-12; **Agency Type:** 1
Schools: 10
    7 Primary; 1 Middle; 1 High; 1 Other Level
    10 Regular; 0 Special Education; 0 Vocational; 0 Alternative

    0 Magnet; 0 Charter; 5 Title I Eligible; 0 School-wide Title I
Students: 6,650   (n/a% male; n/a% female)
    Individual Education Program: 801 (12.0%);
    English Language Learner: n/a; Migrant: 59 (0.9%)
    Eligible for Free Lunch Program: 287 (4.3%)
    Eligible for Reduced-Price Lunch Program: 141 (2.1%)
Teachers: 431.6 (15.4 to 1)
Librarians/Media Specialists: 10.0 (665.0 to 1)
Guidance Counselors: 16.0 (415.6 to 1)
Current Spending: ($ per student per year):
    Total: $10,029; Instruction: $6,855; Support Services: $2,952

Enrollment, Drop-out Rates and Diploma Recipients by Race/Ethnicity

Category	Total	White	Black	Asian	AIAN	Hisp.
Enrollment (%)	100.0	90.3	3.2	3.8	0.2	2.5
Drop-out Rate (%)	1.3	1.3	1.4	3.0	0.0	1.9
H.S. Diplomas (#)	432	398	14	9	0	11

Spring-Ford Area SD
199 Bechtel Rd • Collegeville, PA 19426-2829
(610) 705-6000 • http://mciunix.mciu.k12.pa.us/~sfasdweb
Grade Span: KG-12; **Agency Type:** 1
Schools: 9
    6 Primary; 2 Middle; 1 High; 0 Other Level
    9 Regular; 0 Special Education; 0 Vocational; 0 Alternative
    0 Magnet; 0 Charter; 4 Title I Eligible; 0 School-wide Title I
Students: 6,535   (n/a% male; n/a% female)
    Individual Education Program: 908 (13.9%);
    English Language Learner: n/a; Migrant: 0 (0.0%)
    Eligible for Free Lunch Program: 194 (3.0%)
    Eligible for Reduced-Price Lunch Program: 125 (1.9%)
Teachers: 405.1 (16.1 to 1)
Librarians/Media Specialists: 10.0 (653.5 to 1)
Guidance Counselors: 18.0 (363.1 to 1)
Current Spending: ($ per student per year):
    Total: $9,111; Instruction: $5,710; Support Services: $3,100

Enrollment, Drop-out Rates and Diploma Recipients by Race/Ethnicity

Category	Total	White	Black	Asian	AIAN	Hisp.
Enrollment (%)	100.0	90.1	4.7	3.5	0.1	1.6
Drop-out Rate (%)	1.9	1.9	1.9	0.0	0.0	0.0
H.S. Diplomas (#)	359	331	17	5	0	6

Springfield Township SD
1901 E Paper Mill Rd • Oreland, PA 19075-2499
(215) 233-6000 • http://www.springfield.k12.pa.us
Grade Span: KG-12; **Agency Type:** 1
Schools: 4
    2 Primary; 1 Middle; 1 High; 0 Other Level
    4 Regular; 0 Special Education; 0 Vocational; 0 Alternative
    0 Magnet; 0 Charter; 2 Title I Eligible; 0 School-wide Title I
Students: 2,062   (n/a% male; n/a% female)
    Individual Education Program: 343 (16.6%);
    English Language Learner: n/a; Migrant: 0 (0.0%)
    Eligible for Free Lunch Program: 47 (2.3%)
    Eligible for Reduced-Price Lunch Program: 25 (1.2%)
Teachers: 152.8 (13.5 to 1)
Librarians/Media Specialists: 4.0 (515.5 to 1)
Guidance Counselors: 7.0 (294.6 to 1)
Current Spending: ($ per student per year):
    Total: $11,955; Instruction: $7,034; Support Services: $4,520

Enrollment, Drop-out Rates and Diploma Recipients by Race/Ethnicity

Category	Total	White	Black	Asian	AIAN	Hisp.
Enrollment (%)	100.0	81.8	13.4	3.1	0.1	1.6
Drop-out Rate (%)	1.3	1.1	2.2	4.3	n/a	0.0
H.S. Diplomas (#)	142	116	20	6	0	0

Upper Dublin SD
1580 Fort Washington Ave • Maple Glen, PA 19002
(215) 643-8800 • http://mciu.org/~udsdweb/
Grade Span: KG-12; **Agency Type:** 1
Schools: 6
    4 Primary; 1 Middle; 1 High; 0 Other Level
    6 Regular; 0 Special Education; 0 Vocational; 0 Alternative
    0 Magnet; 0 Charter; 3 Title I Eligible; 0 School-wide Title I
Students: 4,406   (n/a% male; n/a% female)
    Individual Education Program: 526 (11.9%);
    English Language Learner: n/a; Migrant: 0 (0.0%)
    Eligible for Free Lunch Program: 219 (5.0%)
    Eligible for Reduced-Price Lunch Program: 38 (0.9%)
Teachers: 281.1 (15.7 to 1)
Librarians/Media Specialists: 6.0 (734.3 to 1)
Guidance Counselors: 13.0 (338.9 to 1)
Current Spending: ($ per student per year):
    Total: $9,318; Instruction: $6,046; Support Services: $2,992

Enrollment, Drop-out Rates and Diploma Recipients by Race/Ethnicity

Category	Total	White	Black	Asian	AIAN	Hisp.
Enrollment (%)	100.0	82.1	7.4	10.0	0.0	0.4
Drop-out Rate (%)	0.3	0.3	1.9	0.0	0.0	0.0
H.S. Diplomas (#)	345	274	28	40	0	3

Upper Merion Area SD
435 Crossfield Rd · King Of Prussia, PA 19406-2363
(610) 337-6001
Grade Span: KG-12; **Agency Type:** 1
Schools: 6
    4 Primary; 1 Middle; 1 High; 0 Other Level
    6 Regular; 0 Special Education; 0 Vocational; 0 Alternative
    0 Magnet; 0 Charter; 3 Title I Eligible; 0 School-wide Title I
Students: 3,447 (n/a% male; n/a% female)
    Individual Education Program: 486 (14.1%);
    English Language Learner: n/a; Migrant: 0 (0.0%)
    Eligible for Free Lunch Program: 197 (5.7%)
    Eligible for Reduced-Price Lunch Program: 132 (3.8%)
Teachers: 249.4 (13.8 to 1)
Librarians/Media Specialists: 7.5 (459.6 to 1)
Guidance Counselors: 11.0 (313.4 to 1)
Current Spending: ($ per student per year):
    Total: $12,776; Instruction: $7,639; Support Services: $4,692

Enrollment, Drop-out Rates and Diploma Recipients by Race/Ethnicity

Category	Total	White	Black	Asian	AIAN	Hisp.
Enrollment (%)	100.0	79.0	7.7	10.6	0.1	2.6
Drop-out Rate (%)	1.5	1.7	0.0	0.0	0.0	5.6
H.S. Diplomas (#)	212	171	12	24	0	5

Upper Moreland Township SD
2900 Terwood Rd · Willow Grove, PA 19090-1431
(215) 659-6800 · http://www.umsd.k12.pa.us
Grade Span: KG-12; **Agency Type:** 1
Schools: 4
    2 Primary; 1 Middle; 1 High; 0 Other Level
    4 Regular; 0 Special Education; 0 Vocational; 0 Alternative
    0 Magnet; 0 Charter; 3 Title I Eligible; 0 School-wide Title I
Students: 3,108 (n/a% male; n/a% female)
    Individual Education Program: 331 (10.6%);
    English Language Learner: n/a; Migrant: 0 (0.0%)
    Eligible for Free Lunch Program: 188 (6.0%)
    Eligible for Reduced-Price Lunch Program: 91 (2.9%)
Teachers: 196.7 (15.8 to 1)
Librarians/Media Specialists: 4.0 (777.0 to 1)
Guidance Counselors: 8.0 (388.5 to 1)
Current Spending: ($ per student per year):
    Total: $9,772; Instruction: $6,014; Support Services: $3,422

Enrollment, Drop-out Rates and Diploma Recipients by Race/Ethnicity

Category	Total	White	Black	Asian	AIAN	Hisp.
Enrollment (%)	100.0	86.7	7.2	4.2	0.0	1.8
Drop-out Rate (%)	1.3	1.2	2.0	4.5	n/a	0.0
H.S. Diplomas (#)	239	221	10	2	0	6

Upper Perkiomen SD
201 W 5th St · East Greenville, PA 18041-1509
(215) 679-7961 · http://mciunix.mciu.k12.pa.us/~upsd/
Grade Span: KG-12; **Agency Type:** 1
Schools: 4
    2 Primary; 1 Middle; 1 High; 0 Other Level
    4 Regular; 0 Special Education; 0 Vocational; 0 Alternative
    0 Magnet; 0 Charter; 3 Title I Eligible; 0 School-wide Title I
Students: 3,380 (n/a% male; n/a% female)
    Individual Education Program: 417 (12.3%);
    English Language Learner: n/a; Migrant: 3 (0.1%)
    Eligible for Free Lunch Program: 262 (7.8%)
    Eligible for Reduced-Price Lunch Program: 187 (5.5%)
Teachers: 189.7 (17.8 to 1)
Librarians/Media Specialists: 4.0 (845.0 to 1)
Guidance Counselors: 7.0 (482.9 to 1)
Current Spending: ($ per student per year):
    Total: $10,798; Instruction: $7,787; Support Services: $2,645

Enrollment, Drop-out Rates and Diploma Recipients by Race/Ethnicity

Category	Total	White	Black	Asian	AIAN	Hisp.
Enrollment (%)	100.0	94.4	2.0	0.7	0.3	2.5
Drop-out Rate (%)	1.5	1.4	8.3	0.0	0.0	0.0
H.S. Diplomas (#)	266	260	1	2	0	3

Wissahickon SD
601 Knight Rd · Ambler, PA 19002-3441
(215) 619-8000 · http://mciunix.mciu.k12.pa.us:80/~wsdweb/
Grade Span: KG-12; **Agency Type:** 1
Schools: 7
    5 Primary; 1 Middle; 1 High; 0 Other Level
    7 Regular; 0 Special Education; 0 Vocational; 0 Alternative

0 Magnet; 0 Charter; 6 Title I Eligible; 0 School-wide Title I
Students: 4,535 (n/a% male; n/a% female)
    Individual Education Program: 686 (15.1%);
    English Language Learner: n/a; Migrant: 4 (0.1%)
    Eligible for Free Lunch Program: 129 (2.8%)
    Eligible for Reduced-Price Lunch Program: 63 (1.4%)
Teachers: 295.8 (15.3 to 1)
Librarians/Media Specialists: 6.5 (697.7 to 1)
Guidance Counselors: 13.8 (328.6 to 1)
Current Spending: ($ per student per year):
    Total: $11,438; Instruction: $7,330; Support Services: $3,835

Enrollment, Drop-out Rates and Diploma Recipients by Race/Ethnicity

Category	Total	White	Black	Asian	AIAN	Hisp.
Enrollment (%)	100.0	71.8	13.2	12.4	0.1	2.4
Drop-out Rate (%)	1.3	1.2	1.8	1.9	0.0	0.0
H.S. Diplomas (#)	293	213	40	38	0	2

Montour County

Danville Area SD
600 Walnut St · Danville, PA 17821-9131
(570) 271-3268 · http://www.danville.k12.pa.us
Grade Span: KG-12; **Agency Type:** 1
Schools: 6
    4 Primary; 1 Middle; 1 High; 0 Other Level
    6 Regular; 0 Special Education; 0 Vocational; 0 Alternative
    0 Magnet; 0 Charter; 3 Title I Eligible; 0 School-wide Title I
Students: 2,625 (n/a% male; n/a% female)
    Individual Education Program: 321 (12.2%);
    English Language Learner: n/a; Migrant: 0 (0.0%)
    Eligible for Free Lunch Program: 501 (19.1%)
    Eligible for Reduced-Price Lunch Program: 217 (8.3%)
Teachers: 190.0 (13.8 to 1)
Librarians/Media Specialists: 2.0 (1,312.5 to 1)
Guidance Counselors: 7.5 (350.0 to 1)
Current Spending: ($ per student per year):
    Total: $7,699; Instruction: $4,983; Support Services: $2,383

Enrollment, Drop-out Rates and Diploma Recipients by Race/Ethnicity

Category	Total	White	Black	Asian	AIAN	Hisp.
Enrollment (%)	100.0	95.1	1.5	2.3	0.3	0.8
Drop-out Rate (%)	1.3	1.3	0.0	0.0	0.0	0.0
H.S. Diplomas (#)	201	187	3	8	0	3

Northampton County

Bangor Area SD
123 Five Points Richmond Rd · Bangor, PA 18013-5272
(610) 588-2163 · http://www.bangor.k12.pa.us/
Grade Span: KG-12; **Agency Type:** 1
Schools: 5
    2 Primary; 2 Middle; 1 High; 0 Other Level
    5 Regular; 0 Special Education; 0 Vocational; 0 Alternative
    0 Magnet; 0 Charter; 4 Title I Eligible; 0 School-wide Title I
Students: 3,717 (n/a% male; n/a% female)
    Individual Education Program: 541 (14.6%);
    English Language Learner: n/a; Migrant: 0 (0.0%)
    Eligible for Free Lunch Program: 370 (10.0%)
    Eligible for Reduced-Price Lunch Program: 252 (6.8%)
Teachers: 213.7 (17.4 to 1)
Librarians/Media Specialists: 4.0 (929.3 to 1)
Guidance Counselors: 8.0 (464.6 to 1)
Current Spending: ($ per student per year):
    Total: $6,773; Instruction: $3,924; Support Services: $2,555

Enrollment, Drop-out Rates and Diploma Recipients by Race/Ethnicity

Category	Total	White	Black	Asian	AIAN	Hisp.
Enrollment (%)	100.0	95.7	1.2	0.3	0.2	2.4
Drop-out Rate (%)	3.5	3.5	0.0	0.0	0.0	11.1
H.S. Diplomas (#)	220	213	2	3	0	2

Bethlehem Area SD
1516 Sycamore St · Bethlehem, PA 18017-6099
(610) 861-0500 · http://www.beth.k12.pa.us/
Grade Span: KG-12; **Agency Type:** 1
Schools: 22
    16 Primary; 4 Middle; 2 High; 0 Other Level
    22 Regular; 0 Special Education; 0 Vocational; 0 Alternative
    0 Magnet; 0 Charter; 11 Title I Eligible; 4 School-wide Title I
Students: 14,726 (n/a% male; n/a% female)
    Individual Education Program: 1,863 (12.7%);
    English Language Learner: n/a; Migrant: 230 (1.6%)
    Eligible for Free Lunch Program: 3,611 (24.5%)
    Eligible for Reduced-Price Lunch Program: 1,074 (7.3%)
Teachers: 902.8 (16.3 to 1)
Librarians/Media Specialists: 15.1 (975.2 to 1)
Guidance Counselors: 45.0 (327.2 to 1)

Current Spending: ($ per student per year):
Total: $7,516; Instruction: $4,792; Support Services: $2,333
Enrollment, Drop-out Rates and Diploma Recipients by Race/Ethnicity

Category	Total	White	Black	Asian	AIAN	Hisp.
Enrollment (%)	100.0	62.3	6.7	2.2	0.1	28.6
Drop-out Rate (%)	4.4	2.6	4.8	0.0	0.0	10.0
H.S. Diplomas (#)	920	667	42	21	0	190

Easton Area SD
811 Northampton St • Easton, PA 18042-4298
(610) 250-2400 • http://easdnet1.eastonsd.org
Grade Span: KG-12; **Agency Type:** 1
Schools: 9
  6 Primary; 2 Middle; 1 High; 0 Other Level
  9 Regular; 0 Special Education; 0 Vocational; 0 Alternative
  0 Magnet; 0 Charter; 6 Title I Eligible; 0 School-wide Title I
Students: 8,364 (n/a% male; n/a% female)
  Individual Education Program: 1,042 (12.5%);
  English Language Learner: n/a; Migrant: 5 (0.1%)
  Eligible for Free Lunch Program: 1,482 (17.7%)
  Eligible for Reduced-Price Lunch Program: 377 (4.5%)
Teachers: 554.7 (15.1 to 1)
Librarians/Media Specialists: 9.6 (871.3 to 1)
Guidance Counselors: 19.5 (428.9 to 1)
Current Spending: ($ per student per year):
Total: $7,593; Instruction: $4,894; Support Services: $2,490
Enrollment, Drop-out Rates and Diploma Recipients by Race/Ethnicity

Category	Total	White	Black	Asian	AIAN	Hisp.
Enrollment (%)	100.0	70.4	15.7	2.5	0.2	11.2
Drop-out Rate (%)	3.8	3.1	6.0	0.0	0.0	9.0
H.S. Diplomas (#)	502	411	56	9	0	26

Nazareth Area SD
One Education Plaza • Nazareth, PA 18064-2042
(610) 759-1170 • http://www.nazarethasd.k12.pa.us
Grade Span: KG-12; **Agency Type:** 1
Schools: 5
  3 Primary; 1 Middle; 1 High; 0 Other Level
  5 Regular; 0 Special Education; 0 Vocational; 0 Alternative
  0 Magnet; 0 Charter; 2 Title I Eligible; 0 School-wide Title I
Students: 4,424 (n/a% male; n/a% female)
  Individual Education Program: 514 (11.6%);
  English Language Learner: n/a; Migrant: 0 (0.0%)
  Eligible for Free Lunch Program: 179 (4.0%)
  Eligible for Reduced-Price Lunch Program: 86 (1.9%)
Teachers: 271.3 (16.3 to 1)
Librarians/Media Specialists: 3.0 (1,474.7 to 1)
Guidance Counselors: 10.0 (442.4 to 1)
Current Spending: ($ per student per year):
Total: $7,377; Instruction: $4,680; Support Services: $2,435
Enrollment, Drop-out Rates and Diploma Recipients by Race/Ethnicity

Category	Total	White	Black	Asian	AIAN	Hisp.
Enrollment (%)	100.0	96.5	1.0	1.1	0.0	1.4
Drop-out Rate (%)	1.1	1.1	0.0	0.0	n/a	0.0
H.S. Diplomas (#)	254	248	1	3	0	2

Northampton Area SD
2014 Laubach Ave • Northampton, PA 18067-0118
(610) 262-7811 • http://www.northampton.k12.pa.us
Grade Span: KG-12; **Agency Type:** 1
Schools: 6
  4 Primary; 1 Middle; 1 High; 0 Other Level
  6 Regular; 0 Special Education; 0 Vocational; 0 Alternative
  0 Magnet; 0 Charter; 4 Title I Eligible; 0 School-wide Title I
Students: 5,599 (n/a% male; n/a% female)
  Individual Education Program: 807 (14.4%);
  English Language Learner: n/a; Migrant: 0 (0.0%)
  Eligible for Free Lunch Program: 288 (5.1%)
  Eligible for Reduced-Price Lunch Program: 207 (3.7%)
Teachers: 348.5 (16.1 to 1)
Librarians/Media Specialists: 6.0 (933.2 to 1)
Guidance Counselors: 14.5 (386.1 to 1)
Current Spending: ($ per student per year):
Total: $8,127; Instruction: $4,944; Support Services: $2,858
Enrollment, Drop-out Rates and Diploma Recipients by Race/Ethnicity

Category	Total	White	Black	Asian	AIAN	Hisp.
Enrollment (%)	100.0	96.3	1.1	0.7	0.0	1.9
Drop-out Rate (%)	4.1	4.0	0.0	0.0	n/a	20.0
H.S. Diplomas (#)	339	334	0	3	0	2

Pen Argyl Area SD
1620 Teels Rd • Pen Argyl, PA 18072-9734
(610) 863-3191 • http://www.pahs.org
Grade Span: KG-12; **Agency Type:** 1
Schools: 3

1 Primary; 1 Middle; 1 High; 0 Other Level
3 Regular; 0 Special Education; 0 Vocational; 0 Alternative
0 Magnet; 0 Charter; 3 Title I Eligible; 0 School-wide Title I
Students: 1,994 (n/a% male; n/a% female)
  Individual Education Program: 220 (11.0%);
  English Language Learner: n/a; Migrant: 0 (0.0%)
  Eligible for Free Lunch Program: 170 (8.5%)
  Eligible for Reduced-Price Lunch Program: 109 (5.5%)
Teachers: 116.0 (17.2 to 1)
Librarians/Media Specialists: 2.0 (997.0 to 1)
Guidance Counselors: 5.0 (398.8 to 1)
Current Spending: ($ per student per year):
Total: $7,575; Instruction: $4,751; Support Services: $2,559
Enrollment, Drop-out Rates and Diploma Recipients by Race/Ethnicity

Category	Total	White	Black	Asian	AIAN	Hisp.
Enrollment (%)	100.0	95.2	1.0	1.3	0.1	2.4
Drop-out Rate (%)	2.3	2.2	0.0	14.3	0.0	0.0
H.S. Diplomas (#)	137	133	2	2	0	0

Saucon Valley SD
2097 Polk Valley Rd • Hellertown, PA 18055-2400
(610) 838-7026 • http://www.sauconvalley.k12.pa.us
Grade Span: KG-12; **Agency Type:** 1
Schools: 3
  1 Primary; 1 Middle; 1 High; 0 Other Level
  3 Regular; 0 Special Education; 0 Vocational; 0 Alternative
  0 Magnet; 0 Charter; 3 Title I Eligible; 0 School-wide Title I
Students: 2,308 (n/a% male; n/a% female)
  Individual Education Program: 251 (10.9%);
  English Language Learner: n/a; Migrant: 3 (0.1%)
  Eligible for Free Lunch Program: 149 (6.5%)
  Eligible for Reduced-Price Lunch Program: 53 (2.3%)
Teachers: 154.1 (15.0 to 1)
Librarians/Media Specialists: 3.4 (678.8 to 1)
Guidance Counselors: 8.0 (288.5 to 1)
Current Spending: ($ per student per year):
Total: $9,191; Instruction: $5,851; Support Services: $3,051
Enrollment, Drop-out Rates and Diploma Recipients by Race/Ethnicity

Category	Total	White	Black	Asian	AIAN	Hisp.
Enrollment (%)	100.0	97.0	1.0	0.6	0.0	1.3
Drop-out Rate (%)	1.9	2.0	0.0	0.0	0.0	0.0
H.S. Diplomas (#)	174	167	1	1	1	4

Wilson Area SD
2040 Washington Blvd • Easton, PA 18042-3890
(484) 373-6000 • http://www.wilsonareasd.org
Grade Span: KG-12; **Agency Type:** 1
Schools: 5
  3 Primary; 1 Middle; 1 High; 0 Other Level
  5 Regular; 0 Special Education; 0 Vocational; 0 Alternative
  0 Magnet; 0 Charter; 4 Title I Eligible; 0 School-wide Title I
Students: 2,266 (n/a% male; n/a% female)
  Individual Education Program: 359 (15.8%);
  English Language Learner: n/a; Migrant: 2 (0.1%)
  Eligible for Free Lunch Program: 239 (10.5%)
  Eligible for Reduced-Price Lunch Program: 137 (6.0%)
Teachers: 147.8 (15.3 to 1)
Librarians/Media Specialists: 3.5 (647.4 to 1)
Guidance Counselors: 7.0 (323.7 to 1)
Current Spending: ($ per student per year):
Total: $7,637; Instruction: $4,701; Support Services: $2,642
Enrollment, Drop-out Rates and Diploma Recipients by Race/Ethnicity

Category	Total	White	Black	Asian	AIAN	Hisp.
Enrollment (%)	100.0	89.3	4.0	2.3	0.1	4.2
Drop-out Rate (%)	4.7	3.9	10.6	0.0	0.0	17.2
H.S. Diplomas (#)	141	129	7	3	0	2

Northumberland County

Milton Area SD
700 Mahoning St • Milton, PA 17847-2231
(570) 742-7614 • http://www.milton.k12.pa.us
Grade Span: KG-12; **Agency Type:** 1
Schools: 5
  3 Primary; 1 Middle; 1 High; 0 Other Level
  5 Regular; 0 Special Education; 0 Vocational; 0 Alternative
  0 Magnet; 0 Charter; 3 Title I Eligible; 0 School-wide Title I
Students: 2,458 (n/a% male; n/a% female)
  Individual Education Program: 261 (10.6%);
  English Language Learner: n/a; Migrant: 1 (<0.1%)
  Eligible for Free Lunch Program: 632 (25.7%)
  Eligible for Reduced-Price Lunch Program: 223 (9.1%)
Teachers: 173.8 (14.1 to 1)
Librarians/Media Specialists: 3.0 (819.3 to 1)
Guidance Counselors: 8.0 (307.3 to 1)

Current Spending: ($ per student per year):
  Total: $7,553; Instruction: $4,898; Support Services: $2,266

Enrollment, Drop-out Rates and Diploma Recipients by Race/Ethnicity

Category	Total	White	Black	Asian	AIAN	Hisp.
Enrollment (%)	100.0	91.5	3.8	0.7	0.0	3.9
Drop-out Rate (%)	3.7	3.5	5.6	50.0	n/a	5.3
H.S. Diplomas (#)	191	179	5	1	0	6

Mount Carmel Area SD

600 W 5th St • Mount Carmel, PA 17851-1897
(570) 339-3473 • http://www.mca.k12.pa.us
Grade Span: PK-12; Agency Type: 1
Schools: 2
  1 Primary; 0 Middle; 1 High; 0 Other Level
  2 Regular; 0 Special Education; 0 Vocational; 0 Alternative
  0 Magnet; 0 Charter; 2 Title I Eligible; 0 School-wide Title I
Students: 1,794   (n/a% male; n/a% female)
  Individual Education Program: 172 (9.6%);
  English Language Learner: n/a; Migrant: 0 (0.0%)
  Eligible for Free Lunch Program: 507 (28.3%)
  Eligible for Reduced-Price Lunch Program: 195 (10.9%)
Teachers: 113.0 (15.9 to 1)
Librarians/Media Specialists: 2.0 (897.0 to 1)
Guidance Counselors: 3.0 (598.0 to 1)
Current Spending: ($ per student per year):
  Total: $6,284; Instruction: $4,136; Support Services: $1,767

Enrollment, Drop-out Rates and Diploma Recipients by Race/Ethnicity

Category	Total	White	Black	Asian	AIAN	Hisp.
Enrollment (%)	100.0	99.1	0.2	0.3	0.0	0.4
Drop-out Rate (%)	0.9	0.9	n/a	n/a	n/a	0.0
H.S. Diplomas (#)	109	109	0	0	0	0

Shamokin Area SD

2000 W State St • Coal Township, PA 17866-2807
(570) 648-5752 • http://www.indians.k12.pa.us
Grade Span: PK-12; Agency Type: 1
Schools: 2
  1 Primary; 0 Middle; 1 High; 0 Other Level
  2 Regular; 0 Special Education; 0 Vocational; 0 Alternative
  0 Magnet; 0 Charter; 2 Title I Eligible; 0 School-wide Title I
Students: 2,556   (n/a% male; n/a% female)
  Individual Education Program: 381 (14.9%);
  English Language Learner: n/a; Migrant: 0 (0.0%)
  Eligible for Free Lunch Program: 868 (34.0%)
  Eligible for Reduced-Price Lunch Program: 325 (12.7%)
Teachers: 148.0 (17.3 to 1)
Librarians/Media Specialists: 2.0 (1,278.0 to 1)
Guidance Counselors: 4.0 (639.0 to 1)
Current Spending: ($ per student per year):
  Total: $8,090; Instruction: $5,882; Support Services: $1,866

Enrollment, Drop-out Rates and Diploma Recipients by Race/Ethnicity

Category	Total	White	Black	Asian	AIAN	Hisp.
Enrollment (%)	100.0	98.1	0.3	0.2	0.0	1.4
Drop-out Rate (%)	2.2	2.2	n/a	0.0	n/a	0.0
H.S. Diplomas (#)	174	170	0	2	0	2

Shikellamy SD

200 Island Blvd • Sunbury, PA 17801-1028
(570) 286-3720 • http://www.shikbraves.org/
Grade Span: KG-12; Agency Type: 1
Schools: 7
  4 Primary; 2 Middle; 1 High; 0 Other Level
  7 Regular; 0 Special Education; 0 Vocational; 0 Alternative
  0 Magnet; 0 Charter; 5 Title I Eligible; 0 School-wide Title I
Students: 3,270   (n/a% male; n/a% female)
  Individual Education Program: 314 (9.6%);
  English Language Learner: n/a; Migrant: 10 (0.3%)
  Eligible for Free Lunch Program: 648 (19.8%)
  Eligible for Reduced-Price Lunch Program: 285 (8.7%)
Teachers: 201.5 (16.2 to 1)
Librarians/Media Specialists: 5.0 (654.0 to 1)
Guidance Counselors: 7.0 (467.1 to 1)
Current Spending: ($ per student per year):
  Total: $7,141; Instruction: $4,785; Support Services: $2,039

Enrollment, Drop-out Rates and Diploma Recipients by Race/Ethnicity

Category	Total	White	Black	Asian	AIAN	Hisp.
Enrollment (%)	100.0	93.6	2.2	0.5	0.0	3.7
Drop-out Rate (%)	4.3	3.7	23.1	0.0	n/a	19.2
H.S. Diplomas (#)	241	233	3	1	0	4

Warrior Run SD

4800 Susquehanna Tr • Turbotville, PA 17772-9766
(570) 649-5138 • http://www.wrsd.org
Grade Span: KG-12; Agency Type: 1
Schools: 4

---

  2 Primary; 1 Middle; 1 High; 0 Other Level
  4 Regular; 0 Special Education; 0 Vocational; 0 Alternative
  0 Magnet; 0 Charter; 3 Title I Eligible; 0 School-wide Title I
Students: 1,860   (n/a% male; n/a% female)
  Individual Education Program: 240 (12.9%);
  English Language Learner: n/a; Migrant: 0 (0.0%)
  Eligible for Free Lunch Program: 238 (12.8%)
  Eligible for Reduced-Price Lunch Program: 140 (7.5%)
Teachers: 136.2 (13.7 to 1)
Librarians/Media Specialists: 3.0 (620.0 to 1)
Guidance Counselors: 6.0 (310.0 to 1)
Current Spending: ($ per student per year):
  Total: $8,041; Instruction: $5,341; Support Services: $2,378

Enrollment, Drop-out Rates and Diploma Recipients by Race/Ethnicity

Category	Total	White	Black	Asian	AIAN	Hisp.
Enrollment (%)	100.0	97.8	1.2	0.4	0.0	0.5
Drop-out Rate (%)	2.8	2.8	0.0	0.0	n/a	0.0
H.S. Diplomas (#)	148	146	0	2	0	0

Perry County

Susquenita SD

1725 Schoolhouse Rd • Duncannon, PA 17020-9582
(717) 957-2303 • http://www.susq.k12.pa.us
Grade Span: KG-12; Agency Type: 1
Schools: 3
  1 Primary; 1 Middle; 1 High; 0 Other Level
  3 Regular; 0 Special Education; 0 Vocational; 0 Alternative
  0 Magnet; 0 Charter; 3 Title I Eligible; 0 School-wide Title I
Students: 2,283   (n/a% male; n/a% female)
  Individual Education Program: 396 (17.3%);
  English Language Learner: n/a; Migrant: 0 (0.0%)
  Eligible for Free Lunch Program: 295 (12.9%)
  Eligible for Reduced-Price Lunch Program: 174 (7.6%)
Teachers: 149.0 (15.3 to 1)
Librarians/Media Specialists: 2.0 (1,141.5 to 1)
Guidance Counselors: 5.0 (456.6 to 1)
Current Spending: ($ per student per year):
  Total: $7,385; Instruction: $4,389; Support Services: $2,648

Enrollment, Drop-out Rates and Diploma Recipients by Race/Ethnicity

Category	Total	White	Black	Asian	AIAN	Hisp.
Enrollment (%)	100.0	97.9	0.9	0.4	0.0	0.7
Drop-out Rate (%)	4.2	4.3	0.0	0.0	0.0	0.0
H.S. Diplomas (#)	149	146	0	1	0	2

West Perry SD

2606 Shermans Valley Rd • Elliottsburg, PA 17024-9706
(717) 789-3934
Grade Span: KG-12; Agency Type: 1
Schools: 6
  3 Primary; 1 Middle; 2 High; 0 Other Level
  5 Regular; 1 Special Education; 0 Vocational; 0 Alternative
  0 Magnet; 0 Charter; 5 Title I Eligible; 0 School-wide Title I
Students: 2,849   (n/a% male; n/a% female)
  Individual Education Program: 506 (17.8%);
  English Language Learner: n/a; Migrant: 0 (0.0%)
  Eligible for Free Lunch Program: 404 (14.2%)
  Eligible for Reduced-Price Lunch Program: 141 (4.9%)
Teachers: 208.1 (13.7 to 1)
Librarians/Media Specialists: 4.0 (712.3 to 1)
Guidance Counselors: 7.8 (365.3 to 1)
Current Spending: ($ per student per year):
  Total: $7,243; Instruction: $4,399; Support Services: $2,534

Enrollment, Drop-out Rates and Diploma Recipients by Race/Ethnicity

Category	Total	White	Black	Asian	AIAN	Hisp.
Enrollment (%)	100.0	98.1	1.2	0.1	0.0	0.6
Drop-out Rate (%)	2.7	2.5	0.0	50.0	n/a	0.0
H.S. Diplomas (#)	173	171	0	1	0	1

Philadelphia County

Philadelphia City SD

Pkwy At 21st St • Philadelphia, PA 19103-1099
(215) 299-7000 • http://www.philsch.k12.pa.us
Grade Span: KG-12; Agency Type: 1
Schools: 263
  173 Primary; 42 Middle; 39 High; 9 Other Level
  254 Regular; 4 Special Education; 5 Vocational; 0 Alternative
  11 Magnet; 0 Charter; 257 Title I Eligible; 217 School-wide Title I
Students: 189,779   (n/a% male; n/a% female)
  Individual Education Program: 23,604 (12.4%);
  English Language Learner: n/a; Migrant: 727 (0.4%)
  Eligible for Free Lunch Program: 121,650 (64.1%)
  Eligible for Reduced-Price Lunch Program: 13,315 (7.0%)
Teachers: 10,194.0 (18.6 to 1)

Librarians/Media Specialists: 101.0 (1,879.0 to 1)
Guidance Counselors: 365.0 (519.9 to 1)
Current Spending: ($ per student per year):
   Total: $7,554; Instruction: $4,333; Support Services: $2,848
Enrollment, Drop-out Rates and Diploma Recipients by Race/Ethnicity

Category	Total	White	Black	Asian	AIAN	Hisp.
Enrollment (%)	100.0	14.6	65.2	5.3	0.2	14.7
Drop-out Rate (%)	9.8	9.2	9.9	6.7	5.0	12.2
H.S. Diplomas (#)	8,559	1,879	5,193	684	12	791

Pike County

Delaware Valley SD
236 Route 6 And 209 • Milford, PA 18337-9454
(570) 296-1800 • http://dvasdweb.dvasd.k12.pa.us
Grade Span: KG-12; **Agency Type:** 1
Schools: 7
   4 Primary; 2 Middle; 1 High; 0 Other Level
   7 Regular; 0 Special Education; 0 Vocational; 0 Alternative
   0 Magnet; 0 Charter; 4 Title I Eligible; 0 School-wide Title I
Students: 5,378 (n/a% male; n/a% female)
   Individual Education Program: 545 (10.1%);
   English Language Learner: n/a; Migrant: 0 (0.0%)
   Eligible for Free Lunch Program: 563 (10.5%)
   Eligible for Reduced-Price Lunch Program: 289 (5.4%)
Teachers: 325.1 (16.5 to 1)
Librarians/Media Specialists: 6.0 (896.3 to 1)
Guidance Counselors: 12.0 (448.2 to 1)
Current Spending: ($ per student per year):
   Total: $7,407; Instruction: $4,918; Support Services: $2,304
Enrollment, Drop-out Rates and Diploma Recipients by Race/Ethnicity

Category	Total	White	Black	Asian	AIAN	Hisp.
Enrollment (%)	100.0	91.6	3.0	1.0	0.2	4.2
Drop-out Rate (%)	1.2	1.2	0.0	0.0	n/a	2.3
H.S. Diplomas (#)	322	304	7	2	0	9

Schuylkill County

Blue Mountain SD
PO Box 188 • Orwigsburg, PA 17961-0279
(570) 366-0515
Grade Span: KG-12; **Agency Type:** 1
Schools: 5
   3 Primary; 1 Middle; 1 High; 0 Other Level
   5 Regular; 0 Special Education; 0 Vocational; 0 Alternative
   0 Magnet; 0 Charter; 5 Title I Eligible; 0 School-wide Title I
Students: 2,916 (n/a% male; n/a% female)
   Individual Education Program: 400 (13.7%);
   English Language Learner: n/a; Migrant: 0 (0.0%)
   Eligible for Free Lunch Program: 243 (8.3%)
   Eligible for Reduced-Price Lunch Program: 145 (5.0%)
Teachers: 188.5 (15.5 to 1)
Librarians/Media Specialists: 4.0 (729.0 to 1)
Guidance Counselors: 7.0 (416.6 to 1)
Current Spending: ($ per student per year):
   Total: $6,829; Instruction: $4,009; Support Services: $2,516
Enrollment, Drop-out Rates and Diploma Recipients by Race/Ethnicity

Category	Total	White	Black	Asian	AIAN	Hisp.
Enrollment (%)	100.0	96.0	1.1	1.6	0.0	1.2
Drop-out Rate (%)	1.3	1.4	0.0	0.0	n/a	0.0
H.S. Diplomas (#)	206	200	0	6	0	0

North Schuylkill SD
15 Academy Ln Route 61 • Ashland, PA 17921-9301
(570) 874-0466 • http://www.north-schuylkill.k12.pa.us
Grade Span: KG-12; **Agency Type:** 1
Schools: 4
   3 Primary; 0 Middle; 1 High; 0 Other Level
   4 Regular; 0 Special Education; 0 Vocational; 0 Alternative
   0 Magnet; 0 Charter; 4 Title I Eligible; 0 School-wide Title I
Students: 1,994 (n/a% male; n/a% female)
   Individual Education Program: 334 (16.8%);
   English Language Learner: n/a; Migrant: 0 (0.0%)
   Eligible for Free Lunch Program: 432 (21.7%)
   Eligible for Reduced-Price Lunch Program: 214 (10.7%)
Teachers: 107.0 (18.6 to 1)
Librarians/Media Specialists: 2.0 (997.0 to 1)
Guidance Counselors: 4.0 (498.5 to 1)
Current Spending: ($ per student per year):
   Total: $6,888; Instruction: $4,394; Support Services: $2,160
Enrollment, Drop-out Rates and Diploma Recipients by Race/Ethnicity

Category	Total	White	Black	Asian	AIAN	Hisp.
Enrollment (%)	100.0	98.4	0.8	0.2	0.1	0.6
Drop-out Rate (%)	2.5	2.5	0.0	0.0	n/a	0.0
H.S. Diplomas (#)	147	147	0	0	0	0

Pine Grove Area SD
103 School St • Pine Grove, PA 17963-1698
(570) 345-2731 • http://www.pgasd.com
Grade Span: KG-12; **Agency Type:** 1
Schools: 3
   1 Primary; 1 Middle; 1 High; 0 Other Level
   3 Regular; 0 Special Education; 0 Vocational; 0 Alternative
   0 Magnet; 0 Charter; 2 Title I Eligible; 0 School-wide Title I
Students: 1,758 (n/a% male; n/a% female)
   Individual Education Program: 204 (11.6%);
   English Language Learner: n/a; Migrant: 0 (0.0%)
   Eligible for Free Lunch Program: 240 (13.7%)
   Eligible for Reduced-Price Lunch Program: 90 (5.1%)
Teachers: 101.0 (17.4 to 1)
Librarians/Media Specialists: 3.0 (586.0 to 1)
Guidance Counselors: 5.0 (351.6 to 1)
Current Spending: ($ per student per year):
   Total: $6,852; Instruction: $4,048; Support Services: $2,454
Enrollment, Drop-out Rates and Diploma Recipients by Race/Ethnicity

Category	Total	White	Black	Asian	AIAN	Hisp.
Enrollment (%)	100.0	98.7	0.9	0.2	0.1	0.2
Drop-out Rate (%)	2.9	2.9	0.0	n/a	n/a	0.0
H.S. Diplomas (#)	138	136	1	1	0	0

Pottsville Area SD
1501 Laurel Blvd • Pottsville, PA 17901-1498
(570) 621-2900 • http://www.pottsville.k12.pa.us
Grade Span: KG-12; **Agency Type:** 1
Schools: 3
   1 Primary; 1 Middle; 1 High; 0 Other Level
   3 Regular; 0 Special Education; 0 Vocational; 0 Alternative
   0 Magnet; 0 Charter; 2 Title I Eligible; 0 School-wide Title I
Students: 3,060 (n/a% male; n/a% female)
   Individual Education Program: 424 (13.9%);
   English Language Learner: n/a; Migrant: 0 (0.0%)
   Eligible for Free Lunch Program: 710 (23.2%)
   Eligible for Reduced-Price Lunch Program: 206 (6.7%)
Teachers: 159.0 (19.2 to 1)
Librarians/Media Specialists: 3.0 (1,020.0 to 1)
Guidance Counselors: 4.5 (680.0 to 1)
Current Spending: ($ per student per year):
   Total: $6,754; Instruction: $4,200; Support Services: $2,177
Enrollment, Drop-out Rates and Diploma Recipients by Race/Ethnicity

Category	Total	White	Black	Asian	AIAN	Hisp.
Enrollment (%)	100.0	94.1	3.5	0.9	0.3	1.2
Drop-out Rate (%)	5.7	5.4	13.6	10.0	0.0	13.3
H.S. Diplomas (#)	261	246	6	2	1	6

Tamaqua Area SD
PO Box 112 • Tamaqua, PA 18252-0112
(570) 668-2570
Grade Span: KG-12; **Agency Type:** 1
Schools: 5
   3 Primary; 1 Middle; 1 High; 0 Other Level
   5 Regular; 0 Special Education; 0 Vocational; 0 Alternative
   0 Magnet; 0 Charter; 1 Title I Eligible; 0 School-wide Title I
Students: 2,218 (n/a% male; n/a% female)
   Individual Education Program: 356 (16.1%);
   English Language Learner: n/a; Migrant: 0 (0.0%)
   Eligible for Free Lunch Program: 218 (9.8%)
   Eligible for Reduced-Price Lunch Program: 135 (6.1%)
Teachers: 127.9 (17.3 to 1)
Librarians/Media Specialists: 3.0 (739.3 to 1)
Guidance Counselors: 5.0 (443.6 to 1)
Current Spending: ($ per student per year):
   Total: $6,784; Instruction: $4,167; Support Services: $2,323
Enrollment, Drop-out Rates and Diploma Recipients by Race/Ethnicity

Category	Total	White	Black	Asian	AIAN	Hisp.
Enrollment (%)	100.0	96.9	1.1	0.5	0.0	1.5
Drop-out Rate (%)	4.0	3.6	28.6	0.0	n/a	14.3
H.S. Diplomas (#)	132	129	2	1	0	0

Snyder County

Midd-West SD
568 E Main St • Middleburg, PA 17842-1295
(570) 837-0046 • http://www.midd-westsd.k12.pa.us
Grade Span: KG-12; **Agency Type:** 1
Schools: 7
   5 Primary; 0 Middle; 2 High; 0 Other Level
   7 Regular; 0 Special Education; 0 Vocational; 0 Alternative
   0 Magnet; 0 Charter; 5 Title I Eligible; 0 School-wide Title I
Students: 2,486 (n/a% male; n/a% female)
   Individual Education Program: 398 (16.0%);
   English Language Learner: n/a; Migrant: 1 (<0.1%)

Eligible for Free Lunch Program: 483 (19.4%)
Eligible for Reduced-Price Lunch Program: 266 (10.7%)
Teachers: 174.5 (14.2 to 1)
Librarians/Media Specialists: 4.0 (621.5 to 1)
Guidance Counselors: 7.0 (355.1 to 1)
Current Spending: ($ per student per year):
Total: $7,673; Instruction: $4,815; Support Services: $2,492
Enrollment, Drop-out Rates and Diploma Recipients by Race/Ethnicity

Category	Total	White	Black	Asian	AIAN	Hisp.
Enrollment (%)	100.0	98.4	1.0	0.1	0.1	0.4
Drop-out Rate (%)	3.0	3.0	0.0	0.0	n/a	0.0
H.S. Diplomas (#)	174	173	0	1	0	0

Selinsgrove Area SD

401 N 18th St • Selinsgrove, PA 17870-1153
(570) 374-1144 • http://www.selinsgroveasd.k12.pa.us
Grade Span: KG-12; **Agency Type:** 1
Schools: 5
3 Primary; 1 Middle; 1 High; 0 Other Level
5 Regular; 0 Special Education; 0 Vocational; 0 Alternative
0 Magnet; 0 Charter; 3 Title I Eligible; 0 School-wide Title I
Students: 2,890 (n/a% male; n/a% female)
Individual Education Program: 346 (12.0%);
English Language Learner: n/a; Migrant: 0 (0.0%)
Eligible for Free Lunch Program: 486 (16.8%)
Eligible for Reduced-Price Lunch Program: 245 (8.5%)
Teachers: 182.0 (15.9 to 1)
Librarians/Media Specialists: 4.0 (722.5 to 1)
Guidance Counselors: 8.0 (361.3 to 1)
Current Spending: ($ per student per year):
Total: $7,487; Instruction: $4,902; Support Services: $2,294
Enrollment, Drop-out Rates and Diploma Recipients by Race/Ethnicity

Category	Total	White	Black	Asian	AIAN	Hisp.
Enrollment (%)	100.0	94.2	2.7	0.9	0.2	1.9
Drop-out Rate (%)	1.6	1.6	0.0	0.0	n/a	0.0
H.S. Diplomas (#)	203	198	0	2	0	3

Somerset County

Somerset Area SD

645 S Columbia Ave Ste 110 • Somerset, PA 15501-2511
(814) 445-9714
Grade Span: KG-12; **Agency Type:** 1
Schools: 6
3 Primary; 2 Middle; 1 High; 0 Other Level
6 Regular; 0 Special Education; 0 Vocational; 0 Alternative
0 Magnet; 0 Charter; 4 Title I Eligible; 0 School-wide Title I
Students: 2,751 (n/a% male; n/a% female)
Individual Education Program: 397 (14.4%);
English Language Learner: n/a; Migrant: 0 (0.0%)
Eligible for Free Lunch Program: 571 (20.8%)
Eligible for Reduced-Price Lunch Program: 188 (6.8%)
Teachers: 169.4 (16.2 to 1)
Librarians/Media Specialists: 2.0 (1,375.5 to 1)
Guidance Counselors: 5.0 (550.2 to 1)
Current Spending: ($ per student per year):
Total: $7,071; Instruction: $4,399; Support Services: $2,370
Enrollment, Drop-out Rates and Diploma Recipients by Race/Ethnicity

Category	Total	White	Black	Asian	AIAN	Hisp.
Enrollment (%)	100.0	97.8	1.1	0.9	0.1	0.2
Drop-out Rate (%)	3.1	3.2	0.0	0.0	0.0	0.0
H.S. Diplomas (#)	212	209	1	2	0	0

Susquehanna County

Elk Lake SD

PO Box 100 • Dimock, PA 18816-0100
(570) 278-1106
Grade Span: KG-12; **Agency Type:** 1
Schools: 2
1 Primary; 0 Middle; 1 High; 0 Other Level
2 Regular; 0 Special Education; 0 Vocational; 0 Alternative
0 Magnet; 0 Charter; 2 Title I Eligible; 0 School-wide Title I
Students: 1,509 (n/a% male; n/a% female)
Individual Education Program: 233 (15.4%);
English Language Learner: n/a; Migrant: 7 (0.5%)
Eligible for Free Lunch Program: 309 (20.5%)
Eligible for Reduced-Price Lunch Program: 93 (6.2%)
Teachers: 103.9 (14.5 to 1)
Librarians/Media Specialists: 2.0 (754.5 to 1)
Guidance Counselors: 3.0 (503.0 to 1)
Current Spending: ($ per student per year):
Total: $7,662; Instruction: $4,948; Support Services: $2,350

Montrose Area SD

80 High School Rd • Montrose, PA 18801-9501
(570) 278-3731
Grade Span: KG-12; **Agency Type:** 1
Schools: 3
2 Primary; 0 Middle; 1 High; 0 Other Level
3 Regular; 0 Special Education; 0 Vocational; 0 Alternative
0 Magnet; 0 Charter; 1 Title I Eligible; 0 School-wide Title I
Students: 1,917 (n/a% male; n/a% female)
Individual Education Program: 390 (20.3%);
English Language Learner: n/a; Migrant: 1 (0.1%)
Eligible for Free Lunch Program: 366 (19.1%)
Eligible for Reduced-Price Lunch Program: 185 (9.7%)
Teachers: 128.0 (15.0 to 1)
Librarians/Media Specialists: 3.0 (639.0 to 1)
Guidance Counselors: 5.0 (383.4 to 1)
Current Spending: ($ per student per year):
Total: $8,170; Instruction: $5,135; Support Services: $2,730
Enrollment, Drop-out Rates and Diploma Recipients by Race/Ethnicity

Category	Total	White	Black	Asian	AIAN	Hisp.
Enrollment (%)	100.0	97.8	0.8	0.5	0.2	0.7
Drop-out Rate (%)	2.3	2.4	0.0	0.0	n/a	0.0
H.S. Diplomas (#)	121	119	1	1	0	0

Tioga County

Northern Tioga SD

117 Coates Ave • Elkland, PA 16920-1305
(814) 258-5642
Grade Span: KG-12; **Agency Type:** 1
Schools: 6
3 Primary; 0 Middle; 3 High; 0 Other Level
6 Regular; 0 Special Education; 0 Vocational; 0 Alternative
0 Magnet; 0 Charter; 6 Title I Eligible; 0 School-wide Title I
Students: 2,553 (n/a% male; n/a% female)
Individual Education Program: 318 (12.5%);
English Language Learner: n/a; Migrant: 17 (0.7%)
Eligible for Free Lunch Program: 895 (35.1%)
Eligible for Reduced-Price Lunch Program: 325 (12.7%)
Teachers: 200.0 (12.8 to 1)
Librarians/Media Specialists: 4.0 (638.3 to 1)
Guidance Counselors: 4.0 (638.3 to 1)
Current Spending: ($ per student per year):
Total: $8,221; Instruction: $5,178; Support Services: $2,643
Enrollment, Drop-out Rates and Diploma Recipients by Race/Ethnicity

Category	Total	White	Black	Asian	AIAN	Hisp.
Enrollment (%)	100.0	97.9	0.7	0.3	0.2	0.9
Drop-out Rate (%)	2.8	2.7	14.3	0.0	n/a	0.0
H.S. Diplomas (#)	158	155	1	1	0	1

Southern Tioga SD

241 Main St • Blossburg, PA 16912-1125
(570) 638-2183
Grade Span: KG-12; **Agency Type:** 1
Schools: 6
3 Primary; 0 Middle; 3 High; 0 Other Level
6 Regular; 0 Special Education; 0 Vocational; 0 Alternative
0 Magnet; 0 Charter; 4 Title I Eligible; 0 School-wide Title I
Students: 2,228 (n/a% male; n/a% female)
Individual Education Program: 293 (13.2%);
English Language Learner: n/a; Migrant: 24 (1.1%)
Eligible for Free Lunch Program: 627 (28.1%)
Eligible for Reduced-Price Lunch Program: 302 (13.6%)
Teachers: 156.7 (14.2 to 1)
Librarians/Media Specialists: 5.0 (445.6 to 1)
Guidance Counselors: 6.0 (371.3 to 1)
Current Spending: ($ per student per year):
Total: $7,923; Instruction: $4,929; Support Services: $2,619
Enrollment, Drop-out Rates and Diploma Recipients by Race/Ethnicity

Category	Total	White	Black	Asian	AIAN	Hisp.
Enrollment (%)	100.0	97.7	1.0	0.9	0.2	0.3
Drop-out Rate (%)	2.4	2.5	0.0	n/a	0.0	0.0
H.S. Diplomas (#)	174	174	0	0	0	0

Wellsboro Area SD

2 Charles St • Wellsboro, PA 16901-1401
(570) 724-4424 • http://www.wellsborosd.k12.pa.us
Grade Span: KG-12; **Agency Type:** 1
Schools: 4

2 Primary; 1 Middle; 1 High; 0 Other Level
4 Regular; 0 Special Education; 0 Vocational; 0 Alternative
0 Magnet; 0 Charter; 3 Title I Eligible; 0 School-wide Title I
Students: 1,660   (n/a% male; n/a% female)
Individual Education Program: 196 (11.8%);
English Language Learner: n/a; Migrant: 9 (0.5%)
Eligible for Free Lunch Program: 382 (23.0%)
Eligible for Reduced-Price Lunch Program: 165 (9.9%)
Teachers: 121.0 (13.7 to 1)
Librarians/Media Specialists: 3.0 (553.3 to 1)
Guidance Counselors: 4.0 (415.0 to 1)
Current Spending: ($ per student per year):
Total: $8,770; Instruction: $5,616; Support Services: $2,823
Enrollment, Drop-out Rates and Diploma Recipients by Race/Ethnicity

Category	Total	White	Black	Asian	AIAN	Hisp.
Enrollment (%)	100.0	95.8	1.1	1.1	0.2	1.7
Drop-out Rate (%)	2.9	3.1	0.0	0.0	n/a	0.0
H.S. Diplomas (#)	147	145	0	0	0	2

Union County

Lewisburg Area SD
PO Box 351 • Lewisburg, PA 17837-0351
(570) 523-3220 • http://www.dragon.k12.pa.us
Grade Span: KG-12; **Agency Type:** 1
Schools: 4
1 Primary; 2 Middle; 1 High; 0 Other Level
4 Regular; 0 Special Education; 0 Vocational; 0 Alternative
0 Magnet; 0 Charter; 3 Title I Eligible; 0 School-wide Title I
Students: 1,788   (n/a% male; n/a% female)
Individual Education Program: 159 (8.9%);
English Language Learner: n/a; Migrant: 0 (0.0%)
Eligible for Free Lunch Program: 172 (9.6%)
Eligible for Reduced-Price Lunch Program: 57 (3.2%)
Teachers: 122.2 (14.6 to 1)
Librarians/Media Specialists: 4.0 (447.0 to 1)
Guidance Counselors: 7.0 (255.4 to 1)
Current Spending: ($ per student per year):
Total: $8,141; Instruction: $5,105; Support Services: $2,791
Enrollment, Drop-out Rates and Diploma Recipients by Race/Ethnicity

Category	Total	White	Black	Asian	AIAN	Hisp.
Enrollment (%)	100.0	91.8	3.9	2.0	0.0	2.3
Drop-out Rate (%)	1.9	2.0	0.0	0.0	0.0	0.0
H.S. Diplomas (#)	154	148	3	2	0	1

Mifflinburg Area SD
PO Box 285 • Mifflinburg, PA 17844-0285
(570) 966-8200 • http://www.mifflinburg.org
Grade Span: KG-12; **Agency Type:** 1
Schools: 6
4 Primary; 1 Middle; 1 High; 0 Other Level
6 Regular; 0 Special Education; 0 Vocational; 0 Alternative
0 Magnet; 0 Charter; 4 Title I Eligible; 0 School-wide Title I
Students: 2,549   (n/a% male; n/a% female)
Individual Education Program: 271 (10.6%);
English Language Learner: n/a; Migrant: 0 (0.0%)
Eligible for Free Lunch Program: 400 (15.7%)
Eligible for Reduced-Price Lunch Program: 179 (7.0%)
Teachers: 152.1 (16.8 to 1)
Librarians/Media Specialists: 3.0 (849.7 to 1)
Guidance Counselors: 4.0 (637.3 to 1)
Current Spending: ($ per student per year):
Total: $6,526; Instruction: $4,174; Support Services: $2,074
Enrollment, Drop-out Rates and Diploma Recipients by Race/Ethnicity

Category	Total	White	Black	Asian	AIAN	Hisp.
Enrollment (%)	100.0	97.2	1.7	0.2	0.2	0.7
Drop-out Rate (%)	1.9	1.8	100.0	0.0	0.0	0.0
H.S. Diplomas (#)	174	173	0	1	0	0

Venango County

Franklin Area SD
417 13th St • Franklin, PA 16323-1310
(814) 432-8917 • http://www.fasd.k12.pa.us
Grade Span: KG-12; **Agency Type:** 1
Schools: 8
6 Primary; 1 Middle; 1 High; 0 Other Level
8 Regular; 0 Special Education; 0 Vocational; 0 Alternative
0 Magnet; 0 Charter; 7 Title I Eligible; 0 School-wide Title I
Students: 2,332   (n/a% male; n/a% female)
Individual Education Program: 506 (21.7%);
English Language Learner: n/a; Migrant: 0 (0.0%)
Eligible for Free Lunch Program: 637 (27.3%)
Eligible for Reduced-Price Lunch Program: 157 (6.7%)
Teachers: 165.5 (14.1 to 1)

Librarians/Media Specialists: 2.8 (832.9 to 1)
Guidance Counselors: 4.0 (583.0 to 1)
Current Spending: ($ per student per year):
Total: $9,373; Instruction: $6,122; Support Services: $2,957
Enrollment, Drop-out Rates and Diploma Recipients by Race/Ethnicity

Category	Total	White	Black	Asian	AIAN	Hisp.
Enrollment (%)	100.0	93.5	5.2	0.7	0.1	0.5
Drop-out Rate (%)	3.9	4.0	0.0	n/a	0.0	0.0
H.S. Diplomas (#)	196	189	5	1	0	1

Oil City Area SD
825 Grandview Rd • Oil City, PA 16301-0929
(814) 676-1867 • http://www.oilcitysd@mail.ocasd.org
Grade Span: KG-12; **Agency Type:** 1
Schools: 6
4 Primary; 1 Middle; 1 High; 0 Other Level
6 Regular; 0 Special Education; 0 Vocational; 0 Alternative
0 Magnet; 0 Charter; 5 Title I Eligible; 1 School-wide Title I
Students: 2,504   (n/a% male; n/a% female)
Individual Education Program: 540 (21.6%);
English Language Learner: n/a; Migrant: 0 (0.0%)
Eligible for Free Lunch Program: 898 (35.9%)
Eligible for Reduced-Price Lunch Program: 197 (7.9%)
Teachers: 148.0 (16.9 to 1)
Librarians/Media Specialists: 3.0 (834.7 to 1)
Guidance Counselors: 4.0 (626.0 to 1)
Current Spending: ($ per student per year):
Total: $7,612; Instruction: $4,622; Support Services: $2,707
Enrollment, Drop-out Rates and Diploma Recipients by Race/Ethnicity

Category	Total	White	Black	Asian	AIAN	Hisp.
Enrollment (%)	100.0	96.2	2.1	0.4	0.3	1.0
Drop-out Rate (%)	6.0	6.2	0.0	0.0	0.0	0.0
H.S. Diplomas (#)	172	169	1	0	1	1

Titusville Area SD
221 N Washington St • Titusville, PA 16354-1785
(814) 827-2715 • http://www.gorockets.org
Grade Span: PK-12; **Agency Type:** 1
Schools: 7
5 Primary; 1 Middle; 1 High; 0 Other Level
7 Regular; 0 Special Education; 0 Vocational; 0 Alternative
0 Magnet; 0 Charter; 0 Title I Eligible; 0 School-wide Title I
Students: 2,457   (n/a% male; n/a% female)
Individual Education Program: 457 (18.6%);
English Language Learner: n/a; Migrant: 0 (0.0%)
Eligible for Free Lunch Program: 678 (27.6%)
Eligible for Reduced-Price Lunch Program: 170 (6.9%)
Teachers: 157.2 (15.6 to 1)
Librarians/Media Specialists: 3.0 (819.0 to 1)
Guidance Counselors: 4.0 (614.3 to 1)
Current Spending: ($ per student per year):
Total: $7,428; Instruction: $4,594; Support Services: $2,505
Enrollment, Drop-out Rates and Diploma Recipients by Race/Ethnicity

Category	Total	White	Black	Asian	AIAN	Hisp.
Enrollment (%)	100.0	98.1	0.7	0.2	0.2	0.8
Drop-out Rate (%)	2.7	2.7	0.0	0.0	n/a	0.0
H.S. Diplomas (#)	162	161	0	0	0	1

Warren County

Warren County SD
185 Hospital Dr • North Warren, PA 16365-4885
(814) 723-6900 • http://www.wcsdpa.org/
Grade Span: KG-12; **Agency Type:** 1
Schools: 19
13 Primary; 2 Middle; 3 High; 1 Other Level
19 Regular; 0 Special Education; 0 Vocational; 0 Alternative
0 Magnet; 0 Charter; 11 Title I Eligible; 0 School-wide Title I
Students: 6,120   (n/a% male; n/a% female)
Individual Education Program: 1,093 (17.9%);
English Language Learner: n/a; Migrant: 0 (0.0%)
Eligible for Free Lunch Program: 1,202 (19.6%)
Eligible for Reduced-Price Lunch Program: 421 (6.9%)
Teachers: 414.3 (14.8 to 1)
Librarians/Media Specialists: 10.0 (612.0 to 1)
Guidance Counselors: 16.0 (382.5 to 1)
Current Spending: ($ per student per year):
Total: $8,003; Instruction: $4,882; Support Services: $2,872
Enrollment, Drop-out Rates and Diploma Recipients by Race/Ethnicity

Category	Total	White	Black	Asian	AIAN	Hisp.
Enrollment (%)	100.0	98.0	0.7	0.8	0.3	0.3
Drop-out Rate (%)	2.8	2.8	25.0	0.0	0.0	0.0
H.S. Diplomas (#)	499	489	0	4	3	3

Washington County

Burgettstown Area SD
100 Bavington Rd • Burgettstown, PA 15021-2727
(724) 947-3324 • http://www.burgettstown.k12.pa.us
Grade Span: KG-12; **Agency Type:** 1
Schools: 2
  1 Primary; 0 Middle; 1 High; 0 Other Level
  2 Regular; 0 Special Education; 0 Vocational; 0 Alternative
  0 Magnet; 0 Charter; 2 Title I Eligible; 0 School-wide Title I
Students: 1,544   (n/a% male; n/a% female)
  Individual Education Program: 250 (16.2%);
  English Language Learner: n/a; Migrant: 0 (0.0%)
  Eligible for Free Lunch Program: 337 (21.8%)
  Eligible for Reduced-Price Lunch Program: 117 (7.6%)
Teachers: 101.0 (15.3 to 1)
Librarians/Media Specialists: 2.0 (772.0 to 1)
Guidance Counselors: 4.0 (386.0 to 1)
Current Spending: ($ per student per year):
  Total: $7,118; Instruction: $4,744; Support Services: $2,043
Enrollment, Drop-out Rates and Diploma Recipients by Race/Ethnicity

Category	Total	White	Black	Asian	AIAN	Hisp.
Enrollment (%)	100.0	97.1	2.4	0.1	0.2	0.2
Drop-out Rate (%)	5.5	5.2	25.0	0.0	n/a	0.0
H.S. Diplomas (#)	88	86	2	0	0	0

Canon-Mcmillan SD
1 N Jefferson Ave • Canonsburg, PA 15317-1305
(724) 746-2940 • http://www.cmsd.k12.pa.us
Grade Span: KG-12; **Agency Type:** 1
Schools: 11
  7 Primary; 3 Middle; 1 High; 0 Other Level
  11 Regular; 0 Special Education; 0 Vocational; 0 Alternative
  0 Magnet; 0 Charter; 4 Title I Eligible; 0 School-wide Title I
Students: 4,325   (n/a% male; n/a% female)
  Individual Education Program: 484 (11.2%);
  English Language Learner: n/a; Migrant: 6 (0.1%)
  Eligible for Free Lunch Program: 557 (12.9%)
  Eligible for Reduced-Price Lunch Program: 235 (5.4%)
Teachers: 267.5 (16.2 to 1)
Librarians/Media Specialists: 5.0 (865.0 to 1)
Guidance Counselors: 10.0 (432.5 to 1)
Current Spending: ($ per student per year):
  Total: $8,177; Instruction: $5,073; Support Services: $2,776
Enrollment, Drop-out Rates and Diploma Recipients by Race/Ethnicity

Category	Total	White	Black	Asian	AIAN	Hisp.
Enrollment (%)	100.0	92.6	6.1	0.6	0.3	0.4
Drop-out Rate (%)	2.0	1.8	3.3	0.0	0.0	25.0
H.S. Diplomas (#)	244	230	12	2	0	0

Charleroi SD
125 Fecsen Dr • Charleroi, PA 15022-2279
(724) 483-3509
Grade Span: KG-12; **Agency Type:** 1
Schools: 3
  1 Primary; 1 Middle; 1 High; 0 Other Level
  3 Regular; 0 Special Education; 0 Vocational; 0 Alternative
  0 Magnet; 0 Charter; 3 Title I Eligible; 0 School-wide Title I
Students: 1,668   (n/a% male; n/a% female)
  Individual Education Program: 309 (18.5%);
  English Language Learner: n/a; Migrant: 0 (0.0%)
  Eligible for Free Lunch Program: 454 (27.2%)
  Eligible for Reduced-Price Lunch Program: 86 (5.2%)
Teachers: 117.5 (14.2 to 1)
Librarians/Media Specialists: 2.0 (834.0 to 1)
Guidance Counselors: 5.0 (333.6 to 1)
Current Spending: ($ per student per year):
  Total: $6,814; Instruction: $4,163; Support Services: $2,376
Enrollment, Drop-out Rates and Diploma Recipients by Race/Ethnicity

Category	Total	White	Black	Asian	AIAN	Hisp.
Enrollment (%)	100.0	95.6	4.0	0.1	0.1	0.3
Drop-out Rate (%)	2.0	1.9	6.7	0.0	n/a	n/a
H.S. Diplomas (#)	120	118	2	0	0	0

Mcguffey SD
PO Box 431 • Claysville, PA 15323-0431
(724) 663-7745
Grade Span: KG-12; **Agency Type:** 1
Schools: 4
  2 Primary; 1 Middle; 1 High; 0 Other Level
  4 Regular; 0 Special Education; 0 Vocational; 0 Alternative
  0 Magnet; 0 Charter; 1 Title I Eligible; 0 School-wide Title I
Students: 2,357   (n/a% male; n/a% female)
  Individual Education Program: 303 (12.9%);
  English Language Learner: n/a; Migrant: 0 (0.0%)

  Eligible for Free Lunch Program: 336 (14.3%)
  Eligible for Reduced-Price Lunch Program: 152 (6.4%)
Teachers: 148.5 (15.9 to 1)
Librarians/Media Specialists: 2.0 (1,178.5 to 1)
Guidance Counselors: 5.0 (471.4 to 1)
Current Spending: ($ per student per year):
  Total: $8,150; Instruction: $5,252; Support Services: $2,573
Enrollment, Drop-out Rates and Diploma Recipients by Race/Ethnicity

Category	Total	White	Black	Asian	AIAN	Hisp.
Enrollment (%)	100.0	98.8	0.6	0.3	0.0	0.3
Drop-out Rate (%)	1.8	1.7	0.0	0.0	n/a	50.0
H.S. Diplomas (#)	182	181	1	0	0	0

Peters Township SD
631 E Mcmurray Rd • Mcmurray, PA 15317-3430
(724) 941-6251
Grade Span: KG-12; **Agency Type:** 1
Schools: 5
  2 Primary; 2 Middle; 1 High; 0 Other Level
  5 Regular; 0 Special Education; 0 Vocational; 0 Alternative
  0 Magnet; 0 Charter; 4 Title I Eligible; 0 School-wide Title I
Students: 3,937   (n/a% male; n/a% female)
  Individual Education Program: 332 (8.4%);
  English Language Learner: n/a; Migrant: 4 (0.1%)
  Eligible for Free Lunch Program: 67 (1.7%)
  Eligible for Reduced-Price Lunch Program: 13 (0.3%)
Teachers: 220.5 (17.9 to 1)
Librarians/Media Specialists: 5.0 (787.4 to 1)
Guidance Counselors: 9.0 (437.4 to 1)
Current Spending: ($ per student per year):
  Total: $7,208; Instruction: $4,488; Support Services: $2,518
Enrollment, Drop-out Rates and Diploma Recipients by Race/Ethnicity

Category	Total	White	Black	Asian	AIAN	Hisp.
Enrollment (%)	100.0	97.2	0.7	1.5	0.0	0.6
Drop-out Rate (%)	0.4	0.4	0.0	0.0	0.0	0.0
H.S. Diplomas (#)	270	262	2	4	1	1

Ringgold SD
400 Main St • New Eagle, PA 15067-1108
(724) 258-9329
Grade Span: KG-12; **Agency Type:** 1
Schools: 6
  3 Primary; 2 Middle; 1 High; 0 Other Level
  6 Regular; 0 Special Education; 0 Vocational; 0 Alternative
  0 Magnet; 0 Charter; 3 Title I Eligible; 0 School-wide Title I
Students: 3,755   (n/a% male; n/a% female)
  Individual Education Program: 484 (12.9%);
  English Language Learner: n/a; Migrant: 0 (0.0%)
  Eligible for Free Lunch Program: 1,043 (27.8%)
  Eligible for Reduced-Price Lunch Program: 350 (9.3%)
Teachers: 230.0 (16.3 to 1)
Librarians/Media Specialists: 5.0 (751.0 to 1)
Guidance Counselors: 7.0 (536.4 to 1)
Current Spending: ($ per student per year):
  Total: $7,305; Instruction: $4,812; Support Services: $2,223
Enrollment, Drop-out Rates and Diploma Recipients by Race/Ethnicity

Category	Total	White	Black	Asian	AIAN	Hisp.
Enrollment (%)	100.0	89.9	9.0	0.5	0.1	0.5
Drop-out Rate (%)	2.8	2.6	7.0	0.0	0.0	n/a
H.S. Diplomas (#)	270	254	14	2	0	0

Trinity Area SD
231 Park Ave • Washington, PA 15301-5713
(724) 225-9880 • http://www.trinitypride.k12.pa.us
Grade Span: KG-12; **Agency Type:** 1
Schools: 6
  4 Primary; 1 Middle; 1 High; 0 Other Level
  6 Regular; 0 Special Education; 0 Vocational; 0 Alternative
  0 Magnet; 0 Charter; 4 Title I Eligible; 0 School-wide Title I
Students: 3,784   (n/a% male; n/a% female)
  Individual Education Program: 517 (13.7%);
  English Language Learner: n/a; Migrant: 1 (<0.1%)
  Eligible for Free Lunch Program: 503 (13.3%)
  Eligible for Reduced-Price Lunch Program: 174 (4.6%)
Teachers: 232.0 (16.3 to 1)
Librarians/Media Specialists: 6.0 (630.7 to 1)
Guidance Counselors: 7.0 (540.6 to 1)
Current Spending: ($ per student per year):
  Total: $8,078; Instruction: $5,138; Support Services: $2,604
Enrollment, Drop-out Rates and Diploma Recipients by Race/Ethnicity

Category	Total	White	Black	Asian	AIAN	Hisp.
Enrollment (%)	100.0	95.4	3.6	0.3	0.1	0.6
Drop-out Rate (%)	5.4	5.4	8.0	0.0	n/a	0.0
H.S. Diplomas (#)	282	276	5	0	0	1

Washington SD
201 Allison Ave • Washington, PA 15301-4272
(724) 223-5010 • http://www.washington.k12.pa.us
Grade Span: KG-12; **Agency Type:** 1
Schools: 3
   1 Primary; 1 Middle; 1 High; 0 Other Level
   3 Regular; 0 Special Education; 0 Vocational; 0 Alternative
   0 Magnet; 0 Charter; 3 Title I Eligible; 1 School-wide Title I
Students: 2,083 (n/a% male; n/a% female)
   Individual Education Program: 398 (19.1%);
   English Language Learner: n/a; Migrant: 0 (0.0%)
   Eligible for Free Lunch Program: 190 (9.1%)
   Eligible for Reduced-Price Lunch Program: 41 (2.0%)
Teachers: 151.0 (13.8 to 1)
Librarians/Media Specialists: 2.0 (1,041.5 to 1)
Guidance Counselors: 5.0 (416.6 to 1)
Current Spending: ($ per student per year):
   Total: $8,672; Instruction: $5,600; Support Services: $2,632
Enrollment, Drop-out Rates and Diploma Recipients by Race/Ethnicity

Category	Total	White	Black	Asian	AIAN	Hisp.
Enrollment (%)	100.0	67.8	31.5	0.2	0.0	0.4
Drop-out Rate (%)	5.6	5.2	7.1	0.0	n/a	0.0
H.S. Diplomas (#)	127	102	25	0	0	0

Wayne County

Wallenpaupack Area SD
Hc 6 Box 6075 • Hawley, PA 18428-9007
(570) 226-4557 • http://www.paupack.ptd.net
Grade Span: KG-12; **Agency Type:** 1
Schools: 6
   3 Primary; 2 Middle; 1 High; 0 Other Level
   6 Regular; 0 Special Education; 0 Vocational; 0 Alternative
   0 Magnet; 0 Charter; 5 Title I Eligible; 0 School-wide Title I
Students: 3,967 (n/a% male; n/a% female)
   Individual Education Program: 691 (17.4%);
   English Language Learner: n/a; Migrant: 1 (<0.1%)
   Eligible for Free Lunch Program: 929 (23.4%)
   Eligible for Reduced-Price Lunch Program: 439 (11.1%)
Teachers: 283.5 (14.0 to 1)
Librarians/Media Specialists: 5.0 (793.4 to 1)
Guidance Counselors: 9.0 (440.8 to 1)
Current Spending: ($ per student per year):
   Total: $8,976; Instruction: $5,842; Support Services: $2,774
Enrollment, Drop-out Rates and Diploma Recipients by Race/Ethnicity

Category	Total	White	Black	Asian	AIAN	Hisp.
Enrollment (%)	100.0	94.0	2.5	0.4	0.1	3.1
Drop-out Rate (%)	1.8	2.2	0.0	0.0	n/a	0.0
H.S. Diplomas (#)	266	240	8	1	0	17

Wayne Highlands SD
474 Grove St • Honesdale, PA 18431-1099
(570) 253-4661 • http://ns.neiu.k12.pa.us/WWW/WH/index.htm
Grade Span: KG-12; **Agency Type:** 1
Schools: 6
   4 Primary; 1 Middle; 1 High; 0 Other Level
   6 Regular; 0 Special Education; 0 Vocational; 0 Alternative
   0 Magnet; 0 Charter; 5 Title I Eligible; 0 School-wide Title I
Students: 3,281 (n/a% male; n/a% female)
   Individual Education Program: 448 (13.7%);
   English Language Learner: n/a; Migrant: 5 (0.2%)
   Eligible for Free Lunch Program: 759 (23.1%)
   Eligible for Reduced-Price Lunch Program: 375 (11.4%)
Teachers: 209.8 (15.6 to 1)
Librarians/Media Specialists: 4.0 (820.3 to 1)
Guidance Counselors: 9.0 (364.6 to 1)
Current Spending: ($ per student per year):
   Total: $8,312; Instruction: $5,376; Support Services: $2,620
Enrollment, Drop-out Rates and Diploma Recipients by Race/Ethnicity

Category	Total	White	Black	Asian	AIAN	Hisp.
Enrollment (%)	100.0	97.5	0.6	0.4	0.0	1.5
Drop-out Rate (%)	1.9	2.0	0.0	0.0	n/a	0.0
H.S. Diplomas (#)	206	197	2	5	0	2

Western Wayne SD
PO Box 500 • South Canaan, PA 18459-0158
(570) 937-4270 • http://westernwayne.org
Grade Span: PK-12; **Agency Type:** 1
Schools: 5
   3 Primary; 1 Middle; 1 High; 0 Other Level
   5 Regular; 0 Special Education; 0 Vocational; 0 Alternative
   0 Magnet; 0 Charter; 5 Title I Eligible; 0 School-wide Title I
Students: 2,521 (n/a% male; n/a% female)
   Individual Education Program: 320 (12.7%);
   English Language Learner: n/a; Migrant: 0 (0.0%)

   Eligible for Free Lunch Program: 692 (27.4%)
   Eligible for Reduced-Price Lunch Program: 280 (11.1%)
Teachers: 157.3 (16.0 to 1)
Librarians/Media Specialists: 3.0 (840.3 to 1)
Guidance Counselors: 8.0 (315.1 to 1)
Current Spending: ($ per student per year):
   Total: $9,257; Instruction: $5,643; Support Services: $3,263
Enrollment, Drop-out Rates and Diploma Recipients by Race/Ethnicity

Category	Total	White	Black	Asian	AIAN	Hisp.
Enrollment (%)	100.0	95.6	1.9	0.6	0.0	2.0
Drop-out Rate (%)	5.2	5.4	0.0	0.0	n/a	7.7
H.S. Diplomas (#)	150	146	2	0	0	2

Westmoreland County

Belle Vernon Area SD
270 Crest Ave • Belle Vernon, PA 15012-9625
(724) 929-5262 • http://wiu.k12.pa.us/bva/bva.html
Grade Span: KG-12; **Agency Type:** 1
Schools: 5
   2 Primary; 2 Middle; 1 High; 0 Other Level
   5 Regular; 0 Special Education; 0 Vocational; 0 Alternative
   0 Magnet; 0 Charter; 4 Title I Eligible; 0 School-wide Title I
Students: 2,959 (n/a% male; n/a% female)
   Individual Education Program: 382 (12.9%);
   English Language Learner: n/a; Migrant: 0 (0.0%)
   Eligible for Free Lunch Program: 581 (19.6%)
   Eligible for Reduced-Price Lunch Program: 169 (5.7%)
Teachers: 149.0 (19.9 to 1)
Librarians/Media Specialists: 5.0 (591.8 to 1)
Guidance Counselors: 6.0 (493.2 to 1)
Current Spending: ($ per student per year):
   Total: $6,892; Instruction: $4,273; Support Services: $2,314
Enrollment, Drop-out Rates and Diploma Recipients by Race/Ethnicity

Category	Total	White	Black	Asian	AIAN	Hisp.
Enrollment (%)	100.0	95.9	3.2	0.4	0.1	0.3
Drop-out Rate (%)	2.6	2.7	0.0	0.0	n/a	0.0
H.S. Diplomas (#)	190	185	3	1	0	1

Burrell SD
1021 Puckety Church Rd • Lower Burrell, PA 15068-9706
(724) 334-1406 • http://wiu.k12.pa.us/burrell/
Grade Span: KG-12; **Agency Type:** 1
Schools: 4
   2 Primary; 1 Middle; 1 High; 0 Other Level
   4 Regular; 0 Special Education; 0 Vocational; 0 Alternative
   0 Magnet; 0 Charter; 3 Title I Eligible; 0 School-wide Title I
Students: 2,194 (n/a% male; n/a% female)
   Individual Education Program: 262 (11.9%);
   English Language Learner: n/a; Migrant: 0 (0.0%)
   Eligible for Free Lunch Program: 254 (11.6%)
   Eligible for Reduced-Price Lunch Program: 106 (4.8%)
Teachers: 125.0 (17.6 to 1)
Librarians/Media Specialists: 3.0 (731.3 to 1)
Guidance Counselors: 4.0 (548.5 to 1)
Current Spending: ($ per student per year):
   Total: $6,912; Instruction: $3,998; Support Services: $2,619
Enrollment, Drop-out Rates and Diploma Recipients by Race/Ethnicity

Category	Total	White	Black	Asian	AIAN	Hisp.
Enrollment (%)	100.0	97.2	2.1	0.3	0.2	0.3
Drop-out Rate (%)	2.2	2.3	0.0	0.0	n/a	0.0
H.S. Diplomas (#)	164	163	1	0	0	0

Derry Area SD
982 N Chestnut St Ext • Derry, PA 15627-7600
(724) 694-1401 • http://wiu.k12.pa.us/derry/
Grade Span: PK-12; **Agency Type:** 1
Schools: 6
   4 Primary; 1 Middle; 1 High; 0 Other Level
   6 Regular; 0 Special Education; 0 Vocational; 0 Alternative
   0 Magnet; 0 Charter; 5 Title I Eligible; 3 School-wide Title I
Students: 2,757 (n/a% male; n/a% female)
   Individual Education Program: 245 (8.9%);
   English Language Learner: n/a; Migrant: 0 (0.0%)
   Eligible for Free Lunch Program: 754 (27.3%)
   Eligible for Reduced-Price Lunch Program: 316 (11.5%)
Teachers: 167.5 (16.5 to 1)
Librarians/Media Specialists: 3.0 (919.0 to 1)
Guidance Counselors: 5.0 (551.4 to 1)
Current Spending: ($ per student per year):
   Total: $7,365; Instruction: $4,544; Support Services: $2,514

Enrollment, Drop-out Rates and Diploma Recipients by Race/Ethnicity

Category	Total	White	Black	Asian	AIAN	Hisp.
Enrollment (%)	100.0	97.4	1.8	0.1	0.3	0.4
Drop-out Rate (%)	2.1	2.0	7.7	0.0	0.0	0.0
H.S. Diplomas (#)	179	178	1	0	0	0

Franklin Regional SD
3210 School Rd • Murrysville, PA 15668-1553
(724) 327-5456 • http://www.franklinregional.k12.pa.us
Grade Span: KG-12; Agency Type: 1
Schools: 5
  3 Primary; 1 Middle; 1 High; 0 Other Level
  5 Regular; 0 Special Education; 0 Vocational; 0 Alternative
  0 Magnet; 0 Charter; 2 Title I Eligible; 0 School-wide Title I
Students: 3,789 (n/a% male; n/a% female)
  Individual Education Program: 406 (10.7%);
  English Language Learner: n/a; Migrant: 0 (0.0%)
  Eligible for Free Lunch Program: 110 (2.9%)
  Eligible for Reduced-Price Lunch Program: 33 (0.9%)
Teachers: 231.7 (16.4 to 1)
Librarians/Media Specialists: 4.0 (947.3 to 1)
Guidance Counselors: 11.0 (344.5 to 1)
Current Spending: ($ per student per year):
  Total: $7,736; Instruction: $4,857; Support Services: $2,642

Enrollment, Drop-out Rates and Diploma Recipients by Race/Ethnicity

Category	Total	White	Black	Asian	AIAN	Hisp.
Enrollment (%)	100.0	95.4	0.5	3.4	0.4	0.3
Drop-out Rate (%)	0.4	0.4	0.0	0.0	0.0	0.0
H.S. Diplomas (#)	281	268	1	9	0	3

Greater Latrobe SD
410 Main St • Latrobe, PA 15650-1598
(724) 539-4200 • http://wiu.k12.pa.us/latrobe
Grade Span: KG-12; Agency Type: 1
Schools: 5
  3 Primary; 1 Middle; 1 High; 0 Other Level
  5 Regular; 0 Special Education; 0 Vocational; 0 Alternative
  0 Magnet; 0 Charter; 3 Title I Eligible; 0 School-wide Title I
Students: 4,322 (n/a% male; n/a% female)
  Individual Education Program: 439 (10.2%);
  English Language Learner: n/a; Migrant: 0 (0.0%)
  Eligible for Free Lunch Program: 581 (13.4%)
  Eligible for Reduced-Price Lunch Program: 288 (6.7%)
Teachers: 239.8 (18.0 to 1)
Librarians/Media Specialists: 5.0 (864.4 to 1)
Guidance Counselors: 9.0 (480.2 to 1)
Current Spending: ($ per student per year):
  Total: $6,454; Instruction: $4,087; Support Services: $2,082

Enrollment, Drop-out Rates and Diploma Recipients by Race/Ethnicity

Category	Total	White	Black	Asian	AIAN	Hisp.
Enrollment (%)	100.0	97.8	0.6	1.2	0.1	0.4
Drop-out Rate (%)	1.0	1.1	0.0	0.0	n/a	0.0
H.S. Diplomas (#)	284	281	1	2	0	0

Greensburg Salem SD
1 Academy Hill Place • Greensburg, PA 15601-1839
(724) 832-2901
Grade Span: KG-12; Agency Type: 1
Schools: 5
  3 Primary; 1 Middle; 1 High; 0 Other Level
  5 Regular; 0 Special Education; 0 Vocational; 0 Alternative
  0 Magnet; 0 Charter; 3 Title I Eligible; 0 School-wide Title I
Students: 3,506 (n/a% male; n/a% female)
  Individual Education Program: 390 (11.1%);
  English Language Learner: n/a; Migrant: 1 (<0.1%)
  Eligible for Free Lunch Program: 932 (26.6%)
  Eligible for Reduced-Price Lunch Program: 321 (9.2%)
Teachers: 195.0 (18.0 to 1)
Librarians/Media Specialists: 5.0 (701.2 to 1)
Guidance Counselors: 7.0 (500.9 to 1)
Current Spending: ($ per student per year):
  Total: $6,930; Instruction: $4,289; Support Services: $2,329

Enrollment, Drop-out Rates and Diploma Recipients by Race/Ethnicity

Category	Total	White	Black	Asian	AIAN	Hisp.
Enrollment (%)	100.0	91.5	7.4	0.7	0.1	0.3
Drop-out Rate (%)	2.8	2.8	2.6	0.0	n/a	0.0
H.S. Diplomas (#)	250	239	10	1	0	0

Hempfield Area SD
RR 6 Box 76 • Greensburg, PA 15601-9315
(724) 834-2590 • http://wiu.k12.pa.us/hempfield_area
Grade Span: KG-12; Agency Type: 1
Schools: 12
  7 Primary; 3 Middle; 2 High; 0 Other Level
  12 Regular; 0 Special Education; 0 Vocational; 0 Alternative

  0 Magnet; 0 Charter; 6 Title I Eligible; 0 School-wide Title I
Students: 6,616 (n/a% male; n/a% female)
  Individual Education Program: 730 (11.0%);
  English Language Learner: n/a; Migrant: 0 (0.0%)
  Eligible for Free Lunch Program: 670 (10.1%)
  Eligible for Reduced-Price Lunch Program: 318 (4.8%)
Teachers: 412.5 (16.0 to 1)
Librarians/Media Specialists: 10.0 (661.6 to 1)
Guidance Counselors: 17.0 (389.2 to 1)
Current Spending: ($ per student per year):
  Total: $8,107; Instruction: $5,421; Support Services: $2,441

Enrollment, Drop-out Rates and Diploma Recipients by Race/Ethnicity

Category	Total	White	Black	Asian	AIAN	Hisp.
Enrollment (%)	100.0	97.4	1.0	1.0	0.2	0.4
Drop-out Rate (%)	2.1	2.0	11.1	4.5	0.0	0.0
H.S. Diplomas (#)	491	480	5	5	1	0

Kiski Area SD
200 Poplar St • Vandergrift, PA 15690-1466
(724) 845-2022 • http://www.kiskiarea.com
Grade Span: KG-12; Agency Type: 1
Schools: 9
  7 Primary; 1 Middle; 1 High; 0 Other Level
  9 Regular; 0 Special Education; 0 Vocational; 0 Alternative
  0 Magnet; 0 Charter; 6 Title I Eligible; 2 School-wide Title I
Students: 4,502 (n/a% male; n/a% female)
  Individual Education Program: 586 (13.0%);
  English Language Learner: n/a; Migrant: 0 (0.0%)
  Eligible for Free Lunch Program: 817 (18.1%)
  Eligible for Reduced-Price Lunch Program: 346 (7.7%)
Teachers: 234.0 (19.2 to 1)
Librarians/Media Specialists: 3.0 (1,500.7 to 1)
Guidance Counselors: 7.0 (643.1 to 1)
Current Spending: ($ per student per year):
  Total: $7,735; Instruction: $4,880; Support Services: $2,539

Enrollment, Drop-out Rates and Diploma Recipients by Race/Ethnicity

Category	Total	White	Black	Asian	AIAN	Hisp.
Enrollment (%)	100.0	95.2	4.4	0.2	0.0	0.2
Drop-out Rate (%)	2.6	2.7	0.0	0.0	0.0	0.0
H.S. Diplomas (#)	340	323	14	3	0	0

Ligonier Valley SD
339 W Main St • Ligonier, PA 15658-1248
(724) 238-5696 • http://wiu.k12.pa.us/ligonier
Grade Span: KG-12; Agency Type: 1
Schools: 5
  2 Primary; 1 Middle; 2 High; 0 Other Level
  5 Regular; 0 Special Education; 0 Vocational; 0 Alternative
  0 Magnet; 0 Charter; 2 Title I Eligible; 1 School-wide Title I
Students: 2,136 (n/a% male; n/a% female)
  Individual Education Program: 277 (13.0%);
  English Language Learner: n/a; Migrant: 0 (0.0%)
  Eligible for Free Lunch Program: 464 (21.7%)
  Eligible for Reduced-Price Lunch Program: 181 (8.5%)
Teachers: 121.0 (17.7 to 1)
Librarians/Media Specialists: 5.0 (427.2 to 1)
Guidance Counselors: 5.0 (427.2 to 1)
Current Spending: ($ per student per year):
  Total: $7,997; Instruction: $4,352; Support Services: $3,259

Enrollment, Drop-out Rates and Diploma Recipients by Race/Ethnicity

Category	Total	White	Black	Asian	AIAN	Hisp.
Enrollment (%)	100.0	99.0	0.5	0.0	0.0	0.4
Drop-out Rate (%)	2.0	2.1	0.0	0.0	n/a	0.0
H.S. Diplomas (#)	147	146	0	1	0	0

Mount Pleasant Area SD
RR 4 Box 2222 • Mount Pleasant, PA 15666-9041
(724) 547-5706 • http://www.mpasd.net/
Grade Span: KG-12; Agency Type: 1
Schools: 6
  4 Primary; 0 Middle; 1 High; 0 Other Level
  5 Regular; 0 Special Education; 0 Vocational; 0 Alternative
  0 Magnet; 0 Charter; 5 Title I Eligible; 0 School-wide Title I
Students: 2,548 (n/a% male; n/a% female)
  Individual Education Program: 385 (15.1%);
  English Language Learner: n/a; Migrant: 4 (0.2%)
  Eligible for Free Lunch Program: 530 (20.8%)
  Eligible for Reduced-Price Lunch Program: 210 (8.2%)
Teachers: 144.5 (17.6 to 1)
Librarians/Media Specialists: 3.0 (849.3 to 1)
Guidance Counselors: 8.0 (318.5 to 1)
Current Spending: ($ per student per year):
  Total: $7,017; Instruction: $4,127; Support Services: $2,593

Enrollment, Drop-out Rates and Diploma Recipients by Race/Ethnicity

Category	Total	White	Black	Asian	AIAN	Hisp.
Enrollment (%)	100.0	97.5	1.8	0.4		0.3
Drop-out Rate (%)	3.4	3.4	0.0	0.0	0.0	0.0
H.S. Diplomas (#)	186	184	2	0	0	0

New Kensington-Arnold SD
701 Stevenson Blvd • New Kensington, PA 15068-5372
(724) 335-8581 • http://nkasd.wiu.k12.pa.us
Grade Span: PK-12; **Agency Type:** 1
Schools: 6
  3 Primary; 2 Middle; 1 High; 0 Other Level
  6 Regular; 0 Special Education; 0 Vocational; 0 Alternative
  0 Magnet; 0 Charter; 6 Title I Eligible; 1 School-wide Title I
Students: 2,573   (n/a% male; n/a% female)
  Individual Education Program: 455 (17.7%);
  English Language Learner: n/a; Migrant: 0 (0.0%)
  Eligible for Free Lunch Program: 969 (37.7%)
  Eligible for Reduced-Price Lunch Program: 233 (9.1%)
Teachers: 158.5 (16.2 to 1)
Librarians/Media Specialists: 3.0 (857.7 to 1)
Guidance Counselors: 4.0 (643.3 to 1)
Current Spending: ($ per student per year):
  Total: $6,882; Instruction: $4,238; Support Services: $2,308

Enrollment, Drop-out Rates and Diploma Recipients by Race/Ethnicity

Category	Total	White	Black	Asian	AIAN	Hisp.
Enrollment (%)	100.0	69.8	28.3	0.4	0.3	1.1
Drop-out Rate (%)	5.1	5.3	4.3	0.0	0.0	0.0
H.S. Diplomas (#)	143	113	29	0	0	1

Norwin SD
281 Mcmahon Dr • North Huntingdon, PA 15642-2403
(724) 863-5052 • http://wiu.k12.pa.us/norwin
Grade Span: KG-12; **Agency Type:** 1
Schools: 7
  4 Primary; 2 Middle; 1 High; 0 Other Level
  7 Regular; 0 Special Education; 0 Vocational; 0 Alternative
  0 Magnet; 0 Charter; 3 Title I Eligible; 0 School-wide Title I
Students: 5,205   (n/a% male; n/a% female)
  Individual Education Program: 608 (11.7%);
  English Language Learner: n/a; Migrant: 0 (0.0%)
  Eligible for Free Lunch Program: 371 (7.1%)
  Eligible for Reduced-Price Lunch Program: 237 (4.6%)
Teachers: 275.5 (18.9 to 1)
Librarians/Media Specialists: 5.0 (1,041.0 to 1)
Guidance Counselors: 10.0 (520.5 to 1)
Current Spending: ($ per student per year):
  Total: $6,716; Instruction: $4,106; Support Services: $2,280

Enrollment, Drop-out Rates and Diploma Recipients by Race/Ethnicity

Category	Total	White	Black	Asian	AIAN	Hisp.
Enrollment (%)	100.0	98.2	1.0	0.6	0.1	0.1
Drop-out Rate (%)	1.3	1.3	0.0	0.0	0.0	0.0
H.S. Diplomas (#)	373	370	3	0	0	0

Penn-Trafford SD
PO Box 530 • Harrison City, PA 15636-0530
(724) 744-4496 • http://penntrafford.org
Grade Span: KG-12; **Agency Type:** 1
Schools: 8
  5 Primary; 2 Middle; 1 High; 0 Other Level
  8 Regular; 0 Special Education; 0 Vocational; 0 Alternative
  0 Magnet; 0 Charter; 5 Title I Eligible; 0 School-wide Title I
Students: 4,769   (n/a% male; n/a% female)
  Individual Education Program: 439 (9.2%);
  English Language Learner: n/a; Migrant: 0 (0.0%)
  Eligible for Free Lunch Program: 241 (5.1%)
  Eligible for Reduced-Price Lunch Program: 176 (3.7%)
Teachers: 249.5 (19.1 to 1)
Librarians/Media Specialists: 4.0 (1,192.3 to 1)
Guidance Counselors: 6.0 (794.8 to 1)
Current Spending: ($ per student per year):
  Total: $6,157; Instruction: $3,857; Support Services: $2,067

Enrollment, Drop-out Rates and Diploma Recipients by Race/Ethnicity

Category	Total	White	Black	Asian	AIAN	Hisp.
Enrollment (%)	100.0	98.1	0.9	0.6	0.2	0.3
Drop-out Rate (%)	0.6	0.6	0.0	0.0	0.0	0.0
H.S. Diplomas (#)	355	348	2	4	1	0

Southmoreland SD
609 Parker Ave • Scottdale, PA 15683-1026
(724) 887-2000 • http://www.southmoreland.net/
Grade Span: KG-12; **Agency Type:** 1
Schools: 5
  3 Primary; 1 Middle; 1 High; 0 Other Level
  5 Regular; 0 Special Education; 0 Vocational; 0 Alternative

---

  0 Magnet; 0 Charter; 4 Title I Eligible; 0 School-wide Title I
Students: 2,322   (n/a% male; n/a% female)
  Individual Education Program: 417 (18.0%);
  English Language Learner: n/a; Migrant: 0 (0.0%)
  Eligible for Free Lunch Program: 627 (27.0%)
  Eligible for Reduced-Price Lunch Program: 239 (10.3%)
Teachers: 139.5 (16.6 to 1)
Librarians/Media Specialists: 3.0 (774.0 to 1)
Guidance Counselors: 8.0 (290.3 to 1)
Current Spending: ($ per student per year):
  Total: $7,498; Instruction: $4,729; Support Services: $2,409

Enrollment, Drop-out Rates and Diploma Recipients by Race/Ethnicity

Category	Total	White	Black	Asian	AIAN	Hisp.
Enrollment (%)	100.0	97.5	1.7	0.4	0.1	0.3
Drop-out Rate (%)	2.5	2.6	0.0	0.0	0.0	0.0
H.S. Diplomas (#)	153	150	3	0	0	0

Yough SD
99 Lowber Rd • Herminie, PA 15637-1219
(724) 446-7272 • http://www.yough.net
Grade Span: KG-12; **Agency Type:** 1
Schools: 5
  3 Primary; 1 Middle; 1 High; 0 Other Level
  5 Regular; 0 Special Education; 0 Vocational; 0 Alternative
  0 Magnet; 0 Charter; 4 Title I Eligible; 0 School-wide Title I
Students: 2,592   (n/a% male; n/a% female)
  Individual Education Program: 334 (12.9%);
  English Language Learner: n/a; Migrant: 0 (0.0%)
  Eligible for Free Lunch Program: 612 (23.6%)
  Eligible for Reduced-Price Lunch Program: 189 (7.3%)
Teachers: 149.5 (17.3 to 1)
Librarians/Media Specialists: 5.0 (518.4 to 1)
Guidance Counselors: 6.0 (432.0 to 1)
Current Spending: ($ per student per year):
  Total: $7,379; Instruction: $4,906; Support Services: $2,184

Enrollment, Drop-out Rates and Diploma Recipients by Race/Ethnicity

Category	Total	White	Black	Asian	AIAN	Hisp.
Enrollment (%)	100.0	97.3	2.0	0.3	0.1	0.2
Drop-out Rate (%)	1.8	1.9	0.0	0.0	n/a	n/a
H.S. Diplomas (#)	157	157	0	0	0	0

Wyoming County

Tunkhannock Area SD
41 Philadelphia Ave • Tunkhannock, PA 18657-1602
(570) 836-3111
Grade Span: KG-12; **Agency Type:** 1
Schools: 6
  4 Primary; 1 Middle; 1 High; 0 Other Level
  6 Regular; 0 Special Education; 0 Vocational; 0 Alternative
  0 Magnet; 0 Charter; 5 Title I Eligible; 0 School-wide Title I
Students: 3,173   (n/a% male; n/a% female)
  Individual Education Program: 378 (11.9%);
  English Language Learner: n/a; Migrant: 10 (0.3%)
  Eligible for Free Lunch Program: 653 (20.6%)
  Eligible for Reduced-Price Lunch Program: 287 (9.0%)
Teachers: 224.3 (14.1 to 1)
Librarians/Media Specialists: 4.0 (793.3 to 1)
Guidance Counselors: 7.0 (453.3 to 1)
Current Spending: ($ per student per year):
  Total: $8,889; Instruction: $5,511; Support Services: $3,020

Enrollment, Drop-out Rates and Diploma Recipients by Race/Ethnicity

Category	Total	White	Black	Asian	AIAN	Hisp.
Enrollment (%)	100.0	98.0	1.1	0.6	0.1	0.2
Drop-out Rate (%)	1.9	2.0	0.0	0.0	n/a	0.0
H.S. Diplomas (#)	241	237	0	1	0	3

York County

Central York SD
775 Marion Rd • York, PA 17402-1554
(717) 846-6789 • http://www.cysd.k12.pa.us
Grade Span: KG-12; **Agency Type:** 1
Schools: 7
  5 Primary; 1 Middle; 1 High; 0 Other Level
  7 Regular; 0 Special Education; 0 Vocational; 0 Alternative
  0 Magnet; 0 Charter; 4 Title I Eligible; 0 School-wide Title I
Students: 4,732   (n/a% male; n/a% female)
  Individual Education Program: 595 (12.6%);
  English Language Learner: n/a; Migrant: 3 (0.1%)
  Eligible for Free Lunch Program: 386 (8.2%)
  Eligible for Reduced-Price Lunch Program: 195 (4.1%)
Teachers: 286.0 (16.5 to 1)
Librarians/Media Specialists: 5.0 (946.4 to 1)
Guidance Counselors: 12.7 (372.6 to 1)

Current Spending: ($ per student per year):
  Total: $6,885; Instruction: $4,212; Support Services: $2,319
Enrollment, Drop-out Rates and Diploma Recipients by Race/Ethnicity

Category	Total	White	Black	Asian	AIAN	Hisp.
Enrollment (%)	100.0	84.6	7.4	3.7	0.2	4.0
Drop-out Rate (%)	0.6	0.6	0.0	2.3	0.0	0.0
H.S. Diplomas (#)	264	241	11	9	1	2

Dallastown Area SD
700 New School Ln • Dallastown, PA 17313-9242
(717) 244-4021 • http://www.dallastown.k12.pa.us
Grade Span: KG-12; **Agency Type:** 1
Schools: 7
  5 Primary; 1 Middle; 1 High; 0 Other Level
  7 Regular; 0 Special Education; 0 Vocational; 0 Alternative
  0 Magnet; 0 Charter; 4 Title I Eligible; 0 School-wide Title I
Students: 5,287 (n/a% male; n/a% female)
  Individual Education Program: 639 (12.1%);
  English Language Learner: n/a; Migrant: 4 (0.1%)
  Eligible for Free Lunch Program: 295 (5.6%)
  Eligible for Reduced-Price Lunch Program: 171 (3.2%)
Teachers: 341.5 (15.5 to 1)
Librarians/Media Specialists: 6.0 (881.2 to 1)
Guidance Counselors: 12.0 (440.6 to 1)
Current Spending: ($ per student per year):
  Total: $8,415; Instruction: $5,537; Support Services: $2,528
Enrollment, Drop-out Rates and Diploma Recipients by Race/Ethnicity

Category	Total	White	Black	Asian	AIAN	Hisp.
Enrollment (%)	100.0	94.0	2.4	1.4	0.1	2.1
Drop-out Rate (%)	1.3	1.3	0.0	0.0	0.0	4.2
H.S. Diplomas (#)	382	365	8	8	0	1

Dover Area SD
2 School Ln • Dover, PA 17315-1498
(717) 292-3671 • http://www.dover.k12.pa.us
Grade Span: KG-12; **Agency Type:** 1
Schools: 7
  4 Primary; 2 Middle; 1 High; 0 Other Level
  7 Regular; 0 Special Education; 0 Vocational; 0 Alternative
  0 Magnet; 0 Charter; 4 Title I Eligible; 0 School-wide Title I
Students: 3,537 (n/a% male; n/a% female)
  Individual Education Program: 559 (15.8%);
  English Language Learner: n/a; Migrant: 0 (0.0%)
  Eligible for Free Lunch Program: 324 (9.2%)
  Eligible for Reduced-Price Lunch Program: 177 (5.0%)
Teachers: 213.5 (16.6 to 1)
Librarians/Media Specialists: 5.0 (707.4 to 1)
Guidance Counselors: 9.0 (393.0 to 1)
Current Spending: ($ per student per year):
  Total: $6,801; Instruction: $4,205; Support Services: $2,346
Enrollment, Drop-out Rates and Diploma Recipients by Race/Ethnicity

Category	Total	White	Black	Asian	AIAN	Hisp.
Enrollment (%)	100.0	95.9	2.1	0.6	0.0	1.4
Drop-out Rate (%)	3.3	3.4	0.0	0.0	n/a	0.0
H.S. Diplomas (#)	241	235	2	1	0	3

Eastern York SD
PO Box 150 • Wrightsville, PA 17368-0150
(717) 252-1555 • http://www.easternyork.com
Grade Span: KG-12; **Agency Type:** 1
Schools: 5
  3 Primary; 1 Middle; 1 High; 0 Other Level
  5 Regular; 0 Special Education; 0 Vocational; 0 Alternative
  0 Magnet; 0 Charter; 3 Title I Eligible; 0 School-wide Title I
Students: 2,664 (n/a% male; n/a% female)
  Individual Education Program: 515 (19.3%);
  English Language Learner: n/a; Migrant: 4 (0.2%)
  Eligible for Free Lunch Program: 294 (11.0%)
  Eligible for Reduced-Price Lunch Program: 125 (4.7%)
Teachers: 199.0 (13.4 to 1)
Librarians/Media Specialists: 3.0 (888.0 to 1)
Guidance Counselors: 7.5 (355.2 to 1)
Current Spending: ($ per student per year):
  Total: $7,589; Instruction: $4,973; Support Services: $2,253
Enrollment, Drop-out Rates and Diploma Recipients by Race/Ethnicity

Category	Total	White	Black	Asian	AIAN	Hisp.
Enrollment (%)	100.0	95.5	1.7	0.8	0.0	2.0
Drop-out Rate (%)	2.7	2.3	0.0	0.0	n/a	25.0
H.S. Diplomas (#)	176	171	2	3	0	0

Hanover Public SD
403 Moul Ave • Hanover, PA 17331-1541
(717) 637-9000 • http://www.hpsd.k12.pa.us
Grade Span: KG-12; **Agency Type:** 1
Schools: 5

  3 Primary; 1 Middle; 1 High; 0 Other Level
  5 Regular; 0 Special Education; 0 Vocational; 0 Alternative
  0 Magnet; 0 Charter; 3 Title I Eligible; 0 School-wide Title I
Students: 1,711 (n/a% male; n/a% female)
  Individual Education Program: 325 (19.0%);
  English Language Learner: n/a; Migrant: 65 (3.8%)
  Eligible for Free Lunch Program: 278 (16.2%)
  Eligible for Reduced-Price Lunch Program: 103 (6.0%)
Teachers: 115.0 (14.9 to 1)
Librarians/Media Specialists: 3.0 (570.3 to 1)
Guidance Counselors: 5.0 (342.2 to 1)
Current Spending: ($ per student per year):
  Total: $8,199; Instruction: $5,309; Support Services: $2,561
Enrollment, Drop-out Rates and Diploma Recipients by Race/Ethnicity

Category	Total	White	Black	Asian	AIAN	Hisp.
Enrollment (%)	100.0	89.9	2.2	1.9	0.0	6.0
Drop-out Rate (%)	4.2	4.4	0.0	0.0	n/a	0.0
H.S. Diplomas (#)	92	88	0	2	0	2

Northeastern York SD
41 Harding St • Manchester, PA 17345-1119
(717) 266-3667 • http://www.nesd.k12.pa.us
Grade Span: KG-12; **Agency Type:** 1
Schools: 7
  4 Primary; 2 Middle; 1 High; 0 Other Level
  7 Regular; 0 Special Education; 0 Vocational; 0 Alternative
  0 Magnet; 0 Charter; 4 Title I Eligible; 0 School-wide Title I
Students: 3,105 (n/a% male; n/a% female)
  Individual Education Program: 537 (17.3%);
  English Language Learner: n/a; Migrant: 8 (0.3%)
  Eligible for Free Lunch Program: 483 (15.6%)
  Eligible for Reduced-Price Lunch Program: 272 (8.8%)
Teachers: 196.8 (15.8 to 1)
Librarians/Media Specialists: 6.0 (517.5 to 1)
Guidance Counselors: 8.0 (388.1 to 1)
Current Spending: ($ per student per year):
  Total: $7,532; Instruction: $4,725; Support Services: $2,430
Enrollment, Drop-out Rates and Diploma Recipients by Race/Ethnicity

Category	Total	White	Black	Asian	AIAN	Hisp.
Enrollment (%)	100.0	94.4	2.7	0.4	0.2	2.3
Drop-out Rate (%)	2.7	2.6	8.3	0.0	n/a	0.0
H.S. Diplomas (#)	136	133	2	1	0	0

Northern York County SD
149 S Baltimore St • Dillsburg, PA 17019-1035
(717) 432-8691 • http://www.nycsd.k12.pa.us/
Grade Span: KG-12; **Agency Type:** 1
Schools: 6
  4 Primary; 1 Middle; 1 High; 0 Other Level
  6 Regular; 0 Special Education; 0 Vocational; 0 Alternative
  0 Magnet; 0 Charter; 5 Title I Eligible; 0 School-wide Title I
Students: 3,195 (n/a% male; n/a% female)
  Individual Education Program: 365 (11.4%);
  English Language Learner: n/a; Migrant: 2 (0.1%)
  Eligible for Free Lunch Program: 168 (5.3%)
  Eligible for Reduced-Price Lunch Program: 99 (3.1%)
Teachers: 210.3 (15.2 to 1)
Librarians/Media Specialists: 4.0 (798.8 to 1)
Guidance Counselors: 7.0 (456.4 to 1)
Current Spending: ($ per student per year):
  Total: $7,423; Instruction: $4,723; Support Services: $2,455
Enrollment, Drop-out Rates and Diploma Recipients by Race/Ethnicity

Category	Total	White	Black	Asian	AIAN	Hisp.
Enrollment (%)	100.0	96.5	1.0	1.1	0.5	0.9
Drop-out Rate (%)	1.7	1.8	0.0	0.0	0.0	0.0
H.S. Diplomas (#)	185	180	0	4	1	0

Red Lion Area SD
696 Delta Rd • Red Lion, PA 17356-9185
(717) 244-4518 • http://red1.pa.schoolwebpages.com/
Grade Span: KG-12; **Agency Type:** 1
Schools: 10
  8 Primary; 1 Middle; 1 High; 0 Other Level
  10 Regular; 0 Special Education; 0 Vocational; 0 Alternative
  0 Magnet; 0 Charter; 6 Title I Eligible; 0 School-wide Title I
Students: 5,512 (n/a% male; n/a% female)
  Individual Education Program: 807 (14.6%);
  English Language Learner: n/a; Migrant: 1 (<0.1%)
  Eligible for Free Lunch Program: 494 (9.0%)
  Eligible for Reduced-Price Lunch Program: 311 (5.6%)
Teachers: 298.9 (18.4 to 1)
Librarians/Media Specialists: 5.0 (1,102.4 to 1)
Guidance Counselors: 10.0 (551.2 to 1)
Current Spending: ($ per student per year):
  Total: $6,527; Instruction: $4,174; Support Services: $2,038

Enrollment, Drop-out Rates and Diploma Recipients by Race/Ethnicity

Category	Total	White	Black	Asian	AIAN	Hisp.
Enrollment (%)	100.0	97.0	1.2	0.9	0.1	0.9
Drop-out Rate (%)	2.1	2.1	0.0	0.0	0.0	20.0
H.S. Diplomas (#)	306	297	1	8	0	0

South Eastern SD

104 E Main St · Fawn Grove, PA 17321-9545
(717) 382-4843 · http://sesd.k12.pa.us
Grade Span: KG-12; **Agency Type:** 1
Schools: 6
 3 Primary; 2 Middle; 1 High; 0 Other Level
 6 Regular; 0 Special Education; 0 Vocational; 0 Alternative
 0 Magnet; 0 Charter; 4 Title I Eligible; 0 School-wide Title I
Students: 3,292   (n/a% male; n/a% female)
 Individual Education Program: 484 (14.7%);
 English Language Learner: n/a; Migrant: 0 (0.0%)
 Eligible for Free Lunch Program: 174 (5.3%)
 Eligible for Reduced-Price Lunch Program: 106 (3.2%)
Teachers: 200.2 (16.4 to 1)
Librarians/Media Specialists: 4.0 (823.0 to 1)
Guidance Counselors: 8.0 (411.5 to 1)
Current Spending: ($ per student per year):
 Total: $6,653; Instruction: $4,028; Support Services: $2,348

Enrollment, Drop-out Rates and Diploma Recipients by Race/Ethnicity

Category	Total	White	Black	Asian	AIAN	Hisp.
Enrollment (%)	100.0	97.0	1.5	1.0	0.2	0.4
Drop-out Rate (%)	2.7	2.7	0.0	0.0	n/a	0.0
H.S. Diplomas (#)	184	180	2	2	0	0

South Western SD

225 Bowman Rd · Hanover, PA 17331-4213
(717) 632-2500 · http://www.swsd.k12.pa.us
Grade Span: KG-12; **Agency Type:** 1
Schools: 6
 4 Primary; 1 Middle; 1 High; 0 Other Level
 6 Regular; 0 Special Education; 0 Vocational; 0 Alternative
 0 Magnet; 0 Charter; 3 Title I Eligible; 0 School-wide Title I
Students: 4,011   (n/a% male; n/a% female)
 Individual Education Program: 442 (11.0%);
 English Language Learner: n/a; Migrant: 9 (0.2%)
 Eligible for Free Lunch Program: 270 (6.7%)
 Eligible for Reduced-Price Lunch Program: 175 (4.4%)
Teachers: 238.1 (16.8 to 1)
Librarians/Media Specialists: 4.0 (1,002.8 to 1)
Guidance Counselors: 12.0 (334.3 to 1)
Current Spending: ($ per student per year):
 Total: $6,808; Instruction: $4,237; Support Services: $2,279

Enrollment, Drop-out Rates and Diploma Recipients by Race/Ethnicity

Category	Total	White	Black	Asian	AIAN	Hisp.
Enrollment (%)	100.0	95.6	2.0	1.1	0.1	1.2
Drop-out Rate (%)	2.6	2.6	0.0	0.0	n/a	0.0
H.S. Diplomas (#)	276	273	2	1	0	0

Southern York County SD

PO Box 128 · Glen Rock, PA 17327-0128
(717) 235-4811 · http://www.syc.k12.pa.us/
Grade Span: KG-12; **Agency Type:** 1
Schools: 5
 3 Primary; 1 Middle; 1 High; 0 Other Level
 5 Regular; 0 Special Education; 0 Vocational; 0 Alternative
 0 Magnet; 0 Charter; 4 Title I Eligible; 0 School-wide Title I
Students: 3,297   (n/a% male; n/a% female)
 Individual Education Program: 547 (16.6%);
 English Language Learner: n/a; Migrant: 0 (0.0%)
 Eligible for Free Lunch Program: 180 (5.5%)
 Eligible for Reduced-Price Lunch Program: 90 (2.7%)
Teachers: 208.8 (15.8 to 1)
Librarians/Media Specialists: 5.0 (659.4 to 1)
Guidance Counselors: 8.0 (412.1 to 1)
Current Spending: ($ per student per year):
 Total: $7,710; Instruction: $4,858; Support Services: $2,543

Enrollment, Drop-out Rates and Diploma Recipients by Race/Ethnicity

Category	Total	White	Black	Asian	AIAN	Hisp.
Enrollment (%)	100.0	97.1	1.4	0.5	0.1	0.9
Drop-out Rate (%)	2.3	2.4	0.0	0.0	n/a	0.0
H.S. Diplomas (#)	210	206	2	2	0	0

Spring Grove Area SD

100 E College Ave · Spring Grove, PA 17362-1219
(717) 225-4731 · http://www.sgasd.org
Grade Span: KG-12; **Agency Type:** 1
Schools: 6
 3 Primary; 2 Middle; 1 High; 0 Other Level
 6 Regular; 0 Special Education; 0 Vocational; 0 Alternative

0 Magnet; 0 Charter; 4 Title I Eligible; 0 School-wide Title I
Students: 3,851   (n/a% male; n/a% female)
 Individual Education Program: 629 (16.3%);
 English Language Learner: n/a; Migrant: 6 (0.2%)
 Eligible for Free Lunch Program: 317 (8.2%)
 Eligible for Reduced-Price Lunch Program: 185 (4.8%)
Teachers: 240.0 (16.0 to 1)
Librarians/Media Specialists: 5.0 (770.2 to 1)
Guidance Counselors: 10.0 (385.1 to 1)
Current Spending: ($ per student per year):
 Total: $6,810; Instruction: $4,224; Support Services: $2,250

Enrollment, Drop-out Rates and Diploma Recipients by Race/Ethnicity

Category	Total	White	Black	Asian	AIAN	Hisp.
Enrollment (%)	100.0	96.2	1.3	0.4	0.6	1.5
Drop-out Rate (%)	2.0	2.0	0.0	0.0	0.0	0.0
H.S. Diplomas (#)	201	198	2	1	0	0

West Shore SD

PO Box 803 · New Cumberland, PA 17070-0803
(717) 938-9577 · http://www.wssd.k12.pa.us/
Grade Span: KG-12; **Agency Type:** 1
Schools: 16
 10 Primary; 4 Middle; 2 High; 0 Other Level
 16 Regular; 0 Special Education; 0 Vocational; 0 Alternative
 0 Magnet; 0 Charter; 13 Title I Eligible; 0 School-wide Title I
Students: 8,355   (n/a% male; n/a% female)
 Individual Education Program: 1,331 (15.9%);
 English Language Learner: n/a; Migrant: 33 (0.4%)
 Eligible for Free Lunch Program: 581 (7.0%)
 Eligible for Reduced-Price Lunch Program: 299 (3.6%)
Teachers: 513.2 (16.3 to 1)
Librarians/Media Specialists: 13.0 (642.7 to 1)
Guidance Counselors: 20.0 (417.8 to 1)
Current Spending: ($ per student per year):
 Total: $6,835; Instruction: $4,418; Support Services: $2,111

Enrollment, Drop-out Rates and Diploma Recipients by Race/Ethnicity

Category	Total	White	Black	Asian	AIAN	Hisp.
Enrollment (%)	100.0	92.9	2.9	2.0	0.1	2.1
Drop-out Rate (%)	2.3	2.2	8.3	1.6	0.0	2.8
H.S. Diplomas (#)	556	527	6	14	1	8

West York Area SD

2605 W Market St · York, PA 17404-5529
(717) 792-3067 · http://www.wyasd.k12.pa.us
Grade Span: KG-12; **Agency Type:** 1
Schools: 6
 4 Primary; 1 Middle; 1 High; 0 Other Level
 6 Regular; 0 Special Education; 0 Vocational; 0 Alternative
 0 Magnet; 0 Charter; 3 Title I Eligible; 0 School-wide Title I
Students: 3,065   (n/a% male; n/a% female)
 Individual Education Program: 418 (13.6%);
 English Language Learner: n/a; Migrant: 6 (0.2%)
 Eligible for Free Lunch Program: 327 (10.7%)
 Eligible for Reduced-Price Lunch Program: 156 (5.1%)
Teachers: 186.2 (16.5 to 1)
Librarians/Media Specialists: 4.0 (766.3 to 1)
Guidance Counselors: 8.0 (383.1 to 1)
Current Spending: ($ per student per year):
 Total: $6,981; Instruction: $4,198; Support Services: $2,498

Enrollment, Drop-out Rates and Diploma Recipients by Race/Ethnicity

Category	Total	White	Black	Asian	AIAN	Hisp.
Enrollment (%)	100.0	89.6	5.2	1.3	0.2	3.7
Drop-out Rate (%)	2.1	1.7	11.5	0.0	0.0	4.5
H.S. Diplomas (#)	168	158	1	6	0	3

York City SD

PO Box 1927 · York, PA 17405-1927
(717) 845-3571 · http://www.ycs.k12.pa.us/default.html
Grade Span: KG-12; **Agency Type:** 1
Schools: 9
 6 Primary; 2 Middle; 1 High; 0 Other Level
 9 Regular; 0 Special Education; 0 Vocational; 0 Alternative
 0 Magnet; 0 Charter; 9 Title I Eligible; 9 School-wide Title I
Students: 6,691   (n/a% male; n/a% female)
 Individual Education Program: 1,449 (21.7%);
 English Language Learner: n/a; Migrant: 220 (3.3%)
 Eligible for Free Lunch Program: 4,198 (62.7%)
 Eligible for Reduced-Price Lunch Program: 625 (9.3%)
Teachers: 407.0 (16.4 to 1)
Librarians/Media Specialists: 5.0 (1,338.2 to 1)
Guidance Counselors: 14.0 (477.9 to 1)
Current Spending: ($ per student per year):
 Total: $8,335; Instruction: $5,358; Support Services: $2,537

Enrollment, Drop-out Rates and Diploma Recipients by Race/Ethnicity

Category	Total	White	Black	Asian	AIAN	Hisp.
Enrollment (%)	100.0	25.1	43.9	1.0	0.1	29.9
Drop-out Rate (%)	10.0	11.6	8.9	6.7	0.0	10.7
H.S. Diplomas (#)	279	75	119	15	0	70

York Suburban SD
1800 Hollywood Dr • York, PA 17403-4256
(717) 848-2814 • http://www.yshs.k12.pa.us
Grade Span: KG-12; **Agency Type:** 1
Schools: 5
    3 Primary; 1 Middle; 1 High; 0 Other Level
    5 Regular; 0 Special Education; 0 Vocational; 0 Alternative
    0 Magnet; 0 Charter; 2 Title I Eligible; 0 School-wide Title I
Students: 2,706   (n/a% male; n/a% female)
    Individual Education Program: 360 (13.3%);
    English Language Learner: n/a; Migrant: 9 (0.3%)
    Eligible for Free Lunch Program: 149 (5.5%)
    Eligible for Reduced-Price Lunch Program: 81 (3.0%)
Teachers: 179.6 (15.1 to 1)
Librarians/Media Specialists: 4.0 (676.5 to 1)
Guidance Counselors: 9.6 (281.9 to 1)
Current Spending: ($ per student per year):
    Total: $8,924; Instruction: $5,829; Support Services: $2,766
Enrollment, Drop-out Rates and Diploma Recipients by Race/Ethnicity

Category	Total	White	Black	Asian	AIAN	Hisp.
Enrollment (%)	100.0	88.0	5.0	3.2	0.0	3.8
Drop-out Rate (%)	0.2	0.3	0.0	0.0	0.0	0.0
H.S. Diplomas (#)	170	170	0	0	0	0

Number of Schools

Rank	Number	District Name	City
1	263	Philadelphia City SD	Philadelphia
2	92	Pittsburgh SD	Pittsburgh
3	23	Allentown City SD	Allentown
3	23	Central Bucks SD	Doylestown
5	22	Bethlehem Area SD	Bethlehem
6	21	Chambersburg Area SD	Chambersburg
6	21	Erie City SD	Erie
8	19	Lancaster SD	Lancaster
8	19	Reading SD	Reading
8	19	Warren County SD	North Warren
11	18	Central Dauphin SD	Harrisburg
11	18	Scranton SD	Scranton
13	17	North Penn SD	Lansdale
14	16	Pennsbury SD	Fallsington
14	16	West Shore SD	New Cumberland
16	15	Council Rock SD	Newtown
16	15	Harrisburg City SD	Harrisburg
16	15	Mifflin County SD	Lewistown
16	15	West Chester Area SD	West Chester
20	14	Altoona Area SD	Altoona
20	14	Butler Area SD	Butler
20	14	Neshaminy SD	Langhorne
23	13	Armstrong SD	Ford City
23	13	Bristol Township SD	Levittown
23	13	Downingtown Area SD	Downingtown
23	13	Keystone Central SD	Lock Haven
23	13	Millcreek Township SD	Erie
28	12	Coatesville Area SD	Coatesville
28	12	Hempfield Area SD	Greensburg
28	12	Juniata County SD	Mifflintown
28	12	North Allegheny SD	Pittsburgh
28	12	Upper Darby SD	Drexel Hill
33	11	Canon-Mcmillan SD	Canonsburg
33	11	Connellsville Area SD	Connellsville
33	11	East Penn SD	Emmaus
33	11	Norristown Area SD	Norristown
33	11	Pocono Mountain SD	Swiftwater
33	11	State College Area SD	State College
33	11	William Penn SD	Lansdowne
33	11	Williamsport Area SD	Williamsport
41	10	Bensalem Township SD	Bensalem
41	10	Boyertown Area SD	Boyertown
41	10	Carlisle Area SD	Carlisle
41	10	Cumberland Valley SD	Mechanicsburg
41	10	Dubois Area SD	Du Bois
41	10	East Stroudsburg Area SD	E Stroudsburg
41	10	Hempfield SD	Landisville
41	10	Lower Merion SD	Ardmore
41	10	Mt Lebanon SD	Pittsburgh
41	10	Parkland SD	Allentown
41	10	Penn Manor SD	Millersville
41	10	Pennridge SD	Perkasie
41	10	Red Lion Area SD	Red Lion
41	10	Souderton Area SD	Souderton
41	10	Wilson SD	West Lawn
56	9	Abington SD	Abington
56	9	Albert Gallatin Area SD	Uniontown
56	9	Centennial SD	Warminster
56	9	Chester-Upland SD	Chester
56	9	Crawford Central SD	Meadville
56	9	Easton Area SD	Easton
56	9	Hazleton Area SD	Hazleton
56	9	Kiski Area SD	Vandergrift
56	9	Manheim Township SD	Lancaster
56	9	North Hills SD	Pittsburgh
56	9	Punxsutawney Area SD	Punxsutawney
56	9	Quakertown Community SD	Quakertown
56	9	Ridley SD	Folsom
56	9	Seneca Valley SD	Harmony
56	9	Spring-Ford Area SD	Collegeville
56	9	Wilkes-Barre Area SD	Wilkes Barre
56	9	Woodland Hills SD	Pittsburgh
56	9	Wyoming Valley West SD	Kingston
56	9	York City SD	York
75	8	Bethel Park SD	Bethel Park
75	8	Franklin Area SD	Franklin
75	8	Gateway SD	Monroeville
75	8	Hatboro-Horsham SD	Horsham
75	8	Manheim Central SD	Manheim
75	8	Mechanicsburg Area SD	Mechanicsburg
75	8	New Castle Area SD	New Castle
75	8	Penn Hills SD	Pittsburgh
75	8	Penn-Trafford SD	Harrison City
75	8	Shaler Area SD	Glenshaw
75	8	Stroudsburg Area SD	Stroudsburg
75	8	Tredyffrin-Easttown SD	Berwyn
75	8	Uniontown Area SD	Uniontown
88	7	Apollo-Ridge SD	Spring Church
88	7	Athens Area SD	Athens
88	7	Berwick Area SD	Berwick
88	7	Big Spring SD	Newville
88	7	Central York SD	York
88	7	Cheltenham Township SD	Elkins Park
88	7	Colonial SD	Plymouth Meeting
88	7	Conestoga Valley SD	Lancaster
88	7	Corry Area SD	Corry
88	7	Dallastown Area SD	Dallastown
88	7	Delaware Valley SD	Milford
88	7	Donegal SD	Mount Joy
88	7	Dover Area SD	Dover
88	7	Elizabeth Forward SD	Elizabeth
88	7	Elizabethtown Area SD	Elizabethtown
88	7	Ephrata Area SD	Ephrata
88	7	Grove City Area SD	Grove City
88	7	Hamburg Area SD	Hamburg
88	7	Haverford Township SD	Havertown
88	7	Laurel Highlands SD	Uniontown
88	7	Lebanon SD	Lebanon
88	7	Lower Dauphin SD	Hummelstown
88	7	Mckeesport Area SD	Mc Keesport
88	7	Methacton SD	Norristown
88	7	Midd-West SD	Middleburg
88	7	Northeastern York SD	Manchester
88	7	Norwin SD	N Huntingdon
88	7	Penncrest SD	Saegertown
88	7	Perkiomen Valley SD	Collegeville
88	7	Pleasant Valley SD	Brodheadsville
88	7	Plum Borough SD	Plum
88	7	Pottstown SD	Pottstown
88	7	Shikellamy SD	Sunbury
88	7	Solanco SD	Quarryville
88	7	Southeast Delco SD	Folcroft
88	7	Titusville Area SD	Titusville
88	7	Wissahickon SD	Ambler
125	6	Abington Heights SD	Clarks Summit
125	6	Bellefonte Area SD	Bellefonte
125	6	Chichester SD	Boothwyn
125	6	Clearfield Area SD	Clearfield
125	6	Cocalico SD	Denver
125	6	Conneaut SD	Linesville
125	6	Cornwall-Lebanon SD	Lebanon
125	6	Daniel Boone Area SD	Birdsboro
125	6	Danville Area SD	Danville
125	6	Derry Area SD	Derry
125	6	Eastern Lancaster County SD	New Holland
125	6	Eastern Lebanon County SD	Myerstown
125	6	Exeter Township SD	Reading
125	6	Fox Chapel Area SD	Pittsburgh
125	6	Gettysburg Area SD	Gettysburg
125	6	Highlands SD	Natrona Heights
125	6	Hollidaysburg Area SD	Hollidaysburg
125	6	Hopewell Area SD	Aliquippa
125	6	Huntingdon Area SD	Huntingdon
125	6	Indiana Area SD	Indiana
125	6	Interboro SD	Prospect Park
125	6	Jersey Shore Area SD	Jersey Shore
125	6	Kutztown Area SD	Kutztown
125	6	Lehighton Area SD	Lehighton
125	6	Marple Newtown SD	Newtown Square
125	6	Mifflinburg Area SD	Mifflinburg
125	6	Moon Area SD	Moon Township
125	6	Mount Pleasant Area SD	Mount Pleasant
125	6	New Kensington-Arnold SD	New Kensington
125	6	Northampton Area SD	Northampton
125	6	Northern Lebanon SD	Fredericksburg
125	6	Northern Tioga SD	Elkland
125	6	Northern York County SD	Dillsburg
125	6	Oil City Area SD	Oil City
125	6	Owen J Roberts SD	Pottstown
125	6	Penn-Delco SD	Aston
125	6	Philipsburg-Osceola Area SD	Philipsburg
125	6	Phoenixville Area SD	Phoenixville
125	6	Ringgold SD	New Eagle
125	6	Rose Tree Media SD	Media
125	6	Somerset Area SD	Somerset
125	6	South Eastern SD	Fawn Grove
125	6	South Western SD	Hanover
125	6	Southern Tioga SD	Blossburg
125	6	Spring Grove Area SD	Spring Grove
125	6	Towanda Area SD	Towanda
125	6	Trinity Area SD	Washington
125	6	Tunkhannock Area SD	Tunkhannock
125	6	Tuscarora SD	Mercersburg
125	6	Unionville-Chadds Ford SD	Kennett Square
125	6	Upper Dublin SD	Maple Glen
125	6	Upper Merion Area SD	King Of Prussia
125	6	Upper Saint Clair SD	Pittsburgh
125	6	Wallenpaupack Area SD	Hawley
125	6	Wallingford-Swarthmore SD	Wallingford
125	6	Warwick SD	Lititz
125	6	Wayne Highlands SD	Honesdale
125	6	Waynesboro Area SD	Waynesboro
125	6	West Mifflin Area SD	West Mifflin
125	6	West Perry SD	Elliottsburg
125	6	West York Area SD	York
186	5	Ambridge Area SD	Ambridge
186	5	Bald Eagle Area SD	Wingate
186	5	Baldwin-Whitehall SD	Pittsburgh
186	5	Bangor Area SD	Bangor
186	5	Bedford Area SD	Bedford
186	5	Belle Vernon Area SD	Belle Vernon
186	5	Big Beaver Falls Area SD	Beaver Falls
186	5	Blackhawk SD	Beaver Falls
186	5	Blairsville-Saltsburg SD	Blairsville
186	5	Bloomsburg Area SD	Bloomsburg
186	5	Blue Mountain SD	Orwigsburg
186	5	Brandywine Heights Area SD	Topton
186	5	Brownsville Area SD	Brownsville
186	5	Derry Township SD	Hershey
186	5	Eastern York SD	Wrightsville
186	5	Ellwood City Area SD	Ellwood City
186	5	Everett Area SD	Everett
186	5	Fleetwood Area SD	Fleetwood
186	5	Fort Leboeuf SD	Waterford
186	5	Franklin Regional SD	Murrysville
186	5	Freeport Area SD	Freeport
186	5	Garnet Valley SD	Glen Mills
186	5	Governor Mifflin SD	Shillington
186	5	Great Valley SD	Malvern
186	5	Greater Latrobe SD	Latrobe
186	5	Greater Nanticoke Area SD	Nanticoke
186	5	Greensburg Salem SD	Greensburg
186	5	Hampton Township SD	Allison Park
186	5	Hanover Area SD	Wilkes Barre
186	5	Hanover Public SD	Hanover
186	5	Hermitage SD	Hermitage
186	5	Kennett Consolidated SD	Kennett Square
186	5	Keystone Oaks SD	Pittsburgh
186	5	Lampeter-Strasburg SD	Lampeter
186	5	Ligonier Valley SD	Ligonier
186	5	Mars Area SD	Mars
186	5	Middletown Area SD	Middletown
186	5	Milton Area SD	Milton
186	5	Montour SD	Mc Kees Rocks
186	5	Nazareth Area SD	Nazareth
186	5	North Pocono SD	Moscow
186	5	Oxford Area SD	Oxford
186	5	Palisades SD	Kintnersville
186	5	Palmyra Area SD	Palmyra
186	5	Penn Cambria SD	Cresson
186	5	Penns Valley Area SD	Spring Mills
186	5	Pequea Valley SD	Kinzers
186	5	Peters Township SD	Mcmurray
186	5	Pine-Richland SD	Gibsonia
186	5	Pittston Area SD	Pittston
186	5	Pottsgrove SD	Pottstown
186	5	Radnor Township SD	Wayne
186	5	Saint Marys Area SD	Saint Marys
186	5	Selinsgrove Area SD	Selinsgrove
186	5	Shippensburg Area SD	Shippensburg
186	5	Slippery Rock Area SD	Slippery Rock
186	5	Southern Lehigh SD	Center Valley
186	5	Southern York County SD	Glen Rock
186	5	Southmoreland SD	Scottdale
186	5	Spring Cove SD	Roaring Spring
186	5	Steel Valley SD	Munhall
186	5	Susquehanna Township SD	Harrisburg
186	5	Tamaqua Area SD	Tamaqua
186	5	Troy Area SD	Troy
186	5	Twin Valley SD	Elverson
186	5	Upper Adams SD	Biglerville
186	5	West Allegheny SD	Imperial
186	5	West Jefferson Hills SD	Jefferson Hls
186	5	Western Wayne SD	South Canaan
186	5	Wilkinsburg Borough SD	Wilkinsburg
186	5	Wilmington Area SD	New Wilmington
186	5	Wilson Area SD	Easton
186	5	Wyalusing Area SD	Wyalusing
186	5	Wyoming Area SD	Exeter
186	5	York Suburban SD	York
186	5	Yough SD	Herminie
262	4	Annville-Cleona SD	Annville
262	4	Avon Grove SD	West Grove
262	4	Beaver Area SD	Beaver
262	4	Bradford Area SD	Bradford
262	4	Brookville Area SD	Brookville
262	4	Burrell SD	Lower Burrell
262	4	Central Cambria SD	Ebensburg
262	4	Central Greene SD	Waynesburg
262	4	Chartiers Valley SD	Pittsburgh
262	4	Chestnut Ridge SD	Fishertown
262	4	Conewago Valley SD	New Oxford
262	4	Conrad Weiser Area SD	Robesonia
262	4	Crestwood SD	Mountain Top
262	4	Dallas SD	Dallas

Rank	Number	District Name	City
262	4	Deer Lakes SD	Russellton
262	4	East Lycoming SD	Hughesville
262	4	East Pennsboro Area SD	Enola
262	4	Freedom Area SD	Freedom
262	4	General Mclane SD	Edinboro
262	4	Greater Johnstown SD	Johnstown
262	4	Greencastle-Antrim SD	Greencastle
262	4	Harbor Creek SD	Harborcreek
262	4	Jim Thorpe Area SD	Jim Thorpe
262	4	Karns City Area SD	Karns City
262	4	Lake-Lehman SD	Lehman
262	4	Lewisburg Area SD	Lewisburg
262	4	Littlestown Area SD	Littlestown
262	4	Mcguffey SD	Claysville
262	4	Montoursville Area SD	Montoursville
262	4	Mount Union Area SD	Mount Union
262	4	North East SD	North East
262	4	North Schuylkill SD	Ashland
262	4	Northern Lehigh SD	Slatington
262	4	Northwestern SD	Albion
262	4	Northwestern Lehigh SD	New Tripoli
262	4	Octorara Area SD	Atglen
262	4	Palmerton Area SD	Palmerton
262	4	Quaker Valley SD	Sewickley
262	4	Riverside Beaver County SD	Ellwood City
262	4	Salisbury Township SD	Allentown
262	4	Sharon City SD	Sharon
262	4	South Butler County SD	Saxonburg
262	4	South Middleton SD	Boiling Springs
262	4	Springfield SD	Springfield
262	4	Springfield Township SD	Oreland
262	4	Sto-Rox SD	Mckees Rocks
262	4	Upper Moreland Township SD	Willow Grove
262	4	Upper Perkiomen SD	East Greenville
262	4	Valley View SD	Archbald
262	4	Warrior Run SD	Turbotville
262	4	Wellsboro Area SD	Wellsboro
262	4	Whitehall-Coplay SD	Whitehall
314	3	Bermudian Springs SD	York Springs
314	3	Cambria Heights SD	Patton
314	3	Carlynton SD	Carnegie
314	3	Catasauqua Area SD	Catasauqua
314	3	Center Area SD	Monaca
314	3	Central Columbia SD	Bloomsburg
314	3	Charleroi SD	Charleroi
314	3	Dunmore SD	Dunmore
314	3	East Allegheny SD	N Versailles
314	3	Fairview SD	Fairview
314	3	Forest Hills SD	Sidman
314	3	Girard SD	Girard
314	3	Greenville Area SD	Greenville
314	3	Lakeland SD	Jermyn
314	3	Lower Moreland Township SD	Huntingdon Vly
314	3	Marion Center Area SD	Marion Center
314	3	Mercer Area SD	Mercer
314	3	Moniteau SD	West Sunbury
314	3	Montrose Area SD	Montrose
314	3	Muhlenberg SD	Reading
314	3	New Brighton Area SD	New Brighton
314	3	Northgate SD	Pittsburgh
314	3	Oley Valley SD	Oley
314	3	Pen Argyl Area SD	Pen Argyl
314	3	Pine Grove Area SD	Pine Grove
314	3	Pottsville Area SD	Pottsville
314	3	Richland SD	Johnstown
314	3	Saucon Valley SD	Hellertown
314	3	Schuylkill Valley SD	Leesport
314	3	South Allegheny SD	Mc Keesport
314	3	South Fayette Township SD	Mc Donald
314	3	South Park SD	South Park
314	3	Susquenita SD	Duncannon
314	3	Tulpehocken Area SD	Bernville
314	3	Tyrone Area SD	Tyrone
314	3	Washington SD	Washington
314	3	Wattsburg Area SD	Erie
314	3	Westmont Hilltop SD	Johnstown
314	3	Wyomissing Area SD	Wyomissing
353	2	Burgettstown Area SD	Burgettstown
353	2	Elk Lake SD	Dimock
353	2	Mid Valley SD	Throop
353	2	Mohawk Area SD	Bessemer
353	2	Mount Carmel Area SD	Mount Carmel
353	2	Pde Division of Data Services	Harrisburg
353	2	Reynolds SD	Greenville
353	2	Shamokin Area SD	Coal Township
361	1	Pennsylvania Virtual CS	Norristown
361	1	Western Pennsylvania Cyber CS	Midland

Number of Teachers

Rank	Number	District Name	City
1	10,194	Philadelphia City SD	Philadelphia
2	2,686	Pittsburgh SD	Pittsburgh
3	983	Central Bucks SD	Doylestown
4	931	Reading SD	Reading
5	902	Bethlehem Area SD	Bethlehem
6	883	Allentown City SD	Allentown
7	850	North Penn SD	Lansdale
8	827	Erie City SD	Erie
9	793	Council Rock SD	Newtown
10	742	Upper Darby SD	Drexel Hill
11	724	Pocono Mountain SD	Swiftwater
12	722	West Chester Area SD	West Chester
13	719	Central Dauphin SD	Harrisburg
14	706	Lancaster SD	Lancaster
15	690	Pennsbury SD	Fallsington
16	683	Downingtown Area SD	Downingtown
17	629	Scranton SD	Scranton
18	616	Neshaminy SD	Langhorne
19	587	Harrisburg City SD	Harrisburg
20	554	Easton Area SD	Easton
21	553	North Allegheny SD	Pittsburgh
22	527	East Stroudsburg Area SD	E Stroudsburg
23	522	Lower Merion SD	Ardmore
24	514	State College Area SD	State College
25	513	West Shore SD	New Cumberland
26	512	Norristown Area SD	Norristown
27	511	Seneca Valley SD	Harmony
28	498	Parkland SD	Allentown
29	497	Altoona Area SD	Altoona
30	496	Butler Area SD	Butler
31	485	Cumberland Valley SD	Mechanicsburg
32	471	Hazleton Area SD	Hazleton
33	460	Chambersburg Area SD	Chambersburg
34	457	Bristol Township SD	Levittown
35	444	Wilkes-Barre Area SD	Wilkes Barre
36	442	Abington SD	Abington
36	442	Coatesville Area SD	Coatesville
38	442	Armstrong SD	Ford City
39	439	Millcreek Township SD	Erie
40	436	Penn Hills SD	Pittsburgh
41	431	Souderton Area SD	Souderton
42	428	Mifflin County SD	Lewistown
43	423	Williamsport Area SD	Williamsport
44	416	Hempfield SD	Landisville
45	414	Warren County SD	North Warren
46	412	East Penn SD	Emmaus
46	412	Hempfield Area SD	Greensburg
48	409	Pennridge SD	Perkasie
49	407	Boyertown Area SD	Boyertown
50	407	York City SD	York
51	405	Spring-Ford Area SD	Collegeville
52	396	Tredyffrin-Easttown SD	Berwyn
53	396	Ridley SD	Folsom
54	393	Bensalem Township SD	Bensalem
55	382	Pleasant Valley SD	Brodheadsville
56	381	Centennial SD	Warminster
57	380	Shaler Area SD	Glenshaw
58	375	Fox Chapel Area SD	Pittsburgh
59	373	Mt Lebanon SD	Pittsburgh
60	363	Woodland Hills SD	Pittsburgh
61	357	Hatboro-Horsham SD	Horsham
62	356	Keystone Central SD	Lock Haven
63	355	Methacton SD	Norristown
64	355	Bethel Park SD	Bethel Park
65	350	Connellsville Area SD	Connellsville
66	349	Manheim Township SD	Lancaster
67	348	Northampton Area SD	Northampton
68	346	William Penn SD	Lansdowne
69	344	Stroudsburg Area SD	Stroudsburg
70	341	Dallastown Area SD	Dallastown
71	339	Colonial SD	Plymouth Meeting
72	338	Cheltenham Township SD	Elkins Park
73	337	Haverford Township SD	Havertown
74	333	North Hills SD	Pittsburgh
75	331	Carlisle Area SD	Carlisle
76	325	Delaware Valley SD	Milford
77	317	Wilson SD	West Lawn
78	316	Penn Manor SD	Millersville
79	314	Perkiomen Valley SD	Collegeville
80	305	Gateway SD	Monroeville
81	300	Wyoming Valley West SD	Kingston
82	298	Red Lion Area SD	Red Lion
83	298	Garnet Valley SD	Glen Mills
84	295	Wissahickon SD	Ambler
85	295	Dubois Area SD	Du Bois
86	295	Chester-Upland SD	Chester
87	294	Cornwall-Lebanon SD	Lebanon
88	292	Crawford Central SD	Meadville
89	290	Mckeesport Area SD	Mc Keesport
90	289	Rose Tree Media SD	Media
91	289	Warwick SD	Lititz
92	286	Central York SD	York
93	283	Wallenpaupack Area SD	Hawley
94	281	Upper Dublin SD	Maple Glen
95	280	Quakertown Community SD	Quakertown
96	278	Baldwin-Whitehall SD	Pittsburgh
97	276	Avon Grove SD	West Grove
98	275	Norwin SD	N Huntingdon
99	273	Owen J Roberts SD	Pottstown
100	271	Nazareth Area SD	Nazareth
101	267	Canon-Mcmillan SD	Canonsburg
102	266	Lower Dauphin SD	Hummelstown
103	266	Southeast Delco SD	Folcroft
104	262	Pine-Richland SD	Gibsonia
105	261	Upper Saint Clair SD	Pittsburgh
106	261	Governor Mifflin SD	Shillington
107	260	Moon Area SD	Moon Township
108	260	Unionville-Chadds Ford SD	Kennett Square
109	260	Plum Borough SD	Plum
110	256	Wallingford-Swarthmore SD	Wallingford
111	255	Albert Gallatin Area SD	Uniontown
112	254	Waynesboro Area SD	Waynesboro
113	252	Radnor Township SD	Wayne
114	250	Great Valley SD	Malvern
115	249	Penn-Trafford SD	Harrison City
116	249	Interboro SD	Prospect Park
116	249	Upper Merion Area SD	King Of Prussia
118	247	Penncrest SD	Saegertown
119	247	Ephrata Area SD	Ephrata
120	247	Hollidaysburg Area SD	Hollidaysburg
121	244	Lebanon SD	Lebanon
122	243	Marple Newtown SD	Newtown Square
123	242	Mechanicsburg Area SD	Mechanicsburg
124	241	Exeter Township SD	Reading
125	241	Kennett Consolidated SD	Kennett Square
126	240	Berwick Area SD	Berwick
126	240	Spring Grove Area SD	Spring Grove
128	239	Greater Latrobe SD	Latrobe
129	239	Greater Johnstown SD	Johnstown
130	238	South Western SD	Hanover
131	237	New Castle Area SD	New Castle
132	236	Chichester SD	Boothwyn
133	235	Phoenixville Area SD	Phoenixville
134	234	Conestoga Valley SD	Lancaster
135	234	Kiski Area SD	Vandergrift
136	233	Chartiers Valley SD	Pittsburgh
137	232	Indiana Area SD	Indiana
138	232	Trinity Area SD	Washington
139	231	Franklin Regional SD	Murrysville
140	230	Elizabethtown Area SD	Elizabethtown
141	230	Ringgold SD	New Eagle
142	228	Gettysburg Area SD	Gettysburg
143	227	Uniontown Area SD	Uniontown
144	224	Big Spring SD	Newville
145	224	Abington Heights SD	Clarks Summit
146	224	Tunkhannock Area SD	Tunkhannock
147	222	Whitehall-Coplay SD	Whitehall
148	220	Peters Township SD	Mcmurray
149	219	Springfield SD	Springfield
150	218	Oxford Area SD	Oxford
151	217	West Allegheny SD	Imperial
152	215	Daniel Boone Area SD	Birdsboro
153	214	Penn-Delco SD	Aston
154	214	Derry Township SD	Hershey
155	213	Bangor Area SD	Bangor
156	213	Dover Area SD	Dover
157	213	Montour SD	Mc Kees Rocks
158	212	Eastern Lancaster County SD	New Holland
159	211	Pottstown SD	Pottstown
160	211	Solanco SD	Quarryville
161	210	Northern York County SD	Dillsburg
162	210	Cocalico SD	Denver
163	209	Wayne Highlands SD	Honesdale
164	209	Juniata County SD	Mifflintown
165	208	Southern York County SD	Glen Rock
166	208	West Perry SD	Elliottsburg
167	207	Highlands SD	Natrona Heights
168	203	Pottsgrove SD	Pottstown
169	202	Twin Valley SD	Elverson
170	201	Conewago Valley SD	New Oxford
171	201	Jersey Shore Area SD	Jersey Shore
171	201	Shikellamy SD	Sunbury
173	200	Hampton Township SD	Allison Park
174	200	Lampeter-Strasburg SD	Lampeter
175	200	Bellefonte Area SD	Bellefonte
176	200	South Eastern SD	Fawn Grove
177	200	Northern Tioga SD	Elkland
178	199	Eastern York SD	Wrightsville
179	198	Susquehanna Township SD	Harrisburg
180	197	Bradford Area SD	Bradford
181	196	Northeastern York SD	Manchester
181	196	Punxsutawney Area SD	Punxsutawney
183	196	Upper Moreland Township SD	Willow Grove
184	196	Muhlenberg SD	Reading
185	196	North Pocono SD	Moscow
186	195	Greensburg Salem SD	Greensburg
186	195	Laurel Highlands SD	Uniontown

188	193	Manheim Central SD	Manheim
189	192	Middletown Area SD	Middletown
190	191	Ambridge Area SD	Ambridge
190	191	Clearfield Area SD	Clearfield
192	190	Shippensburg Area SD	Shippensburg
193	190	Danville Area SD	Danville
194	189	Upper Perkiomen SD	East Greenville
195	188	Blue Mountain SD	Orwigsburg
196	188	East Pennsboro Area SD	Enola
197	186	Elizabeth Forward SD	Elizabeth
198	186	West York Area SD	York
199	184	Conrad Weiser Area SD	Robesonia
200	184	Conneaut SD	Linesville
201	183	Hopewell Area SD	Aliquippa
202	182	Athens Area SD	Athens
203	182	Selinsgrove Area SD	Selinsgrove
204	181	Pittston Area SD	Pittston
205	180	West Mifflin Area SD	West Mifflin
206	179	York Suburban SD	York
207	178	Corry Area SD	Corry
208	175	Palmyra Area SD	Palmyra
209	174	Midd-West SD	Middleburg
210	174	Southern Lehigh SD	Center Valley
211	174	Lehighton Area SD	Lehighton
212	173	Milton Area SD	Milton
213	173	Mars Area SD	Mars
214	171	Huntingdon Area SD	Huntingdon
215	169	Somerset Area SD	Somerset
216	168	Keystone Oaks SD	Pittsburgh
217	168	Fleetwood Area SD	Fleetwood
217	168	Grove City Area SD	Grove City
219	167	Derry Area SD	Derry
219	167	South Butler County SD	Saxonburg
221	167	Tuscarora SD	Mercersburg
222	165	Blackhawk SD	Beaver Falls
222	165	Franklin Area SD	Franklin
224	163	Donegal SD	Mount Joy
225	161	Central Greene SD	Waynesburg
226	159	Octorara Area SD	Atglen
226	159	West Jefferson Hills SD	Jefferson Hls
228	159	Hamburg Area SD	Hamburg
228	159	Northern Lebanon SD	Fredericksburg
228	159	Pottsville Area SD	Pottsville
231	158	New Kensington-Arnold SD	New Kensington
232	157	General Mclane SD	Edinboro
232	157	Philipsburg-Osceola Area SD	Philipsburg
234	157	Western Wayne SD	South Canaan
235	157	Titusville Area SD	Titusville
236	157	Valley View SD	Archbald
237	156	Southern Tioga SD	Blossburg
238	154	Northwestern Lehigh SD	New Tripoli
239	154	Saucon Valley SD	Hellertown
240	153	Saint Marys Area SD	Saint Marys
240	153	Sharon City SD	Sharon
242	152	Springfield Township SD	Oreland
243	152	South Middleton SD	Boiling Springs
244	152	Mifflinburg Area SD	Mifflinburg
245	152	Wilkinsburg Borough SD	Wilkinsburg
246	151	Washington SD	Washington
247	149	Yough SD	Herminie
248	149	Belle Vernon Area SD	Belle Vernon
248	149	Susquenita SD	Duncannon
250	148	Crestwood SD	Mountain Top
251	148	Mcguffey SD	Claysville
252	148	Slippery Rock Area SD	Slippery Rock
253	148	Oil City Area SD	Oil City
253	148	Shamokin Area SD	Coal Township
255	147	Wilson Area SD	Easton
256	146	Eastern Lebanon County SD	Myerstown
257	146	Harbor Creek SD	Harborcreek
258	145	Dallas SD	Dallas
259	145	Wyoming Area SD	Exeter
260	144	Greencastle-Antrim SD	Greencastle
261	144	Mount Pleasant Area SD	Mount Pleasant
261	144	Palisades SD	Kintnersville
263	144	Big Beaver Falls Area SD	Beaver Falls
264	143	Forest Hills SD	Sidman
265	142	Bedford Area SD	Bedford
266	139	Southmoreland SD	Scottdale
267	139	Oley Valley SD	Oley
267	139	Steel Valley SD	Munhall
269	138	Fort Leboeuf SD	Waterford
270	137	Hermitage SD	Hermitage
271	137	Deer Lakes SD	Russellton
272	137	Bald Eagle Area SD	Wingate
272	137	Central Columbia SD	Bloomsburg
272	137	Littlestown Area SD	Littlestown
275	136	Warrior Run SD	Turbotville
276	136	Montoursville Area SD	Montoursville
277	135	Quaker Valley SD	Sewickley
278	135	Spring Cove SD	Roaring Spring
279	134	Brandywine Heights Area SD	Topton
280	134	Kutztown Area SD	Kutztown
281	134	Blairsville-Saltsburg SD	Blairsville
282	133	Ellwood City Area SD	Ellwood City
283	132	Lake-Lehman SD	Lehman
284	131	Wyomissing Area SD	Wyomissing
285	131	Brownsville Area SD	Brownsville
286	128	Bermudian Springs SD	York Springs
286	128	Center Area SD	Monaca
288	128	Montrose Area SD	Montrose
289	127	Tamaqua Area SD	Tamaqua
290	127	Girard SD	Girard
290	127	Tyrone Area SD	Tyrone
292	127	Freeport Area SD	Freeport
292	127	Pequea Valley SD	Kinzers
294	126	Northern Lehigh SD	Slatington
295	125	Bloomsburg Area SD	Bloomsburg
296	125	Beaver Area SD	Beaver
296	125	Burrell SD	Lower Burrell
296	125	Mohawk Area SD	Bessemer
296	125	Penn Cambria SD	Cresson
296	125	Schuylkill Valley SD	Leesport
301	124	Brookville Area SD	Brookville
302	123	Central Cambria SD	Ebensburg
302	123	East Lycoming SD	Hughesville
302	123	Marion Center Area SD	Marion Center
305	122	Lewisburg Area SD	Lewisburg
306	121	Mount Union Area SD	Mount Union
307	121	Ligonier Valley SD	Ligonier
307	121	South Fayette Township SD	Mc Donald
307	121	Wellsboro Area SD	Wellsboro
310	119	New Brighton Area SD	New Brighton
311	119	Towanda Area SD	Towanda
312	119	Riverside Beaver County SD	Ellwood City
313	118	Salisbury Township SD	Allentown
313	118	South Park SD	South Park
315	118	Catasauqua Area SD	Catasauqua
315	118	Hanover Area SD	Wilkes Barre
315	118	Karns City Area SD	Karns City
318	117	Charleroi SD	Charleroi
319	116	Tulpehocken Area SD	Bernville
320	116	Pen Argyl Area SD	Pen Argyl
320	116	Troy Area SD	Troy
322	115	Cambria Heights SD	Patton
323	115	Hanover Public SD	Hanover
323	115	Lower Moreland Township SD	Huntingdon Vly
325	114	Jim Thorpe Area SD	Jim Thorpe
325	114	South Allegheny SD	Mc Keesport
327	113	Mount Carmel Area SD	Mount Carmel
327	113	Palmerton Area SD	Palmerton
329	112	Upper Adams SD	Biglerville
330	109	Penns Valley Area SD	Spring Mills
331	109	Sto-Rox SD	Mckees Rocks
332	108	East Allegheny SD	N Versailles
332	108	Greater Nanticoke Area SD	Nanticoke
334	108	Chestnut Ridge SD	Fishertown
335	107	North East SD	North East
335	107	Northgate SD	Pittsburgh
337	107	North Schuylkill SD	Ashland
338	106	Northwestern SD	Albion
339	106	Annville-Cleona SD	Annville
340	105	Wilmington Area SD	New Wilmington
341	104	Greenville Area SD	Greenville
342	103	Elk Lake SD	Dimock
343	103	Westmont Hilltop SD	Johnstown
344	103	Carlynton SD	Carnegie
344	103	Freedom Area SD	Freedom
346	101	Burgettstown Area SD	Burgettstown
346	101	Pine Grove Area SD	Pine Grove
348	99	Mid Valley SD	Throop
349	99	Fairview SD	Fairview
350	99	Apollo-Ridge SD	Spring Church
351	96	Wyalusing Area SD	Wyalusing
352	94	Dunmore SD	Dunmore
352	94	Everett Area SD	Everett
354	93	Mercer Area SD	Mercer
355	93	Richland SD	Johnstown
356	93	Moniteau SD	West Sunbury
357	90	Lakeland SD	Jermyn
358	88	Wattsburg Area SD	Erie
359	82	Reynolds SD	Greenville
360	72	Pennsylvania Virtual CS	Norristown
361	39	Western Pennsylvania Cyber CS	Midland
362	n/a	Pde Division of Data Services	Harrisburg

Number of Students

Rank	Number	District Name	City
1	189,779	Philadelphia City SD	Philadelphia
2	34,658	Pittsburgh SD	Pittsburgh
3	19,089	Central Bucks SD	Doylestown
4	16,964	Allentown City SD	Allentown
5	16,515	Reading SD	Reading
6	15,792	Pde Division of Data Services	Harrisburg
7	14,726	Bethlehem Area SD	Bethlehem
8	13,521	North Penn SD	Lansdale
9	12,690	Erie City SD	Erie
10	12,482	Council Rock SD	Newtown
11	12,263	Upper Darby SD	Drexel Hill
12	11,646	West Chester Area SD	West Chester
13	11,207	Pennsbury SD	Fallsington
14	11,190	Pocono Mountain SD	Swiftwater
15	11,104	Central Dauphin SD	Harrisburg
16	11,045	Lancaster SD	Lancaster
17	10,700	Downingtown Area SD	Downingtown
18	9,419	Neshaminy SD	Langhorne
19	9,300	Hazleton Area SD	Hazleton
20	8,940	Scranton SD	Scranton
21	8,695	Parkland SD	Allentown
22	8,390	Altoona Area SD	Altoona
23	8,384	Butler Area SD	Butler
24	8,364	Easton Area SD	Easton
25	8,355	West Shore SD	New Cumberland
26	8,185	North Allegheny SD	Pittsburgh
27	8,022	Chambersburg Area SD	Chambersburg
28	7,883	Harrisburg City SD	Harrisburg
29	7,708	Cumberland Valley SD	Mechanicsburg
30	7,646	Seneca Valley SD	Harmony
31	7,598	East Stroudsburg Area SD	E Stroudsburg
32	7,411	Abington SD	Abington
33	7,343	State College Area SD	State College
34	7,319	Coatesville Area SD	Coatesville
35	7,229	Hempfield SD	Landisville
36	7,116	East Penn SD	Emmaus
37	7,107	Millcreek Township SD	Erie
38	7,085	Pennridge SD	Perkasie
39	6,952	Wilkes-Barre Area SD	Wilkes Barre
40	6,950	Norristown Area SD	Norristown
41	6,934	Boyertown Area SD	Boyertown
42	6,905	Pleasant Valley SD	Brodheadsville
43	6,890	Bristol Township SD	Levittown
44	6,691	York City SD	York
45	6,662	Lower Merion SD	Ardmore
46	6,650	Souderton Area SD	Souderton
47	6,616	Hempfield Area SD	Greensburg
48	6,535	Spring-Ford Area SD	Collegeville
49	6,425	Armstrong SD	Ford City
50	6,360	Bensalem Township SD	Bensalem
51	6,327	Centennial SD	Warminster
52	6,120	Warren County SD	North Warren
53	6,093	Mifflin County SD	Lewistown
54	5,985	Williamsport Area SD	Williamsport
55	5,891	Penn Hills SD	Pittsburgh
56	5,797	Woodland Hills SD	Pittsburgh
57	5,766	Connellsville Area SD	Connellsville
58	5,743	Ridley SD	Folsom
59	5,726	Tredyffrin-Easttown SD	Berwyn
60	5,611	William Penn SD	Lansdowne
61	5,599	Northampton Area SD	Northampton
62	5,595	Shaler Area SD	Glenshaw
63	5,551	Mt Lebanon SD	Pittsburgh
64	5,536	Stroudsburg Area SD	Stroudsburg
65	5,512	Haverford Township SD	Havertown
65	5,512	Red Lion Area SD	Red Lion
67	5,503	Hatboro-Horsham SD	Horsham
68	5,378	Delaware Valley SD	Milford
69	5,369	Manheim Township SD	Lancaster
70	5,342	Penn Manor SD	Millersville
71	5,314	Wilson SD	West Lawn
72	5,287	Dallastown Area SD	Dallastown
73	5,270	Quakertown Community SD	Quakertown
74	5,231	Methacton SD	Norristown
75	5,212	Bethel Park SD	Bethel Park
76	5,205	Norwin SD	N Huntingdon
77	5,152	Wyoming Valley West SD	Kingston
78	5,048	Chester-Upland SD	Chester
79	4,964	Perkiomen Valley SD	Collegeville
80	4,859	North Hills SD	Pittsburgh
81	4,854	Avon Grove SD	West Grove
82	4,820	Carlisle Area SD	Carlisle
83	4,769	Penn-Trafford SD	Harrison City
84	4,734	Cheltenham Township SD	Elkins Park
85	4,732	Central York SD	York
86	4,727	Keystone Central SD	Lock Haven
87	4,714	Cornwall-Lebanon SD	Lebanon
88	4,704	Mckeesport Area SD	Mc Keesport
89	4,644	Fox Chapel Area SD	Pittsburgh
89	4,644	Warwick SD	Lititz
91	4,613	Baldwin-Whitehall SD	Pittsburgh
92	4,612	Colonial SD	Plymouth Meeting
93	4,535	Wissahickon SD	Ambler
94	4,528	Dubois Area SD	Du Bois
95	4,502	Kiski Area SD	Vandergrift
96	4,432	Gateway SD	Monroeville
97	4,424	Nazareth Area SD	Nazareth
98	4,406	Upper Dublin SD	Maple Glen
99	4,397	Plum Borough SD	Plum
100	4,325	Canon-Mcmillan SD	Canonsburg

101	4,322	Greater Latrobe SD	Latrobe
102	4,253	Owen J Roberts SD	Pottstown
103	4,243	Lebanon SD	Lebanon
104	4,236	Crawford Central SD	Meadville
105	4,157	Governor Mifflin SD	Shillington
106	4,127	Upper Saint Clair SD	Pittsburgh
107	4,092	Waynesboro Area SD	Waynesboro
108	4,082	Exeter Township SD	Reading
109	4,081	Albert Gallatin Area SD	Uniontown
110	4,079	Ephrata Area SD	Ephrata
111	4,069	Southeast Delco SD	Folcroft
112	4,038	Kennett Consolidated SD	Kennett Square
113	4,037	Rose Tree Media SD	Media
114	4,011	South Western SD	Hanover
115	3,982	Interboro SD	Prospect Park
116	3,980	Garnet Valley SD	Glen Mills
117	3,969	Whitehall-Coplay SD	Whitehall
118	3,967	Wallenpaupack Area SD	Hawley
119	3,945	Penncrest SD	Saegertown
120	3,939	Solanco SD	Quarryville
121	3,937	Peters Township SD	Mcmurray
122	3,902	Elizabethtown Area SD	Elizabethtown
123	3,900	Lower Dauphin SD	Hummelstown
124	3,884	Conestoga Valley SD	Lancaster
125	3,879	Unionville-Chadds Ford SD	Kennett Square
126	3,851	Spring Grove Area SD	Spring Grove
127	3,839	New Castle Area SD	New Castle
128	3,807	Great Valley SD	Malvern
129	3,793	Hollidaysburg Area SD	Hollidaysburg
130	3,789	Franklin Regional SD	Murrysville
131	3,784	Trinity Area SD	Washington
132	3,755	Ringgold SD	New Eagle
133	3,751	Moon Area SD	Moon Township
134	3,717	Bangor Area SD	Bangor
135	3,715	Pine-Richland SD	Gibsonia
136	3,699	Abington Heights SD	Clarks Summit
137	3,686	Conewago Valley SD	New Oxford
138	3,675	Laurel Highlands SD	Uniontown
139	3,646	Chichester SD	Boothwyn
140	3,578	Greater Johnstown SD	Johnstown
140	3,578	Wallingford-Swarthmore SD	Wallingford
142	3,558	Mechanicsburg Area SD	Mechanicsburg
143	3,543	Uniontown Area SD	Uniontown
144	3,542	Cocalico SD	Denver
145	3,537	Dover Area SD	Dover
146	3,506	Greensburg Salem SD	Greensburg
147	3,489	Daniel Boone Area SD	Birdsboro
148	3,467	Eastern Lancaster County SD	New Holland
149	3,455	Chartiers Valley SD	Pittsburgh
150	3,448	Derry Township SD	Hershey
151	3,447	Upper Merion Area SD	King Of Prussia
152	3,406	Marple Newtown SD	Newtown Square
153	3,396	Berwick Area SD	Berwick
153	3,396	Gettysburg Area SD	Gettysburg
155	3,380	Upper Perkiomen SD	East Greenville
156	3,357	Springfield SD	Springfield
157	3,336	Oxford Area SD	Oxford
158	3,332	Montour SD	Mc Kees Rocks
159	3,330	Pennsylvania Virtual CS	Norristown
160	3,317	Pottstown SD	Pottstown
161	3,315	Penn-Delco SD	Aston
161	3,315	Radnor Township SD	Wayne
163	3,304	Shippensburg Area SD	Shippensburg
164	3,301	West Mifflin Area SD	West Mifflin
165	3,297	Southern York County SD	Glen Rock
166	3,292	South Eastern SD	Fawn Grove
167	3,281	Wayne Highlands SD	Honesdale
168	3,270	Shikellamy SD	Sunbury
169	3,248	North Pocono SD	Moscow
170	3,246	Pottsgrove SD	Pottstown
171	3,233	Indiana Area SD	Indiana
172	3,222	Twin Valley SD	Elverson
173	3,219	Hampton Township SD	Allison Park
174	3,204	West Allegheny SD	Imperial
175	3,201	Lampeter-Strasburg SD	Lampeter
176	3,195	Northern York County SD	Dillsburg
177	3,191	Big Spring SD	Newville
178	3,176	Juniata County SD	Mifflintown
179	3,173	Tunkhannock Area SD	Tunkhannock
180	3,169	Phoenixville Area SD	Phoenixville
181	3,157	Pittston Area SD	Pittston
182	3,121	Susquehanna Township SD	Harrisburg
183	3,108	Upper Moreland Township SD	Willow Grove
184	3,105	Northeastern York SD	Manchester
185	3,087	Manheim Central SD	Manheim
186	3,065	West York Area SD	York
187	3,060	Pottsville Area SD	Pottsville
188	3,043	Ambridge Area SD	Ambridge
189	3,029	Muhlenberg SD	Reading
190	3,022	Jersey Shore Area SD	Jersey Shore
191	3,006	Bellefonte Area SD	Bellefonte
192	2,992	Clearfield Area SD	Clearfield
193	2,986	Crestwood SD	Mountain Top
194	2,965	Bradford Area SD	Bradford
195	2,961	Southern Lehigh SD	Center Valley
196	2,959	Belle Vernon Area SD	Belle Vernon
196	2,959	Elizabeth Forward SD	Elizabeth
198	2,917	South Butler County SD	Saxonburg
199	2,916	Blue Mountain SD	Orwigsburg
200	2,911	Palmyra Area SD	Palmyra
200	2,911	West Jefferson Hills SD	Jefferson Hls
202	2,890	Selinsgrove Area SD	Selinsgrove
203	2,868	Hopewell Area SD	Aliquippa
204	2,849	West Perry SD	Elliottsburg
205	2,821	East Pennsboro Area SD	Enola
206	2,804	Conrad Weiser Area SD	Robesonia
207	2,800	Conneaut SD	Linesville
208	2,788	Grove City Area SD	Grove City
209	2,777	Blackhawk SD	Beaver Falls
210	2,768	Punxsutawney Area SD	Punxsutawney
211	2,757	Derry Area SD	Derry
212	2,751	Mars Area SD	Mars
212	2,751	Somerset Area SD	Somerset
214	2,748	Hamburg Area SD	Hamburg
214	2,748	Highlands SD	Natrona Heights
216	2,706	York Suburban SD	York
217	2,700	Greencastle-Antrim SD	Greencastle
218	2,669	Octorara Area SD	Atglen
219	2,664	Eastern York SD	Wrightsville
220	2,644	Fleetwood Area SD	Fleetwood
221	2,625	Danville Area SD	Danville
222	2,607	Wyoming Area SD	Exeter
223	2,601	Tuscarora SD	Mercersburg
224	2,592	Yough SD	Herminie
225	2,587	Valley View SD	Archbald
226	2,573	New Kensington-Arnold SD	New Kensington
227	2,568	Slippery Rock Area SD	Slippery Rock
228	2,559	Dallas SD	Dallas
229	2,556	Shamokin Area SD	Coal Township
230	2,555	Saint Marys Area SD	Saint Marys
231	2,553	Northern Tioga SD	Elkland
232	2,549	Mifflinburg Area SD	Mifflinburg
233	2,548	Mount Pleasant Area SD	Mount Pleasant
234	2,546	Middletown Area SD	Middletown
235	2,540	Donegal SD	Mount Joy
236	2,537	Keystone Oaks SD	Pittsburgh
237	2,521	Western Wayne SD	South Canaan
238	2,504	Oil City Area SD	Oil City
239	2,486	Midd-West SD	Middleburg
240	2,485	Corry Area SD	Corry
240	2,485	General Mclane SD	Edinboro
242	2,458	Milton Area SD	Milton
243	2,457	Titusville Area SD	Titusville
244	2,454	Northern Lebanon SD	Fredericksburg
245	2,451	Lehighton Area SD	Lehighton
246	2,439	Athens Area SD	Athens
247	2,425	Eastern Lebanon County SD	Myerstown
248	2,407	Sharon City SD	Sharon
249	2,395	Huntingdon Area SD	Huntingdon
250	2,378	Littlestown Area SD	Littlestown
251	2,357	Mcguffey SD	Claysville
252	2,355	Northwestern Lehigh SD	New Tripoli
253	2,351	Fort Leboeuf SD	Waterford
254	2,342	Bedford Area SD	Bedford
255	2,334	Forest Hills SD	Sidman
256	2,332	Franklin Area SD	Franklin
257	2,322	Southmoreland SD	Scottdale
258	2,310	Central Greene SD	Waynesburg
259	2,308	Saucon Valley SD	Hellertown
260	2,297	Hermitage SD	Hermitage
261	2,283	Susquenita SD	Duncannon
262	2,266	Wilson Area SD	Easton
263	2,238	South Park SD	South Park
264	2,228	Southern Tioga SD	Blossburg
265	2,220	Blairsville-Saltsburg SD	Blairsville
266	2,219	Central Columbia SD	Bloomsburg
267	2,218	Tamaqua Area SD	Tamaqua
268	2,206	Ellwood City Area SD	Ellwood City
269	2,194	Burrell SD	Lower Burrell
270	2,176	Lake-Lehman SD	Lehman
271	2,160	Bermudian Springs SD	York Springs
272	2,139	Montoursville Area SD	Montoursville
273	2,136	Ligonier Valley SD	Ligonier
273	2,136	Philipsburg-Osceola Area SD	Philipsburg
275	2,132	Northern Lehigh SD	Slatington
276	2,131	Greater Nanticoke Area SD	Nanticoke
277	2,123	Palisades SD	Kintnersville
278	2,121	Oley Valley SD	Oley
279	2,120	South Middleton SD	Boiling Springs
280	2,116	Steel Valley SD	Munhall
281	2,098	Deer Lakes SD	Russellton
282	2,095	Harbor Creek SD	Harborcreek
283	2,087	Western Pennsylvania Cyber CS	Midland
284	2,083	Washington SD	Washington
285	2,076	Hanover Area SD	Wilkes Barre
286	2,073	Beaver Area SD	Beaver
287	2,062	Springfield Township SD	Oreland
288	2,054	Bald Eagle Area SD	Wingate
289	2,015	Center Area SD	Monaca
290	1,995	Palmerton Area SD	Palmerton
291	1,994	East Allegheny SD	N Versailles
291	1,994	North Schuylkill SD	Ashland
291	1,994	Pen Argyl Area SD	Pen Argyl
294	1,992	Mohawk Area SD	Bessemer
295	1,991	Girard SD	Girard
296	1,983	Brandywine Heights Area SD	Topton
297	1,974	Brownsville Area SD	Brownsville
298	1,965	New Brighton Area SD	New Brighton
299	1,962	Quaker Valley SD	Sewickley
300	1,959	Pequea Valley SD	Kinzers
301	1,953	Tyrone Area SD	Tyrone
302	1,950	Freeport Area SD	Freeport
303	1,939	Spring Cove SD	Roaring Spring
304	1,929	Big Beaver Falls Area SD	Beaver Falls
304	1,929	Riverside Beaver County SD	Ellwood City
306	1,924	North East SD	North East
307	1,917	Montrose Area SD	Montrose
308	1,912	Central Cambria SD	Ebensburg
309	1,908	Schuylkill Valley SD	Leesport
310	1,890	Troy Area SD	Troy
311	1,885	Brookville Area SD	Brookville
312	1,868	South Fayette Township SD	Mc Donald
313	1,867	Penn Cambria SD	Cresson
314	1,860	Warrior Run SD	Turbotville
315	1,858	Wyomissing Area SD	Wyomissing
316	1,854	Northwestern SD	Albion
317	1,853	Towanda Area SD	Towanda
318	1,837	Salisbury Township SD	Allentown
319	1,834	South Allegheny SD	Mc Keesport
320	1,832	Karns City Area SD	Karns City
321	1,828	Chestnut Ridge SD	Fishertown
322	1,822	Jim Thorpe Area SD	Jim Thorpe
323	1,812	Kutztown Area SD	Kutztown
324	1,794	Mount Carmel Area SD	Mount Carmel
325	1,788	Lewisburg Area SD	Lewisburg
326	1,785	Freedom Area SD	Freedom
327	1,781	East Lycoming SD	Hughesville
328	1,780	Bloomsburg Area SD	Bloomsburg
329	1,774	Upper Adams SD	Biglerville
330	1,758	Pine Grove Area SD	Pine Grove
331	1,755	Lower Moreland Township SD	Huntingdon Vly
332	1,724	Dunmore SD	Dunmore
333	1,720	Westmont Hilltop SD	Johnstown
334	1,717	Catasauqua Area SD	Catasauqua
335	1,711	Hanover Public SD	Hanover
336	1,706	Marion Center Area SD	Marion Center
337	1,705	Moniteau SD	West Sunbury
338	1,695	Tulpehocken Area SD	Bernville
339	1,686	Annville-Cleona SD	Annville
340	1,680	Wattsburg Area SD	Erie
341	1,668	Charleroi SD	Charleroi
342	1,661	Wilkinsburg Borough SD	Wilkinsburg
343	1,660	Wellsboro Area SD	Wellsboro
344	1,649	Lakeland SD	Jermyn
345	1,638	Apollo-Ridge SD	Spring Church
346	1,623	Carlynton SD	Carnegie
347	1,615	Penns Valley Area SD	Spring Mills
348	1,602	Greenville Area SD	Greenville
349	1,593	Richland SD	Johnstown
350	1,591	Fairview SD	Fairview
351	1,576	Wilmington Area SD	New Wilmington
352	1,565	Everett Area SD	Everett
353	1,549	Cambria Heights SD	Patton
354	1,545	Mount Union Area SD	Mount Union
355	1,544	Burgettstown Area SD	Burgettstown
356	1,538	Mid Valley SD	Throop
356	1,538	Reynolds SD	Greenville
358	1,529	Mercer Area SD	Mercer
359	1,528	Sto-Rox SD	Mckees Rocks
360	1,526	Northgate SD	Pittsburgh
361	1,509	Elk Lake SD	Dimock
362	1,504	Wyalusing Area SD	Wyalusing

Male Students

Rank	Percent	District Name	City
1	n/a	Abington SD	Abington
1	n/a	Abington Heights SD	Clarks Summit
1	n/a	Albert Gallatin Area SD	Uniontown
1	n/a	Allentown City SD	Allentown
1	n/a	Altoona Area SD	Altoona
1	n/a	Ambridge Area SD	Ambridge
1	n/a	Annville-Cleona SD	Annville
1	n/a	Apollo-Ridge SD	Spring Church
1	n/a	Armstrong SD	Ford City
1	n/a	Athens Area SD	Athens
1	n/a	Avon Grove SD	West Grove

1	n/a	Bald Eagle Area SD	Wingate
1	n/a	Baldwin-Whitehall SD	Pittsburgh
1	n/a	Bangor Area SD	Bangor
1	n/a	Beaver Area SD	Beaver
1	n/a	Bedford Area SD	Bedford
1	n/a	Belle Vernon Area SD	Belle Vernon
1	n/a	Bellefonte Area SD	Bellefonte
1	n/a	Bensalem Township SD	Bensalem
1	n/a	Bermudian Springs SD	York Springs
1	n/a	Berwick Area SD	Berwick
1	n/a	Bethel Park SD	Bethel Park
1	n/a	Bethlehem Area SD	Bethlehem
1	n/a	Big Beaver Falls Area SD	Beaver Falls
1	n/a	Big Spring SD	Newville
1	n/a	Blackhawk SD	Beaver Falls
1	n/a	Blairsville-Saltsburg SD	Blairsville
1	n/a	Bloomsburg Area SD	Bloomsburg
1	n/a	Blue Mountain SD	Orwigsburg
1	n/a	Boyertown Area SD	Boyertown
1	n/a	Bradford Area SD	Bradford
1	n/a	Brandywine Heights Area SD	Topton
1	n/a	Bristol Township SD	Levittown
1	n/a	Brookville Area SD	Brookville
1	n/a	Brownsville Area SD	Brownsville
1	n/a	Burgettstown Area SD	Burgettstown
1	n/a	Burrell SD	Lower Burrell
1	n/a	Butler Area SD	Butler
1	n/a	Cambria Heights SD	Patton
1	n/a	Canon-Mcmillan SD	Canonsburg
1	n/a	Carlisle Area SD	Carlisle
1	n/a	Carlynton SD	Carnegie
1	n/a	Catasauqua Area SD	Catasauqua
1	n/a	Centennial SD	Warminster
1	n/a	Center Area SD	Monaca
1	n/a	Central Bucks SD	Doylestown
1	n/a	Central Cambria SD	Ebensburg
1	n/a	Central Columbia SD	Bloomsburg
1	n/a	Central Dauphin SD	Harrisburg
1	n/a	Central Greene SD	Waynesburg
1	n/a	Central York SD	York
1	n/a	Chambersburg Area SD	Chambersburg
1	n/a	Charleroi SD	Charleroi
1	n/a	Chartiers Valley SD	Pittsburgh
1	n/a	Cheltenham Township SD	Elkins Park
1	n/a	Chester-Upland SD	Chester
1	n/a	Chestnut Ridge SD	Fishertown
1	n/a	Chichester SD	Boothwyn
1	n/a	Clearfield Area SD	Clearfield
1	n/a	Coatesville Area SD	Coatesville
1	n/a	Cocalico SD	Denver
1	n/a	Colonial SD	Plymouth Meeting
1	n/a	Conestoga Valley SD	Lancaster
1	n/a	Conewago Valley SD	New Oxford
1	n/a	Conneaut SD	Linesville
1	n/a	Connellsville Area SD	Connellsville
1	n/a	Conrad Weiser Area SD	Robesonia
1	n/a	Cornwall-Lebanon SD	Lebanon
1	n/a	Corry Area SD	Corry
1	n/a	Council Rock SD	Newtown
1	n/a	Crawford Central SD	Meadville
1	n/a	Crestwood SD	Mountain Top
1	n/a	Cumberland Valley SD	Mechanicsburg
1	n/a	Dallas SD	Dallas
1	n/a	Dallastown Area SD	Dallastown
1	n/a	Daniel Boone Area SD	Birdsboro
1	n/a	Danville Area SD	Danville
1	n/a	Deer Lakes SD	Russellton
1	n/a	Delaware Valley SD	Milford
1	n/a	Derry Area SD	Derry
1	n/a	Derry Township SD	Hershey
1	n/a	Donegal SD	Mount Joy
1	n/a	Dover Area SD	Dover
1	n/a	Downingtown Area SD	Downingtown
1	n/a	Dubois Area SD	Du Bois
1	n/a	Dunmore SD	Dunmore
1	n/a	East Allegheny SD	N Versailles
1	n/a	East Lycoming SD	Hughesville
1	n/a	East Penn SD	Emmaus
1	n/a	East Pennsboro Area SD	Enola
1	n/a	East Stroudsburg Area SD	E Stroudsburg
1	n/a	Eastern Lancaster County SD	New Holland
1	n/a	Eastern Lebanon County SD	Myerstown
1	n/a	Eastern York SD	Wrightsville
1	n/a	Easton Area SD	Easton
1	n/a	Elizabeth Forward SD	Elizabeth
1	n/a	Elizabethtown Area SD	Elizabethtown
1	n/a	Elk Lake SD	Dimock
1	n/a	Ellwood City Area SD	Ellwood City
1	n/a	Ephrata Area SD	Ephrata
1	n/a	Erie City SD	Erie
1	n/a	Everett Area SD	Everett
1	n/a	Exeter Township SD	Reading
1	n/a	Fairview SD	Fairview
1	n/a	Fleetwood Area SD	Fleetwood
1	n/a	Forest Hills SD	Sidman
1	n/a	Fort Leboeuf SD	Waterford
1	n/a	Fox Chapel Area SD	Pittsburgh
1	n/a	Franklin Area SD	Franklin
1	n/a	Franklin Regional SD	Murrysville
1	n/a	Freedom Area SD	Freedom
1	n/a	Freeport Area SD	Freeport
1	n/a	Garnet Valley SD	Glen Mills
1	n/a	Gateway SD	Monroeville
1	n/a	General Mclane SD	Edinboro
1	n/a	Gettysburg Area SD	Gettysburg
1	n/a	Girard SD	Girard
1	n/a	Governor Mifflin SD	Shillington
1	n/a	Great Valley SD	Malvern
1	n/a	Greater Johnstown SD	Johnstown
1	n/a	Greater Latrobe SD	Latrobe
1	n/a	Greater Nanticoke Area SD	Nanticoke
1	n/a	Greencastle-Antrim SD	Greencastle
1	n/a	Greensburg Salem SD	Greensburg
1	n/a	Greenville Area SD	Greenville
1	n/a	Grove City Area SD	Grove City
1	n/a	Hamburg Area SD	Hamburg
1	n/a	Hampton Township SD	Allison Park
1	n/a	Hanover Area SD	Wilkes Barre
1	n/a	Hanover Public SD	Hanover
1	n/a	Harbor Creek SD	Harborcreek
1	n/a	Harrisburg City SD	Harrisburg
1	n/a	Hatboro-Horsham SD	Horsham
1	n/a	Haverford Township SD	Havertown
1	n/a	Hazleton Area SD	Hazleton
1	n/a	Hempfield SD	Landisville
1	n/a	Hempfield Area SD	Greensburg
1	n/a	Hermitage SD	Hermitage
1	n/a	Highlands SD	Natrona Heights
1	n/a	Hollidaysburg Area SD	Hollidaysburg
1	n/a	Hopewell Area SD	Aliquippa
1	n/a	Huntingdon Area SD	Huntingdon
1	n/a	Indiana Area SD	Indiana
1	n/a	Interboro SD	Prospect Park
1	n/a	Jersey Shore Area SD	Jersey Shore
1	n/a	Jim Thorpe Area SD	Jim Thorpe
1	n/a	Juniata County SD	Mifflintown
1	n/a	Karns City Area SD	Karns City
1	n/a	Kennett Consolidated SD	Kennett Square
1	n/a	Keystone Central SD	Lock Haven
1	n/a	Keystone Oaks SD	Pittsburgh
1	n/a	Kiski Area SD	Vandergrift
1	n/a	Kutztown Area SD	Kutztown
1	n/a	Lake-Lehman SD	Lehman
1	n/a	Lakeland SD	Jermyn
1	n/a	Lampeter-Strasburg SD	Lampeter
1	n/a	Lancaster SD	Lancaster
1	n/a	Laurel Highlands SD	Uniontown
1	n/a	Lebanon SD	Lebanon
1	n/a	Lehighton Area SD	Lehighton
1	n/a	Lewisburg Area SD	Lewisburg
1	n/a	Ligonier Valley SD	Ligonier
1	n/a	Littlestown Area SD	Littlestown
1	n/a	Lower Dauphin SD	Hummelstown
1	n/a	Lower Merion SD	Ardmore
1	n/a	Lower Moreland Township SD	Huntingdon Vly
1	n/a	Manheim Central SD	Manheim
1	n/a	Manheim Township SD	Lancaster
1	n/a	Marion Center Area SD	Marion Center
1	n/a	Marple Newtown SD	Newtown Square
1	n/a	Mars Area SD	Mars
1	n/a	Mcguffey SD	Claysville
1	n/a	Mckeesport Area SD	Mc Keesport
1	n/a	Mechanicsburg Area SD	Mechanicsburg
1	n/a	Mercer Area SD	Mercer
1	n/a	Methacton SD	Norristown
1	n/a	Mid Valley SD	Throop
1	n/a	Midd-West SD	Middleburg
1	n/a	Middletown Area SD	Middletown
1	n/a	Mifflin County SD	Lewistown
1	n/a	Mifflinburg Area SD	Mifflinburg
1	n/a	Millcreek Township SD	Erie
1	n/a	Milton Area SD	Milton
1	n/a	Mohawk Area SD	Bessemer
1	n/a	Moniteau SD	West Sunbury
1	n/a	Montour SD	Mc Kees Rocks
1	n/a	Montoursville Area SD	Montoursville
1	n/a	Montrose Area SD	Montrose
1	n/a	Moon Area SD	Moon Township
1	n/a	Mount Carmel Area SD	Mount Carmel
1	n/a	Mount Pleasant Area SD	Mount Pleasant
1	n/a	Mount Union Area SD	Mount Union
1	n/a	Mt Lebanon SD	Pittsburgh
1	n/a	Muhlenberg SD	Reading
1	n/a	Nazareth Area SD	Nazareth
1	n/a	Neshaminy SD	Langhorne
1	n/a	New Brighton Area SD	New Brighton
1	n/a	New Castle Area SD	New Castle
1	n/a	New Kensington-Arnold SD	New Kensington
1	n/a	Norristown Area SD	Norristown
1	n/a	North Allegheny SD	Pittsburgh
1	n/a	North East SD	North East
1	n/a	North Hills SD	Pittsburgh
1	n/a	North Penn SD	Lansdale
1	n/a	North Pocono SD	Moscow
1	n/a	North Schuylkill SD	Ashland
1	n/a	Northampton Area SD	Northampton
1	n/a	Northeastern York SD	Manchester
1	n/a	Northern Lebanon SD	Fredericksburg
1	n/a	Northern Lehigh SD	Slatington
1	n/a	Northern Tioga SD	Elkland
1	n/a	Northern York County SD	Dillsburg
1	n/a	Northgate SD	Pittsburgh
1	n/a	Northwestern SD	Albion
1	n/a	Northwestern Lehigh SD	New Tripoli
1	n/a	Norwin SD	N Huntingdon
1	n/a	Octorara Area SD	Atglen
1	n/a	Oil City Area SD	Oil City
1	n/a	Oley Valley SD	Oley
1	n/a	Owen J Roberts SD	Pottstown
1	n/a	Oxford Area SD	Oxford
1	n/a	Palisades SD	Kintnersville
1	n/a	Palmerton Area SD	Palmerton
1	n/a	Palmyra Area SD	Palmyra
1	n/a	Parkland SD	Allentown
1	n/a	Pde Division of Data Services	Harrisburg
1	n/a	Pen Argyl Area SD	Pen Argyl
1	n/a	Penn Cambria SD	Cresson
1	n/a	Penn Hills SD	Pittsburgh
1	n/a	Penn Manor SD	Millersville
1	n/a	Penn-Delco SD	Aston
1	n/a	Penn-Trafford SD	Harrison City
1	n/a	Penncrest SD	Saegertown
1	n/a	Pennridge SD	Perkasie
1	n/a	Penns Valley Area SD	Spring Mills
1	n/a	Pennsbury SD	Fallsington
1	n/a	Pennsylvania Virtual CS	Norristown
1	n/a	Pequea Valley SD	Kinzers
1	n/a	Perkiomen Valley SD	Collegeville
1	n/a	Peters Township SD	Mcmurray
1	n/a	Philadelphia City SD	Philadelphia
1	n/a	Philipsburg-Osceola Area SD	Philipsburg
1	n/a	Phoenixville Area SD	Phoenixville
1	n/a	Pine Grove Area SD	Pine Grove
1	n/a	Pine-Richland SD	Gibsonia
1	n/a	Pittsburgh SD	Pittsburgh
1	n/a	Pittston Area SD	Pittston
1	n/a	Pleasant Valley SD	Brodheadsville
1	n/a	Plum Borough SD	Plum
1	n/a	Pocono Mountain SD	Swiftwater
1	n/a	Pottsgrove SD	Pottstown
1	n/a	Pottstown SD	Pottstown
1	n/a	Pottsville Area SD	Pottsville
1	n/a	Punxsutawney Area SD	Punxsutawney
1	n/a	Quaker Valley SD	Sewickley
1	n/a	Quakertown Community SD	Quakertown
1	n/a	Radnor Township SD	Wayne
1	n/a	Reading SD	Reading
1	n/a	Red Lion Area SD	Red Lion
1	n/a	Reynolds SD	Greenville
1	n/a	Richland SD	Johnstown
1	n/a	Ridley SD	Folsom
1	n/a	Ringgold SD	New Eagle
1	n/a	Riverside Beaver County SD	Ellwood City
1	n/a	Rose Tree Media SD	Media
1	n/a	Saint Marys Area SD	Saint Marys
1	n/a	Salisbury Township SD	Allentown
1	n/a	Saucon Valley SD	Hellertown
1	n/a	Schuylkill Valley SD	Leesport
1	n/a	Scranton SD	Scranton
1	n/a	Selinsgrove Area SD	Selinsgrove
1	n/a	Seneca Valley SD	Harmony
1	n/a	Shaler Area SD	Glenshaw
1	n/a	Shamokin Area SD	Coal Township
1	n/a	Sharon City SD	Sharon
1	n/a	Shikellamy SD	Sunbury
1	n/a	Shippensburg Area SD	Shippensburg
1	n/a	Slippery Rock Area SD	Slippery Rock
1	n/a	Solanco SD	Quarryville
1	n/a	Somerset Area SD	Somerset
1	n/a	Souderton Area SD	Souderton
1	n/a	South Allegheny SD	Mc Keesport
1	n/a	South Butler County SD	Saxonburg
1	n/a	South Eastern SD	Fawn Grove
1	n/a	South Fayette Township SD	Mc Donald
1	n/a	South Middleton SD	Boiling Springs
1	n/a	South Park SD	South Park
1	n/a	South Western SD	Hanover

1	n/a	Southeast Delco SD	Folcroft
1	n/a	Southern Lehigh SD	Center Valley
1	n/a	Southern Tioga SD	Blossburg
1	n/a	Southern York County SD	Glen Rock
1	n/a	Southmoreland SD	Scottdale
1	n/a	Spring Cove SD	Roaring Spring
1	n/a	Spring Grove Area SD	Spring Grove
1	n/a	Spring-Ford Area SD	Collegeville
1	n/a	Springfield SD	Springfield
1	n/a	Springfield Township SD	Oreland
1	n/a	State College Area SD	State College
1	n/a	Steel Valley SD	Munhall
1	n/a	Sto-Rox SD	Mckees Rocks
1	n/a	Stroudsburg Area SD	Stroudsburg
1	n/a	Susquehanna Township SD	Harrisburg
1	n/a	Susquenita SD	Duncannon
1	n/a	Tamaqua Area SD	Tamaqua
1	n/a	Titusville Area SD	Titusville
1	n/a	Towanda Area SD	Towanda
1	n/a	Tredyffrin-Easttown SD	Berwyn
1	n/a	Trinity Area SD	Washington
1	n/a	Troy Area SD	Troy
1	n/a	Tulpehocken Area SD	Bernville
1	n/a	Tunkhannock Area SD	Tunkhannock
1	n/a	Tuscarora SD	Mercersburg
1	n/a	Twin Valley SD	Elverson
1	n/a	Tyrone Area SD	Tyrone
1	n/a	Uniontown Area SD	Uniontown
1	n/a	Unionville-Chadds Ford SD	Kennett Square
1	n/a	Upper Adams SD	Biglerville
1	n/a	Upper Darby SD	Drexel Hill
1	n/a	Upper Dublin SD	Maple Glen
1	n/a	Upper Merion Area SD	King Of Prussia
1	n/a	Upper Moreland Township SD	Willow Grove
1	n/a	Upper Perkiomen SD	East Greenville
1	n/a	Upper Saint Clair SD	Pittsburgh
1	n/a	Valley View SD	Archbald
1	n/a	Wallenpaupack Area SD	Hawley
1	n/a	Wallingford-Swarthmore SD	Wallingford
1	n/a	Warren County SD	North Warren
1	n/a	Warrior Run SD	Turbotville
1	n/a	Warwick SD	Lititz
1	n/a	Washington SD	Washington
1	n/a	Wattsburg Area SD	Erie
1	n/a	Wayne Highlands SD	Honesdale
1	n/a	Waynesboro Area SD	Waynesboro
1	n/a	Wellsboro Area SD	Wellsboro
1	n/a	West Allegheny SD	Imperial
1	n/a	West Chester Area SD	West Chester
1	n/a	West Jefferson Hills SD	Jefferson Hls
1	n/a	West Mifflin Area SD	West Mifflin
1	n/a	West Perry SD	Elliottsburg
1	n/a	West Shore SD	New Cumberland
1	n/a	West York Area SD	York
1	n/a	Western Pennsylvania Cyber CS	Midland
1	n/a	Western Wayne SD	South Canaan
1	n/a	Westmont Hilltop SD	Johnstown
1	n/a	Whitehall-Coplay SD	Whitehall
1	n/a	Wilkes-Barre Area SD	Wilkes Barre
1	n/a	Wilkinsburg Borough SD	Wilkinsburg
1	n/a	William Penn SD	Lansdowne
1	n/a	Williamsport Area SD	Williamsport
1	n/a	Wilmington Area SD	New Wilmington
1	n/a	Wilson SD	West Lawn
1	n/a	Wilson Area SD	Easton
1	n/a	Wissahickon SD	Ambler
1	n/a	Woodland Hills SD	Pittsburgh
1	n/a	Wyalusing Area SD	Wyalusing
1	n/a	Wyoming Area SD	Exeter
1	n/a	Wyoming Valley West SD	Kingston
1	n/a	Wyomissing Area SD	Wyomissing
1	n/a	York City SD	York
1	n/a	York Suburban SD	York
1	n/a	Yough SD	Herminie

Female Students

Rank	Percent	District Name	City
1	n/a	Abington SD	Abington
1	n/a	Abington Heights SD	Clarks Summit
1	n/a	Albert Gallatin Area SD	Uniontown
1	n/a	Allentown City SD	Allentown
1	n/a	Altoona Area SD	Altoona
1	n/a	Ambridge Area SD	Ambridge
1	n/a	Annville-Cleona SD	Annville
1	n/a	Apollo-Ridge SD	Spring Church
1	n/a	Armstrong SD	Ford City
1	n/a	Athens Area SD	Athens
1	n/a	Avon Grove SD	West Grove
1	n/a	Bald Eagle Area SD	Wingate
1	n/a	Baldwin-Whitehall SD	Pittsburgh
1	n/a	Bangor Area SD	Bangor
1	n/a	Beaver Area SD	Beaver
1	n/a	Bedford Area SD	Bedford
1	n/a	Belle Vernon Area SD	Belle Vernon
1	n/a	Bellefonte Area SD	Bellefonte
1	n/a	Bensalem Township SD	Bensalem
1	n/a	Bermudian Springs SD	York Springs
1	n/a	Berwick Area SD	Berwick
1	n/a	Bethel Park SD	Bethel Park
1	n/a	Bethlehem Area SD	Bethlehem
1	n/a	Big Beaver Falls Area SD	Beaver Falls
1	n/a	Big Spring SD	Newville
1	n/a	Blackhawk SD	Beaver Falls
1	n/a	Blairsville-Saltsburg SD	Blairsville
1	n/a	Bloomsburg Area SD	Bloomsburg
1	n/a	Blue Mountain SD	Orwigsburg
1	n/a	Boyertown Area SD	Boyertown
1	n/a	Bradford Area SD	Bradford
1	n/a	Brandywine Heights Area SD	Topton
1	n/a	Bristol Township SD	Levittown
1	n/a	Brookville Area SD	Brookville
1	n/a	Brownsville Area SD	Brownsville
1	n/a	Burgettstown Area SD	Burgettstown
1	n/a	Burrell SD	Lower Burrell
1	n/a	Butler Area SD	Butler
1	n/a	Cambria Heights SD	Patton
1	n/a	Canon-Mcmillan SD	Canonsburg
1	n/a	Carlisle Area SD	Carlisle
1	n/a	Carlynton SD	Carnegie
1	n/a	Catasauqua Area SD	Catasauqua
1	n/a	Centennial SD	Warminster
1	n/a	Center Area SD	Monaca
1	n/a	Central Bucks SD	Doylestown
1	n/a	Central Cambria SD	Ebensburg
1	n/a	Central Columbia SD	Bloomsburg
1	n/a	Central Dauphin SD	Harrisburg
1	n/a	Central Greene SD	Waynesburg
1	n/a	Central York SD	York
1	n/a	Chambersburg Area SD	Chambersburg
1	n/a	Charleroi SD	Charleroi
1	n/a	Chartiers Valley SD	Pittsburgh
1	n/a	Cheltenham Township SD	Elkins Park
1	n/a	Chester-Upland SD	Chester
1	n/a	Chestnut Ridge SD	Fishertown
1	n/a	Chichester SD	Boothwyn
1	n/a	Clearfield Area SD	Clearfield
1	n/a	Coatesville Area SD	Coatesville
1	n/a	Cocalico SD	Denver
1	n/a	Colonial SD	Plymouth Meeting
1	n/a	Conestoga Valley SD	Lancaster
1	n/a	Conewago Valley SD	New Oxford
1	n/a	Conneaut SD	Linesville
1	n/a	Connellsville Area SD	Connellsville
1	n/a	Conrad Weiser Area SD	Robesonia
1	n/a	Cornwall-Lebanon SD	Lebanon
1	n/a	Corry Area SD	Corry
1	n/a	Council Rock SD	Newtown
1	n/a	Crawford Central SD	Meadville
1	n/a	Crestwood SD	Mountain Top
1	n/a	Cumberland Valley SD	Mechanicsburg
1	n/a	Dallas SD	Dallas
1	n/a	Dallastown Area SD	Dallastown
1	n/a	Daniel Boone Area SD	Birdsboro
1	n/a	Danville Area SD	Danville
1	n/a	Deer Lakes SD	Russellton
1	n/a	Delaware Valley SD	Milford
1	n/a	Derry Area SD	Derry
1	n/a	Derry Township SD	Hershey
1	n/a	Donegal SD	Mount Joy
1	n/a	Dover Area SD	Dover
1	n/a	Downingtown Area SD	Downingtown
1	n/a	Dubois Area SD	Du Bois
1	n/a	Dunmore SD	Dunmore
1	n/a	East Allegheny SD	N Versailles
1	n/a	East Lycoming SD	Hughesville
1	n/a	East Penn SD	Emmaus
1	n/a	East Pennsboro Area SD	Enola
1	n/a	East Stroudsburg Area SD	E Stroudsburg
1	n/a	Eastern Lancaster County SD	New Holland
1	n/a	Eastern Lebanon County SD	Myerstown
1	n/a	Eastern York SD	Wrightsville
1	n/a	Easton Area SD	Easton
1	n/a	Elizabeth Forward SD	Elizabeth
1	n/a	Elizabethtown Area SD	Elizabethtown
1	n/a	Elk Lake SD	Dimock
1	n/a	Ellwood City Area SD	Ellwood City
1	n/a	Ephrata Area SD	Ephrata
1	n/a	Erie City SD	Erie
1	n/a	Everett Area SD	Everett
1	n/a	Exeter Township SD	Reading
1	n/a	Fairview SD	Fairview
1	n/a	Fleetwood Area SD	Fleetwood
1	n/a	Forest Hills SD	Sidman
1	n/a	Fort Leboeuf SD	Waterford
1	n/a	Fox Chapel Area SD	Pittsburgh
1	n/a	Franklin Area SD	Franklin
1	n/a	Franklin Regional SD	Murrysville
1	n/a	Freedom Area SD	Freedom
1	n/a	Freeport Area SD	Freeport
1	n/a	Garnet Valley SD	Glen Mills
1	n/a	Gateway SD	Monroeville
1	n/a	General Mclane SD	Edinboro
1	n/a	Gettysburg Area SD	Gettysburg
1	n/a	Girard SD	Girard
1	n/a	Governor Mifflin SD	Shillington
1	n/a	Great Valley SD	Malvern
1	n/a	Greater Johnstown SD	Johnstown
1	n/a	Greater Latrobe SD	Latrobe
1	n/a	Greater Nanticoke Area SD	Nanticoke
1	n/a	Greencastle-Antrim SD	Greencastle
1	n/a	Greensburg Salem SD	Greensburg
1	n/a	Greenville Area SD	Greenville
1	n/a	Grove City Area SD	Grove City
1	n/a	Hamburg Area SD	Hamburg
1	n/a	Hampton Township SD	Allison Park
1	n/a	Hanover Area SD	Wilkes Barre
1	n/a	Hanover Public SD	Hanover
1	n/a	Harbor Creek SD	Harborcreek
1	n/a	Harrisburg City SD	Harrisburg
1	n/a	Hatboro-Horsham SD	Horsham
1	n/a	Haverford Township SD	Havertown
1	n/a	Hazleton Area SD	Hazleton
1	n/a	Hempfield SD	Landisville
1	n/a	Hempfield Area SD	Greensburg
1	n/a	Hermitage SD	Hermitage
1	n/a	Highlands SD	Natrona Heights
1	n/a	Hollidaysburg Area SD	Hollidaysburg
1	n/a	Hopewell Area SD	Aliquippa
1	n/a	Huntingdon Area SD	Huntingdon
1	n/a	Indiana Area SD	Indiana
1	n/a	Interboro SD	Prospect Park
1	n/a	Jersey Shore Area SD	Jersey Shore
1	n/a	Jim Thorpe Area SD	Jim Thorpe
1	n/a	Juniata County SD	Mifflintown
1	n/a	Karns City Area SD	Karns City
1	n/a	Kennett Consolidated SD	Kennett Square
1	n/a	Keystone Central SD	Lock Haven
1	n/a	Keystone Oaks SD	Pittsburgh
1	n/a	Kiski Area SD	Vandergrift
1	n/a	Kutztown Area SD	Kutztown
1	n/a	Lake-Lehman SD	Lehman
1	n/a	Lakeland SD	Jermyn
1	n/a	Lampeter-Strasburg SD	Lampeter
1	n/a	Lancaster SD	Lancaster
1	n/a	Laurel Highlands SD	Uniontown
1	n/a	Lebanon SD	Lebanon
1	n/a	Lehighton Area SD	Lehighton
1	n/a	Lewisburg Area SD	Lewisburg
1	n/a	Ligonier Valley SD	Ligonier
1	n/a	Littlestown Area SD	Littlestown
1	n/a	Lower Dauphin SD	Hummelstown
1	n/a	Lower Merion SD	Ardmore
1	n/a	Lower Moreland Township SD	Huntingdon Vly
1	n/a	Manheim Central SD	Manheim
1	n/a	Manheim Township SD	Lancaster
1	n/a	Marion Center Area SD	Marion Center
1	n/a	Marple Newtown SD	Newtown Square
1	n/a	Mars Area SD	Mars
1	n/a	Mcguffey SD	Claysville
1	n/a	Mckeesport Area SD	Mc Keesport
1	n/a	Mechanicsburg Area SD	Mechanicsburg
1	n/a	Mercer Area SD	Mercer
1	n/a	Methacton SD	Norristown
1	n/a	Mid Valley SD	Throop
1	n/a	Midd-West SD	Middleburg
1	n/a	Middletown Area SD	Middletown
1	n/a	Mifflin County SD	Lewistown
1	n/a	Mifflinburg Area SD	Mifflinburg
1	n/a	Millcreek Township SD	Erie
1	n/a	Milton Area SD	Milton
1	n/a	Mohawk Area SD	Bessemer
1	n/a	Moniteau SD	West Sunbury
1	n/a	Montour SD	Mc Kees Rocks
1	n/a	Montoursville Area SD	Montoursville
1	n/a	Montrose Area SD	Montrose
1	n/a	Moon Area SD	Moon Township
1	n/a	Mount Carmel Area SD	Mount Carmel
1	n/a	Mount Pleasant Area SD	Mount Pleasant
1	n/a	Mount Union Area SD	Mount Union
1	n/a	Mt Lebanon SD	Pittsburgh
1	n/a	Muhlenberg SD	Reading
1	n/a	Nazareth Area SD	Nazareth
1	n/a	Neshaminy SD	Langhorne
1	n/a	New Brighton Area SD	New Brighton
1	n/a	New Castle Area SD	New Castle
1	n/a	New Kensington-Arnold SD	New Kensington
1	n/a	Norristown Area SD	Norristown

1	n/a	North Allegheny SD	Pittsburgh
1	n/a	North East SD	North East
1	n/a	North Hills SD	Pittsburgh
1	n/a	North Penn SD	Lansdale
1	n/a	North Pocono SD	Moscow
1	n/a	North Schuylkill SD	Ashland
1	n/a	Northampton Area SD	Northampton
1	n/a	Northeastern York SD	Manchester
1	n/a	Northern Lebanon SD	Fredericksburg
1	n/a	Northern Lehigh SD	Slatington
1	n/a	Northern Tioga SD	Elkland
1	n/a	Northern York County SD	Dillsburg
1	n/a	Northgate SD	Pittsburgh
1	n/a	Northwestern SD	Albion
1	n/a	Northwestern Lehigh SD	New Tripoli
1	n/a	Norwin SD	N Huntingdon
1	n/a	Octorara Area SD	Atglen
1	n/a	Oil City Area SD	Oil City
1	n/a	Oley Valley SD	Oley
1	n/a	Owen J Roberts SD	Pottstown
1	n/a	Oxford Area SD	Oxford
1	n/a	Palisades SD	Kintnersville
1	n/a	Palmerton Area SD	Palmerton
1	n/a	Palmyra Area SD	Palmyra
1	n/a	Parkland SD	Allentown
1	n/a	Pde Division of Data Services	Harrisburg
1	n/a	Pen Argyl Area SD	Pen Argyl
1	n/a	Penn Cambria SD	Cresson
1	n/a	Penn Hills SD	Pittsburgh
1	n/a	Penn Manor SD	Millersville
1	n/a	Penn-Delco SD	Aston
1	n/a	Penn-Trafford SD	Harrison City
1	n/a	Penncrest SD	Saegertown
1	n/a	Pennridge SD	Perkasie
1	n/a	Penns Valley Area SD	Spring Mills
1	n/a	Pennsbury SD	Fallsington
1	n/a	Pennsylvania Virtual CS	Norristown
1	n/a	Pequea Valley SD	Kinzers
1	n/a	Perkiomen Valley SD	Collegeville
1	n/a	Peters Township SD	Mcmurray
1	n/a	Philadelphia City SD	Philadelphia
1	n/a	Philipsburg-Osceola Area SD	Philipsburg
1	n/a	Phoenixville Area SD	Phoenixville
1	n/a	Pine Grove Area SD	Pine Grove
1	n/a	Pine-Richland SD	Gibsonia
1	n/a	Pittsburgh SD	Pittsburgh
1	n/a	Pittston Area SD	Pittston
1	n/a	Pleasant Valley SD	Brodheadsville
1	n/a	Plum Borough SD	Plum
1	n/a	Pocono Mountain SD	Swiftwater
1	n/a	Pottsgrove SD	Pottstown
1	n/a	Pottstown SD	Pottstown
1	n/a	Pottsville Area SD	Pottsville
1	n/a	Punxsutawney Area SD	Punxsutawney
1	n/a	Quaker Valley SD	Sewickley
1	n/a	Quakertown Community SD	Quakertown
1	n/a	Radnor Township SD	Wayne
1	n/a	Reading SD	Reading
1	n/a	Red Lion Area SD	Red Lion
1	n/a	Reynolds SD	Greenville
1	n/a	Richland SD	Johnstown
1	n/a	Ridley SD	Folsom
1	n/a	Ringgold SD	New Eagle
1	n/a	Riverside Beaver County SD	Ellwood City
1	n/a	Rose Tree Media SD	Media
1	n/a	Saint Marys Area SD	Saint Marys
1	n/a	Salisbury Township SD	Allentown
1	n/a	Saucon Valley SD	Hellertown
1	n/a	Schuylkill Valley SD	Leesport
1	n/a	Scranton SD	Scranton
1	n/a	Selinsgrove Area SD	Selinsgrove
1	n/a	Seneca Valley SD	Harmony
1	n/a	Shaler Area SD	Glenshaw
1	n/a	Shamokin Area SD	Coal Township
1	n/a	Sharon City SD	Sharon
1	n/a	Shikellamy SD	Sunbury
1	n/a	Shippensburg Area SD	Shippensburg
1	n/a	Slippery Rock Area SD	Slippery Rock
1	n/a	Solanco SD	Quarryville
1	n/a	Somerset Area SD	Somerset
1	n/a	Souderton Area SD	Souderton
1	n/a	South Allegheny SD	Mc Keesport
1	n/a	South Butler County SD	Saxonburg
1	n/a	South Eastern SD	Fawn Grove
1	n/a	South Fayette Township SD	Mc Donald
1	n/a	South Middleton SD	Boiling Springs
1	n/a	South Park SD	South Park
1	n/a	South Western SD	Hanover
1	n/a	Southeast Delco SD	Folcroft
1	n/a	Southern Lehigh SD	Center Valley
1	n/a	Southern Tioga SD	Blossburg
1	n/a	Southern York County SD	Glen Rock
1	n/a	Southmoreland SD	Scottdale
1	n/a	Spring Cove SD	Roaring Spring
1	n/a	Spring Grove Area SD	Spring Grove
1	n/a	Spring-Ford Area SD	Collegeville
1	n/a	Springfield SD	Springfield
1	n/a	Springfield Township SD	Oreland
1	n/a	State College Area SD	State College
1	n/a	Steel Valley SD	Munhall
1	n/a	Sto-Rox SD	Mckees Rocks
1	n/a	Stroudsburg Area SD	Stroudsburg
1	n/a	Susquehanna Township SD	Harrisburg
1	n/a	Susquenita SD	Duncannon
1	n/a	Tamaqua Area SD	Tamaqua
1	n/a	Titusville Area SD	Titusville
1	n/a	Towanda Area SD	Towanda
1	n/a	Tredyffrin-Easttown SD	Berwyn
1	n/a	Trinity Area SD	Washington
1	n/a	Troy Area SD	Troy
1	n/a	Tulpehocken Area SD	Bernville
1	n/a	Tunkhannock Area SD	Tunkhannock
1	n/a	Tuscarora SD	Mercersburg
1	n/a	Twin Valley SD	Elverson
1	n/a	Tyrone Area SD	Tyrone
1	n/a	Uniontown Area SD	Uniontown
1	n/a	Unionville-Chadds Ford SD	Kennett Square
1	n/a	Upper Adams SD	Biglerville
1	n/a	Upper Darby SD	Drexel Hill
1	n/a	Upper Dublin SD	Maple Glen
1	n/a	Upper Merion Area SD	King Of Prussia
1	n/a	Upper Moreland Township SD	Willow Grove
1	n/a	Upper Perkiomen SD	East Greenville
1	n/a	Upper Saint Clair SD	Pittsburgh
1	n/a	Valley View SD	Archbald
1	n/a	Wallenpaupack Area SD	Hawley
1	n/a	Wallingford-Swarthmore SD	Wallingford
1	n/a	Warren County SD	North Warren
1	n/a	Warrior Run SD	Turbotville
1	n/a	Warwick SD	Lititz
1	n/a	Washington SD	Washington
1	n/a	Wattsburg Area SD	Erie
1	n/a	Wayne Highlands SD	Honesdale
1	n/a	Waynesboro Area SD	Waynesboro
1	n/a	Wellsboro Area SD	Wellsboro
1	n/a	West Allegheny SD	Imperial
1	n/a	West Chester Area SD	West Chester
1	n/a	West Jefferson Hills SD	Jefferson Hls
1	n/a	West Mifflin Area SD	West Mifflin
1	n/a	West Perry SD	Elliottsburg
1	n/a	West Shore SD	New Cumberland
1	n/a	West York Area SD	York
1	n/a	Western Pennsylvania Cyber CS	Midland
1	n/a	Western Wayne SD	South Canaan
1	n/a	Westmont Hilltop SD	Johnstown
1	n/a	Whitehall-Coplay SD	Whitehall
1	n/a	Wilkes-Barre Area SD	Wilkes Barre
1	n/a	Wilkinsburg Borough SD	Wilkinsburg
1	n/a	William Penn SD	Lansdowne
1	n/a	Williamsport Area SD	Williamsport
1	n/a	Wilmington Area SD	New Wilmington
1	n/a	Wilson SD	West Lawn
1	n/a	Wilson Area SD	Easton
1	n/a	Wissahickon SD	Ambler
1	n/a	Woodland Hills SD	Pittsburgh
1	n/a	Wyalusing Area SD	Wyalusing
1	n/a	Wyoming Area SD	Exeter
1	n/a	Wyoming Valley West SD	Kingston
1	n/a	Wyomissing Area SD	Wyomissing
1	n/a	York City SD	York
1	n/a	York Suburban SD	York
1	n/a	Yough SD	Herminie

Individual Education Program Students

Rank	Percent	District Name	City
1	25.4	Wilkinsburg Borough SD	Wilkinsburg
2	24.8	Lancaster SD	Lancaster
3	23.4	Sto-Rox SD	Mckees Rocks
4	22.6	Chester-Upland SD	Chester
5	22.2	Central Greene SD	Waynesburg
6	21.7	Franklin Area SD	Franklin
6	21.7	York City SD	York
8	21.6	Oil City Area SD	Oil City
8	21.6	Williamsport Area SD	Williamsport
10	21.3	Southeast Delco SD	Folcroft
11	20.3	Montrose Area SD	Montrose
12	20.0	Erie City SD	Erie
12	20.0	Harrisburg City SD	Harrisburg
14	19.8	Ambridge Area SD	Ambridge
15	19.6	William Penn SD	Lansdowne
16	19.4	Corry Area SD	Corry
16	19.4	Tyrone Area SD	Tyrone
18	19.3	Eastern York SD	Wrightsville
19	19.2	Bristol Township SD	Levittown
20	19.1	Connellsville Area SD	Connellsville
20	19.1	Washington SD	Washington
22	19.0	Hanover Public SD	Hanover
22	19.0	Pottstown SD	Pottstown
24	18.8	Ridley SD	Folsom
25	18.7	Albert Gallatin Area SD	Uniontown
26	18.6	Titusville Area SD	Titusville
27	18.5	Charleroi SD	Charleroi
28	18.4	Athens Area SD	Athens
29	18.3	Garnet Valley SD	Glen Mills
29	18.3	Hanover Area SD	Wilkes Barre
29	18.3	Tulpehocken Area SD	Bernville
32	18.2	Berwick Area SD	Berwick
32	18.2	Lower Merion SD	Ardmore
34	18.1	Scranton SD	Scranton
34	18.1	Wilmington Area SD	New Wilmington
36	18.0	Neshaminy SD	Langhorne
36	18.0	Pittsburgh SD	Pittsburgh
36	18.0	Shaler Area SD	Glenshaw
36	18.0	Southmoreland SD	Scottdale
40	17.9	Mid Valley SD	Throop
40	17.9	Mount Union Area SD	Mount Union
40	17.9	Warren County SD	North Warren
43	17.8	Altoona Area SD	Altoona
43	17.8	Big Spring SD	Newville
43	17.8	Chichester SD	Boothwyn
43	17.8	Kutztown Area SD	Kutztown
43	17.8	West Perry SD	Elliottsburg
48	17.7	Marple Newtown SD	Newtown Square
48	17.7	New Castle Area SD	New Castle
48	17.7	New Kensington-Arnold SD	New Kensington
48	17.7	Tuscarora SD	Mercersburg
52	17.6	Highlands SD	Natrona Heights
52	17.6	Palisades SD	Kintnersville
52	17.6	Punxsutawney Area SD	Punxsutawney
55	17.4	Brownsville Area SD	Brownsville
55	17.4	Centennial SD	Warminster
55	17.4	Middletown Area SD	Middletown
55	17.4	Upper Adams SD	Biglerville
55	17.4	Wallenpaupack Area SD	Hawley
60	17.3	Northeastern York SD	Manchester
60	17.3	Susquenita SD	Duncannon
62	17.2	Crawford Central SD	Meadville
62	17.2	Keystone Central SD	Lock Haven
62	17.2	Norristown Area SD	Norristown
65	17.0	Lebanon SD	Lebanon
66	16.9	Everett Area SD	Everett
66	16.9	Wallingford-Swarthmore SD	Wallingford
68	16.8	Blairsville-Saltsburg SD	Blairsville
68	16.8	Brandywine Heights Area SD	Topton
68	16.8	East Stroudsburg Area SD	E Stroudsburg
68	16.8	North Schuylkill SD	Ashland
68	16.8	Penn-Delco SD	Aston
73	16.7	Donegal SD	Mount Joy
73	16.7	Jersey Shore Area SD	Jersey Shore
73	16.7	Lower Dauphin SD	Hummelstown
73	16.7	Mckeesport Area SD	Mc Keesport
73	16.7	Radnor Township SD	Wayne
73	16.7	Sharon City SD	Sharon
79	16.6	Huntingdon Area SD	Huntingdon
79	16.6	Manheim Central SD	Manheim
79	16.6	Southern York County SD	Glen Rock
79	16.6	Springfield Township SD	Oreland
79	16.6	Susquehanna Township SD	Harrisburg
84	16.5	Chambersburg Area SD	Chambersburg
84	16.5	Jim Thorpe Area SD	Jim Thorpe
86	16.4	Bensalem Township SD	Bensalem
86	16.4	Great Valley SD	Malvern
86	16.4	Greater Nanticoke Area SD	Nanticoke
86	16.4	Haverford Township SD	Havertown
90	16.3	East Allegheny SD	N Versailles
90	16.3	Northwestern SD	Albion
90	16.3	Spring Grove Area SD	Spring Grove
93	16.2	Burgettstown Area SD	Burgettstown
93	16.2	Fort Leboeuf SD	Waterford
93	16.2	Woodland Hills SD	Pittsburgh
96	16.1	Bellefonte Area SD	Bellefonte
96	16.1	Penns Valley Area SD	Spring Mills
96	16.1	Rose Tree Media SD	Media
96	16.1	Spring Cove SD	Roaring Spring
96	16.1	Tamaqua Area SD	Tamaqua
96	16.1	Warwick SD	Lititz
102	16.0	Midd-West SD	Middleburg
103	15.9	Armstrong SD	Ford City
103	15.9	Brookville Area SD	Brookville
103	15.9	Phoenixville Area SD	Phoenixville
103	15.9	West Shore SD	New Cumberland
107	15.8	Bedford Area SD	Bedford
107	15.8	Dover Area SD	Dover
107	15.8	Wilson Area SD	Easton
110	15.7	Butler Area SD	Butler
110	15.7	Catasauqua Area SD	Catasauqua
110	15.7	Greater Johnstown SD	Johnstown
110	15.7	Salisbury Township SD	Allentown

114	15.6	Chestnut Ridge SD	Fishertown
114	15.6	Elizabethtown Area SD	Elizabethtown
114	15.6	Shippensburg Area SD	Shippensburg
117	15.5	Bloomsburg Area SD	Bloomsburg
118	15.4	Conneaut SD	Linesville
118	15.4	Elk Lake SD	Dimock
118	15.4	Wilkes-Barre Area SD	Wilkes Barre
121	15.3	Cocalico SD	Denver
121	15.3	Penn Manor SD	Millersville
123	15.2	Conrad Weiser Area SD	Robesonia
123	15.2	Interboro SD	Prospect Park
123	15.2	Wyoming Valley West SD	Kingston
126	15.1	Hempfield SD	Landisville
126	15.1	Mifflin County SD	Lewistown
126	15.1	Mount Pleasant Area SD	Mount Pleasant
126	15.1	Wissahickon SD	Ambler
130	15.0	Central Cambria SD	Ebensburg
130	15.0	Mercer Area SD	Mercer
132	14.9	Moniteau SD	West Sunbury
132	14.9	Shamokin Area SD	Coal Township
132	14.9	Uniontown Area SD	Uniontown
135	14.8	Coatesville Area SD	Coatesville
135	14.8	Gettysburg Area SD	Gettysburg
135	14.8	Girard SD	Girard
135	14.8	Northwestern Lehigh SD	New Tripoli
135	14.8	Troy Area SD	Troy
140	14.7	Apollo-Ridge SD	Spring Church
140	14.7	Colonial SD	Plymouth Meeting
140	14.7	Palmerton Area SD	Palmerton
140	14.7	Penn Cambria SD	Cresson
140	14.7	South Eastern SD	Fawn Grove
145	14.6	Bangor Area SD	Bangor
145	14.6	Ephrata Area SD	Ephrata
145	14.6	Gateway SD	Monroeville
145	14.6	Greenville Area SD	Greenville
145	14.6	Red Lion Area SD	Red Lion
150	14.5	Carlisle Area SD	Carlisle
151	14.4	Deer Lakes SD	Russellton
151	14.4	Northampton Area SD	Northampton
151	14.4	Penn Hills SD	Pittsburgh
151	14.4	Slippery Rock Area SD	Slippery Rock
151	14.4	Somerset Area SD	Somerset
151	14.4	Towanda Area SD	Towanda
157	14.3	Cambria Heights SD	Patton
157	14.3	Downingtown Area SD	Downingtown
157	14.3	Dubois Area SD	Du Bois
157	14.3	Ellwood City Area SD	Ellwood City
157	14.3	Octorara Area SD	Atglen
157	14.3	Reynolds SD	Greenville
163	14.2	Clearfield Area SD	Clearfield
163	14.2	Moon Area SD	Moon Township
163	14.2	North Penn SD	Lansdale
166	14.1	Elizabeth Forward SD	Elizabeth
166	14.1	Springfield SD	Springfield
166	14.1	Upper Merion Area SD	King Of Prussia
169	14.0	Bradford Area SD	Bradford
169	14.0	Council Rock SD	Newtown
169	14.0	Twin Valley SD	Elverson
169	14.0	Upper Darby SD	Drexel Hill
173	13.9	Annville-Cleona SD	Annville
173	13.9	Penncrest SD	Saegertown
173	13.9	Pottsville Area SD	Pottsville
173	13.9	Spring-Ford Area SD	Collegeville
177	13.8	Philipsburg-Osceola Area SD	Philipsburg
177	13.8	Waynesboro Area SD	Waynesboro
179	13.7	Blue Mountain SD	Orwigsburg
179	13.7	Conewago Valley SD	New Oxford
179	13.7	South Allegheny SD	Mc Keesport
179	13.7	Trinity Area SD	Washington
179	13.7	Wayne Highlands SD	Honesdale
184	13.6	Bald Eagle Area SD	Wingate
184	13.6	East Pennsboro Area SD	Enola
184	13.6	Exeter Township SD	Reading
184	13.6	Lampeter-Strasburg SD	Lampeter
184	13.6	West York Area SD	York
189	13.5	Owen J Roberts SD	Pottstown
189	13.5	Pennsbury SD	Fallsington
189	13.5	Pequea Valley SD	Kinzers
189	13.5	Pottsgrove SD	Pottstown
189	13.5	Seneca Valley SD	Harmony
194	13.4	Eastern Lebanon County SD	Myerstown
194	13.4	Northgate SD	Pittsburgh
196	13.3	Allentown City SD	Allentown
196	13.3	Steel Valley SD	Munhall
196	13.3	Valley View SD	Archbald
196	13.3	York Suburban SD	York
200	13.2	Central Dauphin SD	Harrisburg
200	13.2	Daniel Boone Area SD	Birdsboro
200	13.2	Northern Lebanon SD	Fredericksburg
200	13.2	Northern Lehigh SD	Slatington
200	13.2	Pennridge SD	Perkasie
200	13.2	Quakertown Community SD	Quakertown
200	13.2	Southern Tioga SD	Blossburg
200	13.2	Wattsburg Area SD	Erie
200	13.2	Wyoming Area SD	Exeter
209	13.1	Abington Heights SD	Clarks Summit
209	13.1	Littlestown Area SD	Littlestown
209	13.1	Pocono Mountain SD	Swiftwater
209	13.1	West Mifflin Area SD	West Mifflin
213	13.0	Cheltenham Township SD	Elkins Park
213	13.0	Kiski Area SD	Vandergrift
213	13.0	Ligonier Valley SD	Ligonier
213	13.0	Marion Center Area SD	Marion Center
217	12.9	Belle Vernon Area SD	Belle Vernon
217	12.9	Conestoga Valley SD	Lancaster
217	12.9	Dunmore SD	Dunmore
217	12.9	Mcguffey SD	Claysville
217	12.9	Montour SD	Mc Kees Rocks
217	12.9	Ringgold SD	New Eagle
217	12.9	Warrior Run SD	Turbotville
217	12.9	West Allegheny SD	Imperial
217	12.9	Yough SD	Herminie
226	12.8	Avon Grove SD	West Grove
226	12.8	Boyertown Area SD	Boyertown
226	12.8	Riverside Beaver County SD	Ellwood City
226	12.8	Unionville-Chadds Ford SD	Kennett Square
230	12.7	Bethlehem Area SD	Bethlehem
230	12.7	Tredyffrin-Easttown SD	Berwyn
230	12.7	Western Wayne SD	South Canaan
233	12.6	Central York SD	York
233	12.6	Hollidaysburg Area SD	Hollidaysburg
233	12.6	Keystone Oaks SD	Pittsburgh
233	12.6	Lakeland SD	Jermyn
233	12.6	Oley Valley SD	Oley
233	12.6	Quaker Valley SD	Sewickley
233	12.6	South Middleton SD	Boiling Springs
240	12.5	Cumberland Valley SD	Mechanicsburg
240	12.5	East Lycoming SD	Hughesville
240	12.5	Easton Area SD	Easton
240	12.5	Freedom Area SD	Freedom
240	12.5	Hamburg Area SD	Hamburg
240	12.5	Harbor Creek SD	Harborcreek
240	12.5	Lake-Lehman SD	Lehman
240	12.5	Lehighton Area SD	Lehighton
240	12.5	Northern Tioga SD	Elkland
240	12.5	West Chester Area SD	West Chester
250	12.4	Eastern Lancaster County SD	New Holland
250	12.4	Hopewell Area SD	Aliquippa
250	12.4	Philadelphia City SD	Philadelphia
250	12.4	Saint Marys Area SD	Saint Marys
254	12.3	Big Beaver Falls Area SD	Beaver Falls
254	12.3	Southern Lehigh SD	Center Valley
254	12.3	Upper Perkiomen SD	East Greenville
254	12.3	Wilson SD	West Lawn
258	12.2	Danville Area SD	Danville
258	12.2	General Mclane SD	Edinboro
258	12.2	Muhlenberg SD	Reading
258	12.2	Stroudsburg Area SD	Stroudsburg
262	12.1	Baldwin-Whitehall SD	Pittsburgh
262	12.1	Dallastown Area SD	Dallastown
262	12.1	Governor Mifflin SD	Shillington
262	12.1	Indiana Area SD	Indiana
262	12.1	Kennett Consolidated SD	Kennett Square
262	12.1	North Hills SD	Pittsburgh
268	12.0	Dallas SD	Dallas
268	12.0	Reading SD	Reading
268	12.0	Selinsgrove Area SD	Selinsgrove
268	12.0	Souderton Area SD	Souderton
272	11.9	Burrell SD	Lower Burrell
272	11.9	Greencastle-Antrim SD	Greencastle
272	11.9	Millcreek Township SD	Erie
272	11.9	North Pocono SD	Moscow
272	11.9	Schuylkill Valley SD	Leesport
272	11.9	Tunkhannock Area SD	Tunkhannock
272	11.9	Upper Dublin SD	Maple Glen
279	11.8	Mechanicsburg Area SD	Mechanicsburg
279	11.8	Parkland SD	Allentown
279	11.8	Wellsboro Area SD	Wellsboro
282	11.7	Crestwood SD	Mountain Top
282	11.7	Norwin SD	N Huntingdon
282	11.7	State College Area SD	State College
285	11.6	Abington SD	Abington
285	11.6	Carlynton SD	Carnegie
285	11.6	Hermitage SD	Hermitage
285	11.6	Juniata County SD	Mifflintown
285	11.6	Laurel Highlands SD	Uniontown
285	11.6	Nazareth Area SD	Nazareth
285	11.6	Pine Grove Area SD	Pine Grove
292	11.5	Fox Chapel Area SD	Pittsburgh
292	11.5	Karns City Area SD	Karns City
292	11.5	Manheim Township SD	Lancaster
295	11.4	Bethel Park SD	Bethel Park
295	11.4	Northern York County SD	Dillsburg
295	11.4	Pittston Area SD	Pittston
298	11.3	Fleetwood Area SD	Fleetwood
298	11.3	Grove City Area SD	Grove City
298	11.3	Hatboro-Horsham SD	Horsham
301	11.2	Canon-Mcmillan SD	Canonsburg
301	11.2	Cornwall-Lebanon SD	Lebanon
301	11.2	Hampton Township SD	Allison Park
301	11.2	Lower Moreland Township SD	Huntingdon Vly
301	11.2	Pine-Richland SD	Gibsonia
301	11.2	Pleasant Valley SD	Brodheadsville
307	11.1	Greensburg Salem SD	Greensburg
307	11.1	Whitehall-Coplay SD	Whitehall
309	11.0	Hempfield Area SD	Greensburg
309	11.0	Pen Argyl Area SD	Pen Argyl
309	11.0	South Western SD	Hanover
309	11.0	West Jefferson Hills SD	Jefferson Hls
313	10.9	Saucon Valley SD	Hellertown
314	10.8	Central Columbia SD	Bloomsburg
314	10.8	Mt Lebanon SD	Pittsburgh
314	10.8	Wyalusing Area SD	Wyalusing
317	10.7	Central Bucks SD	Doylestown
317	10.7	Franklin Regional SD	Murrysville
317	10.7	Methacton SD	Norristown
317	10.7	North East SD	North East
321	10.6	Chartiers Valley SD	Pittsburgh
321	10.6	Freeport Area SD	Freeport
321	10.6	Mifflinburg Area SD	Mifflinburg
321	10.6	Milton Area SD	Milton
321	10.6	Mohawk Area SD	Bessemer
321	10.6	Upper Moreland Township SD	Willow Grove
327	10.5	Forest Hills SD	Sidman
328	10.4	Derry Township SD	Hershey
328	10.4	Upper Saint Clair SD	Pittsburgh
330	10.2	Fairview SD	Fairview
330	10.2	Greater Latrobe SD	Latrobe
332	10.1	Delaware Valley SD	Milford
332	10.1	South Park SD	South Park
334	10.0	New Brighton Area SD	New Brighton
334	10.0	Palmyra Area SD	Palmyra
336	9.8	Hazleton Area SD	Hazleton
336	9.8	North Allegheny SD	Pittsburgh
338	9.7	Oxford Area SD	Oxford
338	9.7	Perkiomen Valley SD	Collegeville
338	9.7	Westmont Hilltop SD	Johnstown
341	9.6	Mount Carmel Area SD	Mount Carmel
341	9.6	Shikellamy SD	Sunbury
341	9.6	Solanco SD	Quarryville
344	9.5	Beaver Area SD	Beaver
344	9.5	Montoursville Area SD	Montoursville
344	9.5	Richland SD	Johnstown
347	9.4	Wyomissing Area SD	Wyomissing
348	9.3	East Penn SD	Emmaus
348	9.3	South Fayette Township SD	Mc Donald
350	9.2	Penn-Trafford SD	Harrison City
351	9.1	South Butler County SD	Saxonburg
352	8.9	Center Area SD	Monaca
352	8.9	Derry Area SD	Derry
352	8.9	Lewisburg Area SD	Lewisburg
355	8.8	Bermudian Springs SD	York Springs
356	8.6	Blackhawk SD	Beaver Falls
357	8.5	Plum Borough SD	Plum
358	8.4	Peters Township SD	Mcmurray
359	6.2	Western Pennsylvania Cyber CS	Midland
360	5.9	Pennsylvania Virtual CS	Norristown
361	4.9	Mars Area SD	Mars
362	n/a	Pde Division of Data Services	Harrisburg

English Language Learner Students

Rank	Percent	District Name	City
1	n/a	Abington SD	Abington
1	n/a	Abington Heights SD	Clarks Summit
1	n/a	Albert Gallatin Area SD	Uniontown
1	n/a	Allentown City SD	Allentown
1	n/a	Altoona Area SD	Altoona
1	n/a	Ambridge Area SD	Ambridge
1	n/a	Annville-Cleona SD	Annville
1	n/a	Apollo-Ridge SD	Spring Church
1	n/a	Armstrong SD	Ford City
1	n/a	Athens Area SD	Athens
1	n/a	Avon Grove SD	West Grove
1	n/a	Bald Eagle Area SD	Wingate
1	n/a	Baldwin-Whitehall SD	Pittsburgh
1	n/a	Bangor Area SD	Bangor
1	n/a	Beaver Area SD	Beaver
1	n/a	Bedford Area SD	Bedford
1	n/a	Belle Vernon Area SD	Belle Vernon
1	n/a	Bellefonte Area SD	Bellefonte
1	n/a	Bensalem Township SD	Bensalem
1	n/a	Bermudian Springs SD	York Springs
1	n/a	Berwick Area SD	Berwick
1	n/a	Bethel Park SD	Bethel Park
1	n/a	Bethlehem Area SD	Bethlehem
1	n/a	Big Beaver Falls Area SD	Beaver Falls
1	n/a	Big Spring SD	Newville

1	n/a	Blackhawk SD	Beaver Falls	1	n/a	Great Valley SD	Malvern	1	n/a	Northern Tioga SD	Elkland
1	n/a	Blairsville-Saltsburg SD	Blairsville	1	n/a	Greater Johnstown SD	Johnstown	1	n/a	Northern York County SD	Dillsburg
1	n/a	Bloomsburg Area SD	Bloomsburg	1	n/a	Greater Latrobe SD	Latrobe	1	n/a	Northgate SD	Pittsburgh
1	n/a	Blue Mountain SD	Orwigsburg	1	n/a	Greater Nanticoke Area SD	Nanticoke	1	n/a	Northwestern SD	Albion
1	n/a	Boyertown Area SD	Boyertown	1	n/a	Greencastle-Antrim SD	Greencastle	1	n/a	Northwestern Lehigh SD	New Tripoli
1	n/a	Bradford Area SD	Bradford	1	n/a	Greensburg Salem SD	Greensburg	1	n/a	Norwin SD	N Huntingdon
1	n/a	Brandywine Heights Area SD	Topton	1	n/a	Greenville Area SD	Greenville	1	n/a	Octorara Area SD	Atglen
1	n/a	Bristol Township SD	Levittown	1	n/a	Grove City Area SD	Grove City	1	n/a	Oil City Area SD	Oil City
1	n/a	Brookville Area SD	Brookville	1	n/a	Hamburg Area SD	Hamburg	1	n/a	Oley Valley SD	Oley
1	n/a	Brownsville Area SD	Brownsville	1	n/a	Hampton Township SD	Allison Park	1	n/a	Owen J Roberts SD	Pottstown
1	n/a	Burgettstown Area SD	Burgettstown	1	n/a	Hanover Area SD	Wilkes Barre	1	n/a	Oxford Area SD	Oxford
1	n/a	Burrell SD	Lower Burrell	1	n/a	Hanover Public SD	Hanover	1	n/a	Palisades SD	Kintnersville
1	n/a	Butler Area SD	Butler	1	n/a	Harbor Creek SD	Harborcreek	1	n/a	Palmerton Area SD	Palmerton
1	n/a	Cambria Heights SD	Patton	1	n/a	Harrisburg City SD	Harrisburg	1	n/a	Palmyra Area SD	Palmyra
1	n/a	Canon-Mcmillan SD	Canonsburg	1	n/a	Hatboro-Horsham SD	Horsham	1	n/a	Parkland SD	Allentown
1	n/a	Carlisle Area SD	Carlisle	1	n/a	Haverford Township SD	Havertown	1	n/a	Pde Division of Data Services	Harrisburg
1	n/a	Carlynton SD	Carnegie	1	n/a	Hazleton Area SD	Hazleton	1	n/a	Pen Argyl Area SD	Pen Argyl
1	n/a	Catasauqua Area SD	Catasauqua	1	n/a	Hempfield SD	Landisville	1	n/a	Penn Cambria SD	Cresson
1	n/a	Centennial SD	Warminster	1	n/a	Hempfield Area SD	Greensburg	1	n/a	Penn Hills SD	Pittsburgh
1	n/a	Center Area SD	Monaca	1	n/a	Hermitage SD	Hermitage	1	n/a	Penn Manor SD	Millersville
1	n/a	Central Bucks SD	Doylestown	1	n/a	Highlands SD	Natrona Heights	1	n/a	Penn-Delco SD	Aston
1	n/a	Central Cambria SD	Ebensburg	1	n/a	Hollidaysburg Area SD	Hollidaysburg	1	n/a	Penn-Trafford SD	Harrison City
1	n/a	Central Columbia SD	Bloomsburg	1	n/a	Hopewell Area SD	Aliquippa	1	n/a	Penncrest SD	Saegertown
1	n/a	Central Dauphin SD	Harrisburg	1	n/a	Huntingdon Area SD	Huntingdon	1	n/a	Pennridge SD	Perkasie
1	n/a	Central Greene SD	Waynesburg	1	n/a	Indiana Area SD	Indiana	1	n/a	Penns Valley Area SD	Spring Mills
1	n/a	Central York SD	York	1	n/a	Interboro SD	Prospect Park	1	n/a	Pennsbury SD	Fallsington
1	n/a	Chambersburg Area SD	Chambersburg	1	n/a	Jersey Shore Area SD	Jersey Shore	1	n/a	Pennsylvania Virtual CS	Norristown
1	n/a	Charleroi SD	Charleroi	1	n/a	Jim Thorpe Area SD	Jim Thorpe	1	n/a	Pequea Valley SD	Kinzers
1	n/a	Chartiers Valley SD	Pittsburgh	1	n/a	Juniata County SD	Mifflintown	1	n/a	Perkiomen Valley SD	Collegeville
1	n/a	Cheltenham Township SD	Elkins Park	1	n/a	Karns City Area SD	Karns City	1	n/a	Peters Township SD	Mcmurray
1	n/a	Chester-Upland SD	Chester	1	n/a	Kennett Consolidated SD	Kennett Square	1	n/a	Philadelphia City SD	Philadelphia
1	n/a	Chestnut Ridge SD	Fishertown	1	n/a	Keystone Central SD	Lock Haven	1	n/a	Philipsburg-Osceola Area SD	Philipsburg
1	n/a	Chichester SD	Boothwyn	1	n/a	Keystone Oaks SD	Pittsburgh	1	n/a	Phoenixville Area SD	Phoenixville
1	n/a	Clearfield Area SD	Clearfield	1	n/a	Kiski Area SD	Vandergrift	1	n/a	Pine Grove Area SD	Pine Grove
1	n/a	Coatesville Area SD	Coatesville	1	n/a	Kutztown Area SD	Kutztown	1	n/a	Pine-Richland SD	Gibsonia
1	n/a	Cocalico SD	Denver	1	n/a	Lake-Lehman SD	Lehman	1	n/a	Pittsburgh SD	Pittsburgh
1	n/a	Colonial SD	Plymouth Meeting	1	n/a	Lakeland SD	Jermyn	1	n/a	Pittston Area SD	Pittston
1	n/a	Conestoga Valley SD	Lancaster	1	n/a	Lampeter-Strasburg SD	Lampeter	1	n/a	Pleasant Valley SD	Brodheadsville
1	n/a	Conewago Valley SD	New Oxford	1	n/a	Lancaster SD	Lancaster	1	n/a	Plum Borough SD	Plum
1	n/a	Conneaut SD	Linesville	1	n/a	Laurel Highlands SD	Uniontown	1	n/a	Pocono Mountain SD	Swiftwater
1	n/a	Connellsville Area SD	Connellsville	1	n/a	Lebanon SD	Lebanon	1	n/a	Pottsgrove SD	Pottstown
1	n/a	Conrad Weiser Area SD	Robesonia	1	n/a	Lehighton Area SD	Lehighton	1	n/a	Pottstown SD	Pottstown
1	n/a	Cornwall-Lebanon SD	Lebanon	1	n/a	Lewisburg Area SD	Lewisburg	1	n/a	Pottsville Area SD	Pottsville
1	n/a	Corry Area SD	Corry	1	n/a	Ligonier Valley SD	Ligonier	1	n/a	Punxsutawney Area SD	Punxsutawney
1	n/a	Council Rock SD	Newtown	1	n/a	Littlestown Area SD	Littlestown	1	n/a	Quaker Valley SD	Sewickley
1	n/a	Crawford Central SD	Meadville	1	n/a	Lower Dauphin SD	Hummelstown	1	n/a	Quakertown Community SD	Quakertown
1	n/a	Crestwood SD	Mountain Top	1	n/a	Lower Merion SD	Ardmore	1	n/a	Radnor Township SD	Wayne
1	n/a	Cumberland Valley SD	Mechanicsburg	1	n/a	Lower Moreland Township SD	Huntingdon Vly	1	n/a	Reading SD	Reading
1	n/a	Dallas SD	Dallas	1	n/a	Manheim Central SD	Manheim	1	n/a	Red Lion Area SD	Red Lion
1	n/a	Dallastown Area SD	Dallastown	1	n/a	Manheim Township SD	Lancaster	1	n/a	Reynolds SD	Greenville
1	n/a	Daniel Boone Area SD	Birdsboro	1	n/a	Marion Center Area SD	Marion Center	1	n/a	Richland SD	Johnstown
1	n/a	Danville Area SD	Danville	1	n/a	Marple Newtown SD	Newtown Square	1	n/a	Ridley SD	Folsom
1	n/a	Deer Lakes SD	Russellton	1	n/a	Mars Area SD	Mars	1	n/a	Ringgold SD	New Eagle
1	n/a	Delaware Valley SD	Milford	1	n/a	Mcguffey SD	Claysville	1	n/a	Riverside Beaver County SD	Ellwood City
1	n/a	Derry Area SD	Derry	1	n/a	Mckeesport Area SD	Mc Keesport	1	n/a	Rose Tree Media SD	Media
1	n/a	Derry Township SD	Hershey	1	n/a	Mechanicsburg Area SD	Mechanicsburg	1	n/a	Saint Marys Area SD	Saint Marys
1	n/a	Donegal SD	Mount Joy	1	n/a	Mercer Area SD	Mercer	1	n/a	Salisbury Township SD	Allentown
1	n/a	Dover Area SD	Dover	1	n/a	Methacton SD	Norristown	1	n/a	Saucon Valley SD	Hellertown
1	n/a	Downingtown Area SD	Downingtown	1	n/a	Mid Valley SD	Throop	1	n/a	Schuylkill Valley SD	Leesport
1	n/a	Dubois Area SD	Du Bois	1	n/a	Midd-West SD	Middleburg	1	n/a	Scranton SD	Scranton
1	n/a	Dunmore SD	Dunmore	1	n/a	Middletown Area SD	Middletown	1	n/a	Selinsgrove Area SD	Selinsgrove
1	n/a	East Allegheny SD	N Versailles	1	n/a	Mifflin County SD	Lewistown	1	n/a	Seneca Valley SD	Harmony
1	n/a	East Lycoming SD	Hughesville	1	n/a	Mifflinburg Area SD	Mifflinburg	1	n/a	Shaler Area SD	Glenshaw
1	n/a	East Penn SD	Emmaus	1	n/a	Millcreek Township SD	Erie	1	n/a	Shamokin Area SD	Coal Township
1	n/a	East Pennsboro Area SD	Enola	1	n/a	Milton Area SD	Milton	1	n/a	Sharon City SD	Sharon
1	n/a	East Stroudsburg Area SD	E Stroudsburg	1	n/a	Mohawk Area SD	Bessemer	1	n/a	Shikellamy SD	Sunbury
1	n/a	Eastern Lancaster County SD	New Holland	1	n/a	Moniteau SD	West Sunbury	1	n/a	Shippensburg Area SD	Shippensburg
1	n/a	Eastern Lebanon County SD	Myerstown	1	n/a	Montour SD	Mc Kees Rocks	1	n/a	Slippery Rock Area SD	Slippery Rock
1	n/a	Eastern York SD	Wrightsville	1	n/a	Montoursville Area SD	Montoursville	1	n/a	Solanco SD	Quarryville
1	n/a	Easton Area SD	Easton	1	n/a	Montrose Area SD	Montrose	1	n/a	Somerset Area SD	Somerset
1	n/a	Elizabeth Forward SD	Elizabeth	1	n/a	Moon Area SD	Moon Township	1	n/a	Souderton Area SD	Souderton
1	n/a	Elizabethtown Area SD	Elizabethtown	1	n/a	Mount Carmel Area SD	Mount Carmel	1	n/a	South Allegheny SD	Mc Keesport
1	n/a	Elk Lake SD	Dimock	1	n/a	Mount Pleasant Area SD	Mount Pleasant	1	n/a	South Butler County SD	Saxonburg
1	n/a	Ellwood City Area SD	Ellwood City	1	n/a	Mount Union Area SD	Mount Union	1	n/a	South Eastern SD	Fawn Grove
1	n/a	Ephrata Area SD	Ephrata	1	n/a	Mt Lebanon SD	Pittsburgh	1	n/a	South Fayette Township SD	Mc Donald
1	n/a	Erie City SD	Erie	1	n/a	Muhlenberg SD	Reading	1	n/a	South Middleton SD	Boiling Springs
1	n/a	Exeter Township SD	Reading	1	n/a	Nazareth Area SD	Nazareth	1	n/a	South Park SD	South Park
1	n/a	Fairview SD	Fairview	1	n/a	Neshaminy SD	Langhorne	1	n/a	South Western SD	Hanover
1	n/a	Fleetwood Area SD	Fleetwood	1	n/a	New Brighton Area SD	New Brighton	1	n/a	Southeast Delco SD	Folcroft
1	n/a	Forest Hills SD	Sidman	1	n/a	New Castle Area SD	New Castle	1	n/a	Southern Lehigh SD	Center Valley
1	n/a	Fort Leboeuf SD	Waterford	1	n/a	New Kensington-Arnold SD	New Kensington	1	n/a	Southern Tioga SD	Blossburg
1	n/a	Fox Chapel Area SD	Pittsburgh	1	n/a	Norristown Area SD	Norristown	1	n/a	Southern York County SD	Glen Rock
1	n/a	Franklin Area SD	Franklin	1	n/a	North Allegheny SD	Pittsburgh	1	n/a	Southmoreland SD	Scottdale
1	n/a	Franklin Regional SD	Murrysville	1	n/a	North East SD	North East	1	n/a	Spring Cove SD	Roaring Spring
1	n/a	Freedom Area SD	Freedom	1	n/a	North Hills SD	Pittsburgh	1	n/a	Spring Grove Area SD	Spring Grove
1	n/a	Freeport Area SD	Freeport	1	n/a	North Penn SD	Lansdale	1	n/a	Spring-Ford Area SD	Collegeville
1	n/a	Garnet Valley SD	Glen Mills	1	n/a	North Pocono SD	Moscow	1	n/a	Springfield SD	Springfield
1	n/a	Gateway SD	Monroeville	1	n/a	North Schuylkill SD	Ashland	1	n/a	Springfield Township SD	Oreland
1	n/a	General Mclane SD	Edinboro	1	n/a	Northampton Area SD	Northampton	1	n/a	State College Area SD	State College
1	n/a	Gettysburg Area SD	Gettysburg	1	n/a	Northeastern York SD	Manchester	1	n/a	Steel Valley SD	Munhall
1	n/a	Girard SD	Girard	1	n/a	Northern Lebanon SD	Fredericksburg	1	n/a	Sto-Rox SD	Mckees Rocks
1	n/a	Governor Mifflin SD	Shillington	1	n/a	Northern Lehigh SD	Slatington	1	n/a	Stroudsburg Area SD	Stroudsburg

1	n/a	Susquehanna Township SD	Harrisburg
1	n/a	Susquenita SD	Duncannon
1	n/a	Tamaqua Area SD	Tamaqua
1	n/a	Titusville Area SD	Titusville
1	n/a	Towanda Area SD	Towanda
1	n/a	Tredyffrin-Easttown SD	Berwyn
1	n/a	Trinity Area SD	Washington
1	n/a	Troy Area SD	Troy
1	n/a	Tulpehocken Area SD	Bernville
1	n/a	Tunkhannock Area SD	Tunkhannock
1	n/a	Tuscarora SD	Mercersburg
1	n/a	Twin Valley SD	Elverson
1	n/a	Tyrone Area SD	Tyrone
1	n/a	Uniontown Area SD	Uniontown
1	n/a	Unionville-Chadds Ford SD	Kennett Square
1	n/a	Upper Adams SD	Biglerville
1	n/a	Upper Darby SD	Drexel Hill
1	n/a	Upper Dublin SD	Maple Glen
1	n/a	Upper Merion Area SD	King Of Prussia
1	n/a	Upper Moreland Township SD	Willow Grove
1	n/a	Upper Perkiomen SD	East Greenville
1	n/a	Upper Saint Clair SD	Pittsburgh
1	n/a	Valley View SD	Archbald
1	n/a	Wallenpaupack Area SD	Hawley
1	n/a	Wallingford-Swarthmore SD	Wallingford
1	n/a	Warren County SD	North Warren
1	n/a	Warrior Run SD	Turbotville
1	n/a	Warwick SD	Lititz
1	n/a	Washington SD	Washington
1	n/a	Wattsburg Area SD	Erie
1	n/a	Wayne Highlands SD	Honesdale
1	n/a	Waynesboro Area SD	Waynesboro
1	n/a	Wellsboro Area SD	Wellsboro
1	n/a	West Allegheny SD	Imperial
1	n/a	West Chester Area SD	West Chester
1	n/a	West Jefferson Hills SD	Jefferson Hls
1	n/a	West Mifflin Area SD	West Mifflin
1	n/a	West Perry SD	Elliottsburg
1	n/a	West Shore SD	New Cumberland
1	n/a	West York Area SD	York
1	n/a	Western Pennsylvania Cyber CS	Midland
1	n/a	Western Wayne SD	South Canaan
1	n/a	Westmont Hilltop SD	Johnstown
1	n/a	Whitehall-Coplay SD	Whitehall
1	n/a	Wilkes-Barre Area SD	Wilkes Barre
1	n/a	Wilkinsburg Borough SD	Wilkinsburg
1	n/a	William Penn SD	Lansdowne
1	n/a	Williamsport Area SD	Williamsport
1	n/a	Wilmington Area SD	New Wilmington
1	n/a	Wilson SD	West Lawn
1	n/a	Wilson Area SD	Easton
1	n/a	Wissahickon SD	Ambler
1	n/a	Woodland Hills SD	Pittsburgh
1	n/a	Wyalusing Area SD	Wyalusing
1	n/a	Wyoming Area SD	Exeter
1	n/a	Wyoming Valley West SD	Kingston
1	n/a	Wyomissing Area SD	Wyomissing
1	n/a	York City SD	York
1	n/a	York Suburban SD	York
1	n/a	Yough SD	Herminie

Migrant Students

Rank	Percent	District Name	City
1	15.7	Kennett Consolidated SD	Kennett Square
2	11.2	Lebanon SD	Lebanon
3	11.0	Upper Adams SD	Biglerville
4	9.4	Lancaster SD	Lancaster
5	8.4	Erie City SD	Erie
6	7.5	Reading SD	Reading
7	5.2	Avon Grove SD	West Grove
8	5.0	Bermudian Springs SD	York Springs
9	4.9	Gettysburg Area SD	Gettysburg
10	3.8	Hanover Public SD	Hanover
11	3.7	Conewago Valley SD	New Oxford
12	3.4	Scranton SD	Scranton
13	3.3	Oxford Area SD	Oxford
13	3.3	York City SD	York
15	3.1	Harrisburg City SD	Harrisburg
16	2.8	Chambersburg Area SD	Chambersburg
17	2.5	Allentown City SD	Allentown
18	2.2	Hazleton Area SD	Hazleton
19	2.1	Troy Area SD	Troy
20	2.0	Cornwall-Lebanon SD	Lebanon
21	1.6	Bethlehem Area SD	Bethlehem
21	1.6	Wyalusing Area SD	Wyalusing
23	1.2	Juniata County SD	Mifflintown
24	1.1	Octorara Area SD	Atglen
24	1.1	Southern Tioga SD	Blossburg
24	1.1	Tulpehocken Area SD	Bernville
27	1.0	Central Dauphin SD	Harrisburg
27	1.0	Hempfield SD	Landisville
29	0.9	Athens Area SD	Athens
29	0.9	Carlisle Area SD	Carlisle
29	0.9	Souderton Area SD	Souderton
32	0.8	North Penn SD	Lansdale
33	0.7	Northern Tioga SD	Elkland
34	0.6	Chester-Upland SD	Chester
34	0.6	Coatesville Area SD	Coatesville
34	0.6	Donegal SD	Mount Joy
34	0.6	Tuscarora SD	Mercersburg
38	0.5	East Pennsboro Area SD	Enola
38	0.5	Elk Lake SD	Dimock
38	0.5	Manheim Central SD	Manheim
38	0.5	Millcreek Township SD	Erie
38	0.5	Wellsboro Area SD	Wellsboro
43	0.4	Eastern Lancaster County SD	New Holland
43	0.4	Manheim Township SD	Lancaster
43	0.4	Mechanicsburg Area SD	Mechanicsburg
43	0.4	Mifflin County SD	Lewistown
43	0.4	Norristown Area SD	Norristown
43	0.4	Philadelphia City SD	Philadelphia
43	0.4	Spring Cove SD	Roaring Spring
43	0.4	Susquehanna Township SD	Harrisburg
43	0.4	West Shore SD	New Cumberland
52	0.3	Cocalico SD	Denver
52	0.3	Conestoga Valley SD	Lancaster
52	0.3	Elizabethtown Area SD	Elizabethtown
52	0.3	Ephrata Area SD	Ephrata
52	0.3	Fleetwood Area SD	Fleetwood
52	0.3	Littlestown Area SD	Littlestown
52	0.3	Muhlenberg SD	Reading
52	0.3	Northeastern York SD	Manchester
52	0.3	Shikellamy SD	Sunbury
52	0.3	Tunkhannock Area SD	Tunkhannock
52	0.3	Warwick SD	Lititz
52	0.3	York Suburban SD	York
64	0.2	Abington Heights SD	Clarks Summit
64	0.2	Big Spring SD	Newville
64	0.2	Conneaut SD	Linesville
64	0.2	Eastern Lebanon County SD	Myerstown
64	0.2	Eastern York SD	Wrightsville
64	0.2	Lake-Lehman SD	Lehman
64	0.2	Mid Valley SD	Throop
64	0.2	Mount Pleasant Area SD	Mount Pleasant
64	0.2	North East SD	North East
64	0.2	Solanco SD	Quarryville
64	0.2	South Western SD	Hanover
64	0.2	Spring Grove Area SD	Spring Grove
64	0.2	Wayne Highlands SD	Honesdale
64	0.2	West York Area SD	York
64	0.2	Whitehall-Coplay SD	Whitehall
64	0.2	Wyomissing Area SD	Wyomissing
80	0.1	Brandywine Heights Area SD	Topton
80	0.1	Brookville Area SD	Brookville
80	0.1	Canon-Mcmillan SD	Canonsburg
80	0.1	Central York SD	York
80	0.1	Chestnut Ridge SD	Fishertown
80	0.1	Conrad Weiser Area SD	Robesonia
80	0.1	Cumberland Valley SD	Mechanicsburg
80	0.1	Dallastown Area SD	Dallastown
80	0.1	Derry Township SD	Hershey
80	0.1	Easton Area SD	Easton
80	0.1	Exeter Township SD	Reading
80	0.1	Lower Dauphin SD	Hummelstown
80	0.1	Marion Center Area SD	Marion Center
80	0.1	Montrose Area SD	Montrose
80	0.1	Northern Lebanon SD	Fredericksburg
80	0.1	Northern York County SD	Dillsburg
80	0.1	Northwestern SD	Albion
80	0.1	Palmyra Area SD	Palmyra
80	0.1	Penn Manor SD	Millersville
80	0.1	Pennridge SD	Perkasie
80	0.1	Penns Valley Area SD	Spring Mills
80	0.1	Pequea Valley SD	Kinzers
80	0.1	Peters Township SD	Mcmurray
80	0.1	Punxsutawney Area SD	Punxsutawney
80	0.1	Saucon Valley SD	Hellertown
80	0.1	South Middleton SD	Boiling Springs
80	0.1	Towanda Area SD	Towanda
80	0.1	Tyrone Area SD	Tyrone
80	0.1	Unionville-Chadds Ford SD	Kennett Square
80	0.1	Upper Perkiomen SD	East Greenville
80	0.1	West Chester Area SD	West Chester
80	0.1	Wilson SD	West Lawn
80	0.1	Wilson Area SD	Easton
80	0.1	Wissahickon SD	Ambler
114	0.0	Bedford Area SD	Bedford
114	0.0	Bellefonte Area SD	Bellefonte
114	0.0	Butler Area SD	Butler
114	0.0	Central Bucks SD	Doylestown
114	0.0	East Penn SD	Emmaus
114	0.0	Fort Leboeuf SD	Waterford
114	0.0	Governor Mifflin SD	Shillington
114	0.0	Greensburg Salem SD	Greensburg
114	0.0	Huntingdon Area SD	Huntingdon
114	0.0	Keystone Central SD	Lock Haven
114	0.0	Methacton SD	Norristown
114	0.0	Midd-West SD	Middleburg
114	0.0	Milton Area SD	Milton
114	0.0	Penncrest SD	Saegertown
114	0.0	Pottstown SD	Pottstown
114	0.0	Red Lion Area SD	Red Lion
114	0.0	Shippensburg Area SD	Shippensburg
114	0.0	State College Area SD	State College
114	0.0	Trinity Area SD	Washington
114	0.0	Wallenpaupack Area SD	Hawley
114	0.0	Waynesboro Area SD	Waynesboro
135	0.0	Abington SD	Abington
135	0.0	Albert Gallatin Area SD	Uniontown
135	0.0	Altoona Area SD	Altoona
135	0.0	Ambridge Area SD	Ambridge
135	0.0	Annville-Cleona SD	Annville
135	0.0	Apollo-Ridge SD	Spring Church
135	0.0	Armstrong SD	Ford City
135	0.0	Bald Eagle Area SD	Wingate
135	0.0	Baldwin-Whitehall SD	Pittsburgh
135	0.0	Bangor Area SD	Bangor
135	0.0	Beaver Area SD	Beaver
135	0.0	Belle Vernon Area SD	Belle Vernon
135	0.0	Bensalem Township SD	Bensalem
135	0.0	Berwick Area SD	Berwick
135	0.0	Bethel Park SD	Bethel Park
135	0.0	Big Beaver Falls Area SD	Beaver Falls
135	0.0	Blackhawk SD	Beaver Falls
135	0.0	Blairsville-Saltsburg SD	Blairsville
135	0.0	Bloomsburg Area SD	Bloomsburg
135	0.0	Blue Mountain SD	Orwigsburg
135	0.0	Boyertown Area SD	Boyertown
135	0.0	Bradford Area SD	Bradford
135	0.0	Bristol Township SD	Levittown
135	0.0	Brownsville Area SD	Brownsville
135	0.0	Burgettstown Area SD	Burgettstown
135	0.0	Burrell SD	Lower Burrell
135	0.0	Cambria Heights SD	Patton
135	0.0	Carlynton SD	Carnegie
135	0.0	Catasauqua Area SD	Catasauqua
135	0.0	Centennial SD	Warminster
135	0.0	Center Area SD	Monaca
135	0.0	Central Cambria SD	Ebensburg
135	0.0	Central Columbia SD	Bloomsburg
135	0.0	Central Greene SD	Waynesburg
135	0.0	Charleroi SD	Charleroi
135	0.0	Chartiers Valley SD	Pittsburgh
135	0.0	Cheltenham Township SD	Elkins Park
135	0.0	Chichester SD	Boothwyn
135	0.0	Clearfield Area SD	Clearfield
135	0.0	Colonial SD	Plymouth Meeting
135	0.0	Connellsville Area SD	Connellsville
135	0.0	Corry Area SD	Corry
135	0.0	Council Rock SD	Newtown
135	0.0	Crawford Central SD	Meadville
135	0.0	Crestwood SD	Mountain Top
135	0.0	Dallas SD	Dallas
135	0.0	Daniel Boone Area SD	Birdsboro
135	0.0	Danville Area SD	Danville
135	0.0	Deer Lakes SD	Russellton
135	0.0	Delaware Valley SD	Milford
135	0.0	Derry Area SD	Derry
135	0.0	Dover Area SD	Dover
135	0.0	Downingtown Area SD	Downingtown
135	0.0	Dubois Area SD	Du Bois
135	0.0	Dunmore SD	Dunmore
135	0.0	East Allegheny SD	N Versailles
135	0.0	East Lycoming SD	Hughesville
135	0.0	East Stroudsburg Area SD	E Stroudsburg
135	0.0	Elizabeth Forward SD	Elizabeth
135	0.0	Ellwood City Area SD	Ellwood City
135	0.0	Everett Area SD	Everett
135	0.0	Fairview SD	Fairview
135	0.0	Forest Hills SD	Sidman
135	0.0	Fox Chapel Area SD	Pittsburgh
135	0.0	Franklin Area SD	Franklin
135	0.0	Franklin Regional SD	Murrysville
135	0.0	Freedom Area SD	Freedom
135	0.0	Freeport Area SD	Freeport
135	0.0	Garnet Valley SD	Glen Mills
135	0.0	Gateway SD	Monroeville
135	0.0	General Mclane SD	Edinboro
135	0.0	Girard SD	Girard
135	0.0	Great Valley SD	Malvern
135	0.0	Greater Johnstown SD	Johnstown
135	0.0	Greater Latrobe SD	Latrobe
135	0.0	Greater Nanticoke Area SD	Nanticoke
135	0.0	Greencastle-Antrim SD	Greencastle
135	0.0	Greenville Area SD	Greenville
135	0.0	Grove City Area SD	Grove City
135	0.0	Hamburg Area SD	Hamburg

135	0.0	Hampton Township SD	Allison Park
135	0.0	Hanover Area SD	Wilkes Barre
135	0.0	Harbor Creek SD	Harborcreek
135	0.0	Hatboro-Horsham SD	Horsham
135	0.0	Haverford Township SD	Havertown
135	0.0	Hempfield Area SD	Greensburg
135	0.0	Hermitage SD	Hermitage
135	0.0	Highlands SD	Natrona Heights
135	0.0	Hollidaysburg Area SD	Hollidaysburg
135	0.0	Hopewell Area SD	Aliquippa
135	0.0	Indiana Area SD	Indiana
135	0.0	Interboro SD	Prospect Park
135	0.0	Jersey Shore Area SD	Jersey Shore
135	0.0	Jim Thorpe Area SD	Jim Thorpe
135	0.0	Karns City Area SD	Karns City
135	0.0	Keystone Oaks SD	Pittsburgh
135	0.0	Kiski Area SD	Vandergrift
135	0.0	Kutztown Area SD	Kutztown
135	0.0	Lakeland SD	Jermyn
135	0.0	Lampeter-Strasburg SD	Lampeter
135	0.0	Laurel Highlands SD	Uniontown
135	0.0	Lehighton Area SD	Lehighton
135	0.0	Lewisburg Area SD	Lewisburg
135	0.0	Ligonier Valley SD	Ligonier
135	0.0	Lower Merion SD	Ardmore
135	0.0	Lower Moreland Township SD	Huntingdon Vly
135	0.0	Marple Newtown SD	Newtown Square
135	0.0	Mars Area SD	Mars
135	0.0	Mcguffey SD	Claysville
135	0.0	Mckeesport Area SD	Mc Keesport
135	0.0	Mercer Area SD	Mercer
135	0.0	Middletown Area SD	Middletown
135	0.0	Mifflinburg Area SD	Mifflinburg
135	0.0	Mohawk Area SD	Bessemer
135	0.0	Moniteau SD	West Sunbury
135	0.0	Montour SD	Mc Kees Rocks
135	0.0	Montoursville Area SD	Montoursville
135	0.0	Moon Area SD	Moon Township
135	0.0	Mount Carmel Area SD	Mount Carmel
135	0.0	Mount Union Area SD	Mount Union
135	0.0	Mt Lebanon SD	Pittsburgh
135	0.0	Nazareth Area SD	Nazareth
135	0.0	Neshaminy SD	Langhorne
135	0.0	New Brighton Area SD	New Brighton
135	0.0	New Castle Area SD	New Castle
135	0.0	New Kensington-Arnold SD	New Kensington
135	0.0	North Allegheny SD	Pittsburgh
135	0.0	North Hills SD	Pittsburgh
135	0.0	North Pocono SD	Moscow
135	0.0	North Schuylkill SD	Ashland
135	0.0	Northampton Area SD	Northampton
135	0.0	Northern Lehigh SD	Slatington
135	0.0	Northgate SD	Pittsburgh
135	0.0	Northwestern Lehigh SD	New Tripoli
135	0.0	Norwin SD	N Huntingdon
135	0.0	Oil City Area SD	Oil City
135	0.0	Oley Valley SD	Oley
135	0.0	Owen J Roberts SD	Pottstown
135	0.0	Palisades SD	Kintnersville
135	0.0	Palmerton Area SD	Palmerton
135	0.0	Parkland SD	Allentown
135	0.0	Pen Argyl Area SD	Pen Argyl
135	0.0	Penn Cambria SD	Cresson
135	0.0	Penn Hills SD	Pittsburgh
135	0.0	Penn-Delco SD	Aston
135	0.0	Penn-Trafford SD	Harrison City
135	0.0	Pennsbury SD	Fallsington
135	0.0	Pennsylvania Virtual CS	Norristown
135	0.0	Perkiomen Valley SD	Collegeville
135	0.0	Philipsburg-Osceola Area SD	Philipsburg
135	0.0	Phoenixville Area SD	Phoenixville
135	0.0	Pine Grove Area SD	Pine Grove
135	0.0	Pine-Richland SD	Gibsonia
135	0.0	Pittsburgh SD	Pittsburgh
135	0.0	Pittston Area SD	Pittston
135	0.0	Pleasant Valley SD	Brodheadsville
135	0.0	Plum Borough SD	Plum
135	0.0	Pocono Mountain SD	Swiftwater
135	0.0	Pottsgrove SD	Pottstown
135	0.0	Pottsville Area SD	Pottsville
135	0.0	Quaker Valley SD	Sewickley
135	0.0	Quakertown Community SD	Quakertown
135	0.0	Radnor Township SD	Wayne
135	0.0	Reynolds SD	Greenville
135	0.0	Richland SD	Johnstown
135	0.0	Ridley SD	Folsom
135	0.0	Ringgold SD	New Eagle
135	0.0	Riverside Beaver County SD	Ellwood City
135	0.0	Rose Tree Media SD	Media
135	0.0	Saint Marys Area SD	Saint Marys
135	0.0	Salisbury Township SD	Allentown
135	0.0	Schuylkill Valley SD	Leesport
135	0.0	Selinsgrove Area SD	Selinsgrove
135	0.0	Seneca Valley SD	Harmony
135	0.0	Shaler Area SD	Glenshaw
135	0.0	Shamokin Area SD	Coal Township
135	0.0	Sharon City SD	Sharon
135	0.0	Slippery Rock Area SD	Slippery Rock
135	0.0	Somerset Area SD	Somerset
135	0.0	South Allegheny SD	Mc Keesport
135	0.0	South Butler County SD	Saxonburg
135	0.0	South Eastern SD	Fawn Grove
135	0.0	South Fayette Township SD	Mc Donald
135	0.0	South Park SD	South Park
135	0.0	Southeast Delco SD	Folcroft
135	0.0	Southern Lehigh SD	Center Valley
135	0.0	Southern York County SD	Glen Rock
135	0.0	Southmoreland SD	Scottdale
135	0.0	Spring-Ford Area SD	Collegeville
135	0.0	Springfield SD	Springfield
135	0.0	Springfield Township SD	Oreland
135	0.0	Steel Valley SD	Munhall
135	0.0	Sto-Rox SD	Mckees Rocks
135	0.0	Stroudsburg Area SD	Stroudsburg
135	0.0	Susquenita SD	Duncannon
135	0.0	Tamaqua Area SD	Tamaqua
135	0.0	Titusville Area SD	Titusville
135	0.0	Tredyffrin-Easttown SD	Berwyn
135	0.0	Twin Valley SD	Elverson
135	0.0	Uniontown Area SD	Uniontown
135	0.0	Upper Darby SD	Drexel Hill
135	0.0	Upper Dublin SD	Maple Glen
135	0.0	Upper Merion Area SD	King Of Prussia
135	0.0	Upper Moreland Township SD	Willow Grove
135	0.0	Upper Saint Clair SD	Pittsburgh
135	0.0	Valley View SD	Archbald
135	0.0	Wallingford-Swarthmore SD	Wallingford
135	0.0	Warren County SD	North Warren
135	0.0	Warrior Run SD	Turbotville
135	0.0	Washington SD	Washington
135	0.0	Wattsburg Area SD	Erie
135	0.0	West Allegheny SD	Imperial
135	0.0	West Jefferson Hills SD	Jefferson Hls
135	0.0	West Mifflin Area SD	West Mifflin
135	0.0	West Perry SD	Elliottsburg
135	0.0	Western Pennsylvania Cyber CS	Midland
135	0.0	Western Wayne SD	South Canaan
135	0.0	Westmont Hilltop SD	Johnstown
135	0.0	Wilkes-Barre Area SD	Wilkes Barre
135	0.0	Wilkinsburg Borough SD	Wilkinsburg
135	0.0	William Penn SD	Lansdowne
135	0.0	Williamsport Area SD	Williamsport
135	0.0	Wilmington Area SD	New Wilmington
135	0.0	Woodland Hills SD	Pittsburgh
135	0.0	Wyoming Area SD	Exeter
135	0.0	Wyoming Valley West SD	Kingston
135	0.0	Yough SD	Herminie
362	n/a	Pde Division of Data Services	Harrisburg

Students Eligible for Free Lunch

Rank	Percent	District Name	City
1	71.5	Wilkinsburg Borough SD	Wilkinsburg
2	66.8	Chester-Upland SD	Chester
3	64.1	Philadelphia City SD	Philadelphia
4	62.7	York City SD	York
5	60.1	Erie City SD	Erie
5	60.1	Greater Johnstown SD	Johnstown
7	57.9	Sto-Rox SD	Mckees Rocks
8	56.2	Pittsburgh SD	Pittsburgh
9	55.3	Harrisburg City SD	Harrisburg
9	55.3	Reading SD	Reading
11	53.3	Brownsville Area SD	Brownsville
12	51.5	Lancaster SD	Lancaster
13	48.4	Mckeesport Area SD	Mc Keesport
14	47.9	Sharon City SD	Sharon
15	44.6	Allentown City SD	Allentown
16	44.2	Big Beaver Falls Area SD	Beaver Falls
17	44.0	New Castle Area SD	New Castle
18	43.7	Uniontown Area SD	Uniontown
19	41.0	Woodland Hills SD	Pittsburgh
20	39.9	New Brighton Area SD	New Brighton
21	39.7	Connellsville Area SD	Connellsville
22	37.7	New Kensington-Arnold SD	New Kensington
22	37.7	Norristown Area SD	Norristown
24	37.2	Central Greene SD	Waynesburg
25	36.6	William Penn SD	Lansdowne
26	36.5	Altoona Area SD	Altoona
27	35.9	Laurel Highlands SD	Uniontown
27	35.9	Oil City Area SD	Oil City
29	35.7	Clearfield Area SD	Clearfield
30	35.1	Northern Tioga SD	Elkland
31	35.0	Lebanon SD	Lebanon
32	34.9	Williamsport Area SD	Williamsport
33	34.4	Albert Gallatin Area SD	Uniontown
34	34.0	Shamokin Area SD	Coal Township
35	33.5	Southeast Delco SD	Folcroft
36	33.4	Corry Area SD	Corry
37	33.2	Steel Valley SD	Munhall
38	32.5	Scranton SD	Scranton
39	32.4	Hanover Area SD	Wilkes Barre
40	31.6	Apollo-Ridge SD	Spring Church
41	30.9	East Allegheny SD	N Versailles
41	30.9	Penn Cambria SD	Cresson
43	30.1	Highlands SD	Natrona Heights
44	29.6	Bradford Area SD	Bradford
45	29.5	Marion Center Area SD	Marion Center
46	29.0	Reynolds SD	Greenville
47	28.6	Conneaut SD	Linesville
47	28.6	Pottstown SD	Pottstown
49	28.5	Keystone Central SD	Lock Haven
50	28.3	Mount Carmel Area SD	Mount Carmel
51	28.1	Southern Tioga SD	Blossburg
52	27.8	Ringgold SD	New Eagle
53	27.7	Ellwood City Area SD	Ellwood City
54	27.6	Titusville Area SD	Titusville
55	27.4	Berwick Area SD	Berwick
55	27.4	Western Wayne SD	South Canaan
57	27.3	Derry Area SD	Derry
57	27.3	Franklin Area SD	Franklin
59	27.2	Charleroi SD	Charleroi
60	27.0	Southmoreland SD	Scottdale
61	26.9	Bristol Township SD	Levittown
61	26.9	Dubois Area SD	Du Bois
63	26.7	Towanda Area SD	Towanda
64	26.6	Greensburg Salem SD	Greensburg
64	26.6	Wyoming Valley West SD	Kingston
66	26.4	Blairsville-Saltsburg SD	Blairsville
67	25.9	Coatesville Area SD	Coatesville
67	25.9	Everett Area SD	Everett
69	25.8	Northgate SD	Pittsburgh
69	25.8	Northwestern SD	Albion
71	25.7	Milton Area SD	Milton
72	25.6	Troy Area SD	Troy
73	25.0	Cambria Heights SD	Patton
74	24.8	Crawford Central SD	Meadville
75	24.7	Tyrone Area SD	Tyrone
76	24.6	Greenville Area SD	Greenville
76	24.6	Philipsburg-Osceola Area SD	Philipsburg
78	24.5	Bethlehem Area SD	Bethlehem
79	24.4	Moniteau SD	West Sunbury
80	24.2	Bloomsburg Area SD	Bloomsburg
80	24.2	Penn Hills SD	Pittsburgh
82	23.7	Girard SD	Girard
82	23.7	Upper Adams SD	Biglerville
84	23.6	Yough SD	Herminie
85	23.4	Wallenpaupack Area SD	Hawley
86	23.3	Wilkes-Barre Area SD	Wilkes Barre
87	23.2	Pottsville Area SD	Pottsville
88	23.1	Wayne Highlands SD	Honesdale
89	23.0	Chestnut Ridge SD	Fishertown
89	23.0	Wellsboro Area SD	Wellsboro
91	22.8	Forest Hills SD	Sidman
92	22.7	Mount Union Area SD	Mount Union
93	22.5	Brookville Area SD	Brookville
94	22.4	Mifflin County SD	Lewistown
95	22.2	Karns City Area SD	Karns City
96	21.8	Burgettstown Area SD	Burgettstown
97	21.7	Ligonier Valley SD	Ligonier
97	21.7	North Schuylkill SD	Ashland
99	21.6	Bensalem Township SD	Bensalem
99	21.6	Huntingdon Area SD	Huntingdon
101	21.3	Bald Eagle Area SD	Wingate
102	21.2	Wyalusing Area SD	Wyalusing
103	21.0	Chichester SD	Boothwyn
103	21.0	North East SD	North East
105	20.9	Armstrong SD	Ford City
106	20.8	Mount Pleasant Area SD	Mount Pleasant
106	20.8	Somerset Area SD	Somerset
108	20.6	Tunkhannock Area SD	Tunkhannock
108	20.6	West Mifflin Area SD	West Mifflin
110	20.5	Elk Lake SD	Dimock
110	20.5	Spring Cove SD	Roaring Spring
112	20.3	East Lycoming SD	Hughesville
112	20.3	Riverside Beaver County SD	Ellwood City
114	20.2	Freedom Area SD	Freedom
115	20.0	Penncrest SD	Saegertown
116	19.8	Shikellamy SD	Sunbury
117	19.6	Belle Vernon Area SD	Belle Vernon
117	19.6	Northern Lehigh SD	Slatington
117	19.6	Warren County SD	North Warren
120	19.5	Punxsutawney Area SD	Punxsutawney
121	19.4	Midd-West SD	Middleburg
121	19.4	Pittston Area SD	Pittston
123	19.3	Central Cambria SD	Ebensburg
124	19.2	Mohawk Area SD	Bessemer
125	19.1	Danville Area SD	Danville
125	19.1	Montrose Area SD	Montrose

127	18.9	Mid Valley SD	Throop
128	18.4	Indiana Area SD	Indiana
129	18.3	Oxford Area SD	Oxford
129	18.3	Waynesboro Area SD	Waynesboro
131	18.2	Hazleton Area SD	Hazleton
132	18.1	Kiski Area SD	Vandergrift
133	18.0	Fort Leboeuf SD	Waterford
133	18.0	Wyoming Area SD	Exeter
135	17.8	Jersey Shore Area SD	Jersey Shore
136	17.7	Easton Area SD	Easton
136	17.7	Hermitage SD	Hermitage
136	17.7	Mercer Area SD	Mercer
139	17.6	Jim Thorpe Area SD	Jim Thorpe
140	17.4	Lake-Lehman SD	Lehman
141	17.3	Kennett Consolidated SD	Kennett Square
142	17.0	Butler Area SD	Butler
142	17.0	Lakeland SD	Jermyn
144	16.8	Gettysburg Area SD	Gettysburg
144	16.8	Pocono Mountain SD	Swiftwater
144	16.8	Selinsgrove Area SD	Selinsgrove
144	16.8	Wilmington Area SD	New Wilmington
148	16.6	Upper Darby SD	Drexel Hill
149	16.3	Tuscarora SD	Mercersburg
150	16.2	Ambridge Area SD	Ambridge
150	16.2	Hanover Public SD	Hanover
150	16.2	Juniata County SD	Mifflintown
153	16.1	Chambersburg Area SD	Chambersburg
153	16.1	Dunmore SD	Dunmore
155	15.8	Slippery Rock Area SD	Slippery Rock
156	15.7	Mifflinburg Area SD	Mifflinburg
156	15.7	Valley View SD	Archbald
158	15.6	Hollidaysburg Area SD	Hollidaysburg
158	15.6	Northeastern York SD	Manchester
160	15.3	Bellefonte Area SD	Bellefonte
161	15.1	Conewago Valley SD	New Oxford
162	14.9	Gateway SD	Monroeville
162	14.9	North Pocono SD	Moscow
164	14.8	Wattsburg Area SD	Erie
165	14.7	Lehighton Area SD	Lehighton
165	14.7	Saint Marys Area SD	Saint Marys
167	14.3	Mcguffey SD	Claysville
168	14.2	West Perry SD	Elliottsburg
169	13.9	Cornwall-Lebanon SD	Lebanon
170	13.7	Athens Area SD	Athens
170	13.7	Pine Grove Area SD	Pine Grove
172	13.5	Bedford Area SD	Bedford
173	13.4	Greater Latrobe SD	Latrobe
174	13.3	Keystone Oaks SD	Pittsburgh
174	13.3	Palmerton Area SD	Palmerton
174	13.3	Trinity Area SD	Washington
177	13.2	Chartiers Valley SD	Pittsburgh
178	13.0	South Allegheny SD	Mc Keesport
179	12.9	Canon-Mcmillan SD	Canonsburg
179	12.9	Catasauqua Area SD	Catasauqua
179	12.9	Penns Valley Area SD	Spring Mills
179	12.9	Susquenita SD	Duncannon
183	12.8	Warrior Run SD	Turbotville
184	12.5	Ridley SD	Folsom
184	12.5	Shippensburg Area SD	Shippensburg
186	12.4	Baldwin-Whitehall SD	Pittsburgh
187	12.3	Elizabeth Forward SD	Elizabeth
188	12.2	Stroudsburg Area SD	Stroudsburg
189	12.1	Ephrata Area SD	Ephrata
190	12.0	Carlisle Area SD	Carlisle
190	12.0	Pequea Valley SD	Kinzers
192	11.8	Millcreek Township SD	Erie
193	11.6	Burrell SD	Lower Burrell
194	11.5	Bermudian Springs SD	York Springs
194	11.5	Harbor Creek SD	Harborcreek
194	11.5	Hopewell Area SD	Aliquippa
194	11.5	Interboro SD	Prospect Park
198	11.3	Shaler Area SD	Glenshaw
198	11.3	Susquehanna Township SD	Harrisburg
200	11.2	Greater Nanticoke Area SD	Nanticoke
201	11.1	Donegal SD	Mount Joy
201	11.1	Freeport Area SD	Freeport
201	11.1	General Mclane SD	Edinboro
204	11.0	Central Dauphin SD	Harrisburg
204	11.0	Eastern York SD	Wrightsville
204	11.0	Whitehall-Coplay SD	Whitehall
207	10.9	Littlestown Area SD	Littlestown
208	10.8	Solanco SD	Quarryville
208	10.8	Tulpehocken Area SD	Bernville
210	10.7	West York Area SD	York
211	10.6	East Stroudsburg Area SD	E Stroudsburg
212	10.5	Delaware Valley SD	Milford
212	10.5	Middletown Area SD	Middletown
212	10.5	Wilson Area SD	Easton
215	10.3	Octorara Area SD	Atglen
216	10.2	Grove City Area SD	Grove City
217	10.1	Hempfield Area SD	Greensburg
218	10.0	Bangor Area SD	Bangor
218	10.0	West Allegheny SD	Imperial
220	9.9	Crestwood SD	Mountain Top
220	9.9	Eastern Lancaster County SD	New Holland
222	9.8	Manheim Central SD	Manheim
222	9.8	Pottsgrove SD	Pottstown
222	9.8	Tamaqua Area SD	Tamaqua
225	9.7	Big Spring SD	Newville
226	9.6	Central Columbia SD	Bloomsburg
226	9.6	Lewisburg Area SD	Lewisburg
228	9.4	Centennial SD	Warminster
229	9.3	Blackhawk SD	Beaver Falls
230	9.2	Dover Area SD	Dover
231	9.1	Washington SD	Washington
232	9.0	Red Lion Area SD	Red Lion
233	8.7	Muhlenberg SD	Reading
234	8.6	Phoenixville Area SD	Phoenixville
235	8.5	Pen Argyl Area SD	Pen Argyl
236	8.4	Quaker Valley SD	Sewickley
237	8.3	Blue Mountain SD	Orwigsburg
237	8.3	Westmont Hilltop SD	Johnstown
239	8.2	Central York SD	York
239	8.2	East Pennsboro Area SD	Enola
239	8.2	Spring Grove Area SD	Spring Grove
242	7.9	Northern Lebanon SD	Fredericksburg
242	7.9	State College Area SD	State College
244	7.8	Quakertown Community SD	Quakertown
244	7.8	Richland SD	Johnstown
244	7.8	Upper Perkiomen SD	East Greenville
247	7.7	Cocalico SD	Denver
247	7.7	Fairview SD	Fairview
249	7.6	Lower Dauphin SD	Hummelstown
250	7.4	Mechanicsburg Area SD	Mechanicsburg
251	7.3	Salisbury Township SD	Allentown
252	7.2	Conestoga Valley SD	Lancaster
253	7.1	Eastern Lebanon County SD	Myerstown
253	7.1	Norwin SD	N Huntingdon
253	7.1	Plum Borough SD	Plum
256	7.0	Fox Chapel Area SD	Pittsburgh
256	7.0	Hempfield SD	Landisville
256	7.0	North Hills SD	Pittsburgh
256	7.0	North Penn SD	Lansdale
256	7.0	West Shore SD	New Cumberland
261	6.9	Deer Lakes SD	Russellton
261	6.9	Penn Manor SD	Millersville
263	6.8	Exeter Township SD	Reading
263	6.8	Hamburg Area SD	Hamburg
263	6.8	Montoursville Area SD	Montoursville
266	6.7	South Western SD	Hanover
267	6.5	Saucon Valley SD	Hellertown
268	6.4	Twin Valley SD	Elverson
269	6.3	Kutztown Area SD	Kutztown
270	6.2	Wyomissing Area SD	Wyomissing
271	6.1	Avon Grove SD	West Grove
271	6.1	Brandywine Heights Area SD	Topton
271	6.1	Daniel Boone Area SD	Birdsboro
271	6.1	Warwick SD	Lititz
275	6.0	Pleasant Valley SD	Brodheadsville
275	6.0	Upper Moreland Township SD	Willow Grove
275	6.0	Wilson SD	West Lawn
278	5.9	Abington SD	Abington
278	5.9	Colonial SD	Plymouth Meeting
278	5.9	Moon Area SD	Moon Township
278	5.9	Perkiomen Valley SD	Collegeville
282	5.8	Governor Mifflin SD	Shillington
282	5.8	Seneca Valley SD	Harmony
284	5.7	Neshaminy SD	Langhorne
284	5.7	Schuylkill Valley SD	Leesport
284	5.7	Upper Merion Area SD	King Of Prussia
287	5.6	Annville-Cleona SD	Annville
287	5.6	Boyertown Area SD	Boyertown
287	5.6	Conrad Weiser Area SD	Robesonia
287	5.6	Dallastown Area SD	Dallastown
291	5.5	Owen J Roberts SD	Pottstown
291	5.5	Pennridge SD	Perkasie
291	5.5	Southern York County SD	Glen Rock
291	5.5	York Suburban SD	York
295	5.4	Elizabethtown Area SD	Elizabethtown
296	5.3	Northern York County SD	Dillsburg
296	5.3	South Eastern SD	Fawn Grove
298	5.2	Center Area SD	Monaca
298	5.2	Fleetwood Area SD	Fleetwood
298	5.2	Mars Area SD	Mars
301	5.1	Northampton Area SD	Northampton
301	5.1	Penn-Trafford SD	Harrison City
301	5.1	Pennsbury SD	Fallsington
304	5.0	Upper Dublin SD	Maple Glen
305	4.9	Beaver Area SD	Beaver
305	4.9	Greencastle-Antrim SD	Greencastle
305	4.9	West Chester Area SD	West Chester
308	4.8	South Butler County SD	Saxonburg
308	4.8	West Jefferson Hills SD	Jefferson Hls
310	4.6	Manheim Township SD	Lancaster
310	4.6	South Middleton SD	Boiling Springs
312	4.4	Abington Heights SD	Clarks Summit
313	4.3	Souderton Area SD	Souderton
314	4.2	Dallas SD	Dallas
314	4.2	Montour SD	Mc Kees Rocks
314	4.2	Palmyra Area SD	Palmyra
314	4.2	South Fayette Township SD	Mc Donald
318	4.1	Palisades SD	Kintnersville
319	4.0	Nazareth Area SD	Nazareth
320	3.9	Lampeter-Strasburg SD	Lampeter
320	3.9	South Park SD	South Park
322	3.8	Bethel Park SD	Bethel Park
323	3.7	Hampton Township SD	Allison Park
323	3.7	Northwestern Lehigh SD	New Tripoli
325	3.5	Derry Township SD	Hershey
326	3.4	East Penn SD	Emmaus
326	3.4	Penn-Delco SD	Aston
328	3.2	Cheltenham Township SD	Elkins Park
329	3.1	Cumberland Valley SD	Mechanicsburg
329	3.1	Rose Tree Media SD	Media
331	3.0	Lower Merion SD	Ardmore
331	3.0	Spring-Ford Area SD	Collegeville
331	3.0	Wallingford-Swarthmore SD	Wallingford
334	2.9	Franklin Regional SD	Murrysville
334	2.9	Southern Lehigh SD	Center Valley
334	2.9	Springfield SD	Springfield
337	2.8	Marple Newtown SD	Newtown Square
337	2.8	Wissahickon SD	Ambler
339	2.6	Parkland SD	Allentown
340	2.4	Hatboro-Horsham SD	Horsham
341	2.3	Oley Valley SD	Oley
341	2.3	Springfield Township SD	Oreland
343	2.1	Haverford Township SD	Havertown
344	2.0	Pine-Richland SD	Gibsonia
345	1.9	Central Bucks SD	Doylestown
346	1.7	Peters Township SD	Mcmurray
347	1.5	Downingtown Area SD	Downingtown
347	1.5	Tredyffrin-Easttown SD	Berwyn
349	1.4	Radnor Township SD	Wayne
350	1.3	North Allegheny SD	Pittsburgh
351	1.2	Great Valley SD	Malvern
351	1.2	Methacton SD	Norristown
353	1.0	Lower Moreland Township SD	Huntingdon Vly
353	1.0	Unionville-Chadds Ford SD	Kennett Square
355	0.9	Garnet Valley SD	Glen Mills
355	0.9	Upper Saint Clair SD	Pittsburgh
357	0.8	Council Rock SD	Newtown
358	0.4	Mt Lebanon SD	Pittsburgh
359	0.0	Carlynton SD	Carnegie
359	0.0	Pennsylvania Virtual CS	Norristown
359	0.0	Western Pennsylvania Cyber CS	Midland
362	n/a	Pde Division of Data Services	Harrisburg

Students Eligible for Reduced-Price Lunch

Rank	Percent	District Name	City
1	15.0	Everett Area SD	Everett
2	14.9	New Brighton Area SD	New Brighton
3	14.5	Penn Cambria SD	Cresson
4	13.6	Southern Tioga SD	Blossburg
5	13.5	Girard SD	Girard
5	13.5	Towanda Area SD	Towanda
7	12.9	Hanover Area SD	Wilkes Barre
8	12.8	Marion Center Area SD	Marion Center
9	12.7	Chestnut Ridge SD	Fishertown
9	12.7	Northern Tioga SD	Elkland
9	12.7	Shamokin Area SD	Coal Township
12	12.3	Forest Hills SD	Sidman
13	12.2	Huntingdon Area SD	Huntingdon
14	12.0	Bald Eagle Area SD	Wingate
15	11.8	Big Beaver Falls Area SD	Beaver Falls
16	11.7	Greater Johnstown SD	Johnstown
17	11.5	Connellsville Area SD	Connellsville
17	11.5	Derry Area SD	Derry
19	11.4	Wayne Highlands SD	Honesdale
20	11.2	Bloomsburg Area SD	Bloomsburg
20	11.2	Keystone Central SD	Lock Haven
22	11.1	Tyrone Area SD	Tyrone
22	11.1	Wallenpaupack Area SD	Hawley
22	11.1	Western Wayne SD	South Canaan
25	10.9	Mount Carmel Area SD	Mount Carmel
26	10.8	Conneaut SD	Linesville
26	10.8	Lancaster SD	Lancaster
26	10.8	Sto-Rox SD	Mckees Rocks
29	10.7	Midd-West SD	Middleburg
29	10.7	North Schuylkill SD	Ashland
31	10.6	Highlands SD	Natrona Heights
31	10.6	Jersey Shore Area SD	Jersey Shore
31	10.6	Juniata County SD	Mifflintown
31	10.6	North East SD	North East
35	10.4	Tuscarora SD	Mercersburg
36	10.3	Southmoreland SD	Scottdale

36	10.3	Spring Cove SD	Roaring Spring
36	10.3	Upper Adams SD	Biglerville
39	10.2	Central Cambria SD	Ebensburg
39	10.2	Reynolds SD	Greenville
41	10.1	Berwick Area SD	Berwick
41	10.1	Corry Area SD	Corry
41	10.1	Pottstown SD	Pottstown
41	10.1	Wyalusing Area SD	Wyalusing
45	10.0	Brownsville Area SD	Brownsville
45	10.0	Fort Leboeuf SD	Waterford
47	9.9	Clearfield Area SD	Clearfield
47	9.9	Norristown Area SD	Norristown
47	9.9	Wellsboro Area SD	Wellsboro
50	9.7	Montrose Area SD	Montrose
51	9.6	Apollo-Ridge SD	Spring Church
51	9.6	Philipsburg-Osceola Area SD	Philipsburg
53	9.5	Allentown City SD	Allentown
53	9.5	Altoona Area SD	Altoona
53	9.5	Blairsville-Saltsburg SD	Blairsville
53	9.5	Erie City SD	Erie
53	9.5	Penn Hills SD	Pittsburgh
58	9.3	Armstrong SD	Ford City
58	9.3	Ringgold SD	New Eagle
58	9.3	York City SD	York
61	9.2	Greensburg Salem SD	Greensburg
61	9.2	Mifflin County SD	Lewistown
63	9.1	Milton Area SD	Milton
63	9.1	New Kensington-Arnold SD	New Kensington
63	9.1	Wattsburg Area SD	Erie
66	9.0	Karns City Area SD	Karns City
66	9.0	Mount Union Area SD	Mount Union
66	9.0	Tunkhannock Area SD	Tunkhannock
69	8.9	Moniteau SD	West Sunbury
70	8.8	Dubois Area SD	Du Bois
70	8.8	Northeastern York SD	Manchester
70	8.8	Slippery Rock Area SD	Slippery Rock
70	8.8	Southeast Delco SD	Folcroft
74	8.7	Bellefonte Area SD	Bellefonte
74	8.7	Brookville Area SD	Brookville
74	8.7	Cambria Heights SD	Patton
74	8.7	Riverside Beaver County SD	Ellwood City
74	8.7	Shikellamy SD	Sunbury
79	8.6	Northgate SD	Pittsburgh
79	8.6	Penncrest SD	Saegertown
79	8.6	Sharon City SD	Sharon
79	8.6	Valley View SD	Archbald
83	8.5	Ligonier Valley SD	Ligonier
83	8.5	Selinsgrove Area SD	Selinsgrove
83	8.5	Williamsport Area SD	Williamsport
86	8.4	Keystone Oaks SD	Pittsburgh
86	8.4	Mid Valley SD	Throop
86	8.4	Saint Marys Area SD	Saint Marys
86	8.4	Wilkinsburg Borough SD	Wilkinsburg
90	8.3	Danville Area SD	Danville
90	8.3	Ellwood City Area SD	Ellwood City
90	8.3	Lebanon SD	Lebanon
90	8.3	Northwestern SD	Albion
90	8.3	Woodland Hills SD	Pittsburgh
95	8.2	Hazleton Area SD	Hazleton
95	8.2	Mount Pleasant Area SD	Mount Pleasant
95	8.2	Uniontown Area SD	Uniontown
98	8.1	Central Greene SD	Waynesburg
98	8.1	Waynesboro Area SD	Waynesboro
98	8.1	Wyoming Area SD	Exeter
101	8.0	Bristol Township SD	Levittown
102	7.9	Freeport Area SD	Freeport
102	7.9	Oil City Area SD	Oil City
102	7.9	Punxsutawney Area SD	Punxsutawney
102	7.9	Wyoming Valley West SD	Kingston
106	7.8	Reading SD	Reading
107	7.7	Kiski Area SD	Vandergrift
108	7.6	Burgettstown Area SD	Burgettstown
108	7.6	East Lycoming SD	Hughesville
108	7.6	Freedom Area SD	Freedom
108	7.6	Jim Thorpe Area SD	Jim Thorpe
108	7.6	Susquenita SD	Duncannon
113	7.5	Warrior Run SD	Turbotville
114	7.4	Albert Gallatin Area SD	Uniontown
114	7.4	General Mclane SD	Edinboro
114	7.4	Lehighton Area SD	Lehighton
114	7.4	Mckeesport Area SD	Mc Keesport
114	7.4	Penns Valley Area SD	Spring Mills
114	7.4	Troy Area SD	Troy
120	7.3	Bethlehem Area SD	Bethlehem
120	7.3	Elizabeth Forward SD	Elizabeth
120	7.3	Laurel Highlands SD	Uniontown
120	7.3	Pittston Area SD	Pittston
120	7.3	South Allegheny SD	Mc Keesport
120	7.3	Yough SD	Herminie
126	7.2	Steel Valley SD	Munhall
126	7.2	Susquehanna Township SD	Harrisburg
128	7.1	Hollidaysburg Area SD	Hollidaysburg
128	7.1	Millcreek Township SD	Erie
130	7.0	Conestoga Valley SD	Lancaster
130	7.0	Conewago Valley SD	New Oxford
130	7.0	Gettysburg Area SD	Gettysburg
130	7.0	Middletown Area SD	Middletown
130	7.0	Mifflinburg Area SD	Mifflinburg
130	7.0	Mohawk Area SD	Bessemer
130	7.0	Philadelphia City SD	Philadelphia
137	6.9	East Allegheny SD	N Versailles
137	6.9	Titusville Area SD	Titusville
137	6.9	Warren County SD	North Warren
140	6.8	Bangor Area SD	Bangor
140	6.8	Big Spring SD	Newville
140	6.8	Chichester SD	Boothwyn
140	6.8	Somerset Area SD	Somerset
140	6.8	William Penn SD	Lansdowne
145	6.7	Bedford Area SD	Bedford
145	6.7	Franklin Area SD	Franklin
145	6.7	Greater Latrobe SD	Latrobe
145	6.7	Pottsville Area SD	Pottsville
149	6.6	Athens Area SD	Athens
149	6.6	Bensalem Township SD	Bensalem
149	6.6	Coatesville Area SD	Coatesville
149	6.6	Wilmington Area SD	New Wilmington
153	6.4	Crawford Central SD	Meadville
153	6.4	Mcguffey SD	Claysville
155	6.3	Ephrata Area SD	Ephrata
155	6.3	Littlestown Area SD	Littlestown
155	6.3	Mercer Area SD	Mercer
155	6.3	Whitehall-Coplay SD	Whitehall
155	6.3	Wilkes-Barre Area SD	Wilkes Barre
160	6.2	Elk Lake SD	Dimock
160	6.2	Manheim Central SD	Manheim
160	6.2	Pocono Mountain SD	Swiftwater
160	6.2	Quakertown Community SD	Quakertown
164	6.1	Tamaqua Area SD	Tamaqua
165	6.0	Hanover Public SD	Hanover
165	6.0	Wilson Area SD	Easton
167	5.9	Lake-Lehman SD	Lehman
167	5.9	Palmerton Area SD	Palmerton
167	5.9	Shippensburg Area SD	Shippensburg
170	5.8	Ambridge Area SD	Ambridge
170	5.8	Cornwall-Lebanon SD	Lebanon
170	5.8	Lakeland SD	Jermyn
170	5.8	Scranton SD	Scranton
174	5.7	Belle Vernon Area SD	Belle Vernon
175	5.6	Bermudian Springs SD	York Springs
175	5.6	Central Columbia SD	Bloomsburg
175	5.6	North Hills SD	Pittsburgh
175	5.6	Red Lion Area SD	Red Lion
175	5.6	West Allegheny SD	Imperial
175	5.6	Westmont Hilltop SD	Johnstown
181	5.5	Northern Lebanon SD	Fredericksburg
181	5.5	Pen Argyl Area SD	Pen Argyl
181	5.5	Upper Perkiomen SD	East Greenville
184	5.4	Baldwin-Whitehall SD	Pittsburgh
184	5.4	Canon-Mcmillan SD	Canonsburg
184	5.4	Centennial SD	Warminster
184	5.4	Delaware Valley SD	Milford
184	5.4	Hermitage SD	Hermitage
184	5.4	Indiana Area SD	Indiana
184	5.4	Penn Manor SD	Millersville
191	5.3	Butler Area SD	Butler
191	5.3	Cocalico SD	Denver
191	5.3	Gateway SD	Monroeville
191	5.3	Kennett Consolidated SD	Kennett Square
191	5.3	Oxford Area SD	Oxford
191	5.3	Pequea Valley SD	Kinzers
191	5.3	West Mifflin Area SD	West Mifflin
198	5.2	Charleroi SD	Charleroi
198	5.2	Donegal SD	Mount Joy
198	5.2	Harrisburg City SD	Harrisburg
198	5.2	Muhlenberg SD	Reading
198	5.2	Twin Valley SD	Elverson
203	5.1	Bradford Area SD	Bradford
203	5.1	Central Dauphin SD	Harrisburg
203	5.1	Mechanicsburg Area SD	Mechanicsburg
203	5.1	North Pocono SD	Moscow
203	5.1	Pine Grove Area SD	Pine Grove
203	5.1	Ridley SD	Folsom
203	5.1	West York Area SD	York
210	5.0	Blue Mountain SD	Orwigsburg
210	5.0	Chambersburg Area SD	Chambersburg
210	5.0	Dover Area SD	Dover
213	4.9	Eastern Lancaster County SD	New Holland
213	4.9	Northern Lehigh SD	Slatington
213	4.9	West Perry SD	Elliottsburg
216	4.8	Burrell SD	Lower Burrell
216	4.8	Hempfield Area SD	Greensburg
216	4.8	Phoenixville Area SD	Phoenixville
216	4.8	Spring Grove Area SD	Spring Grove
216	4.8	Tulpehocken Area SD	Bernville
221	4.7	Eastern York SD	Wrightsville
221	4.7	Greater Nanticoke Area SD	Nanticoke
221	4.7	Pittsburgh SD	Pittsburgh
224	4.6	Eastern Lebanon County SD	Myerstown
224	4.6	Interboro SD	Prospect Park
224	4.6	Norwin SD	N Huntingdon
224	4.6	Trinity Area SD	Washington
228	4.5	Easton Area SD	Easton
228	4.5	Shaler Area SD	Glenshaw
228	4.5	Upper Darby SD	Drexel Hill
231	4.4	East Pennsboro Area SD	Enola
231	4.4	Greenville Area SD	Greenville
231	4.4	Grove City Area SD	Grove City
231	4.4	Harbor Creek SD	Harborcreek
231	4.4	Perkiomen Valley SD	Collegeville
231	4.4	Schuylkill Valley SD	Leesport
231	4.4	South Western SD	Hanover
238	4.3	Fleetwood Area SD	Fleetwood
238	4.3	Montoursville Area SD	Montoursville
238	4.3	New Castle Area SD	New Castle
241	4.2	Carlisle Area SD	Carlisle
241	4.2	Chartiers Valley SD	Pittsburgh
241	4.2	Crestwood SD	Mountain Top
241	4.2	East Stroudsburg Area SD	E Stroudsburg
241	4.2	Hopewell Area SD	Aliquippa
246	4.1	Blackhawk SD	Beaver Falls
246	4.1	Catasauqua Area SD	Catasauqua
246	4.1	Central York SD	York
246	4.1	Daniel Boone Area SD	Birdsboro
246	4.1	Solanco SD	Quarryville
251	4.0	Lower Dauphin SD	Hummelstown
251	4.0	Mars Area SD	Mars
253	3.9	Deer Lakes SD	Russellton
253	3.9	Greencastle-Antrim SD	Greencastle
255	3.8	Upper Merion Area SD	King Of Prussia
255	3.8	Warwick SD	Lititz
255	3.8	Wyomissing Area SD	Wyomissing
258	3.7	Chester-Upland SD	Chester
258	3.7	Manheim Township SD	Lancaster
258	3.7	North Penn SD	Lansdale
258	3.7	Northampton Area SD	Northampton
258	3.7	Penn-Trafford SD	Harrison City
258	3.7	Pennridge SD	Perkasie
258	3.7	Richland SD	Johnstown
258	3.7	State College Area SD	State College
266	3.6	Avon Grove SD	West Grove
266	3.6	Boyertown Area SD	Boyertown
266	3.6	Elizabethtown Area SD	Elizabethtown
266	3.6	Kutztown Area SD	Kutztown
266	3.6	Octorara Area SD	Atglen
266	3.6	Palmyra Area SD	Palmyra
266	3.6	Stroudsburg Area SD	Stroudsburg
266	3.6	West Shore SD	New Cumberland
274	3.5	Hempfield SD	Landisville
275	3.4	Annville-Cleona SD	Annville
276	3.3	Exeter Township SD	Reading
276	3.3	Fairview SD	Fairview
276	3.3	Northwestern Lehigh SD	New Tripoli
279	3.2	Dallastown Area SD	Dallastown
279	3.2	Lewisburg Area SD	Lewisburg
279	3.2	South Eastern SD	Fawn Grove
279	3.2	Wilson SD	West Lawn
283	3.1	Bethel Park SD	Bethel Park
283	3.1	Northern York County SD	Dillsburg
285	3.0	Center Area SD	Monaca
285	3.0	West Jefferson Hills SD	Jefferson Hls
285	3.0	York Suburban SD	York
288	2.9	Dunmore SD	Dunmore
288	2.9	Plum Borough SD	Plum
288	2.9	South Fayette Township SD	Mc Donald
288	2.9	Upper Moreland Township SD	Willow Grove
292	2.8	Fox Chapel Area SD	Pittsburgh
292	2.8	Governor Mifflin SD	Shillington
292	2.8	Salisbury Township SD	Allentown
295	2.7	Neshaminy SD	Langhorne
295	2.7	South Butler County SD	Saxonburg
295	2.7	Southern York County SD	Glen Rock
298	2.6	Owen J Roberts SD	Pottstown
299	2.5	Abington SD	Abington
299	2.5	South Park SD	South Park
301	2.4	Colonial SD	Plymouth Meeting
301	2.4	Lampeter-Strasburg SD	Lampeter
301	2.4	Palisades SD	Kintnersville
301	2.4	Seneca Valley SD	Harmony
305	2.3	Conrad Weiser Area SD	Robesonia
305	2.3	Cumberland Valley SD	Mechanicsburg
305	2.3	Derry Township SD	Hershey
305	2.3	Quaker Valley SD	Sewickley
305	2.3	Saucon Valley SD	Hellertown
310	2.2	Brandywine Heights Area SD	Topton
310	2.2	Dallas SD	Dallas
310	2.2	Moon Area SD	Moon Township
310	2.2	Pennsbury SD	Fallsington

310	2.2	Pleasant Valley SD	Brodheadsville
315	2.1	Pottsgrove SD	Pottstown
315	2.1	Souderton Area SD	Souderton
317	2.0	Washington SD	Washington
318	1.9	Abington Heights SD	Clarks Summit
318	1.9	Hamburg Area SD	Hamburg
318	1.9	Hampton Township SD	Allison Park
318	1.9	Nazareth Area SD	Nazareth
318	1.9	Parkland SD	Allentown
318	1.9	Spring-Ford Area SD	Collegeville
324	1.7	Beaver Area SD	Beaver
324	1.7	Penn-Delco SD	Aston
324	1.7	South Middleton SD	Boiling Springs
324	1.7	Southern Lehigh SD	Center Valley
328	1.6	Lower Merion SD	Ardmore
329	1.5	Hatboro-Horsham SD	Horsham
330	1.4	West Chester Area SD	West Chester
330	1.4	Wissahickon SD	Ambler
332	1.3	Cheltenham Township SD	Elkins Park
332	1.3	Pine-Richland SD	Gibsonia
332	1.3	Rose Tree Media SD	Media
335	1.2	Montour SD	Mc Kees Rocks
335	1.2	Oley Valley SD	Oley
335	1.2	Springfield Township SD	Oreland
338	1.1	East Penn SD	Emmaus
338	1.1	Methacton SD	Norristown
338	1.1	Wallingford-Swarthmore SD	Wallingford
341	1.0	Downingtown Area SD	Downingtown
341	1.0	North Allegheny SD	Pittsburgh
343	0.9	Central Bucks SD	Doylestown
343	0.9	Franklin Regional SD	Murrysville
343	0.9	Great Valley SD	Malvern
343	0.9	Haverford Township SD	Havertown
343	0.9	Radnor Township SD	Wayne
343	0.9	Springfield SD	Springfield
343	0.9	Upper Dublin SD	Maple Glen
350	0.8	Marple Newtown SD	Newtown Square
351	0.7	Tredyffrin-Easttown SD	Berwyn
352	0.5	Council Rock SD	Newtown
352	0.5	Unionville-Chadds Ford SD	Kennett Square
354	0.4	Garnet Valley SD	Glen Mills
354	0.4	Upper Saint Clair SD	Pittsburgh
356	0.3	Mt Lebanon SD	Pittsburgh
356	0.3	Peters Township SD	Mcmurray
358	0.2	Lower Moreland Township SD	Huntingdon Vly
359	0.0	Carlynton SD	Carnegie
359	0.0	Pennsylvania Virtual CS	Norristown
359	0.0	Western Pennsylvania Cyber CS	Midland
362	n/a	Pde Division of Data Services	Harrisburg

Student/Teacher Ratio

Rank	Ratio	District Name	City
1	53.2	Western Pennsylvania Cyber CS	Midland
2	46.3	Pennsylvania Virtual CS	Norristown
3	20.1	Crestwood SD	Mountain Top
4	19.9	Belle Vernon Area SD	Belle Vernon
5	19.7	Hazleton Area SD	Hazleton
6	19.6	Greater Nanticoke Area SD	Nanticoke
7	19.4	Central Bucks SD	Doylestown
8	19.2	Allentown City SD	Allentown
8	19.2	Kiski Area SD	Vandergrift
8	19.2	Pottsville Area SD	Pottsville
11	19.1	Penn-Trafford SD	Harrison City
11	19.1	Wattsburg Area SD	Erie
13	18.9	Norwin SD	N Huntingdon
13	18.9	South Park SD	South Park
15	18.8	Laurel Highlands SD	Uniontown
15	18.8	Quakertown Community SD	Quakertown
17	18.7	Greencastle-Antrim SD	Greencastle
18	18.6	North Schuylkill SD	Ashland
18	18.6	Philadelphia City SD	Philadelphia
18	18.6	Reynolds SD	Greenville
18	18.6	Solanco SD	Quarryville
22	18.4	Red Lion Area SD	Red Lion
23	18.3	Conewago Valley SD	New Oxford
23	18.3	Dunmore SD	Dunmore
23	18.3	East Allegheny SD	N Versailles
23	18.3	Moniteau SD	West Sunbury
23	18.3	West Jefferson Hills SD	Jefferson Hls
23	18.3	West Mifflin Area SD	West Mifflin
29	18.2	Lakeland SD	Jermyn
30	18.1	Pleasant Valley SD	Brodheadsville
31	18.0	Greater Latrobe SD	Latrobe
31	18.0	Greensburg Salem SD	Greensburg
31	18.0	Wyoming Area SD	Exeter
34	17.9	North East SD	North East
34	17.9	Peters Township SD	Mcmurray
34	17.9	Whitehall-Coplay SD	Whitehall
37	17.8	Upper Perkiomen SD	East Greenville
38	17.7	Ligonier Valley SD	Ligonier
38	17.7	Palmerton Area SD	Palmerton
38	17.7	Reading SD	Reading
41	17.6	Burrell SD	Lower Burrell
41	17.6	Dallas SD	Dallas
41	17.6	Hanover Area SD	Wilkes Barre
41	17.6	Mount Pleasant Area SD	Mount Pleasant
45	17.5	Avon Grove SD	West Grove
45	17.5	Parkland SD	Allentown
47	17.4	Bangor Area SD	Bangor
47	17.4	Chambersburg Area SD	Chambersburg
47	17.4	Hempfield SD	Landisville
47	17.4	Lebanon SD	Lebanon
47	17.4	Littlestown Area SD	Littlestown
47	17.4	Northwestern SD	Albion
47	17.4	Pine Grove Area SD	Pine Grove
47	17.4	Pittston Area SD	Pittston
47	17.4	Shippensburg Area SD	Shippensburg
47	17.4	South Butler County SD	Saxonburg
57	17.3	East Penn SD	Emmaus
57	17.3	Freedom Area SD	Freedom
57	17.3	Hamburg Area SD	Hamburg
57	17.3	Pennridge SD	Perkasie
57	17.3	Shamokin Area SD	Coal Township
57	17.3	Slippery Rock Area SD	Slippery Rock
57	17.3	Tamaqua Area SD	Tamaqua
57	17.3	Yough SD	Herminie
65	17.2	Pen Argyl Area SD	Pen Argyl
66	17.1	Chester-Upland SD	Chester
66	17.1	Wyoming Valley West SD	Kingston
68	17.0	Boyertown Area SD	Boyertown
68	17.0	Fort Leboeuf SD	Waterford
68	17.0	Richland SD	Johnstown
68	17.0	Southern Lehigh SD	Center Valley
72	16.9	Altoona Area SD	Altoona
72	16.9	Butler Area SD	Butler
72	16.9	Cocalico SD	Denver
72	16.9	Elizabethtown Area SD	Elizabethtown
72	16.9	Exeter Township SD	Reading
72	16.9	Northern Lehigh SD	Slatington
72	16.9	Oil City Area SD	Oil City
72	16.9	Penn Manor SD	Millersville
72	16.9	Plum Borough SD	Plum
81	16.8	Bermudian Springs SD	York Springs
81	16.8	Blackhawk SD	Beaver Falls
81	16.8	Chestnut Ridge SD	Fishertown
81	16.8	Mifflinburg Area SD	Mifflinburg
81	16.8	South Western SD	Hanover
81	16.8	Wilson SD	West Lawn
87	16.7	Abington SD	Abington
87	16.7	Hermitage SD	Hermitage
87	16.7	Kennett Consolidated SD	Kennett Square
87	16.7	Octorara Area SD	Atglen
87	16.7	Saint Marys Area SD	Saint Marys
92	16.6	Baldwin-Whitehall SD	Pittsburgh
92	16.6	Beaver Area SD	Beaver
92	16.6	Blairsville-Saltsburg SD	Blairsville
92	16.6	Centennial SD	Warminster
92	16.6	Conestoga Valley SD	Lancaster
92	16.6	Dover Area SD	Dover
92	16.6	Eastern Lebanon County SD	Myerstown
92	16.6	Everett Area SD	Everett
92	16.6	Grove City Area SD	Grove City
92	16.6	North Pocono SD	Moscow
92	16.6	Palmyra Area SD	Palmyra
92	16.6	Southmoreland SD	Scottdale
92	16.6	Westmont Hilltop SD	Johnstown
105	16.5	Abington Heights SD	Clarks Summit
105	16.5	Apollo-Ridge SD	Spring Church
105	16.5	Central York SD	York
105	16.5	Coatesville Area SD	Coatesville
105	16.5	Connellsville Area SD	Connellsville
105	16.5	Delaware Valley SD	Milford
105	16.5	Derry Area SD	Derry
105	16.5	Ellwood City Area SD	Ellwood City
105	16.5	Ephrata Area SD	Ephrata
105	16.5	Lake-Lehman SD	Lehman
105	16.5	Upper Darby SD	Drexel Hill
105	16.5	Valley View SD	Archbald
105	16.5	West York Area SD	York
118	16.4	Bedford Area SD	Bedford
118	16.4	Franklin Regional SD	Murrysville
118	16.4	New Brighton Area SD	New Brighton
118	16.4	South Eastern SD	Fawn Grove
118	16.4	York City SD	York
123	16.3	Bethlehem Area SD	Bethlehem
123	16.3	Eastern Lancaster County SD	New Holland
123	16.3	Forest Hills SD	Sidman
123	16.3	Haverford Township SD	Havertown
123	16.3	Mercer Area SD	Mercer
123	16.3	Nazareth Area SD	Nazareth
123	16.3	Ringgold SD	New Eagle
123	16.3	Trinity Area SD	Washington
123	16.3	Troy Area SD	Troy
123	16.3	West Shore SD	New Cumberland
133	16.2	Bensalem Township SD	Bensalem
133	16.2	Canon-Mcmillan SD	Canonsburg
133	16.2	Central Columbia SD	Bloomsburg
133	16.2	Daniel Boone Area SD	Birdsboro
133	16.2	Mckeesport Area SD	Mc Keesport
133	16.2	Millcreek Township SD	Erie
133	16.2	New Castle Area SD	New Castle
133	16.2	New Kensington-Arnold SD	New Kensington
133	16.2	Pennsbury SD	Fallsington
133	16.2	Riverside Beaver County SD	Ellwood City
133	16.2	Shikellamy SD	Sunbury
133	16.2	Somerset Area SD	Somerset
133	16.2	William Penn SD	Lansdowne
146	16.1	Derry Township SD	Hershey
146	16.1	Northampton Area SD	Northampton
146	16.1	South Allegheny SD	Mc Keesport
146	16.1	Spring-Ford Area SD	Collegeville
146	16.1	Stroudsburg Area SD	Stroudsburg
146	16.1	Warwick SD	Lititz
146	16.1	Waynesboro Area SD	Waynesboro
146	16.1	West Chester Area SD	West Chester
154	16.0	Albert Gallatin Area SD	Uniontown
154	16.0	Cornwall-Lebanon SD	Lebanon
154	16.0	Fairview SD	Fairview
154	16.0	Hampton Township SD	Allison Park
154	16.0	Hempfield Area SD	Greensburg
154	16.0	Interboro SD	Prospect Park
154	16.0	Jim Thorpe Area SD	Jim Thorpe
154	16.0	Manheim Central SD	Manheim
154	16.0	Pottsgrove SD	Pottstown
154	16.0	Spring Grove Area SD	Spring Grove
154	16.0	Western Wayne SD	South Canaan
165	15.9	Ambridge Area SD	Ambridge
165	15.9	Annville-Cleona SD	Annville
165	15.9	Cumberland Valley SD	Mechanicsburg
165	15.9	Elizabeth Forward SD	Elizabeth
165	15.9	Governor Mifflin SD	Shillington
165	15.9	Lampeter-Strasburg SD	Lampeter
165	15.9	Mars Area SD	Mars
165	15.9	Mcguffey SD	Claysville
165	15.9	Mohawk Area SD	Bessemer
165	15.9	Mount Carmel Area SD	Mount Carmel
165	15.9	North Penn SD	Lansdale
165	15.9	Penncrest SD	Saegertown
165	15.9	Selinsgrove Area SD	Selinsgrove
165	15.9	Twin Valley SD	Elverson
165	15.9	Woodland Hills SD	Pittsburgh
180	15.8	Carlynton SD	Carnegie
180	15.8	General Mclane SD	Edinboro
180	15.8	Northeastern York SD	Manchester
180	15.8	Perkiomen Valley SD	Collegeville
180	15.8	Southern York County SD	Glen Rock
180	15.8	Upper Adams SD	Biglerville
180	15.8	Upper Moreland Township SD	Willow Grove
180	15.8	Upper Saint Clair SD	Pittsburgh
188	15.7	Center Area SD	Monaca
188	15.7	Council Rock SD	Newtown
188	15.7	Downingtown Area SD	Downingtown
188	15.7	Fleetwood Area SD	Fleetwood
188	15.7	Montoursville Area SD	Montoursville
188	15.7	Pottstown SD	Pottstown
188	15.7	Sharon City SD	Sharon
188	15.7	Susquehanna Township SD	Harrisburg
188	15.7	Upper Dublin SD	Maple Glen
188	15.7	Wilkes-Barre Area SD	Wilkes Barre
188	15.7	Wyalusing Area SD	Wyalusing
199	15.6	Clearfield Area SD	Clearfield
199	15.6	Donegal SD	Mount Joy
199	15.6	Girard SD	Girard
199	15.6	Hopewell Area SD	Aliquippa
199	15.6	Lancaster SD	Lancaster
199	15.6	Montour SD	Mc Kees Rocks
199	15.6	Owen J Roberts SD	Pottstown
199	15.6	Titusville Area SD	Titusville
199	15.6	Towanda Area SD	Towanda
199	15.6	Tuscarora SD	Mercersburg
199	15.6	Uniontown Area SD	Uniontown
199	15.6	Wayne Highlands SD	Honesdale
211	15.5	Blue Mountain SD	Orwigsburg
211	15.5	Central Cambria SD	Ebensburg
211	15.5	Dallastown Area SD	Dallastown
211	15.5	Karns City Area SD	Karns City
211	15.5	Penn-Delco SD	Aston
211	15.5	Pocono Mountain SD	Swiftwater
211	15.5	Salisbury Township SD	Allentown
218	15.4	Central Dauphin SD	Harrisburg
218	15.4	Chichester SD	Boothwyn
218	15.4	Freeport Area SD	Freeport
218	15.4	Hatboro-Horsham SD	Horsham
218	15.4	Hollidaysburg Area SD	Hollidaysburg
218	15.4	Manheim Township SD	Lancaster
218	15.4	Mid Valley SD	Throop

218	15.4	Muhlenberg SD	Reading
218	15.4	Northern Lebanon SD	Fredericksburg
218	15.4	Pequea Valley SD	Kinzers
218	15.4	Souderton Area SD	Souderton
218	15.4	South Fayette Township SD	Mc Donald
230	15.3	Burgettstown Area SD	Burgettstown
230	15.3	Deer Lakes SD	Russellton
230	15.3	Dubois Area SD	Du Bois
230	15.3	Erie City SD	Erie
230	15.3	Greenville Area SD	Greenville
230	15.3	Lower Moreland Township SD	Huntingdon Vly
230	15.3	Neshaminy SD	Langhorne
230	15.3	Northwestern Lehigh SD	New Tripoli
230	15.3	Oley Valley SD	Oley
230	15.3	Oxford Area SD	Oxford
230	15.3	Schuylkill Valley SD	Leesport
230	15.3	Southeast Delco SD	Folcroft
230	15.3	Springfield SD	Springfield
230	15.3	Susquenita SD	Duncannon
230	15.3	Tyrone Area SD	Tyrone
230	15.3	Wilson Area SD	Easton
230	15.3	Wissahickon SD	Ambler
247	15.2	Conneaut SD	Linesville
247	15.2	Conrad Weiser Area SD	Robesonia
247	15.2	Great Valley SD	Malvern
247	15.2	Juniata County SD	Mifflintown
247	15.2	Northern York County SD	Dillsburg
247	15.2	Steel Valley SD	Munhall
253	15.1	Bradford Area SD	Bradford
253	15.1	Bristol Township SD	Levittown
253	15.1	Brookville Area SD	Brookville
253	15.1	Brownsville Area SD	Brownsville
253	15.1	Easton Area SD	Easton
253	15.1	Keystone Oaks SD	Pittsburgh
253	15.1	York Suburban SD	York
260	15.0	Bald Eagle Area SD	Wingate
260	15.0	Bellefonte Area SD	Bellefonte
260	15.0	East Pennsboro Area SD	Enola
260	15.0	Greater Johnstown SD	Johnstown
260	15.0	Jersey Shore Area SD	Jersey Shore
260	15.0	Montrose Area SD	Montrose
260	15.0	Saucon Valley SD	Hellertown
260	15.0	Wilmington Area SD	New Wilmington
268	14.9	Hanover Public SD	Hanover
268	14.9	Mt Lebanon SD	Pittsburgh
268	14.9	Penn Cambria SD	Cresson
268	14.9	Seneca Valley SD	Harmony
268	14.9	Unionville-Chadds Ford SD	Kennett Square
273	14.8	Chartiers Valley SD	Pittsburgh
273	14.8	Gettysburg Area SD	Gettysburg
273	14.8	North Allegheny SD	Pittsburgh
273	14.8	Warren County SD	North Warren
273	14.8	West Allegheny SD	Imperial
278	14.7	Bethel Park SD	Bethel Park
278	14.7	Brandywine Heights Area SD	Topton
278	14.7	Mechanicsburg Area SD	Mechanicsburg
278	14.7	Methacton SD	Norristown
278	14.7	Palisades SD	Kintnersville
278	14.7	Penns Valley Area SD	Spring Mills
278	14.7	Shaler Area SD	Glenshaw
285	14.6	Catasauqua Area SD	Catasauqua
285	14.6	Lewisburg Area SD	Lewisburg
285	14.6	Lower Dauphin SD	Hummelstown
285	14.6	North Hills SD	Pittsburgh
289	14.5	Armstrong SD	Ford City
289	14.5	Carlisle Area SD	Carlisle
289	14.5	Crawford Central SD	Meadville
289	14.5	East Lycoming SD	Hughesville
289	14.5	Elk Lake SD	Dimock
289	14.5	Gateway SD	Monroeville
289	14.5	Ridley SD	Folsom
289	14.5	Tulpehocken Area SD	Bernville
297	14.4	East Stroudsburg Area SD	E Stroudsburg
297	14.4	Moon Area SD	Moon Township
297	14.4	Quaker Valley SD	Sewickley
297	14.4	Tredyffrin-Easttown SD	Berwyn
301	14.3	Central Greene SD	Waynesburg
301	14.3	Harbor Creek SD	Harborcreek
301	14.3	Spring Cove SD	Roaring Spring
301	14.3	State College Area SD	State College
305	14.2	Berwick Area SD	Berwick
305	14.2	Big Spring SD	Newville
305	14.2	Bloomsburg Area SD	Bloomsburg
305	14.2	Charleroi SD	Charleroi
305	14.2	Midd-West SD	Middleburg
305	14.2	Mifflin County SD	Lewistown
305	14.2	Northgate SD	Pittsburgh
305	14.2	Scranton SD	Scranton
305	14.2	Southern Tioga SD	Blossburg
305	14.2	Wyomissing Area SD	Wyomissing
315	14.1	Franklin Area SD	Franklin
315	14.1	Lehighton Area SD	Lehighton
315	14.1	Milton Area SD	Milton
315	14.1	Pine-Richland SD	Gibsonia
315	14.1	Punxsutawney Area SD	Punxsutawney
315	14.1	Tunkhannock Area SD	Tunkhannock
315	14.1	Williamsport Area SD	Williamsport
322	14.0	Cheltenham Township SD	Elkins Park
322	14.0	Corry Area SD	Corry
322	14.0	Huntingdon Area SD	Huntingdon
322	14.0	Marple Newtown SD	Newtown Square
322	14.0	Sto-Rox SD	Mckees Rocks
322	14.0	Wallenpaupack Area SD	Hawley
328	13.9	Indiana Area SD	Indiana
328	13.9	Marion Center Area SD	Marion Center
328	13.9	Rose Tree Media SD	Media
328	13.9	South Middleton SD	Boiling Springs
328	13.9	Wallingford-Swarthmore SD	Wallingford
333	13.8	Danville Area SD	Danville
333	13.8	Upper Merion Area SD	King Of Prussia
333	13.8	Washington SD	Washington
336	13.7	Warrior Run SD	Turbotville
336	13.7	Wellsboro Area SD	Wellsboro
336	13.7	West Perry SD	Elliottsburg
339	13.6	Colonial SD	Plymouth Meeting
339	13.6	Norristown Area SD	Norristown
339	13.6	Philipsburg-Osceola Area SD	Philipsburg
342	13.5	Kutztown Area SD	Kutztown
342	13.5	Penn Hills SD	Pittsburgh
342	13.5	Phoenixville Area SD	Phoenixville
342	13.5	Springfield Township SD	Oreland
346	13.4	Athens Area SD	Athens
346	13.4	Big Beaver Falls Area SD	Beaver Falls
346	13.4	Cambria Heights SD	Patton
346	13.4	Eastern York SD	Wrightsville
346	13.4	Harrisburg City SD	Harrisburg
351	13.3	Garnet Valley SD	Glen Mills
351	13.3	Highlands SD	Natrona Heights
351	13.3	Keystone Central SD	Lock Haven
351	13.3	Middletown Area SD	Middletown
355	13.1	Radnor Township SD	Wayne
356	12.9	Pittsburgh SD	Pittsburgh
357	12.8	Lower Merion SD	Ardmore
357	12.8	Northern Tioga SD	Elkland
359	12.7	Mount Union Area SD	Mount Union
360	12.4	Fox Chapel Area SD	Pittsburgh
361	10.9	Wilkinsburg Borough SD	Wilkinsburg
362	n/a	Pde Division of Data Services	Harrisburg

Student/Librarian Ratio

Rank	Ratio	District Name	City
1	5,048.0	Chester-Upland SD	Chester
2	2,871.5	Ridley SD	Folsom
3	2,066.7	Hazleton Area SD	Hazleton
4	1,927.0	Cumberland Valley SD	Mechanicsburg
5	1,879.0	Philadelphia City SD	Philadelphia
6	1,661.0	Wilkinsburg Borough SD	Wilkinsburg
7	1,602.0	Greenville Area SD	Greenville
8	1,586.3	Erie City SD	Erie
9	1,576.0	Wilmington Area SD	New Wilmington
10	1,509.3	Dubois Area SD	Du Bois
11	1,500.7	Kiski Area SD	Vandergrift
12	1,474.7	Nazareth Area SD	Nazareth
13	1,398.3	Altoona Area SD	Altoona
14	1,375.5	Somerset Area SD	Somerset
15	1,338.2	York City SD	York
16	1,313.8	Harrisburg City SD	Harrisburg
17	1,312.5	Danville Area SD	Danville
18	1,303.5	Wyoming Area SD	Exeter
19	1,300.0	Lower Dauphin SD	Hummelstown
20	1,292.2	Millcreek Township SD	Erie
21	1,278.0	Shamokin Area SD	Coal Township
22	1,227.0	Northern Lebanon SD	Fredericksburg
23	1,215.3	Chichester SD	Boothwyn
24	1,203.5	Sharon City SD	Sharon
25	1,197.0	Williamsport Area SD	Williamsport
26	1,192.3	Penn-Trafford SD	Harrison City
27	1,178.5	Mcguffey SD	Claysville
28	1,141.5	Susquenita SD	Duncannon
29	1,132.0	Berwick Area SD	Berwick
30	1,119.0	Pocono Mountain SD	Swiftwater
31	1,103.0	Ellwood City Area SD	Ellwood City
32	1,102.4	Red Lion Area SD	Red Lion
33	1,099.3	Plum Borough SD	Plum
34	1,088.0	Lake-Lehman SD	Lehman
35	1,082.7	North Pocono SD	Moscow
36	1,069.5	Montoursville Area SD	Montoursville
37	1,067.0	Lampeter-Strasburg SD	Lampeter
38	1,065.5	Greater Nanticoke Area SD	Nanticoke
39	1,063.3	Owen J Roberts SD	Pottstown
40	1,060.8	Lebanon SD	Lebanon
41	1,060.3	Allentown City SD	Allentown
42	1,047.5	Harbor Creek SD	Harborcreek
43	1,041.5	Washington SD	Washington
44	1,041.0	Norwin SD	N Huntingdon
45	1,036.5	Beaver Area SD	Beaver
46	1,030.4	Wyoming Valley West SD	Kingston
47	1,027.0	Bald Eagle Area SD	Wingate
48	1,020.3	Albert Gallatin Area SD	Uniontown
49	1,020.0	Pottsville Area SD	Pottsville
50	1,015.5	Mifflin County SD	Lewistown
51	1,009.7	Muhlenberg SD	Reading
52	1,009.3	Rose Tree Media SD	Media
53	1,002.8	South Western SD	Hanover
54	997.5	Palmerton Area SD	Palmerton
55	997.0	East Allegheny SD	N Versailles
55	997.0	North Schuylkill SD	Ashland
55	997.0	Pen Argyl Area SD	Pen Argyl
58	996.0	Mohawk Area SD	Bessemer
59	995.5	Girard SD	Girard
59	995.5	Interboro SD	Prospect Park
61	995.3	Crestwood SD	Mountain Top
62	993.1	Wilkes-Barre Area SD	Wilkes Barre
63	992.3	Whitehall-Coplay SD	Whitehall
64	986.4	Pleasant Valley SD	Brodheadsville
65	986.3	Elizabeth Forward SD	Elizabeth
66	982.5	New Brighton Area SD	New Brighton
67	981.0	Upper Darby SD	Drexel Hill
68	976.5	Tyrone Area SD	Tyrone
69	975.2	Bethlehem Area SD	Bethlehem
70	974.9	Butler Area SD	Butler
71	971.8	North Hills SD	Pittsburgh
72	971.2	Stroudsburg Area SD	Stroudsburg
73	970.8	Avon Grove SD	West Grove
74	970.3	Palmyra Area SD	Palmyra
75	955.8	Seneca Valley SD	Harmony
76	948.3	Hollidaysburg Area SD	Hollidaysburg
77	947.3	Franklin Regional SD	Murrysville
78	946.4	Central York SD	York
79	945.4	Keystone Central SD	Lock Haven
80	933.2	Northampton Area SD	Northampton
81	929.3	Bangor Area SD	Bangor
82	926.9	Carlisle Area SD	Carlisle
83	925.7	Blackhawk SD	Beaver Falls
84	924.8	Abington Heights SD	Clarks Summit
85	921.5	Conewago Valley SD	New Oxford
86	919.0	Derry Area SD	Derry
87	917.5	Reading SD	Reading
88	917.0	South Allegheny SD	Mc Keesport
89	916.0	Highlands SD	Natrona Heights
89	916.0	Karns City Area SD	Karns City
91	900.0	Greencastle-Antrim SD	Greencastle
92	897.0	Mount Carmel Area SD	Mount Carmel
93	896.3	Delaware Valley SD	Milford
94	894.5	Greater Johnstown SD	Johnstown
95	890.3	Penn Manor SD	Millersville
96	889.7	Octorara Area SD	Atglen
97	889.5	East Penn SD	Emmaus
97	889.5	Mechanicsburg Area SD	Mechanicsburg
99	888.0	Eastern York SD	Wrightsville
100	887.0	Upper Adams SD	Biglerville
101	886.4	Gateway SD	Monroeville
102	881.3	Fleetwood Area SD	Fleetwood
103	881.2	Dallastown Area SD	Dallastown
104	872.3	Daniel Boone Area SD	Birdsboro
105	871.3	Easton Area SD	Easton
106	867.0	Tuscarora SD	Mercersburg
107	865.0	Canon-Mcmillan SD	Canonsburg
108	864.4	Greater Latrobe SD	Latrobe
109	863.8	Chartiers Valley SD	Pittsburgh
110	862.3	Valley View SD	Archbald
111	862.0	Dunmore SD	Dunmore
112	860.0	Westmont Hilltop SD	Johnstown
113	857.7	New Kensington-Arnold SD	New Kensington
114	856.0	Slippery Rock Area SD	Slippery Rock
115	853.0	Dallas SD	Dallas
116	852.5	Moniteau SD	West Sunbury
117	851.7	Saint Marys Area SD	Saint Marys
118	849.7	Mifflinburg Area SD	Mifflinburg
119	849.3	Mount Pleasant Area SD	Mount Pleasant
120	845.0	Upper Perkiomen SD	East Greenville
121	844.6	Central Bucks SD	Doylestown
122	844.2	Parkland SD	Allentown
123	841.6	Penn Hills SD	Pittsburgh
124	840.3	Western Wayne SD	South Canaan
125	839.3	Springfield SD	Springfield
126	838.7	Baldwin-Whitehall SD	Pittsburgh
127	834.7	Oil City Area SD	Oil City
128	834.0	Charleroi SD	Charleroi
129	832.9	Franklin Area SD	Franklin
130	831.4	Governor Mifflin SD	Shillington
131	828.8	Penn-Delco SD	Aston
132	828.3	Corry Area SD	Corry
133	827.3	Perkiomen Valley SD	Collegeville
134	826.0	Shippensburg Area SD	Shippensburg
135	824.5	Lakeland SD	Jermyn
136	823.7	Connellsville Area SD	Connellsville
137	823.0	South Eastern SD	Fawn Grove

138	820.3	Wayne Highlands SD	Honesdale
139	819.3	Milton Area SD	Milton
140	819.0	Titusville Area SD	Titusville
141	813.8	Southeast Delco SD	Folcroft
142	811.5	Carlynton SD	Carnegie
143	808.3	Eastern Lebanon County SD	Myerstown
144	807.6	Kennett Consolidated SD	Kennett Square
145	807.5	Penns Valley Area SD	Spring Mills
146	798.8	Northern York County SD	Dillsburg
147	798.5	Downingtown Area SD	Downingtown
148	797.8	Big Spring SD	Newville
149	796.0	Garnet Valley SD	Glen Mills
150	793.4	Wallenpaupack Area SD	Hawley
151	793.3	Tunkhannock Area SD	Tunkhannock
152	792.7	Littlestown Area SD	Littlestown
153	789.3	Pittston Area SD	Pittston
154	787.4	Haverford Township SD	Havertown
154	787.4	Peters Township SD	Mcmurray
156	785.7	Cornwall-Lebanon SD	Lebanon
157	783.7	Fort Leboeuf SD	Waterford
158	782.5	Everett Area SD	Everett
159	780.4	Elizabethtown Area SD	Elizabethtown
160	780.3	Susquehanna Township SD	Harrisburg
161	777.0	Upper Moreland Township SD	Willow Grove
162	776.4	West Chester Area SD	West Chester
163	774.0	Fox Chapel Area SD	Pittsburgh
163	774.0	Southmoreland SD	Scottdale
163	774.0	Warwick SD	Lititz
166	772.5	Mount Union Area SD	Mount Union
167	772.0	Burgettstown Area SD	Burgettstown
168	770.2	Spring Grove Area SD	Spring Grove
169	770.0	Central Greene SD	Waynesburg
170	769.0	Mid Valley SD	Throop
170	769.0	Reynolds SD	Greenville
172	766.3	West York Area SD	York
173	764.5	Mercer Area SD	Mercer
174	763.0	Northgate SD	Pittsburgh
175	761.4	Great Valley SD	Malvern
176	760.8	Ambridge Area SD	Ambridge
177	759.8	East Stroudsburg Area SD	E Stroudsburg
178	754.5	Elk Lake SD	Dimock
179	754.0	Brookville Area SD	Brookville
180	752.0	Wyalusing Area SD	Wyalusing
181	751.5	Bellefonte Area SD	Bellefonte
182	751.0	Ringgold SD	New Eagle
183	750.2	Moon Area SD	Moon Township
184	748.0	Clearfield Area SD	Clearfield
185	747.3	Methacton SD	Norristown
186	747.1	Pennsbury SD	Fallsington
187	746.0	South Park SD	South Park
188	743.0	Pine-Richland SD	Gibsonia
189	739.7	Central Columbia SD	Bloomsburg
190	739.3	Tamaqua Area SD	Tamaqua
191	735.0	Laurel Highlands SD	Uniontown
192	734.3	Upper Dublin SD	Maple Glen
193	731.3	Burrell SD	Lower Burrell
194	729.9	Boyertown Area SD	Boyertown
195	729.3	South Butler County SD	Saxonburg
196	729.0	Blue Mountain SD	Orwigsburg
197	728.7	William Penn SD	Lansdowne
198	727.8	West Jefferson Hills SD	Jefferson Hls
199	724.5	Neshaminy SD	Langhorne
200	722.5	Selinsgrove Area SD	Selinsgrove
201	721.1	Pottstown SD	Pottstown
202	720.0	Bermudian Springs SD	York Springs
203	717.0	Hopewell Area SD	Aliquippa
204	715.6	Wallingford-Swarthmore SD	Wallingford
205	712.3	West Perry SD	Elliottsburg
206	711.6	North Penn SD	Lansdale
207	710.7	Northern Lehigh SD	Slatington
208	708.5	Pennridge SD	Perkasie
209	708.4	Cocalico SD	Denver
210	707.7	Palisades SD	Kintnersville
211	707.4	Dover Area SD	Dover
212	707.0	Oley Valley SD	Oley
213	706.7	Bensalem Township SD	Bensalem
214	706.0	Crawford Central SD	Meadville
215	705.3	East Pennsboro Area SD	Enola
215	705.3	Steel Valley SD	Munhall
217	701.2	Greensburg Salem SD	Greensburg
218	701.0	Conrad Weiser Area SD	Robesonia
219	699.4	Shaler Area SD	Glenshaw
220	697.7	Wissahickon SD	Ambler
221	697.0	Grove City Area SD	Grove City
222	695.0	Norristown Area SD	Norristown
223	693.4	Eastern Lancaster County SD	New Holland
224	692.0	Hanover Area SD	Wilkes Barre
224	692.0	Punxsutawney Area SD	Punxsutawney
226	689.6	Council Rock SD	Newtown
226	689.6	Derry Township SD	Hershey
228	687.8	Mars Area SD	Mars
228	687.8	Upper Saint Clair SD	Pittsburgh
230	687.0	Hamburg Area SD	Hamburg
231	682.0	Waynesboro Area SD	Waynesboro
232	680.5	Unionville-Chadds Ford SD	Kennett Square
233	680.3	Exeter Township SD	Reading
234	679.2	Gettysburg Area SD	Gettysburg
235	678.8	Saucon Valley SD	Hellertown
236	676.5	York Suburban SD	York
237	672.0	Mckeesport Area SD	Mc Keesport
238	671.7	Center Area SD	Monaca
239	671.1	Manheim Central SD	Manheim
240	668.5	Chambersburg Area SD	Chambersburg
241	667.2	Oxford Area SD	Oxford
242	666.4	Montour SD	Mc Kees Rocks
243	666.2	Lower Merion SD	Ardmore
244	665.4	Coatesville Area SD	Coatesville
245	665.0	Souderton Area SD	Souderton
246	664.3	Wilson SD	West Lawn
247	663.0	Hatboro-Horsham SD	Horsham
248	661.6	Hempfield Area SD	Greensburg
249	660.2	West Mifflin Area SD	West Mifflin
250	659.4	Southern York County SD	Glen Rock
251	658.8	Quakertown Community SD	Quakertown
252	657.2	Hempfield SD	Landisville
253	656.5	Solanco SD	Quarryville
254	654.0	Shikellamy SD	Sunbury
255	653.5	Spring-Ford Area SD	Collegeville
256	653.2	Central Dauphin SD	Harrisburg
257	649.2	Pottsgrove SD	Pottstown
258	647.4	Wilson Area SD	Easton
259	647.3	Conestoga Valley SD	Lancaster
260	646.3	Spring Cove SD	Roaring Spring
261	644.4	Twin Valley SD	Elverson
262	643.8	Hampton Township SD	Allison Park
263	643.0	Big Beaver Falls Area SD	Beaver Falls
263	643.0	Riverside Beaver County SD	Ellwood City
265	642.7	West Shore SD	New Cumberland
266	642.5	Armstrong SD	Ford City
267	641.3	North East SD	North East
268	640.8	West Allegheny SD	Imperial
269	639.8	New Castle Area SD	New Castle
270	639.0	Montrose Area SD	Montrose
271	638.6	Scranton SD	Scranton
272	638.3	Northern Tioga SD	Elkland
273	637.3	Central Cambria SD	Ebensburg
274	636.2	Tredyffrin-Easttown SD	Berwyn
275	636.0	Schuylkill Valley SD	Leesport
276	635.2	Juniata County SD	Mifflintown
277	635.0	Donegal SD	Mount Joy
278	634.3	Keystone Oaks SD	Pittsburgh
279	632.7	Centennial SD	Warminster
280	630.7	Trinity Area SD	Washington
281	623.2	Colonial SD	Plymouth Meeting
282	622.7	South Fayette Township SD	Mc Donald
283	621.5	Midd-West SD	Middleburg
284	621.3	General Mclane SD	Edinboro
285	620.0	Warrior Run SD	Turbotville
286	619.7	Northwestern Lehigh SD	New Tripoli
287	619.3	Wyomissing Area SD	Wyomissing
288	618.0	Northwestern SD	Albion
289	617.7	Towanda Area SD	Towanda
290	617.6	Abington SD	Abington
291	616.9	Southern Lehigh SD	Center Valley
292	612.8	Lehighton Area SD	Lehighton
293	612.0	Warren County SD	North Warren
294	611.9	State College Area SD	State College
295	610.2	Woodland Hills SD	Pittsburgh
296	609.3	Chestnut Ridge SD	Fishertown
297	607.3	Jim Thorpe Area SD	Jim Thorpe
298	606.9	Penncrest SD	Saegertown
299	604.4	Jersey Shore Area SD	Jersey Shore
300	599.6	Pittsburgh SD	Pittsburgh
301	598.8	Huntingdon Area SD	Huntingdon
302	595.0	Freedom Area SD	Freedom
303	593.3	Bloomsburg Area SD	Bloomsburg
304	591.8	Belle Vernon Area SD	Belle Vernon
304	591.8	Cheltenham Township SD	Elkins Park
306	590.5	Uniontown Area SD	Uniontown
307	586.0	Pine Grove Area SD	Pine Grove
308	585.5	Bedford Area SD	Bedford
309	585.0	Lower Moreland Township SD	Huntingdon Vly
310	584.6	North Allegheny SD	Pittsburgh
311	583.5	Forest Hills SD	Sidman
312	581.3	Lancaster SD	Lancaster
313	579.1	Bethel Park SD	Bethel Park
314	574.3	Hermitage SD	Hermitage
315	572.3	Catasauqua Area SD	Catasauqua
316	570.3	Hanover Public SD	Hanover
317	568.7	Marion Center Area SD	Marion Center
318	567.7	Marple Newtown SD	Newtown Square
319	565.9	Phoenixville Area SD	Phoenixville
320	565.8	Middletown Area SD	Middletown
321	565.2	Manheim Township SD	Lancaster
322	565.0	Tulpehocken Area SD	Bernville
323	562.0	Annville-Cleona SD	Annville
324	560.0	Wattsburg Area SD	Erie
325	555.1	Mt Lebanon SD	Pittsburgh
326	555.0	Blairsville-Saltsburg SD	Blairsville
327	553.3	Wellsboro Area SD	Wellsboro
328	552.5	Radnor Township SD	Wayne
329	550.8	Brandywine Heights Area SD	Topton
330	546.0	Apollo-Ridge SD	Spring Church
331	543.9	Ephrata Area SD	Ephrata
332	538.8	Indiana Area SD	Indiana
333	531.0	Richland SD	Johnstown
334	530.3	Fairview SD	Fairview
335	530.0	Bristol Township SD	Levittown
335	530.0	South Middleton SD	Boiling Springs
337	524.5	Deer Lakes SD	Russellton
338	518.4	Yough SD	Herminie
339	517.5	Northeastern York SD	Manchester
340	516.3	Cambria Heights SD	Patton
341	515.5	Springfield Township SD	Oreland
342	509.3	Sto-Rox SD	Mckees Rocks
343	493.5	Brownsville Area SD	Brownsville
344	490.5	Quaker Valley SD	Sewickley
345	489.8	Pequea Valley SD	Kinzers
346	487.8	Athens Area SD	Athens
347	487.5	Freeport Area SD	Freeport
348	472.5	Troy Area SD	Troy
349	466.8	Penn Cambria SD	Cresson
350	466.7	Conneaut SD	Linesville
351	459.6	Upper Merion Area SD	King Of Prussia
352	459.3	Salisbury Township SD	Allentown
353	453.0	Kutztown Area SD	Kutztown
354	447.0	Lewisburg Area SD	Lewisburg
355	445.6	Southern Tioga SD	Blossburg
356	427.2	Ligonier Valley SD	Ligonier
356	427.2	Philipsburg-Osceola Area SD	Philipsburg
358	423.6	Bradford Area SD	Bradford
359	n/a	East Lycoming SD	Hughesville
359	n/a	Pde Division of Data Services	Harrisburg
359	n/a	Pennsylvania Virtual CS	Norristown
359	n/a	Western Pennsylvania Cyber CS	Midland

Student/Counselor Ratio

Rank	Ratio	District Name	City
1	2,087.0	Western Pennsylvania Cyber CS	Midland
2	1,279.7	New Castle Area SD	New Castle
3	1,100.3	West Mifflin Area SD	West Mifflin
4	1,052.3	Pittston Area SD	Pittston
5	986.3	Elizabeth Forward SD	Elizabeth
6	942.8	Cornwall-Lebanon SD	Lebanon
7	918.8	Laurel Highlands SD	Uniontown
8	798.3	Huntingdon Area SD	Huntingdon
9	794.8	Penn-Trafford SD	Harrison City
10	789.7	Millcreek Township SD	Erie
11	760.8	Ambridge Area SD	Ambridge
12	735.3	Ellwood City Area SD	Ellwood City
13	727.8	West Jefferson Hills SD	Jefferson Hls
14	715.4	Hazleton Area SD	Hazleton
15	713.9	Armstrong SD	Ford City
16	699.3	Deer Lakes SD	Russellton
17	682.9	Warwick SD	Lititz
18	680.0	Pottsville Area SD	Pottsville
19	679.2	Berwick Area SD	Berwick
20	664.0	Mohawk Area SD	Bessemer
21	651.8	Wyoming Area SD	Exeter
22	644.9	Butler Area SD	Butler
23	643.3	New Kensington-Arnold SD	New Kensington
24	643.1	Kiski Area SD	Vandergrift
25	639.0	Shamokin Area SD	Coal Township
26	638.3	Northern Tioga SD	Elkland
27	637.3	Mifflinburg Area SD	Mifflinburg
28	626.4	Bristol Township SD	Levittown
29	626.0	Oil City Area SD	Oil City
30	625.2	Moon Area SD	Moon Township
31	621.7	Shaler Area SD	Glenshaw
32	617.6	Abington SD	Abington
33	614.3	Conewago Valley SD	New Oxford
33	614.3	Titusville Area SD	Titusville
35	609.8	Athens Area SD	Athens
36	607.3	Jim Thorpe Area SD	Jim Thorpe
37	598.0	Mount Carmel Area SD	Mount Carmel
38	597.2	Crestwood SD	Mountain Top
39	596.3	Greater Johnstown SD	Johnstown
40	595.0	Freedom Area SD	Freedom
41	594.5	Littlestown Area SD	Littlestown
42	593.7	East Lycoming SD	Hughesville
43	592.2	Southern Lehigh SD	Center Valley
44	584.6	Waynesboro Area SD	Waynesboro
45	584.0	Upper Darby SD	Drexel Hill
46	583.4	South Butler County SD	Saxonburg
47	583.0	Franklin Area SD	Franklin
48	579.3	Wilkes-Barre Area SD	Wilkes Barre
49	576.6	Baldwin-Whitehall SD	Pittsburgh

50	574.3	Hermitage SD	Hermitage
50	574.3	Ridley SD	Folsom
52	569.7	East Allegheny SD	N Versailles
53	568.9	Interboro SD	Prospect Park
54	568.3	Moniteau SD	West Sunbury
55	554.8	Central Columbia SD	Bloomsburg
55	554.8	Council Rock SD	Newtown
57	551.4	Derry Area SD	Derry
58	551.2	Red Lion Area SD	Red Lion
59	551.1	Riverside Beaver County SD	Ellwood City
60	550.2	Somerset Area SD	Somerset
61	548.5	Burrell SD	Lower Burrell
62	541.0	Carlynton SD	Carnegie
63	540.6	Trinity Area SD	Washington
64	540.0	Bermudian Springs SD	York Springs
64	540.0	Greencastle-Antrim SD	Greencastle
66	536.5	Hampton Township SD	Allison Park
67	536.4	Ringgold SD	New Eagle
68	534.0	Greenville Area SD	Greenville
69	533.4	Boyertown Area SD	Boyertown
70	532.8	Greater Nanticoke Area SD	Nanticoke
71	531.0	Richland SD	Johnstown
72	530.3	Fairview SD	Fairview
73	525.3	Wilmington Area SD	New Wilmington
74	524.2	Connellsville Area SD	Connellsville
75	522.7	Mckeesport Area SD	Mc Keesport
76	521.7	Everett Area SD	Everett
77	521.2	Bethel Park SD	Bethel Park
78	520.5	Norwin SD	N Huntingdon
79	520.2	Tuscarora SD	Mercersburg
80	519.9	Philadelphia City SD	Philadelphia
81	515.9	Central Bucks SD	Doylestown
82	515.2	Wyoming Valley West SD	Kingston
83	515.0	Mount Union Area SD	Mount Union
84	513.6	Slippery Rock Area SD	Slippery Rock
85	513.2	Oxford Area SD	Oxford
86	512.7	Reynolds SD	Greenville
87	510.1	Albert Gallatin Area SD	Uniontown
88	509.7	Mercer Area SD	Mercer
89	507.8	Mifflin County SD	Lewistown
90	507.4	Keystone Oaks SD	Pittsburgh
91	503.8	Center Area SD	Monaca
92	503.7	Jersey Shore Area SD	Jersey Shore
93	503.0	Elk Lake SD	Dimock
94	502.3	Pittsburgh SD	Pittsburgh
95	501.3	Wyalusing Area SD	Wyalusing
96	500.9	Greensburg Salem SD	Greensburg
97	498.7	Clearfield Area SD	Clearfield
98	498.5	North Schuylkill SD	Ashland
99	497.8	Girard SD	Girard
100	497.0	Corry Area SD	Corry
101	494.2	Bradford Area SD	Bradford
102	493.5	Altoona Area SD	Altoona
103	493.2	Belle Vernon Area SD	Belle Vernon
103	493.2	Pleasant Valley SD	Brodheadsville
105	491.3	New Brighton Area SD	New Brighton
106	488.6	Plum Borough SD	Plum
107	487.5	Freeport Area SD	Freeport
108	485.0	Eastern Lebanon County SD	Myerstown
109	482.9	Upper Perkiomen SD	East Greenville
110	481.9	Hempfield SD	Landisville
111	481.4	Sharon City SD	Sharon
112	480.2	Greater Latrobe SD	Latrobe
113	477.9	York City SD	York
114	472.5	Troy Area SD	Troy
115	472.3	Pennridge SD	Perkasie
116	472.0	Shippensburg Area SD	Shippensburg
117	471.4	Mcguffey SD	Claysville
118	468.4	Bedford Area SD	Bedford
119	467.6	William Penn SD	Lansdowne
120	467.1	Shikellamy SD	Sunbury
121	467.0	South Fayette Township SD	Mc Donald
122	466.8	Forest Hills SD	Sidman
123	466.7	Conneaut SD	Linesville
124	464.7	Grove City Area SD	Grove City
125	464.6	Bangor Area SD	Bangor
126	464.4	Pine-Richland SD	Gibsonia
127	463.5	Northwestern SD	Albion
128	463.4	Seneca Valley SD	Harmony
129	463.3	Towanda Area SD	Towanda
130	462.8	Blackhawk SD	Beaver Falls
131	462.6	Mt Lebanon SD	Pittsburgh
132	462.0	Central Greene SD	Waynesburg
133	459.3	Salisbury Township SD	Allentown
134	458.9	Chester-Upland SD	Chester
135	458.5	Mars Area SD	Mars
136	458.0	Hamburg Area SD	Hamburg
136	458.0	Highlands SD	Natrona Heights
136	458.0	Karns City Area SD	Karns City
139	457.7	West Allegheny SD	Imperial
140	457.3	Lampeter-Strasburg SD	Lampeter
141	457.0	Chestnut Ridge SD	Fishertown
142	456.6	Susquenita SD	Duncannon
143	456.4	Northern York County SD	Dillsburg
144	454.3	Quakertown Community SD	Quakertown
145	453.7	Juniata County SD	Mifflintown
146	453.3	Tunkhannock Area SD	Tunkhannock
147	453.2	Penn Hills SD	Pittsburgh
148	451.3	Perkiomen Valley SD	Collegeville
149	448.4	Norristown Area SD	Norristown
150	448.2	Delaware Valley SD	Milford
151	447.6	South Park SD	South Park
152	446.4	Reading SD	Reading
153	445.0	Bloomsburg Area SD	Bloomsburg
154	443.6	Tamaqua Area SD	Tamaqua
155	443.5	Upper Adams SD	Biglerville
156	443.2	Gateway SD	Monroeville
157	442.8	Cocalico SD	Denver
158	442.4	Nazareth Area SD	Nazareth
159	441.0	Whitehall-Coplay SD	Whitehall
160	440.8	Wallenpaupack Area SD	Hawley
161	440.7	Fleetwood Area SD	Fleetwood
162	440.6	Dallastown Area SD	Dallastown
163	438.3	Penncrest SD	Saegertown
164	437.7	Solanco SD	Quarryville
165	437.6	Erie City SD	Erie
166	437.4	Peters Township SD	Mcmurray
167	436.1	Daniel Boone Area SD	Birdsboro
168	435.2	Lake-Lehman SD	Lehman
169	435.0	Allentown City SD	Allentown
170	433.6	Elizabethtown Area SD	Elizabethtown
171	433.4	Eastern Lancaster County SD	New Holland
172	432.5	Canon-Mcmillan SD	Canonsburg
173	432.0	Yough SD	Herminie
174	431.9	Chartiers Valley SD	Pittsburgh
175	431.0	Dunmore SD	Dunmore
176	428.9	Easton Area SD	Easton
177	428.0	Downingtown Area SD	Downingtown
178	427.2	Ligonier Valley SD	Ligonier
179	426.5	Dallas SD	Dallas
180	426.4	Lancaster SD	Lancaster
181	425.8	Saint Marys Area SD	Saint Marys
181	425.8	Stroudsburg Area SD	Stroudsburg
183	425.7	Scranton SD	Scranton
184	425.5	Big Spring SD	Newville
185	424.0	Haverford Township SD	Havertown
186	423.2	Steel Valley SD	Munhall
187	422.2	Chambersburg Area SD	Chambersburg
188	419.0	Harbor Creek SD	Harborcreek
189	417.8	West Shore SD	New Cumberland
190	416.6	Blue Mountain SD	Orwigsburg
190	416.6	Washington SD	Washington
192	415.9	Palmyra Area SD	Palmyra
193	415.6	Souderton Area SD	Souderton
194	415.3	Wilkinsburg Borough SD	Wilkinsburg
195	415.0	Wellsboro Area SD	Wellsboro
196	414.6	Pottstown SD	Pottstown
197	412.3	Lakeland SD	Jermyn
198	412.1	Southern York County SD	Glen Rock
199	411.6	Dubois Area SD	Du Bois
200	411.5	South Eastern SD	Fawn Grove
201	410.8	Bald Eagle Area SD	Wingate
202	409.7	Hopewell Area SD	Aliquippa
203	409.5	Apollo-Ridge SD	Spring Church
204	409.0	Northern Lebanon SD	Fredericksburg
205	408.5	Lehighton Area SD	Lehighton
206	408.2	Exeter Township SD	Reading
207	407.9	Ephrata Area SD	Ephrata
208	406.9	Southeast Delco SD	Folcroft
209	406.6	Wallingford-Swarthmore SD	Wallingford
210	406.0	North Pocono SD	Moscow
211	403.8	Central Dauphin SD	Harrisburg
211	403.8	Penns Valley Area SD	Spring Mills
213	403.0	East Pennsboro Area SD	Enola
214	402.4	North Penn SD	Lansdale
215	399.9	East Stroudsburg Area SD	E Stroudsburg
216	398.8	Pen Argyl Area SD	Pen Argyl
217	395.7	Penn Manor SD	Millersville
218	395.4	Centennial SD	Warminster
219	394.8	Brownsville Area SD	Brownsville
220	393.9	Keystone Central SD	Lock Haven
221	393.0	Dover Area SD	Dover
222	392.5	Northwestern Lehigh SD	New Tripoli
223	391.8	Fort Leboeuf SD	Waterford
223	391.8	Pequea Valley SD	Kinzers
225	390.1	Susquehanna Township SD	Harrisburg
226	389.4	Abington Heights SD	Clarks Summit
227	389.2	Hempfield Area SD	Greensburg
228	388.7	North Hills SD	Pittsburgh
229	388.5	Upper Moreland Township SD	Willow Grove
230	388.1	Northeastern York SD	Manchester
231	387.8	Spring Cove SD	Roaring Spring
232	387.5	Methacton SD	Norristown
233	386.6	Owen J Roberts SD	Pottstown
234	386.5	Woodland Hills SD	Pittsburgh
235	386.1	Northampton Area SD	Northampton
236	386.0	Burgettstown Area SD	Burgettstown
237	385.9	Manheim Central SD	Manheim
238	385.7	Lebanon SD	Lebanon
239	385.1	Spring Grove Area SD	Spring Grove
240	384.8	North East SD	North East
241	384.6	Kennett Consolidated SD	Kennett Square
242	384.5	Mid Valley SD	Throop
243	383.5	Manheim Township SD	Lancaster
244	383.4	Montrose Area SD	Montrose
245	383.1	Derry Township SD	Hershey
245	383.1	West York Area SD	York
247	382.6	East Penn SD	Emmaus
248	382.5	Warren County SD	North Warren
249	382.4	Central Cambria SD	Ebensburg
250	382.2	Hatboro-Horsham SD	Horsham
251	382.0	Sto-Rox SD	Mckees Rocks
252	381.9	Pottsgrove SD	Pottstown
253	381.6	Schuylkill Valley SD	Leesport
254	381.5	Northgate SD	Pittsburgh
255	379.6	Wilson SD	West Lawn
256	379.3	Hollidaysburg Area SD	Hollidaysburg
257	378.0	Parkland SD	Allentown
258	377.9	Governor Mifflin SD	Shillington
259	377.0	Brookville Area SD	Brookville
260	375.8	Bellefonte Area SD	Bellefonte
261	375.5	Garnet Valley SD	Glen Mills
262	373.6	Pennsbury SD	Fallsington
263	373.0	Springfield SD	Springfield
264	372.6	Central York SD	York
265	372.0	North Allegheny SD	Pittsburgh
266	371.3	Southern Tioga SD	Blossburg
267	370.0	Blairsville-Saltsburg SD	Blairsville
268	369.9	Conestoga Valley SD	Lancaster
269	369.6	Valley View SD	Archbald
270	367.0	Cumberland Valley SD	Mechanicsburg
271	366.8	South Allegheny SD	Mc Keesport
272	365.3	West Perry SD	Elliottsburg
273	364.6	Wayne Highlands SD	Honesdale
274	363.1	Spring-Ford Area SD	Collegeville
275	362.9	Donegal SD	Mount Joy
276	362.4	Kutztown Area SD	Kutztown
277	361.3	Selinsgrove Area SD	Selinsgrove
278	359.2	Indiana Area SD	Indiana
279	358.0	Twin Valley SD	Elverson
280	357.2	Fox Chapel Area SD	Pittsburgh
281	356.5	Montoursville Area SD	Montoursville
282	356.0	Philipsburg-Osceola Area SD	Philipsburg
283	355.8	Mechanicsburg Area SD	Mechanicsburg
284	355.4	Neshaminy SD	Langhorne
285	355.3	Northern Lehigh SD	Slatington
286	355.2	Eastern York SD	Wrightsville
287	355.1	Midd-West SD	Middleburg
287	355.1	Tyrone Area SD	Tyrone
289	355.0	General Mclane SD	Edinboro
290	354.5	Lower Dauphin SD	Hummelstown
291	354.3	Uniontown Area SD	Uniontown
292	353.8	Palisades SD	Kintnersville
293	353.5	Oley Valley SD	Oley
294	353.3	Bensalem Township SD	Bensalem
295	351.6	Pine Grove Area SD	Pine Grove
296	350.0	Danville Area SD	Danville
297	346.1	Great Valley SD	Malvern
298	346.0	Hanover Area SD	Wilkes Barre
298	346.0	Punxsutawney Area SD	Punxsutawney
300	344.5	Franklin Regional SD	Murrysville
301	344.0	Westmont Hilltop SD	Johnstown
302	343.4	Catasauqua Area SD	Catasauqua
303	342.2	Hanover Public SD	Hanover
304	340.6	Marple Newtown SD	Newtown Square
305	339.1	Pocono Mountain SD	Swiftwater
306	338.9	Upper Dublin SD	Maple Glen
307	338.1	Cheltenham Township SD	Elkins Park
308	337.2	Annville-Cleona SD	Annville
309	336.4	Rose Tree Media SD	Media
310	336.0	Wattsburg Area SD	Erie
311	334.3	South Western SD	Hanover
312	333.8	State College Area SD	State College
313	333.6	Charleroi SD	Charleroi
313	333.6	Octorara Area SD	Atglen
315	332.5	Palmerton Area SD	Palmerton
316	331.5	Penn-Delco SD	Aston
317	330.5	Brandywine Heights Area SD	Topton
318	329.9	West Chester Area SD	West Chester
319	329.4	Colonial SD	Plymouth Meeting
320	328.6	Wissahickon SD	Ambler
321	328.5	Harrisburg City SD	Harrisburg
322	327.2	Bethlehem Area SD	Bethlehem
323	327.0	Quaker Valley SD	Sewickley
324	325.8	Crawford Central SD	Meadville
325	323.7	Wilson Area SD	Easton
326	323.6	Avon Grove SD	West Grove

327	323.3	Unionville-Chadds Ford SD	Kennett Square
328	318.5	Mount Pleasant Area SD	Mount Pleasant
329	317.5	Upper Saint Clair SD	Pittsburgh
330	315.1	Western Wayne SD	South Canaan
331	315.0	Williamsport Area SD	Williamsport
332	313.9	Tulpehocken Area SD	Bernville
333	313.4	Upper Merion Area SD	King Of Prussia
334	311.6	Conrad Weiser Area SD	Robesonia
335	311.2	Penn Cambria SD	Cresson
336	311.0	Carlisle Area SD	Carlisle
337	310.0	Warrior Run SD	Turbotville
338	309.8	Cambria Heights SD	Patton
339	308.7	Gettysburg Area SD	Gettysburg
340	307.3	Milton Area SD	Milton
341	305.0	Coatesville Area SD	Coatesville
342	303.8	Chichester SD	Boothwyn
343	302.9	Montour SD	Mc Kees Rocks
343	302.9	South Middleton SD	Boiling Springs
345	301.4	Radnor Township SD	Wayne
346	299.0	Phoenixville Area SD	Phoenixville
347	296.1	Beaver Area SD	Beaver
348	294.6	Springfield Township SD	Oreland
349	292.5	Lower Moreland Township SD	Huntingdon Vly
350	290.3	Southmoreland SD	Scottdale
351	288.5	Saucon Valley SD	Hellertown
352	284.7	Lower Merion SD	Ardmore
353	284.3	Marion Center Area SD	Marion Center
354	282.9	Middletown Area SD	Middletown
355	281.9	York Suburban SD	York
356	275.6	Big Beaver Falls Area SD	Beaver Falls
357	275.4	Muhlenberg SD	Reading
358	272.7	Tredyffrin-Easttown SD	Berwyn
359	265.4	Wyomissing Area SD	Wyomissing
360	255.4	Lewisburg Area SD	Lewisburg
361	n/a	Pde Division of Data Services	Harrisburg
361	n/a	Pennsylvania Virtual CS	Norristown

Current Spending per Student in FY2003

Rank	Dollars	District Name	City
1	16,376	Lower Merion SD	Ardmore
2	13,744	Radnor Township SD	Wayne
3	12,776	Upper Merion Area SD	King Of Prussia
4	12,111	Harrisburg City SD	Harrisburg
5	11,955	Springfield Township SD	Oreland
6	11,943	Cheltenham Township SD	Elkins Park
7	11,780	Colonial SD	Plymouth Meeting
8	11,616	Great Valley SD	Malvern
9	11,438	Wissahickon SD	Ambler
10	11,290	Chester-Upland SD	Chester
11	11,277	Neshaminy SD	Langhorne
12	11,192	Lower Moreland Township SD	Huntingdon Vly
13	11,061	Tredyffrin-Easttown SD	Berwyn
14	10,990	Marple Newtown SD	Newtown Square
15	10,987	Wilkinsburg Borough SD	Wilkinsburg
16	10,979	Rose Tree Media SD	Media
17	10,950	Sto-Rox SD	Mckees Rocks
18	10,902	Pittsburgh SD	Pittsburgh
19	10,851	Salisbury Township SD	Allentown
20	10,804	Owen J Roberts SD	Pottstown
21	10,798	Upper Perkiomen SD	East Greenville
22	10,735	Bristol Township SD	Levittown
23	10,652	Fox Chapel Area SD	Pittsburgh
24	10,578	Gateway SD	Monroeville
25	10,564	Quaker Valley SD	Sewickley
26	10,521	Norristown Area SD	Norristown
27	10,383	Abington SD	Abington
28	10,369	Wallingford-Swarthmore SD	Wallingford
29	10,352	Palisades SD	Kintnersville
30	10,347	Bensalem Township SD	Bensalem
31	10,260	Council Rock SD	Newtown
32	10,252	Moon Area SD	Moon Township
33	10,087	Unionville-Chadds Ford SD	Kennett Square
34	10,029	Souderton Area SD	Souderton
35	10,002	Carlynton SD	Carnegie
36	10,001	Pennsbury SD	Fallsington
37	9,997	Springfield SD	Springfield
38	9,839	West Chester Area SD	West Chester
39	9,833	Keystone Oaks SD	Pittsburgh
40	9,772	Upper Moreland Township SD	Willow Grove
41	9,766	Garnet Valley SD	Glen Mills
42	9,716	Methacton SD	Norristown
42	9,716	North Hills SD	Pittsburgh
44	9,681	Hatboro-Horsham SD	Horsham
45	9,676	Pottstown SD	Pottstown
46	9,666	Keystone Central SD	Lock Haven
46	9,666	Sharon City SD	Sharon
48	9,661	South Fayette Township SD	Mc Donald
49	9,549	Woodland Hills SD	Pittsburgh
50	9,518	William Penn SD	Lansdowne
51	9,515	North Allegheny SD	Pittsburgh
52	9,462	Interboro SD	Prospect Park
53	9,381	North Penn SD	Lansdale
54	9,373	Franklin Area SD	Franklin
55	9,370	Upper Saint Clair SD	Pittsburgh
56	9,348	Indiana Area SD	Indiana
57	9,327	Mt Lebanon SD	Pittsburgh
58	9,318	Upper Dublin SD	Maple Glen
59	9,313	Armstrong SD	Ford City
60	9,287	Punxsutawney Area SD	Punxsutawney
61	9,277	Scranton SD	Scranton
62	9,257	Western Wayne SD	South Canaan
63	9,245	Conestoga Valley SD	Lancaster
64	9,233	Highlands SD	Natrona Heights
65	9,227	Ridley SD	Folsom
66	9,191	Saucon Valley SD	Hellertown
67	9,158	Kutztown Area SD	Kutztown
68	9,151	Deer Lakes SD	Russellton
69	9,147	Haverford Township SD	Havertown
70	9,120	East Stroudsburg Area SD	E Stroudsburg
71	9,111	Spring-Ford Area SD	Collegeville
72	9,106	Schuylkill Valley SD	Leesport
73	9,100	West Allegheny SD	Imperial
74	9,082	Gettysburg Area SD	Gettysburg
75	9,079	Lancaster SD	Lancaster
76	9,071	State College Area SD	State College
77	9,062	Kennett Consolidated SD	Kennett Square
78	8,983	Chichester SD	Boothwyn
79	8,980	Montour SD	Mc Kees Rocks
80	8,977	Penn-Delco SD	Aston
81	8,976	Wallenpaupack Area SD	Hawley
82	8,928	Centennial SD	Warminster
83	8,924	York Suburban SD	York
84	8,895	Coatesville Area SD	Coatesville
85	8,889	Tunkhannock Area SD	Tunkhannock
86	8,887	Bethel Park SD	Bethel Park
87	8,877	Freeport Area SD	Freeport
88	8,861	Quakertown Community SD	Quakertown
89	8,852	Central Greene SD	Waynesburg
90	8,847	Wyomissing Area SD	Wyomissing
91	8,843	Williamsport Area SD	Williamsport
92	8,810	Baldwin-Whitehall SD	Pittsburgh
93	8,797	Wilkes-Barre Area SD	Wilkes Barre
94	8,770	Wellsboro Area SD	Wellsboro
95	8,757	Big Beaver Falls Area SD	Beaver Falls
96	8,749	Perkiomen Valley SD	Collegeville
97	8,739	Tulpehocken Area SD	Bernville
98	8,726	Penncrest SD	Saegertown
99	8,721	Chartiers Valley SD	Pittsburgh
100	8,716	Pottsgrove SD	Pottstown
101	8,714	Athens Area SD	Athens
102	8,700	Cambria Heights SD	Patton
103	8,693	Pennridge SD	Perkasie
104	8,689	Greater Johnstown SD	Johnstown
105	8,678	Downingtown Area SD	Downingtown
106	8,672	Washington SD	Washington
107	8,658	Crawford Central SD	Meadville
108	8,626	Bradford Area SD	Bradford
108	8,626	Penn Cambria SD	Cresson
110	8,615	Twin Valley SD	Elverson
111	8,580	Southeast Delco SD	Folcroft
112	8,569	Octorara Area SD	Atglen
113	8,568	Pequea Valley SD	Kinzers
114	8,559	Fairview SD	Fairview
115	8,510	Central Dauphin SD	Harrisburg
116	8,467	Marion Center Area SD	Marion Center
116	8,467	Shaler Area SD	Glenshaw
118	8,465	Erie City SD	Erie
119	8,451	Brandywine Heights Area SD	Topton
120	8,429	Hanover Area SD	Wilkes Barre
121	8,421	Hampton Township SD	Allison Park
122	8,415	Dallastown Area SD	Dallastown
123	8,408	Mckeesport Area SD	Mc Keesport
123	8,408	Northwestern Lehigh SD	New Tripoli
123	8,408	Towanda Area SD	Towanda
126	8,375	Pittston Area SD	Pittston
127	8,359	Middletown Area SD	Middletown
128	8,342	Pine-Richland SD	Gibsonia
129	8,335	York City SD	York
130	8,312	Wayne Highlands SD	Honesdale
131	8,281	Southern Lehigh SD	Center Valley
132	8,265	Penn Hills SD	Pittsburgh
133	8,248	Conrad Weiser Area SD	Robesonia
134	8,241	Muhlenberg SD	Reading
135	8,226	Mechanicsburg Area SD	Mechanicsburg
136	8,221	Northern Tioga SD	Elkland
137	8,214	Northgate SD	Pittsburgh
138	8,213	Wilson SD	West Lawn
139	8,205	Jersey Shore Area SD	Jersey Shore
140	8,199	Hanover Public SD	Hanover
141	8,197	Harbor Creek SD	Harborcreek
142	8,194	Derry Township SD	Hershey
143	8,177	Canon-Mcmillan SD	Canonsburg
144	8,175	Penns Valley Area SD	Spring Mills
145	8,170	Montrose Area SD	Montrose
146	8,150	Mcguffey SD	Claysville
147	8,141	Lewisburg Area SD	Lewisburg
147	8,141	Uniontown Area SD	Uniontown
149	8,140	Brookville Area SD	Brookville
150	8,135	East Penn SD	Emmaus
151	8,127	Northampton Area SD	Northampton
152	8,109	Stroudsburg Area SD	Stroudsburg
153	8,107	Hempfield Area SD	Greensburg
154	8,097	Wyalusing Area SD	Wyalusing
155	8,096	Catasauqua Area SD	Catasauqua
156	8,094	East Allegheny SD	N Versailles
157	8,090	Shamokin Area SD	Coal Township
158	8,084	Lehighton Area SD	Lehighton
159	8,083	Ambridge Area SD	Ambridge
160	8,082	Brownsville Area SD	Brownsville
161	8,081	Abington Heights SD	Clarks Summit
162	8,078	Central Bucks SD	Doylestown
162	8,078	Trinity Area SD	Washington
164	8,041	Warrior Run SD	Turbotville
165	8,040	East Lycoming SD	Hughesville
165	8,040	Jim Thorpe Area SD	Jim Thorpe
167	8,030	West Mifflin Area SD	West Mifflin
168	8,024	Apollo-Ridge SD	Spring Church
169	8,016	Elizabeth Forward SD	Elizabeth
170	8,009	Parkland SD	Allentown
171	8,003	Warren County SD	North Warren
172	8,000	Everett Area SD	Everett
173	7,999	Central Cambria SD	Ebensburg
174	7,997	Ligonier Valley SD	Ligonier
175	7,990	Blairsville-Saltsburg SD	Blairsville
176	7,965	Manheim Township SD	Lancaster
177	7,959	Karns City Area SD	Karns City
178	7,923	Southern Tioga SD	Blossburg
179	7,916	Carlisle Area SD	Carlisle
180	7,914	Avon Grove SD	West Grove
180	7,914	Hermitage SD	Hermitage
182	7,910	Bald Eagle Area SD	Wingate
183	7,905	Berwick Area SD	Berwick
184	7,858	Bellefonte Area SD	Bellefonte
185	7,839	Eastern Lancaster County SD	New Holland
186	7,834	Millcreek Township SD	Erie
187	7,808	Albert Gallatin Area SD	Uniontown
188	7,796	Lake-Lehman SD	Lehman
189	7,780	Steel Valley SD	Munhall
190	7,776	Bloomsburg Area SD	Bloomsburg
191	7,775	Reynolds SD	Greenville
192	7,771	New Castle Area SD	New Castle
193	7,762	West Jefferson Hills SD	Jefferson Hls
194	7,761	Pocono Mountain SD	Swiftwater
195	7,736	Franklin Regional SD	Murrysville
196	7,735	Kiski Area SD	Vandergrift
196	7,735	Philipsburg-Osceola Area SD	Philipsburg
198	7,728	Oxford Area SD	Oxford
199	7,725	Hollidaysburg Area SD	Hollidaysburg
200	7,722	Connellsville Area SD	Connellsville
201	7,721	Richland SD	Johnstown
201	7,721	Wyoming Valley West SD	Kingston
203	7,711	Fleetwood Area SD	Fleetwood
204	7,710	Southern York County SD	Glen Rock
205	7,705	Lower Dauphin SD	Hummelstown
206	7,699	Danville Area SD	Danville
206	7,699	Manheim Central SD	Manheim
208	7,682	Altoona Area SD	Altoona
209	7,681	Northern Lehigh SD	Slatington
210	7,673	Corry Area SD	Corry
210	7,673	Midd-West SD	Middleburg
212	7,664	Tyrone Area SD	Tyrone
213	7,662	Elk Lake SD	Dimock
214	7,660	Donegal SD	Mount Joy
215	7,656	Tuscarora SD	Mercersburg
216	7,650	Moniteau SD	West Sunbury
217	7,648	Governor Mifflin SD	Shillington
218	7,645	Bedford Area SD	Bedford
219	7,637	Wilson Area SD	Easton
220	7,612	Oil City Area SD	Oil City
221	7,597	South Middleton SD	Boiling Springs
222	7,593	Easton Area SD	Easton
223	7,589	Eastern Lebanon County SD	Myerstown
223	7,589	Eastern York SD	Wrightsville
225	7,575	Pen Argyl Area SD	Pen Argyl
226	7,573	Blackhawk SD	Beaver Falls
227	7,572	Upper Adams SD	Biglerville
228	7,569	Hempfield SD	Landisville
229	7,568	Troy Area SD	Troy
230	7,554	Philadelphia City SD	Philadelphia
231	7,553	Milton Area SD	Milton
232	7,546	Northern Lebanon SD	Fredericksburg
233	7,532	Northeastern York SD	Manchester
234	7,530	Upper Darby SD	Drexel Hill
235	7,516	Bethlehem Area SD	Bethlehem
236	7,513	Mount Union Area SD	Mount Union
237	7,510	Westmont Hilltop SD	Johnstown
238	7,505	Center Area SD	Monaca

239	7,498	North Pocono SD	Moscow
239	7,498	Southmoreland SD	Scottdale
241	7,487	Selinsgrove Area SD	Selinsgrove
242	7,468	Ellwood City Area SD	Ellwood City
243	7,458	Laurel Highlands SD	Uniontown
244	7,447	Oley Valley SD	Oley
245	7,446	Cornwall-Lebanon SD	Lebanon
245	7,446	Hamburg Area SD	Hamburg
247	7,442	Dunmore SD	Dunmore
248	7,439	Riverside Beaver County SD	Ellwood City
249	7,428	Titusville Area SD	Titusville
250	7,427	Susquehanna Township SD	Harrisburg
251	7,423	Northern York County SD	Dillsburg
252	7,416	Hopewell Area SD	Aliquippa
253	7,407	Delaware Valley SD	Milford
254	7,398	South Park SD	South Park
255	7,391	East Pennsboro Area SD	Enola
256	7,385	Susquenita SD	Duncannon
257	7,379	Yough SD	Herminie
258	7,377	Nazareth Area SD	Nazareth
259	7,375	Plum Borough SD	Plum
260	7,366	New Brighton Area SD	New Brighton
261	7,365	Derry Area SD	Derry
262	7,354	Dubois Area SD	Du Bois
263	7,350	Montoursville Area SD	Montoursville
264	7,318	Dallas SD	Dallas
265	7,305	Ringgold SD	New Eagle
266	7,303	Hazleton Area SD	Hazleton
267	7,302	South Allegheny SD	Mc Keesport
268	7,299	Clearfield Area SD	Clearfield
269	7,298	Boyertown Area SD	Boyertown
270	7,287	Palmerton Area SD	Palmerton
271	7,280	Freedom Area SD	Freedom
272	7,279	Butler Area SD	Butler
273	7,270	Mars Area SD	Mars
274	7,263	Big Spring SD	Newville
274	7,263	Grove City Area SD	Grove City
276	7,257	Beaver Area SD	Beaver
277	7,251	Mid Valley SD	Throop
278	7,243	West Perry SD	Elliottsburg
279	7,212	Greater Nanticoke Area SD	Nanticoke
280	7,208	Peters Township SD	Mcmurray
281	7,204	Seneca Valley SD	Harmony
282	7,194	General Mclane SD	Edinboro
283	7,193	Wilmington Area SD	New Wilmington
284	7,188	Greenville Area SD	Greenville
285	7,186	Penn Manor SD	Millersville
286	7,185	Cumberland Valley SD	Mechanicsburg
287	7,184	Mifflin County SD	Lewistown
288	7,165	Saint Marys Area SD	Saint Marys
289	7,141	Shikellamy SD	Sunbury
290	7,137	Wyoming Area SD	Exeter
291	7,129	Waynesboro Area SD	Waynesboro
292	7,126	Chestnut Ridge SD	Fishertown
293	7,118	Burgettstown Area SD	Burgettstown
294	7,114	Exeter Township SD	Reading
295	7,103	Ephrata Area SD	Ephrata
295	7,103	Lampeter-Strasburg SD	Lampeter
297	7,095	Daniel Boone Area SD	Birdsboro
298	7,093	Annville-Cleona SD	Annville
299	7,088	Conneaut SD	Linesville
300	7,071	Somerset Area SD	Somerset
301	7,064	Spring Cove SD	Roaring Spring
302	7,026	Huntingdon Area SD	Huntingdon
303	7,017	Mount Pleasant Area SD	Mount Pleasant
304	6,998	Central Columbia SD	Bloomsburg
305	6,981	West York Area SD	York
306	6,977	Warwick SD	Lititz
307	6,941	Allentown City SD	Allentown
308	6,930	Greensburg Salem SD	Greensburg
309	6,924	Slippery Rock Area SD	Slippery Rock
310	6,912	Burrell SD	Lower Burrell
311	6,898	South Butler County SD	Saxonburg
312	6,892	Belle Vernon Area SD	Belle Vernon
313	6,891	Whitehall-Coplay SD	Whitehall
314	6,888	North Schuylkill SD	Ashland
315	6,885	Central York SD	York
316	6,882	New Kensington-Arnold SD	New Kensington
317	6,863	Forest Hills SD	Sidman
318	6,856	Crestwood SD	Mountain Top
319	6,852	Pine Grove Area SD	Pine Grove
320	6,835	West Shore SD	New Cumberland
321	6,830	Cocalico SD	Denver
322	6,829	Blue Mountain SD	Orwigsburg
323	6,825	Solanco SD	Quarryville
324	6,814	Charleroi SD	Charleroi
325	6,810	Spring Grove Area SD	Spring Grove
326	6,808	South Western SD	Hanover
327	6,801	Dover Area SD	Dover
328	6,784	Tamaqua Area SD	Tamaqua
329	6,773	Bangor Area SD	Bangor
330	6,767	Girard SD	Girard
331	6,754	Pottsville Area SD	Pottsville
332	6,716	Norwin SD	N Huntingdon
333	6,691	North East SD	North East
334	6,664	Wattsburg Area SD	Erie
335	6,653	South Eastern SD	Fawn Grove
336	6,639	Reading SD	Reading
337	6,632	Chambersburg Area SD	Chambersburg
338	6,630	Lakeland SD	Jermyn
339	6,591	Pleasant Valley SD	Brodheadsville
340	6,581	Elizabethtown Area SD	Elizabethtown
341	6,577	Fort Leboeuf SD	Waterford
342	6,575	Mohawk Area SD	Bessemer
343	6,566	Juniata County SD	Mifflintown
344	6,558	Shippensburg Area SD	Shippensburg
345	6,547	Greencastle-Antrim SD	Greencastle
346	6,527	Red Lion Area SD	Red Lion
347	6,526	Mifflinburg Area SD	Mifflinburg
348	6,515	Mercer Area SD	Mercer
349	6,511	Lebanon SD	Lebanon
350	6,490	Valley View SD	Archbald
351	6,454	Greater Latrobe SD	Latrobe
352	6,441	Palmyra Area SD	Palmyra
353	6,325	Littlestown Area SD	Littlestown
354	6,284	Mount Carmel Area SD	Mount Carmel
355	6,211	Conewago Valley SD	New Oxford
356	6,157	Penn-Trafford SD	Harrison City
357	6,141	Bermudian Springs SD	York Springs
358	6,059	Pennsylvania Virtual CS	Norristown
359	5,804	Northwestern SD	Albion
360	4,781	Western Pennsylvania Cyber CS	Midland
361	n/a	Pde Division of Data Services	Harrisburg
361	n/a	Phoenixville Area SD	Phoenixville

Number of Diploma Recipients

Rank	Number	District Name	City
1	8,559	Philadelphia City SD	Philadelphia
2	1,899	Pittsburgh SD	Pittsburgh
3	1,082	Central Bucks SD	Doylestown
4	1,003	North Penn SD	Lansdale
5	920	Bethlehem Area SD	Bethlehem
6	912	Council Rock SD	Newtown
7	876	West Chester Area SD	West Chester
8	796	Neshaminy SD	Langhorne
9	737	Pennsbury SD	Fallsington
10	729	Pocono Mountain SD	Swiftwater
11	706	Central Dauphin SD	Harrisburg
12	694	Upper Darby SD	Drexel Hill
13	686	Allentown City SD	Allentown
14	685	North Allegheny SD	Pittsburgh
15	630	Erie City SD	Erie
16	610	Downingtown Area SD	Downingtown
16	610	State College Area SD	State College
18	600	Parkland SD	Allentown
19	570	Reading SD	Reading
20	567	Altoona Area SD	Altoona
21	558	Butler Area SD	Butler
22	556	Abington SD	Abington
22	556	West Shore SD	New Cumberland
24	546	Hempfield SD	Landisville
25	545	Cumberland Valley SD	Mechanicsburg
26	535	Hazleton Area SD	Hazleton
27	526	Coatesville Area SD	Coatesville
28	525	Scranton SD	Scranton
28	525	Wilkes-Barre Area SD	Wilkes Barre
30	504	Millcreek Township SD	Erie
31	502	Chambersburg Area SD	Chambersburg
31	502	Easton Area SD	Easton
33	500	Bensalem Township SD	Bensalem
34	499	Warren County SD	North Warren
35	497	Seneca Valley SD	Harmony
36	491	Hempfield Area SD	Greensburg
37	490	East Penn SD	Emmaus
38	477	Pennridge SD	Perkasie
39	464	Boyertown Area SD	Boyertown
40	461	Lancaster SD	Lancaster
41	456	Centennial SD	Warminster
42	455	Lower Merion SD	Ardmore
43	452	Mt Lebanon SD	Pittsburgh
44	436	East Stroudsburg Area SD	E Stroudsburg
45	432	Souderton Area SD	Souderton
46	426	Bristol Township SD	Levittown
47	421	Ridley SD	Folsom
48	420	Haverford Township SD	Havertown
49	418	Shaler Area SD	Glenshaw
50	411	Penn Hills SD	Pittsburgh
51	402	Bethel Park SD	Bethel Park
52	396	Norristown Area SD	Norristown
53	395	Baldwin-Whitehall SD	Pittsburgh
54	391	Pleasant Valley SD	Brodheadsville
55	388	Armstrong SD	Ford City
56	385	North Hills SD	Pittsburgh
57	383	Cheltenham Township SD	Elkins Park
58	382	Dallastown Area SD	Dallastown
59	376	Mifflin County SD	Lewistown
60	375	Connellsville Area SD	Connellsville
61	373	Norwin SD	N Huntingdon
62	372	Tredyffrin-Easttown SD	Berwyn
62	372	Williamsport Area SD	Williamsport
64	369	Keystone Central SD	Lock Haven
65	362	Wilson SD	West Lawn
66	359	Spring-Ford Area SD	Collegeville
66	359	Woodland Hills SD	Pittsburgh
68	356	Manheim Township SD	Lancaster
69	355	Hatboro-Horsham SD	Horsham
69	355	Penn-Trafford SD	Harrison City
71	350	Colonial SD	Plymouth Meeting
71	350	Penn Manor SD	Millersville
73	345	Upper Dublin SD	Maple Glen
74	343	Crawford Central SD	Meadville
75	340	Gateway SD	Monroeville
75	340	Kiski Area SD	Vandergrift
77	339	Northampton Area SD	Northampton
78	334	Quakertown Community SD	Quakertown
79	326	Hollidaysburg Area SD	Hollidaysburg
80	324	Plum Borough SD	Plum
81	322	Cornwall-Lebanon SD	Lebanon
81	322	Delaware Valley SD	Milford
83	321	Wyoming Valley West SD	Kingston
84	319	Carlisle Area SD	Carlisle
85	318	Fox Chapel Area SD	Pittsburgh
86	316	Governor Mifflin SD	Shillington
87	308	Upper Saint Clair SD	Pittsburgh
88	306	Red Lion Area SD	Red Lion
88	306	William Penn SD	Lansdowne
90	305	Solanco SD	Quarryville
90	305	Warwick SD	Lititz
92	301	Methacton SD	Norristown
93	299	Penncrest SD	Saegertown
94	298	Stroudsburg Area SD	Stroudsburg
95	294	Rose Tree Media SD	Media
96	293	Waynesboro Area SD	Waynesboro
96	293	Wissahickon SD	Ambler
98	292	Mckeesport Area SD	Mc Keesport
99	289	Albert Gallatin Area SD	Uniontown
99	289	Wallingford-Swarthmore SD	Wallingford
101	285	Chichester SD	Boothwyn
102	284	Greater Latrobe SD	Latrobe
103	283	Interboro SD	Prospect Park
104	282	Trinity Area SD	Washington
105	281	Franklin Regional SD	Murrysville
105	281	Springfield SD	Springfield
107	279	Unionville-Chadds Ford SD	Kennett Square
107	279	York City SD	York
109	278	Abington Heights SD	Clarks Summit
110	277	Marple Newtown SD	Newtown Square
111	276	South Western SD	Hanover
111	276	Whitehall-Coplay SD	Whitehall
113	272	Avon Grove SD	West Grove
114	270	Peters Township SD	Mcmurray
114	270	Ringgold SD	New Eagle
116	269	Ephrata Area SD	Ephrata
117	268	Exeter Township SD	Reading
118	267	Chester-Upland SD	Chester
119	266	Upper Perkiomen SD	East Greenville
119	266	Wallenpaupack Area SD	Hawley
121	264	Central York SD	York
121	264	Indiana Area SD	Indiana
123	261	Owen J Roberts SD	Pottstown
123	261	Pine-Richland SD	Gibsonia
123	261	Pottsville Area SD	Pottsville
126	260	North Pocono SD	Moscow
127	258	General Mclane SD	Edinboro
128	256	Gettysburg Area SD	Gettysburg
128	256	Montour SD	Mc Kees Rocks
130	254	Conestoga Valley SD	Lancaster
130	254	Lower Dauphin SD	Hummelstown
130	254	Nazareth Area SD	Nazareth
133	252	Hampton Township SD	Allison Park
134	250	Greensburg Salem SD	Greensburg
135	247	Derry Township SD	Hershey
136	246	Dubois Area SD	Du Bois
137	245	Pittston Area SD	Pittston
138	244	Canon-Mcmillan SD	Canonsburg
138	244	Elizabethtown Area SD	Elizabethtown
138	244	Laurel Highlands SD	Uniontown
141	241	Dover Area SD	Dover
141	241	Shikellamy SD	Sunbury
141	241	Tunkhannock Area SD	Tunkhannock
144	239	Upper Moreland Township SD	Willow Grove
145	235	Crestwood SD	Mountain Top
146	234	Ambridge Area SD	Ambridge
146	234	Chartiers Valley SD	Pittsburgh
146	234	Eastern Lancaster County SD	New Holland
149	233	Juniata County SD	Mifflintown
150	232	Great Valley SD	Malvern

151	230	Mechanicsburg Area SD	Mechanicsburg
152	229	Radnor Township SD	Wayne
153	228	Hopewell Area SD	Aliquippa
154	223	Conneaut SD	Linesville
155	222	Penn-Delco SD	Aston
155	222	Perkiomen Valley SD	Collegeville
157	221	Blackhawk SD	Beaver Falls
157	221	Manheim Central SD	Manheim
159	220	Bangor Area SD	Bangor
159	220	Moon Area SD	Moon Township
159	220	Pottsgrove SD	Pottstown
159	220	South Butler County SD	Saxonburg
163	219	Harbor Creek SD	Harborcreek
164	218	Bellefonte Area SD	Bellefonte
165	217	Conewago Valley SD	New Oxford
166	216	Uniontown Area SD	Uniontown
167	212	Somerset Area SD	Somerset
167	212	Upper Merion Area SD	King Of Prussia
167	212	West Jefferson Hills SD	Jefferson Hls
170	210	Southern York County SD	Glen Rock
171	209	Big Spring SD	Newville
171	209	Highlands SD	Natrona Heights
173	208	Berwick Area SD	Berwick
173	208	Shippensburg Area SD	Shippensburg
173	208	West Mifflin Area SD	West Mifflin
176	207	Mars Area SD	Mars
176	207	Saint Marys Area SD	Saint Marys
178	206	Blue Mountain SD	Orwigsburg
178	206	Wayne Highlands SD	Honesdale
178	206	West Allegheny SD	Imperial
181	205	Southeast Delco SD	Folcroft
182	203	Cocalico SD	Denver
182	203	Selinsgrove Area SD	Selinsgrove
184	202	Punxsutawney Area SD	Punxsutawney
185	201	Danville Area SD	Danville
185	201	Spring Grove Area SD	Spring Grove
187	199	Harrisburg City SD	Harrisburg
187	199	Muhlenberg SD	Reading
189	198	Garnet Valley SD	Glen Mills
189	198	Keystone Oaks SD	Pittsburgh
189	198	Southern Lehigh SD	Center Valley
192	197	Elizabeth Forward SD	Elizabeth
192	197	Jersey Shore Area SD	Jersey Shore
194	196	Franklin Area SD	Franklin
195	193	Clearfield Area SD	Clearfield
196	192	Lebanon SD	Lebanon
197	191	Milton Area SD	Milton
197	191	Palmyra Area SD	Palmyra
199	190	Belle Vernon Area SD	Belle Vernon
199	190	Susquehanna Township SD	Harrisburg
199	190	Twin Valley SD	Elverson
202	189	Kennett Consolidated SD	Kennett Square
203	187	Grove City Area SD	Grove City
204	186	Bald Eagle Area SD	Wingate
204	186	Mount Pleasant Area SD	Mount Pleasant
206	185	Northern York County SD	Dillsburg
207	184	Phoenixville Area SD	Phoenixville
207	184	South Eastern SD	Fawn Grove
209	183	Lampeter-Strasburg SD	Lampeter
209	183	Valley View SD	Archbald
211	182	Mcguffey SD	Claysville
212	180	Central Cambria SD	Ebensburg
212	180	Hamburg Area SD	Hamburg
212	180	Wyoming Area SD	Exeter
215	179	Derry Area SD	Derry
216	178	Corry Area SD	Corry
217	177	Bradford Area SD	Bradford
217	177	Greater Johnstown SD	Johnstown
219	176	Dallas SD	Dallas
219	176	Eastern York SD	Wrightsville
221	175	Conrad Weiser Area SD	Robesonia
222	174	Fort Leboeuf SD	Waterford
222	174	Midd-West SD	Middleburg
222	174	Mifflinburg Area SD	Mifflinburg
222	174	Saucon Valley SD	Hellertown
222	174	Shamokin Area SD	Coal Township
222	174	Southern Tioga SD	Blossburg
228	173	Middletown Area SD	Middletown
228	173	Penn Cambria SD	Cresson
228	173	West Perry SD	Elliottsburg
231	172	Lehighton Area SD	Lehighton
231	172	Oil City Area SD	Oil City
233	170	Deer Lakes SD	Russellton
233	170	York Suburban SD	York
235	169	Greencastle-Antrim SD	Greencastle
236	168	Montoursville Area SD	Montoursville
236	168	South Park SD	South Park
236	168	West York Area SD	York
239	166	Daniel Boone Area SD	Birdsboro
240	164	Burrell SD	Lower Burrell
240	164	Eastern Lebanon County SD	Myerstown
240	164	Hermitage SD	Hermitage
243	163	New Castle Area SD	New Castle
244	162	Athens Area SD	Athens
244	162	Oxford Area SD	Oxford
244	162	Titusville Area SD	Titusville
247	161	Northern Lebanon SD	Fredericksburg
247	161	Palisades SD	Kintnersville
249	160	Northwestern Lehigh SD	New Tripoli
249	160	Steel Valley SD	Munhall
251	159	Marion Center Area SD	Marion Center
251	159	Spring Cove SD	Roaring Spring
253	158	Fleetwood Area SD	Fleetwood
253	158	Northern Tioga SD	Elkland
255	157	Forest Hills SD	Sidman
255	157	North East SD	North East
255	157	Tuscarora SD	Mercersburg
255	157	Yough SD	Herminie
259	156	Huntingdon Area SD	Huntingdon
260	155	Ellwood City Area SD	Ellwood City
261	154	Lewisburg Area SD	Lewisburg
261	154	South Middleton SD	Boiling Springs
263	153	Beaver Area SD	Beaver
263	153	Southmoreland SD	Scottdale
265	152	Donegal SD	Mount Joy
266	151	Slippery Rock Area SD	Slippery Rock
267	150	Western Wayne SD	South Canaan
268	149	East Pennsboro Area SD	Enola
268	149	Susquenita SD	Duncannon
270	148	Philipsburg-Osceola Area SD	Philipsburg
270	148	Warrior Run SD	Turbotville
272	147	Cambria Heights SD	Patton
272	147	Ligonier Valley SD	Ligonier
272	147	North Schuylkill SD	Ashland
272	147	Wattsburg Area SD	Erie
272	147	Wellsboro Area SD	Wellsboro
277	146	Central Columbia SD	Bloomsburg
277	146	Littlestown Area SD	Littlestown
277	146	Quaker Valley SD	Sewickley
280	145	Central Greene SD	Waynesburg
280	145	Hanover Area SD	Wilkes Barre
280	145	Lake-Lehman SD	Lehman
280	145	Northern Lehigh SD	Slatington
284	143	New Kensington-Arnold SD	New Kensington
284	143	Pottstown SD	Pottstown
286	142	Springfield Township SD	Oreland
287	141	East Lycoming SD	Hughesville
287	141	Octorara Area SD	Atglen
287	141	Schuylkill Valley SD	Leesport
287	141	Wilson Area SD	Easton
291	140	Bermudian Springs SD	York Springs
292	139	Blairsville-Saltsburg SD	Blairsville
292	139	Brownsville Area SD	Brownsville
292	139	Greater Nanticoke Area SD	Nanticoke
292	139	Westmont Hilltop SD	Johnstown
296	138	Chestnut Ridge SD	Fishertown
296	138	Pine Grove Area SD	Pine Grove
298	137	Center Area SD	Monaca
298	137	Pen Argyl Area SD	Pen Argyl
300	136	Bedford Area SD	Bedford
300	136	Northeastern York SD	Manchester
300	136	Richland SD	Johnstown
303	135	Brandywine Heights Area SD	Topton
304	133	Kutztown Area SD	Kutztown
304	133	Riverside Beaver County SD	Ellwood City
304	133	Sharon City SD	Sharon
307	132	Tamaqua Area SD	Tamaqua
308	131	Salisbury Township SD	Allentown
309	130	Karns City Area SD	Karns City
310	129	Freedom Area SD	Freedom
310	129	Palmerton Area SD	Palmerton
310	129	Wilmington Area SD	New Wilmington
313	127	Girard SD	Girard
313	127	Oley Valley SD	Oley
313	127	Washington SD	Washington
316	126	Lower Moreland Township SD	Huntingdon Vly
316	126	Towanda Area SD	Towanda
318	125	Northwestern SD	Albion
319	123	New Brighton Area SD	New Brighton
319	123	South Allegheny SD	Mc Keesport
319	123	Wyomissing Area SD	Wyomissing
322	122	Brookville Area SD	Brookville
322	122	Dunmore SD	Dunmore
322	122	Tyrone Area SD	Tyrone
325	121	Montrose Area SD	Montrose
326	120	Carlynton SD	Carnegie
326	120	Charleroi SD	Charleroi
328	119	Annville-Cleona SD	Annville
328	119	Big Beaver Falls Area SD	Beaver Falls
328	119	East Allegheny SD	N Versailles
328	119	Troy Area SD	Troy
328	119	Tulpehocken Area SD	Bernville
333	118	Lakeland SD	Jermyn
333	118	Mid Valley SD	Throop
335	117	Freeport Area SD	Freeport
336	116	Greenville Area SD	Greenville
337	114	Everett Area SD	Everett
337	114	Fairview SD	Fairview
337	114	Upper Adams SD	Biglerville
340	109	Mohawk Area SD	Bessemer
340	109	Mount Carmel Area SD	Mount Carmel
340	109	Reynolds SD	Greenville
343	108	Pequea Valley SD	Kinzers
344	106	Mercer Area SD	Mercer
345	103	Moniteau SD	West Sunbury
345	103	Penns Valley Area SD	Spring Mills
347	100	Bloomsburg Area SD	Bloomsburg
348	99	Northgate SD	Pittsburgh
348	99	Wyalusing Area SD	Wyalusing
350	96	Catasauqua Area SD	Catasauqua
350	96	Jim Thorpe Area SD	Jim Thorpe
352	95	Mount Union Area SD	Mount Union
353	94	South Fayette Township SD	Mc Donald
354	93	Elk Lake SD	Dimock
355	92	Hanover Public SD	Hanover
356	89	Apollo-Ridge SD	Spring Church
357	88	Burgettstown Area SD	Burgettstown
358	74	Sto-Rox SD	Mckees Rocks
358	74	Wilkinsburg Borough SD	Wilkinsburg
360	57	Western Pennsylvania Cyber CS	Midland
361	0	Pde Division of Data Services	Harrisburg
362	n/a	Pennsylvania Virtual CS	Norristown

High School Drop-out Rate

Rank	Percent	District Name	City
1	25.8	Western Pennsylvania Cyber CS	Midland
2	11.2	Wilkinsburg Borough SD	Wilkinsburg
3	10.7	Lancaster SD	Lancaster
4	10.0	York City SD	York
5	9.8	Philadelphia City SD	Philadelphia
6	9.3	Allentown City SD	Allentown
7	8.7	Reading SD	Reading
8	7.2	Big Beaver Falls Area SD	Beaver Falls
9	6.4	Brownsville Area SD	Brownsville
9	6.4	Lebanon SD	Lebanon
11	6.3	Bloomsburg Area SD	Bloomsburg
12	6.2	Oxford Area SD	Oxford
13	6.0	Oil City Area SD	Oil City
13	6.0	Pottstown SD	Pottstown
15	5.9	Williamsport Area SD	Williamsport
16	5.8	Harrisburg City SD	Harrisburg
17	5.7	Pottsville Area SD	Pottsville
18	5.6	Washington SD	Washington
19	5.5	Burgettstown Area SD	Burgettstown
20	5.4	Northern Lebanon SD	Fredericksburg
20	5.4	Pittsburgh SD	Pittsburgh
20	5.4	Trinity Area SD	Washington
23	5.2	Bradford Area SD	Bradford
23	5.2	Connellsville Area SD	Connellsville
23	5.2	Southeast Delco SD	Folcroft
23	5.2	Western Wayne SD	South Canaan
27	5.1	New Kensington-Arnold SD	New Kensington
27	5.1	Norristown Area SD	Norristown
29	4.9	Athens Area SD	Athens
29	4.9	Berwick Area SD	Berwick
29	4.9	Laurel Highlands SD	Uniontown
32	4.7	Jersey Shore Area SD	Jersey Shore
32	4.7	Sharon City SD	Sharon
32	4.7	Wilson Area SD	Easton
35	4.4	Bethlehem Area SD	Bethlehem
36	4.3	Altoona Area SD	Altoona
36	4.3	Mifflin County SD	Lewistown
36	4.3	New Castle Area SD	New Castle
36	4.3	Shikellamy SD	Sunbury
40	4.2	Hanover Public SD	Hanover
40	4.2	Susquenita SD	Duncannon
40	4.2	Upper Adams SD	Biglerville
40	4.2	Woodland Hills SD	Pittsburgh
44	4.1	Big Spring SD	Newville
44	4.1	Northampton Area SD	Northampton
46	4.0	Catasauqua Area SD	Catasauqua
46	4.0	Daniel Boone Area SD	Birdsboro
46	4.0	Tamaqua Area SD	Tamaqua
46	4.0	William Penn SD	Lansdowne
50	3.9	Derry Township SD	Hershey
50	3.9	Franklin Area SD	Franklin
52	3.8	Easton Area SD	Easton
52	3.8	Erie City SD	Erie
52	3.8	Upper Darby SD	Drexel Hill
55	3.7	East Allegheny SD	N Versailles
55	3.7	Milton Area SD	Milton
57	3.6	Central Greene SD	Waynesburg
57	3.6	Everett Area SD	Everett
59	3.5	Bangor Area SD	Bangor
59	3.5	Butler Area SD	Butler
59	3.5	Conneaut SD	Linesville
59	3.5	Crawford Central SD	Meadville

59	3.5	Saint Marys Area SD	Saint Marys
59	3.5	Wyalusing Area SD	Wyalusing
65	3.4	Albert Gallatin Area SD	Uniontown
65	3.4	Apollo-Ridge SD	Spring Church
65	3.4	Chichester SD	Boothwyn
65	3.4	Littlestown Area SD	Littlestown
65	3.4	Mckeesport Area SD	Mc Keesport
65	3.4	Mount Pleasant Area SD	Mount Pleasant
71	3.3	Dover Area SD	Dover
71	3.3	Scranton SD	Scranton
71	3.3	Wilkes-Barre Area SD	Wilkes Barre
74	3.2	Corry Area SD	Corry
74	3.2	Huntingdon Area SD	Huntingdon
74	3.2	Mount Union Area SD	Mount Union
74	3.2	Muhlenberg SD	Reading
78	3.1	Carlisle Area SD	Carlisle
78	3.1	Girard SD	Girard
78	3.1	Greencastle-Antrim SD	Greencastle
78	3.1	Hazleton Area SD	Hazleton
78	3.1	Somerset Area SD	Somerset
83	3.0	Greater Johnstown SD	Johnstown
83	3.0	Mercer Area SD	Mercer
83	3.0	Midd-West SD	Middleburg
83	3.0	Tulpehocken Area SD	Bernville
83	3.0	Wyoming Area SD	Exeter
88	2.9	Bellefonte Area SD	Bellefonte
88	2.9	Bensalem Township SD	Bensalem
88	2.9	Blairsville-Saltsburg SD	Blairsville
88	2.9	Donegal SD	Mount Joy
88	2.9	Keystone Oaks SD	Pittsburgh
88	2.9	Pine Grove Area SD	Pine Grove
88	2.9	Pleasant Valley SD	Brodheadsville
88	2.9	Waynesboro Area SD	Waynesboro
88	2.9	Wellsboro Area SD	Wellsboro
97	2.8	Bedford Area SD	Bedford
97	2.8	Conestoga Valley SD	Lancaster
97	2.8	Greensburg Salem SD	Greensburg
97	2.8	Middletown Area SD	Middletown
97	2.8	Northern Tioga SD	Elkland
97	2.8	Pottsgrove SD	Pottstown
97	2.8	Ringgold SD	New Eagle
97	2.8	Riverside Beaver County SD	Ellwood City
97	2.8	Warren County SD	North Warren
97	2.8	Warrior Run SD	Turbotville
107	2.7	Chambersburg Area SD	Chambersburg
107	2.7	East Lycoming SD	Hughesville
107	2.7	East Pennsboro Area SD	Enola
107	2.7	Eastern York SD	Wrightsville
107	2.7	Harbor Creek SD	Harborcreek
107	2.7	Millcreek Township SD	Erie
107	2.7	Northeastern York SD	Manchester
107	2.7	Pittston Area SD	Pittston
107	2.7	Quakertown Community SD	Quakertown
107	2.7	South Eastern SD	Fawn Grove
107	2.7	Sto-Rox SD	Mckees Rocks
107	2.7	Titusville Area SD	Titusville
107	2.7	West Perry SD	Elliottsburg
120	2.6	Armstrong SD	Ford City
120	2.6	Belle Vernon Area SD	Belle Vernon
120	2.6	Elk Lake SD	Dimock
120	2.6	Gettysburg Area SD	Gettysburg
120	2.6	Kiski Area SD	Vandergrift
120	2.6	Northwestern SD	Albion
120	2.6	Solanco SD	Quarryville
120	2.6	South Western SD	Hanover
128	2.5	Keystone Central SD	Lock Haven
128	2.5	Lake-Lehman SD	Lehman
128	2.5	Moniteau SD	West Sunbury
128	2.5	North Schuylkill SD	Ashland
128	2.5	Southmoreland SD	Scottdale
128	2.5	Warwick SD	Lititz
134	2.4	Bald Eagle Area SD	Wingate
134	2.4	Bermudian Springs SD	York Springs
134	2.4	East Stroudsburg Area SD	E Stroudsburg
134	2.4	Greater Nanticoke Area SD	Nanticoke
134	2.4	Greenville Area SD	Greenville
134	2.4	Highlands SD	Natrona Heights
134	2.4	Penn Hills SD	Pittsburgh
134	2.4	Southern Tioga SD	Blossburg
134	2.4	Troy Area SD	Troy
134	2.4	Tyrone Area SD	Tyrone
144	2.3	Bristol Township SD	Levittown
144	2.3	East Penn SD	Emmaus
144	2.3	Hamburg Area SD	Hamburg
144	2.3	Montrose Area SD	Montrose
144	2.3	Northgate SD	Pittsburgh
144	2.3	Palisades SD	Kintnersville
144	2.3	Pen Argyl Area SD	Pen Argyl
144	2.3	Penn-Delco SD	Aston
144	2.3	Pequea Valley SD	Kinzers
144	2.3	Pocono Mountain SD	Swiftwater
144	2.3	Southern York County SD	Glen Rock
144	2.3	Twin Valley SD	Elverson
144	2.3	West Shore SD	New Cumberland
157	2.2	Brookville Area SD	Brookville
157	2.2	Burrell SD	Lower Burrell
157	2.2	Carlynton SD	Carnegie
157	2.2	Chestnut Ridge SD	Fishertown
157	2.2	Clearfield Area SD	Clearfield
157	2.2	Ellwood City Area SD	Ellwood City
157	2.2	Hempfield SD	Landisville
157	2.2	Manheim Central SD	Manheim
157	2.2	Shamokin Area SD	Coal Township
157	2.2	Towanda Area SD	Towanda
157	2.2	West Allegheny SD	Imperial
168	2.1	Annville-Cleona SD	Annville
168	2.1	Brandywine Heights Area SD	Topton
168	2.1	Conrad Weiser Area SD	Robesonia
168	2.1	Cornwall-Lebanon SD	Lebanon
168	2.1	Derry Area SD	Derry
168	2.1	Hanover Area SD	Wilkes Barre
168	2.1	Hempfield Area SD	Greensburg
168	2.1	Philipsburg-Osceola Area SD	Philipsburg
168	2.1	Red Lion Area SD	Red Lion
168	2.1	Stroudsburg Area SD	Stroudsburg
168	2.1	West York Area SD	York
179	2.0	Canon-Mcmillan SD	Canonsburg
179	2.0	Charleroi SD	Charleroi
179	2.0	Coatesville Area SD	Coatesville
179	2.0	Fleetwood Area SD	Fleetwood
179	2.0	General Mclane SD	Edinboro
179	2.0	Hollidaysburg Area SD	Hollidaysburg
179	2.0	Indiana Area SD	Indiana
179	2.0	Juniata County SD	Mifflintown
179	2.0	Ligonier Valley SD	Ligonier
179	2.0	Ridley SD	Folsom
179	2.0	Seneca Valley SD	Harmony
179	2.0	South Middleton SD	Boiling Springs
179	2.0	Spring Grove Area SD	Spring Grove
179	2.0	Valley View SD	Archbald
193	1.9	Central Dauphin SD	Harrisburg
193	1.9	Elizabeth Forward SD	Elizabeth
193	1.9	Lewisburg Area SD	Lewisburg
193	1.9	Mifflinburg Area SD	Mifflinburg
193	1.9	Montour SD	Mc Kees Rocks
193	1.9	North East SD	North East
193	1.9	Octorara Area SD	Atglen
193	1.9	Penn Cambria SD	Cresson
193	1.9	Saucon Valley SD	Hellertown
193	1.9	Spring-Ford Area SD	Collegeville
193	1.9	Tunkhannock Area SD	Tunkhannock
193	1.9	Wayne Highlands SD	Honesdale
205	1.8	Avon Grove SD	West Grove
205	1.8	Elizabethtown Area SD	Elizabethtown
205	1.8	Gateway SD	Monroeville
205	1.8	Mcguffey SD	Claysville
205	1.8	Montoursville Area SD	Montoursville
205	1.8	Spring Cove SD	Roaring Spring
205	1.8	Wallenpaupack Area SD	Hawley
205	1.8	Wilson SD	West Lawn
205	1.8	Yough SD	Herminie
214	1.7	Dunmore SD	Dunmore
214	1.7	Jim Thorpe Area SD	Jim Thorpe
214	1.7	Northern York County SD	Dillsburg
214	1.7	Perkiomen Valley SD	Collegeville
214	1.7	Richland SD	Johnstown
214	1.7	Slippery Rock Area SD	Slippery Rock
214	1.7	South Butler County SD	Saxonburg
214	1.7	Steel Valley SD	Munhall
214	1.7	Whitehall-Coplay SD	Whitehall
223	1.6	Blackhawk SD	Beaver Falls
223	1.6	Centennial SD	Warminster
223	1.6	Cheltenham Township SD	Elkins Park
223	1.6	Cumberland Valley SD	Mechanicsburg
223	1.6	Dubois Area SD	Du Bois
223	1.6	Exeter Township SD	Reading
223	1.6	Fairview SD	Fairview
223	1.6	Freedom Area SD	Freedom
223	1.6	Kennett Consolidated SD	Kennett Square
223	1.6	Marple Newtown SD	Newtown Square
223	1.6	Mid Valley SD	Throop
223	1.6	Neshaminy SD	Langhorne
223	1.6	Selinsgrove Area SD	Selinsgrove
223	1.6	Uniontown Area SD	Uniontown
237	1.5	Abington SD	Abington
237	1.5	Boyertown Area SD	Boyertown
237	1.5	Eastern Lebanon County SD	Myerstown
237	1.5	Interboro SD	Prospect Park
237	1.5	Lampeter-Strasburg SD	Lampeter
237	1.5	Mechanicsburg Area SD	Mechanicsburg
237	1.5	Penn Manor SD	Millersville
237	1.5	Shippensburg Area SD	Shippensburg
237	1.5	Upper Merion Area SD	King Of Prussia
237	1.5	Upper Perkiomen SD	East Greenville
247	1.4	Governor Mifflin SD	Shillington
247	1.4	Karns City Area SD	Karns City
247	1.4	Lakeland SD	Jermyn
247	1.4	Owen J Roberts SD	Pottstown
247	1.4	Penncrest SD	Saegertown
247	1.4	West Chester Area SD	West Chester
253	1.3	Blue Mountain SD	Orwigsburg
253	1.3	Cambria Heights SD	Patton
253	1.3	Dallastown Area SD	Dallastown
253	1.3	Danville Area SD	Danville
253	1.3	Eastern Lancaster County SD	New Holland
253	1.3	Ephrata Area SD	Ephrata
253	1.3	Hermitage SD	Hermitage
253	1.3	Hopewell Area SD	Aliquippa
253	1.3	Kutztown Area SD	Kutztown
253	1.3	Lehighton Area SD	Lehighton
253	1.3	Manheim Township SD	Lancaster
253	1.3	Marion Center Area SD	Marion Center
253	1.3	Methacton SD	Norristown
253	1.3	Northern Lehigh SD	Slatington
253	1.3	Norwin SD	N Huntingdon
253	1.3	Pennridge SD	Perkasie
253	1.3	Shaler Area SD	Glenshaw
253	1.3	Souderton Area SD	Souderton
253	1.3	South Park SD	South Park
253	1.3	Springfield Township SD	Oreland
253	1.3	Susquehanna Township SD	Harrisburg
253	1.3	Tuscarora SD	Mercersburg
253	1.3	Upper Moreland Township SD	Willow Grove
253	1.3	West Jefferson Hills SD	Jefferson Hls
253	1.3	Wissahickon SD	Ambler
278	1.2	Ambridge Area SD	Ambridge
278	1.2	Baldwin-Whitehall SD	Pittsburgh
278	1.2	Central Bucks SD	Doylestown
278	1.2	Central Columbia SD	Bloomsburg
278	1.2	Colonial SD	Plymouth Meeting
278	1.2	Crestwood SD	Mountain Top
278	1.2	Delaware Valley SD	Milford
278	1.2	Mohawk Area SD	Bessemer
278	1.2	North Hills SD	Pittsburgh
278	1.2	Wattsburg Area SD	Erie
278	1.2	Wyoming Valley West SD	Kingston
289	1.1	Chartiers Valley SD	Pittsburgh
289	1.1	Conewago Valley SD	New Oxford
289	1.1	Forest Hills SD	Sidman
289	1.1	Fort Leboeuf SD	Waterford
289	1.1	Hatboro-Horsham SD	Horsham
289	1.1	Haverford Township SD	Havertown
289	1.1	Mars Area SD	Mars
289	1.1	Nazareth Area SD	Nazareth
289	1.1	Oley Valley SD	Oley
289	1.1	Punxsutawney Area SD	Punxsutawney
289	1.1	Southern Lehigh SD	Center Valley
300	1.0	Central Cambria SD	Ebensburg
300	1.0	Cocalico SD	Denver
300	1.0	Greater Latrobe SD	Latrobe
300	1.0	North Pocono SD	Moscow
300	1.0	Phoenixville Area SD	Phoenixville
300	1.0	Wyomissing Area SD	Wyomissing
306	0.9	Dallas SD	Dallas
306	0.9	Grove City Area SD	Grove City
306	0.9	Lower Dauphin SD	Hummelstown
306	0.9	Mount Carmel Area SD	Mount Carmel
306	0.9	Palmerton Area SD	Palmerton
306	0.9	Plum Borough SD	Plum
306	0.9	Quaker Valley SD	Sewickley
306	0.9	State College Area SD	State College
306	0.9	Wilmington Area SD	New Wilmington
315	0.8	Chester-Upland SD	Chester
315	0.8	Moon Area SD	Moon Township
315	0.8	North Penn SD	Lansdale
315	0.8	Northwestern Lehigh SD	New Tripoli
315	0.8	Reynolds SD	Greenville
315	0.8	Schuylkill Valley SD	Leesport
315	0.8	South Allegheny SD	Mc Keesport
315	0.8	Springfield SD	Springfield
315	0.8	West Mifflin Area SD	West Mifflin
324	0.7	Fox Chapel Area SD	Pittsburgh
324	0.7	Hampton Township SD	Allison Park
324	0.7	Mt Lebanon SD	Pittsburgh
324	0.7	New Brighton Area SD	New Brighton
324	0.7	Parkland SD	Allentown
324	0.7	Pennsbury SD	Fallsington
330	0.6	Central York SD	York
330	0.6	Garnet Valley SD	Glen Mills
330	0.6	Palmyra Area SD	Palmyra
330	0.6	Penn-Trafford SD	Harrison City
330	0.6	Penns Valley Area SD	Spring Mills
330	0.6	Radnor Township SD	Wayne
330	0.6	Rose Tree Media SD	Media
330	0.6	South Fayette Township SD	Mc Donald
338	0.5	Abington Heights SD	Clarks Summit
338	0.5	Bethel Park SD	Bethel Park
338	0.5	Center Area SD	Monaca

338	0.5	Deer Lakes SD	Russellton
338	0.5	Downingtown Area SD	Downingtown
338	0.5	Freeport Area SD	Freeport
338	0.5	Lower Moreland Township SD	Huntingdon Vly
338	0.5	North Allegheny SD	Pittsburgh
338	0.5	Pine-Richland SD	Gibsonia
338	0.5	Salisbury Township SD	Allentown
338	0.5	Wallingford-Swarthmore SD	Wallingford
349	0.4	Beaver Area SD	Beaver
349	0.4	Franklin Regional SD	Murrysville
349	0.4	Great Valley SD	Malvern
349	0.4	Lower Merion SD	Ardmore
349	0.4	Peters Township SD	Mcmurray
354	0.3	Council Rock SD	Newtown
354	0.3	Upper Dublin SD	Maple Glen
356	0.2	Unionville-Chadds Ford SD	Kennett Square
356	0.2	York Suburban SD	York
358	0.1	Tredyffrin-Easttown SD	Berwyn
359	0.0	Upper Saint Clair SD	Pittsburgh
359	0.0	Westmont Hilltop SD	Johnstown
361	n/a	Pde Division of Data Services	Harrisburg
361	n/a	Pennsylvania Virtual CS	Norristown

Rhode Island

Rhode Island Public School Educational Profile

Category	Value	Category	Value
Schools *(2003-2004)*	341	**Diploma Recipients** *(2002-2003)*	8,828
Instructional Level		White, Non-Hispanic	7,014
Primary	218	Black, Non-Hispanic	635
Middle	58	Asian/Pacific Islander	315
High	55	American Indian/Alaskan Native	35
Other Level	10	Hispanic	829
Curriculum		**High School Drop-out Rate** *(%)* *(2001-2002)*	4.3
Regular	319	White, Non-Hispanic	3.4
Special Education	4	Black, Non-Hispanic	7.1
Vocational	13	Asian/Pacific Islander	4.7
Alternative	5	American Indian/Alaskan Native	6.3
Type		Hispanic	8.5
Magnet	17	**Staff** *(2003-2004)*	
Charter	8	Teachers	11,826.0
Title I Eligible	146	Average Salary[1] ($)	54,809
School-wide Title I	56	Librarians/Media Specialists	0.0
Students *(2003-2004)*	159,342	Guidance Counselors	0.0
Gender (%)		**Ratios** *(2003-2004)*	
Male	51.6	Student/Teacher Ratio	13.5 to 1
Female	48.4	Student/Librarian Ratio	***,***.* to 1
Race/Ethnicity (%)		Student/Counselor Ratio	***,***.* to 1
White, Non-Hispanic	71.3	**College Entrance Exam Scores** *(2005)*	
Black, Non-Hispanic	8.5	Scholastic Aptitude Test (SAT)	
Asian/Pacific Islander	3.2	Participation Rate (%)	72
American Indian/Alaskan Native	0.6	Mean SAT Reasoning Test Verbal Score	503
Hispanic	16.4	Mean SAT Reasoning Test Math Score	505
Classification (%)		American College Testing Program (ACT)	
Individual Education Program (IEP)	21.0	Participation Rate (%)	8
Migrant *(2002-2003)*	0.0	Average Composite Score	21.9
English Language Learner (ELL)	6.1	Average English Score	21.4
Eligible for Free Lunch Program	29.3	Average Math Score	21.7
Eligible for Reduced-Price Lunch Program	6.2	Average Reading Score	22.6
Current Spending *($ per student in FY 2003)*	9,789	Average Science Score	21.3
Instruction	6,178		
Support Services	3,342		

Note: *For an explanation of data, please refer to the User's Guide in the front of the book; (1) AFT estimate*

Rhode Island NAEP 2005 Test Scores

Reading			Mathematics		
Grade/Category	**Value**	**Rank**	**Grade/Category**	**Value**	**Rank**
4th Grade			**4th Grade**		
Average Proficiency	216.4 (1.20)	36/51	Average Proficiency	233.4 (0.93)	38/51
Proficiency by Gender/Race/Ethnicity			Proficiency by Gender/Race/Ethnicity		
Male	212.1 (1.44)	36/51	Male	233.9 (1.06)	39/51
Female	220.8 (1.46)	33/51	Female	232.9 (1.07)	37/51
White, Non-Hispanic	224.2 (1.12)	38/51	White, Non-Hispanic	240.7 (0.80)	42/51
Black, Non-Hispanic	196.6 (3.24)	25/42	Black, Non-Hispanic	210.9 (2.33)	37/42
Asian, Non-Hispanic	218.6 (6.07)	22/27	Asian, Non-Hispanic	240.2 (4.17)	21/25
American Indian, Non-Hispanic	n/a	n/a	American Indian, Non-Hispanic	n/a	n/a
Hispanic	192.0 (2.52)	40/40	Hispanic	211.5 (1.86)	41/41
Proficiency by Class Size			Proficiency by Class Size		
Less than 16 Students	194.8 (7.12)	27/34	Less than 16 Students	n/a	n/a
16 to 18 Students	217.6 (3.09)	17/33	16 to 18 Students	233.7 (2.32)	20/31
19 to 20 Students	223.9 (2.19)	17/38	19 to 20 Students	238.4 (1.28)	24/38
21 to 25 Students	216.6 (1.93)	39/51	21 to 25 Students	235.6 (1.38)	38/51
Greater than 25 Students	212.3 (3.48)	31/36	Greater than 25 Students	228.7 (3.99)	30/33
Percent Attaining Achievement Levels			Percent Attaining Achievement Levels		
Below Basic	38.2 (1.51)	17/51	Below Basic	23.7 (1.31)	15/51
Basic or Above	61.8 (1.51)	35/51	Basic or Above	76.3 (1.31)	37/51
Proficient or Above	29.7 (1.25)	31/51	Proficient or Above	30.5 (1.18)	37/51
Advanced or Above	7.1 (0.81)	23/51	Advanced or Above	3.6 (0.46)	38/51
8th Grade			**8th Grade**		
Average Proficiency	261.0 (0.70)	30/51	Average Proficiency	272.3 (0.77)	38/51
Proficiency by Gender/Race/Ethnicity			Proficiency by Gender/Race/Ethnicity		
Male	256.3 (0.95)	29/51	Male	272.2 (1.02)	39/51
Female	265.6 (1.17)	33/51	Female	272.5 (1.02)	38/51
White, Non-Hispanic	267.9 (0.87)	28/51	White, Non-Hispanic	280.8 (0.78)	41/51
Black, Non-Hispanic	242.9 (2.36)	17/40	Black, Non-Hispanic	248.8 (2.77)	28/41
Asian, Non-Hispanic	257.0 (4.33)	23/24	Asian, Non-Hispanic	278.3 (5.18)	20/23
American Indian, Non-Hispanic	n/a	n/a	American Indian, Non-Hispanic	n/a	n/a
Hispanic	236.6 (2.58)	38/38	Hispanic	243.5 (1.83)	38/38
Proficiency by Parents Highest Level of Ed.			Proficiency by Parents Highest Level of Ed.		
Did Not Finish High School	243.1 (2.97)	33/49	Did Not Finish High School	255.2 (2.66)	37/50
Graduated High School	253.1 (1.65)	27/50	Graduated High School	263.0 (1.85)	37/50
Some Education After High School	263.2 (1.70)	35/50	Some Education After High School	275.7 (1.58)	39/50
Graduated College	272.7 (0.94)	25/50	Graduated College	283.8 (1.00)	37/50
Percent Attaining Achievement Levels			Percent Attaining Achievement Levels		
Below Basic	38.2 (1.51)	17/51	Below Basic	36.5 (1.05)	12/51
Basic or Above	61.8 (1.51)	35/51	Basic or Above	63.5 (1.05)	39/51
Proficient or Above	29.7 (1.25)	31/51	Proficient or Above	23.5 (0.93)	37/51
Advanced or Above	7.1 (0.81)	23/51	Advanced or Above	3.3 (0.50)	40/51

Note: For an explanation of data, please refer to the User's Guide in the front of the book; n/a indicates data not available

Bristol County

Barrington SD
283 County Rd · Barrington, RI 02806
Mailing Address: PO Box 95 · Barrington, RI 02806
(401) 245-5000 · http://www.barringtonschools.org/
Grade Span: PK-12; **Agency Type:** 1
Schools: 6
   3 Primary; 2 Middle; 1 High; 0 Other Level
   6 Regular; 0 Special Education; 0 Vocational; 0 Alternative
   0 Magnet; 0 Charter; 2 Title I Eligible; 0 School-wide Title I
Students: 3,434 (52.5% male; 47.4% female)
   Individual Education Program: 613 (17.9%);
   English Language Learner: 16 (0.5%); Migrant: n/a
   Eligible for Free Lunch Program: 61 (1.8%)
   Eligible for Reduced-Price Lunch Program: 23 (0.7%)
Teachers: 251.0 (13.7 to 1)
Librarians/Media Specialists: n/a
Guidance Counselors: n/a
Current Spending: ($ per student per year):
   Total: $8,843; Instruction: $5,932; Support Services: $2,713
Enrollment, Drop-out Rates and Diploma Recipients by Race/Ethnicity

Category	Total	White	Black	Asian	AIAN	Hisp.
Enrollment (%)	100.0	96.3	0.8	2.1	0.2	0.6
Drop-out Rate (%)	2.3	2.4	0.0	0.0	n/a	0.0
H.S. Diplomas (#)	206	200	1	5	0	0

Bristol Warren RD
151 State St · Bristol, RI 02809
(401) 253-4000 · http://bw.k12.ri.us/
Grade Span: PK-12; **Agency Type:** 1
Schools: 9
   6 Primary; 2 Middle; 1 High; 0 Other Level
   9 Regular; 0 Special Education; 0 Vocational; 0 Alternative
   1 Magnet; 0 Charter; 6 Title I Eligible; 0 School-wide Title I
Students: 3,688 (52.2% male; 47.7% female)
   Individual Education Program: 828 (22.5%);
   English Language Learner: 136 (3.7%); Migrant: n/a
   Eligible for Free Lunch Program: 603 (16.4%)
   Eligible for Reduced-Price Lunch Program: 298 (8.1%)
Teachers: 333.0 (11.1 to 1)
Librarians/Media Specialists: n/a
Guidance Counselors: n/a
Current Spending: ($ per student per year):
   Total: $10,659; Instruction: $6,689; Support Services: $3,731
Enrollment, Drop-out Rates and Diploma Recipients by Race/Ethnicity

Category	Total	White	Black	Asian	AIAN	Hisp.
Enrollment (%)	100.0	95.8	2.4	0.5	0.1	1.2
Drop-out Rate (%)	5.2	5.2	14.3	0.0	n/a	0.0
H.S. Diplomas (#)	205	201	1	3	0	0

Kent County

Coventry SD
9 Foster Dr · Coventry, RI 02816
(401) 822-9400 · http://www.coventryschools.net/
Grade Span: PK-12; **Agency Type:** 1
Schools: 10
   7 Primary; 2 Middle; 1 High; 0 Other Level
   10 Regular; 0 Special Education; 0 Vocational; 0 Alternative
   0 Magnet; 0 Charter; 3 Title I Eligible; 0 School-wide Title I
Students: 5,862 (51.1% male; 48.8% female)
   Individual Education Program: 1,206 (20.6%);
   English Language Learner: 11 (0.2%); Migrant: n/a
   Eligible for Free Lunch Program: 545 (10.9%)
   Eligible for Reduced-Price Lunch Program: 269 (5.4%)
Teachers: 427.0 (11.7 to 1)
Librarians/Media Specialists: n/a
Guidance Counselors: n/a
Current Spending: ($ per student per year):
   Total: $9,272; Instruction: $6,408; Support Services: $2,649
Enrollment, Drop-out Rates and Diploma Recipients by Race/Ethnicity

Category	Total	White	Black	Asian	AIAN	Hisp.
Enrollment (%)	100.0	96.4	1.2	1.0	0.2	1.2
Drop-out Rate (%)	2.5	2.6	0.0	0.0	0.0	0.0
H.S. Diplomas (#)	380	369	3	4	0	4

East Greenwich SD
111 Peirce St · East Greenwich, RI 02818
(401) 885-3300 · http://www.ri.net/schools/East_Greenwich/
Grade Span: PK-12; **Agency Type:** 1
Schools: 6
   2 Primary; 3 Middle; 1 High; 0 Other Level
   6 Regular; 0 Special Education; 0 Vocational; 0 Alternative
   0 Magnet; 0 Charter; 2 Title I Eligible; 0 School-wide Title I
Students: 2,466 (50.2% male; 49.7% female)
   Individual Education Program: 448 (18.2%);
   English Language Learner: 23 (0.9%); Migrant: n/a
   Eligible for Free Lunch Program: 108 (5.0%)
   Eligible for Reduced-Price Lunch Program: 11 (0.5%)
Teachers: 193.0 (11.1 to 1)
Librarians/Media Specialists: n/a
Guidance Counselors: n/a
Current Spending: ($ per student per year):
   Total: $10,192; Instruction: $6,704; Support Services: $3,457
Enrollment, Drop-out Rates and Diploma Recipients by Race/Ethnicity

Category	Total	White	Black	Asian	AIAN	Hisp.
Enrollment (%)	100.0	95.0	1.3	3.0	0.1	0.7
Drop-out Rate (%)	0.9	0.8	0.0	0.0	n/a	50.0
H.S. Diplomas (#)	146	136	1	7	0	2

Exeter-W Greenwich RD
940 Nooseneck Hill Rd · West Greenwich, RI 02817
(401) 397-5125 · http://www.ewg.k12.ri.us/
Grade Span: PK-12; **Agency Type:** 1
Schools: 5
   3 Primary; 1 Middle; 1 High; 0 Other Level
   5 Regular; 0 Special Education; 0 Vocational; 0 Alternative
   0 Magnet; 0 Charter; 2 Title I Eligible; 0 School-wide Title I
Students: 2,204 (49.3% male; 50.6% female)
   Individual Education Program: 418 (19.0%);
   English Language Learner: 6 (0.3%); Migrant: n/a
   Eligible for Free Lunch Program: 142 (6.5%)
   Eligible for Reduced-Price Lunch Program: 75 (3.4%)
Teachers: 182.0 (12.0 to 1)
Librarians/Media Specialists: n/a
Guidance Counselors: n/a
Current Spending: ($ per student per year):
   Total: $9,438; Instruction: $6,036; Support Services: $3,205
Enrollment, Drop-out Rates and Diploma Recipients by Race/Ethnicity

Category	Total	White	Black	Asian	AIAN	Hisp.
Enrollment (%)	100.0	96.2	0.9	0.9	0.5	1.6
Drop-out Rate (%)	1.8	1.7	0.0	0.0	0.0	16.7
H.S. Diplomas (#)	128	124	0	4	0	0

Warwick SD
34 Warwick Lake Ave · Warwick, RI 02889
(401) 734-3100 · http://www.warwickschools.org/
Grade Span: PK-12; **Agency Type:** 1
Schools: 26
   20 Primary; 3 Middle; 3 High; 0 Other Level
   26 Regular; 0 Special Education; 0 Vocational; 0 Alternative
   0 Magnet; 0 Charter; 9 Title I Eligible; 0 School-wide Title I
Students: 11,993 (51.9% male; 48.0% female)
   Individual Education Program: 2,567 (21.4%);
   English Language Learner: 91 (0.8%); Migrant: n/a
   Eligible for Free Lunch Program: 1,602 (13.4%)
   Eligible for Reduced-Price Lunch Program: 723 (6.0%)
Teachers: 1,035.0 (11.6 to 1)
Librarians/Media Specialists: n/a
Guidance Counselors: n/a
Current Spending: ($ per student per year):
   Total: $10,992; Instruction: $7,096; Support Services: $3,645
Enrollment, Drop-out Rates and Diploma Recipients by Race/Ethnicity

Category	Total	White	Black	Asian	AIAN	Hisp.
Enrollment (%)	100.0	93.8	1.8	2.0	0.3	2.2
Drop-out Rate (%)	1.9	1.8	7.7	0.0	0.0	6.0
H.S. Diplomas (#)	782	752	5	8	4	13

West Warwick SD
10 Harris Ave · West Warwick, RI 02893
(401) 821-1180
Grade Span: PK-12; **Agency Type:** 1
Schools: 7
   5 Primary; 1 Middle; 1 High; 0 Other Level
   7 Regular; 0 Special Education; 0 Vocational; 0 Alternative
   0 Magnet; 0 Charter; 2 Title I Eligible; 1 School-wide Title I
Students: 3,838 (51.1% male; 48.8% female)
   Individual Education Program: 884 (23.0%);
   English Language Learner: 87 (2.3%); Migrant: n/a
   Eligible for Free Lunch Program: 958 (25.0%)
   Eligible for Reduced-Price Lunch Program: 311 (8.1%)
Teachers: 280.0 (13.7 to 1)
Librarians/Media Specialists: n/a
Guidance Counselors: n/a
Current Spending: ($ per student per year):
   Total: $9,973; Instruction: $6,387; Support Services: $3,313

Enrollment, Drop-out Rates and Diploma Recipients by Race/Ethnicity

Category	Total	White	Black	Asian	AIAN	Hisp.
Enrollment (%)	100.0	86.9	3.4	2.1	1.0	6.6
Drop-out Rate (%)	5.9	6.3	3.2	0.0	5.3	2.7
H.S. Diplomas (#)	210	190	5	8	2	5

Newport County

Middletown SD

Oliphant School · Middletown, RI 02842
Mailing Address: 26 Oliphant Ln · Middletown, RI 02842
(401) 849-2122 · http://www.ri.net/middletown/
Grade Span: PK-12; **Agency Type:** 1
Schools: 6
    4 Primary; 1 Middle; 1 High; 0 Other Level
    6 Regular; 0 Special Education; 0 Vocational; 0 Alternative
    0 Magnet; 0 Charter; 3 Title I Eligible; 0 School-wide Title I
Students: 2,769   (52.1% male; 47.8% female)
    Individual Education Program: 611 (22.1%);
    English Language Learner: 52 (1.9%); Migrant: n/a
    Eligible for Free Lunch Program: 277 (10.0%)
    Eligible for Reduced-Price Lunch Program: 208 (7.5%)
Teachers: 197.0 (14.1 to 1)
Librarians/Media Specialists: n/a
Guidance Counselors: n/a
Current Spending: ($ per student per year):
    Total: $10,421; Instruction: $6,847; Support Services: $3,334
Enrollment, Drop-out Rates and Diploma Recipients by Race/Ethnicity

Category	Total	White	Black	Asian	AIAN	Hisp.
Enrollment (%)	100.0	84.7	7.7	3.2	0.3	4.0
Drop-out Rate (%)	2.3	1.9	2.1	12.0	0.0	5.3
H.S. Diplomas (#)	169	150	6	7	0	6

Newport SD

437 Broadway · Newport, RI 02840
(401) 847-2100 · http://www.newportrischools.org/
Grade Span: PK-12; **Agency Type:** 1
Schools: 8
    6 Primary; 1 Middle; 1 High; 0 Other Level
    8 Regular; 0 Special Education; 0 Vocational; 0 Alternative
    0 Magnet; 0 Charter; 5 Title I Eligible; 1 School-wide Title I
Students: 2,826   (51.6% male; 48.3% female)
    Individual Education Program: 797 (28.2%);
    English Language Learner: 115 (4.1%); Migrant: n/a
    Eligible for Free Lunch Program: 1,129 (40.8%)
    Eligible for Reduced-Price Lunch Program: 174 (6.3%)
Teachers: 229.0 (12.1 to 1)
Librarians/Media Specialists: n/a
Guidance Counselors: n/a
Current Spending: ($ per student per year):
    Total: $11,949; Instruction: $7,378; Support Services: $4,206
Enrollment, Drop-out Rates and Diploma Recipients by Race/Ethnicity

Category	Total	White	Black	Asian	AIAN	Hisp.
Enrollment (%)	100.0	58.3	24.9	1.9	2.6	12.2
Drop-out Rate (%)	4.3	3.0	8.8	0.0	7.4	6.8
H.S. Diplomas (#)	168	133	26	3	4	2

Portsmouth SD

29 Middle Rd · Portsmouth, RI 02871
(401) 683-1039 · http://portsmouthrischools.tripod.com/
Grade Span: PK-12; **Agency Type:** 1
Schools: 6
    4 Primary; 1 Middle; 1 High; 0 Other Level
    6 Regular; 0 Special Education; 0 Vocational; 0 Alternative
    0 Magnet; 0 Charter; 2 Title I Eligible; 0 School-wide Title I
Students: 3,066   (52.5% male; 47.4% female)
    Individual Education Program: 559 (18.2%);
    English Language Learner: 7 (0.2%); Migrant: n/a
    Eligible for Free Lunch Program: 121 (3.9%)
    Eligible for Reduced-Price Lunch Program: 89 (2.9%)
Teachers: 204.0 (15.0 to 1)
Librarians/Media Specialists: n/a
Guidance Counselors: n/a
Current Spending: ($ per student per year):
    Total: $8,438; Instruction: $5,359; Support Services: $2,853
Enrollment, Drop-out Rates and Diploma Recipients by Race/Ethnicity

Category	Total	White	Black	Asian	AIAN	Hisp.
Enrollment (%)	100.0	94.4	2.1	2.3	0.1	1.2
Drop-out Rate (%)	0.7	0.7	0.0	0.0	0.0	0.0
H.S. Diplomas (#)	184	172	3	8	0	1

Tiverton SD

100 N Brayton Rd · Tiverton, RI 02878
(401) 624-8475 · http://www.tivschools.com/
Grade Span: PK-12; **Agency Type:** 1
Schools: 5
    3 Primary; 1 Middle; 1 High; 0 Other Level
    5 Regular; 0 Special Education; 0 Vocational; 0 Alternative
    0 Magnet; 0 Charter; 2 Title I Eligible; 0 School-wide Title I
Students: 2,224   (51.6% male; 48.3% female)
    Individual Education Program: 500 (22.5%);
    English Language Learner: 0 (0.0%); Migrant: n/a
    Eligible for Free Lunch Program: 219 (9.8%)
    Eligible for Reduced-Price Lunch Program: 101 (4.5%)
Teachers: 195.0 (11.4 to 1)
Librarians/Media Specialists: n/a
Guidance Counselors: n/a
Current Spending: ($ per student per year):
    Total: $8,512; Instruction: $5,534; Support Services: $2,644
Enrollment, Drop-out Rates and Diploma Recipients by Race/Ethnicity

Category	Total	White	Black	Asian	AIAN	Hisp.
Enrollment (%)	100.0	98.7	0.6	0.5	0.0	0.1
Drop-out Rate (%)	3.3	3.3	0.0	0.0	n/a	0.0
H.S. Diplomas (#)	136	134	1	0	0	1

Providence County

Burrillville SD

265 Sayles Ave · Pascoag, RI 02859
(401) 568-1301
Grade Span: PK-12; **Agency Type:** 1
Schools: 5
    3 Primary; 1 Middle; 1 High; 0 Other Level
    5 Regular; 0 Special Education; 0 Vocational; 0 Alternative
    0 Magnet; 0 Charter; 3 Title I Eligible; 0 School-wide Title I
Students: 2,590   (50.5% male; 49.4% female)
    Individual Education Program: 543 (21.0%);
    English Language Learner: 3 (0.1%); Migrant: n/a
    Eligible for Free Lunch Program: 334 (12.9%)
    Eligible for Reduced-Price Lunch Program: 192 (7.4%)
Teachers: 205.0 (12.6 to 1)
Librarians/Media Specialists: n/a
Guidance Counselors: n/a
Current Spending: ($ per student per year):
    Total: $9,472; Instruction: $5,899; Support Services: $3,268
Enrollment, Drop-out Rates and Diploma Recipients by Race/Ethnicity

Category	Total	White	Black	Asian	AIAN	Hisp.
Enrollment (%)	100.0	96.8	0.8	0.6	0.2	1.6
Drop-out Rate (%)	3.5	3.4	0.0	n/a	0.0	25.0
H.S. Diplomas (#)	187	186	0	0	0	1

Central Falls SD

21 Hedley Ave · Central Falls, RI 02863
(401) 727-7700
Grade Span: PK-12; **Agency Type:** 1
Schools: 8
    6 Primary; 1 Middle; 1 High; 0 Other Level
    8 Regular; 0 Special Education; 0 Vocational; 0 Alternative
    0 Magnet; 0 Charter; 7 Title I Eligible; 6 School-wide Title I
Students: 3,734   (51.3% male; 48.6% female)
    Individual Education Program: 934 (25.0%);
    English Language Learner: 1,073 (28.7%); Migrant: n/a
    Eligible for Free Lunch Program: 2,512 (69.2%)
    Eligible for Reduced-Price Lunch Program: 491 (13.5%)
Teachers: 265.0 (13.7 to 1)
Librarians/Media Specialists: n/a
Guidance Counselors: n/a
Current Spending: ($ per student per year):
    Total: $10,706; Instruction: $6,491; Support Services: $3,823
Enrollment, Drop-out Rates and Diploma Recipients by Race/Ethnicity

Category	Total	White	Black	Asian	AIAN	Hisp.
Enrollment (%)	100.0	20.3	11.3	0.3	0.1	68.0
Drop-out Rate (%)	8.8	6.6	12.7	0.0	0.0	9.3
H.S. Diplomas (#)	169	44	17	0	0	108

Cranston SD

845 Park Ave · Cranston, RI 02910
(401) 270-8000 · http://www.cpsed.net/
Grade Span: PK-12; **Agency Type:** 1
Schools: 25
    19 Primary; 3 Middle; 2 High; 1 Other Level
    25 Regular; 0 Special Education; 0 Vocational; 0 Alternative
    0 Magnet; 1 Charter; 7 Title I Eligible; 3 School-wide Title I
Students: 11,222   (51.8% male; 48.1% female)
    Individual Education Program: 2,407 (21.4%);
    English Language Learner: 430 (3.8%); Migrant: n/a

Eligible for Free Lunch Program: 1,850 (16.5%)
Eligible for Reduced-Price Lunch Program: 558 (5.0%)
Teachers: 862.0 (13.0 to 1)
Librarians/Media Specialists: n/a
Guidance Counselors: n/a
Current Spending: ($ per student per year):
Total: $8,693; Instruction: $5,439; Support Services: $3,038
Enrollment, Drop-out Rates and Diploma Recipients by Race/Ethnicity

Category	Total	White	Black	Asian	AIAN	Hisp.
Enrollment (%)	100.0	81.8	4.1	5.9	0.2	7.9
Drop-out Rate (%)	4.1	4.0	5.8	5.1	0.0	3.7
H.S. Diplomas (#)	707	591	28	48	1	39

Cumberland SD

2602 Mendon Rd • Cumberland, RI 02864
(401) 658-1600 • http://www.cumberlandschools.org/
Grade Span: PK-12; **Agency Type:** 1
Schools: 10
7 Primary; 2 Middle; 1 High; 0 Other Level
10 Regular; 0 Special Education; 0 Vocational; 0 Alternative
0 Magnet; 0 Charter; 2 Title I Eligible; 0 School-wide Title I
Students: 5,349 (51.8% male; 48.1% female)
Individual Education Program: 1,263 (23.6%);
English Language Learner: 123 (2.3%); Migrant: n/a
Eligible for Free Lunch Program: 446 (8.3%)
Eligible for Reduced-Price Lunch Program: 207 (3.9%)
Teachers: 414.0 (12.9 to 1)
Librarians/Media Specialists: n/a
Guidance Counselors: n/a
Current Spending: ($ per student per year):
Total: $7,474; Instruction: $4,788; Support Services: $2,491
Enrollment, Drop-out Rates and Diploma Recipients by Race/Ethnicity

Category	Total	White	Black	Asian	AIAN	Hisp.
Enrollment (%)	100.0	92.8	1.9	1.6	0.3	3.4
Drop-out Rate (%)	1.7	1.6	0.0	0.0	0.0	4.3
H.S. Diplomas (#)	304	288	1	0	1	14

East Providence SD

80 Burnside Ave • East Providence, RI 02915
(401) 433-6222 • http://ep.k12.ri.us/
Grade Span: PK-12; **Agency Type:** 1
Schools: 13
9 Primary; 2 Middle; 2 High; 0 Other Level
12 Regular; 0 Special Education; 0 Vocational; 1 Alternative
0 Magnet; 0 Charter; 5 Title I Eligible; 1 School-wide Title I
Students: 6,386 (51.7% male; 48.2% female)
Individual Education Program: 1,461 (22.9%);
English Language Learner: 301 (4.7%); Migrant: n/a
Eligible for Free Lunch Program: 1,404 (22.0%)
Eligible for Reduced-Price Lunch Program: 609 (9.5%)
Teachers: 504.0 (12.7 to 1)
Librarians/Media Specialists: n/a
Guidance Counselors: n/a
Current Spending: ($ per student per year):
Total: $9,701; Instruction: $6,425; Support Services: $3,021
Enrollment, Drop-out Rates and Diploma Recipients by Race/Ethnicity

Category	Total	White	Black	Asian	AIAN	Hisp.
Enrollment (%)	100.0	81.2	12.9	1.3	1.2	3.4
Drop-out Rate (%)	5.5	4.9	10.0	0.0	12.5	2.4
H.S. Diplomas (#)	419	343	64	6	0	6

Foster-Glocester RD

1145 Putnam Pike • Chepachet, RI 02814
Mailing Address: PO Box D • Chepachet, RI 02814
(401) 568-4175
Grade Span: 06-12; **Agency Type:** 1
Schools: 2
0 Primary; 1 Middle; 1 High; 0 Other Level
2 Regular; 0 Special Education; 0 Vocational; 0 Alternative
0 Magnet; 0 Charter; 1 Title I Eligible; 0 School-wide Title I
Students: 1,693 (52.4% male; 47.5% female)
Individual Education Program: 230 (13.6%);
English Language Learner: 0 (0.0%); Migrant: n/a
Eligible for Free Lunch Program: 113 (6.7%)
Eligible for Reduced-Price Lunch Program: 45 (2.7%)
Teachers: 123.0 (13.7 to 1)
Librarians/Media Specialists: n/a
Guidance Counselors: n/a
Current Spending: ($ per student per year):
Total: $8,372; Instruction: $5,420; Support Services: $2,722
Enrollment, Drop-out Rates and Diploma Recipients by Race/Ethnicity

Category	Total	White	Black	Asian	AIAN	Hisp.
Enrollment (%)	100.0	98.6	0.9	0.0	0.0	0.5
Drop-out Rate (%)	2.7	2.7	0.0	0.0	n/a	0.0
H.S. Diplomas (#)	186	182	2	1	0	1

Johnston SD

10 Memorial Ave • Johnston, RI 02919
(401) 233-1900 • http://www.ri.net/schools/Johnston/johnston/
Grade Span: PK-12; **Agency Type:** 1
Schools: 9
7 Primary; 1 Middle; 1 High; 0 Other Level
9 Regular; 0 Special Education; 0 Vocational; 0 Alternative
0 Magnet; 0 Charter; 2 Title I Eligible; 0 School-wide Title I
Students: 3,285 (51.0% male; 48.9% female)
Individual Education Program: 872 (26.5%)
English Language Learner: 38 (1.2%); Migrant: n/a
Eligible for Free Lunch Program: 560 (17.1%)
Eligible for Reduced-Price Lunch Program: 218 (6.6%)
Teachers: 219.0 (15.0 to 1)
Librarians/Media Specialists: n/a
Guidance Counselors: n/a
Current Spending: ($ per student per year):
Total: $10,725; Instruction: $6,758; Support Services: $3,736
Enrollment, Drop-out Rates and Diploma Recipients by Race/Ethnicity

Category	Total	White	Black	Asian	AIAN	Hisp.
Enrollment (%)	100.0	91.0	2.5	1.6	0.3	4.6
Drop-out Rate (%)	1.8	1.9	0.0	0.0	n/a	0.0
H.S. Diplomas (#)	142	142	0	0	0	0

Lincoln SD

1624 Lonsdale Ave • Lincoln, RI 02865
(401) 726-2150 • http://158.123.229.10/
Grade Span: PK-12; **Agency Type:** 1
Schools: 8
6 Primary; 1 Middle; 1 High; 0 Other Level
8 Regular; 0 Special Education; 0 Vocational; 0 Alternative
0 Magnet; 0 Charter; 2 Title I Eligible; 0 School-wide Title I
Students: 3,649 (51.8% male; 48.1% female)
Individual Education Program: 762 (20.9%);
English Language Learner: 35 (1.0%); Migrant: n/a
Eligible for Free Lunch Program: 277 (7.6%)
Eligible for Reduced-Price Lunch Program: 79 (2.2%)
Teachers: 267.0 (13.6 to 1)
Librarians/Media Specialists: n/a
Guidance Counselors: n/a
Current Spending: ($ per student per year):
Total: $9,067; Instruction: $6,069; Support Services: $2,834
Enrollment, Drop-out Rates and Diploma Recipients by Race/Ethnicity

Category	Total	White	Black	Asian	AIAN	Hisp.
Enrollment (%)	100.0	93.0	1.6	2.6	0.1	2.7
Drop-out Rate (%)	0.4	0.4	0.0	0.0	0.0	0.0
H.S. Diplomas (#)	213	200	1	5	0	7

North Providence SD

9 George St • North Providence, RI 02911
(401) 233-1100
Grade Span: PK-12; **Agency Type:** 1
Schools: 9
6 Primary; 2 Middle; 1 High; 0 Other Level
9 Regular; 0 Special Education; 0 Vocational; 0 Alternative
0 Magnet; 0 Charter; 4 Title I Eligible; 0 School-wide Title I
Students: 3,473 (51.6% male; 48.3% female)
Individual Education Program: 679 (19.6%);
English Language Learner: 79 (2.3%); Migrant: n/a
Eligible for Free Lunch Program: 605 (17.4%)
Eligible for Reduced-Price Lunch Program: 204 (5.9%)
Teachers: 283.0 (12.3 to 1)
Librarians/Media Specialists: n/a
Guidance Counselors: n/a
Current Spending: ($ per student per year):
Total: $10,084; Instruction: $6,919; Support Services: $2,867
Enrollment, Drop-out Rates and Diploma Recipients by Race/Ethnicity

Category	Total	White	Black	Asian	AIAN	Hisp.
Enrollment (%)	100.0	83.4	5.3	1.7	0.4	9.2
Drop-out Rate (%)	3.5	3.7	0.0	0.0	0.0	4.5
H.S. Diplomas (#)	213	183	8	6	0	16

North Smithfield SD

450 Greenville Rd • North Smithfield, RI 02896
(401) 769-5492 • http://www.ri.net/schools/North_Smithfield/
Grade Span: PK-12; **Agency Type:** 1
Schools: 4
1 Primary; 2 Middle; 1 High; 0 Other Level
4 Regular; 0 Special Education; 0 Vocational; 0 Alternative
0 Magnet; 0 Charter; 0 Title I Eligible; 0 School-wide Title I
Students: 2,006 (50.4% male; 49.5% female)
Individual Education Program: 356 (17.7%);
English Language Learner: 0 (0.0%); Migrant: n/a
Eligible for Free Lunch Program: 106 (5.3%)
Eligible for Reduced-Price Lunch Program: 79 (3.9%)

Teachers: 141.0 (14.2 to 1)
Librarians/Media Specialists: n/a
Guidance Counselors: n/a
Current Spending: ($ per student per year):
    Total: $8,549; Instruction: $5,417; Support Services: $2,939
Enrollment, Drop-out Rates and Diploma Recipients by Race/Ethnicity

Category	Total	White	Black	Asian	AIAN	Hisp.
Enrollment (%)	100.0	97.9	0.7	0.6	0.0	0.7
Drop-out Rate (%)	1.5	1.5	0.0	0.0	0.0	0.0
H.S. Diplomas (#)	130	129	0	1	0	0

Pawtucket SD

Edward J. Creamer Admin Bldg • Pawtucket, RI 02860
Mailing Address: Park Place/PO Box 388 • Pawtucket, RI 02860
(401) 729-6315
Grade Span: PK-12; **Agency Type:** 1
Schools: 15
    10 Primary; 3 Middle; 2 High; 0 Other Level
    15 Regular; 0 Special Education; 0 Vocational; 0 Alternative
    0 Magnet; 0 Charter; 10 Title I Eligible; 3 School-wide Title I
Students: 9,654   (52.1% male; 47.8% female)
    Individual Education Program: 2,274 (23.6%);
    English Language Learner: 1,118 (11.6%); Migrant: n/a
    Eligible for Free Lunch Program: 5,261 (54.5%)
    Eligible for Reduced-Price Lunch Program: 954 (9.9%)
Teachers: 636.0 (15.2 to 1)
Librarians/Media Specialists: n/a
Guidance Counselors: n/a
Current Spending: ($ per student per year):
    Total: $8,699; Instruction: $5,585; Support Services: $2,810
Enrollment, Drop-out Rates and Diploma Recipients by Race/Ethnicity

Category	Total	White	Black	Asian	AIAN	Hisp.
Enrollment (%)	100.0	49.3	21.1	1.4	0.6	27.5
Drop-out Rate (%)	9.2	10.1	7.0	3.4	37.5	9.1
H.S. Diplomas (#)	394	191	117	2	6	78

Providence SD

797 Westminster St • Providence, RI 02903
(401) 456-9211 • http://www.providenceschools.org/
Grade Span: PK-12; **Agency Type:** 1
Schools: 54
    31 Primary; 9 Middle; 11 High; 3 Other Level
    47 Regular; 2 Special Education; 1 Vocational; 4 Alternative
    16 Magnet; 0 Charter; 34 Title I Eligible; 34 School-wide Title I
Students: 27,900   (50.8% male; 49.1% female)
    Individual Education Program: 5,373 (19.3%);
    English Language Learner: 5,204 (18.7%); Migrant: n/a
    Eligible for Free Lunch Program: 20,105 (73.5%)
    Eligible for Reduced-Price Lunch Program: 1,891 (6.9%)
Teachers: 1,779.0 (15.4 to 1)
Librarians/Media Specialists: n/a
Guidance Counselors: n/a
Current Spending: ($ per student per year):
    Total: $10,555; Instruction: $6,037; Support Services: $4,146
Enrollment, Drop-out Rates and Diploma Recipients by Race/Ethnicity

Category	Total	White	Black	Asian	AIAN	Hisp.
Enrollment (%)	100.0	14.2	22.1	7.6	0.7	55.4
Drop-out Rate (%)	8.2	8.3	7.3	6.6	6.3	9.1
H.S. Diplomas (#)	1,122	231	298	122	5	466

Scituate SD

197 Danielson Pike • North Scituate, RI 02857
Mailing Address: PO Box 188 • North Scituate, RI 02857
(401) 647-4100 • http://www.ScituateRI.net/
Grade Span: PK-12; **Agency Type:** 1
Schools: 5
    3 Primary; 1 Middle; 1 High; 0 Other Level
    5 Regular; 0 Special Education; 0 Vocational; 0 Alternative
    0 Magnet; 0 Charter; 2 Title I Eligible; 0 School-wide Title I
Students: 1,817   (50.0% male; 49.9% female)
    Individual Education Program: 320 (17.6%);
    English Language Learner: 0 (0.0%); Migrant: n/a
    Eligible for Free Lunch Program: 121 (6.7%)
    Eligible for Reduced-Price Lunch Program: 43 (2.4%)
Teachers: 149.0 (12.0 to 1)
Librarians/Media Specialists: n/a
Guidance Counselors: n/a
Current Spending: ($ per student per year):
    Total: $8,510; Instruction: $5,413; Support Services: $2,891
Enrollment, Drop-out Rates and Diploma Recipients by Race/Ethnicity

Category	Total	White	Black	Asian	AIAN	Hisp.
Enrollment (%)	100.0	98.2	0.4	0.8	0.1	0.5
Drop-out Rate (%)	2.3	2.4	0.0	0.0	n/a	0.0
H.S. Diplomas (#)	147	145	0	0	0	2

Smithfield SD

49 Farnum Pike • Esmond, RI 02917
(401) 231-6606 • http://shs.wsbe.org/
Grade Span: PK-12; **Agency Type:** 1
Schools: 6
    4 Primary; 1 Middle; 1 High; 0 Other Level
    6 Regular; 0 Special Education; 0 Vocational; 0 Alternative
    0 Magnet; 0 Charter; 1 Title I Eligible; 0 School-wide Title I
Students: 2,710   (52.1% male; 47.8% female)
    Individual Education Program: 521 (19.2%);
    English Language Learner: 8 (0.3%); Migrant: n/a
    Eligible for Free Lunch Program: 107 (3.9%)
    Eligible for Reduced-Price Lunch Program: 77 (2.8%)
Teachers: 219.0 (12.4 to 1)
Librarians/Media Specialists: n/a
Guidance Counselors: n/a
Current Spending: ($ per student per year):
    Total: $8,361; Instruction: $5,560; Support Services: $2,595
Enrollment, Drop-out Rates and Diploma Recipients by Race/Ethnicity

Category	Total	White	Black	Asian	AIAN	Hisp.
Enrollment (%)	100.0	97.9	0.5	1.0	0.0	0.6
Drop-out Rate (%)	2.0	2.1	0.0	0.0	n/a	0.0
H.S. Diplomas (#)	187	180	2	5	0	0

Woonsocket SD

108 High St • Woonsocket, RI 02895
(401) 767-4600 • http://woonsocketschools.com/
Grade Span: PK-12; **Agency Type:** 1
Schools: 12
    10 Primary; 1 Middle; 1 High; 0 Other Level
    12 Regular; 0 Special Education; 0 Vocational; 0 Alternative
    0 Magnet; 0 Charter; 9 Title I Eligible; 7 School-wide Title I
Students: 6,928   (52.1% male; 47.8% female)
    Individual Education Program: 1,651 (23.8%);
    English Language Learner: 397 (5.7%); Migrant: n/a
    Eligible for Free Lunch Program: 3,438 (49.7%)
    Eligible for Reduced-Price Lunch Program: 769 (11.1%)
Teachers: 499.0 (13.9 to 1)
Librarians/Media Specialists: n/a
Guidance Counselors: n/a
Current Spending: ($ per student per year):
    Total: $8,955; Instruction: $6,122; Support Services: $2,513
Enrollment, Drop-out Rates and Diploma Recipients by Race/Ethnicity

Category	Total	White	Black	Asian	AIAN	Hisp.
Enrollment (%)	100.0	63.9	8.6	7.4	0.4	19.7
Drop-out Rate (%)	8.4	8.4	6.5	6.1	0.0	11.4
H.S. Diplomas (#)	339	237	29	32	0	41

Washington County

Chariho RD

Switch Rd 455a • Wood River Junct., RI 02894
(401) 364-7575
Grade Span: PK-12; **Agency Type:** 1
Schools: 7
    4 Primary; 1 Middle; 1 High; 1 Other Level
    7 Regular; 0 Special Education; 0 Vocational; 0 Alternative
    0 Magnet; 0 Charter; 1 Title I Eligible; 0 School-wide Title I
Students: 3,863   (52.2% male; 47.7% female)
    Individual Education Program: 740 (19.2%);
    English Language Learner: 16 (0.4%); Migrant: n/a
    Eligible for Free Lunch Program: 326 (8.4%)
    Eligible for Reduced-Price Lunch Program: 189 (4.9%)
Teachers: 298.0 (13.0 to 1)
Librarians/Media Specialists: n/a
Guidance Counselors: n/a
Current Spending: ($ per student per year):
    Total: $10,112; Instruction: $6,566; Support Services: $3,327
Enrollment, Drop-out Rates and Diploma Recipients by Race/Ethnicity

Category	Total	White	Black	Asian	AIAN	Hisp.
Enrollment (%)	100.0	96.3	0.8	0.7	1.2	1.0
Drop-out Rate (%)	1.6	1.6	0.0	0.0	5.9	0.0
H.S. Diplomas (#)	280	271	1	2	5	1

Narragansett SD

25 Fifth Ave • Narragansett, RI 02882
(401) 792-9450 • http://www.narragansett.k12.ri.us/
Grade Span: PK-12; **Agency Type:** 1
Schools: 3
    1 Primary; 1 Middle; 1 High; 0 Other Level
    3 Regular; 0 Special Education; 0 Vocational; 0 Alternative
    0 Magnet; 0 Charter; 1 Title I Eligible; 0 School-wide Title I
Students: 1,673   (51.4% male; 48.5% female)
    Individual Education Program: 410 (24.5%);
    English Language Learner: 11 (0.7%); Migrant: n/a

Eligible for Free Lunch Program: 157 (9.4%)
Eligible for Reduced-Price Lunch Program: 54 (3.2%)
Teachers: 160.0 (10.5 to 1)
Librarians/Media Specialists: n/a
Guidance Counselors: n/a
Current Spending: ($ per student per year):
    Total: $12,618; Instruction: $8,139; Support Services: $4,257
Enrollment, Drop-out Rates and Diploma Recipients by Race/Ethnicity

Category	Total	White	Black	Asian	AIAN	Hisp.
Enrollment (%)	100.0	93.6	2.7	1.1	1.4	1.1
Drop-out Rate (%)	3.0	2.9	9.1	0.0	0.0	0.0
H.S. Diplomas (#)	120	117	1	2	0	0

North Kingstown SD
100 Fairway • North Kingstown, RI 02852
(401) 268-6403 • http://www.nksd.net/
Grade Span: PK-12; **Agency Type:** 1
Schools: 10
    7 Primary; 2 Middle; 1 High; 0 Other Level
    10 Regular; 0 Special Education; 0 Vocational; 0 Alternative
    0 Magnet; 0 Charter; 1 Title I Eligible; 0 School-wide Title I
Students: 4,626   (52.1% male; 47.8% female)
    Individual Education Program: 774 (16.7%);
    English Language Learner: 61 (1.3%); Migrant: n/a
    Eligible for Free Lunch Program: 418 (9.0%)
    Eligible for Reduced-Price Lunch Program: 119 (2.6%)
Teachers: 351.0 (13.2 to 1)
Librarians/Media Specialists: n/a
Guidance Counselors: n/a
Current Spending: ($ per student per year):
    Total: $9,716; Instruction: $5,845; Support Services: $3,608
Enrollment, Drop-out Rates and Diploma Recipients by Race/Ethnicity

Category	Total	White	Black	Asian	AIAN	Hisp.
Enrollment (%)	100.0	95.1	1.7	1.3	0.6	1.3
Drop-out Rate (%)	1.9	1.9	4.5	0.0	0.0	0.0
H.S. Diplomas (#)	316	302	5	4	0	5

South Kingstown SD
153 School St • Wakefield, RI 02879
(401) 792-9681 • http://www.skschools.net/
Grade Span: PK-12; **Agency Type:** 1
Schools: 10
    6 Primary; 2 Middle; 1 High; 1 Other Level
    9 Regular; 1 Special Education; 0 Vocational; 0 Alternative
    0 Magnet; 0 Charter; 1 Title I Eligible; 0 School-wide Title I
Students: 4,174   (52.0% male; 47.9% female)
    Individual Education Program: 943 (22.6%);
    English Language Learner: 39 (0.9%); Migrant: n/a
    Eligible for Free Lunch Program: 368 (8.8%)
    Eligible for Reduced-Price Lunch Program: 96 (2.3%)
Teachers: 271.0 (15.4 to 1)
Librarians/Media Specialists: n/a
Guidance Counselors: n/a
Current Spending: ($ per student per year):
    Total: $10,433; Instruction: $6,545; Support Services: $3,660
Enrollment, Drop-out Rates and Diploma Recipients by Race/Ethnicity

Category	Total	White	Black	Asian	AIAN	Hisp.
Enrollment (%)	100.0	90.0	3.1	2.8	2.8	1.4
Drop-out Rate (%)	2.4	2.4	3.1	2.4	5.3	0.0
H.S. Diplomas (#)	301	269	5	14	7	6

Westerly SD
44 Park Ave • Westerly, RI 02891
(401) 348-2700 • http://westerly.k12.ri.us/
Grade Span: PK-12; **Agency Type:** 1
Schools: 7
    5 Primary; 1 Middle; 1 High; 0 Other Level
    7 Regular; 0 Special Education; 0 Vocational; 0 Alternative
    0 Magnet; 0 Charter; 3 Title I Eligible; 0 School-wide Title I
Students: 3,710   (50.5% male; 49.4% female)
    Individual Education Program: 712 (19.2%);
    English Language Learner: 64 (1.7%); Migrant: n/a
    Eligible for Free Lunch Program: 552 (14.9%)
    Eligible for Reduced-Price Lunch Program: 235 (6.3%)
Teachers: 308.0 (12.0 to 1)
Librarians/Media Specialists: n/a
Guidance Counselors: n/a
Current Spending: ($ per student per year):
    Total: $10,467; Instruction: $6,588; Support Services: $3,632
Enrollment, Drop-out Rates and Diploma Recipients by Race/Ethnicity

Category	Total	White	Black	Asian	AIAN	Hisp.
Enrollment (%)	100.0	90.9	2.0	4.2	1.1	1.8
Drop-out Rate (%)	2.0	2.0	6.7	0.0	0.0	0.0
H.S. Diplomas (#)	229	214	4	8	0	3

Number of Schools

Rank	Number	District Name	City
1	54	Providence SD	Providence
2	26	Warwick SD	Warwick
3	25	Cranston SD	Cranston
4	15	Pawtucket SD	Pawtucket
5	13	East Providence SD	E Providence
6	12	Woonsocket SD	Woonsocket
7	10	Coventry SD	Coventry
7	10	Cumberland SD	Cumberland
7	10	North Kingstown SD	N Kingstown
7	10	South Kingstown SD	Wakefield
11	9	Bristol Warren RD	Bristol
11	9	Johnston SD	Johnston
11	9	North Providence SD	N Providence
14	8	Central Falls SD	Central Falls
14	8	Lincoln SD	Lincoln
14	8	Newport SD	Newport
17	7	Chariho RD	Wood River Jct
17	7	West Warwick SD	West Warwick
17	7	Westerly SD	Westerly
20	6	Barrington SD	Barrington
20	6	East Greenwich SD	East Greenwich
20	6	Middletown SD	Middletown
20	6	Portsmouth SD	Portsmouth
20	6	Smithfield SD	Esmond
25	5	Burrillville SD	Pascoag
25	5	Exeter-W Greenwich RD	West Greenwich
25	5	Scituate SD	North Scituate
25	5	Tiverton SD	Tiverton
29	4	North Smithfield SD	N Smithfield
30	3	Narragansett SD	Narragansett
31	2	Foster-Glocester RD	Chepachet

Number of Teachers

Rank	Number	District Name	City
1	1,779	Providence SD	Providence
2	1,035	Warwick SD	Warwick
3	862	Cranston SD	Cranston
4	636	Pawtucket SD	Pawtucket
5	504	East Providence SD	E Providence
6	499	Woonsocket SD	Woonsocket
7	427	Coventry SD	Coventry
8	414	Cumberland SD	Cumberland
9	351	North Kingstown SD	N Kingstown
10	333	Bristol Warren RD	Bristol
11	308	Westerly SD	Westerly
12	298	Chariho RD	Wood River Jct
13	283	North Providence SD	N Providence
14	280	West Warwick SD	West Warwick
15	271	South Kingstown SD	Wakefield
16	267	Lincoln SD	Lincoln
17	265	Central Falls SD	Central Falls
18	251	Barrington SD	Barrington
19	229	Newport SD	Newport
20	219	Johnston SD	Johnston
20	219	Smithfield SD	Esmond
22	205	Burrillville SD	Pascoag
23	204	Portsmouth SD	Portsmouth
24	197	Middletown SD	Middletown
25	195	Tiverton SD	Tiverton
26	193	East Greenwich SD	East Greenwich
27	182	Exeter-W Greenwich RD	West Greenwich
28	160	Narragansett SD	Narragansett
29	149	Scituate SD	North Scituate
30	141	North Smithfield SD	N Smithfield
31	123	Foster-Glocester RD	Chepachet

Number of Students

Rank	Number	District Name	City
1	27,900	Providence SD	Providence
2	11,993	Warwick SD	Warwick
3	11,222	Cranston SD	Cranston
4	9,654	Pawtucket SD	Pawtucket
5	6,928	Woonsocket SD	Woonsocket
6	6,386	East Providence SD	E Providence
7	5,862	Coventry SD	Coventry
8	5,349	Cumberland SD	Cumberland
9	4,626	North Kingstown SD	N Kingstown
10	4,174	South Kingstown SD	Wakefield
11	3,863	Chariho RD	Wood River Jct
12	3,838	West Warwick SD	West Warwick
13	3,734	Central Falls SD	Central Falls
14	3,710	Westerly SD	Westerly
15	3,688	Bristol Warren RD	Bristol
16	3,649	Lincoln SD	Lincoln
17	3,473	North Providence SD	N Providence
18	3,434	Barrington SD	Barrington
19	3,285	Johnston SD	Johnston
20	3,066	Portsmouth SD	Portsmouth
21	2,826	Newport SD	Newport
22	2,769	Middletown SD	Middletown
23	2,710	Smithfield SD	Esmond
24	2,590	Burrillville SD	Pascoag
25	2,466	East Greenwich SD	East Greenwich
26	2,224	Tiverton SD	Tiverton
27	2,204	Exeter-W Greenwich RD	West Greenwich
28	2,006	North Smithfield SD	N Smithfield
29	1,817	Scituate SD	North Scituate
30	1,693	Foster-Glocester RD	Chepachet
31	1,673	Narragansett SD	Narragansett

Male Students

Rank	Percent	District Name	City
1	52.5	Portsmouth SD	Portsmouth
2	52.5	Barrington SD	Barrington
3	52.4	Foster-Glocester RD	Chepachet
4	52.2	Bristol Warren RD	Bristol
5	52.2	Chariho RD	Wood River Jct
6	52.1	Pawtucket SD	Pawtucket
7	52.1	Smithfield SD	Esmond
8	52.1	North Kingstown SD	N Kingstown
9	52.1	Woonsocket SD	Woonsocket
10	52.1	Middletown SD	Middletown
11	52.0	South Kingstown SD	Wakefield
12	51.9	Warwick SD	Warwick
13	51.8	Lincoln SD	Lincoln
14	51.8	Cranston SD	Cranston
15	51.8	Cumberland SD	Cumberland
16	51.7	East Providence SD	E Providence
17	51.6	North Providence SD	N Providence
18	51.6	Newport SD	Newport
19	51.6	Tiverton SD	Tiverton
20	51.4	Narragansett SD	Narragansett
21	51.3	Central Falls SD	Central Falls
22	51.1	Coventry SD	Coventry
23	51.1	West Warwick SD	West Warwick
24	51.0	Johnston SD	Johnston
25	50.8	Providence SD	Providence
26	50.5	Burrillville SD	Pascoag
27	50.5	Westerly SD	Westerly
28	50.4	North Smithfield SD	N Smithfield
29	50.2	East Greenwich SD	East Greenwich
30	50.0	Scituate SD	North Scituate
31	49.3	Exeter-W Greenwich RD	West Greenwich

Female Students

Rank	Percent	District Name	City
1	50.6	Exeter-W Greenwich RD	West Greenwich
2	49.9	Scituate SD	North Scituate
3	49.7	East Greenwich SD	East Greenwich
4	49.5	North Smithfield SD	N Smithfield
5	49.4	Westerly SD	Westerly
6	49.4	Burrillville SD	Pascoag
7	49.1	Providence SD	Providence
8	48.9	Johnston SD	Johnston
9	48.8	West Warwick SD	West Warwick
10	48.8	Coventry SD	Coventry
11	48.6	Central Falls SD	Central Falls
12	48.5	Narragansett SD	Narragansett
13	48.3	Tiverton SD	Tiverton
14	48.3	Newport SD	Newport
15	48.3	North Providence SD	N Providence
16	48.2	East Providence SD	E Providence
17	48.1	Cumberland SD	Cumberland
18	48.1	Cranston SD	Cranston
19	48.1	Lincoln SD	Lincoln
20	48.0	Warwick SD	Warwick
21	47.9	South Kingstown SD	Wakefield
22	47.8	Middletown SD	Middletown
23	47.8	Woonsocket SD	Woonsocket
24	47.8	North Kingstown SD	N Kingstown
25	47.8	Smithfield SD	Esmond
26	47.8	Pawtucket SD	Pawtucket
27	47.7	Chariho RD	Wood River Jct
28	47.7	Bristol Warren RD	Bristol
29	47.5	Foster-Glocester RD	Chepachet
30	47.4	Barrington SD	Barrington
31	47.4	Portsmouth SD	Portsmouth

Individual Education Program Students

Rank	Percent	District Name	City
1	28.2	Newport SD	Newport
2	26.5	Johnston SD	Johnston
3	25.0	Central Falls SD	Central Falls
4	24.5	Narragansett SD	Narragansett
5	23.8	Woonsocket SD	Woonsocket
6	23.6	Cumberland SD	Cumberland
6	23.6	Pawtucket SD	Pawtucket
8	23.0	West Warwick SD	West Warwick

English Language Learner Students

Rank	Percent	District Name	City
1	28.7	Central Falls SD	Central Falls
2	18.7	Providence SD	Providence
3	11.6	Pawtucket SD	Pawtucket
4	5.7	Woonsocket SD	Woonsocket
5	4.7	East Providence SD	E Providence
6	4.1	Newport SD	Newport
7	3.8	Cranston SD	Cranston
8	3.7	Bristol Warren RD	Bristol
9	2.3	Cumberland SD	Cumberland
9	2.3	North Providence SD	N Providence
9	2.3	West Warwick SD	West Warwick
12	1.9	Middletown SD	Middletown
13	1.7	Westerly SD	Westerly
14	1.3	North Kingstown SD	N Kingstown
15	1.2	Johnston SD	Johnston
16	1.0	Lincoln SD	Lincoln
17	0.9	East Greenwich SD	East Greenwich
17	0.9	South Kingstown SD	Wakefield
19	0.8	Warwick SD	Warwick
20	0.7	Narragansett SD	Narragansett
21	0.5	Barrington SD	Barrington
22	0.4	Chariho RD	Wood River Jct
23	0.3	Exeter-W Greenwich RD	West Greenwich
23	0.3	Smithfield SD	Esmond
25	0.2	Coventry SD	Coventry
25	0.2	Portsmouth SD	Portsmouth
27	0.1	Burrillville SD	Pascoag
28	0.0	Foster-Glocester RD	Chepachet
28	0.0	North Smithfield SD	N Smithfield
28	0.0	Scituate SD	North Scituate
28	0.0	Tiverton SD	Tiverton

The following table to the right (of ranks 9-31) continues from above. This column also lists:

Rank	Percent	District Name	City
9	22.9	East Providence SD	E Providence
10	22.6	South Kingstown SD	Wakefield
11	22.5	Bristol Warren RD	Bristol
11	22.5	Tiverton SD	Tiverton
13	22.1	Middletown SD	Middletown
14	21.4	Cranston SD	Cranston
14	21.4	Warwick SD	Warwick
16	21.0	Burrillville SD	Pascoag
17	20.9	Lincoln SD	Lincoln
18	20.6	Coventry SD	Coventry
19	19.6	North Providence SD	N Providence
20	19.3	Providence SD	Providence
21	19.2	Chariho RD	Wood River Jct
21	19.2	Smithfield SD	Esmond
21	19.2	Westerly SD	Westerly
24	19.0	Exeter-W Greenwich RD	West Greenwich
25	18.2	East Greenwich SD	East Greenwich
25	18.2	Portsmouth SD	Portsmouth
27	17.9	Barrington SD	Barrington
28	17.7	North Smithfield SD	N Smithfield
29	17.6	Scituate SD	North Scituate
30	16.7	North Kingstown SD	N Kingstown
31	13.6	Foster-Glocester RD	Chepachet

Migrant Students

Rank	Percent	District Name	City
1	n/a	Barrington SD	Barrington
1	n/a	Bristol Warren RD	Bristol
1	n/a	Burrillville SD	Pascoag
1	n/a	Central Falls SD	Central Falls
1	n/a	Chariho RD	Wood River Jct
1	n/a	Coventry SD	Coventry
1	n/a	Cranston SD	Cranston
1	n/a	Cumberland SD	Cumberland
1	n/a	East Greenwich SD	East Greenwich
1	n/a	East Providence SD	E Providence
1	n/a	Exeter-W Greenwich RD	West Greenwich
1	n/a	Foster-Glocester RD	Chepachet
1	n/a	Johnston SD	Johnston
1	n/a	Lincoln SD	Lincoln
1	n/a	Middletown SD	Middletown
1	n/a	Narragansett SD	Narragansett
1	n/a	Newport SD	Newport
1	n/a	North Kingstown SD	N Kingstown
1	n/a	North Providence SD	N Providence
1	n/a	North Smithfield SD	N Smithfield
1	n/a	Pawtucket SD	Pawtucket
1	n/a	Portsmouth SD	Portsmouth
1	n/a	Providence SD	Providence
1	n/a	Scituate SD	North Scituate
1	n/a	Smithfield SD	Esmond
1	n/a	South Kingstown SD	Wakefield
1	n/a	Tiverton SD	Tiverton
1	n/a	Warwick SD	Warwick
1	n/a	West Warwick SD	West Warwick
1	n/a	Westerly SD	Westerly
1	n/a	Woonsocket SD	Woonsocket

Students Eligible for Free Lunch

Rank	Percent	District Name	City
1	73.5	Providence SD	Providence
2	69.2	Central Falls SD	Central Falls
3	54.5	Pawtucket SD	Pawtucket
4	49.7	Woonsocket SD	Woonsocket
5	40.8	Newport SD	Newport
6	25.0	West Warwick SD	West Warwick
7	22.0	East Providence SD	E Providence
8	17.4	North Providence SD	N Providence
9	17.1	Johnston SD	Johnston
10	16.5	Cranston SD	Cranston
11	16.4	Bristol Warren RD	Bristol
12	14.9	Westerly SD	Westerly
13	13.4	Warwick SD	Warwick
14	12.9	Burrillville SD	Pascoag
15	10.9	Coventry SD	Coventry
16	10.0	Middletown SD	Middletown
17	9.8	Tiverton SD	Tiverton
18	9.4	Narragansett SD	Narragansett
19	9.0	North Kingstown SD	N Kingstown
20	8.8	South Kingstown SD	Wakefield
21	8.4	Chariho RD	Wood River Jct
22	8.3	Cumberland SD	Cumberland
23	7.6	Lincoln SD	Lincoln
24	6.7	Foster-Glocester RD	Chepachet
24	6.7	Scituate SD	North Scituate
26	6.5	Exeter-W Greenwich RD	West Greenwich
27	5.3	North Smithfield SD	N Smithfield
28	5.0	East Greenwich SD	East Greenwich
29	3.9	Portsmouth SD	Portsmouth
29	3.9	Smithfield SD	Esmond
31	1.8	Barrington SD	Barrington

Students Eligible for Reduced-Price Lunch

Rank	Percent	District Name	City
1	13.5	Central Falls SD	Central Falls
2	11.1	Woonsocket SD	Woonsocket
3	9.9	Pawtucket SD	Pawtucket
4	9.5	East Providence SD	E Providence
5	8.1	Bristol Warren RD	Bristol
5	8.1	West Warwick SD	West Warwick
7	7.5	Middletown SD	Middletown
8	7.4	Burrillville SD	Pascoag
9	6.9	Providence SD	Providence
10	6.6	Johnston SD	Johnston
11	6.3	Newport SD	Newport
11	6.3	Westerly SD	Westerly
13	6.0	Warwick SD	Warwick
14	5.9	North Providence SD	N Providence
15	5.4	Coventry SD	Coventry
16	5.0	Cranston SD	Cranston
17	4.9	Chariho RD	Wood River Jct
18	4.5	Tiverton SD	Tiverton
19	3.9	Cumberland SD	Cumberland
19	3.9	North Smithfield SD	N Smithfield
21	3.4	Exeter-W Greenwich RD	West Greenwich
22	3.2	Narragansett SD	Narragansett
23	2.9	Portsmouth SD	Portsmouth
24	2.8	Smithfield SD	Esmond
25	2.7	Foster-Glocester RD	Chepachet
26	2.6	North Kingstown SD	N Kingstown
27	2.4	Scituate SD	North Scituate
28	2.3	South Kingstown SD	Wakefield
29	2.2	Lincoln SD	Lincoln
30	0.7	Barrington SD	Barrington
31	0.5	East Greenwich SD	East Greenwich

Student/Teacher Ratio

Rank	Ratio	District Name	City
1	15.4	Providence SD	Providence
1	15.4	South Kingstown SD	Wakefield
3	15.2	Pawtucket SD	Pawtucket
4	15.0	Johnston SD	Johnston
4	15.0	Portsmouth SD	Portsmouth
6	14.2	North Smithfield SD	N Smithfield
7	14.1	Middletown SD	Middletown
8	13.9	Woonsocket SD	Woonsocket
9	13.7	Barrington SD	Barrington
9	13.7	Central Falls SD	Central Falls
9	13.7	Foster-Glocester RD	Chepachet
9	13.7	West Warwick SD	West Warwick
13	13.6	Lincoln SD	Lincoln
14	13.2	North Kingstown SD	N Kingstown
15	13.0	Chariho RD	Wood River Jct
15	13.0	Cranston SD	Cranston
17	12.9	Cumberland SD	Cumberland
18	12.7	East Providence SD	E Providence
19	12.6	Burrillville SD	Pascoag
20	12.4	Smithfield SD	Esmond

Rank			
21	12.3	North Providence SD	N Providence
22	12.1	Newport SD	Newport
23	12.0	Exeter-W Greenwich RD	West Greenwich
23	12.0	Scituate SD	North Scituate
23	12.0	Westerly SD	Westerly
26	11.7	Coventry SD	Coventry
27	11.6	Warwick SD	Warwick
28	11.4	Tiverton SD	Tiverton
29	11.1	Bristol Warren RD	Bristol
29	11.1	East Greenwich SD	East Greenwich
31	10.5	Narragansett SD	Narragansett

Student/Librarian Ratio

Rank	Ratio	District Name	City
1	n/a	Barrington SD	Barrington
1	n/a	Bristol Warren RD	Bristol
1	n/a	Burrillville SD	Pascoag
1	n/a	Central Falls SD	Central Falls
1	n/a	Chariho RD	Wood River Jct
1	n/a	Coventry SD	Coventry
1	n/a	Cranston SD	Cranston
1	n/a	Cumberland SD	Cumberland
1	n/a	East Greenwich SD	East Greenwich
1	n/a	East Providence SD	E Providence
1	n/a	Exeter-W Greenwich RD	West Greenwich
1	n/a	Foster-Glocester RD	Chepachet
1	n/a	Johnston SD	Johnston
1	n/a	Lincoln SD	Lincoln
1	n/a	Middletown SD	Middletown
1	n/a	Narragansett SD	Narragansett
1	n/a	Newport SD	Newport
1	n/a	North Kingstown SD	N Kingstown
1	n/a	North Providence SD	N Providence
1	n/a	North Smithfield SD	N Smithfield
1	n/a	Pawtucket SD	Pawtucket
1	n/a	Portsmouth SD	Portsmouth
1	n/a	Providence SD	Providence
1	n/a	Scituate SD	North Scituate
1	n/a	Smithfield SD	Esmond
1	n/a	South Kingstown SD	Wakefield
1	n/a	Tiverton SD	Tiverton
1	n/a	Warwick SD	Warwick
1	n/a	West Warwick SD	West Warwick
1	n/a	Westerly SD	Westerly
1	n/a	Woonsocket SD	Woonsocket

Student/Counselor Ratio

Rank	Ratio	District Name	City
1	n/a	Barrington SD	Barrington
1	n/a	Bristol Warren RD	Bristol
1	n/a	Burrillville SD	Pascoag
1	n/a	Central Falls SD	Central Falls
1	n/a	Chariho RD	Wood River Jct
1	n/a	Coventry SD	Coventry
1	n/a	Cranston SD	Cranston
1	n/a	Cumberland SD	Cumberland
1	n/a	East Greenwich SD	East Greenwich
1	n/a	East Providence SD	E Providence
1	n/a	Exeter-W Greenwich RD	West Greenwich
1	n/a	Foster-Glocester RD	Chepachet
1	n/a	Johnston SD	Johnston
1	n/a	Lincoln SD	Lincoln
1	n/a	Middletown SD	Middletown
1	n/a	Narragansett SD	Narragansett
1	n/a	Newport SD	Newport
1	n/a	North Kingstown SD	N Kingstown
1	n/a	North Providence SD	N Providence
1	n/a	North Smithfield SD	N Smithfield
1	n/a	Pawtucket SD	Pawtucket
1	n/a	Portsmouth SD	Portsmouth
1	n/a	Providence SD	Providence
1	n/a	Scituate SD	North Scituate
1	n/a	Smithfield SD	Esmond
1	n/a	South Kingstown SD	Wakefield
1	n/a	Tiverton SD	Tiverton
1	n/a	Warwick SD	Warwick
1	n/a	West Warwick SD	West Warwick
1	n/a	Westerly SD	Westerly
1	n/a	Woonsocket SD	Woonsocket

Current Spending per Student in FY2003

Rank	Dollars	District Name	City
1	12,618	Narragansett SD	Narragansett
2	11,949	Newport SD	Newport
3	10,992	Warwick SD	Warwick
4	10,725	Johnston SD	Johnston
5	10,706	Central Falls SD	Central Falls
6	10,659	Bristol Warren RD	Bristol
7	10,555	Providence SD	Providence
8	10,467	Westerly SD	Westerly
9	10,433	South Kingstown SD	Wakefield
10	10,421	Middletown SD	Middletown
11	10,192	East Greenwich SD	East Greenwich
12	10,112	Chariho RD	Wood River Jct
13	10,084	North Providence SD	N Providence
14	9,973	West Warwick SD	West Warwick
15	9,716	North Kingstown SD	N Kingstown
16	9,701	East Providence SD	E Providence
17	9,472	Burrillville SD	Pascoag
18	9,438	Exeter-W Greenwich RD	West Greenwich
19	9,272	Coventry SD	Coventry
20	9,067	Lincoln SD	Lincoln
21	8,955	Woonsocket SD	Woonsocket
22	8,843	Barrington SD	Barrington
23	8,699	Pawtucket SD	Pawtucket
24	8,693	Cranston SD	Cranston
25	8,549	North Smithfield SD	N Smithfield
26	8,512	Tiverton SD	Tiverton
27	8,510	Scituate SD	North Scituate
28	8,438	Portsmouth SD	Portsmouth
29	8,372	Foster-Glocester RD	Chepachet
30	8,361	Smithfield SD	Esmond
31	7,474	Cumberland SD	Cumberland

Number of Diploma Recipients

Rank	Number	District Name	City
1	1,122	Providence SD	Providence
2	782	Warwick SD	Warwick
3	707	Cranston SD	Cranston
4	419	East Providence SD	E Providence
5	394	Pawtucket SD	Pawtucket
6	380	Coventry SD	Coventry
7	339	Woonsocket SD	Woonsocket
8	316	North Kingstown SD	N Kingstown
9	304	Cumberland SD	Cumberland
10	301	South Kingstown SD	Wakefield
11	280	Chariho RD	Wood River Jct
12	229	Westerly SD	Westerly
13	213	Lincoln SD	Lincoln
13	213	North Providence SD	N Providence
15	210	West Warwick SD	West Warwick
16	206	Barrington SD	Barrington
17	205	Bristol Warren RD	Bristol
18	187	Burrillville SD	Pascoag
18	187	Smithfield SD	Esmond
20	186	Foster-Glocester RD	Chepachet
21	184	Portsmouth SD	Portsmouth
22	169	Central Falls SD	Central Falls
22	169	Middletown SD	Middletown
24	168	Newport SD	Newport
25	147	Scituate SD	North Scituate
26	146	East Greenwich SD	East Greenwich
27	142	Johnston SD	Johnston
28	136	Tiverton SD	Tiverton
29	130	North Smithfield SD	N Smithfield
30	128	Exeter-W Greenwich RD	West Greenwich
31	120	Narragansett SD	Narragansett

High School Drop-out Rate

Rank	Percent	District Name	City
1	9.2	Pawtucket SD	Pawtucket
2	8.8	Central Falls SD	Central Falls
3	8.4	Woonsocket SD	Woonsocket
4	8.2	Providence SD	Providence
5	5.9	West Warwick SD	West Warwick
6	5.5	East Providence SD	E Providence
7	5.2	Bristol Warren RD	Bristol
8	4.3	Newport SD	Newport
9	4.1	Cranston SD	Cranston
10	3.5	Burrillville SD	Pascoag
10	3.5	North Providence SD	N Providence
12	3.3	Tiverton SD	Tiverton
13	3.0	Narragansett SD	Narragansett
14	2.7	Foster-Glocester RD	Chepachet
15	2.5	Coventry SD	Coventry
16	2.4	South Kingstown SD	Wakefield
17	2.3	Barrington SD	Barrington
17	2.3	Middletown SD	Middletown
17	2.3	Scituate SD	North Scituate
20	2.0	Smithfield SD	Esmond
20	2.0	Westerly SD	Westerly
22	1.9	North Kingstown SD	N Kingstown
22	1.9	Warwick SD	Warwick
24	1.8	Exeter-W Greenwich RD	West Greenwich
24	1.8	Johnston SD	Johnston
26	1.7	Cumberland SD	Cumberland
27	1.6	Chariho RD	Wood River Jct
28	1.5	North Smithfield SD	N Smithfield
29	0.9	East Greenwich SD	East Greenwich
30	0.7	Portsmouth SD	Portsmouth
31	0.4	Lincoln SD	Lincoln

South Carolina

South Carolina Public School Educational Profile

Category	Value	Category	Value
Schools *(2003-2004)*	1,162	**Diploma Recipients** *(2002-2003)*	31,302
Instructional Level		White, Non-Hispanic	n/a
Primary	626	Black, Non-Hispanic	n/a
Middle	255	Asian/Pacific Islander	n/a
High	251	American Indian/Alaskan Native	n/a
Other Level	29	Hispanic	n/a
Curriculum		**High School Drop-out Rate** *(%) (2001-2002)*	3.3
Regular	1,092	White, Non-Hispanic	3.1
Special Education	10	Black, Non-Hispanic	3.7
Vocational	40	Asian/Pacific Islander	1.7
Alternative	19	American Indian/Alaskan Native	3.1
Type		Hispanic	3.9
Magnet	60	**Staff** *(2003-2004)*	
Charter	18	Teachers	45,819.5
Title I Eligible	551	Average Salary ($)	41,162
School-wide Title I	502	Librarians/Media Specialists	1,135.4
Students *(2003-2004)*	699,198	Guidance Counselors	1,698.9
Gender (%)		**Ratios** *(2003-2004)*	
Male	51.2	Student/Teacher Ratio	15.3 to 1
Female	48.8	Student/Librarian Ratio	615.8 to 1
Race/Ethnicity (%)		Student/Counselor Ratio	411.6 to 1
White, Non-Hispanic	53.9	**College Entrance Exam Scores** *(2005)*	
Black, Non-Hispanic	41.1	Scholastic Aptitude Test (SAT)	
Asian/Pacific Islander	1.1	Participation Rate (%)	64
American Indian/Alaskan Native	0.3	Mean SAT Reasoning Test Verbal Score	494
Hispanic	3.1	Mean SAT Reasoning Test Math Score	499
Classification (%)		American College Testing Program (ACT)	
Individual Education Program (IEP)	15.7	Participation Rate (%)	38
Migrant *(2002-2003)*	0.0	Average Composite Score	19.4
English Language Learner (ELL)	1.5	Average English Score	18.8
Eligible for Free Lunch Program	43.3	Average Math Score	19.3
Eligible for Reduced-Price Lunch Program	7.7	Average Reading Score	19.6
Current Spending *($ per student in FY 2003)*	7,022	Average Science Score	19.3
Instruction	4,158		
Support Services	2,489		

Note: For an explanation of data, please refer to the User's Guide in the front of the book

South Carolina NAEP 2005 Test Scores

Reading			Mathematics		
Grade/Category	Value	Rank	Grade/Category	Value	Rank
4th Grade			**4th Grade**		
Average Proficiency	213.2 (1.33)	41/51	Average Proficiency	238.3 (0.88)	28/51
Proficiency by Gender/Race/Ethnicity			Proficiency by Gender/Race/Ethnicity		
Male	209.9 (1.41)	40/51	Male	238.4 (1.15)	32/51
Female	216.6 (1.66)	41/51	Female	238.2 (0.93)	23/51
White, Non-Hispanic	224.6 (1.69)	37/51	White, Non-Hispanic	249.6 (0.95)	9/51
Black, Non-Hispanic	197.4 (1.39)	23/42	Black, Non-Hispanic	223.3 (0.96)	13/42
Asian, Non-Hispanic	n/a	n/a	Asian, Non-Hispanic	n/a	n/a
American Indian, Non-Hispanic	n/a	n/a	American Indian, Non-Hispanic	n/a	n/a
Hispanic	215.3 (4.36)	4/40	Hispanic	235.7 (2.30)	1/41
Proficiency by Class Size			Proficiency by Class Size		
Less than 16 Students	n/a	n/a	Less than 16 Students	n/a	n/a
16 to 18 Students	n/a	n/a	16 to 18 Students	n/a	n/a
19 to 20 Students	209.1 (2.16)	35/38	19 to 20 Students	237.7 (2.09)	26/38
21 to 25 Students	217.7 (1.80)	38/51	21 to 25 Students	240.6 (1.27)	28/51
Greater than 25 Students	n/a	n/a	Greater than 25 Students	n/a	n/a
Percent Attaining Achievement Levels			Percent Attaining Achievement Levels		
Below Basic	42.6 (1.73)	10/51	Below Basic	18.5 (1.12)	26/51
Basic or Above	57.4 (1.73)	42/51	Basic or Above	81.5 (1.12)	26/51
Proficient or Above	25.6 (1.28)	40/51	Proficient or Above	35.9 (1.50)	32/51
Advanced or Above	5.8 (0.72)	38/51	Advanced or Above	4.7 (0.62)	24/51
8th Grade			**8th Grade**		
Average Proficiency	257.2 (1.06)	39/51	Average Proficiency	281.2 (0.88)	20/51
Proficiency by Gender/Race/Ethnicity			Proficiency by Gender/Race/Ethnicity		
Male	251.7 (1.34)	38/51	Male	281.7 (1.18)	22/51
Female	262.2 (1.22)	40/51	Female	280.8 (1.08)	20/51
White, Non-Hispanic	266.8 (1.38)	35/51	White, Non-Hispanic	294.2 (0.92)	6/51
Black, Non-Hispanic	242.5 (1.28)	19/40	Black, Non-Hispanic	262.6 (1.26)	7/41
Asian, Non-Hispanic	n/a	n/a	Asian, Non-Hispanic	n/a	n/a
American Indian, Non-Hispanic	n/a	n/a	American Indian, Non-Hispanic	n/a	n/a
Hispanic	n/a	n/a	Hispanic	268.9 (4.42)	4/38
Proficiency by Parents Highest Level of Ed.			Proficiency by Parents Highest Level of Ed.		
Did Not Finish High School	244.5 (3.13)	27/49	Did Not Finish High School	269.6 (2.75)	3/50
Graduated High School	248.2 (1.74)	39/50	Graduated High School	272.9 (1.80)	12/50
Some Education After High School	263.3 (1.68)	34/50	Some Education After High School	284.5 (1.99)	13/50
Graduated College	263.5 (1.34)	41/50	Graduated College	289.3 (1.15)	28/50
Percent Attaining Achievement Levels			Percent Attaining Achievement Levels		
Below Basic	42.6 (1.73)	10/51	Below Basic	28.6 (1.35)	27/51
Basic or Above	57.4 (1.73)	42/51	Basic or Above	71.4 (1.35)	25/51
Proficient or Above	25.6 (1.28)	40/51	Proficient or Above	29.9 (0.88)	25/51
Advanced or Above	5.8 (0.72)	38/51	Advanced or Above	6.7 (0.71)	11/51

Note: *For an explanation of data, please refer to the User's Guide in the front of the book; n/a indicates data not available*

Abbeville County

Abbeville County SD
400 Greenville St • Abbeville, SC 29620-1556
(864) 459-5427 • http://www.acsd.k12.sc.us
Grade Span: PK-12; **Agency Type:** 1
Schools: 11
    5 Primary; 1 Middle; 3 High; 2 Other Level
    10 Regular; 0 Special Education; 1 Vocational; 0 Alternative
    0 Magnet; 1 Charter; 7 Title I Eligible; 7 School-wide Title I
Students: 3,812   (51.9% male; 48.0% female)
    Individual Education Program: 648 (17.0%);
    English Language Learner: 46 (1.2%); Migrant: n/a
    Eligible for Free Lunch Program: 2,094 (54.9%)
    Eligible for Reduced-Price Lunch Program: 291 (7.6%)
Teachers: 262.1 (14.5 to 1)
Librarians/Media Specialists: 9.0 (423.6 to 1)
Guidance Counselors: 9.5 (401.3 to 1)
Current Spending: ($ per student per year):
    Total: $6,883; Instruction: $4,214; Support Services: $2,232
Enrollment, Drop-out Rates and Diploma Recipients by Race/Ethnicity

Category	Total	White	Black	Asian	AIAN	Hisp.
Enrollment (%)	100.0	56.8	41.6	0.4	0.0	1.0
Drop-out Rate (%)	4.5	4.7	4.2	n/a	n/a	0.0
H.S. Diplomas (#)	171	n/a	n/a	n/a	n/a	n/a

Aiken County

Aiken County SD
1000 Brookhaven Dr • Aiken, SC 29803-1137
(803) 641-2700 • http://www.aiken.k12.sc.us
Grade Span: PK-12; **Agency Type:** 1
Schools: 39
    20 Primary; 11 Middle; 8 High; 0 Other Level
    38 Regular; 0 Special Education; 1 Vocational; 0 Alternative
    0 Magnet; 2 Charter; 25 Title I Eligible; 25 School-wide Title I
Students: 25,333   (50.9% male; 49.0% female)
    Individual Education Program: 3,536 (14.0%);
    English Language Learner: 357 (1.4%); Migrant: n/a
    Eligible for Free Lunch Program: 11,191 (44.2%)
    Eligible for Reduced-Price Lunch Program: 1,721 (6.8%)
Teachers: 1,544.3 (16.4 to 1)
Librarians/Media Specialists: 39.6 (639.7 to 1)
Guidance Counselors: 53.1 (477.1 to 1)
Current Spending: ($ per student per year):
    Total: $6,281; Instruction: $3,951; Support Services: $2,028
Enrollment, Drop-out Rates and Diploma Recipients by Race/Ethnicity

Category	Total	White	Black	Asian	AIAN	Hisp.
Enrollment (%)	100.0	59.9	35.6	0.7	0.3	3.3
Drop-out Rate (%)	3.2	3.2	3.2	0.0	0.0	0.8
H.S. Diplomas (#)	1,218	n/a	n/a	n/a	n/a	n/a

Allendale County

Allendale County SD
PO Box 458 • Allendale, SC 29810-0458
(803) 584-4603 • http://www.acs.k12.sc.us/
Grade Span: PK-12; **Agency Type:** 1
Schools: 4
    2 Primary; 1 Middle; 1 High; 0 Other Level
    4 Regular; 0 Special Education; 0 Vocational; 0 Alternative
    0 Magnet; 0 Charter; 3 Title I Eligible; 3 School-wide Title I
Students: 1,873   (51.2% male; 48.7% female)
    Individual Education Program: 406 (21.7%);
    English Language Learner: 10 (0.5%); Migrant: n/a
    Eligible for Free Lunch Program: 1,479 (79.0%)
    Eligible for Reduced-Price Lunch Program: 93 (5.0%)
Teachers: 145.0 (12.9 to 1)
Librarians/Media Specialists: 4.0 (468.3 to 1)
Guidance Counselors: 5.0 (374.6 to 1)
Current Spending: ($ per student per year):
    Total: $10,126; Instruction: $5,227; Support Services: $4,266
Enrollment, Drop-out Rates and Diploma Recipients by Race/Ethnicity

Category	Total	White	Black	Asian	AIAN	Hisp.
Enrollment (%)	100.0	3.0	95.5	0.2	0.0	1.2
Drop-out Rate (%)	1.9	3.2	1.9	0.0	n/a	0.0
H.S. Diplomas (#)	78	n/a	n/a	n/a	n/a	n/a

Anderson County

Anderson County SD 01
Box 99 • Williamston, SC 29697-0099
(864) 847-7344 • http://www.anderson1.k12.sc.us
Grade Span: PK-12; **Agency Type:** 1
Schools: 15

    10 Primary; 3 Middle; 2 High; 0 Other Level
    15 Regular; 0 Special Education; 0 Vocational; 0 Alternative
    0 Magnet; 0 Charter; 3 Title I Eligible; 3 School-wide Title I
Students: 8,314   (51.6% male; 48.3% female)
    Individual Education Program: 1,184 (14.2%);
    English Language Learner: 129 (1.6%); Migrant: n/a
    Eligible for Free Lunch Program: 2,196 (26.4%)
    Eligible for Reduced-Price Lunch Program: 649 (7.8%)
Teachers: 461.2 (18.0 to 1)
Librarians/Media Specialists: 15.0 (554.3 to 1)
Guidance Counselors: 17.5 (475.1 to 1)
Current Spending: ($ per student per year):
    Total: $6,093; Instruction: $3,615; Support Services: $2,183
Enrollment, Drop-out Rates and Diploma Recipients by Race/Ethnicity

Category	Total	White	Black	Asian	AIAN	Hisp.
Enrollment (%)	100.0	88.9	7.7	0.6	0.2	2.4
Drop-out Rate (%)	3.2	3.3	1.9	0.0	n/a	0.0
H.S. Diplomas (#)	380	n/a	n/a	n/a	n/a	n/a

Anderson County SD 02
PO Box 266 • Honea Path, SC 29654-0266
(843) 369-7364 • http://www.anderson2.k12.sc.us
Grade Span: PK-12; **Agency Type:** 1
Schools: 7
    4 Primary; 2 Middle; 1 High; 0 Other Level
    7 Regular; 0 Special Education; 0 Vocational; 0 Alternative
    0 Magnet; 0 Charter; 5 Title I Eligible; 5 School-wide Title I
Students: 3,795   (51.5% male; 48.4% female)
    Individual Education Program: 818 (21.6%);
    English Language Learner: 17 (0.4%); Migrant: n/a
    Eligible for Free Lunch Program: 1,257 (33.1%)
    Eligible for Reduced-Price Lunch Program: 287 (7.6%)
Teachers: 215.1 (17.6 to 1)
Librarians/Media Specialists: 7.0 (542.1 to 1)
Guidance Counselors: 9.0 (421.7 to 1)
Current Spending: ($ per student per year):
    Total: $6,729; Instruction: $4,120; Support Services: $2,261
Enrollment, Drop-out Rates and Diploma Recipients by Race/Ethnicity

Category	Total	White	Black	Asian	AIAN	Hisp.
Enrollment (%)	100.0	78.9	19.4	0.4	0.0	1.2
Drop-out Rate (%)	4.1	4.2	3.9	0.0	n/a	0.0
H.S. Diplomas (#)	177	n/a	n/a	n/a	n/a	n/a

Anderson County SD 03
Box 118 • Iva, SC 29655-0118
(864) 348-6196 • http://www.anderson3.k12.sc.us
Grade Span: PK-12; **Agency Type:** 1
Schools: 4
    2 Primary; 1 Middle; 1 High; 0 Other Level
    4 Regular; 0 Special Education; 0 Vocational; 0 Alternative
    0 Magnet; 0 Charter; 2 Title I Eligible; 2 School-wide Title I
Students: 2,737   (51.3% male; 48.6% female)
    Individual Education Program: 548 (20.0%);
    English Language Learner: 3 (0.1%); Migrant: n/a
    Eligible for Free Lunch Program: 1,221 (44.6%)
    Eligible for Reduced-Price Lunch Program: 251 (9.2%)
Teachers: 163.6 (16.7 to 1)
Librarians/Media Specialists: 4.0 (684.3 to 1)
Guidance Counselors: 5.0 (547.4 to 1)
Current Spending: ($ per student per year):
    Total: $6,218; Instruction: $3,744; Support Services: $2,050
Enrollment, Drop-out Rates and Diploma Recipients by Race/Ethnicity

Category	Total	White	Black	Asian	AIAN	Hisp.
Enrollment (%)	100.0	85.8	13.4	0.2	0.1	0.4
Drop-out Rate (%)	5.0	4.7	7.4	n/a	0.0	n/a
H.S. Diplomas (#)	106	n/a	n/a	n/a	n/a	n/a

Anderson County SD 04
Box 545 • Pendleton, SC 29670-0545
(864) 646-8000 • http://www.anderson4.k12.sc.us
Grade Span: PK-12; **Agency Type:** 1
Schools: 5
    3 Primary; 1 Middle; 1 High; 0 Other Level
    5 Regular; 0 Special Education; 0 Vocational; 0 Alternative
    0 Magnet; 0 Charter; 2 Title I Eligible; 2 School-wide Title I
Students: 2,891   (51.3% male; 48.6% female)
    Individual Education Program: 438 (15.2%);
    English Language Learner: 10 (0.3%); Migrant: n/a
    Eligible for Free Lunch Program: 939 (32.5%)
    Eligible for Reduced-Price Lunch Program: 276 (9.5%)
Teachers: 187.9 (15.4 to 1)
Librarians/Media Specialists: 5.0 (578.2 to 1)
Guidance Counselors: 8.5 (340.1 to 1)
Current Spending: ($ per student per year):
    Total: $6,954; Instruction: $3,985; Support Services: $2,544

Enrollment, Drop-out Rates and Diploma Recipients by Race/Ethnicity

Category	Total	White	Black	Asian	AIAN	Hisp.
Enrollment (%)	100.0	77.0	21.8	0.3	0.1	0.7
Drop-out Rate (%)	0.8	0.0	3.4	0.0	n/a	0.0
H.S. Diplomas (#)	99	n/a	n/a	n/a	n/a	n/a

Anderson County SD 05
Box 439 • Anderson, SC 29622-0439
(864) 260-5000 • http://www.anderson5.net
Grade Span: PK-12; **Agency Type:** 1
Schools: 17
  12 Primary; 3 Middle; 2 High; 0 Other Level
  17 Regular; 0 Special Education; 0 Vocational; 0 Alternative
  0 Magnet; 0 Charter; 3 Title I Eligible; 3 School-wide Title I
Students: 11,943   (50.8% male; 49.1% female)
  Individual Education Program: 2,023 (16.9%);
  English Language Learner: 66 (0.6%); Migrant: n/a
  Eligible for Free Lunch Program: 4,880 (40.9%)
  Eligible for Reduced-Price Lunch Program: 851 (7.1%)
Teachers: 790.0 (15.1 to 1)
Librarians/Media Specialists: 17.0 (702.5 to 1)
Guidance Counselors: 36.5 (327.2 to 1)
Current Spending: ($ per student per year):
  Total: $7,046; Instruction: $4,275; Support Services: $2,431
Enrollment, Drop-out Rates and Diploma Recipients by Race/Ethnicity

Category	Total	White	Black	Asian	AIAN	Hisp.
Enrollment (%)	100.0	60.0	37.3	1.0	0.0	1.5
Drop-out Rate (%)	4.9	4.2	6.7	0.0	0.0	5.3
H.S. Diplomas (#)	542	n/a	n/a	n/a	n/a	n/a

Bamberg County

Bamberg County SD 01
Box 526 • Bamberg, SC 29003-0526
(803) 245-3053
Grade Span: PK-12; **Agency Type:** 1
Schools: 4
  2 Primary; 1 Middle; 1 High; 0 Other Level
  4 Regular; 0 Special Education; 0 Vocational; 0 Alternative
  0 Magnet; 0 Charter; 2 Title I Eligible; 2 School-wide Title I
Students: 1,721   (50.9% male; 49.0% female)
  Individual Education Program: 386 (22.4%);
  English Language Learner: 0 (0.0%); Migrant: n/a
  Eligible for Free Lunch Program: 1,018 (59.2%)
  Eligible for Reduced-Price Lunch Program: 102 (5.9%)
Teachers: 111.0 (15.5 to 1)
Librarians/Media Specialists: 3.0 (573.7 to 1)
Guidance Counselors: 3.7 (465.1 to 1)
Current Spending: ($ per student per year):
  Total: $7,299; Instruction: $4,264; Support Services: $2,545
Enrollment, Drop-out Rates and Diploma Recipients by Race/Ethnicity

Category	Total	White	Black	Asian	AIAN	Hisp.
Enrollment (%)	100.0	41.5	57.4	0.6	0.2	0.4
Drop-out Rate (%)	3.7	4.3	3.5	0.0	n/a	0.0
H.S. Diplomas (#)	95	n/a	n/a	n/a	n/a	n/a

Barnwell County

Barnwell County SD 45
2008 Hagood Ave • Barnwell, SC 29812
(803) 541-1300 • http://www.barnwellweb.com/bsd45
Grade Span: PK-12; **Agency Type:** 1
Schools: 4
  1 Primary; 2 Middle; 1 High; 0 Other Level
  4 Regular; 0 Special Education; 0 Vocational; 0 Alternative
  0 Magnet; 0 Charter; 1 Title I Eligible; 1 School-wide Title I
Students: 2,826   (52.3% male; 47.6% female)
  Individual Education Program: 512 (18.1%);
  English Language Learner: 6 (0.2%); Migrant: n/a
  Eligible for Free Lunch Program: 1,392 (49.3%)
  Eligible for Reduced-Price Lunch Program: 212 (7.5%)
Teachers: 176.4 (16.0 to 1)
Librarians/Media Specialists: 3.0 (942.0 to 1)
Guidance Counselors: 6.0 (471.0 to 1)
Current Spending: ($ per student per year):
  Total: $6,582; Instruction: $4,197; Support Services: $1,948
Enrollment, Drop-out Rates and Diploma Recipients by Race/Ethnicity

Category	Total	White	Black	Asian	AIAN	Hisp.
Enrollment (%)	100.0	53.8	43.8	0.7	0.3	1.3
Drop-out Rate (%)	3.9	4.2	3.6	0.0	0.0	0.0
H.S. Diplomas (#)	125	n/a	n/a	n/a	n/a	n/a

Beaufort County

Beaufort County SD
PO Box 309 • Beaufort, SC 29902-0309
(843) 525-4200 • http://beaufort.schoolnet.com
Grade Span: PK-12; **Agency Type:** 1
Schools: 26
  16 Primary; 6 Middle; 4 High; 0 Other Level
  26 Regular; 0 Special Education; 0 Vocational; 0 Alternative
  11 Magnet; 0 Charter; 14 Title I Eligible; 14 School-wide Title I
Students: 18,328   (50.9% male; 49.0% female)
  Individual Education Program: 2,205 (12.0%);
  English Language Learner: 670 (3.7%); Migrant: n/a
  Eligible for Free Lunch Program: 7,108 (38.8%)
  Eligible for Reduced-Price Lunch Program: 1,520 (8.3%)
Teachers: 1,295.1 (14.2 to 1)
Librarians/Media Specialists: 28.0 (654.6 to 1)
Guidance Counselors: 48.0 (381.8 to 1)
Current Spending: ($ per student per year):
  Total: $7,912; Instruction: $4,481; Support Services: $3,071
Enrollment, Drop-out Rates and Diploma Recipients by Race/Ethnicity

Category	Total	White	Black	Asian	AIAN	Hisp.
Enrollment (%)	100.0	45.9	40.7	1.1	0.2	12.1
Drop-out Rate (%)	1.7	1.6	1.6	2.1	0.0	3.9
H.S. Diplomas (#)	759	n/a	n/a	n/a	n/a	n/a

Berkeley County

Berkeley County SD
PO Box 608 • Moncks Corner, SC 29461-0608
(843) 761-8600 • http://WWW.BERKELEY.K12.SC.US
Grade Span: PK-12; **Agency Type:** 1
Schools: 36
  19 Primary; 11 Middle; 6 High; 0 Other Level
  36 Regular; 0 Special Education; 0 Vocational; 0 Alternative
  2 Magnet; 0 Charter; 27 Title I Eligible; 27 School-wide Title I
Students: 27,899   (51.7% male; 48.2% female)
  Individual Education Program: 4,681 (16.8%);
  English Language Learner: 508 (1.8%); Migrant: n/a
  Eligible for Free Lunch Program: 11,237 (40.3%)
  Eligible for Reduced-Price Lunch Program: 3,148 (11.3%)
Teachers: 1,623.7 (17.2 to 1)
Librarians/Media Specialists: 39.4 (708.1 to 1)
Guidance Counselors: 61.3 (455.1 to 1)
Current Spending: ($ per student per year):
  Total: $6,472; Instruction: $3,736; Support Services: $2,415
Enrollment, Drop-out Rates and Diploma Recipients by Race/Ethnicity

Category	Total	White	Black	Asian	AIAN	Hisp.
Enrollment (%)	100.0	58.5	35.7	1.9	0.3	3.4
Drop-out Rate (%)	4.3	4.7	3.8	2.0	0.0	6.4
H.S. Diplomas (#)	1,302	n/a	n/a	n/a	n/a	n/a

Calhoun County

Calhoun County SD
101 Richland Ave • St Matthews, SC 29135-0215
(803) 655-7310 • http://www.calhoun.k12.sc.us/
Grade Span: PK-12; **Agency Type:** 1
Schools: 4
  1 Primary; 1 Middle; 1 High; 1 Other Level
  4 Regular; 0 Special Education; 0 Vocational; 0 Alternative
  0 Magnet; 0 Charter; 3 Title I Eligible; 3 School-wide Title I
Students: 2,008   (49.7% male; 50.2% female)
  Individual Education Program: 348 (17.3%);
  English Language Learner: 26 (1.3%); Migrant: n/a
  Eligible for Free Lunch Program: 1,452 (72.3%)
  Eligible for Reduced-Price Lunch Program: 168 (8.4%)
Teachers: 144.0 (13.9 to 1)
Librarians/Media Specialists: 4.0 (502.0 to 1)
Guidance Counselors: 5.8 (346.2 to 1)
Current Spending: ($ per student per year):
  Total: $8,647; Instruction: $4,877; Support Services: $3,312
Enrollment, Drop-out Rates and Diploma Recipients by Race/Ethnicity

Category	Total	White	Black	Asian	AIAN	Hisp.
Enrollment (%)	100.0	23.6	73.7	0.0	0.0	2.4
Drop-out Rate (%)	n/a	n/a	n/a	n/a	n/a	n/a
H.S. Diplomas (#)	75	n/a	n/a	n/a	n/a	n/a

Charleston County

Charleston County SD
75 Calhoun St • Charleston, SC 29401-6413
(843) 724-7716 • http://www.charleston.k12.sc.us
Grade Span: PK-12; **Agency Type:** 1
Schools: 80

49 Primary; 15 Middle; 12 High; 4 Other Level
80 Regular; 0 Special Education; 0 Vocational; 0 Alternative
10 Magnet; 4 Charter; 41 Title I Eligible; 41 School-wide Title I
Students: 44,109 (51.2% male; 48.7% female)
Individual Education Program: 6,214 (14.1%);
English Language Learner: 632 (1.4%); Migrant: n/a
Eligible for Free Lunch Program: 19,996 (45.3%)
Eligible for Reduced-Price Lunch Program: 3,059 (6.9%)
Teachers: 3,160.0 (14.0 to 1)
Librarians/Media Specialists: 80.2 (550.0 to 1)
Guidance Counselors: 115.2 (382.9 to 1)
Current Spending: ($ per student per year):
Total: $7,384; Instruction: $4,358; Support Services: $2,623
Enrollment, Drop-out Rates and Diploma Recipients by Race/Ethnicity

Category	Total	White	Black	Asian	AIAN	Hisp.
Enrollment (%)	100.0	39.8	55.3	1.3	0.2	3.1
Drop-out Rate (%)	3.2	2.1	4.1	2.1	0.0	2.1
H.S. Diplomas (#)	1,666	n/a	n/a	n/a	n/a	n/a

Cherokee County

Cherokee County SD
Box 460 • Gaffney, SC 29342-0460
(864) 489-0261 • http://www.cherokee1.k12.sc.us/
Grade Span: PK-12; **Agency Type:** 1
Schools: 19
12 Primary; 4 Middle; 3 High; 0 Other Level
18 Regular; 0 Special Education; 1 Vocational; 0 Alternative
0 Magnet; 0 Charter; 7 Title I Eligible; 7 School-wide Title I
Students: 9,317 (50.5% male; 49.4% female)
Individual Education Program: 1,081 (11.6%);
English Language Learner: 181 (1.9%); Migrant: n/a
Eligible for Free Lunch Program: 4,343 (46.6%)
Eligible for Reduced-Price Lunch Program: 890 (9.6%)
Teachers: 643.2 (14.5 to 1)
Librarians/Media Specialists: 19.0 (490.4 to 1)
Guidance Counselors: 23.0 (405.1 to 1)
Current Spending: ($ per student per year):
Total: $6,907; Instruction: $4,116; Support Services: $2,427
Enrollment, Drop-out Rates and Diploma Recipients by Race/Ethnicity

Category	Total	White	Black	Asian	AIAN	Hisp.
Enrollment (%)	100.0	68.3	28.3	0.5	0.1	2.6
Drop-out Rate (%)	3.5	3.5	3.4	14.3	n/a	2.8
H.S. Diplomas (#)	380	n/a	n/a	n/a	n/a	n/a

Chester County

Chester County SD
109 Hinton St • Chester, SC 29706-2022
(803) 385-6122 • http://www.chester.k12.sc.us
Grade Span: PK-12; **Agency Type:** 1
Schools: 12
5 Primary; 3 Middle; 4 High; 0 Other Level
11 Regular; 0 Special Education; 1 Vocational; 0 Alternative
0 Magnet; 0 Charter; 3 Title I Eligible; 3 School-wide Title I
Students: 6,827 (52.1% male; 47.8% female)
Individual Education Program: 906 (13.3%);
English Language Learner: 2 (<0.1%); Migrant: n/a
Eligible for Free Lunch Program: 3,451 (50.5%)
Eligible for Reduced-Price Lunch Program: 569 (8.3%)
Teachers: 430.7 (15.9 to 1)
Librarians/Media Specialists: 8.0 (853.4 to 1)
Guidance Counselors: 16.0 (426.7 to 1)
Current Spending: ($ per student per year):
Total: $6,986; Instruction: $4,269; Support Services: $2,442
Enrollment, Drop-out Rates and Diploma Recipients by Race/Ethnicity

Category	Total	White	Black	Asian	AIAN	Hisp.
Enrollment (%)	100.0	47.0	51.6	0.4	0.2	0.7
Drop-out Rate (%)	6.7	6.6	6.8	50.0	0.0	0.0
H.S. Diplomas (#)	231	n/a	n/a	n/a	n/a	n/a

Chesterfield County SD
401 W Blvd • Chesterfield, SC 29709-1534
(843) 623-2175 • http://www.chesterfield.k12.sc.us
Grade Span: PK-12; **Agency Type:** 1
Schools: 16
9 Primary; 3 Middle; 4 High; 0 Other Level
16 Regular; 0 Special Education; 0 Vocational; 0 Alternative
0 Magnet; 0 Charter; 9 Title I Eligible; 9 School-wide Title I
Students: 8,242 (50.1% male; 49.8% female)
Individual Education Program: 1,422 (17.3%);
English Language Learner: 119 (1.4%); Migrant: n/a
Eligible for Free Lunch Program: 4,376 (53.1%)
Eligible for Reduced-Price Lunch Program: 774 (9.4%)
Teachers: 538.0 (15.3 to 1)

Librarians/Media Specialists: 15.5 (531.7 to 1)
Guidance Counselors: 17.0 (484.8 to 1)
Current Spending: ($ per student per year):
Total: $6,882; Instruction: $4,106; Support Services: $2,402
Enrollment, Drop-out Rates and Diploma Recipients by Race/Ethnicity

Category	Total	White	Black	Asian	AIAN	Hisp.
Enrollment (%)	100.0	54.9	42.2	0.3	0.3	2.2
Drop-out Rate (%)	4.2	4.1	4.1	0.0	0.0	17.4
H.S. Diplomas (#)	367	n/a	n/a	n/a	n/a	n/a

Clarendon County

Clarendon County SD 02
PO Box 1252 • Manning, SC 29102-1252
(803) 435-4435
Grade Span: PK-12; **Agency Type:** 1
Schools: 6
2 Primary; 2 Middle; 2 High; 0 Other Level
6 Regular; 0 Special Education; 0 Vocational; 0 Alternative
0 Magnet; 1 Charter; 3 Title I Eligible; 3 School-wide Title I
Students: 3,518 (49.5% male; 50.4% female)
Individual Education Program: 636 (18.1%);
English Language Learner: 34 (1.0%); Migrant: n/a
Eligible for Free Lunch Program: 2,383 (67.7%)
Eligible for Reduced-Price Lunch Program: 256 (7.3%)
Teachers: 188.0 (18.7 to 1)
Librarians/Media Specialists: 5.0 (703.6 to 1)
Guidance Counselors: 5.0 (703.6 to 1)
Current Spending: ($ per student per year):
Total: $6,160; Instruction: $3,701; Support Services: $1,984
Enrollment, Drop-out Rates and Diploma Recipients by Race/Ethnicity

Category	Total	White	Black	Asian	AIAN	Hisp.
Enrollment (%)	100.0	30.1	67.1	0.3	0.3	2.1
Drop-out Rate (%)	1.8	3.3	1.1	0.0	n/a	11.1
H.S. Diplomas (#)	167	n/a	n/a	n/a	n/a	n/a

Colleton County

Colleton County SD
PO Box 290 • Walterboro, SC 29488-0290
(843) 549-5715 • http://www.colleton.k12.sc.us
Grade Span: PK-12; **Agency Type:** 1
Schools: 12
7 Primary; 3 Middle; 2 High; 0 Other Level
11 Regular; 0 Special Education; 1 Vocational; 0 Alternative
0 Magnet; 0 Charter; 9 Title I Eligible; 9 School-wide Title I
Students: 6,719 (51.1% male; 48.8% female)
Individual Education Program: 1,071 (15.9%);
English Language Learner: 31 (0.5%); Migrant: n/a
Eligible for Free Lunch Program: 4,357 (64.8%)
Eligible for Reduced-Price Lunch Program: 468 (7.0%)
Teachers: 435.4 (15.4 to 1)
Librarians/Media Specialists: 10.0 (671.9 to 1)
Guidance Counselors: 17.0 (395.2 to 1)
Current Spending: ($ per student per year):
Total: $6,945; Instruction: $4,000; Support Services: $2,557
Enrollment, Drop-out Rates and Diploma Recipients by Race/Ethnicity

Category	Total	White	Black	Asian	AIAN	Hisp.
Enrollment (%)	100.0	39.9	57.3	0.4	0.8	1.3
Drop-out Rate (%)	6.8	8.5	5.6	0.0	0.0	7.7
H.S. Diplomas (#)	266	n/a	n/a	n/a	n/a	n/a

Darlington County

Darlington County SD
PO Box 117 • Darlington, SC 29532-0493
(843) 398-5200 • http://www.darlington.k12.sc.us
Grade Span: PK-12; **Agency Type:** 1
Schools: 22
10 Primary; 7 Middle; 5 High; 0 Other Level
22 Regular; 0 Special Education; 0 Vocational; 0 Alternative
3 Magnet; 1 Charter; 14 Title I Eligible; 14 School-wide Title I
Students: 12,040 (51.7% male; 48.2% female)
Individual Education Program: 2,171 (18.0%);
English Language Learner: 31 (0.3%); Migrant: n/a
Eligible for Free Lunch Program: 7,000 (58.1%)
Eligible for Reduced-Price Lunch Program: 803 (6.7%)
Teachers: 818.8 (14.7 to 1)
Librarians/Media Specialists: 22.0 (547.3 to 1)
Guidance Counselors: 32.0 (376.3 to 1)
Current Spending: ($ per student per year):
Total: $7,292; Instruction: $4,206; Support Services: $2,670

Enrollment, Drop-out Rates and Diploma Recipients by Race/Ethnicity

Category	Total	White	Black	Asian	AIAN	Hisp.
Enrollment (%)	100.0	40.5	58.3	0.3	0.1	0.8
Drop-out Rate (%)	2.7	2.8	2.6	0.0	0.0	7.1
H.S. Diplomas (#)	483	n/a	n/a	n/a	n/a	n/a

Dillon County

Dillon County SD 02
405 W Washington St • Dillon, SC 29536-2855
(843) 774-1200 • http://www.dillon2.k12.sc.us/
Grade Span: PK-12; **Agency Type:** 1
Schools: 6
  3 Primary; 2 Middle; 1 High; 0 Other Level
  6 Regular; 0 Special Education; 0 Vocational; 0 Alternative
  0 Magnet; 0 Charter; 5 Title I Eligible; 5 School-wide Title I
Students: 3,841   (52.2% male; 47.7% female)
  Individual Education Program: 524 (13.6%);
  English Language Learner: 78 (2.0%); Migrant: n/a
  Eligible for Free Lunch Program: 2,789 (72.6%)
  Eligible for Reduced-Price Lunch Program: 282 (7.3%)
Teachers: 209.4 (18.3 to 1)
Librarians/Media Specialists: 6.0 (640.2 to 1)
Guidance Counselors: 9.0 (426.8 to 1)
Current Spending: ($ per student per year):
  Total: $6,114; Instruction: $3,407; Support Services: $2,279
Enrollment, Drop-out Rates and Diploma Recipients by Race/Ethnicity

Category	Total	White	Black	Asian	AIAN	Hisp.
Enrollment (%)	100.0	28.0	66.5	0.4	2.9	2.1
Drop-out Rate (%)	6.5	5.8	6.7	9.1	3.8	28.6
H.S. Diplomas (#)	165	n/a	n/a	n/a	n/a	n/a

Dillon County SD 03
502 N Richardson St • Latta, SC 29565-1415
(843) 752-7101 • http://www.dillon3.k12.sc.us
Grade Span: PK-12; **Agency Type:** 1
Schools: 4
  2 Primary; 1 Middle; 1 High; 0 Other Level
  4 Regular; 0 Special Education; 0 Vocational; 0 Alternative
  0 Magnet; 0 Charter; 2 Title I Eligible; 2 School-wide Title I
Students: 1,594   (50.0% male; 49.9% female)
  Individual Education Program: 248 (15.6%);
  English Language Learner: 0 (0.0%); Migrant: n/a
  Eligible for Free Lunch Program: 994 (62.4%)
  Eligible for Reduced-Price Lunch Program: 115 (7.2%)
Teachers: 97.5 (16.3 to 1)
Librarians/Media Specialists: 3.0 (531.3 to 1)
Guidance Counselors: 4.0 (398.5 to 1)
Current Spending: ($ per student per year):
  Total: $6,658; Instruction: $3,810; Support Services: $2,358
Enrollment, Drop-out Rates and Diploma Recipients by Race/Ethnicity

Category	Total	White	Black	Asian	AIAN	Hisp.
Enrollment (%)	100.0	51.8	45.9	0.1	1.2	0.9
Drop-out Rate (%)	2.4	1.8	3.1	0.0	0.0	0.0
H.S. Diplomas (#)	77	n/a	n/a	n/a	n/a	n/a

Dorchester County

Dorchester County SD 02
102 Greenwave Blvd • Summerville, SC 29483-2455
(843) 873-2901 • http://www.dorchester2.k12.sc.us/
Grade Span: PK-12; **Agency Type:** 1
Schools: 17
  9 Primary; 5 Middle; 2 High; 1 Other Level
  17 Regular; 0 Special Education; 0 Vocational; 0 Alternative
  0 Magnet; 0 Charter; 6 Title I Eligible; 0 School-wide Title I
Students: 18,137   (51.2% male; 48.7% female)
  Individual Education Program: 2,523 (13.9%);
  English Language Learner: 130 (0.7%); Migrant: n/a
  Eligible for Free Lunch Program: 4,246 (23.4%)
  Eligible for Reduced-Price Lunch Program: 1,101 (6.1%)
Teachers: 1,119.5 (16.2 to 1)
Librarians/Media Specialists: 20.0 (906.9 to 1)
Guidance Counselors: 43.0 (421.8 to 1)
Current Spending: ($ per student per year):
  Total: $6,085; Instruction: $3,803; Support Services: $2,044
Enrollment, Drop-out Rates and Diploma Recipients by Race/Ethnicity

Category	Total	White	Black	Asian	AIAN	Hisp.
Enrollment (%)	100.0	66.7	28.6	1.7	0.6	2.2
Drop-out Rate (%)	3.6	3.3	4.3	3.0	6.7	5.6
H.S. Diplomas (#)	883	n/a	n/a	n/a	n/a	n/a

Dorchester County SD 04
500 Ridge St • St George, SC 29477-2452
(843) 563-4535 • http://www.dorchester4.k12.sc.us
Grade Span: PK-12; **Agency Type:** 1
Schools: 4
  2 Primary; 1 Middle; 1 High; 0 Other Level
  4 Regular; 0 Special Education; 0 Vocational; 0 Alternative
  0 Magnet; 0 Charter; 3 Title I Eligible; 3 School-wide Title I
Students: 2,536   (52.7% male; 47.2% female)
  Individual Education Program: 394 (15.5%);
  English Language Learner: 8 (0.3%); Migrant: n/a
  Eligible for Free Lunch Program: 1,666 (65.7%)
  Eligible for Reduced-Price Lunch Program: 254 (10.0%)
Teachers: 176.8 (14.3 to 1)
Librarians/Media Specialists: 4.0 (634.0 to 1)
Guidance Counselors: 5.0 (507.2 to 1)
Current Spending: ($ per student per year):
  Total: $8,231; Instruction: $4,632; Support Services: $3,115
Enrollment, Drop-out Rates and Diploma Recipients by Race/Ethnicity

Category	Total	White	Black	Asian	AIAN	Hisp.
Enrollment (%)	100.0	28.0	67.9	0.4	2.2	1.3
Drop-out Rate (%)	5.7	4.5	5.8	0.0	14.3	50.0
H.S. Diplomas (#)	116	n/a	n/a	n/a	n/a	n/a

Edgefield County

Edgefield County SD
PO Box 608 • Edgefield, SC 29824-0608
(803) 275-4601 • http://www.edgefield.k12.sc.us
Grade Span: PK-12; **Agency Type:** 1
Schools: 9
  4 Primary; 2 Middle; 3 High; 0 Other Level
  8 Regular; 0 Special Education; 1 Vocational; 0 Alternative
  0 Magnet; 0 Charter; 4 Title I Eligible; 4 School-wide Title I
Students: 3,999   (52.1% male; 47.8% female)
  Individual Education Program: 727 (18.2%);
  English Language Learner: 16 (0.4%); Migrant: n/a
  Eligible for Free Lunch Program: 2,006 (50.2%)
  Eligible for Reduced-Price Lunch Program: 361 (9.0%)
Teachers: 277.3 (14.4 to 1)
Librarians/Media Specialists: 8.0 (499.9 to 1)
Guidance Counselors: 9.0 (444.3 to 1)
Current Spending: ($ per student per year):
  Total: $7,145; Instruction: $4,238; Support Services: $2,515
Enrollment, Drop-out Rates and Diploma Recipients by Race/Ethnicity

Category	Total	White	Black	Asian	AIAN	Hisp.
Enrollment (%)	100.0	47.8	50.4	0.2	0.0	1.5
Drop-out Rate (%)	5.6	5.5	5.9	0.0	0.0	0.0
H.S. Diplomas (#)	177	n/a	n/a	n/a	n/a	n/a

Fairfield County

Fairfield County SD
Drawer 622 • Winnsboro, SC 29180-0622
(803) 635-4607 • http://www.fairfield.k12.sc.us
Grade Span: PK-12; **Agency Type:** 1
Schools: 9
  5 Primary; 2 Middle; 2 High; 0 Other Level
  8 Regular; 0 Special Education; 1 Vocational; 0 Alternative
  0 Magnet; 0 Charter; 5 Title I Eligible; 5 School-wide Title I
Students: 3,765   (49.8% male; 50.1% female)
  Individual Education Program: 777 (20.6%);
  English Language Learner: 10 (0.3%); Migrant: n/a
  Eligible for Free Lunch Program: 2,682 (71.2%)
  Eligible for Reduced-Price Lunch Program: 376 (10.0%)
Teachers: 281.0 (13.4 to 1)
Librarians/Media Specialists: 8.0 (470.6 to 1)
Guidance Counselors: 13.0 (289.6 to 1)
Current Spending: ($ per student per year):
  Total: $9,763; Instruction: $5,174; Support Services: $4,141
Enrollment, Drop-out Rates and Diploma Recipients by Race/Ethnicity

Category	Total	White	Black	Asian	AIAN	Hisp.
Enrollment (%)	100.0	13.0	85.6	0.2	0.0	1.2
Drop-out Rate (%)	1.6	2.4	1.5	0.0	n/a	0.0
H.S. Diplomas (#)	159	n/a	n/a	n/a	n/a	n/a

Florence County

Florence County SD 01
319 S Dargan St • Florence, SC 29506-2538
(843) 669-4141 • http://www.fsd1.org
Grade Span: PK-12; **Agency Type:** 1
Schools: 20
  12 Primary; 4 Middle; 4 High; 0 Other Level
  19 Regular; 0 Special Education; 1 Vocational; 0 Alternative

2 Magnet; 0 Charter; 13 Title I Eligible; 13 School-wide Title I
Students: 14,809   (50.9% male; 49.0% female)
    Individual Education Program: 2,435 (16.4%);
    English Language Learner: 92 (0.6%); Migrant: n/a
    Eligible for Free Lunch Program: 6,768 (45.7%)
    Eligible for Reduced-Price Lunch Program: 1,096 (7.4%)
Teachers: 965.1 (15.3 to 1)
Librarians/Media Specialists: 22.0 (673.1 to 1)
Guidance Counselors: 30.0 (493.6 to 1)
Current Spending: ($ per student per year):
    Total: $6,105; Instruction: $3,776; Support Services: $1,990
Enrollment, Drop-out Rates and Diploma Recipients by Race/Ethnicity

Category	Total	White	Black	Asian	AIAN	Hisp.
Enrollment (%)	100.0	45.4	51.8	1.3	0.1	1.1
Drop-out Rate (%)	5.9	4.3	7.6	6.7	0.0	8.3
H.S. Diplomas (#)	721	n/a	n/a	n/a	n/a	n/a

Florence County SD 03
Drawer 1389 • Lake City, SC 29560-1389
(843) 394-8652 • http://www.florence3.k12.sc.us
Grade Span: PK-12; **Agency Type:** 1
Schools: 8
    5 Primary; 2 Middle; 1 High; 0 Other Level
    8 Regular; 0 Special Education; 0 Vocational; 0 Alternative
    0 Magnet; 0 Charter; 7 Title I Eligible; 7 School-wide Title I
Students: 3,977   (52.4% male; 47.5% female)
    Individual Education Program: 919 (23.1%);
    English Language Learner: 14 (0.4%); Migrant: n/a
    Eligible for Free Lunch Program: 3,009 (75.7%)
    Eligible for Reduced-Price Lunch Program: 237 (6.0%)
Teachers: 272.2 (14.6 to 1)
Librarians/Media Specialists: 7.5 (530.3 to 1)
Guidance Counselors: 9.0 (441.9 to 1)
Current Spending: ($ per student per year):
    Total: $7,275; Instruction: $4,166; Support Services: $2,670
Enrollment, Drop-out Rates and Diploma Recipients by Race/Ethnicity

Category	Total	White	Black	Asian	AIAN	Hisp.
Enrollment (%)	100.0	33.4	65.0	0.1	0.1	1.2
Drop-out Rate (%)	4.5	4.6	4.3	0.0	n/a	33.3
H.S. Diplomas (#)	193	n/a	n/a	n/a	n/a	n/a

Florence County SD 05
PO Box 98 • Johnsonville, SC 29555-0098
(843) 386-2358
Grade Span: PK-12; **Agency Type:** 1
Schools: 3
    1 Primary; 1 Middle; 1 High; 0 Other Level
    3 Regular; 0 Special Education; 0 Vocational; 0 Alternative
    0 Magnet; 0 Charter; 2 Title I Eligible; 2 School-wide Title I
Students: 1,507   (51.9% male; 48.0% female)
    Individual Education Program: 361 (24.0%);
    English Language Learner: 9 (0.6%); Migrant: n/a
    Eligible for Free Lunch Program: 703 (46.6%)
    Eligible for Reduced-Price Lunch Program: 129 (8.6%)
Teachers: 94.8 (15.9 to 1)
Librarians/Media Specialists: 3.0 (502.3 to 1)
Guidance Counselors: 3.0 (502.3 to 1)
Current Spending: ($ per student per year):
    Total: $6,879; Instruction: $3,975; Support Services: $2,511
Enrollment, Drop-out Rates and Diploma Recipients by Race/Ethnicity

Category	Total	White	Black	Asian	AIAN	Hisp.
Enrollment (%)	100.0	65.7	32.7	0.3	0.0	1.2
Drop-out Rate (%)	4.1	2.7	7.8	n/a	n/a	0.0
H.S. Diplomas (#)	62	n/a	n/a	n/a	n/a	n/a

Georgetown County

Georgetown County SD
624 Front St • Georgetown, SC 29440-3624
(843) 546-2561 • http://www.gcsd.k12.sc.us
Grade Span: PK-12; **Agency Type:** 1
Schools: 17
    9 Primary; 4 Middle; 4 High; 0 Other Level
    17 Regular; 0 Special Education; 0 Vocational; 0 Alternative
    0 Magnet; 0 Charter; 9 Title I Eligible; 9 School-wide Title I
Students: 10,571   (51.4% male; 48.5% female)
    Individual Education Program: 1,822 (17.2%);
    English Language Learner: 134 (1.3%); Migrant: n/a
    Eligible for Free Lunch Program: 5,899 (55.8%)
    Eligible for Reduced-Price Lunch Program: 775 (7.3%)
Teachers: 739.6 (14.3 to 1)
Librarians/Media Specialists: 18.0 (587.3 to 1)
Guidance Counselors: 29.0 (364.5 to 1)
Current Spending: ($ per student per year):
    Total: $8,140; Instruction: $4,583; Support Services: $3,160

Category	Total	White	Black	Asian	AIAN	Hisp.
Enrollment (%)	100.0	43.8	53.8	0.5	0.2	1.6
Drop-out Rate (%)	2.7	3.1	2.4	0.0	n/a	0.0
H.S. Diplomas (#)	486	n/a	n/a	n/a	n/a	n/a

Greenville County

Greenville County SD
Box 2848 301 Camperdown • Greenville, SC 29602-2848
Mailing Address: Box 2848 301 Camperdown Way • Greenville, SC 29602-2848
(864) 241-3457 • http://www.greenville.k12.sc.us
Grade Span: PK-12; **Agency Type:** 1
Schools: 93
    53 Primary; 19 Middle; 19 High; 2 Other Level
    88 Regular; 1 Special Education; 4 Vocational; 0 Alternative
    12 Magnet; 3 Charter; 18 Title I Eligible; 13 School-wide Title I
Students: 64,245   (51.1% male; 48.8% female)
    Individual Education Program: 10,499 (16.3%);
    English Language Learner: 490 (0.8%); Migrant: n/a
    Eligible for Free Lunch Program: 19,138 (29.8%)
    Eligible for Reduced-Price Lunch Program: 4,600 (7.2%)
Teachers: 3,835.1 (16.8 to 1)
Librarians/Media Specialists: 97.5 (658.9 to 1)
Guidance Counselors: 136.6 (470.3 to 1)
Current Spending: ($ per student per year):
    Total: $6,379; Instruction: $3,785; Support Services: $2,150
Enrollment, Drop-out Rates and Diploma Recipients by Race/Ethnicity

Category	Total	White	Black	Asian	AIAN	Hisp.
Enrollment (%)	100.0	63.7	28.2	1.7	0.1	6.0
Drop-out Rate (%)	2.6	2.2	3.7	0.7	0.0	3.9
H.S. Diplomas (#)	2,934	n/a	n/a	n/a	n/a	n/a

Greenwood County

Greenwood 50 County SD
Box 248 • Greenwood, SC 29648-0248
(864) 223-4348 • http://www.gwd50.k12.sc.us
Grade Span: PK-12; **Agency Type:** 1
Schools: 14
    9 Primary; 3 Middle; 2 High; 0 Other Level
    14 Regular; 0 Special Education; 0 Vocational; 0 Alternative
    0 Magnet; 0 Charter; 9 Title I Eligible; 9 School-wide Title I
Students: 9,522   (50.1% male; 49.8% female)
    Individual Education Program: 1,668 (17.5%);
    English Language Learner: 408 (4.3%); Migrant: n/a
    Eligible for Free Lunch Program: 4,211 (44.2%)
    Eligible for Reduced-Price Lunch Program: 583 (6.1%)
Teachers: 598.7 (15.9 to 1)
Librarians/Media Specialists: 15.0 (634.8 to 1)
Guidance Counselors: 22.5 (423.2 to 1)
Current Spending: ($ per student per year):
    Total: $6,391; Instruction: $4,022; Support Services: $2,007
Enrollment, Drop-out Rates and Diploma Recipients by Race/Ethnicity

Category	Total	White	Black	Asian	AIAN	Hisp.
Enrollment (%)	100.0	49.3	44.3	1.3	0.0	5.0
Drop-out Rate (%)	2.4	1.6	3.4	5.0	n/a	2.4
H.S. Diplomas (#)	427	n/a	n/a	n/a	n/a	n/a

Greenwood 52 County SD
605 Johnston Rd • Ninety Six, SC 29666-1149
(843) 543-3100 • http://www.ninetysix.k12.sc.us
Grade Span: PK-12; **Agency Type:** 1
Schools: 4
    2 Primary; 1 Middle; 1 High; 0 Other Level
    4 Regular; 0 Special Education; 0 Vocational; 0 Alternative
    0 Magnet; 0 Charter; 1 Title I Eligible; 1 School-wide Title I
Students: 1,733   (51.1% male; 48.8% female)
    Individual Education Program: 233 (13.4%);
    English Language Learner: 2 (0.1%); Migrant: n/a
    Eligible for Free Lunch Program: 562 (32.4%)
    Eligible for Reduced-Price Lunch Program: 171 (9.9%)
Teachers: 106.7 (16.2 to 1)
Librarians/Media Specialists: 4.0 (433.3 to 1)
Guidance Counselors: 5.0 (346.6 to 1)
Current Spending: ($ per student per year):
    Total: $6,361; Instruction: $3,912; Support Services: $2,095
Enrollment, Drop-out Rates and Diploma Recipients by Race/Ethnicity

Category	Total	White	Black	Asian	AIAN	Hisp.
Enrollment (%)	100.0	74.4	24.4	0.4	0.2	0.6
Drop-out Rate (%)	1.4	0.9	3.1	0.0	0.0	n/a
H.S. Diplomas (#)	91	n/a	n/a	n/a	n/a	n/a

Hampton County

Hampton 1 County SD
Box 177 • Hampton, SC 29924-0177
(803) 943-4576
Grade Span: PK-12; **Agency Type:** 1
Schools: 7
  5 Primary; 1 Middle; 1 High; 0 Other Level
  7 Regular; 0 Special Education; 0 Vocational; 0 Alternative
  0 Magnet; 0 Charter; 5 Title I Eligible; 5 School-wide Title I
Students: 2,857   (51.4% male; 48.5% female)
  Individual Education Program: 356 (12.5%);
  English Language Learner: 2 (0.1%); Migrant: n/a
  Eligible for Free Lunch Program: 1,509 (52.8%)
  Eligible for Reduced-Price Lunch Program: 346 (12.1%)
Teachers: 183.5 (15.6 to 1)
Librarians/Media Specialists: 5.5 (519.5 to 1)
Guidance Counselors: 7.5 (380.9 to 1)
Current Spending: ($ per student per year):
  Total: $6,730; Instruction: $3,847; Support Services: $2,404
Enrollment, Drop-out Rates and Diploma Recipients by Race/Ethnicity

Category	Total	White	Black	Asian	AIAN	Hisp.
Enrollment (%)	100.0	43.7	55.1	0.4	0.0	0.8
Drop-out Rate (%)	5.6	5.4	5.7	0.0	n/a	0.0
H.S. Diplomas (#)	104	n/a	n/a	n/a	n/a	n/a

Horry County

Horry County SD
1600 Horry St • Conway, SC 29527-4100
(843) 248-2206 • http://www.hcs.k12.sc.us
Grade Span: PK-12; **Agency Type:** 1
Schools: 46
  22 Primary; 11 Middle; 12 High; 1 Other Level
  43 Regular; 0 Special Education; 3 Vocational; 0 Alternative
  0 Magnet; 1 Charter; 27 Title I Eligible; 27 School-wide Title I
Students: 31,648   (51.2% male; 48.7% female)
  Individual Education Program: 5,610 (17.7%);
  English Language Learner: 699 (2.2%); Migrant: n/a
  Eligible for Free Lunch Program: 15,707 (49.6%)
  Eligible for Reduced-Price Lunch Program: 1,945 (6.1%)
Teachers: 2,101.8 (15.1 to 1)
Librarians/Media Specialists: 47.0 (673.4 to 1)
Guidance Counselors: 71.0 (445.7 to 1)
Current Spending: ($ per student per year):
  Total: $7,067; Instruction: $4,200; Support Services: $2,486
Enrollment, Drop-out Rates and Diploma Recipients by Race/Ethnicity

Category	Total	White	Black	Asian	AIAN	Hisp.
Enrollment (%)	100.0	68.7	25.7	1.2	0.3	3.7
Drop-out Rate (%)	2.1	2.0	2.7	2.4	0.0	2.1
H.S. Diplomas (#)	1,335	n/a	n/a	n/a	n/a	n/a

Jasper County

Jasper County SD
Box 848 • Ridgeland, SC 29936-0848
(843) 726-7200
Grade Span: PK-12; **Agency Type:** 1
Schools: 4
  2 Primary; 1 Middle; 1 High; 0 Other Level
  4 Regular; 0 Special Education; 0 Vocational; 0 Alternative
  0 Magnet; 0 Charter; 3 Title I Eligible; 3 School-wide Title I
Students: 3,251   (52.9% male; 47.0% female)
  Individual Education Program: 440 (13.5%);
  English Language Learner: 260 (8.0%); Migrant: n/a
  Eligible for Free Lunch Program: 2,189 (67.3%)
  Eligible for Reduced-Price Lunch Program: 322 (9.9%)
Teachers: 205.5 (15.8 to 1)
Librarians/Media Specialists: 4.0 (812.8 to 1)
Guidance Counselors: 5.5 (591.1 to 1)
Current Spending: ($ per student per year):
  Total: $7,573; Instruction: $4,580; Support Services: $2,607
Enrollment, Drop-out Rates and Diploma Recipients by Race/Ethnicity

Category	Total	White	Black	Asian	AIAN	Hisp.
Enrollment (%)	100.0	13.1	74.7	0.2	0.0	12.1
Drop-out Rate (%)	3.1	11.3	1.5	n/a	n/a	16.7
H.S. Diplomas (#)	85	n/a	n/a	n/a	n/a	n/a

Kershaw County

Kershaw County SD
1301 Dubose Court • Camden, SC 29020-3799
(803) 432-8416 • http://www.kershaw.k12.sc.us
Grade Span: PK-12; **Agency Type:** 1
Schools: 19

  11 Primary; 4 Middle; 4 High; 0 Other Level
  18 Regular; 0 Special Education; 1 Vocational; 0 Alternative
  0 Magnet; 0 Charter; 8 Title I Eligible; 8 School-wide Title I
Students: 10,270   (51.3% male; 48.6% female)
  Individual Education Program: 1,156 (11.3%);
  English Language Learner: 115 (1.1%); Migrant: n/a
  Eligible for Free Lunch Program: 4,068 (39.6%)
  Eligible for Reduced-Price Lunch Program: 998 (9.7%)
Teachers: 634.0 (16.2 to 1)
Librarians/Media Specialists: 19.5 (526.7 to 1)
Guidance Counselors: 24.5 (419.2 to 1)
Current Spending: ($ per student per year):
  Total: $6,798; Instruction: $3,966; Support Services: $2,438
Enrollment, Drop-out Rates and Diploma Recipients by Race/Ethnicity

Category	Total	White	Black	Asian	AIAN	Hisp.
Enrollment (%)	100.0	64.7	32.5	0.3	0.1	2.2
Drop-out Rate (%)	5.1	5.6	4.4	0.0	0.0	0.0
H.S. Diplomas (#)	525	n/a	n/a	n/a	n/a	n/a

Lancaster County

Lancaster County SD
300 S Catawba St • Lancaster, SC 29721-0130
(803) 286-6972
Grade Span: PK-12; **Agency Type:** 1
Schools: 20
  11 Primary; 4 Middle; 5 High; 0 Other Level
  19 Regular; 0 Special Education; 1 Vocational; 0 Alternative
  1 Magnet; 1 Charter; 9 Title I Eligible; 9 School-wide Title I
Students: 11,372   (52.1% male; 47.8% female)
  Individual Education Program: 1,641 (14.4%);
  English Language Learner: 156 (1.4%); Migrant: n/a
  Eligible for Free Lunch Program: 4,844 (42.6%)
  Eligible for Reduced-Price Lunch Program: 898 (7.9%)
Teachers: 725.0 (15.7 to 1)
Librarians/Media Specialists: 19.0 (598.5 to 1)
Guidance Counselors: 25.7 (442.5 to 1)
Current Spending: ($ per student per year):
  Total: $6,437; Instruction: $3,921; Support Services: $2,198
Enrollment, Drop-out Rates and Diploma Recipients by Race/Ethnicity

Category	Total	White	Black	Asian	AIAN	Hisp.
Enrollment (%)	100.0	61.9	34.9	0.5	0.2	2.3
Drop-out Rate (%)	5.4	5.5	4.7	0.0	50.0	20.0
H.S. Diplomas (#)	503	n/a	n/a	n/a	n/a	n/a

Laurens County

Laurens County SD 55
1029 W Main St • Laurens, SC 29360-2654
(864) 984-3568 • http://www.laurens55.k12.sc.us
Grade Span: PK-12; **Agency Type:** 1
Schools: 11
  7 Primary; 3 Middle; 1 High; 0 Other Level
  11 Regular; 0 Special Education; 0 Vocational; 0 Alternative
  0 Magnet; 0 Charter; 5 Title I Eligible; 5 School-wide Title I
Students: 6,146   (51.5% male; 48.4% female)
  Individual Education Program: 1,203 (19.6%);
  English Language Learner: 182 (3.0%); Migrant: n/a
  Eligible for Free Lunch Program: 2,990 (48.6%)
  Eligible for Reduced-Price Lunch Program: 428 (7.0%)
Teachers: 363.2 (16.9 to 1)
Librarians/Media Specialists: 11.0 (558.7 to 1)
Guidance Counselors: 14.1 (435.9 to 1)
Current Spending: ($ per student per year):
  Total: $6,491; Instruction: $3,686; Support Services: $2,450
Enrollment, Drop-out Rates and Diploma Recipients by Race/Ethnicity

Category	Total	White	Black	Asian	AIAN	Hisp.
Enrollment (%)	100.0	61.8	34.4	0.1	0.1	3.3
Drop-out Rate (%)	2.0	2.1	1.7	0.0	n/a	7.1
H.S. Diplomas (#)	229	n/a	n/a	n/a	n/a	n/a

Laurens County SD 56
600 E Florida St • Clinton, SC 29325-2603
(843) 833-0800 • http://www.laurens56.k12.sc.us
Grade Span: PK-12; **Agency Type:** 1
Schools: 7
  4 Primary; 2 Middle; 1 High; 0 Other Level
  7 Regular; 0 Special Education; 0 Vocational; 0 Alternative
  0 Magnet; 0 Charter; 5 Title I Eligible; 5 School-wide Title I
Students: 3,435   (51.4% male; 48.5% female)
  Individual Education Program: 698 (20.3%);
  English Language Learner: 47 (1.4%); Migrant: n/a
  Eligible for Free Lunch Program: 1,870 (54.4%)
  Eligible for Reduced-Price Lunch Program: 376 (10.9%)
Teachers: 219.7 (15.6 to 1)

Librarians/Media Specialists: 7.0 (490.7 to 1)
Guidance Counselors: 8.9 (386.0 to 1)
Current Spending: ($ per student per year):
  Total: $6,960; Instruction: $3,914; Support Services: $2,591
Enrollment, Drop-out Rates and Diploma Recipients by Race/Ethnicity

Category	Total	White	Black	Asian	AIAN	Hisp.
Enrollment (%)	100.0	55.7	42.4	0.3	0.1	1.5
Drop-out Rate (%)	2.3	2.1	2.6	0.0	n/a	0.0
H.S. Diplomas (#)	175	n/a	n/a	n/a	n/a	n/a

Lee County

Lee County SD
PO Box 507 • Bishopville, SC 29010-0507
(803) 484-5327 • http://www.lee.k12.sc.us
Grade Span: PK-12; **Agency Type:** 1
Schools: 7
  3 Primary; 2 Middle; 2 High; 0 Other Level
  6 Regular; 0 Special Education; 1 Vocational; 0 Alternative
  0 Magnet; 0 Charter; 5 Title I Eligible; 5 School-wide Title I
Students: 2,901 (49.8% male; 50.1% female)
  Individual Education Program: 489 (16.9%);
  English Language Learner: 12 (0.4%); Migrant: n/a
  Eligible for Free Lunch Program: 2,222 (76.6%)
  Eligible for Reduced-Price Lunch Program: 197 (6.8%)
Teachers: 197.4 (14.7 to 1)
Librarians/Media Specialists: 6.0 (483.5 to 1)
Guidance Counselors: 8.0 (362.6 to 1)
Current Spending: ($ per student per year):
  Total: $8,097; Instruction: $4,571; Support Services: $2,991
Enrollment, Drop-out Rates and Diploma Recipients by Race/Ethnicity

Category	Total	White	Black	Asian	AIAN	Hisp.
Enrollment (%)	100.0	4.6	94.2	0.2	0.1	0.9
Drop-out Rate (%)	4.6	0.0	5.0	n/a	n/a	0.0
H.S. Diplomas (#)	119	n/a	n/a	n/a	n/a	n/a

Lexington County

Lexington County SD 01
PO Box 1869 • Lexington, SC 29072-1869
(803) 359-4178 • http://www.lexington1.net
Grade Span: PK-12; **Agency Type:** 1
Schools: 20
  10 Primary; 5 Middle; 5 High; 0 Other Level
  19 Regular; 0 Special Education; 1 Vocational; 0 Alternative
  0 Magnet; 0 Charter; 5 Title I Eligible; 3 School-wide Title I
Students: 19,099 (51.5% male; 48.4% female)
  Individual Education Program: 2,991 (15.7%);
  English Language Learner: 235 (1.2%); Migrant: n/a
  Eligible for Free Lunch Program: 4,237 (22.2%)
  Eligible for Reduced-Price Lunch Program: 1,310 (6.9%)
Teachers: 1,277.3 (15.0 to 1)
Librarians/Media Specialists: 23.0 (830.4 to 1)
Guidance Counselors: 42.0 (454.7 to 1)
Current Spending: ($ per student per year):
  Total: $6,963; Instruction: $4,263; Support Services: $2,396
Enrollment, Drop-out Rates and Diploma Recipients by Race/Ethnicity

Category	Total	White	Black	Asian	AIAN	Hisp.
Enrollment (%)	100.0	87.4	8.0	1.5	0.5	2.5
Drop-out Rate (%)	2.4	2.3	4.7	0.0	0.0	3.9
H.S. Diplomas (#)	906	n/a	n/a	n/a	n/a	n/a

Lexington County SD 02
715 Ninth St • W Columbia, SC 29169-7169
(803) 739-4017
Grade Span: PK-12; **Agency Type:** 1
Schools: 16
  10 Primary; 4 Middle; 2 High; 0 Other Level
  16 Regular; 0 Special Education; 0 Vocational; 0 Alternative
  2 Magnet; 0 Charter; 8 Title I Eligible; 8 School-wide Title I
Students: 9,267 (51.2% male; 48.7% female)
  Individual Education Program: 1,426 (15.4%);
  English Language Learner: 249 (2.7%); Migrant: n/a
  Eligible for Free Lunch Program: 3,659 (39.5%)
  Eligible for Reduced-Price Lunch Program: 740 (8.0%)
Teachers: 633.5 (14.6 to 1)
Librarians/Media Specialists: 18.0 (514.8 to 1)
Guidance Counselors: 24.0 (386.1 to 1)
Current Spending: ($ per student per year):
  Total: $7,508; Instruction: $4,545; Support Services: $2,614
Enrollment, Drop-out Rates and Diploma Recipients by Race/Ethnicity

Category	Total	White	Black	Asian	AIAN	Hisp.
Enrollment (%)	100.0	60.4	33.5	1.3	0.2	4.3
Drop-out Rate (%)	3.7	4.3	2.4	0.0	0.0	0.0
H.S. Diplomas (#)	459	n/a	n/a	n/a	n/a	n/a

Lexington County SD 03
121 W Columbia Ave • Batesburg, SC 29006-2124
(803) 532-4423 • http://www.lex3.k12.sc.us
Grade Span: PK-12; **Agency Type:** 1
Schools: 4
  2 Primary; 1 Middle; 1 High; 0 Other Level
  4 Regular; 0 Special Education; 0 Vocational; 0 Alternative
  0 Magnet; 0 Charter; 3 Title I Eligible; 3 School-wide Title I
Students: 2,268 (52.1% male; 47.8% female)
  Individual Education Program: 382 (16.8%);
  English Language Learner: 26 (1.1%); Migrant: n/a
  Eligible for Free Lunch Program: 1,069 (47.1%)
  Eligible for Reduced-Price Lunch Program: 200 (8.8%)
Teachers: 146.4 (15.5 to 1)
Librarians/Media Specialists: 4.0 (567.0 to 1)
Guidance Counselors: 5.0 (453.6 to 1)
Current Spending: ($ per student per year):
  Total: $7,725; Instruction: $4,293; Support Services: $2,969
Enrollment, Drop-out Rates and Diploma Recipients by Race/Ethnicity

Category	Total	White	Black	Asian	AIAN	Hisp.
Enrollment (%)	100.0	53.3	44.3	0.3	0.2	1.6
Drop-out Rate (%)	4.6	6.0	2.6	n/a	0.0	0.0
H.S. Diplomas (#)	125	n/a	n/a	n/a	n/a	n/a

Lexington County SD 04
Box 569 • Swansea, SC 29160-0569
(803) 568-3886 • http://www.lex4.k12.sc.us
Grade Span: PK-12; **Agency Type:** 1
Schools: 6
  3 Primary; 2 Middle; 1 High; 0 Other Level
  6 Regular; 0 Special Education; 0 Vocational; 0 Alternative
  0 Magnet; 0 Charter; 5 Title I Eligible; 0 School-wide Title I
Students: 3,672 (51.5% male; 48.4% female)
  Individual Education Program: 656 (17.9%);
  English Language Learner: 14 (0.4%); Migrant: n/a
  Eligible for Free Lunch Program: 2,037 (55.5%)
  Eligible for Reduced-Price Lunch Program: 358 (9.7%)
Teachers: 216.0 (17.0 to 1)
Librarians/Media Specialists: 5.0 (734.4 to 1)
Guidance Counselors: 4.0 (918.0 to 1)
Current Spending: ($ per student per year):
  Total: $6,372; Instruction: $3,510; Support Services: $2,507
Enrollment, Drop-out Rates and Diploma Recipients by Race/Ethnicity

Category	Total	White	Black	Asian	AIAN	Hisp.
Enrollment (%)	100.0	76.0	21.1	0.3	0.2	2.3
Drop-out Rate (%)	6.3	7.2	2.6	0.0	n/a	0.0
H.S. Diplomas (#)	108	n/a	n/a	n/a	n/a	n/a

Lexington County SD 05
Box 938 • Ballentine, SC 29002-0938
(803) 732-8000 • http://www.lex5.k12.sc.us
Grade Span: PK-12; **Agency Type:** 1
Schools: 18
  11 Primary; 4 Middle; 3 High; 0 Other Level
  18 Regular; 0 Special Education; 0 Vocational; 0 Alternative
  0 Magnet; 0 Charter; 7 Title I Eligible; 0 School-wide Title I
Students: 15,865 (51.7% male; 48.2% female)
  Individual Education Program: 2,095 (13.2%);
  English Language Learner: 228 (1.4%); Migrant: n/a
  Eligible for Free Lunch Program: 2,465 (15.5%)
  Eligible for Reduced-Price Lunch Program: 815 (5.1%)
Teachers: 1,082.8 (14.7 to 1)
Librarians/Media Specialists: 20.0 (793.3 to 1)
Guidance Counselors: 34.5 (459.9 to 1)
Current Spending: ($ per student per year):
  Total: $7,770; Instruction: $4,579; Support Services: $2,859
Enrollment, Drop-out Rates and Diploma Recipients by Race/Ethnicity

Category	Total	White	Black	Asian	AIAN	Hisp.
Enrollment (%)	100.0	69.4	26.4	2.2	0.1	1.5
Drop-out Rate (%)	1.8	1.3	3.3	2.3	0.0	9.1
H.S. Diplomas (#)	1,002	n/a	n/a	n/a	n/a	n/a

Marion County

Marion County SD 01
616 Northside Ave • Marion, SC 29571-2399
(843) 423-1811 • http://www.marion1.k12.sc.us
Grade Span: PK-12; **Agency Type:** 1
Schools: 4
  2 Primary; 1 Middle; 1 High; 0 Other Level
  4 Regular; 0 Special Education; 0 Vocational; 0 Alternative
  0 Magnet; 0 Charter; 4 Title I Eligible; 4 School-wide Title I
Students: 3,256 (51.6% male; 48.3% female)
  Individual Education Program: 432 (13.3%);
  English Language Learner: 1 (<0.1%); Migrant: n/a

Eligible for Free Lunch Program: 2,241 (68.8%)
Eligible for Reduced-Price Lunch Program: 213 (6.5%)
Teachers: 206.0 (15.8 to 1)
Librarians/Media Specialists: 5.0 (651.2 to 1)
Guidance Counselors: 8.0 (407.0 to 1)
Current Spending: ($ per student per year):
Total: $6,679; Instruction: $4,079; Support Services: $2,135
Enrollment, Drop-out Rates and Diploma Recipients by Race/Ethnicity

Category	Total	White	Black	Asian	AIAN	Hisp.
Enrollment (%)	100.0	26.1	72.8	0.2	0.3	0.6
Drop-out Rate (%)	1.2	0.8	1.5	0.0	0.0	n/a
H.S. Diplomas (#)	170	n/a	n/a	n/a	n/a	n/a

Marion County SD 02

Box 689 • Mullins, SC 29574-0689
(843) 464-3700 • http://www.marion2.k12.sc.us
Grade Span: PK-12; **Agency Type:** 1
Schools: 5
2 Primary; 2 Middle; 1 High; 0 Other Level
5 Regular; 0 Special Education; 0 Vocational; 0 Alternative
0 Magnet; 0 Charter; 3 Title I Eligible; 3 School-wide Title I
Students: 2,190   (51.5% male; 48.4% female)
Individual Education Program: 255 (11.6%);
English Language Learner: 6 (0.3%); Migrant: n/a
Eligible for Free Lunch Program: 1,544 (70.5%)
Eligible for Reduced-Price Lunch Program: 192 (8.8%)
Teachers: 135.6 (16.2 to 1)
Librarians/Media Specialists: 4.0 (547.5 to 1)
Guidance Counselors: 5.0 (438.0 to 1)
Current Spending: ($ per student per year):
Total: $6,586; Instruction: $3,944; Support Services: $2,118
Enrollment, Drop-out Rates and Diploma Recipients by Race/Ethnicity

Category	Total	White	Black	Asian	AIAN	Hisp.
Enrollment (%)	100.0	25.9	72.2	0.1	0.3	1.2
Drop-out Rate (%)	2.3	2.2	2.4	0.0	0.0	0.0
H.S. Diplomas (#)	117	n/a	n/a	n/a	n/a	n/a

Marlboro County

Marlboro County SD

PO Box 947 • Bennettsville, SC 29512-4002
(843) 479-4016 • http://www.marlboro.k12.sc.us/
Grade Span: PK-12; **Agency Type:** 1
Schools: 9
6 Primary; 2 Middle; 1 High; 0 Other Level
9 Regular; 0 Special Education; 0 Vocational; 0 Alternative
2 Magnet; 0 Charter; 7 Title I Eligible; 7 School-wide Title I
Students: 5,175   (51.7% male; 48.2% female)
Individual Education Program: 167 (3.2%);
English Language Learner: 1 (<0.1%); Migrant: n/a
Eligible for Free Lunch Program: 3,490 (67.4%)
Eligible for Reduced-Price Lunch Program: 619 (12.0%)
Teachers: 336.0 (15.4 to 1)
Librarians/Media Specialists: 7.0 (739.3 to 1)
Guidance Counselors: 14.0 (369.6 to 1)
Current Spending: ($ per student per year):
Total: $6,963; Instruction: $3,862; Support Services: $2,659
Enrollment, Drop-out Rates and Diploma Recipients by Race/Ethnicity

Category	Total	White	Black	Asian	AIAN	Hisp.
Enrollment (%)	100.0	32.8	62.6	0.2	3.9	0.4
Drop-out Rate (%)	7.1	7.1	7.3	0.0	6.1	0.0
H.S. Diplomas (#)	207	n/a	n/a	n/a	n/a	n/a

Newberry County

Newberry County SD

Box 718 • Newberry, SC 29108-0718
(803) 321-2600 • http://www.newberry.k12.sc.us
Grade Span: PK-12; **Agency Type:** 1
Schools: 14
7 Primary; 3 Middle; 3 High; 1 Other Level
13 Regular; 0 Special Education; 1 Vocational; 0 Alternative
0 Magnet; 0 Charter; 7 Title I Eligible; 7 School-wide Title I
Students: 5,924   (52.1% male; 47.8% female)
Individual Education Program: 1,156 (19.5%);
English Language Learner: 267 (4.5%); Migrant: n/a
Eligible for Free Lunch Program: 2,935 (49.5%)
Eligible for Reduced-Price Lunch Program: 545 (9.2%)
Teachers: 424.1 (14.0 to 1)
Librarians/Media Specialists: 13.0 (455.7 to 1)
Guidance Counselors: 16.5 (359.0 to 1)
Current Spending: ($ per student per year):
Total: $7,757; Instruction: $4,493; Support Services: $2,832

Enrollment, Drop-out Rates and Diploma Recipients by Race/Ethnicity

Category	Total	White	Black	Asian	AIAN	Hisp.
Enrollment (%)	100.0	46.3	46.6	0.1	0.1	6.8
Drop-out Rate (%)	5.8	5.2	6.2	0.0	0.0	11.9
H.S. Diplomas (#)	268	n/a	n/a	n/a	n/a	n/a

Oconee County

Oconee County SD

PO Box 649 • Walhalla, SC 29691-0006
(843) 638-4029 • http://www.oconee.k12.sc.us
Grade Span: PK-12; **Agency Type:** 1
Schools: 21
11 Primary; 5 Middle; 5 High; 0 Other Level
20 Regular; 0 Special Education; 1 Vocational; 0 Alternative
0 Magnet; 0 Charter; 7 Title I Eligible; 7 School-wide Title I
Students: 10,951   (52.1% male; 47.8% female)
Individual Education Program: 2,156 (19.7%);
English Language Learner: 240 (2.2%); Migrant: n/a
Eligible for Free Lunch Program: 4,402 (40.2%)
Eligible for Reduced-Price Lunch Program: 1,062 (9.7%)
Teachers: 786.5 (13.9 to 1)
Librarians/Media Specialists: 20.0 (547.6 to 1)
Guidance Counselors: 29.4 (372.5 to 1)
Current Spending: ($ per student per year):
Total: $7,879; Instruction: $4,625; Support Services: $2,847
Enrollment, Drop-out Rates and Diploma Recipients by Race/Ethnicity

Category	Total	White	Black	Asian	AIAN	Hisp.
Enrollment (%)	100.0	80.7	13.0	0.6	0.2	5.4
Drop-out Rate (%)	4.0	4.2	3.3	0.0	0.0	1.1
H.S. Diplomas (#)	496	n/a	n/a	n/a	n/a	n/a

Orangeburg County

Orangeburg County SD 03

1515 Brant Avenue-PO Box • Holly Hill, SC 29059
Mailing Address: 1515 Brant Avenue-PO Box 98 • Holly Hill, SC 29059
(803) 496-3288 • http://www.obg3.k12.sc.us
Grade Span: PK-12; **Agency Type:** 1
Schools: 8
4 Primary; 1 Middle; 3 High; 0 Other Level
8 Regular; 0 Special Education; 0 Vocational; 0 Alternative
0 Magnet; 0 Charter; 6 Title I Eligible; 6 School-wide Title I
Students: 3,621   (50.0% male; 49.9% female)
Individual Education Program: 715 (19.7%);
English Language Learner: 15 (0.4%); Migrant: n/a
Eligible for Free Lunch Program: 2,866 (79.1%)
Eligible for Reduced-Price Lunch Program: 303 (8.4%)
Teachers: 259.6 (13.9 to 1)
Librarians/Media Specialists: 7.0 (517.3 to 1)
Guidance Counselors: 10.0 (362.1 to 1)
Current Spending: ($ per student per year):
Total: $8,229; Instruction: $4,686; Support Services: $3,086
Enrollment, Drop-out Rates and Diploma Recipients by Race/Ethnicity

Category	Total	White	Black	Asian	AIAN	Hisp.
Enrollment (%)	100.0	9.4	89.5	0.0	0.1	0.9
Drop-out Rate (%)	7.2	14.4	6.5	0.0	0.0	n/a
H.S. Diplomas (#)	154	n/a	n/a	n/a	n/a	n/a

Orangeburg County SD 04

PO Box 69 • Cordova, SC 29039-0006
(803) 534-7420 • http://www.orangeburg4.com
Grade Span: PK-12; **Agency Type:** 1
Schools: 8
4 Primary; 1 Middle; 3 High; 0 Other Level
8 Regular; 0 Special Education; 0 Vocational; 0 Alternative
0 Magnet; 0 Charter; 7 Title I Eligible; 7 School-wide Title I
Students: 4,254   (50.6% male; 49.3% female)
Individual Education Program: 693 (16.3%);
English Language Learner: 2 (<0.1%); Migrant: n/a
Eligible for Free Lunch Program: 2,403 (56.5%)
Eligible for Reduced-Price Lunch Program: 490 (11.5%)
Teachers: 267.2 (15.9 to 1)
Librarians/Media Specialists: 6.0 (709.0 to 1)
Guidance Counselors: 10.0 (425.4 to 1)
Current Spending: ($ per student per year):
Total: $6,972; Instruction: $4,050; Support Services: $2,422
Enrollment, Drop-out Rates and Diploma Recipients by Race/Ethnicity

Category	Total	White	Black	Asian	AIAN	Hisp.
Enrollment (%)	100.0	47.0	52.0	0.2	0.1	0.7
Drop-out Rate (%)	2.4	2.7	2.0	0.0	0.0	20.0
H.S. Diplomas (#)	193	n/a	n/a	n/a	n/a	n/a

Orangeburg County SD 05
578 Ellis Ave • Orangeburg, SC 29115-5022
(803) 534-5454 • http://www.orangeburg5.k12.sc.us
Grade Span: PK-12; **Agency Type:** 1
Schools: 14
    8 Primary; 2 Middle; 2 High; 2 Other Level
    13 Regular; 0 Special Education; 1 Vocational; 0 Alternative
    1 Magnet; 0 Charter; 9 Title I Eligible; 9 School-wide Title I
Students: 7,801 (51.3% male; 48.6% female)
    Individual Education Program: 1,500 (19.2%);
    English Language Learner: 25 (0.3%); Migrant: n/a
    Eligible for Free Lunch Program: 5,488 (70.4%)
    Eligible for Reduced-Price Lunch Program: 685 (8.8%)
Teachers: 572.6 (13.6 to 1)
Librarians/Media Specialists: 15.0 (520.1 to 1)
Guidance Counselors: 22.0 (354.6 to 1)
Current Spending: ($ per student per year):
    Total: $8,314; Instruction: $4,649; Support Services: $3,151
Enrollment, Drop-out Rates and Diploma Recipients by Race/Ethnicity

Category	Total	White	Black	Asian	AIAN	Hisp.
Enrollment (%)	100.0	8.5	90.1	0.8	0.0	0.6
Drop-out Rate (%)	4.6	3.7	4.8	0.0	0.0	0.0
H.S. Diplomas (#)	399	n/a	n/a	n/a	n/a	n/a

Pickens County

Pickens County SD
1348 Griffin Mill Rd • Easley, SC 29640-9808
(864) 855-8150 • http://www.pickens.k12.sc.us
Grade Span: PK-12; **Agency Type:** 1
Schools: 25
    15 Primary; 5 Middle; 5 High; 0 Other Level
    24 Regular; 0 Special Education; 1 Vocational; 0 Alternative
    0 Magnet; 0 Charter; 6 Title I Eligible; 0 School-wide Title I
Students: 16,262 (50.9% male; 49.0% female)
    Individual Education Program: 2,360 (14.5%);
    English Language Learner: 274 (1.7%); Migrant: n/a
    Eligible for Free Lunch Program: 4,841 (29.8%)
    Eligible for Reduced-Price Lunch Program: 1,294 (8.0%)
Teachers: 1,022.4 (15.9 to 1)
Librarians/Media Specialists: 29.0 (560.8 to 1)
Guidance Counselors: 36.2 (449.2 to 1)
Current Spending: ($ per student per year):
    Total: $6,302; Instruction: $3,864; Support Services: $2,084
Enrollment, Drop-out Rates and Diploma Recipients by Race/Ethnicity

Category	Total	White	Black	Asian	AIAN	Hisp.
Enrollment (%)	100.0	87.8	8.9	0.9	0.1	2.1
Drop-out Rate (%)	6.3	6.3	8.4	0.0	0.0	3.7
H.S. Diplomas (#)	755	n/a	n/a	n/a	n/a	n/a

Richland County

Richland County SD 01
1616 Richland St • Columbia, SC 29201-2657
(803) 733-6041 • http://www.richlandone.org/
Grade Span: PK-12; **Agency Type:** 1
Schools: 50
    28 Primary; 10 Middle; 9 High; 3 Other Level
    46 Regular; 3 Special Education; 1 Vocational; 0 Alternative
    8 Magnet; 0 Charter; 23 Title I Eligible; 23 School-wide Title I
Students: 26,990 (50.5% male; 49.4% female)
    Individual Education Program: 3,866 (14.3%);
    English Language Learner: 363 (1.3%); Migrant: n/a
    Eligible for Free Lunch Program: 15,489 (57.4%)
    Eligible for Reduced-Price Lunch Program: 1,349 (5.0%)
Teachers: 1,986.8 (13.6 to 1)
Librarians/Media Specialists: 54.0 (499.8 to 1)
Guidance Counselors: 87.0 (310.2 to 1)
Current Spending: ($ per student per year):
    Total: $8,521; Instruction: $4,952; Support Services: $3,233
Enrollment, Drop-out Rates and Diploma Recipients by Race/Ethnicity

Category	Total	White	Black	Asian	AIAN	Hisp.
Enrollment (%)	100.0	18.5	78.4	0.7	0.1	1.9
Drop-out Rate (%)	3.2	1.6	3.7	0.0	0.0	2.0
H.S. Diplomas (#)	1,178	n/a	n/a	n/a	n/a	n/a

Richland County SD 02
6831 Brookfield Rd • Columbia, SC 29206-2205
(803) 787-1910 • http://www.richland2.org/
Grade Span: PK-12; **Agency Type:** 1
Schools: 23
    16 Primary; 3 Middle; 4 High; 0 Other Level
    23 Regular; 0 Special Education; 0 Vocational; 0 Alternative
    6 Magnet; 0 Charter; 6 Title I Eligible; 6 School-wide Title I
Students: 19,865 (50.4% male; 49.5% female)

    Individual Education Program: 2,488 (12.5%);
    English Language Learner: 519 (2.6%); Migrant: n/a
    Eligible for Free Lunch Program: 5,175 (26.1%)
    Eligible for Reduced-Price Lunch Program: 1,560 (7.9%)
Teachers: 1,332.9 (14.9 to 1)
Librarians/Media Specialists: 23.0 (863.7 to 1)
Guidance Counselors: 45.0 (441.4 to 1)
Current Spending: ($ per student per year):
    Total: $7,144; Instruction: $4,347; Support Services: $2,533
Enrollment, Drop-out Rates and Diploma Recipients by Race/Ethnicity

Category	Total	White	Black	Asian	AIAN	Hisp.
Enrollment (%)	100.0	37.7	55.5	2.7	0.2	3.5
Drop-out Rate (%)	2.6	1.6	3.5	0.0	0.0	2.9
H.S. Diplomas (#)	958	n/a	n/a	n/a	n/a	n/a

Saluda County

Saluda County SD
404 N Wise Rd • Saluda, SC 29138-1024
(843) 445-8441 • http://www.saludak-12.org/
Grade Span: PK-12; **Agency Type:** 1
Schools: 5
    3 Primary; 1 Middle; 1 High; 0 Other Level
    5 Regular; 0 Special Education; 0 Vocational; 0 Alternative
    0 Magnet; 0 Charter; 5 Title I Eligible; 5 School-wide Title I
Students: 2,201 (51.7% male; 48.2% female)
    Individual Education Program: 414 (18.8%);
    English Language Learner: 165 (7.5%); Migrant: n/a
    Eligible for Free Lunch Program: 1,116 (50.7%)
    Eligible for Reduced-Price Lunch Program: 205 (9.3%)
Teachers: 147.5 (14.9 to 1)
Librarians/Media Specialists: 4.0 (550.3 to 1)
Guidance Counselors: 6.0 (366.8 to 1)
Current Spending: ($ per student per year):
    Total: $7,560; Instruction: $4,033; Support Services: $3,057
Enrollment, Drop-out Rates and Diploma Recipients by Race/Ethnicity

Category	Total	White	Black	Asian	AIAN	Hisp.
Enrollment (%)	100.0	50.3	37.1	0.1	0.0	12.4
Drop-out Rate (%)	1.4	0.0	3.5	n/a	n/a	0.0
H.S. Diplomas (#)	79	n/a	n/a	n/a	n/a	n/a

Spartanburg County

Spartanburg County SD 01
Box 218 • Campobello, SC 29322-0218
(864) 468-4542 • http://www.spartanburg1.k12.sc.us/
Grade Span: PK-12; **Agency Type:** 1
Schools: 9
    5 Primary; 2 Middle; 2 High; 0 Other Level
    9 Regular; 0 Special Education; 0 Vocational; 0 Alternative
    0 Magnet; 0 Charter; 5 Title I Eligible; 0 School-wide Title I
Students: 4,574 (51.1% male; 48.8% female)
    Individual Education Program: 816 (17.8%);
    English Language Learner: 57 (1.2%); Migrant: n/a
    Eligible for Free Lunch Program: 1,591 (34.8%)
    Eligible for Reduced-Price Lunch Program: 354 (7.7%)
Teachers: 320.2 (14.3 to 1)
Librarians/Media Specialists: 8.0 (571.8 to 1)
Guidance Counselors: 12.0 (381.2 to 1)
Current Spending: ($ per student per year):
    Total: $6,952; Instruction: $4,264; Support Services: $2,349
Enrollment, Drop-out Rates and Diploma Recipients by Race/Ethnicity

Category	Total	White	Black	Asian	AIAN	Hisp.
Enrollment (%)	100.0	83.1	12.7	1.2	0.2	2.6
Drop-out Rate (%)	2.3	2.5	1.4	0.0	0.0	2.9
H.S. Diplomas (#)	211	n/a	n/a	n/a	n/a	n/a

Spartanburg County SD 02
4606parris Bridge Rd • Spartanburg, SC 29316-6021
(843) 578-0128 • http://www.spartanburg2.k12.sc.us
Grade Span: PK-12; **Agency Type:** 1
Schools: 13
    7 Primary; 3 Middle; 2 High; 1 Other Level
    13 Regular; 0 Special Education; 0 Vocational; 0 Alternative
    0 Magnet; 0 Charter; 4 Title I Eligible; 4 School-wide Title I
Students: 8,853 (52.1% male; 47.8% female)
    Individual Education Program: 1,051 (11.9%);
    English Language Learner: 412 (4.7%); Migrant: n/a
    Eligible for Free Lunch Program: 2,595 (29.3%)
    Eligible for Reduced-Price Lunch Program: 811 (9.2%)
Teachers: 475.7 (18.6 to 1)
Librarians/Media Specialists: 15.0 (590.2 to 1)
Guidance Counselors: 18.0 (491.8 to 1)
Current Spending: ($ per student per year):
    Total: $5,446; Instruction: $3,444; Support Services: $1,688

Enrollment, Drop-out Rates and Diploma Recipients by Race/Ethnicity

Category	Total	White	Black	Asian	AIAN	Hisp.
Enrollment (%)	100.0	79.9	12.1	3.4	0.1	4.2
Drop-out Rate (%)	3.9	3.9	4.2	4.5	0.0	2.6
H.S. Diplomas (#)	409	n/a	n/a	n/a	n/a	n/a

Spartanburg County SD 03
Box 267 • Glendale, SC 29346-0267
(843) 579-8000 • http://www.spa3.K12.sc.us
Grade Span: PK-12; **Agency Type:** 1
Schools: 7
    4 Primary; 2 Middle; 1 High; 0 Other Level
    7 Regular; 0 Special Education; 0 Vocational; 0 Alternative
    0 Magnet; 0 Charter; 4 Title I Eligible; 0 School-wide Title I
Students: 3,210 (51.0% male; 48.9% female)
    Individual Education Program: 504 (15.7%);
    English Language Learner: 113 (3.5%); Migrant: n/a
    Eligible for Free Lunch Program: 1,293 (40.3%)
    Eligible for Reduced-Price Lunch Program: 328 (10.2%)
Teachers: 209.5 (15.3 to 1)
Librarians/Media Specialists: 7.0 (458.6 to 1)
Guidance Counselors: 9.8 (327.6 to 1)
Current Spending: ($ per student per year):
    Total: $8,617; Instruction: $4,944; Support Services: $3,289

Enrollment, Drop-out Rates and Diploma Recipients by Race/Ethnicity

Category	Total	White	Black	Asian	AIAN	Hisp.
Enrollment (%)	100.0	76.8	19.7	1.0	0.2	2.3
Drop-out Rate (%)	1.0	1.0	1.0	0.0	0.0	0.0
H.S. Diplomas (#)	161	n/a	n/a	n/a	n/a	n/a

Spartanburg County SD 04
118 Mcedco Rd • Woodruff, SC 29388-0669
(864) 476-3186
Grade Span: PK-12; **Agency Type:** 1
Schools: 4
    2 Primary; 1 Middle; 1 High; 0 Other Level
    4 Regular; 0 Special Education; 0 Vocational; 0 Alternative
    0 Magnet; 0 Charter; 2 Title I Eligible; 0 School-wide Title I
Students: 2,943 (50.7% male; 49.2% female)
    Individual Education Program: 307 (10.4%);
    English Language Learner: 35 (1.2%); Migrant: n/a
    Eligible for Free Lunch Program: 1,026 (34.9%)
    Eligible for Reduced-Price Lunch Program: 257 (8.7%)
Teachers: 177.0 (16.6 to 1)
Librarians/Media Specialists: 4.0 (735.8 to 1)
Guidance Counselors: 5.0 (588.6 to 1)
Current Spending: ($ per student per year):
    Total: $6,127; Instruction: $3,574; Support Services: $2,190

Enrollment, Drop-out Rates and Diploma Recipients by Race/Ethnicity

Category	Total	White	Black	Asian	AIAN	Hisp.
Enrollment (%)	100.0	75.5	21.2	0.2	0.1	2.8
Drop-out Rate (%)	0.5	0.3	1.4	0.0	n/a	0.0
H.S. Diplomas (#)	101	n/a	n/a	n/a	n/a	n/a

Spartanburg County SD 05
PO Box 307 • Duncan, SC 29334-0307
(864) 949-2350 • http://www.spart5.k12.sc.us
Grade Span: PK-12; **Agency Type:** 1
Schools: 8
    4 Primary; 3 Middle; 1 High; 0 Other Level
    8 Regular; 0 Special Education; 0 Vocational; 0 Alternative
    0 Magnet; 0 Charter; 2 Title I Eligible; 2 School-wide Title I
Students: 6,409 (52.2% male; 47.7% female)
    Individual Education Program: 1,169 (18.2%);
    English Language Learner: 227 (3.5%); Migrant: n/a
    Eligible for Free Lunch Program: 1,967 (30.7%)
    Eligible for Reduced-Price Lunch Program: 577 (9.0%)
Teachers: 439.7 (14.6 to 1)
Librarians/Media Specialists: 8.0 (801.1 to 1)
Guidance Counselors: 15.0 (427.3 to 1)
Current Spending: ($ per student per year):
    Total: $7,080; Instruction: $4,531; Support Services: $2,202

Enrollment, Drop-out Rates and Diploma Recipients by Race/Ethnicity

Category	Total	White	Black	Asian	AIAN	Hisp.
Enrollment (%)	100.0	70.2	23.0	2.1	0.1	4.3
Drop-out Rate (%)	2.7	2.9	2.2	0.0	0.0	0.0
H.S. Diplomas (#)	268	n/a	n/a	n/a	n/a	n/a

Spartanburg County SD 06
1493 W O Ezell Blvd • Spartanburg, SC 29301-2615
(843) 576-4212 • http://www.Spartanburg6.k12.sc.us
Grade Span: PK-12; **Agency Type:** 1
Schools: 14
    9 Primary; 3 Middle; 1 High; 1 Other Level
    14 Regular; 0 Special Education; 0 Vocational; 0 Alternative

    0 Magnet; 0 Charter; 6 Title I Eligible; 6 School-wide Title I
Students: 9,761 (51.0% male; 48.9% female)
    Individual Education Program: 1,266 (13.0%);
    English Language Learner: 417 (4.3%); Migrant: n/a
    Eligible for Free Lunch Program: 3,567 (36.5%)
    Eligible for Reduced-Price Lunch Program: 659 (6.8%)
Teachers: 645.7 (15.1 to 1)
Librarians/Media Specialists: 14.0 (697.2 to 1)
Guidance Counselors: 25.0 (390.4 to 1)
Current Spending: ($ per student per year):
    Total: $6,398; Instruction: $4,128; Support Services: $1,903

Enrollment, Drop-out Rates and Diploma Recipients by Race/Ethnicity

Category	Total	White	Black	Asian	AIAN	Hisp.
Enrollment (%)	100.0	58.3	29.9	3.7	0.5	7.4
Drop-out Rate (%)	1.8	1.2	2.3	2.7	0.0	10.8
H.S. Diplomas (#)	498	n/a	n/a	n/a	n/a	n/a

Spartanburg County SD 07
PO Box 970 610 Dupre • Spartanburg, SC 29304-0970
(864) 594-4400 • http://www.spart7.k12.sc.us
Grade Span: PK-12; **Agency Type:** 1
Schools: 14
    9 Primary; 3 Middle; 1 High; 1 Other Level
    13 Regular; 1 Special Education; 0 Vocational; 0 Alternative
    0 Magnet; 0 Charter; 4 Title I Eligible; 4 School-wide Title I
Students: 8,749 (51.2% male; 48.7% female)
    Individual Education Program: 1,647 (18.8%);
    English Language Learner: 174 (2.0%); Migrant: n/a
    Eligible for Free Lunch Program: 4,962 (56.7%)
    Eligible for Reduced-Price Lunch Program: 588 (6.7%)
Teachers: 698.4 (12.5 to 1)
Librarians/Media Specialists: 15.0 (583.3 to 1)
Guidance Counselors: 21.5 (406.9 to 1)
Current Spending: ($ per student per year):
    Total: $8,936; Instruction: $5,320; Support Services: $3,220

Enrollment, Drop-out Rates and Diploma Recipients by Race/Ethnicity

Category	Total	White	Black	Asian	AIAN	Hisp.
Enrollment (%)	100.0	33.2	61.7	2.7	0.1	2.2
Drop-out Rate (%)	3.8	1.9	5.3	1.8	200.0	2.4
H.S. Diplomas (#)	372	n/a	n/a	n/a	n/a	n/a

Sumter County

Sumter County SD 02
1345 Wilson Hall Rd • Sumter, SC 29150-0002
(803) 469-6900 • http://myschoolonline.com/sc/sumter2
Grade Span: PK-12; **Agency Type:** 1
Schools: 15
    8 Primary; 5 Middle; 2 High; 0 Other Level
    15 Regular; 0 Special Education; 0 Vocational; 0 Alternative
    0 Magnet; 0 Charter; 10 Title I Eligible; 10 School-wide Title I
Students: 9,584 (51.0% male; 48.9% female)
    Individual Education Program: 1,529 (16.0%);
    English Language Learner: 18 (0.2%); Migrant: n/a
    Eligible for Free Lunch Program: 5,397 (56.3%)
    Eligible for Reduced-Price Lunch Program: 1,257 (13.1%)
Teachers: 538.7 (17.8 to 1)
Librarians/Media Specialists: 13.0 (737.2 to 1)
Guidance Counselors: 30.0 (319.5 to 1)
Current Spending: ($ per student per year):
    Total: $6,119; Instruction: $3,293; Support Services: $2,461

Enrollment, Drop-out Rates and Diploma Recipients by Race/Ethnicity

Category	Total	White	Black	Asian	AIAN	Hisp.
Enrollment (%)	100.0	38.0	59.1	0.9	0.3	1.6
Drop-out Rate (%)	1.6	1.5	1.8	3.1	0.0	0.0
H.S. Diplomas (#)	356	n/a	n/a	n/a	n/a	n/a

Sumter County SD 17
PO Box 1180 • Sumter, SC 29150-1180
(803) 469-8536 • http://www.sumter17.k12.sc.us
Grade Span: PK-12; **Agency Type:** 1
Schools: 11
    7 Primary; 3 Middle; 1 High; 0 Other Level
    11 Regular; 0 Special Education; 0 Vocational; 0 Alternative
    0 Magnet; 0 Charter; 8 Title I Eligible; 8 School-wide Title I
Students: 9,316 (50.3% male; 49.6% female)
    Individual Education Program: 1,379 (14.8%);
    English Language Learner: 79 (0.8%); Migrant: n/a
    Eligible for Free Lunch Program: 5,057 (54.3%)
    Eligible for Reduced-Price Lunch Program: 788 (8.5%)
Teachers: 577.1 (16.1 to 1)
Librarians/Media Specialists: 12.0 (776.3 to 1)
Guidance Counselors: 20.3 (458.9 to 1)
Current Spending: ($ per student per year):
    Total: $6,276; Instruction: $3,864; Support Services: $1,962

Enrollment, Drop-out Rates and Diploma Recipients by Race/Ethnicity

Category	Total	White	Black	Asian	AIAN	Hisp.
Enrollment (%)	100.0	31.5	66.2	0.8	0.2	1.3
Drop-out Rate (%)	2.0	1.5	2.2	0.0	0.0	10.0
H.S. Diplomas (#)	416	n/a	n/a	n/a	n/a	n/a

Union County

Union County SD
Box 907 • Union, SC 29379-0907
(864) 429-1740 • http://www.union.k12.sc.us
Grade Span: PK-12; **Agency Type:** 1
Schools: 9
    4 Primary; 2 Middle; 2 High; 1 Other Level
    9 Regular; 0 Special Education; 0 Vocational; 0 Alternative
    0 Magnet; 0 Charter; 4 Title I Eligible; 4 School-wide Title I
Students: 5,111   (50.0% male; 49.9% female)
    Individual Education Program: 1,062 (20.8%);
    English Language Learner: 4 (0.1%); Migrant: n/a
    Eligible for Free Lunch Program: 2,532 (49.5%)
    Eligible for Reduced-Price Lunch Program: 529 (10.4%)
Teachers: 360.5 (14.2 to 1)
Librarians/Media Specialists: 9.0 (567.9 to 1)
Guidance Counselors: 11.5 (444.4 to 1)
Current Spending: ($ per student per year):
    Total: $7,097; Instruction: $4,245; Support Services: $2,441
Enrollment, Drop-out Rates and Diploma Recipients by Race/Ethnicity

Category	Total	White	Black	Asian	AIAN	Hisp.
Enrollment (%)	100.0	59.5	39.6	0.3	0.1	0.3
Drop-out Rate (%)	3.5	3.3	3.8	0.0	n/a	0.0
H.S. Diplomas (#)	234	n/a	n/a	n/a	n/a	n/a

Williamsburg County

Williamsburg County SD
Box 1067 • Kingstree, SC 29556-1067
(843) 354-5571 • http://www.wcsd.k12.sc.us
Grade Span: PK-12; **Agency Type:** 1
Schools: 14
    7 Primary; 2 Middle; 5 High; 0 Other Level
    13 Regular; 0 Special Education; 1 Vocational; 0 Alternative
    0 Magnet; 1 Charter; 13 Title I Eligible; 12 School-wide Title I
Students: 6,085   (51.3% male; 48.6% female)
    Individual Education Program: 1,263 (20.8%);
    English Language Learner: 50 (0.8%); Migrant: n/a
    Eligible for Free Lunch Program: 5,122 (84.2%)
    Eligible for Reduced-Price Lunch Program: 365 (6.0%)
Teachers: 357.0 (17.0 to 1)
Librarians/Media Specialists: 12.6 (482.9 to 1)
Guidance Counselors: 17.0 (357.9 to 1)
Current Spending: ($ per student per year):
    Total: $7,274; Instruction: $4,177; Support Services: $2,624
Enrollment, Drop-out Rates and Diploma Recipients by Race/Ethnicity

Category	Total	White	Black	Asian	AIAN	Hisp.
Enrollment (%)	100.0	7.8	91.7	0.0	0.0	0.4
Drop-out Rate (%)	1.9	1.6	1.9	0.0	n/a	0.0
H.S. Diplomas (#)	271	n/a	n/a	n/a	n/a	n/a

York County

York County SD 01
Box 770 • York, SC 29745-0770
(803) 684-9916 • http://www.york.k12.sc.us
Grade Span: PK-12; **Agency Type:** 1
Schools: 8
    4 Primary; 1 Middle; 2 High; 1 Other Level
    7 Regular; 0 Special Education; 1 Vocational; 0 Alternative
    0 Magnet; 0 Charter; 4 Title I Eligible; 3 School-wide Title I
Students: 5,256   (51.2% male; 48.7% female)
    Individual Education Program: 799 (15.2%);
    English Language Learner: 72 (1.4%); Migrant: n/a
    Eligible for Free Lunch Program: 2,048 (39.0%)
    Eligible for Reduced-Price Lunch Program: 536 (10.2%)
Teachers: 340.3 (15.4 to 1)
Librarians/Media Specialists: 8.0 (657.0 to 1)
Guidance Counselors: 11.6 (453.1 to 1)
Current Spending: ($ per student per year):
    Total: $6,757; Instruction: $4,077; Support Services: $2,269
Enrollment, Drop-out Rates and Diploma Recipients by Race/Ethnicity

Category	Total	White	Black	Asian	AIAN	Hisp.
Enrollment (%)	100.0	73.2	22.4	0.8	0.8	2.6
Drop-out Rate (%)	3.9	3.6	5.1	0.0	0.0	4.0
H.S. Diplomas (#)	242	n/a	n/a	n/a	n/a	n/a

York County SD 02
PO Box 99 • Clover, SC 29710-0099
(803) 222-7191 • http://www.clover.k12.sc.us
Grade Span: PK-12; **Agency Type:** 1
Schools: 8
    5 Primary; 2 Middle; 1 High; 0 Other Level
    8 Regular; 0 Special Education; 0 Vocational; 0 Alternative
    0 Magnet; 0 Charter; 3 Title I Eligible; 0 School-wide Title I
Students: 5,346   (52.2% male; 47.7% female)
    Individual Education Program: 674 (12.6%);
    English Language Learner: 85 (1.6%); Migrant: n/a
    Eligible for Free Lunch Program: 1,284 (24.0%)
    Eligible for Reduced-Price Lunch Program: 366 (6.8%)
Teachers: 363.2 (14.7 to 1)
Librarians/Media Specialists: 10.0 (534.6 to 1)
Guidance Counselors: 13.0 (411.2 to 1)
Current Spending: ($ per student per year):
    Total: $7,814; Instruction: $4,847; Support Services: $2,674
Enrollment, Drop-out Rates and Diploma Recipients by Race/Ethnicity

Category	Total	White	Black	Asian	AIAN	Hisp.
Enrollment (%)	100.0	83.7	12.2	1.9	0.2	2.1
Drop-out Rate (%)	2.4	2.4	1.3	4.8	0.0	7.1
H.S. Diplomas (#)	198	n/a	n/a	n/a	n/a	n/a

York County SD 03
PO Drawer 10072 • Rock Hill, SC 29731-0072
(803) 324-5360 • http://www.rock-hill.k12.sc.us
Grade Span: PK-12; **Agency Type:** 1
Schools: 23
    16 Primary; 4 Middle; 3 High; 0 Other Level
    22 Regular; 0 Special Education; 1 Vocational; 0 Alternative
    0 Magnet; 1 Charter; 8 Title I Eligible; 8 School-wide Title I
Students: 16,307   (51.0% male; 48.9% female)
    Individual Education Program: 2,137 (13.1%);
    English Language Learner: 365 (2.2%); Migrant: n/a
    Eligible for Free Lunch Program: 5,228 (32.1%)
    Eligible for Reduced-Price Lunch Program: 1,123 (6.9%)
Teachers: 996.6 (16.4 to 1)
Librarians/Media Specialists: 23.0 (709.0 to 1)
Guidance Counselors: 39.5 (412.8 to 1)
Current Spending: ($ per student per year):
    Total: $6,966; Instruction: $4,220; Support Services: $2,453
Enrollment, Drop-out Rates and Diploma Recipients by Race/Ethnicity

Category	Total	White	Black	Asian	AIAN	Hisp.
Enrollment (%)	100.0	57.7	35.5	1.6	1.6	3.5
Drop-out Rate (%)	1.7	1.6	1.9	1.3	5.2	0.0
H.S. Diplomas (#)	755	n/a	n/a	n/a	n/a	n/a

York County SD 04
120 E Elliott St • Fort Mill, SC 29715-0369
(803) 548-2527 • http://www.fort-mill.k12.sc.us
Grade Span: PK-12; **Agency Type:** 1
Schools: 8
    4 Primary; 2 Middle; 1 High; 1 Other Level
    8 Regular; 0 Special Education; 0 Vocational; 0 Alternative
    0 Magnet; 0 Charter; 2 Title I Eligible; 0 School-wide Title I
Students: 6,381   (51.8% male; 48.1% female)
    Individual Education Program: 668 (10.5%);
    English Language Learner: 58 (0.9%); Migrant: n/a
    Eligible for Free Lunch Program: 769 (12.1%)
    Eligible for Reduced-Price Lunch Program: 194 (3.0%)
Teachers: 408.4 (15.6 to 1)
Librarians/Media Specialists: 9.0 (709.0 to 1)
Guidance Counselors: 13.0 (490.8 to 1)
Current Spending: ($ per student per year):
    Total: $6,885; Instruction: $4,077; Support Services: $2,519
Enrollment, Drop-out Rates and Diploma Recipients by Race/Ethnicity

Category	Total	White	Black	Asian	AIAN	Hisp.
Enrollment (%)	100.0	85.6	10.2	1.6	0.2	2.2
Drop-out Rate (%)	2.1	2.0	2.4	0.0	0.0	8.3
H.S. Diplomas (#)	299	n/a	n/a	n/a	n/a	n/a

Number of Schools

Rank	Number	District Name	City
1	93	Greenville County SD	Greenville
2	80	Charleston County SD	Charleston
3	50	Richland County SD 01	Columbia
4	46	Horry County SD	Conway
5	39	Aiken County SD	Aiken
6	36	Berkeley County SD	Moncks Corner
7	26	Beaufort County SD	Beaufort
8	25	Pickens County SD	Easley
9	23	Richland County SD 02	Columbia
9	23	York County SD 03	Rock Hill
11	22	Darlington County SD	Darlington
12	21	Oconee County SD	Walhalla
13	20	Florence County SD 01	Florence
13	20	Lancaster County SD	Lancaster
13	20	Lexington County SD 01	Lexington
16	19	Cherokee County SD	Gaffney
16	19	Kershaw County SD	Camden
18	18	Lexington County SD 05	Ballentine
19	17	Anderson County SD 05	Anderson
19	17	Dorchester County SD 02	Summerville
19	17	Georgetown County SD	Georgetown
22	16	Chesterfield County SD	Chesterfield
22	16	Lexington County SD 02	W Columbia
24	15	Anderson County SD 01	Williamston
24	15	Sumter County SD 02	Sumter
26	14	Greenwood 50 County SD	Greenwood
26	14	Newberry County SD	Newberry
26	14	Orangeburg County SD 05	Orangeburg
26	14	Spartanburg County SD 06	Spartanburg
26	14	Spartanburg County SD 07	Spartanburg
26	14	Williamsburg County SD	Kingstree
32	13	Spartanburg County SD 02	Spartanburg
33	12	Chester County SD	Chester
33	12	Colleton County SD	Walterboro
35	11	Abbeville County SD	Abbeville
35	11	Laurens County SD 55	Laurens
35	11	Sumter County SD 17	Sumter
38	9	Edgefield County SD	Edgefield
38	9	Fairfield County SD	Winnsboro
38	9	Marlboro County SD	Bennettsville
38	9	Spartanburg County SD 01	Campobello
38	9	Union County SD	Union
43	8	Florence County SD 03	Lake City
43	8	Orangeburg County SD 03	Holly Hill
43	8	Orangeburg County SD 04	Cordova
43	8	Spartanburg County SD 05	Duncan
43	8	York County SD 01	York
43	8	York County SD 02	Clover
43	8	York County SD 04	Fort Mill
50	7	Anderson County SD 02	Honea Path
50	7	Hampton 1 County SD	Hampton
50	7	Laurens County SD 56	Clinton
50	7	Lee County SD	Bishopville
50	7	Spartanburg County SD 03	Glendale
55	6	Clarendon County SD 02	Manning
55	6	Dillon County SD 02	Dillon
55	6	Lexington County SD 04	Swansea
58	5	Anderson County SD 04	Pendleton
58	5	Marion County SD 02	Mullins
58	5	Saluda County SD	Saluda
61	4	Allendale County SD	Allendale
61	4	Anderson County SD 03	Iva
61	4	Bamberg County SD 01	Bamberg
61	4	Barnwell County SD 45	Barnwell
61	4	Calhoun County SD	St Matthews
61	4	Dillon County SD 03	Latta
61	4	Dorchester County SD 04	St George
61	4	Greenwood 52 County SD	Ninety Six
61	4	Jasper County SD	Ridgeland
61	4	Lexington County SD 03	Batesburg
61	4	Marion County SD 01	Marion
61	4	Spartanburg County SD 04	Woodruff
73	3	Florence County SD 05	Johnsonville

Number of Teachers

Rank	Number	District Name	City
1	3,835	Greenville County SD	Greenville
2	3,160	Charleston County SD	Charleston
3	2,101	Horry County SD	Conway
4	1,986	Richland County SD 01	Columbia
5	1,623	Berkeley County SD	Moncks Corner
6	1,544	Aiken County SD	Aiken
7	1,332	Richland County SD 02	Columbia
8	1,295	Beaufort County SD	Beaufort
9	1,277	Lexington County SD 01	Lexington
10	1,119	Dorchester County SD 02	Summerville
11	1,082	Lexington County SD 05	Ballentine
12	1,022	Pickens County SD	Easley
13	996	York County SD 03	Rock Hill
14	965	Florence County SD 01	Florence
15	818	Darlington County SD	Darlington
16	790	Anderson County SD 05	Anderson
17	786	Oconee County SD	Walhalla
18	739	Georgetown County SD	Georgetown
19	725	Lancaster County SD	Lancaster
20	698	Spartanburg County SD 07	Spartanburg
21	645	Spartanburg County SD 06	Spartanburg
22	643	Cherokee County SD	Gaffney
23	634	Kershaw County SD	Camden
24	633	Lexington County SD 02	W Columbia
25	598	Greenwood 50 County SD	Greenwood
26	577	Sumter County SD 17	Sumter
27	572	Orangeburg County SD 05	Orangeburg
28	538	Sumter County SD 02	Sumter
29	538	Chesterfield County SD	Chesterfield
30	475	Spartanburg County SD 02	Spartanburg
31	461	Anderson County SD 01	Williamston
32	439	Spartanburg County SD 05	Duncan
33	435	Colleton County SD	Walterboro
34	430	Chester County SD	Chester
35	424	Newberry County SD	Newberry
36	408	York County SD 04	Fort Mill
37	363	Laurens County SD 55	Laurens
37	363	York County SD 02	Clover
39	360	Union County SD	Union
40	357	Williamsburg County SD	Kingstree
41	340	York County SD 01	York
42	336	Marlboro County SD	Bennettsville
43	320	Spartanburg County SD 01	Campobello
44	281	Fairfield County SD	Winnsboro
45	277	Edgefield County SD	Edgefield
46	272	Florence County SD 03	Lake City
47	267	Orangeburg County SD 04	Cordova
48	262	Abbeville County SD	Abbeville
49	259	Orangeburg County SD 03	Holly Hill
50	219	Laurens County SD 56	Clinton
51	216	Lexington County SD 04	Swansea
52	215	Anderson County SD 02	Honea Path
53	209	Spartanburg County SD 03	Glendale
54	209	Dillon County SD 02	Dillon
55	206	Marion County SD 01	Marion
56	205	Jasper County SD	Ridgeland
57	197	Lee County SD	Bishopville
58	188	Clarendon County SD 02	Manning
59	187	Anderson County SD 04	Pendleton
60	183	Hampton 1 County SD	Hampton
61	177	Spartanburg County SD 04	Woodruff
62	176	Dorchester County SD 04	St George
63	176	Barnwell County SD 45	Barnwell
64	163	Anderson County SD 03	Iva
65	147	Saluda County SD	Saluda
66	146	Lexington County SD 03	Batesburg
67	145	Allendale County SD	Allendale
68	144	Calhoun County SD	St Matthews
69	135	Marion County SD 02	Mullins
70	111	Bamberg County SD 01	Bamberg
71	106	Greenwood 52 County SD	Ninety Six
72	97	Dillon County SD 03	Latta
73	94	Florence County SD 05	Johnsonville

Number of Students

Rank	Number	District Name	City
1	64,245	Greenville County SD	Greenville
2	44,109	Charleston County SD	Charleston
3	31,648	Horry County SD	Conway
4	27,899	Berkeley County SD	Moncks Corner
5	26,990	Richland County SD 01	Columbia
6	25,333	Aiken County SD	Aiken
7	19,865	Richland County SD 02	Columbia
8	19,099	Lexington County SD 01	Lexington
9	18,328	Beaufort County SD	Beaufort
10	18,137	Dorchester County SD 02	Summerville
11	16,307	York County SD 03	Rock Hill
12	16,262	Pickens County SD	Easley
13	15,865	Lexington County SD 05	Ballentine
14	14,809	Florence County SD 01	Florence
15	12,040	Darlington County SD	Darlington
16	11,943	Anderson County SD 05	Anderson
17	11,372	Lancaster County SD	Lancaster
18	10,951	Oconee County SD	Walhalla
19	10,571	Georgetown County SD	Georgetown
20	10,270	Kershaw County SD	Camden
21	9,761	Spartanburg County SD 06	Spartanburg
22	9,584	Sumter County SD 02	Sumter
23	9,522	Greenwood 50 County SD	Greenwood
24	9,317	Cherokee County SD	Gaffney
25	9,316	Sumter County SD 17	Sumter
26	9,267	Lexington County SD 02	W Columbia
27	8,853	Spartanburg County SD 02	Spartanburg
28	8,749	Spartanburg County SD 07	Spartanburg
29	8,314	Anderson County SD 01	Williamston
30	8,242	Chesterfield County SD	Chesterfield
31	7,801	Orangeburg County SD 05	Orangeburg
32	6,827	Chester County SD	Chester
33	6,719	Colleton County SD	Walterboro
34	6,409	Spartanburg County SD 05	Duncan
35	6,381	York County SD 04	Fort Mill
36	6,146	Laurens County SD 55	Laurens
37	6,085	Williamsburg County SD	Kingstree
38	5,924	Newberry County SD	Newberry
39	5,346	York County SD 02	Clover
40	5,256	York County SD 01	York
41	5,175	Marlboro County SD	Bennettsville
42	5,111	Union County SD	Union
43	4,574	Spartanburg County SD 01	Campobello
44	4,254	Orangeburg County SD 04	Cordova
45	3,999	Edgefield County SD	Edgefield
46	3,977	Florence County SD 03	Lake City
47	3,841	Dillon County SD 02	Dillon
48	3,812	Abbeville County SD	Abbeville
49	3,795	Anderson County SD 02	Honea Path
50	3,765	Fairfield County SD	Winnsboro
51	3,672	Lexington County SD 04	Swansea
52	3,621	Orangeburg County SD 03	Holly Hill
53	3,518	Clarendon County SD 02	Manning
54	3,435	Laurens County SD 56	Clinton
55	3,256	Marion County SD 01	Marion
56	3,251	Jasper County SD	Ridgeland
57	3,210	Spartanburg County SD 03	Glendale
58	2,943	Spartanburg County SD 04	Woodruff
59	2,901	Lee County SD	Bishopville
60	2,891	Anderson County SD 04	Pendleton
61	2,857	Hampton 1 County SD	Hampton
62	2,826	Barnwell County SD 45	Barnwell
63	2,737	Anderson County SD 03	Iva
64	2,536	Dorchester County SD 04	St George
65	2,268	Lexington County SD 03	Batesburg
66	2,201	Saluda County SD	Saluda
67	2,190	Marion County SD 02	Mullins
68	2,008	Calhoun County SD	St Matthews
69	1,873	Allendale County SD	Allendale
70	1,733	Greenwood 52 County SD	Ninety Six
71	1,721	Bamberg County SD 01	Bamberg
72	1,594	Dillon County SD 03	Latta
73	1,507	Florence County SD 05	Johnsonville

Male Students

Rank	Percent	District Name	City
1	52.9	Jasper County SD	Ridgeland
2	52.7	Dorchester County SD 04	St George
3	52.4	Florence County SD 03	Lake City
4	52.3	Barnwell County SD 45	Barnwell
5	52.2	York County SD 02	Clover
6	52.2	Dillon County SD 02	Dillon
7	52.2	Spartanburg County SD 05	Duncan
8	52.1	Chester County SD	Chester
9	52.1	Lexington County SD 03	Batesburg
10	52.1	Lancaster County SD	Lancaster
10	52.1	Oconee County SD	Walhalla
12	52.1	Newberry County SD	Newberry
13	52.1	Spartanburg County SD 02	Spartanburg
14	52.1	Edgefield County SD	Edgefield
15	51.9	Florence County SD 05	Johnsonville
16	51.9	Abbeville County SD	Abbeville
17	51.8	York County SD 04	Fort Mill
18	51.7	Saluda County SD	Saluda
19	51.7	Darlington County SD	Darlington
20	51.7	Berkeley County SD	Moncks Corner
21	51.7	Marlboro County SD	Bennettsville
22	51.7	Lexington County SD 05	Ballentine
23	51.6	Marion County SD 01	Marion
24	51.6	Anderson County SD 01	Williamston
25	51.5	Lexington County SD 04	Swansea
26	51.5	Marion County SD 02	Mullins
27	51.5	Laurens County SD 55	Laurens
28	51.5	Anderson County SD 02	Honea Path
29	51.5	Lexington County SD 01	Lexington
30	51.4	Georgetown County SD	Georgetown
31	51.4	Laurens County SD 56	Clinton
32	51.4	Hampton 1 County SD	Hampton
33	51.3	Kershaw County SD	Camden
34	51.3	Anderson County SD 04	Pendleton
34	51.3	Orangeburg County SD 05	Orangeburg
36	51.3	Williamsburg County SD	Kingstree
37	51.3	Anderson County SD 03	Iva
38	51.2	Dorchester County SD 02	Summerville
39	51.2	Allendale County SD	Allendale
40	51.2	Spartanburg County SD 07	Spartanburg
41	51.2	Lexington County SD 02	W Columbia
42	51.2	York County SD 01	York
43	51.2	Charleston County SD	Charleston
44	51.2	Horry County SD	Conway
45	51.1	Greenville County SD	Greenville

46	51.1	Greenwood 52 County SD	Ninety Six
47	51.1	Colleton County SD	Walterboro
48	51.1	Spartanburg County SD 01	Campobello
49	51.0	Spartanburg County SD 06	Spartanburg
50	51.0	Sumter County SD 02	Sumter
51	51.0	York County SD 03	Rock Hill
52	51.0	Spartanburg County SD 03	Glendale
53	50.9	Florence County SD 01	Florence
54	50.9	Pickens County SD	Easley
55	50.9	Beaufort County SD	Beaufort
56	50.9	Aiken County SD	Aiken
57	50.9	Bamberg County SD 01	Bamberg
58	50.8	Anderson County SD 05	Anderson
59	50.7	Spartanburg County SD 04	Woodruff
60	50.6	Orangeburg County SD 04	Cordova
61	50.5	Richland County SD 01	Columbia
62	50.5	Cherokee County SD	Gaffney
63	50.4	Richland County SD 02	Columbia
64	50.3	Sumter County SD 17	Sumter
65	50.1	Chesterfield County SD	Chesterfield
66	50.1	Greenwood 50 County SD	Greenwood
67	50.0	Dillon County SD 03	Latta
68	50.0	Union County SD	Union
69	50.0	Orangeburg County SD 03	Holly Hill
70	49.8	Lee County SD	Bishopville
71	49.8	Fairfield County SD	Winnsboro
72	49.7	Calhoun County SD	St Matthews
73	49.5	Clarendon County SD 02	Manning

Female Students

Rank	Percent	District Name	City
1	50.4	Clarendon County SD 02	Manning
2	50.2	Calhoun County SD	St Matthews
3	50.1	Fairfield County SD	Winnsboro
4	50.1	Lee County SD	Bishopville
5	49.9	Orangeburg County SD 03	Holly Hill
6	49.9	Union County SD	Union
7	49.9	Dillon County SD 03	Latta
8	49.8	Greenwood 50 County SD	Greenwood
9	49.8	Chesterfield County SD	Chesterfield
10	49.6	Sumter County SD 17	Sumter
11	49.5	Richland County SD 02	Columbia
12	49.4	Cherokee County SD	Gaffney
13	49.4	Richland County SD 01	Columbia
14	49.3	Orangeburg County SD 04	Cordova
15	49.2	Spartanburg County SD 04	Woodruff
16	49.1	Anderson County SD 05	Anderson
17	49.0	Bamberg County SD 01	Bamberg
18	49.0	Aiken County SD	Aiken
19	49.0	Beaufort County SD	Beaufort
20	49.0	Pickens County SD	Easley
21	49.0	Florence County SD 01	Florence
22	48.9	Spartanburg County SD 03	Glendale
23	48.9	York County SD 03	Rock Hill
24	48.9	Sumter County SD 02	Sumter
25	48.9	Spartanburg County SD 06	Spartanburg
26	48.8	Spartanburg County SD 01	Campobello
27	48.8	Colleton County SD	Walterboro
28	48.8	Greenwood 52 County SD	Ninety Six
29	48.8	Greenville County SD	Greenville
30	48.7	Horry County SD	Conway
31	48.7	Charleston County SD	Charleston
32	48.7	York County SD 01	York
33	48.7	Lexington County SD 02	W Columbia
34	48.7	Spartanburg County SD 07	Spartanburg
35	48.7	Allendale County SD	Allendale
36	48.7	Dorchester County SD 02	Summerville
37	48.6	Anderson County SD 03	Iva
38	48.6	Williamsburg County SD	Kingstree
39	48.6	Anderson County SD 04	Pendleton
39	48.6	Orangeburg County SD 05	Orangeburg
41	48.6	Kershaw County SD	Camden
42	48.5	Hampton 1 County SD	Hampton
43	48.5	Laurens County SD 56	Clinton
44	48.5	Georgetown County SD	Georgetown
45	48.4	Lexington County SD 01	Lexington
46	48.4	Anderson County SD 02	Honea Path
47	48.4	Laurens County SD 55	Laurens
48	48.4	Marion County SD 02	Mullins
49	48.4	Lexington County SD 04	Swansea
50	48.3	Anderson County SD 01	Williamston
51	48.3	Marion County SD 01	Marion
52	48.2	Lexington County SD 05	Ballentine
53	48.2	Marlboro County SD	Bennettsville
54	48.2	Berkeley County SD	Moncks Corner
55	48.2	Darlington County SD	Darlington
56	48.2	Saluda County SD	Saluda
57	48.1	York County SD 04	Fort Mill
58	48.0	Abbeville County SD	Abbeville
59	48.0	Florence County SD 05	Johnsonville
60	47.8	Edgefield County SD	Edgefield
61	47.8	Spartanburg County SD 02	Spartanburg
62	47.8	Newberry County SD	Newberry
63	47.8	Lancaster County SD	Lancaster
63	47.8	Oconee County SD	Walhalla
65	47.8	Lexington County SD 03	Batesburg
66	47.8	Chester County SD	Chester
67	47.7	Spartanburg County SD 05	Duncan
68	47.7	Dillon County SD 02	Dillon
69	47.7	York County SD 02	Clover
70	47.6	Barnwell County SD 45	Barnwell
71	47.5	Florence County SD 03	Lake City
72	47.2	Dorchester County SD 04	St George
73	47.0	Jasper County SD	Ridgeland

Individual Education Program Students

Rank	Percent	District Name	City
1	24.0	Florence County SD 05	Johnsonville
2	23.1	Florence County SD 03	Lake City
3	22.4	Bamberg County SD 01	Bamberg
4	21.7	Allendale County SD	Allendale
5	21.6	Anderson County SD 02	Honea Path
6	20.8	Union County SD	Union
6	20.8	Williamsburg County SD	Kingstree
8	20.6	Fairfield County SD	Winnsboro
9	20.3	Laurens County SD 56	Clinton
10	20.0	Anderson County SD 03	Iva
11	19.7	Oconee County SD	Walhalla
11	19.7	Orangeburg County SD 03	Holly Hill
13	19.6	Laurens County SD 55	Laurens
14	19.5	Newberry County SD	Newberry
15	19.2	Orangeburg County SD 05	Orangeburg
16	18.8	Saluda County SD	Saluda
16	18.8	Spartanburg County SD 07	Spartanburg
18	18.2	Edgefield County SD	Edgefield
18	18.2	Spartanburg County SD 05	Duncan
20	18.1	Barnwell County SD 45	Barnwell
20	18.1	Clarendon County SD 02	Manning
22	18.0	Darlington County SD	Darlington
23	17.9	Lexington County SD 04	Swansea
24	17.8	Spartanburg County SD 01	Campobello
25	17.7	Horry County SD	Conway
26	17.5	Greenwood 50 County SD	Greenwood
27	17.3	Calhoun County SD	St Matthews
27	17.3	Chesterfield County SD	Chesterfield
29	17.2	Georgetown County SD	Georgetown
30	17.0	Abbeville County SD	Abbeville
31	16.9	Anderson County SD 05	Anderson
31	16.9	Lee County SD	Bishopville
33	16.8	Berkeley County SD	Moncks Corner
33	16.8	Lexington County SD 03	Batesburg
35	16.4	Florence County SD 01	Florence
36	16.3	Greenville County SD	Greenville
36	16.3	Orangeburg County SD 04	Cordova
38	16.0	Sumter County SD 02	Sumter
39	15.9	Colleton County SD	Walterboro
40	15.7	Lexington County SD 01	Lexington
40	15.7	Spartanburg County SD 03	Glendale
42	15.6	Dillon County SD 03	Latta
43	15.5	Dorchester County SD 04	St George
44	15.4	Lexington County SD 02	W Columbia
45	15.2	Anderson County SD 04	Pendleton
45	15.2	York County SD 01	York
47	14.8	Sumter County SD 17	Sumter
48	14.5	Pickens County SD	Easley
49	14.4	Lancaster County SD	Lancaster
50	14.3	Richland County SD 01	Columbia
51	14.2	Anderson County SD 01	Williamston
52	14.1	Charleston County SD	Charleston
53	14.0	Aiken County SD	Aiken
54	13.9	Dorchester County SD 02	Summerville
55	13.6	Dillon County SD 02	Dillon
56	13.5	Jasper County SD	Ridgeland
57	13.4	Greenwood 52 County SD	Ninety Six
58	13.3	Chester County SD	Chester
58	13.3	Marion County SD 01	Marion
60	13.2	Lexington County SD 05	Ballentine
61	13.1	York County SD 03	Rock Hill
62	13.0	Spartanburg County SD 06	Spartanburg
63	12.6	York County SD 02	Clover
64	12.5	Hampton 1 County SD	Hampton
64	12.5	Richland County SD 02	Columbia
66	12.0	Beaufort County SD	Beaufort
67	11.9	Spartanburg County SD 02	Spartanburg
68	11.6	Cherokee County SD	Gaffney
68	11.6	Marion County SD 02	Mullins
70	11.3	Kershaw County SD	Camden
71	10.5	York County SD 04	Fort Mill
72	10.4	Spartanburg County SD 04	Woodruff
73	3.2	Marlboro County SD	Bennettsville

English Language Learner Students

Rank	Percent	District Name	City
1	8.0	Jasper County SD	Ridgeland
2	7.5	Saluda County SD	Saluda
3	4.7	Spartanburg County SD 02	Spartanburg
4	4.5	Newberry County SD	Newberry
5	4.3	Greenwood 50 County SD	Greenwood
5	4.3	Spartanburg County SD 06	Spartanburg
7	3.7	Beaufort County SD	Beaufort
8	3.5	Spartanburg County SD 03	Glendale
8	3.5	Spartanburg County SD 05	Duncan
10	3.0	Laurens County SD 55	Laurens
11	2.7	Lexington County SD 02	W Columbia
12	2.6	Richland County SD 02	Columbia
13	2.2	Horry County SD	Conway
13	2.2	Oconee County SD	Walhalla
13	2.2	York County SD 03	Rock Hill
16	2.0	Dillon County SD 02	Dillon
16	2.0	Spartanburg County SD 07	Spartanburg
18	1.9	Cherokee County SD	Gaffney
19	1.8	Berkeley County SD	Moncks Corner
20	1.7	Pickens County SD	Easley
21	1.6	Anderson County SD 01	Williamston
21	1.6	York County SD 02	Clover
23	1.4	Aiken County SD	Aiken
23	1.4	Charleston County SD	Charleston
23	1.4	Chesterfield County SD	Chesterfield
23	1.4	Lancaster County SD	Lancaster
23	1.4	Laurens County SD 56	Clinton
23	1.4	Lexington County SD 05	Ballentine
23	1.4	York County SD 01	York
30	1.3	Calhoun County SD	St Matthews
30	1.3	Georgetown County SD	Georgetown
30	1.3	Richland County SD 01	Columbia
33	1.2	Abbeville County SD	Abbeville
33	1.2	Lexington County SD 01	Lexington
33	1.2	Spartanburg County SD 01	Campobello
33	1.2	Spartanburg County SD 04	Woodruff
37	1.1	Kershaw County SD	Camden
37	1.1	Lexington County SD 03	Batesburg
39	1.0	Clarendon County SD 02	Manning
40	0.9	York County SD 04	Fort Mill
41	0.8	Greenville County SD	Greenville
41	0.8	Sumter County SD 17	Sumter
41	0.8	Williamsburg County SD	Kingstree
44	0.7	Dorchester County SD 02	Summerville
45	0.6	Anderson County SD 05	Anderson
45	0.6	Florence County SD 01	Florence
45	0.6	Florence County SD 05	Johnsonville
48	0.5	Allendale County SD	Allendale
48	0.5	Colleton County SD	Walterboro
50	0.4	Anderson County SD 02	Honea Path
50	0.4	Edgefield County SD	Edgefield
50	0.4	Florence County SD 03	Lake City
50	0.4	Lee County SD	Bishopville
50	0.4	Lexington County SD 04	Swansea
50	0.4	Orangeburg County SD 03	Holly Hill
56	0.3	Anderson County SD 04	Pendleton
56	0.3	Darlington County SD	Darlington
56	0.3	Dorchester County SD 04	St George
56	0.3	Fairfield County SD	Winnsboro
56	0.3	Marion County SD 02	Mullins
56	0.3	Orangeburg County SD 05	Orangeburg
62	0.2	Barnwell County SD 45	Barnwell
62	0.2	Sumter County SD 02	Sumter
64	0.1	Anderson County SD 03	Iva
64	0.1	Greenwood 52 County SD	Ninety Six
64	0.1	Hampton 1 County SD	Hampton
64	0.1	Union County SD	Union
68	0.0	Chester County SD	Chester
68	0.0	Marion County SD 01	Marion
68	0.0	Marlboro County SD	Bennettsville
68	0.0	Orangeburg County SD 04	Cordova
72	0.0	Bamberg County SD 01	Bamberg
72	0.0	Dillon County SD 03	Latta

Migrant Students

Rank	Percent	District Name	City
1	n/a	Abbeville County SD	Abbeville
1	n/a	Aiken County SD	Aiken
1	n/a	Allendale County SD	Allendale
1	n/a	Anderson County SD 01	Williamston
1	n/a	Anderson County SD 02	Honea Path
1	n/a	Anderson County SD 03	Iva
1	n/a	Anderson County SD 04	Pendleton
1	n/a	Anderson County SD 05	Anderson
1	n/a	Bamberg County SD 01	Bamberg
1	n/a	Barnwell County SD 45	Barnwell
1	n/a	Beaufort County SD	Beaufort
1	n/a	Berkeley County SD	Moncks Corner
1	n/a	Calhoun County SD	St Matthews
1	n/a	Charleston County SD	Charleston
1	n/a	Cherokee County SD	Gaffney
1	n/a	Chester County SD	Chester

1	n/a	Chesterfield County SD	Chesterfield
1	n/a	Clarendon County SD 02	Manning
1	n/a	Colleton County SD	Walterboro
1	n/a	Darlington County SD	Darlington
1	n/a	Dillon County SD 02	Dillon
1	n/a	Dillon County SD 03	Latta
1	n/a	Dorchester County SD 02	Summerville
1	n/a	Dorchester County SD 04	St George
1	n/a	Edgefield County SD	Edgefield
1	n/a	Fairfield County SD	Winnsboro
1	n/a	Florence County SD 01	Florence
1	n/a	Florence County SD 03	Lake City
1	n/a	Florence County SD 05	Johnsonville
1	n/a	Georgetown County SD	Georgetown
1	n/a	Greenville County SD	Greenville
1	n/a	Greenwood 50 County SD	Greenwood
1	n/a	Greenwood 52 County SD	Ninety Six
1	n/a	Hampton 1 County SD	Hampton
1	n/a	Horry County SD	Conway
1	n/a	Jasper County SD	Ridgeland
1	n/a	Kershaw County SD	Camden
1	n/a	Lancaster County SD	Lancaster
1	n/a	Laurens County SD 55	Laurens
1	n/a	Laurens County SD 56	Clinton
1	n/a	Lee County SD	Bishopville
1	n/a	Lexington County SD 01	Lexington
1	n/a	Lexington County SD 02	W Columbia
1	n/a	Lexington County SD 03	Batesburg
1	n/a	Lexington County SD 04	Swansea
1	n/a	Lexington County SD 05	Ballentine
1	n/a	Marion County SD 01	Marion
1	n/a	Marion County SD 02	Mullins
1	n/a	Marlboro County SD	Bennettsville
1	n/a	Newberry County SD	Newberry
1	n/a	Oconee County SD	Walhalla
1	n/a	Orangeburg County SD 03	Holly Hill
1	n/a	Orangeburg County SD 04	Cordova
1	n/a	Orangeburg County SD 05	Orangeburg
1	n/a	Pickens County SD	Easley
1	n/a	Richland County SD 01	Columbia
1	n/a	Richland County SD 02	Columbia
1	n/a	Saluda County SD	Saluda
1	n/a	Spartanburg County SD 01	Campobello
1	n/a	Spartanburg County SD 02	Spartanburg
1	n/a	Spartanburg County SD 03	Glendale
1	n/a	Spartanburg County SD 04	Woodruff
1	n/a	Spartanburg County SD 05	Duncan
1	n/a	Spartanburg County SD 06	Spartanburg
1	n/a	Spartanburg County SD 07	Spartanburg
1	n/a	Sumter County SD 02	Sumter
1	n/a	Sumter County SD 17	Sumter
1	n/a	Union County SD	Union
1	n/a	Williamsburg County SD	Kingstree
1	n/a	York County SD 01	York
1	n/a	York County SD 02	Clover
1	n/a	York County SD 03	Rock Hill
1	n/a	York County SD 04	Fort Mill

Students Eligible for Free Lunch

Rank	Percent	District Name	City
1	84.2	Williamsburg County SD	Kingstree
2	79.1	Orangeburg County SD 03	Holly Hill
3	79.0	Allendale County SD	Allendale
4	76.6	Lee County SD	Bishopville
5	75.7	Florence County SD 03	Lake City
6	72.6	Dillon County SD 02	Dillon
7	72.3	Calhoun County SD	St Matthews
8	71.2	Fairfield County SD	Winnsboro
9	70.5	Marion County SD 02	Mullins
10	70.4	Orangeburg County SD 05	Orangeburg
11	68.8	Marion County SD 01	Marion
12	67.7	Clarendon County SD 02	Manning
13	67.4	Marlboro County SD	Bennettsville
14	67.3	Jasper County SD	Ridgeland
15	65.7	Dorchester County SD 04	St George
16	64.8	Colleton County SD	Walterboro
17	62.4	Dillon County SD 03	Latta
18	59.2	Bamberg County SD 01	Bamberg
19	58.1	Darlington County SD	Darlington
20	57.4	Richland County SD 01	Columbia
21	56.7	Spartanburg County SD 07	Spartanburg
22	56.5	Orangeburg County SD 04	Cordova
23	56.3	Sumter County SD 02	Sumter
24	55.8	Georgetown County SD	Georgetown
25	55.5	Lexington County SD 04	Swansea
26	54.9	Abbeville County SD	Abbeville
27	54.4	Laurens County SD 56	Clinton
28	54.3	Sumter County SD 17	Sumter
29	53.1	Chesterfield County SD	Chesterfield
30	52.8	Hampton 1 County SD	Hampton
31	50.7	Saluda County SD	Saluda
32	50.5	Chester County SD	Chester
33	50.2	Edgefield County SD	Edgefield
34	49.6	Horry County SD	Conway
35	49.5	Newberry County SD	Newberry
35	49.5	Union County SD	Union
37	49.3	Barnwell County SD 45	Barnwell
38	48.6	Laurens County SD 55	Laurens
39	47.1	Lexington County SD 03	Batesburg
40	46.6	Cherokee County SD	Gaffney
40	46.6	Florence County SD 05	Johnsonville
42	45.7	Florence County SD 01	Florence
43	45.3	Charleston County SD	Charleston
44	44.6	Anderson County SD 03	Iva
45	44.2	Aiken County SD	Aiken
45	44.2	Greenwood 50 County SD	Greenwood
47	42.6	Lancaster County SD	Lancaster
48	40.9	Anderson County SD 05	Anderson
49	40.3	Berkeley County SD	Moncks Corner
49	40.3	Spartanburg County SD 03	Glendale
51	40.2	Oconee County SD	Walhalla
52	39.6	Kershaw County SD	Camden
53	39.5	Lexington County SD 02	W Columbia
54	39.0	York County SD 01	York
55	38.8	Beaufort County SD	Beaufort
56	36.5	Spartanburg County SD 06	Spartanburg
57	34.9	Spartanburg County SD 04	Woodruff
58	34.8	Spartanburg County SD 01	Campobello
59	33.1	Anderson County SD 02	Honea Path
60	32.5	Anderson County SD 04	Pendleton
61	32.4	Greenwood 52 County SD	Ninety Six
62	32.1	York County SD 03	Rock Hill
63	30.7	Spartanburg County SD 05	Duncan
64	29.8	Greenville County SD	Greenville
64	29.8	Pickens County SD	Easley
66	29.3	Spartanburg County SD 02	Spartanburg
67	26.4	Anderson County SD 01	Williamston
68	26.1	Richland County SD 02	Columbia
69	24.0	York County SD 02	Clover
70	23.4	Dorchester County SD 02	Summerville
71	22.2	Lexington County SD 01	Lexington
72	15.5	Lexington County SD 05	Ballentine
73	12.1	York County SD 04	Fort Mill

Students Eligible for Reduced-Price Lunch

Rank	Percent	District Name	City
1	13.1	Sumter County SD 02	Sumter
2	12.1	Hampton 1 County SD	Hampton
3	12.0	Marlboro County SD	Bennettsville
4	11.5	Orangeburg County SD 04	Cordova
5	11.3	Berkeley County SD	Moncks Corner
6	10.9	Laurens County SD 56	Clinton
7	10.4	Union County SD	Union
8	10.2	Spartanburg County SD 03	Glendale
8	10.2	York County SD 01	York
10	10.0	Dorchester County SD 04	St George
10	10.0	Fairfield County SD	Winnsboro
12	9.9	Greenwood 52 County SD	Ninety Six
12	9.9	Jasper County SD	Ridgeland
14	9.7	Kershaw County SD	Camden
14	9.7	Lexington County SD 04	Swansea
14	9.7	Oconee County SD	Walhalla
17	9.6	Cherokee County SD	Gaffney
18	9.5	Anderson County SD 04	Pendleton
19	9.4	Chesterfield County SD	Chesterfield
20	9.3	Saluda County SD	Saluda
21	9.2	Anderson County SD 03	Iva
21	9.2	Newberry County SD	Newberry
21	9.2	Spartanburg County SD 02	Spartanburg
24	9.0	Edgefield County SD	Edgefield
24	9.0	Spartanburg County SD 05	Duncan
26	8.8	Lexington County SD 03	Batesburg
26	8.8	Marion County SD 02	Mullins
26	8.8	Orangeburg County SD 05	Orangeburg
29	8.7	Spartanburg County SD 04	Woodruff
30	8.6	Florence County SD 05	Johnsonville
31	8.5	Sumter County SD 17	Sumter
32	8.4	Calhoun County SD	St Matthews
32	8.4	Orangeburg County SD 03	Holly Hill
34	8.3	Beaufort County SD	Beaufort
34	8.3	Chester County SD	Chester
36	8.0	Lexington County SD 02	W Columbia
36	8.0	Pickens County SD	Easley
38	7.9	Lancaster County SD	Lancaster
38	7.9	Richland County SD 02	Columbia
40	7.8	Anderson County SD 01	Williamston
41	7.7	Spartanburg County SD 01	Campobello
42	7.6	Abbeville County SD	Abbeville
42	7.6	Anderson County SD 02	Honea Path
44	7.5	Barnwell County SD 45	Barnwell
45	7.4	Florence County SD 01	Florence
46	7.3	Clarendon County SD 02	Manning
46	7.3	Dillon County SD 02	Dillon
46	7.3	Georgetown County SD	Georgetown
49	7.2	Dillon County SD 03	Latta
49	7.2	Greenville County SD	Greenville
51	7.1	Anderson County SD 05	Anderson
52	7.0	Colleton County SD	Walterboro
52	7.0	Laurens County SD 55	Laurens
54	6.9	Charleston County SD	Charleston
54	6.9	Lexington County SD 01	Lexington
54	6.9	York County SD 03	Rock Hill
57	6.8	Aiken County SD	Aiken
57	6.8	Lee County SD	Bishopville
57	6.8	Spartanburg County SD 06	Spartanburg
57	6.8	York County SD 02	Clover
61	6.7	Darlington County SD	Darlington
61	6.7	Spartanburg County SD 07	Spartanburg
63	6.5	Marion County SD 01	Marion
64	6.1	Dorchester County SD 02	Summerville
64	6.1	Greenwood 50 County SD	Greenwood
64	6.1	Horry County SD	Conway
67	6.0	Florence County SD 03	Lake City
67	6.0	Williamsburg County SD	Kingstree
69	5.9	Bamberg County SD 01	Bamberg
70	5.1	Lexington County SD 05	Ballentine
71	5.0	Allendale County SD	Allendale
71	5.0	Richland County SD 01	Columbia
73	3.0	York County SD 04	Fort Mill

Student/Teacher Ratio

Rank	Ratio	District Name	City
1	18.7	Clarendon County SD 02	Manning
2	18.6	Spartanburg County SD 02	Spartanburg
3	18.3	Dillon County SD 02	Dillon
4	18.0	Anderson County SD 01	Williamston
5	17.8	Sumter County SD 02	Sumter
6	17.6	Anderson County SD 02	Honea Path
7	17.2	Berkeley County SD	Moncks Corner
8	17.0	Lexington County SD 04	Swansea
8	17.0	Williamsburg County SD	Kingstree
10	16.9	Laurens County SD 55	Laurens
11	16.8	Greenville County SD	Greenville
12	16.7	Anderson County SD 03	Iva
13	16.6	Spartanburg County SD 04	Woodruff
14	16.4	Aiken County SD	Aiken
14	16.4	York County SD 03	Rock Hill
16	16.3	Dillon County SD 03	Latta
17	16.2	Dorchester County SD 02	Summerville
17	16.2	Greenwood 52 County SD	Ninety Six
17	16.2	Kershaw County SD	Camden
17	16.2	Marion County SD 02	Mullins
21	16.1	Sumter County SD 17	Sumter
22	16.0	Barnwell County SD 45	Barnwell
23	15.9	Chester County SD	Chester
23	15.9	Florence County SD 05	Johnsonville
23	15.9	Greenwood 50 County SD	Greenwood
23	15.9	Orangeburg County SD 04	Cordova
23	15.9	Pickens County SD	Easley
28	15.8	Jasper County SD	Ridgeland
28	15.8	Marion County SD 01	Marion
30	15.7	Lancaster County SD	Lancaster
31	15.6	Hampton 1 County SD	Hampton
31	15.6	Laurens County SD 56	Clinton
31	15.6	York County SD 04	Fort Mill
34	15.5	Bamberg County SD 01	Bamberg
34	15.5	Lexington County SD 03	Batesburg
36	15.4	Anderson County SD 04	Pendleton
36	15.4	Colleton County SD	Walterboro
36	15.4	Marlboro County SD	Bennettsville
36	15.4	York County SD 01	York
40	15.3	Chesterfield County SD	Chesterfield
40	15.3	Florence County SD 01	Florence
40	15.3	Spartanburg County SD 03	Glendale
43	15.1	Anderson County SD 05	Anderson
43	15.1	Horry County SD	Conway
43	15.1	Spartanburg County SD 06	Spartanburg
46	15.0	Lexington County SD 01	Lexington
47	14.9	Richland County SD 02	Columbia
47	14.9	Saluda County SD	Saluda
49	14.7	Darlington County SD	Darlington
49	14.7	Lee County SD	Bishopville
49	14.7	Lexington County SD 05	Ballentine
49	14.7	York County SD 02	Clover
53	14.6	Florence County SD 03	Lake City
53	14.6	Lexington County SD 02	W Columbia
53	14.6	Spartanburg County SD 05	Duncan
56	14.5	Abbeville County SD	Abbeville
56	14.5	Cherokee County SD	Gaffney
58	14.4	Edgefield County SD	Edgefield
59	14.3	Dorchester County SD 04	St George
59	14.3	Georgetown County SD	Georgetown
59	14.3	Spartanburg County SD 01	Campobello
62	14.2	Beaufort County SD	Beaufort

62	14.2	Union County SD	Union
64	14.0	Charleston County SD	Charleston
64	14.0	Newberry County SD	Newberry
66	13.9	Calhoun County SD	St Matthews
66	13.9	Oconee County SD	Walhalla
66	13.9	Orangeburg County SD 03	Holly Hill
69	13.6	Orangeburg County SD 05	Orangeburg
69	13.6	Richland County SD 01	Columbia
71	13.4	Fairfield County SD	Winnsboro
72	12.9	Allendale County SD	Allendale
73	12.5	Spartanburg County SD 07	Spartanburg

Student/Librarian Ratio

Rank	Ratio	District Name	City
1	942.0	Barnwell County SD 45	Barnwell
2	906.9	Dorchester County SD 02	Summerville
3	863.7	Richland County SD 02	Columbia
4	853.4	Chester County SD	Chester
5	830.4	Lexington County SD 01	Lexington
6	812.8	Jasper County SD	Ridgeland
7	801.1	Spartanburg County SD 05	Duncan
8	793.3	Lexington County SD 05	Ballentine
9	776.3	Sumter County SD 17	Sumter
10	739.3	Marlboro County SD	Bennettsville
11	737.2	Sumter County SD 02	Sumter
12	735.8	Spartanburg County SD 04	Woodruff
13	734.4	Lexington County SD 04	Swansea
14	709.0	Orangeburg County SD 04	Cordova
14	709.0	York County SD 03	Rock Hill
14	709.0	York County SD 04	Fort Mill
17	708.1	Berkeley County SD	Moncks Corner
18	703.6	Clarendon County SD 02	Manning
19	702.5	Anderson County SD 05	Anderson
20	697.2	Spartanburg County SD 06	Spartanburg
21	684.3	Anderson County SD 03	Iva
22	673.4	Horry County SD	Conway
23	673.1	Florence County SD 01	Florence
24	671.9	Colleton County SD	Walterboro
25	658.9	Greenville County SD	Greenville
26	657.0	York County SD 01	York
27	654.6	Beaufort County SD	Beaufort
28	651.2	Marion County SD 01	Marion
29	640.2	Dillon County SD 02	Dillon
30	639.7	Aiken County SD	Aiken
31	634.8	Greenwood 50 County SD	Greenwood
32	634.0	Dorchester County SD 04	St George
33	598.5	Lancaster County SD	Lancaster
34	590.2	Spartanburg County SD 02	Spartanburg
35	587.3	Georgetown County SD	Georgetown
36	583.3	Spartanburg County SD 07	Spartanburg
37	578.2	Anderson County SD 04	Pendleton
38	573.7	Bamberg County SD 01	Bamberg
39	571.8	Spartanburg County SD 01	Campobello
40	567.9	Union County SD	Union
41	567.0	Lexington County SD 03	Batesburg
42	560.8	Pickens County SD	Easley
43	558.7	Laurens County SD 55	Laurens
44	554.3	Anderson County SD 01	Williamston
45	550.3	Saluda County SD	Saluda
46	550.0	Charleston County SD	Charleston
47	547.6	Oconee County SD	Walhalla
48	547.5	Marion County SD 02	Mullins
49	547.3	Darlington County SD	Darlington
50	542.1	Anderson County SD 02	Honea Path
51	534.6	York County SD 02	Clover
52	531.7	Chesterfield County SD	Chesterfield
53	531.3	Dillon County SD 03	Latta
54	530.3	Florence County SD 03	Lake City
55	526.7	Kershaw County SD	Camden
56	520.1	Orangeburg County SD 05	Orangeburg
57	519.5	Hampton 1 County SD	Hampton
58	517.3	Orangeburg County SD 03	Holly Hill
59	514.8	Lexington County SD 02	W Columbia
60	502.3	Florence County SD 05	Johnsonville
61	502.0	Calhoun County SD	St Matthews
62	499.9	Edgefield County SD	Edgefield
63	499.8	Richland County SD 01	Columbia
64	490.7	Laurens County SD 56	Clinton
65	490.4	Cherokee County SD	Gaffney
66	483.5	Lee County SD	Bishopville
67	482.9	Williamsburg County SD	Kingstree
68	470.6	Fairfield County SD	Winnsboro
69	468.3	Allendale County SD	Allendale
70	458.6	Spartanburg County SD 03	Glendale
71	455.7	Newberry County SD	Newberry
72	433.3	Greenwood 52 County SD	Ninety Six
73	423.6	Abbeville County SD	Abbeville

Student/Counselor Ratio

Rank	Ratio	District Name	City
1	918.0	Lexington County SD 04	Swansea
2	703.6	Clarendon County SD 02	Manning
3	591.1	Jasper County SD	Ridgeland
4	588.6	Spartanburg County SD 04	Woodruff
5	547.4	Anderson County SD 03	Iva
6	507.2	Dorchester County SD 04	St George
7	502.3	Florence County SD 05	Johnsonville
8	493.6	Florence County SD 01	Florence
9	491.8	Spartanburg County SD 02	Spartanburg
10	490.8	York County SD 04	Fort Mill
11	484.8	Chesterfield County SD	Chesterfield
12	477.1	Aiken County SD	Aiken
13	475.1	Anderson County SD 01	Williamston
14	471.0	Barnwell County SD 45	Barnwell
15	470.3	Greenville County SD	Greenville
16	465.1	Bamberg County SD 01	Bamberg
17	459.9	Lexington County SD 05	Ballentine
18	458.9	Sumter County SD 17	Sumter
19	455.1	Berkeley County SD	Moncks Corner
20	454.7	Lexington County SD 01	Lexington
21	453.6	Lexington County SD 03	Batesburg
22	453.1	York County SD 01	York
23	449.2	Pickens County SD	Easley
24	445.7	Horry County SD	Conway
25	444.4	Union County SD	Union
26	444.3	Edgefield County SD	Edgefield
27	442.5	Lancaster County SD	Lancaster
28	441.9	Florence County SD 03	Lake City
29	441.4	Richland County SD 02	Columbia
30	438.0	Marion County SD 02	Mullins
31	435.9	Laurens County SD 55	Laurens
32	427.3	Spartanburg County SD 05	Duncan
33	426.8	Dillon County SD 02	Dillon
34	426.7	Chester County SD	Chester
35	425.4	Orangeburg County SD 04	Cordova
36	423.2	Greenwood 50 County SD	Greenwood
37	421.8	Dorchester County SD 02	Summerville
38	421.7	Anderson County SD 02	Honea Path
39	419.2	Kershaw County SD	Camden
40	412.8	York County SD 03	Rock Hill
41	411.2	York County SD 02	Clover
42	407.0	Marion County SD 01	Marion
43	406.9	Spartanburg County SD 07	Spartanburg
44	405.1	Cherokee County SD	Gaffney
45	401.3	Abbeville County SD	Abbeville
46	398.5	Dillon County SD 03	Latta
47	395.2	Colleton County SD	Walterboro
48	390.4	Spartanburg County SD 06	Spartanburg
49	386.1	Lexington County SD 02	W Columbia
50	386.0	Laurens County SD 56	Clinton
51	382.9	Charleston County SD	Charleston
52	381.8	Beaufort County SD	Beaufort
53	381.2	Spartanburg County SD 01	Campobello
54	380.9	Hampton 1 County SD	Hampton
55	376.3	Darlington County SD	Darlington
56	374.6	Allendale County SD	Allendale
57	372.5	Oconee County SD	Walhalla
58	369.6	Marlboro County SD	Bennettsville
59	366.8	Saluda County SD	Saluda
60	364.5	Georgetown County SD	Georgetown
61	362.6	Lee County SD	Bishopville
62	362.1	Orangeburg County SD 03	Holly Hill
63	359.0	Newberry County SD	Newberry
64	357.9	Williamsburg County SD	Kingstree
65	354.6	Orangeburg County SD 05	Orangeburg
66	346.6	Greenwood 52 County SD	Ninety Six
67	346.2	Calhoun County SD	St Matthews
68	340.1	Anderson County SD 04	Pendleton
69	327.6	Spartanburg County SD 03	Glendale
70	327.2	Anderson County SD 05	Anderson
71	319.5	Sumter County SD 02	Sumter
72	310.2	Richland County SD 01	Columbia
73	289.6	Fairfield County SD	Winnsboro

Current Spending per Student in FY2003

Rank	Dollars	District Name	City
1	10,126	Allendale County SD	Allendale
2	9,763	Fairfield County SD	Winnsboro
3	8,936	Spartanburg County SD 07	Spartanburg
4	8,647	Calhoun County SD	St Matthews
5	8,617	Spartanburg County SD 03	Glendale
6	8,521	Richland County SD 01	Columbia
7	8,314	Orangeburg County SD 05	Orangeburg
8	8,231	Dorchester County SD 04	St George
9	8,229	Orangeburg County SD 03	Holly Hill
10	8,140	Georgetown County SD	Georgetown
11	8,097	Lee County SD	Bishopville
12	7,912	Beaufort County SD	Beaufort
13	7,879	Oconee County SD	Walhalla
14	7,814	York County SD 02	Clover
15	7,770	Lexington County SD 05	Ballentine
16	7,757	Newberry County SD	Newberry
17	7,725	Lexington County SD 03	Batesburg
18	7,573	Jasper County SD	Ridgeland
19	7,560	Saluda County SD	Saluda
20	7,508	Lexington County SD 02	W Columbia
21	7,384	Charleston County SD	Charleston
22	7,299	Bamberg County SD 01	Bamberg
23	7,292	Darlington County SD	Darlington
24	7,275	Florence County SD 03	Lake City
25	7,274	Williamsburg County SD	Kingstree
26	7,145	Edgefield County SD	Edgefield
27	7,144	Richland County SD 02	Columbia
28	7,097	Union County SD	Union
29	7,080	Spartanburg County SD 05	Duncan
30	7,067	Horry County SD	Conway
31	7,046	Anderson County SD 05	Anderson
32	6,986	Chester County SD	Chester
33	6,972	Orangeburg County SD 04	Cordova
34	6,966	York County SD 03	Rock Hill
35	6,963	Lexington County SD 01	Lexington
35	6,963	Marlboro County SD	Bennettsville
37	6,960	Laurens County SD 56	Clinton
38	6,954	Anderson County SD 04	Pendleton
39	6,952	Spartanburg County SD 01	Campobello
40	6,945	Colleton County SD	Walterboro
41	6,907	Cherokee County SD	Gaffney
42	6,885	York County SD 04	Fort Mill
43	6,883	Abbeville County SD	Abbeville
44	6,882	Chesterfield County SD	Chesterfield
45	6,879	Florence County SD 05	Johnsonville
46	6,798	Kershaw County SD	Camden
47	6,757	York County SD 01	York
48	6,730	Hampton 1 County SD	Hampton
49	6,729	Anderson County SD 02	Honea Path
50	6,679	Marion County SD 01	Marion
51	6,658	Dillon County SD 03	Latta
52	6,586	Marion County SD 02	Mullins
53	6,582	Barnwell County SD 45	Barnwell
54	6,491	Laurens County SD 55	Laurens
55	6,472	Berkeley County SD	Moncks Corner
56	6,437	Lancaster County SD	Lancaster
57	6,398	Spartanburg County SD 06	Spartanburg
58	6,391	Greenwood 50 County SD	Greenwood
59	6,379	Greenville County SD	Greenville
60	6,372	Lexington County SD 04	Swansea
61	6,361	Greenwood 52 County SD	Ninety Six
62	6,302	Pickens County SD	Easley
63	6,281	Aiken County SD	Aiken
64	6,276	Sumter County SD 17	Sumter
65	6,218	Anderson County SD 03	Iva
66	6,160	Clarendon County SD 02	Manning
67	6,127	Spartanburg County SD 04	Woodruff
68	6,119	Sumter County SD 02	Sumter
69	6,114	Dillon County SD 02	Dillon
70	6,105	Florence County SD 01	Florence
71	6,093	Anderson County SD 01	Williamston
72	6,085	Dorchester County SD 02	Summerville
73	5,446	Spartanburg County SD 02	Spartanburg

Number of Diploma Recipients

Rank	Number	District Name	City
1	2,934	Greenville County SD	Greenville
2	1,666	Charleston County SD	Charleston
3	1,335	Horry County SD	Conway
4	1,302	Berkeley County SD	Moncks Corner
5	1,218	Aiken County SD	Aiken
6	1,178	Richland County SD 01	Columbia
7	1,002	Lexington County SD 05	Ballentine
8	958	Richland County SD 02	Columbia
9	906	Lexington County SD 01	Lexington
10	883	Dorchester County SD 02	Summerville
11	759	Beaufort County SD	Beaufort
12	755	Pickens County SD	Easley
12	755	York County SD 03	Rock Hill
14	721	Florence County SD 01	Florence
15	542	Anderson County SD 05	Anderson
16	525	Kershaw County SD	Camden
17	503	Lancaster County SD	Lancaster
18	498	Spartanburg County SD 06	Spartanburg
19	496	Oconee County SD	Walhalla
20	486	Georgetown County SD	Georgetown
21	483	Darlington County SD	Darlington
22	459	Lexington County SD 02	W Columbia
23	427	Greenwood 50 County SD	Greenwood
24	416	Sumter County SD 17	Sumter
25	409	Spartanburg County SD 02	Spartanburg
26	399	Orangeburg County SD 05	Orangeburg
27	380	Anderson County SD 01	Williamston
27	380	Cherokee County SD	Gaffney
29	372	Spartanburg County SD 07	Spartanburg
30	367	Chesterfield County SD	Chesterfield
31	356	Sumter County SD 02	Sumter
32	299	York County SD 04	Fort Mill
33	271	Williamsburg County SD	Kingstree

34	268	Newberry County SD	Newberry
34	268	Spartanburg County SD 05	Duncan
36	266	Colleton County SD	Walterboro
37	242	York County SD 01	York
38	234	Union County SD	Union
39	231	Chester County SD	Chester
40	229	Laurens County SD 55	Laurens
41	211	Spartanburg County SD 01	Campobello
42	207	Marlboro County SD	Bennettsville
43	198	York County SD 02	Clover
44	193	Florence County SD 03	Lake City
44	193	Orangeburg County SD 04	Cordova
46	177	Anderson County SD 02	Honea Path
46	177	Edgefield County SD	Edgefield
48	175	Laurens County SD 56	Clinton
49	171	Abbeville County SD	Abbeville
50	170	Marion County SD 01	Marion
51	167	Clarendon County SD 02	Manning
52	165	Dillon County SD 02	Dillon
53	161	Spartanburg County SD 03	Glendale
54	159	Fairfield County SD	Winnsboro
55	154	Orangeburg County SD 03	Holly Hill
56	125	Barnwell County SD 45	Barnwell
56	125	Lexington County SD 03	Batesburg
58	119	Lee County SD	Bishopville
59	117	Marion County SD 02	Mullins
60	116	Dorchester County SD 04	St George
61	108	Lexington County SD 04	Swansea
62	106	Anderson County SD 03	Iva
63	104	Hampton 1 County SD	Hampton
64	101	Spartanburg County SD 04	Woodruff
65	99	Anderson County SD 04	Pendleton
66	95	Bamberg County SD 01	Bamberg
67	91	Greenwood 52 County SD	Ninety Six
68	85	Jasper County SD	Ridgeland
69	79	Saluda County SD	Saluda
70	78	Allendale County SD	Allendale
71	77	Dillon County SD 03	Latta
72	75	Calhoun County SD	St Matthews
73	62	Florence County SD 05	Johnsonville

High School Drop-out Rate

Rank	Percent	District Name	City
1	7.2	Orangeburg County SD 03	Holly Hill
2	7.1	Marlboro County SD	Bennettsville
3	6.8	Colleton County SD	Walterboro
4	6.7	Chester County SD	Chester
5	6.5	Dillon County SD 02	Dillon
6	6.3	Lexington County SD 04	Swansea
6	6.3	Pickens County SD	Easley
8	5.9	Florence County SD 01	Florence
9	5.8	Newberry County SD	Newberry
10	5.7	Dorchester County SD 04	St George
11	5.6	Edgefield County SD	Edgefield
11	5.6	Hampton 1 County SD	Hampton
13	5.4	Lancaster County SD	Lancaster
14	5.1	Kershaw County SD	Camden
15	5.0	Anderson County SD 03	Iva
16	4.9	Anderson County SD 05	Anderson
17	4.6	Lee County SD	Bishopville
17	4.6	Lexington County SD 03	Batesburg
17	4.6	Orangeburg County SD 05	Orangeburg
20	4.5	Abbeville County SD	Abbeville
20	4.5	Florence County SD 03	Lake City
22	4.3	Berkeley County SD	Moncks Corner
23	4.2	Chesterfield County SD	Chesterfield
24	4.1	Anderson County SD 02	Honea Path
24	4.1	Florence County SD 05	Johnsonville
26	4.0	Oconee County SD	Walhalla
27	3.9	Barnwell County SD 45	Barnwell
27	3.9	Spartanburg County SD 02	Spartanburg
27	3.9	York County SD 01	York
30	3.8	Spartanburg County SD 07	Spartanburg
31	3.7	Bamberg County SD 01	Bamberg
31	3.7	Lexington County SD 02	W Columbia
33	3.6	Dorchester County SD 02	Summerville
34	3.5	Cherokee County SD	Gaffney
34	3.5	Union County SD	Union
36	3.2	Aiken County SD	Aiken
36	3.2	Anderson County SD 01	Williamston
36	3.2	Charleston County SD	Charleston
36	3.2	Richland County SD 01	Columbia
40	3.1	Jasper County SD	Ridgeland
41	2.7	Darlington County SD	Darlington
41	2.7	Georgetown County SD	Georgetown
41	2.7	Spartanburg County SD 05	Duncan
44	2.6	Greenville County SD	Greenville
44	2.6	Richland County SD 02	Columbia
46	2.4	Dillon County SD 03	Latta
46	2.4	Greenwood 50 County SD	Greenwood
46	2.4	Lexington County SD 01	Lexington
46	2.4	Orangeburg County SD 04	Cordova
46	2.4	York County SD 02	Clover
51	2.3	Laurens County SD 56	Clinton
51	2.3	Marion County SD 02	Mullins
51	2.3	Spartanburg County SD 01	Campobello
54	2.1	Horry County SD	Conway
54	2.1	York County SD 04	Fort Mill
56	2.0	Laurens County SD 55	Laurens
56	2.0	Sumter County SD 17	Sumter
58	1.9	Allendale County SD	Allendale
58	1.9	Williamsburg County SD	Kingstree
60	1.8	Clarendon County SD 02	Manning
60	1.8	Lexington County SD 05	Ballentine
60	1.8	Spartanburg County SD 06	Spartanburg
63	1.7	Beaufort County SD	Beaufort
63	1.7	York County SD 03	Rock Hill
65	1.6	Fairfield County SD	Winnsboro
65	1.6	Sumter County SD 02	Sumter
67	1.4	Greenwood 52 County SD	Ninety Six
67	1.4	Saluda County SD	Saluda
69	1.2	Marion County SD 01	Marion
70	1.0	Spartanburg County SD 03	Glendale
71	0.8	Anderson County SD 04	Pendleton
72	0.5	Spartanburg County SD 04	Woodruff
73	n/a	Calhoun County SD	St Matthews

South Dakota

South Dakota Public School Educational Profile

Category	Value	Category	Value
Schools *(2003-2004)*	741	**Diploma Recipients** *(2002-2003)*	8,649
Instructional Level		White, Non-Hispanic	8,098
Primary	363	Black, Non-Hispanic	49
Middle	173	Asian/Pacific Islander	99
High	185	American Indian/Alaskan Native	342
Other Level	19	Hispanic	61
Curriculum		**High School Drop-out Rate** (%) *(2001-2002)*	2.8
Regular	710	White, Non-Hispanic	2.0
Special Education	6	Black, Non-Hispanic	7.3
Vocational	0	Asian/Pacific Islander	1.9
Alternative	24	American Indian/Alaskan Native	13.1
Type		Hispanic	6.2
Magnet	0	**Staff** *(2003-2004)*	
Charter	0	Teachers	9,243.7
Title I Eligible	336	Average Salary ($)	33,236
School-wide Title I	123	Librarians/Media Specialists	146.0
Students *(2003-2004)*	125,538	Guidance Counselors	327.7
Gender (%)		**Ratios** *(2003-2004)*	
Male	51.7	Student/Teacher Ratio	13.6 to 1
Female	48.3	Student/Librarian Ratio	859.8 to 1
Race/Ethnicity (%)		Student/Counselor Ratio	383.1 to 1
White, Non-Hispanic	84.9	**College Entrance Exam Scores** *(2005)*	
Black, Non-Hispanic	1.5	Scholastic Aptitude Test (SAT)	
Asian/Pacific Islander	1.0	Participation Rate (%)	5
American Indian/Alaskan Native	10.7	Mean SAT Reasoning Test Verbal Score	589
Hispanic	1.8	Mean SAT Reasoning Test Math Score	589
Classification (%)		American College Testing Program (ACT)	
Individual Education Program (IEP)	13.6	Participation Rate (%)	76
Migrant *(2002-2003)*	0.7	Average Composite Score	21.5
English Language Learner (ELL)	3.6	Average English Score	20.8
Eligible for Free Lunch Program	22.8	Average Math Score	21.3
Eligible for Reduced-Price Lunch Program	8.6	Average Reading Score	21.7
Current Spending *($ per student in FY 2003)*	6,517	Average Science Score	21.6
Instruction	3,902		
Support Services	2,311		

Note: *For an explanation of data, please refer to the User's Guide in the front of the book*

South Dakota NAEP 2005 Test Scores

Reading			Mathematics		
Grade/Category	Value	Rank	Grade/Category	Value	Rank
4th Grade			**4th Grade**		
Average Proficiency	222.4 (0.54)	18/51	Average Proficiency	241.6 (0.51)	14/51
Proficiency by Gender/Race/Ethnicity			Proficiency by Gender/Race/Ethnicity		
Male	218.5 (0.83)	19/51	Male	243.4 (0.74)	11/51
Female	226.8 (1.05)	12/51	Female	239.7 (0.69)	17/51
White, Non-Hispanic	226.2 (0.59)	28/51	White, Non-Hispanic	245.0 (0.59)	22/51
Black, Non-Hispanic	n/a	n/a	Black, Non-Hispanic	n/a	n/a
Asian, Non-Hispanic	n/a	n/a	Asian, Non-Hispanic	n/a	n/a
American Indian, Non-Hispanic	201.4 (2.28)	3/7	American Indian, Non-Hispanic	220.7 (1.74)	5/7
Hispanic	n/a	n/a	Hispanic	n/a	n/a
Proficiency by Class Size			Proficiency by Class Size		
Less than 16 Students	215.3 (1.80)	9/34	Less than 16 Students	236.9 (1.12)	8/35
16 to 18 Students	221.6 (1.63)	10/33	16 to 18 Students	240.7 (1.39)	10/31
19 to 20 Students	224.4 (1.97)	16/38	19 to 20 Students	241.7 (1.50)	14/38
21 to 25 Students	224.8 (1.04)	17/51	21 to 25 Students	242.9 (0.78)	14/51
Greater than 25 Students	224.2 (1.70)	9/36	Greater than 25 Students	243.3 (1.26)	4/33
Percent Attaining Achievement Levels			Percent Attaining Achievement Levels		
Below Basic	30.2 (1.11)	39/51	Below Basic	13.6 (0.78)	42/51
Basic or Above	69.8 (1.11)	13/51	Basic or Above	86.4 (0.78)	9/51
Proficient or Above	32.9 (1.28)	22/51	Proficient or Above	40.6 (1.28)	12/51
Advanced or Above	6.3 (0.66)	34/51	Advanced or Above	4.1 (0.42)	31/51
8th Grade			**8th Grade**		
Average Proficiency	268.5 (0.63)	8/51	Average Proficiency	287.3 (0.61)	4/51
Proficiency by Gender/Race/Ethnicity			Proficiency by Gender/Race/Ethnicity		
Male	264.0 (1.05)	7/51	Male	287.4 (0.83)	3/51
Female	273.2 (0.88)	9/51	Female	287.2 (0.91)	4/51
White, Non-Hispanic	271.6 (0.64)	16/51	White, Non-Hispanic	291.1 (0.66)	14/51
Black, Non-Hispanic	n/a	n/a	Black, Non-Hispanic	n/a	n/a
Asian, Non-Hispanic	n/a	n/a	Asian, Non-Hispanic	n/a	n/a
American Indian, Non-Hispanic	245.3 (2.40)	6/9	American Indian, Non-Hispanic	259.9 (2.30)	7/10
Hispanic	n/a	n/a	Hispanic	n/a	n/a
Proficiency by Parents Highest Level of Ed.			Proficiency by Parents Highest Level of Ed.		
Did Not Finish High School	246.2 (4.00)	21/49	Did Not Finish High School	267.2 (2.24)	6/50
Graduated High School	261.5 (1.55)	3/50	Graduated High School	275.9 (1.72)	5/50
Some Education After High School	269.4 (1.50)	11/50	Some Education After High School	287.2 (1.32)	4/50
Graduated College	274.5 (0.88)	17/50	Graduated College	294.8 (0.94)	7/50
Percent Attaining Achievement Levels			Percent Attaining Achievement Levels		
Below Basic	30.2 (1.11)	39/51	Below Basic	19.7 (0.79)	50/51
Basic or Above	69.8 (1.11)	13/51	Basic or Above	80.3 (0.79)	2/51
Proficient or Above	32.9 (1.28)	22/51	Proficient or Above	36.5 (1.04)	4/51
Advanced or Above	6.3 (0.66)	34/51	Advanced or Above	6.5 (0.72)	14/51

Note: *For an explanation of data, please refer to the User's Guide in the front of the book; n/a indicates data not available*

Beadle County

Huron SD 02-2
88 3rd St SE • Huron, SD 57350-0949
Mailing Address: PO Box 949 • Huron, SD 57350-0949
(605) 353-6990
Grade Span: PK-12; **Agency Type:** 1
Schools: 9
　6 Primary; 1 Middle; 1 High; 1 Other Level
　8 Regular; 0 Special Education; 0 Vocational; 1 Alternative
　0 Magnet; 0 Charter; 2 Title I Eligible; 2 School-wide Title I
Students: 2,103　(50.6% male; 49.3% female)
　Individual Education Program: 293 (13.9%);
　English Language Learner: 51 (2.4%); Migrant: 58 (2.8%)
　Eligible for Free Lunch Program: 462 (22.0%)
　Eligible for Reduced-Price Lunch Program: 212 (10.1%)
Teachers: 136.9 (15.4 to 1)
Librarians/Media Specialists: 2.0 (1,051.5 to 1)
Guidance Counselors: 4.0 (525.8 to 1)
Current Spending: ($ per student per year):
　Total: $6,310; Instruction: $3,688; Support Services: $2,175
Enrollment, Drop-out Rates and Diploma Recipients by Race/Ethnicity

Category	Total	White	Black	Asian	AIAN	Hisp.
Enrollment (%)	100.0	92.0	2.5	0.5	3.3	1.7
Drop-out Rate (%)	3.0	3.0	12.5	0.0	0.0	0.0
H.S. Diplomas (#)	157	154	0	3	0	0

Brookings County

Brookings SD 05-1
2130 8th St S • Brookings, SD 57006-3507
(605) 696-4703 • http://www.bpsce.org/bsshp.htm
Grade Span: PK-12; **Agency Type:** 1
Schools: 5
　3 Primary; 1 Middle; 1 High; 0 Other Level
　5 Regular; 0 Special Education; 0 Vocational; 0 Alternative
　0 Magnet; 0 Charter; 3 Title I Eligible; 0 School-wide Title I
Students: 2,730　(51.1% male; 48.8% female)
　Individual Education Program: 327 (12.0%);
　English Language Learner: 30 (1.1%); Migrant: 0 (0.0%)
　Eligible for Free Lunch Program: 353 (12.9%)
　Eligible for Reduced-Price Lunch Program: 120 (4.4%)
Teachers: 178.2 (15.3 to 1)
Librarians/Media Specialists: 4.5 (606.7 to 1)
Guidance Counselors: 8.0 (341.3 to 1)
Current Spending: ($ per student per year):
　Total: $5,845; Instruction: $3,770; Support Services: $1,841
Enrollment, Drop-out Rates and Diploma Recipients by Race/Ethnicity

Category	Total	White	Black	Asian	AIAN	Hisp.
Enrollment (%)	100.0	89.5	1.5	3.0	2.8	3.2
Drop-out Rate (%)	2.1	2.0	0.0	0.0	12.5	0.0
H.S. Diplomas (#)	231	220	0	7	2	2

Brown County

Aberdeen SD 06-1
314 S Main St • Aberdeen, SD 57401-4146
(605) 725-7111 • http://www.aberdeen.k12.sd.us/
Grade Span: PK-12; **Agency Type:** 1
Schools: 10
　5 Primary; 2 Middle; 2 High; 1 Other Level
　8 Regular; 0 Special Education; 0 Vocational; 2 Alternative
　0 Magnet; 0 Charter; 4 Title I Eligible; 1 School-wide Title I
Students: 3,819　(51.3% male; 48.6% female)
　Individual Education Program: 601 (15.7%);
　English Language Learner: 9 (0.2%); Migrant: 0 (0.0%)
　Eligible for Free Lunch Program: 614 (16.1%)
　Eligible for Reduced-Price Lunch Program: 221 (5.8%)
Teachers: 226.6 (16.9 to 1)
Librarians/Media Specialists: 4.0 (954.8 to 1)
Guidance Counselors: 10.7 (356.9 to 1)
Current Spending: ($ per student per year):
　Total: $5,771; Instruction: $3,486; Support Services: $1,990
Enrollment, Drop-out Rates and Diploma Recipients by Race/Ethnicity

Category	Total	White	Black	Asian	AIAN	Hisp.
Enrollment (%)	100.0	89.4	0.9	1.0	7.7	1.1
Drop-out Rate (%)	3.9	3.4	0.0	0.0	11.7	14.3
H.S. Diplomas (#)	289	273	1	6	9	0

Codington County

Watertown SD 14-4
200 NE 9th St • Watertown, SD 57201-0730
Mailing Address: PO Box 730 • Watertown, SD 57201-0730
(605) 882-6312
Grade Span: PK-12; **Agency Type:** 1
Schools: 8
　6 Primary; 1 Middle; 1 High; 0 Other Level
　8 Regular; 0 Special Education; 0 Vocational; 0 Alternative
　0 Magnet; 0 Charter; 4 Title I Eligible; 0 School-wide Title I
Students: 3,862　(51.3% male; 48.6% female)
　Individual Education Program: 475 (12.3%);
　English Language Learner: 5 (0.1%); Migrant: 1 (<0.1%)
　Eligible for Free Lunch Program: 528 (13.7%)
　Eligible for Reduced-Price Lunch Program: 330 (8.5%)
Teachers: 238.3 (16.2 to 1)
Librarians/Media Specialists: 2.0 (1,931.0 to 1)
Guidance Counselors: 7.0 (551.7 to 1)
Current Spending: ($ per student per year):
　Total: $5,598; Instruction: $3,585; Support Services: $1,761
Enrollment, Drop-out Rates and Diploma Recipients by Race/Ethnicity

Category	Total	White	Black	Asian	AIAN	Hisp.
Enrollment (%)	100.0	94.4	0.3	0.8	3.3	1.3
Drop-out Rate (%)	2.7	2.8	0.0	0.0	0.0	0.0
H.S. Diplomas (#)	1	1	0	0	0	0

Davison County

Mitchell SD 17-2
800 W 10th Ave • Mitchell, SD 57301-7760
Mailing Address: PO Box 7760 • Mitchell, SD 57301-7760
(605) 995-3010 • http://www.mitchell.k12.sd.us/
Grade Span: PK-12; **Agency Type:** 1
Schools: 7
　5 Primary; 1 Middle; 1 High; 0 Other Level
　7 Regular; 0 Special Education; 0 Vocational; 0 Alternative
　0 Magnet; 0 Charter; 5 Title I Eligible; 0 School-wide Title I
Students: 2,581　(51.2% male; 48.7% female)
　Individual Education Program: 390 (15.1%);
　English Language Learner: 28 (1.1%); Migrant: 32 (1.2%)
　Eligible for Free Lunch Program: 525 (20.3%)
　Eligible for Reduced-Price Lunch Program: 197 (7.6%)
Teachers: 175.2 (14.7 to 1)
Librarians/Media Specialists: 1.0 (2,581.0 to 1)
Guidance Counselors: 6.4 (403.3 to 1)
Current Spending: ($ per student per year):
　Total: $6,255; Instruction: $3,842; Support Services: $2,064
Enrollment, Drop-out Rates and Diploma Recipients by Race/Ethnicity

Category	Total	White	Black	Asian	AIAN	Hisp.
Enrollment (%)	100.0	91.3	0.5	1.0	5.2	1.9
Drop-out Rate (%)	1.2	1.3	n/a	0.0	0.0	0.0
H.S. Diplomas (#)	224	218	0	3	2	1

Hughes County

Pierre SD 32-2
211 S Poplar Ave • Pierre, SD 57501-1845
(605) 773-7300
Grade Span: PK-12; **Agency Type:** 1
Schools: 7
　5 Primary; 1 Middle; 1 High; 0 Other Level
　7 Regular; 0 Special Education; 0 Vocational; 0 Alternative
　0 Magnet; 0 Charter; 3 Title I Eligible; 0 School-wide Title I
Students: 2,670　(52.1% male; 47.8% female)
　Individual Education Program: 284 (10.6%);
　English Language Learner: 18 (0.7%); Migrant: 0 (0.0%)
　Eligible for Free Lunch Program: 331 (12.4%)
　Eligible for Reduced-Price Lunch Program: 126 (4.7%)
Teachers: 162.0 (16.5 to 1)
Librarians/Media Specialists: 1.0 (2,670.0 to 1)
Guidance Counselors: 8.0 (333.8 to 1)
Current Spending: ($ per student per year):
　Total: $5,641; Instruction: $3,511; Support Services: $1,857
Enrollment, Drop-out Rates and Diploma Recipients by Race/Ethnicity

Category	Total	White	Black	Asian	AIAN	Hisp.
Enrollment (%)	100.0	85.9	0.2	0.5	12.4	1.0
Drop-out Rate (%)	1.2	0.6	0.0	0.0	10.2	0.0
H.S. Diplomas (#)	225	214	2	3	4	2

Lawrence County

Spearfish SD 40-2
525 E Illinois St • Spearfish, SD 57783-2521
(605) 717-1229 • http://spearfish.k12.sd.us/
Grade Span: PK-12; **Agency Type:** 1
Schools: 4
  2 Primary; 1 Middle; 1 High; 0 Other Level
  4 Regular; 0 Special Education; 0 Vocational; 0 Alternative
  0 Magnet; 0 Charter; 2 Title I Eligible; 0 School-wide Title I
Students: 2,003 (53.2% male; 46.7% female)
  Individual Education Program: 263 (13.1%);
  English Language Learner: 7 (0.3%); Migrant: 6 (0.3%)
  Eligible for Free Lunch Program: 292 (14.6%)
  Eligible for Reduced-Price Lunch Program: 146 (7.3%)
Teachers: 126.0 (15.9 to 1)
Librarians/Media Specialists: 2.0 (1,001.5 to 1)
Guidance Counselors: 4.5 (445.1 to 1)
Current Spending: ($ per student per year):
  Total: $5,955; Instruction: $3,715; Support Services: $2,006
Enrollment, Drop-out Rates and Diploma Recipients by Race/Ethnicity

Category	Total	White	Black	Asian	AIAN	Hisp.
Enrollment (%)	100.0	92.6	0.4	1.2	3.5	2.3
Drop-out Rate (%)	3.4	3.0	0.0	0.0	21.1	0.0
H.S. Diplomas (#)	174	164	1	1	6	2

Meade County

Meade SD 46-1
1230 Douglas St • Sturgis, SD 57785-1869
(605) 347-2523 • http://meade.k12.sd.us/
Grade Span: PK-12; **Agency Type:** 1
Schools: 13
  11 Primary; 1 Middle; 1 High; 0 Other Level
  13 Regular; 0 Special Education; 0 Vocational; 0 Alternative
  0 Magnet; 0 Charter; 4 Title I Eligible; 0 School-wide Title I
Students: 2,664 (52.4% male; 47.5% female)
  Individual Education Program: 301 (11.3%);
  English Language Learner: 5 (0.2%); Migrant: 1 (<0.1%)
  Eligible for Free Lunch Program: 497 (18.7%)
  Eligible for Reduced-Price Lunch Program: 251 (9.4%)
Teachers: 191.6 (13.9 to 1)
Librarians/Media Specialists: 2.0 (1,332.0 to 1)
Guidance Counselors: 7.9 (337.2 to 1)
Current Spending: ($ per student per year):
  Total: $5,608; Instruction: $3,527; Support Services: $1,802
Enrollment, Drop-out Rates and Diploma Recipients by Race/Ethnicity

Category	Total	White	Black	Asian	AIAN	Hisp.
Enrollment (%)	100.0	92.4	1.0	1.1	4.0	1.5
Drop-out Rate (%)	2.3	2.2	0.0	0.0	5.3	12.5
H.S. Diplomas (#)	188	178	3	1	5	1

Minnehaha County

Brandon Valley SD 49-2
301 S Splitrock Blvd • Brandon, SD 57005-1651
(605) 582-2049 • http://www.splitrocktel.net/~bvsdco/
Grade Span: PK-12; **Agency Type:** 1
Schools: 5
  3 Primary; 1 Middle; 1 High; 0 Other Level
  5 Regular; 0 Special Education; 0 Vocational; 0 Alternative
  0 Magnet; 0 Charter; 2 Title I Eligible; 0 School-wide Title I
Students: 2,685 (51.0% male; 48.9% female)
  Individual Education Program: 251 (9.3%);
  English Language Learner: 6 (0.2%); Migrant: 0 (0.0%)
  Eligible for Free Lunch Program: 155 (5.8%)
  Eligible for Reduced-Price Lunch Program: 109 (4.1%)
Teachers: 148.1 (18.1 to 1)
Librarians/Media Specialists: 3.0 (895.0 to 1)
Guidance Counselors: 4.9 (548.0 to 1)
Current Spending: ($ per student per year):
  Total: $5,289; Instruction: $2,989; Support Services: $1,968
Enrollment, Drop-out Rates and Diploma Recipients by Race/Ethnicity

Category	Total	White	Black	Asian	AIAN	Hisp.
Enrollment (%)	100.0	97.0	0.8	0.9	0.9	0.4
Drop-out Rate (%)	0.0	0.0	0.0	0.0	0.0	0.0
H.S. Diplomas (#)	195	191	1	2	0	1

Sioux Falls SD 49-5
201 E 38th St • Sioux Falls, SD 57105-5898
(605) 367-7920 • http://www.sf.k12.sd.us/
Grade Span: PK-12; **Agency Type:** 1
Schools: 44
  25 Primary; 5 Middle; 8 High; 5 Other Level
  33 Regular; 1 Special Education; 0 Vocational; 9 Alternative

---

  0 Magnet; 0 Charter; 7 Title I Eligible; 7 School-wide Title I
Students: 20,053 (51.7% male; 48.2% female)
  Individual Education Program: 2,682 (13.4%);
  English Language Learner: 757 (3.8%); Migrant: 378 (1.9%)
  Eligible for Free Lunch Program: 4,041 (20.2%)
  Eligible for Reduced-Price Lunch Program: 1,520 (7.6%)
Teachers: 1,241.0 (16.2 to 1)
Librarians/Media Specialists: 19.1 (1,049.9 to 1)
Guidance Counselors: 47.9 (418.6 to 1)
Current Spending: ($ per student per year):
  Total: $6,152; Instruction: $3,741; Support Services: $2,140
Enrollment, Drop-out Rates and Diploma Recipients by Race/Ethnicity

Category	Total	White	Black	Asian	AIAN	Hisp.
Enrollment (%)	100.0	84.1	5.1	2.3	3.9	4.6
Drop-out Rate (%)	4.2	3.5	7.9	2.4	16.9	10.9
H.S. Diplomas (#)	1,131	1,051	24	23	15	18

Pennington County

Douglas SD 51-1
400 Patriot Dr • Box Elder, SD 57719-2218
(605) 923-0000 • http://www.dsdk12.net/
Grade Span: PK-12; **Agency Type:** 1
Schools: 6
  3 Primary; 2 Middle; 1 High; 0 Other Level
  6 Regular; 0 Special Education; 0 Vocational; 0 Alternative
  0 Magnet; 0 Charter; 3 Title I Eligible; 0 School-wide Title I
Students: 2,539 (52.5% male; 47.4% female)
  Individual Education Program: 466 (18.4%);
  English Language Learner: 7 (0.3%); Migrant: 3 (0.1%)
  Eligible for Free Lunch Program: 499 (19.7%)
  Eligible for Reduced-Price Lunch Program: 410 (16.1%)
Teachers: 198.0 (12.8 to 1)
Librarians/Media Specialists: 3.0 (846.3 to 1)
Guidance Counselors: 7.0 (362.7 to 1)
Current Spending: ($ per student per year):
  Total: $7,524; Instruction: $4,695; Support Services: $2,559
Enrollment, Drop-out Rates and Diploma Recipients by Race/Ethnicity

Category	Total	White	Black	Asian	AIAN	Hisp.
Enrollment (%)	100.0	84.7	3.7	1.7	5.9	4.1
Drop-out Rate (%)	4.3	4.3	0.0	0.0	9.7	4.8
H.S. Diplomas (#)	96	79	4	5	5	3

Rapid City Area SD 51-4
300 6th St • Rapid City, SD 57701-2724
(605) 394-4031 • http://www.rcas.org/
Grade Span: PK-12; **Agency Type:** 1
Schools: 25
  16 Primary; 5 Middle; 3 High; 1 Other Level
  23 Regular; 1 Special Education; 0 Vocational; 1 Alternative
  0 Magnet; 0 Charter; 10 Title I Eligible; 8 School-wide Title I
Students: 13,167 (51.3% male; 48.6% female)
  Individual Education Program: 1,705 (12.9%);
  English Language Learner: 37 (0.3%); Migrant: 167 (1.3%)
  Eligible for Free Lunch Program: 3,010 (22.9%)
  Eligible for Reduced-Price Lunch Program: 713 (5.4%)
Teachers: 797.0 (16.5 to 1)
Librarians/Media Specialists: 17.5 (752.3 to 1)
Guidance Counselors: 23.0 (572.4 to 1)
Current Spending: ($ per student per year):
  Total: $5,787; Instruction: $3,559; Support Services: $2,011
Enrollment, Drop-out Rates and Diploma Recipients by Race/Ethnicity

Category	Total	White	Black	Asian	AIAN	Hisp.
Enrollment (%)	100.0	79.0	1.7	1.2	16.1	2.0
Drop-out Rate (%)	3.4	2.1	14.3	6.5	10.3	5.9
H.S. Diplomas (#)	1,186	1,069	5	15	87	10

Todd County

Todd County SD 66-1
E Denver Dr • Mission, SD 57555-0087
Mailing Address: PO Box 87 • Mission, SD 57555-0087
(605) 856-4457 • http://www.tcsdk12.org/
Grade Span: PK-12; **Agency Type:** 1
Schools: 12
  8 Primary; 2 Middle; 1 High; 1 Other Level
  11 Regular; 1 Special Education; 0 Vocational; 0 Alternative
  0 Magnet; 0 Charter; 12 Title I Eligible; 12 School-wide Title I
Students: 2,124 (52.4% male; 47.5% female)
  Individual Education Program: 324 (15.3%);
  English Language Learner: 1,905 (89.7%); Migrant: 1 (<0.1%)
  Eligible for Free Lunch Program: 2,067 (97.3%)
  Eligible for Reduced-Price Lunch Program: 0 (0.0%)
Teachers: 202.0 (10.5 to 1)
Librarians/Media Specialists: 2.0 (1,062.0 to 1)

Guidance Counselors: 15.0 (141.6 to 1)
Current Spending: ($ per student per year):
    Total: $11,532; Instruction: $6,365; Support Services: $4,754
Enrollment, Drop-out Rates and Diploma Recipients by Race/Ethnicity

Category	Total	White	Black	Asian	AIAN	Hisp.
Enrollment (%)	100.0	4.7	0.3	0.1	94.9	0.0
Drop-out Rate (%)	18.3	0.0	n/a	n/a	19.7	0.0
H.S. Diplomas (#)	54	6	0	0	48	0

Yankton County

Yankton SD 63-3
1900 Ferdig • Yankton, SD 57078-0738
Mailing Address: PO Box 738 • Yankton, SD 57078-0738
(605) 665-3998 • http://www.ysd.k12.sd.us/
Grade Span: PK-12; **Agency Type:** 1
Schools: 6
    4 Primary; 1 Middle; 1 High; 0 Other Level
    6 Regular; 0 Special Education; 0 Vocational; 0 Alternative
    0 Magnet; 0 Charter; 3 Title I Eligible; 0 School-wide Title I
Students: 3,114   (51.2% male; 48.7% female)
    Individual Education Program: 444 (14.3%);
    English Language Learner: 25 (0.8%); Migrant: 0 (0.0%)
    Eligible for Free Lunch Program: 574 (18.4%)
    Eligible for Reduced-Price Lunch Program: 266 (8.5%)
Teachers: 179.5 (17.3 to 1)
Librarians/Media Specialists: 1.9 (1,638.9 to 1)
Guidance Counselors: 8.0 (389.3 to 1)
Current Spending: ($ per student per year):
    Total: $5,854; Instruction: $3,475; Support Services: $2,048
Enrollment, Drop-out Rates and Diploma Recipients by Race/Ethnicity

Category	Total	White	Black	Asian	AIAN	Hisp.
Enrollment (%)	100.0	92.5	1.0	0.9	3.2	2.5
Drop-out Rate (%)	3.4	3.2	25.0	0.0	11.8	0.0
H.S. Diplomas (#)	229	224	1	2	2	0

Number of Schools

Rank	Number	District Name	City
1	44	Sioux Falls SD 49-5	Sioux Falls
2	25	Rapid City Area SD 51-4	Rapid City
3	13	Meade SD 46-1	Sturgis
4	12	Todd County SD 66-1	Mission
5	10	Aberdeen SD 06-1	Aberdeen
6	9	Huron SD 02-2	Huron
7	8	Watertown SD 14-4	Watertown
8	7	Mitchell SD 17-2	Mitchell
8	7	Pierre SD 32-2	Pierre
10	6	Douglas SD 51-1	Box Elder
10	6	Yankton SD 63-3	Yankton
12	5	Brandon Valley SD 49-2	Brandon
12	5	Brookings SD 05-1	Brookings
14	4	Spearfish SD 40-2	Spearfish

Number of Teachers

Rank	Number	District Name	City
1	1,241	Sioux Falls SD 49-5	Sioux Falls
2	797	Rapid City Area SD 51-4	Rapid City
3	238	Watertown SD 14-4	Watertown
4	226	Aberdeen SD 06-1	Aberdeen
5	202	Todd County SD 66-1	Mission
6	198	Douglas SD 51-1	Box Elder
7	191	Meade SD 46-1	Sturgis
8	179	Yankton SD 63-3	Yankton
9	178	Brookings SD 05-1	Brookings
10	175	Mitchell SD 17-2	Mitchell
11	162	Pierre SD 32-2	Pierre
12	148	Brandon Valley SD 49-2	Brandon
13	136	Huron SD 02-2	Huron
14	126	Spearfish SD 40-2	Spearfish

Number of Students

Rank	Number	District Name	City
1	20,053	Sioux Falls SD 49-5	Sioux Falls
2	13,167	Rapid City Area SD 51-4	Rapid City
3	3,862	Watertown SD 14-4	Watertown
4	3,819	Aberdeen SD 06-1	Aberdeen
5	3,114	Yankton SD 63-3	Yankton
6	2,730	Brookings SD 05-1	Brookings
7	2,685	Brandon Valley SD 49-2	Brandon
8	2,670	Pierre SD 32-2	Pierre
9	2,664	Meade SD 46-1	Sturgis
10	2,581	Mitchell SD 17-2	Mitchell
11	2,539	Douglas SD 51-1	Box Elder
12	2,124	Todd County SD 66-1	Mission
13	2,103	Huron SD 02-2	Huron
14	2,003	Spearfish SD 40-2	Spearfish

Male Students

Rank	Percent	District Name	City
1	53.2	Spearfish SD 40-2	Spearfish
2	52.5	Douglas SD 51-1	Box Elder
3	52.4	Todd County SD 66-1	Mission
4	52.4	Meade SD 46-1	Sturgis
5	52.1	Pierre SD 32-2	Pierre
6	51.7	Sioux Falls SD 49-5	Sioux Falls
7	51.3	Aberdeen SD 06-1	Aberdeen
8	51.3	Rapid City Area SD 51-4	Rapid City
9	51.3	Watertown SD 14-4	Watertown
10	51.2	Mitchell SD 17-2	Mitchell
11	51.2	Yankton SD 63-3	Yankton
12	51.1	Brookings SD 05-1	Brookings
13	51.0	Brandon Valley SD 49-2	Brandon
14	50.6	Huron SD 02-2	Huron

Female Students

Rank	Percent	District Name	City
1	49.3	Huron SD 02-2	Huron
2	48.9	Brandon Valley SD 49-2	Brandon
3	48.8	Brookings SD 05-1	Brookings
4	48.7	Yankton SD 63-3	Yankton
5	48.7	Mitchell SD 17-2	Mitchell
6	48.6	Watertown SD 14-4	Watertown
7	48.6	Rapid City Area SD 51-4	Rapid City
8	48.6	Aberdeen SD 06-1	Aberdeen
9	48.2	Sioux Falls SD 49-5	Sioux Falls
10	47.8	Pierre SD 32-2	Pierre
11	47.5	Meade SD 46-1	Sturgis
12	47.5	Todd County SD 66-1	Mission
13	47.4	Douglas SD 51-1	Box Elder
14	46.7	Spearfish SD 40-2	Spearfish

Individual Education Program Students

Rank	Percent	District Name	City
1	18.4	Douglas SD 51-1	Box Elder
2	15.7	Aberdeen SD 06-1	Aberdeen
3	15.3	Todd County SD 66-1	Mission
4	15.1	Mitchell SD 17-2	Mitchell
5	14.3	Yankton SD 63-3	Yankton
6	13.9	Huron SD 02-2	Huron
7	13.4	Sioux Falls SD 49-5	Sioux Falls
8	13.1	Spearfish SD 40-2	Spearfish
9	12.9	Rapid City Area SD 51-4	Rapid City
10	12.3	Watertown SD 14-4	Watertown
11	12.0	Brookings SD 05-1	Brookings
12	11.3	Meade SD 46-1	Sturgis
13	10.6	Pierre SD 32-2	Pierre
14	9.3	Brandon Valley SD 49-2	Brandon

English Language Learner Students

Rank	Percent	District Name	City
1	89.7	Todd County SD 66-1	Mission
2	3.8	Sioux Falls SD 49-5	Sioux Falls
3	2.4	Huron SD 02-2	Huron
4	1.1	Brookings SD 05-1	Brookings
4	1.1	Mitchell SD 17-2	Mitchell
6	0.8	Yankton SD 63-3	Yankton
7	0.7	Pierre SD 32-2	Pierre
8	0.3	Douglas SD 51-1	Box Elder
8	0.3	Rapid City Area SD 51-4	Rapid City
8	0.3	Spearfish SD 40-2	Spearfish
11	0.2	Aberdeen SD 06-1	Aberdeen
11	0.2	Brandon Valley SD 49-2	Brandon
11	0.2	Meade SD 46-1	Sturgis
14	0.1	Watertown SD 14-4	Watertown

Migrant Students

Rank	Percent	District Name	City
1	2.8	Huron SD 02-2	Huron
2	1.9	Sioux Falls SD 49-5	Sioux Falls
3	1.3	Rapid City Area SD 51-4	Rapid City
4	1.2	Mitchell SD 17-2	Mitchell
5	0.3	Spearfish SD 40-2	Spearfish
6	0.1	Douglas SD 51-1	Box Elder
7	0.0	Meade SD 46-1	Sturgis
7	0.0	Todd County SD 66-1	Mission
7	0.0	Watertown SD 14-4	Watertown
10	0.0	Aberdeen SD 06-1	Aberdeen
10	0.0	Brandon Valley SD 49-2	Brandon
10	0.0	Brookings SD 05-1	Brookings
10	0.0	Pierre SD 32-2	Pierre
10	0.0	Yankton SD 63-3	Yankton

Students Eligible for Free Lunch

Rank	Percent	District Name	City
1	97.3	Todd County SD 66-1	Mission
2	22.9	Rapid City Area SD 51-4	Rapid City
3	22.0	Huron SD 02-2	Huron
4	20.3	Mitchell SD 17-2	Mitchell
5	20.2	Sioux Falls SD 49-5	Sioux Falls
6	19.7	Douglas SD 51-1	Box Elder
7	18.7	Meade SD 46-1	Sturgis
8	18.4	Yankton SD 63-3	Yankton
9	16.1	Aberdeen SD 06-1	Aberdeen
10	14.6	Spearfish SD 40-2	Spearfish
11	13.7	Watertown SD 14-4	Watertown
12	12.9	Brookings SD 05-1	Brookings
13	12.4	Pierre SD 32-2	Pierre
14	5.8	Brandon Valley SD 49-2	Brandon

Students Eligible for Reduced-Price Lunch

Rank	Percent	District Name	City
1	16.1	Douglas SD 51-1	Box Elder
2	10.1	Huron SD 02-2	Huron
3	9.4	Meade SD 46-1	Sturgis
4	8.5	Watertown SD 14-4	Watertown
4	8.5	Yankton SD 63-3	Yankton
6	7.6	Mitchell SD 17-2	Mitchell
6	7.6	Sioux Falls SD 49-5	Sioux Falls
8	7.3	Spearfish SD 40-2	Spearfish
9	5.8	Aberdeen SD 06-1	Aberdeen
10	5.4	Rapid City Area SD 51-4	Rapid City
11	4.7	Pierre SD 32-2	Pierre
12	4.4	Brookings SD 05-1	Brookings
13	4.1	Brandon Valley SD 49-2	Brandon
14	0.0	Todd County SD 66-1	Mission

Student/Teacher Ratio

Rank	Ratio	District Name	City
1	18.1	Brandon Valley SD 49-2	Brandon
2	17.3	Yankton SD 63-3	Yankton
3	16.9	Aberdeen SD 06-1	Aberdeen
4	16.5	Pierre SD 32-2	Pierre
4	16.5	Rapid City Area SD 51-4	Rapid City
6	16.2	Sioux Falls SD 49-5	Sioux Falls
6	16.2	Watertown SD 14-4	Watertown
8	15.9	Spearfish SD 40-2	Spearfish
9	15.4	Huron SD 02-2	Huron
10	15.3	Brookings SD 05-1	Brookings
11	14.7	Mitchell SD 17-2	Mitchell
12	13.9	Meade SD 46-1	Sturgis
13	12.8	Douglas SD 51-1	Box Elder
14	10.5	Todd County SD 66-1	Mission

Student/Librarian Ratio

Rank	Ratio	District Name	City
1	2,670.0	Pierre SD 32-2	Pierre
2	2,581.0	Mitchell SD 17-2	Mitchell
3	1,931.0	Watertown SD 14-4	Watertown
4	1,638.9	Yankton SD 63-3	Yankton
5	1,232.0	Meade SD 46-1	Sturgis
6	1,062.0	Todd County SD 66-1	Mission
7	1,051.5	Huron SD 02-2	Huron
8	1,049.5	Sioux Falls SD 49-5	Sioux Falls
9	1,001.5	Spearfish SD 40-2	Spearfish
10	954.8	Aberdeen SD 06-1	Aberdeen
11	895.0	Brandon Valley SD 49-2	Brandon
12	846.3	Douglas SD 51-1	Box Elder
13	752.3	Rapid City Area SD 51-4	Rapid City
14	606.7	Brookings SD 05-1	Brookings

Student/Counselor Ratio

Rank	Ratio	District Name	City
1	572.4	Rapid City Area SD 51-4	Rapid City
2	551.7	Watertown SD 14-4	Watertown
3	548.0	Brandon Valley SD 49-2	Brandon
4	525.8	Huron SD 02-2	Huron
5	445.1	Spearfish SD 40-2	Spearfish
6	418.6	Sioux Falls SD 49-5	Sioux Falls
7	403.3	Mitchell SD 17-2	Mitchell
8	389.3	Yankton SD 63-3	Yankton
9	362.7	Douglas SD 51-1	Box Elder
10	356.9	Aberdeen SD 06-1	Aberdeen
11	341.3	Brookings SD 05-1	Brookings
12	337.2	Meade SD 46-1	Sturgis
13	333.8	Pierre SD 32-2	Pierre
14	141.6	Todd County SD 66-1	Mission

Current Spending per Student in FY2003

Rank	Dollars	District Name	City
1	11,532	Todd County SD 66-1	Mission
2	7,524	Douglas SD 51-1	Box Elder
3	6,310	Huron SD 02-2	Huron
4	6,255	Mitchell SD 17-2	Mitchell
5	6,152	Sioux Falls SD 49-5	Sioux Falls
6	5,955	Spearfish SD 40-2	Spearfish
7	5,854	Yankton SD 63-3	Yankton
8	5,845	Brookings SD 05-1	Brookings
9	5,787	Rapid City Area SD 51-4	Rapid City
10	5,771	Aberdeen SD 06-1	Aberdeen
11	5,641	Pierre SD 32-2	Pierre
12	5,598	Meade SD 46-1	Sturgis
13	5,598	Watertown SD 14-4	Watertown
14	5,289	Brandon Valley SD 49-2	Brandon

Number of Diploma Recipients

Rank	Number	District Name	City
1	1,186	Rapid City Area SD 51-4	Rapid City
2	1,131	Sioux Falls SD 49-5	Sioux Falls
3	289	Aberdeen SD 06-1	Aberdeen
4	231	Brookings SD 05-1	Brookings
5	229	Yankton SD 63-3	Yankton
6	225	Pierre SD 32-2	Pierre
7	224	Mitchell SD 17-2	Mitchell
8	195	Brandon Valley SD 49-2	Brandon
9	188	Meade SD 46-1	Sturgis
10	174	Spearfish SD 40-2	Spearfish
11	157	Huron SD 02-2	Huron
12	96	Douglas SD 51-1	Box Elder
13	54	Todd County SD 66-1	Mission
14	1	Watertown SD 14-4	Watertown

High School Drop-out Rate

Rank	Percent	District Name	City
1	18.3	Todd County SD 66-1	Mission
2	4.3	Douglas SD 51-1	Box Elder
3	4.2	Sioux Falls SD 49-5	Sioux Falls
4	3.9	Aberdeen SD 06-1	Aberdeen
5	3.4	Rapid City Area SD 51-4	Rapid City

5	3.4	Spearfish SD 40-2	Spearfish
5	3.4	Yankton SD 63-3	Yankton
8	3.0	Huron SD 02-2	Huron
9	2.7	Watertown SD 14-4	Watertown
10	2.3	Meade SD 46-1	Sturgis
11	2.1	Brookings SD 05-1	Brookings
12	1.2	Mitchell SD 17-2	Mitchell
12	1.2	Pierre SD 32-2	Pierre
14	0.0	Brandon Valley SD 49-2	Brandon

Tennessee

Tennessee Public School Educational Profile

Category	Value	Category	Value
Schools *(2003-2004)*	1,677	**Diploma Recipients** *(2002-2003)*	40,825
Instructional Level		White, Non-Hispanic	n/a
Primary	982	Black, Non-Hispanic	n/a
Middle	306	Asian/Pacific Islander	n/a
High	318	American Indian/Alaskan Native	n/a
Other Level	71	Hispanic	n/a
Curriculum		**High School Drop-out Rate** (%) *(2001-2002)*	3.8
Regular	1,611	White, Non-Hispanic	n/a
Special Education	16	Black, Non-Hispanic	n/a
Vocational	23	Asian/Pacific Islander	n/a
Alternative	27	American Indian/Alaskan Native	n/a
Type		Hispanic	n/a
Magnet	30	**Staff** *(2003-2004)*	
Charter	4	Teachers	59,584.1
Title I Eligible	899	Average Salary[1] ($)	40,318
School-wide Title I	714	Librarians/Media Specialists	1,544.9
Students *(2003-2004)*	911,636	Guidance Counselors	1,918.6
Gender (%)		**Ratios** *(2003-2004)*	
Male	n/a	Student/Teacher Ratio	15.3 to 1
Female	n/a	Student/Librarian Ratio	590.1 to 1
Race/Ethnicity (%)		Student/Counselor Ratio	475.2 to 1
White, Non-Hispanic	n/a	**College Entrance Exam Scores** *(2005)*	
Black, Non-Hispanic	n/a	Scholastic Aptitude Test (SAT)	
Asian/Pacific Islander	n/a	Participation Rate (%)	16
American Indian/Alaskan Native	n/a	Mean SAT Reasoning Test Verbal Score	572
Hispanic	n/a	Mean SAT Reasoning Test Math Score	563
Classification (%)		American College Testing Program (ACT)	
Individual Education Program (IEP)	18.8	Participation Rate (%)	92
Migrant *(2002-2003)*	n/a	Average Composite Score	20.5
English Language Learner (ELL)	n/a	Average English Score	20.6
Eligible for Free Lunch Program	n/a	Average Math Score	19.7
Eligible for Reduced-Price Lunch Program	n/a	Average Reading Score	20.8
Current Spending *($ per student in FY 2003)*	6,197	Average Science Score	20.2
Instruction	4,000		
Support Services	1,895		

Note: *For an explanation of data, please refer to the User's Guide in the front of the book; (1) Includes extra-duty pay*

Tennessee NAEP 2005 Test Scores

Reading			Mathematics		
Grade/Category	Value	Rank	Grade/Category	Value	Rank
4th Grade			**4th Grade**		
Average Proficiency	214.2 (1.44)	39/51	Average Proficiency	231.7 (1.22)	40/51
Proficiency by Gender/Race/Ethnicity			Proficiency by Gender/Race/Ethnicity		
Male	210.5 (1.73)	39/51	Male	232.6 (1.46)	42/51
Female	217.8 (1.52)	39/51	Female	230.8 (1.26)	41/51
White, Non-Hispanic	221.6 (1.54)	46/51	White, Non-Hispanic	238.3 (1.18)	46/51
Black, Non-Hispanic	194.9 (2.48)	30/42	Black, Non-Hispanic	213.8 (1.94)	34/42
Asian, Non-Hispanic	n/a	n/a	Asian, Non-Hispanic	n/a	n/a
American Indian, Non-Hispanic	n/a	n/a	American Indian, Non-Hispanic	n/a	n/a
Hispanic	199.3 (4.92)	32/40	Hispanic	229.2 (3.87)	13/41
Proficiency by Class Size			Proficiency by Class Size		
Less than 16 Students	n/a	n/a	Less than 16 Students	225.1 (4.50)	16/35
16 to 18 Students	205.1 (3.06)	31/33	16 to 18 Students	225.6 (2.32)	28/31
19 to 20 Students	214.3 (5.11)	30/38	19 to 20 Students	231.0 (3.23)	33/38
21 to 25 Students	216.3 (2.14)	40/51	21 to 25 Students	233.5 (1.75)	41/51
Greater than 25 Students	n/a	n/a	Greater than 25 Students	n/a	n/a
Percent Attaining Achievement Levels			Percent Attaining Achievement Levels		
Below Basic	40.8 (1.71)	13/51	Below Basic	26.2 (1.49)	9/51
Basic or Above	59.2 (1.71)	39/51	Basic or Above	73.8 (1.49)	43/51
Proficient or Above	26.7 (1.77)	37/51	Proficient or Above	27.7 (1.67)	42/51
Advanced or Above	5.8 (0.79)	38/51	Advanced or Above	3.0 (0.47)	41/51
8th Grade			**8th Grade**		
Average Proficiency	259.1 (0.94)	34/51	Average Proficiency	270.5 (1.13)	42/51
Proficiency by Gender/Race/Ethnicity			Proficiency by Gender/Race/Ethnicity		
Male	254.7 (1.12)	33/51	Male	270.1 (1.38)	43/51
Female	263.8 (1.21)	36/51	Female	270.9 (1.38)	42/51
White, Non-Hispanic	264.6 (1.11)	42/51	White, Non-Hispanic	277.9 (1.07)	46/51
Black, Non-Hispanic	240.1 (1.84)	26/40	Black, Non-Hispanic	246.1 (1.84)	36/41
Asian, Non-Hispanic	n/a	n/a	Asian, Non-Hispanic	n/a	n/a
American Indian, Non-Hispanic	n/a	n/a	American Indian, Non-Hispanic	n/a	n/a
Hispanic	n/a	n/a	Hispanic	n/a	n/a
Proficiency by Parents Highest Level of Ed.			Proficiency by Parents Highest Level of Ed.		
Did Not Finish High School	247.2 (2.38)	19/49	Did Not Finish High School	258.5 (2.14)	32/50
Graduated High School	250.1 (1.64)	32/50	Graduated High School	262.5 (1.58)	39/50
Some Education After High School	263.0 (1.96)	37/50	Some Education After High School	274.6 (1.88)	42/50
Graduated College	267.3 (1.45)	34/50	Graduated College	279.1 (1.70)	43/50
Percent Attaining Achievement Levels			Percent Attaining Achievement Levels		
Below Basic	40.8 (1.71)	13/51	Below Basic	39.0 (1.58)	10/51
Basic or Above	59.2 (1.71)	39/51	Basic or Above	61.0 (1.58)	42/51
Proficient or Above	26.7 (1.77)	37/51	Proficient or Above	20.6 (1.29)	43/51
Advanced or Above	5.8 (0.79)	38/51	Advanced or Above	2.9 (0.38)	43/51

Note: For an explanation of data, please refer to the User's Guide in the front of the book; n/a indicates data not available

Anderson County

Anderson County School Distrct
Ste 500 101 S Main • Clinton, TN 37716-3619
(865) 463-8631 • http://www.acorns.k12.tn.us/
Grade Span: KG-12; **Agency Type:** 1
Schools: 17
9 Primary; 4 Middle; 3 High; 1 Other Level
15 Regular; 0 Special Education; 1 Vocational; 1 Alternative
0 Magnet; 0 Charter; 8 Title I Eligible; 8 School-wide Title I
Students: 6,840 (n/a% male; n/a% female)
Individual Education Program: 1,797 (26.3%);
English Language Learner: n/a; Migrant: n/a
Eligible for Free Lunch Program: n/a
Eligible for Reduced-Price Lunch Program: n/a
Teachers: 499.7 (13.7 to 1)
Librarians/Media Specialists: 13.0 (526.2 to 1)
Guidance Counselors: 18.0 (380.0 to 1)
Current Spending: ($ per student per year):
Total: $6,296; Instruction: $4,046; Support Services: $1,921
Enrollment, Drop-out Rates and Diploma Recipients by Race/Ethnicity

Category	Total	White	Black	Asian	AIAN	Hisp.
Enrollment (%)	100.0	0.0	0.0	0.0	0.0	0.0
Drop-out Rate (%)	2.6	n/a	n/a	n/a	n/a	n/a
H.S. Diplomas (#)	431	n/a	n/a	n/a	n/a	n/a

Oak Ridge City SD
304new York Ave PO Box 658 • Oak Ridge, TN 37831-3221
(865) 425-9001 • http://www.ortn.edu/
Grade Span: PK-12; **Agency Type:** 1
Schools: 8
5 Primary; 2 Middle; 1 High; 0 Other Level
8 Regular; 0 Special Education; 0 Vocational; 0 Alternative
0 Magnet; 0 Charter; 0 Title I Eligible; 0 School-wide Title I
Students: 4,360 (n/a% male; n/a% female)
Individual Education Program: 1,249 (28.6%);
English Language Learner: n/a; Migrant: n/a
Eligible for Free Lunch Program: n/a
Eligible for Reduced-Price Lunch Program: n/a
Teachers: 331.0 (13.2 to 1)
Librarians/Media Specialists: 8.0 (545.0 to 1)
Guidance Counselors: 15.0 (290.7 to 1)
Current Spending: ($ per student per year):
Total: $8,866; Instruction: $5,607; Support Services: $2,912
Enrollment, Drop-out Rates and Diploma Recipients by Race/Ethnicity

Category	Total	White	Black	Asian	AIAN	Hisp.
Enrollment (%)	100.0	n/a	n/a	n/a	n/a	n/a
Drop-out Rate (%)	3.6	n/a	n/a	n/a	n/a	n/a
H.S. Diplomas (#)	281	n/a	n/a	n/a	n/a	n/a

Bedford County

Bedford County SD
500 Madison St • Shelbyville, TN 37160-3341
(931) 684-3284 • http://www.bedfordk12tn.com/
Grade Span: KG-12; **Agency Type:** 1
Schools: 12
6 Primary; 2 Middle; 3 High; 1 Other Level
12 Regular; 0 Special Education; 0 Vocational; 0 Alternative
0 Magnet; 0 Charter; 6 Title I Eligible; 2 School-wide Title I
Students: 6,689 (n/a% male; n/a% female)
Individual Education Program: 1,081 (16.2%);
English Language Learner: n/a; Migrant: n/a
Eligible for Free Lunch Program: n/a
Eligible for Reduced-Price Lunch Program: n/a
Teachers: 427.3 (15.7 to 1)
Librarians/Media Specialists: 11.0 (608.1 to 1)
Guidance Counselors: 13.0 (514.5 to 1)
Current Spending: ($ per student per year):
Total: $5,143; Instruction: $3,337; Support Services: $1,525
Enrollment, Drop-out Rates and Diploma Recipients by Race/Ethnicity

Category	Total	White	Black	Asian	AIAN	Hisp.
Enrollment (%)	100.0	n/a	n/a	n/a	n/a	n/a
Drop-out Rate (%)	2.2	n/a	n/a	n/a	n/a	n/a
H.S. Diplomas (#)	272	n/a	n/a	n/a	n/a	n/a

Benton County

Benton County SD
197 Briarwood St • Camden, TN 38320-1381
(731) 584-6111 • http://www.benton-lea.benton.k12.tn.us/
Grade Span: KG-12; **Agency Type:** 1
Schools: 8
3 Primary; 1 Middle; 3 High; 1 Other Level
7 Regular; 0 Special Education; 1 Vocational; 0 Alternative
0 Magnet; 0 Charter; 5 Title I Eligible; 5 School-wide Title I
Students: 2,438 (n/a% male; n/a% female)
Individual Education Program: 515 (21.1%);
English Language Learner: n/a; Migrant: n/a
Eligible for Free Lunch Program: n/a
Eligible for Reduced-Price Lunch Program: n/a
Teachers: 176.8 (13.8 to 1)
Librarians/Media Specialists: 5.0 (487.6 to 1)
Guidance Counselors: 6.5 (375.1 to 1)
Current Spending: ($ per student per year):
Total: $5,910; Instruction: $4,065; Support Services: $1,815
Enrollment, Drop-out Rates and Diploma Recipients by Race/Ethnicity

Category	Total	White	Black	Asian	AIAN	Hisp.
Enrollment (%)	100.0	0.0	0.0	0.0	0.0	0.0
Drop-out Rate (%)	1.2	n/a	n/a	n/a	n/a	n/a
H.S. Diplomas (#)	95	n/a	n/a	n/a	n/a	n/a

Bledsoe County

Bledsoe County SD
PO Box 369 • Pikeville, TN 37367-0369
(423) 447-2914 • http://WWW.BLEDSOE.K12.TN.US/
Grade Span: KG-12; **Agency Type:** 1
Schools: 6
3 Primary; 1 Middle; 2 High; 0 Other Level
5 Regular; 0 Special Education; 1 Vocational; 0 Alternative
0 Magnet; 0 Charter; 4 Title I Eligible; 3 School-wide Title I
Students: 1,794 (n/a% male; n/a% female)
Individual Education Program: 535 (29.8%);
English Language Learner: n/a; Migrant: n/a
Eligible for Free Lunch Program: n/a
Eligible for Reduced-Price Lunch Program: n/a
Teachers: 121.5 (14.8 to 1)
Librarians/Media Specialists: 3.0 (598.0 to 1)
Guidance Counselors: 3.0 (598.0 to 1)
Current Spending: ($ per student per year):
Total: $5,808; Instruction: $3,505; Support Services: $1,881
Enrollment, Drop-out Rates and Diploma Recipients by Race/Ethnicity

Category	Total	White	Black	Asian	AIAN	Hisp.
Enrollment (%)	100.0	0.0	0.0	0.0	0.0	0.0
Drop-out Rate (%)	4.9	n/a	n/a	n/a	n/a	n/a
H.S. Diplomas (#)	55	n/a	n/a	n/a	n/a	n/a

Blount County

Blount County SD
831 Grandview Dr • Maryville, TN 37803-5312
(865) 984-1212 • http://www.blountk12.org/
Grade Span: KG-12; **Agency Type:** 1
Schools: 19
11 Primary; 4 Middle; 3 High; 1 Other Level
18 Regular; 1 Special Education; 0 Vocational; 0 Alternative
0 Magnet; 0 Charter; 8 Title I Eligible; 0 School-wide Title I
Students: 10,944 (n/a% male; n/a% female)
Individual Education Program: 2,279 (20.8%);
English Language Learner: n/a; Migrant: n/a
Eligible for Free Lunch Program: n/a
Eligible for Reduced-Price Lunch Program: n/a
Teachers: 649.6 (16.8 to 1)
Librarians/Media Specialists: 18.5 (591.6 to 1)
Guidance Counselors: 23.1 (473.8 to 1)
Current Spending: ($ per student per year):
Total: $6,149; Instruction: $4,001; Support Services: $1,791
Enrollment, Drop-out Rates and Diploma Recipients by Race/Ethnicity

Category	Total	White	Black	Asian	AIAN	Hisp.
Enrollment (%)	100.0	n/a	n/a	n/a	n/a	n/a
Drop-out Rate (%)	3.8	n/a	n/a	n/a	n/a	n/a
H.S. Diplomas (#)	509	n/a	n/a	n/a	n/a	n/a

Maryville City SD
833 Lawrence Ave • Maryville, TN 37801-4857
(865) 982-7122 • http://www.ci.maryville.tn.us/schools/
Grade Span: KG-12; **Agency Type:** 1
Schools: 7
4 Primary; 2 Middle; 1 High; 0 Other Level
7 Regular; 0 Special Education; 0 Vocational; 0 Alternative
0 Magnet; 0 Charter; 4 Title I Eligible; 0 School-wide Title I
Students: 4,598 (n/a% male; n/a% female)
Individual Education Program: 816 (17.7%);
English Language Learner: n/a; Migrant: n/a
Eligible for Free Lunch Program: n/a
Eligible for Reduced-Price Lunch Program: n/a
Teachers: 291.5 (15.8 to 1)
Librarians/Media Specialists: 7.0 (656.9 to 1)
Guidance Counselors: 11.0 (418.0 to 1)

Current Spending: ($ per student per year):
Total: $7,494; Instruction: $5,189; Support Services: $1,898
Enrollment, Drop-out Rates and Diploma Recipients by Race/Ethnicity

Category	Total	White	Black	Asian	AIAN	Hisp.
Enrollment (%)	100.0	n/a	n/a	n/a	n/a	n/a
Drop-out Rate (%)	0.8	n/a	n/a	n/a	n/a	n/a
H.S. Diplomas (#)	230	n/a	n/a	n/a	n/a	n/a

Bradley County

Bradley County SD
800 S Lee Hwy • Cleveland, TN 37311-5853
(423) 476-0620 • http://www.bradleyschools.org/
Grade Span: KG-12; **Agency Type:** 1
Schools: 16
11 Primary; 2 Middle; 2 High; 1 Other Level
15 Regular; 0 Special Education; 0 Vocational; 1 Alternative
0 Magnet; 0 Charter; 9 Title I Eligible; 9 School-wide Title I
Students: 9,184 (n/a% male; n/a% female)
Individual Education Program: 1,274 (13.9%);
English Language Learner: n/a; Migrant: n/a
Eligible for Free Lunch Program: n/a
Eligible for Reduced-Price Lunch Program: n/a
Teachers: 560.2 (16.4 to 1)
Librarians/Media Specialists: 15.0 (612.3 to 1)
Guidance Counselors: 21.0 (437.3 to 1)
Current Spending: ($ per student per year):
Total: $5,242; Instruction: $3,502; Support Services: $1,417
Enrollment, Drop-out Rates and Diploma Recipients by Race/Ethnicity

Category	Total	White	Black	Asian	AIAN	Hisp.
Enrollment (%)	100.0	n/a	n/a	n/a	n/a	n/a
Drop-out Rate (%)	3.4	n/a	n/a	n/a	n/a	n/a
H.S. Diplomas (#)	401	n/a	n/a	n/a	n/a	n/a

Cleveland City SD
4300 Mouse Creek Rd NW • Cleveland, TN 37312-3303
(423) 472-9571 • http://www.clevelandschools.org
Grade Span: KG-12; **Agency Type:** 1
Schools: 8
6 Primary; 1 Middle; 1 High; 0 Other Level
8 Regular; 0 Special Education; 0 Vocational; 0 Alternative
0 Magnet; 0 Charter; 3 Title I Eligible; 3 School-wide Title I
Students: 4,393 (n/a% male; n/a% female)
Individual Education Program: 846 (19.3%);
English Language Learner: n/a; Migrant: n/a
Eligible for Free Lunch Program: n/a
Eligible for Reduced-Price Lunch Program: n/a
Teachers: 304.6 (14.4 to 1)
Librarians/Media Specialists: 8.0 (549.1 to 1)
Guidance Counselors: 12.0 (366.1 to 1)
Current Spending: ($ per student per year):
Total: $6,717; Instruction: $4,373; Support Services: $1,989
Enrollment, Drop-out Rates and Diploma Recipients by Race/Ethnicity

Category	Total	White	Black	Asian	AIAN	Hisp.
Enrollment (%)	100.0	n/a	n/a	n/a	n/a	n/a
Drop-out Rate (%)	0.9	n/a	n/a	n/a	n/a	n/a
H.S. Diplomas (#)	185	n/a	n/a	n/a	n/a	n/a

Campbell County

Campbell County School Distrct
522 Main St PO Box 445 • Jacksboro, TN 37757-0445
(423) 562-8377 • http://www.campbell.k12.tn.us/
Grade Span: KG-12; **Agency Type:** 1
Schools: 16
10 Primary; 2 Middle; 3 High; 1 Other Level
16 Regular; 0 Special Education; 0 Vocational; 0 Alternative
0 Magnet; 0 Charter; 12 Title I Eligible; 12 School-wide Title I
Students: 6,046 (n/a% male; n/a% female)
Individual Education Program: 1,031 (17.1%);
English Language Learner: n/a; Migrant: n/a
Eligible for Free Lunch Program: n/a
Eligible for Reduced-Price Lunch Program: n/a
Teachers: 396.3 (16.6 to 1)
Librarians/Media Specialists: 11.0 (599.6 to 1)
Guidance Counselors: 11.0 (599.6 to 1)
Current Spending: ($ per student per year):
Total: $5,531; Instruction: $3,556; Support Services: $1,552
Enrollment, Drop-out Rates and Diploma Recipients by Race/Ethnicity

Category	Total	White	Black	Asian	AIAN	Hisp.
Enrollment (%)	100.0	n/a	n/a	n/a	n/a	n/a
Drop-out Rate (%)	2.2	n/a	n/a	n/a	n/a	n/a
H.S. Diplomas (#)	255	n/a	n/a	n/a	n/a	n/a

Cannon County

Cannon County SD
301 W Main St • Woodbury, TN 37190-1100
(615) 563-5752
Grade Span: KG-12; **Agency Type:** 1
Schools: 7
6 Primary; 0 Middle; 1 High; 0 Other Level
7 Regular; 0 Special Education; 0 Vocational; 0 Alternative
0 Magnet; 0 Charter; 4 Title I Eligible; 2 School-wide Title I
Students: 2,136 (n/a% male; n/a% female)
Individual Education Program: 445 (20.8%);
English Language Learner: n/a; Migrant: n/a
Eligible for Free Lunch Program: n/a
Eligible for Reduced-Price Lunch Program: n/a
Teachers: 147.6 (14.5 to 1)
Librarians/Media Specialists: 4.0 (534.0 to 1)
Guidance Counselors: 5.0 (427.2 to 1)
Current Spending: ($ per student per year):
Total: $5,417; Instruction: $3,587; Support Services: $1,488
Enrollment, Drop-out Rates and Diploma Recipients by Race/Ethnicity

Category	Total	White	Black	Asian	AIAN	Hisp.
Enrollment (%)	100.0	n/a	n/a	n/a	n/a	n/a
Drop-out Rate (%)	2.4	n/a	n/a	n/a	n/a	n/a
H.S. Diplomas (#)	99	n/a	n/a	n/a	n/a	n/a

Carter County

Carter County SD
305 Academy St • Elizabethton, TN 37643-2208
(423) 547-4000 • http://www.elizabethton-lea.carter.k12.tn.us/Carter/
Grade Span: KG-12; **Agency Type:** 1
Schools: 17
10 Primary; 1 Middle; 5 High; 1 Other Level
16 Regular; 0 Special Education; 0 Vocational; 1 Alternative
0 Magnet; 0 Charter; 10 Title I Eligible; 10 School-wide Title I
Students: 5,858 (n/a% male; n/a% female)
Individual Education Program: 1,124 (19.2%);
English Language Learner: n/a; Migrant: n/a
Eligible for Free Lunch Program: n/a
Eligible for Reduced-Price Lunch Program: n/a
Teachers: 436.7 (13.4 to 1)
Librarians/Media Specialists: 13.0 (450.6 to 1)
Guidance Counselors: 12.0 (488.2 to 1)
Current Spending: ($ per student per year):
Total: $6,049; Instruction: $3,957; Support Services: $1,736
Enrollment, Drop-out Rates and Diploma Recipients by Race/Ethnicity

Category	Total	White	Black	Asian	AIAN	Hisp.
Enrollment (%)	100.0	n/a	n/a	n/a	n/a	n/a
Drop-out Rate (%)	1.9	n/a	n/a	n/a	n/a	n/a
H.S. Diplomas (#)	149	n/a	n/a	n/a	n/a	n/a

Elizabethton City SD
804 S Watauga Ave • Elizabethton, TN 37643-4207
(423) 547-8000 • http://ecschools.net/
Grade Span: KG-12; **Agency Type:** 1
Schools: 5
3 Primary; 1 Middle; 1 High; 0 Other Level
5 Regular; 0 Special Education; 0 Vocational; 0 Alternative
0 Magnet; 0 Charter; 2 Title I Eligible; 2 School-wide Title I
Students: 2,209 (n/a% male; n/a% female)
Individual Education Program: 358 (16.2%);
English Language Learner: n/a; Migrant: n/a
Eligible for Free Lunch Program: n/a
Eligible for Reduced-Price Lunch Program: n/a
Teachers: 153.2 (14.4 to 1)
Librarians/Media Specialists: 6.0 (368.2 to 1)
Guidance Counselors: 6.0 (368.2 to 1)
Current Spending: ($ per student per year):
Total: $6,638; Instruction: $4,439; Support Services: $1,862
Enrollment, Drop-out Rates and Diploma Recipients by Race/Ethnicity

Category	Total	White	Black	Asian	AIAN	Hisp.
Enrollment (%)	100.0	n/a	n/a	n/a	n/a	n/a
Drop-out Rate (%)	2.3	n/a	n/a	n/a	n/a	n/a
H.S. Diplomas (#)	168	n/a	n/a	n/a	n/a	n/a

Cheatham County

Cheatham County School Distrct
102 Elizabeth St • Ashland City, TN 37015-1101
(615) 792-5664 • http://www.cheatham-lea.k12.tn.us/
Grade Span: KG-12; **Agency Type:** 1
Schools: 14
7 Primary; 3 Middle; 4 High; 0 Other Level
14 Regular; 0 Special Education; 0 Vocational; 0 Alternative

0 Magnet; 0 Charter; 5 Title I Eligible; 0 School-wide Title I
Students: 6,931 (n/a% male; n/a% female)
Individual Education Program: 973 (14.0%);
English Language Learner: n/a; Migrant: n/a
Eligible for Free Lunch Program: n/a
Eligible for Reduced-Price Lunch Program: n/a
Teachers: 436.4 (15.7 to 1)
Librarians/Media Specialists: 13.0 (528.4 to 1)
Guidance Counselors: 19.0 (361.5 to 1)
Current Spending: ($ per student per year):
Total: $5,358; Instruction: $3,542; Support Services: $1,529
Enrollment, Drop-out Rates and Diploma Recipients by Race/Ethnicity

Category	Total	White	Black	Asian	AIAN	Hisp.
Enrollment (%)	100.0	n/a	n/a	n/a	n/a	n/a
Drop-out Rate (%)	0.7	n/a	n/a	n/a	n/a	n/a
H.S. Diplomas (#)	329	n/a	n/a	n/a	n/a	n/a

Chester County

Chester County SD
PO Box 327 • Henderson, TN 38340-0327
(731) 989-5134
Grade Span: KG-12; **Agency Type:** 1
Schools: 6
3 Primary; 2 Middle; 1 High; 0 Other Level
6 Regular; 0 Special Education; 0 Vocational; 0 Alternative
0 Magnet; 0 Charter; 4 Title I Eligible; 4 School-wide Title I
Students: 2,524 (n/a% male; n/a% female)
Individual Education Program: 272 (10.8%);
English Language Learner: n/a; Migrant: n/a
Eligible for Free Lunch Program: n/a
Eligible for Reduced-Price Lunch Program: n/a
Teachers: 142.7 (17.7 to 1)
Librarians/Media Specialists: 4.0 (631.0 to 1)
Guidance Counselors: 4.0 (631.0 to 1)
Current Spending: ($ per student per year):
Total: $4,831; Instruction: $3,090; Support Services: $1,413
Enrollment, Drop-out Rates and Diploma Recipients by Race/Ethnicity

Category	Total	White	Black	Asian	AIAN	Hisp.
Enrollment (%)	100.0	n/a	n/a	n/a	n/a	n/a
Drop-out Rate (%)	2.7	n/a	n/a	n/a	n/a	n/a
H.S. Diplomas (#)	105	n/a	n/a	n/a	n/a	n/a

Claiborne County

Claiborne County SD
PO Box 179 • Tazewell, TN 37879-0179
(423) 626-3543
Grade Span: PK-12; **Agency Type:** 1
Schools: 14
8 Primary; 2 Middle; 4 High; 0 Other Level
13 Regular; 0 Special Education; 0 Vocational; 1 Alternative
0 Magnet; 0 Charter; 9 Title I Eligible; 9 School-wide Title I
Students: 4,648 (n/a% male; n/a% female)
Individual Education Program: 1,071 (23.0%);
English Language Learner: n/a; Migrant: n/a
Eligible for Free Lunch Program: n/a
Eligible for Reduced-Price Lunch Program: n/a
Teachers: 348.2 (13.3 to 1)
Librarians/Media Specialists: 7.5 (619.7 to 1)
Guidance Counselors: 13.2 (352.1 to 1)
Current Spending: ($ per student per year):
Total: $5,800; Instruction: $3,998; Support Services: $1,598
Enrollment, Drop-out Rates and Diploma Recipients by Race/Ethnicity

Category	Total	White	Black	Asian	AIAN	Hisp.
Enrollment (%)	100.0	0.0	0.0	0.0	0.0	0.0
Drop-out Rate (%)	1.1	n/a	n/a	n/a	n/a	n/a
H.S. Diplomas (#)	172	n/a	n/a	n/a	n/a	n/a

Cocke County

Cocke County SD
305 Hedrick Dr • Newport, TN 37821-2908
(423) 623-7821 • http://www.cocke-lea.cocke.k12.tn.us/
Grade Span: KG-12; **Agency Type:** 1
Schools: 12
9 Primary; 0 Middle; 3 High; 0 Other Level
12 Regular; 0 Special Education; 0 Vocational; 0 Alternative
0 Magnet; 0 Charter; 9 Title I Eligible; 9 School-wide Title I
Students: 4,723 (n/a% male; n/a% female)
Individual Education Program: 915 (19.4%);
English Language Learner: n/a; Migrant: n/a
Eligible for Free Lunch Program: n/a
Eligible for Reduced-Price Lunch Program: n/a
Teachers: 314.6 (15.0 to 1)

Librarians/Media Specialists: 10.5 (449.8 to 1)
Guidance Counselors: 11.8 (400.3 to 1)
Current Spending: ($ per student per year):
Total: $5,543; Instruction: $3,515; Support Services: $1,582
Enrollment, Drop-out Rates and Diploma Recipients by Race/Ethnicity

Category	Total	White	Black	Asian	AIAN	Hisp.
Enrollment (%)	100.0	n/a	n/a	n/a	n/a	n/a
Drop-out Rate (%)	0.8	n/a	n/a	n/a	n/a	n/a
H.S. Diplomas (#)	277	n/a	n/a	n/a	n/a	n/a

Coffee County

Coffee County SD
1343 Mcarthur St • Manchester, TN 37355-1785
(931) 723-5150 • http://www.coffeecountyschools.com/
Grade Span: KG-12; **Agency Type:** 1
Schools: 8
5 Primary; 1 Middle; 2 High; 0 Other Level
7 Regular; 0 Special Education; 0 Vocational; 1 Alternative
0 Magnet; 0 Charter; 5 Title I Eligible; 5 School-wide Title I
Students: 4,129 (n/a% male; n/a% female)
Individual Education Program: 847 (20.5%);
English Language Learner: n/a; Migrant: n/a
Eligible for Free Lunch Program: n/a
Eligible for Reduced-Price Lunch Program: n/a
Teachers: 273.1 (15.1 to 1)
Librarians/Media Specialists: 8.0 (516.1 to 1)
Guidance Counselors: 10.0 (412.9 to 1)
Current Spending: ($ per student per year):
Total: $5,611; Instruction: $3,674; Support Services: $1,595
Enrollment, Drop-out Rates and Diploma Recipients by Race/Ethnicity

Category	Total	White	Black	Asian	AIAN	Hisp.
Enrollment (%)	100.0	0.0	0.0	0.0	0.0	0.0
Drop-out Rate (%)	1.3	n/a	n/a	n/a	n/a	n/a
H.S. Diplomas (#)	254	n/a	n/a	n/a	n/a	n/a

Tullahoma City SD
510 S Jackson St • Tullahoma, TN 37388-3468
(931) 454-2600 • http://www.tullahomacityschools.net/
Grade Span: KG-12; **Agency Type:** 1
Schools: 7
4 Primary; 2 Middle; 1 High; 0 Other Level
7 Regular; 0 Special Education; 0 Vocational; 0 Alternative
0 Magnet; 0 Charter; 3 Title I Eligible; 2 School-wide Title I
Students: 3,597 (n/a% male; n/a% female)
Individual Education Program: 757 (21.0%);
English Language Learner: n/a; Migrant: n/a
Eligible for Free Lunch Program: n/a
Eligible for Reduced-Price Lunch Program: n/a
Teachers: 230.6 (15.6 to 1)
Librarians/Media Specialists: 8.0 (449.6 to 1)
Guidance Counselors: 9.0 (399.7 to 1)
Current Spending: ($ per student per year):
Total: $6,235; Instruction: $4,172; Support Services: $1,712
Enrollment, Drop-out Rates and Diploma Recipients by Race/Ethnicity

Category	Total	White	Black	Asian	AIAN	Hisp.
Enrollment (%)	100.0	n/a	n/a	n/a	n/a	n/a
Drop-out Rate (%)	1.6	n/a	n/a	n/a	n/a	n/a
H.S. Diplomas (#)	236	n/a	n/a	n/a	n/a	n/a

Crockett County

Crockett County SD
102 N Cavalier Dr • Alamo, TN 38001-9699
(731) 696-2604 • http://www.ccetc.org/
Grade Span: KG-12; **Agency Type:** 1
Schools: 5
3 Primary; 1 Middle; 1 High; 0 Other Level
5 Regular; 0 Special Education; 0 Vocational; 0 Alternative
0 Magnet; 0 Charter; 3 Title I Eligible; 0 School-wide Title I
Students: 1,782 (n/a% male; n/a% female)
Individual Education Program: 310 (17.4%);
English Language Learner: n/a; Migrant: n/a
Eligible for Free Lunch Program: n/a
Eligible for Reduced-Price Lunch Program: n/a
Teachers: 117.5 (15.2 to 1)
Librarians/Media Specialists: 2.0 (891.0 to 1)
Guidance Counselors: 3.0 (594.0 to 1)
Current Spending: ($ per student per year):
Total: $5,363; Instruction: $3,208; Support Services: $1,810
Enrollment, Drop-out Rates and Diploma Recipients by Race/Ethnicity

Category	Total	White	Black	Asian	AIAN	Hisp.
Enrollment (%)	100.0	n/a	n/a	n/a	n/a	n/a
Drop-out Rate (%)	1.7	n/a	n/a	n/a	n/a	n/a
H.S. Diplomas (#)	141	n/a	n/a	n/a	n/a	n/a

Cumberland County

Cumberland County SD
756 Stanley St • Crossville, TN 38555-4790
(931) 484-6135 • http://cumberland-lea.k12tn.net/
Grade Span: KG-12; **Agency Type:** 1
Schools: 10
  9 Primary; 0 Middle; 1 High; 0 Other Level
  10 Regular; 0 Special Education; 0 Vocational; 0 Alternative
  0 Magnet; 0 Charter; 9 Title I Eligible; 9 School-wide Title I
Students: 6,899 (n/a% male; n/a% female)
  Individual Education Program: 1,354 (19.6%);
  English Language Learner: n/a; Migrant: n/a
  Eligible for Free Lunch Program: n/a
  Eligible for Reduced-Price Lunch Program: n/a
Teachers: 400.4 (17.2 to 1)
Librarians/Media Specialists: 8.8 (784.0 to 1)
Guidance Counselors: 10.3 (669.8 to 1)
Current Spending: ($ per student per year):
  Total: $5,314; Instruction: $3,556; Support Services: $1,415
Enrollment, Drop-out Rates and Diploma Recipients by Race/Ethnicity

Category	Total	White	Black	Asian	AIAN	Hisp.
Enrollment (%)	100.0	n/a	n/a	n/a	n/a	n/a
Drop-out Rate (%)	3.2	n/a	n/a	n/a	n/a	n/a
H.S. Diplomas (#)	301	n/a	n/a	n/a	n/a	n/a

Davidson County

Nashville-Davidson County SD
2601 Bransford Ave • Nashville, TN 37204-2811
(615) 259-8419 • http://www.mnps.org/site3.aspx
Grade Span: KG-12; **Agency Type:** 1
Schools: 126
  69 Primary; 35 Middle; 18 High; 4 Other Level
  119 Regular; 3 Special Education; 0 Vocational; 4 Alternative
  14 Magnet; 1 Charter; 67 Title I Eligible; 67 School-wide Title I
Students: 68,651 (n/a% male; n/a% female)
  Individual Education Program: 13,514 (19.7%);
  English Language Learner: n/a; Migrant: n/a
  Eligible for Free Lunch Program: n/a
  Eligible for Reduced-Price Lunch Program: n/a
Teachers: 4,857.6 (14.1 to 1)
Librarians/Media Specialists: 119.0 (576.9 to 1)
Guidance Counselors: 180.5 (380.3 to 1)
Current Spending: ($ per student per year):
  Total: $7,614; Instruction: $4,782; Support Services: $2,510
Enrollment, Drop-out Rates and Diploma Recipients by Race/Ethnicity

Category	Total	White	Black	Asian	AIAN	Hisp.
Enrollment (%)	100.0	0.0	0.0	0.0	0.0	0.0
Drop-out Rate (%)	7.6	n/a	n/a	n/a	n/a	n/a
H.S. Diplomas (#)	2,609	n/a	n/a	n/a	n/a	n/a

De Kalb County

Dekalb County SD
110 S Public Square • Smithville, TN 37166-1723
(615) 597-4084 • http://www.dekalbschools.com
Grade Span: KG-12; **Agency Type:** 1
Schools: 5
  3 Primary; 1 Middle; 1 High; 0 Other Level
  5 Regular; 0 Special Education; 0 Vocational; 0 Alternative
  0 Magnet; 0 Charter; 4 Title I Eligible; 4 School-wide Title I
Students: 2,584 (n/a% male; n/a% female)
  Individual Education Program: 641 (24.8%);
  English Language Learner: n/a; Migrant: n/a
  Eligible for Free Lunch Program: n/a
  Eligible for Reduced-Price Lunch Program: n/a
Teachers: 179.3 (14.4 to 1)
Librarians/Media Specialists: 5.0 (516.8 to 1)
Guidance Counselors: 5.0 (516.8 to 1)
Current Spending: ($ per student per year):
  Total: $5,367; Instruction: $3,450; Support Services: $1,583
Enrollment, Drop-out Rates and Diploma Recipients by Race/Ethnicity

Category	Total	White	Black	Asian	AIAN	Hisp.
Enrollment (%)	100.0	n/a	n/a	n/a	n/a	n/a
Drop-out Rate (%)	2.7	n/a	n/a	n/a	n/a	n/a
H.S. Diplomas (#)	108	n/a	n/a	n/a	n/a	n/a

Dickson County

Dickson County SD
817 N Charlotte St • Dickson, TN 37055-1008
(615) 446-7571 • http://www.dicksoncountyschools.org/
Grade Span: KG-12; **Agency Type:** 1
Schools: 14

8 Primary; 3 Middle; 2 High; 1 Other Level
  13 Regular; 0 Special Education; 0 Vocational; 1 Alternative
  0 Magnet; 0 Charter; 7 Title I Eligible; 5 School-wide Title I
Students: 8,111 (n/a% male; n/a% female)
  Individual Education Program: 1,859 (22.9%);
  English Language Learner: n/a; Migrant: n/a
  Eligible for Free Lunch Program: n/a
  Eligible for Reduced-Price Lunch Program: n/a
Teachers: 528.1 (15.4 to 1)
Librarians/Media Specialists: 12.5 (648.9 to 1)
Guidance Counselors: 15.1 (537.2 to 1)
Current Spending: ($ per student per year):
  Total: $5,852; Instruction: $3,754; Support Services: $1,766
Enrollment, Drop-out Rates and Diploma Recipients by Race/Ethnicity

Category	Total	White	Black	Asian	AIAN	Hisp.
Enrollment (%)	100.0	n/a	n/a	n/a	n/a	n/a
Drop-out Rate (%)	5.5	n/a	n/a	n/a	n/a	n/a
H.S. Diplomas (#)	396	n/a	n/a	n/a	n/a	n/a

Dyer County

Dyer County SD
159 Everett Ave • Dyersburg, TN 38024-5119
(731) 285-6712 • http://www.dyer-lea.dyer.k12.tn.us/
Grade Span: KG-12; **Agency Type:** 1
Schools: 8
  5 Primary; 2 Middle; 1 High; 0 Other Level
  8 Regular; 0 Special Education; 0 Vocational; 0 Alternative
  0 Magnet; 0 Charter; 5 Title I Eligible; 1 School-wide Title I
Students: 3,205 (n/a% male; n/a% female)
  Individual Education Program: 784 (24.5%);
  English Language Learner: n/a; Migrant: n/a
  Eligible for Free Lunch Program: n/a
  Eligible for Reduced-Price Lunch Program: n/a
Teachers: 206.1 (15.6 to 1)
Librarians/Media Specialists: 3.0 (1,068.3 to 1)
Guidance Counselors: 5.0 (641.0 to 1)
Current Spending: ($ per student per year):
  Total: $6,632; Instruction: $3,848; Support Services: $2,378
Enrollment, Drop-out Rates and Diploma Recipients by Race/Ethnicity

Category	Total	White	Black	Asian	AIAN	Hisp.
Enrollment (%)	100.0	n/a	n/a	n/a	n/a	n/a
Drop-out Rate (%)	1.2	n/a	n/a	n/a	n/a	n/a
H.S. Diplomas (#)	194	n/a	n/a	n/a	n/a	n/a

Dyersburg City SD
PO Box 1507 • Dyersburg, TN 38025-1507
(731) 286-3600 • http://www.dyersburg-lea.dyer.k12.tn.us/
Grade Span: KG-12; **Agency Type:** 1
Schools: 4
  2 Primary; 1 Middle; 1 High; 0 Other Level
  4 Regular; 0 Special Education; 0 Vocational; 0 Alternative
  0 Magnet; 0 Charter; 3 Title I Eligible; 3 School-wide Title I
Students: 3,555 (n/a% male; n/a% female)
  Individual Education Program: 644 (18.1%);
  English Language Learner: n/a; Migrant: n/a
  Eligible for Free Lunch Program: n/a
  Eligible for Reduced-Price Lunch Program: n/a
Teachers: 219.2 (16.2 to 1)
Librarians/Media Specialists: 5.0 (711.0 to 1)
Guidance Counselors: 6.0 (592.5 to 1)
Current Spending: ($ per student per year):
  Total: $6,158; Instruction: $4,169; Support Services: $1,624
Enrollment, Drop-out Rates and Diploma Recipients by Race/Ethnicity

Category	Total	White	Black	Asian	AIAN	Hisp.
Enrollment (%)	100.0	n/a	n/a	n/a	n/a	n/a
Drop-out Rate (%)	5.4	n/a	n/a	n/a	n/a	n/a
H.S. Diplomas (#)	197	n/a	n/a	n/a	n/a	n/a

Fayette County

Fayette County SD
126 W Market St • Somerville, TN 38068-0009
(901) 465-5260
Grade Span: KG-12; **Agency Type:** 1
Schools: 10
  7 Primary; 2 Middle; 1 High; 0 Other Level
  10 Regular; 0 Special Education; 0 Vocational; 0 Alternative
  0 Magnet; 0 Charter; 10 Title I Eligible; 10 School-wide Title I
Students: 3,213 (n/a% male; n/a% female)
  Individual Education Program: 637 (19.8%);
  English Language Learner: n/a; Migrant: n/a
  Eligible for Free Lunch Program: n/a
  Eligible for Reduced-Price Lunch Program: n/a
Teachers: 260.0 (12.4 to 1)

Librarians/Media Specialists: 10.0 (321.3 to 1)
Guidance Counselors: 7.0 (459.0 to 1)
Current Spending: ($ per student per year):
   Total: $7,161; Instruction: $4,267; Support Services: $2,315
Enrollment, Drop-out Rates and Diploma Recipients by Race/Ethnicity

Category	Total	White	Black	Asian	AIAN	Hisp.
Enrollment (%)	100.0	n/a	n/a	n/a	n/a	n/a
Drop-out Rate (%)	9.7	n/a	n/a	n/a	n/a	n/a
H.S. Diplomas (#)	138	n/a	n/a	n/a	n/a	n/a

Fentress County

Fentress County School Distrct
PO Box 963 • Jamestown, TN 38556-0963
(931) 879-9218
Grade Span: KG-12; **Agency Type:** 1
Schools: 6
   4 Primary; 0 Middle; 2 High; 0 Other Level
   6 Regular; 0 Special Education; 0 Vocational; 0 Alternative
   0 Magnet; 0 Charter; 4 Title I Eligible; 4 School-wide Title I
Students: 2,252 (n/a% male; n/a% female)
   Individual Education Program: 409 (18.2%);
   English Language Learner: n/a; Migrant: n/a
   Eligible for Free Lunch Program: n/a
   Eligible for Reduced-Price Lunch Program: n/a
Teachers: 161.5 (13.9 to 1)
Librarians/Media Specialists: 5.0 (450.4 to 1)
Guidance Counselors: 4.0 (563.0 to 1)
Current Spending: ($ per student per year):
   Total: $5,625; Instruction: $3,751; Support Services: $1,513
Enrollment, Drop-out Rates and Diploma Recipients by Race/Ethnicity

Category	Total	White	Black	Asian	AIAN	Hisp.
Enrollment (%)	100.0	n/a	n/a	n/a	n/a	n/a
Drop-out Rate (%)	2.9	n/a	n/a	n/a	n/a	n/a
H.S. Diplomas (#)	150	n/a	n/a	n/a	n/a	n/a

Franklin County

Franklin County School Distrct
215 S College St • Winchester, TN 37398-1519
(931) 967-0626 • http://www.fssd.org/
Grade Span: KG-12; **Agency Type:** 1
Schools: 12
   8 Primary; 2 Middle; 1 High; 1 Other Level
   12 Regular; 0 Special Education; 0 Vocational; 0 Alternative
   0 Magnet; 0 Charter; 4 Title I Eligible; 4 School-wide Title I
Students: 5,776 (n/a% male; n/a% female)
   Individual Education Program: 1,226 (21.2%);
   English Language Learner: n/a; Migrant: n/a
   Eligible for Free Lunch Program: n/a
   Eligible for Reduced-Price Lunch Program: n/a
Teachers: 392.0 (14.7 to 1)
Librarians/Media Specialists: 12.0 (481.3 to 1)
Guidance Counselors: 12.0 (481.3 to 1)
Current Spending: ($ per student per year):
   Total: $5,575; Instruction: $3,644; Support Services: $1,748
Enrollment, Drop-out Rates and Diploma Recipients by Race/Ethnicity

Category	Total	White	Black	Asian	AIAN	Hisp.
Enrollment (%)	100.0	n/a	n/a	n/a	n/a	n/a
Drop-out Rate (%)	5.2	n/a	n/a	n/a	n/a	n/a
H.S. Diplomas (#)	306	n/a	n/a	n/a	n/a	n/a

Gibson County

Gibson Special District
135 Hwy 45 W Box D • Dyer, TN 38330
(731) 692-3803 • http://volweb.utk.edu/school/gibson/gcsd99.html
Grade Span: KG-12; **Agency Type:** 1
Schools: 7
   5 Primary; 1 Middle; 1 High; 0 Other Level
   7 Regular; 0 Special Education; 0 Vocational; 0 Alternative
   0 Magnet; 0 Charter; 4 Title I Eligible; 0 School-wide Title I
Students: 2,640 (n/a% male; n/a% female)
   Individual Education Program: 493 (18.7%);
   English Language Learner: n/a; Migrant: n/a
   Eligible for Free Lunch Program: n/a
   Eligible for Reduced-Price Lunch Program: n/a
Teachers: 161.9 (16.3 to 1)
Librarians/Media Specialists: 6.0 (440.0 to 1)
Guidance Counselors: 5.0 (528.0 to 1)
Current Spending: ($ per student per year):
   Total: $4,910; Instruction: $3,190; Support Services: $1,376

Category	Total	White	Black	Asian	AIAN	Hisp.
Enrollment (%)	100.0	n/a	n/a	n/a	n/a	n/a
Drop-out Rate (%)	2.7	n/a	n/a	n/a	n/a	n/a
H.S. Diplomas (#)	126	n/a	n/a	n/a	n/a	n/a

Milan City Special SD
PO Box 528 2048 S First • Milan, TN 38358-0528
(731) 686-0844 • http://www.milanssd.org/
Grade Span: KG-12; **Agency Type:** 1
Schools: 3
   1 Primary; 1 Middle; 1 High; 0 Other Level
   3 Regular; 0 Special Education; 0 Vocational; 0 Alternative
   0 Magnet; 0 Charter; 1 Title I Eligible; 1 School-wide Title I
Students: 2,022 (n/a% male; n/a% female)
   Individual Education Program: 379 (18.7%);
   English Language Learner: n/a; Migrant: n/a
   Eligible for Free Lunch Program: n/a
   Eligible for Reduced-Price Lunch Program: n/a
Teachers: 135.6 (14.9 to 1)
Librarians/Media Specialists: 4.0 (505.5 to 1)
Guidance Counselors: 5.0 (404.4 to 1)
Current Spending: ($ per student per year):
   Total: $5,486; Instruction: $3,572; Support Services: $1,573
Enrollment, Drop-out Rates and Diploma Recipients by Race/Ethnicity

Category	Total	White	Black	Asian	AIAN	Hisp.
Enrollment (%)	100.0	n/a	n/a	n/a	n/a	n/a
Drop-out Rate (%)	1.1	n/a	n/a	n/a	n/a	n/a
H.S. Diplomas (#)	123	n/a	n/a	n/a	n/a	n/a

Giles County

Giles County SD
270 Richland Dr • Pulaski, TN 38478-2609
(931) 363-4558 • http://www.giles-lea.giles.k12.tn.us
Grade Span: KG-12; **Agency Type:** 1
Schools: 8
   5 Primary; 1 Middle; 1 High; 1 Other Level
   8 Regular; 0 Special Education; 0 Vocational; 0 Alternative
   0 Magnet; 0 Charter; 6 Title I Eligible; 0 School-wide Title I
Students: 4,432 (n/a% male; n/a% female)
   Individual Education Program: 753 (17.0%);
   English Language Learner: n/a; Migrant: n/a
   Eligible for Free Lunch Program: n/a
   Eligible for Reduced-Price Lunch Program: n/a
Teachers: 291.7 (15.2 to 1)
Librarians/Media Specialists: 10.0 (443.2 to 1)
Guidance Counselors: 10.0 (443.2 to 1)
Current Spending: ($ per student per year):
   Total: $5,788; Instruction: $3,662; Support Services: $1,768
Enrollment, Drop-out Rates and Diploma Recipients by Race/Ethnicity

Category	Total	White	Black	Asian	AIAN	Hisp.
Enrollment (%)	100.0	n/a	n/a	n/a	n/a	n/a
Drop-out Rate (%)	4.2	n/a	n/a	n/a	n/a	n/a
H.S. Diplomas (#)	233	n/a	n/a	n/a	n/a	n/a

Grainger County

Grainger County School Distrct
PO Box 38 • Rutledge, TN 37861-0038
(865) 828-3611 • http://www.grainger.k12.tn.us
Grade Span: KG-12; **Agency Type:** 1
Schools: 7
   4 Primary; 0 Middle; 2 High; 1 Other Level
   7 Regular; 0 Special Education; 0 Vocational; 0 Alternative
   0 Magnet; 0 Charter; 5 Title I Eligible; 5 School-wide Title I
Students: 3,336 (n/a% male; n/a% female)
   Individual Education Program: 719 (21.6%);
   English Language Learner: n/a; Migrant: n/a
   Eligible for Free Lunch Program: n/a
   Eligible for Reduced-Price Lunch Program: n/a
Teachers: 204.2 (16.3 to 1)
Librarians/Media Specialists: 5.0 (667.2 to 1)
Guidance Counselors: 4.6 (725.2 to 1)
Current Spending: ($ per student per year):
   Total: $5,444; Instruction: $3,757; Support Services: $1,352
Enrollment, Drop-out Rates and Diploma Recipients by Race/Ethnicity

Category	Total	White	Black	Asian	AIAN	Hisp.
Enrollment (%)	100.0	n/a	n/a	n/a	n/a	n/a
Drop-out Rate (%)	1.3	n/a	n/a	n/a	n/a	n/a
H.S. Diplomas (#)	170	n/a	n/a	n/a	n/a	n/a

Greene County

Greene County SD
910 W Summer St • Greeneville, TN 37743-3016
(423) 639-4194 • http://www.greene.xtn.net/~gcs/
Grade Span: KG-12; **Agency Type:** 1
Schools: 15
   11 Primary; 0 Middle; 4 High; 0 Other Level
   15 Regular; 0 Special Education; 0 Vocational; 0 Alternative
   0 Magnet; 0 Charter; 11 Title I Eligible; 11 School-wide Title I
Students: 6,976 (n/a% male; n/a% female)
   Individual Education Program: 1,624 (23.3%);
   English Language Learner: n/a; Migrant: n/a
   Eligible for Free Lunch Program: n/a
   Eligible for Reduced-Price Lunch Program: n/a
Teachers: 451.0 (15.5 to 1)
Librarians/Media Specialists: 11.0 (634.2 to 1)
Guidance Counselors: 14.0 (498.3 to 1)
Current Spending: ($ per student per year):
   Total: $5,405; Instruction: $3,490; Support Services: $1,527
Enrollment, Drop-out Rates and Diploma Recipients by Race/Ethnicity

Category	Total	White	Black	Asian	AIAN	Hisp.
Enrollment (%)	100.0	n/a	n/a	n/a	n/a	n/a
Drop-out Rate (%)	2.2	n/a	n/a	n/a	n/a	n/a
H.S. Diplomas (#)	339	n/a	n/a	n/a	n/a	n/a

Greeneville City SD
PO Box 1420 • Greeneville, TN 37744-1420
(423) 787-8000 • http://www.gcschools.net/
Grade Span: KG-12; **Agency Type:** 1
Schools: 7
   4 Primary; 1 Middle; 2 High; 0 Other Level
   6 Regular; 0 Special Education; 1 Vocational; 0 Alternative
   0 Magnet; 0 Charter; 3 Title I Eligible; 1 School-wide Title I
Students: 2,676 (n/a% male; n/a% female)
   Individual Education Program: 708 (26.5%);
   English Language Learner: n/a; Migrant: n/a
   Eligible for Free Lunch Program: n/a
   Eligible for Reduced-Price Lunch Program: n/a
Teachers: 193.0 (13.9 to 1)
Librarians/Media Specialists: 6.0 (446.0 to 1)
Guidance Counselors: 10.0 (267.6 to 1)
Current Spending: ($ per student per year):
   Total: $7,775; Instruction: $4,935; Support Services: $2,486
Enrollment, Drop-out Rates and Diploma Recipients by Race/Ethnicity

Category	Total	White	Black	Asian	AIAN	Hisp.
Enrollment (%)	100.0	0.0	0.0	0.0	0.0	0.0
Drop-out Rate (%)	0.9	n/a	n/a	n/a	n/a	n/a
H.S. Diplomas (#)	121	n/a	n/a	n/a	n/a	n/a

Grundy County

Grundy County SD
PO Box 97 • Altamont, TN 37301-0097
(931) 692-3467 •
http://volweb.utk.edu/Schools/grundyco/grundy.index.html
Grade Span: KG-12; **Agency Type:** 1
Schools: 7
   6 Primary; 0 Middle; 1 High; 0 Other Level
   7 Regular; 0 Special Education; 0 Vocational; 0 Alternative
   0 Magnet; 0 Charter; 6 Title I Eligible; 6 School-wide Title I
Students: 2,255 (n/a% male; n/a% female)
   Individual Education Program: 650 (28.8%);
   English Language Learner: n/a; Migrant: n/a
   Eligible for Free Lunch Program: n/a
   Eligible for Reduced-Price Lunch Program: n/a
Teachers: 183.5 (12.3 to 1)
Librarians/Media Specialists: 2.0 (1,127.5 to 1)
Guidance Counselors: 3.0 (751.7 to 1)
Current Spending: ($ per student per year):
   Total: $5,793; Instruction: $3,905; Support Services: $1,682
Enrollment, Drop-out Rates and Diploma Recipients by Race/Ethnicity

Category	Total	White	Black	Asian	AIAN	Hisp.
Enrollment (%)	100.0	n/a	n/a	n/a	n/a	n/a
Drop-out Rate (%)	1.7	n/a	n/a	n/a	n/a	n/a
H.S. Diplomas (#)	123	n/a	n/a	n/a	n/a	n/a

Hamblen County

Hamblen County SD
210 E Morris Blvd • Morristown, TN 37813-2341
(423) 586-7700 • http://www.hcboe.net
Grade Span: PK-12; **Agency Type:** 1
Schools: 18
   11 Primary; 4 Middle; 2 High; 1 Other Level
   17 Regular; 0 Special Education; 0 Vocational; 1 Alternative
   0 Magnet; 0 Charter; 10 Title I Eligible; 10 School-wide Title I
Students: 9,145 (n/a% male; n/a% female)
   Individual Education Program: 1,494 (16.3%);
   English Language Learner: n/a; Migrant: n/a
   Eligible for Free Lunch Program: n/a
   Eligible for Reduced-Price Lunch Program: n/a
Teachers: 593.2 (15.4 to 1)
Librarians/Media Specialists: 20.0 (457.3 to 1)
Guidance Counselors: 17.5 (522.6 to 1)
Current Spending: ($ per student per year):
   Total: $6,008; Instruction: $4,105; Support Services: $1,541
Enrollment, Drop-out Rates and Diploma Recipients by Race/Ethnicity

Category	Total	White	Black	Asian	AIAN	Hisp.
Enrollment (%)	100.0	n/a	n/a	n/a	n/a	n/a
Drop-out Rate (%)	1.8	n/a	n/a	n/a	n/a	n/a
H.S. Diplomas (#)	434	n/a	n/a	n/a	n/a	n/a

Hamilton County

Hamilton County School Distrct
6703 Bonny Oaks Dr • Chattanooga, TN 37421
(423) 209-8400 • http://www.hcde.org/
Grade Span: KG-12; **Agency Type:** 1
Schools: 81
   48 Primary; 15 Middle; 13 High; 5 Other Level
   76 Regular; 1 Special Education; 3 Vocational; 1 Alternative
   3 Magnet; 0 Charter; 34 Title I Eligible; 34 School-wide Title I
Students: 40,100 (n/a% male; n/a% female)
   Individual Education Program: 8,557 (21.3%);
   English Language Learner: n/a; Migrant: n/a
   Eligible for Free Lunch Program: n/a
   Eligible for Reduced-Price Lunch Program: n/a
Teachers: 2,738.9 (14.6 to 1)
Librarians/Media Specialists: 82.0 (489.0 to 1)
Guidance Counselors: 85.5 (469.0 to 1)
Current Spending: ($ per student per year):
   Total: $6,901; Instruction: $4,461; Support Services: $2,116
Enrollment, Drop-out Rates and Diploma Recipients by Race/Ethnicity

Category	Total	White	Black	Asian	AIAN	Hisp.
Enrollment (%)	100.0	0.0	0.0	0.0	0.0	0.0
Drop-out Rate (%)	5.8	n/a	n/a	n/a	n/a	n/a
H.S. Diplomas (#)	1,715	n/a	n/a	n/a	n/a	n/a

Hardeman County

Hardeman County School Distrct
PO Box 112 • Bolivar, TN 38008-0112
(731) 658-2508
Grade Span: KG-12; **Agency Type:** 1
Schools: 9
   6 Primary; 1 Middle; 2 High; 0 Other Level
   9 Regular; 0 Special Education; 0 Vocational; 0 Alternative
   0 Magnet; 0 Charter; 7 Title I Eligible; 6 School-wide Title I
Students: 4,465 (n/a% male; n/a% female)
   Individual Education Program: 969 (21.7%);
   English Language Learner: n/a; Migrant: n/a
   Eligible for Free Lunch Program: n/a
   Eligible for Reduced-Price Lunch Program: n/a
Teachers: 332.0 (13.4 to 1)
Librarians/Media Specialists: 8.0 (558.1 to 1)
Guidance Counselors: 9.0 (496.1 to 1)
Current Spending: ($ per student per year):
   Total: $5,206; Instruction: $3,757; Support Services: $1,437
Enrollment, Drop-out Rates and Diploma Recipients by Race/Ethnicity

Category	Total	White	Black	Asian	AIAN	Hisp.
Enrollment (%)	100.0	n/a	n/a	n/a	n/a	n/a
Drop-out Rate (%)	6.6	n/a	n/a	n/a	n/a	n/a
H.S. Diplomas (#)	179	n/a	n/a	n/a	n/a	n/a

Hardin County

Hardin County SD
155 N Guinn St • Savannah, TN 38372-2026
(731) 925-3943 • http://www.hardin.k12.tn.us/
Grade Span: KG-12; **Agency Type:** 1
Schools: 10
   8 Primary; 1 Middle; 1 High; 0 Other Level
   10 Regular; 0 Special Education; 0 Vocational; 0 Alternative
   0 Magnet; 0 Charter; 8 Title I Eligible; 7 School-wide Title I
Students: 3,753 (n/a% male; n/a% female)
   Individual Education Program: 684 (18.2%);
   English Language Learner: n/a; Migrant: n/a
   Eligible for Free Lunch Program: n/a
   Eligible for Reduced-Price Lunch Program: n/a

Teachers: 267.9 (14.0 to 1)
Librarians/Media Specialists: 8.0 (469.1 to 1)
Guidance Counselors: 12.0 (312.8 to 1)
Current Spending: ($ per student per year):
   Total: $5,769; Instruction: $3,747; Support Services: $1,579
Enrollment, Drop-out Rates and Diploma Recipients by Race/Ethnicity

Category	Total	White	Black	Asian	AIAN	Hisp.
Enrollment (%)	100.0	n/a	n/a	n/a	n/a	n/a
Drop-out Rate (%)	3.5	n/a	n/a	n/a	n/a	n/a
H.S. Diplomas (#)	217	n/a	n/a	n/a	n/a	n/a

Hawkins County

Hawkins County SD
200 N Depot St • Rogersville, TN 37857-2639
(423) 272-7629 • http://www.hawkins.k12.tn.us/central/
Grade Span: KG-12; **Agency Type:** 1
Schools: 17
   11 Primary; 3 Middle; 2 High; 1 Other Level
   17 Regular; 0 Special Education; 0 Vocational; 0 Alternative
   0 Magnet; 0 Charter; 12 Title I Eligible; 12 School-wide Title I
Students: 7,235 (n/a% male; n/a% female)
   Individual Education Program: 1,715 (23.7%);
   English Language Learner: n/a; Migrant: n/a
   Eligible for Free Lunch Program: n/a
   Eligible for Reduced-Price Lunch Program: n/a
Teachers: 506.0 (14.3 to 1)
Librarians/Media Specialists: 16.0 (452.2 to 1)
Guidance Counselors: 16.0 (452.2 to 1)
Current Spending: ($ per student per year):
   Total: $5,658; Instruction: $3,718; Support Services: $1,591
Enrollment, Drop-out Rates and Diploma Recipients by Race/Ethnicity

Category	Total	White	Black	Asian	AIAN	Hisp.
Enrollment (%)	100.0	n/a	n/a	n/a	n/a	n/a
Drop-out Rate (%)	5.1	n/a	n/a	n/a	n/a	n/a
H.S. Diplomas (#)	323	n/a	n/a	n/a	n/a	n/a

Haywood County

Haywood County SD
900 E Main Str • Brownsville, TN 38012-2647
(731) 772-9613
Grade Span: KG-12; **Agency Type:** 1
Schools: 7
   3 Primary; 2 Middle; 1 High; 1 Other Level
   5 Regular; 1 Special Education; 0 Vocational; 1 Alternative
   0 Magnet; 0 Charter; 4 Title I Eligible; 4 School-wide Title I
Students: 3,511 (n/a% male; n/a% female)
   Individual Education Program: 661 (18.8%);
   English Language Learner: n/a; Migrant: n/a
   Eligible for Free Lunch Program: n/a
   Eligible for Reduced-Price Lunch Program: n/a
Teachers: 242.7 (14.5 to 1)
Librarians/Media Specialists: 7.0 (501.6 to 1)
Guidance Counselors: 7.0 (501.6 to 1)
Current Spending: ($ per student per year):
   Total: $6,179; Instruction: $3,938; Support Services: $1,765
Enrollment, Drop-out Rates and Diploma Recipients by Race/Ethnicity

Category	Total	White	Black	Asian	AIAN	Hisp.
Enrollment (%)	100.0	n/a	n/a	n/a	n/a	n/a
Drop-out Rate (%)	4.1	n/a	n/a	n/a	n/a	n/a
H.S. Diplomas (#)	162	n/a	n/a	n/a	n/a	n/a

Henderson County

Henderson County SD
35 E Wilson St PO Box 190 • Lexington, TN 38351
(731) 968-3661 • http://www.henderson-lea.henderson.k12.tn.us/
Grade Span: KG-12; **Agency Type:** 1
Schools: 10
   7 Primary; 0 Middle; 2 High; 1 Other Level
   9 Regular; 0 Special Education; 0 Vocational; 1 Alternative
   0 Magnet; 0 Charter; 7 Title I Eligible; 0 School-wide Title I
Students: 3,382 (n/a% male; n/a% female)
   Individual Education Program: 659 (19.5%);
   English Language Learner: n/a; Migrant: n/a
   Eligible for Free Lunch Program: n/a
   Eligible for Reduced-Price Lunch Program: n/a
Teachers: 232.0 (14.6 to 1)
Librarians/Media Specialists: 9.0 (375.8 to 1)
Guidance Counselors: 9.0 (375.8 to 1)
Current Spending: ($ per student per year):
   Total: $5,428; Instruction: $3,860; Support Services: $1,520

Enrollment, Drop-out Rates and Diploma Recipients by Race/Ethnicity

Category	Total	White	Black	Asian	AIAN	Hisp.
Enrollment (%)	100.0	0.0	0.0	0.0	0.0	0.0
Drop-out Rate (%)	3.2	n/a	n/a	n/a	n/a	n/a
H.S. Diplomas (#)	55	n/a	n/a	n/a	n/a	n/a

Henry County

Henry County SD
217 Grove Blvd • Paris, TN 38242-4711
(731) 642-9733 • http://www.henry.k12.tn.us/
Grade Span: KG-12; **Agency Type:** 1
Schools: 6
   4 Primary; 0 Middle; 1 High; 1 Other Level
   6 Regular; 0 Special Education; 0 Vocational; 0 Alternative
   0 Magnet; 0 Charter; 5 Title I Eligible; 5 School-wide Title I
Students: 3,155 (n/a% male; n/a% female)
   Individual Education Program: 589 (18.7%);
   English Language Learner: n/a; Migrant: n/a
   Eligible for Free Lunch Program: n/a
   Eligible for Reduced-Price Lunch Program: n/a
Teachers: 207.3 (15.2 to 1)
Librarians/Media Specialists: 5.0 (631.0 to 1)
Guidance Counselors: 9.0 (350.6 to 1)
Current Spending: ($ per student per year):
   Total: $5,853; Instruction: $3,568; Support Services: $1,883
Enrollment, Drop-out Rates and Diploma Recipients by Race/Ethnicity

Category	Total	White	Black	Asian	AIAN	Hisp.
Enrollment (%)	100.0	n/a	n/a	n/a	n/a	n/a
Drop-out Rate (%)	2.8	n/a	n/a	n/a	n/a	n/a
H.S. Diplomas (#)	221	n/a	n/a	n/a	n/a	n/a

Hickman County

Hickman County SD
115 Murphree Ave • Centerville, TN 37033-1430
(931) 729-3391 • http://www.hickman.k12.tn.us/
Grade Span: KG-12; **Agency Type:** 1
Schools: 7
   4 Primary; 2 Middle; 1 High; 0 Other Level
   7 Regular; 0 Special Education; 0 Vocational; 0 Alternative
   0 Magnet; 0 Charter; 4 Title I Eligible; 0 School-wide Title I
Students: 3,813 (n/a% male; n/a% female)
   Individual Education Program: 834 (21.9%);
   English Language Learner: n/a; Migrant: n/a
   Eligible for Free Lunch Program: n/a
   Eligible for Reduced-Price Lunch Program: n/a
Teachers: 240.9 (15.8 to 1)
Librarians/Media Specialists: 7.0 (544.7 to 1)
Guidance Counselors: 8.0 (476.6 to 1)
Current Spending: ($ per student per year):
   Total: $5,213; Instruction: $3,419; Support Services: $1,489
Enrollment, Drop-out Rates and Diploma Recipients by Race/Ethnicity

Category	Total	White	Black	Asian	AIAN	Hisp.
Enrollment (%)	100.0	n/a	n/a	n/a	n/a	n/a
Drop-out Rate (%)	1.3	n/a	n/a	n/a	n/a	n/a
H.S. Diplomas (#)	175	n/a	n/a	n/a	n/a	n/a

Humphreys County

Humphreys County SD
2443 Hwy 70 E • Waverly, TN 37185-2223
(931) 296-2568
Grade Span: KG-12; **Agency Type:** 1
Schools: 7
   3 Primary; 2 Middle; 2 High; 0 Other Level
   7 Regular; 0 Special Education; 0 Vocational; 0 Alternative
   0 Magnet; 0 Charter; 2 Title I Eligible; 2 School-wide Title I
Students: 3,000 (n/a% male; n/a% female)
   Individual Education Program: 593 (19.8%);
   English Language Learner: n/a; Migrant: n/a
   Eligible for Free Lunch Program: n/a
   Eligible for Reduced-Price Lunch Program: n/a
Teachers: 197.7 (15.2 to 1)
Librarians/Media Specialists: 6.0 (500.0 to 1)
Guidance Counselors: 6.0 (500.0 to 1)
Current Spending: ($ per student per year):
   Total: $5,690; Instruction: $3,661; Support Services: $1,623
Enrollment, Drop-out Rates and Diploma Recipients by Race/Ethnicity

Category	Total	White	Black	Asian	AIAN	Hisp.
Enrollment (%)	100.0	n/a	n/a	n/a	n/a	n/a
Drop-out Rate (%)	1.5	n/a	n/a	n/a	n/a	n/a
H.S. Diplomas (#)	159	n/a	n/a	n/a	n/a	n/a

Jackson County

Jackson County SD
205 W Gibson Ave • Gainsboro, TN 38562-9399
(931) 268-0268 • http://volweb.utk.edu/school/jackson/
Grade Span: KG-12; **Agency Type:** 1
Schools: 5
   2 Primary; 1 Middle; 2 High; 0 Other Level
   4 Regular; 0 Special Education; 1 Vocational; 0 Alternative
   0 Magnet; 0 Charter; 3 Title I Eligible; 3 School-wide Title I
Students: 1,668 (n/a% male; n/a% female)
   Individual Education Program: 337 (20.2%);
   English Language Learner: n/a; Migrant: n/a
   Eligible for Free Lunch Program: n/a
   Eligible for Reduced-Price Lunch Program: n/a
Teachers: 116.8 (14.3 to 1)
Librarians/Media Specialists: 3.0 (556.0 to 1)
Guidance Counselors: 3.0 (556.0 to 1)
Current Spending: ($ per student per year):
   Total: $5,911; Instruction: $3,673; Support Services: $1,825
Enrollment, Drop-out Rates and Diploma Recipients by Race/Ethnicity

Category	Total	White	Black	Asian	AIAN	Hisp.
Enrollment (%)	100.0	0.0	0.0	0.0	0.0	0.0
Drop-out Rate (%)	1.6	n/a	n/a	n/a	n/a	n/a
H.S. Diplomas (#)	76	n/a	n/a	n/a	n/a	n/a

Jefferson County

Jefferson County SD
PO Box 190 • Dandridge, TN 37725-0190
(865) 397-3194 • http://208.183.128.3/
Grade Span: KG-12; **Agency Type:** 1
Schools: 10
   7 Primary; 2 Middle; 1 High; 0 Other Level
   10 Regular; 0 Special Education; 0 Vocational; 0 Alternative
   0 Magnet; 0 Charter; 7 Title I Eligible; 7 School-wide Title I
Students: 7,036 (n/a% male; n/a% female)
   Individual Education Program: 1,541 (21.9%);
   English Language Learner: n/a; Migrant: n/a
   Eligible for Free Lunch Program: n/a
   Eligible for Reduced-Price Lunch Program: n/a
Teachers: 440.7 (16.0 to 1)
Librarians/Media Specialists: 11.0 (639.6 to 1)
Guidance Counselors: 16.6 (423.9 to 1)
Current Spending: ($ per student per year):
   Total: $5,807; Instruction: $3,735; Support Services: $1,753
Enrollment, Drop-out Rates and Diploma Recipients by Race/Ethnicity

Category	Total	White	Black	Asian	AIAN	Hisp.
Enrollment (%)	100.0	n/a	n/a	n/a	n/a	n/a
Drop-out Rate (%)	0.4	n/a	n/a	n/a	n/a	n/a
H.S. Diplomas (#)	374	n/a	n/a	n/a	n/a	n/a

Johnson County

Johnson County SD
211 N Church St • Mountain City, TN 37683-1325
(423) 727-2640 • http://www.jocoed@k12tn.net
Grade Span: KG-12; **Agency Type:** 1
Schools: 7
   5 Primary; 1 Middle; 1 High; 0 Other Level
   7 Regular; 0 Special Education; 0 Vocational; 0 Alternative
   0 Magnet; 0 Charter; 5 Title I Eligible; 5 School-wide Title I
Students: 2,285 (n/a% male; n/a% female)
   Individual Education Program: 489 (21.4%);
   English Language Learner: n/a; Migrant: n/a
   Eligible for Free Lunch Program: n/a
   Eligible for Reduced-Price Lunch Program: n/a
Teachers: 161.3 (14.2 to 1)
Librarians/Media Specialists: 5.0 (457.0 to 1)
Guidance Counselors: 4.5 (507.8 to 1)
Current Spending: ($ per student per year):
   Total: $6,382; Instruction: $3,959; Support Services: $2,011
Enrollment, Drop-out Rates and Diploma Recipients by Race/Ethnicity

Category	Total	White	Black	Asian	AIAN	Hisp.
Enrollment (%)	100.0	n/a	n/a	n/a	n/a	n/a
Drop-out Rate (%)	3.2	n/a	n/a	n/a	n/a	n/a
H.S. Diplomas (#)	125	n/a	n/a	n/a	n/a	n/a

Knox County

Knox County SD
PO Box 2188 912 S Gay Str • Knoxville, TN 37902-2188
(865) 594-1801 • http://www.korrnet.org/kcschool/
Grade Span: KG-12; **Agency Type:** 1
Schools: 88

   53 Primary; 14 Middle; 17 High; 4 Other Level
   79 Regular; 4 Special Education; 2 Vocational; 3 Alternative
   4 Magnet; 0 Charter; 14 Title I Eligible; 14 School-wide Title I
Students: 52,659 (n/a% male; n/a% female)
   Individual Education Program: 8,547 (16.2%);
   English Language Learner: n/a; Migrant: n/a
   Eligible for Free Lunch Program: n/a
   Eligible for Reduced-Price Lunch Program: n/a
Teachers: 3,609.4 (14.6 to 1)
Librarians/Media Specialists: 88.9 (592.3 to 1)
Guidance Counselors: 92.7 (568.1 to 1)
Current Spending: ($ per student per year):
   Total: $6,148; Instruction: $3,923; Support Services: $1,944
Enrollment, Drop-out Rates and Diploma Recipients by Race/Ethnicity

Category	Total	White	Black	Asian	AIAN	Hisp.
Enrollment (%)	100.0	0.0	0.0	0.0	0.0	0.0
Drop-out Rate (%)	3.0	n/a	n/a	n/a	n/a	n/a
H.S. Diplomas (#)	2,553	n/a	n/a	n/a	n/a	n/a

Lauderdale County

Lauderdale County SD
402 S Washington St • Ripley, TN 38063-0350
(731) 635-2941 • http://www.lced.net/
Grade Span: KG-12; **Agency Type:** 1
Schools: 7
   3 Primary; 2 Middle; 2 High; 0 Other Level
   7 Regular; 0 Special Education; 0 Vocational; 0 Alternative
   0 Magnet; 0 Charter; 5 Title I Eligible; 5 School-wide Title I
Students: 4,544 (n/a% male; n/a% female)
   Individual Education Program: 1,088 (23.9%);
   English Language Learner: n/a; Migrant: n/a
   Eligible for Free Lunch Program: n/a
   Eligible for Reduced-Price Lunch Program: n/a
Teachers: 305.0 (14.9 to 1)
Librarians/Media Specialists: 8.0 (568.0 to 1)
Guidance Counselors: 9.0 (504.9 to 1)
Current Spending: ($ per student per year):
   Total: $5,549; Instruction: $3,572; Support Services: $1,555
Enrollment, Drop-out Rates and Diploma Recipients by Race/Ethnicity

Category	Total	White	Black	Asian	AIAN	Hisp.
Enrollment (%)	100.0	n/a	n/a	n/a	n/a	n/a
Drop-out Rate (%)	3.9	n/a	n/a	n/a	n/a	n/a
H.S. Diplomas (#)	193	n/a	n/a	n/a	n/a	n/a

Lawrence County

Lawrence County School Distrct
700 Mahr Ave • Lawrenceburg, TN 38464-3110
(931) 762-3581
Grade Span: KG-12; **Agency Type:** 1
Schools: 13
   8 Primary; 1 Middle; 4 High; 0 Other Level
   13 Regular; 0 Special Education; 0 Vocational; 0 Alternative
   0 Magnet; 0 Charter; 6 Title I Eligible; 1 School-wide Title I
Students: 6,710 (n/a% male; n/a% female)
   Individual Education Program: 1,377 (20.5%);
   English Language Learner: n/a; Migrant: n/a
   Eligible for Free Lunch Program: n/a
   Eligible for Reduced-Price Lunch Program: n/a
Teachers: 461.1 (14.6 to 1)
Librarians/Media Specialists: 13.0 (516.2 to 1)
Guidance Counselors: 13.0 (516.2 to 1)
Current Spending: ($ per student per year):
   Total: $5,659; Instruction: $3,779; Support Services: $1,463
Enrollment, Drop-out Rates and Diploma Recipients by Race/Ethnicity

Category	Total	White	Black	Asian	AIAN	Hisp.
Enrollment (%)	100.0	n/a	n/a	n/a	n/a	n/a
Drop-out Rate (%)	6.1	n/a	n/a	n/a	n/a	n/a
H.S. Diplomas (#)	383	n/a	n/a	n/a	n/a	n/a

Lewis County

Lewis County SD
206 S Court St • Hohenwald, TN 38462-1736
(931) 796-3264 • http://volweb.utk.edu/Schools/lewisco/lewisco
Grade Span: KG-12; **Agency Type:** 1
Schools: 4
   2 Primary; 1 Middle; 1 High; 0 Other Level
   4 Regular; 0 Special Education; 0 Vocational; 0 Alternative
   0 Magnet; 0 Charter; 3 Title I Eligible; 0 School-wide Title I
Students: 1,969 (n/a% male; n/a% female)
   Individual Education Program: 324 (16.5%);
   English Language Learner: n/a; Migrant: n/a
   Eligible for Free Lunch Program: n/a

Eligible for Reduced-Price Lunch Program: n/a
Teachers: 129.5 (15.2 to 1)
Librarians/Media Specialists: 4.0 (492.3 to 1)
Guidance Counselors: 3.9 (504.9 to 1)
Current Spending: ($ per student per year):
   Total: $5,029; Instruction: $3,228; Support Services: $1,462
Enrollment, Drop-out Rates and Diploma Recipients by Race/Ethnicity

Category	Total	White	Black	Asian	AIAN	Hisp.
Enrollment (%)	100.0	n/a	n/a	n/a	n/a	n/a
Drop-out Rate (%)	2.6	n/a	n/a	n/a	n/a	n/a
H.S. Diplomas (#)	93	n/a	n/a	n/a	n/a	n/a

Lincoln County

Lincoln County SD
206 E Davidson Dr • Fayetteville, TN 37334-3581
(931) 433-3565 • http://www.lcdoe.org/
Grade Span: KG-12; **Agency Type:** 1
Schools: 8
   6 Primary; 0 Middle; 1 High; 1 Other Level
   8 Regular; 0 Special Education; 0 Vocational; 0 Alternative
   0 Magnet; 0 Charter; 4 Title I Eligible; 2 School-wide Title I
Students: 3,986 (n/a% male; n/a% female)
   Individual Education Program: 613 (15.4%);
   English Language Learner: n/a; Migrant: n/a
   Eligible for Free Lunch Program: n/a
   Eligible for Reduced-Price Lunch Program: n/a
Teachers: 254.9 (15.6 to 1)
Librarians/Media Specialists: 10.0 (398.6 to 1)
Guidance Counselors: 8.9 (447.9 to 1)
Current Spending: ($ per student per year):
   Total: $5,315; Instruction: $3,784; Support Services: $1,513
Enrollment, Drop-out Rates and Diploma Recipients by Race/Ethnicity

Category	Total	White	Black	Asian	AIAN	Hisp.
Enrollment (%)	100.0	n/a	n/a	n/a	n/a	n/a
Drop-out Rate (%)	5.6	n/a	n/a	n/a	n/a	n/a
H.S. Diplomas (#)	266	n/a	n/a	n/a	n/a	n/a

Loudon County

Lenoir City SD
2145 Harrison Ave • Lenoir City, TN 37771-6623
(865) 986-8058
Grade Span: KG-12; **Agency Type:** 1
Schools: 3
   1 Primary; 1 Middle; 1 High; 0 Other Level
   3 Regular; 0 Special Education; 0 Vocational; 0 Alternative
   0 Magnet; 0 Charter; 1 Title I Eligible; 1 School-wide Title I
Students: 2,030 (n/a% male; n/a% female)
   Individual Education Program: 313 (15.4%);
   English Language Learner: n/a; Migrant: n/a
   Eligible for Free Lunch Program: n/a
   Eligible for Reduced-Price Lunch Program: n/a
Teachers: 125.0 (16.2 to 1)
Librarians/Media Specialists: 3.0 (676.7 to 1)
Guidance Counselors: 5.0 (406.0 to 1)
Current Spending: ($ per student per year):
   Total: $5,934; Instruction: $4,074; Support Services: $1,833
Enrollment, Drop-out Rates and Diploma Recipients by Race/Ethnicity

Category	Total	White	Black	Asian	AIAN	Hisp.
Enrollment (%)	100.0	n/a	n/a	n/a	n/a	n/a
Drop-out Rate (%)	2.1	n/a	n/a	n/a	n/a	n/a
H.S. Diplomas (#)	201	n/a	n/a	n/a	n/a	n/a

Loudon County SD
100 River Rd Box 113 • Loudon, TN 37774-1042
(865) 458-5411 • http://k12.loudoncounty.org
Grade Span: KG-12; **Agency Type:** 1
Schools: 9
   5 Primary; 2 Middle; 1 High; 1 Other Level
   9 Regular; 0 Special Education; 0 Vocational; 0 Alternative
   0 Magnet; 0 Charter; 5 Title I Eligible; 4 School-wide Title I
Students: 4,852 (n/a% male; n/a% female)
   Individual Education Program: 632 (13.0%);
   English Language Learner: n/a; Migrant: n/a
   Eligible for Free Lunch Program: n/a
   Eligible for Reduced-Price Lunch Program: n/a
Teachers: 282.7 (17.2 to 1)
Librarians/Media Specialists: 9.0 (539.1 to 1)
Guidance Counselors: 8.1 (599.0 to 1)
Current Spending: ($ per student per year):
   Total: $5,613; Instruction: $4,012; Support Services: $1,432

Enrollment, Drop-out Rates and Diploma Recipients by Race/Ethnicity

Category	Total	White	Black	Asian	AIAN	Hisp.
Enrollment (%)	100.0	n/a	n/a	n/a	n/a	n/a
Drop-out Rate (%)	3.4	n/a	n/a	n/a	n/a	n/a
H.S. Diplomas (#)	160	n/a	n/a	n/a	n/a	n/a

Macon County

Macon County SD
501 College St • Lafayette, TN 37083-1706
(615) 666-2125 • http://maconcountyschools.com
Grade Span: KG-12; **Agency Type:** 1
Schools: 7
   3 Primary; 2 Middle; 1 High; 1 Other Level
   7 Regular; 0 Special Education; 0 Vocational; 0 Alternative
   0 Magnet; 0 Charter; 5 Title I Eligible; 3 School-wide Title I
Students: 3,547 (n/a% male; n/a% female)
   Individual Education Program: 544 (15.3%);
   English Language Learner: n/a; Migrant: n/a
   Eligible for Free Lunch Program: n/a
   Eligible for Reduced-Price Lunch Program: n/a
Teachers: 213.7 (16.6 to 1)
Librarians/Media Specialists: 7.0 (506.7 to 1)
Guidance Counselors: 6.0 (591.2 to 1)
Current Spending: ($ per student per year):
   Total: $5,115; Instruction: $3,554; Support Services: $1,552
Enrollment, Drop-out Rates and Diploma Recipients by Race/Ethnicity

Category	Total	White	Black	Asian	AIAN	Hisp.
Enrollment (%)	100.0	n/a	n/a	n/a	n/a	n/a
Drop-out Rate (%)	4.2	n/a	n/a	n/a	n/a	n/a
H.S. Diplomas (#)	188	n/a	n/a	n/a	n/a	n/a

Madison County

Jackson-Madison Consolidated
310 N Pkwy • Jackson, TN 38305-2712
(731) 664-2500 • http://www.jmcss.net/default.htm
Grade Span: KG-12; **Agency Type:** 1
Schools: 28
   14 Primary; 8 Middle; 6 High; 0 Other Level
   26 Regular; 0 Special Education; 0 Vocational; 2 Alternative
   5 Magnet; 0 Charter; 7 Title I Eligible; 7 School-wide Title I
Students: 13,609 (n/a% male; n/a% female)
   Individual Education Program: 3,233 (23.8%);
   English Language Learner: n/a; Migrant: n/a
   Eligible for Free Lunch Program: n/a
   Eligible for Reduced-Price Lunch Program: n/a
Teachers: 1,001.2 (13.6 to 1)
Librarians/Media Specialists: 25.7 (529.5 to 1)
Guidance Counselors: 35.0 (388.8 to 1)
Current Spending: ($ per student per year):
   Total: $6,504; Instruction: $4,254; Support Services: $1,909
Enrollment, Drop-out Rates and Diploma Recipients by Race/Ethnicity

Category	Total	White	Black	Asian	AIAN	Hisp.
Enrollment (%)	100.0	n/a	n/a	n/a	n/a	n/a
Drop-out Rate (%)	4.8	n/a	n/a	n/a	n/a	n/a
H.S. Diplomas (#)	683	n/a	n/a	n/a	n/a	n/a

Marion County

Marion County SD
204 Betsy Pack Dr • Jasper, TN 37347-3024
(423) 942-3434
Grade Span: KG-12; **Agency Type:** 1
Schools: 9
   4 Primary; 2 Middle; 3 High; 0 Other Level
   9 Regular; 0 Special Education; 0 Vocational; 0 Alternative
   0 Magnet; 0 Charter; 4 Title I Eligible; 4 School-wide Title I
Students: 4,102 (n/a% male; n/a% female)
   Individual Education Program: 724 (17.6%);
   English Language Learner: n/a; Migrant: n/a
   Eligible for Free Lunch Program: n/a
   Eligible for Reduced-Price Lunch Program: n/a
Teachers: 270.4 (15.2 to 1)
Librarians/Media Specialists: 9.0 (455.8 to 1)
Guidance Counselors: 8.6 (477.0 to 1)
Current Spending: ($ per student per year):
   Total: $5,472; Instruction: $3,470; Support Services: $1,636
Enrollment, Drop-out Rates and Diploma Recipients by Race/Ethnicity

Category	Total	White	Black	Asian	AIAN	Hisp.
Enrollment (%)	100.0	n/a	n/a	n/a	n/a	n/a
Drop-out Rate (%)	2.7	n/a	n/a	n/a	n/a	n/a
H.S. Diplomas (#)	188	n/a	n/a	n/a	n/a	n/a

Marshall County

Marshall County School Distrct
700 Jones Circle • Lewisburg, TN 37091-2427
(931) 359-1581 • http://www.mcs.k12.tn.us/
Grade Span: KG-12; **Agency Type:** 1
Schools: 9
  5 Primary; 1 Middle; 1 High; 2 Other Level
  9 Regular; 0 Special Education; 0 Vocational; 0 Alternative
  0 Magnet; 0 Charter; 3 Title I Eligible; 1 School-wide Title I
Students: 4,829   (n/a% male; n/a% female)
  Individual Education Program: 885 (18.3%);
  English Language Learner: n/a; Migrant: n/a
  Eligible for Free Lunch Program: n/a
  Eligible for Reduced-Price Lunch Program: n/a
Teachers: 295.3 (16.4 to 1)
Librarians/Media Specialists: 9.0 (536.6 to 1)
Guidance Counselors: 8.8 (548.8 to 1)
Current Spending: ($ per student per year):
  Total: $5,872; Instruction: $3,623; Support Services: $1,879
Enrollment, Drop-out Rates and Diploma Recipients by Race/Ethnicity

Category	Total	White	Black	Asian	AIAN	Hisp.
Enrollment (%)	100.0	n/a	n/a	n/a	n/a	n/a
Drop-out Rate (%)	2.4	n/a	n/a	n/a	n/a	n/a
H.S. Diplomas (#)	246	n/a	n/a	n/a	n/a	n/a

Maury County

Maury County SD
501 W Eight St • Columbia, TN 38401-3191
(931) 388-8403 • http://www.maury-lea.maury.k12.tn.us/
Grade Span: KG-12; **Agency Type:** 1
Schools: 18
  9 Primary; 3 Middle; 3 High; 3 Other Level
  18 Regular; 0 Special Education; 0 Vocational; 0 Alternative
  0 Magnet; 0 Charter; 6 Title I Eligible; 3 School-wide Title I
Students: 11,141   (n/a% male; n/a% female)
  Individual Education Program: 2,152 (19.3%);
  English Language Learner: n/a; Migrant: n/a
  Eligible for Free Lunch Program: n/a
  Eligible for Reduced-Price Lunch Program: n/a
Teachers: 763.2 (14.6 to 1)
Librarians/Media Specialists: 17.9 (622.4 to 1)
Guidance Counselors: 25.0 (445.6 to 1)
Current Spending: ($ per student per year):
  Total: $6,436; Instruction: $4,185; Support Services: $1,915
Enrollment, Drop-out Rates and Diploma Recipients by Race/Ethnicity

Category	Total	White	Black	Asian	AIAN	Hisp.
Enrollment (%)	100.0	n/a	n/a	n/a	n/a	n/a
Drop-out Rate (%)	2.7	n/a	n/a	n/a	n/a	n/a
H.S. Diplomas (#)	490	n/a	n/a	n/a	n/a	n/a

Mcminn County

Athens City Elementary SD
943 Crestway Dr • Athens, TN 37303-4130
(423) 745-2863 • http://www.athens-lea.mcminn.k12.tn.us/
Grade Span: KG-09; **Agency Type:** 1
Schools: 5
  2 Primary; 3 Middle; 0 High; 0 Other Level
  5 Regular; 0 Special Education; 0 Vocational; 0 Alternative
  0 Magnet; 0 Charter; 5 Title I Eligible; 0 School-wide Title I
Students: 1,680   (n/a% male; n/a% female)
  Individual Education Program: 341 (20.3%);
  English Language Learner: n/a; Migrant: n/a
  Eligible for Free Lunch Program: n/a
  Eligible for Reduced-Price Lunch Program: n/a
Teachers: 108.7 (15.5 to 1)
Librarians/Media Specialists: 5.0 (336.0 to 1)
Guidance Counselors: 4.0 (420.0 to 1)
Current Spending: ($ per student per year):
  Total: $6,547; Instruction: $4,138; Support Services: $1,973
Enrollment, Drop-out Rates and Diploma Recipients by Race/Ethnicity

Category	Total	White	Black	Asian	AIAN	Hisp.
Enrollment (%)	100.0	n/a	n/a	n/a	n/a	n/a
Drop-out Rate (%)	0.0	n/a	n/a	n/a	n/a	n/a
H.S. Diplomas (#)	n/a	n/a	n/a	n/a	n/a	n/a

Mcminn County SD
216 N Jackson • Athens, TN 37303-3640
(423) 745-1612 • http://www.mcminn-lea.mcminn.k12.tn.us/
Grade Span: KG-12; **Agency Type:** 1
Schools: 9
  7 Primary; 0 Middle; 2 High; 0 Other Level
  9 Regular; 0 Special Education; 0 Vocational; 0 Alternative
  0 Magnet; 0 Charter; 7 Title I Eligible; 7 School-wide Title I
Students: 5,829   (n/a% male; n/a% female)
  Individual Education Program: 1,221 (20.9%);
  English Language Learner: n/a; Migrant: n/a
  Eligible for Free Lunch Program: n/a
  Eligible for Reduced-Price Lunch Program: n/a
Teachers: 348.9 (16.7 to 1)
Librarians/Media Specialists: 10.0 (582.9 to 1)
Guidance Counselors: 11.0 (529.9 to 1)
Current Spending: ($ per student per year):
  Total: $5,241; Instruction: $3,429; Support Services: $1,511
Enrollment, Drop-out Rates and Diploma Recipients by Race/Ethnicity

Category	Total	White	Black	Asian	AIAN	Hisp.
Enrollment (%)	100.0	n/a	n/a	n/a	n/a	n/a
Drop-out Rate (%)	2.1	n/a	n/a	n/a	n/a	n/a
H.S. Diplomas (#)	351	n/a	n/a	n/a	n/a	n/a

Mcnairy County

Mcnairy County SD
170 W Court Ave • Selmer, TN 38375
(731) 645-3267 • http://www.mcnairy.org
Grade Span: KG-12; **Agency Type:** 1
Schools: 8
  5 Primary; 1 Middle; 2 High; 0 Other Level
  8 Regular; 0 Special Education; 0 Vocational; 0 Alternative
  0 Magnet; 0 Charter; 5 Title I Eligible; 5 School-wide Title I
Students: 4,233   (n/a% male; n/a% female)
  Individual Education Program: 626 (14.8%);
  English Language Learner: n/a; Migrant: n/a
  Eligible for Free Lunch Program: n/a
  Eligible for Reduced-Price Lunch Program: n/a
Teachers: 289.3 (14.6 to 1)
Librarians/Media Specialists: 8.0 (529.1 to 1)
Guidance Counselors: 7.0 (604.7 to 1)
Current Spending: ($ per student per year):
  Total: $5,280; Instruction: $3,639; Support Services: $1,285
Enrollment, Drop-out Rates and Diploma Recipients by Race/Ethnicity

Category	Total	White	Black	Asian	AIAN	Hisp.
Enrollment (%)	100.0	n/a	n/a	n/a	n/a	n/a
Drop-out Rate (%)	1.4	n/a	n/a	n/a	n/a	n/a
H.S. Diplomas (#)	181	n/a	n/a	n/a	n/a	n/a

Meigs County

Meigs County SD
PO Box 1039 • Decatur, TN 37322-1039
(423) 334-5793
Grade Span: KG-12; **Agency Type:** 1
Schools: 4
  2 Primary; 1 Middle; 1 High; 0 Other Level
  4 Regular; 0 Special Education; 0 Vocational; 0 Alternative
  0 Magnet; 0 Charter; 3 Title I Eligible; 2 School-wide Title I
Students: 1,841   (n/a% male; n/a% female)
  Individual Education Program: 353 (19.2%);
  English Language Learner: n/a; Migrant: n/a
  Eligible for Free Lunch Program: n/a
  Eligible for Reduced-Price Lunch Program: n/a
Teachers: 116.0 (15.9 to 1)
Librarians/Media Specialists: 2.0 (920.5 to 1)
Guidance Counselors: 4.9 (375.7 to 1)
Current Spending: ($ per student per year):
  Total: $5,206; Instruction: $3,536; Support Services: $1,296
Enrollment, Drop-out Rates and Diploma Recipients by Race/Ethnicity

Category	Total	White	Black	Asian	AIAN	Hisp.
Enrollment (%)	100.0	n/a	n/a	n/a	n/a	n/a
Drop-out Rate (%)	1.2	n/a	n/a	n/a	n/a	n/a
H.S. Diplomas (#)	98	n/a	n/a	n/a	n/a	n/a

Monroe County

Monroe County SD
205 Oak Grove Rd • Madisonville, TN 37354-5930
(423) 442-2373 • http://www.monroe.k12.tn.us
Grade Span: KG-12; **Agency Type:** 1
Schools: 11
  6 Primary; 2 Middle; 3 High; 0 Other Level
  11 Regular; 0 Special Education; 0 Vocational; 0 Alternative
  0 Magnet; 0 Charter; 6 Title I Eligible; 6 School-wide Title I
Students: 5,188   (n/a% male; n/a% female)
  Individual Education Program: 917 (17.7%);
  English Language Learner: n/a; Migrant: n/a
  Eligible for Free Lunch Program: n/a
  Eligible for Reduced-Price Lunch Program: n/a
Teachers: 302.1 (17.2 to 1)

Librarians/Media Specialists: 10.0 (518.8 to 1)
Guidance Counselors: 10.0 (518.8 to 1)
Current Spending: ($ per student per year):
Total: $5,666; Instruction: $3,565; Support Services: $1,691
Enrollment, Drop-out Rates and Diploma Recipients by Race/Ethnicity

Category	Total	White	Black	Asian	AIAN	Hisp.
Enrollment (%)	100.0	n/a	n/a	n/a	n/a	n/a
Drop-out Rate (%)	2.4	n/a	n/a	n/a	n/a	n/a
H.S. Diplomas (#)	84	n/a	n/a	n/a	n/a	n/a

Montgomery County

Montgomery County Schools
621 Gracey Ave · Clarksville, TN 37040
(931) 648-5600 · http://www.cmcss.org/
Grade Span: KG-12; **Agency Type:** 1
Schools: 30
17 Primary; 7 Middle; 6 High; 0 Other Level
30 Regular; 0 Special Education; 0 Vocational; 0 Alternative
0 Magnet; 0 Charter; 8 Title I Eligible; 8 School-wide Title I
Students: 24,924 (n/a% male; n/a% female)
Individual Education Program: 4,242 (17.0%);
English Language Learner: n/a; Migrant: n/a
Eligible for Free Lunch Program: n/a
Eligible for Reduced-Price Lunch Program: n/a
Teachers: 1,558.4 (16.0 to 1)
Librarians/Media Specialists: 35.0 (712.1 to 1)
Guidance Counselors: 54.0 (461.6 to 1)
Current Spending: ($ per student per year):
Total: $5,170; Instruction: $3,123; Support Services: $1,748
Enrollment, Drop-out Rates and Diploma Recipients by Race/Ethnicity

Category	Total	White	Black	Asian	AIAN	Hisp.
Enrollment (%)	100.0	n/a	n/a	n/a	n/a	n/a
Drop-out Rate (%)	3.3	n/a	n/a	n/a	n/a	n/a
H.S. Diplomas (#)	1,063	n/a	n/a	n/a	n/a	n/a

Morgan County

Morgan County SD
136 Flat Fork Rd · Wartburg, TN 37887-0348
(423) 346-6214
Grade Span: KG-12; **Agency Type:** 1
Schools: 8
3 Primary; 0 Middle; 2 High; 3 Other Level
7 Regular; 0 Special Education; 1 Vocational; 0 Alternative
0 Magnet; 0 Charter; 7 Title I Eligible; 7 School-wide Title I
Students: 3,250 (n/a% male; n/a% female)
Individual Education Program: 643 (19.8%);
English Language Learner: n/a; Migrant: n/a
Eligible for Free Lunch Program: n/a
Eligible for Reduced-Price Lunch Program: n/a
Teachers: 226.0 (14.4 to 1)
Librarians/Media Specialists: 5.0 (650.0 to 1)
Guidance Counselors: 6.0 (541.7 to 1)
Current Spending: ($ per student per year):
Total: $5,751; Instruction: $3,735; Support Services: $1,687
Enrollment, Drop-out Rates and Diploma Recipients by Race/Ethnicity

Category	Total	White	Black	Asian	AIAN	Hisp.
Enrollment (%)	100.0	0.0	0.0	0.0	0.0	0.0
Drop-out Rate (%)	2.6	n/a	n/a	n/a	n/a	n/a
H.S. Diplomas (#)	186	n/a	n/a	n/a	n/a	n/a

Obion County

Obion County SD
316 S Third St · Union City, TN 38261-3724
(731) 885-9743 · http://www.obioncountyschools.com
Grade Span: KG-12; **Agency Type:** 1
Schools: 8
5 Primary; 0 Middle; 2 High; 1 Other Level
7 Regular; 0 Special Education; 1 Vocational; 0 Alternative
0 Magnet; 0 Charter; 5 Title I Eligible; 1 School-wide Title I
Students: 3,966 (n/a% male; n/a% female)
Individual Education Program: 773 (19.5%);
English Language Learner: n/a; Migrant: n/a
Eligible for Free Lunch Program: n/a
Eligible for Reduced-Price Lunch Program: n/a
Teachers: 256.0 (15.5 to 1)
Librarians/Media Specialists: 7.0 (566.6 to 1)
Guidance Counselors: 8.0 (495.8 to 1)
Current Spending: ($ per student per year):
Total: $5,567; Instruction: $3,599; Support Services: $1,629

Enrollment, Drop-out Rates and Diploma Recipients by Race/Ethnicity

Category	Total	White	Black	Asian	AIAN	Hisp.
Enrollment (%)	100.0	0.0	0.0	0.0	0.0	0.0
Drop-out Rate (%)	3.3	n/a	n/a	n/a	n/a	n/a
H.S. Diplomas (#)	206	n/a	n/a	n/a	n/a	n/a

Overton County

Overton County SD
112 Bussell St · Livingston, TN 38570
(931) 823-1287
Grade Span: KG-12; **Agency Type:** 1
Schools: 9
5 Primary; 1 Middle; 3 High; 0 Other Level
9 Regular; 0 Special Education; 0 Vocational; 0 Alternative
0 Magnet; 0 Charter; 6 Title I Eligible; 6 School-wide Title I
Students: 3,291 (n/a% male; n/a% female)
Individual Education Program: 784 (23.8%);
English Language Learner: n/a; Migrant: n/a
Eligible for Free Lunch Program: n/a
Eligible for Reduced-Price Lunch Program: n/a
Teachers: 221.3 (14.9 to 1)
Librarians/Media Specialists: 5.3 (620.9 to 1)
Guidance Counselors: 8.0 (411.4 to 1)
Current Spending: ($ per student per year):
Total: $5,452; Instruction: $3,475; Support Services: $1,605
Enrollment, Drop-out Rates and Diploma Recipients by Race/Ethnicity

Category	Total	White	Black	Asian	AIAN	Hisp.
Enrollment (%)	100.0	n/a	n/a	n/a	n/a	n/a
Drop-out Rate (%)	1.1	n/a	n/a	n/a	n/a	n/a
H.S. Diplomas (#)	181	n/a	n/a	n/a	n/a	n/a

Polk County

Polk County SD
PO Box A · Benton, TN 37307-1001
(423) 338-4506
Grade Span: KG-12; **Agency Type:** 1
Schools: 8
5 Primary; 1 Middle; 2 High; 0 Other Level
8 Regular; 0 Special Education; 0 Vocational; 0 Alternative
0 Magnet; 0 Charter; 5 Title I Eligible; 4 School-wide Title I
Students: 2,532 (n/a% male; n/a% female)
Individual Education Program: 326 (12.9%);
English Language Learner: n/a; Migrant: n/a
Eligible for Free Lunch Program: n/a
Eligible for Reduced-Price Lunch Program: n/a
Teachers: 161.0 (21.7 to 1)
Librarians/Media Specialists: 3.0 (1,165.0 to 1)
Guidance Counselors: 2.0 (1,747.5 to 1)
Current Spending: ($ per student per year):
Total: $5,652; Instruction: $3,812; Support Services: $1,491
Enrollment, Drop-out Rates and Diploma Recipients by Race/Ethnicity

Category	Total	White	Black	Asian	AIAN	Hisp.
Enrollment (%)	100.0	n/a	n/a	n/a	n/a	n/a
Drop-out Rate (%)	5.2	n/a	n/a	n/a	n/a	n/a
H.S. Diplomas (#)	91	n/a	n/a	n/a	n/a	n/a

Putnam County

Putnam County SD
1400 E Spring St · Cookeville, TN 38506-4313
(931) 526-9777 · http://www.putnam.k12.tn.us/
Grade Span: KG-12; **Agency Type:** 1
Schools: 17
8 Primary; 4 Middle; 4 High; 1 Other Level
16 Regular; 0 Special Education; 0 Vocational; 1 Alternative
0 Magnet; 0 Charter; 7 Title I Eligible; 1 School-wide Title I
Students: 9,872 (n/a% male; n/a% female)
Individual Education Program: 2,062 (20.9%);
English Language Learner: n/a; Migrant: n/a
Eligible for Free Lunch Program: n/a
Eligible for Reduced-Price Lunch Program: n/a
Teachers: 591.8 (15.1 to 1)
Librarians/Media Specialists: 18.9 (471.4 to 1)
Guidance Counselors: 25.4 (350.7 to 1)
Current Spending: ($ per student per year):
Total: $5,734; Instruction: $3,699; Support Services: $1,704
Enrollment, Drop-out Rates and Diploma Recipients by Race/Ethnicity

Category	Total	White	Black	Asian	AIAN	Hisp.
Enrollment (%)	100.0	n/a	n/a	n/a	n/a	n/a
Drop-out Rate (%)	1.7	n/a	n/a	n/a	n/a	n/a
H.S. Diplomas (#)	425	n/a	n/a	n/a	n/a	n/a

Rhea County

Rhea County SD
305 California Ave • Dayton, TN 37321-1409
(423) 775-7813 • http://www.rhea.k12.tn.us/
Grade Span: KG-12; **Agency Type:** 1
Schools: 6
  4 Primary; 1 Middle; 1 High; 0 Other Level
  6 Regular; 0 Special Education; 0 Vocational; 0 Alternative
  0 Magnet; 0 Charter; 3 Title I Eligible; 3 School-wide Title I
Students: 3,836 (n/a% male; n/a% female)
  Individual Education Program: 529 (13.8%);
  English Language Learner: n/a; Migrant: n/a
  Eligible for Free Lunch Program: n/a
  Eligible for Reduced-Price Lunch Program: n/a
Teachers: 246.4 (15.6 to 1)
Librarians/Media Specialists: 5.0 (767.2 to 1)
Guidance Counselors: 7.0 (548.0 to 1)
Current Spending: ($ per student per year):
  Total: $4,775; Instruction: $3,242; Support Services: $1,205
Enrollment, Drop-out Rates and Diploma Recipients by Race/Ethnicity

Category	Total	White	Black	Asian	AIAN	Hisp.
Enrollment (%)	100.0	n/a	n/a	n/a	n/a	n/a
Drop-out Rate (%)	2.6	n/a	n/a	n/a	n/a	n/a
H.S. Diplomas (#)	243	n/a	n/a	n/a	n/a	n/a

Roane County

Roane County SD
105 Bluff Rd • Kingston, TN 37763-7209
(865) 376-5592 • http://www.roane-lea.roane.k12.tn.us/
Grade Span: KG-12; **Agency Type:** 1
Schools: 18
  8 Primary; 4 Middle; 5 High; 1 Other Level
  17 Regular; 0 Special Education; 1 Vocational; 0 Alternative
  0 Magnet; 0 Charter; 8 Title I Eligible; 8 School-wide Title I
Students: 7,397 (n/a% male; n/a% female)
  Individual Education Program: 1,585 (21.4%);
  English Language Learner: n/a; Migrant: n/a
  Eligible for Free Lunch Program: n/a
  Eligible for Reduced-Price Lunch Program: n/a
Teachers: 479.2 (15.4 to 1)
Librarians/Media Specialists: 15.0 (493.1 to 1)
Guidance Counselors: 12.0 (616.4 to 1)
Current Spending: ($ per student per year):
  Total: $6,072; Instruction: $3,972; Support Services: $1,756
Enrollment, Drop-out Rates and Diploma Recipients by Race/Ethnicity

Category	Total	White	Black	Asian	AIAN	Hisp.
Enrollment (%)	100.0	n/a	n/a	n/a	n/a	n/a
Drop-out Rate (%)	3.6	n/a	n/a	n/a	n/a	n/a
H.S. Diplomas (#)	332	n/a	n/a	n/a	n/a	n/a

Robertson County

Robertson County SD
2121 Woodland St PO Box 130 • Springfield, TN 37172-3736
(615) 384-5588 • http://www.robcoschools.k12.tn.us/
Grade Span: KG-12; **Agency Type:** 1
Schools: 16
  9 Primary; 2 Middle; 2 High; 3 Other Level
  16 Regular; 0 Special Education; 0 Vocational; 0 Alternative
  0 Magnet; 0 Charter; 4 Title I Eligible; 2 School-wide Title I
Students: 9,693 (n/a% male; n/a% female)
  Individual Education Program: 2,068 (21.3%);
  English Language Learner: n/a; Migrant: n/a
  Eligible for Free Lunch Program: n/a
  Eligible for Reduced-Price Lunch Program: n/a
Teachers: 623.8 (15.5 to 1)
Librarians/Media Specialists: 15.0 (646.2 to 1)
Guidance Counselors: 16.5 (587.5 to 1)
Current Spending: ($ per student per year):
  Total: $5,658; Instruction: $4,044; Support Services: $1,597
Enrollment, Drop-out Rates and Diploma Recipients by Race/Ethnicity

Category	Total	White	Black	Asian	AIAN	Hisp.
Enrollment (%)	100.0	n/a	n/a	n/a	n/a	n/a
Drop-out Rate (%)	3.9	n/a	n/a	n/a	n/a	n/a
H.S. Diplomas (#)	410	n/a	n/a	n/a	n/a	n/a

Rutherford County

Murfreesboro City Elem SD
2552 S Church St • Murfreesboro, TN 37127-6342
(615) 893-2313 • http://www.cityschools.net/
Grade Span: KG-06; **Agency Type:** 1
Schools: 10

  10 Primary; 0 Middle; 0 High; 0 Other Level
  10 Regular; 0 Special Education; 0 Vocational; 0 Alternative
  0 Magnet; 0 Charter; 8 Title I Eligible; 1 School-wide Title I
Students: 5,965 (n/a% male; n/a% female)
  Individual Education Program: 865 (14.5%);
  English Language Learner: n/a; Migrant: n/a
  Eligible for Free Lunch Program: n/a
  Eligible for Reduced-Price Lunch Program: n/a
Teachers: 395.5 (15.1 to 1)
Librarians/Media Specialists: 10.0 (596.5 to 1)
Guidance Counselors: 12.0 (497.1 to 1)
Current Spending: ($ per student per year):
  Total: $5,954; Instruction: $4,182; Support Services: $1,749
Enrollment, Drop-out Rates and Diploma Recipients by Race/Ethnicity

Category	Total	White	Black	Asian	AIAN	Hisp.
Enrollment (%)	100.0	n/a	n/a	n/a	n/a	n/a
Drop-out Rate (%)	n/a	n/a	n/a	n/a	n/a	n/a
H.S. Diplomas (#)	n/a	n/a	n/a	n/a	n/a	n/a

Rutherford County SD
2240 S Park Blvd • Murfreesboro, TN 37128
(615) 893-5812 • http://www.rcs.k12.tn.us/
Grade Span: KG-12; **Agency Type:** 1
Schools: 38
  20 Primary; 7 Middle; 8 High; 3 Other Level
  37 Regular; 1 Special Education; 0 Vocational; 0 Alternative
  1 Magnet; 0 Charter; 8 Title I Eligible; 4 School-wide Title I
Students: 29,529 (n/a% male; n/a% female)
  Individual Education Program: 5,179 (17.5%);
  English Language Learner: n/a; Migrant: n/a
  Eligible for Free Lunch Program: n/a
  Eligible for Reduced-Price Lunch Program: n/a
Teachers: 1,792.3 (16.5 to 1)
Librarians/Media Specialists: 40.0 (738.2 to 1)
Guidance Counselors: 60.0 (492.2 to 1)
Current Spending: ($ per student per year):
  Total: $5,301; Instruction: $3,711; Support Services: $1,580
Enrollment, Drop-out Rates and Diploma Recipients by Race/Ethnicity

Category	Total	White	Black	Asian	AIAN	Hisp.
Enrollment (%)	100.0	n/a	n/a	n/a	n/a	n/a
Drop-out Rate (%)	2.2	n/a	n/a	n/a	n/a	n/a
H.S. Diplomas (#)	1,506	n/a	n/a	n/a	n/a	n/a

Scott County

Scott County SD
PO Box 37 208 Court St • Huntsville, TN 37756-0037
(423) 663-2159 • http://www.scottcounty.net/
Grade Span: KG-12; **Agency Type:** 1
Schools: 7
  5 Primary; 1 Middle; 1 High; 0 Other Level
  7 Regular; 0 Special Education; 0 Vocational; 0 Alternative
  0 Magnet; 0 Charter; 7 Title I Eligible; 6 School-wide Title I
Students: 2,622 (n/a% male; n/a% female)
  Individual Education Program: 381 (14.5%);
  English Language Learner: n/a; Migrant: n/a
  Eligible for Free Lunch Program: n/a
  Eligible for Reduced-Price Lunch Program: n/a
Teachers: 199.7 (13.1 to 1)
Librarians/Media Specialists: 6.0 (437.0 to 1)
Guidance Counselors: 4.0 (655.5 to 1)
Current Spending: ($ per student per year):
  Total: $6,155; Instruction: $4,130; Support Services: $1,587
Enrollment, Drop-out Rates and Diploma Recipients by Race/Ethnicity

Category	Total	White	Black	Asian	AIAN	Hisp.
Enrollment (%)	100.0	n/a	n/a	n/a	n/a	n/a
Drop-out Rate (%)	4.3	n/a	n/a	n/a	n/a	n/a
H.S. Diplomas (#)	97	n/a	n/a	n/a	n/a	n/a

Sequatchie County

Sequatchie County SD
PO Box 488 24 Spring St • Dunlap, TN 37327-0488
(423) 949-3617
Grade Span: KG-12; **Agency Type:** 1
Schools: 3
  1 Primary; 1 Middle; 1 High; 0 Other Level
  3 Regular; 0 Special Education; 0 Vocational; 0 Alternative
  0 Magnet; 0 Charter; 2 Title I Eligible; 2 School-wide Title I
Students: 1,914 (n/a% male; n/a% female)
  Individual Education Program: 459 (24.0%);
  English Language Learner: n/a; Migrant: n/a
  Eligible for Free Lunch Program: n/a
  Eligible for Reduced-Price Lunch Program: n/a
Teachers: 134.5 (14.2 to 1)

Librarians/Media Specialists: 3.0 (638.0 to 1)
Guidance Counselors: 3.0 (638.0 to 1)
Current Spending: ($ per student per year):
   Total: $5,255; Instruction: $3,484; Support Services: $1,451
Enrollment, Drop-out Rates and Diploma Recipients by Race/Ethnicity

Category	Total	White	Black	Asian	AIAN	Hisp.
Enrollment (%)	100.0	n/a	n/a	n/a	n/a	n/a
Drop-out Rate (%)	2.8	n/a	n/a	n/a	n/a	n/a
H.S. Diplomas (#)	80	n/a	n/a	n/a	n/a	n/a

Sevier County

Sevier County SD
226 Cedar St • Sevierville, TN 37862-3803
(865) 453-4671 • http://www.sevier.org/
Grade Span: KG-12; **Agency Type:** 1
Schools: 24
   13 Primary; 4 Middle; 6 High; 1 Other Level
   22 Regular; 1 Special Education; 0 Vocational; 1 Alternative
   0 Magnet; 0 Charter; 12 Title I Eligible; 12 School-wide Title I
Students: 13,054 (n/a% male; n/a% female)
   Individual Education Program: 2,517 (19.3%);
   English Language Learner: n/a; Migrant: n/a
   Eligible for Free Lunch Program: n/a
   Eligible for Reduced-Price Lunch Program: n/a
Teachers: 839.5 (15.5 to 1)
Librarians/Media Specialists: 20.5 (636.8 to 1)
Guidance Counselors: 27.5 (474.7 to 1)
Current Spending: ($ per student per year):
   Total: $6,235; Instruction: $4,001; Support Services: $1,876
Enrollment, Drop-out Rates and Diploma Recipients by Race/Ethnicity

Category	Total	White	Black	Asian	AIAN	Hisp.
Enrollment (%)	100.0	n/a	n/a	n/a	n/a	n/a
Drop-out Rate (%)	2.4	n/a	n/a	n/a	n/a	n/a
H.S. Diplomas (#)	614	n/a	n/a	n/a	n/a	n/a

Shelby County

Memphis City SD
2597 Avery Ave • Memphis, TN 38112-4818
(901) 325-5300 • http://www.memphis-schools.k12.tn.us/
Grade Span: KG-12; **Agency Type:** 1
Schools: 185
   114 Primary; 31 Middle; 37 High; 3 Other Level
   177 Regular; 1 Special Education; 6 Vocational; 1 Alternative
   1 Magnet; 3 Charter; 180 Title I Eligible; 180 School-wide Title I
Students: 116,224 (n/a% male; n/a% female)
   Individual Education Program: 16,545 (14.2%);
   English Language Learner: n/a; Migrant: n/a
   Eligible for Free Lunch Program: n/a
   Eligible for Reduced-Price Lunch Program: n/a
Teachers: 7,274.9 (16.0 to 1)
Librarians/Media Specialists: 167.8 (692.6 to 1)
Guidance Counselors: 221.1 (525.7 to 1)
Current Spending: ($ per student per year):
   Total: $7,005; Instruction: $4,262; Support Services: $2,357
Enrollment, Drop-out Rates and Diploma Recipients by Race/Ethnicity

Category	Total	White	Black	Asian	AIAN	Hisp.
Enrollment (%)	100.0	0.0	0.0	0.0	0.0	0.0
Drop-out Rate (%)	8.6	n/a	n/a	n/a	n/a	n/a
H.S. Diplomas (#)	3,933	n/a	n/a	n/a	n/a	n/a

Shelby County SD
160 S Hollywood • Memphis, TN 38112-4801
(901) 321-2500 • http://www.scs.k12.tn.us
Grade Span: KG-12; **Agency Type:** 1
Schools: 49
   28 Primary; 13 Middle; 7 High; 1 Other Level
   48 Regular; 0 Special Education; 0 Vocational; 1 Alternative
   0 Magnet; 0 Charter; 9 Title I Eligible; 9 School-wide Title I
Students: 46,808 (n/a% male; n/a% female)
   Individual Education Program: 10,507 (22.4%);
   English Language Learner: n/a; Migrant: n/a
   Eligible for Free Lunch Program: n/a
   Eligible for Reduced-Price Lunch Program: n/a
Teachers: 2,649.3 (17.7 to 1)
Librarians/Media Specialists: 55.9 (837.4 to 1)
Guidance Counselors: 90.9 (514.9 to 1)
Current Spending: ($ per student per year):
   Total: $5,891; Instruction: $4,027; Support Services: $1,712
Enrollment, Drop-out Rates and Diploma Recipients by Race/Ethnicity

Category	Total	White	Black	Asian	AIAN	Hisp.
Enrollment (%)	100.0	0.0	0.0	0.0	0.0	0.0
Drop-out Rate (%)	2.1	n/a	n/a	n/a	n/a	n/a
H.S. Diplomas (#)	2,550	n/a	n/a	n/a	n/a	n/a

Smith County

Smith County SD
207 N Main St B • Carthage, TN 37030-0155
(615) 735-9625 • http://boe.smithcounty.com/
Grade Span: KG-12; **Agency Type:** 1
Schools: 11
   7 Primary; 1 Middle; 2 High; 1 Other Level
   10 Regular; 0 Special Education; 1 Vocational; 0 Alternative
   0 Magnet; 0 Charter; 5 Title I Eligible; 0 School-wide Title I
Students: 3,144 (n/a% male; n/a% female)
   Individual Education Program: 545 (17.3%);
   English Language Learner: n/a; Migrant: n/a
   Eligible for Free Lunch Program: n/a
   Eligible for Reduced-Price Lunch Program: n/a
Teachers: 199.6 (15.8 to 1)
Librarians/Media Specialists: 5.0 (628.8 to 1)
Guidance Counselors: 5.0 (628.8 to 1)
Current Spending: ($ per student per year):
   Total: $4,958; Instruction: $3,314; Support Services: $1,290
Enrollment, Drop-out Rates and Diploma Recipients by Race/Ethnicity

Category	Total	White	Black	Asian	AIAN	Hisp.
Enrollment (%)	100.0	0.0	0.0	0.0	0.0	0.0
Drop-out Rate (%)	1.2	n/a	n/a	n/a	n/a	n/a
H.S. Diplomas (#)	160	n/a	n/a	n/a	n/a	n/a

Stewart County

Stewart County SD
PO Box 433 1031 Spring St • Dover, TN 37058-0433
(931) 232-5176
Grade Span: KG-12; **Agency Type:** 1
Schools: 3
   2 Primary; 0 Middle; 1 High; 0 Other Level
   3 Regular; 0 Special Education; 0 Vocational; 0 Alternative
   0 Magnet; 0 Charter; 2 Title I Eligible; 2 School-wide Title I
Students: 2,106 (n/a% male; n/a% female)
   Individual Education Program: 450 (21.4%);
   English Language Learner: n/a; Migrant: n/a
   Eligible for Free Lunch Program: n/a
   Eligible for Reduced-Price Lunch Program: n/a
Teachers: 125.7 (16.8 to 1)
Librarians/Media Specialists: 3.0 (702.0 to 1)
Guidance Counselors: 3.5 (601.7 to 1)
Current Spending: ($ per student per year):
   Total: $5,582; Instruction: $3,279; Support Services: $1,955
Enrollment, Drop-out Rates and Diploma Recipients by Race/Ethnicity

Category	Total	White	Black	Asian	AIAN	Hisp.
Enrollment (%)	100.0	n/a	n/a	n/a	n/a	n/a
Drop-out Rate (%)	2.2	n/a	n/a	n/a	n/a	n/a
H.S. Diplomas (#)	111	n/a	n/a	n/a	n/a	n/a

Sullivan County

Bristol City SD
615 Edgemont Ave • Bristol, TN 37620-2315
(423) 652-9451 • http://www.btcs.org/
Grade Span: KG-12; **Agency Type:** 1
Schools: 8
   6 Primary; 1 Middle; 1 High; 0 Other Level
   8 Regular; 0 Special Education; 0 Vocational; 0 Alternative
   0 Magnet; 0 Charter; 3 Title I Eligible; 3 School-wide Title I
Students: 3,655 (n/a% male; n/a% female)
   Individual Education Program: 618 (16.9%);
   English Language Learner: n/a; Migrant: n/a
   Eligible for Free Lunch Program: n/a
   Eligible for Reduced-Price Lunch Program: n/a
Teachers: 253.9 (14.4 to 1)
Librarians/Media Specialists: 6.8 (537.5 to 1)
Guidance Counselors: 10.0 (365.5 to 1)
Current Spending: ($ per student per year):
   Total: $7,540; Instruction: $4,756; Support Services: $2,414
Enrollment, Drop-out Rates and Diploma Recipients by Race/Ethnicity

Category	Total	White	Black	Asian	AIAN	Hisp.
Enrollment (%)	100.0	n/a	n/a	n/a	n/a	n/a
Drop-out Rate (%)	2.3	n/a	n/a	n/a	n/a	n/a
H.S. Diplomas (#)	205	n/a	n/a	n/a	n/a	n/a

Kingsport City SD
1701 E Center St • Kingsport, TN 37664-2608
(423) 378-2100 • http://www.kpt.k12.tn.us
Grade Span: PK-12; **Agency Type:** 1
Schools: 11
   8 Primary; 2 Middle; 1 High; 0 Other Level
   10 Regular; 1 Special Education; 0 Vocational; 0 Alternative

0 Magnet; 0 Charter; 5 Title I Eligible; 5 School-wide Title I
Students: 6,381 (n/a% male; n/a% female)
  Individual Education Program: 1,173 (18.4%);
  English Language Learner: n/a; Migrant: n/a
  Eligible for Free Lunch Program: n/a
  Eligible for Reduced-Price Lunch Program: n/a
Teachers: 442.2 (14.4 to 1)
Librarians/Media Specialists: 11.0 (580.1 to 1)
Guidance Counselors: 13.1 (487.1 to 1)
Current Spending: ($ per student per year):
  Total: $7,276; Instruction: $4,747; Support Services: $2,146
Enrollment, Drop-out Rates and Diploma Recipients by Race/Ethnicity

Category	Total	White	Black	Asian	AIAN	Hisp.
Enrollment (%)	100.0	n/a	n/a	n/a	n/a	n/a
Drop-out Rate (%)	1.7	n/a	n/a	n/a	n/a	n/a
H.S. Diplomas (#)	297	n/a	n/a	n/a	n/a	n/a

Sullivan County School Distrct
PO Box 306 • Blountville, TN 37617-0306
(423) 279-2300 • http://www.scde.k12.tn.us
Grade Span: KG-12; **Agency Type:** 1
Schools: 29
  17 Primary; 7 Middle; 4 High; 1 Other Level
  28 Regular; 1 Special Education; 0 Vocational; 0 Alternative
  0 Magnet; 0 Charter; 13 Title I Eligible; 0 School-wide Title I
Students: 13,003 (n/a% male; n/a% female)
  Individual Education Program: 2,846 (21.9%);
  English Language Learner: n/a; Migrant: n/a
  Eligible for Free Lunch Program: n/a
  Eligible for Reduced-Price Lunch Program: n/a
Teachers: 852.1 (15.3 to 1)
Librarians/Media Specialists: 27.4 (474.6 to 1)
Guidance Counselors: 29.8 (436.3 to 1)
Current Spending: ($ per student per year):
  Total: $6,489; Instruction: $4,171; Support Services: $1,922
Enrollment, Drop-out Rates and Diploma Recipients by Race/Ethnicity

Category	Total	White	Black	Asian	AIAN	Hisp.
Enrollment (%)	100.0	n/a	n/a	n/a	n/a	n/a
Drop-out Rate (%)	3.3	n/a	n/a	n/a	n/a	n/a
H.S. Diplomas (#)	610	n/a	n/a	n/a	n/a	n/a

Sumner County

Sumner County SD
695 E Main St • Gallatin, TN 37066-2908
(615) 451-5200 • http://www.sumnerschools.org
Grade Span: KG-12; **Agency Type:** 1
Schools: 42
  23 Primary; 10 Middle; 8 High; 1 Other Level
  41 Regular; 0 Special Education; 0 Vocational; 1 Alternative
  1 Magnet; 0 Charter; 8 Title I Eligible; 0 School-wide Title I
Students: 24,002 (n/a% male; n/a% female)
  Individual Education Program: 4,778 (19.9%);
  English Language Learner: n/a; Migrant: n/a
  Eligible for Free Lunch Program: n/a
  Eligible for Reduced-Price Lunch Program: n/a
Teachers: 1,575.5 (15.2 to 1)
Librarians/Media Specialists: 40.0 (600.1 to 1)
Guidance Counselors: 47.5 (505.3 to 1)
Current Spending: ($ per student per year):
  Total: $5,740; Instruction: $3,806; Support Services: $1,637
Enrollment, Drop-out Rates and Diploma Recipients by Race/Ethnicity

Category	Total	White	Black	Asian	AIAN	Hisp.
Enrollment (%)	100.0	n/a	n/a	n/a	n/a	n/a
Drop-out Rate (%)	1.4	n/a	n/a	n/a	n/a	n/a
H.S. Diplomas (#)	1,477	n/a	n/a	n/a	n/a	n/a

Tipton County

Tipton County SD
PO Box 486 • Covington, TN 38019-0486
(901) 476-7148 • http://www.tipton-county.com/
Grade Span: KG-12; **Agency Type:** 1
Schools: 12
  5 Primary; 3 Middle; 3 High; 1 Other Level
  11 Regular; 0 Special Education; 0 Vocational; 1 Alternative
  1 Magnet; 0 Charter; 5 Title I Eligible; 4 School-wide Title I
Students: 11,153 (n/a% male; n/a% female)
  Individual Education Program: 2,083 (18.7%);
  English Language Learner: n/a; Migrant: n/a
  Eligible for Free Lunch Program: n/a
  Eligible for Reduced-Price Lunch Program: n/a
Teachers: 673.2 (16.6 to 1)
Librarians/Media Specialists: 11.0 (1,013.9 to 1)
Guidance Counselors: 15.0 (743.5 to 1)

Current Spending: ($ per student per year):
  Total: $5,347; Instruction: $3,628; Support Services: $1,382
Enrollment, Drop-out Rates and Diploma Recipients by Race/Ethnicity

Category	Total	White	Black	Asian	AIAN	Hisp.
Enrollment (%)	100.0	n/a	n/a	n/a	n/a	n/a
Drop-out Rate (%)	3.6	n/a	n/a	n/a	n/a	n/a
H.S. Diplomas (#)	522	n/a	n/a	n/a	n/a	n/a

Unicoi County

Unicoi SD
600 N Elm Ave • Erwin, TN 37650-1310
(423) 743-1600
Grade Span: KG-12; **Agency Type:** 1
Schools: 6
  4 Primary; 1 Middle; 1 High; 0 Other Level
  6 Regular; 0 Special Education; 0 Vocational; 0 Alternative
  0 Magnet; 0 Charter; 4 Title I Eligible; 4 School-wide Title I
Students: 2,540 (n/a% male; n/a% female)
  Individual Education Program: 742 (29.2%);
  English Language Learner: n/a; Migrant: n/a
  Eligible for Free Lunch Program: n/a
  Eligible for Reduced-Price Lunch Program: n/a
Teachers: 154.0 (16.5 to 1)
Librarians/Media Specialists: 5.0 (508.0 to 1)
Guidance Counselors: 5.0 (508.0 to 1)
Current Spending: ($ per student per year):
  Total: $5,306; Instruction: $3,411; Support Services: $1,605
Enrollment, Drop-out Rates and Diploma Recipients by Race/Ethnicity

Category	Total	White	Black	Asian	AIAN	Hisp.
Enrollment (%)	100.0	n/a	n/a	n/a	n/a	n/a
Drop-out Rate (%)	1.4	n/a	n/a	n/a	n/a	n/a
H.S. Diplomas (#)	161	n/a	n/a	n/a	n/a	n/a

Union County

Union County SD
Box 10 635 Main St • Maynardville, TN 37807-0010
(865) 992-5466 • http://www.union-city-hs.obion.k12.tn.us/
Grade Span: KG-12; **Agency Type:** 1
Schools: 7
  4 Primary; 1 Middle; 2 High; 0 Other Level
  6 Regular; 0 Special Education; 0 Vocational; 1 Alternative
  0 Magnet; 0 Charter; 4 Title I Eligible; 4 School-wide Title I
Students: 3,054 (n/a% male; n/a% female)
  Individual Education Program: 736 (24.1%);
  English Language Learner: n/a; Migrant: n/a
  Eligible for Free Lunch Program: n/a
  Eligible for Reduced-Price Lunch Program: n/a
Teachers: 216.3 (14.1 to 1)
Librarians/Media Specialists: 4.0 (763.5 to 1)
Guidance Counselors: 4.9 (623.3 to 1)
Current Spending: ($ per student per year):
  Total: $5,506; Instruction: $3,625; Support Services: $1,531
Enrollment, Drop-out Rates and Diploma Recipients by Race/Ethnicity

Category	Total	White	Black	Asian	AIAN	Hisp.
Enrollment (%)	100.0	n/a	n/a	n/a	n/a	n/a
Drop-out Rate (%)	0.6	n/a	n/a	n/a	n/a	n/a
H.S. Diplomas (#)	105	n/a	n/a	n/a	n/a	n/a

Warren County

Warren County SD
2548 Morrison St • Mcminnville, TN 37110-2545
(931) 668-4022 • http://www.warrenschools.com/
Grade Span: KG-12; **Agency Type:** 1
Schools: 11
  8 Primary; 1 Middle; 1 High; 1 Other Level
  10 Regular; 0 Special Education; 0 Vocational; 1 Alternative
  0 Magnet; 0 Charter; 9 Title I Eligible; 4 School-wide Title I
Students: 5,999 (n/a% male; n/a% female)
  Individual Education Program: 1,496 (24.9%);
  English Language Learner: n/a; Migrant: n/a
  Eligible for Free Lunch Program: n/a
  Eligible for Reduced-Price Lunch Program: n/a
Teachers: 413.2 (14.5 to 1)
Librarians/Media Specialists: 10.0 (599.9 to 1)
Guidance Counselors: 14.0 (428.5 to 1)
Current Spending: ($ per student per year):
  Total: $5,611; Instruction: $3,578; Support Services: $1,724

Enrollment, Drop-out Rates and Diploma Recipients by Race/Ethnicity

Category	Total	White	Black	Asian	AIAN	Hisp.
Enrollment (%)	100.0	n/a	n/a	n/a	n/a	n/a
Drop-out Rate (%)	0.8	n/a	n/a	n/a	n/a	n/a
H.S. Diplomas (#)	341	n/a	n/a	n/a	n/a	n/a

Washington County

Johnson City SD
PO Box 1517 • Johnson City, TN 37605-1517
(423) 434-5200 • http://www.jcschools.org
Grade Span: KG-12; **Agency Type:** 1
Schools: 10
   8 Primary; 1 Middle; 1 High; 0 Other Level
   10 Regular; 0 Special Education; 0 Vocational; 0 Alternative
   0 Magnet; 0 Charter; 5 Title I Eligible; 5 School-wide Title I
Students: 6,880 (n/a% male; n/a% female)
   Individual Education Program: 1,356 (19.7%);
   English Language Learner: n/a; Migrant: n/a
   Eligible for Free Lunch Program: n/a
   Eligible for Reduced-Price Lunch Program: n/a
Teachers: 449.9 (15.3 to 1)
Librarians/Media Specialists: 9.0 (764.4 to 1)
Guidance Counselors: 14.0 (491.4 to 1)
Current Spending: ($ per student per year):
   Total: $6,366; Instruction: $4,139; Support Services: $1,888
Enrollment, Drop-out Rates and Diploma Recipients by Race/Ethnicity

Category	Total	White	Black	Asian	AIAN	Hisp.
Enrollment (%)	100.0	n/a	n/a	n/a	n/a	n/a
Drop-out Rate (%)	0.4	n/a	n/a	n/a	n/a	n/a
H.S. Diplomas (#)	340	n/a	n/a	n/a	n/a	n/a

Washington County SD
405 W College St • Jonesborough, TN 37659-1009
(423) 753-1100 • http://www.wcde.org/
Grade Span: KG-12; **Agency Type:** 1
Schools: 13
   8 Primary; 2 Middle; 2 High; 1 Other Level
   13 Regular; 0 Special Education; 0 Vocational; 0 Alternative
   0 Magnet; 0 Charter; 9 Title I Eligible; 0 School-wide Title I
Students: 8,744 (n/a% male; n/a% female)
   Individual Education Program: 1,456 (16.7%);
   English Language Learner: n/a; Migrant: n/a
   Eligible for Free Lunch Program: n/a
   Eligible for Reduced-Price Lunch Program: n/a
Teachers: 539.3 (16.2 to 1)
Librarians/Media Specialists: 15.0 (582.9 to 1)
Guidance Counselors: 17.0 (514.4 to 1)
Current Spending: ($ per student per year):
   Total: $5,254; Instruction: $3,708; Support Services: $1,523
Enrollment, Drop-out Rates and Diploma Recipients by Race/Ethnicity

Category	Total	White	Black	Asian	AIAN	Hisp.
Enrollment (%)	100.0	n/a	n/a	n/a	n/a	n/a
Drop-out Rate (%)	3.2	n/a	n/a	n/a	n/a	n/a
H.S. Diplomas (#)	387	n/a	n/a	n/a	n/a	n/a

Wayne County

Wayne County SD
PO Box 658 • Waynesboro, TN 38485-0658
(931) 722-3548 • http://www.wayne-lea.wayne.k12.tn.us/
Grade Span: KG-12; **Agency Type:** 1
Schools: 8
   2 Primary; 2 Middle; 3 High; 1 Other Level
   7 Regular; 0 Special Education; 1 Vocational; 0 Alternative
   0 Magnet; 0 Charter; 5 Title I Eligible; 5 School-wide Title I
Students: 2,554 (n/a% male; n/a% female)
   Individual Education Program: 547 (21.4%);
   English Language Learner: n/a; Migrant: n/a
   Eligible for Free Lunch Program: n/a
   Eligible for Reduced-Price Lunch Program: n/a
Teachers: 194.8 (13.1 to 1)
Librarians/Media Specialists: 6.5 (392.9 to 1)
Guidance Counselors: 4.0 (638.5 to 1)
Current Spending: ($ per student per year):
   Total: $5,483; Instruction: $3,882; Support Services: $1,555
Enrollment, Drop-out Rates and Diploma Recipients by Race/Ethnicity

Category	Total	White	Black	Asian	AIAN	Hisp.
Enrollment (%)	100.0	n/a	n/a	n/a	n/a	n/a
Drop-out Rate (%)	2.2	n/a	n/a	n/a	n/a	n/a
H.S. Diplomas (#)	143	n/a	n/a	n/a	n/a	n/a

Weakley County

Weakley County SD
8319 Hwy 22 Ste A • Dresden, TN 38225
(731) 364-2247 • http://www.weakley-lea.weakley.k12.tn.us/
Grade Span: KG-12; **Agency Type:** 1
Schools: 11
   4 Primary; 2 Middle; 3 High; 2 Other Level
   11 Regular; 0 Special Education; 0 Vocational; 0 Alternative
   0 Magnet; 0 Charter; 7 Title I Eligible; 7 School-wide Title I
Students: 4,759 (n/a% male; n/a% female)
   Individual Education Program: 854 (17.9%);
   English Language Learner: n/a; Migrant: n/a
   Eligible for Free Lunch Program: n/a
   Eligible for Reduced-Price Lunch Program: n/a
Teachers: 316.9 (15.0 to 1)
Librarians/Media Specialists: 9.5 (500.9 to 1)
Guidance Counselors: 11.0 (432.6 to 1)
Current Spending: ($ per student per year):
   Total: $5,279; Instruction: $3,541; Support Services: $1,409
Enrollment, Drop-out Rates and Diploma Recipients by Race/Ethnicity

Category	Total	White	Black	Asian	AIAN	Hisp.
Enrollment (%)	100.0	n/a	n/a	n/a	n/a	n/a
Drop-out Rate (%)	1.0	n/a	n/a	n/a	n/a	n/a
H.S. Diplomas (#)	270	n/a	n/a	n/a	n/a	n/a

White County

White County SD
136 Baker St • Sparta, TN 38583-1700
(931) 836-2229
Grade Span: KG-12; **Agency Type:** 1
Schools: 9
   7 Primary; 1 Middle; 1 High; 0 Other Level
   9 Regular; 0 Special Education; 0 Vocational; 0 Alternative
   0 Magnet; 0 Charter; 7 Title I Eligible; 7 School-wide Title I
Students: 3,898 (n/a% male; n/a% female)
   Individual Education Program: 744 (19.1%);
   English Language Learner: n/a; Migrant: n/a
   Eligible for Free Lunch Program: n/a
   Eligible for Reduced-Price Lunch Program: n/a
Teachers: 249.7 (15.6 to 1)
Librarians/Media Specialists: 7.0 (556.9 to 1)
Guidance Counselors: 9.0 (433.1 to 1)
Current Spending: ($ per student per year):
   Total: $4,918; Instruction: $3,307; Support Services: $1,277
Enrollment, Drop-out Rates and Diploma Recipients by Race/Ethnicity

Category	Total	White	Black	Asian	AIAN	Hisp.
Enrollment (%)	100.0	n/a	n/a	n/a	n/a	n/a
Drop-out Rate (%)	1.2	n/a	n/a	n/a	n/a	n/a
H.S. Diplomas (#)	202	n/a	n/a	n/a	n/a	n/a

Williamson County

Franklin City Elementary SD
507 New Hwy 96 W • Franklin, TN 37064-2470
(615) 794-6624
Grade Span: KG-08; **Agency Type:** 1
Schools: 8
   5 Primary; 3 Middle; 0 High; 0 Other Level
   8 Regular; 0 Special Education; 0 Vocational; 0 Alternative
   0 Magnet; 0 Charter; 1 Title I Eligible; 0 School-wide Title I
Students: 3,703 (n/a% male; n/a% female)
   Individual Education Program: 746 (20.1%);
   English Language Learner: n/a; Migrant: n/a
   Eligible for Free Lunch Program: n/a
   Eligible for Reduced-Price Lunch Program: n/a
Teachers: 295.5 (12.5 to 1)
Librarians/Media Specialists: 8.0 (462.9 to 1)
Guidance Counselors: 10.0 (370.3 to 1)
Current Spending: ($ per student per year):
   Total: $8,599; Instruction: $5,555; Support Services: $2,728
Enrollment, Drop-out Rates and Diploma Recipients by Race/Ethnicity

Category	Total	White	Black	Asian	AIAN	Hisp.
Enrollment (%)	100.0	n/a	n/a	n/a	n/a	n/a
Drop-out Rate (%)	n/a	n/a	n/a	n/a	n/a	n/a
H.S. Diplomas (#)	n/a	n/a	n/a	n/a	n/a	n/a

Williamson County SD
1320 W Main Ste 202 • Franklin, TN 37064-3736
(615) 472-4000 • http://www.wcs.edu
Grade Span: KG-12; **Agency Type:** 1
Schools: 33
   20 Primary; 6 Middle; 6 High; 1 Other Level
   33 Regular; 0 Special Education; 0 Vocational; 0 Alternative

0 Magnet; 0 Charter; 7 Title I Eligible; 0 School-wide Title I
Students: 21,956   (n/a% male; n/a% female)
  Individual Education Program: 3,976 (18.1%);
  English Language Learner: n/a; Migrant: n/a
  Eligible for Free Lunch Program: n/a
  Eligible for Reduced-Price Lunch Program: n/a
Teachers: 1,360.9 (16.1 to 1)
Librarians/Media Specialists: 35.5 (618.5 to 1)
Guidance Counselors: 50.9 (431.4 to 1)
Current Spending: ($ per student per year):
  Total: $6,816; Instruction: $4,381; Support Services: $2,165
Enrollment, Drop-out Rates and Diploma Recipients by Race/Ethnicity

Category	Total	White	Black	Asian	AIAN	Hisp.
Enrollment (%)	100.0	n/a	n/a	n/a	n/a	n/a
Drop-out Rate (%)	1.7	n/a	n/a	n/a	n/a	n/a
H.S. Diplomas (#)	745	n/a	n/a	n/a	n/a	n/a

Wilson County

Lebanon City Elementary SD
701 Coles Ferry Pike • Lebanon, TN 37087-5631
(615) 449-6060
Grade Span: KG-08; **Agency Type:** 1
Schools: 5
  3 Primary; 2 Middle; 0 High; 0 Other Level
  5 Regular; 0 Special Education; 0 Vocational; 0 Alternative
  0 Magnet; 0 Charter; 2 Title I Eligible; 1 School-wide Title I
Students: 3,007   (n/a% male; n/a% female)
  Individual Education Program: 571 (19.0%);
  English Language Learner: n/a; Migrant: n/a
  Eligible for Free Lunch Program: n/a
  Eligible for Reduced-Price Lunch Program: n/a
Teachers: 204.0 (14.7 to 1)
Librarians/Media Specialists: 4.0 (751.8 to 1)
Guidance Counselors: 5.0 (601.4 to 1)
Current Spending: ($ per student per year):
  Total: $5,824; Instruction: $3,746; Support Services: $1,776
Enrollment, Drop-out Rates and Diploma Recipients by Race/Ethnicity

Category	Total	White	Black	Asian	AIAN	Hisp.
Enrollment (%)	100.0	n/a	n/a	n/a	n/a	n/a
Drop-out Rate (%)	n/a	n/a	n/a	n/a	n/a	n/a
H.S. Diplomas (#)	n/a	n/a	n/a	n/a	n/a	n/a

Wilson County SD
351 Stumpy Ln • Lebanon, TN 37090
(615) 444-3282 • http://www.wcschools.com/
Grade Span: KG-12; **Agency Type:** 1
Schools: 19
  11 Primary; 2 Middle; 6 High; 0 Other Level
  18 Regular; 0 Special Education; 1 Vocational; 0 Alternative
  0 Magnet; 0 Charter; 4 Title I Eligible; 0 School-wide Title I
Students: 12,542   (n/a% male; n/a% female)
  Individual Education Program: 1,719 (13.7%);
  English Language Learner: n/a; Migrant: n/a
  Eligible for Free Lunch Program: n/a
  Eligible for Reduced-Price Lunch Program: n/a
Teachers: 742.5 (16.9 to 1)
Librarians/Media Specialists: 17.0 (737.8 to 1)
Guidance Counselors: 30.0 (418.1 to 1)
Current Spending: ($ per student per year):
  Total: $6,113; Instruction: $3,576; Support Services: $2,207
Enrollment, Drop-out Rates and Diploma Recipients by Race/Ethnicity

Category	Total	White	Black	Asian	AIAN	Hisp.
Enrollment (%)	100.0	0.0	0.0	0.0	0.0	0.0
Drop-out Rate (%)	2.3	n/a	n/a	n/a	n/a	n/a
H.S. Diplomas (#)	648	n/a	n/a	n/a	n/a	n/a

Number of Schools

Rank	Number	District Name	City
1	185	Memphis City SD	Memphis
2	126	Nashville-Davidson County SD	Nashville
3	88	Knox County SD	Knoxville
4	81	Hamilton County School Distrct	Chattanooga
5	49	Shelby County SD	Memphis
6	42	Sumner County SD	Gallatin
7	38	Rutherford County SD	Murfreesboro
8	33	Williamson County SD	Franklin
9	30	Montgomery County Schools	Clarksville
10	29	Sullivan County School Distrct	Blountville
11	28	Jackson-Madison Consolidated	Jackson
12	24	Sevier County SD	Sevierville
13	19	Blount County SD	Maryville
13	19	Wilson County SD	Lebanon
15	18	Hamblen County SD	Morristown
15	18	Maury County SD	Columbia
15	18	Roane County SD	Kingston
18	17	Anderson County School Distrct	Clinton
18	17	Carter County SD	Elizabethton
18	17	Hawkins County SD	Rogersville
18	17	Putnam County SD	Cookeville
22	16	Bradley County SD	Cleveland
22	16	Campbell County School Distrct	Jacksboro
22	16	Robertson County SD	Springfield
25	15	Greene County SD	Greeneville
26	14	Cheatham County School Distrct	Ashland City
26	14	Claiborne County SD	Tazewell
26	14	Dickson County SD	Dickson
29	13	Lawrence County School Distrct	Lawrenceburg
29	13	Washington County SD	Jonesborough
31	12	Bedford County SD	Shelbyville
31	12	Cocke County SD	Newport
31	12	Franklin County School Distrct	Winchester
31	12	Tipton County SD	Covington
35	11	Kingsport City SD	Kingsport
35	11	Monroe County SD	Madisonville
35	11	Smith County SD	Carthage
35	11	Warren County SD	Mcminnville
35	11	Weakley County SD	Dresden
40	10	Cumberland County SD	Crossville
40	10	Fayette County SD	Somerville
40	10	Hardin County SD	Savannah
40	10	Henderson County SD	Lexington
40	10	Jefferson County SD	Dandridge
40	10	Johnson City SD	Johnson City
40	10	Murfreesboro City Elem SD	Murfreesboro
47	9	Hardeman County School Distrct	Bolivar
47	9	Loudon County SD	Loudon
47	9	Marion County SD	Jasper
47	9	Marshall County School Distrct	Lewisburg
47	9	Mcminn County SD	Athens
47	9	Overton County SD	Livingston
47	9	White County SD	Sparta
54	8	Benton County SD	Camden
54	8	Bristol City SD	Bristol
54	8	Cleveland City SD	Cleveland
54	8	Coffee County SD	Manchester
54	8	Dyer County SD	Dyersburg
54	8	Franklin City Elementary SD	Franklin
54	8	Giles County SD	Pulaski
54	8	Lincoln County SD	Fayetteville
54	8	Mcnairy County SD	Selmer
54	8	Morgan County SD	Wartburg
54	8	Oak Ridge City SD	Oak Ridge
54	8	Obion County SD	Union City
54	8	Polk County SD	Benton
54	8	Wayne County SD	Waynesboro
68	7	Cannon County SD	Woodbury
68	7	Gibson Special District	Dyer
68	7	Grainger County School Distrct	Rutledge
68	7	Greeneville City SD	Greeneville
68	7	Grundy County SD	Altamont
68	7	Haywood County SD	Brownsville
68	7	Hickman County SD	Centerville
68	7	Humphreys County SD	Waverly
68	7	Johnson County SD	Mountain City
68	7	Lauderdale County SD	Ripley
68	7	Macon County SD	Lafayette
68	7	Maryville City SD	Maryville
68	7	Scott County SD	Huntsville
68	7	Tullahoma City SD	Tullahoma
68	7	Union County SD	Maynardville
83	6	Bledsoe County SD	Pikeville
83	6	Chester County SD	Henderson
83	6	Fentress County School Distrct	Jamestown
83	6	Henry County SD	Paris
83	6	Rhea County SD	Dayton
83	6	Unicoi SD	Erwin
89	5	Athens City Elementary SD	Athens
89	5	Crockett County SD	Alamo
89	5	Dekalb County SD	Smithville
89	5	Elizabethton City SD	Elizabethton
89	5	Jackson County SD	Gainsboro
89	5	Lebanon City Elementary SD	Lebanon
95	4	Dyersburg City SD	Dyersburg
95	4	Lewis County SD	Hohenwald
95	4	Meigs County SD	Decatur
98	3	Lenoir City SD	Lenoir City
98	3	Milan City Special SD	Milan
98	3	Sequatchie County SD	Dunlap
98	3	Stewart County SD	Dover

Number of Teachers

Rank	Number	District Name	City
1	7,274	Memphis City SD	Memphis
2	4,857	Nashville-Davidson County SD	Nashville
3	3,609	Knox County SD	Knoxville
4	2,738	Hamilton County School Distrct	Chattanooga
5	2,649	Shelby County SD	Memphis
6	1,792	Rutherford County SD	Murfreesboro
7	1,575	Sumner County SD	Gallatin
8	1,558	Montgomery County Schools	Clarksville
9	1,360	Williamson County SD	Franklin
10	1,001	Jackson-Madison Consolidated	Jackson
11	852	Sullivan County School Distrct	Blountville
12	839	Sevier County SD	Sevierville
13	763	Maury County SD	Columbia
14	742	Wilson County SD	Lebanon
15	673	Tipton County SD	Covington
16	649	Blount County SD	Maryville
17	623	Robertson County SD	Springfield
18	593	Hamblen County SD	Morristown
19	591	Putnam County SD	Cookeville
20	560	Bradley County SD	Cleveland
21	539	Washington County SD	Jonesborough
22	528	Dickson County SD	Dickson
23	506	Hawkins County SD	Rogersville
24	499	Anderson County School Distrct	Clinton
25	479	Roane County SD	Kingston
26	461	Lawrence County School Distrct	Lawrenceburg
27	451	Greene County SD	Greeneville
28	449	Johnson City SD	Johnson City
29	442	Kingsport City SD	Kingsport
30	440	Jefferson County SD	Dandridge
31	436	Carter County SD	Elizabethton
32	436	Cheatham County School Distrct	Ashland City
33	427	Bedford County SD	Shelbyville
34	413	Warren County SD	Mcminnville
35	400	Cumberland County SD	Crossville
36	396	Campbell County School Distrct	Jacksboro
37	395	Murfreesboro City Elem SD	Murfreesboro
38	392	Franklin County School Distrct	Winchester
39	348	Mcminn County SD	Athens
40	348	Claiborne County SD	Tazewell
41	332	Hardeman County School Distrct	Bolivar
42	331	Oak Ridge City SD	Oak Ridge
43	316	Weakley County SD	Dresden
44	314	Cocke County SD	Newport
45	305	Lauderdale County SD	Ripley
46	304	Cleveland City SD	Cleveland
47	302	Monroe County SD	Madisonville
48	295	Franklin City Elementary SD	Franklin
49	295	Marshall County School Distrct	Lewisburg
50	291	Giles County SD	Pulaski
51	291	Maryville City SD	Maryville
52	289	Mcnairy County SD	Selmer
53	282	Loudon County SD	Loudon
54	273	Coffee County SD	Manchester
55	270	Marion County SD	Jasper
56	267	Hardin County SD	Savannah
57	260	Fayette County SD	Somerville
58	256	Obion County SD	Union City
59	254	Lincoln County SD	Fayetteville
60	253	Bristol City SD	Bristol
61	249	White County SD	Sparta
62	246	Rhea County SD	Dayton
63	242	Haywood County SD	Brownsville
64	240	Hickman County SD	Centerville
65	232	Henderson County SD	Lexington
66	230	Tullahoma City SD	Tullahoma
67	226	Morgan County SD	Wartburg
68	221	Overton County SD	Livingston
69	219	Dyersburg City SD	Dyersburg
70	216	Union County SD	Maynardville
71	213	Macon County SD	Lafayette
72	207	Henry County SD	Paris
73	206	Dyer County SD	Dyersburg
74	204	Grainger County School Distrct	Rutledge
75	204	Lebanon City Elementary SD	Lebanon
76	199	Scott County SD	Huntsville
77	199	Smith County SD	Carthage
78	197	Humphreys County SD	Waverly
79	194	Wayne County SD	Waynesboro
80	193	Greeneville City SD	Greeneville
81	183	Grundy County SD	Altamont
82	179	Dekalb County SD	Smithville
83	176	Benton County SD	Camden
84	161	Gibson Special District	Dyer
85	161	Fentress County School Distrct	Jamestown
86	161	Johnson County SD	Mountain City
87	161	Polk County SD	Benton
88	154	Unicoi SD	Erwin
89	153	Elizabethton City SD	Elizabethton
90	147	Cannon County SD	Woodbury
91	142	Chester County SD	Henderson
92	135	Milan City Special SD	Milan
93	134	Sequatchie County SD	Dunlap
94	129	Lewis County SD	Hohenwald
95	125	Stewart County SD	Dover
96	125	Lenoir City SD	Lenoir City
97	121	Bledsoe County SD	Pikeville
98	117	Crockett County SD	Alamo
99	116	Jackson County SD	Gainsboro
100	116	Meigs County SD	Decatur
101	108	Athens City Elementary SD	Athens

Number of Students

Rank	Number	District Name	City
1	116,224	Memphis City SD	Memphis
2	68,651	Nashville-Davidson County SD	Nashville
3	52,659	Knox County SD	Knoxville
4	46,808	Shelby County SD	Memphis
5	40,100	Hamilton County School Distrct	Chattanooga
6	29,529	Rutherford County SD	Murfreesboro
7	24,924	Montgomery County Schools	Clarksville
8	24,002	Sumner County SD	Gallatin
9	21,956	Williamson County SD	Franklin
10	13,609	Jackson-Madison Consolidated	Jackson
11	13,054	Sevier County SD	Sevierville
12	13,003	Sullivan County School Distrct	Blountville
13	12,542	Wilson County SD	Lebanon
14	11,153	Tipton County SD	Covington
15	11,141	Maury County SD	Columbia
16	10,944	Blount County SD	Maryville
17	9,872	Putnam County SD	Cookeville
18	9,693	Robertson County SD	Springfield
19	9,184	Bradley County SD	Cleveland
20	9,145	Hamblen County SD	Morristown
21	8,744	Washington County SD	Jonesborough
22	8,111	Dickson County SD	Dickson
23	7,397	Roane County SD	Kingston
24	7,235	Hawkins County SD	Rogersville
25	7,036	Jefferson County SD	Dandridge
26	6,976	Greene County SD	Greeneville
27	6,931	Cheatham County School Distrct	Ashland City
28	6,899	Cumberland County SD	Crossville
29	6,880	Johnson City SD	Johnson City
30	6,840	Anderson County School Distrct	Clinton
31	6,710	Lawrence County School Distrct	Lawrenceburg
32	6,689	Bedford County SD	Shelbyville
33	6,381	Kingsport City SD	Kingsport
34	6,046	Campbell County School Distrct	Jacksboro
35	5,999	Warren County SD	Mcminnville
36	5,965	Murfreesboro City Elem SD	Murfreesboro
37	5,858	Carter County SD	Elizabethton
38	5,829	Mcminn County SD	Athens
39	5,776	Franklin County School Distrct	Winchester
40	5,188	Monroe County SD	Madisonville
41	4,852	Loudon County SD	Loudon
42	4,829	Marshall County School Distrct	Lewisburg
43	4,759	Weakley County SD	Dresden
44	4,723	Cocke County SD	Newport
45	4,648	Claiborne County SD	Tazewell
46	4,598	Maryville City SD	Maryville
47	4,544	Lauderdale County SD	Ripley
48	4,465	Hardeman County School Distrct	Bolivar
49	4,432	Giles County SD	Pulaski
50	4,393	Cleveland City SD	Cleveland
51	4,360	Oak Ridge City SD	Oak Ridge
52	4,233	Mcnairy County SD	Selmer
53	4,129	Coffee County SD	Manchester
54	4,102	Marion County SD	Jasper
55	3,986	Lincoln County SD	Fayetteville
56	3,966	Obion County SD	Union City
57	3,898	White County SD	Sparta
58	3,836	Rhea County SD	Dayton
59	3,813	Hickman County SD	Centerville
60	3,753	Hardin County SD	Savannah
61	3,703	Franklin City Elementary SD	Franklin
62	3,655	Bristol City SD	Bristol
63	3,597	Tullahoma City SD	Tullahoma
64	3,555	Dyersburg City SD	Dyersburg
65	3,547	Macon County SD	Lafayette
66	3,511	Haywood County SD	Brownsville

67	3,382	Henderson County SD	Lexington
68	3,336	Grainger County School Distrct	Rutledge
69	3,291	Overton County SD	Livingston
70	3,250	Morgan County SD	Wartburg
71	3,213	Fayette County SD	Somerville
72	3,205	Dyer County SD	Dyersburg
73	3,155	Henry County SD	Paris
74	3,144	Smith County SD	Carthage
75	3,054	Union County SD	Maynardville
76	3,007	Lebanon City Elementary SD	Lebanon
77	3,000	Humphreys County SD	Waverly
78	2,676	Greeneville City SD	Greeneville
79	2,640	Gibson Special District	Dyer
80	2,622	Scott County SD	Huntsville
81	2,584	Dekalb County SD	Smithville
82	2,554	Wayne County SD	Waynesboro
83	2,540	Unicoi SD	Erwin
84	2,532	Polk County SD	Benton
85	2,524	Chester County SD	Henderson
86	2,438	Benton County SD	Camden
87	2,285	Johnson County SD	Mountain City
88	2,255	Grundy County SD	Altamont
89	2,252	Fentress County School Distrct	Jamestown
90	2,209	Elizabethton City SD	Elizabethton
91	2,136	Cannon County SD	Woodbury
92	2,106	Stewart County SD	Dover
93	2,030	Lenoir City SD	Lenoir City
94	2,022	Milan City Special SD	Milan
95	1,969	Lewis County SD	Hohenwald
96	1,914	Sequatchie County SD	Dunlap
97	1,841	Meigs County SD	Decatur
98	1,794	Bledsoe County SD	Pikeville
99	1,782	Crockett County SD	Alamo
100	1,680	Athens City Elementary SD	Athens
101	1,668	Jackson County SD	Gainsboro

Male Students

Rank	Percent	District Name	City
1	n/a	Anderson County School Distrct	Clinton
1	n/a	Athens City Elementary SD	Athens
1	n/a	Bedford County SD	Shelbyville
1	n/a	Benton County SD	Camden
1	n/a	Bledsoe County SD	Pikeville
1	n/a	Blount County SD	Maryville
1	n/a	Bradley County SD	Cleveland
1	n/a	Bristol City SD	Bristol
1	n/a	Campbell County School Distrct	Jacksboro
1	n/a	Cannon County SD	Woodbury
1	n/a	Carter County SD	Elizabethton
1	n/a	Cheatham County School Distrct	Ashland City
1	n/a	Chester County SD	Henderson
1	n/a	Claiborne County SD	Tazewell
1	n/a	Cleveland City SD	Cleveland
1	n/a	Cocke County SD	Newport
1	n/a	Coffee County SD	Manchester
1	n/a	Crockett County SD	Alamo
1	n/a	Cumberland County SD	Crossville
1	n/a	Dekalb County SD	Smithville
1	n/a	Dickson County SD	Dickson
1	n/a	Dyer County SD	Dyersburg
1	n/a	Dyersburg City SD	Dyersburg
1	n/a	Elizabethton City SD	Elizabethton
1	n/a	Fayette County SD	Somerville
1	n/a	Fentress County School Distrct	Jamestown
1	n/a	Franklin City Elementary SD	Franklin
1	n/a	Franklin County School Distrct	Winchester
1	n/a	Gibson Special District	Dyer
1	n/a	Giles County SD	Pulaski
1	n/a	Grainger County School Distrct	Rutledge
1	n/a	Greene County SD	Greeneville
1	n/a	Greeneville City SD	Greeneville
1	n/a	Grundy County SD	Altamont
1	n/a	Hamblen County SD	Morristown
1	n/a	Hamilton County School Distrct	Chattanooga
1	n/a	Hardeman County School Distrct	Bolivar
1	n/a	Hardin County SD	Savannah
1	n/a	Hawkins County SD	Rogersville
1	n/a	Haywood County SD	Brownsville
1	n/a	Henderson County SD	Lexington
1	n/a	Henry County SD	Paris
1	n/a	Hickman County SD	Centerville
1	n/a	Humphreys County SD	Waverly
1	n/a	Jackson County SD	Gainsboro
1	n/a	Jackson-Madison Consolidated	Jackson
1	n/a	Jefferson County SD	Dandridge
1	n/a	Johnson City SD	Johnson City
1	n/a	Johnson County SD	Mountain City
1	n/a	Kingsport City SD	Kingsport
1	n/a	Knox County SD	Knoxville
1	n/a	Lauderdale County SD	Ripley
1	n/a	Lawrence County School Distrct	Lawrenceburg
1	n/a	Lebanon City Elementary SD	Lebanon
1	n/a	Lenoir City SD	Lenoir City
1	n/a	Lewis County SD	Hohenwald
1	n/a	Lincoln County SD	Fayetteville
1	n/a	Loudon County SD	Loudon
1	n/a	Macon County SD	Lafayette
1	n/a	Marion County SD	Jasper
1	n/a	Marshall County School Distrct	Lewisburg
1	n/a	Maryville City SD	Maryville
1	n/a	Maury County SD	Columbia
1	n/a	Mcminn County SD	Athens
1	n/a	Mcnairy County SD	Selmer
1	n/a	Meigs County SD	Decatur
1	n/a	Memphis City SD	Memphis
1	n/a	Milan City Special SD	Milan
1	n/a	Monroe County SD	Madisonville
1	n/a	Montgomery County Schools	Clarksville
1	n/a	Morgan County SD	Wartburg
1	n/a	Murfreesboro City Elem SD	Murfreesboro
1	n/a	Nashville-Davidson County SD	Nashville
1	n/a	Oak Ridge City SD	Oak Ridge
1	n/a	Obion County SD	Union City
1	n/a	Overton County SD	Livingston
1	n/a	Polk County SD	Benton
1	n/a	Putnam County SD	Cookeville
1	n/a	Rhea County SD	Dayton
1	n/a	Roane County SD	Kingston
1	n/a	Robertson County SD	Springfield
1	n/a	Rutherford County SD	Murfreesboro
1	n/a	Scott County SD	Huntsville
1	n/a	Sequatchie County SD	Dunlap
1	n/a	Sevier County SD	Sevierville
1	n/a	Shelby County SD	Memphis
1	n/a	Smith County SD	Carthage
1	n/a	Stewart County SD	Dover
1	n/a	Sullivan County School Distrct	Blountville
1	n/a	Sumner County SD	Gallatin
1	n/a	Tipton County SD	Covington
1	n/a	Tullahoma City SD	Tullahoma
1	n/a	Unicoi SD	Erwin
1	n/a	Union County SD	Maynardville
1	n/a	Warren County SD	Mcminnville
1	n/a	Washington County SD	Jonesborough
1	n/a	Wayne County SD	Waynesboro
1	n/a	Weakley County SD	Dresden
1	n/a	White County SD	Sparta
1	n/a	Williamson County SD	Franklin
1	n/a	Wilson County SD	Lebanon

Female Students

Rank	Percent	District Name	City
1	n/a	Anderson County School Distrct	Clinton
1	n/a	Athens City Elementary SD	Athens
1	n/a	Bedford County SD	Shelbyville
1	n/a	Benton County SD	Camden
1	n/a	Bledsoe County SD	Pikeville
1	n/a	Blount County SD	Maryville
1	n/a	Bradley County SD	Cleveland
1	n/a	Bristol City SD	Bristol
1	n/a	Campbell County School Distrct	Jacksboro
1	n/a	Cannon County SD	Woodbury
1	n/a	Carter County SD	Elizabethton
1	n/a	Cheatham County School Distrct	Ashland City
1	n/a	Chester County SD	Henderson
1	n/a	Claiborne County SD	Tazewell
1	n/a	Cleveland City SD	Cleveland
1	n/a	Cocke County SD	Newport
1	n/a	Coffee County SD	Manchester
1	n/a	Crockett County SD	Alamo
1	n/a	Cumberland County SD	Crossville
1	n/a	Dekalb County SD	Smithville
1	n/a	Dickson County SD	Dickson
1	n/a	Dyer County SD	Dyersburg
1	n/a	Dyersburg City SD	Dyersburg
1	n/a	Elizabethton City SD	Elizabethton
1	n/a	Fayette County SD	Somerville
1	n/a	Fentress County School Distrct	Jamestown
1	n/a	Franklin City Elementary SD	Franklin
1	n/a	Franklin County School Distrct	Winchester
1	n/a	Gibson Special District	Dyer
1	n/a	Giles County SD	Pulaski
1	n/a	Grainger County School Distrct	Rutledge
1	n/a	Greene County SD	Greeneville
1	n/a	Greeneville City SD	Greeneville
1	n/a	Grundy County SD	Altamont
1	n/a	Hamblen County SD	Morristown
1	n/a	Hamilton County School Distrct	Chattanooga
1	n/a	Hardeman County School Distrct	Bolivar
1	n/a	Hardin County SD	Savannah
1	n/a	Hawkins County SD	Rogersville
1	n/a	Haywood County SD	Brownsville
1	n/a	Henderson County SD	Lexington
1	n/a	Henry County SD	Paris
1	n/a	Hickman County SD	Centerville
1	n/a	Humphreys County SD	Waverly
1	n/a	Jackson County SD	Gainsboro
1	n/a	Jackson-Madison Consolidated	Jackson
1	n/a	Jefferson County SD	Dandridge
1	n/a	Johnson City SD	Johnson City
1	n/a	Johnson County SD	Mountain City
1	n/a	Kingsport City SD	Kingsport
1	n/a	Knox County SD	Knoxville
1	n/a	Lauderdale County SD	Ripley
1	n/a	Lawrence County School Distrct	Lawrenceburg
1	n/a	Lebanon City Elementary SD	Lebanon
1	n/a	Lenoir City SD	Lenoir City
1	n/a	Lewis County SD	Hohenwald
1	n/a	Lincoln County SD	Fayetteville
1	n/a	Loudon County SD	Loudon
1	n/a	Macon County SD	Lafayette
1	n/a	Marion County SD	Jasper
1	n/a	Marshall County School Distrct	Lewisburg
1	n/a	Maryville City SD	Maryville
1	n/a	Maury County SD	Columbia
1	n/a	Mcminn County SD	Athens
1	n/a	Mcnairy County SD	Selmer
1	n/a	Meigs County SD	Decatur
1	n/a	Memphis City SD	Memphis
1	n/a	Milan City Special SD	Milan
1	n/a	Monroe County SD	Madisonville
1	n/a	Montgomery County Schools	Clarksville
1	n/a	Morgan County SD	Wartburg
1	n/a	Murfreesboro City Elem SD	Murfreesboro
1	n/a	Nashville-Davidson County SD	Nashville
1	n/a	Oak Ridge City SD	Oak Ridge
1	n/a	Obion County SD	Union City
1	n/a	Overton County SD	Livingston
1	n/a	Polk County SD	Benton
1	n/a	Putnam County SD	Cookeville
1	n/a	Rhea County SD	Dayton
1	n/a	Roane County SD	Kingston
1	n/a	Robertson County SD	Springfield
1	n/a	Rutherford County SD	Murfreesboro
1	n/a	Scott County SD	Huntsville
1	n/a	Sequatchie County SD	Dunlap
1	n/a	Sevier County SD	Sevierville
1	n/a	Shelby County SD	Memphis
1	n/a	Smith County SD	Carthage
1	n/a	Stewart County SD	Dover
1	n/a	Sullivan County School Distrct	Blountville
1	n/a	Sumner County SD	Gallatin
1	n/a	Tipton County SD	Covington
1	n/a	Tullahoma City SD	Tullahoma
1	n/a	Unicoi SD	Erwin
1	n/a	Union County SD	Maynardville
1	n/a	Warren County SD	Mcminnville
1	n/a	Washington County SD	Jonesborough
1	n/a	Wayne County SD	Waynesboro
1	n/a	Weakley County SD	Dresden
1	n/a	White County SD	Sparta
1	n/a	Williamson County SD	Franklin
1	n/a	Wilson County SD	Lebanon

Individual Education Program Students

Rank	Percent	District Name	City
1	29.8	Bledsoe County SD	Pikeville
2	29.2	Unicoi SD	Erwin
3	28.8	Grundy County SD	Altamont
4	28.6	Oak Ridge City SD	Oak Ridge
5	26.5	Greeneville City SD	Greeneville
6	26.3	Anderson County School Distrct	Clinton
7	24.9	Warren County SD	Mcminnville
8	24.8	Dekalb County SD	Smithville
9	24.5	Dyer County SD	Dyersburg
10	24.1	Union County SD	Maynardville
11	24.0	Sequatchie County SD	Dunlap
12	23.9	Lauderdale County SD	Ripley
13	23.8	Jackson-Madison Consolidated	Jackson
13	23.8	Overton County SD	Livingston
15	23.7	Hawkins County SD	Rogersville
16	23.3	Greene County SD	Greeneville
17	23.0	Claiborne County SD	Tazewell
18	22.9	Dickson County SD	Dickson
19	22.4	Shelby County SD	Memphis
20	21.9	Hickman County SD	Centerville
20	21.9	Jefferson County SD	Dandridge
20	21.9	Sullivan County School Distrct	Blountville
23	21.7	Hardeman County School Distrct	Bolivar
24	21.6	Grainger County School Distrct	Rutledge
25	21.4	Johnson County SD	Mountain City
25	21.4	Roane County SD	Kingston
25	21.4	Stewart County SD	Dover
25	21.4	Wayne County SD	Waynesboro
29	21.3	Hamilton County School Distrct	Chattanooga
29	21.3	Robertson County SD	Springfield

31	21.2	Franklin County School Distrct	Winchester
32	21.1	Benton County SD	Camden
33	21.0	Tullahoma City SD	Tullahoma
34	20.9	Mcminn County SD	Athens
34	20.9	Putnam County SD	Cookeville
36	20.8	Blount County SD	Maryville
36	20.8	Cannon County SD	Woodbury
38	20.5	Coffee County SD	Manchester
38	20.5	Lawrence County School Distrct	Lawrenceburg
40	20.3	Athens City Elementary SD	Athens
41	20.2	Jackson County SD	Gainsboro
42	20.1	Franklin City Elementary SD	Franklin
43	19.9	Sumner County SD	Gallatin
44	19.8	Fayette County SD	Somerville
44	19.8	Humphreys County SD	Waverly
44	19.8	Morgan County SD	Wartburg
47	19.7	Johnson City SD	Johnson City
47	19.7	Nashville-Davidson County SD	Nashville
49	19.6	Cumberland County SD	Crossville
50	19.5	Henderson County SD	Lexington
50	19.5	Obion County SD	Union City
52	19.4	Cocke County SD	Newport
53	19.3	Cleveland City SD	Cleveland
53	19.3	Maury County SD	Columbia
53	19.3	Sevier County SD	Sevierville
56	19.2	Carter County SD	Elizabethton
56	19.2	Meigs County SD	Decatur
58	19.1	White County SD	Sparta
59	19.0	Lebanon City Elementary SD	Lebanon
60	18.8	Haywood County SD	Brownsville
61	18.7	Gibson Special District	Dyer
61	18.7	Henry County SD	Paris
61	18.7	Milan City Special SD	Milan
61	18.7	Tipton County SD	Covington
65	18.4	Kingsport City SD	Kingsport
66	18.3	Marshall County School Distrct	Lewisburg
67	18.2	Fentress County School Distrct	Jamestown
67	18.2	Hardin County SD	Savannah
69	18.1	Dyersburg City SD	Dyersburg
69	18.1	Williamson County SD	Franklin
71	17.9	Weakley County SD	Dresden
72	17.7	Maryville City SD	Maryville
72	17.7	Monroe County SD	Madisonville
74	17.6	Marion County SD	Jasper
75	17.5	Rutherford County SD	Murfreesboro
76	17.4	Crockett County SD	Alamo
77	17.3	Smith County SD	Carthage
78	17.1	Campbell County School Distrct	Jacksboro
79	17.0	Giles County SD	Pulaski
79	17.0	Montgomery County Schools	Clarksville
81	16.9	Bristol City SD	Bristol
82	16.7	Washington County SD	Jonesborough
83	16.5	Lewis County SD	Hohenwald
84	16.3	Hamblen County SD	Morristown
85	16.2	Bedford County SD	Shelbyville
85	16.2	Elizabethton City SD	Elizabethton
85	16.2	Knox County SD	Knoxville
88	15.4	Lenoir City SD	Lenoir City
88	15.4	Lincoln County SD	Fayetteville
90	15.3	Macon County SD	Lafayette
91	14.8	Mcnairy County SD	Selmer
92	14.5	Murfreesboro City Elem SD	Murfreesboro
92	14.5	Scott County SD	Huntsville
94	14.2	Memphis City SD	Memphis
95	14.0	Cheatham County School Distrct	Ashland City
96	13.9	Bradley County SD	Cleveland
97	13.8	Rhea County SD	Dayton
98	13.7	Wilson County SD	Lebanon
99	13.0	Loudon County SD	Loudon
100	12.9	Polk County SD	Benton
101	10.8	Chester County SD	Henderson

English Language Learner Students

Rank	Percent	District Name	City
1	n/a	Anderson County School Distrct	Clinton
1	n/a	Athens City Elementary SD	Athens
1	n/a	Bedford County SD	Shelbyville
1	n/a	Benton County SD	Camden
1	n/a	Bledsoe County SD	Pikeville
1	n/a	Blount County SD	Maryville
1	n/a	Bradley County SD	Cleveland
1	n/a	Bristol City SD	Bristol
1	n/a	Campbell County School Distrct	Jacksboro
1	n/a	Cannon County SD	Woodbury
1	n/a	Carter County SD	Elizabethton
1	n/a	Cheatham County School Distrct	Ashland City
1	n/a	Chester County SD	Henderson
1	n/a	Claiborne County SD	Tazewell
1	n/a	Cleveland City SD	Cleveland
1	n/a	Cocke County SD	Newport
1	n/a	Coffee County SD	Manchester
1	n/a	Crockett County SD	Alamo
1	n/a	Cumberland County SD	Crossville
1	n/a	Dekalb County SD	Smithville
1	n/a	Dickson County SD	Dickson
1	n/a	Dyer County SD	Dyersburg
1	n/a	Dyersburg City SD	Dyersburg
1	n/a	Elizabethton City SD	Elizabethton
1	n/a	Fayette County SD	Somerville
1	n/a	Fentress County School Distrct	Jamestown
1	n/a	Franklin City Elementary SD	Franklin
1	n/a	Franklin County School Distrct	Winchester
1	n/a	Gibson Special District	Dyer
1	n/a	Giles County SD	Pulaski
1	n/a	Grainger County School Distrct	Rutledge
1	n/a	Greene County SD	Greeneville
1	n/a	Greeneville City SD	Greeneville
1	n/a	Grundy County SD	Altamont
1	n/a	Hamblen County SD	Morristown
1	n/a	Hamilton County School Distrct	Chattanooga
1	n/a	Hardeman County School Distrct	Bolivar
1	n/a	Hardin County SD	Savannah
1	n/a	Hawkins County SD	Rogersville
1	n/a	Haywood County SD	Brownsville
1	n/a	Henderson County SD	Lexington
1	n/a	Henry County SD	Paris
1	n/a	Hickman County SD	Centerville
1	n/a	Humphreys County SD	Waverly
1	n/a	Jackson County SD	Gainsboro
1	n/a	Jackson-Madison Consolidated	Jackson
1	n/a	Jefferson County SD	Dandridge
1	n/a	Johnson City SD	Johnson City
1	n/a	Johnson County SD	Mountain City
1	n/a	Kingsport City SD	Kingsport
1	n/a	Knox County SD	Knoxville
1	n/a	Lauderdale County SD	Ripley
1	n/a	Lawrence County School Distrct	Lawrenceburg
1	n/a	Lebanon City Elementary SD	Lebanon
1	n/a	Lenoir City SD	Lenoir City
1	n/a	Lewis County SD	Hohenwald
1	n/a	Lincoln County SD	Fayetteville
1	n/a	Loudon County SD	Loudon
1	n/a	Macon County SD	Lafayette
1	n/a	Marion County SD	Jasper
1	n/a	Marshall County School Distrct	Lewisburg
1	n/a	Maryville City SD	Maryville
1	n/a	Maury County SD	Columbia
1	n/a	Mcminn County SD	Athens
1	n/a	Mcnairy County SD	Selmer
1	n/a	Meigs County SD	Decatur
1	n/a	Memphis City SD	Memphis
1	n/a	Milan City Special SD	Milan
1	n/a	Monroe County SD	Madisonville
1	n/a	Montgomery County Schools	Clarksville
1	n/a	Morgan County SD	Wartburg
1	n/a	Murfreesboro City Elem SD	Murfreesboro
1	n/a	Nashville-Davidson County SD	Nashville
1	n/a	Oak Ridge City SD	Oak Ridge
1	n/a	Obion County SD	Union City
1	n/a	Overton County SD	Livingston
1	n/a	Polk County SD	Benton
1	n/a	Putnam County SD	Cookeville
1	n/a	Rhea County SD	Dayton
1	n/a	Roane County SD	Kingston
1	n/a	Robertson County SD	Springfield
1	n/a	Rutherford County SD	Murfreesboro
1	n/a	Scott County SD	Huntsville
1	n/a	Sequatchie County SD	Dunlap
1	n/a	Sevier County SD	Sevierville
1	n/a	Shelby County SD	Memphis
1	n/a	Smith County SD	Carthage
1	n/a	Stewart County SD	Dover
1	n/a	Sullivan County School Distrct	Blountville
1	n/a	Sumner County SD	Gallatin
1	n/a	Tipton County SD	Covington
1	n/a	Tullahoma City SD	Tullahoma
1	n/a	Unicoi SD	Erwin
1	n/a	Union County SD	Maynardville
1	n/a	Warren County SD	Mcminnville
1	n/a	Washington County SD	Jonesborough
1	n/a	Wayne County SD	Waynesboro
1	n/a	Weakley County SD	Dresden
1	n/a	White County SD	Sparta
1	n/a	Williamson County SD	Franklin
1	n/a	Wilson County SD	Lebanon

Migrant Students

Rank	Percent	District Name	City
1	n/a	Anderson County School Distrct	Clinton
1	n/a	Athens City Elementary SD	Athens
1	n/a	Bedford County SD	Shelbyville
1	n/a	Benton County SD	Camden
1	n/a	Bledsoe County SD	Pikeville
1	n/a	Blount County SD	Maryville
1	n/a	Bradley County SD	Cleveland
1	n/a	Bristol City SD	Bristol
1	n/a	Campbell County School Distrct	Jacksboro
1	n/a	Cannon County SD	Woodbury
1	n/a	Carter County SD	Elizabethton
1	n/a	Cheatham County School Distrct	Ashland City
1	n/a	Chester County SD	Henderson
1	n/a	Claiborne County SD	Tazewell
1	n/a	Cleveland City SD	Cleveland
1	n/a	Cocke County SD	Newport
1	n/a	Coffee County SD	Manchester
1	n/a	Crockett County SD	Alamo
1	n/a	Cumberland County SD	Crossville
1	n/a	Dekalb County SD	Smithville
1	n/a	Dickson County SD	Dickson
1	n/a	Dyer County SD	Dyersburg
1	n/a	Dyersburg City SD	Dyersburg
1	n/a	Elizabethton City SD	Elizabethton
1	n/a	Fayette County SD	Somerville
1	n/a	Fentress County School Distrct	Jamestown
1	n/a	Franklin City Elementary SD	Franklin
1	n/a	Franklin County School Distrct	Winchester
1	n/a	Gibson Special District	Dyer
1	n/a	Giles County SD	Pulaski
1	n/a	Grainger County School Distrct	Rutledge
1	n/a	Greene County SD	Greeneville
1	n/a	Greeneville City SD	Greeneville
1	n/a	Grundy County SD	Altamont
1	n/a	Hamblen County SD	Morristown
1	n/a	Hamilton County School Distrct	Chattanooga
1	n/a	Hardeman County School Distrct	Bolivar
1	n/a	Hardin County SD	Savannah
1	n/a	Hawkins County SD	Rogersville
1	n/a	Haywood County SD	Brownsville
1	n/a	Henderson County SD	Lexington
1	n/a	Henry County SD	Paris
1	n/a	Hickman County SD	Centerville
1	n/a	Humphreys County SD	Waverly
1	n/a	Jackson County SD	Gainsboro
1	n/a	Jackson-Madison Consolidated	Jackson
1	n/a	Jefferson County SD	Dandridge
1	n/a	Johnson City SD	Johnson City
1	n/a	Johnson County SD	Mountain City
1	n/a	Kingsport City SD	Kingsport
1	n/a	Knox County SD	Knoxville
1	n/a	Lauderdale County SD	Ripley
1	n/a	Lawrence County School Distrct	Lawrenceburg
1	n/a	Lebanon City Elementary SD	Lebanon
1	n/a	Lenoir City SD	Lenoir City
1	n/a	Lewis County SD	Hohenwald
1	n/a	Lincoln County SD	Fayetteville
1	n/a	Loudon County SD	Loudon
1	n/a	Macon County SD	Lafayette
1	n/a	Marion County SD	Jasper
1	n/a	Marshall County School Distrct	Lewisburg
1	n/a	Maryville City SD	Maryville
1	n/a	Maury County SD	Columbia
1	n/a	Mcminn County SD	Athens
1	n/a	Mcnairy County SD	Selmer
1	n/a	Meigs County SD	Decatur
1	n/a	Memphis City SD	Memphis
1	n/a	Milan City Special SD	Milan
1	n/a	Monroe County SD	Madisonville
1	n/a	Montgomery County Schools	Clarksville
1	n/a	Morgan County SD	Wartburg
1	n/a	Murfreesboro City Elem SD	Murfreesboro
1	n/a	Nashville-Davidson County SD	Nashville
1	n/a	Oak Ridge City SD	Oak Ridge
1	n/a	Obion County SD	Union City
1	n/a	Overton County SD	Livingston
1	n/a	Polk County SD	Benton
1	n/a	Putnam County SD	Cookeville
1	n/a	Rhea County SD	Dayton
1	n/a	Roane County SD	Kingston
1	n/a	Robertson County SD	Springfield
1	n/a	Rutherford County SD	Murfreesboro
1	n/a	Scott County SD	Huntsville
1	n/a	Sequatchie County SD	Dunlap
1	n/a	Sevier County SD	Sevierville
1	n/a	Shelby County SD	Memphis
1	n/a	Smith County SD	Carthage
1	n/a	Stewart County SD	Dover
1	n/a	Sullivan County School Distrct	Blountville
1	n/a	Sumner County SD	Gallatin
1	n/a	Tipton County SD	Covington
1	n/a	Tullahoma City SD	Tullahoma
1	n/a	Unicoi SD	Erwin
1	n/a	Union County SD	Maynardville
1	n/a	Warren County SD	Mcminnville
1	n/a	Washington County SD	Jonesborough
1	n/a	Wayne County SD	Waynesboro
1	n/a	Weakley County SD	Dresden

1	n/a	White County SD	Sparta
1	n/a	Williamson County SD	Franklin
1	n/a	Wilson County SD	Lebanon

Students Eligible for Free Lunch

Rank	Percent	District Name	City
1	n/a	Anderson County School Distrct	Clinton
1	n/a	Athens City Elementary SD	Athens
1	n/a	Bedford County SD	Shelbyville
1	n/a	Benton County SD	Camden
1	n/a	Bledsoe County SD	Pikeville
1	n/a	Blount County SD	Maryville
1	n/a	Bradley County SD	Cleveland
1	n/a	Bristol City SD	Bristol
1	n/a	Campbell County School Distrct	Jacksboro
1	n/a	Cannon County SD	Woodbury
1	n/a	Carter County SD	Elizabethton
1	n/a	Cheatham County School Distrct	Ashland City
1	n/a	Chester County SD	Henderson
1	n/a	Claiborne County SD	Tazewell
1	n/a	Cleveland City SD	Cleveland
1	n/a	Cocke County SD	Newport
1	n/a	Coffee County SD	Manchester
1	n/a	Crockett County SD	Alamo
1	n/a	Cumberland County SD	Crossville
1	n/a	Dekalb County SD	Smithville
1	n/a	Dickson County SD	Dickson
1	n/a	Dyer County SD	Dyersburg
1	n/a	Dyersburg City SD	Dyersburg
1	n/a	Elizabethton City SD	Elizabethton
1	n/a	Fayette County SD	Somerville
1	n/a	Fentress County School Distrct	Jamestown
1	n/a	Franklin City Elementary SD	Franklin
1	n/a	Franklin County School Distrct	Winchester
1	n/a	Gibson Special District	Dyer
1	n/a	Giles County SD	Pulaski
1	n/a	Grainger County School Distrct	Rutledge
1	n/a	Greene County SD	Greeneville
1	n/a	Greeneville City SD	Greeneville
1	n/a	Grundy County SD	Altamont
1	n/a	Hamblen County SD	Morristown
1	n/a	Hamilton County School Distrct	Chattanooga
1	n/a	Hardeman County School Distrct	Bolivar
1	n/a	Hardin County SD	Savannah
1	n/a	Hawkins County SD	Rogersville
1	n/a	Haywood County SD	Brownsville
1	n/a	Henderson County SD	Lexington
1	n/a	Henry County SD	Paris
1	n/a	Hickman County SD	Centerville
1	n/a	Humphreys County SD	Waverly
1	n/a	Jackson County SD	Gainsboro
1	n/a	Jackson-Madison Consolidated	Jackson
1	n/a	Jefferson County SD	Dandridge
1	n/a	Johnson City SD	Johnson City
1	n/a	Johnson County SD	Mountain City
1	n/a	Kingsport City SD	Kingsport
1	n/a	Knox County SD	Knoxville
1	n/a	Lauderdale County SD	Ripley
1	n/a	Lawrence County School Distrct	Lawrenceburg
1	n/a	Lebanon City Elementary SD	Lebanon
1	n/a	Lenoir City SD	Lenoir City
1	n/a	Lewis County SD	Hohenwald
1	n/a	Lincoln County SD	Fayetteville
1	n/a	Loudon County SD	Loudon
1	n/a	Macon County SD	Lafayette
1	n/a	Marion County SD	Jasper
1	n/a	Marshall County School Distrct	Lewisburg
1	n/a	Maryville City SD	Maryville
1	n/a	Maury County SD	Columbia
1	n/a	Mcminn County SD	Athens
1	n/a	Mcnairy County SD	Selmer
1	n/a	Meigs County SD	Decatur
1	n/a	Memphis City SD	Memphis
1	n/a	Milan City Special SD	Milan
1	n/a	Monroe County SD	Madisonville
1	n/a	Montgomery County Schools	Clarksville
1	n/a	Morgan County SD	Wartburg
1	n/a	Murfreesboro City Elem SD	Murfreesboro
1	n/a	Nashville-Davidson County SD	Nashville
1	n/a	Oak Ridge City SD	Oak Ridge
1	n/a	Obion County SD	Union City
1	n/a	Overton County SD	Livingston
1	n/a	Polk County SD	Benton
1	n/a	Putnam County SD	Cookeville
1	n/a	Rhea County SD	Dayton
1	n/a	Roane County SD	Kingston
1	n/a	Robertson County SD	Springfield
1	n/a	Rutherford County SD	Murfreesboro
1	n/a	Scott County SD	Huntsville
1	n/a	Sequatchie County SD	Dunlap
1	n/a	Sevier County SD	Sevierville
1	n/a	Shelby County SD	Memphis
1	n/a	Smith County SD	Carthage
1	n/a	Stewart County SD	Dover
1	n/a	Sullivan County School Distrct	Blountville
1	n/a	Sumner County SD	Gallatin
1	n/a	Tipton County SD	Covington
1	n/a	Tullahoma City SD	Tullahoma
1	n/a	Unicoi SD	Erwin
1	n/a	Union County SD	Maynardville
1	n/a	Warren County SD	Mcminnville
1	n/a	Washington County SD	Jonesborough
1	n/a	Wayne County SD	Waynesboro
1	n/a	Weakley County SD	Dresden
1	n/a	White County SD	Sparta
1	n/a	Williamson County SD	Franklin
1	n/a	Wilson County SD	Lebanon

Students Eligible for Reduced-Price Lunch

Rank	Percent	District Name	City
1	n/a	Anderson County School Distrct	Clinton
1	n/a	Athens City Elementary SD	Athens
1	n/a	Bedford County SD	Shelbyville
1	n/a	Benton County SD	Camden
1	n/a	Bledsoe County SD	Pikeville
1	n/a	Blount County SD	Maryville
1	n/a	Bradley County SD	Cleveland
1	n/a	Bristol City SD	Bristol
1	n/a	Campbell County School Distrct	Jacksboro
1	n/a	Cannon County SD	Woodbury
1	n/a	Carter County SD	Elizabethton
1	n/a	Cheatham County School Distrct	Ashland City
1	n/a	Chester County SD	Henderson
1	n/a	Claiborne County SD	Tazewell
1	n/a	Cleveland City SD	Cleveland
1	n/a	Cocke County SD	Newport
1	n/a	Coffee County SD	Manchester
1	n/a	Crockett County SD	Alamo
1	n/a	Cumberland County SD	Crossville
1	n/a	Dekalb County SD	Smithville
1	n/a	Dickson County SD	Dickson
1	n/a	Dyer County SD	Dyersburg
1	n/a	Dyersburg City SD	Dyersburg
1	n/a	Elizabethton City SD	Elizabethton
1	n/a	Fayette County SD	Somerville
1	n/a	Fentress County School Distrct	Jamestown
1	n/a	Franklin City Elementary SD	Franklin
1	n/a	Franklin County School Distrct	Winchester
1	n/a	Gibson Special District	Dyer
1	n/a	Giles County SD	Pulaski
1	n/a	Grainger County School Distrct	Rutledge
1	n/a	Greene County SD	Greeneville
1	n/a	Greeneville City SD	Greeneville
1	n/a	Grundy County SD	Altamont
1	n/a	Hamblen County SD	Morristown
1	n/a	Hamilton County School Distrct	Chattanooga
1	n/a	Hardeman County School Distrct	Bolivar
1	n/a	Hardin County SD	Savannah
1	n/a	Hawkins County SD	Rogersville
1	n/a	Haywood County SD	Brownsville
1	n/a	Henderson County SD	Lexington
1	n/a	Henry County SD	Paris
1	n/a	Hickman County SD	Centerville
1	n/a	Humphreys County SD	Waverly
1	n/a	Jackson County SD	Gainsboro
1	n/a	Jackson-Madison Consolidated	Jackson
1	n/a	Jefferson County SD	Dandridge
1	n/a	Johnson City SD	Johnson City
1	n/a	Johnson County SD	Mountain City
1	n/a	Kingsport City SD	Kingsport
1	n/a	Knox County SD	Knoxville
1	n/a	Lauderdale County SD	Ripley
1	n/a	Lawrence County School Distrct	Lawrenceburg
1	n/a	Lebanon City Elementary SD	Lebanon
1	n/a	Lenoir City SD	Lenoir City
1	n/a	Lewis County SD	Hohenwald
1	n/a	Lincoln County SD	Fayetteville
1	n/a	Loudon County SD	Loudon
1	n/a	Macon County SD	Lafayette
1	n/a	Marion County SD	Jasper
1	n/a	Marshall County School Distrct	Lewisburg
1	n/a	Maryville City SD	Maryville
1	n/a	Maury County SD	Columbia
1	n/a	Mcminn County SD	Athens
1	n/a	Mcnairy County SD	Selmer
1	n/a	Meigs County SD	Decatur
1	n/a	Memphis City SD	Memphis
1	n/a	Milan City Special SD	Milan
1	n/a	Monroe County SD	Madisonville
1	n/a	Montgomery County Schools	Clarksville
1	n/a	Morgan County SD	Wartburg
1	n/a	Murfreesboro City Elem SD	Murfreesboro
1	n/a	Nashville-Davidson County SD	Nashville
1	n/a	Oak Ridge City SD	Oak Ridge
1	n/a	Obion County SD	Union City
1	n/a	Overton County SD	Livingston
1	n/a	Polk County SD	Benton
1	n/a	Putnam County SD	Cookeville
1	n/a	Rhea County SD	Dayton
1	n/a	Roane County SD	Kingston
1	n/a	Robertson County SD	Springfield
1	n/a	Rutherford County SD	Murfreesboro
1	n/a	Scott County SD	Huntsville
1	n/a	Sequatchie County SD	Dunlap
1	n/a	Sevier County SD	Sevierville
1	n/a	Shelby County SD	Memphis
1	n/a	Smith County SD	Carthage
1	n/a	Stewart County SD	Dover
1	n/a	Sullivan County School Distrct	Blountville
1	n/a	Sumner County SD	Gallatin
1	n/a	Tipton County SD	Covington
1	n/a	Tullahoma City SD	Tullahoma
1	n/a	Unicoi SD	Erwin
1	n/a	Union County SD	Maynardville
1	n/a	Warren County SD	Mcminnville
1	n/a	Washington County SD	Jonesborough
1	n/a	Wayne County SD	Waynesboro
1	n/a	Weakley County SD	Dresden
1	n/a	White County SD	Sparta
1	n/a	Williamson County SD	Franklin
1	n/a	Wilson County SD	Lebanon

Student/Teacher Ratio

Rank	Ratio	District Name	City
1	21.7	Polk County SD	Benton
2	17.7	Chester County SD	Henderson
2	17.7	Shelby County SD	Memphis
4	17.2	Cumberland County SD	Crossville
4	17.2	Loudon County SD	Loudon
4	17.2	Monroe County SD	Madisonville
7	16.9	Wilson County SD	Lebanon
8	16.8	Blount County SD	Maryville
8	16.8	Stewart County SD	Dover
10	16.7	Mcminn County SD	Athens
11	16.6	Campbell County School Distrct	Jacksboro
11	16.6	Macon County SD	Lafayette
11	16.6	Tipton County SD	Covington
14	16.5	Rutherford County SD	Murfreesboro
14	16.5	Unicoi SD	Erwin
16	16.4	Bradley County SD	Cleveland
16	16.4	Marshall County School Distrct	Lewisburg
18	16.3	Gibson Special District	Dyer
18	16.3	Grainger County School Distrct	Rutledge
20	16.2	Dyersburg City SD	Dyersburg
20	16.2	Lenoir City SD	Lenoir City
20	16.2	Washington County SD	Jonesborough
23	16.1	Williamson County SD	Franklin
24	16.0	Jefferson County SD	Dandridge
24	16.0	Memphis City SD	Memphis
24	16.0	Montgomery County Schools	Clarksville
27	15.9	Meigs County SD	Decatur
28	15.8	Hickman County SD	Centerville
28	15.8	Maryville City SD	Maryville
28	15.8	Smith County SD	Carthage
31	15.7	Bedford County SD	Shelbyville
31	15.7	Cheatham County School Distrct	Ashland City
33	15.6	Dyer County SD	Dyersburg
33	15.6	Lincoln County SD	Fayetteville
33	15.6	Rhea County SD	Dayton
33	15.6	Tullahoma City SD	Tullahoma
33	15.6	White County SD	Sparta
38	15.5	Athens City Elementary SD	Athens
38	15.5	Greene County SD	Greeneville
38	15.5	Obion County SD	Union City
38	15.5	Robertson County SD	Springfield
38	15.5	Sevier County SD	Sevierville
43	15.4	Dickson County SD	Dickson
43	15.4	Hamblen County SD	Morristown
43	15.4	Roane County SD	Kingston
46	15.3	Johnson City SD	Johnson City
46	15.3	Sullivan County School Distrct	Blountville
48	15.2	Crockett County SD	Alamo
48	15.2	Giles County SD	Pulaski
48	15.2	Henry County SD	Paris
48	15.2	Humphreys County SD	Waverly
48	15.2	Lewis County SD	Hohenwald
48	15.2	Marion County SD	Jasper
48	15.2	Sumner County SD	Gallatin
55	15.1	Coffee County SD	Manchester
55	15.1	Murfreesboro City Elem SD	Murfreesboro
55	15.1	Putnam County SD	Cookeville
58	15.0	Cocke County SD	Newport
58	15.0	Weakley County SD	Dresden
60	14.9	Lauderdale County SD	Ripley

60	14.9	Milan City Special SD	Milan
60	14.9	Overton County SD	Livingston
63	14.8	Bledsoe County SD	Pikeville
64	14.7	Franklin County School Distrct	Winchester
64	14.7	Lebanon City Elementary SD	Lebanon
66	14.6	Hamilton County School Distrct	Chattanooga
66	14.6	Henderson County SD	Lexington
66	14.6	Knox County SD	Knoxville
66	14.6	Lawrence County School Distrct	Lawrenceburg
66	14.6	Maury County SD	Columbia
66	14.6	Mcnairy County SD	Selmer
72	14.5	Cannon County SD	Woodbury
72	14.5	Haywood County SD	Brownsville
72	14.5	Warren County SD	Mcminnville
75	14.4	Bristol City SD	Bristol
75	14.4	Cleveland City SD	Cleveland
75	14.4	Dekalb County SD	Smithville
75	14.4	Elizabethton City SD	Elizabethton
75	14.4	Kingsport City SD	Kingsport
75	14.4	Morgan County SD	Wartburg
81	14.3	Hawkins County SD	Rogersville
81	14.3	Jackson County SD	Gainsboro
83	14.2	Johnson County SD	Mountain City
83	14.2	Sequatchie County SD	Dunlap
85	14.1	Nashville-Davidson County SD	Nashville
85	14.1	Union County SD	Maynardville
87	14.0	Hardin County SD	Savannah
88	13.9	Fentress County School Distrct	Jamestown
88	13.9	Greeneville City SD	Greeneville
90	13.8	Benton County SD	Camden
91	13.7	Anderson County School Distrct	Clinton
92	13.6	Jackson-Madison Consolidated	Jackson
93	13.4	Carter County SD	Elizabethton
93	13.4	Hardeman County School Distrct	Bolivar
95	13.3	Claiborne County SD	Tazewell
96	13.2	Oak Ridge City SD	Oak Ridge
97	13.1	Scott County SD	Huntsville
97	13.1	Wayne County SD	Waynesboro
99	12.5	Franklin City Elementary SD	Franklin
100	12.4	Fayette County SD	Somerville
101	12.3	Grundy County SD	Altamont

Student/Librarian Ratio

Rank	Ratio	District Name	City
1	1,165.0	Polk County SD	Benton
2	1,127.5	Grundy County SD	Altamont
3	1,068.3	Dyer County SD	Dyersburg
4	1,013.9	Tipton County SD	Covington
5	920.5	Meigs County SD	Decatur
6	891.0	Crockett County SD	Alamo
7	837.4	Shelby County SD	Memphis
8	784.0	Cumberland County SD	Crossville
9	767.2	Rhea County SD	Dayton
10	764.4	Johnson City SD	Johnson City
11	763.5	Union County SD	Maynardville
12	751.8	Lebanon City Elementary SD	Lebanon
13	738.2	Rutherford County SD	Murfreesboro
14	737.8	Wilson County SD	Lebanon
15	712.1	Montgomery County Schools	Clarksville
16	711.0	Dyersburg City SD	Dyersburg
17	702.0	Stewart County SD	Dover
18	692.6	Memphis City SD	Memphis
19	676.7	Lenoir City SD	Lenoir City
20	667.2	Grainger County School Distrct	Rutledge
21	656.9	Maryville City SD	Maryville
22	650.0	Morgan County SD	Wartburg
23	648.9	Dickson County SD	Dickson
24	646.2	Robertson County SD	Springfield
25	639.6	Jefferson County SD	Dandridge
26	638.0	Sequatchie County SD	Dunlap
27	636.8	Sevier County SD	Sevierville
28	634.2	Greene County SD	Greeneville
29	631.0	Chester County SD	Henderson
29	631.0	Henry County SD	Paris
31	628.8	Smith County SD	Carthage
32	622.4	Maury County SD	Columbia
33	620.9	Overton County SD	Livingston
34	619.7	Claiborne County SD	Tazewell
35	618.5	Williamson County SD	Franklin
36	612.3	Bradley County SD	Cleveland
37	608.1	Bedford County SD	Shelbyville
38	600.1	Sumner County SD	Gallatin
39	599.9	Warren County SD	Mcminnville
40	599.6	Campbell County School Distrct	Jacksboro
41	598.0	Bledsoe County SD	Pikeville
42	596.5	Murfreesboro City Elem SD	Murfreesboro
43	592.3	Knox County SD	Knoxville
44	591.6	Blount County SD	Maryville
45	582.9	Mcminn County SD	Athens
45	582.9	Washington County SD	Jonesborough
47	580.1	Kingsport City SD	Kingsport
48	576.9	Nashville-Davidson County SD	Nashville
49	568.0	Lauderdale County SD	Ripley
50	566.6	Obion County SD	Union City
51	558.1	Hardeman County School Distrct	Bolivar
52	556.9	White County SD	Sparta
53	556.0	Jackson County SD	Gainsboro
54	549.1	Cleveland City SD	Cleveland
55	545.0	Oak Ridge City SD	Oak Ridge
56	544.7	Hickman County SD	Centerville
57	539.1	Loudon County SD	Loudon
58	537.5	Bristol City SD	Bristol
59	536.6	Marshall County School Distrct	Lewisburg
60	534.0	Cannon County SD	Woodbury
61	529.5	Jackson-Madison Consolidated	Jackson
62	529.1	Mcnairy County SD	Selmer
63	528.4	Cheatham County School Distrct	Ashland City
64	526.2	Anderson County School Distrct	Clinton
65	518.8	Monroe County SD	Madisonville
66	516.8	Dekalb County SD	Smithville
67	516.2	Lawrence County School Distrct	Lawrenceburg
68	516.1	Coffee County SD	Manchester
69	508.0	Unicoi SD	Erwin
70	506.7	Macon County SD	Lafayette
71	505.5	Milan City Special SD	Milan
72	501.6	Haywood County SD	Brownsville
73	500.9	Weakley County SD	Dresden
74	500.0	Humphreys County SD	Waverly
75	493.1	Roane County SD	Kingston
76	492.3	Lewis County SD	Hohenwald
77	489.0	Hamilton County School Distrct	Chattanooga
78	487.6	Benton County SD	Camden
79	481.3	Franklin County School Distrct	Winchester
80	474.6	Sullivan County School Distrct	Blountville
81	471.4	Putnam County SD	Cookeville
82	469.1	Hardin County SD	Savannah
83	462.9	Franklin City Elementary SD	Franklin
84	457.3	Hamblen County SD	Morristown
85	457.0	Johnson County SD	Mountain City
86	455.8	Marion County SD	Jasper
87	452.2	Hawkins County SD	Rogersville
88	450.6	Carter County SD	Elizabethton
89	450.4	Fentress County School Distrct	Jamestown
90	449.8	Cocke County SD	Newport
91	449.6	Tullahoma City SD	Tullahoma
92	446.0	Greeneville City SD	Greeneville
93	443.2	Giles County SD	Pulaski
94	440.0	Gibson Special District	Dyer
95	437.0	Scott County SD	Huntsville
96	398.6	Lincoln County SD	Fayetteville
97	392.9	Wayne County SD	Waynesboro
98	375.8	Henderson County SD	Lexington
99	368.2	Elizabethton City SD	Elizabethton
100	336.0	Athens City Elementary SD	Athens
101	321.3	Fayette County SD	Somerville

Student/Counselor Ratio

Rank	Ratio	District Name	City
1	1,747.5	Polk County SD	Benton
2	751.7	Grundy County SD	Altamont
3	743.5	Tipton County SD	Covington
4	725.2	Grainger County School Distrct	Rutledge
5	669.8	Cumberland County SD	Crossville
6	655.5	Scott County SD	Huntsville
7	641.0	Dyer County SD	Dyersburg
8	638.5	Wayne County SD	Waynesboro
9	638.0	Sequatchie County SD	Dunlap
10	631.0	Chester County SD	Henderson
11	628.8	Smith County SD	Carthage
12	623.3	Union County SD	Maynardville
13	616.4	Roane County SD	Kingston
14	604.7	Mcnairy County SD	Selmer
15	601.7	Stewart County SD	Dover
16	601.4	Lebanon City Elementary SD	Lebanon
17	599.6	Campbell County School Distrct	Jacksboro
18	599.0	Loudon County SD	Loudon
19	598.0	Bledsoe County SD	Pikeville
20	594.0	Crockett County SD	Alamo
21	592.5	Dyersburg City SD	Dyersburg
22	591.2	Macon County SD	Lafayette
23	587.5	Robertson County SD	Springfield
24	568.1	Knox County SD	Knoxville
25	563.0	Fentress County School Distrct	Jamestown
26	556.0	Jackson County SD	Gainsboro
27	548.8	Marshall County School Distrct	Lewisburg
28	548.0	Rhea County SD	Dayton
29	541.7	Morgan County SD	Wartburg
30	537.2	Dickson County SD	Dickson
31	529.9	Mcminn County SD	Athens
32	528.0	Gibson Special District	Dyer
33	525.7	Memphis City SD	Memphis
34	522.6	Hamblen County SD	Morristown
35	518.8	Monroe County SD	Madisonville
36	516.8	Dekalb County SD	Smithville
37	516.2	Lawrence County School Distrct	Lawrenceburg
38	514.9	Shelby County SD	Memphis
39	514.5	Bedford County SD	Shelbyville
40	514.4	Washington County SD	Jonesborough
41	508.0	Unicoi SD	Erwin
42	507.8	Johnson County SD	Mountain City
43	505.3	Sumner County SD	Gallatin
44	504.9	Lauderdale County SD	Ripley
44	504.9	Lewis County SD	Hohenwald
46	501.6	Haywood County SD	Brownsville
47	500.0	Humphreys County SD	Waverly
48	498.3	Greene County SD	Greeneville
49	497.1	Murfreesboro City Elem SD	Murfreesboro
50	496.1	Hardeman County School Distrct	Bolivar
51	495.8	Obion County SD	Union City
52	492.2	Rutherford County SD	Murfreesboro
53	491.4	Johnson City SD	Johnson City
54	488.2	Carter County SD	Elizabethton
55	487.1	Kingsport City SD	Kingsport
56	481.3	Franklin County School Distrct	Winchester
57	477.0	Marion County SD	Jasper
58	476.6	Hickman County SD	Centerville
59	474.7	Sevier County SD	Sevierville
60	473.8	Blount County SD	Maryville
61	469.0	Hamilton County School Distrct	Chattanooga
62	461.6	Montgomery County Schools	Clarksville
63	459.0	Fayette County SD	Somerville
64	452.2	Hawkins County SD	Rogersville
65	447.9	Lincoln County SD	Fayetteville
66	445.6	Maury County SD	Columbia
67	443.2	Giles County SD	Pulaski
68	437.3	Bradley County SD	Cleveland
69	436.3	Sullivan County School Distrct	Blountville
70	433.1	White County SD	Sparta
71	432.6	Weakley County SD	Dresden
72	431.4	Williamson County SD	Franklin
73	428.5	Warren County SD	Mcminnville
74	427.2	Cannon County SD	Woodbury
75	423.9	Jefferson County SD	Dandridge
76	420.0	Athens City Elementary SD	Athens
77	418.1	Wilson County SD	Lebanon
78	418.0	Maryville City SD	Maryville
79	412.9	Coffee County SD	Manchester
80	411.4	Overton County SD	Livingston
81	406.0	Lenoir City SD	Lenoir City
82	404.4	Milan City Special SD	Milan
83	400.3	Cocke County SD	Newport
84	399.7	Tullahoma City SD	Tullahoma
85	388.8	Jackson-Madison Consolidated	Jackson
86	380.3	Nashville-Davidson County SD	Nashville
87	380.0	Anderson County School Distrct	Clinton
88	375.8	Henderson County SD	Lexington
89	375.7	Meigs County SD	Decatur
90	375.1	Benton County SD	Camden
91	370.3	Franklin City Elementary SD	Franklin
92	368.2	Elizabethton City SD	Elizabethton
93	366.1	Cleveland City SD	Cleveland
94	365.5	Bristol City SD	Bristol
95	361.5	Cheatham County School Distrct	Ashland City
96	352.1	Claiborne County SD	Tazewell
97	350.7	Putnam County SD	Cookeville
98	350.6	Henry County SD	Paris
99	312.8	Hardin County SD	Savannah
100	290.7	Oak Ridge City SD	Oak Ridge
101	267.6	Greeneville City SD	Greeneville

Current Spending per Student in FY2003

Rank	Dollars	District Name	City
1	8,866	Oak Ridge City SD	Oak Ridge
2	8,599	Franklin City Elementary SD	Franklin
3	7,775	Greeneville City SD	Greeneville
4	7,614	Nashville-Davidson County SD	Nashville
5	7,540	Bristol City SD	Bristol
6	7,494	Maryville City SD	Maryville
7	7,276	Kingsport City SD	Kingsport
8	7,161	Fayette County SD	Somerville
9	7,005	Memphis City SD	Memphis
10	6,901	Hamilton County School Distrct	Chattanooga
11	6,816	Williamson County SD	Franklin
12	6,717	Cleveland City SD	Cleveland
13	6,638	Elizabethton City SD	Elizabethton
14	6,632	Dyer County SD	Dyersburg
15	6,547	Athens City Elementary SD	Athens
16	6,504	Jackson-Madison Consolidated	Jackson
17	6,489	Sullivan County School Distrct	Blountville
18	6,436	Maury County SD	Columbia
19	6,382	Johnson County SD	Mountain City
20	6,366	Johnson City SD	Johnson City
21	6,296	Anderson County School Distrct	Clinton
22	6,235	Sevier County SD	Sevierville
22	6,235	Tullahoma City SD	Tullahoma
24	6,179	Haywood County SD	Brownsville

25	6,158	Dyersburg City SD	Dyersburg
26	6,155	Scott County SD	Huntsville
27	6,149	Blount County SD	Maryville
28	6,148	Knox County SD	Knoxville
29	6,113	Wilson County SD	Lebanon
30	6,072	Roane County SD	Kingston
31	6,049	Carter County SD	Elizabethton
32	6,008	Hamblen County SD	Morristown
33	5,954	Murfreesboro City Elem SD	Murfreesboro
34	5,934	Lenoir City SD	Lenoir City
35	5,911	Jackson County SD	Gainsboro
36	5,910	Benton County SD	Camden
37	5,891	Shelby County SD	Memphis
38	5,872	Marshall County School Distrct	Lewisburg
39	5,853	Henry County SD	Paris
40	5,852	Dickson County SD	Dickson
41	5,824	Lebanon City Elementary SD	Lebanon
42	5,808	Bledsoe County SD	Pikeville
43	5,807	Jefferson County SD	Dandridge
44	5,800	Claiborne County SD	Tazewell
45	5,793	Grundy County SD	Altamont
46	5,788	Giles County SD	Pulaski
47	5,769	Hardin County SD	Savannah
48	5,751	Morgan County SD	Wartburg
49	5,740	Sumner County SD	Gallatin
50	5,734	Putnam County SD	Cookeville
51	5,690	Humphreys County SD	Waverly
52	5,666	Monroe County SD	Madisonville
53	5,659	Lawrence County School Distrct	Lawrenceburg
54	5,658	Hawkins County SD	Rogersville
54	5,658	Robertson County SD	Springfield
56	5,652	Polk County SD	Benton
57	5,625	Fentress County School Distrct	Jamestown
58	5,613	Loudon County SD	Loudon
59	5,611	Coffee County SD	Manchester
59	5,611	Warren County SD	Mcminnville
61	5,582	Stewart County SD	Dover
62	5,575	Franklin County School Distrct	Winchester
63	5,567	Obion County SD	Union City
64	5,549	Lauderdale County SD	Ripley
65	5,543	Cocke County SD	Newport
66	5,531	Campbell County School Distrct	Jacksboro
67	5,506	Union County SD	Maynardville
68	5,486	Milan City Special SD	Milan
69	5,483	Wayne County SD	Waynesboro
70	5,472	Marion County SD	Jasper
71	5,452	Overton County SD	Livingston
72	5,444	Grainger County School Distrct	Rutledge
73	5,428	Henderson County SD	Lexington
74	5,417	Cannon County SD	Woodbury
75	5,405	Greene County SD	Greeneville
76	5,367	Dekalb County SD	Smithville
77	5,363	Crockett County SD	Alamo
78	5,358	Cheatham County School Distrct	Ashland City
79	5,347	Tipton County SD	Covington
80	5,315	Lincoln County SD	Fayetteville
81	5,314	Cumberland County SD	Crossville
82	5,306	Unicoi SD	Erwin
83	5,301	Rutherford County SD	Murfreesboro
84	5,280	Mcnairy County SD	Selmer
85	5,279	Weakley County SD	Dresden
86	5,255	Sequatchie County SD	Dunlap
87	5,254	Washington County SD	Jonesborough
88	5,242	Bradley County SD	Cleveland
89	5,241	Mcminn County SD	Athens
90	5,213	Hickman County SD	Centerville
91	5,206	Hardeman County School Distrct	Bolivar
91	5,206	Meigs County SD	Decatur
93	5,170	Montgomery County Schools	Clarksville
94	5,143	Bedford County SD	Shelbyville
95	5,115	Macon County SD	Lafayette
96	5,029	Lewis County SD	Hohenwald
97	4,958	Smith County SD	Carthage
98	4,918	White County SD	Sparta
99	4,910	Gibson Special District	Dyer
100	4,831	Chester County SD	Henderson
101	4,775	Rhea County SD	Dayton

Number of Diploma Recipients

Rank	Number	District Name	City
1	3,933	Memphis City SD	Memphis
2	2,609	Nashville-Davidson County SD	Nashville
3	2,553	Knox County SD	Knoxville
4	2,550	Shelby County SD	Memphis
5	1,715	Hamilton County School Distrct	Chattanooga
6	1,506	Rutherford County SD	Murfreesboro
7	1,477	Sumner County SD	Gallatin
8	1,063	Montgomery County Schools	Clarksville
9	745	Williamson County SD	Franklin
10	683	Jackson-Madison Consolidated	Jackson
11	648	Wilson County SD	Lebanon
12	614	Sevier County SD	Sevierville
13	610	Sullivan County School Distrct	Blountville
14	522	Tipton County SD	Covington
15	509	Blount County SD	Maryville
16	490	Maury County SD	Columbia
17	434	Hamblen County SD	Morristown
18	431	Anderson County School Distrct	Clinton
19	425	Putnam County SD	Cookeville
20	410	Robertson County SD	Springfield
21	401	Bradley County SD	Cleveland
22	396	Dickson County SD	Dickson
23	387	Washington County SD	Jonesborough
24	383	Lawrence County School Distrct	Lawrenceburg
25	374	Jefferson County SD	Dandridge
26	351	Mcminn County SD	Athens
27	341	Warren County SD	Mcminnville
28	340	Johnson City SD	Johnson City
29	339	Greene County SD	Greeneville
30	332	Roane County SD	Kingston
31	329	Cheatham County School Distrct	Ashland City
32	323	Hawkins County SD	Rogersville
33	306	Franklin County School Distrct	Winchester
34	301	Cumberland County SD	Crossville
35	297	Kingsport City SD	Kingsport
36	281	Oak Ridge City SD	Oak Ridge
37	277	Cocke County SD	Newport
38	272	Bedford County SD	Shelbyville
39	270	Weakley County SD	Dresden
40	266	Lincoln County SD	Fayetteville
41	255	Campbell County School Distrct	Jacksboro
42	254	Coffee County SD	Manchester
43	246	Marshall County School Distrct	Lewisburg
44	243	Rhea County SD	Dayton
45	236	Tullahoma City SD	Tullahoma
46	233	Giles County SD	Pulaski
47	230	Maryville City SD	Maryville
48	221	Henry County SD	Paris
49	217	Hardin County SD	Savannah
50	206	Obion County SD	Union City
51	205	Bristol City SD	Bristol
52	202	White County SD	Sparta
53	201	Lenoir City SD	Lenoir City
54	197	Dyersburg City SD	Dyersburg
55	194	Dyer County SD	Dyersburg
56	193	Lauderdale County SD	Ripley
57	188	Macon County SD	Lafayette
57	188	Marion County SD	Jasper
59	186	Morgan County SD	Wartburg
60	185	Cleveland City SD	Cleveland
61	181	Mcnairy County SD	Selmer
61	181	Overton County SD	Livingston
63	179	Hardeman County School Distrct	Bolivar
64	175	Hickman County SD	Centerville
65	172	Claiborne County SD	Tazewell
66	170	Grainger County School Distrct	Rutledge
67	168	Elizabethton City SD	Elizabethton
68	162	Haywood County SD	Brownsville
69	161	Unicoi SD	Erwin
70	160	Loudon County SD	Loudon
70	160	Smith County SD	Carthage
72	159	Humphreys County SD	Waverly
73	150	Fentress County School Distrct	Jamestown
74	149	Carter County SD	Elizabethton
75	143	Wayne County SD	Waynesboro
76	141	Crockett County SD	Alamo
77	138	Fayette County SD	Somerville
78	126	Gibson Special District	Dyer
79	125	Johnson County SD	Mountain City
80	123	Grundy County SD	Altamont
80	123	Milan City Special SD	Milan
82	121	Greeneville City SD	Greeneville
83	111	Stewart County SD	Dover
84	108	Dekalb County SD	Smithville
85	105	Chester County SD	Henderson
85	105	Union County SD	Maynardville
87	99	Cannon County SD	Woodbury
88	98	Meigs County SD	Decatur
89	97	Scott County SD	Huntsville
90	95	Benton County SD	Camden
91	93	Lewis County SD	Hohenwald
92	91	Polk County SD	Benton
93	84	Monroe County SD	Madisonville
94	80	Sequatchie County SD	Dunlap
95	76	Jackson County SD	Gainsboro
96	55	Bledsoe County SD	Pikeville
96	55	Henderson County SD	Lexington
98	n/a	Athens City Elementary SD	Athens
98	n/a	Franklin City Elementary SD	Franklin
98	n/a	Lebanon City Elementary SD	Lebanon
98	n/a	Murfreesboro City Elem SD	Murfreesboro

High School Drop-out Rate

Rank	Percent	District Name	City
1	9.7	Fayette County SD	Somerville
2	8.6	Memphis City SD	Memphis
3	7.6	Nashville-Davidson County SD	Nashville
4	6.6	Hardeman County School Distrct	Bolivar
5	6.1	Lawrence County School Distrct	Lawrenceburg
6	5.8	Hamilton County School Distrct	Chattanooga
7	5.6	Lincoln County SD	Fayetteville
8	5.5	Dickson County SD	Dickson
9	5.4	Dyersburg City SD	Dyersburg
10	5.2	Franklin County School Distrct	Winchester
10	5.2	Polk County SD	Benton
12	5.1	Hawkins County SD	Rogersville
13	4.9	Bledsoe County SD	Pikeville
14	4.8	Jackson-Madison Consolidated	Jackson
15	4.3	Scott County SD	Huntsville
16	4.2	Giles County SD	Pulaski
16	4.2	Macon County SD	Lafayette
18	4.1	Haywood County SD	Brownsville
19	3.9	Lauderdale County SD	Ripley
19	3.9	Robertson County SD	Springfield
21	3.8	Blount County SD	Maryville
22	3.6	Oak Ridge City SD	Oak Ridge
22	3.6	Roane County SD	Kingston
22	3.6	Tipton County SD	Covington
25	3.5	Hardin County SD	Savannah
26	3.4	Bradley County SD	Cleveland
26	3.4	Loudon County SD	Loudon
28	3.3	Montgomery County Schools	Clarksville
28	3.3	Obion County SD	Union City
28	3.3	Sullivan County School Distrct	Blountville
31	3.2	Cumberland County SD	Crossville
31	3.2	Henderson County SD	Lexington
31	3.2	Johnson County SD	Mountain City
31	3.2	Washington County SD	Jonesborough
35	3.0	Knox County SD	Knoxville
36	2.9	Fentress County School Distrct	Jamestown
37	2.8	Henry County SD	Paris
37	2.8	Sequatchie County SD	Dunlap
39	2.7	Chester County SD	Henderson
39	2.7	Dekalb County SD	Smithville
39	2.7	Gibson Special District	Dyer
39	2.7	Marion County SD	Jasper
39	2.7	Maury County SD	Columbia
44	2.6	Anderson County School Distrct	Clinton
44	2.6	Lewis County SD	Hohenwald
44	2.6	Morgan County SD	Wartburg
44	2.6	Rhea County SD	Dayton
48	2.4	Cannon County SD	Woodbury
48	2.4	Marshall County School Distrct	Lewisburg
48	2.4	Monroe County SD	Madisonville
48	2.4	Sevier County SD	Sevierville
52	2.3	Bristol City SD	Bristol
52	2.3	Elizabethton City SD	Elizabethton
52	2.3	Wilson County SD	Lebanon
55	2.2	Bedford County SD	Shelbyville
55	2.2	Campbell County School Distrct	Jacksboro
55	2.2	Greene County SD	Greeneville
55	2.2	Rutherford County SD	Murfreesboro
55	2.2	Stewart County SD	Dover
55	2.2	Wayne County SD	Waynesboro
61	2.1	Lenoir City SD	Lenoir City
61	2.1	Mcminn County SD	Athens
61	2.1	Shelby County SD	Memphis
64	1.9	Carter County SD	Elizabethton
65	1.8	Hamblen County SD	Morristown
66	1.7	Crockett County SD	Alamo
66	1.7	Grundy County SD	Altamont
66	1.7	Kingsport City SD	Kingsport
66	1.7	Putnam County SD	Cookeville
66	1.7	Williamson County SD	Franklin
71	1.6	Jackson County SD	Gainsboro
71	1.6	Tullahoma City SD	Tullahoma
73	1.5	Humphreys County SD	Waverly
74	1.4	Mcnairy County SD	Selmer
74	1.4	Sumner County SD	Gallatin
74	1.4	Unicoi SD	Erwin
77	1.3	Coffee County SD	Manchester
77	1.3	Grainger County School Distrct	Rutledge
77	1.3	Hickman County SD	Centerville
80	1.2	Benton County SD	Camden
80	1.2	Dyer County SD	Dyersburg
80	1.2	Meigs County SD	Decatur
80	1.2	Smith County SD	Carthage
80	1.2	White County SD	Sparta
85	1.1	Claiborne County SD	Tazewell
85	1.1	Milan City Special SD	Milan
85	1.1	Overton County SD	Livingston
88	1.0	Weakley County SD	Dresden
89	0.9	Cleveland City SD	Cleveland
89	0.9	Greeneville City SD	Greeneville
91	0.8	Cocke County SD	Newport
91	0.8	Maryville City SD	Maryville

91	0.8	Warren County SD	Mcminnville
94	0.7	Cheatham County School Distrct	Ashland City
95	0.6	Union County SD	Maynardville
96	0.4	Jefferson County SD	Dandridge
96	0.4	Johnson City SD	Johnson City
98	0.0	Athens City Elementary SD	Athens
99	n/a	Franklin City Elementary SD	Franklin
99	n/a	Lebanon City Elementary SD	Lebanon
99	n/a	Murfreesboro City Elem SD	Murfreesboro

Texas

Texas Public School Educational Profile

Category	Value	Category	Value
Schools *(2003-2004)*	8,110	**Diploma Recipients** *(2002-2003)*	225,155
Instructional Level		White, Non-Hispanic	112,379
Primary	4,001	Black, Non-Hispanic	30,028
Middle	1,591	Asian/Pacific Islander	7,707
High	1,445	American Indian/Alaskan Native	578
Other Level	941	Hispanic	74,463
Curriculum		**High School Drop-out Rate** (%) *(2001-2002)*	3.8
Regular	6,884	White, Non-Hispanic	2.2
Special Education	119	Black, Non-Hispanic	4.9
Vocational	30	Asian/Pacific Islander	1.6
Alternative	945	American Indian/Alaskan Native	4.1
Type		Hispanic	5.5
Magnet	0	**Staff** *(2003-2004)*	
Charter	274	Teachers	289,480.1
Title I Eligible	5,010	Average Salary ($)	40,476
School-wide Title I	4,567	Librarians/Media Specialists	4,864.2
Students *(2003-2004)*	4,331,751	Guidance Counselors	9,938.7
Gender (%)		**Ratios** *(2003-2004)*	
Male	51.4	Student/Teacher Ratio	15.0 to 1
Female	48.6	Student/Librarian Ratio	890.5 to 1
Race/Ethnicity (%)		Student/Counselor Ratio	435.8 to 1
White, Non-Hispanic	38.7	**College Entrance Exam Scores** *(2005)*	
Black, Non-Hispanic	14.3	Scholastic Aptitude Test (SAT)	
Asian/Pacific Islander	2.9	Participation Rate (%)	54
American Indian/Alaskan Native	0.3	Mean SAT Reasoning Test Verbal Score	493
Hispanic	43.8	Mean SAT Reasoning Test Math Score	502
Classification (%)		American College Testing Program (ACT)	
Individual Education Program (IEP)	11.8	Participation Rate (%)	29
Migrant *(2002-2003)*	2.6	Average Composite Score	20.2
English Language Learner (ELL)	15.3	Average English Score	19.3
Eligible for Free Lunch Program	39.4	Average Math Score	20.3
Eligible for Reduced-Price Lunch Program	7.4	Average Reading Score	20.3
Current Spending *($ per student in FY 2003)*	6,986	Average Science Score	20.2
Instruction	4,266		
Support Services	2,375		

Note: *For an explanation of data, please refer to the User's Guide in the front of the book*

Texas NAEP 2005 Test Scores

Reading			Mathematics		
Grade/Category	Value	Rank	Grade/Category	Value	Rank
4th Grade			**4th Grade**		
Average Proficiency	218.7 (0.80)	29/51	Average Proficiency	242.0 (0.58)	11/51
Proficiency by Gender/Race/Ethnicity			Proficiency by Gender/Race/Ethnicity		
Male	215.6 (0.96)	30/51	Male	243.8 (0.74)	9/51
Female	221.9 (0.93)	28/51	Female	240.1 (0.62)	15/51
White, Non-Hispanic	231.7 (1.00)	10/51	White, Non-Hispanic	253.5 (0.84)	2/51
Black, Non-Hispanic	206.1 (1.65)	9/42	Black, Non-Hispanic	228.2 (1.19)	2/42
Asian, Non-Hispanic	234.0 (3.62)	9/27	Asian, Non-Hispanic	263.7 (2.51)	2/25
American Indian, Non-Hispanic	n/a	n/a	American Indian, Non-Hispanic	n/a	n/a
Hispanic	209.7 (1.15)	11/40	Hispanic	235.0 (0.57)	2/41
Proficiency by Class Size			Proficiency by Class Size		
Less than 16 Students	214.8 (2.92)	10/34	Less than 16 Students	240.6 (2.40)	4/35
16 to 18 Students	216.1 (1.62)	20/33	16 to 18 Students	238.3 (1.41)	14/31
19 to 20 Students	219.2 (1.66)	21/38	19 to 20 Students	244.4 (1.31)	7/38
21 to 25 Students	221.4 (1.73)	27/51	21 to 25 Students	242.7 (1.36)	16/51
Greater than 25 Students	n/a	n/a	Greater than 25 Students	n/a	n/a
Percent Attaining Achievement Levels			Percent Attaining Achievement Levels		
Below Basic	36.1 (1.13)	22/51	Below Basic	13.3 (0.62)	44/51
Basic or Above	63.9 (1.13)	30/51	Basic or Above	86.7 (0.62)	8/51
Proficient or Above	29.0 (0.94)	36/51	Proficient or Above	40.0 (0.94)	16/51
Advanced or Above	6.0 (0.51)	37/51	Advanced or Above	5.1 (0.43)	19/51
8th Grade			**8th Grade**		
Average Proficiency	258.2 (0.64)	36/51	Average Proficiency	281.1 (0.62)	21/51
Proficiency by Gender/Race/Ethnicity			Proficiency by Gender/Race/Ethnicity		
Male	253.8 (0.89)	35/51	Male	282.8 (0.83)	18/51
Female	262.7 (0.85)	38/51	Female	279.4 (0.72)	26/51
White, Non-Hispanic	270.4 (1.06)	21/51	White, Non-Hispanic	294.9 (0.76)	4/51
Black, Non-Hispanic	246.1 (1.71)	10/40	Black, Non-Hispanic	263.6 (1.70)	4/41
Asian, Non-Hispanic	279.5 (3.29)	6/24	Asian, Non-Hispanic	307.6 (3.82)	3/23
American Indian, Non-Hispanic	n/a	n/a	American Indian, Non-Hispanic	n/a	n/a
Hispanic	248.1 (0.88)	15/38	Hispanic	270.8 (1.05)	2/38
Proficiency by Parents Highest Level of Ed.			Proficiency by Parents Highest Level of Ed.		
Did Not Finish High School	244.6 (1.57)	26/49	Did Not Finish High School	268.4 (1.32)	5/50
Graduated High School	249.4 (1.36)	37/50	Graduated High School	271.5 (1.23)	18/50
Some Education After High School	264.6 (1.21)	30/50	Some Education After High School	285.9 (1.24)	8/50
Graduated College	269.3 (0.95)	33/50	Graduated College	292.9 (0.96)	17/50
Percent Attaining Achievement Levels			Percent Attaining Achievement Levels		
Below Basic	36.1 (1.13)	22/51	Below Basic	27.9 (0.72)	28/51
Basic or Above	63.9 (1.13)	30/51	Basic or Above	72.1 (0.72)	24/51
Proficient or Above	29.0 (0.94)	36/51	Proficient or Above	30.7 (0.84)	22/51
Advanced or Above	6.0 (0.51)	37/51	Advanced or Above	6.2 (0.42)	18/51

Note: *For an explanation of data, please refer to the User's Guide in the front of the book; n/a indicates data not available*

Anderson County

Palestine ISD
1600 S Loop 256 • Palestine, TX 75801-5847
(903) 731-8001
Grade Span: PK-12; **Agency Type:** 1
Schools: 7
    4 Primary; 2 Middle; 1 High; 0 Other Level
    7 Regular; 0 Special Education; 0 Vocational; 0 Alternative
    0 Magnet; 0 Charter; 7 Title I Eligible; 7 School-wide Title I
Students: 3,316 (51.7% male; 48.2% female)
    Individual Education Program: 326 (9.8%);
    English Language Learner: 282 (8.5%); Migrant: 2 (0.1%)
    Eligible for Free Lunch Program: 1,802 (54.3%)
    Eligible for Reduced-Price Lunch Program: 231 (7.0%)
Teachers: 253.2 (13.1 to 1)
Librarians/Media Specialists: 4.0 (829.0 to 1)
Guidance Counselors: 9.0 (368.4 to 1)
Current Spending: ($ per student per year):
    Total: $6,948; Instruction: $4,273; Support Services: $2,285
Enrollment, Drop-out Rates and Diploma Recipients by Race/Ethnicity

Category	Total	White	Black	Asian	AIAN	Hisp.
Enrollment (%)	100.0	40.4	31.5	0.8	0.2	27.1
Drop-out Rate (%)	2.9	1.4	4.1	0.0	n/a	4.5
H.S. Diplomas (#)	201	112	63	3	0	23

Westwood ISD
4524 W Oak • Palestine, TX 75801-5453
Mailing Address: PO Box 260 • Palestine, TX 75802-0260
(903) 729-1776
Grade Span: PK-12; **Agency Type:** 1
Schools: 4
    2 Primary; 1 Middle; 1 High; 0 Other Level
    4 Regular; 0 Special Education; 0 Vocational; 0 Alternative
    0 Magnet; 0 Charter; 2 Title I Eligible; 2 School-wide Title I
Students: 1,785 (50.7% male; 49.2% female)
    Individual Education Program: 266 (14.9%);
    English Language Learner: 23 (1.3%); Migrant: 0 (0.0%)
    Eligible for Free Lunch Program: 623 (34.9%)
    Eligible for Reduced-Price Lunch Program: 104 (5.8%)
Teachers: 117.6 (15.2 to 1)
Librarians/Media Specialists: 1.0 (1,785.0 to 1)
Guidance Counselors: 4.0 (446.3 to 1)
Current Spending: ($ per student per year):
    Total: $6,209; Instruction: $3,897; Support Services: $1,952
Enrollment, Drop-out Rates and Diploma Recipients by Race/Ethnicity

Category	Total	White	Black	Asian	AIAN	Hisp.
Enrollment (%)	100.0	71.2	16.9	0.7	0.2	11.0
Drop-out Rate (%)	1.2	1.5	0.0	0.0	0.0	0.0
H.S. Diplomas (#)	91	75	11	0	1	4

Andrews County

Andrews ISD
405 NW 3rd St • Andrews, TX 79714-5098
(432) 523-3640 • http://andrews.esc18.net/
Grade Span: PK-12; **Agency Type:** 1
Schools: 7
    4 Primary; 1 Middle; 1 High; 1 Other Level
    6 Regular; 0 Special Education; 0 Vocational; 1 Alternative
    0 Magnet; 0 Charter; 6 Title I Eligible; 0 School-wide Title I
Students: 2,966 (52.0% male; 47.9% female)
    Individual Education Program: 540 (18.2%);
    English Language Learner: 303 (10.2%); Migrant: 79 (2.7%)
    Eligible for Free Lunch Program: 814 (27.4%)
    Eligible for Reduced-Price Lunch Program: 269 (9.1%)
Teachers: 213.0 (13.9 to 1)
Librarians/Media Specialists: 5.1 (581.6 to 1)
Guidance Counselors: 5.5 (539.3 to 1)
Current Spending: ($ per student per year):
    Total: $8,615; Instruction: $5,345; Support Services: $2,841
Enrollment, Drop-out Rates and Diploma Recipients by Race/Ethnicity

Category	Total	White	Black	Asian	AIAN	Hisp.
Enrollment (%)	100.0	42.5	1.7	0.6	0.1	55.1
Drop-out Rate (%)	2.5	2.2	0.0	0.0	50.0	2.7
H.S. Diplomas (#)	221	117	2	2	0	100

Angelina County

Central ISD
7622 US Hwy 69 N • Pollok, TX 75969-9710
(936) 853-2216
Grade Span: PK-12; **Agency Type:** 1
Schools: 5
    2 Primary; 1 Middle; 2 High; 0 Other Level
    4 Regular; 0 Special Education; 0 Vocational; 1 Alternative
    0 Magnet; 0 Charter; 3 Title I Eligible; 3 School-wide Title I
Students: 1,692 (49.9% male; 50.0% female)
    Individual Education Program: 303 (17.9%);
    English Language Learner: 54 (3.2%); Migrant: 0 (0.0%)
    Eligible for Free Lunch Program: 548 (32.4%)
    Eligible for Reduced-Price Lunch Program: 150 (8.9%)
Teachers: 117.5 (14.4 to 1)
Librarians/Media Specialists: 2.0 (846.0 to 1)
Guidance Counselors: 5.0 (338.4 to 1)
Current Spending: ($ per student per year):
    Total: $5,977; Instruction: $3,720; Support Services: $1,872
Enrollment, Drop-out Rates and Diploma Recipients by Race/Ethnicity

Category	Total	White	Black	Asian	AIAN	Hisp.
Enrollment (%)	100.0	83.6	3.6	0.6	0.2	11.9
Drop-out Rate (%)	3.7	4.1	0.0	0.0	n/a	0.0
H.S. Diplomas (#)	107	99	2	1	0	5

Diboll ISD
401 Dennis • Diboll, TX 75941-0550
Mailing Address: PO Box 550 • Diboll, TX 75941-0550
(936) 829-4718
Grade Span: PK-12; **Agency Type:** 1
Schools: 5
    2 Primary; 1 Middle; 2 High; 0 Other Level
    4 Regular; 0 Special Education; 0 Vocational; 1 Alternative
    0 Magnet; 0 Charter; 4 Title I Eligible; 4 School-wide Title I
Students: 1,932 (54.2% male; 45.7% female)
    Individual Education Program: 244 (12.6%);
    English Language Learner: 321 (16.6%); Migrant: 0 (0.0%)
    Eligible for Free Lunch Program: 1,014 (52.5%)
    Eligible for Reduced-Price Lunch Program: 293 (15.2%)
Teachers: 146.3 (13.2 to 1)
Librarians/Media Specialists: 2.2 (878.2 to 1)
Guidance Counselors: 4.0 (483.0 to 1)
Current Spending: ($ per student per year):
    Total: $7,501; Instruction: $4,689; Support Services: $2,438
Enrollment, Drop-out Rates and Diploma Recipients by Race/Ethnicity

Category	Total	White	Black	Asian	AIAN	Hisp.
Enrollment (%)	100.0	40.9	14.4	0.1	0.1	44.4
Drop-out Rate (%)	18.9	17.6	27.3	n/a	0.0	16.8
H.S. Diplomas (#)	104	41	22	0	0	41

Hudson ISD
6735 Ted Trout Dr • Lufkin, TX 75904-8600
(936) 875-3351
Grade Span: PK-12; **Agency Type:** 1
Schools: 5
    2 Primary; 1 Middle; 2 High; 0 Other Level
    4 Regular; 0 Special Education; 0 Vocational; 1 Alternative
    0 Magnet; 0 Charter; 5 Title I Eligible; 5 School-wide Title I
Students: 2,352 (51.4% male; 48.5% female)
    Individual Education Program: 256 (10.9%);
    English Language Learner: 139 (5.9%); Migrant: 2 (0.1%)
    Eligible for Free Lunch Program: 1,029 (43.8%)
    Eligible for Reduced-Price Lunch Program: 241 (10.2%)
Teachers: 167.4 (14.1 to 1)
Librarians/Media Specialists: 3.0 (784.0 to 1)
Guidance Counselors: 5.0 (470.4 to 1)
Current Spending: ($ per student per year):
    Total: $6,130; Instruction: $3,488; Support Services: $2,243
Enrollment, Drop-out Rates and Diploma Recipients by Race/Ethnicity

Category	Total	White	Black	Asian	AIAN	Hisp.
Enrollment (%)	100.0	75.0	3.9	0.4	0.3	20.3
Drop-out Rate (%)	3.8	3.2	4.8	0.0	0.0	6.5
H.S. Diplomas (#)	131	111	4	0	0	16

Huntington ISD
908 Main St • Huntington, TX 75949-0328
Mailing Address: PO Box 328 • Huntington, TX 75949-0328
(936) 876-4287
Grade Span: PK-12; **Agency Type:** 1
Schools: 5
    1 Primary; 2 Middle; 2 High; 0 Other Level
    4 Regular; 0 Special Education; 0 Vocational; 1 Alternative
    0 Magnet; 0 Charter; 4 Title I Eligible; 4 School-wide Title I
Students: 1,659 (52.9% male; 47.0% female)
    Individual Education Program: 298 (18.0%);
    English Language Learner: 24 (1.4%); Migrant: 4 (0.2%)
    Eligible for Free Lunch Program: 575 (34.7%)
    Eligible for Reduced-Price Lunch Program: 104 (6.3%)
Teachers: 124.9 (13.3 to 1)
Librarians/Media Specialists: 2.0 (829.5 to 1)
Guidance Counselors: 3.6 (460.8 to 1)
Current Spending: ($ per student per year):
    Total: $6,822; Instruction: $4,173; Support Services: $2,218

Enrollment, Drop-out Rates and Diploma Recipients by Race/Ethnicity

Category	Total	White	Black	Asian	AIAN	Hisp.
Enrollment (%)	100.0	92.0	4.2	0.2	0.1	3.4
Drop-out Rate (%)	3.9	3.7	0.0	33.3	0.0	9.5
H.S. Diplomas (#)	108	97	8	0	0	3

Lufkin ISD

101 Cotton Sq • Lufkin, TX 75904
Mailing Address: PO Box 1407 • Lufkin, TX 75902-1407
(936) 634-6696 • http://www.lufkinisd.org/
Grade Span: PK-12; Agency Type: 1
Schools: 18
  11 Primary; 1 Middle; 2 High; 4 Other Level
  13 Regular; 2 Special Education; 0 Vocational; 3 Alternative
  0 Magnet; 0 Charter; 11 Title I Eligible; 11 School-wide Title I
Students: 8,282 (49.7% male; 50.2% female)
  Individual Education Program: 1,192 (14.4%);
  English Language Learner: 1,009 (12.2%); Migrant: 125 (1.5%)
  Eligible for Free Lunch Program: 4,417 (53.3%)
  Eligible for Reduced-Price Lunch Program: 548 (6.6%)
Teachers: 594.2 (13.9 to 1)
Librarians/Media Specialists: 9.0 (920.2 to 1)
Guidance Counselors: 20.0 (414.1 to 1)
Current Spending: ($ per student per year):
  Total: $6,507; Instruction: $3,969; Support Services: $2,165
Enrollment, Drop-out Rates and Diploma Recipients by Race/Ethnicity

Category	Total	White	Black	Asian	AIAN	Hisp.
Enrollment (%)	100.0	39.8	31.4	0.9	0.1	27.7
Drop-out Rate (%)	4.6	3.7	3.7	0.0	20.0	8.6
H.S. Diplomas (#)	476	240	161	4	1	70

Aransas County

Aransas County ISD

1700 Omohundro St • Rockport, TX 78382
Mailing Address: PO Box 907 • Rockport, TX 78381-0907
(361) 790-2212 • http://www.acisd.org/
Grade Span: PK-12; Agency Type: 1
Schools: 5
  2 Primary; 2 Middle; 1 High; 0 Other Level
  5 Regular; 0 Special Education; 0 Vocational; 0 Alternative
  0 Magnet; 0 Charter; 5 Title I Eligible; 5 School-wide Title I
Students: 3,343 (51.9% male; 48.0% female)
  Individual Education Program: 515 (15.4%);
  English Language Learner: 153 (4.6%); Migrant: 8 (0.2%)
  Eligible for Free Lunch Program: 1,595 (47.7%)
  Eligible for Reduced-Price Lunch Program: 226 (6.8%)
Teachers: 234.9 (14.2 to 1)
Librarians/Media Specialists: 2.4 (1,392.9 to 1)
Guidance Counselors: 13.2 (253.3 to 1)
Current Spending: ($ per student per year):
  Total: $7,375; Instruction: $4,257; Support Services: $2,753
Enrollment, Drop-out Rates and Diploma Recipients by Race/Ethnicity

Category	Total	White	Black	Asian	AIAN	Hisp.
Enrollment (%)	100.0	59.6	2.6	4.0	0.2	33.5
Drop-out Rate (%)	2.5	2.7	0.0	1.6	0.0	2.4
H.S. Diplomas (#)	210	140	4	14	0	52

Atascosa County

Lytle ISD

15437 Cottage St • Lytle, TX 78052-0745
Mailing Address: PO Box 745 • Lytle, TX 78052-0745
(830) 709-5100
Grade Span: PK-12; Agency Type: 1
Schools: 6
  2 Primary; 2 Middle; 1 High; 1 Other Level
  5 Regular; 0 Special Education; 0 Vocational; 1 Alternative
  0 Magnet; 0 Charter; 2 Title I Eligible; 2 School-wide Title I
Students: 1,542 (53.7% male; 46.2% female)
  Individual Education Program: 190 (12.3%)
  English Language Learner: 139 (9.0%); Migrant: 65 (4.2%)
  Eligible for Free Lunch Program: 887 (57.5%)
  Eligible for Reduced-Price Lunch Program: 136 (8.8%)
Teachers: 103.9 (14.8 to 1)
Librarians/Media Specialists: 0.0 (n/a to 1)
Guidance Counselors: 4.0 (385.5 to 1)
Current Spending: ($ per student per year):
  Total: $6,949; Instruction: $4,012; Support Services: $2,523
Enrollment, Drop-out Rates and Diploma Recipients by Race/Ethnicity

Category	Total	White	Black	Asian	AIAN	Hisp.
Enrollment (%)	100.0	26.9	0.2	0.3	0.4	72.2
Drop-out Rate (%)	3.4	0.0	50.0	0.0	0.0	5.1
H.S. Diplomas (#)	90	42	0	1	0	47

Pleasanton ISD

831 Stadium Dr • Pleasanton, TX 78064-2499
(830) 569-1200
Grade Span: PK-12; Agency Type: 1
Schools: 8
  3 Primary; 2 Middle; 2 High; 1 Other Level
  6 Regular; 0 Special Education; 0 Vocational; 2 Alternative
  0 Magnet; 0 Charter; 6 Title I Eligible; 6 School-wide Title I
Students: 3,498 (51.5% male; 48.4% female)
  Individual Education Program: 635 (18.2%);
  English Language Learner: 92 (2.6%); Migrant: 47 (1.3%)
  Eligible for Free Lunch Program: 1,792 (51.2%)
  Eligible for Reduced-Price Lunch Program: 304 (8.7%)
Teachers: 256.1 (13.7 to 1)
Librarians/Media Specialists: 3.0 (1,166.0 to 1)
Guidance Counselors: 11.0 (318.0 to 1)
Current Spending: ($ per student per year):
  Total: $7,468; Instruction: $4,426; Support Services: $2,614
Enrollment, Drop-out Rates and Diploma Recipients by Race/Ethnicity

Category	Total	White	Black	Asian	AIAN	Hisp.
Enrollment (%)	100.0	34.4	1.0	0.5	0.1	64.0
Drop-out Rate (%)	3.8	2.7	0.0	0.0	0.0	4.7
H.S. Diplomas (#)	215	97	2	0	1	115

Poteet ISD

1100 School Dr • Poteet, TX 78065-0138
Mailing Address: PO Box 138 • Poteet, TX 78065-0138
(830) 742-3567
Grade Span: PK-12; Agency Type: 1
Schools: 5
  1 Primary; 2 Middle; 1 High; 1 Other Level
  4 Regular; 0 Special Education; 0 Vocational; 1 Alternative
  0 Magnet; 0 Charter; 3 Title I Eligible; 3 School-wide Title I
Students: 1,686 (49.7% male; 50.2% female)
  Individual Education Program: 251 (14.9%);
  English Language Learner: 98 (5.8%); Migrant: 17 (1.0%)
  Eligible for Free Lunch Program: 1,029 (61.0%)
  Eligible for Reduced-Price Lunch Program: 190 (11.3%)
Teachers: 126.1 (13.4 to 1)
Librarians/Media Specialists: 3.0 (562.0 to 1)
Guidance Counselors: 3.7 (455.7 to 1)
Current Spending: ($ per student per year):
  Total: $7,443; Instruction: $4,606; Support Services: $2,402
Enrollment, Drop-out Rates and Diploma Recipients by Race/Ethnicity

Category	Total	White	Black	Asian	AIAN	Hisp.
Enrollment (%)	100.0	16.1	0.5	0.2	0.3	83.0
Drop-out Rate (%)	3.1	1.1	0.0	0.0	n/a	3.6
H.S. Diplomas (#)	99	22	0	0	0	77

Austin County

Bellville ISD

404 E Main St • Bellville, TX 77418-1599
(979) 865-3133 • http://www.bellville.k12.tx.us/
Grade Span: PK-12; Agency Type: 1
Schools: 6
  2 Primary; 2 Middle; 1 High; 0 Other Level
  5 Regular; 0 Special Education; 0 Vocational; 0 Alternative
  0 Magnet; 0 Charter; 2 Title I Eligible; 2 School-wide Title I
Students: 2,141 (51.1% male; 48.8% female)
  Individual Education Program: 296 (13.8%);
  English Language Learner: 136 (6.4%); Migrant: 3 (0.1%)
  Eligible for Free Lunch Program: 514 (24.0%)
  Eligible for Reduced-Price Lunch Program: 114 (5.3%)
Teachers: 154.3 (13.9 to 1)
Librarians/Media Specialists: 2.5 (856.4 to 1)
Guidance Counselors: 5.2 (411.7 to 1)
Current Spending: ($ per student per year):
  Total: $6,405; Instruction: $3,909; Support Services: $2,165
Enrollment, Drop-out Rates and Diploma Recipients by Race/Ethnicity

Category	Total	White	Black	Asian	AIAN	Hisp.
Enrollment (%)	100.0	68.0	13.9	0.4	0.2	17.5
Drop-out Rate (%)	0.3	0.0	1.2	n/a	0.0	1.3
H.S. Diplomas (#)	147	117	17	0	1	12

Sealy ISD

939 Tiger Ln • Sealy, TX 77474-3211
(979) 885-3516
Grade Span: PK-12; Agency Type: 1
Schools: 4
  1 Primary; 2 Middle; 1 High; 0 Other Level
  4 Regular; 0 Special Education; 0 Vocational; 0 Alternative
  0 Magnet; 0 Charter; 2 Title I Eligible; 2 School-wide Title I
Students: 2,384 (51.7% male; 48.2% female)
  Individual Education Program: 329 (13.8%);

English Language Learner: 205 (8.6%); Migrant: 6 (0.3%)
Eligible for Free Lunch Program: 883 (37.0%)
Eligible for Reduced-Price Lunch Program: 170 (7.1%)
Teachers: 171.4 (13.9 to 1)
Librarians/Media Specialists: 2.0 (1,192.0 to 1)
Guidance Counselors: 8.6 (277.2 to 1)
Current Spending: ($ per student per year):
Total: $7,030; Instruction: $4,651; Support Services: $2,042
Enrollment, Drop-out Rates and Diploma Recipients by Race/Ethnicity

Category	Total	White	Black	Asian	AIAN	Hisp.
Enrollment (%)	100.0	51.6	14.8	0.7	0.2	32.8
Drop-out Rate (%)	2.4	1.7	6.1	0.0	0.0	2.3
H.S. Diplomas (#)	128	89	11	1	0	27

Bandera County

Bandera ISD

2303 State Hwy 16 S • Bandera, TX 78003-0727
Mailing Address: PO Box 727 • Bandera, TX 78003-0727
(830) 796-3313
Grade Span: PK-12; **Agency Type:** 1
Schools: 4
2 Primary; 1 Middle; 1 High; 0 Other Level
4 Regular; 0 Special Education; 0 Vocational; 0 Alternative
0 Magnet; 0 Charter; 1 Title I Eligible; 1 School-wide Title I
Students: 2,665   (50.6% male; 49.3% female)
Individual Education Program: 406 (15.2%);
English Language Learner: 72 (2.7%); Migrant: 0 (0.0%)
Eligible for Free Lunch Program: 854 (32.0%)
Eligible for Reduced-Price Lunch Program: 222 (8.3%)
Teachers: 199.4 (13.4 to 1)
Librarians/Media Specialists: 4.0 (666.3 to 1)
Guidance Counselors: 7.0 (380.7 to 1)
Current Spending: ($ per student per year):
Total: $7,196; Instruction: $4,337; Support Services: $2,533
Enrollment, Drop-out Rates and Diploma Recipients by Race/Ethnicity

Category	Total	White	Black	Asian	AIAN	Hisp.
Enrollment (%)	100.0	77.1	1.0	0.5	0.6	20.8
Drop-out Rate (%)	3.8	4.0	0.0	n/a	0.0	3.1
H.S. Diplomas (#)	146	127	0	0	1	18

Bastrop County

Bastrop ISD

906 Farm St • Bastrop, TX 78602-3310
(512) 321-2292 • http://www.bastrop.isd.tenet.edu/
Grade Span: PK-12; **Agency Type:** 1
Schools: 12
4 Primary; 4 Middle; 2 High; 2 Other Level
9 Regular; 0 Special Education; 0 Vocational; 3 Alternative
0 Magnet; 0 Charter; 6 Title I Eligible; 0 School-wide Title I
Students: 7,565   (51.5% male; 48.4% female)
Individual Education Program: 942 (12.5%);
English Language Learner: 611 (8.1%); Migrant: 300 (4.0%)
Eligible for Free Lunch Program: 2,867 (37.9%)
Eligible for Reduced-Price Lunch Program: 771 (10.2%)
Teachers: 516.2 (14.7 to 1)
Librarians/Media Specialists: 8.0 (945.6 to 1)
Guidance Counselors: 21.5 (351.9 to 1)
Current Spending: ($ per student per year):
Total: $7,207; Instruction: $4,174; Support Services: $2,641
Enrollment, Drop-out Rates and Diploma Recipients by Race/Ethnicity

Category	Total	White	Black	Asian	AIAN	Hisp.
Enrollment (%)	100.0	54.1	10.4	0.8	0.5	34.2
Drop-out Rate (%)	4.3	3.7	5.3	0.0	0.0	5.6
H.S. Diplomas (#)	340	228	34	2	3	73

Elgin ISD

900 W 2nd St • Elgin, TX 78621-2515
Mailing Address: PO Box 351 • Elgin, TX 78621-0351
(512) 281-3434 • http://www.elginisd.net/
Grade Span: PK-12; **Agency Type:** 1
Schools: 5
2 Primary; 1 Middle; 2 High; 0 Other Level
4 Regular; 0 Special Education; 0 Vocational; 1 Alternative
0 Magnet; 0 Charter; 4 Title I Eligible; 4 School-wide Title I
Students: 3,084   (50.4% male; 49.5% female)
Individual Education Program: 361 (11.7%);
English Language Learner: 507 (16.4%); Migrant: 116 (3.8%)
Eligible for Free Lunch Program: 1,436 (46.6%)
Eligible for Reduced-Price Lunch Program: 227 (7.4%)
Teachers: 215.5 (14.3 to 1)
Librarians/Media Specialists: 3.7 (833.5 to 1)
Guidance Counselors: 7.0 (440.6 to 1)

Current Spending: ($ per student per year):
Total: $6,678; Instruction: $4,058; Support Services: $2,249
Enrollment, Drop-out Rates and Diploma Recipients by Race/Ethnicity

Category	Total	White	Black	Asian	AIAN	Hisp.
Enrollment (%)	100.0	40.7	13.5	0.5	0.4	44.9
Drop-out Rate (%)	2.0	1.1	0.9	0.0	n/a	3.5
H.S. Diplomas (#)	164	82	25	1	0	56

Smithville ISD

901 NE 6th St • Smithville, TX 78957-0479
Mailing Address: PO Box 479 • Smithville, TX 78957-0479
(512) 237-2487
Grade Span: PK-12; **Agency Type:** 1
Schools: 5
2 Primary; 1 Middle; 1 High; 1 Other Level
4 Regular; 0 Special Education; 0 Vocational; 1 Alternative
0 Magnet; 0 Charter; 3 Title I Eligible; 2 School-wide Title I
Students: 1,904   (52.4% male; 47.5% female)
Individual Education Program: 275 (14.4%);
English Language Learner: 65 (3.4%); Migrant: 54 (2.8%)
Eligible for Free Lunch Program: 750 (39.4%)
Eligible for Reduced-Price Lunch Program: 161 (8.5%)
Teachers: 144.3 (13.2 to 1)
Librarians/Media Specialists: 4.0 (476.0 to 1)
Guidance Counselors: 5.0 (380.8 to 1)
Current Spending: ($ per student per year):
Total: $7,003; Instruction: $4,273; Support Services: $2,365
Enrollment, Drop-out Rates and Diploma Recipients by Race/Ethnicity

Category	Total	White	Black	Asian	AIAN	Hisp.
Enrollment (%)	100.0	70.2	10.2	0.5	0.2	19.0
Drop-out Rate (%)	2.6	2.5	3.8	0.0	0.0	2.2
H.S. Diplomas (#)	103	76	10	0	0	17

Bee County

Beeville ISD

2400 N Saint Mary's St • Beeville, TX 78102-2494
(361) 358-7111 • http://www.beevilleisd.esc2.net/
Grade Span: PK-12; **Agency Type:** 1
Schools: 8
4 Primary; 2 Middle; 2 High; 0 Other Level
7 Regular; 0 Special Education; 0 Vocational; 1 Alternative
0 Magnet; 0 Charter; 8 Title I Eligible; 8 School-wide Title I
Students: 3,779   (50.5% male; 49.4% female)
Individual Education Program: 418 (11.1%);
English Language Learner: 75 (2.0%); Migrant: 0 (0.0%)
Eligible for Free Lunch Program: 2,105 (55.7%)
Eligible for Reduced-Price Lunch Program: 435 (11.5%)
Teachers: 247.6 (15.3 to 1)
Librarians/Media Specialists: 2.3 (1,643.0 to 1)
Guidance Counselors: 13.0 (290.7 to 1)
Current Spending: ($ per student per year):
Total: $7,102; Instruction: $4,334; Support Services: $2,300
Enrollment, Drop-out Rates and Diploma Recipients by Race/Ethnicity

Category	Total	White	Black	Asian	AIAN	Hisp.
Enrollment (%)	100.0	21.4	2.9	0.6	0.2	74.9
Drop-out Rate (%)	4.1	2.4	4.3	0.0	0.0	4.9
H.S. Diplomas (#)	223	81	8	4	0	130

Bell County

Belton ISD

616 E 6th Ave • Belton, TX 76513-2707
Mailing Address: PO Box 269 • Belton, TX 76513-0269
(254) 939-1881 • http://www.bisd.net/
Grade Span: PK-12; **Agency Type:** 1
Schools: 12
6 Primary; 3 Middle; 2 High; 1 Other Level
10 Regular; 0 Special Education; 0 Vocational; 2 Alternative
0 Magnet; 0 Charter; 7 Title I Eligible; 7 School-wide Title I
Students: 7,114   (52.1% male; 47.8% female)
Individual Education Program: 1,115 (15.7%);
English Language Learner: 441 (6.2%); Migrant: 25 (0.4%)
Eligible for Free Lunch Program: 2,606 (36.6%)
Eligible for Reduced-Price Lunch Program: 697 (9.8%)
Teachers: 468.2 (15.2 to 1)
Librarians/Media Specialists: 4.3 (1,654.4 to 1)
Guidance Counselors: 16.5 (431.2 to 1)
Current Spending: ($ per student per year):
Total: $6,686; Instruction: $3,925; Support Services: $2,383
Enrollment, Drop-out Rates and Diploma Recipients by Race/Ethnicity

Category	Total	White	Black	Asian	AIAN	Hisp.
Enrollment (%)	100.0	65.4	5.9	0.9	0.8	27.0
Drop-out Rate (%)	1.7	1.6	2.1	0.0	0.0	2.5
H.S. Diplomas (#)	463	345	23	8	6	81

Killeen ISD
200 NW S Young Dr • Killeen, TX 76543-4025
Mailing Address: PO Box 967 • Killeen, TX 76540-0967
(254) 501-0006 • http://www.killeenisd.org/
Grade Span: PK-12; **Agency Type:** 1
Schools: 49
  28 Primary; 10 Middle; 6 High; 4 Other Level
  41 Regular; 0 Special Education; 0 Vocational; 7 Alternative
  0 Magnet; 0 Charter; 25 Title I Eligible; 19 School-wide Title I
Students: 32,583 (51.2% male; 48.7% female)
  Individual Education Program: 4,346 (13.3%);
  English Language Learner: 1,879 (5.8%); Migrant: 57 (0.2%)
  Eligible for Free Lunch Program: 10,845 (33.3%)
  Eligible for Reduced-Price Lunch Program: 5,034 (15.5%)
Teachers: 2,302.9 (14.1 to 1)
Librarians/Media Specialists: 40.0 (813.0 to 1)
Guidance Counselors: 71.2 (456.8 to 1)
Current Spending: ($ per student per year):
  Total: $7,552; Instruction: $4,598; Support Services: $2,619
Enrollment, Drop-out Rates and Diploma Recipients by Race/Ethnicity

Category	Total	White	Black	Asian	AIAN	Hisp.
Enrollment (%)	100.0	35.7	40.4	4.4	0.7	18.9
Drop-out Rate (%)	3.5	3.4	3.6	2.8	2.1	3.7
H.S. Diplomas (#)	1,358	442	551	92	4	269

Temple ISD
200 N 23rd St • Temple, TX 76504-2486
Mailing Address: PO Box 788 • Temple, TX 76503-0788
(254) 778-6721 • http://www.tisd.org/
Grade Span: PK-12; **Agency Type:** 1
Schools: 17
  10 Primary; 3 Middle; 1 High; 3 Other Level
  14 Regular; 0 Special Education; 0 Vocational; 3 Alternative
  0 Magnet; 0 Charter; 13 Title I Eligible; 13 School-wide Title I
Students: 8,254 (51.1% male; 48.8% female)
  Individual Education Program: 1,376 (16.7%);
  English Language Learner: 541 (6.6%); Migrant: 56 (0.7%)
  Eligible for Free Lunch Program: 3,882 (47.0%)
  Eligible for Reduced-Price Lunch Program: 693 (8.4%)
Teachers: 618.8 (13.3 to 1)
Librarians/Media Specialists: 13.0 (634.9 to 1)
Guidance Counselors: 19.9 (414.8 to 1)
Current Spending: ($ per student per year):
  Total: $7,326; Instruction: $4,362; Support Services: $2,582
Enrollment, Drop-out Rates and Diploma Recipients by Race/Ethnicity

Category	Total	White	Black	Asian	AIAN	Hisp.
Enrollment (%)	100.0	41.4	28.7	1.5	0.4	28.0
Drop-out Rate (%)	3.0	1.5	5.5	0.0	0.0	3.6
H.S. Diplomas (#)	441	226	121	8	0	86

Bexar County

Alamo Heights ISD
7101 Broadway St • San Antonio, TX 78209-3797
(210) 824-2483 • http://www.ahisd.net/
Grade Span: PK-12; **Agency Type:** 1
Schools: 6
  3 Primary; 1 Middle; 1 High; 1 Other Level
  5 Regular; 0 Special Education; 0 Vocational; 1 Alternative
  0 Magnet; 0 Charter; 3 Title I Eligible; 0 School-wide Title I
Students: 4,356 (51.5% male; 48.4% female)
  Individual Education Program: 437 (10.0%);
  English Language Learner: 216 (5.0%); Migrant: 0 (0.0%)
  Eligible for Free Lunch Program: 678 (15.6%)
  Eligible for Reduced-Price Lunch Program: 204 (4.7%)
Teachers: 308.0 (14.1 to 1)
Librarians/Media Specialists: 4.0 (1,089.0 to 1)
Guidance Counselors: 12.8 (340.3 to 1)
Current Spending: ($ per student per year):
  Total: $7,852; Instruction: $5,133; Support Services: $2,430
Enrollment, Drop-out Rates and Diploma Recipients by Race/Ethnicity

Category	Total	White	Black	Asian	AIAN	Hisp.
Enrollment (%)	100.0	67.8	2.0	1.4	0.2	28.7
Drop-out Rate (%)	1.1	0.5	8.0	0.0	0.0	2.1
H.S. Diplomas (#)	347	243	5	2	0	97

East Central ISD
6634 New Sulphur Springs Rd • San Antonio, TX 78263-9701
(210) 648-7861 • http://www.ecisd.net/
Grade Span: PK-12; **Agency Type:** 1
Schools: 13
  6 Primary; 3 Middle; 1 High; 3 Other Level
  10 Regular; 0 Special Education; 0 Vocational; 3 Alternative
  0 Magnet; 0 Charter; 6 Title I Eligible; 6 School-wide Title I
Students: 7,917 (52.0% male; 47.9% female)

  Individual Education Program: 1,026 (13.0%);
  English Language Learner: 334 (4.2%); Migrant: 24 (0.3%)
  Eligible for Free Lunch Program: 3,316 (41.9%)
  Eligible for Reduced-Price Lunch Program: 933 (11.8%)
Teachers: 491.8 (16.1 to 1)
Librarians/Media Specialists: 9.0 (879.7 to 1)
Guidance Counselors: 17.5 (452.4 to 1)
Current Spending: ($ per student per year):
  Total: $7,104; Instruction: $4,281; Support Services: $2,454
Enrollment, Drop-out Rates and Diploma Recipients by Race/Ethnicity

Category	Total	White	Black	Asian	AIAN	Hisp.
Enrollment (%)	100.0	37.4	10.9	0.4	0.3	51.0
Drop-out Rate (%)	2.6	2.3	1.3	0.0	0.0	3.3
H.S. Diplomas (#)	492	228	58	3	1	202

Edgewood ISD
5358 W Commerce St • San Antonio, TX 78237-1354
(210) 444-4500 • http://www.edgewood.esc7.net/
Grade Span: PK-12; **Agency Type:** 1
Schools: 25
  13 Primary; 4 Middle; 3 High; 3 Other Level
  20 Regular; 0 Special Education; 0 Vocational; 3 Alternative
  0 Magnet; 0 Charter; 21 Title I Eligible; 21 School-wide Title I
Students: 12,894 (50.8% male; 49.1% female)
  Individual Education Program: 1,837 (14.2%);
  English Language Learner: 2,627 (20.4%); Migrant: 394 (3.1%)
  Eligible for Free Lunch Program: 1,533 (11.9%)
  Eligible for Reduced-Price Lunch Program: 87 (0.7%)
Teachers: 754.2 (17.1 to 1)
Librarians/Media Specialists: 18.3 (704.6 to 1)
Guidance Counselors: 28.2 (457.2 to 1)
Current Spending: ($ per student per year):
  Total: $7,239; Instruction: $4,270; Support Services: $2,485
Enrollment, Drop-out Rates and Diploma Recipients by Race/Ethnicity

Category	Total	White	Black	Asian	AIAN	Hisp.
Enrollment (%)	100.0	1.1	1.5	0.1	0.1	97.3
Drop-out Rate (%)	6.1	4.5	7.3	0.0	0.0	6.2
H.S. Diplomas (#)	622	10	13	2	2	595

Harlandale ISD
102 Genevieve St • San Antonio, TX 78214-2997
(210) 921-4300 • http://www.harlandale.k12.tx.us/
Grade Span: PK-12; **Agency Type:** 1
Schools: 30
  16 Primary; 7 Middle; 6 High; 1 Other Level
  20 Regular; 3 Special Education; 0 Vocational; 7 Alternative
  0 Magnet; 0 Charter; 22 Title I Eligible; 21 School-wide Title I
Students: 14,088 (51.8% male; 48.1% female)
  Individual Education Program: 2,215 (15.7%);
  English Language Learner: 2,113 (15.0%); Migrant: 199 (1.4%)
  Eligible for Free Lunch Program: 3,322 (23.6%)
  Eligible for Reduced-Price Lunch Program: 530 (3.8%)
Teachers: 942.0 (15.0 to 1)
Librarians/Media Specialists: 17.9 (787.0 to 1)
Guidance Counselors: 36.5 (386.0 to 1)
Current Spending: ($ per student per year):
  Total: $7,764; Instruction: $4,400; Support Services: $2,894
Enrollment, Drop-out Rates and Diploma Recipients by Race/Ethnicity

Category	Total	White	Black	Asian	AIAN	Hisp.
Enrollment (%)	100.0	4.4	0.5	0.1	0.1	94.8
Drop-out Rate (%)	4.4	3.8	7.1	0.0	0.0	4.4
H.S. Diplomas (#)	800	62	1	0	0	737

Judson ISD
8012 Shin Oak • San Antonio, TX 78233-2457
(210) 659-9600 •
http://www.judsonisd.org/education/district/district.php?sectionid=1
Grade Span: PK-12; **Agency Type:** 1
Schools: 22
  14 Primary; 3 Middle; 2 High; 3 Other Level
  19 Regular; 0 Special Education; 0 Vocational; 3 Alternative
  0 Magnet; 0 Charter; 14 Title I Eligible; 12 School-wide Title I
Students: 17,981 (52.0% male; 47.9% female)
  Individual Education Program: 1,853 (10.3%);
  English Language Learner: 812 (4.5%); Migrant: 5 (<0.1%)
  Eligible for Free Lunch Program: 6,817 (37.9%)
  Eligible for Reduced-Price Lunch Program: 2,074 (11.5%)
Teachers: 1,228.9 (14.6 to 1)
Librarians/Media Specialists: 19.0 (946.4 to 1)
Guidance Counselors: 35.2 (510.8 to 1)
Current Spending: ($ per student per year):
  Total: $6,486; Instruction: $4,071; Support Services: $2,132

Enrollment, Drop-out Rates and Diploma Recipients by Race/Ethnicity

Category	Total	White	Black	Asian	AIAN	Hisp.
Enrollment (%)	100.0	29.5	25.5	2.6	0.4	42.0
Drop-out Rate (%)	2.9	2.5	2.4	2.0	0.0	3.8
H.S. Diplomas (#)	842	348	191	24	3	276

North East ISD
8961 Tesoro Dr • San Antonio, TX 78217-6225
(210) 804-7000 • http://www.neisd.net/index.html
Grade Span: PK-12; **Agency Type:** 1
Schools: 65
  39 Primary; 12 Middle; 9 High; 5 Other Level
  56 Regular; 2 Special Education; 0 Vocational; 7 Alternative
  0 Magnet; 0 Charter; 20 Title I Eligible; 20 School-wide Title I
Students: 56,298   (50.9% male; 49.0% female)
  Individual Education Program: 8,732 (15.5%);
  English Language Learner: 2,680 (4.8%); Migrant: 43 (0.1%)
  Eligible for Free Lunch Program: 15,740 (28.0%)
  Eligible for Reduced-Price Lunch Program: 4,055 (7.2%)
Teachers: 3,670.7 (15.3 to 1)
Librarians/Media Specialists: 60.7 (927.5 to 1)
Guidance Counselors: 144.0 (391.0 to 1)
Current Spending: ($ per student per year):
  Total: $6,951; Instruction: $4,392; Support Services: $2,277

Enrollment, Drop-out Rates and Diploma Recipients by Race/Ethnicity

Category	Total	White	Black	Asian	AIAN	Hisp.
Enrollment (%)	100.0	45.4	9.5	3.0	0.2	41.8
Drop-out Rate (%)	1.8	1.3	1.9	0.9	3.0	2.5
H.S. Diplomas (#)	3,208	1,705	266	102	6	1,129

Northside ISD
5900 Evers Rd • San Antonio, TX 78238-1699
(210) 706-8770 • http://www.nisd.net/
Grade Span: PK-12; **Agency Type:** 1
Schools: 93
  53 Primary; 15 Middle; 12 High; 13 Other Level
  71 Regular; 9 Special Education; 0 Vocational; 13 Alternative
  0 Magnet; 0 Charter; 30 Title I Eligible; 30 School-wide Title I
Students: 71,798   (51.6% male; 48.3% female)
  Individual Education Program: 10,669 (14.9%);
  English Language Learner: 4,354 (6.1%); Migrant: 238 (0.3%)
  Eligible for Free Lunch Program: 24,166 (33.7%)
  Eligible for Reduced-Price Lunch Program: 6,861 (9.6%)
Teachers: 4,594.2 (15.6 to 1)
Librarians/Media Specialists: 71.8 (1,000.0 to 1)
Guidance Counselors: 204.0 (352.0 to 1)
Current Spending: ($ per student per year):
  Total: $6,808; Instruction: $4,084; Support Services: $2,404

Enrollment, Drop-out Rates and Diploma Recipients by Race/Ethnicity

Category	Total	White	Black	Asian	AIAN	Hisp.
Enrollment (%)	100.0	31.3	7.2	2.5	0.3	58.7
Drop-out Rate (%)	3.0	2.0	3.3	1.3	0.0	3.7
H.S. Diplomas (#)	3,928	1,583	296	110	12	1,927

San Antonio ISD
141 Lavaca St • San Antonio, TX 78210-1039
(210) 299-5500 • http://www.saisd.net/
Grade Span: PK-12; **Agency Type:** 1
Schools: 107
  67 Primary; 19 Middle; 13 High; 8 Other Level
  89 Regular; 4 Special Education; 0 Vocational; 14 Alternative
  0 Magnet; 0 Charter; 90 Title I Eligible; 90 School-wide Title I
Students: 56,914   (51.0% male; 48.9% female)
  Individual Education Program: 7,350 (12.9%);
  English Language Learner: 9,633 (16.9%); Migrant: 2,416 (4.2%)
  Eligible for Free Lunch Program: 16,615 (29.2%)
  Eligible for Reduced-Price Lunch Program: 1,283 (2.3%)
Teachers: 3,526.9 (16.1 to 1)
Librarians/Media Specialists: 71.6 (794.9 to 1)
Guidance Counselors: 149.5 (380.7 to 1)
Current Spending: ($ per student per year):
  Total: $7,880; Instruction: $4,612; Support Services: $2,803

Enrollment, Drop-out Rates and Diploma Recipients by Race/Ethnicity

Category	Total	White	Black	Asian	AIAN	Hisp.
Enrollment (%)	100.0	3.6	8.8	0.3	0.1	87.2
Drop-out Rate (%)	7.1	7.2	6.9	2.6	0.0	7.2
H.S. Diplomas (#)	2,727	124	258	14	0	2,331

Somerset ISD
19644 Somerset Rd • Somerset, TX 78069-0279
Mailing Address: PO Box 279 • Somerset, TX 78069-0279
(866) 852-9858
Grade Span: PK-12; **Agency Type:** 1
Schools: 7
  3 Primary; 1 Middle; 1 High; 1 Other Level

  5 Regular; 0 Special Education; 0 Vocational; 1 Alternative
  0 Magnet; 0 Charter; 4 Title I Eligible; 4 School-wide Title I
Students: 3,284   (51.4% male; 48.5% female)
  Individual Education Program: 413 (12.6%);
  English Language Learner: 287 (8.7%); Migrant: 89 (2.7%)
  Eligible for Free Lunch Program: 2,021 (61.5%)
  Eligible for Reduced-Price Lunch Program: 420 (12.8%)
Teachers: 209.4 (15.7 to 1)
Librarians/Media Specialists: 2.1 (1,563.8 to 1)
Guidance Counselors: 7.0 (469.1 to 1)
Current Spending: ($ per student per year):
  Total: $7,351; Instruction: $4,224; Support Services: $2,603

Enrollment, Drop-out Rates and Diploma Recipients by Race/Ethnicity

Category	Total	White	Black	Asian	AIAN	Hisp.
Enrollment (%)	100.0	16.1	1.6	0.2	0.1	82.0
Drop-out Rate (%)	3.2	1.2	0.0	0.0	0.0	3.7
H.S. Diplomas (#)	127	33	0	1	1	92

South San Antonio ISD
2515 Bobcat Ln • San Antonio, TX 78224-1268
(210) 977-7000 • http://www.southsanisd.net
Grade Span: PK-12; **Agency Type:** 1
Schools: 19
  10 Primary; 3 Middle; 4 High; 1 Other Level
  15 Regular; 0 Special Education; 0 Vocational; 3 Alternative
  0 Magnet; 0 Charter; 17 Title I Eligible; 17 School-wide Title I
Students: 9,951   (52.4% male; 47.5% female)
  Individual Education Program: 1,080 (10.9%);
  English Language Learner: 1,779 (17.9%); Migrant: 269 (2.7%)
  Eligible for Free Lunch Program: 6,396 (64.3%)
  Eligible for Reduced-Price Lunch Program: 876 (8.8%)
Teachers: 660.4 (15.1 to 1)
Librarians/Media Specialists: 12.0 (829.3 to 1)
Guidance Counselors: 25.0 (398.0 to 1)
Current Spending: ($ per student per year):
  Total: $7,155; Instruction: $4,539; Support Services: $2,147

Enrollment, Drop-out Rates and Diploma Recipients by Race/Ethnicity

Category	Total	White	Black	Asian	AIAN	Hisp.
Enrollment (%)	100.0	2.9	1.5	0.2	0.1	95.3
Drop-out Rate (%)	5.6	4.9	4.5	25.0	n/a	5.6
H.S. Diplomas (#)	474	16	5	1	0	452

Southside ISD
1460 Martinez Losoya Rd • San Antonio, TX 78221-9648
(210) 882-1600
Grade Span: PK-12; **Agency Type:** 1
Schools: 8
  3 Primary; 2 Middle; 1 High; 2 Other Level
  6 Regular; 0 Special Education; 0 Vocational; 2 Alternative
  0 Magnet; 0 Charter; 6 Title I Eligible; 6 School-wide Title I
Students: 4,676   (50.9% male; 49.0% female)
  Individual Education Program: 696 (14.9%);
  English Language Learner: 455 (9.7%); Migrant: 123 (2.6%)
  Eligible for Free Lunch Program: 3,190 (68.2%)
  Eligible for Reduced-Price Lunch Program: 555 (11.9%)
Teachers: 306.0 (15.3 to 1)
Librarians/Media Specialists: 4.7 (994.9 to 1)
Guidance Counselors: 13.0 (359.7 to 1)
Current Spending: ($ per student per year):
  Total: $6,659; Instruction: $3,848; Support Services: $2,385

Enrollment, Drop-out Rates and Diploma Recipients by Race/Ethnicity

Category	Total	White	Black	Asian	AIAN	Hisp.
Enrollment (%)	100.0	15.3	1.5	0.9	0.1	82.2
Drop-out Rate (%)	4.8	5.4	0.0	7.7	0.0	4.8
H.S. Diplomas (#)	264	36	2	7	1	218

Southwest ISD
11914 Dragon Ln • San Antonio, TX 78252-2647
(210) 622-4300 • http://www.swisd.net/
Grade Span: PK-12; **Agency Type:** 1
Schools: 14
  9 Primary; 3 Middle; 1 High; 1 Other Level
  13 Regular; 0 Special Education; 0 Vocational; 1 Alternative
  0 Magnet; 0 Charter; 13 Title I Eligible; 13 School-wide Title I
Students: 9,684   (50.9% male; 49.0% female)
  Individual Education Program: 1,365 (14.1%);
  English Language Learner: 1,226 (12.7%); Migrant: 230 (2.4%)
  Eligible for Free Lunch Program: 6,412 (66.2%)
  Eligible for Reduced-Price Lunch Program: 1,227 (12.7%)
Teachers: 643.3 (15.1 to 1)
Librarians/Media Specialists: 6.0 (1,614.0 to 1)
Guidance Counselors: 24.0 (403.5 to 1)
Current Spending: ($ per student per year):
  Total: $6,736; Instruction: $4,069; Support Services: $2,291

Enrollment, Drop-out Rates and Diploma Recipients by Race/Ethnicity

Category	Total	White	Black	Asian	AIAN	Hisp.
Enrollment (%)	100.0	9.4	3.7	0.4	0.1	86.5
Drop-out Rate (%)	5.5	2.1	2.4	0.0	0.0	6.3
H.S. Diplomas (#)	476	72	25	3	0	376

Bowie County

Liberty-Eylau ISD
2901 Leopard Dr • Texarkana, TX 75501-7817
(903) 832-1535
Grade Span: PK-12; **Agency Type:** 1
Schools: 7
  3 Primary; 1 Middle; 2 High; 1 Other Level
  5 Regular; 0 Special Education; 0 Vocational; 2 Alternative
  0 Magnet; 0 Charter; 3 Title I Eligible; 3 School-wide Title I
Students: 2,725 (52.4% male; 47.5% female)
  Individual Education Program: 448 (16.4%);
  English Language Learner: 10 (0.4%); Migrant: 8 (0.3%)
  Eligible for Free Lunch Program: 1,495 (54.9%)
  Eligible for Reduced-Price Lunch Program: 199 (7.3%)
Teachers: 204.3 (13.3 to 1)
Librarians/Media Specialists: 2.0 (1,362.5 to 1)
Guidance Counselors: 7.8 (349.4 to 1)
Current Spending: ($ per student per year):
  Total: $7,006; Instruction: $4,453; Support Services: $2,178
Enrollment, Drop-out Rates and Diploma Recipients by Race/Ethnicity

Category	Total	White	Black	Asian	AIAN	Hisp.
Enrollment (%)	100.0	51.1	47.2	0.2	0.2	1.3
Drop-out Rate (%)	3.2	4.3	2.4	n/a	0.0	0.0
H.S. Diplomas (#)	164	80	77	0	1	6

Pleasant Grove ISD
8500 N Kings Hwy • Texarkana, TX 75503-4893
(903) 831-4086
Grade Span: PK-12; **Agency Type:** 1
Schools: 3
  1 Primary; 1 Middle; 1 High; 0 Other Level
  3 Regular; 0 Special Education; 0 Vocational; 0 Alternative
  0 Magnet; 0 Charter; 1 Title I Eligible; 0 School-wide Title I
Students: 1,925 (52.2% male; 47.7% female)
  Individual Education Program: 164 (8.5%);
  English Language Learner: 31 (1.6%); Migrant: 0 (0.0%)
  Eligible for Free Lunch Program: 197 (10.2%)
  Eligible for Reduced-Price Lunch Program: 63 (3.3%)
Teachers: 133.7 (14.4 to 1)
Librarians/Media Specialists: 2.0 (962.5 to 1)
Guidance Counselors: 4.0 (481.3 to 1)
Current Spending: ($ per student per year):
  Total: $5,836; Instruction: $3,651; Support Services: $1,931
Enrollment, Drop-out Rates and Diploma Recipients by Race/Ethnicity

Category	Total	White	Black	Asian	AIAN	Hisp.
Enrollment (%)	100.0	86.1	8.4	2.8	0.3	2.4
Drop-out Rate (%)	1.3	1.4	0.0	0.0	n/a	0.0
H.S. Diplomas (#)	130	116	10	2	0	2

Texarkana ISD
4241 Summerhill Rd • Texarkana, TX 75503-2733
(903) 794-3651 • http://www.txkisd.net/
Grade Span: PK-12; **Agency Type:** 1
Schools: 11
  7 Primary; 1 Middle; 2 High; 1 Other Level
  9 Regular; 0 Special Education; 0 Vocational; 2 Alternative
  0 Magnet; 0 Charter; 7 Title I Eligible; 7 School-wide Title I
Students: 5,719 (50.4% male; 49.5% female)
  Individual Education Program: 976 (17.1%);
  English Language Learner: 107 (1.9%); Migrant: 5 (0.1%)
  Eligible for Free Lunch Program: 3,067 (53.6%)
  Eligible for Reduced-Price Lunch Program: 413 (7.2%)
Teachers: 389.9 (14.7 to 1)
Librarians/Media Specialists: 2.0 (2,859.5 to 1)
Guidance Counselors: 17.0 (336.4 to 1)
Current Spending: ($ per student per year):
  Total: $6,502; Instruction: $3,946; Support Services: $2,146
Enrollment, Drop-out Rates and Diploma Recipients by Race/Ethnicity

Category	Total	White	Black	Asian	AIAN	Hisp.
Enrollment (%)	100.0	44.0	50.0	0.8	0.4	4.9
Drop-out Rate (%)	5.1	3.8	6.9	5.9	0.0	2.6
H.S. Diplomas (#)	276	162	107	4	0	3

Brazoria County

Alvin ISD
301 E House St • Alvin, TX 77511-3581
(281) 388-1130 • http://www.alvin.isd.tenet.edu/
Grade Span: PK-12; **Agency Type:** 1
Schools: 17
  8 Primary; 6 Middle; 1 High; 2 Other Level
  14 Regular; 1 Special Education; 0 Vocational; 2 Alternative
  0 Magnet; 0 Charter; 15 Title I Eligible; 15 School-wide Title I
Students: 12,131 (52.5% male; 47.4% female)
  Individual Education Program: 1,516 (12.5%);
  English Language Learner: 1,224 (10.1%); Migrant: 81 (0.7%)
  Eligible for Free Lunch Program: 4,552 (37.5%)
  Eligible for Reduced-Price Lunch Program: 1,070 (8.8%)
Teachers: 788.2 (15.4 to 1)
Librarians/Media Specialists: 14.0 (866.5 to 1)
Guidance Counselors: 23.9 (507.6 to 1)
Current Spending: ($ per student per year):
  Total: $6,726; Instruction: $4,099; Support Services: $2,275
Enrollment, Drop-out Rates and Diploma Recipients by Race/Ethnicity

Category	Total	White	Black	Asian	AIAN	Hisp.
Enrollment (%)	100.0	54.4	3.9	2.1	0.2	39.4
Drop-out Rate (%)	5.1	4.2	2.4	0.0	0.0	7.3
H.S. Diplomas (#)	509	355	19	9	0	126

Angleton ISD
1900 N Downing Rd • Angleton, TX 77515-3799
(979) 849-8594 • http://www.aisd.net/
Grade Span: PK-12; **Agency Type:** 1
Schools: 13
  5 Primary; 2 Middle; 2 High; 4 Other Level
  9 Regular; 0 Special Education; 0 Vocational; 4 Alternative
  0 Magnet; 0 Charter; 8 Title I Eligible; 7 School-wide Title I
Students: 6,506 (52.1% male; 47.8% female)
  Individual Education Program: 887 (13.6%);
  English Language Learner: 384 (5.9%); Migrant: 13 (0.2%)
  Eligible for Free Lunch Program: 2,312 (35.5%)
  Eligible for Reduced-Price Lunch Program: 488 (7.5%)
Teachers: 381.4 (17.1 to 1)
Librarians/Media Specialists: 8.0 (813.3 to 1)
Guidance Counselors: 13.9 (468.1 to 1)
Current Spending: ($ per student per year):
  Total: $5,963; Instruction: $3,737; Support Services: $1,902
Enrollment, Drop-out Rates and Diploma Recipients by Race/Ethnicity

Category	Total	White	Black	Asian	AIAN	Hisp.
Enrollment (%)	100.0	50.7	15.1	0.9	0.3	33.0
Drop-out Rate (%)	1.3	1.5	1.2	5.3	0.0	0.8
H.S. Diplomas (#)	318	187	51	4	1	75

Brazosport ISD
PO Drawer Z • Freeport, TX 77541-1926
(979) 730-7000 • http://www.brazosport.isd.tenet.edu/
Grade Span: PK-12; **Agency Type:** 1
Schools: 21
  11 Primary; 5 Middle; 2 High; 3 Other Level
  18 Regular; 0 Special Education; 0 Vocational; 3 Alternative
  0 Magnet; 0 Charter; 11 Title I Eligible; 11 School-wide Title I
Students: 13,180 (51.8% male; 48.1% female)
  Individual Education Program: 1,817 (13.8%);
  English Language Learner: 1,028 (7.8%); Migrant: 535 (4.1%)
  Eligible for Free Lunch Program: 5,188 (39.4%)
  Eligible for Reduced-Price Lunch Program: 894 (6.8%)
Teachers: 811.9 (16.2 to 1)
Librarians/Media Specialists: 18.5 (712.4 to 1)
Guidance Counselors: 32.5 (405.5 to 1)
Current Spending: ($ per student per year):
  Total: $6,577; Instruction: $3,992; Support Services: $2,207
Enrollment, Drop-out Rates and Diploma Recipients by Race/Ethnicity

Category	Total	White	Black	Asian	AIAN	Hisp.
Enrollment (%)	100.0	50.2	9.9	1.4	0.2	38.2
Drop-out Rate (%)	4.1	2.9	5.0	0.0	0.0	6.4
H.S. Diplomas (#)	733	449	53	14	3	214

Columbia-Brazoria ISD
521 S 16th St • West Columbia, TX 77486-0158
Mailing Address: PO Box 158 • West Columbia, TX 77486-0158
(979) 345-5147 • http://www.columbia-brazoria.isd.tenet.edu/
Grade Span: PK-12; **Agency Type:** 1
Schools: 7
  3 Primary; 2 Middle; 1 High; 1 Other Level
  6 Regular; 0 Special Education; 0 Vocational; 1 Alternative
  0 Magnet; 0 Charter; 4 Title I Eligible; 4 School-wide Title I
Students: 3,123   (50.4% male; 49.5% female)
  Individual Education Program: 403 (12.9%);

English Language Learner: 108 (3.5%); Migrant: 16 (0.5%)
Eligible for Free Lunch Program: 1,082 (34.6%)
Eligible for Reduced-Price Lunch Program: 217 (6.9%)
Teachers: 204.5 (15.3 to 1)
Librarians/Media Specialists: 3.1 (1,007.4 to 1)
Guidance Counselors: 6.0 (520.5 to 1)
Current Spending: ($ per student per year):
Total: $7,046; Instruction: $4,192; Support Services: $2,454
Enrollment, Drop-out Rates and Diploma Recipients by Race/Ethnicity

Category	Total	White	Black	Asian	AIAN	Hisp.
Enrollment (%)	100.0	63.4	16.1	0.7	0.5	19.3
Drop-out Rate (%)	4.7	4.8	5.3	0.0	0.0	3.8
H.S. Diplomas (#)	185	123	39	1	0	22

Pearland ISD

2337 N Galveston Ave • Pearland, TX 77581-4245
Mailing Address: PO Box 7 • Pearland, TX 77581-4209
(281) 485-3203 • http://www.pearlandisd.org/pisd/default.htm
Grade Span: PK-12; **Agency Type:** 1
Schools: 18
8 Primary; 7 Middle; 1 High; 2 Other Level
16 Regular; 0 Special Education; 0 Vocational; 2 Alternative
0 Magnet; 0 Charter; 6 Title I Eligible; 0 School-wide Title I
Students: 13,096 (51.0% male; 48.9% female)
Individual Education Program: 1,189 (9.1%);
English Language Learner: 742 (5.7%); Migrant: 10 (0.1%)
Eligible for Free Lunch Program: 1,851 (14.1%)
Eligible for Reduced-Price Lunch Program: 546 (4.2%)
Teachers: 839.1 (15.6 to 1)
Librarians/Media Specialists: 17.0 (770.4 to 1)
Guidance Counselors: 30.0 (436.5 to 1)
Current Spending: ($ per student per year):
Total: $6,474; Instruction: $3,742; Support Services: $2,456
Enrollment, Drop-out Rates and Diploma Recipients by Race/Ethnicity

Category	Total	White	Black	Asian	AIAN	Hisp.
Enrollment (%)	100.0	56.6	12.5	8.2	0.2	22.5
Drop-out Rate (%)	2.9	2.5	1.3	1.1	0.0	5.2
H.S. Diplomas (#)	628	426	54	29	2	117

Sweeny ISD

1310 N Elm St • Sweeny, TX 77480-1399
(979) 491-8000
Grade Span: PK-12; **Agency Type:** 1
Schools: 4
1 Primary; 1 Middle; 1 High; 1 Other Level
3 Regular; 0 Special Education; 0 Vocational; 1 Alternative
0 Magnet; 0 Charter; 2 Title I Eligible; 2 School-wide Title I
Students: 2,098 (54.0% male; 45.9% female)
Individual Education Program: 247 (11.8%);
English Language Learner: 51 (2.4%); Migrant: 0 (0.0%)
Eligible for Free Lunch Program: 607 (28.9%)
Eligible for Reduced-Price Lunch Program: 150 (7.1%)
Teachers: 137.0 (15.3 to 1)
Librarians/Media Specialists: 2.0 (1,049.0 to 1)
Guidance Counselors: 4.0 (524.5 to 1)
Current Spending: ($ per student per year):
Total: $7,464; Instruction: $4,459; Support Services: $2,684
Enrollment, Drop-out Rates and Diploma Recipients by Race/Ethnicity

Category	Total	White	Black	Asian	AIAN	Hisp.
Enrollment (%)	100.0	66.5	18.6	0.2	0.1	14.5
Drop-out Rate (%)	1.0	0.8	1.7	0.0	0.0	1.3
H.S. Diplomas (#)	156	107	31	2	1	15

Brazos County

Bryan ISD

101 N Texas Ave • Bryan, TX 77803-5398
(979) 209-1000 • http://www.bryanisd.org/
Grade Span: PK-12; **Agency Type:** 1
Schools: 25
16 Primary; 3 Middle; 3 High; 3 Other Level
21 Regular; 0 Special Education; 0 Vocational; 4 Alternative
0 Magnet; 0 Charter; 16 Title I Eligible; 15 School-wide Title I
Students: 14,213 (51.8% male; 48.1% female)
Individual Education Program: 1,547 (10.9%);
English Language Learner: 1,644 (11.6%); Migrant: 460 (3.2%)
Eligible for Free Lunch Program: 7,674 (54.0%)
Eligible for Reduced-Price Lunch Program: 1,086 (7.6%)
Teachers: 935.3 (15.2 to 1)
Librarians/Media Specialists: 19.0 (748.1 to 1)
Guidance Counselors: 35.1 (404.9 to 1)
Current Spending: ($ per student per year):
Total: $6,662; Instruction: $3,962; Support Services: $2,307

Enrollment, Drop-out Rates and Diploma Recipients by Race/Ethnicity

Category	Total	White	Black	Asian	AIAN	Hisp.
Enrollment (%)	100.0	36.1	24.9	0.6	0.1	38.3
Drop-out Rate (%)	1.9	0.9	1.5	6.7	50.0	3.5
H.S. Diplomas (#)	699	365	143	5	1	185

College Station ISD

1812 Welsh Ave • College Station, TX 77840-4851
(979) 764-5400 • http://www.csisd.org/
Grade Span: PK-12; **Agency Type:** 1
Schools: 11
5 Primary; 4 Middle; 2 High; 0 Other Level
10 Regular; 0 Special Education; 0 Vocational; 1 Alternative
0 Magnet; 0 Charter; 3 Title I Eligible; 3 School-wide Title I
Students: 7,931 (51.8% male; 48.1% female)
Individual Education Program: 696 (8.8%);
English Language Learner: 380 (4.8%); Migrant: 17 (0.2%)
Eligible for Free Lunch Program: 1,083 (13.7%)
Eligible for Reduced-Price Lunch Program: 349 (4.4%)
Teachers: 526.7 (15.1 to 1)
Librarians/Media Specialists: 8.1 (979.1 to 1)
Guidance Counselors: 13.5 (587.5 to 1)
Current Spending: ($ per student per year):
Total: $6,905; Instruction: $4,284; Support Services: $2,300
Enrollment, Drop-out Rates and Diploma Recipients by Race/Ethnicity

Category	Total	White	Black	Asian	AIAN	Hisp.
Enrollment (%)	100.0	66.2	11.8	9.2	0.1	12.7
Drop-out Rate (%)	1.7	1.3	3.6	0.7	0.0	3.5
H.S. Diplomas (#)	512	401	44	33	0	34

Brooks County

Brooks County ISD

221 S Henry St • Falfurrias, TX 78355-4321
Mailing Address: PO Box 589 • Falfurrias, TX 78355-0589
(361) 325-5681
Grade Span: PK-12; **Agency Type:** 1
Schools: 4
2 Primary; 1 Middle; 1 High; 0 Other Level
4 Regular; 0 Special Education; 0 Vocational; 0 Alternative
0 Magnet; 0 Charter; 4 Title I Eligible; 4 School-wide Title I
Students: 1,648 (53.2% male; 46.7% female)
Individual Education Program: 263 (16.0%);
English Language Learner: 76 (4.6%); Migrant: 191 (11.6%)
Eligible for Free Lunch Program: 1,391 (84.4%)
Eligible for Reduced-Price Lunch Program: 167 (10.1%)
Teachers: 129.3 (12.7 to 1)
Librarians/Media Specialists: 1.0 (1,648.0 to 1)
Guidance Counselors: 3.0 (549.3 to 1)
Current Spending: ($ per student per year):
Total: $8,300; Instruction: $5,113; Support Services: $2,673
Enrollment, Drop-out Rates and Diploma Recipients by Race/Ethnicity

Category	Total	White	Black	Asian	AIAN	Hisp.
Enrollment (%)	100.0	3.9	0.0	0.1	0.1	95.9
Drop-out Rate (%)	4.5	4.2	0.0	n/a	n/a	4.5
H.S. Diplomas (#)	111	3	1	0	0	107

Brown County

Brownwood ISD

2707 Southside • Brownwood, TX 76801-6148
Mailing Address: PO Box 730 • Brownwood, TX 76804-0730
(325) 643-5644 • http://www.brownwoodisd.com/
Grade Span: PK-12; **Agency Type:** 1
Schools: 8
3 Primary; 3 Middle; 1 High; 1 Other Level
7 Regular; 0 Special Education; 0 Vocational; 1 Alternative
0 Magnet; 0 Charter; 6 Title I Eligible; 6 School-wide Title I
Students: 3,599 (51.1% male; 48.8% female)
Individual Education Program: 421 (11.7%);
English Language Learner: 109 (3.0%); Migrant: 18 (0.5%)
Eligible for Free Lunch Program: 1,585 (44.0%)
Eligible for Reduced-Price Lunch Program: 334 (9.3%)
Teachers: 272.5 (13.2 to 1)
Librarians/Media Specialists: 1.1 (3,271.8 to 1)
Guidance Counselors: 8.0 (449.9 to 1)
Current Spending: ($ per student per year):
Total: $6,544; Instruction: $4,260; Support Services: $1,966
Enrollment, Drop-out Rates and Diploma Recipients by Race/Ethnicity

Category	Total	White	Black	Asian	AIAN	Hisp.
Enrollment (%)	100.0	59.2	7.0	0.3	0.1	33.4
Drop-out Rate (%)	4.4	3.8	5.9	0.0	0.0	5.3
H.S. Diplomas (#)	250	162	20	1	0	67

Burleson County

Caldwell ISD
203 N Gray St • Caldwell, TX 77836-1549
(979) 567-9000
Grade Span: PK-12; **Agency Type:** 1
Schools: 5
  2 Primary; 1 Middle; 1 High; 1 Other Level
  4 Regular; 0 Special Education; 0 Vocational; 1 Alternative
  0 Magnet; 0 Charter; 3 Title I Eligible; 3 School-wide Title I
Students: 1,909 (53.1% male; 46.8% female)
  Individual Education Program: 258 (13.5%);
  English Language Learner: 121 (6.3%); Migrant: 22 (1.2%)
  Eligible for Free Lunch Program: 717 (37.6%)
  Eligible for Reduced-Price Lunch Program: 140 (7.3%)
Teachers: 137.2 (13.9 to 1)
Librarians/Media Specialists: 1.0 (1,909.0 to 1)
Guidance Counselors: 6.0 (318.2 to 1)
Current Spending: ($ per student per year):
  Total: $7,880; Instruction: $4,401; Support Services: $3,102
Enrollment, Drop-out Rates and Diploma Recipients by Race/Ethnicity

Category	Total	White	Black	Asian	AIAN	Hisp.
Enrollment (%)	100.0	62.8	13.4	0.2	0.4	23.3
Drop-out Rate (%)	3.6	3.6	1.1	0.0	n/a	6.2
H.S. Diplomas (#)	124	94	17	0	0	13

Burnet County

Burnet Cons ISD
208 E Brier Ln • Burnet, TX 78611-0180
(512) 756-2124 • http://www.burnet.txed.net/
Grade Span: PK-12; **Agency Type:** 1
Schools: 6
  2 Primary; 2 Middle; 2 High; 0 Other Level
  5 Regular; 0 Special Education; 0 Vocational; 1 Alternative
  0 Magnet; 0 Charter; 5 Title I Eligible; 5 School-wide Title I
Students: 3,083 (50.8% male; 49.1% female)
  Individual Education Program: 492 (16.0%);
  English Language Learner: 129 (4.2%); Migrant: 33 (1.1%)
  Eligible for Free Lunch Program: 1,028 (33.3%)
  Eligible for Reduced-Price Lunch Program: 298 (9.7%)
Teachers: 212.0 (14.5 to 1)
Librarians/Media Specialists: 2.5 (1,233.2 to 1)
Guidance Counselors: 8.0 (385.4 to 1)
Current Spending: ($ per student per year):
  Total: $7,211; Instruction: $4,329; Support Services: $2,551
Enrollment, Drop-out Rates and Diploma Recipients by Race/Ethnicity

Category	Total	White	Black	Asian	AIAN	Hisp.
Enrollment (%)	100.0	77.9	1.2	0.5	0.7	19.7
Drop-out Rate (%)	1.3	1.0	0.0	0.0	n/a	2.8
H.S. Diplomas (#)	169	139	4	0	0	26

Marble Falls ISD
2001 Broadway St • Marble Falls, TX 78654-4803
(830) 693-4357
Grade Span: PK-12; **Agency Type:** 1
Schools: 5
  3 Primary; 1 Middle; 1 High; 0 Other Level
  5 Regular; 0 Special Education; 0 Vocational; 0 Alternative
  0 Magnet; 0 Charter; 5 Title I Eligible; 5 School-wide Title I
Students: 3,703 (48.8% male; 51.1% female)
  Individual Education Program: 412 (11.1%);
  English Language Learner: 369 (10.0%); Migrant: 65 (1.8%)
  Eligible for Free Lunch Program: 1,399 (37.8%)
  Eligible for Reduced-Price Lunch Program: 324 (8.7%)
Teachers: 264.2 (14.0 to 1)
Librarians/Media Specialists: 4.0 (925.8 to 1)
Guidance Counselors: 10.0 (370.3 to 1)
Current Spending: ($ per student per year):
  Total: $7,665; Instruction: $4,523; Support Services: $2,791
Enrollment, Drop-out Rates and Diploma Recipients by Race/Ethnicity

Category	Total	White	Black	Asian	AIAN	Hisp.
Enrollment (%)	100.0	66.5	1.8	0.6	0.6	30.5
Drop-out Rate (%)	3.3	2.5	0.0	0.0	0.0	6.4
H.S. Diplomas (#)	193	155	2	1	2	33

Caldwell County

Lockhart ISD
105 S Colorado • Lockhart, TX 78644-2730
Mailing Address: PO Box 120 • Lockhart, TX 78644-0120
(512) 398-0000 • http://www.lockhart.k12.tx.us/
Grade Span: PK-12; **Agency Type:** 1
Schools: 8
  4 Primary; 1 Middle; 2 High; 1 Other Level

  7 Regular; 0 Special Education; 0 Vocational; 1 Alternative
  0 Magnet; 0 Charter; 4 Title I Eligible; 4 School-wide Title I
Students: 4,495 (51.7% male; 48.2% female)
  Individual Education Program: 659 (14.7%);
  English Language Learner: 191 (4.2%); Migrant: 11 (0.2%)
  Eligible for Free Lunch Program: 1,838 (40.9%)
  Eligible for Reduced-Price Lunch Program: 519 (11.5%)
Teachers: 303.1 (14.8 to 1)
Librarians/Media Specialists: 7.0 (642.1 to 1)
Guidance Counselors: 12.0 (374.6 to 1)
Current Spending: ($ per student per year):
  Total: $6,933; Instruction: $4,220; Support Services: $2,390
Enrollment, Drop-out Rates and Diploma Recipients by Race/Ethnicity

Category	Total	White	Black	Asian	AIAN	Hisp.
Enrollment (%)	100.0	39.0	7.9	0.5	0.2	52.4
Drop-out Rate (%)	2.7	2.2	1.5	0.0	0.0	3.6
H.S. Diplomas (#)	285	141	31	2	0	111

Luling ISD
212 E Bowie St • Luling, TX 78648-2904
(830) 875-3191
Grade Span: PK-12; **Agency Type:** 1
Schools: 5
  3 Primary; 1 Middle; 1 High; 0 Other Level
  5 Regular; 0 Special Education; 0 Vocational; 0 Alternative
  0 Magnet; 0 Charter; 5 Title I Eligible; 5 School-wide Title I
Students: 1,615 (50.1% male; 49.8% female)
  Individual Education Program: 172 (10.7%);
  English Language Learner: 115 (7.1%); Migrant: 78 (4.8%)
  Eligible for Free Lunch Program: 888 (55.0%)
  Eligible for Reduced-Price Lunch Program: 154 (9.5%)
Teachers: 114.8 (14.1 to 1)
Librarians/Media Specialists: 1.0 (1,615.0 to 1)
Guidance Counselors: 4.0 (403.8 to 1)
Current Spending: ($ per student per year):
  Total: $6,555; Instruction: $4,359; Support Services: $1,804
Enrollment, Drop-out Rates and Diploma Recipients by Race/Ethnicity

Category	Total	White	Black	Asian	AIAN	Hisp.
Enrollment (%)	100.0	39.1	8.8	0.4	0.1	51.6
Drop-out Rate (%)	4.4	2.5	5.7	0.0	n/a	6.1
H.S. Diplomas (#)	86	44	6	0	0	36

Calhoun County

Calhoun County ISD
525 N Commerce St • Port Lavaca, TX 77979-3034
(361) 552-9728
Grade Span: PK-12; **Agency Type:** 1
Schools: 9
  5 Primary; 1 Middle; 2 High; 1 Other Level
  7 Regular; 0 Special Education; 0 Vocational; 2 Alternative
  0 Magnet; 0 Charter; 5 Title I Eligible; 5 School-wide Title I
Students: 4,298 (51.8% male; 48.1% female)
  Individual Education Program: 545 (12.7%);
  English Language Learner: 326 (7.6%); Migrant: 43 (1.0%)
  Eligible for Free Lunch Program: 2,006 (46.7%)
  Eligible for Reduced-Price Lunch Program: 370 (8.6%)
Teachers: 273.6 (15.7 to 1)
Librarians/Media Specialists: 4.0 (1,074.5 to 1)
Guidance Counselors: 10.8 (398.0 to 1)
Current Spending: ($ per student per year):
  Total: $7,529; Instruction: $4,534; Support Services: $2,606
Enrollment, Drop-out Rates and Diploma Recipients by Race/Ethnicity

Category	Total	White	Black	Asian	AIAN	Hisp.
Enrollment (%)	100.0	38.9	2.4	4.1	0.0	54.7
Drop-out Rate (%)	3.6	2.7	2.7	0.0	n/a	4.9
H.S. Diplomas (#)	225	112	7	15	0	91

Cameron County

Brownsville ISD
1900 Price Rd • Brownsville, TX 78521-2417
(956) 548-8000 • http://www.bisd.us/
Grade Span: PK-12; **Agency Type:** 1
Schools: 52
  32 Primary; 10 Middle; 5 High; 4 Other Level
  47 Regular; 0 Special Education; 0 Vocational; 4 Alternative
  0 Magnet; 0 Charter; 49 Title I Eligible; 49 School-wide Title I
Students: 45,923 (51.1% male; 48.8% female)
  Individual Education Program: 5,947 (12.9%);
  English Language Learner: 22,983 (50.0%); Migrant: 4,649 (10.1%)
  Eligible for Free Lunch Program: 2,742 (6.0%)
  Eligible for Reduced-Price Lunch Program: 276 (0.6%)
Teachers: 3,014.3 (15.2 to 1)
Librarians/Media Specialists: 52.0 (883.1 to 1)

Guidance Counselors: 138.6 (331.3 to 1)
Current Spending: ($ per student per year):
   Total: $7,515; Instruction: $4,520; Support Services: $2,534
Enrollment, Drop-out Rates and Diploma Recipients by Race/Ethnicity

Category	Total	White	Black	Asian	AIAN	Hisp.
Enrollment (%)	100.0	1.8	0.1	0.3	0.0	97.7
Drop-out Rate (%)	4.1	1.3	0.0	0.0	0.0	4.2
H.S. Diplomas (#)	1,854	63	5	5	0	1,781

Harlingen Cons ISD
1409 E Harrison St • Harlingen, TX 78550-7129
(956) 427-3400 • http://www.harlingen.isd.tenet.edu/
Grade Span: PK-12; **Agency Type:** 1
Schools: 26
   15 Primary; 4 Middle; 3 High; 3 Other Level
   22 Regular; 0 Special Education; 0 Vocational; 3 Alternative
   0 Magnet; 0 Charter; 22 Title I Eligible; 21 School-wide Title I
Students: 17,051   (51.7% male; 48.2% female)
   Individual Education Program: 1,758 (10.3%);
   English Language Learner: 2,318 (13.6%); Migrant: 1,995 (11.7%)
   Eligible for Free Lunch Program: 11,104 (65.1%)
   Eligible for Reduced-Price Lunch Program: 1,104 (6.5%)
Teachers: 1,048.9 (16.3 to 1)
Librarians/Media Specialists: 20.0 (852.6 to 1)
Guidance Counselors: 46.1 (369.9 to 1)
Current Spending: ($ per student per year):
   Total: $6,845; Instruction: $4,256; Support Services: $2,175
Enrollment, Drop-out Rates and Diploma Recipients by Race/Ethnicity

Category	Total	White	Black	Asian	AIAN	Hisp.
Enrollment (%)	100.0	10.8	0.7	0.6	0.0	87.8
Drop-out Rate (%)	4.8	2.3	9.1	0.0	0.0	5.2
H.S. Diplomas (#)	807	140	7	6	0	654

La Feria ISD
203 E Oleander • La Feria, TX 78559-1159
Mailing Address: PO Box 1159 • La Feria, TX 78559-1159
(956) 797-2612
Grade Span: PK-12; **Agency Type:** 1
Schools: 8
   3 Primary; 2 Middle; 1 High; 2 Other Level
   6 Regular; 0 Special Education; 0 Vocational; 2 Alternative
   0 Magnet; 0 Charter; 6 Title I Eligible; 6 School-wide Title I
Students: 2,899   (51.2% male; 48.7% female)
   Individual Education Program: 269 (9.3%);
   English Language Learner: 383 (13.2%); Migrant: 141 (4.9%)
   Eligible for Free Lunch Program: 1,396 (48.2%)
   Eligible for Reduced-Price Lunch Program: 156 (5.4%)
Teachers: 203.0 (14.3 to 1)
Librarians/Media Specialists: 3.0 (966.3 to 1)
Guidance Counselors: 6.0 (483.2 to 1)
Current Spending: ($ per student per year):
   Total: $7,022; Instruction: $4,723; Support Services: $1,916
Enrollment, Drop-out Rates and Diploma Recipients by Race/Ethnicity

Category	Total	White	Black	Asian	AIAN	Hisp.
Enrollment (%)	100.0	8.8	0.3	0.1	0.0	90.7
Drop-out Rate (%)	2.3	1.1	0.0	0.0	n/a	2.5
H.S. Diplomas (#)	167	20	1	0	0	146

Los Fresnos Cons ISD
600 N Mesquite St • Los Fresnos, TX 78566-3634
Mailing Address: PO Box 309 • Los Fresnos, TX 78566-0309
(956) 233-4407 • http://www.lfcisd.net/
Grade Span: PK-12; **Agency Type:** 1
Schools: 10
   6 Primary; 2 Middle; 1 High; 1 Other Level
   9 Regular; 0 Special Education; 0 Vocational; 1 Alternative
   0 Magnet; 0 Charter; 9 Title I Eligible; 9 School-wide Title I
Students: 7,510   (51.6% male; 48.3% female)
   Individual Education Program: 885 (11.8%);
   English Language Learner: 1,978 (26.3%); Migrant: 596 (7.9%)
   Eligible for Free Lunch Program: 2,511 (33.4%)
   Eligible for Reduced-Price Lunch Program: 317 (4.2%)
Teachers: 455.1 (16.5 to 1)
Librarians/Media Specialists: 11.0 (682.7 to 1)
Guidance Counselors: 17.0 (441.8 to 1)
Current Spending: ($ per student per year):
   Total: $6,931; Instruction: $3,998; Support Services: $2,426
Enrollment, Drop-out Rates and Diploma Recipients by Race/Ethnicity

Category	Total	White	Black	Asian	AIAN	Hisp.
Enrollment (%)	100.0	6.1	0.3	0.3	0.1	93.2
Drop-out Rate (%)	3.3	1.8	45.5	50.0	50.0	3.1
H.S. Diplomas (#)	369	36	2	0	1	330

Point Isabel ISD
Drawer A H • Port Isabel, TX 78578-2433
(956) 943-0005
Grade Span: PK-12; **Agency Type:** 1
Schools: 4
   2 Primary; 1 Middle; 1 High; 0 Other Level
   4 Regular; 0 Special Education; 0 Vocational; 0 Alternative
   0 Magnet; 0 Charter; 4 Title I Eligible; 4 School-wide Title I
Students: 2,556   (50.9% male; 49.0% female)
   Individual Education Program: 287 (11.2%);
   English Language Learner: 725 (28.4%); Migrant: 165 (6.5%)
   Eligible for Free Lunch Program: 1,254 (49.1%)
   Eligible for Reduced-Price Lunch Program: 144 (5.6%)
Teachers: 162.3 (15.7 to 1)
Librarians/Media Specialists: 4.0 (639.0 to 1)
Guidance Counselors: 7.5 (340.8 to 1)
Current Spending: ($ per student per year):
   Total: $7,651; Instruction: $4,364; Support Services: $2,767
Enrollment, Drop-out Rates and Diploma Recipients by Race/Ethnicity

Category	Total	White	Black	Asian	AIAN	Hisp.
Enrollment (%)	100.0	14.6	0.3	0.2	0.0	84.8
Drop-out Rate (%)	3.3	3.2	0.0	0.0	0.0	3.4
H.S. Diplomas (#)	149	30	1	1	0	117

Rio Hondo ISD
215 W Colorado • Rio Hondo, TX 78583-0220
Mailing Address: PO Box 220 • Rio Hondo, TX 78583-0220
(956) 748-1000
Grade Span: PK-12; **Agency Type:** 1
Schools: 5
   2 Primary; 1 Middle; 1 High; 1 Other Level
   4 Regular; 0 Special Education; 0 Vocational; 1 Alternative
   0 Magnet; 0 Charter; 4 Title I Eligible; 4 School-wide Title I
Students: 2,177   (51.8% male; 48.1% female)
   Individual Education Program: 348 (16.0%);
   English Language Learner: 285 (13.1%); Migrant: 236 (10.8%)
   Eligible for Free Lunch Program: 829 (38.1%)
   Eligible for Reduced-Price Lunch Program: 135 (6.2%)
Teachers: 134.9 (16.1 to 1)
Librarians/Media Specialists: 1.0 (2,177.0 to 1)
Guidance Counselors: 5.5 (395.8 to 1)
Current Spending: ($ per student per year):
   Total: $7,586; Instruction: $4,420; Support Services: $2,651
Enrollment, Drop-out Rates and Diploma Recipients by Race/Ethnicity

Category	Total	White	Black	Asian	AIAN	Hisp.
Enrollment (%)	100.0	4.6	0.1	0.0	0.1	95.1
Drop-out Rate (%)	3.4	0.0	n/a	n/a	n/a	3.7
H.S. Diplomas (#)	109	6	0	0	0	103

San Benito Cons ISD
240 N Crockett St • San Benito, TX 78586-4608
(956) 361-6110 • http://www.sanbenito.k12.tx.us/
Grade Span: PK-12; **Agency Type:** 1
Schools: 18
   10 Primary; 2 Middle; 1 High; 5 Other Level
   14 Regular; 0 Special Education; 0 Vocational; 4 Alternative
   0 Magnet; 0 Charter; 15 Title I Eligible; 15 School-wide Title I
Students: 9,886   (51.9% male; 48.0% female)
   Individual Education Program: 1,186 (12.0%);
   English Language Learner: 2,485 (25.1%); Migrant: 1,462 (14.8%)
   Eligible for Free Lunch Program: 1,818 (18.4%)
   Eligible for Reduced-Price Lunch Program: 212 (2.1%)
Teachers: 576.5 (17.1 to 1)
Librarians/Media Specialists: 13.0 (760.5 to 1)
Guidance Counselors: 27.0 (366.1 to 1)
Current Spending: ($ per student per year):
   Total: $6,847; Instruction: $3,894; Support Services: $2,470
Enrollment, Drop-out Rates and Diploma Recipients by Race/Ethnicity

Category	Total	White	Black	Asian	AIAN	Hisp.
Enrollment (%)	100.0	1.9	0.2	0.1	0.0	97.9
Drop-out Rate (%)	5.4	5.5	0.0	0.0	n/a	5.4
H.S. Diplomas (#)	399	8	1	0	0	390

South Texas ISD
100 Med High Dr • Mercedes, TX 78570-9702
(956) 565-2454
Grade Span: 01-12; **Agency Type:** 1
Schools: 6
   0 Primary; 0 Middle; 3 High; 1 Other Level
   3 Regular; 0 Special Education; 1 Vocational; 0 Alternative
   0 Magnet; 0 Charter; 4 Title I Eligible; 4 School-wide Title I
Students: 2,090   (46.6% male; 53.3% female)
   Individual Education Program: 140 (6.7%);
   English Language Learner: 74 (3.5%); Migrant: 71 (3.4%)
   Eligible for Free Lunch Program: 895 (42.8%)

Eligible for Reduced-Price Lunch Program: 214 (10.2%)
Teachers: 162.7 (12.8 to 1)
Librarians/Media Specialists: 4.1 (509.8 to 1)
Guidance Counselors: 8.0 (261.3 to 1)
Current Spending: ($ per student per year):
   Total: $11,767; Instruction: $6,247; Support Services: $5,131
Enrollment, Drop-out Rates and Diploma Recipients by Race/Ethnicity

Category	Total	White	Black	Asian	AIAN	Hisp.
Enrollment (%)	100.0	16.1	0.9	6.5	0.1	76.4
Drop-out Rate (%)	0.4	0.3	0.0	0.0	0.0	0.5
H.S. Diplomas (#)	353	70	1	23	0	259

Camp County

Pittsburg ISD
402 Broach St • Pittsburg, TX 75686-1039
Mailing Address: PO Box 1189 • Pittsburg, TX 75686-0621
(903) 856-3628
Grade Span: PK-12; **Agency Type:** 1
Schools: 5
   2 Primary; 2 Middle; 1 High; 0 Other Level
   5 Regular; 0 Special Education; 0 Vocational; 0 Alternative
   0 Magnet; 0 Charter; 3 Title I Eligible; 3 School-wide Title I
Students: 2,333   (52.5% male; 47.4% female)
   Individual Education Program: 376 (16.1%);
   English Language Learner: 280 (12.0%); Migrant: 219 (9.4%)
   Eligible for Free Lunch Program: 1,270 (54.4%)
   Eligible for Reduced-Price Lunch Program: 202 (8.7%)
Teachers: 169.2 (13.8 to 1)
Librarians/Media Specialists: 3.0 (777.7 to 1)
Guidance Counselors: 5.0 (466.6 to 1)
Current Spending: ($ per student per year):
   Total: $6,504; Instruction: $4,318; Support Services: $1,849
Enrollment, Drop-out Rates and Diploma Recipients by Race/Ethnicity

Category	Total	White	Black	Asian	AIAN	Hisp.
Enrollment (%)	100.0	50.5	22.5	0.5	0.3	26.1
Drop-out Rate (%)	2.9	2.2	1.8	0.0	0.0	6.7
H.S. Diplomas (#)	105	63	30	1	0	11

Cass County

Atlanta ISD
315 Buckner St • Atlanta, TX 75551-2211
(903) 796-4194
Grade Span: PK-12; **Agency Type:** 1
Schools: 5
   2 Primary; 1 Middle; 1 High; 1 Other Level
   4 Regular; 0 Special Education; 0 Vocational; 1 Alternative
   0 Magnet; 0 Charter; 4 Title I Eligible; 4 School-wide Title I
Students: 1,947   (52.0% male; 47.9% female)
   Individual Education Program: 360 (18.5%);
   English Language Learner: 13 (0.7%); Migrant: 47 (2.4%)
   Eligible for Free Lunch Program: 889 (45.7%)
   Eligible for Reduced-Price Lunch Program: 215 (11.0%)
Teachers: 154.3 (12.6 to 1)
Librarians/Media Specialists: 3.0 (649.0 to 1)
Guidance Counselors: 5.0 (389.4 to 1)
Current Spending: ($ per student per year):
   Total: $7,517; Instruction: $4,739; Support Services: $2,379
Enrollment, Drop-out Rates and Diploma Recipients by Race/Ethnicity

Category	Total	White	Black	Asian	AIAN	Hisp.
Enrollment (%)	100.0	61.4	35.4	0.2	0.2	2.8
Drop-out Rate (%)	0.5	0.8	0.0	n/a	0.0	0.0
H.S. Diplomas (#)	135	81	53	0	0	1

Chambers County

Barbers Hill ISD
9600 Eagle Dr • Mt Belvieu, TX 77580-1108
Mailing Address: PO Box 1108 • Mont Belvieu, TX 77580-1108
(281) 576-2221
Grade Span: PK-12; **Agency Type:** 1
Schools: 8
   2 Primary; 2 Middle; 2 High; 2 Other Level
   5 Regular; 1 Special Education; 0 Vocational; 2 Alternative
   0 Magnet; 0 Charter; 1 Title I Eligible; 1 School-wide Title I
Students: 3,020   (51.4% male; 48.5% female)
   Individual Education Program: 227 (7.5%);
   English Language Learner: 77 (2.5%); Migrant: 1 (<0.1%)
   Eligible for Free Lunch Program: 428 (14.2%)
   Eligible for Reduced-Price Lunch Program: 135 (4.5%)
Teachers: 209.8 (14.4 to 1)
Librarians/Media Specialists: 5.0 (604.0 to 1)
Guidance Counselors: 6.0 (503.3 to 1)

Current Spending: ($ per student per year):
   Total: $7,576; Instruction: $4,489; Support Services: $2,737
Enrollment, Drop-out Rates and Diploma Recipients by Race/Ethnicity

Category	Total	White	Black	Asian	AIAN	Hisp.
Enrollment (%)	100.0	84.3	2.9	0.3	0.2	12.2
Drop-out Rate (%)	0.8	0.7	0.0	n/a	0.0	1.5
H.S. Diplomas (#)	143	127	3	0	0	13

Cherokee County

Jacksonville ISD
1547 E Pine St • Jacksonville, TX 75766-5408
Mailing Address: PO Box 631 • Jacksonville, TX 75766-0631
(903) 586-6511
Grade Span: PK-12; **Agency Type:** 1
Schools: 8
   4 Primary; 2 Middle; 1 High; 1 Other Level
   7 Regular; 0 Special Education; 0 Vocational; 1 Alternative
   0 Magnet; 0 Charter; 8 Title I Eligible; 8 School-wide Title I
Students: 4,823   (51.8% male; 48.1% female)
   Individual Education Program: 635 (13.2%);
   English Language Learner: 813 (16.9%); Migrant: 5 (0.1%)
   Eligible for Free Lunch Program: 2,970 (61.6%)
   Eligible for Reduced-Price Lunch Program: 290 (6.0%)
Teachers: 341.9 (14.1 to 1)
Librarians/Media Specialists: 4.7 (1,026.2 to 1)
Guidance Counselors: 12.0 (401.9 to 1)
Current Spending: ($ per student per year):
   Total: $6,810; Instruction: $4,180; Support Services: $2,215
Enrollment, Drop-out Rates and Diploma Recipients by Race/Ethnicity

Category	Total	White	Black	Asian	AIAN	Hisp.
Enrollment (%)	100.0	45.0	22.2	0.5	0.3	32.0
Drop-out Rate (%)	2.1	1.6	1.9	0.0	0.0	3.6
H.S. Diplomas (#)	239	148	49	2	0	40

Rusk ISD
203 E 7th St • Rusk, TX 75785-1122
(903) 683-5592
Grade Span: PK-12; **Agency Type:** 1
Schools: 5
   2 Primary; 2 Middle; 1 High; 0 Other Level
   5 Regular; 0 Special Education; 0 Vocational; 0 Alternative
   0 Magnet; 0 Charter; 4 Title I Eligible; 4 School-wide Title I
Students: 1,959   (50.3% male; 49.6% female)
   Individual Education Program: 282 (14.4%);
   English Language Learner: 75 (3.8%); Migrant: 14 (0.7%)
   Eligible for Free Lunch Program: 837 (42.7%)
   Eligible for Reduced-Price Lunch Program: 170 (8.7%)
Teachers: 150.2 (13.0 to 1)
Librarians/Media Specialists: 0.4 (4,897.5 to 1)
Guidance Counselors: 4.6 (425.9 to 1)
Current Spending: ($ per student per year):
   Total: $6,848; Instruction: $4,278; Support Services: $2,213
Enrollment, Drop-out Rates and Diploma Recipients by Race/Ethnicity

Category	Total	White	Black	Asian	AIAN	Hisp.
Enrollment (%)	100.0	74.2	14.8	0.5	0.3	10.3
Drop-out Rate (%)	3.8	3.6	5.3	0.0	0.0	2.5
H.S. Diplomas (#)	104	72	21	2	1	8

Collin County

Allen ISD
601 E Main St • Allen, TX 75002-2837
Mailing Address: PO Box 13 • Allen, TX 75013-0013
(972) 727-0511 • http://www.allenisd.org/
Grade Span: PK-12; **Agency Type:** 1
Schools: 17
   11 Primary; 2 Middle; 1 High; 2 Other Level
   15 Regular; 0 Special Education; 0 Vocational; 1 Alternative
   0 Magnet; 0 Charter; 3 Title I Eligible; 0 School-wide Title I
Students: 13,864   (51.4% male; 48.5% female)
   Individual Education Program: 1,560 (11.3%);
   English Language Learner: 677 (4.9%); Migrant: 7 (0.1%)
   Eligible for Free Lunch Program: 810 (5.8%)
   Eligible for Reduced-Price Lunch Program: 288 (2.1%)
Teachers: 872.4 (15.9 to 1)
Librarians/Media Specialists: 12.9 (1,074.7 to 1)
Guidance Counselors: 20.7 (669.8 to 1)
Current Spending: ($ per student per year):
   Total: $6,238; Instruction: $3,786; Support Services: $2,214
Enrollment, Drop-out Rates and Diploma Recipients by Race/Ethnicity

Category	Total	White	Black	Asian	AIAN	Hisp.
Enrollment (%)	100.0	75.9	8.1	5.7	0.6	9.7
Drop-out Rate (%)	0.5	0.4	0.0	0.0	0.0	1.4
H.S. Diplomas (#)	739	636	35	20	4	44

Frisco ISD

6942 W Maple • Frisco, TX 75034-3401
Mailing Address: PO Box 910 • Frisco, TX 75034-0910
(469) 633-6000 • http://www.friscoisd.org/
Grade Span: PK-12; Agency Type: 1
Schools: 22
   15 Primary; 4 Middle; 2 High; 1 Other Level
   20 Regular; 0 Special Education; 0 Vocational; 2 Alternative
   0 Magnet; 0 Charter; 5 Title I Eligible; 0 School-wide Title I
Students: 13,411   (50.4% male; 49.5% female)
   Individual Education Program: 1,425 (10.6%);
   English Language Learner: 623 (4.6%); Migrant: 12 (0.1%)
   Eligible for Free Lunch Program: 920 (6.9%)
   Eligible for Reduced-Price Lunch Program: 289 (2.2%)
Teachers: 932.1 (14.4 to 1)
Librarians/Media Specialists: 21.0 (638.6 to 1)
Guidance Counselors: 31.4 (427.1 to 1)
Current Spending: ($ per student per year):
   Total: $6,977; Instruction: $4,180; Support Services: $2,462
Enrollment, Drop-out Rates and Diploma Recipients by Race/Ethnicity

Category	Total	White	Black	Asian	AIAN	Hisp.
Enrollment (%)	100.0	71.1	8.1	6.8	0.9	13.0
Drop-out Rate (%)	0.6	0.3	0.0	0.0	6.7	2.0
H.S. Diplomas (#)	334	256	14	8	3	53

Mckinney ISD

#1 Duvall St • Mckinney, TX 75069-3211
(469) 742-4070 • http://www.mckinneyisd.net/
Grade Span: PK-12; Agency Type: 1
Schools: 25
   15 Primary; 3 Middle; 4 High; 3 Other Level
   21 Regular; 0 Special Education; 0 Vocational; 4 Alternative
   0 Magnet; 0 Charter; 5 Title I Eligible; 5 School-wide Title I
Students: 16,663   (51.9% male; 48.0% female)
   Individual Education Program: 1,865 (11.2%);
   English Language Learner: 1,447 (8.7%); Migrant: 11 (0.1%)
   Eligible for Free Lunch Program: 2,945 (17.7%)
   Eligible for Reduced-Price Lunch Program: 600 (3.6%)
Teachers: 1,101.9 (15.1 to 1)
Librarians/Media Specialists: 20.0 (833.2 to 1)
Guidance Counselors: 33.4 (498.9 to 1)
Current Spending: ($ per student per year):
   Total: $6,724; Instruction: $4,128; Support Services: $2,328
Enrollment, Drop-out Rates and Diploma Recipients by Race/Ethnicity

Category	Total	White	Black	Asian	AIAN	Hisp.
Enrollment (%)	100.0	66.8	9.2	2.2	0.5	21.2
Drop-out Rate (%)	2.7	1.3	8.3	0.0	7.7	5.5
H.S. Diplomas (#)	604	460	47	8	4	85

Plano ISD

2700 W 15th • Plano, TX 75075-5898
(469) 752-8100 • http://www.pisd.edu/
Grade Span: PK-12; Agency Type: 1
Schools: 72
   46 Primary; 12 Middle; 3 High; 8 Other Level
   63 Regular; 0 Special Education; 0 Vocational; 6 Alternative
   0 Magnet; 0 Charter; 18 Title I Eligible; 7 School-wide Title I
Students: 51,869   (51.3% male; 48.6% female)
   Individual Education Program: 6,158 (11.9%);
   English Language Learner: 5,489 (10.6%); Migrant: 0 (0.0%)
   Eligible for Free Lunch Program: 6,336 (12.2%)
   Eligible for Reduced-Price Lunch Program: 1,647 (3.2%)
Teachers: 3,825.6 (13.6 to 1)
Librarians/Media Specialists: 66.6 (778.8 to 1)
Guidance Counselors: 133.9 (387.4 to 1)
Current Spending: ($ per student per year):
   Total: $7,073; Instruction: $4,565; Support Services: $2,236
Enrollment, Drop-out Rates and Diploma Recipients by Race/Ethnicity

Category	Total	White	Black	Asian	AIAN	Hisp.
Enrollment (%)	100.0	62.3	8.8	15.6	0.3	13.0
Drop-out Rate (%)	1.5	1.3	2.4	0.8	5.3	3.1
H.S. Diplomas (#)	2,795	2,010	192	418	5	170

Princeton ISD

321 Panther Pkwy • Princeton, TX 75407-1002
(972) 736-3503
Grade Span: PK-12; Agency Type: 1
Schools: 6
   1 Primary; 2 Middle; 1 High; 1 Other Level
   4 Regular; 0 Special Education; 0 Vocational; 1 Alternative
   0 Magnet; 0 Charter; 2 Title I Eligible; 2 School-wide Title I
Students: 2,254   (52.7% male; 47.2% female)
   Individual Education Program: 304 (13.5%);
   English Language Learner: 143 (6.3%); Migrant: 11 (0.5%)
   Eligible for Free Lunch Program: 657 (29.1%)

   Eligible for Reduced-Price Lunch Program: 203 (9.0%)
Teachers: 145.6 (15.5 to 1)
Librarians/Media Specialists: 3.0 (751.3 to 1)
Guidance Counselors: 3.0 (751.3 to 1)
Current Spending: ($ per student per year):
   Total: $6,385; Instruction: $3,864; Support Services: $2,142
Enrollment, Drop-out Rates and Diploma Recipients by Race/Ethnicity

Category	Total	White	Black	Asian	AIAN	Hisp.
Enrollment (%)	100.0	77.2	1.5	0.3	0.6	20.4
Drop-out Rate (%)	2.6	2.7	7.1	20.0	0.0	0.0
H.S. Diplomas (#)	97	85	3	0	1	8

Wylie ISD

951 S Ballard • Wylie, TX 75098-4175
Mailing Address: PO Box 490 • Wylie, TX 75098-0490
(972) 442-5444 • http://www.wylieisd.net/default.wspx
Grade Span: PK-12; Agency Type: 1
Schools: 11
   5 Primary; 3 Middle; 1 High; 1 Other Level
   9 Regular; 0 Special Education; 0 Vocational; 1 Alternative
   0 Magnet; 0 Charter; 5 Title I Eligible; 0 School-wide Title I
Students: 6,661   (51.5% male; 48.4% female)
   Individual Education Program: 767 (11.5%);
   English Language Learner: 384 (5.8%); Migrant: 6 (0.1%)
   Eligible for Free Lunch Program: 990 (15.0%)
   Eligible for Reduced-Price Lunch Program: 348 (5.3%)
Teachers: 449.4 (14.7 to 1)
Librarians/Media Specialists: 3.0 (2,205.0 to 1)
Guidance Counselors: 12.8 (516.8 to 1)
Current Spending: ($ per student per year):
   Total: $7,341; Instruction: $4,333; Support Services: $2,678
Enrollment, Drop-out Rates and Diploma Recipients by Race/Ethnicity

Category	Total	White	Black	Asian	AIAN	Hisp.
Enrollment (%)	100.0	72.0	8.0	2.6	1.2	16.0
Drop-out Rate (%)	1.9	1.6	4.0	0.0	14.3	3.5
H.S. Diplomas (#)	235	206	11	2	1	15

Colorado County

Columbus ISD

105 Cardinal Ln • Columbus, TX 78934-0578
(979) 732-5704
Grade Span: PK-12; Agency Type: 1
Schools: 3
   1 Primary; 1 Middle; 1 High; 0 Other Level
   3 Regular; 0 Special Education; 0 Vocational; 0 Alternative
   0 Magnet; 0 Charter; 1 Title I Eligible; 1 School-wide Title I
Students: 1,565   (50.3% male; 49.6% female)
   Individual Education Program: 206 (13.2%);
   English Language Learner: 105 (6.7%); Migrant: 4 (0.3%)
   Eligible for Free Lunch Program: 510 (32.6%)
   Eligible for Reduced-Price Lunch Program: 118 (7.5%)
Teachers: 113.5 (13.8 to 1)
Librarians/Media Specialists: 3.0 (521.7 to 1)
Guidance Counselors: 4.0 (391.3 to 1)
Current Spending: ($ per student per year):
   Total: $6,389; Instruction: $4,149; Support Services: $1,918
Enrollment, Drop-out Rates and Diploma Recipients by Race/Ethnicity

Category	Total	White	Black	Asian	AIAN	Hisp.
Enrollment (%)	100.0	63.5	13.9	0.5	0.1	22.0
Drop-out Rate (%)	0.2	0.3	0.0	0.0	n/a	0.0
H.S. Diplomas (#)	98	77	9	0	0	12

Comal County

Comal ISD

1421 N Business 35 • New Braunfels, TX 78130-3240
(830) 221-2000 • http://www.comalisd.org/
Grade Span: PK-12; Agency Type: 1
Schools: 20
   10 Primary; 5 Middle; 3 High; 2 Other Level
   17 Regular; 0 Special Education; 0 Vocational; 3 Alternative
   0 Magnet; 0 Charter; 6 Title I Eligible; 0 School-wide Title I
Students: 11,989   (52.3% male; 47.6% female)
   Individual Education Program: 1,634 (13.6%);
   English Language Learner: 380 (3.2%); Migrant: 81 (0.7%)
   Eligible for Free Lunch Program: 2,555 (21.3%)
   Eligible for Reduced-Price Lunch Program: 797 (6.6%)
Teachers: 766.4 (15.6 to 1)
Librarians/Media Specialists: 17.0 (705.2 to 1)
Guidance Counselors: 24.0 (499.5 to 1)
Current Spending: ($ per student per year):
   Total: $7,033; Instruction: $4,249; Support Services: $2,471

Enrollment, Drop-out Rates and Diploma Recipients by Race/Ethnicity

Category	Total	White	Black	Asian	AIAN	Hisp.
Enrollment (%)	100.0	73.6	1.5	0.6	0.3	24.0
Drop-out Rate (%)	2.6	2.0	5.0	0.0	33.3	5.0
H.S. Diplomas (#)	681	553	9	3	0	116

New Braunfels ISD

430 W Mill • New Braunfels, TX 78130-7993
Mailing Address: Box 311688 • New Braunfels, TX 78131-1688
(830) 643-5700 • http://www.newbraunfels.txed.net/
Grade Span: PK-12; **Agency Type:** 1
Schools: 12
  6 Primary; 3 Middle; 1 High; 2 Other Level
  10 Regular; 0 Special Education; 0 Vocational; 2 Alternative
  0 Magnet; 0 Charter; 9 Title I Eligible; 7 School-wide Title I
Students: 6,360 (50.1% male; 49.8% female)
  Individual Education Program: 729 (11.5%);
  English Language Learner: 460 (7.2%); Migrant: 113 (1.8%)
  Eligible for Free Lunch Program: 1,764 (27.7%)
  Eligible for Reduced-Price Lunch Program: 545 (8.6%)
Teachers: 409.8 (15.5 to 1)
Librarians/Media Specialists: 6.4 (993.8 to 1)
Guidance Counselors: 15.0 (424.0 to 1)
Current Spending: ($ per student per year):
  Total: $6,130; Instruction: $3,792; Support Services: $2,037
Enrollment, Drop-out Rates and Diploma Recipients by Race/Ethnicity

Category	Total	White	Black	Asian	AIAN	Hisp.
Enrollment (%)	100.0	54.5	1.6	0.5	0.2	43.3
Drop-out Rate (%)	3.6	1.7	3.4	0.0	0.0	6.5
H.S. Diplomas (#)	413	265	6	1	0	141

Cooke County

Gainesville ISD

1201 Lindsay St • Gainesville, TX 76240-5621
(940) 665-4362
Grade Span: PK-12; **Agency Type:** 1
Schools: 8
  3 Primary; 2 Middle; 1 High; 2 Other Level
  6 Regular; 0 Special Education; 0 Vocational; 2 Alternative
  0 Magnet; 0 Charter; 4 Title I Eligible; 4 School-wide Title I
Students: 2,993 (50.7% male; 49.2% female)
  Individual Education Program: 459 (15.3%);
  English Language Learner: 421 (14.1%); Migrant: 95 (3.2%)
  Eligible for Free Lunch Program: 1,440 (48.1%)
  Eligible for Reduced-Price Lunch Program: 200 (6.7%)
Teachers: 211.9 (14.1 to 1)
Librarians/Media Specialists: 2.8 (1,068.9 to 1)
Guidance Counselors: 9.0 (332.6 to 1)
Current Spending: ($ per student per year):
  Total: $7,129; Instruction: $4,459; Support Services: $2,302
Enrollment, Drop-out Rates and Diploma Recipients by Race/Ethnicity

Category	Total	White	Black	Asian	AIAN	Hisp.
Enrollment (%)	100.0	57.2	9.7	0.4	0.9	31.7
Drop-out Rate (%)	4.2	3.8	3.4	0.0	0.0	6.3
H.S. Diplomas (#)	146	102	18	1	2	23

Coryell County

Copperas Cove ISD

703 W Ave D • Copperas Cove, TX 76522-0580
(254) 547-1227 • http://www.ccisd.com/
Grade Span: PK-12; **Agency Type:** 1
Schools: 13
  7 Primary; 4 Middle; 2 High; 0 Other Level
  12 Regular; 0 Special Education; 0 Vocational; 1 Alternative
  0 Magnet; 0 Charter; 9 Title I Eligible; 9 School-wide Title I
Students: 7,466 (51.0% male; 48.9% female)
  Individual Education Program: 948 (12.7%);
  English Language Learner: 64 (0.9%); Migrant: 16 (0.2%)
  Eligible for Free Lunch Program: 1,881 (25.2%)
  Eligible for Reduced-Price Lunch Program: 832 (11.1%)
Teachers: 523.9 (14.3 to 1)
Librarians/Media Specialists: 13.0 (574.3 to 1)
Guidance Counselors: 18.0 (414.8 to 1)
Current Spending: ($ per student per year):
  Total: $7,108; Instruction: $4,494; Support Services: $2,302
Enrollment, Drop-out Rates and Diploma Recipients by Race/Ethnicity

Category	Total	White	Black	Asian	AIAN	Hisp.
Enrollment (%)	100.0	57.9	25.0	2.9	1.0	13.3
Drop-out Rate (%)	2.8	2.9	2.9	3.1	7.7	2.2
H.S. Diplomas (#)	449	248	121	32	2	46

Gatesville ISD

311 S Lovers Ln • Gatesville, TX 76528-0759
(254) 865-7251
Grade Span: PK-12; **Agency Type:** 1
Schools: 5
  2 Primary; 2 Middle; 1 High; 0 Other Level
  5 Regular; 0 Special Education; 0 Vocational; 0 Alternative
  0 Magnet; 0 Charter; 2 Title I Eligible; 2 School-wide Title I
Students: 2,616 (52.2% male; 47.7% female)
  Individual Education Program: 488 (18.7%);
  English Language Learner: 42 (1.6%); Migrant: 6 (0.2%)
  Eligible for Free Lunch Program: 697 (26.6%)
  Eligible for Reduced-Price Lunch Program: 241 (9.2%)
Teachers: 177.5 (14.7 to 1)
Librarians/Media Specialists: 3.6 (726.7 to 1)
Guidance Counselors: 6.0 (436.0 to 1)
Current Spending: ($ per student per year):
  Total: $5,669; Instruction: $3,515; Support Services: $1,804
Enrollment, Drop-out Rates and Diploma Recipients by Race/Ethnicity

Category	Total	White	Black	Asian	AIAN	Hisp.
Enrollment (%)	100.0	82.6	4.1	0.7	0.4	12.2
Drop-out Rate (%)	3.2	3.5	0.0	0.0	0.0	2.4
H.S. Diplomas (#)	157	134	4	1	2	16

Dallam County

Dalhart ISD

315 Rock Is Ave • Dalhart, TX 79022-2639
(806) 244-7810 • http://www.dalhart.k12.tx.us/
Grade Span: PK-12; **Agency Type:** 1
Schools: 5
  1 Primary; 2 Middle; 2 High; 0 Other Level
  4 Regular; 0 Special Education; 0 Vocational; 1 Alternative
  0 Magnet; 0 Charter; 5 Title I Eligible; 5 School-wide Title I
Students: 1,625 (53.4% male; 46.5% female)
  Individual Education Program: 242 (14.9%);
  English Language Learner: 128 (7.9%); Migrant: 231 (14.2%)
  Eligible for Free Lunch Program: 696 (42.8%)
  Eligible for Reduced-Price Lunch Program: 212 (13.0%)
Teachers: 125.1 (13.0 to 1)
Librarians/Media Specialists: 1.0 (1,625.0 to 1)
Guidance Counselors: 4.0 (406.3 to 1)
Current Spending: ($ per student per year):
  Total: $6,965; Instruction: $4,272; Support Services: $2,302
Enrollment, Drop-out Rates and Diploma Recipients by Race/Ethnicity

Category	Total	White	Black	Asian	AIAN	Hisp.
Enrollment (%)	100.0	61.0	2.8	0.7	0.2	35.3
Drop-out Rate (%)	4.6	4.9	0.0	0.0	n/a	4.0
H.S. Diplomas (#)	67	53	2	0	0	12

Dallas County

Carrollton-Farmers Branch

1445 N Perry Rd • Carrollton, TX 75006-6134
Mailing Address: PO Box 115186 • Carrollton, TX 75011-5186
(972) 466-6100 • http://www.cfbisd.edu/
Grade Span: PK-12; **Agency Type:** 1
Schools: 41
  25 Primary; 6 Middle; 4 High; 4 Other Level
  35 Regular; 1 Special Education; 0 Vocational; 3 Alternative
  0 Magnet; 0 Charter; 21 Title I Eligible; 17 School-wide Title I
Students: 25,638 (51.3% male; 48.6% female)
  Individual Education Program: 2,536 (9.9%);
  English Language Learner: 5,854 (22.8%); Migrant: 46 (0.2%)
  Eligible for Free Lunch Program: 9,023 (35.2%)
  Eligible for Reduced-Price Lunch Program: 2,341 (9.1%)
Teachers: 1,742.2 (14.7 to 1)
Librarians/Media Specialists: 34.9 (734.6 to 1)
Guidance Counselors: 45.8 (559.8 to 1)
Current Spending: ($ per student per year):
  Total: $6,957; Instruction: $4,146; Support Services: $2,530
Enrollment, Drop-out Rates and Diploma Recipients by Race/Ethnicity

Category	Total	White	Black	Asian	AIAN	Hisp.
Enrollment (%)	100.0	33.3	13.1	12.0	0.5	41.1
Drop-out Rate (%)	2.1	1.4	1.1	1.0	0.0	4.1
H.S. Diplomas (#)	1,277	695	123	201	1	257

Cedar Hill ISD

270 S Hwy 67 • Cedar Hill, TX 75104-0248
(972) 291-1581 • http://www.chisd.com/
Grade Span: PK-12; **Agency Type:** 1
Schools: 12
  6 Primary; 4 Middle; 1 High; 1 Other Level
  11 Regular; 0 Special Education; 0 Vocational; 1 Alternative
  0 Magnet; 0 Charter; 4 Title I Eligible; 0 School-wide Title I

Students: 7,564 (52.4% male; 47.5% female)
    Individual Education Program: 835 (11.0%);
    English Language Learner: 308 (4.1%); Migrant: 2 (<0.1%)
    Eligible for Free Lunch Program: 1,376 (18.2%)
    Eligible for Reduced-Price Lunch Program: 609 (8.1%)
Teachers: 447.4 (16.9 to 1)
Librarians/Media Specialists: 9.0 (840.4 to 1)
Guidance Counselors: 18.0 (420.2 to 1)
Current Spending: ($ per student per year):
    Total: $6,127; Instruction: $3,841; Support Services: $1,995
Enrollment, Drop-out Rates and Diploma Recipients by Race/Ethnicity

Category	Total	White	Black	Asian	AIAN	Hisp.
Enrollment (%)	100.0	25.2	55.3	1.8	0.5	17.3
Drop-out Rate (%)	1.6	1.1	1.6	2.1	14.3	2.2
H.S. Diplomas (#)	382	177	136	9	1	59

Coppell ISD
200 S Denton Tap Rd • Coppell, TX 75019-3205
(214) 496-6000 • http://www.coppellisd.com/
Grade Span: PK-12; **Agency Type:** 1
Schools: 16
    10 Primary; 3 Middle; 1 High; 1 Other Level
    14 Regular; 0 Special Education; 0 Vocational; 1 Alternative
    0 Magnet; 0 Charter; 7 Title I Eligible; 7 School-wide Title I
Students: 10,003 (51.7% male; 48.2% female)
    Individual Education Program: 877 (8.8%);
    English Language Learner: 578 (5.8%); Migrant: 0 (0.0%)
    Eligible for Free Lunch Program: 322 (3.2%)
    Eligible for Reduced-Price Lunch Program: 145 (1.4%)
Teachers: 670.2 (14.9 to 1)
Librarians/Media Specialists: 11.7 (855.0 to 1)
Guidance Counselors: 24.0 (416.8 to 1)
Current Spending: ($ per student per year):
    Total: $6,588; Instruction: $4,201; Support Services: $2,065
Enrollment, Drop-out Rates and Diploma Recipients by Race/Ethnicity

Category	Total	White	Black	Asian	AIAN	Hisp.
Enrollment (%)	100.0	71.3	4.5	15.5	0.3	8.4
Drop-out Rate (%)	0.5	0.6	0.0	0.3	0.0	1.0
H.S. Diplomas (#)	542	396	17	86	3	40

Dallas ISD
3700 Ross Ave • Dallas, TX 75204-5491
(972) 925-3700 • http://www.dallasisd.org/
Grade Span: PK-12; **Agency Type:** 1
Schools: 227
    148 Primary; 39 Middle; 38 High; 2 Other Level
    214 Regular; 1 Special Education; 2 Vocational; 10 Alternative
    0 Magnet; 0 Charter; 191 Title I Eligible; 191 School-wide Title I
Students: 160,584 (50.5% male; 49.4% female)
    Individual Education Program: 12,722 (7.9%);
    English Language Learner: 50,658 (31.5%); Migrant: 1,200 (0.7%)
    Eligible for Free Lunch Program: 112,447 (70.1%)
    Eligible for Reduced-Price Lunch Program: 13,277 (8.3%)
Teachers: 10,323.0 (15.5 to 1)
Librarians/Media Specialists: 213.0 (753.1 to 1)
Guidance Counselors: 418.4 (383.4 to 1)
Current Spending: ($ per student per year):
    Total: $7,435; Instruction: $4,655; Support Services: $2,439
Enrollment, Drop-out Rates and Diploma Recipients by Race/Ethnicity

Category	Total	White	Black	Asian	AIAN	Hisp.
Enrollment (%)	100.0	6.3	31.3	1.1	0.3	61.0
Drop-out Rate (%)	5.1	4.7	5.1	2.6	8.3	5.2
H.S. Diplomas (#)	6,532	710	2,764	159	23	2,876

Desoto ISD
200 E Belt Line Rd • Desoto, TX 75115-5795
(972) 223-6666 • http://www.desotoisd.org/disd/home.nsf/home?open
Grade Span: PK-12; **Agency Type:** 1
Schools: 12
    5 Primary; 4 Middle; 1 High; 2 Other Level
    11 Regular; 0 Special Education; 0 Vocational; 1 Alternative
    0 Magnet; 0 Charter; 2 Title I Eligible; 2 School-wide Title I
Students: 7,651 (50.2% male; 49.7% female)
    Individual Education Program: 958 (12.5%);
    English Language Learner: 316 (4.1%); Migrant: 5 (0.1%)
    Eligible for Free Lunch Program: 2,143 (28.0%)
    Eligible for Reduced-Price Lunch Program: 670 (8.8%)
Teachers: 517.3 (14.8 to 1)
Librarians/Media Specialists: 10.0 (765.1 to 1)
Guidance Counselors: 14.8 (517.0 to 1)
Current Spending: ($ per student per year):
    Total: $6,171; Instruction: $3,766; Support Services: $2,082

Enrollment, Drop-out Rates and Diploma Recipients by Race/Ethnicity

Category	Total	White	Black	Asian	AIAN	Hisp.
Enrollment (%)	100.0	16.1	69.6	1.0	0.2	13.1
Drop-out Rate (%)	1.3	1.5	1.0	0.0	0.0	3.4
H.S. Diplomas (#)	386	149	205	3	2	27

Duncanville ISD
802 S Main St • Duncanville, TX 75137-2316
(972) 708-2000 • http://www.duncanvilleisd.org/
Grade Span: PK-12; **Agency Type:** 1
Schools: 19
    9 Primary; 5 Middle; 2 High; 3 Other Level
    16 Regular; 0 Special Education; 0 Vocational; 3 Alternative
    0 Magnet; 0 Charter; 8 Title I Eligible; 8 School-wide Title I
Students: 11,368 (51.3% male; 48.6% female)
    Individual Education Program: 1,368 (12.0%);
    English Language Learner: 1,129 (9.9%); Migrant: 6 (0.1%)
    Eligible for Free Lunch Program: 4,286 (37.7%)
    Eligible for Reduced-Price Lunch Program: 1,287 (11.3%)
Teachers: 699.9 (16.2 to 1)
Librarians/Media Specialists: 17.0 (668.7 to 1)
Guidance Counselors: 38.0 (299.2 to 1)
Current Spending: ($ per student per year):
    Total: $6,552; Instruction: $3,910; Support Services: $2,315
Enrollment, Drop-out Rates and Diploma Recipients by Race/Ethnicity

Category	Total	White	Black	Asian	AIAN	Hisp.
Enrollment (%)	100.0	21.4	44.5	2.6	0.3	31.2
Drop-out Rate (%)	1.0	0.8	0.6	1.1	0.0	2.7
H.S. Diplomas (#)	707	298	278	16	1	114

Garland ISD
501 S Jupiter • Garland, TX 75042-7108
(972) 494-8201 • http://www.garlandisd.net/
Grade Span: PK-12; **Agency Type:** 1
Schools: 70
    45 Primary; 13 Middle; 7 High; 4 Other Level
    63 Regular; 2 Special Education; 0 Vocational; 4 Alternative
    0 Magnet; 0 Charter; 28 Title I Eligible; 24 School-wide Title I
Students: 55,114 (51.4% male; 48.5% female)
    Individual Education Program: 6,270 (11.4%);
    English Language Learner: 12,124 (22.0%); Migrant: 159 (0.3%)
    Eligible for Free Lunch Program: 18,049 (32.7%)
    Eligible for Reduced-Price Lunch Program: 4,000 (7.3%)
Teachers: 3,509.4 (15.7 to 1)
Librarians/Media Specialists: 74.0 (744.8 to 1)
Guidance Counselors: 121.9 (452.1 to 1)
Current Spending: ($ per student per year):
    Total: $5,763; Instruction: $3,634; Support Services: $1,846
Enrollment, Drop-out Rates and Diploma Recipients by Race/Ethnicity

Category	Total	White	Black	Asian	AIAN	Hisp.
Enrollment (%)	100.0	39.5	18.2	7.0	0.5	34.9
Drop-out Rate (%)	1.7	1.3	1.3	1.5	2.8	2.9
H.S. Diplomas (#)	2,689	1,489	448	201	20	531

Grand Prairie ISD
2602 S Belt Line Rd • Grand Prairie, TX 75052-5344
Mailing Address: Box 531170 • Grand Prairie, TX 75053-1170
(972) 264-6141 • http://www.gpisd.org/
Grade Span: PK-12; **Agency Type:** 1
Schools: 33
    21 Primary; 6 Middle; 3 High; 3 Other Level
    29 Regular; 0 Special Education; 0 Vocational; 4 Alternative
    0 Magnet; 0 Charter; 16 Title I Eligible; 16 School-wide Title I
Students: 22,132 (51.0% male; 48.9% female)
    Individual Education Program: 2,835 (12.8%);
    English Language Learner: 3,950 (17.8%); Migrant: 107 (0.5%)
    Eligible for Free Lunch Program: 9,986 (45.2%)
    Eligible for Reduced-Price Lunch Program: 2,629 (11.9%)
Teachers: 1,477.5 (14.9 to 1)
Librarians/Media Specialists: 31.0 (712.3 to 1)
Guidance Counselors: 47.6 (463.9 to 1)
Current Spending: ($ per student per year):
    Total: $6,751; Instruction: $4,237; Support Services: $2,149
Enrollment, Drop-out Rates and Diploma Recipients by Race/Ethnicity

Category	Total	White	Black	Asian	AIAN	Hisp.
Enrollment (%)	100.0	25.3	15.0	4.0	0.8	54.9
Drop-out Rate (%)	3.7	2.8	2.9	1.2	9.1	5.0
H.S. Diplomas (#)	1,035	400	158	63	9	405

Highland Park ISD
7015 Westchester Dr • Dallas, TX 75205-1061
(214) 780-3000 • http://www.hpisd.org/
Grade Span: PK-12; **Agency Type:** 1
Schools: 7
    4 Primary; 2 Middle; 1 High; 0 Other Level

7 Regular; 0 Special Education; 0 Vocational; 0 Alternative
0 Magnet; 0 Charter; 0 Title I Eligible; 0 School-wide Title I
Students: 6,074 (50.0% male; 49.9% female)
  Individual Education Program: 552 (9.1%);
  English Language Learner: 34 (0.6%); Migrant: 0 (0.0%)
  Eligible for Free Lunch Program: 0 (0.0%)
  Eligible for Reduced-Price Lunch Program: 0 (0.0%)
Teachers: 391.4 (15.5 to 1)
Librarians/Media Specialists: 7.0 (867.7 to 1)
Guidance Counselors: 15.0 (404.9 to 1)
Current Spending: ($ per student per year):
  Total: $7,101; Instruction: $4,589; Support Services: $2,363

Enrollment, Drop-out Rates and Diploma Recipients by Race/Ethnicity

Category	Total	White	Black	Asian	AIAN	Hisp.
Enrollment (%)	100.0	96.4	0.2	1.6	0.1	1.6
Drop-out Rate (%)	0.3	0.3	0.0	0.0	0.0	0.0
H.S. Diplomas (#)	414	402	0	6	1	5

Honors Academy
4300 Macarthur Ave Ste 160 • Dallas, TX 75209
(214) 521-6365
Grade Span: PK-12; **Agency Type:** 7
Schools: 10
  0 Primary; 0 Middle; 4 High; 4 Other Level
  1 Regular; 0 Special Education; 0 Vocational; 7 Alternative
  0 Magnet; 8 Charter; 1 Title I Eligible; 1 School-wide Title I
Students: 1,896 (49.6% male; 50.3% female)
  Individual Education Program: 202 (10.7%);
  English Language Learner: 0 (0.0%); Migrant: 6 (0.3%)
  Eligible for Free Lunch Program: 632 (33.3%)
  Eligible for Reduced-Price Lunch Program: 112 (5.9%)
Teachers: 59.7 (31.8 to 1)
Librarians/Media Specialists: 0.0 (n/a to 1)
Guidance Counselors: 0.0 (n/a to 1)
Current Spending: ($ per student per year):
  Total: $4,097; Instruction: $1,744; Support Services: $2,139

Enrollment, Drop-out Rates and Diploma Recipients by Race/Ethnicity

Category	Total	White	Black	Asian	AIAN	Hisp.
Enrollment (%)	100.0	38.2	43.7	0.9	0.5	16.8
Drop-out Rate (%)	9.5	6.4	11.7	6.7	0.0	13.6
H.S. Diplomas (#)	225	131	63	6	0	25

Irving ISD
901 N O'connor Rd • Irving, TX 75061-4596
Mailing Address: PO Box 152637 • Irving, TX 75015-2637
(972) 215-5000 • http://www.irvingisd.net/
Grade Span: PK-12; **Agency Type:** 1
Schools: 39
  23 Primary; 7 Middle; 4 High; 5 Other Level
  34 Regular; 0 Special Education; 0 Vocational; 5 Alternative
  0 Magnet; 0 Charter; 35 Title I Eligible; 35 School-wide Title I
Students: 31,249 (51.5% male; 48.4% female)
  Individual Education Program: 3,030 (9.7%);
  English Language Learner: 10,560 (33.8%); Migrant: 290 (0.9%)
  Eligible for Free Lunch Program: 15,637 (50.0%)
  Eligible for Reduced-Price Lunch Program: 3,515 (11.2%)
Teachers: 2,087.9 (15.0 to 1)
Librarians/Media Specialists: 35.4 (882.7 to 1)
Guidance Counselors: 78.3 (399.1 to 1)
Current Spending: ($ per student per year):
  Total: $6,637; Instruction: $4,356; Support Services: $1,986

Enrollment, Drop-out Rates and Diploma Recipients by Race/Ethnicity

Category	Total	White	Black	Asian	AIAN	Hisp.
Enrollment (%)	100.0	24.3	12.7	4.8	0.5	57.8
Drop-out Rate (%)	3.3	2.3	2.2	2.6	4.7	4.7
H.S. Diplomas (#)	1,308	581	202	100	3	422

Lancaster ISD
1201 N Dallas Ave • Lancaster, TX 75146-1621
Mailing Address: PO Box 400 • Lancaster, TX 75146-0400
(972) 227-4141 • http://www.lancasterisd.org/home.htm
Grade Span: PK-12; **Agency Type:** 1
Schools: 10
  5 Primary; 2 Middle; 1 High; 1 Other Level
  8 Regular; 0 Special Education; 0 Vocational; 1 Alternative
  0 Magnet; 0 Charter; 7 Title I Eligible; 7 School-wide Title I
Students: 4,754 (50.9% male; 49.0% female)
  Individual Education Program: 520 (10.9%);
  English Language Learner: 320 (6.7%); Migrant: 9 (0.2%)
  Eligible for Free Lunch Program: 2,095 (44.1%)
  Eligible for Reduced-Price Lunch Program: 520 (10.9%)
Teachers: 299.7 (15.9 to 1)
Librarians/Media Specialists: 7.0 (678.9 to 1)
Guidance Counselors: 10.0 (475.2 to 1)
Current Spending: ($ per student per year):
  Total: $6,793; Instruction: $4,064; Support Services: $2,389

Category	Total	White	Black	Asian	AIAN	Hisp.
Enrollment (%)	100.0	9.0	73.7	0.3	0.3	16.8
Drop-out Rate (%)	1.7	2.6	1.4	0.0	0.0	2.0
H.S. Diplomas (#)	252	59	169	2	0	22

Mesquite ISD
405 E Davis St • Mesquite, TX 75149-4701
(972) 288-6411 • http://www.mesquiteisd.org/misdweb/index.html
Grade Span: PK-12; **Agency Type:** 1
Schools: 44
  30 Primary; 7 Middle; 5 High; 2 Other Level
  42 Regular; 0 Special Education; 0 Vocational; 2 Alternative
  0 Magnet; 0 Charter; 11 Title I Eligible; 11 School-wide Title I
Students: 34,414 (50.7% male; 49.2% female)
  Individual Education Program: 4,903 (14.2%);
  English Language Learner: 3,521 (10.2%); Migrant: 94 (0.3%)
  Eligible for Free Lunch Program: 10,162 (29.5%)
  Eligible for Reduced-Price Lunch Program: 2,662 (7.7%)
Teachers: 2,149.6 (16.0 to 1)
Librarians/Media Specialists: 44.0 (782.1 to 1)
Guidance Counselors: 70.0 (491.6 to 1)
Current Spending: ($ per student per year):
  Total: $6,287; Instruction: $3,863; Support Services: $2,103

Enrollment, Drop-out Rates and Diploma Recipients by Race/Ethnicity

Category	Total	White	Black	Asian	AIAN	Hisp.
Enrollment (%)	100.0	45.8	21.3	3.6	0.8	28.5
Drop-out Rate (%)	2.9	2.7	2.6	1.0	4.8	4.0
H.S. Diplomas (#)	1,956	1,226	324	99	14	293

Richardson ISD
400 S Greenville Ave • Richardson, TX 75081-4198
(469) 593-0000 • http://www.richardson.k12.tx.us/
Grade Span: PK-12; **Agency Type:** 1
Schools: 57
  40 Primary; 9 Middle; 5 High; 3 Other Level
  54 Regular; 0 Special Education; 0 Vocational; 3 Alternative
  0 Magnet; 0 Charter; 20 Title I Eligible; 20 School-wide Title I
Students: 34,536 (51.6% male; 48.3% female)
  Individual Education Program: 4,302 (12.5%);
  English Language Learner: 6,395 (18.5%); Migrant: 31 (0.1%)
  Eligible for Free Lunch Program: 11,901 (34.6%)
  Eligible for Reduced-Price Lunch Program: 2,342 (6.8%)
Teachers: 2,419.2 (14.2 to 1)
Librarians/Media Specialists: 48.0 (717.6 to 1)
Guidance Counselors: 96.2 (358.0 to 1)
Current Spending: ($ per student per year):
  Total: $6,677; Instruction: $4,086; Support Services: $2,339

Enrollment, Drop-out Rates and Diploma Recipients by Race/Ethnicity

Category	Total	White	Black	Asian	AIAN	Hisp.
Enrollment (%)	100.0	40.1	25.1	8.6	0.5	25.7
Drop-out Rate (%)	2.0	1.2	3.3	2.4	0.0	3.0
H.S. Diplomas (#)	1,891	1,263	276	202	8	142

Wilmer-Hutchins ISD
3820 E Illinois Ave • Dallas, TX 75216-4140
(214) 376-7311
Grade Span: PK-12; **Agency Type:** 1
Schools: 10
  6 Primary; 1 Middle; 2 High; 1 Other Level
  9 Regular; 0 Special Education; 0 Vocational; 1 Alternative
  0 Magnet; 0 Charter; 9 Title I Eligible; 9 School-wide Title I
Students: 3,070 (51.5% male; 48.4% female)
  Individual Education Program: 219 (7.1%);
  English Language Learner: 366 (11.9%); Migrant: 9 (0.3%)
  Eligible for Free Lunch Program: 1,905 (62.1%)
  Eligible for Reduced-Price Lunch Program: 240 (7.8%)
Teachers: 207.9 (14.8 to 1)
Librarians/Media Specialists: 3.0 (1,023.3 to 1)
Guidance Counselors: 9.0 (341.1 to 1)
Current Spending: ($ per student per year):
  Total: $8,790; Instruction: $4,918; Support Services: $3,449

Enrollment, Drop-out Rates and Diploma Recipients by Race/Ethnicity

Category	Total	White	Black	Asian	AIAN	Hisp.
Enrollment (%)	100.0	3.8	69.1	0.0	0.2	26.8
Drop-out Rate (%)	4.2	8.0	3.2	n/a	n/a	8.4
H.S. Diplomas (#)	102	1	90	0	0	11

Dawson County

Lamesa ISD

212 N Houston • Lamesa, TX 79331-5442
Mailing Address: PO Box 261 • Lamesa, TX 79331-0261
(806) 872-5461 • http://lamesa.esc17.net/
Grade Span: PK-12; **Agency Type:** 1
Schools: 4
  2 Primary; 1 Middle; 1 High; 0 Other Level
  4 Regular; 0 Special Education; 0 Vocational; 0 Alternative
  0 Magnet; 0 Charter; 4 Title I Eligible; 4 School-wide Title I
Students: 2,127 (52.0% male; 47.9% female)
  Individual Education Program: 255 (12.0%);
  English Language Learner: 185 (8.7%); Migrant: 195 (9.2%)
  Eligible for Free Lunch Program: 1,213 (57.0%)
  Eligible for Reduced-Price Lunch Program: 183 (8.6%)
Teachers: 155.0 (13.7 to 1)
Librarians/Media Specialists: 2.0 (1,063.5 to 1)
Guidance Counselors: 3.8 (559.7 to 1)
Current Spending: ($ per student per year):
  Total: $6,987; Instruction: $4,412; Support Services: $2,153
Enrollment, Drop-out Rates and Diploma Recipients by Race/Ethnicity

Category	Total	White	Black	Asian	AIAN	Hisp.
Enrollment (%)	100.0	23.3	5.0	0.4	0.0	71.2
Drop-out Rate (%)	2.3	0.9	7.1	0.0	0.0	2.7
H.S. Diplomas (#)	171	68	7	0	0	96

De Witt County

Cuero ISD

405 Park Hts Dr • Cuero, TX 77954-2132
(361) 275-3832
Grade Span: PK-12; **Agency Type:** 1
Schools: 6
  2 Primary; 1 Middle; 1 High; 2 Other Level
  4 Regular; 1 Special Education; 0 Vocational; 1 Alternative
  0 Magnet; 0 Charter; 2 Title I Eligible; 2 School-wide Title I
Students: 1,949 (51.6% male; 48.3% female)
  Individual Education Program: 273 (14.0%);
  English Language Learner: 15 (0.8%); Migrant: 15 (0.8%)
  Eligible for Free Lunch Program: 773 (39.7%)
  Eligible for Reduced-Price Lunch Program: 215 (11.0%)
Teachers: 148.6 (13.1 to 1)
Librarians/Media Specialists: 3.0 (649.7 to 1)
Guidance Counselors: 5.0 (389.8 to 1)
Current Spending: ($ per student per year):
  Total: $8,240; Instruction: $5,089; Support Services: $2,810
Enrollment, Drop-out Rates and Diploma Recipients by Race/Ethnicity

Category	Total	White	Black	Asian	AIAN	Hisp.
Enrollment (%)	100.0	50.6	13.3	0.2	0.1	35.7
Drop-out Rate (%)	4.7	1.8	10.1	0.0	0.0	8.7
H.S. Diplomas (#)	158	109	14	0	1	34

Yoakum ISD

102 Mc Kinnon St • Yoakum, TX 77995-1623
Mailing Address: PO Box 737 • Yoakum, TX 77995-0737
(361) 293-3162
Grade Span: PK-12; **Agency Type:** 1
Schools: 5
  2 Primary; 1 Middle; 1 High; 1 Other Level
  4 Regular; 1 Special Education; 0 Vocational; 0 Alternative
  0 Magnet; 0 Charter; 2 Title I Eligible; 2 School-wide Title I
Students: 1,567 (51.6% male; 48.3% female)
  Individual Education Program: 235 (15.0%);
  English Language Learner: 101 (6.4%); Migrant: 16 (1.0%)
  Eligible for Free Lunch Program: 696 (44.4%)
  Eligible for Reduced-Price Lunch Program: 146 (9.3%)
Teachers: 119.9 (13.1 to 1)
Librarians/Media Specialists: 1.8 (870.6 to 1)
Guidance Counselors: 3.8 (412.4 to 1)
Current Spending: ($ per student per year):
  Total: $7,137; Instruction: $4,852; Support Services: $1,913
Enrollment, Drop-out Rates and Diploma Recipients by Race/Ethnicity

Category	Total	White	Black	Asian	AIAN	Hisp.
Enrollment (%)	100.0	48.7	12.4	0.4	0.0	38.5
Drop-out Rate (%)	0.6	0.6	0.0	n/a	n/a	0.8
H.S. Diplomas (#)	88	63	10	0	0	15

Deaf Smith County

Hereford ISD

601 N 25 Mile Ave • Hereford, TX 79045-4406
(806) 364-0606 • http://www.hisd.net/
Grade Span: PK-12; **Agency Type:** 1
Schools: 8

  4 Primary; 3 Middle; 1 High; 0 Other Level
  8 Regular; 0 Special Education; 0 Vocational; 0 Alternative
  0 Magnet; 0 Charter; 8 Title I Eligible; 8 School-wide Title I
Students: 3,939 (52.8% male; 47.1% female)
  Individual Education Program: 514 (13.0%);
  English Language Learner: 498 (12.6%); Migrant: 1,821 (46.2%)
  Eligible for Free Lunch Program: 2,438 (61.9%)
  Eligible for Reduced-Price Lunch Program: 339 (8.6%)
Teachers: 278.4 (14.1 to 1)
Librarians/Media Specialists: 8.0 (492.4 to 1)
Guidance Counselors: 11.0 (358.1 to 1)
Current Spending: ($ per student per year):
  Total: $6,552; Instruction: $4,116; Support Services: $2,082
Enrollment, Drop-out Rates and Diploma Recipients by Race/Ethnicity

Category	Total	White	Black	Asian	AIAN	Hisp.
Enrollment (%)	100.0	18.7	1.3	0.2	0.1	79.7
Drop-out Rate (%)	3.4	1.4	3.4	0.0	0.0	4.2
H.S. Diplomas (#)	268	92	4	0	0	172

Denton County

Denton ISD

1307 N Locust St • Denton, TX 76201-3037
(940) 369-0000 • http://www.dentonisd.org/index.htm
Grade Span: PK-12; **Agency Type:** 1
Schools: 25
  14 Primary; 4 Middle; 3 High; 4 Other Level
  20 Regular; 0 Special Education; 0 Vocational; 5 Alternative
  0 Magnet; 0 Charter; 10 Title I Eligible; 9 School-wide Title I
Students: 15,951 (51.5% male; 48.4% female)
  Individual Education Program: 2,151 (13.5%);
  English Language Learner: 2,369 (14.9%); Migrant: 106 (0.7%)
  Eligible for Free Lunch Program: 5,027 (31.5%)
  Eligible for Reduced-Price Lunch Program: 794 (5.0%)
Teachers: 1,169.7 (13.6 to 1)
Librarians/Media Specialists: 20.4 (781.9 to 1)
Guidance Counselors: 38.0 (419.8 to 1)
Current Spending: ($ per student per year):
  Total: $7,300; Instruction: $4,483; Support Services: $2,538
Enrollment, Drop-out Rates and Diploma Recipients by Race/Ethnicity

Category	Total	White	Black	Asian	AIAN	Hisp.
Enrollment (%)	100.0	58.5	11.5	2.1	0.5	27.4
Drop-out Rate (%)	4.7	3.5	6.9	1.3	11.8	7.9
H.S. Diplomas (#)	720	548	66	13	1	92

Lake Dallas ISD

315 E Hundley Dr • Lake Dallas, TX 75065-2629
Mailing Address: PO Box 548 • Lake Dallas, TX 75065-0548
(940) 497-4039 • http://www.ldisd.net/
Grade Span: PK-12; **Agency Type:** 1
Schools: 7
  3 Primary; 2 Middle; 1 High; 1 Other Level
  6 Regular; 0 Special Education; 0 Vocational; 1 Alternative
  0 Magnet; 0 Charter; 1 Title I Eligible; 0 School-wide Title I
Students: 3,578 (52.5% male; 47.4% female)
  Individual Education Program: 476 (13.3%);
  English Language Learner: 150 (4.2%); Migrant: 4 (0.1%)
  Eligible for Free Lunch Program: 520 (14.5%)
  Eligible for Reduced-Price Lunch Program: 106 (3.0%)
Teachers: 251.1 (14.2 to 1)
Librarians/Media Specialists: 6.0 (596.3 to 1)
Guidance Counselors: 6.9 (518.6 to 1)
Current Spending: ($ per student per year):
  Total: $6,779; Instruction: $4,393; Support Services: $2,134
Enrollment, Drop-out Rates and Diploma Recipients by Race/Ethnicity

Category	Total	White	Black	Asian	AIAN	Hisp.
Enrollment (%)	100.0	78.7	5.9	2.3	1.0	12.1
Drop-out Rate (%)	0.9	1.1	0.0	0.0	0.0	0.0
H.S. Diplomas (#)	168	137	5	4	2	20

Lewisville ISD

1800 Timber Creek Rd • Flower Mound, TX 75028-1198
Mailing Address: PO Box 217 • Lewisville, TX 75067-0217
(972) 539-1551 • http://www.lisd.net/
Grade Span: PK-12; **Agency Type:** 1
Schools: 58
  36 Primary; 13 Middle; 6 High; 3 Other Level
  55 Regular; 0 Special Education; 0 Vocational; 3 Alternative
  0 Magnet; 0 Charter; 14 Title I Eligible; 3 School-wide Title I
Students: 44,024 (51.1% male; 48.8% female)
  Individual Education Program: 4,980 (11.3%);
  English Language Learner: 3,900 (8.9%); Migrant: 57 (0.1%)
  Eligible for Free Lunch Program: 4,190 (9.6%)
  Eligible for Reduced-Price Lunch Program: 1,248 (2.8%)
Teachers: 3,063.2 (14.3 to 1)
Librarians/Media Specialists: 59.6 (735.2 to 1)

Guidance Counselors: 124.3 (352.5 to 1)
Current Spending: ($ per student per year):
    Total: $6,762; Instruction: $4,316; Support Services: $2,157
Enrollment, Drop-out Rates and Diploma Recipients by Race/Ethnicity

Category	Total	White	Black	Asian	AIAN	Hisp.
Enrollment (%)	100.0	68.6	8.3	6.6	0.5	16.0
Drop-out Rate (%)	1.1	0.8	1.7	0.4	4.7	2.7
H.S. Diplomas (#)	2,267	1,785	164	88	8	222

Little Elm ISD
500 Lobo Ln • Little Elm, TX 75068-5220
(972) 292-1847 •
http://www.arlington.k12.tx.us/schools/elementary/little/jblittle.htm
Grade Span: PK-12; Agency Type: 1
Schools: 8
    4 Primary; 2 Middle; 1 High; 1 Other Level
    7 Regular; 0 Special Education; 0 Vocational; 1 Alternative
    0 Magnet; 0 Charter; 5 Title I Eligible; 5 School-wide Title I
Students: 3,484   (51.6% male; 48.3% female)
    Individual Education Program: 436 (12.5%);
    English Language Learner: 471 (13.5%); Migrant: 175 (5.0%)
    Eligible for Free Lunch Program: 962 (27.6%)
    Eligible for Reduced-Price Lunch Program: 298 (8.6%)
Teachers: 238.7 (14.6 to 1)
Librarians/Media Specialists: 4.0 (871.0 to 1)
Guidance Counselors: 7.0 (497.7 to 1)
Current Spending: ($ per student per year):
    Total: $7,235; Instruction: $4,170; Support Services: $2,644
Enrollment, Drop-out Rates and Diploma Recipients by Race/Ethnicity

Category	Total	White	Black	Asian	AIAN	Hisp.
Enrollment (%)	100.0	57.8	7.8	1.3	0.5	32.5
Drop-out Rate (%)	1.8	0.6	12.5	0.0	0.0	3.8
H.S. Diplomas (#)	104	78	2	2	0	22

Northwest ISD
1800 Hwy 114 • Fort Worth, TX 76177-0070
Mailing Address: PO Box 77070 • Fort Worth, TX 76177-0070
(817) 490-6473 • http://www.northwest.k12.tx.us/index.htm
Grade Span: PK-12; Agency Type: 1
Schools: 14
    8 Primary; 3 Middle; 2 High; 0 Other Level
    12 Regular; 0 Special Education; 0 Vocational; 1 Alternative
    0 Magnet; 0 Charter; 3 Title I Eligible; 3 School-wide Title I
Students: 6,917   (52.0% male; 47.9% female)
    Individual Education Program: 789 (11.4%);
    English Language Learner: 256 (3.7%); Migrant: 3 (<0.1%)
    Eligible for Free Lunch Program: 986 (14.3%)
    Eligible for Reduced-Price Lunch Program: 325 (4.7%)
Teachers: 474.5 (14.6 to 1)
Librarians/Media Specialists: 10.3 (671.6 to 1)
Guidance Counselors: 15.1 (458.1 to 1)
Current Spending: ($ per student per year):
    Total: $8,336; Instruction: $4,810; Support Services: $3,239
Enrollment, Drop-out Rates and Diploma Recipients by Race/Ethnicity

Category	Total	White	Black	Asian	AIAN	Hisp.
Enrollment (%)	100.0	82.7	2.6	1.6	0.8	12.3
Drop-out Rate (%)	2.4	2.1	11.1	0.0	0.0	4.5
H.S. Diplomas (#)	285	257	1	6	2	19

Sanger ISD
601 Elm St • Sanger, TX 76266-9635
Mailing Address: PO Box 2399 • Sanger, TX 76266-0188
(940) 458-7438
Grade Span: PK-12; Agency Type: 1
Schools: 6
    2 Primary; 2 Middle; 1 High; 1 Other Level
    5 Regular; 0 Special Education; 0 Vocational; 1 Alternative
    0 Magnet; 0 Charter; 6 Title I Eligible; 6 School-wide Title I
Students: 2,150   (53.9% male; 46.0% female)
    Individual Education Program: 362 (16.8%);
    English Language Learner: 75 (3.5%); Migrant: 19 (0.9%)
    Eligible for Free Lunch Program: 475 (22.1%)
    Eligible for Reduced-Price Lunch Program: 122 (5.7%)
Teachers: 165.5 (13.0 to 1)
Librarians/Media Specialists: 1.0 (2,150.0 to 1)
Guidance Counselors: 6.5 (330.8 to 1)
Current Spending: ($ per student per year):
    Total: $8,682; Instruction: $4,987; Support Services: $3,321
Enrollment, Drop-out Rates and Diploma Recipients by Race/Ethnicity

Category	Total	White	Black	Asian	AIAN	Hisp.
Enrollment (%)	100.0	81.9	2.1	0.8	0.5	14.7
Drop-out Rate (%)	2.1	2.1	0.0	0.0	0.0	3.8
H.S. Diplomas (#)	155	138	3	1	2	11

Dimmit County

Carrizo Springs Cons ISD
300 N Seventh St • Carrizo Springs, TX 78834-3102
(830) 876-3503
Grade Span: PK-12; Agency Type: 1
Schools: 6
    3 Primary; 2 Middle; 1 High; 0 Other Level
    6 Regular; 0 Special Education; 0 Vocational; 0 Alternative
    0 Magnet; 0 Charter; 6 Title I Eligible; 6 School-wide Title I
Students: 2,485   (51.6% male; 48.3% female)
    Individual Education Program: 254 (10.2%);
    English Language Learner: 249 (10.0%); Migrant: 338 (13.6%)
    Eligible for Free Lunch Program: 1,224 (49.3%)
    Eligible for Reduced-Price Lunch Program: 240 (9.7%)
Teachers: 172.5 (14.4 to 1)
Librarians/Media Specialists: 1.0 (2,485.0 to 1)
Guidance Counselors: 8.0 (310.6 to 1)
Current Spending: ($ per student per year):
    Total: $7,752; Instruction: $4,713; Support Services: $2,511
Enrollment, Drop-out Rates and Diploma Recipients by Race/Ethnicity

Category	Total	White	Black	Asian	AIAN	Hisp.
Enrollment (%)	100.0	8.2	1.0	0.3	0.0	90.5
Drop-out Rate (%)	6.8	5.3	0.0	0.0	0.0	7.1
H.S. Diplomas (#)	135	11	0	0	0	124

Duval County

San Diego ISD
609 W Labbe St • San Diego, TX 78384-3499
(361) 279-3382
Grade Span: PK-12; Agency Type: 1
Schools: 4
    2 Primary; 1 Middle; 1 High; 0 Other Level
    4 Regular; 0 Special Education; 0 Vocational; 0 Alternative
    0 Magnet; 0 Charter; 4 Title I Eligible; 4 School-wide Title I
Students: 1,545   (49.0% male; 50.9% female)
    Individual Education Program: 158 (10.2%);
    English Language Learner: 205 (13.3%); Migrant: 142 (9.2%)
    Eligible for Free Lunch Program: 1,101 (71.3%)
    Eligible for Reduced-Price Lunch Program: 229 (14.8%)
Teachers: 112.7 (13.7 to 1)
Librarians/Media Specialists: 1.0 (1,545.0 to 1)
Guidance Counselors: 3.3 (468.2 to 1)
Current Spending: ($ per student per year):
    Total: $7,584; Instruction: $4,490; Support Services: $2,664
Enrollment, Drop-out Rates and Diploma Recipients by Race/Ethnicity

Category	Total	White	Black	Asian	AIAN	Hisp.
Enrollment (%)	100.0	0.8	0.1	0.0	0.0	99.1
Drop-out Rate (%)	2.9	10.0	n/a	n/a	n/a	2.5
H.S. Diplomas (#)	91	1	0	0	0	90

Ector County

Ector County ISD
802 N Sam Houston • Odessa, TX 79760-3912
Mailing Address: PO Box 3912 • Odessa, TX 79760-3912
(432) 332-9151 • http://www.ector-county.k12.tx.us/
Grade Span: PK-12; Agency Type: 1
Schools: 42
    28 Primary; 5 Middle; 7 High; 2 Other Level
    37 Regular; 1 Special Education; 0 Vocational; 4 Alternative
    0 Magnet; 0 Charter; 26 Title I Eligible; 26 School-wide Title I
Students: 26,090   (51.2% male; 48.7% female)
    Individual Education Program: 3,038 (11.6%);
    English Language Learner: 3,312 (12.7%); Migrant: 522 (2.0%)
    Eligible for Free Lunch Program: 13,005 (49.8%)
    Eligible for Reduced-Price Lunch Program: 2,356 (9.0%)
Teachers: 1,671.4 (15.6 to 1)
Librarians/Media Specialists: 34.0 (767.4 to 1)
Guidance Counselors: 68.0 (383.7 to 1)
Current Spending: ($ per student per year):
    Total: $6,138; Instruction: $3,734; Support Services: $2,108
Enrollment, Drop-out Rates and Diploma Recipients by Race/Ethnicity

Category	Total	White	Black	Asian	AIAN	Hisp.
Enrollment (%)	100.0	35.4	5.4	0.7	0.7	57.8
Drop-out Rate (%)	9.0	6.0	9.9	3.6	2.7	11.5
H.S. Diplomas (#)	1,478	702	73	7	8	688

El Paso County

Canutillo ISD
7965 Artcraft • El Paso, TX 79932
Mailing Address: PO Box 100 • Canutillo, TX 79835-0100
(915) 877-7400
Grade Span: PK-12; **Agency Type:** 1
Schools: 6
    4 Primary; 1 Middle; 1 High; 0 Other Level
    6 Regular; 0 Special Education; 0 Vocational; 0 Alternative
    0 Magnet; 0 Charter; 6 Title I Eligible; 6 School-wide Title I
Students: 4,830 (52.6% male; 47.3% female)
    Individual Education Program: 486 (10.1%);
    English Language Learner: 1,964 (40.7%); Migrant: 355 (7.3%)
    Eligible for Free Lunch Program: 3,521 (72.9%)
    Eligible for Reduced-Price Lunch Program: 466 (9.6%)
Teachers: 353.6 (13.7 to 1)
Librarians/Media Specialists: 6.0 (805.0 to 1)
Guidance Counselors: 9.2 (525.0 to 1)
Current Spending: ($ per student per year):
    Total: $7,765; Instruction: $4,406; Support Services: $2,879
Enrollment, Drop-out Rates and Diploma Recipients by Race/Ethnicity

Category	Total	White	Black	Asian	AIAN	Hisp.
Enrollment (%)	100.0	3.8	0.2	0.1	0.0	95.8
Drop-out Rate (%)	5.3	4.2	0.0	0.0	0.0	5.4
H.S. Diplomas (#)	233	13	0	0	1	219

Clint ISD
14521 Horizon Blvd • El Paso, TX 79928
(915) 926-4000 • http://www.clintweb.net/index.cfm
Grade Span: PK-12; **Agency Type:** 1
Schools: 11
    5 Primary; 3 Middle; 2 High; 1 Other Level
    11 Regular; 0 Special Education; 0 Vocational; 0 Alternative
    0 Magnet; 0 Charter; 11 Title I Eligible; 11 School-wide Title I
Students: 8,564 (50.6% male; 49.3% female)
    Individual Education Program: 791 (9.2%);
    English Language Learner: 3,976 (46.4%); Migrant: 285 (3.3%)
    Eligible for Free Lunch Program: 6,870 (80.2%)
    Eligible for Reduced-Price Lunch Program: 687 (8.0%)
Teachers: 496.3 (17.3 to 1)
Librarians/Media Specialists: 5.0 (1,712.8 to 1)
Guidance Counselors: 15.9 (538.6 to 1)
Current Spending: ($ per student per year):
    Total: $6,235; Instruction: $3,642; Support Services: $2,286
Enrollment, Drop-out Rates and Diploma Recipients by Race/Ethnicity

Category	Total	White	Black	Asian	AIAN	Hisp.
Enrollment (%)	100.0	3.9	0.4	0.1	0.1	95.5
Drop-out Rate (%)	4.2	2.0	0.0	n/a	0.0	4.3
H.S. Diplomas (#)	406	19	4	0	0	383

El Paso ISD
6531 Boeing Dr • El Paso, TX 79925
Mailing Address: PO Box 20100 • El Paso, TX 79998-0100
(915) 779-3781 • http://www.episd.org/District/
Grade Span: PK-12; **Agency Type:** 1
Schools: 93
    56 Primary; 16 Middle; 16 High; 4 Other Level
    82 Regular; 1 Special Education; 1 Vocational; 8 Alternative
    0 Magnet; 0 Charter; 75 Title I Eligible; 75 School-wide Title I
Students: 63,200 (51.0% male; 48.9% female)
    Individual Education Program: 5,690 (9.0%);
    English Language Learner: 19,276 (30.5%); Migrant: 2,475 (3.9%)
    Eligible for Free Lunch Program: 37,566 (59.4%)
    Eligible for Reduced-Price Lunch Program: 5,275 (8.3%)
Teachers: 4,504.9 (14.0 to 1)
Librarians/Media Specialists: 92.6 (682.5 to 1)
Guidance Counselors: 149.0 (424.2 to 1)
Current Spending: ($ per student per year):
    Total: $7,198; Instruction: $4,418; Support Services: $2,406
Enrollment, Drop-out Rates and Diploma Recipients by Race/Ethnicity

Category	Total	White	Black	Asian	AIAN	Hisp.
Enrollment (%)	100.0	13.3	4.4	1.3	0.3	80.6
Drop-out Rate (%)	4.1	2.1	4.8	1.3	6.9	4.6
H.S. Diplomas (#)	3,353	687	133	53	1	2,479

Fabens ISD
821 NE Ave G • Fabens, TX 79838-0697
Mailing Address: PO Box 697 • Fabens, TX 79838-0697
(915) 764-2025
Grade Span: PK-12; **Agency Type:** 1
Schools: 5
    2 Primary; 2 Middle; 1 High; 0 Other Level
    5 Regular; 0 Special Education; 0 Vocational; 0 Alternative
    0 Magnet; 0 Charter; 5 Title I Eligible; 5 School-wide Title I

Students: 2,774 (50.4% male; 49.5% female)
    Individual Education Program: 223 (8.0%);
    English Language Learner: 1,229 (44.3%); Migrant: 368 (13.3%)
    Eligible for Free Lunch Program: 1,114 (40.2%)
    Eligible for Reduced-Price Lunch Program: 236 (8.5%)
Teachers: 176.5 (15.7 to 1)
Librarians/Media Specialists: 2.1 (1,321.0 to 1)
Guidance Counselors: 6.2 (447.4 to 1)
Current Spending: ($ per student per year):
    Total: $7,575; Instruction: $4,731; Support Services: $2,427
Enrollment, Drop-out Rates and Diploma Recipients by Race/Ethnicity

Category	Total	White	Black	Asian	AIAN	Hisp.
Enrollment (%)	100.0	2.1	0.1	0.1	0.0	97.7
Drop-out Rate (%)	4.2	20.0	0.0	0.0	n/a	3.8
H.S. Diplomas (#)	163	2	1	0	0	160

San Elizario ISD
1050 Chicken Ranch Rd • San Elizario, TX 79849-0920
Mailing Address: PO Box 920 • San Elizario, TX 79849-0920
(915) 872-3900
Grade Span: PK-12; **Agency Type:** 1
Schools: 7
    4 Primary; 1 Middle; 1 High; 1 Other Level
    6 Regular; 0 Special Education; 0 Vocational; 1 Alternative
    0 Magnet; 0 Charter; 6 Title I Eligible; 6 School-wide Title I
Students: 3,711 (52.0% male; 47.9% female)
    Individual Education Program: 452 (12.2%);
    English Language Learner: 2,005 (54.0%); Migrant: 675 (18.2%)
    Eligible for Free Lunch Program: 3,283 (88.5%)
    Eligible for Reduced-Price Lunch Program: 272 (7.3%)
Teachers: 240.8 (15.4 to 1)
Librarians/Media Specialists: 6.0 (618.5 to 1)
Guidance Counselors: 11.0 (337.4 to 1)
Current Spending: ($ per student per year):
    Total: $7,609; Instruction: $4,103; Support Services: $2,994
Enrollment, Drop-out Rates and Diploma Recipients by Race/Ethnicity

Category	Total	White	Black	Asian	AIAN	Hisp.
Enrollment (%)	100.0	0.5	0.3	0.0	0.1	99.2
Drop-out Rate (%)	4.6	0.0	n/a	n/a	0.0	4.7
H.S. Diplomas (#)	157	1	0	0	0	156

Socorro ISD
12300 Eastlake Dr • El Paso, TX 79928-5400
Mailing Address: PO Box 292800 • El Paso, TX 79929-2800
(915) 937-0000 • http://www.sisd.net/
Grade Span: PK-12; **Agency Type:** 1
Schools: 34
    22 Primary; 7 Middle; 3 High; 2 Other Level
    32 Regular; 0 Special Education; 0 Vocational; 2 Alternative
    0 Magnet; 0 Charter; 33 Title I Eligible; 33 School-wide Title I
Students: 32,241 (51.2% male; 48.7% female)
    Individual Education Program: 3,291 (10.2%);
    English Language Learner: 9,640 (29.9%); Migrant: 761 (2.4%)
    Eligible for Free Lunch Program: 19,413 (60.2%)
    Eligible for Reduced-Price Lunch Program: 4,098 (12.7%)
Teachers: 1,910.7 (16.9 to 1)
Librarians/Media Specialists: 33.9 (951.1 to 1)
Guidance Counselors: 77.1 (418.2 to 1)
Current Spending: ($ per student per year):
    Total: $6,284; Instruction: $3,765; Support Services: $2,216
Enrollment, Drop-out Rates and Diploma Recipients by Race/Ethnicity

Category	Total	White	Black	Asian	AIAN	Hisp.
Enrollment (%)	100.0	5.4	1.3	0.4	0.3	92.6
Drop-out Rate (%)	1.9	1.6	1.0	0.0	0.0	2.0
H.S. Diplomas (#)	1,533	120	16	13	1	1,383

Ysleta ISD
9600 Sims Dr • El Paso, TX 79925-7225
(915) 434-0000 • http://www.yisd.net/home/home.jsp
Grade Span: PK-12; **Agency Type:** 1
Schools: 64
    37 Primary; 13 Middle; 11 High; 2 Other Level
    55 Regular; 0 Special Education; 0 Vocational; 8 Alternative
    0 Magnet; 0 Charter; 59 Title I Eligible; 57 School-wide Title I
Students: 46,668 (51.2% male; 48.7% female)
    Individual Education Program: 5,298 (11.4%);
    English Language Learner: 11,441 (24.5%); Migrant: 530 (1.1%)
    Eligible for Free Lunch Program: 18,774 (40.2%)
    Eligible for Reduced-Price Lunch Program: 4,880 (10.5%)
Teachers: 2,999.6 (15.6 to 1)
Librarians/Media Specialists: 51.5 (906.2 to 1)
Guidance Counselors: 83.8 (556.9 to 1)
Current Spending: ($ per student per year):
    Total: $6,756; Instruction: $4,195; Support Services: $2,265

Enrollment, Drop-out Rates and Diploma Recipients by Race/Ethnicity

Category	Total	White	Black	Asian	AIAN	Hisp.
Enrollment (%)	100.0	6.8	2.2	0.4	0.5	90.1
Drop-out Rate (%)	5.6	3.0	5.6	2.5	8.0	5.9
H.S. Diplomas (#)	2,842	285	78	15	18	2,446

Ellis County

Ennis ISD
303 W Knox • Ennis, TX 75119-3957
Mailing Address: PO Box 1420 • Ennis, TX 75120-1420
(972) 875-9027 • http://districtweb1.ednet10.net/ennis/home/index.html
Grade Span: PK-12; Agency Type: 1
Schools: 9
　5 Primary; 3 Middle; 1 High; 0 Other Level
　9 Regular; 0 Special Education; 0 Vocational; 0 Alternative
　0 Magnet; 0 Charter; 9 Title I Eligible; 2 School-wide Title I
Students: 5,393　(51.3% male; 48.6% female)
　Individual Education Program: 858 (15.9%);
　English Language Learner: 764 (14.2%); Migrant: 25 (0.5%)
　Eligible for Free Lunch Program: 2,494 (46.2%)
　Eligible for Reduced-Price Lunch Program: 446 (8.3%)
Teachers: 359.8 (15.0 to 1)
Librarians/Media Specialists: 5.0 (1,078.6 to 1)
Guidance Counselors: 16.0 (337.1 to 1)
Current Spending: ($ per student per year):
　Total: $6,987; Instruction: $4,405; Support Services: $2,196
Enrollment, Drop-out Rates and Diploma Recipients by Race/Ethnicity

Category	Total	White	Black	Asian	AIAN	Hisp.
Enrollment (%)	100.0	43.8	15.4	0.3	0.1	40.4
Drop-out Rate (%)	1.8	1.0	2.6	n/a	0.0	2.6
H.S. Diplomas (#)	260	142	52	0	0	66

Ferris ISD
303 E 5th St • Ferris, TX 75125-2225
Mailing Address: PO Box 459 • Ferris, TX 75125-0459
(972) 544-3858 • http://ferris.ednet10.net/
Grade Span: PK-12; Agency Type: 1
Schools: 5
　2 Primary; 2 Middle; 1 High; 0 Other Level
　5 Regular; 0 Special Education; 0 Vocational; 0 Alternative
　0 Magnet; 0 Charter; 2 Title I Eligible; 2 School-wide Title I
Students: 2,277　(50.4% male; 49.5% female)
　Individual Education Program: 383 (16.8%);
　English Language Learner: 214 (9.4%); Migrant: 17 (0.7%)
　Eligible for Free Lunch Program: 1,009 (44.3%)
　Eligible for Reduced-Price Lunch Program: 283 (12.4%)
Teachers: 156.8 (14.5 to 1)
Librarians/Media Specialists: 2.0 (1,138.5 to 1)
Guidance Counselors: 6.0 (379.5 to 1)
Current Spending: ($ per student per year):
　Total: $7,083; Instruction: $4,321; Support Services: $2,402
Enrollment, Drop-out Rates and Diploma Recipients by Race/Ethnicity

Category	Total	White	Black	Asian	AIAN	Hisp.
Enrollment (%)	100.0	43.2	10.3	0.2	0.3	46.0
Drop-out Rate (%)	2.5	2.0	3.3	n/a	0.0	2.9
H.S. Diplomas (#)	98	48	20	0	0	30

Midlothian ISD
100 Walter Stephenson Rd • Midlothian, TX 76065-3418
(972) 775-8296 • http://www.midlothian-isd.net/
Grade Span: PK-12; Agency Type: 1
Schools: 7
　4 Primary; 2 Middle; 1 High; 0 Other Level
　7 Regular; 0 Special Education; 0 Vocational; 0 Alternative
　0 Magnet; 0 Charter; 2 Title I Eligible; 0 School-wide Title I
Students: 5,396　(51.7% male; 48.2% female)
　Individual Education Program: 770 (14.3%);
　English Language Learner: 166 (3.1%); Migrant: 29 (0.5%)
　Eligible for Free Lunch Program: 593 (11.0%)
　Eligible for Reduced-Price Lunch Program: 248 (4.6%)
Teachers: 372.7 (14.5 to 1)
Librarians/Media Specialists: 4.0 (1,349.0 to 1)
Guidance Counselors: 11.0 (490.5 to 1)
Current Spending: ($ per student per year):
　Total: $7,480; Instruction: $4,391; Support Services: $2,833
Enrollment, Drop-out Rates and Diploma Recipients by Race/Ethnicity

Category	Total	White	Black	Asian	AIAN	Hisp.
Enrollment (%)	100.0	83.7	2.7	0.8	0.5	12.4
Drop-out Rate (%)	2.1	1.8	2.6	0.0	0.0	5.3
H.S. Diplomas (#)	258	229	7	2	1	19

Red Oak ISD
156 Louise Ritter Blvd • Red Oak, TX 75154-9000
Mailing Address: PO Box 9000 • Red Oak, TX 75154-9000
(972) 617-2941
Grade Span: PK-12; Agency Type: 1
Schools: 8
　4 Primary; 2 Middle; 1 High; 1 Other Level
　7 Regular; 0 Special Education; 0 Vocational; 1 Alternative
　0 Magnet; 0 Charter; 1 Title I Eligible; 0 School-wide Title I
Students: 4,803　(51.2% male; 48.7% female)
　Individual Education Program: 717 (14.9%);
　English Language Learner: 198 (4.1%); Migrant: 0 (0.0%)
　Eligible for Free Lunch Program: 787 (16.4%)
　Eligible for Reduced-Price Lunch Program: 206 (4.3%)
Teachers: 308.4 (15.6 to 1)
Librarians/Media Specialists: 5.2 (923.7 to 1)
Guidance Counselors: 14.6 (329.0 to 1)
Current Spending: ($ per student per year):
　Total: $6,264; Instruction: $3,875; Support Services: $2,081
Enrollment, Drop-out Rates and Diploma Recipients by Race/Ethnicity

Category	Total	White	Black	Asian	AIAN	Hisp.
Enrollment (%)	100.0	72.7	6.8	0.5	0.7	19.3
Drop-out Rate (%)	2.8	2.4	3.9	0.0	0.0	4.5
H.S. Diplomas (#)	249	205	16	1	1	26

Waxahachie ISD
411 N Gibson St • Waxahachie, TX 75165-3007
(972) 923-4631 • http://www.wisd.org/
Grade Span: PK-12; Agency Type: 1
Schools: 10
　5 Primary; 2 Middle; 2 High; 1 Other Level
　9 Regular; 0 Special Education; 0 Vocational; 1 Alternative
　0 Magnet; 0 Charter; 6 Title I Eligible; 0 School-wide Title I
Students: 5,859　(50.6% male; 49.3% female)
　Individual Education Program: 889 (15.2%);
　English Language Learner: 366 (6.2%); Migrant: 70 (1.2%)
　Eligible for Free Lunch Program: 1,974 (33.7%)
　Eligible for Reduced-Price Lunch Program: 479 (8.2%)
Teachers: 377.6 (15.5 to 1)
Librarians/Media Specialists: 2.1 (2,790.0 to 1)
Guidance Counselors: 10.6 (552.7 to 1)
Current Spending: ($ per student per year):
　Total: $6,970; Instruction: $4,208; Support Services: $2,407
Enrollment, Drop-out Rates and Diploma Recipients by Race/Ethnicity

Category	Total	White	Black	Asian	AIAN	Hisp.
Enrollment (%)	100.0	57.6	15.3	0.4	0.5	26.3
Drop-out Rate (%)	1.8	1.5	2.3	0.0	0.0	2.4
H.S. Diplomas (#)	390	251	68	2	2	67

Erath County

Stephenville
2655 W Overhill • Stephenville, TX 76401-3003
(254) 968-7990
Grade Span: PK-12; Agency Type: 1
Schools: 6
　3 Primary; 2 Middle; 1 High; 0 Other Level
　6 Regular; 0 Special Education; 0 Vocational; 0 Alternative
　0 Magnet; 0 Charter; 5 Title I Eligible; 5 School-wide Title I
Students: 3,530　(51.5% male; 48.4% female)
　Individual Education Program: 396 (11.2%);
　English Language Learner: 188 (5.3%); Migrant: 6 (0.2%)
　Eligible for Free Lunch Program: 997 (28.2%)
　Eligible for Reduced-Price Lunch Program: 284 (8.0%)
Teachers: 222.9 (15.8 to 1)
Librarians/Media Specialists: 4.0 (882.5 to 1)
Guidance Counselors: 7.6 (464.5 to 1)
Current Spending: ($ per student per year):
　Total: $6,021; Instruction: $3,941; Support Services: $1,802
Enrollment, Drop-out Rates and Diploma Recipients by Race/Ethnicity

Category	Total	White	Black	Asian	AIAN	Hisp.
Enrollment (%)	100.0	77.1	1.2	0.7	0.5	20.5
Drop-out Rate (%)	0.9	0.5	0.0	0.0	0.0	3.0
H.S. Diplomas (#)	224	197	1	3	0	23

Fannin County

Bonham ISD
220 W 11th • Bonham, TX 75418-3028
Mailing Address: PO Box 490 • Bonham, TX 75418-0490
(903) 583-5526
Grade Span: PK-12; Agency Type: 1
Schools: 6
　2 Primary; 2 Middle; 1 High; 1 Other Level
　5 Regular; 0 Special Education; 0 Vocational; 1 Alternative

0 Magnet; 0 Charter; 4 Title I Eligible; 4 School-wide Title I
Students: 2,009 (50.3% male; 49.6% female)
  Individual Education Program: 338 (16.8%);
  English Language Learner: 92 (4.6%); Migrant: 29 (1.4%)
  Eligible for Free Lunch Program: 629 (31.3%)
  Eligible for Reduced-Price Lunch Program: 130 (6.5%)
Teachers: 142.3 (14.1 to 1)
Librarians/Media Specialists: 1.7 (1,181.8 to 1)
Guidance Counselors: 5.0 (401.8 to 1)
Current Spending: ($ per student per year):
  Total: $7,486; Instruction: $4,521; Support Services: $2,600
Enrollment, Drop-out Rates and Diploma Recipients by Race/Ethnicity

Category	Total	White	Black	Asian	AIAN	Hisp.
Enrollment (%)	100.0	78.8	8.8	0.7	1.5	10.2
Drop-out Rate (%)	2.8	2.4	6.1	0.0	0.0	5.6
H.S. Diplomas (#)	106	91	13	2	0	0

Fayette County

La Grange ISD

641 E Milam • La Grange, TX 78945-2819
Mailing Address: PO Box 100 • La Grange, TX 78945-0100
(979) 968-7000 •
http://lagrange.fais.net/New_City_site/schools/schools.htm
Grade Span: PK-12; **Agency Type:** 1
Schools: 4
  1 Primary; 2 Middle; 1 High; 0 Other Level
  4 Regular; 0 Special Education; 0 Vocational; 0 Alternative
  0 Magnet; 0 Charter; 3 Title I Eligible; 3 School-wide Title I
Students: 1,945 (51.4% male; 48.5% female)
  Individual Education Program: 235 (12.1%);
  English Language Learner: 136 (7.0%); Migrant: 3 (0.2%)
  Eligible for Free Lunch Program: 650 (33.4%)
  Eligible for Reduced-Price Lunch Program: 157 (8.1%)
Teachers: 138.0 (14.1 to 1)
Librarians/Media Specialists: 2.0 (972.5 to 1)
Guidance Counselors: 4.0 (486.3 to 1)
Current Spending: ($ per student per year):
  Total: $6,754; Instruction: $4,219; Support Services: $2,135
Enrollment, Drop-out Rates and Diploma Recipients by Race/Ethnicity

Category	Total	White	Black	Asian	AIAN	Hisp.
Enrollment (%)	100.0	65.6	10.5	0.4	0.4	23.1
Drop-out Rate (%)	2.0	1.0	8.8	0.0	0.0	2.9
H.S. Diplomas (#)	130	103	11	0	0	16

Fort Bend County

Fort Bend ISD

16431 Lexington Blvd • Sugar Land, TX 77479-2308
(281) 634-1000 • http://www.fortbend.k12.tx.us/
Grade Span: PK-12; **Agency Type:** 1
Schools: 59
  36 Primary; 11 Middle; 10 High; 2 Other Level
  56 Regular; 0 Special Education; 0 Vocational; 3 Alternative
  0 Magnet; 0 Charter; 15 Title I Eligible; 14 School-wide Title I
Students: 61,248 (51.7% male; 48.2% female)
  Individual Education Program: 6,110 (10.0%);
  English Language Learner: 6,194 (10.1%); Migrant: 5 (<0.1%)
  Eligible for Free Lunch Program: 12,984 (21.2%)
  Eligible for Reduced-Price Lunch Program: 3,001 (4.9%)
Teachers: 3,719.7 (16.5 to 1)
Librarians/Media Specialists: 63.4 (966.1 to 1)
Guidance Counselors: 127.5 (480.4 to 1)
Current Spending: ($ per student per year):
  Total: $6,500; Instruction: $4,114; Support Services: $2,151
Enrollment, Drop-out Rates and Diploma Recipients by Race/Ethnicity

Category	Total	White	Black	Asian	AIAN	Hisp.
Enrollment (%)	100.0	31.7	29.8	18.2	0.2	20.2
Drop-out Rate (%)	2.2	1.3	2.8	1.4	0.0	4.6
H.S. Diplomas (#)	3,630	1,457	971	743	0	459

Lamar Consolidated ISD

3911 Ave I • Rosenberg, TX 77471-3960
(281) 341-3100 • http://www.lcisd.org/
Grade Span: PK-12; **Agency Type:** 1
Schools: 28
  16 Primary; 5 Middle; 3 High; 4 Other Level
  25 Regular; 1 Special Education; 0 Vocational; 2 Alternative
  0 Magnet; 0 Charter; 17 Title I Eligible; 15 School-wide Title I
Students: 17,864 (50.6% male; 49.3% female)
  Individual Education Program: 2,145 (12.0%);
  English Language Learner: 1,949 (10.9%); Migrant: 0 (0.0%)
  Eligible for Free Lunch Program: 6,914 (38.7%)
  Eligible for Reduced-Price Lunch Program: 1,241 (6.9%)
Teachers: 1,155.4 (15.5 to 1)

Librarians/Media Specialists: 24.0 (744.3 to 1)
Guidance Counselors: 49.8 (358.7 to 1)
Current Spending: ($ per student per year):
  Total: $7,067; Instruction: $4,277; Support Services: $2,408
Enrollment, Drop-out Rates and Diploma Recipients by Race/Ethnicity

Category	Total	White	Black	Asian	AIAN	Hisp.
Enrollment (%)	100.0	35.6	14.1	2.6	0.1	47.5
Drop-out Rate (%)	3.2	1.4	4.8	0.0	0.0	4.5
H.S. Diplomas (#)	796	366	98	9	2	321

Needville ISD

16227 Hwy 36 • Needville, TX 77461-0412
Mailing Address: PO Box 412 • Needville, TX 77461-0412
(979) 793-4308
Grade Span: PK-12; **Agency Type:** 1
Schools: 5
  2 Primary; 2 Middle; 1 High; 0 Other Level
  5 Regular; 0 Special Education; 0 Vocational; 0 Alternative
  0 Magnet; 0 Charter; 3 Title I Eligible; 0 School-wide Title I
Students: 2,466 (51.6% male; 48.3% female)
  Individual Education Program: 320 (13.0%);
  English Language Learner: 116 (4.7%); Migrant: 3 (0.1%)
  Eligible for Free Lunch Program: 566 (23.0%)
  Eligible for Reduced-Price Lunch Program: 137 (5.6%)
Teachers: 162.7 (15.2 to 1)
Librarians/Media Specialists: 3.0 (822.0 to 1)
Guidance Counselors: 7.0 (352.3 to 1)
Current Spending: ($ per student per year):
  Total: $6,792; Instruction: $4,326; Support Services: $2,157
Enrollment, Drop-out Rates and Diploma Recipients by Race/Ethnicity

Category	Total	White	Black	Asian	AIAN	Hisp.
Enrollment (%)	100.0	60.9	6.3	0.2	0.1	32.4
Drop-out Rate (%)	2.6	1.8	4.3	0.0	0.0	4.8
H.S. Diplomas (#)	170	121	11	0	1	37

Stafford Municipal School

1625 Staffordshire Rd • Stafford, TX 77477-6326
(281) 261-9200
Grade Span: PK-12; **Agency Type:** 1
Schools: 7
  2 Primary; 2 Middle; 1 High; 2 Other Level
  5 Regular; 0 Special Education; 0 Vocational; 2 Alternative
  0 Magnet; 0 Charter; 4 Title I Eligible; 0 School-wide Title I
Students: 2,838 (52.1% male; 47.8% female)
  Individual Education Program: 271 (9.5%);
  English Language Learner: 352 (12.4%); Migrant: 0 (0.0%)
  Eligible for Free Lunch Program: 789 (27.8%)
  Eligible for Reduced-Price Lunch Program: 234 (8.2%)
Teachers: 197.6 (14.4 to 1)
Librarians/Media Specialists: 3.0 (946.0 to 1)
Guidance Counselors: 6.0 (473.0 to 1)
Current Spending: ($ per student per year):
  Total: $7,348; Instruction: $4,523; Support Services: $2,394
Enrollment, Drop-out Rates and Diploma Recipients by Race/Ethnicity

Category	Total	White	Black	Asian	AIAN	Hisp.
Enrollment (%)	100.0	17.2	29.0	19.9	0.2	33.7
Drop-out Rate (%)	1.6	2.2	1.0	1.2	n/a	2.0
H.S. Diplomas (#)	179	41	45	44	0	49

Freestone County

Fairfield ISD

615 Post Oak Rd • Fairfield, TX 75840-2005
(903) 389-2532 • http://www.fairfield.k12.tx.us/
Grade Span: PK-12; **Agency Type:** 1
Schools: 4
  1 Primary; 1 Middle; 1 High; 1 Other Level
  3 Regular; 0 Special Education; 0 Vocational; 1 Alternative
  0 Magnet; 0 Charter; 2 Title I Eligible; 2 School-wide Title I
Students: 1,677 (51.5% male; 48.4% female)
  Individual Education Program: 244 (14.5%);
  English Language Learner: 75 (4.5%); Migrant: 0 (0.0%)
  Eligible for Free Lunch Program: 605 (36.1%)
  Eligible for Reduced-Price Lunch Program: 106 (6.3%)
Teachers: 121.1 (13.8 to 1)
Librarians/Media Specialists: 2.0 (838.5 to 1)
Guidance Counselors: 5.8 (289.1 to 1)
Current Spending: ($ per student per year):
  Total: $8,764; Instruction: $5,170; Support Services: $3,250
Enrollment, Drop-out Rates and Diploma Recipients by Race/Ethnicity

Category	Total	White	Black	Asian	AIAN	Hisp.
Enrollment (%)	100.0	62.7	23.2	0.7	0.9	12.5
Drop-out Rate (%)	1.0	0.9	1.7	0.0	0.0	0.0
H.S. Diplomas (#)	104	79	22	0	1	2

Frio County

Pearsall ISD
318 Berry Ranch Rd • Pearsall, TX 78061-3315
(830) 334-8001
Grade Span: PK-12; **Agency Type:** 1
Schools: 6
  2 Primary; 1 Middle; 1 High; 2 Other Level
  4 Regular; 0 Special Education; 0 Vocational; 2 Alternative
  0 Magnet; 0 Charter; 4 Title I Eligible; 4 School-wide Title I
Students: 2,287 (51.0% male; 48.9% female)
  Individual Education Program: 233 (10.2%);
  English Language Learner: 266 (11.6%); Migrant: 346 (15.1%)
  Eligible for Free Lunch Program: 1,581 (69.1%)
  Eligible for Reduced-Price Lunch Program: 200 (8.7%)
Teachers: 166.8 (13.7 to 1)
Librarians/Media Specialists: 0.0 (n/a to 1)
Guidance Counselors: 10.0 (228.7 to 1)
Current Spending: ($ per student per year):
  Total: $7,310; Instruction: $4,224; Support Services: $2,680
Enrollment, Drop-out Rates and Diploma Recipients by Race/Ethnicity

Category	Total	White	Black	Asian	AIAN	Hisp.
Enrollment (%)	100.0	10.7	0.3	0.5	0.0	88.5
Drop-out Rate (%)	3.0	1.4	0.0	0.0	n/a	3.3
H.S. Diplomas (#)	120	20	1	0	0	99

Gaines County

Seminole ISD
207 SW 6th St • Seminole, TX 79360-4305
(432) 758-3662
Grade Span: PK-12; **Agency Type:** 1
Schools: 6
  2 Primary; 2 Middle; 1 High; 1 Other Level
  5 Regular; 0 Special Education; 0 Vocational; 1 Alternative
  0 Magnet; 0 Charter; 6 Title I Eligible; 6 School-wide Title I
Students: 2,192 (51.8% male; 48.1% female)
  Individual Education Program: 365 (16.7%);
  English Language Learner: 286 (13.0%); Migrant: 11 (0.5%)
  Eligible for Free Lunch Program: 1,072 (48.9%)
  Eligible for Reduced-Price Lunch Program: 155 (7.1%)
Teachers: 162.8 (13.5 to 1)
Librarians/Media Specialists: 3.0 (730.7 to 1)
Guidance Counselors: 5.9 (371.5 to 1)
Current Spending: ($ per student per year):
  Total: $9,509; Instruction: $5,632; Support Services: $3,368
Enrollment, Drop-out Rates and Diploma Recipients by Race/Ethnicity

Category	Total	White	Black	Asian	AIAN	Hisp.
Enrollment (%)	100.0	58.1	2.1	0.2	0.5	39.1
Drop-out Rate (%)	1.6	0.8	4.8	n/a	0.0	2.4
H.S. Diplomas (#)	128	66	7	0	0	55

Galveston County

Clear Creek ISD
2425 E Main St • League City, TX 77573-2799
Mailing Address: PO Box 799 • League City, TX 77574-0799
(281) 332-2828 • http://www.ccisd.net/
Grade Span: PK-12; **Agency Type:** 1
Schools: 38
  22 Primary; 8 Middle; 3 High; 5 Other Level
  33 Regular; 0 Special Education; 0 Vocational; 5 Alternative
  0 Magnet; 0 Charter; 6 Title I Eligible; 6 School-wide Title I
Students: 32,810 (51.3% male; 48.6% female)
  Individual Education Program: 2,999 (9.1%);
  English Language Learner: 2,186 (6.7%); Migrant: 0 (0.0%)
  Eligible for Free Lunch Program: 3,788 (11.5%)
  Eligible for Reduced-Price Lunch Program: 1,164 (3.5%)
Teachers: 1,995.6 (16.4 to 1)
Librarians/Media Specialists: 34.0 (965.0 to 1)
Guidance Counselors: 64.9 (505.5 to 1)
Current Spending: ($ per student per year):
  Total: $6,151; Instruction: $3,939; Support Services: $1,959
Enrollment, Drop-out Rates and Diploma Recipients by Race/Ethnicity

Category	Total	White	Black	Asian	AIAN	Hisp.
Enrollment (%)	100.0	67.2	7.4	9.4	0.3	15.6
Drop-out Rate (%)	1.8	1.6	2.4	0.4	0.0	4.0
H.S. Diplomas (#)	1,844	1,292	134	231	3	184

Dickinson ISD
4512 Hwy 3 • Dickinson, TX 77539-2026
Mailing Address: PO Box Z • Dickinson, TX 77539-2026
(281) 534-3581 • http://www.dickinsonisd.org/mainindex.html
Grade Span: PK-12; **Agency Type:** 1
Schools: 10

  4 Primary; 2 Middle; 1 High; 3 Other Level
  7 Regular; 0 Special Education; 0 Vocational; 3 Alternative
  0 Magnet; 0 Charter; 5 Title I Eligible; 5 School-wide Title I
Students: 6,539 (51.8% male; 48.1% female)
  Individual Education Program: 704 (10.8%);
  English Language Learner: 963 (14.7%); Migrant: 37 (0.6%)
  Eligible for Free Lunch Program: 3,173 (48.5%)
  Eligible for Reduced-Price Lunch Program: 505 (7.7%)
Teachers: 403.5 (16.2 to 1)
Librarians/Media Specialists: 7.0 (934.1 to 1)
Guidance Counselors: 9.2 (710.8 to 1)
Current Spending: ($ per student per year):
  Total: $6,500; Instruction: $3,966; Support Services: $2,167
Enrollment, Drop-out Rates and Diploma Recipients by Race/Ethnicity

Category	Total	White	Black	Asian	AIAN	Hisp.
Enrollment (%)	100.0	46.0	12.3	3.9	0.4	37.3
Drop-out Rate (%)	7.6	5.6	9.5	0.0	100.0	11.5
H.S. Diplomas (#)	247	149	27	13	0	58

Friendswood ISD
302 Laurel Dr • Friendswood, TX 77546-3923
(281) 482-1267 • http://www.friendswood.isd.tenet.edu/
Grade Span: PK-12; **Agency Type:** 1
Schools: 7
  2 Primary; 3 Middle; 1 High; 0 Other Level
  6 Regular; 0 Special Education; 0 Vocational; 0 Alternative
  0 Magnet; 0 Charter; 2 Title I Eligible; 0 School-wide Title I
Students: 5,527 (50.8% male; 49.1% female)
  Individual Education Program: 495 (9.0%);
  English Language Learner: 39 (0.7%); Migrant: 0 (0.0%)
  Eligible for Free Lunch Program: 131 (2.4%)
  Eligible for Reduced-Price Lunch Program: 33 (0.6%)
Teachers: 338.9 (16.3 to 1)
Librarians/Media Specialists: 5.0 (1,105.4 to 1)
Guidance Counselors: 9.3 (594.3 to 1)
Current Spending: ($ per student per year):
  Total: $6,168; Instruction: $3,804; Support Services: $2,127
Enrollment, Drop-out Rates and Diploma Recipients by Race/Ethnicity

Category	Total	White	Black	Asian	AIAN	Hisp.
Enrollment (%)	100.0	86.4	2.1	3.6	0.1	7.9
Drop-out Rate (%)	0.8	0.7	0.0	0.0	0.0	2.9
H.S. Diplomas (#)	381	336	8	10	1	26

Galveston ISD
3904 Ave T • Galveston, TX 77550-8643
Mailing Address: PO Box 660 • Galveston, TX 77553-0660
(409) 766-5100 • http://www.Galveston-Schools.org/
Grade Span: PK-12; **Agency Type:** 1
Schools: 17
  10 Primary; 3 Middle; 1 High; 3 Other Level
  13 Regular; 1 Special Education; 0 Vocational; 3 Alternative
  0 Magnet; 0 Charter; 13 Title I Eligible; 13 School-wide Title I
Students: 9,170 (50.8% male; 49.1% female)
  Individual Education Program: 1,036 (11.3%);
  English Language Learner: 1,080 (11.8%); Migrant: 0 (0.0%)
  Eligible for Free Lunch Program: 5,059 (55.2%)
  Eligible for Reduced-Price Lunch Program: 649 (7.1%)
Teachers: 584.0 (15.7 to 1)
Librarians/Media Specialists: 10.1 (907.9 to 1)
Guidance Counselors: 14.9 (615.4 to 1)
Current Spending: ($ per student per year):
  Total: $7,467; Instruction: $4,292; Support Services: $2,815
Enrollment, Drop-out Rates and Diploma Recipients by Race/Ethnicity

Category	Total	White	Black	Asian	AIAN	Hisp.
Enrollment (%)	100.0	26.6	32.2	2.7	0.3	38.2
Drop-out Rate (%)	6.7	4.8	8.1	0.0	0.0	7.4
H.S. Diplomas (#)	419	145	149	10	1	114

La Marque ISD
1727 Bayou Rd • La Marque, TX 77568-5209
Mailing Address: PO Box 7 • La Marque, TX 77568-0007
(409) 938-4251 • http://www.la-marque.isd.tenet.edu/
Grade Span: PK-12; **Agency Type:** 1
Schools: 8
  5 Primary; 1 Middle; 1 High; 1 Other Level
  7 Regular; 0 Special Education; 0 Vocational; 1 Alternative
  0 Magnet; 0 Charter; 7 Title I Eligible; 7 School-wide Title I
Students: 3,750 (50.9% male; 49.0% female)
  Individual Education Program: 465 (12.4%);
  English Language Learner: 80 (2.1%); Migrant: 2 (0.1%)
  Eligible for Free Lunch Program: 1,784 (47.6%)
  Eligible for Reduced-Price Lunch Program: 251 (6.7%)
Teachers: 244.5 (15.3 to 1)
Librarians/Media Specialists: 6.0 (625.0 to 1)
Guidance Counselors: 8.8 (426.1 to 1)

Current Spending: ($ per student per year):
Total: $6,997; Instruction: $3,807; Support Services: $2,747
Enrollment, Drop-out Rates and Diploma Recipients by Race/Ethnicity

Category	Total	White	Black	Asian	AIAN	Hisp.
Enrollment (%)	100.0	15.5	67.8	0.2	0.3	16.3
Drop-out Rate (%)	4.3	5.2	3.9	0.0	0.0	6.1
H.S. Diplomas (#)	241	41	181	2	0	17

Santa Fe ISD

13304 Hwy 6 • Santa Fe, TX 77510-0370
Mailing Address: PO Box 370 • Santa Fe, TX 77510-0370
(409) 925-3526
Grade Span: PK-12; **Agency Type:** 1
Schools: 7
2 Primary; 3 Middle; 1 High; 1 Other Level
6 Regular; 0 Special Education; 0 Vocational; 1 Alternative
0 Magnet; 0 Charter; 5 Title I Eligible; 0 School-wide Title I
Students: 4,475 (52.7% male; 47.2% female)
Individual Education Program: 446 (10.0%);
English Language Learner: 82 (1.8%); Migrant: 0 (0.0%)
Eligible for Free Lunch Program: 848 (18.9%)
Eligible for Reduced-Price Lunch Program: 207 (4.6%)
Teachers: 272.7 (16.4 to 1)
Librarians/Media Specialists: 5.0 (895.0 to 1)
Guidance Counselors: 9.0 (497.2 to 1)
Current Spending: ($ per student per year):
Total: $5,812; Instruction: $3,511; Support Services: $2,007
Enrollment, Drop-out Rates and Diploma Recipients by Race/Ethnicity

Category	Total	White	Black	Asian	AIAN	Hisp.
Enrollment (%)	100.0	88.6	0.4	0.2	0.3	10.6
Drop-out Rate (%)	4.9	4.9	n/a	0.0	0.0	4.8
H.S. Diplomas (#)	241	220	0	1	0	20

Texas City ISD

1401 9th Ave N • Texas City, TX 77590-5495
Mailing Address: PO Box 1150 • Texas City, TX 77592-1150
(409) 942-2713 • http://www.texascity.isd.tenet.edu/
Grade Span: PK-12; **Agency Type:** 1
Schools: 9
4 Primary; 2 Middle; 1 High; 2 Other Level
7 Regular; 0 Special Education; 0 Vocational; 2 Alternative
0 Magnet; 0 Charter; 4 Title I Eligible; 4 School-wide Title I
Students: 5,804 (51.2% male; 48.7% female)
Individual Education Program: 603 (10.4%);
English Language Learner: 383 (6.6%); Migrant: 0 (0.0%)
Eligible for Free Lunch Program: 2,743 (47.3%)
Eligible for Reduced-Price Lunch Program: 431 (7.4%)
Teachers: 369.2 (15.7 to 1)
Librarians/Media Specialists: 7.1 (817.5 to 1)
Guidance Counselors: 13.0 (446.5 to 1)
Current Spending: ($ per student per year):
Total: $7,379; Instruction: $4,228; Support Services: $2,728
Enrollment, Drop-out Rates and Diploma Recipients by Race/Ethnicity

Category	Total	White	Black	Asian	AIAN	Hisp.
Enrollment (%)	100.0	47.5	19.6	0.6	0.2	32.1
Drop-out Rate (%)	6.7	5.4	7.8	0.0	0.0	8.6
H.S. Diplomas (#)	264	151	47	5	0	61

Gillespie County

Fredericksburg ISD

234 Friendship Ln • Fredericksburg, TX 78624-5053
(830) 997-9551 • http://www.fisd.org/
Grade Span: PK-12; **Agency Type:** 1
Schools: 6
3 Primary; 1 Middle; 2 High; 0 Other Level
5 Regular; 0 Special Education; 0 Vocational; 1 Alternative
0 Magnet; 0 Charter; 3 Title I Eligible; 2 School-wide Title I
Students: 2,848 (50.2% male; 49.7% female)
Individual Education Program: 311 (10.9%);
English Language Learner: 236 (8.3%); Migrant: 32 (1.1%)
Eligible for Free Lunch Program: 915 (32.1%)
Eligible for Reduced-Price Lunch Program: 265 (9.3%)
Teachers: 212.4 (13.4 to 1)
Librarians/Media Specialists: 2.0 (1,424.0 to 1)
Guidance Counselors: 8.0 (356.0 to 1)
Current Spending: ($ per student per year):
Total: $7,185; Instruction: $4,278; Support Services: $2,588
Enrollment, Drop-out Rates and Diploma Recipients by Race/Ethnicity

Category	Total	White	Black	Asian	AIAN	Hisp.
Enrollment (%)	100.0	62.7	0.6	0.2	0.2	36.2
Drop-out Rate (%)	1.3	0.5	0.0	0.0	0.0	3.8
H.S. Diplomas (#)	219	178	1	1	0	39

Gonzales County

Gonzales ISD

926 St Lawrence • Gonzales, TX 78629-4151
(830) 672-9551
Grade Span: PK-12; **Agency Type:** 1
Schools: 6
2 Primary; 2 Middle; 2 High; 0 Other Level
5 Regular; 0 Special Education; 0 Vocational; 1 Alternative
0 Magnet; 0 Charter; 5 Title I Eligible; 5 School-wide Title I
Students: 2,627 (51.4% male; 48.5% female)
Individual Education Program: 323 (12.3%);
English Language Learner: 214 (8.1%); Migrant: 53 (2.0%)
Eligible for Free Lunch Program: 1,433 (54.5%)
Eligible for Reduced-Price Lunch Program: 241 (9.2%)
Teachers: 180.3 (14.6 to 1)
Librarians/Media Specialists: 1.8 (1,459.4 to 1)
Guidance Counselors: 4.7 (558.9 to 1)
Current Spending: ($ per student per year):
Total: $6,599; Instruction: $3,988; Support Services: $2,331
Enrollment, Drop-out Rates and Diploma Recipients by Race/Ethnicity

Category	Total	White	Black	Asian	AIAN	Hisp.
Enrollment (%)	100.0	38.0	12.4	0.3	0.0	49.3
Drop-out Rate (%)	2.2	1.9	0.0	0.0	0.0	3.1
H.S. Diplomas (#)	147	67	28	1	1	50

Gray County

Pampa ISD

321 W Albert St • Pampa, TX 79065-7801
(806) 669-4700 • http://www.pampaisd.net/
Grade Span: PK-12; **Agency Type:** 1
Schools: 7
4 Primary; 1 Middle; 2 High; 0 Other Level
6 Regular; 0 Special Education; 0 Vocational; 1 Alternative
0 Magnet; 0 Charter; 5 Title I Eligible; 5 School-wide Title I
Students: 3,289 (50.4% male; 49.5% female)
Individual Education Program: 391 (11.9%);
English Language Learner: 188 (5.7%); Migrant: 8 (0.2%)
Eligible for Free Lunch Program: 1,220 (37.1%)
Eligible for Reduced-Price Lunch Program: 230 (7.0%)
Teachers: 236.9 (13.9 to 1)
Librarians/Media Specialists: 1.6 (2,055.6 to 1)
Guidance Counselors: 9.1 (361.4 to 1)
Current Spending: ($ per student per year):
Total: $6,641; Instruction: $4,282; Support Services: $2,042
Enrollment, Drop-out Rates and Diploma Recipients by Race/Ethnicity

Category	Total	White	Black	Asian	AIAN	Hisp.
Enrollment (%)	100.0	68.1	4.2	0.5	0.5	26.6
Drop-out Rate (%)	3.9	3.4	7.0	0.0	6.7	5.4
H.S. Diplomas (#)	253	207	9	4	4	29

Denison ISD

1201 S Rusk Ave • Denison, TX 75020-6340
(903) 462-7000 • http://www.denisonisd.net/
Grade Span: PK-12; **Agency Type:** 1
Schools: 11
7 Primary; 1 Middle; 2 High; 0 Other Level
9 Regular; 0 Special Education; 0 Vocational; 1 Alternative
0 Magnet; 0 Charter; 7 Title I Eligible; 7 School-wide Title I
Students: 4,561 (51.9% male; 48.0% female)
Individual Education Program: 872 (19.1%);
English Language Learner: 144 (3.2%); Migrant: 11 (0.2%)
Eligible for Free Lunch Program: 1,849 (40.5%)
Eligible for Reduced-Price Lunch Program: 400 (8.8%)
Teachers: 308.8 (14.8 to 1)
Librarians/Media Specialists: 2.0 (2,280.5 to 1)
Guidance Counselors: 15.6 (292.4 to 1)
Current Spending: ($ per student per year):
Total: $6,761; Instruction: $4,162; Support Services: $2,213
Enrollment, Drop-out Rates and Diploma Recipients by Race/Ethnicity

Category	Total	White	Black	Asian	AIAN	Hisp.
Enrollment (%)	100.0	77.3	11.6	0.9	2.3	8.0
Drop-out Rate (%)	5.4	5.0	8.2	9.1	5.6	5.2
H.S. Diplomas (#)	226	188	24	2	2	10

Sherman ISD

120 W King St • Sherman, TX 75090-7133
Mailing Address: PO Box 1176 • Sherman, TX 75091-1176
(903) 891-6400 • http://www.shermanisd.net/default.asp
Grade Span: PK-12; **Agency Type:** 1
Schools: 13
6 Primary; 2 Middle; 2 High; 3 Other Level
10 Regular; 0 Special Education; 0 Vocational; 3 Alternative
0 Magnet; 0 Charter; 8 Title I Eligible; 8 School-wide Title I

Students: 6,363 (51.7% male; 48.2% female)
  Individual Education Program: 993 (15.6%)
  English Language Learner: 601 (9.4%); Migrant: 27 (0.4%)
  Eligible for Free Lunch Program: 2,639 (41.5%)
  Eligible for Reduced-Price Lunch Program: 447 (7.0%)
Teachers: 465.0 (13.7 to 1)
Librarians/Media Specialists: 5.1 (1,247.6 to 1)
Guidance Counselors: 16.0 (397.7 to 1)
Current Spending: ($ per student per year):
  Total: $6,734; Instruction: $4,183; Support Services: $2,207

Enrollment, Drop-out Rates and Diploma Recipients by Race/Ethnicity

Category	Total	White	Black	Asian	AIAN	Hisp.
Enrollment (%)	100.0	61.1	16.4	1.1	1.3	20.1
Drop-out Rate (%)	3.1	2.6	5.1	0.0	7.7	3.5
H.S. Diplomas (#)	300	231	45	2	3	19

Whitesboro ISD
115 Fourth St • Whitesboro, TX 76273-0130
(903) 564-4200
Grade Span: PK-12; **Agency Type:** 1
Schools: 4
  2 Primary; 1 Middle; 1 High; 0 Other Level
  4 Regular; 0 Special Education; 0 Vocational; 0 Alternative
  0 Magnet; 0 Charter; 2 Title I Eligible; 2 School-wide Title I
Students: 1,609 (52.2% male; 47.7% female)
  Individual Education Program: 261 (16.2%)
  English Language Learner: 26 (1.6%); Migrant: 4 (0.2%)
  Eligible for Free Lunch Program: 455 (28.3%)
  Eligible for Reduced-Price Lunch Program: 129 (8.0%)
Teachers: 110.2 (14.6 to 1)
Librarians/Media Specialists: 2.0 (804.5 to 1)
Guidance Counselors: 5.0 (321.8 to 1)
Current Spending: ($ per student per year):
  Total: $6,599; Instruction: $4,180; Support Services: $2,044

Enrollment, Drop-out Rates and Diploma Recipients by Race/Ethnicity

Category	Total	White	Black	Asian	AIAN	Hisp.
Enrollment (%)	100.0	91.0	0.2	0.9	2.4	5.5
Drop-out Rate (%)	1.1	1.2	n/a	0.0	0.0	0.0
H.S. Diplomas (#)	88	86	0	0	1	1

Gregg County

Gladewater ISD
500 W Quitman • Gladewater, TX 75647-2011
(903) 845-6991 • http://gladewaterisd.com/
Grade Span: PK-12; **Agency Type:** 1
Schools: 6
  2 Primary; 2 Middle; 1 High; 1 Other Level
  6 Regular; 0 Special Education; 0 Vocational; 0 Alternative
  0 Magnet; 0 Charter; 5 Title I Eligible; 5 School-wide Title I
Students: 2,265 (52.2% male; 47.7% female)
  Individual Education Program: 425 (18.8%)
  English Language Learner: 42 (1.9%); Migrant: 1 (<0.1%)
  Eligible for Free Lunch Program: 1,021 (45.1%)
  Eligible for Reduced-Price Lunch Program: 165 (7.3%)
Teachers: 157.2 (14.4 to 1)
Librarians/Media Specialists: 4.0 (566.3 to 1)
Guidance Counselors: 7.0 (323.6 to 1)
Current Spending: ($ per student per year):
  Total: $6,896; Instruction: $4,301; Support Services: $2,145

Enrollment, Drop-out Rates and Diploma Recipients by Race/Ethnicity

Category	Total	White	Black	Asian	AIAN	Hisp.
Enrollment (%)	100.0	72.9	19.5	0.6	0.5	6.5
Drop-out Rate (%)	2.2	1.7	2.8	0.0	n/a	6.7
H.S. Diplomas (#)	133	108	21	0	0	4

Kilgore ISD
301 N Kilgore St • Kilgore, TX 75662-5499
(903) 984-2073 • http://www.kisd.org/
Grade Span: PK-12; **Agency Type:** 1
Schools: 7
  2 Primary; 2 Middle; 2 High; 1 Other Level
  5 Regular; 0 Special Education; 0 Vocational; 2 Alternative
  0 Magnet; 0 Charter; 3 Title I Eligible; 0 School-wide Title I
Students: 3,669 (49.6% male; 50.3% female)
  Individual Education Program: 493 (13.4%)
  English Language Learner: 277 (7.5%); Migrant: 7 (0.2%)
  Eligible for Free Lunch Program: 1,638 (44.6%)
  Eligible for Reduced-Price Lunch Program: 249 (6.8%)
Teachers: 276.6 (13.3 to 1)
Librarians/Media Specialists: 1.0 (3,669.0 to 1)
Guidance Counselors: 4.5 (815.3 to 1)
Current Spending: ($ per student per year):
  Total: $6,360; Instruction: $4,011; Support Services: $2,023

Enrollment, Drop-out Rates and Diploma Recipients by Race/Ethnicity

Category	Total	White	Black	Asian	AIAN	Hisp.
Enrollment (%)	100.0	63.1	20.5	0.9	0.3	15.3
Drop-out Rate (%)	5.3	3.9	8.7	0.0	n/a	9.3
H.S. Diplomas (#)	227	166	42	0	0	19

Longview ISD
1301 E Young St • Longview, TX 75602
Mailing Address: PO Box 3268 • Longview, TX 75606-3268
(903) 381-2200 • http://www.lisd.org/www2/Main/default.asp
Grade Span: PK-12; **Agency Type:** 1
Schools: 18
  11 Primary; 3 Middle; 1 High; 3 Other Level
  15 Regular; 1 Special Education; 0 Vocational; 2 Alternative
  0 Magnet; 0 Charter; 11 Title I Eligible; 11 School-wide Title I
Students: 8,291 (51.5% male; 48.4% female)
  Individual Education Program: 1,263 (15.2%)
  English Language Learner: 894 (10.8%); Migrant: 1 (<0.1%)
  Eligible for Free Lunch Program: 4,736 (57.1%)
  Eligible for Reduced-Price Lunch Program: 468 (5.6%)
Teachers: 573.5 (14.5 to 1)
Librarians/Media Specialists: 15.0 (552.7 to 1)
Guidance Counselors: 20.0 (414.6 to 1)
Current Spending: ($ per student per year):
  Total: $7,167; Instruction: $4,367; Support Services: $2,353

Enrollment, Drop-out Rates and Diploma Recipients by Race/Ethnicity

Category	Total	White	Black	Asian	AIAN	Hisp.
Enrollment (%)	100.0	29.0	49.5	0.8	0.2	20.5
Drop-out Rate (%)	3.3	1.5	4.2	6.9	0.0	5.2
H.S. Diplomas (#)	406	175	203	5	0	23

Pine Tree ISD
1001 W Fairmont St • Longview, TX 75604-3511
Mailing Address: PO Box 5878 • Longview, TX 75608-5878
(903) 295-5000
Grade Span: PK-12; **Agency Type:** 1
Schools: 7
  3 Primary; 2 Middle; 1 High; 1 Other Level
  7 Regular; 0 Special Education; 0 Vocational; 0 Alternative
  0 Magnet; 0 Charter; 3 Title I Eligible; 3 School-wide Title I
Students: 4,643 (51.9% male; 48.0% female)
  Individual Education Program: 524 (11.3%)
  English Language Learner: 285 (6.1%); Migrant: 3 (0.1%)
  Eligible for Free Lunch Program: 1,389 (29.9%)
  Eligible for Reduced-Price Lunch Program: 275 (5.9%)
Teachers: 321.7 (14.4 to 1)
Librarians/Media Specialists: 5.1 (910.4 to 1)
Guidance Counselors: 10.0 (464.3 to 1)
Current Spending: ($ per student per year):
  Total: $6,163; Instruction: $3,942; Support Services: $1,906

Enrollment, Drop-out Rates and Diploma Recipients by Race/Ethnicity

Category	Total	White	Black	Asian	AIAN	Hisp.
Enrollment (%)	100.0	68.8	13.0	1.9	0.4	15.9
Drop-out Rate (%)	1.5	1.1	3.4	0.0	0.0	3.2
H.S. Diplomas (#)	300	253	16	8	3	20

Spring Hill ISD
3101 Spring Hill Rd • Longview, TX 75605-2822
(903) 759-4404
Grade Span: PK-12; **Agency Type:** 1
Schools: 5
  2 Primary; 2 Middle; 1 High; 0 Other Level
  5 Regular; 0 Special Education; 0 Vocational; 0 Alternative
  0 Magnet; 0 Charter; 2 Title I Eligible; 0 School-wide Title I
Students: 1,727 (50.8% male; 49.1% female)
  Individual Education Program: 152 (8.8%)
  English Language Learner: 29 (1.7%); Migrant: 0 (0.0%)
  Eligible for Free Lunch Program: 308 (17.8%)
  Eligible for Reduced-Price Lunch Program: 72 (4.2%)
Teachers: 117.3 (14.7 to 1)
Librarians/Media Specialists: 3.0 (575.7 to 1)
Guidance Counselors: 3.5 (493.4 to 1)
Current Spending: ($ per student per year):
  Total: $5,618; Instruction: $3,721; Support Services: $1,606

Enrollment, Drop-out Rates and Diploma Recipients by Race/Ethnicity

Category	Total	White	Black	Asian	AIAN	Hisp.
Enrollment (%)	100.0	87.3	6.0	1.7	0.3	4.6
Drop-out Rate (%)	1.9	1.6	0.0	0.0	n/a	7.7
H.S. Diplomas (#)	109	100	2	1	0	6

Grimes County

Navasota ISD
705 E Washington Ave • Navasota, TX 77868-3005
Mailing Address: PO Box 511 • Navasota, TX 77868-0511
(936) 825-4200 • http://www.navasota.k12.tx.us/
Grade Span: PK-12; **Agency Type:** 1
Schools: 7
   2 Primary; 2 Middle; 2 High; 1 Other Level
   5 Regular; 0 Special Education; 0 Vocational; 2 Alternative
   0 Magnet; 0 Charter; 3 Title I Eligible; 3 School-wide Title I
Students: 3,003   (50.4% male; 49.5% female)
   Individual Education Program: 320 (10.7%);
   English Language Learner: 261 (8.7%); Migrant: 36 (1.2%)
   Eligible for Free Lunch Program: 1,505 (50.1%)
   Eligible for Reduced-Price Lunch Program: 317 (10.6%)
Teachers: 204.7 (14.7 to 1)
Librarians/Media Specialists: 2.1 (1,430.0 to 1)
Guidance Counselors: 7.0 (429.0 to 1)
Current Spending: ($ per student per year):
   Total: $6,854; Instruction: $3,969; Support Services: $2,462
Enrollment, Drop-out Rates and Diploma Recipients by Race/Ethnicity

Category	Total	White	Black	Asian	AIAN	Hisp.
Enrollment (%)	100.0	39.2	28.4	0.4	0.2	31.9
Drop-out Rate (%)	2.4	1.2	3.4	0.0	25.0	3.1
H.S. Diplomas (#)	197	98	57	1	0	41

Guadalupe County

Schertz-Cibolo-U City ISD
1060 Elbel Rd • Schertz, TX 78154-2099
(210) 945-6200 • http://www.scuc.txed.net/
Grade Span: PK-12; **Agency Type:** 1
Schools: 12
   6 Primary; 4 Middle; 2 High; 0 Other Level
   11 Regular; 0 Special Education; 0 Vocational; 1 Alternative
   0 Magnet; 0 Charter; 4 Title I Eligible; 3 School-wide Title I
Students: 7,257   (51.5% male; 48.4% female)
   Individual Education Program: 855 (11.8%);
   English Language Learner: 189 (2.6%); Migrant: 13 (0.2%)
   Eligible for Free Lunch Program: 1,377 (19.0%)
   Eligible for Reduced-Price Lunch Program: 414 (5.7%)
Teachers: 467.7 (15.5 to 1)
Librarians/Media Specialists: 11.0 (659.7 to 1)
Guidance Counselors: 18.4 (394.4 to 1)
Current Spending: ($ per student per year):
   Total: $6,245; Instruction: $3,818; Support Services: $2,212
Enrollment, Drop-out Rates and Diploma Recipients by Race/Ethnicity

Category	Total	White	Black	Asian	AIAN	Hisp.
Enrollment (%)	100.0	61.9	10.2	2.1	0.3	25.5
Drop-out Rate (%)	2.6	2.3	1.9	2.2	0.0	3.7
H.S. Diplomas (#)	467	312	48	10	2	95

Seguin ISD
1221 E Kingsbury • Seguin, TX 78155
(830) 372-5771 • http://www.seguin.k12.tx.us/
Grade Span: PK-12; **Agency Type:** 1
Schools: 16
   8 Primary; 3 Middle; 2 High; 3 Other Level
   13 Regular; 0 Special Education; 0 Vocational; 3 Alternative
   0 Magnet; 0 Charter; 11 Title I Eligible; 11 School-wide Title I
Students: 7,595   (51.3% male; 48.6% female)
   Individual Education Program: 1,017 (13.4%);
   English Language Learner: 659 (8.7%); Migrant: 428 (5.6%)
   Eligible for Free Lunch Program: 3,665 (48.3%)
   Eligible for Reduced-Price Lunch Program: 716 (9.4%)
Teachers: 552.2 (13.8 to 1)
Librarians/Media Specialists: 10.3 (737.4 to 1)
Guidance Counselors: 21.0 (361.7 to 1)
Current Spending: ($ per student per year):
   Total: $6,918; Instruction: $4,321; Support Services: $2,227
Enrollment, Drop-out Rates and Diploma Recipients by Race/Ethnicity

Category	Total	White	Black	Asian	AIAN	Hisp.
Enrollment (%)	100.0	31.9	7.7	0.7	0.3	59.5
Drop-out Rate (%)	3.8	1.9	4.5	0.0	0.0	5.2
H.S. Diplomas (#)	384	169	36	8	0	171

Hale County

Plainview ISD
912 Portland St • Plainview, TX 79072-7060
Mailing Address: PO Box 1540 • Plainview, TX 79073-1540
(806) 296-6392 • http://www.plainview.k12.tx.us/
Grade Span: PK-12; **Agency Type:** 1
Schools: 13

---

   6 Primary; 3 Middle; 1 High; 3 Other Level
   11 Regular; 0 Special Education; 0 Vocational; 2 Alternative
   0 Magnet; 0 Charter; 10 Title I Eligible; 10 School-wide Title I
Students: 6,091   (50.9% male; 49.0% female)
   Individual Education Program: 872 (14.3%);
   English Language Learner: 592 (9.7%); Migrant: 717 (11.8%)
   Eligible for Free Lunch Program: 3,159 (51.9%)
   Eligible for Reduced-Price Lunch Program: 470 (7.7%)
Teachers: 403.3 (15.1 to 1)
Librarians/Media Specialists: 8.9 (684.4 to 1)
Guidance Counselors: 16.0 (380.7 to 1)
Current Spending: ($ per student per year):
   Total: $6,224; Instruction: $3,863; Support Services: $2,063
Enrollment, Drop-out Rates and Diploma Recipients by Race/Ethnicity

Category	Total	White	Black	Asian	AIAN	Hisp.
Enrollment (%)	100.0	25.5	5.9	0.5	0.3	67.7
Drop-out Rate (%)	4.8	1.8	7.6	0.0	0.0	6.2
H.S. Diplomas (#)	374	132	32	2	2	206

Hardin County

Hardin-Jefferson ISD
520 W Herring • Sour Lake, TX 77659-0490
Mailing Address: PO Box 490 • Sour Lake, TX 77659-0490
(409) 981-6400 • http://www.esc05.k12.tx.us/hjisd/index.htm
Grade Span: PK-12; **Agency Type:** 1
Schools: 6
   2 Primary; 1 Middle; 1 High; 0 Other Level
   4 Regular; 0 Special Education; 0 Vocational; 0 Alternative
   0 Magnet; 0 Charter; 2 Title I Eligible; 2 School-wide Title I
Students: 2,130   (53.6% male; 46.3% female)
   Individual Education Program: 304 (14.3%);
   English Language Learner: 32 (1.5%); Migrant: 3 (0.1%)
   Eligible for Free Lunch Program: 517 (24.3%)
   Eligible for Reduced-Price Lunch Program: 161 (7.6%)
Teachers: 151.0 (14.1 to 1)
Librarians/Media Specialists: 0.0 (n/a to 1)
Guidance Counselors: 5.0 (426.0 to 1)
Current Spending: ($ per student per year):
   Total: $6,934; Instruction: $4,189; Support Services: $2,394
Enrollment, Drop-out Rates and Diploma Recipients by Race/Ethnicity

Category	Total	White	Black	Asian	AIAN	Hisp.
Enrollment (%)	100.0	83.1	12.9	0.4	0.2	3.4
Drop-out Rate (%)	1.5	1.8	0.0	0.0	0.0	0.0
H.S. Diplomas (#)	139	122	12	1	0	4

Lumberton ISD
121 S Main • Lumberton, TX 77657-0123
Mailing Address: PO Box 8123 • Lumberton, TX 77657-0123
(409) 755-4993
Grade Span: PK-12; **Agency Type:** 1
Schools: 6
   2 Primary; 2 Middle; 1 High; 1 Other Level
   5 Regular; 0 Special Education; 1 Vocational; 0 Alternative
   0 Magnet; 0 Charter; 2 Title I Eligible; 0 School-wide Title I
Students: 3,466   (51.6% male; 48.3% female)
   Individual Education Program: 424 (12.2%);
   English Language Learner: 14 (0.4%); Migrant: 0 (0.0%)
   Eligible for Free Lunch Program: 757 (21.8%)
   Eligible for Reduced-Price Lunch Program: 225 (6.5%)
Teachers: 232.2 (14.9 to 1)
Librarians/Media Specialists: 4.0 (866.5 to 1)
Guidance Counselors: 8.0 (433.3 to 1)
Current Spending: ($ per student per year):
   Total: $6,363; Instruction: $3,846; Support Services: $2,147
Enrollment, Drop-out Rates and Diploma Recipients by Race/Ethnicity

Category	Total	White	Black	Asian	AIAN	Hisp.
Enrollment (%)	100.0	96.9	0.1	0.3	0.2	2.4
Drop-out Rate (%)	0.7	0.7	n/a	0.0	0.0	0.0
H.S. Diplomas (#)	222	217	0	1	0	4

Silsbee ISD
415 W Ave N • Silsbee, TX 77656-4799
(409) 385-5286
Grade Span: PK-12; **Agency Type:** 1
Schools: 7
   3 Primary; 2 Middle; 1 High; 1 Other Level
   6 Regular; 0 Special Education; 0 Vocational; 1 Alternative
   0 Magnet; 0 Charter; 5 Title I Eligible; 5 School-wide Title I
Students: 3,097   (52.0% male; 47.9% female)
   Individual Education Program: 532 (17.2%);
   English Language Learner: 18 (0.6%); Migrant: 8 (0.3%)
   Eligible for Free Lunch Program: 957 (30.9%)
   Eligible for Reduced-Price Lunch Program: 189 (6.1%)
Teachers: 203.8 (15.2 to 1)
Librarians/Media Specialists: 2.1 (1,474.8 to 1)

Guidance Counselors: 8.4 (368.7 to 1)
Current Spending: ($ per student per year):
    Total: $7,261; Instruction: $4,423; Support Services: $2,506
Enrollment, Drop-out Rates and Diploma Recipients by Race/Ethnicity

Category	Total	White	Black	Asian	AIAN	Hisp.
Enrollment (%)	100.0	78.0	19.2	0.5	0.1	2.3
Drop-out Rate (%)	3.1	3.5	1.6	0.0	0.0	0.0
H.S. Diplomas (#)	208	155	50	1	0	2

Harris County

Aldine ISD
14910 Aldine Westfield Rd • Houston, TX 77032-3099
(281) 449-1011 • http://www.aldine.k12.tx.us/
Grade Span: PK-12; **Agency Type:** 1
Schools: 66
    34 Primary; 17 Middle; 6 High; 9 Other Level
    61 Regular; 1 Special Education; 0 Vocational; 4 Alternative
    0 Magnet; 0 Charter; 65 Title I Eligible; 65 School-wide Title I
Students: 56,292   (51.3% male; 48.6% female)
    Individual Education Program: 5,524 (9.8%);
    English Language Learner: 13,958 (24.8%); Migrant: 75 (0.1%)
    Eligible for Free Lunch Program: 36,874 (65.5%)
    Eligible for Reduced-Price Lunch Program: 5,925 (10.5%)
Teachers: 3,616.4 (15.6 to 1)
Librarians/Media Specialists: 60.0 (938.2 to 1)
Guidance Counselors: 127.2 (442.5 to 1)
Current Spending: ($ per student per year):
    Total: $7,326; Instruction: $4,547; Support Services: $2,388
Enrollment, Drop-out Rates and Diploma Recipients by Race/Ethnicity

Category	Total	White	Black	Asian	AIAN	Hisp.
Enrollment (%)	100.0	6.5	33.1	2.4	0.1	58.0
Drop-out Rate (%)	5.8	5.2	4.6	3.1	0.0	7.1
H.S. Diplomas (#)	2,149	286	834	74	0	955

Alief ISD
12302 High Star • Houston, TX 77072-1124
Mailing Address: PO Box 68 • Alief, TX 77411-0068
(281) 498-8110 • http://www.aliefisd.net/
Grade Span: PK-12; **Agency Type:** 1
Schools: 41
    22 Primary; 12 Middle; 4 High; 2 Other Level
    38 Regular; 1 Special Education; 0 Vocational; 1 Alternative
    0 Magnet; 0 Charter; 20 Title I Eligible; 20 School-wide Title I
Students: 45,344   (51.1% male; 48.8% female)
    Individual Education Program: 5,324 (11.7%);
    English Language Learner: 14,288 (31.5%); Migrant: 0 (0.0%)
    Eligible for Free Lunch Program: 23,500 (51.8%)
    Eligible for Reduced-Price Lunch Program: 3,499 (7.7%)
Teachers: 2,977.1 (15.2 to 1)
Librarians/Media Specialists: 43.2 (1,049.6 to 1)
Guidance Counselors: 97.9 (463.2 to 1)
Current Spending: ($ per student per year):
    Total: $6,588; Instruction: $4,291; Support Services: $1,947
Enrollment, Drop-out Rates and Diploma Recipients by Race/Ethnicity

Category	Total	White	Black	Asian	AIAN	Hisp.
Enrollment (%)	100.0	6.7	36.8	13.3	0.1	43.1
Drop-out Rate (%)	3.3	2.5	2.5	2.9	0.0	4.5
H.S. Diplomas (#)	1,960	279	626	485	0	570

Channelview ISD
1403 Sheldon Rd • Channelview, TX 77530-2603
(281) 452-8008 • http://www.channelview.isd.esc4.net/
Grade Span: PK-12; **Agency Type:** 1
Schools: 11
    5 Primary; 2 Middle; 1 High; 3 Other Level
    8 Regular; 0 Special Education; 0 Vocational; 3 Alternative
    0 Magnet; 0 Charter; 9 Title I Eligible; 7 School-wide Title I
Students: 7,451   (51.7% male; 48.2% female)
    Individual Education Program: 883 (11.9%);
    English Language Learner: 1,626 (21.8%); Migrant: 24 (0.3%)
    Eligible for Free Lunch Program: 3,915 (52.5%)
    Eligible for Reduced-Price Lunch Program: 826 (11.1%)
Teachers: 434.6 (17.1 to 1)
Librarians/Media Specialists: 3.0 (2,483.7 to 1)
Guidance Counselors: 15.0 (496.7 to 1)
Current Spending: ($ per student per year):
    Total: $6,421; Instruction: $4,052; Support Services: $2,024
Enrollment, Drop-out Rates and Diploma Recipients by Race/Ethnicity

Category	Total	White	Black	Asian	AIAN	Hisp.
Enrollment (%)	100.0	28.0	16.0	1.5	0.1	54.4
Drop-out Rate (%)	3.0	2.5	2.7	0.0	n/a	3.8
H.S. Diplomas (#)	301	133	48	6	0	114

Crosby ISD
706 Runneburg • Crosby, TX 77532-8009
Mailing Address: PO Box 2009 • Crosby, TX 77532-8009
(281) 328-9200 • http://www.crosby.isd.esc4.net/
Grade Span: PK-12; **Agency Type:** 1
Schools: 6
    3 Primary; 2 Middle; 1 High; 0 Other Level
    6 Regular; 0 Special Education; 0 Vocational; 0 Alternative
    0 Magnet; 0 Charter; 4 Title I Eligible; 1 School-wide Title I
Students: 4,278   (52.1% male; 47.8% female)
    Individual Education Program: 552 (12.9%);
    English Language Learner: 211 (4.9%); Migrant: 0 (0.0%)
    Eligible for Free Lunch Program: 1,348 (31.5%)
    Eligible for Reduced-Price Lunch Program: 264 (6.2%)
Teachers: 251.7 (17.0 to 1)
Librarians/Media Specialists: 5.0 (855.6 to 1)
Guidance Counselors: 7.0 (611.1 to 1)
Current Spending: ($ per student per year):
    Total: $6,896; Instruction: $3,984; Support Services: $2,533
Enrollment, Drop-out Rates and Diploma Recipients by Race/Ethnicity

Category	Total	White	Black	Asian	AIAN	Hisp.
Enrollment (%)	100.0	60.9	23.2	0.4	0.2	15.3
Drop-out Rate (%)	3.0	2.5	4.8	12.5	0.0	1.6
H.S. Diplomas (#)	219	146	49	4	0	20

Cypress-Fairbanks ISD
10300 Jones Rd • Houston, TX 77065-4208
Mailing Address: PO Box 692003 • Houston, TX 77269-2003
(281) 897-4000 • http://www.cfisd.net/
Grade Span: PK-12; **Agency Type:** 1
Schools: 60
    38 Primary; 12 Middle; 8 High; 2 Other Level
    57 Regular; 0 Special Education; 0 Vocational; 3 Alternative
    0 Magnet; 0 Charter; 12 Title I Eligible; 12 School-wide Title I
Students: 74,877   (51.3% male; 48.6% female)
    Individual Education Program: 6,985 (9.3%);
    English Language Learner: 9,676 (12.9%); Migrant: 12 (<0.1%)
    Eligible for Free Lunch Program: 14,483 (19.3%)
    Eligible for Reduced-Price Lunch Program: 4,568 (6.1%)
Teachers: 4,884.1 (15.3 to 1)
Librarians/Media Specialists: 68.6 (1,091.5 to 1)
Guidance Counselors: 154.5 (484.6 to 1)
Current Spending: ($ per student per year):
    Total: $6,799; Instruction: $4,485; Support Services: $2,050
Enrollment, Drop-out Rates and Diploma Recipients by Race/Ethnicity

Category	Total	White	Black	Asian	AIAN	Hisp.
Enrollment (%)	100.0	51.9	11.1	8.2	0.2	28.7
Drop-out Rate (%)	1.1	0.9	1.6	0.5	0.0	1.9
H.S. Diplomas (#)	3,938	2,490	388	353	6	701

Deer Park ISD
203 Ivy • Deer Park, TX 77536-2747
(832) 668-7000 • http://www.dpisd.org/index.html
Grade Span: PK-12; **Agency Type:** 1
Schools: 13
    7 Primary; 4 Middle; 1 High; 1 Other Level
    12 Regular; 0 Special Education; 0 Vocational; 1 Alternative
    0 Magnet; 0 Charter; 3 Title I Eligible; 3 School-wide Title I
Students: 11,819   (50.6% male; 49.3% female)
    Individual Education Program: 1,247 (10.6%);
    English Language Learner: 1,064 (9.0%); Migrant: 1 (<0.1%)
    Eligible for Free Lunch Program: 2,649 (22.4%)
    Eligible for Reduced-Price Lunch Program: 743 (6.3%)
Teachers: 716.3 (16.5 to 1)
Librarians/Media Specialists: 13.0 (909.2 to 1)
Guidance Counselors: 25.5 (463.5 to 1)
Current Spending: ($ per student per year):
    Total: $6,739; Instruction: $4,049; Support Services: $2,384
Enrollment, Drop-out Rates and Diploma Recipients by Race/Ethnicity

Category	Total	White	Black	Asian	AIAN	Hisp.
Enrollment (%)	100.0	62.5	1.4	2.1	0.3	33.7
Drop-out Rate (%)	1.2	1.0	2.5	1.3	0.0	1.8
H.S. Diplomas (#)	678	523	2	18	1	134

Galena Park ISD
14705 Woodforest Blvd • Houston, TX 77015
Mailing Address: PO Box 565 • Galena Park, TX 77547-0565
(832) 386-1000 • http://www.galenaparkisd.com/
Grade Span: PK-12; **Agency Type:** 1
Schools: 23
    13 Primary; 5 Middle; 2 High; 3 Other Level
    21 Regular; 0 Special Education; 0 Vocational; 2 Alternative
    0 Magnet; 0 Charter; 20 Title I Eligible; 20 School-wide Title I
Students: 20,454   (50.7% male; 49.2% female)
    Individual Education Program: 2,394 (11.7%);

English Language Learner: 5,180 (25.3%); Migrant: 274 (1.3%)
Eligible for Free Lunch Program: 12,070 (59.1%)
Eligible for Reduced-Price Lunch Program: 2,015 (9.9%)
Teachers: 1,460.9 (14.0 to 1)
Librarians/Media Specialists: 16.5 (1,237.6 to 1)
Guidance Counselors: 42.7 (478.2 to 1)
Current Spending: ($ per student per year):
Total: $6,992; Instruction: $4,098; Support Services: $2,535
Enrollment, Drop-out Rates and Diploma Recipients by Race/Ethnicity

Category	Total	White	Black	Asian	AIAN	Hisp.
Enrollment (%)	100.0	11.2	21.3	1.5	0.1	65.9
Drop-out Rate (%)	3.0	1.6	2.5	2.4	n/a	3.8
H.S. Diplomas (#)	1,077	175	273	28	0	601

Goose Creek CISD

4544 Interstate 10 E • Baytown, TX 77521
Mailing Address: PO Box 30 • Baytown, TX 77522-0030
(281) 420-4800 • http://www.goosecreek.cisd.esc4.net/right.htm
Grade Span: PK-12; **Agency Type:** 1
Schools: 27
14 Primary; 5 Middle; 5 High; 2 Other Level
21 Regular; 1 Special Education; 0 Vocational; 0 Alternative
0 Magnet; 0 Charter; 14 Title I Eligible; 14 School-wide Title I
Students: 19,247 (51.1% male; 48.8% female)
Individual Education Program: 1,946 (10.1%);
English Language Learner: 2,761 (14.3%); Migrant: 1,181 (6.1%)
Eligible for Free Lunch Program: 9,295 (48.3%)
Eligible for Reduced-Price Lunch Program: 1,834 (9.5%)
Teachers: 1,217.3 (15.8 to 1)
Librarians/Media Specialists: 23.0 (836.8 to 1)
Guidance Counselors: 38.2 (503.8 to 1)
Current Spending: ($ per student per year):
Total: $7,234; Instruction: $4,239; Support Services: $2,592
Enrollment, Drop-out Rates and Diploma Recipients by Race/Ethnicity

Category	Total	White	Black	Asian	AIAN	Hisp.
Enrollment (%)	100.0	35.5	17.6	1.2	0.2	45.6
Drop-out Rate (%)	5.1	3.5	4.3	1.7	25.0	7.3
H.S. Diplomas (#)	899	476	151	12	1	259

Houston ISD

3830 Richmond Ave • Houston, TX 77027-5838
(713) 892-6000 • http://www.houstonisd.org/
Grade Span: PK-12; **Agency Type:** 1
Schools: 308
209 Primary; 50 Middle; 37 High; 12 Other Level
284 Regular; 3 Special Education; 2 Vocational; 19 Alternative
0 Magnet; 0 Charter; 280 Title I Eligible; 280 School-wide Title I
Students: 211,499 (51.0% male; 48.9% female)
Individual Education Program: 21,339 (10.1%);
English Language Learner: 61,144 (28.9%); Migrant: 1,957 (0.9%)
Eligible for Free Lunch Program: 138,455 (65.5%)
Eligible for Reduced-Price Lunch Program: 20,795 (9.8%)
Teachers: 12,276.8 (17.2 to 1)
Librarians/Media Specialists: 233.1 (907.1 to 1)
Guidance Counselors: 270.7 (781.1 to 1)
Current Spending: ($ per student per year):
Total: $7,236; Instruction: $4,277; Support Services: $2,610
Enrollment, Drop-out Rates and Diploma Recipients by Race/Ethnicity

Category	Total	White	Black	Asian	AIAN	Hisp.
Enrollment (%)	100.0	9.1	29.7	3.0	0.1	58.1
Drop-out Rate (%)	6.0	2.8	5.2	1.5	8.0	7.7
H.S. Diplomas (#)	7,945	1,255	2,754	380	5	3,551

Huffman ISD

24302 F M 2100 • Huffman, TX 77336-2390
Mailing Address: PO Box 2390 • Huffman, TX 77336-2390
(281) 324-1871
Grade Span: PK-12; **Agency Type:** 1
Schools: 5
1 Primary; 2 Middle; 1 High; 1 Other Level
4 Regular; 0 Special Education; 0 Vocational; 1 Alternative
0 Magnet; 0 Charter; 2 Title I Eligible; 1 School-wide Title I
Students: 2,869 (52.7% male; 47.2% female)
Individual Education Program: 331 (11.5%);
English Language Learner: 42 (1.5%); Migrant: 0 (0.0%)
Eligible for Free Lunch Program: 537 (18.7%)
Eligible for Reduced-Price Lunch Program: 157 (5.5%)
Teachers: 171.0 (16.8 to 1)
Librarians/Media Specialists: 4.0 (717.3 to 1)
Guidance Counselors: 5.0 (573.8 to 1)
Current Spending: ($ per student per year):
Total: $6,631; Instruction: $3,752; Support Services: $2,597

Enrollment, Drop-out Rates and Diploma Recipients by Race/Ethnicity

Category	Total	White	Black	Asian	AIAN	Hisp.
Enrollment (%)	100.0	90.1	1.3	0.5	0.3	7.8
Drop-out Rate (%)	1.7	1.8	0.0	0.0	0.0	0.0
H.S. Diplomas (#)	182	170	0	1	1	10

Humble ISD

20200 Eastway Village Dr • Humble, TX 77347-2000
Mailing Address: PO Box 2000 • Humble, TX 77347-2000
(281) 641-1000 • http://www.humble.k12.tx.us/
Grade Span: PK-12; **Agency Type:** 1
Schools: 30
20 Primary; 6 Middle; 3 High; 1 Other Level
28 Regular; 0 Special Education; 0 Vocational; 2 Alternative
0 Magnet; 0 Charter; 4 Title I Eligible; 4 School-wide Title I
Students: 27,009 (51.4% male; 48.5% female)
Individual Education Program: 2,704 (10.0%);
English Language Learner: 1,560 (5.8%); Migrant: 1 (<0.1%)
Eligible for Free Lunch Program: 4,042 (15.0%)
Eligible for Reduced-Price Lunch Program: 1,124 (4.2%)
Teachers: 1,744.8 (15.5 to 1)
Librarians/Media Specialists: 31.9 (846.7 to 1)
Guidance Counselors: 59.0 (457.8 to 1)
Current Spending: ($ per student per year):
Total: $6,227; Instruction: $3,858; Support Services: $2,128
Enrollment, Drop-out Rates and Diploma Recipients by Race/Ethnicity

Category	Total	White	Black	Asian	AIAN	Hisp.
Enrollment (%)	100.0	65.7	12.3	3.4	0.4	18.2
Drop-out Rate (%)	1.7	1.4	2.6	3.8	0.0	2.5
H.S. Diplomas (#)	1,653	1,253	149	63	3	185

Katy ISD

6301 S Stadium Ln • Katy, TX 77494-1057
Mailing Address: PO Box 159 • Katy, TX 77492-0159
(281) 396-6000 • http://www.katy.isd.tenet.edu/
Grade Span: PK-12; **Agency Type:** 1
Schools: 42
23 Primary; 9 Middle; 6 High; 4 Other Level
37 Regular; 1 Special Education; 0 Vocational; 4 Alternative
0 Magnet; 0 Charter; 12 Title I Eligible; 2 School-wide Title I
Students: 42,116 (51.1% male; 48.8% female)
Individual Education Program: 4,228 (10.0%);
English Language Learner: 4,013 (9.5%); Migrant: 0 (0.0%)
Eligible for Free Lunch Program: 5,587 (13.3%)
Eligible for Reduced-Price Lunch Program: 1,640 (3.9%)
Teachers: 2,801.5 (15.0 to 1)
Librarians/Media Specialists: 36.9 (1,141.4 to 1)
Guidance Counselors: 74.7 (563.8 to 1)
Current Spending: ($ per student per year):
Total: $6,660; Instruction: $4,281; Support Services: $2,108
Enrollment, Drop-out Rates and Diploma Recipients by Race/Ethnicity

Category	Total	White	Black	Asian	AIAN	Hisp.
Enrollment (%)	100.0	63.6	6.7	7.4	0.2	22.1
Drop-out Rate (%)	1.1	0.9	1.9	0.6	6.3	2.3
H.S. Diplomas (#)	2,112	1,602	111	139	4	256

Klein ISD

7200 Spring-Cypress Rd • Klein, TX 77379-3299
(832) 249-4000 • http://www.kleinisd.net/
Grade Span: PK-12; **Agency Type:** 1
Schools: 34
20 Primary; 7 Middle; 4 High; 3 Other Level
31 Regular; 1 Special Education; 0 Vocational; 2 Alternative
0 Magnet; 0 Charter; 5 Title I Eligible; 5 School-wide Title I
Students: 35,558 (51.6% male; 48.3% female)
Individual Education Program: 3,731 (10.5%);
English Language Learner: 3,508 (9.9%); Migrant: 0 (0.0%)
Eligible for Free Lunch Program: 6,629 (18.6%)
Eligible for Reduced-Price Lunch Program: 1,530 (4.3%)
Teachers: 2,219.4 (16.0 to 1)
Librarians/Media Specialists: 48.4 (734.7 to 1)
Guidance Counselors: 68.9 (516.1 to 1)
Current Spending: ($ per student per year):
Total: $6,272; Instruction: $3,827; Support Services: $2,123
Enrollment, Drop-out Rates and Diploma Recipients by Race/Ethnicity

Category	Total	White	Black	Asian	AIAN	Hisp.
Enrollment (%)	100.0	54.4	13.7	7.9	0.3	23.8
Drop-out Rate (%)	2.5	2.0	2.8	2.7	0.0	4.1
H.S. Diplomas (#)	2,112	1,374	259	190	10	279

La Porte ISD

1002 San Jacinto St • La Porte, TX 77571-6496
(281) 604-7015 • http://www.laporte.isd.esc4.net/
Grade Span: PK-12; **Agency Type:** 1
Schools: 13

6 Primary; 3 Middle; 1 High; 2 Other Level
10 Regular; 0 Special Education; 0 Vocational; 2 Alternative
0 Magnet; 0 Charter; 4 Title I Eligible; 3 School-wide Title I
Students: 7,695   (52.7% male; 47.2% female)
   Individual Education Program: 791 (10.3%);
   English Language Learner: 348 (4.5%); Migrant: 2 (<0.1%)
   Eligible for Free Lunch Program: 1,771 (23.0%)
   Eligible for Reduced-Price Lunch Program: 664 (8.6%)
Teachers: 468.1 (16.4 to 1)
Librarians/Media Specialists: 9.5 (810.0 to 1)
Guidance Counselors: 15.0 (513.0 to 1)
Current Spending: ($ per student per year):
   Total: $7,127; Instruction: $4,231; Support Services: $2,500

Enrollment, Drop-out Rates and Diploma Recipients by Race/Ethnicity

Category	Total	White	Black	Asian	AIAN	Hisp.
Enrollment (%)	100.0	61.7	8.9	1.0	0.3	28.1
Drop-out Rate (%)	2.5	3.0	1.4	0.0	0.0	1.6
H.S. Diplomas (#)	472	324	41	6	2	99

North Forest ISD
7201 Langley • Houston, TX 77016
Mailing Address: PO Box 23278 • Houston, TX 77228-3278
(713) 633-1600 • http://www.northforestschools.org/
Grade Span: PK-12; **Agency Type:** 1
Schools: 18
8 Primary; 4 Middle; 3 High; 3 Other Level
14 Regular; 0 Special Education; 0 Vocational; 4 Alternative
0 Magnet; 0 Charter; 14 Title I Eligible; 14 School-wide Title I
Students: 10,818   (50.9% male; 49.0% female)
   Individual Education Program: 812 (7.5%);
   English Language Learner: 1,302 (12.0%); Migrant: 0 (0.0%)
   Eligible for Free Lunch Program: 5,024 (46.4%)
   Eligible for Reduced-Price Lunch Program: 345 (3.2%)
Teachers: 708.4 (15.3 to 1)
Librarians/Media Specialists: 12.9 (838.6 to 1)
Guidance Counselors: 30.4 (355.9 to 1)
Current Spending: ($ per student per year):
   Total: $7,059; Instruction: $3,845; Support Services: $2,775

Enrollment, Drop-out Rates and Diploma Recipients by Race/Ethnicity

Category	Total	White	Black	Asian	AIAN	Hisp.
Enrollment (%)	100.0	0.8	75.6	0.1	0.0	23.5
Drop-out Rate (%)	7.0	25.0	6.2	0.0	n/a	11.6
H.S. Diplomas (#)	505	1	455	1	0	48

Pasadena ISD
1515 Cherrybrook • Pasadena, TX 77502-4099
(713) 740-0000 • http://www.pasadenaisd.org/
Grade Span: PK-12; **Agency Type:** 1
Schools: 56
33 Primary; 13 Middle; 8 High; 2 Other Level
49 Regular; 0 Special Education; 0 Vocational; 7 Alternative
0 Magnet; 0 Charter; 38 Title I Eligible; 38 School-wide Title I
Students: 46,142   (51.3% male; 48.6% female)
   Individual Education Program: 3,610 (7.8%);
   English Language Learner: 11,789 (25.5%); Migrant: 436 (0.9%)
   Eligible for Free Lunch Program: 24,476 (53.1%)
   Eligible for Reduced-Price Lunch Program: 4,613 (10.0%)
Teachers: 2,680.6 (17.2 to 1)
Librarians/Media Specialists: 54.7 (842.0 to 1)
Guidance Counselors: 85.5 (538.7 to 1)
Current Spending: ($ per student per year):
   Total: $6,215; Instruction: $3,847; Support Services: $2,015

Enrollment, Drop-out Rates and Diploma Recipients by Race/Ethnicity

Category	Total	White	Black	Asian	AIAN	Hisp.
Enrollment (%)	100.0	19.4	6.4	3.2	0.2	70.8
Drop-out Rate (%)	5.4	3.6	4.0	3.3	0.0	6.6
H.S. Diplomas (#)	2,028	693	103	110	8	1,114

Sheldon ISD
11411 C E King Pkwy • Houston, TX 77044-2002
(281) 727-2000
Grade Span: PK-12; **Agency Type:** 1
Schools: 7
3 Primary; 2 Middle; 2 High; 0 Other Level
6 Regular; 0 Special Education; 0 Vocational; 1 Alternative
0 Magnet; 0 Charter; 6 Title I Eligible; 6 School-wide Title I
Students: 4,539   (50.4% male; 49.5% female)
   Individual Education Program: 545 (12.0%);
   English Language Learner: 703 (15.5%); Migrant: 0 (0.0%)
   Eligible for Free Lunch Program: 2,480 (54.6%)
   Eligible for Reduced-Price Lunch Program: 488 (10.8%)
Teachers: 279.4 (16.2 to 1)
Librarians/Media Specialists: 4.2 (1,080.7 to 1)
Guidance Counselors: 11.0 (412.6 to 1)
Current Spending: ($ per student per year):
   Total: $8,126; Instruction: $4,766; Support Services: $2,983

Enrollment, Drop-out Rates and Diploma Recipients by Race/Ethnicity

Category	Total	White	Black	Asian	AIAN	Hisp.
Enrollment (%)	100.0	28.7	25.0	0.7	0.1	45.5
Drop-out Rate (%)	4.1	5.7	3.3	0.0	0.0	3.0
H.S. Diplomas (#)	199	82	52	2	0	63

Spring Branch ISD
955 Campbell Rd • Houston, TX 77024-2803
(713) 464-1511 • http://www.springbranchisd.com/
Grade Span: PK-12; **Agency Type:** 1
Schools: 50
32 Primary; 8 Middle; 6 High; 3 Other Level
45 Regular; 1 Special Education; 0 Vocational; 3 Alternative
0 Magnet; 0 Charter; 30 Title I Eligible; 30 School-wide Title I
Students: 33,005   (51.2% male; 48.7% female)
   Individual Education Program: 3,638 (11.0%);
   English Language Learner: 10,055 (30.5%); Migrant: 18 (0.1%)
   Eligible for Free Lunch Program: 15,768 (47.8%)
   Eligible for Reduced-Price Lunch Program: 1,991 (6.0%)
Teachers: 2,226.2 (14.8 to 1)
Librarians/Media Specialists: 28.6 (1,154.0 to 1)
Guidance Counselors: 69.8 (472.9 to 1)
Current Spending: ($ per student per year):
   Total: $7,512; Instruction: $4,602; Support Services: $2,592

Enrollment, Drop-out Rates and Diploma Recipients by Race/Ethnicity

Category	Total	White	Black	Asian	AIAN	Hisp.
Enrollment (%)	100.0	34.7	6.3	6.2	0.1	52.7
Drop-out Rate (%)	3.2	1.5	5.7	1.4	0.0	5.0
H.S. Diplomas (#)	1,751	866	95	175	4	611

Spring ISD
16717 Ella Blvd • Houston, TX 77090-4299
(281) 586-1100 • http://www.springisd.org/
Grade Span: PK-12; **Agency Type:** 1
Schools: 27
16 Primary; 5 Middle; 2 High; 4 Other Level
23 Regular; 1 Special Education; 0 Vocational; 3 Alternative
0 Magnet; 0 Charter; 11 Title I Eligible; 11 School-wide Title I
Students: 26,768   (51.1% male; 48.8% female)
   Individual Education Program: 2,816 (10.5%);
   English Language Learner: 3,586 (13.4%); Migrant: 0 (0.0%)
   Eligible for Free Lunch Program: 9,886 (36.9%)
   Eligible for Reduced-Price Lunch Program: 2,529 (9.4%)
Teachers: 1,787.4 (15.0 to 1)
Librarians/Media Specialists: 28.0 (956.0 to 1)
Guidance Counselors: 60.1 (445.4 to 1)
Current Spending: ($ per student per year):
   Total: $6,661; Instruction: $4,248; Support Services: $2,061

Enrollment, Drop-out Rates and Diploma Recipients by Race/Ethnicity

Category	Total	White	Black	Asian	AIAN	Hisp.
Enrollment (%)	100.0	31.0	31.8	5.7	0.2	31.2
Drop-out Rate (%)	2.9	2.6	3.1	1.1	0.0	3.8
H.S. Diplomas (#)	1,334	622	354	95	3	260

Tomball ISD
221 W Main St • Tomball, TX 77375-5529
(281) 357-3100 • http://www.tomballisd.net/
Grade Span: PK-12; **Agency Type:** 1
Schools: 13
5 Primary; 5 Middle; 1 High; 2 Other Level
11 Regular; 0 Special Education; 0 Vocational; 2 Alternative
0 Magnet; 0 Charter; 4 Title I Eligible; 4 School-wide Title I
Students: 8,415   (51.2% male; 48.7% female)
   Individual Education Program: 772 (9.2%);
   English Language Learner: 595 (7.1%); Migrant: 0 (0.0%)
   Eligible for Free Lunch Program: 1,194 (14.2%)
   Eligible for Reduced-Price Lunch Program: 300 (3.6%)
Teachers: 532.9 (15.8 to 1)
Librarians/Media Specialists: 9.3 (904.8 to 1)
Guidance Counselors: 13.8 (609.8 to 1)
Current Spending: ($ per student per year):
   Total: $6,599; Instruction: $3,889; Support Services: $2,464

Enrollment, Drop-out Rates and Diploma Recipients by Race/Ethnicity

Category	Total	White	Black	Asian	AIAN	Hisp.
Enrollment (%)	100.0	75.3	5.6	2.8	0.3	15.9
Drop-out Rate (%)	2.0	1.9	3.4	0.0	0.0	3.2
H.S. Diplomas (#)	435	373	20	9	3	30

Hallsville ISD
Green St • Hallsville, TX 75650-0810
Mailing Address: PO Box 810 • Hallsville, TX 75650-0810
(903) 668-5990
Grade Span: PK-12; **Agency Type:** 1
Schools: 7
3 Primary; 2 Middle; 1 High; 1 Other Level

6 Regular; 0 Special Education; 0 Vocational; 1 Alternative
0 Magnet; 0 Charter; 2 Title I Eligible; 2 School-wide Title I
Students: 3,732   (52.0% male; 47.9% female)
  Individual Education Program: 387 (10.4%);
  English Language Learner: 59 (1.6%); Migrant: 0 (0.0%)
  Eligible for Free Lunch Program: 993 (26.6%)
  Eligible for Reduced-Price Lunch Program: 293 (7.9%)
Teachers: 249.8 (14.9 to 1)
Librarians/Media Specialists: 2.2 (1,696.4 to 1)
Guidance Counselors: 9.5 (392.8 to 1)
Current Spending: ($ per student per year):
  Total: $6,570; Instruction: $3,820; Support Services: $2,428
Enrollment, Drop-out Rates and Diploma Recipients by Race/Ethnicity

Category	Total	White	Black	Asian	AIAN	Hisp.
Enrollment (%)	100.0	87.1	7.4	0.5	0.3	4.7
Drop-out Rate (%)	1.7	1.9	0.0	0.0	n/a	2.8
H.S. Diplomas (#)	237	210	21	4	0	2

Marshall ISD
1305 E Pinecrest Dr • Marshall, TX 75670-7349
Mailing Address: PO Box 879 • Marshall, TX 75671-0879
(903) 927-8701 • http://www.marshallisd.com/
Grade Span: PK-12; **Agency Type:** 1
Schools: 13
  7 Primary; 3 Middle; 1 High; 2 Other Level
  11 Regular; 0 Special Education; 0 Vocational; 2 Alternative
  0 Magnet; 0 Charter; 12 Title I Eligible; 12 School-wide Title I
Students: 5,880   (51.0% male; 48.9% female)
  Individual Education Program: 875 (14.9%);
  English Language Learner: 566 (9.6%); Migrant: 0 (0.0%)
  Eligible for Free Lunch Program: 2,979 (50.7%)
  Eligible for Reduced-Price Lunch Program: 404 (6.9%)
Teachers: 428.7 (13.7 to 1)
Librarians/Media Specialists: 3.0 (1,960.0 to 1)
Guidance Counselors: 10.0 (588.0 to 1)
Current Spending: ($ per student per year):
  Total: $6,277; Instruction: $3,937; Support Services: $1,959
Enrollment, Drop-out Rates and Diploma Recipients by Race/Ethnicity

Category	Total	White	Black	Asian	AIAN	Hisp.
Enrollment (%)	100.0	42.6	40.9	0.5	0.1	15.9
Drop-out Rate (%)	5.5	3.8	6.0	14.3	0.0	12.9
H.S. Diplomas (#)	374	188	162	1	1	22

Hays County

Dripping Springs ISD
510 Mercer • Dripping Springs, TX 78620-3867
Mailing Address: PO Box 479 • Dripping Springs, TX 78620-0479
(512) 858-4905 • http://www.dripping-springs.k12.tx.us/
Grade Span: PK-12; **Agency Type:** 1
Schools: 4
  1 Primary; 2 Middle; 1 High; 0 Other Level
  4 Regular; 0 Special Education; 0 Vocational; 0 Alternative
  0 Magnet; 0 Charter; 3 Title I Eligible; 3 School-wide Title I
Students: 3,280   (51.4% male; 48.5% female)
  Individual Education Program: 434 (13.2%);
  English Language Learner: 74 (2.3%); Migrant: 18 (0.5%)
  Eligible for Free Lunch Program: 235 (7.2%)
  Eligible for Reduced-Price Lunch Program: 64 (2.0%)
Teachers: 219.6 (14.9 to 1)
Librarians/Media Specialists: 4.0 (820.0 to 1)
Guidance Counselors: 11.6 (282.8 to 1)
Current Spending: ($ per student per year):
  Total: $6,727; Instruction: $3,829; Support Services: $2,563
Enrollment, Drop-out Rates and Diploma Recipients by Race/Ethnicity

Category	Total	White	Black	Asian	AIAN	Hisp.
Enrollment (%)	100.0	86.7	0.7	0.5	0.5	11.6
Drop-out Rate (%)	0.7	0.6	0.0	0.0	0.0	0.9
H.S. Diplomas (#)	230	207	1	2	2	18

Hays Cons ISD
21003 Ih 35 • Kyle, TX 78640-9530
(512) 268-2141
Grade Span: PK-12; **Agency Type:** 1
Schools: 15
  7 Primary; 3 Middle; 2 High; 2 Other Level
  11 Regular; 0 Special Education; 0 Vocational; 3 Alternative
  0 Magnet; 0 Charter; 5 Title I Eligible; 5 School-wide Title I
Students: 9,052   (52.3% male; 47.6% female)
  Individual Education Program: 1,183 (13.1%);
  English Language Learner: 809 (8.9%); Migrant: 10 (0.1%)
  Eligible for Free Lunch Program: 2,735 (30.2%)
  Eligible for Reduced-Price Lunch Program: 846 (9.3%)
Teachers: 588.7 (15.4 to 1)
Librarians/Media Specialists: 11.8 (767.1 to 1)
Guidance Counselors: 21.5 (421.0 to 1)

Current Spending: ($ per student per year):
  Total: $6,950; Instruction: $3,959; Support Services: $2,702
Enrollment, Drop-out Rates and Diploma Recipients by Race/Ethnicity

Category	Total	White	Black	Asian	AIAN	Hisp.
Enrollment (%)	100.0	42.6	4.3	0.6	0.2	52.4
Drop-out Rate (%)	3.2	2.5	2.2	0.0	0.0	4.0
H.S. Diplomas (#)	485	258	20	1	2	204

San Marcos Cons ISD
501 S Lbj Dr • San Marcos, TX 78666-6821
Mailing Address: PO Box 1087 • San Marcos, TX 78667-1087
(512) 393-6700 • http://www.san-marcos.isd.tenet.edu/
Grade Span: PK-12; **Agency Type:** 1
Schools: 11
  5 Primary; 3 Middle; 2 High; 1 Other Level
  9 Regular; 0 Special Education; 0 Vocational; 2 Alternative
  0 Magnet; 0 Charter; 8 Title I Eligible; 8 School-wide Title I
Students: 7,052   (51.4% male; 48.5% female)
  Individual Education Program: 769 (10.9%);
  English Language Learner: 434 (6.2%); Migrant: 34 (0.5%)
  Eligible for Free Lunch Program: 3,389 (48.1%)
  Eligible for Reduced-Price Lunch Program: 962 (13.6%)
Teachers: 484.2 (14.6 to 1)
Librarians/Media Specialists: 8.0 (881.5 to 1)
Guidance Counselors: 13.0 (542.5 to 1)
Current Spending: ($ per student per year):
  Total: $7,089; Instruction: $4,295; Support Services: $2,481
Enrollment, Drop-out Rates and Diploma Recipients by Race/Ethnicity

Category	Total	White	Black	Asian	AIAN	Hisp.
Enrollment (%)	100.0	26.8	4.6	0.7	0.1	67.8
Drop-out Rate (%)	4.0	3.8	4.7	0.0	100.0	3.9
H.S. Diplomas (#)	407	150	22	6	0	229

Wimberley ISD
14401 Ranch Rd 12 • Wimberley, TX 78676-6216
(512) 847-2414
Grade Span: PK-12; **Agency Type:** 1
Schools: 4
  2 Primary; 1 Middle; 1 High; 0 Other Level
  4 Regular; 0 Special Education; 0 Vocational; 0 Alternative
  0 Magnet; 0 Charter; 3 Title I Eligible; 0 School-wide Title I
Students: 1,880   (53.7% male; 46.2% female)
  Individual Education Program: 248 (13.2%);
  English Language Learner: 62 (3.3%); Migrant: 0 (0.0%)
  Eligible for Free Lunch Program: 242 (12.9%)
  Eligible for Reduced-Price Lunch Program: 75 (4.0%)
Teachers: 141.4 (13.3 to 1)
Librarians/Media Specialists: 2.0 (940.0 to 1)
Guidance Counselors: 3.7 (508.1 to 1)
Current Spending: ($ per student per year):
  Total: $7,419; Instruction: $4,453; Support Services: $2,616
Enrollment, Drop-out Rates and Diploma Recipients by Race/Ethnicity

Category	Total	White	Black	Asian	AIAN	Hisp.
Enrollment (%)	100.0	88.5	1.0	0.2	0.6	9.7
Drop-out Rate (%)	0.5	0.6	0.0	0.0	0.0	0.0
H.S. Diplomas (#)	147	136	1	1	1	8

Henderson County

Athens ISD
104 Hawn St • Athens, TX 75751-2423
(903) 677-6900
Grade Span: PK-12; **Agency Type:** 1
Schools: 7
  3 Primary; 3 Middle; 1 High; 0 Other Level
  7 Regular; 0 Special Education; 0 Vocational; 0 Alternative
  0 Magnet; 0 Charter; 6 Title I Eligible; 6 School-wide Title I
Students: 3,500   (51.7% male; 48.2% female)
  Individual Education Program: 417 (11.9%);
  English Language Learner: 587 (16.8%); Migrant: 2 (0.1%)
  Eligible for Free Lunch Program: 1,594 (45.5%)
  Eligible for Reduced-Price Lunch Program: 286 (8.2%)
Teachers: 243.2 (14.4 to 1)
Librarians/Media Specialists: 2.2 (1,590.9 to 1)
Guidance Counselors: 8.9 (393.3 to 1)
Current Spending: ($ per student per year):
  Total: $6,687; Instruction: $4,210; Support Services: $2,143
Enrollment, Drop-out Rates and Diploma Recipients by Race/Ethnicity

Category	Total	White	Black	Asian	AIAN	Hisp.
Enrollment (%)	100.0	55.1	16.2	0.2	0.0	28.5
Drop-out Rate (%)	3.3	2.8	5.3	16.7	0.0	3.2
H.S. Diplomas (#)	192	129	26	2	1	34

Brownsboro ISD
Hwy 31 W • Brownsboro, TX 75756-0465
Mailing Address: PO Box 465 • Brownsboro, TX 75756-0465
(903) 852-3701 • http://www.brownsboro.k12.tx.us/
Grade Span: PK-12; Agency Type: 1
Schools: 7
   3 Primary; 2 Middle; 2 High; 0 Other Level
   6 Regular; 0 Special Education; 0 Vocational; 1 Alternative
   0 Magnet; 0 Charter; 5 Title I Eligible; 5 School-wide Title I
Students: 2,721   (52.0% male; 47.9% female)
   Individual Education Program: 340 (12.5%);
   English Language Learner: 92 (3.4%); Migrant: 0 (0.0%)
   Eligible for Free Lunch Program: 961 (35.3%)
   Eligible for Reduced-Price Lunch Program: 224 (8.2%)
Teachers: 176.7 (15.4 to 1)
Librarians/Media Specialists: 0.0 (n/a to 1)
Guidance Counselors: 9.6 (283.4 to 1)
Current Spending: ($ per student per year):
   Total: $6,789; Instruction: $4,032; Support Services: $2,398

Enrollment, Drop-out Rates and Diploma Recipients by Race/Ethnicity

Category	Total	White	Black	Asian	AIAN	Hisp.
Enrollment (%)	100.0	81.6	8.7	0.3	0.3	9.2
Drop-out Rate (%)	2.4	2.9	0.0	0.0	0.0	0.0
H.S. Diplomas (#)	143	123	17	0	0	3

Eustace ISD
316 S Fm 316 • Eustace, TX 75124-0188
Mailing Address: PO Box 188 • Eustace, TX 75124-0188
(903) 425-5151
Grade Span: PK-12; Agency Type: 1
Schools: 4
   2 Primary; 1 Middle; 1 High; 0 Other Level
   4 Regular; 0 Special Education; 0 Vocational; 0 Alternative
   0 Magnet; 0 Charter; 4 Title I Eligible; 4 School-wide Title I
Students: 1,513   (50.8% male; 49.1% female)
   Individual Education Program: 311 (20.6%);
   English Language Learner: 15 (1.0%); Migrant: 0 (0.0%)
   Eligible for Free Lunch Program: 683 (45.1%)
   Eligible for Reduced-Price Lunch Program: 160 (10.6%)
Teachers: 114.0 (13.3 to 1)
Librarians/Media Specialists: 2.0 (756.5 to 1)
Guidance Counselors: 2.0 (756.5 to 1)
Current Spending: ($ per student per year):
   Total: $6,501; Instruction: $4,109; Support Services: $2,008

Enrollment, Drop-out Rates and Diploma Recipients by Race/Ethnicity

Category	Total	White	Black	Asian	AIAN	Hisp.
Enrollment (%)	100.0	91.3	1.5	0.1	0.6	6.5
Drop-out Rate (%)	2.5	2.7	0.0	n/a	0.0	0.0
H.S. Diplomas (#)	75	70	1	0	1	3

Hidalgo County

Donna ISD
116 N 10th St • Donna, TX 78537-2799
(956) 464-1600 • http://www.esconett.org/donnaisd/
Grade Span: PK-12; Agency Type: 1
Schools: 18
   12 Primary; 2 Middle; 1 High; 3 Other Level
   16 Regular; 0 Special Education; 0 Vocational; 2 Alternative
   0 Magnet; 0 Charter; 16 Title I Eligible; 16 School-wide Title I
Students: 11,700   (51.4% male; 48.5% female)
   Individual Education Program: 1,125 (9.6%);
   English Language Learner: 6,124 (52.3%); Migrant: 3,422 (29.2%)
   Eligible for Free Lunch Program: 5,950 (50.9%)
   Eligible for Reduced-Price Lunch Program: 534 (4.6%)
Teachers: 791.6 (14.8 to 1)
Librarians/Media Specialists: 16.0 (731.3 to 1)
Guidance Counselors: 35.8 (326.8 to 1)
Current Spending: ($ per student per year):
   Total: $7,980; Instruction: $4,560; Support Services: $2,922

Enrollment, Drop-out Rates and Diploma Recipients by Race/Ethnicity

Category	Total	White	Black	Asian	AIAN	Hisp.
Enrollment (%)	100.0	0.9	0.1	0.0	0.1	98.9
Drop-out Rate (%)	6.5	6.7	0.0	0.0	n/a	6.5
H.S. Diplomas (#)	429	5	0	1	0	423

Edcouch-Elsa ISD
920 Santa Rosa • Edcouch, TX 78538-0127
Mailing Address: PO Box 127 • Edcouch, TX 78538-0127
(956) 262-6000 • http://www.eeisd.org/
Grade Span: PK-12; Agency Type: 1
Schools: 9
   5 Primary; 2 Middle; 1 High; 1 Other Level
   8 Regular; 0 Special Education; 0 Vocational; 1 Alternative
   0 Magnet; 0 Charter; 8 Title I Eligible; 8 School-wide Title I

Students: 5,366   (51.0% male; 48.9% female)
   Individual Education Program: 519 (9.7%);
   English Language Learner: 2,310 (43.0%); Migrant: 1,680 (31.3%)
   Eligible for Free Lunch Program: 826 (15.4%)
   Eligible for Reduced-Price Lunch Program: 55 (1.0%)
Teachers: 316.9 (16.9 to 1)
Librarians/Media Specialists: 5.0 (1,073.2 to 1)
Guidance Counselors: 13.0 (412.8 to 1)
Current Spending: ($ per student per year):
   Total: $7,587; Instruction: $4,403; Support Services: $2,593

Enrollment, Drop-out Rates and Diploma Recipients by Race/Ethnicity

Category	Total	White	Black	Asian	AIAN	Hisp.
Enrollment (%)	100.0	0.4	0.1	0.0	0.0	99.4
Drop-out Rate (%)	7.2	0.0	0.0	n/a	n/a	7.2
H.S. Diplomas (#)	279	3	0	0	0	276

Edinburg CISD
101 N 8th St • Edinburg, TX 78539-3303
Mailing Address: PO Box 990 • Edinburg, TX 78540-0990
(956) 289-2300 • http://www.ecisd.us/
Grade Span: PK-12; Agency Type: 1
Schools: 37
   27 Primary; 4 Middle; 3 High; 3 Other Level
   34 Regular; 0 Special Education; 0 Vocational; 3 Alternative
   0 Magnet; 0 Charter; 34 Title I Eligible; 34 School-wide Title I
Students: 25,373   (51.4% male; 48.5% female)
   Individual Education Program: 2,318 (9.1%);
   English Language Learner: 7,823 (30.8%); Migrant: 3,910 (15.4%)
   Eligible for Free Lunch Program: 6,706 (26.4%)
   Eligible for Reduced-Price Lunch Program: 654 (2.6%)
Teachers: 1,631.5 (15.6 to 1)
Librarians/Media Specialists: 35.0 (724.9 to 1)
Guidance Counselors: 68.0 (373.1 to 1)
Current Spending: ($ per student per year):
   Total: $7,312; Instruction: $4,413; Support Services: $2,417

Enrollment, Drop-out Rates and Diploma Recipients by Race/Ethnicity

Category	Total	White	Black	Asian	AIAN	Hisp.
Enrollment (%)	100.0	2.6	0.2	0.4	0.0	96.8
Drop-out Rate (%)	3.5	3.0	0.0	0.0	n/a	3.5
H.S. Diplomas (#)	1,038	64	1	5	1	967

Hidalgo ISD
PO Drawer D • Hidalgo, TX 78557-3004
(956) 843-3100
Grade Span: PK-12; Agency Type: 1
Schools: 6
   3 Primary; 1 Middle; 2 High; 0 Other Level
   5 Regular; 0 Special Education; 0 Vocational; 1 Alternative
   0 Magnet; 0 Charter; 6 Title I Eligible; 6 School-wide Title I
Students: 3,157   (50.9% male; 49.0% female)
   Individual Education Program: 199 (6.3%);
   English Language Learner: 1,706 (54.0%); Migrant: 503 (15.9%)
   Eligible for Free Lunch Program: 442 (14.0%)
   Eligible for Reduced-Price Lunch Program: 14 (0.4%)
Teachers: 223.8 (14.1 to 1)
Librarians/Media Specialists: 5.0 (631.4 to 1)
Guidance Counselors: 11.8 (267.5 to 1)
Current Spending: ($ per student per year):
   Total: $8,528; Instruction: $5,102; Support Services: $2,843

Enrollment, Drop-out Rates and Diploma Recipients by Race/Ethnicity

Category	Total	White	Black	Asian	AIAN	Hisp.
Enrollment (%)	100.0	0.1	0.0	0.2	0.0	99.7
Drop-out Rate (%)	2.9	0.0	0.0	n/a	n/a	3.0
H.S. Diplomas (#)	150	2	0	0	0	148

La Joya ISD
201 E Expy 83 • La Joya, TX 78560-2009
(956) 580-5441 • http://www.lajoyaisd.com/
Grade Span: PK-12; Agency Type: 1
Schools: 27
   16 Primary; 4 Middle; 3 High; 4 Other Level
   24 Regular; 0 Special Education; 0 Vocational; 3 Alternative
   0 Magnet; 0 Charter; 25 Title I Eligible; 25 School-wide Title I
Students: 21,765   (51.4% male; 48.5% female)
   Individual Education Program: 2,289 (10.5%);
   English Language Learner: 10,361 (47.6%); Migrant: 6,030 (27.7%)
   Eligible for Free Lunch Program: 11,161 (51.3%)
   Eligible for Reduced-Price Lunch Program: 657 (3.0%)
Teachers: 1,365.6 (15.9 to 1)
Librarians/Media Specialists: 24.0 (906.9 to 1)
Guidance Counselors: 68.9 (315.9 to 1)
Current Spending: ($ per student per year):
   Total: $6,963; Instruction: $4,152; Support Services: $2,389

Enrollment, Drop-out Rates and Diploma Recipients by Race/Ethnicity

Category	Total	White	Black	Asian	AIAN	Hisp.
Enrollment (%)	100.0	0.3	0.0	0.0	0.0	99.6
Drop-out Rate (%)	7.6	5.0	0.0	0.0	n/a	7.6
H.S. Diplomas (#)	765	6	0	1	0	758

Mcallen ISD

2000 N 23rd St • Mcallen, TX 78501-2000
(956) 618-6000 • http://www.mcallenisd.org/home.asp
Grade Span: PK-12; **Agency Type:** 1
Schools: 32
   20 Primary; 6 Middle; 4 High; 2 Other Level
   29 Regular; 0 Special Education; 0 Vocational; 3 Alternative
   0 Magnet; 0 Charter; 28 Title I Eligible; 27 School-wide Title I
Students: 23,492 (50.6% male; 49.3% female)
   Individual Education Program: 1,981 (8.4%);
   English Language Learner: 8,481 (36.1%); Migrant: 2,066 (8.8%)
   Eligible for Free Lunch Program: 9,368 (40.0%)
   Eligible for Reduced-Price Lunch Program: 1,589 (6.8%)
Teachers: 1,540.5 (15.2 to 1)
Librarians/Media Specialists: 30.4 (770.4 to 1)
Guidance Counselors: 100.8 (232.4 to 1)
Current Spending: ($ per student per year):
   Total: $7,153; Instruction: $4,224; Support Services: $2,546
Enrollment, Drop-out Rates and Diploma Recipients by Race/Ethnicity

Category	Total	White	Black	Asian	AIAN	Hisp.
Enrollment (%)	100.0	8.2	0.6	1.9	0.0	89.3
Drop-out Rate (%)	4.8	1.5	4.5	4.2	0.0	5.3
H.S. Diplomas (#)	1,270	174	7	20	1	1,068

Mercedes ISD

206 E 6th St • Mercedes, TX 78570-3504
Mailing Address: PO Box 419 • Mercedes, TX 78570-0419
(956) 514-2000 • http://www.mercedes.k12.tx.us/
Grade Span: PK-12; **Agency Type:** 1
Schools: 10
   4 Primary; 2 Middle; 2 High; 2 Other Level
   7 Regular; 0 Special Education; 0 Vocational; 3 Alternative
   0 Magnet; 0 Charter; 8 Title I Eligible; 8 School-wide Title I
Students: 5,342 (51.1% male; 48.8% female)
   Individual Education Program: 477 (8.9%);
   English Language Learner: 1,710 (32.0%); Migrant: 1,222 (22.9%)
   Eligible for Free Lunch Program: 890 (16.7%)
   Eligible for Reduced-Price Lunch Program: 75 (1.4%)
Teachers: 350.1 (15.3 to 1)
Librarians/Media Specialists: 8.0 (667.8 to 1)
Guidance Counselors: 15.0 (356.1 to 1)
Current Spending: ($ per student per year):
   Total: $8,409; Instruction: $4,843; Support Services: $3,088
Enrollment, Drop-out Rates and Diploma Recipients by Race/Ethnicity

Category	Total	White	Black	Asian	AIAN	Hisp.
Enrollment (%)	100.0	0.7	0.3	0.0	0.0	98.9
Drop-out Rate (%)	5.6	0.0	0.0	n/a	n/a	5.7
H.S. Diplomas (#)	256	6	1	0	0	249

Mission Cons ISD

1201 Bryce Dr • Mission, TX 78572-4399
(956) 580-5500 • http://www.mission-cons.k12.tx.us/
Grade Span: PK-12; **Agency Type:** 1
Schools: 21
   13 Primary; 3 Middle; 3 High; 2 Other Level
   18 Regular; 0 Special Education; 0 Vocational; 3 Alternative
   0 Magnet; 0 Charter; 18 Title I Eligible; 18 School-wide Title I
Students: 14,094 (51.2% male; 48.7% female)
   Individual Education Program: 884 (6.3%);
   English Language Learner: 3,875 (27.5%); Migrant: 2,118 (15.1%)
   Eligible for Free Lunch Program: 743 (5.3%)
   Eligible for Reduced-Price Lunch Program: 61 (0.4%)
Teachers: 914.4 (15.4 to 1)
Librarians/Media Specialists: 21.0 (668.6 to 1)
Guidance Counselors: 41.8 (335.9 to 1)
Current Spending: ($ per student per year):
   Total: $7,432; Instruction: $4,561; Support Services: $2,486
Enrollment, Drop-out Rates and Diploma Recipients by Race/Ethnicity

Category	Total	White	Black	Asian	AIAN	Hisp.
Enrollment (%)	100.0	2.0	0.2	0.0	0.0	97.7
Drop-out Rate (%)	6.1	4.6	0.0	0.0	n/a	6.2
H.S. Diplomas (#)	569	27	0	0	0	542

Pharr-San Juan-Alamo ISD

804 E Hwy 83 • Pharr, TX 78577-1225
Mailing Address: PO Box Y • Pharr, TX 78577-1225
(956) 702-5600 • http://www.psja.k12.tx.us/
Grade Span: PK-12; **Agency Type:** 1
Schools: 36

   25 Primary; 5 Middle; 5 High; 1 Other Level
   33 Regular; 0 Special Education; 0 Vocational; 3 Alternative
   0 Magnet; 0 Charter; 35 Title I Eligible; 35 School-wide Title I
Students: 26,493 (50.6% male; 49.3% female)
   Individual Education Program: 2,298 (8.7%);
   English Language Learner: 10,607 (40.0%); Migrant: 4,444 (16.8%)
   Eligible for Free Lunch Program: 4,576 (17.3%)
   Eligible for Reduced-Price Lunch Program: 398 (1.5%)
Teachers: 1,579.5 (16.8 to 1)
Librarians/Media Specialists: 33.0 (802.8 to 1)
Guidance Counselors: 60.2 (440.1 to 1)
Current Spending: ($ per student per year):
   Total: $7,368; Instruction: $4,446; Support Services: $2,485
Enrollment, Drop-out Rates and Diploma Recipients by Race/Ethnicity

Category	Total	White	Black	Asian	AIAN	Hisp.
Enrollment (%)	100.0	1.2	0.2	0.1	0.0	98.6
Drop-out Rate (%)	6.1	2.8	0.0	0.0	n/a	6.1
H.S. Diplomas (#)	1,045	12	2	1	0	1,030

Progreso ISD

F M Rd 1015 • Progreso, TX 78579-0610
Mailing Address: PO Box 610 • Progreso, TX 78579-0610
(956) 565-6203
Grade Span: PK-12; **Agency Type:** 1
Schools: 5
   2 Primary; 1 Middle; 1 High; 1 Other Level
   4 Regular; 0 Special Education; 0 Vocational; 1 Alternative
   0 Magnet; 0 Charter; 4 Title I Eligible; 4 School-wide Title I
Students: 2,112 (52.3% male; 47.6% female)
   Individual Education Program: 132 (6.3%);
   English Language Learner: 1,001 (47.4%); Migrant: 885 (41.9%)
   Eligible for Free Lunch Program: 1,094 (51.8%)
   Eligible for Reduced-Price Lunch Program: 27 (1.3%)
Teachers: 148.0 (14.3 to 1)
Librarians/Media Specialists: 4.0 (528.0 to 1)
Guidance Counselors: 6.0 (352.0 to 1)
Current Spending: ($ per student per year):
   Total: $7,688; Instruction: $4,485; Support Services: $2,671
Enrollment, Drop-out Rates and Diploma Recipients by Race/Ethnicity

Category	Total	White	Black	Asian	AIAN	Hisp.
Enrollment (%)	100.0	0.0	0.0	0.0	0.0	100.0
Drop-out Rate (%)	5.2	100.0	n/a	n/a	n/a	4.6
H.S. Diplomas (#)	91	0	0	0	0	91

Sharyland ISD

1106 N Shary Rd • Mission, TX 78572-4652
(956) 580-5200 • http://www.sharyland.k12.tx.us/index.html
Grade Span: PK-12; **Agency Type:** 1
Schools: 10
   5 Primary; 1 Middle; 3 High; 0 Other Level
   7 Regular; 0 Special Education; 0 Vocational; 2 Alternative
   0 Magnet; 0 Charter; 7 Title I Eligible; 7 School-wide Title I
Students: 6,751 (52.2% male; 47.7% female)
   Individual Education Program: 540 (8.0%);
   English Language Learner: 1,671 (24.8%); Migrant: 152 (2.3%)
   Eligible for Free Lunch Program: 2,994 (44.3%)
   Eligible for Reduced-Price Lunch Program: 547 (8.1%)
Teachers: 395.7 (17.1 to 1)
Librarians/Media Specialists: 7.0 (964.4 to 1)
Guidance Counselors: 21.4 (315.5 to 1)
Current Spending: ($ per student per year):
   Total: $6,261; Instruction: $3,866; Support Services: $2,076
Enrollment, Drop-out Rates and Diploma Recipients by Race/Ethnicity

Category	Total	White	Black	Asian	AIAN	Hisp.
Enrollment (%)	100.0	13.0	0.6	1.6	0.0	84.8
Drop-out Rate (%)	2.1	1.9	33.3	0.0	0.0	2.1
H.S. Diplomas (#)	257	64	0	4	0	189

Valley View ISD

61/2 Mi S Jackson Rd • Pharr, TX 78577-9999
Mailing Address: Rt 1 Box 122 • Pharr, TX 78577-9705
(956) 843-8825
Grade Span: PK-12; **Agency Type:** 1
Schools: 5
   3 Primary; 1 Middle; 1 High; 0 Other Level
   5 Regular; 0 Special Education; 0 Vocational; 0 Alternative
   0 Magnet; 0 Charter; 5 Title I Eligible; 5 School-wide Title I
Students: 2,956 (50.8% male; 49.1% female)
   Individual Education Program: 289 (9.8%);
   English Language Learner: 1,606 (54.3%); Migrant: 375 (12.7%)
   Eligible for Free Lunch Program: 298 (10.1%)
   Eligible for Reduced-Price Lunch Program: 28 (0.9%)
Teachers: 189.0 (15.6 to 1)
Librarians/Media Specialists: 3.0 (985.3 to 1)
Guidance Counselors: 6.9 (428.4 to 1)

Current Spending: ($ per student per year):
    Total: $7,112; Instruction: $4,183; Support Services: $2,373

Enrollment, Drop-out Rates and Diploma Recipients by Race/Ethnicity

Category	Total	White	Black	Asian	AIAN	Hisp.
Enrollment (%)	100.0	0.1	0.0	0.0	0.0	99.9
Drop-out Rate (%)	3.5	n/a	n/a	n/a	n/a	3.5
H.S. Diplomas (#)	91	0	0	0	0	91

Weslaco ISD

319 W 4th St • Weslaco, TX 78596-6047
Mailing Address: PO Box 266 • Weslaco, TX 78599-0266
(956) 969-6500 • http://www.wisd.us/
Grade Span: PK-12; **Agency Type:** 1
Schools: 21
    10 Primary; 4 Middle; 4 High; 3 Other Level
    16 Regular; 0 Special Education; 1 Vocational; 4 Alternative
    0 Magnet; 0 Charter; 17 Title I Eligible; 17 School-wide Title I
Students: 14,977   (51.4% male; 48.5% female)
    Individual Education Program: 1,374 (9.2%);
    English Language Learner: 4,042 (27.0%); Migrant: 4,957 (33.1%)
    Eligible for Free Lunch Program: 5,330 (35.6%)
    Eligible for Reduced-Price Lunch Program: 347 (2.3%)
Teachers: 968.5 (15.5 to 1)
Librarians/Media Specialists: 18.2 (822.9 to 1)
Guidance Counselors: 44.3 (338.1 to 1)
Current Spending: ($ per student per year):
    Total: $7,163; Instruction: $4,139; Support Services: $2,557

Enrollment, Drop-out Rates and Diploma Recipients by Race/Ethnicity

Category	Total	White	Black	Asian	AIAN	Hisp.
Enrollment (%)	100.0	2.2	0.2	0.2	0.0	97.4
Drop-out Rate (%)	5.2	2.8	25.0	0.0	n/a	5.3
H.S. Diplomas (#)	611	28	0	3	0	580

Hill County

Hillsboro ISD

121 E Franklin St • Hillsboro, TX 76645-2137
(254) 582-8585
Grade Span: PK-12; **Agency Type:** 1
Schools: 7
    2 Primary; 2 Middle; 1 High; 2 Other Level
    5 Regular; 0 Special Education; 0 Vocational; 2 Alternative
    0 Magnet; 0 Charter; 5 Title I Eligible; 5 School-wide Title I
Students: 1,818   (51.2% male; 48.7% female)
    Individual Education Program: 292 (16.1%);
    English Language Learner: 261 (14.4%); Migrant: 5 (0.3%)
    Eligible for Free Lunch Program: 1,093 (60.1%)
    Eligible for Reduced-Price Lunch Program: 139 (7.6%)
Teachers: 140.0 (13.0 to 1)
Librarians/Media Specialists: 2.0 (909.0 to 1)
Guidance Counselors: 7.0 (259.7 to 1)
Current Spending: ($ per student per year):
    Total: $8,118; Instruction: $4,776; Support Services: $2,864

Enrollment, Drop-out Rates and Diploma Recipients by Race/Ethnicity

Category	Total	White	Black	Asian	AIAN	Hisp.
Enrollment (%)	100.0	36.7	20.8	0.6	0.2	41.7
Drop-out Rate (%)	6.5	6.1	3.8	0.0	0.0	9.3
H.S. Diplomas (#)	113	59	23	1	0	30

Whitney ISD

305 S San Jacinto St • Whitney, TX 76692-2391
Mailing Address: PO Box 518 • Whitney, TX 76692-0518
(254) 694-2254
Grade Span: PK-12; **Agency Type:** 1
Schools: 4
    2 Primary; 1 Middle; 1 High; 0 Other Level
    4 Regular; 0 Special Education; 0 Vocational; 0 Alternative
    0 Magnet; 0 Charter; 1 Title I Eligible; 1 School-wide Title I
Students: 1,548   (50.9% male; 49.0% female)
    Individual Education Program: 194 (12.5%);
    English Language Learner: 15 (1.0%); Migrant: 6 (0.4%)
    Eligible for Free Lunch Program: 602 (38.9%)
    Eligible for Reduced-Price Lunch Program: 129 (8.3%)
Teachers: 107.6 (14.4 to 1)
Librarians/Media Specialists: 1.0 (1,548.0 to 1)
Guidance Counselors: 3.0 (516.0 to 1)
Current Spending: ($ per student per year):
    Total: $7,344; Instruction: $4,310; Support Services: $2,611

Enrollment, Drop-out Rates and Diploma Recipients by Race/Ethnicity

Category	Total	White	Black	Asian	AIAN	Hisp.
Enrollment (%)	100.0	86.4	3.1	0.1	0.1	10.3
Drop-out Rate (%)	2.6	2.8	0.0	0.0	0.0	2.6
H.S. Diplomas (#)	100	83	5	0	3	9

Hockley County

Levelland ISD

704 11th St • Levelland, TX 79336-5424
(806) 894-9628
Grade Span: PK-12; **Agency Type:** 1
Schools: 7
    4 Primary; 0 Middle; 1 High; 2 Other Level
    7 Regular; 0 Special Education; 0 Vocational; 0 Alternative
    0 Magnet; 0 Charter; 7 Title I Eligible; 7 School-wide Title I
Students: 3,099   (51.6% male; 48.3% female)
    Individual Education Program: 493 (15.9%);
    English Language Learner: 111 (3.6%); Migrant: 494 (15.9%)
    Eligible for Free Lunch Program: 1,533 (49.5%)
    Eligible for Reduced-Price Lunch Program: 302 (9.7%)
Teachers: 244.8 (12.7 to 1)
Librarians/Media Specialists: 7.0 (442.7 to 1)
Guidance Counselors: 11.0 (281.7 to 1)
Current Spending: ($ per student per year):
    Total: $7,800; Instruction: $4,931; Support Services: $2,558

Enrollment, Drop-out Rates and Diploma Recipients by Race/Ethnicity

Category	Total	White	Black	Asian	AIAN	Hisp.
Enrollment (%)	100.0	36.9	5.6	0.3	0.4	57.0
Drop-out Rate (%)	4.3	2.4	1.9	n/a	0.0	6.3
H.S. Diplomas (#)	199	109	12	0	0	78

Hood County

Granbury ISD

600 W Pearl St • Granbury, TX 76048-2046
(817) 408-4000 • http://www.granbury.k12.tx.us/
Grade Span: PK-12; **Agency Type:** 1
Schools: 13
    4 Primary; 5 Middle; 2 High; 2 Other Level
    10 Regular; 0 Special Education; 0 Vocational; 3 Alternative
    0 Magnet; 0 Charter; 7 Title I Eligible; 6 School-wide Title I
Students: 6,607   (51.3% male; 48.6% female)
    Individual Education Program: 866 (13.1%);
    English Language Learner: 352 (5.3%); Migrant: 0 (0.0%)
    Eligible for Free Lunch Program: 1,875 (28.4%)
    Eligible for Reduced-Price Lunch Program: 434 (6.6%)
Teachers: 451.6 (14.6 to 1)
Librarians/Media Specialists: 8.8 (750.8 to 1)
Guidance Counselors: 16.1 (410.4 to 1)
Current Spending: ($ per student per year):
    Total: $6,512; Instruction: $3,774; Support Services: $2,423

Enrollment, Drop-out Rates and Diploma Recipients by Race/Ethnicity

Category	Total	White	Black	Asian	AIAN	Hisp.
Enrollment (%)	100.0	85.3	0.9	0.7	0.5	12.7
Drop-out Rate (%)	3.4	3.0	0.0	0.0	0.0	7.3
H.S. Diplomas (#)	346	313	3	2	1	27

Hopkins County

Sulphur Springs ISD

631 Connally St • Sulphur Springs, TX 75482-2401
(903) 885-2153
Grade Span: PK-12; **Agency Type:** 1
Schools: 8
    5 Primary; 2 Middle; 1 High; 0 Other Level
    8 Regular; 0 Special Education; 0 Vocational; 0 Alternative
    0 Magnet; 0 Charter; 6 Title I Eligible; 6 School-wide Title I
Students: 4,159   (50.6% male; 49.3% female)
    Individual Education Program: 588 (14.1%);
    English Language Learner: 264 (6.3%); Migrant: 113 (2.7%)
    Eligible for Free Lunch Program: 1,506 (36.2%)
    Eligible for Reduced-Price Lunch Program: 310 (7.5%)
Teachers: 301.3 (13.8 to 1)
Librarians/Media Specialists: 1.1 (3,780.9 to 1)
Guidance Counselors: 8.0 (519.9 to 1)
Current Spending: ($ per student per year):
    Total: $6,936; Instruction: $4,430; Support Services: $2,129

Enrollment, Drop-out Rates and Diploma Recipients by Race/Ethnicity

Category	Total	White	Black	Asian	AIAN	Hisp.
Enrollment (%)	100.0	69.8	13.3	0.4	0.2	16.3
Drop-out Rate (%)	1.4	1.2	0.7	0.0	0.0	4.0
H.S. Diplomas (#)	254	193	40	1	0	20

Houston County

Crockett ISD

704 Burnet Ave • Crockett, TX 75835-2111
(936) 544-2125 • http://www.crockettisd.net/
Grade Span: PK-12; **Agency Type:** 1
Schools: 6

2 Primary; 2 Middle; 1 High; 1 Other Level
5 Regular; 0 Special Education; 0 Vocational; 1 Alternative
0 Magnet; 0 Charter; 4 Title I Eligible; 4 School-wide Title I
Students: 1,689 (50.7% male; 49.2% female)
Individual Education Program: 210 (12.4%);
English Language Learner: 87 (5.2%); Migrant: 65 (3.8%)
Eligible for Free Lunch Program: 1,070 (63.4%)
Eligible for Reduced-Price Lunch Program: 117 (6.9%)
Teachers: 142.7 (11.8 to 1)
Librarians/Media Specialists: 1.5 (1,126.0 to 1)
Guidance Counselors: 4.7 (359.4 to 1)
Current Spending: ($ per student per year):
Total: $7,699; Instruction: $4,917; Support Services: $2,339
Enrollment, Drop-out Rates and Diploma Recipients by Race/Ethnicity

Category	Total	White	Black	Asian	AIAN	Hisp.
Enrollment (%)	100.0	27.0	58.4	0.3	0.7	13.6
Drop-out Rate (%)	6.1	5.9	5.9	0.0	0.0	8.7
H.S. Diplomas (#)	116	32	69	3	0	12

Howard County

Big Spring ISD
708 E 11th Pl • Big Spring, TX 79720-4696
(432) 264-3600 • http://bsisd.esc18.net/
Grade Span: PK-12; **Agency Type:** 1
Schools: 9
5 Primary; 2 Middle; 1 High; 1 Other Level
8 Regular; 0 Special Education; 0 Vocational; 1 Alternative
0 Magnet; 0 Charter; 8 Title I Eligible; 8 School-wide Title I
Students: 3,931 (51.5% male; 48.4% female)
Individual Education Program: 445 (11.3%);
English Language Learner: 87 (2.2%); Migrant: 6 (0.2%)
Eligible for Free Lunch Program: 1,815 (46.2%)
Eligible for Reduced-Price Lunch Program: 468 (11.9%)
Teachers: 273.8 (14.4 to 1)
Librarians/Media Specialists: 0.6 (6,551.7 to 1)
Guidance Counselors: 6.6 (595.6 to 1)
Current Spending: ($ per student per year):
Total: $6,624; Instruction: $4,114; Support Services: $2,081
Enrollment, Drop-out Rates and Diploma Recipients by Race/Ethnicity

Category	Total	White	Black	Asian	AIAN	Hisp.
Enrollment (%)	100.0	41.3	6.5	0.6	0.5	51.0
Drop-out Rate (%)	4.5	3.2	4.9	0.0	0.0	6.2
H.S. Diplomas (#)	227	135	12	3	0	77

Hunt County

Commerce ISD
604 Culver • Commerce, TX 75428-3608
Mailing Address: PO Box 1251 • Commerce, TX 75429-1251
(903) 886-3755 • http://commerce.ednet10.net/
Grade Span: PK-12; **Agency Type:** 1
Schools: 5
2 Primary; 1 Middle; 2 High; 0 Other Level
4 Regular; 0 Special Education; 0 Vocational; 1 Alternative
0 Magnet; 0 Charter; 2 Title I Eligible; 2 School-wide Title I
Students: 1,829 (52.2% male; 47.7% female)
Individual Education Program: 332 (18.2%);
English Language Learner: 94 (5.1%); Migrant: 5 (0.3%)
Eligible for Free Lunch Program: 944 (51.6%)
Eligible for Reduced-Price Lunch Program: 122 (6.7%)
Teachers: 123.6 (14.8 to 1)
Librarians/Media Specialists: 3.0 (609.7 to 1)
Guidance Counselors: 7.0 (261.3 to 1)
Current Spending: ($ per student per year):
Total: $7,854; Instruction: $4,311; Support Services: $3,127
Enrollment, Drop-out Rates and Diploma Recipients by Race/Ethnicity

Category	Total	White	Black	Asian	AIAN	Hisp.
Enrollment (%)	100.0	63.3	23.7	1.9	0.8	10.3
Drop-out Rate (%)	1.3	1.3	0.9	0.0	0.0	3.0
H.S. Diplomas (#)	117	86	22	0	0	9

Greenville ISD
3504 King St • Greenville, TX 75401-5103
Mailing Address: PO Box 1022 • Greenville, TX 75403-1022
(903) 457-2500 • http://districtweb1.ednet10.net/greenville/
Grade Span: PK-12; **Agency Type:** 1
Schools: 12
6 Primary; 2 Middle; 2 High; 2 Other Level
9 Regular; 0 Special Education; 0 Vocational; 3 Alternative
0 Magnet; 0 Charter; 7 Title I Eligible; 7 School-wide Title I
Students: 5,288 (51.0% male; 48.9% female)
Individual Education Program: 607 (11.5%);
English Language Learner: 545 (10.3%); Migrant: 2 (<0.1%)
Eligible for Free Lunch Program: 2,264 (42.8%)

Eligible for Reduced-Price Lunch Program: 399 (7.5%)
Teachers: 365.8 (14.5 to 1)
Librarians/Media Specialists: 5.9 (896.1 to 1)
Guidance Counselors: 12.4 (426.4 to 1)
Current Spending: ($ per student per year):
Total: $6,922; Instruction: $4,477; Support Services: $2,122
Enrollment, Drop-out Rates and Diploma Recipients by Race/Ethnicity

Category	Total	White	Black	Asian	AIAN	Hisp.
Enrollment (%)	100.0	50.9	24.4	0.9	0.4	23.3
Drop-out Rate (%)	7.3	4.4	14.0	0.0	0.0	8.3
H.S. Diplomas (#)	289	193	64	2	0	30

Quinlan ISD
301 E Main St • Quinlan, TX 75474-9690
(903) 356-3293
Grade Span: PK-12; **Agency Type:** 1
Schools: 6
2 Primary; 2 Middle; 1 High; 1 Other Level
5 Regular; 0 Special Education; 0 Vocational; 1 Alternative
0 Magnet; 0 Charter; 5 Title I Eligible; 5 School-wide Title I
Students: 2,871 (51.6% male; 48.3% female)
Individual Education Program: 539 (18.8%);
English Language Learner: 62 (2.2%); Migrant: 0 (0.0%)
Eligible for Free Lunch Program: 1,062 (37.0%)
Eligible for Reduced-Price Lunch Program: 228 (7.9%)
Teachers: 191.3 (15.0 to 1)
Librarians/Media Specialists: 3.0 (957.0 to 1)
Guidance Counselors: 5.0 (574.2 to 1)
Current Spending: ($ per student per year):
Total: $7,103; Instruction: $3,964; Support Services: $2,718
Enrollment, Drop-out Rates and Diploma Recipients by Race/Ethnicity

Category	Total	White	Black	Asian	AIAN	Hisp.
Enrollment (%)	100.0	90.4	1.1	0.5	1.0	7.1
Drop-out Rate (%)	2.6	2.8	0.0	0.0	0.0	0.0
H.S. Diplomas (#)	162	143	1	0	3	15

Hutchinson County

Borger ISD
200 E 9th St • Borger, TX 79007-3612
(806) 273-6481 • http://www.borgerisd.net/
Grade Span: PK-12; **Agency Type:** 1
Schools: 6
3 Primary; 1 Middle; 2 High; 0 Other Level
5 Regular; 0 Special Education; 0 Vocational; 1 Alternative
0 Magnet; 0 Charter; 4 Title I Eligible; 4 School-wide Title I
Students: 2,882 (51.1% male; 48.8% female)
Individual Education Program: 406 (14.1%);
English Language Learner: 194 (6.7%); Migrant: 14 (0.5%)
Eligible for Free Lunch Program: 978 (33.9%)
Eligible for Reduced-Price Lunch Program: 223 (7.7%)
Teachers: 210.7 (13.7 to 1)
Librarians/Media Specialists: 4.0 (720.5 to 1)
Guidance Counselors: 5.2 (554.2 to 1)
Current Spending: ($ per student per year):
Total: $6,712; Instruction: $4,255; Support Services: $2,167
Enrollment, Drop-out Rates and Diploma Recipients by Race/Ethnicity

Category	Total	White	Black	Asian	AIAN	Hisp.
Enrollment (%)	100.0	62.8	4.8	0.6	0.6	31.2
Drop-out Rate (%)	3.2	2.5	8.3	0.0	0.0	4.5
H.S. Diplomas (#)	201	149	12	1	1	38

Jackson County

Edna ISD
1307 W Gayle St • Edna, TX 77957-1504
Mailing Address: PO Box 919 • Edna, TX 77957-0919
(361) 782-3573
Grade Span: PK-12; **Agency Type:** 1
Schools: 5
2 Primary; 1 Middle; 1 High; 1 Other Level
4 Regular; 0 Special Education; 0 Vocational; 1 Alternative
0 Magnet; 0 Charter; 5 Title I Eligible; 5 School-wide Title I
Students: 1,555 (50.3% male; 49.6% female)
Individual Education Program: 175 (11.3%);
English Language Learner: 107 (6.9%); Migrant: 7 (0.5%)
Eligible for Free Lunch Program: 643 (41.4%)
Eligible for Reduced-Price Lunch Program: 91 (5.9%)
Teachers: 105.0 (14.8 to 1)
Librarians/Media Specialists: 1.0 (1,555.0 to 1)
Guidance Counselors: 3.0 (518.3 to 1)
Current Spending: ($ per student per year):
Total: $6,683; Instruction: $4,299; Support Services: $2,102

Enrollment, Drop-out Rates and Diploma Recipients by Race/Ethnicity

Category	Total	White	Black	Asian	AIAN	Hisp.
Enrollment (%)	100.0	50.9	13.8	0.2	0.0	35.1
Drop-out Rate (%)	3.6	2.5	3.3	n/a	n/a	5.8
H.S. Diplomas (#)	108	64	12	0	0	32

Jasper County

Buna ISD

Hwy 62 & 253 • Buna, TX 77612-1087
Mailing Address: PO Box 1087 • Buna, TX 77612-1087
(409) 994-5101
Grade Span: PK-12; **Agency Type:** 1
Schools: 3
  1 Primary; 1 Middle; 1 High; 0 Other Level
  3 Regular; 0 Special Education; 0 Vocational; 0 Alternative
  0 Magnet; 0 Charter; 1 Title I Eligible; 1 School-wide Title I
Students: 1,589   (50.5% male; 49.4% female)
  Individual Education Program: 263 (16.6%);
  English Language Learner: 3 (0.2%); Migrant: 3 (0.2%)
  Eligible for Free Lunch Program: 418 (26.3%)
  Eligible for Reduced-Price Lunch Program: 126 (7.9%)
Teachers: 127.8 (12.4 to 1)
Librarians/Media Specialists: 0.3 (5,296.7 to 1)
Guidance Counselors: 4.3 (369.5 to 1)
Current Spending: ($ per student per year):
  Total: $7,293; Instruction: $4,523; Support Services: $2,519
Enrollment, Drop-out Rates and Diploma Recipients by Race/Ethnicity

Category	Total	White	Black	Asian	AIAN	Hisp.
Enrollment (%)	100.0	93.5	3.5	0.4	0.9	1.7
Drop-out Rate (%)	2.7	2.8	0.0	0.0	0.0	10.0
H.S. Diplomas (#)	96	82	10	0	1	3

Jasper ISD

128 Park St • Jasper, TX 75951-3466
(409) 384-2401 • http://www.jasperisd.net/jasper.htm
Grade Span: PK-12; **Agency Type:** 1
Schools: 5
  2 Primary; 2 Middle; 1 High; 0 Other Level
  5 Regular; 0 Special Education; 0 Vocational; 0 Alternative
  0 Magnet; 0 Charter; 4 Title I Eligible; 1 School-wide Title I
Students: 3,115   (51.1% male; 48.8% female)
  Individual Education Program: 423 (13.6%);
  English Language Learner: 131 (4.2%); Migrant: 0 (0.0%)
  Eligible for Free Lunch Program: 1,683 (54.0%)
  Eligible for Reduced-Price Lunch Program: 278 (8.9%)
Teachers: 230.9 (13.5 to 1)
Librarians/Media Specialists: 2.1 (1,483.3 to 1)
Guidance Counselors: 6.0 (519.2 to 1)
Current Spending: ($ per student per year):
  Total: $7,016; Instruction: $4,085; Support Services: $2,490
Enrollment, Drop-out Rates and Diploma Recipients by Race/Ethnicity

Category	Total	White	Black	Asian	AIAN	Hisp.
Enrollment (%)	100.0	49.7	42.5	0.6	0.4	6.9
Drop-out Rate (%)	2.1	2.1	1.9	0.0	0.0	3.5
H.S. Diplomas (#)	192	111	67	1	1	12

Kirbyville CISD

206 E Main St • Kirbyville, TX 75956-2128
(409) 423-2284
Grade Span: PK-12; **Agency Type:** 1
Schools: 3
  1 Primary; 1 Middle; 1 High; 0 Other Level
  3 Regular; 0 Special Education; 0 Vocational; 0 Alternative
  0 Magnet; 0 Charter; 1 Title I Eligible; 1 School-wide Title I
Students: 1,598   (51.3% male; 48.6% female)
  Individual Education Program: 252 (15.8%);
  English Language Learner: 21 (1.3%); Migrant: 11 (0.7%)
  Eligible for Free Lunch Program: 665 (41.6%)
  Eligible for Reduced-Price Lunch Program: 114 (7.1%)
Teachers: 108.5 (14.7 to 1)
Librarians/Media Specialists: 1.0 (1,598.0 to 1)
Guidance Counselors: 3.6 (443.9 to 1)
Current Spending: ($ per student per year):
  Total: $6,177; Instruction: $3,804; Support Services: $2,068
Enrollment, Drop-out Rates and Diploma Recipients by Race/Ethnicity

Category	Total	White	Black	Asian	AIAN	Hisp.
Enrollment (%)	100.0	82.0	15.3	0.0	0.1	2.5
Drop-out Rate (%)	1.9	2.1	1.1	n/a	0.0	0.0
H.S. Diplomas (#)	119	87	28	0	1	3

Jefferson County

Beaumont ISD

3395 Harrison Ave • Beaumont, TX 77706-5009
(409) 899-9972 • http://www.beaumont.k12.tx.us/
Grade Span: PK-12; **Agency Type:** 1
Schools: 36
  21 Primary; 7 Middle; 5 High; 3 Other Level
  30 Regular; 1 Special Education; 0 Vocational; 5 Alternative
  0 Magnet; 0 Charter; 24 Title I Eligible; 14 School-wide Title I
Students: 20,732   (50.2% male; 49.7% female)
  Individual Education Program: 2,420 (11.7%);
  English Language Learner: 1,130 (5.5%); Migrant: 0 (0.0%)
  Eligible for Free Lunch Program: 11,309 (54.5%)
  Eligible for Reduced-Price Lunch Program: 1,137 (5.5%)
Teachers: 1,456.2 (14.2 to 1)
Librarians/Media Specialists: 8.7 (2,383.0 to 1)
Guidance Counselors: 43.1 (481.0 to 1)
Current Spending: ($ per student per year):
  Total: $6,864; Instruction: $4,172; Support Services: $2,292
Enrollment, Drop-out Rates and Diploma Recipients by Race/Ethnicity

Category	Total	White	Black	Asian	AIAN	Hisp.
Enrollment (%)	100.0	22.1	63.9	2.8	0.2	11.0
Drop-out Rate (%)	4.4	2.6	5.1	2.4	9.1	5.9
H.S. Diplomas (#)	1,153	338	713	40	1	61

Hamshire-Fannett ISD

12702 Second St • Hamshire, TX 77622-0223
Mailing Address: PO Box 223 • Hamshire, TX 77622-0223
(409) 243-2514 • http://www.hfisd.net/
Grade Span: PK-12; **Agency Type:** 1
Schools: 5
  1 Primary; 2 Middle; 1 High; 0 Other Level
  4 Regular; 0 Special Education; 0 Vocational; 0 Alternative
  0 Magnet; 0 Charter; 2 Title I Eligible; 0 School-wide Title I
Students: 1,785   (51.8% male; 48.1% female)
  Individual Education Program: 227 (12.7%);
  English Language Learner: 40 (2.2%); Migrant: 3 (0.2%)
  Eligible for Free Lunch Program: 343 (19.2%)
  Eligible for Reduced-Price Lunch Program: 102 (5.7%)
Teachers: 122.1 (14.6 to 1)
Librarians/Media Specialists: 3.9 (457.7 to 1)
Guidance Counselors: 4.0 (446.3 to 1)
Current Spending: ($ per student per year):
  Total: $6,450; Instruction: $3,777; Support Services: $2,325
Enrollment, Drop-out Rates and Diploma Recipients by Race/Ethnicity

Category	Total	White	Black	Asian	AIAN	Hisp.
Enrollment (%)	100.0	85.5	5.3	0.7	0.1	8.4
Drop-out Rate (%)	0.7	0.8	0.0	0.0	n/a	0.0
H.S. Diplomas (#)	120	110	3	2	0	5

Nederland ISD

220 N 17th St • Nederland, TX 77627-5029
(409) 724-2391 • http://www.nederland.k12.tx.us/
Grade Span: PK-12; **Agency Type:** 1
Schools: 9
  4 Primary; 2 Middle; 1 High; 2 Other Level
  7 Regular; 1 Special Education; 0 Vocational; 1 Alternative
  0 Magnet; 0 Charter; 5 Title I Eligible; 1 School-wide Title I
Students: 5,066   (51.9% male; 48.0% female)
  Individual Education Program: 796 (15.7%);
  English Language Learner: 137 (2.7%); Migrant: 0 (0.0%)
  Eligible for Free Lunch Program: 911 (18.0%)
  Eligible for Reduced-Price Lunch Program: 294 (5.8%)
Teachers: 325.1 (15.6 to 1)
Librarians/Media Specialists: 4.9 (1,033.9 to 1)
Guidance Counselors: 10.1 (501.6 to 1)
Current Spending: ($ per student per year):
  Total: $6,139; Instruction: $3,796; Support Services: $2,044
Enrollment, Drop-out Rates and Diploma Recipients by Race/Ethnicity

Category	Total	White	Black	Asian	AIAN	Hisp.
Enrollment (%)	100.0	85.4	3.1	4.9	0.1	6.6
Drop-out Rate (%)	3.2	3.3	0.0	2.9	0.0	3.0
H.S. Diplomas (#)	326	295	3	13	0	15

Port Arthur ISD

733 5th St • Port Arthur, TX 77640-6599
Mailing Address: PO Box 1388 • Port Arthur, TX 77641-1388
(409) 989-6244 • http://paisd.k12.tx.us.clickmyschool.com/
Grade Span: PK-12; **Agency Type:** 1
Schools: 19
  9 Primary; 3 Middle; 1 High; 3 Other Level
  14 Regular; 1 Special Education; 0 Vocational; 1 Alternative
  0 Magnet; 0 Charter; 11 Title I Eligible; 11 School-wide Title I
Students: 10,357   (50.5% male; 49.4% female)

Individual Education Program: 974 (9.4%);
English Language Learner: 1,431 (13.8%); Migrant: 152 (1.5%)
Eligible for Free Lunch Program: 7,714 (74.5%)
Eligible for Reduced-Price Lunch Program: 592 (5.7%)
Teachers: 607.3 (17.1 to 1)
Librarians/Media Specialists: 14.0 (739.8 to 1)
Guidance Counselors: 27.1 (382.2 to 1)
Current Spending: ($ per student per year):
Total: $7,398; Instruction: $4,385; Support Services: $2,597
Enrollment, Drop-out Rates and Diploma Recipients by Race/Ethnicity

Category	Total	White	Black	Asian	AIAN	Hisp.
Enrollment (%)	100.0	7.4	55.7	7.5	0.1	29.2
Drop-out Rate (%)	4.9	4.1	5.0	3.1	0.0	5.9
H.S. Diplomas (#)	547	79	350	47	0	71

Port Neches-Groves ISD
620 Ave C • Port Neches, TX 77651-3092
(409) 722-4244
Grade Span: PK-12; **Agency Type:** 1
Schools: 12
5 Primary; 4 Middle; 1 High; 2 Other Level
10 Regular; 0 Special Education; 0 Vocational; 2 Alternative
0 Magnet; 0 Charter; 7 Title I Eligible; 1 School-wide Title I
Students: 4,753 (51.0% male; 48.9% female)
Individual Education Program: 552 (11.6%);
English Language Learner: 75 (1.6%); Migrant: 1 (<0.1%)
Eligible for Free Lunch Program: 419 (8.8%)
Eligible for Reduced-Price Lunch Program: 277 (5.8%)
Teachers: 323.2 (14.7 to 1)
Librarians/Media Specialists: 10.0 (475.3 to 1)
Guidance Counselors: 13.0 (365.6 to 1)
Current Spending: ($ per student per year):
Total: $6,955; Instruction: $4,283; Support Services: $2,332
Enrollment, Drop-out Rates and Diploma Recipients by Race/Ethnicity

Category	Total	White	Black	Asian	AIAN	Hisp.
Enrollment (%)	100.0	86.7	1.8	3.0	0.5	7.9
Drop-out Rate (%)	1.6	1.7	0.0	0.0	33.3	0.0
H.S. Diplomas (#)	374	342	1	9	0	22

Jim Wells County

Alice ISD
1801 E Main St • Alice, TX 78332-4140
(361) 664-0981 • http://www.aliceisd.net/home.asp
Grade Span: PK-12; **Agency Type:** 1
Schools: 10
6 Primary; 3 Middle; 1 High; 0 Other Level
10 Regular; 0 Special Education; 0 Vocational; 0 Alternative
0 Magnet; 0 Charter; 10 Title I Eligible; 10 School-wide Title I
Students: 5,702 (51.1% male; 48.8% female)
Individual Education Program: 640 (11.2%);
English Language Learner: 260 (4.6%); Migrant: 469 (8.2%)
Eligible for Free Lunch Program: 3,334 (58.5%)
Eligible for Reduced-Price Lunch Program: 494 (8.7%)
Teachers: 373.6 (15.3 to 1)
Librarians/Media Specialists: 10.8 (528.0 to 1)
Guidance Counselors: 17.0 (335.4 to 1)
Current Spending: ($ per student per year):
Total: $6,962; Instruction: $4,140; Support Services: $2,448
Enrollment, Drop-out Rates and Diploma Recipients by Race/Ethnicity

Category	Total	White	Black	Asian	AIAN	Hisp.
Enrollment (%)	100.0	8.9	0.5	0.6	0.1	89.9
Drop-out Rate (%)	5.4	3.1	0.0	0.0	n/a	5.7
H.S. Diplomas (#)	269	41	3	2	0	223

Orange Grove ISD
504 S Dibrell • Orange Grove, TX 78372-0534
Mailing Address: PO Box 534 • Orange Grove, TX 78372-0534
(361) 384-2495
Grade Span: PK-12; **Agency Type:** 1
Schools: 4
2 Primary; 1 Middle; 1 High; 0 Other Level
4 Regular; 0 Special Education; 0 Vocational; 0 Alternative
0 Magnet; 0 Charter; 3 Title I Eligible; 3 School-wide Title I
Students: 1,632 (48.2% male; 51.7% female)
Individual Education Program: 191 (11.7%);
English Language Learner: 44 (2.7%); Migrant: 117 (7.2%)
Eligible for Free Lunch Program: 866 (53.1%)
Eligible for Reduced-Price Lunch Program: 170 (10.4%)
Teachers: 110.6 (14.8 to 1)
Librarians/Media Specialists: 0.2 (8,160.0 to 1)
Guidance Counselors: 3.0 (544.0 to 1)
Current Spending: ($ per student per year):
Total: $6,844; Instruction: $4,052; Support Services: $2,330

Category	Total	White	Black	Asian	AIAN	Hisp.
Enrollment (%)	100.0	42.3	0.6	0.2	0.1	56.8
Drop-out Rate (%)	2.3	2.5	0.0	0.0	n/a	2.1
H.S. Diplomas (#)	96	41	1	0	1	53

Johnson County

Alvarado ISD
110 N Bill Jackson Dr • Alvarado, TX 76009-4206
Mailing Address: PO Box 387 • Alvarado, TX 76009-0387
(817) 783-6800 • http://www.alvarado.isd.tenet.edu/
Grade Span: PK-12; **Agency Type:** 1
Schools: 7
3 Primary; 2 Middle; 1 High; 1 Other Level
6 Regular; 0 Special Education; 0 Vocational; 1 Alternative
0 Magnet; 0 Charter; 5 Title I Eligible; 5 School-wide Title I
Students: 3,437 (51.2% male; 48.7% female)
Individual Education Program: 430 (12.5%);
English Language Learner: 149 (4.3%); Migrant: 5 (0.1%)
Eligible for Free Lunch Program: 1,229 (35.8%)
Eligible for Reduced-Price Lunch Program: 380 (11.1%)
Teachers: 215.9 (15.9 to 1)
Librarians/Media Specialists: 2.1 (1,636.7 to 1)
Guidance Counselors: 4.1 (838.3 to 1)
Current Spending: ($ per student per year):
Total: $6,007; Instruction: $3,765; Support Services: $1,884
Enrollment, Drop-out Rates and Diploma Recipients by Race/Ethnicity

Category	Total	White	Black	Asian	AIAN	Hisp.
Enrollment (%)	100.0	76.6	4.1	0.2	0.4	18.7
Drop-out Rate (%)	4.5	4.6	2.2	0.0	0.0	5.0
H.S. Diplomas (#)	196	170	10	0	1	15

Burleson ISD
1160 SW Wilshire Blvd • Burleson, TX 76028-5719
(817) 447-5730 • http://www.burlesonisd.net/
Grade Span: PK-12; **Agency Type:** 1
Schools: 11
7 Primary; 2 Middle; 2 High; 0 Other Level
10 Regular; 0 Special Education; 0 Vocational; 1 Alternative
0 Magnet; 0 Charter; 5 Title I Eligible; 5 School-wide Title I
Students: 7,279 (53.6% male; 46.3% female)
Individual Education Program: 593 (8.1%);
English Language Learner: 45 (0.6%); Migrant: 2 (<0.1%)
Eligible for Free Lunch Program: 965 (13.3%)
Eligible for Reduced-Price Lunch Program: 497 (6.8%)
Teachers: 444.9 (16.4 to 1)
Librarians/Media Specialists: 5.0 (1,455.8 to 1)
Guidance Counselors: 12.5 (582.3 to 1)
Current Spending: ($ per student per year):
Total: $6,206; Instruction: $3,947; Support Services: $1,937
Enrollment, Drop-out Rates and Diploma Recipients by Race/Ethnicity

Category	Total	White	Black	Asian	AIAN	Hisp.
Enrollment (%)	100.0	89.4	1.4	0.5	0.6	8.1
Drop-out Rate (%)	1.1	1.2	0.0	0.0	0.0	0.0
H.S. Diplomas (#)	413	387	1	3	1	21

Cleburne ISD
103 S Walnut St • Cleburne, TX 76033-5422
(817) 202-1100 • http://www.cleburne.k12.tx.us/
Grade Span: PK-12; **Agency Type:** 1
Schools: 11
6 Primary; 2 Middle; 2 High; 1 Other Level
9 Regular; 0 Special Education; 0 Vocational; 2 Alternative
0 Magnet; 0 Charter; 8 Title I Eligible; 4 School-wide Title I
Students: 6,413 (50.5% male; 49.4% female)
Individual Education Program: 793 (12.4%);
English Language Learner: 729 (11.4%); Migrant: 7 (0.1%)
Eligible for Free Lunch Program: 2,429 (37.9%)
Eligible for Reduced-Price Lunch Program: 467 (7.3%)
Teachers: 423.9 (15.1 to 1)
Librarians/Media Specialists: 2.0 (3,206.5 to 1)
Guidance Counselors: 15.0 (427.5 to 1)
Current Spending: ($ per student per year):
Total: $6,466; Instruction: $4,162; Support Services: $1,959
Enrollment, Drop-out Rates and Diploma Recipients by Race/Ethnicity

Category	Total	White	Black	Asian	AIAN	Hisp.
Enrollment (%)	100.0	64.5	5.4	0.9	0.3	28.9
Drop-out Rate (%)	2.0	1.2	2.2	0.0	0.0	4.7
H.S. Diplomas (#)	311	235	15	2	0	59

Joshua ISD

310 E 18th St • Joshua, TX 76058-3110
Mailing Address: PO Box 40 • Joshua, TX 76058-0040
(817) 558-3703
Grade Span: PK-12; **Agency Type:** 1
Schools: 8
   3 Primary; 2 Middle; 2 High; 1 Other Level
   6 Regular; 0 Special Education; 0 Vocational; 2 Alternative
   0 Magnet; 0 Charter; 3 Title I Eligible; 3 School-wide Title I
Students: 4,427 (51.7% male; 48.2% female)
   Individual Education Program: 550 (12.4%);
   English Language Learner: 136 (3.1%); Migrant: 4 (0.1%)
   Eligible for Free Lunch Program: 1,402 (31.7%)
   Eligible for Reduced-Price Lunch Program: 392 (8.9%)
Teachers: 310.3 (14.3 to 1)
Librarians/Media Specialists: 5.0 (885.4 to 1)
Guidance Counselors: 10.0 (442.7 to 1)
Current Spending: ($ per student per year):
   Total: $6,442; Instruction: $4,154; Support Services: $1,958
Enrollment, Drop-out Rates and Diploma Recipients by Race/Ethnicity

Category	Total	White	Black	Asian	AIAN	Hisp.
Enrollment (%)	100.0	86.1	1.1	0.4	0.3	12.2
Drop-out Rate (%)	5.2	5.2	16.7	0.0	0.0	4.7
H.S. Diplomas (#)	249	214	4	5	1	25

Venus ISD

401 S Hickory St • Venus, TX 76084-0364
Mailing Address: PO Box 364 • Venus, TX 76084-0364
(972) 366-3448
Grade Span: PK-12; **Agency Type:** 1
Schools: 5
   2 Primary; 1 Middle; 2 High; 0 Other Level
   4 Regular; 0 Special Education; 0 Vocational; 1 Alternative
   0 Magnet; 0 Charter; 4 Title I Eligible; 4 School-wide Title I
Students: 1,826 (53.7% male; 46.2% female)
   Individual Education Program: 407 (22.3%);
   English Language Learner: 191 (10.5%); Migrant: 196 (10.7%)
   Eligible for Free Lunch Program: 905 (49.6%)
   Eligible for Reduced-Price Lunch Program: 245 (13.4%)
Teachers: 132.0 (13.8 to 1)
Librarians/Media Specialists: 1.0 (1,826.0 to 1)
Guidance Counselors: 4.0 (456.5 to 1)
Current Spending: ($ per student per year):
   Total: $6,185; Instruction: $3,890; Support Services: $1,874
Enrollment, Drop-out Rates and Diploma Recipients by Race/Ethnicity

Category	Total	White	Black	Asian	AIAN	Hisp.
Enrollment (%)	100.0	61.2	2.7	2.9	0.4	32.7
Drop-out Rate (%)	0.6	0.9	0.0	0.0	0.0	0.0
H.S. Diplomas (#)	100	61	3	5	1	30

Kaufman County

Crandall ISD

300 W Lewis St • Crandall, TX 75114-0128
Mailing Address: PO Box 128 • Crandall, TX 75114-0128
(972) 427-8004 • http://www.crandall-isd.net/
Grade Span: PK-12; **Agency Type:** 1
Schools: 5
   2 Primary; 1 Middle; 1 High; 1 Other Level
   4 Regular; 0 Special Education; 0 Vocational; 1 Alternative
   0 Magnet; 0 Charter; 2 Title I Eligible; 2 School-wide Title I
Students: 2,079 (51.8% male; 48.1% female)
   Individual Education Program: 267 (12.8%);
   English Language Learner: 52 (2.5%); Migrant: 0 (0.0%)
   Eligible for Free Lunch Program: 353 (17.0%)
   Eligible for Reduced-Price Lunch Program: 88 (4.2%)
Teachers: 141.9 (14.7 to 1)
Librarians/Media Specialists: 4.0 (519.8 to 1)
Guidance Counselors: 4.0 (519.8 to 1)
Current Spending: ($ per student per year):
   Total: $6,966; Instruction: $4,158; Support Services: $2,528
Enrollment, Drop-out Rates and Diploma Recipients by Race/Ethnicity

Category	Total	White	Black	Asian	AIAN	Hisp.
Enrollment (%)	100.0	85.3	4.3	0.3	0.6	9.4
Drop-out Rate (%)	0.9	0.6	3.4	0.0	0.0	3.6
H.S. Diplomas (#)	122	112	4	1	0	5

Forney ISD

600 S Bois D'arc St • Forney, TX 75126-9682
(972) 564-4055 • http://forney.ednet10.net/prod_site/index.html
Grade Span: PK-12; **Agency Type:** 1
Schools: 7
   4 Primary; 1 Middle; 1 High; 1 Other Level
   6 Regular; 0 Special Education; 0 Vocational; 1 Alternative
   0 Magnet; 0 Charter; 5 Title I Eligible; 0 School-wide Title I

Students: 3,805 (51.7% male; 48.2% female)
   Individual Education Program: 469 (12.3%);
   English Language Learner: 85 (2.2%); Migrant: 12 (0.3%)
   Eligible for Free Lunch Program: 382 (10.0%)
   Eligible for Reduced-Price Lunch Program: 113 (3.0%)
Teachers: 256.8 (14.8 to 1)
Librarians/Media Specialists: 2.4 (1,585.4 to 1)
Guidance Counselors: 8.0 (475.6 to 1)
Current Spending: ($ per student per year):
   Total: $6,735; Instruction: $3,978; Support Services: $2,424
Enrollment, Drop-out Rates and Diploma Recipients by Race/Ethnicity

Category	Total	White	Black	Asian	AIAN	Hisp.
Enrollment (%)	100.0	81.0	5.9	0.7	0.7	11.8
Drop-out Rate (%)	0.2	0.1	0.0	0.0	0.0	1.8
H.S. Diplomas (#)	176	158	10	0	0	8

Kaufman ISD

1000 S Houston St • Kaufman, TX 75142-2298
(972) 932-2622 • http://kaufman.ednet10.net/
Grade Span: PK-12; **Agency Type:** 1
Schools: 7
   3 Primary; 2 Middle; 2 High; 0 Other Level
   6 Regular; 0 Special Education; 0 Vocational; 1 Alternative
   0 Magnet; 0 Charter; 4 Title I Eligible; 4 School-wide Title I
Students: 3,407 (50.4% male; 49.5% female)
   Individual Education Program: 431 (12.7%);
   English Language Learner: 416 (12.2%); Migrant: 28 (0.8%)
   Eligible for Free Lunch Program: 1,342 (39.4%)
   Eligible for Reduced-Price Lunch Program: 238 (7.0%)
Teachers: 231.3 (14.7 to 1)
Librarians/Media Specialists: 1.1 (3,097.3 to 1)
Guidance Counselors: 4.8 (709.8 to 1)
Current Spending: ($ per student per year):
   Total: $6,690; Instruction: $4,101; Support Services: $2,293
Enrollment, Drop-out Rates and Diploma Recipients by Race/Ethnicity

Category	Total	White	Black	Asian	AIAN	Hisp.
Enrollment (%)	100.0	62.1	6.8	0.7	0.7	29.8
Drop-out Rate (%)	1.6	1.6	1.7	0.0	0.0	1.8
H.S. Diplomas (#)	155	109	16	2	0	28

Kemp ISD

202 W 17th St • Kemp, TX 75143-9155
(903) 498-1314
Grade Span: PK-12; **Agency Type:** 1
Schools: 4
   2 Primary; 1 Middle; 1 High; 0 Other Level
   4 Regular; 0 Special Education; 0 Vocational; 0 Alternative
   0 Magnet; 0 Charter; 3 Title I Eligible; 3 School-wide Title I
Students: 1,708 (53.2% male; 46.7% female)
   Individual Education Program: 248 (14.5%);
   English Language Learner: 30 (1.8%); Migrant: 0 (0.0%)
   Eligible for Free Lunch Program: 594 (34.8%)
   Eligible for Reduced-Price Lunch Program: 110 (6.4%)
Teachers: 116.6 (14.6 to 1)
Librarians/Media Specialists: 2.0 (854.0 to 1)
Guidance Counselors: 4.0 (427.0 to 1)
Current Spending: ($ per student per year):
   Total: $6,852; Instruction: $3,906; Support Services: $2,608
Enrollment, Drop-out Rates and Diploma Recipients by Race/Ethnicity

Category	Total	White	Black	Asian	AIAN	Hisp.
Enrollment (%)	100.0	89.2	3.6	0.1	0.9	6.2
Drop-out Rate (%)	2.6	2.4	0.0	0.0	50.0	4.8
H.S. Diplomas (#)	82	74	4	0	0	4

Mabank ISD

124 E Market St • Mabank, TX 75147-8377
(903) 887-9311
Grade Span: PK-12; **Agency Type:** 1
Schools: 6
   3 Primary; 1 Middle; 1 High; 1 Other Level
   5 Regular; 0 Special Education; 0 Vocational; 1 Alternative
   0 Magnet; 0 Charter; 3 Title I Eligible; 3 School-wide Title I
Students: 3,259 (52.1% male; 47.8% female)
   Individual Education Program: 522 (16.0%);
   English Language Learner: 45 (1.4%); Migrant: 0 (0.0%)
   Eligible for Free Lunch Program: 1,356 (41.6%)
   Eligible for Reduced-Price Lunch Program: 305 (9.4%)
Teachers: 229.6 (14.2 to 1)
Librarians/Media Specialists: 5.0 (651.8 to 1)
Guidance Counselors: 6.7 (486.4 to 1)
Current Spending: ($ per student per year):
   Total: $6,743; Instruction: $4,145; Support Services: $2,246

Enrollment, Drop-out Rates and Diploma Recipients by Race/Ethnicity

Category	Total	White	Black	Asian	AIAN	Hisp.
Enrollment (%)	100.0	88.2	2.3	0.7	0.5	8.3
Drop-out Rate (%)	1.4	1.1	0.0	0.0	0.0	8.2
H.S. Diplomas (#)	177	160	5	0	2	10

Terrell ISD

700 N Catherine St • Terrell, TX 75160-2659
(972) 563-7504
Grade Span: PK-12; **Agency Type:** 1
Schools: 7
  3 Primary; 2 Middle; 1 High; 1 Other Level
  6 Regular; 1 Special Education; 0 Vocational; 0 Alternative
  0 Magnet; 0 Charter; 6 Title I Eligible; 6 School-wide Title I
Students: 4,175 (52.7% male; 47.2% female)
  Individual Education Program: 660 (15.8%);
  English Language Learner: 519 (12.4%); Migrant: 15 (0.4%)
  Eligible for Free Lunch Program: 2,184 (52.3%)
  Eligible for Reduced-Price Lunch Program: 283 (6.8%)
Teachers: 298.5 (14.0 to 1)
Librarians/Media Specialists: 6.0 (695.7 to 1)
Guidance Counselors: 9.0 (463.8 to 1)
Current Spending: ($ per student per year):
  Total: $7,319; Instruction: $4,348; Support Services: $2,643

Enrollment, Drop-out Rates and Diploma Recipients by Race/Ethnicity

Category	Total	White	Black	Asian	AIAN	Hisp.
Enrollment (%)	100.0	41.7	32.3	1.4	0.3	24.3
Drop-out Rate (%)	3.5	3.0	2.8	0.0	0.0	6.7
H.S. Diplomas (#)	208	102	80	0	0	26

Kendall County

Boerne ISD

123 W John's Rd • Boerne, TX 78006-2023
(830) 249-5000 • http://www.boerne-isd.net/
Grade Span: PK-12; **Agency Type:** 1
Schools: 9
  4 Primary; 2 Middle; 1 High; 2 Other Level
  7 Regular; 0 Special Education; 0 Vocational; 2 Alternative
  0 Magnet; 0 Charter; 3 Title I Eligible; 0 School-wide Title I
Students: 5,380 (52.1% male; 47.8% female)
  Individual Education Program: 706 (13.1%);
  English Language Learner: 195 (3.6%); Migrant: 1 (<0.1%)
  Eligible for Free Lunch Program: 730 (13.6%)
  Eligible for Reduced-Price Lunch Program: 261 (4.9%)
Teachers: 384.8 (14.0 to 1)
Librarians/Media Specialists: 7.0 (768.6 to 1)
Guidance Counselors: 12.0 (448.3 to 1)
Current Spending: ($ per student per year):
  Total: $7,096; Instruction: $4,344; Support Services: $2,453

Enrollment, Drop-out Rates and Diploma Recipients by Race/Ethnicity

Category	Total	White	Black	Asian	AIAN	Hisp.
Enrollment (%)	100.0	79.5	0.6	0.6	0.3	19.0
Drop-out Rate (%)	0.6	0.7	0.0	0.0	0.0	0.4
H.S. Diplomas (#)	353	285	2	0	0	66

Kerr County

Ingram ISD

510 College St • Ingram, TX 78025-4100
(830) 367-5517
Grade Span: PK-12; **Agency Type:** 1
Schools: 3
  1 Primary; 1 Middle; 1 High; 0 Other Level
  3 Regular; 0 Special Education; 0 Vocational; 0 Alternative
  0 Magnet; 0 Charter; 3 Title I Eligible; 3 School-wide Title I
Students: 1,513 (51.1% male; 48.8% female)
  Individual Education Program: 169 (11.2%);
  English Language Learner: 109 (7.2%); Migrant: 4 (0.3%)
  Eligible for Free Lunch Program: 709 (46.9%)
  Eligible for Reduced-Price Lunch Program: 153 (10.1%)
Teachers: 123.5 (12.3 to 1)
Librarians/Media Specialists: 1.1 (1,375.5 to 1)
Guidance Counselors: 3.1 (488.1 to 1)
Current Spending: ($ per student per year):
  Total: $7,613; Instruction: $4,703; Support Services: $2,487

Enrollment, Drop-out Rates and Diploma Recipients by Race/Ethnicity

Category	Total	White	Black	Asian	AIAN	Hisp.
Enrollment (%)	100.0	67.4	1.5	1.0	0.5	29.6
Drop-out Rate (%)	2.9	2.4	0.0	0.0	0.0	4.8
H.S. Diplomas (#)	87	73	0	0	0	14

Kerrville ISD

1009 Barnett St • Kerrville, TX 78028-4614
(830) 257-2200 • http://www.kerrvilleisd.net/
Grade Span: PK-12; **Agency Type:** 1
Schools: 12
  6 Primary; 2 Middle; 1 High; 3 Other Level
  9 Regular; 0 Special Education; 0 Vocational; 3 Alternative
  0 Magnet; 0 Charter; 6 Title I Eligible; 6 School-wide Title I
Students: 4,771 (51.9% male; 48.0% female)
  Individual Education Program: 646 (13.5%);
  English Language Learner: 180 (3.8%); Migrant: 7 (0.1%)
  Eligible for Free Lunch Program: 1,731 (36.3%)
  Eligible for Reduced-Price Lunch Program: 428 (9.0%)
Teachers: 335.8 (14.2 to 1)
Librarians/Media Specialists: 2.0 (2,385.5 to 1)
Guidance Counselors: 14.1 (338.4 to 1)
Current Spending: ($ per student per year):
  Total: $6,527; Instruction: $4,137; Support Services: $2,115

Enrollment, Drop-out Rates and Diploma Recipients by Race/Ethnicity

Category	Total	White	Black	Asian	AIAN	Hisp.
Enrollment (%)	100.0	58.2	4.0	0.7	0.5	36.6
Drop-out Rate (%)	5.3	3.4	7.7	0.0	0.0	9.5
H.S. Diplomas (#)	302	221	6	4	2	69

Kleberg County

Kingsville ISD

207 N Third St • Kingsville, TX 78363-4401
Mailing Address: PO Box 871 • Kingsville, TX 78364-0871
(361) 592-3387 • http://www.kvisd.esc2.net/
Grade Span: PK-12; **Agency Type:** 1
Schools: 14
  7 Primary; 2 Middle; 3 High; 2 Other Level
  10 Regular; 1 Special Education; 0 Vocational; 3 Alternative
  0 Magnet; 0 Charter; 7 Title I Eligible; 7 School-wide Title I
Students: 4,544 (52.0% male; 47.9% female)
  Individual Education Program: 675 (14.9%);
  English Language Learner: 487 (10.7%); Migrant: 143 (3.1%)
  Eligible for Free Lunch Program: 2,564 (56.4%)
  Eligible for Reduced-Price Lunch Program: 433 (9.5%)
Teachers: 304.9 (14.9 to 1)
Librarians/Media Specialists: 5.0 (908.8 to 1)
Guidance Counselors: 16.3 (278.8 to 1)
Current Spending: ($ per student per year):
  Total: $7,378; Instruction: $4,467; Support Services: $2,543

Enrollment, Drop-out Rates and Diploma Recipients by Race/Ethnicity

Category	Total	White	Black	Asian	AIAN	Hisp.
Enrollment (%)	100.0	14.5	4.4	0.9	0.2	79.9
Drop-out Rate (%)	4.6	3.3	5.8	0.0	0.0	5.0
H.S. Diplomas (#)	358	77	12	4	0	265

Lamar County

North Lamar ISD

3201 Lewis Ln • Paris, TX 75462-2092
(903) 737-2000 • http://www.northlamar.net/
Grade Span: PK-12; **Agency Type:** 1
Schools: 7
  3 Primary; 2 Middle; 1 High; 0 Other Level
  6 Regular; 0 Special Education; 0 Vocational; 0 Alternative
  0 Magnet; 0 Charter; 4 Title I Eligible; 4 School-wide Title I
Students: 3,182 (51.7% male; 48.2% female)
  Individual Education Program: 466 (14.6%);
  English Language Learner: 27 (0.8%); Migrant: 20 (0.6%)
  Eligible for Free Lunch Program: 881 (27.7%)
  Eligible for Reduced-Price Lunch Program: 159 (5.0%)
Teachers: 231.0 (13.8 to 1)
Librarians/Media Specialists: 3.0 (1,060.7 to 1)
Guidance Counselors: 6.5 (489.5 to 1)
Current Spending: ($ per student per year):
  Total: $5,968; Instruction: $3,939; Support Services: $1,671

Enrollment, Drop-out Rates and Diploma Recipients by Race/Ethnicity

Category	Total	White	Black	Asian	AIAN	Hisp.
Enrollment (%)	100.0	89.5	5.2	0.5	1.4	3.4
Drop-out Rate (%)	2.4	2.3	2.9	0.0	10.0	0.0
H.S. Diplomas (#)	203	183	10	2	3	5

Paris ISD

1920 Clarksville • Paris, TX 75460-1159
(903) 737-7473 • http://www.parisisd.net/
Grade Span: PK-12; **Agency Type:** 1
Schools: 9
  3 Primary; 1 Middle; 2 High; 3 Other Level
  7 Regular; 0 Special Education; 1 Vocational; 1 Alternative
  0 Magnet; 0 Charter; 3 Title I Eligible; 3 School-wide Title I

Students: 3,945   (51.4% male; 48.5% female)
  Individual Education Program: 613 (15.5%);
  English Language Learner: 119 (3.0%); Migrant: 84 (2.1%)
  Eligible for Free Lunch Program: 2,194 (55.6%)
  Eligible for Reduced-Price Lunch Program: 250 (6.3%)
Teachers: 305.0 (12.9 to 1)
Librarians/Media Specialists: 3.6 (1,095.8 to 1)
Guidance Counselors: 10.7 (368.7 to 1)
Current Spending: ($ per student per year):
  Total: $7,346; Instruction: $4,596; Support Services: $2,306
Enrollment, Drop-out Rates and Diploma Recipients by Race/Ethnicity

Category	Total	White	Black	Asian	AIAN	Hisp.
Enrollment (%)	100.0	50.4	41.3	0.6	1.4	6.4
Drop-out Rate (%)	1.3	1.0	1.8	0.0	0.0	0.0
H.S. Diplornas (#)	175	85	87	1	0	2

Lampasas County

Lampasas ISD

207 W 8th St • Lampasas, TX 76550-3125
(512) 556-6224 • http://www.lampasas.k12.tx.us/
Grade Span: PK-12; **Agency Type:** 1
Schools: 4
  2 Primary; 1 Middle; 1 High; 0 Other Level
  4 Regular; 0 Special Education; 0 Vocational; 0 Alternative
  0 Magnet; 0 Charter; 3 Title I Eligible; 3 School-wide Title I
Students: 3,250   (52.6% male; 47.3% female)
  Individual Education Program: 481 (14.8%);
  English Language Learner: 91 (2.8%); Migrant: 71 (2.2%)
  Eligible for Free Lunch Program: 1,129 (34.7%)
  Eligible for Reduced-Price Lunch Program: 276 (8.5%)
Teachers: 219.7 (14.8 to 1)
Librarians/Media Specialists: 4.0 (812.5 to 1)
Guidance Counselors: 5.0 (650.0 to 1)
Current Spending: ($ per student per year):
  Total: $6,520; Instruction: $3,925; Support Services: $2,270
Enrollment, Drop-out Rates and Diploma Recipients by Race/Ethnicity

Category	Total	White	Black	Asian	AIAN	Hisp.
Enrollment (%)	100.0	74.6	4.4	0.8	1.1	19.1
Drop-out Rate (%)	5.7	5.3	2.9	0.0	0.0	8.8
H.S. Diplomas (#)	212	163	11	4	2	32

Lee County

Giddings ISD

2249 N Main • Giddings, TX 78942-0389
Mailing Address: PO Box 389 2249 N Main • Giddings, TX 78942-0389
(979) 542-2854 • http://www.giddings.txed.net/
Grade Span: PK-12; **Agency Type:** 1
Schools: 5
  1 Primary; 2 Middle; 2 High; 0 Other Level
  4 Regular; 0 Special Education; 0 Vocational; 1 Alternative
  0 Magnet; 0 Charter; 5 Title I Eligible; 5 School-wide Title I
Students: 1,825   (50.8% male; 49.1% female)
  Individual Education Program: 183 (10.0%);
  English Language Learner: 227 (12.4%); Migrant: 19 (1.0%)
  Eligible for Free Lunch Program: 699 (38.3%)
  Eligible for Reduced-Price Lunch Program: 130 (7.1%)
Teachers: 140.7 (13.0 to 1)
Librarians/Media Specialists: 3.0 (608.3 to 1)
Guidance Counselors: 5.0 (365.0 to 1)
Current Spending: ($ per student per year):
  Total: $7,424; Instruction: $4,565; Support Services: $2,450
Enrollment, Drop-out Rates and Diploma Recipients by Race/Ethnicity

Category	Total	White	Black	Asian	AIAN	Hisp.
Enrollment (%)	100.0	44.8	14.2	0.4	0.2	40.5
Drop-out Rate (%)	0.4	0.0	2.7	0.0	n/a	0.0
H.S. Diplomas (#)	123	75	15	2	0	31

Liberty County

Cleveland ISD

316 E Dallas St • Cleveland, TX 77327-4709
(281) 592-8717
Grade Span: PK-12; **Agency Type:** 1
Schools: 8
  3 Primary; 2 Middle; 2 High; 1 Other Level
  6 Regular; 0 Special Education; 0 Vocational; 2 Alternative
  0 Magnet; 0 Charter; 6 Title I Eligible; 6 School-wide Title I
Students: 3,329   (50.4% male; 49.5% female)
  Individual Education Program: 368 (11.1%);
  English Language Learner: 504 (15.1%); Migrant: 15 (0.5%)
  Eligible for Free Lunch Program: 1,812 (54.4%)
  Eligible for Reduced-Price Lunch Program: 243 (7.3%)
Teachers: 215.8 (15.4 to 1)

Librarians/Media Specialists: 4.5 (739.8 to 1)
Guidance Counselors: 5.1 (652.7 to 1)
Current Spending: ($ per student per year):
  Total: $7,021; Instruction: $3,910; Support Services: $2,755
Enrollment, Drop-out Rates and Diploma Recipients by Race/Ethnicity

Category	Total	White	Black	Asian	AIAN	Hisp.
Enrollment (%)	100.0	54.6	15.6	0.6	0.4	28.8
Drop-out Rate (%)	3.0	3.1	2.5	0.0	0.0	3.6
H.S. Diplomas (#)	162	97	37	1	3	24

Dayton ISD

209 W Hwy 90 • Dayton, TX 77535-2639
Mailing Address: PO Box 248 • Dayton, TX 77535-0248
(936) 258-2667 • http://www.dayton.isd.esc4.net/
Grade Span: PK-12; **Agency Type:** 1
Schools: 8
  2 Primary; 3 Middle; 2 High; 1 Other Level
  6 Regular; 0 Special Education; 0 Vocational; 2 Alternative
  0 Magnet; 0 Charter; 5 Title I Eligible; 5 School-wide Title I
Students: 5,116   (52.0% male; 47.9% female)
  Individual Education Program: 603 (11.8%);
  English Language Learner: 232 (4.5%); Migrant: 0 (0.0%)
  Eligible for Free Lunch Program: 1,798 (35.1%)
  Eligible for Reduced-Price Lunch Program: 428 (8.4%)
Teachers: 298.3 (17.2 to 1)
Librarians/Media Specialists: 5.0 (1,023.2 to 1)
Guidance Counselors: 7.0 (730.9 to 1)
Current Spending: ($ per student per year):
  Total: $5,920; Instruction: $3,509; Support Services: $2,082
Enrollment, Drop-out Rates and Diploma Recipients by Race/Ethnicity

Category	Total	White	Black	Asian	AIAN	Hisp.
Enrollment (%)	100.0	74.2	10.7	0.7	0.2	14.3
Drop-out Rate (%)	4.4	4.4	2.0	0.0	0.0	6.8
H.S. Diplomas (#)	247	202	26	2	0	17

Liberty ISD

1600 Grand Ave • Liberty, TX 77575-4725
(936) 336-7213 • http://www.liberty.isd.esc4.net/
Grade Span: PK-12; **Agency Type:** 1
Schools: 6
  2 Primary; 1 Middle; 1 High; 2 Other Level
  4 Regular; 1 Special Education; 0 Vocational; 1 Alternative
  0 Magnet; 0 Charter; 4 Title I Eligible; 4 School-wide Title I
Students: 2,347   (50.4% male; 49.5% female)
  Individual Education Program: 294 (12.5%);
  English Language Learner: 211 (9.0%); Migrant: 0 (0.0%)
  Eligible for Free Lunch Program: 1,005 (42.8%)
  Eligible for Reduced-Price Lunch Program: 148 (6.3%)
Teachers: 164.9 (14.2 to 1)
Librarians/Media Specialists: 2.0 (1,173.5 to 1)
Guidance Counselors: 6.0 (391.2 to 1)
Current Spending: ($ per student per year):
  Total: $7,645; Instruction: $4,606; Support Services: $2,651
Enrollment, Drop-out Rates and Diploma Recipients by Race/Ethnicity

Category	Total	White	Black	Asian	AIAN	Hisp.
Enrollment (%)	100.0	58.2	21.2	0.6	0.1	19.8
Drop-out Rate (%)	1.1	1.1	0.7	0.0	0.0	1.6
H.S. Diplomas (#)	153	93	34	1	1	24

Tarkington ISD

F M 163 • Cleveland, TX 77327-8811
Mailing Address: Rt 6 Box 130 • Cleveland, TX 77327-8811
(281) 592-8781
Grade Span: PK-12; **Agency Type:** 1
Schools: 4
  2 Primary; 1 Middle; 1 High; 0 Other Level
  4 Regular; 0 Special Education; 0 Vocational; 0 Alternative
  0 Magnet; 0 Charter; 2 Title I Eligible; 2 School-wide Title I
Students: 1,857   (51.4% male; 48.5% female)
  Individual Education Program: 173 (9.3%);
  English Language Learner: 10 (0.5%); Migrant: 0 (0.0%)
  Eligible for Free Lunch Program: 431 (23.2%)
  Eligible for Reduced-Price Lunch Program: 107 (5.8%)
Teachers: 136.2 (13.6 to 1)
Librarians/Media Specialists: 2.2 (844.1 to 1)
Guidance Counselors: 4.0 (464.3 to 1)
Current Spending: ($ per student per year):
  Total: $6,244; Instruction: $3,904; Support Services: $1,980
Enrollment, Drop-out Rates and Diploma Recipients by Race/Ethnicity

Category	Total	White	Black	Asian	AIAN	Hisp.
Enrollment (%)	100.0	95.4	0.9	0.0	0.3	3.4
Drop-out Rate (%)	1.6	1.7	0.0	n/a	n/a	0.0
H.S. Diplomas (#)	120	118	1	0	0	1

Limestone County

Groesbeck ISD
1202 N Ellis • Groesbeck, TX 76642-0559
Mailing Address: PO Box 559 • Groesbeck, TX 76642-0559
(254) 729-4100
Grade Span: PK-12; **Agency Type:** 1
Schools: 5
  1 Primary; 1 Middle; 2 High; 1 Other Level
  3 Regular; 0 Special Education; 0 Vocational; 2 Alternative
  0 Magnet; 0 Charter; 1 Title I Eligible; 1 School-wide Title I
Students: 1,656 (51.8% male; 48.1% female)
  Individual Education Program: 249 (15.0%);
  English Language Learner: 74 (4.5%); Migrant: 4 (0.2%)
  Eligible for Free Lunch Program: 723 (43.7%)
  Eligible for Reduced-Price Lunch Program: 126 (7.6%)
Teachers: 129.1 (12.8 to 1)
Librarians/Media Specialists: 3.0 (552.0 to 1)
Guidance Counselors: 3.0 (552.0 to 1)
Current Spending: ($ per student per year):
  Total: $8,120; Instruction: $4,780; Support Services: $2,978
Enrollment, Drop-out Rates and Diploma Recipients by Race/Ethnicity

Category	Total	White	Black	Asian	AIAN	Hisp.
Enrollment (%)	100.0	69.8	12.7	0.1	0.4	17.0
Drop-out Rate (%)	1.4	1.0	0.0	n/a	0.0	5.4
H.S. Diplomas (#)	113	85	14	0	1	13

Mexia ISD
405 E Milam • Mexia, TX 76667-2452
Mailing Address: PO Box 2000 • Mexia, TX 76667-2452
(254) 562-4000
Grade Span: PK-12; **Agency Type:** 1
Schools: 6
  2 Primary; 1 Middle; 2 High; 1 Other Level
  4 Regular; 0 Special Education; 0 Vocational; 2 Alternative
  0 Magnet; 0 Charter; 3 Title I Eligible; 3 School-wide Title I
Students: 2,336 (52.3% male; 47.6% female)
  Individual Education Program: 405 (17.3%);
  English Language Learner: 161 (6.9%); Migrant: 11 (0.5%)
  Eligible for Free Lunch Program: 1,279 (54.8%)
  Eligible for Reduced-Price Lunch Program: 167 (7.1%)
Teachers: 162.6 (14.4 to 1)
Librarians/Media Specialists: 3.0 (778.7 to 1)
Guidance Counselors: 4.0 (584.0 to 1)
Current Spending: ($ per student per year):
  Total: $8,034; Instruction: $5,062; Support Services: $2,623
Enrollment, Drop-out Rates and Diploma Recipients by Race/Ethnicity

Category	Total	White	Black	Asian	AIAN	Hisp.
Enrollment (%)	100.0	42.2	34.9	0.3	0.2	22.4
Drop-out Rate (%)	4.5	3.1	3.4	0.0	0.0	10.5
H.S. Diplomas (#)	124	64	47	0	0	13

Llano County

Llano ISD
200 E Lampasas • Llano, TX 78643-2734
(325) 247-4747 • http://www.llano.k12.tx.us/
Grade Span: PK-12; **Agency Type:** 1
Schools: 4
  2 Primary; 1 Middle; 1 High; 0 Other Level
  4 Regular; 0 Special Education; 0 Vocational; 0 Alternative
  0 Magnet; 0 Charter; 2 Title I Eligible; 2 School-wide Title I
Students: 1,916 (52.6% male; 47.3% female)
  Individual Education Program: 335 (17.5%);
  English Language Learner: 53 (2.8%); Migrant: 7 (0.4%)
  Eligible for Free Lunch Program: 635 (33.1%)
  Eligible for Reduced-Price Lunch Program: 202 (10.5%)
Teachers: 139.6 (13.7 to 1)
Librarians/Media Specialists: 2.5 (766.4 to 1)
Guidance Counselors: 4.0 (479.0 to 1)
Current Spending: ($ per student per year):
  Total: $8,539; Instruction: $5,226; Support Services: $2,915
Enrollment, Drop-out Rates and Diploma Recipients by Race/Ethnicity

Category	Total	White	Black	Asian	AIAN	Hisp.
Enrollment (%)	100.0	84.8	0.4	0.4	0.8	13.6
Drop-out Rate (%)	2.8	2.9	0.0	0.0	100.0	0.0
H.S. Diplomas (#)	92	81	1	0	0	10

Lubbock County

Frenship ISD
300 Main St • Wolfforth, TX 79382-0100
Mailing Address: PO Box 100 • Wolfforth, TX 79382-0100
(806) 866-9541 • http://www.frenship.k12.tx.us/
Grade Span: PK-12; **Agency Type:** 1
Schools: 9
  4 Primary; 2 Middle; 1 High; 2 Other Level
  7 Regular; 0 Special Education; 0 Vocational; 2 Alternative
  0 Magnet; 0 Charter; 4 Title I Eligible; 4 School-wide Title I
Students: 5,506 (50.6% male; 49.3% female)
  Individual Education Program: 648 (11.8%);
  English Language Learner: 117 (2.1%); Migrant: 23 (0.4%)
  Eligible for Free Lunch Program: 1,490 (27.1%)
  Eligible for Reduced-Price Lunch Program: 411 (7.5%)
Teachers: 364.7 (15.1 to 1)
Librarians/Media Specialists: 4.0 (1,376.5 to 1)
Guidance Counselors: 14.5 (379.7 to 1)
Current Spending: ($ per student per year):
  Total: $6,073; Instruction: $3,660; Support Services: $2,161
Enrollment, Drop-out Rates and Diploma Recipients by Race/Ethnicity

Category	Total	White	Black	Asian	AIAN	Hisp.
Enrollment (%)	100.0	65.0	4.8	1.8	0.5	28.0
Drop-out Rate (%)	1.0	0.9	1.8	0.0	0.0	1.5
H.S. Diplomas (#)	334	240	18	3	1	72

Lubbock ISD
1628 19th St • Lubbock, TX 79401-4895
(806) 766-1000 • http://www.lubbock.k12.tx.us/lbb/
Grade Span: PK-12; **Agency Type:** 1
Schools: 57
  39 Primary; 9 Middle; 5 High; 4 Other Level
  52 Regular; 1 Special Education; 0 Vocational; 4 Alternative
  0 Magnet; 0 Charter; 29 Title I Eligible; 29 School-wide Title I
Students: 29,020 (50.8% male; 49.1% female)
  Individual Education Program: 4,403 (15.2%);
  English Language Learner: 709 (2.4%); Migrant: 704 (2.5%)
  Eligible for Free Lunch Program: 13,309 (46.7%)
  Eligible for Reduced-Price Lunch Program: 2,552 (9.0%)
Teachers: 2,073.7 (13.7 to 1)
Librarians/Media Specialists: 31.7 (898.8 to 1)
Guidance Counselors: 72.0 (395.7 to 1)
Current Spending: ($ per student per year):
  Total: $6,991; Instruction: $4,388; Support Services: $2,308
Enrollment, Drop-out Rates and Diploma Recipients by Race/Ethnicity

Category	Total	White	Black	Asian	AIAN	Hisp.
Enrollment (%)	100.0	38.1	14.8	1.5	0.3	45.3
Drop-out Rate (%)	3.8	1.5	5.4	0.0	4.3	5.9
H.S. Diplomas (#)	1,737	894	232	26	2	583

Lubbock-Cooper ISD
16302 Loop 493 • Lubbock, TX 79423-9530
(806) 863-2282
Grade Span: PK-12; **Agency Type:** 1
Schools: 6
  2 Primary; 2 Middle; 1 High; 1 Other Level
  5 Regular; 0 Special Education; 0 Vocational; 1 Alternative
  0 Magnet; 0 Charter; 3 Title I Eligible; 3 School-wide Title I
Students: 2,408 (53.6% male; 46.3% female)
  Individual Education Program: 421 (17.5%);
  English Language Learner: 65 (2.7%); Migrant: 29 (1.2%)
  Eligible for Free Lunch Program: 831 (34.5%)
  Eligible for Reduced-Price Lunch Program: 198 (8.2%)
Teachers: 168.2 (14.3 to 1)
Librarians/Media Specialists: 4.0 (602.0 to 1)
Guidance Counselors: 7.0 (344.0 to 1)
Current Spending: ($ per student per year):
  Total: $6,929; Instruction: $4,092; Support Services: $2,354
Enrollment, Drop-out Rates and Diploma Recipients by Race/Ethnicity

Category	Total	White	Black	Asian	AIAN	Hisp.
Enrollment (%)	100.0	65.9	1.9	0.3	0.3	31.6
Drop-out Rate (%)	n/a	n/a	n/a	n/a	n/a	n/a
H.S. Diplomas (#)	111	88	0	0	0	23

Madison County

Madisonville Cons ISD
718 Bacon St • Madisonville, TX 77864-2540
Mailing Address: PO Box 879 • Madisonville, TX 77864-0879
(936) 348-2797 • http://www.madisonvilleisd.org/
Grade Span: PK-12; **Agency Type:** 1
Schools: 4
  2 Primary; 1 Middle; 1 High; 0 Other Level
  4 Regular; 0 Special Education; 0 Vocational; 0 Alternative

0 Magnet; 0 Charter; 3 Title I Eligible; 3 School-wide Title I
Students: 2,177   (52.1% male; 47.8% female)
   Individual Education Program: 270 (12.4%);
   English Language Learner: 239 (11.0%); Migrant: 30 (1.4%)
   Eligible for Free Lunch Program: 1,150 (52.8%)
   Eligible for Reduced-Price Lunch Program: 193 (8.9%)
Teachers: 150.9 (14.4 to 1)
Librarians/Media Specialists: 1.0 (2,177.0 to 1)
Guidance Counselors: 4.1 (531.0 to 1)
Current Spending: ($ per student per year):
   Total: $6,891; Instruction: $4,048; Support Services: $2,389
Enrollment, Drop-out Rates and Diploma Recipients by Race/Ethnicity

Category	Total	White	Black	Asian	AIAN	Hisp.
Enrollment (%)	100.0	56.0	21.9	0.4	0.2	21.5
Drop-out Rate (%)	2.2	1.2	4.2	0.0	0.0	3.6
H.S. Diplomas (#)	115	65	35	0	1	14

Matagorda County

Bay City ISD
520 7th St • Bay City, TX 77414-3610
(979) 245-5766
Grade Span: PK-12; **Agency Type:** 1
Schools: 8
   3 Primary; 3 Middle; 1 High; 1 Other Level
   7 Regular; 0 Special Education; 0 Vocational; 1 Alternative
   0 Magnet; 0 Charter; 7 Title I Eligible; 7 School-wide Title I
Students: 4,258   (51.5% male; 48.4% female)
   Individual Education Program: 586 (13.8%);
   English Language Learner: 293 (6.9%); Migrant: 16 (0.4%)
   Eligible for Free Lunch Program: 2,303 (54.1%)
   Eligible for Reduced-Price Lunch Program: 319 (7.5%)
Teachers: 278.9 (15.3 to 1)
Librarians/Media Specialists: 5.0 (851.6 to 1)
Guidance Counselors: 12.0 (354.8 to 1)
Current Spending: ($ per student per year):
   Total: $7,164; Instruction: $4,242; Support Services: $2,576
Enrollment, Drop-out Rates and Diploma Recipients by Race/Ethnicity

Category	Total	White	Black	Asian	AIAN	Hisp.
Enrollment (%)	100.0	35.7	18.4	0.9	0.1	44.9
Drop-out Rate (%)	2.2	1.3	3.2	0.0	n/a	2.7
H.S. Diplomas (#)	271	122	66	3	0	80

Palacios ISD
1209 12th St • Palacios, TX 77465-3799
(361) 972-5491 • http://www.palacios.k12.tx.us/
Grade Span: PK-12; **Agency Type:** 1
Schools: 5
   1 Primary; 2 Middle; 1 High; 1 Other Level
   4 Regular; 0 Special Education; 0 Vocational; 1 Alternative
   0 Magnet; 0 Charter; 4 Title I Eligible; 4 School-wide Title I
Students: 1,681   (50.7% male; 49.2% female)
   Individual Education Program: 170 (10.1%);
   English Language Learner: 230 (13.7%); Migrant: 16 (1.0%)
   Eligible for Free Lunch Program: 952 (56.6%)
   Eligible for Reduced-Price Lunch Program: 143 (8.5%)
Teachers: 124.8 (13.5 to 1)
Librarians/Media Specialists: 3.3 (509.4 to 1)
Guidance Counselors: 3.1 (542.3 to 1)
Current Spending: ($ per student per year):
   Total: $7,956; Instruction: $4,977; Support Services: $2,584
Enrollment, Drop-out Rates and Diploma Recipients by Race/Ethnicity

Category	Total	White	Black	Asian	AIAN	Hisp.
Enrollment (%)	100.0	27.4	4.2	13.1	0.2	55.0
Drop-out Rate (%)	2.1	1.3	0.0	3.5	0.0	2.2
H.S. Diplomas (#)	113	41	4	25	0	43

Maverick County

Eagle Pass ISD
1420 Eidson Rd • Eagle Pass, TX 78852-5604
(830) 773-5181 • http://www.eagle-pass.k12.tx.us/
Grade Span: PK-12; **Agency Type:** 1
Schools: 24
   18 Primary; 2 Middle; 3 High; 1 Other Level
   22 Regular; 0 Special Education; 0 Vocational; 2 Alternative
   0 Magnet; 0 Charter; 24 Title I Eligible; 24 School-wide Title I
Students: 13,496   (51.0% male; 48.9% female)
   Individual Education Program: 1,162 (8.6%);
   English Language Learner: 5,068 (37.6%); Migrant: 2,231 (16.5%)
   Eligible for Free Lunch Program: 9,551 (70.8%)
   Eligible for Reduced-Price Lunch Program: 1,153 (8.5%)
Teachers: 770.1 (17.5 to 1)
Librarians/Media Specialists: 3.2 (4,217.5 to 1)
Guidance Counselors: 33.2 (406.5 to 1)

Current Spending: ($ per student per year):
   Total: $6,587; Instruction: $3,977; Support Services: $2,131
Enrollment, Drop-out Rates and Diploma Recipients by Race/Ethnicity

Category	Total	White	Black	Asian	AIAN	Hisp.
Enrollment (%)	100.0	1.3	0.1	0.2	1.3	97.1
Drop-out Rate (%)	5.5	4.5	n/a	9.1	25.0	5.3
H.S. Diplomas (#)	582	12	0	2	1	567

McLennan County

China Spring ISD
6301 Sylvia St • Waco, TX 76708-5817
Mailing Address: PO Box 250 • China Spring, TX 76633-0250
(254) 836-1115
Grade Span: PK-12; **Agency Type:** 1
Schools: 8
   1 Primary; 2 Middle; 2 High; 2 Other Level
   4 Regular; 1 Special Education; 0 Vocational; 2 Alternative
   0 Magnet; 0 Charter; 1 Title I Eligible; 1 School-wide Title I
Students: 1,800   (48.6% male; 51.3% female)
   Individual Education Program: 352 (19.6%);
   English Language Learner: 12 (0.7%); Migrant: 0 (0.0%)
   Eligible for Free Lunch Program: 234 (13.0%)
   Eligible for Reduced-Price Lunch Program: 92 (5.1%)
Teachers: 109.2 (16.5 to 1)
Librarians/Media Specialists: 2.0 (900.0 to 1)
Guidance Counselors: 4.0 (450.0 to 1)
Current Spending: ($ per student per year):
   Total: $5,354; Instruction: $3,313; Support Services: $1,745
Enrollment, Drop-out Rates and Diploma Recipients by Race/Ethnicity

Category	Total	White	Black	Asian	AIAN	Hisp.
Enrollment (%)	100.0	87.1	1.3	0.5	1.3	9.8
Drop-out Rate (%)	0.6	0.6	0.0	0.0	0.0	0.0
H.S. Diplomas (#)	123	115	1	0	0	7

Connally ISD
200 Cadet Way • Waco, TX 76705-1199
(254) 296-6460 • http://www.connally.org/
Grade Span: PK-12; **Agency Type:** 1
Schools: 8
   3 Primary; 2 Middle; 1 High; 2 Other Level
   6 Regular; 0 Special Education; 0 Vocational; 2 Alternative
   0 Magnet; 0 Charter; 6 Title I Eligible; 6 School-wide Title I
Students: 2,634   (52.9% male; 47.0% female)
   Individual Education Program: 407 (15.5%);
   English Language Learner: 88 (3.3%); Migrant: 7 (0.3%)
   Eligible for Free Lunch Program: 1,166 (44.3%)
   Eligible for Reduced-Price Lunch Program: 293 (11.1%)
Teachers: 175.7 (15.0 to 1)
Librarians/Media Specialists: 5.0 (526.8 to 1)
Guidance Counselors: 5.5 (478.9 to 1)
Current Spending: ($ per student per year):
   Total: $7,750; Instruction: $4,552; Support Services: $2,733
Enrollment, Drop-out Rates and Diploma Recipients by Race/Ethnicity

Category	Total	White	Black	Asian	AIAN	Hisp.
Enrollment (%)	100.0	55.4	23.0	0.7	0.5	20.3
Drop-out Rate (%)	3.1	3.0	1.5	0.0	0.0	5.4
H.S. Diplomas (#)	147	92	26	2	1	26

La Vega ISD
3100 Bellmead Dr • Waco, TX 76705-3096
(254) 799-4963 • http://www.lavegaisd.org/
Grade Span: PK-12; **Agency Type:** 1
Schools: 8
   2 Primary; 2 Middle; 2 High; 2 Other Level
   6 Regular; 0 Special Education; 0 Vocational; 2 Alternative
   0 Magnet; 0 Charter; 4 Title I Eligible; 4 School-wide Title I
Students: 2,629   (51.0% male; 48.9% female)
   Individual Education Program: 381 (14.5%);
   English Language Learner: 232 (8.8%); Migrant: 48 (1.8%)
   Eligible for Free Lunch Program: 1,490 (56.7%)
   Eligible for Reduced-Price Lunch Program: 304 (11.6%)
Teachers: 187.0 (14.1 to 1)
Librarians/Media Specialists: 3.0 (876.3 to 1)
Guidance Counselors: 7.0 (375.6 to 1)
Current Spending: ($ per student per year):
   Total: $7,791; Instruction: $4,476; Support Services: $2,878
Enrollment, Drop-out Rates and Diploma Recipients by Race/Ethnicity

Category	Total	White	Black	Asian	AIAN	Hisp.
Enrollment (%)	100.0	40.6	23.4	1.0	0.3	34.8
Drop-out Rate (%)	8.3	8.4	2.7	25.0	0.0	13.8
H.S. Diplomas (#)	127	57	41	2	0	27

Lorena ISD

Lorena Isd • Lorena, TX 76655-9656
Mailing Address: PO Box 97 • Lorena, TX 76655-0097
(254) 857-3239
Grade Span: PK-12; **Agency Type:** 1
Schools: 6
  1 Primary; 1 Middle; 2 High; 2 Other Level
  3 Regular; 1 Special Education; 0 Vocational; 2 Alternative
  0 Magnet; 0 Charter; 1 Title I Eligible; 0 School-wide Title I
Students: 1,557 (54.7% male; 45.2% female)
  Individual Education Program: 266 (17.1%);
  English Language Learner: 9 (0.6%); Migrant: 0 (0.0%)
  Eligible for Free Lunch Program: 196 (12.6%)
  Eligible for Reduced-Price Lunch Program: 58 (3.7%)
Teachers: 95.4 (16.3 to 1)
Librarians/Media Specialists: 2.0 (778.5 to 1)
Guidance Counselors: 3.6 (432.5 to 1)
Current Spending: ($ per student per year):
  Total: $4,986; Instruction: $3,250; Support Services: $1,460
Enrollment, Drop-out Rates and Diploma Recipients by Race/Ethnicity

Category	Total	White	Black	Asian	AIAN	Hisp.
Enrollment (%)	100.0	90.1	0.7	0.3	0.1	8.8
Drop-out Rate (%)	1.4	1.5	0.0	0.0	0.0	0.0
H.S. Diplomas (#)	101	87	1	0	1	12

Midway ISD

1205 Foundation Dr • Waco, TX 76712-6821
(254) 761-5610 • http://www.midwayisd.org/
Grade Span: PK-12; **Agency Type:** 1
Schools: 9
  5 Primary; 0 Middle; 1 High; 3 Other Level
  8 Regular; 0 Special Education; 0 Vocational; 1 Alternative
  0 Magnet; 0 Charter; 4 Title I Eligible; 1 School-wide Title I
Students: 5,881 (51.0% male; 48.9% female)
  Individual Education Program: 604 (10.3%);
  English Language Learner: 98 (1.7%); Migrant: 0 (0.0%)
  Eligible for Free Lunch Program: 672 (11.4%)
  Eligible for Reduced-Price Lunch Program: 331 (5.6%)
Teachers: 361.8 (16.3 to 1)
Librarians/Media Specialists: 9.0 (653.4 to 1)
Guidance Counselors: 14.1 (417.1 to 1)
Current Spending: ($ per student per year):
  Total: $6,232; Instruction: $3,912; Support Services: $2,052
Enrollment, Drop-out Rates and Diploma Recipients by Race/Ethnicity

Category	Total	White	Black	Asian	AIAN	Hisp.
Enrollment (%)	100.0	76.6	8.2	3.4	0.4	11.3
Drop-out Rate (%)	0.8	0.6	0.9	3.7	0.0	1.9
H.S. Diplomas (#)	382	310	20	13	1	38

Robinson ISD

500 W Lyndale • Robinson, TX 76706-5505
(254) 662-0194
Grade Span: PK-12; **Agency Type:** 1
Schools: 7
  2 Primary; 2 Middle; 2 High; 0 Other Level
  5 Regular; 0 Special Education; 0 Vocational; 1 Alternative
  0 Magnet; 0 Charter; 5 Title I Eligible; 5 School-wide Title I
Students: 2,056 (52.3% male; 47.6% female)
  Individual Education Program: 312 (15.2%);
  English Language Learner: 15 (0.7%); Migrant: 10 (0.5%)
  Eligible for Free Lunch Program: 291 (14.2%)
  Eligible for Reduced-Price Lunch Program: 154 (7.5%)
Teachers: 156.0 (13.2 to 1)
Librarians/Media Specialists: 1.3 (1,581.5 to 1)
Guidance Counselors: 7.1 (289.6 to 1)
Current Spending: ($ per student per year):
  Total: $6,782; Instruction: $4,292; Support Services: $2,193
Enrollment, Drop-out Rates and Diploma Recipients by Race/Ethnicity

Category	Total	White	Black	Asian	AIAN	Hisp.
Enrollment (%)	100.0	82.1	3.9	0.5	0.5	13.0
Drop-out Rate (%)	0.4	0.2	0.0	0.0	0.0	1.9
H.S. Diplomas (#)	153	119	8	0	0	26

Waco ISD

501 Franklin • Waco, TX 76701-0027
Mailing Address: PO Box 27 • Waco, TX 76703-0027
(254) 755-9420 • http://www.wacoisd.org/
Grade Span: PK-12; **Agency Type:** 1
Schools: 37
  21 Primary; 6 Middle; 3 High; 6 Other Level
  32 Regular; 0 Special Education; 0 Vocational; 4 Alternative
  0 Magnet; 0 Charter; 30 Title I Eligible; 30 School-wide Title I
Students: 15,669 (51.2% male; 48.7% female)
  Individual Education Program: 2,172 (13.9%);
  English Language Learner: 1,816 (11.6%); Migrant: 21 (0.1%)

  Eligible for Free Lunch Program: 11,103 (70.9%)
  Eligible for Reduced-Price Lunch Program: 1,494 (9.5%)
Teachers: 1,041.0 (15.1 to 1)
Librarians/Media Specialists: 13.0 (1,205.3 to 1)
Guidance Counselors: 40.0 (391.7 to 1)
Current Spending: ($ per student per year):
  Total: $6,737; Instruction: $3,893; Support Services: $2,425
Enrollment, Drop-out Rates and Diploma Recipients by Race/Ethnicity

Category	Total	White	Black	Asian	AIAN	Hisp.
Enrollment (%)	100.0	16.9	36.9	0.4	0.1	45.8
Drop-out Rate (%)	8.1	6.6	7.2	5.0	14.3	9.8
H.S. Diplomas (#)	588	120	232	2	1	233

West ISD

801 N Reagan • West, TX 76691-1198
(254) 826-7500
Grade Span: PK-12; **Agency Type:** 1
Schools: 8
  1 Primary; 2 Middle; 2 High; 2 Other Level
  4 Regular; 0 Special Education; 0 Vocational; 3 Alternative
  0 Magnet; 0 Charter; 2 Title I Eligible; 2 School-wide Title I
Students: 1,551 (54.8% male; 45.1% female)
  Individual Education Program: 357 (23.0%);
  English Language Learner: 26 (1.7%); Migrant: 8 (0.5%)
  Eligible for Free Lunch Program: 422 (27.2%)
  Eligible for Reduced-Price Lunch Program: 130 (8.4%)
Teachers: 97.0 (16.0 to 1)
Librarians/Media Specialists: 2.0 (775.5 to 1)
Guidance Counselors: 4.0 (387.8 to 1)
Current Spending: ($ per student per year):
  Total: $5,710; Instruction: $3,404; Support Services: $1,937
Enrollment, Drop-out Rates and Diploma Recipients by Race/Ethnicity

Category	Total	White	Black	Asian	AIAN	Hisp.
Enrollment (%)	100.0	86.8	3.6	0.1	0.6	8.9
Drop-out Rate (%)	1.2	0.6	8.7	n/a	0.0	4.2
H.S. Diplomas (#)	140	131	3	0	0	6

Medina County

Devine ISD

205 W College • Devine, TX 78016-6080
(830) 663-3611
Grade Span: PK-12; **Agency Type:** 1
Schools: 5
  2 Primary; 1 Middle; 1 High; 1 Other Level
  4 Regular; 0 Special Education; 0 Vocational; 1 Alternative
  0 Magnet; 0 Charter; 3 Title I Eligible; 3 School-wide Title I
Students: 1,980 (50.6% male; 49.3% female)
  Individual Education Program: 251 (12.7%);
  English Language Learner: 67 (3.4%); Migrant: 2 (0.1%)
  Eligible for Free Lunch Program: 903 (45.6%)
  Eligible for Reduced-Price Lunch Program: 235 (11.9%)
Teachers: 139.9 (14.2 to 1)
Librarians/Media Specialists: 2.0 (990.0 to 1)
Guidance Counselors: 5.0 (396.0 to 1)
Current Spending: ($ per student per year):
  Total: $7,225; Instruction: $4,348; Support Services: $2,523
Enrollment, Drop-out Rates and Diploma Recipients by Race/Ethnicity

Category	Total	White	Black	Asian	AIAN	Hisp.
Enrollment (%)	100.0	46.5	1.4	0.1	0.3	51.7
Drop-out Rate (%)	2.7	0.7	0.0	0.0	0.0	5.2
H.S. Diplomas (#)	139	75	2	1	3	58

Hondo ISD

2604 Ave E • Hondo, TX 78861-3137
Mailing Address: PO Box 308 • Hondo, TX 78861-0308
(830) 426-3027
Grade Span: PK-12; **Agency Type:** 1
Schools: 5
  2 Primary; 1 Middle; 1 High; 1 Other Level
  4 Regular; 0 Special Education; 0 Vocational; 1 Alternative
  0 Magnet; 0 Charter; 4 Title I Eligible; 4 School-wide Title I
Students: 2,175 (51.6% male; 48.3% female)
  Individual Education Program: 256 (11.8%);
  English Language Learner: 79 (3.6%); Migrant: 16 (0.7%)
  Eligible for Free Lunch Program: 579 (26.6%)
  Eligible for Reduced-Price Lunch Program: 237 (10.9%)
Teachers: 171.0 (12.7 to 1)
Librarians/Media Specialists: 4.0 (543.8 to 1)
Guidance Counselors: 6.0 (362.5 to 1)
Current Spending: ($ per student per year):
  Total: $7,105; Instruction: $4,583; Support Services: $2,230

Enrollment, Drop-out Rates and Diploma Recipients by Race/Ethnicity

Category	Total	White	Black	Asian	AIAN	Hisp.
Enrollment (%)	100.0	35.0	1.5	0.4	0.1	63.0
Drop-out Rate (%)	1.8	2.9	0.0	0.0	0.0	1.1
H.S. Diplomas (#)	125	61	1	1	0	62

Medina Valley ISD

8449 F M 471 S • Castroville, TX 78009-9531
(830) 931-2243
Grade Span: PK-12; **Agency Type:** 1
Schools: 6
    3 Primary; 1 Middle; 1 High; 1 Other Level
    5 Regular; 0 Special Education; 0 Vocational; 1 Alternative
    0 Magnet; 0 Charter; 3 Title I Eligible; 3 School-wide Title I
Students: 3,003   (52.6% male; 47.3% female)
    Individual Education Program: 376 (12.5%);
    English Language Learner: 172 (5.7%); Migrant: 71 (2.4%)
    Eligible for Free Lunch Program: 1,063 (35.4%)
    Eligible for Reduced-Price Lunch Program: 251 (8.4%)
Teachers: 184.7 (16.3 to 1)
Librarians/Media Specialists: 1.0 (3,003.0 to 1)
Guidance Counselors: 6.1 (492.3 to 1)
Current Spending: ($ per student per year):
    Total: $6,978; Instruction: $4,023; Support Services: $2,556

Enrollment, Drop-out Rates and Diploma Recipients by Race/Ethnicity

Category	Total	White	Black	Asian	AIAN	Hisp.
Enrollment (%)	100.0	48.0	1.3	0.5	0.6	49.6
Drop-out Rate (%)	3.3	2.9	0.0	0.0	0.0	3.9
H.S. Diplomas (#)	202	116	1	0	2	83

Midland County

Greenwood ISD

2700 Fm 1379 • Midland, TX 79706-5330
(915) 685-7800
Grade Span: PK-12; **Agency Type:** 1
Schools: 4
    1 Primary; 2 Middle; 1 High; 0 Other Level
    4 Regular; 0 Special Education; 0 Vocational; 0 Alternative
    0 Magnet; 0 Charter; 2 Title I Eligible; 0 School-wide Title I
Students: 1,503   (52.8% male; 47.1% female)
    Individual Education Program: 179 (11.9%);
    English Language Learner: 74 (4.9%); Migrant: 0 (0.0%)
    Eligible for Free Lunch Program: 294 (19.6%)
    Eligible for Reduced-Price Lunch Program: 89 (5.9%)
Teachers: 99.8 (15.1 to 1)
Librarians/Media Specialists: 2.0 (751.5 to 1)
Guidance Counselors: 3.0 (501.0 to 1)
Current Spending: ($ per student per year):
    Total: $6,048; Instruction: $3,982; Support Services: $1,793

Enrollment, Drop-out Rates and Diploma Recipients by Race/Ethnicity

Category	Total	White	Black	Asian	AIAN	Hisp.
Enrollment (%)	100.0	72.6	0.1	0.3	0.2	26.8
Drop-out Rate (%)	0.6	0.7	0.0	0.0	n/a	0.0
H.S. Diplomas (#)	133	115	0	0	0	18

Midland ISD

615 W Missouri Ave • Midland, TX 79701-5017
(432) 689-1000 • http://www.midland.k12.tx.us/
Grade Span: PK-12; **Agency Type:** 1
Schools: 36
    25 Primary; 5 Middle; 3 High; 3 Other Level
    34 Regular; 0 Special Education; 0 Vocational; 2 Alternative
    0 Magnet; 0 Charter; 19 Title I Eligible; 19 School-wide Title I
Students: 20,921   (50.5% male; 49.4% female)
    Individual Education Program: 2,185 (10.4%);
    English Language Learner: 1,873 (9.0%); Migrant: 309 (1.5%)
    Eligible for Free Lunch Program: 8,273 (39.5%)
    Eligible for Reduced-Price Lunch Program: 1,576 (7.5%)
Teachers: 1,361.7 (15.4 to 1)
Librarians/Media Specialists: 26.1 (801.6 to 1)
Guidance Counselors: 40.9 (511.5 to 1)
Current Spending: ($ per student per year):
    Total: $6,656; Instruction: $4,126; Support Services: $2,173

Enrollment, Drop-out Rates and Diploma Recipients by Race/Ethnicity

Category	Total	White	Black	Asian	AIAN	Hisp.
Enrollment (%)	100.0	42.7	9.8	0.9	0.5	46.2
Drop-out Rate (%)	5.5	3.0	8.6	3.4	8.3	8.4
H.S. Diplomas (#)	1,207	716	97	10	9	375

Milam County

Cameron ISD

304 E 12th • Cameron, TX 76520-2751
Mailing Address: Box 712 • Cameron, TX 76520-0712
(254) 697-3512
Grade Span: PK-12; **Agency Type:** 1
Schools: 4
    2 Primary; 1 Middle; 1 High; 0 Other Level
    4 Regular; 0 Special Education; 0 Vocational; 0 Alternative
    0 Magnet; 0 Charter; 4 Title I Eligible; 4 School-wide Title I
Students: 1,639   (53.6% male; 46.3% female)
    Individual Education Program: 203 (12.4%);
    English Language Learner: 104 (6.3%); Migrant: 34 (2.1%)
    Eligible for Free Lunch Program: 946 (57.7%)
    Eligible for Reduced-Price Lunch Program: 125 (7.6%)
Teachers: 127.5 (12.9 to 1)
Librarians/Media Specialists: 2.0 (819.5 to 1)
Guidance Counselors: 5.0 (327.8 to 1)
Current Spending: ($ per student per year):
    Total: $7,051; Instruction: $4,611; Support Services: $2,116

Enrollment, Drop-out Rates and Diploma Recipients by Race/Ethnicity

Category	Total	White	Black	Asian	AIAN	Hisp.
Enrollment (%)	100.0	42.2	21.8	0.0	0.1	36.0
Drop-out Rate (%)	1.7	1.1	3.0	0.0	n/a	1.9
H.S. Diplomas (#)	119	67	14	1	0	37

Rockdale ISD

520 Davilla • Rockdale, TX 76567-0632
Mailing Address: PO Box 632 • Rockdale, TX 76567-0632
(512) 430-6000
Grade Span: PK-12; **Agency Type:** 1
Schools: 4
    1 Primary; 1 Middle; 1 High; 1 Other Level
    3 Regular; 0 Special Education; 0 Vocational; 1 Alternative
    0 Magnet; 0 Charter; 1 Title I Eligible; 1 School-wide Title I
Students: 1,882   (52.1% male; 47.8% female)
    Individual Education Program: 304 (16.2%);
    English Language Learner: 88 (4.7%); Migrant: 5 (0.3%)
    Eligible for Free Lunch Program: 883 (46.9%)
    Eligible for Reduced-Price Lunch Program: 82 (4.4%)
Teachers: 123.5 (15.2 to 1)
Librarians/Media Specialists: 1.0 (1,882.0 to 1)
Guidance Counselors: 5.0 (376.4 to 1)
Current Spending: ($ per student per year):
    Total: $6,682; Instruction: $4,001; Support Services: $2,366

Enrollment, Drop-out Rates and Diploma Recipients by Race/Ethnicity

Category	Total	White	Black	Asian	AIAN	Hisp.
Enrollment (%)	100.0	56.9	14.0	0.3	0.2	28.6
Drop-out Rate (%)	3.3	2.5	4.3	0.0	n/a	4.5
H.S. Diplomas (#)	96	58	14	0	0	24

Montague County

Bowie ISD

100 W Wichita St • Bowie, TX 76230-1168
Mailing Address: PO Box 1168 • Bowie, TX 76230-1168
(940) 872-1151 • http://www.esc9.net/bowie/
Grade Span: PK-12; **Agency Type:** 1
Schools: 4
    1 Primary; 2 Middle; 1 High; 0 Other Level
    4 Regular; 0 Special Education; 0 Vocational; 0 Alternative
    0 Magnet; 0 Charter; 2 Title I Eligible; 2 School-wide Title I
Students: 1,651   (52.2% male; 47.7% female)
    Individual Education Program: 202 (12.2%);
    English Language Learner: 33 (2.0%); Migrant: 106 (6.4%)
    Eligible for Free Lunch Program: 502 (30.4%)
    Eligible for Reduced-Price Lunch Program: 127 (7.7%)
Teachers: 121.2 (13.6 to 1)
Librarians/Media Specialists: 3.0 (550.3 to 1)
Guidance Counselors: 3.0 (550.3 to 1)
Current Spending: ($ per student per year):
    Total: $6,438; Instruction: $4,196; Support Services: $1,927

Enrollment, Drop-out Rates and Diploma Recipients by Race/Ethnicity

Category	Total	White	Black	Asian	AIAN	Hisp.
Enrollment (%)	100.0	89.7	0.3	0.3	0.7	9.0
Drop-out Rate (%)	3.2	3.3	0.0	0.0	0.0	2.9
H.S. Diplomas (#)	97	93	0	0	0	4

Montgomery County

Conroe ISD
3205 W Davis • Conroe, TX 77304
(936) 756-7751 • http://www.conroe.isd.tenet.edu/
Grade Span: PK-12; **Agency Type:** 1
Schools: 46
   23 Primary; 13 Middle; 5 High; 5 Other Level
   42 Regular; 1 Special Education; 0 Vocational; 3 Alternative
   0 Magnet; 0 Charter; 15 Title I Eligible; 12 School-wide Title I
Students: 39,246 (51.3% male; 48.6% female)
   Individual Education Program: 4,192 (10.7%);
   English Language Learner: 3,808 (9.7%); Migrant: 41 (0.1%)
   Eligible for Free Lunch Program: 9,202 (23.4%)
   Eligible for Reduced-Price Lunch Program: 1,714 (4.4%)
Teachers: 2,496.4 (15.7 to 1)
Librarians/Media Specialists: 44.2 (887.9 to 1)
Guidance Counselors: 87.5 (448.5 to 1)
Current Spending: ($ per student per year):
   Total: $6,549; Instruction: $3,908; Support Services: $2,408
Enrollment, Drop-out Rates and Diploma Recipients by Race/Ethnicity

Category	Total	White	Black	Asian	AIAN	Hisp.
Enrollment (%)	100.0	70.7	5.4	2.4	0.5	20.9
Drop-out Rate (%)	1.8	1.4	3.1	0.9	0.0	3.5
H.S. Diplomas (#)	2,202	1,753	99	65	6	279

Magnolia ISD
829 S Magnolia St • Magnolia, TX 77355-8547
Mailing Address: PO Box 88 • Magnolia, TX 77353-0088
(281) 356-3571 • http://www.magnoliaisd.org/
Grade Span: PK-12; **Agency Type:** 1
Schools: 14
   6 Primary; 4 Middle; 2 High; 2 Other Level
   11 Regular; 0 Special Education; 0 Vocational; 3 Alternative
   0 Magnet; 0 Charter; 4 Title I Eligible; 4 School-wide Title I
Students: 9,135 (52.4% male; 47.5% female)
   Individual Education Program: 1,092 (12.0%);
   English Language Learner: 720 (7.9%); Migrant: 13 (0.1%)
   Eligible for Free Lunch Program: 2,280 (25.0%)
   Eligible for Reduced-Price Lunch Program: 517 (5.7%)
Teachers: 599.5 (15.2 to 1)
Librarians/Media Specialists: 8.0 (1,141.9 to 1)
Guidance Counselors: 19.0 (480.8 to 1)
Current Spending: ($ per student per year):
   Total: $6,517; Instruction: $4,016; Support Services: $2,198
Enrollment, Drop-out Rates and Diploma Recipients by Race/Ethnicity

Category	Total	White	Black	Asian	AIAN	Hisp.
Enrollment (%)	100.0	79.9	2.9	0.3	0.4	16.5
Drop-out Rate (%)	2.3	2.1	1.9	0.0	0.0	3.8
H.S. Diplomas (#)	428	370	6	4	1	47

Montgomery ISD
13159 Walden Rd • Montgomery, TX 77356-1475
Mailing Address: PO Box 1475 • Montgomery, TX 77356-1475
(936) 582-1333
Grade Span: PK-12; **Agency Type:** 1
Schools: 7
   2 Primary; 2 Middle; 1 High; 2 Other Level
   6 Regular; 0 Special Education; 0 Vocational; 1 Alternative
   0 Magnet; 0 Charter; 4 Title I Eligible; 0 School-wide Title I
Students: 4,640 (52.8% male; 47.1% female)
   Individual Education Program: 539 (11.6%);
   English Language Learner: 113 (2.4%); Migrant: 0 (0.0%)
   Eligible for Free Lunch Program: 820 (17.7%)
   Eligible for Reduced-Price Lunch Program: 224 (4.8%)
Teachers: 290.0 (16.0 to 1)
Librarians/Media Specialists: 5.0 (928.0 to 1)
Guidance Counselors: 8.0 (580.0 to 1)
Current Spending: ($ per student per year):
   Total: $7,360; Instruction: $4,540; Support Services: $2,445
Enrollment, Drop-out Rates and Diploma Recipients by Race/Ethnicity

Category	Total	White	Black	Asian	AIAN	Hisp.
Enrollment (%)	100.0	85.6	6.1	0.6	0.3	7.3
Drop-out Rate (%)	1.5	1.4	2.5	0.0	0.0	1.7
H.S. Diplomas (#)	204	186	14	1	0	3

New Caney ISD
21580 Loop 494 • New Caney, TX 77357-9115
(281) 354-1166 • http://www.newcaneyisd.org/
Grade Span: PK-12; **Agency Type:** 1
Schools: 11
   4 Primary; 2 Middle; 1 High; 4 Other Level
   8 Regular; 1 Special Education; 0 Vocational; 2 Alternative
   0 Magnet; 0 Charter; 7 Title I Eligible; 7 School-wide Title I
Students: 7,282 (51.7% male; 48.2% female)

   Individual Education Program: 1,025 (14.1%);
   English Language Learner: 704 (9.7%); Migrant: 16 (0.2%)
   Eligible for Free Lunch Program: 2,735 (37.6%)
   Eligible for Reduced-Price Lunch Program: 657 (9.0%)
Teachers: 498.1 (14.6 to 1)
Librarians/Media Specialists: 6.4 (1,137.8 to 1)
Guidance Counselors: 15.2 (479.1 to 1)
Current Spending: ($ per student per year):
   Total: $6,563; Instruction: $3,853; Support Services: $2,326
Enrollment, Drop-out Rates and Diploma Recipients by Race/Ethnicity

Category	Total	White	Black	Asian	AIAN	Hisp.
Enrollment (%)	100.0	72.8	2.1	0.9	0.2	24.0
Drop-out Rate (%)	3.3	3.1	6.5	10.0	0.0	3.3
H.S. Diplomas (#)	277	238	7	1	1	30

Splendora ISD
23419 Fm 2090 • Splendora, TX 77372-6210
(281) 689-3128
Grade Span: PK-12; **Agency Type:** 1
Schools: 5
   2 Primary; 1 Middle; 1 High; 1 Other Level
   4 Regular; 0 Special Education; 0 Vocational; 1 Alternative
   0 Magnet; 0 Charter; 4 Title I Eligible; 4 School-wide Title I
Students: 3,135 (51.8% male; 48.1% female)
   Individual Education Program: 246 (7.8%);
   English Language Learner: 148 (4.7%); Migrant: 6 (0.2%)
   Eligible for Free Lunch Program: 1,364 (43.5%)
   Eligible for Reduced-Price Lunch Program: 328 (10.5%)
Teachers: 209.0 (15.0 to 1)
Librarians/Media Specialists: 4.0 (783.8 to 1)
Guidance Counselors: 9.0 (348.3 to 1)
Current Spending: ($ per student per year):
   Total: $6,651; Instruction: $4,062; Support Services: $2,195
Enrollment, Drop-out Rates and Diploma Recipients by Race/Ethnicity

Category	Total	White	Black	Asian	AIAN	Hisp.
Enrollment (%)	100.0	85.1	0.8	0.3	0.3	13.5
Drop-out Rate (%)	5.4	5.4	0.0	n/a	0.0	5.4
H.S. Diplomas (#)	125	110	1	0	0	14

Willis ISD
204 W Rogers St • Willis, TX 77378-9239
(936) 856-1200
Grade Span: PK-12; **Agency Type:** 1
Schools: 9
   4 Primary; 2 Middle; 1 High; 2 Other Level
   7 Regular; 0 Special Education; 0 Vocational; 2 Alternative
   0 Magnet; 0 Charter; 5 Title I Eligible; 5 School-wide Title I
Students: 4,741 (52.1% male; 47.8% female)
   Individual Education Program: 607 (12.8%);
   English Language Learner: 478 (10.1%); Migrant: 19 (0.4%)
   Eligible for Free Lunch Program: 1,759 (37.1%)
   Eligible for Reduced-Price Lunch Program: 485 (10.2%)
Teachers: 301.1 (15.7 to 1)
Librarians/Media Specialists: 6.2 (764.7 to 1)
Guidance Counselors: 12.0 (395.1 to 1)
Current Spending: ($ per student per year):
   Total: $6,598; Instruction: $3,718; Support Services: $2,538
Enrollment, Drop-out Rates and Diploma Recipients by Race/Ethnicity

Category	Total	White	Black	Asian	AIAN	Hisp.
Enrollment (%)	100.0	69.4	7.9	0.4	0.6	21.7
Drop-out Rate (%)	1.7	1.3	3.7	0.0	0.0	2.8
H.S. Diplomas (#)	259	205	23	1	0	30

Moore County

Dumas ISD
421 W 4th St • Dumas, TX 79029-0615
Mailing Address: PO Box 615 • Dumas, TX 79029-0615
(806) 935-6461 • http://www.dumas-k12.net/
Grade Span: PK-12; **Agency Type:** 1
Schools: 8
   5 Primary; 1 Middle; 2 High; 0 Other Level
   7 Regular; 0 Special Education; 0 Vocational; 1 Alternative
   0 Magnet; 0 Charter; 6 Title I Eligible; 6 School-wide Title I
Students: 4,195 (52.2% male; 47.7% female)
   Individual Education Program: 410 (9.8%);
   English Language Learner: 1,052 (25.1%); Migrant: 1,878 (44.8%)
   Eligible for Free Lunch Program: 1,949 (46.5%)
   Eligible for Reduced-Price Lunch Program: 381 (9.1%)
Teachers: 298.9 (14.0 to 1)
Librarians/Media Specialists: 7.0 (599.3 to 1)
Guidance Counselors: 8.0 (524.4 to 1)
Current Spending: ($ per student per year):
   Total: $6,035; Instruction: $3,929; Support Services: $1,807

Enrollment, Drop-out Rates and Diploma Recipients by Race/Ethnicity

Category	Total	White	Black	Asian	AIAN	Hisp.
Enrollment (%)	100.0	30.6	0.8	1.0	0.4	67.2
Drop-out Rate (%)	2.9	1.8	14.3	0.0	0.0	3.8
H.S. Diplomas (#)	243	111	2	3	0	127

Morris County

Daingerfield-Lone Star Is
200 Tiger Dr • Daingerfield, TX 75638-0851
(903) 645-2239
Grade Span: PK-12; **Agency Type:** 1
Schools: 5
   3 Primary; 1 Middle; 1 High; 0 Other Level
   5 Regular; 0 Special Education; 0 Vocational; 0 Alternative
   0 Magnet; 0 Charter; 5 Title I Eligible; 5 School-wide Title I
Students: 1,566 (52.6% male; 47.3% female)
   Individual Education Program: 231 (14.8%);
   English Language Learner: 51 (3.3%); Migrant: 69 (4.4%)
   Eligible for Free Lunch Program: 809 (51.7%)
   Eligible for Reduced-Price Lunch Program: 128 (8.2%)
Teachers: 127.4 (12.3 to 1)
Librarians/Media Specialists: 4.1 (382.0 to 1)
Guidance Counselors: 5.0 (313.2 to 1)
Current Spending: ($ per student per year):
   Total: $7,730; Instruction: $4,676; Support Services: $2,621

Enrollment, Drop-out Rates and Diploma Recipients by Race/Ethnicity

Category	Total	White	Black	Asian	AIAN	Hisp.
Enrollment (%)	100.0	49.6	42.0	0.1	0.6	7.8
Drop-out Rate (%)	5.2	4.2	5.5	n/a	0.0	12.5
H.S. Diplomas (#)	89	53	29	0	1	6

Nacogdoches County

Nacogdoches ISD
Drawer 631521 • Nacogdoches, TX 75963-1521
(936) 569-5000 • http://www.nacogdoches.k12.tx.us/
Grade Span: PK-12; **Agency Type:** 1
Schools: 10
   6 Primary; 2 Middle; 1 High; 1 Other Level
   9 Regular; 0 Special Education; 0 Vocational; 1 Alternative
   0 Magnet; 0 Charter; 7 Title I Eligible; 7 School-wide Title I
Students: 6,384 (51.3% male; 48.6% female)
   Individual Education Program: 551 (8.6%);
   English Language Learner: 1,027 (16.1%); Migrant: 217 (3.4%)
   Eligible for Free Lunch Program: 3,730 (58.4%)
   Eligible for Reduced-Price Lunch Program: 434 (6.8%)
Teachers: 410.4 (15.6 to 1)
Librarians/Media Specialists: 6.0 (1,064.0 to 1)
Guidance Counselors: 11.0 (580.4 to 1)
Current Spending: ($ per student per year):
   Total: $6,582; Instruction: $3,802; Support Services: $2,362

Enrollment, Drop-out Rates and Diploma Recipients by Race/Ethnicity

Category	Total	White	Black	Asian	AIAN	Hisp.
Enrollment (%)	100.0	35.9	30.7	1.0	0.2	32.2
Drop-out Rate (%)	4.3	3.2	4.4	0.0	33.3	7.5
H.S. Diplomas (#)	399	240	95	8	0	56

Navarro County

Corsicana ISD
601 N 13th St • Corsicana, TX 75110-3298
(903) 874-7441 • https://www.edline.net/pages/Corsicana_ISD
Grade Span: PK-12; **Agency Type:** 1
Schools: 8
   4 Primary; 2 Middle; 1 High; 1 Other Level
   8 Regular; 0 Special Education; 0 Vocational; 0 Alternative
   0 Magnet; 0 Charter; 6 Title I Eligible; 6 School-wide Title I
Students: 5,480 (51.0% male; 48.9% female)
   Individual Education Program: 783 (14.3%);
   English Language Learner: 698 (12.7%); Migrant: 215 (3.9%)
   Eligible for Free Lunch Program: 2,645 (48.3%)
   Eligible for Reduced-Price Lunch Program: 374 (6.8%)
Teachers: 366.1 (15.0 to 1)
Librarians/Media Specialists: 4.0 (1,370.0 to 1)
Guidance Counselors: 15.0 (365.3 to 1)
Current Spending: ($ per student per year):
   Total: $6,344; Instruction: $3,906; Support Services: $2,042

Enrollment, Drop-out Rates and Diploma Recipients by Race/Ethnicity

Category	Total	White	Black	Asian	AIAN	Hisp.
Enrollment (%)	100.0	40.8	24.7	1.3	0.2	33.0
Drop-out Rate (%)	4.5	4.2	5.0	0.0	33.3	4.5
H.S. Diplomas (#)	270	137	85	4	0	44

Nolan County

Sweetwater ISD
207 Musgrove St • Sweetwater, TX 79556-5321
(325) 235-8601
Grade Span: PK-12; **Agency Type:** 1
Schools: 7
   3 Primary; 2 Middle; 2 High; 0 Other Level
   6 Regular; 0 Special Education; 0 Vocational; 1 Alternative
   0 Magnet; 0 Charter; 3 Title I Eligible; 3 School-wide Title I
Students: 2,218 (50.9% male; 49.0% female)
   Individual Education Program: 324 (14.6%);
   English Language Learner: 17 (0.8%); Migrant: 44 (2.0%)
   Eligible for Free Lunch Program: 1,010 (45.5%)
   Eligible for Reduced-Price Lunch Program: 241 (10.9%)
Teachers: 190.9 (11.6 to 1)
Librarians/Media Specialists: 0.4 (5,545.0 to 1)
Guidance Counselors: 4.5 (492.9 to 1)
Current Spending: ($ per student per year):
   Total: $7,868; Instruction: $4,785; Support Services: $2,600

Enrollment, Drop-out Rates and Diploma Recipients by Race/Ethnicity

Category	Total	White	Black	Asian	AIAN	Hisp.
Enrollment (%)	100.0	52.8	7.9	0.0	0.1	39.1
Drop-out Rate (%)	6.0	4.4	5.1	n/a	n/a	8.9
H.S. Diplomas (#)	150	101	7	0	0	42

Nueces County

Calallen ISD
4205 Wildcat Dr • Corpus Christi, TX 78410-5198
(361) 242-5600 • http://www.calallen.k12.tx.us/
Grade Span: PK-12; **Agency Type:** 1
Schools: 6
   3 Primary; 1 Middle; 1 High; 0 Other Level
   5 Regular; 0 Special Education; 0 Vocational; 0 Alternative
   0 Magnet; 0 Charter; 3 Title I Eligible; 3 School-wide Title I
Students: 3,924 (51.3% male; 48.6% female)
   Individual Education Program: 503 (12.8%);
   English Language Learner: 63 (1.6%); Migrant: 0 (0.0%)
   Eligible for Free Lunch Program: 1,081 (27.5%)
   Eligible for Reduced-Price Lunch Program: 242 (6.2%)
Teachers: 249.2 (15.7 to 1)
Librarians/Media Specialists: 3.0 (1,308.0 to 1)
Guidance Counselors: 9.0 (436.0 to 1)
Current Spending: ($ per student per year):
   Total: $6,360; Instruction: $3,762; Support Services: $2,245

Enrollment, Drop-out Rates and Diploma Recipients by Race/Ethnicity

Category	Total	White	Black	Asian	AIAN	Hisp.
Enrollment (%)	100.0	54.5	2.4	0.5	0.2	42.4
Drop-out Rate (%)	2.3	1.6	4.2	0.0	0.0	3.8
H.S. Diplomas (#)	321	229	4	4	2	82

Corpus Christi ISD
801 Leopard St • Corpus Christi, TX 78401-2421
Mailing Address: PO Box 110 • Corpus Christi, TX 78403-0110
(361) 886-9002 • http://corpuschristiisd.org/
Grade Span: PK-12; **Agency Type:** 1
Schools: 63
   40 Primary; 12 Middle; 6 High; 4 Other Level
   58 Regular; 0 Special Education; 0 Vocational; 4 Alternative
   0 Magnet; 0 Charter; 33 Title I Eligible; 33 School-wide Title I
Students: 39,310 (51.5% male; 48.4% female)
   Individual Education Program: 5,671 (14.4%);
   English Language Learner: 3,454 (8.8%); Migrant: 1,138 (2.9%)
   Eligible for Free Lunch Program: 19,331 (49.3%)
   Eligible for Reduced-Price Lunch Program: 3,215 (8.2%)
Teachers: 2,408.6 (16.3 to 1)
Librarians/Media Specialists: 39.2 (999.6 to 1)
Guidance Counselors: 105.3 (372.1 to 1)
Current Spending: ($ per student per year):
   Total: $6,872; Instruction: $4,196; Support Services: $2,400

Enrollment, Drop-out Rates and Diploma Recipients by Race/Ethnicity

Category	Total	White	Black	Asian	AIAN	Hisp.
Enrollment (%)	100.0	20.2	5.5	1.5	0.3	72.5
Drop-out Rate (%)	4.8	2.8	5.3	1.4	0.0	5.5
H.S. Diplomas (#)	2,119	605	130	24	6	1,354

Flour Bluff ISD
2505 Waldron Rd • Corpus Christi, TX 78418-4798
(361) 694-9200 • http://www.flourbluffschools.net/
Grade Span: PK-12; **Agency Type:** 1
Schools: 7
   3 Primary; 2 Middle; 1 High; 1 Other Level
   6 Regular; 0 Special Education; 0 Vocational; 1 Alternative
   0 Magnet; 0 Charter; 4 Title I Eligible; 4 School-wide Title I

Students: 5,066   (51.1% male; 48.8% female)
   Individual Education Program: 647 (12.8%);
   English Language Learner: 115 (2.3%); Migrant: 5 (0.1%)
   Eligible for Free Lunch Program: 1,749 (34.5%)
   Eligible for Reduced-Price Lunch Program: 532 (10.5%)
Teachers: 318.5 (15.9 to 1)
Librarians/Media Specialists: 5.0 (1,013.2 to 1)
Guidance Counselors: 14.0 (361.9 to 1)
Current Spending: ($ per student per year):
   Total: $6,697; Instruction: $3,990; Support Services: $2,333
Enrollment, Drop-out Rates and Diploma Recipients by Race/Ethnicity

Category	Total	White	Black	Asian	AIAN	Hisp.
Enrollment (%)	100.0	61.8	6.2	3.9	1.1	27.1
Drop-out Rate (%)	2.4	2.6	1.3	0.0	0.0	2.7
H.S. Diplomas (#)	324	231	15	16	2	60

Robstown ISD
801 N 1st St • Robstown, TX 78380-2608
(361) 767-6600
Grade Span: PK-12; **Agency Type:** 1
Schools: 10
   4 Primary; 2 Middle; 2 High; 2 Other Level
   7 Regular; 0 Special Education; 0 Vocational; 3 Alternative
   0 Magnet; 0 Charter; 9 Title I Eligible; 9 School-wide Title I
Students: 3,944   (51.9% male; 48.0% female)
   Individual Education Program: 640 (16.2%);
   English Language Learner: 213 (5.4%); Migrant: 3,574 (90.6%)
   Eligible for Free Lunch Program: 3,338 (84.6%)
   Eligible for Reduced-Price Lunch Program: 250 (6.3%)
Teachers: 274.3 (14.4 to 1)
Librarians/Media Specialists: 6.0 (657.3 to 1)
Guidance Counselors: 14.0 (281.7 to 1)
Current Spending: ($ per student per year):
   Total: $7,685; Instruction: $4,495; Support Services: $2,651
Enrollment, Drop-out Rates and Diploma Recipients by Race/Ethnicity

Category	Total	White	Black	Asian	AIAN	Hisp.
Enrollment (%)	100.0	1.3	0.9	0.1	0.0	97.8
Drop-out Rate (%)	8.2	0.0	0.0	0.0	n/a	8.4
H.S. Diplomas (#)	199	3	2	0	0	194

Tuloso-Midway ISD
9760 La Branch • Corpus Christi, TX 78460-0900
Mailing Address: PO Box 10900 • Corpus Christi, TX 78460-0900
(361) 241-3286
Grade Span: PK-12; **Agency Type:** 1
Schools: 6
   2 Primary; 1 Middle; 2 High; 0 Other Level
   4 Regular; 0 Special Education; 0 Vocational; 1 Alternative
   0 Magnet; 0 Charter; 5 Title I Eligible; 0 School-wide Title I
Students: 3,367   (49.5% male; 50.4% female)
   Individual Education Program: 399 (11.9%);
   English Language Learner: 148 (4.4%); Migrant: 3 (0.1%)
   Eligible for Free Lunch Program: 1,303 (38.7%)
   Eligible for Reduced-Price Lunch Program: 236 (7.0%)
Teachers: 195.5 (17.2 to 1)
Librarians/Media Specialists: 3.0 (1,122.3 to 1)
Guidance Counselors: 8.0 (420.9 to 1)
Current Spending: ($ per student per year):
   Total: $6,497; Instruction: $3,744; Support Services: $2,435
Enrollment, Drop-out Rates and Diploma Recipients by Race/Ethnicity

Category	Total	White	Black	Asian	AIAN	Hisp.
Enrollment (%)	100.0	39.3	1.8	0.5	0.1	58.4
Drop-out Rate (%)	1.1	0.6	0.0	0.0	n/a	1.7
H.S. Diplomas (#)	223	113	9	1	1	99

West Oso ISD
5050 Rockford Dr • Corpus Christi, TX 78416-2530
(361) 855-3321
Grade Span: PK-12; **Agency Type:** 1
Schools: 5
   2 Primary; 1 Middle; 1 High; 0 Other Level
   4 Regular; 0 Special Education; 0 Vocational; 0 Alternative
   0 Magnet; 0 Charter; 4 Title I Eligible; 4 School-wide Title I
Students: 1,902   (53.9% male; 46.0% female)
   Individual Education Program: 238 (12.5%);
   English Language Learner: 160 (8.4%); Migrant: 71 (3.7%)
   Eligible for Free Lunch Program: 768 (40.4%)
   Eligible for Reduced-Price Lunch Program: 125 (6.6%)
Teachers: 128.9 (14.8 to 1)
Librarians/Media Specialists: 3.0 (634.0 to 1)
Guidance Counselors: 5.0 (380.4 to 1)
Current Spending: ($ per student per year):
   Total: $7,624; Instruction: $4,591; Support Services: $2,608

Enrollment, Drop-out Rates and Diploma Recipients by Race/Ethnicity

Category	Total	White	Black	Asian	AIAN	Hisp.
Enrollment (%)	100.0	3.0	13.2	0.2	0.2	83.4
Drop-out Rate (%)	4.1	7.1	4.2	0.0	n/a	3.9
H.S. Diplomas (#)	56	1	7	0	0	48

Ochiltree County

Perryton ISD
821 SW 17th Ave • Perryton, TX 79070-1048
(806) 435-5478
Grade Span: PK-12; **Agency Type:** 1
Schools: 6
   2 Primary; 2 Middle; 2 High; 0 Other Level
   5 Regular; 0 Special Education; 0 Vocational; 1 Alternative
   0 Magnet; 0 Charter; 4 Title I Eligible; 4 School-wide Title I
Students: 1,984   (52.0% male; 47.9% female)
   Individual Education Program: 188 (9.5%);
   English Language Learner: 396 (20.0%); Migrant: 380 (19.2%)
   Eligible for Free Lunch Program: 814 (41.0%)
   Eligible for Reduced-Price Lunch Program: 237 (11.9%)
Teachers: 144.5 (13.7 to 1)
Librarians/Media Specialists: 1.1 (1,803.6 to 1)
Guidance Counselors: 2.8 (708.6 to 1)
Current Spending: ($ per student per year):
   Total: $7,021; Instruction: $4,613; Support Services: $2,029
Enrollment, Drop-out Rates and Diploma Recipients by Race/Ethnicity

Category	Total	White	Black	Asian	AIAN	Hisp.
Enrollment (%)	100.0	48.0	0.4	0.5	0.5	50.7
Drop-out Rate (%)	2.2	2.3	n/a	0.0	0.0	2.0
H.S. Diplomas (#)	128	99	0	0	0	29

Orange County

Bridge City ISD
1031 W Roundbunch Rd • Bridge City, TX 77611-0847
(409) 735-1602
Grade Span: PK-12; **Agency Type:** 1
Schools: 5
   2 Primary; 2 Middle; 1 High; 0 Other Level
   5 Regular; 0 Special Education; 0 Vocational; 0 Alternative
   0 Magnet; 0 Charter; 3 Title I Eligible; 0 School-wide Title I
Students: 2,589   (51.4% male; 48.5% female)
   Individual Education Program: 331 (12.8%);
   English Language Learner: 88 (3.4%); Migrant: 12 (0.5%)
   Eligible for Free Lunch Program: 692 (26.7%)
   Eligible for Reduced-Price Lunch Program: 129 (5.0%)
Teachers: 179.6 (14.4 to 1)
Librarians/Media Specialists: 4.3 (602.1 to 1)
Guidance Counselors: 7.0 (369.9 to 1)
Current Spending: ($ per student per year):
   Total: $6,119; Instruction: $3,738; Support Services: $2,119
Enrollment, Drop-out Rates and Diploma Recipients by Race/Ethnicity

Category	Total	White	Black	Asian	AIAN	Hisp.
Enrollment (%)	100.0	89.6	0.3	3.1	0.5	6.5
Drop-out Rate (%)	2.2	1.8	n/a	0.0	0.0	13.8
H.S. Diplomas (#)	198	185	0	5	1	7

Little Cypress-Mauricevil
6586 Fm 1130 • Orange, TX 77632-0708
(409) 883-2232 • http://www.lcmcisd.org/
Grade Span: PK-12; **Agency Type:** 1
Schools: 6
   3 Primary; 2 Middle; 1 High; 0 Other Level
   6 Regular; 0 Special Education; 0 Vocational; 0 Alternative
   0 Magnet; 0 Charter; 5 Title I Eligible; 5 School-wide Title I
Students: 3,699   (51.8% male; 48.1% female)
   Individual Education Program: 599 (16.2%);
   English Language Learner: 49 (1.3%); Migrant: 0 (0.0%)
   Eligible for Free Lunch Program: 866 (23.4%)
   Eligible for Reduced-Price Lunch Program: 163 (4.4%)
Teachers: 245.2 (15.1 to 1)
Librarians/Media Specialists: 5.0 (739.8 to 1)
Guidance Counselors: 7.0 (528.4 to 1)
Current Spending: ($ per student per year):
   Total: $6,471; Instruction: $3,734; Support Services: $2,384
Enrollment, Drop-out Rates and Diploma Recipients by Race/Ethnicity

Category	Total	White	Black	Asian	AIAN	Hisp.
Enrollment (%)	100.0	89.1	4.9	0.8	0.4	4.8
Drop-out Rate (%)	1.0	1.1	0.0	0.0	0.0	0.0
H.S. Diplomas (#)	273	246	16	5	1	5

Orangefield ISD

9974 Fm 105 • Orangefield, TX 77639-0228
Mailing Address: PO Box 228 • Orangefield, TX 77639-0228
(409) 735-5337
Grade Span: PK-12; **Agency Type:** 1
Schools: 3
  1 Primary; 1 Middle; 1 High; 0 Other Level
  3 Regular; 0 Special Education; 0 Vocational; 0 Alternative
  0 Magnet; 0 Charter; 1 Title I Eligible; 1 School-wide Title I
Students: 1,644 (52.3% male; 47.6% female)
  Individual Education Program: 215 (13.1%);
  English Language Learner: 20 (1.2%); Migrant: 0 (0.0%)
  Eligible for Free Lunch Program: 189 (11.5%)
  Eligible for Reduced-Price Lunch Program: 75 (4.6%)
Teachers: 113.9 (14.4 to 1)
Librarians/Media Specialists: 1.0 (1,644.0 to 1)
Guidance Counselors: 4.0 (411.0 to 1)
Current Spending: ($ per student per year):
  Total: $6,413; Instruction: $3,886; Support Services: $2,147
Enrollment, Drop-out Rates and Diploma Recipients by Race/Ethnicity

Category	Total	White	Black	Asian	AIAN	Hisp.
Enrollment (%)	100.0	93.5	0.5	1.8	0.5	3.6
Drop-out Rate (%)	2.0	2.0	0.0	0.0	0.0	3.8
H.S. Diplomas (#)	100	93	0	1	1	5

Vidor ISD

120 E Bolivar St • Vidor, TX 77662-4907
(409) 769-2143 • http://www.vidor.k12.tx.us/
Grade Span: PK-12; **Agency Type:** 1
Schools: 7
  3 Primary; 2 Middle; 2 High; 0 Other Level
  6 Regular; 0 Special Education; 0 Vocational; 1 Alternative
  0 Magnet; 0 Charter; 4 Title I Eligible; 0 School-wide Title I
Students: 5,228 (51.2% male; 48.7% female)
  Individual Education Program: 961 (18.4%);
  English Language Learner: 30 (0.6%); Migrant: 2 (<0.1%)
  Eligible for Free Lunch Program: 2,027 (38.8%)
  Eligible for Reduced-Price Lunch Program: 480 (9.2%)
Teachers: 358.8 (14.6 to 1)
Librarians/Media Specialists: 6.0 (871.3 to 1)
Guidance Counselors: 13.0 (402.2 to 1)
Current Spending: ($ per student per year):
  Total: $6,667; Instruction: $4,191; Support Services: $2,150
Enrollment, Drop-out Rates and Diploma Recipients by Race/Ethnicity

Category	Total	White	Black	Asian	AIAN	Hisp.
Enrollment (%)	100.0	96.3	0.2	0.7	0.1	2.8
Drop-out Rate (%)	2.7	2.8	0.0	0.0	0.0	0.0
H.S. Diplomas (#)	337	327	0	2	0	8

West Orange-Cove Cons ISD

505 N 15th St • Orange, TX 77631-1107
Mailing Address: PO Box 1107 • Orange, TX 77631-1107
(409) 882-5500
Grade Span: PK-12; **Agency Type:** 1
Schools: 7
  4 Primary; 1 Middle; 2 High; 0 Other Level
  7 Regular; 0 Special Education; 0 Vocational; 0 Alternative
  0 Magnet; 0 Charter; 5 Title I Eligible; 5 School-wide Title I
Students: 3,222 (51.7% male; 48.2% female)
  Individual Education Program: 558 (17.3%);
  English Language Learner: 40 (1.2%); Migrant: 0 (0.0%)
  Eligible for Free Lunch Program: 1,963 (60.9%)
  Eligible for Reduced-Price Lunch Program: 180 (5.6%)
Teachers: 228.6 (14.1 to 1)
Librarians/Media Specialists: 4.5 (716.0 to 1)
Guidance Counselors: 6.0 (537.0 to 1)
Current Spending: ($ per student per year):
  Total: $8,869; Instruction: $5,188; Support Services: $3,289
Enrollment, Drop-out Rates and Diploma Recipients by Race/Ethnicity

Category	Total	White	Black	Asian	AIAN	Hisp.
Enrollment (%)	100.0	35.0	59.8	0.7	0.2	4.3
Drop-out Rate (%)	5.1	5.3	5.1	0.0	0.0	3.3
H.S. Diplomas (#)	181	86	90	0	0	5

Palo Pinto County

Mineral Wells ISD

906 SW 5th Ave • Mineral Wells, TX 76067-4895
(940) 325-6404 • http://www.mwisd.esc11.net/
Grade Span: PK-12; **Agency Type:** 1
Schools: 6
  2 Primary; 2 Middle; 2 High; 0 Other Level
  5 Regular; 0 Special Education; 0 Vocational; 1 Alternative
  0 Magnet; 0 Charter; 5 Title I Eligible; 4 School-wide Title I
Students: 3,684 (51.8% male; 48.1% female)

  Individual Education Program: 660 (17.9%);
  English Language Learner: 232 (6.3%); Migrant: 13 (0.4%)
  Eligible for Free Lunch Program: 1,656 (45.0%)
  Eligible for Reduced-Price Lunch Program: 370 (10.0%)
Teachers: 272.9 (13.5 to 1)
Librarians/Media Specialists: 3.7 (995.7 to 1)
Guidance Counselors: 10.5 (350.9 to 1)
Current Spending: ($ per student per year):
  Total: $7,570; Instruction: $4,644; Support Services: $2,542
Enrollment, Drop-out Rates and Diploma Recipients by Race/Ethnicity

Category	Total	White	Black	Asian	AIAN	Hisp.
Enrollment (%)	100.0	68.2	4.6	0.5	0.8	25.9
Drop-out Rate (%)	3.6	3.6	4.2	0.0	0.0	4.2
H.S. Diplomas (#)	190	153	10	1	0	26

Panola County

Carthage ISD

#1 Bulldog Dr • Carthage, TX 75633-2370
(903) 693-3806
Grade Span: PK-12; **Agency Type:** 1
Schools: 5
  2 Primary; 2 Middle; 1 High; 0 Other Level
  5 Regular; 0 Special Education; 0 Vocational; 0 Alternative
  0 Magnet; 0 Charter; 4 Title I Eligible; 4 School-wide Title I
Students: 2,912 (52.2% male; 47.7% female)
  Individual Education Program: 432 (14.8%);
  English Language Learner: 58 (2.0%); Migrant: 7 (0.2%)
  Eligible for Free Lunch Program: 1,078 (37.0%)
  Eligible for Reduced-Price Lunch Program: 182 (6.3%)
Teachers: 198.9 (14.6 to 1)
Librarians/Media Specialists: 2.9 (1,004.1 to 1)
Guidance Counselors: 5.9 (493.6 to 1)
Current Spending: ($ per student per year):
  Total: $7,429; Instruction: $4,924; Support Services: $2,125
Enrollment, Drop-out Rates and Diploma Recipients by Race/Ethnicity

Category	Total	White	Black	Asian	AIAN	Hisp.
Enrollment (%)	100.0	64.7	27.1	0.4	0.2	7.5
Drop-out Rate (%)	0.8	0.8	0.5	0.0	0.0	2.3
H.S. Diplomas (#)	196	149	36	1	0	10

Parker County

Aledo ISD

1008 Bailey Ranch Rd • Aledo, TX 76008-4407
(817) 441-8327 • http://www.aledo.k12.tx.us/aisdweb/index.htm
Grade Span: PK-12; **Agency Type:** 1
Schools: 7
  3 Primary; 2 Middle; 1 High; 1 Other Level
  6 Regular; 0 Special Education; 0 Vocational; 1 Alternative
  0 Magnet; 0 Charter; 3 Title I Eligible; 3 School-wide Title I
Students: 3,495 (51.7% male; 48.2% female)
  Individual Education Program: 336 (9.6%);
  English Language Learner: 53 (1.5%); Migrant: 14 (0.4%)
  Eligible for Free Lunch Program: 233 (6.7%)
  Eligible for Reduced-Price Lunch Program: 52 (1.5%)
Teachers: 237.9 (14.7 to 1)
Librarians/Media Specialists: 4.0 (873.8 to 1)
Guidance Counselors: 8.0 (436.9 to 1)
Current Spending: ($ per student per year):
  Total: $6,928; Instruction: $4,141; Support Services: $2,453
Enrollment, Drop-out Rates and Diploma Recipients by Race/Ethnicity

Category	Total	White	Black	Asian	AIAN	Hisp.
Enrollment (%)	100.0	92.6	0.7	0.7	0.5	5.5
Drop-out Rate (%)	0.1	0.1	0.0	0.0	0.0	0.0
H.S. Diplomas (#)	218	207	0	3	0	8

Springtown ISD

101 E Second St • Springtown, TX 76082-2566
(817) 220-7243
Grade Span: PK-12; **Agency Type:** 1
Schools: 8
  3 Primary; 1 Middle; 2 High; 2 Other Level
  6 Regular; 0 Special Education; 0 Vocational; 2 Alternative
  0 Magnet; 0 Charter; 4 Title I Eligible; 4 School-wide Title I
Students: 3,565 (52.0% male; 47.9% female)
  Individual Education Program: 485 (13.6%);
  English Language Learner: 74 (2.1%); Migrant: 8 (0.2%)
  Eligible for Free Lunch Program: 1,066 (29.9%)
  Eligible for Reduced-Price Lunch Program: 330 (9.3%)
Teachers: 254.6 (14.0 to 1)
Librarians/Media Specialists: 6.0 (594.2 to 1)
Guidance Counselors: 12.4 (287.5 to 1)
Current Spending: ($ per student per year):
  Total: $6,797; Instruction: $4,068; Support Services: $2,401

Enrollment, Drop-out Rates and Diploma Recipients by Race/Ethnicity

Category	Total	White	Black	Asian	AIAN	Hisp.
Enrollment (%)	100.0	90.4	0.6	0.3	1.0	7.8
Drop-out Rate (%)	3.2	3.2	0.0	0.0	0.0	3.8
H.S. Diplomas (#)	174	162	0	0	2	10

Weatherford ISD
1100 Longhorn Dr • Weatherford, TX 76086-9999
(817) 598-2800 • http://www.weatherfordisd.com/
Grade Span: PK-12; **Agency Type:** 1
Schools: 12
   7 Primary; 2 Middle; 2 High; 1 Other Level
   11 Regular; 0 Special Education; 0 Vocational; 1 Alternative
   0 Magnet; 0 Charter; 4 Title I Eligible; 4 School-wide Title I
Students: 6,987 (52.6% male; 47.3% female)
   Individual Education Program: 896 (12.8%);
   English Language Learner: 342 (4.9%); Migrant: 27 (0.4%)
   Eligible for Free Lunch Program: 1,925 (27.6%)
   Eligible for Reduced-Price Lunch Program: 474 (6.8%)
Teachers: 468.5 (14.9 to 1)
Librarians/Media Specialists: 10.1 (691.8 to 1)
Guidance Counselors: 17.0 (411.0 to 1)
Current Spending: ($ per student per year):
   Total: $6,802; Instruction: $4,001; Support Services: $2,444
Enrollment, Drop-out Rates and Diploma Recipients by Race/Ethnicity

Category	Total	White	Black	Asian	AIAN	Hisp.
Enrollment (%)	100.0	80.7	1.8	0.9	0.7	15.8
Drop-out Rate (%)	2.4	1.8	5.9	0.0	0.0	7.9
H.S. Diplomas (#)	410	379	4	5	0	22

Pecos County

Ft Stockton ISD
101 W Division St • Ft Stockton, TX 79735-7107
(432) 336-4000 • http://www.fort-stockton.k12.tx.us/
Grade Span: PK-12; **Agency Type:** 1
Schools: 6
   2 Primary; 2 Middle; 2 High; 0 Other Level
   5 Regular; 0 Special Education; 0 Vocational; 1 Alternative
   0 Magnet; 0 Charter; 5 Title I Eligible; 5 School-wide Title I
Students: 2,291 (51.6% male; 48.3% female)
   Individual Education Program: 237 (10.3%);
   English Language Learner: 278 (12.1%); Migrant: 218 (9.5%)
   Eligible for Free Lunch Program: 1,215 (53.0%)
   Eligible for Reduced-Price Lunch Program: 285 (12.4%)
Teachers: 154.2 (14.9 to 1)
Librarians/Media Specialists: 2.0 (1,145.5 to 1)
Guidance Counselors: 5.8 (395.0 to 1)
Current Spending: ($ per student per year):
   Total: $8,164; Instruction: $4,844; Support Services: $2,854
Enrollment, Drop-out Rates and Diploma Recipients by Race/Ethnicity

Category	Total	White	Black	Asian	AIAN	Hisp.
Enrollment (%)	100.0	18.6	0.4	0.4	0.0	80.6
Drop-out Rate (%)	4.1	4.9	0.0	0.0	n/a	3.9
H.S. Diplomas (#)	172	42	0	2	0	128

Polk County

Livingston ISD
1412 S Houston • Livingston, TX 77351-1297
Mailing Address: PO Box 1297 • Livingston, TX 77351-1297
(936) 328-2100 • http://www.lioncountry.org/
Grade Span: PK-12; **Agency Type:** 1
Schools: 5
   2 Primary; 2 Middle; 1 High; 0 Other Level
   5 Regular; 0 Special Education; 0 Vocational; 0 Alternative
   0 Magnet; 0 Charter; 3 Title I Eligible; 3 School-wide Title I
Students: 4,048 (51.4% male; 48.5% female)
   Individual Education Program: 713 (17.6%);
   English Language Learner: 167 (4.1%); Migrant: 3 (0.1%)
   Eligible for Free Lunch Program: 1,439 (35.5%)
   Eligible for Reduced-Price Lunch Program: 238 (5.9%)
Teachers: 257.4 (15.7 to 1)
Librarians/Media Specialists: 3.0 (1,349.3 to 1)
Guidance Counselors: 18.0 (224.9 to 1)
Current Spending: ($ per student per year):
   Total: $7,033; Instruction: $4,140; Support Services: $2,537
Enrollment, Drop-out Rates and Diploma Recipients by Race/Ethnicity

Category	Total	White	Black	Asian	AIAN	Hisp.
Enrollment (%)	100.0	72.0	13.4	0.9	0.7	13.0
Drop-out Rate (%)	3.2	3.2	2.1	0.0	0.0	5.0
H.S. Diplomas (#)	250	208	20	3	2	17

Potter County

Amarillo ISD
7200 I-40 W • Amarillo, TX 79106-2598
(806) 354-4200 • http://www.amaisd.org/
Grade Span: PK-12; **Agency Type:** 1
Schools: 52
   37 Primary; 8 Middle; 6 High; 1 Other Level
   51 Regular; 0 Special Education; 0 Vocational; 1 Alternative
   0 Magnet; 0 Charter; 33 Title I Eligible; 33 School-wide Title I
Students: 29,527 (51.2% male; 48.7% female)
   Individual Education Program: 3,769 (12.8%);
   English Language Learner: 2,692 (9.1%); Migrant: 2,125 (7.2%)
   Eligible for Free Lunch Program: 13,883 (47.0%)
   Eligible for Reduced-Price Lunch Program: 2,701 (9.1%)
Teachers: 2,025.7 (14.6 to 1)
Librarians/Media Specialists: 34.5 (855.9 to 1)
Guidance Counselors: 80.4 (367.3 to 1)
Current Spending: ($ per student per year):
   Total: $6,595; Instruction: $4,159; Support Services: $2,104
Enrollment, Drop-out Rates and Diploma Recipients by Race/Ethnicity

Category	Total	White	Black	Asian	AIAN	Hisp.
Enrollment (%)	100.0	48.7	10.6	2.5	0.3	37.9
Drop-out Rate (%)	3.1	2.5	4.2	2.1	5.9	4.1
H.S. Diplomas (#)	1,544	1,013	134	60	2	335

Presidio County

Presidio ISD
100 Market St • Presidio, TX 79845-1401
Mailing Address: PO Box 1401 • Presidio, TX 79845-1401
(432) 229-3275
Grade Span: PK-12; **Agency Type:** 1
Schools: 3
   1 Primary; 1 Middle; 1 High; 0 Other Level
   3 Regular; 0 Special Education; 0 Vocational; 0 Alternative
   0 Magnet; 0 Charter; 3 Title I Eligible; 3 School-wide Title I
Students: 1,525 (53.2% male; 46.7% female)
   Individual Education Program: 137 (9.0%);
   English Language Learner: 811 (53.2%); Migrant: 380 (24.9%)
   Eligible for Free Lunch Program: 1,066 (69.9%)
   Eligible for Reduced-Price Lunch Program: 90 (5.9%)
Teachers: 103.9 (14.7 to 1)
Librarians/Media Specialists: 0.3 (5,083.3 to 1)
Guidance Counselors: 2.0 (762.5 to 1)
Current Spending: ($ per student per year):
   Total: $6,987; Instruction: $4,035; Support Services: $2,510
Enrollment, Drop-out Rates and Diploma Recipients by Race/Ethnicity

Category	Total	White	Black	Asian	AIAN	Hisp.
Enrollment (%)	100.0	1.6	0.0	0.1	0.1	98.2
Drop-out Rate (%)	7.1	0.0	n/a	n/a	n/a	7.2
H.S. Diplomas (#)	89	2	0	0	0	87

Rains County

Rains ISD
1759 W US Hwy 69 • Emory, TX 75440-0247
Mailing Address: PO Box 247 • Emory, TX 75440-0247
(903) 473-2222
Grade Span: PK-12; **Agency Type:** 1
Schools: 4
   1 Primary; 2 Middle; 1 High; 0 Other Level
   4 Regular; 0 Special Education; 0 Vocational; 0 Alternative
   0 Magnet; 0 Charter; 3 Title I Eligible; 0 School-wide Title I
Students: 1,554 (53.0% male; 46.9% female)
   Individual Education Program: 259 (16.7%);
   English Language Learner: 75 (4.8%); Migrant: 2 (0.1%)
   Eligible for Free Lunch Program: 581 (37.4%)
   Eligible for Reduced-Price Lunch Program: 149 (9.6%)
Teachers: 127.0 (12.2 to 1)
Librarians/Media Specialists: 2.0 (777.0 to 1)
Guidance Counselors: 3.0 (518.0 to 1)
Current Spending: ($ per student per year):
   Total: $7,284; Instruction: $4,238; Support Services: $2,568
Enrollment, Drop-out Rates and Diploma Recipients by Race/Ethnicity

Category	Total	White	Black	Asian	AIAN	Hisp.
Enrollment (%)	100.0	85.8	3.0	0.8	1.1	9.3
Drop-out Rate (%)	1.2	1.0	0.0	0.0	0.0	4.2
H.S. Diplomas (#)	93	83	7	0	1	2

Randall County

Canyon ISD

508 16th St • Canyon, TX 79015-0899
Mailing Address: PO Box 899 • Canyon, TX 79015-0899
(806) 677-2600 • http://www.canyonisd.net/
Grade Span: PK-12; **Agency Type:** 1
Schools: 13
   7 Primary; 3 Middle; 2 High; 1 Other Level
   12 Regular; 0 Special Education; 0 Vocational; 1 Alternative
   0 Magnet; 0 Charter; 5 Title I Eligible; 4 School-wide Title I
Students: 7,721 (52.0% male; 47.9% female)
   Individual Education Program: 931 (12.1%);
   English Language Learner: 30 (0.4%); Migrant: 2 (<0.1%)
   Eligible for Free Lunch Program: 1,308 (16.9%)
   Eligible for Reduced-Price Lunch Program: 340 (4.4%)
Teachers: 481.5 (16.0 to 1)
Librarians/Media Specialists: 12.0 (643.4 to 1)
Guidance Counselors: 18.3 (421.9 to 1)
Current Spending: ($ per student per year):
   Total: $5,655; Instruction: $3,592; Support Services: $1,820
Enrollment, Drop-out Rates and Diploma Recipients by Race/Ethnicity

Category	Total	White	Black	Asian	AIAN	Hisp.
Enrollment (%)	100.0	84.0	1.9	0.9	0.6	12.6
Drop-out Rate (%)	1.8	1.8	5.9	0.0	0.0	1.6
H.S. Diplomas (#)	497	434	6	2	4	51

Reeves County

Pecos-Barstow-Toyah ISD

1302 S Park St • Pecos, TX 79772-5718
Mailing Address: PO Box 869 • Pecos, TX 79772-0869
(432) 447-7201
Grade Span: PK-12; **Agency Type:** 1
Schools: 6
   2 Primary; 2 Middle; 1 High; 1 Other Level
   5 Regular; 0 Special Education; 0 Vocational; 1 Alternative
   0 Magnet; 0 Charter; 5 Title I Eligible; 5 School-wide Title I
Students: 2,346 (52.9% male; 47.0% female)
   Individual Education Program: 295 (12.6%);
   English Language Learner: 226 (9.6%); Migrant: 61 (2.6%)
   Eligible for Free Lunch Program: 1,428 (60.9%)
   Eligible for Reduced-Price Lunch Program: 206 (8.8%)
Teachers: 159.0 (14.8 to 1)
Librarians/Media Specialists: 4.0 (586.5 to 1)
Guidance Counselors: 6.0 (391.0 to 1)
Current Spending: ($ per student per year):
   Total: $7,213; Instruction: $4,400; Support Services: $2,360
Enrollment, Drop-out Rates and Diploma Recipients by Race/Ethnicity

Category	Total	White	Black	Asian	AIAN	Hisp.
Enrollment (%)	100.0	9.7	2.6	0.3	0.1	87.3
Drop-out Rate (%)	4.1	0.0	0.0	0.0	0.0	4.8
H.S. Diplomas (#)	183	16	1	0	1	165

Rockwall County

Rockwall ISD

1050 Williams • Rockwall, TX 75087-3832
(972) 771-0605 • http://www.rockwallisd.com/
Grade Span: PK-12; **Agency Type:** 1
Schools: 14
   9 Primary; 2 Middle; 2 High; 1 Other Level
   13 Regular; 0 Special Education; 0 Vocational; 1 Alternative
   0 Magnet; 0 Charter; 4 Title I Eligible; 2 School-wide Title I
Students: 10,096 (52.2% male; 47.7% female)
   Individual Education Program: 1,052 (10.4%);
   English Language Learner: 538 (5.3%); Migrant: 16 (0.2%)
   Eligible for Free Lunch Program: 1,260 (12.5%)
   Eligible for Reduced-Price Lunch Program: 346 (3.4%)
Teachers: 593.9 (17.0 to 1)
Librarians/Media Specialists: 11.4 (885.6 to 1)
Guidance Counselors: 22.5 (448.7 to 1)
Current Spending: ($ per student per year):
   Total: $6,074; Instruction: $3,605; Support Services: $2,216
Enrollment, Drop-out Rates and Diploma Recipients by Race/Ethnicity

Category	Total	White	Black	Asian	AIAN	Hisp.
Enrollment (%)	100.0	77.7	5.8	1.9	0.3	14.3
Drop-out Rate (%)	2.2	2.1	1.0	0.0	0.0	4.1
H.S. Diplomas (#)	492	428	15	15	1	33

Royse City ISD

115 E I-30 • Royse City, TX 75189-0479
Mailing Address: PO Box 479 • Royse City, TX 75189-0479
(972) 636-2413
Grade Span: PK-12; **Agency Type:** 1
Schools: 6
   3 Primary; 1 Middle; 1 High; 1 Other Level
   5 Regular; 0 Special Education; 0 Vocational; 1 Alternative
   0 Magnet; 0 Charter; 3 Title I Eligible; 0 School-wide Title I
Students: 2,694 (53.9% male; 46.0% female)
   Individual Education Program: 384 (14.3%);
   English Language Learner: 202 (7.5%); Migrant: 9 (0.3%)
   Eligible for Free Lunch Program: 788 (29.3%)
   Eligible for Reduced-Price Lunch Program: 185 (6.9%)
Teachers: 195.6 (13.8 to 1)
Librarians/Media Specialists: 4.0 (673.5 to 1)
Guidance Counselors: 5.0 (538.8 to 1)
Current Spending: ($ per student per year):
   Total: $6,838; Instruction: $3,931; Support Services: $2,513
Enrollment, Drop-out Rates and Diploma Recipients by Race/Ethnicity

Category	Total	White	Black	Asian	AIAN	Hisp.
Enrollment (%)	100.0	69.8	5.4	0.6	0.2	24.1
Drop-out Rate (%)	5.3	4.7	0.0	14.3	33.3	7.6
H.S. Diplomas (#)	127	87	9	3	0	28

Rusk County

Henderson ISD

200 N High St • Henderson, TX 75652-3103
Mailing Address: PO Box 728 • Henderson, TX 75653-0728
(903) 657-8511 • http://www.hen.sprnet.org/
Grade Span: PK-12; **Agency Type:** 1
Schools: 7
   4 Primary; 2 Middle; 1 High; 0 Other Level
   7 Regular; 0 Special Education; 0 Vocational; 0 Alternative
   0 Magnet; 0 Charter; 6 Title I Eligible; 6 School-wide Title I
Students: 3,485 (52.5% male; 47.4% female)
   Individual Education Program: 577 (16.6%);
   English Language Learner: 331 (9.5%); Migrant: 5 (0.1%)
   Eligible for Free Lunch Program: 1,446 (41.5%)
   Eligible for Reduced-Price Lunch Program: 271 (7.8%)
Teachers: 263.4 (13.2 to 1)
Librarians/Media Specialists: 5.0 (697.0 to 1)
Guidance Counselors: 10.5 (331.9 to 1)
Current Spending: ($ per student per year):
   Total: $7,313; Instruction: $4,475; Support Services: $2,417
Enrollment, Drop-out Rates and Diploma Recipients by Race/Ethnicity

Category	Total	White	Black	Asian	AIAN	Hisp.
Enrollment (%)	100.0	58.3	23.8	0.4	0.1	17.4
Drop-out Rate (%)	2.3	2.0	3.8	0.0	n/a	0.8
H.S. Diplomas (#)	230	143	63	1	0	23

San Jacinto County

Coldspring-Oakhurst Cons

121 Commercial Ave • Coldspring, TX 77331-0039
Mailing Address: PO Box 39 • Coldspring, TX 77331-0039
(936) 653-1115
Grade Span: PK-12; **Agency Type:** 1
Schools: 4
   2 Primary; 1 Middle; 1 High; 0 Other Level
   4 Regular; 0 Special Education; 0 Vocational; 0 Alternative
   0 Magnet; 0 Charter; 4 Title I Eligible; 4 School-wide Title I
Students: 1,794 (54.1% male; 45.8% female)
   Individual Education Program: 241 (13.4%);
   English Language Learner: 4 (0.2%); Migrant: 0 (0.0%)
   Eligible for Free Lunch Program: 896 (49.9%)
   Eligible for Reduced-Price Lunch Program: 124 (6.9%)
Teachers: 131.8 (13.6 to 1)
Librarians/Media Specialists: 1.0 (1,794.0 to 1)
Guidance Counselors: 4.0 (448.5 to 1)
Current Spending: ($ per student per year):
   Total: $6,920; Instruction: $3,824; Support Services: $2,714
Enrollment, Drop-out Rates and Diploma Recipients by Race/Ethnicity

Category	Total	White	Black	Asian	AIAN	Hisp.
Enrollment (%)	100.0	70.0	24.6	0.6	0.7	4.2
Drop-out Rate (%)	4.2	3.7	5.9	0.0	n/a	0.0
H.S. Diplomas (#)	91	54	36	0	0	1

Shepherd ISD

1401 S Byrd Ave • Shepherd, TX 77371-0429
(936) 628-3396
Grade Span: PK-12; **Agency Type:** 1
Schools: 4
   2 Primary; 1 Middle; 1 High; 0 Other Level

4 Regular; 0 Special Education; 0 Vocational; 0 Alternative
0 Magnet; 0 Charter; 3 Title I Eligible; 3 School-wide Title I
Students: 1,923 (54.1% male; 45.8% female)
  Individual Education Program: 269 (14.0%);
  English Language Learner: 92 (4.8%); Migrant: 5 (0.3%)
  Eligible for Free Lunch Program: 932 (48.5%)
  Eligible for Reduced-Price Lunch Program: 181 (9.4%)
Teachers: 140.7 (13.7 to 1)
Librarians/Media Specialists: 0.9 (2,136.7 to 1)
Guidance Counselors: 2.4 (801.3 to 1)
Current Spending: ($ per student per year):
  Total: $6,730; Instruction: $4,043; Support Services: $2,302
Enrollment, Drop-out Rates and Diploma Recipients by Race/Ethnicity

Category	Total	White	Black	Asian	AIAN	Hisp.
Enrollment (%)	100.0	76.1	10.3	1.1	0.5	11.9
Drop-out Rate (%)	1.3	1.7	0.0	0.0	0.0	0.0
H.S. Diplomas (#)	94	75	12	1	0	6

San Patricio County

Aransas Pass ISD
244 W Harrison Blvd • Aransas Pass, TX 78336-2442
(361) 758-3466 • http://www.aransas-pass.k12.tx.us/
Grade Span: PK-12; **Agency Type:** 1
Schools: 6
  2 Primary; 2 Middle; 1 High; 1 Other Level
  5 Regular; 1 Special Education; 0 Vocational; 0 Alternative
  0 Magnet; 0 Charter; 5 Title I Eligible; 5 School-wide Title I
Students: 2,103 (51.6% male; 48.3% female)
  Individual Education Program: 354 (16.8%);
  English Language Learner: 148 (7.0%); Migrant: 1 (<0.1%)
  Eligible for Free Lunch Program: 921 (43.8%)
  Eligible for Reduced-Price Lunch Program: 220 (10.5%)
Teachers: 153.8 (13.7 to 1)
Librarians/Media Specialists: 1.6 (1,314.4 to 1)
Guidance Counselors: 6.1 (344.8 to 1)
Current Spending: ($ per student per year):
  Total: $7,500; Instruction: $4,499; Support Services: $2,662
Enrollment, Drop-out Rates and Diploma Recipients by Race/Ethnicity

Category	Total	White	Black	Asian	AIAN	Hisp.
Enrollment (%)	100.0	47.5	3.8	0.8	0.4	47.5
Drop-out Rate (%)	2.9	2.4	0.0	0.0	0.0	3.9
H.S. Diplomas (#)	131	71	3	1	1	55

Gregory-Portland ISD
308 N Gregory Ave • Gregory, TX 78359-0338
Mailing Address: PO Box 338 • Gregory, TX 78359-0338
(361) 643-6566 • http://www.gpisd.esc2.net/
Grade Span: PK-12; **Agency Type:** 1
Schools: 8
  4 Primary; 2 Middle; 1 High; 0 Other Level
  7 Regular; 0 Special Education; 0 Vocational; 0 Alternative
  0 Magnet; 0 Charter; 4 Title I Eligible; 4 School-wide Title I
Students: 4,302 (52.3% male; 47.6% female)
  Individual Education Program: 509 (11.8%);
  English Language Learner: 97 (2.3%); Migrant: 7 (0.2%)
  Eligible for Free Lunch Program: 970 (22.5%)
  Eligible for Reduced-Price Lunch Program: 510 (11.9%)
Teachers: 253.6 (17.0 to 1)
Librarians/Media Specialists: 3.1 (1,387.7 to 1)
Guidance Counselors: 9.3 (462.6 to 1)
Current Spending: ($ per student per year):
  Total: $5,606; Instruction: $3,386; Support Services: $1,904
Enrollment, Drop-out Rates and Diploma Recipients by Race/Ethnicity

Category	Total	White	Black	Asian	AIAN	Hisp.
Enrollment (%)	100.0	53.1	3.7	1.3	0.3	41.4
Drop-out Rate (%)	2.2	1.7	8.1	8.7	0.0	2.5
H.S. Diplomas (#)	274	173	7	6	2	86

Ingleside ISD
2807 Mustang Dr • Ingleside, TX 78362-1313
Mailing Address: PO Box 1320 • Ingleside, TX 78362-1313
(361) 776-7631 • http://www.inglesideisd.esc2.net/
Grade Span: PK-12; **Agency Type:** 1
Schools: 5
  2 Primary; 2 Middle; 1 High; 0 Other Level
  5 Regular; 0 Special Education; 0 Vocational; 0 Alternative
  0 Magnet; 0 Charter; 3 Title I Eligible; 3 School-wide Title I
Students: 2,330 (52.0% male; 47.9% female)
  Individual Education Program: 298 (12.8%);
  English Language Learner: 92 (3.9%); Migrant: 4 (0.2%)
  Eligible for Free Lunch Program: 598 (25.7%)
  Eligible for Reduced-Price Lunch Program: 248 (10.6%)
Teachers: 140.7 (16.6 to 1)
Librarians/Media Specialists: 2.0 (1,165.0 to 1)
Guidance Counselors: 5.0 (466.0 to 1)

Current Spending: ($ per student per year):
  Total: $5,966; Instruction: $3,852; Support Services: $1,854
Enrollment, Drop-out Rates and Diploma Recipients by Race/Ethnicity

Category	Total	White	Black	Asian	AIAN	Hisp.
Enrollment (%)	100.0	58.5	3.2	2.8	0.6	34.9
Drop-out Rate (%)	1.3	0.6	0.0	0.0	0.0	2.9
H.S. Diplomas (#)	126	80	7	3	1	35

Mathis ISD
602 E San Patricio Ave • Mathis, TX 78368-2429
Mailing Address: PO Box 1179 • Mathis, TX 78368-1179
(361) 547-3378 • http://www.mathisisd.esc2.net/
Grade Span: PK-12; **Agency Type:** 1
Schools: 4
  1 Primary; 2 Middle; 1 High; 0 Other Level
  4 Regular; 0 Special Education; 0 Vocational; 0 Alternative
  0 Magnet; 0 Charter; 4 Title I Eligible; 4 School-wide Title I
Students: 1,894 (49.1% male; 50.8% female)
  Individual Education Program: 203 (10.7%);
  English Language Learner: 105 (5.5%); Migrant: 756 (39.9%)
  Eligible for Free Lunch Program: 1,346 (71.1%)
  Eligible for Reduced-Price Lunch Program: 185 (9.8%)
Teachers: 137.0 (13.8 to 1)
Librarians/Media Specialists: 3.0 (631.3 to 1)
Guidance Counselors: 6.0 (315.7 to 1)
Current Spending: ($ per student per year):
  Total: $7,876; Instruction: $4,813; Support Services: $2,560
Enrollment, Drop-out Rates and Diploma Recipients by Race/Ethnicity

Category	Total	White	Black	Asian	AIAN	Hisp.
Enrollment (%)	100.0	11.6	0.9	0.1	0.0	87.5
Drop-out Rate (%)	5.5	4.2	0.0	n/a	n/a	5.8
H.S. Diplomas (#)	125	23	2	0	0	100

Sinton ISD
322 S Archer • Sinton, TX 78387-1337
(361) 364-6801
Grade Span: PK-12; **Agency Type:** 1
Schools: 7
  2 Primary; 2 Middle; 1 High; 2 Other Level
  5 Regular; 0 Special Education; 0 Vocational; 2 Alternative
  0 Magnet; 0 Charter; 5 Title I Eligible; 5 School-wide Title I
Students: 2,142 (53.8% male; 46.1% female)
  Individual Education Program: 306 (14.3%);
  English Language Learner: 50 (2.3%); Migrant: 187 (8.7%)
  Eligible for Free Lunch Program: 1,220 (57.0%)
  Eligible for Reduced-Price Lunch Program: 179 (8.4%)
Teachers: 151.3 (14.2 to 1)
Librarians/Media Specialists: 2.0 (1,071.0 to 1)
Guidance Counselors: 7.5 (285.6 to 1)
Current Spending: ($ per student per year):
  Total: $7,689; Instruction: $4,594; Support Services: $2,696
Enrollment, Drop-out Rates and Diploma Recipients by Race/Ethnicity

Category	Total	White	Black	Asian	AIAN	Hisp.
Enrollment (%)	100.0	20.4	1.4	0.2	0.1	77.8
Drop-out Rate (%)	2.9	0.7	0.0	0.0	0.0	3.7
H.S. Diplomas (#)	111	23	4	0	0	84

Scurry County

Snyder ISD
2901 37th St • Snyder, TX 79549-5226
(325) 573-5401
Grade Span: PK-12; **Agency Type:** 1
Schools: 8
  5 Primary; 1 Middle; 2 High; 0 Other Level
  7 Regular; 0 Special Education; 0 Vocational; 1 Alternative
  0 Magnet; 0 Charter; 5 Title I Eligible; 5 School-wide Title I
Students: 2,608 (51.5% male; 48.4% female)
  Individual Education Program: 413 (15.8%);
  English Language Learner: 142 (5.4%); Migrant: 52 (2.0%)
  Eligible for Free Lunch Program: 1,113 (42.7%)
  Eligible for Reduced-Price Lunch Program: 207 (7.9%)
Teachers: 198.3 (13.2 to 1)
Librarians/Media Specialists: 2.0 (1,304.0 to 1)
Guidance Counselors: 5.0 (521.6 to 1)
Current Spending: ($ per student per year):
  Total: $7,157; Instruction: $4,423; Support Services: $2,386
Enrollment, Drop-out Rates and Diploma Recipients by Race/Ethnicity

Category	Total	White	Black	Asian	AIAN	Hisp.
Enrollment (%)	100.0	47.7	4.8	0.3	0.5	46.7
Drop-out Rate (%)	3.1	1.3	9.1	0.0	0.0	5.1
H.S. Diplomas (#)	172	107	4	1	0	60

Shelby County

Center ISD
404 Mosby St • Center, TX 75935-3864
(936) 598-5642 • http://www.centerisd.org/
Grade Span: PK-12; **Agency Type:** 1
Schools: 5
   2 Primary; 2 Middle; 1 High; 0 Other Level
   5 Regular; 0 Special Education; 0 Vocational; 0 Alternative
   0 Magnet; 0 Charter; 4 Title I Eligible; 4 School-wide Title I
Students: 2,470   (49.2% male; 50.7% female)
   Individual Education Program: 259 (10.5%)
   English Language Learner: 410 (16.6%); Migrant: 192 (7.8%)
   Eligible for Free Lunch Program: 1,292 (52.3%)
   Eligible for Reduced-Price Lunch Program: 182 (7.4%)
Teachers: 170.5 (14.5 to 1)
Librarians/Media Specialists: 3.0 (823.3 to 1)
Guidance Counselors: 5.0 (494.0 to 1)
Current Spending: ($ per student per year):
   Total: $6,439; Instruction: $3,989; Support Services: $2,083
Enrollment, Drop-out Rates and Diploma Recipients by Race/Ethnicity

Category	Total	White	Black	Asian	AIAN	Hisp.
Enrollment (%)	100.0	48.9	27.2	0.4	0.1	23.3
Drop-out Rate (%)	2.1	0.6	4.3	0.0	0.0	3.6
H.S. Diplomas (#)	129	68	49	0	0	12

Smith County

Bullard ISD
218 Schoolhouse Rd • Bullard, TX 75757-0250
Mailing Address: PO Box 250 • Bullard, TX 75757-0250
(903) 894-6639
Grade Span: PK-12; **Agency Type:** 1
Schools: 5
   2 Primary; 1 Middle; 1 High; 1 Other Level
   4 Regular; 1 Special Education; 0 Vocational; 0 Alternative
   0 Magnet; 0 Charter; 1 Title I Eligible; 0 School-wide Title I
Students: 1,564   (53.4% male; 46.5% female)
   Individual Education Program: 199 (12.7%);
   English Language Learner: 16 (1.0%); Migrant: 0 (0.0%)
   Eligible for Free Lunch Program: 392 (25.1%)
   Eligible for Reduced-Price Lunch Program: 128 (8.2%)
Teachers: 107.2 (14.6 to 1)
Librarians/Media Specialists: 0.3 (5,213.3 to 1)
Guidance Counselors: 4.0 (391.0 to 1)
Current Spending: ($ per student per year):
   Total: $6,038; Instruction: $3,642; Support Services: $2,053
Enrollment, Drop-out Rates and Diploma Recipients by Race/Ethnicity

Category	Total	White	Black	Asian	AIAN	Hisp.
Enrollment (%)	100.0	90.3	5.0	0.3	0.6	3.8
Drop-out Rate (%)	2.9	3.0	3.8	0.0	0.0	0.0
H.S. Diplomas (#)	81	69	6	0	0	6

Chapel Hill ISD
11134 Cr 2249 • Tyler, TX 75707-9752
(903) 566-2441
Grade Span: PK-12; **Agency Type:** 1
Schools: 8
   3 Primary; 1 Middle; 1 High; 2 Other Level
   5 Regular; 1 Special Education; 0 Vocational; 1 Alternative
   0 Magnet; 0 Charter; 3 Title I Eligible; 3 School-wide Title I
Students: 3,047   (52.4% male; 47.5% female)
   Individual Education Program: 254 (8.3%);
   English Language Learner: 267 (8.8%); Migrant: 3 (0.1%)
   Eligible for Free Lunch Program: 1,353 (44.4%)
   Eligible for Reduced-Price Lunch Program: 198 (6.5%)
Teachers: 221.3 (13.8 to 1)
Librarians/Media Specialists: 2.0 (1,523.5 to 1)
Guidance Counselors: 9.0 (338.6 to 1)
Current Spending: ($ per student per year):
   Total: $6,578; Instruction: $4,070; Support Services: $2,162
Enrollment, Drop-out Rates and Diploma Recipients by Race/Ethnicity

Category	Total	White	Black	Asian	AIAN	Hisp.
Enrollment (%)	100.0	49.5	26.8	0.4	0.3	23.0
Drop-out Rate (%)	2.4	1.4	3.8	0.0	0.0	4.1
H.S. Diplomas (#)	202	131	43	1	0	27

Lindale ISD
505 Pierce St • Lindale, TX 75771-3336
Mailing Address: PO Box 370 • Lindale, TX 75771-0370
(903) 881-4001 • http://www.lind.sprnet.org/
Grade Span: PK-12; **Agency Type:** 1
Schools: 7
   3 Primary; 2 Middle; 1 High; 1 Other Level
   6 Regular; 1 Special Education; 0 Vocational; 0 Alternative

   0 Magnet; 0 Charter; 4 Title I Eligible; 4 School-wide Title I
Students: 3,109   (50.8% male; 49.1% female)
   Individual Education Program: 397 (12.8%);
   English Language Learner: 72 (2.3%); Migrant: 4 (0.1%)
   Eligible for Free Lunch Program: 786 (25.3%)
   Eligible for Reduced-Price Lunch Program: 222 (7.1%)
Teachers: 222.7 (14.0 to 1)
Librarians/Media Specialists: 4.0 (777.3 to 1)
Guidance Counselors: 7.6 (409.1 to 1)
Current Spending: ($ per student per year):
   Total: $6,337; Instruction: $3,930; Support Services: $2,064
Enrollment, Drop-out Rates and Diploma Recipients by Race/Ethnicity

Category	Total	White	Black	Asian	AIAN	Hisp.
Enrollment (%)	100.0	83.2	8.5	1.2	0.6	6.6
Drop-out Rate (%)	0.5	0.1	0.0	37.5	0.0	0.0
H.S. Diplomas (#)	172	152	12	2	4	2

Tyler ISD
1319 W Eighth St • Tyler, TX 75701-3800
Mailing Address: PO Box 2035 • Tyler, TX 75710-2035
(903) 531-3500 • http://www.tylerisd.org/
Grade Span: PK-12; **Agency Type:** 1
Schools: 29
   17 Primary; 6 Middle; 2 High; 4 Other Level
   24 Regular; 1 Special Education; 0 Vocational; 4 Alternative
   0 Magnet; 0 Charter; 20 Title I Eligible; 20 School-wide Title I
Students: 17,394   (51.4% male; 48.5% female)
   Individual Education Program: 2,253 (13.0%);
   English Language Learner: 2,860 (16.4%); Migrant: 13 (0.1%)
   Eligible for Free Lunch Program: 8,337 (47.9%)
   Eligible for Reduced-Price Lunch Program: 1,177 (6.8%)
Teachers: 1,253.1 (13.9 to 1)
Librarians/Media Specialists: 21.9 (794.2 to 1)
Guidance Counselors: 38.0 (457.7 to 1)
Current Spending: ($ per student per year):
   Total: $6,715; Instruction: $4,255; Support Services: $2,125
Enrollment, Drop-out Rates and Diploma Recipients by Race/Ethnicity

Category	Total	White	Black	Asian	AIAN	Hisp.
Enrollment (%)	100.0	32.9	34.0	1.2	0.2	31.7
Drop-out Rate (%)	4.4	2.5	4.8	5.1	11.1	6.9
H.S. Diplomas (#)	901	427	316	8	1	149

Whitehouse ISD
106 W Wildcat Dr • Whitehouse, TX 75791-3130
(903) 839-5500
Grade Span: PK-12; **Agency Type:** 1
Schools: 8
   3 Primary; 2 Middle; 1 High; 2 Other Level
   6 Regular; 0 Special Education; 0 Vocational; 2 Alternative
   0 Magnet; 0 Charter; 3 Title I Eligible; 3 School-wide Title I
Students: 4,096   (52.2% male; 47.7% female)
   Individual Education Program: 386 (9.4%);
   English Language Learner: 75 (1.8%); Migrant: 0 (0.0%)
   Eligible for Free Lunch Program: 815 (19.9%)
   Eligible for Reduced-Price Lunch Program: 277 (6.8%)
Teachers: 253.7 (16.1 to 1)
Librarians/Media Specialists: 3.5 (1,170.3 to 1)
Guidance Counselors: 9.0 (455.1 to 1)
Current Spending: ($ per student per year):
   Total: $5,664; Instruction: $3,471; Support Services: $1,911
Enrollment, Drop-out Rates and Diploma Recipients by Race/Ethnicity

Category	Total	White	Black	Asian	AIAN	Hisp.
Enrollment (%)	100.0	83.7	9.4	1.4	0.3	5.2
Drop-out Rate (%)	2.6	2.7	1.0	0.0	0.0	6.3
H.S. Diplomas (#)	264	222	25	5	1	11

Somervell County

Glen Rose ISD
1102 Stadium Dr • Glen Rose, TX 76043-2129
Mailing Address: PO Box 2129 • Glen Rose, TX 76043-2129
(254) 897-2517 • http://www.grisd.net/
Grade Span: PK-12; **Agency Type:** 1
Schools: 4
   2 Primary; 1 Middle; 1 High; 0 Other Level
   4 Regular; 0 Special Education; 0 Vocational; 0 Alternative
   0 Magnet; 0 Charter; 2 Title I Eligible; 2 School-wide Title I
Students: 1,596   (52.7% male; 47.2% female)
   Individual Education Program: 232 (14.5%);
   English Language Learner: 105 (6.6%); Migrant: 2 (0.1%)
   Eligible for Free Lunch Program: 533 (33.4%)
   Eligible for Reduced-Price Lunch Program: 131 (8.2%)
Teachers: 135.7 (11.8 to 1)
Librarians/Media Specialists: 1.8 (886.7 to 1)
Guidance Counselors: 4.5 (354.7 to 1)

Current Spending: ($ per student per year):
Total: $8,908; Instruction: $5,257; Support Services: $3,229
Enrollment, Drop-out Rates and Diploma Recipients by Race/Ethnicity

Category	Total	White	Black	Asian	AIAN	Hisp.
Enrollment (%)	100.0	78.0	0.2	0.3	1.1	20.4
Drop-out Rate (%)	2.0	1.6	0.0	0.0	0.0	3.8
H.S. Diplomas (#)	103	83	1	0	0	19

Starr County

Rio Grande City CISD
Fort Ringgold • Rio Grande City, TX 78582-4799
(956) 716-6700 • http://www.angelfire.com/tx/rgccisd/
Grade Span: PK-12; **Agency Type:** 1
Schools: 11
    8 Primary; 2 Middle; 1 High; 0 Other Level
    11 Regular; 0 Special Education; 0 Vocational; 0 Alternative
    0 Magnet; 0 Charter; 11 Title I Eligible; 11 School-wide Title I
Students: 9,526   (50.9% male; 49.0% female)
    Individual Education Program: 1,219 (12.8%);
    English Language Learner: 4,786 (50.2%); Migrant: 2,913 (30.6%)
    Eligible for Free Lunch Program: 7,524 (79.0%)
    Eligible for Reduced-Price Lunch Program: 266 (2.8%)
Teachers: 637.2 (14.9 to 1)
Librarians/Media Specialists: 8.9 (1,070.3 to 1)
Guidance Counselors: 32.9 (289.5 to 1)
Current Spending: ($ per student per year):
Total: $8,108; Instruction: $4,763; Support Services: $2,819
Enrollment, Drop-out Rates and Diploma Recipients by Race/Ethnicity

Category	Total	White	Black	Asian	AIAN	Hisp.
Enrollment (%)	100.0	0.2	0.0	0.2	0.0	99.6
Drop-out Rate (%)	8.8	0.0	0.0	0.0	n/a	8.9
H.S. Diplomas (#)	420	2	2	0	0	416

Roma ISD
703 N Gladiator Blvd • Roma, TX 78584-0187
Mailing Address: PO Box 187 • Roma, TX 78584-0187
(956) 849-1377 • http://www.roma.k12.tx.us/
Grade Span: PK-12; **Agency Type:** 1
Schools: 10
    5 Primary; 2 Middle; 2 High; 1 Other Level
    8 Regular; 0 Special Education; 1 Vocational; 1 Alternative
    0 Magnet; 0 Charter; 10 Title I Eligible; 10 School-wide Title I
Students: 6,223   (50.6% male; 49.3% female)
    Individual Education Program: 515 (8.3%);
    English Language Learner: 2,921 (46.9%); Migrant: 1,818 (29.2%)
    Eligible for Free Lunch Program: 472 (7.6%)
    Eligible for Reduced-Price Lunch Program: 39 (0.6%)
Teachers: 411.1 (15.1 to 1)
Librarians/Media Specialists: 8.0 (777.9 to 1)
Guidance Counselors: 14.6 (426.2 to 1)
Current Spending: ($ per student per year):
Total: $7,232; Instruction: $4,508; Support Services: $2,213
Enrollment, Drop-out Rates and Diploma Recipients by Race/Ethnicity

Category	Total	White	Black	Asian	AIAN	Hisp.
Enrollment (%)	100.0	0.2	0.0	0.0	0.0	99.8
Drop-out Rate (%)	7.8	0.0	n/a	n/a	0.0	7.9
H.S. Diplomas (#)	291	2	0	0	0	289

Stephens County

Breckenridge ISD
208 N Miller • Breckenridge, TX 76424-3492
Mailing Address: PO Box 1738 • Breckenridge, TX 76424-1738
(254) 559-2278
Grade Span: PK-12; **Agency Type:** 1
Schools: 6
    2 Primary; 2 Middle; 1 High; 1 Other Level
    5 Regular; 0 Special Education; 0 Vocational; 1 Alternative
    0 Magnet; 0 Charter; 3 Title I Eligible; 3 School-wide Title I
Students: 1,598   (51.3% male; 48.6% female)
    Individual Education Program: 216 (13.5%);
    English Language Learner: 116 (7.3%); Migrant: 5 (0.3%)
    Eligible for Free Lunch Program: 778 (48.7%)
    Eligible for Reduced-Price Lunch Program: 117 (7.3%)
Teachers: 119.0 (13.4 to 1)
Librarians/Media Specialists: 3.0 (532.7 to 1)
Guidance Counselors: 4.0 (399.5 to 1)
Current Spending: ($ per student per year):
Total: $7,016; Instruction: $4,429; Support Services: $2,170
Enrollment, Drop-out Rates and Diploma Recipients by Race/Ethnicity

Category	Total	White	Black	Asian	AIAN	Hisp.
Enrollment (%)	100.0	69.0	2.4	0.5	0.5	27.7
Drop-out Rate (%)	4.8	4.3	0.0	0.0	0.0	7.1
H.S. Diplomas (#)	119	93	0	0	1	25

Tarrant County

Arlington ISD
1203 W Pioneer Pkwy • Arlington, TX 76013-6246
(817) 460-4611 • http://www.arlington.k12.tx.us/
Grade Span: PK-12; **Agency Type:** 1
Schools: 77
    52 Primary; 13 Middle; 8 High; 4 Other Level
    71 Regular; 0 Special Education; 0 Vocational; 6 Alternative
    0 Magnet; 0 Charter; 33 Title I Eligible; 31 School-wide Title I
Students: 62,454   (50.9% male; 49.0% female)
    Individual Education Program: 6,091 (9.8%);
    English Language Learner: 10,181 (16.3%); Migrant: 23 (<0.1%)
    Eligible for Free Lunch Program: 24,536 (39.3%)
    Eligible for Reduced-Price Lunch Program: 4,258 (6.8%)
Teachers: 3,991.3 (15.6 to 1)
Librarians/Media Specialists: 63.8 (978.9 to 1)
Guidance Counselors: 126.6 (493.3 to 1)
Current Spending: ($ per student per year):
Total: $6,115; Instruction: $3,942; Support Services: $1,873
Enrollment, Drop-out Rates and Diploma Recipients by Race/Ethnicity

Category	Total	White	Black	Asian	AIAN	Hisp.
Enrollment (%)	100.0	39.5	22.7	6.9	0.5	30.5
Drop-out Rate (%)	2.7	1.6	3.0	1.4	5.4	5.9
H.S. Diplomas (#)	2,875	1,661	533	281	12	388

Azle ISD
300 Roe St • Azle, TX 76020-3194
(817) 444-3235 • http://www.azle.esc11.net/
Grade Span: PK-12; **Agency Type:** 1
Schools: 11
    5 Primary; 4 Middle; 1 High; 1 Other Level
    10 Regular; 0 Special Education; 0 Vocational; 1 Alternative
    0 Magnet; 0 Charter; 7 Title I Eligible; 7 School-wide Title I
Students: 5,882   (52.8% male; 47.1% female)
    Individual Education Program: 768 (13.1%);
    English Language Learner: 67 (1.1%); Migrant: 3 (0.1%)
    Eligible for Free Lunch Program: 1,397 (23.8%)
    Eligible for Reduced-Price Lunch Program: 416 (7.1%)
Teachers: 391.2 (15.0 to 1)
Librarians/Media Specialists: 4.0 (1,470.5 to 1)
Guidance Counselors: 9.5 (619.2 to 1)
Current Spending: ($ per student per year):
Total: $6,416; Instruction: $3,956; Support Services: $2,063
Enrollment, Drop-out Rates and Diploma Recipients by Race/Ethnicity

Category	Total	White	Black	Asian	AIAN	Hisp.
Enrollment (%)	100.0	89.4	0.7	0.9	0.7	8.3
Drop-out Rate (%)	3.3	3.2	0.0	0.0	0.0	5.8
H.S. Diplomas (#)	355	319	3	2	3	28

Birdville ISD
6125 E Belknap St • Haltom City, TX 76117-4204
(817) 547-5700 • http://www.birdville.k12.tx.us/
Grade Span: PK-12; **Agency Type:** 1
Schools: 33
    20 Primary; 7 Middle; 4 High; 1 Other Level
    30 Regular; 1 Special Education; 0 Vocational; 1 Alternative
    0 Magnet; 0 Charter; 13 Title I Eligible; 9 School-wide Title I
Students: 22,507   (51.9% male; 48.0% female)
    Individual Education Program: 3,039 (13.5%);
    English Language Learner: 1,847 (8.2%); Migrant: 11 (<0.1%)
    Eligible for Free Lunch Program: 6,315 (28.1%)
    Eligible for Reduced-Price Lunch Program: 1,999 (8.9%)
Teachers: 1,355.0 (16.6 to 1)
Librarians/Media Specialists: 30.0 (750.2 to 1)
Guidance Counselors: 46.8 (480.9 to 1)
Current Spending: ($ per student per year):
Total: $6,484; Instruction: $4,197; Support Services: $1,950
Enrollment, Drop-out Rates and Diploma Recipients by Race/Ethnicity

Category	Total	White	Black	Asian	AIAN	Hisp.
Enrollment (%)	100.0	65.4	6.1	5.6	0.5	22.3
Drop-out Rate (%)	1.9	1.7	1.8	2.2	0.0	2.8
H.S. Diplomas (#)	1,164	902	37	78	1	146

Carroll ISD
3051 Dove Rd • Grapevine, TX 76051
(817) 949-8222 • http://www.southlakecarroll.edu/
Grade Span: PK-12; **Agency Type:** 1
Schools: 11
    5 Primary; 4 Middle; 1 High; 1 Other Level
    11 Regular; 0 Special Education; 0 Vocational; 0 Alternative
    0 Magnet; 0 Charter; 3 Title I Eligible; 0 School-wide Title I
Students: 7,304   (52.5% male; 47.4% female)
    Individual Education Program: 738 (10.1%);
    English Language Learner: 5 (0.1%); Migrant: 0 (0.0%)

Eligible for Free Lunch Program: 86 (1.2%)
Eligible for Reduced-Price Lunch Program: 24 (0.3%)
Teachers: 511.7 (14.3 to 1)
Librarians/Media Specialists: 11.0 (664.0 to 1)
Guidance Counselors: 17.0 (429.6 to 1)
Current Spending: ($ per student per year):
Total: $7,241; Instruction: $4,278; Support Services: $2,650
Enrollment, Drop-out Rates and Diploma Recipients by Race/Ethnicity

Category	Total	White	Black	Asian	AIAN	Hisp.
Enrollment (%)	100.0	90.3	1.9	3.7	0.3	3.8
Drop-out Rate (%)	0.3	0.3	0.0	0.0	0.0	0.0
H.S. Diplomas (#)	439	408	4	14	1	12

Castleberry ISD
315 Churchill Rd • Fort Worth, TX 76114-3729
(817) 252-2000 • http://www.castleberryisd.net/
Grade Span: PK-12; **Agency Type:** 1
Schools: 8
2 Primary; 2 Middle; 2 High; 2 Other Level
5 Regular; 0 Special Education; 0 Vocational; 3 Alternative
0 Magnet; 0 Charter; 5 Title I Eligible; 4 School-wide Title I
Students: 3,233 (49.9% male; 50.0% female)
Individual Education Program: 316 (9.8%);
English Language Learner: 579 (17.9%); Migrant: 10 (0.3%)
Eligible for Free Lunch Program: 1,596 (49.4%)
Eligible for Reduced-Price Lunch Program: 308 (9.5%)
Teachers: 195.6 (16.5 to 1)
Librarians/Media Specialists: 3.0 (1,077.7 to 1)
Guidance Counselors: 8.0 (404.1 to 1)
Current Spending: ($ per student per year):
Total: $6,564; Instruction: $3,894; Support Services: $2,331
Enrollment, Drop-out Rates and Diploma Recipients by Race/Ethnicity

Category	Total	White	Black	Asian	AIAN	Hisp.
Enrollment (%)	100.0	45.4	1.9	0.6	0.3	51.8
Drop-out Rate (%)	4.8	5.4	0.0	0.0	0.0	4.2
H.S. Diplomas (#)	178	118	2	1	0	57

Crowley ISD
1008 Hwy 1187 • Crowley, TX 76036-0688
Mailing Address: PO Box 688 • Crowley, TX 76036-0688
(817) 297-5800 • http://www.crowley.k12.tx.us/
Grade Span: PK-12; **Agency Type:** 1
Schools: 15
8 Primary; 2 Middle; 2 High; 3 Other Level
14 Regular; 0 Special Education; 0 Vocational; 1 Alternative
0 Magnet; 0 Charter; 5 Title I Eligible; 4 School-wide Title I
Students: 11,819 (51.3% male; 48.6% female)
Individual Education Program: 1,480 (12.5%);
English Language Learner: 598 (5.1%); Migrant: 7 (0.1%)
Eligible for Free Lunch Program: 2,492 (21.1%)
Eligible for Reduced-Price Lunch Program: 881 (7.5%)
Teachers: 759.8 (15.6 to 1)
Librarians/Media Specialists: 13.0 (909.2 to 1)
Guidance Counselors: 21.5 (549.7 to 1)
Current Spending: ($ per student per year):
Total: $6,497; Instruction: $4,471; Support Services: $1,758
Enrollment, Drop-out Rates and Diploma Recipients by Race/Ethnicity

Category	Total	White	Black	Asian	AIAN	Hisp.
Enrollment (%)	100.0	50.6	27.4	4.4	0.7	17.0
Drop-out Rate (%)	1.4	1.5	0.9	0.0	5.6	1.9
H.S. Diplomas (#)	603	396	129	26	1	51

Eagle Mt-Saginaw ISD
1200 Old Decatur Rd • Fort Worth, TX 76179-9160
(817) 232-0880 • http://www.emsisd.com/index.html
Grade Span: PK-12; **Agency Type:** 1
Schools: 13
7 Primary; 2 Middle; 2 High; 2 Other Level
10 Regular; 0 Special Education; 0 Vocational; 3 Alternative
0 Magnet; 0 Charter; 4 Title I Eligible; 0 School-wide Title I
Students: 8,517 (51.4% male; 48.5% female)
Individual Education Program: 730 (8.6%);
English Language Learner: 355 (4.2%); Migrant: 1 (<0.1%)
Eligible for Free Lunch Program: 1,309 (15.4%)
Eligible for Reduced-Price Lunch Program: 509 (6.0%)
Teachers: 490.7 (17.4 to 1)
Librarians/Media Specialists: 10.0 (851.7 to 1)
Guidance Counselors: 20.8 (409.5 to 1)
Current Spending: ($ per student per year):
Total: $6,032; Instruction: $3,866; Support Services: $1,878
Enrollment, Drop-out Rates and Diploma Recipients by Race/Ethnicity

Category	Total	White	Black	Asian	AIAN	Hisp.
Enrollment (%)	100.0	68.4	3.8	5.1	0.2	22.5
Drop-out Rate (%)	2.8	2.4	3.2	5.0	0.0	4.3
H.S. Diplomas (#)	406	323	11	15	0	57

Everman ISD
608 Townley Dr • Everman, TX 76140-5206
(817) 568-3500 • http://www.eisd.org/
Grade Span: PK-12; **Agency Type:** 1
Schools: 7
4 Primary; 1 Middle; 1 High; 0 Other Level
6 Regular; 0 Special Education; 0 Vocational; 0 Alternative
0 Magnet; 0 Charter; 5 Title I Eligible; 0 School-wide Title I
Students: 3,832 (50.3% male; 49.6% female)
Individual Education Program: 565 (14.7%);
English Language Learner: 539 (14.1%); Migrant: 5 (0.1%)
Eligible for Free Lunch Program: 2 (0.1%)
Eligible for Reduced-Price Lunch Program: 0 (0.0%)
Teachers: 245.3 (15.6 to 1)
Librarians/Media Specialists: 3.0 (1,277.3 to 1)
Guidance Counselors: 7.2 (532.2 to 1)
Current Spending: ($ per student per year):
Total: $6,312; Instruction: $4,025; Support Services: $1,911
Enrollment, Drop-out Rates and Diploma Recipients by Race/Ethnicity

Category	Total	White	Black	Asian	AIAN	Hisp.
Enrollment (%)	100.0	14.7	51.4	1.3	0.1	32.5
Drop-out Rate (%)	2.2	1.4	0.9	0.0	0.0	6.7
H.S. Diplomas (#)	127	28	75	1	0	23

Fort Worth ISD
100 N University Dr • Fort Worth, TX 76107-3010
(817) 871-2000 • http://www.fortworthisd.org/
Grade Span: PK-12; **Agency Type:** 1
Schools: 145
81 Primary; 30 Middle; 20 High; 14 Other Level
114 Regular; 3 Special Education; 1 Vocational; 27 Alternative
0 Magnet; 0 Charter; 80 Title I Eligible; 80 School-wide Title I
Students: 80,335 (50.8% male; 49.1% female)
Individual Education Program: 7,669 (9.5%);
English Language Learner: 21,342 (26.6%); Migrant: 167 (0.2%)
Eligible for Free Lunch Program: 50,688 (63.1%)
Eligible for Reduced-Price Lunch Program: 5,025 (6.3%)
Teachers: 4,792.6 (16.8 to 1)
Librarians/Media Specialists: 109.0 (737.0 to 1)
Guidance Counselors: 194.4 (413.2 to 1)
Current Spending: ($ per student per year):
Total: $7,034; Instruction: $4,112; Support Services: $2,575
Enrollment, Drop-out Rates and Diploma Recipients by Race/Ethnicity

Category	Total	White	Black	Asian	AIAN	Hisp.
Enrollment (%)	100.0	17.8	28.1	1.8	0.2	52.1
Drop-out Rate (%)	6.5	4.6	6.6	3.1	10.5	7.7
H.S. Diplomas (#)	3,222	909	1,053	112	3	1,145

Grapevine-Colleyville ISD
3051 Ira E Woods Ave • Grapevine, TX 76051-3897
(817) 488-9588 • http://www.gcisd-k12.org/
Grade Span: PK-12; **Agency Type:** 1
Schools: 19
11 Primary; 4 Middle; 3 High; 1 Other Level
17 Regular; 0 Special Education; 0 Vocational; 2 Alternative
0 Magnet; 0 Charter; 8 Title I Eligible; 0 School-wide Title I
Students: 13,777 (50.2% male; 49.7% female)
Individual Education Program: 1,017 (7.4%);
English Language Learner: 600 (4.4%); Migrant: 0 (0.0%)
Eligible for Free Lunch Program: 1,106 (8.0%)
Eligible for Reduced-Price Lunch Program: 248 (1.8%)
Teachers: 877.6 (15.7 to 1)
Librarians/Media Specialists: 13.2 (1,043.7 to 1)
Guidance Counselors: 30.0 (459.2 to 1)
Current Spending: ($ per student per year):
Total: $6,640; Instruction: $4,114; Support Services: $2,239
Enrollment, Drop-out Rates and Diploma Recipients by Race/Ethnicity

Category	Total	White	Black	Asian	AIAN	Hisp.
Enrollment (%)	100.0	80.0	3.2	5.9	0.5	10.5
Drop-out Rate (%)	1.6	1.2	3.3	1.9	0.0	6.8
H.S. Diplomas (#)	956	842	25	37	3	49

Hurst-Euless-Bedford ISD
1849a Central Dr • Bedford, TX 76022-6096
(817) 283-4461 • http://www.hebisd.edu/
Grade Span: PK-12; **Agency Type:** 1
Schools: 32
19 Primary; 5 Middle; 4 High; 3 Other Level
26 Regular; 1 Special Education; 0 Vocational; 4 Alternative
0 Magnet; 0 Charter; 13 Title I Eligible; 8 School-wide Title I
Students: 19,527 (51.3% male; 48.6% female)
Individual Education Program: 2,042 (10.5%);
English Language Learner: 1,920 (9.8%); Migrant: 11 (0.1%)
Eligible for Free Lunch Program: 5,753 (29.5%)
Eligible for Reduced-Price Lunch Program: 1,649 (8.4%)

Teachers: 1,271.6 (15.4 to 1)
Librarians/Media Specialists: 25.2 (774.9 to 1)
Guidance Counselors: 40.0 (488.2 to 1)
Current Spending: ($ per student per year):
   Total: $6,680; Instruction: $4,082; Support Services: $2,293
Enrollment, Drop-out Rates and Diploma Recipients by Race/Ethnicity

Category	Total	White	Black	Asian	AIAN	Hisp.
Enrollment (%)	100.0	59.5	11.9	9.3	0.9	18.3
Drop-out Rate (%)	1.9	1.6	1.9	2.0	8.6	3.2
H.S. Diplomas (#)	1,227	900	96	109	7	115

Keller ISD

350 Keller Pkwy · Keller, TX 76248-3447
(817) 744-1000 · http://www.kellerisd.com/
Grade Span: PK-12; **Agency Type:** 1
Schools: 26
  13 Primary; 8 Middle; 3 High; 1 Other Level
  24 Regular; 0 Special Education; 0 Vocational; 1 Alternative
  0 Magnet; 0 Charter; 10 Title I Eligible; 0 School-wide Title I
Students: 21,803 (51.7% male; 48.2% female)
  Individual Education Program: 1,691 (7.8%);
  English Language Learner: 705 (3.2%); Migrant: 7 (<0.1%)
  Eligible for Free Lunch Program: 1,800 (8.3%)
  Eligible for Reduced-Price Lunch Program: 679 (3.1%)
Teachers: 1,248.8 (17.5 to 1)
Librarians/Media Specialists: 18.6 (1,172.2 to 1)
Guidance Counselors: 32.9 (662.7 to 1)
Current Spending: ($ per student per year):
   Total: $5,591; Instruction: $3,484; Support Services: $1,847
Enrollment, Drop-out Rates and Diploma Recipients by Race/Ethnicity

Category	Total	White	Black	Asian	AIAN	Hisp.
Enrollment (%)	100.0	77.3	5.1	5.9	0.4	11.3
Drop-out Rate (%)	2.2	2.1	2.1	2.8	0.0	3.2
H.S. Diplomas (#)	1,013	821	43	67	1	81

Kennedale ISD

120 W Mansfield Hwy · Kennedale, TX 76060-0467
Mailing Address: PO Box 467 · Kennedale, TX 76060-0467
(817) 483-3600 · http://www.kennedale.net/
Grade Span: PK-12; **Agency Type:** 1
Schools: 7
  2 Primary; 2 Middle; 1 High; 1 Other Level
  5 Regular; 0 Special Education; 0 Vocational; 1 Alternative
  0 Magnet; 0 Charter; 3 Title I Eligible; 0 School-wide Title I
Students: 2,938 (50.7% male; 49.2% female)
  Individual Education Program: 287 (9.8%);
  English Language Learner: 93 (3.2%); Migrant: 0 (0.0%)
  Eligible for Free Lunch Program: 410 (14.0%)
  Eligible for Reduced-Price Lunch Program: 191 (6.5%)
Teachers: 184.9 (15.9 to 1)
Librarians/Media Specialists: 3.0 (979.3 to 1)
Guidance Counselors: 6.0 (489.7 to 1)
Current Spending: ($ per student per year):
   Total: $5,723; Instruction: $3,668; Support Services: $1,794
Enrollment, Drop-out Rates and Diploma Recipients by Race/Ethnicity

Category	Total	White	Black	Asian	AIAN	Hisp.
Enrollment (%)	100.0	69.9	12.7	2.6	0.4	14.4
Drop-out Rate (%)	2.8	3.7	0.0	0.0	0.0	1.1
H.S. Diplomas (#)	134	105	14	2	0	13

Lake Worth ISD

6800 Telephone Rd · Lake Worth, TX 76135-2899
(817) 237-1491 ·
http://www.lake-worth.k12.tx.us/education/district/district.php?sectionid=
1
Grade Span: PK-12; **Agency Type:** 1
Schools: 7
  3 Primary; 1 Middle; 2 High; 1 Other Level
  4 Regular; 0 Special Education; 0 Vocational; 3 Alternative
  0 Magnet; 0 Charter; 5 Title I Eligible; 5 School-wide Title I
Students: 2,392 (53.6% male; 46.3% female)
  Individual Education Program: 217 (9.1%);
  English Language Learner: 306 (12.8%); Migrant: 0 (0.0%)
  Eligible for Free Lunch Program: 1,682 (70.3%)
  Eligible for Reduced-Price Lunch Program: 169 (7.1%)
Teachers: 172.1 (13.9 to 1)
Librarians/Media Specialists: 3.0 (797.3 to 1)
Guidance Counselors: 3.0 (797.3 to 1)
Current Spending: ($ per student per year):
   Total: $7,180; Instruction: $4,190; Support Services: $2,518
Enrollment, Drop-out Rates and Diploma Recipients by Race/Ethnicity

Category	Total	White	Black	Asian	AIAN	Hisp.
Enrollment (%)	100.0	45.3	7.1	1.2	0.8	45.7
Drop-out Rate (%)	3.4	3.0	3.6	0.0	0.0	4.2
H.S. Diplomas (#)	117	69	8	0	1	39

Mansfield ISD

605 E Broad St · Mansfield, TX 76063-1794
(817) 473-5600 · http://www.mansfieldisd.org/
Grade Span: PK-12; **Agency Type:** 1
Schools: 23
  12 Primary; 6 Middle; 3 High; 1 Other Level
  20 Regular; 0 Special Education; 0 Vocational; 2 Alternative
  0 Magnet; 0 Charter; 2 Title I Eligible; 2 School-wide Title I
Students: 21,060 (51.6% male; 48.3% female)
  Individual Education Program: 2,337 (11.1%);
  English Language Learner: 1,258 (6.0%); Migrant: 1 (<0.1%)
  Eligible for Free Lunch Program: 3,663 (17.5%)
  Eligible for Reduced-Price Lunch Program: 1,416 (6.7%)
Teachers: 1,367.4 (15.3 to 1)
Librarians/Media Specialists: 16.2 (1,295.4 to 1)
Guidance Counselors: 41.1 (510.6 to 1)
Current Spending: ($ per student per year):
   Total: $6,121; Instruction: $3,922; Support Services: $1,964
Enrollment, Drop-out Rates and Diploma Recipients by Race/Ethnicity

Category	Total	White	Black	Asian	AIAN	Hisp.
Enrollment (%)	100.0	59.9	19.4	4.5	0.5	15.7
Drop-out Rate (%)	2.1	1.8	1.8	1.1	7.1	4.8
H.S. Diplomas (#)	791	566	110	38	2	75

White Settlement ISD

401 S Cherry Ln · White Settlement, TX 76108-2521
(817) 367-1350
Grade Span: PK-12; **Agency Type:** 1
Schools: 10
  4 Primary; 2 Middle; 2 High; 1 Other Level
  7 Regular; 0 Special Education; 0 Vocational; 2 Alternative
  0 Magnet; 0 Charter; 5 Title I Eligible; 5 School-wide Title I
Students: 4,828 (51.8% male; 48.1% female)
  Individual Education Program: 597 (12.4%);
  English Language Learner: 201 (4.2%); Migrant: 5 (0.1%)
  Eligible for Free Lunch Program: 1,571 (32.5%)
  Eligible for Reduced-Price Lunch Program: 361 (7.5%)
Teachers: 316.0 (15.3 to 1)
Librarians/Media Specialists: 3.2 (1,508.8 to 1)
Guidance Counselors: 9.3 (519.1 to 1)
Current Spending: ($ per student per year):
   Total: $6,377; Instruction: $3,964; Support Services: $2,062
Enrollment, Drop-out Rates and Diploma Recipients by Race/Ethnicity

Category	Total	White	Black	Asian	AIAN	Hisp.
Enrollment (%)	100.0	67.8	7.2	2.5	0.7	21.8
Drop-out Rate (%)	4.8	5.0	0.9	6.5	0.0	5.8
H.S. Diplomas (#)	283	215	26	8	3	31

Taylor County

Abilene ISD

842 N Mockingbird · Abilene, TX 79603-5729
Mailing Address: PO Box 981 · Abilene, TX 79604-0981
(325) 677-1444 · http://www.aisd.org/
Grade Span: PK-12; **Agency Type:** 1
Schools: 41
  19 Primary; 7 Middle; 3 High; 9 Other Level
  24 Regular; 4 Special Education; 0 Vocational; 10 Alternative
  0 Magnet; 0 Charter; 9 Title I Eligible; 9 School-wide Title I
Students: 17,036 (51.1% male; 48.8% female)
  Individual Education Program: 3,077 (18.1%);
  English Language Learner: 390 (2.3%); Migrant: 0 (0.0%)
  Eligible for Free Lunch Program: 7,719 (45.3%)
  Eligible for Reduced-Price Lunch Program: 1,705 (10.0%)
Teachers: 1,294.6 (13.2 to 1)
Librarians/Media Specialists: 25.5 (668.1 to 1)
Guidance Counselors: 47.0 (362.5 to 1)
Current Spending: ($ per student per year):
   Total: $6,979; Instruction: $4,527; Support Services: $2,105
Enrollment, Drop-out Rates and Diploma Recipients by Race/Ethnicity

Category	Total	White	Black	Asian	AIAN	Hisp.
Enrollment (%)	100.0	54.1	12.7	1.2	0.5	31.5
Drop-out Rate (%)	4.9	3.4	5.9	1.4	6.3	8.4
H.S. Diplomas (#)	1,032	688	109	21	1	213

Wylie ISD

7049 Buffalo Gap Rd · Abilene, TX 79606-5448
(325) 692-4353
Grade Span: PK-12; **Agency Type:** 1
Schools: 7
  3 Primary; 2 Middle; 1 High; 0 Other Level
  6 Regular; 0 Special Education; 0 Vocational; 0 Alternative
  0 Magnet; 0 Charter; 4 Title I Eligible; 0 School-wide Title I
Students: 2,804 (49.1% male; 50.8% female)
  Individual Education Program: 328 (11.7%);

English Language Learner: 5 (0.2%); Migrant: 0 (0.0%)
Eligible for Free Lunch Program: 153 (5.5%)
Eligible for Reduced-Price Lunch Program: 110 (3.9%)
Teachers: 173.1 (16.2 to 1)
Librarians/Media Specialists: 2.0 (1,402.0 to 1)
Guidance Counselors: 6.4 (438.1 to 1)
Current Spending: ($ per student per year):
Total: $4,913; Instruction: $3,220; Support Services: $1,466
Enrollment, Drop-out Rates and Diploma Recipients by Race/Ethnicity

Category	Total	White	Black	Asian	AIAN	Hisp.
Enrollment (%)	100.0	87.7	2.9	1.9	0.5	7.0
Drop-out Rate (%)	1.1	1.2	0.0	0.0	0.0	0.0
H.S. Diplomas (#)	194	175	7	4	1	7

Terry County

Brownfield ISD

601 Tahoka Rd • Brownfield, TX 79316-3631
(806) 637-2591 • http://www.brownfield.k12.tx.us/
Grade Span: PK-12; **Agency Type:** 1
Schools: 4
2 Primary; 1 Middle; 1 High; 0 Other Level
4 Regular; 0 Special Education; 0 Vocational; 0 Alternative
0 Magnet; 0 Charter; 4 Title I Eligible; 2 School-wide Title I
Students: 1,947 (51.0% male; 48.9% female)
Individual Education Program: 295 (15.2%);
English Language Learner: 103 (5.3%); Migrant: 305 (15.7%)
Eligible for Free Lunch Program: 1,131 (58.1%)
Eligible for Reduced-Price Lunch Program: 164 (8.4%)
Teachers: 152.9 (12.7 to 1)
Librarians/Media Specialists: 3.0 (649.0 to 1)
Guidance Counselors: 5.9 (330.0 to 1)
Current Spending: ($ per student per year):
Total: $7,825; Instruction: $4,865; Support Services: $2,617
Enrollment, Drop-out Rates and Diploma Recipients by Race/Ethnicity

Category	Total	White	Black	Asian	AIAN	Hisp.
Enrollment (%)	100.0	31.4	4.8	0.4	0.2	63.2
Drop-out Rate (%)	2.8	0.4	12.1	0.0	n/a	3.2
H.S. Diplomas (#)	163	68	8	3	0	84

Titus County

Mount Pleasant ISD

105 N Riddle • Mount Pleasant, TX 75455
Mailing Address: PO Box 1117 • Mount Pleasant, TX 75456-1117
(903) 575-2000 • http://www.mpisd.net/
Grade Span: PK-12; **Agency Type:** 1
Schools: 10
6 Primary; 1 Middle; 2 High; 1 Other Level
8 Regular; 0 Special Education; 0 Vocational; 2 Alternative
0 Magnet; 0 Charter; 6 Title I Eligible; 6 School-wide Title I
Students: 5,129 (52.0% male; 47.9% female)
Individual Education Program: 738 (14.4%);
English Language Learner: 1,748 (34.1%); Migrant: 1,242 (24.2%)
Eligible for Free Lunch Program: 3,068 (59.8%)
Eligible for Reduced-Price Lunch Program: 532 (10.4%)
Teachers: 376.7 (13.6 to 1)
Librarians/Media Specialists: 2.0 (2,564.5 to 1)
Guidance Counselors: 14.0 (366.4 to 1)
Current Spending: ($ per student per year):
Total: $7,352; Instruction: $4,488; Support Services: $2,477
Enrollment, Drop-out Rates and Diploma Recipients by Race/Ethnicity

Category	Total	White	Black	Asian	AIAN	Hisp.
Enrollment (%)	100.0	31.1	15.4	0.5	0.4	52.6
Drop-out Rate (%)	2.8	2.0	1.6	0.0	33.3	4.1
H.S. Diplomas (#)	270	151	39	2	0	78

Tom Green County

San Angelo ISD

1621 University Ave • San Angelo, TX 76904-5164
(325) 947-3700 • http://www.saisd.org/
Grade Span: PK-12; **Agency Type:** 1
Schools: 27
19 Primary; 4 Middle; 2 High; 2 Other Level
25 Regular; 0 Special Education; 0 Vocational; 2 Alternative
0 Magnet; 0 Charter; 16 Title I Eligible; 16 School-wide Title I
Students: 15,126 (51.0% male; 48.9% female)
Individual Education Program: 1,974 (13.1%);
English Language Learner: 797 (5.3%); Migrant: 309 (2.0%)
Eligible for Free Lunch Program: 6,254 (41.3%)
Eligible for Reduced-Price Lunch Program: 1,535 (10.1%)
Teachers: 971.1 (15.6 to 1)
Librarians/Media Specialists: 16.0 (945.4 to 1)
Guidance Counselors: 39.0 (387.8 to 1)

Current Spending: ($ per student per year):
Total: $6,190; Instruction: $3,924; Support Services: $1,965
Enrollment, Drop-out Rates and Diploma Recipients by Race/Ethnicity

Category	Total	White	Black	Asian	AIAN	Hisp.
Enrollment (%)	100.0	44.2	6.3	1.1	0.2	48.2
Drop-out Rate (%)	4.3	2.8	3.8	1.8	0.0	6.3
H.S. Diplomas (#)	960	527	55	17	2	359

Travis County

Austin ISD

1111 W 6th St • Austin, TX 78703-5399
(512) 414-1700 • http://www.austin.isd.tenet.edu/
Grade Span: PK-12; **Agency Type:** 1
Schools: 111
75 Primary; 17 Middle; 12 High; 7 Other Level
104 Regular; 0 Special Education; 0 Vocational; 7 Alternative
0 Magnet; 0 Charter; 67 Title I Eligible; 66 School-wide Title I
Students: 79,007 (51.5% male; 48.4% female)
Individual Education Program: 9,739 (12.3%);
English Language Learner: 17,259 (21.8%); Migrant: 96 (0.1%)
Eligible for Free Lunch Program: 37,178 (47.2%)
Eligible for Reduced-Price Lunch Program: 6,657 (8.4%)
Teachers: 5,354.4 (14.7 to 1)
Librarians/Media Specialists: 98.9 (796.8 to 1)
Guidance Counselors: 162.1 (486.2 to 1)
Current Spending: ($ per student per year):
Total: $7,580; Instruction: $4,420; Support Services: $2,837
Enrollment, Drop-out Rates and Diploma Recipients by Race/Ethnicity

Category	Total	White	Black	Asian	AIAN	Hisp.
Enrollment (%)	100.0	30.2	13.6	2.7	0.2	53.2
Drop-out Rate (%)	6.0	2.9	8.6	3.1	4.5	8.0
H.S. Diplomas (#)	3,705	1,755	562	117	8	1,263

Del Valle ISD

5301 Ross Rd • Del Valle, TX 78617-9404
(512) 386-3000 • http://www.del-valle.k12.tx.us/
Grade Span: PK-12; **Agency Type:** 1
Schools: 11
6 Primary; 2 Middle; 2 High; 1 Other Level
9 Regular; 0 Special Education; 0 Vocational; 2 Alternative
0 Magnet; 0 Charter; 10 Title I Eligible; 10 School-wide Title I
Students: 7,656 (51.2% male; 48.7% female)
Individual Education Program: 1,134 (14.8%);
English Language Learner: 1,533 (20.0%); Migrant: 15 (0.2%)
Eligible for Free Lunch Program: 4,521 (59.1%)
Eligible for Reduced-Price Lunch Program: 918 (12.0%)
Teachers: 526.3 (14.5 to 1)
Librarians/Media Specialists: 9.0 (850.7 to 1)
Guidance Counselors: 20.0 (382.8 to 1)
Current Spending: ($ per student per year):
Total: $7,198; Instruction: $4,227; Support Services: $2,565
Enrollment, Drop-out Rates and Diploma Recipients by Race/Ethnicity

Category	Total	White	Black	Asian	AIAN	Hisp.
Enrollment (%)	100.0	14.4	14.9	1.2	0.5	69.0
Drop-out Rate (%)	4.8	5.2	4.5	0.0	0.0	4.9
H.S. Diplomas (#)	302	66	67	7	5	157

Eanes ISD

601 Camp Craft Rd • Austin, TX 78746-6511
(512) 732-9001 •
http://www.eanes.k12.tx.us/education/district/district.php?sectionid=1
Grade Span: PK-12; **Agency Type:** 1
Schools: 10
6 Primary; 2 Middle; 2 High; 0 Other Level
9 Regular; 0 Special Education; 0 Vocational; 1 Alternative
0 Magnet; 0 Charter; 4 Title I Eligible; 0 School-wide Title I
Students: 7,091 (52.0% male; 47.9% female)
Individual Education Program: 760 (10.7%);
English Language Learner: 125 (1.8%); Migrant: 0 (0.0%)
Eligible for Free Lunch Program: 69 (1.0%)
Eligible for Reduced-Price Lunch Program: 27 (0.4%)
Teachers: 510.5 (13.9 to 1)
Librarians/Media Specialists: 9.0 (787.9 to 1)
Guidance Counselors: 21.8 (325.3 to 1)
Current Spending: ($ per student per year):
Total: $7,546; Instruction: $4,620; Support Services: $2,576
Enrollment, Drop-out Rates and Diploma Recipients by Race/Ethnicity

Category	Total	White	Black	Asian	AIAN	Hisp.
Enrollment (%)	100.0	86.9	0.6	6.8	0.3	5.4
Drop-out Rate (%)	0.7	0.8	0.0	0.6	0.0	0.0
H.S. Diplomas (#)	528	466	2	33	2	25

Lake Travis ISD
3322 Ranch Rd 620 S • Austin, TX 78738-6801
(512) 533-6000
Grade Span: PK-12; Agency Type: 1
Schools: 8
  3 Primary; 2 Middle; 1 High; 0 Other Level
  6 Regular; 0 Special Education; 0 Vocational; 0 Alternative
  0 Magnet; 0 Charter; 1 Title I Eligible; 0 School-wide Title I
Students: 4,818 (53.5% male; 46.4% female)
  Individual Education Program: 516 (10.7%);
  English Language Learner: 216 (4.5%); Migrant: 0 (0.0%)
  Eligible for Free Lunch Program: 393 (8.2%)
  Eligible for Reduced-Price Lunch Program: 103 (2.1%)
Teachers: 321.3 (15.0 to 1)
Librarians/Media Specialists: 7.0 (688.3 to 1)
Guidance Counselors: 13.0 (370.6 to 1)
Current Spending: ($ per student per year):
  Total: $6,793; Instruction: $4,234; Support Services: $2,316
Enrollment, Drop-out Rates and Diploma Recipients by Race/Ethnicity

Category	Total	White	Black	Asian	AIAN	Hisp.
Enrollment (%)	100.0	83.7	1.0	2.2	0.5	12.6
Drop-out Rate (%)	1.4	1.4	0.0	0.0	0.0	1.6
H.S. Diplomas (#)	269	234	0	3	0	32

Manor ISD
312 Murray Ave • Manor, TX 78653-0679
Mailing Address: PO Box 359 • Manor, TX 78653-0359
(512) 278-4000 • http://mustang.manor.isd.tenet.edu/
Grade Span: PK-12; Agency Type: 1
Schools: 7
  3 Primary; 1 Middle; 1 High; 2 Other Level
  5 Regular; 0 Special Education; 0 Vocational; 2 Alternative
  0 Magnet; 0 Charter; 6 Title I Eligible; 6 School-wide Title I
Students: 3,227 (51.1% male; 48.8% female)
  Individual Education Program: 459 (14.2%);
  English Language Learner: 620 (19.2%); Migrant: 35 (1.1%)
  Eligible for Free Lunch Program: 1,637 (50.7%)
  Eligible for Reduced-Price Lunch Program: 360 (11.2%)
Teachers: 214.9 (15.0 to 1)
Librarians/Media Specialists: 5.0 (645.4 to 1)
Guidance Counselors: 7.0 (461.0 to 1)
Current Spending: ($ per student per year):
  Total: $7,826; Instruction: $4,414; Support Services: $2,965
Enrollment, Drop-out Rates and Diploma Recipients by Race/Ethnicity

Category	Total	White	Black	Asian	AIAN	Hisp.
Enrollment (%)	100.0	26.6	21.7	1.7	0.1	49.9
Drop-out Rate (%)	4.5	3.1	3.6	0.0	0.0	6.6
H.S. Diplomas (#)	141	54	39	2	1	45

Pflugerville ISD
1401 W Pecan St • Pflugerville, TX 78660-2518
(512) 594-0000 • http://www.pflugervilleisd.net/
Grade Span: PK-12; Agency Type: 1
Schools: 24
  14 Primary; 5 Middle; 3 High; 2 Other Level
  21 Regular; 0 Special Education; 0 Vocational; 3 Alternative
  0 Magnet; 0 Charter; 8 Title I Eligible; 0 School-wide Title I
Students: 16,592 (51.8% male; 48.1% female)
  Individual Education Program: 1,889 (11.4%);
  English Language Learner: 1,702 (10.3%); Migrant: 3 (<0.1%)
  Eligible for Free Lunch Program: 4,137 (24.9%)
  Eligible for Reduced-Price Lunch Program: 1,630 (9.8%)
Teachers: 1,028.7 (16.1 to 1)
Librarians/Media Specialists: 19.8 (838.0 to 1)
Guidance Counselors: 32.5 (510.5 to 1)
Current Spending: ($ per student per year):
  Total: $6,267; Instruction: $3,848; Support Services: $2,135
Enrollment, Drop-out Rates and Diploma Recipients by Race/Ethnicity

Category	Total	White	Black	Asian	AIAN	Hisp.
Enrollment (%)	100.0	40.7	21.0	8.3	0.4	29.6
Drop-out Rate (%)	1.8	1.8	1.1	1.6	9.1	2.3
H.S. Diplomas (#)	864	463	138	78	2	183

Upshur County

Gilmer ISD
500 So Trinity • Gilmer, TX 75644-0040
(903) 843-2525
Grade Span: PK-12; Agency Type: 1
Schools: 4
  2 Primary; 1 Middle; 1 High; 0 Other Level
  4 Regular; 0 Special Education; 0 Vocational; 0 Alternative
  0 Magnet; 0 Charter; 4 Title I Eligible; 4 School-wide Title I
Students: 2,276 (53.0% male; 46.9% female)
  Individual Education Program: 355 (15.6%);

  English Language Learner: 84 (3.7%); Migrant: 8 (0.4%)
  Eligible for Free Lunch Program: 942 (41.4%)
  Eligible for Reduced-Price Lunch Program: 219 (9.6%)
Teachers: 174.1 (13.1 to 1)
Librarians/Media Specialists: 4.0 (569.0 to 1)
Guidance Counselors: 5.0 (455.2 to 1)
Current Spending: ($ per student per year):
  Total: $6,994; Instruction: $4,343; Support Services: $2,287
Enrollment, Drop-out Rates and Diploma Recipients by Race/Ethnicity

Category	Total	White	Black	Asian	AIAN	Hisp.
Enrollment (%)	100.0	72.2	19.3	0.5	0.7	7.2
Drop-out Rate (%)	2.9	2.8	3.7	n/a	0.0	3.1
H.S. Diplomas (#)	166	131	27	0	1	7

Uvalde County

Uvalde Cons ISD
1000 N Getty • Uvalde, TX 78801-4206
Mailing Address: PO Box 1909 • Uvalde, TX 78802-1909
(830) 278-6655 • http://www.uvalde-cons.k12.tx.us/
Grade Span: PK-12; Agency Type: 1
Schools: 10
  5 Primary; 3 Middle; 2 High; 0 Other Level
  9 Regular; 0 Special Education; 0 Vocational; 1 Alternative
  0 Magnet; 0 Charter; 10 Title I Eligible; 10 School-wide Title I
Students: 5,282 (52.0% male; 47.9% female)
  Individual Education Program: 597 (11.3%);
  English Language Learner: 485 (9.2%); Migrant: 858 (16.2%)
  Eligible for Free Lunch Program: 3,497 (66.2%)
  Eligible for Reduced-Price Lunch Program: 444 (8.4%)
Teachers: 365.3 (14.5 to 1)
Librarians/Media Specialists: 6.0 (880.3 to 1)
Guidance Counselors: 16.0 (330.1 to 1)
Current Spending: ($ per student per year):
  Total: $7,136; Instruction: $4,281; Support Services: $2,463
Enrollment, Drop-out Rates and Diploma Recipients by Race/Ethnicity

Category	Total	White	Black	Asian	AIAN	Hisp.
Enrollment (%)	100.0	13.3	0.4	0.4	0.1	85.7
Drop-out Rate (%)	6.1	1.7	0.0	0.0	0.0	7.2
H.S. Diplomas (#)	273	66	0	1	0	206

Val Verde County

San Felipe-Del Rio Cons I
PO Drawer 428002 • Del Rio, TX 78842-0128
(830) 778-4007 • http://www.sfdr-cisd.org/
Grade Span: PK-12; Agency Type: 1
Schools: 15
  8 Primary; 1 Middle; 1 High; 4 Other Level
  14 Regular; 0 Special Education; 0 Vocational; 0 Alternative
  0 Magnet; 0 Charter; 14 Title I Eligible; 14 School-wide Title I
Students: 10,461 (51.0% male; 48.9% female)
  Individual Education Program: 1,258 (12.0%);
  English Language Learner: 1,907 (18.2%); Migrant: 3,790 (36.2%)
  Eligible for Free Lunch Program: 6,591 (63.0%)
  Eligible for Reduced-Price Lunch Program: 1,107 (10.6%)
Teachers: 573.7 (18.2 to 1)
Librarians/Media Specialists: 10.9 (959.7 to 1)
Guidance Counselors: 23.1 (452.9 to 1)
Current Spending: ($ per student per year):
  Total: $7,006; Instruction: $4,283; Support Services: $2,368
Enrollment, Drop-out Rates and Diploma Recipients by Race/Ethnicity

Category	Total	White	Black	Asian	AIAN	Hisp.
Enrollment (%)	100.0	9.4	1.2	0.3	0.1	89.0
Drop-out Rate (%)	4.8	3.1	11.1	0.0	100.0	4.9
H.S. Diplomas (#)	482	52	6	1	1	422

Van Zandt County

Canton ISD
225 W Elm St • Canton, TX 75103-1799
(903) 567-4179
Grade Span: PK-12; Agency Type: 1
Schools: 4
  2 Primary; 1 Middle; 1 High; 0 Other Level
  4 Regular; 0 Special Education; 0 Vocational; 0 Alternative
  0 Magnet; 0 Charter; 3 Title I Eligible; 0 School-wide Title I
Students: 1,798 (50.9% male; 49.0% female)
  Individual Education Program: 166 (9.2%);
  English Language Learner: 47 (2.6%); Migrant: 0 (0.0%)
  Eligible for Free Lunch Program: 417 (23.2%)
  Eligible for Reduced-Price Lunch Program: 114 (6.3%)
Teachers: 125.1 (14.4 to 1)
Librarians/Media Specialists: 2.0 (899.0 to 1)
Guidance Counselors: 3.0 (599.3 to 1)

Current Spending: ($ per student per year):
Total: $6,442; Instruction: $4,238; Support Services: $1,891
Enrollment, Drop-out Rates and Diploma Recipients by Race/Ethnicity

Category	Total	White	Black	Asian	AIAN	Hisp.
Enrollment (%)	100.0	88.9	2.9	1.1	0.1	7.0
Drop-out Rate (%)	1.2	1.1	6.3	0.0	0.0	0.0
H.S. Diplomas (#)	105	93	7	2	0	3

Van ISD

549 E Texas St · Van, TX 75790-0697
Mailing Address: PO Box 697 · Van, TX 75790-0697
(903) 963-8328
Grade Span: PK-12; **Agency Type:** 1
Schools: 4
2 Primary; 1 Middle; 1 High; 0 Other Level
4 Regular; 0 Special Education; 0 Vocational; 0 Alternative
0 Magnet; 0 Charter; 2 Title I Eligible; 2 School-wide Title I
Students: 2,168   (51.3% male; 48.6% female)
Individual Education Program: 286 (13.2%);
English Language Learner: 132 (6.1%); Migrant: 0 (0.0%)
Eligible for Free Lunch Program: 763 (35.2%)
Eligible for Reduced-Price Lunch Program: 170 (7.8%)
Teachers: 155.3 (14.0 to 1)
Librarians/Media Specialists: 2.0 (1,084.0 to 1)
Guidance Counselors: 6.0 (361.3 to 1)
Current Spending: ($ per student per year):
Total: $6,692; Instruction: $4,078; Support Services: $2,233
Enrollment, Drop-out Rates and Diploma Recipients by Race/Ethnicity

Category	Total	White	Black	Asian	AIAN	Hisp.
Enrollment (%)	100.0	85.2	3.8	0.4	0.4	10.2
Drop-out Rate (%)	2.4	2.4	0.0	0.0	0.0	4.8
H.S. Diplomas (#)	121	111	4	0	0	6

Wills Point ISD

338 W N Commerce St · Wills Point, TX 75169-2504
(903) 873-3161
Grade Span: PK-12; **Agency Type:** 1
Schools: 5
2 Primary; 2 Middle; 1 High; 0 Other Level
5 Regular; 0 Special Education; 0 Vocational; 0 Alternative
0 Magnet; 0 Charter; 5 Title I Eligible; 5 School-wide Title I
Students: 2,711   (51.3% male; 48.6% female)
Individual Education Program: 377 (13.9%);
English Language Learner: 96 (3.5%); Migrant: 15 (0.6%)
Eligible for Free Lunch Program: 1,043 (38.5%)
Eligible for Reduced-Price Lunch Program: 270 (10.0%)
Teachers: 174.4 (15.5 to 1)
Librarians/Media Specialists: 3.0 (903.7 to 1)
Guidance Counselors: 5.0 (542.2 to 1)
Current Spending: ($ per student per year):
Total: $6,476; Instruction: $3,997; Support Services: $2,129
Enrollment, Drop-out Rates and Diploma Recipients by Race/Ethnicity

Category	Total	White	Black	Asian	AIAN	Hisp.
Enrollment (%)	100.0	82.1	7.0	0.1	0.6	10.1
Drop-out Rate (%)	1.7	1.8	2.3	0.0	0.0	0.0
H.S. Diplomas (#)	159	123	27	0	1	8

Victoria County

Victoria ISD

102 Profit Dr · Victoria, TX 77901-7346
Mailing Address: PO Box 1759 · Victoria, TX 77902-1759
(361) 576-3131 · http://www.visd.com/
Grade Span: PK-12; **Agency Type:** 1
Schools: 26
17 Primary; 2 Middle; 2 High; 4 Other Level
20 Regular; 0 Special Education; 0 Vocational; 5 Alternative
0 Magnet; 0 Charter; 12 Title I Eligible; 12 School-wide Title I
Students: 14,437   (51.8% male; 48.1% female)
Individual Education Program: 1,731 (12.0%);
English Language Learner: 435 (3.0%); Migrant: 22 (0.2%)
Eligible for Free Lunch Program: 6,268 (43.4%)
Eligible for Reduced-Price Lunch Program: 1,270 (8.8%)
Teachers: 969.7 (14.9 to 1)
Librarians/Media Specialists: 16.4 (880.3 to 1)
Guidance Counselors: 39.1 (369.2 to 1)
Current Spending: ($ per student per year):
Total: $6,842; Instruction: $4,107; Support Services: $2,415
Enrollment, Drop-out Rates and Diploma Recipients by Race/Ethnicity

Category	Total	White	Black	Asian	AIAN	Hisp.
Enrollment (%)	100.0	37.2	8.4	0.9	0.3	53.2
Drop-out Rate (%)	4.3	2.2	4.3	0.0	0.0	6.5
H.S. Diplomas (#)	867	448	67	12	1	339

Walker County

Huntsville ISD

441 Fm 2821 E · Huntsville, TX 77320-9298
(936) 295-3421 · http://www.huntsville-isd.org/
Grade Span: PK-12; **Agency Type:** 1
Schools: 10
5 Primary; 2 Middle; 3 High; 0 Other Level
8 Regular; 0 Special Education; 0 Vocational; 2 Alternative
0 Magnet; 0 Charter; 6 Title I Eligible; 6 School-wide Title I
Students: 6,746   (50.1% male; 49.8% female)
Individual Education Program: 783 (11.6%);
English Language Learner: 449 (6.7%); Migrant: 50 (0.7%)
Eligible for Free Lunch Program: 2,246 (33.3%)
Eligible for Reduced-Price Lunch Program: 710 (10.5%)
Teachers: 430.6 (15.7 to 1)
Librarians/Media Specialists: 8.9 (758.0 to 1)
Guidance Counselors: 14.0 (481.9 to 1)
Current Spending: ($ per student per year):
Total: $6,220; Instruction: $3,513; Support Services: $2,381
Enrollment, Drop-out Rates and Diploma Recipients by Race/Ethnicity

Category	Total	White	Black	Asian	AIAN	Hisp.
Enrollment (%)	100.0	50.0	28.8	1.2	0.3	19.6
Drop-out Rate (%)	2.7	2.5	2.4	0.0	0.0	4.4
H.S. Diplomas (#)	357	221	87	2	1	46

Waller County

Royal ISD

2520 Durkin Rd · Brookshire, TX 77423-9418
Mailing Address: PO Box 489 · Pattison, TX 77466-0489
(281) 934-2248
Grade Span: PK-12; **Agency Type:** 1
Schools: 4
2 Primary; 1 Middle; 1 High; 0 Other Level
4 Regular; 0 Special Education; 0 Vocational; 0 Alternative
0 Magnet; 0 Charter; 4 Title I Eligible; 4 School-wide Title I
Students: 1,684   (51.3% male; 48.6% female)
Individual Education Program: 196 (11.6%);
English Language Learner: 260 (15.4%); Migrant: 5 (0.3%)
Eligible for Free Lunch Program: 1,104 (65.6%)
Eligible for Reduced-Price Lunch Program: 124 (7.4%)
Teachers: 126.9 (13.3 to 1)
Librarians/Media Specialists: 2.9 (580.7 to 1)
Guidance Counselors: 3.3 (510.3 to 1)
Current Spending: ($ per student per year):
Total: $7,618; Instruction: $4,392; Support Services: $2,828
Enrollment, Drop-out Rates and Diploma Recipients by Race/Ethnicity

Category	Total	White	Black	Asian	AIAN	Hisp.
Enrollment (%)	100.0	18.1	30.3	0.5	0.1	51.0
Drop-out Rate (%)	2.3	1.1	2.3	0.0	n/a	3.2
H.S. Diplomas (#)	70	15	26	1	0	28

Waller ISD

2214 Waller St · Waller, TX 77484-1918
(936) 931-3685
Grade Span: PK-12; **Agency Type:** 1
Schools: 8
4 Primary; 2 Middle; 1 High; 1 Other Level
7 Regular; 0 Special Education; 0 Vocational; 1 Alternative
0 Magnet; 0 Charter; 7 Title I Eligible; 7 School-wide Title I
Students: 4,830   (51.7% male; 48.2% female)
Individual Education Program: 453 (9.4%);
English Language Learner: 619 (12.8%); Migrant: 0 (0.0%)
Eligible for Free Lunch Program: 1,842 (38.1%)
Eligible for Reduced-Price Lunch Program: 386 (8.0%)
Teachers: 318.0 (15.2 to 1)
Librarians/Media Specialists: 5.8 (832.8 to 1)
Guidance Counselors: 9.2 (525.0 to 1)
Current Spending: ($ per student per year):
Total: $6,909; Instruction: $4,047; Support Services: $2,533
Enrollment, Drop-out Rates and Diploma Recipients by Race/Ethnicity

Category	Total	White	Black	Asian	AIAN	Hisp.
Enrollment (%)	100.0	53.6	16.4	1.0	0.6	28.4
Drop-out Rate (%)	2.9	2.5	3.1	0.0	0.0	4.2
H.S. Diplomas (#)	281	174	52	3	0	52

Ward County

Monahans-Wickett-Pyote Is

606 S Betty Ave · Monahans, TX 79756-5018
(432) 943-6711
Grade Span: PK-12; **Agency Type:** 1
Schools: 8
3 Primary; 2 Middle; 2 High; 1 Other Level

7 Regular; 0 Special Education; 0 Vocational; 1 Alternative
0 Magnet; 0 Charter; 4 Title I Eligible; 4 School-wide Title I
Students: 1,964 (50.4% male; 49.5% female)
Individual Education Program: 291 (14.8%);
English Language Learner: 79 (4.0%); Migrant: 0 (0.0%)
Eligible for Free Lunch Program: 598 (30.4%)
Eligible for Reduced-Price Lunch Program: 184 (9.4%)
Teachers: 142.3 (13.8 to 1)
Librarians/Media Specialists: 0.9 (2,182.2 to 1)
Guidance Counselors: 1.8 (1,091.1 to 1)
Current Spending: ($ per student per year):
Total: $7,114; Instruction: $4,392; Support Services: $2,327
Enrollment, Drop-out Rates and Diploma Recipients by Race/Ethnicity

Category	Total	White	Black	Asian	AIAN	Hisp.
Enrollment (%)	100.0	43.6	7.2	0.4	0.1	48.7
Drop-out Rate (%)	5.1	2.9	6.5	0.0	0.0	7.4
H.S. Diplomas (#)	139	70	7	2	0	60

Washington County

Brenham ISD
711 Mansfield • Brenham, TX 77833-4732
Mailing Address: PO Box 1147 • Brenham, TX 77834-1147
(979) 277-6500
Grade Span: PK-12; **Agency Type:** 1
Schools: 10
3 Primary; 4 Middle; 1 High; 2 Other Level
6 Regular; 1 Special Education; 0 Vocational; 3 Alternative
0 Magnet; 0 Charter; 4 Title I Eligible; 4 School-wide Title I
Students: 4,837 (51.3% male; 48.6% female)
Individual Education Program: 583 (12.1%);
English Language Learner: 306 (6.3%); Migrant: 7 (0.1%)
Eligible for Free Lunch Program: 1,801 (37.2%)
Eligible for Reduced-Price Lunch Program: 302 (6.2%)
Teachers: 351.3 (13.8 to 1)
Librarians/Media Specialists: 3.5 (1,382.0 to 1)
Guidance Counselors: 12.1 (399.8 to 1)
Current Spending: ($ per student per year):
Total: $7,159; Instruction: $4,446; Support Services: $2,296
Enrollment, Drop-out Rates and Diploma Recipients by Race/Ethnicity

Category	Total	White	Black	Asian	AIAN	Hisp.
Enrollment (%)	100.0	54.0	28.0	1.3	0.2	16.5
Drop-out Rate (%)	2.9	1.3	5.3	4.2	0.0	5.8
H.S. Diplomas (#)	338	230	74	7	1	26

Webb County

Laredo ISD
1702 Houston St • Laredo, TX 78040-4906
(956) 795-3200 • http://www.laredoisd.org/
Grade Span: PK-12; **Agency Type:** 1
Schools: 29
20 Primary; 4 Middle; 3 High; 2 Other Level
27 Regular; 0 Special Education; 0 Vocational; 2 Alternative
0 Magnet; 0 Charter; 27 Title I Eligible; 27 School-wide Title I
Students: 24,846 (50.6% male; 49.3% female)
Individual Education Program: 3,386 (13.6%);
English Language Learner: 15,416 (62.0%); Migrant: 476 (1.9%)
Eligible for Free Lunch Program: 10,742 (43.2%)
Eligible for Reduced-Price Lunch Program: 670 (2.7%)
Teachers: 1,552.6 (16.0 to 1)
Librarians/Media Specialists: 27.9 (890.5 to 1)
Guidance Counselors: 60.5 (410.7 to 1)
Current Spending: ($ per student per year):
Total: $6,949; Instruction: $4,394; Support Services: $2,232
Enrollment, Drop-out Rates and Diploma Recipients by Race/Ethnicity

Category	Total	White	Black	Asian	AIAN	Hisp.
Enrollment (%)	100.0	0.5	0.1	0.2	0.0	99.2
Drop-out Rate (%)	4.6	1.4	0.0	0.0	0.0	4.6
H.S. Diplomas (#)	1,080	11	1	0	0	1,068

United ISD
201 Lindenwood Rd • Laredo, TX 78045-2499
(956) 717-6201 • http://www.uisd.net/
Grade Span: PK-12; **Agency Type:** 1
Schools: 37
22 Primary; 8 Middle; 4 High; 3 Other Level
35 Regular; 0 Special Education; 0 Vocational; 2 Alternative
0 Magnet; 0 Charter; 34 Title I Eligible; 33 School-wide Title I
Students: 32,262 (51.2% male; 48.7% female)
Individual Education Program: 4,063 (12.6%);
English Language Learner: 14,602 (45.3%); Migrant: 380 (1.2%)
Eligible for Free Lunch Program: 20,278 (62.9%)
Eligible for Reduced-Price Lunch Program: 3,367 (10.4%)
Teachers: 1,953.2 (16.5 to 1)

Librarians/Media Specialists: 31.7 (1,017.7 to 1)
Guidance Counselors: 68.7 (469.6 to 1)
Current Spending: ($ per student per year):
Total: $6,496; Instruction: $3,908; Support Services: $2,189
Enrollment, Drop-out Rates and Diploma Recipients by Race/Ethnicity

Category	Total	White	Black	Asian	AIAN	Hisp.
Enrollment (%)	100.0	2.1	0.2	0.4	0.0	97.2
Drop-out Rate (%)	1.8	0.4	0.0	0.0	0.0	1.9
H.S. Diplomas (#)	1,360	59	2	11	0	1,288

Wharton County

El Campo ISD
700 W Norris St • El Campo, TX 77437-2499
(979) 543-6771 • http://www.ecisd.org/
Grade Span: PK-12; **Agency Type:** 1
Schools: 5
2 Primary; 2 Middle; 1 High; 0 Other Level
5 Regular; 0 Special Education; 0 Vocational; 0 Alternative
0 Magnet; 0 Charter; 3 Title I Eligible; 3 School-wide Title I
Students: 3,496   (51.9% male; 48.0% female)
Individual Education Program: 446 (12.8%);
English Language Learner: 264 (7.6%); Migrant: 209 (6.0%)
Eligible for Free Lunch Program: 1,735 (49.6%)
Eligible for Reduced-Price Lunch Program: 367 (10.5%)
Teachers: 250.2 (14.0 to 1)
Librarians/Media Specialists: 3.0 (1,165.3 to 1)
Guidance Counselors: 12.0 (291.3 to 1)
Current Spending: ($ per student per year):
Total: $6,835; Instruction: $4,401; Support Services: $2,127
Enrollment, Drop-out Rates and Diploma Recipients by Race/Ethnicity

Category	Total	White	Black	Asian	AIAN	Hisp.
Enrollment (%)	100.0	35.8	14.3	0.2	0.0	49.7
Drop-out Rate (%)	1.9	0.7	1.4	0.0	50.0	3.4
H.S. Diplomas (#)	239	136	30	3	0	70

Wharton ISD
2100 N Fulton St • Wharton, TX 77488-3146
(979) 532-6201
Grade Span: PK-12; **Agency Type:** 1
Schools: 5
2 Primary; 1 Middle; 2 High; 0 Other Level
5 Regular; 0 Special Education; 0 Vocational; 0 Alternative
0 Magnet; 0 Charter; 5 Title I Eligible; 5 School-wide Title I
Students: 2,510   (51.3% male; 48.6% female)
Individual Education Program: 332 (13.2%);
English Language Learner: 151 (6.0%); Migrant: 7 (0.3%)
Eligible for Free Lunch Program: 1,298 (51.7%)
Eligible for Reduced-Price Lunch Program: 212 (8.4%)
Teachers: 180.9 (13.9 to 1)
Librarians/Media Specialists: 4.0 (627.5 to 1)
Guidance Counselors: 6.0 (418.3 to 1)
Current Spending: ($ per student per year):
Total: $7,242; Instruction: $4,649; Support Services: $2,266
Enrollment, Drop-out Rates and Diploma Recipients by Race/Ethnicity

Category	Total	White	Black	Asian	AIAN	Hisp.
Enrollment (%)	100.0	29.4	29.2	0.9	0.0	40.4
Drop-out Rate (%)	1.7	0.3	0.8	0.0	n/a	4.1
H.S. Diplomas (#)	179	67	65	1	0	46

Wichita County

Burkburnett ISD
416 Glendale St • Burkburnett, TX 76354-2499
(940) 569-3326
Grade Span: PK-12; **Agency Type:** 1
Schools: 6
3 Primary; 1 Middle; 2 High; 0 Other Level
5 Regular; 0 Special Education; 0 Vocational; 1 Alternative
0 Magnet; 0 Charter; 2 Title I Eligible; 2 School-wide Title I
Students: 3,619   (52.0% male; 47.9% female)
Individual Education Program: 435 (12.0%);
English Language Learner: 22 (0.6%); Migrant: 0 (0.0%)
Eligible for Free Lunch Program: 893 (24.7%)
Eligible for Reduced-Price Lunch Program: 427 (11.8%)
Teachers: 278.9 (13.0 to 1)
Librarians/Media Specialists: 5.0 (723.8 to 1)
Guidance Counselors: 8.0 (452.4 to 1)
Current Spending: ($ per student per year):
Total: $6,765; Instruction: $4,372; Support Services: $2,048
Enrollment, Drop-out Rates and Diploma Recipients by Race/Ethnicity

Category	Total	White	Black	Asian	AIAN	Hisp.
Enrollment (%)	100.0	80.8	7.6	2.1	1.7	7.8
Drop-out Rate (%)	3.3	3.4	1.4	0.0	0.0	6.7
H.S. Diplomas (#)	230	187	18	6	2	17

Iowa Park Cons ISD
413 E Cash • Iowa Park, TX 76367-2014
Mailing Address: PO Box 898 • Iowa Park, TX 76367-0898
(940) 592-4193 • http://www.ipcisd.net/
Grade Span: PK-12; **Agency Type:** 1
Schools: 4
  2 Primary; 1 Middle; 1 High; 0 Other Level
  4 Regular; 0 Special Education; 0 Vocational; 0 Alternative
  0 Magnet; 0 Charter; 2 Title I Eligible; 2 School-wide Title I
Students: 1,820 (51.3% male; 48.6% female)
  Individual Education Program: 172 (9.5%);
  English Language Learner: 2 (0.1%); Migrant: 0 (0.0%)
  Eligible for Free Lunch Program: 339 (18.6%)
  Eligible for Reduced-Price Lunch Program: 219 (12.0%)
Teachers: 118.2 (15.4 to 1)
Librarians/Media Specialists: 2.9 (627.6 to 1)
Guidance Counselors: 5.0 (364.0 to 1)
Current Spending: ($ per student per year):
  Total: $5,968; Instruction: $3,859; Support Services: $1,819
Enrollment, Drop-out Rates and Diploma Recipients by Race/Ethnicity

Category	Total	White	Black	Asian	AIAN	Hisp.
Enrollment (%)	100.0	93.5	0.1	0.3	1.9	4.3
Drop-out Rate (%)	3.7	3.6	0.0	0.0	16.7	3.2
H.S. Diplomas (#)	136	134	0	1	0	1

Wichita Falls ISD
1104 Broad St • Wichita Falls, TX 76301-4412
Mailing Address: PO Box 97533 • Wichita Falls, TX 76307-2570
(940) 720-3303 • http://www.wfisd.net/
Grade Span: PK-12; **Agency Type:** 1
Schools: 36
  23 Primary; 4 Middle; 5 High; 4 Other Level
  32 Regular; 1 Special Education; 0 Vocational; 3 Alternative
  0 Magnet; 0 Charter; 23 Title I Eligible; 23 School-wide Title I
Students: 15,063 (51.0% male; 48.9% female)
  Individual Education Program: 2,082 (13.8%);
  English Language Learner: 654 (4.3%); Migrant: 59 (0.4%)
  Eligible for Free Lunch Program: 6,218 (41.3%)
  Eligible for Reduced-Price Lunch Program: 1,440 (9.6%)
Teachers: 1,113.0 (13.5 to 1)
Librarians/Media Specialists: 20.2 (745.7 to 1)
Guidance Counselors: 32.1 (469.3 to 1)
Current Spending: ($ per student per year):
  Total: $6,908; Instruction: $4,325; Support Services: $2,236
Enrollment, Drop-out Rates and Diploma Recipients by Race/Ethnicity

Category	Total	White	Black	Asian	AIAN	Hisp.
Enrollment (%)	100.0	56.8	17.5	2.5	0.9	22.3
Drop-out Rate (%)	1.9	1.5	2.7	0.7	4.3	3.2
H.S. Diplomas (#)	1,071	736	141	33	6	155

Vernon ISD
1713 Wilbarger St #203 • Vernon, TX 76384-4741
(940) 553-1900
Grade Span: PK-12; **Agency Type:** 1
Schools: 6
  2 Primary; 2 Middle; 1 High; 1 Other Level
  5 Regular; 0 Special Education; 0 Vocational; 1 Alternative
  0 Magnet; 0 Charter; 5 Title I Eligible; 5 School-wide Title I
Students: 2,343 (53.0% male; 46.9% female)
  Individual Education Program: 396 (16.9%)
  English Language Learner: 100 (4.3%); Migrant: 159 (6.8%)
  Eligible for Free Lunch Program: 1,087 (46.4%)
  Eligible for Reduced-Price Lunch Program: 221 (9.4%)
Teachers: 177.6 (13.2 to 1)
Librarians/Media Specialists: 2.0 (1,171.5 to 1)
Guidance Counselors: 6.5 (360.5 to 1)
Current Spending: ($ per student per year):
  Total: $6,874; Instruction: $4,539; Support Services: $2,034
Enrollment, Drop-out Rates and Diploma Recipients by Race/Ethnicity

Category	Total	White	Black	Asian	AIAN	Hisp.
Enrollment (%)	100.0	53.1	10.1	0.8	0.3	35.7
Drop-out Rate (%)	3.3	1.8	4.7	0.0	0.0	5.9
H.S. Diplomas (#)	158	105	14	1	3	35

Lyford CISD
Simon Gomez Blvd • Lyford, TX 78569-9999
Mailing Address: PO Box 220 • Lyford, TX 78569-0220
(956) 347-3521
Grade Span: PK-12; **Agency Type:** 1
Schools: 4
  2 Primary; 1 Middle; 1 High; 0 Other Level

  4 Regular; 0 Special Education; 0 Vocational; 0 Alternative
  0 Magnet; 0 Charter; 4 Title I Eligible; 4 School-wide Title I
Students: 1,505 (51.8% male; 48.1% female)
  Individual Education Program: 156 (10.4%);
  English Language Learner: 230 (15.3%); Migrant: 384 (25.5%)
  Eligible for Free Lunch Program: 36 (2.4%)
  Eligible for Reduced-Price Lunch Program: 2 (0.1%)
Teachers: 108.6 (13.9 to 1)
Librarians/Media Specialists: 1.0 (1,505.0 to 1)
Guidance Counselors: 5.0 (301.0 to 1)
Current Spending: ($ per student per year):
  Total: $8,516; Instruction: $5,013; Support Services: $2,986
Enrollment, Drop-out Rates and Diploma Recipients by Race/Ethnicity

Category	Total	White	Black	Asian	AIAN	Hisp.
Enrollment (%)	100.0	3.1	0.3	0.0	0.0	96.5
Drop-out Rate (%)	3.6	0.0	0.0	n/a	n/a	3.8
H.S. Diplomas (#)	117	6	1	0	0	110

Raymondville ISD
One Bearkat Blvd • Raymondville, TX 78580-3351
(956) 689-2471
Grade Span: PK-12; **Agency Type:** 1
Schools: 4
  2 Primary; 1 Middle; 1 High; 0 Other Level
  4 Regular; 0 Special Education; 0 Vocational; 0 Alternative
  0 Magnet; 0 Charter; 4 Title I Eligible; 4 School-wide Title I
Students: 2,512 (52.1% male; 47.8% female)
  Individual Education Program: 274 (10.9%);
  English Language Learner: 330 (13.1%); Migrant: 1,020 (40.6%)
  Eligible for Free Lunch Program: 1,223 (48.7%)
  Eligible for Reduced-Price Lunch Program: 100 (4.0%)
Teachers: 171.3 (14.7 to 1)
Librarians/Media Specialists: 3.0 (837.3 to 1)
Guidance Counselors: 6.0 (418.7 to 1)
Current Spending: ($ per student per year):
  Total: $7,266; Instruction: $4,180; Support Services: $2,578
Enrollment, Drop-out Rates and Diploma Recipients by Race/Ethnicity

Category	Total	White	Black	Asian	AIAN	Hisp.
Enrollment (%)	100.0	3.1	0.2	0.2	0.0	96.5
Drop-out Rate (%)	5.9	3.0	0.0	n/a	n/a	6.1
H.S. Diplomas (#)	164	7	1	0	0	156

Georgetown ISD
603 Lakeway Dr • Georgetown, TX 78628-2843
(512) 943-5000 • http://www.georgetown.txed.net/
Grade Span: PK-12; **Agency Type:** 1
Schools: 17
  8 Primary; 3 Middle; 2 High; 4 Other Level
  13 Regular; 0 Special Education; 0 Vocational; 4 Alternative
  0 Magnet; 0 Charter; 9 Title I Eligible; 4 School-wide Title I
Students: 8,662 (51.6% male; 48.3% female)
  Individual Education Program: 835 (9.6%);
  English Language Learner: 586 (6.8%); Migrant: 91 (1.1%)
  Eligible for Free Lunch Program: 2,144 (24.8%)
  Eligible for Reduced-Price Lunch Program: 707 (8.2%)
Teachers: 667.9 (13.0 to 1)
Librarians/Media Specialists: 13.0 (666.3 to 1)
Guidance Counselors: 22.0 (393.7 to 1)
Current Spending: ($ per student per year):
  Total: $7,105; Instruction: $4,488; Support Services: $2,232
Enrollment, Drop-out Rates and Diploma Recipients by Race/Ethnicity

Category	Total	White	Black	Asian	AIAN	Hisp.
Enrollment (%)	100.0	67.7	3.8	0.7	0.3	27.4
Drop-out Rate (%)	2.6	1.7	3.5	15.4	0.0	5.4
H.S. Diplomas (#)	530	450	13	2	2	63

Hutto ISD
302 College • Hutto, TX 78634-0430
Mailing Address: PO Box 430 • Hutto, TX 78634-0430
(512) 759-3771
Grade Span: PK-12; **Agency Type:** 1
Schools: 4
  2 Primary; 1 Middle; 1 High; 0 Other Level
  4 Regular; 0 Special Education; 0 Vocational; 0 Alternative
  0 Magnet; 0 Charter; 2 Title I Eligible; 0 School-wide Title I
Students: 1,982 (50.2% male; 49.7% female)
  Individual Education Program: 202 (10.2%);
  English Language Learner: 110 (5.5%); Migrant: 3 (0.2%)
  Eligible for Free Lunch Program: 316 (15.9%)
  Eligible for Reduced-Price Lunch Program: 247 (12.5%)
Teachers: 137.3 (14.4 to 1)
Librarians/Media Specialists: 3.0 (660.7 to 1)
Guidance Counselors: 4.0 (495.5 to 1)

Current Spending: ($ per student per year):
    Total: $7,152; Instruction: $4,284; Support Services: $2,484

Enrollment, Drop-out Rates and Diploma Recipients by Race/Ethnicity

Category	Total	White	Black	Asian	AIAN	Hisp.
Enrollment (%)	100.0	62.0	9.0	1.1	0.2	27.7
Drop-out Rate (%)	1.9	2.0	0.0	0.0	0.0	1.7
H.S. Diplomas (#)	70	62	1	0	0	7

Leander ISD

204 W S St • Leander, TX 78641-1806
Mailing Address: PO Box 218 • Leander, TX 78646-0218
(512) 434-5000 • http://www.leanderisd.org/
Grade Span: PK-12; **Agency Type:** 1
Schools: 23
    12 Primary; 4 Middle; 5 High; 2 Other Level
    19 Regular; 1 Special Education; 0 Vocational; 3 Alternative
    0 Magnet; 0 Charter; 8 Title I Eligible; 0 School-wide Title I
Students: 18,201 (52.1% male; 47.8% female)
    Individual Education Program: 2,153 (11.8%);
    English Language Learner: 724 (4.0%); Migrant: 27 (0.1%)
    Eligible for Free Lunch Program: 2,551 (14.0%)
    Eligible for Reduced-Price Lunch Program: 1,045 (5.7%)
Teachers: 1,216.4 (15.0 to 1)
Librarians/Media Specialists: 19.1 (952.9 to 1)
Guidance Counselors: 37.8 (481.5 to 1)
Current Spending: ($ per student per year):
    Total: $6,571; Instruction: $3,867; Support Services: $2,367

Enrollment, Drop-out Rates and Diploma Recipients by Race/Ethnicity

Category	Total	White	Black	Asian	AIAN	Hisp.
Enrollment (%)	100.0	74.0	5.0	3.2	0.6	17.2
Drop-out Rate (%)	2.0	1.9	1.2	0.0	4.3	2.6
H.S. Diplomas (#)	765	609	35	18	4	99

Liberty Hill ISD

14001 W Hwy 29 • Liberty Hill, TX 78642-0068
Mailing Address: PO Box 68 • Liberty Hill, TX 78642-0068
(512) 260-5580
Grade Span: PK-12; **Agency Type:** 1
Schools: 6
    2 Primary; 1 Middle; 1 High; 2 Other Level
    4 Regular; 0 Special Education; 0 Vocational; 2 Alternative
    0 Magnet; 0 Charter; 1 Title I Eligible; 0 School-wide Title I
Students: 1,797 (51.7% male; 48.2% female)
    Individual Education Program: 196 (10.9%)
    English Language Learner: 77 (4.3%); Migrant: 29 (1.6%)
    Eligible for Free Lunch Program: 315 (17.5%)
    Eligible for Reduced-Price Lunch Program: 156 (8.7%)
Teachers: 131.8 (13.6 to 1)
Librarians/Media Specialists: 0.0 (n/a to 1)
Guidance Counselors: 2.2 (816.8 to 1)
Current Spending: ($ per student per year):
    Total: $7,003; Instruction: $4,361; Support Services: $2,293

Enrollment, Drop-out Rates and Diploma Recipients by Race/Ethnicity

Category	Total	White	Black	Asian	AIAN	Hisp.
Enrollment (%)	100.0	82.4	1.2	0.7	0.3	15.4
Drop-out Rate (%)	0.9	0.8	0.0	0.0	0.0	1.4
H.S. Diplomas (#)	83	69	2	1	0	11

Round Rock ISD

1311 Round Rock Ave • Round Rock, TX 78681-4999
(512) 464-5000 • http://www.roundrockisd.org/home/index.asp
Grade Span: PK-12; **Agency Type:** 1
Schools: 47
    28 Primary; 8 Middle; 6 High; 3 Other Level
    40 Regular; 0 Special Education; 0 Vocational; 5 Alternative
    0 Magnet; 0 Charter; 11 Title I Eligible; 6 School-wide Title I
Students: 35,553 (51.2% male; 48.7% female)
    Individual Education Program: 3,621 (10.2%);
    English Language Learner: 2,293 (6.4%); Migrant: 94 (0.3%)
    Eligible for Free Lunch Program: 5,368 (15.1%)
    Eligible for Reduced-Price Lunch Program: 1,865 (5.2%)
Teachers: 2,344.3 (15.2 to 1)
Librarians/Media Specialists: 44.0 (808.0 to 1)
Guidance Counselors: 77.7 (457.6 to 1)
Current Spending: ($ per student per year):
    Total: $6,745; Instruction: $4,043; Support Services: $2,397

Enrollment, Drop-out Rates and Diploma Recipients by Race/Ethnicity

Category	Total	White	Black	Asian	AIAN	Hisp.
Enrollment (%)	100.0	60.4	9.6	8.5	0.4	21.0
Drop-out Rate (%)	2.1	1.6	2.9	0.3	3.0	4.8
H.S. Diplomas (#)	1,977	1,421	157	123	8	268

Taylor ISD

602 W 12th St • Taylor, TX 76574-2998
(512) 365-1391
Grade Span: PK-12; **Agency Type:** 1
Schools: 8
    3 Primary; 2 Middle; 1 High; 1 Other Level
    5 Regular; 0 Special Education; 0 Vocational; 2 Alternative
    0 Magnet; 0 Charter; 4 Title I Eligible; 4 School-wide Title I
Students: 3,041 (53.0% male; 46.9% female)
    Individual Education Program: 403 (13.3%);
    English Language Learner: 250 (8.2%); Migrant: 180 (5.9%)
    Eligible for Free Lunch Program: 1,512 (49.7%)
    Eligible for Reduced-Price Lunch Program: 237 (7.8%)
Teachers: 213.3 (14.3 to 1)
Librarians/Media Specialists: 4.0 (760.3 to 1)
Guidance Counselors: 6.9 (440.7 to 1)
Current Spending: ($ per student per year):
    Total: $7,480; Instruction: $4,450; Support Services: $2,653

Enrollment, Drop-out Rates and Diploma Recipients by Race/Ethnicity

Category	Total	White	Black	Asian	AIAN	Hisp.
Enrollment (%)	100.0	33.7	15.6	0.2	0.5	50.0
Drop-out Rate (%)	2.2	1.0	2.2	0.0	0.0	3.4
H.S. Diplomas (#)	174	89	28	1	0	56

Wilson County

Floresville ISD

908 10th St • Floresville, TX 78114-1852
(830) 393-5300 • http://www.floresville.isd.tenet.edu/
Grade Span: PK-12; **Agency Type:** 1
Schools: 8
    3 Primary; 1 Middle; 1 High; 3 Other Level
    5 Regular; 0 Special Education; 0 Vocational; 3 Alternative
    0 Magnet; 0 Charter; 4 Title I Eligible; 4 School-wide Title I
Students: 3,566 (50.4% male; 49.5% female)
    Individual Education Program: 478 (13.4%);
    English Language Learner: 138 (3.9%); Migrant: 16 (0.4%)
    Eligible for Free Lunch Program: 1,387 (38.9%)
    Eligible for Reduced-Price Lunch Program: 444 (12.5%)
Teachers: 249.5 (14.3 to 1)
Librarians/Media Specialists: 3.0 (1,188.7 to 1)
Guidance Counselors: 10.0 (356.6 to 1)
Current Spending: ($ per student per year):
    Total: $7,560; Instruction: $4,499; Support Services: $2,671

Enrollment, Drop-out Rates and Diploma Recipients by Race/Ethnicity

Category	Total	White	Black	Asian	AIAN	Hisp.
Enrollment (%)	100.0	39.7	2.0	0.4	0.1	57.8
Drop-out Rate (%)	2.8	2.0	0.0	0.0	0.0	3.6
H.S. Diplomas (#)	207	95	7	2	0	103

La Vernia ISD

13600 US Hwy 87 W • La Vernia, TX 78121-9554
(830) 779-2181
Grade Span: PK-12; **Agency Type:** 1
Schools: 7
    2 Primary; 1 Middle; 2 High; 2 Other Level
    4 Regular; 0 Special Education; 0 Vocational; 3 Alternative
    0 Magnet; 0 Charter; 1 Title I Eligible; 0 School-wide Title I
Students: 2,419 (52.6% male; 47.3% female)
    Individual Education Program: 339 (14.0%);
    English Language Learner: 74 (3.1%); Migrant: 5 (0.2%)
    Eligible for Free Lunch Program: 505 (20.9%)
    Eligible for Reduced-Price Lunch Program: 167 (6.9%)
Teachers: 154.5 (15.7 to 1)
Librarians/Media Specialists: 3.2 (755.9 to 1)
Guidance Counselors: 5.9 (410.0 to 1)
Current Spending: ($ per student per year):
    Total: $6,418; Instruction: $3,902; Support Services: $2,156

Enrollment, Drop-out Rates and Diploma Recipients by Race/Ethnicity

Category	Total	White	Black	Asian	AIAN	Hisp.
Enrollment (%)	100.0	78.6	1.2	0.2	0.2	19.8
Drop-out Rate (%)	2.1	2.2	0.0	0.0	n/a	2.2
H.S. Diplomas (#)	141	126	2	0	0	13

Wise County

Bridgeport ISD

2107 15th St • Bridgeport, TX 76426-0036
(940) 683-5124
Grade Span: PK-12; **Agency Type:** 1
Schools: 6
    2 Primary; 1 Middle; 2 High; 1 Other Level
    4 Regular; 0 Special Education; 0 Vocational; 2 Alternative
    0 Magnet; 0 Charter; 3 Title I Eligible; 3 School-wide Title I
Students: 2,228 (51.9% male; 48.0% female)

Individual Education Program: 336 (15.1%);
English Language Learner: 186 (8.3%); Migrant: 41 (1.8%)
Eligible for Free Lunch Program: 689 (30.9%)
Eligible for Reduced-Price Lunch Program: 123 (5.5%)
Teachers: 146.7 (15.2 to 1)
Librarians/Media Specialists: 3.0 (742.7 to 1)
Guidance Counselors: 7.5 (297.1 to 1)
Current Spending: ($ per student per year):
Total: $7,698; Instruction: $4,555; Support Services: $2,761
Enrollment, Drop-out Rates and Diploma Recipients by Race/Ethnicity

Category	Total	White	Black	Asian	AIAN	Hisp.
Enrollment (%)	100.0	71.5	0.5	0.2	0.5	27.2
Drop-out Rate (%)	2.0	2.1	0.0	0.0	0.0	1.7
H.S. Diplomas (#)	137	111	1	0	0	25

Decatur ISD

501 E Collins • Decatur, TX 76234-2360
(940) 627-3215 • http://www.decatur.esc11.net/
Grade Span: PK-12; **Agency Type:** 1
Schools: 6
2 Primary; 2 Middle; 2 High; 0 Other Level
5 Regular; 0 Special Education; 0 Vocational; 1 Alternative
0 Magnet; 0 Charter; 3 Title I Eligible; 3 School-wide Title I
Students: 2,846   (51.1% male; 48.8% female)
Individual Education Program: 309 (10.9%);
English Language Learner: 323 (11.3%); Migrant: 36 (1.3%)
Eligible for Free Lunch Program: 756 (26.6%)
Eligible for Reduced-Price Lunch Program: 183 (6.4%)
Teachers: 207.5 (13.7 to 1)
Librarians/Media Specialists: 3.5 (813.1 to 1)
Guidance Counselors: 5.6 (508.2 to 1)
Current Spending: ($ per student per year):
Total: $6,553; Instruction: $4,228; Support Services: $1,947
Enrollment, Drop-out Rates and Diploma Recipients by Race/Ethnicity

Category	Total	White	Black	Asian	AIAN	Hisp.
Enrollment (%)	100.0	71.3	1.7	1.1	0.6	25.5
Drop-out Rate (%)	1.1	0.5	6.7	0.0	0.0	2.7
H.S. Diplomas (#)	178	145	3	3	3	24

Wood County

Mineola ISD

1000 W Loop • Mineola, TX 75773-1617
(903) 569-2448
Grade Span: PK-12; **Agency Type:** 1
Schools: 4
2 Primary; 1 Middle; 1 High; 0 Other Level
4 Regular; 0 Special Education; 0 Vocational; 0 Alternative
0 Magnet; 0 Charter; 4 Title I Eligible; 4 School-wide Title I
Students: 1,601   (49.9% male; 50.0% female)
Individual Education Program: 245 (15.3%);
English Language Learner: 118 (7.4%); Migrant: 3 (0.2%)
Eligible for Free Lunch Program: 738 (46.1%)
Eligible for Reduced-Price Lunch Program: 120 (7.5%)
Teachers: 112.9 (14.2 to 1)
Librarians/Media Specialists: 2.0 (800.5 to 1)
Guidance Counselors: 3.0 (533.7 to 1)
Current Spending: ($ per student per year):
Total: $6,416; Instruction: $4,216; Support Services: $1,880
Enrollment, Drop-out Rates and Diploma Recipients by Race/Ethnicity

Category	Total	White	Black	Asian	AIAN	Hisp.
Enrollment (%)	100.0	69.4	10.1	0.3	0.3	19.9
Drop-out Rate (%)	2.5	3.0	2.0	0.0	0.0	0.0
H.S. Diplomas (#)	94	67	17	0	1	9

Young County

Graham ISD

400 3rd St • Graham, TX 76450-3011
(940) 549-0595
Grade Span: PK-12; **Agency Type:** 1
Schools: 6
2 Primary; 2 Middle; 2 High; 0 Other Level
5 Regular; 0 Special Education; 0 Vocational; 1 Alternative
0 Magnet; 0 Charter; 5 Title I Eligible; 5 School-wide Title I
Students: 2,421   (50.9% male; 49.0% female)
Individual Education Program: 308 (12.7%);
English Language Learner: 135 (5.6%); Migrant: 24 (1.0%)
Eligible for Free Lunch Program: 793 (32.8%)
Eligible for Reduced-Price Lunch Program: 213 (8.8%)
Teachers: 169.0 (14.3 to 1)
Librarians/Media Specialists: 1.0 (2,421.0 to 1)
Guidance Counselors: 5.0 (484.2 to 1)
Current Spending: ($ per student per year):
Total: $6,082; Instruction: $3,987; Support Services: $1,769

Category	Total	White	Black	Asian	AIAN	Hisp.
Enrollment (%)	100.0	79.7	1.2	0.6	0.2	18.3
Drop-out Rate (%)	0.9	0.8	0.0	0.0	0.0	1.7
H.S. Diplomas (#)	153	134	2	0	1	16

Zapata County

Zapata County ISD

17th & Carla St • Zapata, TX 78076-0158
Mailing Address: PO Box 158 • Zapata, TX 78076-0158
(956) 765-6546
Grade Span: PK-12; **Agency Type:** 1
Schools: 6
4 Primary; 1 Middle; 1 High; 0 Other Level
6 Regular; 0 Special Education; 0 Vocational; 0 Alternative
0 Magnet; 0 Charter; 6 Title I Eligible; 6 School-wide Title I
Students: 3,163   (51.5% male; 48.4% female)
Individual Education Program: 325 (10.3%);
English Language Learner: 1,200 (37.9%); Migrant: 178 (5.6%)
Eligible for Free Lunch Program: 1,352 (42.7%)
Eligible for Reduced-Price Lunch Program: 154 (4.9%)
Teachers: 245.4 (12.9 to 1)
Librarians/Media Specialists: 5.0 (632.6 to 1)
Guidance Counselors: 11.0 (287.5 to 1)
Current Spending: ($ per student per year):
Total: $8,735; Instruction: $5,473; Support Services: $2,812
Enrollment, Drop-out Rates and Diploma Recipients by Race/Ethnicity

Category	Total	White	Black	Asian	AIAN	Hisp.
Enrollment (%)	100.0	2.2	0.1	0.2	0.0	97.5
Drop-out Rate (%)	8.0	0.0	n/a	0.0	n/a	8.5
H.S. Diplomas (#)	184	13	0	0	0	171

Zavala County

Crystal City ISD

805 E Crockett St • Crystal City, TX 78839-2799
(830) 374-2367 • http://www.crystal-city.k12.tx.us/
Grade Span: PK-12; **Agency Type:** 1
Schools: 5
2 Primary; 2 Middle; 1 High; 0 Other Level
5 Regular; 0 Special Education; 0 Vocational; 0 Alternative
0 Magnet; 0 Charter; 4 Title I Eligible; 4 School-wide Title I
Students: 2,071   (50.2% male; 49.7% female)
Individual Education Program: 222 (10.7%);
English Language Learner: 397 (19.2%); Migrant: 542 (26.2%)
Eligible for Free Lunch Program: 1,284 (62.0%)
Eligible for Reduced-Price Lunch Program: 92 (4.4%)
Teachers: 125.9 (16.4 to 1)
Librarians/Media Specialists: 2.0 (1,035.5 to 1)
Guidance Counselors: 7.0 (295.9 to 1)
Current Spending: ($ per student per year):
Total: $7,969; Instruction: $4,643; Support Services: $2,828
Enrollment, Drop-out Rates and Diploma Recipients by Race/Ethnicity

Category	Total	White	Black	Asian	AIAN	Hisp.
Enrollment (%)	100.0	1.0	1.0	0.0	0.0	98.0
Drop-out Rate (%)	8.1	10.0	100.0	n/a	0.0	7.9
H.S. Diplomas (#)	87	1	0	0	0	86

Number of Schools

Rank	Number	District Name	City
1	308	Houston ISD	Houston
2	227	Dallas ISD	Dallas
3	145	Fort Worth ISD	Fort Worth
4	111	Austin ISD	Austin
5	107	San Antonio ISD	San Antonio
6	93	El Paso ISD	El Paso
6	93	Northside ISD	San Antonio
8	77	Arlington ISD	Arlington
9	72	Plano ISD	Plano
10	70	Garland ISD	Garland
11	66	Aldine ISD	Houston
12	65	North East ISD	San Antonio
13	64	Ysleta ISD	El Paso
14	63	Corpus Christi ISD	Corpus Christi
15	60	Cypress-Fairbanks ISD	Houston
16	59	Fort Bend ISD	Sugar Land
17	58	Lewisville ISD	Flower Mound
18	57	Lubbock ISD	Lubbock
18	57	Richardson ISD	Richardson
20	56	Pasadena ISD	Pasadena
21	52	Amarillo ISD	Amarillo
21	52	Brownsville ISD	Brownsville
23	50	Spring Branch ISD	Houston
24	49	Killeen ISD	Killeen
25	47	Round Rock ISD	Round Rock
26	46	Conroe ISD	Conroe
27	44	Mesquite ISD	Mesquite
28	42	Ector County ISD	Odessa
28	42	Katy ISD	Katy
30	41	Abilene ISD	Abilene
30	41	Alief ISD	Houston
30	41	Carrollton-Farmers Branch	Carrollton
33	39	Irving ISD	Irving
34	38	Clear Creek ISD	League City
35	37	Edinburg CISD	Edinburg
35	37	United ISD	Laredo
35	37	Waco ISD	Waco
38	36	Beaumont ISD	Beaumont
38	36	Midland ISD	Midland
38	36	Pharr-San Juan-Alamo ISD	Pharr
38	36	Wichita Falls ISD	Wichita Falls
42	34	Klein ISD	Klein
42	34	Socorro ISD	El Paso
44	33	Birdville ISD	Haltom City
44	33	Grand Prairie ISD	Grand Prairie
46	32	Hurst-Euless-Bedford ISD	Bedford
46	32	Mcallen ISD	Mcallen
48	30	Harlandale ISD	San Antonio
48	30	Humble ISD	Humble
50	29	Laredo ISD	Laredo
50	29	Tyler ISD	Tyler
52	28	Lamar Consolidated ISD	Rosenberg
53	27	Goose Creek CISD	Baytown
53	27	La Joya ISD	La Joya
53	27	San Angelo ISD	San Angelo
53	27	Spring ISD	Houston
57	26	Harlingen Cons ISD	Harlingen
57	26	Keller ISD	Keller
57	26	Victoria ISD	Victoria
60	25	Bryan ISD	Bryan
60	25	Denton ISD	Denton
60	25	Edgewood ISD	San Antonio
60	25	Mckinney ISD	Mckinney
64	24	Eagle Pass ISD	Eagle Pass
64	24	Pflugerville ISD	Pflugerville
66	23	Galena Park ISD	Houston
66	23	Leander ISD	Leander
66	23	Mansfield ISD	Mansfield
69	22	Frisco ISD	Frisco
69	22	Judson ISD	San Antonio
71	21	Brazosport ISD	Freeport
71	21	Mission Cons ISD	Mission
71	21	Weslaco ISD	Weslaco
74	20	Comal ISD	New Braunfels
75	19	Duncanville ISD	Duncanville
75	19	Grapevine-Colleyville ISD	Grapevine
75	19	Port Arthur ISD	Port Arthur
75	19	South San Antonio ISD	San Antonio
79	18	Donna ISD	Donna
79	18	Longview ISD	Longview
79	18	Lufkin ISD	Lufkin
79	18	North Forest ISD	Houston
79	18	Pearland ISD	Pearland
79	18	San Benito Cons ISD	San Benito
85	17	Allen ISD	Allen
85	17	Alvin ISD	Alvin
85	17	Galveston ISD	Galveston
85	17	Georgetown ISD	Georgetown
85	17	Temple ISD	Temple
90	16	Coppell ISD	Coppell
90	16	Seguin ISD	Seguin
92	15	Crowley ISD	Crowley
92	15	Hays Cons ISD	Kyle
92	15	San Felipe-Del Rio Cons I	Del Rio
95	14	Kingsville ISD	Kingsville
95	14	Magnolia ISD	Magnolia
95	14	Northwest ISD	Fort Worth
95	14	Rockwall ISD	Rockwall
95	14	Southwest ISD	San Antonio
100	13	Angleton ISD	Angleton
100	13	Canyon ISD	Canyon
100	13	Copperas Cove ISD	Copperas Cove
100	13	Deer Park ISD	Deer Park
100	13	Eagle Mt-Saginaw ISD	Fort Worth
100	13	East Central ISD	San Antonio
100	13	Granbury ISD	Granbury
100	13	La Porte ISD	La Porte
100	13	Marshall ISD	Marshall
100	13	Plainview ISD	Plainview
100	13	Sherman ISD	Sherman
100	13	Tomball ISD	Tomball
112	12	Bastrop ISD	Bastrop
112	12	Belton ISD	Belton
112	12	Cedar Hill ISD	Cedar Hill
112	12	Desoto ISD	Desoto
112	12	Greenville ISD	Greenville
112	12	Kerrville ISD	Kerrville
112	12	New Braunfels ISD	New Braunfels
112	12	Port Neches-Groves ISD	Port Neches
112	12	Schertz-Cibolo-U City ISD	Schertz
112	12	Weatherford ISD	Weatherford
122	11	Azle ISD	Azle
122	11	Burleson ISD	Burleson
122	11	Carroll ISD	Grapevine
122	11	Channelview ISD	Channelview
122	11	Cleburne ISD	Cleburne
122	11	Clint ISD	El Paso
122	11	College Station ISD	College Station
122	11	Del Valle ISD	Del Valle
122	11	Denison ISD	Denison
122	11	New Caney ISD	New Caney
122	11	Rio Grande City CISD	Rio Grande City
122	11	San Marcos Cons ISD	San Marcos
122	11	Texarkana ISD	Texarkana
122	11	Wylie ISD	Wylie
136	10	Alice ISD	Alice
136	10	Brenham ISD	Brenham
136	10	Dickinson ISD	Dickinson
136	10	Eanes ISD	Austin
136	10	Honors Academy	Dallas
136	10	Huntsville ISD	Huntsville
136	10	Lancaster ISD	Lancaster
136	10	Los Fresnos Cons ISD	Los Fresnos
136	10	Mercedes ISD	Mercedes
136	10	Mount Pleasant ISD	Mt Pleasant
136	10	Nacogdoches ISD	Nacogdoches
136	10	Robstown ISD	Robstown
136	10	Roma ISD	Roma
136	10	Sharyland ISD	Mission
136	10	Uvalde Cons ISD	Uvalde
136	10	Waxahachie ISD	Waxahachie
136	10	White Settlement ISD	White Settlement
136	10	Wilmer-Hutchins ISD	Dallas
154	9	Big Spring ISD	Big Spring
154	9	Boerne ISD	Boerne
154	9	Calhoun County ISD	Port Lavaca
154	9	Edcouch-Elsa ISD	Edcouch
154	9	Ennis ISD	Ennis
154	9	Frenship ISD	Wolfforth
154	9	Midway ISD	Waco
154	9	Nederland ISD	Nederland
154	9	Paris ISD	Paris
154	9	Texas City ISD	Texas City
154	9	Willis ISD	Willis
165	8	Barbers Hill ISD	Mt Belvieu
165	8	Bay City ISD	Bay City
165	8	Beeville ISD	Beeville
165	8	Brownwood ISD	Brownwood
165	8	Castleberry ISD	Fort Worth
165	8	Chapel Hill ISD	Tyler
165	8	China Spring ISD	Waco
165	8	Cleveland ISD	Cleveland
165	8	Connally ISD	Waco
165	8	Corsicana ISD	Corsicana
165	8	Dayton ISD	Dayton
165	8	Dumas ISD	Dumas
165	8	Floresville ISD	Floresville
165	8	Gainesville ISD	Gainesville
165	8	Gregory-Portland ISD	Gregory
165	8	Hereford ISD	Hereford
165	8	Jacksonville ISD	Jacksonville
165	8	Joshua ISD	Joshua
165	8	La Feria ISD	La Feria
165	8	La Marque ISD	La Marque
165	8	La Vega ISD	Waco
165	8	Lake Travis ISD	Austin
165	8	Little Elm ISD	Little Elm
165	8	Lockhart ISD	Lockhart
165	8	Monahans-Wickett-Pyote Is	Monahans
165	8	Pleasanton ISD	Pleasanton
165	8	Red Oak ISD	Red Oak
165	8	Snyder ISD	Snyder
165	8	Southside ISD	San Antonio
165	8	Springtown ISD	Springtown
165	8	Sulphur Springs ISD	Sulphur Springs
165	8	Taylor ISD	Taylor
165	8	Waller ISD	Waller
165	8	West ISD	West
165	8	Whitehouse ISD	Whitehouse
200	7	Aledo ISD	Aledo
200	7	Alvarado ISD	Alvarado
200	7	Andrews ISD	Andrews
200	7	Athens ISD	Athens
200	7	Brownsboro ISD	Brownsboro
200	7	Columbia-Brazoria ISD	West Columbia
200	7	Everman ISD	Everman
200	7	Flour Bluff ISD	Corpus Christi
200	7	Forney ISD	Forney
200	7	Friendswood ISD	Friendswood
200	7	Hallsville ISD	Hallsville
200	7	Henderson ISD	Henderson
200	7	Highland Park ISD	Dallas
200	7	Hillsboro ISD	Hillsboro
200	7	Kaufman ISD	Kaufman
200	7	Kennedale ISD	Kennedale
200	7	Kilgore ISD	Kilgore
200	7	La Vernia ISD	La Vernia
200	7	Lake Dallas ISD	Lake Dallas
200	7	Lake Worth ISD	Lake Worth
200	7	Levelland ISD	Levelland
200	7	Liberty-Eylau ISD	Texarkana
200	7	Lindale ISD	Lindale
200	7	Manor ISD	Manor
200	7	Midlothian ISD	Midlothian
200	7	Montgomery ISD	Montgomery
200	7	Navasota ISD	Navasota
200	7	North Lamar ISD	Paris
200	7	Palestine ISD	Palestine
200	7	Pampa ISD	Pampa
200	7	Pine Tree ISD	Longview
200	7	Robinson ISD	Robinson
200	7	San Elizario ISD	San Elizario
200	7	Santa Fe ISD	Santa Fe
200	7	Sheldon ISD	Houston
200	7	Silsbee ISD	Silsbee
200	7	Sinton ISD	Sinton
200	7	Somerset ISD	Somerset
200	7	Stafford Municipal School	Stafford
200	7	Sweetwater ISD	Sweetwater
200	7	Terrell ISD	Terrell
200	7	Vidor ISD	Vidor
200	7	West Orange-Cove Cons ISD	Orange
200	7	Wylie ISD	Abilene
244	6	Alamo Heights ISD	San Antonio
244	6	Aransas Pass ISD	Aransas Pass
244	6	Bellville ISD	Bellville
244	6	Bonham ISD	Bonham
244	6	Borger ISD	Borger
244	6	Breckenridge ISD	Breckenridge
244	6	Bridgeport ISD	Bridgeport
244	6	Burkburnett ISD	Burkburnett
244	6	Burnet Cons ISD	Burnet
244	6	Calallen ISD	Corpus Christi
244	6	Canutillo ISD	El Paso
244	6	Carrizo Springs Cons ISD	Carrizo Springs
244	6	Crockett ISD	Crockett
244	6	Crosby ISD	Crosby
244	6	Cuero ISD	Cuero
244	6	Decatur ISD	Decatur
244	6	Fredericksburg ISD	Fredericksburg
244	6	Ft Stockton ISD	Ft Stockton
244	6	Gladewater ISD	Gladewater
244	6	Gonzales ISD	Gonzales
244	6	Graham ISD	Graham
244	6	Hardin-Jefferson ISD	Sour Lake
244	6	Hidalgo ISD	Hidalgo
244	6	Liberty Hill ISD	Liberty Hill
244	6	Liberty ISD	Liberty
244	6	Little Cypress-Mauricevil	Orange
244	6	Lorena ISD	Lorena
244	6	Lubbock-Cooper ISD	Lubbock
244	6	Lumberton ISD	Lumberton
244	6	Lytle ISD	Lytle
244	6	Mabank ISD	Mabank
244	6	Medina Valley ISD	Castroville

Rank		District Name	City
244	6	Mexia ISD	Mexia
244	6	Mineral Wells ISD	Mineral Wells
244	6	Pearsall ISD	Pearsall
244	6	Pecos-Barstow-Toyah ISD	Pecos
244	6	Perryton ISD	Perryton
244	6	Princeton ISD	Princeton
244	6	Quinlan ISD	Quinlan
244	6	Royse City ISD	Royse City
244	6	Sanger ISD	Sanger
244	6	Seminole ISD	Seminole
244	6	South Texas ISD	Mercedes
244	6	Stephenville	Stephenville
244	6	Tuloso-Midway ISD	Corpus Christi
244	6	Vernon ISD	Vernon
244	6	Zapata County ISD	Zapata
291	5	Aransas County ISD	Rockport
291	5	Atlanta ISD	Atlanta
291	5	Bridge City ISD	Bridge City
291	5	Bullard ISD	Bullard
291	5	Caldwell ISD	Caldwell
291	5	Carthage ISD	Carthage
291	5	Center ISD	Center
291	5	Central ISD	Pollok
291	5	Commerce ISD	Commerce
291	5	Crandall ISD	Crandall
291	5	Crystal City ISD	Crystal City
291	5	Daingerfield-Lone Star Is	Daingerfield
291	5	Dalhart ISD	Dalhart
291	5	Devine ISD	Devine
291	5	Diboll ISD	Diboll
291	5	Edna ISD	Edna
291	5	El Campo ISD	El Campo
291	5	Elgin ISD	Elgin
291	5	Fabens ISD	Fabens
291	5	Ferris ISD	Ferris
291	5	Gatesville ISD	Gatesville
291	5	Giddings ISD	Giddings
291	5	Groesbeck ISD	Groesbeck
291	5	Hamshire-Fannett ISD	Hamshire
291	5	Hondo ISD	Hondo
291	5	Hudson ISD	Lufkin
291	5	Huffman ISD	Huffman
291	5	Huntington ISD	Huntington
291	5	Ingleside ISD	Ingleside
291	5	Jasper ISD	Jasper
291	5	Livingston ISD	Livingston
291	5	Luling ISD	Luling
291	5	Marble Falls ISD	Marble Falls
291	5	Needville ISD	Needville
291	5	Palacios ISD	Palacios
291	5	Pittsburg ISD	Pittsburg
291	5	Poteet ISD	Poteet
291	5	Progreso ISD	Progreso
291	5	Rio Hondo ISD	Rio Hondo
291	5	Rusk ISD	Rusk
291	5	Smithville ISD	Smithville
291	5	Splendora ISD	Splendora
291	5	Spring Hill ISD	Longview
291	5	Valley View ISD	Pharr
291	5	Venus ISD	Venus
291	5	West Oso ISD	Corpus Christi
291	5	Wharton ISD	Wharton
291	5	Wills Point ISD	Wills Point
291	5	Yoakum ISD	Yoakum
340	4	Bandera ISD	Bandera
340	4	Bowie ISD	Bowie
340	4	Brooks County ISD	Falfurrias
340	4	Brownfield ISD	Brownfield
340	4	Cameron ISD	Cameron
340	4	Canton ISD	Canton
340	4	Coldspring-Oakhurst Cons	Coldspring
340	4	Dripping Springs ISD	Dripping Spgs
340	4	Eustace ISD	Eustace
340	4	Fairfield ISD	Fairfield
340	4	Gilmer ISD	Gilmer
340	4	Glen Rose ISD	Glen Rose
340	4	Greenwood ISD	Midland
340	4	Hutto ISD	Hutto
340	4	Iowa Park Cons ISD	Iowa Park
340	4	Kemp ISD	Kemp
340	4	La Grange ISD	La Grange
340	4	Lamesa ISD	Lamesa
340	4	Lampasas ISD	Lampasas
340	4	Llano ISD	Llano
340	4	Lyford CISD	Lyford
340	4	Madisonville Cons ISD	Madisonville
340	4	Mathis ISD	Mathis
340	4	Mineola ISD	Mineola
340	4	Orange Grove ISD	Orange Grove
340	4	Point Isabel ISD	Port Isabel
340	4	Rains ISD	Emory
340	4	Raymondville ISD	Raymondville
340	4	Rockdale ISD	Rockdale
340	4	Royal ISD	Brookshire
340	4	San Diego ISD	San Diego
340	4	Sealy ISD	Sealy
340	4	Shepherd ISD	Shepherd
340	4	Sweeny ISD	Sweeny
340	4	Tarkington ISD	Cleveland
340	4	Van ISD	Van
340	4	Westwood ISD	Palestine
340	4	Whitesboro ISD	Whitesboro
340	4	Whitney ISD	Whitney
340	4	Wimberley ISD	Wimberley
380	3	Buna ISD	Buna
380	3	Columbus ISD	Columbus
380	3	Ingram ISD	Ingram
380	3	Kirbyville CISD	Kirbyville
380	3	Orangefield ISD	Orangefield
380	3	Pleasant Grove ISD	Texarkana
380	3	Presidio ISD	Presidio

Number of Teachers

Rank	Number	District Name	City
1	12,276	Houston ISD	Houston
2	10,323	Dallas ISD	Dallas
3	5,354	Austin ISD	Austin
4	4,884	Cypress-Fairbanks ISD	Houston
5	4,792	Fort Worth ISD	Fort Worth
6	4,594	Northside ISD	San Antonio
7	4,504	El Paso ISD	El Paso
8	3,991	Arlington ISD	Arlington
9	3,825	Plano ISD	Plano
10	3,719	Fort Bend ISD	Sugar Land
11	3,670	North East ISD	San Antonio
12	3,616	Aldine ISD	Houston
13	3,526	San Antonio ISD	San Antonio
14	3,509	Garland ISD	Garland
15	3,063	Lewisville ISD	Flower Mound
16	3,014	Brownsville ISD	Brownsville
17	2,999	Ysleta ISD	El Paso
18	2,977	Alief ISD	Houston
19	2,801	Katy ISD	Katy
20	2,680	Pasadena ISD	Pasadena
21	2,496	Conroe ISD	Conroe
22	2,419	Richardson ISD	Richardson
23	2,408	Corpus Christi ISD	Corpus Christi
24	2,344	Round Rock ISD	Round Rock
25	2,302	Killeen ISD	Killeen
26	2,226	Spring Branch ISD	Houston
27	2,219	Klein ISD	Klein
28	2,149	Mesquite ISD	Mesquite
29	2,087	Irving ISD	Irving
30	2,073	Lubbock ISD	Lubbock
31	2,025	Amarillo ISD	Amarillo
32	1,995	Clear Creek ISD	League City
33	1,953	United ISD	Laredo
34	1,910	Socorro ISD	El Paso
35	1,787	Spring ISD	Houston
36	1,744	Humble ISD	Humble
37	1,742	Carrollton-Farmers Branch	Carrollton
38	1,671	Ector County ISD	Odessa
39	1,631	Edinburg CISD	Edinburg
40	1,579	Pharr-San Juan-Alamo ISD	Pharr
41	1,552	Laredo ISD	Laredo
42	1,540	Mcallen ISD	Mcallen
43	1,477	Grand Prairie ISD	Grand Prairie
44	1,460	Galena Park ISD	Houston
45	1,456	Beaumont ISD	Beaumont
46	1,367	Mansfield ISD	Mansfield
47	1,365	La Joya ISD	La Joya
48	1,361	Midland ISD	Midland
49	1,355	Birdville ISD	Haltom City
50	1,294	Abilene ISD	Abilene
51	1,271	Hurst-Euless-Bedford ISD	Bedford
52	1,253	Tyler ISD	Tyler
53	1,248	Keller ISD	Keller
54	1,228	Judson ISD	San Antonio
55	1,217	Goose Creek CISD	Baytown
56	1,216	Leander ISD	Leander
57	1,169	Denton ISD	Denton
58	1,155	Lamar Consolidated ISD	Rosenberg
59	1,113	Wichita Falls ISD	Wichita Falls
60	1,101	Mckinney ISD	Mckinney
61	1,048	Harlingen Cons ISD	Harlingen
62	1,041	Waco ISD	Waco
63	1,028	Pflugerville ISD	Pflugerville
64	971	San Angelo ISD	San Angelo
65	969	Victoria ISD	Victoria
66	968	Weslaco ISD	Weslaco
67	942	Harlandale ISD	San Antonio
68	935	Bryan ISD	Bryan
69	932	Frisco ISD	Frisco
70	914	Mission Cons ISD	Mission
71	877	Grapevine-Colleyville ISD	Grapevine
72	872	Allen ISD	Allen
73	839	Pearland ISD	Pearland
74	811	Brazosport ISD	Freeport
75	791	Donna ISD	Donna
76	788	Alvin ISD	Alvin
77	770	Eagle Pass ISD	Eagle Pass
78	766	Comal ISD	New Braunfels
79	759	Crowley ISD	Crowley
80	754	Edgewood ISD	San Antonio
81	716	Deer Park ISD	Deer Park
82	708	North Forest ISD	Houston
83	699	Duncanville ISD	Duncanville
84	670	Coppell ISD	Coppell
85	667	Georgetown ISD	Georgetown
86	660	South San Antonio ISD	San Antonio
87	643	Southwest ISD	San Antonio
88	637	Rio Grande City CISD	Rio Grande City
89	618	Temple ISD	Temple
90	607	Port Arthur ISD	Port Arthur
91	599	Magnolia ISD	Magnolia
92	594	Lufkin ISD	Lufkin
93	593	Rockwall ISD	Rockwall
94	588	Hays Cons ISD	Kyle
95	584	Galveston ISD	Galveston
96	576	San Benito Cons ISD	San Benito
97	573	San Felipe-Del Rio Cons I	Del Rio
98	573	Longview ISD	Longview
99	552	Seguin ISD	Seguin
100	532	Tomball ISD	Tomball
101	526	College Station ISD	College Station
102	526	Del Valle ISD	Del Valle
103	523	Copperas Cove ISD	Copperas Cove
104	517	Desoto ISD	Desoto
105	516	Bastrop ISD	Bastrop
106	511	Carroll ISD	Grapevine
107	510	Eanes ISD	Austin
108	498	New Caney ISD	New Caney
109	496	Clint ISD	El Paso
110	491	East Central ISD	San Antonio
111	490	Eagle Mt-Saginaw ISD	Fort Worth
112	484	San Marcos Cons ISD	San Marcos
113	481	Canyon ISD	Canyon
114	474	Northwest ISD	Fort Worth
115	468	Weatherford ISD	Weatherford
116	468	Belton ISD	Belton
117	468	La Porte ISD	La Porte
118	467	Schertz-Cibolo-U City ISD	Schertz
119	465	Sherman ISD	Sherman
120	455	Los Fresnos Cons ISD	Los Fresnos
121	451	Granbury ISD	Granbury
122	449	Wylie ISD	Wylie
123	447	Cedar Hill ISD	Cedar Hill
124	444	Burleson ISD	Burleson
125	434	Channelview ISD	Channelview
126	430	Huntsville ISD	Huntsville
127	428	Marshall ISD	Marshall
128	423	Cleburne ISD	Cleburne
129	411	Roma ISD	Roma
130	410	Nacogdoches ISD	Nacogdoches
131	409	New Braunfels ISD	New Braunfels
132	403	Dickinson ISD	Dickinson
133	403	Plainview ISD	Plainview
134	395	Sharyland ISD	Mission
135	391	Highland Park ISD	Dallas
136	391	Azle ISD	Azle
137	389	Texarkana ISD	Texarkana
138	384	Boerne ISD	Boerne
139	381	Angleton ISD	Angleton
140	377	Waxahachie ISD	Waxahachie
141	376	Mount Pleasant ISD	Mt Pleasant
142	373	Alice ISD	Alice
143	372	Midlothian ISD	Midlothian
144	369	Texas City ISD	Texas City
145	366	Corsicana ISD	Corsicana
146	365	Greenville ISD	Greenville
147	365	Uvalde Cons ISD	Uvalde
148	364	Frenship ISD	Wolfforth
149	361	Midway ISD	Waco
150	359	Ennis ISD	Ennis
151	358	Vidor ISD	Vidor
152	353	Canutillo ISD	El Paso
153	351	Brenham ISD	Brenham
154	350	Mercedes ISD	Mercedes
155	341	Jacksonville ISD	Jacksonville
156	338	Friendswood ISD	Friendswood
157	335	Kerrville ISD	Kerrville
158	325	Nederland ISD	Nederland
159	323	Port Neches-Groves ISD	Port Neches
160	321	Pine Tree ISD	Longview
161	321	Lake Travis ISD	Austin
162	318	Flour Bluff ISD	Corpus Christi

Rank	Number	District Name	City
163	318	Waller ISD	Waller
164	316	Edcouch-Elsa ISD	Edcouch
165	316	White Settlement ISD	White Settlement
166	310	Joshua ISD	Joshua
167	308	Denison ISD	Denison
168	308	Red Oak ISD	Red Oak
169	308	Alamo Heights ISD	San Antonio
170	306	Southside ISD	San Antonio
171	305	Paris ISD	Paris
172	304	Kingsville ISD	Kingsville
173	303	Lockhart ISD	Lockhart
174	301	Sulphur Springs ISD	Sulphur Springs
175	301	Willis ISD	Willis
176	299	Lancaster ISD	Lancaster
177	298	Dumas ISD	Dumas
178	298	Terrell ISD	Terrell
179	298	Dayton ISD	Dayton
180	290	Montgomery ISD	Montgomery
181	279	Sheldon ISD	Houston
182	278	Bay City ISD	Bay City
182	278	Burkburnett ISD	Burkburnett
184	278	Hereford ISD	Hereford
185	276	Kilgore ISD	Kilgore
186	274	Robstown ISD	Robstown
187	273	Big Spring ISD	Big Spring
188	273	Calhoun County ISD	Port Lavaca
189	272	Mineral Wells ISD	Mineral Wells
190	272	Santa Fe ISD	Santa Fe
191	272	Brownwood ISD	Brownwood
192	264	Marble Falls ISD	Marble Falls
193	263	Henderson ISD	Henderson
194	257	Livingston ISD	Livingston
195	256	Forney ISD	Forney
196	256	Pleasanton ISD	Pleasanton
197	254	Springtown ISD	Springtown
198	253	Whitehouse ISD	Whitehouse
199	253	Gregory-Portland ISD	Gregory
200	253	Palestine ISD	Palestine
201	251	Crosby ISD	Crosby
202	251	Lake Dallas ISD	Lake Dallas
203	250	El Campo ISD	El Campo
204	249	Hallsville ISD	Hallsville
205	249	Floresville ISD	Floresville
206	249	Calallen ISD	Corpus Christi
207	247	Beeville ISD	Beeville
208	245	Zapata County ISD	Zapata
209	245	Everman ISD	Everman
210	245	Little Cypress-Mauricevil	Orange
211	244	Levelland ISD	Levelland
212	244	La Marque ISD	La Marque
213	243	Athens ISD	Athens
214	240	San Elizario ISD	San Elizario
215	238	Little Elm ISD	Little Elm
216	237	Aledo ISD	Aledo
217	236	Pampa ISD	Pampa
218	234	Aransas County ISD	Rockport
219	232	Lumberton ISD	Lumberton
220	231	Kaufman ISD	Kaufman
221	231	North Lamar ISD	Paris
222	230	Jasper ISD	Jasper
223	229	Mabank ISD	Mabank
224	228	West Orange-Cove Cons ISD	Orange
225	223	Hidalgo ISD	Hidalgo
226	222	Stephenville	Stephenville
227	222	Lindale ISD	Lindale
228	221	Chapel Hill ISD	Tyler
229	219	Lampasas ISD	Lampasas
230	219	Dripping Springs ISD	Dripping Spgs
231	215	Alvarado ISD	Alvarado
232	215	Cleveland ISD	Cleveland
233	215	Elgin ISD	Elgin
234	214	Manor ISD	Manor
235	213	Taylor ISD	Taylor
236	213	Andrews ISD	Andrews
237	212	Fredericksburg ISD	Fredericksburg
238	212	Burnet Cons ISD	Burnet
239	211	Gainesville ISD	Gainesville
240	210	Borger ISD	Borger
241	209	Barbers Hill ISD	Mt Belvieu
242	209	Somerset ISD	Somerset
243	209	Splendora ISD	Splendora
244	207	Wilmer-Hutchins ISD	Dallas
245	207	Decatur ISD	Decatur
246	204	Navasota ISD	Navasota
247	204	Columbia-Brazoria ISD	West Columbia
248	204	Liberty-Eylau ISD	Texarkana
249	203	Silsbee ISD	Silsbee
250	203	La Feria ISD	La Feria
251	199	Bandera ISD	Bandera
252	198	Carthage ISD	Carthage
253	198	Snyder ISD	Snyder
254	197	Stafford Municipal School	Stafford
255	195	Castleberry ISD	Fort Worth
255	195	Royse City ISD	Royse City
257	195	Tuloso-Midway ISD	Corpus Christi
258	191	Quinlan ISD	Quinlan
259	190	Sweetwater ISD	Sweetwater
260	189	Valley View ISD	Pharr
261	187	La Vega ISD	Waco
262	184	Kennedale ISD	Kennedale
263	184	Medina Valley ISD	Castroville
264	180	Wharton ISD	Wharton
265	180	Gonzales ISD	Gonzales
266	179	Bridge City ISD	Bridge City
267	177	Vernon ISD	Vernon
268	177	Gatesville ISD	Gatesville
269	176	Brownsboro ISD	Brownsboro
270	176	Fabens ISD	Fabens
271	175	Connally ISD	Waco
272	174	Wills Point ISD	Wills Point
273	174	Gilmer ISD	Gilmer
274	173	Wylie ISD	Abilene
275	172	Carrizo Springs Cons ISD	Carrizo Springs
276	172	Lake Worth ISD	Lake Worth
277	171	Sealy ISD	Sealy
278	171	Raymondville ISD	Raymondville
279	171	Hondo ISD	Hondo
279	171	Huffman ISD	Huffman
281	170	Center ISD	Center
282	169	Pittsburg ISD	Pittsburg
283	169	Graham ISD	Graham
284	168	Lubbock-Cooper ISD	Lubbock
285	167	Hudson ISD	Lufkin
286	166	Pearsall ISD	Pearsall
287	165	Sanger ISD	Sanger
288	164	Liberty ISD	Liberty
289	162	Seminole ISD	Seminole
290	162	Needville ISD	Needville
290	162	South Texas ISD	Mercedes
292	162	Mexia ISD	Mexia
293	162	Point Isabel ISD	Port Isabel
294	159	Pecos-Barstow-Toyah ISD	Pecos
295	157	Gladewater ISD	Gladewater
296	156	Ferris ISD	Ferris
297	156	Robinson ISD	Robinson
298	155	Van ISD	Van
299	155	Lamesa ISD	Lamesa
300	154	La Vernia ISD	La Vernia
301	154	Atlanta ISD	Atlanta
301	154	Bellville ISD	Bellville
303	154	Ft Stockton ISD	Ft Stockton
304	153	Aransas Pass ISD	Aransas Pass
305	152	Brownfield ISD	Brownfield
306	151	Sinton ISD	Sinton
307	151	Hardin-Jefferson ISD	Sour Lake
308	150	Madisonville Cons ISD	Madisonville
309	150	Rusk ISD	Rusk
310	148	Cuero ISD	Cuero
311	148	Progreso ISD	Progreso
312	146	Bridgeport ISD	Bridgeport
313	146	Diboll ISD	Diboll
314	145	Princeton ISD	Princeton
315	144	Perryton ISD	Perryton
316	144	Smithville ISD	Smithville
317	142	Crockett ISD	Crockett
318	142	Bonham ISD	Bonham
318	142	Monahans-Wickett-Pyote Is	Monahans
320	141	Crandall ISD	Crandall
321	141	Wimberley ISD	Wimberley
322	140	Giddings ISD	Giddings
322	140	Ingleside ISD	Ingleside
322	140	Shepherd ISD	Shepherd
325	140	Hillsboro ISD	Hillsboro
326	139	Devine ISD	Devine
327	139	Llano ISD	Llano
328	138	La Grange ISD	La Grange
329	137	Hutto ISD	Hutto
330	137	Caldwell ISD	Caldwell
331	137	Mathis ISD	Mathis
331	137	Sweeny ISD	Sweeny
333	136	Tarkington ISD	Cleveland
334	135	Glen Rose ISD	Glen Rose
335	134	Rio Hondo ISD	Rio Hondo
336	133	Pleasant Grove ISD	Texarkana
337	132	Venus ISD	Venus
338	131	Coldspring-Oakhurst Cons	Coldspring
338	131	Liberty Hill ISD	Liberty Hill
340	129	Brooks County ISD	Falfurrias
341	129	Groesbeck ISD	Groesbeck
342	128	West Oso ISD	Corpus Christi
343	127	Buna ISD	Buna
344	127	Cameron ISD	Cameron
345	127	Daingerfield-Lone Star Is	Daingerfield
346	127	Rains ISD	Emory
347	126	Royal ISD	Brookshire
348	126	Poteet ISD	Poteet
349	125	Crystal City ISD	Crystal City
350	125	Canton ISD	Canton
350	125	Dalhart ISD	Dalhart
352	124	Huntington ISD	Huntington
353	124	Palacios ISD	Palacios
354	123	Commerce ISD	Commerce
355	123	Ingram ISD	Ingram
355	123	Rockdale ISD	Rockdale
357	122	Hamshire-Fannett ISD	Hamshire
358	121	Bowie ISD	Bowie
359	121	Fairfield ISD	Fairfield
360	119	Yoakum ISD	Yoakum
361	119	Breckenridge ISD	Breckenridge
362	118	Iowa Park Cons ISD	Iowa Park
363	117	Westwood ISD	Palestine
364	117	Central ISD	Pollok
365	117	Spring Hill ISD	Longview
366	116	Kemp ISD	Kemp
367	114	Luling ISD	Luling
368	114	Eustace ISD	Eustace
369	113	Orangefield ISD	Orangefield
370	113	Columbus ISD	Columbus
371	112	Mineola ISD	Mineola
372	112	San Diego ISD	San Diego
373	110	Orange Grove ISD	Orange Grove
374	110	Whitesboro ISD	Whitesboro
375	109	China Spring ISD	Waco
376	108	Lyford CISD	Lyford
377	108	Kirbyville CISD	Kirbyville
378	107	Whitney ISD	Whitney
379	107	Bullard ISD	Bullard
380	105	Edna ISD	Edna
381	103	Lytle ISD	Lytle
381	103	Presidio ISD	Presidio
383	99	Greenwood ISD	Midland
384	97	West ISD	West
385	95	Lorena ISD	Lorena
386	59	Honors Academy	Dallas

Number of Students

Rank	Number	District Name	City
1	211,499	Houston ISD	Houston
2	160,584	Dallas ISD	Dallas
3	80,335	Fort Worth ISD	Fort Worth
4	79,007	Austin ISD	Austin
5	74,877	Cypress-Fairbanks ISD	Houston
6	71,798	Northside ISD	San Antonio
7	63,200	El Paso ISD	El Paso
8	62,454	Arlington ISD	Arlington
9	61,248	Fort Bend ISD	Sugar Land
10	56,914	San Antonio ISD	San Antonio
11	56,298	North East ISD	San Antonio
12	56,292	Aldine ISD	Houston
13	55,114	Garland ISD	Garland
14	51,869	Plano ISD	Plano
15	46,668	Ysleta ISD	El Paso
16	46,142	Pasadena ISD	Pasadena
17	45,923	Brownsville ISD	Brownsville
18	45,344	Alief ISD	Houston
19	44,024	Lewisville ISD	Flower Mound
20	42,116	Katy ISD	Katy
21	39,310	Corpus Christi ISD	Corpus Christi
22	39,246	Conroe ISD	Conroe
23	35,558	Klein ISD	Klein
24	35,553	Round Rock ISD	Round Rock
25	34,536	Richardson ISD	Richardson
26	34,414	Mesquite ISD	Mesquite
27	33,005	Spring Branch ISD	Houston
28	32,810	Clear Creek ISD	League City
29	32,583	Killeen ISD	Killeen
30	32,262	United ISD	Laredo
31	32,241	Socorro ISD	El Paso
32	31,249	Irving ISD	Irving
33	29,527	Amarillo ISD	Amarillo
34	29,020	Lubbock ISD	Lubbock
35	27,009	Humble ISD	Humble
36	26,768	Spring ISD	Houston
37	26,493	Pharr-San Juan-Alamo ISD	Pharr
38	26,090	Ector County ISD	Odessa
39	25,638	Carrollton-Farmers Branch	Carrollton
40	25,373	Edinburg CISD	Edinburg
41	24,846	Laredo ISD	Laredo
42	23,492	Mcallen ISD	Mcallen
43	22,507	Birdville ISD	Haltom City
44	22,132	Grand Prairie ISD	Grand Prairie
45	21,803	Keller ISD	Keller
46	21,765	La Joya ISD	La Joya
47	21,060	Mansfield ISD	Mansfield
48	20,921	Midland ISD	Midland
49	20,732	Beaumont ISD	Beaumont
50	20,454	Galena Park ISD	Houston

51	19,527	Hurst-Euless-Bedford ISD	Bedford	144	5,506	Frenship ISD	Wolfforth	236	3,109	Lindale ISD	Lindale
52	19,247	Goose Creek CISD	Baytown	145	5,480	Corsicana ISD	Corsicana	237	3,099	Levelland ISD	Levelland
53	18,201	Leander ISD	Leander	146	5,396	Midlothian ISD	Midlothian	238	3,097	Silsbee ISD	Silsbee
54	17,981	Judson ISD	San Antonio	147	5,393	Ennis ISD	Ennis	239	3,084	Elgin ISD	Elgin
55	17,864	Lamar Consolidated ISD	Rosenberg	148	5,380	Boerne ISD	Boerne	240	3,083	Burnet Cons ISD	Burnet
56	17,394	Tyler ISD	Tyler	149	5,366	Edcouch-Elsa ISD	Edcouch	241	3,070	Wilmer-Hutchins ISD	Dallas
57	17,051	Harlingen Cons ISD	Harlingen	150	5,342	Mercedes ISD	Mercedes	242	3,047	Chapel Hill ISD	Tyler
58	17,036	Abilene ISD	Abilene	151	5,288	Greenville ISD	Greenville	243	3,041	Taylor ISD	Taylor
59	16,663	Mckinney ISD	Mckinney	152	5,282	Uvalde Cons ISD	Uvalde	244	3,020	Barbers Hill ISD	Mt Belvieu
60	16,592	Pflugerville ISD	Pflugerville	153	5,228	Vidor ISD	Vidor	245	3,003	Medina Valley ISD	Castroville
61	15,951	Denton ISD	Denton	154	5,129	Mount Pleasant ISD	Mt Pleasant	245	3,003	Navasota ISD	Navasota
62	15,669	Waco ISD	Waco	155	5,116	Dayton ISD	Dayton	247	2,993	Gainesville ISD	Gainesville
63	15,126	San Angelo ISD	San Angelo	156	5,066	Flour Bluff ISD	Corpus Christi	248	2,966	Andrews ISD	Andrews
64	15,063	Wichita Falls ISD	Wichita Falls	157	5,066	Nederland ISD	Nederland	249	2,956	Valley View ISD	Pharr
65	14,977	Weslaco ISD	Weslaco	158	4,837	Brenham ISD	Brenham	250	2,938	Kennedale ISD	Kennedale
66	14,437	Victoria ISD	Victoria	159	4,830	Canutillo ISD	El Paso	251	2,912	Carthage ISD	Carthage
67	14,213	Bryan ISD	Bryan	159	4,830	Waller ISD	Waller	252	2,899	La Feria ISD	La Feria
68	14,094	Mission Cons ISD	Mission	161	4,828	White Settlement ISD	White Settlement	253	2,882	Borger ISD	Borger
69	14,088	Harlandale ISD	San Antonio	162	4,823	Jacksonville ISD	Jacksonville	254	2,871	Quinlan ISD	Quinlan
70	13,864	Allen ISD	Allen	163	4,818	Lake Travis ISD	Austin	255	2,869	Huffman ISD	Huffman
71	13,777	Grapevine-Colleyville ISD	Grapevine	164	4,803	Red Oak ISD	Red Oak	256	2,848	Fredericksburg ISD	Fredericksburg
72	13,496	Eagle Pass ISD	Eagle Pass	165	4,771	Kerrville ISD	Kerrville	257	2,846	Decatur ISD	Decatur
73	13,411	Frisco ISD	Frisco	166	4,754	Lancaster ISD	Lancaster	258	2,838	Stafford Municipal School	Stafford
74	13,180	Brazosport ISD	Freeport	167	4,753	Port Neches-Groves ISD	Port Neches	259	2,804	Wylie ISD	Abilene
75	13,096	Pearland ISD	Pearland	168	4,741	Willis ISD	Willis	260	2,774	Fabens ISD	Fabens
76	12,894	Edgewood ISD	San Antonio	169	4,676	Southside ISD	San Antonio	261	2,725	Liberty-Eylau ISD	Texarkana
77	12,131	Alvin ISD	Alvin	170	4,643	Pine Tree ISD	Longview	262	2,721	Brownsboro ISD	Brownsboro
78	11,989	Comal ISD	New Braunfels	171	4,640	Montgomery ISD	Montgomery	263	2,711	Wills Point ISD	Wills Point
79	11,819	Crowley ISD	Crowley	172	4,561	Denison ISD	Denison	264	2,694	Royse City ISD	Royse City
79	11,819	Deer Park ISD	Deer Park	173	4,544	Kingsville ISD	Kingsville	265	2,665	Bandera ISD	Bandera
81	11,700	Donna ISD	Donna	174	4,539	Sheldon ISD	Houston	266	2,634	Connally ISD	Waco
82	11,368	Duncanville ISD	Duncanville	175	4,495	Lockhart ISD	Lockhart	267	2,629	La Vega ISD	Waco
83	10,818	North Forest ISD	Houston	176	4,475	Santa Fe ISD	Santa Fe	268	2,627	Gonzales ISD	Gonzales
84	10,461	San Felipe-Del Rio Cons I	Del Rio	177	4,427	Joshua ISD	Joshua	269	2,616	Gatesville ISD	Gatesville
85	10,357	Port Arthur ISD	Port Arthur	178	4,356	Alamo Heights ISD	San Antonio	270	2,608	Snyder ISD	Snyder
86	10,096	Rockwall ISD	Rockwall	179	4,302	Gregory-Portland ISD	Gregory	271	2,589	Bridge City ISD	Bridge City
87	10,003	Coppell ISD	Coppell	180	4,298	Calhoun County ISD	Port Lavaca	272	2,556	Point Isabel ISD	Point Isabel
88	9,951	South San Antonio ISD	San Antonio	181	4,278	Crosby ISD	Crosby	273	2,512	Raymondville ISD	Raymondville
89	9,886	San Benito Cons ISD	San Benito	182	4,258	Bay City ISD	Bay City	274	2,510	Wharton ISD	Wharton
90	9,684	Southwest ISD	San Antonio	183	4,195	Dumas ISD	Dumas	275	2,485	Carrizo Springs Cons ISD	Carrizo Springs
91	9,526	Rio Grande City CISD	Rio Grande City	184	4,175	Terrell ISD	Terrell	276	2,470	Center ISD	Center
92	9,170	Galveston ISD	Galveston	185	4,159	Sulphur Springs ISD	Sulphur Springs	277	2,466	Needville ISD	Needville
93	9,135	Magnolia ISD	Magnolia	186	4,096	Whitehouse ISD	Whitehouse	278	2,421	Graham ISD	Graham
94	9,052	Hays Cons ISD	Kyle	187	4,048	Livingston ISD	Livingston	279	2,419	La Vernia ISD	La Vernia
95	8,662	Georgetown ISD	Georgetown	188	3,945	Paris ISD	Paris	280	2,408	Lubbock-Cooper ISD	Lubbock
96	8,564	Clint ISD	El Paso	189	3,944	Robstown ISD	Robstown	281	2,392	Lake Worth ISD	Lake Worth
97	8,517	Eagle Mt-Saginaw ISD	Fort Worth	190	3,939	Hereford ISD	Hereford	282	2,384	Sealy ISD	Sealy
98	8,415	Tomball ISD	Tomball	191	3,931	Big Spring ISD	Big Spring	283	2,352	Hudson ISD	Lufkin
99	8,291	Longview ISD	Longview	192	3,924	Calallen ISD	Corpus Christi	284	2,347	Liberty ISD	Liberty
100	8,282	Lufkin ISD	Lufkin	193	3,832	Everman ISD	Everman	285	2,346	Pecos-Barstow-Toyah ISD	Pecos
101	8,254	Temple ISD	Temple	194	3,805	Forney ISD	Forney	286	2,343	Vernon ISD	Vernon
102	7,931	College Station ISD	College Station	195	3,779	Beeville ISD	Beeville	287	2,336	Mexia ISD	Mexia
103	7,917	East Central ISD	San Antonio	196	3,750	La Marque ISD	La Marque	288	2,333	Pittsburg ISD	Pittsburg
104	7,721	Canyon ISD	Canyon	197	3,732	Hallsville ISD	Hallsville	289	2,330	Ingleside ISD	Ingleside
105	7,695	La Porte ISD	La Porte	198	3,711	San Elizario ISD	San Elizario	290	2,201	Ft Stockton ISD	Ft Stockton
106	7,656	Del Valle ISD	Del Valle	199	3,703	Marble Falls ISD	Marble Falls	291	2,287	Pearsall ISD	Pearsall
107	7,651	Desoto ISD	Desoto	200	3,699	Little Cypress-Mauricevil	Orange	292	2,277	Ferris ISD	Ferris
108	7,595	Seguin ISD	Seguin	201	3,684	Mineral Wells ISD	Mineral Wells	293	2,276	Gilmer ISD	Gilmer
109	7,565	Bastrop ISD	Bastrop	202	3,669	Kilgore ISD	Kilgore	294	2,265	Gladewater ISD	Gladewater
110	7,564	Cedar Hill ISD	Cedar Hill	203	3,619	Burkburnett ISD	Burkburnett	295	2,254	Princeton ISD	Princeton
111	7,510	Los Fresnos Cons ISD	Los Fresnos	204	3,599	Brownwood ISD	Brownwood	296	2,228	Bridgeport ISD	Bridgeport
112	7,466	Copperas Cove ISD	Copperas Cove	205	3,578	Lake Dallas ISD	Lake Dallas	297	2,218	Sweetwater ISD	Sweetwater
113	7,451	Channelview ISD	Channelview	206	3,566	Floresville ISD	Floresville	298	2,192	Seminole ISD	Seminole
114	7,304	Carroll ISD	Grapevine	207	3,565	Springtown ISD	Springtown	299	2,177	Madisonville Cons ISD	Madisonville
115	7,282	New Caney ISD	New Caney	208	3,530	Stephenville ISD	Stephenville	299	2,177	Rio Hondo ISD	Rio Hondo
116	7,279	Burleson ISD	Burleson	209	3,500	Athens ISD	Athens	301	2,175	Hondo ISD	Hondo
117	7,257	Schertz-Cibolo-U City ISD	Schertz	210	3,496	Pleasanton ISD	Pleasanton	302	2,168	Van ISD	Van
118	7,114	Belton ISD	Belton	211	3,496	El Campo ISD	El Campo	303	2,150	Sanger ISD	Sanger
119	7,091	Eanes ISD	Austin	212	3,495	Aledo ISD	Aledo	304	2,142	Sinton ISD	Sinton
120	7,052	San Marcos Cons ISD	San Marcos	213	3,485	Henderson ISD	Henderson	305	2,141	Bellville ISD	Bellville
121	6,987	Weatherford ISD	Weatherford	214	3,484	Little Elm ISD	Little Elm	306	2,130	Hardin-Jefferson ISD	Sour Lake
122	6,917	Northwest ISD	Fort Worth	215	3,466	Lumberton ISD	Lumberton	307	2,127	Lamesa ISD	Lamesa
123	6,751	Sharyland ISD	Mission	216	3,437	Alvarado ISD	Alvarado	308	2,112	Progreso ISD	Progreso
124	6,746	Huntsville ISD	Huntsville	217	3,407	Kaufman ISD	Kaufman	309	2,103	Aransas Pass ISD	Aransas Pass
125	6,661	Wylie ISD	Wylie	218	3,367	Tuloso-Midway ISD	Corpus Christi	310	2,098	Sweeny ISD	Sweeny
126	6,607	Granbury ISD	Granbury	219	3,343	Aransas County ISD	Rockport	311	2,090	South Texas ISD	Mercedes
127	6,539	Dickinson ISD	Dickinson	220	3,329	Cleveland ISD	Cleveland	312	2,079	Crandall ISD	Crandall
128	6,506	Angleton ISD	Angleton	221	3,316	Palestine ISD	Palestine	313	2,071	Crystal City ISD	Crystal City
129	6,413	Cleburne ISD	Cleburne	222	3,289	Pampa ISD	Pampa	314	2,056	Robinson ISD	Robinson
130	6,384	Nacogdoches ISD	Nacogdoches	223	3,284	Somerset ISD	Somerset	315	2,009	Bonham ISD	Bonham
131	6,363	Sherman ISD	Sherman	224	3,280	Dripping Springs ISD	Dripping Spgs	316	1,984	Perryton ISD	Perryton
132	6,360	New Braunfels ISD	New Braunfels	225	3,259	Mabank ISD	Mabank	317	1,982	Hutto ISD	Hutto
133	6,223	Roma ISD	Roma	226	3,250	Lampasas ISD	Lampasas	318	1,980	Devine ISD	Devine
134	6,091	Plainview ISD	Plainview	227	3,233	Castleberry ISD	Fort Worth	319	1,964	Monahans-Wickett-Pyote Is	Monahans
135	6,074	Highland Park ISD	Dallas	228	3,227	Manor ISD	Manor	320	1,959	Rusk ISD	Rusk
136	5,882	Azle ISD	Azle	229	3,222	West Orange-Cove Cons ISD	Orange	321	1,949	Cuero ISD	Cuero
137	5,881	Midway ISD	Waco	230	3,182	North Lamar ISD	Paris	322	1,947	Atlanta ISD	Atlanta
138	5,880	Marshall ISD	Marshall	231	3,163	Zapata County ISD	Zapata	322	1,947	Brownfield ISD	Brownfield
139	5,859	Waxahachie ISD	Waxahachie	232	3,157	Hidalgo ISD	Hidalgo	324	1,945	La Grange ISD	La Grange
140	5,804	Texas City ISD	Texas City	233	3,135	Splendora ISD	Splendora	325	1,932	Diboll ISD	Diboll
141	5,719	Texarkana ISD	Texarkana	234	3,123	Columbia-Brazoria ISD	West Columbia	326	1,925	Pleasant Grove ISD	Texarkana
142	5,702	Alice ISD	Alice	235	3,115	Jasper ISD	Jasper	327	1,923	Shepherd ISD	Shepherd
143	5,527	Friendswood ISD	Friendswood					328	1,916	Llano ISD	Llano

Rank	Percent	District Name	City
329	1,909	Caldwell ISD	Caldwell
330	1,904	Smithville ISD	Smithville
331	1,902	West Oso ISD	Corpus Christi
332	1,896	Honors Academy	Dallas
333	1,894	Mathis ISD	Mathis
334	1,882	Rockdale ISD	Rockdale
335	1,880	Wimberley ISD	Wimberley
336	1,857	Tarkington ISD	Cleveland
337	1,829	Commerce ISD	Commerce
338	1,826	Venus ISD	Venus
339	1,825	Giddings ISD	Giddings
340	1,820	Iowa Park Cons ISD	Iowa Park
341	1,818	Hillsboro ISD	Hillsboro
342	1,800	China Spring ISD	Waco
343	1,798	Canton ISD	Canton
344	1,797	Liberty Hill ISD	Liberty Hill
345	1,794	Coldspring-Oakhurst Cons	Coldspring
346	1,785	Hamshire-Fannett ISD	Hamshire
346	1,785	Westwood ISD	Palestine
348	1,727	Spring Hill ISD	Longview
349	1,708	Kemp ISD	Kemp
350	1,692	Central ISD	Pollok
351	1,689	Crockett ISD	Crockett
352	1,686	Poteet ISD	Poteet
353	1,684	Royal ISD	Brookshire
354	1,681	Palacios ISD	Palacios
355	1,677	Fairfield ISD	Fairfield
356	1,659	Huntington ISD	Huntington
357	1,656	Groesbeck ISD	Groesbeck
358	1,651	Bowie ISD	Bowie
359	1,648	Brooks County ISD	Falfurrias
360	1,644	Orangefield ISD	Orangefield
361	1,639	Cameron ISD	Cameron
362	1,632	Orange Grove ISD	Orange Grove
363	1,625	Dalhart ISD	Dalhart
364	1,615	Luling ISD	Luling
365	1,609	Whitesboro ISD	Whitesboro
366	1,601	Mineola ISD	Mineola
367	1,598	Breckenridge ISD	Breckenridge
367	1,598	Kirbyville CISD	Kirbyville
369	1,596	Glen Rose ISD	Glen Rose
370	1,589	Buna ISD	Buna
371	1,567	Yoakum ISD	Yoakum
372	1,566	Daingerfield-Lone Star Is	Daingerfield
373	1,565	Columbus ISD	Columbus
374	1,564	Bullard ISD	Bullard
375	1,557	Lorena ISD	Lorena
376	1,555	Edna ISD	Edna
377	1,554	Rains ISD	Emory
378	1,551	West ISD	West
379	1,548	Whitney ISD	Whitney
380	1,545	San Diego ISD	San Diego
381	1,542	Lytle ISD	Lytle
382	1,525	Presidio ISD	Presidio
383	1,513	Eustace ISD	Eustace
383	1,513	Ingram ISD	Ingram
385	1,505	Lyford CISD	Lyford
386	1,503	Greenwood ISD	Midland

Male Students

Rank	Percent	District Name	City
1	54.8	West ISD	West
2	54.7	Lorena ISD	Lorena
3	54.2	Diboll ISD	Diboll
4	54.1	Shepherd ISD	Shepherd
5	54.1	Coldspring-Oakhurst Cons	Coldspring
6	54.0	Sweeny ISD	Sweeny
7	53.9	Sanger ISD	Sanger
8	53.9	West Oso ISD	Corpus Christi
9	53.9	Royse City ISD	Royse City
10	53.8	Sinton ISD	Sinton
11	53.7	Wimberley ISD	Wimberley
12	53.7	Lytle ISD	Lytle
13	53.7	Venus ISD	Venus
14	53.6	Cameron ISD	Cameron
15	53.6	Hardin-Jefferson ISD	Sour Lake
16	53.6	Lake Worth ISD	Lake Worth
17	53.6	Burleson ISD	Burleson
18	53.6	Lubbock-Cooper ISD	Lubbock
19	53.5	Lake Travis ISD	Austin
20	53.4	Dalhart ISD	Dalhart
21	53.4	Bullard ISD	Bullard
22	53.2	Presidio ISD	Presidio
23	53.2	Kemp ISD	Kemp
24	53.2	Brooks County ISD	Falfurrias
25	53.1	Caldwell ISD	Caldwell
26	53.0	Gilmer ISD	Gilmer
27	53.0	Vernon ISD	Vernon
28	53.0	Rains ISD	Emory
29	53.0	Taylor ISD	Taylor
30	52.9	Pecos-Barstow-Toyah ISD	Pecos
31	52.9	Connally ISD	Waco
32	52.9	Huntington ISD	Huntington
33	52.9	Greenwood ISD	Midland
34	52.8	Montgomery ISD	Montgomery
35	52.8	Hereford ISD	Hereford
36	52.8	Azle ISD	Azle
37	52.7	La Porte ISD	La Porte
38	52.7	Santa Fe ISD	Santa Fe
39	52.7	Glen Rose ISD	Glen Rose
40	52.7	Terrell ISD	Terrell
41	52.7	Princeton ISD	Princeton
42	52.7	Huffman ISD	Huffman
43	52.6	Weatherford ISD	Weatherford
44	52.6	Canutillo ISD	El Paso
45	52.6	Medina Valley ISD	Castroville
46	52.6	Lampasas ISD	Lampasas
47	52.6	Llano ISD	Llano
48	52.6	La Vernia ISD	La Vernia
49	52.6	Daingerfield-Lone Star Is	Daingerfield
50	52.5	Lake Dallas ISD	Lake Dallas
51	52.5	Henderson ISD	Henderson
52	52.5	Pittsburg ISD	Pittsburg
53	52.5	Alvin ISD	Alvin
54	52.5	Carroll ISD	Grapevine
55	52.4	Chapel Hill ISD	Tyler
56	52.4	Liberty-Eylau ISD	Texarkana
57	52.4	Smithville ISD	Smithville
58	52.4	Cedar Hill ISD	Cedar Hill
59	52.4	South San Antonio ISD	San Antonio
60	52.4	Magnolia ISD	Magnolia
61	52.3	Robinson ISD	Robinson
62	52.3	Hays Cons ISD	Kyle
63	52.3	Gregory-Portland ISD	Gregory
64	52.3	Progreso ISD	Progreso
65	52.3	Comal ISD	New Braunfels
66	52.3	Mexia ISD	Mexia
67	52.3	Orangefield ISD	Orangefield
68	52.2	Gatesville ISD	Gatesville
69	52.2	Sharyland ISD	Mission
70	52.2	Whitehouse ISD	Whitehouse
71	52.2	Commerce ISD	Commerce
72	52.2	Carthage ISD	Carthage
73	52.2	Pleasant Grove ISD	Texarkana
74	52.2	Rockwall ISD	Rockwall
75	52.2	Gladewater ISD	Gladewater
76	52.2	Bowie ISD	Bowie
77	52.2	Whitesboro ISD	Whitesboro
78	52.2	Dumas ISD	Dumas
79	52.1	Madisonville Cons ISD	Madisonville
80	52.1	Raymondville ISD	Raymondville
81	52.1	Willis ISD	Willis
82	52.1	Mabank ISD	Mabank
83	52.1	Crosby ISD	Crosby
84	52.1	Rockdale ISD	Rockdale
85	52.1	Angleton ISD	Angleton
86	52.1	Stafford Municipal School	Stafford
87	52.1	Belton ISD	Belton
88	52.1	Leander ISD	Leander
89	52.1	Boerne ISD	Boerne
90	52.0	Kingsville ISD	Kingsville
91	52.0	Hallsville ISD	Hallsville
92	52.0	San Elizario ISD	San Elizario
93	52.0	Burkburnett ISD	Burkburnett
94	52.0	Atlanta ISD	Atlanta
95	52.0	Northwest ISD	Fort Worth
96	52.0	Ingleside ISD	Ingleside
97	52.0	Andrews ISD	Andrews
98	52.0	Dayton ISD	Dayton
99	52.0	Silsbee ISD	Silsbee
100	52.0	Judson ISD	San Antonio
101	52.0	Lamesa ISD	Lamesa
102	52.0	East Central ISD	San Antonio
103	52.0	Brownsboro ISD	Brownsboro
104	52.0	Eanes ISD	Austin
105	52.0	Mount Pleasant ISD	Mt Pleasant
106	52.0	Springtown ISD	Springtown
107	52.0	Perryton ISD	Perryton
108	52.0	Canyon ISD	Canyon
109	52.0	Uvalde Cons ISD	Uvalde
110	51.9	Nederland ISD	Nederland
111	51.9	El Campo ISD	El Campo
112	51.9	Aransas County ISD	Rockport
113	51.9	Mckinney ISD	Mckinney
114	51.9	Pine Tree ISD	Longview
115	51.9	Denison ISD	Denison
116	51.9	Kerrville ISD	Kerrville
117	51.9	Birdville ISD	Haltom City
118	51.9	Bridgeport ISD	Bridgeport
119	51.9	Robstown ISD	Robstown
120	51.9	San Benito Cons ISD	San Benito
121	51.8	Splendora ISD	Splendora
122	51.8	College Station ISD	College Station
123	51.8	Jacksonville ISD	Jacksonville
124	51.8	Harlandale ISD	San Antonio
125	51.8	Calhoun County ISD	Port Lavaca
126	51.8	Little Cypress-Mauricevil	Orange
127	51.8	Hamshire-Fannett ISD	Hamshire
128	51.8	Brazosport ISD	Freeport
129	51.8	Victoria ISD	Victoria
130	51.8	White Settlement ISD	White Settlement
131	51.8	Crandall ISD	Crandall
132	51.8	Mineral Wells ISD	Mineral Wells
133	51.8	Dickinson ISD	Dickinson
134	51.8	Lyford CISD	Lyford
135	51.8	Bryan ISD	Bryan
136	51.8	Seminole ISD	Seminole
137	51.8	Rio Hondo ISD	Rio Hondo
138	51.8	Groesbeck ISD	Groesbeck
139	51.8	Pflugerville ISD	Pflugerville
140	51.7	Aledo ISD	Aledo
141	51.7	Harlingen Cons ISD	Harlingen
142	51.7	Palestine ISD	Palestine
143	51.7	Forney ISD	Forney
144	51.7	Joshua ISD	Joshua
145	51.7	New Caney ISD	New Caney
146	51.7	West Orange-Cove Cons ISD	Orange
147	51.7	Channelview ISD	Channelview
148	51.7	Midlothian ISD	Midlothian
149	51.7	Waller ISD	Waller
150	51.7	Liberty Hill ISD	Liberty Hill
151	51.7	Sherman ISD	Sherman
152	51.7	Lockhart ISD	Lockhart
153	51.7	Fort Bend ISD	Sugar Land
154	51.7	North Lamar ISD	Paris
155	51.7	Coppell ISD	Coppell
156	51.7	Sealy ISD	Sealy
157	51.7	Athens ISD	Athens
158	51.7	Keller ISD	Keller
159	51.6	Georgetown ISD	Georgetown
160	51.6	Richardson ISD	Richardson
161	51.6	Levelland ISD	Levelland
162	51.6	Northside ISD	San Antonio
163	51.6	Aransas Pass ISD	Aransas Pass
164	51.6	Hondo ISD	Hondo
165	51.6	Carrizo Springs Cons ISD	Carrizo Springs
166	51.6	Cuero ISD	Cuero
167	51.6	Little Elm ISD	Little Elm
168	51.6	Needville ISD	Needville
169	51.6	Quinlan ISD	Quinlan
170	51.6	Los Fresnos Cons ISD	Los Fresnos
171	51.6	Ft Stockton ISD	Ft Stockton
171	51.6	Klein ISD	Klein
173	51.6	Mansfield ISD	Mansfield
174	51.6	Yoakum ISD	Yoakum
175	51.6	Lumberton ISD	Lumberton
176	51.5	Austin ISD	Austin
177	51.5	Stephenville	Stephenville
178	51.5	Corpus Christi ISD	Corpus Christi
179	51.5	Snyder ISD	Snyder
180	51.5	Zapata County ISD	Zapata
181	51.5	Wilmer-Hutchins ISD	Dallas
182	51.5	Longview ISD	Longview
183	51.5	Alamo Heights ISD	San Antonio
184	51.5	Wylie ISD	Wylie
185	51.5	Irving ISD	Irving
186	51.5	Big Spring ISD	Big Spring
187	51.5	Denton ISD	Denton
188	51.5	Schertz-Cibolo-U City ISD	Schertz
189	51.5	Fairfield ISD	Fairfield
190	51.5	Pleasanton ISD	Pleasanton
191	51.5	Bastrop ISD	Bastrop
192	51.5	Bay City ISD	Bay City
193	51.4	Dripping Springs ISD	Dripping Spgs
194	51.4	Somerset ISD	Somerset
195	51.4	San Marcos Cons ISD	San Marcos
196	51.4	Bridge City ISD	Bridge City
197	51.4	La Joya ISD	La Joya
198	51.4	Tarkington ISD	Cleveland
199	51.4	Donna ISD	Donna
200	51.4	Gonzales ISD	Gonzales
201	51.4	La Grange ISD	La Grange
202	51.4	Allen ISD	Allen
203	51.4	Livingston ISD	Livingston
203	51.4	Paris ISD	Paris
205	51.4	Barbers Hill ISD	Mt Belvieu
206	51.4	Edinburg CISD	Edinburg
207	51.4	Eagle Mt-Saginaw ISD	Fort Worth
208	51.4	Garland ISD	Garland
209	51.4	Weslaco ISD	Weslaco
210	51.4	Humble ISD	Humble
211	51.4	Tyler ISD	Tyler
212	51.4	Hudson ISD	Lufkin
213	51.3	Brenham ISD	Brenham
214	51.3	Wharton ISD	Wharton
215	51.3	Pasadena ISD	Pasadena
216	51.3	Cypress-Fairbanks ISD	Houston

Rank	Percent	District Name	City
217	51.3	Breckenridge ISD	Breckenridge
217	51.3	Kirbyville CISD	Kirbyville
219	51.3	Hurst-Euless-Bedford ISD	Bedford
220	51.3	Plano ISD	Plano
221	51.3	Iowa Park Cons ISD	Iowa Park
222	51.3	Royal ISD	Brookshire
223	51.3	Aldine ISD	Houston
224	51.3	Calallen ISD	Corpus Christi
225	51.3	Crowley ISD	Crowley
226	51.3	Clear Creek ISD	League City
227	51.3	Wills Point ISD	Wills Point
228	51.3	Granbury ISD	Granbury
229	51.3	Van ISD	Van
230	51.3	Carrollton-Farmers Branch	Carrollton
231	51.3	Seguin ISD	Seguin
232	51.3	Duncanville ISD	Duncanville
233	51.3	Conroe ISD	Conroe
234	51.3	Ennis ISD	Ennis
235	51.3	Nacogdoches ISD	Nacogdoches
236	51.2	Mission Cons ISD	Mission
237	51.2	Alvarado ISD	Alvarado
238	51.2	Del Valle ISD	Del Valle
239	51.2	Round Rock ISD	Round Rock
240	51.2	Spring Branch ISD	Houston
241	51.2	Tomball ISD	Tomball
242	51.2	Socorro ISD	El Paso
243	51.2	United ISD	Laredo
244	51.2	Hillsboro ISD	Hillsboro
245	51.2	La Feria ISD	La Feria
246	51.2	Ector County ISD	Odessa
247	51.2	Amarillo ISD	Amarillo
248	51.2	Vidor ISD	Vidor
249	51.2	Red Oak ISD	Red Oak
250	51.2	Ysleta ISD	El Paso
251	51.2	Waco ISD	Waco
252	51.2	Killeen ISD	Killeen
253	51.2	Texas City ISD	Texas City
254	51.1	Decatur ISD	Decatur
255	51.1	Alice ISD	Alice
256	51.1	Brownwood ISD	Brownwood
257	51.1	Katy ISD	Katy
258	51.1	Jasper ISD	Jasper
259	51.1	Ingram ISD	Ingram
260	51.1	Brownsville ISD	Brownsville
261	51.1	Lewisville ISD	Flower Mound
262	51.1	Borger ISD	Borger
263	51.1	Bellville ISD	Bellville
264	51.1	Flour Bluff ISD	Corpus Christi
265	51.1	Mercedes ISD	Mercedes
266	51.1	Temple ISD	Temple
267	51.1	Goose Creek CISD	Baytown
268	51.1	Alief ISD	Houston
269	51.1	Spring ISD	Houston
270	51.1	Abilene ISD	Abilene
271	51.1	Manor ISD	Manor
272	51.0	San Antonio ISD	San Antonio
273	51.0	Eagle Pass ISD	Eagle Pass
274	51.0	Corsicana ISD	Corsicana
275	51.0	Pearland ISD	Pearland
276	51.0	Midway ISD	Waco
277	51.0	El Paso ISD	El Paso
278	51.0	Pearsall ISD	Pearsall
279	51.0	Port Neches-Groves ISD	Port Neches
280	51.0	Brownfield ISD	Brownfield
281	51.0	Copperas Cove ISD	Copperas Cove
282	51.0	Edcouch-Elsa ISD	Edcouch
283	51.0	Wichita Falls ISD	Wichita Falls
284	51.0	Marshall ISD	Marshall
285	51.0	Grand Prairie ISD	Grand Prairie
286	51.0	San Angelo ISD	San Angelo
287	51.0	Greenville ISD	Greenville
288	51.0	San Felipe-Del Rio Cons I	Del Rio
289	51.0	Houston ISD	Houston
290	51.0	La Vega ISD	Waco
291	50.9	North Forest ISD	Houston
292	50.9	Hidalgo ISD	Hidalgo
293	50.9	Plainview ISD	Plainview
294	50.9	La Marque ISD	La Marque
295	50.9	Southside ISD	San Antonio
296	50.9	Point Isabel ISD	Port Isabel
297	50.9	Graham ISD	Graham
298	50.9	Arlington ISD	Arlington
299	50.9	Sweetwater ISD	Sweetwater
300	50.9	North East ISD	San Antonio
301	50.9	Canton ISD	Canton
302	50.9	Rio Grande City CISD	Rio Grande City
303	50.9	Southwest ISD	San Antonio
304	50.9	Lancaster ISD	Lancaster
305	50.9	Whitney ISD	Whitney
306	50.8	Spring Hill ISD	Longview
307	50.8	Galveston ISD	Galveston
308	50.8	Eustace ISD	Eustace
309	50.8	Burnet Cons ISD	Burnet
310	50.8	Fort Worth ISD	Fort Worth
311	50.8	Lindale ISD	Lindale
311	50.8	Lubbock ISD	Lubbock
313	50.8	Friendswood ISD	Friendswood
314	50.8	Giddings ISD	Giddings
315	50.8	Valley View ISD	Pharr
316	50.8	Edgewood ISD	San Antonio
317	50.7	Crockett ISD	Crockett
318	50.7	Galena Park ISD	Houston
319	50.7	Westwood ISD	Palestine
320	50.7	Gainesville ISD	Gainesville
321	50.7	Palacios ISD	Palacios
322	50.7	Mesquite ISD	Mesquite
323	50.7	Kennedale ISD	Kennedale
324	50.6	Laredo ISD	Laredo
325	50.6	Sulphur Springs ISD	Sulphur Springs
326	50.6	Deer Park ISD	Deer Park
327	50.6	Clint ISD	El Paso
328	50.6	Waxahachie ISD	Waxahachie
329	50.6	Frenship ISD	Wolfforth
330	50.6	Mcallen ISD	Mcallen
331	50.6	Roma ISD	Roma
332	50.6	Lamar Consolidated ISD	Rosenberg
333	50.6	Bandera ISD	Bandera
334	50.6	Pharr-San Juan-Alamo ISD	Pharr
335	50.6	Devine ISD	Devine
336	50.5	Buna ISD	Buna
337	50.5	Beeville ISD	Beeville
338	50.5	Midland ISD	Midland
339	50.5	Cleburne ISD	Cleburne
340	50.5	Dallas ISD	Dallas
341	50.5	Port Arthur ISD	Port Arthur
342	50.4	Columbia-Brazoria ISD	West Columbia
343	50.4	Navasota ISD	Navasota
344	50.4	Floresville ISD	Floresville
345	50.4	Pampa ISD	Pampa
346	50.4	Kaufman ISD	Kaufman
347	50.4	Sheldon ISD	Houston
348	50.4	Texarkana ISD	Texarkana
349	50.4	Frisco ISD	Frisco
350	50.4	Fabens ISD	Fabens
351	50.4	Elgin ISD	Elgin
352	50.4	Brownsville ISD	Brownsville
353	50.4	Monahans-Wickett-Pyote Is	Monahans
354	50.4	Cleveland ISD	Cleveland
355	50.4	Liberty ISD	Liberty
356	50.3	Everman ISD	Everman
357	50.3	Edna ISD	Edna
358	50.3	Columbus ISD	Columbus
359	50.3	Rusk ISD	Rusk
360	50.3	Bonham ISD	Bonham
361	50.2	Grapevine-Colleyville ISD	Grapevine
362	50.2	Fredericksburg ISD	Fredericksburg
363	50.2	Beaumont ISD	Beaumont
364	50.2	Crystal City ISD	Crystal City
365	50.2	Desoto ISD	Desoto
366	50.2	Hutto ISD	Hutto
367	50.1	Huntsville ISD	Huntsville
368	50.1	New Braunfels ISD	New Braunfels
369	50.1	Luling ISD	Luling
370	50.0	Highland Park ISD	Dallas
371	49.9	Mineola ISD	Mineola
372	49.9	Central ISD	Pollok
373	49.9	Castleberry ISD	Fort Worth
374	49.7	Lufkin ISD	Lufkin
375	49.7	Poteet ISD	Poteet
376	49.6	Kilgore ISD	Kilgore
377	49.6	Honors Academy	Dallas
378	49.5	Tuloso-Midway ISD	Corpus Christi
379	49.2	Center ISD	Center
380	49.1	Wylie ISD	Abilene
381	49.1	Mathis ISD	Mathis
382	49.0	San Diego ISD	San Diego
383	48.8	Marble Falls ISD	Marble Falls
384	48.6	China Spring ISD	Waco
385	48.2	Orange Grove ISD	Orange Grove
386	46.6	South Texas ISD	Mercedes

Female Students

Rank	Percent	District Name	City
1	53.3	South Texas ISD	Mercedes
2	51.7	Orange Grove ISD	Orange Grove
3	51.3	China Spring ISD	Waco
4	51.1	Marble Falls ISD	Marble Falls
5	50.9	San Diego ISD	San Diego
6	50.8	Mathis ISD	Mathis
7	50.8	Wylie ISD	Abilene
8	50.7	Center ISD	Center
9	50.4	Tuloso-Midway ISD	Corpus Christi
10	50.3	Honors Academy	Dallas
11	50.3	Kilgore ISD	Kilgore
12	50.2	Poteet ISD	Poteet
13	50.2	Lufkin ISD	Lufkin
14	50.0	Castleberry ISD	Fort Worth
15	50.0	Central ISD	Pollok
16	50.0	Mineola ISD	Mineola
17	49.9	Highland Park ISD	Dallas
18	49.8	Luling ISD	Luling
19	49.8	New Braunfels ISD	New Braunfels
20	49.8	Huntsville ISD	Huntsville
21	49.7	Hutto ISD	Hutto
22	49.7	Desoto ISD	Desoto
23	49.7	Crystal City ISD	Crystal City
24	49.7	Beaumont ISD	Beaumont
25	49.7	Fredericksburg ISD	Fredericksburg
26	49.7	Grapevine-Colleyville ISD	Grapevine
27	49.6	Bonham ISD	Bonham
28	49.6	Rusk ISD	Rusk
29	49.6	Columbus ISD	Columbus
30	49.6	Edna ISD	Edna
31	49.6	Everman ISD	Everman
32	49.6	Liberty ISD	Liberty
33	49.5	Cleveland ISD	Cleveland
34	49.5	Monahans-Wickett-Pyote Is	Monahans
35	49.5	Ferris ISD	Ferris
36	49.5	Elgin ISD	Elgin
37	49.5	Fabens ISD	Fabens
38	49.5	Frisco ISD	Frisco
39	49.5	Texarkana ISD	Texarkana
40	49.5	Sheldon ISD	Houston
41	49.5	Kaufman ISD	Kaufman
42	49.5	Pampa ISD	Pampa
43	49.5	Floresville ISD	Floresville
44	49.5	Navasota ISD	Navasota
45	49.5	Columbia-Brazoria ISD	West Columbia
46	49.4	Port Arthur ISD	Port Arthur
47	49.4	Dallas ISD	Dallas
48	49.4	Cleburne ISD	Cleburne
49	49.4	Midland ISD	Midland
50	49.4	Beeville ISD	Beeville
51	49.4	Buna ISD	Buna
52	49.3	Devine ISD	Devine
53	49.3	Pharr-San Juan-Alamo ISD	Pharr
54	49.3	Bandera ISD	Bandera
55	49.3	Lamar Consolidated ISD	Rosenberg
56	49.3	Roma ISD	Roma
57	49.3	Mcallen ISD	Mcallen
58	49.3	Frenship ISD	Wolfforth
59	49.3	Waxahachie ISD	Waxahachie
60	49.3	Clint ISD	El Paso
61	49.3	Deer Park ISD	Deer Park
62	49.3	Sulphur Springs ISD	Sulphur Springs
63	49.3	Laredo ISD	Laredo
64	49.2	Kennedale ISD	Kennedale
65	49.2	Mesquite ISD	Mesquite
66	49.2	Palacios ISD	Palacios
67	49.2	Gainesville ISD	Gainesville
68	49.2	Westwood ISD	Palestine
69	49.2	Galena Park ISD	Houston
70	49.2	Crockett ISD	Crockett
71	49.1	Edgewood ISD	San Antonio
72	49.1	Valley View ISD	Pharr
73	49.1	Giddings ISD	Giddings
74	49.1	Friendswood ISD	Friendswood
75	49.1	Lindale ISD	Lindale
75	49.1	Lubbock ISD	Lubbock
77	49.1	Fort Worth ISD	Fort Worth
78	49.1	Burnet Cons ISD	Burnet
79	49.1	Eustace ISD	Eustace
80	49.1	Galveston ISD	Galveston
81	49.1	Spring Hill ISD	Longview
82	49.0	Whitney ISD	Whitney
83	49.0	Lancaster ISD	Lancaster
84	49.0	Southwest ISD	San Antonio
85	49.0	Rio Grande City CISD	Rio Grande City
86	49.0	Canton ISD	Canton
87	49.0	North East ISD	San Antonio
88	49.0	Sweetwater ISD	Sweetwater
89	49.0	Arlington ISD	Arlington
90	49.0	Graham ISD	Graham
91	49.0	Point Isabel ISD	Port Isabel
92	49.0	Southside ISD	San Antonio
93	49.0	La Marque ISD	La Marque
94	49.0	Plainview ISD	Plainview
95	49.0	Hidalgo ISD	Hidalgo
96	49.0	North Forest ISD	Houston
97	48.9	La Vega ISD	Waco
98	48.9	Houston ISD	Houston
99	48.9	San Felipe-Del Rio Cons I	Del Rio
100	48.9	Greenville ISD	Greenville
101	48.9	San Angelo ISD	San Angelo
102	48.9	Grand Prairie ISD	Grand Prairie
103	48.9	Marshall ISD	Marshall

104	48.9	Wichita Falls ISD	Wichita Falls	197	48.4	Pleasanton ISD	Pleasanton	289	47.9	Dayton ISD	Dayton
105	48.9	Edcouch-Elsa ISD	Edcouch	198	48.4	Fairfield ISD	Fairfield	290	47.9	Andrews ISD	Andrews
106	48.9	Copperas Cove ISD	Copperas Cove	199	48.4	Schertz-Cibolo-U City ISD	Schertz	291	47.9	Ingleside ISD	Ingleside
107	48.9	Brownfield ISD	Brownfield	200	48.4	Denton ISD	Denton	292	47.9	Northwest ISD	Fort Worth
108	48.9	Port Neches-Groves ISD	Port Neches	201	48.4	Big Spring ISD	Big Spring	293	47.9	Atlanta ISD	Atlanta
109	48.9	Pearsall ISD	Pearsall	202	48.4	Irving ISD	Irving	294	47.9	Burkburnett ISD	Burkburnett
110	48.9	El Paso ISD	El Paso	203	48.4	Wylie ISD	Wylie	295	47.9	San Elizario ISD	San Elizario
111	48.9	Midway ISD	Waco	204	48.4	Alamo Heights ISD	San Antonio	296	47.9	Hallsville ISD	Hallsville
112	48.9	Pearland ISD	Pearland	205	48.4	Longview ISD	Longview	297	47.9	Kingsville ISD	Kingsville
113	48.9	Corsicana ISD	Corsicana	206	48.4	Wilmer-Hutchins ISD	Dallas	298	47.8	Boerne ISD	Boerne
114	48.9	Eagle Pass ISD	Eagle Pass	207	48.4	Zapata County ISD	Zapata	299	47.8	Leander ISD	Leander
115	48.9	San Antonio ISD	San Antonio	208	48.4	Snyder ISD	Snyder	300	47.8	Belton ISD	Belton
116	48.8	Manor ISD	Manor	209	48.4	Corpus Christi ISD	Corpus Christi	301	47.8	Stafford Municipal School	Stafford
117	48.8	Abilene ISD	Abilene	210	48.4	Stephenville	Stephenville	302	47.8	Angleton ISD	Angleton
118	48.8	Spring ISD	Houston	211	48.4	Austin ISD	Austin	303	47.8	Rockdale ISD	Rockdale
119	48.8	Alief ISD	Houston	212	48.3	Lumberton ISD	Lumberton	304	47.8	Crosby ISD	Crosby
120	48.8	Goose Creek CISD	Baytown	213	48.3	Yoakum ISD	Yoakum	305	47.8	Mabank ISD	Mabank
121	48.8	Temple ISD	Temple	214	48.3	Mansfield ISD	Mansfield	306	47.8	Willis ISD	Willis
122	48.8	Mercedes ISD	Mercedes	215	48.3	Ft Stockton ISD	Ft Stockton	307	47.8	Raymondville ISD	Raymondville
123	48.8	Flour Bluff ISD	Corpus Christi	215	48.3	Klein ISD	Klein	308	47.8	Madisonville Cons ISD	Madisonville
124	48.8	Bellville ISD	Bellville	217	48.3	Los Fresnos Cons ISD	Los Fresnos	309	47.7	Dumas ISD	Dumas
125	48.8	Borger ISD	Borger	218	48.3	Quinlan ISD	Quinlan	310	47.7	Whitesboro ISD	Whitesboro
126	48.8	Lewisville ISD	Flower Mound	219	48.3	Needville ISD	Needville	311	47.7	Bowie ISD	Bowie
127	48.8	Brownsville ISD	Brownsville	220	48.3	Little Elm ISD	Little Elm	312	47.7	Gladewater ISD	Gladewater
128	48.8	Ingram ISD	Ingram	221	48.3	Cuero ISD	Cuero	313	47.7	Rockwall ISD	Rockwall
129	48.8	Jasper ISD	Jasper	222	48.3	Carrizo Springs Cons ISD	Carrizo Springs	314	47.7	Pleasant Grove ISD	Texarkana
130	48.8	Katy ISD	Katy	223	48.3	Hondo ISD	Hondo	315	47.7	Carthage ISD	Carthage
131	48.8	Brownwood ISD	Brownwood	224	48.3	Aransas Pass ISD	Aransas Pass	316	47.7	Commerce ISD	Commerce
132	48.8	Alice ISD	Alice	225	48.3	Northside ISD	San Antonio	317	47.7	Whitehouse ISD	Whitehouse
133	48.8	Decatur ISD	Decatur	226	48.3	Levelland ISD	Levelland	318	47.7	Sharyland ISD	Mission
134	48.7	Texas City ISD	Texas City	227	48.3	Richardson ISD	Richardson	319	47.7	Gatesville ISD	Gatesville
135	48.7	Killeen ISD	Killeen	228	48.3	Georgetown ISD	Georgetown	320	47.6	Orangefield ISD	Orangefield
136	48.7	Waco ISD	Waco	229	48.2	Keller ISD	Keller	321	47.6	Mexia ISD	Mexia
137	48.7	Ysleta ISD	El Paso	230	48.2	Athens ISD	Athens	322	47.6	Comal ISD	New Braunfels
138	48.7	Red Oak ISD	Red Oak	231	48.2	Sealy ISD	Sealy	323	47.6	Progreso ISD	Progreso
139	48.7	Vidor ISD	Vidor	232	48.2	Coppell ISD	Coppell	324	47.6	Gregory-Portland ISD	Gregory
140	48.7	Amarillo ISD	Amarillo	233	48.2	North Lamar ISD	Paris	325	47.6	Hays Cons ISD	Kyle
141	48.7	Ector County ISD	Odessa	234	48.2	Fort Bend ISD	Sugar Land	326	47.6	Robinson ISD	Robinson
142	48.7	La Feria ISD	La Feria	235	48.2	Lockhart ISD	Lockhart	327	47.5	Magnolia ISD	Magnolia
143	48.7	Hillsboro ISD	Hillsboro	236	48.2	Sherman ISD	Sherman	328	47.5	South San Antonio ISD	San Antonio
144	48.7	United ISD	Laredo	237	48.2	Liberty Hill ISD	Liberty Hill	329	47.5	Cedar Hill ISD	Cedar Hill
145	48.7	Socorro ISD	El Paso	238	48.2	Waller ISD	Waller	330	47.5	Smithville ISD	Smithville
146	48.7	Tomball ISD	Tomball	239	48.2	Midlothian ISD	Midlothian	331	47.5	Liberty-Eylau ISD	Texarkana
147	48.7	Spring Branch ISD	Houston	240	48.2	Channelview ISD	Channelview	332	47.5	Chapel Hill ISD	Tyler
148	48.7	Round Rock ISD	Round Rock	241	48.2	West Orange-Cove Cons ISD	Orange	333	47.4	Carroll ISD	Grapevine
149	48.7	Del Valle ISD	Del Valle	242	48.2	New Caney ISD	New Caney	334	47.4	Alvin ISD	Alvin
150	48.7	Alvarado ISD	Alvarado	243	48.2	Joshua ISD	Joshua	335	47.4	Pittsburg ISD	Pittsburg
151	48.7	Mission Cons ISD	Mission	244	48.2	Forney ISD	Forney	336	47.4	Henderson ISD	Henderson
152	48.6	Nacogdoches ISD	Nacogdoches	245	48.2	Palestine ISD	Palestine	337	47.4	Lake Dallas ISD	Lake Dallas
153	48.6	Ennis ISD	Ennis	246	48.2	Harlingen Cons ISD	Harlingen	338	47.3	Daingerfield-Lone Star Is	Daingerfield
154	48.6	Conroe ISD	Conroe	247	48.2	Aledo ISD	Aledo	339	47.3	La Vernia ISD	La Vernia
155	48.6	Duncanville ISD	Duncanville	248	48.1	Pflugerville ISD	Pflugerville	340	47.3	Llano ISD	Llano
156	48.6	Seguin ISD	Seguin	249	48.1	Groesbeck ISD	Groesbeck	341	47.3	Lampasas ISD	Lampasas
157	48.6	Carrollton-Farmers Branch	Carrollton	250	48.1	Rio Hondo ISD	Rio Hondo	342	47.3	Medina Valley ISD	Castroville
158	48.6	Van ISD	Van	251	48.1	Seminole ISD	Seminole	343	47.3	Canutillo ISD	El Paso
159	48.6	Granbury ISD	Granbury	252	48.1	Bryan ISD	Bryan	344	47.3	Weatherford ISD	Weatherford
160	48.6	Wills Point ISD	Wills Point	253	48.1	Lyford CISD	Lyford	345	47.2	Huffman ISD	Huffman
161	48.6	Clear Creek ISD	League City	254	48.1	Dickinson ISD	Dickinson	346	47.2	Princeton ISD	Princeton
162	48.6	Crowley ISD	Crowley	255	48.1	Mineral Wells ISD	Mineral Wells	347	47.2	Terrell ISD	Terrell
163	48.6	Calallen ISD	Corpus Christi	256	48.1	Crandall ISD	Crandall	348	47.2	Glen Rose ISD	Glen Rose
164	48.6	Aldine ISD	Houston	257	48.1	White Settlement ISD	White Settlement	349	47.2	Santa Fe ISD	Santa Fe
165	48.6	Royal ISD	Brookshire	258	48.1	Victoria ISD	Victoria	350	47.2	La Porte ISD	La Porte
166	48.6	Iowa Park Cons ISD	Iowa Park	259	48.1	Brazosport ISD	Freeport	351	47.1	Azle ISD	Azle
167	48.6	Plano ISD	Plano	260	48.1	Hamshire-Fannett ISD	Hamshire	352	47.1	Hereford ISD	Hereford
168	48.6	Hurst-Euless-Bedford ISD	Bedford	261	48.1	Little Cypress-Mauricevil	Orange	353	47.1	Montgomery ISD	Montgomery
169	48.6	Breckenridge ISD	Breckenridge	262	48.1	Calhoun County ISD	Port Lavaca	354	47.1	Greenwood ISD	Midland
169	48.6	Kirbyville CISD	Kirbyville	263	48.1	Harlandale ISD	San Antonio	355	47.0	Huntington ISD	Huntington
171	48.6	Cypress-Fairbanks ISD	Houston	264	48.1	Jacksonville ISD	Jacksonville	356	47.0	Connally ISD	Waco
172	48.6	Pasadena ISD	Pasadena	265	48.1	College Station ISD	College Station	357	47.0	Pecos-Barstow-Toyah ISD	Pecos
173	48.6	Wharton ISD	Wharton	266	48.1	Splendora ISD	Splendora	358	46.9	Taylor ISD	Taylor
174	48.6	Brenham ISD	Brenham	267	48.0	San Benito Cons ISD	San Benito	359	46.9	Rains ISD	Emory
175	48.5	Hudson ISD	Lufkin	268	48.0	Robstown ISD	Robstown	360	46.9	Vernon ISD	Vernon
176	48.5	Tyler ISD	Tyler	269	48.0	Bridgeport ISD	Bridgeport	361	46.9	Gilmer ISD	Gilmer
177	48.5	Humble ISD	Humble	270	48.0	Birdville ISD	Haltom City	362	46.8	Caldwell ISD	Caldwell
178	48.5	Weslaco ISD	Weslaco	271	48.0	Kerrville ISD	Kerrville	363	46.7	Brooks County ISD	Falfurrias
179	48.5	Garland ISD	Garland	272	48.0	Denison ISD	Denison	364	46.7	Kemp ISD	Kemp
180	48.5	Eagle Mt-Saginaw ISD	Fort Worth	273	48.0	Pine Tree ISD	Longview	365	46.7	Presidio ISD	Presidio
181	48.5	Edinburg CISD	Edinburg	274	48.0	Mckinney ISD	Mckinney	366	46.5	Bullard ISD	Bullard
182	48.5	Barbers Hill ISD	Mt Belvieu	275	48.0	Aransas County ISD	Rockport	367	46.5	Dalhart ISD	Dalhart
183	48.5	Livingston ISD	Livingston	276	48.0	El Campo ISD	El Campo	368	46.4	Lake Travis ISD	Austin
183	48.5	Paris ISD	Paris	277	48.0	Nederland ISD	Nederland	369	46.3	Lubbock-Cooper ISD	Lubbock
185	48.5	Allen ISD	Allen	278	47.9	Uvalde Cons ISD	Uvalde	370	46.3	Burleson ISD	Burleson
186	48.5	La Grange ISD	La Grange	279	47.9	Canyon ISD	Canyon	371	46.3	Lake Worth ISD	Lake Worth
187	48.5	Gonzales ISD	Gonzales	280	47.9	Perryton ISD	Perryton	372	46.3	Hardin-Jefferson ISD	Sour Lake
188	48.5	Donna ISD	Donna	281	47.9	Springtown ISD	Springtown	373	46.3	Cameron ISD	Cameron
189	48.5	Tarkington ISD	Cleveland	282	47.9	Mount Pleasant ISD	Mt Pleasant	374	46.2	Venus ISD	Venus
190	48.5	La Joya ISD	La Joya	283	47.9	Eanes ISD	Austin	375	46.2	Lytle ISD	Lytle
191	48.5	Bridge City ISD	Bridge City	284	47.9	Brownsboro ISD	Brownsboro	376	46.2	Wimberley ISD	Wimberley
192	48.5	San Marcos Cons ISD	San Marcos	285	47.9	East Central ISD	San Antonio	377	46.1	Sinton ISD	Sinton
193	48.5	Somerset ISD	Somerset	286	47.9	Lamesa ISD	Lamesa	378	46.0	Royse City ISD	Royse City
194	48.5	Dripping Springs ISD	Dripping Spgs	287	47.9	Judson ISD	San Antonio	379	46.0	West Oso ISD	Corpus Christi
195	48.4	Bay City ISD	Bay City	288	47.9	Silsbee ISD	Silsbee	380	46.0	Sanger ISD	Sanger
196	48.4	Bastrop ISD	Bastrop								

381	45.9	Sweeny ISD	Sweeny
382	45.8	Coldspring-Oakhurst Cons	Coldspring
383	45.8	Shepherd ISD	Shepherd
384	45.7	Diboll ISD	Diboll
385	45.2	Lorena ISD	Lorena
386	45.1	West ISD	West

Individual Education Program Students

Rank	Percent	District Name	City
1	23.0	West ISD	West
2	22.3	Venus ISD	Venus
3	20.6	Eustace ISD	Eustace
4	19.6	China Spring ISD	Waco
5	19.1	Denison ISD	Denison
6	18.8	Gladewater ISD	Gladewater
6	18.8	Quinlan ISD	Quinlan
8	18.7	Gatesville ISD	Gatesville
9	18.5	Atlanta ISD	Atlanta
10	18.4	Vidor ISD	Vidor
11	18.2	Andrews ISD	Andrews
11	18.2	Commerce ISD	Commerce
11	18.2	Pleasanton ISD	Pleasanton
14	18.1	Abilene ISD	Abilene
15	18.0	Huntington ISD	Huntington
16	17.9	Central ISD	Pollok
16	17.9	Mineral Wells ISD	Mineral Wells
18	17.6	Livingston ISD	Livingston
19	17.5	Llano ISD	Llano
19	17.5	Lubbock-Cooper ISD	Lubbock
21	17.3	Mexia ISD	Mexia
21	17.3	West Orange-Cove Cons ISD	Orange
23	17.2	Silsbee ISD	Silsbee
24	17.1	Lorena ISD	Lorena
24	17.1	Texarkana ISD	Texarkana
26	16.9	Vernon ISD	Vernon
27	16.8	Aransas Pass ISD	Aransas Pass
27	16.8	Bonham ISD	Bonham
27	16.8	Ferris ISD	Ferris
27	16.8	Sanger ISD	Sanger
31	16.7	Rains ISD	Emory
31	16.7	Seminole ISD	Seminole
31	16.7	Temple ISD	Temple
34	16.6	Buna ISD	Buna
34	16.6	Henderson ISD	Henderson
36	16.4	Liberty-Eylau ISD	Texarkana
37	16.2	Little Cypress-Mauricevil	Orange
37	16.2	Robstown ISD	Robstown
37	16.2	Rockdale ISD	Rockdale
37	16.2	Whitesboro ISD	Whitesboro
41	16.1	Hillsboro ISD	Hillsboro
41	16.1	Pittsburg ISD	Pittsburg
43	16.0	Brooks County ISD	Falfurrias
43	16.0	Burnet Cons ISD	Burnet
43	16.0	Mabank ISD	Mabank
43	16.0	Rio Hondo ISD	Rio Hondo
47	15.9	Ennis ISD	Ennis
47	15.9	Levelland ISD	Levelland
49	15.8	Kirbyville CISD	Kirbyville
49	15.8	Snyder ISD	Snyder
49	15.8	Terrell ISD	Terrell
52	15.7	Belton ISD	Belton
52	15.7	Harlandale ISD	San Antonio
52	15.7	Nederland ISD	Nederland
55	15.6	Gilmer ISD	Gilmer
55	15.6	Sherman ISD	Sherman
57	15.5	Connally ISD	Waco
57	15.5	North East ISD	San Antonio
57	15.5	Paris ISD	Paris
60	15.4	Aransas County ISD	Rockport
61	15.3	Gainesville ISD	Gainesville
61	15.3	Mineola ISD	Mineola
63	15.2	Bandera ISD	Bandera
63	15.2	Brownfield ISD	Brownfield
63	15.2	Longview ISD	Longview
63	15.2	Lubbock ISD	Lubbock
63	15.2	Robinson ISD	Robinson
63	15.2	Waxahachie ISD	Waxahachie
69	15.1	Bridgeport ISD	Bridgeport
70	15.0	Groesbeck ISD	Groesbeck
70	15.0	Yoakum ISD	Yoakum
72	14.9	Dalhart ISD	Dalhart
72	14.9	Kingsville ISD	Kingsville
72	14.9	Marshall ISD	Marshall
72	14.9	Northside ISD	San Antonio
72	14.9	Poteet ISD	Poteet
72	14.9	Red Oak ISD	Red Oak
72	14.9	Southside ISD	San Antonio
72	14.9	Westwood ISD	Palestine
80	14.8	Carthage ISD	Carthage
80	14.8	Daingerfield-Lone Star Is	Daingerfield
80	14.8	Del Valle ISD	Del Valle
80	14.8	Lampasas ISD	Lampasas
80	14.8	Monahans-Wickett-Pyote Is	Monahans
85	14.7	Everman ISD	Everman
85	14.7	Lockhart ISD	Lockhart
87	14.6	North Lamar ISD	Paris
87	14.6	Sweetwater ISD	Sweetwater
89	14.5	Fairfield ISD	Fairfield
89	14.5	Glen Rose ISD	Glen Rose
89	14.5	Kemp ISD	Kemp
89	14.5	La Vega ISD	Waco
93	14.4	Corpus Christi ISD	Corpus Christi
93	14.4	Lufkin ISD	Lufkin
93	14.4	Mount Pleasant ISD	Mt Pleasant
93	14.4	Rusk ISD	Rusk
93	14.4	Smithville ISD	Smithville
98	14.3	Corsicana ISD	Corsicana
98	14.3	Hardin-Jefferson ISD	Sour Lake
98	14.3	Midlothian ISD	Midlothian
98	14.3	Plainview ISD	Plainview
98	14.3	Royse City ISD	Royse City
98	14.3	Sinton ISD	Sinton
104	14.2	Edgewood ISD	San Antonio
104	14.2	Manor ISD	Manor
104	14.2	Mesquite ISD	Mesquite
107	14.1	Borger ISD	Borger
107	14.1	New Caney ISD	New Caney
107	14.1	Southwest ISD	San Antonio
107	14.1	Sulphur Springs ISD	Sulphur Springs
111	14.0	Cuero ISD	Cuero
111	14.0	La Vernia ISD	La Vernia
111	14.0	Shepherd ISD	Shepherd
114	13.9	Waco ISD	Waco
114	13.9	Wills Point ISD	Wills Point
116	13.8	Bay City ISD	Bay City
116	13.8	Bellville ISD	Bellville
116	13.8	Brazosport ISD	Freeport
116	13.8	Sealy ISD	Sealy
116	13.8	Wichita Falls ISD	Wichita Falls
121	13.6	Angleton ISD	Angleton
121	13.6	Comal ISD	New Braunfels
121	13.6	Jasper ISD	Jasper
121	13.6	Laredo ISD	Laredo
121	13.6	Springtown ISD	Springtown
126	13.5	Birdville ISD	Haltom City
126	13.5	Breckenridge ISD	Breckenridge
126	13.5	Caldwell ISD	Caldwell
126	13.5	Denton ISD	Denton
126	13.5	Kerrville ISD	Kerrville
126	13.5	Princeton ISD	Princeton
132	13.4	Coldspring-Oakhurst Cons	Coldspring
132	13.4	Floresville ISD	Floresville
132	13.4	Kilgore ISD	Kilgore
132	13.4	Seguin ISD	Seguin
136	13.3	Killeen ISD	Killeen
136	13.3	Lake Dallas ISD	Lake Dallas
136	13.3	Taylor ISD	Taylor
139	13.2	Columbus ISD	Columbus
139	13.2	Dripping Springs ISD	Dripping Spgs
139	13.2	Jacksonville ISD	Jacksonville
139	13.2	Van ISD	Van
139	13.2	Wharton ISD	Wharton
139	13.2	Wimberley ISD	Wimberley
145	13.1	Azle ISD	Azle
145	13.1	Boerne ISD	Boerne
145	13.1	Granbury ISD	Granbury
145	13.1	Hays Cons ISD	Kyle
145	13.1	Orangefield ISD	Orangefield
145	13.1	San Angelo ISD	San Angelo
151	13.0	East Central ISD	San Antonio
151	13.0	Hereford ISD	Hereford
151	13.0	Needville ISD	Needville
151	13.0	Tyler ISD	Tyler
155	12.9	Brownsville ISD	Brownsville
155	12.9	Columbia-Brazoria ISD	West Columbia
155	12.9	Crosby ISD	Crosby
155	12.9	San Antonio ISD	San Antonio
159	12.8	Amarillo ISD	Amarillo
159	12.8	Bridge City ISD	Bridge City
159	12.8	Calallen ISD	Corpus Christi
159	12.8	Crandall ISD	Crandall
159	12.8	El Campo ISD	El Campo
159	12.8	Flour Bluff ISD	Corpus Christi
159	12.8	Grand Prairie ISD	Grand Prairie
159	12.8	Ingleside ISD	Ingleside
159	12.8	Lindale ISD	Lindale
159	12.8	Rio Grande City CISD	Rio Grande City
159	12.8	Weatherford ISD	Weatherford
159	12.8	Willis ISD	Willis
171	12.7	Bullard ISD	Bullard
171	12.7	Calhoun County ISD	Port Lavaca
171	12.7	Copperas Cove ISD	Copperas Cove
171	12.7	Devine ISD	Devine
171	12.7	Graham ISD	Graham
171	12.7	Hamshire-Fannett ISD	Hamshire
171	12.7	Kaufman ISD	Kaufman
178	12.6	Diboll ISD	Diboll
178	12.6	Pecos-Barstow-Toyah ISD	Pecos
178	12.6	Somerset ISD	Somerset
178	12.6	United ISD	Laredo
182	12.5	Alvarado ISD	Alvarado
182	12.5	Alvin ISD	Alvin
182	12.5	Bastrop ISD	Bastrop
182	12.5	Brownsboro ISD	Brownsboro
182	12.5	Crowley ISD	Crowley
182	12.5	Desoto ISD	Desoto
182	12.5	Liberty ISD	Liberty
182	12.5	Little Elm ISD	Little Elm
182	12.5	Medina Valley ISD	Castroville
182	12.5	Richardson ISD	Richardson
182	12.5	West Oso ISD	Corpus Christi
182	12.5	Whitney ISD	Whitney
194	12.4	Cameron ISD	Cameron
194	12.4	Cleburne ISD	Cleburne
194	12.4	Crockett ISD	Crockett
194	12.4	Joshua ISD	Joshua
194	12.4	La Marque ISD	La Marque
194	12.4	Madisonville Cons ISD	Madisonville
194	12.4	White Settlement ISD	White Settlement
201	12.3	Austin ISD	Austin
201	12.3	Forney ISD	Forney
201	12.3	Gonzales ISD	Gonzales
201	12.3	Lytle ISD	Lytle
205	12.2	Bowie ISD	Bowie
205	12.2	Lumberton ISD	Lumberton
205	12.2	San Elizario ISD	San Elizario
208	12.1	Brenham ISD	Brenham
208	12.1	Canyon ISD	Canyon
208	12.1	La Grange ISD	La Grange
211	12.0	Burkburnett ISD	Burkburnett
211	12.0	Duncanville ISD	Duncanville
211	12.0	Lamar Consolidated ISD	Rosenberg
211	12.0	Lamesa ISD	Lamesa
211	12.0	Magnolia ISD	Magnolia
211	12.0	San Benito Cons ISD	San Benito
211	12.0	San Felipe-Del Rio Cons I	Del Rio
211	12.0	Sheldon ISD	Houston
211	12.0	Victoria ISD	Victoria
220	11.9	Athens ISD	Athens
220	11.9	Channelview ISD	Channelview
220	11.9	Greenwood ISD	Midland
220	11.9	Pampa ISD	Pampa
220	11.9	Plano ISD	Plano
220	11.9	Tuloso-Midway ISD	Corpus Christi
226	11.8	Dayton ISD	Dayton
226	11.8	Frenship ISD	Wolfforth
226	11.8	Gregory-Portland ISD	Gregory
226	11.8	Hondo ISD	Hondo
226	11.8	Leander ISD	Leander
226	11.8	Los Fresnos Cons ISD	Los Fresnos
226	11.8	Schertz-Cibolo-U City ISD	Schertz
226	11.8	Sweeny ISD	Sweeny
234	11.7	Alief ISD	Houston
234	11.7	Beaumont ISD	Beaumont
234	11.7	Brownwood ISD	Brownwood
234	11.7	Elgin ISD	Elgin
234	11.7	Galena Park ISD	Houston
234	11.7	Orange Grove ISD	Orange Grove
234	11.7	Wylie ISD	Abilene
241	11.6	Ector County ISD	Odessa
241	11.6	Huntsville ISD	Huntsville
241	11.6	Montgomery ISD	Montgomery
241	11.6	Port Neches-Groves ISD	Port Neches
241	11.6	Royal ISD	Brookshire
246	11.5	Greenville ISD	Greenville
246	11.5	Huffman ISD	Huffman
246	11.5	New Braunfels ISD	New Braunfels
246	11.5	Wylie ISD	Wylie
250	11.4	Garland ISD	Garland
250	11.4	Northwest ISD	Fort Worth
250	11.4	Pflugerville ISD	Pflugerville
250	11.4	Ysleta ISD	El Paso
254	11.3	Allen ISD	Allen
254	11.3	Big Spring ISD	Big Spring
254	11.3	Edna ISD	Edna
254	11.3	Galveston ISD	Galveston
254	11.3	Lewisville ISD	Flower Mound
254	11.3	Pine Tree ISD	Longview
254	11.3	Uvalde Cons ISD	Uvalde
261	11.2	Alice ISD	Alice
261	11.2	Ingram ISD	Ingram
261	11.2	Mckinney ISD	Mckinney
261	11.2	Point Isabel ISD	Point Isabel
261	11.2	Stephenville	Stephenville
266	11.1	Beeville ISD	Beeville
266	11.1	Cleveland ISD	Cleveland
266	11.1	Mansfield ISD	Mansfield

266	11.1	Marble Falls ISD	Marble Falls
270	11.0	Cedar Hill ISD	Cedar Hill
270	11.0	Spring Branch ISD	Houston
272	10.9	Bryan ISD	Bryan
272	10.9	Decatur ISD	Decatur
272	10.9	Fredericksburg ISD	Fredericksburg
272	10.9	Hudson ISD	Lufkin
272	10.9	Lancaster ISD	Lancaster
272	10.9	Liberty Hill ISD	Liberty Hill
272	10.9	Raymondville ISD	Raymondville
272	10.9	San Marcos Cons ISD	San Marcos
272	10.9	South San Antonio ISD	San Antonio
281	10.8	Dickinson ISD	Dickinson
282	10.7	Conroe ISD	Conroe
282	10.7	Crystal City ISD	Crystal City
282	10.7	Eanes ISD	Austin
282	10.7	Honors Academy	Dallas
282	10.7	Lake Travis ISD	Austin
282	10.7	Luling ISD	Luling
282	10.7	Mathis ISD	Mathis
282	10.7	Navasota ISD	Navasota
290	10.6	Deer Park ISD	Deer Park
290	10.6	Frisco ISD	Frisco
292	10.5	Center ISD	Center
292	10.5	Hurst-Euless-Bedford ISD	Bedford
292	10.5	Klein ISD	Klein
292	10.5	La Joya ISD	La Joya
292	10.5	Spring ISD	Houston
297	10.4	Hallsville ISD	Hallsville
297	10.4	Lyford CISD	Lyford
297	10.4	Midland ISD	Midland
297	10.4	Rockwall ISD	Rockwall
297	10.4	Texas City ISD	Texas City
302	10.3	Ft Stockton ISD	Ft Stockton
302	10.3	Harlingen Cons ISD	Harlingen
302	10.3	Judson ISD	San Antonio
302	10.3	La Porte ISD	La Porte
302	10.3	Midway ISD	Waco
302	10.3	Zapata County ISD	Zapata
308	10.2	Carrizo Springs Cons ISD	Carrizo Springs
308	10.2	Hutto ISD	Hutto
308	10.2	Pearsall ISD	Pearsall
308	10.2	Round Rock ISD	Round Rock
308	10.2	San Diego ISD	San Diego
308	10.2	Socorro ISD	El Paso
314	10.1	Canutillo ISD	El Paso
314	10.1	Carroll ISD	Grapevine
314	10.1	Goose Creek CISD	Baytown
314	10.1	Houston ISD	Houston
314	10.1	Palacios ISD	Palacios
319	10.0	Alamo Heights ISD	San Antonio
319	10.0	Fort Bend ISD	Sugar Land
319	10.0	Giddings ISD	Giddings
319	10.0	Humble ISD	Humble
319	10.0	Katy ISD	Katy
319	10.0	Santa Fe ISD	Santa Fe
325	9.9	Carrollton-Farmers Branch	Carrollton
326	9.8	Aldine ISD	Houston
326	9.8	Arlington ISD	Arlington
326	9.8	Castleberry ISD	Fort Worth
326	9.8	Dumas ISD	Dumas
326	9.8	Kennedale ISD	Kennedale
326	9.8	Palestine ISD	Palestine
326	9.8	Valley View ISD	Pharr
333	9.7	Edcouch-Elsa ISD	Edcouch
333	9.7	Irving ISD	Irving
335	9.6	Aledo ISD	Aledo
335	9.6	Donna ISD	Donna
335	9.6	Georgetown ISD	Georgetown
338	9.5	Fort Worth ISD	Fort Worth
338	9.5	Iowa Park Cons ISD	Iowa Park
338	9.5	Perryton ISD	Perryton
338	9.5	Stafford Municipal School	Stafford
342	9.4	Port Arthur ISD	Port Arthur
342	9.4	Waller ISD	Waller
342	9.4	Whitehouse ISD	Whitehouse
345	9.3	Cypress-Fairbanks ISD	Houston
345	9.3	La Feria ISD	La Feria
345	9.3	Tarkington ISD	Cleveland
348	9.2	Canton ISD	Canton
348	9.2	Clint ISD	El Paso
348	9.2	Tomball ISD	Tomball
348	9.2	Weslaco ISD	Weslaco
352	9.1	Clear Creek ISD	League City
352	9.1	Edinburg CISD	Edinburg
352	9.1	Highland Park ISD	Dallas
352	9.1	Lake Worth ISD	Lake Worth
352	9.1	Pearland ISD	Pearland
357	9.0	El Paso ISD	El Paso
357	9.0	Friendswood ISD	Friendswood
357	9.0	Presidio ISD	Presidio
360	8.9	Mercedes ISD	Mercedes
361	8.8	College Station ISD	College Station
361	8.8	Coppell ISD	Coppell
361	8.8	Spring Hill ISD	Longview
364	8.7	Pharr-San Juan-Alamo ISD	Pharr
365	8.6	Eagle Mt-Saginaw ISD	Fort Worth
365	8.6	Eagle Pass ISD	Eagle Pass
365	8.6	Nacogdoches ISD	Nacogdoches
368	8.5	Pleasant Grove ISD	Texarkana
369	8.4	Mcallen ISD	Mcallen
370	8.3	Chapel Hill ISD	Tyler
370	8.3	Roma ISD	Roma
372	8.1	Burleson ISD	Burleson
373	8.0	Fabens ISD	Fabens
373	8.0	Sharyland ISD	Mission
375	7.9	Dallas ISD	Dallas
376	7.8	Keller ISD	Keller
376	7.8	Pasadena ISD	Pasadena
376	7.8	Splendora ISD	Splendora
379	7.5	Barbers Hill ISD	Mt Belvieu
379	7.5	North Forest ISD	Houston
381	7.4	Grapevine-Colleyville ISD	Grapevine
382	7.1	Wilmer-Hutchins ISD	Dallas
383	6.7	South Texas ISD	Mercedes
384	6.3	Hidalgo ISD	Hidalgo
384	6.3	Mission Cons ISD	Mission
384	6.3	Progreso ISD	Progreso

English Language Learner Students

Rank	Percent	District Name	City
1	62.0	Laredo ISD	Laredo
2	54.3	Valley View ISD	Pharr
3	54.0	Hidalgo ISD	Hidalgo
3	54.0	San Elizario ISD	San Elizario
5	53.2	Presidio ISD	Presidio
6	52.3	Donna ISD	Donna
7	50.2	Rio Grande City CISD	Rio Grande City
8	50.0	Brownsville ISD	Brownsville
9	47.6	La Joya ISD	La Joya
10	47.4	Progreso ISD	Progreso
11	46.9	Roma ISD	Roma
12	46.4	Clint ISD	El Paso
13	45.3	United ISD	Laredo
14	44.3	Fabens ISD	Fabens
15	43.0	Edcouch-Elsa ISD	Edcouch
16	40.7	Canutillo ISD	El Paso
17	40.0	Pharr-San Juan-Alamo ISD	Pharr
18	37.9	Zapata County ISD	Zapata
19	37.6	Eagle Pass ISD	Eagle Pass
20	36.1	Mcallen ISD	Mcallen
21	34.1	Mount Pleasant ISD	Mt Pleasant
22	33.8	Irving ISD	Irving
23	32.0	Mercedes ISD	Mercedes
24	31.5	Alief ISD	Houston
24	31.5	Dallas ISD	Dallas
26	30.8	Edinburg CISD	Edinburg
27	30.5	El Paso ISD	El Paso
27	30.5	Spring Branch ISD	Houston
29	29.9	Socorro ISD	El Paso
30	28.9	Houston ISD	Houston
31	28.4	Point Isabel ISD	Port Isabel
32	27.5	Mission Cons ISD	Mission
33	27.0	Weslaco ISD	Weslaco
34	26.6	Fort Worth ISD	Fort Worth
35	26.3	Los Fresnos Cons ISD	Los Fresnos
36	25.5	Pasadena ISD	Pasadena
37	25.3	Galena Park ISD	Houston
38	25.1	Dumas ISD	Dumas
38	25.1	San Benito Cons ISD	San Benito
40	24.8	Aldine ISD	Houston
40	24.8	Sharyland ISD	Mission
42	24.5	Ysleta ISD	El Paso
43	22.8	Carrollton-Farmers Branch	Carrollton
44	22.0	Garland ISD	Garland
45	21.8	Austin ISD	Austin
45	21.8	Channelview ISD	Channelview
47	20.4	Edgewood ISD	San Antonio
48	20.0	Del Valle ISD	Del Valle
48	20.0	Perryton ISD	Perryton
50	19.2	Crystal City ISD	Crystal City
50	19.2	Manor ISD	Manor
52	18.5	Richardson ISD	Richardson
53	18.2	San Felipe-Del Rio Cons I	Del Rio
54	17.9	Castleberry ISD	Fort Worth
54	17.9	South San Antonio ISD	San Antonio
56	17.8	Grand Prairie ISD	Grand Prairie
57	16.9	Jacksonville ISD	Jacksonville
57	16.9	San Antonio ISD	San Antonio
59	16.8	Athens ISD	Athens
60	16.6	Center ISD	Center
60	16.6	Diboll ISD	Diboll
62	16.4	Elgin ISD	Elgin
62	16.4	Tyler ISD	Tyler
64	16.3	Arlington ISD	Arlington
65	16.1	Nacogdoches ISD	Nacogdoches
66	15.5	Sheldon ISD	Houston
67	15.4	Royal ISD	Brookshire
68	15.3	Lyford CISD	Lyford
69	15.1	Cleveland ISD	Cleveland
70	15.0	Harlandale ISD	San Antonio
71	14.9	Denton ISD	Denton
72	14.7	Dickinson ISD	Dickinson
73	14.4	Hillsboro ISD	Hillsboro
74	14.3	Goose Creek CISD	Baytown
75	14.2	Ennis ISD	Ennis
76	14.1	Everman ISD	Everman
76	14.1	Gainesville ISD	Gainesville
78	13.8	Port Arthur ISD	Port Arthur
79	13.7	Palacios ISD	Palacios
80	13.6	Harlingen Cons ISD	Harlingen
81	13.5	Little Elm ISD	Little Elm
82	13.4	Spring ISD	Houston
83	13.3	San Diego ISD	San Diego
84	13.2	La Feria ISD	La Feria
85	13.1	Raymondville ISD	Raymondville
85	13.1	Rio Hondo ISD	Rio Hondo
87	13.0	Seminole ISD	Seminole
88	12.9	Cypress-Fairbanks ISD	Houston
89	12.8	Lake Worth ISD	Lake Worth
89	12.8	Waller ISD	Waller
91	12.7	Corsicana ISD	Corsicana
91	12.7	Ector County ISD	Odessa
91	12.7	Southwest ISD	San Antonio
94	12.6	Hereford ISD	Hereford
95	12.4	Giddings ISD	Giddings
95	12.4	Stafford Municipal School	Stafford
95	12.4	Terrell ISD	Terrell
98	12.2	Kaufman ISD	Kaufman
98	12.2	Lufkin ISD	Lufkin
100	12.1	Ft Stockton ISD	Ft Stockton
101	12.0	North Forest ISD	Houston
101	12.0	Pittsburg ISD	Pittsburg
103	11.9	Wilmer-Hutchins ISD	Dallas
104	11.8	Galveston ISD	Galveston
105	11.6	Bryan ISD	Bryan
105	11.6	Pearsall ISD	Pearsall
105	11.6	Waco ISD	Waco
108	11.4	Cleburne ISD	Cleburne
109	11.3	Decatur ISD	Decatur
110	11.0	Madisonville Cons ISD	Madisonville
111	10.9	Lamar Consolidated ISD	Rosenberg
112	10.8	Longview ISD	Longview
113	10.7	Kingsville ISD	Kingsville
114	10.6	Plano ISD	Plano
115	10.5	Venus ISD	Venus
116	10.3	Greenville ISD	Greenville
116	10.3	Pflugerville ISD	Pflugerville
118	10.2	Andrews ISD	Andrews
118	10.2	Mesquite ISD	Mesquite
120	10.1	Alvin ISD	Alvin
120	10.1	Fort Bend ISD	Sugar Land
120	10.1	Willis ISD	Willis
123	10.0	Carrizo Springs Cons ISD	Carrizo Springs
123	10.0	Marble Falls ISD	Marble Falls
125	9.9	Duncanville ISD	Duncanville
125	9.9	Klein ISD	Klein
127	9.8	Hurst-Euless-Bedford ISD	Bedford
128	9.7	Conroe ISD	Conroe
128	9.7	New Caney ISD	New Caney
128	9.7	Plainview ISD	Plainview
128	9.7	Southside ISD	San Antonio
132	9.6	Marshall ISD	Marshall
132	9.6	Pecos-Barstow-Toyah ISD	Pecos
134	9.5	Henderson ISD	Henderson
134	9.5	Katy ISD	Katy
136	9.4	Ferris ISD	Ferris
136	9.4	Sherman ISD	Sherman
138	9.2	Uvalde Cons ISD	Uvalde
139	9.1	Amarillo ISD	Amarillo
140	9.0	Deer Park ISD	Deer Park
140	9.0	Liberty ISD	Liberty
140	9.0	Lytle ISD	Lytle
140	9.0	Midland ISD	Midland
144	8.9	Hays Cons ISD	Kyle
144	8.9	Lewisville ISD	Flower Mound
146	8.8	Chapel Hill ISD	Tyler
146	8.8	Corpus Christi ISD	Corpus Christi
146	8.8	La Vega ISD	Waco
149	8.7	Lamesa ISD	Lamesa
149	8.7	Mckinney ISD	Mckinney
149	8.7	Navasota ISD	Navasota
149	8.7	Seguin ISD	Seguin
149	8.7	Somerset ISD	Somerset
154	8.6	Sealy ISD	Sealy
155	8.5	Palestine ISD	Palestine
156	8.4	West Oso ISD	Corpus Christi

Rank	Value	District Name	City
157	8.3	Bridgeport ISD	Bridgeport
157	8.3	Fredericksburg ISD	Fredericksburg
159	8.2	Birdville ISD	Haltom City
159	8.2	Taylor ISD	Taylor
161	8.1	Bastrop ISD	Bastrop
161	8.1	Gonzales ISD	Gonzales
163	7.9	Dalhart ISD	Dalhart
163	7.9	Magnolia ISD	Magnolia
165	7.8	Brazosport ISD	Freeport
166	7.6	Calhoun County ISD	Port Lavaca
166	7.6	El Campo ISD	El Campo
168	7.5	Kilgore ISD	Kilgore
168	7.5	Royse City ISD	Royse City
170	7.4	Mineola ISD	Mineola
171	7.3	Breckenridge ISD	Breckenridge
172	7.2	Ingram ISD	Ingram
172	7.2	New Braunfels ISD	New Braunfels
174	7.1	Luling ISD	Luling
174	7.1	Tomball ISD	Tomball
176	7.0	Aransas Pass ISD	Aransas Pass
176	7.0	La Grange ISD	La Grange
178	6.9	Bay City ISD	Bay City
178	6.9	Edna ISD	Edna
178	6.9	Mexia ISD	Mexia
181	6.8	Georgetown ISD	Georgetown
182	6.7	Borger ISD	Borger
182	6.7	Clear Creek ISD	League City
182	6.7	Columbus ISD	Columbus
182	6.7	Huntsville ISD	Huntsville
182	6.7	Lancaster ISD	Lancaster
187	6.6	Glen Rose ISD	Glen Rose
187	6.6	Temple ISD	Temple
187	6.6	Texas City ISD	Texas City
190	6.4	Bellville ISD	Bellville
190	6.4	Round Rock ISD	Round Rock
190	6.4	Yoakum ISD	Yoakum
193	6.3	Brenham ISD	Brenham
193	6.3	Caldwell ISD	Caldwell
193	6.3	Cameron ISD	Cameron
193	6.3	Mineral Wells ISD	Mineral Wells
193	6.3	Princeton ISD	Princeton
193	6.3	Sulphur Springs ISD	Sulphur Springs
199	6.2	Belton ISD	Belton
199	6.2	San Marcos Cons ISD	San Marcos
199	6.2	Waxahachie ISD	Waxahachie
202	6.1	Northside ISD	San Antonio
202	6.1	Pine Tree ISD	Longview
202	6.1	Van ISD	Van
205	6.0	Mansfield ISD	Mansfield
205	6.0	Wharton ISD	Wharton
207	5.9	Angleton ISD	Angleton
207	5.9	Hudson ISD	Lufkin
209	5.8	Coppell ISD	Coppell
209	5.8	Humble ISD	Humble
209	5.8	Killeen ISD	Killeen
209	5.8	Poteet ISD	Poteet
209	5.8	Wylie ISD	Wylie
214	5.7	Medina Valley ISD	Castroville
214	5.7	Pampa ISD	Pampa
214	5.7	Pearland ISD	Pearland
217	5.6	Graham ISD	Graham
218	5.5	Beaumont ISD	Beaumont
218	5.5	Hutto ISD	Hutto
218	5.5	Mathis ISD	Mathis
221	5.4	Robstown ISD	Robstown
221	5.4	Snyder ISD	Snyder
223	5.3	Brownfield ISD	Brownfield
223	5.3	Granbury ISD	Granbury
223	5.3	Rockwall ISD	Rockwall
223	5.3	San Angelo ISD	San Angelo
223	5.3	Stephenville	Stephenville
228	5.2	Crockett ISD	Crockett
229	5.1	Commerce ISD	Commerce
229	5.1	Crowley ISD	Crowley
231	5.0	Alamo Heights ISD	San Antonio
232	4.9	Allen ISD	Allen
232	4.9	Crosby ISD	Crosby
232	4.9	Greenwood ISD	Midland
232	4.9	Weatherford ISD	Weatherford
236	4.8	College Station ISD	College Station
236	4.8	North East ISD	San Antonio
236	4.8	Rains ISD	Emory
236	4.8	Shepherd ISD	Shepherd
240	4.7	Needville ISD	Needville
240	4.7	Rockdale ISD	Rockdale
240	4.7	Splendora ISD	Splendora
243	4.6	Alice ISD	Alice
243	4.6	Aransas County ISD	Rockport
243	4.6	Bonham ISD	Bonham
243	4.6	Brooks County ISD	Falfurrias
243	4.6	Frisco ISD	Frisco
248	4.5	Dayton ISD	Dayton
248	4.5	Fairfield ISD	Fairfield
248	4.5	Groesbeck ISD	Groesbeck
248	4.5	Judson ISD	San Antonio
248	4.5	La Porte ISD	La Porte
248	4.5	Lake Travis ISD	Austin
254	4.4	Grapevine-Colleyville ISD	Grapevine
254	4.4	Tuloso-Midway ISD	Corpus Christi
256	4.3	Alvarado ISD	Alvarado
256	4.3	Liberty Hill ISD	Liberty Hill
256	4.3	Vernon ISD	Vernon
256	4.3	Wichita Falls ISD	Wichita Falls
260	4.2	Burnet Cons ISD	Burnet
260	4.2	Eagle Mt-Saginaw ISD	Fort Worth
260	4.2	East Central ISD	San Antonio
260	4.2	Jasper ISD	Jasper
260	4.2	Lake Dallas ISD	Lake Dallas
260	4.2	Lockhart ISD	Lockhart
260	4.2	White Settlement ISD	White Settlement
267	4.1	Cedar Hill ISD	Cedar Hill
267	4.1	Desoto ISD	Desoto
267	4.1	Livingston ISD	Livingston
267	4.1	Red Oak ISD	Red Oak
271	4.0	Leander ISD	Leander
271	4.0	Monahans-Wickett-Pyote Is	Monahans
273	3.9	Floresville ISD	Floresville
273	3.9	Ingleside ISD	Ingleside
275	3.8	Kerrville ISD	Kerrville
275	3.8	Rusk ISD	Rusk
277	3.7	Gilmer ISD	Gilmer
277	3.7	Northwest ISD	Fort Worth
279	3.6	Boerne ISD	Boerne
279	3.6	Hondo ISD	Hondo
279	3.6	Levelland ISD	Levelland
282	3.5	Columbia-Brazoria ISD	West Columbia
282	3.5	Sanger ISD	Sanger
282	3.5	South Texas ISD	Mercedes
282	3.5	Wills Point ISD	Wills Point
286	3.4	Bridge City ISD	Bridge City
286	3.4	Brownsboro ISD	Brownsboro
286	3.4	Devine ISD	Devine
286	3.4	Smithville ISD	Smithville
290	3.3	Connally ISD	Waco
290	3.3	Daingerfield-Lone Star Is	Daingerfield
290	3.3	Wimberley ISD	Wimberley
293	3.2	Central ISD	Pollok
293	3.2	Comal ISD	New Braunfels
293	3.2	Denison ISD	Denison
293	3.2	Keller ISD	Keller
293	3.2	Kennedale ISD	Kennedale
298	3.1	Joshua ISD	Joshua
298	3.1	La Vernia ISD	La Vernia
298	3.1	Midlothian ISD	Midlothian
301	3.0	Brownwood ISD	Brownwood
301	3.0	Paris ISD	Paris
301	3.0	Victoria ISD	Victoria
304	2.8	Lampasas ISD	Lampasas
304	2.8	Llano ISD	Llano
306	2.7	Bandera ISD	Bandera
306	2.7	Lubbock-Cooper ISD	Lubbock
306	2.7	Nederland ISD	Nederland
306	2.7	Orange Grove ISD	Orange Grove
310	2.6	Canton ISD	Canton
310	2.6	Pleasanton ISD	Pleasanton
310	2.6	Schertz-Cibolo-U City ISD	Schertz
313	2.5	Barbers Hill ISD	Mt Belvieu
313	2.5	Crandall ISD	Crandall
315	2.4	Lubbock ISD	Lubbock
315	2.4	Montgomery ISD	Montgomery
315	2.4	Sweeny ISD	Sweeny
318	2.3	Abilene ISD	Abilene
318	2.3	Dripping Springs ISD	Dripping Spgs
318	2.3	Flour Bluff ISD	Corpus Christi
318	2.3	Gregory-Portland ISD	Gregory
318	2.3	Lindale ISD	Lindale
318	2.3	Sinton ISD	Sinton
324	2.2	Big Spring ISD	Big Spring
324	2.2	Forney ISD	Forney
324	2.2	Hamshire-Fannett ISD	Hamshire
324	2.2	Quinlan ISD	Quinlan
328	2.1	Frenship ISD	Wolfforth
328	2.1	La Marque ISD	La Marque
328	2.1	Springtown ISD	Springtown
331	2.0	Beeville ISD	Beeville
331	2.0	Bowie ISD	Bowie
331	2.0	Carthage ISD	Carthage
334	1.9	Gladewater ISD	Gladewater
334	1.9	Texarkana ISD	Texarkana
336	1.8	Eanes ISD	Austin
336	1.8	Kemp ISD	Kemp
336	1.8	Santa Fe ISD	Santa Fe
336	1.8	Whitehouse ISD	Whitehouse
340	1.7	Midway ISD	Waco
340	1.7	Spring Hill ISD	Longview
340	1.7	West ISD	West
343	1.6	Calallen ISD	Corpus Christi
343	1.6	Gatesville ISD	Gatesville
343	1.6	Hallsville ISD	Hallsville
343	1.6	Pleasant Grove ISD	Texarkana
343	1.6	Port Neches-Groves ISD	Port Neches
343	1.6	Whitesboro ISD	Whitesboro
349	1.5	Aledo ISD	Aledo
349	1.5	Hardin-Jefferson ISD	Sour Lake
349	1.5	Huffman ISD	Huffman
352	1.4	Huntington ISD	Huntington
352	1.4	Mabank ISD	Mabank
354	1.3	Kirbyville CISD	Kirbyville
354	1.3	Little Cypress-Mauricevil	Orange
354	1.3	Westwood ISD	Palestine
357	1.2	Orangefield ISD	Orangefield
357	1.2	West Orange-Cove Cons ISD	Orange
359	1.1	Azle ISD	Azle
360	1.0	Bullard ISD	Bullard
360	1.0	Eustace ISD	Eustace
360	1.0	Whitney ISD	Whitney
363	0.9	Copperas Cove ISD	Copperas Cove
364	0.8	Cuero ISD	Cuero
364	0.8	North Lamar ISD	Paris
364	0.8	Sweetwater ISD	Sweetwater
367	0.7	Atlanta ISD	Atlanta
367	0.7	China Spring ISD	Waco
367	0.7	Friendswood ISD	Friendswood
367	0.7	Robinson ISD	Robinson
371	0.6	Burkburnett ISD	Burkburnett
371	0.6	Burleson ISD	Burleson
371	0.6	Highland Park ISD	Dallas
371	0.6	Lorena ISD	Lorena
371	0.6	Silsbee ISD	Silsbee
371	0.6	Vidor ISD	Vidor
377	0.5	Tarkington ISD	Cleveland
378	0.4	Canyon ISD	Canyon
378	0.4	Liberty-Eylau ISD	Texarkana
378	0.4	Lumberton ISD	Lumberton
381	0.2	Buna ISD	Buna
381	0.2	Coldspring-Oakhurst Cons	Coldspring
381	0.2	Wylie ISD	Abilene
384	0.1	Carroll ISD	Grapevine
384	0.1	Iowa Park Cons ISD	Iowa Park
386	0.0	Honors Academy	Dallas

Migrant Students

Rank	Percent	District Name	City
1	90.6	Robstown ISD	Robstown
2	46.2	Hereford ISD	Hereford
3	44.8	Dumas ISD	Dumas
4	41.9	Progreso ISD	Progreso
5	40.6	Raymondville ISD	Raymondville
6	39.9	Mathis ISD	Mathis
7	36.2	San Felipe-Del Rio Cons I	Del Rio
8	33.1	Weslaco ISD	Weslaco
9	31.3	Edcouch-Elsa ISD	Edcouch
10	30.6	Rio Grande City CISD	Rio Grande City
11	29.2	Donna ISD	Donna
11	29.2	Roma ISD	Roma
13	27.7	La Joya ISD	La Joya
14	26.2	Crystal City ISD	Crystal City
15	25.5	Lyford CISD	Lyford
16	24.9	Presidio ISD	Presidio
17	24.2	Mount Pleasant ISD	Mt Pleasant
18	22.9	Mercedes ISD	Mercedes
19	19.2	Perryton ISD	Perryton
20	18.2	San Elizario ISD	San Elizario
21	16.8	Pharr-San Juan-Alamo ISD	Pharr
22	16.5	Eagle Pass ISD	Eagle Pass
23	16.2	Uvalde Cons ISD	Uvalde
24	15.9	Hidalgo ISD	Hidalgo
24	15.9	Levelland ISD	Levelland
26	15.7	Brownfield ISD	Brownfield
27	15.4	Edinburg CISD	Edinburg
28	15.1	Mission Cons ISD	Mission
28	15.1	Pearsall ISD	Pearsall
30	14.8	San Benito Cons ISD	San Benito
31	14.2	Dalhart ISD	Dalhart
32	13.6	Carrizo Springs Cons ISD	Carrizo Springs
33	13.3	Fabens ISD	Fabens
34	12.7	Valley View ISD	Pharr
35	11.8	Plainview ISD	Plainview
36	11.7	Harlingen Cons ISD	Harlingen
37	11.6	Brooks County ISD	Falfurrias
38	10.8	Rio Hondo ISD	Rio Hondo
39	10.7	Venus ISD	Venus
40	10.1	Brownsville ISD	Brownsville
41	9.5	Ft Stockton ISD	Ft Stockton
42	9.4	Pittsburg ISD	Pittsburg
43	9.2	Lamesa ISD	Lamesa
43	9.2	San Diego ISD	San Diego

Rank	Value	District	City
45	8.8	Mcallen ISD	Mcallen
46	8.7	Sinton ISD	Sinton
47	8.2	Alice ISD	Alice
48	7.9	Los Fresnos Cons ISD	Los Fresnos
49	7.8	Center ISD	Center
50	7.3	Canutillo ISD	El Paso
51	7.2	Amarillo ISD	Amarillo
51	7.2	Orange Grove ISD	Orange Grove
53	6.8	Vernon ISD	Vernon
54	6.5	Point Isabel ISD	Port Isabel
55	6.4	Bowie ISD	Bowie
56	6.1	Goose Creek CISD	Baytown
57	6.0	El Campo ISD	El Campo
58	5.9	Taylor ISD	Taylor
59	5.6	Seguin ISD	Seguin
59	5.6	Zapata County ISD	Zapata
61	5.0	Little Elm ISD	Little Elm
62	4.9	La Feria ISD	La Feria
63	4.8	Luling ISD	Luling
64	4.4	Daingerfield-Lone Star Is	Daingerfield
65	4.2	Lytle ISD	Lytle
65	4.2	San Antonio ISD	San Antonio
67	4.1	Brazosport ISD	Freeport
68	4.0	Bastrop ISD	Bastrop
69	3.9	Corsicana ISD	Corsicana
69	3.9	El Paso ISD	El Paso
71	3.8	Crockett ISD	Crockett
71	3.8	Elgin ISD	Elgin
73	3.7	West Oso ISD	Corpus Christi
74	3.4	Nacogdoches ISD	Nacogdoches
74	3.4	South Texas ISD	Mercedes
76	3.3	Clint ISD	El Paso
77	3.2	Bryan ISD	Bryan
77	3.2	Gainesville ISD	Gainesville
79	3.1	Edgewood ISD	San Antonio
79	3.1	Kingsville ISD	Kingsville
81	2.9	Corpus Christi ISD	Corpus Christi
82	2.8	Smithville ISD	Smithville
83	2.7	Andrews ISD	Andrews
83	2.7	Somerset ISD	Somerset
83	2.7	South San Antonio ISD	San Antonio
83	2.7	Sulphur Springs ISD	Sulphur Springs
87	2.6	Pecos-Barstow-Toyah ISD	Pecos
87	2.6	Southside ISD	San Antonio
89	2.5	Lubbock ISD	Lubbock
90	2.4	Atlanta ISD	Atlanta
90	2.4	Medina Valley ISD	Castroville
90	2.4	Socorro ISD	El Paso
90	2.4	Southwest ISD	San Antonio
94	2.3	Sharyland ISD	Mission
95	2.2	Lampasas ISD	Lampasas
96	2.1	Cameron ISD	Cameron
96	2.1	Paris ISD	Paris
98	2.0	Ector County ISD	Odessa
98	2.0	Gonzales ISD	Gonzales
98	2.0	San Angelo ISD	San Angelo
98	2.0	Snyder ISD	Snyder
98	2.0	Sweetwater ISD	Sweetwater
103	1.9	Laredo ISD	Laredo
104	1.8	Bridgeport ISD	Bridgeport
104	1.8	La Vega ISD	Waco
104	1.8	Marble Falls ISD	Marble Falls
104	1.8	New Braunfels ISD	New Braunfels
108	1.6	Liberty Hill ISD	Liberty Hill
109	1.5	Lufkin ISD	Lufkin
109	1.5	Midland ISD	Midland
109	1.5	Port Arthur ISD	Port Arthur
112	1.4	Bonham ISD	Bonham
112	1.4	Harlandale ISD	San Antonio
112	1.4	Madisonville Cons ISD	Madisonville
115	1.3	Decatur ISD	Decatur
115	1.3	Galena Park ISD	Houston
115	1.3	Pleasanton ISD	Pleasanton
118	1.2	Caldwell ISD	Caldwell
118	1.2	Lubbock-Cooper ISD	Lubbock
118	1.2	Navasota ISD	Navasota
118	1.2	United ISD	Laredo
118	1.2	Waxahachie ISD	Waxahachie
123	1.1	Burnet Cons ISD	Burnet
123	1.1	Fredericksburg ISD	Fredericksburg
123	1.1	Georgetown ISD	Georgetown
123	1.1	Manor ISD	Manor
123	1.1	Ysleta ISD	El Paso
128	1.0	Calhoun County ISD	Port Lavaca
128	1.0	Giddings ISD	Giddings
128	1.0	Graham ISD	Graham
128	1.0	Palacios ISD	Palacios
128	1.0	Poteet ISD	Poteet
128	1.0	Yoakum ISD	Yoakum
134	0.9	Houston ISD	Houston
134	0.9	Irving ISD	Irving
134	0.9	Pasadena ISD	Pasadena
134	0.9	Sanger ISD	Sanger
138	0.8	Cuero ISD	Cuero
138	0.8	Kaufman ISD	Kaufman
140	0.7	Alvin ISD	Alvin
140	0.7	Comal ISD	New Braunfels
140	0.7	Dallas ISD	Dallas
140	0.7	Denton ISD	Denton
140	0.7	Ferris ISD	Ferris
140	0.7	Hondo ISD	Hondo
140	0.7	Huntsville ISD	Huntsville
140	0.7	Kirbyville CISD	Kirbyville
140	0.7	Rusk ISD	Rusk
140	0.7	Temple ISD	Temple
150	0.6	Dickinson ISD	Dickinson
150	0.6	North Lamar ISD	Paris
150	0.6	Wills Point ISD	Wills Point
153	0.5	Borger ISD	Borger
153	0.5	Bridge City ISD	Bridge City
153	0.5	Brownwood ISD	Brownwood
153	0.5	Cleveland ISD	Cleveland
153	0.5	Columbia-Brazoria ISD	West Columbia
153	0.5	Dripping Springs ISD	Dripping Spgs
153	0.5	Edna ISD	Edna
153	0.5	Ennis ISD	Ennis
153	0.5	Grand Prairie ISD	Grand Prairie
153	0.5	Mexia ISD	Mexia
153	0.5	Midlothian ISD	Midlothian
153	0.5	Princeton ISD	Princeton
153	0.5	Robinson ISD	Robinson
153	0.5	San Marcos Cons ISD	San Marcos
153	0.5	Seminole ISD	Seminole
153	0.5	West ISD	West
169	0.4	Aledo ISD	Aledo
169	0.4	Bay City ISD	Bay City
169	0.4	Belton ISD	Belton
169	0.4	Floresville ISD	Floresville
169	0.4	Frenship ISD	Wolfforth
169	0.4	Gilmer ISD	Gilmer
169	0.4	Llano ISD	Llano
169	0.4	Mineral Wells ISD	Mineral Wells
169	0.4	Sherman ISD	Sherman
169	0.4	Terrell ISD	Terrell
169	0.4	Weatherford ISD	Weatherford
169	0.4	Whitney ISD	Whitney
169	0.4	Wichita Falls ISD	Wichita Falls
169	0.4	Willis ISD	Willis
183	0.3	Breckenridge ISD	Breckenridge
183	0.3	Castleberry ISD	Fort Worth
183	0.3	Channelview ISD	Channelview
183	0.3	Columbus ISD	Columbus
183	0.3	Commerce ISD	Commerce
183	0.3	Connally ISD	Waco
183	0.3	East Central ISD	San Antonio
183	0.3	Forney ISD	Forney
183	0.3	Garland ISD	Garland
183	0.3	Hillsboro ISD	Hillsboro
183	0.3	Honors Academy	Dallas
183	0.3	Ingram ISD	Ingram
183	0.3	Liberty-Eylau ISD	Texarkana
183	0.3	Mesquite ISD	Mesquite
183	0.3	Northside ISD	San Antonio
183	0.3	Rockdale ISD	Rockdale
183	0.3	Round Rock ISD	Round Rock
183	0.3	Royal ISD	Brookshire
183	0.3	Royse City ISD	Royse City
183	0.3	Sealy ISD	Sealy
183	0.3	Shepherd ISD	Shepherd
183	0.3	Silsbee ISD	Silsbee
183	0.3	Wharton ISD	Wharton
183	0.3	Wilmer-Hutchins ISD	Dallas
207	0.2	Angleton ISD	Angleton
207	0.2	Aransas County ISD	Rockport
207	0.2	Big Spring ISD	Big Spring
207	0.2	Buna ISD	Buna
207	0.2	Carrollton-Farmers Branch	Carrollton
207	0.2	Carthage ISD	Carthage
207	0.2	College Station ISD	College Station
207	0.2	Copperas Cove ISD	Copperas Cove
207	0.2	Del Valle ISD	Del Valle
207	0.2	Denison ISD	Denison
207	0.2	Fort Worth ISD	Fort Worth
207	0.2	Gatesville ISD	Gatesville
207	0.2	Gregory-Portland ISD	Gregory
207	0.2	Groesbeck ISD	Groesbeck
207	0.2	Hamshire-Fannett ISD	Hamshire
207	0.2	Huntington ISD	Huntington
207	0.2	Hutto ISD	Hutto
207	0.2	Ingleside ISD	Ingleside
207	0.2	Kilgore ISD	Kilgore
207	0.2	Killeen ISD	Killeen
207	0.2	La Grange ISD	La Grange
207	0.2	La Vernia ISD	La Vernia
207	0.2	Lancaster ISD	Lancaster
207	0.2	Lockhart ISD	Lockhart
207	0.2	Mineola ISD	Mineola
207	0.2	New Caney ISD	New Caney
207	0.2	Pampa ISD	Pampa
207	0.2	Rockwall ISD	Rockwall
207	0.2	Schertz-Cibolo-U City ISD	Schertz
207	0.2	Splendora ISD	Splendora
207	0.2	Springtown ISD	Springtown
207	0.2	Stephenville ISD	Stephenville
207	0.2	Victoria ISD	Victoria
207	0.2	Whitesboro ISD	Whitesboro
241	0.1	Aldine ISD	Houston
241	0.1	Allen ISD	Allen
241	0.1	Alvarado ISD	Alvarado
241	0.1	Athens ISD	Athens
241	0.1	Austin ISD	Austin
241	0.1	Azle ISD	Azle
241	0.1	Bellville ISD	Bellville
241	0.1	Brenham ISD	Brenham
241	0.1	Chapel Hill ISD	Tyler
241	0.1	Cleburne ISD	Cleburne
241	0.1	Conroe ISD	Conroe
241	0.1	Crowley ISD	Crowley
241	0.1	Desoto ISD	Desoto
241	0.1	Devine ISD	Devine
241	0.1	Duncanville ISD	Duncanville
241	0.1	Everman ISD	Everman
241	0.1	Flour Bluff ISD	Corpus Christi
241	0.1	Frisco ISD	Frisco
241	0.1	Glen Rose ISD	Glen Rose
241	0.1	Hardin-Jefferson ISD	Sour Lake
241	0.1	Hays Cons ISD	Kyle
241	0.1	Henderson ISD	Henderson
241	0.1	Hudson ISD	Lufkin
241	0.1	Hurst-Euless-Bedford ISD	Bedford
241	0.1	Jacksonville ISD	Jacksonville
241	0.1	Joshua ISD	Joshua
241	0.1	Kerrville ISD	Kerrville
241	0.1	La Marque ISD	La Marque
241	0.1	Lake Dallas ISD	Lake Dallas
241	0.1	Leander ISD	Leander
241	0.1	Lewisville ISD	Flower Mound
241	0.1	Lindale ISD	Lindale
241	0.1	Livingston ISD	Livingston
241	0.1	Magnolia ISD	Magnolia
241	0.1	Mckinney ISD	Mckinney
241	0.1	Needville ISD	Needville
241	0.1	North East ISD	San Antonio
241	0.1	Palestine ISD	Palestine
241	0.1	Pearland ISD	Pearland
241	0.1	Pine Tree ISD	Longview
241	0.1	Rains ISD	Emory
241	0.1	Richardson ISD	Richardson
241	0.1	Spring Branch ISD	Houston
241	0.1	Texarkana ISD	Texarkana
241	0.1	Tuloso-Midway ISD	Corpus Christi
241	0.1	Tyler ISD	Tyler
241	0.1	Waco ISD	Waco
241	0.1	White Settlement ISD	White Settlement
241	0.1	Wylie ISD	Wylie
290	0.0	Aransas Pass ISD	Aransas Pass
290	0.0	Arlington ISD	Arlington
290	0.0	Barbers Hill ISD	Mt Belvieu
290	0.0	Birdville ISD	Haltom City
290	0.0	Boerne ISD	Boerne
290	0.0	Burleson ISD	Burleson
290	0.0	Canyon ISD	Canyon
290	0.0	Cedar Hill ISD	Cedar Hill
290	0.0	Cypress-Fairbanks ISD	Houston
290	0.0	Deer Park ISD	Deer Park
290	0.0	Eagle Mt-Saginaw ISD	Fort Worth
290	0.0	Fort Bend ISD	Sugar Land
290	0.0	Gladewater ISD	Gladewater
290	0.0	Greenville ISD	Greenville
290	0.0	Humble ISD	Humble
290	0.0	Judson ISD	San Antonio
290	0.0	Keller ISD	Keller
290	0.0	La Porte ISD	La Porte
290	0.0	Longview ISD	Longview
290	0.0	Mansfield ISD	Mansfield
290	0.0	Northwest ISD	Fort Worth
290	0.0	Pflugerville ISD	Pflugerville
290	0.0	Port Neches-Groves ISD	Port Neches
290	0.0	Vidor ISD	Vidor
314	0.0	Abilene ISD	Abilene
314	0.0	Alamo Heights ISD	San Antonio
314	0.0	Alief ISD	Houston
314	0.0	Bandera ISD	Bandera
314	0.0	Beaumont ISD	Beaumont
314	0.0	Beeville ISD	Beeville
314	0.0	Brownsboro ISD	Brownsboro
314	0.0	Bullard ISD	Bullard
314	0.0	Burkburnett ISD	Burkburnett

Rank	Percent	District Name	City
314	0.0	Calallen ISD	Corpus Christi
314	0.0	Canton ISD	Canton
314	0.0	Carroll ISD	Grapevine
314	0.0	Central ISD	Pollok
314	0.0	China Spring ISD	Waco
314	0.0	Clear Creek ISD	League City
314	0.0	Coldspring-Oakhurst Cons	Coldspring
314	0.0	Coppell ISD	Coppell
314	0.0	Crandall ISD	Crandall
314	0.0	Crosby ISD	Crosby
314	0.0	Dayton ISD	Dayton
314	0.0	Diboll ISD	Diboll
314	0.0	Eanes ISD	Austin
314	0.0	Eustace ISD	Eustace
314	0.0	Fairfield ISD	Fairfield
314	0.0	Friendswood ISD	Friendswood
314	0.0	Galveston ISD	Galveston
314	0.0	Granbury ISD	Granbury
314	0.0	Grapevine-Colleyville ISD	Grapevine
314	0.0	Greenwood ISD	Midland
314	0.0	Hallsville ISD	Hallsville
314	0.0	Highland Park ISD	Dallas
314	0.0	Huffman ISD	Huffman
314	0.0	Iowa Park Cons ISD	Iowa Park
314	0.0	Jasper ISD	Jasper
314	0.0	Katy ISD	Katy
314	0.0	Kemp ISD	Kemp
314	0.0	Kennedale ISD	Kennedale
314	0.0	Klein ISD	Klein
314	0.0	Lake Travis ISD	Austin
314	0.0	Lake Worth ISD	Lake Worth
314	0.0	Lamar Consolidated ISD	Rosenberg
314	0.0	Liberty ISD	Liberty
314	0.0	Little Cypress-Mauricevil	Orange
314	0.0	Lorena ISD	Lorena
314	0.0	Lumberton ISD	Lumberton
314	0.0	Mabank ISD	Mabank
314	0.0	Marshall ISD	Marshall
314	0.0	Midway ISD	Waco
314	0.0	Monahans-Wickett-Pyote Is	Monahans
314	0.0	Montgomery ISD	Montgomery
314	0.0	Nederland ISD	Nederland
314	0.0	North Forest ISD	Houston
314	0.0	Orangefield ISD	Orangefield
314	0.0	Plano ISD	Plano
314	0.0	Pleasant Grove ISD	Texarkana
314	0.0	Quinlan ISD	Quinlan
314	0.0	Red Oak ISD	Red Oak
314	0.0	Santa Fe ISD	Santa Fe
314	0.0	Sheldon ISD	Houston
314	0.0	Spring Hill ISD	Longview
314	0.0	Spring ISD	Houston
314	0.0	Stafford Municipal School	Stafford
314	0.0	Sweeny ISD	Sweeny
314	0.0	Tarkington ISD	Cleveland
314	0.0	Texas City ISD	Texas City
314	0.0	Tomball ISD	Tomball
314	0.0	Van ISD	Van
314	0.0	Waller ISD	Waller
314	0.0	West Orange-Cove Cons ISD	Orange
314	0.0	Westwood ISD	Palestine
314	0.0	Whitehouse ISD	Whitehouse
314	0.0	Wimberley ISD	Wimberley
314	0.0	Wylie ISD	Abilene

Students Eligible for Free Lunch

Rank	Percent	District Name	City
1	88.5	San Elizario ISD	San Elizario
2	84.6	Robstown ISD	Robstown
3	84.4	Brooks County ISD	Falfurrias
4	80.2	Clint ISD	El Paso
5	79.0	Rio Grande City CISD	Rio Grande City
6	74.5	Port Arthur ISD	Port Arthur
7	72.9	Canutillo ISD	El Paso
8	71.3	San Diego ISD	San Diego
9	71.1	Mathis ISD	Mathis
10	70.9	Waco ISD	Waco
11	70.8	Eagle Pass ISD	Eagle Pass
12	70.3	Lake Worth ISD	Lake Worth
13	70.1	Dallas ISD	Dallas
14	69.9	Presidio ISD	Presidio
15	69.1	Pearsall ISD	Pearsall
16	68.2	Southside ISD	San Antonio
17	66.2	Southwest ISD	San Antonio
17	66.2	Uvalde Cons ISD	Uvalde
19	65.6	Royal ISD	Brookshire
20	65.5	Aldine ISD	Houston
20	65.5	Houston ISD	Houston
22	65.1	Harlingen Cons ISD	Harlingen
23	64.3	South San Antonio ISD	San Antonio
24	63.4	Crockett ISD	Crockett
25	63.1	Fort Worth ISD	Fort Worth
26	63.0	San Felipe-Del Rio Cons I	Del Rio
27	62.9	United ISD	Laredo
28	62.1	Wilmer-Hutchins ISD	Dallas
29	62.0	Crystal City ISD	Crystal City
30	61.9	Hereford ISD	Hereford
31	61.6	Jacksonville ISD	Jacksonville
32	61.5	Somerset ISD	Somerset
33	61.0	Poteet ISD	Poteet
34	60.9	Pecos-Barstow-Toyah ISD	Pecos
34	60.9	West Orange-Cove Cons ISD	Orange
36	60.2	Socorro ISD	El Paso
37	60.1	Hillsboro ISD	Hillsboro
38	59.8	Mount Pleasant ISD	Mt Pleasant
39	59.4	El Paso ISD	El Paso
40	59.1	Del Valle ISD	Del Valle
40	59.1	Galena Park ISD	Houston
42	58.5	Alice ISD	Alice
43	58.4	Nacogdoches ISD	Nacogdoches
44	58.1	Brownfield ISD	Brownfield
45	57.7	Cameron ISD	Cameron
46	57.5	Lytle ISD	Lytle
47	57.1	Longview ISD	Longview
48	57.0	Lamesa ISD	Lamesa
48	57.0	Sinton ISD	Sinton
50	56.7	La Vega ISD	Waco
51	56.6	Palacios ISD	Palacios
52	56.4	Kingsville ISD	Kingsville
53	55.7	Beeville ISD	Beeville
54	55.6	Paris ISD	Paris
55	55.2	Galveston ISD	Galveston
56	55.0	Luling ISD	Luling
57	54.9	Liberty-Eylau ISD	Texarkana
58	54.8	Mexia ISD	Mexia
59	54.6	Sheldon ISD	Houston
60	54.5	Beaumont ISD	Beaumont
60	54.5	Gonzales ISD	Gonzales
62	54.4	Cleveland ISD	Cleveland
62	54.4	Pittsburg ISD	Pittsburg
64	54.3	Palestine ISD	Palestine
65	54.1	Bay City ISD	Bay City
66	54.0	Bryan ISD	Bryan
66	54.0	Jasper ISD	Jasper
68	53.6	Texarkana ISD	Texarkana
69	53.3	Lufkin ISD	Lufkin
70	53.1	Orange Grove ISD	Orange Grove
70	53.1	Pasadena ISD	Pasadena
72	53.0	Ft Stockton ISD	Ft Stockton
73	52.8	Madisonville Cons ISD	Madisonville
74	52.5	Channelview ISD	Channelview
74	52.5	Diboll ISD	Diboll
76	52.3	Center ISD	Center
76	52.3	Terrell ISD	Terrell
78	51.9	Plainview ISD	Plainview
79	51.8	Alief ISD	Houston
79	51.8	Progreso ISD	Progreso
81	51.7	Daingerfield-Lone Star Is	Daingerfield
81	51.7	Wharton ISD	Wharton
83	51.6	Commerce ISD	Commerce
84	51.3	La Joya ISD	La Joya
85	51.2	Pleasanton ISD	Pleasanton
86	50.9	Donna ISD	Donna
87	50.7	Manor ISD	Manor
87	50.7	Marshall ISD	Marshall
89	50.7	Navasota ISD	Navasota
90	50.0	Irving ISD	Irving
91	49.9	Coldspring-Oakhurst Cons	Coldspring
92	49.8	Ector County ISD	Odessa
93	49.7	Taylor ISD	Taylor
94	49.6	El Campo ISD	El Campo
94	49.6	Venus ISD	Venus
96	49.5	Levelland ISD	Levelland
97	49.4	Castleberry ISD	Fort Worth
98	49.3	Carrizo Springs Cons ISD	Carrizo Springs
98	49.3	Corpus Christi ISD	Corpus Christi
100	49.1	Point Isabel ISD	Port Isabel
101	48.9	Seminole ISD	Seminole
102	48.7	Breckenridge ISD	Breckenridge
102	48.7	Raymondville ISD	Raymondville
104	48.5	Dickinson ISD	Dickinson
104	48.5	Shepherd ISD	Shepherd
106	48.3	Corsicana ISD	Corsicana
106	48.3	Goose Creek CISD	Baytown
106	48.3	Seguin ISD	Seguin
109	48.2	La Feria ISD	La Feria
110	48.1	Gainesville ISD	Gainesville
110	48.1	San Marcos Cons ISD	San Marcos
112	47.9	Tyler ISD	Tyler
113	47.8	Spring Branch ISD	Houston
114	47.7	Aransas County ISD	Rockport
115	47.6	La Marque ISD	La Marque
116	47.3	Texas City ISD	Texas City
117	47.2	Austin ISD	Austin
118	47.0	Amarillo ISD	Amarillo
118	47.0	Temple ISD	Temple
120	46.9	Ingram ISD	Ingram
120	46.9	Rockdale ISD	Rockdale
122	46.7	Calhoun County ISD	Port Lavaca
122	46.7	Lubbock ISD	Lubbock
124	46.6	Elgin ISD	Elgin
125	46.5	Dumas ISD	Dumas
126	46.4	North Forest ISD	Houston
126	46.4	Vernon ISD	Vernon
128	46.2	Big Spring ISD	Big Spring
128	46.2	Ennis ISD	Ennis
130	46.1	Mineola ISD	Mineola
131	45.7	Atlanta ISD	Atlanta
132	45.6	Devine ISD	Devine
133	45.5	Athens ISD	Athens
133	45.5	Sweetwater ISD	Sweetwater
135	45.3	Abilene ISD	Abilene
136	45.2	Grand Prairie ISD	Grand Prairie
137	45.1	Eustace ISD	Eustace
137	45.1	Gladewater ISD	Gladewater
139	45.0	Mineral Wells ISD	Mineral Wells
140	44.6	Kilgore ISD	Kilgore
141	44.4	Chapel Hill ISD	Tyler
141	44.4	Yoakum ISD	Yoakum
143	44.3	Connally ISD	Waco
143	44.3	Ferris ISD	Ferris
143	44.3	Sharyland ISD	Mission
146	44.1	Lancaster ISD	Lancaster
147	44.0	Brownwood ISD	Brownwood
148	43.8	Aransas Pass ISD	Aransas Pass
148	43.8	Hudson ISD	Lufkin
150	43.7	Groesbeck ISD	Groesbeck
151	43.5	Splendora ISD	Splendora
152	43.4	Victoria ISD	Victoria
153	43.2	Laredo ISD	Laredo
154	42.8	Dalhart ISD	Dalhart
154	42.8	Greenville ISD	Greenville
154	42.8	Liberty ISD	Liberty
154	42.8	South Texas ISD	Mercedes
158	42.7	Rusk ISD	Rusk
158	42.7	Snyder ISD	Snyder
158	42.7	Zapata County ISD	Zapata
161	41.9	East Central ISD	San Antonio
162	41.6	Kirbyville CISD	Kirbyville
162	41.6	Mabank ISD	Mabank
164	41.5	Henderson ISD	Henderson
164	41.5	Sherman ISD	Sherman
166	41.4	Edna ISD	Edna
166	41.4	Gilmer ISD	Gilmer
168	41.3	San Angelo ISD	San Angelo
168	41.3	Wichita Falls ISD	Wichita Falls
170	41.0	Perryton ISD	Perryton
171	40.9	Lockhart ISD	Lockhart
172	40.5	Denison ISD	Denison
173	40.4	West Oso ISD	Corpus Christi
174	40.2	Fabens ISD	Fabens
174	40.2	Ysleta ISD	El Paso
176	40.0	Mcallen ISD	Mcallen
177	39.7	Cuero ISD	Cuero
178	39.5	Midland ISD	Midland
179	39.4	Brazosport ISD	Freeport
179	39.4	Kaufman ISD	Kaufman
179	39.4	Smithville ISD	Smithville
182	39.3	Arlington ISD	Arlington
183	38.9	Floresville ISD	Floresville
183	38.9	Whitney ISD	Whitney
185	38.8	Vidor ISD	Vidor
186	38.7	Lamar Consolidated ISD	Rosenberg
186	38.7	Tuloso-Midway ISD	Corpus Christi
188	38.5	Wills Point ISD	Wills Point
189	38.3	Giddings ISD	Giddings
190	38.1	Rio Hondo ISD	Rio Hondo
190	38.1	Waller ISD	Waller
192	37.9	Bastrop ISD	Bastrop
192	37.9	Cleburne ISD	Cleburne
192	37.9	Judson ISD	San Antonio
195	37.8	Marble Falls ISD	Marble Falls
196	37.7	Duncanville ISD	Duncanville
197	37.6	Caldwell ISD	Caldwell
197	37.6	New Caney ISD	New Caney
199	37.5	Alvin ISD	Alvin
200	37.4	Rains ISD	Emory
201	37.2	Brenham ISD	Brenham
202	37.1	Pampa ISD	Pampa
202	37.1	Willis ISD	Willis
204	37.0	Carthage ISD	Carthage
204	37.0	Quinlan ISD	Quinlan
204	37.0	Sealy ISD	Sealy
207	36.9	Spring ISD	Houston
208	36.6	Belton ISD	Belton
209	36.3	Kerrville ISD	Kerrville
210	36.2	Sulphur Springs ISD	Sulphur Springs

Rank	Percent	District Name	City
211	36.1	Fairfield ISD	Fairfield
212	35.8	Alvarado ISD	Alvarado
213	35.6	Weslaco ISD	Weslaco
214	35.5	Angleton ISD	Angleton
214	35.5	Livingston ISD	Livingston
216	35.4	Medina Valley ISD	Castroville
217	35.3	Brownsboro ISD	Brownsboro
218	35.2	Carrollton-Farmers Branch	Carrollton
218	35.2	Van ISD	Van
220	35.1	Dayton ISD	Dayton
221	34.9	Westwood ISD	Palestine
222	34.8	Kemp ISD	Kemp
223	34.7	Huntington ISD	Huntington
223	34.7	Lampasas ISD	Lampasas
225	34.6	Columbia-Brazoria ISD	West Columbia
225	34.6	Richardson ISD	Richardson
227	34.5	Flour Bluff ISD	Corpus Christi
227	34.5	Lubbock-Cooper ISD	Lubbock
229	33.9	Borger ISD	Borger
230	33.7	Northside ISD	San Antonio
230	33.7	Waxahachie ISD	Waxahachie
232	33.4	Glen Rose ISD	Glen Rose
232	33.4	La Grange ISD	La Grange
232	33.4	Los Fresnos Cons ISD	Los Fresnos
235	33.3	Burnet Cons ISD	Burnet
235	33.3	Honors Academy	Dallas
235	33.3	Huntsville ISD	Huntsville
235	33.3	Killeen ISD	Killeen
239	33.1	Llano ISD	Llano
240	32.8	Graham ISD	Graham
241	32.7	Garland ISD	Garland
242	32.6	Columbus ISD	Columbus
243	32.5	White Settlement ISD	White Settlement
244	32.4	Central ISD	Pollok
245	32.1	Fredericksburg ISD	Fredericksburg
246	32.0	Bandera ISD	Bandera
247	31.7	Joshua ISD	Joshua
248	31.5	Crosby ISD	Crosby
248	31.5	Denton ISD	Denton
250	31.3	Bonham ISD	Bonham
251	30.9	Bridgeport ISD	Bridgeport
251	30.9	Silsbee ISD	Silsbee
253	30.4	Bowie ISD	Bowie
253	30.4	Monahans-Wickett-Pyote Is	Monahans
255	30.2	Hays Cons ISD	Kyle
256	29.9	Pine Tree ISD	Longview
256	29.9	Springtown ISD	Springtown
258	29.5	Hurst-Euless-Bedford ISD	Bedford
258	29.5	Mesquite ISD	Mesquite
260	29.3	Royse City ISD	Royse City
261	29.2	San Antonio ISD	San Antonio
262	29.1	Princeton ISD	Princeton
263	28.9	Sweeny ISD	Sweeny
264	28.4	Granbury ISD	Granbury
265	28.3	Whitesboro ISD	Whitesboro
266	28.3	Stephenville	Stephenville
267	28.1	Birdville ISD	Haltom City
268	28.0	Desoto ISD	Desoto
268	28.0	North East ISD	San Antonio
270	27.8	Stafford Municipal School	Stafford
271	27.7	New Braunfels ISD	New Braunfels
271	27.7	North Lamar ISD	Paris
273	27.6	Little Elm ISD	Little Elm
273	27.6	Weatherford ISD	Weatherford
275	27.5	Calallen ISD	Corpus Christi
276	27.4	Andrews ISD	Andrews
277	27.2	West ISD	West
278	27.1	Frenship ISD	Wolfforth
279	26.7	Bridge City ISD	Bridge City
280	26.6	Decatur ISD	Decatur
280	26.6	Gatesville ISD	Gatesville
280	26.6	Hallsville ISD	Hallsville
280	26.6	Hondo ISD	Hondo
284	26.4	Edinburg CISD	Edinburg
285	26.3	Buna ISD	Buna
286	25.7	Ingleside ISD	Ingleside
287	25.3	Lindale ISD	Lindale
288	25.2	Copperas Cove ISD	Copperas Cove
289	25.1	Bullard ISD	Bullard
290	25.0	Magnolia ISD	Magnolia
291	24.9	Pflugerville ISD	Pflugerville
292	24.8	Georgetown ISD	Georgetown
293	24.7	Burkburnett ISD	Burkburnett
294	24.3	Hardin-Jefferson ISD	Sour Lake
295	24.0	Bellville ISD	Bellville
296	23.8	Azle ISD	Azle
297	23.6	Harlandale ISD	San Antonio
298	23.4	Conroe ISD	Conroe
298	23.4	Little Cypress-Mauricevil	Orange
300	23.2	Canton ISD	Canton
300	23.2	Tarkington ISD	Cleveland
302	23.0	La Porte ISD	La Porte
302	23.0	Needville ISD	Needville
304	22.5	Gregory-Portland ISD	Gregory
305	22.4	Deer Park ISD	Deer Park
306	22.1	Sanger ISD	Sanger
307	21.8	Lumberton ISD	Lumberton
308	21.3	Comal ISD	New Braunfels
309	21.2	Fort Bend ISD	Sugar Land
310	21.1	Crowley ISD	Crowley
311	20.9	La Vernia ISD	La Vernia
312	19.9	Whitehouse ISD	Whitehouse
313	19.6	Greenwood ISD	Midland
314	19.3	Cypress-Fairbanks ISD	Houston
315	19.2	Hamshire-Fannett ISD	Hamshire
316	19.0	Schertz-Cibolo-U City ISD	Schertz
317	18.9	Santa Fe ISD	Santa Fe
318	18.7	Huffman ISD	Huffman
319	18.6	Iowa Park Cons ISD	Iowa Park
319	18.6	Klein ISD	Klein
321	18.4	San Benito Cons ISD	San Benito
322	18.2	Cedar Hill ISD	Cedar Hill
323	18.0	Nederland ISD	Nederland
324	17.8	Spring Hill ISD	Longview
325	17.7	Mckinney ISD	Mckinney
325	17.7	Montgomery ISD	Montgomery
327	17.5	Liberty Hill ISD	Liberty Hill
327	17.5	Mansfield ISD	Mansfield
329	17.3	Pharr-San Juan-Alamo ISD	Pharr
330	17.0	Crandall ISD	Crandall
331	16.9	Canyon ISD	Canyon
332	16.7	Mercedes ISD	Mercedes
333	16.4	Red Oak ISD	Red Oak
334	15.9	Hutto ISD	Hutto
335	15.6	Alamo Heights ISD	San Antonio
336	15.4	Eagle Mt-Saginaw ISD	Fort Worth
336	15.4	Edcouch-Elsa ISD	Edcouch
338	15.1	Round Rock ISD	Round Rock
339	15.0	Humble ISD	Humble
339	15.0	Wylie ISD	Wylie
341	14.5	Lake Dallas ISD	Lake Dallas
342	14.3	Northwest ISD	Fort Worth
343	14.2	Barbers Hill ISD	Mt Belvieu
343	14.2	Robinson ISD	Robinson
343	14.2	Tomball ISD	Tomball
346	14.1	Pearland ISD	Pearland
347	14.0	Hidalgo ISD	Hidalgo
347	14.0	Kennedale ISD	Kennedale
347	14.0	Leander ISD	Leander
350	13.7	College Station ISD	College Station
351	13.6	Boerne ISD	Boerne
352	13.3	Burleson ISD	Burleson
352	13.3	Katy ISD	Katy
354	13.0	China Spring ISD	Waco
355	12.9	Wimberley ISD	Wimberley
356	12.6	Lorena ISD	Lorena
357	12.5	Rockwall ISD	Rockwall
358	12.2	Plano ISD	Plano
359	11.9	Edgewood ISD	San Antonio
360	11.5	Clear Creek ISD	League City
360	11.5	Orangefield ISD	Orangefield
362	11.4	Midway ISD	Waco
363	11.0	Midlothian ISD	Midlothian
364	10.2	Pleasant Grove ISD	Texarkana
365	10.1	Valley View ISD	Pharr
366	10.0	Forney ISD	Forney
367	9.6	Lewisville ISD	Flower Mound
368	8.8	Port Neches-Groves ISD	Port Neches
369	8.3	Keller ISD	Keller
370	8.2	Lake Travis ISD	Austin
371	8.0	Grapevine-Colleyville ISD	Grapevine
372	7.6	Roma ISD	Roma
373	7.2	Dripping Springs ISD	Dripping Spgs
374	6.9	Frisco ISD	Frisco
375	6.7	Aledo ISD	Aledo
376	6.0	Brownsville ISD	Brownsville
377	5.8	Allen ISD	Allen
378	5.5	Wylie ISD	Abilene
379	5.3	Mission Cons ISD	Mission
380	3.2	Coppell ISD	Coppell
381	2.4	Friendswood ISD	Friendswood
381	2.4	Lyford CISD	Lyford
383	1.2	Carroll ISD	Grapevine
384	1.0	Eanes ISD	Austin
385	0.1	Everman ISD	Everman
386	0.0	Highland Park ISD	Dallas

Students Eligible for Reduced-Price Lunch

Rank	Percent	District Name	City
1	15.5	Killeen ISD	Killeen
2	15.2	Diboll ISD	Diboll
3	14.8	San Diego ISD	San Diego
4	13.6	San Marcos Cons ISD	San Marcos
5	13.4	Venus ISD	Venus
6	13.0	Dalhart ISD	Dalhart
7	12.8	Somerset ISD	Somerset
8	12.7	Socorro ISD	El Paso
8	12.7	Southwest ISD	San Antonio
10	12.5	Floresville ISD	Floresville
10	12.5	Hutto ISD	Hutto
12	12.4	Ferris ISD	Ferris
12	12.4	Ft Stockton ISD	Ft Stockton
14	12.0	Del Valle ISD	Del Valle
14	12.0	Iowa Park Cons ISD	Iowa Park
16	11.9	Big Spring ISD	Big Spring
16	11.9	Devine ISD	Devine
16	11.9	Grand Prairie ISD	Grand Prairie
16	11.9	Gregory-Portland ISD	Gregory
16	11.9	Perryton ISD	Perryton
16	11.9	Southside ISD	San Antonio
22	11.8	Burkburnett ISD	Burkburnett
22	11.8	East Central ISD	San Antonio
24	11.6	La Vega ISD	Waco
25	11.5	Beeville ISD	Beeville
25	11.5	Judson ISD	San Antonio
25	11.5	Lockhart ISD	Lockhart
28	11.3	Duncanville ISD	Duncanville
28	11.3	Poteet ISD	Poteet
30	11.2	Irving ISD	Irving
30	11.2	Manor ISD	Manor
32	11.1	Alvarado ISD	Alvarado
32	11.1	Channelview ISD	Channelview
32	11.1	Connally ISD	Waco
32	11.1	Copperas Cove ISD	Copperas Cove
36	11.0	Atlanta ISD	Atlanta
36	11.0	Cuero ISD	Cuero
38	10.9	Hondo ISD	Hondo
38	10.9	Lancaster ISD	Lancaster
38	10.9	Sweetwater ISD	Sweetwater
41	10.8	Sheldon ISD	Houston
42	10.6	Eustace ISD	Eustace
42	10.6	Ingleside ISD	Ingleside
42	10.6	Navasota ISD	Navasota
42	10.6	San Felipe-Del Rio Cons I	Del Rio
46	10.5	Aldine ISD	Houston
46	10.5	Aransas Pass ISD	Aransas Pass
46	10.5	El Campo ISD	El Campo
46	10.5	Flour Bluff ISD	Corpus Christi
46	10.5	Huntsville ISD	Huntsville
46	10.5	Llano ISD	Llano
46	10.5	Splendora ISD	Splendora
46	10.5	Ysleta ISD	El Paso
54	10.4	Mount Pleasant ISD	Mt Pleasant
54	10.4	Orange Grove ISD	Orange Grove
54	10.4	United ISD	Laredo
57	10.2	Bastrop ISD	Bastrop
57	10.2	Hudson ISD	Lufkin
57	10.2	South Texas ISD	Mercedes
57	10.2	Willis ISD	Willis
61	10.1	Brooks County ISD	Falfurrias
61	10.1	Ingram ISD	Ingram
61	10.1	San Angelo ISD	San Angelo
64	10.0	Abilene ISD	Abilene
64	10.0	Mineral Wells ISD	Mineral Wells
64	10.0	Pasadena ISD	Pasadena
64	10.0	Wills Point ISD	Wills Point
68	9.9	Galena Park ISD	Houston
69	9.8	Belton ISD	Belton
69	9.8	Houston ISD	Houston
69	9.8	Mathis ISD	Mathis
69	9.8	Pflugerville ISD	Pflugerville
73	9.7	Burnet Cons ISD	Burnet
73	9.7	Carrizo Springs Cons ISD	Carrizo Springs
73	9.7	Levelland ISD	Levelland
76	9.6	Canutillo ISD	El Paso
76	9.6	Gilmer ISD	Gilmer
76	9.6	Northside ISD	San Antonio
76	9.6	Rains ISD	Emory
76	9.6	Wichita Falls ISD	Wichita Falls
81	9.5	Castleberry ISD	Fort Worth
81	9.5	Goose Creek CISD	Baytown
81	9.5	Kingsville ISD	Kingsville
81	9.5	Luling ISD	Luling
81	9.5	Waco ISD	Waco
86	9.4	Mabank ISD	Mabank
86	9.4	Monahans-Wickett-Pyote Is	Monahans
86	9.4	Seguin ISD	Seguin
86	9.4	Shepherd ISD	Shepherd
86	9.4	Spring ISD	Houston
86	9.4	Vernon ISD	Vernon
92	9.3	Brownwood ISD	Brownwood
92	9.3	Fredericksburg ISD	Fredericksburg
92	9.3	Hays Cons ISD	Kyle
92	9.3	Springtown ISD	Springtown
92	9.3	Yoakum ISD	Yoakum

Rank	Score	District	City
97	9.2	Gatesville ISD	Gatesville
97	9.2	Gonzales ISD	Gonzales
97	9.2	Vidor ISD	Vidor
100	9.1	Amarillo ISD	Amarillo
100	9.1	Andrews ISD	Andrews
100	9.1	Carrollton-Farmers Branch	Carrollton
100	9.1	Dumas ISD	Dumas
104	9.0	Ector County ISD	Odessa
104	9.0	Kerrville ISD	Kerrville
104	9.0	Lubbock ISD	Lubbock
104	9.0	New Caney ISD	New Caney
104	9.0	Princeton ISD	Princeton
109	8.9	Birdville ISD	Haltom City
109	8.9	Central ISD	Pollok
109	8.9	Jasper ISD	Jasper
109	8.9	Joshua ISD	Joshua
109	8.9	Madisonville Cons ISD	Madisonville
114	8.8	Alvin ISD	Alvin
114	8.8	Denison ISD	Denison
114	8.8	Desoto ISD	Desoto
114	8.8	Graham ISD	Graham
114	8.8	Lytle ISD	Lytle
114	8.8	Pecos-Barstow-Toyah ISD	Pecos
114	8.8	South San Antonio ISD	San Antonio
114	8.8	Victoria ISD	Victoria
122	8.7	Alice ISD	Alice
122	8.7	Liberty Hill ISD	Liberty Hill
122	8.7	Marble Falls ISD	Marble Falls
122	8.7	Pearsall ISD	Pearsall
122	8.7	Pittsburg ISD	Pittsburg
122	8.7	Pleasanton ISD	Pleasanton
122	8.7	Rusk ISD	Rusk
129	8.6	Calhoun County ISD	Port Lavaca
129	8.6	Hereford ISD	Hereford
129	8.6	La Porte ISD	La Porte
129	8.6	Lamesa ISD	Lamesa
129	8.6	Little Elm ISD	Little Elm
129	8.6	New Braunfels ISD	New Braunfels
135	8.5	Eagle Pass ISD	Eagle Pass
135	8.5	Fabens ISD	Fabens
135	8.5	Lampasas ISD	Lampasas
135	8.5	Palacios ISD	Palacios
135	8.5	Smithville ISD	Smithville
140	8.4	Austin ISD	Austin
140	8.4	Brownfield ISD	Brownfield
140	8.4	Dayton ISD	Dayton
140	8.4	Hurst-Euless-Bedford ISD	Bedford
140	8.4	Medina Valley ISD	Castroville
140	8.4	Sinton ISD	Sinton
140	8.4	Temple ISD	Temple
140	8.4	Uvalde Cons ISD	Uvalde
140	8.4	West ISD	West
140	8.4	Wharton ISD	Wharton
150	8.3	Bandera ISD	Bandera
150	8.3	Dallas ISD	Dallas
150	8.3	El Paso ISD	El Paso
150	8.3	Ennis ISD	Ennis
150	8.3	Whitney ISD	Whitney
155	8.2	Athens ISD	Athens
155	8.2	Brownsboro ISD	Brownsboro
155	8.2	Bullard ISD	Bullard
155	8.2	Corpus Christi ISD	Corpus Christi
155	8.2	Daingerfield-Lone Star Is	Daingerfield
155	8.2	Georgetown ISD	Georgetown
155	8.2	Glen Rose ISD	Glen Rose
155	8.2	Lubbock-Cooper ISD	Lubbock
155	8.2	Stafford Municipal School	Stafford
155	8.2	Waxahachie ISD	Waxahachie
165	8.1	Cedar Hill ISD	Cedar Hill
165	8.1	La Grange ISD	La Grange
165	8.1	Sharyland ISD	Mission
168	8.0	Clint ISD	El Paso
168	8.0	Stephenville ISD	Stephenville
168	8.0	Waller ISD	Waller
168	8.0	Whitesboro ISD	Whitesboro
172	7.9	Buna ISD	Buna
172	7.9	Hallsville ISD	Hallsville
172	7.9	Quinlan ISD	Quinlan
172	7.9	Snyder ISD	Snyder
176	7.8	Henderson ISD	Henderson
176	7.8	Taylor ISD	Taylor
176	7.8	Van ISD	Van
176	7.8	Wilmer-Hutchins ISD	Dallas
180	7.7	Alief ISD	Houston
180	7.7	Borger ISD	Borger
180	7.7	Bowie ISD	Bowie
180	7.7	Dickinson ISD	Dickinson
180	7.7	Mesquite ISD	Mesquite
180	7.7	Plainview ISD	Plainview
186	7.6	Bryan ISD	Bryan
186	7.6	Cameron ISD	Cameron
186	7.6	Groesbeck ISD	Groesbeck
186	7.6	Hardin-Jefferson ISD	Sour Lake
186	7.6	Hillsboro ISD	Hillsboro
191	7.5	Angleton ISD	Angleton
191	7.5	Bay City ISD	Bay City
191	7.5	Columbus ISD	Columbus
191	7.5	Crowley ISD	Crowley
191	7.5	Frenship ISD	Wolfforth
191	7.5	Greenville ISD	Greenville
191	7.5	Midland ISD	Midland
191	7.5	Mineola ISD	Mineola
191	7.5	Robinson ISD	Robinson
191	7.5	Sulphur Springs ISD	Sulphur Springs
191	7.5	White Settlement ISD	White Settlement
202	7.4	Center ISD	Center
202	7.4	Elgin ISD	Elgin
202	7.4	Royal ISD	Brookshire
202	7.4	Texas City ISD	Texas City
206	7.3	Breckenridge ISD	Breckenridge
206	7.3	Caldwell ISD	Caldwell
206	7.3	Cleburne ISD	Cleburne
206	7.3	Cleveland ISD	Cleveland
206	7.3	Garland ISD	Garland
206	7.3	Gladewater ISD	Gladewater
206	7.3	Liberty-Eylau ISD	Texarkana
206	7.3	San Elizario ISD	San Elizario
214	7.2	North East ISD	San Antonio
214	7.2	Texarkana ISD	Texarkana
216	7.1	Azle ISD	Azle
216	7.1	Galveston ISD	Galveston
216	7.1	Giddings ISD	Giddings
216	7.1	Kirbyville CISD	Kirbyville
216	7.1	Lake Worth ISD	Lake Worth
216	7.1	Lindale ISD	Lindale
216	7.1	Mexia ISD	Mexia
216	7.1	Sealy ISD	Sealy
216	7.1	Seminole ISD	Seminole
216	7.1	Sweeny ISD	Sweeny
226	7.0	Kaufman ISD	Kaufman
226	7.0	Palestine ISD	Palestine
226	7.0	Pampa ISD	Pampa
226	7.0	Sherman ISD	Sherman
226	7.0	Tuloso-Midway ISD	Corpus Christi
231	6.9	Coldspring-Oakhurst Cons	Coldspring
231	6.9	Columbia-Brazoria ISD	West Columbia
231	6.9	Crockett ISD	Crockett
231	6.9	La Vernia ISD	La Vernia
231	6.9	Lamar Consolidated ISD	Rosenberg
231	6.9	Marshall ISD	Marshall
231	6.9	Royse City ISD	Royse City
238	6.8	Aransas County ISD	Rockport
238	6.8	Arlington ISD	Arlington
238	6.8	Brazosport ISD	Freeport
238	6.8	Burleson ISD	Burleson
238	6.8	Corsicana ISD	Corsicana
238	6.8	Kilgore ISD	Kilgore
238	6.8	Mcallen ISD	Mcallen
238	6.8	Nacogdoches ISD	Nacogdoches
238	6.8	Richardson ISD	Richardson
238	6.8	Terrell ISD	Terrell
238	6.8	Tyler ISD	Tyler
238	6.8	Weatherford ISD	Weatherford
238	6.8	Whitehouse ISD	Whitehouse
251	6.7	Commerce ISD	Commerce
251	6.7	Gainesville ISD	Gainesville
251	6.7	La Marque ISD	La Marque
251	6.7	Mansfield ISD	Mansfield
255	6.6	Comal ISD	New Braunfels
255	6.6	Granbury ISD	Granbury
255	6.6	Lufkin ISD	Lufkin
255	6.6	West Oso ISD	Corpus Christi
259	6.5	Bonham ISD	Bonham
259	6.5	Chapel Hill ISD	Tyler
259	6.5	Harlingen Cons ISD	Harlingen
259	6.5	Kennedale ISD	Kennedale
259	6.5	Lumberton ISD	Lumberton
264	6.4	Decatur ISD	Decatur
264	6.4	Kemp ISD	Kemp
266	6.3	Canton ISD	Canton
266	6.3	Carthage ISD	Carthage
266	6.3	Deer Park ISD	Deer Park
266	6.3	Fairfield ISD	Fairfield
266	6.3	Fort Worth ISD	Fort Worth
266	6.3	Huntington ISD	Huntington
266	6.3	Liberty ISD	Liberty
266	6.3	Paris ISD	Paris
266	6.3	Robstown ISD	Robstown
275	6.2	Brenham ISD	Brenham
275	6.2	Calallen ISD	Corpus Christi
275	6.2	Crosby ISD	Crosby
275	6.2	Rio Hondo ISD	Rio Hondo
279	6.1	Cypress-Fairbanks ISD	Houston
279	6.1	Silsbee ISD	Silsbee
281	6.0	Eagle Mt-Saginaw ISD	Fort Worth
281	6.0	Jacksonville ISD	Jacksonville
281	6.0	Spring Branch ISD	Houston
284	5.9	Edna ISD	Edna
284	5.9	Greenwood ISD	Midland
284	5.9	Honors Academy	Dallas
284	5.9	Livingston ISD	Livingston
284	5.9	Pine Tree ISD	Longview
284	5.9	Presidio ISD	Presidio
290	5.8	Nederland ISD	Nederland
290	5.8	Port Neches-Groves ISD	Port Neches
290	5.8	Tarkington ISD	Cleveland
290	5.8	Westwood ISD	Palestine
294	5.7	Hamshire-Fannett ISD	Hamshire
294	5.7	Leander ISD	Leander
294	5.7	Magnolia ISD	Magnolia
294	5.7	Port Arthur ISD	Port Arthur
294	5.7	Sanger ISD	Sanger
294	5.7	Schertz-Cibolo-U City ISD	Schertz
300	5.6	Longview ISD	Longview
300	5.6	Midway ISD	Waco
300	5.6	Needville ISD	Needville
300	5.6	Point Isabel ISD	Port Isabel
300	5.6	West Orange-Cove Cons ISD	Orange
305	5.5	Beaumont ISD	Beaumont
305	5.5	Bridgeport ISD	Bridgeport
305	5.5	Huffman ISD	Huffman
308	5.4	La Feria ISD	La Feria
309	5.3	Bellville ISD	Bellville
309	5.3	Wylie ISD	Wylie
311	5.2	Round Rock ISD	Round Rock
312	5.1	China Spring ISD	Waco
313	5.0	Bridge City ISD	Bridge City
313	5.0	Denton ISD	Denton
313	5.0	North Lamar ISD	Paris
316	4.9	Boerne ISD	Boerne
316	4.9	Fort Bend ISD	Sugar Land
316	4.9	Zapata County ISD	Zapata
319	4.8	Montgomery ISD	Montgomery
320	4.7	Alamo Heights ISD	San Antonio
320	4.7	Northwest ISD	Fort Worth
322	4.6	Donna ISD	Donna
322	4.6	Midlothian ISD	Midlothian
322	4.6	Orangefield ISD	Orangefield
322	4.6	Santa Fe ISD	Santa Fe
326	4.5	Barbers Hill ISD	Mt Belvieu
327	4.4	Canyon ISD	Canyon
327	4.4	College Station ISD	College Station
327	4.4	Conroe ISD	Conroe
327	4.4	Crystal City ISD	Crystal City
327	4.4	Little Cypress-Mauricevil	Orange
327	4.4	Rockdale ISD	Rockdale
333	4.3	Klein ISD	Klein
333	4.3	Red Oak ISD	Red Oak
335	4.2	Crandall ISD	Crandall
335	4.2	Humble ISD	Humble
335	4.2	Los Fresnos Cons ISD	Los Fresnos
335	4.2	Pearland ISD	Pearland
335	4.2	Spring Hill ISD	Longview
340	4.0	Raymondville ISD	Raymondville
340	4.0	Wimberley ISD	Wimberley
342	3.9	Katy ISD	Katy
342	3.9	Wylie ISD	Abilene
344	3.8	Harlandale ISD	San Antonio
345	3.7	Lorena ISD	Lorena
346	3.6	Mckinney ISD	Mckinney
346	3.6	Tomball ISD	Tomball
348	3.5	Clear Creek ISD	League City
349	3.4	Rockwall ISD	Rockwall
350	3.3	Pleasant Grove ISD	Texarkana
351	3.2	North Forest ISD	Houston
351	3.2	Plano ISD	Plano
353	3.1	Keller ISD	Keller
354	3.0	Forney ISD	Forney
354	3.0	La Joya ISD	La Joya
354	3.0	Lake Dallas ISD	Lake Dallas
357	2.8	Lewisville ISD	Flower Mound
357	2.8	Rio Grande City CISD	Rio Grande City
359	2.7	Laredo ISD	Laredo
360	2.6	Edinburg CISD	Edinburg
361	2.3	San Antonio ISD	San Antonio
361	2.3	Weslaco ISD	Weslaco
363	2.2	Frisco ISD	Frisco
364	2.1	Allen ISD	Allen
364	2.1	Lake Travis ISD	Austin
364	2.1	San Benito Cons ISD	San Benito
367	2.0	Dripping Springs ISD	Dripping Spgs
368	1.8	Grapevine-Colleyville ISD	Grapevine
369	1.5	Aledo ISD	Aledo
369	1.5	Pharr-San Juan-Alamo ISD	Pharr
371	1.4	Coppell ISD	Coppell
371	1.4	Mercedes ISD	Mercedes
373	1.3	Progreso ISD	Progreso

Rank		District Name	City
374	1.0	Edcouch-Elsa ISD	Edcouch
375	0.9	Valley View ISD	Pharr
376	0.7	Edgewood ISD	San Antonio
377	0.6	Brownsville ISD	Brownsville
377	0.6	Friendswood ISD	Friendswood
377	0.6	Roma ISD	Roma
380	0.4	Eanes ISD	Austin
380	0.4	Hidalgo ISD	Hidalgo
380	0.4	Mission Cons ISD	Mission
383	0.3	Carroll ISD	Grapevine
384	0.1	Lyford CISD	Lyford
385	0.0	Everman ISD	Everman
385	0.0	Highland Park ISD	Dallas

Student/Teacher Ratio

Rank	Ratio	District Name	City
1	31.8	Honors Academy	Dallas
2	18.2	San Felipe-Del Rio Cons I	Del Rio
3	17.5	Eagle Pass ISD	Eagle Pass
3	17.5	Keller ISD	Keller
5	17.4	Eagle Mt-Saginaw ISD	Fort Worth
6	17.3	Clint ISD	El Paso
7	17.2	Dayton ISD	Dayton
7	17.2	Houston ISD	Houston
7	17.2	Pasadena ISD	Pasadena
7	17.2	Tuloso-Midway ISD	Corpus Christi
11	17.1	Angleton ISD	Angleton
11	17.1	Channelview ISD	Channelview
11	17.1	Edgewood ISD	San Antonio
11	17.1	Port Arthur ISD	Port Arthur
11	17.1	San Benito Cons ISD	San Benito
11	17.1	Sharyland ISD	Mission
17	17.0	Crosby ISD	Crosby
17	17.0	Gregory-Portland ISD	Gregory
17	17.0	Rockwall ISD	Rockwall
20	16.9	Cedar Hill ISD	Cedar Hill
20	16.9	Edcouch-Elsa ISD	Edcouch
20	16.9	Socorro ISD	El Paso
23	16.8	Fort Worth ISD	Fort Worth
23	16.8	Huffman ISD	Huffman
23	16.8	Pharr-San Juan-Alamo ISD	Pharr
26	16.6	Birdville ISD	Haltom City
26	16.6	Ingleside ISD	Ingleside
28	16.5	Castleberry ISD	Fort Worth
28	16.5	China Spring ISD	Waco
28	16.5	Deer Park ISD	Deer Park
28	16.5	Fort Bend ISD	Sugar Land
28	16.5	Los Fresnos Cons ISD	Los Fresnos
28	16.5	United ISD	Laredo
34	16.4	Burleson ISD	Burleson
34	16.4	Clear Creek ISD	League City
34	16.4	Crystal City ISD	Crystal City
34	16.4	La Porte ISD	La Porte
34	16.4	Santa Fe ISD	Santa Fe
39	16.3	Corpus Christi ISD	Corpus Christi
39	16.3	Friendswood ISD	Friendswood
39	16.3	Harlingen Cons ISD	Harlingen
39	16.3	Lorena ISD	Lorena
39	16.3	Medina Valley ISD	Castroville
39	16.3	Midway ISD	Waco
45	16.2	Brazosport ISD	Freeport
45	16.2	Dickinson ISD	Dickinson
45	16.2	Duncanville ISD	Duncanville
45	16.2	Sheldon ISD	Houston
45	16.2	Wylie ISD	Abilene
50	16.1	East Central ISD	San Antonio
50	16.1	Pflugerville ISD	Pflugerville
50	16.1	Rio Hondo ISD	Rio Hondo
50	16.1	San Antonio ISD	San Antonio
50	16.1	Whitehouse ISD	Whitehouse
55	16.0	Canyon ISD	Canyon
55	16.0	Klein ISD	Klein
55	16.0	Laredo ISD	Laredo
55	16.0	Mesquite ISD	Mesquite
55	16.0	Montgomery ISD	Montgomery
55	16.0	West ISD	West
61	15.9	Allen ISD	Allen
61	15.9	Alvarado ISD	Alvarado
61	15.9	Flour Bluff ISD	Corpus Christi
61	15.9	Kennedale ISD	Kennedale
61	15.9	La Joya ISD	La Joya
61	15.9	Lancaster ISD	Lancaster
67	15.8	Goose Creek CISD	Baytown
67	15.8	Stephenville ISD	Stephenville
67	15.8	Tomball ISD	Tomball
70	15.7	Calallen ISD	Corpus Christi
70	15.7	Calhoun County ISD	Port Lavaca
70	15.7	Conroe ISD	Conroe
70	15.7	Fabens ISD	Fabens
70	15.7	Galveston ISD	Galveston
70	15.7	Garland ISD	Garland
70	15.7	Grapevine-Colleyville ISD	Grapevine
70	15.7	Huntsville ISD	Huntsville
70	15.7	La Vernia ISD	La Vernia
70	15.7	Livingston ISD	Livingston
70	15.7	Point Isabel ISD	Port Isabel
70	15.7	Somerset ISD	Somerset
70	15.7	Texas City ISD	Texas City
70	15.7	Willis ISD	Willis
84	15.6	Aldine ISD	Houston
84	15.6	Arlington ISD	Arlington
84	15.6	Comal ISD	New Braunfels
84	15.6	Crowley ISD	Crowley
84	15.6	Ector County ISD	Odessa
84	15.6	Edinburg CISD	Edinburg
84	15.6	Everman ISD	Everman
84	15.6	Nacogdoches ISD	Nacogdoches
84	15.6	Nederland ISD	Nederland
84	15.6	Northside ISD	San Antonio
84	15.6	Pearland ISD	Pearland
84	15.6	Red Oak ISD	Red Oak
84	15.6	San Angelo ISD	San Angelo
84	15.6	Valley View ISD	Pharr
84	15.6	Ysleta ISD	El Paso
99	15.5	Highland Park ISD	Dallas
99	15.5	Humble ISD	Humble
99	15.5	Lamar Consolidated ISD	Rosenberg
99	15.5	New Braunfels ISD	New Braunfels
99	15.5	Princeton ISD	Princeton
99	15.5	Schertz-Cibolo-U City ISD	Schertz
99	15.5	Waxahachie ISD	Waxahachie
99	15.5	Weslaco ISD	Weslaco
99	15.5	Wills Point ISD	Wills Point
109	15.4	Alvin ISD	Alvin
109	15.4	Brownsboro ISD	Brownsboro
109	15.4	Cleveland ISD	Cleveland
109	15.4	Hays Cons ISD	Kyle
109	15.4	Hurst-Euless-Bedford ISD	Bedford
109	15.4	Iowa Park Cons ISD	Iowa Park
109	15.4	Midland ISD	Midland
109	15.4	Mission Cons ISD	Mission
109	15.4	San Elizario ISD	San Elizario
118	15.3	Alice ISD	Alice
118	15.3	Bay City ISD	Bay City
118	15.3	Beeville ISD	Beeville
118	15.3	Columbia-Brazoria ISD	West Columbia
118	15.3	Cypress-Fairbanks ISD	Houston
118	15.3	La Marque ISD	La Marque
118	15.3	Mansfield ISD	Mansfield
118	15.3	Mercedes ISD	Mercedes
118	15.3	North East ISD	San Antonio
118	15.3	North Forest ISD	Houston
118	15.3	Southside ISD	San Antonio
118	15.3	Sweeny ISD	Sweeny
118	15.3	White Settlement ISD	White Settlement
131	15.2	Alief ISD	Houston
131	15.2	Belton ISD	Belton
131	15.2	Bridgeport ISD	Bridgeport
131	15.2	Brownsville ISD	Brownsville
131	15.2	Bryan ISD	Bryan
131	15.2	Magnolia ISD	Magnolia
131	15.2	Mcallen ISD	Mcallen
131	15.2	Needville ISD	Needville
131	15.2	Rockdale ISD	Rockdale
131	15.2	Round Rock ISD	Round Rock
131	15.2	Silsbee ISD	Silsbee
131	15.2	Waller ISD	Waller
131	15.2	Westwood ISD	Palestine
144	15.1	Cleburne ISD	Cleburne
144	15.1	College Station ISD	College Station
144	15.1	Frenship ISD	Wolfforth
144	15.1	Greenwood ISD	Midland
144	15.1	Little Cypress-Mauricevil	Orange
144	15.1	Mckinney ISD	Mckinney
144	15.1	Plainview ISD	Plainview
144	15.1	Roma ISD	Roma
144	15.1	South San Antonio ISD	San Antonio
144	15.1	Southwest ISD	San Antonio
144	15.1	Waco ISD	Waco
155	15.0	Azle ISD	Azle
155	15.0	Connally ISD	Waco
155	15.0	Corsicana ISD	Corsicana
155	15.0	Ennis ISD	Ennis
155	15.0	Harlandale ISD	San Antonio
155	15.0	Irving ISD	Irving
155	15.0	Katy ISD	Katy
155	15.0	Lake Travis ISD	Austin
155	15.0	Leander ISD	Leander
155	15.0	Manor ISD	Manor
155	15.0	Quinlan ISD	Quinlan
155	15.0	Splendora ISD	Splendora
155	15.0	Spring ISD	Houston
168	14.9	Coppell ISD	Coppell
168	14.9	Dripping Springs ISD	Dripping Spgs
168	14.9	Ft Stockton ISD	Ft Stockton
168	14.9	Grand Prairie ISD	Grand Prairie
168	14.9	Hallsville ISD	Hallsville
168	14.9	Kingsville ISD	Kingsville
168	14.9	Lumberton ISD	Lumberton
168	14.9	Rio Grande City CISD	Rio Grande City
168	14.9	Victoria ISD	Victoria
168	14.9	Weatherford ISD	Weatherford
178	14.8	Commerce ISD	Commerce
178	14.8	Denison ISD	Denison
178	14.8	Desoto ISD	Desoto
178	14.8	Donna ISD	Donna
178	14.8	Edna ISD	Edna
178	14.8	Forney ISD	Forney
178	14.8	Lampasas ISD	Lampasas
178	14.8	Lockhart ISD	Lockhart
178	14.8	Lytle ISD	Lytle
178	14.8	Orange Grove ISD	Orange Grove
178	14.8	Pecos-Barstow-Toyah ISD	Pecos
178	14.8	Spring Branch ISD	Houston
178	14.8	West Oso ISD	Corpus Christi
178	14.8	Wilmer-Hutchins ISD	Dallas
192	14.7	Aledo ISD	Aledo
192	14.7	Austin ISD	Austin
192	14.7	Bastrop ISD	Bastrop
192	14.7	Carrollton-Farmers Branch	Carrollton
192	14.7	Crandall ISD	Crandall
192	14.7	Gatesville ISD	Gatesville
192	14.7	Kaufman ISD	Kaufman
192	14.7	Kirbyville CISD	Kirbyville
192	14.7	Navasota ISD	Navasota
192	14.7	Port Neches-Groves ISD	Port Neches
192	14.7	Presidio ISD	Presidio
192	14.7	Raymondville ISD	Raymondville
192	14.7	Spring Hill ISD	Longview
192	14.7	Texarkana ISD	Texarkana
192	14.7	Wylie ISD	Wylie
207	14.6	Amarillo ISD	Amarillo
207	14.6	Bullard ISD	Bullard
207	14.6	Carthage ISD	Carthage
207	14.6	Gonzales ISD	Gonzales
207	14.6	Granbury ISD	Granbury
207	14.6	Hamshire-Fannett ISD	Hamshire
207	14.6	Judson ISD	San Antonio
207	14.6	Kemp ISD	Kemp
207	14.6	Little Elm ISD	Little Elm
207	14.6	New Caney ISD	New Caney
207	14.6	Northwest ISD	Fort Worth
207	14.6	San Marcos Cons ISD	San Marcos
207	14.6	Vidor ISD	Vidor
207	14.6	Whitesboro ISD	Whitesboro
221	14.5	Burnet Cons ISD	Burnet
221	14.5	Center ISD	Center
221	14.5	Del Valle ISD	Del Valle
221	14.5	Ferris ISD	Ferris
221	14.5	Greenville ISD	Greenville
221	14.5	Longview ISD	Longview
221	14.5	Midlothian ISD	Midlothian
221	14.5	Uvalde Cons ISD	Uvalde
229	14.4	Athens ISD	Athens
229	14.4	Barbers Hill ISD	Mt Belvieu
229	14.4	Big Spring ISD	Big Spring
229	14.4	Bridge City ISD	Bridge City
229	14.4	Canton ISD	Canton
229	14.4	Carrizo Springs Cons ISD	Carrizo Springs
229	14.4	Central ISD	Pollok
229	14.4	Frisco ISD	Frisco
229	14.4	Gladewater ISD	Gladewater
229	14.4	Hutto ISD	Hutto
229	14.4	Madisonville Cons ISD	Madisonville
229	14.4	Mexia ISD	Mexia
229	14.4	Orangefield ISD	Orangefield
229	14.4	Pine Tree ISD	Longview
229	14.4	Pleasant Grove ISD	Texarkana
229	14.4	Robstown ISD	Robstown
229	14.4	Stafford Municipal School	Stafford
229	14.4	Whitney ISD	Whitney
247	14.3	Carroll ISD	Grapevine
247	14.3	Copperas Cove ISD	Copperas Cove
247	14.3	Elgin ISD	Elgin
247	14.3	Floresville ISD	Floresville
247	14.3	Graham ISD	Graham
247	14.3	Joshua ISD	Joshua
247	14.3	La Feria ISD	La Feria
247	14.3	Lewisville ISD	Flower Mound
247	14.3	Lubbock-Cooper ISD	Lubbock
247	14.3	Progreso ISD	Progreso
247	14.3	Taylor ISD	Taylor
258	14.2	Aransas County ISD	Rockport
258	14.2	Beaumont ISD	Beaumont
258	14.2	Devine ISD	Devine

258	14.2	Kerrville ISD	Kerrville
258	14.2	Lake Dallas ISD	Lake Dallas
258	14.2	Liberty ISD	Liberty
258	14.2	Mabank ISD	Mabank
258	14.2	Mineola ISD	Mineola
258	14.2	Richardson ISD	Richardson
258	14.2	Sinton ISD	Sinton
268	14.1	Alamo Heights ISD	San Antonio
268	14.1	Bonham ISD	Bonham
268	14.1	Gainesville ISD	Gainesville
268	14.1	Hardin-Jefferson ISD	Sour Lake
268	14.1	Hereford ISD	Hereford
268	14.1	Hidalgo ISD	Hidalgo
268	14.1	Hudson ISD	Lufkin
268	14.1	Jacksonville ISD	Jacksonville
268	14.1	Killeen ISD	Killeen
268	14.1	La Grange ISD	La Grange
268	14.1	La Vega ISD	Waco
268	14.1	Luling ISD	Luling
268	14.1	West Orange-Cove Cons ISD	Orange
281	14.0	Boerne ISD	Boerne
281	14.0	Dumas ISD	Dumas
281	14.0	El Campo ISD	El Campo
281	14.0	El Paso ISD	El Paso
281	14.0	Galena Park ISD	Houston
281	14.0	Lindale ISD	Lindale
281	14.0	Marble Falls ISD	Marble Falls
281	14.0	Springtown ISD	Springtown
281	14.0	Terrell ISD	Terrell
281	14.0	Van ISD	Van
291	13.9	Andrews ISD	Andrews
291	13.9	Bellville ISD	Bellville
291	13.9	Caldwell ISD	Caldwell
291	13.9	Eanes ISD	Austin
291	13.9	Lake Worth ISD	Lake Worth
291	13.9	Lufkin ISD	Lufkin
291	13.9	Lyford CISD	Lyford
291	13.9	Pampa ISD	Pampa
291	13.9	Sealy ISD	Sealy
291	13.9	Tyler ISD	Tyler
291	13.9	Wharton ISD	Wharton
302	13.8	Brenham ISD	Brenham
302	13.8	Chapel Hill ISD	Tyler
302	13.8	Columbus ISD	Columbus
302	13.8	Fairfield ISD	Fairfield
302	13.8	Mathis ISD	Mathis
302	13.8	Monahans-Wickett-Pyote Is	Monahans
302	13.8	North Lamar ISD	Paris
302	13.8	Pittsburg ISD	Pittsburg
302	13.8	Royse City ISD	Royse City
302	13.8	Seguin ISD	Seguin
302	13.8	Sulphur Springs ISD	Sulphur Springs
302	13.8	Venus ISD	Venus
314	13.7	Aransas Pass ISD	Aransas Pass
314	13.7	Borger ISD	Borger
314	13.7	Canutillo ISD	El Paso
314	13.7	Decatur ISD	Decatur
314	13.7	Lamesa ISD	Lamesa
314	13.7	Llano ISD	Llano
314	13.7	Lubbock ISD	Lubbock
314	13.7	Marshall ISD	Marshall
314	13.7	Pearsall ISD	Pearsall
314	13.7	Perryton ISD	Perryton
314	13.7	Pleasanton ISD	Pleasanton
314	13.7	San Diego ISD	San Diego
314	13.7	Shepherd ISD	Shepherd
314	13.7	Sherman ISD	Sherman
328	13.6	Bowie ISD	Bowie
328	13.6	Coldspring-Oakhurst Cons	Coldspring
328	13.6	Denton ISD	Denton
328	13.6	Liberty Hill ISD	Liberty Hill
328	13.6	Mount Pleasant ISD	Mt Pleasant
328	13.6	Plano ISD	Plano
328	13.6	Tarkington ISD	Cleveland
335	13.5	Jasper ISD	Jasper
335	13.5	Mineral Wells ISD	Mineral Wells
335	13.5	Palacios ISD	Palacios
335	13.5	Seminole ISD	Seminole
335	13.5	Wichita Falls ISD	Wichita Falls
340	13.4	Bandera ISD	Bandera
340	13.4	Breckenridge ISD	Breckenridge
340	13.4	Fredericksburg ISD	Fredericksburg
340	13.4	Poteet ISD	Poteet
344	13.3	Eustace ISD	Eustace
344	13.3	Huntington ISD	Huntington
344	13.3	Kilgore ISD	Kilgore
344	13.3	Liberty-Eylau ISD	Texarkana
344	13.3	Royal ISD	Brookshire
344	13.3	Temple ISD	Temple
344	13.3	Wimberley ISD	Wimberley
351	13.2	Abilene ISD	Abilene
351	13.2	Brownwood ISD	Brownwood
351	13.2	Diboll ISD	Diboll
351	13.2	Henderson ISD	Henderson
351	13.2	Robinson ISD	Robinson
351	13.2	Smithville ISD	Smithville
351	13.2	Snyder ISD	Snyder
351	13.2	Vernon ISD	Vernon
359	13.1	Cuero ISD	Cuero
359	13.1	Gilmer ISD	Gilmer
359	13.1	Palestine ISD	Palestine
359	13.1	Yoakum ISD	Yoakum
363	13.0	Burkburnett ISD	Burkburnett
363	13.0	Dalhart ISD	Dalhart
363	13.0	Georgetown ISD	Georgetown
363	13.0	Giddings ISD	Giddings
363	13.0	Hillsboro ISD	Hillsboro
363	13.0	Rusk ISD	Rusk
363	13.0	Sanger ISD	Sanger
370	12.9	Cameron ISD	Cameron
370	12.9	Paris ISD	Paris
370	12.9	Zapata County ISD	Zapata
373	12.8	Groesbeck ISD	Groesbeck
373	12.8	South Texas ISD	Mercedes
375	12.7	Brooks County ISD	Falfurrias
375	12.7	Brownfield ISD	Brownfield
375	12.7	Hondo ISD	Hondo
375	12.7	Levelland ISD	Levelland
379	12.6	Atlanta ISD	Atlanta
380	12.4	Buna ISD	Buna
381	12.3	Daingerfield-Lone Star Is	Daingerfield
381	12.3	Ingram ISD	Ingram
383	12.2	Rains ISD	Emory
384	11.8	Crockett ISD	Crockett
384	11.8	Glen Rose ISD	Glen Rose
386	11.6	Sweetwater ISD	Sweetwater

Student/Librarian Ratio

Rank	Ratio	District Name	City
1	8,160.0	Orange Grove ISD	Orange Grove
2	6,551.7	Big Spring ISD	Big Spring
3	5,545.0	Sweetwater ISD	Sweetwater
4	5,296.7	Buna ISD	Buna
5	5,213.3	Bullard ISD	Bullard
6	5,083.3	Presidio ISD	Presidio
7	4,897.5	Rusk ISD	Rusk
8	4,217.5	Eagle Pass ISD	Eagle Pass
9	3,780.9	Sulphur Springs ISD	Sulphur Springs
10	3,669.0	Kilgore ISD	Kilgore
11	3,271.8	Brownwood ISD	Brownwood
12	3,206.5	Cleburne ISD	Cleburne
13	3,097.3	Kaufman ISD	Kaufman
14	3,003.0	Medina Valley ISD	Castroville
15	2,859.5	Texarkana ISD	Texarkana
16	2,790.0	Waxahachie ISD	Waxahachie
17	2,564.5	Mount Pleasant ISD	Mt Pleasant
18	2,485.0	Carrizo Springs Cons ISD	Carrizo Springs
19	2,483.7	Channelview ISD	Channelview
20	2,421.0	Graham ISD	Graham
21	2,385.5	Kerrville ISD	Kerrville
22	2,383.0	Beaumont ISD	Beaumont
23	2,280.5	Denison ISD	Denison
24	2,205.0	Wylie ISD	Wylie
25	2,182.2	Monahans-Wickett-Pyote Is	Monahans
26	2,177.0	Madisonville Cons ISD	Madisonville
26	2,177.0	Rio Hondo ISD	Rio Hondo
28	2,150.0	Sanger ISD	Sanger
29	2,136.7	Shepherd ISD	Shepherd
30	2,055.6	Pampa ISD	Pampa
31	1,960.0	Marshall ISD	Marshall
32	1,909.0	Caldwell ISD	Caldwell
33	1,882.0	Rockdale ISD	Rockdale
34	1,826.0	Venus ISD	Venus
35	1,803.6	Perryton ISD	Perryton
36	1,794.0	Coldspring-Oakhurst Cons	Coldspring
37	1,785.0	Westwood ISD	Palestine
38	1,712.8	Clint ISD	El Paso
39	1,696.4	Hallsville ISD	Hallsville
40	1,654.4	Belton ISD	Belton
41	1,648.0	Brooks County ISD	Falfurrias
42	1,644.0	Orangefield ISD	Orangefield
43	1,643.0	Beeville ISD	Beeville
44	1,636.7	Alvarado ISD	Alvarado
45	1,625.0	Dalhart ISD	Dalhart
46	1,615.0	Luling ISD	Luling
47	1,614.0	Southwest ISD	San Antonio
48	1,598.0	Kirbyville CISD	Kirbyville
49	1,590.9	Athens ISD	Athens
50	1,585.4	Forney ISD	Forney
51	1,581.5	Robinson ISD	Robinson
52	1,563.8	Somerset ISD	Somerset
53	1,555.0	Edna ISD	Edna
54	1,548.0	Whitney ISD	Whitney
55	1,545.0	San Diego ISD	San Diego
56	1,523.5	Chapel Hill ISD	Tyler
57	1,508.8	White Settlement ISD	White Settlement
58	1,505.0	Lyford CISD	Lyford
59	1,483.3	Jasper ISD	Jasper
60	1,474.8	Silsbee ISD	Silsbee
61	1,470.5	Azle ISD	Azle
62	1,459.4	Gonzales ISD	Gonzales
63	1,455.8	Burleson ISD	Burleson
64	1,430.0	Navasota ISD	Navasota
65	1,424.0	Fredericksburg ISD	Fredericksburg
66	1,402.0	Wylie ISD	Abilene
67	1,392.9	Aransas County ISD	Rockport
68	1,387.7	Gregory-Portland ISD	Gregory
69	1,382.0	Brenham ISD	Brenham
70	1,376.5	Frenship ISD	Wolfforth
71	1,375.5	Ingram ISD	Ingram
72	1,370.0	Corsicana ISD	Corsicana
73	1,362.5	Liberty-Eylau ISD	Texarkana
74	1,349.3	Livingston ISD	Livingston
75	1,349.0	Midlothian ISD	Midlothian
76	1,321.0	Fabens ISD	Fabens
77	1,314.4	Aransas Pass ISD	Aransas Pass
78	1,308.0	Calallen ISD	Corpus Christi
79	1,304.0	Snyder ISD	Snyder
80	1,295.4	Mansfield ISD	Mansfield
81	1,277.3	Everman ISD	Everman
82	1,247.6	Sherman ISD	Sherman
83	1,237.6	Galena Park ISD	Houston
84	1,233.2	Burnet Cons ISD	Burnet
85	1,205.3	Waco ISD	Waco
86	1,192.0	Sealy ISD	Sealy
87	1,188.7	Floresville ISD	Floresville
88	1,181.8	Bonham ISD	Bonham
89	1,173.5	Liberty ISD	Liberty
90	1,172.2	Keller ISD	Keller
91	1,171.5	Vernon ISD	Vernon
92	1,170.3	Whitehouse ISD	Whitehouse
93	1,166.0	Pleasanton ISD	Pleasanton
94	1,165.3	El Campo ISD	El Campo
95	1,165.0	Ingleside ISD	Ingleside
96	1,154.0	Spring Branch ISD	Houston
97	1,145.5	Ft Stockton ISD	Ft Stockton
98	1,141.9	Magnolia ISD	Magnolia
99	1,141.4	Katy ISD	Katy
100	1,138.5	Ferris ISD	Ferris
101	1,137.8	New Caney ISD	New Caney
102	1,126.0	Crockett ISD	Crockett
103	1,122.3	Tuloso-Midway ISD	Corpus Christi
104	1,105.4	Friendswood ISD	Friendswood
105	1,095.8	Paris ISD	Paris
106	1,091.5	Cypress-Fairbanks ISD	Houston
107	1,089.0	Alamo Heights ISD	San Antonio
108	1,084.0	Van ISD	Van
109	1,080.7	Sheldon ISD	Houston
110	1,078.6	Ennis ISD	Ennis
111	1,077.7	Castleberry ISD	Fort Worth
112	1,074.7	Allen ISD	Allen
113	1,074.5	Calhoun County ISD	Port Lavaca
114	1,073.2	Edcouch-Elsa ISD	Edcouch
115	1,071.0	Sinton ISD	Sinton
116	1,070.3	Rio Grande City CISD	Rio Grande City
117	1,068.9	Gainesville ISD	Gainesville
118	1,064.0	Nacogdoches ISD	Nacogdoches
119	1,063.5	Lamesa ISD	Lamesa
120	1,060.7	North Lamar ISD	Paris
121	1,049.6	Alief ISD	Houston
122	1,049.0	Sweeny ISD	Sweeny
123	1,043.7	Grapevine-Colleyville ISD	Grapevine
124	1,035.5	Crystal City ISD	Crystal City
125	1,033.9	Nederland ISD	Nederland
126	1,026.2	Jacksonville ISD	Jacksonville
127	1,023.3	Wilmer-Hutchins ISD	Dallas
128	1,023.2	Dayton ISD	Dayton
129	1,017.7	United ISD	Laredo
130	1,013.2	Flour Bluff ISD	Corpus Christi
131	1,007.4	Columbia-Brazoria ISD	West Columbia
132	1,004.1	Carthage ISD	Carthage
133	1,000.0	Northside ISD	San Antonio
134	999.6	Corpus Christi ISD	Corpus Christi
135	995.7	Mineral Wells ISD	Mineral Wells
136	994.9	Southside ISD	San Antonio
137	993.8	New Braunfels ISD	New Braunfels
138	990.0	Devine ISD	Devine
139	985.3	Valley View ISD	Pharr
140	979.3	Kennedale ISD	Kennedale
141	979.1	College Station ISD	College Station
142	978.9	Arlington ISD	Arlington
143	972.5	La Grange ISD	La Grange
144	966.3	La Feria ISD	La Feria
145	966.1	Fort Bend ISD	Sugar Land
146	965.0	Clear Creek ISD	League City
147	964.4	Sharyland ISD	Mission
148	962.5	Pleasant Grove ISD	Texarkana
149	959.7	San Felipe-Del Rio Cons I	Del Rio

Rank	Value	District Name	City
150	957.0	Quinlan ISD	Quinlan
151	956.0	Spring ISD	Houston
152	952.9	Leander ISD	Leander
153	951.1	Socorro ISD	El Paso
154	946.4	Judson ISD	San Antonio
155	946.0	Stafford Municipal School	Stafford
156	945.6	Bastrop ISD	Bastrop
157	945.4	San Angelo ISD	San Angelo
158	940.0	Wimberley ISD	Wimberley
159	938.2	Aldine ISD	Houston
160	934.1	Dickinson ISD	Dickinson
161	928.0	Montgomery ISD	Montgomery
162	927.5	North East ISD	San Antonio
163	925.8	Marble Falls ISD	Marble Falls
164	923.7	Red Oak ISD	Red Oak
165	920.2	Lufkin ISD	Lufkin
166	910.4	Pine Tree ISD	Longview
167	909.2	Crowley ISD	Crowley
167	909.2	Deer Park ISD	Deer Park
169	909.0	Hillsboro ISD	Hillsboro
170	908.8	Kingsville ISD	Kingsville
171	907.9	Galveston ISD	Galveston
172	907.1	Houston ISD	Houston
173	906.9	La Joya ISD	La Joya
174	906.2	Ysleta ISD	El Paso
175	904.8	Tomball ISD	Tomball
176	903.7	Wills Point ISD	Wills Point
177	900.0	China Spring ISD	Waco
178	899.0	Canton ISD	Canton
179	898.8	Lubbock ISD	Lubbock
180	896.1	Greenville ISD	Greenville
181	895.0	Santa Fe ISD	Santa Fe
182	890.5	Laredo ISD	Laredo
183	887.9	Conroe ISD	Conroe
184	886.7	Glen Rose ISD	Glen Rose
185	885.6	Rockwall ISD	Rockwall
186	885.4	Joshua ISD	Joshua
187	883.1	Brownsville ISD	Brownsville
188	882.7	Irving ISD	Irving
189	882.5	Stephenville	Stephenville
190	881.5	San Marcos Cons ISD	San Marcos
191	880.3	Uvalde Cons ISD	Uvalde
191	880.3	Victoria ISD	Victoria
193	879.7	East Central ISD	San Antonio
194	878.2	Diboll ISD	Diboll
195	876.3	La Vega ISD	Waco
196	873.8	Aledo ISD	Aledo
197	871.3	Vidor ISD	Vidor
198	871.0	Little Elm ISD	Little Elm
199	870.6	Yoakum ISD	Yoakum
200	867.7	Highland Park ISD	Dallas
201	866.5	Alvin ISD	Alvin
201	866.5	Lumberton ISD	Lumberton
203	856.4	Bellville ISD	Bellville
204	855.9	Amarillo ISD	Amarillo
205	855.6	Crosby ISD	Crosby
206	855.0	Coppell ISD	Coppell
207	854.0	Kemp ISD	Kemp
208	852.6	Harlingen Cons ISD	Harlingen
209	851.7	Eagle Mt-Saginaw ISD	Fort Worth
210	851.6	Bay City ISD	Bay City
211	850.7	Del Valle ISD	Del Valle
212	846.7	Humble ISD	Humble
213	846.0	Central ISD	Pollok
214	844.1	Tarkington ISD	Cleveland
215	842.0	Pasadena ISD	Pasadena
216	840.4	Cedar Hill ISD	Cedar Hill
217	838.6	North Forest ISD	Houston
218	838.5	Fairfield ISD	Fairfield
219	838.0	Pflugerville ISD	Pflugerville
220	837.3	Raymondville ISD	Raymondville
221	836.8	Goose Creek CISD	Baytown
222	833.5	Elgin ISD	Elgin
223	833.2	Mckinney ISD	Mckinney
224	832.8	Waller ISD	Waller
225	829.5	Huntington ISD	Huntington
226	829.3	South San Antonio ISD	San Antonio
227	829.0	Palestine ISD	Palestine
228	823.3	Center ISD	Center
229	822.9	Weslaco ISD	Weslaco
230	822.0	Needville ISD	Needville
231	820.0	Dripping Springs ISD	Dripping Spgs
232	819.5	Cameron ISD	Cameron
233	817.5	Texas City ISD	Texas City
234	813.3	Angleton ISD	Angleton
235	813.1	Decatur ISD	Decatur
236	813.0	Killeen ISD	Killeen
237	812.5	Lampasas ISD	Lampasas
238	810.0	La Porte ISD	La Porte
239	808.0	Round Rock ISD	Round Rock
240	805.0	Canutillo ISD	El Paso
241	804.5	Whitesboro ISD	Whitesboro
242	802.8	Pharr-San Juan-Alamo ISD	Pharr
243	801.6	Midland ISD	Midland
244	800.5	Mineola ISD	Mineola
245	797.3	Lake Worth ISD	Lake Worth
246	796.8	Austin ISD	Austin
247	794.9	San Antonio ISD	San Antonio
248	794.2	Tyler ISD	Tyler
249	787.9	Eanes ISD	Austin
250	787.0	Harlandale ISD	San Antonio
251	784.0	Hudson ISD	Lufkin
252	783.8	Splendora ISD	Splendora
253	782.1	Mesquite ISD	Mesquite
254	781.9	Denton ISD	Denton
255	778.8	Plano ISD	Plano
256	778.7	Mexia ISD	Mexia
257	778.5	Lorena ISD	Lorena
258	777.9	Roma ISD	Roma
259	777.7	Pittsburg ISD	Pittsburg
260	777.3	Lindale ISD	Lindale
261	777.0	Rains ISD	Emory
262	775.5	West ISD	West
263	774.9	Hurst-Euless-Bedford ISD	Bedford
264	770.4	Mcallen ISD	Mcallen
264	770.4	Pearland ISD	Pearland
266	768.6	Boerne ISD	Boerne
267	767.4	Ector County ISD	Odessa
268	767.1	Hays Cons ISD	Kyle
269	766.4	Llano ISD	Llano
270	765.1	Desoto ISD	Desoto
271	764.7	Willis ISD	Willis
272	760.5	San Benito Cons ISD	San Benito
273	760.3	Taylor ISD	Taylor
274	758.0	Huntsville ISD	Huntsville
275	756.5	Eustace ISD	Eustace
276	755.9	La Vernia ISD	La Vernia
277	753.1	Dallas ISD	Dallas
278	751.5	Greenwood ISD	Midland
279	751.3	Princeton ISD	Princeton
280	750.8	Granbury ISD	Granbury
281	750.2	Birdville ISD	Haltom City
282	748.1	Bryan ISD	Bryan
283	745.7	Wichita Falls ISD	Wichita Falls
284	744.8	Garland ISD	Garland
285	744.3	Lamar Consolidated ISD	Rosenberg
286	742.7	Bridgeport ISD	Bridgeport
287	739.8	Cleveland ISD	Cleveland
287	739.8	Little Cypress-Mauricevil	Orange
287	739.8	Port Arthur ISD	Port Arthur
290	737.4	Seguin ISD	Seguin
291	737.0	Fort Worth ISD	Fort Worth
292	735.2	Lewisville ISD	Flower Mound
293	734.7	Klein ISD	Klein
294	734.6	Carrollton-Farmers Branch	Carrollton
295	731.3	Donna ISD	Donna
296	730.7	Seminole ISD	Seminole
297	726.7	Gatesville ISD	Gatesville
298	724.9	Edinburg CISD	Edinburg
299	723.8	Burkburnett ISD	Burkburnett
300	720.5	Borger ISD	Borger
301	717.6	Richardson ISD	Richardson
302	717.3	Huffman ISD	Huffman
303	716.0	West Orange-Cove Cons ISD	Orange
304	712.4	Brazosport ISD	Freeport
305	712.3	Grand Prairie ISD	Grand Prairie
306	705.2	Comal ISD	New Braunfels
307	704.6	Edgewood ISD	San Antonio
308	697.0	Henderson ISD	Henderson
309	695.7	Terrell ISD	Terrell
310	691.8	Weatherford ISD	Weatherford
311	688.3	Lake Travis ISD	Austin
312	684.4	Plainview ISD	Plainview
313	682.7	Los Fresnos Cons ISD	Los Fresnos
314	682.5	El Paso ISD	El Paso
315	678.9	Lancaster ISD	Lancaster
316	673.5	Royse City ISD	Royse City
317	671.6	Northwest ISD	Fort Worth
318	668.7	Duncanville ISD	Duncanville
319	668.6	Mission Cons ISD	Mission
320	668.1	Abilene ISD	Abilene
321	667.8	Mercedes ISD	Mercedes
322	666.3	Bandera ISD	Bandera
322	666.3	Georgetown ISD	Georgetown
324	664.0	Carroll ISD	Grapevine
325	660.7	Hutto ISD	Hutto
326	659.7	Schertz-Cibolo-U City ISD	Schertz
327	657.3	Robstown ISD	Robstown
328	653.4	Midway ISD	Waco
329	651.8	Mabank ISD	Mabank
330	649.7	Cuero ISD	Cuero
331	649.0	Atlanta ISD	Atlanta
331	649.0	Brownfield ISD	Brownfield
333	645.4	Manor ISD	Manor
334	643.4	Canyon ISD	Canyon
335	642.1	Lockhart ISD	Lockhart
336	639.0	Point Isabel ISD	Port Isabel
337	638.5	Frisco ISD	Frisco
338	634.9	Temple ISD	Temple
339	634.0	West Oso ISD	Corpus Christi
340	632.6	Zapata County ISD	Zapata
341	631.4	Hidalgo ISD	Hidalgo
342	631.3	Mathis ISD	Mathis
343	627.6	Iowa Park Cons ISD	Iowa Park
344	627.5	Wharton ISD	Wharton
345	625.0	La Marque ISD	La Marque
346	618.5	San Elizario ISD	San Elizario
347	609.7	Commerce ISD	Commerce
348	608.3	Giddings ISD	Giddings
349	604.0	Barbers Hill ISD	Mt Belvieu
350	602.1	Bridge City ISD	Bridge City
351	602.0	Lubbock-Cooper ISD	Lubbock
352	599.3	Dumas ISD	Dumas
353	596.3	Lake Dallas ISD	Lake Dallas
354	594.2	Springtown ISD	Springtown
355	586.5	Pecos-Barstow-Toyah ISD	Pecos
356	581.6	Andrews ISD	Andrews
357	580.7	Royal ISD	Brookshire
358	575.7	Spring Hill ISD	Longview
359	574.3	Copperas Cove ISD	Copperas Cove
360	569.0	Gilmer ISD	Gilmer
361	566.3	Gladewater ISD	Gladewater
362	562.0	Poteet ISD	Poteet
363	552.7	Longview ISD	Longview
364	552.0	Groesbeck ISD	Groesbeck
365	550.3	Bowie ISD	Bowie
366	543.8	Hondo ISD	Hondo
367	532.7	Breckenridge ISD	Breckenridge
368	528.0	Alice ISD	Alice
368	528.0	Progreso ISD	Progreso
370	526.8	Connally ISD	Waco
371	521.7	Columbus ISD	Columbus
372	519.8	Crandall ISD	Crandall
373	509.8	South Texas ISD	Mercedes
374	509.4	Palacios ISD	Palacios
375	492.4	Hereford ISD	Hereford
376	476.0	Smithville ISD	Smithville
377	475.3	Port Neches-Groves ISD	Port Neches
378	457.7	Hamshire-Fannett ISD	Hamshire
379	442.7	Levelland ISD	Levelland
380	382.0	Daingerfield-Lone Star Is	Daingerfield
381	n/a	Brownsboro ISD	Brownsboro
381	n/a	Hardin-Jefferson ISD	Sour Lake
381	n/a	Honors Academy	Dallas
381	n/a	Liberty Hill ISD	Liberty Hill
381	n/a	Lytle ISD	Lytle
381	n/a	Pearsall ISD	Pearsall

Student/Counselor Ratio

Rank	Ratio	District Name	City
1	1,091.1	Monahans-Wickett-Pyote Is	Monahans
2	838.3	Alvarado ISD	Alvarado
3	816.8	Liberty Hill ISD	Liberty Hill
4	815.3	Kilgore ISD	Kilgore
5	801.3	Shepherd ISD	Shepherd
6	797.3	Lake Worth ISD	Lake Worth
7	781.1	Houston ISD	Houston
8	762.5	Presidio ISD	Presidio
9	756.5	Eustace ISD	Eustace
10	751.3	Princeton ISD	Princeton
11	730.9	Dayton ISD	Dayton
12	710.8	Dickinson ISD	Dickinson
13	709.8	Kaufman ISD	Kaufman
14	708.6	Perryton ISD	Perryton
15	669.8	Allen ISD	Allen
16	662.7	Keller ISD	Keller
17	652.7	Cleveland ISD	Cleveland
18	650.0	Lampasas ISD	Lampasas
19	619.2	Azle ISD	Azle
20	615.4	Galveston ISD	Galveston
21	611.1	Crosby ISD	Crosby
22	609.8	Tomball ISD	Tomball
23	599.3	Canton ISD	Canton
24	595.6	Big Spring ISD	Big Spring
25	594.3	Friendswood ISD	Friendswood
26	588.0	Marshall ISD	Marshall
27	587.5	College Station ISD	College Station
28	584.0	Mexia ISD	Mexia
29	582.3	Burleson ISD	Burleson
30	580.4	Nacogdoches ISD	Nacogdoches
31	580.0	Montgomery ISD	Montgomery
32	574.2	Quinlan ISD	Quinlan
33	573.8	Huffman ISD	Huffman
34	563.6	Katy ISD	Katy
35	559.8	Carrollton-Farmers Branch	Carrollton
36	559.7	Lamesa ISD	Lamesa
37	558.9	Gonzales ISD	Gonzales

Rank	Score	District	City
38	556.9	Ysleta ISD	El Paso
39	554.2	Borger ISD	Borger
40	552.7	Waxahachie ISD	Waxahachie
41	552.0	Groesbeck ISD	Groesbeck
42	550.3	Bowie ISD	Bowie
43	549.7	Crowley ISD	Crowley
44	549.3	Brooks County ISD	Falfurrias
45	544.0	Orange Grove ISD	Orange Grove
46	542.5	San Marcos Cons ISD	San Marcos
47	542.3	Palacios ISD	Palacios
48	542.2	Wills Point ISD	Wills Point
49	539.3	Andrews ISD	Andrews
50	538.8	Royse City ISD	Royse City
51	538.7	Pasadena ISD	Pasadena
52	538.6	Clint ISD	El Paso
53	537.0	West Orange-Cove Cons ISD	Orange
54	533.7	Mineola ISD	Mineola
55	532.2	Everman ISD	Everman
56	531.0	Madisonville Cons ISD	Madisonville
57	528.4	Little Cypress-Mauricevil	Orange
58	525.0	Canutillo ISD	El Paso
58	525.0	Waller ISD	Waller
60	524.5	Sweeny ISD	Sweeny
61	524.4	Dumas ISD	Dumas
62	521.6	Snyder ISD	Snyder
63	520.5	Columbia-Brazoria ISD	West Columbia
64	519.9	Sulphur Springs ISD	Sulphur Springs
65	519.8	Crandall ISD	Crandall
66	519.2	Jasper ISD	Jasper
67	519.1	White Settlement ISD	White Settlement
68	518.6	Lake Dallas ISD	Lake Dallas
69	518.3	Edna ISD	Edna
70	518.0	Rains ISD	Emory
71	517.0	Desoto ISD	Desoto
72	516.8	Wylie ISD	Wylie
73	516.1	Klein ISD	Klein
74	516.0	Whitney ISD	Whitney
75	513.0	La Porte ISD	La Porte
76	511.5	Midland ISD	Midland
77	510.8	Judson ISD	San Antonio
78	510.6	Mansfield ISD	Mansfield
79	510.5	Pflugerville ISD	Pflugerville
80	510.3	Royal ISD	Brookshire
81	508.2	Decatur ISD	Decatur
82	508.1	Wimberley ISD	Wimberley
83	507.6	Alvin ISD	Alvin
84	505.5	Clear Creek ISD	League City
85	503.8	Goose Creek CISD	Baytown
86	503.3	Barbers Hill ISD	Mt Belvieu
87	501.6	Nederland ISD	Nederland
88	501.0	Greenwood ISD	Midland
89	499.5	Comal ISD	New Braunfels
90	498.9	Mckinney ISD	Mckinney
91	497.7	Little Elm ISD	Little Elm
92	497.2	Santa Fe ISD	Santa Fe
93	496.7	Channelview ISD	Channelview
94	495.5	Hutto ISD	Hutto
95	494.0	Center ISD	Center
96	493.6	Carthage ISD	Carthage
97	493.4	Spring Hill ISD	Longview
98	493.3	Arlington ISD	Arlington
99	492.9	Sweetwater ISD	Sweetwater
100	492.3	Medina Valley ISD	Castroville
101	491.6	Mesquite ISD	Mesquite
102	490.5	Midlothian ISD	Midlothian
103	489.7	Kennedale ISD	Kennedale
104	489.5	North Lamar ISD	Paris
105	488.2	Hurst-Euless-Bedford ISD	Bedford
106	488.1	Ingram ISD	Ingram
107	486.4	Mabank ISD	Mabank
108	486.3	La Grange ISD	La Grange
109	486.2	Austin ISD	Austin
110	484.6	Cypress-Fairbanks ISD	Houston
111	484.2	Graham ISD	Graham
112	483.2	La Feria ISD	La Feria
113	483.0	Diboll ISD	Diboll
114	481.9	Huntsville ISD	Huntsville
115	481.5	Leander ISD	Leander
116	481.3	Pleasant Grove ISD	Texarkana
117	481.0	Beaumont ISD	Beaumont
118	480.9	Birdville ISD	Haltom City
119	480.8	Magnolia ISD	Magnolia
120	480.4	Fort Bend ISD	Sugar Land
121	479.1	New Caney ISD	New Caney
122	479.0	Llano ISD	Llano
123	478.9	Connally ISD	Waco
124	478.2	Galena Park ISD	Houston
125	475.6	Forney ISD	Forney
126	475.2	Lancaster ISD	Lancaster
127	473.0	Stafford Municipal School	Stafford
128	472.9	Spring Branch ISD	Houston
129	470.4	Hudson ISD	Lufkin
130	469.6	United ISD	Laredo
131	469.3	Wichita Falls ISD	Wichita Falls
132	469.1	Somerset ISD	Somerset
133	468.2	San Diego ISD	San Diego
134	468.1	Angleton ISD	Angleton
135	466.6	Pittsburg ISD	Pittsburg
136	466.0	Ingleside ISD	Ingleside
137	464.5	Stephenville ISD	Stephenville
138	464.3	Pine Tree ISD	Longview
138	464.3	Tarkington ISD	Cleveland
140	463.9	Grand Prairie ISD	Grand Prairie
141	463.8	Terrell ISD	Terrell
142	463.5	Deer Park ISD	Deer Park
143	463.2	Alief ISD	Houston
144	462.6	Gregory-Portland ISD	Gregory
145	461.0	Manor ISD	Manor
146	460.8	Huntington ISD	Huntington
147	459.2	Grapevine-Colleyville ISD	Grapevine
148	458.1	Northwest ISD	Fort Worth
149	457.8	Humble ISD	Humble
150	457.7	Tyler ISD	Tyler
151	457.6	Round Rock ISD	Round Rock
152	457.2	Edgewood ISD	San Antonio
153	456.8	Killeen ISD	Killeen
154	456.5	Venus ISD	Venus
155	455.7	Poteet ISD	Poteet
156	455.2	Gilmer ISD	Gilmer
157	455.1	Whitehouse ISD	Whitehouse
158	452.9	San Felipe-Del Rio Cons I	Del Rio
159	452.4	Burkburnett ISD	Burkburnett
159	452.4	East Central ISD	San Antonio
161	452.1	Garland ISD	Garland
162	450.0	China Spring ISD	Waco
163	449.9	Brownwood ISD	Brownwood
164	448.7	Rockwall ISD	Rockwall
165	448.5	Coldspring-Oakhurst Cons	Coldspring
165	448.5	Conroe ISD	Conroe
167	448.3	Boerne ISD	Boerne
168	447.4	Fabens ISD	Fabens
169	446.5	Texas City ISD	Texas City
170	446.3	Hamshire-Fannett ISD	Hamshire
170	446.3	Westwood ISD	Palestine
172	445.4	Spring ISD	Houston
173	443.9	Kirbyville CISD	Kirbyville
174	442.7	Joshua ISD	Joshua
175	442.5	Aldine ISD	Houston
176	441.8	Los Fresnos Cons ISD	Los Fresnos
177	440.7	Taylor ISD	Taylor
178	440.6	Elgin ISD	Elgin
179	440.1	Pharr-San Juan-Alamo ISD	Pharr
180	438.1	Wylie ISD	Abilene
181	436.9	Aledo ISD	Aledo
182	436.5	Pearland ISD	Pearland
183	436.0	Calallen ISD	Corpus Christi
183	436.0	Gatesville ISD	Gatesville
185	433.3	Lumberton ISD	Lumberton
186	432.5	Lorena ISD	Lorena
187	431.2	Belton ISD	Belton
188	429.6	Carroll ISD	Grapevine
189	429.0	Navasota ISD	Navasota
190	428.4	Valley View ISD	Pharr
191	427.5	Cleburne ISD	Cleburne
192	427.1	Frisco ISD	Frisco
193	427.0	Kemp ISD	Kemp
194	426.4	Greenville ISD	Greenville
195	426.2	Roma ISD	Roma
196	426.1	La Marque ISD	La Marque
197	426.0	Hardin-Jefferson ISD	Sour Lake
198	425.9	Rusk ISD	Rusk
199	424.2	El Paso ISD	El Paso
200	424.0	New Braunfels ISD	New Braunfels
201	421.9	Canyon ISD	Canyon
202	421.0	Hays Cons ISD	Kyle
203	420.9	Tuloso-Midway ISD	Corpus Christi
204	420.2	Cedar Hill ISD	Cedar Hill
205	419.8	Denton ISD	Denton
206	418.7	Raymondville ISD	Raymondville
207	418.3	Wharton ISD	Wharton
208	418.2	Socorro ISD	El Paso
209	417.1	Midway ISD	Waco
210	416.8	Coppell ISD	Coppell
211	414.8	Copperas Cove ISD	Copperas Cove
211	414.8	Temple ISD	Temple
213	414.6	Longview ISD	Longview
214	414.1	Lufkin ISD	Lufkin
215	413.2	Fort Worth ISD	Fort Worth
216	412.8	Edcouch-Elsa ISD	Edcouch
217	412.6	Sheldon ISD	Houston
218	412.4	Yoakum ISD	Yoakum
219	411.7	Bellville ISD	Bellville
220	411.0	Orangefield ISD	Orangefield
220	411.0	Weatherford ISD	Weatherford
222	410.7	Laredo ISD	Laredo
223	410.4	Granbury ISD	Granbury
224	410.0	La Vernia ISD	La Vernia
225	409.5	Eagle Mt-Saginaw ISD	Fort Worth
226	409.1	Lindale ISD	Lindale
227	406.5	Eagle Pass ISD	Eagle Pass
228	406.3	Dalhart ISD	Dalhart
229	405.5	Brazosport ISD	Freeport
230	404.9	Bryan ISD	Bryan
230	404.9	Highland Park ISD	Dallas
232	404.1	Castleberry ISD	Fort Worth
233	403.8	Luling ISD	Luling
234	403.5	Southwest ISD	San Antonio
235	402.2	Vidor ISD	Vidor
236	401.9	Jacksonville ISD	Jacksonville
237	401.8	Bonham ISD	Bonham
238	399.8	Brenham ISD	Brenham
239	399.5	Breckenridge ISD	Breckenridge
240	399.1	Irving ISD	Irving
241	398.0	Calhoun County ISD	Port Lavaca
241	398.0	South San Antonio ISD	San Antonio
243	397.7	Sherman ISD	Sherman
244	396.0	Devine ISD	Devine
245	395.8	Rio Hondo ISD	Rio Hondo
246	395.7	Lubbock ISD	Lubbock
247	395.1	Willis ISD	Willis
248	395.0	Ft Stockton ISD	Ft Stockton
249	394.4	Schertz-Cibolo-U City ISD	Schertz
250	393.7	Georgetown ISD	Georgetown
251	393.3	Athens ISD	Athens
252	392.8	Hallsville ISD	Hallsville
253	391.7	Waco ISD	Waco
254	391.3	Columbus ISD	Columbus
255	391.2	Liberty ISD	Liberty
256	391.0	Bullard ISD	Bullard
256	391.0	North East ISD	San Antonio
256	391.0	Pecos-Barstow-Toyah ISD	Pecos
259	389.8	Cuero ISD	Cuero
260	389.4	Atlanta ISD	Atlanta
261	387.8	San Angelo ISD	San Angelo
261	387.8	West ISD	West
263	387.4	Plano ISD	Plano
264	386.0	Harlandale ISD	San Antonio
265	385.5	Lytle ISD	Lytle
266	385.4	Burnet Cons ISD	Burnet
267	383.7	Ector County ISD	Odessa
268	383.4	Dallas ISD	Dallas
269	382.8	Del Valle ISD	Del Valle
270	382.2	Port Arthur ISD	Port Arthur
271	380.8	Smithville ISD	Smithville
272	380.7	Bandera ISD	Bandera
272	380.7	Plainview ISD	Plainview
272	380.7	San Antonio ISD	San Antonio
275	380.4	West Oso ISD	Corpus Christi
276	379.7	Frenship ISD	Wolfforth
277	379.5	Ferris ISD	Ferris
278	376.4	Rockdale ISD	Rockdale
279	375.6	La Vega ISD	Waco
280	374.6	Lockhart ISD	Lockhart
281	373.1	Edinburg CISD	Edinburg
282	372.1	Corpus Christi ISD	Corpus Christi
283	371.5	Seminole ISD	Seminole
284	370.6	Lake Travis ISD	Austin
285	370.3	Marble Falls ISD	Marble Falls
286	369.9	Bridge City ISD	Bridge City
286	369.9	Harlingen Cons ISD	Harlingen
288	369.5	Buna ISD	Buna
289	369.2	Victoria ISD	Victoria
290	368.7	Paris ISD	Paris
290	368.7	Silsbee ISD	Silsbee
292	368.4	Palestine ISD	Palestine
293	367.3	Amarillo ISD	Amarillo
294	366.4	Mount Pleasant ISD	Mt Pleasant
295	366.1	San Benito Cons ISD	San Benito
296	365.6	Port Neches-Groves ISD	Port Neches
297	365.3	Corsicana ISD	Corsicana
298	365.0	Giddings ISD	Giddings
299	364.0	Iowa Park Cons ISD	Iowa Park
300	362.5	Abilene ISD	Abilene
300	362.5	Hondo ISD	Hondo
302	361.9	Flour Bluff ISD	Corpus Christi
303	361.7	Seguin ISD	Seguin
304	361.4	Pampa ISD	Pampa
305	361.3	Van ISD	Van
306	360.5	Vernon ISD	Vernon
307	359.7	Southside ISD	San Antonio
308	359.4	Crockett ISD	Crockett
309	358.7	Lamar Consolidated ISD	Rosenberg
310	358.1	Hereford ISD	Hereford
311	358.0	Richardson ISD	Richardson
312	356.6	Floresville ISD	Floresville
313	356.1	Mercedes ISD	Mercedes
314	356.0	Fredericksburg ISD	Fredericksburg

315	355.9	North Forest ISD	Houston
316	354.8	Bay City ISD	Bay City
317	354.7	Glen Rose ISD	Glen Rose
318	352.5	Lewisville ISD	Flower Mound
319	352.3	Needville ISD	Needville
320	352.0	Northside ISD	San Antonio
320	352.0	Progreso ISD	Progreso
322	351.9	Bastrop ISD	Bastrop
323	350.9	Mineral Wells ISD	Mineral Wells
324	349.4	Liberty-Eylau ISD	Texarkana
325	348.3	Splendora ISD	Splendora
326	344.8	Aransas Pass ISD	Aransas Pass
327	344.0	Lubbock-Cooper ISD	Lubbock
328	341.1	Wilmer-Hutchins ISD	Dallas
329	340.8	Point Isabel ISD	Port Isabel
330	340.3	Alamo Heights ISD	San Antonio
331	338.6	Chapel Hill ISD	Tyler
332	338.4	Central ISD	Pollok
332	338.4	Kerrville ISD	Kerrville
334	338.1	Weslaco ISD	Weslaco
335	337.4	San Elizario ISD	San Elizario
336	337.1	Ennis ISD	Ennis
337	336.4	Texarkana ISD	Texarkana
338	335.9	Mission Cons ISD	Mission
339	335.4	Alice ISD	Alice
340	332.6	Gainesville ISD	Gainesville
341	331.9	Henderson ISD	Henderson
342	331.3	Brownsville ISD	Brownsville
343	330.8	Sanger ISD	Sanger
344	330.1	Uvalde Cons ISD	Uvalde
345	330.0	Brownfield ISD	Brownfield
346	329.0	Red Oak ISD	Red Oak
347	327.8	Cameron ISD	Cameron
348	326.8	Donna ISD	Donna
349	325.3	Eanes ISD	Austin
350	323.6	Gladewater ISD	Gladewater
351	321.8	Whitesboro ISD	Whitesboro
352	318.2	Caldwell ISD	Caldwell
353	318.0	Pleasanton ISD	Pleasanton
354	315.9	La Joya ISD	La Joya
355	315.7	Mathis ISD	Mathis
356	315.5	Sharyland ISD	Mission
357	313.2	Daingerfield-Lone Star Is	Daingerfield
358	310.6	Carrizo Springs Cons ISD	Carrizo Springs
359	301.0	Lyford CISD	Lyford
360	299.2	Duncanville ISD	Duncanville
361	297.1	Bridgeport ISD	Bridgeport
362	295.9	Crystal City ISD	Crystal City
363	292.4	Denison ISD	Denison
364	291.3	El Campo ISD	El Campo
365	290.7	Beeville ISD	Beeville
366	289.6	Robinson ISD	Robinson
367	289.5	Rio Grande City CISD	Rio Grande City
368	289.1	Fairfield ISD	Fairfield
369	287.5	Springtown ISD	Springtown
369	287.5	Zapata County ISD	Zapata
371	285.6	Sinton ISD	Sinton
372	283.4	Brownsboro ISD	Brownsboro
373	282.8	Dripping Springs ISD	Dripping Spgs
374	281.7	Levelland ISD	Levelland
374	281.7	Robstown ISD	Robstown
376	278.8	Kingsville ISD	Kingsville
377	277.2	Sealy ISD	Sealy
378	267.5	Hidalgo ISD	Hidalgo
379	261.3	Commerce ISD	Commerce
379	261.3	South Texas ISD	Mercedes
381	259.7	Hillsboro ISD	Hillsboro
382	253.3	Aransas County ISD	Rockport
383	232.4	Mcallen ISD	Mcallen
384	228.7	Pearsall ISD	Pearsall
385	224.9	Livingston ISD	Livingston
386	n/a	Honors Academy	Dallas

Current Spending per Student in FY2003

Rank	Dollars	District Name	City
1	11,767	South Texas ISD	Mercedes
2	9,509	Seminole ISD	Seminole
3	8,908	Glen Rose ISD	Glen Rose
4	8,869	West Orange-Cove Cons ISD	Orange
5	8,790	Wilmer-Hutchins ISD	Dallas
6	8,764	Fairfield ISD	Fairfield
7	8,735	Zapata County ISD	Zapata
8	8,682	Sanger ISD	Sanger
9	8,615	Andrews ISD	Andrews
10	8,539	Llano ISD	Llano
11	8,528	Hidalgo ISD	Hidalgo
12	8,516	Lyford CISD	Lyford
13	8,409	Mercedes ISD	Mercedes
14	8,336	Northwest ISD	Fort Worth
15	8,300	Brooks County ISD	Falfurrias
16	8,240	Cuero ISD	Cuero
17	8,164	Ft Stockton ISD	Ft Stockton
18	8,126	Sheldon ISD	Houston
19	8,120	Groesbeck ISD	Groesbeck
20	8,118	Hillsboro ISD	Hillsboro
21	8,108	Rio Grande City CISD	Rio Grande City
22	8,034	Mexia ISD	Mexia
23	7,980	Donna ISD	Donna
24	7,969	Crystal City ISD	Crystal City
25	7,956	Palacios ISD	Palacios
26	7,880	Caldwell ISD	Caldwell
26	7,880	San Antonio ISD	San Antonio
28	7,876	Mathis ISD	Mathis
29	7,868	Sweetwater ISD	Sweetwater
30	7,854	Commerce ISD	Commerce
31	7,852	Alamo Heights ISD	San Antonio
32	7,826	Manor ISD	Manor
33	7,825	Brownfield ISD	Brownfield
34	7,800	Levelland ISD	Levelland
35	7,791	La Vega ISD	Waco
36	7,765	Canutillo ISD	El Paso
37	7,764	Harlandale ISD	San Antonio
38	7,752	Carrizo Springs Cons ISD	Carrizo Springs
39	7,750	Connally ISD	Waco
40	7,730	Daingerfield-Lone Star Is	Daingerfield
41	7,699	Crockett ISD	Crockett
42	7,698	Bridgeport ISD	Bridgeport
43	7,689	Sinton ISD	Sinton
44	7,688	Progreso ISD	Progreso
45	7,685	Robstown ISD	Robstown
46	7,665	Marble Falls ISD	Marble Falls
47	7,651	Point Isabel ISD	Port Isabel
48	7,645	Liberty ISD	Liberty
49	7,624	West Oso ISD	Corpus Christi
50	7,618	Royal ISD	Brookshire
51	7,613	Ingram ISD	Ingram
52	7,609	San Elizario ISD	San Elizario
53	7,587	Edcouch-Elsa ISD	Edcouch
54	7,586	Rio Hondo ISD	Rio Hondo
55	7,584	San Diego ISD	San Diego
56	7,580	Austin ISD	Austin
57	7,576	Barbers Hill ISD	Mt Belvieu
58	7,575	Fabens ISD	Fabens
59	7,570	Mineral Wells ISD	Mineral Wells
60	7,560	Floresville ISD	Floresville
61	7,552	Killeen ISD	Killeen
62	7,546	Eanes ISD	Austin
63	7,529	Calhoun County ISD	Port Lavaca
64	7,517	Atlanta ISD	Atlanta
65	7,515	Brownsville ISD	Brownsville
66	7,512	Spring Branch ISD	Houston
67	7,501	Diboll ISD	Diboll
68	7,500	Aransas Pass ISD	Aransas Pass
69	7,486	Bonham ISD	Bonham
70	7,480	Midlothian ISD	Midlothian
70	7,480	Taylor ISD	Taylor
72	7,468	Pleasanton ISD	Pleasanton
73	7,467	Galveston ISD	Galveston
74	7,464	Sweeny ISD	Sweeny
75	7,443	Poteet ISD	Poteet
76	7,435	Dallas ISD	Dallas
77	7,432	Mission Cons ISD	Mission
78	7,429	Carthage ISD	Carthage
79	7,424	Giddings ISD	Giddings
80	7,419	Wimberley ISD	Wimberley
81	7,398	Port Arthur ISD	Port Arthur
82	7,379	Texas City ISD	Texas City
83	7,378	Kingsville ISD	Kingsville
84	7,375	Aransas County ISD	Rockport
85	7,368	Pharr-San Juan-Alamo ISD	Pharr
86	7,360	Montgomery ISD	Montgomery
87	7,352	Mount Pleasant ISD	Mt Pleasant
88	7,351	Somerset ISD	Somerset
89	7,348	Stafford Municipal School	Stafford
90	7,346	Paris ISD	Paris
91	7,344	Whitney ISD	Whitney
92	7,341	Wylie ISD	Wylie
93	7,326	Aldine ISD	Houston
93	7,326	Temple ISD	Temple
95	7,319	Terrell ISD	Terrell
96	7,313	Henderson ISD	Henderson
97	7,312	Edinburg CISD	Edinburg
98	7,310	Pearsall ISD	Pearsall
99	7,300	Denton ISD	Denton
100	7,293	Buna ISD	Buna
101	7,284	Rains ISD	Emory
102	7,266	Raymondville ISD	Raymondville
103	7,261	Silsbee ISD	Silsbee
104	7,242	Wharton ISD	Wharton
105	7,241	Carroll ISD	Grapevine
106	7,239	Edgewood ISD	San Antonio
107	7,236	Houston ISD	Houston
108	7,235	Little Elm ISD	Little Elm
109	7,234	Goose Creek CISD	Baytown
110	7,232	Roma ISD	Roma
111	7,225	Devine ISD	Devine
112	7,213	Pecos-Barstow-Toyah ISD	Pecos
113	7,211	Burnet Cons ISD	Burnet
114	7,207	Bastrop ISD	Bastrop
115	7,198	Del Valle ISD	Del Valle
115	7,198	El Paso ISD	El Paso
117	7,196	Bandera ISD	Bandera
118	7,185	Fredericksburg ISD	Fredericksburg
119	7,180	Lake Worth ISD	Lake Worth
120	7,167	Longview ISD	Longview
121	7,164	Bay City ISD	Bay City
122	7,163	Weslaco ISD	Weslaco
123	7,159	Brenham ISD	Brenham
124	7,157	Snyder ISD	Snyder
125	7,155	South San Antonio ISD	San Antonio
126	7,153	Mcallen ISD	Mcallen
127	7,152	Hutto ISD	Hutto
128	7,137	Yoakum ISD	Yoakum
129	7,136	Uvalde Cons ISD	Uvalde
130	7,129	Gainesville ISD	Gainesville
131	7,127	La Porte ISD	La Porte
132	7,114	Monahans-Wickett-Pyote Is	Monahans
133	7,112	Valley View ISD	Pharr
134	7,108	Copperas Cove ISD	Copperas Cove
135	7,105	Georgetown ISD	Georgetown
135	7,105	Hondo ISD	Hondo
137	7,104	East Central ISD	San Antonio
138	7,103	Quinlan ISD	Quinlan
139	7,102	Beeville ISD	Beeville
140	7,101	Highland Park ISD	Dallas
141	7,096	Boerne ISD	Boerne
142	7,089	San Marcos Cons ISD	San Marcos
143	7,083	Ferris ISD	Ferris
144	7,073	Plano ISD	Plano
145	7,067	Lamar Consolidated ISD	Rosenberg
146	7,059	North Forest ISD	Houston
147	7,051	Cameron ISD	Cameron
148	7,046	Columbia-Brazoria ISD	West Columbia
149	7,034	Fort Worth ISD	Fort Worth
150	7,033	Comal ISD	New Braunfels
150	7,033	Livingston ISD	Livingston
152	7,030	Sealy ISD	Sealy
153	7,022	La Feria ISD	La Feria
154	7,021	Cleveland ISD	Cleveland
154	7,021	Perryton ISD	Perryton
156	7,016	Breckenridge ISD	Breckenridge
156	7,016	Jasper ISD	Jasper
158	7,006	Liberty-Eylau ISD	Texarkana
158	7,006	San Felipe-Del Rio Cons I	Del Rio
160	7,003	Liberty Hill ISD	Liberty Hill
160	7,003	Smithville ISD	Smithville
162	6,997	La Marque ISD	La Marque
163	6,994	Gilmer ISD	Gilmer
164	6,992	Galena Park ISD	Houston
165	6,991	Lubbock ISD	Lubbock
166	6,987	Ennis ISD	Ennis
166	6,987	Lamesa ISD	Lamesa
166	6,987	Presidio ISD	Presidio
169	6,979	Abilene ISD	Abilene
170	6,978	Medina Valley ISD	Castroville
171	6,977	Frisco ISD	Frisco
172	6,970	Waxahachie ISD	Waxahachie
173	6,966	Crandall ISD	Crandall
174	6,965	Dalhart ISD	Dalhart
175	6,963	La Joya ISD	La Joya
176	6,962	Alice ISD	Alice
177	6,957	Carrollton-Farmers Branch	Carrollton
178	6,955	Port Neches-Groves ISD	Port Neches
179	6,951	North East ISD	San Antonio
180	6,950	Hays Cons ISD	Kyle
181	6,949	Laredo ISD	Laredo
181	6,949	Lytle ISD	Lytle
183	6,948	Palestine ISD	Palestine
184	6,936	Sulphur Springs ISD	Sulphur Springs
185	6,934	Hardin-Jefferson ISD	Sour Lake
186	6,933	Lockhart ISD	Lockhart
187	6,931	Los Fresnos Cons ISD	Los Fresnos
188	6,929	Lubbock-Cooper ISD	Lubbock
189	6,928	Aledo ISD	Aledo
190	6,922	Greenville ISD	Greenville
191	6,920	Coldspring-Oakhurst Cons	Coldspring
192	6,918	Seguin ISD	Seguin
193	6,909	Waller ISD	Waller
194	6,908	Wichita Falls ISD	Wichita Falls
195	6,905	College Station ISD	College Station
196	6,896	Crosby ISD	Crosby
196	6,896	Gladewater ISD	Gladewater
198	6,891	Madisonville Cons ISD	Madisonville
199	6,874	Vernon ISD	Vernon
200	6,872	Corpus Christi ISD	Corpus Christi
201	6,864	Beaumont ISD	Beaumont
202	6,854	Navasota ISD	Navasota

Rank	Number	District Name	City
203	6,852	Kemp ISD	Kemp
204	6,848	Rusk ISD	Rusk
205	6,847	San Benito Cons ISD	San Benito
206	6,845	Harlingen Cons ISD	Harlingen
207	6,844	Orange Grove ISD	Orange Grove
208	6,842	Victoria ISD	Victoria
209	6,838	Royse City ISD	Royse City
210	6,835	El Campo ISD	El Campo
211	6,822	Huntington ISD	Huntington
212	6,810	Jacksonville ISD	Jacksonville
213	6,808	Northside ISD	San Antonio
214	6,802	Weatherford ISD	Weatherford
215	6,799	Cypress-Fairbanks ISD	Houston
216	6,797	Springtown ISD	Springtown
217	6,793	Lake Travis ISD	Austin
217	6,793	Lancaster ISD	Lancaster
219	6,792	Needville ISD	Needville
220	6,789	Brownsboro ISD	Brownsboro
221	6,782	Robinson ISD	Robinson
222	6,779	Lake Dallas ISD	Lake Dallas
223	6,765	Burkburnett ISD	Burkburnett
224	6,762	Lewisville ISD	Flower Mound
225	6,761	Denison ISD	Denison
226	6,756	Ysleta ISD	El Paso
227	6,754	La Grange ISD	La Grange
228	6,751	Grand Prairie ISD	Grand Prairie
229	6,745	Round Rock ISD	Round Rock
230	6,743	Mabank ISD	Mabank
231	6,739	Deer Park ISD	Deer Park
232	6,737	Waco ISD	Waco
233	6,736	Southwest ISD	San Antonio
234	6,735	Forney ISD	Forney
235	6,734	Sherman ISD	Sherman
236	6,730	Shepherd ISD	Shepherd
237	6,727	Dripping Springs ISD	Dripping Spgs
238	6,726	Alvin ISD	Alvin
239	6,724	Mckinney ISD	Mckinney
240	6,715	Tyler ISD	Tyler
241	6,712	Borger ISD	Borger
242	6,697	Flour Bluff ISD	Corpus Christi
243	6,692	Van ISD	Van
244	6,690	Kaufman ISD	Kaufman
245	6,687	Athens ISD	Athens
246	6,686	Belton ISD	Belton
247	6,683	Edna ISD	Edna
248	6,682	Rockdale ISD	Rockdale
249	6,680	Hurst-Euless-Bedford ISD	Bedford
250	6,678	Elgin ISD	Elgin
251	6,677	Richardson ISD	Richardson
252	6,667	Vidor ISD	Vidor
253	6,662	Bryan ISD	Bryan
254	6,661	Spring ISD	Houston
255	6,660	Katy ISD	Katy
256	6,659	Southside ISD	San Antonio
257	6,656	Midland ISD	Midland
258	6,651	Splendora ISD	Splendora
259	6,641	Pampa ISD	Pampa
260	6,640	Grapevine-Colleyville ISD	Grapevine
261	6,637	Irving ISD	Irving
262	6,631	Huffman ISD	Huffman
263	6,624	Big Spring ISD	Big Spring
264	6,599	Gonzales ISD	Gonzales
264	6,599	Tomball ISD	Tomball
264	6,599	Whitesboro ISD	Whitesboro
267	6,598	Willis ISD	Willis
268	6,595	Amarillo ISD	Amarillo
269	6,588	Alief ISD	Houston
269	6,588	Coppell ISD	Coppell
271	6,587	Eagle Pass ISD	Eagle Pass
272	6,582	Nacogdoches ISD	Nacogdoches
273	6,578	Chapel Hill ISD	Tyler
274	6,577	Brazosport ISD	Freeport
275	6,571	Leander ISD	Leander
276	6,570	Hallsville ISD	Hallsville
277	6,564	Castleberry ISD	Fort Worth
278	6,563	New Caney ISD	New Caney
279	6,555	Luling ISD	Luling
280	6,553	Decatur ISD	Decatur
281	6,552	Duncanville ISD	Duncanville
281	6,552	Hereford ISD	Hereford
283	6,549	Conroe ISD	Conroe
284	6,544	Brownwood ISD	Brownwood
285	6,527	Kerrville ISD	Kerrville
286	6,520	Lampasas ISD	Lampasas
287	6,517	Magnolia ISD	Magnolia
288	6,512	Granbury ISD	Granbury
289	6,507	Lufkin ISD	Lufkin
290	6,504	Pittsburg ISD	Pittsburg
291	6,502	Texarkana ISD	Texarkana
292	6,501	Eustace ISD	Eustace
293	6,500	Dickinson ISD	Dickinson
293	6,500	Fort Bend ISD	Sugar Land
295	6,497	Crowley ISD	Crowley
295	6,497	Tuloso-Midway ISD	Corpus Christi
297	6,496	United ISD	Laredo
298	6,486	Judson ISD	San Antonio
299	6,484	Birdville ISD	Haltom City
300	6,476	Wills Point ISD	Wills Point
301	6,474	Pearland ISD	Pearland
302	6,471	Little Cypress-Mauricevil	Orange
303	6,466	Cleburne ISD	Cleburne
304	6,450	Hamshire-Fannett ISD	Hamshire
305	6,442	Canton ISD	Canton
305	6,442	Joshua ISD	Joshua
307	6,439	Center ISD	Center
308	6,438	Bowie ISD	Bowie
309	6,421	Channelview ISD	Channelview
310	6,418	La Vernia ISD	La Vernia
311	6,416	Azle ISD	Azle
311	6,416	Mineola ISD	Mineola
313	6,413	Orangefield ISD	Orangefield
314	6,405	Bellville ISD	Bellville
315	6,389	Columbus ISD	Columbus
316	6,385	Princeton ISD	Princeton
317	6,377	White Settlement ISD	White Settlement
318	6,363	Lumberton ISD	Lumberton
319	6,360	Calallen ISD	Corpus Christi
319	6,360	Kilgore ISD	Kilgore
321	6,344	Corsicana ISD	Corsicana
322	6,337	Lindale ISD	Lindale
323	6,312	Everman ISD	Everman
324	6,287	Mesquite ISD	Mesquite
325	6,284	Socorro ISD	El Paso
326	6,277	Marshall ISD	Marshall
327	6,272	Klein ISD	Klein
328	6,267	Pflugerville ISD	Pflugerville
329	6,264	Red Oak ISD	Red Oak
330	6,261	Sharyland ISD	Mission
331	6,245	Schertz-Cibolo-U City ISD	Schertz
332	6,244	Tarkington ISD	Cleveland
333	6,238	Allen ISD	Allen
334	6,235	Clint ISD	El Paso
335	6,232	Midway ISD	Waco
336	6,227	Humble ISD	Humble
337	6,224	Plainview ISD	Plainview
338	6,220	Huntsville ISD	Huntsville
339	6,215	Pasadena ISD	Pasadena
340	6,209	Westwood ISD	Palestine
341	6,206	Burleson ISD	Burleson
342	6,190	San Angelo ISD	San Angelo
343	6,185	Venus ISD	Venus
344	6,177	Kirbyville CISD	Kirbyville
345	6,171	Desoto ISD	Desoto
346	6,168	Friendswood ISD	Friendswood
347	6,163	Pine Tree ISD	Longview
348	6,151	Clear Creek ISD	League City
349	6,139	Nederland ISD	Nederland
350	6,138	Ector County ISD	Odessa
351	6,130	Hudson ISD	Lufkin
351	6,130	New Braunfels ISD	New Braunfels
353	6,127	Cedar Hill ISD	Cedar Hill
354	6,121	Mansfield ISD	Mansfield
355	6,119	Bridge City ISD	Bridge City
356	6,115	Arlington ISD	Arlington
357	6,082	Graham ISD	Graham
358	6,074	Rockwall ISD	Rockwall
359	6,073	Frenship ISD	Wolfforth
360	6,048	Greenwood ISD	Midland
361	6,038	Bullard ISD	Bullard
362	6,035	Dumas ISD	Dumas
363	6,032	Eagle Mt-Saginaw ISD	Fort Worth
364	6,021	Stephenville ISD	Stephenville
365	6,007	Alvarado ISD	Alvarado
366	5,977	Central ISD	Pollok
367	5,968	Iowa Park Cons ISD	Iowa Park
367	5,968	North Lamar ISD	Paris
369	5,966	Ingleside ISD	Ingleside
370	5,963	Angleton ISD	Angleton
371	5,920	Dayton ISD	Dayton
372	5,836	Pleasant Grove ISD	Texarkana
373	5,812	Santa Fe ISD	Santa Fe
374	5,763	Garland ISD	Garland
375	5,723	Kennedale ISD	Kennedale
376	5,710	West ISD	West
377	5,669	Gatesville ISD	Gatesville
378	5,664	Whitehouse ISD	Whitehouse
379	5,655	Canyon ISD	Canyon
380	5,618	Spring Hill ISD	Longview
381	5,606	Gregory-Portland ISD	Gregory
382	5,591	Keller ISD	Keller
383	5,354	China Spring ISD	Waco
384	4,986	Lorena ISD	Lorena
385	4,913	Wylie ISD	Abilene
386	4,097	Honors Academy	Dallas

Number of Diploma Recipients

Rank	Number	District Name	City
1	7,945	Houston ISD	Houston
2	6,532	Dallas ISD	Dallas
3	3,938	Cypress-Fairbanks ISD	Houston
4	3,928	Northside ISD	San Antonio
5	3,705	Austin ISD	Austin
6	3,630	Fort Bend ISD	Sugar Land
7	3,353	El Paso ISD	El Paso
8	3,222	Fort Worth ISD	Fort Worth
9	3,208	North East ISD	San Antonio
10	2,875	Arlington ISD	Arlington
11	2,842	Ysleta ISD	El Paso
12	2,795	Plano ISD	Plano
13	2,727	San Antonio ISD	San Antonio
14	2,689	Garland ISD	Garland
15	2,267	Lewisville ISD	Flower Mound
16	2,202	Conroe ISD	Conroe
17	2,149	Aldine ISD	Houston
18	2,119	Corpus Christi ISD	Corpus Christi
19	2,112	Katy ISD	Katy
19	2,112	Klein ISD	Klein
21	2,028	Pasadena ISD	Pasadena
22	1,977	Round Rock ISD	Round Rock
23	1,960	Alief ISD	Houston
24	1,956	Mesquite ISD	Mesquite
25	1,891	Richardson ISD	Richardson
26	1,854	Brownsville ISD	Brownsville
27	1,844	Clear Creek ISD	League City
28	1,751	Spring Branch ISD	Houston
29	1,737	Lubbock ISD	Lubbock
30	1,653	Humble ISD	Humble
31	1,544	Amarillo ISD	Amarillo
32	1,533	Socorro ISD	El Paso
33	1,478	Ector County ISD	Odessa
34	1,360	United ISD	Laredo
35	1,358	Killeen ISD	Killeen
36	1,334	Spring ISD	Houston
37	1,308	Irving ISD	Irving
38	1,277	Carrollton-Farmers Branch	Carrollton
39	1,270	Mcallen ISD	Mcallen
40	1,227	Hurst-Euless-Bedford ISD	Bedford
41	1,207	Midland ISD	Midland
42	1,164	Birdville ISD	Haltom City
43	1,153	Beaumont ISD	Beaumont
44	1,080	Laredo ISD	Laredo
45	1,077	Galena Park ISD	Houston
46	1,071	Wichita Falls ISD	Wichita Falls
47	1,045	Pharr-San Juan-Alamo ISD	Pharr
48	1,038	Edinburg CISD	Edinburg
49	1,035	Grand Prairie ISD	Grand Prairie
50	1,032	Abilene ISD	Abilene
51	1,013	Keller ISD	Keller
52	960	San Angelo ISD	San Angelo
53	956	Grapevine-Colleyville ISD	Grapevine
54	901	Tyler ISD	Tyler
55	899	Goose Creek CISD	Baytown
56	867	Victoria ISD	Victoria
57	864	Pflugerville ISD	Pflugerville
58	842	Judson ISD	San Antonio
59	807	Harlingen Cons ISD	Harlingen
60	800	Harlandale ISD	San Antonio
61	796	Lamar Consolidated ISD	Rosenberg
62	791	Mansfield ISD	Mansfield
63	765	La Joya ISD	La Joya
63	765	Leander ISD	Leander
65	739	Allen ISD	Allen
66	733	Brazosport ISD	Freeport
67	720	Denton ISD	Denton
68	707	Duncanville ISD	Duncanville
69	699	Bryan ISD	Bryan
70	681	Comal ISD	New Braunfels
71	678	Deer Park ISD	Deer Park
72	628	Pearland ISD	Pearland
73	622	Edgewood ISD	San Antonio
74	611	Weslaco ISD	Weslaco
75	604	Mckinney ISD	Mckinney
76	603	Crowley ISD	Crowley
77	588	Waco ISD	Waco
78	582	Eagle Pass ISD	Eagle Pass
79	569	Mission Cons ISD	Mission
80	547	Port Arthur ISD	Port Arthur
81	542	Coppell ISD	Coppell
82	530	Georgetown ISD	Georgetown
83	528	Eanes ISD	Austin
84	512	College Station ISD	College Station
85	509	Alvin ISD	Alvin
86	505	North Forest ISD	Houston
87	497	Canyon ISD	Canyon
88	492	East Central ISD	San Antonio
88	492	Rockwall ISD	Rockwall
90	485	Hays Cons ISD	Kyle

Rank		District	City
91	482	San Felipe-Del Rio Cons I	Del Rio
92	476	Lufkin ISD	Lufkin
92	476	Southwest ISD	San Antonio
94	474	South San Antonio ISD	San Antonio
95	472	La Porte ISD	La Porte
96	467	Schertz-Cibolo-U City ISD	Schertz
97	463	Belton ISD	Belton
98	449	Copperas Cove ISD	Copperas Cove
99	441	Temple ISD	Temple
100	439	Carroll ISD	Grapevine
101	435	Tomball ISD	Tomball
102	429	Donna ISD	Donna
103	428	Magnolia ISD	Magnolia
104	420	Rio Grande City CISD	Rio Grande City
105	419	Galveston ISD	Galveston
106	414	Highland Park ISD	Dallas
107	413	Burleson ISD	Burleson
107	413	New Braunfels ISD	New Braunfels
109	410	Weatherford ISD	Weatherford
110	407	San Marcos Cons ISD	San Marcos
111	406	Clint ISD	El Paso
111	406	Eagle Mt-Saginaw ISD	Fort Worth
111	406	Longview ISD	Longview
114	399	Nacogdoches ISD	Nacogdoches
114	399	San Benito Cons ISD	San Benito
116	390	Waxahachie ISD	Waxahachie
117	386	Desoto ISD	Desoto
118	384	Seguin ISD	Seguin
119	382	Cedar Hill ISD	Cedar Hill
119	382	Midway ISD	Waco
121	381	Friendswood ISD	Friendswood
122	374	Marshall ISD	Marshall
122	374	Plainview ISD	Plainview
122	374	Port Neches-Groves ISD	Port Neches
125	369	Los Fresnos Cons ISD	Los Fresnos
126	358	Kingsville ISD	Kingsville
127	357	Huntsville ISD	Huntsville
128	355	Azle ISD	Azle
129	353	Boerne ISD	Boerne
129	353	South Texas ISD	Mercedes
131	347	Alamo Heights ISD	San Antonio
132	346	Granbury ISD	Granbury
133	340	Bastrop ISD	Bastrop
134	338	Brenham ISD	Brenham
135	337	Vidor ISD	Vidor
136	334	Frenship ISD	Wolfforth
136	334	Frisco ISD	Frisco
138	326	Nederland ISD	Nederland
139	324	Flour Bluff ISD	Corpus Christi
140	321	Calallen ISD	Corpus Christi
141	318	Angleton ISD	Angleton
142	311	Cleburne ISD	Cleburne
143	302	Del Valle ISD	Del Valle
143	302	Kerrville ISD	Kerrville
145	301	Channelview ISD	Channelview
146	300	Pine Tree ISD	Longview
146	300	Sherman ISD	Sherman
148	291	Roma ISD	Roma
149	289	Greenville ISD	Greenville
150	285	Lockhart ISD	Lockhart
150	285	Northwest ISD	Fort Worth
152	283	White Settlement ISD	White Settlement
153	281	Waller ISD	Waller
154	279	Edcouch-Elsa ISD	Edcouch
155	277	New Caney ISD	New Caney
156	276	Texarkana ISD	Texarkana
157	274	Gregory-Portland ISD	Gregory
158	273	Little Cypress-Mauricevil	Orange
158	273	Uvalde Cons ISD	Uvalde
160	271	Bay City ISD	Bay City
161	270	Corsicana ISD	Corsicana
161	270	Mount Pleasant ISD	Mt Pleasant
163	269	Alice ISD	Alice
163	269	Lake Travis ISD	Austin
165	268	Hereford ISD	Hereford
166	264	Southside ISD	San Antonio
166	264	Texas City ISD	Texas City
166	264	Whitehouse ISD	Whitehouse
169	260	Ennis ISD	Ennis
170	259	Willis ISD	Willis
171	258	Midlothian ISD	Midlothian
172	257	Sharyland ISD	Mission
173	256	Mercedes ISD	Mercedes
174	254	Sulphur Springs ISD	Sulphur Springs
175	253	Pampa ISD	Pampa
176	252	Lancaster ISD	Lancaster
177	250	Brownwood ISD	Brownwood
177	250	Livingston ISD	Livingston
179	249	Joshua ISD	Joshua
179	249	Red Oak ISD	Red Oak
181	247	Dayton ISD	Dayton
181	247	Dickinson ISD	Dickinson
183	243	Dumas ISD	Dumas
184	241	La Marque ISD	La Marque
184	241	Santa Fe ISD	Santa Fe
186	239	El Campo ISD	El Campo
186	239	Jacksonville ISD	Jacksonville
188	237	Hallsville ISD	Hallsville
189	235	Wylie ISD	Wylie
190	233	Canutillo ISD	El Paso
191	230	Burkburnett ISD	Burkburnett
191	230	Dripping Springs ISD	Dripping Spgs
191	230	Henderson ISD	Henderson
194	227	Big Spring ISD	Big Spring
194	227	Kilgore ISD	Kilgore
196	226	Denison ISD	Denison
197	225	Calhoun County ISD	Port Lavaca
197	225	Honors Academy	Dallas
199	224	Stephenville ISD	Stephenville
200	223	Beeville ISD	Beeville
200	223	Tuloso-Midway ISD	Corpus Christi
202	222	Lumberton ISD	Lumberton
203	221	Andrews ISD	Andrews
204	219	Crosby ISD	Crosby
204	219	Fredericksburg ISD	Fredericksburg
206	218	Aledo ISD	Aledo
207	215	Pleasanton ISD	Pleasanton
208	212	Lampasas ISD	Lampasas
209	210	Aransas County ISD	Rockport
210	208	Silsbee ISD	Silsbee
210	208	Terrell ISD	Terrell
212	207	Floresville ISD	Floresville
213	204	Montgomery ISD	Montgomery
214	203	North Lamar ISD	Paris
215	202	Chapel Hill ISD	Tyler
215	202	Medina Valley ISD	Castroville
217	201	Borger ISD	Borger
217	201	Palestine ISD	Palestine
219	199	Levelland ISD	Levelland
219	199	Robstown ISD	Robstown
219	199	Sheldon ISD	Houston
222	198	Bridge City ISD	Bridge City
223	197	Navasota ISD	Navasota
224	196	Alvarado ISD	Alvarado
224	196	Carthage ISD	Carthage
226	194	Wylie ISD	Abilene
227	193	Marble Falls ISD	Marble Falls
228	192	Athens ISD	Athens
228	192	Jasper ISD	Jasper
230	190	Mineral Wells ISD	Mineral Wells
231	185	Columbia-Brazoria ISD	West Columbia
232	184	Zapata County ISD	Zapata
233	183	Pecos-Barstow-Toyah ISD	Pecos
234	182	Huffman ISD	Huffman
235	181	West Orange-Cove Cons ISD	Orange
236	179	Stafford Municipal School	Stafford
236	179	Wharton ISD	Wharton
238	178	Castleberry ISD	Fort Worth
238	178	Decatur ISD	Decatur
240	177	Mabank ISD	Mabank
241	176	Forney ISD	Forney
242	175	Paris ISD	Paris
243	174	Springtown ISD	Springtown
243	174	Taylor ISD	Taylor
245	172	Ft Stockton ISD	Ft Stockton
245	172	Lindale ISD	Lindale
245	172	Snyder ISD	Snyder
248	171	Lamesa ISD	Lamesa
249	170	Needville ISD	Needville
250	169	Burnet Cons ISD	Burnet
251	168	Lake Dallas ISD	Lake Dallas
252	167	La Feria ISD	La Feria
253	166	Gilmer ISD	Gilmer
254	164	Elgin ISD	Elgin
254	164	Liberty-Eylau ISD	Texarkana
254	164	Raymondville ISD	Raymondville
257	163	Brownfield ISD	Brownfield
257	163	Fabens ISD	Fabens
259	162	Cleveland ISD	Cleveland
259	162	Quinlan ISD	Quinlan
261	159	Wills Point ISD	Wills Point
262	158	Cuero ISD	Cuero
262	158	Vernon ISD	Vernon
264	157	Gatesville ISD	Gatesville
264	157	San Elizario ISD	San Elizario
266	156	Sweeny ISD	Sweeny
267	155	Kaufman ISD	Kaufman
267	155	Sanger ISD	Sanger
269	153	Graham ISD	Graham
269	153	Liberty ISD	Liberty
269	153	Robinson ISD	Robinson
272	150	Hidalgo ISD	Hidalgo
272	150	Sweetwater ISD	Sweetwater
274	149	Point Isabel ISD	Port Isabel
275	147	Bellville ISD	Bellville
275	147	Connally ISD	Waco
275	147	Gonzales ISD	Gonzales
275	147	Wimberley ISD	Wimberley
279	146	Bandera ISD	Bandera
279	146	Gainesville ISD	Gainesville
281	143	Barbers Hill ISD	Mt Belvieu
281	143	Brownsboro ISD	Brownsboro
283	141	La Vernia ISD	La Vernia
283	141	Manor ISD	Manor
285	140	West ISD	West
286	139	Devine ISD	Devine
286	139	Hardin-Jefferson ISD	Sour Lake
286	139	Monahans-Wickett-Pyote Is	Monahans
289	137	Bridgeport ISD	Bridgeport
290	136	Iowa Park Cons ISD	Iowa Park
291	135	Atlanta ISD	Atlanta
291	135	Carrizo Springs Cons ISD	Carrizo Springs
293	134	Kennedale ISD	Kennedale
294	133	Gladewater ISD	Gladewater
294	133	Greenwood ISD	Midland
296	131	Aransas Pass ISD	Aransas Pass
296	131	Hudson ISD	Lufkin
298	130	La Grange ISD	La Grange
298	130	Pleasant Grove ISD	Texarkana
300	129	Center ISD	Center
301	128	Perryton ISD	Perryton
301	128	Sealy ISD	Sealy
301	128	Seminole ISD	Seminole
304	127	Everman ISD	Everman
304	127	La Vega ISD	Waco
304	127	Royse City ISD	Royse City
304	127	Somerset ISD	Somerset
308	126	Ingleside ISD	Ingleside
309	125	Hondo ISD	Hondo
309	125	Mathis ISD	Mathis
309	125	Splendora ISD	Splendora
312	124	Caldwell ISD	Caldwell
312	124	Mexia ISD	Mexia
314	123	China Spring ISD	Waco
314	123	Giddings ISD	Giddings
316	122	Crandall ISD	Crandall
317	121	Van ISD	Van
318	120	Hamshire-Fannett ISD	Hamshire
318	120	Pearsall ISD	Pearsall
318	120	Tarkington ISD	Cleveland
321	119	Breckenridge ISD	Breckenridge
321	119	Cameron ISD	Cameron
321	119	Kirbyville CISD	Kirbyville
324	117	Commerce ISD	Commerce
324	117	Lake Worth ISD	Lake Worth
324	117	Lyford CISD	Lyford
327	116	Crockett ISD	Crockett
328	115	Madisonville Cons ISD	Madisonville
329	113	Groesbeck ISD	Groesbeck
329	113	Hillsboro ISD	Hillsboro
329	113	Palacios ISD	Palacios
332	111	Brooks County ISD	Falfurrias
332	111	Lubbock-Cooper ISD	Lubbock
332	111	Sinton ISD	Sinton
335	109	Rio Hondo ISD	Rio Hondo
335	109	Spring Hill ISD	Longview
337	108	Edna ISD	Edna
337	108	Huntington ISD	Huntington
339	107	Central ISD	Pollok
340	106	Bonham ISD	Bonham
341	105	Canton ISD	Canton
341	105	Pittsburg ISD	Pittsburg
343	104	Diboll ISD	Diboll
343	104	Fairfield ISD	Fairfield
343	104	Little Elm ISD	Little Elm
343	104	Rusk ISD	Rusk
347	103	Glen Rose ISD	Glen Rose
347	103	Smithville ISD	Smithville
349	102	Wilmer-Hutchins ISD	Dallas
350	101	Lorena ISD	Lorena
351	100	Orangefield ISD	Orangefield
351	100	Venus ISD	Venus
351	100	Whitney ISD	Whitney
354	99	Poteet ISD	Poteet
355	98	Columbus ISD	Columbus
355	98	Ferris ISD	Ferris
357	97	Bowie ISD	Bowie
357	97	Princeton ISD	Princeton
359	96	Buna ISD	Buna
359	96	Orange Grove ISD	Orange Grove
359	96	Rockdale ISD	Rockdale
362	94	Mineola ISD	Mineola
362	94	Shepherd ISD	Shepherd
364	93	Rains ISD	Emory
365	92	Llano ISD	Llano
366	91	Coldspring-Oakhurst Cons	Coldspring
366	91	Progreso ISD	Progreso

Rank		District Name	City
366	91	San Diego ISD	San Diego
366	91	Valley View ISD	Pharr
366	91	Westwood ISD	Palestine
371	90	Lytle ISD	Lytle
372	89	Daingerfield-Lone Star Is	Daingerfield
372	89	Presidio ISD	Presidio
374	88	Whitesboro ISD	Whitesboro
374	88	Yoakum ISD	Yoakum
376	87	Crystal City ISD	Crystal City
376	87	Ingram ISD	Ingram
378	86	Luling ISD	Luling
379	83	Liberty Hill ISD	Liberty Hill
380	82	Kemp ISD	Kemp
381	81	Bullard ISD	Bullard
382	75	Eustace ISD	Eustace
383	70	Hutto ISD	Hutto
383	70	Royal ISD	Brookshire
385	67	Dalhart ISD	Dalhart
386	56	West Oso ISD	Corpus Christi

High School Drop-out Rate

Rank	Percent	District Name	City
1	18.9	Diboll ISD	Diboll
2	9.5	Honors Academy	Dallas
3	9.0	Ector County ISD	Odessa
4	8.8	Rio Grande City CISD	Rio Grande City
5	8.3	La Vega ISD	Waco
6	8.2	Robstown ISD	Robstown
7	8.1	Crystal City ISD	Crystal City
7	8.1	Waco ISD	Waco
9	8.0	Zapata County ISD	Zapata
10	7.8	Roma ISD	Roma
11	7.6	Dickinson ISD	Dickinson
11	7.6	La Joya ISD	La Joya
13	7.3	Greenville ISD	Greenville
14	7.2	Edcouch-Elsa ISD	Edcouch
15	7.1	Presidio ISD	Presidio
15	7.1	San Antonio ISD	San Antonio
17	7.0	North Forest ISD	Houston
18	6.8	Carrizo Springs Cons ISD	Carrizo Springs
19	6.7	Galveston ISD	Galveston
19	6.7	Texas City ISD	Texas City
21	6.5	Donna ISD	Donna
21	6.5	Fort Worth ISD	Fort Worth
21	6.5	Hillsboro ISD	Hillsboro
24	6.1	Crockett ISD	Crockett
24	6.1	Edgewood ISD	San Antonio
24	6.1	Mission Cons ISD	Mission
24	6.1	Pharr-San Juan-Alamo ISD	Pharr
24	6.1	Uvalde Cons ISD	Uvalde
29	6.0	Austin ISD	Austin
29	6.0	Houston ISD	Houston
29	6.0	Sweetwater ISD	Sweetwater
32	5.9	Raymondville ISD	Raymondville
33	5.8	Aldine ISD	Houston
34	5.7	Lampasas ISD	Lampasas
35	5.6	Mercedes ISD	Mercedes
35	5.6	South San Antonio ISD	San Antonio
35	5.6	Ysleta ISD	El Paso
38	5.5	Eagle Pass ISD	Eagle Pass
38	5.5	Marshall ISD	Marshall
38	5.5	Mathis ISD	Mathis
38	5.5	Midland ISD	Midland
38	5.5	Southwest ISD	San Antonio
43	5.4	Alice ISD	Alice
43	5.4	Denison ISD	Denison
43	5.4	Pasadena ISD	Pasadena
43	5.4	San Benito Cons ISD	San Benito
43	5.4	Splendora ISD	Splendora
48	5.3	Canutillo ISD	El Paso
48	5.3	Kerrville ISD	Kerrville
48	5.3	Kilgore ISD	Kilgore
48	5.3	Royse City ISD	Royse City
52	5.2	Daingerfield-Lone Star Is	Daingerfield
52	5.2	Joshua ISD	Joshua
52	5.2	Progreso ISD	Progreso
52	5.2	Weslaco ISD	Weslaco
56	5.1	Alvin ISD	Alvin
56	5.1	Dallas ISD	Dallas
56	5.1	Goose Creek CISD	Baytown
56	5.1	Monahans-Wickett-Pyote Is	Monahans
56	5.1	Texarkana ISD	Texarkana
56	5.1	West Orange-Cove Cons ISD	Orange
62	4.9	Abilene ISD	Abilene
62	4.9	Port Arthur ISD	Port Arthur
62	4.9	Santa Fe ISD	Santa Fe
65	4.8	Breckenridge ISD	Breckenridge
65	4.8	Castleberry ISD	Fort Worth
65	4.8	Corpus Christi ISD	Corpus Christi
65	4.8	Del Valle ISD	Del Valle
65	4.8	Harlingen Cons ISD	Harlingen
65	4.8	Mcallen ISD	Mcallen
65	4.8	Plainview ISD	Plainview
65	4.8	San Felipe-Del Rio Cons I	Del Rio
65	4.8	Southside ISD	San Antonio
65	4.8	White Settlement ISD	White Settlement
75	4.7	Columbia-Brazoria ISD	West Columbia
75	4.7	Cuero ISD	Cuero
75	4.7	Denton ISD	Denton
78	4.6	Dalhart ISD	Dalhart
78	4.6	Kingsville ISD	Kingsville
78	4.6	Laredo ISD	Laredo
78	4.6	Lufkin ISD	Lufkin
78	4.6	San Elizario ISD	San Elizario
83	4.5	Alvarado ISD	Alvarado
83	4.5	Big Spring ISD	Big Spring
83	4.5	Brooks County ISD	Falfurrias
83	4.5	Corsicana ISD	Corsicana
83	4.5	Manor ISD	Manor
83	4.5	Mexia ISD	Mexia
89	4.4	Beaumont ISD	Beaumont
89	4.4	Brownwood ISD	Brownwood
89	4.4	Dayton ISD	Dayton
89	4.4	Harlandale ISD	San Antonio
89	4.4	Luling ISD	Luling
89	4.4	Tyler ISD	Tyler
95	4.3	Bastrop ISD	Bastrop
95	4.3	La Marque ISD	La Marque
95	4.3	Levelland ISD	Levelland
95	4.3	Nacogdoches ISD	Nacogdoches
95	4.3	San Angelo ISD	San Angelo
95	4.3	Victoria ISD	Victoria
101	4.2	Clint ISD	El Paso
101	4.2	Coldspring-Oakhurst Cons	Coldspring
101	4.2	Fabens ISD	Fabens
101	4.2	Gainesville ISD	Gainesville
101	4.2	Wilmer-Hutchins ISD	Dallas
106	4.1	Beeville ISD	Beeville
106	4.1	Brazosport ISD	Freeport
106	4.1	Brownsville ISD	Brownsville
106	4.1	El Paso ISD	El Paso
106	4.1	Ft Stockton ISD	Ft Stockton
106	4.1	Pecos-Barstow-Toyah ISD	Pecos
106	4.1	Sheldon ISD	Houston
106	4.1	West Oso ISD	Corpus Christi
114	4.0	San Marcos Cons ISD	San Marcos
115	3.9	Huntington ISD	Huntington
115	3.9	Pampa ISD	Pampa
117	3.8	Bandera ISD	Bandera
117	3.8	Hudson ISD	Lufkin
117	3.8	Lubbock ISD	Lubbock
117	3.8	Pleasanton ISD	Pleasanton
117	3.8	Rusk ISD	Rusk
117	3.8	Seguin ISD	Seguin
123	3.7	Central ISD	Pollok
123	3.7	Grand Prairie ISD	Grand Prairie
123	3.7	Iowa Park Cons ISD	Iowa Park
126	3.6	Caldwell ISD	Caldwell
126	3.6	Calhoun County ISD	Port Lavaca
126	3.6	Edna ISD	Edna
126	3.6	Lyford CISD	Lyford
126	3.6	Mineral Wells ISD	Mineral Wells
126	3.6	New Braunfels ISD	New Braunfels
132	3.5	Edinburg CISD	Edinburg
132	3.5	Killeen ISD	Killeen
132	3.5	Terrell ISD	Terrell
132	3.5	Valley View ISD	Pharr
136	3.4	Granbury ISD	Granbury
136	3.4	Hereford ISD	Hereford
136	3.4	Lake Worth ISD	Lake Worth
136	3.4	Lytle ISD	Lytle
136	3.4	Rio Hondo ISD	Rio Hondo
141	3.3	Alief ISD	Houston
141	3.3	Athens ISD	Athens
141	3.3	Azle ISD	Azle
141	3.3	Burkburnett ISD	Burkburnett
141	3.3	Irving ISD	Irving
141	3.3	Longview ISD	Longview
141	3.3	Los Fresnos Cons ISD	Los Fresnos
141	3.3	Marble Falls ISD	Marble Falls
141	3.3	Medina Valley ISD	Castroville
141	3.3	New Caney ISD	New Caney
141	3.3	Point Isabel ISD	Port Isabel
141	3.3	Rockdale ISD	Rockdale
141	3.3	Vernon ISD	Vernon
154	3.2	Borger ISD	Borger
154	3.2	Bowie ISD	Bowie
154	3.2	Gatesville ISD	Gatesville
154	3.2	Hays Cons ISD	Kyle
154	3.2	Lamar Consolidated ISD	Rosenberg
154	3.2	Liberty-Eylau ISD	Texarkana
154	3.2	Livingston ISD	Livingston
154	3.2	Nederland ISD	Nederland
154	3.2	Somerset ISD	Somerset
154	3.2	Spring Branch ISD	Houston
154	3.2	Springtown ISD	Springtown
165	3.1	Amarillo ISD	Amarillo
165	3.1	Connally ISD	Waco
165	3.1	Poteet ISD	Poteet
165	3.1	Sherman ISD	Sherman
165	3.1	Silsbee ISD	Silsbee
165	3.1	Snyder ISD	Snyder
171	3.0	Channelview ISD	Channelview
171	3.0	Cleveland ISD	Cleveland
171	3.0	Crosby ISD	Crosby
171	3.0	Galena Park ISD	Houston
171	3.0	Northside ISD	San Antonio
171	3.0	Pearsall ISD	Pearsall
171	3.0	Temple ISD	Temple
178	2.9	Aransas Pass ISD	Aransas Pass
178	2.9	Brenham ISD	Brenham
178	2.9	Bullard ISD	Bullard
178	2.9	Dumas ISD	Dumas
178	2.9	Gilmer ISD	Gilmer
178	2.9	Hidalgo ISD	Hidalgo
178	2.9	Ingram ISD	Ingram
178	2.9	Judson ISD	San Antonio
178	2.9	Mesquite ISD	Mesquite
178	2.9	Palestine ISD	Palestine
178	2.9	Pearland ISD	Pearland
178	2.9	Pittsburg ISD	Pittsburg
178	2.9	San Diego ISD	San Diego
178	2.9	Sinton ISD	Sinton
178	2.9	Spring ISD	Houston
178	2.9	Waller ISD	Waller
194	2.8	Bonham ISD	Bonham
194	2.8	Brownfield ISD	Brownfield
194	2.8	Copperas Cove ISD	Copperas Cove
194	2.8	Eagle Mt-Saginaw ISD	Fort Worth
194	2.8	Floresville ISD	Floresville
194	2.8	Kennedale ISD	Kennedale
194	2.8	Llano ISD	Llano
194	2.8	Mount Pleasant ISD	Mt Pleasant
194	2.8	Red Oak ISD	Red Oak
203	2.7	Arlington ISD	Arlington
203	2.7	Buna ISD	Buna
203	2.7	Devine ISD	Devine
203	2.7	Huntsville ISD	Huntsville
203	2.7	Lockhart ISD	Lockhart
203	2.7	Mckinney ISD	Mckinney
203	2.7	Vidor ISD	Vidor
210	2.6	Comal ISD	New Braunfels
210	2.6	East Central ISD	San Antonio
210	2.6	Georgetown ISD	Georgetown
210	2.6	Kemp ISD	Kemp
210	2.6	Needville ISD	Needville
210	2.6	Princeton ISD	Princeton
210	2.6	Quinlan ISD	Quinlan
210	2.6	Schertz-Cibolo-U City ISD	Schertz
210	2.6	Smithville ISD	Smithville
210	2.6	Whitehouse ISD	Whitehouse
210	2.6	Whitney ISD	Whitney
221	2.5	Andrews ISD	Andrews
221	2.5	Aransas County ISD	Rockport
221	2.5	Eustace ISD	Eustace
221	2.5	Ferris ISD	Ferris
221	2.5	Klein ISD	Klein
221	2.5	La Porte ISD	La Porte
221	2.5	Mineola ISD	Mineola
228	2.4	Brownsboro ISD	Brownsboro
228	2.4	Chapel Hill ISD	Tyler
228	2.4	Flour Bluff ISD	Corpus Christi
228	2.4	Navasota ISD	Navasota
228	2.4	North Lamar ISD	Paris
228	2.4	Northwest ISD	Fort Worth
228	2.4	Sealy ISD	Sealy
228	2.4	Van ISD	Van
228	2.4	Weatherford ISD	Weatherford
237	2.3	Calallen ISD	Corpus Christi
237	2.3	Henderson ISD	Henderson
237	2.3	La Feria ISD	La Feria
237	2.3	Lamesa ISD	Lamesa
237	2.3	Magnolia ISD	Magnolia
237	2.3	Orange Grove ISD	Orange Grove
237	2.3	Royal ISD	Brookshire
244	2.2	Bay City ISD	Bay City
244	2.2	Bridge City ISD	Bridge City
244	2.2	Everman ISD	Everman
244	2.2	Fort Bend ISD	Sugar Land
244	2.2	Gladewater ISD	Gladewater
244	2.2	Gonzales ISD	Gonzales
244	2.2	Gregory-Portland ISD	Gregory
244	2.2	Keller ISD	Keller
244	2.2	Madisonville Cons ISD	Madisonville
244	2.2	Perryton ISD	Perryton
244	2.2	Rockwall ISD	Rockwall

244	2.2	Taylor ISD	Taylor
256	2.1	Carrollton-Farmers Branch	Carrollton
256	2.1	Center ISD	Center
256	2.1	Jacksonville ISD	Jacksonville
256	2.1	Jasper ISD	Jasper
256	2.1	La Vernia ISD	La Vernia
256	2.1	Mansfield ISD	Mansfield
256	2.1	Midlothian ISD	Midlothian
256	2.1	Palacios ISD	Palacios
256	2.1	Round Rock ISD	Round Rock
256	2.1	Sanger ISD	Sanger
256	2.1	Sharyland ISD	Mission
267	2.0	Bridgeport ISD	Bridgeport
267	2.0	Cleburne ISD	Cleburne
267	2.0	Elgin ISD	Elgin
267	2.0	Glen Rose ISD	Glen Rose
267	2.0	La Grange ISD	La Grange
267	2.0	Leander ISD	Leander
267	2.0	Orangefield ISD	Orangefield
267	2.0	Richardson ISD	Richardson
267	2.0	Tomball ISD	Tomball
276	1.9	Birdville ISD	Haltom City
276	1.9	Bryan ISD	Bryan
276	1.9	El Campo ISD	El Campo
276	1.9	Hurst-Euless-Bedford ISD	Bedford
276	1.9	Hutto ISD	Hutto
276	1.9	Kirbyville CISD	Kirbyville
276	1.9	Socorro ISD	El Paso
276	1.9	Spring Hill ISD	Longview
276	1.9	Wichita Falls ISD	Wichita Falls
276	1.9	Wylie ISD	Wylie
286	1.8	Canyon ISD	Canyon
286	1.8	Clear Creek ISD	League City
286	1.8	Conroe ISD	Conroe
286	1.8	Ennis ISD	Ennis
286	1.8	Hondo ISD	Hondo
286	1.8	Little Elm ISD	Little Elm
286	1.8	North East ISD	San Antonio
286	1.8	Pflugerville ISD	Pflugerville
286	1.8	United ISD	Laredo
286	1.8	Waxahachie ISD	Waxahachie
296	1.7	Belton ISD	Belton
296	1.7	Cameron ISD	Cameron
296	1.7	College Station ISD	College Station
296	1.7	Garland ISD	Garland
296	1.7	Hallsville ISD	Hallsville
296	1.7	Huffman ISD	Huffman
296	1.7	Humble ISD	Humble
296	1.7	Lancaster ISD	Lancaster
296	1.7	Wharton ISD	Wharton
296	1.7	Willis ISD	Willis
296	1.7	Wills Point ISD	Wills Point
307	1.6	Cedar Hill ISD	Cedar Hill
307	1.6	Grapevine-Colleyville ISD	Grapevine
307	1.6	Kaufman ISD	Kaufman
307	1.6	Port Neches-Groves ISD	Port Neches
307	1.6	Seminole ISD	Seminole
307	1.6	Stafford Municipal School	Stafford
307	1.6	Tarkington ISD	Cleveland
314	1.5	Hardin-Jefferson ISD	Sour Lake
314	1.5	Montgomery ISD	Montgomery
314	1.5	Pine Tree ISD	Longview
314	1.5	Plano ISD	Plano
318	1.4	Crowley ISD	Crowley
318	1.4	Groesbeck ISD	Groesbeck
318	1.4	Lake Travis ISD	Austin
318	1.4	Lorena ISD	Lorena
318	1.4	Mabank ISD	Mabank
318	1.4	Sulphur Springs ISD	Sulphur Springs
324	1.3	Angleton ISD	Angleton
324	1.3	Burnet Cons ISD	Burnet
324	1.3	Commerce ISD	Commerce
324	1.3	Desoto ISD	Desoto
324	1.3	Fredericksburg ISD	Fredericksburg
324	1.3	Ingleside ISD	Ingleside
324	1.3	Paris ISD	Paris
324	1.3	Pleasant Grove ISD	Texarkana
324	1.3	Shepherd ISD	Shepherd
333	1.2	Canton ISD	Canton
333	1.2	Deer Park ISD	Deer Park
333	1.2	Rains ISD	Emory
333	1.2	West ISD	West
333	1.2	Westwood ISD	Palestine
338	1.1	Alamo Heights ISD	San Antonio
338	1.1	Burleson ISD	Burleson
338	1.1	Cypress-Fairbanks ISD	Houston
338	1.1	Decatur ISD	Decatur
338	1.1	Katy ISD	Katy
338	1.1	Lewisville ISD	Flower Mound
338	1.1	Liberty ISD	Liberty
338	1.1	Tuloso-Midway ISD	Corpus Christi
338	1.1	Whitesboro ISD	Whitesboro
338	1.1	Wylie ISD	Abilene
348	1.0	Duncanville ISD	Duncanville
348	1.0	Fairfield ISD	Fairfield
348	1.0	Frenship ISD	Wolfforth
348	1.0	Little Cypress-Mauricevil	Orange
348	1.0	Sweeny ISD	Sweeny
353	0.9	Crandall ISD	Crandall
353	0.9	Graham ISD	Graham
353	0.9	Lake Dallas ISD	Lake Dallas
353	0.9	Liberty Hill ISD	Liberty Hill
353	0.9	Stephenville	Stephenville
358	0.8	Barbers Hill ISD	Mt Belvieu
358	0.8	Carthage ISD	Carthage
358	0.8	Friendswood ISD	Friendswood
358	0.8	Midway ISD	Waco
362	0.7	Dripping Springs ISD	Dripping Spgs
362	0.7	Eanes ISD	Austin
362	0.7	Hamshire-Fannett ISD	Hamshire
362	0.7	Lumberton ISD	Lumberton
366	0.6	Boerne ISD	Boerne
366	0.6	China Spring ISD	Waco
366	0.6	Frisco ISD	Frisco
366	0.6	Greenwood ISD	Midland
366	0.6	Venus ISD	Venus
366	0.6	Yoakum ISD	Yoakum
372	0.5	Allen ISD	Allen
372	0.5	Atlanta ISD	Atlanta
372	0.5	Coppell ISD	Coppell
372	0.5	Lindale ISD	Lindale
372	0.5	Wimberley ISD	Wimberley
377	0.4	Giddings ISD	Giddings
377	0.4	Robinson ISD	Robinson
377	0.4	South Texas ISD	Mercedes
380	0.3	Bellville ISD	Bellville
380	0.3	Carroll ISD	Grapevine
380	0.3	Highland Park ISD	Dallas
383	0.2	Columbus ISD	Columbus
383	0.2	Forney ISD	Forney
385	0.1	Aledo ISD	Aledo
386	n/a	Lubbock-Cooper ISD	Lubbock

Utah

Utah Public School Educational Profile

Category	Value	Category	Value
Schools (2003-2004)	887	**Diploma Recipients** (2002-2003)	30,182
Instructional Level		White, Non-Hispanic	27,306
Primary	501	Black, Non-Hispanic	172
Middle	142	Asian/Pacific Islander	817
High	187	American Indian/Alaskan Native	313
Other Level	56	Hispanic	1,574
Curriculum		**High School Drop-out Rate** (%) (2001-2002)	3.7
Regular	753	White, Non-Hispanic	3.1
Special Education	41	Black, Non-Hispanic	8.8
Vocational	2	Asian/Pacific Islander	5.2
Alternative	90	American Indian/Alaskan Native	8.1
Type		Hispanic	8.2
Magnet	4	**Staff** (2003-2004)	
Charter	19	Teachers	22,270.7
Title I Eligible	220	Average Salary ($)	38,976
School-wide Title I	160	Librarians/Media Specialists	279.4
Students (2003-2004)	491,206	Guidance Counselors	683.2
Gender (%)		**Ratios** (2003-2004)	
Male	51.5	Student/Teacher Ratio	22.1 to 1
Female	48.5	Student/Librarian Ratio	1,758.1 to 1
Race/Ethnicity (%)		Student/Counselor Ratio	719.0 to 1
White, Non-Hispanic	83.2	**College Entrance Exam Scores** (2005)	
Black, Non-Hispanic	1.1	Scholastic Aptitude Test (SAT)	
Asian/Pacific Islander	2.9	Participation Rate (%)	7
American Indian/Alaskan Native	1.5	Mean SAT Reasoning Test Verbal Score	566
Hispanic	11.0	Mean SAT Reasoning Test Math Score	557
Classification (%)		American College Testing Program (ACT)	
Individual Education Program (IEP)	11.8	Participation Rate (%)	68
Migrant (2002-2003)	0.0	Average Composite Score	21.5
English Language Learner (ELL)	10.1	Average English Score	21.1
Eligible for Free Lunch Program	23.1	Average Math Score	21.0
Eligible for Reduced-Price Lunch Program	9.3	Average Reading Score	22.2
Current Spending ($ per student in FY 2003)	4,859	Average Science Score	21.4
Instruction	3,122		
Support Services	1,460		

Note: For an explanation of data, please refer to the User's Guide in the front of the book

Utah NAEP 2005 Test Scores

Reading			Mathematics		
Grade/Category	Value	Rank	Grade/Category	Value	Rank
4th Grade			**4th Grade**		
Average Proficiency	221.3 (1.05)	21/51	Average Proficiency	238.8 (0.78)	26/51
Proficiency by Gender/Race/Ethnicity			Proficiency by Gender/Race/Ethnicity		
Male	216.3 (1.37)	28/51	Male	240.3 (0.87)	24/51
Female	226.4 (1.45)	15/51	Female	237.2 (0.97)	28/51
White, Non-Hispanic	225.9 (1.02)	30/51	White, Non-Hispanic	242.3 (0.77)	37/51
Black, Non-Hispanic	n/a	n/a	Black, Non-Hispanic	n/a	n/a
Asian, Non-Hispanic	217.6 (4.24)	23/27	Asian, Non-Hispanic	235.3 (3.76)	24/25
American Indian, Non-Hispanic	n/a	n/a	American Indian, Non-Hispanic	n/a	n/a
Hispanic	198.7 (2.44)	34/40	Hispanic	220.2 (1.59)	31/41
Proficiency by Class Size			Proficiency by Class Size		
Less than 16 Students	n/a	n/a	Less than 16 Students	n/a	n/a
16 to 18 Students	n/a	n/a	16 to 18 Students	n/a	n/a
19 to 20 Students	n/a	n/a	19 to 20 Students	n/a	n/a
21 to 25 Students	221.6 (2.08)	26/51	21 to 25 Students	240.1 (1.46)	30/51
Greater than 25 Students	223.4 (1.38)	13/36	Greater than 25 Students	239.7 (1.08)	15/33
Percent Attaining Achievement Levels			Percent Attaining Achievement Levels		
Below Basic	32.3 (1.32)	31/51	Below Basic	17.4 (0.97)	29/51
Basic or Above	67.7 (1.32)	20/51	Basic or Above	82.6 (0.97)	23/51
Proficient or Above	34.1 (1.31)	17/51	Proficient or Above	36.8 (1.47)	27/51
Advanced or Above	7.5 (0.83)	17/51	Advanced or Above	4.1 (0.58)	31/51
8th Grade			**8th Grade**		
Average Proficiency	261.9 (0.75)	28/51	Average Proficiency	279.2 (0.68)	29/51
Proficiency by Gender/Race/Ethnicity			Proficiency by Gender/Race/Ethnicity		
Male	255.0 (1.00)	32/51	Male	280.0 (0.99)	29/51
Female	268.5 (0.95)	26/51	Female	278.3 (0.92)	29/51
White, Non-Hispanic	264.7 (0.92)	41/51	White, Non-Hispanic	282.9 (0.71)	38/51
Black, Non-Hispanic	n/a	n/a	Black, Non-Hispanic	n/a	n/a
Asian, Non-Hispanic	266.1 (3.15)	17/24	Asian, Non-Hispanic	273.5 (4.49)	21/23
American Indian, Non-Hispanic	n/a	n/a	American Indian, Non-Hispanic	n/a	n/a
Hispanic	242.8 (2.50)	33/38	Hispanic	255.4 (2.30)	33/38
Proficiency by Parents Highest Level of Ed.			Proficiency by Parents Highest Level of Ed.		
Did Not Finish High School	239.7 (3.50)	39/49	Did Not Finish High School	259.0 (2.78)	31/50
Graduated High School	247.9 (2.32)	41/50	Graduated High School	262.1 (1.52)	41/50
Some Education After High School	261.9 (1.66)	40/50	Some Education After High School	279.5 (1.54)	30/50
Graduated College	270.3 (1.13)	30/50	Graduated College	289.4 (0.90)	27/50
Percent Attaining Achievement Levels			Percent Attaining Achievement Levels		
Below Basic	32.3 (1.32)	31/51	Below Basic	28.9 (1.03)	26/51
Basic or Above	67.7 (1.32)	20/51	Basic or Above	71.1 (1.03)	26/51
Proficient or Above	34.1 (1.31)	17/51	Proficient or Above	29.5 (1.05)	29/51
Advanced or Above	7.5 (0.83)	17/51	Advanced or Above	4.7 (0.57)	30/51

Note: *For an explanation of data, please refer to the User's Guide in the front of the book; n/a indicates data not available*

Box Elder County

Box Elder SD
960 S Main • Brigham City, UT 84302-2598
(435) 734-4800 • http://www.boxelder.k12.ut.us
Grade Span: PK-12; **Agency Type:** 1
Schools: 29
   17 Primary; 3 Middle; 4 High; 5 Other Level
   25 Regular; 1 Special Education; 0 Vocational; 3 Alternative
   0 Magnet; 0 Charter; 4 Title I Eligible; 4 School-wide Title I
Students: 10,498   (51.9% male; 48.0% female)
   Individual Education Program: 1,401 (13.3%);
   English Language Learner: 291 (2.8%); Migrant: n/a
   Eligible for Free Lunch Program: 2,154 (20.5%)
   Eligible for Reduced-Price Lunch Program: 1,433 (13.6%)
Teachers: 503.5 (20.9 to 1)
Librarians/Media Specialists: 6.0 (1,752.3 to 1)
Guidance Counselors: 17.6 (597.4 to 1)
Current Spending: ($ per student per year):
   Total: $4,728; Instruction: $3,013; Support Services: $1,451
Enrollment, Drop-out Rates and Diploma Recipients by Race/Ethnicity

Category	Total	White	Black	Asian	AIAN	Hisp.
Enrollment (%)	100.0	90.0	0.5	1.0	0.8	7.7
Drop-out Rate (%)	2.0	1.7	0.0	2.3	8.7	6.9
H.S. Diplomas (#)	805	762	2	10	3	28

Cache County

Cache SD
2063 N 1200 E • Logan, UT 84341-2099
(435) 752-3925 • http://www.cache.k12.ut.us
Grade Span: KG-12; **Agency Type:** 1
Schools: 25
   13 Primary; 4 Middle; 6 High; 2 Other Level
   20 Regular; 1 Special Education; 0 Vocational; 4 Alternative
   0 Magnet; 0 Charter; 7 Title I Eligible; 6 School-wide Title I
Students: 13,156   (51.0% male; 48.9% female)
   Individual Education Program: 1,686 (12.8%);
   English Language Learner: 752 (5.7%); Migrant: n/a
   Eligible for Free Lunch Program: 2,207 (16.8%)
   Eligible for Reduced-Price Lunch Program: 1,556 (11.8%)
Teachers: 582.6 (22.6 to 1)
Librarians/Media Specialists: 18.9 (696.1 to 1)
Guidance Counselors: 15.1 (871.3 to 1)
Current Spending: ($ per student per year):
   Total: $4,973; Instruction: $3,204; Support Services: $1,477
Enrollment, Drop-out Rates and Diploma Recipients by Race/Ethnicity

Category	Total	White	Black	Asian	AIAN	Hisp.
Enrollment (%)	100.0	92.3	0.4	0.9	0.3	6.1
Drop-out Rate (%)	3.5	3.2	0.0	0.0	12.5	11.8
H.S. Diplomas (#)	895	859	0	5	0	31

Logan SD
101 W Center • Logan, UT 84321-4563
(435) 755-2300 • http://www.lcsd.logan.k12.ut.us
Grade Span: KG-12; **Agency Type:** 1
Schools: 10
   5 Primary; 1 Middle; 3 High; 1 Other Level
   7 Regular; 0 Special Education; 0 Vocational; 3 Alternative
   0 Magnet; 0 Charter; 4 Title I Eligible; 4 School-wide Title I
Students: 5,738   (51.3% male; 48.6% female)
   Individual Education Program: 670 (11.7%);
   English Language Learner: 799 (13.9%); Migrant: n/a
   Eligible for Free Lunch Program: 1,811 (31.6%)
   Eligible for Reduced-Price Lunch Program: 597 (10.4%)
Teachers: 285.1 (20.1 to 1)
Librarians/Media Specialists: 3.1 (1,851.0 to 1)
Guidance Counselors: 7.0 (819.7 to 1)
Current Spending: ($ per student per year):
   Total: $4,871; Instruction: $3,446; Support Services: $1,140
Enrollment, Drop-out Rates and Diploma Recipients by Race/Ethnicity

Category	Total	White	Black	Asian	AIAN	Hisp.
Enrollment (%)	100.0	76.2	1.1	4.4	1.4	16.9
Drop-out Rate (%)	4.4	3.1	12.5	3.4	0.0	16.0
H.S. Diplomas (#)	405	345	6	22	3	29

Carbon County

Carbon SD
251 W 400 N • Price, UT 84501-1438
Mailing Address: PO Box 1438 • Price, UT 84501-1438
(435) 637-1732 • http://www.carbon.k12.ut.us
Grade Span: KG-12; **Agency Type:** 1
Schools: 12
   5 Primary; 2 Middle; 3 High; 2 Other Level

   9 Regular; 1 Special Education; 0 Vocational; 2 Alternative
   0 Magnet; 0 Charter; 6 Title I Eligible; 5 School-wide Title I
Students: 3,622   (50.1% male; 49.8% female)
   Individual Education Program: 694 (19.2%);
   English Language Learner: 30 (0.8%); Migrant: n/a
   Eligible for Free Lunch Program: 1,250 (34.5%)
   Eligible for Reduced-Price Lunch Program: 347 (9.6%)
Teachers: 204.7 (17.7 to 1)
Librarians/Media Specialists: 2.0 (1,811.0 to 1)
Guidance Counselors: 9.7 (373.4 to 1)
Current Spending: ($ per student per year):
   Total: $6,268; Instruction: $4,087; Support Services: $1,875
Enrollment, Drop-out Rates and Diploma Recipients by Race/Ethnicity

Category	Total	White	Black	Asian	AIAN	Hisp.
Enrollment (%)	100.0	86.6	0.6	0.6	1.3	11.0
Drop-out Rate (%)	2.0	1.6	0.0	0.0	0.0	5.5
H.S. Diplomas (#)	273	240	0	2	3	28

Davis County

Davis SD
45 E State St • Farmington, UT 84025-2344
(801) 402-5261 • http://www.davis.k12.ut.us
Grade Span: PK-12; **Agency Type:** 1
Schools: 96
   56 Primary; 17 Middle; 20 High; 3 Other Level
   77 Regular; 5 Special Education; 2 Vocational; 12 Alternative
   0 Magnet; 0 Charter; 14 Title I Eligible; 10 School-wide Title I
Students: 60,749   (51.3% male; 48.6% female)
   Individual Education Program: 5,903 (9.7%);
   English Language Learner: 3,196 (5.3%); Migrant: n/a
   Eligible for Free Lunch Program: 9,130 (15.0%)
   Eligible for Reduced-Price Lunch Program: 5,048 (8.3%)
Teachers: 2,627.1 (23.1 to 1)
Librarians/Media Specialists: 19.7 (3,083.7 to 1)
Guidance Counselors: 107.9 (563.0 to 1)
Current Spending: ($ per student per year):
   Total: $4,692; Instruction: $2,997; Support Services: $1,325
Enrollment, Drop-out Rates and Diploma Recipients by Race/Ethnicity

Category	Total	White	Black	Asian	AIAN	Hisp.
Enrollment (%)	100.0	88.9	1.4	2.1	0.5	5.8
Drop-out Rate (%)	2.4	2.2	2.9	1.9	5.9	6.1
H.S. Diplomas (#)	3,765	3,524	24	91	14	112

Duchesne County

Duchesne SD
90 E 100 S • Duchesne, UT 84021-0446
Mailing Address: PO Box 446 • Duchesne, UT 84021-0446
(435) 738-2411
Grade Span: KG-12; **Agency Type:** 1
Schools: 15
   6 Primary; 2 Middle; 5 High; 1 Other Level
   12 Regular; 2 Special Education; 0 Vocational; 0 Alternative
   0 Magnet; 0 Charter; 7 Title I Eligible; 0 School-wide Title I
Students: 3,900   (51.0% male; 49.0% female)
   Individual Education Program: 620 (15.9%);
   English Language Learner: 97 (2.5%); Migrant: n/a
   Eligible for Free Lunch Program: 1,149 (29.5%)
   Eligible for Reduced-Price Lunch Program: 543 (13.9%)
Teachers: 213.1 (18.3 to 1)
Librarians/Media Specialists: 6.7 (582.1 to 1)
Guidance Counselors: 5.8 (672.4 to 1)
Current Spending: ($ per student per year):
   Total: $5,778; Instruction: $3,483; Support Services: $2,014
Enrollment, Drop-out Rates and Diploma Recipients by Race/Ethnicity

Category	Total	White	Black	Asian	AIAN	Hisp.
Enrollment (%)	100.0	88.0	0.2	0.5	8.4	2.9
Drop-out Rate (%)	5.9	4.7	n/a	0.0	17.6	12.1
H.S. Diplomas (#)	303	289	0	1	8	5

Emery County

Emery SD
130 N Main • Huntington, UT 84528
Mailing Address: PO Box 120 • Huntington, UT 84528
(435) 687-9846 • http://www.emery.k12.ut.us
Grade Span: PK-12; **Agency Type:** 1
Schools: 10
   6 Primary; 2 Middle; 2 High; 0 Other Level
   10 Regular; 0 Special Education; 0 Vocational; 0 Alternative
   0 Magnet; 0 Charter; 4 Title I Eligible; 1 School-wide Title I
Students: 2,436   (52.4% male; 47.5% female)
   Individual Education Program: 405 (16.6%);
   English Language Learner: 85 (3.5%); Migrant: n/a

Eligible for Free Lunch Program: 766 (31.4%)
Eligible for Reduced-Price Lunch Program: 396 (16.3%)
Teachers: 129.9 (18.8 to 1)
Librarians/Media Specialists: 1.5 (1,624.0 to 1)
Guidance Counselors: 2.0 (1,218.0 to 1)
Current Spending: ($ per student per year):
Total: $6,269; Instruction: $4,072; Support Services: $1,882
Enrollment, Drop-out Rates and Diploma Recipients by Race/Ethnicity

Category	Total	White	Black	Asian	AIAN	Hisp.
Enrollment (%)	100.0	92.6	0.7	0.7	0.5	5.5
Drop-out Rate (%)	1.2	1.0	n/a	0.0	0.0	8.0
H.S. Diplomas (#)	219	212	0	1	1	5

Iron County

Iron SD
2077 W Royal Hunte Dr • Cedar City, UT 84720-0120
(435) 586-2804 • http://www.iron.k12.ut.us
Grade Span: PK-12; **Agency Type:** 1
Schools: 15
7 Primary; 2 Middle; 4 High; 2 Other Level
12 Regular; 0 Special Education; 0 Vocational; 3 Alternative
0 Magnet; 0 Charter; 5 Title I Eligible; 3 School-wide Title I
Students: 7,457 (52.3% male; 47.6% female)
Individual Education Program: 1,012 (13.6%);
English Language Learner: 475 (6.4%); Migrant: n/a
Eligible for Free Lunch Program: 2,089 (28.0%)
Eligible for Reduced-Price Lunch Program: 887 (11.9%)
Teachers: 341.9 (21.8 to 1)
Librarians/Media Specialists: 3.0 (2,485.7 to 1)
Guidance Counselors: 7.9 (943.9 to 1)
Current Spending: ($ per student per year):
Total: $5,081; Instruction: $3,245; Support Services: $1,559
Enrollment, Drop-out Rates and Diploma Recipients by Race/Ethnicity

Category	Total	White	Black	Asian	AIAN	Hisp.
Enrollment (%)	100.0	89.1	0.7	1.0	3.5	5.7
Drop-out Rate (%)	1.2	1.3	0.0	0.0	1.2	0.0
H.S. Diplomas (#)	482	445	3	5	12	17

Juab County

Juab SD
346 E 600 N • Nephi, UT 84648-1531
(435) 623-1940 • http://utahreach.usu.edu/juab/schools/district.htm
Grade Span: KG-12; **Agency Type:** 1
Schools: 5
2 Primary; 2 Middle; 1 High; 0 Other Level
5 Regular; 0 Special Education; 0 Vocational; 0 Alternative
0 Magnet; 0 Charter; 2 Title I Eligible; 1 School-wide Title I
Students: 1,939 (50.2% male; 49.7% female)
Individual Education Program: 268 (13.8%);
English Language Learner: 1 (0.1%); Migrant: n/a
Eligible for Free Lunch Program: 392 (20.2%)
Eligible for Reduced-Price Lunch Program: 304 (15.7%)
Teachers: 82.2 (23.6 to 1)
Librarians/Media Specialists: 0.0 (n/a to 1)
Guidance Counselors: 1.7 (1,140.6 to 1)
Current Spending: ($ per student per year):
Total: $4,686; Instruction: $2,978; Support Services: $1,387
Enrollment, Drop-out Rates and Diploma Recipients by Race/Ethnicity

Category	Total	White	Black	Asian	AIAN	Hisp.
Enrollment (%)	100.0	97.2	0.4	0.7	0.5	1.3
Drop-out Rate (%)	1.0	1.0	n/a	0.0	0.0	0.0
H.S. Diplomas (#)	124	121	0	1	1	1

Millard County

Millard SD
285 E 450 N • Delta, UT 84624-0666
(435) 864-5600 • http://www.millard.k12.ut.us
Grade Span: KG-12; **Agency Type:** 1
Schools: 10
4 Primary; 3 Middle; 3 High; 0 Other Level
10 Regular; 0 Special Education; 0 Vocational; 0 Alternative
0 Magnet; 0 Charter; 5 Title I Eligible; 2 School-wide Title I
Students: 3,177 (51.8% male; 48.1% female)
Individual Education Program: 433 (13.6%);
English Language Learner: 351 (11.0%); Migrant: n/a
Eligible for Free Lunch Program: 957 (30.1%)
Eligible for Reduced-Price Lunch Program: 501 (15.8%)
Teachers: 170.4 (18.6 to 1)
Librarians/Media Specialists: 3.7 (858.6 to 1)
Guidance Counselors: 4.0 (794.3 to 1)
Current Spending: ($ per student per year):
Total: $6,560; Instruction: $4,068; Support Services: $2,123

Enrollment, Drop-out Rates and Diploma Recipients by Race/Ethnicity

Category	Total	White	Black	Asian	AIAN	Hisp.
Enrollment (%)	100.0	86.5	0.2	1.1	1.4	10.9
Drop-out Rate (%)	0.9	0.9	0.0	0.0	0.0	1.5
H.S. Diplomas (#)	263	247	0	1	2	13

Morgan County

Morgan SD
240 E Young St • Morgan, UT 84050-0530
Mailing Address: PO Box 530 • Morgan, UT 84050-0530
(801) 829-3411 • http://www.morgan.k12.ut.us
Grade Span: PK-12; **Agency Type:** 1
Schools: 3
1 Primary; 1 Middle; 1 High; 0 Other Level
3 Regular; 0 Special Education; 0 Vocational; 0 Alternative
0 Magnet; 0 Charter; 1 Title I Eligible; 0 School-wide Title I
Students: 1,989 (51.9% male; 48.0% female)
Individual Education Program: 150 (7.5%);
English Language Learner: 6 (0.3%); Migrant: n/a
Eligible for Free Lunch Program: 206 (10.4%)
Eligible for Reduced-Price Lunch Program: 181 (9.1%)
Teachers: 96.7 (20.6 to 1)
Librarians/Media Specialists: 1.2 (1,657.5 to 1)
Guidance Counselors: 2.4 (828.8 to 1)
Current Spending: ($ per student per year):
Total: $4,829; Instruction: $3,180; Support Services: $1,319
Enrollment, Drop-out Rates and Diploma Recipients by Race/Ethnicity

Category	Total	White	Black	Asian	AIAN	Hisp.
Enrollment (%)	100.0	97.7	0.2	0.7	0.2	1.3
Drop-out Rate (%)	1.1	1.1	0.0	0.0	0.0	0.0
H.S. Diplomas (#)	174	170	0	1	0	3

Salt Lake County

Granite SD
340 E 3545 S • Salt Lake City, UT 84115-4697
(801) 685-5000 • http://www.granite.k12.ut.us
Grade Span: PK-12; **Agency Type:** 1
Schools: 109
64 Primary; 20 Middle; 19 High; 6 Other Level
89 Regular; 6 Special Education; 0 Vocational; 14 Alternative
0 Magnet; 0 Charter; 16 Title I Eligible; 16 School-wide Title I
Students: 70,771 (51.3% male; 48.6% female)
Individual Education Program: 8,206 (11.6%);
English Language Learner: 13,244 (18.7%); Migrant: n/a
Eligible for Free Lunch Program: 21,210 (30.0%)
Eligible for Reduced-Price Lunch Program: 6,818 (9.6%)
Teachers: 3,206.2 (22.1 to 1)
Librarians/Media Specialists: 24.7 (2,865.2 to 1)
Guidance Counselors: 96.4 (734.1 to 1)
Current Spending: ($ per student per year):
Total: $4,595; Instruction: $2,961; Support Services: $1,409
Enrollment, Drop-out Rates and Diploma Recipients by Race/Ethnicity

Category	Total	White	Black	Asian	AIAN	Hisp.
Enrollment (%)	100.0	71.6	1.6	6.4	1.2	19.1
Drop-out Rate (%)	6.0	5.8	9.5	5.8	6.2	7.4
H.S. Diplomas (#)	4,170	3,464	28	273	27	378

Jordan SD
9361 S 300 E • Sandy, UT 84070-2998
(801) 567-8100 • http://www.jordandistrict.org
Grade Span: KG-12; **Agency Type:** 1
Schools: 85
57 Primary; 15 Middle; 11 High; 2 Other Level
77 Regular; 4 Special Education; 0 Vocational; 4 Alternative
0 Magnet; 0 Charter; 5 Title I Eligible; 5 School-wide Title I
Students: 74,761 (51.3% male; 48.6% female)
Individual Education Program: 8,026 (10.7%);
English Language Learner: 4,465 (6.0%); Migrant: n/a
Eligible for Free Lunch Program: 10,493 (14.0%)
Eligible for Reduced-Price Lunch Program: 5,044 (6.7%)
Teachers: 3,053.9 (24.5 to 1)
Librarians/Media Specialists: 26.9 (2,779.2 to 1)
Guidance Counselors: 70.9 (1,054.5 to 1)
Current Spending: ($ per student per year):
Total: $4,520; Instruction: $2,880; Support Services: $1,387
Enrollment, Drop-out Rates and Diploma Recipients by Race/Ethnicity

Category	Total	White	Black	Asian	AIAN	Hisp.
Enrollment (%)	100.0	90.2	0.7	2.4	0.6	6.0
Drop-out Rate (%)	4.4	3.9	14.8	6.9	23.4	10.1
H.S. Diplomas (#)	4,916	4,662	13	80	14	147

Murray SD
147 E 5065 S • Murray, UT 84107-4898
(801) 264-7400 • http://www.mury.k12.ut.us
Grade Span: KG-12; **Agency Type:** 1
Schools: 12
  7 Primary; 2 Middle; 2 High; 1 Other Level
  10 Regular; 0 Special Education; 0 Vocational; 2 Alternative
  0 Magnet; 0 Charter; 4 Title I Eligible; 0 School-wide Title I
Students: 6,482 (50.7% male; 49.2% female)
  Individual Education Program: 541 (8.3%);
  English Language Learner: 493 (7.6%); Migrant: n/a
  Eligible for Free Lunch Program: 1,085 (16.7%)
  Eligible for Reduced-Price Lunch Program: 491 (7.6%)
Teachers: 300.1 (21.6 to 1)
Librarians/Media Specialists: 3.0 (2,160.7 to 1)
Guidance Counselors: 8.5 (762.6 to 1)
Current Spending: ($ per student per year):
  Total: $5,002; Instruction: $3,052; Support Services: $1,684
Enrollment, Drop-out Rates and Diploma Recipients by Race/Ethnicity

Category	Total	White	Black	Asian	AIAN	Hisp.
Enrollment (%)	100.0	83.3	2.2	3.1	1.0	10.5
Drop-out Rate (%)	3.0	2.8	3.7	2.8	5.9	3.9
H.S. Diplomas (#)	480	434	2	14	3	27

Salt Lake City SD
440 E 100 S • Salt Lake City, UT 84111-1898
(801) 578-8599 • http://www.slc.k12.ut.us
Grade Span: PK-12; **Agency Type:** 1
Schools: 44
  29 Primary; 6 Middle; 5 High; 4 Other Level
  37 Regular; 6 Special Education; 0 Vocational; 1 Alternative
  1 Magnet; 0 Charter; 17 Title I Eligible; 16 School-wide Title I
Students: 24,443 (51.4% male; 48.5% female)
  Individual Education Program: 3,100 (12.7%);
  English Language Learner: 9,273 (37.9%); Migrant: n/a
  Eligible for Free Lunch Program: 12,031 (49.2%)
  Eligible for Reduced-Price Lunch Program: 2,275 (9.3%)
Teachers: 1,229.7 (19.9 to 1)
Librarians/Media Specialists: 40.8 (599.1 to 1)
Guidance Counselors: 39.7 (615.7 to 1)
Current Spending: ($ per student per year):
  Total: $5,714; Instruction: $3,677; Support Services: $1,714
Enrollment, Drop-out Rates and Diploma Recipients by Race/Ethnicity

Category	Total	White	Black	Asian	AIAN	Hisp.
Enrollment (%)	100.0	50.3	3.9	10.1	1.9	33.7
Drop-out Rate (%)	11.2	9.0	14.6	10.1	20.0	16.1
H.S. Diplomas (#)	1,202	849	41	113	17	182

San Juan SD
200 N Main St • Blanding, UT 84511-3600
(435) 678-1200 • http://www.sanjuan.k12.ut.us
Grade Span: PK-12; **Agency Type:** 1
Schools: 13
  7 Primary; 1 Middle; 5 High; 0 Other Level
  13 Regular; 0 Special Education; 0 Vocational; 0 Alternative
  0 Magnet; 0 Charter; 8 Title I Eligible; 8 School-wide Title I
Students: 2,979 (51.9% male; 48.0% female)
  Individual Education Program: 330 (11.1%);
  English Language Learner: 1,465 (49.2%); Migrant: n/a
  Eligible for Free Lunch Program: 1,887 (63.3%)
  Eligible for Reduced-Price Lunch Program: 288 (9.7%)
Teachers: 199.0 (15.0 to 1)
Librarians/Media Specialists: 9.0 (331.0 to 1)
Guidance Counselors: 5.9 (504.9 to 1)
Current Spending: ($ per student per year):
  Total: $9,647; Instruction: $5,280; Support Services: $3,940
Enrollment, Drop-out Rates and Diploma Recipients by Race/Ethnicity

Category	Total	White	Black	Asian	AIAN	Hisp.
Enrollment (%)	100.0	40.8	0.2	0.5	56.1	2.4
Drop-out Rate (%)	2.9	0.7	n/a	0.0	4.6	2.9
H.S. Diplomas (#)	199	99	0	0	93	7

N Sanpete SD
220 E 700 S • Mt Pleasant, UT 84647-1327
(435) 462-2485 • http://www.nsanpete.k12.ut.us
Grade Span: PK-12; **Agency Type:** 1
Schools: 8
  5 Primary; 1 Middle; 2 High; 0 Other Level
  7 Regular; 0 Special Education; 0 Vocational; 1 Alternative
  0 Magnet; 0 Charter; 5 Title I Eligible; 4 School-wide Title I
Students: 2,376 (50.2% male; 49.7% female)

  Individual Education Program: 337 (14.2%);
  English Language Learner: 212 (8.9%); Migrant: n/a
  Eligible for Free Lunch Program: 734 (30.9%)
  Eligible for Reduced-Price Lunch Program: 444 (18.7%)
Teachers: 114.4 (20.8 to 1)
Librarians/Media Specialists: 1.0 (2,376.0 to 1)
Guidance Counselors: 2.0 (1,188.0 to 1)
Current Spending: ($ per student per year):
  Total: $5,595; Instruction: $3,258; Support Services: $2,007
Enrollment, Drop-out Rates and Diploma Recipients by Race/Ethnicity

Category	Total	White	Black	Asian	AIAN	Hisp.
Enrollment (%)	100.0	88.5	0.5	0.8	0.8	9.4
Drop-out Rate (%)	3.5	3.6	0.0	0.0	0.0	3.8
H.S. Diplomas (#)	175	161	0	1	0	13

S Sanpete SD
39 S Main • Manti, UT 84642-1398
(435) 835-2261 • http://www.ssanpete.k12.ut.us
Grade Span: PK-12; **Agency Type:** 1
Schools: 9
  3 Primary; 2 Middle; 2 High; 2 Other Level
  7 Regular; 0 Special Education; 0 Vocational; 2 Alternative
  0 Magnet; 0 Charter; 3 Title I Eligible; 3 School-wide Title I
Students: 2,792 (52.8% male; 47.1% female)
  Individual Education Program: 476 (17.0%);
  English Language Learner: 152 (5.4%); Migrant: n/a
  Eligible for Free Lunch Program: 949 (34.0%)
  Eligible for Reduced-Price Lunch Program: 465 (16.7%)
Teachers: 149.7 (18.7 to 1)
Librarians/Media Specialists: 0.0 (n/a to 1)
Guidance Counselors: 3.5 (797.7 to 1)
Current Spending: ($ per student per year):
  Total: $5,733; Instruction: $3,872; Support Services: $1,535
Enrollment, Drop-out Rates and Diploma Recipients by Race/Ethnicity

Category	Total	White	Black	Asian	AIAN	Hisp.
Enrollment (%)	100.0	89.8	0.3	1.3	1.1	7.5
Drop-out Rate (%)	1.1	1.1	0.0	0.0	0.0	2.2
H.S. Diplomas (#)	226	211	0	5	3	7

Sevier SD
195 E 500 N • Richfield, UT 84701-1899
(435) 896-8214
Grade Span: PK-12; **Agency Type:** 1
Schools: 15
  5 Primary; 4 Middle; 6 High; 0 Other Level
  12 Regular; 0 Special Education; 0 Vocational; 3 Alternative
  0 Magnet; 0 Charter; 3 Title I Eligible; 0 School-wide Title I
Students: 4,436 (50.8% male; 49.1% female)
  Individual Education Program: 568 (12.8%);
  English Language Learner: 55 (1.2%); Migrant: n/a
  Eligible for Free Lunch Program: 1,274 (28.7%)
  Eligible for Reduced-Price Lunch Program: 661 (14.9%)
Teachers: 220.0 (20.2 to 1)
Librarians/Media Specialists: 0.0 (n/a to 1)
Guidance Counselors: 3.8 (1,167.4 to 1)
Current Spending: ($ per student per year):
  Total: $5,291; Instruction: $3,376; Support Services: $1,633
Enrollment, Drop-out Rates and Diploma Recipients by Race/Ethnicity

Category	Total	White	Black	Asian	AIAN	Hisp.
Enrollment (%)	100.0	92.1	0.2	0.5	4.4	2.8
Drop-out Rate (%)	6.4	5.9	50.0	0.0	33.3	0.0
H.S. Diplomas (#)	305	296	0	3	3	3

Park City SD
2700 Kearns Blvd • Park City, UT 84060-7476
(435) 645-5600 • http://www.parkcity.k12.ut.us
Grade Span: PK-12; **Agency Type:** 1
Schools: 8
  4 Primary; 2 Middle; 2 High; 0 Other Level
  7 Regular; 0 Special Education; 0 Vocational; 1 Alternative
  0 Magnet; 1 Charter; 2 Title I Eligible; 0 School-wide Title I
Students: 4,123 (52.6% male; 47.3% female)
  Individual Education Program: 399 (9.7%);
  English Language Learner: 404 (9.8%); Migrant: n/a
  Eligible for Free Lunch Program: 333 (8.1%)
  Eligible for Reduced-Price Lunch Program: 75 (1.8%)
Teachers: 218.7 (18.9 to 1)
Librarians/Media Specialists: 6.0 (687.2 to 1)
Guidance Counselors: 8.4 (490.8 to 1)
Current Spending: ($ per student per year):
  Total: $6,351; Instruction: $3,863; Support Services: $2,234

Enrollment, Drop-out Rates and Diploma Recipients by Race/Ethnicity

Category	Total	White	Black	Asian	AIAN	Hisp.
Enrollment (%)	100.0	87.4	0.4	1.4	0.2	10.5
Drop-out Rate (%)	3.0	1.9	0.0	0.0	0.0	16.7
H.S. Diplomas (#)	282	263	0	4	1	14

Tooele County

Tooele SD
66 W Vine • Tooele, UT 84074-2035
(435) 833-1900 • http://tcsd.tooele.k12.ut.us
Grade Span: KG-12; **Agency Type:** 1
Schools: 21
   13 Primary; 2 Middle; 5 High; 1 Other Level
   19 Regular; 0 Special Education; 0 Vocational; 2 Alternative
   0 Magnet; 0 Charter; 8 Title I Eligible; 2 School-wide Title I
Students: 10,508 (51.1% male; 48.8% female)
   Individual Education Program: 1,400 (13.3%);
   English Language Learner: 394 (3.7%); Migrant: n/a
   Eligible for Free Lunch Program: 2,535 (24.1%)
   Eligible for Reduced-Price Lunch Program: 1,234 (11.7%)
Teachers: 458.9 (22.9 to 1)
Librarians/Media Specialists: 6.0 (1,751.3 to 1)
Guidance Counselors: 13.0 (808.3 to 1)
Current Spending: ($ per student per year):
   Total: $4,374; Instruction: $2,779; Support Services: $1,326

Enrollment, Drop-out Rates and Diploma Recipients by Race/Ethnicity

Category	Total	White	Black	Asian	AIAN	Hisp.
Enrollment (%)	100.0	86.0	1.1	1.1	1.6	10.2
Drop-out Rate (%)	2.6	2.0	0.0	3.0	3.6	7.2
H.S. Diplomas (#)	513	430	5	10	9	59

Uintah County

Uintah SD
635 W 200 S • Vernal, UT 84078-3099
(435) 781-3100 • http://server1.do.uintah.k12.ut.us
Grade Span: KG-12; **Agency Type:** 1
Schools: 12
   6 Primary; 3 Middle; 2 High; 1 Other Level
   11 Regular; 0 Special Education; 0 Vocational; 1 Alternative
   0 Magnet; 0 Charter; 6 Title I Eligible; 5 School-wide Title I
Students: 5,607 (52.4% male; 47.5% female)
   Individual Education Program: 873 (15.6%);
   English Language Learner: 726 (12.9%); Migrant: n/a
   Eligible for Free Lunch Program: 1,617 (28.8%)
   Eligible for Reduced-Price Lunch Program: 819 (14.6%)
Teachers: 296.0 (18.9 to 1)
Librarians/Media Specialists: 2.0 (2,803.5 to 1)
Guidance Counselors: 7.0 (801.0 to 1)
Current Spending: ($ per student per year):
   Total: $5,799; Instruction: $3,700; Support Services: $1,777

Enrollment, Drop-out Rates and Diploma Recipients by Race/Ethnicity

Category	Total	White	Black	Asian	AIAN	Hisp.
Enrollment (%)	100.0	84.7	0.1	0.6	11.9	2.7
Drop-out Rate (%)	4.2	3.6	50.0	7.1	7.0	9.1
H.S. Diplomas (#)	393	368	1	3	8	13

Utah County

Alpine SD
575 N 100 E • American Fork, UT 84003-1700
(801) 756-8400 • http://www.alpine.k12.ut.us
Grade Span: KG-12; **Agency Type:** 1
Schools: 63
   42 Primary; 9 Middle; 10 High; 2 Other Level
   57 Regular; 3 Special Education; 0 Vocational; 3 Alternative
   0 Magnet; 0 Charter; 9 Title I Eligible; 7 School-wide Title I
Students: 51,240 (51.4% male; 48.5% female)
   Individual Education Program: 5,216 (10.2%);
   English Language Learner: 2,965 (5.8%); Migrant: n/a
   Eligible for Free Lunch Program: 8,870 (17.3%)
   Eligible for Reduced-Price Lunch Program: 4,021 (7.8%)
Teachers: 2,117.0 (24.2 to 1)
Librarians/Media Specialists: 15.9 (3,222.6 to 1)
Guidance Counselors: 56.3 (910.1 to 1)
Current Spending: ($ per student per year):
   Total: $4,413; Instruction: $2,937; Support Services: $1,224

Enrollment, Drop-out Rates and Diploma Recipients by Race/Ethnicity

Category	Total	White	Black	Asian	AIAN	Hisp.
Enrollment (%)	100.0	90.1	0.6	1.9	0.6	6.8
Drop-out Rate (%)	2.1	1.9	7.5	2.8	7.6	4.6
H.S. Diplomas (#)	2,726	2,598	1	41	15	71

Nebo SD
350 S Main • Spanish Fork, UT 84660-2499
(801) 354-7400 • http://www.nebo.edu
Grade Span: PK-12; **Agency Type:** 1
Schools: 35
   22 Primary; 4 Middle; 5 High; 4 Other Level
   32 Regular; 1 Special Education; 0 Vocational; 2 Alternative
   0 Magnet; 0 Charter; 9 Title I Eligible; 7 School-wide Title I
Students: 24,129 (52.1% male; 47.8% female)
   Individual Education Program: 3,163 (13.1%);
   English Language Learner: 1,092 (4.5%); Migrant: n/a
   Eligible for Free Lunch Program: 4,577 (19.0%)
   Eligible for Reduced-Price Lunch Program: 2,228 (9.2%)
Teachers: 1,007.4 (24.0 to 1)
Librarians/Media Specialists: 10.0 (2,412.9 to 1)
Guidance Counselors: 32.8 (735.6 to 1)
Current Spending: ($ per student per year):
   Total: $4,339; Instruction: $2,739; Support Services: $1,378

Enrollment, Drop-out Rates and Diploma Recipients by Race/Ethnicity

Category	Total	White	Black	Asian	AIAN	Hisp.
Enrollment (%)	100.0	91.7	0.4	1.0	0.8	6.1
Drop-out Rate (%)	2.0	2.0	0.0	0.0	4.7	2.2
H.S. Diplomas (#)	1,303	1,237	3	14	9	40

Provo SD
280 W 940 N • Provo, UT 84604-3394
(801) 374-4800 • http://www.provo.k12.ut.us
Grade Span: KG-12; **Agency Type:** 1
Schools: 26
   13 Primary; 3 Middle; 6 High; 4 Other Level
   18 Regular; 1 Special Education; 0 Vocational; 7 Alternative
   0 Magnet; 0 Charter; 4 Title I Eligible; 4 School-wide Title I
Students: 13,145 (51.4% male; 48.5% female)
   Individual Education Program: 1,610 (12.2%);
   English Language Learner: 2,589 (19.7%); Migrant: n/a
   Eligible for Free Lunch Program: 4,418 (33.6%)
   Eligible for Reduced-Price Lunch Program: 1,272 (9.7%)
Teachers: 668.0 (19.7 to 1)
Librarians/Media Specialists: 16.3 (806.4 to 1)
Guidance Counselors: 15.0 (876.3 to 1)
Current Spending: ($ per student per year):
   Total: $5,611; Instruction: $3,982; Support Services: $1,370

Enrollment, Drop-out Rates and Diploma Recipients by Race/Ethnicity

Category	Total	White	Black	Asian	AIAN	Hisp.
Enrollment (%)	100.0	73.7	0.8	4.3	1.3	19.8
Drop-out Rate (%)	1.4	1.2	0.0	0.5	2.7	2.4
H.S. Diplomas (#)	763	647	4	34	7	71

Wasatch County

Wasatch SD
101 E 200 N • Heber City, UT 84032-1708
(435) 654-0280 • http://www.wasatch.k12.ut.us
Grade Span: KG-12; **Agency Type:** 1
Schools: 7
   3 Primary; 1 Middle; 2 High; 1 Other Level
   6 Regular; 0 Special Education; 0 Vocational; 1 Alternative
   0 Magnet; 0 Charter; 3 Title I Eligible; 0 School-wide Title I
Students: 4,022 (52.1% male; 47.8% female)
   Individual Education Program: 550 (13.7%);
   English Language Learner: 281 (7.0%); Migrant: n/a
   Eligible for Free Lunch Program: 704 (17.5%)
   Eligible for Reduced-Price Lunch Program: 294 (7.3%)
Teachers: 189.8 (21.2 to 1)
Librarians/Media Specialists: 2.5 (1,608.8 to 1)
Guidance Counselors: 7.7 (522.3 to 1)
Current Spending: ($ per student per year):
   Total: $4,891; Instruction: $3,283; Support Services: $1,392

Enrollment, Drop-out Rates and Diploma Recipients by Race/Ethnicity

Category	Total	White	Black	Asian	AIAN	Hisp.
Enrollment (%)	100.0	89.3	0.4	0.5	0.3	9.4
Drop-out Rate (%)	1.7	1.6	0.0	0.0	0.0	5.4
H.S. Diplomas (#)	277	265	0	1	1	10

Washington County

Washington SD
121 W Tabernacle • St George, UT 84770-3390
(435) 673-3553 • http://www.wash.k12.ut.us
Grade Span: PK-12; **Agency Type:** 1
Schools: 35
   19 Primary; 4 Middle; 10 High; 2 Other Level
   31 Regular; 0 Special Education; 0 Vocational; 4 Alternative
   0 Magnet; 0 Charter; 12 Title I Eligible; 12 School-wide Title I
Students: 20,482 (51.4% male; 48.5% female)

Individual Education Program: 2,340 (11.4%);
English Language Learner: 1,267 (6.2%); Migrant: n/a
Eligible for Free Lunch Program: 4,426 (21.6%)
Eligible for Reduced-Price Lunch Program: 2,093 (10.2%)
Teachers: 892.3 (23.0 to 1)
Librarians/Media Specialists: 10.0 (2,048.2 to 1)
Guidance Counselors: 33.6 (609.6 to 1)
Current Spending: ($ per student per year):
Total: $4,524; Instruction: $2,969; Support Services: $1,335
Enrollment, Drop-out Rates and Diploma Recipients by Race/Ethnicity

Category	Total	White	Black	Asian	AIAN	Hisp.
Enrollment (%)	100.0	88.1	0.6	1.6	2.3	7.3
Drop-out Rate (%)	0.8	0.9	0.0	0.0	1.9	0.4
H.S. Diplomas (#)	1,214	1,132	0	31	13	38

Weber County

Ogden SD

1950 Monroe Blvd • Ogden, UT 84401-0619
(801) 737-7300 • http://www.ogden.k12.ut.us
Grade Span: KG-12; **Agency Type:** 1
Schools: 32
16 Primary; 4 Middle; 10 High; 2 Other Level
21 Regular; 2 Special Education; 0 Vocational; 9 Alternative
0 Magnet; 0 Charter; 12 Title I Eligible; 12 School-wide Title I
Students: 12,963   (51.4% male; 48.5% female)
Individual Education Program: 1,531 (11.8%);
English Language Learner: 3,168 (24.4%); Migrant: n/a
Eligible for Free Lunch Program: 7,217 (55.7%)
Eligible for Reduced-Price Lunch Program: 1,199 (9.2%)
Teachers: 624.4 (20.8 to 1)
Librarians/Media Specialists: 19.2 (675.2 to 1)
Guidance Counselors: 27.2 (476.6 to 1)
Current Spending: ($ per student per year):
Total: $5,371; Instruction: $3,229; Support Services: $1,762
Enrollment, Drop-out Rates and Diploma Recipients by Race/Ethnicity

Category	Total	White	Black	Asian	AIAN	Hisp.
Enrollment (%)	100.0	53.9	3.0	1.9	1.5	39.7
Drop-out Rate (%)	5.8	4.6	5.4	6.5	3.5	8.7
H.S. Diplomas (#)	656	479	21	15	8	133

Weber SD

5320 S Adams Ave Pkwy • Ogden, UT 84405-6913
(801) 476-7800 • http://www.weber.k12.ut.us
Grade Span: KG-12; **Agency Type:** 1
Schools: 48
28 Primary; 10 Middle; 6 High; 4 Other Level
40 Regular; 5 Special Education; 0 Vocational; 3 Alternative
0 Magnet; 0 Charter; 4 Title I Eligible; 4 School-wide Title I
Students: 28,196   (51.6% male; 48.3% female)
Individual Education Program: 3,887 (13.8%);
English Language Learner: 737 (2.6%); Migrant: n/a
Eligible for Free Lunch Program: 4,298 (15.2%)
Eligible for Reduced-Price Lunch Program: 2,591 (9.2%)
Teachers: 1,236.7 (22.8 to 1)
Librarians/Media Specialists: 11.8 (2,389.5 to 1)
Guidance Counselors: 53.5 (527.0 to 1)
Current Spending: ($ per student per year):
Total: $4,521; Instruction: $2,951; Support Services: $1,294
Enrollment, Drop-out Rates and Diploma Recipients by Race/Ethnicity

Category	Total	White	Black	Asian	AIAN	Hisp.
Enrollment (%)	100.0	89.8	1.2	1.6	0.5	6.5
Drop-out Rate (%)	2.2	1.9	5.1	3.2	14.3	5.2
H.S. Diplomas (#)	1,898	1,771	17	31	12	67

Number of Schools

Rank	Number	District Name	City
1	109	Granite SD	Salt Lake City
2	96	Davis SD	Farmington
3	85	Jordan SD	Sandy
4	63	Alpine SD	American Fork
5	48	Weber SD	Ogden
6	44	Salt Lake City SD	Salt Lake City
7	35	Nebo SD	Spanish Fork
7	35	Washington SD	St George
9	32	Ogden SD	Ogden
10	29	Box Elder SD	Brigham City
11	26	Provo SD	Provo
12	25	Cache SD	Logan
13	21	Tooele SD	Tooele
14	15	Duchesne SD	Duchesne
14	15	Iron SD	Cedar City
14	15	Sevier SD	Richfield
17	13	San Juan SD	Blanding
18	12	Carbon SD	Price
18	12	Murray SD	Murray
18	12	Uintah SD	Vernal
21	10	Emery SD	Huntington
21	10	Logan SD	Logan
21	10	Millard SD	Delta
24	9	S Sanpete SD	Manti
25	8	N Sanpete SD	Mt Pleasant
25	8	Park City SD	Park City
27	7	Wasatch SD	Heber City
28	5	Juab SD	Nephi
29	3	Morgan SD	Morgan

Number of Teachers

Rank	Number	District Name	City
1	3,206	Granite SD	Salt Lake City
2	3,053	Jordan SD	Sandy
3	2,627	Davis SD	Farmington
4	2,117	Alpine SD	American Fork
5	1,236	Weber SD	Ogden
6	1,229	Salt Lake City SD	Salt Lake City
7	1,007	Nebo SD	Spanish Fork
8	892	Washington SD	St George
9	668	Provo SD	Provo
10	624	Ogden SD	Ogden
11	582	Cache SD	Logan
12	503	Box Elder SD	Brigham City
13	458	Tooele SD	Tooele
14	341	Iron SD	Cedar City
15	300	Murray SD	Murray
16	296	Uintah SD	Vernal
17	285	Logan SD	Logan
18	220	Sevier SD	Richfield
19	218	Park City SD	Park City
20	213	Duchesne SD	Duchesne
21	204	Carbon SD	Price
22	199	San Juan SD	Blanding
23	189	Wasatch SD	Heber City
24	170	Millard SD	Delta
25	149	S Sanpete SD	Manti
26	129	Emery SD	Huntington
27	114	N Sanpete SD	Mt Pleasant
28	96	Morgan SD	Morgan
29	82	Juab SD	Nephi

Number of Students

Rank	Number	District Name	City
1	74,761	Jordan SD	Sandy
2	70,771	Granite SD	Salt Lake City
3	60,749	Davis SD	Farmington
4	51,240	Alpine SD	American Fork
5	28,196	Weber SD	Ogden
6	24,443	Salt Lake City SD	Salt Lake City
7	24,129	Nebo SD	Spanish Fork
8	20,482	Washington SD	St George
9	13,156	Cache SD	Logan
10	13,145	Provo SD	Provo
11	12,963	Ogden SD	Ogden
12	10,508	Tooele SD	Tooele
13	10,498	Box Elder SD	Brigham City
14	7,457	Iron SD	Cedar City
15	6,482	Murray SD	Murray
16	5,738	Logan SD	Logan
17	5,607	Uintah SD	Vernal
18	4,436	Sevier SD	Richfield
19	4,123	Park City SD	Park City
20	4,022	Wasatch SD	Heber City
21	3,900	Duchesne SD	Duchesne
22	3,622	Carbon SD	Price
23	3,177	Millard SD	Delta
24	2,979	San Juan SD	Blanding
25	2,792	S Sanpete SD	Manti
26	2,436	Emery SD	Huntington
27	2,376	N Sanpete SD	Mt Pleasant
28	1,989	Morgan SD	Morgan
29	1,939	Juab SD	Nephi

Male Students

Rank	Percent	District Name	City
1	52.8	S Sanpete SD	Manti
2	52.6	Park City SD	Park City
3	52.4	Uintah SD	Vernal
4	52.4	Emery SD	Huntington
5	52.3	Iron SD	Cedar City
6	52.1	Nebo SD	Spanish Fork
7	52.1	Wasatch SD	Heber City
8	51.9	San Juan SD	Blanding
9	51.9	Morgan SD	Morgan
10	51.9	Box Elder SD	Brigham City
11	51.8	Millard SD	Delta
12	51.6	Weber SD	Ogden
13	51.4	Salt Lake City SD	Salt Lake City
14	51.4	Washington SD	St George
15	51.4	Ogden SD	Ogden
16	51.4	Alpine SD	American Fork
17	51.4	Provo SD	Provo
18	51.3	Jordan SD	Sandy
19	51.3	Logan SD	Logan
20	51.3	Davis SD	Farmington
21	51.3	Granite SD	Salt Lake City
22	51.1	Tooele SD	Tooele
23	51.0	Cache SD	Logan
24	51.0	Duchesne SD	Duchesne
25	50.8	Sevier SD	Richfield
26	50.7	Murray SD	Murray
27	50.2	Juab SD	Nephi
28	50.2	N Sanpete SD	Mt Pleasant
29	50.1	Carbon SD	Price

Female Students

Rank	Percent	District Name	City
1	49.8	Carbon SD	Price
2	49.7	N Sanpete SD	Mt Pleasant
3	49.7	Juab SD	Nephi
4	49.2	Murray SD	Murray
5	49.1	Sevier SD	Richfield
6	49.0	Duchesne SD	Duchesne
7	48.9	Cache SD	Logan
8	48.8	Tooele SD	Tooele
9	48.6	Granite SD	Salt Lake City
10	48.6	Davis SD	Farmington
11	48.6	Logan SD	Logan
12	48.6	Jordan SD	Sandy
13	48.5	Provo SD	Provo
14	48.5	Alpine SD	American Fork
15	48.5	Ogden SD	Ogden
16	48.5	Washington SD	St George
17	48.5	Salt Lake City SD	Salt Lake City
18	48.3	Weber SD	Ogden
19	48.1	Millard SD	Delta
20	48.0	Box Elder SD	Brigham City
21	48.0	Morgan SD	Morgan
22	48.0	San Juan SD	Blanding
23	47.8	Wasatch SD	Heber City
24	47.8	Nebo SD	Spanish Fork
25	47.6	Iron SD	Cedar City
26	47.5	Emery SD	Huntington
27	47.5	Uintah SD	Vernal
28	47.3	Park City SD	Park City
29	47.1	S Sanpete SD	Manti

Individual Education Program Students

Rank	Percent	District Name	City
1	19.2	Carbon SD	Price
2	17.0	S Sanpete SD	Manti
3	16.6	Emery SD	Huntington
4	15.9	Duchesne SD	Duchesne
5	15.6	Uintah SD	Vernal
6	14.2	N Sanpete SD	Mt Pleasant
7	13.8	Juab SD	Nephi
7	13.8	Weber SD	Ogden
9	13.7	Wasatch SD	Heber City
10	13.6	Iron SD	Cedar City
10	13.6	Millard SD	Delta
12	13.3	Box Elder SD	Brigham City
12	13.3	Tooele SD	Tooele
14	13.1	Nebo SD	Spanish Fork
15	12.8	Cache SD	Logan
15	12.8	Sevier SD	Richfield
17	12.7	Salt Lake City SD	Salt Lake City
18	12.2	Provo SD	Provo

19	11.8	Ogden SD	Ogden
20	11.7	Logan SD	Logan
21	11.6	Granite SD	Salt Lake City
22	11.4	Washington SD	St George
23	11.1	San Juan SD	Blanding
24	10.7	Jordan SD	Sandy
25	10.2	Alpine SD	American Fork
26	9.7	Davis SD	Farmington
26	9.7	Park City SD	Park City
28	8.3	Murray SD	Murray
29	7.5	Morgan SD	Morgan

English Language Learner Students

Rank	Percent	District Name	City
1	49.2	San Juan SD	Blanding
2	37.9	Salt Lake City SD	Salt Lake City
3	24.4	Ogden SD	Ogden
4	19.7	Provo SD	Provo
5	18.7	Granite SD	Salt Lake City
6	13.9	Logan SD	Logan
7	12.9	Uintah SD	Vernal
8	11.0	Millard SD	Delta
9	9.8	Park City SD	Park City
10	8.9	N Sanpete SD	Mt Pleasant
11	7.6	Murray SD	Murray
12	7.0	Wasatch SD	Heber City
13	6.4	Iron SD	Cedar City
14	6.2	Washington SD	St George
15	6.0	Jordan SD	Sandy
16	5.8	Alpine SD	American Fork
17	5.7	Cache SD	Logan
18	5.4	S Sanpete SD	Manti
19	5.3	Davis SD	Farmington
20	4.5	Nebo SD	Spanish Fork
21	3.7	Tooele SD	Tooele
22	3.5	Emery SD	Huntington
23	2.8	Box Elder SD	Brigham City
24	2.6	Weber SD	Ogden
25	2.5	Duchesne SD	Duchesne
26	1.2	Sevier SD	Richfield
27	0.8	Carbon SD	Price
28	0.3	Morgan SD	Morgan
29	0.1	Juab SD	Nephi

Migrant Students

Rank	Percent	District Name	City
1	n/a	Alpine SD	American Fork
1	n/a	Box Elder SD	Brigham City
1	n/a	Cache SD	Logan
1	n/a	Carbon SD	Price
1	n/a	Davis SD	Farmington
1	n/a	Duchesne SD	Duchesne
1	n/a	Emery SD	Huntington
1	n/a	Granite SD	Salt Lake City
1	n/a	Iron SD	Cedar City
1	n/a	Jordan SD	Sandy
1	n/a	Juab SD	Nephi
1	n/a	Logan SD	Logan
1	n/a	Millard SD	Delta
1	n/a	Morgan SD	Morgan
1	n/a	Murray SD	Murray
1	n/a	N Sanpete SD	Mt Pleasant
1	n/a	Nebo SD	Spanish Fork
1	n/a	Ogden SD	Ogden
1	n/a	Park City SD	Park City
1	n/a	Provo SD	Provo
1	n/a	S Sanpete SD	Manti
1	n/a	Salt Lake City SD	Salt Lake City
1	n/a	San Juan SD	Blanding
1	n/a	Sevier SD	Richfield
1	n/a	Tooele SD	Tooele
1	n/a	Uintah SD	Vernal
1	n/a	Wasatch SD	Heber City
1	n/a	Washington SD	St George
1	n/a	Weber SD	Ogden

Students Eligible for Free Lunch

Rank	Percent	District Name	City
1	63.3	San Juan SD	Blanding
2	55.7	Ogden SD	Ogden
3	49.2	Salt Lake City SD	Salt Lake City
4	34.5	Carbon SD	Price
5	34.0	S Sanpete SD	Manti
6	33.6	Provo SD	Provo
7	31.6	Logan SD	Logan
8	31.4	Emery SD	Huntington
9	30.9	N Sanpete SD	Mt Pleasant
10	30.1	Millard SD	Delta
11	30.0	Granite SD	Salt Lake City
12	29.5	Duchesne SD	Duchesne

Rank		District Name	City
13	28.8	Uintah SD	Vernal
14	28.7	Sevier SD	Richfield
15	28.0	Iron SD	Cedar City
16	24.1	Tooele SD	Tooele
17	21.6	Washington SD	St George
18	20.5	Box Elder SD	Brigham City
19	20.2	Juab SD	Nephi
20	19.0	Nebo SD	Spanish Fork
21	17.5	Wasatch SD	Heber City
22	17.3	Alpine SD	American Fork
23	16.8	Cache SD	Logan
24	16.7	Murray SD	Murray
25	15.2	Weber SD	Ogden
26	15.0	Davis SD	Farmington
27	14.0	Jordan SD	Sandy
28	10.4	Morgan SD	Morgan
29	8.1	Park City SD	Park City

Students Eligible for Reduced-Price Lunch

Rank	Percent	District Name	City
1	18.7	N Sanpete SD	Mt Pleasant
2	16.7	S Sanpete SD	Manti
3	16.3	Emery SD	Huntington
4	15.8	Millard SD	Delta
5	15.7	Juab SD	Nephi
6	14.9	Sevier SD	Richfield
7	14.6	Uintah SD	Vernal
8	13.9	Duchesne SD	Duchesne
9	13.6	Box Elder SD	Brigham City
10	11.9	Iron SD	Cedar City
11	11.8	Cache SD	Logan
12	11.7	Tooele SD	Tooele
13	10.4	Logan SD	Logan
14	10.2	Washington SD	St George
15	9.7	Provo SD	Provo
15	9.7	San Juan SD	Blanding
17	9.6	Carbon SD	Price
17	9.6	Granite SD	Salt Lake City
19	9.3	Salt Lake City SD	Salt Lake City
20	9.2	Nebo SD	Spanish Fork
20	9.2	Ogden SD	Ogden
20	9.2	Weber SD	Ogden
23	9.1	Morgan SD	Morgan
24	8.3	Davis SD	Farmington
25	7.8	Alpine SD	American Fork
26	7.6	Murray SD	Murray
27	7.3	Wasatch SD	Heber City
28	6.7	Jordan SD	Sandy
29	1.8	Park City SD	Park City

Student/Teacher Ratio

Rank	Ratio	District Name	City
1	24.5	Jordan SD	Sandy
2	24.2	Alpine SD	American Fork
3	24.0	Nebo SD	Spanish Fork
4	23.6	Juab SD	Nephi
5	23.1	Davis SD	Farmington
6	23.0	Washington SD	St George
7	22.9	Tooele SD	Tooele
8	22.8	Weber SD	Ogden
9	22.6	Cache SD	Logan
10	22.1	Granite SD	Salt Lake City
11	21.8	Iron SD	Cedar City
12	21.6	Murray SD	Murray
13	21.2	Wasatch SD	Heber City
14	20.9	Box Elder SD	Brigham City
15	20.8	N Sanpete SD	Mt Pleasant
15	20.8	Ogden SD	Ogden
17	20.6	Morgan SD	Morgan
18	20.2	Sevier SD	Richfield
19	20.1	Logan SD	Logan
20	19.9	Salt Lake City SD	Salt Lake City
21	19.7	Provo SD	Provo
22	18.9	Park City SD	Park City
22	18.9	Uintah SD	Vernal
24	18.8	Emery SD	Huntington
25	18.7	S Sanpete SD	Manti
26	18.6	Millard SD	Delta
27	18.3	Duchesne SD	Duchesne
28	17.7	Carbon SD	Price
29	15.0	San Juan SD	Blanding

Student/Librarian Ratio

Rank	Ratio	District Name	City
1	3,222.6	Alpine SD	American Fork
2	3,083.7	Davis SD	Farmington
3	2,865.2	Granite SD	Salt Lake City
4	2,803.5	Uintah SD	Vernal
5	2,779.2	Jordan SD	Sandy

Rank	Ratio	District Name	City
6	2,485.7	Iron SD	Cedar City
7	2,412.9	Nebo SD	Spanish Fork
8	2,389.5	Weber SD	Ogden
9	2,376.0	N Sanpete SD	Mt Pleasant
10	2,160.7	Murray SD	Murray
11	2,048.2	Washington SD	St George
12	1,851.0	Logan SD	Logan
13	1,811.0	Carbon SD	Price
14	1,752.3	Box Elder SD	Brigham City
15	1,751.3	Tooele SD	Tooele
16	1,657.5	Morgan SD	Morgan
17	1,624.0	Emery SD	Huntington
18	1,608.8	Wasatch SD	Heber City
19	858.6	Millard SD	Delta
20	806.4	Provo SD	Provo
21	696.1	Cache SD	Logan
22	687.2	Park City SD	Park City
23	675.2	Ogden SD	Ogden
24	599.1	Salt Lake City SD	Salt Lake City
25	582.1	Duchesne SD	Duchesne
26	331.0	San Juan SD	Blanding
27	n/a	Juab SD	Nephi
27	n/a	S Sanpete SD	Manti
27	n/a	Sevier SD	Richfield

Student/Counselor Ratio

Rank	Ratio	District Name	City
1	1,218.0	Emery SD	Huntington
2	1,188.0	N Sanpete SD	Mt Pleasant
3	1,167.4	Sevier SD	Richfield
4	1,140.6	Juab SD	Nephi
5	1,054.5	Jordan SD	Sandy
6	943.9	Iron SD	Cedar City
7	910.1	Alpine SD	American Fork
8	876.3	Provo SD	Provo
9	871.3	Cache SD	Logan
10	828.8	Morgan SD	Morgan
11	819.7	Logan SD	Logan
12	808.3	Tooele SD	Tooele
13	801.0	Uintah SD	Vernal
14	797.7	S Sanpete SD	Manti
15	794.3	Millard SD	Delta
16	762.6	Murray SD	Murray
17	735.6	Nebo SD	Spanish Fork
18	734.1	Granite SD	Salt Lake City
19	672.4	Duchesne SD	Duchesne
20	615.7	Salt Lake City SD	Salt Lake City
21	609.6	Washington SD	St George
22	597.4	Box Elder SD	Brigham City
23	563.0	Davis SD	Farmington
24	527.0	Weber SD	Ogden
25	522.3	Wasatch SD	Heber City
26	504.9	San Juan SD	Blanding
27	490.8	Park City SD	Park City
28	476.6	Ogden SD	Ogden
29	373.4	Carbon SD	Price

Current Spending per Student in FY2003

Rank	Dollars	District Name	City
1	9,647	San Juan SD	Blanding
2	6,560	Millard SD	Delta
3	6,351	Park City SD	Park City
4	6,269	Emery SD	Huntington
5	6,268	Carbon SD	Price
6	5,799	Uintah SD	Vernal
7	5,778	Duchesne SD	Duchesne
8	5,733	S Sanpete SD	Manti
9	5,714	Salt Lake City SD	Salt Lake City
10	5,611	Provo SD	Provo
11	5,595	N Sanpete SD	Mt Pleasant
12	5,371	Ogden SD	Ogden
13	5,291	Sevier SD	Richfield
14	5,081	Iron SD	Cedar City
15	5,002	Murray SD	Murray
16	4,973	Cache SD	Logan
17	4,891	Wasatch SD	Heber City
18	4,871	Logan SD	Logan
19	4,829	Morgan SD	Morgan
20	4,728	Box Elder SD	Brigham City
21	4,692	Davis SD	Farmington
22	4,686	Juab SD	Nephi
23	4,595	Granite SD	Salt Lake City
24	4,524	Washington SD	St George
25	4,521	Weber SD	Ogden
26	4,520	Jordan SD	Sandy
27	4,413	Alpine SD	American Fork
28	4,374	Tooele SD	Tooele
29	4,339	Nebo SD	Spanish Fork

Number of Diploma Recipients

Rank	Number	District Name	City
1	4,916	Jordan SD	Sandy
2	4,170	Granite SD	Salt Lake City
3	3,765	Davis SD	Farmington
4	2,726	Alpine SD	American Fork
5	1,898	Weber SD	Ogden
6	1,303	Nebo SD	Spanish Fork
7	1,214	Washington SD	St George
8	1,202	Salt Lake City SD	Salt Lake City
9	895	Cache SD	Logan
10	805	Box Elder SD	Brigham City
11	763	Provo SD	Provo
12	656	Ogden SD	Ogden
13	513	Tooele SD	Tooele
14	482	Iron SD	Cedar City
15	480	Murray SD	Murray
16	405	Logan SD	Logan
17	393	Uintah SD	Vernal
18	305	Sevier SD	Richfield
19	303	Duchesne SD	Duchesne
20	282	Park City SD	Park City
21	277	Wasatch SD	Heber City
22	273	Carbon SD	Price
23	263	Millard SD	Delta
24	226	S Sanpete SD	Manti
25	219	Emery SD	Huntington
26	199	San Juan SD	Blanding
27	175	N Sanpete SD	Mt Pleasant
28	174	Morgan SD	Morgan
29	124	Juab SD	Nephi

High School Drop-out Rate

Rank	Percent	District Name	City
1	11.2	Salt Lake City SD	Salt Lake City
2	6.4	Sevier SD	Richfield
3	6.0	Granite SD	Salt Lake City
4	5.9	Duchesne SD	Duchesne
5	5.8	Ogden SD	Ogden
6	4.4	Jordan SD	Sandy
6	4.4	Logan SD	Logan
8	4.2	Uintah SD	Vernal
9	3.5	Cache SD	Logan
9	3.5	N Sanpete SD	Mt Pleasant
11	3.0	Murray SD	Murray
11	3.0	Park City SD	Park City
13	2.9	San Juan SD	Blanding
14	2.6	Tooele SD	Tooele
15	2.4	Davis SD	Farmington
16	2.2	Weber SD	Ogden
17	2.1	Alpine SD	American Fork
18	2.0	Box Elder SD	Brigham City
18	2.0	Carbon SD	Price
18	2.0	Nebo SD	Spanish Fork
21	1.7	Wasatch SD	Heber City
22	1.4	Provo SD	Provo
23	1.2	Emery SD	Huntington
23	1.2	Iron SD	Cedar City
25	1.1	Morgan SD	Morgan
25	1.1	S Sanpete SD	Manti
27	1.0	Juab SD	Nephi
28	0.9	Millard SD	Delta
29	0.8	Washington SD	St George

Vermont

Vermont Public School Educational Profile

Category	Value	Category	Value
Schools (2003-2004)	393	**Diploma Recipients** (2002-2003)	7,083
Instructional Level		White, Non-Hispanic	n/a
Primary	259	Black, Non-Hispanic	n/a
Middle	25	Asian/Pacific Islander	n/a
High	61	American Indian/Alaskan Native	n/a
Other Level	48	Hispanic	n/a
Curriculum		**High School Drop-out Rate** (%) (2001-2002)	4.0
Regular	316	White, Non-Hispanic	3.9
Special Education	61	Black, Non-Hispanic	7.3
Vocational	14	Asian/Pacific Islander	2.2
Alternative	2	American Indian/Alaskan Native	5.9
Type		Hispanic	9.0
Magnet	0	**Staff** (2003-2004)	
Charter	0	Teachers	8,750.4
Title I Eligible	210	Average Salary[1] ($)	43,009
School-wide Title I	82	Librarians/Media Specialists	226.1
Students (2003-2004)	99,103	Guidance Counselors	426.5
Gender (%)		**Ratios** (2003-2004)	
Male	51.6	Student/Teacher Ratio	11.3 to 1
Female	48.4	Student/Librarian Ratio	438.3 to 1
Race/Ethnicity (%)		Student/Counselor Ratio	232.4 to 1
White, Non-Hispanic	95.4	**College Entrance Exam Scores** (2005)	
Black, Non-Hispanic	1.2	Scholastic Aptitude Test (SAT)	
Asian/Pacific Islander	1.5	Participation Rate (%)	67
American Indian/Alaskan Native	0.6	Mean SAT Reasoning Test Verbal Score	521
Hispanic	0.8	Mean SAT Reasoning Test Math Score	517
Classification (%)		American College Testing Program (ACT)	
Individual Education Program (IEP)	14.9	Participation Rate (%)	16
Migrant (2002-2003)	0.8	Average Composite Score	22.6
English Language Learner (ELL)	2.0	Average English Score	22.3
Eligible for Free Lunch Program	20.0	Average Math Score	22.1
Eligible for Reduced-Price Lunch Program	7.4	Average Reading Score	23.5
Current Spending ($ per student in FY 2003)	9,790	Average Science Score	22.1
Instruction	6,503		
Support Services	2,998		

Note: For an explanation of data, please refer to the User's Guide in the front of the book; (1) Includes extra-duty pay

Vermont NAEP 2005 Test Scores

Reading			Mathematics		
Grade/Category	Value	Rank	Grade/Category	Value	Rank
4th Grade			**4th Grade**		
Average Proficiency	226.9 (0.88)	3/51	Average Proficiency	243.5 (0.53)	6/51
Proficiency by Gender/Race/Ethnicity			Proficiency by Gender/Race/Ethnicity		
Male	223.2 (1.14)	4/51	Male	245.9 (0.73)	5/51
Female	230.3 (1.19)	3/51	Female	240.8 (0.76)	10/51
White, Non-Hispanic	226.7 (0.87)	22/51	White, Non-Hispanic	243.7 (0.54)	31/51
Black, Non-Hispanic	n/a	n/a	Black, Non-Hispanic	n/a	n/a
Asian, Non-Hispanic	n/a	n/a	Asian, Non-Hispanic	n/a	n/a
American Indian, Non-Hispanic	n/a	n/a	American Indian, Non-Hispanic	n/a	n/a
Hispanic	n/a	n/a	Hispanic	n/a	n/a
Proficiency by Class Size			Proficiency by Class Size		
Less than 16 Students	222.8 (1.78)	2/34	Less than 16 Students	243.2 (1.07)	2/35
16 to 18 Students	227.5 (1.47)	1/33	16 to 18 Students	242.8 (1.33)	5/31
19 to 20 Students	228.4 (1.75)	2/38	19 to 20 Students	243.4 (1.27)	9/38
21 to 25 Students	228.4 (1.76)	5/51	21 to 25 Students	245.4 (1.30)	7/51
Greater than 25 Students	n/a	n/a	Greater than 25 Students	n/a	n/a
Percent Attaining Achievement Levels			Percent Attaining Achievement Levels		
Below Basic	27.6 (1.27)	48/51	Below Basic	13.1 (0.76)	45/51
Basic or Above	72.4 (1.27)	4/51	Basic or Above	86.9 (0.76)	7/51
Proficient or Above	38.5 (1.20)	3/51	Proficient or Above	43.5 (1.08)	6/51
Advanced or Above	10.2 (1.00)	4/51	Advanced or Above	6.1 (0.60)	11/51
8th Grade			**8th Grade**		
Average Proficiency	268.8 (0.75)	7/51	Average Proficiency	287.4 (0.75)	3/51
Proficiency by Gender/Race/Ethnicity			Proficiency by Gender/Race/Ethnicity		
Male	262.2 (1.08)	12/51	Male	287.3 (1.03)	5/51
Female	275.6 (1.24)	3/51	Female	287.4 (1.04)	3/51
White, Non-Hispanic	269.0 (0.74)	25/51	White, Non-Hispanic	288.3 (0.78)	24/51
Black, Non-Hispanic	n/a	n/a	Black, Non-Hispanic	n/a	n/a
Asian, Non-Hispanic	n/a	n/a	Asian, Non-Hispanic	n/a	n/a
American Indian, Non-Hispanic	n/a	n/a	American Indian, Non-Hispanic	n/a	n/a
Hispanic	n/a	n/a	Hispanic	n/a	n/a
Proficiency by Parents Highest Level of Ed.			Proficiency by Parents Highest Level of Ed.		
Did Not Finish High School	240.0 (3.78)	36/49	Did Not Finish High School	264.7 (3.77)	12/50
Graduated High School	256.9 (1.82)	15/50	Graduated High School	274.6 (1.44)	7/50
Some Education After High School	264.4 (2.14)	31/50	Some Education After High School	284.9 (1.78)	11/50
Graduated College	278.5 (1.01)	2/50	Graduated College	298.2 (1.10)	3/50
Percent Attaining Achievement Levels			Percent Attaining Achievement Levels		
Below Basic	27.6 (1.27)	48/51	Below Basic	22.5 (0.98)	46/51
Basic or Above	72.4 (1.27)	4/51	Basic or Above	77.5 (0.98)	6/51
Proficient or Above	38.5 (1.20)	3/51	Proficient or Above	37.8 (1.07)	3/51
Advanced or Above	10.2 (1.00)	4/51	Advanced or Above	8.8 (0.72)	3/51

Note: *For an explanation of data, please refer to the User's Guide in the front of the book; n/a indicates data not available*

Bennington County

Mount Anthony Uhsd 14
301 Park St Ex. • Bennington, VT 05201-5011
Mailing Address: Park St • Bennington, VT 05201-5011
(802) 447-7511
Grade Span: 07-12; Agency Type: 2
Schools: 3
   0 Primary; 1 Middle; 2 High; 0 Other Level
   2 Regular; 0 Special Education; 1 Vocational; 0 Alternative
   0 Magnet; 0 Charter; 0 Title I Eligible; 0 School-wide Title I
Students: 1,817   (50.7% male; 49.2% female)
   Individual Education Program: 0 (0.0%);
   English Language Learner: 17 (0.9%); Migrant: 3 (0.2%)
   Eligible for Free Lunch Program: 399 (22.0%)
   Eligible for Reduced-Price Lunch Program: 59 (3.2%)
Teachers: 136.0 (13.4 to 1)
Librarians/Media Specialists: 2.0 (908.5 to 1)
Guidance Counselors: 12.0 (151.4 to 1)
Current Spending: ($ per student per year):
   Total: $7,287; Instruction: $4,345; Support Services: $2,938

Enrollment, Drop-out Rates and Diploma Recipients by Race/Ethnicity

Category	Total	White	Black	Asian	AIAN	Hisp.
Enrollment (%)	100.0	97.6	0.9	1.2	0.0	0.4
Drop-out Rate (%)	4.9	4.7	27.3	6.7	0.0	0.0
H.S. Diplomas (#)	285	n/a	n/a	n/a	n/a	n/a

Chittenden County

Burlington SD
150 Colchester Ave • Burlington, VT 05401
(802) 864-8461 • http://burlington.k12.vt.us/
Grade Span: PK-12; Agency Type: 2
Schools: 12
   7 Primary; 2 Middle; 2 High; 1 Other Level
   9 Regular; 1 Special Education; 1 Vocational; 1 Alternative
   0 Magnet; 0 Charter; 8 Title I Eligible; 3 School-wide Title I
Students: 3,621   (52.2% male; 47.7% female)
   Individual Education Program: 654 (18.1%);
   English Language Learner: 434 (12.0%); Migrant: 2 (0.1%)
   Eligible for Free Lunch Program: 1,320 (36.5%)
   Eligible for Reduced-Price Lunch Program: 265 (7.3%)
Teachers: 299.7 (12.1 to 1)
Librarians/Media Specialists: 8.4 (431.1 to 1)
Guidance Counselors: 16.1 (224.9 to 1)
Current Spending: ($ per student per year):
   Total: $10,918; Instruction: $6,913; Support Services: $3,562

Enrollment, Drop-out Rates and Diploma Recipients by Race/Ethnicity

Category	Total	White	Black	Asian	AIAN	Hisp.
Enrollment (%)	100.0	84.8	5.6	6.1	0.3	2.1
Drop-out Rate (%)	5.6	5.5	5.1	6.3	0.0	8.3
H.S. Diplomas (#)	199	n/a	n/a	n/a	n/a	n/a

Colchester SD
125 Laker Ln • Colchester, VT 05446-0055
Mailing Address: Box 27 • Colchester, VT 05446-0055
(802) 658-4047 • http://www.colchestersd.k12.vt.us/
Grade Span: PK-12; Agency Type: 2
Schools: 5
   3 Primary; 1 Middle; 1 High; 0 Other Level
   5 Regular; 0 Special Education; 0 Vocational; 0 Alternative
   0 Magnet; 0 Charter; 3 Title I Eligible; 0 School-wide Title I
Students: 2,412   (51.8% male; 48.1% female)
   Individual Education Program: 251 (10.4%);
   English Language Learner: 62 (2.6%); Migrant: 1 (<0.1%)
   Eligible for Free Lunch Program: 205 (8.5%)
   Eligible for Reduced-Price Lunch Program: 94 (3.9%)
Teachers: 157.3 (15.3 to 1)
Librarians/Media Specialists: 5.0 (482.4 to 1)
Guidance Counselors: 9.8 (246.1 to 1)
Current Spending: ($ per student per year):
   Total: $8,536; Instruction: $5,179; Support Services: $3,077

Enrollment, Drop-out Rates and Diploma Recipients by Race/Ethnicity

Category	Total	White	Black	Asian	AIAN	Hisp.
Enrollment (%)	100.0	96.4	1.4	1.3	0.2	0.7
Drop-out Rate (%)	2.4	2.3	0.0	14.3	0.0	0.0
H.S. Diplomas (#)	159	n/a	n/a	n/a	n/a	n/a

Essex Community Education Ctr
2 Educational Dr • Essex Junction, VT 05452-3167
(802) 879-5500
Grade Span: 09-12; Agency Type: 2
Schools: 2
   0 Primary; 0 Middle; 2 High; 0 Other Level
   1 Regular; 0 Special Education; 1 Vocational; 0 Alternative

   0 Magnet; 0 Charter; 0 Title I Eligible; 0 School-wide Title I
Students: 1,596   (53.6% male; 46.3% female)
   Individual Education Program: 126 (7.9%);
   English Language Learner: 53 (3.3%); Migrant: 2 (0.1%)
   Eligible for Free Lunch Program: 103 (6.5%)
   Eligible for Reduced-Price Lunch Program: 48 (3.0%)
Teachers: 147.0 (10.9 to 1)
Librarians/Media Specialists: 1.0 (1,596.0 to 1)
Guidance Counselors: 9.4 (169.8 to 1)
Current Spending: ($ per student per year):
   Total: $12,372; Instruction: $8,249; Support Services: $3,567

Enrollment, Drop-out Rates and Diploma Recipients by Race/Ethnicity

Category	Total	White	Black	Asian	AIAN	Hisp.
Enrollment (%)	100.0	93.3	1.7	2.7	0.3	1.3
Drop-out Rate (%)	3.9	3.8	7.7	7.3	25.0	0.0
H.S. Diplomas (#)	337	n/a	n/a	n/a	n/a	n/a

Milton Id SD
42 Herrick Ave • Milton, VT 05468-0018
(802) 893-3210
Grade Span: PK-12; Agency Type: 2
Schools: 3
   1 Primary; 1 Middle; 1 High; 0 Other Level
   3 Regular; 0 Special Education; 0 Vocational; 0 Alternative
   0 Magnet; 0 Charter; 2 Title I Eligible; 2 School-wide Title I
Students: 1,876   (52.5% male; 47.4% female)
   Individual Education Program: 400 (21.3%);
   English Language Learner: 15 (0.8%); Migrant: 0 (0.0%)
   Eligible for Free Lunch Program: 242 (12.9%)
   Eligible for Reduced-Price Lunch Program: 106 (5.7%)
Teachers: 145.0 (12.9 to 1)
Librarians/Media Specialists: 3.0 (625.3 to 1)
Guidance Counselors: 11.0 (170.5 to 1)
Current Spending: ($ per student per year):
   Total: $8,334; Instruction: $5,096; Support Services: $3,049

Enrollment, Drop-out Rates and Diploma Recipients by Race/Ethnicity

Category	Total	White	Black	Asian	AIAN	Hisp.
Enrollment (%)	100.0	98.3	0.5	0.5	0.3	0.4
Drop-out Rate (%)	4.1	4.2	0.0	0.0	0.0	0.0
H.S. Diplomas (#)	114	n/a	n/a	n/a	n/a	n/a

Mount Mansfield Usd 17
211 Browns Tace Rd • Jericho, VT 05465-9498
Mailing Address: 211 Browns Trace • Jericho, VT 05465-9498
(802) 899-4690
Grade Span: 05-12; Agency Type: 2
Schools: 3
   0 Primary; 2 Middle; 1 High; 0 Other Level
   3 Regular; 0 Special Education; 0 Vocational; 0 Alternative
   0 Magnet; 0 Charter; 1 Title I Eligible; 0 School-wide Title I
Students: 1,982   (50.6% male; 49.3% female)
   Individual Education Program: 109 (5.5%);
   English Language Learner: 3 (0.2%); Migrant: 1 (0.1%)
   Eligible for Free Lunch Program: 98 (4.9%)
   Eligible for Reduced-Price Lunch Program: 65 (3.3%)
Teachers: 126.1 (15.7 to 1)
Librarians/Media Specialists: 3.0 (660.7 to 1)
Guidance Counselors: 8.0 (247.8 to 1)
Current Spending: ($ per student per year):
   Total: $6,958; Instruction: $4,601; Support Services: $2,013

Enrollment, Drop-out Rates and Diploma Recipients by Race/Ethnicity

Category	Total	White	Black	Asian	AIAN	Hisp.
Enrollment (%)	100.0	97.3	0.8	0.8	0.2	0.6
Drop-out Rate (%)	1.6	1.6	0.0	0.0	0.0	0.0
H.S. Diplomas (#)	247	n/a	n/a	n/a	n/a	n/a

South Burlington SD
550 Dorset St • South Burlington, VT 05403-6296
(802) 652-7250
Grade Span: KG-12; Agency Type: 2
Schools: 5
   3 Primary; 1 Middle; 1 High; 0 Other Level
   5 Regular; 0 Special Education; 0 Vocational; 0 Alternative
   0 Magnet; 0 Charter; 1 Title I Eligible; 0 School-wide Title I
Students: 2,667   (51.2% male; 48.7% female)
   Individual Education Program: 290 (10.9%);
   English Language Learner: 235 (8.8%); Migrant: 1 (<0.1%)
   Eligible for Free Lunch Program: 236 (8.8%)
   Eligible for Reduced-Price Lunch Program: 110 (4.1%)
Teachers: 199.5 (13.4 to 1)
Librarians/Media Specialists: 4.8 (555.6 to 1)
Guidance Counselors: 10.2 (261.5 to 1)
Current Spending: ($ per student per year):
   Total: $10,648; Instruction: $6,984; Support Services: $3,263

Enrollment, Drop-out Rates and Diploma Recipients by Race/Ethnicity

Category	Total	White	Black	Asian	AIAN	Hisp.
Enrollment (%)	100.0	90.0	1.9	6.5	0.0	1.2
Drop-out Rate (%)	1.8	1.7	0.0	0.0	0.0	50.0
H.S. Diplomas (#)	195	n/a	n/a	n/a	n/a	n/a

Rutland County

Rutland City SD
6 Church St • Rutland, VT 05701-0969
(802) 773-1900
Grade Span: KG-12; **Agency Type:** 2
Schools: 6
   3 Primary; 1 Middle; 2 High; 0 Other Level
   5 Regular; 0 Special Education; 1 Vocational; 0 Alternative
   0 Magnet; 0 Charter; 4 Title I Eligible; 4 School-wide Title I
Students: 2,801   (49.8% male; 50.1% female)
   Individual Education Program: 381 (13.6%);
   English Language Learner: 13 (0.5%); Migrant: 5 (0.2%)
   Eligible for Free Lunch Program: 822 (29.3%)
   Eligible for Reduced-Price Lunch Program: 237 (8.5%)
Teachers: 237.5 (11.8 to 1)
Librarians/Media Specialists: 2.0 (1,400.5 to 1)
Guidance Counselors: 13.0 (215.5 to 1)
Current Spending: ($ per student per year):
   Total: $10,223; Instruction: $7,360; Support Services: $2,474

Enrollment, Drop-out Rates and Diploma Recipients by Race/Ethnicity

Category	Total	White	Black	Asian	AIAN	Hisp.
Enrollment (%)	100.0	96.6	1.2	1.0	0.1	0.7
Drop-out Rate (%)	4.9	4.9	6.3	0.0	25.0	0.0
H.S. Diplomas (#)	238	n/a	n/a	n/a	n/a	n/a

Windsor County

Hartford SD
73 Highland Ave • White River Junction, VT 05001-8018
(802) 295-8600
Grade Span: PK-12; **Agency Type:** 2
Schools: 6
   3 Primary; 1 Middle; 2 High; 0 Other Level
   5 Regular; 0 Special Education; 1 Vocational; 0 Alternative
   0 Magnet; 0 Charter; 3 Title I Eligible; 0 School-wide Title I
Students: 1,928   (51.0% male; 48.9% female)
   Individual Education Program: 247 (12.8%);
   English Language Learner: 13 (0.7%); Migrant: 1 (0.1%)
   Eligible for Free Lunch Program: 210 (10.9%)
   Eligible for Reduced-Price Lunch Program: 45 (2.3%)
Teachers: 176.3 (10.9 to 1)
Librarians/Media Specialists: 5.0 (385.6 to 1)
Guidance Counselors: 10.3 (187.2 to 1)
Current Spending: ($ per student per year):
   Total: $10,151; Instruction: $6,391; Support Services: $3,525

Enrollment, Drop-out Rates and Diploma Recipients by Race/Ethnicity

Category	Total	White	Black	Asian	AIAN	Hisp.
Enrollment (%)	100.0	96.7	1.0	1.1	0.4	0.5
Drop-out Rate (%)	4.7	4.3	n/a	n/a	n/a	0.0
H.S. Diplomas (#)	181	n/a	n/a	n/a	n/a	n/a

Number of Schools

Rank	Number	District Name	City
1	12	Burlington SD	Burlington
2	6	Hartford SD	White River Jct
2	6	Rutland City SD	Rutland
4	5	Colchester SD	Colchester
4	5	South Burlington SD	S Burlington
6	3	Milton Id SD	Milton
6	3	Mount Anthony Uhsd 14	Bennington
6	3	Mount Mansfield Usd 17	Jericho
9	2	Essex Community Education Ctr	Essex Junction

Number of Teachers

Rank	Number	District Name	City
1	299	Burlington SD	Burlington
2	237	Rutland City SD	Rutland
3	199	South Burlington SD	S Burlington
4	176	Hartford SD	White River Jct
5	157	Colchester SD	Colchester
6	147	Essex Community Education Ctr	Essex Junction
7	145	Milton Id SD	Milton
8	136	Mount Anthony Uhsd 14	Bennington
9	126	Mount Mansfield Usd 17	Jericho

Number of Students

Rank	Number	District Name	City
1	3,621	Burlington SD	Burlington
2	2,801	Rutland City SD	Rutland
3	2,667	South Burlington SD	S Burlington
4	2,412	Colchester SD	Colchester
5	1,982	Mount Mansfield Usd 17	Jericho
6	1,928	Hartford SD	White River Jct
7	1,876	Milton Id SD	Milton
8	1,817	Mount Anthony Uhsd 14	Bennington
9	1,596	Essex Community Education Ctr	Essex Junction

Male Students

Rank	Percent	District Name	City
1	53.6	Essex Community Education Ctr	Essex Junction
2	52.5	Milton Id SD	Milton
3	52.2	Burlington SD	Burlington
4	51.8	Colchester SD	Colchester
5	51.2	South Burlington SD	S Burlington
6	51.0	Hartford SD	White River Jct
7	50.7	Mount Anthony Uhsd 14	Bennington
8	50.6	Mount Mansfield Usd 17	Jericho
9	49.8	Rutland City SD	Rutland

Female Students

Rank	Percent	District Name	City
1	50.1	Rutland City SD	Rutland
2	49.3	Mount Mansfield Usd 17	Jericho
3	49.2	Mount Anthony Uhsd 14	Bennington
4	48.9	Hartford SD	White River Jct
5	48.7	South Burlington SD	S Burlington
6	48.1	Colchester SD	Colchester
7	47.7	Burlington SD	Burlington
8	47.4	Milton Id SD	Milton
9	46.3	Essex Community Education Ctr	Essex Junction

Individual Education Program Students

Rank	Percent	District Name	City
1	21.3	Milton Id SD	Milton
2	18.1	Burlington SD	Burlington
3	13.6	Rutland City SD	Rutland
4	12.8	Hartford SD	White River Jct
5	10.9	South Burlington SD	S Burlington
6	10.4	Colchester SD	Colchester
7	7.9	Essex Community Education Ctr	Essex Junction
8	5.5	Mount Mansfield Usd 17	Jericho
9	0.0	Mount Anthony Uhsd 14	Bennington

English Language Learner Students

Rank	Percent	District Name	City
1	12.0	Burlington SD	Burlington
2	8.8	South Burlington SD	S Burlington
3	3.3	Essex Community Education Ctr	Essex Junction
4	2.6	Colchester SD	Colchester
5	0.9	Mount Anthony Uhsd 14	Bennington
6	0.8	Milton Id SD	Milton
7	0.7	Hartford SD	White River Jct
8	0.5	Rutland City SD	Rutland
9	0.2	Mount Mansfield Usd 17	Jericho

Migrant Students

Rank	Percent	District Name	City

	0.2	Mount Anthony Uhsd 14	Bennington
1	0.2	Rutland City SD	Rutland
3	0.1	Burlington SD	Burlington
3	0.1	Essex Community Education Ctr	Essex Junction
3	0.1	Hartford SD	White River Jct
3	0.1	Mount Mansfield Usd 17	Jericho
7	0.0	Colchester SD	Colchester
7	0.0	South Burlington SD	S Burlington
9	0.0	Milton Id SD	Milton

Students Eligible for Free Lunch

Rank	Percent	District Name	City
1	36.5	Burlington SD	Burlington
2	29.3	Rutland City SD	Rutland
3	22.0	Mount Anthony Uhsd 14	Bennington
4	12.9	Milton Id SD	Milton
5	10.9	Hartford SD	White River Jct
6	8.8	South Burlington SD	S Burlington
7	8.5	Colchester SD	Colchester
8	6.5	Essex Community Education Ctr	Essex Junction
9	4.9	Mount Mansfield Usd 17	Jericho

Students Eligible for Reduced-Price Lunch

Rank	Percent	District Name	City
1	8.5	Rutland City SD	Rutland
2	7.3	Burlington SD	Burlington
3	5.7	Milton Id SD	Milton
4	4.1	South Burlington SD	S Burlington
5	3.9	Colchester SD	Colchester
6	3.3	Mount Mansfield Usd 17	Jericho
7	3.2	Mount Anthony Uhsd 14	Bennington
8	3.0	Essex Community Education Ctr	Essex Junction
9	2.3	Hartford SD	White River Jct

Student/Teacher Ratio

Rank	Ratio	District Name	City
1	15.7	Mount Mansfield Usd 17	Jericho
2	15.3	Colchester SD	Colchester
3	13.4	Mount Anthony Uhsd 14	Bennington
3	13.4	South Burlington SD	S Burlington
5	12.9	Milton Id SD	Milton
6	12.1	Burlington SD	Burlington
7	11.8	Rutland City SD	Rutland
8	10.9	Essex Community Education Ctr	Essex Junction
8	10.9	Hartford SD	White River Jct

Student/Librarian Ratio

Rank	Ratio	District Name	City
1	1,596.0	Essex Community Education Ctr	Essex Junction
2	1,400.5	Rutland City SD	Rutland
3	908.5	Mount Anthony Uhsd 14	Bennington
4	660.7	Mount Mansfield Usd 17	Jericho
5	625.3	Milton Id SD	Milton
6	555.6	South Burlington SD	S Burlington
7	482.4	Colchester SD	Colchester
8	431.1	Burlington SD	Burlington
9	385.6	Hartford SD	White River Jct

Student/Counselor Ratio

Rank	Ratio	District Name	City
1	261.5	South Burlington SD	S Burlington
2	247.8	Mount Mansfield Usd 17	Jericho
3	246.1	Colchester SD	Colchester
4	224.9	Burlington SD	Burlington
5	215.5	Rutland City SD	Rutland
6	187.2	Hartford SD	White River Jct
7	170.5	Milton Id SD	Milton
8	169.8	Essex Community Education Ctr	Essex Junction
9	151.4	Mount Anthony Uhsd 14	Bennington

Current Spending per Student in FY2003

Rank	Dollars	District Name	City
1	12,372	Essex Community Education Ctr	Essex Junction
2	10,918	Burlington SD	Burlington
3	10,648	South Burlington SD	S Burlington
4	10,223	Rutland City SD	Rutland
5	10,151	Hartford SD	White River Jct
6	8,536	Colchester SD	Colchester
7	8,334	Milton Id SD	Milton
8	7,287	Mount Anthony Uhsd 14	Bennington
9	6,958	Mount Mansfield Usd 17	Jericho

Number of Diploma Recipients

Rank	Number	District Name	City
1	337	Essex Community Education Ctr	Essex Junction
2	285	Mount Anthony Uhsd 14	Bennington
3	247	Mount Mansfield Usd 17	Jericho
4	238	Rutland City SD	Rutland
5	199	Burlington SD	Burlington
6	195	South Burlington SD	S Burlington
7	181	Hartford SD	White River Jct
8	159	Colchester SD	Colchester
9	114	Milton Id SD	Milton

High School Drop-out Rate

Rank	Percent	District Name	City
1	5.6	Burlington SD	Burlington
2	4.9	Mount Anthony Uhsd 14	Bennington
2	4.9	Rutland City SD	Rutland
4	4.7	Hartford SD	White River Jct
5	4.1	Milton Id SD	Milton
6	3.9	Essex Community Education Ctr	Essex Junction
7	2.4	Colchester SD	Colchester
8	1.8	South Burlington SD	S Burlington
9	1.6	Mount Mansfield Usd 17	Jericho

Virginia

Virginia Public School Educational Profile

Category	Value	Category	Value
Schools *(2003-2004)*	2,074	**Diploma Recipients** *(2002-2003)*	66,519
Instructional Level		White, Non-Hispanic	45,485
Primary	1,173	Black, Non-Hispanic	15,084
Middle	340	Asian/Pacific Islander	3,353
High	339	American Indian/Alaskan Native	143
Other Level	218	Hispanic	2,454
Curriculum		**High School Drop-out Rate** (%) *(2001-2002)*	2.9
Regular	1,835	White, Non-Hispanic	2.3
Special Education	56	Black, Non-Hispanic	4.0
Vocational	48	Asian/Pacific Islander	2.0
Alternative	131	American Indian/Alaskan Native	4.1
Type		Hispanic	5.8
Magnet	192	**Staff** *(2003-2004)*	
Charter	6	Teachers	91,373.3
Title I Eligible	800	Average Salary ($)	43,936
School-wide Title I	301	Librarians/Media Specialists	1,986.1
Students *(2003-2004)*	1,192,094	Guidance Counselors	2,565.4
Gender (%)		**Ratios** *(2003-2004)*	
Male	51.4	Student/Teacher Ratio	13.0 to 1
Female	48.6	Student/Librarian Ratio	600.2 to 1
Race/Ethnicity (%)		Student/Counselor Ratio	464.7 to 1
White, Non-Hispanic	60.6	**College Entrance Exam Scores** *(2005)*	
Black, Non-Hispanic	26.9	Scholastic Aptitude Test (SAT)	
Asian/Pacific Islander	4.7	Participation Rate (%)	73
American Indian/Alaskan Native	0.3	Mean SAT Reasoning Test Verbal Score	516
Hispanic	6.5	Mean SAT Reasoning Test Math Score	514
Classification (%)		American College Testing Program (ACT)	
Individual Education Program (IEP)	14.5	Participation Rate (%)	14
Migrant *(2002-2003)*	0.1	Average Composite Score	20.8
English Language Learner (ELL)	5.1	Average English Score	20.5
Eligible for Free Lunch Program	23.3	Average Math Score	20.6
Eligible for Reduced-Price Lunch Program	6.9	Average Reading Score	21.2
Current Spending *($ per student in FY 2003)*	7,833	Average Science Score	20.6
Instruction	4,816		
Support Services	2,708		

Note: For an explanation of data, please refer to the User's Guide in the front of the book

Virginia NAEP 2005 Test Scores

Reading			Mathematics		
Grade/Category	Value	Rank	Grade/Category	Value	Rank
4th Grade			**4th Grade**		
Average Proficiency	225.8 (0.81)	4/51	Average Proficiency	240.5 (0.93)	20/51
Proficiency by Gender/Race/Ethnicity			Proficiency by Gender/Race/Ethnicity		
Male	223.3 (1.14)	3/51	Male	242.0 (1.21)	17/51
Female	228.1 (1.02)	8/51	Female	239.0 (0.98)	19/51
White, Non-Hispanic	232.8 (0.99)	5/51	White, Non-Hispanic	247.1 (0.95)	15/51
Black, Non-Hispanic	207.2 (1.20)	6/42	Black, Non-Hispanic	223.5 (1.40)	12/42
Asian, Non-Hispanic	238.7 (2.69)	5/27	Asian, Non-Hispanic	256.0 (2.33)	9/25
American Indian, Non-Hispanic	n/a	n/a	American Indian, Non-Hispanic	n/a	n/a
Hispanic	217.7 (2.24)	2/40	Hispanic	230.5 (2.89)	10/41
Proficiency by Class Size			Proficiency by Class Size		
Less than 16 Students	213.2 (3.91)	11/34	Less than 16 Students	231.3 (3.53)	12/35
16 to 18 Students	217.6 (2.28)	17/33	16 to 18 Students	232.8 (2.27)	22/31
19 to 20 Students	225.9 (2.51)	8/38	19 to 20 Students	239.5 (2.23)	20/38
21 to 25 Students	228.7 (1.50)	3/51	21 to 25 Students	243.6 (1.63)	11/51
Greater than 25 Students	n/a	n/a	Greater than 25 Students	n/a	n/a
Percent Attaining Achievement Levels			Percent Attaining Achievement Levels		
Below Basic	28.1 (1.52)	47/51	Below Basic	17.2 (1.05)	30/51
Basic or Above	71.9 (1.52)	5/51	Basic or Above	82.8 (1.05)	22/51
Proficient or Above	36.9 (1.39)	7/51	Proficient or Above	39.3 (1.53)	18/51
Advanced or Above	8.2 (0.79)	11/51	Advanced or Above	5.6 (0.79)	14/51
8th Grade			**8th Grade**		
Average Proficiency	267.8 (1.04)	11/51	Average Proficiency	284.4 (1.13)	10/51
Proficiency by Gender/Race/Ethnicity			Proficiency by Gender/Race/Ethnicity		
Male	262.9 (1.36)	9/51	Male	285.5 (1.50)	8/51
Female	272.6 (1.09)	12/51	Female	283.3 (1.34)	12/51
White, Non-Hispanic	275.1 (1.26)	5/51	White, Non-Hispanic	293.2 (1.21)	8/51
Black, Non-Hispanic	251.4 (1.85)	5/40	Black, Non-Hispanic	262.7 (1.46)	6/41
Asian, Non-Hispanic	282.2 (3.39)	3/24	Asian, Non-Hispanic	300.4 (3.83)	8/23
American Indian, Non-Hispanic	n/a	n/a	American Indian, Non-Hispanic	n/a	n/a
Hispanic	258.8 (2.27)	1/38	Hispanic	270.0 (3.27)	3/38
Proficiency by Parents Highest Level of Ed.			Proficiency by Parents Highest Level of Ed.		
Did Not Finish High School	255.9 (2.37)	3/49	Did Not Finish High School	265.7 (2.22)	9/50
Graduated High School	257.4 (1.73)	14/50	Graduated High School	270.6 (1.86)	21/50
Some Education After High School	269.8 (1.75)	9/50	Some Education After High School	282.0 (2.57)	26/50
Graduated College	276.1 (1.18)	7/50	Graduated College	294.9 (1.32)	6/50
Percent Attaining Achievement Levels			Percent Attaining Achievement Levels		
Below Basic	28.1 (1.52)	47/51	Below Basic	25.4 (1.20)	38/51
Basic or Above	71.9 (1.52)	5/51	Basic or Above	74.6 (1.20)	14/51
Proficient or Above	36.9 (1.39)	7/51	Proficient or Above	33.4 (1.49)	16/51
Advanced or Above	8.2 (0.79)	11/51	Advanced or Above	7.9 (0.88)	6/51

Note: *For an explanation of data, please refer to the User's Guide in the front of the book; n/a indicates data not available*

Accomack County

Accomack County Public Schools
23296 Courthouse Ave • Accomac, VA 23301-0330
Mailing Address: PO Box 330 • Accomac, VA 23301-0330
(757) 787-5754 • http://www.sbo.accomack.k12.va.us/public/
Grade Span: PK-12; **Agency Type:** 1
Schools: 15
  5 Primary; 3 Middle; 2 High; 5 Other Level
  12 Regular; 0 Special Education; 2 Vocational; 1 Alternative
  0 Magnet; 0 Charter; 4 Title I Eligible; 4 School-wide Title I
Students: 5,390   (51.9% male; 48.0% female)
  Individual Education Program: 675 (12.5%);
  English Language Learner: 346 (6.4%); Migrant: 264 (4.9%)
  Eligible for Free Lunch Program: 2,682 (49.8%)
  Eligible for Reduced-Price Lunch Program: 488 (9.1%)
Teachers: 434.0 (12.4 to 1)
Librarians/Media Specialists: 12.0 (449.2 to 1)
Guidance Counselors: 13.0 (414.6 to 1)
Current Spending: ($ per student per year):
  Total: $7,552; Instruction: $4,692; Support Services: $2,504
Enrollment, Drop-out Rates and Diploma Recipients by Race/Ethnicity

Category	Total	White	Black	Asian	AIAN	Hisp.
Enrollment (%)	100.0	43.8	45.8	0.4	0.0	9.9
Drop-out Rate (%)	5.0	5.7	4.2	0.0	0.0	8.5
H.S. Diplomas (#)	255	125	121	0	2	7

Albemarle County

Albemarle County Public Schools
401 Mcintire Rd • Charlottesville, VA 22902-4596
(434) 296-5826 • http://k12.albemarle.org/
Grade Span: PK-12; **Agency Type:** 1
Schools: 25
  16 Primary; 5 Middle; 4 High; 0 Other Level
  25 Regular; 0 Special Education; 0 Vocational; 0 Alternative
  0 Magnet; 1 Charter; 12 Title I Eligible; 0 School-wide Title I
Students: 12,565   (50.8% male; 49.1% female)
  Individual Education Program: 1,948 (15.5%);
  English Language Learner: 636 (5.1%); Migrant: 34 (0.3%)
  Eligible for Free Lunch Program: 1,652 (13.2%)
  Eligible for Reduced-Price Lunch Program: 530 (4.2%)
Teachers: 1,074.5 (11.7 to 1)
Librarians/Media Specialists: 22.8 (550.3 to 1)
Guidance Counselors: 24.4 (514.2 to 1)
Current Spending: ($ per student per year):
  Total: $8,269; Instruction: $4,912; Support Services: $3,069
Enrollment, Drop-out Rates and Diploma Recipients by Race/Ethnicity

Category	Total	White	Black	Asian	AIAN	Hisp.
Enrollmont (%)	100.0	79.5	12.9	3.7	0.2	3.7
Drop-out Rate (%)	1.2	1.1	1.7	0.0	0.0	3.3
H.S. Diplomas (#)	762	649	78	23	0	12

Alexandria City

Alexandria City Public Schools
2000 N Beauregard St • Alexandria, VA 22311-1712
(703) 824-6610 • http://www.acps.k12.va.us/
Grade Span: PK-12; **Agency Type:** 1
Schools: 16
  13 Primary; 2 Middle; 1 High; 0 Other Level
  16 Regular; 0 Special Education; 0 Vocational; 0 Alternative
  3 Magnet; 0 Charter; 9 Title I Eligible; 0 School-wide Title I
Students: 10,902   (51.4% male; 48.5% female)
  Individual Education Program: 1,970 (18.1%);
  English Language Learner: 2,650 (24.3%); Migrant: 0 (0.0%)
  Eligible for Free Lunch Program: 4,062 (37.3%)
  Eligible for Reduced-Price Lunch Program: 1,092 (10.0%)
Teachers: 1,035.4 (10.5 to 1)
Librarians/Media Specialists: 22.0 (495.5 to 1)
Guidance Counselors: 23.0 (474.0 to 1)
Current Spending: ($ per student per year):
  Total: $12,736; Instruction: $7,903; Support Services: $4,472
Enrollment, Drop-out Rates and Diploma Recipients by Race/Ethnicity

Category	Total	White	Black	Asian	AIAN	Hisp.
Enrollment (%)	100.0	22.9	42.9	6.7	0.3	27.0
Drop-out Rate (%)	3.7	1.4	3.8	2.3	0.0	6.4
H.S. Diplomas (#)	533	191	224	38	1	79

Alleghany County

Alleghany County Public Schools
110 Rosedale Ave • Covington, VA 24426-1296
(540) 965-1800 • http://www.alleghany.k12.va.us/
Grade Span: PK-12; **Agency Type:** 1
Schools: 7
  5 Primary; 1 Middle; 1 High; 0 Other Level
  7 Regular; 0 Special Education; 0 Vocational; 0 Alternative
  0 Magnet; 0 Charter; 4 Title I Eligible; 0 School-wide Title I
Students: 2,881   (51.4% male; 48.5% female)
  Individual Education Program: 486 (16.9%);
  English Language Learner: 3 (0.1%); Migrant: 0 (0.0%)
  Eligible for Free Lunch Program: 760 (26.4%)
  Eligible for Reduced-Price Lunch Program: 220 (7.6%)
Teachers: 228.8 (12.6 to 1)
Librarians/Media Specialists: 7.0 (411.6 to 1)
Guidance Counselors: 7.0 (411.6 to 1)
Current Spending: ($ per student per year):
  Total: $7,551; Instruction: $4,511; Support Services: $2,762
Enrollment, Drop-out Rates and Diploma Recipients by Race/Ethnicity

Category	Total	White	Black	Asian	AIAN	Hisp.
Enrollment (%)	100.0	92.2	7.2	0.1	0.2	0.2
Drop-out Rate (%)	4.2	4.3	3.3	0.0	0.0	0.0
H.S. Diplomas (#)	173	163	10	0	0	0

Amelia County

Amelia County Public Schools
8701 Otterburn Rd Ste 101 • Amelia, VA 23002
(804) 561-2621 • http://eclipse.achs.amelia.k12.va.us/public
Grade Span: PK-12; **Agency Type:** 1
Schools: 3
  1 Primary; 1 Middle; 1 High; 0 Other Level
  3 Regular; 0 Special Education; 0 Vocational; 0 Alternative
  0 Magnet; 0 Charter; 1 Title I Eligible; 0 School-wide Title I
Students: 1,724   (52.1% male; 47.8% female)
  Individual Education Program: 305 (17.7%);
  English Language Learner: 6 (0.3%); Migrant: 1 (0.1%)
  Eligible for Free Lunch Program: 462 (26.8%)
  Eligible for Reduced-Price Lunch Program: 156 (9.0%)
Teachers: 130.5 (13.2 to 1)
Librarians/Media Specialists: 0.0 (n/a to 1)
Guidance Counselors: 0.0 (n/a to 1)
Current Spending: ($ per student per year):
  Total: $6,907; Instruction: $3,860; Support Services: $2,730
Enrollment, Drop-out Rates and Diploma Recipients by Race/Ethnicity

Category	Total	White	Black	Asian	AIAN	Hisp.
Enrollment (%)	100.0	65.5	33.4	0.1	0.2	0.8
Drop-out Rate (%)	3.7	4.1	3.1	0.0	n/a	0.0
H.S. Diplomas (#)	109	55	53	1	0	0

Amherst County

Amherst County Public Schools
153 Washington St • Amherst, VA 24521-1257
Mailing Address: PO Box 1257 • Amherst, VA 24521-1257
(434) 946-9387 • http://www.amherst.k12.va.us/
Grade Span: PK-12; **Agency Type:** 1
Schools: 10
  7 Primary; 2 Middle; 1 High; 0 Other Level
  10 Regular; 0 Special Education; 0 Vocational; 0 Alternative
  0 Magnet; 0 Charter; 6 Title I Eligible; 0 School-wide Title I
Students: 4,542   (52.0% male; 47.9% female)
  Individual Education Program: 576 (12.7%);
  English Language Learner: 11 (0.2%); Migrant: 1 (<0.1%)
  Eligible for Free Lunch Program: 1,292 (27.7%)
  Eligible for Reduced-Price Lunch Program: 313 (6.7%)
Teachers: 373.7 (12.5 to 1)
Librarians/Media Specialists: 10.0 (467.1 to 1)
Guidance Counselors: 9.5 (491.7 to 1)
Current Spending: ($ per student per year):
  Total: $6,601; Instruction: $4,243; Support Services: $2,070
Enrollment, Drop-out Rates and Diploma Recipients by Race/Ethnicity

Category	Total	White	Black	Asian	AIAN	Hisp.
Enrollment (%)	100.0	70.8	26.4	0.7	1.0	1.1
Drop-out Rate (%)	2.6	2.5	2.8	0.0	0.0	0.0
H.S. Diplomas (#)	266	193	66	1	6	0

Appomattox County

Appomattox County Public Schools
124 Court St • Appomattox, VA 24522-0548
(434) 352-8251 • http://www.appomattox.k12.va.us/acps/index.aspx
Grade Span: PK-12; Agency Type: 1
Schools: 4
  2 Primary; 1 Middle; 1 High; 0 Other Level
  4 Regular; 0 Special Education; 0 Vocational; 0 Alternative
  0 Magnet; 0 Charter; 2 Title I Eligible; 0 School-wide Title I
Students: 2,327 (53.0% male; 46.9% female)
  Individual Education Program: 365 (15.7%);
  English Language Learner: 2 (0.1%); Migrant: 0 (0.0%)
  Eligible for Free Lunch Program: 685 (29.4%)
  Eligible for Reduced-Price Lunch Program: 170 (7.3%)
Teachers: 188.5 (12.3 to 1)
Librarians/Media Specialists: 4.0 (581.8 to 1)
Guidance Counselors: 4.0 (581.8 to 1)
Current Spending: ($ per student per year):
  Total: $6,292; Instruction: $4,059; Support Services: $1,932

Enrollment, Drop-out Rates and Diploma Recipients by Race/Ethnicity

Category	Total	White	Black	Asian	AIAN	Hisp.
Enrollment (%)	100.0	69.0	30.3	0.2	0.0	0.3
Drop-out Rate (%)	5.6	5.0	6.8	n/a	n/a	25.0
H.S. Diplomas (#)	140	107	32	0	0	1

Arlington County

Arlington County Public Schools
1426 N Quincy St • Arlington, VA 22207-3646
(703) 228-6010 • http://www.arlington.k12.va.us/
Grade Span: PK-12; Agency Type: 1
Schools: 32
  22 Primary; 5 Middle; 3 High; 2 Other Level
  30 Regular; 1 Special Education; 1 Vocational; 0 Alternative
  5 Magnet; 0 Charter; 16 Title I Eligible; 3 School-wide Title I
Students: 19,158 (51.5% male; 48.4% female)
  Individual Education Program: 3,238 (16.9%);
  English Language Learner: 6,020 (31.4%); Migrant: 0 (0.0%)
  Eligible for Free Lunch Program: 5,100 (26.6%)
  Eligible for Reduced-Price Lunch Program: 1,885 (9.8%)
Teachers: 1,774.6 (10.8 to 1)
Librarians/Media Specialists: 38.5 (497.6 to 1)
Guidance Counselors: 57.3 (334.3 to 1)
Current Spending: ($ per student per year):
  Total: $13,334; Instruction: $8,018; Support Services: $5,018

Enrollment, Drop-out Rates and Diploma Recipients by Race/Ethnicity

Category	Total	White	Black	Asian	AIAN	Hisp.
Enrollment (%)	100.0	42.3	14.5	10.2	0.1	32.8
Drop-out Rate (%)	3.0	1.0	4.5	1.7	0.0	5.1
H.S. Diplomas (#)	923	460	133	111	1	218

Augusta County

Augusta County Public Schools
6 John Lewis Rd • Fishersville, VA 22939-9610
(540) 245-5100 • http://www.augusta.k12.va.us/
Grade Span: PK-12; Agency Type: 1
Schools: 20
  12 Primary; 3 Middle; 5 High; 0 Other Level
  20 Regular; 0 Special Education; 0 Vocational; 0 Alternative
  0 Magnet; 0 Charter; 8 Title I Eligible; 0 School-wide Title I
Students: 10,714 (51.2% male; 48.7% female)
  Individual Education Program: 1,597 (14.9%);
  English Language Learner: 142 (1.3%); Migrant: 16 (0.1%)
  Eligible for Free Lunch Program: 1,791 (16.7%)
  Eligible for Reduced-Price Lunch Program: 783 (7.3%)
Teachers: 834.0 (12.8 to 1)
Librarians/Media Specialists: 18.0 (595.2 to 1)
Guidance Counselors: 19.0 (563.9 to 1)
Current Spending: ($ per student per year):
  Total: $6,818; Instruction: $4,452; Support Services: $2,105

Enrollment, Drop-out Rates and Diploma Recipients by Race/Ethnicity

Category	Total	White	Black	Asian	AIAN	Hisp.
Enrollment (%)	100.0	94.7	3.1	0.4	0.1	1.7
Drop-out Rate (%)	2.9	2.8	5.1	6.3	0.0	4.7
H.S. Diplomas (#)	713	679	25	3	0	6

Bedford County

Bedford County Public Schools
310 S Bridge St • Bedford, VA 24523-0748
Mailing Address: PO Box 748 • Bedford, VA 24523-0748
(540) 586-1045 • http://www.bedford.k12.va.us/
Grade Span: PK-12; Agency Type: 1
Schools: 22
  15 Primary; 3 Middle; 3 High; 1 Other Level
  21 Regular; 0 Special Education; 1 Vocational; 0 Alternative
  0 Magnet; 0 Charter; 10 Title I Eligible; 0 School-wide Title I
Students: 10,872 (52.0% male; 47.9% female)
  Individual Education Program: 1,421 (13.1%);
  English Language Learner: 31 (0.3%); Migrant: 0 (0.0%)
  Eligible for Free Lunch Program: 2,240 (20.6%)
  Eligible for Reduced-Price Lunch Program: 707 (6.5%)
Teachers: 815.8 (13.3 to 1)
Librarians/Media Specialists: 22.0 (494.2 to 1)
Guidance Counselors: 22.0 (494.2 to 1)
Current Spending: ($ per student per year):
  Total: $6,090; Instruction: $3,827; Support Services: $1,953

Enrollment, Drop-out Rates and Diploma Recipients by Race/Ethnicity

Category	Total	White	Black	Asian	AIAN	Hisp.
Enrollment (%)	100.0	88.1	10.0	0.7	0.3	0.9
Drop-out Rate (%)	1.8	1.6	3.2	0.0	0.0	0.0
H.S. Diplomas (#)	669	600	62	5	0	2

Botetourt County

Botetourt County Public Schools
143 Poor Farm Rd • Fincastle, VA 24090-0309
(540) 473-8263 • http://www.bcps.k12.va.us/
Grade Span: PK-12; Agency Type: 1
Schools: 12
  7 Primary; 2 Middle; 2 High; 1 Other Level
  11 Regular; 0 Special Education; 1 Vocational; 0 Alternative
  0 Magnet; 0 Charter; 4 Title I Eligible; 0 School-wide Title I
Students: 4,761 (51.0% male; 48.9% female)
  Individual Education Program: 837 (17.6%);
  English Language Learner: 11 (0.2%); Migrant: 0 (0.0%)
  Eligible for Free Lunch Program: 412 (8.7%)
  Eligible for Reduced-Price Lunch Program: 132 (2.8%)
Teachers: 376.9 (12.6 to 1)
Librarians/Media Specialists: 11.0 (432.8 to 1)
Guidance Counselors: 11.0 (432.8 to 1)
Current Spending: ($ per student per year):
  Total: $7,089; Instruction: $4,650; Support Services: $2,193

Enrollment, Drop-out Rates and Diploma Recipients by Race/Ethnicity

Category	Total	White	Black	Asian	AIAN	Hisp.
Enrollment (%)	100.0	95.3	3.0	0.6	0.3	0.3
Drop-out Rate (%)	2.8	2.9	0.0	0.0	0.0	0.0
H.S. Diplomas (#)	313	300	9	1	1	2

Bristol City

Bristol City Public Schools
222 Oak St • Bristol, VA 24201-4198
(276) 821-5600 • http://www.bristolvaschools.org/
Grade Span: PK-12; Agency Type: 1
Schools: 7
  4 Primary; 1 Middle; 1 High; 1 Other Level
  6 Regular; 1 Special Education; 0 Vocational; 0 Alternative
  0 Magnet; 0 Charter; 4 Title I Eligible; 0 School-wide Title I
Students: 2,324 (51.5% male; 48.4% female)
  Individual Education Program: 444 (19.1%);
  English Language Learner: 16 (0.7%); Migrant: 0 (0.0%)
  Eligible for Free Lunch Program: 981 (42.2%)
  Eligible for Reduced-Price Lunch Program: 137 (5.9%)
Teachers: 207.0 (11.2 to 1)
Librarians/Media Specialists: 6.0 (387.3 to 1)
Guidance Counselors: 6.0 (387.3 to 1)
Current Spending: ($ per student per year):
  Total: $7,877; Instruction: $5,229; Support Services: $2,300

Enrollment, Drop-out Rates and Diploma Recipients by Race/Ethnicity

Category	Total	White	Black	Asian	AIAN	Hisp.
Enrollment (%)	100.0	87.4	10.2	0.6	0.0	1.4
Drop-out Rate (%)	4.4	4.1	9.8	0.0	n/a	0.0
H.S. Diplomas (#)	123	112	10	0	0	1

Brunswick County

Brunswick County Public Schools
219 N Main St • Lawrenceville, VA 23868-0309
Mailing Address: PO Box 309 • Lawrenceville, VA 23868-0309
(434) 848-3138 • http://www.brun.k12.va.us/
Grade Span: PK-12; Agency Type: 1
Schools: 6
  4 Primary; 1 Middle; 1 High; 0 Other Level
  6 Regular; 0 Special Education; 0 Vocational; 0 Alternative
  0 Magnet; 0 Charter; 4 Title I Eligible; 0 School-wide Title I
Students: 2,433   (52.0% male; 47.9% female)
  Individual Education Program: 315 (12.9%);
  English Language Learner: 13 (0.5%); Migrant: 0 (0.0%)
  Eligible for Free Lunch Program: 1,403 (57.7%)
  Eligible for Reduced-Price Lunch Program: 300 (12.3%)
Teachers: 203.0 (12.0 to 1)
Librarians/Media Specialists: 6.0 (405.5 to 1)
Guidance Counselors: 4.0 (608.3 to 1)
Current Spending: ($ per student per year):
  Total: $7,761; Instruction: $4,126; Support Services: $3,224
Enrollment, Drop-out Rates and Diploma Recipients by Race/Ethnicity

Category	Total	White	Black	Asian	AIAN	Hisp.
Enrollment (%)	100.0	19.9	79.0	0.1	0.0	0.9
Drop-out Rate (%)	7.4	9.2	6.9	n/a	n/a	0.0
H.S. Diplomas (#)	154	36	117	0	0	1

Buchanan County

Buchanan County Public Schools
Rt 83 Slate Creek Rd • Grundy, VA 24614-0833
Mailing Address: Slate Creek Rd Rt 83 • Grundy, VA 24614-0833
(276) 935-4551 • http://www.buc.k12.va.us/
Grade Span: PK-12; Agency Type: 1
Schools: 11
  6 Primary; 0 Middle; 4 High; 1 Other Level
  10 Regular; 0 Special Education; 1 Vocational; 0 Alternative
  0 Magnet; 0 Charter; 6 Title I Eligible; 2 School-wide Title I
Students: 3,649   (52.3% male; 47.6% female)
  Individual Education Program: 757 (20.7%);
  English Language Learner: n/a; Migrant: 0 (0.0%)
  Eligible for Free Lunch Program: 1,909 (52.3%)
  Eligible for Reduced-Price Lunch Program: 585 (16.0%)
Teachers: 329.0 (11.1 to 1)
Librarians/Media Specialists: 11.0 (331.7 to 1)
Guidance Counselors: 9.0 (405.4 to 1)
Current Spending: ($ per student per year):
  Total: $7,277; Instruction: $4,517; Support Services: $2,403
Enrollment, Drop-out Rates and Diploma Recipients by Race/Ethnicity

Category	Total	White	Black	Asian	AIAN	Hisp.
Enrollment (%)	100.0	99.8	0.1	0.0	0.0	0.1
Drop-out Rate (%)	5.1	5.1	0.0	n/a	n/a	n/a
H.S. Diplomas (#)	260	258	2	0	0	0

Buckingham County

Buckingham County Public Schools
Rte 60 • Buckingham, VA 23921-0024
Mailing Address: PO Box 24 • Buckingham, VA 23921-0024
(434) 969-6100 • http://www.bchs.k12.va.us/
Grade Span: PK-12; Agency Type: 1
Schools: 6
  3 Primary; 2 Middle; 1 High; 0 Other Level
  6 Regular; 0 Special Education; 0 Vocational; 0 Alternative
  0 Magnet; 0 Charter; 3 Title I Eligible; 3 School-wide Title I
Students: 2,265   (51.4% male; 48.5% female)
  Individual Education Program: 338 (14.9%);
  English Language Learner: 2 (0.1%); Migrant: 1 (<0.1%)
  Eligible for Free Lunch Program: 990 (43.7%)
  Eligible for Reduced-Price Lunch Program: 252 (11.1%)
Teachers: 182.0 (12.4 to 1)
Librarians/Media Specialists: 6.0 (377.5 to 1)
Guidance Counselors: 3.0 (755.0 to 1)
Current Spending: ($ per student per year):
  Total: $7,129; Instruction: $4,409; Support Services: $2,420
Enrollment, Drop-out Rates and Diploma Recipients by Race/Ethnicity

Category	Total	White	Black	Asian	AIAN	Hisp.
Enrollment (%)	100.0	51.5	47.3	0.4	0.2	0.6
Drop-out Rate (%)	8.3	7.8	9.2	0.0	0.0	0.0
H.S. Diplomas (#)	111	74	35	0	0	2

Campbell County

Campbell County Public Schools
684 Village Hwy • Rustburg, VA 24588-0099
Mailing Address: PO Box 99 • Rustburg, VA 24588-0099
(434) 332-8201 • http://www.campbell.k12.va.us/
Grade Span: PK-12; Agency Type: 1
Schools: 16
  8 Primary; 2 Middle; 2 High; 4 Other Level
  14 Regular; 0 Special Education; 1 Vocational; 1 Alternative
  0 Magnet; 0 Charter; 6 Title I Eligible; 0 School-wide Title I
Students: 8,815   (51.5% male; 48.4% female)
  Individual Education Program: 1,058 (12.0%);
  English Language Learner: 31 (0.4%); Migrant: 0 (0.0%)
  Eligible for Free Lunch Program: 2,043 (23.2%)
  Eligible for Reduced-Price Lunch Program: 656 (7.4%)
Teachers: 653.0 (13.5 to 1)
Librarians/Media Specialists: 0.1 (88,150.0 to 1)
Guidance Counselors: 0.2 (44,075.0 to 1)
Current Spending: ($ per student per year):
  Total: $6,445; Instruction: $4,089; Support Services: $2,068
Enrollment, Drop-out Rates and Diploma Recipients by Race/Ethnicity

Category	Total	White	Black	Asian	AIAN	Hisp.
Enrollment (%)	100.0	79.1	18.8	1.1	0.1	0.8
Drop-out Rate (%)	1.6	1.0	4.1	0.0	0.0	10.0
H.S. Diplomas (#)	486	405	75	6	0	0

Caroline County

Caroline County Public Schools
16221 Richmond Turnpike • Bowling Green, VA 22427-2203
(804) 633-5088 • http://www.caroline.k12.va.us/
Grade Span: PK-12; Agency Type: 1
Schools: 6
  4 Primary; 1 Middle; 1 High; 0 Other Level
  6 Regular; 0 Special Education; 0 Vocational; 0 Alternative
  0 Magnet; 0 Charter; 2 Title I Eligible; 1 School-wide Title I
Students: 3,752   (51.2% male; 48.7% female)
  Individual Education Program: 503 (13.4%);
  English Language Learner: 32 (0.9%); Migrant: 0 (0.0%)
  Eligible for Free Lunch Program: 1,157 (30.8%)
  Eligible for Reduced-Price Lunch Program: 298 (7.9%)
Teachers: 242.0 (15.5 to 1)
Librarians/Media Specialists: 6.0 (625.3 to 1)
Guidance Counselors: 7.0 (536.0 to 1)
Current Spending: ($ per student per year):
  Total: $6,678; Instruction: $4,128; Support Services: $2,249
Enrollment, Drop-out Rates and Diploma Recipients by Race/Ethnicity

Category	Total	White	Black	Asian	AIAN	Hisp.
Enrollment (%)	100.0	55.1	41.9	0.4	0.4	1.8
Drop-out Rate (%)	7.9	7.3	8.1	0.0	42.9	14.3
H.S. Diplomas (#)	200	117	82	1	0	0

Carroll County

Carroll County Public Schools
605-9 N Pine St • Hillsville, VA 24343-1453
(276) 728-3191 • http://www.ccpsd.k12.va.us/
Grade Span: PK-12; Agency Type: 1
Schools: 10
  8 Primary; 0 Middle; 1 High; 1 Other Level
  10 Regular; 0 Special Education; 0 Vocational; 0 Alternative
  0 Magnet; 0 Charter; 8 Title I Eligible; 1 School-wide Title I
Students: 4,082   (52.4% male; 47.5% female)
  Individual Education Program: 711 (17.4%);
  English Language Learner: 57 (1.4%); Migrant: 55 (1.3%)
  Eligible for Free Lunch Program: 1,530 (37.5%)
  Eligible for Reduced-Price Lunch Program: 491 (12.0%)
Teachers: 328.8 (12.4 to 1)
Librarians/Media Specialists: 10.0 (408.2 to 1)
Guidance Counselors: 10.0 (408.2 to 1)
Current Spending: ($ per student per year):
  Total: $6,947; Instruction: $4,250; Support Services: $2,340
Enrollment, Drop-out Rates and Diploma Recipients by Race/Ethnicity

Category	Total	White	Black	Asian	AIAN	Hisp.
Enrollment (%)	100.0	95.7	0.7	0.3	0.0	3.2
Drop-out Rate (%)	2.4	2.3	12.5	0.0	0.0	0.0
H.S. Diplomas (#)	211	208	0	1	0	2

Charlotte County

Charlotte County Public Schools
250 Legrande Ave Ste E • Charlotte Court House, VA 23923-0790
Mailing Address: PO Box 790 • Charlotte Court House, VA 23923-0790
(434) 542-5151
Grade Span: PK-12; **Agency Type:** 1
Schools: 7
  5 Primary; 1 Middle; 1 High; 0 Other Level
  7 Regular; 0 Special Education; 0 Vocational; 0 Alternative
  0 Magnet; 0 Charter; 2 Title I Eligible; 0 School-wide Title I
Students: 2,287   (49.6% male; 50.3% female)
  Individual Education Program: 322 (14.1%);
  English Language Learner: 7 (0.3%); Migrant: 0 (0.0%)
  Eligible for Free Lunch Program: 861 (37.6%)
  Eligible for Reduced-Price Lunch Program: 293 (12.8%)
Teachers: 169.0 (13.5 to 1)
Librarians/Media Specialists: 5.0 (457.4 to 1)
Guidance Counselors: 3.0 (762.3 to 1)
Current Spending: ($ per student per year):
  Total: $6,742; Instruction: $4,181; Support Services: $2,223
Enrollment, Drop-out Rates and Diploma Recipients by Race/Ethnicity

Category	Total	White	Black	Asian	AIAN	Hisp.
Enrollment (%)	100.0	59.9	38.1	0.4	0.3	1.3
Drop-out Rate (%)	2.5	2.0	3.4	n/a	0.0	0.0
H.S. Diplomas (#)	135	76	58	1	0	0

Charlottesville City Public Schools
1562 Dairy Rd • Charlottesville, VA 22903-1304
(434) 245-2400 • http://www.ccs.k12.va.us/
Grade Span: PK-12; **Agency Type:** 1
Schools: 10
  6 Primary; 2 Middle; 1 High; 1 Other Level
  9 Regular; 0 Special Education; 0 Vocational; 1 Alternative
  0 Magnet; 0 Charter; 6 Title I Eligible; 5 School-wide Title I
Students: 4,422   (51.1% male; 48.8% female)
  Individual Education Program: 794 (18.0%);
  English Language Learner: 175 (4.0%); Migrant: 0 (0.0%)
  Eligible for Free Lunch Program: 1,784 (40.3%)
  Eligible for Reduced-Price Lunch Program: 329 (7.4%)
Teachers: 403.5 (11.0 to 1)
Librarians/Media Specialists: 9.0 (491.3 to 1)
Guidance Counselors: 13.0 (340.2 to 1)
Current Spending: ($ per student per year):
  Total: $10,833; Instruction: $6,477; Support Services: $4,045
Enrollment, Drop-out Rates and Diploma Recipients by Race/Ethnicity

Category	Total	White	Black	Asian	AIAN	Hisp.
Enrollment (%)	100.0	43.8	47.9	1.9	0.1	2.9
Drop-out Rate (%)	2.9	1.5	4.6	8.7	n/a	0.0
H.S. Diplomas (#)	194	108	82	1	0	3

Chesapeake City

Chesapeake City Public Schools
312 Cedar Rd • Chesapeake, VA 23322
Mailing Address: PO Box 16496 • Chesapeake, VA 23328-5204
(757) 547-0165 • http://eclipse.cps.k12.va.us/
Grade Span: PK-12; **Agency Type:** 1
Schools: 46
  27 Primary; 11 Middle; 6 High; 2 Other Level
  44 Regular; 0 Special Education; 0 Vocational; 2 Alternative
  0 Magnet; 0 Charter; 11 Title I Eligible; 7 School-wide Title I
Students: 39,412   (51.2% male; 48.7% female)
  Individual Education Program: 7,068 (17.9%);
  English Language Learner: 252 (0.6%); Migrant: 0 (0.0%)
  Eligible for Free Lunch Program: 7,534 (19.1%)
  Eligible for Reduced-Price Lunch Program: 2,138 (5.4%)
Teachers: 2,877.2 (13.7 to 1)
Librarians/Media Specialists: 56.0 (703.8 to 1)
Guidance Counselors: 88.2 (446.8 to 1)
Current Spending: ($ per student per year):
  Total: $7,433; Instruction: $4,714; Support Services: $2,490
Enrollment, Drop-out Rates and Diploma Recipients by Race/Ethnicity

Category	Total	White	Black	Asian	AIAN	Hisp.
Enrollment (%)	100.0	59.8	35.1	2.2	0.3	2.0
Drop-out Rate (%)	2.8	2.3	3.8	1.3	3.6	1.9
H.S. Diplomas (#)	2,298	1,464	739	56	7	32

Chesterfield County

Chesterfield County Public Schools
9900 Krause Rd • Chesterfield, VA 23832-0001
Mailing Address: PO Box 10 • Chesterfield, VA 23832-0001
(804) 748-1411 • http://chesterfield.k12.va.us/
Grade Span: PK-12; **Agency Type:** 1
Schools: 60
  37 Primary; 12 Middle; 10 High; 1 Other Level
  57 Regular; 0 Special Education; 1 Vocational; 2 Alternative
  1 Magnet; 0 Charter; 14 Title I Eligible; 5 School-wide Title I
Students: 55,393   (51.4% male; 48.5% female)
  Individual Education Program: 8,308 (15.0%);
  English Language Learner: 1,379 (2.5%); Migrant: 0 (0.0%)
  Eligible for Free Lunch Program: 5,083 (9.2%)
  Eligible for Reduced-Price Lunch Program: 2,109 (3.8%)
Teachers: 3,845.8 (14.4 to 1)
Librarians/Media Specialists: 75.2 (736.6 to 1)
Guidance Counselors: 89.5 (618.9 to 1)
Current Spending: ($ per student per year):
  Total: $6,711; Instruction: $4,249; Support Services: $2,216
Enrollment, Drop-out Rates and Diploma Recipients by Race/Ethnicity

Category	Total	White	Black	Asian	AIAN	Hisp.
Enrollment (%)	100.0	67.1	25.0	2.8	0.5	4.2
Drop-out Rate (%)	4.3	3.8	5.4	3.8	6.3	10.3
H.S. Diplomas (#)	3,292	2,392	725	103	14	58

Clarke County

Clarke County Public Schools
309 W Main St • Berryville, VA 22611-1230
(540) 955-6100 • http://www.clarke.k12.va.us/
Grade Span: PK-12; **Agency Type:** 1
Schools: 5
  3 Primary; 1 Middle; 1 High; 0 Other Level
  5 Regular; 0 Special Education; 0 Vocational; 0 Alternative
  0 Magnet; 0 Charter; 3 Title I Eligible; 0 School-wide Title I
Students: 2,071   (51.2% male; 48.7% female)
  Individual Education Program: 210 (10.1%);
  English Language Learner: 32 (1.5%); Migrant: 0 (0.0%)
  Eligible for Free Lunch Program: 221 (10.7%)
  Eligible for Reduced-Price Lunch Program: 62 (3.0%)
Teachers: 161.5 (12.8 to 1)
Librarians/Media Specialists: 5.0 (414.2 to 1)
Guidance Counselors: 3.5 (591.7 to 1)
Current Spending: ($ per student per year):
  Total: $7,604; Instruction: $4,696; Support Services: $2,647
Enrollment, Drop-out Rates and Diploma Recipients by Race/Ethnicity

Category	Total	White	Black	Asian	AIAN	Hisp.
Enrollment (%)	100.0	91.0	6.1	0.8	0.3	1.8
Drop-out Rate (%)	1.9	1.8	2.3	0.0	n/a	16.7
H.S. Diplomas (#)	144	134	10	0	0	0

Colonial Heights County

Colonial Heights City Public Schools
512 Blvd • Colonial Heights, VA 23834-3798
(804) 524-3400 • http://www.colonialhts.net/
Grade Span: PK-12; **Agency Type:** 1
Schools: 5
  3 Primary; 1 Middle; 1 High; 0 Other Level
  5 Regular; 0 Special Education; 0 Vocational; 0 Alternative
  0 Magnet; 0 Charter; 3 Title I Eligible; 0 School-wide Title I
Students: 2,796   (53.1% male; 46.8% female)
  Individual Education Program: 413 (14.8%);
  English Language Learner: 29 (1.0%); Migrant: 0 (0.0%)
  Eligible for Free Lunch Program: 307 (11.0%)
  Eligible for Reduced-Price Lunch Program: 147 (5.3%)
Teachers: 246.6 (11.3 to 1)
Librarians/Media Specialists: 5.0 (559.2 to 1)
Guidance Counselors: 6.0 (466.0 to 1)
Current Spending: ($ per student per year):
  Total: $8,212; Instruction: $5,544; Support Services: $2,408
Enrollment, Drop-out Rates and Diploma Recipients by Race/Ethnicity

Category	Total	White	Black	Asian	AIAN	Hisp.
Enrollment (%)	100.0	85.3	9.0	4.1	0.0	1.5
Drop-out Rate (%)	4.7	4.7	5.2	6.5	0.0	0.0
H.S. Diplomas (#)	166	147	11	7	0	1

Culpeper County

Culpeper County Public Schools
450 Radio Ln • Culpeper, VA 22701-1542
(540) 825-3677 • http://culpeperschools.org/
Grade Span: PK-12; **Agency Type:** 1
Schools: 9
   6 Primary; 2 Middle; 1 High; 0 Other Level
   9 Regular; 0 Special Education; 0 Vocational; 0 Alternative
   0 Magnet; 0 Charter; 4 Title I Eligible; 0 School-wide Title I
Students: 6,227   (50.9% male; 49.0% female)
   Individual Education Program: 725 (11.6%);
   English Language Learner: 120 (1.9%); Migrant: 0 (0.0%)
   Eligible for Free Lunch Program: 773 (12.4%)
   Eligible for Reduced-Price Lunch Program: 344 (5.5%)
Teachers: 494.8 (12.6 to 1)
Librarians/Media Specialists: 8.0 (778.4 to 1)
Guidance Counselors: 15.0 (415.1 to 1)
Current Spending: ($ per student per year):
   Total: $6,930; Instruction: $4,578; Support Services: $2,052
Enrollment, Drop-out Rates and Diploma Recipients by Race/Ethnicity

Category	Total	White	Black	Asian	AIAN	Hisp.
Enrollment (%)	100.0	75.4	19.7	0.7	0.1	4.1
Drop-out Rate (%)	6.2	5.3	10.2	6.7	0.0	6.5
H.S. Diplomas (#)	309	257	44	2	0	6

Danville City

Danville City Public Schools
313 Municipal Bldg • Danville, VA 24541
Mailing Address: 313 Municipal Building • Danville, VA 24543-9600
(434) 799-6400 • http://web.dps.k12.va.us/dps/default.htm
Grade Span: PK-12; **Agency Type:** 1
Schools: 17
   10 Primary; 3 Middle; 2 High; 2 Other Level
   15 Regular; 0 Special Education; 0 Vocational; 2 Alternative
   11 Magnet; 0 Charter; 10 Title I Eligible; 9 School-wide Title I
Students: 7,384   (51.0% male; 48.9% female)
   Individual Education Program: 946 (12.8%);
   English Language Learner: 152 (2.1%); Migrant: 0 (0.0%)
   Eligible for Free Lunch Program: 3,674 (49.8%)
   Eligible for Reduced-Price Lunch Program: 494 (6.7%)
Teachers: 615.8 (12.0 to 1)
Librarians/Media Specialists: 16.0 (461.5 to 1)
Guidance Counselors: 16.0 (461.5 to 1)
Current Spending: ($ per student per year):
   Total: $7,626; Instruction: $4,761; Support Services: $2,491
Enrollment, Drop-out Rates and Diploma Recipients by Race/Ethnicity

Category	Total	White	Black	Asian	AIAN	Hisp.
Enrollment (%)	100.0	28.0	68.9	0.6	0.2	2.3
Drop-out Rate (%)	5.3	3.2	6.6	0.0	0.0	3.6
H.S. Diplomas (#)	397	191	202	3	0	1

Dickenson County

Dickenson County Public Schools
Volunteer St • Clintwood, VA 24228-1127
Mailing Address: PO Box 1127 • Clintwood, VA 24228-1127
(276) 926-4643 • http://www.dickenson.k12.va.us/
Grade Span: PK-12; **Agency Type:** 1
Schools: 9
   5 Primary; 0 Middle; 3 High; 1 Other Level
   8 Regular; 0 Special Education; 1 Vocational; 0 Alternative
   0 Magnet; 0 Charter; 5 Title I Eligible; 4 School-wide Title I
Students: 2,601   (51.2% male; 48.7% female)
   Individual Education Program: 434 (16.7%);
   English Language Learner: n/a; Migrant: 0 (0.0%)
   Eligible for Free Lunch Program: 1,091 (41.9%)
   Eligible for Reduced-Price Lunch Program: 373 (14.3%)
Teachers: 221.0 (11.8 to 1)
Librarians/Media Specialists: 8.0 (325.1 to 1)
Guidance Counselors: 7.0 (371.6 to 1)
Current Spending: ($ per student per year):
   Total: $7,451; Instruction: $4,336; Support Services: $2,623
Enrollment, Drop-out Rates and Diploma Recipients by Race/Ethnicity

Category	Total	White	Black	Asian	AIAN	Hisp.
Enrollment (%)	100.0	99.3	0.6	0.0	0.0	0.0
Drop-out Rate (%)	3.4	3.4	0.0	0.0	n/a	n/a
H.S. Diplomas (#)	189	189	0	0	0	0

Dinwiddie County

Dinwiddie County Public Schools
14016 Boydton Plank Rd • Dinwiddie, VA 23841-0007
Mailing Address: PO Box 7 • Dinwiddie, VA 23841-0007
(804) 469-4190 • http://www.dinwiddie.k12.va.us/
Grade Span: PK-12; **Agency Type:** 1
Schools: 7
   5 Primary; 1 Middle; 1 High; 0 Other Level
   7 Regular; 0 Special Education; 0 Vocational; 0 Alternative
   0 Magnet; 0 Charter; 4 Title I Eligible; 0 School-wide Title I
Students: 4,469   (52.3% male; 47.6% female)
   Individual Education Program: 621 (13.9%);
   English Language Learner: 34 (0.8%); Migrant: 0 (0.0%)
   Eligible for Free Lunch Program: 1,321 (29.6%)
   Eligible for Reduced-Price Lunch Program: 378 (8.5%)
Teachers: 334.0 (13.4 to 1)
Librarians/Media Specialists: 8.0 (558.6 to 1)
Guidance Counselors: 9.0 (496.6 to 1)
Current Spending: ($ per student per year):
   Total: $6,875; Instruction: $4,062; Support Services: $2,543
Enrollment, Drop-out Rates and Diploma Recipients by Race/Ethnicity

Category	Total	White	Black	Asian	AIAN	Hisp.
Enrollment (%)	100.0	56.1	41.6	0.4	0.2	1.8
Drop-out Rate (%)	4.4	2.9	6.7	0.0	0.0	0.0
H.S. Diplomas (#)	203	124	78	1	0	0

Essex County

Essex County Public Schools
109 N Cross St • Tappahannock, VA 22560-0756
Mailing Address: PO Box 756 • Tappahannock, VA 22560-0756
(804) 443-4366 • http://www.essex.k12.va.us/
Grade Span: PK-12; **Agency Type:** 1
Schools: 3
   1 Primary; 1 Middle; 1 High; 0 Other Level
   3 Regular; 0 Special Education; 0 Vocational; 0 Alternative
   0 Magnet; 0 Charter; 2 Title I Eligible; 0 School-wide Title I
Students: 1,701   (49.0% male; 50.9% female)
   Individual Education Program: 310 (18.2%);
   English Language Learner: 17 (1.0%); Migrant: 0 (0.0%)
   Eligible for Free Lunch Program: 996 (58.6%)
   Eligible for Reduced-Price Lunch Program: 159 (9.3%)
Teachers: 142.0 (12.0 to 1)
Librarians/Media Specialists: 3.0 (567.0 to 1)
Guidance Counselors: 3.0 (567.0 to 1)
Current Spending: ($ per student per year):
   Total: $7,339; Instruction: $4,747; Support Services: $2,275
Enrollment, Drop-out Rates and Diploma Recipients by Race/Ethnicity

Category	Total	White	Black	Asian	AIAN	Hisp.
Enrollment (%)	100.0	42.4	55.6	0.5	0.2	1.4
Drop-out Rate (%)	3.1	3.9	2.3	0.0	n/a	n/a
H.S. Diplomas (#)	105	48	56	1	0	0

Fairfax County

Fairfax County Public Schools
10700 Page Ave • Fairfax, VA 22030-4006
(703) 246-2631 • http://www.fcps.k12.va.us/
Grade Span: PK-12; **Agency Type:** 1
Schools: 204
   137 Primary; 23 Middle; 28 High; 16 Other Level
   184 Regular; 8 Special Education; 1 Vocational; 11 Alternative
   70 Magnet; 0 Charter; 37 Title I Eligible; 27 School-wide Title I
Students: 164,235   (52.0% male; 47.9% female)
   Individual Education Program: 23,233 (14.1%);
   English Language Learner: 26,886 (16.4%); Migrant: 0 (0.0%)
   Eligible for Free Lunch Program: 22,170 (13.5%)
   Eligible for Reduced-Price Lunch Program: 9,104 (5.5%)
Teachers: 12,293.0 (13.4 to 1)
Librarians/Media Specialists: 226.5 (725.1 to 1)
Guidance Counselors: 426.5 (385.1 to 1)
Current Spending: ($ per student per year):
   Total: $9,488; Instruction: $5,757; Support Services: $3,324
Enrollment, Drop-out Rates and Diploma Recipients by Race/Ethnicity

Category	Total	White	Black	Asian	AIAN	Hisp.
Enrollment (%)	100.0	52.8	10.7	16.8	0.4	15.1
Drop-out Rate (%)	2.7	1.5	4.6	2.2	7.0	7.0
H.S. Diplomas (#)	10,450	6,715	1,055	1,757	16	907

Falls Church City

Falls Church City Public Schools
803 W Broad St Ste 300 • Falls Church, VA 22046-3432
(703) 248-5601 • http://www.fccps.k12.va.us/
Grade Span: PK-12; **Agency Type:** 1
Schools: 4
  2 Primary; 1 Middle; 1 High; 0 Other Level
  4 Regular; 0 Special Education; 0 Vocational; 0 Alternative
  0 Magnet; 0 Charter; 1 Title I Eligible; 0 School-wide Title I
Students: 1,874 (52.7% male; 47.2% female)
  Individual Education Program: 275 (14.7%);
  English Language Learner: 185 (9.9%); Migrant: 0 (0.0%)
  Eligible for Free Lunch Program: 74 (3.9%)
  Eligible for Reduced-Price Lunch Program: 29 (1.5%)
Teachers: 174.1 (10.8 to 1)
Librarians/Media Specialists: 4.0 (468.5 to 1)
Guidance Counselors: 4.6 (407.4 to 1)
Current Spending: ($ per student per year):
  Total: $12,960; Instruction: $7,490; Support Services: $4,863
Enrollment, Drop-out Rates and Diploma Recipients by Race/Ethnicity

Category	Total	White	Black	Asian	AIAN	Hisp.
Enrollment (%)	100.0	76.5	5.0	9.7	0.2	8.6
Drop-out Rate (%)	0.4	0.2	4.0	0.0	0.0	0.0
H.S. Diplomas (#)	117	93	7	8	0	9

Fauquier County

Fauquier County Public Schools
320 Hospital Dr • Warrenton, VA 20186-3037
(540) 351-1000 • http://www.fcps1.org/
Grade Span: PK-12; **Agency Type:** 1
Schools: 18
  10 Primary; 4 Middle; 2 High; 1 Other Level
  16 Regular; 0 Special Education; 0 Vocational; 1 Alternative
  0 Magnet; 0 Charter; 7 Title I Eligible; 0 School-wide Title I
Students: 10,327 (51.0% male; 48.9% female)
  Individual Education Program: 1,374 (13.3%);
  English Language Learner: 169 (1.6%); Migrant: 4 (<0.1%)
  Eligible for Free Lunch Program: 1,105 (10.7%)
  Eligible for Reduced-Price Lunch Program: 433 (4.2%)
Teachers: 822.2 (12.6 to 1)
Librarians/Media Specialists: 18.5 (558.2 to 1)
Guidance Counselors: 19.5 (529.6 to 1)
Current Spending: ($ per student per year):
  Total: $7,932; Instruction: $5,061; Support Services: $2,570
Enrollment, Drop-out Rates and Diploma Recipients by Race/Ethnicity

Category	Total	White	Black	Asian	AIAN	Hisp.
Enrollment (%)	100.0	85.3	10.2	1.0	0.3	3.2
Drop-out Rate (%)	3.0	2.7	5.5	0.0	0.0	6.7
H.S. Diplomas (#)	651	586	52	9	0	4

Floyd County

Floyd County Public Schools
140 Harris Hart Rd NE • Floyd, VA 24091-9710
(540) 745-9400 • http://www.floyd.k12.va.us/
Grade Span: PK-12; **Agency Type:** 1
Schools: 5
  4 Primary; 0 Middle; 1 High; 0 Other Level
  5 Regular; 0 Special Education; 0 Vocational; 0 Alternative
  0 Magnet; 0 Charter; 3 Title I Eligible; 0 School-wide Title I
Students: 2,103 (49.2% male; 50.7% female)
  Individual Education Program: 384 (18.3%);
  English Language Learner: 39 (1.9%); Migrant: 10 (0.5%)
  Eligible for Free Lunch Program: 514 (24.4%)
  Eligible for Reduced-Price Lunch Program: 171 (8.1%)
Teachers: 165.0 (12.7 to 1)
Librarians/Media Specialists: 5.0 (420.6 to 1)
Guidance Counselors: 5.0 (420.6 to 1)
Current Spending: ($ per student per year):
  Total: $6,917; Instruction: $4,477; Support Services: $2,292
Enrollment, Drop-out Rates and Diploma Recipients by Race/Ethnicity

Category	Total	White	Black	Asian	AIAN	Hisp.
Enrollment (%)	100.0	94.3	3.1	0.2	0.0	2.1
Drop-out Rate (%)	2.9	2.7	10.0	n/a	n/a	0.0
H.S. Diplomas (#)	115	114	1	0	0	0

Fluvanna County

Fluvanna County Public Schools
14455 James Madison Hwy • Palmyra, VA 22963-0419
Mailing Address: PO Box 419 • Palmyra, VA 22963-0419
(434) 589-8208 • http://www.fluco.org/
Grade Span: PK-12; **Agency Type:** 1
Schools: 5
  3 Primary; 1 Middle; 1 High; 0 Other Level
  5 Regular; 0 Special Education; 0 Vocational; 0 Alternative
  0 Magnet; 0 Charter; 3 Title I Eligible; 0 School-wide Title I
Students: 3,336 (50.5% male; 49.4% female)
  Individual Education Program: 500 (15.0%);
  English Language Learner: 4 (0.1%); Migrant: 3 (0.1%)
  Eligible for Free Lunch Program: 440 (13.2%)
  Eligible for Reduced-Price Lunch Program: 155 (4.6%)
Teachers: 255.0 (13.1 to 1)
Librarians/Media Specialists: 6.0 (556.0 to 1)
Guidance Counselors: 4.8 (695.0 to 1)
Current Spending: ($ per student per year):
  Total: $6,837; Instruction: $4,515; Support Services: $2,259
Enrollment, Drop-out Rates and Diploma Recipients by Race/Ethnicity

Category	Total	White	Black	Asian	AIAN	Hisp.
Enrollment (%)	100.0	75.7	19.8	0.7	0.1	1.3
Drop-out Rate (%)	3.1	2.9	4.0	0.0	n/a	0.0
H.S. Diplomas (#)	183	148	34	0	0	1

Franklin County

Franklin County Public Schools
25 Bernard Rd • Rocky Mount, VA 24151-6614
(540) 483-5138 • http://www.franklincity.k12.va.us/
Grade Span: PK-12; **Agency Type:** 1
Schools: 15
  11 Primary; 2 Middle; 1 High; 1 Other Level
  15 Regular; 0 Special Education; 0 Vocational; 0 Alternative
  0 Magnet; 0 Charter; 8 Title I Eligible; 8 School-wide Title I
Students: 7,270 (50.9% male; 49.0% female)
  Individual Education Program: 1,372 (18.9%);
  English Language Learner: 51 (0.7%); Migrant: 0 (0.0%)
  Eligible for Free Lunch Program: 2,201 (30.3%)
  Eligible for Reduced-Price Lunch Program: 646 (8.9%)
Teachers: 540.3 (13.5 to 1)
Librarians/Media Specialists: 14.0 (519.3 to 1)
Guidance Counselors: 14.0 (519.3 to 1)
Current Spending: ($ per student per year):
  Total: $6,744; Instruction: $4,073; Support Services: $2,355
Enrollment, Drop-out Rates and Diploma Recipients by Race/Ethnicity

Category	Total	White	Black	Asian	AIAN	Hisp.
Enrollment (%)	100.0	84.7	12.4	0.7	0.2	2.1
Drop-out Rate (%)	4.3	4.5	3.8	0.0	0.0	0.0
H.S. Diplomas (#)	418	362	49	4	0	3

Frederick County

Frederick County Public Schools
1415 Amherst St • Winchester, VA 22601
Mailing Address: PO Box 3508 • Winchester, VA 22604-2546
(540) 662-3888 • http://www.frederick.k12.va.us/
Grade Span: PK-12; **Agency Type:** 1
Schools: 16
  10 Primary; 3 Middle; 3 High; 0 Other Level
  16 Regular; 0 Special Education; 0 Vocational; 0 Alternative
  0 Magnet; 0 Charter; 8 Title I Eligible; 0 School-wide Title I
Students: 11,357 (50.8% male; 49.1% female)
  Individual Education Program: 1,797 (15.8%);
  English Language Learner: 278 (2.4%); Migrant: 59 (0.5%)
  Eligible for Free Lunch Program: 1,304 (11.5%)
  Eligible for Reduced-Price Lunch Program: 534 (4.7%)
Teachers: 873.6 (13.0 to 1)
Librarians/Media Specialists: 19.0 (597.7 to 1)
Guidance Counselors: 28.5 (398.5 to 1)
Current Spending: ($ per student per year):
  Total: $7,646; Instruction: $4,730; Support Services: $2,653
Enrollment, Drop-out Rates and Diploma Recipients by Race/Ethnicity

Category	Total	White	Black	Asian	AIAN	Hisp.
Enrollment (%)	100.0	90.4	4.1	1.2	0.2	3.8
Drop-out Rate (%)	3.1	3.1	5.7	0.0	0.0	3.8
H.S. Diplomas (#)	548	510	20	6	1	11

Fredericksburg City Public Schools
817 Princess Anne St • Fredericksburg, VA 22401-5819
(540) 372-1130 • http://www.cityschools.com/
Grade Span: PK-12; **Agency Type:** 1
Schools: 4

2 Primary; 1 Middle; 1 High; 0 Other Level
3 Regular; 1 Special Education; 0 Vocational; 0 Alternative
0 Magnet; 0 Charter; 2 Title I Eligible; 2 School-wide Title I
Students: 2,450   (50.1% male; 49.8% female)
  Individual Education Program: 360 (14.7%);
  English Language Learner: 128 (5.2%); Migrant: 0 (0.0%)
  Eligible for Free Lunch Program: 785 (32.0%)
  Eligible for Reduced-Price Lunch Program: 108 (4.4%)
Teachers: 198.4 (12.3 to 1)
Librarians/Media Specialists: 3.0 (816.7 to 1)
Guidance Counselors: 5.0 (490.0 to 1)
Current Spending: ($ per student per year):
  Total: $9,202; Instruction: $6,018; Support Services: $2,823
Enrollment, Drop-out Rates and Diploma Recipients by Race/Ethnicity

Category	Total	White	Black	Asian	AIAN	Hisp.
Enrollment (%)	100.0	44.8	45.0	1.6	0.1	8.4
Drop-out Rate (%)	2.0	1.5	3.4	0.0	n/a	0.0
H.S. Diplomas (#)	114	72	35	4	0	3

Giles County

Giles County Public Schools
151 School Rd • Pearisburg, VA 24134-9725
(540) 921-1421 • http://sbo.gilesk12.org/
Grade Span: PK-12; **Agency Type:** 1
Schools: 6
  3 Primary; 0 Middle; 2 High; 1 Other Level
  5 Regular; 0 Special Education; 1 Vocational; 0 Alternative
  0 Magnet; 0 Charter; 3 Title I Eligible; 0 School-wide Title I
Students: 2,545   (51.6% male; 48.3% female)
  Individual Education Program: 363 (14.3%);
  English Language Learner: 0 (0.0%); Migrant: 0 (0.0%)
  Eligible for Free Lunch Program: 586 (23.0%)
  Eligible for Reduced-Price Lunch Program: 231 (9.1%)
Teachers: 193.0 (13.2 to 1)
Librarians/Media Specialists: 5.0 (509.0 to 1)
Guidance Counselors: 6.0 (424.2 to 1)
Current Spending: ($ per student per year):
  Total: $6,985; Instruction: $4,353; Support Services: $2,377
Enrollment, Drop-out Rates and Diploma Recipients by Race/Ethnicity

Category	Total	White	Black	Asian	AIAN	Hisp.
Enrollment (%)	100.0	97.2	1.6	0.6	0.0	0.6
Drop-out Rate (%)	2.1	2.1	0.0	0.0	0.0	0.0
H.S. Diplomas (#)	149	144	4	0	0	1

Gloucester County

Gloucester County Public Schools
6489 Main St • Gloucester, VA 23061-2320
(804) 693-5300 • http://gets.gc.k12.va.us/
Grade Span: PK-12; **Agency Type:** 1
Schools: 10
  6 Primary; 3 Middle; 1 High; 0 Other Level
  10 Regular; 0 Special Education; 0 Vocational; 0 Alternative
  0 Magnet; 0 Charter; 6 Title I Eligible; 0 School-wide Title I
Students: 6,257   (52.4% male; 47.5% female)
  Individual Education Program: 766 (12.2%);
  English Language Learner: 1 (<0.1%); Migrant: 0 (0.0%)
  Eligible for Free Lunch Program: 811 (13.0%)
  Eligible for Reduced-Price Lunch Program: 319 (5.1%)
Teachers: 466.6 (13.4 to 1)
Librarians/Media Specialists: 10.0 (625.7 to 1)
Guidance Counselors: 10.0 (625.7 to 1)
Current Spending: ($ per student per year):
  Total: $6,863; Instruction: $4,139; Support Services: $2,453
Enrollment, Drop-out Rates and Diploma Recipients by Race/Ethnicity

Category	Total	White	Black	Asian	AIAN	Hisp.
Enrollment (%)	100.0	86.0	11.2	0.8	0.3	1.6
Drop-out Rate (%)	2.4	2.4	2.4	0.0	0.0	0.0
H.S. Diplomas (#)	374	322	40	5	1	6

Goochland County

Goochland County Public Schools
2938 River Rd W • Goochland, VA 23063-0169
Mailing Address: PO Box 169 • Goochland, VA 23063-0169
(804) 556-5601 • http://www.glnd.k12.va.us/
Grade Span: PK-12; **Agency Type:** 1
Schools: 5
  3 Primary; 1 Middle; 1 High; 0 Other Level
  5 Regular; 0 Special Education; 0 Vocational; 0 Alternative
  0 Magnet; 0 Charter; 2 Title I Eligible; 0 School-wide Title I
Students: 2,115   (52.8% male; 47.1% female)
  Individual Education Program: 374 (17.7%);
  English Language Learner: 9 (0.4%); Migrant: 0 (0.0%)

Eligible for Free Lunch Program: 93 (4.4%)
  Eligible for Reduced-Price Lunch Program: 26 (1.2%)
Teachers: 176.2 (12.0 to 1)
Librarians/Media Specialists: 5.0 (423.0 to 1)
Guidance Counselors: 5.0 (423.0 to 1)
Current Spending: ($ per student per year):
  Total: $8,207; Instruction: $4,859; Support Services: $3,257
Enrollment, Drop-out Rates and Diploma Recipients by Race/Ethnicity

Category	Total	White	Black	Asian	AIAN	Hisp.
Enrollment (%)	100.0	67.3	30.4	0.8	0.1	1.4
Drop-out Rate (%)	3.8	3.2	5.6	0.0	0.0	0.0
H.S. Diplomas (#)	130	76	53	1	0	0

Grayson County

Grayson County Public Schools
412 E Main St • Independence, VA 24348-0888
Mailing Address: PO Box 888 • Independence, VA 24348-0888
(276) 773-2832 • http://www.grayson.k12.va.us/
Grade Span: PK-12; **Agency Type:** 1
Schools: 11
  6 Primary; 2 Middle; 1 High; 2 Other Level
  10 Regular; 0 Special Education; 1 Vocational; 0 Alternative
  0 Magnet; 0 Charter; 6 Title I Eligible; 3 School-wide Title I
Students: 2,254   (50.1% male; 49.8% female)
  Individual Education Program: 310 (13.8%);
  English Language Learner: 3 (0.1%); Migrant: 0 (0.0%)
  Eligible for Free Lunch Program: 764 (33.9%)
  Eligible for Reduced-Price Lunch Program: 238 (10.6%)
Teachers: 201.3 (11.2 to 1)
Librarians/Media Specialists: 8.0 (281.8 to 1)
Guidance Counselors: 4.4 (512.3 to 1)
Current Spending: ($ per student per year):
  Total: $7,378; Instruction: $4,443; Support Services: $2,690
Enrollment, Drop-out Rates and Diploma Recipients by Race/Ethnicity

Category	Total	White	Black	Asian	AIAN	Hisp.
Enrollment (%)	100.0	94.5	3.3	0.1	0.1	2.0
Drop-out Rate (%)	1.7	1.3	16.7	n/a	n/a	0.0
H.S. Diplomas (#)	115	113	2	0	0	0

Greene County

Greene County Public Schools
40 Celt Rd • Stanardsville, VA 22973-1140
Mailing Address: PO Box 1140 • Stanardsville, VA 22973-1140
(434) 985-5254 • http://www.greenecountyschools.com/
Grade Span: PK-12; **Agency Type:** 1
Schools: 7
  3 Primary; 1 Middle; 1 High; 2 Other Level
  6 Regular; 0 Special Education; 1 Vocational; 0 Alternative
  0 Magnet; 1 Charter; 3 Title I Eligible; 0 School-wide Title I
Students: 2,700   (51.8% male; 48.1% female)
  Individual Education Program: 514 (19.0%);
  English Language Learner: 33 (1.2%); Migrant: 0 (0.0%)
  Eligible for Free Lunch Program: 312 (11.6%)
  Eligible for Reduced-Price Lunch Program: 97 (3.6%)
Teachers: 245.5 (11.0 to 1)
Librarians/Media Specialists: 5.0 (540.0 to 1)
Guidance Counselors: 6.0 (450.0 to 1)
Current Spending: ($ per student per year):
  Total: $7,489; Instruction: $4,968; Support Services: $2,428
Enrollment, Drop-out Rates and Diploma Recipients by Race/Ethnicity

Category	Total	White	Black	Asian	AIAN	Hisp.
Enrollment (%)	100.0	86.4	10.3	0.6	0.4	2.3
Drop-out Rate (%)	4.8	4.9	4.8	0.0	0.0	0.0
H.S. Diplomas (#)	144	125	16	0	0	3

Greensville County

Greensville County Public Schools
105 Ruffin St • Emporia, VA 23847-1156
(434) 634-3748 • http://www.greensville.k12.va.us/
Grade Span: PK-12; **Agency Type:** 3
Schools: 5
  1 Primary; 2 Middle; 2 High; 0 Other Level
  4 Regular; 0 Special Education; 0 Vocational; 1 Alternative
  0 Magnet; 0 Charter; 3 Title I Eligible; 3 School-wide Title I
Students: 2,634   (51.2% male; 48.7% female)
  Individual Education Program: 424 (16.1%);
  English Language Learner: 16 (0.6%); Migrant: 0 (0.0%)
  Eligible for Free Lunch Program: 1,257 (47.7%)
  Eligible for Reduced-Price Lunch Program: 221 (8.4%)
Teachers: 213.0 (12.4 to 1)
Librarians/Media Specialists: 4.0 (658.5 to 1)
Guidance Counselors: 6.0 (439.0 to 1)

Current Spending: ($ per student per year):
Total: $6,978; Instruction: $4,384; Support Services: $2,294
Enrollment, Drop-out Rates and Diploma Recipients by Race/Ethnicity

Category	Total	White	Black	Asian	AIAN	Hisp.
Enrollment (%)	100.0	26.9	71.7	0.3	0.2	0.8
Drop-out Rate (%)	2.2	2.3	2.1	0.0	n/a	0.0
H.S. Diplomas (#)	152	45	107	0	0	0

Halifax County

Halifax County Public Schools
Mary Bethune Ofc Complex • Halifax, VA 24558-1849
Mailing Address: PO Box 1849 • Halifax, VA 24558-1849
(434) 476-2171 • http://www.halifax.k12.va.us/
Grade Span: PK-12; **Agency Type:** 1
Schools: 15
  11 Primary; 2 Middle; 2 High; 0 Other Level
  14 Regular; 0 Special Education; 0 Vocational; 1 Alternative
  0 Magnet; 0 Charter; 11 Title I Eligible; 0 School-wide Title I
Students: 5,908   (50.5% male; 49.4% female)
  Individual Education Program: 1,172 (19.8%);
  English Language Learner: 12 (0.2%); Migrant: 9 (0.2%)
  Eligible for Free Lunch Program: 2,662 (45.1%)
  Eligible for Reduced-Price Lunch Program: 616 (10.4%)
Teachers: 507.0 (11.7 to 1)
Librarians/Media Specialists: 15.0 (393.9 to 1)
Guidance Counselors: 15.0 (393.9 to 1)
Current Spending: ($ per student per year):
  Total: $7,637; Instruction: $4,570; Support Services: $2,665
Enrollment, Drop-out Rates and Diploma Recipients by Race/Ethnicity

Category	Total	White	Black	Asian	AIAN	Hisp.
Enrollment (%)	100.0	49.4	48.8	0.3	0.1	1.3
Drop-out Rate (%)	1.4	0.8	1.9	0.0	0.0	14.3
H.S. Diplomas (#)	347	183	160	1	1	2

Hampton City

Hampton City Public Schools
1 Franklin St • Hampton, VA 23669-3570
(757) 727-2000 • http://www.sbo.hampton.k12.va.us/
Grade Span: PK-12; **Agency Type:** 1
Schools: 37
  24 Primary; 6 Middle; 4 High; 2 Other Level
  35 Regular; 0 Special Education; 0 Vocational; 1 Alternative
  2 Magnet; 1 Charter; 16 Title I Eligible; 10 School-wide Title I
Students: 23,009   (51.7% male; 48.2% female)
  Individual Education Program: 3,268 (14.2%);
  English Language Learner: 219 (1.0%); Migrant: 0 (0.0%)
  Eligible for Free Lunch Program: 7,407 (32.2%)
  Eligible for Reduced-Price Lunch Program: 2,093 (9.1%)
Teachers: 1,868.0 (12.3 to 1)
Librarians/Media Specialists: 44.0 (522.9 to 1)
Guidance Counselors: 55.0 (418.3 to 1)
Current Spending: ($ per student per year):
  Total: $7,252; Instruction: $4,413; Support Services: $2,511
Enrollment, Drop-out Rates and Diploma Recipients by Race/Ethnicity

Category	Total	White	Black	Asian	AIAN	Hisp.
Enrollment (%)	100.0	35.0	60.5	1.8	0.3	2.4
Drop-out Rate (%)	3.7	3.3	4.0	2.1	4.5	3.3
H.S. Diplomas (#)	1,279	540	692	22	4	21

Hanover County

Hanover County Public Schools
200 Berkley St • Ashland, VA 23005-1399
(804) 365-4500 • http://hcps2.hanover.k12.va.us/
Grade Span: PK-12; **Agency Type:** 1
Schools: 21
  13 Primary; 4 Middle; 4 High; 0 Other Level
  21 Regular; 0 Special Education; 0 Vocational; 0 Alternative
  0 Magnet; 0 Charter; 4 Title I Eligible; 0 School-wide Title I
Students: 18,139   (51.7% male; 48.2% female)
  Individual Education Program: 2,774 (15.3%);
  English Language Learner: 137 (0.8%); Migrant: 0 (0.0%)
  Eligible for Free Lunch Program: 1,164 (6.4%)
  Eligible for Reduced-Price Lunch Program: 430 (2.4%)
Teachers: 1,404.0 (12.9 to 1)
Librarians/Media Specialists: 27.0 (671.8 to 1)
Guidance Counselors: 34.0 (533.5 to 1)
Current Spending: ($ per student per year):
  Total: $6,348; Instruction: $4,282; Support Services: $1,774

Category	Total	White	Black	Asian	AIAN	Hisp.
Enrollment (%)	100.0	86.5	10.2	1.4	0.3	1.1
Drop-out Rate (%)	0.7	0.6	1.7	0.0	11.1	0.0
H.S. Diplomas (#)	1,060	956	90	5	3	6

Harrisonburg City

Harrisonburg City Public Schools
317 S Main St • Harrisonburg, VA 22801-3606
(540) 434-9916 • http://www.harrisonburg.k12.va.us/
Grade Span: PK-12; **Agency Type:** 1
Schools: 6
  4 Primary; 1 Middle; 1 High; 0 Other Level
  6 Regular; 0 Special Education; 0 Vocational; 0 Alternative
  0 Magnet; 0 Charter; 4 Title I Eligible; 0 School-wide Title I
Students: 4,031   (51.5% male; 48.4% female)
  Individual Education Program: 634 (15.7%);
  English Language Learner: 1,264 (31.4%); Migrant: 123 (3.1%)
  Eligible for Free Lunch Program: 1,592 (39.5%)
  Eligible for Reduced-Price Lunch Program: 323 (8.0%)
Teachers: 377.7 (10.7 to 1)
Librarians/Media Specialists: 7.0 (575.9 to 1)
Guidance Counselors: 7.5 (537.5 to 1)
Current Spending: ($ per student per year):
  Total: $8,777; Instruction: $5,758; Support Services: $2,549
Enrollment, Drop-out Rates and Diploma Recipients by Race/Ethnicity

Category	Total	White	Black	Asian	AIAN	Hisp.
Enrollment (%)	100.0	58.7	12.5	3.9	0.1	24.8
Drop-out Rate (%)	0.9	0.7	0.8	0.0	n/a	2.1
H.S. Diplomas (#)	244	186	23	8	0	27

Henrico County

Henrico County Public Schools
3820 Nine Mile Rd • Richmond, VA 23223-0420
(804) 652-3717 • http://www.henrico.k12.va.us/
Grade Span: PK-12; **Agency Type:** 1
Schools: 66
  43 Primary; 10 Middle; 8 High; 5 Other Level
  61 Regular; 1 Special Education; 2 Vocational; 2 Alternative
  7 Magnet; 0 Charter; 13 Title I Eligible; 5 School-wide Title I
Students: 45,354   (51.4% male; 48.5% female)
  Individual Education Program: 6,482 (14.3%);
  English Language Learner: 1,455 (3.2%); Migrant: 0 (0.0%)
  Eligible for Free Lunch Program: 6,114 (13.5%)
  Eligible for Reduced-Price Lunch Program: 2,015 (4.4%)
Teachers: 3,175.2 (14.3 to 1)
Librarians/Media Specialists: 77.0 (589.0 to 1)
Guidance Counselors: 84.9 (534.2 to 1)
Current Spending: ($ per student per year):
  Total: $6,757; Instruction: $4,151; Support Services: $2,345
Enrollment, Drop-out Rates and Diploma Recipients by Race/Ethnicity

Category	Total	White	Black	Asian	AIAN	Hisp.
Enrollment (%)	100.0	55.2	35.4	4.3	0.2	2.9
Drop-out Rate (%)	2.3	1.8	2.7	4.6	11.1	9.1
H.S. Diplomas (#)	2,400	1,515	713	119	3	50

Henry County

Henry County Public Schools
3300 Kings Mountain Rd • Collinsville, VA 24078-8958
Mailing Address: PO Box 8958 • Collinsville, VA 24078-8958
(276) 634-4712 •
http://henryva.schoolwires.com/henrycounty/site/default.asp
Grade Span: PK-12; **Agency Type:** 1
Schools: 20
  12 Primary; 4 Middle; 4 High; 0 Other Level
  20 Regular; 0 Special Education; 0 Vocational; 0 Alternative
  0 Magnet; 0 Charter; 10 Title I Eligible; 10 School-wide Title I
Students: 8,180   (50.1% male; 49.8% female)
  Individual Education Program: 1,566 (19.1%);
  English Language Learner: 239 (2.9%); Migrant: 0 (0.0%)
  Eligible for Free Lunch Program: 3,125 (38.2%)
  Eligible for Reduced-Price Lunch Program: 529 (6.5%)
Teachers: 682.7 (12.0 to 1)
Librarians/Media Specialists: 19.0 (430.5 to 1)
Guidance Counselors: 19.0 (430.5 to 1)
Current Spending: ($ per student per year):
  Total: $6,821; Instruction: $4,246; Support Services: $2,235

Enrollment, Drop-out Rates and Diploma Recipients by Race/Ethnicity

Category	Total	White	Black	Asian	AIAN	Hisp.
Enrollment (%)	100.0	66.9	28.0	0.5	0.0	4.6
Drop-out Rate (%)	3.5	3.8	3.2	0.0	n/a	2.4
H.S. Diplomas (#)	512	349	154	4	0	5

Hopewell City

Hopewell City Public Schools
103 N 12th Ave • Hopewell, VA 23860-3758
(804) 541-6400 • http://www.hopewell.k12.va.us/
Grade Span: PK-12; **Agency Type:** 1
Schools: 8
 4 Primary; 1 Middle; 1 High; 2 Other Level
 6 Regular; 0 Special Education; 0 Vocational; 2 Alternative
 0 Magnet; 0 Charter; 3 Title I Eligible; 3 School-wide Title I
Students: 3,886 (50.4% male; 49.5% female)
 Individual Education Program: 718 (18.5%);
 English Language Learner: 37 (1.0%); Migrant: 0 (0.0%)
 Eligible for Free Lunch Program: 1,923 (49.5%)
 Eligible for Reduced-Price Lunch Program: 360 (9.3%)
Teachers: 313.0 (12.4 to 1)
Librarians/Media Specialists: 5.0 (777.2 to 1)
Guidance Counselors: 10.0 (388.6 to 1)
Current Spending: ($ per student per year):
 Total: $8,056; Instruction: $5,164; Support Services: $2,539

Enrollment, Drop-out Rates and Diploma Recipients by Race/Ethnicity

Category	Total	White	Black	Asian	AIAN	Hisp.
Enrollment (%)	100.0	42.8	52.5	0.6	0.1	4.0
Drop-out Rate (%)	9.7	6.4	13.1	16.7	0.0	4.8
H.S. Diplomas (#)	217	123	88	1	0	5

Isle Of Wight County

Isle of Wight County Public Schools
17124 Monument Circle • Isle Of Wight, VA 23397-0078
Mailing Address: PO Box 78 • Isle Of Wight, VA 23397-0078
(757) 357-0449 • http://www.iwcs.k12.va.us/
Grade Span: PK-12; **Agency Type:** 1
Schools: 8
 4 Primary; 2 Middle; 2 High; 0 Other Level
 8 Regular; 0 Special Education; 0 Vocational; 0 Alternative
 0 Magnet; 0 Charter; 4 Title I Eligible; 0 School-wide Title I
Students: 5,063 (51.7% male; 48.2% female)
 Individual Education Program: 705 (13.9%);
 English Language Learner: 19 (<0.1%); Migrant: 0 (0.0%)
 Eligible for Free Lunch Program: 1,249 (24.7%)
 Eligible for Reduced-Price Lunch Program: 324 (6.4%)
Teachers: 361.5 (14.0 to 1)
Librarians/Media Specialists: 1.0 (5,063.0 to 1)
Guidance Counselors: 0.0 (n/a to 1)
Current Spending: ($ per student per year):
 Total: $6,831; Instruction: $4,332; Support Services: $2,218

Enrollment, Drop-out Rates and Diploma Recipients by Race/Ethnicity

Category	Total	White	Black	Asian	AIAN	Hisp.
Enrollment (%)	100.0	63.8	33.8	0.7	0.7	1.0
Drop-out Rate (%)	3.9	4.0	3.8	0.0	0.0	0.0
H.S. Diplomas (#)	273	200	69	2	1	1

King George County

King George County Public Schools
9100 St Anthony's Rd • King George, VA 22485-0021
Mailing Address: PO Box 1239 • King George, VA 22485-0021
(540) 775-5833 • http://www.kgcs.k12.va.us/
Grade Span: PK-12; **Agency Type:** 1
Schools: 4
 2 Primary; 1 Middle; 1 High; 0 Other Level
 4 Regular; 0 Special Education; 0 Vocational; 0 Alternative
 0 Magnet; 0 Charter; 2 Title I Eligible; 0 School-wide Title I
Students: 3,203 (51.4% male; 48.5% female)
 Individual Education Program: 457 (14.3%);
 English Language Learner: 19 (0.6%); Migrant: 0 (0.0%)
 Eligible for Free Lunch Program: 549 (17.1%)
 Eligible for Reduced-Price Lunch Program: 121 (3.8%)
Teachers: 242.8 (13.2 to 1)
Librarians/Media Specialists: 4.0 (800.8 to 1)
Guidance Counselors: 3.0 (1,067.7 to 1)
Current Spending: ($ per student per year):
 Total: $6,912; Instruction: $4,243; Support Services: $2,431

Enrollment, Drop-out Rates and Diploma Recipients by Race/Ethnicity

Category	Total	White	Black	Asian	AIAN	Hisp.
Enrollment (%)	100.0	73.1	23.2	1.4	0.3	1.7
Drop-out Rate (%)	2.0	1.5	3.7	0.0	0.0	0.0
H.S. Diplomas (#)	216	160	48	4	1	3

King William County

King William County Public Schools
18548 King William Rd • King William, VA 23086-0185
Mailing Address: PO Box 185 • King William, VA 23086-0185
(804) 769-3434 • http://www.kwcps.k12.va.us/
Grade Span: PK-12; **Agency Type:** 1
Schools: 4
 2 Primary; 1 Middle; 1 High; 0 Other Level
 4 Regular; 0 Special Education; 0 Vocational; 0 Alternative
 0 Magnet; 0 Charter; 3 Title I Eligible; 0 School-wide Title I
Students: 1,866 (52.0% male; 47.9% female)
 Individual Education Program: 332 (17.8%);
 English Language Learner: 4 (0.2%); Migrant: 0 (0.0%)
 Eligible for Free Lunch Program: 384 (20.6%)
 Eligible for Reduced-Price Lunch Program: 151 (8.1%)
Teachers: 167.0 (11.2 to 1)
Librarians/Media Specialists: 4.0 (466.5 to 1)
Guidance Counselors: 4.0 (466.5 to 1)
Current Spending: ($ per student per year):
 Total: $6,890; Instruction: $4,539; Support Services: $2,325

Enrollment, Drop-out Rates and Diploma Recipients by Race/Ethnicity

Category	Total	White	Black	Asian	AIAN	Hisp.
Enrollment (%)	100.0	69.7	27.0	0.2	2.4	0.8
Drop-out Rate (%)	0.6	0.9	0.0	0.0	0.0	0.0
H.S. Diplomas (#)	110	62	46	0	2	0

Lee County

Lee County Public Schools
5 Park St • Jonesville, VA 24263-1201
(276) 346-2107 • http://www.leectysch.com/
Grade Span: PK-12; **Agency Type:** 1
Schools: 14
 9 Primary; 2 Middle; 2 High; 1 Other Level
 13 Regular; 0 Special Education; 0 Vocational; 0 Alternative
 0 Magnet; 0 Charter; 11 Title I Eligible; 10 School-wide Title I
Students: 3,732 (50.6% male; 49.3% female)
 Individual Education Program: 790 (21.2%);
 English Language Learner: 1 (<0.1%); Migrant: 0 (0.0%)
 Eligible for Free Lunch Program: 1,959 (52.5%)
 Eligible for Reduced-Price Lunch Program: 388 (10.4%)
Teachers: 363.5 (10.3 to 1)
Librarians/Media Specialists: 11.0 (339.3 to 1)
Guidance Counselors: 11.5 (324.5 to 1)
Current Spending: ($ per student per year):
 Total: $7,472; Instruction: $4,930; Support Services: $2,210

Enrollment, Drop-out Rates and Diploma Recipients by Race/Ethnicity

Category	Total	White	Black	Asian	AIAN	Hisp.
Enrollment (%)	100.0	98.5	0.6	0.1	0.1	0.5
Drop-out Rate (%)	5.7	5.7	0.0	0.0	n/a	0.0
H.S. Diplomas (#)	184	183	1	0	0	0

Loudoun County

Loudoun County Public Schools
102 N St NW • Leesburg, VA 20176-2203
(703) 771-6400 • http://www.loudoun.k12.va.us/
Grade Span: PK-12; **Agency Type:** 1
Schools: 61
 41 Primary; 9 Middle; 6 High; 5 Other Level
 59 Regular; 0 Special Education; 1 Vocational; 1 Alternative
 0 Magnet; 0 Charter; 17 Title I Eligible; 0 School-wide Title I
Students: 40,750 (51.3% male; 48.6% female)
 Individual Education Program: 4,367 (10.7%);
 English Language Learner: 1,869 (4.6%); Migrant: 0 (0.0%)
 Eligible for Free Lunch Program: 2,899 (7.1%)
 Eligible for Reduced-Price Lunch Program: 1,407 (3.5%)
Teachers: 3,016.6 (13.5 to 1)
Librarians/Media Specialists: 74.0 (550.7 to 1)
Guidance Counselors: 105.0 (388.1 to 1)
Current Spending: ($ per student per year):
 Total: $9,477; Instruction: $6,066; Support Services: $3,150

Enrollment, Drop-out Rates and Diploma Recipients by Race/Ethnicity

Category	Total	White	Black	Asian	AIAN	Hisp.
Enrollment (%)	100.0	72.2	8.4	8.7	0.3	9.9
Drop-out Rate (%)	1.1	0.9	1.8	1.0	5.0	2.4
H.S. Diplomas (#)	1,766	1,385	134	136	2	109

Louisa County

Louisa County Public Schools
953 Davis Hwy • Mineral, VA 23117-0007
Mailing Address: PO Box 7 • Mineral, VA 23117-0007
(540) 894-5115 • http://www.lcps.k12.va.us/
Grade Span: PK-12; **Agency Type:** 1
Schools: 5
    3 Primary; 1 Middle; 1 High; 0 Other Level
    5 Regular; 0 Special Education; 0 Vocational; 0 Alternative
    0 Magnet; 0 Charter; 2 Title I Eligible; 1 School-wide Title I
Students: 4,321   (52.0% male; 47.9% female)
    Individual Education Program: 604 (14.0%);
    English Language Learner: 17 (0.4%); Migrant: 0 (0.0%)
    Eligible for Free Lunch Program: 1,108 (25.6%)
    Eligible for Reduced-Price Lunch Program: 351 (8.1%)
Teachers: 331.5 (13.0 to 1)
Librarians/Media Specialists: 7.0 (617.3 to 1)
Guidance Counselors: 8.0 (540.1 to 1)
Current Spending: ($ per student per year):
    Total: $7,280; Instruction: $3,986; Support Services: $2,977
Enrollment, Drop-out Rates and Diploma Recipients by Race/Ethnicity

Category	Total	White	Black	Asian	AIAN	Hisp.
Enrollment (%)	100.0	71.6	26.5	0.2	0.3	0.9
Drop-out Rate (%)	2.9	2.5	4.0	0.0	0.0	0.0
H.S. Diplomas (#)	303	232	67	2	0	2

Lunenburg County

Lunenburg County Public Schools
1615 Eighth St • Victoria, VA 23974-0649
Mailing Address: PO Box X • Victoria, VA 23974-0649
(434) 696-2116 • http://www.ssvawebs.com/lunweb/index.htm
Grade Span: PK-12; **Agency Type:** 1
Schools: 4
    2 Primary; 1 Middle; 1 High; 0 Other Level
    4 Regular; 0 Special Education; 0 Vocational; 0 Alternative
    0 Magnet; 0 Charter; 2 Title I Eligible; 0 School-wide Title I
Students: 1,710   (48.7% male; 51.2% female)
    Individual Education Program: 317 (18.5%);
    English Language Learner: 5 (0.3%); Migrant: 1 (0.1%)
    Eligible for Free Lunch Program: 903 (52.8%)
    Eligible for Reduced-Price Lunch Program: 200 (11.7%)
Teachers: 150.1 (11.4 to 1)
Librarians/Media Specialists: 4.0 (427.5 to 1)
Guidance Counselors: 5.0 (342.0 to 1)
Current Spending: ($ per student per year):
    Total: $7,656; Instruction: $4,772; Support Services: $2,528
Enrollment, Drop-out Rates and Diploma Recipients by Race/Ethnicity

Category	Total	White	Black	Asian	AIAN	Hisp.
Enrollment (%)	100.0	49.8	48.2	0.3	0.5	1.2
Drop-out Rate (%)	5.4	5.0	6.0	0.0	n/a	0.0
H.S. Diplomas (#)	116	61	55	0	0	0

Lynchburg City

Lynchburg City Public Schools
915 Court St • Lynchburg, VA 24504
Mailing Address: PO Box 1599 • Lynchburg, VA 24505-1599
(434) 522-3700 • http://www.lynchburg.org/
Grade Span: PK-12; **Agency Type:** 1
Schools: 17
    11 Primary; 3 Middle; 2 High; 1 Other Level
    16 Regular; 0 Special Education; 0 Vocational; 1 Alternative
    3 Magnet; 0 Charter; 14 Title I Eligible; 11 School-wide Title I
Students: 8,775   (50.9% male; 49.0% female)
    Individual Education Program: 1,388 (15.8%);
    English Language Learner: 43 (0.5%); Migrant: 0 (0.0%)
    Eligible for Free Lunch Program: 3,865 (44.0%)
    Eligible for Reduced-Price Lunch Program: 397 (4.5%)
Teachers: 701.9 (12.5 to 1)
Librarians/Media Specialists: 18.0 (487.5 to 1)
Guidance Counselors: 23.5 (373.4 to 1)
Current Spending: ($ per student per year):
    Total: $7,686; Instruction: $4,757; Support Services: $2,681
Enrollment, Drop-out Rates and Diploma Recipients by Race/Ethnicity

Category	Total	White	Black	Asian	AIAN	Hisp.
Enrollment (%)	100.0	44.8	50.8	1.5	0.1	1.2
Drop-out Rate (%)	3.2	2.1	4.2	6.7	40.0	0.0
H.S. Diplomas (#)	504	289	199	12	0	4

Madison County

Madison County Public Schools
60 School Board Court • Madison, VA 22727-0647
Mailing Address: PO Box 647 • Madison, VA 22727-0647
(540) 948-3780 • http://www.madisonschools.k12.va.us/
Grade Span: PK-12; **Agency Type:** 1
Schools: 4
    2 Primary; 1 Middle; 1 High; 0 Other Level
    4 Regular; 0 Special Education; 0 Vocational; 0 Alternative
    0 Magnet; 0 Charter; 2 Title I Eligible; 0 School-wide Title I
Students: 1,865   (48.9% male; 51.0% female)
    Individual Education Program: 235 (12.6%);
    English Language Learner: 5 (0.3%); Migrant: 0 (0.0%)
    Eligible for Free Lunch Program: 283 (15.2%)
    Eligible for Reduced-Price Lunch Program: 101 (5.4%)
Teachers: 152.0 (12.3 to 1)
Librarians/Media Specialists: 4.0 (466.3 to 1)
Guidance Counselors: 4.0 (466.3 to 1)
Current Spending: ($ per student per year):
    Total: $7,570; Instruction: $4,551; Support Services: $2,755
Enrollment, Drop-out Rates and Diploma Recipients by Race/Ethnicity

Category	Total	White	Black	Asian	AIAN	Hisp.
Enrollment (%)	100.0	83.3	15.4	0.4	0.1	0.8
Drop-out Rate (%)	2.8	2.4	4.0	0.0	0.0	100.0
H.S. Diplomas (#)	146	123	20	1	1	1

Manassas City

Manassas City Public Schools
9000 Tudor Ln • Manassas, VA 20110-5700
(703) 257-8808 • http://www.manassas.k12.va.us/
Grade Span: PK-12; **Agency Type:** 1
Schools: 8
    5 Primary; 1 Middle; 1 High; 1 Other Level
    7 Regular; 0 Special Education; 0 Vocational; 1 Alternative
    0 Magnet; 0 Charter; 2 Title I Eligible; 0 School-wide Title I
Students: 6,803   (51.8% male; 48.1% female)
    Individual Education Program: 779 (11.5%);
    English Language Learner: 1,400 (20.6%); Migrant: 0 (0.0%)
    Eligible for Free Lunch Program: 1,169 (17.2%)
    Eligible for Reduced-Price Lunch Program: 399 (5.9%)
Teachers: 506.6 (13.4 to 1)
Librarians/Media Specialists: 9.5 (716.1 to 1)
Guidance Counselors: 11.0 (618.5 to 1)
Current Spending: ($ per student per year):
    Total: $8,491; Instruction: $5,331; Support Services: $2,914
Enrollment, Drop-out Rates and Diploma Recipients by Race/Ethnicity

Category	Total	White	Black	Asian	AIAN	Hisp.
Enrollment (%)	100.0	51.2	17.0	4.6	0.3	27.0
Drop-out Rate (%)	1.5	1.2	1.4	2.1	0.0	2.8
H.S. Diplomas (#)	355	269	39	16	0	31

Manassas Park City

Manassas Park City Public Schools
One Park Center Ct Ste A • Manassas Park, VA 20111-2395
(703) 335-8850 • http://www.mpark.net/
Grade Span: PK-12; **Agency Type:** 1
Schools: 4
    1 Primary; 2 Middle; 1 High; 0 Other Level
    4 Regular; 0 Special Education; 0 Vocational; 0 Alternative
    0 Magnet; 0 Charter; 2 Title I Eligible; 0 School-wide Title I
Students: 2,288   (51.0% male; 48.9% female)
    Individual Education Program: 282 (12.3%);
    English Language Learner: 531 (23.2%); Migrant: 0 (0.0%)
    Eligible for Free Lunch Program: 519 (22.7%)
    Eligible for Reduced-Price Lunch Program: 185 (8.1%)
Teachers: 199.1 (11.5 to 1)
Librarians/Media Specialists: 4.0 (572.0 to 1)
Guidance Counselors: 5.0 (457.6 to 1)
Current Spending: ($ per student per year):
    Total: $7,924; Instruction: $4,852; Support Services: $2,804
Enrollment, Drop-out Rates and Diploma Recipients by Race/Ethnicity

Category	Total	White	Black	Asian	AIAN	Hisp.
Enrollment (%)	100.0	46.8	14.3	7.4	0.2	30.9
Drop-out Rate (%)	2.0	1.5	3.4	3.2	0.0	1.8
H.S. Diplomas (#)	91	46	14	4	1	26

Martinsville City

Martinsville City Public Schools
202 Cleveland Ave • Martinsville, VA 24115-5548
(276) 632-6313 • http://www.martinsville.k12.va.us/
Grade Span: PK-12; **Agency Type:** 1
Schools: 6
   4 Primary; 1 Middle; 1 High; 0 Other Level
   6 Regular; 0 Special Education; 0 Vocational; 0 Alternative
   0 Charter; 0 Magnet; 3 Title I Eligible; 3 School-wide Title I
Students: 2,611   (50.5% male; 49.4% female)
   Individual Education Program: 385 (14.7%);
   English Language Learner: 56 (2.1%); Migrant: 0 (0.0%)
   Eligible for Free Lunch Program: 904 (34.6%)
   Eligible for Reduced-Price Lunch Program: 134 (5.1%)
Teachers: 229.3 (11.4 to 1)
Librarians/Media Specialists: 6.0 (435.2 to 1)
Guidance Counselors: 7.0 (373.0 to 1)
Current Spending: ($ per student per year):
   Total: $7,883; Instruction: $4,856; Support Services: $2,676

Enrollment, Drop-out Rates and Diploma Recipients by Race/Ethnicity

Category	Total	White	Black	Asian	AIAN	Hisp.
Enrollment (%)	100.0	37.7	59.0	0.9	0.0	2.3
Drop-out Rate (%)	1.4	0.5	2.0	0.0	n/a	11.1
H.S. Diplomas (#)	158	71	86	0	0	1

Mecklenburg County

Mecklenburg County Public Schools
939 Jefferson St • Boydton, VA 23917-0190
(434) 738-6111 • http://www.meck.k12.va.us/
Grade Span: PK-12; **Agency Type:** 1
Schools: 11
   7 Primary; 2 Middle; 2 High; 0 Other Level
   11 Regular; 0 Special Education; 0 Vocational; 0 Alternative
   0 Magnet; 0 Charter; 7 Title I Eligible; 3 School-wide Title I
Students: 4,785   (51.8% male; 48.1% female)
   Individual Education Program: 818 (17.1%);
   English Language Learner: 32 (0.7%); Migrant: 0 (0.0%)
   Eligible for Free Lunch Program: 2,259 (47.2%)
   Eligible for Reduced-Price Lunch Program: 555 (11.6%)
Teachers: 362.6 (13.2 to 1)
Librarians/Media Specialists: 8.5 (562.9 to 1)
Guidance Counselors: 8.0 (598.1 to 1)
Current Spending: ($ per student per year):
   Total: $6,732; Instruction: $4,196; Support Services: $2,198

Enrollment, Drop-out Rates and Diploma Recipients by Race/Ethnicity

Category	Total	White	Black	Asian	AIAN	Hisp.
Enrollment (%)	100.0	50.4	47.9	0.4	0.1	1.3
Drop-out Rate (%)	2.5	1.5	3.7	0.0	n/a	0.0
H.S. Diplomas (#)	279	164	112	0	0	3

Montgomery County

Montgomery County Public Schools
200 Junkin St • Christiansburg, VA 24073-3098
(540) 382-5100 • http://www.mcps.org/
Grade Span: PK-12; **Agency Type:** 1
Schools: 21
   12 Primary; 4 Middle; 4 High; 1 Other Level
   20 Regular; 0 Special Education; 0 Vocational; 1 Alternative
   0 Magnet; 0 Charter; 10 Title I Eligible; 3 School-wide Title I
Students: 9,467   (51.3% male; 48.6% female)
   Individual Education Program: 1,274 (13.5%);
   English Language Learner: 199 (2.1%); Migrant: 0 (0.0%)
   Eligible for Free Lunch Program: 2,202 (23.3%)
   Eligible for Reduced-Price Lunch Program: 642 (6.8%)
Teachers: 846.0 (11.2 to 1)
Librarians/Media Specialists: 22.0 (430.3 to 1)
Guidance Counselors: 24.0 (394.5 to 1)
Current Spending: ($ per student per year):
   Total: $7,431; Instruction: $4,594; Support Services: $2,520

Enrollment, Drop-out Rates and Diploma Recipients by Race/Ethnicity

Category	Total	White	Black	Asian	AIAN	Hisp.
Enrollment (%)	100.0	89.3	5.3	3.1	0.4	1.5
Drop-out Rate (%)	4.0	3.9	8.5	0.0	0.0	3.3
H.S. Diplomas (#)	563	520	22	15	0	6

Nelson County

Nelson County Public Schools
84 Courthouse Square • Lovingston, VA 22949-0276
Mailing Address: PO Box 276 • Lovingston, VA 22949-0276
(434) 263-7100 • http://www.nelson.k12.va.us/
Grade Span: PK-12; **Agency Type:** 1
Schools: 4
   2 Primary; 1 Middle; 1 High; 0 Other Level
   4 Regular; 0 Special Education; 0 Vocational; 0 Alternative
   0 Magnet; 0 Charter; 2 Title I Eligible; 0 School-wide Title I
Students: 2,015   (52.0% male; 47.9% female)
   Individual Education Program: 379 (18.8%);
   English Language Learner: 38 (1.9%); Migrant: 12 (0.6%)
   Eligible for Free Lunch Program: 545 (27.0%)
   Eligible for Reduced-Price Lunch Program: 242 (12.0%)
Teachers: 168.3 (12.0 to 1)
Librarians/Media Specialists: 4.0 (503.8 to 1)
Guidance Counselors: 4.0 (503.8 to 1)
Current Spending: ($ per student per year):
   Total: $8,012; Instruction: $4,513; Support Services: $3,160

Enrollment, Drop-out Rates and Diploma Recipients by Race/Ethnicity

Category	Total	White	Black	Asian	AIAN	Hisp.
Enrollment (%)	100.0	77.7	19.8	0.3	0.1	2.2
Drop-out Rate (%)	1.4	1.3	1.6	0.0	n/a	0.0
H.S. Diplomas (#)	129	97	30	0	0	2

New Kent County

New Kent County Public Schools
12007 Courthouse Cir • New Kent, VA 23124-0110
Mailing Address: PO Box 110 • New Kent, VA 23124-0110
(804) 966-9650 • http://www.newkentschools.org/
Grade Span: PK-12; **Agency Type:** 1
Schools: 4
   2 Primary; 1 Middle; 1 High; 0 Other Level
   4 Regular; 0 Special Education; 0 Vocational; 0 Alternative
   0 Magnet; 0 Charter; 1 Title I Eligible; 0 School-wide Title I
Students: 2,546   (52.0% male; 47.9% female)
   Individual Education Program: 491 (19.3%);
   English Language Learner: 4 (0.2%); Migrant: 0 (0.0%)
   Eligible for Free Lunch Program: 319 (12.5%)
   Eligible for Reduced-Price Lunch Program: 95 (3.7%)
Teachers: 207.5 (12.3 to 1)
Librarians/Media Specialists: 4.0 (636.5 to 1)
Guidance Counselors: 5.0 (509.2 to 1)
Current Spending: ($ per student per year):
   Total: $6,571; Instruction: $4,014; Support Services: $2,388

Enrollment, Drop-out Rates and Diploma Recipients by Race/Ethnicity

Category	Total	White	Black	Asian	AIAN	Hisp.
Enrollment (%)	100.0	80.8	16.1	0.4	1.5	1.3
Drop-out Rate (%)	1.6	1.5	2.3	0.0	0.0	0.0
H.S. Diplomas (#)	144	113	26	3	1	1

Newport News City

Newport News City Public Schools
12465 Warwick Blvd • Newport News, VA 23606-3041
(757) 591-4545 • http://www.sbo.nn.k12.va.us/
Grade Span: PK-12; **Agency Type:** 1
Schools: 48
   31 Primary; 8 Middle; 5 High; 4 Other Level
   44 Regular; 0 Special Education; 0 Vocational; 4 Alternative
   12 Magnet; 0 Charter; 21 Title I Eligible; 0 School-wide Title I
Students: 32,893   (50.5% male; 49.4% female)
   Individual Education Program: 4,272 (13.0%);
   English Language Learner: 462 (1.4%); Migrant: 0 (0.0%)
   Eligible for Free Lunch Program: 12,100 (36.8%)
   Eligible for Reduced-Price Lunch Program: 3,420 (10.4%)
Teachers: 2,425.4 (13.6 to 1)
Librarians/Media Specialists: 43.0 (765.0 to 1)
Guidance Counselors: 76.3 (431.1 to 1)
Current Spending: ($ per student per year):
   Total: $7,220; Instruction: $4,452; Support Services: $2,440

Enrollment, Drop-out Rates and Diploma Recipients by Race/Ethnicity

Category	Total	White	Black	Asian	AIAN	Hisp.
Enrollment (%)	100.0	34.9	56.9	2.5	0.9	4.8
Drop-out Rate (%)	3.0	2.6	3.5	1.3	1.5	2.7
H.S. Diplomas (#)	1,570	640	811	51	7	61

Norfolk City

Norfolk City Public Schools
800 E City Hall Ave • Norfolk, VA 23510
Mailing Address: PO Box 1357 • Norfolk, VA 23501
(757) 628-3830 • http://www.nps.k12.va.us/
Grade Span: PK-12; **Agency Type:** 1
Schools: 58
   39 Primary; 9 Middle; 5 High; 5 Other Level
   51 Regular; 2 Special Education; 2 Vocational; 3 Alternative
   3 Magnet; 0 Charter; 20 Title I Eligible; 20 School-wide Title I
Students: 36,724 (50.8% male; 49.1% female)
   Individual Education Program: 5,181 (14.1%);
   English Language Learner: 192 (0.5%); Migrant: 0 (0.0%)
   Eligible for Free Lunch Program: 17,099 (46.6%)
   Eligible for Reduced-Price Lunch Program: 4,083 (11.1%)
Teachers: 2,586.0 (14.2 to 1)
Librarians/Media Specialists: 48.0 (765.1 to 1)
Guidance Counselors: 76.0 (483.2 to 1)
Current Spending: ($ per student per year):
   Total: $7,608; Instruction: $4,715; Support Services: $2,568
Enrollment, Drop-out Rates and Diploma Recipients by Race/Ethnicity

Category	Total	White	Black	Asian	AIAN	Hisp.
Enrollment (%)	100.0	26.4	68.6	2.0	0.2	2.8
Drop-out Rate (%)	4.6	3.3	5.4	1.8	5.0	3.1
H.S. Diplomas (#)	1,348	503	759	49	2	35

Northampton County

Northampton County Public Schools
7207 Young St • Machipongo, VA 23405-0360
(757) 678-5151 • http://www.ncps.k12.va.us/
Grade Span: PK-12; **Agency Type:** 1
Schools: 5
   2 Primary; 1 Middle; 1 High; 1 Other Level
   4 Regular; 0 Special Education; 0 Vocational; 1 Alternative
   0 Magnet; 0 Charter; 2 Title I Eligible; 2 School-wide Title I
Students: 2,029 (50.4% male; 49.5% female)
   Individual Education Program: 289 (14.2%);
   English Language Learner: 82 (4.0%); Migrant: 107 (5.3%)
   Eligible for Free Lunch Program: 1,248 (61.5%)
   Eligible for Reduced-Price Lunch Program: 180 (8.9%)
Teachers: 180.0 (11.3 to 1)
Librarians/Media Specialists: 4.0 (507.3 to 1)
Guidance Counselors: 4.0 (507.3 to 1)
Current Spending: ($ per student per year):
   Total: $8,109; Instruction: $4,973; Support Services: $2,875
Enrollment, Drop-out Rates and Diploma Recipients by Race/Ethnicity

Category	Total	White	Black	Asian	AIAN	Hisp.
Enrollment (%)	100.0	38.9	54.0	0.4	0.1	6.7
Drop-out Rate (%)	7.0	8.1	5.7	33.3	0.0	13.0
H.S. Diplomas (#)	134	63	69	1	0	1

Nottoway County

Nottoway County Public Schools
Hwy 460 • Nottoway, VA 23955-0047
(434) 645-9596 • http://nottowaynt.k12.nottoway.state.va.us/
Grade Span: PK-12; **Agency Type:** 1
Schools: 7
   3 Primary; 2 Middle; 1 High; 1 Other Level
   6 Regular; 0 Special Education; 0 Vocational; 1 Alternative
   0 Magnet; 0 Charter; 4 Title I Eligible; 4 School-wide Title I
Students: 2,447 (51.4% male; 48.5% female)
   Individual Education Program: 448 (18.3%);
   English Language Learner: 28 (1.1%); Migrant: 22 (0.9%)
   Eligible for Free Lunch Program: 979 (40.0%)
   Eligible for Reduced-Price Lunch Program: 237 (9.7%)
Teachers: 184.0 (13.3 to 1)
Librarians/Media Specialists: 4.1 (596.8 to 1)
Guidance Counselors: 4.0 (611.8 to 1)
Current Spending: ($ per student per year):
   Total: $6,847; Instruction: $4,181; Support Services: $2,268
Enrollment, Drop-out Rates and Diploma Recipients by Race/Ethnicity

Category	Total	White	Black	Asian	AIAN	Hisp.
Enrollment (%)	100.0	50.8	46.8	0.1	0.0	2.1
Drop-out Rate (%)	5.1	7.1	3.4	0.0	n/a	0.0
H.S. Diplomas (#)	144	70	70	1	0	3

Orange County

Orange County Public Schools
437 Waugh Blvd • Orange, VA 22960-1859
(540) 661-4550 • http://www.ocss-va.org/
Grade Span: PK-12; **Agency Type:** 1
Schools: 8
   5 Primary; 2 Middle; 1 High; 0 Other Level
   8 Regular; 0 Special Education; 0 Vocational; 0 Alternative
   0 Magnet; 0 Charter; 4 Title I Eligible; 3 School-wide Title I
Students: 4,090 (50.0% male; 49.9% female)
   Individual Education Program: 568 (13.9%);
   English Language Learner: 40 (1.0%); Migrant: 0 (0.0%)
   Eligible for Free Lunch Program: 911 (22.3%)
   Eligible for Reduced-Price Lunch Program: 282 (6.9%)
Teachers: 327.0 (12.5 to 1)
Librarians/Media Specialists: 9.0 (454.4 to 1)
Guidance Counselors: 6.0 (681.7 to 1)
Current Spending: ($ per student per year):
   Total: $7,608; Instruction: $4,759; Support Services: $2,572
Enrollment, Drop-out Rates and Diploma Recipients by Race/Ethnicity

Category	Total	White	Black	Asian	AIAN	Hisp.
Enrollment (%)	100.0	78.3	19.0	0.5	0.0	1.9
Drop-out Rate (%)	1.4	1.6	0.8	0.0	0.0	0.0
H.S. Diplomas (#)	256	201	51	0	1	3

Page County

Page County Public Schools
735 W Main St • Luray, VA 22835-1030
(540) 743-6533 • http://eclipse.pagecounty.k12.va.us/~pcps/index.html
Grade Span: PK-12; **Agency Type:** 1
Schools: 8
   5 Primary; 0 Middle; 2 High; 1 Other Level
   7 Regular; 0 Special Education; 1 Vocational; 0 Alternative
   0 Magnet; 0 Charter; 5 Title I Eligible; 0 School-wide Title I
Students: 3,584 (51.2% male; 48.7% female)
   Individual Education Program: 414 (11.6%);
   English Language Learner: 19 (0.5%); Migrant: 10 (0.3%)
   Eligible for Free Lunch Program: 1,060 (29.6%)
   Eligible for Reduced-Price Lunch Program: 308 (8.6%)
Teachers: 261.0 (13.7 to 1)
Librarians/Media Specialists: 7.0 (512.0 to 1)
Guidance Counselors: 8.0 (448.0 to 1)
Current Spending: ($ per student per year):
   Total: $6,085; Instruction: $4,056; Support Services: $1,746
Enrollment, Drop-out Rates and Diploma Recipients by Race/Ethnicity

Category	Total	White	Black	Asian	AIAN	Hisp.
Enrollment (%)	100.0	96.2	2.7	0.1	0.0	0.9
Drop-out Rate (%)	3.7	3.5	7.5	0.0	0.0	6.7
H.S. Diplomas (#)	206	196	6	2	0	2

Patrick County

Patrick County Public Schools
PO Box 346 • Stuart, VA 24171-0346
(276) 694-3163 • http://www.patrick-county.org/
Grade Span: PK-12; **Agency Type:** 1
Schools: 7
   5 Primary; 1 Middle; 1 High; 0 Other Level
   7 Regular; 0 Special Education; 0 Vocational; 0 Alternative
   0 Magnet; 0 Charter; 6 Title I Eligible; 0 School-wide Title I
Students: 2,586 (50.4% male; 49.5% female)
   Individual Education Program: 445 (17.2%);
   English Language Learner: 34 (1.3%); Migrant: 38 (1.5%)
   Eligible for Free Lunch Program: 984 (38.1%)
   Eligible for Reduced-Price Lunch Program: 179 (6.9%)
Teachers: 217.5 (11.9 to 1)
Librarians/Media Specialists: 6.0 (431.0 to 1)
Guidance Counselors: 6.0 (431.0 to 1)
Current Spending: ($ per student per year):
   Total: $6,544; Instruction: $4,122; Support Services: $2,092
Enrollment, Drop-out Rates and Diploma Recipients by Race/Ethnicity

Category	Total	White	Black	Asian	AIAN	Hisp.
Enrollment (%)	100.0	88.8	7.4	0.3	0.1	3.2
Drop-out Rate (%)	2.4	2.2	1.9	0.0	n/a	15.4
H.S. Diplomas (#)	170	155	15	0	0	0

Petersburg City

Petersburg City Public Schools
141 E Wythe St • Petersburg, VA 23803-4535
(804) 732-0510 • http://www.ppsk12.com/
Grade Span: PK-12; **Agency Type:** 1
Schools: 10

7 Primary; 2 Middle; 1 High; 0 Other Level
10 Regular; 0 Special Education; 0 Vocational; 0 Alternative
0 Magnet; 0 Charter; 9 Title I Eligible; 7 School-wide Title I
Students: 5,363   (50.2% male; 49.7% female)
Individual Education Program: 752 (14.0%);
English Language Learner: 31 (0.6%); Migrant: 0 (0.0%)
Eligible for Free Lunch Program: 3,428 (63.9%)
Eligible for Reduced-Price Lunch Program: 490 (9.1%)
Teachers: 400.0 (13.4 to 1)
Librarians/Media Specialists: 11.0 (487.5 to 1)
Guidance Counselors: 8.0 (670.4 to 1)
Current Spending: ($ per student per year):
Total: $7,597; Instruction: $4,334; Support Services: $2,851
Enrollment, Drop-out Rates and Diploma Recipients by Race/Ethnicity

Category	Total	White	Black	Asian	AIAN	Hisp.
Enrollment (%)	100.0	1.9	96.3	0.2	0.1	1.5
Drop-out Rate (%)	7.5	3.1	7.6	0.0	n/a	16.7
H.S. Diplomas (#)	237	2	235	0	0	0

Pittsylvania County

Pittsylvania County Public Schools
39 Bank St SE • Chatham, VA 24531-0232
Mailing Address: PO Box 232 • Chatham, VA 24531-0232
(434) 432-2761 • http://www.pcs.k12.va.us/public/
Grade Span: PK-12; **Agency Type:** 1
Schools: 19
9 Primary; 4 Middle; 4 High; 2 Other Level
17 Regular; 0 Special Education; 1 Vocational; 1 Alternative
0 Magnet; 0 Charter; 11 Title I Eligible; 8 School-wide Title I
Students: 9,264   (51.8% male; 48.1% female)
Individual Education Program: 1,292 (13.9%);
English Language Learner: 111 (1.2%); Migrant: 37 (0.4%)
Eligible for Free Lunch Program: 2,814 (30.4%)
Eligible for Reduced-Price Lunch Program: 691 (7.5%)
Teachers: 683.8 (13.5 to 1)
Librarians/Media Specialists: 16.0 (579.0 to 1)
Guidance Counselors: 25.0 (370.6 to 1)
Current Spending: ($ per student per year):
Total: $6,316; Instruction: $3,900; Support Services: $2,095
Enrollment, Drop-out Rates and Diploma Recipients by Race/Ethnicity

Category	Total	White	Black	Asian	AIAN	Hisp.
Enrollment (%)	100.0	67.6	30.4	0.2	0.1	1.7
Drop-out Rate (%)	3.1	2.2	5.3	0.0	0.0	0.0
H.S. Diplomas (#)	581	416	163	1	0	1

Poquoson City

Poquoson City Public Schools
500 City Hall Ave • Poquoson, VA 23662-0068
(757) 868-3055 • http://www.sbo.poquoson.k12.va.us/
Grade Span: PK-12; **Agency Type:** 1
Schools: 4
2 Primary; 1 Middle; 1 High; 0 Other Level
4 Regular; 0 Special Education; 0 Vocational; 0 Alternative
0 Magnet; 0 Charter; 2 Title I Eligible; 0 School-wide Title I
Students: 2,544   (53.4% male; 46.5% female)
Individual Education Program: 279 (11.0%);
English Language Learner: 13 (0.5%); Migrant: 0 (0.0%)
Eligible for Free Lunch Program: 102 (4.0%)
Eligible for Reduced-Price Lunch Program: 38 (1.5%)
Teachers: 192.8 (13.2 to 1)
Librarians/Media Specialists: 4.0 (636.0 to 1)
Guidance Counselors: 4.0 (636.0 to 1)
Current Spending: ($ per student per year):
Total: $6,299; Instruction: $4,047; Support Services: $2,155
Enrollment, Drop-out Rates and Diploma Recipients by Race/Ethnicity

Category	Total	White	Black	Asian	AIAN	Hisp.
Enrollment (%)	100.0	95.3	0.5	2.4	0.8	0.9
Drop-out Rate (%)	1.1	1.1	0.0	0.0	n/a	0.0
H.S. Diplomas (#)	180	171	1	8	0	0

Portsmouth City

Portsmouth City Public Schools
801 Crawford St • Portsmouth, VA 23704-3822
Mailing Address: PO Box 998 • Portsmouth, VA 23705-0998
(757) 393-8742 • http://pps.k12.va.us/
Grade Span: PK-12; **Agency Type:** 1
Schools: 27
17 Primary; 4 Middle; 4 High; 2 Other Level
23 Regular; 1 Special Education; 1 Vocational; 2 Alternative
6 Magnet; 0 Charter; 14 Title I Eligible; 14 School-wide Title I
Students: 16,545   (50.8% male; 49.1% female)
Individual Education Program: 2,284 (13.8%);

English Language Learner: 16 (0.1%); Migrant: 0 (0.0%)
Eligible for Free Lunch Program: 7,319 (44.2%)
Eligible for Reduced-Price Lunch Program: 1,302 (7.9%)
Teachers: 1,155.0 (14.3 to 1)
Librarians/Media Specialists: 28.0 (590.9 to 1)
Guidance Counselors: 44.0 (376.0 to 1)
Current Spending: ($ per student per year):
Total: $7,356; Instruction: $4,329; Support Services: $2,597
Enrollment, Drop-out Rates and Diploma Recipients by Race/Ethnicity

Category	Total	White	Black	Asian	AIAN	Hisp.
Enrollment (%)	100.0	26.8	71.3	0.8	0.1	1.1
Drop-out Rate (%)	3.3	2.1	3.9	2.4	0.0	5.3
H.S. Diplomas (#)	736	224	500	4	4	4

Powhatan County

Powhatan County Public Schools
2320 Skaggs Rd • Powhatan, VA 23139-5713
(804) 598-5700 • http://www.powhatan.k12.va.us/
Grade Span: PK-12; **Agency Type:** 1
Schools: 6
2 Primary; 2 Middle; 1 High; 1 Other Level
5 Regular; 0 Special Education; 1 Vocational; 0 Alternative
0 Magnet; 0 Charter; 2 Title I Eligible; 0 School-wide Title I
Students: 4,051   (51.9% male; 48.0% female)
Individual Education Program: 643 (15.9%);
English Language Learner: 9 (0.2%); Migrant: 0 (0.0%)
Eligible for Free Lunch Program: 332 (8.2%)
Eligible for Reduced-Price Lunch Program: 155 (3.8%)
Teachers: 304.9 (13.3 to 1)
Librarians/Media Specialists: 6.0 (675.2 to 1)
Guidance Counselors: 9.0 (450.1 to 1)
Current Spending: ($ per student per year):
Total: $7,047; Instruction: $4,332; Support Services: $2,513
Enrollment, Drop-out Rates and Diploma Recipients by Race/Ethnicity

Category	Total	White	Black	Asian	AIAN	Hisp.
Enrollment (%)	100.0	87.3	11.3	0.3	0.1	1.0
Drop-out Rate (%)	2.6	2.7	1.6	0.0	0.0	20.0
H.S. Diplomas (#)	207	183	21	0	1	2

Prince Edward County

Prince Edward County Public Schools
35 Eagle Dr • Farmville, VA 23901-9011
(434) 392-2100 • http://www.pecps.k12.va.us/
Grade Span: PK-12; **Agency Type:** 1
Schools: 3
1 Primary; 1 Middle; 1 High; 0 Other Level
3 Regular; 0 Special Education; 0 Vocational; 0 Alternative
0 Magnet; 0 Charter; 3 Title I Eligible; 3 School-wide Title I
Students: 2,852   (52.2% male; 47.7% female)
Individual Education Program: 560 (19.6%);
English Language Learner: 2 (0.1%); Migrant: 2 (0.1%)
Eligible for Free Lunch Program: 1,409 (49.4%)
Eligible for Reduced-Price Lunch Program: 307 (10.8%)
Teachers: 210.7 (13.5 to 1)
Librarians/Media Specialists: 3.0 (950.7 to 1)
Guidance Counselors: 6.0 (475.3 to 1)
Current Spending: ($ per student per year):
Total: $6,705; Instruction: $4,125; Support Services: $2,320
Enrollment, Drop-out Rates and Diploma Recipients by Race/Ethnicity

Category	Total	White	Black	Asian	AIAN	Hisp.
Enrollment (%)	100.0	39.4	58.8	0.7	0.4	0.7
Drop-out Rate (%)	5.1	3.7	6.4	0.0	n/a	0.0
H.S. Diplomas (#)	131	64	64	1	0	2

Prince George County

Prince George County Public Schools
6410 Courts Rd • Prince George, VA 23875
Mailing Address: PO Box 400 • Prince George, VA 23875
(804) 733-2700 • http://pgs.k12.va.us/
Grade Span: PK-12; **Agency Type:** 1
Schools: 8
5 Primary; 1 Middle; 1 High; 1 Other Level
8 Regular; 0 Special Education; 0 Vocational; 0 Alternative
0 Magnet; 0 Charter; 5 Title I Eligible; 0 School-wide Title I
Students: 6,090   (51.9% male; 48.0% female)
Individual Education Program: 713 (11.7%);
English Language Learner: 28 (0.5%); Migrant: 0 (0.0%)
Eligible for Free Lunch Program: 866 (14.2%)
Eligible for Reduced-Price Lunch Program: 538 (8.8%)
Teachers: 412.0 (14.8 to 1)
Librarians/Media Specialists: 11.0 (553.6 to 1)
Guidance Counselors: 14.0 (435.0 to 1)

Current Spending: ($ per student per year):
Total: $6,530; Instruction: $3,877; Support Services: $2,376

Enrollment, Drop-out Rates and Diploma Recipients by Race/Ethnicity

Category	Total	White	Black	Asian	AIAN	Hisp.
Enrollment (%)	100.0	54.4	37.8	1.2	0.2	4.1
Drop-out Rate (%)	3.1	3.2	2.9	0.0	0.0	4.5
H.S. Diplomas (#)	312	197	105	1	0	9

Prince William County

Prince William County Public Schools
14800 Joplin Rd · Manassas, VA 20112
Mailing Address: PO Box 389 · Manassas, VA 20108-0389
(703) 791-8712 · http://www.pwcs.edu/
Grade Span: PK-12; **Agency Type:** 1
Schools: 76
   49 Primary; 13 Middle; 8 High; 5 Other Level
   69 Regular; 3 Special Education; 0 Vocational; 3 Alternative
   25 Magnet; 0 Charter; 18 Title I Eligible; 1 School-wide Title I
Students: 63,404   (51.4% male; 48.5% female)
   Individual Education Program: 7,463 (11.8%);
   English Language Learner: 6,890 (10.9%); Migrant: 0 (0.0%)
   Eligible for Free Lunch Program: 10,897 (17.2%)
   Eligible for Reduced-Price Lunch Program: 4,267 (6.7%)
Teachers: 4,125.0 (15.4 to 1)
Librarians/Media Specialists: 82.5 (768.5 to 1)
Guidance Counselors: 111.0 (571.2 to 1)
Current Spending: ($ per student per year):
   Total: $7,670; Instruction: $4,468; Support Services: $2,897

Enrollment, Drop-out Rates and Diploma Recipients by Race/Ethnicity

Category	Total	White	Black	Asian	AIAN	Hisp.
Enrollment (%)	100.0	50.0	23.1	5.6	0.4	17.6
Drop-out Rate (%)	4.0	3.2	4.4	3.0	5.1	8.0
H.S. Diplomas (#)	3,196	2,031	753	155	18	239

Pulaski County

Pulaski County Public Schools
44 Third St NW · Pulaski, VA 24301-5008
(540) 643-0200 · http://admin.sbo.pulaski.k12.va.us/
Grade Span: PK-12; **Agency Type:** 1
Schools: 11
   8 Primary; 2 Middle; 1 High; 0 Other Level
   11 Regular; 0 Special Education; 0 Vocational; 0 Alternative
   0 Magnet; 0 Charter; 5 Title I Eligible; 2 School-wide Title I
Students: 4,887   (51.5% male; 48.4% female)
   Individual Education Program: 902 (18.5%);
   English Language Learner: 28 (0.6%); Migrant: 0 (0.0%)
   Eligible for Free Lunch Program: 1,449 (29.7%)
   Eligible for Reduced-Price Lunch Program: 389 (8.0%)
Teachers: 385.5 (12.7 to 1)
Librarians/Media Specialists: 10.0 (488.7 to 1)
Guidance Counselors: 13.0 (375.9 to 1)
Current Spending: ($ per student per year):
   Total: $6,829; Instruction: $4,075; Support Services: $2,412

Enrollment, Drop-out Rates and Diploma Recipients by Race/Ethnicity

Category	Total	White	Black	Asian	AIAN	Hisp.
Enrollment (%)	100.0	91.4	7.4	0.4	0.1	0.7
Drop-out Rate (%)	2.7	2.5	7.0	0.0	0.0	0.0
H.S. Diplomas (#)	329	301	23	5	0	0

Radford City

Radford City Public Schools
1612 Wadsworth St · Radford, VA 24143-3698
Mailing Address: PO Box 3698 · Radford, VA 24143-3698
(540) 731-3647 · http://www.rcps.org/
Grade Span: PK-12; **Agency Type:** 1
Schools: 4
   1 Primary; 2 Middle; 1 High; 0 Other Level
   4 Regular; 0 Special Education; 0 Vocational; 0 Alternative
   0 Magnet; 0 Charter; 2 Title I Eligible; 0 School-wide Title I
Students: 1,537   (49.8% male; 50.1% female)
   Individual Education Program: 232 (15.1%);
   English Language Learner: 10 (0.7%); Migrant: 0 (0.0%)
   Eligible for Free Lunch Program: 227 (14.8%)
   Eligible for Reduced-Price Lunch Program: 34 (2.2%)
Teachers: 122.2 (12.6 to 1)
Librarians/Media Specialists: 3.0 (512.3 to 1)
Guidance Counselors: 3.0 (512.3 to 1)
Current Spending: ($ per student per year):
   Total: $6,891; Instruction: $4,368; Support Services: $2,265

Category	Total	White	Black	Asian	AIAN	Hisp.
Enrollment (%)	100.0	85.4	12.0	2.0	0.0	0.5
Drop-out Rate (%)	2.6	2.1	7.4	0.0	n/a	0.0
H.S. Diplomas (#)	102	86	14	2	0	0

Richmond City

Richmond City Public Schools
301 N 9th St · Richmond, VA 23219-3913
(804) 780-7700 · http://www.richmond.k12.va.us/
Grade Span: PK-12; **Agency Type:** 1
Schools: 59
   32 Primary; 9 Middle; 8 High; 10 Other Level
   50 Regular; 4 Special Education; 1 Vocational; 4 Alternative
   0 Magnet; 0 Charter; 39 Title I Eligible; 39 School-wide Title I
Students: 25,399   (50.2% male; 49.7% female)
   Individual Education Program: 4,314 (17.0%);
   English Language Learner: 406 (1.6%); Migrant: 0 (0.0%)
   Eligible for Free Lunch Program: 15,853 (62.4%)
   Eligible for Reduced-Price Lunch Program: 2,297 (9.0%)
Teachers: 1,891.9 (13.4 to 1)
Librarians/Media Specialists: 50.0 (508.0 to 1)
Guidance Counselors: 77.0 (329.9 to 1)
Current Spending: ($ per student per year):
   Total: $9,808; Instruction: $5,574; Support Services: $3,875

Enrollment, Drop-out Rates and Diploma Recipients by Race/Ethnicity

Category	Total	White	Black	Asian	AIAN	Hisp.
Enrollment (%)	100.0	7.0	89.9	0.6	0.1	2.4
Drop-out Rate (%)	3.1	3.6	3.0	2.7	0.0	6.7
H.S. Diplomas (#)	1,058	46	998	7	0	7

Roanoke County

Roanoke County Public Schools
5937 Cove Rd NW · Roanoke, VA 24019-2403
(540) 562-3900 · http://www.rcs.k12.va.us/
Grade Span: PK-12; **Agency Type:** 1
Schools: 29
   17 Primary; 5 Middle; 5 High; 2 Other Level
   27 Regular; 0 Special Education; 1 Vocational; 1 Alternative
   5 Magnet; 0 Charter; 8 Title I Eligible; 0 School-wide Title I
Students: 14,537   (51.2% male; 48.7% female)
   Individual Education Program: 2,363 (16.3%);
   English Language Learner: 156 (1.1%); Migrant: 0 (0.0%)
   Eligible for Free Lunch Program: 1,458 (10.0%)
   Eligible for Reduced-Price Lunch Program: 750 (5.2%)
Teachers: 1,244.5 (11.7 to 1)
Librarians/Media Specialists: 30.0 (484.6 to 1)
Guidance Counselors: 31.0 (468.9 to 1)
Current Spending: ($ per student per year):
   Total: $7,318; Instruction: $4,623; Support Services: $2,427

Enrollment, Drop-out Rates and Diploma Recipients by Race/Ethnicity

Category	Total	White	Black	Asian	AIAN	Hisp.
Enrollment (%)	100.0	90.5	5.4	2.7	0.1	1.4
Drop-out Rate (%)	1.7	1.6	2.2	2.2	0.0	5.0
H.S. Diplomas (#)	929	859	47	16	0	7

Roanoke City Public Schools
40 Douglas Ave NW · Roanoke, VA 24012-4699
Mailing Address: PO Box 13145 · Roanoke, VA 24031
(540) 853-2381 · http://www.roanoke.k12.va.us/
Grade Span: PK-12; **Agency Type:** 1
Schools: 31
   21 Primary; 6 Middle; 3 High; 1 Other Level
   30 Regular; 0 Special Education; 0 Vocational; 1 Alternative
   14 Magnet; 1 Charter; 15 Title I Eligible; 15 School-wide Title I
Students: 13,567   (50.8% male; 49.1% female)
   Individual Education Program: 2,234 (16.5%);
   English Language Learner: 498 (3.7%); Migrant: 0 (0.0%)
   Eligible for Free Lunch Program: 7,194 (53.0%)
   Eligible for Reduced-Price Lunch Program: 964 (7.1%)
Teachers: 1,191.0 (11.4 to 1)
Librarians/Media Specialists: 30.0 (452.2 to 1)
Guidance Counselors: 33.0 (411.1 to 1)
Current Spending: ($ per student per year):
   Total: $7,784; Instruction: $4,908; Support Services: $2,563

Enrollment, Drop-out Rates and Diploma Recipients by Race/Ethnicity

Category	Total	White	Black	Asian	AIAN	Hisp.
Enrollment (%)	100.0	49.1	46.3	1.8	0.1	2.7
Drop-out Rate (%)	7.2	5.9	8.2	6.0	0.0	24.5
H.S. Diplomas (#)	498	267	214	12	1	4

Rockbridge County

Rockbridge County Public Schools
1972 Big Spring Dr • Lexington, VA 24450-2738
(540) 463-7386 • http://www.rcs.rang.k12.va.us/
Grade Span: PK-12; **Agency Type:** 1
Schools: 8
  5 Primary; 2 Middle; 1 High; 0 Other Level
  8 Regular; 0 Special Education; 0 Vocational; 0 Alternative
  0 Magnet; 0 Charter; 4 Title I Eligible; 0 School-wide Title I
Students: 2,930 (51.8% male; 48.1% female)
  Individual Education Program: 407 (13.9%);
  English Language Learner: 8 (0.3%); Migrant: 3 (0.1%)
  Eligible for Free Lunch Program: 649 (22.2%)
  Eligible for Reduced-Price Lunch Program: 229 (7.8%)
Teachers: 261.0 (11.2 to 1)
Librarians/Media Specialists: 9.0 (325.6 to 1)
Guidance Counselors: 8.0 (366.3 to 1)
Current Spending: ($ per student per year):
  Total: $7,385; Instruction: $4,642; Support Services: $2,455
Enrollment, Drop-out Rates and Diploma Recipients by Race/Ethnicity

Category	Total	White	Black	Asian	AIAN	Hisp.
Enrollment (%)	100.0	94.1	4.0	0.6	0.4	1.0
Drop-out Rate (%)	3.1	2.5	12.1	0.0	25.0	0.0
H.S. Diplomas (#)	210	198	9	2	0	1

Rockingham County

Rockingham County Public Schools
2 S Main St • Harrisonburg, VA 22801
(540) 564-3230 • http://www.rockingham.k12.va.us/
Grade Span: PK-12; **Agency Type:** 1
Schools: 20
  13 Primary; 4 Middle; 3 High; 0 Other Level
  20 Regular; 0 Special Education; 0 Vocational; 0 Alternative
  0 Magnet; 0 Charter; 8 Title I Eligible; 0 School-wide Title I
Students: 11,185 (51.7% male; 48.2% female)
  Individual Education Program: 1,393 (12.5%);
  English Language Learner: 627 (5.6%); Migrant: 135 (1.2%)
  Eligible for Free Lunch Program: 2,225 (19.9%)
  Eligible for Reduced-Price Lunch Program: 882 (7.9%)
Teachers: 887.4 (12.6 to 1)
Librarians/Media Specialists: 24.0 (466.0 to 1)
Guidance Counselors: 23.0 (486.3 to 1)
Current Spending: ($ per student per year):
  Total: $7,155; Instruction: $4,499; Support Services: $2,361
Enrollment, Drop-out Rates and Diploma Recipients by Race/Ethnicity

Category	Total	White	Black	Asian	AIAN	Hisp.
Enrollment (%)	100.0	91.5	1.8	0.5	0.0	6.2
Drop-out Rate (%)	2.9	2.7	4.6	0.0	0.0	7.2
H.S. Diplomas (#)	686	652	15	3	0	16

Russell County

Russell County Public Schools
1 School Board Dr • Lebanon, VA 24266-0008
(276) 889-6500 • http://www.russell.k12.va.us/
Grade Span: PK-12; **Agency Type:** 1
Schools: 13
  8 Primary; 1 Middle; 3 High; 1 Other Level
  12 Regular; 0 Special Education; 1 Vocational; 0 Alternative
  0 Magnet; 0 Charter; 9 Title I Eligible; 6 School-wide Title I
Students: 4,208 (50.3% male; 49.6% female)
  Individual Education Program: 718 (17.1%);
  English Language Learner: 2 (<0.1%); Migrant: 0 (0.0%)
  Eligible for Free Lunch Program: 1,555 (37.0%)
  Eligible for Reduced-Price Lunch Program: 385 (9.1%)
Teachers: 305.5 (13.8 to 1)
Librarians/Media Specialists: 8.0 (526.0 to 1)
Guidance Counselors: 10.5 (400.8 to 1)
Current Spending: ($ per student per year):
  Total: $6,427; Instruction: $3,962; Support Services: $2,160
Enrollment, Drop-out Rates and Diploma Recipients by Race/Ethnicity

Category	Total	White	Black	Asian	AIAN	Hisp.
Enrollment (%)	100.0	99.0	0.7	0.1	0.0	0.2
Drop-out Rate (%)	2.5	2.5	0.0	n/a	n/a	0.0
H.S. Diplomas (#)	270	269	1	0	0	0

Salem City

Salem City Public Schools
510 S College Ave • Salem, VA 24153-5054
(540) 389-0130 • http://www.salem.k12.va.us/
Grade Span: PK-12; **Agency Type:** 1
Schools: 6

  4 Primary; 1 Middle; 1 High; 0 Other Level
  6 Regular; 0 Special Education; 0 Vocational; 0 Alternative
  0 Magnet; 0 Charter; 2 Title I Eligible; 0 School-wide Title I
Students: 3,910 (52.0% male; 47.9% female)
  Individual Education Program: 476 (12.2%);
  English Language Learner: 32 (0.8%); Migrant: 0 (0.0%)
  Eligible for Free Lunch Program: 476 (12.2%)
  Eligible for Reduced-Price Lunch Program: 186 (4.8%)
Teachers: 307.9 (12.7 to 1)
Librarians/Media Specialists: 7.0 (558.6 to 1)
Guidance Counselors: 7.7 (507.8 to 1)
Current Spending: ($ per student per year):
  Total: $7,212; Instruction: $4,824; Support Services: $2,091
Enrollment, Drop-out Rates and Diploma Recipients by Race/Ethnicity

Category	Total	White	Black	Asian	AIAN	Hisp.
Enrollment (%)	100.0	88.4	8.4	2.1	0.2	0.8
Drop-out Rate (%)	2.0	1.9	4.7	0.0	n/a	0.0
H.S. Diplomas (#)	267	235	17	11	0	4

Scott County

Scott County Public Schools
261 E Jackson St • Gate City, VA 24251-3422
(276) 386-6118 • http://scott.k12.va.us/
Grade Span: PK-12; **Agency Type:** 1
Schools: 14
  7 Primary; 3 Middle; 3 High; 1 Other Level
  13 Regular; 0 Special Education; 1 Vocational; 0 Alternative
  0 Magnet; 0 Charter; 8 Title I Eligible; 4 School-wide Title I
Students: 3,734 (50.8% male; 49.1% female)
  Individual Education Program: 669 (17.9%);
  English Language Learner: 2 (0.1%); Migrant: 0 (0.0%)
  Eligible for Free Lunch Program: 1,439 (38.5%)
  Eligible for Reduced-Price Lunch Program: 462 (12.4%)
Teachers: 293.5 (12.7 to 1)
Librarians/Media Specialists: 11.0 (339.5 to 1)
Guidance Counselors: 7.0 (533.4 to 1)
Current Spending: ($ per student per year):
  Total: $6,539; Instruction: $4,137; Support Services: $2,071
Enrollment, Drop-out Rates and Diploma Recipients by Race/Ethnicity

Category	Total	White	Black	Asian	AIAN	Hisp.
Enrollment (%)	100.0	98.2	0.8	0.2	0.2	0.6
Drop-out Rate (%)	1.4	1.2	0.0	0.0	n/a	300.0
H.S. Diplomas (#)	219	217	2	0	0	0

Shenandoah County

Shenandoah County Public Schools
600 N Main St #200 • Woodstock, VA 22664-1855
(540) 459-6222 • http://www.shenandoah.k12.va.us/
Grade Span: PK-12; **Agency Type:** 1
Schools: 10
  3 Primary; 3 Middle; 3 High; 1 Other Level
  9 Regular; 0 Special Education; 1 Vocational; 0 Alternative
  0 Magnet; 0 Charter; 3 Title I Eligible; 0 School-wide Title I
Students: 5,827 (51.8% male; 48.1% female)
  Individual Education Program: 826 (14.2%);
  English Language Learner: 139 (2.4%); Migrant: 143 (2.5%)
  Eligible for Free Lunch Program: 1,113 (19.1%)
  Eligible for Reduced-Price Lunch Program: 359 (6.2%)
Teachers: 474.0 (12.3 to 1)
Librarians/Media Specialists: 10.0 (582.7 to 1)
Guidance Counselors: 12.0 (485.6 to 1)
Current Spending: ($ per student per year):
  Total: $6,867; Instruction: $4,347; Support Services: $2,299
Enrollment, Drop-out Rates and Diploma Recipients by Race/Ethnicity

Category	Total	White	Black	Asian	AIAN	Hisp.
Enrollment (%)	100.0	91.2	1.7	0.5	0.1	6.5
Drop-out Rate (%)	2.6	2.1	12.0	0.0	n/a	12.7
H.S. Diplomas (#)	357	339	5	3	0	10

Smyth County

Smyth County Public Schools
121 Bagley Cir Ste 300 • Marion, VA 24354-3140
(276) 783-3791 • http://www.scsb.org/
Grade Span: PK-12; **Agency Type:** 1
Schools: 14
  7 Primary; 3 Middle; 3 High; 1 Other Level
  13 Regular; 0 Special Education; 1 Vocational; 0 Alternative
  0 Magnet; 0 Charter; 7 Title I Eligible; 0 School-wide Title I
Students: 5,084 (51.8% male; 48.1% female)
  Individual Education Program: 952 (18.7%);
  English Language Learner: 19 (0.4%); Migrant: 0 (0.0%)
  Eligible for Free Lunch Program: 1,812 (35.6%)

Eligible for Reduced-Price Lunch Program: 439 (8.6%)
Teachers: 463.0 (11.0 to 1)
Librarians/Media Specialists: 12.0 (423.7 to 1)
Guidance Counselors: 10.0 (508.4 to 1)
Current Spending: ($ per student per year):
   Total: $6,771; Instruction: $4,614; Support Services: $1,970
Enrollment, Drop-out Rates and Diploma Recipients by Race/Ethnicity

Category	Total	White	Black	Asian	AIAN	Hisp.
Enrollment (%)	100.0	96.9	1.6	0.4	0.2	1.0
Drop-out Rate (%)	0.8	0.7	4.5	0.0	0.0	0.0
H.S. Diplomas (#)	302	296	3	0	1	2

Southampton County

Southampton County Public Schools
21308 Plank Rd • Courtland, VA 23837-0096
Mailing Address: PO Box 96 • Courtland, VA 23837-0096
(757) 653-2692 • http://www.southampton.k12.va.us/
Grade Span: PK-12; **Agency Type:** 1
Schools: 6
   4 Primary; 1 Middle; 1 High; 0 Other Level
   6 Regular; 0 Special Education; 0 Vocational; 0 Alternative
   0 Magnet; 0 Charter; 4 Title I Eligible; 0 School-wide Title I
Students: 2,853 (52.7% male; 47.2% female)
   Individual Education Program: 515 (18.1%);
   English Language Learner: 1 (<0.1%); Migrant: 0 (0.0%)
   Eligible for Free Lunch Program: 942 (33.0%)
   Eligible for Reduced-Price Lunch Program: 243 (8.5%)
Teachers: 221.0 (12.9 to 1)
Librarians/Media Specialists: 6.0 (475.5 to 1)
Guidance Counselors: 7.0 (407.6 to 1)
Current Spending: ($ per student per year):
   Total: $7,585; Instruction: $4,454; Support Services: $2,736
Enrollment, Drop-out Rates and Diploma Recipients by Race/Ethnicity

Category	Total	White	Black	Asian	AIAN	Hisp.
Enrollment (%)	100.0	49.1	49.4	0.3	0.3	0.7
Drop-out Rate (%)	3.1	2.0	4.1	0.0	n/a	50.0
H.S. Diplomas (#)	152	89	61	1	0	1

Spotsylvania County

Spotsylvania County Public Schools
6717 Smith Station Rd • Spotsylvania, VA 22553-1803
(540) 898-6032 • http://205.174.118.254/index.htm
Grade Span: PK-12; **Agency Type:** 1
Schools: 30
   16 Primary; 7 Middle; 6 High; 1 Other Level
   27 Regular; 0 Special Education; 1 Vocational; 2 Alternative
   0 Magnet; 0 Charter; 15 Title I Eligible; 0 School-wide Title I
Students: 22,075 (51.1% male; 48.8% female)
   Individual Education Program: 3,219 (14.6%);
   English Language Learner: 313 (1.4%); Migrant: 1 (<0.1%)
   Eligible for Free Lunch Program: 2,919 (13.2%)
   Eligible for Reduced-Price Lunch Program: 1,012 (4.6%)
Teachers: 1,663.2 (13.3 to 1)
Librarians/Media Specialists: 32.0 (689.8 to 1)
Guidance Counselors: 35.0 (630.7 to 1)
Current Spending: ($ per student per year):
   Total: $6,891; Instruction: $4,345; Support Services: $2,294
Enrollment, Drop-out Rates and Diploma Recipients by Race/Ethnicity

Category	Total	White	Black	Asian	AIAN	Hisp.
Enrollment (%)	100.0	75.4	18.0	2.1	0.3	4.2
Drop-out Rate (%)	2.2	2.1	2.7	1.0	0.0	4.7
H.S. Diplomas (#)	1,119	862	180	25	8	44

Stafford County

Stafford County Public Schools
31 Stafford Ave • Stafford, VA 22554-7213
(540) 658-6000 • http://www.pen.k12.va.us/Div/Stafford/
Grade Span: PK-12; **Agency Type:** 1
Schools: 24
   14 Primary; 6 Middle; 4 High; 0 Other Level
   24 Regular; 0 Special Education; 0 Vocational; 0 Alternative
   0 Magnet; 0 Charter; 7 Title I Eligible; 0 School-wide Title I
Students: 24,869 (51.4% male; 48.5% female)
   Individual Education Program: 2,707 (10.9%);
   English Language Learner: 315 (1.3%); Migrant: 0 (0.0%)
   Eligible for Free Lunch Program: 2,109 (8.5%)
   Eligible for Reduced-Price Lunch Program: 821 (3.3%)
Teachers: 1,735.7 (14.3 to 1)
Librarians/Media Specialists: 29.0 (857.6 to 1)
Guidance Counselors: 35.8 (694.7 to 1)
Current Spending: ($ per student per year):
   Total: $6,737; Instruction: $4,341; Support Services: $2,127

Enrollment, Drop-out Rates and Diploma Recipients by Race/Ethnicity

Category	Total	White	Black	Asian	AIAN	Hisp.
Enrollment (%)	100.0	72.3	19.3	2.5	0.4	4.5
Drop-out Rate (%)	2.5	2.4	2.5	1.8	0.0	4.0
H.S. Diplomas (#)	1,359	1,031	188	45	1	94

Staunton City

Staunton City Public Schools
116 W Beverly St • Staunton, VA 24401-4203
Mailing Address: PO Box 900 • Staunton, VA 24402-0900
(540) 332-3920 • http://www.staunton.k12.va.us/
Grade Span: PK-12; **Agency Type:** 1
Schools: 6
   4 Primary; 1 Middle; 1 High; 0 Other Level
   6 Regular; 0 Special Education; 0 Vocational; 0 Alternative
   0 Magnet; 0 Charter; 4 Title I Eligible; 0 School-wide Title I
Students: 2,684 (51.3% male; 48.6% female)
   Individual Education Program: 454 (16.9%);
   English Language Learner: 16 (0.6%); Migrant: 0 (0.0%)
   Eligible for Free Lunch Program: 897 (33.4%)
   Eligible for Reduced-Price Lunch Program: 205 (7.6%)
Teachers: 250.3 (10.7 to 1)
Librarians/Media Specialists: 6.0 (447.3 to 1)
Guidance Counselors: 7.0 (383.4 to 1)
Current Spending: ($ per student per year):
   Total: $8,792; Instruction: $5,849; Support Services: $2,666
Enrollment, Drop-out Rates and Diploma Recipients by Race/Ethnicity

Category	Total	White	Black	Asian	AIAN	Hisp.
Enrollment (%)	100.0	74.7	23.0	0.7	0.1	1.5
Drop-out Rate (%)	3.9	4.5	2.0	14.3	n/a	0.0
H.S. Diplomas (#)	169	129	37	1	0	2

Suffolk City

Suffolk City Public Schools
524 N Main St • Suffolk, VA 23434-1549
Mailing Address: PO Box 1549 • Suffolk, VA 23439-1549
(757) 925-5500 • http://www.sps.k12.va.us/
Grade Span: PK-12; **Agency Type:** 1
Schools: 21
   12 Primary; 4 Middle; 2 High; 2 Other Level
   18 Regular; 0 Special Education; 0 Vocational; 2 Alternative
   0 Magnet; 0 Charter; 12 Title I Eligible; 0 School-wide Title I
Students: 13,273 (51.8% male; 48.1% female)
   Individual Education Program: 1,503 (11.3%);
   English Language Learner: 14 (0.1%); Migrant: 0 (0.0%)
   Eligible for Free Lunch Program: 4,213 (31.7%)
   Eligible for Reduced-Price Lunch Program: 1,064 (8.0%)
Teachers: 911.3 (14.6 to 1)
Librarians/Media Specialists: 20.0 (663.7 to 1)
Guidance Counselors: 23.0 (577.1 to 1)
Current Spending: ($ per student per year):
   Total: $6,733; Instruction: $4,291; Support Services: $2,120
Enrollment, Drop-out Rates and Diploma Recipients by Race/Ethnicity

Category	Total	White	Black	Asian	AIAN	Hisp.
Enrollment (%)	100.0	40.4	57.0	0.9	0.2	1.3
Drop-out Rate (%)	3.1	2.1	3.9	3.3	0.0	0.0
H.S. Diplomas (#)	531	262	264	2	0	3

Tazewell County

Tazewell County Public Schools
209 W Fincastle • Tazewell, VA 24651-0927
(276) 988-5511 • http://www.tazewell.k12.va.us/web1/index.html
Grade Span: PK-12; **Agency Type:** 1
Schools: 17
   9 Primary; 3 Middle; 3 High; 2 Other Level
   16 Regular; 0 Special Education; 1 Vocational; 0 Alternative
   0 Magnet; 0 Charter; 9 Title I Eligible; 1 School-wide Title I
Students: 6,986 (50.9% male; 49.0% female)
   Individual Education Program: 1,084 (15.5%);
   English Language Learner: 1 (<0.1%); Migrant: 0 (0.0%)
   Eligible for Free Lunch Program: 2,833 (40.6%)
   Eligible for Reduced-Price Lunch Program: 653 (9.3%)
Teachers: 570.0 (12.3 to 1)
Librarians/Media Specialists: 14.5 (481.8 to 1)
Guidance Counselors: 12.6 (554.4 to 1)
Current Spending: ($ per student per year):
   Total: $6,660; Instruction: $4,267; Support Services: $1,979

Enrollment, Drop-out Rates and Diploma Recipients by Race/Ethnicity

Category	Total	White	Black	Asian	AIAN	Hisp.
Enrollment (%)	100.0	95.9	2.7	1.1	0.0	0.1
Drop-out Rate (%)	3.3	3.1	10.3	0.0	0.0	0.0
H.S. Diplomas (#)	447	429	15	2	1	0

Virginia Beach City

Virginia Beach City Public Schools
2512 George Mason Dr • Virginia Beach, VA 23456-6038
Mailing Address: PO Box 6038 • Virginia Beach, VA 23456-6038
(757) 427-4585 • http://www.vbschools.com/
Grade Span: PK-12; **Agency Type:** 1
Schools: 86
    55 Primary; 14 Middle; 11 High; 6 Other Level
    80 Regular; 0 Special Education; 2 Vocational; 4 Alternative
    6 Magnet; 0 Charter; 16 Title I Eligible; 4 School-wide Title I
Students: 76,304   (51.3% male; 48.6% female)
    Individual Education Program: 10,685 (14.0%);
    English Language Learner: 844 (1.1%); Migrant: 0 (0.0%)
    Eligible for Free Lunch Program: 14,980 (19.6%)
    Eligible for Reduced-Price Lunch Program: 8,674 (11.4%)
Teachers: 5,555.4 (13.7 to 1)
Librarians/Media Specialists: 109.0 (700.0 to 1)
Guidance Counselors: 142.2 (536.6 to 1)
Current Spending: ($ per student per year):
    Total: $7,268; Instruction: $4,336; Support Services: $2,672
Enrollment, Drop-out Rates and Diploma Recipients by Race/Ethnicity

Category	Total	White	Black	Asian	AIAN	Hisp.
Enrollment (%)	100.0	60.0	28.6	5.7	0.3	4.6
Drop-out Rate (%)	1.2	1.2	1.3	0.2	0.0	1.3
H.S. Diplomas (#)	4,455	2,914	1,042	340	16	143

Warren County

Warren County Public Schools
210 N Commerce Ave • Front Royal, VA 22630-4419
(540) 635-2171 • http://www.wcps.k12.va.us/
Grade Span: PK-12; **Agency Type:** 1
Schools: 8
    5 Primary; 2 Middle; 1 High; 0 Other Level
    8 Regular; 0 Special Education; 0 Vocational; 0 Alternative
    0 Magnet; 0 Charter; 5 Title I Eligible; 0 School-wide Title I
Students: 5,076   (51.5% male; 48.4% female)
    Individual Education Program: 762 (15.0%);
    English Language Learner: 110 (2.2%); Migrant: 0 (0.0%)
    Eligible for Free Lunch Program: 937 (18.5%)
    Eligible for Reduced-Price Lunch Program: 223 (4.4%)
Teachers: 357.0 (14.2 to 1)
Librarians/Media Specialists: 8.0 (634.5 to 1)
Guidance Counselors: 11.0 (461.5 to 1)
Current Spending: ($ per student per year):
    Total: $6,464; Instruction: $3,783; Support Services: $2,410
Enrollment, Drop-out Rates and Diploma Recipients by Race/Ethnicity

Category	Total	White	Black	Asian	AIAN	Hisp.
Enrollment (%)	100.0	89.4	6.8	1.1	0.2	2.5
Drop-out Rate (%)	2.8	2.5	7.1	0.0	0.0	5.9
H.S. Diplomas (#)	261	239	17	2	0	3

Washington County

Washington County Public Schools
812 Thompson Dr • Abingdon, VA 24210-2354
(276) 628-1826 • http://www.wcs.k12.va.us/
Grade Span: PK-12; **Agency Type:** 1
Schools: 17
    7 Primary; 4 Middle; 4 High; 2 Other Level
    15 Regular; 0 Special Education; 2 Vocational; 0 Alternative
    0 Magnet; 0 Charter; 6 Title I Eligible; 0 School-wide Title I
Students: 7,312   (50.6% male; 49.3% female)
    Individual Education Program: 1,012 (13.8%);
    English Language Learner: 13 (0.2%); Migrant: 0 (0.0%)
    Eligible for Free Lunch Program: 1,979 (27.1%)
    Eligible for Reduced-Price Lunch Program: 551 (7.5%)
Teachers: 518.1 (14.1 to 1)
Librarians/Media Specialists: 10.0 (731.2 to 1)
Guidance Counselors: 14.0 (522.3 to 1)
Current Spending: ($ per student per year):
    Total: $6,755; Instruction: $4,096; Support Services: $2,329
Enrollment, Drop-out Rates and Diploma Recipients by Race/Ethnicity

Category	Total	White	Black	Asian	AIAN	Hisp.
Enrollment (%)	100.0	97.3	1.6	0.4	0.1	0.4
Drop-out Rate (%)	2.4	2.4	2.2	0.0	0.0	0.0
H.S. Diplomas (#)	494	481	6	4	0	3

Waynesboro City

Waynesboro City Public Schools
301 Pine Ave • Waynesboro, VA 22980-4761
(540) 946-4600 • http://www.waynesboro.k12.va.us/
Grade Span: PK-12; **Agency Type:** 1
Schools: 6
    4 Primary; 1 Middle; 1 High; 0 Other Level
    6 Regular; 0 Special Education; 0 Vocational; 0 Alternative
    0 Magnet; 0 Charter; 3 Title I Eligible; 2 School-wide Title I
Students: 3,017   (51.2% male; 48.7% female)
    Individual Education Program: 315 (10.4%);
    English Language Learner: 111 (3.7%); Migrant: 0 (0.0%)
    Eligible for Free Lunch Program: 1,076 (35.7%)
    Eligible for Reduced-Price Lunch Program: 234 (7.8%)
Teachers: 234.4 (12.9 to 1)
Librarians/Media Specialists: 6.0 (502.8 to 1)
Guidance Counselors: 6.0 (502.8 to 1)
Current Spending: ($ per student per year):
    Total: $7,327; Instruction: $4,539; Support Services: $2,482
Enrollment, Drop-out Rates and Diploma Recipients by Race/Ethnicity

Category	Total	White	Black	Asian	AIAN	Hisp.
Enrollment (%)	100.0	76.1	15.8	1.2	0.6	6.4
Drop-out Rate (%)	1.5	1.2	3.4	0.0	0.0	0.0
H.S. Diplomas (#)	162	142	14	1	0	5

Westmoreland County

Westmoreland County Public Schools
141 Opal Ln • Montross, VA 22520-1060
(804) 493-8018 • http://www.wmlcps.org/
Grade Span: PK-12; **Agency Type:** 1
Schools: 4
    2 Primary; 1 Middle; 1 High; 0 Other Level
    4 Regular; 0 Special Education; 0 Vocational; 0 Alternative
    0 Magnet; 0 Charter; 2 Title I Eligible; 2 School-wide Title I
Students: 2,043   (51.8% male; 48.1% female)
    Individual Education Program: 237 (11.6%);
    English Language Learner: 78 (3.8%); Migrant: 101 (4.9%)
    Eligible for Free Lunch Program: 644 (31.5%)
    Eligible for Reduced-Price Lunch Program: 109 (5.3%)
Teachers: 156.0 (13.1 to 1)
Librarians/Media Specialists: 4.0 (510.8 to 1)
Guidance Counselors: 4.0 (510.8 to 1)
Current Spending: ($ per student per year):
    Total: $6,522; Instruction: $3,830; Support Services: $2,337
Enrollment, Drop-out Rates and Diploma Recipients by Race/Ethnicity

Category	Total	White	Black	Asian	AIAN	Hisp.
Enrollment (%)	100.0	39.4	53.1	0.4	0.0	7.0
Drop-out Rate (%)	1.1	0.0	2.1	0.0	n/a	0.0
H.S. Diplomas (#)	135	57	74	0	0	4

Williamsburg City

Williamsburg-James City County Public Schools
101-D Mounts Bay Rd • Williamsburg, VA 23185-8783
(757) 253-6777 • http://www.wjcc.k12.va.us/
Grade Span: PK-12; **Agency Type:** 3
Schools: 12
    7 Primary; 3 Middle; 2 High; 0 Other Level
    12 Regular; 0 Special Education; 0 Vocational; 0 Alternative
    0 Magnet; 0 Charter; 6 Title I Eligible; 0 School-wide Title I
Students: 8,961   (50.6% male; 49.3% female)
    Individual Education Program: 1,249 (13.9%);
    English Language Learner: 178 (2.0%); Migrant: 0 (0.0%)
    Eligible for Free Lunch Program: 1,255 (14.0%)
    Eligible for Reduced-Price Lunch Program: 359 (4.0%)
Teachers: 765.9 (11.7 to 1)
Librarians/Media Specialists: 15.0 (597.4 to 1)
Guidance Counselors: 16.0 (560.1 to 1)
Current Spending: ($ per student per year):
    Total: $8,635; Instruction: $5,291; Support Services: $3,066
Enrollment, Drop-out Rates and Diploma Recipients by Race/Ethnicity

Category	Total	White	Black	Asian	AIAN	Hisp.
Enrollment (%)	100.0	71.7	21.9	2.4	0.7	3.2
Drop-out Rate (%)	1.5	1.1	3.5	0.0	0.0	0.0
H.S. Diplomas (#)	525	406	90	17	1	11

Winchester City

Winchester City Public Schools
12 N Washington St • Winchester, VA 22601
Mailing Address: PO Box 551 • Winchester, VA 22604-0551
(540) 667-4253 • http://www.wps.k12.va.us/
Grade Span: PK-12; Agency Type: 1
Schools: 6
  4 Primary; 1 Middle; 1 High; 0 Other Level
  6 Regular; 0 Special Education; 0 Vocational; 0 Alternative
  0 Magnet; 0 Charter; 4 Title I Eligible; 0 School-wide Title I
Students: 3,624 (52.1% male; 47.8% female)
  Individual Education Program: 706 (19.5%);
  English Language Learner: 386 (10.7%); Migrant: 51 (1.4%)
  Eligible for Free Lunch Program: 1,026 (28.3%)
  Eligible for Reduced-Price Lunch Program: 312 (8.6%)
Teachers: 312.6 (11.6 to 1)
Librarians/Media Specialists: 5.0 (724.8 to 1)
Guidance Counselors: 7.0 (517.7 to 1)
Current Spending: ($ per student per year):
  Total: $9,524; Instruction: $6,125; Support Services: $3,060
Enrollment, Drop-out Rates and Diploma Recipients by Race/Ethnicity

Category	Total	White	Black	Asian	AIAN	Hisp.
Enrollment (%)	100.0	67.7	17.7	2.3	0.5	11.7
Drop-out Rate (%)	3.7	3.2	3.7	3.4	0.0	13.3
H.S. Diplomas (#)	181	151	26	2	0	2

Wise County

Wise County Public Schools
628 Lake St • Wise, VA 24293-1217
Mailing Address: PO Box 1217 • Wise, VA 24293-1217
(276) 328-8017 • http://www.wise.k12.va.us/
Grade Span: PK-12; Agency Type: 1
Schools: 17
  6 Primary; 3 Middle; 6 High; 2 Other Level
  15 Regular; 0 Special Education; 1 Vocational; 1 Alternative
  0 Magnet; 0 Charter; 6 Title I Eligible; 1 School-wide Title I
Students: 6,818 (51.2% male; 48.7% female)
  Individual Education Program: 986 (14.5%);
  English Language Learner: 19 (0.3%); Migrant: 0 (0.0%)
  Eligible for Free Lunch Program: 2,764 (40.5%)
  Eligible for Reduced-Price Lunch Program: 582 (8.5%)
Teachers: 572.9 (11.9 to 1)
Librarians/Media Specialists: 14.9 (457.6 to 1)
Guidance Counselors: 16.5 (413.2 to 1)
Current Spending: ($ per student per year):
  Total: $6,888; Instruction: $4,354; Support Services: $2,252
Enrollment, Drop-out Rates and Diploma Recipients by Race/Ethnicity

Category	Total	White	Black	Asian	AIAN	Hisp.
Enrollment (%)	100.0	97.6	1.6	0.3	0.0	0.5
Drop-out Rate (%)	2.8	2.8	4.9	0.0	0.0	11.1
H.S. Diplomas (#)	463	446	14	1	0	2

Wythe County

Wythe County Public Schools
1570 W Reservoir St • Wytheville, VA 24382-1500
(276) 228-5411 • http://wcps.wythe.k12.va.us/public/
Grade Span: PK-12; Agency Type: 1
Schools: 13
  6 Primary; 3 Middle; 3 High; 1 Other Level
  12 Regular; 0 Special Education; 1 Vocational; 0 Alternative
  3 Magnet; 0 Charter; 6 Title I Eligible; 0 School-wide Title I
Students: 4,274 (51.3% male; 48.6% female)
  Individual Education Program: 514 (12.0%);
  English Language Learner: 3 (0.1%); Migrant: 0 (0.0%)
  Eligible for Free Lunch Program: 1,328 (31.1%)
  Eligible for Reduced-Price Lunch Program: 372 (8.7%)
Teachers: 336.9 (12.7 to 1)
Librarians/Media Specialists: 12.0 (356.2 to 1)
Guidance Counselors: 12.0 (356.2 to 1)
Current Spending: ($ per student per year):
  Total: $6,803; Instruction: $4,317; Support Services: $2,208
Enrollment, Drop-out Rates and Diploma Recipients by Race/Ethnicity

Category	Total	White	Black	Asian	AIAN	Hisp.
Enrollment (%)	100.0	94.8	3.9	0.5	0.0	0.7
Drop-out Rate (%)	2.6	2.6	4.5	0.0	n/a	0.0
H.S. Diplomas (#)	273	266	5	1	0	1

York County

York County Public Schools
302 Dare Rd • Yorktown, VA 23692-2795
(757) 898-0300 • http://yorkcountyschools.org/
Grade Span: PK-12; Agency Type: 1
Schools: 19
  10 Primary; 4 Middle; 4 High; 1 Other Level
  19 Regular; 0 Special Education; 0 Vocational; 0 Alternative
  3 Magnet; 1 Charter; 5 Title I Eligible; 0 School-wide Title I
Students: 12,417 (51.7% male; 48.2% female)
  Individual Education Program: 1,144 (9.2%);
  English Language Learner: 120 (1.0%); Migrant: 0 (0.0%)
  Eligible for Free Lunch Program: 977 (7.9%)
  Eligible for Reduced-Price Lunch Program: 751 (6.0%)
Teachers: 844.5 (14.7 to 1)
Librarians/Media Specialists: 18.0 (689.8 to 1)
Guidance Counselors: 26.0 (477.6 to 1)
Current Spending: ($ per student per year):
  Total: $6,840; Instruction: $4,029; Support Services: $2,597
Enrollment, Drop-out Rates and Diploma Recipients by Race/Ethnicity

Category	Total	White	Black	Asian	AIAN	Hisp.
Enrollment (%)	100.0	75.5	15.3	5.2	0.6	3.3
Drop-out Rate (%)	1.1	0.9	2.9	0.0	7.1	0.0
H.S. Diplomas (#)	835	652	105	50	2	26

Number of Schools

Rank	Number	District Name	City
1	204	Fairfax County Public Schools	Fairfax
2	86	Virginia Beach City Public Schls	Virginia Beach
3	76	Prince William Co Public Schools	Manassas
4	66	Henrico County Public Schools	Richmond
5	61	Loudoun County Public Schools	Leesburg
6	60	Chesterfield County Public Schools	Chesterfield
7	59	Richmond City Public Schools	Richmond
8	58	Norfolk City Public Schools	Norfolk
9	48	Newport News City Public Schools	Newport News
10	46	Chesapeake City Public Schools	Chesapeake
11	37	Hampton City Public Schools	Hampton
12	32	Arlington County Public Schools	Arlington
13	31	Roanoke City Public Schools	Roanoke
14	30	Spotsylvania Co Public Schools	Spotsylvania
15	29	Roanoke County Public Schools	Roanoke
16	27	Portsmouth City Public Schools	Portsmouth
17	25	Albemarle County Public Schools	Charlottesville
18	24	Stafford County Public Schools	Stafford
19	22	Bedford County Public Schools	Bedford
20	21	Hanover County Public Schools	Ashland
20	21	Montgomery County Public Schools	Christiansburg
20	21	Suffolk City Public Schools	Suffolk
23	20	Augusta County Public Schools	Fishersville
23	20	Henry County Public Schools	Collinsville
23	20	Rockingham County Public Schools	Harrisonburg
26	19	Pittsylvania County Public Schools	Chatham
26	19	York County Public Schools	Yorktown
28	18	Fauquier County Public Schools	Warrenton
29	17	Danville City Public Schools	Danville
29	17	Lynchburg City Public Schools	Lynchburg
29	17	Tazewell County Public Schools	Tazewell
29	17	Washington County Public Schools	Abingdon
29	17	Wise County Public Schools	Wise
34	16	Alexandria City Public Schools	Alexandria
34	16	Campbell County Public Schools	Rustburg
34	16	Frederick County Public Schools	Winchester
37	15	Accomack County Public Schools	Accomac
37	15	Franklin County Public Schools	Rocky Mount
37	15	Halifax County Public Schools	Halifax
40	14	Lee County Public Schools	Jonesville
40	14	Scott County Public Schools	Gate City
40	14	Smyth County Public Schools	Marion
43	13	Russell County Public Schools	Lebanon
43	13	Wythe County Public Schools	Wytheville
45	12	Botetourt County Public Schools	Fincastle
45	12	Williamsburg-James City Co PS	Williamsburg
47	11	Buchanan County Public Schools	Grundy
47	11	Grayson County Public Schools	Independence
47	11	Mecklenburg County Public Schools	Boydton
47	11	Pulaski County Public Schools	Pulaski
51	10	Amherst County Public Schools	Amherst
51	10	Carroll County Public Schools	Hillsville
51	10	Charlottesville City Pub Schools	Charlottesville
51	10	Gloucester County Public Schools	Gloucester
51	10	Petersburg City Public Schools	Petersburg
51	10	Shenandoah County Public Schools	Woodstock
57	9	Culpeper County Public Schools	Culpeper
57	9	Dickenson County Public Schools	Clintwood
59	8	Hopewell City Public Schools	Hopewell
59	8	Isle of Wight Co Public Schools	Isle Of Wight
59	8	Manassas City Public Schools	Manassas
59	8	Orange County Public Schools	Orange
59	8	Page County Public Schools	Luray
59	8	Prince George Co Public Schools	Prince George
59	8	Rockbridge County Public Schools	Lexington
59	8	Warren County Public Schools	Front Royal
67	7	Alleghany County Public Schools	Covington
67	7	Bristol City Public Schools	Bristol
67	7	Charlotte County Public Schools	Charlotte Ct Hse
67	7	Dinwiddie County Public Schools	Dinwiddie
67	7	Greene County Public Schools	Stanardsville
67	7	Nottoway County Public Schools	Nottoway
67	7	Patrick County Public Schools	Stuart
74	6	Brunswick County Public Schools	Lawrenceville
74	6	Buckingham County Public Schools	Buckingham
74	6	Caroline County Public Schools	Bowling Green
74	6	Giles County Public Schools	Pearisburg
74	6	Harrisonburg City Public Schools	Harrisonburg
74	6	Martinsville City Public Schools	Martinsville
74	6	Powhatan County Public Schools	Powhatan
74	6	Salem City Public Schools	Salem
74	6	Southampton County Public Schools	Courtland
74	6	Staunton City Public Schools	Staunton
74	6	Waynesboro City Public Schools	Waynesboro
74	6	Winchester City Public Schools	Winchester
86	5	Clarke County Public Schools	Berryville
86	5	Colonial Hgts City Public Schools	Colonial Hgts
86	5	Floyd County Public Schools	Floyd
86	5	Fluvanna County Public Schools	Palmyra
86	5	Goochland County Public Schools	Goochland
86	5	Greensville County Public Schools	Emporia
86	5	Louisa County Public Schools	Mineral
86	5	Northampton County Public Schools	Machipongo
94	4	Appomattox County Public Schools	Appomattox
94	4	Falls Church City Public Schools	Falls Church
94	4	Fredericksburg City Public Schools	Fredericksburg
94	4	King George County Public Schools	King George
94	4	King William County Public Schools	King William
94	4	Lunenburg County Public Schools	Victoria
94	4	Madison County Public Schools	Madison
94	4	Manassas Park City Public Schools	Manassas Park
94	4	Nelson County Public Schools	Lovingston
94	4	New Kent County Public Schools	New Kent
94	4	Poquoson City Public Schools	Poquoson
94	4	Radford City Public Schools	Radford
94	4	Westmoreland Co Public Schools	Montross
107	3	Amelia County Public Schools	Amelia
107	3	Essex County Public Schools	Tappahannock
107	3	Prince Edward Co Public Schools	Farmville

Number of Teachers

Rank	Number	District Name	City
1	12,293	Fairfax County Public Schools	Fairfax
2	5,555	Virginia Beach City Public Schls	Virginia Beach
3	4,125	Prince William Co Public Schools	Manassas
4	3,845	Chesterfield County Public Schools	Chesterfield
5	3,175	Henrico County Public Schools	Richmond
6	3,016	Loudoun County Public Schools	Leesburg
7	2,877	Chesapeake City Public Schools	Chesapeake
8	2,586	Norfolk City Public Schools	Norfolk
9	2,425	Newport News City Public Schools	Newport News
10	1,891	Richmond City Public Schools	Richmond
11	1,868	Hampton City Public Schools	Hampton
12	1,774	Arlington County Public Schools	Arlington
13	1,735	Stafford County Public Schools	Stafford
14	1,663	Spotsylvania Co Public Schools	Spotsylvania
15	1,404	Hanover County Public Schools	Ashland
16	1,244	Roanoke County Public Schools	Roanoke
17	1,191	Roanoke City Public Schools	Roanoke
18	1,155	Portsmouth City Public Schools	Portsmouth
19	1,074	Albemarle County Public Schools	Charlottesville
20	1,035	Alexandria City Public Schools	Alexandria
21	911	Suffolk City Public Schools	Suffolk
22	887	Rockingham County Public Schools	Harrisonburg
23	873	Frederick County Public Schools	Winchester
24	846	Montgomery County Public Schools	Christiansburg
25	844	York County Public Schools	Yorktown
26	834	Augusta County Public Schools	Fishersville
27	822	Fauquier County Public Schools	Warrenton
28	815	Bedford County Public Schools	Bedford
29	765	Williamsburg-James City Co PS	Williamsburg
30	701	Lynchburg City Public Schools	Lynchburg
31	683	Pittsylvania County Public Schools	Chatham
32	682	Henry County Public Schools	Collinsville
33	653	Campbell County Public Schools	Rustburg
34	615	Danville City Public Schools	Danville
35	572	Wise County Public Schools	Wise
36	570	Tazewell County Public Schools	Tazewell
37	540	Franklin County Public Schools	Rocky Mount
38	518	Washington County Public Schools	Abingdon
39	507	Halifax County Public Schools	Halifax
40	506	Manassas City Public Schools	Manassas
41	494	Culpeper County Public Schools	Culpeper
42	474	Shenandoah County Public Schools	Woodstock
43	466	Gloucester County Public Schools	Gloucester
44	463	Smyth County Public Schools	Marion
45	434	Accomack County Public Schools	Accomac
46	412	Prince George Co Public Schools	Prince George
47	403	Charlottesville City Pub Schools	Charlottesville
48	400	Petersburg City Public Schools	Petersburg
49	385	Pulaski County Public Schools	Pulaski
50	377	Harrisonburg City Public Schools	Harrisonburg
51	376	Botetourt County Public Schools	Fincastle
52	373	Amherst County Public Schools	Amherst
53	363	Lee County Public Schools	Jonesville
54	362	Mecklenburg County Public Schools	Boydton
55	361	Isle of Wight Co Public Schools	Isle Of Wight
56	357	Warren County Public Schools	Front Royal
57	336	Wythe County Public Schools	Wytheville
58	334	Dinwiddie County Public Schools	Dinwiddie
59	331	Louisa County Public Schools	Mineral
60	329	Buchanan County Public Schools	Grundy
61	328	Carroll County Public Schools	Hillsville
62	327	Orange County Public Schools	Orange
63	313	Hopewell City Public Schools	Hopewell
64	312	Winchester City Public Schools	Winchester
65	307	Salem City Public Schools	Salem
66	305	Russell County Public Schools	Lebanon
67	304	Powhatan County Public Schools	Powhatan
68	293	Scott County Public Schools	Gate City
69	261	Page County Public Schools	Luray
69	261	Rockbridge County Public Schools	Lexington
71	255	Fluvanna County Public Schools	Palmyra
72	250	Staunton City Public Schools	Staunton
73	246	Colonial Hgts City Public Schools	Colonial Hgts
74	245	Greene County Public Schools	Stanardsville
75	242	King George County Public Schools	King George
76	242	Caroline County Public Schools	Bowling Green
77	234	Waynesboro City Public Schools	Waynesboro
78	229	Martinsville City Public Schools	Martinsville
79	228	Alleghany County Public Schools	Covington
80	221	Dickenson County Public Schools	Clintwood
80	221	Southampton County Public Schools	Courtland
82	217	Patrick County Public Schools	Stuart
83	213	Greensville County Public Schools	Emporia
84	210	Prince Edward Co Public Schools	Farmville
85	207	New Kent County Public Schools	New Kent
86	207	Bristol City Public Schools	Bristol
87	203	Brunswick County Public Schools	Lawrenceville
88	201	Grayson County Public Schools	Independence
89	199	Manassas Park City Public Schools	Manassas Park
90	198	Fredericksburg City Public Schools	Fredericksburg
91	193	Giles County Public Schools	Pearisburg
92	192	Poquoson City Public Schools	Poquoson
93	188	Appomattox County Public Schools	Appomattox
94	184	Nottoway County Public Schools	Nottoway
95	182	Buckingham County Public Schools	Buckingham
96	180	Northampton County Public Schools	Machipongo
97	176	Goochland County Public Schools	Goochland
98	174	Falls Church City Public Schools	Falls Church
99	169	Charlotte County Public Schools	Charlotte Ct Hse
100	168	Nelson County Public Schools	Lovingston
101	167	King William County Public Schools	King William
102	165	Floyd County Public Schools	Floyd
103	161	Clarke County Public Schools	Berryville
104	156	Westmoreland Co Public Schools	Montross
105	152	Madison County Public Schools	Madison
106	150	Lunenburg County Public Schools	Victoria
107	142	Essex County Public Schools	Tappahannock
108	130	Amelia County Public Schools	Amelia
109	122	Radford City Public Schools	Radford

Number of Students

Rank	Number	District Name	City
1	164,235	Fairfax County Public Schools	Fairfax
2	76,304	Virginia Beach City Public Schls	Virginia Beach
3	63,404	Prince William Co Public Schools	Manassas
4	55,393	Chesterfield County Public Schools	Chesterfield
5	45,354	Henrico County Public Schools	Richmond
6	40,750	Loudoun County Public Schools	Leesburg
7	39,412	Chesapeake City Public Schools	Chesapeake
8	36,724	Norfolk City Public Schools	Norfolk
9	32,893	Newport News City Public Schools	Newport News
10	25,399	Richmond City Public Schools	Richmond
11	24,869	Stafford County Public Schools	Stafford
12	23,009	Hampton City Public Schools	Hampton
13	22,075	Spotsylvania Co Public Schools	Spotsylvania
14	19,158	Arlington County Public Schools	Arlington
15	18,139	Hanover County Public Schools	Ashland
16	16,545	Portsmouth City Public Schools	Portsmouth
17	14,537	Roanoke County Public Schools	Roanoke
18	13,567	Roanoke City Public Schools	Roanoke
19	13,273	Suffolk City Public Schools	Suffolk
20	12,565	Albemarle County Public Schools	Charlottesville
21	12,417	York County Public Schools	Yorktown
22	11,357	Frederick County Public Schools	Winchester
23	11,185	Rockingham County Public Schools	Harrisonburg
24	10,902	Alexandria City Public Schools	Alexandria
25	10,872	Bedford County Public Schools	Bedford
26	10,714	Augusta County Public Schools	Fishersville
27	10,327	Fauquier County Public Schools	Warrenton
28	9,467	Montgomery County Public Schools	Christiansburg
29	9,264	Pittsylvania County Public Schools	Chatham
30	8,961	Williamsburg-James City Co PS	Williamsburg
31	8,815	Campbell County Public Schools	Rustburg
32	8,775	Lynchburg City Public Schools	Lynchburg
33	8,180	Henry County Public Schools	Collinsville
34	7,384	Danville City Public Schools	Danville
35	7,312	Washington County Public Schools	Abingdon
36	7,270	Franklin County Public Schools	Rocky Mount
37	6,986	Tazewell County Public Schools	Tazewell
38	6,818	Wise County Public Schools	Wise
39	6,803	Manassas City Public Schools	Manassas
40	6,257	Gloucester County Public Schools	Gloucester
41	6,227	Culpeper County Public Schools	Culpeper
42	6,090	Prince George Co Public Schools	Prince George
43	5,908	Halifax County Public Schools	Halifax
44	5,827	Shenandoah County Public Schools	Woodstock
45	5,390	Accomack County Public Schools	Accomac
46	5,363	Petersburg City Public Schools	Petersburg
47	5,084	Smyth County Public Schools	Marion
48	5,076	Warren County Public Schools	Front Royal
49	5,063	Isle of Wight Co Public Schools	Isle Of Wight
50	4,887	Pulaski County Public Schools	Pulaski

51	4,785	Mecklenburg County Public Schools	Boydton
52	4,761	Botetourt County Public Schools	Fincastle
53	4,542	Amherst County Public Schools	Amherst
54	4,469	Dinwiddie County Public Schools	Dinwiddie
55	4,422	Charlottesville City Pub Schools	Charlottesville
56	4,321	Louisa County Public Schools	Mineral
57	4,274	Wythe County Public Schools	Wytheville
58	4,208	Russell County Public Schools	Lebanon
59	4,090	Orange County Public Schools	Orange
60	4,082	Carroll County Public Schools	Hillsville
61	4,051	Powhatan County Public Schools	Powhatan
62	4,031	Harrisonburg City Public Schools	Harrisonburg
63	3,910	Salem City Public Schools	Salem
64	3,886	Hopewell City Public Schools	Hopewell
65	3,752	Caroline County Public Schools	Bowling Green
66	3,734	Scott County Public Schools	Gate City
67	3,732	Lee County Public Schools	Jonesville
68	3,649	Buchanan County Public Schools	Grundy
69	3,624	Winchester City Public Schools	Winchester
70	3,584	Page County Public Schools	Luray
71	3,336	Fluvanna County Public Schools	Palmyra
72	3,203	King George County Public Schools	King George
73	3,017	Waynesboro City Public Schools	Waynesboro
74	2,930	Rockbridge County Public Schools	Lexington
75	2,881	Alleghany County Public Schools	Covington
76	2,853	Southampton County Public Schools	Courtland
77	2,852	Prince Edward Co Public Schools	Farmville
78	2,796	Colonial Hgts City Public Schools	Colonial Hgts
79	2,700	Greene County Public Schools	Stanardsville
80	2,684	Staunton City Public Schools	Staunton
81	2,634	Greensville County Public Schools	Emporia
82	2,611	Martinsville City Public Schools	Martinsville
83	2,601	Dickenson County Public Schools	Clintwood
84	2,586	Patrick County Public Schools	Stuart
85	2,546	New Kent County Public Schools	New Kent
86	2,545	Giles County Public Schools	Pearisburg
87	2,544	Poquoson City Public Schools	Poquoson
88	2,450	Fredericksburg City Public Schools	Fredericksburg
89	2,447	Nottoway County Public Schools	Nottoway
90	2,433	Brunswick County Public Schools	Lawrenceville
91	2,327	Appomattox County Public Schools	Appomattox
92	2,324	Bristol City Public Schools	Bristol
93	2,288	Manassas Park City Public Schools	Manassas Park
94	2,287	Charlotte County Public Schools	Charlotte Ct Hse
95	2,265	Buckingham County Public Schools	Buckingham
96	2,254	Grayson County Public Schools	Independence
97	2,115	Goochland County Public Schools	Goochland
98	2,103	Floyd County Public Schools	Floyd
99	2,071	Clarke County Public Schools	Berryville
100	2,043	Westmoreland Co Public Schools	Montross
101	2,029	Northampton County Public Schools	Machipongo
102	2,015	Nelson County Public Schools	Lovingston
103	1,874	Falls Church City Public Schools	Falls Church
104	1,866	King William County Public Schools	King William
105	1,865	Madison County Public Schools	Madison
106	1,724	Amelia County Public Schools	Amelia
107	1,710	Lunenburg County Public Schools	Victoria
108	1,701	Essex County Public Schools	Tappahannock
109	1,537	Radford City Public Schools	Radford

Male Students

Rank	Percent	District Name	City
1	53.4	Poquoson City Public Schools	Poquoson
2	53.1	Colonial Hgts City Public Schools	Colonial Hgts
3	53.0	Appomattox County Public Schools	Appomattox
4	52.8	Goochland County Public Schools	Goochland
5	52.7	Falls Church City Public Schools	Falls Church
6	52.7	Southampton County Public Schools	Courtland
7	52.4	Carroll County Public Schools	Hillsville
8	52.4	Gloucester County Public Schools	Gloucester
9	52.3	Buchanan County Public Schools	Grundy
10	52.3	Dinwiddie County Public Schools	Dinwiddie
11	52.2	Prince Edward Co Public Schools	Farmville
12	52.1	Winchester City Public Schools	Winchester
13	52.1	Amelia County Public Schools	Amelia
14	52.0	King William County Public Schools	King William
15	52.0	Salem City Public Schools	Salem
16	52.0	Nelson County Public Schools	Lovingston
17	52.0	Louisa County Public Schools	Mineral
18	52.0	Fairfax County Public Schools	Fairfax
19	52.0	Brunswick County Public Schools	Lawrenceville
20	52.0	Bedford County Public Schools	Bedford
21	52.0	New Kent County Public Schools	New Kent
22	52.0	Amherst County Public Schools	Amherst
23	51.9	Prince George Co Public Schools	Prince George
24	51.9	Powhatan County Public Schools	Powhatan
25	51.9	Accomack County Public Schools	Accomac
26	51.8	Mecklenburg County Public Schools	Boydton
27	51.8	Suffolk City Public Schools	Suffolk
28	51.8	Manassas City Public Schools	Manassas
29	51.8	Smyth County Public Schools	Marion
30	51.8	Pittsylvania County Public Schools	Chatham
31	51.8	Rockbridge County Public Schools	Lexington
32	51.8	Greene County Public Schools	Stanardsville
33	51.8	Westmoreland Co Public Schools	Montross
34	51.8	Shenandoah County Public Schools	Woodstock
35	51.7	Isle of Wight Co Public Schools	Isle Of Wight
36	51.7	Hampton City Public Schools	Hampton
37	51.7	Rockingham County Public Schools	Harrisonburg
38	51.7	Hanover County Public Schools	Ashland
39	51.7	York County Public Schools	Yorktown
40	51.6	Giles County Public Schools	Pearisburg
41	51.5	Arlington County Public Schools	Arlington
42	51.5	Pulaski County Public Schools	Pulaski
43	51.5	Bristol City Public Schools	Bristol
44	51.5	Harrisonburg City Public Schools	Harrisonburg
45	51.5	Warren County Public Schools	Front Royal
46	51.5	Campbell County Public Schools	Rustburg
47	51.4	Alleghany County Public Schools	Covington
48	51.4	King George County Public Schools	King George
49	51.4	Alexandria City Public Schools	Alexandria
50	51.4	Prince William Co Public Schools	Manassas
51	51.4	Henrico County Public Schools	Richmond
52	51.4	Chesterfield County Public Schools	Chesterfield
53	51.4	Buckingham County Public Schools	Buckingham
54	51.4	Nottoway County Public Schools	Nottoway
55	51.4	Stafford County Public Schools	Stafford
56	51.3	Loudoun County Public Schools	Leesburg
57	51.3	Montgomery County Public Schools	Christiansburg
58	51.3	Wythe County Public Schools	Wytheville
59	51.3	Virginia Beach City Public Schls	Virginia Beach
60	51.3	Staunton City Public Schools	Staunton
61	51.2	Page County Public Schools	Luray
62	51.2	Greensville County Public Schools	Emporia
63	51.2	Caroline County Public Schools	Bowling Green
64	51.2	Wise County Public Schools	Wise
65	51.2	Dickenson County Public Schools	Clintwood
66	51.2	Chesapeake City Public Schools	Chesapeake
67	51.2	Clarke County Public Schools	Berryville
68	51.2	Roanoke County Public Schools	Roanoke
69	51.2	Waynesboro City Public Schools	Waynesboro
70	51.2	Augusta County Public Schools	Fishersville
71	51.1	Spotsylvania Co Public Schools	Spotsylvania
72	51.1	Charlottesville City Pub Schools	Charlottesville
73	51.0	Botetourt County Public Schools	Fincastle
74	51.0	Danville City Public Schools	Danville
75	51.0	Manassas Park City Public Schools	Manassas Park
76	51.0	Fauquier County Public Schools	Warrenton
77	50.9	Franklin County Public Schools	Rocky Mount
78	50.9	Culpeper County Public Schools	Culpeper
79	50.9	Lynchburg City Public Schools	Lynchburg
80	50.9	Tazewell County Public Schools	Tazewell
81	50.8	Norfolk City Public Schools	Norfolk
82	50.8	Frederick County Public Schools	Winchester
83	50.8	Scott County Public Schools	Gate City
84	50.8	Albemarle County Public Schools	Charlottesville
85	50.8	Roanoke City Public Schools	Roanoke
86	50.8	Portsmouth City Public Schools	Portsmouth
87	50.6	Washington County Public Schools	Abingdon
88	50.6	Lee County Public Schools	Jonesville
89	50.6	Williamsburg-James City Co PS	Williamsburg
90	50.5	Newport News City Public Schools	Newport News
91	50.5	Halifax County Public Schools	Halifax
92	50.5	Martinsville City Public Schools	Martinsville
93	50.5	Fluvanna County Public Schools	Palmyra
94	50.4	Northampton County Public Schools	Machipongo
95	50.4	Patrick County Public Schools	Stuart
96	50.4	Hopewell City Public Schools	Hopewell
97	50.3	Russell County Public Schools	Lebanon
98	50.2	Petersburg City Public Schools	Petersburg
99	50.2	Richmond City Public Schools	Richmond
100	50.1	Fredericksburg City Public Schools	Fredericksburg
101	50.1	Grayson County Public Schools	Independence
102	50.1	Henry County Public Schools	Collinsville
103	50.0	Orange County Public Schools	Orange
104	49.8	Radford City Public Schools	Radford
105	49.6	Charlotte County Public Schools	Charlotte Ct Hse
106	49.2	Floyd County Public Schools	Floyd
107	49.0	Essex County Public Schools	Tappahannock
108	48.9	Madison County Public Schools	Madison
109	48.7	Lunenburg County Public Schools	Victoria

Female Students

Rank	Percent	District Name	City
1	51.2	Lunenburg County Public Schools	Victoria
2	51.0	Madison County Public Schools	Madison
3	50.9	Essex County Public Schools	Tappahannock
4	50.7	Floyd County Public Schools	Floyd
5	50.3	Charlotte County Public Schools	Charlotte Ct Hse
6	50.1	Radford City Public Schools	Radford
7	49.9	Orange County Public Schools	Orange
8	49.8	Henry County Public Schools	Collinsville
9	49.8	Grayson County Public Schools	Independence
10	49.8	Fredericksburg City Public Schools	Fredericksburg
11	49.7	Richmond City Public Schools	Richmond
12	49.7	Petersburg City Public Schools	Petersburg
13	49.6	Russell County Public Schools	Lebanon
14	49.5	Hopewell City Public Schools	Hopewell
15	49.5	Patrick County Public Schools	Stuart
16	49.5	Northampton County Public Schools	Machipongo
17	49.4	Fluvanna County Public Schools	Palmyra
18	49.4	Martinsville City Public Schools	Martinsville
19	49.4	Halifax County Public Schools	Halifax
20	49.4	Newport News City Public Schools	Newport News
21	49.3	Williamsburg-James City Co PS	Williamsburg
22	49.3	Lee County Public Schools	Jonesville
23	49.3	Washington County Public Schools	Abingdon
24	49.1	Portsmouth City Public Schools	Portsmouth
25	49.1	Roanoke City Public Schools	Roanoke
26	49.1	Albemarle County Public Schools	Charlottesville
27	49.1	Scott County Public Schools	Gate City
28	49.1	Frederick County Public Schools	Winchester
29	49.1	Norfolk City Public Schools	Norfolk
30	49.0	Tazewell County Public Schools	Tazewell
31	49.0	Lynchburg City Public Schools	Lynchburg
32	49.0	Culpeper County Public Schools	Culpeper
33	49.0	Franklin County Public Schools	Rocky Mount
34	48.9	Fauquier County Public Schools	Warrenton
35	48.9	Manassas Park City Public Schools	Manassas Park
36	48.9	Danville City Public Schools	Danville
37	48.9	Botetourt County Public Schools	Fincastle
38	48.8	Charlottesville City Pub Schools	Charlottesville
39	48.8	Spotsylvania Co Public Schools	Spotsylvania
40	48.7	Augusta County Public Schools	Fishersville
41	48.7	Waynesboro City Public Schools	Waynesboro
42	48.7	Roanoke County Public Schools	Roanoke
43	48.7	Clarke County Public Schools	Berryville
44	48.7	Chesapeake City Public Schools	Chesapeake
45	48.7	Dickenson County Public Schools	Clintwood
46	48.7	Wise County Public Schools	Wise
47	48.7	Caroline County Public Schools	Bowling Green
48	48.7	Greensville County Public Schools	Emporia
49	48.7	Page County Public Schools	Luray
50	48.6	Staunton City Public Schools	Staunton
51	48.6	Virginia Beach City Public Schls	Virginia Beach
52	48.6	Wythe County Public Schools	Wytheville
53	48.6	Montgomery County Public Schools	Christiansburg
54	48.6	Loudoun County Public Schools	Leesburg
55	48.5	Stafford County Public Schools	Stafford
56	48.5	Nottoway County Public Schools	Nottoway
57	48.5	Buckingham County Public Schools	Buckingham
58	48.5	Chesterfield County Public Schools	Chesterfield
59	48.5	Henrico County Public Schools	Richmond
60	48.5	Prince William Co Public Schools	Manassas
61	48.5	Alexandria City Public Schools	Alexandria
62	48.5	King George County Public Schools	King George
63	48.5	Alleghany County Public Schools	Covington
64	48.4	Campbell County Public Schools	Rustburg
65	48.4	Warren County Public Schools	Front Royal
66	48.4	Harrisonburg City Public Schools	Harrisonburg
67	48.4	Bristol City Public Schools	Bristol
68	48.4	Pulaski County Public Schools	Pulaski
69	48.4	Arlington County Public Schools	Arlington
70	48.3	Giles County Public Schools	Pearisburg
71	48.2	York County Public Schools	Yorktown
72	48.2	Hanover County Public Schools	Ashland
73	48.2	Rockingham County Public Schools	Harrisonburg
74	48.2	Hampton City Public Schools	Hampton
75	48.2	Isle of Wight Co Public Schools	Isle Of Wight
76	48.1	Shenandoah County Public Schools	Woodstock
77	48.1	Westmoreland Co Public Schools	Montross
78	48.1	Greene County Public Schools	Stanardsville
79	48.1	Rockbridge County Public Schools	Lexington
80	48.1	Pittsylvania County Public Schools	Chatham
81	48.1	Smyth County Public Schools	Marion
82	48.1	Manassas City Public Schools	Manassas
83	48.1	Suffolk City Public Schools	Suffolk
84	48.1	Mecklenburg County Public Schools	Boydton
85	48.0	Accomack County Public Schools	Accomac
86	48.0	Powhatan County Public Schools	Powhatan
87	48.0	Prince George Co Public Schools	Prince George
88	47.9	Amherst County Public Schools	Amherst
89	47.9	New Kent County Public Schools	New Kent
90	47.9	Bedford County Public Schools	Bedford
91	47.9	Brunswick County Public Schools	Lawrenceville
92	47.9	Fairfax County Public Schools	Fairfax
93	47.9	Louisa County Public Schools	Mineral
94	47.9	Nelson County Public Schools	Lovingston
95	47.9	Salem City Public Schools	Salem
96	47.9	King William County Public Schools	King William
97	47.8	Amelia County Public Schools	Amelia
98	47.8	Winchester City Public Schools	Winchester
99	47.7	Prince Edward Co Public Schools	Farmville
100	47.6	Dinwiddie County Public Schools	Dinwiddie
101	47.6	Buchanan County Public Schools	Grundy
102	47.5	Gloucester County Public Schools	Gloucester

103	47.5	Carroll County Public Schools	Hillsville
104	47.2	Southampton County Public Schools	Courtland
105	47.2	Falls Church City Public Schools	Falls Church
106	47.1	Goochland County Public Schools	Goochland
107	46.9	Appomattox County Public Schools	Appomattox
108	46.8	Colonial Hgts City Public Schools	Colonial Hgts
109	46.5	Poquoson City Public Schools	Poquoson

Individual Education Program Students

Rank	Percent	District Name	City
1	21.2	Lee County Public Schools	Jonesville
2	20.7	Buchanan County Public Schools	Grundy
3	19.8	Halifax County Public Schools	Halifax
4	19.6	Prince Edward Co Public Schools	Farmville
5	19.5	Winchester City Public Schools	Winchester
6	19.3	New Kent County Public Schools	New Kent
7	19.1	Bristol City Public Schools	Bristol
7	19.1	Henry County Public Schools	Collinsville
9	19.0	Greene County Public Schools	Stanardsville
10	18.9	Franklin County Public Schools	Rocky Mount
11	18.8	Nelson County Public Schools	Lovingston
12	18.7	Smyth County Public Schools	Marion
13	18.5	Hopewell City Public Schools	Hopewell
13	18.5	Lunenburg County Public Schools	Victoria
13	18.5	Pulaski County Public Schools	Pulaski
16	18.3	Floyd County Public Schools	Floyd
16	18.3	Nottoway County Public Schools	Nottoway
18	18.2	Essex County Public Schools	Tappahannock
19	18.1	Alexandria City Public Schools	Alexandria
19	18.1	Southampton County Public Schools	Courtland
21	18.0	Charlottesville City Pub Schools	Charlottesville
22	17.9	Chesapeake City Public Schools	Chesapeake
22	17.9	Scott County Public Schools	Gate City
24	17.8	King William County Public Schools	King William
25	17.7	Amelia County Public Schools	Amelia
25	17.7	Goochland County Public Schools	Goochland
27	17.6	Botetourt County Public Schools	Fincastle
28	17.4	Carroll County Public Schools	Hillsville
29	17.2	Patrick County Public Schools	Stuart
30	17.1	Mecklenburg County Public Schools	Boydton
30	17.1	Russell County Public Schools	Lebanon
32	17.0	Richmond City Public Schools	Richmond
33	16.9	Alleghany County Public Schools	Covington
33	16.9	Arlington County Public Schools	Arlington
33	16.9	Staunton City Public Schools	Staunton
36	16.7	Dickenson County Public Schools	Clintwood
37	16.5	Roanoke City Public Schools	Roanoke
38	16.3	Roanoke County Public Schools	Roanoke
39	16.1	Greensville County Public Schools	Emporia
40	15.9	Powhatan County Public Schools	Powhatan
41	15.8	Frederick County Public Schools	Winchester
41	15.8	Lynchburg City Public Schools	Lynchburg
43	15.7	Appomattox County Public Schools	Appomattox
43	15.7	Harrisonburg City Public Schools	Harrisonburg
45	15.5	Albemarle County Public Schools	Charlottesville
45	15.5	Tazewell County Public Schools	Tazewell
47	15.3	Hanover County Public Schools	Ashland
48	15.1	Radford City Public Schools	Radford
49	15.0	Chesterfield County Public Schools	Chesterfield
49	15.0	Fluvanna County Public Schools	Palmyra
49	15.0	Warren County Public Schools	Front Royal
52	14.9	Augusta County Public Schools	Fishersville
52	14.9	Buckingham County Public Schools	Buckingham
54	14.8	Colonial Hgts City Public Schools	Colonial Hgts
55	14.7	Falls Church City Public Schools	Falls Church
55	14.7	Fredericksburg City Public Schools	Fredericksburg
55	14.7	Martinsville City Public Schools	Martinsville
58	14.6	Spotsylvania Co Public Schools	Spotsylvania
59	14.5	Wise County Public Schools	Wise
60	14.3	Giles County Public Schools	Pearisburg
60	14.3	Henrico County Public Schools	Richmond
60	14.3	King George County Public Schools	King George
63	14.2	Hampton City Public Schools	Hampton
63	14.2	Northampton County Public Schools	Machipongo
63	14.2	Shenandoah County Public Schools	Woodstock
66	14.1	Charlotte County Public Schools	Charlotte Ct Hse
66	14.1	Fairfax County Public Schools	Fairfax
66	14.1	Norfolk City Public Schools	Norfolk
69	14.0	Louisa County Public Schools	Mineral
69	14.0	Petersburg City Public Schools	Petersburg
69	14.0	Virginia Beach City Public Schls	Virginia Beach
72	13.9	Dinwiddie County Public Schools	Dinwiddie
72	13.9	Isle of Wight Co Public Schools	Isle Of Wight
72	13.9	Orange County Public Schools	Orange
72	13.9	Pittsylvania County Public Schools	Chatham
72	13.9	Rockbridge County Public Schools	Lexington
72	13.9	Williamsburg-James City Co PS	Williamsburg
78	13.8	Grayson County Public Schools	Independence
78	13.8	Portsmouth City Public Schools	Portsmouth
78	13.8	Washington County Public Schools	Abingdon
81	13.5	Montgomery County Public Schools	Christiansburg
82	13.4	Caroline County Public Schools	Bowling Green
83	13.3	Fauquier County Public Schools	Warrenton
84	13.1	Bedford County Public Schools	Bedford
85	13.0	Newport News City Public Schools	Newport News
86	12.9	Brunswick County Public Schools	Lawrenceville
87	12.8	Danville City Public Schools	Danville
88	12.7	Amherst County Public Schools	Amherst
89	12.6	Madison County Public Schools	Madison
90	12.5	Accomack County Public Schools	Accomac
90	12.5	Rockingham County Public Schools	Harrisonburg
92	12.3	Manassas Park City Public Schools	Manassas Park
93	12.2	Gloucester County Public Schools	Gloucester
93	12.2	Salem City Public Schools	Salem
95	12.0	Campbell County Public Schools	Rustburg
95	12.0	Wythe County Public Schools	Wytheville
97	11.8	Prince William Co Public Schools	Manassas
98	11.7	Prince George Co Public Schools	Prince George
99	11.6	Culpeper County Public Schools	Culpeper
99	11.6	Page County Public Schools	Luray
99	11.6	Westmoreland Co Public Schools	Montross
102	11.5	Manassas City Public Schools	Manassas
103	11.3	Suffolk City Public Schools	Suffolk
104	11.0	Poquoson City Public Schools	Poquoson
105	10.9	Stafford County Public Schools	Stafford
106	10.7	Loudoun County Public Schools	Leesburg
107	10.4	Waynesboro City Public Schools	Waynesboro
108	10.1	Clarke County Public Schools	Berryville
109	9.2	York County Public Schools	Yorktown

English Language Learner Students

Rank	Percent	District Name	City
1	31.4	Arlington County Public Schools	Arlington
1	31.4	Harrisonburg City Public Schools	Harrisonburg
3	24.3	Alexandria City Public Schools	Alexandria
4	23.2	Manassas Park City Public Schools	Manassas Park
5	20.6	Manassas City Public Schools	Manassas
6	16.4	Fairfax County Public Schools	Fairfax
7	10.9	Prince William Co Public Schools	Manassas
8	10.7	Winchester City Public Schools	Winchester
9	9.9	Falls Church City Public Schools	Falls Church
10	6.4	Accomack County Public Schools	Accomac
11	5.6	Rockingham County Public Schools	Harrisonburg
12	5.2	Fredericksburg City Public Schools	Fredericksburg
13	5.1	Albemarle County Public Schools	Charlottesville
14	4.6	Loudoun County Public Schools	Leesburg
15	4.0	Charlottesville City Pub Schools	Charlottesville
15	4.0	Northampton County Public Schools	Machipongo
17	3.8	Westmoreland Co Public Schools	Montross
18	3.7	Roanoke City Public Schools	Roanoke
18	3.7	Waynesboro City Public Schools	Waynesboro
20	3.2	Henrico County Public Schools	Richmond
21	2.9	Henry County Public Schools	Collinsville
22	2.5	Chesterfield County Public Schools	Chesterfield
23	2.4	Frederick County Public Schools	Winchester
23	2.4	Shenandoah County Public Schools	Woodstock
25	2.2	Warren County Public Schools	Front Royal
26	2.1	Danville City Public Schools	Danville
26	2.1	Martinsville City Public Schools	Martinsville
26	2.1	Montgomery County Public Schools	Christiansburg
29	2.0	Williamsburg-James City Co PS	Williamsburg
30	1.9	Culpeper County Public Schools	Culpeper
30	1.9	Floyd County Public Schools	Floyd
30	1.9	Nelson County Public Schools	Lovingston
33	1.6	Fauquier County Public Schools	Warrenton
33	1.6	Richmond City Public Schools	Richmond
35	1.5	Clarke County Public Schools	Berryville
36	1.4	Carroll County Public Schools	Hillsville
36	1.4	Newport News City Public Schools	Newport News
36	1.4	Spotsylvania Co Public Schools	Spotsylvania
39	1.3	Augusta County Public Schools	Fishersville
39	1.3	Patrick County Public Schools	Stuart
39	1.3	Stafford County Public Schools	Stafford
42	1.2	Greene County Public Schools	Stanardsville
42	1.2	Pittsylvania County Public Schools	Chatham
44	1.1	Nottoway County Public Schools	Nottoway
44	1.1	Roanoke County Public Schools	Roanoke
44	1.1	Virginia Beach City Public Schls	Virginia Beach
47	1.0	Colonial Hgts City Public Schools	Colonial Hgts
47	1.0	Essex County Public Schools	Tappahannock
47	1.0	Hampton City Public Schools	Hampton
47	1.0	Hopewell City Public Schools	Hopewell
47	1.0	Orange County Public Schools	Orange
47	1.0	York County Public Schools	Yorktown
53	0.9	Caroline County Public Schools	Bowling Green
54	0.8	Dinwiddie County Public Schools	Dinwiddie
54	0.8	Hanover County Public Schools	Ashland
54	0.8	Salem City Public Schools	Salem
57	0.7	Bristol City Public Schools	Bristol
57	0.7	Franklin County Public Schools	Rocky Mount
57	0.7	Mecklenburg County Public Schools	Boydton
57	0.7	Radford City Public Schools	Radford
61	0.6	Chesapeake City Public Schools	Chesapeake
61	0.6	Greensville County Public Schools	Emporia
61	0.6	King George County Public Schools	King George
61	0.6	Petersburg City Public Schools	Petersburg
61	0.6	Pulaski County Public Schools	Pulaski
61	0.6	Staunton City Public Schools	Staunton
67	0.5	Brunswick County Public Schools	Lawrenceville
67	0.5	Lynchburg City Public Schools	Lynchburg
67	0.5	Norfolk City Public Schools	Norfolk
67	0.5	Page County Public Schools	Luray
67	0.5	Poquoson City Public Schools	Poquoson
67	0.5	Prince George Co Public Schools	Prince George
73	0.4	Campbell County Public Schools	Rustburg
73	0.4	Goochland County Public Schools	Goochland
73	0.4	Isle of Wight Co Public Schools	Isle Of Wight
73	0.4	Louisa County Public Schools	Mineral
73	0.4	Smyth County Public Schools	Marion
78	0.3	Amelia County Public Schools	Amelia
78	0.3	Bedford County Public Schools	Bedford
78	0.3	Charlotte County Public Schools	Charlotte Ct Hse
78	0.3	Lunenburg County Public Schools	Victoria
78	0.3	Madison County Public Schools	Madison
78	0.3	Rockbridge County Public Schools	Lexington
78	0.3	Wise County Public Schools	Wise
85	0.2	Amherst County Public Schools	Amherst
85	0.2	Botetourt County Public Schools	Fincastle
85	0.2	Halifax County Public Schools	Halifax
85	0.2	King William County Public Schools	King William
85	0.2	New Kent County Public Schools	New Kent
85	0.2	Powhatan County Public Schools	Powhatan
85	0.2	Washington County Public Schools	Abingdon
92	0.1	Alleghany County Public Schools	Covington
92	0.1	Appomattox County Public Schools	Appomattox
92	0.1	Buckingham County Public Schools	Buckingham
92	0.1	Fluvanna County Public Schools	Palmyra
92	0.1	Grayson County Public Schools	Independence
92	0.1	Portsmouth City Public Schools	Portsmouth
92	0.1	Prince Edward Co Public Schools	Farmville
92	0.1	Scott County Public Schools	Gate City
92	0.1	Suffolk City Public Schools	Suffolk
92	0.1	Wythe County Public Schools	Wytheville
102	0.0	Gloucester County Public Schools	Gloucester
102	0.0	Lee County Public Schools	Jonesville
102	0.0	Russell County Public Schools	Lebanon
102	0.0	Southampton County Public Schools	Courtland
102	0.0	Tazewell County Public Schools	Tazewell
107	0.0	Giles County Public Schools	Pearisburg
108	n/a	Buchanan County Public Schools	Grundy
108	n/a	Dickenson County Public Schools	Clintwood

Migrant Students

Rank	Percent	District Name	City
1	5.3	Northampton County Public Schools	Machipongo
2	4.9	Accomack County Public Schools	Accomac
2	4.9	Westmoreland Co Public Schools	Montross
4	3.1	Harrisonburg City Public Schools	Harrisonburg
5	2.5	Shenandoah County Public Schools	Woodstock
6	1.5	Patrick County Public Schools	Stuart
7	1.4	Winchester City Public Schools	Winchester
8	1.3	Carroll County Public Schools	Hillsville
9	1.2	Rockingham County Public Schools	Harrisonburg
10	0.9	Nottoway County Public Schools	Nottoway
11	0.6	Nelson County Public Schools	Lovingston
12	0.5	Floyd County Public Schools	Floyd
12	0.5	Frederick County Public Schools	Winchester
14	0.4	Pittsylvania County Public Schools	Chatham
15	0.3	Albemarle County Public Schools	Charlottesville
15	0.3	Page County Public Schools	Luray
17	0.2	Halifax County Public Schools	Halifax
18	0.1	Amelia County Public Schools	Amelia
18	0.1	Augusta County Public Schools	Fishersville
18	0.1	Fluvanna County Public Schools	Palmyra
18	0.1	Lunenburg County Public Schools	Victoria
18	0.1	Prince Edward Co Public Schools	Farmville
18	0.1	Rockbridge County Public Schools	Lexington
24	0.0	Amherst County Public Schools	Amherst
24	0.0	Buckingham County Public Schools	Buckingham
24	0.0	Fauquier County Public Schools	Warrenton
24	0.0	Spotsylvania Co Public Schools	Spotsylvania
28	0.0	Alexandria City Public Schools	Alexandria
28	0.0	Alleghany County Public Schools	Covington
28	0.0	Appomattox County Public Schools	Appomattox
28	0.0	Arlington County Public Schools	Arlington
28	0.0	Bedford County Public Schools	Bedford
28	0.0	Botetourt County Public Schools	Fincastle
28	0.0	Bristol City Public Schools	Bristol
28	0.0	Brunswick County Public Schools	Lawrenceville
28	0.0	Buchanan County Public Schools	Grundy
28	0.0	Campbell County Public Schools	Rustburg
28	0.0	Caroline County Public Schools	Bowling Green
28	0.0	Charlotte County Public Schools	Charlotte Ct Hse
28	0.0	Charlottesville City Pub Schools	Charlottesville
28	0.0	Chesapeake City Public Schools	Chesapeake
28	0.0	Chesterfield County Public Schools	Chesterfield

28	0.0	Clarke County Public Schools	Berryville
28	0.0	Colonial Hgts City Public Schools	Colonial Hgts
28	0.0	Culpeper County Public Schools	Culpeper
28	0.0	Danville City Public Schools	Danville
28	0.0	Dickenson County Public Schools	Clintwood
28	0.0	Dinwiddie County Public Schools	Dinwiddie
28	0.0	Essex County Public Schools	Tappahannock
28	0.0	Fairfax County Public Schools	Fairfax
28	0.0	Falls Church City Public Schools	Falls Church
28	0.0	Franklin County Public Schools	Rocky Mount
28	0.0	Fredericksburg City Public Schools	Fredericksburg
28	0.0	Giles County Public Schools	Pearisburg
28	0.0	Gloucester County Public Schools	Gloucester
28	0.0	Goochland County Public Schools	Goochland
28	0.0	Grayson County Public Schools	Independence
28	0.0	Greene County Public Schools	Stanardsville
28	0.0	Greensville County Public Schools	Emporia
28	0.0	Hampton City Public Schools	Hampton
28	0.0	Hanover County Public Schools	Ashland
28	0.0	Henrico County Public Schools	Richmond
28	0.0	Henry County Public Schools	Collinsville
28	0.0	Hopewell City Public Schools	Hopewell
28	0.0	Isle of Wight Co Public Schools	Isle Of Wight
28	0.0	King George County Public Schools	King George
28	0.0	King William County Public Schools	King William
28	0.0	Lee County Public Schools	Jonesville
28	0.0	Loudoun County Public Schools	Leesburg
28	0.0	Louisa County Public Schools	Mineral
28	0.0	Lynchburg City Public Schools	Lynchburg
28	0.0	Madison County Public Schools	Madison
28	0.0	Manassas City Public Schools	Manassas
28	0.0	Manassas Park City Public Schools	Manassas Park
28	0.0	Martinsville City Public Schools	Martinsville
28	0.0	Mecklenburg County Public Schools	Boydton
28	0.0	Montgomery County Public Schools	Christiansburg
28	0.0	New Kent County Public Schools	New Kent
28	0.0	Newport News City Public Schools	Newport News
28	0.0	Norfolk City Public Schools	Norfolk
28	0.0	Orange County Public Schools	Orange
28	0.0	Petersburg City Public Schools	Petersburg
28	0.0	Poquoson City Public Schools	Poquoson
28	0.0	Portsmouth City Public Schools	Portsmouth
28	0.0	Powhatan County Public Schools	Powhatan
28	0.0	Prince George Co Public Schools	Prince George
28	0.0	Prince William Co Public Schools	Manassas
28	0.0	Pulaski County Public Schools	Pulaski
28	0.0	Radford City Public Schools	Radford
28	0.0	Richmond City Public Schools	Richmond
28	0.0	Roanoke City Public Schools	Roanoke
28	0.0	Roanoke County Public Schools	Roanoke
28	0.0	Russell County Public Schools	Lebanon
28	0.0	Salem City Public Schools	Salem
28	0.0	Scott County Public Schools	Gate City
28	0.0	Smyth County Public Schools	Marion
28	0.0	Southampton County Public Schools	Courtland
28	0.0	Stafford County Public Schools	Stafford
28	0.0	Staunton City Public Schools	Staunton
28	0.0	Suffolk City Public Schools	Suffolk
28	0.0	Tazewell County Public Schools	Tazewell
28	0.0	Virginia Beach City Public Schls	Virginia Beach
28	0.0	Warren County Public Schools	Front Royal
28	0.0	Washington County Public Schools	Abingdon
28	0.0	Waynesboro City Public Schools	Waynesboro
28	0.0	Williamsburg-James City Co PS	Williamsburg
28	0.0	Wise County Public Schools	Wise
28	0.0	Wythe County Public Schools	Wytheville
28	0.0	York County Public Schools	Yorktown

Students Eligible for Free Lunch

Rank	Percent	District Name	City
1	63.9	Petersburg City Public Schools	Petersburg
2	62.4	Richmond City Public Schools	Richmond
3	61.5	Northampton County Public Schools	Machipongo
4	58.6	Essex County Public Schools	Tappahannock
5	57.7	Brunswick County Public Schools	Lawrenceville
6	53.0	Roanoke City Public Schools	Roanoke
7	52.8	Lunenburg County Public Schools	Victoria
8	52.5	Lee County Public Schools	Jonesville
9	52.3	Buchanan County Public Schools	Grundy
10	49.8	Accomack County Public Schools	Accomac
10	49.8	Danville City Public Schools	Danville
12	49.5	Hopewell City Public Schools	Hopewell
13	49.4	Prince Edward Co Public Schools	Farmville
14	47.7	Greensville County Public Schools	Emporia
15	47.2	Mecklenburg County Public Schools	Boydton
16	46.6	Norfolk City Public Schools	Norfolk
17	45.1	Halifax County Public Schools	Halifax
18	44.2	Portsmouth City Public Schools	Portsmouth
19	44.0	Lynchburg City Public Schools	Lynchburg
20	43.7	Buckingham County Public Schools	Buckingham
21	42.2	Bristol City Public Schools	Bristol
22	41.9	Dickenson County Public Schools	Clintwood
23	40.6	Tazewell County Public Schools	Tazewell
24	40.5	Wise County Public Schools	Wise
25	40.3	Charlottesville City Pub Schools	Charlottesville
26	40.0	Nottoway County Public Schools	Nottoway
27	39.5	Harrisonburg City Public Schools	Harrisonburg
28	38.5	Scott County Public Schools	Gate City
29	38.2	Henry County Public Schools	Collinsville
30	38.1	Patrick County Public Schools	Stuart
31	37.6	Charlotte County Public Schools	Charlotte Ct Hse
32	37.5	Carroll County Public Schools	Hillsville
33	37.3	Alexandria City Public Schools	Alexandria
34	37.0	Russell County Public Schools	Lebanon
35	36.8	Newport News City Public Schools	Newport News
36	35.7	Waynesboro City Public Schools	Waynesboro
37	35.6	Smyth County Public Schools	Marion
38	34.6	Martinsville City Public Schools	Martinsville
39	33.9	Grayson County Public Schools	Independence
40	33.4	Staunton City Public Schools	Staunton
41	33.0	Southampton County Public Schools	Courtland
42	32.2	Hampton City Public Schools	Hampton
43	32.0	Fredericksburg City Public Schools	Fredericksburg
44	31.7	Suffolk City Public Schools	Suffolk
45	31.5	Westmoreland Co Public Schools	Montross
46	31.1	Wythe County Public Schools	Wytheville
47	30.8	Caroline County Public Schools	Bowling Green
48	30.4	Pittsylvania County Public Schools	Chatham
49	30.3	Franklin County Public Schools	Rocky Mount
50	29.7	Pulaski County Public Schools	Pulaski
51	29.6	Dinwiddie County Public Schools	Dinwiddie
51	29.6	Page County Public Schools	Luray
53	29.4	Appomattox County Public Schools	Appomattox
54	28.3	Winchester City Public Schools	Winchester
55	27.7	Amherst County Public Schools	Amherst
56	27.1	Washington County Public Schools	Abingdon
57	27.0	Nelson County Public Schools	Lovingston
58	26.8	Amelia County Public Schools	Amelia
59	26.6	Arlington County Public Schools	Arlington
60	26.4	Alleghany County Public Schools	Covington
61	25.6	Louisa County Public Schools	Mineral
62	24.7	Isle of Wight Co Public Schools	Isle Of Wight
63	24.4	Floyd County Public Schools	Floyd
64	23.3	Montgomery County Public Schools	Christiansburg
65	23.2	Campbell County Public Schools	Rustburg
66	23.0	Giles County Public Schools	Pearisburg
67	22.7	Manassas Park City Public Schools	Manassas Park
68	22.3	Orange County Public Schools	Orange
69	22.2	Rockbridge County Public Schools	Lexington
70	20.6	Bedford County Public Schools	Bedford
70	20.6	King William County Public Schools	King William
72	19.9	Rockingham County Public Schools	Harrisonburg
73	19.6	Virginia Beach City Public Schls	Virginia Beach
74	19.1	Chesapeake City Public Schools	Chesapeake
74	19.1	Shenandoah County Public Schools	Woodstock
76	18.5	Warren County Public Schools	Front Royal
77	17.2	Manassas City Public Schools	Manassas
77	17.2	Prince William Co Public Schools	Manassas
79	17.1	King George County Public Schools	King George
80	16.7	Augusta County Public Schools	Fishersville
81	15.2	Madison County Public Schools	Madison
82	14.8	Radford City Public Schools	Radford
83	14.2	Prince George Co Public Schools	Prince George
84	14.0	Williamsburg-James City Co PS	Williamsburg
85	13.5	Fairfax County Public Schools	Fairfax
85	13.5	Henrico County Public Schools	Richmond
87	13.2	Albemarle County Public Schools	Charlottesville
87	13.2	Fluvanna County Public Schools	Palmyra
87	13.2	Spotsylvania Co Public Schools	Spotsylvania
90	13.0	Gloucester County Public Schools	Gloucester
91	12.5	New Kent County Public Schools	New Kent
92	12.4	Culpeper County Public Schools	Culpeper
93	12.2	Salem City Public Schools	Salem
94	11.6	Greene County Public Schools	Stanardsville
95	11.5	Frederick County Public Schools	Winchester
96	11.0	Colonial Hgts City Public Schools	Colonial Hgts
97	10.7	Clarke County Public Schools	Berryville
97	10.7	Fauquier County Public Schools	Warrenton
99	10.0	Roanoke County Public Schools	Roanoke
100	9.2	Chesterfield County Public Schools	Chesterfield
101	8.7	Botetourt County Public Schools	Fincastle
102	8.5	Stafford County Public Schools	Stafford
103	8.2	Powhatan County Public Schools	Powhatan
104	7.9	York County Public Schools	Yorktown
105	7.1	Loudoun County Public Schools	Leesburg
106	6.4	Hanover County Public Schools	Ashland
107	4.4	Goochland County Public Schools	Goochland
108	4.0	Poquoson City Public Schools	Poquoson
109	3.9	Falls Church City Public Schools	Falls Church

Students Eligible for Reduced-Price Lunch

Rank	Percent	District Name	City
1	16.0	Buchanan County Public Schools	Grundy
2	14.3	Dickenson County Public Schools	Clintwood
3	12.8	Charlotte County Public Schools	Charlotte Ct Hse
4	12.4	Scott County Public Schools	Gate City
5	12.3	Brunswick County Public Schools	Lawrenceville
6	12.0	Carroll County Public Schools	Hillsville
6	12.0	Nelson County Public Schools	Lovingston
8	11.7	Lunenburg County Public Schools	Victoria
9	11.6	Mecklenburg County Public Schools	Boydton
10	11.4	Virginia Beach City Public Schls	Virginia Beach
11	11.1	Buckingham County Public Schools	Buckingham
11	11.1	Norfolk City Public Schools	Norfolk
13	10.8	Prince Edward Co Public Schools	Farmville
14	10.6	Grayson County Public Schools	Independence
15	10.4	Halifax County Public Schools	Halifax
15	10.4	Lee County Public Schools	Jonesville
15	10.4	Newport News City Public Schools	Newport News
18	10.0	Alexandria City Public Schools	Alexandria
19	9.8	Arlington County Public Schools	Arlington
20	9.7	Nottoway County Public Schools	Nottoway
21	9.3	Essex County Public Schools	Tappahannock
21	9.3	Hopewell City Public Schools	Hopewell
21	9.3	Tazewell County Public Schools	Tazewell
24	9.1	Accomack County Public Schools	Accomac
24	9.1	Giles County Public Schools	Pearisburg
24	9.1	Hampton City Public Schools	Hampton
24	9.1	Petersburg City Public Schools	Petersburg
24	9.1	Russell County Public Schools	Lebanon
29	9.0	Amelia County Public Schools	Amelia
29	9.0	Richmond City Public Schools	Richmond
31	8.9	Franklin County Public Schools	Rocky Mount
31	8.9	Northampton County Public Schools	Machipongo
33	8.8	Prince George Co Public Schools	Prince George
34	8.7	Wythe County Public Schools	Wytheville
35	8.6	Page County Public Schools	Luray
35	8.6	Smyth County Public Schools	Marion
35	8.6	Winchester City Public Schools	Winchester
38	8.5	Dinwiddie County Public Schools	Dinwiddie
38	8.5	Southampton County Public Schools	Courtland
38	8.5	Wise County Public Schools	Wise
41	8.4	Greensville County Public Schools	Emporia
42	8.1	Floyd County Public Schools	Floyd
42	8.1	King William County Public Schools	King William
42	8.1	Louisa County Public Schools	Mineral
42	8.1	Manassas Park City Public Schools	Manassas Park
46	8.0	Harrisonburg City Public Schools	Harrisonburg
46	8.0	Pulaski County Public Schools	Pulaski
46	8.0	Suffolk City Public Schools	Suffolk
49	7.9	Caroline County Public Schools	Bowling Green
49	7.9	Portsmouth City Public Schools	Portsmouth
49	7.9	Rockingham County Public Schools	Harrisonburg
52	7.8	Rockbridge County Public Schools	Lexington
52	7.8	Waynesboro City Public Schools	Waynesboro
54	7.6	Alleghany County Public Schools	Covington
54	7.6	Staunton City Public Schools	Staunton
56	7.5	Pittsylvania County Public Schools	Chatham
56	7.5	Washington County Public Schools	Abingdon
58	7.4	Campbell County Public Schools	Rustburg
58	7.4	Charlottesville City Pub Schools	Charlottesville
60	7.3	Appomattox County Public Schools	Appomattox
60	7.3	Augusta County Public Schools	Fishersville
62	7.1	Roanoke City Public Schools	Roanoke
63	6.9	Orange County Public Schools	Orange
63	6.9	Patrick County Public Schools	Stuart
65	6.8	Montgomery County Public Schools	Christiansburg
66	6.7	Amherst County Public Schools	Amherst
66	6.7	Danville City Public Schools	Danville
66	6.7	Prince William Co Public Schools	Manassas
69	6.5	Bedford County Public Schools	Bedford
69	6.5	Henry County Public Schools	Collinsville
71	6.4	Isle of Wight Co Public Schools	Isle Of Wight
72	6.2	Shenandoah County Public Schools	Woodstock
73	6.0	York County Public Schools	Yorktown
74	5.9	Bristol City Public Schools	Bristol
74	5.9	Manassas City Public Schools	Manassas
76	5.5	Culpeper County Public Schools	Culpeper
76	5.5	Fairfax County Public Schools	Fairfax
78	5.4	Chesapeake City Public Schools	Chesapeake
78	5.4	Madison County Public Schools	Madison
80	5.3	Colonial Hgts City Public Schools	Colonial Hgts
80	5.3	Westmoreland Co Public Schools	Montross
82	5.2	Roanoke County Public Schools	Roanoke
83	5.1	Gloucester County Public Schools	Gloucester
83	5.1	Martinsville City Public Schools	Martinsville
85	4.8	Salem City Public Schools	Salem
86	4.7	Frederick County Public Schools	Winchester
87	4.6	Fluvanna County Public Schools	Palmyra
87	4.6	Spotsylvania Co Public Schools	Spotsylvania
89	4.5	Lynchburg City Public Schools	Lynchburg
90	4.4	Fredericksburg City Public Schools	Fredericksburg
90	4.4	Henrico County Public Schools	Richmond
90	4.4	Warren County Public Schools	Front Royal

93	4.2	Albemarle County Public Schools	Charlottesville
93	4.2	Fauquier County Public Schools	Warrenton
95	4.0	Williamsburg-James City Co PS	Williamsburg
96	3.8	Chesterfield County Public Schools	Chesterfield
96	3.8	King George County Public Schools	King George
96	3.8	Powhatan County Public Schools	Powhatan
99	3.7	New Kent County Public Schools	New Kent
100	3.6	Greene County Public Schools	Stanardsville
101	3.5	Loudoun County Public Schools	Leesburg
102	3.3	Stafford County Public Schools	Stafford
103	3.0	Clarke County Public Schools	Berryville
104	2.8	Botetourt County Public Schools	Fincastle
105	2.4	Hanover County Public Schools	Ashland
106	2.2	Radford City Public Schools	Radford
107	1.5	Falls Church City Public Schools	Falls Church
107	1.5	Poquoson City Public Schools	Poquoson
109	1.2	Goochland County Public Schools	Goochland

Student/Teacher Ratio

Rank	Ratio	District Name	City
1	15.5	Caroline County Public Schools	Bowling Green
2	15.4	Prince William Co Public Schools	Manassas
3	14.8	Prince George Co Public Schools	Prince George
4	14.7	York County Public Schools	Yorktown
5	14.6	Suffolk City Public Schools	Suffolk
6	14.4	Chesterfield County Public Schools	Chesterfield
7	14.3	Henrico County Public Schools	Richmond
7	14.3	Portsmouth City Public Schools	Portsmouth
7	14.3	Stafford County Public Schools	Stafford
10	14.2	Norfolk City Public Schools	Norfolk
10	14.2	Warren County Public Schools	Front Royal
12	14.1	Washington County Public Schools	Abingdon
13	14.0	Isle of Wight Co Public Schools	Isle Of Wight
14	13.8	Russell County Public Schools	Lebanon
15	13.7	Chesapeake City Public Schools	Chesapeake
15	13.7	Page County Public Schools	Luray
15	13.7	Virginia Beach City Public Schls	Virginia Beach
18	13.6	Newport News City Public Schools	Newport News
19	13.5	Campbell County Public Schools	Rustburg
19	13.5	Charlotte County Public Schools	Charlotte Ct Hse
19	13.5	Franklin County Public Schools	Rocky Mount
19	13.5	Loudoun County Public Schools	Leesburg
19	13.5	Pittsylvania County Public Schools	Chatham
19	13.5	Prince Edward Co Public Schools	Farmville
25	13.4	Dinwiddie County Public Schools	Dinwiddie
25	13.4	Fairfax County Public Schools	Fairfax
25	13.4	Gloucester County Public Schools	Gloucester
25	13.4	Manassas City Public Schools	Manassas
25	13.4	Petersburg City Public Schools	Petersburg
25	13.4	Richmond City Public Schools	Richmond
31	13.3	Bedford County Public Schools	Bedford
31	13.3	Nottoway County Public Schools	Nottoway
31	13.3	Powhatan County Public Schools	Powhatan
31	13.3	Spotsylvania Co Public Schools	Spotsylvania
35	13.2	Amelia County Public Schools	Amelia
35	13.2	Giles County Public Schools	Pearisburg
35	13.2	King George County Public Schools	King George
35	13.2	Mecklenburg County Public Schools	Boydton
35	13.2	Poquoson City Public Schools	Poquoson
40	13.1	Fluvanna County Public Schools	Palmyra
40	13.1	Westmoreland Co Public Schools	Montross
42	13.0	Frederick County Public Schools	Winchester
42	13.0	Louisa County Public Schools	Mineral
44	12.9	Hanover County Public Schools	Ashland
44	12.9	Southampton County Public Schools	Courtland
44	12.9	Waynesboro City Public Schools	Waynesboro
47	12.8	Augusta County Public Schools	Fishersville
47	12.8	Clarke County Public Schools	Berryville
49	12.7	Floyd County Public Schools	Floyd
49	12.7	Pulaski County Public Schools	Pulaski
49	12.7	Salem City Public Schools	Salem
49	12.7	Scott County Public Schools	Gate City
49	12.7	Wythe County Public Schools	Wytheville
54	12.6	Alleghany County Public Schools	Covington
54	12.6	Botetourt County Public Schools	Fincastle
54	12.6	Culpeper County Public Schools	Culpeper
54	12.6	Fauquier County Public Schools	Warrenton
54	12.6	Radford City Public Schools	Radford
54	12.6	Rockingham County Public Schools	Harrisonburg
60	12.5	Amherst County Public Schools	Amherst
60	12.5	Lynchburg City Public Schools	Lynchburg
60	12.5	Orange County Public Schools	Orange
63	12.4	Accomack County Public Schools	Accomac
63	12.4	Buckingham County Public Schools	Buckingham
63	12.4	Carroll County Public Schools	Hillsville
63	12.4	Greensville County Public Schools	Emporia
63	12.4	Hopewell City Public Schools	Hopewell
68	12.3	Appomattox County Public Schools	Appomattox
68	12.3	Fredericksburg City Public Schools	Fredericksburg
68	12.3	Hampton City Public Schools	Hampton
68	12.3	Madison County Public Schools	Madison
68	12.3	New Kent County Public Schools	New Kent
68	12.3	Shenandoah County Public Schools	Woodstock
68	12.3	Tazewell County Public Schools	Tazewell
75	12.0	Brunswick County Public Schools	Lawrenceville
75	12.0	Danville City Public Schools	Danville
75	12.0	Essex County Public Schools	Tappahannock
75	12.0	Goochland County Public Schools	Goochland
75	12.0	Henry County Public Schools	Collinsville
75	12.0	Nelson County Public Schools	Lovingston
81	11.9	Patrick County Public Schools	Stuart
81	11.9	Wise County Public Schools	Wise
83	11.8	Dickenson County Public Schools	Clintwood
84	11.7	Albemarle County Public Schools	Charlottesville
84	11.7	Halifax County Public Schools	Halifax
84	11.7	Roanoke County Public Schools	Roanoke
84	11.7	Williamsburg-James City Co PS	Williamsburg
88	11.6	Winchester City Public Schools	Winchester
89	11.5	Manassas Park City Public Schools	Manassas Park
90	11.4	Lunenburg County Public Schools	Victoria
90	11.4	Martinsville City Public Schools	Martinsville
90	11.4	Roanoke City Public Schools	Roanoke
93	11.3	Colonial Hgts City Public Schools	Colonial Hgts
93	11.3	Northampton County Public Schools	Machipongo
95	11.2	Bristol City Public Schools	Bristol
95	11.2	Grayson County Public Schools	Independence
95	11.2	King William County Public Schools	King William
95	11.2	Montgomery County Public Schools	Christiansburg
95	11.2	Rockbridge County Public Schools	Lexington
100	11.1	Buchanan County Public Schools	Grundy
101	11.0	Charlottesville City Pub Schools	Charlottesville
101	11.0	Greene County Public Schools	Stanardsville
101	11.0	Smyth County Public Schools	Marion
104	10.8	Arlington County Public Schools	Arlington
104	10.8	Falls Church City Public Schools	Falls Church
106	10.7	Harrisonburg City Public Schools	Harrisonburg
106	10.7	Staunton City Public Schools	Staunton
108	10.5	Alexandria City Public Schools	Alexandria
109	10.3	Lee County Public Schools	Jonesville

Student/Librarian Ratio

Rank	Ratio	District Name	City
1	88,150.0	Campbell County Public Schools	Rustburg
2	5,063.0	Isle of Wight Co Public Schools	Isle Of Wight
3	950.7	Prince Edward Co Public Schools	Farmville
4	857.6	Stafford County Public Schools	Stafford
5	816.7	Fredericksburg City Public Schools	Fredericksburg
6	800.8	King George County Public Schools	King George
7	778.4	Culpeper County Public Schools	Culpeper
8	777.2	Hopewell City Public Schools	Hopewell
9	768.5	Prince William Co Public Schools	Manassas
10	765.1	Norfolk City Public Schools	Norfolk
11	765.0	Newport News City Public Schools	Newport News
12	736.6	Chesterfield County Public Schools	Chesterfield
13	731.2	Washington County Public Schools	Abingdon
14	725.1	Fairfax County Public Schools	Fairfax
15	724.8	Winchester City Public Schools	Winchester
16	716.1	Manassas City Public Schools	Manassas
17	703.8	Chesapeake City Public Schools	Chesapeake
18	700.0	Virginia Beach City Public Schls	Virginia Beach
19	689.8	Spotsylvania Co Public Schools	Spotsylvania
19	689.8	York County Public Schools	Yorktown
21	675.2	Powhatan County Public Schools	Powhatan
22	671.8	Hanover County Public Schools	Ashland
23	663.7	Suffolk City Public Schools	Suffolk
24	658.5	Greensville County Public Schools	Emporia
25	636.5	New Kent County Public Schools	New Kent
26	636.0	Poquoson City Public Schools	Poquoson
27	634.5	Warren County Public Schools	Front Royal
28	625.7	Gloucester County Public Schools	Gloucester
29	625.3	Caroline County Public Schools	Bowling Green
30	617.3	Louisa County Public Schools	Mineral
31	597.7	Frederick County Public Schools	Winchester
32	597.4	Williamsburg-James City Co PS	Williamsburg
33	596.8	Nottoway County Public Schools	Nottoway
34	595.2	Augusta County Public Schools	Fishersville
35	590.9	Portsmouth City Public Schools	Portsmouth
36	589.0	Henrico County Public Schools	Richmond
37	582.7	Shenandoah County Public Schools	Woodstock
38	581.8	Appomattox County Public Schools	Appomattox
39	579.0	Pittsylvania County Public Schools	Chatham
40	575.9	Harrisonburg City Public Schools	Harrisonburg
41	572.0	Manassas Park City Public Schools	Manassas Park
42	567.0	Essex County Public Schools	Tappahannock
43	562.9	Mecklenburg County Public Schools	Boydton
44	559.2	Colonial Hgts City Public Schools	Colonial Hgts
45	558.6	Dinwiddie County Public Schools	Dinwiddie
45	558.6	Salem City Public Schools	Salem
47	558.2	Fauquier County Public Schools	Warrenton
48	556.0	Fluvanna County Public Schools	Palmyra
49	553.6	Prince George Co Public Schools	Prince George
50	550.7	Loudoun County Public Schools	Leesburg
51	550.3	Albemarle County Public Schools	Charlottesville
52	540.0	Greene County Public Schools	Stanardsville
53	526.0	Russell County Public Schools	Lebanon
54	522.9	Hampton City Public Schools	Hampton
55	519.3	Franklin County Public Schools	Rocky Mount
56	512.3	Radford City Public Schools	Radford
57	512.0	Page County Public Schools	Luray
58	510.8	Westmoreland Co Public Schools	Montross
59	509.0	Giles County Public Schools	Pearisburg
60	508.0	Richmond City Public Schools	Richmond
61	507.3	Northampton County Public Schools	Machipongo
62	503.8	Nelson County Public Schools	Lovingston
63	502.8	Waynesboro City Public Schools	Waynesboro
64	497.6	Arlington County Public Schools	Arlington
65	495.5	Alexandria City Public Schools	Alexandria
66	494.2	Bedford County Public Schools	Bedford
67	491.3	Charlottesville City Pub Schools	Charlottesville
68	488.7	Pulaski County Public Schools	Pulaski
69	487.5	Lynchburg City Public Schools	Lynchburg
69	487.5	Petersburg City Public Schools	Petersburg
71	484.6	Roanoke County Public Schools	Roanoke
72	481.8	Tazewell County Public Schools	Tazewell
73	475.5	Southampton County Public Schools	Courtland
74	468.5	Falls Church City Public Schools	Falls Church
75	467.1	Amherst County Public Schools	Amherst
76	466.5	King William County Public Schools	King William
77	466.3	Madison County Public Schools	Madison
78	466.0	Rockingham County Public Schools	Harrisonburg
79	461.5	Danville City Public Schools	Danville
80	457.6	Wise County Public Schools	Wise
81	457.4	Charlotte County Public Schools	Charlotte Ct Hse
82	454.4	Orange County Public Schools	Orange
83	452.2	Roanoke City Public Schools	Roanoke
84	449.2	Accomack County Public Schools	Accomac
85	447.3	Staunton City Public Schools	Staunton
86	435.2	Martinsville City Public Schools	Martinsville
87	432.8	Botetourt County Public Schools	Fincastle
88	431.0	Patrick County Public Schools	Stuart
89	430.5	Henry County Public Schools	Collinsville
90	430.3	Montgomery County Public Schools	Christiansburg
91	427.5	Lunenburg County Public Schools	Victoria
92	423.7	Smyth County Public Schools	Marion
93	423.0	Goochland County Public Schools	Goochland
94	420.6	Floyd County Public Schools	Floyd
95	414.2	Clarke County Public Schools	Berryville
96	411.6	Alleghany County Public Schools	Covington
97	408.2	Carroll County Public Schools	Hillsville
98	405.5	Brunswick County Public Schools	Lawrenceville
99	393.9	Halifax County Public Schools	Halifax
100	387.3	Bristol City Public Schools	Bristol
101	377.5	Buckingham County Public Schools	Buckingham
102	356.2	Wythe County Public Schools	Wytheville
103	339.5	Scott County Public Schools	Gate City
104	339.3	Lee County Public Schools	Jonesville
105	331.7	Buchanan County Public Schools	Grundy
106	325.6	Rockbridge County Public Schools	Lexington
107	325.1	Dickenson County Public Schools	Clintwood
108	281.8	Grayson County Public Schools	Independence
109	n/a	Amelia County Public Schools	Amelia

Student/Counselor Ratio

Rank	Ratio	District Name	City
1	44,075.0	Campbell County Public Schools	Rustburg
2	1,067.7	King George County Public Schools	King George
3	762.3	Charlotte County Public Schools	Charlotte Ct Hse
4	755.0	Buckingham County Public Schools	Buckingham
5	695.0	Fluvanna County Public Schools	Palmyra
6	694.7	Stafford County Public Schools	Stafford
7	681.7	Orange County Public Schools	Orange
8	670.4	Petersburg City Public Schools	Petersburg
9	636.0	Poquoson City Public Schools	Poquoson
10	630.7	Spotsylvania Co Public Schools	Spotsylvania
11	625.7	Gloucester County Public Schools	Gloucester
12	618.9	Chesterfield County Public Schools	Chesterfield
13	618.5	Manassas City Public Schools	Manassas
14	611.8	Nottoway County Public Schools	Nottoway
15	608.3	Brunswick County Public Schools	Lawrenceville
16	598.1	Mecklenburg County Public Schools	Boydton
17	591.7	Clarke County Public Schools	Berryville
18	581.8	Appomattox County Public Schools	Appomattox
19	577.1	Suffolk City Public Schools	Suffolk
20	571.2	Prince William Co Public Schools	Manassas
21	567.0	Essex County Public Schools	Tappahannock
22	563.9	Augusta County Public Schools	Fishersville
23	560.1	Williamsburg-James City Co PS	Williamsburg
24	554.4	Tazewell County Public Schools	Tazewell
25	540.1	Louisa County Public Schools	Mineral
26	537.5	Harrisonburg City Public Schools	Harrisonburg
27	536.6	Virginia Beach City Public Schls	Virginia Beach
28	536.0	Caroline County Public Schools	Bowling Green
29	534.2	Henrico County Public Schools	Richmond
30	533.5	Hanover County Public Schools	Ashland
31	533.4	Scott County Public Schools	Gate City
32	529.6	Fauquier County Public Schools	Warrenton

33	522.3	Washington County Public Schools	Abingdon
34	519.3	Franklin County Public Schools	Rocky Mount
35	517.7	Winchester City Public Schools	Winchester
36	514.2	Albemarle County Public Schools	Charlottesville
37	512.3	Grayson County Public Schools	Independence
37	512.3	Radford City Public Schools	Radford
39	510.8	Westmoreland Co Public Schools	Montross
40	509.2	New Kent County Public Schools	New Kent
41	508.4	Smyth County Public Schools	Marion
42	507.8	Salem City Public Schools	Salem
43	507.3	Northampton County Public Schools	Machipongo
44	503.8	Nelson County Public Schools	Lovingston
45	502.8	Waynesboro City Public Schools	Waynesboro
46	496.6	Dinwiddie County Public Schools	Dinwiddie
47	494.2	Bedford County Public Schools	Bedford
48	491.7	Amherst County Public Schools	Amherst
49	490.0	Fredericksburg City Public Schools	Fredericksburg
50	486.3	Rockingham County Public Schools	Harrisonburg
51	485.6	Shenandoah County Public Schools	Woodstock
52	483.2	Norfolk City Public Schools	Norfolk
53	477.6	York County Public Schools	Yorktown
54	475.3	Prince Edward Co Public Schools	Farmville
55	474.0	Alexandria City Public Schools	Alexandria
56	468.9	Roanoke County Public Schools	Roanoke
57	466.5	King William County Public Schools	King William
58	466.3	Madison County Public Schools	Madison
59	466.0	Colonial Hgts City Public Schools	Colonial Hgts
60	461.5	Danville City Public Schools	Danville
60	461.5	Warren County Public Schools	Front Royal
62	457.6	Manassas Park City Public Schools	Manassas Park
63	450.1	Powhatan County Public Schools	Powhatan
64	450.0	Greene County Public Schools	Stanardsville
65	448.0	Page County Public Schools	Luray
66	446.8	Chesapeake City Public Schools	Chesapeake
67	439.0	Greensville County Public Schools	Emporia
68	435.0	Prince George Co Public Schools	Prince George
69	432.8	Botetourt County Public Schools	Fincastle
70	431.1	Newport News City Public Schools	Newport News
71	431.0	Patrick County Public Schools	Stuart
72	430.5	Henry County Public Schools	Collinsville
73	424.2	Giles County Public Schools	Pearisburg
74	423.0	Goochland County Public Schools	Goochland
75	420.6	Floyd County Public Schools	Floyd
76	418.3	Hampton City Public Schools	Hampton
77	415.1	Culpeper County Public Schools	Culpeper
78	414.6	Accomack County Public Schools	Accomac
79	413.2	Wise County Public Schools	Wise
80	411.6	Alleghany County Public Schools	Covington
81	411.1	Roanoke City Public Schools	Roanoke
82	408.2	Carroll County Public Schools	Hillsville
83	407.6	Southampton County Public Schools	Courtland
84	407.4	Falls Church City Public Schools	Falls Church
85	405.4	Buchanan County Public Schools	Grundy
86	400.8	Russell County Public Schools	Lebanon
87	398.5	Frederick County Public Schools	Winchester
88	394.5	Montgomery County Public Schools	Christiansburg
89	393.9	Halifax County Public Schools	Halifax
90	388.6	Hopewell City Public Schools	Hopewell
91	388.1	Loudoun County Public Schools	Leesburg
92	387.3	Bristol City Public Schools	Bristol
93	385.1	Fairfax County Public Schools	Fairfax
94	383.4	Staunton City Public Schools	Staunton
95	376.0	Portsmouth City Public Schools	Portsmouth
96	375.9	Pulaski County Public Schools	Pulaski
97	373.4	Lynchburg City Public Schools	Lynchburg
98	373.0	Martinsville City Public Schools	Martinsville
99	371.6	Dickenson County Public Schools	Clintwood
100	370.6	Pittsylvania County Public Schools	Chatham
101	366.3	Rockbridge County Public Schools	Lexington
102	356.2	Wythe County Public Schools	Wytheville
103	342.0	Lunenburg County Public Schools	Victoria
104	340.2	Charlottesville City Pub Schools	Charlottesville
105	334.3	Arlington County Public Schools	Arlington
106	329.9	Richmond City Public Schools	Richmond
107	324.5	Lee County Public Schools	Jonesville
108	n/a	Amelia County Public Schools	Amelia
108	n/a	Isle of Wight Co Public Schools	Isle Of Wight

Current Spending per Student in FY2003

Rank	Dollars	District Name	City
1	13,334	Arlington County Public Schools	Arlington
2	12,960	Falls Church City Public Schools	Falls Church
3	12,736	Alexandria City Public Schools	Alexandria
4	10,833	Charlottesville City Pub Schools	Charlottesville
5	9,808	Richmond City Public Schools	Richmond
6	9,524	Winchester City Public Schools	Winchester
7	9,488	Fairfax County Public Schools	Fairfax
8	9,477	Loudoun County Public Schools	Leesburg
9	9,202	Fredericksburg City Public Schools	Fredericksburg
10	8,792	Staunton City Public Schools	Staunton
11	8,777	Harrisonburg City Public Schools	Harrisonburg
12	8,635	Williamsburg-James City Co PS	Williamsburg
13	8,491	Manassas City Public Schools	Manassas
14	8,269	Albemarle County Public Schools	Charlottesville
15	8,212	Colonial Hgts City Public Schools	Colonial Hgts
16	8,207	Goochland County Public Schools	Goochland
17	8,109	Northampton County Public Schools	Machipongo
18	8,056	Hopewell City Public Schools	Hopewell
19	8,012	Nelson County Public Schools	Lovingston
20	7,932	Fauquier County Public Schools	Warrenton
21	7,924	Manassas Park City Public Schools	Manassas Park
22	7,883	Martinsville City Public Schools	Martinsville
23	7,877	Bristol City Public Schools	Bristol
24	7,784	Roanoke City Public Schools	Roanoke
25	7,761	Brunswick County Public Schools	Lawrenceville
26	7,686	Lynchburg City Public Schools	Lynchburg
27	7,670	Prince William Co Public Schools	Manassas
28	7,656	Lunenburg County Public Schools	Victoria
29	7,646	Frederick County Public Schools	Winchester
30	7,637	Halifax County Public Schools	Halifax
31	7,626	Danville City Public Schools	Danville
32	7,608	Norfolk City Public Schools	Norfolk
32	7,608	Orange County Public Schools	Orange
34	7,604	Clarke County Public Schools	Berryville
35	7,597	Petersburg City Public Schools	Petersburg
36	7,585	Southampton County Public Schools	Courtland
37	7,570	Madison County Public Schools	Madison
38	7,552	Accomack County Public Schools	Accomac
39	7,551	Alleghany County Public Schools	Covington
40	7,489	Greene County Public Schools	Stanardsville
41	7,472	Lee County Public Schools	Jonesville
42	7,451	Dickenson County Public Schools	Clintwood
43	7,433	Chesapeake City Public Schools	Chesapeake
44	7,431	Montgomery County Public Schools	Christiansburg
45	7,385	Rockbridge County Public Schools	Lexington
46	7,378	Grayson County Public Schools	Independence
47	7,356	Portsmouth City Public Schools	Portsmouth
48	7,339	Essex County Public Schools	Tappahannock
49	7,327	Waynesboro City Public Schools	Waynesboro
50	7,318	Roanoke County Public Schools	Roanoke
51	7,280	Louisa County Public Schools	Mineral
52	7,277	Buchanan County Public Schools	Grundy
53	7,268	Virginia Beach City Public Schls	Virginia Beach
54	7,252	Hampton City Public Schools	Hampton
55	7,220	Newport News City Public Schools	Newport News
56	7,212	Salem City Public Schools	Salem
57	7,155	Rockingham County Public Schools	Harrisonburg
58	7,129	Buckingham County Public Schools	Buckingham
59	7,089	Botetourt County Public Schools	Fincastle
60	7,047	Powhatan County Public Schools	Powhatan
61	6,985	Giles County Public Schools	Pearisburg
62	6,978	Greensville County Public Schools	Emporia
63	6,947	Carroll County Public Schools	Hillsville
64	6,930	Culpeper County Public Schools	Culpeper
65	6,917	Floyd County Public Schools	Floyd
66	6,912	King George County Public Schools	King George
67	6,907	Amelia County Public Schools	Amelia
68	6,891	Radford City Public Schools	Radford
68	6,891	Spotsylvania Co Public Schools	Spotsylvania
70	6,890	King William County Public Schools	King William
71	6,888	Wise County Public Schools	Wise
72	6,875	Dinwiddie County Public Schools	Dinwiddie
73	6,867	Shenandoah County Public Schools	Woodstock
74	6,863	Gloucester County Public Schools	Gloucester
75	6,847	Nottoway County Public Schools	Nottoway
76	6,840	York County Public Schools	Yorktown
77	6,837	Fluvanna County Public Schools	Palmyra
78	6,831	Isle of Wight Co Public Schools	Isle Of Wight
79	6,829	Pulaski County Public Schools	Pulaski
80	6,821	Henry County Public Schools	Collinsville
81	6,818	Augusta County Public Schools	Fishersville
82	6,803	Wythe County Public Schools	Wytheville
83	6,771	Smyth County Public Schools	Marion
84	6,757	Henrico County Public Schools	Richmond
85	6,755	Washington County Public Schools	Abingdon
86	6,744	Franklin County Public Schools	Rocky Mount
87	6,742	Charlotte County Public Schools	Charlotte Ct Hse
88	6,737	Stafford County Public Schools	Stafford
89	6,733	Suffolk City Public Schools	Suffolk
90	6,732	Mecklenburg County Public Schools	Boydton
91	6,711	Chesterfield County Public Schools	Chesterfield
92	6,705	Prince Edward Co Public Schools	Farmville
93	6,678	Caroline County Public Schools	Bowling Green
94	6,660	Tazewell County Public Schools	Tazewell
95	6,601	Amherst County Public Schools	Amherst
96	6,571	New Kent County Public Schools	New Kent
97	6,544	Patrick County Public Schools	Stuart
98	6,539	Scott County Public Schools	Gate City
99	6,530	Prince George Co Public Schools	Prince George
100	6,522	Westmoreland Co Public Schools	Montross
101	6,464	Warren County Public Schools	Front Royal
102	6,445	Campbell County Public Schools	Rustburg
103	6,427	Russell County Public Schools	Lebanon
104	6,348	Hanover County Public Schools	Ashland
105	6,316	Pittsylvania County Public Schools	Chatham
106	6,299	Poquoson City Public Schools	Poquoson
107	6,292	Appomattox County Public Schools	Appomattox
108	6,090	Bedford County Public Schools	Bedford
109	6,085	Page County Public Schools	Luray

Number of Diploma Recipients

Rank	Number	District Name	City
1	10,450	Fairfax County Public Schools	Fairfax
2	4,455	Virginia Beach City Public Schls	Virginia Beach
3	3,292	Chesterfield County Public Schools	Chesterfield
4	3,196	Prince William Co Public Schools	Manassas
5	2,400	Henrico County Public Schools	Richmond
6	2,298	Chesapeake City Public Schools	Chesapeake
7	1,766	Loudoun County Public Schools	Leesburg
8	1,570	Newport News City Public Schools	Newport News
9	1,359	Stafford County Public Schools	Stafford
10	1,348	Norfolk City Public Schools	Norfolk
11	1,279	Hampton City Public Schools	Hampton
12	1,119	Spotsylvania Co Public Schools	Spotsylvania
13	1,060	Hanover County Public Schools	Ashland
14	1,058	Richmond City Public Schools	Richmond
15	929	Roanoke County Public Schools	Roanoke
16	923	Arlington County Public Schools	Arlington
17	835	York County Public Schools	Yorktown
18	762	Albemarle County Public Schools	Charlottesville
19	736	Portsmouth City Public Schools	Portsmouth
20	713	Augusta County Public Schools	Fishersville
21	686	Rockingham County Public Schools	Harrisonburg
22	669	Bedford County Public Schools	Bedford
23	651	Fauquier County Public Schools	Warrenton
24	581	Pittsylvania County Public Schools	Chatham
25	563	Montgomery County Public Schools	Christiansburg
26	548	Frederick County Public Schools	Winchester
27	533	Alexandria City Public Schools	Alexandria
28	531	Suffolk City Public Schools	Suffolk
29	525	Williamsburg-James City Co PS	Williamsburg
30	512	Henry County Public Schools	Collinsville
31	504	Lynchburg City Public Schools	Lynchburg
32	498	Roanoke City Public Schools	Roanoke
33	494	Washington County Public Schools	Abingdon
34	486	Campbell County Public Schools	Rustburg
35	463	Wise County Public Schools	Wise
36	447	Tazewell County Public Schools	Tazewell
37	418	Franklin County Public Schools	Rocky Mount
38	397	Danville City Public Schools	Danville
39	374	Gloucester County Public Schools	Gloucester
40	357	Shenandoah County Public Schools	Woodstock
41	355	Manassas City Public Schools	Manassas
42	347	Halifax County Public Schools	Halifax
43	329	Pulaski County Public Schools	Pulaski
44	313	Botetourt County Public Schools	Fincastle
45	312	Prince George Co Public Schools	Prince George
46	309	Culpeper County Public Schools	Culpeper
47	303	Louisa County Public Schools	Mineral
48	302	Smyth County Public Schools	Marion
49	279	Mecklenburg County Public Schools	Boydton
50	273	Isle of Wight Co Public Schools	Isle Of Wight
50	273	Wythe County Public Schools	Wytheville
52	270	Russell County Public Schools	Lebanon
53	267	Salem City Public Schools	Salem
54	266	Amherst County Public Schools	Amherst
55	261	Warren County Public Schools	Front Royal
56	260	Buchanan County Public Schools	Grundy
57	256	Orange County Public Schools	Orange
58	255	Accomack County Public Schools	Accomac
59	244	Harrisonburg City Public Schools	Harrisonburg
60	237	Petersburg City Public Schools	Petersburg
61	219	Scott County Public Schools	Gate City
62	217	Hopewell City Public Schools	Hopewell
63	216	King George County Public Schools	King George
64	211	Carroll County Public Schools	Hillsville
65	210	Rockbridge County Public Schools	Lexington
66	207	Powhatan County Public Schools	Powhatan
67	206	Page County Public Schools	Luray
68	203	Dinwiddie County Public Schools	Dinwiddie
69	200	Caroline County Public Schools	Bowling Green
70	194	Charlottesville City Pub Schools	Charlottesville
71	189	Dickenson County Public Schools	Clintwood
72	184	Lee County Public Schools	Jonesville
73	183	Fluvanna County Public Schools	Palmyra
74	181	Winchester City Public Schools	Winchester
75	180	Poquoson City Public Schools	Poquoson
76	173	Alleghany County Public Schools	Covington
77	170	Patrick County Public Schools	Stuart
78	169	Staunton City Public Schools	Staunton
79	166	Colonial Hgts City Public Schools	Colonial Hgts
80	162	Waynesboro City Public Schools	Waynesboro
81	158	Martinsville City Public Schools	Martinsville
82	154	Brunswick County Public Schools	Lawrenceville
83	152	Greensville County Public Schools	Emporia
83	152	Southampton County Public Schools	Courtland

85	149	Giles County Public Schools	Pearisburg
86	146	Madison County Public Schools	Madison
87	144	Clarke County Public Schools	Berryville
87	144	Greene County Public Schools	Stanardsville
87	144	New Kent County Public Schools	New Kent
87	144	Nottoway County Public Schools	Nottoway
91	140	Appomattox County Public Schools	Appomattox
92	135	Charlotte County Public Schools	Charlotte Ct Hse
92	135	Westmoreland Co Public Schools	Montross
94	134	Northampton County Public Schools	Machipongo
95	131	Prince Edward Co Public Schools	Farmville
96	130	Goochland County Public Schools	Goochland
97	129	Nelson County Public Schools	Lovingston
98	123	Bristol City Public Schools	Bristol
99	117	Falls Church City Public Schools	Falls Church
100	116	Lunenburg County Public Schools	Victoria
101	115	Floyd County Public Schools	Floyd
101	115	Grayson County Public Schools	Independence
103	114	Fredericksburg City Public Schools	Fredericksburg
104	111	Buckingham County Public Schools	Buckingham
105	110	King William County Public Schools	King William
106	109	Amelia County Public Schools	Amelia
107	105	Essex County Public Schools	Tappahannock
108	102	Radford City Public Schools	Radford
109	91	Manassas Park City Public Schools	Manassas Park

High School Drop-out Rate

Rank	Percent	District Name	City
1	9.7	Hopewell City Public Schools	Hopewell
2	8.3	Buckingham County Public Schools	Buckingham
3	7.9	Caroline County Public Schools	Bowling Green
4	7.5	Petersburg City Public Schools	Petersburg
5	7.4	Brunswick County Public Schools	Lawrenceville
6	7.2	Roanoke City Public Schools	Roanoke
7	7.0	Northampton County Public Schools	Machipongo
8	6.2	Culpeper County Public Schools	Culpeper
9	5.7	Lee County Public Schools	Jonesville
10	5.6	Appomattox County Public Schools	Appomattox
11	5.4	Lunenburg County Public Schools	Victoria
12	5.3	Danville City Public Schools	Danville
13	5.1	Buchanan County Public Schools	Grundy
13	5.1	Nottoway County Public Schools	Nottoway
13	5.1	Prince Edward Co Public Schools	Farmville
16	5.0	Accomack County Public Schools	Accomac
17	4.8	Greene County Public Schools	Stanardsville
18	4.7	Colonial Hgts City Public Schools	Colonial Hgts
19	4.6	Norfolk City Public Schools	Norfolk
20	4.4	Bristol City Public Schools	Bristol
20	4.4	Dinwiddie County Public Schools	Dinwiddie
22	4.3	Chesterfield County Public Schools	Chesterfield
22	4.3	Franklin County Public Schools	Rocky Mount
24	4.2	Alleghany County Public Schools	Covington
25	4.0	Montgomery County Public Schools	Christiansburg
25	4.0	Prince William Co Public Schools	Manassas
27	3.9	Isle of Wight Co Public Schools	Isle Of Wight
27	3.9	Staunton City Public Schools	Staunton
29	3.8	Goochland County Public Schools	Goochland
30	3.7	Alexandria City Public Schools	Alexandria
30	3.7	Amelia County Public Schools	Amelia
30	3.7	Hampton City Public Schools	Hampton
30	3.7	Page County Public Schools	Luray
30	3.7	Winchester City Public Schools	Winchester
35	3.5	Henry County Public Schools	Collinsville
36	3.4	Dickenson County Public Schools	Clintwood
37	3.3	Portsmouth City Public Schools	Portsmouth
37	3.3	Tazewell County Public Schools	Tazewell
39	3.2	Lynchburg City Public Schools	Lynchburg
40	3.1	Essex County Public Schools	Tappahannock
40	3.1	Fluvanna County Public Schools	Palmyra
40	3.1	Frederick County Public Schools	Winchester
40	3.1	Pittsylvania County Public Schools	Chatham
40	3.1	Prince George Co Public Schools	Prince George
40	3.1	Richmond City Public Schools	Richmond
40	3.1	Rockbridge County Public Schools	Lexington
40	3.1	Southampton County Public Schools	Courtland
40	3.1	Suffolk City Public Schools	Suffolk
49	3.0	Arlington County Public Schools	Arlington
49	3.0	Fauquier County Public Schools	Warrenton
49	3.0	Newport News City Public Schools	Newport News
52	2.9	Augusta County Public Schools	Fishersville
52	2.9	Charlottesville City Pub Schools	Charlottesville
52	2.9	Floyd County Public Schools	Floyd
52	2.9	Louisa County Public Schools	Mineral
52	2.9	Rockingham County Public Schools	Harrisonburg
57	2.8	Botetourt County Public Schools	Fincastle
57	2.8	Chesapeake City Public Schools	Chesapeake
57	2.8	Madison County Public Schools	Madison
57	2.8	Warren County Public Schools	Front Royal
57	2.8	Wise County Public Schools	Wise
62	2.7	Fairfax County Public Schools	Fairfax
62	2.7	Pulaski County Public Schools	Pulaski
64	2.6	Amherst County Public Schools	Amherst
64	2.6	Powhatan County Public Schools	Powhatan
64	2.6	Radford City Public Schools	Radford
64	2.6	Shenandoah County Public Schools	Woodstock
64	2.6	Wythe County Public Schools	Wytheville
69	2.5	Charlotte County Public Schools	Charlotte Ct Hse
69	2.5	Mecklenburg County Public Schools	Boydton
69	2.5	Russell County Public Schools	Lebanon
69	2.5	Stafford County Public Schools	Stafford
73	2.4	Carroll County Public Schools	Hillsville
73	2.4	Gloucester County Public Schools	Gloucester
73	2.4	Patrick County Public Schools	Stuart
73	2.4	Washington County Public Schools	Abingdon
77	2.3	Henrico County Public Schools	Richmond
78	2.2	Greensville County Public Schools	Emporia
78	2.2	Spotsylvania Co Public Schools	Spotsylvania
80	2.1	Giles County Public Schools	Pearisburg
81	2.0	Fredericksburg City Public Schools	Fredericksburg
81	2.0	King George County Public Schools	King George
81	2.0	Manassas Park City Public Schools	Manassas Park
81	2.0	Salem City Public Schools	Salem
85	1.9	Clarke County Public Schools	Berryville
86	1.8	Bedford County Public Schools	Bedford
87	1.7	Grayson County Public Schools	Independence
87	1.7	Roanoke County Public Schools	Roanoke
89	1.6	Campbell County Public Schools	Rustburg
89	1.6	New Kent County Public Schools	New Kent
91	1.5	Manassas City Public Schools	Manassas
91	1.5	Waynesboro City Public Schools	Waynesboro
91	1.5	Williamsburg-James City Co PS	Williamsburg
94	1.4	Halifax County Public Schools	Halifax
94	1.4	Martinsville City Public Schools	Martinsville
94	1.4	Nelson County Public Schools	Lovingston
94	1.4	Orange County Public Schools	Orange
94	1.4	Scott County Public Schools	Gate City
99	1.2	Albemarle County Public Schools	Charlottesville
99	1.2	Virginia Beach City Public Schls	Virginia Beach
101	1.1	Loudoun County Public Schools	Leesburg
101	1.1	Poquoson City Public Schools	Poquoson
101	1.1	Westmoreland Co Public Schools	Montross
101	1.1	York County Public Schools	Yorktown
105	0.9	Harrisonburg City Public Schools	Harrisonburg
106	0.8	Smyth County Public Schools	Marion
107	0.7	Hanover County Public Schools	Ashland
108	0.6	King William County Public Schools	King William
109	0.4	Falls Church City Public Schools	Falls Church

Washington

Washington Public School Educational Profile

Category	Value	Category	Value
Schools *(2003-2004)*	2,251	**Diploma Recipients** *(2002-2003)*	58,311
Instructional Level		White, Non-Hispanic	45,918
Primary	1,188	Black, Non-Hispanic	2,306
Middle	358	Asian/Pacific Islander	5,030
High	464	American Indian/Alaskan Native	1,120
Other Level	241	Hispanic	3,937
Curriculum		**High School Drop-out Rate** *(%) (2001-2002)*	7.1
Regular	1,891	White, Non-Hispanic	5.6
Special Education	84	Black, Non-Hispanic	16.8
Vocational	10	Asian/Pacific Islander	6.6
Alternative	266	American Indian/Alaskan Native	15.2
Type		Hispanic	12.3
Magnet	0	**Staff** *(2003-2004)*	
Charter	0	Teachers	52,823.1
Title I Eligible	1,016	Average Salary ($)	45,437
School-wide Title I	486	Librarians/Media Specialists	1,308.7
Students *(2003-2004)*	1,021,349	Guidance Counselors	1,954.3
Gender (%)		**Ratios** *(2003-2004)*	
Male	51.6	Student/Teacher Ratio	19.3 to 1
Female	48.4	Student/Librarian Ratio	780.4 to 1
Race/Ethnicity (%)		Student/Counselor Ratio	522.6 to 1
White, Non-Hispanic	71.5	**College Entrance Exam Scores** *(2005)*	
Black, Non-Hispanic	5.7	Scholastic Aptitude Test (SAT)	
Asian/Pacific Islander	7.9	Participation Rate (%)	55
American Indian/Alaskan Native	2.7	Mean SAT Reasoning Test Verbal Score	532
Hispanic	12.3	Mean SAT Reasoning Test Math Score	534
Classification (%)		American College Testing Program (ACT)	
Individual Education Program (IEP)	10.8	Participation Rate (%)	16
Migrant *(2002-2003)*	0.0	Average Composite Score	22.7
English Language Learner (ELL)	5.7	Average English Score	22.3
Eligible for Free Lunch Program	26.8	Average Math Score	22.4
Eligible for Reduced-Price Lunch Program	8.7	Average Reading Score	23.5
Current Spending *($ per student in FY 2003)*	7,101	Average Science Score	22.3
Instruction	4,270		
Support Services	2,478		

Note: For an explanation of data, please refer to the User's Guide in the front of the book

Washington NAEP 2005 Test Scores

Reading			Mathematics		
Grade/Category	**Value**	**Rank**	**Grade/Category**	**Value**	**Rank**
4th Grade			**4th Grade**		
Average Proficiency	223.5 (1.13)	12/51	Average Proficiency	241.7 (0.92)	12/51
Proficiency by Gender/Race/Ethnicity			Proficiency by Gender/Race/Ethnicity		
Male	218.8 (1.43)	17/51	Male	242.4 (1.13)	16/51
Female	228.2 (1.22)	7/51	Female	241.0 (1.01)	8/51
White, Non-Hispanic	227.9 (1.09)	16/51	White, Non-Hispanic	246.4 (0.95)	19/51
Black, Non-Hispanic	211.7 (2.83)	2/42	Black, Non-Hispanic	230.9 (2.24)	1/42
Asian, Non-Hispanic	229.6 (2.56)	15/27	Asian, Non-Hispanic	244.6 (2.25)	16/25
American Indian, Non-Hispanic	n/a	n/a	American Indian, Non-Hispanic	n/a	n/a
Hispanic	202.0 (2.53)	27/40	Hispanic	223.9 (1.50)	24/41
Proficiency by Class Size			Proficiency by Class Size		
Less than 16 Students	n/a	n/a	Less than 16 Students	n/a	n/a
16 to 18 Students	n/a	n/a	16 to 18 Students	n/a	n/a
19 to 20 Students	n/a	n/a	19 to 20 Students	239.2 (2.83)	21/38
21 to 25 Students	224.6 (1.11)	18/51	21 to 25 Students	242.4 (1.25)	18/51
Greater than 25 Students	223.6 (2.48)	12/36	Greater than 25 Students	242.2 (1.68)	6/33
Percent Attaining Achievement Levels			Percent Attaining Achievement Levels		
Below Basic	30.1 (1.37)	40/51	Below Basic	16.0 (1.07)	34/51
Basic or Above	69.9 (1.37)	12/51	Basic or Above	84.0 (1.07)	17/51
Proficient or Above	35.5 (1.43)	11/51	Proficient or Above	41.6 (1.49)	10/51
Advanced or Above	8.2 (0.88)	11/51	Advanced or Above	6.0 (0.69)	13/51
8th Grade			**8th Grade**		
Average Proficiency	264.7 (1.26)	21/51	Average Proficiency	285.1 (1.02)	8/51
Proficiency by Gender/Race/Ethnicity			Proficiency by Gender/Race/Ethnicity		
Male	259.9 (1.67)	21/51	Male	284.9 (1.28)	11/51
Female	269.4 (1.43)	24/51	Female	285.2 (1.34)	7/51
White, Non-Hispanic	267.9 (1.33)	28/51	White, Non-Hispanic	288.8 (1.00)	22/51
Black, Non-Hispanic	255.0 (4.06)	1/40	Black, Non-Hispanic	265.4 (4.77)	2/41
Asian, Non-Hispanic	269.9 (2.99)	14/24	Asian, Non-Hispanic	293.7 (3.34)	14/23
American Indian, Non-Hispanic	255.4 (5.85)	1/9	American Indian, Non-Hispanic	273.2 (4.27)	2/10
Hispanic	245.3 (3.34)	26/38	Hispanic	262.3 (2.74)	19/38
Proficiency by Parents Highest Level of Ed.			Proficiency by Parents Highest Level of Ed.		
Did Not Finish High School	238.7 (3.18)	42/49	Did Not Finish High School	264.0 (2.99)	15/50
Graduated High School	256.2 (2.02)	21/50	Graduated High School	276.9 (1.74)	3/50
Some Education After High School	269.0 (1.62)	13/50	Some Education After High School	286.9 (1.51)	5/50
Graduated College	273.6 (1.29)	19/50	Graduated College	295.4 (1.30)	4/50
Percent Attaining Achievement Levels			Percent Attaining Achievement Levels		
Below Basic	30.1 (1.37)	40/51	Below Basic	24.7 (1.20)	40/51
Basic or Above	69.9 (1.37)	12/51	Basic or Above	75.3 (1.20)	12/51
Proficient or Above	35.5 (1.43)	11/51	Proficient or Above	36.0 (1.37)	5/51
Advanced or Above	8.2 (0.88)	11/51	Advanced or Above	8.7 (0.83)	4/51

Note: For an explanation of data, please refer to the User's Guide in the front of the book; n/a indicates data not available

Adams County

Othello SD 147
615 E Juniper St • Othello, WA 99344-1463
(509) 488-2659 • http://www.othello.wednet.edu/
Grade Span: KG-12; **Agency Type:** 1
Schools: 5
　3 Primary; 1 Middle; 1 High; 0 Other Level
　5 Regular; 0 Special Education; 0 Vocational; 0 Alternative
　0 Magnet; 0 Charter; 5 Title I Eligible; 4 School-wide Title I
Students: 3,096　(50.6% male; 49.3% female)
　Individual Education Program: 323 (10.4%);
　English Language Learner: 40 (1.3%); Migrant: n/a
　Eligible for Free Lunch Program: 1,823 (58.9%)
　Eligible for Reduced-Price Lunch Program: 504 (16.3%)
Teachers: 168.2 (18.4 to 1)
Librarians/Media Specialists: 5.0 (619.2 to 1)
Guidance Counselors: 5.0 (619.2 to 1)
Current Spending: ($ per student per year):
　Total: $6,786; Instruction: $4,258; Support Services: $2,109
Enrollment, Drop-out Rates and Diploma Recipients by Race/Ethnicity

Category	Total	White	Black	Asian	AIAN	Hisp.
Enrollment (%)	100.0	24.4	0.5	0.5	0.2	74.5
Drop-out Rate (%)	6.3	3.5	0.0	0.0	n/a	7.8
H.S. Diplomas (#)	161	62	1	0	0	98

Asotin County

Clarkston SD 250
1294 Chestnut • Clarkston, WA 99403-2557
(509) 758-2531 • http://jawbone.clarkston.wednet.edu/
Grade Span: PK-12; **Agency Type:** 1
Schools: 9
　5 Primary; 1 Middle; 1 High; 2 Other Level
　6 Regular; 1 Special Education; 0 Vocational; 2 Alternative
　0 Magnet; 0 Charter; 4 Title I Eligible; 3 School-wide Title I
Students: 2,832　(52.1% male; 47.8% female)
　Individual Education Program: 415 (14.7%);
　English Language Learner: 227 (8.0%); Migrant: n/a
　Eligible for Free Lunch Program: 1,001 (35.3%)
　Eligible for Reduced-Price Lunch Program: 238 (8.4%)
Teachers: 134.7 (21.0 to 1)
Librarians/Media Specialists: 2.0 (1,416.0 to 1)
Guidance Counselors: 3.0 (944.0 to 1)
Current Spending: ($ per student per year):
　Total: $7,027; Instruction: $4,280; Support Services: $2,361
Enrollment, Drop-out Rates and Diploma Recipients by Race/Ethnicity

Category	Total	White	Black	Asian	AIAN	Hisp.
Enrollment (%)	100.0	92.8	0.7	0.6	2.7	3.2
Drop-out Rate (%)	10.0	9.9	0.0	0.0	23.3	8.0
H.S. Diplomas (#)	157	150	1	3	0	3

Benton County

Kennewick SD 17
524 S Auburn St • Kennewick, WA 99336-5601
(509) 585-3020 • http://www.ksd.org/ksd.org/htmls/index2.htm
Grade Span: PK-12; **Agency Type:** 1
Schools: 25
　15 Primary; 4 Middle; 5 High; 1 Other Level
　22 Regular; 0 Special Education; 1 Vocational; 2 Alternative
　0 Magnet; 0 Charter; 5 Title I Eligible; 3 School-wide Title I
Students: 14,987　(52.0% male; 47.9% female)
　Individual Education Program: 1,410 (9.4%);
　English Language Learner: 457 (3.0%); Migrant: n/a
　Eligible for Free Lunch Program: 4,289 (28.6%)
　Eligible for Reduced-Price Lunch Program: 1,169 (7.8%)
Teachers: 730.5 (20.5 to 1)
Librarians/Media Specialists: 20.4 (734.7 to 1)
Guidance Counselors: 32.0 (468.3 to 1)
Current Spending: ($ per student per year):
　Total: $6,923; Instruction: $4,353; Support Services: $2,221
Enrollment, Drop-out Rates and Diploma Recipients by Race/Ethnicity

Category	Total	White	Black	Asian	AIAN	Hisp.
Enrollment (%)	100.0	72.9	2.3	2.0	0.5	22.2
Drop-out Rate (%)	5.9	4.4	12.5	4.3	0.0	13.8
H.S. Diplomas (#)	977	824	12	25	2	114

Kiona-Benton SD 52
1107 Grace • Benton City, WA 99320-9704
(509) 588-3717 • http://www.owt.com/kibe/
Grade Span: PK-12; **Agency Type:** 1
Schools: 4
　1 Primary; 2 Middle; 1 High; 0 Other Level
　4 Regular; 0 Special Education; 0 Vocational; 0 Alternative

　0 Magnet; 0 Charter; 3 Title I Eligible; 3 School-wide Title I
Students: 1,656　(51.2% male; 48.7% female)
　Individual Education Program: 205 (12.4%);
　English Language Learner: 68 (4.1%); Migrant: n/a
　Eligible for Free Lunch Program: 569 (34.4%)
　Eligible for Reduced-Price Lunch Program: 167 (10.1%)
Teachers: 82.9 (20.0 to 1)
Librarians/Media Specialists: 2.0 (828.0 to 1)
Guidance Counselors: 3.0 (552.0 to 1)
Current Spending: ($ per student per year):
　Total: $6,858; Instruction: $4,038; Support Services: $2,457
Enrollment, Drop-out Rates and Diploma Recipients by Race/Ethnicity

Category	Total	White	Black	Asian	AIAN	Hisp.
Enrollment (%)	100.0	76.6	0.9	1.3	0.6	20.7
Drop-out Rate (%)	4.8	3.6	0.0	0.0	n/a	11.2
H.S. Diplomas (#)	99	87	0	0	1	11

Prosser SD 116
823 Park Ave • Prosser, WA 99350-1264
(509) 786-3323 • http://www.prosserschools.org/
Grade Span: PK-12; **Agency Type:** 1
Schools: 6
　3 Primary; 1 Middle; 2 High; 0 Other Level
　5 Regular; 0 Special Education; 0 Vocational; 1 Alternative
　0 Magnet; 0 Charter; 5 Title I Eligible; 4 School-wide Title I
Students: 2,864　(50.7% male; 49.2% female)
　Individual Education Program: 267 (9.3%);
　English Language Learner: 24 (0.8%); Migrant: n/a
　Eligible for Free Lunch Program: 1,222 (42.7%)
　Eligible for Reduced-Price Lunch Program: 278 (9.7%)
Teachers: 139.6 (20.5 to 1)
Librarians/Media Specialists: 4.5 (636.4 to 1)
Guidance Counselors: 6.9 (415.1 to 1)
Current Spending: ($ per student per year):
　Total: $7,247; Instruction: $4,186; Support Services: $2,607
Enrollment, Drop-out Rates and Diploma Recipients by Race/Ethnicity

Category	Total	White	Black	Asian	AIAN	Hisp.
Enrollment (%)	100.0	52.4	0.9	1.1	0.2	45.4
Drop-out Rate (%)	2.8	1.8	0.0	0.0	0.0	4.3
H.S. Diplomas (#)	165	103	0	0	0	62

Richland SD 400
615 Snow Ave • Richland, WA 99352-3899
(509) 942-2400 • http://www.rsd.edu/
Grade Span: PK-12; **Agency Type:** 1
Schools: 15
　8 Primary; 3 Middle; 4 High; 0 Other Level
　14 Regular; 0 Special Education; 0 Vocational; 1 Alternative
　0 Magnet; 0 Charter; 7 Title I Eligible; 0 School-wide Title I
Students: 9,790　(51.0% male; 48.9% female)
　Individual Education Program: 1,082 (11.1%);
　English Language Learner: 0 (0.0%); Migrant: n/a
　Eligible for Free Lunch Program: 1,618 (16.5%)
　Eligible for Reduced-Price Lunch Program: 575 (5.9%)
Teachers: 485.7 (20.2 to 1)
Librarians/Media Specialists: 14.0 (699.3 to 1)
Guidance Counselors: 21.9 (447.0 to 1)
Current Spending: ($ per student per year):
　Total: $6,551; Instruction: $3,890; Support Services: $2,320
Enrollment, Drop-out Rates and Diploma Recipients by Race/Ethnicity

Category	Total	White	Black	Asian	AIAN	Hisp.
Enrollment (%)	100.0	85.9	2.7	4.5	0.8	6.0
Drop-out Rate (%)	3.9	3.7	8.6	0.9	16.7	8.5
H.S. Diplomas (#)	743	671	10	40	3	19

Chelan County

Cashmere SD 222
210 S Division St • Cashmere, WA 98815-1133
(509) 782-3355 • http://www.cashmere.wednet.edu/
Grade Span: PK-12; **Agency Type:** 1
Schools: 3
　1 Primary; 1 Middle; 1 High; 0 Other Level
　3 Regular; 0 Special Education; 0 Vocational; 0 Alternative
　0 Magnet; 0 Charter; 2 Title I Eligible; 0 School-wide Title I
Students: 1,516　(51.3% male; 48.6% female)
　Individual Education Program: 119 (7.8%);
　English Language Learner: 985 (65.0%); Migrant: n/a
　Eligible for Free Lunch Program: 460 (30.3%)
　Eligible for Reduced-Price Lunch Program: 194 (12.8%)
Teachers: 78.1 (19.4 to 1)
Librarians/Media Specialists: 1.6 (947.5 to 1)
Guidance Counselors: 2.9 (522.8 to 1)
Current Spending: ($ per student per year):
　Total: $6,593; Instruction: $4,055; Support Services: $2,121

Enrollment, Drop-out Rates and Diploma Recipients by Race/Ethnicity

Category	Total	White	Black	Asian	AIAN	Hisp.
Enrollment (%)	100.0	70.1	0.3	0.6	0.8	28.2
Drop-out Rate (%)	3.6	1.9	n/a	0.0	0.0	10.0
H.S. Diplomas (#)	96	81	0	0	0	15

Wenatchee SD 246

235 Sunset Ave • Wenatchee, WA 98801-1999
(509) 663-8161 • http://home.wsd.wednet.edu/
Grade Span: PK-12; Agency Type: 1
Schools: 16
   7 Primary; 3 Middle; 3 High; 3 Other Level
   13 Regular; 1 Special Education; 0 Vocational; 2 Alternative
   0 Magnet; 0 Charter; 6 Title I Eligible; 3 School-wide Title I
Students: 7,505 (51.0% male; 48.9% female)
   Individual Education Program: 607 (8.1%);
   English Language Learner: 826 (11.0%); Migrant: n/a
   Eligible for Free Lunch Program: 2,797 (37.3%)
   Eligible for Reduced-Price Lunch Program: 564 (7.5%)
Teachers: 367.3 (20.4 to 1)
Librarians/Media Specialists: 10.8 (694.9 to 1)
Guidance Counselors: 15.5 (484.2 to 1)
Current Spending: ($ per student per year):
   Total: $6,602; Instruction: $4,085; Support Services: $2,153

Enrollment, Drop-out Rates and Diploma Recipients by Race/Ethnicity

Category	Total	White	Black	Asian	AIAN	Hisp.
Enrollment (%)	100.0	63.3	0.6	1.3	1.4	33.4
Drop-out Rate (%)	12.2	10.2	66.7	8.3	16.7	17.3
H.S. Diplomas (#)	432	320	0	10	5	97

Clallam County

Port Angeles SD 121

216 E 4th St • Port Angeles, WA 98362-3023
(360) 457-8575 • http://www.pasd.wednet.edu/
Grade Span: PK-12; Agency Type: 1
Schools: 13
   6 Primary; 2 Middle; 3 High; 2 Other Level
   9 Regular; 1 Special Education; 1 Vocational; 2 Alternative
   0 Magnet; 0 Charter; 8 Title I Eligible; 6 School-wide Title I
Students: 4,799 (52.6% male; 47.3% female)
   Individual Education Program: 681 (14.2%);
   English Language Learner: 62 (1.3%); Migrant: n/a
   Eligible for Free Lunch Program: 1,433 (29.9%)
   Eligible for Reduced-Price Lunch Program: 447 (9.3%)
Teachers: 252.0 (19.0 to 1)
Librarians/Media Specialists: 2.8 (1,713.9 to 1)
Guidance Counselors: 4.5 (1,066.4 to 1)
Current Spending: ($ per student per year):
   Total: $7,006; Instruction: $4,334; Support Services: $2,354

Enrollment, Drop-out Rates and Diploma Recipients by Race/Ethnicity

Category	Total	White	Black	Asian	AIAN	Hisp.
Enrollment (%)	100.0	86.4	1.7	2.0	7.8	2.2
Drop-out Rate (%)	3.9	3.7	0.0	10.5	4.8	6.5
H.S. Diplomas (#)	121	104	2	7	5	3

Sequim SD 323

503 N Sequim Ave • Sequim, WA 98382-3161
(360) 582-3260 • http://www.sequimschools.wednet.edu/
Grade Span: PK-12; Agency Type: 1
Schools: 5
   2 Primary; 1 Middle; 1 High; 1 Other Level
   4 Regular; 0 Special Education; 0 Vocational; 1 Alternative
   0 Magnet; 0 Charter; 2 Title I Eligible; 0 School-wide Title I
Students: 2,889 (52.1% male; 47.8% female)
   Individual Education Program: 262 (9.1%);
   English Language Learner: 0 (0.0%); Migrant: n/a
   Eligible for Free Lunch Program: 570 (19.7%)
   Eligible for Reduced-Price Lunch Program: 236 (8.2%)
Teachers: 137.1 (21.1 to 1)
Librarians/Media Specialists: 4.0 (722.3 to 1)
Guidance Counselors: 6.0 (481.5 to 1)
Current Spending: ($ per student per year):
   Total: $6,273; Instruction: $4,031; Support Services: $1,851

Enrollment, Drop-out Rates and Diploma Recipients by Race/Ethnicity

Category	Total	White	Black	Asian	AIAN	Hisp.
Enrollment (%)	100.0	85.7	0.9	3.7	4.6	5.2
Drop-out Rate (%)	2.5	2.4	0.0	0.0	8.2	2.1
H.S. Diplomas (#)	203	180	1	7	7	8

Clark County

Battle Ground SD 119

11104 NE 149th St • Brush Prairie, WA 98606-9565
(360) 885-5302 • http://www.bgsd.k12.wa.us/
Grade Span: PK-12; Agency Type: 1
Schools: 18
   7 Primary; 5 Middle; 3 High; 3 Other Level
   13 Regular; 1 Special Education; 0 Vocational; 4 Alternative
   0 Magnet; 0 Charter; 3 Title I Eligible; 0 School-wide Title I
Students: 12,504 (51.5% male; 48.4% female)
   Individual Education Program: 1,266 (10.1%);
   English Language Learner: 20 (0.2%); Migrant: n/a
   Eligible for Free Lunch Program: 1,941 (15.5%)
   Eligible for Reduced-Price Lunch Program: 1,049 (8.4%)
Teachers: 567.8 (22.0 to 1)
Librarians/Media Specialists: 13.1 (954.5 to 1)
Guidance Counselors: 9.0 (1,389.3 to 1)
Current Spending: ($ per student per year):
   Total: $6,237; Instruction: $3,636; Support Services: $2,281

Enrollment, Drop-out Rates and Diploma Recipients by Race/Ethnicity

Category	Total	White	Black	Asian	AIAN	Hisp.
Enrollment (%)	100.0	92.4	1.0	2.2	1.0	3.5
Drop-out Rate (%)	7.5	7.2	19.4	11.1	12.1	12.0
H.S. Diplomas (#)	843	793	3	17	6	24

Camas SD 117

1919 NE Ione St • Camas, WA 98607-1145
(360) 817-4400 • http://www.camas.wednet.edu/
Grade Span: PK-12; Agency Type: 1
Schools: 7
   5 Primary; 1 Middle; 0 High; 1 Other Level
   7 Regular; 0 Special Education; 0 Vocational; 0 Alternative
   0 Magnet; 0 Charter; 5 Title I Eligible; 0 School-wide Title I
Students: 4,739 (52.3% male; 47.6% female)
   Individual Education Program: 463 (9.8%);
   English Language Learner: 31 (0.7%); Migrant: n/a
   Eligible for Free Lunch Program: 682 (14.4%)
   Eligible for Reduced-Price Lunch Program: 304 (6.4%)
Teachers: 235.8 (20.1 to 1)
Librarians/Media Specialists: 7.0 (677.0 to 1)
Guidance Counselors: 8.3 (571.0 to 1)
Current Spending: ($ per student per year):
   Total: $6,434; Instruction: $3,827; Support Services: $2,300

Enrollment, Drop-out Rates and Diploma Recipients by Race/Ethnicity

Category	Total	White	Black	Asian	AIAN	Hisp.
Enrollment (%)	100.0	89.5	1.6	4.9	1.0	3.0
Drop-out Rate (%)	3.9	3.7	0.0	4.9	20.0	6.9
H.S. Diplomas (#)	203	190	1	5	1	6

Evergreen SD 114

13501 NE 28th St • Vancouver, WA 98668-8910
(360) 604-4005 • http://www.egreen.wednet.edu/
Grade Span: PK-12; Agency Type: 1
Schools: 35
   21 Primary; 6 Middle; 7 High; 1 Other Level
   28 Regular; 1 Special Education; 1 Vocational; 5 Alternative
   0 Magnet; 0 Charter; 12 Title I Eligible; 0 School-wide Title I
Students: 23,979 (51.1% male; 48.8% female)
   Individual Education Program: 2,574 (10.7%);
   English Language Learner: 640 (2.7%); Migrant: n/a
   Eligible for Free Lunch Program: 5,976 (24.9%)
   Eligible for Reduced-Price Lunch Program: 2,516 (10.5%)
Teachers: 1,287.7 (18.6 to 1)
Librarians/Media Specialists: 29.0 (826.9 to 1)
Guidance Counselors: 49.2 (487.4 to 1)
Current Spending: ($ per student per year):
   Total: $6,732; Instruction: $3,942; Support Services: $2,462

Enrollment, Drop-out Rates and Diploma Recipients by Race/Ethnicity

Category	Total	White	Black	Asian	AIAN	Hisp.
Enrollment (%)	100.0	81.6	4.1	7.7	1.1	5.5
Drop-out Rate (%)	6.3	5.8	15.5	4.0	21.3	9.4
H.S. Diplomas (#)	1,147	973	31	101	5	37

Hockinson SD 98

15916 NE 182nd Ave • Brush Prairie, WA 98606-9765
(360) 256-5270
Grade Span: KG-09; Agency Type: 1
Schools: 4
   2 Primary; 1 Middle; 1 High; 0 Other Level
   4 Regular; 0 Special Education; 0 Vocational; 0 Alternative
   0 Magnet; 0 Charter; 0 Title I Eligible; 0 School-wide Title I
Students: 1,742 (52.6% male; 47.3% female)
   Individual Education Program: 157 (9.0%);
   English Language Learner: 0 (0.0%); Migrant: n/a

Eligible for Free Lunch Program: 207 (11.9%)
Eligible for Reduced-Price Lunch Program: 104 (6.0%)
Teachers: 80.2 (21.7 to 1)
Librarians/Media Specialists: 2.0 (871.0 to 1)
Guidance Counselors: 1.0 (1,742.0 to 1)
Current Spending: ($ per student per year):
Total: $5,840; Instruction: $3,571; Support Services: $2,014

Enrollment, Drop-out Rates and Diploma Recipients by Race/Ethnicity

Category	Total	White	Black	Asian	AIAN	Hisp.
Enrollment (%)	100.0	95.9	0.5	1.5	0.1	2.0
Drop-out Rate (%)	n/a	n/a	n/a	n/a	n/a	n/a
H.S. Diplomas (#)	n/a	n/a	n/a	n/a	n/a	n/a

Ridgefield SD 122

2724 S Hillhurst Rd • Ridgefield, WA 98642-9088
(360) 887-0200 • http://www.ridge.k12.wa.us/
Grade Span: KG-12; **Agency Type:** 1
Schools: 4
2 Primary; 1 Middle; 1 High; 0 Other Level
4 Regular; 0 Special Education; 0 Vocational; 0 Alternative
0 Magnet; 0 Charter; 1 Title I Eligible; 0 School-wide Title I
Students: 1,843 (52.5% male; 47.4% female)
Individual Education Program: 187 (10.1%);
English Language Learner: 0 (0.0%); Migrant: n/a
Eligible for Free Lunch Program: 375 (20.3%)
Eligible for Reduced-Price Lunch Program: 146 (7.9%)
Teachers: 83.8 (22.0 to 1)
Librarians/Media Specialists: 1.0 (1,843.0 to 1)
Guidance Counselors: 2.0 (921.5 to 1)
Current Spending: ($ per student per year):
Total: $6,011; Instruction: $3,929; Support Services: $1,720

Enrollment, Drop-out Rates and Diploma Recipients by Race/Ethnicity

Category	Total	White	Black	Asian	AIAN	Hisp.
Enrollment (%)	100.0	90.0	0.8	3.1	1.5	4.6
Drop-out Rate (%)	0.5	0.4	0.0	0.0	10.0	0.0
H.S. Diplomas (#)	108	100	0	3	3	2

Vancouver SD 37

2901 Falk Rd • Vancouver, WA 98661-5683
(360) 313-1200 • http://www.vannet.k12.wa.us/
Grade Span: PK-12; **Agency Type:** 1
Schools: 37
22 Primary; 4 Middle; 6 High; 5 Other Level
33 Regular; 1 Special Education; 0 Vocational; 3 Alternative
0 Magnet; 0 Charter; 16 Title I Eligible; 16 School-wide Title I
Students: 22,119 (51.4% male; 48.5% female)
Individual Education Program: 2,678 (12.1%);
English Language Learner: 114 (0.5%); Migrant: n/a
Eligible for Free Lunch Program: 7,561 (34.2%)
Eligible for Reduced-Price Lunch Program: 2,006 (9.1%)
Teachers: 1,139.5 (19.4 to 1)
Librarians/Media Specialists: 28.0 (790.0 to 1)
Guidance Counselors: 41.2 (536.9 to 1)
Current Spending: ($ per student per year):
Total: $7,075; Instruction: $4,170; Support Services: $2,604

Enrollment, Drop-out Rates and Diploma Recipients by Race/Ethnicity

Category	Total	White	Black	Asian	AIAN	Hisp.
Enrollment (%)	100.0	77.7	5.2	4.9	2.1	10.0
Drop-out Rate (%)	10.5	9.7	16.1	9.6	17.5	16.6
H.S. Diplomas (#)	1,170	996	32	77	15	50

Washougal SD 112-6

2349 B St • Washougal, WA 98671-2497
(360) 954-3000 • http://www.washougal.k12.wa.us/
Grade Span: PK-12; **Agency Type:** 1
Schools: 8
4 Primary; 2 Middle; 2 High; 0 Other Level
7 Regular; 1 Special Education; 0 Vocational; 0 Alternative
0 Magnet; 0 Charter; 3 Title I Eligible; 0 School-wide Title I
Students: 2,775 (51.5% male; 48.4% female)
Individual Education Program: 268 (9.7%);
English Language Learner: n/a; Migrant: n/a
Eligible for Free Lunch Program: 673 (24.3%)
Eligible for Reduced-Price Lunch Program: 200 (7.2%)
Teachers: 136.7 (20.3 to 1)
Librarians/Media Specialists: 1.0 (2,775.0 to 1)
Guidance Counselors: 2.0 (1,387.5 to 1)
Current Spending: ($ per student per year):
Total: $6,701; Instruction: $3,985; Support Services: $2,354

Enrollment, Drop-out Rates and Diploma Recipients by Race/Ethnicity

Category	Total	White	Black	Asian	AIAN	Hisp.
Enrollment (%)	100.0	91.7	1.2	2.4	1.4	3.2
Drop-out Rate (%)	2.9	2.8	0.0	7.7	16.7	0.0
H.S. Diplomas (#)	124	121	0	2	0	1

Kelso SD 458

601 Crawford St • Kelso, WA 98626-4398
(360) 501-1927 • http://www.kelso.wednet.edu/
Grade Span: PK-12; **Agency Type:** 1
Schools: 13
7 Primary; 2 Middle; 2 High; 2 Other Level
12 Regular; 1 Special Education; 0 Vocational; 0 Alternative
0 Magnet; 0 Charter; 3 Title I Eligible; 3 School-wide Title I
Students: 5,250 (51.1% male; 48.8% female)
Individual Education Program: 555 (10.6%);
English Language Learner: 404 (7.7%); Migrant: n/a
Eligible for Free Lunch Program: 1,758 (33.5%)
Eligible for Reduced-Price Lunch Program: 589 (11.2%)
Teachers: 267.3 (19.6 to 1)
Librarians/Media Specialists: 8.8 (596.6 to 1)
Guidance Counselors: 7.4 (709.5 to 1)
Current Spending: ($ per student per year):
Total: $7,040; Instruction: $4,225; Support Services: $2,430

Enrollment, Drop-out Rates and Diploma Recipients by Race/Ethnicity

Category	Total	White	Black	Asian	AIAN	Hisp.
Enrollment (%)	100.0	84.6	1.1	1.5	6.2	6.6
Drop-out Rate (%)	1.8	1.5	5.9	0.0	5.0	1.4
H.S. Diplomas (#)	283	248	2	3	22	8

Longview SD 122

2715 Lilac St • Longview, WA 98632-3596
(360) 575-7016 • http://www.longview.k12.wa.us/
Grade Span: PK-12; **Agency Type:** 1
Schools: 14
10 Primary; 2 Middle; 2 High; 0 Other Level
12 Regular; 2 Special Education; 0 Vocational; 0 Alternative
0 Magnet; 0 Charter; 5 Title I Eligible; 5 School-wide Title I
Students: 7,576 (51.2% male; 48.7% female)
Individual Education Program: 904 (11.9%);
English Language Learner: 510 (6.7%); Migrant: n/a
Eligible for Free Lunch Program: 2,736 (36.1%)
Eligible for Reduced-Price Lunch Program: 523 (6.9%)
Teachers: 376.7 (20.1 to 1)
Librarians/Media Specialists: 11.8 (642.0 to 1)
Guidance Counselors: 18.9 (400.8 to 1)
Current Spending: ($ per student per year):
Total: $7,621; Instruction: $4,530; Support Services: $2,745

Enrollment, Drop-out Rates and Diploma Recipients by Race/Ethnicity

Category	Total	White	Black	Asian	AIAN	Hisp.
Enrollment (%)	100.0	81.0	1.9	3.2	3.5	10.3
Drop-out Rate (%)	11.9	11.3	24.0	8.0	19.2	17.5
H.S. Diplomas (#)	360	319	2	23	4	12

Woodland SD 404

800 3rd St • Woodland, WA 98674-8467
(360) 225-9451 • http://www.woodland.wednet.edu/
Grade Span: PK-12; **Agency Type:** 1
Schools: 6
2 Primary; 1 Middle; 2 High; 1 Other Level
5 Regular; 0 Special Education; 0 Vocational; 1 Alternative
0 Magnet; 0 Charter; 2 Title I Eligible; 0 School-wide Title I
Students: 2,039 (52.5% male; 47.4% female)
Individual Education Program: 198 (9.7%);
English Language Learner: 0 (0.0%); Migrant: n/a
Eligible for Free Lunch Program: 447 (21.9%)
Eligible for Reduced-Price Lunch Program: 211 (10.3%)
Teachers: 97.5 (20.9 to 1)
Librarians/Media Specialists: 3.0 (679.7 to 1)
Guidance Counselors: 3.0 (679.7 to 1)
Current Spending: ($ per student per year):
Total: $6,981; Instruction: $3,948; Support Services: $2,644

Enrollment, Drop-out Rates and Diploma Recipients by Race/Ethnicity

Category	Total	White	Black	Asian	AIAN	Hisp.
Enrollment (%)	100.0	88.0	1.5	1.7	1.4	7.3
Drop-out Rate (%)	6.4	5.5	0.0	0.0	0.0	28.0
H.S. Diplomas (#)	102	97	0	2	0	3

Eastmont SD 206

460 9th St NE • East Wenatchee, WA 98802-4443
(509) 884-7169 • http://www.eastmont.wednet.edu/
Grade Span: KG-12; **Agency Type:** 1
Schools: 10
5 Primary; 1 Middle; 2 High; 2 Other Level
9 Regular; 0 Special Education; 1 Vocational; 0 Alternative
0 Magnet; 0 Charter; 6 Title I Eligible; 1 School-wide Title I
Students: 5,476 (51.1% male; 48.8% female)

Individual Education Program: 607 (11.1%);
English Language Learner: 0 (0.0%); Migrant: n/a
Eligible for Free Lunch Program: 1,712 (31.3%)
Eligible for Reduced-Price Lunch Program: 495 (9.0%)
Teachers: 272.1 (20.1 to 1)
Librarians/Media Specialists: 8.3 (659.8 to 1)
Guidance Counselors: 6.5 (842.5 to 1)
Current Spending: ($ per student per year):
Total: $6,645; Instruction: $4,291; Support Services: $2,009
Enrollment, Drop-out Rates and Diploma Recipients by Race/Ethnicity

Category	Total	White	Black	Asian	AIAN	Hisp.
Enrollment (%)	100.0	69.2	0.8	1.3	1.3	27.5
Drop-out Rate (%)	5.9	3.9	9.1	4.3	18.8	12.4
H.S. Diplomas (#)	343	271	0	3	5	64

Franklin County

North Franklin SD 51
1100 W Clark St • Connell, WA 99326-0829
(509) 234-2021 • http://www.nfsd.k12.wa.us/
Grade Span: PK-12; **Agency Type:** 1
Schools: 8
4 Primary; 1 Middle; 2 High; 1 Other Level
7 Regular; 1 Special Education; 0 Vocational; 0 Alternative
0 Magnet; 0 Charter; 7 Title I Eligible; 4 School-wide Title I
Students: 1,942 (52.4% male; 47.5% female)
Individual Education Program: 188 (9.7%);
English Language Learner: 0 (0.0%); Migrant: n/a
Eligible for Free Lunch Program: 1,130 (58.2%)
Eligible for Reduced-Price Lunch Program: 180 (9.3%)
Teachers: 107.0 (18.1 to 1)
Librarians/Media Specialists: 3.3 (588.5 to 1)
Guidance Counselors: 3.4 (571.2 to 1)
Current Spending: ($ per student per year):
Total: $7,288; Instruction: $4,321; Support Services: $2,613
Enrollment, Drop-out Rates and Diploma Recipients by Race/Ethnicity

Category	Total	White	Black	Asian	AIAN	Hisp.
Enrollment (%)	100.0	38.9	0.5	1.5	0.3	58.8
Drop-out Rate (%)	2.7	1.1	0.0	0.0	0.0	4.4
H.S. Diplomas (#)	112	60	0	1	0	51

Pasco SD 001
1215 W Lewis St • Pasco, WA 99301-5472
(509) 543-6700 • http://www.pasco.wednet.edu/
Grade Span: KG-12; **Agency Type:** 1
Schools: 16
11 Primary; 2 Middle; 2 High; 1 Other Level
14 Regular; 0 Special Education; 0 Vocational; 2 Alternative
0 Magnet; 0 Charter; 14 Title I Eligible; 14 School-wide Title I
Students: 10,477 (51.6% male; 48.3% female)
Individual Education Program: 986 (9.4%);
English Language Learner: 0 (0.0%); Migrant: n/a
Eligible for Free Lunch Program: 5,702 (54.4%)
Eligible for Reduced-Price Lunch Program: 1,061 (10.1%)
Teachers: 533.2 (19.6 to 1)
Librarians/Media Specialists: 11.0 (952.5 to 1)
Guidance Counselors: 20.5 (511.1 to 1)
Current Spending: ($ per student per year):
Total: $7,196; Instruction: $4,255; Support Services: $2,527
Enrollment, Drop-out Rates and Diploma Recipients by Race/Ethnicity

Category	Total	White	Black	Asian	AIAN	Hisp.
Enrollment (%)	100.0	27.6	2.8	1.5	0.5	67.7
Drop-out Rate (%)	6.0	4.4	7.2	3.8	9.1	7.0
H.S. Diplomas (#)	325	175	11	11	2	126

Grant County

Ephrata SD 165
499 C St NW • Ephrata, WA 98823-1690
(509) 754-2474 • http://www.esd165.org/
Grade Span: PK-12; **Agency Type:** 1
Schools: 7
3 Primary; 2 Middle; 2 High; 0 Other Level
6 Regular; 1 Special Education; 0 Vocational; 0 Alternative
0 Magnet; 0 Charter; 4 Title I Eligible; 0 School-wide Title I
Students: 2,278 (51.4% male; 48.5% female)
Individual Education Program: 232 (10.2%);
English Language Learner: 87 (3.8%); Migrant: n/a
Eligible for Free Lunch Program: 625 (27.4%)
Eligible for Reduced-Price Lunch Program: 254 (11.2%)
Teachers: 112.4 (20.3 to 1)
Librarians/Media Specialists: 3.0 (759.3 to 1)
Guidance Counselors: 5.8 (392.8 to 1)
Current Spending: ($ per student per year):
Total: $6,849; Instruction: $3,950; Support Services: $2,588

Enrollment, Drop-out Rates and Diploma Recipients by Race/Ethnicity

Category	Total	White	Black	Asian	AIAN	Hisp.
Enrollment (%)	100.0	79.4	0.8	1.6	0.7	17.4
Drop-out Rate (%)	1.0	0.8	0.0	0.0	0.0	3.1
H.S. Diplomas (#)	163	144	0	3	1	15

Moses Lake SD 161
920 W Ivy Ave • Moses Lake, WA 98837-2047
(509) 766-2650 • http://www.moseslakeschools.org/
Grade Span: PK-12; **Agency Type:** 1
Schools: 12
8 Primary; 2 Middle; 1 High; 1 Other Level
12 Regular; 0 Special Education; 0 Vocational; 0 Alternative
0 Magnet; 0 Charter; 7 Title I Eligible; 3 School-wide Title I
Students: 6,974 (51.3% male; 48.6% female)
Individual Education Program: 643 (9.2%);
English Language Learner: 393 (5.6%); Migrant: n/a
Eligible for Free Lunch Program: 2,845 (40.8%)
Eligible for Reduced-Price Lunch Program: 728 (10.4%)
Teachers: 349.5 (20.0 to 1)
Librarians/Media Specialists: 3.6 (1,937.2 to 1)
Guidance Counselors: 11.6 (601.2 to 1)
Current Spending: ($ per student per year):
Total: $6,694; Instruction: $4,216; Support Services: $2,107
Enrollment, Drop-out Rates and Diploma Recipients by Race/Ethnicity

Category	Total	White	Black	Asian	AIAN	Hisp.
Enrollment (%)	100.0	64.4	2.2	1.5	1.3	30.6
Drop-out Rate (%)	9.2	7.3	26.8	0.0	37.5	13.8
H.S. Diplomas (#)	353	273	2	11	1	66

Quincy SD 144
119 J St SW • Quincy, WA 98848-1330
(509) 787-4571 • http://www.qsd.wednet.edu/
Grade Span: PK-12; **Agency Type:** 1
Schools: 8
3 Primary; 2 Middle; 2 High; 1 Other Level
6 Regular; 1 Special Education; 0 Vocational; 1 Alternative
0 Magnet; 0 Charter; 5 Title I Eligible; 3 School-wide Title I
Students: 2,350 (53.0% male; 46.9% female)
Individual Education Program: 235 (10.0%);
English Language Learner: 32 (1.4%); Migrant: n/a
Eligible for Free Lunch Program: 1,134 (48.3%)
Eligible for Reduced-Price Lunch Program: 273 (11.6%)
Teachers: 134.9 (17.4 to 1)
Librarians/Media Specialists: 1.0 (2,350.0 to 1)
Guidance Counselors: 5.0 (470.0 to 1)
Current Spending: ($ per student per year):
Total: $7,188; Instruction: $4,680; Support Services: $2,144
Enrollment, Drop-out Rates and Diploma Recipients by Race/Ethnicity

Category	Total	White	Black	Asian	AIAN	Hisp.
Enrollment (%)	100.0	29.0	0.2	0.3	0.5	70.0
Drop-out Rate (%)	6.0	2.5	0.0	50.0	n/a	9.0
H.S. Diplomas (#)	117	67	0	0	0	50

Wahluke SD 73
411 E Saddle Mt Dr • Mattawa, WA 99349-0952
(509) 932-4565
Grade Span: PK-12; **Agency Type:** 1
Schools: 5
2 Primary; 1 Middle; 2 High; 0 Other Level
4 Regular; 0 Special Education; 0 Vocational; 1 Alternative
0 Magnet; 0 Charter; 5 Title I Eligible; 4 School-wide Title I
Students: 1,754 (51.6% male; 48.3% female)
Individual Education Program: 181 (10.3%);
English Language Learner: 0 (0.0%); Migrant: n/a
Eligible for Free Lunch Program: 1,281 (73.0%)
Eligible for Reduced-Price Lunch Program: 190 (10.8%)
Teachers: 100.8 (17.4 to 1)
Librarians/Media Specialists: 2.0 (877.0 to 1)
Guidance Counselors: 4.3 (407.9 to 1)
Current Spending: ($ per student per year):
Total: $7,649; Instruction: $4,708; Support Services: $2,538
Enrollment, Drop-out Rates and Diploma Recipients by Race/Ethnicity

Category	Total	White	Black	Asian	AIAN	Hisp.
Enrollment (%)	100.0	12.5	0.0	0.4	0.7	86.3
Drop-out Rate (%)	8.9	1.0	n/a	0.0	0.0	12.0
H.S. Diplomas (#)	72	31	0	0	0	41

Grays Harbor County

Aberdeen SD 5
216 N G St • Aberdeen, WA 98520-5297
(360) 538-2006 • http://www.asd5.org/
Grade Span: PK-12; **Agency Type:** 1
Schools: 12

7 Primary; 1 Middle; 2 High; 2 Other Level
11 Regular; 0 Special Education; 0 Vocational; 1 Alternative
0 Magnet; 0 Charter; 7 Title I Eligible; 7 School-wide Title I
Students: 4,140   (51.2% male; 48.7% female)
   Individual Education Program: 492 (11.9%)
   English Language Learner: 619 (15.0%); Migrant: n/a
   Eligible for Free Lunch Program: 1,889 (45.6%)
   Eligible for Reduced-Price Lunch Program: 409 (9.9%)
Teachers: 217.5 (19.0 to 1)
Librarians/Media Specialists: 2.0 (2,070.0 to 1)
Guidance Counselors: 11.0 (376.4 to 1)
Current Spending: ($ per student per year):
   Total: $7,142; Instruction: $4,428; Support Services: $2,269
Enrollment, Drop-out Rates and Diploma Recipients by Race/Ethnicity

Category	Total	White	Black	Asian	AIAN	Hisp.
Enrollment (%)	100.0	75.0	1.4	4.4	7.1	12.1
Drop-out Rate (%)	11.9	11.2	18.8	12.7	15.3	14.4
H.S. Diplomas (#)	273	230	4	10	23	6

Elma SD 68
1235 Monte Elma Rd • Elma, WA 98541-9038
(360) 482-2822 • http://wonders.eburg.wednet.edu/
Grade Span: KG-12; **Agency Type:** 1
Schools: 4
1 Primary; 1 Middle; 2 High; 0 Other Level
3 Regular; 0 Special Education; 0 Vocational; 1 Alternative
0 Magnet; 0 Charter; 1 Title I Eligible; 1 School-wide Title I
Students: 1,912   (51.8% male; 48.1% female)
   Individual Education Program: 216 (11.3%)
   English Language Learner: 119 (6.2%); Migrant: n/a
   Eligible for Free Lunch Program: 592 (31.0%)
   Eligible for Reduced-Price Lunch Program: 179 (9.4%)
Teachers: 99.4 (19.2 to 1)
Librarians/Media Specialists: 0.0 (n/a to 1)
Guidance Counselors: 4.0 (478.0 to 1)
Current Spending: ($ per student per year):
   Total: $6,929; Instruction: $4,409; Support Services: $2,138
Enrollment, Drop-out Rates and Diploma Recipients by Race/Ethnicity

Category	Total	White	Black	Asian	AIAN	Hisp.
Enrollment (%)	100.0	86.7	1.4	1.6	4.6	5.8
Drop-out Rate (%)	12.0	12.1	0.0	20.0	7.9	10.7
H.S. Diplomas (#)	171	149	2	5	7	8

Hoquiam SD 28
305 Simpson Ave • Hoquiam, WA 98550-2419
(360) 538-8200 • http://www.hoquiam.k12.wa.us/
Grade Span: KG-12; **Agency Type:** 1
Schools: 6
4 Primary; 1 Middle; 1 High; 0 Other Level
6 Regular; 0 Special Education; 0 Vocational; 0 Alternative
0 Magnet; 0 Charter; 5 Title I Eligible; 5 School-wide Title I
Students: 2,128   (53.1% male; 46.8% female)
   Individual Education Program: 211 (9.9%)
   English Language Learner: 31 (1.5%); Migrant: n/a
   Eligible for Free Lunch Program: 897 (42.2%)
   Eligible for Reduced-Price Lunch Program: 242 (11.4%)
Teachers: 106.0 (20.1 to 1)
Librarians/Media Specialists: 1.0 (2,128.0 to 1)
Guidance Counselors: 3.0 (709.3 to 1)
Current Spending: ($ per student per year):
   Total: $7,499; Instruction: $4,451; Support Services: $2,583
Enrollment, Drop-out Rates and Diploma Recipients by Race/Ethnicity

Category	Total	White	Black	Asian	AIAN	Hisp.
Enrollment (%)	100.0	80.5	1.0	2.1	6.9	9.5
Drop-out Rate (%)	9.7	10.0	40.0	5.3	5.3	7.0
H.S. Diplomas (#)	114	96	1	6	3	8

Island County

Oak Harbor SD 201
350 S Oak Harbor St • Oak Harbor, WA 98277-5015
(360) 279-5006 • http://www.ohsd.net/
Grade Span: PK-12; **Agency Type:** 1
Schools: 13
6 Primary; 2 Middle; 3 High; 2 Other Level
10 Regular; 2 Special Education; 0 Vocational; 1 Alternative
0 Magnet; 0 Charter; 4 Title I Eligible; 0 School-wide Title I
Students: 6,257   (52.6% male; 47.3% female)
   Individual Education Program: 580 (9.3%)
   English Language Learner: 0 (0.0%); Migrant: n/a
   Eligible for Free Lunch Program: 1,092 (17.5%)
   Eligible for Reduced-Price Lunch Program: 739 (11.8%)
Teachers: 307.4 (20.4 to 1)
Librarians/Media Specialists: 8.8 (711.0 to 1)
Guidance Counselors: 13.9 (450.1 to 1)

Current Spending: ($ per student per year):
   Total: $6,442; Instruction: $4,013; Support Services: $2,148
Enrollment, Drop-out Rates and Diploma Recipients by Race/Ethnicity

Category	Total	White	Black	Asian	AIAN	Hisp.
Enrollment (%)	100.0	72.0	7.3	13.8	1.3	5.6
Drop-out Rate (%)	10.5	10.3	16.7	11.1	6.7	6.9
H.S. Diplomas (#)	378	284	8	64	3	19

South Whidbey SD 206
721 Camano Ave • Langley, WA 98260-9577
(360) 221-6100 • http://www.islandweb.org/schools/swsd.htm
Grade Span: PK-12; **Agency Type:** 1
Schools: 7
2 Primary; 1 Middle; 2 High; 2 Other Level
4 Regular; 1 Special Education; 0 Vocational; 2 Alternative
0 Magnet; 0 Charter; 2 Title I Eligible; 0 School-wide Title I
Students: 2,284   (49.4% male; 50.5% female)
   Individual Education Program: 219 (9.6%)
   English Language Learner: 58 (2.5%); Migrant: n/a
   Eligible for Free Lunch Program: 308 (13.5%)
   Eligible for Reduced-Price Lunch Program: 122 (5.3%)
Teachers: 116.7 (19.6 to 1)
Librarians/Media Specialists: 3.2 (713.8 to 1)
Guidance Counselors: 5.2 (439.2 to 1)
Current Spending: ($ per student per year):
   Total: $6,990; Instruction: $4,184; Support Services: $2,526
Enrollment, Drop-out Rates and Diploma Recipients by Race/Ethnicity

Category	Total	White	Black	Asian	AIAN	Hisp.
Enrollment (%)	100.0	91.2	1.1	3.4	1.8	2.5
Drop-out Rate (%)	6.9	6.7	16.7	0.0	0.0	23.8
H.S. Diplomas (#)	168	162	1	4	0	1

Jefferson County

Port Townsend SD 50
450 Fir St Lincoln Bldg • Port Townsend, WA 98368-6441
(360) 379-4501 • http://www.ptsd.wednet.edu/
Grade Span: PK-12; **Agency Type:** 1
Schools: 5
2 Primary; 1 Middle; 0 High; 2 Other Level
4 Regular; 0 Special Education; 0 Vocational; 1 Alternative
0 Magnet; 0 Charter; 2 Title I Eligible; 0 School-wide Title I
Students: 1,637   (50.8% male; 49.1% female)
   Individual Education Program: 172 (10.5%)
   English Language Learner: 0 (0.0%); Migrant: n/a
   Eligible for Free Lunch Program: 419 (25.6%)
   Eligible for Reduced-Price Lunch Program: 209 (12.8%)
Teachers: 83.8 (19.5 to 1)
Librarians/Media Specialists: 2.8 (584.6 to 1)
Guidance Counselors: 4.4 (372.0 to 1)
Current Spending: ($ per student per year):
   Total: $7,041; Instruction: $4,284; Support Services: $2,293
Enrollment, Drop-out Rates and Diploma Recipients by Race/Ethnicity

Category	Total	White	Black	Asian	AIAN	Hisp.
Enrollment (%)	100.0	88.3	1.8	3.7	3.2	2.9
Drop-out Rate (%)	2.2	2.2	0.0	0.0	7.7	0.0
H.S. Diplomas (#)	161	154	1	3	3	0

King County

Auburn SD 408
915 4th St NE • Auburn, WA 98002-4499
(253) 931-4914 • http://www.auburn.wednet.edu/
Grade Span: PK-12; **Agency Type:** 1
Schools: 20
12 Primary; 4 Middle; 3 High; 1 Other Level
18 Regular; 1 Special Education; 0 Vocational; 1 Alternative
0 Magnet; 0 Charter; 9 Title I Eligible; 5 School-wide Title I
Students: 13,910   (51.4% male; 48.5% female)
   Individual Education Program: 1,263 (9.1%)
   English Language Learner: 223 (1.6%); Migrant: n/a
   Eligible for Free Lunch Program: 4,145 (29.8%)
   Eligible for Reduced-Price Lunch Program: 1,276 (9.2%)
Teachers: 707.0 (19.7 to 1)
Librarians/Media Specialists: 18.0 (772.8 to 1)
Guidance Counselors: 32.1 (433.3 to 1)
Current Spending: ($ per student per year):
   Total: $6,540; Instruction: $4,052; Support Services: $2,152
Enrollment, Drop-out Rates and Diploma Recipients by Race/Ethnicity

Category	Total	White	Black	Asian	AIAN	Hisp.
Enrollment (%)	100.0	71.7	5.5	7.9	4.4	10.5
Drop-out Rate (%)	4.2	3.6	6.9	2.5	16.1	4.9
H.S. Diplomas (#)	836	717	19	50	16	34

Bellevue SD 405

12111 NE 1st St • Bellevue, WA 98005-3183
(425) 456-4172 • http://belnet.bellevue.k12.wa.us/
Grade Span: PK-12; **Agency Type:** 1
Schools: 32
  16 Primary; 6 Middle; 7 High; 3 Other Level
  26 Regular; 1 Special Education; 0 Vocational; 5 Alternative
  0 Magnet; 0 Charter; 10 Title I Eligible; 3 School-wide Title I
Students: 16,125 (52.0% male; 47.9% female)
  Individual Education Program: 1,412 (8.8%);
  English Language Learner: 497 (3.1%); Migrant: n/a
  Eligible for Free Lunch Program: 2,046 (12.7%)
  Eligible for Reduced-Price Lunch Program: 749 (4.6%)
Teachers: 863.3 (18.7 to 1)
Librarians/Media Specialists: 21.0 (767.9 to 1)
Guidance Counselors: 32.2 (500.8 to 1)
Current Spending: ($ per student per year):
  Total: $7,395; Instruction: $4,433; Support Services: $2,606
Enrollment, Drop-out Rates and Diploma Recipients by Race/Ethnicity

Category	Total	White	Black	Asian	AIAN	Hisp.
Enrollment (%)	100.0	66.0	2.5	22.9	0.4	8.2
Drop-out Rate (%)	2.5	1.0	2.6	1.3	0.0	19.9
H.S. Diplomas (#)	1,090	773	33	253	1	30

Enumclaw SD 216

2929 Mcdougall Ave • Enumclaw, WA 98022-7499
(360) 802-7100 • http://www.enumclaw.wednet.edu/
Grade Span: PK-12; **Agency Type:** 1
Schools: 9
  6 Primary; 2 Middle; 1 High; 0 Other Level
  9 Regular; 0 Special Education; 0 Vocational; 0 Alternative
  0 Magnet; 0 Charter; 3 Title I Eligible; 0 School-wide Title I
Students: 4,985 (51.6% male; 48.3% female)
  Individual Education Program: 533 (10.7%);
  English Language Learner: 0 (0.0%); Migrant: n/a
  Eligible for Free Lunch Program: 721 (14.5%)
  Eligible for Reduced-Price Lunch Program: 276 (5.5%)
Teachers: 248.8 (20.0 to 1)
Librarians/Media Specialists: 4.4 (1,133.0 to 1)
Guidance Counselors: 12.0 (415.4 to 1)
Current Spending: ($ per student per year):
  Total: $6,885; Instruction: $4,112; Support Services: $2,431
Enrollment, Drop-out Rates and Diploma Recipients by Race/Ethnicity

Category	Total	White	Black	Asian	AIAN	Hisp.
Enrollment (%)	100.0	91.1	0.8	1.4	1.6	5.2
Drop-out Rate (%)	1.3	1.2	0.0	0.0	0.0	5.1
H.S. Diplomas (#)	316	299	3	5	2	7

Federal Way SD 210

31405 18th Ave S • Federal Way, WA 98003-5433
(253) 945-2000 • http://www.fwsd.wednet.edu/
Grade Span: PK-12; **Agency Type:** 1
Schools: 46
  24 Primary; 6 Middle; 7 High; 9 Other Level
  34 Regular; 3 Special Education; 0 Vocational; 9 Alternative
  0 Magnet; 0 Charter; 11 Title I Eligible; 7 School-wide Title I
Students: 22,538 (51.6% male; 48.3% female)
  Individual Education Program: 2,422 (10.7%);
  English Language Learner: 0 (0.0%); Migrant: n/a
  Eligible for Free Lunch Program: 5,996 (26.6%)
  Eligible for Reduced-Price Lunch Program: 2,311 (10.3%)
Teachers: 1,125.6 (20.0 to 1)
Librarians/Media Specialists: 31.4 (717.8 to 1)
Guidance Counselors: 38.1 (591.5 to 1)
Current Spending: ($ per student per year):
  Total: $6,548; Instruction: $4,053; Support Services: $2,149
Enrollment, Drop-out Rates and Diploma Recipients by Race/Ethnicity

Category	Total	White	Black	Asian	AIAN	Hisp.
Enrollment (%)	100.0	57.4	13.0	16.7	1.4	11.6
Drop-out Rate (%)	5.9	4.9	11.7	4.3	6.5	10.6
H.S. Diplomas (#)	1,151	805	100	188	11	47

Highline SD 401

15675 Ambaum Bldv SW • Seattle, WA 98166-0100
(206) 433-2217 • http://www.hsd401.org/
Grade Span: KG-12; **Agency Type:** 1
Schools: 32
  22 Primary; 4 Middle; 6 High; 0 Other Level
  30 Regular; 0 Special Education; 1 Vocational; 1 Alternative
  0 Magnet; 0 Charter; 22 Title I Eligible; 17 School-wide Title I
Students: 17,711 (51.4% male; 48.5% female)
  Individual Education Program: 1,928 (10.9%);
  English Language Learner: 3,468 (19.6%); Migrant: n/a
  Eligible for Free Lunch Program: 7,788 (44.0%)
  Eligible for Reduced-Price Lunch Program: 1,928 (10.9%)

Teachers: 937.6 (18.9 to 1)
Librarians/Media Specialists: 32.0 (553.5 to 1)
Guidance Counselors: 45.1 (392.7 to 1)
Current Spending: ($ per student per year):
  Total: $7,417; Instruction: $4,348; Support Services: $2,743
Enrollment, Drop-out Rates and Diploma Recipients by Race/Ethnicity

Category	Total	White	Black	Asian	AIAN	Hisp.
Enrollment (%)	100.0	43.7	13.6	20.8	2.2	19.8
Drop-out Rate (%)	10.0	7.7	14.9	9.1	20.7	16.5
H.S. Diplomas (#)	984	625	58	215	16	70

Issaquah SD 411

565 NW Holly St • Issaquah, WA 98027-2899
(425) 837-7002 • http://www.issaquah.wednet.edu/
Grade Span: PK-12; **Agency Type:** 1
Schools: 23
  12 Primary; 4 Middle; 5 High; 2 Other Level
  21 Regular; 1 Special Education; 0 Vocational; 1 Alternative
  0 Magnet; 0 Charter; 7 Title I Eligible; 0 School-wide Title I
Students: 15,146 (51.8% male; 48.1% female)
  Individual Education Program: 1,464 (9.7%);
  English Language Learner: 0 (0.0%); Migrant: n/a
  Eligible for Free Lunch Program: 563 (3.7%)
  Eligible for Reduced-Price Lunch Program: 319 (2.1%)
Teachers: 729.5 (20.8 to 1)
Librarians/Media Specialists: 20.0 (757.3 to 1)
Guidance Counselors: 25.9 (584.8 to 1)
Current Spending: ($ per student per year):
  Total: $6,629; Instruction: $3,908; Support Services: $2,343
Enrollment, Drop-out Rates and Diploma Recipients by Race/Ethnicity

Category	Total	White	Black	Asian	AIAN	Hisp.
Enrollment (%)	100.0	80.5	1.8	13.4	0.7	3.6
Drop-out Rate (%)	6.6	5.0	42.0	3.3	52.3	21.9
H.S. Diplomas (#)	896	769	11	97	3	16

Kent SD 415

12033 SE 256th St • Kent, WA 98031-6643
(253) 373-7200 • http://www.kent.wednet.edu/
Grade Span: PK-12; **Agency Type:** 1
Schools: 42
  28 Primary; 7 Middle; 6 High; 1 Other Level
  39 Regular; 0 Special Education; 0 Vocational; 3 Alternative
  0 Magnet; 0 Charter; 15 Title I Eligible; 13 School-wide Title I
Students: 26,860 (51.9% male; 48.0% female)
  Individual Education Program: 2,919 (10.9%);
  English Language Learner: 3,419 (12.7%); Migrant: n/a
  Eligible for Free Lunch Program: 6,461 (24.1%)
  Eligible for Reduced-Price Lunch Program: 2,234 (8.3%)
Teachers: 1,371.4 (19.6 to 1)
Librarians/Media Specialists: 25.3 (1,061.7 to 1)
Guidance Counselors: 49.8 (539.4 to 1)
Current Spending: ($ per student per year):
  Total: $6,736; Instruction: $4,097; Support Services: $2,302
Enrollment, Drop-out Rates and Diploma Recipients by Race/Ethnicity

Category	Total	White	Black	Asian	AIAN	Hisp.
Enrollment (%)	100.0	64.9	10.4	15.4	1.2	8.1
Drop-out Rate (%)	2.7	2.3	5.7	1.9	5.6	4.8
H.S. Diplomas (#)	1,535	1,122	114	228	13	58

Lake Washington SD 414

16250 NE 74th St • Redmond, WA 98052-7817
(425) 702-3257 • http://www.lkwash.wednet.edu/
Grade Span: PK-12; **Agency Type:** 1
Schools: 49
  29 Primary; 9 Middle; 8 High; 3 Other Level
  37 Regular; 1 Special Education; 0 Vocational; 11 Alternative
  0 Magnet; 0 Charter; 10 Title I Eligible; 0 School-wide Title I
Students: 24,144 (52.0% male; 47.9% female)
  Individual Education Program: 2,050 (8.5%);
  English Language Learner: 2,074 (8.6%); Migrant: n/a
  Eligible for Free Lunch Program: 2,476 (10.3%)
  Eligible for Reduced-Price Lunch Program: 760 (3.1%)
Teachers: 1,186.7 (20.3 to 1)
Librarians/Media Specialists: 36.8 (656.1 to 1)
Guidance Counselors: 44.2 (546.2 to 1)
Current Spending: ($ per student per year):
  Total: $6,473; Instruction: $4,048; Support Services: $2,116
Enrollment, Drop-out Rates and Diploma Recipients by Race/Ethnicity

Category	Total	White	Black	Asian	AIAN	Hisp.
Enrollment (%)	100.0	77.9	2.6	12.5	0.8	6.2
Drop-out Rate (%)	1.8	1.7	1.4	0.8	6.1	4.2
H.S. Diplomas (#)	1,651	1,386	32	171	9	53

Mercer Island SD 400

4160 86th Ave SE • Mercer Island, WA 98040-4196
(206) 236-3300 • http://www.misd.wednet.edu/
Grade Span: KG-12; **Agency Type:** 1
Schools: 6
    4 Primary; 1 Middle; 1 High; 0 Other Level
    5 Regular; 1 Special Education; 0 Vocational; 0 Alternative
    0 Magnet; 0 Charter; 2 Title I Eligible; 0 School-wide Title I
Students: 4,163   (52.0% male; 47.9% female)
    Individual Education Program: 365 (8.8%);
    English Language Learner: 0 (0.0%); Migrant: n/a
    Eligible for Free Lunch Program: 36 (0.9%)
    Eligible for Reduced-Price Lunch Program: 32 (0.8%)
Teachers: 207.5 (20.1 to 1)
Librarians/Media Specialists: 5.0 (832.6 to 1)
Guidance Counselors: 7.4 (562.6 to 1)
Current Spending: ($ per student per year):
    Total: $7,260; Instruction: $3,894; Support Services: $2,901
Enrollment, Drop-out Rates and Diploma Recipients by Race/Ethnicity

Category	Total	White	Black	Asian	AIAN	Hisp.
Enrollment (%)	100.0	79.1	1.3	17.7	0.3	1.7
Drop-out Rate (%)	0.7	0.5	4.0	0.4	0.0	10.0
H.S. Diplomas (#)	330	268	8	50	1	3

Northshore SD 417

18315 Bothell Way NE • Bothell, WA 98011-1983
(425) 489-6353 • http://www.nsd.org/
Grade Span: PK-12; **Agency Type:** 1
Schools: 35
    21 Primary; 7 Middle; 5 High; 2 Other Level
    31 Regular; 1 Special Education; 0 Vocational; 3 Alternative
    0 Magnet; 0 Charter; 11 Title I Eligible; 0 School-wide Title I
Students: 20,088   (51.8% male; 48.1% female)
    Individual Education Program: 2,365 (11.8%);
    English Language Learner: 0 (0.0%); Migrant: n/a
    Eligible for Free Lunch Program: 1,482 (7.4%)
    Eligible for Reduced-Price Lunch Program: 648 (3.2%)
Teachers: 1,012.2 (19.8 to 1)
Librarians/Media Specialists: 32.6 (616.2 to 1)
Guidance Counselors: 30.0 (669.6 to 1)
Current Spending: ($ per student per year):
    Total: $7,084; Instruction: $4,308; Support Services: $2,446
Enrollment, Drop-out Rates and Diploma Recipients by Race/Ethnicity

Category	Total	White	Black	Asian	AIAN	Hisp.
Enrollment (%)	100.0	80.8	2.5	9.8	1.1	5.8
Drop-out Rate (%)	1.3	1.2	2.8	0.4	6.3	2.5
H.S. Diplomas (#)	1,413	1,247	18	96	12	40

Renton SD 403

Kohlwes Educ Ctr 300 SW 7th • Renton, WA 98055-2307
(425) 204-2340 • http://www.renton.wednet.edu/
Grade Span: PK-12; **Agency Type:** 1
Schools: 26
    15 Primary; 3 Middle; 5 High; 3 Other Level
    20 Regular; 4 Special Education; 0 Vocational; 2 Alternative
    0 Magnet; 0 Charter; 10 Title I Eligible; 3 School-wide Title I
Students: 13,280   (51.6% male; 48.3% female)
    Individual Education Program: 1,482 (11.2%);
    English Language Learner: 76 (0.6%); Migrant: n/a
    Eligible for Free Lunch Program: 4,132 (31.1%)
    Eligible for Reduced-Price Lunch Program: 1,387 (10.4%)
Teachers: 663.6 (20.0 to 1)
Librarians/Media Specialists: 19.9 (667.3 to 1)
Guidance Counselors: 29.8 (445.6 to 1)
Current Spending: ($ per student per year):
    Total: $6,732; Instruction: $4,004; Support Services: $2,417
Enrollment, Drop-out Rates and Diploma Recipients by Race/Ethnicity

Category	Total	White	Black	Asian	AIAN	Hisp.
Enrollment (%)	100.0	48.1	18.4	21.2	1.4	10.9
Drop-out Rate (%)	14.8	11.5	24.4	10.7	28.8	27.4
H.S. Diplomas (#)	651	357	101	148	15	30

Riverview Special Services

32240 NE 50th St • Carnation, WA 98014-6332
(425) 844-4504 • http://www.riverview.wednet.edu/
Grade Span: PK-12; **Agency Type:** 1
Schools: 8
    4 Primary; 1 Middle; 2 High; 1 Other Level
    6 Regular; 0 Special Education; 0 Vocational; 2 Alternative
    0 Magnet; 0 Charter; 2 Title I Eligible; 0 School-wide Title I
Students: 2,914   (50.9% male; 49.0% female)
    Individual Education Program: 304 (10.4%);
    English Language Learner: 0 (0.0%); Migrant: n/a
    Eligible for Free Lunch Program: 227 (7.8%)
    Eligible for Reduced-Price Lunch Program: 127 (4.4%)

Teachers: 148.4 (19.6 to 1)
Librarians/Media Specialists: 5.0 (582.8 to 1)
Guidance Counselors: 5.4 (539.6 to 1)
Current Spending: ($ per student per year):
    Total: $6,794; Instruction: $3,982; Support Services: $2,404
Enrollment, Drop-out Rates and Diploma Recipients by Race/Ethnicity

Category	Total	White	Black	Asian	AIAN	Hisp.
Enrollment (%)	100.0	90.0	0.6	3.0	1.2	5.2
Drop-out Rate (%)	1.9	1.2	0.0	8.3	12.5	8.1
H.S. Diplomas (#)	150	135	0	3	4	8

Seattle SD 1

815 4th Ave N • Seattle, WA 98109-3902
(206) 252-0100 • http://www.seattleschools.org/area/main/index.dxml
Grade Span: PK-12; **Agency Type:** 1
Schools: 129
    72 Primary; 11 Middle; 17 High; 29 Other Level
    88 Regular; 8 Special Education; 0 Vocational; 33 Alternative
    0 Magnet; 0 Charter; 42 Title I Eligible; 39 School-wide Title I
Students: 47,588   (51.3% male; 48.6% female)
    Individual Education Program: 5,362 (11.3%);
    English Language Learner: 0 (0.0%); Migrant: n/a
    Eligible for Free Lunch Program: 15,731 (33.1%)
    Eligible for Reduced-Price Lunch Program: 3,188 (6.7%)
Teachers: 2,577.3 (18.5 to 1)
Librarians/Media Specialists: 69.4 (685.7 to 1)
Guidance Counselors: 83.5 (569.9 to 1)
Current Spending: ($ per student per year):
    Total: $8,649; Instruction: $5,028; Support Services: $3,319
Enrollment, Drop-out Rates and Diploma Recipients by Race/Ethnicity

Category	Total	White	Black	Asian	AIAN	Hisp.
Enrollment (%)	100.0	40.7	22.8	23.0	2.4	11.2
Drop-out Rate (%)	24.4	17.0	40.3	18.0	43.6	28.2
H.S. Diplomas (#)	2,629	1,046	542	779	60	202

Shoreline SD 412

18560 1st Ave NE • Shoreline, WA 98155-2118
(206) 361-4203 • http://www.shorelineschools.org/
Grade Span: PK-12; **Agency Type:** 1
Schools: 21
    13 Primary; 2 Middle; 4 High; 2 Other Level
    16 Regular; 2 Special Education; 0 Vocational; 3 Alternative
    0 Magnet; 0 Charter; 7 Title I Eligible; 0 School-wide Title I
Students: 10,010   (52.2% male; 47.7% female)
    Individual Education Program: 1,175 (11.7%);
    English Language Learner: 280 (2.8%); Migrant: n/a
    Eligible for Free Lunch Program: 1,328 (13.3%)
    Eligible for Reduced-Price Lunch Program: 567 (5.7%)
Teachers: 530.9 (18.9 to 1)
Librarians/Media Specialists: 16.2 (617.9 to 1)
Guidance Counselors: 14.1 (709.9 to 1)
Current Spending: ($ per student per year):
    Total: $7,200; Instruction: $4,314; Support Services: $2,459
Enrollment, Drop-out Rates and Diploma Recipients by Race/Ethnicity

Category	Total	White	Black	Asian	AIAN	Hisp.
Enrollment (%)	100.0	68.9	6.8	17.6	1.3	5.4
Drop-out Rate (%)	4.6	4.5	7.8	2.4	4.9	13.9
H.S. Diplomas (#)	746	540	16	160	6	24

Snoqualmie SD 410

8001 Silva Ave SE • Snoqualmie, WA 98065-0400
(425) 831-8000 • http://www.snoqualmie.k12.wa.us/
Grade Span: PK-12; **Agency Type:** 1
Schools: 8
    4 Primary; 2 Middle; 2 High; 0 Other Level
    7 Regular; 0 Special Education; 0 Vocational; 1 Alternative
    0 Magnet; 0 Charter; 4 Title I Eligible; 0 School-wide Title I
Students: 4,901   (52.2% male; 47.7% female)
    Individual Education Program: 440 (9.0%);
    English Language Learner: 0 (0.0%); Migrant: n/a
    Eligible for Free Lunch Program: 463 (9.4%)
    Eligible for Reduced-Price Lunch Program: 196 (4.0%)
Teachers: 236.6 (20.7 to 1)
Librarians/Media Specialists: 5.5 (891.1 to 1)
Guidance Counselors: 8.1 (605.1 to 1)
Current Spending: ($ per student per year):
    Total: $6,293; Instruction: $3,716; Support Services: $2,226
Enrollment, Drop-out Rates and Diploma Recipients by Race/Ethnicity

Category	Total	White	Black	Asian	AIAN	Hisp.
Enrollment (%)	100.0	91.4	1.2	2.9	1.4	3.0
Drop-out Rate (%)	5.2	4.9	15.4	4.2	7.4	10.5
H.S. Diplomas (#)	240	221	0	4	2	13

Tahoma SD 409

25720 Maple Valley Blk Diam • Maple Valley, WA 98038-8313
(425) 413-3400 • http://www.tahoma.wednet.edu/
Grade Span: PK-12; **Agency Type:** 1
Schools: 9
    4 Primary; 1 Middle; 2 High; 2 Other Level
    8 Regular; 0 Special Education; 0 Vocational; 1 Alternative
    0 Magnet; 0 Charter; 2 Title I Eligible; 0 School-wide Title I
Students: 6,408 (50.8% male; 49.1% female)
    Individual Education Program: 744 (11.6%);
    English Language Learner: 0 (0.0%); Migrant: n/a
    Eligible for Free Lunch Program: 448 (7.0%)
    Eligible for Reduced-Price Lunch Program: 280 (4.4%)
Teachers: 311.1 (20.6 to 1)
Librarians/Media Specialists: 4.5 (1,424.0 to 1)
Guidance Counselors: 8.8 (728.2 to 1)
Current Spending: ($ per student per year):
    Total: $6,368; Instruction: $3,836; Support Services: $2,241
Enrollment, Drop-out Rates and Diploma Recipients by Race/Ethnicity

Category	Total	White	Black	Asian	AIAN	Hisp.
Enrollment (%)	100.0	90.5	1.9	3.0	1.1	3.4
Drop-out Rate (%)	7.4	7.1	7.1	1.9	20.0	23.1
H.S. Diplomas (#)	351	328	6	13	1	3

Tukwila SD 406

4640 S 144th St • Tukwila, WA 98168-4134
(206) 901-8000 • http://www.tukwila.wednet.edu/
Grade Span: PK-12; **Agency Type:** 1
Schools: 5
    3 Primary; 1 Middle; 1 High; 0 Other Level
    5 Regular; 0 Special Education; 0 Vocational; 0 Alternative
    0 Magnet; 0 Charter; 5 Title I Eligible; 5 School-wide Title I
Students: 2,726 (51.4% male; 48.5% female)
    Individual Education Program: 249 (9.1%);
    English Language Learner: 0 (0.0%); Migrant: n/a
    Eligible for Free Lunch Program: 1,395 (51.2%)
    Eligible for Reduced-Price Lunch Program: 306 (11.2%)
Teachers: 136.9 (19.9 to 1)
Librarians/Media Specialists: 5.0 (545.2 to 1)
Guidance Counselors: 4.0 (681.5 to 1)
Current Spending: ($ per student per year):
    Total: $6,918; Instruction: $3,997; Support Services: $2,618
Enrollment, Drop-out Rates and Diploma Recipients by Race/Ethnicity

Category	Total	White	Black	Asian	AIAN	Hisp.
Enrollment (%)	100.0	34.0	21.4	19.7	1.8	23.2
Drop-out Rate (%)	9.6	7.3	10.5	10.2	12.5	14.4
H.S. Diplomas (#)	139	78	15	30	5	11

Vashon Island SD 402

20414 Vashon Hwy SW • Vashon, WA 98070-6503
(206) 463-6000 • http://www.vashonsd.wednet.edu/
Grade Span: PK-12; **Agency Type:** 1
Schools: 5
    1 Primary; 1 Middle; 2 High; 1 Other Level
    3 Regular; 0 Special Education; 0 Vocational; 2 Alternative
    0 Magnet; 0 Charter; 1 Title I Eligible; 0 School-wide Title I
Students: 1,605 (51.2% male; 48.7% female)
    Individual Education Program: 144 (9.0%);
    English Language Learner: 200 (12.5%); Migrant: n/a
    Eligible for Free Lunch Program: 84 (5.2%)
    Eligible for Reduced-Price Lunch Program: 47 (2.9%)
Teachers: 84.2 (19.1 to 1)
Librarians/Media Specialists: 3.0 (535.0 to 1)
Guidance Counselors: 3.5 (458.6 to 1)
Current Spending: ($ per student per year):
    Total: $6,984; Instruction: $4,003; Support Services: $2,596
Enrollment, Drop-out Rates and Diploma Recipients by Race/Ethnicity

Category	Total	White	Black	Asian	AIAN	Hisp.
Enrollment (%)	100.0	90.8	1.2	3.0	1.1	3.9
Drop-out Rate (%)	3.5	3.2	18.2	0.0	0.0	5.6
H.S. Diplomas (#)	132	119	3	4	2	4

Kitsap County

Bainbridge Island SD 303

8489 Madison Ave NE • Bainbridge Isl, WA 98110-2999
(206) 780-1050 • http://www.bainbridge.wednet.edu/
Grade Span: PK-12; **Agency Type:** 1
Schools: 11
    5 Primary; 2 Middle; 2 High; 2 Other Level
    7 Regular; 2 Special Education; 0 Vocational; 2 Alternative
    0 Magnet; 0 Charter; 3 Title I Eligible; 0 School-wide Title I
Students: 4,211 (51.4% male; 48.5% female)
    Individual Education Program: 465 (11.0%);
    English Language Learner: 278 (6.6%); Migrant: n/a

    Eligible for Free Lunch Program: 127 (3.0%)
    Eligible for Reduced-Price Lunch Program: 74 (1.8%)
Teachers: 200.4 (21.0 to 1)
Librarians/Media Specialists: 6.0 (701.8 to 1)
Guidance Counselors: 10.7 (393.6 to 1)
Current Spending: ($ per student per year):
    Total: $6,543; Instruction: $3,823; Support Services: $2,452
Enrollment, Drop-out Rates and Diploma Recipients by Race/Ethnicity

Category	Total	White	Black	Asian	AIAN	Hisp.
Enrollment (%)	100.0	89.6	1.6	4.7	1.4	2.7
Drop-out Rate (%)	0.9	1.0	0.0	0.0	0.0	0.0
H.S. Diplomas (#)	294	268	5	18	1	2

Bremerton SD 100

1111 Carr Blvd • Bremerton, WA 98312-2212
(360) 478-5100 • http://bhs1.bremerton.wednet.edu/
Grade Span: KG-12; **Agency Type:** 1
Schools: 14
    8 Primary; 1 Middle; 4 High; 1 Other Level
    11 Regular; 0 Special Education; 1 Vocational; 2 Alternative
    0 Magnet; 0 Charter; 10 Title I Eligible; 10 School-wide Title I
Students: 5,703 (51.2% male; 48.7% female)
    Individual Education Program: 656 (11.5%);
    English Language Learner: 482 (8.5%); Migrant: n/a
    Eligible for Free Lunch Program: 2,060 (36.1%)
    Eligible for Reduced-Price Lunch Program: 693 (12.2%)
Teachers: 329.8 (17.3 to 1)
Librarians/Media Specialists: 10.0 (570.3 to 1)
Guidance Counselors: 10.8 (528.1 to 1)
Current Spending: ($ per student per year):
    Total: $7,757; Instruction: $4,742; Support Services: $2,648
Enrollment, Drop-out Rates and Diploma Recipients by Race/Ethnicity

Category	Total	White	Black	Asian	AIAN	Hisp.
Enrollment (%)	100.0	66.4	11.1	11.9	4.1	6.6
Drop-out Rate (%)	13.1	12.4	14.6	10.4	31.3	13.8
H.S. Diplomas (#)	265	197	32	19	5	12

Central Kitsap SD 401

9210 Silverdale Way NW • Silverdale, WA 98383-9197
(360) 692-3100 • http://www.cksd.wednet.edu/
Grade Span: PK-12; **Agency Type:** 1
Schools: 24
    14 Primary; 4 Middle; 5 High; 1 Other Level
    20 Regular; 0 Special Education; 0 Vocational; 4 Alternative
    0 Magnet; 0 Charter; 9 Title I Eligible; 1 School-wide Title I
Students: 13,202 (51.7% male; 48.2% female)
    Individual Education Program: 1,554 (11.8%);
    English Language Learner: 139 (1.1%); Migrant: n/a
    Eligible for Free Lunch Program: 1,606 (12.2%)
    Eligible for Reduced-Price Lunch Program: 1,202 (9.1%)
Teachers: 687.2 (19.2 to 1)
Librarians/Media Specialists: 21.5 (614.0 to 1)
Guidance Counselors: 17.2 (767.6 to 1)
Current Spending: ($ per student per year):
    Total: $7,119; Instruction: $4,390; Support Services: $2,375
Enrollment, Drop-out Rates and Diploma Recipients by Race/Ethnicity

Category	Total	White	Black	Asian	AIAN	Hisp.
Enrollment (%)	100.0	77.0	5.4	12.4	1.2	4.0
Drop-out Rate (%)	3.8	4.2	5.4	2.1	6.3	0.0
H.S. Diplomas (#)	972	787	23	148	14	0

North Kitsap SD 400

18360 Caldart Ave NE • Poulsbo, WA 98370-8775
(360) 779-8702 • http://www.nksd.wednet.edu/
Grade Span: PK-12; **Agency Type:** 1
Schools: 14
    7 Primary; 3 Middle; 2 High; 2 Other Level
    11 Regular; 1 Special Education; 0 Vocational; 2 Alternative
    0 Magnet; 0 Charter; 5 Title I Eligible; 0 School-wide Title I
Students: 7,075 (52.1% male; 47.8% female)
    Individual Education Program: 758 (10.7%);
    English Language Learner: 0 (0.0%); Migrant: n/a
    Eligible for Free Lunch Program: 997 (14.1%)
    Eligible for Reduced-Price Lunch Program: 427 (6.0%)
Teachers: 363.2 (19.5 to 1)
Librarians/Media Specialists: 10.0 (707.5 to 1)
Guidance Counselors: 15.7 (450.6 to 1)
Current Spending: ($ per student per year):
    Total: $6,755; Instruction: $3,957; Support Services: $2,464
Enrollment, Drop-out Rates and Diploma Recipients by Race/Ethnicity

Category	Total	White	Black	Asian	AIAN	Hisp.
Enrollment (%)	100.0	82.1	1.9	4.3	7.2	4.5
Drop-out Rate (%)	3.4	3.3	9.8	1.0	6.4	0.0
H.S. Diplomas (#)	401	342	8	26	13	12

South Kitsap SD 402

1962 Hoover Ave SE • Port Orchard, WA 98366-3098
(360) 874-7380 • http://www.skitsap.wednet.edu/
Grade Span: PK-12; **Agency Type:** 1
Schools: 17
   10 Primary; 3 Middle; 2 High; 2 Other Level
   14 Regular; 1 Special Education; 0 Vocational; 2 Alternative
   0 Magnet; 0 Charter; 8 Title I Eligible; 1 School-wide Title I
Students: 11,051   (51.6% male; 48.3% female)
   Individual Education Program: 1,361 (12.3%);
   English Language Learner: 275 (2.5%); Migrant: n/a
   Eligible for Free Lunch Program: 2,032 (18.4%)
   Eligible for Reduced-Price Lunch Program: 903 (8.2%)
Teachers: 585.5 (18.9 to 1)
Librarians/Media Specialists: 9.0 (1,227.9 to 1)
Guidance Counselors: 21.5 (514.0 to 1)
Current Spending: ($ per student per year):
   Total: $6,733; Instruction: $3,880; Support Services: $2,553
Enrollment, Drop-out Rates and Diploma Recipients by Race/Ethnicity

Category	Total	White	Black	Asian	AIAN	Hisp.
Enrollment (%)	100.0	82.9	3.2	7.2	3.0	3.7
Drop-out Rate (%)	7.6	7.3	10.3	9.1	9.3	8.6
H.S. Diplomas (#)	625	526	15	50	18	16

Kittitas County

Ellensburg SD 401

506 N Sprague St • Ellensburg, WA 98926-3195
(509) 925-8010 • http://wonders.eburg.wednet.edu/
Grade Span: KG-12; **Agency Type:** 1
Schools: 6
   4 Primary; 1 Middle; 1 High; 0 Other Level
   6 Regular; 0 Special Education; 0 Vocational; 0 Alternative
   0 Magnet; 0 Charter; 4 Title I Eligible; 1 School-wide Title I
Students: 2,949   (52.5% male; 47.4% female)
   Individual Education Program: 296 (10.0%);
   English Language Learner: 123 (4.2%); Migrant: n/a
   Eligible for Free Lunch Program: 687 (23.3%)
   Eligible for Reduced-Price Lunch Program: 225 (7.6%)
Teachers: 145.9 (20.2 to 1)
Librarians/Media Specialists: 5.0 (589.8 to 1)
Guidance Counselors: 7.9 (373.3 to 1)
Current Spending: ($ per student per year):
   Total: $6,837; Instruction: $4,099; Support Services: $2,370
Enrollment, Drop-out Rates and Diploma Recipients by Race/Ethnicity

Category	Total	White	Black	Asian	AIAN	Hisp.
Enrollment (%)	100.0	84.4	1.2	1.8	1.2	11.4
Drop-out Rate (%)	4.8	4.8	0.0	0.0	20.0	6.3
H.S. Diplomas (#)	227	207	2	3	2	13

Lewis County

Centralia SD 401

2320 Borst Ave • Centralia, WA 98531-1498
(360) 330-7600 • http://www.centralia1.wednet.edu/firstpage.htm
Grade Span: KG-12; **Agency Type:** 1
Schools: 7
   4 Primary; 2 Middle; 1 High; 0 Other Level
   7 Regular; 0 Special Education; 0 Vocational; 0 Alternative
   0 Magnet; 0 Charter; 6 Title I Eligible; 6 School-wide Title I
Students: 3,363   (50.8% male; 49.1% female)
   Individual Education Program: 367 (10.9%);
   English Language Learner: 362 (10.8%); Migrant: n/a
   Eligible for Free Lunch Program: 1,363 (40.5%)
   Eligible for Reduced-Price Lunch Program: 305 (9.1%)
Teachers: 175.2 (19.2 to 1)
Librarians/Media Specialists: 2.0 (1,681.5 to 1)
Guidance Counselors: 9.3 (361.6 to 1)
Current Spending: ($ per student per year):
   Total: $6,838; Instruction: $4,222; Support Services: $2,246
Enrollment, Drop-out Rates and Diploma Recipients by Race/Ethnicity

Category	Total	White	Black	Asian	AIAN	Hisp.
Enrollment (%)	100.0	81.4	1.0	1.6	1.0	15.0
Drop-out Rate (%)	8.1	7.5	0.0	10.0	18.2	10.9
H.S. Diplomas (#)	179	162	0	6	2	9

Chehalis SD 302

310 SW 16th St • Chehalis, WA 98532-3809
(360) 748-8681 • http://www.chehalis.k12.wa.us/
Grade Span: KG-12; **Agency Type:** 1
Schools: 7
   2 Primary; 2 Middle; 2 High; 1 Other Level
   7 Regular; 0 Special Education; 0 Vocational; 0 Alternative
   0 Magnet; 0 Charter; 4 Title I Eligible; 2 School-wide Title I
Students: 2,952   (53.5% male; 46.4% female)

   Individual Education Program: 318 (10.8%);
   English Language Learner: 26 (0.9%); Migrant: n/a
   Eligible for Free Lunch Program: 602 (20.4%)
   Eligible for Reduced-Price Lunch Program: 249 (8.4%)
Teachers: 160.7 (18.4 to 1)
Librarians/Media Specialists: 4.5 (656.0 to 1)
Guidance Counselors: 4.0 (738.0 to 1)
Current Spending: ($ per student per year):
   Total: $7,489; Instruction: $4,503; Support Services: $2,602
Enrollment, Drop-out Rates and Diploma Recipients by Race/Ethnicity

Category	Total	White	Black	Asian	AIAN	Hisp.
Enrollment (%)	100.0	86.1	2.5	1.5	1.6	8.2
Drop-out Rate (%)	3.2	3.4	0.0	0.0	4.2	5.3
H.S. Diplomas (#)	210	190	3	7	1	9

Mason County

North Mason SD 403

71 E Campus Dr • Belfair, WA 98528-8305
(360) 277-2300 • http://www.nmsd.wednet.edu/
Grade Span: KG-12; **Agency Type:** 1
Schools: 6
   2 Primary; 1 Middle; 2 High; 1 Other Level
   4 Regular; 0 Special Education; 0 Vocational; 2 Alternative
   0 Magnet; 0 Charter; 2 Title I Eligible; 0 School-wide Title I
Students: 2,386   (51.7% male; 48.2% female)
   Individual Education Program: 271 (11.4%);
   English Language Learner: 0 (0.0%); Migrant: n/a
   Eligible for Free Lunch Program: 596 (25.0%)
   Eligible for Reduced-Price Lunch Program: 240 (10.1%)
Teachers: 126.6 (18.8 to 1)
Librarians/Media Specialists: 4.0 (596.5 to 1)
Guidance Counselors: 4.0 (596.5 to 1)
Current Spending: ($ per student per year):
   Total: $6,861; Instruction: $4,007; Support Services: $2,442
Enrollment, Drop-out Rates and Diploma Recipients by Race/Ethnicity

Category	Total	White	Black	Asian	AIAN	Hisp.
Enrollment (%)	100.0	86.7	2.5	3.6	2.7	4.4
Drop-out Rate (%)	3.9	3.8	10.0	5.0	7.7	0.0
H.S. Diplomas (#)	166	156	1	7	1	1

Shelton SD 309

700 S 1st St • Shelton, WA 98584-3602
(360) 426-1687 • http://www.shelton.wednet.edu/
Grade Span: PK-12; **Agency Type:** 1
Schools: 9
   3 Primary; 2 Middle; 3 High; 1 Other Level
   6 Regular; 0 Special Education; 0 Vocational; 3 Alternative
   0 Magnet; 0 Charter; 3 Title I Eligible; 3 School-wide Title I
Students: 4,201   (51.6% male; 48.3% female)
   Individual Education Program: 511 (12.2%);
   English Language Learner: 0 (0.0%); Migrant: n/a
   Eligible for Free Lunch Program: 1,614 (38.4%)
   Eligible for Reduced-Price Lunch Program: 393 (9.4%)
Teachers: 216.4 (19.4 to 1)
Librarians/Media Specialists: 3.3 (1,273.0 to 1)
Guidance Counselors: 9.4 (446.9 to 1)
Current Spending: ($ per student per year):
   Total: $7,108; Instruction: $4,098; Support Services: $2,599
Enrollment, Drop-out Rates and Diploma Recipients by Race/Ethnicity

Category	Total	White	Black	Asian	AIAN	Hisp.
Enrollment (%)	100.0	77.2	0.5	2.6	9.1	10.5
Drop-out Rate (%)	8.7	8.1	28.6	2.6	11.7	13.3
H.S. Diplomas (#)	318	270	2	7	30	9

Okanogan County

Omak SD 19

619 W Bartlett Ave • Omak, WA 98841-9700
(509) 826-7681 • http://www.omaksd.wednet.edu/
Grade Span: PK-12; **Agency Type:** 1
Schools: 5
   2 Primary; 1 Middle; 2 High; 0 Other Level
   4 Regular; 0 Special Education; 0 Vocational; 1 Alternative
   0 Magnet; 0 Charter; 3 Title I Eligible; 2 School-wide Title I
Students: 1,861   (50.8% male; 49.1% female)
   Individual Education Program: 245 (13.2%);
   English Language Learner: 37 (2.0%); Migrant: n/a
   Eligible for Free Lunch Program: 721 (38.7%)
   Eligible for Reduced-Price Lunch Program: 211 (11.3%)
Teachers: 101.0 (18.4 to 1)
Librarians/Media Specialists: 0.7 (2,658.6 to 1)
Guidance Counselors: 5.6 (332.3 to 1)
Current Spending: ($ per student per year):
   Total: $8,005; Instruction: $4,735; Support Services: $2,894

Enrollment, Drop-out Rates and Diploma Recipients by Race/Ethnicity

Category	Total	White	Black	Asian	AIAN	Hisp.
Enrollment (%)	100.0	57.7	0.5	1.5	27.5	12.7
Drop-out Rate (%)	14.1	7.3	50.0	0.0	31.1	17.1
H.S. Diplomas (#)	109	76	1	1	23	8

Pierce County

Bethel SD 403
516 176th St E • Spanaway, WA 98387-8399
(253) 539-6024 • http://www.bethel.wednet.edu/
Grade Span: PK-12; **Agency Type:** 1
Schools: 29
    21 Primary; 5 Middle; 3 High; 0 Other Level
    28 Regular; 0 Special Education; 0 Vocational; 1 Alternative
    0 Magnet; 0 Charter; 12 Title I Eligible; 5 School-wide Title I
Students: 17,397   (52.1% male; 47.8% female)
    Individual Education Program: 2,111 (12.1%);
    English Language Learner: 7,792 (44.8%); Migrant: n/a
    Eligible for Free Lunch Program: 4,113 (23.6%)
    Eligible for Reduced-Price Lunch Program: 1,970 (11.3%)
Teachers: 825.3 (21.1 to 1)
Librarians/Media Specialists: 21.0 (828.4 to 1)
Guidance Counselors: 21.5 (809.2 to 1)
Current Spending: ($ per student per year):
    Total: $6,703; Instruction: $3,812; Support Services: $2,578
Enrollment, Drop-out Rates and Diploma Recipients by Race/Ethnicity

Category	Total	White	Black	Asian	AIAN	Hisp.
Enrollment (%)	100.0	70.6	10.2	9.7	3.3	6.2
Drop-out Rate (%)	7.1	7.7	6.5	2.2	11.2	7.2
H.S. Diplomas (#)	975	668	110	125	33	39

Clover Park SD 400
10903 Gravelly Lake Dr SW • Lakewood, WA 98499-1341
(253) 589-7500 • http://cpsd.cloverpark.k12.wa.us/
Grade Span: PK-12; **Agency Type:** 1
Schools: 33
    19 Primary; 5 Middle; 4 High; 5 Other Level
    27 Regular; 2 Special Education; 0 Vocational; 4 Alternative
    0 Magnet; 0 Charter; 17 Title I Eligible; 17 School-wide Title I
Students: 13,217   (52.0% male; 47.9% female)
    Individual Education Program: 1,665 (12.6%);
    English Language Learner: 0 (0.0%); Migrant: n/a
    Eligible for Free Lunch Program: 4,684 (35.4%)
    Eligible for Reduced-Price Lunch Program: 2,077 (15.7%)
Teachers: 703.6 (18.8 to 1)
Librarians/Media Specialists: 25.0 (528.7 to 1)
Guidance Counselors: 30.9 (427.7 to 1)
Current Spending: ($ per student per year):
    Total: $7,785; Instruction: $4,520; Support Services: $2,911
Enrollment, Drop-out Rates and Diploma Recipients by Race/Ethnicity

Category	Total	White	Black	Asian	AIAN	Hisp.
Enrollment (%)	100.0	53.6	22.5	9.3	1.8	12.8
Drop-out Rate (%)	13.9	13.4	13.8	11.5	20.3	19.2
H.S. Diplomas (#)	455	231	104	72	13	35

Eatonville SD 404
208 Lynch St • Eatonville, WA 98328-0698
(360) 879-1000 • http://cruiser.eatonville.wednet.edu/
Grade Span: KG-12; **Agency Type:** 1
Schools: 5
    3 Primary; 1 Middle; 1 High; 0 Other Level
    5 Regular; 0 Special Education; 0 Vocational; 0 Alternative
    0 Magnet; 0 Charter; 2 Title I Eligible; 0 School-wide Title I
Students: 2,091   (53.2% male; 46.7% female)
    Individual Education Program: 225 (10.8%);
    English Language Learner: 0 (0.0%); Migrant: n/a
    Eligible for Free Lunch Program: 393 (18.8%)
    Eligible for Reduced-Price Lunch Program: 251 (12.0%)
Teachers: 108.7 (19.2 to 1)
Librarians/Media Specialists: 2.0 (1,045.5 to 1)
Guidance Counselors: 4.0 (522.8 to 1)
Current Spending: ($ per student per year):
    Total: $6,742; Instruction: $3,853; Support Services: $2,569
Enrollment, Drop-out Rates and Diploma Recipients by Race/Ethnicity

Category	Total	White	Black	Asian	AIAN	Hisp.
Enrollment (%)	100.0	91.4	1.1	1.6	2.6	3.3
Drop-out Rate (%)	5.5	5.4	n/a	5.6	5.0	10.5
H.S. Diplomas (#)	126	120	0	2	0	4

Fife SD 417
5802 20th St E • Tacoma, WA 98424-2000
(253) 284-1000 • http://www.fifeschools.com/
Grade Span: KG-12; **Agency Type:** 1
Schools: 7

    3 Primary; 1 Middle; 2 High; 1 Other Level
    6 Regular; 0 Special Education; 0 Vocational; 1 Alternative
    0 Magnet; 0 Charter; 3 Title I Eligible; 0 School-wide Title I
Students: 3,247   (50.6% male; 49.3% female)
    Individual Education Program: 258 (7.9%);
    English Language Learner: 0 (0.0%); Migrant: n/a
    Eligible for Free Lunch Program: 727 (22.4%)
    Eligible for Reduced-Price Lunch Program: 290 (8.9%)
Teachers: 160.8 (20.2 to 1)
Librarians/Media Specialists: 6.0 (541.2 to 1)
Guidance Counselors: 4.9 (662.7 to 1)
Current Spending: ($ per student per year):
    Total: $6,821; Instruction: $4,043; Support Services: $2,369
Enrollment, Drop-out Rates and Diploma Recipients by Race/Ethnicity

Category	Total	White	Black	Asian	AIAN	Hisp.
Enrollment (%)	100.0	74.0	4.7	7.9	3.6	9.9
Drop-out Rate (%)	4.7	4.0	7.1	4.4	12.8	6.0
H.S. Diplomas (#)	202	176	5	5	8	8

Franklin Pierce SD 402
315 129th St S • Tacoma, WA 98444-5099
(253) 537-0211 • http://www.fp.k12.wa.us/
Grade Span: PK-12; **Agency Type:** 1
Schools: 15
    8 Primary; 2 Middle; 4 High; 1 Other Level
    12 Regular; 0 Special Education; 0 Vocational; 3 Alternative
    0 Magnet; 0 Charter; 8 Title I Eligible; 8 School-wide Title I
Students: 7,843   (51.1% male; 48.8% female)
    Individual Education Program: 878 (11.2%);
    English Language Learner: 723 (9.2%); Migrant: n/a
    Eligible for Free Lunch Program: 2,648 (33.8%)
    Eligible for Reduced-Price Lunch Program: 995 (12.7%)
Teachers: 393.5 (19.9 to 1)
Librarians/Media Specialists: 7.0 (1,120.4 to 1)
Guidance Counselors: 15.9 (493.3 to 1)
Current Spending: ($ per student per year):
    Total: $6,881; Instruction: $4,209; Support Services: $2,366
Enrollment, Drop-out Rates and Diploma Recipients by Race/Ethnicity

Category	Total	White	Black	Asian	AIAN	Hisp.
Enrollment (%)	100.0	61.4	15.2	12.0	2.4	9.0
Drop-out Rate (%)	9.8	8.8	12.0	11.0	13.2	14.7
H.S. Diplomas (#)	407	294	36	54	11	12

Orting SD 344
120 Washington Ave N • Orting, WA 98360-8403
(360) 893-6500 • http://www.orting.wednet.edu/
Grade Span: PK-12; **Agency Type:** 1
Schools: 4
    2 Primary; 1 Middle; 1 High; 0 Other Level
    4 Regular; 0 Special Education; 0 Vocational; 0 Alternative
    0 Magnet; 0 Charter; 2 Title I Eligible; 0 School-wide Title I
Students: 1,912   (52.6% male; 47.3% female)
    Individual Education Program: 242 (12.7%);
    English Language Learner: 1,366 (71.4%); Migrant: n/a
    Eligible for Free Lunch Program: 314 (16.4%)
    Eligible for Reduced-Price Lunch Program: 145 (7.6%)
Teachers: 102.4 (18.7 to 1)
Librarians/Media Specialists: 2.0 (956.0 to 1)
Guidance Counselors: 1.9 (1,006.3 to 1)
Current Spending: ($ per student per year):
    Total: $6,645; Instruction: $3,984; Support Services: $2,356
Enrollment, Drop-out Rates and Diploma Recipients by Race/Ethnicity

Category	Total	White	Black	Asian	AIAN	Hisp.
Enrollment (%)	100.0	91.9	1.2	2.0	0.8	4.0
Drop-out Rate (%)	4.6	4.2	25.0	0.0	33.3	7.7
H.S. Diplomas (#)	95	84	0	1	0	10

Peninsula SD 401
14015 62nd Ave NW • Gig Harbor, WA 98332-8698
(253) 857-3525 • http://www.peninsula.wednet.edu/
Grade Span: PK-12; **Agency Type:** 1
Schools: 16
    8 Primary; 4 Middle; 3 High; 1 Other Level
    14 Regular; 0 Special Education; 0 Vocational; 2 Alternative
    0 Magnet; 0 Charter; 7 Title I Eligible; 1 School-wide Title I
Students: 9,726   (52.0% male; 47.9% female)
    Individual Education Program: 1,053 (10.8%);
    English Language Learner: 3,976 (40.9%); Migrant: n/a
    Eligible for Free Lunch Program: 1,294 (13.3%)
    Eligible for Reduced-Price Lunch Program: 616 (6.3%)
Teachers: 466.5 (20.8 to 1)
Librarians/Media Specialists: 5.1 (1,907.1 to 1)
Guidance Counselors: 27.6 (352.4 to 1)
Current Spending: ($ per student per year):
    Total: $6,710; Instruction: $4,021; Support Services: $2,369

Enrollment, Drop-out Rates and Diploma Recipients by Race/Ethnicity

Category	Total	White	Black	Asian	AIAN	Hisp.
Enrollment (%)	100.0	88.3	1.9	3.5	3.0	3.2
Drop-out Rate (%)	0.9	0.8	2.2	2.3	2.0	0.0
H.S. Diplomas (#)	604	553	4	11	16	20

Puyallup SD 3
302 2nd St SE • Puyallup, WA 98372-3220
(253) 841-8769 • http://www.puyallup.k12.wa.us/
Grade Span: PK-12; **Agency Type:** 1
Schools: 32
   21 Primary; 6 Middle; 4 High; 1 Other Level
   31 Regular; 0 Special Education; 0 Vocational; 1 Alternative
   0 Magnet; 0 Charter; 9 Title I Eligible; 1 School-wide Title I
Students: 20,043   (51.3% male; 48.6% female)
   Individual Education Program: 2,121 (10.6%);
   English Language Learner: 0 (0.0%); Migrant: n/a
   Eligible for Free Lunch Program: 2,775 (13.8%)
   Eligible for Reduced-Price Lunch Program: 1,478 (7.4%)
Teachers: 1,020.6 (19.6 to 1)
Librarians/Media Specialists: 26.3 (762.1 to 1)
Guidance Counselors: 44.7 (448.4 to 1)
Current Spending: ($ per student per year):
   Total: $6,756; Instruction: $4,038; Support Services: $2,402

Enrollment, Drop-out Rates and Diploma Recipients by Race/Ethnicity

Category	Total	White	Black	Asian	AIAN	Hisp.
Enrollment (%)	100.0	81.8	4.4	6.3	1.8	5.6
Drop-out Rate (%)	7.4	6.7	10.8	4.9	40.2	11.2
H.S. Diplomas (#)	1,153	985	27	71	35	35

Steilacoom Historical SD
510 Chambers St • Steilacoom, WA 98388-3311
(253) 983-2200 • http://steilacoom.k12.wa.us/
Grade Span: PK-12; **Agency Type:** 1
Schools: 7
   5 Primary; 1 Middle; 1 High; 0 Other Level
   7 Regular; 0 Special Education; 0 Vocational; 0 Alternative
   0 Magnet; 0 Charter; 3 Title I Eligible; 0 School-wide Title I
Students: 2,170   (51.7% male; 48.2% female)
   Individual Education Program: 234 (10.8%);
   English Language Learner: 13 (0.6%); Migrant: n/a
   Eligible for Free Lunch Program: 152 (7.0%)
   Eligible for Reduced-Price Lunch Program: 97 (4.5%)
Teachers: 106.8 (20.3 to 1)
Librarians/Media Specialists: 2.0 (1,085.0 to 1)
Guidance Counselors: 6.0 (361.7 to 1)
Current Spending: ($ per student per year):
   Total: $7,021; Instruction: $3,906; Support Services: $2,721

Enrollment, Drop-out Rates and Diploma Recipients by Race/Ethnicity

Category	Total	White	Black	Asian	AIAN	Hisp.
Enrollment (%)	100.0	66.5	14.2	12.0	1.0	6.4
Drop-out Rate (%)	5.3	4.4	13.2	2.4	21.4	3.2
H.S. Diplomas (#)	125	87	13	15	2	8

Sumner SD #320
1202 Wood Ave • Sumner, WA 98390-1933
(253) 891-6080 • http://www.sumner.wednet.edu/
Grade Span: PK-12; **Agency Type:** 1
Schools: 13
   8 Primary; 3 Middle; 1 High; 1 Other Level
   12 Regular; 1 Special Education; 0 Vocational; 0 Alternative
   0 Magnet; 0 Charter; 7 Title I Eligible; 0 School-wide Title I
Students: 8,088   (51.8% male; 48.1% female)
   Individual Education Program: 905 (11.2%);
   English Language Learner: 89 (1.1%); Migrant: n/a
   Eligible for Free Lunch Program: 1,249 (15.4%)
   Eligible for Reduced-Price Lunch Program: 636 (7.9%)
Teachers: 383.0 (21.1 to 1)
Librarians/Media Specialists: 9.0 (898.7 to 1)
Guidance Counselors: 11.4 (709.5 to 1)
Current Spending: ($ per student per year):
   Total: $6,439; Instruction: $3,731; Support Services: $2,389

Enrollment, Drop-out Rates and Diploma Recipients by Race/Ethnicity

Category	Total	White	Black	Asian	AIAN	Hisp.
Enrollment (%)	100.0	87.3	1.8	2.9	2.3	5.6
Drop-out Rate (%)	2.8	2.7	0.0	4.6	7.8	1.2
H.S. Diplomas (#)	396	372	2	10	5	7

Tacoma SD 10
601 S 8th Zip 98405 • Tacoma, WA 98401-1357
(253) 571-1010 • http://www.tacoma.k12.wa.us/
Grade Span: PK-12; **Agency Type:** 1
Schools: 61
   36 Primary; 11 Middle; 11 High; 3 Other Level
   53 Regular; 1 Special Education; 0 Vocational; 7 Alternative

   0 Magnet; 0 Charter; 23 Title I Eligible; 23 School-wide Title I
Students: 33,605   (51.4% male; 48.5% female)
   Individual Education Program: 4,013 (11.9%);
   English Language Learner: 0 (0.0%); Migrant: n/a
   Eligible for Free Lunch Program: 13,680 (40.7%)
   Eligible for Reduced-Price Lunch Program: 3,579 (10.7%)
Teachers: 1,764.7 (19.0 to 1)
Librarians/Media Specialists: 52.9 (635.3 to 1)
Guidance Counselors: 77.6 (433.1 to 1)
Current Spending: ($ per student per year):
   Total: $7,591; Instruction: $4,434; Support Services: $2,802

Enrollment, Drop-out Rates and Diploma Recipients by Race/Ethnicity

Category	Total	White	Black	Asian	AIAN	Hisp.
Enrollment (%)	100.0	52.8	22.3	12.8	2.0	10.0
Drop-out Rate (%)	5.0	4.4	6.1	4.3	9.2	7.3
H.S. Diplomas (#)	1,462	876	268	221	23	74

University Place SD 83
3717 Grandview Dr W • University Pla, WA 98466-2138
(253) 566-5600 • http://www.upsd.wednet.edu/
Grade Span: PK-12; **Agency Type:** 1
Schools: 10
   4 Primary; 3 Middle; 2 High; 1 Other Level
   8 Regular; 1 Special Education; 0 Vocational; 1 Alternative
   0 Magnet; 0 Charter; 4 Title I Eligible; 0 School-wide Title I
Students: 5,346   (50.8% male; 49.1% female)
   Individual Education Program: 558 (10.4%);
   English Language Learner: 875 (16.4%); Migrant: n/a
   Eligible for Free Lunch Program: 858 (16.0%)
   Eligible for Reduced-Price Lunch Program: 495 (9.3%)
Teachers: 279.6 (19.1 to 1)
Librarians/Media Specialists: 6.0 (891.0 to 1)
Guidance Counselors: 9.6 (556.9 to 1)
Current Spending: ($ per student per year):
   Total: $6,848; Instruction: $3,998; Support Services: $2,452

Enrollment, Drop-out Rates and Diploma Recipients by Race/Ethnicity

Category	Total	White	Black	Asian	AIAN	Hisp.
Enrollment (%)	100.0	67.6	14.5	12.6	1.0	4.3
Drop-out Rate (%)	3.1	2.4	6.5	2.4	8.7	5.8
H.S. Diplomas (#)	410	285	45	63	3	14

White River SD 416
240 N A St • Buckley, WA 98321-2050
(360) 829-0600 • http://www.whiteriver.wednet.edu/index.shtml
Grade Span: PK-12; **Agency Type:** 1
Schools: 8
   5 Primary; 1 Middle; 1 High; 1 Other Level
   7 Regular; 0 Special Education; 0 Vocational; 1 Alternative
   0 Magnet; 0 Charter; 3 Title I Eligible; 0 School-wide Title I
Students: 4,436   (50.0% male; 49.9% female)
   Individual Education Program: 505 (11.4%);
   English Language Learner: 11 (0.2%); Migrant: n/a
   Eligible for Free Lunch Program: 680 (15.3%)
   Eligible for Reduced-Price Lunch Program: 313 (7.1%)
Teachers: 223.8 (19.8 to 1)
Librarians/Media Specialists: 6.0 (739.3 to 1)
Guidance Counselors: 9.5 (466.9 to 1)
Current Spending: ($ per student per year):
   Total: $6,729; Instruction: $4,174; Support Services: $2,204

Enrollment, Drop-out Rates and Diploma Recipients by Race/Ethnicity

Category	Total	White	Black	Asian	AIAN	Hisp.
Enrollment (%)	100.0	91.0	0.9	1.8	3.0	3.3
Drop-out Rate (%)	15.4	14.9	14.3	22.2	10.0	46.2
H.S. Diplomas (#)	232	219	0	6	5	2

Skagit County

Anacortes SD 103
2200 M Ave • Anacortes, WA 98221-3794
(360) 293-1200 • http://www.anacortes.k12.wa.us/
Grade Span: KG-12; **Agency Type:** 1
Schools: 11
   4 Primary; 1 Middle; 4 High; 2 Other Level
   6 Regular; 1 Special Education; 0 Vocational; 4 Alternative
   0 Magnet; 0 Charter; 5 Title I Eligible; 0 School-wide Title I
Students: 3,120   (51.9% male; 48.0% female)
   Individual Education Program: 319 (10.2%);
   English Language Learner: 0 (0.0%); Migrant: n/a
   Eligible for Free Lunch Program: 539 (17.3%)
   Eligible for Reduced-Price Lunch Program: 238 (7.6%)
Teachers: 150.3 (20.8 to 1)
Librarians/Media Specialists: 5.0 (624.0 to 1)
Guidance Counselors: 7.2 (433.3 to 1)
Current Spending: ($ per student per year):
   Total: $7,136; Instruction: $4,492; Support Services: $2,332

Enrollment, Drop-out Rates and Diploma Recipients by Race/Ethnicity

Category	Total	White	Black	Asian	AIAN	Hisp.
Enrollment (%)	100.0	88.9	1.2	4.4	1.7	3.8
Drop-out Rate (%)	5.6	5.6	18.2	2.2	0.0	9.7
H.S. Diplomas (#)	197	179	3	9	2	4

Burlington-Edison SD 100

927 E Fairhaven Ave • Burlington, WA 98233-1900
(360) 757-3311 • http://www.be.wednet.edu/
Grade Span: PK-12; **Agency Type:** 1
Schools: 8
  6 Primary; 0 Middle; 2 High; 0 Other Level
  6 Regular; 0 Special Education; 0 Vocational; 2 Alternative
  0 Magnet; 0 Charter; 3 Title I Eligible; 0 School-wide Title I
Students: 3,665 (50.0% male; 49.9% female)
  Individual Education Program: 381 (10.4%);
  English Language Learner: 62 (1.7%); Migrant: n/a
  Eligible for Free Lunch Program: 931 (25.4%)
  Eligible for Reduced-Price Lunch Program: 275 (7.5%)
Teachers: 175.3 (20.9 to 1)
Librarians/Media Specialists: 2.0 (1,832.5 to 1)
Guidance Counselors: 8.0 (458.1 to 1)
Current Spending: ($ per student per year):
  Total: $6,703; Instruction: $4,005; Support Services: $2,326
Enrollment, Drop-out Rates and Diploma Recipients by Race/Ethnicity

Category	Total	White	Black	Asian	AIAN	Hisp.
Enrollment (%)	100.0	72.1	0.8	2.4	1.1	23.6
Drop-out Rate (%)	3.7	2.9	0.0	6.5	0.0	8.9
H.S. Diplomas (#)	203	181	0	6	1	15

Mount Vernon SD 320

124 E Lawrence St • Mount Vernon, WA 98273-2999
(360) 428-6181 • http://www.mv.k12.wa.us/
Grade Span: KG-12; **Agency Type:** 1
Schools: 10
  6 Primary; 2 Middle; 1 High; 1 Other Level
  9 Regular; 1 Special Education; 0 Vocational; 0 Alternative
  0 Magnet; 0 Charter; 8 Title I Eligible; 8 School-wide Title I
Students: 5,935 (50.8% male; 49.1% female)
  Individual Education Program: 674 (11.4%)
  English Language Learner: 1,178 (19.8%); Migrant: n/a
  Eligible for Free Lunch Program: 2,740 (46.2%)
  Eligible for Reduced-Price Lunch Program: 562 (9.5%)
Teachers: 293.4 (20.2 to 1)
Librarians/Media Specialists: 9.0 (659.4 to 1)
Guidance Counselors: 14.0 (423.9 to 1)
Current Spending: ($ per student per year):
  Total: $7,281; Instruction: $4,555; Support Services: $2,300
Enrollment, Drop-out Rates and Diploma Recipients by Race/Ethnicity

Category	Total	White	Black	Asian	AIAN	Hisp.
Enrollment (%)	100.0	54.1	1.6	2.5	1.3	40.5
Drop-out Rate (%)	8.5	6.5	0.0	7.1	7.1	14.7
H.S. Diplomas (#)	293	239	1	7	2	44

Sedro-Woolley SD 101

801 Tr Rd • Sedro Woolley, WA 98284-9387
(360) 855-3500 • http://www.swsd.wednet.edu/
Grade Span: PK-12; **Agency Type:** 1
Schools: 11
  7 Primary; 1 Middle; 1 High; 2 Other Level
  9 Regular; 1 Special Education; 0 Vocational; 1 Alternative
  0 Magnet; 0 Charter; 5 Title I Eligible; 1 School-wide Title I
Students: 4,656 (52.5% male; 47.4% female)
  Individual Education Program: 534 (11.5%);
  English Language Learner: 50 (1.1%); Migrant: n/a
  Eligible for Free Lunch Program: 1,308 (28.1%)
  Eligible for Reduced-Price Lunch Program: 405 (8.7%)
Teachers: 243.7 (19.1 to 1)
Librarians/Media Specialists: 5.9 (789.2 to 1)
Guidance Counselors: 9.6 (485.0 to 1)
Current Spending: ($ per student per year):
  Total: $6,986; Instruction: $4,053; Support Services: $2,597
Enrollment, Drop-out Rates and Diploma Recipients by Race/Ethnicity

Category	Total	White	Black	Asian	AIAN	Hisp.
Enrollment (%)	100.0	84.5	1.5	1.3	3.1	9.6
Drop-out Rate (%)	13.5	11.0	52.8	16.4	23.3	24.6
H.S. Diplomas (#)	310	258	5	19	7	21

Snohomish County

Arlington SD 16

315 N French Ave • Arlington, WA 98223-1317
(360) 435-2156 • http://www.asd.wednet.edu/
Grade Span: KG-12; **Agency Type:** 1
Schools: 9

---

  5 Primary; 1 Middle; 2 High; 1 Other Level
  7 Regular; 0 Special Education; 0 Vocational; 2 Alternative
  0 Magnet; 0 Charter; 3 Title I Eligible; 0 School-wide Title I
Students: 5,306 (51.0% male; 48.9% female)
  Individual Education Program: 590 (11.1%);
  English Language Learner: 0 (0.0%); Migrant: n/a
  Eligible for Free Lunch Program: 789 (14.9%)
  Eligible for Reduced-Price Lunch Program: 378 (7.1%)
Teachers: 266.0 (19.9 to 1)
Librarians/Media Specialists: 4.1 (1,294.1 to 1)
Guidance Counselors: 10.0 (530.6 to 1)
Current Spending: ($ per student per year):
  Total: $6,571; Instruction: $4,152; Support Services: $2,161
Enrollment, Drop-out Rates and Diploma Recipients by Race/Ethnicity

Category	Total	White	Black	Asian	AIAN	Hisp.
Enrollment (%)	100.0	90.0	1.2	2.3	1.6	5.0
Drop-out Rate (%)	10.2	10.1	22.2	2.5	4.5	20.0
H.S. Diplomas (#)	270	248	0	8	4	10

Edmonds SD 15

20420 68th Ave W • Lynnwood, WA 98036-7400
(425) 670-7003 • http://www.edmonds.wednet.edu/
Grade Span: PK-12; **Agency Type:** 1
Schools: 42
  26 Primary; 4 Middle; 7 High; 5 Other Level
  31 Regular; 3 Special Education; 0 Vocational; 8 Alternative
  0 Magnet; 0 Charter; 16 Title I Eligible; 3 School-wide Title I
Students: 21,984 (51.4% male; 48.5% female)
  Individual Education Program: 2,321 (10.6%);
  English Language Learner: 235 (1.1%); Migrant: n/a
  Eligible for Free Lunch Program: 3,691 (16.8%)
  Eligible for Reduced-Price Lunch Program: 1,737 (7.9%)
Teachers: 1,071.0 (20.5 to 1)
Librarians/Media Specialists: 34.8 (631.7 to 1)
Guidance Counselors: 32.8 (670.2 to 1)
Current Spending: ($ per student per year):
  Total: $6,721; Instruction: $4,106; Support Services: $2,329
Enrollment, Drop-out Rates and Diploma Recipients by Race/Ethnicity

Category	Total	White	Black	Asian	AIAN	Hisp.
Enrollment (%)	100.0	72.5	5.5	13.5	1.6	7.0
Drop-out Rate (%)	6.9	6.8	10.8	4.7	12.2	10.5
H.S. Diplomas (#)	1,111	855	27	183	16	30

Everett SD 2

4730 Colby Ave • Everett, WA 98203-2999
(425) 339-4205 • http://www.everett.k12.wa.us/
Grade Span: PK-12; **Agency Type:** 1
Schools: 31
  17 Primary; 5 Middle; 6 High; 3 Other Level
  24 Regular; 3 Special Education; 0 Vocational; 4 Alternative
  0 Magnet; 0 Charter; 7 Title I Eligible; 6 School-wide Title I
Students: 18,610 (51.7% male; 48.2% female)
  Individual Education Program: 1,888 (10.1%);
  English Language Learner: 1,766 (9.5%); Migrant: n/a
  Eligible for Free Lunch Program: 4,119 (22.1%)
  Eligible for Reduced-Price Lunch Program: 1,356 (7.3%)
Teachers: 874.0 (21.3 to 1)
Librarians/Media Specialists: 24.0 (775.4 to 1)
Guidance Counselors: 38.0 (489.7 to 1)
Current Spending: ($ per student per year):
  Total: $6,940; Instruction: $4,173; Support Services: $2,458
Enrollment, Drop-out Rates and Diploma Recipients by Race/Ethnicity

Category	Total	White	Black	Asian	AIAN	Hisp.
Enrollment (%)	100.0	75.5	4.5	11.1	1.8	7.2
Drop-out Rate (%)	11.6	11.2	18.6	7.0	36.5	12.7
H.S. Diplomas (#)	885	718	18	105	9	35

Granite Falls SD 332

307 N Alder Ave • Granite Falls, WA 98252-8908
(360) 691-7717 • http://www.gfalls.wednet.edu/
Grade Span: KG-12; **Agency Type:** 1
Schools: 4
  2 Primary; 1 Middle; 1 High; 0 Other Level
  4 Regular; 0 Special Education; 0 Vocational; 0 Alternative
  0 Magnet; 0 Charter; 1 Title I Eligible; 0 School-wide Title I
Students: 2,405 (51.3% male; 48.6% female)
  Individual Education Program: 311 (12.9%);
  English Language Learner: 0 (0.0%); Migrant: n/a
  Eligible for Free Lunch Program: 466 (19.4%)
  Eligible for Reduced-Price Lunch Program: 295 (12.3%)
Teachers: 120.5 (20.0 to 1)
Librarians/Media Specialists: 3.0 (801.7 to 1)
Guidance Counselors: 5.0 (481.0 to 1)
Current Spending: ($ per student per year):
  Total: $6,291; Instruction: $3,581; Support Services: $2,363

Enrollment, Drop-out Rates and Diploma Recipients by Race/Ethnicity

Category	Total	White	Black	Asian	AIAN	Hisp.
Enrollment (%)	100.0	91.0	0.8	1.5	2.8	3.9
Drop-out Rate (%)	8.3	7.4	50.0	11.1	25.0	11.1
H.S. Diplomas (#)	104	93	0	4	4	3

Lake Stevens SD 4
12309 22nd St NE • Lake Stevens, WA 98258-9500
(425) 335-1553 • http://www.lkstevens.wednet.edu/
Grade Span: PK-12; **Agency Type:** 1
Schools: 11
  6 Primary; 2 Middle; 2 High; 1 Other Level
  9 Regular; 0 Special Education; 0 Vocational; 2 Alternative
  0 Magnet; 0 Charter; 3 Title I Eligible; 0 School-wide Title I
Students: 7,489   (50.7% male; 49.2% female)
  Individual Education Program: 797 (10.6%);
  English Language Learner: 0 (0.0%); Migrant: n/a
  Eligible for Free Lunch Program: 1,023 (13.7%)
  Eligible for Reduced-Price Lunch Program: 514 (6.9%)
Teachers: 346.1 (21.6 to 1)
Librarians/Media Specialists: 9.0 (832.1 to 1)
Guidance Counselors: 15.4 (486.3 to 1)
Current Spending: ($ per student per year):
  Total: $6,007; Instruction: $3,710; Support Services: $1,991
Enrollment, Drop-out Rates and Diploma Recipients by Race/Ethnicity

Category	Total	White	Black	Asian	AIAN	Hisp.
Enrollment (%)	100.0	88.3	1.9	3.9	1.2	4.7
Drop-out Rate (%)	2.8	2.9	0.0	0.0	24.1	1.1
H.S. Diplomas (#)	373	346	2	10	8	7

Lakewood SD 306
17110 16th Dr NE • North Lakewood, WA 98259-0220
(360) 652-4500 • http://www.lwsd.wednet.edu/
Grade Span: PK-12; **Agency Type:** 1
Schools: 5
  3 Primary; 1 Middle; 1 High; 0 Other Level
  5 Regular; 0 Special Education; 0 Vocational; 0 Alternative
  0 Magnet; 0 Charter; 3 Title I Eligible; 0 School-wide Title I
Students: 2,645   (51.6% male; 48.3% female)
  Individual Education Program: 301 (11.4%);
  English Language Learner: 0 (0.0%); Migrant: n/a
  Eligible for Free Lunch Program: 444 (16.8%)
  Eligible for Reduced-Price Lunch Program: 261 (9.9%)
Teachers: 125.5 (21.1 to 1)
Librarians/Media Specialists: 4.0 (661.3 to 1)
Guidance Counselors: 7.9 (334.8 to 1)
Current Spending: ($ per student per year):
  Total: $6,779; Instruction: $3,793; Support Services: $2,622
Enrollment, Drop-out Rates and Diploma Recipients by Race/Ethnicity

Category	Total	White	Black	Asian	AIAN	Hisp.
Enrollment (%)	100.0	85.1	4.3	4.0	1.2	5.3
Drop-out Rate (%)	6.6	6.2	11.1	0.0	25.0	10.3
H.S. Diplomas (#)	129	118	2	1	2	6

Marysville SD 25
4220 80th St NE • Marysville, WA 98270-3498
(360) 653-0800 • http://www.msvl.wednet.edu/
Grade Span: PK-12; **Agency Type:** 1
Schools: 21
  11 Primary; 3 Middle; 3 High; 4 Other Level
  15 Regular; 1 Special Education; 0 Vocational; 5 Alternative
  0 Magnet; 0 Charter; 0 Title I Eligible; 0 School-wide Title I
Students: 11,382   (51.9% male; 48.0% female)
  Individual Education Program: 1,202 (10.6%);
  English Language Learner: 0 (0.0%); Migrant: n/a
  Eligible for Free Lunch Program: 2,150 (18.9%)
  Eligible for Reduced-Price Lunch Program: 1,091 (9.6%)
Teachers: 555.6 (20.5 to 1)
Librarians/Media Specialists: 11.8 (964.6 to 1)
Guidance Counselors: 21.7 (524.5 to 1)
Current Spending: ($ per student per year):
  Total: $6,665; Instruction: $3,962; Support Services: $2,379
Enrollment, Drop-out Rates and Diploma Recipients by Race/Ethnicity

Category	Total	White	Black	Asian	AIAN	Hisp.
Enrollment (%)	100.0	77.8	1.7	6.3	8.2	5.9
Drop-out Rate (%)	6.6	5.9	5.8	5.7	14.7	5.9
H.S. Diplomas (#)	601	495	9	49	25	23

Monroe SD 103
200 E Fremont St • Monroe, WA 98272-2336
(360) 794-3000 • http://www.monroe.wednet.edu/
Grade Span: PK-12; **Agency Type:** 1
Schools: 15
  5 Primary; 3 Middle; 3 High; 4 Other Level
  9 Regular; 4 Special Education; 0 Vocational; 2 Alternative

  0 Magnet; 0 Charter; 3 Title I Eligible; 0 School-wide Title I
Students: 6,375   (50.5% male; 49.4% female)
  Individual Education Program: 612 (9.6%);
  English Language Learner: 191 (3.0%); Migrant: n/a
  Eligible for Free Lunch Program: 880 (13.8%)
  Eligible for Reduced-Price Lunch Program: 418 (6.6%)
Teachers: 286.2 (22.3 to 1)
Librarians/Media Specialists: 8.1 (787.0 to 1)
Guidance Counselors: 14.4 (442.7 to 1)
Current Spending: ($ per student per year):
  Total: $6,666; Instruction: $4,059; Support Services: $2,284
Enrollment, Drop-out Rates and Diploma Recipients by Race/Ethnicity

Category	Total	White	Black	Asian	AIAN	Hisp.
Enrollment (%)	100.0	84.8	1.3	3.8	1.0	9.2
Drop-out Rate (%)	4.2	3.9	0.0	3.2	5.6	9.7
H.S. Diplomas (#)	353	327	2	12	1	11

Mukilteo SD 6
9401 Sharon Dr • Everett, WA 98204-2699
(425) 356-1220 • http://www.mukilteo.wednet.edu/
Grade Span: PK-12; **Agency Type:** 1
Schools: 23
  14 Primary; 4 Middle; 4 High; 1 Other Level
  19 Regular; 1 Special Education; 1 Vocational; 2 Alternative
  0 Magnet; 0 Charter; 10 Title I Eligible; 10 School-wide Title I
Students: 14,197   (51.8% male; 48.1% female)
  Individual Education Program: 1,328 (9.4%);
  English Language Learner: 389 (2.7%); Migrant: n/a
  Eligible for Free Lunch Program: 3,679 (25.9%)
  Eligible for Reduced-Price Lunch Program: 1,220 (8.6%)
Teachers: 715.0 (19.9 to 1)
Librarians/Media Specialists: 17.0 (835.1 to 1)
Guidance Counselors: 16.5 (860.4 to 1)
Current Spending: ($ per student per year):
  Total: $6,791; Instruction: $4,307; Support Services: $2,131
Enrollment, Drop-out Rates and Diploma Recipients by Race/Ethnicity

Category	Total	White	Black	Asian	AIAN	Hisp.
Enrollment (%)	100.0	68.4	5.2	13.8	1.7	10.9
Drop-out Rate (%)	4.5	4.0	3.4	4.8	8.8	8.0
H.S. Diplomas (#)	745	530	28	132	10	45

Snohomish SD 201
1601 Ave D • Snohomish, WA 98290-1799
(360) 563-7280 • http://www.sno.wednet.edu/
Grade Span: KG-12; **Agency Type:** 1
Schools: 19
  9 Primary; 3 Middle; 3 High; 4 Other Level
  16 Regular; 1 Special Education; 0 Vocational; 2 Alternative
  0 Magnet; 0 Charter; 7 Title I Eligible; 0 School-wide Title I
Students: 9,010   (51.9% male; 48.0% female)
  Individual Education Program: 934 (10.4%);
  English Language Learner: 7,722 (85.7%); Migrant: n/a
  Eligible for Free Lunch Program: 775 (8.6%)
  Eligible for Reduced-Price Lunch Program: 297 (3.3%)
Teachers: 414.5 (21.7 to 1)
Librarians/Media Specialists: 12.4 (726.6 to 1)
Guidance Counselors: 13.8 (652.9 to 1)
Current Spending: ($ per student per year):
  Total: $6,283; Instruction: $3,773; Support Services: $2,257
Enrollment, Drop-out Rates and Diploma Recipients by Race/Ethnicity

Category	Total	White	Black	Asian	AIAN	Hisp.
Enrollment (%)	100.0	90.2	1.0	3.9	1.0	3.9
Drop-out Rate (%)	5.5	5.3	8.7	4.9	33.3	7.7
H.S. Diplomas (#)	557	526	7	15	0	9

Stanwood-Camano SD 401
9307 271st St NW • Stanwood, WA 98292-8072
(360) 629-1200 • http://www.stanwood.wednet.edu/
Grade Span: KG-12; **Agency Type:** 1
Schools: 9
  5 Primary; 2 Middle; 2 High; 0 Other Level
  8 Regular; 0 Special Education; 0 Vocational; 1 Alternative
  0 Magnet; 0 Charter; 3 Title I Eligible; 0 School-wide Title I
Students: 5,421   (51.7% male; 48.2% female)
  Individual Education Program: 648 (12.0%);
  English Language Learner: 655 (12.1%); Migrant: n/a
  Eligible for Free Lunch Program: 778 (14.4%)
  Eligible for Reduced-Price Lunch Program: 359 (6.6%)
Teachers: 278.6 (19.5 to 1)
Librarians/Media Specialists: 8.0 (677.6 to 1)
Guidance Counselors: 9.4 (576.7 to 1)
Current Spending: ($ per student per year):
  Total: $6,037; Instruction: $3,723; Support Services: $2,032

Enrollment, Drop-out Rates and Diploma Recipients by Race/Ethnicity

Category	Total	White	Black	Asian	AIAN	Hisp.
Enrollment (%)	100.0	92.5	0.8	2.0	1.2	3.5
Drop-out Rate (%)	8.3	8.0	5.3	14.3	17.9	13.5
H.S. Diplomas (#)	318	297	6	5	4	6

Sultan Home School

514 4th St • Sultan, WA 98294-0399
(360) 793-9804 • http://www.sultan.k12.wa.us/
Grade Span: PK-12; **Agency Type:** 1
Schools: 5
   3 Primary; 1 Middle; 1 High; 0 Other Level
   4 Regular; 1 Special Education; 0 Vocational; 0 Alternative
   0 Magnet; 0 Charter; 2 Title I Eligible; 0 School-wide Title I
Students: 2,305   (52.2% male; 47.7% female)
   Individual Education Program: 305 (13.2%);
   English Language Learner: 934 (40.5%); Migrant: n/a
   Eligible for Free Lunch Program: 630 (27.3%)
   Eligible for Reduced-Price Lunch Program: 225 (9.8%)
Teachers: 114.7 (20.1 to 1)
Librarians/Media Specialists: 4.0 (576.3 to 1)
Guidance Counselors: 3.0 (768.3 to 1)
Current Spending: ($ per student per year):
   Total: $6,761; Instruction: $4,152; Support Services: $2,267

Enrollment, Drop-out Rates and Diploma Recipients by Race/Ethnicity

Category	Total	White	Black	Asian	AIAN	Hisp.
Enrollment (%)	100.0	85.2	0.9	2.8	2.3	8.9
Drop-out Rate (%)	7.4	6.4	0.0	0.0	35.7	16.7
H.S. Diplomas (#)	85	77	1	1	0	6

Spokane County

Central Valley SD 356

19307 E Cataldo Ave • Greenacres, WA 99016-9404
(509) 228-5404 • http://www.cvsd.org/
Grade Span: PK-12; **Agency Type:** 1
Schools: 23
   13 Primary; 5 Middle; 2 High; 3 Other Level
   21 Regular; 0 Special Education; 0 Vocational; 2 Alternative
   0 Magnet; 0 Charter; 9 Title I Eligible; 0 School-wide Title I
Students: 11,482   (51.6% male; 48.3% female)
   Individual Education Program: 1,351 (11.8%);
   English Language Learner: 656 (5.7%); Migrant: n/a
   Eligible for Free Lunch Program: 2,089 (18.2%)
   Eligible for Reduced-Price Lunch Program: 1,124 (9.8%)
Teachers: 633.3 (18.1 to 1)
Librarians/Media Specialists: 20.0 (574.1 to 1)
Guidance Counselors: 26.0 (441.6 to 1)
Current Spending: ($ per student per year):
   Total: $6,945; Instruction: $4,271; Support Services: $2,322

Enrollment, Drop-out Rates and Diploma Recipients by Race/Ethnicity

Category	Total	White	Black	Asian	AIAN	Hisp.
Enrollment (%)	100.0	92.0	1.8	2.2	1.6	2.4
Drop-out Rate (%)	0.6	0.6	0.0	0.0	0.0	0.0
H.S. Diplomas (#)	756	713	9	18	9	7

Cheney SD 360

520 4th St • Cheney, WA 99004-1695
(509) 235-6205 • http://www.cheneysd.org/
Grade Span: PK-12; **Agency Type:** 1
Schools: 9
   6 Primary; 1 Middle; 2 High; 0 Other Level
   7 Regular; 1 Special Education; 0 Vocational; 1 Alternative
   0 Magnet; 0 Charter; 6 Title I Eligible; 1 School-wide Title I
Students: 3,436   (50.0% male; 50.0% female)
   Individual Education Program: 447 (13.0%);
   English Language Learner: 0 (0.0%); Migrant: n/a
   Eligible for Free Lunch Program: 929 (27.0%)
   Eligible for Reduced-Price Lunch Program: 377 (11.0%)
Teachers: 195.2 (17.6 to 1)
Librarians/Media Specialists: 6.5 (528.6 to 1)
Guidance Counselors: 7.9 (434.9 to 1)
Current Spending: ($ per student per year):
   Total: $7,476; Instruction: $4,585; Support Services: $2,614

Enrollment, Drop-out Rates and Diploma Recipients by Race/Ethnicity

Category	Total	White	Black	Asian	AIAN	Hisp.
Enrollment (%)	100.0	87.2	2.4	4.1	2.6	3.7
Drop-out Rate (%)	5.5	5.4	15.0	2.9	5.0	3.4
H.S. Diplomas (#)	4	4	0	0	0	0

Deer Park SD 414

908 E Crawford • Deer Park, WA 99006-0490
(509) 276-5051 • http://www.dpsd.org/
Grade Span: PK-12; **Agency Type:** 1
Schools: 5

   2 Primary; 1 Middle; 1 High; 1 Other Level
   4 Regular; 0 Special Education; 0 Vocational; 1 Alternative
   0 Magnet; 0 Charter; 4 Title I Eligible; 0 School-wide Title I
Students: 2,107   (51.4% male; 48.5% female)
   Individual Education Program: 261 (12.4%);
   English Language Learner: 301 (14.3%); Migrant: n/a
   Eligible for Free Lunch Program: 779 (37.0%)
   Eligible for Reduced-Price Lunch Program: 328 (15.6%)
Teachers: 98.5 (21.4 to 1)
Librarians/Media Specialists: 2.2 (957.7 to 1)
Guidance Counselors: 3.9 (540.3 to 1)
Current Spending: ($ per student per year):
   Total: $6,885; Instruction: $4,250; Support Services: $2,282

Enrollment, Drop-out Rates and Diploma Recipients by Race/Ethnicity

Category	Total	White	Black	Asian	AIAN	Hisp.
Enrollment (%)	100.0	94.4	0.7	0.8	2.0	2.1
Drop-out Rate (%)	3.1	3.1	0.0	0.0	0.0	0.0
H.S. Diplomas (#)	133	128	2	0	1	2

East Valley SD 361

12325 E Grace Ave • Spokane, WA 99216-3716
(509) 924-1830 • http://www.evsd.org/
Grade Span: PK-12; **Agency Type:** 1
Schools: 12
   7 Primary; 2 Middle; 3 High; 0 Other Level
   9 Regular; 0 Special Education; 0 Vocational; 3 Alternative
   0 Magnet; 0 Charter; 5 Title I Eligible; 1 School-wide Title I
Students: 4,469   (52.0% male; 47.9% female)
   Individual Education Program: 477 (10.7%);
   English Language Learner: 39 (0.9%); Migrant: n/a
   Eligible for Free Lunch Program: 1,257 (28.1%)
   Eligible for Reduced-Price Lunch Program: 579 (13.0%)
Teachers: 229.4 (19.5 to 1)
Librarians/Media Specialists: 7.1 (629.4 to 1)
Guidance Counselors: 7.0 (638.4 to 1)
Current Spending: ($ per student per year):
   Total: $7,079; Instruction: $4,295; Support Services: $2,374

Enrollment, Drop-out Rates and Diploma Recipients by Race/Ethnicity

Category	Total	White	Black	Asian	AIAN	Hisp.
Enrollment (%)	100.0	90.3	1.9	2.9	2.6	2.3
Drop-out Rate (%)	3.2	3.2	0.0	0.0	6.3	8.3
H.S. Diplomas (#)	299	275	2	11	6	5

Mead SD 354

12828 N Newport Hwy • Mead, WA 99021-9600
(509) 465-6000 • http://coldfusion.mead.k12.wa.us/index.cfm
Grade Span: KG-12; **Agency Type:** 1
Schools: 13
   7 Primary; 2 Middle; 3 High; 1 Other Level
   11 Regular; 0 Special Education; 0 Vocational; 2 Alternative
   0 Magnet; 0 Charter; 3 Title I Eligible; 0 School-wide Title I
Students: 8,731   (50.4% male; 49.5% female)
   Individual Education Program: 911 (10.4%);
   English Language Learner: 328 (3.8%); Migrant: n/a
   Eligible for Free Lunch Program: 1,015 (11.6%)
   Eligible for Reduced-Price Lunch Program: 707 (8.1%)
Teachers: 430.2 (20.3 to 1)
Librarians/Media Specialists: 11.0 (793.7 to 1)
Guidance Counselors: 10.8 (808.4 to 1)
Current Spending: ($ per student per year):
   Total: $6,734; Instruction: $4,018; Support Services: $2,268

Enrollment, Drop-out Rates and Diploma Recipients by Race/Ethnicity

Category	Total	White	Black	Asian	AIAN	Hisp.
Enrollment (%)	100.0	93.1	1.5	2.5	1.0	1.9
Drop-out Rate (%)	2.2	2.2	3.3	0.0	0.0	3.6
H.S. Diplomas (#)	679	633	5	19	6	16

Medical Lake SD 326

116 W Third St • Medical Lake, WA 99022-0128
(509) 565-3100 • http://www.mlsd.org/mlsd/
Grade Span: PK-12; **Agency Type:** 1
Schools: 5
   2 Primary; 2 Middle; 1 High; 0 Other Level
   5 Regular; 0 Special Education; 0 Vocational; 0 Alternative
   0 Magnet; 0 Charter; 2 Title I Eligible; 0 School-wide Title I
Students: 2,298   (53.6% male; 46.3% female)
   Individual Education Program: 226 (9.8%);
   English Language Learner: 0 (0.0%); Migrant: n/a
   Eligible for Free Lunch Program: 419 (18.2%)
   Eligible for Reduced-Price Lunch Program: 381 (16.6%)
Teachers: 123.1 (18.7 to 1)
Librarians/Media Specialists: 3.5 (656.6 to 1)
Guidance Counselors: 4.0 (574.5 to 1)
Current Spending: ($ per student per year):
   Total: $7,229; Instruction: $4,352; Support Services: $2,504

Enrollment, Drop-out Rates and Diploma Recipients by Race/Ethnicity

Category	Total	White	Black	Asian	AIAN	Hisp.
Enrollment (%)	100.0	85.5	4.3	4.1	1.6	4.6
Drop-out Rate (%)	1.5	1.4	2.9	0.0	0.0	5.0
H.S. Diplomas (#)	140	127	6	3	3	1

Nine Mile Falls SD 325/179

10110 W Charles Rd • Nine Mile Fall, WA 99026-8623
(509) 466-5512 • http://www.9mile.org/
Grade Span: PK-12; **Agency Type:** 1
Schools: 5
   2 Primary; 1 Middle; 2 High; 0 Other Level
   4 Regular; 0 Special Education; 0 Vocational; 1 Alternative
   0 Magnet; 0 Charter; 4 Title I Eligible; 0 School-wide Title I
Students: 1,651   (52.0% male; 47.9% female)
   Individual Education Program: 179 (10.8%);
   English Language Learner: 31 (1.9%); Migrant: n/a
   Eligible for Free Lunch Program: 255 (15.4%)
   Eligible for Reduced-Price Lunch Program: 177 (10.7%)
Teachers: 83.5 (19.8 to 1)
Librarians/Media Specialists: 2.0 (825.5 to 1)
Guidance Counselors: 2.1 (786.2 to 1)
Current Spending: ($ per student per year):
   Total: $7,022; Instruction: $4,106; Support Services: $2,436

Enrollment, Drop-out Rates and Diploma Recipients by Race/Ethnicity

Category	Total	White	Black	Asian	AIAN	Hisp.
Enrollment (%)	100.0	95.1	1.0	1.4	1.0	1.6
Drop-out Rate (%)	1.0	1.1	0.0	0.0	0.0	0.0
H.S. Diplomas (#)	132	130	1	1	0	0

Riverside SD 416

34515 N Newport Hwy • Chattaroy, WA 99003-7706
(509) 464-8201 • http://www.riversidesd.org/
Grade Span: PK-12; **Agency Type:** 1
Schools: 6
   2 Primary; 1 Middle; 2 High; 1 Other Level
   4 Regular; 0 Special Education; 0 Vocational; 2 Alternative
   0 Magnet; 0 Charter; 4 Title I Eligible; 0 School-wide Title I
Students: 1,949   (50.7% male; 49.2% female)
   Individual Education Program: 209 (10.7%);
   English Language Learner: 588 (30.2%); Migrant: n/a
   Eligible for Free Lunch Program: 552 (28.3%)
   Eligible for Reduced-Price Lunch Program: 234 (12.0%)
Teachers: 94.5 (20.6 to 1)
Librarians/Media Specialists: 1.0 (1,949.0 to 1)
Guidance Counselors: 5.0 (389.8 to 1)
Current Spending: ($ per student per year):
   Total: $6,982; Instruction: $4,043; Support Services: $2,581

Enrollment, Drop-out Rates and Diploma Recipients by Race/Ethnicity

Category	Total	White	Black	Asian	AIAN	Hisp.
Enrollment (%)	100.0	95.0	0.4	0.6	2.4	1.6
Drop-out Rate (%)	2.8	2.9	0.0	0.0	0.0	0.0
H.S. Diplomas (#)	10	9	0	0	0	1

Spokane SD 81

200 N Bernard St • Spokane, WA 99201-0282
(509) 354-7364 • http://www.sd81.k12.wa.us/
Grade Span: PK-12; **Agency Type:** 1
Schools: 66
   37 Primary; 6 Middle; 14 High; 9 Other Level
   47 Regular; 5 Special Education; 1 Vocational; 13 Alternative
   0 Magnet; 0 Charter; 17 Title I Eligible; 12 School-wide Title I
Students: 31,068   (50.9% male; 49.0% female)
   Individual Education Program: 3,631 (11.7%);
   English Language Learner: 1,442 (4.6%); Migrant: n/a
   Eligible for Free Lunch Program: 11,222 (36.1%)
   Eligible for Reduced-Price Lunch Program: 3,743 (12.0%)
Teachers: 1,753.0 (17.7 to 1)
Librarians/Media Specialists: 46.4 (669.6 to 1)
Guidance Counselors: 71.0 (437.6 to 1)
Current Spending: ($ per student per year):
   Total: $7,638; Instruction: $4,703; Support Services: $2,585

Enrollment, Drop-out Rates and Diploma Recipients by Race/Ethnicity

Category	Total	White	Black	Asian	AIAN	Hisp.
Enrollment (%)	100.0	85.3	5.0	2.8	3.8	3.1
Drop-out Rate (%)	3.9	3.6	6.9	4.2	8.1	4.9
H.S. Diplomas (#)	1,793	1,584	58	83	31	37

West Valley SD 363

2805 N Argonne Rd • Spokane, WA 99212-2245
(509) 924-2150 • http://www.wvsd.com/
Grade Span: PK-12; **Agency Type:** 1
Schools: 13
   5 Primary; 3 Middle; 4 High; 1 Other Level
   8 Regular; 0 Special Education; 0 Vocational; 5 Alternative

   0 Magnet; 0 Charter; 5 Title I Eligible; 3 School-wide Title I
Students: 3,795   (51.0% male; 48.9% female)
   Individual Education Program: 377 (9.9%);
   English Language Learner: 852 (22.5%); Migrant: n/a
   Eligible for Free Lunch Program: 1,176 (31.0%)
   Eligible for Reduced-Price Lunch Program: 472 (12.4%)
Teachers: 166.5 (22.8 to 1)
Librarians/Media Specialists: 5.0 (759.0 to 1)
Guidance Counselors: 8.5 (446.5 to 1)
Current Spending: ($ per student per year):
   Total: $7,230; Instruction: $4,167; Support Services: $2,694

Enrollment, Drop-out Rates and Diploma Recipients by Race/Ethnicity

Category	Total	White	Black	Asian	AIAN	Hisp.
Enrollment (%)	100.0	88.5	2.7	1.4	2.9	4.4
Drop-out Rate (%)	22.6	22.1	44.4	22.2	22.9	23.5
H.S. Diplomas (#)	283	260	1	4	7	11

Stevens County

Colville SD 115

217 S Hofstetter St • Colville, WA 99114-3239
(509) 684-7850 • http://www.colsd.org/
Grade Span: KG-12; **Agency Type:** 1
Schools: 5
   2 Primary; 2 Middle; 1 High; 0 Other Level
   5 Regular; 0 Special Education; 0 Vocational; 0 Alternative
   0 Magnet; 0 Charter; 5 Title I Eligible; 0 School-wide Title I
Students: 2,099   (50.5% male; 49.4% female)
   Individual Education Program: 243 (11.6%);
   English Language Learner: 0 (0.0%); Migrant: n/a
   Eligible for Free Lunch Program: 727 (34.6%)
   Eligible for Reduced-Price Lunch Program: 261 (12.4%)
Teachers: 111.8 (18.8 to 1)
Librarians/Media Specialists: 2.7 (777.4 to 1)
Guidance Counselors: 3.2 (655.9 to 1)
Current Spending: ($ per student per year):
   Total: $7,286; Instruction: $4,132; Support Services: $2,769

Enrollment, Drop-out Rates and Diploma Recipients by Race/Ethnicity

Category	Total	White	Black	Asian	AIAN	Hisp.
Enrollment (%)	100.0	91.9	0.6	2.5	3.2	1.7
Drop-out Rate (%)	1.5	1.4	0.0	0.0	0.0	16.7
H.S. Diplomas (#)	170	165	0	3	2	0

Thurston County

North Thurston SD 3

305 College St NE • Lacey, WA 98516-5390
(360) 412-4413 • http://www.ntsd.wednet.edu/
Grade Span: PK-12; **Agency Type:** 1
Schools: 19
   12 Primary; 3 Middle; 4 High; 0 Other Level
   18 Regular; 0 Special Education; 0 Vocational; 1 Alternative
   0 Magnet; 0 Charter; 7 Title I Eligible; 2 School-wide Title I
Students: 13,079   (51.3% male; 48.6% female)
   Individual Education Program: 1,588 (12.1%);
   English Language Learner: 341 (2.6%); Migrant: n/a
   Eligible for Free Lunch Program: 2,595 (19.8%)
   Eligible for Reduced-Price Lunch Program: 1,404 (10.7%)
Teachers: 729.4 (17.9 to 1)
Librarians/Media Specialists: 17.6 (743.1 to 1)
Guidance Counselors: 26.6 (491.7 to 1)
Current Spending: ($ per student per year):
   Total: $6,983; Instruction: $4,358; Support Services: $2,288

Enrollment, Drop-out Rates and Diploma Recipients by Race/Ethnicity

Category	Total	White	Black	Asian	AIAN	Hisp.
Enrollment (%)	100.0	67.4	8.9	13.1	2.7	7.9
Drop-out Rate (%)	4.7	4.2	5.3	5.0	8.3	7.9
H.S. Diplomas (#)	822	578	81	117	11	35

Olympia SD 111

1113 Legion Way SE • Olympia, WA 98501-1697
(360) 753-8850 • http://kids.osd.wednet.edu/
Grade Span: KG-12; **Agency Type:** 1
Schools: 18
   11 Primary; 4 Middle; 3 High; 0 Other Level
   17 Regular; 0 Special Education; 0 Vocational; 1 Alternative
   0 Magnet; 0 Charter; 8 Title I Eligible; 4 School-wide Title I
Students: 9,234   (51.5% male; 48.4% female)
   Individual Education Program: 980 (10.6%);
   English Language Learner: 106 (1.1%); Migrant: n/a
   Eligible for Free Lunch Program: 1,237 (13.4%)
   Eligible for Reduced-Price Lunch Program: 481 (5.2%)
Teachers: 457.1 (20.2 to 1)
Librarians/Media Specialists: 12.0 (769.5 to 1)
Guidance Counselors: 11.4 (810.0 to 1)

Current Spending: ($ per student per year):
   Total: $7,157; Instruction: $4,427; Support Services: $2,327
Enrollment, Drop-out Rates and Diploma Recipients by Race/Ethnicity

Category	Total	White	Black	Asian	AIAN	Hisp.
Enrollment (%)	100.0	80.6	3.4	9.8	1.4	4.7
Drop-out Rate (%)	4.0	3.7	11.1	2.3	10.3	8.3
H.S. Diplomas (#)	681	583	9	61	2	26

Rochester SD 401

9917 Hwy 12 SW • Rochester, WA 98579-9601
(360) 273-5536
Grade Span: KG-12; **Agency Type:** 1
Schools: 6
   2 Primary; 1 Middle; 3 High; 0 Other Level
   5 Regular; 0 Special Education; 0 Vocational; 1 Alternative
   0 Magnet; 0 Charter; 4 Title I Eligible; 0 School-wide Title I
Students: 2,269   (56.5% male; 43.4% female)
   Individual Education Program: 338 (14.9%);
   English Language Learner: 0 (0.0%); Migrant: n/a
   Eligible for Free Lunch Program: 632 (27.9%)
   Eligible for Reduced-Price Lunch Program: 235 (10.4%)
Teachers: 120.2 (18.9 to 1)
Librarians/Media Specialists: 1.0 (2,269.0 to 1)
Guidance Counselors: 6.0 (378.2 to 1)
Current Spending: ($ per student per year):
   Total: $7,495; Instruction: $4,601; Support Services: $2,528
Enrollment, Drop-out Rates and Diploma Recipients by Race/Ethnicity

Category	Total	White	Black	Asian	AIAN	Hisp.
Enrollment (%)	100.0	79.3	2.1	1.5	4.7	12.4
Drop-out Rate (%)	4.5	4.9	0.0	0.0	2.6	5.9
H.S. Diplomas (#)	106	94	1	2	4	5

Tumwater SD 33

419 Linwood Ave SW • Tumwater, WA 98512-8499
(360) 709-7000 • http://www.tumwater.k12.wa.us/
Grade Span: KG-12; **Agency Type:** 1
Schools: 13
   6 Primary; 2 Middle; 3 High; 2 Other Level
   11 Regular; 0 Special Education; 1 Vocational; 1 Alternative
   0 Magnet; 0 Charter; 4 Title I Eligible; 0 School-wide Title I
Students: 6,161   (51.3% male; 48.6% female)
   Individual Education Program: 651 (10.6%);
   English Language Learner: 0 (0.0%); Migrant: n/a
   Eligible for Free Lunch Program: 1,160 (18.8%)
   Eligible for Reduced-Price Lunch Program: 499 (8.1%)
Teachers: 323.7 (19.0 to 1)
Librarians/Media Specialists: 9.9 (622.3 to 1)
Guidance Counselors: 13.0 (473.9 to 1)
Current Spending: ($ per student per year):
   Total: $7,208; Instruction: $4,189; Support Services: $2,634
Enrollment, Drop-out Rates and Diploma Recipients by Race/Ethnicity

Category	Total	White	Black	Asian	AIAN	Hisp.
Enrollment (%)	100.0	88.5	2.2	3.4	2.0	3.8
Drop-out Rate (%)	8.0	7.6	10.9	7.6	18.4	10.0
H.S. Diplomas (#)	341	316	4	7	4	10

Yelm Community Schools

404 Yelm Ave W • Yelm, WA 98597-7678
(360) 458-6114 • http://www.ycs.wednet.edu/
Grade Span: PK-12; **Agency Type:** 1
Schools: 8
   4 Primary; 2 Middle; 1 High; 1 Other Level
   7 Regular; 0 Special Education; 0 Vocational; 1 Alternative
   0 Magnet; 0 Charter; 5 Title I Eligible; 0 School-wide Title I
Students: 4,737   (51.2% male; 48.7% female)
   Individual Education Program: 514 (10.9%);
   English Language Learner: 68 (1.4%); Migrant: n/a
   Eligible for Free Lunch Program: 1,173 (24.8%)
   Eligible for Reduced-Price Lunch Program: 548 (11.6%)
Teachers: 244.8 (19.4 to 1)
Librarians/Media Specialists: 4.7 (1,007.9 to 1)
Guidance Counselors: 11.5 (411.9 to 1)
Current Spending: ($ per student per year):
   Total: $6,863; Instruction: $3,990; Support Services: $2,469
Enrollment, Drop-out Rates and Diploma Recipients by Race/Ethnicity

Category	Total	White	Black	Asian	AIAN	Hisp.
Enrollment (%)	100.0	86.0	2.4	3.2	3.1	5.3
Drop-out Rate (%)	5.9	5.8	8.6	4.1	11.9	3.6
H.S. Diplomas (#)	266	233	8	7	9	9

Walla Walla County

Walla Walla SD 140

364 S Park St • Walla Walla, WA 99362-3249
(509) 527-3000 • http://www.wwps.org/
Grade Span: PK-12; **Agency Type:** 1
Schools: 14
   8 Primary; 2 Middle; 3 High; 1 Other Level
   11 Regular; 0 Special Education; 0 Vocational; 3 Alternative
   0 Magnet; 0 Charter; 6 Title I Eligible; 5 School-wide Title I
Students: 6,261   (51.4% male; 48.5% female)
   Individual Education Program: 688 (11.0%);
   English Language Learner: 106 (1.7%); Migrant: n/a
   Eligible for Free Lunch Program: 2,346 (37.5%)
   Eligible for Reduced-Price Lunch Program: 541 (8.6%)
Teachers: 332.6 (18.8 to 1)
Librarians/Media Specialists: 9.0 (695.7 to 1)
Guidance Counselors: 8.9 (703.5 to 1)
Current Spending: ($ per student per year):
   Total: $7,200; Instruction: $4,452; Support Services: $2,337
Enrollment, Drop-out Rates and Diploma Recipients by Race/Ethnicity

Category	Total	White	Black	Asian	AIAN	Hisp.
Enrollment (%)	100.0	66.6	1.5	1.8	1.0	29.0
Drop-out Rate (%)	7.9	6.6	17.2	2.1	26.7	11.7
H.S. Diplomas (#)	457	366	6	10	2	73

Whatcom County

Bellingham SD 501

1306 Dupont St • Bellingham, WA 98225-3198
(360) 676-6501 • http://www.bham.wednet.edu/
Grade Span: PK-12; **Agency Type:** 1
Schools: 27
   13 Primary; 4 Middle; 6 High; 4 Other Level
   20 Regular; 2 Special Education; 0 Vocational; 5 Alternative
   0 Magnet; 0 Charter; 7 Title I Eligible; 6 School-wide Title I
Students: 10,537   (50.9% male; 49.0% female)
   Individual Education Program: 1,211 (11.5%);
   English Language Learner: 192 (1.8%); Migrant: n/a
   Eligible for Free Lunch Program: 2,242 (21.3%)
   Eligible for Reduced-Price Lunch Program: 764 (7.3%)
Teachers: 545.1 (19.3 to 1)
Librarians/Media Specialists: 19.0 (554.6 to 1)
Guidance Counselors: 16.8 (627.2 to 1)
Current Spending: ($ per student per year):
   Total: $7,030; Instruction: $4,289; Support Services: $2,382
Enrollment, Drop-out Rates and Diploma Recipients by Race/Ethnicity

Category	Total	White	Black	Asian	AIAN	Hisp.
Enrollment (%)	100.0	81.5	2.3	6.0	2.5	7.7
Drop-out Rate (%)	5.0	4.7	3.6	4.6	13.2	6.9
H.S. Diplomas (#)	710	628	12	42	5	23

Blaine SD 503

770 Mitchell Ave • Blaine, WA 98230-9149
(360) 332-5881 • http://www.blaine.wednet.edu/
Grade Span: PK-12; **Agency Type:** 1
Schools: 6
   3 Primary; 1 Middle; 1 High; 1 Other Level
   6 Regular; 0 Special Education; 0 Vocational; 0 Alternative
   0 Magnet; 0 Charter; 4 Title I Eligible; 0 School-wide Title I
Students: 2,151   (52.0% male; 47.9% female)
   Individual Education Program: 209 (9.7%);
   English Language Learner: 284 (13.2%); Migrant: n/a
   Eligible for Free Lunch Program: 658 (30.6%)
   Eligible for Reduced-Price Lunch Program: 223 (10.4%)
Teachers: 101.4 (21.2 to 1)
Librarians/Media Specialists: 3.0 (717.0 to 1)
Guidance Counselors: 6.0 (358.5 to 1)
Current Spending: ($ per student per year):
   Total: $7,059; Instruction: $4,269; Support Services: $2,398
Enrollment, Drop-out Rates and Diploma Recipients by Race/Ethnicity

Category	Total	White	Black	Asian	AIAN	Hisp.
Enrollment (%)	100.0	84.9	2.1	4.1	2.3	6.6
Drop-out Rate (%)	7.4	7.5	0.0	0.0	15.4	11.4
H.S. Diplomas (#)	107	92	3	8	1	3

Ferndale SD 502

6041 Vista Dr • Ferndale, WA 98248-9317
(360) 383-9207 • http://www.ferndale.wednet.edu/
Grade Span: PK-12; **Agency Type:** 1
Schools: 10
   7 Primary; 2 Middle; 1 High; 0 Other Level
   10 Regular; 0 Special Education; 0 Vocational; 0 Alternative
   0 Magnet; 0 Charter; 6 Title I Eligible; 1 School-wide Title I
Students: 5,096   (51.7% male; 48.2% female)

Individual Education Program: 626 (12.3%);
English Language Learner: 52 (1.0%); Migrant: n/a
Eligible for Free Lunch Program: 1,665 (32.7%)
Eligible for Reduced-Price Lunch Program: 621 (12.2%)
Teachers: 294.2 (17.3 to 1)
Librarians/Media Specialists: 9.0 (566.2 to 1)
Guidance Counselors: 10.5 (485.3 to 1)
Current Spending: ($ per student per year):
Total: $7,409; Instruction: $4,576; Support Services: $2,494
Enrollment, Drop-out Rates and Diploma Recipients by Race/Ethnicity

Category	Total	White	Black	Asian	AIAN	Hisp.
Enrollment (%)	100.0	76.1	1.3	2.4	11.8	8.4
Drop-out Rate (%)	7.0	5.0	0.0	8.7	17.4	14.7
H.S. Diplomas (#)	259	217	1	1	24	16

Lynden SD 504
1203 Bradley Rd • Lynden, WA 98264-9514
(360) 354-4443 • http://www.lynden.wednet.edu/
Grade Span: PK-12; **Agency Type:** 1
Schools: 7
2 Primary; 1 Middle; 2 High; 2 Other Level
6 Regular; 1 Special Education; 0 Vocational; 0 Alternative
0 Magnet; 0 Charter; 4 Title I Eligible; 0 School-wide Title I
Students: 2,678 (50.6% male; 49.3% female)
Individual Education Program: 201 (7.5%);
English Language Learner: 46 (1.7%); Migrant: n/a
Eligible for Free Lunch Program: 650 (24.3%)
Eligible for Reduced-Price Lunch Program: 246 (9.2%)
Teachers: 132.1 (20.3 to 1)
Librarians/Media Specialists: 1.0 (2,678.0 to 1)
Guidance Counselors: 5.8 (461.7 to 1)
Current Spending: ($ per student per year):
Total: $6,283; Instruction: $3,998; Support Services: $1,930
Enrollment, Drop-out Rates and Diploma Recipients by Race/Ethnicity

Category	Total	White	Black	Asian	AIAN	Hisp.
Enrollment (%)	100.0	78.0	0.7	4.0	1.8	15.5
Drop-out Rate (%)	2.6	1.9	0.0	0.0	0.0	8.2
H.S. Diplomas (#)	158	132	0	6	1	19

Meridian SD 505
214 W Laurel Rd • Bellingham, WA 98226-9623
(360) 398-7111 • http://www.meridian.wednet.edu/
Grade Span: PK-12; **Agency Type:** 1
Schools: 6
2 Primary; 2 Middle; 2 High; 0 Other Level
6 Regular; 0 Special Education; 0 Vocational; 0 Alternative
0 Magnet; 0 Charter; 3 Title I Eligible; 1 School-wide Title I
Students: 1,572 (52.8% male; 47.1% female)
Individual Education Program: 192 (12.2%);
English Language Learner: 0 (0.0%); Migrant: n/a
Eligible for Free Lunch Program: 429 (27.3%)
Eligible for Reduced-Price Lunch Program: 170 (10.8%)
Teachers: 83.1 (18.9 to 1)
Librarians/Media Specialists: 1.0 (1,572.0 to 1)
Guidance Counselors: 3.0 (524.0 to 1)
Current Spending: ($ per student per year):
Total: $6,849; Instruction: $4,133; Support Services: $2,328
Enrollment, Drop-out Rates and Diploma Recipients by Race/Ethnicity

Category	Total	White	Black	Asian	AIAN	Hisp.
Enrollment (%)	100.0	83.9	1.1	3.4	1.5	10.2
Drop-out Rate (%)	7.6	7.5	0.0	3.8	0.0	14.3
H.S. Diplomas (#)	97	86	0	6	1	4

Mount Baker SD 507
4936 Deming Rd • Deming, WA 98244-0095
(360) 383-2000 • http://www.mtbaker.wednet.edu/
Grade Span: KG-12; **Agency Type:** 1
Schools: 6
3 Primary; 1 Middle; 2 High; 0 Other Level
5 Regular; 0 Special Education; 0 Vocational; 1 Alternative
0 Magnet; 0 Charter; 3 Title I Eligible; 3 School-wide Title I
Students: 2,460 (50.0% male; 49.9% female)
Individual Education Program: 300 (12.2%);
English Language Learner: 199 (8.1%); Migrant: n/a
Eligible for Free Lunch Program: 919 (37.4%)
Eligible for Reduced-Price Lunch Program: 260 (10.6%)
Teachers: 129.1 (19.1 to 1)
Librarians/Media Specialists: 2.0 (1,230.0 to 1)
Guidance Counselors: 4.4 (559.1 to 1)
Current Spending: ($ per student per year):
Total: $6,840; Instruction: $4,084; Support Services: $2,269

Enrollment, Drop-out Rates and Diploma Recipients by Race/Ethnicity

Category	Total	White	Black	Asian	AIAN	Hisp.
Enrollment (%)	100.0	84.6	0.7	1.7	7.2	5.9
Drop-out Rate (%)	3.9	3.4	50.0	0.0	5.6	3.6
H.S. Diplomas (#)	135	119	0	2	12	2

Nooksack Valley SD 506
3326 E Badger Rd • Everson, WA 98247-9232
(360) 988-4754 • http://www.nv.k12.wa.us/
Grade Span: PK-12; **Agency Type:** 1
Schools: 7
4 Primary; 1 Middle; 2 High; 0 Other Level
6 Regular; 1 Special Education; 0 Vocational; 0 Alternative
0 Magnet; 0 Charter; 3 Title I Eligible; 3 School-wide Title I
Students: 1,870 (48.8% male; 51.1% female)
Individual Education Program: 204 (10.9%);
English Language Learner: 0 (0.0%); Migrant: n/a
Eligible for Free Lunch Program: 610 (32.6%)
Eligible for Reduced-Price Lunch Program: 259 (13.9%)
Teachers: 100.7 (18.6 to 1)
Librarians/Media Specialists: 1.0 (1,870.0 to 1)
Guidance Counselors: 4.0 (467.5 to 1)
Current Spending: ($ per student per year):
Total: $7,386; Instruction: $4,427; Support Services: $2,563
Enrollment, Drop-out Rates and Diploma Recipients by Race/Ethnicity

Category	Total	White	Black	Asian	AIAN	Hisp.
Enrollment (%)	100.0	71.8	0.7	1.7	6.4	19.5
Drop-out Rate (%)	2.6	2.6	0.0	0.0	0.0	4.5
H.S. Diplomas (#)	117	98	1	4	5	9

Whitman County

Pullman SD 267
240 SE Dexter St • Pullman, WA 99163-3585
(509) 332-3581 • http://www.psd267.wednet.edu/
Grade Span: KG-12; **Agency Type:** 1
Schools: 5
3 Primary; 1 Middle; 1 High; 0 Other Level
5 Regular; 0 Special Education; 0 Vocational; 0 Alternative
0 Magnet; 0 Charter; 3 Title I Eligible; 0 School-wide Title I
Students: 2,272 (51.4% male; 48.5% female)
Individual Education Program: 241 (10.6%);
English Language Learner: 0 (0.0%); Migrant: n/a
Eligible for Free Lunch Program: 456 (20.1%)
Eligible for Reduced-Price Lunch Program: 129 (5.7%)
Teachers: 114.2 (19.9 to 1)
Librarians/Media Specialists: 2.0 (1,136.0 to 1)
Guidance Counselors: 4.3 (528.4 to 1)
Current Spending: ($ per student per year):
Total: $7,031; Instruction: $4,279; Support Services: $2,336
Enrollment, Drop-out Rates and Diploma Recipients by Race/Ethnicity

Category	Total	White	Black	Asian	AIAN	Hisp.
Enrollment (%)	100.0	76.1	4.4	11.4	1.5	6.7
Drop-out Rate (%)	3.9	2.9	5.0	1.5	30.8	19.2
H.S. Diplomas (#)	166	144	4	10	3	5

Yakima County

East Valley SD 90
2002 Beaudry Rd • Yakima, WA 98901-8012
(509) 573-7320 • http://www.ysd.wednet.edu/
Grade Span: KG-12; **Agency Type:** 1
Schools: 5
2 Primary; 2 Middle; 1 High; 0 Other Level
5 Regular; 0 Special Education; 0 Vocational; 0 Alternative
0 Magnet; 0 Charter; 3 Title I Eligible; 2 School-wide Title I
Students: 2,449 (51.3% male; 48.6% female)
Individual Education Program: 281 (11.5%);
English Language Learner: 412 (16.8%); Migrant: n/a
Eligible for Free Lunch Program: 743 (30.3%)
Eligible for Reduced-Price Lunch Program: 326 (13.3%)
Teachers: 122.6 (20.0 to 1)
Librarians/Media Specialists: 1.5 (1,632.7 to 1)
Guidance Counselors: 5.0 (489.8 to 1)
Current Spending: ($ per student per year):
Total: $6,707; Instruction: $4,094; Support Services: $2,253
Enrollment, Drop-out Rates and Diploma Recipients by Race/Ethnicity

Category	Total	White	Black	Asian	AIAN	Hisp.
Enrollment (%)	100.0	68.9	1.3	0.6	1.9	27.3
Drop-out Rate (%)	10.8	9.4	14.3	0.0	28.6	15.4
H.S. Diplomas (#)	121	96	0	2	0	23

Grandview SD 200

913 W 2nd St • Grandview, WA 98930-1202
(509) 882-2271 • http://www.grandview.wednet.edu/
Grade Span: PK-12; **Agency Type:** 1
Schools: 8
    3 Primary; 0 Middle; 4 High; 1 Other Level
    6 Regular; 0 Special Education; 0 Vocational; 2 Alternative
    0 Magnet; 0 Charter; 5 Title I Eligible; 4 School-wide Title I
Students: 3,250 (50.9% male; 49.0% female)
    Individual Education Program: 322 (9.9%);
    English Language Learner: 0 (0.0%); Migrant: n/a
    Eligible for Free Lunch Program: 2,187 (67.3%)
    Eligible for Reduced-Price Lunch Program: 378 (11.6%)
Teachers: 166.6 (19.5 to 1)
Librarians/Media Specialists: 5.0 (650.0 to 1)
Guidance Counselors: 7.0 (464.3 to 1)
Current Spending: ($ per student per year):
    Total: $6,700; Instruction: $4,338; Support Services: $1,975

Enrollment, Drop-out Rates and Diploma Recipients by Race/Ethnicity

Category	Total	White	Black	Asian	AIAN	Hisp.
Enrollment (%)	100.0	18.0	0.5	0.5	0.3	80.6
Drop-out Rate (%)	4.3	3.9	0.0	0.0	0.0	4.6
H.S. Diplomas (#)	182	44	0	4	2	132

Naches Valley SD 3

24 Shafer Ave • Naches, WA 98937-9744
(509) 653-2220 • http://www.esd105.wednet.edu/
Grade Span: KG-12; **Agency Type:** 1
Schools: 3
    2 Primary; 0 Middle; 1 High; 0 Other Level
    3 Regular; 0 Special Education; 0 Vocational; 0 Alternative
    0 Magnet; 0 Charter; 2 Title I Eligible; 0 School-wide Title I
Students: 1,593 (53.2% male; 46.7% female)
    Individual Education Program: 132 (8.3%);
    English Language Learner: 0 (0.0%); Migrant: n/a
    Eligible for Free Lunch Program: 322 (20.2%)
    Eligible for Reduced-Price Lunch Program: 134 (8.4%)
Teachers: 82.5 (19.3 to 1)
Librarians/Media Specialists: 3.0 (531.0 to 1)
Guidance Counselors: 2.4 (663.8 to 1)
Current Spending: ($ per student per year):
    Total: $6,172; Instruction: $3,720; Support Services: $2,171

Enrollment, Drop-out Rates and Diploma Recipients by Race/Ethnicity

Category	Total	White	Black	Asian	AIAN	Hisp.
Enrollment (%)	100.0	84.2	1.4	0.6	0.8	13.1
Drop-out Rate (%)	1.8	2.0	0.0	0.0	0.0	0.0
H.S. Diplomas (#)	90	83	0	0	0	7

Selah SD 119

105 W Bartlett Ave • Selah, WA 98942-1117
(509) 697-0706 • http://www.selah.k12.wa.us/Index.cfm
Grade Span: PK-12; **Agency Type:** 1
Schools: 7
    3 Primary; 1 Middle; 2 High; 1 Other Level
    5 Regular; 1 Special Education; 0 Vocational; 1 Alternative
    0 Magnet; 0 Charter; 2 Title I Eligible; 1 School-wide Title I
Students: 3,587 (51.7% male; 48.2% female)
    Individual Education Program: 399 (11.1%);
    English Language Learner: 0 (0.0%); Migrant: n/a
    Eligible for Free Lunch Program: 1,158 (32.3%)
    Eligible for Reduced-Price Lunch Program: 409 (11.4%)
Teachers: 177.7 (20.2 to 1)
Librarians/Media Specialists: 5.0 (717.4 to 1)
Guidance Counselors: 7.3 (491.4 to 1)
Current Spending: ($ per student per year):
    Total: $6,702; Instruction: $4,274; Support Services: $2,119

Enrollment, Drop-out Rates and Diploma Recipients by Race/Ethnicity

Category	Total	White	Black	Asian	AIAN	Hisp.
Enrollment (%)	100.0	79.5	1.3	0.9	1.9	16.3
Drop-out Rate (%)	3.2	3.0	0.0	5.6	0.0	5.4
H.S. Diplomas (#)	214	186	1	7	1	19

Sunnyside SD 201

1110 S 6th St • Sunnyside, WA 98944-2197
(509) 836-6532 • http://www.sunnyside.wednet.edu/
Grade Span: PK-12; **Agency Type:** 1
Schools: 8
    4 Primary; 2 Middle; 2 High; 0 Other Level
    6 Regular; 0 Special Education; 0 Vocational; 2 Alternative
    0 Magnet; 0 Charter; 8 Title I Eligible; 5 School-wide Title I
Students: 5,681 (51.4% male; 48.5% female)
    Individual Education Program: 594 (10.5%);
    English Language Learner: 489 (8.6%); Migrant: n/a
    Eligible for Free Lunch Program: 3,935 (69.3%)
    Eligible for Reduced-Price Lunch Program: 487 (8.6%)

Teachers: 294.5 (19.3 to 1)
Librarians/Media Specialists: 6.0 (946.8 to 1)
Guidance Counselors: 17.0 (334.2 to 1)
Current Spending: ($ per student per year):
    Total: $6,917; Instruction: $4,124; Support Services: $2,459

Enrollment, Drop-out Rates and Diploma Recipients by Race/Ethnicity

Category	Total	White	Black	Asian	AIAN	Hisp.
Enrollment (%)	100.0	17.2	0.2	0.5	0.2	81.9
Drop-out Rate (%)	17.1	12.8	0.0	9.1	0.0	19.0
H.S. Diplomas (#)	279	85	1	6	0	187

Toppenish SD 202

106 Franklin Ave • Toppenish, WA 98948-1248
(509) 865-4455 • http://www.toppenish.wednet.edu/
Grade Span: PK-12; **Agency Type:** 1
Schools: 8
    4 Primary; 1 Middle; 2 High; 1 Other Level
    6 Regular; 1 Special Education; 0 Vocational; 1 Alternative
    0 Magnet; 0 Charter; 7 Title I Eligible; 7 School-wide Title I
Students: 3,391 (51.1% male; 48.8% female)
    Individual Education Program: 344 (10.1%);
    English Language Learner: 0 (0.0%); Migrant: n/a
    Eligible for Free Lunch Program: 2,464 (72.7%)
    Eligible for Reduced-Price Lunch Program: 425 (12.5%)
Teachers: 188.7 (18.0 to 1)
Librarians/Media Specialists: 6.0 (565.2 to 1)
Guidance Counselors: 9.9 (342.5 to 1)
Current Spending: ($ per student per year):
    Total: $7,801; Instruction: $4,679; Support Services: $2,690

Enrollment, Drop-out Rates and Diploma Recipients by Race/Ethnicity

Category	Total	White	Black	Asian	AIAN	Hisp.
Enrollment (%)	100.0	5.7	0.2	0.4	15.0	78.7
Drop-out Rate (%)	13.6	8.9	0.0	0.0	26.2	11.7
H.S. Diplomas (#)	142	19	0	1	20	102

Wapato SD 207

212 W 3rd St • Wapato, WA 98951-1308
(509) 877-4181 • http://www.wapato.k12.wa.us/
Grade Span: KG-12; **Agency Type:** 1
Schools: 6
    3 Primary; 1 Middle; 1 High; 1 Other Level
    5 Regular; 0 Special Education; 0 Vocational; 1 Alternative
    0 Magnet; 0 Charter; 6 Title I Eligible; 6 School-wide Title I
Students: 3,490 (51.1% male; 48.8% female)
    Individual Education Program: 348 (10.0%);
    English Language Learner: 22 (0.6%); Migrant: n/a
    Eligible for Free Lunch Program: 2,607 (74.7%)
    Eligible for Reduced-Price Lunch Program: 354 (10.1%)
Teachers: 175.4 (19.9 to 1)
Librarians/Media Specialists: 4.5 (775.6 to 1)
Guidance Counselors: 7.9 (441.8 to 1)
Current Spending: ($ per student per year):
    Total: $7,244; Instruction: $4,053; Support Services: $2,725

Enrollment, Drop-out Rates and Diploma Recipients by Race/Ethnicity

Category	Total	White	Black	Asian	AIAN	Hisp.
Enrollment (%)	100.0	8.8	0.4	2.4	26.0	62.4
Drop-out Rate (%)	22.1	12.2	0.0	0.0	36.9	19.1
H.S. Diplomas (#)	147	27	1	2	20	97

West Valley SD 208

8902 Zier Rd • Yakima, WA 98908-9240
(509) 972-6000 • http://www.esd105.wednet.edu/WestValley/
Grade Span: KG-12; **Agency Type:** 1
Schools: 9
    6 Primary; 1 Middle; 1 High; 1 Other Level
    9 Regular; 0 Special Education; 0 Vocational; 0 Alternative
    0 Magnet; 0 Charter; 4 Title I Eligible; 0 School-wide Title I
Students: 4,680 (52.2% male; 47.7% female)
    Individual Education Program: 482 (10.3%);
    English Language Learner: 371 (7.9%); Migrant: n/a
    Eligible for Free Lunch Program: 890 (19.0%)
    Eligible for Reduced-Price Lunch Program: 413 (8.8%)
Teachers: 218.7 (21.4 to 1)
Librarians/Media Specialists: 3.0 (1,560.0 to 1)
Guidance Counselors: 13.0 (360.0 to 1)
Current Spending: ($ per student per year):
    Total: $6,325; Instruction: $3,786; Support Services: $2,209

Enrollment, Drop-out Rates and Diploma Recipients by Race/Ethnicity

Category	Total	White	Black	Asian	AIAN	Hisp.
Enrollment (%)	100.0	80.1	1.2	2.5	1.9	14.2
Drop-out Rate (%)	1.8	1.4	10.0	0.0	0.0	5.8
H.S. Diplomas (#)	332	288	1	12	1	30

Yakima SD 7
104 N 4th Ave • Yakima, WA 98902-2636
(509) 573-7001 • http://www.ysd.wednet.edu/
Grade Span: PK-12; **Agency Type:** 1
Schools: 24
   14 Primary; 4 Middle; 4 High; 2 Other Level
   22 Regular; 0 Special Education; 1 Vocational; 1 Alternative
   0 Magnet; 0 Charter; 21 Title I Eligible; 21 School-wide Title I
Students: 14,528   (51.3% male; 48.6% female)
   Individual Education Program: 1,556 (10.7%);
   English Language Learner: 57 (0.4%); Migrant: n/a
   Eligible for Free Lunch Program: 7,867 (54.2%)
   Eligible for Reduced-Price Lunch Program: 1,694 (11.7%)
Teachers: 777.5 (18.7 to 1)
Librarians/Media Specialists: 17.8 (816.2 to 1)
Guidance Counselors: 31.7 (458.3 to 1)
Current Spending: ($ per student per year):
   Total: $7,474; Instruction: $4,819; Support Services: $2,299
Enrollment, Drop-out Rates and Diploma Recipients by Race/Ethnicity

Category	Total	White	Black	Asian	AIAN	Hisp.
Enrollment (%)	100.0	37.5	3.3	1.2	2.4	55.7
Drop-out Rate (%)	18.4	15.7	14.4	5.4	28.3	21.7
H.S. Diplomas (#)	616	366	26	19	5	200

Number of Schools

Rank	Number	District Name	City
1	129	Seattle SD 1	Seattle
2	66	Spokane SD 81	Spokane
3	61	Tacoma SD 10	Tacoma
4	49	Lake Washington SD 414	Redmond
5	46	Federal Way SD 210	Federal Way
6	42	Edmonds SD 15	Lynnwood
6	42	Kent SD 415	Kent
8	37	Vancouver SD 37	Vancouver
9	35	Evergreen SD 114	Vancouver
9	35	Northshore SD 417	Bothell
11	33	Clover Park SD 400	Lakewood
12	32	Bellevue SD 405	Bellevue
12	32	Highline SD 401	Seattle
12	32	Puyallup SD 3	Puyallup
15	31	Everett SD 2	Everett
16	29	Bethel SD 403	Spanaway
17	27	Bellingham SD 501	Bellingham
18	26	Renton SD 403	Renton
19	25	Kennewick SD 17	Kennewick
20	24	Central Kitsap SD 401	Silverdale
20	24	Yakima SD 7	Yakima
22	23	Central Valley SD 356	Greenacres
22	23	Issaquah SD 411	Issaquah
22	23	Mukilteo SD 6	Everett
25	21	Marysville SD 25	Marysville
25	21	Shoreline SD 412	Shoreline
27	20	Auburn SD 408	Auburn
28	19	North Thurston SD 3	Lacey
28	19	Snohomish SD 201	Snohomish
30	18	Battle Ground SD 119	Brush Prairie
30	18	Olympia SD 111	Olympia
32	17	South Kitsap SD 402	Port Orchard
33	16	Pasco SD 001	Pasco
33	16	Peninsula SD 401	Gig Harbor
33	16	Wenatchee SD 246	Wenatchee
36	15	Franklin Pierce SD 402	Tacoma
36	15	Monroe SD 103	Monroe
36	15	Richland SD 400	Richland
39	14	Bremerton SD 100	Bremerton
39	14	Longview SD 122	Longview
39	14	North Kitsap SD 400	Poulsbo
39	14	Walla Walla SD 140	Walla Walla
43	13	Kelso SD 458	Kelso
43	13	Mead SD 354	Mead
43	13	Oak Harbor SD 201	Oak Harbor
43	13	Port Angeles SD 121	Port Angeles
43	13	Sumner SD #320	Sumner
43	13	Tumwater SD 33	Tumwater
43	13	West Valley SD 363	Spokane
50	12	Aberdeen SD 5	Aberdeen
50	12	East Valley SD 361	Spokane
50	12	Moses Lake SD 161	Moses Lake
53	11	Anacortes SD 103	Anacortes
53	11	Bainbridge Island SD 303	Bainbridge Isl
53	11	Lake Stevens SD 4	Lake Stevens
53	11	Sedro-Woolley SD 101	Sedro Woolley
57	10	Eastmont SD 206	East Wenatchee
57	10	Ferndale SD 502	Ferndale
57	10	Mount Vernon SD 320	Mount Vernon
57	10	University Place SD 83	Univ Place
61	9	Arlington SD 16	Arlington
61	9	Cheney SD 360	Cheney
61	9	Clarkston SD 250	Clarkston
61	9	Enumclaw SD 216	Enumclaw
61	9	Shelton SD 309	Shelton
61	9	Stanwood-Camano SD 401	Stanwood
61	9	Tahoma SD 409	Maple Valley
61	9	West Valley SD 208	Yakima
69	8	Burlington-Edison SD 100	Burlington
69	8	Grandview SD 200	Grandview
69	8	North Franklin SD 51	Connell
69	8	Quincy SD 144	Quincy
69	8	Riverview Special Services	Carnation
69	8	Snoqualmie SD 410	Snoqualmie
69	8	Sunnyside SD 201	Sunnyside
69	8	Toppenish SD 202	Toppenish
69	8	Washougal SD 112-6	Washougal
69	8	White River SD 416	Buckley
69	8	Yelm Community Schools	Yelm
80	7	Camas SD 117	Camas
80	7	Centralia SD 401	Centralia
80	7	Chehalis SD 302	Chehalis
80	7	Ephrata SD 165	Ephrata
80	7	Fife SD 417	Tacoma
80	7	Lynden SD 504	Lynden
80	7	Nooksack Valley SD 506	Everson
80	7	Selah SD 119	Selah
80	7	South Whidbey SD 206	Langley
80	7	Steilacoom Historical SD	Steilacoom
90	6	Blaine SD 503	Blaine
90	6	Ellensburg SD 401	Ellensburg
90	6	Hoquiam SD 28	Hoquiam
90	6	Mercer Island SD 400	Mercer Island
90	6	Meridian SD 505	Bellingham
90	6	Mount Baker SD 507	Deming
90	6	North Mason SD 403	Belfair
90	6	Prosser SD 116	Prosser
90	6	Riverside SD 416	Chattaroy
90	6	Rochester SD 401	Rochester
90	6	Wapato SD 207	Wapato
90	6	Woodland SD 404	Woodland
102	5	Colville SD 115	Colville
102	5	Deer Park SD 414	Deer Park
102	5	East Valley SD 90	Yakima
102	5	Eatonville SD 404	Eatonville
102	5	Lakewood SD 306	North Lakewood
102	5	Medical Lake SD 326	Medical Lake
102	5	Nine Mile Falls SD 325/179	Nine Mile Fall
102	5	Omak SD 19	Omak
102	5	Othello SD 147	Othello
102	5	Port Townsend SD 50	Port Townsend
102	5	Pullman SD 267	Pullman
102	5	Sequim SD 323	Sequim
102	5	Sultan Home School	Sultan
102	5	Tukwila SD 406	Tukwila
102	5	Vashon Island SD 402	Vashon
102	5	Wahluke SD 73	Mattawa
118	4	Elma SD 68	Elma
118	4	Granite Falls SD 332	Granite Falls
118	4	Hockinson SD 98	Brush Prairie
118	4	Kiona-Benton SD 52	Benton City
118	4	Orting SD 344	Orting
118	4	Ridgefield SD 122	Ridgefield
124	3	Cashmere SD 222	Cashmere
124	3	Naches Valley SD 3	Naches

Number of Teachers

Rank	Number	District Name	City
1	2,577	Seattle SD 1	Seattle
2	1,764	Tacoma SD 10	Tacoma
3	1,753	Spokane SD 81	Spokane
4	1,371	Kent SD 415	Kent
5	1,287	Evergreen SD 114	Vancouver
6	1,186	Lake Washington SD 414	Redmond
7	1,139	Vancouver SD 37	Vancouver
8	1,125	Federal Way SD 210	Federal Way
9	1,071	Edmonds SD 15	Lynnwood
10	1,020	Puyallup SD 3	Puyallup
11	1,012	Northshore SD 417	Bothell
12	937	Highline SD 401	Seattle
13	874	Everett SD 2	Everett
14	863	Bellevue SD 405	Bellevue
15	825	Bethel SD 403	Spanaway
16	777	Yakima SD 7	Yakima
17	730	Kennewick SD 17	Kennewick
18	729	Issaquah SD 411	Issaquah
19	729	North Thurston SD 3	Lacey
20	715	Mukilteo SD 6	Everett
21	707	Auburn SD 408	Auburn
22	703	Clover Park SD 400	Lakewood
23	687	Central Kitsap SD 401	Silverdale
24	663	Renton SD 403	Renton
25	633	Central Valley SD 356	Greenacres
26	585	South Kitsap SD 402	Port Orchard
27	567	Battle Ground SD 119	Brush Prairie
28	555	Marysville SD 25	Marysville
29	545	Bellingham SD 501	Bellingham
30	533	Pasco SD 001	Pasco
31	530	Shoreline SD 412	Shoreline
32	485	Richland SD 400	Richland
33	466	Peninsula SD 401	Gig Harbor
34	457	Olympia SD 111	Olympia
35	430	Mead SD 354	Mead
36	414	Snohomish SD 201	Snohomish
37	393	Franklin Pierce SD 402	Tacoma
38	383	Sumner SD #320	Sumner
39	376	Longview SD 122	Longview
40	367	Wenatchee SD 246	Wenatchee
41	363	North Kitsap SD 400	Poulsbo
42	349	Moses Lake SD 161	Moses Lake
43	346	Lake Stevens SD 4	Lake Stevens
44	332	Walla Walla SD 140	Walla Walla
45	329	Bremerton SD 100	Bremerton
46	323	Tumwater SD 33	Tumwater
47	311	Tahoma SD 409	Maple Valley
48	307	Oak Harbor SD 201	Oak Harbor
49	294	Sunnyside SD 201	Sunnyside
50	294	Ferndale SD 502	Ferndale
51	293	Mount Vernon SD 320	Mount Vernon
52	286	Monroe SD 103	Monroe
53	279	University Place SD 83	Univ Place
54	278	Stanwood-Camano SD 401	Stanwood
55	272	Eastmont SD 206	East Wenatchee
56	267	Kelso SD 458	Kelso
57	266	Arlington SD 16	Arlington
58	252	Port Angeles SD 121	Port Angeles
59	248	Enumclaw SD 216	Enumclaw
60	244	Yelm Community Schools	Yelm
61	243	Sedro-Woolley SD 101	Sedro Woolley
62	236	Snoqualmie SD 410	Snoqualmie
63	235	Camas SD 117	Camas
64	229	East Valley SD 361	Spokane
65	223	White River SD 416	Buckley
66	218	West Valley SD 208	Yakima
67	217	Aberdeen SD 5	Aberdeen
68	216	Shelton SD 309	Shelton
69	207	Mercer Island SD 400	Mercer Island
70	200	Bainbridge Island SD 303	Bainbridge Isl
71	195	Cheney SD 360	Cheney
72	188	Toppenish SD 202	Toppenish
73	177	Selah SD 119	Selah
74	175	Wapato SD 207	Wapato
75	175	Burlington-Edison SD 100	Burlington
76	175	Centralia SD 401	Centralia
77	168	Othello SD 147	Othello
78	166	Grandview SD 200	Grandview
79	166	West Valley SD 363	Spokane
80	160	Fife SD 417	Tacoma
81	160	Chehalis SD 302	Chehalis
82	150	Anacortes SD 103	Anacortes
83	148	Riverview Special Services	Carnation
84	145	Ellensburg SD 401	Ellensburg
85	139	Prosser SD 116	Prosser
86	137	Sequim SD 323	Sequim
87	136	Tukwila SD 406	Tukwila
88	136	Washougal SD 112-6	Washougal
89	134	Quincy SD 144	Quincy
90	134	Clarkston SD 250	Clarkston
91	132	Lynden SD 504	Lynden
92	129	Mount Baker SD 507	Deming
93	126	North Mason SD 403	Belfair
94	125	Lakewood SD 306	North Lakewood
95	123	Medical Lake SD 326	Medical Lake
96	122	East Valley SD 90	Yakima
97	120	Granite Falls SD 332	Granite Falls
98	120	Rochester SD 401	Rochester
99	116	South Whidbey SD 206	Langley
100	114	Sultan Home School	Sultan
101	114	Pullman SD 267	Pullman
102	112	Ephrata SD 165	Ephrata
103	111	Colville SD 115	Colville
104	108	Eatonville SD 404	Eatonville
105	107	North Franklin SD 51	Connell
106	106	Steilacoom Historical SD	Steilacoom
107	106	Hoquiam SD 28	Hoquiam
108	102	Orting SD 344	Orting
109	101	Blaine SD 503	Blaine
110	101	Omak SD 19	Omak
111	100	Wahluke SD 73	Mattawa
112	100	Nooksack Valley SD 506	Everson
113	99	Elma SD 68	Elma
114	98	Deer Park SD 414	Deer Park
115	97	Woodland SD 404	Woodland
116	94	Riverside SD 416	Chattaroy
117	84	Vashon Island SD 402	Vashon
118	83	Port Townsend SD 50	Port Townsend
118	83	Ridgefield SD 122	Ridgefield
120	83	Nine Mile Falls SD 325/179	Nine Mile Fall
121	83	Meridian SD 505	Bellingham
122	82	Kiona-Benton SD 52	Benton City
123	82	Naches Valley SD 3	Naches
124	80	Hockinson SD 98	Brush Prairie
125	78	Cashmere SD 222	Cashmere

Number of Students

Rank	Number	District Name	City
1	47,588	Seattle SD 1	Seattle
2	33,605	Tacoma SD 10	Tacoma
3	31,068	Spokane SD 81	Spokane
4	26,860	Kent SD 415	Kent
5	24,144	Lake Washington SD 414	Redmond
6	23,979	Evergreen SD 114	Vancouver
7	22,538	Federal Way SD 210	Federal Way
8	22,119	Vancouver SD 37	Vancouver
9	21,984	Edmonds SD 15	Lynnwood
10	20,088	Northshore SD 417	Bothell
11	20,043	Puyallup SD 3	Puyallup
12	18,610	Everett SD 2	Everett
13	17,711	Highline SD 401	Seattle
14	17,397	Bethel SD 403	Spanaway
15	16,125	Bellevue SD 405	Bellevue
16	15,146	Issaquah SD 411	Issaquah
17	14,987	Kennewick SD 17	Kennewick
18	14,528	Yakima SD 7	Yakima

19	14,197	Mukilteo SD 6	Everett
20	13,910	Auburn SD 408	Auburn
21	13,280	Renton SD 403	Renton
22	13,217	Clover Park SD 400	Lakewood
23	13,202	Central Kitsap SD 401	Silverdale
24	13,079	North Thurston SD 3	Lacey
25	12,504	Battle Ground SD 119	Brush Prairie
26	11,482	Central Valley SD 356	Greenacres
27	11,382	Marysville SD 25	Marysville
28	11,051	South Kitsap SD 402	Port Orchard
29	10,537	Bellingham SD 501	Bellingham
30	10,477	Pasco SD 001	Pasco
31	10,010	Shoreline SD 412	Shoreline
32	9,790	Richland SD 400	Richland
33	9,726	Peninsula SD 401	Gig Harbor
34	9,234	Olympia SD 111	Olympia
35	9,010	Snohomish SD 201	Snohomish
36	8,731	Mead SD 354	Mead
37	8,088	Sumner SD #320	Sumner
38	7,843	Franklin Pierce SD 402	Tacoma
39	7,576	Longview SD 122	Longview
40	7,505	Wenatchee SD 246	Wenatchee
41	7,489	Lake Stevens SD 4	Lake Stevens
42	7,075	North Kitsap SD 400	Poulsbo
43	6,974	Moses Lake SD 161	Moses Lake
44	6,408	Tahoma SD 409	Maple Valley
45	6,375	Monroe SD 103	Monroe
46	6,261	Walla Walla SD 140	Walla Walla
47	6,257	Oak Harbor SD 201	Oak Harbor
48	6,161	Tumwater SD 33	Tumwater
49	5,935	Mount Vernon SD 320	Mount Vernon
50	5,703	Bremerton SD 100	Bremerton
51	5,681	Sunnyside SD 201	Sunnyside
52	5,476	Eastmont SD 206	East Wenatchee
53	5,421	Stanwood-Camano SD 401	Stanwood
54	5,346	University Place SD 83	Univ Place
55	5,306	Arlington SD 16	Arlington
56	5,250	Kelso SD 458	Kelso
57	5,096	Ferndale SD 502	Ferndale
58	4,985	Enumclaw SD 216	Enumclaw
59	4,901	Snoqualmie SD 410	Snoqualmie
60	4,799	Port Angeles SD 121	Port Angeles
61	4,739	Camas SD 117	Camas
62	4,737	Yelm Community Schools	Yelm
63	4,680	West Valley SD 208	Yakima
64	4,656	Sedro-Woolley SD 101	Sedro Woolley
65	4,469	East Valley SD 361	Spokane
66	4,436	White River SD 416	Buckley
67	4,211	Bainbridge Island SD 303	Bainbridge Isl
68	4,201	Shelton SD 309	Shelton
69	4,163	Mercer Island SD 400	Mercer Island
70	4,140	Aberdeen SD 5	Aberdeen
71	3,795	West Valley SD 363	Spokane
72	3,665	Burlington-Edison SD 100	Burlington
73	3,587	Selah SD 119	Selah
74	3,490	Wapato SD 207	Wapato
75	3,436	Cheney SD 360	Cheney
76	3,391	Toppenish SD 202	Toppenish
77	3,363	Centralia SD 401	Centralia
78	3,250	Grandview SD 200	Grandview
79	3,247	Fife SD 417	Tacoma
80	3,120	Anacortes SD 103	Anacortes
81	3,096	Othello SD 147	Othello
82	2,952	Chehalis SD 302	Chehalis
83	2,949	Ellensburg SD 401	Ellensburg
84	2,914	Riverview Special Services	Carnation
85	2,889	Sequim SD 323	Sequim
86	2,864	Prosser SD 116	Prosser
87	2,832	Clarkston SD 250	Clarkston
88	2,775	Washougal SD 112-6	Washougal
89	2,726	Tukwila SD 406	Tukwila
90	2,678	Lynden SD 504	Lynden
91	2,645	Lakewood SD 306	North Lakewood
92	2,460	Mount Baker SD 507	Deming
93	2,449	East Valley SD 90	Yakima
94	2,405	Granite Falls SD 332	Granite Falls
95	2,386	North Mason SD 403	Belfair
96	2,350	Quincy SD 144	Quincy
97	2,305	Sultan Home School	Sultan
98	2,298	Medical Lake SD 326	Medical Lake
99	2,284	South Whidbey SD 206	Langley
100	2,278	Ephrata SD 165	Ephrata
101	2,272	Pullman SD 267	Pullman
102	2,269	Rochester SD 401	Rochester
103	2,170	Steilacoom Historical SD	Steilacoom
104	2,151	Blaine SD 503	Blaine
105	2,128	Hoquiam SD 28	Hoquiam
106	2,107	Deer Park SD 414	Deer Park
107	2,099	Colville SD 115	Colville
108	2,091	Eatonville SD 404	Eatonville
109	2,039	Woodland SD 404	Woodland
110	1,949	Riverside SD 416	Chattaroy
111	1,942	North Franklin SD 51	Connell
112	1,912	Elma SD 68	Elma
112	1,912	Orting SD 344	Orting
114	1,870	Nooksack Valley SD 506	Everson
115	1,861	Omak SD 19	Omak
116	1,843	Ridgefield SD 122	Ridgefield
117	1,754	Wahluke SD 73	Mattawa
118	1,742	Hockinson SD 98	Brush Prairie
119	1,656	Kiona-Benton SD 52	Benton City
120	1,651	Nine Mile Falls SD 325/179	Nine Mile Fall
121	1,637	Port Townsend SD 50	Port Townsend
122	1,605	Vashon Island SD 402	Vashon
123	1,593	Naches Valley SD 3	Naches
124	1,572	Meridian SD 505	Bellingham
125	1,516	Cashmere SD 222	Cashmere

Male Students

Rank	Percent	District Name	City
1	56.5	Rochester SD 401	Rochester
2	53.6	Medical Lake SD 326	Medical Lake
3	53.5	Chehalis SD 302	Chehalis
4	53.2	Naches Valley SD 3	Naches
5	53.2	Eatonville SD 404	Eatonville
6	53.1	Hoquiam SD 28	Hoquiam
7	53.0	Quincy SD 144	Quincy
8	52.8	Meridian SD 505	Bellingham
9	52.6	Port Angeles SD 121	Port Angeles
10	52.6	Hockinson SD 98	Brush Prairie
11	52.6	Oak Harbor SD 201	Oak Harbor
12	52.6	Orting SD 344	Orting
13	52.5	Ridgefield SD 122	Ridgefield
13	52.5	Sedro-Woolley SD 101	Sedro Woolley
15	52.5	Ellensburg SD 401	Ellensburg
16	52.5	Woodland SD 404	Woodland
17	52.4	North Franklin SD 51	Connell
18	52.3	Camas SD 117	Camas
19	52.2	Snoqualmie SD 410	Snoqualmie
20	52.2	West Valley SD 208	Yakima
21	52.2	Shoreline SD 412	Shoreline
22	52.2	Sultan Home School	Sultan
23	52.1	North Kitsap SD 400	Poulsbo
24	52.1	Clarkston SD 250	Clarkston
25	52.1	Sequim SD 323	Sequim
26	52.1	Bethel SD 403	Spanaway
27	52.0	Nine Mile Falls SD 325/179	Nine Mile Fall
28	52.0	Mercer Island SD 400	Mercer Island
29	52.0	Clover Park SD 400	Lakewood
30	52.0	Blaine SD 503	Blaine
31	52.0	Lake Washington SD 414	Redmond
32	52.0	Bellevue SD 405	Bellevue
33	52.0	Peninsula SD 401	Gig Harbor
34	52.0	East Valley SD 361	Spokane
35	52.0	Kennewick SD 17	Kennewick
36	51.9	Anacortes SD 103	Anacortes
37	51.9	Snohomish SD 201	Snohomish
38	51.9	Kent SD 415	Kent
39	51.9	Marysville SD 25	Marysville
40	51.8	Mukilteo SD 6	Everett
41	51.8	Sumner SD #320	Sumner
42	51.8	Elma SD 68	Elma
43	51.8	Issaquah SD 411	Issaquah
44	51.8	Northshore SD 417	Bothell
45	51.7	Steilacoom Historical SD	Steilacoom
46	51.7	Stanwood-Camano SD 401	Stanwood
47	51.7	Everett SD 2	Everett
48	51.7	Central Kitsap SD 401	Silverdale
49	51.7	Ferndale SD 502	Ferndale
50	51.7	North Mason SD 403	Belfair
51	51.7	Selah SD 119	Selah
52	51.6	South Kitsap SD 402	Port Orchard
53	51.6	Shelton SD 309	Shelton
54	51.6	Pasco SD 001	Pasco
55	51.6	Wahluke SD 73	Mattawa
56	51.6	Lakewood SD 306	North Lakewood
57	51.6	Central Valley SD 356	Greenacres
58	51.6	Enumclaw SD 216	Enumclaw
59	51.6	Federal Way SD 210	Federal Way
60	51.6	Renton SD 403	Renton
61	51.5	Washougal SD 112-6	Washougal
62	51.5	Battle Ground SD 119	Brush Prairie
63	51.5	Olympia SD 111	Olympia
64	51.4	Highline SD 401	Seattle
65	51.4	Ephrata SD 165	Ephrata
66	51.4	Edmonds SD 15	Lynnwood
67	51.4	Vancouver SD 37	Vancouver
68	51.4	Tukwila SD 406	Tukwila
69	51.4	Auburn SD 408	Auburn
70	51.4	Walla Walla SD 140	Walla Walla
71	51.4	Tacoma SD 10	Tacoma
72	51.4	Pullman SD 267	Pullman
73	51.4	Sunnyside SD 201	Sunnyside
74	51.4	Deer Park SD 414	Deer Park
75	51.4	Bainbridge Island SD 303	Bainbridge Isl
76	51.3	Yakima SD 7	Yakima
77	51.3	Tumwater SD 33	Tumwater
78	51.3	East Valley SD 90	Yakima
79	51.3	Granite Falls SD 332	Granite Falls
80	51.3	Seattle SD 1	Seattle
81	51.3	Puyallup SD 3	Puyallup
82	51.3	Moses Lake SD 161	Moses Lake
83	51.3	Cashmere SD 222	Cashmere
84	51.3	North Thurston SD 3	Lacey
85	51.2	Kiona-Benton SD 52	Benton City
86	51.2	Bremerton SD 100	Bremerton
87	51.2	Yelm Community Schools	Yelm
88	51.2	Aberdeen SD 5	Aberdeen
89	51.2	Vashon Island SD 402	Vashon
90	51.2	Longview SD 122	Longview
91	51.1	Franklin Pierce SD 402	Tacoma
92	51.1	Toppenish SD 202	Toppenish
93	51.1	Kelso SD 458	Kelso
94	51.1	Wapato SD 207	Wapato
95	51.1	Eastmont SD 206	East Wenatchee
96	51.1	Evergreen SD 114	Vancouver
97	51.0	West Valley SD 363	Spokane
98	51.0	Wenatchee SD 246	Wenatchee
99	51.0	Arlington SD 16	Arlington
100	51.0	Richland SD 400	Richland
101	50.9	Grandview SD 200	Grandview
102	50.9	Bellingham SD 501	Bellingham
103	50.9	Riverview Special Services	Carnation
104	50.9	Spokane SD 81	Spokane
105	50.8	Port Townsend SD 50	Port Townsend
106	50.8	Tahoma SD 409	Maple Valley
107	50.8	Mount Vernon SD 320	Mount Vernon
108	50.8	University Place SD 83	Univ Place
109	50.8	Omak SD 19	Omak
110	50.8	Centralia SD 401	Centralia
111	50.7	Riverside SD 416	Chattaroy
112	50.7	Lake Stevens SD 4	Lake Stevens
113	50.7	Prosser SD 116	Prosser
114	50.6	Othello SD 147	Othello
115	50.6	Fife SD 417	Tacoma
116	50.6	Lynden SD 504	Lynden
117	50.5	Monroe SD 103	Monroe
118	50.5	Colville SD 115	Colville
119	50.4	Mead SD 354	Mead
120	50.0	White River SD 416	Buckley
121	50.0	Mount Baker SD 507	Deming
122	50.0	Burlington-Edison SD 100	Burlington
123	50.0	Cheney SD 360	Cheney
124	49.4	South Whidbey SD 206	Langley
125	48.8	Nooksack Valley SD 506	Everson

Female Students

Rank	Percent	District Name	City
1	51.1	Nooksack Valley SD 506	Everson
2	50.5	South Whidbey SD 206	Langley
3	50.0	Cheney SD 360	Cheney
4	49.9	Burlington-Edison SD 100	Burlington
5	49.9	Mount Baker SD 507	Deming
6	49.9	White River SD 416	Buckley
7	49.5	Mead SD 354	Mead
8	49.4	Colville SD 115	Colville
9	49.4	Monroe SD 103	Monroe
10	49.3	Lynden SD 504	Lynden
11	49.3	Fife SD 417	Tacoma
12	49.3	Othello SD 147	Othello
13	49.2	Prosser SD 116	Prosser
14	49.2	Lake Stevens SD 4	Lake Stevens
15	49.2	Riverside SD 416	Chattaroy
16	49.1	Centralia SD 401	Centralia
17	49.1	Omak SD 19	Omak
18	49.1	University Place SD 83	Univ Place
19	49.1	Mount Vernon SD 320	Mount Vernon
20	49.1	Tahoma SD 409	Maple Valley
21	49.1	Port Townsend SD 50	Port Townsend
22	49.0	Spokane SD 81	Spokane
23	49.0	Riverview Special Services	Carnation
24	49.0	Bellingham SD 501	Bellingham
25	49.0	Grandview SD 200	Grandview
26	48.9	Richland SD 400	Richland
27	48.9	Arlington SD 16	Arlington
28	48.9	Wenatchee SD 246	Wenatchee
29	48.9	West Valley SD 363	Spokane
30	48.8	Evergreen SD 114	Vancouver
31	48.8	Eastmont SD 206	East Wenatchee
32	48.8	Wapato SD 207	Wapato
33	48.8	Kelso SD 458	Kelso
34	48.8	Toppenish SD 202	Toppenish
35	48.8	Franklin Pierce SD 402	Tacoma
36	48.7	Longview SD 122	Longview
37	48.7	Vashon Island SD 402	Vashon
38	48.7	Aberdeen SD 5	Aberdeen

39	48.7	Yelm Community Schools	Yelm
40	48.7	Bremerton SD 100	Bremerton
41	48.7	Kiona-Benton SD 52	Benton City
42	48.6	North Thurston SD 3	Lacey
43	48.6	Cashmere SD 222	Cashmere
44	48.6	Moses Lake SD 161	Moses Lake
45	48.6	Puyallup SD 3	Puyallup
46	48.6	Seattle SD 1	Seattle
47	48.6	Granite Falls SD 332	Granite Falls
48	48.6	East Valley SD 90	Yakima
49	48.6	Tumwater SD 33	Tumwater
50	48.6	Yakima SD 7	Yakima
51	48.5	Bainbridge Island SD 303	Bainbridge Isl
52	48.5	Deer Park SD 414	Deer Park
53	48.5	Sunnyside SD 201	Sunnyside
54	48.5	Pullman SD 267	Pullman
55	48.5	Tacoma SD 10	Tacoma
56	48.5	Walla Walla SD 140	Walla Walla
57	48.5	Auburn SD 408	Auburn
58	48.5	Tukwila SD 406	Tukwila
59	48.5	Vancouver SD 37	Vancouver
60	48.5	Edmonds SD 15	Lynnwood
61	48.5	Ephrata SD 165	Ephrata
62	48.5	Highline SD 401	Seattle
63	48.4	Olympia SD 111	Olympia
64	48.4	Battle Ground SD 119	Brush Prairie
65	48.4	Washougal SD 112-6	Washougal
66	48.3	Renton SD 403	Renton
67	48.3	Federal Way SD 210	Federal Way
68	48.3	Enumclaw SD 216	Enumclaw
69	48.3	Central Valley SD 356	Greenacres
70	48.3	Lakewood SD 306	North Lakewood
71	48.3	Wahluke SD 73	Mattawa
72	48.3	Pasco SD 001	Pasco
73	48.3	Shelton SD 309	Shelton
74	48.3	South Kitsap SD 402	Port Orchard
75	48.2	Selah SD 119	Selah
76	48.2	North Mason SD 403	Belfair
77	48.2	Ferndale SD 502	Ferndale
78	48.2	Central Kitsap SD 401	Silverdale
79	48.2	Everett SD 2	Everett
80	48.2	Stanwood-Camano SD 401	Stanwood
81	48.2	Steilacoom Historical SD	Steilacoom
82	48.1	Northshore SD 417	Bothell
83	48.1	Issaquah SD 411	Issaquah
84	48.1	Elma SD 68	Elma
85	48.1	Sumner SD #320	Sumner
86	48.1	Mukilteo SD 6	Everett
87	48.0	Marysville SD 25	Marysville
88	48.0	Kent SD 415	Kent
89	48.0	Snohomish SD 201	Snohomish
90	48.0	Anacortes SD 103	Anacortes
91	47.9	Kennewick SD 17	Kennewick
92	47.9	East Valley SD 361	Spokane
93	47.9	Peninsula SD 401	Gig Harbor
94	47.9	Bellevue SD 405	Bellevue
95	47.9	Lake Washington SD 414	Redmond
96	47.9	Blaine SD 503	Blaine
97	47.9	Clover Park SD 400	Lakewood
98	47.9	Mercer Island SD 400	Mercer Island
99	47.9	Nine Mile Falls SD 325/179	Nine Mile Fall
100	47.8	Bethel SD 403	Spanaway
101	47.8	Sequim SD 323	Sequim
102	47.8	Clarkston SD 250	Clarkston
103	47.8	North Kitsap SD 400	Poulsbo
104	47.7	Sultan Home School	Sultan
105	47.7	Shoreline SD 412	Shoreline
106	47.7	West Valley SD 208	Yakima
107	47.7	Snoqualmie SD 410	Snoqualmie
108	47.6	Camas SD 117	Camas
109	47.5	North Franklin SD 51	Connell
110	47.4	Woodland SD 404	Woodland
111	47.4	Ellensburg SD 401	Ellensburg
112	47.4	Ridgefield SD 122	Ridgefield
112	47.4	Sedro-Woolley SD 101	Sedro Woolley
114	47.3	Orting SD 344	Orting
115	47.3	Oak Harbor SD 201	Oak Harbor
116	47.3	Hockinson SD 98	Brush Prairie
117	47.3	Port Angeles SD 121	Port Angeles
118	47.1	Meridian SD 505	Bellingham
119	46.9	Quincy SD 144	Quincy
120	46.8	Hoquiam SD 28	Hoquiam
121	46.7	Eatonville SD 404	Eatonville
122	46.7	Naches Valley SD 3	Naches
123	46.4	Chehalis SD 302	Chehalis
124	46.3	Medical Lake SD 326	Medical Lake
125	43.4	Rochester SD 401	Rochester

Individual Education Program Students

Rank	Percent	District Name	City
1	14.9	Rochester SD 401	Rochester
2	14.7	Clarkston SD 250	Clarkston
3	14.2	Port Angeles SD 121	Port Angeles
4	13.2	Omak SD 19	Omak
4	13.2	Sultan Home School	Sultan
6	13.0	Cheney SD 360	Cheney
7	12.9	Granite Falls SD 332	Granite Falls
8	12.7	Orting SD 344	Orting
9	12.6	Clover Park SD 400	Lakewood
10	12.4	Deer Park SD 414	Deer Park
10	12.4	Kiona-Benton SD 52	Benton City
12	12.3	Ferndale SD 502	Ferndale
12	12.3	South Kitsap SD 402	Port Orchard
14	12.2	Meridian SD 505	Bellingham
14	12.2	Mount Baker SD 507	Deming
14	12.2	Shelton SD 309	Shelton
17	12.1	Bethel SD 403	Spanaway
17	12.1	North Thurston SD 3	Lacey
17	12.1	Vancouver SD 37	Vancouver
20	12.0	Stanwood-Camano SD 401	Stanwood
21	11.9	Aberdeen SD 5	Aberdeen
21	11.9	Longview SD 122	Longview
21	11.9	Tacoma SD 10	Tacoma
24	11.8	Central Kitsap SD 401	Silverdale
24	11.8	Central Valley SD 356	Greenacres
24	11.8	Northshore SD 417	Bothell
27	11.7	Shoreline SD 412	Shoreline
27	11.7	Spokane SD 81	Spokane
29	11.6	Colville SD 115	Colville
29	11.6	Tahoma SD 409	Maple Valley
31	11.5	Bellingham SD 501	Bellingham
31	11.5	Bremerton SD 100	Bremerton
31	11.5	East Valley SD 90	Yakima
31	11.5	Sedro-Woolley SD 101	Sedro Woolley
35	11.4	Lakewood SD 306	North Lakewood
35	11.4	Mount Vernon SD 320	Mount Vernon
35	11.4	North Mason SD 403	Belfair
35	11.4	White River SD 416	Buckley
39	11.3	Elma SD 68	Elma
39	11.3	Seattle SD 1	Seattle
41	11.2	Franklin Pierce SD 402	Tacoma
41	11.2	Renton SD 403	Renton
41	11.2	Sumner SD #320	Sumner
44	11.1	Arlington SD 16	Arlington
44	11.1	Eastmont SD 206	East Wenatchee
44	11.1	Richland SD 400	Richland
44	11.1	Selah SD 119	Selah
48	11.0	Bainbridge Island SD 303	Bainbridge Isl
48	11.0	Walla Walla SD 140	Walla Walla
50	10.9	Centralia SD 401	Centralia
50	10.9	Highline SD 401	Seattle
50	10.9	Kent SD 415	Kent
50	10.9	Nooksack Valley SD 506	Everson
50	10.9	Yelm Community Schools	Yelm
55	10.8	Chehalis SD 302	Chehalis
55	10.8	Eatonville SD 404	Eatonville
55	10.8	Nine Mile Falls SD 325/179	Nine Mile Fall
55	10.8	Peninsula SD 401	Gig Harbor
55	10.8	Steilacoom Historical SD	Steilacoom
60	10.7	East Valley SD 361	Spokane
60	10.7	Enumclaw SD 216	Enumclaw
60	10.7	Evergreen SD 114	Vancouver
60	10.7	Federal Way SD 210	Federal Way
60	10.7	North Kitsap SD 400	Poulsbo
60	10.7	Riverside SD 416	Chattaroy
60	10.7	Yakima SD 7	Yakima
67	10.6	Edmonds SD 15	Lynnwood
67	10.6	Kelso SD 458	Kelso
67	10.6	Lake Stevens SD 4	Lake Stevens
67	10.6	Marysville SD 25	Marysville
67	10.6	Olympia SD 111	Olympia
67	10.6	Pullman SD 267	Pullman
67	10.6	Puyallup SD 3	Puyallup
67	10.6	Tumwater SD 33	Tumwater
75	10.5	Port Townsend SD 50	Port Townsend
75	10.5	Sunnyside SD 201	Sunnyside
77	10.4	Burlington-Edison SD 100	Burlington
77	10.4	Mead SD 354	Mead
77	10.4	Othello SD 147	Othello
77	10.4	Riverview Special Services	Carnation
77	10.4	Snohomish SD 201	Snohomish
77	10.4	University Place SD 83	Univ Place
83	10.3	Wahluke SD 73	Mattawa
83	10.3	West Valley SD 208	Yakima
85	10.2	Anacortes SD 103	Anacortes
85	10.2	Ephrata SD 165	Ephrata
87	10.1	Battle Ground SD 119	Brush Prairie
87	10.1	Everett SD 2	Everett
87	10.1	Ridgefield SD 122	Ridgefield
87	10.1	Toppenish SD 202	Toppenish
91	10.0	Ellensburg SD 401	Ellensburg
91	10.0	Quincy SD 144	Quincy
91	10.0	Wapato SD 207	Wapato
94	9.9	Grandview SD 200	Grandview
94	9.9	Hoquiam SD 28	Hoquiam
94	9.9	West Valley SD 363	Spokane
97	9.8	Camas SD 117	Camas
97	9.8	Medical Lake SD 326	Medical Lake
99	9.7	Blaine SD 503	Blaine
99	9.7	Issaquah SD 411	Issaquah
99	9.7	North Franklin SD 51	Connell
99	9.7	Washougal SD 112-6	Washougal
99	9.7	Woodland SD 404	Woodland
104	9.6	Monroe SD 103	Monroe
104	9.6	South Whidbey SD 206	Langley
106	9.4	Kennewick SD 17	Kennewick
106	9.4	Mukilteo SD 6	Everett
106	9.4	Pasco SD 001	Pasco
109	9.3	Oak Harbor SD 201	Oak Harbor
109	9.3	Prosser SD 116	Prosser
111	9.2	Moses Lake SD 161	Moses Lake
112	9.1	Auburn SD 408	Auburn
112	9.1	Sequim SD 323	Sequim
112	9.1	Tukwila SD 406	Tukwila
115	9.0	Hockinson SD 98	Brush Prairie
115	9.0	Snoqualmie SD 410	Snoqualmie
115	9.0	Vashon Island SD 402	Vashon
118	8.8	Bellevue SD 405	Bellevue
118	8.8	Mercer Island SD 400	Mercer Island
120	8.5	Lake Washington SD 414	Redmond
121	8.3	Naches Valley SD 3	Naches
122	8.1	Wenatchee SD 246	Wenatchee
123	7.9	Fife SD 417	Tacoma
124	7.8	Cashmere SD 222	Cashmere
125	7.5	Lynden SD 504	Lynden

English Language Learner Students

Rank	Percent	District Name	City
1	85.7	Snohomish SD 201	Snohomish
2	71.4	Orting SD 344	Orting
3	65.0	Cashmere SD 222	Cashmere
4	44.8	Bethel SD 403	Spanaway
5	40.9	Peninsula SD 401	Gig Harbor
6	40.5	Sultan Home School	Sultan
7	30.2	Riverside SD 416	Chattaroy
8	22.5	West Valley SD 363	Spokane
9	19.8	Mount Vernon SD 320	Mount Vernon
10	19.6	Highline SD 401	Seattle
11	16.8	East Valley SD 90	Yakima
12	16.4	University Place SD 83	Univ Place
13	15.0	Aberdeen SD 5	Aberdeen
14	14.3	Deer Park SD 414	Deer Park
15	13.2	Blaine SD 503	Blaine
16	12.7	Kent SD 415	Kent
17	12.5	Vashon Island SD 402	Vashon
18	12.1	Stanwood-Camano SD 401	Stanwood
19	11.0	Wenatchee SD 246	Wenatchee
20	10.8	Centralia SD 401	Centralia
21	9.5	Everett SD 2	Everett
22	9.2	Franklin Pierce SD 402	Tacoma
23	8.6	Lake Washington SD 414	Redmond
23	8.6	Sunnyside SD 201	Sunnyside
25	8.5	Bremerton SD 100	Bremerton
26	8.1	Mount Baker SD 507	Deming
27	8.0	Clarkston SD 250	Clarkston
28	7.9	West Valley SD 208	Yakima
29	7.7	Kelso SD 458	Kelso
30	6.7	Longview SD 122	Longview
31	6.6	Bainbridge Island SD 303	Bainbridge Isl
32	6.2	Elma SD 68	Elma
33	5.7	Central Valley SD 356	Greenacres
34	5.6	Moses Lake SD 161	Moses Lake
35	4.6	Spokane SD 81	Spokane
36	4.2	Ellensburg SD 401	Ellensburg
37	4.1	Kiona-Benton SD 52	Benton City
38	3.8	Ephrata SD 165	Ephrata
38	3.8	Mead SD 354	Mead
40	3.1	Bellevue SD 405	Bellevue
41	3.0	Kennewick SD 17	Kennewick
41	3.0	Monroe SD 103	Monroe
43	2.8	Shoreline SD 412	Shoreline
44	2.7	Evergreen SD 114	Vancouver
44	2.7	Mukilteo SD 6	Everett
46	2.6	North Thurston SD 3	Lacey
47	2.5	South Kitsap SD 402	Port Orchard
47	2.5	South Whidbey SD 206	Langley
49	2.0	Omak SD 19	Omak
50	1.9	Nine Mile Falls SD 325/179	Nine Mile Fall
51	1.8	Bellingham SD 501	Bellingham
52	1.7	Burlington-Edison SD 100	Burlington
52	1.7	Lynden SD 504	Lynden
52	1.7	Walla Walla SD 140	Walla Walla
55	1.6	Auburn SD 408	Auburn
56	1.5	Hoquiam SD 28	Hoquiam
57	1.4	Quincy SD 144	Quincy
57	1.4	Yelm Community Schools	Yelm
59	1.3	Othello SD 147	Othello

Rank	Percent	District Name	City
59	1.3	Port Angeles SD 121	Port Angeles
61	1.1	Central Kitsap SD 401	Silverdale
61	1.1	Edmonds SD 15	Lynnwood
61	1.1	Olympia SD 111	Olympia
61	1.1	Sedro-Woolley SD 101	Sedro Woolley
61	1.1	Sumner SD #320	Sumner
66	1.0	Ferndale SD 502	Ferndale
67	0.9	Chehalis SD 302	Chehalis
67	0.9	East Valley SD 361	Spokane
69	0.8	Prosser SD 116	Prosser
70	0.7	Camas SD 117	Camas
71	0.6	Renton SD 403	Renton
71	0.6	Steilacoom Historical SD	Steilacoom
71	0.6	Wapato SD 207	Wapato
74	0.5	Vancouver SD 37	Vancouver
75	0.4	Yakima SD 7	Yakima
76	0.2	Battle Ground SD 119	Brush Prairie
76	0.2	White River SD 416	Buckley
78	0.0	Anacortes SD 103	Anacortes
78	0.0	Arlington SD 16	Arlington
78	0.0	Cheney SD 360	Cheney
78	0.0	Clover Park SD 400	Lakewood
78	0.0	Colville SD 115	Colville
78	0.0	Eastmont SD 206	East Wenatchee
78	0.0	Eatonville SD 404	Eatonville
78	0.0	Enumclaw SD 216	Enumclaw
78	0.0	Federal Way SD 210	Federal Way
78	0.0	Fife SD 417	Tacoma
78	0.0	Grandview SD 200	Grandview
78	0.0	Granite Falls SD 332	Granite Falls
78	0.0	Hockinson SD 98	Brush Prairie
78	0.0	Issaquah SD 411	Issaquah
78	0.0	Lake Stevens SD 4	Lake Stevens
78	0.0	Lakewood SD 306	North Lakewood
78	0.0	Marysville SD 25	Marysville
78	0.0	Medical Lake SD 326	Medical Lake
78	0.0	Mercer Island SD 400	Mercer Island
78	0.0	Meridian SD 505	Bellingham
78	0.0	Naches Valley SD 3	Naches
78	0.0	Nooksack Valley SD 506	Everson
78	0.0	North Franklin SD 51	Connell
78	0.0	North Kitsap SD 400	Poulsbo
78	0.0	North Mason SD 403	Belfair
78	0.0	Northshore SD 417	Bothell
78	0.0	Oak Harbor SD 201	Oak Harbor
78	0.0	Pasco SD 001	Pasco
78	0.0	Port Townsend SD 50	Port Townsend
78	0.0	Pullman SD 267	Pullman
78	0.0	Puyallup SD 3	Puyallup
78	0.0	Richland SD 400	Richland
78	0.0	Ridgefield SD 122	Ridgefield
78	0.0	Riverview Special Services	Carnation
78	0.0	Rochester SD 401	Rochester
78	0.0	Seattle SD 1	Seattle
70	0.0	Selah SD 119	Selah
78	0.0	Sequim SD 323	Sequim
78	0.0	Shelton SD 309	Shelton
78	0.0	Snoqualmie SD 410	Snoqualmie
78	0.0	Tacoma SD 10	Tacoma
78	0.0	Tahoma SD 409	Maple Valley
78	0.0	Toppenish SD 202	Toppenish
78	0.0	Tukwila SD 406	Tukwila
78	0.0	Tumwater SD 33	Tumwater
78	0.0	Wahluke SD 73	Mattawa
78	0.0	Woodland SD 404	Woodland
125	n/a	Washougal SD 112-6	Washougal

Migrant Students

Rank	Percent	District Name	City
1	n/a	Aberdeen SD 5	Aberdeen
1	n/a	Anacortes SD 103	Anacortes
1	n/a	Arlington SD 16	Arlington
1	n/a	Auburn SD 408	Auburn
1	n/a	Bainbridge Island SD 303	Bainbridge Isl
1	n/a	Battle Ground SD 119	Brush Prairie
1	n/a	Bellevue SD 405	Bellevue
1	n/a	Bellingham SD 501	Bellingham
1	n/a	Bethel SD 403	Spanaway
1	n/a	Blaine SD 503	Blaine
1	n/a	Bremerton SD 100	Bremerton
1	n/a	Burlington-Edison SD 100	Burlington
1	n/a	Camas SD 117	Camas
1	n/a	Cashmere SD 222	Cashmere
1	n/a	Central Kitsap SD 401	Silverdale
1	n/a	Central Valley SD 356	Greenacres
1	n/a	Centralia SD 401	Centralia
1	n/a	Chehalis SD 302	Chehalis
1	n/a	Cheney SD 360	Cheney
1	n/a	Clarkston SD 250	Clarkston
1	n/a	Clover Park SD 400	Lakewood
1	n/a	Colville SD 115	Colville
1	n/a	Deer Park SD 414	Deer Park
1	n/a	East Valley SD 361	Spokane
1	n/a	East Valley SD 90	Yakima
1	n/a	Eastmont SD 206	East Wenatchee
1	n/a	Eatonville SD 404	Eatonville
1	n/a	Edmonds SD 15	Lynnwood
1	n/a	Ellensburg SD 401	Ellensburg
1	n/a	Elma SD 68	Elma
1	n/a	Enumclaw SD 216	Enumclaw
1	n/a	Ephrata SD 165	Ephrata
1	n/a	Everett SD 2	Everett
1	n/a	Evergreen SD 114	Vancouver
1	n/a	Federal Way SD 210	Federal Way
1	n/a	Ferndale SD 502	Ferndale
1	n/a	Fife SD 417	Tacoma
1	n/a	Franklin Pierce SD 402	Tacoma
1	n/a	Grandview SD 200	Grandview
1	n/a	Granite Falls SD 332	Granite Falls
1	n/a	Highline SD 401	Seattle
1	n/a	Hockinson SD 98	Brush Prairie
1	n/a	Hoquiam SD 28	Hoquiam
1	n/a	Issaquah SD 411	Issaquah
1	n/a	Kelso SD 458	Kelso
1	n/a	Kennewick SD 17	Kennewick
1	n/a	Kent SD 415	Kent
1	n/a	Kiona-Benton SD 52	Benton City
1	n/a	Lake Stevens SD 4	Lake Stevens
1	n/a	Lake Washington SD 414	Redmond
1	n/a	Lakewood SD 306	North Lakewood
1	n/a	Longview SD 122	Longview
1	n/a	Lynden SD 504	Lynden
1	n/a	Marysville SD 25	Marysville
1	n/a	Mead SD 354	Mead
1	n/a	Medical Lake SD 326	Medical Lake
1	n/a	Mercer Island SD 400	Mercer Island
1	n/a	Meridian SD 505	Bellingham
1	n/a	Monroe SD 103	Monroe
1	n/a	Moses Lake SD 161	Moses Lake
1	n/a	Mount Baker SD 507	Deming
1	n/a	Mount Vernon SD 320	Mount Vernon
1	n/a	Mukilteo SD 6	Everett
1	n/a	Naches Valley SD 3	Naches
1	n/a	Nine Mile Falls SD 325/179	Nine Mile Fall
1	n/a	Nooksack Valley SD 506	Everson
1	n/a	North Franklin SD 51	Connell
1	n/a	North Kitsap SD 400	Poulsbo
1	n/a	North Mason SD 403	Belfair
1	n/a	North Thurston SD 3	Lacey
1	n/a	Northshore SD 417	Bothell
1	n/a	Oak Harbor SD 201	Oak Harbor
1	n/a	Olympia SD 111	Olympia
1	n/a	Omak SD 19	Omak
1	n/a	Orting SD 344	Orting
1	n/a	Othello SD 147	Othello
1	n/a	Pasco SD 001	Pasco
1	n/a	Peninsula SD 401	Gig Harbor
1	n/a	Port Angeles SD 121	Port Angeles
1	n/a	Port Townsend SD 50	Port Townsend
1	n/a	Prosser SD 116	Prosser
1	n/a	Pullman SD 267	Pullman
1	n/a	Puyallup SD 3	Puyallup
1	n/a	Quincy SD 144	Quincy
1	n/a	Renton SD 403	Renton
1	n/a	Richland SD 400	Richland
1	n/a	Ridgefield SD 122	Ridgefield
1	n/a	Riverside SD 416	Chattaroy
1	n/a	Riverview Special Services	Carnation
1	n/a	Rochester SD 401	Rochester
1	n/a	Seattle SD 1	Seattle
1	n/a	Sedro-Woolley SD 101	Sedro Woolley
1	n/a	Selah SD 119	Selah
1	n/a	Sequim SD 323	Sequim
1	n/a	Shelton SD 309	Shelton
1	n/a	Shoreline SD 412	Shoreline
1	n/a	Snohomish SD 201	Snohomish
1	n/a	Snoqualmie SD 410	Snoqualmie
1	n/a	South Kitsap SD 402	Port Orchard
1	n/a	South Whidbey SD 206	Langley
1	n/a	Spokane SD 81	Spokane
1	n/a	Stanwood-Camano SD 401	Stanwood
1	n/a	Steilacoom Historical SD	Steilacoom
1	n/a	Sultan Home School	Sultan
1	n/a	Sumner SD #320	Sumner
1	n/a	Sunnyside SD 201	Sunnyside
1	n/a	Tacoma SD 10	Tacoma
1	n/a	Tahoma SD 409	Maple Valley
1	n/a	Toppenish SD 202	Toppenish
1	n/a	Tukwila SD 406	Tukwila
1	n/a	Tumwater SD 33	Tumwater
1	n/a	University Place SD 83	Univ Place
1	n/a	Vancouver SD 37	Vancouver
1	n/a	Vashon Island SD 402	Vashon
1	n/a	Wahluke SD 73	Mattawa
1	n/a	Walla Walla SD 140	Walla Walla
1	n/a	Wapato SD 207	Wapato
1	n/a	Washougal SD 112-6	Washougal
1	n/a	Wenatchee SD 246	Wenatchee
1	n/a	West Valley SD 208	Yakima
1	n/a	West Valley SD 363	Spokane
1	n/a	White River SD 416	Buckley
1	n/a	Woodland SD 404	Woodland
1	n/a	Yakima SD 7	Yakima
1	n/a	Yelm Community Schools	Yelm

Students Eligible for Free Lunch

Rank	Percent	District Name	City
1	74.7	Wapato SD 207	Wapato
2	73.0	Wahluke SD 73	Mattawa
3	72.7	Toppenish SD 202	Toppenish
4	69.3	Sunnyside SD 201	Sunnyside
5	67.3	Grandview SD 200	Grandview
6	58.9	Othello SD 147	Othello
7	58.2	North Franklin SD 51	Connell
8	54.4	Pasco SD 001	Pasco
9	54.2	Yakima SD 7	Yakima
10	51.2	Tukwila SD 406	Tukwila
11	48.3	Quincy SD 144	Quincy
12	46.2	Mount Vernon SD 320	Mount Vernon
13	45.6	Aberdeen SD 5	Aberdeen
14	44.0	Highline SD 401	Seattle
15	42.7	Prosser SD 116	Prosser
16	42.2	Hoquiam SD 28	Hoquiam
17	40.8	Moses Lake SD 161	Moses Lake
18	40.7	Tacoma SD 10	Tacoma
19	40.5	Centralia SD 401	Centralia
20	38.7	Omak SD 19	Omak
21	38.4	Shelton SD 309	Shelton
22	37.5	Walla Walla SD 140	Walla Walla
23	37.4	Mount Baker SD 507	Deming
24	37.3	Wenatchee SD 246	Wenatchee
25	37.0	Deer Park SD 414	Deer Park
26	36.1	Bremerton SD 100	Bremerton
26	36.1	Longview SD 122	Longview
26	36.1	Spokane SD 81	Spokane
29	35.4	Clover Park SD 400	Lakewood
30	35.3	Clarkston SD 250	Clarkston
31	34.6	Colville SD 115	Colville
32	34.4	Kiona-Benton SD 52	Benton City
33	34.2	Vancouver SD 37	Vancouver
34	33.8	Franklin Pierce SD 402	Tacoma
35	33.5	Kelso SD 458	Kelso
36	33.1	Seattle SD 1	Seattle
37	32.7	Ferndale SD 502	Ferndale
38	32.6	Nooksack Valley SD 506	Everson
39	32.3	Selah SD 119	Selah
40	31.3	Eastmont SD 206	East Wenatchee
41	31.1	Renton SD 403	Renton
42	31.0	Elma SD 68	Elma
42	31.0	West Valley SD 363	Spokane
44	30.6	Blaine SD 503	Blaine
45	30.3	Cashmere SD 222	Cashmere
45	30.3	East Valley SD 90	Yakima
47	29.9	Port Angeles SD 121	Port Angeles
48	29.8	Auburn SD 408	Auburn
49	28.6	Kennewick SD 17	Kennewick
50	28.3	Riverside SD 416	Chattaroy
51	28.1	East Valley SD 361	Spokane
51	28.1	Sedro-Woolley SD 101	Sedro Woolley
53	27.9	Rochester SD 401	Rochester
54	27.4	Ephrata SD 165	Ephrata
55	27.3	Meridian SD 505	Bellingham
55	27.3	Sultan Home School	Sultan
57	27.0	Cheney SD 360	Cheney
58	26.6	Federal Way SD 210	Federal Way
59	25.9	Mukilteo SD 6	Everett
60	25.6	Port Townsend SD 50	Port Townsend
61	25.4	Burlington-Edison SD 100	Burlington
62	25.0	North Mason SD 403	Belfair
63	24.9	Evergreen SD 114	Vancouver
64	24.8	Yelm Community Schools	Yelm
65	24.3	Lynden SD 504	Lynden
65	24.3	Washougal SD 112-6	Washougal
67	24.1	Kent SD 415	Kent
68	23.6	Bethel SD 403	Spanaway
69	23.3	Ellensburg SD 401	Ellensburg
70	22.4	Fife SD 417	Tacoma
71	22.1	Everett SD 2	Everett
72	21.9	Woodland SD 404	Woodland
73	21.3	Bellingham SD 501	Bellingham
74	20.4	Chehalis SD 302	Chehalis
75	20.3	Ridgefield SD 122	Ridgefield
76	20.2	Naches Valley SD 3	Naches
77	20.1	Pullman SD 267	Pullman
78	19.8	North Thurston SD 3	Lacey
79	19.7	Sequim SD 323	Sequim

80	19.4	Granite Falls SD 332	Granite Falls
81	19.0	West Valley SD 208	Yakima
82	18.9	Marysville SD 25	Marysville
83	18.8	Eatonville SD 404	Eatonville
83	18.8	Tumwater SD 33	Tumwater
85	18.4	South Kitsap SD 402	Port Orchard
86	18.2	Central Valley SD 356	Greenacres
86	18.2	Medical Lake SD 326	Medical Lake
88	17.5	Oak Harbor SD 201	Oak Harbor
89	17.3	Anacortes SD 103	Anacortes
90	16.8	Edmonds SD 15	Lynnwood
90	16.8	Lakewood SD 306	North Lakewood
92	16.5	Richland SD 400	Richland
93	16.4	Orting SD 344	Orting
94	16.0	University Place SD 83	Univ Place
95	15.5	Battle Ground SD 119	Brush Prairie
96	15.4	Nine Mile Falls SD 325/179	Nine Mile Fall
96	15.4	Sumner SD #320	Sumner
98	15.3	White River SD 416	Buckley
99	14.9	Arlington SD 16	Arlington
100	14.5	Enumclaw SD 216	Enumclaw
101	14.4	Camas SD 117	Camas
101	14.4	Stanwood-Camano SD 401	Stanwood
103	14.1	North Kitsap SD 400	Poulsbo
104	13.8	Monroe SD 103	Monroe
104	13.8	Puyallup SD 3	Puyallup
106	13.7	Lake Stevens SD 4	Lake Stevens
107	13.5	South Whidbey SD 206	Langley
108	13.4	Olympia SD 111	Olympia
109	13.3	Peninsula SD 401	Gig Harbor
109	13.3	Shoreline SD 412	Shoreline
111	12.7	Bellevue SD 405	Bellevue
112	12.2	Central Kitsap SD 401	Silverdale
113	11.9	Hockinson SD 98	Brush Prairie
114	11.6	Mead SD 354	Mead
115	10.3	Lake Washington SD 414	Redmond
116	9.4	Snoqualmie SD 410	Snoqualmie
117	8.6	Snohomish SD 201	Snohomish
118	7.8	Riverview Special Services	Carnation
119	7.4	Northshore SD 417	Bothell
120	7.0	Steilacoom Historical SD	Steilacoom
120	7.0	Tahoma SD 409	Maple Valley
122	5.2	Vashon Island SD 402	Vashon
123	3.7	Issaquah SD 411	Issaquah
124	3.0	Bainbridge Island SD 303	Bainbridge Isl
125	0.9	Mercer Island SD 400	Mercer Island

Students Eligible for Reduced-Price Lunch

Rank	Percent	District Name	City
1	16.6	Medical Lake SD 326	Medical Lake
2	16.3	Othello SD 147	Othello
3	15.7	Clover Park SD 400	Lakewood
4	15.6	Deer Park SD 414	Deer Park
5	13.9	Nooksack Valley SD 506	Everson
6	13.3	East Valley SD 90	Yakima
7	13.0	East Valley SD 361	Spokane
8	12.8	Cashmere SD 222	Cashmere
8	12.8	Port Townsend SD 50	Port Townsend
10	12.7	Franklin Pierce SD 402	Tacoma
11	12.5	Toppenish SD 202	Toppenish
12	12.4	Colville SD 115	Colville
12	12.4	West Valley SD 363	Spokane
14	12.3	Granite Falls SD 332	Granite Falls
15	12.2	Bremerton SD 100	Bremerton
15	12.2	Ferndale SD 502	Ferndale
17	12.0	Eatonville SD 404	Eatonville
17	12.0	Riverside SD 416	Chattaroy
17	12.0	Spokane SD 81	Spokane
20	11.8	Oak Harbor SD 201	Oak Harbor
21	11.7	Yakima SD 7	Yakima
22	11.6	Grandview SD 200	Grandview
22	11.6	Quincy SD 144	Quincy
22	11.6	Yelm Community Schools	Yelm
25	11.4	Hoquiam SD 28	Hoquiam
25	11.4	Selah SD 119	Selah
27	11.3	Bethel SD 403	Spanaway
27	11.3	Omak SD 19	Omak
29	11.2	Ephrata SD 165	Ephrata
29	11.2	Kelso SD 458	Kelso
29	11.2	Tukwila SD 406	Tukwila
32	11.0	Cheney SD 360	Cheney
33	10.9	Highline SD 401	Seattle
34	10.8	Meridian SD 505	Bellingham
34	10.8	Wahluke SD 73	Mattawa
36	10.7	Nine Mile Falls SD 325/179	Nine Mile Fall
36	10.7	North Thurston SD 3	Lacey
36	10.7	Tacoma SD 10	Tacoma
39	10.6	Mount Baker SD 507	Deming
40	10.5	Evergreen SD 114	Vancouver
41	10.4	Blaine SD 503	Blaine
41	10.4	Moses Lake SD 161	Moses Lake
41	10.4	Renton SD 403	Renton
41	10.4	Rochester SD 401	Rochester
45	10.3	Federal Way SD 210	Federal Way
45	10.3	Woodland SD 404	Woodland
47	10.1	Kiona-Benton SD 52	Benton City
47	10.1	North Mason SD 403	Belfair
47	10.1	Pasco SD 001	Pasco
47	10.1	Wapato SD 207	Wapato
51	9.9	Aberdeen SD 5	Aberdeen
51	9.9	Lakewood SD 306	North Lakewood
53	9.8	Central Valley SD 356	Greenacres
53	9.8	Sultan Home School	Sultan
55	9.7	Prosser SD 116	Prosser
56	9.6	Marysville SD 25	Marysville
57	9.5	Mount Vernon SD 320	Mount Vernon
58	9.4	Elma SD 68	Elma
58	9.4	Shelton SD 309	Shelton
60	9.3	North Franklin SD 51	Connell
60	9.3	Port Angeles SD 121	Port Angeles
60	9.3	University Place SD 83	Univ Place
63	9.2	Auburn SD 408	Auburn
63	9.2	Lynden SD 504	Lynden
65	9.1	Central Kitsap SD 401	Silverdale
65	9.1	Centralia SD 401	Centralia
65	9.1	Vancouver SD 37	Vancouver
68	9.0	Eastmont SD 206	East Wenatchee
69	8.9	Fife SD 417	Tacoma
70	8.8	West Valley SD 208	Yakima
71	8.7	Sedro-Woolley SD 101	Sedro Woolley
72	8.6	Mukilteo SD 6	Everett
72	8.6	Sunnyside SD 201	Sunnyside
72	8.6	Walla Walla SD 140	Walla Walla
75	8.4	Battle Ground SD 119	Brush Prairie
75	8.4	Chehalis SD 302	Chehalis
75	8.4	Clarkston SD 250	Clarkston
75	8.4	Naches Valley SD 3	Naches
79	8.3	Kent SD 415	Kent
80	8.2	Sequim SD 323	Sequim
80	8.2	South Kitsap SD 402	Port Orchard
82	8.1	Mead SD 354	Mead
82	8.1	Tumwater SD 33	Tumwater
84	7.9	Edmonds SD 15	Lynnwood
84	7.9	Ridgefield SD 122	Ridgefield
84	7.9	Sumner SD #320	Sumner
87	7.8	Kennewick SD 17	Kennewick
88	7.6	Anacortes SD 103	Anacortes
88	7.6	Ellensburg SD 401	Ellensburg
88	7.6	Orting SD 344	Orting
91	7.5	Burlington-Edison SD 100	Burlington
91	7.5	Wenatchee SD 246	Wenatchee
93	7.4	Puyallup SD 3	Puyallup
94	7.3	Bellingham SD 501	Bellingham
94	7.3	Everett SD 2	Everett
96	7.2	Washougal SD 112-6	Washougal
97	7.1	Arlington SD 16	Arlington
97	7.1	White River SD 416	Buckley
99	6.9	Lake Stevens SD 4	Lake Stevens
99	6.9	Longview SD 122	Longview
101	6.7	Seattle SD 1	Seattle
102	6.6	Monroe SD 103	Monroe
102	6.6	Stanwood-Camano SD 401	Stanwood
104	6.4	Camas SD 117	Camas
105	6.3	Peninsula SD 401	Gig Harbor
106	6.0	Hockinson SD 98	Brush Prairie
106	6.0	North Kitsap SD 400	Poulsbo
108	5.9	Richland SD 400	Richland
109	5.7	Pullman SD 267	Pullman
109	5.7	Shoreline SD 412	Shoreline
111	5.5	Enumclaw SD 216	Enumclaw
112	5.3	South Whidbey SD 206	Langley
113	5.2	Olympia SD 111	Olympia
114	4.6	Bellevue SD 405	Bellevue
115	4.5	Steilacoom Historical SD	Steilacoom
116	4.4	Riverview Special Services	Carnation
116	4.4	Tahoma SD 409	Maple Valley
118	4.0	Snoqualmie SD 410	Snoqualmie
119	3.3	Snohomish SD 201	Snohomish
120	3.2	Northshore SD 417	Bothell
121	3.1	Lake Washington SD 414	Redmond
122	2.9	Vashon Island SD 402	Vashon
123	2.1	Issaquah SD 411	Issaquah
124	1.8	Bainbridge Island SD 303	Bainbridge Isl
125	0.8	Mercer Island SD 400	Mercer Island

Student/Teacher Ratio

Rank	Ratio	District Name	City
1	22.8	West Valley SD 363	Spokane
2	22.3	Monroe SD 103	Monroe
3	22.0	Battle Ground SD 119	Brush Prairie
3	22.0	Ridgefield SD 122	Ridgefield
5	21.7	Hockinson SD 98	Brush Prairie
5	21.7	Snohomish SD 201	Snohomish
7	21.6	Lake Stevens SD 4	Lake Stevens
8	21.4	Deer Park SD 414	Deer Park
8	21.4	West Valley SD 208	Yakima
10	21.3	Everett SD 2	Everett
11	21.2	Blaine SD 503	Blaine
12	21.1	Bethel SD 403	Spanaway
12	21.1	Lakewood SD 306	North Lakewood
12	21.1	Sequim SD 323	Sequim
12	21.1	Sumner SD #320	Sumner
16	21.0	Bainbridge Island SD 303	Bainbridge Isl
16	21.0	Clarkston SD 250	Clarkston
18	20.9	Burlington-Edison SD 100	Burlington
18	20.9	Woodland SD 404	Woodland
20	20.8	Anacortes SD 103	Anacortes
20	20.8	Issaquah SD 411	Issaquah
20	20.8	Peninsula SD 401	Gig Harbor
23	20.7	Snoqualmie SD 410	Snoqualmie
24	20.6	Riverside SD 416	Chattaroy
24	20.6	Tahoma SD 409	Maple Valley
26	20.5	Edmonds SD 15	Lynnwood
26	20.5	Kennewick SD 17	Kennewick
26	20.5	Marysville SD 25	Marysville
26	20.5	Prosser SD 116	Prosser
30	20.4	Oak Harbor SD 201	Oak Harbor
30	20.4	Wenatchee SD 246	Wenatchee
32	20.3	Ephrata SD 165	Ephrata
32	20.3	Lake Washington SD 414	Redmond
32	20.3	Lynden SD 504	Lynden
32	20.3	Mead SD 354	Mead
32	20.3	Steilacoom Historical SD	Steilacoom
32	20.3	Washougal SD 112-6	Washougal
38	20.2	Ellensburg SD 401	Ellensburg
38	20.2	Fife SD 417	Tacoma
38	20.2	Mount Vernon SD 320	Mount Vernon
38	20.2	Olympia SD 111	Olympia
38	20.2	Richland SD 400	Richland
38	20.2	Selah SD 119	Selah
44	20.1	Camas SD 117	Camas
44	20.1	Eastmont SD 206	East Wenatchee
44	20.1	Hoquiam SD 28	Hoquiam
44	20.1	Longview SD 122	Longview
44	20.1	Mercer Island SD 400	Mercer Island
44	20.1	Sultan Home School	Sultan
50	20.0	East Valley SD 90	Yakima
50	20.0	Enumclaw SD 216	Enumclaw
50	20.0	Federal Way SD 210	Federal Way
50	20.0	Granite Falls SD 332	Granite Falls
50	20.0	Kiona-Benton SD 52	Benton City
50	20.0	Moses Lake SD 161	Moses Lake
50	20.0	Renton SD 403	Renton
57	19.9	Arlington SD 16	Arlington
57	19.9	Franklin Pierce SD 402	Tacoma
57	19.9	Mukilteo SD 6	Everett
57	19.9	Pullman SD 267	Pullman
57	19.9	Tukwila SD 406	Tukwila
57	19.9	Wapato SD 207	Wapato
63	19.8	Nine Mile Falls SD 325/179	Nine Mile Fall
63	19.8	Northshore SD 417	Bothell
63	19.8	White River SD 416	Buckley
66	19.7	Auburn SD 408	Auburn
67	19.6	Kelso SD 458	Kelso
67	19.6	Kent SD 415	Kent
67	19.6	Pasco SD 001	Pasco
67	19.6	Puyallup SD 3	Puyallup
67	19.6	Riverview Special Services	Carnation
67	19.6	South Whidbey SD 206	Langley
73	19.5	East Valley SD 361	Spokane
73	19.5	Grandview SD 200	Grandview
73	19.5	North Kitsap SD 400	Poulsbo
73	19.5	Port Townsend SD 50	Port Townsend
73	19.5	Stanwood-Camano SD 401	Stanwood
78	19.4	Cashmere SD 222	Cashmere
78	19.4	Shelton SD 309	Shelton
78	19.4	Vancouver SD 37	Vancouver
78	19.4	Yelm Community Schools	Yelm
82	19.3	Bellingham SD 501	Bellingham
82	19.3	Naches Valley SD 3	Naches
82	19.3	Sunnyside SD 201	Sunnyside
85	19.2	Central Kitsap SD 401	Silverdale
85	19.2	Centralia SD 401	Centralia
85	19.2	Eatonville SD 404	Eatonville
85	19.2	Elma SD 68	Elma
89	19.1	Mount Baker SD 507	Deming
89	19.1	Sedro-Woolley SD 101	Sedro Woolley
89	19.1	University Place SD 83	Univ Place
89	19.1	Vashon Island SD 402	Vashon
93	19.0	Aberdeen SD 5	Aberdeen
93	19.0	Port Angeles SD 121	Port Angeles
93	19.0	Tacoma SD 10	Tacoma
93	19.0	Tumwater SD 33	Tumwater
97	18.9	Highline SD 401	Seattle
97	18.9	Meridian SD 505	Bellingham

97	18.9	Rochester SD 401	Rochester
97	18.9	Shoreline SD 412	Shoreline
97	18.9	South Kitsap SD 402	Port Orchard
102	18.8	Clover Park SD 400	Lakewood
102	18.8	Colville SD 115	Colville
102	18.8	North Mason SD 403	Belfair
102	18.8	Walla Walla SD 140	Walla Walla
106	18.7	Bellevue SD 405	Bellevue
106	18.7	Medical Lake SD 326	Medical Lake
106	18.7	Orting SD 344	Orting
106	18.7	Yakima SD 7	Yakima
110	18.6	Evergreen SD 114	Vancouver
110	18.6	Nooksack Valley SD 506	Everson
112	18.5	Seattle SD 1	Seattle
113	18.4	Chehalis SD 302	Chehalis
113	18.4	Omak SD 19	Omak
113	18.4	Othello SD 147	Othello
116	18.1	Central Valley SD 356	Greenacres
116	18.1	North Franklin SD 51	Connell
118	18.0	Toppenish SD 202	Toppenish
119	17.9	North Thurston SD 3	Lacey
120	17.7	Spokane SD 81	Spokane
121	17.6	Cheney SD 360	Cheney
122	17.4	Quincy SD 144	Quincy
122	17.4	Wahluke SD 73	Mattawa
124	17.3	Bremerton SD 100	Bremerton
124	17.3	Ferndale SD 502	Ferndale

Student/Librarian Ratio

Rank	Ratio	District Name	City
1	2,775.0	Washougal SD 112-6	Washougal
2	2,678.0	Lynden SD 504	Lynden
3	2,658.6	Omak SD 19	Omak
4	2,350.0	Quincy SD 144	Quincy
5	2,269.0	Rochester SD 401	Rochester
6	2,128.0	Hoquiam SD 28	Hoquiam
7	2,070.0	Aberdeen SD 5	Aberdeen
8	1,949.0	Riverside SD 416	Chattaroy
9	1,937.2	Moses Lake SD 161	Moses Lake
10	1,907.1	Peninsula SD 401	Gig Harbor
11	1,870.0	Nooksack Valley SD 506	Everson
12	1,843.0	Ridgefield SD 122	Ridgefield
13	1,832.5	Burlington-Edison SD 100	Burlington
14	1,713.9	Port Angeles SD 121	Port Angeles
15	1,681.5	Centralia SD 401	Centralia
16	1,632.7	East Valley SD 90	Yakima
17	1,572.0	Meridian SD 505	Bellingham
18	1,560.0	West Valley SD 208	Yakima
19	1,424.0	Tahoma SD 409	Maple Valley
20	1,416.0	Clarkston SD 250	Clarkston
21	1,294.1	Arlington SD 16	Arlington
22	1,273.0	Shelton SD 309	Shelton
23	1,230.0	Mount Baker SD 507	Deming
24	1,227.9	South Kitsap SD 402	Port Orchard
25	1,136.0	Pullman SD 267	Pullman
26	1,133.0	Enumclaw SD 216	Enumclaw
27	1,120.4	Franklin Pierce SD 402	Tacoma
28	1,085.0	Steilacoom Historical SD	Steilacoom
29	1,061.7	Kent SD 415	Kent
30	1,045.5	Eatonville SD 404	Eatonville
31	1,007.9	Yelm Community Schools	Yelm
32	964.6	Marysville SD 25	Marysville
33	957.7	Deer Park SD 414	Deer Park
34	956.0	Orting SD 344	Orting
35	954.5	Battle Ground SD 119	Brush Prairie
36	952.5	Pasco SD 001	Pasco
37	947.5	Cashmere SD 222	Cashmere
38	946.8	Sunnyside SD 201	Sunnyside
39	898.7	Sumner SD #320	Sumner
40	891.1	Snoqualmie SD 410	Snoqualmie
41	891.0	University Place SD 83	Univ Place
42	877.0	Wahluke SD 73	Mattawa
43	871.0	Hockinson SD 98	Brush Prairie
44	835.1	Mukilteo SD 6	Everett
45	832.6	Mercer Island SD 400	Mercer Island
46	832.1	Lake Stevens SD 4	Lake Stevens
47	828.4	Bethel SD 403	Spanaway
48	828.0	Kiona-Benton SD 52	Benton City
49	826.9	Evergreen SD 114	Vancouver
50	825.5	Nine Mile Falls SD 325/179	Nine Mile Fall
51	816.2	Yakima SD 7	Yakima
52	801.7	Granite Falls SD 332	Granite Falls
53	793.7	Mead SD 354	Mead
54	790.0	Vancouver SD 37	Vancouver
55	789.2	Sedro-Woolley SD 101	Sedro Woolley
56	787.0	Monroe SD 103	Monroe
57	777.4	Colville SD 115	Colville
58	775.6	Wapato SD 207	Wapato
59	775.4	Everett SD 2	Everett
60	772.8	Auburn SD 408	Auburn
61	769.5	Olympia SD 111	Olympia
62	767.9	Bellevue SD 405	Bellevue
63	762.1	Puyallup SD 3	Puyallup
64	759.3	Ephrata SD 165	Ephrata
65	759.0	West Valley SD 363	Spokane
66	757.3	Issaquah SD 411	Issaquah
67	743.1	North Thurston SD 3	Lacey
68	739.3	White River SD 416	Buckley
69	734.7	Kennewick SD 17	Kennewick
70	726.6	Snohomish SD 201	Snohomish
71	722.3	Sequim SD 323	Sequim
72	717.8	Federal Way SD 210	Federal Way
73	717.4	Selah SD 119	Selah
74	717.0	Blaine SD 503	Blaine
75	713.8	South Whidbey SD 206	Langley
76	711.0	Oak Harbor SD 201	Oak Harbor
77	707.5	North Kitsap SD 400	Poulsbo
78	701.8	Bainbridge Island SD 303	Bainbridge Isl
79	699.3	Richland SD 400	Richland
80	695.7	Walla Walla SD 140	Walla Walla
81	694.9	Wenatchee SD 246	Wenatchee
82	685.7	Seattle SD 1	Seattle
83	679.7	Woodland SD 404	Woodland
84	677.6	Stanwood-Camano SD 401	Stanwood
85	677.0	Camas SD 117	Camas
86	669.6	Spokane SD 81	Spokane
87	667.3	Renton SD 403	Renton
88	661.3	Lakewood SD 306	North Lakewood
89	659.8	Eastmont SD 206	East Wenatchee
90	659.4	Mount Vernon SD 320	Mount Vernon
91	656.6	Medical Lake SD 326	Medical Lake
92	656.1	Lake Washington SD 414	Redmond
93	656.0	Chehalis SD 302	Chehalis
94	650.0	Grandview SD 200	Grandview
95	642.0	Longview SD 122	Longview
96	636.4	Prosser SD 116	Prosser
97	635.3	Tacoma SD 10	Tacoma
98	631.7	Edmonds SD 15	Lynnwood
99	629.4	East Valley SD 361	Spokane
100	624.0	Anacortes SD 103	Anacortes
101	622.3	Tumwater SD 33	Tumwater
102	619.2	Othello SD 147	Othello
103	617.9	Shoreline SD 412	Shoreline
104	616.2	Northshore SD 417	Bothell
105	614.0	Central Kitsap SD 401	Silverdale
106	596.6	Kelso SD 458	Kelso
107	596.5	North Mason SD 403	Belfair
108	589.8	Ellensburg SD 401	Ellensburg
109	588.5	North Franklin SD 51	Connell
110	584.6	Port Townsend SD 50	Port Townsend
111	582.8	Riverview Special Services	Carnation
112	576.3	Sultan Home School	Sultan
113	574.1	Central Valley SD 356	Greenacres
114	570.3	Bremerton SD 100	Bremerton
115	566.2	Ferndale SD 502	Ferndale
116	565.2	Toppenish SD 202	Toppenish
117	554.6	Bellingham SD 501	Bellingham
118	553.5	Highline SD 401	Seattle
119	545.2	Tukwila SD 406	Tukwila
120	541.2	Fife SD 417	Tacoma
121	535.0	Vashon Island SD 402	Vashon
122	531.0	Naches Valley SD 3	Naches
123	528.7	Clover Park SD 400	Lakewood
124	528.6	Cheney SD 360	Cheney
125	n/a	Elma SD 68	Elma

Student/Counselor Ratio

Rank	Ratio	District Name	City
1	1,742.0	Hockinson SD 98	Brush Prairie
2	1,389.3	Battle Ground SD 119	Brush Prairie
3	1,387.5	Washougal SD 112-6	Washougal
4	1,066.4	Port Angeles SD 121	Port Angeles
5	1,006.3	Orting SD 344	Orting
6	944.0	Clarkston SD 250	Clarkston
7	921.5	Ridgefield SD 122	Ridgefield
8	860.4	Mukilteo SD 6	Everett
9	842.5	Eastmont SD 206	East Wenatchee
10	810.0	Olympia SD 111	Olympia
11	809.2	Bethel SD 403	Spanaway
12	808.4	Mead SD 354	Mead
13	786.2	Nine Mile Falls SD 325/179	Nine Mile Fall
14	768.3	Sultan Home School	Sultan
15	767.6	Central Kitsap SD 401	Silverdale
16	738.0	Chehalis SD 302	Chehalis
17	728.2	Tahoma SD 409	Maple Valley
18	709.9	Shoreline SD 412	Shoreline
19	709.5	Kelso SD 458	Kelso
19	709.5	Sumner SD #320	Sumner
21	709.3	Hoquiam SD 28	Hoquiam
22	703.5	Walla Walla SD 140	Walla Walla
23	681.5	Tukwila SD 406	Tukwila
24	679.7	Woodland SD 404	Woodland
25	670.2	Edmonds SD 15	Lynnwood
26	669.6	Northshore SD 417	Bothell
27	663.8	Naches Valley SD 3	Naches
28	662.7	Fife SD 417	Tacoma
29	655.9	Colville SD 115	Colville
30	652.9	Snohomish SD 201	Snohomish
31	638.4	East Valley SD 361	Spokane
32	627.2	Bellingham SD 501	Bellingham
33	619.2	Othello SD 147	Othello
34	605.1	Snoqualmie SD 410	Snoqualmie
35	601.2	Moses Lake SD 161	Moses Lake
36	596.5	North Mason SD 403	Belfair
37	591.5	Federal Way SD 210	Federal Way
38	584.8	Issaquah SD 411	Issaquah
39	576.7	Stanwood-Camano SD 401	Stanwood
40	574.5	Medical Lake SD 326	Medical Lake
41	571.2	North Franklin SD 51	Connell
42	571.0	Camas SD 117	Camas
43	569.9	Seattle SD 1	Seattle
44	562.6	Mercer Island SD 400	Mercer Island
45	559.1	Mount Baker SD 507	Deming
46	556.9	University Place SD 83	Univ Place
47	552.0	Kiona-Benton SD 52	Benton City
48	546.2	Lake Washington SD 414	Redmond
49	540.3	Deer Park SD 414	Deer Park
50	539.6	Riverview Special Services	Carnation
51	539.4	Kent SD 415	Kent
52	536.9	Vancouver SD 37	Vancouver
53	530.6	Arlington SD 16	Arlington
54	528.4	Pullman SD 267	Pullman
55	528.1	Bremerton SD 100	Bremerton
56	524.5	Marysville SD 25	Marysville
57	524.0	Meridian SD 505	Bellingham
58	522.8	Cashmere SD 222	Cashmere
58	522.8	Eatonville SD 404	Eatonville
60	514.0	South Kitsap SD 402	Port Orchard
61	511.1	Pasco SD 001	Pasco
62	500.8	Bellevue SD 405	Bellevue
63	493.3	Franklin Pierce SD 402	Tacoma
64	491.7	North Thurston SD 3	Lacey
65	491.4	Selah SD 119	Selah
66	489.8	East Valley SD 90	Yakima
67	489.7	Everett SD 2	Everett
68	487.4	Evergreen SD 114	Vancouver
69	486.3	Lake Stevens SD 4	Lake Stevens
70	485.3	Ferndale SD 502	Ferndale
71	485.0	Sedro-Woolley SD 101	Sedro Woolley
72	484.2	Wenatchee SD 246	Wenatchee
73	481.5	Sequim SD 323	Sequim
74	481.0	Granite Falls SD 332	Granite Falls
75	478.0	Elma SD 68	Elma
76	473.9	Tumwater SD 33	Tumwater
77	470.0	Quincy SD 144	Quincy
78	468.3	Kennewick SD 17	Kennewick
79	467.5	Nooksack Valley SD 506	Everson
80	466.9	White River SD 416	Buckley
81	464.3	Grandview SD 200	Grandview
82	461.7	Lynden SD 504	Lynden
83	458.6	Vashon Island SD 402	Vashon
84	458.3	Yakima SD 7	Yakima
85	458.1	Burlington-Edison SD 100	Burlington
86	450.6	North Kitsap SD 400	Poulsbo
87	450.1	Oak Harbor SD 201	Oak Harbor
88	448.4	Puyallup SD 3	Puyallup
89	447.0	Richland SD 400	Richland
90	446.9	Shelton SD 309	Shelton
91	446.5	West Valley SD 363	Spokane
92	445.6	Renton SD 403	Renton
93	442.7	Monroe SD 103	Monroe
94	441.8	Wapato SD 207	Wapato
95	441.6	Central Valley SD 356	Greenacres
96	439.2	South Whidbey SD 206	Langley
97	437.6	Spokane SD 81	Spokane
98	434.9	Cheney SD 360	Cheney
99	433.3	Anacortes SD 103	Anacortes
99	433.3	Auburn SD 408	Auburn
101	433.1	Tacoma SD 10	Tacoma
102	427.7	Clover Park SD 400	Lakewood
103	423.9	Mount Vernon SD 320	Mount Vernon
104	415.4	Enumclaw SD 216	Enumclaw
105	415.1	Prosser SD 116	Prosser
106	411.9	Yelm Community Schools	Yelm
107	407.9	Wahluke SD 73	Mattawa
108	400.8	Longview SD 122	Longview
109	393.6	Bainbridge Island SD 303	Bainbridge Isl
110	392.8	Ephrata SD 165	Ephrata
111	392.7	Highline SD 401	Seattle
112	389.8	Riverside SD 416	Chattaroy
113	378.2	Rochester SD 401	Rochester
114	376.4	Aberdeen SD 5	Aberdeen
115	373.3	Ellensburg SD 401	Ellensburg
116	372.0	Port Townsend SD 50	Port Townsend
117	361.7	Steilacoom Historical SD	Steilacoom
118	361.6	Centralia SD 401	Centralia
119	360.0	West Valley SD 208	Yakima

120	358.5	Blaine SD 503	Blaine
121	352.4	Peninsula SD 401	Gig Harbor
122	342.5	Toppenish SD 202	Toppenish
123	334.8	Lakewood SD 306	North Lakewood
124	334.2	Sunnyside SD 201	Sunnyside
125	332.3	Omak SD 19	Omak

Current Spending per Student in FY2003

Rank	Dollars	District Name	City
1	8,649	Seattle SD 1	Seattle
2	8,005	Omak SD 19	Omak
3	7,801	Toppenish SD 202	Toppenish
4	7,785	Clover Park SD 400	Lakewood
5	7,757	Bremerton SD 100	Bremerton
6	7,649	Wahluke SD 73	Mattawa
7	7,638	Spokane SD 81	Spokane
8	7,621	Longview SD 122	Longview
9	7,591	Tacoma SD 10	Tacoma
10	7,499	Hoquiam SD 28	Hoquiam
11	7,495	Rochester SD 401	Rochester
12	7,489	Chehalis SD 302	Chehalis
13	7,476	Cheney SD 360	Cheney
14	7,474	Yakima SD 7	Yakima
15	7,417	Highline SD 401	Seattle
16	7,409	Ferndale SD 502	Ferndale
17	7,395	Bellevue SD 405	Bellevue
18	7,386	Nooksack Valley SD 506	Everson
19	7,288	North Franklin SD 51	Connell
20	7,286	Colville SD 115	Colville
21	7,281	Mount Vernon SD 320	Mount Vernon
22	7,260	Mercer Island SD 400	Mercer Island
23	7,247	Prosser SD 116	Prosser
24	7,244	Wapato SD 207	Wapato
25	7,230	West Valley SD 363	Spokane
26	7,229	Medical Lake SD 326	Medical Lake
27	7,208	Tumwater SD 33	Tumwater
28	7,200	Shoreline SD 412	Shoreline
28	7,200	Walla Walla SD 140	Walla Walla
30	7,196	Pasco SD 001	Pasco
31	7,188	Quincy SD 144	Quincy
32	7,157	Olympia SD 111	Olympia
33	7,142	Aberdeen SD 5	Aberdeen
34	7,136	Anacortes SD 103	Anacortes
35	7,119	Central Kitsap SD 401	Silverdale
36	7,108	Shelton SD 309	Shelton
37	7,084	Northshore SD 417	Bothell
38	7,079	East Valley SD 361	Spokane
39	7,075	Vancouver SD 37	Vancouver
40	7,059	Blaine SD 503	Blaine
41	7,041	Port Townsend SD 50	Port Townsend
42	7,040	Kelso SD 458	Kelso
43	7,031	Pullman SD 267	Pullman
44	7,030	Bellingham SD 501	Bellingham
45	7,027	Clarkston SD 250	Clarkston
46	7,022	Nine Mile Falls SD 325/179	Nine Mile Fall
47	7,021	Steilacoom Historical SD	Steilacoom
48	7,006	Port Angeles SD 121	Port Angeles
49	6,990	South Whidbey SD 206	Langley
50	6,986	Sedro-Woolley SD 101	Sedro Woolley
51	6,984	Vashon Island SD 402	Vashon
52	6,983	North Thurston SD 3	Lacey
53	6,982	Riverside SD 416	Chattaroy
54	6,981	Woodland SD 404	Woodland
55	6,945	Central Valley SD 356	Greenacres
56	6,940	Everett SD 2	Everett
57	6,929	Elma SD 68	Elma
58	6,923	Kennewick SD 17	Kennewick
59	6,918	Tukwila SD 406	Tukwila
60	6,917	Sunnyside SD 201	Sunnyside
61	6,885	Deer Park SD 414	Deer Park
61	6,885	Enumclaw SD 216	Enumclaw
63	6,881	Franklin Pierce SD 402	Tacoma
64	6,863	Yelm Community Schools	Yelm
65	6,861	North Mason SD 403	Belfair
66	6,858	Kiona-Benton SD 52	Benton City
67	6,849	Ephrata SD 165	Ephrata
67	6,849	Meridian SD 505	Bellingham
69	6,848	University Place SD 83	Univ Place
70	6,840	Mount Baker SD 507	Deming
71	6,838	Centralia SD 401	Centralia
72	6,837	Ellensburg SD 401	Ellensburg
73	6,821	Fife SD 417	Tacoma
74	6,794	Riverview Special Services	Carnation
75	6,791	Mukilteo SD 6	Everett
76	6,786	Othello SD 147	Othello
77	6,779	Lakewood SD 306	North Lakewood
78	6,761	Sultan Home School	Sultan
79	6,756	Puyallup SD 3	Puyallup
80	6,755	North Kitsap SD 400	Poulsbo
81	6,742	Eatonville SD 404	Eatonville
82	6,736	Kent SD 415	Kent
83	6,734	Mead SD 354	Mead
84	6,733	South Kitsap SD 402	Port Orchard
85	6,732	Evergreen SD 114	Vancouver
85	6,732	Renton SD 403	Renton
87	6,729	White River SD 416	Buckley
88	6,721	Edmonds SD 15	Lynnwood
89	6,710	Peninsula SD 401	Gig Harbor
90	6,707	East Valley SD 90	Yakima
91	6,703	Bethel SD 403	Spanaway
91	6,703	Burlington-Edison SD 100	Burlington
93	6,702	Selah SD 119	Selah
94	6,701	Washougal SD 112-6	Washougal
95	6,700	Grandview SD 200	Grandview
96	6,694	Moses Lake SD 161	Moses Lake
97	6,666	Monroe SD 103	Monroe
98	6,665	Marysville SD 25	Marysville
99	6,645	Eastmont SD 206	East Wenatchee
99	6,645	Orting SD 344	Orting
101	6,629	Issaquah SD 411	Issaquah
102	6,602	Wenatchee SD 246	Wenatchee
103	6,593	Cashmere SD 222	Cashmere
104	6,571	Arlington SD 16	Arlington
105	6,551	Richland SD 400	Richland
106	6,548	Federal Way SD 210	Federal Way
107	6,543	Bainbridge Island SD 303	Bainbridge Isl
108	6,540	Auburn SD 408	Auburn
109	6,473	Lake Washington SD 414	Redmond
110	6,442	Oak Harbor SD 201	Oak Harbor
111	6,439	Sumner SD #320	Sumner
112	6,434	Camas SD 117	Camas
113	6,368	Tahoma SD 409	Maple Valley
114	6,325	West Valley SD 208	Yakima
115	6,293	Snoqualmie SD 410	Snoqualmie
116	6,291	Granite Falls SD 332	Granite Falls
117	6,283	Lynden SD 504	Lynden
117	6,283	Snohomish SD 201	Snohomish
119	6,273	Sequim SD 323	Sequim
120	6,237	Battle Ground SD 119	Brush Prairie
121	6,172	Naches Valley SD 3	Naches
122	6,037	Stanwood-Camano SD 401	Stanwood
123	6,011	Ridgefield SD 122	Ridgefield
124	6,007	Lake Stevens SD 4	Lake Stevens
125	5,840	Hockinson SD 98	Brush Prairie

Number of Diploma Recipients

Rank	Number	District Name	City
1	2,629	Seattle SD 1	Seattle
2	1,793	Spokane SD 81	Spokane
3	1,651	Lake Washington SD 414	Redmond
4	1,535	Kent SD 415	Kent
5	1,462	Tacoma SD 10	Tacoma
6	1,413	Northshore SD 417	Bothell
7	1,170	Vancouver SD 37	Vancouver
8	1,153	Puyallup SD 3	Puyallup
9	1,151	Federal Way SD 210	Federal Way
10	1,147	Evergreen SD 114	Vancouver
11	1,111	Edmonds SD 15	Lynnwood
12	1,090	Bellevue SD 405	Bellevue
13	984	Highline SD 401	Seattle
14	977	Kennewick SD 17	Kennewick
15	975	Bethel SD 403	Spanaway
16	972	Central Kitsap SD 401	Silverdale
17	896	Issaquah SD 411	Issaquah
18	885	Everett SD 2	Everett
19	843	Battle Ground SD 119	Brush Prairie
20	836	Auburn SD 408	Auburn
21	822	North Thurston SD 3	Lacey
22	756	Central Valley SD 356	Greenacres
23	746	Shoreline SD 412	Shoreline
24	745	Mukilteo SD 6	Everett
25	743	Richland SD 400	Richland
26	710	Bellingham SD 501	Bellingham
27	681	Olympia SD 111	Olympia
28	679	Mead SD 354	Mead
29	651	Renton SD 403	Renton
30	625	South Kitsap SD 402	Port Orchard
31	616	Yakima SD 7	Yakima
32	604	Peninsula SD 401	Gig Harbor
33	601	Marysville SD 25	Marysville
34	557	Snohomish SD 201	Snohomish
35	457	Walla Walla SD 140	Walla Walla
36	455	Clover Park SD 400	Lakewood
37	432	Wenatchee SD 246	Wenatchee
38	410	University Place SD 83	Univ Place
39	407	Franklin Pierce SD 402	Tacoma
40	401	North Kitsap SD 400	Poulsbo
41	396	Sumner SD #320	Sumner
42	378	Oak Harbor SD 201	Oak Harbor
43	373	Lake Stevens SD 4	Lake Stevens
44	360	Longview SD 122	Longview
45	353	Monroe SD 103	Monroe
45	353	Moses Lake SD 161	Moses Lake
47	351	Tahoma SD 409	Maple Valley
48	343	Eastmont SD 206	East Wenatchee
49	341	Tumwater SD 33	Tumwater
50	332	West Valley SD 208	Yakima
51	330	Mercer Island SD 400	Mercer Island
52	325	Pasco SD 001	Pasco
53	318	Shelton SD 309	Shelton
53	318	Stanwood-Camano SD 401	Stanwood
55	316	Enumclaw SD 216	Enumclaw
56	310	Sedro-Woolley SD 101	Sedro Woolley
57	299	East Valley SD 361	Spokane
58	294	Bainbridge Island SD 303	Bainbridge Isl
59	293	Mount Vernon SD 320	Mount Vernon
60	283	Kelso SD 458	Kelso
60	283	West Valley SD 363	Spokane
62	279	Sunnyside SD 201	Sunnyside
63	273	Aberdeen SD 5	Aberdeen
64	270	Arlington SD 16	Arlington
65	266	Yelm Community Schools	Yelm
66	265	Bremerton SD 100	Bremerton
67	259	Ferndale SD 502	Ferndale
68	240	Snoqualmie SD 410	Snoqualmie
69	232	White River SD 416	Buckley
70	227	Ellensburg SD 401	Ellensburg
71	214	Selah SD 119	Selah
72	210	Chehalis SD 302	Chehalis
73	203	Burlington-Edison SD 100	Burlington
73	203	Camas SD 117	Camas
73	203	Sequim SD 323	Sequim
76	202	Fife SD 417	Tacoma
77	197	Anacortes SD 103	Anacortes
78	182	Grandview SD 200	Grandview
79	179	Centralia SD 401	Centralia
80	171	Elma SD 68	Elma
81	170	Colville SD 115	Colville
82	168	South Whidbey SD 206	Langley
83	166	North Mason SD 403	Belfair
83	166	Pullman SD 267	Pullman
85	165	Prosser SD 116	Prosser
86	163	Ephrata SD 165	Ephrata
87	161	Othello SD 147	Othello
87	161	Port Townsend SD 50	Port Townsend
89	158	Lynden SD 504	Lynden
90	157	Clarkston SD 250	Clarkston
91	150	Riverview Special Services	Carnation
92	147	Wapato SD 207	Wapato
93	142	Toppenish SD 202	Toppenish
94	140	Medical Lake SD 326	Medical Lake
95	139	Tukwila SD 406	Tukwila
96	135	Mount Baker SD 507	Deming
97	133	Deer Park SD 414	Deer Park
98	132	Nine Mile Falls SD 325/179	Nine Mile Fall
98	132	Vashon Island SD 402	Vashon
100	129	Lakewood SD 306	North Lakewood
101	126	Eatonville SD 404	Eatonville
102	125	Steilacoom Historical SD	Steilacoom
103	124	Washougal SD 112-6	Washougal
104	121	East Valley SD 90	Yakima
104	121	Port Angeles SD 121	Port Angeles
106	117	Nooksack Valley SD 506	Everson
106	117	Quincy SD 144	Quincy
108	114	Hoquiam SD 28	Hoquiam
109	112	North Franklin SD 51	Connell
110	109	Omak SD 19	Omak
111	108	Ridgefield SD 122	Ridgefield
112	107	Blaine SD 503	Blaine
113	106	Rochester SD 401	Rochester
114	104	Granite Falls SD 332	Granite Falls
115	102	Woodland SD 404	Woodland
116	99	Kiona-Benton SD 52	Benton City
117	97	Meridian SD 505	Bellingham
118	96	Cashmere SD 222	Cashmere
119	95	Orting SD 344	Orting
120	90	Naches Valley SD 3	Naches
121	85	Sultan Home School	Sultan
122	72	Wahluke SD 73	Mattawa
123	10	Riverside SD 416	Chattaroy
124	4	Cheney SD 360	Cheney
125	n/a	Hockinson SD 98	Brush Prairie

High School Drop-out Rate

Rank	Percent	District Name	City
1	24.4	Seattle SD 1	Seattle
2	22.6	West Valley SD 363	Spokane
3	22.1	Wapato SD 207	Wapato
4	18.4	Yakima SD 7	Yakima
5	17.1	Sunnyside SD 201	Sunnyside
6	15.4	White River SD 416	Buckley
7	14.8	Renton SD 403	Renton
8	14.1	Omak SD 19	Omak
9	13.9	Clover Park SD 400	Lakewood
10	13.6	Toppenish SD 202	Toppenish
11	13.5	Sedro-Woolley SD 101	Sedro Woolley

Rank	Score	District	City
12	13.1	Bremerton SD 100	Bremerton
13	12.2	Wenatchee SD 246	Wenatchee
14	12.0	Elma SD 68	Elma
15	11.9	Aberdeen SD 5	Aberdeen
15	11.9	Longview SD 122	Longview
17	11.6	Everett SD 2	Everett
18	10.8	East Valley SD 90	Yakima
19	10.5	Oak Harbor SD 201	Oak Harbor
19	10.5	Vancouver SD 37	Vancouver
21	10.2	Arlington SD 16	Arlington
22	10.0	Clarkston SD 250	Clarkston
22	10.0	Highline SD 401	Seattle
24	9.8	Franklin Pierce SD 402	Tacoma
25	9.7	Hoquiam SD 28	Hoquiam
26	9.6	Tukwila SD 406	Tukwila
27	9.2	Moses Lake SD 161	Moses Lake
28	8.9	Wahluke SD 73	Mattawa
29	8.7	Shelton SD 309	Shelton
30	8.5	Mount Vernon SD 320	Mount Vernon
31	8.3	Granite Falls SD 332	Granite Falls
31	8.3	Stanwood-Camano SD 401	Stanwood
33	8.1	Centralia SD 401	Centralia
34	8.0	Tumwater SD 33	Tumwater
35	7.9	Walla Walla SD 140	Walla Walla
36	7.6	Meridian SD 505	Bellingham
36	7.6	South Kitsap SD 402	Port Orchard
38	7.5	Battle Ground SD 119	Brush Prairie
39	7.4	Blaine SD 503	Blaine
39	7.4	Puyallup SD 3	Puyallup
39	7.4	Sultan Home School	Sultan
39	7.4	Tahoma SD 409	Maple Valley
43	7.1	Bethel SD 403	Spanaway
44	7.0	Ferndale SD 502	Ferndale
45	6.9	Edmonds SD 15	Lynnwood
45	6.9	South Whidbey SD 206	Langley
47	6.6	Issaquah SD 411	Issaquah
47	6.6	Lakewood SD 306	North Lakewood
47	6.6	Marysville SD 25	Marysville
50	6.4	Woodland SD 404	Woodland
51	6.3	Evergreen SD 114	Vancouver
51	6.3	Othello SD 147	Othello
53	6.0	Pasco SD 001	Pasco
53	6.0	Quincy SD 144	Quincy
55	5.9	Eastmont SD 206	East Wenatchee
55	5.9	Federal Way SD 210	Federal Way
55	5.9	Kennewick SD 17	Kennewick
55	5.9	Yelm Community Schools	Yelm
59	5.6	Anacortes SD 103	Anacortes
60	5.5	Cheney SD 360	Cheney
60	5.5	Eatonville SD 404	Eatonville
60	5.5	Snohomish SD 201	Snohomish
63	5.3	Steilacoom Historical SD	Steilacoom
64	5.2	Snoqualmie SD 410	Snoqualmie
65	5.0	Bellingham SD 501	Bellingham
65	5.0	Tacoma SD 10	Tacoma
67	4.8	Ellensburg SD 401	Ellensburg
67	4.8	Kiona-Benton SD 52	Benton City
69	4.7	Fife SD 417	Tacoma
69	4.7	North Thurston SD 3	Lacey
71	4.6	Orting SD 344	Orting
71	4.6	Shoreline SD 412	Shoreline
73	4.5	Mukilteo SD 6	Everett
73	4.5	Rochester SD 401	Rochester
75	4.3	Grandview SD 200	Grandview
76	4.2	Auburn SD 408	Auburn
76	4.2	Monroe SD 103	Monroe
78	4.0	Olympia SD 111	Olympia
79	3.9	Camas SD 117	Camas
79	3.9	Mount Baker SD 507	Deming
79	3.9	North Mason SD 403	Belfair
79	3.9	Port Angeles SD 121	Port Angeles
79	3.9	Pullman SD 267	Pullman
79	3.9	Richland SD 400	Richland
79	3.9	Spokane SD 81	Spokane
86	3.8	Central Kitsap SD 401	Silverdale
87	3.7	Burlington-Edison SD 100	Burlington
88	3.6	Cashmere SD 222	Cashmere
89	3.5	Vashon Island SD 402	Vashon
90	3.4	North Kitsap SD 400	Poulsbo
91	3.2	Chehalis SD 302	Chehalis
91	3.2	East Valley SD 361	Spokane
91	3.2	Selah SD 119	Selah
94	3.1	Deer Park SD 414	Deer Park
94	3.1	University Place SD 83	Univ Place
96	2.9	Washougal SD 112-6	Washougal
97	2.8	Lake Stevens SD 4	Lake Stevens
97	2.8	Prosser SD 116	Prosser
97	2.8	Riverside SD 416	Chattaroy
97	2.8	Sumner SD #320	Sumner
101	2.7	Kent SD 415	Kent
101	2.7	North Franklin SD 51	Connell
103	2.6	Lynden SD 504	Lynden
103	2.6	Nooksack Valley SD 506	Everson
105	2.5	Bellevue SD 405	Bellevue
105	2.5	Sequim SD 323	Sequim
107	2.2	Mead SD 354	Mead
107	2.2	Port Townsend SD 50	Port Townsend
109	1.9	Riverview Special Services	Carnation
110	1.8	Kelso SD 458	Kelso
110	1.8	Lake Washington SD 414	Redmond
110	1.8	Naches Valley SD 3	Naches
110	1.8	West Valley SD 208	Yakima
114	1.5	Colville SD 115	Colville
114	1.5	Medical Lake SD 326	Medical Lake
116	1.3	Enumclaw SD 216	Enumclaw
116	1.3	Northshore SD 417	Bothell
118	1.0	Ephrata SD 165	Ephrata
118	1.0	Nine Mile Falls SD 325/179	Nine Mile Fall
120	0.9	Bainbridge Island SD 303	Bainbridge Isl
120	0.9	Peninsula SD 401	Gig Harbor
122	0.7	Mercer Island SD 400	Mercer Island
123	0.6	Central Valley SD 356	Greenacres
124	0.5	Ridgefield SD 122	Ridgefield
125	n/a	Hockinson SD 98	Brush Prairie

West Virginia

West Virginia Public School Educational Profile

Category	Value	Category	Value
Schools *(2003-2004)*	799	**Diploma Recipients** *(2002-2003)*	17,128
Instructional Level		White, Non-Hispanic	16,281
Primary	479	Black, Non-Hispanic	600
Middle	128	Asian/Pacific Islander	148
High	157	American Indian/Alaskan Native	29
Other Level	29	Hispanic	70
Curriculum		**High School Drop-out Rate** *(%) (2001-2002)*	3.7
Regular	727	White, Non-Hispanic	3.7
Special Education	9	Black, Non-Hispanic	3.9
Vocational	33	Asian/Pacific Islander	1.8
Alternative	24	American Indian/Alaskan Native	8.9
Type		Hispanic	1.8
Magnet	0	**Staff** *(2003-2004)*	
Charter	0	Teachers	20,019.9
Title I Eligible	432	Average Salary ($)	38,496
School-wide Title I	350	Librarians/Media Specialists	386.1
Students *(2003-2004)*	281,209	Guidance Counselors	659.7
Gender (%)		**Ratios** *(2003-2004)*	
Male	51.7	Student/Teacher Ratio	14.0 to 1
Female	48.3	Student/Librarian Ratio	728.3 to 1
Race/Ethnicity (%)		Student/Counselor Ratio	426.3 to 1
White, Non-Hispanic	94.1	**College Entrance Exam Scores** *(2005)*	
Black, Non-Hispanic	4.6	Scholastic Aptitude Test (SAT)	
Asian/Pacific Islander	0.6	Participation Rate (%)	20
American Indian/Alaskan Native	0.1	Mean SAT Reasoning Test Verbal Score	523
Hispanic	0.5	Mean SAT Reasoning Test Math Score	511
Classification (%)		American College Testing Program (ACT)	
Individual Education Program (IEP)	18.0	Participation Rate (%)	65
Migrant *(2002-2003)*	0.1	Average Composite Score	20.4
English Language Learner (ELL)	0.5	Average English Score	20.5
Eligible for Free Lunch Program	38.8	Average Math Score	19.3
Eligible for Reduced-Price Lunch Program	10.5	Average Reading Score	20.9
Current Spending *($ per student in FY 2003)*	8,218	Average Science Score	20.4
Instruction	5,044		
Support Services	2,706		

Note: *For an explanation of data, please refer to the User's Guide in the front of the book*

West Virginia NAEP 2005 Test Scores

Reading			Mathematics		
Grade/Category	Value	Rank	Grade/Category	Value	Rank
4th Grade			**4th Grade**		
Average Proficiency	214.8 (0.83)	37/51	Average Proficiency	230.8 (0.74)	42/51
Proficiency by Gender/Race/Ethnicity			Proficiency by Gender/Race/Ethnicity		
Male	211.4 (1.19)	37/51	Male	232.3 (0.85)	43/51
Female	218.2 (0.98)	37/51	Female	229.3 (0.95)	43/51
White, Non-Hispanic	215.4 (0.83)	51/51	White, Non-Hispanic	231.0 (0.74)	51/51
Black, Non-Hispanic	202.4 (3.22)	13/42	Black, Non-Hispanic	225.8 (2.62)	6/42
Asian, Non-Hispanic	n/a	n/a	Asian, Non-Hispanic	n/a	n/a
American Indian, Non-Hispanic	n/a	n/a	American Indian, Non-Hispanic	n/a	n/a
Hispanic	n/a	n/a	Hispanic	n/a	n/a
Proficiency by Class Size			Proficiency by Class Size		
Less than 16 Students	208.6 (2.58)	18/34	Less than 16 Students	225.0 (2.43)	17/35
16 to 18 Students	216.2 (2.54)	19/33	16 to 18 Students	228.2 (1.84)	27/31
19 to 20 Students	214.0 (2.38)	31/38	19 to 20 Students	229.4 (2.25)	34/38
21 to 25 Students	215.1 (1.38)	42/51	21 to 25 Students	232.2 (1.29)	42/51
Greater than 25 Students	n/a	n/a	Greater than 25 Students	n/a	n/a
Percent Attaining Achievement Levels			Percent Attaining Achievement Levels		
Below Basic	39.5 (1.14)	15/51	Below Basic	24.6 (1.14)	13/51
Basic or Above	60.5 (1.14)	37/51	Basic or Above	75.4 (1.14)	39/51
Proficient or Above	25.6 (0.95)	40/51	Proficient or Above	25.1 (1.33)	46/51
Advanced or Above	4.9 (0.72)	43/51	Advanced or Above	1.5 (0.25)	49/51
8th Grade			**8th Grade**		
Average Proficiency	255.1 (1.22)	42/51	Average Proficiency	269.1 (0.96)	44/51
Proficiency by Gender/Race/Ethnicity			Proficiency by Gender/Race/Ethnicity		
Male	249.8 (1.69)	41/51	Male	268.5 (1.30)	45/51
Female	260.8 (1.44)	42/51	Female	269.8 (1.07)	43/51
White, Non-Hispanic	255.8 (1.24)	51/51	White, Non-Hispanic	269.6 (0.88)	51/51
Black, Non-Hispanic	236.1 (3.70)	38/40	Black, Non-Hispanic	251.4 (4.18)	23/41
Asian, Non-Hispanic	n/a	n/a	Asian, Non-Hispanic	n/a	n/a
American Indian, Non-Hispanic	n/a	n/a	American Indian, Non-Hispanic	n/a	n/a
Hispanic	n/a	n/a	Hispanic	n/a	n/a
Proficiency by Parents Highest Level of Ed.			Proficiency by Parents Highest Level of Ed.		
Did Not Finish High School	236.3 (2.79)	48/49	Did Not Finish High School	251.0 (2.41)	46/50
Graduated High School	249.9 (1.73)	33/50	Graduated High School	262.6 (1.38)	38/50
Some Education After High School	259.2 (1.55)	44/50	Some Education After High School	273.4 (1.33)	45/50
Graduated College	264.9 (1.73)	38/50	Graduated College	278.8 (1.40)	44/50
Percent Attaining Achievement Levels			Percent Attaining Achievement Levels		
Below Basic	39.5 (1.14)	15/51	Below Basic	40.0 (1.49)	8/51
Basic or Above	60.5 (1.14)	37/51	Basic or Above	60.0 (1.49)	44/51
Proficient or Above	25.6 (0.95)	40/51	Proficient or Above	17.9 (1.04)	46/51
Advanced or Above	4.9 (0.72)	43/51	Advanced or Above	1.4 (0.31)	49/51

Note: *For an explanation of data, please refer to the User's Guide in the front of the book; n/a indicates data not available*

Barbour County

Barbour County SD
105 S Railroad St • Philippi, WV 26416-1177
(304) 457-3030
Grade Span: PK-12; **Agency Type:** 1
Schools: 9
    6 Primary; 2 Middle; 1 High; 0 Other Level
    9 Regular; 0 Special Education; 0 Vocational; 0 Alternative
    0 Magnet; 0 Charter; 8 Title I Eligible; 8 School-wide Title I
Students: 2,573   (53.5% male; 46.4% female)
    Individual Education Program: 485 (18.8%);
    English Language Learner: 3 (0.1%); Migrant: 0 (0.0%)
    Eligible for Free Lunch Program: 1,312 (51.0%)
    Eligible for Reduced-Price Lunch Program: 396 (15.4%)
Teachers: 186.8 (13.8 to 1)
Librarians/Media Specialists: 3.8 (677.1 to 1)
Guidance Counselors: 4.0 (643.3 to 1)
Current Spending: ($ per student per year):
    Total: $7,487; Instruction: $4,637; Support Services: $2,379
Enrollment, Drop-out Rates and Diploma Recipients by Race/Ethnicity

Category	Total	White	Black	Asian	AIAN	Hisp.
Enrollment (%)	100.0	97.4	0.9	0.3	1.1	0.3
Drop-out Rate (%)	4.3	4.3	16.7	0.0	0.0	0.0
H.S. Diplomas (#)	161	156	2	2	1	0

Berkeley County

Berkeley County SD
401 S Queen St • Martinsburg, WV 25401-3285
(304) 267-3500 • http://boe.berk.k12.wv.us/
Grade Span: PK-12; **Agency Type:** 1
Schools: 28
    17 Primary; 7 Middle; 4 High; 0 Other Level
    26 Regular; 1 Special Education; 1 Vocational; 0 Alternative
    0 Magnet; 0 Charter; 19 Title I Eligible; 2 School-wide Title I
Students: 14,277   (50.9% male; 49.0% female)
    Individual Education Program: 2,527 (17.7%);
    English Language Learner: 173 (1.2%); Migrant: 65 (0.5%)
    Eligible for Free Lunch Program: 3,708 (26.0%)
    Eligible for Reduced-Price Lunch Program: 1,510 (10.6%)
Teachers: 1,019.3 (14.0 to 1)
Librarians/Media Specialists: 21.5 (664.0 to 1)
Guidance Counselors: 36.0 (396.6 to 1)
Current Spending: ($ per student per year):
    Total: $8,014; Instruction: $4,819; Support Services: $2,691
Enrollment, Drop-out Rates and Diploma Recipients by Race/Ethnicity

Category	Total	White	Black	Asian	AIAN	Hisp.
Enrollment (%)	100.0	88.1	8.2	0.7	0.2	2.8
Drop-out Rate (%)	5.5	5.7	4.3	0.0	0.0	1.7
H.S. Diplomas (#)	710	636	43	16	1	14

Boone County

Boone County SD
69 Ave B • Madison, WV 25130-1162
(304) 369-3131 • http://www.boonecountyboe.org/
Grade Span: PK-12; **Agency Type:** 1
Schools: 17
    10 Primary; 2 Middle; 4 High; 1 Other Level
    15 Regular; 0 Special Education; 1 Vocational; 1 Alternative
    0 Magnet; 0 Charter; 10 Title I Eligible; 9 School-wide Title I
Students: 4,584   (52.3% male; 47.6% female)
    Individual Education Program: 925 (20.2%);
    English Language Learner: 1 (<0.1%); Migrant: 0 (0.0%)
    Eligible for Free Lunch Program: 2,039 (44.5%)
    Eligible for Reduced-Price Lunch Program: 494 (10.8%)
Teachers: 357.0 (12.8 to 1)
Librarians/Media Specialists: 4.0 (1,146.0 to 1)
Guidance Counselors: 8.0 (573.0 to 1)
Current Spending: ($ per student per year):
    Total: $9,095; Instruction: $5,385; Support Services: $3,191
Enrollment, Drop-out Rates and Diploma Recipients by Race/Ethnicity

Category	Total	White	Black	Asian	AIAN	Hisp.
Enrollment (%)	100.0	98.6	1.0	0.0	0.1	0.3
Drop-out Rate (%)	5.4	5.3	14.3	0.0	0.0	0.0
H.S. Diplomas (#)	256	253	2	1	0	0

Braxton County

Braxton County SD
411 N Hill Rd • Sutton, WV 26601-1147
(304) 765-7101 • http://boe.brax.k12.wv.us/INDEX.HTM
Grade Span: PK-12; **Agency Type:** 1
Schools: 8

    6 Primary; 1 Middle; 1 High; 0 Other Level
    8 Regular; 0 Special Education; 0 Vocational; 0 Alternative
    0 Magnet; 0 Charter; 8 Title I Eligible; 8 School-wide Title I
Students: 2,555   (51.0% male; 48.9% female)
    Individual Education Program: 516 (20.2%);
    English Language Learner: 2 (0.1%); Migrant: 0 (0.0%)
    Eligible for Free Lunch Program: 1,242 (48.6%)
    Eligible for Reduced-Price Lunch Program: 234 (9.2%)
Teachers: 190.5 (13.4 to 1)
Librarians/Media Specialists: 2.0 (1,277.5 to 1)
Guidance Counselors: 6.5 (393.1 to 1)
Current Spending: ($ per student per year):
    Total: $7,850; Instruction: $4,875; Support Services: $2,563
Enrollment, Drop-out Rates and Diploma Recipients by Race/Ethnicity

Category	Total	White	Black	Asian	AIAN	Hisp.
Enrollment (%)	100.0	99.2	0.4	0.2	0.0	0.2
Drop-out Rate (%)	4.1	4.1	0.0	0.0	0.0	n/a
H.S. Diplomas (#)	148	147	1	0	0	0

Brooke County

Brooke County SD
1201 Pleasant Ave • Wellsburg, WV 26070-1497
(304) 737-3481
Grade Span: PK-12; **Agency Type:** 1
Schools: 12
    9 Primary; 2 Middle; 1 High; 0 Other Level
    12 Regular; 0 Special Education; 0 Vocational; 0 Alternative
    0 Magnet; 0 Charter; 7 Title I Eligible; 6 School-wide Title I
Students: 3,596   (49.8% male; 50.1% female)
    Individual Education Program: 709 (19.7%);
    English Language Learner: 0 (0.0%); Migrant: 0 (0.0%)
    Eligible for Free Lunch Program: 923 (25.7%)
    Eligible for Reduced-Price Lunch Program: 355 (9.9%)
Teachers: 257.0 (14.0 to 1)
Librarians/Media Specialists: 4.0 (899.0 to 1)
Guidance Counselors: 7.0 (513.7 to 1)
Current Spending: ($ per student per year):
    Total: $8,548; Instruction: $5,131; Support Services: $2,868
Enrollment, Drop-out Rates and Diploma Recipients by Race/Ethnicity

Category	Total	White	Black	Asian	AIAN	Hisp.
Enrollment (%)	100.0	97.6	1.6	0.3	0.1	0.3
Drop-out Rate (%)	4.1	4.1	0.0	0.0	0.0	0.0
H.S. Diplomas (#)	279	274	4	1	0	0

Cabell County

Cabell County SD
620 20th St • Huntington, WV 25703
(304) 528-5000 • http://boe.cabe.k12.wv.us/
Grade Span: PK-12; **Agency Type:** 1
Schools: 31
    20 Primary; 7 Middle; 4 High; 0 Other Level
    28 Regular; 0 Special Education; 1 Vocational; 2 Alternative
    0 Magnet; 0 Charter; 13 Title I Eligible; 13 School-wide Title I
Students: 12,217   (51.6% male; 48.3% female)
    Individual Education Program: 2,089 (17.1%);
    English Language Learner: 94 (0.8%); Migrant: 0 (0.0%)
    Eligible for Free Lunch Program: 4,971 (40.7%)
    Eligible for Reduced-Price Lunch Program: 1,206 (9.9%)
Teachers: 857.6 (14.2 to 1)
Librarians/Media Specialists: 11.0 (1,110.6 to 1)
Guidance Counselors: 28.0 (436.3 to 1)
Current Spending: ($ per student per year):
    Total: $8,297; Instruction: $4,976; Support Services: $2,865
Enrollment, Drop-out Rates and Diploma Recipients by Race/Ethnicity

Category	Total	White	Black	Asian	AIAN	Hisp.
Enrollment (%)	100.0	91.2	7.2	0.8	0.3	0.5
Drop-out Rate (%)	4.6	4.5	5.8	0.0	6.7	9.5
H.S. Diplomas (#)	688	635	37	6	6	4

Clay County

Clay County SD
1 Gump St • Clay, WV 25043-0120
Mailing Address: PO Box 120 • Clay, WV 25043-0120
(304) 587-4266
Grade Span: PK-12; **Agency Type:** 1
Schools: 7
    5 Primary; 1 Middle; 1 High; 0 Other Level
    7 Regular; 0 Special Education; 0 Vocational; 0 Alternative
    0 Magnet; 0 Charter; 6 Title I Eligible; 6 School-wide Title I
Students: 2,099   (49.2% male; 50.7% female)
    Individual Education Program: 409 (19.5%);
    English Language Learner: 0 (0.0%); Migrant: 0 (0.0%)

Eligible for Free Lunch Program: 1,272 (60.6%)
Eligible for Reduced-Price Lunch Program: 319 (15.2%)
Teachers: 158.1 (13.3 to 1)
Librarians/Media Specialists: 3.0 (699.7 to 1)
Guidance Counselors: 3.0 (699.7 to 1)
Current Spending: ($ per student per year):
Total: $8,153; Instruction: $5,018; Support Services: $2,494
Enrollment, Drop-out Rates and Diploma Recipients by Race/Ethnicity

Category	Total	White	Black	Asian	AIAN	Hisp.
Enrollment (%)	100.0	99.4	0.5	0.0	0.0	0.0
Drop-out Rate (%)	3.8	3.8	0.0	n/a	n/a	0.0
H.S. Diplomas (#)	121	120	0	0	0	1

Fayette County

Fayette County SD
111 Fayette Ave • Fayetteville, WV 25840-1219
(304) 574-1176 • http://boe.faye.k12.wv.us/
Grade Span: PK-12; **Agency Type:** 1
Schools: 26
13 Primary; 5 Middle; 6 High; 2 Other Level
25 Regular; 0 Special Education; 1 Vocational; 0 Alternative
0 Magnet; 0 Charter; 14 Title I Eligible; 13 School-wide Title I
Students: 7,001 (53.2% male; 46.7% female)
Individual Education Program: 1,102 (15.7%);
English Language Learner: 7 (0.1%); Migrant: 0 (0.0%)
Eligible for Free Lunch Program: 3,100 (44.3%)
Eligible for Reduced-Price Lunch Program: 783 (11.2%)
Teachers: 520.0 (13.5 to 1)
Librarians/Media Specialists: 7.0 (1,000.1 to 1)
Guidance Counselors: 15.0 (466.7 to 1)
Current Spending: ($ per student per year):
Total: $8,473; Instruction: $5,464; Support Services: $2,549
Enrollment, Drop-out Rates and Diploma Recipients by Race/Ethnicity

Category	Total	White	Black	Asian	AIAN	Hisp.
Enrollment (%)	100.0	92.4	7.0	0.1	0.1	0.3
Drop-out Rate (%)	4.9	5.0	3.4	0.0	33.3	0.0
H.S. Diplomas (#)	442	405	36	0	0	1

Grant County

Grant County SD
204 Jefferson Ave • Petersburg, WV 26847-1628
(304) 257-1011
Grade Span: PK-12; **Agency Type:** 1
Schools: 6
3 Primary; 0 Middle; 2 High; 1 Other Level
5 Regular; 0 Special Education; 1 Vocational; 0 Alternative
0 Magnet; 0 Charter; 3 Title I Eligible; 0 School-wide Title I
Students: 1,984 (50.9% male; 49.0% female)
Individual Education Program: 406 (20.5%);
English Language Learner: 0 (0.0%); Migrant: 0 (0.0%)
Eligible for Free Lunch Program: 695 (35.0%)
Eligible for Reduced-Price Lunch Program: 298 (15.0%)
Teachers: 138.2 (14.4 to 1)
Librarians/Media Specialists: 3.0 (661.3 to 1)
Guidance Counselors: 2.8 (708.6 to 1)
Current Spending: ($ per student per year):
Total: $7,802; Instruction: $4,771; Support Services: $2,528
Enrollment, Drop-out Rates and Diploma Recipients by Race/Ethnicity

Category	Total	White	Black	Asian	AIAN	Hisp.
Enrollment (%)	100.0	98.2	1.3	0.3	0.1	0.1
Drop-out Rate (%)	3.3	3.1	33.3	0.0	n/a	0.0
H.S. Diplomas (#)	128	126	1	0	0	1

Greenbrier County

Greenbrier County SD
202 Chestnut St • Lewisburg, WV 24901-1108
(304) 647-6457 • http://boe.gree.k12.wv.us/
Grade Span: PK-12; **Agency Type:** 1
Schools: 14
10 Primary; 2 Middle; 2 High; 0 Other Level
14 Regular; 0 Special Education; 0 Vocational; 0 Alternative
0 Magnet; 0 Charter; 10 Title I Eligible; 10 School-wide Title I
Students: 5,381 (52.4% male; 47.5% female)
Individual Education Program: 1,073 (19.9%);
English Language Learner: 2 (<0.1%); Migrant: 0 (0.0%)
Eligible for Free Lunch Program: 2,240 (41.6%)
Eligible for Reduced-Price Lunch Program: 761 (14.1%)
Teachers: 371.1 (14.5 to 1)
Librarians/Media Specialists: 5.0 (1,076.2 to 1)
Guidance Counselors: 15.0 (358.7 to 1)
Current Spending: ($ per student per year):
Total: $8,043; Instruction: $5,304; Support Services: $2,276

Enrollment, Drop-out Rates and Diploma Recipients by Race/Ethnicity

Category	Total	White	Black	Asian	AIAN	Hisp.
Enrollment (%)	100.0	95.8	3.5	0.1	0.0	0.6
Drop-out Rate (%)	3.5	3.5	3.2	0.0	50.0	0.0
H.S. Diplomas (#)	329	314	14	1	0	0

Hampshire County

Hampshire County SD
46 S High St • Romney, WV 26757-1812
(304) 822-3528
Grade Span: PK-12; **Agency Type:** 1
Schools: 10
6 Primary; 2 Middle; 2 High; 0 Other Level
9 Regular; 0 Special Education; 1 Vocational; 0 Alternative
0 Magnet; 0 Charter; 6 Title I Eligible; 1 School-wide Title I
Students: 3,577 (52.0% male; 47.9% female)
Individual Education Program: 683 (19.1%);
English Language Learner: 0 (0.0%); Migrant: 0 (0.0%)
Eligible for Free Lunch Program: 1,319 (36.9%)
Eligible for Reduced-Price Lunch Program: 579 (16.2%)
Teachers: 245.2 (14.6 to 1)
Librarians/Media Specialists: 2.8 (1,277.5 to 1)
Guidance Counselors: 8.0 (447.1 to 1)
Current Spending: ($ per student per year):
Total: $7,397; Instruction: $4,638; Support Services: $2,351
Enrollment, Drop-out Rates and Diploma Recipients by Race/Ethnicity

Category	Total	White	Black	Asian	AIAN	Hisp.
Enrollment (%)	100.0	97.8	1.0	0.3	0.1	0.8
Drop-out Rate (%)	4.6	4.5	5.9	0.0	n/a	50.0
H.S. Diplomas (#)	198	193	5	0	0	0

Hancock County

Hancock County SD
104 N Court St • New Cumberland, WV 26047-1300
Mailing Address: PO Box 1300 • New Cumberland, WV 26047-1300
(304) 564-3411 • http://boe.hanc.k12.wv.us/
Grade Span: PK-12; **Agency Type:** 1
Schools: 13
6 Primary; 2 Middle; 3 High; 0 Other Level
10 Regular; 0 Special Education; 1 Vocational; 0 Alternative
0 Magnet; 0 Charter; 6 Title I Eligible; 0 School-wide Title I
Students: 4,297 (52.2% male; 47.7% female)
Individual Education Program: 789 (18.4%);
English Language Learner: 0 (0.0%); Migrant: 0 (0.0%)
Eligible for Free Lunch Program: 1,184 (27.6%)
Eligible for Reduced-Price Lunch Program: 383 (8.9%)
Teachers: 300.2 (14.3 to 1)
Librarians/Media Specialists: 3.8 (1,130.8 to 1)
Guidance Counselors: 8.0 (537.1 to 1)
Current Spending: ($ per student per year):
Total: $8,108; Instruction: $5,021; Support Services: $2,765
Enrollment, Drop-out Rates and Diploma Recipients by Race/Ethnicity

Category	Total	White	Black	Asian	AIAN	Hisp.
Enrollment (%)	100.0	95.0	4.1	0.3	0.2	0.4
Drop-out Rate (%)	4.1	4.0	1.9	28.6	0.0	0.0
H.S. Diplomas (#)	274	263	9	1	0	1

Hardy County

Hardy County SD
510 Ashby St • Moorefield, WV 26836-1001
(304) 538-2348 • http://www.hardycountyschools.com/
Grade Span: PK-12; **Agency Type:** 1
Schools: 5
2 Primary; 1 Middle; 2 High; 0 Other Level
5 Regular; 0 Special Education; 0 Vocational; 0 Alternative
0 Magnet; 0 Charter; 3 Title I Eligible; 2 School-wide Title I
Students: 2,342 (50.9% male; 49.0% female)
Individual Education Program: 440 (18.8%);
English Language Learner: 13 (0.6%); Migrant: 108 (4.6%)
Eligible for Free Lunch Program: 790 (33.7%)
Eligible for Reduced-Price Lunch Program: 414 (17.7%)
Teachers: 157.1 (14.9 to 1)
Librarians/Media Specialists: 5.0 (468.4 to 1)
Guidance Counselors: 5.0 (468.4 to 1)
Current Spending: ($ per student per year):
Total: $6,853; Instruction: $4,148; Support Services: $2,184
Enrollment, Drop-out Rates and Diploma Recipients by Race/Ethnicity

Category	Total	White	Black	Asian	AIAN	Hisp.
Enrollment (%)	100.0	97.0	2.1	0.1	0.0	0.8
Drop-out Rate (%)	0.7	0.7	0.0	n/a	n/a	0.0
H.S. Diplomas (#)	121	116	5	0	0	0

Harrison County

Harrison County SD
408 E.B. Saunders Way • Clarksburg, WV 26301
Mailing Address: PO Box 1370 • Clarksburg, WV 26302-1370
(304) 624-3300
Grade Span: PK-12; **Agency Type:** 1
Schools: 29
  14 Primary; 6 Middle; 7 High; 2 Other Level
  25 Regular; 2 Special Education; 1 Vocational; 1 Alternative
  0 Magnet; 0 Charter; 12 Title I Eligible; 8 School-wide Title I
Students: 11,583 (50.9% male; 49.0% female)
  Individual Education Program: 2,047 (17.7%);
  English Language Learner: 28 (0.2%); Migrant: 0 (0.0%)
  Eligible for Free Lunch Program: 4,557 (39.3%)
  Eligible for Reduced-Price Lunch Program: 1,107 (9.6%)
Teachers: 767.1 (15.1 to 1)
Librarians/Media Specialists: 22.0 (526.5 to 1)
Guidance Counselors: 22.0 (526.5 to 1)
Current Spending: ($ per student per year):
  Total: $7,995; Instruction: $4,954; Support Services: $2,616
Enrollment, Drop-out Rates and Diploma Recipients by Race/Ethnicity

Category	Total	White	Black	Asian	AIAN	Hisp.
Enrollment (%)	100.0	96.4	2.6	0.6	0.1	0.3
Drop-out Rate (%)	2.7	2.8	1.3	0.0	0.0	0.0
H.S. Diplomas (#)	709	683	15	6	0	5

Jackson County

Jackson County SD
#1 School St • Ripley, WV 25271-0770
Mailing Address: PO Box 770 • Ripley, WV 25271-0770
(304) 372-7300
Grade Span: PK-12; **Agency Type:** 1
Schools: 13
  8 Primary; 2 Middle; 3 High; 0 Other Level
  12 Regular; 0 Special Education; 1 Vocational; 0 Alternative
  0 Magnet; 0 Charter; 8 Title I Eligible; 8 School-wide Title I
Students: 5,065 (51.9% male; 48.0% female)
  Individual Education Program: 885 (17.5%)
  English Language Learner: 16 (0.3%); Migrant: 0 (0.0%)
  Eligible for Free Lunch Program: 1,759 (34.7%)
  Eligible for Reduced-Price Lunch Program: 450 (8.9%)
Teachers: 348.7 (14.5 to 1)
Librarians/Media Specialists: 4.0 (1,266.3 to 1)
Guidance Counselors: 12.0 (422.1 to 1)
Current Spending: ($ per student per year):
  Total: $8,127; Instruction: $4,869; Support Services: $2,893
Enrollment, Drop-out Rates and Diploma Recipients by Race/Ethnicity

Category	Total	White	Black	Asian	AIAN	Hisp
Enrollment (%)	100.0	98.9	0.4	0.5	0.1	0.1
Drop-out Rate (%)	3.7	3.8	0.0	0.0	0.0	0.0
H.S. Diplomas (#)	309	293	1	12	1	2

Jefferson County

Jefferson County SD
110mordington Ave • Charles Town, WV 25414-0987
Mailing Address: PO Box 987 • Charles Town, WV 25414-0987
(304) 725-9741
Grade Span: PK-12; **Agency Type:** 1
Schools: 13
  9 Primary; 3 Middle; 1 High; 0 Other Level
  13 Regular; 0 Special Education; 0 Vocational; 0 Alternative
  0 Magnet; 0 Charter; 3 Title I Eligible; 2 School-wide Title I
Students: 7,414 (51.4% male; 48.5% female)
  Individual Education Program: 1,223 (16.5%);
  English Language Learner: 155 (2.1%); Migrant: 23 (0.3%)
  Eligible for Free Lunch Program: 1,679 (22.6%)
  Eligible for Reduced-Price Lunch Program: 736 (9.9%)
Teachers: 502.3 (14.8 to 1)
Librarians/Media Specialists: 14.0 (529.6 to 1)
Guidance Counselors: 17.5 (423.7 to 1)
Current Spending: ($ per student per year):
  Total: $7,510; Instruction: $4,713; Support Services: $2,394
Enrollment, Drop-out Rates and Diploma Recipients by Race/Ethnicity

Category	Total	White	Black	Asian	AIAN	Hisp.
Enrollment (%)	100.0	86.1	9.3	0.9	0.3	3.4
Drop-out Rate (%)	2.7	2.8	1.3	0.0	0.0	2.8
H.S. Diplomas (#)	418	378	34	3	1	2

Kanawha County

Kanawha County SD
200 Elizabeth St • Charleston, WV 25311-2119
(304) 348-7732 • http://kcs.kana.k12.wv.us/
Grade Span: PK-12; **Agency Type:** 1
Schools: 71
  47 Primary; 13 Middle; 11 High; 0 Other Level
  66 Regular; 1 Special Education; 2 Vocational; 2 Alternative
  0 Magnet; 0 Charter; 28 Title I Eligible; 26 School-wide Title I
Students: 28,306 (52.0% male; 47.9% female)
  Individual Education Program: 4,668 (16.5%)
  English Language Learner: 357 (1.3%); Migrant: 0 (0.0%)
  Eligible for Free Lunch Program: 10,757 (38.0%)
  Eligible for Reduced-Price Lunch Program: 2,483 (8.8%)
Teachers: 1,934.0 (14.6 to 1)
Librarians/Media Specialists: 64.0 (442.3 to 1)
Guidance Counselors: 83.9 (337.4 to 1)
Current Spending: ($ per student per year):
  Total: $8,304; Instruction: $5,147; Support Services: $2,626
Enrollment, Drop-out Rates and Diploma Recipients by Race/Ethnicity

Category	Total	White	Black	Asian	AIAN	Hisp.
Enrollment (%)	100.0	86.6	11.7	1.1	0.1	0.5
Drop-out Rate (%)	5.3	5.2	6.3	4.0	0.0	0.0
H.S. Diplomas (#)	1,630	1,458	134	25	4	9

Lewis County

Lewis County SD
322 E 3rd St • Weston, WV 26452-2002
(304) 269-8300 • http://boe.lewi.k12.wv.us/
Grade Span: PK-12; **Agency Type:** 1
Schools: 7
  5 Primary; 1 Middle; 1 High; 0 Other Level
  7 Regular; 0 Special Education; 0 Vocational; 0 Alternative
  0 Magnet; 0 Charter; 5 Title I Eligible; 5 School-wide Title I
Students: 2,799 (52.3% male; 47.6% female)
  Individual Education Program: 614 (21.9%);
  English Language Learner: 3 (0.1%); Migrant: 7 (0.3%)
  Eligible for Free Lunch Program: 1,177 (42.1%)
  Eligible for Reduced-Price Lunch Program: 337 (12.0%)
Teachers: 197.5 (14.2 to 1)
Librarians/Media Specialists: 4.0 (699.8 to 1)
Guidance Counselors: 6.0 (466.5 to 1)
Current Spending: ($ per student per year):
  Total: $8,148; Instruction: $4,813; Support Services: $2,808
Enrollment, Drop-out Rates and Diploma Recipients by Race/Ethnicity

Category	Total	White	Black	Asian	AIAN	Hisp.
Enrollment (%)	100.0	98.7	0.8	0.1	0.1	0.3
Drop-out Rate (%)	3.0	3.0	0.0	0.0	0.0	0.0
H.S. Diplomas (#)	192	189	0	2	1	0

Lincoln County

Lincoln County SD
10 Marland Ave • Hamlin, WV 25523-1099
(304) 824-3033
Grade Span: PK-12; **Agency Type:** 1
Schools: 12
  7 Primary; 0 Middle; 5 High; 0 Other Level
  11 Regular; 0 Special Education; 1 Vocational; 0 Alternative
  0 Magnet; 0 Charter; 7 Title I Eligible; 7 School-wide Title I
Students: 3,826 (52.1% male; 47.8% female)
  Individual Education Program: 836 (21.9%);
  English Language Learner: 0 (0.0%); Migrant: 0 (0.0%)
  Eligible for Free Lunch Program: 1,887 (49.3%)
  Eligible for Reduced-Price Lunch Program: 429 (11.2%)
Teachers: 291.0 (13.1 to 1)
Librarians/Media Specialists: 5.0 (765.2 to 1)
Guidance Counselors: 6.0 (637.7 to 1)
Current Spending: ($ per student per year):
  Total: $8,318; Instruction: $5,106; Support Services: $2,623
Enrollment, Drop-out Rates and Diploma Recipients by Race/Ethnicity

Category	Total	White	Black	Asian	AIAN	Hisp.
Enrollment (%)	100.0	99.6	0.2	0.1	0.0	0.1
Drop-out Rate (%)	3.8	3.8	0.0	n/a	n/a	0.0
H.S. Diplomas (#)	231	231	0	0	0	0

Logan County

Logan County SD
506 Holly Ave • Logan, WV 25601-0477
Mailing Address: PO Box 477 • Logan, WV 25601-0477
(304) 792-2060 • http://lc2.boe.loga.k12.wv.us/
Grade Span: PK-12; **Agency Type:** 1
Schools: 18
    11 Primary; 2 Middle; 4 High; 1 Other Level
    16 Regular; 1 Special Education; 1 Vocational; 0 Alternative
    0 Magnet; 0 Charter; 12 Title I Eligible; 12 School-wide Title I
Students: 6,077 (50.9% male; 49.0% female)
    Individual Education Program: 1,040 (17.1%);
    English Language Learner: 27 (0.4%); Migrant: 0 (0.0%)
    Eligible for Free Lunch Program: 2,809 (46.2%)
    Eligible for Reduced-Price Lunch Program: 516 (8.5%)
Teachers: 447.5 (13.6 to 1)
Librarians/Media Specialists: 6.0 (1,012.8 to 1)
Guidance Counselors: 11.0 (552.5 to 1)
Current Spending: ($ per student per year):
    Total: $7,867; Instruction: $5,005; Support Services: $2,398
Enrollment, Drop-out Rates and Diploma Recipients by Race/Ethnicity

Category	Total	White	Black	Asian	AIAN	Hisp.
Enrollment (%)	100.0	96.1	3.2	0.3	0.0	0.4
Drop-out Rate (%)	5.0	5.2	1.9	0.0	0.0	0.0
H.S. Diplomas (#)	402	383	11	2	1	5

Marion County

Marion County SD
200 Gaston Ave • Fairmont, WV 26554-2739
(304) 367-2100 • http://www.marion.k12.ky.us/
Grade Span: PK-12; **Agency Type:** 1
Schools: 22
    11 Primary; 6 Middle; 5 High; 0 Other Level
    20 Regular; 0 Special Education; 1 Vocational; 1 Alternative
    0 Magnet; 0 Charter; 11 Title I Eligible; 9 School-wide Title I
Students: 8,244 (51.6% male; 48.3% female)
    Individual Education Program: 1,352 (16.4%);
    English Language Learner: 1 (<0.1%); Migrant: 0 (0.0%)
    Eligible for Free Lunch Program: 2,985 (36.2%)
    Eligible for Reduced-Price Lunch Program: 660 (8.0%)
Teachers: 619.0 (13.3 to 1)
Librarians/Media Specialists: 18.0 (458.0 to 1)
Guidance Counselors: 19.0 (433.9 to 1)
Current Spending: ($ per student per year):
    Total: $8,698; Instruction: $5,224; Support Services: $3,082
Enrollment, Drop-out Rates and Diploma Recipients by Race/Ethnicity

Category	Total	White	Black	Asian	AIAN	Hisp.
Enrollment (%)	100.0	93.4	5.7	0.4	0.2	0.4
Drop-out Rate (%)	2.3	2.3	4.1	0.0	0.0	0.0
H.S. Diplomas (#)	634	600	26	5	1	2

Marshall County

Marshall County SD
2700 E 4th St • Moundsville, WV 26041-0578
Mailing Address: PO Box 578 • Moundsville, WV 26041-0578
(304) 843-4400 • http://boe.mars.k12.wv.us/
Grade Span: PK-12; **Agency Type:** 1
Schools: 15
    11 Primary; 2 Middle; 2 High; 0 Other Level
    15 Regular; 0 Special Education; 0 Vocational; 0 Alternative
    0 Magnet; 0 Charter; 8 Title I Eligible; 8 School-wide Title I
Students: 5,329 (51.5% male; 48.4% female)
    Individual Education Program: 1,059 (19.9%);
    English Language Learner: 2 (<0.1%); Migrant: 0 (0.0%)
    Eligible for Free Lunch Program: 1,940 (36.4%)
    Eligible for Reduced-Price Lunch Program: 585 (11.0%)
Teachers: 347.2 (15.3 to 1)
Librarians/Media Specialists: 4.0 (1,332.3 to 1)
Guidance Counselors: 14.0 (380.6 to 1)
Current Spending: ($ per student per year):
    Total: $8,617; Instruction: $5,463; Support Services: $2,725
Enrollment, Drop-out Rates and Diploma Recipients by Race/Ethnicity

Category	Total	White	Black	Asian	AIAN	Hisp.
Enrollment (%)	100.0	98.4	1.0	0.2	0.1	0.2
Drop-out Rate (%)	3.0	3.0	10.0	0.0	0.0	0.0
H.S. Diplomas (#)	411	403	1	4	1	2

Mason County

Mason County SD
307 8th St • Point Pleasant, WV 25550-1298
(304) 675-4540 • http://boe.maso.k12.wv.us/
Grade Span: PK-12; **Agency Type:** 1
Schools: 13
    8 Primary; 1 Middle; 4 High; 0 Other Level
    12 Regular; 0 Special Education; 1 Vocational; 0 Alternative
    0 Magnet; 0 Charter; 6 Title I Eligible; 4 School-wide Title I
Students: 4,202 (53.4% male; 46.5% female)
    Individual Education Program: 889 (21.2%);
    English Language Learner: 3 (0.1%); Migrant: 0 (0.0%)
    Eligible for Free Lunch Program: 1,689 (40.2%)
    Eligible for Reduced-Price Lunch Program: 413 (9.8%)
Teachers: 308.2 (13.6 to 1)
Librarians/Media Specialists: 4.0 (1,050.5 to 1)
Guidance Counselors: 12.0 (350.2 to 1)
Current Spending: ($ per student per year):
    Total: $8,223; Instruction: $5,174; Support Services: $2,576
Enrollment, Drop-out Rates and Diploma Recipients by Race/Ethnicity

Category	Total	White	Black	Asian	AIAN	Hisp.
Enrollment (%)	100.0	98.2	1.4	0.2	0.1	0.1
Drop-out Rate (%)	3.6	3.7	0.0	0.0	n/a	0.0
H.S. Diplomas (#)	271	270	0	0	0	1

Mcdowell County

Mcdowell County SD
30 Central Ave • Welch, WV 24801-2008
(304) 436-8441 • http://boe.mcdo.k12.wv.us/
Grade Span: PK-12; **Agency Type:** 1
Schools: 18
    11 Primary; 2 Middle; 4 High; 0 Other Level
    16 Regular; 0 Special Education; 1 Vocational; 0 Alternative
    0 Magnet; 0 Charter; 13 Title I Eligible; 13 School-wide Title I
Students: 4,253 (52.4% male; 47.5% female)
    Individual Education Program: 911 (21.4%);
    English Language Learner: 0 (0.0%); Migrant: 0 (0.0%)
    Eligible for Free Lunch Program: 3,060 (71.9%)
    Eligible for Reduced-Price Lunch Program: 445 (10.5%)
Teachers: 334.0 (12.7 to 1)
Librarians/Media Specialists: 3.0 (1,417.7 to 1)
Guidance Counselors: 12.0 (354.4 to 1)
Current Spending: ($ per student per year):
    Total: $9,525; Instruction: $6,162; Support Services: $2,860
Enrollment, Drop-out Rates and Diploma Recipients by Race/Ethnicity

Category	Total	White	Black	Asian	AIAN	Hisp.
Enrollment (%)	100.0	87.0	12.8	0.1	0.0	0.1
Drop-out Rate (%)	1.4	1.4	1.2	n/a	n/a	n/a
H.S. Diplomas (#)	237	210	27	0	0	0

Mercer County

Mercer County SD
1403 Honaker Ave • Princeton, WV 24740-3065
(304) 487-1551 • http://boe.merc.k12.wv.us/
Grade Span: PK-12; **Agency Type:** 1
Schools: 26
    19 Primary; 2 Middle; 5 High; 0 Other Level
    25 Regular; 0 Special Education; 1 Vocational; 0 Alternative
    0 Magnet; 0 Charter; 14 Title I Eligible; 12 School-wide Title I
Students: 9,395 (51.8% male; 48.1% female)
    Individual Education Program: 1,639 (17.4%);
    English Language Learner: 12 (0.1%); Migrant: 0 (0.0%)
    Eligible for Free Lunch Program: 4,333 (46.1%)
    Eligible for Reduced-Price Lunch Program: 981 (10.4%)
Teachers: 685.5 (13.7 to 1)
Librarians/Media Specialists: 21.0 (447.4 to 1)
Guidance Counselors: 22.0 (427.0 to 1)
Current Spending: ($ per student per year):
    Total: $7,961; Instruction: $4,884; Support Services: $2,567
Enrollment, Drop-out Rates and Diploma Recipients by Race/Ethnicity

Category	Total	White	Black	Asian	AIAN	Hisp.
Enrollment (%)	100.0	90.2	9.0	0.5	0.1	0.2
Drop-out Rate (%)	3.7	3.7	3.2	0.0	0.0	0.0
H.S. Diplomas (#)	527	482	36	7	1	1

Mineral County

Mineral County SD
1 Baker Pl • Keyser, WV 26726-2898
(304) 788-4200 • http://mctc.mine.tec.wv.us/
Grade Span: PK-12; **Agency Type:** 1
Schools: 14

9 Primary; 1 Middle; 4 High; 0 Other Level
12 Regular; 0 Special Education; 2 Vocational; 0 Alternative
0 Magnet; 0 Charter; 7 Title I Eligible; 2 School-wide Title I
Students: 4,555 (51.0% male; 48.9% female)
Individual Education Program: 790 (17.3%);
English Language Learner: 8 (0.2%); Migrant: 0 (0.0%)
Eligible for Free Lunch Program: 1,374 (30.2%)
Eligible for Reduced-Price Lunch Program: 550 (12.1%)
Teachers: 322.0 (14.1 to 1)
Librarians/Media Specialists: 5.5 (828.2 to 1)
Guidance Counselors: 10.0 (455.5 to 1)
Current Spending: ($ per student per year):
Total: $8,048; Instruction: $4,705; Support Services: $2,857
Enrollment, Drop-out Rates and Diploma Recipients by Race/Ethnicity

Category	Total	White	Black	Asian	AIAN	Hisp.
Enrollment (%)	100.0	95.5	4.0	0.1	0.0	0.5
Drop-out Rate (%)	2.3	2.5	0.0	0.0	n/a	0.0
H.S. Diplomas (#)	283	262	18	2	0	1

Mingo County

Mingo County SD
815 Alderson St • Williamson, WV 25661-9746
Mailing Address: Rt 2 Box 310 • Williamson, WV 25661-9746
(304) 235-3333
Grade Span: PK-12; **Agency Type:** 1
Schools: 18
8 Primary; 4 Middle; 6 High; 0 Other Level
17 Regular; 0 Special Education; 1 Vocational; 0 Alternative
0 Magnet; 0 Charter; 12 Title I Eligible; 12 School-wide Title I
Students: 4,705 (51.9% male; 48.0% female)
Individual Education Program: 906 (19.3%);
English Language Learner: 0 (0.0%); Migrant: 0 (0.0%)
Eligible for Free Lunch Program: 2,621 (55.7%)
Eligible for Reduced-Price Lunch Program: 534 (11.3%)
Teachers: 341.0 (13.8 to 1)
Librarians/Media Specialists: 4.2 (1,120.2 to 1)
Guidance Counselors: 10.0 (470.5 to 1)
Current Spending: ($ per student per year):
Total: $9,223; Instruction: $5,643; Support Services: $3,124
Enrollment, Drop-out Rates and Diploma Recipients by Race/Ethnicity

Category	Total	White	Black	Asian	AIAN	Hisp.
Enrollment (%)	100.0	97.1	2.7	0.1	0.0	0.0
Drop-out Rate (%)	3.9	4.0	0.0	0.0	0.0	0.0
H.S. Diplomas (#)	320	311	6	1	1	1

Monongalia County

Monongalia SD
13 S High St • Morgantown, WV 26501-7546
(304) 291-9210 • http://boe.mono.k12.wv.us/
Grade Span: PK-12; **Agency Type:** 1
Schools: 25
17 Primary; 4 Middle; 4 High; 0 Other Level
24 Regular; 0 Special Education; 1 Vocational; 0 Alternative
0 Magnet; 0 Charter; 9 Title I Eligible; 8 School-wide Title I
Students: 10,206 (51.6% male; 48.3% female)
Individual Education Program: 1,570 (15.4%);
English Language Learner: 404 (4.0%); Migrant: 0 (0.0%)
Eligible for Free Lunch Program: 2,793 (27.4%)
Eligible for Reduced-Price Lunch Program: 891 (8.7%)
Teachers: 700.2 (14.6 to 1)
Librarians/Media Specialists: 19.0 (537.2 to 1)
Guidance Counselors: 22.5 (453.6 to 1)
Current Spending: ($ per student per year):
Total: $8,199; Instruction: $5,014; Support Services: $2,768
Enrollment, Drop-out Rates and Diploma Recipients by Race/Ethnicity

Category	Total	White	Black	Asian	AIAN	Hisp.
Enrollment (%)	100.0	91.2	4.8	3.0	0.2	0.8
Drop-out Rate (%)	2.8	2.8	3.7	0.0	25.0	0.0
H.S. Diplomas (#)	629	602	16	11	0	0

Monroe County

Monroe County SD
Willow Bend Rd • Union, WV 24983-0330
Mailing Address: PO Box 330 • Union, WV 24983-0330
(304) 772-3094 • http://www.monroecountyschoolswv.org/
Grade Span: PK-12; **Agency Type:** 1
Schools: 5
2 Primary; 1 Middle; 2 High; 0 Other Level
4 Regular; 0 Special Education; 1 Vocational; 0 Alternative
0 Magnet; 0 Charter; 2 Title I Eligible; 2 School-wide Title I
Students: 2,031 (51.2% male; 48.7% female)
Individual Education Program: 416 (20.5%);

English Language Learner: 0 (0.0%); Migrant: 0 (0.0%)
Eligible for Free Lunch Program: 783 (38.6%)
Eligible for Reduced-Price Lunch Program: 354 (17.4%)
Teachers: 150.8 (13.5 to 1)
Librarians/Media Specialists: 1.0 (2,031.0 to 1)
Guidance Counselors: 4.9 (414.5 to 1)
Current Spending: ($ per student per year):
Total: $7,768; Instruction: $4,796; Support Services: $2,575
Enrollment, Drop-out Rates and Diploma Recipients by Race/Ethnicity

Category	Total	White	Black	Asian	AIAN	Hisp.
Enrollment (%)	100.0	98.4	1.1	0.1	0.1	0.1
Drop-out Rate (%)	2.9	3.0	0.0	0.0	0.0	0.0
H.S. Diplomas (#)	96	95	1	0	0	0

Morgan County

Morgan County SD
714 S Washington St • Berkeley Springs, WV 25411-1099
(304) 258-2430
Grade Span: PK-12; **Agency Type:** 1
Schools: 11
6 Primary; 1 Middle; 2 High; 0 Other Level
9 Regular; 0 Special Education; 0 Vocational; 0 Alternative
0 Magnet; 0 Charter; 4 Title I Eligible; 3 School-wide Title I
Students: 2,564 (51.6% male; 48.3% female)
Individual Education Program: 412 (16.1%);
English Language Learner: 3 (0.1%); Migrant: 0 (0.0%)
Eligible for Free Lunch Program: 739 (28.8%)
Eligible for Reduced-Price Lunch Program: 320 (12.5%)
Teachers: 173.5 (14.8 to 1)
Librarians/Media Specialists: 4.0 (641.0 to 1)
Guidance Counselors: 6.4 (400.6 to 1)
Current Spending: ($ per student per year):
Total: $7,415; Instruction: $4,366; Support Services: $2,588
Enrollment, Drop-out Rates and Diploma Recipients by Race/Ethnicity

Category	Total	White	Black	Asian	AIAN	Hisp.
Enrollment (%)	100.0	97.8	1.1	0.2	0.1	0.9
Drop-out Rate (%)	4.1	4.3	0.0	0.0	0.0	0.0
H.S. Diplomas (#)	137	131	2	3	1	0

Nicholas County

Nicholas County SD
400 Old Main Dr • Summersville, WV 26651-1360
(304) 872-3611 • http://boe.nich.k12.wv.us/
Grade Span: PK-12; **Agency Type:** 1
Schools: 16
11 Primary; 2 Middle; 2 High; 1 Other Level
15 Regular; 0 Special Education; 1 Vocational; 0 Alternative
0 Magnet; 0 Charter; 8 Title I Eligible; 8 School-wide Title I
Students: 4,303 (52.1% male; 47.8% female)
Individual Education Program: 885 (20.6%);
English Language Learner: 11 (0.3%); Migrant: 0 (0.0%)
Eligible for Free Lunch Program: 1,937 (45.0%)
Eligible for Reduced-Price Lunch Program: 491 (11.4%)
Teachers: 320.5 (13.4 to 1)
Librarians/Media Specialists: 4.0 (1,075.8 to 1)
Guidance Counselors: 9.5 (452.9 to 1)
Current Spending: ($ per student per year):
Total: $8,698; Instruction: $5,245; Support Services: $2,899
Enrollment, Drop-out Rates and Diploma Recipients by Race/Ethnicity

Category	Total	White	Black	Asian	AIAN	Hisp.
Enrollment (%)	100.0	99.1	0.4	0.1	0.0	0.3
Drop-out Rate (%)	3.5	3.6	0.0	0.0	0.0	0.0
H.S. Diplomas (#)	276	274	0	1	0	1

Ohio County

Ohio County SD
2203 National Rd • Wheeling, WV 26003-5203
(304) 243-0300 • http://wphs.ohio.k12.wv.us/ocbe/
Grade Span: PK-12; **Agency Type:** 1
Schools: 13
9 Primary; 3 Middle; 1 High; 0 Other Level
13 Regular; 0 Special Education; 0 Vocational; 0 Alternative
0 Magnet; 0 Charter; 7 Title I Eligible; 4 School-wide Title I
Students: 5,451 (51.7% male; 48.2% female)
Individual Education Program: 886 (16.3%);
English Language Learner: 21 (0.4%); Migrant: 0 (0.0%)
Eligible for Free Lunch Program: 1,851 (34.0%)
Eligible for Reduced-Price Lunch Program: 455 (8.3%)
Teachers: 375.0 (14.5 to 1)
Librarians/Media Specialists: 9.0 (605.7 to 1)
Guidance Counselors: 12.0 (454.3 to 1)

Current Spending: ($ per student per year):
Total: $8,643; Instruction: $5,109; Support Services: $3,128
Enrollment, Drop-out Rates and Diploma Recipients by Race/Ethnicity

Category	Total	White	Black	Asian	AIAN	Hisp.
Enrollment (%)	100.0	91.2	7.7	0.8	0.1	0.2
Drop-out Rate (%)	3.4	3.1	5.6	12.5	25.0	0.0
H.S. Diplomas (#)	341	317	19	3	2	0

Preston County

Preston County SD
300 Preston Dr · Kingwood, WV 26537-0566
Mailing Address: PO Box 566 · Kingwood, WV 26537-0566
(304) 329-0580 · http://www.prestonboe.com/
Grade Span: PK-12; **Agency Type:** 1
Schools: 12
    8 Primary; 3 Middle; 1 High; 0 Other Level
    12 Regular; 0 Special Education; 0 Vocational; 0 Alternative
    0 Magnet; 0 Charter; 7 Title I Eligible; 6 School-wide Title I
Students: 4,790   (50.8% male; 49.1% female)
    Individual Education Program: 935 (19.5%);
    English Language Learner: 3 (0.1%); Migrant: 0 (0.0%)
    Eligible for Free Lunch Program: 1,925 (40.2%)
    Eligible for Reduced-Price Lunch Program: 729 (15.2%)
Teachers: 329.8 (14.5 to 1)
Librarians/Media Specialists: 4.5 (1,064.4 to 1)
Guidance Counselors: 9.0 (532.2 to 1)
Current Spending: ($ per student per year):
    Total: $7,628; Instruction: $4,895; Support Services: $2,328
Enrollment, Drop-out Rates and Diploma Recipients by Race/Ethnicity

Category	Total	White	Black	Asian	AIAN	Hisp.
Enrollment (%)	100.0	99.0	0.6	0.1	0.1	0.1
Drop-out Rate (%)	5.7	5.6	11.1	0.0	33.3	0.0
H.S. Diplomas (#)	311	306	2	2	0	1

Putnam County

Putnam County SD
9 Courthouse Dr · Winfield, WV 25213-9347
(304) 586-0500 · http://boe.putn.k12.wv.us/boe/index.html
Grade Span: PK-12; **Agency Type:** 1
Schools: 22
    13 Primary; 4 Middle; 5 High; 0 Other Level
    21 Regular; 0 Special Education; 1 Vocational; 0 Alternative
    0 Magnet; 0 Charter; 8 Title I Eligible; 8 School-wide Title I
Students: 8,782   (52.1% male; 47.8% female)
    Individual Education Program: 1,635 (18.6%);
    English Language Learner: 23 (0.3%); Migrant: 0 (0.0%)
    Eligible for Free Lunch Program: 1,971 (22.4%)
    Eligible for Reduced-Price Lunch Program: 681 (7.8%)
Teachers: 607.0 (14.5 to 1)
Librarians/Media Specialists: 8.0 (1,097.8 to 1)
Guidance Counselors: 21.0 (418.2 to 1)
Current Spending: ($ per student per year):
    Total: $7,933; Instruction: $4,951; Support Services: $2,491
Enrollment, Drop-out Rates and Diploma Recipients by Race/Ethnicity

Category	Total	White	Black	Asian	AIAN	Hisp.
Enrollment (%)	100.0	97.6	1.4	0.7	0.1	0.2
Drop-out Rate (%)	3.0	3.0	0.0	0.0	25.0	0.0
H.S. Diplomas (#)	495	488	1	3	2	1

Raleigh County

Raleigh County SD
105 Adair St · Beckley, WV 25801-3733
(304) 256-4500 · http://boe.rale.k12.wv.us/
Grade Span: PK-12; **Agency Type:** 1
Schools: 33
    20 Primary; 5 Middle; 7 High; 0 Other Level
    29 Regular; 0 Special Education; 2 Vocational; 1 Alternative
    0 Magnet; 0 Charter; 18 Title I Eligible; 16 School-wide Title I
Students: 11,881   (52.1% male; 47.8% female)
    Individual Education Program: 1,916 (16.1%);
    English Language Learner: 37 (0.3%); Migrant: 0 (0.0%)
    Eligible for Free Lunch Program: 5,280 (44.4%)
    Eligible for Reduced-Price Lunch Program: 1,310 (11.0%)
Teachers: 808.3 (14.7 to 1)
Librarians/Media Specialists: 10.0 (1,188.1 to 1)
Guidance Counselors: 33.0 (360.0 to 1)
Current Spending: ($ per student per year):
    Total: $8,491; Instruction: $4,844; Support Services: $3,195

Enrollment, Drop-out Rates and Diploma Recipients by Race/Ethnicity

Category	Total	White	Black	Asian	AIAN	Hisp.
Enrollment (%)	100.0	88.2	10.5	0.8	0.1	0.4
Drop-out Rate (%)	3.2	3.3	3.0	0.0	0.0	0.0
H.S. Diplomas (#)	728	653	66	6	2	1

Randolph County

Randolph County SD
40 11th St · Elkins, WV 26241-3512
(304) 636-9150
Grade Span: PK-12; **Agency Type:** 1
Schools: 16
    9 Primary; 1 Middle; 2 High; 4 Other Level
    14 Regular; 0 Special Education; 1 Vocational; 1 Alternative
    0 Magnet; 0 Charter; 10 Title I Eligible; 6 School-wide Title I
Students: 4,480   (51.1% male; 48.8% female)
    Individual Education Program: 732 (16.3%);
    English Language Learner: 0 (0.0%); Migrant: 0 (0.0%)
    Eligible for Free Lunch Program: 1,762 (39.3%)
    Eligible for Reduced-Price Lunch Program: 645 (14.4%)
Teachers: 340.5 (13.2 to 1)
Librarians/Media Specialists: 3.0 (1,493.3 to 1)
Guidance Counselors: 13.0 (344.6 to 1)
Current Spending: ($ per student per year):
    Total: $7,669; Instruction: $5,071; Support Services: $2,159
Enrollment, Drop-out Rates and Diploma Recipients by Race/Ethnicity

Category	Total	White	Black	Asian	AIAN	Hisp.
Enrollment (%)	100.0	98.7	0.5	0.4	0.2	0.2
Drop-out Rate (%)	3.1	3.0	25.0	0.0	0.0	0.0
H.S. Diplomas (#)	273	264	3	3	1	2

Ritchie County

Ritchie County SD
134 S Penn Ave · Harrisville, WV 26362-1370
(304) 643-2991
Grade Span: PK-12; **Agency Type:** 1
Schools: 6
    4 Primary; 1 Middle; 1 High; 0 Other Level
    6 Regular; 0 Special Education; 0 Vocational; 0 Alternative
    0 Magnet; 0 Charter; 4 Title I Eligible; 3 School-wide Title I
Students: 1,650   (50.1% male; 49.8% female)
    Individual Education Program: 333 (20.2%);
    English Language Learner: 0 (0.0%); Migrant: 0 (0.0%)
    Eligible for Free Lunch Program: 666 (40.4%)
    Eligible for Reduced-Price Lunch Program: 216 (13.1%)
Teachers: 115.0 (14.3 to 1)
Librarians/Media Specialists: 1.0 (1,650.0 to 1)
Guidance Counselors: 2.0 (825.0 to 1)
Current Spending: ($ per student per year):
    Total: $7,932; Instruction: $4,999; Support Services: $2,456
Enrollment, Drop-out Rates and Diploma Recipients by Race/Ethnicity

Category	Total	White	Black	Asian	AIAN	Hisp.
Enrollment (%)	100.0	98.4	0.4	0.3	0.1	0.8
Drop-out Rate (%)	3.2	3.2	n/a	0.0	n/a	0.0
H.S. Diplomas (#)	113	113	0	0	0	0

Roane County

Roane County SD
Bowman St · Spencer, WV 25276-0609
Mailing Address: PO Box 609 · Spencer, WV 25276-0609
(304) 927-6400 · http://boe.roan.k12.wv.us/
Grade Span: PK-12; **Agency Type:** 1
Schools: 6
    4 Primary; 1 Middle; 1 High; 0 Other Level
    6 Regular; 0 Special Education; 0 Vocational; 0 Alternative
    0 Magnet; 0 Charter; 5 Title I Eligible; 5 School-wide Title I
Students: 2,593   (52.2% male; 47.7% female)
    Individual Education Program: 518 (20.0%);
    English Language Learner: 3 (0.1%); Migrant: 0 (0.0%)
    Eligible for Free Lunch Program: 1,231 (47.5%)
    Eligible for Reduced-Price Lunch Program: 367 (14.2%)
Teachers: 186.8 (13.9 to 1)
Librarians/Media Specialists: 2.0 (1,296.5 to 1)
Guidance Counselors: 5.0 (518.6 to 1)
Current Spending: ($ per student per year):
    Total: $7,501; Instruction: $4,610; Support Services: $2,410
Enrollment, Drop-out Rates and Diploma Recipients by Race/Ethnicity

Category	Total	White	Black	Asian	AIAN	Hisp.
Enrollment (%)	100.0	98.3	0.4	0.6	0.2	0.6
Drop-out Rate (%)	6.3	6.3	n/a	0.0	n/a	0.0
H.S. Diplomas (#)	174	172	0	1	0	1

Summers County

Summers County SD
116 Main St • Hinton, WV 25951-2439
(304) 466-6000
Grade Span: PK-12; **Agency Type:** 1
Schools: 5
   3 Primary; 1 Middle; 1 High; 0 Other Level
   5 Regular; 0 Special Education; 0 Vocational; 0 Alternative
   0 Magnet; 0 Charter; 3 Title I Eligible; 3 School-wide Title I
Students: 1,610 (50.6% male; 49.3% female)
   Individual Education Program: 361 (22.4%);
   English Language Learner: 0 (0.0%); Migrant: 0 (0.0%)
   Eligible for Free Lunch Program: 840 (52.2%)
   Eligible for Reduced-Price Lunch Program: 171 (10.6%)
Teachers: 109.5 (14.7 to 1)
Librarians/Media Specialists: 1.0 (1,610.0 to 1)
Guidance Counselors: 4.0 (402.5 to 1)
Current Spending: ($ per student per year):
   Total: $7,927; Instruction: $4,823; Support Services: $2,648

Enrollment, Drop-out Rates and Diploma Recipients by Race/Ethnicity

Category	Total	White	Black	Asian	AIAN	Hisp.
Enrollment (%)	100.0	95.7	3.2	0.3	0.3	0.4
Drop-out Rate (%)	5.8	6.0	0.0	0.0	0.0	0.0
H.S. Diplomas (#)	97	92	5	0	0	0

Taylor County

Taylor County SD
306 Beech St • Grafton, WV 26354-1836
(304) 265-2497 • http://www.wvonline.com/taylorcounty/index.htm
Grade Span: PK-12; **Agency Type:** 1
Schools: 7
   4 Primary; 1 Middle; 2 High; 0 Other Level
   6 Regular; 0 Special Education; 1 Vocational; 0 Alternative
   0 Magnet; 0 Charter; 4 Title I Eligible; 1 School-wide Title I
Students: 2,432 (51.6% male; 48.3% female)
   Individual Education Program: 431 (17.7%);
   English Language Learner: 1 (<0.1%); Migrant: 0 (0.0%)
   Eligible for Free Lunch Program: 917 (37.7%)
   Eligible for Reduced-Price Lunch Program: 273 (11.2%)
Teachers: 162.0 (15.0 to 1)
Librarians/Media Specialists: 4.0 (608.0 to 1)
Guidance Counselors: 5.5 (442.2 to 1)
Current Spending: ($ per student per year):
   Total: $8,202; Instruction: $4,864; Support Services: $2,909

Enrollment, Drop-out Rates and Diploma Recipients by Race/Ethnicity

Category	Total	White	Black	Asian	AIAN	Hisp.
Enrollment (%)	100.0	98.5	0.8	0.3	0.2	0.2
Drop-out Rate (%)	3.8	3.8	0.0	0.0	0.0	0.0
H.S. Diplomas (#)	143	139	1	3	0	0

Tyler County

Tyler County SD
1993 Silver Knight St • Sistersville, WV 26175-0025
Mailing Address: PO Box 25 • Middlebourne, WV 26149-0025
(304) 758-2145
Grade Span: PK-12; **Agency Type:** 1
Schools: 4
   2 Primary; 1 Middle; 1 High; 0 Other Level
   4 Regular; 0 Special Education; 0 Vocational; 0 Alternative
   0 Magnet; 0 Charter; 3 Title I Eligible; 0 School-wide Title I
Students: 1,571 (49.6% male; 50.3% female)
   Individual Education Program: 331 (21.1%);
   English Language Learner: 0 (0.0%); Migrant: 0 (0.0%)
   Eligible for Free Lunch Program: 663 (42.2%)
   Eligible for Reduced-Price Lunch Program: 170 (10.8%)
Teachers: 120.0 (13.1 to 1)
Librarians/Media Specialists: 2.0 (785.5 to 1)
Guidance Counselors: 4.0 (392.8 to 1)
Current Spending: ($ per student per year):
   Total: $8,624; Instruction: $5,174; Support Services: $2,994

Enrollment, Drop-out Rates and Diploma Recipients by Race/Ethnicity

Category	Total	White	Black	Asian	AIAN	Hisp.
Enrollment (%)	100.0	99.4	0.3	0.2	0.0	0.1
Drop-out Rate (%)	2.2	2.2	n/a	n/a	n/a	0.0
H.S. Diplomas (#)	100	98	0	0	0	2

Upshur County

Upshur County SD
102 Smithfield St • Buckhannon, WV 26201-2620
(304) 472-5480
Grade Span: PK-12; **Agency Type:** 1
Schools: 12
   9 Primary; 1 Middle; 2 High; 0 Other Level
   11 Regular; 0 Special Education; 1 Vocational; 0 Alternative
   0 Magnet; 0 Charter; 8 Title I Eligible; 8 School-wide Title I
Students: 3,841 (51.6% male; 48.3% female)
   Individual Education Program: 793 (20.6%);
   English Language Learner: 0 (0.0%); Migrant: 0 (0.0%)
   Eligible for Free Lunch Program: 1,543 (40.2%)
   Eligible for Reduced-Price Lunch Program: 478 (12.4%)
Teachers: 291.0 (13.2 to 1)
Librarians/Media Specialists: 2.0 (1,920.5 to 1)
Guidance Counselors: 9.0 (426.8 to 1)
Current Spending: ($ per student per year):
   Total: $8,031; Instruction: $4,933; Support Services: $2,651

Enrollment, Drop-out Rates and Diploma Recipients by Race/Ethnicity

Category	Total	White	Black	Asian	AIAN	Hisp.
Enrollment (%)	100.0	98.3	0.8	0.4	0.2	0.3
Drop-out Rate (%)	3.9	3.9	0.0	0.0	n/a	0.0
H.S. Diplomas (#)	244	241	1	2	0	0

Wayne County

Wayne County SD
212 N Court St • Wayne, WV 25570-0070
Mailing Address: PO Box 70 • Wayne, WV 25570-0070
(304) 272-5116
Grade Span: PK-12; **Agency Type:** 1
Schools: 21
   12 Primary; 6 Middle; 3 High; 0 Other Level
   21 Regular; 0 Special Education; 0 Vocational; 0 Alternative
   0 Magnet; 0 Charter; 12 Title I Eligible; 11 School-wide Title I
Students: 7,445 (52.1% male; 47.8% female)
   Individual Education Program: 1,447 (19.4%);
   English Language Learner: 3 (<0.1%); Migrant: 0 (0.0%)
   Eligible for Free Lunch Program: 3,245 (43.6%)
   Eligible for Reduced-Price Lunch Program: 799 (10.7%)
Teachers: 535.3 (13.9 to 1)
Librarians/Media Specialists: 9.0 (827.2 to 1)
Guidance Counselors: 13.2 (564.0 to 1)
Current Spending: ($ per student per year):
   Total: $8,125; Instruction: $5,050; Support Services: $2,621

Enrollment, Drop-out Rates and Diploma Recipients by Race/Ethnicity

Category	Total	White	Black	Asian	AIAN	Hisp.
Enrollment (%)	100.0	99.1	0.4	0.3	0.1	0.1
Drop-out Rate (%)	2.6	2.6	0.0	0.0	0.0	0.0
H.S. Diplomas (#)	395	391	0	3	0	1

Webster County

Webster County SD
315 S Main St • Webster Springs, WV 26288-1187
(304) 847-5638 • http://glade.webs.k12.wv.us/WebsterBdOff.htm
Grade Span: PK-12; **Agency Type:** 1
Schools: 6
   4 Primary; 1 Middle; 1 High; 0 Other Level
   6 Regular; 0 Special Education; 0 Vocational; 0 Alternative
   0 Magnet; 0 Charter; 3 Title I Eligible; 3 School-wide Title I
Students: 1,673 (51.6% male; 48.3% female)
   Individual Education Program: 297 (17.8%);
   English Language Learner: 0 (0.0%); Migrant: 0 (0.0%)
   Eligible for Free Lunch Program: 935 (55.9%)
   Eligible for Reduced-Price Lunch Program: 199 (11.9%)
Teachers: 127.8 (13.1 to 1)
Librarians/Media Specialists: 1.0 (1,673.0 to 1)
Guidance Counselors: 4.0 (418.3 to 1)
Current Spending: ($ per student per year):
   Total: $8,639; Instruction: $5,567; Support Services: $2,676

Enrollment, Drop-out Rates and Diploma Recipients by Race/Ethnicity

Category	Total	White	Black	Asian	AIAN	Hisp.
Enrollment (%)	100.0	99.6	0.4	0.0	0.0	0.1
Drop-out Rate (%)	2.5	2.5	0.0	0.0	n/a	n/a
H.S. Diplomas (#)	115	115	0	0	0	0

Wetzel County

Wetzel County SD
333 Foundry St • New Martinsville, WV 26155-1141
(304) 455-2441
Grade Span: PK-12; **Agency Type:** 1
Schools: 9
  5 Primary; 0 Middle; 4 High; 0 Other Level
  9 Regular; 0 Special Education; 0 Vocational; 0 Alternative
  0 Magnet; 0 Charter; 4 Title I Eligible; 3 School-wide Title I
Students: 3,320   (51.1% male; 48.8% female)
  Individual Education Program: 688 (20.7%);
  English Language Learner: 14 (0.4%); Migrant: 0 (0.0%)
  Eligible for Free Lunch Program: 1,253 (37.7%)
  Eligible for Reduced-Price Lunch Program: 354 (10.7%)
Teachers: 239.5 (13.9 to 1)
Librarians/Media Specialists: 4.5 (737.8 to 1)
Guidance Counselors: 8.0 (415.0 to 1)
Current Spending: ($ per student per year):
  Total: $7,970; Instruction: $4,942; Support Services: $2,675
Enrollment, Drop-out Rates and Diploma Recipients by Race/Ethnicity

Category	Total	White	Black	Asian	AIAN	Hisp.
Enrollment (%)	100.0	98.3	0.8	0.7	0.1	0.2
Drop-out Rate (%)	2.2	2.1	n/a	25.0	n/a	0.0
H.S. Diplomas (#)	223	222	0	0	0	1

Wood County

Wood County SD
1210 13th St • Parkersburg, WV 26101-4144
(304) 420-9663 • http://www.netassoc.net/wcboe/
Grade Span: PK-12; **Agency Type:** 1
Schools: 29
  19 Primary; 5 Middle; 4 High; 1 Other Level
  27 Regular; 1 Special Education; 1 Vocational; 0 Alternative
  0 Magnet; 0 Charter; 9 Title I Eligible; 9 School-wide Title I
Students: 13,738   (51.0% male; 48.9% female)
  Individual Education Program: 2,038 (14.8%);
  English Language Learner: 47 (0.3%); Migrant: 0 (0.0%)
  Eligible for Free Lunch Program: 4,510 (32.8%)
  Eligible for Reduced-Price Lunch Program: 1,041 (7.6%)
Teachers: 929.5 (14.8 to 1)
Librarians/Media Specialists: 24.0 (572.4 to 1)
Guidance Counselors: 26.0 (528.3 to 1)
Current Spending: ($ per student per year):
  Total: $8,172; Instruction: $4,979; Support Services: $2,721
Enrollment, Drop-out Rates and Diploma Recipients by Race/Ethnicity

Category	Total	White	Black	Asian	AIAN	Hisp.
Enrollment (%)	100.0	97.2	1.9	0.6	0.1	0.3
Drop-out Rate (%)	3.3	3.4	2.7	4.2	0.0	0.0
H.S. Diplomas (#)	778	757	9	8	1	3

Wyoming County

Wyoming County SD
Main St • Pineville, WV 24874-0069
Mailing Address: PO Box 69 • Pineville, WV 24874-0069
(304) 732-6262
Grade Span: PK-12; **Agency Type:** 1
Schools: 14
  8 Primary; 3 Middle; 3 High; 0 Other Level
  13 Regular; 0 Special Education; 1 Vocational; 0 Alternative
  0 Magnet; 0 Charter; 11 Title I Eligible; 6 School-wide Title I
Students: 4,259   (52.4% male; 47.5% female)
  Individual Education Program: 763 (17.9%);
  English Language Learner: 0 (0.0%); Migrant: 0 (0.0%)
  Eligible for Free Lunch Program: 2,257 (53.0%)
  Eligible for Reduced-Price Lunch Program: 451 (10.6%)
Teachers: 339.5 (12.5 to 1)
Librarians/Media Specialists: 2.0 (2,129.5 to 1)
Guidance Counselors: 7.0 (608.4 to 1)
Current Spending: ($ per student per year):
  Total: $8,936; Instruction: $5,892; Support Services: $2,443
Enrollment, Drop-out Rates and Diploma Recipients by Race/Ethnicity

Category	Total	White	Black	Asian	AIAN	Hisp.
Enrollment (%)	100.0	98.3	1.2	0.1	0.1	0.2
Drop-out Rate (%)	3.3	3.4	0.0	0.0	n/a	n/a
H.S. Diplomas (#)	309	306	2	1	0	0

Number of Schools

Rank	Number	District Name	City
1	71	Kanawha County SD	Charleston
2	33	Raleigh County SD	Beckley
3	31	Cabell County SD	Huntington
4	29	Harrison County SD	Clarksburg
4	29	Wood County SD	Parkersburg
6	28	Berkeley County SD	Martinsburg
7	26	Fayette County SD	Fayetteville
7	26	Mercer County SD	Princeton
9	25	Monongalia SD	Morgantown
10	22	Marion County SD	Fairmont
10	22	Putnam County SD	Winfield
12	21	Wayne County SD	Wayne
13	18	Logan County SD	Logan
13	18	Mcdowell County SD	Welch
13	18	Mingo County SD	Williamson
16	17	Boone County SD	Madison
17	16	Nicholas County SD	Summersville
17	16	Randolph County SD	Elkins
19	15	Marshall County SD	Moundsville
20	14	Greenbrier County SD	Lewisburg
20	14	Mineral County SD	Keyser
20	14	Wyoming County SD	Pineville
23	13	Hancock County SD	New Cumberland
23	13	Jackson County SD	Ripley
23	13	Jefferson County SD	Charles Town
23	13	Mason County SD	Point Pleasant
23	13	Ohio County SD	Wheeling
28	12	Brooke County SD	Wellsburg
28	12	Lincoln County SD	Hamlin
28	12	Preston County SD	Kingwood
28	12	Upshur County SD	Buckhannon
32	11	Morgan County SD	Berkeley Spgs
33	10	Hampshire County SD	Romney
34	9	Barbour County SD	Philippi
34	9	Wetzel County SD	New Martinsville
36	8	Braxton County SD	Sutton
37	7	Clay County SD	Clay
37	7	Lewis County SD	Weston
37	7	Taylor County SD	Grafton
40	6	Grant County SD	Petersburg
40	6	Ritchie County SD	Harrisville
40	6	Roane County SD	Spencer
40	6	Webster County SD	Webster Spgs
44	5	Hardy County SD	Moorefield
44	5	Monroe County SD	Union
44	5	Summers County SD	Hinton
47	4	Tyler County SD	Sistersville

Number of Teachers

Rank	Number	District Name	City
1	1,934	Kanawha County SD	Charleston
2	1,019	Berkeley County SD	Martinsburg
3	929	Wood County SD	Parkersburg
4	857	Cabell County SD	Huntington
5	808	Raleigh County SD	Beckley
6	767	Harrison County SD	Clarksburg
7	700	Monongalia SD	Morgantown
8	685	Mercer County SD	Princeton
9	619	Marion County SD	Fairmont
10	607	Putnam County SD	Winfield
11	535	Wayne County SD	Wayne
12	520	Fayette County SD	Fayetteville
13	502	Jefferson County SD	Charles Town
14	447	Logan County SD	Logan
15	375	Ohio County SD	Wheeling
16	371	Greenbrier County SD	Lewisburg
17	357	Boone County SD	Madison
18	348	Jackson County SD	Ripley
19	347	Marshall County SD	Moundsville
20	341	Mingo County SD	Williamson
21	340	Randolph County SD	Elkins
22	339	Wyoming County SD	Pineville
23	334	Mcdowell County SD	Welch
24	329	Preston County SD	Kingwood
25	322	Mineral County SD	Keyser
26	320	Nicholas County SD	Summersville
27	308	Mason County SD	Point Pleasant
28	300	Hancock County SD	New Cumberland
29	291	Lincoln County SD	Hamlin
29	291	Upshur County SD	Buckhannon
31	257	Brooke County SD	Wellsburg
32	245	Hampshire County SD	Romney
33	239	Wetzel County SD	New Martinsville
34	197	Lewis County SD	Weston
35	190	Braxton County SD	Sutton
36	186	Barbour County SD	Philippi
36	186	Roane County SD	Spencer
38	173	Morgan County SD	Berkeley Spgs
39	162	Taylor County SD	Grafton

40	158	Clay County SD	Clay
41	157	Hardy County SD	Moorefield
42	150	Monroe County SD	Union
43	138	Grant County SD	Petersburg
44	127	Webster County SD	Webster Spgs
45	120	Tyler County SD	Sistersville
46	115	Ritchie County SD	Harrisville
47	109	Summers County SD	Hinton

Number of Students

Rank	Number	District Name	City
1	28,306	Kanawha County SD	Charleston
2	14,277	Berkeley County SD	Martinsburg
3	13,738	Wood County SD	Parkersburg
4	12,217	Cabell County SD	Huntington
5	11,881	Raleigh County SD	Beckley
6	11,583	Harrison County SD	Clarksburg
7	10,206	Monongalia SD	Morgantown
8	9,395	Mercer County SD	Princeton
9	8,782	Putnam County SD	Winfield
10	8,244	Marion County SD	Fairmont
11	7,445	Wayne County SD	Wayne
12	7,414	Jefferson County SD	Charles Town
13	7,001	Fayette County SD	Fayetteville
14	6,077	Logan County SD	Logan
15	5,451	Ohio County SD	Wheeling
16	5,381	Greenbrier County SD	Lewisburg
17	5,329	Marshall County SD	Moundsville
18	5,065	Jackson County SD	Ripley
19	4,790	Preston County SD	Kingwood
20	4,705	Mingo County SD	Williamson
21	4,584	Boone County SD	Madison
22	4,555	Mineral County SD	Keyser
23	4,480	Randolph County SD	Elkins
24	4,303	Nicholas County SD	Summersville
25	4,297	Hancock County SD	New Cumberland
26	4,259	Wyoming County SD	Pineville
27	4,253	Mcdowell County SD	Welch
28	4,202	Mason County SD	Point Pleasant
29	3,841	Upshur County SD	Buckhannon
30	3,826	Lincoln County SD	Hamlin
31	3,596	Brooke County SD	Wellsburg
32	3,577	Hampshire County SD	Romney
33	3,320	Wetzel County SD	New Martinsville
34	2,799	Lewis County SD	Weston
35	2,593	Roane County SD	Spencer
36	2,573	Barbour County SD	Philippi
37	2,564	Morgan County SD	Berkeley Spgs
38	2,555	Braxton County SD	Sutton
39	2,432	Taylor County SD	Grafton
40	2,342	Hardy County SD	Moorefield
41	2,099	Clay County SD	Clay
42	2,031	Monroe County SD	Union
43	1,984	Grant County SD	Petersburg
44	1,673	Webster County SD	Webster Spgs
45	1,650	Ritchie County SD	Harrisville
46	1,610	Summers County SD	Hinton
47	1,571	Tyler County SD	Sistersville

Male Students

Rank	Percent	District Name	City
1	53.5	Barbour County SD	Philippi
2	53.4	Mason County SD	Point Pleasant
3	53.2	Fayette County SD	Fayetteville
4	52.4	Wyoming County SD	Pineville
5	52.4	Greenbrier County SD	Lewisburg
6	52.4	Mcdowell County SD	Welch
7	52.3	Boone County SD	Madison
8	52.3	Lewis County SD	Weston
9	52.2	Hancock County SD	New Cumberland
10	52.2	Roane County SD	Spencer
11	52.1	Lincoln County SD	Hamlin
12	52.1	Nicholas County SD	Summersville
13	52.1	Raleigh County SD	Beckley
14	52.1	Wayne County SD	Wayne
15	52.1	Putnam County SD	Winfield
16	52.0	Kanawha County SD	Charleston
17	52.0	Hampshire County SD	Romney
18	51.9	Mingo County SD	Williamson
19	51.9	Jackson County SD	Ripley
20	51.8	Mercer County SD	Princeton
21	51.7	Ohio County SD	Wheeling
22	51.6	Taylor County SD	Grafton
23	51.6	Morgan County SD	Berkeley Spgs
24	51.6	Cabell County SD	Huntington
24	51.6	Marion County SD	Fairmont
26	51.6	Monongalia SD	Morgantown
27	51.6	Webster County SD	Webster Spgs
28	51.6	Upshur County SD	Buckhannon
29	51.5	Marshall County SD	Moundsville
30	51.4	Jefferson County SD	Charles Town

31	51.2	Monroe County SD	Union
32	51.1	Wetzel County SD	New Martinsville
33	51.1	Randolph County SD	Elkins
34	51.0	Wood County SD	Parkersburg
35	51.0	Braxton County SD	Sutton
36	51.0	Mineral County SD	Keyser
37	50.9	Harrison County SD	Clarksburg
38	50.9	Logan County SD	Logan
39	50.9	Hardy County SD	Moorefield
40	50.9	Berkeley County SD	Martinsburg
41	50.9	Grant County SD	Petersburg
42	50.8	Preston County SD	Kingwood
43	50.6	Summers County SD	Hinton
44	50.1	Ritchie County SD	Harrisville
45	49.8	Brooke County SD	Wellsburg
46	49.6	Tyler County SD	Sistersville
47	49.2	Clay County SD	Clay

Female Students

Rank	Percent	District Name	City
1	50.7	Clay County SD	Clay
2	50.3	Tyler County SD	Sistersville
3	50.1	Brooke County SD	Wellsburg
4	49.8	Ritchie County SD	Harrisville
5	49.3	Summers County SD	Hinton
6	49.1	Preston County SD	Kingwood
7	49.0	Grant County SD	Petersburg
8	49.0	Berkeley County SD	Martinsburg
9	49.0	Hardy County SD	Moorefield
10	49.0	Logan County SD	Logan
11	49.0	Harrison County SD	Clarksburg
12	48.9	Mineral County SD	Keyser
13	48.9	Braxton County SD	Sutton
14	48.9	Wood County SD	Parkersburg
15	48.8	Randolph County SD	Elkins
16	48.8	Wetzel County SD	New Martinsville
17	48.7	Monroe County SD	Union
18	48.5	Jefferson County SD	Charles Town
19	48.4	Marshall County SD	Moundsville
20	48.3	Upshur County SD	Buckhannon
21	48.3	Webster County SD	Webster Spgs
22	48.3	Monongalia SD	Morgantown
23	48.3	Cabell County SD	Huntington
23	48.3	Marion County SD	Fairmont
25	48.3	Morgan County SD	Berkeley Spgs
26	48.3	Taylor County SD	Grafton
27	48.2	Ohio County SD	Wheeling
28	48.1	Mercer County SD	Princeton
29	48.0	Jackson County SD	Ripley
30	48.0	Mingo County SD	Williamson
31	47.9	Hampshire County SD	Romney
32	47.9	Kanawha County SD	Charleston
33	47.8	Putnam County SD	Winfield
34	47.8	Wayne County SD	Wayne
35	47.8	Raleigh County SD	Beckley
36	47.8	Nicholas County SD	Summersville
37	47.8	Lincoln County SD	Hamlin
38	47.7	Roane County SD	Spencer
39	47.7	Hancock County SD	New Cumberland
40	47.6	Lewis County SD	Weston
41	47.6	Boone County SD	Madison
42	47.5	Mcdowell County SD	Welch
43	47.5	Greenbrier County SD	Lewisburg
44	47.5	Wyoming County SD	Pineville
45	46.7	Fayette County SD	Fayetteville
46	46.5	Mason County SD	Point Pleasant
47	46.4	Barbour County SD	Philippi

Individual Education Program Students

Rank	Percent	District Name	City
1	22.4	Summers County SD	Hinton
2	21.9	Lewis County SD	Weston
2	21.9	Lincoln County SD	Hamlin
4	21.4	Mcdowell County SD	Welch
5	21.2	Mason County SD	Point Pleasant
6	21.1	Tyler County SD	Sistersville
7	20.7	Wetzel County SD	New Martinsville
8	20.6	Nicholas County SD	Summersville
8	20.6	Upshur County SD	Buckhannon
10	20.5	Grant County SD	Petersburg
10	20.5	Monroe County SD	Union
12	20.2	Boone County SD	Madison
12	20.2	Braxton County SD	Sutton
12	20.2	Ritchie County SD	Harrisville
15	20.0	Roane County SD	Spencer
16	19.9	Greenbrier County SD	Lewisburg
16	19.9	Marshall County SD	Moundsville
18	19.7	Brooke County SD	Wellsburg
19	19.5	Clay County SD	Clay
19	19.5	Preston County SD	Kingwood
21	19.4	Wayne County SD	Wayne

22	19.3	Mingo County SD	Williamson
23	19.1	Hampshire County SD	Romney
24	18.8	Barbour County SD	Philippi
24	18.8	Hardy County SD	Moorefield
26	18.6	Putnam County SD	Winfield
27	18.4	Hancock County SD	New Cumberland
28	17.9	Wyoming County SD	Pineville
29	17.8	Webster County SD	Webster Spgs
30	17.7	Berkeley County SD	Martinsburg
30	17.7	Harrison County SD	Clarksburg
30	17.7	Taylor County SD	Grafton
33	17.5	Jackson County SD	Ripley
34	17.4	Mercer County SD	Princeton
35	17.3	Mineral County SD	Keyser
36	17.1	Cabell County SD	Huntington
36	17.1	Logan County SD	Logan
38	16.5	Jefferson County SD	Charles Town
38	16.5	Kanawha County SD	Charleston
40	16.4	Marion County SD	Fairmont
41	16.3	Ohio County SD	Wheeling
41	16.3	Randolph County SD	Elkins
43	16.1	Morgan County SD	Berkeley Spgs
43	16.1	Raleigh County SD	Beckley
45	15.7	Fayette County SD	Fayetteville
46	15.4	Monongalia SD	Morgantown
47	14.8	Wood County SD	Parkersburg

English Language Learner Students

Rank	Percent	District Name	City
1	4.0	Monongalia SD	Morgantown
2	2.1	Jefferson County SD	Charles Town
3	1.3	Kanawha County SD	Charleston
4	1.2	Berkeley County SD	Martinsburg
5	0.8	Cabell County SD	Huntington
6	0.6	Hardy County SD	Moorefield
7	0.4	Logan County SD	Logan
7	0.4	Ohio County SD	Wheeling
7	0.4	Wetzel County SD	New Martinsville
10	0.3	Jackson County SD	Ripley
10	0.3	Nicholas County SD	Summersville
10	0.3	Putnam County SD	Winfield
10	0.3	Raleigh County SD	Beckley
10	0.3	Wood County SD	Parkersburg
15	0.2	Harrison County SD	Clarksburg
15	0.2	Mineral County SD	Keyser
17	0.1	Barbour County SD	Philippi
17	0.1	Braxton County SD	Sutton
17	0.1	Fayette County SD	Fayetteville
17	0.1	Lewis County SD	Weston
17	0.1	Mason County SD	Point Pleasant
17	0.1	Mercer County SD	Princeton
17	0.1	Morgan County SD	Berkeley Spgs
17	0.1	Preston County SD	Kingwood
17	0.1	Roane County SD	Spencer
26	0.0	Boone County SD	Madison
26	0.0	Greenbrier County SD	Lewisburg
26	0.0	Marion County SD	Fairmont
26	0.0	Marshall County SD	Moundsville
26	0.0	Taylor County SD	Grafton
26	0.0	Wayne County SD	Wayne
32	0.0	Brooke County SD	Wellsburg
32	0.0	Clay County SD	Clay
32	0.0	Grant County SD	Petersburg
32	0.0	Hampshire County SD	Romney
32	0.0	Hancock County SD	New Cumberland
32	0.0	Lincoln County SD	Hamlin
32	0.0	Mcdowell County SD	Welch
32	0.0	Mingo County SD	Williamson
32	0.0	Monroe County SD	Union
32	0.0	Randolph County SD	Elkins
32	0.0	Ritchie County SD	Harrisville
32	0.0	Summers County SD	Hinton
32	0.0	Tyler County SD	Sistersville
32	0.0	Upshur County SD	Buckhannon
32	0.0	Webster County SD	Webster Spgs
32	0.0	Wyoming County SD	Pineville

Migrant Students

Rank	Percent	District Name	City
1	4.6	Hardy County SD	Moorefield
2	0.5	Berkeley County SD	Martinsburg
3	0.3	Jefferson County SD	Charles Town
3	0.3	Lewis County SD	Weston
5	0.0	Barbour County SD	Philippi
5	0.0	Boone County SD	Madison
5	0.0	Braxton County SD	Sutton
5	0.0	Brooke County SD	Wellsburg
5	0.0	Cabell County SD	Huntington
5	0.0	Clay County SD	Clay
5	0.0	Fayette County SD	Fayetteville
5	0.0	Grant County SD	Petersburg
5	0.0	Greenbrier County SD	Lewisburg
5	0.0	Hampshire County SD	Romney
5	0.0	Hancock County SD	New Cumberland
5	0.0	Harrison County SD	Clarksburg
5	0.0	Jackson County SD	Ripley
5	0.0	Kanawha County SD	Charleston
5	0.0	Lincoln County SD	Hamlin
5	0.0	Logan County SD	Logan
5	0.0	Marion County SD	Fairmont
5	0.0	Marshall County SD	Moundsville
5	0.0	Mason County SD	Point Pleasant
5	0.0	Mcdowell County SD	Welch
5	0.0	Mercer County SD	Princeton
5	0.0	Mineral County SD	Keyser
5	0.0	Mingo County SD	Williamson
5	0.0	Monongalia SD	Morgantown
5	0.0	Monroe County SD	Union
5	0.0	Morgan County SD	Berkeley Spgs
5	0.0	Nicholas County SD	Summersville
5	0.0	Ohio County SD	Wheeling
5	0.0	Preston County SD	Kingwood
5	0.0	Putnam County SD	Winfield
5	0.0	Raleigh County SD	Beckley
5	0.0	Randolph County SD	Elkins
5	0.0	Ritchie County SD	Harrisville
5	0.0	Roane County SD	Spencer
5	0.0	Summers County SD	Hinton
5	0.0	Taylor County SD	Grafton
5	0.0	Tyler County SD	Sistersville
5	0.0	Upshur County SD	Buckhannon
5	0.0	Wayne County SD	Wayne
5	0.0	Webster County SD	Webster Spgs
5	0.0	Wetzel County SD	New Martinsville
5	0.0	Wood County SD	Parkersburg
5	0.0	Wyoming County SD	Pineville

Students Eligible for Free Lunch

Rank	Percent	District Name	City
1	71.9	Mcdowell County SD	Welch
2	60.6	Clay County SD	Clay
3	55.9	Webster County SD	Webster Spgs
4	55.7	Mingo County SD	Williamson
5	53.0	Wyoming County SD	Pineville
6	52.2	Summers County SD	Hinton
7	51.0	Barbour County SD	Philippi
8	49.3	Lincoln County SD	Hamlin
9	48.6	Braxton County SD	Sutton
10	47.5	Roane County SD	Spencer
11	46.2	Logan County SD	Logan
12	46.1	Mercer County SD	Princeton
13	45.0	Nicholas County SD	Summersville
14	44.5	Boone County SD	Madison
15	44.4	Raleigh County SD	Beckley
16	44.3	Fayette County SD	Fayetteville
17	43.6	Wayne County SD	Wayne
18	42.2	Tyler County SD	Sistersville
19	42.1	Lewis County SD	Weston
20	41.6	Greenbrier County SD	Lewisburg
21	40.7	Cabell County SD	Huntington
22	40.4	Ritchie County SD	Harrisville
23	40.2	Mason County SD	Point Pleasant
23	40.2	Preston County SD	Kingwood
23	40.2	Upshur County SD	Buckhannon
26	39.3	Harrison County SD	Clarksburg
26	39.3	Randolph County SD	Elkins
28	38.6	Monroe County SD	Union
29	38.0	Kanawha County SD	Charleston
30	37.7	Taylor County SD	Grafton
30	37.7	Wetzel County SD	New Martinsville
32	36.9	Hampshire County SD	Romney
33	36.4	Marshall County SD	Moundsville
34	36.2	Marion County SD	Fairmont
35	35.0	Grant County SD	Petersburg
36	34.7	Jackson County SD	Ripley
37	34.0	Ohio County SD	Wheeling
38	33.7	Hardy County SD	Moorefield
39	32.8	Wood County SD	Parkersburg
40	30.2	Mineral County SD	Keyser
41	28.8	Morgan County SD	Berkeley Spgs
42	27.6	Hancock County SD	New Cumberland
43	27.4	Monongalia SD	Morgantown
44	26.0	Berkeley County SD	Martinsburg
45	25.7	Brooke County SD	Wellsburg
46	22.6	Jefferson County SD	Charles Town
47	22.4	Putnam County SD	Winfield

Students Eligible for Reduced-Price Lunch

Rank	Percent	District Name	City
1	17.7	Hardy County SD	Moorefield
2	17.4	Monroe County SD	Union
3	16.2	Hampshire County SD	Romney
4	15.4	Barbour County SD	Philippi
5	15.2	Clay County SD	Clay
5	15.2	Preston County SD	Kingwood
7	15.0	Grant County SD	Petersburg
8	14.4	Randolph County SD	Elkins
9	14.2	Roane County SD	Spencer
10	14.1	Greenbrier County SD	Lewisburg
11	13.1	Ritchie County SD	Harrisville
12	12.5	Morgan County SD	Berkeley Spgs
13	12.4	Upshur County SD	Buckhannon
14	12.1	Mineral County SD	Keyser
15	12.0	Lewis County SD	Weston
16	11.9	Webster County SD	Webster Spgs
17	11.4	Nicholas County SD	Summersville
18	11.3	Mingo County SD	Williamson
19	11.2	Fayette County SD	Fayetteville
19	11.2	Lincoln County SD	Hamlin
19	11.2	Taylor County SD	Grafton
22	11.0	Marshall County SD	Moundsville
22	11.0	Raleigh County SD	Beckley
24	10.8	Boone County SD	Madison
24	10.8	Tyler County SD	Sistersville
26	10.7	Wayne County SD	Wayne
26	10.7	Wetzel County SD	New Martinsville
28	10.6	Berkeley County SD	Martinsburg
28	10.6	Summers County SD	Hinton
28	10.6	Wyoming County SD	Pineville
31	10.5	Mcdowell County SD	Welch
32	10.4	Mercer County SD	Princeton
33	9.9	Brooke County SD	Wellsburg
33	9.9	Cabell County SD	Huntington
33	9.9	Jefferson County SD	Charles Town
36	9.8	Mason County SD	Point Pleasant
37	9.6	Harrison County SD	Clarksburg
38	9.2	Braxton County SD	Sutton
39	8.9	Hancock County SD	New Cumberland
39	8.9	Jackson County SD	Ripley
41	8.8	Kanawha County SD	Charleston
42	8.7	Monongalia SD	Morgantown
43	8.5	Logan County SD	Logan
44	8.3	Ohio County SD	Wheeling
45	8.0	Marion County SD	Fairmont
46	7.8	Putnam County SD	Winfield
47	7.6	Wood County SD	Parkersburg

Student/Teacher Ratio

Rank	Ratio	District Name	City
1	15.3	Marshall County SD	Moundsville
2	15.1	Harrison County SD	Clarksburg
3	15.0	Taylor County SD	Grafton
4	14.9	Hardy County SD	Moorefield
5	14.8	Jefferson County SD	Charles Town
5	14.8	Morgan County SD	Berkeley Spgs
5	14.8	Wood County SD	Parkersburg
8	14.7	Raleigh County SD	Beckley
8	14.7	Summers County SD	Hinton
10	14.6	Hampshire County SD	Romney
10	14.6	Kanawha County SD	Charleston
10	14.6	Monongalia SD	Morgantown
13	14.5	Greenbrier County SD	Lewisburg
13	14.5	Jackson County SD	Ripley
13	14.5	Ohio County SD	Wheeling
13	14.5	Preston County SD	Kingwood
13	14.5	Putnam County SD	Winfield
18	14.4	Grant County SD	Petersburg
19	14.3	Hancock County SD	New Cumberland
19	14.3	Ritchie County SD	Harrisville
21	14.2	Cabell County SD	Huntington
21	14.2	Lewis County SD	Weston
23	14.1	Mineral County SD	Keyser
24	14.0	Berkeley County SD	Martinsburg
24	14.0	Brooke County SD	Wellsburg
26	13.9	Roane County SD	Spencer
26	13.9	Wayne County SD	Wayne
26	13.9	Wetzel County SD	New Martinsville
29	13.8	Barbour County SD	Philippi
29	13.8	Mingo County SD	Williamson
31	13.7	Mercer County SD	Princeton
32	13.6	Logan County SD	Logan
32	13.6	Mason County SD	Point Pleasant
34	13.5	Fayette County SD	Fayetteville
34	13.5	Monroe County SD	Union
36	13.4	Braxton County SD	Sutton
36	13.4	Nicholas County SD	Summersville
38	13.3	Clay County SD	Clay
38	13.3	Marion County SD	Fairmont
40	13.2	Randolph County SD	Elkins
40	13.2	Upshur County SD	Buckhannon
42	13.1	Lincoln County SD	Hamlin
42	13.1	Tyler County SD	Sistersville
42	13.1	Webster County SD	Webster Spgs

45	12.8	Boone County SD	Madison
46	12.7	Mcdowell County SD	Welch
47	12.5	Wyoming County SD	Pineville

Student/Librarian Ratio

Rank	Ratio	District Name	City
1	2,129.5	Wyoming County SD	Pineville
2	2,031.0	Monroe County SD	Union
3	1,920.5	Upshur County SD	Buckhannon
4	1,673.0	Webster County SD	Webster Spgs
5	1,650.0	Ritchie County SD	Harrisville
6	1,610.0	Summers County SD	Hinton
7	1,493.3	Randolph County SD	Elkins
8	1,417.7	Mcdowell County SD	Welch
9	1,332.3	Marshall County SD	Moundsville
10	1,296.5	Roane County SD	Spencer
11	1,277.5	Braxton County SD	Sutton
11	1,277.5	Hampshire County SD	Romney
13	1,266.3	Jackson County SD	Ripley
14	1,188.1	Raleigh County SD	Beckley
15	1,146.0	Boone County SD	Madison
16	1,130.8	Hancock County SD	New Cumberland
17	1,120.2	Mingo County SD	Williamson
18	1,110.6	Cabell County SD	Huntington
19	1,097.8	Putnam County SD	Winfield
20	1,076.2	Greenbrier County SD	Lewisburg
21	1,075.8	Nicholas County SD	Summersville
22	1,064.2	Preston County SD	Kingwood
23	1,050.5	Mason County SD	Point Pleasant
24	1,012.8	Logan County SD	Logan
25	1,000.1	Fayette County SD	Fayetteville
26	899.0	Brooke County SD	Wellsburg
27	828.2	Mineral County SD	Keyser
28	827.2	Wayne County SD	Wayne
29	785.5	Tyler County SD	Sistersville
30	765.2	Lincoln County SD	Hamlin
31	737.8	Wetzel County SD	New Martinsville
32	699.8	Lewis County SD	Weston
33	699.7	Clay County SD	Clay
34	677.1	Barbour County SD	Philippi
35	664.0	Berkeley County SD	Martinsburg
36	661.3	Grant County SD	Petersburg
37	641.0	Morgan County SD	Berkeley Spgs
38	608.0	Taylor County SD	Grafton
39	605.7	Ohio County SD	Wheeling
40	572.4	Wood County SD	Parkersburg
41	537.2	Monongalia SD	Morgantown
42	529.6	Jefferson County SD	Charles Town
43	526.5	Harrison County SD	Clarksburg
44	468.4	Hardy County SD	Moorefield
45	458.0	Marion County SD	Fairmont
46	447.4	Mercer County SD	Princeton
47	442.3	Kanawha County SD	Charleston

Student/Counselor Ratio

Rank	Ratio	District Name	City
1	825.0	Ritchie County SD	Harrisville
2	708.6	Grant County SD	Petersburg
3	699.7	Clay County SD	Clay
4	643.3	Barbour County SD	Philippi
5	637.7	Lincoln County SD	Hamlin
6	608.4	Wyoming County SD	Pineville
7	573.0	Boone County SD	Madison
8	564.0	Wayne County SD	Wayne
9	552.5	Logan County SD	Logan
10	537.1	Hancock County SD	New Cumberland
11	532.2	Preston County SD	Kingwood
12	528.3	Wood County SD	Parkersburg
13	526.5	Harrison County SD	Clarksburg
14	518.6	Roane County SD	Spencer
15	513.7	Brooke County SD	Wellsburg
16	470.5	Mingo County SD	Williamson
17	468.4	Hardy County SD	Moorefield
18	466.7	Fayette County SD	Fayetteville
19	466.5	Lewis County SD	Weston
20	455.5	Mineral County SD	Keyser
21	454.3	Ohio County SD	Wheeling
22	453.6	Monongalia SD	Morgantown
23	452.9	Nicholas County SD	Summersville
24	447.1	Hampshire County SD	Romney
25	442.2	Taylor County SD	Grafton
26	436.3	Cabell County SD	Huntington
27	433.9	Marion County SD	Fairmont
28	427.0	Mercer County SD	Princeton
29	426.8	Upshur County SD	Buckhannon
30	423.7	Jefferson County SD	Charles Town
31	422.1	Jackson County SD	Ripley
32	418.3	Webster County SD	Webster Spgs
33	418.2	Putnam County SD	Winfield
34	415.0	Wetzel County SD	New Martinsville
35	414.5	Monroe County SD	Union

36	402.5	Summers County SD	Hinton
37	400.6	Morgan County SD	Berkeley Spgs
38	396.6	Berkeley County SD	Martinsburg
39	393.1	Braxton County SD	Sutton
40	392.8	Tyler County SD	Sistersville
41	380.6	Marshall County SD	Moundsville
42	360.0	Raleigh County SD	Beckley
43	358.7	Greenbrier County SD	Lewisburg
44	354.4	Mcdowell County SD	Welch
45	350.2	Mason County SD	Point Pleasant
46	344.6	Randolph County SD	Elkins
47	337.4	Kanawha County SD	Charleston

Current Spending per Student in FY2003

Rank	Dollars	District Name	City
1	9,525	Mcdowell County SD	Welch
2	9,223	Mingo County SD	Williamson
3	9,095	Boone County SD	Madison
4	8,936	Wyoming County SD	Pineville
5	8,698	Marion County SD	Fairmont
5	8,698	Nicholas County SD	Summersville
7	8,643	Ohio County SD	Wheeling
8	8,639	Webster County SD	Webster Spgs
9	8,624	Tyler County SD	Sistersville
10	8,617	Marshall County SD	Moundsville
11	8,548	Brooke County SD	Wellsburg
12	8,491	Raleigh County SD	Beckley
13	8,473	Fayette County SD	Fayetteville
14	8,318	Lincoln County SD	Hamlin
15	8,304	Kanawha County SD	Charleston
16	8,297	Cabell County SD	Huntington
17	8,223	Mason County SD	Point Pleasant
18	8,202	Taylor County SD	Grafton
19	8,199	Monongalia SD	Morgantown
20	8,172	Wood County SD	Parkersburg
21	8,153	Clay County SD	Clay
22	8,148	Lewis County SD	Weston
23	8,127	Jackson County SD	Ripley
24	8,125	Wayne County SD	Wayne
25	8,108	Hancock County SD	New Cumberland
26	8,048	Mineral County SD	Keyser
27	8,043	Greenbrier County SD	Lewisburg
28	8,031	Upshur County SD	Buckhannon
29	8,014	Berkeley County SD	Martinsburg
30	7,995	Harrison County SD	Clarksburg
31	7,970	Wetzel County SD	New Martinsville
32	7,961	Mercer County SD	Princeton
33	7,933	Putnam County SD	Winfield
34	7,932	Ritchie County SD	Harrisville
35	7,927	Summers County SD	Hinton
36	7,867	Logan County SD	Logan
37	7,850	Braxton County SD	Sutton
38	7,802	Grant County SD	Petersburg
39	7,768	Monroe County SD	Union
40	7,669	Randolph County SD	Elkins
41	7,628	Preston County SD	Kingwood
42	7,510	Jefferson County SD	Charles Town
43	7,501	Roane County SD	Spencer
44	7,487	Barbour County SD	Philippi
45	7,415	Morgan County SD	Berkeley Spgs
46	7,397	Hampshire County SD	Romney
47	6,853	Hardy County SD	Moorefield

Number of Diploma Recipients

Rank	Number	District Name	City
1	1,630	Kanawha County SD	Charleston
2	778	Wood County SD	Parkersburg
3	728	Raleigh County SD	Beckley
4	710	Berkeley County SD	Martinsburg
5	709	Harrison County SD	Clarksburg
6	688	Cabell County SD	Huntington
7	634	Marion County SD	Fairmont
8	629	Monongalia SD	Morgantown
9	527	Mercer County SD	Princeton
10	495	Putnam County SD	Winfield
11	442	Fayette County SD	Fayetteville
12	418	Jefferson County SD	Charles Town
13	411	Marshall County SD	Moundsville
14	402	Logan County SD	Logan
15	395	Wayne County SD	Wayne
16	341	Ohio County SD	Wheeling
17	329	Greenbrier County SD	Lewisburg
18	320	Mingo County SD	Williamson
19	311	Preston County SD	Kingwood
20	309	Jackson County SD	Ripley
20	309	Wyoming County SD	Pineville
22	283	Mineral County SD	Keyser
23	279	Brooke County SD	Wellsburg
24	276	Nicholas County SD	Summersville
25	274	Hancock County SD	New Cumberland
26	273	Randolph County SD	Elkins

27	271	Mason County SD	Point Pleasant
28	256	Boone County SD	Madison
29	244	Upshur County SD	Buckhannon
30	237	Mcdowell County SD	Welch
31	231	Lincoln County SD	Hamlin
32	223	Wetzel County SD	New Martinsville
33	198	Hampshire County SD	Romney
34	192	Lewis County SD	Weston
35	174	Roane County SD	Spencer
36	161	Barbour County SD	Philippi
37	148	Braxton County SD	Sutton
38	143	Taylor County SD	Grafton
39	137	Morgan County SD	Berkeley Spgs
40	128	Grant County SD	Petersburg
41	121	Clay County SD	Clay
41	121	Hardy County SD	Moorefield
43	115	Webster County SD	Webster Spgs
44	113	Ritchie County SD	Harrisville
45	100	Tyler County SD	Sistersville
46	97	Summers County SD	Hinton
47	96	Monroe County SD	Union

High School Drop-out Rate

Rank	Percent	District Name	City
1	6.3	Roane County SD	Spencer
2	5.8	Summers County SD	Hinton
3	5.7	Preston County SD	Kingwood
4	5.5	Berkeley County SD	Martinsburg
5	5.4	Boone County SD	Madison
6	5.3	Kanawha County SD	Charleston
7	5.0	Logan County SD	Logan
8	4.9	Fayette County SD	Fayetteville
9	4.6	Cabell County SD	Huntington
9	4.6	Hampshire County SD	Romney
11	4.3	Barbour County SD	Philippi
12	4.1	Braxton County SD	Sutton
12	4.1	Brooke County SD	Wellsburg
12	4.1	Hancock County SD	New Cumberland
12	4.1	Morgan County SD	Berkeley Spgs
16	3.9	Mingo County SD	Williamson
16	3.9	Upshur County SD	Buckhannon
18	3.8	Clay County SD	Clay
18	3.8	Lincoln County SD	Hamlin
18	3.8	Taylor County SD	Grafton
21	3.7	Jackson County SD	Ripley
21	3.7	Mercer County SD	Princeton
23	3.6	Mason County SD	Point Pleasant
24	3.5	Greenbrier County SD	Lewisburg
24	3.5	Nicholas County SD	Summersville
26	3.4	Ohio County SD	Wheeling
27	3.3	Grant County SD	Petersburg
27	3.3	Wood County SD	Parkersburg
27	3.3	Wyoming County SD	Pineville
30	3.2	Raleigh County SD	Beckley
30	3.2	Ritchie County SD	Harrisville
32	3.1	Randolph County SD	Elkins
33	3.0	Lewis County SD	Weston
33	3.0	Marshall County SD	Moundsville
33	3.0	Putnam County SD	Winfield
36	2.9	Monroe County SD	Union
37	2.8	Monongalia SD	Morgantown
38	2.7	Harrison County SD	Clarksburg
38	2.7	Jefferson County SD	Charles Town
40	2.6	Wayne County SD	Wayne
41	2.5	Webster County SD	Webster Spgs
42	2.3	Marion County SD	Fairmont
42	2.3	Mineral County SD	Keyser
44	2.2	Tyler County SD	Sistersville
44	2.2	Wetzel County SD	New Martinsville
46	1.4	Mcdowell County SD	Welch
47	0.7	Hardy County SD	Moorefield

Wisconsin

Wisconsin Public School Educational Profile

Category	Value	Category	Value
Schools *(2003-2004)*	2,250	**Diploma Recipients** *(2002-2003)*	60,575
Instructional Level		White, Non-Hispanic	53,255
Primary	1,239	Black, Non-Hispanic	3,148
Middle	388	Asian/Pacific Islander	1,757
High	514	American Indian/Alaskan Native	623
Other Level	81	Hispanic	1,792
Curriculum		**High School Drop-out Rate** (%) *(2001-2002)*	1.9
Regular	2,020	White, Non-Hispanic	1.2
Special Education	10	Black, Non-Hispanic	8.3
Vocational	1	Asian/Pacific Islander	1.8
Alternative	191	American Indian/Alaskan Native	4.1
Type		Hispanic	5.6
Magnet	0	**Staff** *(2003-2004)*	
Charter	137	Teachers	60,373.4
Title I Eligible	1,097	Average Salary ($)	41,687
School-wide Title I	302	Librarians/Media Specialists	1,246.9
Students *(2003-2004)*	880,031	Guidance Counselors	1,953.0
Gender (%)		**Ratios** *(2003-2004)*	
Male	51.6	Student/Teacher Ratio	14.6 to 1
Female	48.4	Student/Librarian Ratio	705.8 to 1
Race/Ethnicity (%)		Student/Counselor Ratio	450.6 to 1
White, Non-Hispanic	78.8	**College Entrance Exam Scores** *(2005)*	
Black, Non-Hispanic	10.5	Scholastic Aptitude Test (SAT)	
Asian/Pacific Islander	3.4	Participation Rate (%)	6
American Indian/Alaskan Native	1.4	Mean SAT Reasoning Test Verbal Score	592
Hispanic	5.8	Mean SAT Reasoning Test Math Score	599
Classification (%)		American College Testing Program (ACT)	
Individual Education Program (IEP)	14.4	Participation Rate (%)	69
Migrant *(2002-2003)*	0.1	Average Composite Score	22.2
English Language Learner (ELL)	3.0	Average English Score	21.5
Eligible for Free Lunch Program	0.0	Average Math Score	22.0
Eligible for Reduced-Price Lunch Program	0.0	Average Reading Score	22.4
Current Spending *($ per student in FY 2003)*	8,965	Average Science Score	22.3
Instruction	5,512		
Support Services	3,141		

Note: *For an explanation of data, please refer to the User's Guide in the front of the book*

Wisconsin NAEP 2005 Test Scores

Reading			Mathematics		
Grade/Category	Value	Rank	Grade/Category	Value	Rank
4th Grade			**4th Grade**		
Average Proficiency	221.2 (0.99)	22/51	Average Proficiency	240.6 (0.94)	17/51
Proficiency by Gender/Race/Ethnicity			Proficiency by Gender/Race/Ethnicity		
Male	218.5 (1.20)	19/51	Male	242.0 (1.11)	17/51
Female	223.9 (1.16)	23/51	Female	239.1 (1.02)	18/51
White, Non-Hispanic	226.7 (1.01)	22/51	White, Non-Hispanic	246.9 (0.76)	17/51
Black, Non-Hispanic	193.8 (2.45)	33/42	Black, Non-Hispanic	210.0 (3.03)	41/42
Asian, Non-Hispanic	225.8 (4.49)	16/27	Asian, Non-Hispanic	235.9 (3.78)	23/25
American Indian, Non-Hispanic	n/a	n/a	American Indian, Non-Hispanic	n/a	n/a
Hispanic	208.3 (3.45)	13/40	Hispanic	224.1 (2.42)	23/41
Proficiency by Class Size			Proficiency by Class Size		
Less than 16 Students	211.3 (4.14)	14/34	Less than 16 Students	229.8 (4.56)	15/35
16 to 18 Students	215.9 (2.55)	22/33	16 to 18 Students	239.6 (2.91)	12/31
19 to 20 Students	225.7 (3.12)	9/38	19 to 20 Students	241.8 (2.24)	13/38
21 to 25 Students	225.1 (1.45)	16/51	21 to 25 Students	243.3 (1.37)	12/51
Greater than 25 Students	216.7 (3.19)	26/36	Greater than 25 Students	236.8 (3.21)	21/33
Percent Attaining Achievement Levels			Percent Attaining Achievement Levels		
Below Basic	32.8 (1.30)	29/51	Below Basic	16.2 (1.20)	32/51
Basic or Above	67.2 (1.30)	23/51	Basic or Above	83.8 (1.20)	19/51
Proficient or Above	33.1 (1.41)	20/51	Proficient or Above	40.3 (1.44)	15/51
Advanced or Above	7.1 (0.68)	23/51	Advanced or Above	5.0 (0.64)	21/51
8th Grade			**8th Grade**		
Average Proficiency	266.2 (1.12)	17/51	Average Proficiency	284.5 (1.15)	9/51
Proficiency by Gender/Race/Ethnicity			Proficiency by Gender/Race/Ethnicity		
Male	260.5 (1.41)	19/51	Male	284.6 (1.37)	12/51
Female	272.6 (1.24)	12/51	Female	284.4 (1.46)	10/51
White, Non-Hispanic	271.4 (1.02)	17/51	White, Non-Hispanic	291.3 (1.01)	12/51
Black, Non-Hispanic	236.4 (4.06)	36/40	Black, Non-Hispanic	246.0 (3.94)	37/41
Asian, Non-Hispanic	261.5 (3.43)	21/24	Asian, Non-Hispanic	285.5 (5.80)	17/23
American Indian, Non-Hispanic	n/a	n/a	American Indian, Non-Hispanic	n/a	n/a
Hispanic	247.5 (5.12)	16/38	Hispanic	265.4 (3.55)	9/38
Proficiency by Parents Highest Level of Ed.			Proficiency by Parents Highest Level of Ed.		
Did Not Finish High School	239.6 (4.20)	40/49	Did Not Finish High School	263.6 (3.83)	18/50
Graduated High School	259.6 (2.23)	10/50	Graduated High School	276.4 (1.66)	4/50
Some Education After High School	269.7 (1.75)	10/50	Some Education After High School	287.6 (2.01)	3/50
Graduated College	272.8 (1.16)	24/50	Graduated College	293.0 (1.28)	16/50
Percent Attaining Achievement Levels			Percent Attaining Achievement Levels		
Below Basic	32.8 (1.30)	29/51	Below Basic	23.9 (1.37)	42/51
Basic or Above	67.2 (1.30)	23/51	Basic or Above	76.1 (1.37)	10/51
Proficient or Above	33.1 (1.41)	20/51	Proficient or Above	35.8 (1.44)	8/51
Advanced or Above	7.1 (0.68)	23/51	Advanced or Above	6.7 (0.71)	11/51

Note: For an explanation of data, please refer to the User's Guide in the front of the book; n/a indicates data not available

Adams County

Adams-Friendship Area
201 W 6th St · Friendship, WI 53934-9135
(608) 339-3213 · http://www.af.k12.wi.us
Grade Span: PK-12; **Agency Type:** 1
Schools: 8
    4 Primary; 1 Middle; 2 High; 1 Other Level
    7 Regular; 0 Special Education; 0 Vocational; 1 Alternative
    0 Magnet; 0 Charter; 6 Title I Eligible; 5 School-wide Title I
Students: 2,059 (53.0% male; 46.9% female)
    Individual Education Program: 414 (20.1%);
    English Language Learner: 0 (0.0%); Migrant: 0 (0.0%)
    Eligible for Free Lunch Program: n/a
    Eligible for Reduced-Price Lunch Program: n/a
Teachers: 161.7 (12.7 to 1)
Librarians/Media Specialists: 1.0 (2,059.0 to 1)
Guidance Counselors: 7.0 (294.1 to 1)
Current Spending: ($ per student per year):
    Total: $9,070; Instruction: $5,587; Support Services: $3,052

Enrollment, Drop-out Rates and Diploma Recipients by Race/Ethnicity

Category	Total	White	Black	Asian	AIAN	Hisp.
Enrollment (%)	100.0	93.1	0.6	0.1	1.2	5.0
Drop-out Rate (%)	1.0	1.1	0.0	0.0	0.0	0.0
H.S. Diplomas (#)	162	160	0	1	0	1

Ashland County

Ashland
502 Main St W 3rd Floor · Ashland, WI 54806-1512
(715) 682-7080 · http://www.ashland.k12.wi.us
Grade Span: PK-12; **Agency Type:** 1
Schools: 5
    3 Primary; 1 Middle; 1 High; 0 Other Level
    5 Regular; 0 Special Education; 0 Vocational; 0 Alternative
    0 Magnet; 0 Charter; 4 Title I Eligible; 0 School-wide Title I
Students: 2,286 (52.7% male; 47.2% female)
    Individual Education Program: 303 (13.3%);
    English Language Learner: 0 (0.0%); Migrant: 0 (0.0%)
    Eligible for Free Lunch Program: n/a
    Eligible for Reduced-Price Lunch Program: n/a
Teachers: 173.7 (13.2 to 1)
Librarians/Media Specialists: 4.0 (571.5 to 1)
Guidance Counselors: 6.0 (381.0 to 1)
Current Spending: ($ per student per year):
    Total: $8,851; Instruction: $5,298; Support Services: $3,196

Enrollment, Drop-out Rates and Diploma Recipients by Race/Ethnicity

Category	Total	White	Black	Asian	AIAN	Hisp.
Enrollment (%)	100.0	77.7	0.3	1.1	20.4	0.4
Drop-out Rate (%)	1.2	1.3	0.0	0.0	0.8	0.0
H.S. Diplomas (#)	172	156	0	0	16	0

Barron County

Rice Lake Area
700 Augusta St · Rice Lake, WI 54868-1996
(715) 234-9007 · http://www.ricelake.k12.wi.us
Grade Span: PK-12; **Agency Type:** 1
Schools: 12
    8 Primary; 1 Middle; 2 High; 1 Other Level
    10 Regular; 1 Special Education; 0 Vocational; 1 Alternative
    0 Magnet; 1 Charter; 5 Title I Eligible; 0 School-wide Title I
Students: 2,634 (50.9% male; 49.0% female)
    Individual Education Program: 362 (13.7%);
    English Language Learner: 0 (0.0%); Migrant: 0 (0.0%)
    Eligible for Free Lunch Program: n/a
    Eligible for Reduced-Price Lunch Program: n/a
Teachers: 178.4 (14.8 to 1)
Librarians/Media Specialists: 4.0 (658.5 to 1)
Guidance Counselors: 8.0 (329.3 to 1)
Current Spending: ($ per student per year):
    Total: $8,496; Instruction: $5,116; Support Services: $3,052

Enrollment, Drop-out Rates and Diploma Recipients by Race/Ethnicity

Category	Total	White	Black	Asian	AIAN	Hisp.
Enrollment (%)	100.0	96.0	0.5	1.5	0.5	1.5
Drop-out Rate (%)	1.5	1.4	0.0	0.0	0.0	18.2
H.S. Diplomas (#)	220	213	1	5	1	0

Brown County

Ashwaubenon
1055 Griffiths Ln · Green Bay, WI 54304-5599
(920) 492-2905 · http://www.ashwaubenon.k12.wi.us
Grade Span: PK-12; **Agency Type:** 1
Schools: 5
    3 Primary; 1 Middle; 1 High; 0 Other Level
    5 Regular; 0 Special Education; 0 Vocational; 0 Alternative
    0 Magnet; 0 Charter; 2 Title I Eligible; 0 School-wide Title I
Students: 3,122 (52.7% male; 47.2% female)
    Individual Education Program: 497 (15.9%);
    English Language Learner: 0 (0.0%); Migrant: 0 (0.0%)
    Eligible for Free Lunch Program: n/a
    Eligible for Reduced-Price Lunch Program: n/a
Teachers: 209.8 (14.9 to 1)
Librarians/Media Specialists: 4.0 (780.5 to 1)
Guidance Counselors: 8.2 (380.7 to 1)
Current Spending: ($ per student per year):
    Total: $8,606; Instruction: $5,388; Support Services: $2,870

Enrollment, Drop-out Rates and Diploma Recipients by Race/Ethnicity

Category	Total	White	Black	Asian	AIAN	Hisp.
Enrollment (%)	100.0	90.6	2.6	3.2	1.6	2.1
Drop-out Rate (%)	0.5	0.4	0.0	0.0	8.3	0.0
H.S. Diplomas (#)	260	251	3	4	1	1

De Pere
1700 Chicago St · De Pere, WI 54115-3499
(920) 337-1032 · http://www.depere.k12.wi.us
Grade Span: PK-12; **Agency Type:** 1
Schools: 5
    2 Primary; 2 Middle; 1 High; 0 Other Level
    5 Regular; 0 Special Education; 0 Vocational; 0 Alternative
    0 Magnet; 0 Charter; 2 Title I Eligible; 0 School-wide Title I
Students: 3,266 (51.4% male; 48.5% female)
    Individual Education Program: 337 (10.3%);
    English Language Learner: 0 (0.0%); Migrant: 0 (0.0%)
    Eligible for Free Lunch Program: n/a
    Eligible for Reduced-Price Lunch Program: n/a
Teachers: 214.9 (15.2 to 1)
Librarians/Media Specialists: 5.1 (640.4 to 1)
Guidance Counselors: 8.0 (408.3 to 1)
Current Spending: ($ per student per year):
    Total: $7,628; Instruction: $4,240; Support Services: $3,032

Enrollment, Drop-out Rates and Diploma Recipients by Race/Ethnicity

Category	Total	White	Black	Asian	AIAN	Hisp.
Enrollment (%)	100.0	95.3	1.6	1.1	0.9	1.2
Drop-out Rate (%)	0.3	0.3	0.0	0.0	0.0	0.0
H.S. Diplomas (#)	231	225	3	1	1	1

Denmark
450 N Wall St · Denmark, WI 54208-9416
(920) 863-2176 · http://www.denmark.k12.wi.us
Grade Span: PK-12; **Agency Type:** 1
Schools: 5
    2 Primary; 1 Middle; 2 High; 0 Other Level
    4 Regular; 0 Special Education; 0 Vocational; 1 Alternative
    0 Magnet; 1 Charter; 3 Title I Eligible; 0 School-wide Title I
Students: 1,615 (53.2% male; 46.7% female)
    Individual Education Program: 245 (15.2%);
    English Language Learner: 0 (0.0%); Migrant: 0 (0.0%)
    Eligible for Free Lunch Program: n/a
    Eligible for Reduced-Price Lunch Program: n/a
Teachers: 109.4 (14.8 to 1)
Librarians/Media Specialists: 3.0 (538.3 to 1)
Guidance Counselors: 4.0 (403.8 to 1)
Current Spending: ($ per student per year):
    Total: $7,351; Instruction: $4,660; Support Services: $2,400

Enrollment, Drop-out Rates and Diploma Recipients by Race/Ethnicity

Category	Total	White	Black	Asian	AIAN	Hisp.
Enrollment (%)	100.0	95.6	0.5	1.7	0.7	1.5
Drop-out Rate (%)	0.7	0.7	0.0	0.0	0.0	0.0
H.S. Diplomas (#)	131	130	0	1	0	0

Green Bay Area
200 S Broadway · Green Bay, WI 54303
Mailing Address: PO Box 23387 · Green Bay, WI 54305-3387
(920) 448-2100 · http://www.greenbay.k12.wi.us
Grade Span: PK-12; **Agency Type:** 1
Schools: 36
    27 Primary; 4 Middle; 4 High; 1 Other Level
    36 Regular; 0 Special Education; 0 Vocational; 0 Alternative
    0 Magnet; 0 Charter; 13 Title I Eligible; 10 School-wide Title I
Students: 20,297 (51.4% male; 48.5% female)
    Individual Education Program: 3,882 (19.1%);
    English Language Learner: 2,266 (11.2%); Migrant: 341 (1.7%)
    Eligible for Free Lunch Program: n/a
    Eligible for Reduced-Price Lunch Program: n/a
Teachers: 1,463.3 (13.9 to 1)
Librarians/Media Specialists: 25.5 (796.0 to 1)
Guidance Counselors: 49.4 (410.9 to 1)
Current Spending: ($ per student per year):
    Total: $8,767; Instruction: $5,581; Support Services: $2,881

Enrollment, Drop-out Rates and Diploma Recipients by Race/Ethnicity

Category	Total	White	Black	Asian	AIAN	Hisp.
Enrollment (%)	100.0	69.9	4.5	8.4	5.0	12.2
Drop-out Rate (%)	1.6	1.2	2.5	1.4	3.6	4.4
H.S. Diplomas (#)	1,131	952	12	93	33	41

Howard-Suamico
2700 Lineville Rd • Green Bay, WI 54313-7197
(920) 662-7878 • http://www.hssd.k12.wi.us
Grade Span: PK-12; **Agency Type:** 1
Schools: 7
  4 Primary; 2 Middle; 1 High; 0 Other Level
  7 Regular; 0 Special Education; 0 Vocational; 0 Alternative
  0 Magnet; 0 Charter; 2 Title I Eligible; 0 School-wide Title I
Students: 4,778   (51.3% male; 48.6% female)
  Individual Education Program: 618 (12.9%);
  English Language Learner: 38 (0.8%); Migrant: 0 (0.0%)
  Eligible for Free Lunch Program: n/a
  Eligible for Reduced-Price Lunch Program: n/a
Teachers: 293.3 (16.3 to 1)
Librarians/Media Specialists: 7.0 (682.6 to 1)
Guidance Counselors: 12.6 (379.2 to 1)
Current Spending: ($ per student per year):
  Total: $7,311; Instruction: $4,452; Support Services: $2,583

Enrollment, Drop-out Rates and Diploma Recipients by Race/Ethnicity

Category	Total	White	Black	Asian	AIAN	Hisp.
Enrollment (%)	100.0	95.6	1.2	1.4	0.9	0.9
Drop-out Rate (%)	1.1	1.0	12.5	0.0	0.0	0.0
H.S. Diplomas (#)	271	259	5	3	2	2

Pulaski Community
143 W Green Bay St • Pulaski, WI 54162-0036
Mailing Address: PO Box 36 • Pulaski, WI 54162-0036
(920) 822-6000 • http://www.pulaski.k12.wi.us
Grade Span: PK-12; **Agency Type:** 1
Schools: 7
  5 Primary; 1 Middle; 1 High; 0 Other Level
  7 Regular; 0 Special Education; 0 Vocational; 0 Alternative
  0 Magnet; 0 Charter; 3 Title I Eligible; 0 School-wide Title I
Students: 3,550   (51.4% male; 48.5% female)
  Individual Education Program: 511 (14.4%);
  English Language Learner: 0 (0.0%); Migrant: 0 (0.0%)
  Eligible for Free Lunch Program: n/a
  Eligible for Reduced-Price Lunch Program: n/a
Teachers: 238.0 (14.9 to 1)
Librarians/Media Specialists: 4.0 (887.5 to 1)
Guidance Counselors: 6.7 (529.9 to 1)
Current Spending: ($ per student per year):
  Total: $7,999; Instruction: $4,823; Support Services: $2,805

Enrollment, Drop-out Rates and Diploma Recipients by Race/Ethnicity

Category	Total	White	Black	Asian	AIAN	Hisp.
Enrollment (%)	100.0	94.8	0.6	0.8	2.9	0.8
Drop-out Rate (%)	0.5	0.5	0.0	0.0	2.8	0.0
H.S. Diplomas (#)	232	221	0	2	8	1

West De Pere
930 Oak St • De Pere, WI 54115-1014
(920) 337-1393 • http://www.netnet.net/wdpschools
Grade Span: PK-12; **Agency Type:** 1
Schools: 3
  1 Primary; 1 Middle; 1 High; 0 Other Level
  3 Regular; 0 Special Education; 0 Vocational; 0 Alternative
  0 Magnet; 0 Charter; 3 Title I Eligible; 0 School-wide Title I
Students: 2,029   (53.9% male; 46.0% female)
  Individual Education Program: 289 (14.2%);
  English Language Learner: 0 (0.0%); Migrant: 0 (0.0%)
  Eligible for Free Lunch Program: n/a
  Eligible for Reduced-Price Lunch Program: n/a
Teachers: 135.2 (15.0 to 1)
Librarians/Media Specialists: 0.8 (2,536.3 to 1)
Guidance Counselors: 4.0 (507.3 to 1)
Current Spending: ($ per student per year):
  Total: $8,414; Instruction: $5,186; Support Services: $2,938

Enrollment, Drop-out Rates and Diploma Recipients by Race/Ethnicity

Category	Total	White	Black	Asian	AIAN	Hisp.
Enrollment (%)	100.0	85.5	1.6	1.3	10.3	1.3
Drop-out Rate (%)	0.6	0.4	16.7	0.0	1.8	0.0
H.S. Diplomas (#)	134	119	2	0	13	0

Chippewa County

Chippewa Falls Area
1130 Miles St • Chippewa Falls, WI 54729-1923
(715) 726-2417 • http://cfsd.chipfalls.k12.wi.us
Grade Span: PK-12; **Agency Type:** 1
Schools: 8
  6 Primary; 1 Middle; 1 High; 0 Other Level
  8 Regular; 0 Special Education; 0 Vocational; 0 Alternative
  0 Magnet; 0 Charter; 6 Title I Eligible; 0 School-wide Title I
Students: 4,491   (52.0% male; 47.9% female)
  Individual Education Program: 618 (13.8%);
  English Language Learner: 0 (0.0%); Migrant: 0 (0.0%)
  Eligible for Free Lunch Program: n/a
  Eligible for Reduced-Price Lunch Program: n/a
Teachers: 293.6 (15.3 to 1)
Librarians/Media Specialists: 9.0 (499.0 to 1)
Guidance Counselors: 11.0 (408.3 to 1)
Current Spending: ($ per student per year):
  Total: $8,286; Instruction: $4,859; Support Services: $3,139

Enrollment, Drop-out Rates and Diploma Recipients by Race/Ethnicity

Category	Total	White	Black	Asian	AIAN	Hisp.
Enrollment (%)	100.0	95.5	1.0	2.1	0.7	0.7
Drop-out Rate (%)	2.1	2.1	0.0	0.0	0.0	0.0
H.S. Diplomas (#)	363	359	0	1	2	1

Columbia County

Lodi
115 School St • Lodi, WI 53555-1046
(608) 592-3851 • http://www.lodi.k12.wi.us/
Grade Span: PK-12; **Agency Type:** 1
Schools: 5
  2 Primary; 1 Middle; 2 High; 0 Other Level
  4 Regular; 0 Special Education; 0 Vocational; 1 Alternative
  0 Magnet; 1 Charter; 2 Title I Eligible; 0 School-wide Title I
Students: 1,683   (51.5% male; 48.4% female)
  Individual Education Program: 210 (12.5%);
  English Language Learner: 0 (0.0%); Migrant: 0 (0.0%)
  Eligible for Free Lunch Program: n/a
  Eligible for Reduced-Price Lunch Program: n/a
Teachers: 115.8 (14.5 to 1)
Librarians/Media Specialists: 3.2 (525.9 to 1)
Guidance Counselors: 4.3 (391.4 to 1)
Current Spending: ($ per student per year):
  Total: $8,236; Instruction: $4,790; Support Services: $3,143

Enrollment, Drop-out Rates and Diploma Recipients by Race/Ethnicity

Category	Total	White	Black	Asian	AIAN	Hisp.
Enrollment (%)	100.0	97.2	0.7	0.9	0.3	0.9
Drop-out Rate (%)	0.0	0.0	0.0	0.0	0.0	0.0
H.S. Diplomas (#)	114	114	0	0	0	0

Portage Community
904 De Witt St • Portage, WI 53901-1726
(608) 742-4879 • http://www.portage.k12.wi.us
Grade Span: PK-12; **Agency Type:** 1
Schools: 10
  6 Primary; 2 Middle; 2 High; 0 Other Level
  8 Regular; 0 Special Education; 0 Vocational; 2 Alternative
  0 Magnet; 2 Charter; 3 Title I Eligible; 0 School-wide Title I
Students: 2,561   (51.8% male; 48.1% female)
  Individual Education Program: 423 (16.5%);
  English Language Learner: 0 (0.0%); Migrant: 10 (0.4%)
  Eligible for Free Lunch Program: n/a
  Eligible for Reduced-Price Lunch Program: n/a
Teachers: 180.6 (14.2 to 1)
Librarians/Media Specialists: 2.0 (1,280.5 to 1)
Guidance Counselors: 7.5 (341.5 to 1)
Current Spending: ($ per student per year):
  Total: $8,085; Instruction: $4,813; Support Services: $2,919

Enrollment, Drop-out Rates and Diploma Recipients by Race/Ethnicity

Category	Total	White	Black	Asian	AIAN	Hisp.
Enrollment (%)	100.0	94.6	0.9	0.7	0.8	2.9
Drop-out Rate (%)	0.8	0.7	50.0	0.0	0.0	0.0
H.S. Diplomas (#)	170	167	0	1	0	2

Dane County

De Forest Area
520 E Holum St • De Forest, WI 53532-1395
(608) 842-6577 • http://www.deforest.k12.wi.us
Grade Span: PK-12; **Agency Type:** 1
Schools: 7
  5 Primary; 1 Middle; 1 High; 0 Other Level
  7 Regular; 0 Special Education; 0 Vocational; 0 Alternative

0 Magnet; 0 Charter; 3 Title I Eligible; 0 School-wide Title I
Students: 3,151 (50.5% male; 49.4% female)
   Individual Education Program: 435 (13.8%);
   English Language Learner: 34 (1.1%); Migrant: 0 (0.0%)
   Eligible for Free Lunch Program: n/a
   Eligible for Reduced-Price Lunch Program: n/a
Teachers: 220.4 (14.3 to 1)
Librarians/Media Specialists: 4.7 (670.4 to 1)
Guidance Counselors: 8.0 (393.9 to 1)
Current Spending: ($ per student per year):
   Total: $8,613; Instruction: $5,239; Support Services: $3,057
Enrollment, Drop-out Rates and Diploma Recipients by Race/Ethnicity

Category	Total	White	Black	Asian	AIAN	Hisp.
Enrollment (%)	100.0	92.3	2.4	2.3	0.6	2.4
Drop-out Rate (%)	0.1	0.1	0.0	0.0	0.0	0.0
H.S. Diplomas (#)	200	196	0	2	1	1

Madison Metropolitan
545 W Dayton St • Madison, WI 53703-1967
(608) 663-1607 • http://www.madison.k12.wi.us
Grade Span: PK-12; **Agency Type:** 1
Schools: 52
   31 Primary; 11 Middle; 8 High; 1 Other Level
   45 Regular; 0 Special Education; 0 Vocational; 6 Alternative
   0 Magnet; 1 Charter; 17 Title I Eligible; 10 School-wide Title I
Students: 24,913 (50.3% male; 49.6% female)
   Individual Education Program: 4,592 (18.4%);
   English Language Learner: 3,005 (12.1%); Migrant: 80 (0.3%)
   Eligible for Free Lunch Program: n/a
   Eligible for Reduced-Price Lunch Program: n/a
Teachers: 1,992.3 (12.5 to 1)
Librarians/Media Specialists: 48.5 (513.7 to 1)
Guidance Counselors: 41.8 (596.0 to 1)
Current Spending: ($ per student per year):
   Total: $11,396; Instruction: $6,854; Support Services: $4,239
Enrollment, Drop-out Rates and Diploma Recipients by Race/Ethnicity

Category	Total	White	Black	Asian	AIAN	Hisp.
Enrollment (%)	100.0	59.3	19.8	10.1	0.7	10.1
Drop-out Rate (%)	3.0	1.9	6.1	1.4	8.8	8.1
H.S. Diplomas (#)	1,607	1,231	154	140	4	78

Mcfarland
5101 Farwell St • Mc Farland, WI 53558-9216
(608) 838-3169
Grade Span: PK-12; **Agency Type:** 1
Schools: 5
   3 Primary; 1 Middle; 1 High; 0 Other Level
   5 Regular; 0 Special Education; 0 Vocational; 0 Alternative
   0 Magnet; 0 Charter; 2 Title I Eligible; 0 School-wide Title I
Students: 1,004 (51.5% male; 40.4% female)
   Individual Education Program: 308 (15.7%);
   English Language Learner: 0 (0.0%); Migrant: 0 (0.0%)
   Eligible for Free Lunch Program: n/a
   Eligible for Reduced-Price Lunch Program: n/a
Teachers: 136.8 (14.4 to 1)
Librarians/Media Specialists: 4.0 (491.0 to 1)
Guidance Counselors: 6.3 (311.7 to 1)
Current Spending: ($ per student per year):
   Total: $8,688; Instruction: $5,384; Support Services: $2,934
Enrollment, Drop-out Rates and Diploma Recipients by Race/Ethnicity

Category	Total	White	Black	Asian	AIAN	Hisp.
Enrollment (%)	100.0	92.7	2.2	2.7	0.3	2.0
Drop-out Rate (%)	0.5	0.5	0.0	0.0	0.0	0.0
H.S. Diplomas (#)	153	145	0	4	0	4

Middleton-Cross Plains
7106 S Ave • Middleton, WI 53562-3263
(608) 829-9004 • http://www.mcpasd.k12.wi.us/home.cfm
Grade Span: PK-12; **Agency Type:** 1
Schools: 10
   6 Primary; 2 Middle; 2 High; 0 Other Level
   9 Regular; 0 Special Education; 0 Vocational; 1 Alternative
   0 Magnet; 1 Charter; 3 Title I Eligible; 0 School-wide Title I
Students: 5,500 (50.8% male; 49.1% female)
   Individual Education Program: 773 (14.1%);
   English Language Learner: 0 (0.0%); Migrant: 0 (0.0%)
   Eligible for Free Lunch Program: n/a
   Eligible for Reduced-Price Lunch Program: n/a
Teachers: 400.8 (13.7 to 1)
Librarians/Media Specialists: 9.5 (578.8 to 1)
Guidance Counselors: 13.0 (423.0 to 1)
Current Spending: ($ per student per year):
   Total: $9,135; Instruction: $5,902; Support Services: $2,881

Enrollment, Drop-out Rates and Diploma Recipients by Race/Ethnicity

Category	Total	White	Black	Asian	AIAN	Hisp.
Enrollment (%)	100.0	88.4	5.0	3.0	0.3	3.3
Drop-out Rate (%)	0.7	0.6	7.7	0.0	0.0	0.0
H.S. Diplomas (#)	385	360	5	12	0	8

Monona Grove
5301 Monona Dr • Monona, WI 53716-3126
(608) 221-7660 • http://www.mgsd.k12.wi.us
Grade Span: PK-12; **Agency Type:** 1
Schools: 7
   4 Primary; 1 Middle; 2 High; 0 Other Level
   6 Regular; 0 Special Education; 0 Vocational; 1 Alternative
   0 Magnet; 1 Charter; 3 Title I Eligible; 0 School-wide Title I
Students: 2,817 (51.5% male; 48.4% female)
   Individual Education Program: 326 (11.6%);
   English Language Learner: 0 (0.0%); Migrant: 0 (0.0%)
   Eligible for Free Lunch Program: n/a
   Eligible for Reduced-Price Lunch Program: n/a
Teachers: 218.8 (12.9 to 1)
Librarians/Media Specialists: 6.0 (468.7 to 1)
Guidance Counselors: 6.0 (468.7 to 1)
Current Spending: ($ per student per year):
   Total: $9,165; Instruction: $5,403; Support Services: $3,476
Enrollment, Drop-out Rates and Diploma Recipients by Race/Ethnicity

Category	Total	White	Black	Asian	AIAN	Hisp.
Enrollment (%)	100.0	91.3	3.6	1.8	0.2	3.0
Drop-out Rate (%)	0.4	0.3	3.3	0.0	0.0	0.0
H.S. Diplomas (#)	178	167	3	2	0	6

Mount Horeb Area
1304 E Lincoln St • Mount Horeb, WI 53572-0087
Mailing Address: PO Box 87 • Mount Horeb, WI 53572-0087
(608) 437-2400 • http://www.mhasd.k12.wi.us
Grade Span: PK-12; **Agency Type:** 1
Schools: 5
   3 Primary; 1 Middle; 1 High; 0 Other Level
   5 Regular; 0 Special Education; 0 Vocational; 0 Alternative
   0 Magnet; 0 Charter; 2 Title I Eligible; 0 School-wide Title I
Students: 2,057 (50.0% male; 49.9% female)
   Individual Education Program: 247 (12.0%);
   English Language Learner: 0 (0.0%); Migrant: 0 (0.0%)
   Eligible for Free Lunch Program: n/a
   Eligible for Reduced-Price Lunch Program: n/a
Teachers: 140.3 (14.6 to 1)
Librarians/Media Specialists: 3.5 (586.3 to 1)
Guidance Counselors: 5.0 (410.4 to 1)
Current Spending: ($ per student per year):
   Total: $7,725; Instruction: $4,707; Support Services: $2,751
Enrollment, Drop-out Rates and Diploma Recipients by Race/Ethnicity

Category	Total	White	Black	Asian	AIAN	Hisp.
Enrollment (%)	100.0	96.5	1.5	0.8	0.2	1.0
Drop-out Rate (%)	0.2	0.0	0.0	0.0	33.3	0.0
H.S. Diplomas (#)	126	123	2	0	0	1

Oregon
200 N Main St • Oregon, WI 53575-1447
(608) 835-4003 • http://www.oregon.k12.wi.us
Grade Span: PK-12; **Agency Type:** 1
Schools: 6
   3 Primary; 2 Middle; 1 High; 0 Other Level
   6 Regular; 0 Special Education; 0 Vocational; 0 Alternative
   0 Magnet; 0 Charter; 2 Title I Eligible; 0 School-wide Title I
Students: 3,468 (51.1% male; 48.8% female)
   Individual Education Program: 481 (13.9%);
   English Language Learner: 0 (0.0%); Migrant: 0 (0.0%)
   Eligible for Free Lunch Program: n/a
   Eligible for Reduced-Price Lunch Program: n/a
Teachers: 248.7 (13.9 to 1)
Librarians/Media Specialists: 6.0 (577.5 to 1)
Guidance Counselors: 8.5 (407.6 to 1)
Current Spending: ($ per student per year):
   Total: $9,170; Instruction: $5,330; Support Services: $3,491
Enrollment, Drop-out Rates and Diploma Recipients by Race/Ethnicity

Category	Total	White	Black	Asian	AIAN	Hisp.
Enrollment (%)	100.0	94.8	1.8	1.3	0.4	1.7
Drop-out Rate (%)	0.5	0.5	0.0	0.0	0.0	0.0
H.S. Diplomas (#)	228	222	2	2	1	1

Stoughton Area
320 N St • Stoughton, WI 53589-1733
(608) 877-5001 • http://www.stoughton.k12.wi.us
Grade Span: PK-12; **Agency Type:** 1
Schools: 6
   3 Primary; 2 Middle; 1 High; 0 Other Level

6 Regular; 0 Special Education; 0 Vocational; 0 Alternative
0 Magnet; 0 Charter; 4 Title I Eligible; 0 School-wide Title I
Students: 3,591 (51.8% male; 48.1% female)
Individual Education Program: 702 (19.5%);
English Language Learner: 0 (0.0%); Migrant: 0 (0.0%)
Eligible for Free Lunch Program: n/a
Eligible for Reduced-Price Lunch Program: n/a
Teachers: 252.7 (14.2 to 1)
Librarians/Media Specialists: 6.0 (597.7 to 1)
Guidance Counselors: 7.5 (478.1 to 1)
Current Spending: ($ per student per year):
Total: $7,870; Instruction: $5,049; Support Services: $2,637
Enrollment, Drop-out Rates and Diploma Recipients by Race/Ethnicity

Category	Total	White	Black	Asian	AIAN	Hisp.
Enrollment (%)	100.0	93.1	3.2	1.6	0.5	1.6
Drop-out Rate (%)	0.4	0.4	0.0	0.0	0.0	3.8
H.S. Diplomas (#)	254	239	2	3	1	9

Sun Prairie Area
501 S Bird St • Sun Prairie, WI 53590-2803
(608) 834-6502 • http://www.spasd.k12.wi.us
Grade Span: PK-12; **Agency Type:** 1
Schools: 10
5 Primary; 2 Middle; 3 High; 0 Other Level
8 Regular; 0 Special Education; 0 Vocational; 2 Alternative
0 Magnet; 2 Charter; 4 Title I Eligible; 0 School-wide Title I
Students: 5,240 (51.2% male; 48.7% female)
Individual Education Program: 788 (15.0%);
English Language Learner: 85 (1.6%); Migrant: 0 (0.0%)
Eligible for Free Lunch Program: n/a
Eligible for Reduced-Price Lunch Program: n/a
Teachers: 373.9 (14.0 to 1)
Librarians/Media Specialists: 8.0 (655.0 to 1)
Guidance Counselors: 11.0 (476.4 to 1)
Current Spending: ($ per student per year):
Total: $8,886; Instruction: $5,596; Support Services: $3,000
Enrollment, Drop-out Rates and Diploma Recipients by Race/Ethnicity

Category	Total	White	Black	Asian	AIAN	Hisp.
Enrollment (%)	100.0	83.6	9.0	3.3	0.6	3.5
Drop-out Rate (%)	2.3	2.2	3.1	0.0	0.0	12.0
H.S. Diplomas (#)	347	330	6	5	1	5

Verona Area
700 N Main St • Verona, WI 53593-1153
(608) 845-4310 • http://www.verona.k12.wi.us
Grade Span: PK-12; **Agency Type:** 1
Schools: 9
6 Primary; 2 Middle; 1 High; 0 Other Level
7 Regular; 0 Special Education; 0 Vocational; 2 Alternative
0 Magnet; 2 Charter; 3 Title I Eligible; 0 School-wide Title I
Students: 4,498 (52.2% male; 47.7% female)
Individual Education Program: 569 (12.7%);
English Language Learner: 0 (0.0%); Migrant: 0 (0.0%)
Eligible for Free Lunch Program: n/a
Eligible for Reduced-Price Lunch Program: n/a
Teachers: 360.1 (12.5 to 1)
Librarians/Media Specialists: 5.0 (899.4 to 1)
Guidance Counselors: 12.6 (356.9 to 1)
Current Spending: ($ per student per year):
Total: $9,098; Instruction: $5,973; Support Services: $2,809
Enrollment, Drop-out Rates and Diploma Recipients by Race/Ethnicity

Category	Total	White	Black	Asian	AIAN	Hisp.
Enrollment (%)	100.0	80.6	8.8	3.8	0.8	6.0
Drop-out Rate (%)	0.0	0.0	0.0	0.0	0.0	0.0
H.S. Diplomas (#)	280	256	8	7	1	8

Waunakee Community
101 School Dr • Waunakee, WI 53597-1637
(608) 849-2000 • http://www.waunakee.k12.wi.us
Grade Span: PK-12; **Agency Type:** 1
Schools: 5
2 Primary; 2 Middle; 1 High; 0 Other Level
5 Regular; 0 Special Education; 0 Vocational; 0 Alternative
0 Magnet; 0 Charter; 0 Title I Eligible; 0 School-wide Title I
Students: 3,031 (51.7% male; 48.2% female)
Individual Education Program: 418 (13.8%);
English Language Learner: 0 (0.0%); Migrant: 0 (0.0%)
Eligible for Free Lunch Program: n/a
Eligible for Reduced-Price Lunch Program: n/a
Teachers: 212.5 (14.2 to 1)
Librarians/Media Specialists: 5.9 (513.1 to 1)
Guidance Counselors: 7.0 (432.4 to 1)
Current Spending: ($ per student per year):
Total: $7,991; Instruction: $4,718; Support Services: $3,006

Enrollment, Drop-out Rates and Diploma Recipients by Race/Ethnicity

Category	Total	White	Black	Asian	AIAN	Hisp.
Enrollment (%)	100.0	96.8	0.9	0.9	0.3	1.1
Drop-out Rate (%)	0.9	0.9	0.0	0.0	0.0	0.0
H.S. Diplomas (#)	188	183	3	1	0	1

Dodge County

Beaver Dam
705 Mckinley St • Beaver Dam, WI 53916-1941
(920) 885-7309 • http://www.beaverdam.k12.wi.us
Grade Span: PK-12; **Agency Type:** 1
Schools: 10
7 Primary; 1 Middle; 1 High; 1 Other Level
9 Regular; 0 Special Education; 0 Vocational; 1 Alternative
0 Magnet; 1 Charter; 7 Title I Eligible; 0 School-wide Title I
Students: 3,443 (52.5% male; 47.4% female)
Individual Education Program: 596 (17.3%);
English Language Learner: 94 (2.7%); Migrant: 10 (0.3%)
Eligible for Free Lunch Program: n/a
Eligible for Reduced-Price Lunch Program: n/a
Teachers: 244.3 (14.1 to 1)
Librarians/Media Specialists: 4.0 (860.8 to 1)
Guidance Counselors: 7.5 (459.1 to 1)
Current Spending: ($ per student per year):
Total: $9,021; Instruction: $5,635; Support Services: $3,096
Enrollment, Drop-out Rates and Diploma Recipients by Race/Ethnicity

Category	Total	White	Black	Asian	AIAN	Hisp.
Enrollment (%)	100.0	89.4	1.2	1.5	0.4	7.5
Drop-out Rate (%)	0.3	0.2	0.0	0.0	0.0	2.4
H.S. Diplomas (#)	299	290	0	2	2	5

Douglas County

Superior
3025 Tower Ave • Superior, WI 54880-5369
(715) 394-8710 • http://www.superior.k12.wi.us
Grade Span: PK-12; **Agency Type:** 1
Schools: 8
6 Primary; 1 Middle; 1 High; 0 Other Level
8 Regular; 0 Special Education; 0 Vocational; 0 Alternative
0 Magnet; 0 Charter; 7 Title I Eligible; 4 School-wide Title I
Students: 4,938 (52.2% male; 47.7% female)
Individual Education Program: 622 (12.6%);
English Language Learner: 0 (0.0%); Migrant: 0 (0.0%)
Eligible for Free Lunch Program: n/a
Eligible for Reduced-Price Lunch Program: n/a
Teachers: 323.4 (15.3 to 1)
Librarians/Media Specialists: 7.0 (705.4 to 1)
Guidance Counselors: 15.0 (329.2 to 1)
Current Spending: ($ per student per year):
Total: $8,669; Instruction: $5,250; Support Services: $3,076
Enrollment, Drop-out Rates and Diploma Recipients by Race/Ethnicity

Category	Total	White	Black	Asian	AIAN	Hisp.
Enrollment (%)	100.0	90.2	2.0	1.7	5.1	1.1
Drop-out Rate (%)	2.8	2.5	6.7	3.1	5.5	9.1
H.S. Diplomas (#)	338	312	2	1	21	2

Dunn County

Menomonie Area
215 Pine Ave NE • Menomonie, WI 54751-1511
(715) 232-1642 • http://msd.k12.wi.us
Grade Span: PK-12; **Agency Type:** 1
Schools: 8
5 Primary; 1 Middle; 2 High; 0 Other Level
7 Regular; 0 Special Education; 0 Vocational; 1 Alternative
0 Magnet; 1 Charter; 6 Title I Eligible; 2 School-wide Title I
Students: 3,312 (50.1% male; 49.8% female)
Individual Education Program: 442 (13.3%);
English Language Learner: 133 (4.0%); Migrant: 0 (0.0%)
Eligible for Free Lunch Program: n/a
Eligible for Reduced-Price Lunch Program: n/a
Teachers: 226.7 (14.6 to 1)
Librarians/Media Specialists: 4.0 (828.0 to 1)
Guidance Counselors: 9.7 (341.4 to 1)
Current Spending: ($ per student per year):
Total: $8,684; Instruction: $5,191; Support Services: $3,060
Enrollment, Drop-out Rates and Diploma Recipients by Race/Ethnicity

Category	Total	White	Black	Asian	AIAN	Hisp.
Enrollment (%)	100.0	87.7	1.4	9.6	0.6	0.6
Drop-out Rate (%)	1.1	1.3	0.0	0.0	0.0	0.0
H.S. Diplomas (#)	258	225	0	23	1	9

Eau Claire County

Eau Claire Area
500 Main St • Eau Claire, WI 54701-3770
(715) 833-3465 • http://www.ecasd.k12.wi.us
Grade Span: PK-12; **Agency Type:** 1
Schools: 22
    15 Primary; 3 Middle; 4 High; 0 Other Level
    19 Regular; 0 Special Education; 0 Vocational; 3 Alternative
    0 Magnet; 3 Charter; 12 Title I Eligible; 4 School-wide Title I
Students: 10,753 (51.3% male; 48.6% female)
    Individual Education Program: 1,486 (13.8%);
    English Language Learner: 416 (3.9%); Migrant: 0 (0.0%)
    Eligible for Free Lunch Program: n/a
    Eligible for Reduced-Price Lunch Program: n/a
Teachers: 779.4 (13.8 to 1)
Librarians/Media Specialists: 16.0 (672.1 to 1)
Guidance Counselors: 32.7 (328.8 to 1)
Current Spending: ($ per student per year):
    Total: $9,413; Instruction: $5,934; Support Services: $3,127
Enrollment, Drop-out Rates and Diploma Recipients by Race/Ethnicity

Category	Total	White	Black	Asian	AIAN	Hisp.
Enrollment (%)	100.0	86.6	1.8	9.2	1.1	1.2
Drop-out Rate (%)	0.7	0.6	4.9	1.0	7.7	0.0
H.S. Diplomas (#)	978	865	10	74	20	9

Fond Du Lac County

Campbellsport
114 W Sheboygan St • Campbellsport, WI 53010-2791
(920) 533-8381 • http://www.csd.k12.wi.us
Grade Span: PK-12; **Agency Type:** 1
Schools: 4
    2 Primary; 1 Middle; 1 High; 0 Other Level
    4 Regular; 0 Special Education; 0 Vocational; 0 Alternative
    0 Magnet; 0 Charter; 2 Title I Eligible; 0 School-wide Title I
Students: 1,534 (52.6% male; 47.3% female)
    Individual Education Program: 240 (15.6%);
    English Language Learner: 0 (0.0%); Migrant: 0 (0.0%)
    Eligible for Free Lunch Program: n/a
    Eligible for Reduced-Price Lunch Program: n/a
Teachers: 101.3 (15.1 to 1)
Librarians/Media Specialists: 2.0 (767.0 to 1)
Guidance Counselors: 4.5 (340.9 to 1)
Current Spending: ($ per student per year):
    Total: $7,508; Instruction: $4,477; Support Services: $2,730
Enrollment, Drop-out Rates and Diploma Recipients by Race/Ethnicity

Category	Total	White	Black	Asian	AIAN	Hisp.
Enrollment (%)	100.0	98.2	0.6	0.0	0.1	1.1
Drop-out Rate (%)	1.0	1.0	n/a	0.0	n/a	0.0
H.S. Diplomas (#)	130	129	0	1	0	0

Fond Du Lac
72 W 9th St • Fond Du Lac, WI 54935-4972
(920) 929-2760 • http://www.fonddulac.k12.wi.us
Grade Span: PK-12; **Agency Type:** 1
Schools: 13
    9 Primary; 2 Middle; 1 High; 1 Other Level
    13 Regular; 0 Special Education; 0 Vocational; 0 Alternative
    0 Magnet; 0 Charter; 6 Title I Eligible; 0 School-wide Title I
Students: 7,278 (51.1% male; 48.8% female)
    Individual Education Program: 1,142 (15.7%);
    English Language Learner: 117 (1.6%); Migrant: 4 (0.1%)
    Eligible for Free Lunch Program: n/a
    Eligible for Reduced-Price Lunch Program: n/a
Teachers: 478.4 (15.2 to 1)
Librarians/Media Specialists: 13.0 (559.8 to 1)
Guidance Counselors: 14.0 (519.9 to 1)
Current Spending: ($ per student per year):
    Total: $8,183; Instruction: $5,158; Support Services: $2,721
Enrollment, Drop-out Rates and Diploma Recipients by Race/Ethnicity

Category	Total	White	Black	Asian	AIAN	Hisp.
Enrollment (%)	100.0	90.1	1.8	2.8	0.5	4.8
Drop-out Rate (%)	3.4	3.2	11.1	1.4	0.0	7.5
H.S. Diplomas (#)	463	440	4	14	1	4

Ripon
1120 Metomen St • Ripon, WI 54971-0991
Mailing Address: PO Box 991 • Ripon, WI 54971-0991
(920) 748-4600 • http://www.ripon.k12.wi.us
Grade Span: PK-12; **Agency Type:** 1
Schools: 4
    2 Primary; 1 Middle; 1 High; 0 Other Level
    4 Regular; 0 Special Education; 0 Vocational; 0 Alternative
    0 Magnet; 0 Charter; 2 Title I Eligible; 0 School-wide Title I

Students: 1,694 (52.2% male; 47.7% female)
    Individual Education Program: 251 (14.8%);
    English Language Learner: 0 (0.0%); Migrant: 0 (0.0%)
    Eligible for Free Lunch Program: n/a
    Eligible for Reduced-Price Lunch Program: n/a
Teachers: 117.5 (14.4 to 1)
Librarians/Media Specialists: 3.0 (564.7 to 1)
Guidance Counselors: 4.5 (376.4 to 1)
Current Spending: ($ per student per year):
    Total: $8,480; Instruction: $5,058; Support Services: $3,085
Enrollment, Drop-out Rates and Diploma Recipients by Race/Ethnicity

Category	Total	White	Black	Asian	AIAN	Hisp.
Enrollment (%)	100.0	94.2	0.5	0.6	0.4	4.3
Drop-out Rate (%)	0.7	0.8	0.0	0.0	0.0	0.0
H.S. Diplomas (#)	132	126	0	2	0	4

Waupun
950 Wilcox St • Waupun, WI 53963-2242
(920) 324-9341 • http://www.waupun.k12.wi.us
Grade Span: PK-12; **Agency Type:** 1
Schools: 7
    4 Primary; 1 Middle; 1 High; 1 Other Level
    6 Regular; 0 Special Education; 0 Vocational; 1 Alternative
    0 Magnet; 1 Charter; 3 Title I Eligible; 0 School-wide Title I
Students: 2,284 (52.3% male; 47.6% female)
    Individual Education Program: 358 (15.7%);
    English Language Learner: 0 (0.0%); Migrant: 7 (0.3%)
    Eligible for Free Lunch Program: n/a
    Eligible for Reduced-Price Lunch Program: n/a
Teachers: 165.5 (13.8 to 1)
Librarians/Media Specialists: 3.0 (761.3 to 1)
Guidance Counselors: 6.4 (356.9 to 1)
Current Spending: ($ per student per year):
    Total: $9,317; Instruction: $5,992; Support Services: $3,022
Enrollment, Drop-out Rates and Diploma Recipients by Race/Ethnicity

Category	Total	White	Black	Asian	AIAN	Hisp.
Enrollment (%)	100.0	95.6	0.6	0.3	0.2	3.2
Drop-out Rate (%)	2.7	2.8	0.0	0.0	n/a	0.0
H.S. Diplomas (#)	184	180	0	1	0	3

Grant County

Platteville
780 N 2nd St • Platteville, WI 53818-1847
(608) 342-4000 • http://www.platteville.k12.wi.us
Grade Span: PK-12; **Agency Type:** 1
Schools: 5
    3 Primary; 1 Middle; 1 High; 0 Other Level
    5 Regular; 0 Special Education; 0 Vocational; 0 Alternative
    0 Magnet; 0 Charter; 3 Title I Eligible; 0 School-wide Title I
Students: 1,560 (50.8% male; 49.1% female)
    Individual Education Program: 245 (15.7%);
    English Language Learner: 0 (0.0%); Migrant: 0 (0.0%)
    Eligible for Free Lunch Program: n/a
    Eligible for Reduced-Price Lunch Program: n/a
Teachers: 104.3 (15.0 to 1)
Librarians/Media Specialists: 1.5 (1,040.0 to 1)
Guidance Counselors: 2.1 (742.9 to 1)
Current Spending: ($ per student per year):
    Total: $8,854; Instruction: $5,372; Support Services: $3,119
Enrollment, Drop-out Rates and Diploma Recipients by Race/Ethnicity

Category	Total	White	Black	Asian	AIAN	Hisp.
Enrollment (%)	100.0	93.7	2.5	2.2	0.3	1.2
Drop-out Rate (%)	1.0	1.1	0.0	0.0	n/a	0.0
H.S. Diplomas (#)	146	141	1	3	0	1

Green County

Monroe
925 16th Ave Ste 3 • Monroe, WI 53566-1763
(608) 328-7171 • http://www.monroeschools.com
Grade Span: PK-12; **Agency Type:** 1
Schools: 7
    3 Primary; 1 Middle; 3 High; 0 Other Level
    5 Regular; 0 Special Education; 0 Vocational; 2 Alternative
    0 Magnet; 2 Charter; 2 Title I Eligible; 0 School-wide Title I
Students: 2,587 (48.9% male; 51.0% female)
    Individual Education Program: 423 (16.4%);
    English Language Learner: 0 (0.0%); Migrant: 11 (0.4%)
    Eligible for Free Lunch Program: n/a
    Eligible for Reduced-Price Lunch Program: n/a
Teachers: 212.6 (12.2 to 1)
Librarians/Media Specialists: 5.1 (507.3 to 1)
Guidance Counselors: 8.1 (319.4 to 1)

Current Spending: ($ per student per year):
Total: $9,575; Instruction: $6,260; Support Services: $3,025
Enrollment, Drop-out Rates and Diploma Recipients by Race/Ethnicity

Category	Total	White	Black	Asian	AIAN	Hisp.
Enrollment (%)	100.0	95.6	1.2	0.7	0.9	1.6
Drop-out Rate (%)	1.3	1.1	0.0	0.0	22.2	0.0
H.S. Diplomas (#)	190	186	1	2	1	0

Berlin Area
295 E Marquette St • Berlin, WI 54923-1272
(920) 361-2004 • http://www.berlin.k12.wi.us
Grade Span: PK-12; **Agency Type:** 1
Schools: 4
2 Primary; 1 Middle; 1 High; 0 Other Level
4 Regular; 0 Special Education; 0 Vocational; 0 Alternative
0 Magnet; 0 Charter; 1 Title I Eligible; 0 School-wide Title I
Students: 1,742   (50.6% male; 49.3% female)
Individual Education Program: 251 (14.4%);
English Language Learner: 0 (0.0%); Migrant: 100 (5.8%)
Eligible for Free Lunch Program: n/a
Eligible for Reduced-Price Lunch Program: n/a
Teachers: 119.8 (14.5 to 1)
Librarians/Media Specialists: 3.0 (579.0 to 1)
Guidance Counselors: 5.5 (315.8 to 1)
Current Spending: ($ per student per year):
Total: $7,771; Instruction: $4,724; Support Services: $2,802
Enrollment, Drop-out Rates and Diploma Recipients by Race/Ethnicity

Category	Total	White	Black	Asian	AIAN	Hisp.
Enrollment (%)	100.0	87.8	0.3	2.0	0.0	9.8
Drop-out Rate (%)	0.2	0.2	0.0	0.0	0.0	0.0
H.S. Diplomas (#)	143	139	0	2	0	2

Jackson County

Black River Falls
301 N 4th St • Black River Fls, WI 54615-1227
(715) 284-4357 • http://www.brf.org
Grade Span: PK-12; **Agency Type:** 1
Schools: 5
3 Primary; 1 Middle; 1 High; 0 Other Level
5 Regular; 0 Special Education; 0 Vocational; 0 Alternative
0 Magnet; 0 Charter; 2 Title I Eligible; 1 School-wide Title I
Students: 1,918   (51.6% male; 48.3% female)
Individual Education Program: 302 (15.7%);
English Language Learner: 0 (0.0%); Migrant: 0 (0.0%)
Eligible for Free Lunch Program: n/a
Eligible for Reduced-Price Lunch Program: n/a
Teachers: 144.6 (13.3 to 1)
Librarians/Media Specialists: 2.9 (661.4 to 1)
Guidance Counselors: 5.0 (383.6 to 1)
Current Spending: ($ per student per year):
Total: $8,314; Instruction: $5,236; Support Services: $2,704
Enrollment, Drop-out Rates and Diploma Recipients by Race/Ethnicity

Category	Total	White	Black	Asian	AIAN	Hisp.
Enrollment (%)	100.0	79.5	0.6	0.8	17.9	1.1
Drop-out Rate (%)	1.4	1.1	n/a	0.0	3.2	0.0
H.S. Diplomas (#)	149	128	0	0	19	2

Jefferson County

Fort Atkinson
201 Park St • Fort Atkinson, WI 53538-2155
(920) 563-7807 • http://www.fortschools.org
Grade Span: PK-12; **Agency Type:** 1
Schools: 7
4 Primary; 1 Middle; 2 High; 0 Other Level
6 Regular; 0 Special Education; 0 Vocational; 1 Alternative
0 Magnet; 0 Charter; 3 Title I Eligible; 0 School-wide Title I
Students: 2,633   (51.8% male; 48.1% female)
Individual Education Program: 372 (14.1%);
English Language Learner: 0 (0.0%); Migrant: 0 (0.0%)
Eligible for Free Lunch Program: n/a
Eligible for Reduced-Price Lunch Program: n/a
Teachers: 185.3 (14.2 to 1)
Librarians/Media Specialists: 5.0 (526.6 to 1)
Guidance Counselors: 5.0 (526.6 to 1)
Current Spending: ($ per student per year):
Total: $9,022; Instruction: $5,362; Support Services: $3,318
Enrollment, Drop-out Rates and Diploma Recipients by Race/Ethnicity

Category	Total	White	Black	Asian	AIAN	Hisp.
Enrollment (%)	100.0	93.2	0.7	1.1	0.3	4.6
Drop-out Rate (%)	1.9	2.0	0.0	0.0	0.0	0.0
H.S. Diplomas (#)	219	213	0	1	0	5

Jefferson
206 S Taft Ave • Jefferson, WI 53549-1453
(920) 675-1000 • http://www.jefferson.k12.wi.us
Grade Span: PK-12; **Agency Type:** 1
Schools: 6
3 Primary; 1 Middle; 2 High; 0 Other Level
5 Regular; 0 Special Education; 0 Vocational; 1 Alternative
0 Magnet; 1 Charter; 3 Title I Eligible; 0 School-wide Title I
Students: 1,728   (52.3% male; 47.6% female)
Individual Education Program: 279 (16.1%);
English Language Learner: 0 (0.0%); Migrant: 0 (0.0%)
Eligible for Free Lunch Program: n/a
Eligible for Reduced-Price Lunch Program: n/a
Teachers: 131.6 (13.1 to 1)
Librarians/Media Specialists: 3.5 (493.7 to 1)
Guidance Counselors: 4.4 (392.7 to 1)
Current Spending: ($ per student per year):
Total: $9,383; Instruction: $5,657; Support Services: $3,364
Enrollment, Drop-out Rates and Diploma Recipients by Race/Ethnicity

Category	Total	White	Black	Asian	AIAN	Hisp.
Enrollment (%)	100.0	90.3	0.5	0.5	1.2	7.5
Drop-out Rate (%)	1.2	1.0	0.0	0.0	n/a	3.8
H.S. Diplomas (#)	101	98	0	1	0	2

Watertown
111 Dodge St • Watertown, WI 53094-4470
(920) 262-1460 • http://www.watertown.k12.wi.us
Grade Span: PK-12; **Agency Type:** 1
Schools: 7
5 Primary; 1 Middle; 1 High; 0 Other Level
7 Regular; 0 Special Education; 0 Vocational; 0 Alternative
0 Magnet; 0 Charter; 4 Title I Eligible; 0 School-wide Title I
Students: 3,672   (51.5% male; 48.4% female)
Individual Education Program: 656 (17.9%);
English Language Learner: 0 (0.0%); Migrant: 44 (1.2%)
Eligible for Free Lunch Program: n/a
Eligible for Reduced-Price Lunch Program: n/a
Teachers: 230.2 (16.0 to 1)
Librarians/Media Specialists: 4.8 (765.0 to 1)
Guidance Counselors: 8.5 (432.0 to 1)
Current Spending: ($ per student per year):
Total: $9,008; Instruction: $5,431; Support Services: $3,182
Enrollment, Drop-out Rates and Diploma Recipients by Race/Ethnicity

Category	Total	White	Black	Asian	AIAN	Hisp.
Enrollment (%)	100.0	88.0	1.1	1.0	0.7	9.2
Drop-out Rate (%)	2.2	2.1	0.0	5.0	0.0	3.6
H.S. Diplomas (#)	288	273	1	4	2	8

Juneau County

Mauston
510 Grayside Ave • Mauston, WI 53948-1952
(608) 847-5451 • http://www.mauston.k12.wi.us
Grade Span: PK-12; **Agency Type:** 1
Schools: 6
3 Primary; 2 Middle; 1 High; 0 Other Level
5 Regular; 0 Special Education; 0 Vocational; 1 Alternative
0 Magnet; 1 Charter; 3 Title I Eligible; 0 School-wide Title I
Students: 1,618   (52.4% male; 47.5% female)
Individual Education Program: 267 (16.5%);
English Language Learner: 0 (0.0%); Migrant: 0 (0.0%)
Eligible for Free Lunch Program: n/a
Eligible for Reduced-Price Lunch Program: n/a
Teachers: 127.8 (12.6 to 1)
Librarians/Media Specialists: 3.9 (414.4 to 1)
Guidance Counselors: 4.0 (404.0 to 1)
Current Spending: ($ per student per year):
Total: $9,284; Instruction: $5,507; Support Services: $3,339
Enrollment, Drop-out Rates and Diploma Recipients by Race/Ethnicity

Category	Total	White	Black	Asian	AIAN	Hisp.
Enrollment (%)	100.0	93.7	1.5	1.3	2.0	1.5
Drop-out Rate (%)	3.8	3.7	0.0	0.0	7.7	9.1
H.S. Diplomas (#)	116	110	2	3	0	1

Kenosha County

Kenosha
3600 52nd St • Kenosha, WI 53144
Mailing Address: PO Box 340 • Kenosha, WI 53141-0340
(262) 653-6320 • http://www.kusd.edu
Grade Span: PK-12; **Agency Type:** 1
Schools: 41
27 Primary; 7 Middle; 6 High; 1 Other Level
36 Regular; 0 Special Education; 1 Vocational; 4 Alternative
0 Magnet; 3 Charter; 18 Title I Eligible; 12 School-wide Title I

Students: 21,426 (52.2% male; 47.7% female)
  Individual Education Program: 3,013 (14.1%);
  English Language Learner: 858 (4.0%); Migrant: 0 (0.0%)
  Eligible for Free Lunch Program: n/a
  Eligible for Reduced-Price Lunch Program: n/a
Teachers: 1,444.0 (14.8 to 1)
Librarians/Media Specialists: 39.0 (549.4 to 1)
Guidance Counselors: 55.3 (387.5 to 1)
Current Spending: ($ per student per year):
  Total: $8,761; Instruction: $5,474; Support Services: $3,031
Enrollment, Drop-out Rates and Diploma Recipients by Race/Ethnicity

Category	Total	White	Black	Asian	AIAN	Hisp.
Enrollment (%)	100.0	69.1	14.4	1.7	0.4	14.5
Drop-out Rate (%)	3.3	2.3	8.9	2.4	9.5	4.9
H.S. Diplomas (#)	1,305	1,071	100	22	1	111

Kewaunee County

Luxemburg-Casco
318 N Main St • Luxemburg, WI 54217-0070
Mailing Address: PO Box 70 • Luxemburg, WI 54217-0070
(920) 845-2391 • http://www.luxcasco.k12.wi.us
Grade Span: PK-12; **Agency Type:** 1
Schools: 4
  2 Primary; 1 Middle; 1 High; 0 Other Level
  4 Regular; 0 Special Education; 0 Vocational; 0 Alternative
  0 Magnet; 0 Charter; 2 Title I Eligible; 0 School-wide Title I
Students: 1,907 (52.7% male; 47.2% female)
  Individual Education Program: 242 (12.7%);
  English Language Learner: 0 (0.0%); Migrant: 0 (0.0%)
  Eligible for Free Lunch Program: n/a
  Eligible for Reduced-Price Lunch Program: n/a
Teachers: 125.1 (15.2 to 1)
Librarians/Media Specialists: 4.0 (476.8 to 1)
Guidance Counselors: 4.5 (423.8 to 1)
Current Spending: ($ per student per year):
  Total: $8,050; Instruction: $4,589; Support Services: $3,145
Enrollment, Drop-out Rates and Diploma Recipients by Race/Ethnicity

Category	Total	White	Black	Asian	AIAN	Hisp.
Enrollment (%)	100.0	97.5	0.6	0.6	0.4	0.9
Drop-out Rate (%)	0.3	0.1	0.0	0.0	33.3	0.0
H.S. Diplomas (#)	165	163	0	1	1	0

La Crosse County

Holmen
502 N Main St • Holmen, WI 54636-0580
Mailing Address: PO Box 580 • Holmen, WI 54636-0580
(608) 526-1301 • http://www.holmen.k12.wi.us
Grade Span: PK-12; **Agency Type:** 1
Schools: 6
  4 Primary; 1 Middle; 1 High; 0 Other Level
  6 Regular; 0 Special Education; 0 Vocational; 0 Alternative
  0 Magnet; 0 Charter; 2 Title I Eligible; 0 School-wide Title I
Students: 3,149 (51.5% male; 48.4% female)
  Individual Education Program: 389 (12.4%);
  English Language Learner: 150 (4.8%); Migrant: 0 (0.0%)
  Eligible for Free Lunch Program: n/a
  Eligible for Reduced-Price Lunch Program: n/a
Teachers: 225.5 (14.0 to 1)
Librarians/Media Specialists: 7.0 (449.9 to 1)
Guidance Counselors: 7.8 (403.7 to 1)
Current Spending: ($ per student per year):
  Total: $8,310; Instruction: $4,943; Support Services: $2,955
Enrollment, Drop-out Rates and Diploma Recipients by Race/Ethnicity

Category	Total	White	Black	Asian	AIAN	Hisp.
Enrollment (%)	100.0	90.9	1.0	6.7	0.6	0.8
Drop-out Rate (%)	0.2	0.1	0.0	2.4	0.0	0.0
H.S. Diplomas (#)	228	211	2	13	2	0

La Crosse
Hogan Admin Center • La Crosse, WI 54601-4982
(608) 789-7628 • http://www.centuryinter.net/hogan
Grade Span: PK-12; **Agency Type:** 1
Schools: 24
  14 Primary; 5 Middle; 5 High; 0 Other Level
  19 Regular; 0 Special Education; 0 Vocational; 5 Alternative
  0 Magnet; 5 Charter; 13 Title I Eligible; 4 School-wide Title I
Students: 7,498 (51.8% male; 48.1% female)
  Individual Education Program: 1,088 (14.5%);
  English Language Learner: 472 (6.3%); Migrant: 0 (0.0%)
  Eligible for Free Lunch Program: n/a
  Eligible for Reduced-Price Lunch Program: n/a
Teachers: 566.6 (13.2 to 1)
Librarians/Media Specialists: 19.0 (394.6 to 1)

Guidance Counselors: 19.0 (394.6 to 1)
Current Spending: ($ per student per year):
  Total: $10,263; Instruction: $6,404; Support Services: $3,363
Enrollment, Drop-out Rates and Diploma Recipients by Race/Ethnicity

Category	Total	White	Black	Asian	AIAN	Hisp.
Enrollment (%)	100.0	81.0	4.1	12.6	1.1	1.2
Drop-out Rate (%)	1.5	1.5	3.8	1.0	0.0	5.6
H.S. Diplomas (#)	499	422	10	57	5	5

Onalaska
1821 E Main St • Onalaska, WI 54650-0429
Mailing Address: PO Box 429 • Onalaska, WI 54650-0429
(608) 781-9700 • http://www.onalaska.k12.wi.us
Grade Span: PK-12; **Agency Type:** 1
Schools: 6
  4 Primary; 1 Middle; 1 High; 0 Other Level
  6 Regular; 0 Special Education; 0 Vocational; 0 Alternative
  0 Magnet; 0 Charter; 3 Title I Eligible; 0 School-wide Title I
Students: 2,749 (51.1% male; 48.8% female)
  Individual Education Program: 276 (10.0%);
  English Language Learner: 51 (1.9%); Migrant: 0 (0.0%)
  Eligible for Free Lunch Program: n/a
  Eligible for Reduced-Price Lunch Program: n/a
Teachers: 186.3 (14.8 to 1)
Librarians/Media Specialists: 5.5 (499.8 to 1)
Guidance Counselors: 7.0 (392.7 to 1)
Current Spending: ($ per student per year):
  Total: $8,264; Instruction: $4,902; Support Services: $3,039
Enrollment, Drop-out Rates and Diploma Recipients by Race/Ethnicity

Category	Total	White	Black	Asian	AIAN	Hisp.
Enrollment (%)	100.0	86.8	2.3	9.1	0.1	1.6
Drop-out Rate (%)	2.1	2.2	10.0	0.0	n/a	0.0
H.S. Diplomas (#)	228	220	2	6	0	0

West Salem
450 N Mark St • West Salem, WI 54669-1224
(608) 786-0700 • http://www.cesa4.wi.us/cesaschools/26districts/
Grade Span: PK-12; **Agency Type:** 1
Schools: 3
  1 Primary; 1 Middle; 1 High; 0 Other Level
  3 Regular; 0 Special Education; 0 Vocational; 0 Alternative
  0 Magnet; 0 Charter; 1 Title I Eligible; 0 School-wide Title I
Students: 1,626 (49.7% male; 50.2% female)
  Individual Education Program: 191 (11.7%);
  English Language Learner: 0 (0.0%); Migrant: 0 (0.0%)
  Eligible for Free Lunch Program: n/a
  Eligible for Reduced-Price Lunch Program: n/a
Teachers: 115.0 (14.1 to 1)
Librarians/Media Specialists: 4.0 (406.5 to 1)
Guidance Counselors: 0.0 (542.0 to 1)
Current Spending: ($ per student per year):
  Total: $8,005; Instruction: $4,897; Support Services: $2,744
Enrollment, Drop-out Rates and Diploma Recipients by Race/Ethnicity

Category	Total	White	Black	Asian	AIAN	Hisp.
Enrollment (%)	100.0	96.7	0.9	1.5	0.7	0.2
Drop-out Rate (%)	0.2	0.2	0.0	0.0	0.0	0.0
H.S. Diplomas (#)	110	105	0	3	0	2

Langlade County

Antigo
120 S Dorr St • Antigo, WI 54409-1220
(715) 627-4355 • http://www.antigoschools.k12.wi.us
Grade Span: PK-12; **Agency Type:** 1
Schools: 10
  8 Primary; 1 Middle; 1 High; 0 Other Level
  10 Regular; 0 Special Education; 0 Vocational; 0 Alternative
  0 Magnet; 0 Charter; 7 Title I Eligible; 3 School-wide Title I
Students: 2,855 (52.8% male; 47.1% female)
  Individual Education Program: 512 (17.9%);
  English Language Learner: 0 (0.0%); Migrant: 0 (0.0%)
  Eligible for Free Lunch Program: n/a
  Eligible for Reduced-Price Lunch Program: n/a
Teachers: 218.7 (13.1 to 1)
Librarians/Media Specialists: 3.0 (951.7 to 1)
Guidance Counselors: 8.0 (356.9 to 1)
Current Spending: ($ per student per year):
  Total: $9,763; Instruction: $5,731; Support Services: $3,572
Enrollment, Drop-out Rates and Diploma Recipients by Race/Ethnicity

Category	Total	White	Black	Asian	AIAN	Hisp.
Enrollment (%)	100.0	96.0	0.7	0.5	1.8	1.1
Drop-out Rate (%)	0.9	0.9	0.0	0.0	4.3	0.0
H.S. Diplomas (#)	307	295	2	3	6	1

Lincoln County

Merrill Area
1111 N Sales St • Merrill, WI 54452-3198
(715) 536-4581 • http://www.maps.k12.wi.us
Grade Span: PK-12; **Agency Type:** 1
Schools: 10
8 Primary; 1 Middle; 1 High; 0 Other Level
10 Regular; 0 Special Education; 0 Vocational; 0 Alternative
0 Magnet; 0 Charter; 6 Title I Eligible; 0 School-wide Title I
Students: 3,314 (52.3% male; 47.6% female)
Individual Education Program: 430 (13.0%);
English Language Learner: 0 (0.0%); Migrant: 0 (0.0%)
Eligible for Free Lunch Program: n/a
Eligible for Reduced-Price Lunch Program: n/a
Teachers: 224.8 (14.7 to 1)
Librarians/Media Specialists: 3.0 (1,104.7 to 1)
Guidance Counselors: 8.0 (414.3 to 1)
Current Spending: ($ per student per year):
Total: $8,650; Instruction: $5,395; Support Services: $2,908
Enrollment, Drop-out Rates and Diploma Recipients by Race/Ethnicity

Category	Total	White	Black	Asian	AIAN	Hisp.
Enrollment (%)	100.0	96.8	0.5	1.3	0.5	0.9
Drop-out Rate (%)	2.9	2.8	0.0	5.6	0.0	0.0
H.S. Diplomas (#)	258	251	0	1	4	2

Tomahawk
328 N 4th St • Tomahawk, WI 54487-1370
(715) 453-5551 • http://www.tomahawk.k12.wi.us/
Grade Span: PK-12; **Agency Type:** 1
Schools: 3
1 Primary; 1 Middle; 1 High; 0 Other Level
3 Regular; 0 Special Education; 0 Vocational; 0 Alternative
0 Magnet; 0 Charter; 1 Title I Eligible; 0 School-wide Title I
Students: 1,635 (49.6% male; 50.3% female)
Individual Education Program: 203 (12.4%);
English Language Learner: 0 (0.0%); Migrant: 0 (0.0%)
Eligible for Free Lunch Program: n/a
Eligible for Reduced-Price Lunch Program: n/a
Teachers: 110.3 (14.8 to 1)
Librarians/Media Specialists: 3.0 (545.0 to 1)
Guidance Counselors: 4.0 (408.8 to 1)
Current Spending: ($ per student per year):
Total: $8,600; Instruction: $5,074; Support Services: $3,171
Enrollment, Drop-out Rates and Diploma Recipients by Race/Ethnicity

Category	Total	White	Black	Asian	AIAN	Hisp.
Enrollment (%)	100.0	97.8	0.5	0.9	0.4	0.4
Drop-out Rate (%)	0.8	0.8	n/a	0.0	0.0	0.0
H.S. Diplomas (#)	136	132	0	2	1	1

Manitowoc County

Manitowoc
1820 S 30 St • Manitowoc, WI 54220
Mailing Address: PO Box 1657 • Manitowoc, WI 54221-1657
(920) 686-4781 • http://www.mpsd.k12.wi.us
Grade Span: PK-12; **Agency Type:** 1
Schools: 10
7 Primary; 2 Middle; 1 High; 0 Other Level
10 Regular; 0 Special Education; 0 Vocational; 0 Alternative
0 Magnet; 0 Charter; 6 Title I Eligible; 0 School-wide Title I
Students: 5,329 (50.7% male; 49.2% female)
Individual Education Program: 646 (12.1%);
English Language Learner: 354 (6.6%); Migrant: 0 (0.0%)
Eligible for Free Lunch Program: n/a
Eligible for Reduced-Price Lunch Program: n/a
Teachers: 352.5 (15.1 to 1)
Librarians/Media Specialists: 4.0 (1,332.3 to 1)
Guidance Counselors: 10.0 (532.9 to 1)
Current Spending: ($ per student per year):
Total: $7,997; Instruction: $4,940; Support Services: $3,032
Enrollment, Drop-out Rates and Diploma Recipients by Race/Ethnicity

Category	Total	White	Black	Asian	AIAN	Hisp.
Enrollment (%)	100.0	83.4	1.5	10.1	0.8	4.2
Drop-out Rate (%)	3.5	3.0	10.0	7.4	11.1	5.3
H.S. Diplomas (#)	377	345	2	21	3	6

Two Rivers
4521 Lincoln Ave • Two Rivers, WI 54241-2134
(920) 793-4560 • http://www.trschools.k12.wi.us
Grade Span: PK-12; **Agency Type:** 1
Schools: 5
3 Primary; 1 Middle; 1 High; 0 Other Level
5 Regular; 0 Special Education; 0 Vocational; 0 Alternative
0 Magnet; 0 Charter; 2 Title I Eligible; 0 School-wide Title I

Students: 2,108 (54.0% male; 45.9% female)
Individual Education Program: 345 (16.4%);
English Language Learner: 63 (3.0%); Migrant: 0 (0.0%)
Eligible for Free Lunch Program: n/a
Eligible for Reduced-Price Lunch Program: n/a
Teachers: 157.8 (13.4 to 1)
Librarians/Media Specialists: 2.0 (1,054.0 to 1)
Guidance Counselors: 7.0 (301.1 to 1)
Current Spending: ($ per student per year):
Total: $8,403; Instruction: $5,141; Support Services: $2,961
Enrollment, Drop-out Rates and Diploma Recipients by Race/Ethnicity

Category	Total	White	Black	Asian	AIAN	Hisp.
Enrollment (%)	100.0	92.6	0.4	5.3	0.6	1.0
Drop-out Rate (%)	0.7	0.8	0.0	0.0	0.0	0.0
H.S. Diplomas (#)	165	150	1	11	2	1

Marathon County

D C Everest Area
6300 Alderson St • Weston, WI 54476-3908
(715) 359-4221 • http://www.dce.k12.wi.us/
Grade Span: PK-12; **Agency Type:** 1
Schools: 10
7 Primary; 1 Middle; 1 High; 1 Other Level
10 Regular; 0 Special Education; 0 Vocational; 0 Alternative
0 Magnet; 0 Charter; 3 Title I Eligible; 0 School-wide Title I
Students: 5,213 (51.5% male; 48.4% female)
Individual Education Program: 632 (12.1%);
English Language Learner: 324 (6.2%); Migrant: 0 (0.0%)
Eligible for Free Lunch Program: n/a
Eligible for Reduced-Price Lunch Program: n/a
Teachers: 348.2 (15.0 to 1)
Librarians/Media Specialists: 8.0 (651.6 to 1)
Guidance Counselors: 12.6 (413.7 to 1)
Current Spending: ($ per student per year):
Total: $8,258; Instruction: $5,069; Support Services: $2,885
Enrollment, Drop-out Rates and Diploma Recipients by Race/Ethnicity

Category	Total	White	Black	Asian	AIAN	Hisp.
Enrollment (%)	100.0	87.4	0.5	10.8	0.5	0.7
Drop-out Rate (%)	0.7	0.8	0.0	0.0	0.0	0.0
H.S. Diplomas (#)	390	352	2	34	2	0

Mosinee
591 W State Hwy 153 • Mosinee, WI 54455-7499
(715) 693-2530 • http://www.mosinee.k12.wi.us
Grade Span: PK-12; **Agency Type:** 1
Schools: 3
1 Primary; 1 Middle; 1 High; 0 Other Level
3 Regular; 0 Special Education; 0 Vocational; 0 Alternative
0 Magnet; 0 Charter; 2 Title I Eligible; 0 School-wide Title I
Students: 2,014 (52.0% male; 47.9% female)
Individual Education Program: 268 (13.3%);
English Language Learner: 0 (0.0%); Migrant: 0 (0.0%)
Eligible for Free Lunch Program: n/a
Eligible for Reduced-Price Lunch Program: n/a
Teachers: 133.3 (15.1 to 1)
Librarians/Media Specialists: 2.0 (1,007.0 to 1)
Guidance Counselors: 4.0 (503.5 to 1)
Current Spending: ($ per student per year):
Total: $8,811; Instruction: $5,344; Support Services: $3,137
Enrollment, Drop-out Rates and Diploma Recipients by Race/Ethnicity

Category	Total	White	Black	Asian	AIAN	Hisp.
Enrollment (%)	100.0	96.9	1.0	0.6	0.1	1.3
Drop-out Rate (%)	1.0	1.1	0.0	0.0	0.0	0.0
H.S. Diplomas (#)	158	155	0	1	1	1

Wausau
650 S 7th Ave • Wausau, WI 54401
Mailing Address: PO Box 359 • Wausau, WI 54402-0359
(715) 261-2561 • http://www.wausau.k12.wi.us
Grade Span: PK-12; **Agency Type:** 1
Schools: 19
15 Primary; 1 Middle; 2 High; 1 Other Level
18 Regular; 0 Special Education; 0 Vocational; 1 Alternative
0 Magnet; 1 Charter; 7 Title I Eligible; 0 School-wide Title I
Students: 8,746 (52.9% male; 47.0% female)
Individual Education Program: 1,151 (13.2%);
English Language Learner: 1,480 (16.9%); Migrant: 0 (0.0%)
Eligible for Free Lunch Program: n/a
Eligible for Reduced-Price Lunch Program: n/a
Teachers: 613.9 (14.2 to 1)
Librarians/Media Specialists: 10.8 (809.8 to 1)
Guidance Counselors: 21.5 (406.8 to 1)
Current Spending: ($ per student per year):
Total: $9,630; Instruction: $5,858; Support Services: $3,422

Enrollment, Drop-out Rates and Diploma Recipients by Race/Ethnicity

Category	Total	White	Black	Asian	AIAN	Hisp.
Enrollment (%)	100.0	72.4	1.6	23.7	0.9	1.3
Drop-out Rate (%)	1.7	1.2	9.1	2.8	5.9	6.3
H.S. Diplomas (#)	586	484	2	94	2	4

Marinette County

Marinette
2139 Pierce Ave • Marinette, WI 54143-3998
(715) 732-7905 • http://www.marinette.k12.wi.us
Grade Span: PK-12; **Agency Type:** 1
Schools: 6
  5 Primary; 0 Middle; 1 High; 0 Other Level
  6 Regular; 0 Special Education; 0 Vocational; 0 Alternative
  0 Magnet; 0 Charter; 3 Title I Eligible; 0 School-wide Title I
Students: 2,486   (51.3% male; 48.6% female)
  Individual Education Program: 338 (13.6%);
  English Language Learner: 0 (0.0%); Migrant: 0 (0.0%)
  Eligible for Free Lunch Program: n/a
  Eligible for Reduced-Price Lunch Program: n/a
Teachers: 159.6 (15.6 to 1)
Librarians/Media Specialists: 3.0 (828.7 to 1)
Guidance Counselors: 5.0 (497.2 to 1)
Current Spending: ($ per student per year):
  Total: $8,115; Instruction: $4,967; Support Services: $2,817

Enrollment, Drop-out Rates and Diploma Recipients by Race/Ethnicity

Category	Total	White	Black	Asian	AIAN	Hisp.
Enrollment (%)	100.0	97.4	0.9	0.2	0.8	0.6
Drop-out Rate (%)	0.9	0.9	0.0	0.0	0.0	0.0
H.S. Diplomas (#)	214	210	0	2	0	2

Milwaukee County

Brown Deer
8200 N 60th St • Brown Deer, WI 53223-3598
(414) 371-6767 • http://www.bdsd.k12.wi.us
Grade Span: PK-12; **Agency Type:** 1
Schools: 4
  2 Primary; 1 Middle; 1 High; 0 Other Level
  4 Regular; 0 Special Education; 0 Vocational; 0 Alternative
  0 Magnet; 0 Charter; 1 Title I Eligible; 0 School-wide Title I
Students: 1,861   (54.5% male; 45.4% female)
  Individual Education Program: 188 (10.1%);
  English Language Learner: 0 (0.0%); Migrant: 0 (0.0%)
  Eligible for Free Lunch Program: n/a
  Eligible for Reduced-Price Lunch Program: n/a
Teachers: 118.8 (15.7 to 1)
Librarians/Media Specialists: 0.0 (n/a to 1)
Guidance Counselors: 6.0 (310.2 to 1)
Current Spending: ($ per student per year):
  Total: $9,261; Instruction: $5,219; Support Services: $3,739

Enrollment, Drop-out Rates and Diploma Recipients by Race/Ethnicity

Category	Total	White	Black	Asian	AIAN	Hisp.
Enrollment (%)	100.0	56.1	34.9	4.6	0.8	3.6
Drop-out Rate (%)	0.5	0.7	0.0	0.0	0.0	0.0
H.S. Diplomas (#)	127	98	22	4	0	3

Cudahy
2915 E Ramsey Ave • Cudahy, WI 53110-2559
(414) 294-7402 • http://www.cudahy.k12.wi.us/
Grade Span: PK-12; **Agency Type:** 1
Schools: 7
  5 Primary; 1 Middle; 1 High; 0 Other Level
  7 Regular; 0 Special Education; 0 Vocational; 0 Alternative
  0 Magnet; 0 Charter; 3 Title I Eligible; 0 School-wide Title I
Students: 2,849   (52.0% male; 47.9% female)
  Individual Education Program: 458 (16.1%);
  English Language Learner: 0 (0.0%); Migrant: 0 (0.0%)
  Eligible for Free Lunch Program: n/a
  Eligible for Reduced-Price Lunch Program: n/a
Teachers: 203.1 (14.0 to 1)
Librarians/Media Specialists: 3.0 (948.0 to 1)
Guidance Counselors: 7.0 (406.3 to 1)
Current Spending: ($ per student per year):
  Total: $9,344; Instruction: $5,971; Support Services: $3,116

Enrollment, Drop-out Rates and Diploma Recipients by Race/Ethnicity

Category	Total	White	Black	Asian	AIAN	Hisp.
Enrollment (%)	100.0	82.2	3.2	3.3	1.6	9.8
Drop-out Rate (%)	0.8	0.7	0.0	0.0	0.0	3.7
H.S. Diplomas (#)	203	159	12	17	4	11

Franklin Public
8255 W Forest Hill Ave • Franklin, WI 53132-9705
(414) 529-8269 • http://www.franklin.k12.wi.us
Grade Span: PK-12; **Agency Type:** 1
Schools: 7
  5 Primary; 1 Middle; 1 High; 0 Other Level
  7 Regular; 0 Special Education; 0 Vocational; 0 Alternative
  0 Magnet; 0 Charter; 0 Title I Eligible; 0 School-wide Title I
Students: 3,956   (51.2% male; 48.7% female)
  Individual Education Program: 420 (10.6%);
  English Language Learner: 197 (5.0%); Migrant: 0 (0.0%)
  Eligible for Free Lunch Program: n/a
  Eligible for Reduced-Price Lunch Program: n/a
Teachers: 263.8 (15.0 to 1)
Librarians/Media Specialists: 7.0 (565.1 to 1)
Guidance Counselors: 11.0 (359.6 to 1)
Current Spending: ($ per student per year):
  Total: $9,703; Instruction: $5,994; Support Services: $3,399

Enrollment, Drop-out Rates and Diploma Recipients by Race/Ethnicity

Category	Total	White	Black	Asian	AIAN	Hisp.
Enrollment (%)	100.0	82.1	5.8	7.2	0.9	4.0
Drop-out Rate (%)	0.1	0.1	1.6	0.0	0.0	0.0
H.S. Diplomas (#)	329	287	9	25	0	8

Greendale
5900 S 51st St • Greendale, WI 53129-2699
(414) 423-2700 • http://www.greendale.k12.wi.us
Grade Span: PK-12; **Agency Type:** 1
Schools: 6
  4 Primary; 1 Middle; 1 High; 0 Other Level
  5 Regular; 0 Special Education; 0 Vocational; 1 Alternative
  0 Magnet; 1 Charter; 3 Title I Eligible; 0 School-wide Title I
Students: 2,376   (50.4% male; 49.5% female)
  Individual Education Program: 234 (9.8%);
  English Language Learner: 0 (0.0%); Migrant: 0 (0.0%)
  Eligible for Free Lunch Program: n/a
  Eligible for Reduced-Price Lunch Program: n/a
Teachers: 148.6 (16.0 to 1)
Librarians/Media Specialists: 2.8 (848.6 to 1)
Guidance Counselors: 5.0 (475.2 to 1)
Current Spending: ($ per student per year):
  Total: $9,560; Instruction: $5,751; Support Services: $3,547

Enrollment, Drop-out Rates and Diploma Recipients by Race/Ethnicity

Category	Total	White	Black	Asian	AIAN	Hisp.
Enrollment (%)	100.0	88.0	2.6	4.2	0.4	4.8
Drop-out Rate (%)	0.4	0.4	0.0	0.0	0.0	0.0
H.S. Diplomas (#)	180	161	7	9	0	3

Greenfield
8500 W Chapman Ave • Greenfield, WI 53228-2915
(414) 529-9090 • http://www.greenfield.k12.wi.us
Grade Span: PK-12; **Agency Type:** 1
Schools: 6
  4 Primary; 1 Middle; 1 High; 0 Other Level
  6 Regular; 0 Special Education; 0 Vocational; 0 Alternative
  0 Magnet; 0 Charter; 4 Title I Eligible; 0 School-wide Title I
Students: 3,397   (51.1% male; 48.8% female)
  Individual Education Program: 411 (12.1%);
  English Language Learner: 0 (0.0%); Migrant: 0 (0.0%)
  Eligible for Free Lunch Program: n/a
  Eligible for Reduced-Price Lunch Program: n/a
Teachers: 214.6 (15.8 to 1)
Librarians/Media Specialists: 5.4 (629.1 to 1)
Guidance Counselors: 10.8 (314.5 to 1)
Current Spending: ($ per student per year):
  Total: $8,718; Instruction: $5,337; Support Services: $3,074

Enrollment, Drop-out Rates and Diploma Recipients by Race/Ethnicity

Category	Total	White	Black	Asian	AIAN	Hisp.
Enrollment (%)	100.0	78.7	4.1	6.5	1.7	9.1
Drop-out Rate (%)	0.9	0.9	6.7	0.0	0.0	0.0
H.S. Diplomas (#)	234	200	4	5	0	25

Milwaukee
5225 W Vliet St • Milwaukee, WI 53208
Mailing Address: PO Box 2181 • Milwaukee, WI 53201-2181
(414) 475-8001 • http://www.milwaukee.k12.wi.us
Grade Span: PK-12; **Agency Type:** 1
Schools: 233
  134 Primary; 32 Middle; 42 High; 15 Other Level
  192 Regular; 1 Special Education; 0 Vocational; 30 Alternative
  0 Magnet; 25 Charter; 170 Title I Eligible; 167 School-wide Title I
Students: 97,359   (50.7% male; 49.2% female)
  Individual Education Program: 16,017 (16.5%);
  English Language Learner: 6,438 (6.6%); Migrant: 50 (0.1%)
  Eligible for Free Lunch Program: n/a

Eligible for Reduced-Price Lunch Program: n/a
Teachers: 5,929.5 (16.4 to 1)
Librarians/Media Specialists: 57.8 (1,684.4 to 1)
Guidance Counselors: 86.0 (1,132.1 to 1)
Current Spending: ($ per student per year):
    Total: $10,352; Instruction: $6,156; Support Services: $3,841
Enrollment, Drop-out Rates and Diploma Recipients by Race/Ethnicity

Category	Total	White	Black	Asian	AIAN	Hisp.
Enrollment (%)	100.0	17.3	59.4	4.4	0.9	18.0
Drop-out Rate (%)	9.0	6.7	9.9	4.9	12.3	9.4
H.S. Diplomas (#)	3,912	995	2,102	199	49	567

Oak Creek-Franklin
7630 S 10th St • Oak Creek, WI 53154-1912
(414) 768-5886 • http://www.oakcreek.k12.wi.us
Grade Span: PK-12; **Agency Type:** 1
Schools: 8
    5 Primary; 2 Middle; 1 High; 0 Other Level
    8 Regular; 0 Special Education; 0 Vocational; 0 Alternative
    0 Magnet; 0 Charter; 0 Title I Eligible; 0 School-wide Title I
Students: 5,063   (51.1% male; 48.8% female)
    Individual Education Program: 608 (12.0%);
    English Language Learner: 0 (0.0%); Migrant: 0 (0.0%)
    Eligible for Free Lunch Program: n/a
    Eligible for Reduced-Price Lunch Program: n/a
Teachers: 306.1 (16.5 to 1)
Librarians/Media Specialists: 5.0 (1,011.0 to 1)
Guidance Counselors: 13.0 (388.8 to 1)
Current Spending: ($ per student per year):
    Total: $8,410; Instruction: $5,031; Support Services: $3,080
Enrollment, Drop-out Rates and Diploma Recipients by Race/Ethnicity

Category	Total	White	Black	Asian	AIAN	Hisp.
Enrollment (%)	100.0	80.8	5.0	4.6	1.3	8.3
Drop-out Rate (%)	0.8	0.7	1.4	0.0	13.3	1.0
H.S. Diplomas (#)	382	335	12	14	3	18

Shorewood
1701 E Capitol Dr • Shorewood, WI 53211-1996
(414) 963-6901 • http://www.shorewoodschools.org
Grade Span: PK-12; **Agency Type:** 1
Schools: 4
    2 Primary; 1 Middle; 1 High; 0 Other Level
    4 Regular; 0 Special Education; 0 Vocational; 0 Alternative
    0 Magnet; 0 Charter; 4 Title I Eligible; 0 School-wide Title I
Students: 2,161   (49.8% male; 50.1% female)
    Individual Education Program: 190 (8.8%);
    English Language Learner: 183 (8.5%); Migrant: 0 (0.0%)
    Eligible for Free Lunch Program: n/a
    Eligible for Reduced-Price Lunch Program: n/a
Teachers: 148.5 (14.6 to 1)
Librarians/Media Specialists: 4.0 (540.3 to 1)
Guidance Counselors: 5.0 (432.2 to 1)
Current Spending: ($ per student per year):
    Total: $9,484; Instruction: $6,083; Support Services: $3,217
Enrollment, Drop-out Rates and Diploma Recipients by Race/Ethnicity

Category	Total	White	Black	Asian	AIAN	Hisp.
Enrollment (%)	100.0	75.1	14.1	5.6	0.8	4.5
Drop-out Rate (%)	0.0	0.0	0.0	0.0	0.0	0.0
H.S. Diplomas (#)	179	142	20	8	1	8

South Milwaukee
1225 Memorial Dr • South Milwaukee, WI 53172-1625
(414) 768-6300 • http://www.sdsm.k12.wi.us
Grade Span: PK-12; **Agency Type:** 1
Schools: 7
    4 Primary; 1 Middle; 2 High; 0 Other Level
    6 Regular; 0 Special Education; 0 Vocational; 1 Alternative
    0 Magnet; 1 Charter; 4 Title I Eligible; 0 School-wide Title I
Students: 3,532   (51.8% male; 48.1% female)
    Individual Education Program: 404 (11.4%);
    English Language Learner: 0 (0.0%); Migrant: 0 (0.0%)
    Eligible for Free Lunch Program: n/a
    Eligible for Reduced-Price Lunch Program: n/a
Teachers: 232.2 (15.2 to 1)
Librarians/Media Specialists: 3.0 (1,177.3 to 1)
Guidance Counselors: 9.0 (392.4 to 1)
Current Spending: ($ per student per year):
    Total: $8,852; Instruction: $5,574; Support Services: $2,954
Enrollment, Drop-out Rates and Diploma Recipients by Race/Ethnicity

Category	Total	White	Black	Asian	AIAN	Hisp.
Enrollment (%)	100.0	84.8	4.9	2.4	0.9	7.0
Drop-out Rate (%)	0.9	1.0	1.6	0.0	0.0	0.0
H.S. Diplomas (#)	252	217	11	9	0	15

Wauwatosa
12121 W N Ave • Wauwatosa, WI 53226-2096
(414) 773-1010 • http://www.wauwatosaschools.org
Grade Span: PK-12; **Agency Type:** 1
Schools: 17
    9 Primary; 2 Middle; 2 High; 4 Other Level
    13 Regular; 0 Special Education; 0 Vocational; 4 Alternative
    0 Magnet; 0 Charter; 7 Title I Eligible; 0 School-wide Title I
Students: 7,040   (51.7% male; 48.2% female)
    Individual Education Program: 745 (10.6%);
    English Language Learner: 0 (0.0%); Migrant: 0 (0.0%)
    Eligible for Free Lunch Program: n/a
    Eligible for Reduced-Price Lunch Program: n/a
Teachers: 464.2 (15.2 to 1)
Librarians/Media Specialists: 13.0 (541.5 to 1)
Guidance Counselors: 13.5 (521.5 to 1)
Current Spending: ($ per student per year):
    Total: $8,594; Instruction: $5,329; Support Services: $3,081
Enrollment, Drop-out Rates and Diploma Recipients by Race/Ethnicity

Category	Total	White	Black	Asian	AIAN	Hisp.
Enrollment (%)	100.0	77.4	13.3	5.1	0.7	3.5
Drop-out Rate (%)	0.2	0.2	0.0	0.0	0.0	1.5
H.S. Diplomas (#)	496	406	48	25	3	14

West Allis
9333 W Lincoln Ave • West Allis, WI 53227-2395
(414) 604-3005 • http://www.wawm.k12.wi.us
Grade Span: PK-12; **Agency Type:** 1
Schools: 18
    11 Primary; 1 Middle; 4 High; 2 Other Level
    16 Regular; 0 Special Education; 0 Vocational; 2 Alternative
    0 Magnet; 1 Charter; 9 Title I Eligible; 1 School-wide Title I
Students: 8,827   (51.6% male; 48.3% female)
    Individual Education Program: 1,272 (14.4%);
    English Language Learner: 221 (2.5%); Migrant: 0 (0.0%)
    Eligible for Free Lunch Program: n/a
    Eligible for Reduced-Price Lunch Program: n/a
Teachers: 589.4 (15.0 to 1)
Librarians/Media Specialists: 12.0 (735.6 to 1)
Guidance Counselors: 11.0 (802.5 to 1)
Current Spending: ($ per student per year):
    Total: $8,795; Instruction: $5,230; Support Services: $3,325
Enrollment, Drop-out Rates and Diploma Recipients by Race/Ethnicity

Category	Total	White	Black	Asian	AIAN	Hisp.
Enrollment (%)	100.0	83.1	5.5	2.7	1.5	7.2
Drop-out Rate (%)	1.6	1.5	2.0	0.0	7.1	3.6
H.S. Diplomas (#)	637	587	17	14	4	15

Whitefish Bay
1200 E Fairmount Ave • Whitefish Bay, WI 53217-6099
(414) 963-3921 • http://www.wfbschools.com
Grade Span: PK-12; **Agency Type:** 1
Schools: 4
    2 Primary; 1 Middle; 1 High; 0 Other Level
    4 Regular; 0 Special Education; 0 Vocational; 0 Alternative
    0 Magnet; 0 Charter; 4 Title I Eligible; 0 School-wide Title I
Students: 2,941   (50.3% male; 49.6% female)
    Individual Education Program: 214 (7.3%);
    English Language Learner: 0 (0.0%); Migrant: 0 (0.0%)
    Eligible for Free Lunch Program: n/a
    Eligible for Reduced-Price Lunch Program: n/a
Teachers: 190.6 (15.4 to 1)
Librarians/Media Specialists: 3.0 (980.3 to 1)
Guidance Counselors: 10.3 (285.5 to 1)
Current Spending: ($ per student per year):
    Total: $8,779; Instruction: $5,122; Support Services: $3,645
Enrollment, Drop-out Rates and Diploma Recipients by Race/Ethnicity

Category	Total	White	Black	Asian	AIAN	Hisp.
Enrollment (%)	100.0	81.4	10.7	5.0	0.0	2.8
Drop-out Rate (%)	0.2	0.1	1.0	0.0	0.0	0.0
H.S. Diplomas (#)	211	165	31	7	2	6

Whitnall
5000 S 116th St • Greenfield, WI 53228-3197
(414) 525-8402 • http://www.whitnall.com
Grade Span: PK-12; **Agency Type:** 1
Schools: 4
    2 Primary; 1 Middle; 1 High; 0 Other Level
    4 Regular; 0 Special Education; 0 Vocational; 0 Alternative
    0 Magnet; 0 Charter; 0 Title I Eligible; 0 School-wide Title I
Students: 2,501   (52.1% male; 47.8% female)
    Individual Education Program: 300 (12.0%);
    English Language Learner: 64 (2.6%); Migrant: 0 (0.0%)
    Eligible for Free Lunch Program: n/a
    Eligible for Reduced-Price Lunch Program: n/a

Teachers: 146.6 (17.1 to 1)
Librarians/Media Specialists: 3.0 (833.7 to 1)
Guidance Counselors: 5.0 (500.2 to 1)
Current Spending: ($ per student per year):
    Total: $8,800; Instruction: $5,004; Support Services: $3,442
Enrollment, Drop-out Rates and Diploma Recipients by Race/Ethnicity

Category	Total	White	Black	Asian	AIAN	Hisp.
Enrollment (%)	100.0	88.5	3.5	4.9	0.4	2.7
Drop-out Rate (%)	0.0	0.0	0.0	0.0	0.0	0.0
H.S. Diplomas (#)	206	191	5	8	1	1

Monroe County

Sparta Area
201 E Franklin St • Sparta, WI 54656-1803
Mailing Address: 506 N Black River St • Sparta, WI 54656-1548
(608) 269-3151 • http://www.spartan.org/education.html
Grade Span: PK-12; **Agency Type:** 1
Schools: 13
    7 Primary; 2 Middle; 3 High; 0 Other Level
    9 Regular; 0 Special Education; 0 Vocational; 3 Alternative
    0 Magnet; 2 Charter; 6 Title I Eligible; 0 School-wide Title I
Students: 2,647　(51.7% male; 48.2% female)
    Individual Education Program: 385 (14.5%);
    English Language Learner: 0 (0.0%); Migrant: 0 (0.0%)
    Eligible for Free Lunch Program: n/a
    Eligible for Reduced-Price Lunch Program: n/a
Teachers: 194.4 (13.6 to 1)
Librarians/Media Specialists: 5.0 (529.4 to 1)
Guidance Counselors: 7.9 (335.1 to 1)
Current Spending: ($ per student per year):
    Total: $8,683; Instruction: $4,897; Support Services: $3,402
Enrollment, Drop-out Rates and Diploma Recipients by Race/Ethnicity

Category	Total	White	Black	Asian	AIAN	Hisp.
Enrollment (%)	100.0	94.6	1.4	1.5	0.3	2.2
Drop-out Rate (%)	1.6	1.5	0.0	0.0	0.0	20.0
H.S. Diplomas (#)	206	204	0	2	0	0

Tomah Area
129 W Clifton St • Tomah, WI 54660-2507
(608) 374-7210 • http://www.tomah.k12.wi.us/
Grade Span: PK-12; **Agency Type:** 1
Schools: 10
    6 Primary; 2 Middle; 1 High; 1 Other Level
    9 Regular; 0 Special Education; 0 Vocational; 1 Alternative
    0 Magnet; 0 Charter; 7 Title I Eligible; 0 School-wide Title I
Students: 2,935　(50.8% male; 49.1% female)
    Individual Education Program: 359 (12.2%);
    English Language Learner: 0 (0.0%); Migrant: 0 (0.0%)
    Eligible for Free Lunch Program: n/a
    Eligible for Reduced-Price Lunch Program: n/a
Teachers: 216.9 (13.5 to 1)
Librarians/Media Specialists: 4.9 (599.0 to 1)
Guidance Counselors: 8.0 (366.9 to 1)
Current Spending: ($ per student per year):
    Total: $8,045; Instruction: $4,888; Support Services: $2,810
Enrollment, Drop-out Rates and Diploma Recipients by Race/Ethnicity

Category	Total	White	Black	Asian	AIAN	Hisp.
Enrollment (%)	100.0	92.8	1.6	0.7	3.4	1.4
Drop-out Rate (%)	0.4	0.5	0.0	0.0	0.0	0.0
H.S. Diplomas (#)	225	210	1	2	10	2

Oconto County

Oconto Falls
200 N Farm Rd • Oconto Falls, WI 54154-1221
(920) 848-4471 • http://www.ocontofalls.k12.wi.us
Grade Span: PK-12; **Agency Type:** 1
Schools: 6
    2 Primary; 1 Middle; 2 High; 1 Other Level
    4 Regular; 0 Special Education; 0 Vocational; 2 Alternative
    0 Magnet; 2 Charter; 2 Title I Eligible; 0 School-wide Title I
Students: 1,966　(51.1% male; 48.8% female)
    Individual Education Program: 308 (15.7%);
    English Language Learner: 0 (0.0%); Migrant: 0 (0.0%)
    Eligible for Free Lunch Program: n/a
    Eligible for Reduced-Price Lunch Program: n/a
Teachers: 136.4 (14.4 to 1)
Librarians/Media Specialists: 2.9 (677.9 to 1)
Guidance Counselors: 6.0 (327.7 to 1)
Current Spending: ($ per student per year):
    Total: $8,151; Instruction: $5,055; Support Services: $2,747

Oneida County

Rhinelander
315 S Oneida Ave • Rhinelander, WI 54501-3422
(715) 365-9750 • http://www.rhinelander.k12.wi.us
Grade Span: PK-12; **Agency Type:** 1
Schools: 11
    8 Primary; 1 Middle; 1 High; 0 Other Level
    10 Regular; 0 Special Education; 0 Vocational; 0 Alternative
    0 Magnet; 0 Charter; 5 Title I Eligible; 0 School-wide Title I
Students: 3,146　(51.3% male; 48.6% female)
    Individual Education Program: 404 (12.8%);
    English Language Learner: 0 (0.0%); Migrant: 0 (0.0%)
    Eligible for Free Lunch Program: n/a
    Eligible for Reduced-Price Lunch Program: n/a
Teachers: 212.5 (14.8 to 1)
Librarians/Media Specialists: 2.0 (1,573.0 to 1)
Guidance Counselors: 8.1 (388.4 to 1)
Current Spending: ($ per student per year):
    Total: $9,290; Instruction: $5,440; Support Services: $3,535
Enrollment, Drop-out Rates and Diploma Recipients by Race/Ethnicity

Category	Total	White	Black	Asian	AIAN	Hisp.
Enrollment (%)	100.0	95.2	1.1	0.9	1.8	1.0
Drop-out Rate (%)	3.0	2.8	0.0	0.0	37.5	0.0
H.S. Diplomas (#)	234	231	0	2	1	0

Outagamie County

Appleton Area
10 College Ave Ste 214 • Appleton, WI 54911
Mailing Address: PO Box 2019 • Appleton, WI 54912-2019
(920) 832-6126 • http://www.aasd.k12.wi.us
Grade Span: PK-12; **Agency Type:** 1
Schools: 33
    19 Primary; 6 Middle; 8 High; 0 Other Level
    24 Regular; 0 Special Education; 0 Vocational; 9 Alternative
    0 Magnet; 9 Charter; 10 Title I Eligible; 2 School-wide Title I
Students: 15,275　(51.8% male; 48.1% female)
    Individual Education Program: 2,182 (14.3%);
    English Language Learner: 1,292 (8.5%); Migrant: 0 (0.0%)
    Eligible for Free Lunch Program: n/a
    Eligible for Reduced-Price Lunch Program: n/a
Teachers: 948.1 (16.1 to 1)
Librarians/Media Specialists: 21.1 (723.9 to 1)
Guidance Counselors: 30.3 (504.1 to 1)
Current Spending: ($ per student per year):
    Total: $8,499; Instruction: $5,524; Support Services: $2,745
Enrollment, Drop-out Rates and Diploma Recipients by Race/Ethnicity

Category	Total	White	Black	Asian	AIAN	Hisp.
Enrollment (%)	100.0	82.4	2.4	10.2	0.9	4.2
Drop-out Rate (%)	0.8	0.6	1.5	1.6	3.8	3.7
H.S. Diplomas (#)	1,109	990	8	88	4	19

Freedom Area
N4021 County Rd E • Freedom, WI 54131-1008
Mailing Address: PO Box 1008 • Freedom, WI 54131-1008
(920) 788-7944 • http://www.freedomschools.k12.wi.us
Grade Span: PK-12; **Agency Type:** 1
Schools: 3
    1 Primary; 1 Middle; 1 High; 0 Other Level
    3 Regular; 0 Special Education; 0 Vocational; 0 Alternative
    0 Magnet; 0 Charter; 1 Title I Eligible; 0 School-wide Title I
Students: 1,557　(52.7% male; 47.2% female)
    Individual Education Program: 219 (14.1%);
    English Language Learner: 0 (0.0%); Migrant: 0 (0.0%)
    Eligible for Free Lunch Program: n/a
    Eligible for Reduced-Price Lunch Program: n/a
Teachers: 100.9 (15.4 to 1)
Librarians/Media Specialists: 2.0 (778.5 to 1)
Guidance Counselors: 3.5 (444.9 to 1)
Current Spending: ($ per student per year):
    Total: $7,563; Instruction: $4,725; Support Services: $2,571
Enrollment, Drop-out Rates and Diploma Recipients by Race/Ethnicity

Category	Total	White	Black	Asian	AIAN	Hisp.
Enrollment (%)	100.0	92.9	0.6	0.0	5.4	1.0
Drop-out Rate (%)	0.8	0.6	n/a	33.3	0.0	0.0
H.S. Diplomas (#)	147	141	0	0	6	0

Hortonville
246 N Olk St • Hortonville, WI 54944-0070
Mailing Address: PO Box 70 • Hortonville, WI 54944-0070
(920) 779-7900 • http://www.hasd.org
Grade Span: PK-12; Agency Type: 1
Schools: 5
  2 Primary; 2 Middle; 1 High; 0 Other Level
  5 Regular; 0 Special Education; 0 Vocational; 0 Alternative
  0 Magnet; 0 Charter; 1 Title I Eligible; 0 School-wide Title I
Students: 3,003 (52.2% male; 47.7% female)
  Individual Education Program: 411 (13.7%);
  English Language Learner: 0 (0.0%); Migrant: 0 (0.0%)
  Eligible for Free Lunch Program: n/a
  Eligible for Reduced-Price Lunch Program: n/a
Teachers: 206.1 (14.6 to 1)
Librarians/Media Specialists: 2.0 (1,501.5 to 1)
Guidance Counselors: 7.0 (429.0 to 1)
Current Spending: ($ per student per year):
  Total: $7,289; Instruction: $4,509; Support Services: $2,494
Enrollment, Drop-out Rates and Diploma Recipients by Race/Ethnicity

Category	Total	White	Black	Asian	AIAN	Hisp.
Enrollment (%)	100.0	95.3	0.3	1.7	0.6	2.1
Drop-out Rate (%)	0.2	0.2	0.0	0.0	0.0	0.0
H.S. Diplomas (#)	177	173	0	2	0	2

Kaukauna Area
112 Main Ave • Kaukauna, WI 54130-2437
(920) 766-6100 • http://kaukauna.k12.wi.us
Grade Span: PK-12; Agency Type: 1
Schools: 7
  5 Primary; 1 Middle; 1 High; 0 Other Level
  7 Regular; 0 Special Education; 0 Vocational; 0 Alternative
  0 Magnet; 0 Charter; 0 Title I Eligible; 0 School-wide Title I
Students: 3,727 (51.1% male; 48.8% female)
  Individual Education Program: 520 (14.0%);
  English Language Learner: 109 (2.9%); Migrant: 0 (0.0%)
  Eligible for Free Lunch Program: n/a
  Eligible for Reduced-Price Lunch Program: n/a
Teachers: 248.0 (15.0 to 1)
Librarians/Media Specialists: 4.0 (931.8 to 1)
Guidance Counselors: 7.8 (477.8 to 1)
Current Spending: ($ per student per year):
  Total: $8,196; Instruction: $5,267; Support Services: $2,689
Enrollment, Drop-out Rates and Diploma Recipients by Race/Ethnicity

Category	Total	White	Black	Asian	AIAN	Hisp.
Enrollment (%)	100.0	94.0	0.9	2.5	1.1	1.6
Drop-out Rate (%)	1.1	1.1	0.0	0.0	0.0	0.0
H.S. Diplomas (#)	246	241	0	3	1	1

Kimberly Area
217 E Kimberly Ave • Kimberly, WI 54136-1404
(920) 788-7900 • http://www.kimberly.k12.wi.us
Grade Span: PK-12; Agency Type: 1
Schools: 6
  4 Primary; 1 Middle; 1 High; 0 Other Level
  6 Regular; 0 Special Education; 0 Vocational; 0 Alternative
  0 Magnet; 0 Charter; 0 Title I Eligible; 0 School-wide Title I
Students: 3,750 (52.0% male; 48.0% female)
  Individual Education Program: 394 (10.5%);
  English Language Learner: 0 (0.0%); Migrant: 0 (0.0%)
  Eligible for Free Lunch Program: n/a
  Eligible for Reduced-Price Lunch Program: n/a
Teachers: 225.9 (16.6 to 1)
Librarians/Media Specialists: 2.8 (1,339.3 to 1)
Guidance Counselors: 8.8 (426.1 to 1)
Current Spending: ($ per student per year):
  Total: $7,232; Instruction: $4,360; Support Services: $2,696
Enrollment, Drop-out Rates and Diploma Recipients by Race/Ethnicity

Category	Total	White	Black	Asian	AIAN	Hisp.
Enrollment (%)	100.0	95.4	0.6	2.0	0.4	1.6
Drop-out Rate (%)	0.1	0.1	0.0	0.0	0.0	0.0
H.S. Diplomas (#)	181	179	0	2	0	0

Little Chute Area
325 Meulemans St Ste A • Little Chute, WI 54140-3300
(920) 788-7605
Grade Span: PK-12; Agency Type: 1
Schools: 3
  1 Primary; 1 Middle; 1 High; 0 Other Level
  3 Regular; 0 Special Education; 0 Vocational; 0 Alternative
  0 Magnet; 0 Charter; 1 Title I Eligible; 0 School-wide Title I
Students: 1,500 (54.4% male; 45.5% female)
  Individual Education Program: 186 (12.4%);
  English Language Learner: 0 (0.0%); Migrant: 0 (0.0%)
  Eligible for Free Lunch Program: n/a

Eligible for Reduced-Price Lunch Program: n/a
Teachers: 97.4 (15.4 to 1)
Librarians/Media Specialists: 2.3 (652.2 to 1)
Guidance Counselors: 4.6 (326.1 to 1)
Current Spending: ($ per student per year):
  Total: $7,414; Instruction: $4,748; Support Services: $2,453
Enrollment, Drop-out Rates and Diploma Recipients by Race/Ethnicity

Category	Total	White	Black	Asian	AIAN	Hisp.
Enrollment (%)	100.0	92.7	1.3	2.1	0.4	3.6
Drop-out Rate (%)	0.5	0.5	0.0	0.0	n/a	0.0
H.S. Diplomas (#)	127	124	0	1	0	2

Seymour Community
10 Circle Dr • Seymour, WI 54165-1678
(920) 833-2304 • http://www.seymour.k12.wi.us
Grade Span: PK-12; Agency Type: 1
Schools: 4
  2 Primary; 1 Middle; 1 High; 0 Other Level
  4 Regular; 0 Special Education; 0 Vocational; 0 Alternative
  0 Magnet; 0 Charter; 2 Title I Eligible; 0 School-wide Title I
Students: 2,472 (51.6% male; 48.3% female)
  Individual Education Program: 345 (14.0%);
  English Language Learner: 0 (0.0%); Migrant: 0 (0.0%)
  Eligible for Free Lunch Program: n/a
  Eligible for Reduced-Price Lunch Program: n/a
Teachers: 152.1 (16.3 to 1)
Librarians/Media Specialists: 4.0 (618.0 to 1)
Guidance Counselors: 6.0 (412.0 to 1)
Current Spending: ($ per student per year):
  Total: $7,668; Instruction: $4,678; Support Services: $2,684
Enrollment, Drop-out Rates and Diploma Recipients by Race/Ethnicity

Category	Total	White	Black	Asian	AIAN	Hisp.
Enrollment (%)	100.0	83.8	0.3	1.6	13.2	1.1
Drop-out Rate (%)	0.0	0.0	0.0	0.0	0.0	0.0
H.S. Diplomas (#)	190	171	0	1	17	1

Ozaukee County

Cedarburg
W68n611 Evergreen Blvd • Cedarburg, WI 53012-1899
(262) 376-6115 • http://www.cedarburg.k12.wi.us
Grade Span: PK-12; Agency Type: 1
Schools: 5
  3 Primary; 1 Middle; 1 High; 0 Other Level
  5 Regular; 0 Special Education; 0 Vocational; 0 Alternative
  0 Magnet; 0 Charter; 3 Title I Eligible; 0 School-wide Title I
Students: 3,119 (51.7% male; 48.2% female)
  Individual Education Program: 343 (11.0%);
  English Language Learner: 0 (0.0%); Migrant: 0 (0.0%)
  Eligible for Free Lunch Program: n/a
  Eligible for Reduced-Price Lunch Program: n/a
Teachers: 188.0 (16.6 to 1)
Librarians/Media Specialists: 5.0 (623.8 to 1)
Guidance Counselors: 9.6 (324.9 to 1)
Current Spending: ($ per student per year):
  Total: $8,786; Instruction: $5,350; Support Services: $3,235
Enrollment, Drop-out Rates and Diploma Recipients by Race/Ethnicity

Category	Total	White	Black	Asian	AIAN	Hisp.
Enrollment (%)	100.0	97.6	0.6	1.0	0.1	0.8
Drop-out Rate (%)	0.3	0.3	0.0	0.0	0.0	0.0
H.S. Diplomas (#)	222	219	1	1	0	1

Grafton
1900 Washington St • Grafton, WI 53024-2198
(262) 376-5440 • http://www.grafton.k12.wi.us
Grade Span: PK-12; Agency Type: 1
Schools: 5
  3 Primary; 1 Middle; 1 High; 0 Other Level
  5 Regular; 0 Special Education; 0 Vocational; 0 Alternative
  0 Magnet; 0 Charter; 3 Title I Eligible; 0 School-wide Title I
Students: 2,003 (52.9% male; 47.0% female)
  Individual Education Program: 287 (14.3%);
  English Language Learner: 0 (0.0%); Migrant: 0 (0.0%)
  Eligible for Free Lunch Program: n/a
  Eligible for Reduced-Price Lunch Program: n/a
Teachers: 137.8 (14.5 to 1)
Librarians/Media Specialists: 5.0 (400.6 to 1)
Guidance Counselors: 5.0 (400.6 to 1)
Current Spending: ($ per student per year):
  Total: $9,439; Instruction: $6,057; Support Services: $3,174
Enrollment, Drop-out Rates and Diploma Recipients by Race/Ethnicity

Category	Total	White	Black	Asian	AIAN	Hisp.
Enrollment (%)	100.0	96.7	0.8	1.1	0.1	1.3
Drop-out Rate (%)	0.4	0.4	0.0	0.0	n/a	0.0
H.S. Diplomas (#)	185	178	0	1	0	6

Mequon-Thiensville
5000 W Mequon Rd • Mequon, WI 53092-2044
(262) 238-8503 • http://www.mtsd.k12.wi.us
Grade Span: PK-12; **Agency Type:** 1
Schools: 7
   4 Primary; 2 Middle; 1 High; 0 Other Level
   7 Regular; 0 Special Education; 0 Vocational; 0 Alternative
   0 Magnet; 0 Charter; 4 Title I Eligible; 0 School-wide Title I
Students: 4,120   (52.6% male; 47.3% female)
   Individual Education Program: 463 (11.2%);
   English Language Learner: 0 (0.0%); Migrant: 0 (0.0%)
   Eligible for Free Lunch Program: n/a
   Eligible for Reduced-Price Lunch Program: n/a
Teachers: 264.4 (15.6 to 1)
Librarians/Media Specialists: 4.5 (915.6 to 1)
Guidance Counselors: 11.0 (374.5 to 1)
Current Spending: ($ per student per year):
   Total: $9,670; Instruction: $6,052; Support Services: $3,324
Enrollment, Drop-out Rates and Diploma Recipients by Race/Ethnicity

Category	Total	White	Black	Asian	AIAN	Hisp.
Enrollment (%)	100.0	88.3	6.0	4.1	0.2	1.5
Drop-out Rate (%)	0.0	0.0	0.0	0.0	0.0	0.0
H.S. Diplomas (#)	356	326	7	18	1	4

Port Washington-Saukville
100 W Monroe St • Port Washington, WI 53074-1267
(262) 268-6005 • http://www.pwssd.k12.wi.us
Grade Span: PK-12; **Agency Type:** 1
Schools: 5
   3 Primary; 1 Middle; 1 High; 0 Other Level
   5 Regular; 0 Special Education; 0 Vocational; 0 Alternative
   0 Magnet; 0 Charter; 3 Title I Eligible; 0 School-wide Title I
Students: 2,628   (53.0% male; 46.9% female)
   Individual Education Program: 359 (13.7%);
   English Language Learner: 0 (0.0%); Migrant: 0 (0.0%)
   Eligible for Free Lunch Program: n/a
   Eligible for Reduced-Price Lunch Program: n/a
Teachers: 166.1 (15.8 to 1)
Librarians/Media Specialists: 2.0 (1,314.0 to 1)
Guidance Counselors: 7.0 (375.4 to 1)
Current Spending: ($ per student per year):
   Total: $9,492; Instruction: $5,951; Support Services: $3,240
Enrollment, Drop-out Rates and Diploma Recipients by Race/Ethnicity

Category	Total	White	Black	Asian	AIAN	Hisp.
Enrollment (%)	100.0	93.3	2.7	0.6	0.6	2.7
Drop-out Rate (%)	0.9	0.9	0.0	0.0	0.0	0.0
H.S. Diplomas (#)	186	184	1	1	0	0

Pierce County

Ellsworth Community
300 Hillcrest St • Ellsworth, WI 54011-1500
Mailing Address: PO Box 1500 • Ellsworth, WI 54011-1500
(715) 273-3900 • http://www.ellsworth.k12.wi.us
Grade Span: PK-12; **Agency Type:** 1
Schools: 6
   4 Primary; 1 Middle; 1 High; 0 Other Level
   6 Regular; 0 Special Education; 0 Vocational; 0 Alternative
   0 Magnet; 0 Charter; 4 Title I Eligible; 0 School-wide Title I
Students: 1,746   (52.5% male; 47.4% female)
   Individual Education Program: 223 (12.8%);
   English Language Learner: 0 (0.0%); Migrant: 0 (0.0%)
   Eligible for Free Lunch Program: n/a
   Eligible for Reduced-Price Lunch Program: n/a
Teachers: 120.8 (14.5 to 1)
Librarians/Media Specialists: 2.5 (698.4 to 1)
Guidance Counselors: 4.6 (379.6 to 1)
Current Spending: ($ per student per year):
   Total: $9,018; Instruction: $5,671; Support Services: $2,927
Enrollment, Drop-out Rates and Diploma Recipients by Race/Ethnicity

Category	Total	White	Black	Asian	AIAN	Hisp.
Enrollment (%)	100.0	97.0	0.5	0.9	0.7	0.9
Drop-out Rate (%)	1.0	1.1	0.0	0.0	0.0	0.0
H.S. Diplomas (#)	156	149	1	3	2	1

River Falls
852 E Division St • River Falls, WI 54022-2599
(715) 425-1800 • http://www.rfsd.k12.wi.us
Grade Span: PK-12; **Agency Type:** 1
Schools: 7
   4 Primary; 1 Middle; 2 High; 0 Other Level
   5 Regular; 0 Special Education; 0 Vocational; 2 Alternative
   0 Magnet; 2 Charter; 4 Title I Eligible; 0 School-wide Title I
Students: 2,984   (52.0% male; 47.9% female)
   Individual Education Program: 366 (12.3%);

English Language Learner: 0 (0.0%); Migrant: 0 (0.0%)
   Eligible for Free Lunch Program: n/a
   Eligible for Reduced-Price Lunch Program: n/a
Teachers: 191.8 (15.6 to 1)
Librarians/Media Specialists: 5.0 (596.8 to 1)
Guidance Counselors: 7.5 (397.9 to 1)
Current Spending: ($ per student per year):
   Total: $8,320; Instruction: $5,389; Support Services: $2,569
Enrollment, Drop-out Rates and Diploma Recipients by Race/Ethnicity

Category	Total	White	Black	Asian	AIAN	Hisp.
Enrollment (%)	100.0	94.1	1.9	1.5	1.0	1.4
Drop-out Rate (%)	0.5	0.5	0.0	0.0	0.0	0.0
H.S. Diplomas (#)	217	208	4	3	0	2

Polk County

Amery
543 Minneapolis Ave S • Amery, WI 54001-1522
(715) 268-0272 • http://www.amerysd.k12.wi.us
Grade Span: PK-12; **Agency Type:** 1
Schools: 4
   2 Primary; 1 Middle; 1 High; 0 Other Level
   4 Regular; 0 Special Education; 0 Vocational; 0 Alternative
   0 Magnet; 0 Charter; 2 Title I Eligible; 0 School-wide Title I
Students: 1,856   (50.8% male; 49.1% female)
   Individual Education Program: 263 (14.2%);
   English Language Learner: 0 (0.0%); Migrant: 0 (0.0%)
   Eligible for Free Lunch Program: n/a
   Eligible for Reduced-Price Lunch Program: n/a
Teachers: 124.5 (14.9 to 1)
Librarians/Media Specialists: 2.5 (742.4 to 1)
Guidance Counselors: 4.5 (412.4 to 1)
Current Spending: ($ per student per year):
   Total: $8,323; Instruction: $5,158; Support Services: $2,755
Enrollment, Drop-out Rates and Diploma Recipients by Race/Ethnicity

Category	Total	White	Black	Asian	AIAN	Hisp.
Enrollment (%)	100.0	96.0	0.6	0.4	1.5	1.5
Drop-out Rate (%)	0.0	0.0	0.0	0.0	0.0	0.0
H.S. Diplomas (#)	147	141	0	0	4	2

Osceola
331 Middle School Dr • Osceola, WI 54020-0128
Mailing Address: PO Box 128 • Osceola, WI 54020-0128
(715) 294-4140 • http://www.osceola.k12.wi.us
Grade Span: PK-12; **Agency Type:** 1
Schools: 4
   2 Primary; 1 Middle; 1 High; 0 Other Level
   4 Regular; 0 Special Education; 0 Vocational; 0 Alternative
   0 Magnet; 0 Charter; 2 Title I Eligible; 0 School-wide Title I
Students: 1,780   (49.7% male; 50.2% female)
   Individual Education Program: 195 (11.0%);
   English Language Learner: 0 (0.0%); Migrant: 2 (0.1%)
   Eligible for Free Lunch Program: n/a
   Eligible for Reduced-Price Lunch Program: n/a
Teachers: 105.4 (16.9 to 1)
Librarians/Media Specialists: 2.0 (890.0 to 1)
Guidance Counselors: 4.0 (445.0 to 1)
Current Spending: ($ per student per year):
   Total: $7,659; Instruction: $4,363; Support Services: $2,984
Enrollment, Drop-out Rates and Diploma Recipients by Race/Ethnicity

Category	Total	White	Black	Asian	AIAN	Hisp.
Enrollment (%)	100.0	95.6	1.0	1.1	0.7	1.7
Drop-out Rate (%)	0.9	0.9	0.0	0.0	0.0	0.0
H.S. Diplomas (#)	139	138	0	1	0	0

Portage County

Stevens Point Area
1900 Polk St • Stevens Point, WI 54481-5875
(715) 345-5444 • http://www.wisp.k12.wi.us
Grade Span: PK-12; **Agency Type:** 1
Schools: 19
   11 Primary; 3 Middle; 5 High; 0 Other Level
   10 Regular; 1 Special Education; 0 Vocational; 8 Alternative
   0 Magnet; 6 Charter; 6 Title I Eligible; 0 School-wide Title I
Students: 7,592   (51.6% male; 48.3% female)
   Individual Education Program: 1,006 (13.3%);
   English Language Learner: 331 (4.4%); Migrant: 0 (0.0%)
   Eligible for Free Lunch Program: n/a
   Eligible for Reduced-Price Lunch Program: n/a
Teachers: 482.7 (15.7 to 1)
Librarians/Media Specialists: 7.0 (1,084.6 to 1)
Guidance Counselors: 8.0 (949.0 to 1)
Current Spending: ($ per student per year):
   Total: $8,989; Instruction: $5,862; Support Services: $2,879

Enrollment, Drop-out Rates and Diploma Recipients by Race/Ethnicity

Category	Total	White	Black	Asian	AIAN	Hisp.
Enrollment (%)	100.0	87.2	1.0	7.8	0.6	3.3
Drop-out Rate (%)	2.0	2.0	0.0	3.4	0.0	0.0
H.S. Diplomas (#)	676	626	6	33	5	6

Racine County

Burlington Area
100 N Kane St • Burlington, WI 53105-1896
(262) 763-0210 • http://basd.k12.wi.us
Grade Span: PK-12; **Agency Type:** 1
Schools: 8
  5 Primary; 2 Middle; 1 High; 0 Other Level
  8 Regular; 0 Special Education; 0 Vocational; 0 Alternative
  0 Magnet; 0 Charter; 3 Title I Eligible; 0 School-wide Title I
Students: 3,650 (51.2% male; 48.7% female)
  Individual Education Program: 503 (13.8%);
  English Language Learner: 80 (2.2%); Migrant: 0 (0.0%)
  Eligible for Free Lunch Program: n/a
  Eligible for Reduced-Price Lunch Program: n/a
Teachers: 239.8 (15.2 to 1)
Librarians/Media Specialists: 5.1 (715.7 to 1)
Guidance Counselors: 9.4 (388.3 to 1)
Current Spending: ($ per student per year):
  Total: $7,354; Instruction: $4,635; Support Services: $2,424
Enrollment, Drop-out Rates and Diploma Recipients by Race/Ethnicity

Category	Total	White	Black	Asian	AIAN	Hisp.
Enrollment (%)	100.0	92.4	1.1	0.8	0.2	5.5
Drop-out Rate (%)	0.7	0.7	12.5	0.0	0.0	0.0
H.S. Diplomas (#)	248	230	1	3	0	14

Racine
2220 Northwestern Ave • Racine, WI 53404-2597
(262) 631-7064 • http://www.racine.k12.wi.us
Grade Span: PK-12; **Agency Type:** 1
Schools: 35
  23 Primary; 6 Middle; 4 High; 2 Other Level
  30 Regular; 0 Special Education; 0 Vocational; 5 Alternative
  0 Magnet; 2 Charter; 13 Title I Eligible; 12 School-wide Title I
Students: 21,457 (51.6% male; 48.3% female)
  Individual Education Program: 3,691 (17.2%);
  English Language Learner: 1,046 (4.9%); Migrant: 7 (<0.1%)
  Eligible for Free Lunch Program: n/a
  Eligible for Reduced-Price Lunch Program: n/a
Teachers: 1,323.9 (16.2 to 1)
Librarians/Media Specialists: 31.1 (689.9 to 1)
Guidance Counselors: 39.5 (543.2 to 1)
Current Spending: ($ per student per year):
  Total: $9,216; Instruction: $5,904; Support Services: $3,039
Enrollment, Drop-out Rates and Diploma Recipients by Race/Ethnicity

Category	Total	White	Black	Asian	AIAN	Hisp.
Enrollment (%)	100.0	56.3	26.3	1.3	0.3	15.9
Drop-out Rate (%)	5.2	3.6	9.5	0.0	4.8	6.6
H.S. Diplomas (#)	1,163	890	170	10	0	93

Waterford Graded J1
819 W Main St • Waterford, WI 53185-4073
(262) 514-8250
Grade Span: KG-08; **Agency Type:** 1
Schools: 4
  3 Primary; 1 Middle; 0 High; 0 Other Level
  4 Regular; 0 Special Education; 0 Vocational; 0 Alternative
  0 Magnet; 0 Charter; 0 Title I Eligible; 0 School-wide Title I
Students: 1,514 (53.3% male; 46.6% female)
  Individual Education Program: 214 (14.1%);
  English Language Learner: 0 (0.0%); Migrant: 0 (0.0%)
  Eligible for Free Lunch Program: n/a
  Eligible for Reduced-Price Lunch Program: n/a
Teachers: 100.3 (15.1 to 1)
Librarians/Media Specialists: 2.5 (605.6 to 1)
Guidance Counselors: 3.0 (504.7 to 1)
Current Spending: ($ per student per year):
  Total: $6,992; Instruction: $4,013; Support Services: $2,737
Enrollment, Drop-out Rates and Diploma Recipients by Race/Ethnicity

Category	Total	White	Black	Asian	AIAN	Hisp.
Enrollment (%)	100.0	96.7	0.2	0.5	0.4	2.2
Drop-out Rate (%)	n/a	n/a	n/a	n/a	n/a	n/a
H.S. Diplomas (#)	n/a	n/a	n/a	n/a	n/a	n/a

Richland County

Richland
26221 Starlight Ln Ste A • Richland Center, WI 53581-4048
(608) 647-6106 • http://www.richland.k12.wi.us
Grade Span: PK-12; **Agency Type:** 1
Schools: 6
  3 Primary; 1 Middle; 2 High; 0 Other Level
  5 Regular; 0 Special Education; 0 Vocational; 1 Alternative
  0 Magnet; 1 Charter; 3 Title I Eligible; 0 School-wide Title I
Students: 1,514 (50.0% male; 49.9% female)
  Individual Education Program: 339 (22.4%);
  English Language Learner: 0 (0.0%); Migrant: 0 (0.0%)
  Eligible for Free Lunch Program: n/a
  Eligible for Reduced-Price Lunch Program: n/a
Teachers: 111.7 (13.6 to 1)
Librarians/Media Specialists: 3.0 (504.7 to 1)
Guidance Counselors: 6.0 (252.3 to 1)
Current Spending: ($ per student per year):
  Total: $9,886; Instruction: $5,890; Support Services: $3,591
Enrollment, Drop-out Rates and Diploma Recipients by Race/Ethnicity

Category	Total	White	Black	Asian	AIAN	Hisp.
Enrollment (%)	100.0	96.8	1.1	0.3	0.5	1.3
Drop-out Rate (%)	1.0	1.0	0.0	0.0	n/a	0.0
H.S. Diplomas (#)	143	142	0	0	0	1

Rock County

Beloit
1633 Keeler Ave • Beloit, WI 53511-4799
(608) 361-4017 • http://www.sdb.k12.wi.us
Grade Span: PK-12; **Agency Type:** 1
Schools: 17
  13 Primary; 3 Middle; 1 High; 0 Other Level
  16 Regular; 0 Special Education; 0 Vocational; 1 Alternative
  0 Magnet; 1 Charter; 9 Title I Eligible; 9 School-wide Title I
Students: 6,941 (51.2% male; 48.7% female)
  Individual Education Program: 1,308 (18.8%);
  English Language Learner: 529 (7.6%); Migrant: 0 (0.0%)
  Eligible for Free Lunch Program: n/a
  Eligible for Reduced-Price Lunch Program: n/a
Teachers: 471.2 (14.7 to 1)
Librarians/Media Specialists: 9.5 (730.6 to 1)
Guidance Counselors: 11.8 (588.2 to 1)
Current Spending: ($ per student per year):
  Total: $9,411; Instruction: $5,965; Support Services: $3,162
Enrollment, Drop-out Rates and Diploma Recipients by Race/Ethnicity

Category	Total	White	Black	Asian	AIAN	Hisp.
Enrollment (%)	100.0	55.0	27.3	1.0	0.4	16.3
Drop-out Rate (%)	3.6	2.7	4.7	3.7	50.0	5.8
H.S. Diplomas (#)	357	237	90	9	0	21

Edgerton
200 Elm High Dr • Edgerton, WI 53534-1498
(608) 884-9402 • http://www.edgerton.k12.wi.us
Grade Span: PK-12; **Agency Type:** 1
Schools: 4
  2 Primary; 1 Middle; 1 High; 0 Other Level
  4 Regular; 0 Special Education; 0 Vocational; 0 Alternative
  0 Magnet; 0 Charter; 2 Title I Eligible; 0 School-wide Title I
Students: 1,855 (52.4% male; 47.5% female)
  Individual Education Program: 346 (18.7%);
  English Language Learner: 0 (0.0%); Migrant: 0 (0.0%)
  Eligible for Free Lunch Program: n/a
  Eligible for Reduced-Price Lunch Program: n/a
Teachers: 124.9 (14.9 to 1)
Librarians/Media Specialists: 3.0 (618.3 to 1)
Guidance Counselors: 4.0 (463.8 to 1)
Current Spending: ($ per student per year):
  Total: $8,793; Instruction: $5,109; Support Services: $3,499
Enrollment, Drop-out Rates and Diploma Recipients by Race/Ethnicity

Category	Total	White	Black	Asian	AIAN	Hisp.
Enrollment (%)	100.0	94.9	0.6	0.9	0.4	3.1
Drop-out Rate (%)	0.0	0.0	0.0	0.0	0.0	0.0
H.S. Diplomas (#)	137	135	0	1	0	1

Evansville Community
340 Fair St • Evansville, WI 53536-1299
(608) 882-5224 • http://evansvilleschools.org
Grade Span: PK-12; **Agency Type:** 1
Schools: 4
  2 Primary; 1 Middle; 1 High; 0 Other Level
  4 Regular; 0 Special Education; 0 Vocational; 0 Alternative
  0 Magnet; 0 Charter; 3 Title I Eligible; 0 School-wide Title I
Students: 1,668 (51.7% male; 48.2% female)

Individual Education Program: 246 (14.7%);
English Language Learner: 29 (1.7%); Migrant: 0 (0.0%)
Eligible for Free Lunch Program: n/a
Eligible for Reduced-Price Lunch Program: n/a
Teachers: 120.2 (13.9 to 1)
Librarians/Media Specialists: 3.0 (556.0 to 1)
Guidance Counselors: 3.5 (476.6 to 1)
Current Spending: ($ per student per year):
Total: $8,379; Instruction: $5,279; Support Services: $2,819
Enrollment, Drop-out Rates and Diploma Recipients by Race/Ethnicity

Category	Total	White	Black	Asian	AIAN	Hisp.
Enrollment (%)	100.0	94.7	0.9	1.0	0.4	3.1
Drop-out Rate (%)	1.3	0.9	0.0	0.0	0.0	20.0
H.S. Diplomas (#)	94	91	0	1	1	1

Janesville
527 S Franklin St • Janesville, WI 53545-4823
(608) 743-5050 • http://www.inwave.com/schools/jps
Grade Span: PK-12; **Agency Type:** 1
Schools: 18
12 Primary; 3 Middle; 3 High; 0 Other Level
17 Regular; 0 Special Education; 0 Vocational; 1 Alternative
0 Magnet; 1 Charter; 9 Title I Eligible; 1 School-wide Title I
Students: 10,667   (51.8% male; 48.1% female)
Individual Education Program: 1,776 (16.6%);
English Language Learner: 294 (2.8%); Migrant: 0 (0.0%)
Eligible for Free Lunch Program: n/a
Eligible for Reduced-Price Lunch Program: n/a
Teachers: 765.5 (13.9 to 1)
Librarians/Media Specialists: 20.5 (520.3 to 1)
Guidance Counselors: 26.0 (410.3 to 1)
Current Spending: ($ per student per year):
Total: $8,490; Instruction: $5,511; Support Services: $2,762
Enrollment, Drop-out Rates and Diploma Recipients by Race/Ethnicity

Category	Total	White	Black	Asian	AIAN	Hisp.
Enrollment (%)	100.0	88.5	4.6	1.9	0.5	4.5
Drop-out Rate (%)	1.8	1.7	4.4	0.0	0.0	6.3
H.S. Diplomas (#)	673	646	6	9	2	10

Milton
430 E High St Ste 2 • Milton, WI 53563-1502
(608) 868-9200 • http://www.milton.k12.wi.us
Grade Span: PK-12; **Agency Type:** 1
Schools: 6
3 Primary; 1 Middle; 1 High; 1 Other Level
6 Regular; 0 Special Education; 0 Vocational; 0 Alternative
0 Magnet; 0 Charter; 3 Title I Eligible; 0 School-wide Title I
Students: 2,953   (53.1% male; 46.8% female)
Individual Education Program: 301 (10.2%);
English Language Learner: 0 (0.0%); Migrant: 0 (0.0%)
Eligible for Free Lunch Program: n/a
Eligible for Reduced-Price Lunch Program: n/a
Teachers: 186.2 (15.9 to 1)
Librarians/Media Specialists: 5.0 (590.6 to 1)
Guidance Counselors: 7.5 (393.7 to 1)
Current Spending: ($ per student per year):
Total: $7,727; Instruction: $4,963; Support Services: $2,475
Enrollment, Drop-out Rates and Diploma Recipients by Race/Ethnicity

Category	Total	White	Black	Asian	AIAN	Hisp.
Enrollment (%)	100.0	96.4	0.8	1.3	0.2	1.3
Drop-out Rate (%)	2.0	1.9	0.0	0.0	0.0	12.5
H.S. Diplomas (#)	199	195	1	3	0	0

Sauk County

Baraboo
101 2nd Ave • Baraboo, WI 53913-2494
(608) 355-3950 • http://www.baraboo.k12.wi.us
Grade Span: PK-12; **Agency Type:** 1
Schools: 8
6 Primary; 1 Middle; 1 High; 0 Other Level
8 Regular; 0 Special Education; 0 Vocational; 0 Alternative
0 Magnet; 0 Charter; 6 Title I Eligible; 0 School-wide Title I
Students: 3,013   (51.0% male; 48.9% female)
Individual Education Program: 455 (15.1%);
English Language Learner: 0 (0.0%); Migrant: 0 (0.0%)
Eligible for Free Lunch Program: n/a
Eligible for Reduced-Price Lunch Program: n/a
Teachers: 200.1 (15.1 to 1)
Librarians/Media Specialists: 3.0 (1,004.3 to 1)
Guidance Counselors: 7.6 (396.4 to 1)
Current Spending: ($ per student per year):
Total: $7,960; Instruction: $4,967; Support Services: $2,688

Enrollment, Drop-out Rates and Diploma Recipients by Race/Ethnicity

Category	Total	White	Black	Asian	AIAN	Hisp.
Enrollment (%)	100.0	92.2	1.5	1.3	2.6	2.4
Drop-out Rate (%)	2.2	1.9	20.0	0.0	4.0	18.2
H.S. Diplomas (#)	214	207	0	0	5	2

Reedsburg
710 N Webb Ave • Reedsburg, WI 53959-1198
(608) 524-2401 • http://www.rsd.k12.wi.us
Grade Span: PK-12; **Agency Type:** 1
Schools: 8
6 Primary; 1 Middle; 1 High; 0 Other Level
8 Regular; 0 Special Education; 0 Vocational; 0 Alternative
0 Magnet; 0 Charter; 5 Title I Eligible; 0 School-wide Title I
Students: 2,469   (50.9% male; 49.0% female)
Individual Education Program: 393 (15.9%);
English Language Learner: 0 (0.0%); Migrant: 0 (0.0%)
Eligible for Free Lunch Program: n/a
Eligible for Reduced-Price Lunch Program: n/a
Teachers: 172.3 (14.3 to 1)
Librarians/Media Specialists: 3.0 (823.0 to 1)
Guidance Counselors: 5.0 (493.8 to 1)
Current Spending: ($ per student per year):
Total: $8,321; Instruction: $5,212; Support Services: $2,696
Enrollment, Drop-out Rates and Diploma Recipients by Race/Ethnicity

Category	Total	White	Black	Asian	AIAN	Hisp.
Enrollment (%)	100.0	96.1	0.4	0.5	1.1	1.9
Drop-out Rate (%)	1.4	1.4	0.0	0.0	0.0	0.0
H.S. Diplomas (#)	173	171	0	1	0	1

Sauk Prairie
213 Maple St • Sauk City, WI 53583-1097
(608) 643-5981 • http://www.saukpr.k12.wi.us
Grade Span: PK-12; **Agency Type:** 1
Schools: 7
5 Primary; 1 Middle; 1 High; 0 Other Level
7 Regular; 0 Special Education; 0 Vocational; 0 Alternative
0 Magnet; 0 Charter; 5 Title I Eligible; 1 School-wide Title I
Students: 2,639   (50.7% male; 49.2% female)
Individual Education Program: 406 (15.4%);
English Language Learner: 100 (3.8%); Migrant: 0 (0.0%)
Eligible for Free Lunch Program: n/a
Eligible for Reduced-Price Lunch Program: n/a
Teachers: 197.7 (13.3 to 1)
Librarians/Media Specialists: 4.5 (586.4 to 1)
Guidance Counselors: 6.3 (418.9 to 1)
Current Spending: ($ per student per year):
Total: $8,836; Instruction: $5,439; Support Services: $3,036
Enrollment, Drop-out Rates and Diploma Recipients by Race/Ethnicity

Category	Total	White	Black	Asian	AIAN	Hisp.
Enrollment (%)	100.0	92.2	0.6	0.9	0.5	5.9
Drop-out Rate (%)	1.3	1.2	0.0	0.0	0.0	5.0
H.S. Diplomas (#)	159	156	1	1	1	0

Wisconsin Dells
811 County Rd H • Wisconsin Dells, WI 53965-9636
(608) 254-7769 • http://www.sdwd.k12.wi.us/
Grade Span: PK-12; **Agency Type:** 1
Schools: 6
3 Primary; 1 Middle; 2 High; 0 Other Level
5 Regular; 0 Special Education; 0 Vocational; 1 Alternative
0 Magnet; 1 Charter; 2 Title I Eligible; 0 School-wide Title I
Students: 1,724   (48.6% male; 51.3% female)
Individual Education Program: 218 (12.6%);
English Language Learner: 0 (0.0%); Migrant: 1 (0.1%)
Eligible for Free Lunch Program: n/a
Eligible for Reduced-Price Lunch Program: n/a
Teachers: 122.7 (14.1 to 1)
Librarians/Media Specialists: 1.0 (1,724.0 to 1)
Guidance Counselors: 5.0 (344.8 to 1)
Current Spending: ($ per student per year):
Total: $8,178; Instruction: $5,085; Support Services: $2,745
Enrollment, Drop-out Rates and Diploma Recipients by Race/Ethnicity

Category	Total	White	Black	Asian	AIAN	Hisp.
Enrollment (%)	100.0	86.5	1.4	0.3	8.3	3.5
Drop-out Rate (%)	2.0	2.2	0.0	0.0	0.0	5.6
H.S. Diplomas (#)	118	107	2	3	4	2

Sawyer County

Hayward Community
15930 W 5th St • Hayward, WI 54843-0860
Mailing Address: PO Box 860 • Hayward, WI 54843-0860
(715) 634-2619 • http://www.hayward.k12.wi.us
Grade Span: PK-12; **Agency Type:** 1
Schools: 8
    4 Primary; 1 Middle; 1 High; 2 Other Level
    5 Regular; 0 Special Education; 0 Vocational; 3 Alternative
    0 Magnet; 2 Charter; 4 Title I Eligible; 4 School-wide Title I
Students: 2,005 (51.2% male; 48.7% female)
    Individual Education Program: 294 (14.7%);
    English Language Learner: 0 (0.0%); Migrant: 0 (0.0%)
    Eligible for Free Lunch Program: n/a
    Eligible for Reduced-Price Lunch Program: n/a
Teachers: 151.2 (13.3 to 1)
Librarians/Media Specialists: 2.9 (691.4 to 1)
Guidance Counselors: 4.0 (501.3 to 1)
Current Spending: ($ per student per year):
    Total: $8,895; Instruction: $4,892; Support Services: $3,637
Enrollment, Drop-out Rates and Diploma Recipients by Race/Ethnicity

Category	Total	White	Black	Asian	AIAN	Hisp.
Enrollment (%)	100.0	74.2	0.4	0.6	24.2	0.6
Drop-out Rate (%)	2.2	1.6	0.0	0.0	4.0	33.3
H.S. Diplomas (#)	109	92	0	0	17	0

Shawano County

Shawano-Gresham
218 County Rd B • Shawano, WI 54166-7054
(715) 526-3194 • http://www.sgsd.k12.wi.us
Grade Span: PK-12; **Agency Type:** 1
Schools: 6
    3 Primary; 1 Middle; 2 High; 0 Other Level
    6 Regular; 0 Special Education; 0 Vocational; 0 Alternative
    0 Magnet; 0 Charter; 3 Title I Eligible; 0 School-wide Title I
Students: 2,947 (51.7% male; 48.2% female)
    Individual Education Program: 471 (16.0%);
    English Language Learner: 0 (0.0%); Migrant: 0 (0.0%)
    Eligible for Free Lunch Program: n/a
    Eligible for Reduced-Price Lunch Program: n/a
Teachers: 198.1 (14.9 to 1)
Librarians/Media Specialists: 4.0 (736.8 to 1)
Guidance Counselors: 7.7 (382.7 to 1)
Current Spending: ($ per student per year):
    Total: $8,033; Instruction: $5,113; Support Services: $2,627
Enrollment, Drop-out Rates and Diploma Recipients by Race/Ethnicity

Category	Total	White	Black	Asian	AIAN	Hisp.
Enrollment (%)	100.0	80.8	0.6	0.6	15.7	2.3
Drop-out Rate (%)	1.5	1.5	0.0	0.0	0.6	8.0
H.S. Diplomas (#)	187	160	0	1	24	2

Sheboygan County

Plymouth
125 S Highland Ave • Plymouth, WI 53073-2599
(920) 892-2661 • http://www.plymouth.k12.wi.us
Grade Span: PK-12; **Agency Type:** 1
Schools: 7
    5 Primary; 1 Middle; 1 High; 0 Other Level
    7 Regular; 0 Special Education; 0 Vocational; 0 Alternative
    0 Magnet; 0 Charter; 4 Title I Eligible; 0 School-wide Title I
Students: 2,474 (50.7% male; 49.2% female)
    Individual Education Program: 369 (14.9%);
    English Language Learner: 3 (0.1%); Migrant: 0 (0.0%)
    Eligible for Free Lunch Program: n/a
    Eligible for Reduced-Price Lunch Program: n/a
Teachers: 166.3 (14.9 to 1)
Librarians/Media Specialists: 2.8 (883.6 to 1)
Guidance Counselors: 7.5 (329.9 to 1)
Current Spending: ($ per student per year):
    Total: $7,973; Instruction: $4,774; Support Services: $2,893
Enrollment, Drop-out Rates and Diploma Recipients by Race/Ethnicity

Category	Total	White	Black	Asian	AIAN	Hisp.
Enrollment (%)	100.0	96.3	0.2	0.8	0.8	1.9
Drop-out Rate (%)	1.4	1.3	0.0	0.0	0.0	14.3
H.S. Diplomas (#)	202	195	0	3	2	2

Sheboygan Area
830 Virginia Ave • Sheboygan, WI 53081-4427
(920) 459-3511 • http://www.sheboygan.k12.wi.us
Grade Span: PK-12; **Agency Type:** 1
Schools: 18
    13 Primary; 3 Middle; 2 High; 0 Other Level
    18 Regular; 0 Special Education; 0 Vocational; 0 Alternative
    0 Magnet; 0 Charter; 6 Title I Eligible; 4 School-wide Title I
Students: 10,231 (50.6% male; 49.3% female)
    Individual Education Program: 1,682 (16.4%);
    English Language Learner: 1,976 (19.3%); Migrant: 0 (0.0%)
    Eligible for Free Lunch Program: n/a
    Eligible for Reduced-Price Lunch Program: n/a
Teachers: 719.5 (14.2 to 1)
Librarians/Media Specialists: 13.6 (752.3 to 1)
Guidance Counselors: 24.2 (422.8 to 1)
Current Spending: ($ per student per year):
    Total: $8,866; Instruction: $5,915; Support Services: $2,715
Enrollment, Drop-out Rates and Diploma Recipients by Race/Ethnicity

Category	Total	White	Black	Asian	AIAN	Hisp.
Enrollment (%)	100.0	70.2	2.2	16.6	0.6	10.4
Drop-out Rate (%)	1.9	1.4	7.1	3.9	0.0	2.8
H.S. Diplomas (#)	768	597	7	111	6	47

Sheboygan Falls
220 Amherst Ave • Sheboygan Falls, WI 53085-1799
(920) 467-7893 • http://www.sheboyganfalls.k12.wi.us
Grade Span: PK-12; **Agency Type:** 1
Schools: 3
    1 Primary; 1 Middle; 1 High; 0 Other Level
    3 Regular; 0 Special Education; 0 Vocational; 0 Alternative
    0 Magnet; 0 Charter; 2 Title I Eligible; 0 School-wide Title I
Students: 1,689 (52.1% male; 47.8% female)
    Individual Education Program: 215 (12.7%);
    English Language Learner: 0 (0.0%); Migrant: 0 (0.0%)
    Eligible for Free Lunch Program: n/a
    Eligible for Reduced-Price Lunch Program: n/a
Teachers: 117.5 (14.4 to 1)
Librarians/Media Specialists: 2.0 (844.5 to 1)
Guidance Counselors: 4.8 (351.9 to 1)
Current Spending: ($ per student per year):
    Total: $8,193; Instruction: $4,998; Support Services: $2,874
Enrollment, Drop-out Rates and Diploma Recipients by Race/Ethnicity

Category	Total	White	Black	Asian	AIAN	Hisp.
Enrollment (%)	100.0	96.1	1.2	0.4	0.7	1.6
Drop-out Rate (%)	0.9	0.7	20.0	0.0	0.0	0.0
H.S. Diplomas (#)	133	130	1	1	0	1

St. Croix County

Hudson
1401 Vine St • Hudson, WI 54016-1880
(715) 386-4901 • http://www.hudson.k12.wi.us
Grade Span: PK-12; **Agency Type:** 1
Schools: 7
    5 Primary; 1 Middle; 1 High; 0 Other Level
    7 Regular; 0 Special Education; 0 Vocational; 0 Alternative
    0 Magnet; 0 Charter; 3 Title I Eligible; 0 School-wide Title I
Students: 4,578 (52.3% male; 47.6% female)
    Individual Education Program: 653 (14.3%);
    English Language Learner: 0 (0.0%); Migrant: 0 (0.0%)
    Eligible for Free Lunch Program: n/a
    Eligible for Reduced-Price Lunch Program: n/a
Teachers: 299.5 (15.3 to 1)
Librarians/Media Specialists: 7.0 (654.0 to 1)
Guidance Counselors: 12.4 (369.2 to 1)
Current Spending: ($ per student per year):
    Total: $8,056; Instruction: $4,948; Support Services: $2,733
Enrollment, Drop-out Rates and Diploma Recipients by Race/Ethnicity

Category	Total	White	Black	Asian	AIAN	Hisp.
Enrollment (%)	100.0	95.3	1.0	2.0	0.4	1.3
Drop-out Rate (%)	0.0	0.0	0.0	0.0	0.0	0.0
H.S. Diplomas (#)	314	309	0	2	0	3

New Richmond
701 E 11th St • New Richmond, WI 54017-2355
(715) 243-7411 • http://www.newrichmond.k12.wi.us
Grade Span: PK-12; **Agency Type:** 1
Schools: 4
    3 Primary; 0 Middle; 1 High; 0 Other Level
    4 Regular; 0 Special Education; 0 Vocational; 0 Alternative
    0 Magnet; 0 Charter; 2 Title I Eligible; 0 School-wide Title I
Students: 2,507 (50.0% male; 49.9% female)
    Individual Education Program: 318 (12.7%);
    English Language Learner: 0 (0.0%); Migrant: 0 (0.0%)
    Eligible for Free Lunch Program: n/a
    Eligible for Reduced-Price Lunch Program: n/a
Teachers: 151.3 (16.6 to 1)
Librarians/Media Specialists: 3.8 (659.7 to 1)
Guidance Counselors: 5.8 (432.2 to 1)
Current Spending: ($ per student per year):
    Total: $8,289; Instruction: $4,880; Support Services: $3,044

Enrollment, Drop-out Rates and Diploma Recipients by Race/Ethnicity

Category	Total	White	Black	Asian	AIAN	Hisp.
Enrollment (%)	100.0	96.0	0.8	1.1	0.6	1.6
Drop-out Rate (%)	0.8	0.7	25.0	0.0	0.0	0.0
H.S. Diplomas (#)	189	183	2	3	0	1

Taylor County

Medford Area
124 W State St • Medford, WI 54451-1771
(715) 748-4620 • http://www.medford.k12.wi.us
Grade Span: PK-12; **Agency Type:** 1
Schools: 4
  2 Primary; 1 Middle; 1 High; 0 Other Level
  4 Regular; 0 Special Education; 0 Vocational; 0 Alternative
  0 Magnet; 0 Charter; 2 Title I Eligible; 0 School-wide Title I
Students: 2,274   (52.3% male; 47.6% female)
  Individual Education Program: 249 (10.9%);
  English Language Learner: 0 (0.0%); Migrant: 0 (0.0%)
  Eligible for Free Lunch Program: n/a
  Eligible for Reduced-Price Lunch Program: n/a
Teachers: 147.4 (15.4 to 1)
Librarians/Media Specialists: 3.0 (758.0 to 1)
Guidance Counselors: 4.6 (494.3 to 1)
Current Spending: ($ per student per year):
  Total: $8,046; Instruction: $4,909; Support Services: $2,795
Enrollment, Drop-out Rates and Diploma Recipients by Race/Ethnicity

Category	Total	White	Black	Asian	AIAN	Hisp.
Enrollment (%)	100.0	96.7	0.6	1.1	0.2	1.3
Drop-out Rate (%)	1.2	1.1	50.0	0.0	0.0	0.0
H.S. Diplomas (#)	219	218	0	1	0	0

Vilas County

Northland Pines
1780 Pleasure Island Rd • Eagle River, WI 54521-8927
(715) 479-6487 • http://www.fen.com/wi/npsd
Grade Span: PK-12; **Agency Type:** 1
Schools: 5
  3 Primary; 1 Middle; 1 High; 0 Other Level
  5 Regular; 0 Special Education; 0 Vocational; 0 Alternative
  0 Magnet; 0 Charter; 3 Title I Eligible; 0 School-wide Title I
Students: 1,532   (52.8% male; 47.1% female)
  Individual Education Program: 228 (14.9%);
  English Language Learner: 0 (0.0%); Migrant: 0 (0.0%)
  Eligible for Free Lunch Program: n/a
  Eligible for Reduced-Price Lunch Program: n/a
Teachers: 117.6 (13.0 to 1)
Librarians/Media Specialists: 2.0 (766.0 to 1)
Guidance Counselors: 6.0 (255.0 to 1)
Current Spending: ($ per student per year):
  Total: $9,858; Instruction: $5,788; Support Services: $3,738
Enrollment, Drop-out Rates and Diploma Recipients by Race/Ethnicity

Category	Total	White	Black	Asian	AIAN	Hisp.
Enrollment (%)	100.0	97.1	0.4	0.4	1.0	1.0
Drop-out Rate (%)	1.1	0.9	n/a	0.0	33.3	0.0
H.S. Diplomas (#)	116	114	0	1	1	0

Walworth County

Delavan-Darien
324 Beloit St • Delavan, WI 53115-1606
(262) 728-2642 • http://www.ddschools.org
Grade Span: PK-12; **Agency Type:** 1
Schools: 5
  3 Primary; 1 Middle; 1 High; 0 Other Level
  5 Regular; 0 Special Education; 0 Vocational; 0 Alternative
  0 Magnet; 0 Charter; 2 Title I Eligible; 0 School-wide Title I
Students: 2,819   (52.2% male; 47.7% female)
  Individual Education Program: 351 (12.5%);
  English Language Learner: 346 (12.3%); Migrant: 0 (0.0%)
  Eligible for Free Lunch Program: n/a
  Eligible for Reduced-Price Lunch Program: n/a
Teachers: 172.0 (16.3 to 1)
Librarians/Media Specialists: 4.0 (698.8 to 1)
Guidance Counselors: 6.0 (465.8 to 1)
Current Spending: ($ per student per year):
  Total: $7,313; Instruction: $4,368; Support Services: $2,630
Enrollment, Drop-out Rates and Diploma Recipients by Race/Ethnicity

Category	Total	White	Black	Asian	AIAN	Hisp.
Enrollment (%)	100.0	66.4	2.9	0.8	0.5	29.3
Drop-out Rate (%)	3.4	2.0	30.8	0.0	0.0	7.3
H.S. Diplomas (#)	207	171	2	2	1	31

East Troy Community
2043 Division St • East Troy, WI 53120-1238
(262) 642-6710 • http://www.easttroy.k12.wi.us
Grade Span: KG-12; **Agency Type:** 1
Schools: 5
  3 Primary; 1 Middle; 1 High; 0 Other Level
  5 Regular; 0 Special Education; 0 Vocational; 0 Alternative
  0 Magnet; 0 Charter; 3 Title I Eligible; 0 School-wide Title I
Students: 1,682   (51.1% male; 48.8% female)
  Individual Education Program: 167 (9.9%);
  English Language Learner: 0 (0.0%); Migrant: 0 (0.0%)
  Eligible for Free Lunch Program: n/a
  Eligible for Reduced-Price Lunch Program: n/a
Teachers: 109.3 (15.4 to 1)
Librarians/Media Specialists: 2.0 (841.0 to 1)
Guidance Counselors: 4.0 (420.5 to 1)
Current Spending: ($ per student per year):
  Total: $7,645; Instruction: $4,855; Support Services: $2,551
Enrollment, Drop-out Rates and Diploma Recipients by Race/Ethnicity

Category	Total	White	Black	Asian	AIAN	Hisp.
Enrollment (%)	100.0	96.1	0.7	0.4	0.4	2.5
Drop-out Rate (%)	0.9	1.0	0.0	0.0	0.0	0.0
H.S. Diplomas (#)	145	143	1	0	0	1

Elkhorn Area
3 N Jackson St • Elkhorn, WI 53121-1905
(262) 723-3160 • http://www.elkhorn.k12.wi.us
Grade Span: KG-12; **Agency Type:** 1
Schools: 6
  2 Primary; 2 Middle; 2 High; 0 Other Level
  5 Regular; 0 Special Education; 0 Vocational; 1 Alternative
  0 Magnet; 1 Charter; 3 Title I Eligible; 0 School-wide Title I
Students: 2,596   (51.3% male; 48.6% female)
  Individual Education Program: 284 (10.9%);
  English Language Learner: 157 (6.0%); Migrant: 0 (0.0%)
  Eligible for Free Lunch Program: n/a
  Eligible for Reduced-Price Lunch Program: n/a
Teachers: 163.9 (15.8 to 1)
Librarians/Media Specialists: 4.0 (649.0 to 1)
Guidance Counselors: 6.0 (432.7 to 1)
Current Spending: ($ per student per year):
  Total: $7,903; Instruction: $4,730; Support Services: $2,927
Enrollment, Drop-out Rates and Diploma Recipients by Race/Ethnicity

Category	Total	White	Black	Asian	AIAN	Hisp.
Enrollment (%)	100.0	90.0	0.8	1.4	0.3	7.4
Drop-out Rate (%)	0.4	0.4	0.0	0.0	n/a	0.0
H.S. Diplomas (#)	181	169	0	3	0	9

Lake Geneva J1
200 E 8 St • Lake Geneva, WI 53147-2436
(262) 348-1000 • http://lakegenevaschools.com/
Grade Span: KG-08; **Agency Type:** 1
Schools: 4
  3 Primary; 1 Middle; 0 High; 0 Other Level
  4 Regular; 0 Special Education; 0 Vocational; 0 Alternative
  0 Magnet; 0 Charter; 2 Title I Eligible; 0 School-wide Title I
Students: 1,746   (51.2% male; 48.7% female)
  Individual Education Program: 252 (14.4%);
  English Language Learner: 221 (12.7%); Migrant: 0 (0.0%)
  Eligible for Free Lunch Program: n/a
  Eligible for Reduced-Price Lunch Program: n/a
Teachers: 122.9 (14.2 to 1)
Librarians/Media Specialists: 2.0 (873.0 to 1)
Guidance Counselors: 4.0 (436.5 to 1)
Current Spending: ($ per student per year):
  Total: $7,867; Instruction: $4,957; Support Services: $2,635
Enrollment, Drop-out Rates and Diploma Recipients by Race/Ethnicity

Category	Total	White	Black	Asian	AIAN	Hisp.
Enrollment (%)	100.0	77.8	2.1	1.1	0.9	18.2
Drop-out Rate (%)	n/a	n/a	n/a	n/a	n/a	n/a
H.S. Diplomas (#)	n/a	n/a	n/a	n/a	n/a	n/a

Whitewater
419 S Elizabeth St • Whitewater, WI 53190-1632
(262) 472-8708 • http://www.whitewater.k12.wi.us
Grade Span: PK-12; **Agency Type:** 1
Schools: 5
  3 Primary; 1 Middle; 1 High; 0 Other Level
  5 Regular; 0 Special Education; 0 Vocational; 0 Alternative
  0 Magnet; 0 Charter; 2 Title I Eligible; 0 School-wide Title I
Students: 2,051   (51.7% male; 48.2% female)
  Individual Education Program: 278 (13.6%);
  English Language Learner: 214 (10.4%); Migrant: 0 (0.0%)
  Eligible for Free Lunch Program: n/a
  Eligible for Reduced-Price Lunch Program: n/a

Teachers: 140.3 (14.6 to 1)
Librarians/Media Specialists: 2.9 (707.2 to 1)
Guidance Counselors: 5.0 (410.2 to 1)
Current Spending: ($ per student per year):
   Total: $8,186; Instruction: $4,721; Support Services: $3,098
Enrollment, Drop-out Rates and Diploma Recipients by Race/Ethnicity

Category	Total	White	Black	Asian	AIAN	Hisp.
Enrollment (%)	100.0	81.9	1.9	1.2	0.5	14.5
Drop-out Rate (%)	2.0	2.0	0.0	0.0	0.0	2.7
H.S. Diplomas (#)	144	129	0	3	0	12

Washburn County

Spooner
500 College St • Spooner, WI 54801-1298
(715) 635-2171 • http://www.spooner.k12.wi.us
Grade Span: PK-12; **Agency Type:** 1
Schools: 3
   1 Primary; 1 Middle; 1 High; 0 Other Level
   3 Regular; 0 Special Education; 0 Vocational; 0 Alternative
   0 Magnet; 0 Charter; 2 Title I Eligible; 1 School-wide Title I
Students: 1,512   (55.2% male; 44.7% female)
   Individual Education Program: 208 (13.8%);
   English Language Learner: 0 (0.0%); Migrant: 0 (0.0%)
   Eligible for Free Lunch Program: n/a
   Eligible for Reduced-Price Lunch Program: n/a
Teachers: 108.1 (14.0 to 1)
Librarians/Media Specialists: 3.0 (504.0 to 1)
Guidance Counselors: 3.1 (487.7 to 1)
Current Spending: ($ per student per year):
   Total: $8,953; Instruction: $5,657; Support Services: $3,059
Enrollment, Drop-out Rates and Diploma Recipients by Race/Ethnicity

Category	Total	White	Black	Asian	AIAN	Hisp.
Enrollment (%)	100.0	94.0	1.6	0.9	2.5	1.1
Drop-out Rate (%)	0.8	0.7	33.3	0.0	0.0	0.0
H.S. Diplomas (#)	153	147	2	3	1	0

Washington County

Germantown
N104w13840 Donges Bay Rd • Germantown, WI 53022-4499
(262) 253-3904 • http://www.germantown.k12.wi.us
Grade Span: PK-12; **Agency Type:** 1
Schools: 6
   4 Primary; 1 Middle; 1 High; 0 Other Level
   6 Regular; 0 Special Education; 0 Vocational; 0 Alternative
   0 Magnet; 0 Charter; 3 Title I Eligible; 0 School-wide Title I
Students: 3,716   (52.2% male; 47.7% female)
   Individual Education Program: 418 (11.2%);
   English Language Learner: 0 (0.0%); Migrant: 0 (0.0%)
   Eligible for Free Lunch Program: n/a
   Eligible for Reduced-Price Lunch Program: n/a
Teachers: 242.2 (15.3 to 1)
Librarians/Media Specialists: 3.0 (1,238.7 to 1)
Guidance Counselors: 9.4 (395.3 to 1)
Current Spending: ($ per student per year):
   Total: $9,172; Instruction: $5,237; Support Services: $3,654
Enrollment, Drop-out Rates and Diploma Recipients by Race/Ethnicity

Category	Total	White	Black	Asian	AIAN	Hisp.
Enrollment (%)	100.0	93.6	2.1	2.4	0.4	1.5
Drop-out Rate (%)	0.3	0.3	0.0	0.0	0.0	0.0
H.S. Diplomas (#)	271	262	2	4	1	2

Hartford J1
675 E Rossman St • Hartford, WI 53027-1333
(262) 673-3155 • http://www.hartfordjt1.k12.wi.us
Grade Span: PK-08; **Agency Type:** 1
Schools: 3
   2 Primary; 1 Middle; 0 High; 0 Other Level
   3 Regular; 0 Special Education; 0 Vocational; 0 Alternative
   0 Magnet; 0 Charter; 1 Title I Eligible; 0 School-wide Title I
Students: 1,624   (50.6% male; 49.3% female)
   Individual Education Program: 291 (17.9%);
   English Language Learner: 0 (0.0%); Migrant: 0 (0.0%)
   Eligible for Free Lunch Program: n/a
   Eligible for Reduced-Price Lunch Program: n/a
Teachers: 116.1 (14.0 to 1)
Librarians/Media Specialists: 3.0 (541.3 to 1)
Guidance Counselors: 3.0 (541.3 to 1)
Current Spending: ($ per student per year):
   Total: $9,057; Instruction: $5,940; Support Services: $2,743

Category	Total	White	Black	Asian	AIAN	Hisp.
Enrollment (%)	100.0	92.0	1.3	0.9	0.9	4.9
Drop-out Rate (%)	n/a	n/a	n/a	n/a	n/a	n/a
H.S. Diplomas (#)	n/a	n/a	n/a	n/a	n/a	n/a

Hartford Uhs
805 Cedar St • Hartford, WI 53027-2399
(262) 673-8950 • http://www.huhs.org
Grade Span: 09-12; **Agency Type:** 1
Schools: 1
   0 Primary; 0 Middle; 1 High; 0 Other Level
   1 Regular; 0 Special Education; 0 Vocational; 0 Alternative
   0 Magnet; 0 Charter; 1 Title I Eligible; 0 School-wide Title I
Students: 1,684   (53.0% male; 46.9% female)
   Individual Education Program: 196 (11.6%);
   English Language Learner: 0 (0.0%); Migrant: 0 (0.0%)
   Eligible for Free Lunch Program: n/a
   Eligible for Reduced-Price Lunch Program: n/a
Teachers: 109.9 (15.3 to 1)
Librarians/Media Specialists: 1.5 (1,122.7 to 1)
Guidance Counselors: 5.0 (336.8 to 1)
Current Spending: ($ per student per year):
   Total: $9,335; Instruction: $5,420; Support Services: $3,610
Enrollment, Drop-out Rates and Diploma Recipients by Race/Ethnicity

Category	Total	White	Black	Asian	AIAN	Hisp.
Enrollment (%)	100.0	95.6	0.4	1.2	0.2	2.6
Drop-out Rate (%)	1.3	1.2	0.0	0.0	0.0	7.1
H.S. Diplomas (#)	379	366	1	4	0	8

Kewaskum
1455 School St • Kewaskum, WI 53040-0037
Mailing Address: PO Box 37 • Kewaskum, WI 53040-0037
(262) 626-8427 • http://www.ksd.k12.wi.us
Grade Span: PK-12; **Agency Type:** 1
Schools: 5
   3 Primary; 1 Middle; 1 High; 0 Other Level
   5 Regular; 0 Special Education; 0 Vocational; 0 Alternative
   0 Magnet; 0 Charter; 1 Title I Eligible; 0 School-wide Title I
Students: 1,874   (49.1% male; 50.8% female)
   Individual Education Program: 219 (11.7%);
   English Language Learner: 0 (0.0%); Migrant: 0 (0.0%)
   Eligible for Free Lunch Program: n/a
   Eligible for Reduced-Price Lunch Program: n/a
Teachers: 118.7 (15.8 to 1)
Librarians/Media Specialists: 2.0 (937.0 to 1)
Guidance Counselors: 5.0 (374.8 to 1)
Current Spending: ($ per student per year):
   Total: $8,324; Instruction: $5,214; Support Services: $2,788
Enrollment, Drop-out Rates and Diploma Recipients by Race/Ethnicity

Category	Total	White	Black	Asian	AIAN	Hisp.
Enrollment (%)	100.0	97.1	0.1	0.2	0.9	1.8
Drop-out Rate (%)	1.6	1.6	n/a	0.0	0.0	0.0
H.S. Diplomas (#)	144	141	0	0	1	2

Slinger
207 Polk St • Slinger, WI 53086-9585
(262) 644-9615 • http://www.slinger.k12.wi.us
Grade Span: PK-12; **Agency Type:** 1
Schools: 5
   3 Primary; 1 Middle; 1 High; 0 Other Level
   5 Regular; 0 Special Education; 0 Vocational; 0 Alternative
   0 Magnet; 0 Charter; 3 Title I Eligible; 0 School-wide Title I
Students: 2,847   (51.1% male; 48.8% female)
   Individual Education Program: 336 (11.8%);
   English Language Learner: 0 (0.0%); Migrant: 0 (0.0%)
   Eligible for Free Lunch Program: n/a
   Eligible for Reduced-Price Lunch Program: n/a
Teachers: 167.1 (17.0 to 1)
Librarians/Media Specialists: 3.0 (949.0 to 1)
Guidance Counselors: 8.0 (355.9 to 1)
Current Spending: ($ per student per year):
   Total: $7,456; Instruction: $4,725; Support Services: $2,430
Enrollment, Drop-out Rates and Diploma Recipients by Race/Ethnicity

Category	Total	White	Black	Asian	AIAN	Hisp.
Enrollment (%)	100.0	97.6	0.4	0.5	0.1	1.3
Drop-out Rate (%)	1.9	1.7	0.0	0.0	0.0	25.0
H.S. Diplomas (#)	189	185	0	1	0	3

West Bend
735 S Main • West Bend, WI 53095-3939
(262) 335-5435 • http://www.west-bend.k12.wi.us
Grade Span: PK-12; **Agency Type:** 1
Schools: 11
   7 Primary; 2 Middle; 2 High; 0 Other Level

11 Regular; 0 Special Education; 0 Vocational; 0 Alternative
0 Magnet; 0 Charter; 5 Title I Eligible; 0 School-wide Title I
Students: 6,824   (52.8% male; 47.1% female)
   Individual Education Program: 844 (12.4%);
   English Language Learner: 0 (0.0%); Migrant: 0 (0.0%)
   Eligible for Free Lunch Program: n/a
   Eligible for Reduced-Price Lunch Program: n/a
Teachers: 419.0 (16.3 to 1)
Librarians/Media Specialists: 10.0 (682.4 to 1)
Guidance Counselors: 16.0 (426.5 to 1)
Current Spending: ($ per student per year):
   Total: $8,037; Instruction: $5,232; Support Services: $2,503
Enrollment, Drop-out Rates and Diploma Recipients by Race/Ethnicity

Category	Total	White	Black	Asian	AIAN	Hisp.
Enrollment (%)	100.0	95.1	1.2	0.7	0.7	2.3
Drop-out Rate (%)	0.9	0.8	0.0	7.1	8.3	5.6
H.S. Diplomas (#)	603	589	1	6	1	6

Waukesha County

Arrowhead Uhs
700 N Ave • Hartland, WI 53029-9502
(262) 369-3611 • http://www.ahs.k12.wi.us
Grade Span: 09-12; **Agency Type:** 1
Schools: 1
   0 Primary; 0 Middle; 1 High; 0 Other Level
   1 Regular; 0 Special Education; 0 Vocational; 0 Alternative
   0 Magnet; 0 Charter; 1 Title I Eligible; 0 School-wide Title I
Students: 2,281   (51.3% male; 48.6% female)
   Individual Education Program: 159 (7.0%);
   English Language Learner: 0 (0.0%); Migrant: 0 (0.0%)
   Eligible for Free Lunch Program: n/a
   Eligible for Reduced-Price Lunch Program: n/a
Teachers: 135.3 (16.9 to 1)
Librarians/Media Specialists: 2.0 (1,140.5 to 1)
Guidance Counselors: 6.0 (380.2 to 1)
Current Spending: ($ per student per year):
   Total: $9,773; Instruction: $5,941; Support Services: $3,574
Enrollment, Drop-out Rates and Diploma Recipients by Race/Ethnicity

Category	Total	White	Black	Asian	AIAN	Hisp.
Enrollment (%)	100.0	98.4	0.3	0.5	0.1	0.7
Drop-out Rate (%)	0.5	0.5	0.0	0.0	0.0	0.0
H.S. Diplomas (#)	457	450	0	4	1	2

Elmbrook
13780 Hope St • Brookfield, WI 53005-1700
Mailing Address: PO Box 1830 • Brookfield, WI 53008-1830
(262) 781-3030 • http://www.elmbrook.k12.wi.us
Grade Span: PK-12; **Agency Type:** 1
Schools: 11
   6 Primary; 2 Middle; 2 High; 1 Other Level
   10 Regular; 1 Special Education; 0 Vocational; 0 Alternative
   0 Magnet; 0 Charter; 5 Title I Eligible; 0 School-wide Title I
Students: 7,664   (51.0% male; 48.9% female)
   Individual Education Program: 842 (11.0%);
   English Language Learner: 0 (0.0%); Migrant: 0 (0.0%)
   Eligible for Free Lunch Program: n/a
   Eligible for Reduced-Price Lunch Program: n/a
Teachers: 498.4 (15.4 to 1)
Librarians/Media Specialists: 9.0 (851.6 to 1)
Guidance Counselors: 14.0 (547.4 to 1)
Current Spending: ($ per student per year):
   Total: $10,038; Instruction: $6,311; Support Services: $3,432
Enrollment, Drop-out Rates and Diploma Recipients by Race/Ethnicity

Category	Total	White	Black	Asian	AIAN	Hisp.
Enrollment (%)	100.0	87.1	4.7	6.2	0.1	1.9
Drop-out Rate (%)	0.2	0.2	0.0	0.0	0.0	0.0
H.S. Diplomas (#)	589	526	25	27	0	11

Hamilton
W220n6151 Town Line Rd • Sussex, WI 53089-3999
(262) 246-1973 • http://www.hamiltondist.k12.wi.us
Grade Span: PK-12; **Agency Type:** 1
Schools: 8
   5 Primary; 2 Middle; 1 High; 0 Other Level
   7 Regular; 0 Special Education; 0 Vocational; 1 Alternative
   0 Magnet; 1 Charter; 5 Title I Eligible; 0 School-wide Title I
Students: 4,075   (51.5% male; 48.4% female)
   Individual Education Program: 396 (9.7%);
   English Language Learner: 0 (0.0%); Migrant: 0 (0.0%)
   Eligible for Free Lunch Program: n/a
   Eligible for Reduced-Price Lunch Program: n/a
Teachers: 255.9 (15.9 to 1)
Librarians/Media Specialists: 5.9 (690.7 to 1)
Guidance Counselors: 9.0 (452.8 to 1)

Current Spending: ($ per student per year):
   Total: $8,212; Instruction: $4,952; Support Services: $3,050
Enrollment, Drop-out Rates and Diploma Recipients by Race/Ethnicity

Category	Total	White	Black	Asian	AIAN	Hisp.
Enrollment (%)	100.0	92.0	2.3	3.2	0.6	2.0
Drop-out Rate (%)	0.3	0.3	0.0	0.0	0.0	0.0
H.S. Diplomas (#)	280	252	6	14	3	5

Kettle Moraine
563 A J Allen Cir • Wales, WI 53183-0901
Mailing Address: PO Box 901 • Wales, WI 53183-0901
(262) 968-6330 • http://www.kmsd.edu
Grade Span: PK-12; **Agency Type:** 1
Schools: 6
   4 Primary; 1 Middle; 1 High; 0 Other Level
   6 Regular; 0 Special Education; 0 Vocational; 0 Alternative
   0 Magnet; 0 Charter; 0 Title I Eligible; 0 School-wide Title I
Students: 4,378   (50.4% male; 49.5% female)
   Individual Education Program: 574 (13.1%);
   English Language Learner: 0 (0.0%); Migrant: 12 (0.3%)
   Eligible for Free Lunch Program: n/a
   Eligible for Reduced-Price Lunch Program: n/a
Teachers: 270.6 (16.2 to 1)
Librarians/Media Specialists: 6.0 (729.7 to 1)
Guidance Counselors: 9.7 (451.3 to 1)
Current Spending: ($ per student per year):
   Total: $9,065; Instruction: $5,638; Support Services: $3,055
Enrollment, Drop-out Rates and Diploma Recipients by Race/Ethnicity

Category	Total	White	Black	Asian	AIAN	Hisp.
Enrollment (%)	100.0	96.5	0.6	1.0	0.3	1.6
Drop-out Rate (%)	0.6	0.6	n/a	0.0	0.0	0.0
H.S. Diplomas (#)	342	326	0	4	2	10

Menomonee Falls
N84w16579 Menomonee Ave • Menomonee Falls, WI 53051-3040
(262) 255-8440 • http://www.sdmf.k12.wi.us
Grade Span: PK-12; **Agency Type:** 1
Schools: 7
   4 Primary; 1 Middle; 1 High; 1 Other Level
   7 Regular; 0 Special Education; 0 Vocational; 0 Alternative
   0 Magnet; 0 Charter; 3 Title I Eligible; 0 School-wide Title I
Students: 4,455   (51.2% male; 48.7% female)
   Individual Education Program: 539 (12.1%);
   English Language Learner: 0 (0.0%); Migrant: 0 (0.0%)
   Eligible for Free Lunch Program: n/a
   Eligible for Reduced-Price Lunch Program: n/a
Teachers: 303.9 (14.7 to 1)
Librarians/Media Specialists: 9.0 (495.0 to 1)
Guidance Counselors: 11.6 (384.1 to 1)
Current Spending: ($ per student per year):
   Total: $9,191; Instruction: $5,556; Support Services: $3,365
Enrollment, Drop-out Rates and Diploma Recipients by Race/Ethnicity

Category	Total	White	Black	Asian	AIAN	Hisp.
Enrollment (%)	100.0	83.9	8.7	4.0	0.6	2.8
Drop-out Rate (%)	0.2	0.2	0.0	0.0	0.0	0.0
H.S. Diplomas (#)	275	243	15	10	2	5

Mukwonago
423 Division St • Mukwonago, WI 53149-1294
(262) 363-6304 • http://www.mukwonago.k12.wi.us
Grade Span: PK-12; **Agency Type:** 1
Schools: 8
   5 Primary; 1 Middle; 1 High; 0 Other Level
   7 Regular; 0 Special Education; 0 Vocational; 0 Alternative
   0 Magnet; 0 Charter; 0 Title I Eligible; 0 School-wide Title I
Students: 5,041   (51.3% male; 48.6% female)
   Individual Education Program: 643 (12.8%);
   English Language Learner: 0 (0.0%); Migrant: 0 (0.0%)
   Eligible for Free Lunch Program: n/a
   Eligible for Reduced-Price Lunch Program: n/a
Teachers: 309.0 (16.3 to 1)
Librarians/Media Specialists: 6.9 (730.6 to 1)
Guidance Counselors: 9.0 (560.1 to 1)
Current Spending: ($ per student per year):
   Total: $8,139; Instruction: $5,281; Support Services: $2,555
Enrollment, Drop-out Rates and Diploma Recipients by Race/Ethnicity

Category	Total	White	Black	Asian	AIAN	Hisp.
Enrollment (%)	100.0	96.1	0.7	0.8	0.5	1.9
Drop-out Rate (%)	0.3	0.3	0.0	0.0	0.0	0.0
H.S. Diplomas (#)	415	401	1	2	2	9

Muskego-Norway
S87w18763 Woods Rd • Muskego, WI 53150-9374
(262) 679-5400 • http://www.mnsd.k12.wi.us
Grade Span: PK-12; **Agency Type:** 1
Schools: 8
    5 Primary; 2 Middle; 1 High; 0 Other Level
    8 Regular; 0 Special Education; 0 Vocational; 0 Alternative
    0 Magnet; 0 Charter; 3 Title I Eligible; 0 School-wide Title I
Students: 4,640 (50.4% male; 49.5% female)
    Individual Education Program: 590 (12.7%);
    English Language Learner: 0 (0.0%); Migrant: 0 (0.0%)
    Eligible for Free Lunch Program: n/a
    Eligible for Reduced-Price Lunch Program: n/a
Teachers: 282.8 (16.4 to 1)
Librarians/Media Specialists: 6.4 (725.0 to 1)
Guidance Counselors: 11.4 (407.0 to 1)
Current Spending: ($ per student per year):
    Total: $8,891; Instruction: $5,599; Support Services: $3,048
Enrollment, Drop-out Rates and Diploma Recipients by Race/Ethnicity

Category	Total	White	Black	Asian	AIAN	Hisp.
Enrollment (%)	100.0	95.9	0.5	1.0	0.7	1.9
Drop-out Rate (%)	0.2	0.1	0.0	0.0	0.0	3.8
H.S. Diplomas (#)	299	289	2	3	0	5

New Berlin
4333 S Sunnyslope Rd • New Berlin, WI 53151-6844
(262) 789-6220 • http://www.nbps.k12.wi.us
Grade Span: PK-12; **Agency Type:** 1
Schools: 10
    6 Primary; 2 Middle; 2 High; 0 Other Level
    10 Regular; 0 Special Education; 0 Vocational; 0 Alternative
    0 Magnet; 0 Charter; 5 Title I Eligible; 0 School-wide Title I
Students: 4,592 (50.8% male; 49.1% female)
    Individual Education Program: 570 (12.4%);
    English Language Learner: 0 (0.0%); Migrant: 0 (0.0%)
    Eligible for Free Lunch Program: n/a
    Eligible for Reduced-Price Lunch Program: n/a
Teachers: 307.4 (14.9 to 1)
Librarians/Media Specialists: 8.0 (574.0 to 1)
Guidance Counselors: 7.0 (656.0 to 1)
Current Spending: ($ per student per year):
    Total: $10,443; Instruction: $6,217; Support Services: $3,970
Enrollment, Drop-out Rates and Diploma Recipients by Race/Ethnicity

Category	Total	White	Black	Asian	AIAN	Hisp.
Enrollment (%)	100.0	90.5	1.3	5.6	0.4	2.2
Drop-out Rate (%)	0.3	0.3	6.7	0.0	0.0	0.0
H.S. Diplomas (#)	382	356	5	15	1	5

Oconomowoc Area
W360n7077 Brown St • Oconomowoc, WI 53066-1197
(262) 560-2111 • http://www.oasd.k12.wi.us
Grade Span: PK-12; **Agency Type:** 1
Schools: 7
    5 Primary; 1 Middle; 1 High; 0 Other Level
    7 Regular; 0 Special Education; 0 Vocational; 0 Alternative
    0 Magnet; 0 Charter; 4 Title I Eligible; 0 School-wide Title I
Students: 4,210 (50.7% male; 49.2% female)
    Individual Education Program: 651 (15.5%);
    English Language Learner: 0 (0.0%); Migrant: 0 (0.0%)
    Eligible for Free Lunch Program: n/a
    Eligible for Reduced-Price Lunch Program: n/a
Teachers: 269.1 (15.6 to 1)
Librarians/Media Specialists: 2.5 (1,684.0 to 1)
Guidance Counselors: 8.5 (495.3 to 1)
Current Spending: ($ per student per year):
    Total: $9,396; Instruction: $5,853; Support Services: $3,285
Enrollment, Drop-out Rates and Diploma Recipients by Race/Ethnicity

Category	Total	White	Black	Asian	AIAN	Hisp.
Enrollment (%)	100.0	96.1	0.8	0.9	0.4	1.8
Drop-out Rate (%)	1.5	1.5	0.0	0.0	0.0	0.0
H.S. Diplomas (#)	321	315	1	3	1	1

Pewaukee
404 Lake St • Pewaukee, WI 53072-3630
(262) 691-2100 • http://www.pewaukee.k12.wi.us
Grade Span: PK-12; **Agency Type:** 1
Schools: 4
    1 Primary; 2 Middle; 1 High; 0 Other Level
    4 Regular; 0 Special Education; 0 Vocational; 0 Alternative
    0 Magnet; 0 Charter; 4 Title I Eligible; 0 School-wide Title I
Students: 2,160 (51.5% male; 48.4% female)
    Individual Education Program: 258 (11.9%);
    English Language Learner: 0 (0.0%); Migrant: 0 (0.0%)
    Eligible for Free Lunch Program: n/a
    Eligible for Reduced-Price Lunch Program: n/a

Teachers: 143.1 (15.1 to 1)
Librarians/Media Specialists: 3.5 (617.1 to 1)
Guidance Counselors: 5.0 (432.0 to 1)
Current Spending: ($ per student per year):
    Total: $9,069; Instruction: $5,351; Support Services: $3,410
Enrollment, Drop-out Rates and Diploma Recipients by Race/Ethnicity

Category	Total	White	Black	Asian	AIAN	Hisp.
Enrollment (%)	100.0	92.4	2.0	3.1	0.4	2.2
Drop-out Rate (%)	0.2	0.2	0.0	0.0	0.0	0.0
H.S. Diplomas (#)	127	125	0	2	0	0

Waukesha
222 Maple Ave • Waukesha, WI 53186-4725
(262) 970-1012 • http://www.waukesha.k12.wi.us
Grade Span: PK-12; **Agency Type:** 1
Schools: 27
    17 Primary; 3 Middle; 5 High; 0 Other Level
    23 Regular; 0 Special Education; 0 Vocational; 2 Alternative
    0 Magnet; 2 Charter; 7 Title I Eligible; 2 School-wide Title I
Students: 12,892 (51.4% male; 48.5% female)
    Individual Education Program: 1,707 (13.2%);
    English Language Learner: 842 (6.5%); Migrant: 0 (0.0%)
    Eligible for Free Lunch Program: n/a
    Eligible for Reduced-Price Lunch Program: n/a
Teachers: 849.7 (15.2 to 1)
Librarians/Media Specialists: 13.5 (955.0 to 1)
Guidance Counselors: 27.0 (477.5 to 1)
Current Spending: ($ per student per year):
    Total: $9,048; Instruction: $5,755; Support Services: $3,051
Enrollment, Drop-out Rates and Diploma Recipients by Race/Ethnicity

Category	Total	White	Black	Asian	AIAN	Hisp.
Enrollment (%)	100.0	82.8	2.6	2.5	0.5	11.5
Drop-out Rate (%)	0.4	0.4	0.0	1.4	0.0	0.6
H.S. Diplomas (#)	1,043	911	18	12	7	95

Waupaca County

Clintonville
45 W Green Tree Rd • Clintonville, WI 54929-1595
(715) 823-7215 • http://www.clintonville.k12.wi.us
Grade Span: PK-12; **Agency Type:** 1
Schools: 5
    3 Primary; 1 Middle; 1 High; 0 Other Level
    5 Regular; 0 Special Education; 0 Vocational; 0 Alternative
    0 Magnet; 0 Charter; 3 Title I Eligible; 0 School-wide Title I
Students: 1,586 (52.7% male; 47.2% female)
    Individual Education Program: 236 (14.9%);
    English Language Learner: 0 (0.0%); Migrant: 0 (0.0%)
    Eligible for Free Lunch Program: n/a
    Eligible for Reduced-Price Lunch Program: n/a
Teachers: 122.8 (12.9 to 1)
Librarians/Media Specialists: 3.0 (528.7 to 1)
Guidance Counselors: 4.3 (368.8 to 1)
Current Spending: ($ per student per year):
    Total: $9,573; Instruction: $6,053; Support Services: $3,130
Enrollment, Drop-out Rates and Diploma Recipients by Race/Ethnicity

Category	Total	White	Black	Asian	AIAN	Hisp.
Enrollment (%)	100.0	94.5	0.8	0.9	0.9	3.0
Drop-out Rate (%)	2.0	1.6	0.0	0.0	0.0	21.4
H.S. Diplomas (#)	108	103	0	2	1	2

New London
901 W Washington St • New London, WI 54961-1698
(920) 982-8530 • http://www.newlondon.k12.wi.us
Grade Span: PK-12; **Agency Type:** 1
Schools: 7
    4 Primary; 1 Middle; 2 High; 0 Other Level
    6 Regular; 0 Special Education; 0 Vocational; 1 Alternative
    0 Magnet; 1 Charter; 3 Title I Eligible; 0 School-wide Title I
Students: 2,516 (51.9% male; 48.0% female)
    Individual Education Program: 323 (12.8%);
    English Language Learner: 60 (2.4%); Migrant: 0 (0.0%)
    Eligible for Free Lunch Program: n/a
    Eligible for Reduced-Price Lunch Program: n/a
Teachers: 168.8 (14.9 to 1)
Librarians/Media Specialists: 3.0 (838.0 to 1)
Guidance Counselors: 7.0 (359.1 to 1)
Current Spending: ($ per student per year):
    Total: $8,108; Instruction: $4,890; Support Services: $2,805
Enrollment, Drop-out Rates and Diploma Recipients by Race/Ethnicity

Category	Total	White	Black	Asian	AIAN	Hisp.
Enrollment (%)	100.0	94.6	0.5	0.8	0.2	4.0
Drop-out Rate (%)	1.5	1.4	0.0	20.0	0.0	0.0
H.S. Diplomas (#)	186	181	1	0	1	3

Waupaca
515 School St • Waupaca, WI 54981-1658
(715) 258-4121 • http://wsd.waupaca.k12.wi.us
Grade Span: PK-12; **Agency Type:** 1
Schools: 7
  4 Primary; 1 Middle; 2 High; 0 Other Level
  6 Regular; 0 Special Education; 0 Vocational; 1 Alternative
  0 Magnet; 0 Charter; 4 Title I Eligible; 0 School-wide Title I
Students: 2,585   (52.5% male; 47.4% female)
  Individual Education Program: 329 (12.7%);
  English Language Learner: 0 (0.0%); Migrant: 0 (0.0%)
  Eligible for Free Lunch Program: n/a
  Eligible for Reduced-Price Lunch Program: n/a
Teachers: 195.8 (13.2 to 1)
Librarians/Media Specialists: 4.0 (645.3 to 1)
Guidance Counselors: 5.0 (516.2 to 1)
Current Spending: ($ per student per year):
  Total: $7,584; Instruction: $4,586; Support Services: $2,662
Enrollment, Drop-out Rates and Diploma Recipients by Race/Ethnicity

Category	Total	White	Black	Asian	AIAN	Hisp.
Enrollment (%)	100.0	94.1	0.9	0.6	1.3	3.1
Drop-out Rate (%)	0.2	0.2	0.0	0.0	0.0	0.0
H.S. Diplomas (#)	183	176	1	2	0	4

Waushara County

Wautoma Area
556 S Cambridge St • Wautoma, WI 54982-0870
Mailing Address: PO Box 870 • Wautoma, WI 54982-0870
(920) 787-7112 • http://www.wautoma.k12.wi.us
Grade Span: PK-12; **Agency Type:** 1
Schools: 4
  2 Primary; 1 Middle; 1 High; 0 Other Level
  4 Regular; 0 Special Education; 0 Vocational; 0 Alternative
  0 Magnet; 0 Charter; 3 Title I Eligible; 3 School-wide Title I
Students: 1,592   (53.3% male; 46.6% female)
  Individual Education Program: 194 (12.2%);
  English Language Learner: 182 (11.4%); Migrant: 90 (5.7%)
  Eligible for Free Lunch Program: n/a
  Eligible for Reduced-Price Lunch Program: n/a
Teachers: 117.4 (13.6 to 1)
Librarians/Media Specialists: 3.0 (530.7 to 1)
Guidance Counselors: 4.0 (398.0 to 1)
Current Spending: ($ per student per year):
  Total: $7,861; Instruction: $4,900; Support Services: $2,614
Enrollment, Drop-out Rates and Diploma Recipients by Race/Ethnicity

Category	Total	White	Black	Asian	AIAN	Hisp.
Enrollment (%)	100.0	83.7	0.9	0.6	0.7	14.1
Drop-out Rate (%)	0.0	0.0	n/a	0.0	0.0	0.0
H.S. Diplomas (#)	130	110	0	1	0	0

Winnebago County

Menasha
328 Sixth St • Menasha, WI 54952-0360
Mailing Address: PO Box 360 • Menasha, WI 54952-0360
(920) 967-1401 • http://www.mjsd.k12.wi.us
Grade Span: PK-12; **Agency Type:** 1
Schools: 9
  6 Primary; 2 Middle; 1 High; 0 Other Level
  8 Regular; 0 Special Education; 0 Vocational; 1 Alternative
  0 Magnet; 1 Charter; 5 Title I Eligible; 0 School-wide Title I
Students: 3,589   (51.1% male; 48.8% female)
  Individual Education Program: 494 (13.8%);
  English Language Learner: 373 (10.4%); Migrant: 0 (0.0%)
  Eligible for Free Lunch Program: n/a
  Eligible for Reduced-Price Lunch Program: n/a
Teachers: 239.9 (15.0 to 1)
Librarians/Media Specialists: 5.0 (717.8 to 1)
Guidance Counselors: 9.0 (398.8 to 1)
Current Spending: ($ per student per year):
  Total: $8,243; Instruction: $5,136; Support Services: $2,848
Enrollment, Drop-out Rates and Diploma Recipients by Race/Ethnicity

Category	Total	White	Black	Asian	AIAN	Hisp.
Enrollment (%)	100.0	81.8	2.0	4.3	0.8	11.2
Drop-out Rate (%)	2.8	2.3	26.7	3.9	9.1	3.1
H.S. Diplomas (#)	236	213	3	7	1	12

Neenah
410 S Commercial St • Neenah, WI 54956-2593
(920) 751-6800 • http://neenah.k12.wi.us
Grade Span: PK-12; **Agency Type:** 1
Schools: 14
  10 Primary; 2 Middle; 1 High; 0 Other Level
  13 Regular; 0 Special Education; 0 Vocational; 0 Alternative

  0 Magnet; 0 Charter; 7 Title I Eligible; 0 School-wide Title I
Students: 6,387   (51.3% male; 48.6% female)
  Individual Education Program: 898 (14.1%);
  English Language Learner: 195 (3.1%); Migrant: 0 (0.0%)
  Eligible for Free Lunch Program: n/a
  Eligible for Reduced-Price Lunch Program: n/a
Teachers: 403.3 (15.8 to 1)
Librarians/Media Specialists: 13.0 (491.3 to 1)
Guidance Counselors: 15.5 (412.1 to 1)
Current Spending: ($ per student per year):
  Total: $8,553; Instruction: $5,852; Support Services: $2,498
Enrollment, Drop-out Rates and Diploma Recipients by Race/Ethnicity

Category	Total	White	Black	Asian	AIAN	Hisp.
Enrollment (%)	100.0	92.8	1.4	2.3	0.8	2.6
Drop-out Rate (%)	1.1	1.1	4.8	2.4	0.0	0.0
H.S. Diplomas (#)	439	426	3	5	2	3

Oshkosh Area
215 S Eagle St • Oshkosh, WI 54902
Mailing Address: PO Box 3048 • Oshkosh, WI 54903-3048
(920) 424-0160 • http://www.oshkosh.k12.wi.us
Grade Span: PK-12; **Agency Type:** 1
Schools: 29
  18 Primary; 6 Middle; 2 High; 0 Other Level
  24 Regular; 0 Special Education; 0 Vocational; 2 Alternative
  0 Magnet; 2 Charter; 13 Title I Eligible; 1 School-wide Title I
Students: 10,419   (51.3% male; 48.6% female)
  Individual Education Program: 1,589 (15.3%);
  English Language Learner: 484 (4.6%); Migrant: 0 (0.0%)
  Eligible for Free Lunch Program: n/a
  Eligible for Reduced-Price Lunch Program: n/a
Teachers: 684.9 (15.2 to 1)
Librarians/Media Specialists: 13.7 (760.5 to 1)
Guidance Counselors: 20.2 (515.8 to 1)
Current Spending: ($ per student per year):
  Total: $8,195; Instruction: $5,434; Support Services: $2,548
Enrollment, Drop-out Rates and Diploma Recipients by Race/Ethnicity

Category	Total	White	Black	Asian	AIAN	Hisp.
Enrollment (%)	100.0	87.3	2.4	8.2	0.3	1.8
Drop-out Rate (%)	2.5	2.4	4.7	2.0	7.1	3.1
H.S. Diplomas (#)	671	615	6	38	1	11

Winneconne Community
233 S 3rd Ave • Winneconne, WI 54986-5000
Mailing Address: PO Box 5000 • Winneconne, WI 54986-5000
(920) 582-5802 • http://www.winneconne.k12.wi.us/district/index.html
Grade Span: PK-12; **Agency Type:** 1
Schools: 4
  2 Primary; 1 Middle; 1 High; 0 Other Level
  4 Regular; 0 Special Education; 0 Vocational; 0 Alternative
  0 Magnet; 0 Charter; 1 Title I Eligible; 0 School-wide Title I
Students: 1,525   (53.2% male; 46.7% female)
  Individual Education Program: 215 (14.1%);
  English Language Learner: 0 (0.0%); Migrant: 0 (0.0%)
  Eligible for Free Lunch Program: n/a
  Eligible for Reduced-Price Lunch Program: n/a
Teachers: 111.2 (13.7 to 1)
Librarians/Media Specialists: 2.8 (544.6 to 1)
Guidance Counselors: 4.5 (338.9 to 1)
Current Spending: ($ per student per year):
  Total: $8,075; Instruction: $4,704; Support Services: $3,079
Enrollment, Drop-out Rates and Diploma Recipients by Race/Ethnicity

Category	Total	White	Black	Asian	AIAN	Hisp.
Enrollment (%)	100.0	98.1	0.2	0.6	0.6	0.5
Drop-out Rate (%)	0.2	0.2	n/a	0.0	0.0	n/a
H.S. Diplomas (#)	127	126	0	1	0	0

Wood County

Marshfield
1010 E 4th St • Marshfield, WI 54449-4538
(715) 387-1101 • http://marshfield.k12.wi.us
Grade Span: PK-12; **Agency Type:** 1
Schools: 7
  5 Primary; 1 Middle; 1 High; 0 Other Level
  7 Regular; 0 Special Education; 0 Vocational; 0 Alternative
  0 Magnet; 0 Charter; 5 Title I Eligible; 0 School-wide Title I
Students: 4,050   (51.7% male; 48.2% female)
  Individual Education Program: 553 (13.7%);
  English Language Learner: 0 (0.0%); Migrant: 0 (0.0%)
  Eligible for Free Lunch Program: n/a
  Eligible for Reduced-Price Lunch Program: n/a
Teachers: 252.0 (16.1 to 1)
Librarians/Media Specialists: 6.0 (675.0 to 1)
Guidance Counselors: 6.5 (623.1 to 1)

Current Spending: ($ per student per year):
    Total: $8,499; Instruction: $5,517; Support Services: $2,747

Enrollment, Drop-out Rates and Diploma Recipients by Race/Ethnicity

Category	Total	White	Black	Asian	AIAN	Hisp.
Enrollment (%)	100.0	95.2	1.2	2.1	0.5	1.0
Drop-out Rate (%)	0.4	0.4	0.0	0.0	0.0	0.0
H.S. Diplomas (#)	352	342	1	4	1	4

Wisconsin Rapids
2510 Industrial St • Wis Rapids, WI 54495-2292
Mailing Address: 510 Peach St • Wisconsin Rapids, WI 54494-4698
(715) 422-6003 • http://www.wrps.org
Grade Span: PK-12; **Agency Type:** 1
Schools: 16
    10 Primary; 2 Middle; 2 High; 0 Other Level
    13 Regular; 0 Special Education; 0 Vocational; 1 Alternative
    0 Magnet; 1 Charter; 6 Title I Eligible; 0 School-wide Title I
Students: 5,704   (51.4% male; 48.5% female)
    Individual Education Program: 817 (14.3%);
    English Language Learner: 250 (4.4%); Migrant: 9 (0.2%)
    Eligible for Free Lunch Program: n/a
    Eligible for Reduced-Price Lunch Program: n/a
Teachers: 417.2 (13.7 to 1)
Librarians/Media Specialists: 10.8 (528.1 to 1)
Guidance Counselors: 16.0 (356.5 to 1)
Current Spending: ($ per student per year):
    Total: $9,357; Instruction: $5,877; Support Services: $3,185

Enrollment, Drop-out Rates and Diploma Recipients by Race/Ethnicity

Category	Total	White	Black	Asian	AIAN	Hisp.
Enrollment (%)	100.0	90.9	0.8	5.3	1.3	1.7
Drop-out Rate (%)	1.2	1.1	9.1	0.0	3.8	4.2
H.S. Diplomas (#)	501	466	2	22	5	6

Number of Schools

Rank	Number	District Name	City
1	233	Milwaukee	Milwaukee
2	52	Madison Metropolitan	Madison
3	41	Kenosha	Kenosha
4	36	Green Bay Area	Green Bay
5	35	Racine	Racine
6	33	Appleton Area	Appleton
7	29	Oshkosh Area	Oshkosh
8	27	Waukesha	Waukesha
9	24	La Crosse	La Crosse
10	22	Eau Claire Area	Eau Claire
11	19	Stevens Point Area	Stevens Point
11	19	Wausau	Wausau
13	18	Janesville	Janesville
13	18	Sheboygan Area	Sheboygan
13	18	West Allis	West Allis
16	17	Beloit	Beloit
16	17	Wauwatosa	Wauwatosa
18	16	Wisconsin Rapids	Wis Rapids
19	14	Neenah	Neenah
20	13	Fond Du Lac	Fond Du Lac
20	13	Sparta Area	Sparta
22	12	Rice Lake Area	Rice Lake
23	11	Elmbrook	Brookfield
23	11	Rhinelander	Rhinelander
23	11	West Bend	West Bend
26	10	Antigo	Antigo
26	10	Beaver Dam	Beaver Dam
26	10	D C Everest Area	Weston
26	10	Manitowoc	Manitowoc
26	10	Merrill Area	Merrill
26	10	Middleton-Cross Plains	Middleton
26	10	New Berlin	New Berlin
26	10	Portage Community	Portage
26	10	Sun Prairie Area	Sun Prairie
26	10	Tomah Area	Tomah
36	9	Menasha	Menasha
36	9	Verona Area	Verona
38	8	Adams-Friendship Area	Friendship
38	8	Baraboo	Baraboo
38	8	Burlington Area	Burlington
38	8	Chippewa Falls Area	Chippewa Falls
38	8	Hamilton	Sussex
38	8	Hayward Community	Hayward
38	8	Menomonie Area	Menomonie
38	8	Mukwonago	Mukwonago
38	8	Muskego-Norway	Muskego
38	8	Oak Creek-Franklin	Oak Creek
38	8	Reedsburg	Reedsburg
38	8	Superior	Superior
50	7	Cudahy	Cudahy
50	7	De Forest Area	De Forest
50	7	Fort Atkinson	Fort Atkinson
50	7	Franklin Public	Franklin
50	7	Howard-Suamico	Green Bay
50	7	Hudson	Hudson
50	7	Kaukauna Area	Kaukauna
50	7	Marshfield	Marshfield
50	7	Menomonee Falls	Menomonee Fls
50	7	Mequon-Thiensville	Mequon
50	7	Monona Grove	Monona
50	7	Monroe	Monroe
50	7	New London	New London
50	7	Oconomowoc Area	Oconomowoc
50	7	Plymouth	Plymouth
50	7	Pulaski Community	Pulaski
50	7	River Falls	River Falls
50	7	Sauk Prairie	Sauk City
50	7	South Milwaukee	S Milwaukee
50	7	Watertown	Watertown
50	7	Waupaca	Waupaca
50	7	Waupun	Waupun
72	6	Elkhorn Area	Elkhorn
72	6	Ellsworth Community	Ellsworth
72	6	Germantown	Germantown
72	6	Greendale	Greendale
72	6	Greenfield	Greenfield
72	6	Holmen	Holmen
72	6	Jefferson	Jefferson
72	6	Kettle Moraine	Wales
72	6	Kimberly Area	Kimberly
72	6	Marinette	Marinette
72	6	Mauston	Mauston
72	6	Milton	Milton
72	6	Oconto Falls	Oconto Falls
72	6	Onalaska	Onalaska
72	6	Oregon	Oregon
72	6	Richland	Richland Ctr
72	6	Shawano-Gresham	Shawano
72	6	Stoughton Area	Stoughton
72	6	Wisconsin Dells	Wisconsin Dells

Rank	Number	District Name	City
91	5	Ashland	Ashland
91	5	Ashwaubenon	Green Bay
91	5	Black River Falls	Black River Fls
91	5	Cedarburg	Cedarburg
91	5	Clintonville	Clintonville
91	5	De Pere	De Pere
91	5	Delavan-Darien	Delavan
91	5	Denmark	Denmark
91	5	East Troy Community	East Troy
91	5	Grafton	Grafton
91	5	Hortonville	Hortonville
91	5	Kewaskum	Kewaskum
91	5	Lodi	Lodi
91	5	Mcfarland	Mc Farland
91	5	Mount Horeb Area	Mount Horeb
91	5	Northland Pines	Eagle River
91	5	Platteville	Platteville
91	5	Port Washington-Saukville	Pt Washington
91	5	Slinger	Slinger
91	5	Two Rivers	Two Rivers
91	5	Waunakee Community	Waunakee
91	5	Whitewater	Whitewater
113	4	Amery	Amery
113	4	Berlin Area	Berlin
113	4	Brown Deer	Brown Deer
113	4	Campbellsport	Campbellsport
113	4	Edgerton	Edgerton
113	4	Evansville Community	Evansville
113	4	Lake Geneva J1	Lake Geneva
113	4	Luxemburg-Casco	Luxemburg
113	4	Medford Area	Medford
113	4	New Richmond	New Richmond
113	4	Osceola	Osceola
113	4	Pewaukee	Pewaukee
113	4	Ripon	Ripon
113	4	Seymour Community	Seymour
113	4	Shorewood	Shorewood
113	4	Waterford Graded J1	Waterford
113	4	Wautoma Area	Wautoma
113	4	Whitefish Bay	Whitefish Bay
113	4	Whitnall	Greenfield
113	4	Winneconne Community	Winneconne
133	3	Freedom Area	Freedom
133	3	Hartford J1	Hartford
133	3	Little Chute Area	Little Chute
133	3	Mosinee	Mosinee
133	3	Sheboygan Falls	Sheboygan Fls
133	3	Spooner	Spooner
133	3	Tomahawk	Tomahawk
133	3	West De Pere	De Pere
133	3	West Salem	West Salem
142	1	Arrowhead Uhs	Hartland
142	1	Hartford Uhs	Hartford

Number of Teachers

Rank	Number	District Name	City
1	5,929	Milwaukee	Milwaukee
2	1,992	Madison Metropolitan	Madison
3	1,463	Green Bay Area	Green Bay
4	1,444	Kenosha	Kenosha
5	1,323	Racine	Racine
6	948	Appleton Area	Appleton
7	849	Waukesha	Waukesha
8	779	Eau Claire Area	Eau Claire
9	765	Janesville	Janesville
10	719	Sheboygan Area	Sheboygan
11	684	Oshkosh Area	Oshkosh
12	613	Wausau	Wausau
13	589	West Allis	West Allis
14	566	La Crosse	La Crosse
15	498	Elmbrook	Brookfield
16	482	Stevens Point Area	Stevens Point
17	478	Fond Du Lac	Fond Du Lac
18	471	Beloit	Beloit
19	464	Wauwatosa	Wauwatosa
20	419	West Bend	West Bend
21	417	Wisconsin Rapids	Wis Rapids
22	403	Neenah	Neenah
23	400	Middleton-Cross Plains	Middleton
24	373	Sun Prairie Area	Sun Prairie
25	360	Verona Area	Verona
26	352	Manitowoc	Manitowoc
27	348	D C Everest Area	Weston
28	323	Superior	Superior
29	309	Mukwonago	Mukwonago
30	307	New Berlin	New Berlin
31	306	Oak Creek-Franklin	Oak Creek
32	303	Menomonee Falls	Menomonee Fls
33	299	Hudson	Hudson
34	293	Chippewa Falls Area	Chippewa Falls
35	293	Howard-Suamico	Green Bay
36	282	Muskego-Norway	Muskego

Rank	Number	District Name	City
37	270	Kettle Moraine	Wales
38	269	Oconomowoc Area	Oconomowoc
39	264	Mequon-Thiensville	Mequon
40	263	Franklin Public	Franklin
41	255	Hamilton	Sussex
42	252	Stoughton Area	Stoughton
43	252	Marshfield	Marshfield
44	248	Oregon	Oregon
45	248	Kaukauna Area	Kaukauna
46	244	Beaver Dam	Beaver Dam
47	242	Germantown	Germantown
48	239	Menasha	Menasha
49	239	Burlington Area	Burlington
50	238	Pulaski Community	Pulaski
51	232	South Milwaukee	S Milwaukee
52	230	Watertown	Watertown
53	226	Menomonie Area	Menomonie
54	225	Kimberly Area	Kimberly
55	225	Holmen	Holmen
56	224	Merrill Area	Merrill
57	220	De Forest Area	De Forest
58	218	Monona Grove	Monona
59	218	Antigo	Antigo
60	216	Tomah Area	Tomah
61	214	De Pere	De Pere
62	214	Greenfield	Greenfield
63	212	Monroe	Monroe
64	212	Rhinelander	Rhinelander
64	212	Waunakee Community	Waunakee
66	209	Ashwaubenon	Green Bay
67	206	Hortonville	Hortonville
68	203	Cudahy	Cudahy
69	200	Baraboo	Baraboo
70	198	Shawano-Gresham	Shawano
71	197	Sauk Prairie	Sauk City
72	195	Waupaca	Waupaca
73	194	Sparta Area	Sparta
74	191	River Falls	River Falls
75	190	Whitefish Bay	Whitefish Bay
76	188	Cedarburg	Cedarburg
77	186	Onalaska	Onalaska
78	186	Milton	Milton
79	185	Fort Atkinson	Fort Atkinson
80	180	Portage Community	Portage
81	178	Rice Lake Area	Rice Lake
82	173	Ashland	Ashland
83	172	Reedsburg	Reedsburg
84	172	Delavan-Darien	Delavan
85	168	New London	New London
86	167	Slinger	Slinger
87	166	Plymouth	Plymouth
88	166	Port Washington-Saukville	Pt Washington
89	165	Waupun	Waupun
90	162	Elkhorn Area	Elkhorn
91	161	Adams-Friendship Area	Friendship
92	159	Marinette	Marinette
93	157	Two Rivers	Two Rivers
94	152	Seymour Community	Seymour
95	151	New Richmond	New Richmond
96	151	Hayward Community	Hayward
97	148	Greendale	Greendale
98	148	Shorewood	Shorewood
99	147	Medford Area	Medford
100	146	Whitnall	Greenfield
101	144	Black River Falls	Black River Fls
102	143	Pewaukee	Pewaukee
103	140	Mount Horeb Area	Mount Horeb
103	140	Whitewater	Whitewater
105	137	Grafton	Grafton
106	136	Mcfarland	Mc Farland
107	136	Oconto Falls	Oconto Falls
108	135	Arrowhead Uhs	Hartland
109	135	West De Pere	De Pere
110	133	Mosinee	Mosinee
111	131	Jefferson	Jefferson
112	127	Mauston	Mauston
113	125	Luxemburg-Casco	Luxemburg
114	124	Edgerton	Edgerton
115	124	Amery	Amery
116	122	Lake Geneva J1	Lake Geneva
117	122	Clintonville	Clintonville
118	122	Wisconsin Dells	Wisconsin Dells
119	120	Ellsworth Community	Ellsworth
120	120	Evansville Community	Evansville
121	119	Berlin Area	Berlin
122	118	Brown Deer	Brown Deer
123	118	Kewaskum	Kewaskum
124	117	Northland Pines	Eagle River
125	117	Ripon	Ripon
125	117	Sheboygan Falls	Sheboygan Fls
127	117	Wautoma Area	Wautoma
128	116	Hartford J1	Hartford

Rank	Number	District Name	City
129	115	Lodi	Lodi
130	115	West Salem	West Salem
131	111	Richland	Richland Ctr
132	111	Winneconne Community	Winneconne
133	110	Tomahawk	Tomahawk
134	109	Hartford Uhs	Hartford
135	109	Denmark	Denmark
136	109	East Troy Community	East Troy
137	108	Spooner	Spooner
138	105	Osceola	Osceola
139	104	Platteville	Platteville
140	101	Campbellsport	Campbellsport
141	100	Freedom Area	Freedom
142	100	Waterford Graded J1	Waterford
143	97	Little Chute Area	Little Chute

Number of Students

Rank	Number	District Name	City
1	97,359	Milwaukee	Milwaukee
2	24,913	Madison Metropolitan	Madison
3	21,457	Racine	Racine
4	21,426	Kenosha	Kenosha
5	20,297	Green Bay Area	Green Bay
6	15,275	Appleton Area	Appleton
7	12,892	Waukesha	Waukesha
8	10,753	Eau Claire Area	Eau Claire
9	10,667	Janesville	Janesville
10	10,419	Oshkosh Area	Oshkosh
11	10,231	Sheboygan Area	Sheboygan
12	8,827	West Allis	West Allis
13	8,746	Wausau	Wausau
14	7,664	Elmbrook	Brookfield
15	7,592	Stevens Point Area	Stevens Point
16	7,498	La Crosse	La Crosse
17	7,278	Fond Du Lac	Fond Du Lac
18	7,040	Wauwatosa	Wauwatosa
19	6,941	Beloit	Beloit
20	6,824	West Bend	West Bend
21	6,387	Neenah	Neenah
22	5,704	Wisconsin Rapids	Wis Rapids
23	5,500	Middleton-Cross Plains	Middleton
24	5,329	Manitowoc	Manitowoc
25	5,240	Sun Prairie Area	Sun Prairie
26	5,213	D C Everest Area	Weston
27	5,063	Oak Creek-Franklin	Oak Creek
28	5,041	Mukwonago	Mukwonago
29	4,938	Superior	Superior
30	4,778	Howard-Suamico	Green Bay
31	4,640	Muskego-Norway	Muskego
32	4,592	New Berlin	New Berlin
33	4,578	Hudson	Hudson
34	4,498	Verona Area	Verona
35	4,491	Chippewa Falls Area	Chippewa Falls
36	4,455	Menomonee Falls	Menomonee Fls
37	4,378	Kettle Moraine	Wales
38	4,210	Oconomowoc Area	Oconomowoc
39	4,120	Mequon-Thiensville	Mequon
40	4,075	Hamilton	Sussex
41	4,050	Marshfield	Marshfield
42	3,956	Franklin Public	Franklin
43	3,750	Kimberly Area	Kimberly
44	3,727	Kaukauna Area	Kaukauna
45	3,716	Germantown	Germantown
46	3,672	Watertown	Watertown
47	3,650	Burlington Area	Burlington
48	3,591	Stoughton Area	Stoughton
49	3,589	Menasha	Menasha
50	3,550	Pulaski Community	Pulaski
51	3,532	South Milwaukee	S Milwaukee
52	3,468	Oregon	Oregon
53	3,443	Beaver Dam	Beaver Dam
54	3,397	Greenfield	Greenfield
55	3,314	Merrill Area	Merrill
56	3,312	Menomonie Area	Menomonie
57	3,266	De Pere	De Pere
58	3,151	De Forest Area	De Forest
59	3,149	Holmen	Holmen
60	3,146	Rhinelander	Rhinelander
61	3,122	Ashwaubenon	Green Bay
62	3,119	Cedarburg	Cedarburg
63	3,031	Waunakee Community	Waunakee
64	3,013	Baraboo	Baraboo
65	3,003	Hortonville	Hortonville
66	2,984	River Falls	River Falls
67	2,953	Milton	Milton
68	2,947	Shawano-Gresham	Shawano
69	2,941	Whitefish Bay	Whitefish Bay
70	2,935	Tomah Area	Tomah
71	2,855	Antigo	Antigo
72	2,849	Cudahy	Cudahy
73	2,847	Slinger	Slinger
74	2,819	Delavan-Darien	Delavan
75	2,817	Monona Grove	Monona
76	2,749	Onalaska	Onalaska
77	2,647	Sparta Area	Sparta
78	2,639	Sauk Prairie	Sauk City
79	2,634	Rice Lake Area	Rice Lake
80	2,633	Fort Atkinson	Fort Atkinson
81	2,628	Port Washington-Saukville	Pt Washington
82	2,596	Elkhorn Area	Elkhorn
83	2,587	Monroe	Monroe
84	2,585	Waupaca	Waupaca
85	2,561	Portage Community	Portage
86	2,516	New London	New London
87	2,507	New Richmond	New Richmond
88	2,501	Whitnall	Greenfield
89	2,486	Marinette	Marinette
90	2,474	Plymouth	Plymouth
91	2,472	Seymour Community	Seymour
92	2,469	Reedsburg	Reedsburg
93	2,376	Greendale	Greendale
94	2,286	Ashland	Ashland
95	2,284	Waupun	Waupun
96	2,281	Arrowhead Uhs	Hartland
97	2,274	Medford Area	Medford
98	2,161	Shorewood	Shorewood
99	2,160	Pewaukee	Pewaukee
100	2,108	Two Rivers	Two Rivers
101	2,059	Adams-Friendship Area	Friendship
102	2,057	Mount Horeb Area	Mount Horeb
103	2,051	Whitewater	Whitewater
104	2,029	West De Pere	De Pere
105	2,014	Mosinee	Mosinee
106	2,005	Hayward Community	Hayward
107	2,003	Grafton	Grafton
108	1,966	Oconto Falls	Oconto Falls
109	1,964	Mcfarland	Mc Farland
110	1,918	Black River Falls	Black River Fls
111	1,907	Luxemburg-Casco	Luxemburg
112	1,874	Kewaskum	Kewaskum
113	1,861	Brown Deer	Brown Deer
114	1,856	Amery	Amery
115	1,855	Edgerton	Edgerton
116	1,780	Osceola	Osceola
117	1,746	Ellsworth Community	Ellsworth
117	1,746	Lake Geneva J1	Lake Geneva
119	1,742	Berlin Area	Berlin
120	1,728	Jefferson	Jefferson
121	1,724	Wisconsin Dells	Wisconsin Dells
122	1,694	Ripon	Ripon
123	1,689	Sheboygan Falls	Sheboygan Fls
124	1,684	Hartford Uhs	Hartford
125	1,683	Lodi	Lodi
126	1,682	East Troy Community	East Troy
127	1,668	Evansville Community	Evansville
128	1,635	Tomahawk	Tomahawk
129	1,626	West Salem	West Salem
130	1,624	Hartford J1	Hartford
131	1,618	Mauston	Mauston
132	1,615	Denmark	Denmark
133	1,592	Wautoma Area	Wautoma
134	1,586	Clintonville	Clintonville
135	1,560	Platteville	Platteville
136	1,557	Freedom Area	Freedom
137	1,534	Campbellsport	Campbellsport
138	1,532	Northland Pines	Eagle River
139	1,525	Winneconne Community	Winneconne
140	1,514	Richland	Richland Ctr
140	1,514	Waterford Graded J1	Waterford
142	1,512	Spooner	Spooner
143	1,500	Little Chute Area	Little Chute

Male Students

Rank	Percent	District Name	City
1	55.2	Spooner	Spooner
2	54.5	Brown Deer	Brown Deer
3	54.4	Little Chute Area	Little Chute
4	54.0	Two Rivers	Two Rivers
5	53.9	West De Pere	De Pere
6	53.3	Wautoma Area	Wautoma
7	53.3	Waterford Graded J1	Waterford
8	53.2	Denmark	Denmark
9	53.2	Winneconne Community	Winneconne
10	53.1	Milton	Milton
11	53.0	Adams-Friendship Area	Friendship
12	53.0	Port Washington-Saukville	Pt Washington
13	53.0	Hartford Uhs	Hartford
14	52.9	Wausau	Wausau
15	52.9	Grafton	Grafton
16	52.8	West Bend	West Bend
17	52.8	Antigo	Antigo
18	52.8	Northland Pines	Eagle River
19	52.7	Ashland	Ashland
20	52.7	Freedom Area	Freedom
21	52.7	Ashwaubenon	Green Bay
22	52.7	Clintonville	Clintonville
23	52.7	Luxemburg-Casco	Luxemburg
24	52.6	Mequon-Thiensville	Mequon
25	52.6	Campbellsport	Campbellsport
26	52.5	Ellsworth Community	Ellsworth
27	52.5	Waupaca	Waupaca
28	52.5	Beaver Dam	Beaver Dam
29	52.4	Edgerton	Edgerton
30	52.4	Mauston	Mauston
31	52.3	Jefferson	Jefferson
32	52.3	Waupun	Waupun
33	52.3	Hudson	Hudson
34	52.3	Merrill Area	Merrill
35	52.3	Medford Area	Medford
36	52.2	Kenosha	Kenosha
37	52.2	Hortonville	Hortonville
38	52.2	Superior	Superior
39	52.2	Verona Area	Verona
40	52.2	Ripon	Ripon
41	52.2	Germantown	Germantown
42	52.2	Delavan-Darien	Delavan
43	52.1	Whitnall	Greenfield
44	52.1	Sheboygan Falls	Sheboygan Fls
45	52.0	River Falls	River Falls
46	52.0	Chippewa Falls Area	Chippewa Falls
47	52.0	Mosinee	Mosinee
48	52.0	Cudahy	Cudahy
49	52.0	Kimberly Area	Kimberly
50	51.9	New London	New London
51	51.8	Portage Community	Portage
52	51.8	Fort Atkinson	Fort Atkinson
53	51.8	Stoughton Area	Stoughton
54	51.8	Janesville	Janesville
55	51.8	Appleton Area	Appleton
56	51.8	La Crosse	La Crosse
57	51.8	South Milwaukee	S Milwaukee
58	51.7	Evansville Community	Evansville
59	51.7	Sparta Area	Sparta
60	51.7	Whitewater	Whitewater
61	51.7	Cedarburg	Cedarburg
62	51.7	Marshfield	Marshfield
63	51.7	Shawano-Gresham	Shawano
64	51.7	Wauwatosa	Wauwatosa
65	51.7	Waunakee Community	Waunakee
66	51.6	Stevens Point Area	Stevens Point
67	51.6	Racine	Racine
68	51.6	Seymour Community	Seymour
69	51.6	Black River Falls	Black River Fls
70	51.6	West Allis	West Allis
71	51.5	D C Everest Area	Weston
72	51.5	Watertown	Watertown
73	51.5	Holmen	Holmen
74	51.5	Monona Grove	Monona
75	51.5	Pewaukee	Pewaukee
76	51.5	Mcfarland	Mc Farland
77	51.5	Lodi	Lodi
78	51.5	Hamilton	Sussex
79	51.4	Green Bay Area	Green Bay
80	51.4	Wisconsin Rapids	Wis Rapids
81	51.4	Pulaski Community	Pulaski
82	51.4	De Pere	De Pere
83	51.4	Waukesha	Waukesha
84	51.3	Rhinelander	Rhinelander
85	51.3	Eau Claire Area	Eau Claire
86	51.3	Elkhorn Area	Elkhorn
87	51.3	Arrowhead Uhs	Hartland
88	51.3	Mukwonago	Mukwonago
89	51.3	Oshkosh Area	Oshkosh
90	51.3	Howard-Suamico	Green Bay
91	51.3	Neenah	Neenah
92	51.3	Marinette	Marinette
93	51.2	Beloit	Beloit
94	51.2	Lake Geneva J1	Lake Geneva
95	51.2	Menomonee Falls	Menomonee Fls
96	51.2	Hayward Community	Hayward
97	51.2	Sun Prairie Area	Sun Prairie
98	51.2	Franklin Public	Franklin
99	51.2	Burlington Area	Burlington
100	51.1	Slinger	Slinger
101	51.1	Oconto Falls	Oconto Falls
102	51.1	Oregon	Oregon
103	51.1	Kaukauna Area	Kaukauna
104	51.1	Oak Creek-Franklin	Oak Creek
105	51.1	East Troy Community	East Troy
106	51.1	Fond Du Lac	Fond Du Lac
107	51.1	Onalaska	Onalaska
108	51.1	Greenfield	Greenfield
109	51.1	Menasha	Menasha
110	51.0	Elmbrook	Brookfield
111	51.0	Baraboo	Baraboo
112	50.9	Rice Lake Area	Rice Lake
113	50.9	Reedsburg	Reedsburg

Rank	Percent	District Name	City
114	50.8	New Berlin	New Berlin
115	50.8	Middleton-Cross Plains	Middleton
116	50.8	Platteville	Platteville
117	50.8	Amery	Amery
118	50.8	Tomah Area	Tomah
119	50.7	Manitowoc	Manitowoc
120	50.7	Sauk Prairie	Sauk City
121	50.7	Oconomowoc Area	Oconomowoc
122	50.7	Milwaukee	Milwaukee
123	50.7	Plymouth	Plymouth
124	50.6	Sheboygan Area	Sheboygan
125	50.6	Berlin Area	Berlin
126	50.6	Hartford J1	Hartford
127	50.5	De Forest Area	De Forest
128	50.4	Greendale	Greendale
129	50.4	Kettle Moraine	Wales
130	50.4	Muskego-Norway	Muskego
131	50.3	Madison Metropolitan	Madison
132	50.3	Whitefish Bay	Whitefish Bay
133	50.1	Menomonie Area	Menomonie
134	50.0	Mount Horeb Area	Mount Horeb
135	50.0	Richland	Richland Ctr
136	50.0	New Richmond	New Richmond
137	49.8	Shorewood	Shorewood
138	49.7	West Salem	West Salem
139	49.7	Osceola	Osceola
140	49.6	Tomahawk	Tomahawk
141	49.1	Kewaskum	Kewaskum
142	48.9	Monroe	Monroe
143	48.6	Wisconsin Dells	Wisconsin Dells

Female Students

Rank	Percent	District Name	City
1	51.3	Wisconsin Dells	Wisconsin Dells
2	51.0	Monroe	Monroe
3	50.8	Kewaskum	Kewaskum
4	50.3	Tomahawk	Tomahawk
5	50.2	Osceola	Osceola
6	50.2	West Salem	West Salem
7	50.1	Shorewood	Shorewood
8	49.9	New Richmond	New Richmond
9	49.9	Richland	Richland Ctr
10	49.9	Mount Horeb Area	Mount Horeb
11	49.8	Menomonie Area	Menomonie
12	49.6	Whitefish Bay	Whitefish Bay
13	49.6	Madison Metropolitan	Madison
14	49.5	Muskego-Norway	Muskego
15	49.5	Kettle Moraine	Wales
16	49.5	Greendale	Greendale
17	49.4	De Forest Area	De Forest
18	49.3	Hartford J1	Hartford
19	49.3	Berlin Area	Berlin
20	49.3	Sheboygan Area	Sheboygan
21	49.2	Plymouth	Plymouth
22	49.2	Milwaukee	Milwaukee
23	49.2	Oconomowoc Area	Oconomowoc
24	49.2	Sauk Prairie	Sauk City
25	49.2	Manitowoc	Manitowoc
26	49.1	Tomah Area	Tomah
27	49.1	Amery	Amery
28	49.1	Platteville	Platteville
29	49.1	Middleton-Cross Plains	Middleton
30	49.1	New Berlin	New Berlin
31	49.0	Reedsburg	Reedsburg
32	49.0	Rice Lake Area	Rice Lake
33	48.9	Baraboo	Baraboo
34	48.9	Elmbrook	Brookfield
35	48.8	Menasha	Menasha
36	48.8	Greenfield	Greenfield
37	48.8	Onalaska	Onalaska
38	48.8	Fond Du Lac	Fond Du Lac
39	48.8	East Troy Community	East Troy
40	48.8	Oak Creek-Franklin	Oak Creek
41	48.8	Kaukauna Area	Kaukauna
42	48.8	Oregon	Oregon
43	48.8	Oconto Falls	Oconto Falls
44	48.8	Slinger	Slinger
45	48.7	Burlington Area	Burlington
46	48.7	Franklin Public	Franklin
47	48.7	Sun Prairie Area	Sun Prairie
48	48.7	Hayward Community	Hayward
49	48.7	Menomonee Falls	Menomonee Fls
50	48.7	Lake Geneva J1	Lake Geneva
51	48.7	Beloit	Beloit
52	48.6	Marinette	Marinette
53	48.6	Neenah	Neenah
54	48.6	Howard-Suamico	Green Bay
55	48.6	Oshkosh Area	Oshkosh
56	48.6	Mukwonago	Mukwonago
57	48.6	Arrowhead Uhs	Hartland
58	48.6	Elkhorn Area	Elkhorn
59	48.6	Eau Claire Area	Eau Claire
60	48.6	Rhinelander	Rhinelander
61	48.5	Waukesha	Waukesha
62	48.5	De Pere	De Pere
63	48.5	Pulaski Community	Pulaski
64	48.5	Wisconsin Rapids	Wis Rapids
65	48.5	Green Bay Area	Green Bay
66	48.4	Hamilton	Sussex
67	48.4	Lodi	Lodi
68	48.4	Mcfarland	Mc Farland
69	48.4	Pewaukee	Pewaukee
70	48.4	Monona Grove	Monona
71	48.4	Holmen	Holmen
72	48.4	Watertown	Watertown
73	48.4	D C Everest Area	Weston
74	48.3	West Allis	West Allis
75	48.3	Black River Falls	Black River Fls
76	48.3	Seymour Community	Seymour
77	48.3	Racine	Racine
78	48.3	Stevens Point Area	Stevens Point
79	48.2	Waunakee Community	Waunakee
80	48.2	Wauwatosa	Wauwatosa
81	48.2	Shawano-Gresham	Shawano
82	48.2	Marshfield	Marshfield
83	48.2	Cedarburg	Cedarburg
84	48.2	Whitewater	Whitewater
85	48.2	Sparta Area	Sparta
86	48.2	Evansville Community	Evansville
87	48.1	South Milwaukee	S Milwaukee
88	48.1	La Crosse	La Crosse
89	48.1	Appleton Area	Appleton
90	48.1	Janesville	Janesville
91	48.1	Stoughton Area	Stoughton
92	48.1	Fort Atkinson	Fort Atkinson
93	48.1	Portage Community	Portage
94	48.0	New London	New London
95	48.0	Kimberly Area	Kimberly
96	47.9	Cudahy	Cudahy
97	47.9	Mosinee	Mosinee
98	47.9	Chippewa Falls Area	Chippewa Falls
99	47.9	River Falls	River Falls
100	47.8	Sheboygan Falls	Sheboygan Fls
101	47.8	Whitnall	Greenfield
102	47.7	Delavan-Darien	Delavan
103	47.7	Germantown	Germantown
104	47.7	Ripon	Ripon
105	47.7	Verona Area	Verona
106	47.7	Superior	Superior
107	47.7	Hortonville	Hortonville
108	47.7	Kenosha	Kenosha
109	47.6	Medford Area	Medford
110	47.6	Merrill Area	Merrill
111	47.6	Hudson	Hudson
112	47.6	Waupun	Waupun
113	47.6	Jefferson	Jefferson
114	47.5	Mauston	Mauston
115	47.5	Edgerton	Edgerton
116	47.4	Beaver Dam	Beaver Dam
117	47.4	Waupaca	Waupaca
118	47.4	Ellsworth Community	Ellsworth
119	47.3	Campbellsport	Campbellsport
120	47.3	Mequon-Thiensville	Mequon
121	47.2	Luxemburg-Casco	Luxemburg
122	47.2	Clintonville	Clintonville
123	47.2	Ashwaubenon	Green Bay
124	47.2	Freedom Area	Freedom
125	47.2	Ashland	Ashland
126	47.1	Northland Pines	Eagle River
127	47.1	Antigo	Antigo
128	47.1	West Bend	West Bend
129	47.0	Grafton	Grafton
130	47.0	Wausau	Wausau
131	46.9	Hartford Uhs	Hartford
132	46.9	Port Washington-Saukville	Pt Washington
133	46.9	Adams-Friendship Area	Friendship
134	46.8	Milton	Milton
135	46.7	Winneconne Community	Winneconne
136	46.7	Denmark	Denmark
137	46.6	Waterford Graded J1	Waterford
138	46.6	Wautoma Area	Wautoma
139	46.0	West De Pere	De Pere
140	45.9	Two Rivers	Two Rivers
141	45.5	Little Chute Area	Little Chute
142	45.4	Brown Deer	Brown Deer
143	44.7	Spooner	Spooner

Individual Education Program Students

Rank	Percent	District Name	City
1	22.4	Richland	Richland Ctr
2	20.1	Adams-Friendship Area	Friendship
3	19.5	Stoughton Area	Stoughton
4	19.1	Green Bay Area	Green Bay
5	18.8	Beloit	Beloit
6	18.7	Edgerton	Edgerton
7	18.4	Madison Metropolitan	Madison
8	17.9	Antigo	Antigo
8	17.9	Hartford J1	Hartford
8	17.9	Watertown	Watertown
11	17.3	Beaver Dam	Beaver Dam
12	17.2	Racine	Racine
13	16.6	Janesville	Janesville
14	16.5	Mauston	Mauston
14	16.5	Milwaukee	Milwaukee
14	16.5	Portage Community	Portage
17	16.4	Monroe	Monroe
17	16.4	Sheboygan Area	Sheboygan
17	16.4	Two Rivers	Two Rivers
20	16.1	Cudahy	Cudahy
20	16.1	Jefferson	Jefferson
22	16.0	Shawano-Gresham	Shawano
23	15.9	Ashwaubenon	Green Bay
23	15.9	Reedsburg	Reedsburg
25	15.7	Black River Falls	Black River Fls
25	15.7	Fond Du Lac	Fond Du Lac
25	15.7	Mcfarland	Mc Farland
25	15.7	Oconto Falls	Oconto Falls
25	15.7	Platteville	Platteville
25	15.7	Waupun	Waupun
31	15.6	Campbellsport	Campbellsport
32	15.5	Oconomowoc Area	Oconomowoc
33	15.4	Sauk Prairie	Sauk City
34	15.3	Oshkosh Area	Oshkosh
35	15.2	Denmark	Denmark
36	15.1	Baraboo	Baraboo
37	15.0	Sun Prairie Area	Sun Prairie
38	14.9	Clintonville	Clintonville
38	14.9	Northland Pines	Eagle River
38	14.9	Plymouth	Plymouth
41	14.8	Ripon	Ripon
42	14.7	Evansville Community	Evansville
42	14.7	Hayward Community	Hayward
44	14.5	La Crosse	La Crosse
44	14.5	Sparta Area	Sparta
46	14.4	Berlin Area	Berlin
46	14.4	Lake Geneva J1	Lake Geneva
46	14.4	Pulaski Community	Pulaski
46	14.4	West Allis	West Allis
50	14.3	Appleton Area	Appleton
50	14.3	Grafton	Grafton
50	14.3	Hudson	Hudson
50	14.3	Wisconsin Rapids	Wis Rapids
54	14.2	Amery	Amery
54	14.2	West De Pere	De Pere
56	14.1	Fort Atkinson	Fort Atkinson
56	14.1	Freedom Area	Freedom
56	14.1	Kenosha	Kenosha
56	14.1	Middleton-Cross Plains	Middleton
56	14.1	Neenah	Neenah
56	14.1	Waterford Graded J1	Waterford
56	14.1	Winneconne Community	Winneconne
63	14.0	Kaukauna Area	Kaukauna
63	14.0	Seymour Community	Seymour
65	13.9	Oregon	Oregon
66	13.8	Burlington Area	Burlington
66	13.8	Chippewa Falls Area	Chippewa Falls
66	13.8	De Forest Area	De Forest
66	13.8	Eau Claire Area	Eau Claire
66	13.8	Menasha	Menasha
66	13.8	Spooner	Spooner
66	13.8	Waunakee Community	Waunakee
73	13.7	Hortonville	Hortonville
73	13.7	Marshfield	Marshfield
73	13.7	Port Washington-Saukville	Pt Washington
73	13.7	Rice Lake Area	Rice Lake
77	13.6	Marinette	Marinette
77	13.6	Whitewater	Whitewater
79	13.3	Ashland	Ashland
79	13.3	Menomonie Area	Menomonie
79	13.3	Mosinee	Mosinee
79	13.3	Stevens Point Area	Stevens Point
83	13.2	Waukesha	Waukesha
83	13.2	Wausau	Wausau
85	13.1	Kettle Moraine	Wales
86	13.0	Merrill Area	Merrill
87	12.9	Howard-Suamico	Green Bay
88	12.8	Ellsworth Community	Ellsworth
88	12.8	Mukwonago	Mukwonago
88	12.8	New London	New London
88	12.8	Rhinelander	Rhinelander
92	12.7	Luxemburg-Casco	Luxemburg
92	12.7	Muskego-Norway	Muskego
92	12.7	New Richmond	New Richmond
92	12.7	Sheboygan Falls	Sheboygan Fls
92	12.7	Verona Area	Verona
92	12.7	Waupaca	Waupaca

Rank	Percent	District Name	City
98	12.6	Superior	Superior
98	12.6	Wisconsin Dells	Wisconsin Dells
100	12.5	Delavan-Darien	Delavan
100	12.5	Lodi	Lodi
102	12.4	Holmen	Holmen
102	12.4	Little Chute Area	Little Chute
102	12.4	New Berlin	New Berlin
102	12.4	Tomahawk	Tomahawk
102	12.4	West Bend	West Bend
107	12.3	River Falls	River Falls
108	12.2	Tomah Area	Tomah
108	12.2	Wautoma Area	Wautoma
110	12.1	D C Everest Area	Weston
110	12.1	Greenfield	Greenfield
110	12.1	Manitowoc	Manitowoc
110	12.1	Menomonee Falls	Menomonee Fls
114	12.0	Mount Horeb Area	Mount Horeb
114	12.0	Oak Creek-Franklin	Oak Creek
114	12.0	Whitnall	Greenfield
117	11.9	Pewaukee	Pewaukee
118	11.8	Slinger	Slinger
119	11.7	Kewaskum	Kewaskum
119	11.7	West Salem	West Salem
121	11.6	Hartford Uhs	Hartford
121	11.6	Monona Grove	Monona
123	11.4	South Milwaukee	S Milwaukee
124	11.2	Germantown	Germantown
124	11.2	Mequon-Thiensville	Mequon
126	11.0	Cedarburg	Cedarburg
126	11.0	Elmbrook	Brookfield
126	11.0	Osceola	Osceola
129	10.9	Elkhorn Area	Elkhorn
129	10.9	Medford Area	Medford
131	10.6	Franklin Public	Franklin
131	10.6	Wauwatosa	Wauwatosa
133	10.5	Kimberly Area	Kimberly
134	10.3	De Pere	De Pere
135	10.2	Milton	Milton
136	10.1	Brown Deer	Brown Deer
137	10.0	Onalaska	Onalaska
138	9.9	East Troy Community	East Troy
139	9.8	Greendale	Greendale
140	9.7	Hamilton	Sussex
141	8.8	Shorewood	Shorewood
142	7.3	Whitefish Bay	Whitefish Bay
143	7.0	Arrowhead Uhs	Hartland

English Language Learner Students

Rank	Percent	District Name	City
1	19.3	Sheboygan Area	Sheboygan
2	16.9	Wausau	Wausau
3	12.7	Lake Geneva J1	Lake Geneva
4	12.3	Delavan-Darien	Delavan
5	12.1	Madison Metropolitan	Madison
6	11.4	Wautoma Area	Wautoma
7	11.2	Green Bay Area	Green Bay
8	10.4	Menasha	Menasha
8	10.4	Whitewater	Whitewater
10	8.5	Appleton Area	Appleton
10	8.5	Shorewood	Shorewood
12	7.6	Beloit	Beloit
13	6.6	Manitowoc	Manitowoc
13	6.6	Milwaukee	Milwaukee
15	6.5	Waukesha	Waukesha
16	6.3	La Crosse	La Crosse
17	6.2	D C Everest Area	Weston
18	6.0	Elkhorn Area	Elkhorn
19	5.0	Franklin Public	Franklin
20	4.9	Racine	Racine
21	4.8	Holmen	Holmen
22	4.6	Oshkosh Area	Oshkosh
23	4.4	Stevens Point Area	Stevens Point
23	4.4	Wisconsin Rapids	Wis Rapids
25	4.0	Kenosha	Kenosha
25	4.0	Menomonie Area	Menomonie
27	3.9	Eau Claire Area	Eau Claire
28	3.8	Sauk Prairie	Sauk City
29	3.1	Neenah	Neenah
30	3.0	Two Rivers	Two Rivers
31	2.9	Kaukauna Area	Kaukauna
32	2.8	Janesville	Janesville
33	2.7	Beaver Dam	Beaver Dam
34	2.6	Whitnall	Greenfield
35	2.5	West Allis	West Allis
36	2.4	New London	New London
37	2.2	Burlington Area	Burlington
38	1.9	Onalaska	Onalaska
39	1.7	Evansville Community	Evansville
40	1.6	Fond Du Lac	Fond Du Lac
40	1.6	Sun Prairie Area	Sun Prairie
42	1.1	De Forest Area	De Forest
43	0.8	Howard-Suamico	Green Bay
44	0.1	Plymouth	Plymouth
45	0.0	Adams-Friendship Area	Friendship
45	0.0	Amery	Amery
45	0.0	Antigo	Antigo
45	0.0	Arrowhead Uhs	Hartland
45	0.0	Ashland	Ashland
45	0.0	Ashwaubenon	Green Bay
45	0.0	Baraboo	Baraboo
45	0.0	Berlin Area	Berlin
45	0.0	Black River Falls	Black River Fls
45	0.0	Brown Deer	Brown Deer
45	0.0	Campbellsport	Campbellsport
45	0.0	Cedarburg	Cedarburg
45	0.0	Chippewa Falls Area	Chippewa Falls
45	0.0	Clintonville	Clintonville
45	0.0	Cudahy	Cudahy
45	0.0	De Pere	De Pere
45	0.0	Denmark	Denmark
45	0.0	East Troy Community	East Troy
45	0.0	Edgerton	Edgerton
45	0.0	Ellsworth Community	Ellsworth
45	0.0	Elmbrook	Brookfield
45	0.0	Fort Atkinson	Fort Atkinson
45	0.0	Freedom Area	Freedom
45	0.0	Germantown	Germantown
45	0.0	Grafton	Grafton
45	0.0	Greendale	Greendale
45	0.0	Greenfield	Greenfield
45	0.0	Hamilton	Sussex
45	0.0	Hartford J1	Hartford
45	0.0	Hartford Uhs	Hartford
45	0.0	Hayward Community	Hayward
45	0.0	Hortonville	Hortonville
45	0.0	Hudson	Hudson
45	0.0	Jefferson	Jefferson
45	0.0	Kettle Moraine	Wales
45	0.0	Kewaskum	Kewaskum
45	0.0	Kimberly Area	Kimberly
45	0.0	Little Chute Area	Little Chute
45	0.0	Lodi	Lodi
45	0.0	Luxemburg-Casco	Luxemburg
45	0.0	Marinette	Marinette
45	0.0	Marshfield	Marshfield
45	0.0	Mauston	Mauston
45	0.0	Mcfarland	Mc Farland
45	0.0	Medford Area	Medford
45	0.0	Menomonee Falls	Menomonee Fls
45	0.0	Mequon-Thiensville	Mequon
45	0.0	Merrill Area	Merrill
45	0.0	Middleton-Cross Plains	Middleton
45	0.0	Milton	Milton
45	0.0	Monona Grove	Monona
45	0.0	Monroe	Monroe
45	0.0	Mosinee	Mosinee
45	0.0	Mount Horeb Area	Mount Horeb
45	0.0	Mukwonago	Mukwonago
45	0.0	Muskego-Norway	Muskego
45	0.0	New Berlin	New Berlin
45	0.0	New Richmond	New Richmond
45	0.0	Northland Pines	Eagle River
45	0.0	Oak Creek-Franklin	Oak Creek
45	0.0	Oconomowoc Area	Oconomowoc
45	0.0	Oconto Falls	Oconto Falls
45	0.0	Oregon	Oregon
45	0.0	Osceola	Osceola
45	0.0	Pewaukee	Pewaukee
45	0.0	Platteville	Platteville
45	0.0	Port Washington-Saukville	Pt Washington
45	0.0	Portage Community	Portage
45	0.0	Pulaski Community	Pulaski
45	0.0	Reedsburg	Reedsburg
45	0.0	Rhinelander	Rhinelander
45	0.0	Rice Lake Area	Rice Lake
45	0.0	Richland	Richland Ctr
45	0.0	Ripon	Ripon
45	0.0	River Falls	River Falls
45	0.0	Seymour Community	Seymour
45	0.0	Shawano-Gresham	Shawano
45	0.0	Sheboygan Falls	Sheboygan Fls
45	0.0	Slinger	Slinger
45	0.0	South Milwaukee	S Milwaukee
45	0.0	Sparta Area	Sparta
45	0.0	Spooner	Spooner
45	0.0	Stoughton Area	Stoughton
45	0.0	Superior	Superior
45	0.0	Tomah Area	Tomah
45	0.0	Tomahawk	Tomahawk
45	0.0	Verona Area	Verona
45	0.0	Waterford Graded J1	Waterford
45	0.0	Watertown	Watertown
45	0.0	Waunakee Community	Waunakee
45	0.0	Waupaca	Waupaca
45	0.0	Waupun	Waupun
45	0.0	Wauwatosa	Wauwatosa
45	0.0	West Bend	West Bend
45	0.0	West De Pere	De Pere
45	0.0	West Salem	West Salem
45	0.0	Whitefish Bay	Whitefish Bay
45	0.0	Winneconne Community	Winneconne
45	0.0	Wisconsin Dells	Wisconsin Dells

Migrant Students

Rank	Percent	District Name	City
1	5.8	Berlin Area	Berlin
2	5.7	Wautoma Area	Wautoma
3	1.7	Green Bay Area	Green Bay
4	1.2	Watertown	Watertown
5	0.4	Monroe	Monroe
5	0.4	Portage Community	Portage
7	0.3	Beaver Dam	Beaver Dam
7	0.3	Kettle Moraine	Wales
7	0.3	Madison Metropolitan	Madison
7	0.3	Waupun	Waupun
11	0.2	Wisconsin Rapids	Wis Rapids
12	0.1	Fond Du Lac	Fond Du Lac
12	0.1	Milwaukee	Milwaukee
12	0.1	Osceola	Osceola
12	0.1	Wisconsin Dells	Wisconsin Dells
16	0.0	Racine	Racine
17	0.0	Adams-Friendship Area	Friendship
17	0.0	Amery	Amery
17	0.0	Antigo	Antigo
17	0.0	Appleton Area	Appleton
17	0.0	Arrowhead Uhs	Hartland
17	0.0	Ashland	Ashland
17	0.0	Ashwaubenon	Green Bay
17	0.0	Baraboo	Baraboo
17	0.0	Beloit	Beloit
17	0.0	Black River Falls	Black River Fls
17	0.0	Brown Deer	Brown Deer
17	0.0	Burlington Area	Burlington
17	0.0	Campbellsport	Campbellsport
17	0.0	Cedarburg	Cedarburg
17	0.0	Chippewa Falls Area	Chippewa Falls
17	0.0	Clintonville	Clintonville
17	0.0	Cudahy	Cudahy
17	0.0	D C Everest Area	Weston
17	0.0	De Forest Area	De Forest
17	0.0	De Pere	De Pere
17	0.0	Delavan-Darien	Delavan
17	0.0	Denmark	Denmark
17	0.0	East Troy Community	East Troy
17	0.0	Eau Claire Area	Eau Claire
17	0.0	Edgerton	Edgerton
17	0.0	Elkhorn Area	Elkhorn
17	0.0	Ellsworth Community	Ellsworth
17	0.0	Elmbrook	Brookfield
17	0.0	Evansville Community	Evansville
17	0.0	Fort Atkinson	Fort Atkinson
17	0.0	Franklin Public	Franklin
17	0.0	Freedom Area	Freedom
17	0.0	Germantown	Germantown
17	0.0	Grafton	Grafton
17	0.0	Greendale	Greendale
17	0.0	Greenfield	Greenfield
17	0.0	Hamilton	Sussex
17	0.0	Hartford J1	Hartford
17	0.0	Hartford Uhs	Hartford
17	0.0	Hayward Community	Hayward
17	0.0	Holmen	Holmen
17	0.0	Hortonville	Hortonville
17	0.0	Howard-Suamico	Green Bay
17	0.0	Hudson	Hudson
17	0.0	Janesville	Janesville
17	0.0	Jefferson	Jefferson
17	0.0	Kaukauna Area	Kaukauna
17	0.0	Kenosha	Kenosha
17	0.0	Kewaskum	Kewaskum
17	0.0	Kimberly Area	Kimberly
17	0.0	La Crosse	La Crosse
17	0.0	Lake Geneva J1	Lake Geneva
17	0.0	Little Chute Area	Little Chute
17	0.0	Lodi	Lodi
17	0.0	Luxemburg-Casco	Luxemburg
17	0.0	Manitowoc	Manitowoc
17	0.0	Marinette	Marinette
17	0.0	Marshfield	Marshfield
17	0.0	Mauston	Mauston
17	0.0	Mcfarland	Mc Farland
17	0.0	Medford Area	Medford
17	0.0	Menasha	Menasha
17	0.0	Menomonee Falls	Menomonee Fls
17	0.0	Menomonie Area	Menomonie
17	0.0	Mequon-Thiensville	Mequon
17	0.0	Merrill Area	Merrill

Rank	Percent	District Name	City
17	0.0	Middleton-Cross Plains	Middleton
17	0.0	Milton	Milton
17	0.0	Monona Grove	Monona
17	0.0	Mosinee	Mosinee
17	0.0	Mount Horeb Area	Mount Horeb
17	0.0	Mukwonago	Mukwonago
17	0.0	Muskego-Norway	Muskego
17	0.0	Neenah	Neenah
17	0.0	New Berlin	New Berlin
17	0.0	New London	New London
17	0.0	New Richmond	New Richmond
17	0.0	Northland Pines	Eagle River
17	0.0	Oak Creek-Franklin	Oak Creek
17	0.0	Oconomowoc Area	Oconomowoc
17	0.0	Oconto Falls	Oconto Falls
17	0.0	Onalaska	Onalaska
17	0.0	Oregon	Oregon
17	0.0	Oshkosh Area	Oshkosh
17	0.0	Pewaukee	Pewaukee
17	0.0	Platteville	Platteville
17	0.0	Plymouth	Plymouth
17	0.0	Port Washington-Saukville	Pt Washington
17	0.0	Pulaski Community	Pulaski
17	0.0	Reedsburg	Reedsburg
17	0.0	Rhinelander	Rhinelander
17	0.0	Rice Lake Area	Rice Lake
17	0.0	Richland	Richland Ctr
17	0.0	Ripon	Ripon
17	0.0	River Falls	River Falls
17	0.0	Sauk Prairie	Sauk City
17	0.0	Seymour Community	Seymour
17	0.0	Shawano-Gresham	Shawano
17	0.0	Sheboygan Area	Sheboygan
17	0.0	Sheboygan Falls	Sheboygan Fls
17	0.0	Shorewood	Shorewood
17	0.0	Slinger	Slinger
17	0.0	South Milwaukee	S Milwaukee
17	0.0	Sparta Area	Sparta
17	0.0	Spooner	Spooner
17	0.0	Stevens Point Area	Stevens Point
17	0.0	Stoughton Area	Stoughton
17	0.0	Sun Prairie Area	Sun Prairie
17	0.0	Superior	Superior
17	0.0	Tomah Area	Tomah
17	0.0	Tomahawk	Tomahawk
17	0.0	Two Rivers	Two Rivers
17	0.0	Verona Area	Verona
17	0.0	Waterford Graded J1	Waterford
17	0.0	Waukesha	Waukesha
17	0.0	Waunakee Community	Waunakee
17	0.0	Waupaca	Waupaca
17	0.0	Wausau	Wausau
17	0.0	Wauwatosa	Wauwatosa
17	0.0	West Allis	West Allis
17	0.0	West Bend	West Bend
17	0.0	West De Pere	De Pere
17	0.0	West Salem	West Salem
17	0.0	Whitefish Bay	Whitefish Bay
17	0.0	Whitnall	Greenfield
17	0.0	Whitewater	Whitewater
17	0.0	Winneconne Community	Winneconne

Students Eligible for Free Lunch

Rank	Percent	District Name	City
1	n/a	Adams-Friendship Area	Friendship
1	n/a	Amery	Amery
1	n/a	Antigo	Antigo
1	n/a	Appleton Area	Appleton
1	n/a	Arrowhead Uhs	Hartland
1	n/a	Ashland	Ashland
1	n/a	Ashwaubenon	Green Bay
1	n/a	Baraboo	Baraboo
1	n/a	Beaver Dam	Beaver Dam
1	n/a	Beloit	Beloit
1	n/a	Berlin Area	Berlin
1	n/a	Black River Falls	Black River Fls
1	n/a	Brown Deer	Brown Deer
1	n/a	Burlington Area	Burlington
1	n/a	Campbellsport	Campbellsport
1	n/a	Cedarburg	Cedarburg
1	n/a	Chippewa Falls Area	Chippewa Falls
1	n/a	Clintonville	Clintonville
1	n/a	Cudahy	Cudahy
1	n/a	D C Everest Area	Weston
1	n/a	De Forest Area	De Forest
1	n/a	De Pere	De Pere
1	n/a	Delavan-Darien	Delavan
1	n/a	Denmark	Denmark
1	n/a	East Troy Community	East Troy
1	n/a	Eau Claire Area	Eau Claire
1	n/a	Edgerton	Edgerton
1	n/a	Elkhorn Area	Elkhorn
1	n/a	Ellsworth Community	Ellsworth
1	n/a	Elmbrook	Brookfield
1	n/a	Evansville Community	Evansville
1	n/a	Fond Du Lac	Fond Du Lac
1	n/a	Fort Atkinson	Fort Atkinson
1	n/a	Franklin Public	Franklin
1	n/a	Freedom Area	Freedom
1	n/a	Germantown	Germantown
1	n/a	Grafton	Grafton
1	n/a	Green Bay Area	Green Bay
1	n/a	Greendale	Greendale
1	n/a	Greenfield	Greenfield
1	n/a	Hamilton	Sussex
1	n/a	Hartford J1	Hartford
1	n/a	Hartford Uhs	Hartford
1	n/a	Hayward Community	Hayward
1	n/a	Holmen	Holmen
1	n/a	Hortonville	Hortonville
1	n/a	Howard-Suamico	Green Bay
1	n/a	Hudson	Hudson
1	n/a	Janesville	Janesville
1	n/a	Jefferson	Jefferson
1	n/a	Kaukauna Area	Kaukauna
1	n/a	Kenosha	Kenosha
1	n/a	Kettle Moraine	Wales
1	n/a	Kewaskum	Kewaskum
1	n/a	Kimberly Area	Kimberly
1	n/a	La Crosse	La Crosse
1	n/a	Lake Geneva J1	Lake Geneva
1	n/a	Little Chute Area	Little Chute
1	n/a	Lodi	Lodi
1	n/a	Luxemburg-Casco	Luxemburg
1	n/a	Madison Metropolitan	Madison
1	n/a	Manitowoc	Manitowoc
1	n/a	Marinette	Marinette
1	n/a	Marshfield	Marshfield
1	n/a	Mauston	Mauston
1	n/a	Mcfarland	Mc Farland
1	n/a	Medford Area	Medford
1	n/a	Menasha	Menasha
1	n/a	Menomonee Falls	Menomonee Fls
1	n/a	Menomonie Area	Menomonie
1	n/a	Mequon-Thiensville	Mequon
1	n/a	Merrill Area	Merrill
1	n/a	Middleton-Cross Plains	Middleton
1	n/a	Milton	Milton
1	n/a	Milwaukee	Milwaukee
1	n/a	Monona Grove	Monona
1	n/a	Monroe	Monroe
1	n/a	Mosinee	Mosinee
1	n/a	Mount Horeb Area	Mount Horeb
1	n/a	Mukwonago	Mukwonago
1	n/a	Muskego-Norway	Muskego
1	n/a	Neenah	Neenah
1	n/a	New Berlin	New Berlin
1	n/a	New London	New London
1	n/a	New Richmond	New Richmond
1	n/a	Northland Pines	Eagle River
1	n/a	Oak Creek-Franklin	Oak Creek
1	n/a	Oconomowoc Area	Oconomowoc
1	n/a	Oconto Falls	Oconto Falls
1	n/a	Onalaska	Onalaska
1	n/a	Oregon	Oregon
1	n/a	Osceola	Osceola
1	n/a	Oshkosh Area	Oshkosh
1	n/a	Pewaukee	Pewaukee
1	n/a	Platteville	Platteville
1	n/a	Plymouth	Plymouth
1	n/a	Port Washington-Saukville	Pt Washington
1	n/a	Portage Community	Portage
1	n/a	Pulaski Community	Pulaski
1	n/a	Racine	Racine
1	n/a	Reedsburg	Reedsburg
1	n/a	Rhinelander	Rhinelander
1	n/a	Rice Lake Area	Rice Lake
1	n/a	Richland	Richland Ctr
1	n/a	Ripon	Ripon
1	n/a	River Falls	River Falls
1	n/a	Sauk Prairie	Sauk City
1	n/a	Seymour Community	Seymour
1	n/a	Shawano-Gresham	Shawano
1	n/a	Sheboygan Area	Sheboygan
1	n/a	Sheboygan Falls	Sheboygan Fls
1	n/a	Shorewood	Shorewood
1	n/a	Slinger	Slinger
1	n/a	South Milwaukee	S Milwaukee
1	n/a	Sparta Area	Sparta
1	n/a	Spooner	Spooner
1	n/a	Stevens Point Area	Stevens Point
1	n/a	Stoughton Area	Stoughton
1	n/a	Sun Prairie Area	Sun Prairie
1	n/a	Superior	Superior
1	n/a	Tomah Area	Tomah
1	n/a	Tomahawk	Tomahawk
1	n/a	Two Rivers	Two Rivers
1	n/a	Verona Area	Verona
1	n/a	Waterford Graded J1	Waterford
1	n/a	Watertown	Watertown
1	n/a	Waukesha	Waukesha
1	n/a	Waunakee Community	Waunakee
1	n/a	Waupaca	Waupaca
1	n/a	Waupun	Waupun
1	n/a	Wausau	Wausau
1	n/a	Wautoma Area	Wautoma
1	n/a	Wauwatosa	Wauwatosa
1	n/a	West Allis	West Allis
1	n/a	West Bend	West Bend
1	n/a	West De Pere	De Pere
1	n/a	West Salem	West Salem
1	n/a	Whitefish Bay	Whitefish Bay
1	n/a	Whitewater	Whitewater
1	n/a	Whitnall	Greenfield
1	n/a	Winneconne Community	Winneconne
1	n/a	Wisconsin Dells	Wisconsin Dells
1	n/a	Wisconsin Rapids	Wis Rapids

Students Eligible for Reduced-Price Lunch

Rank	Percent	District Name	City
1	n/a	Adams-Friendship Area	Friendship
1	n/a	Amery	Amery
1	n/a	Antigo	Antigo
1	n/a	Appleton Area	Appleton
1	n/a	Arrowhead Uhs	Hartland
1	n/a	Ashland	Ashland
1	n/a	Ashwaubenon	Green Bay
1	n/a	Baraboo	Baraboo
1	n/a	Beaver Dam	Beaver Dam
1	n/a	Beloit	Beloit
1	n/a	Berlin Area	Berlin
1	n/a	Black River Falls	Black River Fls
1	n/a	Brown Deer	Brown Deer
1	n/a	Burlington Area	Burlington
1	n/a	Campbellsport	Campbellsport
1	n/a	Cedarburg	Cedarburg
1	n/a	Chippewa Falls Area	Chippewa Falls
1	n/a	Clintonville	Clintonville
1	n/a	Cudahy	Cudahy
1	n/a	D C Everest Area	Weston
1	n/a	De Forest Area	De Forest
1	n/a	De Pere	De Pere
1	n/a	Delavan-Darien	Delavan
1	n/a	Denmark	Denmark
1	n/a	East Troy Community	East Troy
1	n/a	Eau Claire Area	Eau Claire
1	n/a	Edgerton	Edgerton
1	n/a	Elkhorn Area	Elkhorn
1	n/a	Ellsworth Community	Ellsworth
1	n/a	Elmbrook	Brookfield
1	n/a	Evansville Community	Evansville
1	n/a	Fond Du Lac	Fond Du Lac
1	n/a	Fort Atkinson	Fort Atkinson
1	n/a	Franklin Public	Franklin
1	n/a	Freedom Area	Freedom
1	n/a	Germantown	Germantown
1	n/a	Grafton	Grafton
1	n/a	Green Bay Area	Green Bay
1	n/a	Greendale	Greendale
1	n/a	Greenfield	Greenfield
1	n/a	Hamilton	Sussex
1	n/a	Hartford J1	Hartford
1	n/a	Hartford Uhs	Hartford
1	n/a	Hayward Community	Hayward
1	n/a	Holmen	Holmen
1	n/a	Hortonville	Hortonville
1	n/a	Howard-Suamico	Green Bay
1	n/a	Hudson	Hudson
1	n/a	Janesville	Janesville
1	n/a	Jefferson	Jefferson
1	n/a	Kaukauna Area	Kaukauna
1	n/a	Kenosha	Kenosha
1	n/a	Kettle Moraine	Wales
1	n/a	Kewaskum	Kewaskum
1	n/a	Kimberly Area	Kimberly
1	n/a	La Crosse	La Crosse
1	n/a	Lake Geneva J1	Lake Geneva
1	n/a	Little Chute Area	Little Chute
1	n/a	Lodi	Lodi
1	n/a	Luxemburg-Casco	Luxemburg
1	n/a	Madison Metropolitan	Madison
1	n/a	Manitowoc	Manitowoc
1	n/a	Marinette	Marinette
1	n/a	Marshfield	Marshfield

Rank	Ratio	District Name	City
1	n/a	Mauston	Mauston
1	n/a	Mcfarland	Mc Farland
1	n/a	Medford Area	Medford
1	n/a	Menasha	Menasha
1	n/a	Menomonee Falls	Menomonee Fls
1	n/a	Menomonie Area	Menomonie
1	n/a	Mequon-Thiensville	Mequon
1	n/a	Merrill Area	Merrill
1	n/a	Middleton-Cross Plains	Middleton
1	n/a	Milton	Milton
1	n/a	Milwaukee	Milwaukee
1	n/a	Monona Grove	Monona
1	n/a	Monroe	Monroe
1	n/a	Mosinee	Mosinee
1	n/a	Mount Horeb Area	Mount Horeb
1	n/a	Mukwonago	Mukwonago
1	n/a	Muskego-Norway	Muskego
1	n/a	Neenah	Neenah
1	n/a	New Berlin	New Berlin
1	n/a	New London	New London
1	n/a	New Richmond	New Richmond
1	n/a	Northland Pines	Eagle River
1	n/a	Oak Creek-Franklin	Oak Creek
1	n/a	Oconomowoc Area	Oconomowoc
1	n/a	Oconto Falls	Oconto Falls
1	n/a	Onalaska	Onalaska
1	n/a	Oregon	Oregon
1	n/a	Osceola	Osceola
1	n/a	Oshkosh Area	Oshkosh
1	n/a	Pewaukee	Pewaukee
1	n/a	Platteville	Platteville
1	n/a	Plymouth	Plymouth
1	n/a	Port Washington-Saukville	Pt Washington
1	n/a	Portage Community	Portage
1	n/a	Pulaski Community	Pulaski
1	n/a	Racine	Racine
1	n/a	Reedsburg	Reedsburg
1	n/a	Rhinelander	Rhinelander
1	n/a	Rice Lake Area	Rice Lake
1	n/a	Richland	Richland Ctr
1	n/a	Ripon	Ripon
1	n/a	River Falls	River Falls
1	n/a	Sauk Prairie	Sauk City
1	n/a	Seymour Community	Seymour
1	n/a	Shawano-Gresham	Shawano
1	n/a	Sheboygan Area	Sheboygan
1	n/a	Sheboygan Falls	Sheboygan Fls
1	n/a	Shorewood	Shorewood
1	n/a	Slinger	Slinger
1	n/a	South Milwaukee	S Milwaukee
1	n/a	Sparta Area	Sparta
1	n/a	Spooner	Spooner
1	n/a	Stevens Point Area	Stevens Point
1	n/a	Stoughton Area	Stoughton
1	n/a	Sun Prairie Area	Sun Prairie
1	n/a	Superior	Superior
1	n/a	Tomah Area	Tomah
1	n/a	Tomahawk	Tomahawk
1	n/a	Two Rivers	Two Rivers
1	n/a	Verona Area	Verona
1	n/a	Waterford Graded J1	Waterford
1	n/a	Watertown	Watertown
1	n/a	Waukesha	Waukesha
1	n/a	Waunakee Community	Waunakee
1	n/a	Waupaca	Waupaca
1	n/a	Waupun	Waupun
1	n/a	Wausau	Wausau
1	n/a	Wautoma Area	Wautoma
1	n/a	Wauwatosa	Wauwatosa
1	n/a	West Allis	West Allis
1	n/a	West Bend	West Bend
1	n/a	West De Pere	De Pere
1	n/a	West Salem	West Salem
1	n/a	Whitefish Bay	Whitefish Bay
1	n/a	Whitewater	Whitewater
1	n/a	Whitnall	Greenfield
1	n/a	Winneconne Community	Winneconne
1	n/a	Wisconsin Dells	Wisconsin Dells
1	n/a	Wisconsin Rapids	Wis Rapids

Student/Teacher Ratio

Rank	Ratio	District Name	City
1	17.1	Whitnall	Greenfield
2	17.0	Slinger	Slinger
3	16.9	Arrowhead Uhs	Hartland
3	16.9	Osceola	Osceola
5	16.6	Cedarburg	Cedarburg
5	16.6	Kimberly Area	Kimberly
5	16.6	New Richmond	New Richmond
8	16.5	Oak Creek-Franklin	Oak Creek
9	16.4	Milwaukee	Milwaukee
9	16.4	Muskego-Norway	Muskego
11	16.3	Delavan-Darien	Delavan
11	16.3	Howard-Suamico	Green Bay
11	16.3	Mukwonago	Mukwonago
11	16.3	Seymour Community	Seymour
11	16.3	West Bend	West Bend
16	16.2	Kettle Moraine	Wales
16	16.2	Racine	Racine
18	16.1	Appleton Area	Appleton
18	16.1	Marshfield	Marshfield
20	16.0	Greendale	Greendale
20	16.0	Watertown	Watertown
22	15.9	Hamilton	Sussex
22	15.9	Milton	Milton
24	15.8	Elkhorn Area	Elkhorn
24	15.8	Greenfield	Greenfield
24	15.8	Kewaskum	Kewaskum
24	15.8	Neenah	Neenah
24	15.8	Port Washington-Saukville	Pt Washington
29	15.7	Brown Deer	Brown Deer
29	15.7	Stevens Point Area	Stevens Point
31	15.6	Marinette	Marinette
31	15.6	Mequon-Thiensville	Mequon
31	15.6	Oconomowoc Area	Oconomowoc
31	15.6	River Falls	River Falls
35	15.4	East Troy Community	East Troy
35	15.4	Elmbrook	Brookfield
35	15.4	Freedom Area	Freedom
35	15.4	Little Chute Area	Little Chute
35	15.4	Medford Area	Medford
35	15.4	Whitefish Bay	Whitefish Bay
41	15.3	Chippewa Falls Area	Chippewa Falls
41	15.3	Germantown	Germantown
41	15.3	Hartford Uhs	Hartford
41	15.3	Hudson	Hudson
41	15.3	Superior	Superior
46	15.2	Burlington Area	Burlington
46	15.2	De Pere	De Pere
46	15.2	Fond Du Lac	Fond Du Lac
46	15.2	Luxemburg-Casco	Luxemburg
46	15.2	Oshkosh Area	Oshkosh
46	15.2	South Milwaukee	S Milwaukee
46	15.2	Waukesha	Waukesha
46	15.2	Wauwatosa	Wauwatosa
54	15.1	Baraboo	Baraboo
54	15.1	Campbellsport	Campbellsport
54	15.1	Manitowoc	Manitowoc
54	15.1	Mosinee	Mosinee
54	15.1	Pewaukee	Pewaukee
54	15.1	Waterford Graded J1	Waterford
60	15.0	D C Everest Area	Weston
60	15.0	Franklin Public	Franklin
60	15.0	Kaukauna Area	Kaukauna
60	15.0	Menasha	Menasha
60	15.0	Platteville	Platteville
60	15.0	West Allis	West Allis
60	15.0	West De Pere	De Pere
67	14.9	Amery	Amery
67	14.9	Ashwaubenon	Green Bay
67	14.9	Edgerton	Edgerton
67	14.9	New Berlin	New Berlin
67	14.9	New London	New London
67	14.9	Plymouth	Plymouth
67	14.9	Pulaski Community	Pulaski
67	14.9	Shawano-Gresham	Shawano
75	14.8	Denmark	Denmark
75	14.8	Kenosha	Kenosha
75	14.8	Onalaska	Onalaska
75	14.8	Rhinelander	Rhinelander
75	14.8	Rice Lake Area	Rice Lake
75	14.8	Tomahawk	Tomahawk
81	14.7	Beloit	Beloit
81	14.7	Menomonee Falls	Menomonee Fls
81	14.7	Merrill Area	Merrill
84	14.6	Hortonville	Hortonville
84	14.6	Menomonie Area	Menomonie
84	14.6	Mount Horeb Area	Mount Horeb
84	14.6	Shorewood	Shorewood
84	14.6	Whitewater	Whitewater
89	14.5	Berlin Area	Berlin
89	14.5	Ellsworth Community	Ellsworth
89	14.5	Grafton	Grafton
89	14.5	Lodi	Lodi
93	14.4	Mcfarland	Mc Farland
93	14.4	Oconto Falls	Oconto Falls
93	14.4	Ripon	Ripon
93	14.4	Sheboygan Falls	Sheboygan Fls
97	14.3	De Forest Area	De Forest
97	14.3	Reedsburg	Reedsburg
99	14.2	Fort Atkinson	Fort Atkinson
99	14.2	Lake Geneva J1	Lake Geneva
99	14.2	Portage Community	Portage
99	14.2	Sheboygan Area	Sheboygan
99	14.2	Stoughton Area	Stoughton
99	14.2	Waunakee Community	Waunakee
99	14.2	Wausau	Wausau
106	14.1	Beaver Dam	Beaver Dam
106	14.1	West Salem	West Salem
106	14.1	Wisconsin Dells	Wisconsin Dells
109	14.0	Cudahy	Cudahy
109	14.0	Hartford J1	Hartford
109	14.0	Holmen	Holmen
109	14.0	Spooner	Spooner
109	14.0	Sun Prairie Area	Sun Prairie
114	13.9	Evansville Community	Evansville
114	13.9	Green Bay Area	Green Bay
114	13.9	Janesville	Janesville
114	13.9	Oregon	Oregon
118	13.8	Eau Claire Area	Eau Claire
118	13.8	Waupun	Waupun
120	13.7	Middleton-Cross Plains	Middleton
120	13.7	Winneconne Community	Winneconne
120	13.7	Wisconsin Rapids	Wis Rapids
123	13.6	Richland	Richland Ctr
123	13.6	Sparta Area	Sparta
123	13.6	Wautoma Area	Wautoma
126	13.5	Tomah Area	Tomah
127	13.4	Two Rivers	Two Rivers
128	13.3	Black River Falls	Black River Fls
128	13.3	Hayward Community	Hayward
128	13.3	Sauk Prairie	Sauk City
131	13.2	Ashland	Ashland
131	13.2	La Crosse	La Crosse
131	13.2	Waupaca	Waupaca
134	13.1	Antigo	Antigo
134	13.1	Jefferson	Jefferson
136	13.0	Northland Pines	Eagle River
137	12.9	Clintonville	Clintonville
137	12.9	Monona Grove	Monona
139	12.7	Adams-Friendship Area	Friendship
140	12.6	Mauston	Mauston
141	12.5	Madison Metropolitan	Madison
141	12.5	Verona Area	Verona
143	12.2	Monroe	Monroe

Student/Librarian Ratio

Rank	Ratio	District Name	City
1	2,536.3	West De Pere	De Pere
2	2,059.0	Adams-Friendship Area	Friendship
3	1,724.0	Wisconsin Dells	Wisconsin Dells
4	1,684.4	Milwaukee	Milwaukee
5	1,684.0	Oconomowoc Area	Oconomowoc
6	1,573.0	Rhinelander	Rhinelander
7	1,501.5	Hortonville	Hortonville
8	1,339.3	Kimberly Area	Kimberly
9	1,332.3	Manitowoc	Manitowoc
10	1,314.0	Port Washington-Saukville	Pt Washington
11	1,280.5	Portage Community	Portage
12	1,238.7	Germantown	Germantown
13	1,177.3	South Milwaukee	S Milwaukee
14	1,140.5	Arrowhead Uhs	Hartland
15	1,122.7	Hartford Uhs	Hartford
16	1,104.7	Merrill Area	Merrill
17	1,084.6	Stevens Point Area	Stevens Point
18	1,054.0	Two Rivers	Two Rivers
19	1,040.0	Platteville	Platteville
20	1,011.0	Oak Creek-Franklin	Oak Creek
21	1,007.0	Mosinee	Mosinee
22	1,004.3	Baraboo	Baraboo
23	980.3	Whitefish Bay	Whitefish Bay
24	955.0	Waukesha	Waukesha
25	951.7	Antigo	Antigo
26	949.0	Slinger	Slinger
27	948.0	Cudahy	Cudahy
28	937.0	Kewaskum	Kewaskum
29	931.8	Kaukauna Area	Kaukauna
30	915.6	Mequon-Thiensville	Mequon
31	899.4	Verona Area	Verona
32	890.0	Osceola	Osceola
33	887.5	Pulaski Community	Pulaski
34	883.6	Plymouth	Plymouth
35	873.0	Lake Geneva J1	Lake Geneva
36	860.8	Beaver Dam	Beaver Dam
37	851.6	Elmbrook	Brookfield
38	848.6	Greendale	Greendale
39	844.5	Sheboygan Falls	Sheboygan Fls
40	841.0	East Troy Community	East Troy
41	838.0	New London	New London
42	833.7	Whitnall	Greenfield
43	828.7	Marinette	Marinette
44	828.0	Menomonie Area	Menomonie
45	823.0	Reedsburg	Reedsburg
46	809.8	Wausau	Wausau
47	796.0	Green Bay Area	Green Bay
48	780.5	Ashwaubenon	Green Bay

49	778.5	Freedom Area	Freedom
50	767.0	Campbellsport	Campbellsport
51	766.0	Northland Pines	Eagle River
52	765.0	Watertown	Watertown
53	761.3	Waupun	Waupun
54	760.5	Oshkosh Area	Oshkosh
55	758.0	Medford Area	Medford
56	752.3	Sheboygan Area	Sheboygan
57	742.4	Amery	Amery
58	736.8	Shawano-Gresham	Shawano
59	735.6	West Allis	West Allis
60	730.6	Beloit	Beloit
60	730.6	Mukwonago	Mukwonago
62	729.7	Kettle Moraine	Wales
63	725.0	Muskego-Norway	Muskego
64	723.9	Appleton Area	Appleton
65	717.8	Menasha	Menasha
66	715.7	Burlington Area	Burlington
67	707.2	Whitewater	Whitewater
68	705.4	Superior	Superior
69	698.8	Delavan-Darien	Delavan
70	698.4	Ellsworth Community	Ellsworth
71	691.4	Hayward Community	Hayward
72	690.7	Hamilton	Sussex
73	689.9	Racine	Racine
74	682.6	Howard-Suamico	Green Bay
75	682.4	West Bend	West Bend
76	677.9	Oconto Falls	Oconto Falls
77	675.0	Marshfield	Marshfield
78	672.1	Eau Claire Area	Eau Claire
79	670.4	De Forest Area	De Forest
80	661.4	Black River Falls	Black River Fls
81	659.7	New Richmond	New Richmond
82	658.5	Rice Lake Area	Rice Lake
83	655.0	Sun Prairie Area	Sun Prairie
84	654.0	Hudson	Hudson
85	652.2	Little Chute Area	Little Chute
86	651.6	D C Everest Area	Weston
87	649.0	Elkhorn Area	Elkhorn
88	645.3	Waupaca	Waupaca
89	640.4	De Pere	De Pere
90	629.1	Greenfield	Greenfield
91	623.8	Cedarburg	Cedarburg
92	618.3	Edgerton	Edgerton
93	618.0	Seymour Community	Seymour
94	617.1	Pewaukee	Pewaukee
95	605.6	Waterford Graded J1	Waterford
96	599.0	Tomah Area	Tomah
97	597.7	Stoughton Area	Stoughton
98	596.8	River Falls	River Falls
99	590.6	Milton	Milton
100	586.4	Sauk Prairie	Sauk City
101	586.3	Mount Horeb Area	Mount Horeb
102	579.0	Berlin Area	Berlin
103	578.8	Middleton-Cross Plains	Middleton
104	577.5	Oregon	Oregon
105	574.0	New Berlin	New Berlin
106	571.5	Ashland	Ashland
107	565.1	Franklin Public	Franklin
108	564.7	Ripon	Ripon
109	559.8	Fond Du Lac	Fond Du Lac
110	556.0	Evansville Community	Evansville
111	549.4	Kenosha	Kenosha
112	545.0	Tomahawk	Tomahawk
113	544.6	Winneconne Community	Winneconne
114	541.5	Wauwatosa	Wauwatosa
115	541.3	Hartford J1	Hartford
116	540.3	Shorewood	Shorewood
117	538.3	Denmark	Denmark
118	530.7	Wautoma Area	Wautoma
119	529.4	Sparta Area	Sparta
120	528.7	Clintonville	Clintonville
121	528.1	Wisconsin Rapids	Wis Rapids
122	526.6	Fort Atkinson	Fort Atkinson
123	525.9	Lodi	Lodi
124	520.3	Janesville	Janesville
125	513.7	Madison Metropolitan	Madison
126	513.1	Waunakee Community	Waunakee
127	507.3	Monroe	Monroe
128	504.7	Richland	Richland Ctr
129	504.0	Spooner	Spooner
130	499.8	Onalaska	Onalaska
131	499.0	Chippewa Falls Area	Chippewa Falls
132	495.0	Menomonee Falls	Menomonee Fls
133	493.7	Jefferson	Jefferson
134	491.3	Neenah	Neenah
135	491.0	Mcfarland	Mc Farland
136	476.8	Luxemburg-Casco	Luxemburg
137	468.7	Monona Grove	Monona
138	449.9	Holmen	Holmen
139	414.4	Mauston	Mauston
140	406.5	West Salem	West Salem
141	400.6	Grafton	Grafton
142	394.6	La Crosse	La Crosse
143	n/a	Brown Deer	Brown Deer

Student/Counselor Ratio

Rank	Ratio	District Name	City
1	1,132.1	Milwaukee	Milwaukee
2	949.0	Stevens Point Area	Stevens Point
3	802.5	West Allis	West Allis
4	742.9	Platteville	Platteville
5	656.0	New Berlin	New Berlin
6	623.1	Marshfield	Marshfield
7	596.0	Madison Metropolitan	Madison
8	588.2	Beloit	Beloit
9	560.1	Mukwonago	Mukwonago
10	547.4	Elmbrook	Brookfield
11	543.2	Racine	Racine
12	542.0	West Salem	West Salem
13	541.3	Hartford J1	Hartford
14	532.9	Manitowoc	Manitowoc
15	529.9	Pulaski Community	Pulaski
16	526.6	Fort Atkinson	Fort Atkinson
17	521.5	Wauwatosa	Wauwatosa
18	519.9	Fond Du Lac	Fond Du Lac
19	516.2	Waupaca	Waupaca
20	515.8	Oshkosh Area	Oshkosh
21	507.3	West De Pere	De Pere
22	504.7	Waterford Graded J1	Waterford
23	504.1	Appleton Area	Appleton
24	503.5	Mosinee	Mosinee
25	501.3	Hayward Community	Hayward
26	500.2	Whitnall	Greenfield
27	497.2	Marinette	Marinette
28	495.3	Oconomowoc Area	Oconomowoc
29	494.3	Medford Area	Medford
30	493.8	Reedsburg	Reedsburg
31	487.7	Spooner	Spooner
32	478.1	Stoughton Area	Stoughton
33	477.8	Kaukauna Area	Kaukauna
34	477.5	Waukesha	Waukesha
35	476.6	Evansville Community	Evansville
36	476.4	Sun Prairie Area	Sun Prairie
37	475.2	Greendale	Greendale
38	468.7	Monona Grove	Monona
39	465.8	Delavan-Darien	Delavan
40	463.8	Edgerton	Edgerton
41	459.1	Beaver Dam	Beaver Dam
42	452.8	Hamilton	Sussex
43	451.3	Kettle Moraine	Wales
44	445.0	Osceola	Osceola
45	444.9	Freedom Area	Freedom
46	436.5	Lake Geneva J1	Lake Geneva
47	432.7	Elkhorn Area	Elkhorn
48	432.4	Waunakee Community	Waunakee
49	432.2	New Richmond	New Richmond
49	432.2	Shorewood	Shorewood
51	432.0	Pewaukee	Pewaukee
51	432.0	Watertown	Watertown
53	429.0	Hortonville	Hortonville
54	426.5	West Bend	West Bend
55	426.1	Kimberly Area	Kimberly
56	423.8	Luxemburg-Casco	Luxemburg
57	423.0	Middleton-Cross Plains	Middleton
58	422.8	Sheboygan Area	Sheboygan
59	420.5	East Troy Community	East Troy
60	418.9	Sauk Prairie	Sauk City
61	414.3	Merrill Area	Merrill
62	413.7	D C Everest Area	Weston
63	412.4	Amery	Amery
64	412.1	Neenah	Neenah
65	412.0	Seymour Community	Seymour
66	410.9	Green Bay Area	Green Bay
67	410.4	Mount Horeb Area	Mount Horeb
68	410.3	Janesville	Janesville
69	410.2	Whitewater	Whitewater
70	408.8	Tomahawk	Tomahawk
71	408.3	Chippewa Falls Area	Chippewa Falls
71	408.3	De Pere	De Pere
73	407.6	Oregon	Oregon
74	407.0	Muskego-Norway	Muskego
75	406.8	Wausau	Wausau
76	406.3	Cudahy	Cudahy
77	404.0	Mauston	Mauston
78	403.8	Denmark	Denmark
79	403.7	Holmen	Holmen
80	400.6	Grafton	Grafton
81	398.8	Menasha	Menasha
82	398.0	Wautoma Area	Wautoma
83	397.9	River Falls	River Falls
84	396.4	Baraboo	Baraboo
85	395.3	Germantown	Germantown
86	394.6	La Crosse	La Crosse
87	393.9	De Forest Area	De Forest
88	393.7	Milton	Milton
89	392.7	Jefferson	Jefferson
89	392.7	Onalaska	Onalaska
91	392.4	South Milwaukee	S Milwaukee
92	391.4	Lodi	Lodi
93	388.8	Oak Creek-Franklin	Oak Creek
94	388.4	Rhinelander	Rhinelander
95	388.3	Burlington Area	Burlington
96	387.5	Kenosha	Kenosha
97	384.1	Menomonee Falls	Menomonee Fls
98	383.6	Black River Falls	Black River Fls
99	382.7	Shawano-Gresham	Shawano
100	381.0	Ashland	Ashland
101	380.7	Ashwaubenon	Green Bay
102	380.2	Arrowhead Uhs	Hartland
103	379.6	Ellsworth Community	Ellsworth
104	379.2	Howard-Suamico	Green Bay
105	376.4	Ripon	Ripon
106	375.4	Port Washington-Saukville	Pt Washington
107	374.8	Kewaskum	Kewaskum
108	374.5	Mequon-Thiensville	Mequon
109	369.2	Hudson	Hudson
110	368.8	Clintonville	Clintonville
111	366.9	Tomah Area	Tomah
112	359.6	Franklin Public	Franklin
113	359.1	New London	New London
114	356.9	Antigo	Antigo
114	356.9	Verona Area	Verona
114	356.9	Waupun	Waupun
117	356.5	Wisconsin Rapids	Wis Rapids
118	355.9	Slinger	Slinger
119	351.9	Sheboygan Falls	Sheboygan Fls
120	344.8	Wisconsin Dells	Wisconsin Dells
121	341.5	Portage Community	Portage
122	341.4	Menomonie Area	Menomonie
123	340.9	Campbellsport	Campbellsport
124	338.9	Winneconne Community	Winneconne
125	336.8	Hartford Uhs	Hartford
126	335.1	Sparta Area	Sparta
127	329.9	Plymouth	Plymouth
128	329.3	Rice Lake Area	Rice Lake
129	329.2	Superior	Superior
130	328.8	Eau Claire Area	Eau Claire
131	327.7	Oconto Falls	Oconto Falls
132	326.1	Little Chute Area	Little Chute
133	324.9	Cedarburg	Cedarburg
134	319.4	Monroe	Monroe
135	315.8	Berlin Area	Berlin
136	314.5	Greenfield	Greenfield
137	311.7	Mcfarland	Mc Farland
138	310.2	Brown Deer	Brown Deer
139	301.1	Two Rivers	Two Rivers
140	294.1	Adams-Friendship Area	Friendship
141	285.5	Whitefish Bay	Whitefish Bay
142	255.3	Northland Pines	Eagle River
143	252.3	Richland	Richland Ctr

Current Spending per Student in FY2003

Rank	Dollars	District Name	City
1	11,396	Madison Metropolitan	Madison
2	10,443	New Berlin	New Berlin
3	10,352	Milwaukee	Milwaukee
4	10,263	La Crosse	La Crosse
5	10,038	Elmbrook	Brookfield
6	9,886	Richland	Richland Ctr
7	9,858	Northland Pines	Eagle River
8	9,773	Arrowhead Uhs	Hartland
9	9,763	Antigo	Antigo
10	9,703	Franklin Public	Franklin
11	9,670	Mequon-Thiensville	Mequon
12	9,630	Wausau	Wausau
13	9,575	Monroe	Monroe
14	9,573	Clintonville	Clintonville
15	9,560	Greendale	Greendale
16	9,492	Port Washington-Saukville	Pt Washington
17	9,484	Shorewood	Shorewood
18	9,439	Grafton	Grafton
19	9,413	Eau Claire Area	Eau Claire
20	9,411	Beloit	Beloit
21	9,396	Oconomowoc Area	Oconomowoc
22	9,383	Jefferson	Jefferson
23	9,357	Wisconsin Rapids	Wis Rapids
24	9,344	Cudahy	Cudahy
25	9,335	Hartford Uhs	Hartford
26	9,317	Waupun	Waupun
27	9,290	Rhinelander	Rhinelander
28	9,284	Mauston	Mauston
29	9,261	Brown Deer	Brown Deer
30	9,216	Racine	Racine
31	9,191	Menomonee Falls	Menomonee Fls
32	9,172	Germantown	Germantown

33	9,170	Oregon	Oregon
34	9,165	Monona Grove	Monona
35	9,135	Middleton-Cross Plains	Middleton
36	9,098	Verona Area	Verona
37	9,070	Adams-Friendship Area	Friendship
38	9,069	Pewaukee	Pewaukee
39	9,065	Kettle Moraine	Wales
40	9,057	Hartford J1	Hartford
41	9,048	Waukesha	Waukesha
42	9,022	Fort Atkinson	Fort Atkinson
43	9,021	Beaver Dam	Beaver Dam
44	9,018	Ellsworth Community	Ellsworth
45	9,008	Watertown	Watertown
46	8,989	Stevens Point Area	Stevens Point
47	8,953	Spooner	Spooner
48	8,895	Hayward Community	Hayward
49	8,891	Muskego-Norway	Muskego
50	8,886	Sun Prairie Area	Sun Prairie
51	8,866	Sheboygan Area	Sheboygan
52	8,854	Platteville	Platteville
53	8,852	South Milwaukee	S Milwaukee
54	8,851	Ashland	Ashland
55	8,836	Sauk Prairie	Sauk City
56	8,811	Mosinee	Mosinee
57	8,800	Whitnall	Greenfield
58	8,795	West Allis	West Allis
59	8,793	Edgerton	Edgerton
60	8,786	Cedarburg	Cedarburg
61	8,779	Whitefish Bay	Whitefish Bay
62	8,767	Green Bay Area	Green Bay
63	8,761	Kenosha	Kenosha
64	8,718	Greenfield	Greenfield
65	8,688	Mcfarland	Mc Farland
66	8,684	Menomonie Area	Menomonie
67	8,683	Sparta Area	Sparta
68	8,669	Superior	Superior
69	8,650	Merrill Area	Merrill
70	8,613	De Forest Area	De Forest
71	8,606	Ashwaubenon	Green Bay
72	8,600	Tomahawk	Tomahawk
73	8,594	Wauwatosa	Wauwatosa
74	8,553	Neenah	Neenah
75	8,499	Appleton Area	Appleton
75	8,499	Marshfield	Marshfield
77	8,496	Rice Lake Area	Rice Lake
78	8,490	Janesville	Janesville
79	8,480	Ripon	Ripon
80	8,414	West De Pere	De Pere
81	8,410	Oak Creek-Franklin	Oak Creek
82	8,403	Two Rivers	Two Rivers
83	8,379	Evansville Community	Evansville
84	8,324	Kewaskum	Kewaskum
85	8,323	Amery	Amery
86	8,321	Reedsburg	Reedsburg
87	8,320	River Falls	River Falls
88	8,314	Black River Falls	Black River Fls
89	8,310	Holmen	Holmen
90	8,289	New Richmond	New Richmond
91	8,286	Chippewa Falls Area	Chippewa Falls
92	8,264	Onalaska	Onalaska
93	8,258	D C Everest Area	Weston
94	8,243	Menasha	Menasha
95	8,236	Lodi	Lodi
96	8,212	Hamilton	Sussex
97	8,196	Kaukauna Area	Kaukauna
98	8,195	Oshkosh Area	Oshkosh
99	8,193	Sheboygan Falls	Sheboygan Fls
100	8,186	Whitewater	Whitewater
101	8,183	Fond Du Lac	Fond Du Lac
102	8,178	Wisconsin Dells	Wisconsin Dells
103	8,151	Oconto Falls	Oconto Falls
104	8,139	Mukwonago	Mukwonago
105	8,115	Marinette	Marinette
106	8,108	New London	New London
107	8,085	Portage Community	Portage
108	8,075	Winneconne Community	Winneconne
109	8,056	Hudson	Hudson
110	8,050	Luxemburg-Casco	Luxemburg
111	8,046	Medford Area	Medford
112	8,045	Tomah Area	Tomah
113	8,037	West Bend	West Bend
114	8,033	Shawano-Gresham	Shawano
115	8,005	West Salem	West Salem
116	7,999	Pulaski Community	Pulaski
117	7,997	Manitowoc	Manitowoc
118	7,991	Waunakee Community	Waunakee
119	7,973	Plymouth	Plymouth
120	7,960	Baraboo	Baraboo
121	7,903	Elkhorn Area	Elkhorn
122	7,870	Stoughton Area	Stoughton
123	7,867	Lake Geneva J1	Lake Geneva
124	7,861	Wautoma Area	Wautoma
125	7,771	Berlin Area	Berlin
126	7,727	Milton	Milton
127	7,725	Mount Horeb Area	Mount Horeb
128	7,668	Seymour Community	Seymour
129	7,659	Osceola	Osceola
130	7,645	East Troy Community	East Troy
131	7,628	De Pere	De Pere
132	7,584	Waupaca	Waupaca
133	7,563	Freedom Area	Freedom
134	7,508	Campbellsport	Campbellsport
135	7,456	Slinger	Slinger
136	7,414	Little Chute Area	Little Chute
137	7,354	Burlington Area	Burlington
138	7,351	Denmark	Denmark
139	7,313	Delavan-Darien	Delavan
140	7,311	Howard-Suamico	Green Bay
141	7,289	Hortonville	Hortonville
142	7,232	Kimberly Area	Kimberly
143	6,992	Waterford Graded J1	Waterford

Number of Diploma Recipients

Rank	Number	District Name	City
1	3,912	Milwaukee	Milwaukee
2	1,607	Madison Metropolitan	Madison
3	1,305	Kenosha	Kenosha
4	1,163	Racine	Racine
5	1,131	Green Bay Area	Green Bay
6	1,109	Appleton Area	Appleton
7	1,043	Waukesha	Waukesha
8	978	Eau Claire Area	Eau Claire
9	768	Sheboygan Area	Sheboygan
10	676	Stevens Point Area	Stevens Point
11	673	Janesville	Janesville
12	671	Oshkosh Area	Oshkosh
13	637	West Allis	West Allis
14	603	West Bend	West Bend
15	589	Elmbrook	Brookfield
16	586	Wausau	Wausau
17	501	Wisconsin Rapids	Wis Rapids
18	499	La Crosse	La Crosse
19	496	Wauwatosa	Wauwatosa
20	463	Fond Du Lac	Fond Du Lac
21	457	Arrowhead Uhs	Hartland
22	439	Neenah	Neenah
23	415	Mukwonago	Mukwonago
24	390	D C Everest Area	Weston
25	385	Middleton-Cross Plains	Middleton
26	382	New Berlin	New Berlin
26	382	Oak Creek-Franklin	Oak Creek
28	379	Hartford Uhs	Hartford
29	377	Manitowoc	Manitowoc
30	363	Chippewa Falls Area	Chippewa Falls
31	357	Beloit	Beloit
32	356	Mequon-Thiensville	Mequon
33	352	Marshfield	Marshfield
34	347	Sun Prairie Area	Sun Prairie
35	342	Kettle Moraine	Wales
36	338	Superior	Superior
37	329	Franklin Public	Franklin
38	321	Oconomowoc Area	Oconomowoc
39	314	Hudson	Hudson
40	307	Antigo	Antigo
41	299	Beaver Dam	Beaver Dam
41	299	Muskego-Norway	Muskego
43	288	Watertown	Watertown
44	280	Hamilton	Sussex
44	280	Verona Area	Verona
46	275	Menomonee Falls	Menomonee Fls
47	271	Germantown	Germantown
47	271	Howard-Suamico	Green Bay
49	260	Ashwaubenon	Green Bay
50	258	Menomonie Area	Menomonie
50	258	Merrill Area	Merrill
52	254	Stoughton Area	Stoughton
53	252	South Milwaukee	S Milwaukee
54	248	Burlington Area	Burlington
55	246	Kaukauna Area	Kaukauna
56	236	Menasha	Menasha
57	234	Greenfield	Greenfield
57	234	Rhinelander	Rhinelander
59	232	Pulaski Community	Pulaski
60	231	De Pere	De Pere
61	228	Holmen	Holmen
61	228	Onalaska	Onalaska
61	228	Oregon	Oregon
64	225	Tomah Area	Tomah
65	222	Cedarburg	Cedarburg
66	220	Rice Lake Area	Rice Lake
67	219	Fort Atkinson	Fort Atkinson
67	219	Medford Area	Medford
69	217	River Falls	River Falls
70	214	Baraboo	Baraboo
70	214	Marinette	Marinette
72	211	Whitefish Bay	Whitefish Bay
73	207	Delavan-Darien	Delavan
74	206	Sparta Area	Sparta
74	206	Whitnall	Greenfield
76	203	Cudahy	Cudahy
77	202	Plymouth	Plymouth
78	200	De Forest Area	De Forest
79	199	Milton	Milton
80	190	Monroe	Monroe
80	190	Seymour Community	Seymour
82	189	New Richmond	New Richmond
82	189	Slinger	Slinger
84	188	Waunakee Community	Waunakee
85	187	Shawano-Gresham	Shawano
86	186	New London	New London
86	186	Port Washington-Saukville	Pt Washington
88	185	Grafton	Grafton
89	184	Waupun	Waupun
90	183	Waupaca	Waupaca
91	181	Elkhorn Area	Elkhorn
91	181	Kimberly Area	Kimberly
93	180	Greendale	Greendale
94	179	Shorewood	Shorewood
95	178	Monona Grove	Monona
96	177	Hortonville	Hortonville
97	173	Reedsburg	Reedsburg
98	172	Ashland	Ashland
99	170	Portage Community	Portage
100	165	Luxemburg-Casco	Luxemburg
100	165	Two Rivers	Two Rivers
102	162	Adams-Friendship Area	Friendship
103	159	Sauk Prairie	Sauk City
104	158	Mosinee	Mosinee
105	156	Ellsworth Community	Ellsworth
106	153	Mcfarland	Mc Farland
106	153	Spooner	Spooner
108	149	Black River Falls	Black River Fls
109	147	Amery	Amery
109	147	Freedom Area	Freedom
111	146	Platteville	Platteville
112	145	East Troy Community	East Troy
113	144	Kewaskum	Kewaskum
113	144	Whitewater	Whitewater
115	143	Berlin Area	Berlin
115	143	Richland	Richland Ctr
117	139	Osceola	Osceola
118	137	Edgerton	Edgerton
119	136	Oconto Falls	Oconto Falls
119	136	Tomahawk	Tomahawk
121	134	West De Pere	De Pere
122	133	Sheboygan Falls	Sheboygan Fls
123	132	Ripon	Ripon
124	131	Denmark	Denmark
125	130	Campbellsport	Campbellsport
126	127	Brown Deer	Brown Deer
126	127	Little Chute Area	Little Chute
126	127	Pewaukee	Pewaukee
126	127	Winneconne Community	Winneconne
130	126	Mount Horeb Area	Mount Horeb
131	120	Wautoma Area	Wautoma
132	118	Wisconsin Dells	Wisconsin Dells
133	116	Mauston	Mauston
133	116	Northland Pines	Eagle River
135	114	Lodi	Lodi
136	110	West Salem	West Salem
137	109	Hayward Community	Hayward
138	108	Clintonville	Clintonville
139	101	Jefferson	Jefferson
140	94	Evansville Community	Evansville
141	n/a	Hartford J1	Hartford
141	n/a	Lake Geneva J1	Lake Geneva
141	n/a	Waterford Graded J1	Waterford

High School Drop-out Rate

Rank	Percent	District Name	City
1	9.0	Milwaukee	Milwaukee
2	5.2	Racine	Racine
3	3.8	Mauston	Mauston
4	3.6	Beloit	Beloit
5	3.5	Manitowoc	Manitowoc
6	3.4	Delavan-Darien	Delavan
6	3.4	Fond Du Lac	Fond Du Lac
8	3.3	Kenosha	Kenosha
9	3.0	Madison Metropolitan	Madison
9	3.0	Rhinelander	Rhinelander
11	2.9	Merrill Area	Merrill
12	2.8	Menasha	Menasha
12	2.8	Superior	Superior
14	2.7	Waupun	Waupun
15	2.5	Oshkosh Area	Oshkosh
16	2.3	Sun Prairie Area	Sun Prairie
17	2.2	Baraboo	Baraboo

17	2.2	Hayward Community	Hayward
17	2.2	Watertown	Watertown
20	2.1	Chippewa Falls Area	Chippewa Falls
20	2.1	Onalaska	Onalaska
22	2.0	Clintonville	Clintonville
22	2.0	Milton	Milton
22	2.0	Stevens Point Area	Stevens Point
22	2.0	Whitewater	Whitewater
22	2.0	Wisconsin Dells	Wisconsin Dells
27	1.9	Fort Atkinson	Fort Atkinson
27	1.9	Sheboygan Area	Sheboygan
27	1.9	Slinger	Slinger
30	1.8	Janesville	Janesville
31	1.7	Wausau	Wausau
32	1.6	Green Bay Area	Green Bay
32	1.6	Kewaskum	Kewaskum
32	1.6	Sparta Area	Sparta
32	1.6	West Allis	West Allis
36	1.5	La Crosse	La Crosse
36	1.5	New London	New London
36	1.5	Oconomowoc Area	Oconomowoc
36	1.5	Rice Lake Area	Rice Lake
36	1.5	Shawano-Gresham	Shawano
41	1.4	Black River Falls	Black River Fls
41	1.4	Plymouth	Plymouth
41	1.4	Reedsburg	Reedsburg
44	1.3	Evansville Community	Evansville
44	1.3	Hartford Uhs	Hartford
44	1.3	Monroe	Monroe
44	1.3	Sauk Prairie	Sauk City
48	1.2	Ashland	Ashland
48	1.2	Jefferson	Jefferson
48	1.2	Medford Area	Medford
48	1.2	Wisconsin Rapids	Wis Rapids
52	1.1	Howard-Suamico	Green Bay
52	1.1	Kaukauna Area	Kaukauna
52	1.1	Menomonie Area	Menomonie
52	1.1	Neenah	Neenah
52	1.1	Northland Pines	Eagle River
57	1.0	Adams-Friendship Area	Friendship
57	1.0	Campbellsport	Campbellsport
57	1.0	Ellsworth Community	Ellsworth
57	1.0	Mosinee	Mosinee
57	1.0	Platteville	Platteville
57	1.0	Richland	Richland Ctr
63	0.9	Antigo	Antigo
63	0.9	East Troy Community	East Troy
63	0.9	Greenfield	Greenfield
63	0.9	Marinette	Marinette
63	0.9	Osceola	Osceola
63	0.9	Port Washington-Saukville	Pt Washington
63	0.9	Sheboygan Falls	Sheboygan Fls
63	0.9	South Milwaukee	S Milwaukee
63	0.9	Waunakee Community	Waunakee
63	0.9	West Bend	West Bend
73	0.8	Appleton Area	Appleton
73	0.8	Cudahy	Cudahy
73	0.8	Freedom Area	Freedom
73	0.8	New Richmond	New Richmond
73	0.8	Oak Creek-Franklin	Oak Creek
73	0.8	Portage Community	Portage
73	0.8	Spooner	Spooner
73	0.8	Tomahawk	Tomahawk
81	0.7	Burlington Area	Burlington
81	0.7	D C Everest Area	Weston
81	0.7	Denmark	Denmark
81	0.7	Eau Claire Area	Eau Claire
81	0.7	Middleton-Cross Plains	Middleton
81	0.7	Ripon	Ripon
81	0.7	Two Rivers	Two Rivers
88	0.6	Kettle Moraine	Wales
88	0.6	West De Pere	De Pere
90	0.5	Arrowhead Uhs	Hartland
90	0.5	Ashwaubenon	Green Bay
90	0.5	Brown Deer	Brown Deer
90	0.5	Little Chute Area	Little Chute
90	0.5	Mcfarland	Mc Farland
90	0.5	Oconto Falls	Oconto Falls
90	0.5	Oregon	Oregon
90	0.5	Pulaski Community	Pulaski
90	0.5	River Falls	River Falls
99	0.4	Elkhorn Area	Elkhorn
99	0.4	Grafton	Grafton
99	0.4	Greendale	Greendale
99	0.4	Marshfield	Marshfield
99	0.4	Monona Grove	Monona
99	0.4	Stoughton Area	Stoughton
99	0.4	Tomah Area	Tomah
99	0.4	Waukesha	Waukesha
107	0.3	Beaver Dam	Beaver Dam
107	0.3	Cedarburg	Cedarburg
107	0.3	De Pere	De Pere
107	0.3	Germantown	Germantown
107	0.3	Hamilton	Sussex
107	0.3	Luxemburg-Casco	Luxemburg
107	0.3	Mukwonago	Mukwonago
107	0.3	New Berlin	New Berlin
115	0.2	Berlin Area	Berlin
115	0.2	Elmbrook	Brookfield
115	0.2	Holmen	Holmen
115	0.2	Hortonville	Hortonville
115	0.2	Menomonee Falls	Menomonee Fls
115	0.2	Mount Horeb Area	Mount Horeb
115	0.2	Muskego-Norway	Muskego
115	0.2	Pewaukee	Pewaukee
115	0.2	Waupaca	Waupaca
115	0.2	Wauwatosa	Wauwatosa
115	0.2	West Salem	West Salem
115	0.2	Whitefish Bay	Whitefish Bay
115	0.2	Winneconne Community	Winneconne
128	0.1	De Forest Area	De Forest
128	0.1	Franklin Public	Franklin
128	0.1	Kimberly Area	Kimberly
131	0.0	Amery	Amery
131	0.0	Edgerton	Edgerton
131	0.0	Hudson	Hudson
131	0.0	Lodi	Lodi
131	0.0	Mequon-Thiensville	Mequon
131	0.0	Seymour Community	Seymour
131	0.0	Shorewood	Shorewood
131	0.0	Verona Area	Verona
131	0.0	Wautoma Area	Wautoma
131	0.0	Whitnall	Greenfield
141	n/a	Hartford J1	Hartford
141	n/a	Lake Geneva J1	Lake Geneva
141	n/a	Waterford Graded J1	Waterford

Wyoming

Wyoming Public School Educational Profile

Category	Value	Category	Value
Schools (2003-2004)	380	**Diploma Recipients** (2002-2003)	6,106
Instructional Level		White, Non-Hispanic	5,569
Primary	210	Black, Non-Hispanic	60
Middle	76	Asian/Pacific Islander	51
High	76	American Indian/Alaskan Native	102
Other Level	18	Hispanic	324
Curriculum		**High School Drop-out Rate** (%) (2001-2002)	5.8
Regular	353	White, Non-Hispanic	5.2
Special Education	0	Black, Non-Hispanic	9.9
Vocational	0	Asian/Pacific Islander	2.7
Alternative	27	American Indian/Alaskan Native	13.0
Type		Hispanic	12.3
Magnet	0	**Staff** (2003-2004)	
Charter	1	Teachers	6,567.7
Title I Eligible	194	Average Salary ($)	39,537
School-wide Title I	57	Librarians/Media Specialists	131.1
Students (2003-2004)	87,462	Guidance Counselors	394.6
Gender (%)		**Ratios** (2003-2004)	
Male	51.8	Student/Teacher Ratio	13.3 to 1
Female	48.2	Student/Librarian Ratio	667.1 to 1
Race/Ethnicity (%)		Student/Counselor Ratio	221.6 to 1
White, Non-Hispanic	86.0	**College Entrance Exam Scores** (2005)	
Black, Non-Hispanic	1.4	Scholastic Aptitude Test (SAT)	
Asian/Pacific Islander	1.0	Participation Rate (%)	12
American Indian/Alaskan Native	3.4	Mean SAT Reasoning Test Verbal Score	544
Hispanic	8.2	Mean SAT Reasoning Test Math Score	543
Classification (%)		American College Testing Program (ACT)	
Individual Education Program (IEP)	15.4	Participation Rate (%)	69
Migrant (2002-2003)	0.3	Average Composite Score	21.4
English Language Learner (ELL)	4.0	Average English Score	20.6
Eligible for Free Lunch Program	21.8	Average Math Score	21.0
Eligible for Reduced-Price Lunch Program	9.4	Average Reading Score	22.0
Current Spending ($ per student in FY 2003)	9,202	Average Science Score	21.4
Instruction	5,507		
Support Services	3,400		

Note: *For an explanation of data, please refer to the User's Guide in the front of the book*

Wyoming NAEP 2005 Test Scores

Reading			Mathematics		
Grade/Category	Value	Rank	Grade/Category	Value	Rank
4th Grade			**4th Grade**		
Average Proficiency	223.3 (0.74)	13/51	Average Proficiency	243.0 (0.61)	7/51
Proficiency by Gender/Race/Ethnicity			Proficiency by Gender/Race/Ethnicity		
Male	221.0 (1.19)	11/51	Male	244.2 (0.83)	7/51
Female	225.6 (1.03)	18/51	Female	241.7 (0.99)	6/51
White, Non-Hispanic	226.6 (0.79)	24/51	White, Non-Hispanic	244.7 (0.64)	26/51
Black, Non-Hispanic	n/a	n/a	Black, Non-Hispanic	n/a	n/a
Asian, Non-Hispanic	n/a	n/a	Asian, Non-Hispanic	n/a	n/a
American Indian, Non-Hispanic	n/a	n/a	American Indian, Non-Hispanic	n/a	n/a
Hispanic	203.8 (3.26)	20/40	Hispanic	234.1 (2.35)	4/41
Proficiency by Class Size			Proficiency by Class Size		
Less than 16 Students	216.3 (2.13)	8/34	Less than 16 Students	238.6 (1.62)	6/35
16 to 18 Students	225.5 (1.52)	3/33	16 to 18 Students	243.2 (1.02)	4/31
19 to 20 Students	225.6 (1.92)	11/38	19 to 20 Students	247.8 (1.80)	4/38
21 to 25 Students	224.2 (1.18)	19/51	21 to 25 Students	242.9 (0.98)	14/51
Greater than 25 Students	223.2 (3.02)	15/36	Greater than 25 Students	241.6 (2.64)	8/33
Percent Attaining Achievement Levels			Percent Attaining Achievement Levels		
Below Basic	29.2 (1.20)	42/51	Below Basic	12.9 (0.91)	46/51
Basic or Above	70.8 (1.20)	10/51	Basic or Above	87.1 (0.91)	6/51
Proficient or Above	34.5 (1.38)	14/51	Proficient or Above	42.6 (1.43)	7/51
Advanced or Above	7.1 (0.63)	23/51	Advanced or Above	5.1 (0.68)	19/51
8th Grade			**8th Grade**		
Average Proficiency	268.1 (0.68)	10/51	Average Proficiency	282.1 (0.75)	17/51
Proficiency by Gender/Race/Ethnicity			Proficiency by Gender/Race/Ethnicity		
Male	264.3 (1.04)	5/51	Male	282.8 (0.90)	18/51
Female	271.9 (0.95)	14/51	Female	281.3 (1.08)	18/51
White, Non-Hispanic	269.9 (0.77)	23/51	White, Non-Hispanic	284.5 (0.83)	33/51
Black, Non-Hispanic	n/a	n/a	Black, Non-Hispanic	n/a	n/a
Asian, Non-Hispanic	n/a	n/a	Asian, Non-Hispanic	n/a	n/a
American Indian, Non-Hispanic	250.9 (3.72)	3/9	American Indian, Non-Hispanic	262.4 (2.82)	5/10
Hispanic	255.7 (3.06)	4/38	Hispanic	264.5 (2.82)	15/38
Proficiency by Parents Highest Level of Ed.			Proficiency by Parents Highest Level of Ed.		
Did Not Finish High School	253.1 (2.70)	4/49	Did Not Finish High School	261.5 (3.64)	27/50
Graduated High School	257.9 (1.69)	13/50	Graduated High School	274.1 (1.45)	9/50
Some Education After High School	272.1 (1.63)	2/50	Some Education After High School	283.3 (1.52)	19/50
Graduated College	275.5 (1.13)	9/50	Graduated College	290.4 (1.07)	23/50
Percent Attaining Achievement Levels			Percent Attaining Achievement Levels		
Below Basic	29.2 (1.20)	42/51	Below Basic	23.7 (1.14)	43/51
Basic or Above	70.8 (1.20)	10/51	Basic or Above	76.3 (1.14)	9/51
Proficient or Above	34.5 (1.38)	14/51	Proficient or Above	29.0 (1.41)	31/51
Advanced or Above	7.1 (0.63)	23/51	Advanced or Above	3.5 (0.40)	38/51

Note: *For an explanation of data, please refer to the User's Guide in the front of the book; n/a indicates data not available*

Albany County

Albany County SD #1
1948 Grand Ave • Laramie, WY 82070-4317
(307) 721-4400 • http://sage.ac1.k12.wy.us
Grade Span: KG-12; **Agency Type:** 1
Schools: 20
  14 Primary; 2 Middle; 3 High; 1 Other Level
  19 Regular; 0 Special Education; 0 Vocational; 1 Alternative
  0 Magnet; 1 Charter; 7 Title I Eligible; 1 School-wide Title I
Students: 3,735 (53.4% male; 46.5% female)
  Individual Education Program: 666 (17.8%);
  English Language Learner: 40 (1.1%); Migrant: 0 (0.0%)
  Eligible for Free Lunch Program: 668 (18.2%)
  Eligible for Reduced-Price Lunch Program: 262 (7.1%)
Teachers: 308.5 (11.9 to 1)
Librarians/Media Specialists: 6.2 (592.4 to 1)
Guidance Counselors: 22.3 (164.7 to 1)
Current Spending: ($ per student per year):
  Total: $9,680; Instruction: $5,785; Support Services: $3,584
Enrollment, Drop-out Rates and Diploma Recipients by Race/Ethnicity

Category	Total	White	Black	Asian	AIAN	Hisp.
Enrollment (%)	100.0	81.2	2.2	2.8	1.6	12.2
Drop-out Rate (%)	6.4	6.0	18.8	5.3	30.8	5.9
H.S. Diplomas (#)	277	242	4	2	6	23

Campbell County

Campbell County SD #1
1000 W 8th St • Gillette, WY 82717-3033
Mailing Address: PO Box 3033 • Gillette, WY 82717-3033
(307) 682-5171 • http://www.ccsd.k12.wy.us
Grade Span: KG-12; **Agency Type:** 1
Schools: 20
  15 Primary; 2 Middle; 3 High; 0 Other Level
  19 Regular; 0 Special Education; 0 Vocational; 1 Alternative
  0 Magnet; 0 Charter; 9 Title I Eligible; 3 School-wide Title I
Students: 7,326 (51.6% male; 48.3% female)
  Individual Education Program: 852 (11.6%);
  English Language Learner: 230 (3.1%); Migrant: 0 (0.0%)
  Eligible for Free Lunch Program: 1,042 (14.4%)
  Eligible for Reduced-Price Lunch Program: 596 (8.2%)
Teachers: 536.7 (13.5 to 1)
Librarians/Media Specialists: 12.0 (602.8 to 1)
Guidance Counselors: 32.0 (226.1 to 1)
Current Spending: ($ per student per year):
  Total: $8,419; Instruction: $4,844; Support Services: $3,276
Enrollment, Drop-out Rates and Diploma Recipients by Race/Ethnicity

Category	Total	White	Black	Asian	AIAN	Hisp.
Enrollment (%)	100.0	93.1	0.4	0.6	1.6	4.3
Drop-out Rate (%)	4.5	4.3	n/a	0.0	8.3	10.8
H.S. Diplomas (#)	534	515	0	2	4	13

Carbon County

Carbon County SD #1
615 Rodeo St • Rawlins, WY 82301-0160
Mailing Address: PO Box 160 • Rawlins, WY 82301-0160
(307) 328-9200
Grade Span: KG-12; **Agency Type:** 1
Schools: 9
  5 Primary; 1 Middle; 2 High; 1 Other Level
  7 Regular; 0 Special Education; 0 Vocational; 2 Alternative
  0 Magnet; 0 Charter; 4 Title I Eligible; 3 School-wide Title I
Students: 1,796 (51.9% male; 48.0% female)
  Individual Education Program: 361 (20.1%);
  English Language Learner: 30 (1.7%); Migrant: 0 (0.0%)
  Eligible for Free Lunch Program: 345 (20.0%)
  Eligible for Reduced-Price Lunch Program: 140 (8.1%)
Teachers: 135.4 (12.8 to 1)
Librarians/Media Specialists: 3.0 (576.0 to 1)
Guidance Counselors: 5.6 (308.6 to 1)
Current Spending: ($ per student per year):
  Total: $8,234; Instruction: $5,049; Support Services: $2,952
Enrollment, Drop-out Rates and Diploma Recipients by Race/Ethnicity

Category	Total	White	Black	Asian	AIAN	Hisp.
Enrollment (%)	100.0	76.1	1.0	1.4	0.6	20.8
Drop-out Rate (%)	5.6	3.7	0.0	0.0	0.0	14.2
H.S. Diplomas (#)	164	126	0	7	1	30

Converse County

Converse County SD #1
615 Hamilton St • Douglas, WY 82633-2615
(307) 358-2942 • http://www.ccsd1.k12.wy.us/
Grade Span: KG-12; **Agency Type:** 1
Schools: 8
  6 Primary; 1 Middle; 1 High; 0 Other Level
  8 Regular; 0 Special Education; 0 Vocational; 0 Alternative
  0 Magnet; 0 Charter; 5 Title I Eligible; 0 School-wide Title I
Students: 1,633 (50.8% male; 49.1% female)
  Individual Education Program: 257 (15.7%);
  English Language Learner: 9 (0.6%); Migrant: 0 (0.0%)
  Eligible for Free Lunch Program: 331 (20.8%)
  Eligible for Reduced-Price Lunch Program: 123 (7.7%)
Teachers: 127.4 (12.5 to 1)
Librarians/Media Specialists: 3.0 (531.0 to 1)
Guidance Counselors: 7.2 (221.3 to 1)
Current Spending: ($ per student per year):
  Total: $8,363; Instruction: $5,373; Support Services: $2,665
Enrollment, Drop-out Rates and Diploma Recipients by Race/Ethnicity

Category	Total	White	Black	Asian	AIAN	Hisp.
Enrollment (%)	100.0	90.5	0.4	0.9	0.9	7.2
Drop-out Rate (%)	2.7	3.0	0.0	0.0	0.0	0.0
H.S. Diplomas (#)	118	110	1	0	1	6

Fremont County

Fremont County SD # 1
400 Baldwin Creek Rd • Lander, WY 82520
(307) 332-4711 • http://www.fre1.k12.wy.us
Grade Span: KG-12; **Agency Type:** 1
Schools: 8
  5 Primary; 1 Middle; 2 High; 0 Other Level
  7 Regular; 0 Special Education; 0 Vocational; 1 Alternative
  0 Magnet; 0 Charter; 5 Title I Eligible; 2 School-wide Title I
Students: 1,906 (53.8% male; 46.1% female)
  Individual Education Program: 305 (16.0%);
  English Language Learner: 346 (18.2%); Migrant: 0 (0.0%)
  Eligible for Free Lunch Program: 434 (23.4%)
  Eligible for Reduced-Price Lunch Program: 129 (7.0%)
Teachers: 128.2 (14.5 to 1)
Librarians/Media Specialists: 4.0 (463.8 to 1)
Guidance Counselors: 9.0 (206.1 to 1)
Current Spending: ($ per student per year):
  Total: $9,394; Instruction: $5,899; Support Services: $3,316
Enrollment, Drop-out Rates and Diploma Recipients by Race/Ethnicity

Category	Total	White	Black	Asian	AIAN	Hisp.
Enrollment (%)	100.0	76.9	0.8	1.1	17.9	3.3
Drop-out Rate (%)	6.2	5.3	n/a	0.0	9.1	9.5
H.S. Diplomas (#)	144	117	0	0	25	2

Fremont County SD #25
121 N 5th St W • Riverton, WY 82501-9407
(307) 856-9407 • http://www.fremont25.k12.wy.us/
Grade Span: KG-12; **Agency Type:** 1
Schools: 6
  3 Primary; 2 Middle; 1 High; 0 Other Level
  6 Regular; 0 Special Education; 0 Vocational; 0 Alternative
  0 Magnet; 0 Charter; 4 Title I Eligible; 3 School-wide Title I
Students: 2,507 (49.0% male; 50.9% female)
  Individual Education Program: 483 (19.3%);
  English Language Learner: 376 (15.0%); Migrant: 0 (0.0%)
  Eligible for Free Lunch Program: 687 (28.3%)
  Eligible for Reduced-Price Lunch Program: 221 (9.1%)
Teachers: 157.8 (15.4 to 1)
Librarians/Media Specialists: 1.0 (2,425.0 to 1)
Guidance Counselors: 12.5 (194.0 to 1)
Current Spending: ($ per student per year):
  Total: $8,376; Instruction: $5,133; Support Services: $2,968
Enrollment, Drop-out Rates and Diploma Recipients by Race/Ethnicity

Category	Total	White	Black	Asian	AIAN	Hisp.
Enrollment (%)	100.0	78.6	0.5	0.5	13.8	6.6
Drop-out Rate (%)	5.2	3.4	100.0	0.0	16.3	7.3
H.S. Diplomas (#)	176	154	0	2	10	10

Goshen County

Goshen County SD #1
2602 W E St • Torrington, WY 82240-1821
(307) 532-2171 • http://www.goshen.k12.wy.us
Grade Span: KG-12; **Agency Type:** 1
Schools: 11
  5 Primary; 3 Middle; 3 High; 0 Other Level
  11 Regular; 0 Special Education; 0 Vocational; 0 Alternative

0 Magnet; 0 Charter; 5 Title I Eligible; 5 School-wide Title I
Students: 1,899 (51.9% male; 48.0% female)
  Individual Education Program: 305 (16.1%);
  English Language Learner: 57 (3.0%); Migrant: 119 (6.4%)
  Eligible for Free Lunch Program: 608 (32.7%)
  Eligible for Reduced-Price Lunch Program: 271 (14.6%)
Teachers: 163.7 (11.4 to 1)
Librarians/Media Specialists: 4.5 (412.9 to 1)
Guidance Counselors: 9.0 (206.4 to 1)
Current Spending: ($ per student per year):
  Total: $9,785; Instruction: $6,015; Support Services: $3,472
Enrollment, Drop-out Rates and Diploma Recipients by Race/Ethnicity

Category	Total	White	Black	Asian	AIAN	Hisp.
Enrollment (%)	100.0	84.6	0.2	0.1	1.3	13.8
Drop-out Rate (%)	4.0	3.7	0.0	0.0	0.0	7.8
H.S. Diplomas (#)	138	123	1	2	1	11

Laramie County

Laramie County SD #1
2810 House Ave • Cheyenne, WY 82001-2860
(307) 771-2100 • http://www.laramie1.k12.wy.us
Grade Span: KG-12; **Agency Type:** 1
Schools: 32
  25 Primary; 4 Middle; 3 High; 0 Other Level
  31 Regular; 0 Special Education; 0 Vocational; 1 Alternative
  0 Magnet; 0 Charter; 12 Title I Eligible; 11 School-wide Title I
Students: 13,344 (51.2% male; 48.7% female)
  Individual Education Program: 1,865 (14.0%);
  English Language Learner: 154 (1.2%); Migrant: 0 (0.0%)
  Eligible for Free Lunch Program: 2,813 (21.5%)
  Eligible for Reduced-Price Lunch Program: 1,250 (9.6%)
Teachers: 876.4 (14.9 to 1)
Librarians/Media Specialists: 10.0 (1,306.5 to 1)
Guidance Counselors: 54.3 (240.6 to 1)
Current Spending: ($ per student per year):
  Total: $8,169; Instruction: $4,977; Support Services: $2,928
Enrollment, Drop-out Rates and Diploma Recipients by Race/Ethnicity

Category	Total	White	Black	Asian	AIAN	Hisp.
Enrollment (%)	100.0	77.5	4.5	1.7	1.4	14.9
Drop-out Rate (%)	8.2	7.4	9.0	5.5	11.8	14.2
H.S. Diplomas (#)	783	653	36	9	4	81

Lincoln County

Lincoln County SD #2
222e. 4th Ave • Afton, WY 83110-0219
Mailing Address: PO Box 219 • Afton, WY 83110-0219
(307) 885-3811 • http://www.lcsd2.org
Grade Span: KG-12; **Agency Type:** 1
Schools: 9
  3 Primary; 3 Middle; 3 High; 0 Other Level
  8 Regular; 0 Special Education; 0 Vocational; 1 Alternative
  0 Magnet; 0 Charter; 4 Title I Eligible; 1 School-wide Title I
Students: 2,513 (51.3% male; 48.6% female)
  Individual Education Program: 342 (13.6%);
  English Language Learner: 29 (1.2%); Migrant: 0 (0.0%)
  Eligible for Free Lunch Program: 431 (17.6%)
  Eligible for Reduced-Price Lunch Program: 325 (13.3%)
Teachers: 159.3 (15.4 to 1)
Librarians/Media Specialists: 2.9 (844.5 to 1)
Guidance Counselors: 5.6 (437.3 to 1)
Current Spending: ($ per student per year):
  Total: $7,865; Instruction: $4,924; Support Services: $2,662
Enrollment, Drop-out Rates and Diploma Recipients by Race/Ethnicity

Category	Total	White	Black	Asian	AIAN	Hisp.
Enrollment (%)	100.0	96.5	0.1	0.8	0.6	2.0
Drop-out Rate (%)	2.5	2.3	0.0	0.0	n/a	22.2
H.S. Diplomas (#)	179	175	0	2	0	2

Natrona County

Natrona County SD #1
970 N Glenn Rd • Casper, WY 82601-1635
(307) 577-0200 • http://www.trib.com/WYOMING/NCSD/
Grade Span: KG-12; **Agency Type:** 1
Schools: 36
  28 Primary; 4 Middle; 3 High; 1 Other Level
  36 Regular; 0 Special Education; 0 Vocational; 0 Alternative
  0 Magnet; 0 Charter; 15 Title I Eligible; 12 School-wide Title I
Students: 12,028 (51.9% male; 48.0% female)
  Individual Education Program: 1,803 (15.0%);
  English Language Learner: 119 (1.0%); Migrant: 0 (0.0%)
  Eligible for Free Lunch Program: 2,870 (24.2%)
  Eligible for Reduced-Price Lunch Program: 1,005 (8.5%)

Teachers: 803.7 (14.7 to 1)
Librarians/Media Specialists: 8.1 (1,463.2 to 1)
Guidance Counselors: 55.4 (213.9 to 1)
Current Spending: ($ per student per year):
  Total: $8,363; Instruction: $5,248; Support Services: $2,877
Enrollment, Drop-out Rates and Diploma Recipients by Race/Ethnicity

Category	Total	White	Black	Asian	AIAN	Hisp.
Enrollment (%)	100.0	90.6	1.8	0.6	1.2	5.8
Drop-out Rate (%)	10.0	9.1	17.3	6.7	38.9	19.4
H.S. Diplomas (#)	733	693	8	5	2	25

Park County

Park County SD # 1
160 N Evarts • Powell, WY 82435-2730
(307) 754-2215
Grade Span: KG-12; **Agency Type:** 1
Schools: 7
  4 Primary; 1 Middle; 2 High; 0 Other Level
  6 Regular; 0 Special Education; 0 Vocational; 1 Alternative
  0 Magnet; 0 Charter; 7 Title I Eligible; 0 School-wide Title I
Students: 1,597 (50.6% male; 49.3% female)
  Individual Education Program: 215 (13.5%);
  English Language Learner: 12 (0.8%); Migrant: 17 (1.1%)
  Eligible for Free Lunch Program: 320 (20.5%)
  Eligible for Reduced-Price Lunch Program: 168 (10.7%)
Teachers: 115.1 (13.6 to 1)
Librarians/Media Specialists: 3.0 (521.0 to 1)
Guidance Counselors: 7.0 (223.3 to 1)
Current Spending: ($ per student per year):
  Total: $8,548; Instruction: $4,910; Support Services: $3,389
Enrollment, Drop-out Rates and Diploma Recipients by Race/Ethnicity

Category	Total	White	Black	Asian	AIAN	Hisp.
Enrollment (%)	100.0	89.4	0.4	0.7	0.4	9.1
Drop-out Rate (%)	3.9	3.9	0.0	0.0	n/a	5.2
H.S. Diplomas (#)	122	110	0	0	0	12

Park County SD # 6
919 Cody Ave • Cody, WY 82414-4115
(307) 587-4253 • http://www.park6.org/
Grade Span: KG-12; **Agency Type:** 1
Schools: 7
  5 Primary; 1 Middle; 1 High; 0 Other Level
  7 Regular; 0 Special Education; 0 Vocational; 0 Alternative
  0 Magnet; 0 Charter; 3 Title I Eligible; 0 School-wide Title I
Students: 2,303 (51.0% male; 48.9% female)
  Individual Education Program: 287 (12.5%);
  English Language Learner: 1 (<0.1%); Migrant: 0 (0.0%)
  Eligible for Free Lunch Program: 307 (13.6%)
  Eligible for Reduced-Price Lunch Program: 175 (7.8%)
Teachers: 158.0 (14.3 to 1)
Librarians/Media Specialists: 5.0 (450.4 to 1)
Guidance Counselors: 10.3 (218.6 to 1)
Current Spending: ($ per student per year):
  Total: $7,961; Instruction: $4,847; Support Services: $2,960
Enrollment, Drop-out Rates and Diploma Recipients by Race/Ethnicity

Category	Total	White	Black	Asian	AIAN	Hisp.
Enrollment (%)	100.0	95.9	0.2	0.8	0.5	2.6
Drop-out Rate (%)	1.5	1.3	n/a	10.0	20.0	0.0
H.S. Diplomas (#)	196	190	0	1	1	4

Sheridan County

Sheridan County SD #2
1470 Sugarland Dr Suites 2 & • Sheridan, WY 82801-0919
Mailing Address: PO Box 919 • Sheridan, WY 82801-0919
(307) 674-7405 • http://web.sheridan2.k12.wy.us
Grade Span: KG-12; **Agency Type:** 1
Schools: 12
  7 Primary; 2 Middle; 2 High; 1 Other Level
  10 Regular; 0 Special Education; 0 Vocational; 2 Alternative
  0 Magnet; 0 Charter; 7 Title I Eligible; 3 School-wide Title I
Students: 3,135 (50.8% male; 49.1% female)
  Individual Education Program: 453 (14.4%);
  English Language Learner: 12 (0.4%); Migrant: 3 (0.1%)
  Eligible for Free Lunch Program: 601 (19.6%)
  Eligible for Reduced-Price Lunch Program: 332 (10.8%)
Teachers: 259.0 (11.8 to 1)
Librarians/Media Specialists: 3.0 (1,021.7 to 1)
Guidance Counselors: 16.0 (191.6 to 1)
Current Spending: ($ per student per year):
  Total: $8,749; Instruction: $5,668; Support Services: $2,809

Enrollment, Drop-out Rates and Diploma Recipients by Race/Ethnicity

Category	Total	White	Black	Asian	AIAN	Hisp.
Enrollment (%)	100.0	92.8	0.6	1.1	1.7	3.8
Drop-out Rate (%)	4.3	4.6	0.0	0.0	0.0	0.0
H.S. Diplomas (#)	232	216	3	6	5	2

Sweetwater County

Sweetwater County SD #1
3550 Foothill Blvd • Rock Springs, WY 82902-1089
Mailing Address: PO Box 1089 • Rock Springs, WY 82902-1089
(307) 352-3400 • http://www.sw1.k12.wy.us/
Grade Span: KG-12; **Agency Type:** 1
Schools: 14
  7 Primary; 4 Middle; 3 High; 0 Other Level
  13 Regular; 0 Special Education; 0 Vocational; 1 Alternative
  0 Magnet; 0 Charter; 7 Title I Eligible; 0 School-wide Title I
Students: 4,318 (51.5% male; 48.4% female)
  Individual Education Program: 780 (18.1%);
  English Language Learner: 108 (2.5%); Migrant: 0 (0.0%)
  Eligible for Free Lunch Program: 886 (21.1%)
  Eligible for Reduced-Price Lunch Program: 354 (8.4%)
Teachers: 293.5 (14.3 to 1)
Librarians/Media Specialists: 6.0 (698.8 to 1)
Guidance Counselors: 26.5 (158.2 to 1)
Current Spending: ($ per student per year):
  Total: $9,585; Instruction: $5,556; Support Services: $3,787

Enrollment, Drop-out Rates and Diploma Recipients by Race/Ethnicity

Category	Total	White	Black	Asian	AIAN	Hisp.
Enrollment (%)	100.0	84.1	1.9	0.8	1.3	11.9
Drop-out Rate (%)	7.5	6.6	0.0	0.0	28.6	17.8
H.S. Diplomas (#)	270	241	3	4	0	22

Sweetwater County SD #2
320 Monroe Ave • Green River, WY 82935-4223
(307) 872-5500 • http://www.sw2.k12.wy.us/
Grade Span: KG-12; **Agency Type:** 1
Schools: 11
  7 Primary; 2 Middle; 2 High; 0 Other Level
  10 Regular; 0 Special Education; 0 Vocational; 1 Alternative
  0 Magnet; 0 Charter; 7 Title I Eligible; 0 School-wide Title I
Students: 2,694 (52.1% male; 47.8% female)
  Individual Education Program: 449 (16.7%);
  English Language Learner: 102 (3.8%); Migrant: 0 (0.0%)
  Eligible for Free Lunch Program: 324 (12.2%)
  Eligible for Reduced-Price Lunch Program: 185 (7.0%)
Teachers: 182.9 (14.5 to 1)
Librarians/Media Specialists: 4.0 (662.5 to 1)
Guidance Counselors: 13.0 (203.8 to 1)
Current Spending: ($ per student per year):
  Total: $9,078; Instruction: $5,257; Support Services: $3,563

Enrollment, Drop-out Rates and Diploma Recipients by Race/Ethnicity

Category	Total	White	Black	Asian	AIAN	Hisp.
Enrollment (%)	100.0	87.4	0.4	0.5	1.0	10.7
Drop-out Rate (%)	7.2	7.7	33.3	0.0	16.7	2.1
H.S. Diplomas (#)	212	186	1	1	1	23

Teton County

Teton County SD #1
220 S Glenwood • Jackson, WY 83001-0568
Mailing Address: PO Box 568 • Jackson, WY 83001-0568
(307) 733-2704 • http://www.tcsd.org
Grade Span: KG-12; **Agency Type:** 1
Schools: 9
  6 Primary; 1 Middle; 2 High; 0 Other Level
  8 Regular; 0 Special Education; 0 Vocational; 1 Alternative
  0 Magnet; 0 Charter; 3 Title I Eligible; 0 School-wide Title I
Students: 2,328 (52.5% male; 47.4% female)
  Individual Education Program: 272 (11.7%);
  English Language Learner: 224 (9.6%); Migrant: 0 (0.0%)
  Eligible for Free Lunch Program: 175 (7.6%)
  Eligible for Reduced-Price Lunch Program: 87 (3.8%)
Teachers: 163.3 (14.1 to 1)
Librarians/Media Specialists: 2.0 (1,148.0 to 1)
Guidance Counselors: 9.0 (255.1 to 1)
Current Spending: ($ per student per year):
  Total: $10,047; Instruction: $5,732; Support Services: $4,004

Enrollment, Drop-out Rates and Diploma Recipients by Race/Ethnicity

Category	Total	White	Black	Asian	AIAN	Hisp.
Enrollment (%)	100.0	86.5	0.2	1.2	0.2	12.0
Drop-out Rate (%)	2.7	1.2	n/a	n/a	n/a	27.5
H.S. Diplomas (#)	152	149	0	0	0	3

Uinta County

Uinta County SD #1
537 Tenth St • Evanston, WY 82931-6002
Mailing Address: PO Box 6002 • Evanston, WY 82931-6002
(307) 789-7571 • http://www.uinta1.k12.wy.us
Grade Span: KG-12; **Agency Type:** 1
Schools: 7
  4 Primary; 2 Middle; 1 High; 0 Other Level
  7 Regular; 0 Special Education; 0 Vocational; 0 Alternative
  0 Magnet; 0 Charter; 2 Title I Eligible; 2 School-wide Title I
Students: 2,943 (52.9% male; 47.0% female)
  Individual Education Program: 497 (16.9%);
  English Language Learner: 43 (1.5%); Migrant: 0 (0.0%)
  Eligible for Free Lunch Program: 810 (27.9%)
  Eligible for Reduced-Price Lunch Program: 439 (15.1%)
Teachers: 222.6 (13.0 to 1)
Librarians/Media Specialists: 8.0 (362.8 to 1)
Guidance Counselors: 11.3 (256.8 to 1)
Current Spending: ($ per student per year):
  Total: $8,137; Instruction: $4,870; Support Services: $2,920

Enrollment, Drop-out Rates and Diploma Recipients by Race/Ethnicity

Category	Total	White	Black	Asian	AIAN	Hisp.
Enrollment (%)	100.0	89.4	0.6	1.1	0.6	8.3
Drop-out Rate (%)	6.7	6.3	0.0	0.0	8.3	16.7
H.S. Diplomas (#)	215	204	0	1	1	9

Number of Schools

Rank	Number	District Name	City
1	36	Natrona County SD #1	Casper
2	32	Laramie County SD #1	Cheyenne
3	20	Albany County SD #1	Laramie
3	20	Campbell County SD #1	Gillette
5	14	Sweetwater County SD #1	Rock Springs
6	12	Sheridan County SD #2	Sheridan
7	11	Goshen County SD #1	Torrington
7	11	Sweetwater County SD #2	Green River
9	9	Carbon County SD #1	Rawlins
9	9	Lincoln County SD #2	Afton
9	9	Teton County SD #1	Jackson
12	8	Converse County SD #1	Douglas
12	8	Fremont County SD # 1	Lander
14	7	Park County SD # 1	Powell
14	7	Park County SD # 6	Cody
14	7	Uinta County SD #1	Evanston
17	6	Fremont County SD #25	Riverton

Number of Teachers

Rank	Number	District Name	City
1	876	Laramie County SD #1	Cheyenne
2	803	Natrona County SD #1	Casper
3	536	Campbell County SD #1	Gillette
4	308	Albany County SD #1	Laramie
5	293	Sweetwater County SD #1	Rock Springs
6	259	Sheridan County SD #2	Sheridan
7	222	Uinta County SD #1	Evanston
8	182	Sweetwater County SD #2	Green River
9	163	Goshen County SD #1	Torrington
10	163	Teton County SD #1	Jackson
11	159	Lincoln County SD #2	Afton
12	158	Park County SD # 6	Cody
13	157	Fremont County SD #25	Riverton
14	135	Carbon County SD #1	Rawlins
15	128	Fremont County SD # 1	Lander
16	127	Converse County SD #1	Douglas
17	115	Park County SD # 1	Powell

Number of Students

Rank	Number	District Name	City
1	13,344	Laramie County SD #1	Cheyenne
2	12,028	Natrona County SD #1	Casper
3	7,326	Campbell County SD #1	Gillette
4	4,318	Sweetwater County SD #1	Rock Springs
5	3,735	Albany County SD #1	Laramie
6	3,135	Sheridan County SD #2	Sheridan
7	2,943	Uinta County SD #1	Evanston
8	2,694	Sweetwater County SD #2	Green River
9	2,513	Lincoln County SD #2	Afton
10	2,507	Fremont County SD #25	Riverton
11	2,328	Teton County SD #1	Jackson
12	2,303	Park County SD # 6	Cody
13	1,906	Fremont County SD # 1	Lander
14	1,899	Goshen County SD #1	Torrington
15	1,796	Carbon County SD #1	Rawlins
16	1,633	Converse County SD #1	Douglas
17	1,597	Park County SD # 1	Powell

Male Students

Rank	Percent	District Name	City
1	53.8	Fremont County SD # 1	Lander
2	53.4	Albany County SD #1	Laramie
3	52.9	Uinta County SD #1	Evanston
4	52.5	Teton County SD #1	Jackson
5	52.1	Sweetwater County SD #2	Green River
6	51.9	Goshen County SD #1	Torrington
7	51.9	Carbon County SD #1	Rawlins
8	51.9	Natrona County SD #1	Casper
9	51.6	Campbell County SD #1	Gillette
10	51.5	Sweetwater County SD #1	Rock Springs
11	51.3	Lincoln County SD #2	Afton
12	51.2	Laramie County SD #1	Cheyenne
13	51.0	Park County SD # 6	Cody
14	50.8	Sheridan County SD #2	Sheridan
15	50.8	Converse County SD #1	Douglas
16	50.6	Park County SD # 1	Powell
17	49.0	Fremont County SD #25	Riverton

Female Students

Rank	Percent	District Name	City
1	50.9	Fremont County SD #25	Riverton
2	49.3	Park County SD # 1	Powell
3	49.1	Converse County SD #1	Douglas
4	49.1	Sheridan County SD #2	Sheridan
5	48.9	Park County SD # 6	Cody
6	48.7	Laramie County SD #1	Cheyenne
7	48.6	Lincoln County SD #2	Afton
8	48.4	Sweetwater County SD #1	Rock Springs
9	48.3	Campbell County SD #1	Gillette
10	48.0	Natrona County SD #1	Casper
11	48.0	Carbon County SD #1	Rawlins
12	48.0	Goshen County SD #1	Torrington
13	47.8	Sweetwater County SD #2	Green River
14	47.4	Teton County SD #1	Jackson
15	47.0	Uinta County SD #1	Evanston
16	46.5	Albany County SD #1	Laramie
17	46.1	Fremont County SD # 1	Lander

Individual Education Program Students

Rank	Percent	District Name	City
1	20.1	Carbon County SD #1	Rawlins
2	19.3	Fremont County SD #25	Riverton
3	18.1	Sweetwater County SD #1	Rock Springs
4	17.8	Albany County SD #1	Laramie
5	16.9	Uinta County SD #1	Evanston
6	16.7	Sweetwater County SD #2	Green River
7	16.1	Goshen County SD #1	Torrington
8	16.0	Fremont County SD # 1	Lander
9	15.7	Converse County SD #1	Douglas
10	15.0	Natrona County SD #1	Casper
11	14.4	Sheridan County SD #2	Sheridan
12	14.0	Laramie County SD #1	Cheyenne
13	13.6	Lincoln County SD #2	Afton
14	13.5	Park County SD # 1	Powell
15	12.5	Park County SD # 6	Cody
16	11.7	Teton County SD #1	Jackson
17	11.6	Campbell County SD #1	Gillette

English Language Learner Students

Rank	Percent	District Name	City
1	18.2	Fremont County SD # 1	Lander
2	15.0	Fremont County SD #25	Riverton
3	9.6	Teton County SD #1	Jackson
4	3.8	Sweetwater County SD #2	Green River
5	3.1	Campbell County SD #1	Gillette
6	3.0	Goshen County SD #1	Torrington
7	2.5	Sweetwater County SD #1	Rock Springs
8	1.7	Carbon County SD #1	Rawlins
9	1.5	Uinta County SD #1	Evanston
10	1.2	Laramie County SD #1	Cheyenne
10	1.2	Lincoln County SD #2	Afton
12	1.1	Albany County SD #1	Laramie
13	1.0	Natrona County SD #1	Casper
14	0.8	Park County SD # 1	Powell
15	0.6	Converse County SD #1	Douglas
16	0.4	Sheridan County SD #2	Sheridan
17	0.0	Park County SD # 6	Cody

Migrant Students

Rank	Percent	District Name	City
1	6.4	Goshen County SD #1	Torrington
2	1.1	Park County SD # 1	Powell
3	0.1	Sheridan County SD #2	Sheridan
4	0.0	Albany County SD #1	Laramie
4	0.0	Campbell County SD #1	Gillette
4	0.0	Carbon County SD #1	Rawlins
4	0.0	Converse County SD #1	Douglas
4	0.0	Fremont County SD # 1	Lander
4	0.0	Fremont County SD #25	Riverton
4	0.0	Laramie County SD #1	Cheyenne
4	0.0	Lincoln County SD #2	Afton
4	0.0	Natrona County SD #1	Casper
4	0.0	Park County SD # 6	Cody
4	0.0	Sweetwater County SD #1	Rock Springs
4	0.0	Sweetwater County SD #2	Green River
4	0.0	Teton County SD #1	Jackson
4	0.0	Uinta County SD #1	Evanston

Students Eligible for Free Lunch

Rank	Percent	District Name	City
1	32.7	Goshen County SD #1	Torrington
2	28.3	Fremont County SD #25	Riverton
3	27.9	Uinta County SD #1	Evanston
4	24.2	Natrona County SD #1	Casper
5	23.4	Fremont County SD # 1	Lander
6	21.5	Laramie County SD #1	Cheyenne
7	21.1	Sweetwater County SD #1	Rock Springs
8	20.8	Converse County SD #1	Douglas
9	20.5	Park County SD # 1	Powell
10	20.0	Carbon County SD #1	Rawlins
11	19.6	Sheridan County SD #2	Sheridan
12	18.2	Albany County SD #1	Laramie
13	17.6	Lincoln County SD #2	Afton
14	14.4	Campbell County SD #1	Gillette
15	13.6	Park County SD # 6	Cody
16	12.2	Sweetwater County SD #2	Green River
17	7.6	Teton County SD #1	Jackson

Students Eligible for Reduced-Price Lunch

Rank	Percent	District Name	City
1	15.1	Uinta County SD #1	Evanston
2	14.6	Goshen County SD #1	Torrington
3	13.3	Lincoln County SD #2	Afton
4	10.8	Sheridan County SD #2	Sheridan
5	10.7	Park County SD # 1	Powell
6	9.6	Laramie County SD #1	Cheyenne
7	9.1	Fremont County SD #25	Riverton
8	8.5	Natrona County SD #1	Casper
9	8.4	Sweetwater County SD #1	Rock Springs
10	8.2	Campbell County SD #1	Gillette
11	8.1	Carbon County SD #1	Rawlins
12	7.8	Park County SD # 6	Cody
13	7.7	Converse County SD #1	Douglas
14	7.1	Albany County SD #1	Laramie
15	7.0	Fremont County SD # 1	Lander
15	7.0	Sweetwater County SD #2	Green River
17	3.8	Teton County SD #1	Jackson

Student/Teacher Ratio

Rank	Ratio	District Name	City
1	15.4	Fremont County SD #25	Riverton
1	15.4	Lincoln County SD #2	Afton
3	14.9	Laramie County SD #1	Cheyenne
4	14.7	Natrona County SD #1	Casper
5	14.5	Fremont County SD # 1	Lander
5	14.5	Sweetwater County SD #2	Green River
7	14.3	Park County SD # 6	Cody
7	14.3	Sweetwater County SD #1	Rock Springs
9	14.1	Teton County SD #1	Jackson
10	13.6	Park County SD # 1	Powell
11	13.5	Campbell County SD #1	Gillette
12	13.0	Uinta County SD #1	Evanston
13	12.8	Carbon County SD #1	Rawlins
14	12.5	Converse County SD #1	Douglas
15	11.9	Albany County SD #1	Laramie
16	11.8	Sheridan County SD #2	Sheridan
17	11.4	Goshen County SD #1	Torrington

Student/Librarian Ratio

Rank	Ratio	District Name	City
1	2,425.0	Fremont County SD #25	Riverton
2	1,463.2	Natrona County SD #1	Casper
3	1,306.5	Laramie County SD #1	Cheyenne
4	1,148.0	Teton County SD #1	Jackson
5	1,021.7	Sheridan County SD #2	Sheridan
6	844.5	Lincoln County SD #2	Afton
7	698.8	Sweetwater County SD #1	Rock Springs
8	662.5	Sweetwater County SD #2	Green River
9	602.8	Campbell County SD #1	Gillette
10	592.4	Albany County SD #1	Laramie
11	576.0	Carbon County SD #1	Rawlins
12	531.0	Converse County SD #1	Douglas
13	521.0	Park County SD # 1	Powell
14	463.8	Fremont County SD # 1	Lander
15	450.4	Park County SD # 6	Cody
16	412.9	Goshen County SD #1	Torrington
17	362.8	Uinta County SD #1	Evanston

Student/Counselor Ratio

Rank	Ratio	District Name	City
1	437.3	Lincoln County SD #2	Afton
2	308.6	Carbon County SD #1	Rawlins
3	256.8	Uinta County SD #1	Evanston
4	255.1	Teton County SD #1	Jackson
5	240.6	Laramie County SD #1	Cheyenne
6	226.1	Campbell County SD #1	Gillette
7	223.3	Park County SD # 1	Powell
8	221.3	Converse County SD #1	Douglas
9	218.6	Park County SD # 6	Cody
10	213.9	Natrona County SD #1	Casper
11	206.4	Goshen County SD #1	Torrington
12	206.1	Fremont County SD # 1	Lander
13	203.8	Sweetwater County SD #2	Green River
14	194.0	Fremont County SD #25	Riverton
15	191.6	Sheridan County SD #2	Sheridan
16	164.7	Albany County SD #1	Laramie
17	158.2	Sweetwater County SD #1	Rock Springs

Current Spending per Student in FY2003

Rank	Dollars	District Name	City
1	10,047	Teton County SD #1	Jackson
2	9,785	Goshen County SD #1	Torrington

3	9,680	Albany County SD #1	Laramie
4	9,585	Sweetwater County SD #1	Rock Springs
5	9,394	Fremont County SD # 1	Lander
6	9,078	Sweetwater County SD #2	Green River
7	8,749	Sheridan County SD #2	Sheridan
8	8,548	Park County SD # 1	Powell
9	8,419	Campbell County SD #1	Gillette
10	8,376	Fremont County SD #25	Riverton
11	8,363	Converse County SD #1	Douglas
11	8,363	Natrona County SD #1	Casper
13	8,234	Carbon County SD #1	Rawlins
14	8,169	Laramie County SD #1	Cheyenne
15	8,137	Uinta County SD #1	Evanston
16	7,961	Park County SD # 6	Cody
17	7,865	Lincoln County SD #2	Afton

Number of Diploma Recipients

Rank	Number	District Name	City
1	783	Laramie County SD #1	Cheyenne
2	733	Natrona County SD #1	Casper
3	534	Campbell County SD #1	Gillette
4	277	Albany County SD #1	Laramie
5	270	Sweetwater County SD #1	Rock Springs
6	232	Sheridan County SD #2	Sheridan
7	215	Uinta County SD #1	Evanston
8	212	Sweetwater County SD #2	Green River
9	196	Park County SD # 6	Cody
10	179	Lincoln County SD #2	Afton
11	176	Fremont County SD #25	Riverton
12	164	Carbon County SD #1	Rawlins
13	152	Teton County SD #1	Jackson
14	144	Fremont County SD # 1	Lander
15	138	Goshen County SD #1	Torrington
16	122	Park County SD # 1	Powell
17	118	Converse County SD #1	Douglas

High School Drop-out Rate

Rank	Percent	District Name	City
1	10.0	Natrona County SD #1	Casper
2	8.2	Laramie County SD #1	Cheyenne
3	7.5	Sweetwater County SD #1	Rock Springs
4	7.2	Sweetwater County SD #2	Green River
5	6.7	Uinta County SD #1	Evanston
6	6.4	Albany County SD #1	Laramie
7	6.2	Fremont County SD # 1	Lander
8	5.6	Carbon County SD #1	Rawlins
9	5.2	Fremont County SD #25	Riverton
10	4.5	Campbell County SD #1	Gillette
11	4.3	Sheridan County SD #2	Sheridan
12	4.0	Goshen County SD #1	Torrington
13	3.9	Park County SD # 1	Powell
14	2.7	Converse County SD #1	Douglas
14	2.7	Teton County SD #1	Jackson
16	2.5	Lincoln County SD #2	Afton
17	1.5	Park County SD # 6	Cody

NATIONAL PUBLIC
SCHOOL DATA

National Public School Educational Profile

Category	Value	Category	Value
Schools (2003-2004)	96,143	**Diploma Recipients** (2002-2003)	2,619,492
Instructional Level		White, Non-Hispanic	1,727,483
Primary	52,951	Black, Non-Hispanic	324,889
Middle	16,212	Asian/Pacific Islander	130,578
High	18,732	American Indian/Alaskan Native	26,521
Other Level	7,831	Hispanic	311,058
Curriculum		**High School Drop-out Rate** (%) (2001-2002)	4.5
Regular	86,340	White, Non-Hispanic	3.3
Special Education	2,328	Black, Non-Hispanic	7.3
Vocational	1,100	Asian/Pacific Islander	3.6
Alternative	5,958	American Indian/Alaskan Native	8.8
Type		Hispanic	7.9
Magnet	2,108	**Staff** (2003-2004)	
Charter	2,977	Teachers	3,033,463.0
Title I Eligible	51,029	Average Salary ($)	46,597
School-wide Title I	27,297	Librarians/Media Specialists	54,105.2
Students (2003-2004)	48,506,317	Guidance Counselors	98,865.6
Gender (%)		**Ratios** (2003-2004)	
Male	51.4	Student/Teacher Ratio	16.0 to 1
Female	48.6	Student/Librarian Ratio	896.5 to 1
Race/Ethnicity (%)		Student/Counselor Ratio	490.6 to 1
White, Non-Hispanic	57.1	**College Entrance Exam Scores** (2005)	
Black, Non-Hispanic	16.7	Scholastic Aptitude Test (SAT)	
Asian/Pacific Islander	4.4	Participation Rate (%)	49
American Indian/Alaskan Native	1.2	Mean SAT Reasoning Test Verbal Score	508
Hispanic	18.4	Mean SAT Reasoning Test Math Score	520
Classification (%)		American College Testing Program (ACT)	
Individual Education Program (IEP)	12.8	Participation Rate (%)	40
Migrant (2002-2003)	1.2	Average Composite Score	20.9
English Language Learner (ELL)	7.8	Average English Score	20.9
Eligible for Free Lunch Program	28.8	Average Math Score	20.9
Eligible for Reduced-Price Lunch Program	6.7	Average Reading Score	20.9
Current Spending ($ per student in FY 2003)	7,919	Average Science Score	20.9
Instruction	4,890		
Support Services	2,707		

Note: For an explanation of data, please refer to the User's Guide in the front of the book

National Public School NAEP 2005 Test Scores

Reading		Mathematics	
Grade/Category	Value	Grade/Category	Value
4th Grade		**4th Grade**	
Average Proficiency	217.3 (0.22)	Average Proficiency	237.1 (0.16)
Proficiency by Gender/Race/Ethnicity		Proficiency by Gender/Race/Ethnicity	
Male	214.2 (0.25)	Male	238.3 (0.18)
Female	220.5 (0.27)	Female	235.9 (0.18)
White, Non-Hispanic	227.6 (0.19)	White, Non-Hispanic	245.7 (0.15)
Black, Non-Hispanic	198.9 (0.33)	Black, Non-Hispanic	219.7 (0.26)
Asian, Non-Hispanic	227.2 (0.85)	Asian, Non-Hispanic	250.8 (0.69)
American Indian, Non-Hispanic	204.6 (1.32)	American Indian, Non-Hispanic	227.1 (0.99)
Hispanic	201.3 (0.49)	Hispanic	225.1 (0.30)
Proficiency by Class Size		Proficiency by Class Size	
Less than 16 Students	204.8 (0.75)	Less than 16 Students	226.7 (0.62)
16 to 18 Students	215.0 (0.63)	16 to 18 Students	235.9 (0.63)
19 to 20 Students	219.9 (0.59)	19 to 20 Students	239.6 (0.45)
21 to 25 Students	221.3 (0.35)	21 to 25 Students	239.8 (0.30)
Greater than 25 Students	214.8 (0.53)	Greater than 25 Students	234.9 (0.43)
Percent Attaining Achievement Levels		Percent Attaining Achievement Levels	
Below Basic	37.5 (0.31)	Below Basic	20.5 (0.17)
Basic or Above	62.5 (0.31)	Basic or Above	79.5 (0.17)
Proficient or Above	29.8 (0.24)	Proficient or Above	35.3 (0.24)
Advanced or Above	6.8 (0.12)	Advanced or Above	4.8 (0.11)
8th Grade		**8th Grade**	
Average Proficiency	260.4 (0.19)	Average Proficiency	277.5 (0.18)
Proficiency by Gender/Race/Ethnicity		Proficiency by Gender/Race/Ethnicity	
Male	255.2 (0.23)	Male	278.2 (0.24)
Female	265.6 (0.21)	Female	276.8 (0.22)
White, Non-Hispanic	269.4 (0.17)	White, Non-Hispanic	287.6 (0.18)
Black, Non-Hispanic	242.0 (0.44)	Black, Non-Hispanic	254.2 (0.41)
Asian, Non-Hispanic	269.7 (0.81)	Asian, Non-Hispanic	294.5 (0.99)
American Indian, Non-Hispanic	250.7 (1.22)	American Indian, Non-Hispanic	265.6 (0.95)
Hispanic	244.9 (0.44)	Hispanic	261.1 (0.43)
Proficiency by Parents Highest Level of Ed.		Proficiency by Parents Highest Level of Ed.	
Did Not Finish High School	243.6 (0.51)	Did Not Finish High School	259.3 (0.46)
Graduated High School	251.7 (0.34)	Graduated High School	267.1 (0.34)
Some Education After High School	264.7 (0.24)	Some Education After High School	280.1 (0.33)
Graduated College	270.2 (0.24)	Graduated College	288.9 (0.25)
Percent Attaining Achievement Levels		Percent Attaining Achievement Levels	
Below Basic	37.5 (0.31)	Below Basic	32.1 (0.24)
Basic or Above	62.5 (0.31)	Basic or Above	67.9 (0.24)
Proficient or Above	29.8 (0.24)	Proficient or Above	28.5 (0.22)
Advanced or Above	6.8 (0.12)	Advanced or Above	5.6 (0.10)

Note: *For an explanation of data, please refer to the User's Guide in the front of the book; n/a indicates data not available*

Number of Schools
School districts ranked in *descending* order

Rank	Number	District Name	City, State	Rank	Number	District Name	City, State
1	1,225	New York City Public Schools	Brooklyn, NY	61	97	Portland SD 1J	Portland, OR
2	693	Los Angeles Unified	Los Angeles, CA	62	96	Davis SD	Farmington, UT
3	633	City of Chicago SD 299	Chicago, IL	63	95	Anchorage SD	Anchorage, AK
4	375	Dade County SD	Miami, FL	64	93	El Paso ISD	El Paso, TX
5	308	Houston ISD	Houston, TX	64	93	Greenville County SD	Greenville, SC
6	298	Clark County SD	Las Vegas, NV	64	93	Northside ISD	San Antonio, TX
7	284	Hawaii Department of Education	Honolulu, HI	67	92	Indianapolis Public Schools	Indianapolis, IN
8	264	Broward County SD	Fort Lauderdale, FL	67	92	Pittsburgh SD	Pittsburgh, PA
9	263	Philadelphia City SD	Philadelphia, PA	69	91	Long Beach Unified	Long Beach, CA
10	261	Detroit City SD	Detroit, MI	69	91	Mesa Unified District	Mesa, AZ
11	237	Hillsborough County SD	Tampa, FL	71	90	Wichita	Wichita, KS
12	233	Milwaukee	Milwaukee, WI	72	89	Kansas City 33	Kansas City, MO
13	227	Dallas ISD	Dallas, TX	72	89	Oklahoma City	Oklahoma City, OK
14	213	Palm Beach County SD	West Palm Beach, FL	74	88	Grand Rapids Public Schools	Grand Rapids, MI
15	204	Fairfax County Public Schools	Fairfax, VA	74	88	Knox County SD	Knoxville, TN
16	203	Prince Georges Co Public Schools	Upper Marlboro, MD	74	88	Sacramento City Unified	Sacramento, CA
17	194	Montgomery County Public Schls	Rockville, MD	77	87	Fulton County	Atlanta, GA
18	190	Orange County SD	Orlando, FL	77	87	Volusia County SD	Deland, FL
19	189	Baltimore City Public Schools Sys	Baltimore, MD	79	86	Cincinnati City SD	Cincinnati, OH
20	185	Memphis City SD	Memphis, TN	79	86	Tulsa	Tulsa, OK
20	185	San Diego Unified	San Diego, CA	79	86	Virginia Beach City Public Schls	Virginia Beach, VA
22	180	Intermediate SD 287	Plymouth, MN	82	85	Cumberland County Schools	Fayetteville, NC
23	179	Duval County SD	Jacksonville, FL	82	85	Jordan SD	Sandy, UT
24	173	Jefferson County	Louisville, KY	84	84	Jefferson Parish School Board	Harvey, LA
25	170	District of Columbia Pub Schls	Washington, DC	84	84	Omaha Public Schools	Omaha, NE
26	169	Pinellas County SD	Largo, FL	84	84	San Juan Unified	Carmichael, CA
27	167	Baltimore County Public Schls	Towson, MD	87	83	Lee County SD	Fort Myers, FL
27	167	Jefferson County R-1	Golden, CO	88	81	Hamilton County School Distrct	Chattanooga, TN
29	153	Columbus Public Schools	Columbus, OH	89	80	Birmingham City	Birmingham, AL
30	148	Albuquerque Public Schools	Albuquerque, NM	89	80	Charleston County SD	Charleston, SC
31	147	Polk County SD	Bartow, FL	91	77	Arlington ISD	Arlington, TX
32	145	Denver County 1	Denver, CO	91	77	Escambia County SD	Pensacola, FL
32	145	Fort Worth ISD	Fort Worth, TX	91	77	Newark City	Newark, NJ
34	142	Minneapolis	Minneapolis, MN	94	76	Prince William Co Public Schools	Manassas, VA
35	141	Dekalb County	Decatur, GA	95	75	Caddo Parish School Board	Shreveport, LA
36	137	Charlotte-Mecklenburg Schools	Charlotte, NC	96	73	Manatee County SD	Bradenton, FL
37	136	Boston	Boston, MA	96	73	Pasco County SD	Land O' Lakes, FL
38	129	Orleans Parish School Board	New Orleans, LA	98	72	Plano ISD	Plano, TX
38	129	Seattle SD 1	Seattle, WA	98	72	Seminole County SD	Sanford, FL
40	126	Nashville-Davidson County SD	Nashville, TN	100	71	Howard County Pub Schls System	Ellicott City, MD
40	126	Tucson Unified District	Tucson, AZ	100	71	Kanawha County SD	Charleston, WV
40	126	Wake County Schools	Raleigh, NC	102	70	Garland ISD	Garland, TX
43	123	St. Paul	St. Paul, MN	103	69	Forsyth County Schools	Winston Salem, NC
44	122	Cleveland Municipal City SD	Cleveland, OH	104	68	Buffalo City SD	Buffalo, NY
45	119	Anne Arundel County Pub Schls	Annapolis, MD	105	67	Garden Grove Unified	Garden Grove, CA
46	118	Oakland Unified	Oakland, CA	105	67	Salem-Keizer SD 24J	Salem, OR
46	118	San Francisco Unified	San Francisco, CA	105	67	Toledo City SD	Toledo, OH
48	111	Austin ISD	Austin, TX	108	66	Alachua County SD	Gainesville, FL
49	109	Granite SD	Salt Lake City, UT	108	66	Aldine ISD	Houston, TX
50	108	Brevard County SD	Viera, FL	108	66	Henrico County Public Schools	Richmond, VA
50	108	St. Louis City	St Louis, MO	108	66	Lincoln Public Schools	Lincoln, NE
52	107	San Antonio ISD	San Antonio, TX	108	66	Spokane SD 81	Spokane, WA
53	106	Cobb County	Marietta, GA	113	65	Colorado Springs 11	Colorado Spgs, CO
54	105	Atlanta City	Atlanta, GA	113	65	Marion County SD	Ocala, FL
54	105	Guilford County Schools	Greensboro, NC	113	65	North East ISD	San Antonio, TX
56	104	Mobile County	Mobile, AL	113	65	San Bernardino City Unified	San Bernardino, CA
57	103	Fresno Unified	Fresno, CA	113	65	West Contra Costa Unified	Richmond, CA
58	102	Washoe County SD	Reno, NV	118	64	Ysleta ISD	El Paso, TX
59	98	E Baton Rouge Parish SB	Baton Rouge, LA	119	63	Akron Public Schools	Akron, OH
59	98	Gwinnett County	Lawrenceville, GA	119	63	Alpine SD	American Fork, UT

This section ranks 120 school districts at both the "top" and "bottom" of each category for a total of 240 districts per category. The "top" list (descending order) appears first, followed by the "bottom" list (ascending order). Ranking tables cover public school districts serving 1,500 or more students.

Number of Schools

School districts ranked in *ascending* order

Rank	Number	District Name	City, State	Rank	Number	District Name	City, State
1	1	Adlai E Stevenson Dist 125	Lincolnshire, IL	45	2	Elk Lake SD	Dimock, PA
1	1	Argo Community HSD 217	Summit, IL	45	2	Essex Community Education Ctr	Essex Junction, VT
1	1	Arrowhead UHS	Hartland, WI	45	2	Exeter Region Cooperative SD	Exeter, NH
1	1	Boces Eastern Suffolk (Suffolk I)	Patchogue, NY	45	2	Fairfax Elementary	Bakersfield, CA
1	1	Boces Nassau	Garden City, NY	45	2	Flathead HS	Kalispell, MT
1	1	Bozeman HS	Bozeman, MT	45	2	Floral Park-Bellerose Union Free SD	Floral Park, NY
1	1	Bradley Bourbonnais CHSD 307	Bradley, IL	45	2	Florida State Univ Lab School	Tallahassee, FL
1	1	Butte HS	Butte, MT	45	2	Florida Virtual School	Orlando, FL
1	1	Community High SD 94	West Chicago, IL	45	2	Foster-Glocester RD	Chepachet, RI
1	1	Edison-Friendship Public Charter	Washington, DC	45	2	Freetown-Lakeville	Lakeville, MA
1	1	Electronic Classrm of Tomorrow	Columbus, OH	45	2	Fremont SD 79	Mundelein, IL
1	1	Evanston Twp HSD 202	Evanston, IL	45	2	Great Falls HS	Great Falls, MT
1	1	Fenton Community HSD 100	Bensenville, IL	45	2	Greater Egg Harbor Reg	Mays Landing, NJ
1	1	Grayslake Community High SD 127	Grayslake, IL	45	2	Hampton Bays Union Free SD	Hampton Bays, NY
1	1	Greater Lowell Voc Tec	Tyngsborough, MA	45	2	Hazlehurst City SD	Hazlehurst, MS
1	1	Greater New Bedford	New Bedford, MA	45	2	Helena HS	Helena, MT
1	1	Hartford UHS	Hartford, WI	45	2	Hinsdale Twp HSD 86	Hinsdale, IL
1	1	High Point Regional	Sussex, NJ	45	2	Jacksonville City	Jacksonville, AL
1	1	Homewood Flossmoor CHSD 233	Flossmoor, IL	45	2	King Philip	Wrentham, MA
1	1	Hononegah Community HSD 207	Rockton, IL	45	2	Kingsway Regional	Woolwich Twp, NJ
1	1	Hunterdon Central Reg	Flemington, NJ	45	2	Leyden Community HSD 212	Franklin Park, IL
1	1	Lake Forest Community HS Dist 115	Lake Forest, IL	45	2	Lincoln Way Community HSD 210	New Lenox, IL
1	1	Lake Park Community HSD 108	Roselle, IL	45	2	Little Egg Harbor Twp	Little Egg Hbr, NJ
1	1	Lockport Twp HSD 205	Lockport, IL	45	2	Los Gatos-Saratoga Jt Union High	Los Gatos, CA
1	1	Lyons Twp HSD 204	La Grange, IL	45	2	Lower Cape May Regional	Cape May, NJ
1	1	Mainland Regional	Linwood, NJ	45	2	Manasquan Boro	Manasquan, NJ
1	1	Minooka Community HS District 111	Minooka, IL	45	2	Masconomet	Topsfield, MA
1	1	Mundelein Cons High SD 120	Mundelein, IL	45	2	Mattituck-Cutchogue Union Free SD	Cutchogue, NY
1	1	Norwich Free Academy	Norwich, CT	45	2	Mchenry Community HSD 156	Mc Henry, IL
1	1	O Fallon Twp High SD 203	Ofallon, IL	45	2	Mid Valley SD	Throop, PA
1	1	Oak Lawn Community HSD 229	Oak Lawn, IL	45	2	Millstone Twp	Clarksburg, NJ
1	1	Oak Park & River Forest Dist 200	Oak Park, IL	45	2	Mohawk Area SD	Bessemer, PA
1	1	Ohio Virtual Academy	Maumee, OH	45	2	Morris Hills Regional	Rockaway, NJ
1	1	Ottawa Twp HSD 140	Ottawa, IL	45	2	Mount Carmel Area SD	Mount Carmel, PA
1	1	Passaic County Vocational	Wayne, NJ	45	2	N Hunt/Voorhees Regional	Annandale, NJ
1	1	Pekin Community HSD 303	Pekin, IL	45	2	Nauset	Orleans, MA
1	1	Pennsylvania Virtual CS	Norristown, PA	45	2	New Trier Twp HSD 203	Northfield, IL
1	1	Pinkerton Academy SD	Derry, NH	45	2	Niles Twp Community High SD 219	Skokie, IL
1	1	Reavis Twp HSD 220	Burbank, IL	45	2	Northern Burlington Reg	Columbus, NJ
1	1	United Twp HS District 30	East Moline, IL	45	2	Northern Valley Regional	Demarest, NJ
1	1	Warren Twp High SD 121	Gages Lake, IL	45	2	Oro Grande Elementary	Oro Grande, CA
1	1	Watchung Hills Regional	Warren, NJ	45	2	Palisades Park	Palisades Park, NJ
1	1	Western Pennsylvania Cyber CS	Midland, PA	45	2	Paoli Community School Corp	Paoli, IN
1	1	Zion-Benton Twp HSD 126	Zion, IL	45	2	Pascack Valley Regional	Montvale, NJ
45	2	Acton-Boxborough	Acton, MA	45	2	Pde Division of Data Services	Harrisburg, PA
45	2	Amherst-Pelham	Amherst, MA	45	2	Pinelands Regional	Tuckerton, NJ
45	2	Brooklyn Center	Brooklyn Center, MN	45	2	Proviso Twp HSD 209	Maywood, IL
45	2	Burgettstown Area SD	Burgettstown, PA	45	2	Ramapo-Indian Hill Reg	Franklin Lakes, NJ
45	2	Burlington County Vocational	Westampton Twp, NJ	45	2	Rancocas Valley Regional	Mount Holly, NJ
45	2	Camden County Vocational	Sicklerville, NJ	45	2	Reynolds SD	Greenville, PA
45	2	Central Regional	Bayville, NJ	45	2	Romoland Elementary	Homeland, CA
45	2	Clearview Regional	Mullica Hill, NJ	45	2	San Benito High	Hollister, CA
45	2	Colorado River Union High SD	Fort Mojave, AZ	45	2	Santa Paula Union High	Santa Paula, CA
45	2	Community High SD 128	Libertyville, IL	45	2	Schuylerville Central SD	Schuylerville, NY
45	2	Community High SD 99	Downers Grove, IL	45	2	Shamokin Area SD	Coal Township, PA
45	2	Crete Public Schools	Crete, NE	45	2	Silver Lake	Kingston, MA
45	2	Delsea Regional H.S District	Franklinville, NJ	45	2	South Ripley Com Sch Corp	Versailles, IN
45	2	Detroit Acad of Arts & Sciences	Detroit, MI	45	2	Southern Regional	Manahawkin, NJ
45	2	Du Page High SD 88	Villa Park, IL	45	2	Township High SD 113	Highland Park, IL
45	2	Eastern Camden County Reg	Voorhees, NJ	45	2	United Local SD	Hanoverton, OH

This section ranks 120 school districts at both the "top" and "bottom" of each category for a total of 240 districts per category. The "top" list (descending order) appears first, followed by the "bottom" list (ascending order). Ranking tables cover public school districts serving 1,500 or more students.

Number of Teachers

School districts ranked in *descending* order

Rank	Number	District Name	City, State	Rank	Number	District Name	City, State
1	70,171	New York City Public Schools	Brooklyn, NY	61	3,719	Fort Bend ISD	Sugar Land, TX
2	35,492	Los Angeles Unified	Los Angeles, CA	62	3,704	Mesa Unified District	Mesa, AZ
3	22,950	City of Chicago SD 299	Chicago, IL	63	3,692	Atlanta City	Atlanta, GA
4	18,887	Dade County SD	Miami, FL	64	3,687	Newark City	Newark, NJ
5	14,264	Broward County SD	Fort Lauderdale, FL	65	3,670	North East ISD	San Antonio, TX
6	13,483	Clark County SD	Las Vegas, NV	66	3,624	Lee County SD	Fort Myers, FL
7	12,293	Fairfax County Public Schools	Fairfax, VA	67	3,616	Aldine ISD	Houston, TX
8	12,276	Houston ISD	Houston, TX	68	3,614	Washoe County SD	Reno, NV
9	11,128	Hawaii Department of Education	Honolulu, HI	69	3,609	Knox County SD	Knoxville, TN
10	11,020	Hillsborough County SD	Tampa, FL	70	3,526	San Antonio ISD	San Antonio, TX
11	10,323	Dallas ISD	Dallas, TX	71	3,509	Garland ISD	Garland, TX
12	10,194	Philadelphia City SD	Philadelphia, PA	72	3,371	Jefferson Parish School Board	Harvey, LA
13	9,495	Orange County SD	Orlando, FL	73	3,355	Tucson Unified District	Tucson, AZ
14	9,359	Palm Beach County SD	West Palm Beach, FL	74	3,323	Howard County Pub Schls System	Ellicott City, MD
15	9,007	Montgomery County Public Schls	Rockville, MD	75	3,255	Cumberland County Schools	Fayetteville, NC
16	8,220	Gwinnett County	Lawrenceville, GA	76	3,251	Forsyth County Schools	Winston Salem, NC
17	8,119	Prince Georges Co Public Schools	Upper Marlboro, MD	77	3,227	St. Louis City	St Louis, MO
18	7,420	San Diego Unified	San Diego, CA	78	3,206	Granite SD	Salt Lake City, UT
19	7,350	Charlotte-Mecklenburg Schools	Charlotte, NC	79	3,196	Pasco County SD	Land O' Lakes, FL
20	7,302	Wake County Schools	Raleigh, NC	80	3,175	Henrico County Public Schools	Richmond, VA
21	7,291	Baltimore County Public Schls	Towson, MD	81	3,160	Charleston County SD	Charleston, SC
22	7,274	Memphis City SD	Memphis, TN	82	3,139	San Francisco Unified	San Francisco, CA
23	6,976	Duval County SD	Jacksonville, FL	83	3,137	E Baton Rouge Parish SB	Baton Rouge, LA
24	6,867	Cobb County	Marietta, GA	84	3,133	Akron Public Schools	Akron, OH
25	6,719	Detroit City SD	Detroit, MI	85	3,132	Cincinnati City SD	Cincinnati, OH
26	6,632	Pinellas County SD	Largo, FL	86	3,100	Omaha Public Schools	Omaha, NE
27	6,408	Dekalb County	Decatur, GA	87	3,069	Wichita	Wichita, KS
28	6,268	Baltimore City Public Schools Sys	Baltimore, MD	88	3,063	Lewisville ISD	Flower Mound, TX
29	6,191	Albuquerque Public Schools	Albuquerque, NM	89	3,053	Jordan SD	Sandy, UT
30	5,929	Milwaukee	Milwaukee, WI	90	3,024	Minneapolis	Minneapolis, MN
31	5,656	Jefferson County	Louisville, KY	91	3,022	Buffalo City SD	Buffalo, NY
32	5,555	Virginia Beach City Public Schls	Virginia Beach, VA	92	3,016	Loudoun County Public Schools	Leesburg, VA
33	5,354	Austin ISD	Austin, TX	93	3,014	Brownsville ISD	Brownsville, TX
34	5,284	Polk County SD	Bartow, FL	94	2,999	Ysleta ISD	El Paso, TX
35	5,108	Cleveland Municipal City SD	Cleveland, OH	95	2,977	Alief ISD	Houston, TX
36	4,898	District of Columbia Pub Schls	Washington, DC	96	2,954	Clayton County	Jonesboro, GA
37	4,891	Fulton County	Atlanta, GA	97	2,927	Caddo Parish School Board	Shreveport, LA
38	4,884	Cypress-Fairbanks ISD	Houston, TX	98	2,877	Chesapeake City Public Schools	Chesapeake, VA
39	4,857	Nashville-Davidson County SD	Nashville, TN	99	2,833	Santa Ana Unified	Santa Ana, CA
40	4,792	Fort Worth ISD	Fort Worth, TX	100	2,833	Rochester City SD	Rochester, NY
41	4,764	Jefferson County R-1	Golden, CO	101	2,832	Anchorage SD	Anchorage, AK
42	4,656	Orleans Parish School Board	New Orleans, LA	102	2,801	Katy ISD	Katy, TX
43	4,594	Northside ISD	San Antonio, TX	103	2,769	Indianapolis Public Schools	Indianapolis, IN
44	4,504	El Paso ISD	El Paso, TX	104	2,754	St. Paul	St. Paul, MN
45	4,501	Anne Arundel County Pub Schls	Annapolis, MD	105	2,738	Hamilton County School Distrct	Chattanooga, TN
46	4,439	Long Beach Unified	Long Beach, CA	106	2,737	Cherry Creek 5	Greenwood Vlg, CO
47	4,390	Guilford County Schools	Greensboro, NC	107	2,701	Jersey City	Jersey City, NJ
48	4,303	Brevard County SD	Viera, FL	108	2,691	San Bernardino City Unified	San Bernardino, CA
49	4,236	Mobile County	Mobile, AL	109	2,686	Pittsburgh SD	Pittsburgh, PA
50	4,217	Denver County 1	Denver, CO	110	2,684	Portland SD 1J	Portland, OR
51	4,125	Prince William Co Public Schools	Manassas, VA	111	2,680	Pasadena ISD	Pasadena, TX
52	3,991	Arlington ISD	Arlington, TX	112	2,660	Elk Grove Unified	Elk Grove, CA
53	3,926	Fresno Unified	Fresno, CA	113	2,659	Sacramento City Unified	Sacramento, CA
54	3,926	Boston	Boston, MA	114	2,649	Shelby County SD	Memphis, TN
55	3,845	Chesterfield County Public Schools	Chesterfield, VA	115	2,627	Davis SD	Farmington, UT
56	3,838	Columbus Public Schools	Columbus, OH	116	2,600	Kansas City 33	Kansas City, MO
57	3,835	Greenville County SD	Greenville, SC	117	2,586	Norfolk City Public Schools	Norfolk, VA
58	3,825	Plano ISD	Plano, TX	118	2,577	Seattle SD 1	Seattle, WA
59	3,807	Volusia County SD	Deland, FL	119	2,566	Tulsa	Tulsa, OK
60	3,788	Seminole County SD	Sanford, FL	120	2,544	Oakland Unified	Oakland, CA

This section ranks 120 school districts at both the "top" and "bottom" of each category for a total of 240 districts per category. The "top" list (descending order) appears first, followed by the "bottom" list (ascending order). Ranking tables cover public school districts serving 1,500 or more students.

Number of Teachers

School districts ranked in *ascending* order

Rank	Number	District Name	City, State	Rank	Number	District Name	City, State
1	16	Mason Consol Schools (Monroe)	Erie, MI	61	83	Minooka Community HS District 111	Minooka, IL
2	20	Peach Springs Unified District	Peach Springs, AZ	62	83	Port Townsend SD 50	Port Townsend, WA
3	35	Northview Public SD	Grand Rapids, MI	62	83	Ridgefield SD 122	Ridgefield, WA
4	39	Western Pennsylvania Cyber CS	Midland, PA	64	84	Chowchilla Elementary	Chowchilla, CA
5	51	Washtenaw ISD	Ann Arbor, MI	64	84	Clare Public Schools	Clare, MI
6	53	Ohio Virtual Academy	Maumee, OH	64	84	Meridian Public Schools	Sanford, MI
7	59	Honors Academy	Dallas, TX	64	84	Montague Area Public Schools	Montague, MI
8	60	Fern Ridge SD 28J	Elmira, OR	64	84	North Knox School Corp	Bicknell, IN
9	61	North Branch Area Schools	North Branch, MI	64	84	Piner-Olivet Union Elementary	Santa Rosa, CA
10	62	Galena City SD	Galena, AK	64	84	Zane Trace Local SD	Chillicothe, OH
11	64	Santa Paula Union High	Santa Paula, CA	71	84	Fruitland District	Fruitland, ID
12	67	Gorman Elementary	Gorman, CA	71	84	Vashon Island SD 402	Vashon, WA
13	67	Westwood Unified	Westwood, CA	73	84	Earlimart Elementary	Earlimart, CA
14	68	Nuview Union Elementary	Nuevo, CA	73	84	Ridgewood Local SD	West Lafayette, OH
15	70	Lake Fenton Community Schools	Fenton, MI	75	85	Bradley SD 61	Bradley, IL
16	71	Edison-Friendship Public Charter	Washington, DC	75	85	Quincy Community SD	Quincy, MI
17	71	Fairfax Elementary	Bakersfield, CA	75	85	Vassar Public Schools	Vassar, MI
18	72	Pennsylvania Virtual CS	Norristown, PA	78	85	Carlinville CUSD 1	Carlinville, IL
19	73	Saginaw ISD	Saginaw, MI	79	85	Brookville Local SD	Brookville, OH
20	73	Sutherlin SD 130	Sutherlin, OR	80	85	Switzerland County School Corp	Vevay, IN
21	73	Sonora Union High	Sonora, CA	81	85	West Bonner County District	Sandpoint, ID
22	75	Romoland Elementary	Homeland, CA	82	86	M S D Bluffton-Harrison	Bluffton, IN
23	75	Porter Township School Corp	Valparaiso, IN	83	86	Bayless	St Louis, MO
24	75	Jamul-Dulzura Union Elementary	Jamul, CA	84	86	Virginia	Virginia, MN
25	76	Butte County Joint District	Arco, ID	85	87	Bangor Public Schools (Van Buren)	Bangor, MI
26	77	Florida Virtual School	Orlando, FL	85	87	North College Hill City SD	Cincinnati, OH
26	77	Michigan Center SD	Michigan Center, MI	85	87	Tawas Area Schools	Tawas City, MI
28	77	Brawley Union High	Brawley, CA	88	87	Pike-Delta-York Local SD	Delta, OH
29	77	Mohave Valley Elementary District	Mohave Valley, AZ	89	87	Manchester Community Schools	N Manchester, IN
30	78	Dooly County	Vienna, GA	89	87	Willows Unified	Willows, CA
30	78	Hanover Community School Corp	Cedar Lake, IN	91	87	North Marion SD 15	Aurora, OR
30	78	Northwestern Con School Corp	Fairland, IN	91	87	Winston-Dillard SD 116	Winston, OR
33	78	Cashmere SD 222	Cashmere, WA	93	88	Wattsburg Area SD	Erie, PA
34	78	Junction City SD 69	Junction City, OR	94	88	Fremont SD 79	Mundelein, IL
35	79	Pembroke	Pembroke, MA	94	88	Gallatin County	Warsaw, KY
36	79	Mother Lode Union Elementary	Placerville, CA	96	88	Lacrescent-Hokah	Lacrescent, MN
37	79	Cascade Union Elementary	Anderson, CA	96	88	Live Oak Unified	Live Oak, CA
37	79	Riverdale Joint Unified	Riverdale, CA	98	88	Acton-Agua Dulce Unified	Acton, CA
39	79	Lake Local SD	Millbury, OH	99	88	Circle	Towanda, KS
40	80	Manchester Local SD	Akron, OH	100	88	Ballard County	Barlow, KY
40	80	South Ripley Com Sch Corp	Versailles, IN	101	89	Almont Community Schools	Almont, MI
42	80	Hockinson SD 98	Brush Prairie, WA	101	89	Bradley Bourbonnais CHSD 307	Bradley, IL
43	80	Cloverdale Unified	Cloverdale, CA	101	89	Colorado River Union High SD	Fort Mojave, AZ
44	80	Greenfield Union Elementary	Greenfield, CA	101	89	East Jackson Community Schools	Jackson, MI
45	81	Elk Rapids Schools	Elk Rapids, MI	101	89	East Washington School Corp	Pekin, IN
45	81	Millington Community Schools	Millington, MI	101	89	Flat Rock Community Schools	Flat Rock, MI
47	81	Posen-Robbins El SD 143-5	Posen, IL	101	89	Maricopa County Regional District	Phoenix, AZ
48	81	Julian Union Elementary	Julian, CA	101	89	Oak Lawn Community HSD 229	Oak Lawn, IL
49	82	Mark West Union Elementary	Santa Rosa, CA	101	89	Ovid-Elsie Area Schools	Elsie, MI
49	82	Woodlake Union Elementary	Woodlake, CA	101	89	Union Township School Corp	Valparaiso, IN
51	82	Juab SD	Nephi, UT	111	89	John Swett Unified	Crockett, CA
52	82	Naches Valley SD 3	Naches, WA	112	89	Byron	Byron, MN
52	82	Reynolds SD	Greenville, PA	112	89	Philomath SD 17J	Philomath, OR
54	82	Kiona-Benton SD 52	Benton City, WA	114	89	Genoa Area Local SD	Genoa, OH
54	82	Siuslaw SD 97J	Florence, OR	114	89	Seaside SD 10	Seaside, OR
56	83	Carterville CUSD 5	Carterville, IL	114	89	Wilmington CUSD 209U	Wilmington, IL
56	83	United Local SD	Hanoverton, OH	117	89	Swanton Local SD	Swanton, OH
58	83	Meridian SD 505	Bellingham, WA	118	89	Bellevue Union Elementary	Santa Rosa, CA
58	83	Southeast Dubois County Sch Corp	Ferdinand, IN	119	90	Freeland Community SD	Freeland, MI
60	83	Nine Mile Falls SD 325/179	Nine Mile Fall, WA	119	90	Weiser District	Weiser, ID

This section ranks 120 school districts at both the "top" and "bottom" of each category for a total of 240 districts per category. The "top" list (descending order) appears first, followed by the "bottom" list (ascending order). Ranking tables cover public school districts serving 1,500 or more students.

Number of Students

School districts ranked in *descending* order

Rank	Number	District Name	City, State	Rank	Number	District Name	City, State
1	1,023,674	New York City Public Schools	Brooklyn, NY	61	62,874	Santa Ana Unified	Santa Ana, CA
2	747,009	Los Angeles Unified	Los Angeles, CA	62	62,454	Arlington ISD	Arlington, TX
3	434,419	City of Chicago SD 299	Chicago, IL	63	62,103	Washoe County SD	Reno, NV
4	371,785	Dade County SD	Miami, FL	64	61,448	Tucson Unified District	Tucson, AZ
5	272,835	Broward County SD	Fort Lauderdale, FL	65	61,248	Fort Bend ISD	Sugar Land, TX
6	270,529	Clark County SD	Las Vegas, NV	66	60,749	Davis SD	Farmington, UT
7	211,499	Houston ISD	Houston, TX	67	60,150	Boston	Boston, MA
8	189,779	Philadelphia City SD	Philadelphia, PA	68	57,818	San Bernardino City Unified	San Bernardino, CA
9	183,609	Hawaii Department of Education	Honolulu, HI	69	57,805	San Francisco Unified	San Francisco, CA
10	181,900	Hillsborough County SD	Tampa, FL	70	57,510	Pasco County SD	Land O' Lakes, FL
11	170,260	Palm Beach County SD	West Palm Beach, FL	71	56,914	San Antonio ISD	San Antonio, TX
12	165,992	Orange County SD	Orlando, FL	72	56,298	North East ISD	San Antonio, TX
13	164,235	Fairfax County Public Schools	Fairfax, VA	73	56,292	Aldine ISD	Houston, TX
14	160,584	Dallas ISD	Dallas, TX	74	55,613	Elk Grove Unified	Elk Grove, CA
15	153,034	Detroit City SD	Detroit, MI	75	55,393	Chesterfield County Public Schools	Chesterfield, VA
16	139,201	Montgomery County Public Schls	Rockville, MD	76	55,114	Garland ISD	Garland, TX
17	137,960	San Diego Unified	San Diego, CA	77	53,159	Cumberland County Schools	Fayetteville, NC
18	137,285	Prince Georges Co Public Schools	Upper Marlboro, MD	78	52,659	Knox County SD	Knoxville, TN
19	129,557	Duval County SD	Jacksonville, FL	79	52,103	Atlanta City	Atlanta, GA
20	129,014	Gwinnett County	Lawrenceville, GA	79	52,103	Sacramento City Unified	Sacramento, CA
21	116,224	Memphis City SD	Memphis, TN	81	51,869	Plano ISD	Plano, TX
22	114,510	Pinellas County SD	Largo, FL	82	51,453	Jefferson Parish School Board	Harvey, LA
23	114,071	Charlotte-Mecklenburg Schools	Charlotte, NC	83	51,240	Alpine SD	American Fork, UT
24	109,424	Wake County Schools	Raleigh, NC	84	50,906	San Juan Unified	Carmichael, CA
25	108,523	Baltimore County Public Schls	Towson, MD	85	50,555	Clayton County	Jonesboro, GA
26	102,034	Cobb County	Marietta, GA	86	50,437	Oakland Unified	Oakland, CA
27	99,550	Dekalb County	Decatur, GA	87	50,172	Garden Grove Unified	Garden Grove, CA
28	97,560	Long Beach Unified	Long Beach, CA	88	49,746	Capistrano Unified	San Juan Capis, CA
29	97,359	Milwaukee	Milwaukee, WI	89	49,722	Anchorage SD	Anchorage, AK
30	95,582	Jefferson County	Louisville, KY	90	48,894	Wichita	Wichita, KS
31	94,049	Baltimore City Public Schools Sys	Baltimore, MD	91	48,344	Portland SD 1J	Portland, OR
32	90,537	Albuquerque Public Schools	Albuquerque, NM	92	47,833	Howard County Pub Schls System	Ellicott City, MD
33	87,172	Jefferson County R-1	Golden, CO	93	47,788	Forsyth County Schools	Winston Salem, NC
34	84,135	Polk County SD	Bartow, FL	94	47,588	Seattle SD 1	Seattle, WA
35	81,408	Fresno Unified	Fresno, CA	95	46,926	Newark City	Newark, NJ
36	80,335	Fort Worth ISD	Fort Worth, TX	96	46,808	Shelby County SD	Memphis, TN
37	79,007	Austin ISD	Austin, TX	97	46,668	Ysleta ISD	El Paso, TX
38	76,304	Virginia Beach City Public Schls	Virginia Beach, VA	98	46,644	E Baton Rouge Parish SB	Baton Rouge, LA
39	75,401	Mesa Unified District	Mesa, AZ	99	46,594	Cherry Creek 5	Greenwood Vlg, CO
40	74,877	Cypress-Fairbanks ISD	Houston, TX	100	46,142	Pasadena ISD	Pasadena, TX
41	74,761	Jordan SD	Sandy, UT	101	46,035	Omaha Public Schools	Omaha, NE
42	74,508	Anne Arundel County Pub Schls	Annapolis, MD	102	45,923	Brownsville ISD	Brownsville, TX
43	73,901	Brevard County SD	Viera, FL	103	45,354	Henrico County Public Schools	Richmond, VA
44	73,319	Fulton County	Atlanta, GA	104	45,344	Alief ISD	Houston, TX
45	72,100	Denver County 1	Denver, CO	105	44,473	Caddo Parish School Board	Shreveport, LA
46	71,798	Northside ISD	San Antonio, TX	106	44,109	Charleston County SD	Charleston, SC
47	70,771	Granite SD	Salt Lake City, UT	107	44,024	Lewisville ISD	Flower Mound, TX
48	69,655	Cleveland Municipal City SD	Cleveland, OH	108	43,998	Corona-Norco Unified	Norco, CA
49	68,651	Nashville-Davidson County SD	Nashville, TN	108	43,998	Escambia County SD	Pensacola, FL
50	67,922	Orleans Parish School Board	New Orleans, LA	110	43,911	Osceola County SD	Kissimmee, FL
51	66,971	Guilford County Schools	Greensboro, NC	111	43,397	Minneapolis	Minneapolis, MN
52	66,466	Lee County SD	Fort Myers, FL	112	42,510	St. Paul	St. Paul, MN
53	65,099	District of Columbia Pub Schls	Washington, DC	113	42,280	Tulsa	Tulsa, OK
54	64,904	Seminole County SD	Sanford, FL	114	42,116	Katy ISD	Katy, TX
55	64,774	Mobile County	Mobile, AL	115	42,012	Riverside Unified	Riverside, CA
56	64,245	Greenville County SD	Greenville, SC	116	41,924	Douglas County Re 1	Castle Rock, CO
57	64,089	Volusia County SD	Deland, FL	117	41,343	Fontana Unified	Fontana, CA
58	63,404	Prince William Co Public Schools	Manassas, VA	118	41,254	Anoka-Hennepin	Coon Rapids, MN
59	63,200	El Paso ISD	El Paso, TX	119	41,089	Buffalo City SD	Buffalo, NY
60	63,098	Columbus Public Schools	Columbus, OH	120	40,827	St. Louis City	St Louis, MO

This section ranks 120 school districts at both the "top" and "bottom" of each category for a total of 240 districts per category. The "top" list (descending order) appears first, followed by the "bottom" list (ascending order). Ranking tables cover public school districts serving 1,500 or more students.

Number of Students

School districts ranked in *ascending* order

Rank	Number	District Name	City, State	Rank	Number	District Name	City, State
1	1,500	Carle Place Union Free SD	Carle Place, NY	59	1,522	Mason Consol Schools (Monroe)	Erie, MI
1	1,500	Little Chute Area	Little Chute, WI	59	1,522	Northeast School Corp	Hymera, IN
1	1,500	Montague Area Public Schools	Montague, MI	63	1,523	Crete Public Schools	Crete, NE
4	1,501	Chatham Central SD	Chatham, NY	63	1,523	Macomb ISD	Clinton Twp, MI
4	1,501	Fenton Community HSD 100	Bensenville, IL	63	1,523	Nuview Union Elementary	Nuevo, CA
4	1,501	Ridgewood Local SD	West Lafayette, OH	63	1,523	Pinon Unified District	Pinon, AZ
4	1,501	Salem R-80	Salem, MO	67	1,524	Sitka Borough SD	Sitka, AK
8	1,502	Lake Fenton Community Schools	Fenton, MI	67	1,524	Watkins Glen Central SD	Watkins Glen, NY
8	1,502	Valley Stream 30 Union Free SD	Valley Stream, NY	69	1,525	Presidio ISD	Presidio, TX
10	1,503	Clearview Local SD	Lorain, OH	69	1,525	Winneconne Community	Winneconne, WI
10	1,503	Greenwood ISD	Midland, TX	71	1,526	Northgate SD	Pittsburgh, PA
10	1,503	Red Lake	Red Lake, MN	72	1,527	Bangor Public Schools (Van Buren)	Bangor, MI
13	1,504	Hanover Twp	Whippany, NJ	72	1,527	Howard-Winneshiek Community SD	Cresco, IA
13	1,504	Independence Community SD	Independence, IA	74	1,528	Sto-Rox SD	Mckees Rocks, PA
13	1,504	Wilson Central SD	Wilson, NY	75	1,529	Lansing Central SD	Lansing, NY
13	1,504	Wyalusing Area SD	Wyalusing, PA	75	1,529	M S D Bluffton-Harrison	Bluffton, IN
17	1,505	Lyford CISD	Lyford, TX	75	1,529	Mercer Area SD	Mercer, PA
18	1,506	Franklin Twp	Franklinville, NJ	75	1,529	Mohawk Trail	Shelburne Falls, MA
19	1,507	Florence County SD 05	Johnsonville, SC	75	1,529	Prospect Heights SD 23	Prospect Hgts, IL
19	1,507	MSAD 05 Rockland	Rockland, ME	75	1,529	Tawas Area Schools	Tawas City, MI
19	1,507	Oak Hill United School Corp	Converse, IN	81	1,530	Warsaw R-IX	Warsaw, MO
22	1,508	Flora Community Unit SD 35	Flora, IL	81	1,530	White Cloud Public Schools	White Cloud, MI
22	1,508	Madeira City SD	Cincinnati, OH	83	1,531	Cheektowaga-Sloan Union Free SD	Sloan, NY
24	1,509	Cresskill Boro	Cresskill, NJ	83	1,531	Monmouth Unit SD 38	Monmouth, IL
24	1,509	Elk Lake SD	Dimock, PA	85	1,532	Gowanda Central SD	Gowanda, NY
24	1,509	Gwinn Area Community Schools	Gwinn, MI	85	1,532	Newfound Area SD	Bristol, NH
24	1,509	Libby K-12 Schools	Libby, MT	85	1,532	Northland Pines	Eagle River, WI
28	1,511	Cedar Grove Twp	Cedar Grove, NJ	88	1,534	Campbellsport	Campbellsport, WI
29	1,512	Southeast Dubois County Sch Corp	Ferdinand, IN	88	1,534	Checotah	Checotah, OK
29	1,512	Spooner	Spooner, WI	88	1,534	Minooka Community HS District 111	Minooka, IL
29	1,512	Waldwick Boro	Waldwick, NJ	91	1,535	Shaker Regional SD	Belmont, NH
32	1,513	Atlantic Community SD	Atlantic, IA	92	1,536	Mountain Grove R-III	Mountain Grove, MO
32	1,513	Canton Central SD	Canton, NY	93	1,537	Ballard County	Barlow, KY
32	1,513	Eustace ISD	Eustace, TX	93	1,537	Brandywine Public SD	Niles, MI
32	1,513	Hartford Public SD	Hartford, MI	93	1,537	Circle	Towanda, KS
32	1,513	Ingram ISD	Ingram, TX	93	1,537	Porter Township School Corp	Valparaiso, IN
32	1,513	Iola	Iola, KS	93	1,537	Radford City Public Schools	Radford, VA
32	1,513	Salamanca City SD	Salamanca, NY	93	1,537	United Local SD	Hanoverton, OH
32	1,513	South Ripley Com Sch Corp	Versailles, IN	99	1,538	Mid Valley SD	Throop, PA
40	1,514	Palisades Park	Palisades Park, NJ	99	1,538	North College Hill City SD	Cincinnati, OH
40	1,514	Richland	Richland Ctr, WI	99	1,538	Reynolds SD	Greenville, PA
40	1,514	Wahpeton 37	Wahpeton, ND	102	1,539	Northwestern Con School Corp	Fairland, IN
40	1,514	Waterford Graded J1	Waterford, WI	102	1,539	Quincy Community SD	Quincy, MI
44	1,516	Cashmere SD 222	Cashmere, WA	104	1,540	Cobre Consolidated Schools	Bayard, NM
44	1,516	Taylor Community School Corp	Kokomo, IN	104	1,540	High Point Regional	Sussex, NJ
46	1,517	Carrollton SD	Saginaw, MI	104	1,540	Wabash City Schools	Wabash, IN
46	1,517	Crookston	Crookston, MN	107	1,541	Alleghany County Schools	Sparta, NC
46	1,517	Locust Grove	Locust Grove, OK	108	1,542	Lytle ISD	Lytle, TX
49	1,518	Mantua Twp	Sewell, NJ	108	1,542	Posen-Robbins El SD 143-5	Posen, IL
49	1,518	Pana Community Unit SD 8	Pana, IL	108	1,542	Valley View SD	Jonesboro, AR
49	1,518	Salem City	Salem, NJ	108	1,542	Wells-Ogunquit CSD	Wells, ME
49	1,518	Wilmington CUSD 209U	Wilmington, IL	112	1,543	Dollarway SD	Pine Bluff, AR
53	1,519	Trinidad 1	Trinidad, CO	112	1,543	Eastern Local SD	Sardinia, OH
54	1,520	Manchester Local SD	Akron, OH	112	1,543	Lebanon SD	Lebanon, CT
54	1,520	Newton Falls Ex Vill SD	Newton Falls, OH	115	1,544	Blackwell	Blackwell, OK
56	1,521	Dekalb County Eastern Com SD	Butler, IN	115	1,544	Burgettstown Area SD	Burgettstown, PA
56	1,521	Monroe Local SD	Monroe, OH	115	1,544	Colts Neck Twp	Colts Neck, NJ
56	1,521	North Knox School Corp	Bicknell, IN	115	1,544	Monson	Monson, MA
59	1,522	Harwich	Harwich, MA	115	1,544	Washington Twp	Robbinsville, NJ
59	1,522	Martins Ferry City SD	Martins Ferry, OH	120	1,545	Hatch Valley Public Schools	Hatch, NM

This section ranks 120 school districts at both the "top" and "bottom" of each category for a total of 240 districts per category. The "top" list (descending order) appears first, followed by the "bottom" list (ascending order). Ranking tables cover public school districts serving 1,500 or more students.

Male Students

School districts ranked in *descending* order

Rank	Percent	District Name	City, State	Rank	Percent	District Name	City, State
1	91.4	Corrections SD 428 Dept of	Springfield, IL	61	54.5	Brown Deer	Brown Deer, WI
2	75.8	Boces Nassau	Garden City, NY	62	54.4	Litchfield SD	Litchfield, NH
3	74.0	Boces Eastern Suffolk (Suffolk I)	Patchogue, NY	63	54.4	Southeast Local SD	Apple Creek, OH
4	73.5	San Bernardino Co Off of Education	San Bernardino, CA	64	54.4	Little Chute Area	Little Chute, WI
5	71.6	Burlington County Spec Serv	Mount Holly, NJ	65	54.4	Franklin County SD	Meadville, MS
6	71.4	Macomb ISD	Clinton Twp, MI	66	54.4	Highland Central SD	Highland, NY
7	71.0	Mercer County Special Service	Trenton, NJ	67	54.4	Mercer County	Harrodsburg, KY
8	69.3	Los Angeles Co Office of Education	Downey, CA	68	54.3	St Marys City SD	Saint Marys, OH
9	69.0	Specl. Sch. Dst. St. Louis Co.	Town & Ctry, MO	69	54.3	Monroe County	Tompkinsville, KY
10	68.6	Coxsackie-Athens Central SD	Coxsackie, NY	70	54.3	Orrville City SD	Orrville, OH
11	67.7	Kern County Office of Education	Bakersfield, CA	71	54.3	Cameron R-I	Cameron, MO
12	67.7	Santa Clara Co Off of Education	San Jose, CA	72	54.3	Tallmadge City Schools	Tallmadge, OH
13	67.2	Fresno County Office of Education	Fresno, CA	73	54.3	Cascade Union Elementary	Anderson, CA
14	66.9	Taos Municipal Schools	Taos, NM	74	54.2	Clio Area SD	Clio, MI
15	66.0	Tulare County Office of Education	Visalia, CA	75	54.2	Genoa Area Local SD	Genoa, OH
16	64.4	Bergen County Special Service	Paramus, NJ	76	54.2	Diboll ISD	Diboll, TX
17	64.1	State Vocational-Technical Schools	Middletown, CT	77	54.2	Sullivan	Sullivan, MO
18	61.2	San Joaquin Co Off of Education	Stockton, CA	78	54.2	Franklin Twp	Franklinville, NJ
19	60.8	Orange County Office of Education	Costa Mesa, CA	79	54.1	Union Local SD	Morristown, OH
20	60.4	Riverside Co Office of Education	Riverside, CA	80	54.1	Evans County	Claxton, GA
21	60.3	Maricopa County Regional District	Phoenix, AZ	81	54.1	Logan-Rogersville R-VIII	Rogersville, MO
22	59.3	Area Coop Educational Services	North Haven, CT	82	54.1	El Dorado	El Dorado, KS
23	59.0	San Diego Co Office of Education	San Diego, CA	83	54.1	Shepherd ISD	Shepherd, TX
24	58.4	Middlesex County Vocational	E Brunswick, NJ	84	54.1	Coldspring-Oakhurst Cons	Coldspring, TX
25	58.0	Vassar Public Schools	Vassar, MI	85	54.0	Bloomfield SD	Bloomfield, CT
26	58.0	Fremont County Joint District	St. Anthony, ID	86	54.0	Mannheim SD 83	Franklin Park, IL
27	57.7	Intermediate SD 287	Plymouth, MN	87	54.0	Jacksonville City	Jacksonville, AL
28	56.5	Rochester SD 401	Rochester, WA	88	54.0	Aspen 1	Aspen, CO
29	56.3	Broadalbin-Perth Central SD	Broadalbin, NY	89	54.0	Sweeny ISD	Sweeny, TX
30	56.1	Hudson City SD	Hudson, NY	90	54.0	Western Maricopa Ed Ctr (West-Mec)	Phoenix, AZ
31	56.1	Martin County	Inez, KY	91	54.0	Two Rivers	Two Rivers, WI
32	55.8	East Valley Institute of Tech	Mesa, AZ	92	53.9	Atlantic Community SD	Atlantic, IA
33	55.5	Monmouth County Vocational	Colts Neck, NJ	93	53.9	Moraga Elementary	Moraga, CA
34	55.5	Washtenaw ISD	Ann Arbor, MI	94	53.9	North Arlington Boro	North Arlington, NJ
35	55.2	Berlin SD	Berlin, NH	95	53.9	Beachwood City SD	Beachwood, OH
36	55.2	Fonda-Fultonville Central SD	Fonda, NY	96	53.9	Tecumseh	Tecumseh, OK
37	55.2	Mantua Twp	Sewell, NJ	97	53.9	Wilton SD	Wilton, CT
38	55.2	Watkins Glen Central SD	Watkins Glen, NY	98	53.9	Plattsmouth Community Schools	Plattsmouth, NE
39	55.2	Pike County	Troy, AL	99	53.9	Winters Joint Unified	Winters, CA
40	55.2	Spooner	Spooner, WI	100	53.9	Canton Local SD	Canton, OH
41	55.2	Lower Twp	Cape May, NJ	101	53.9	Caledonia Community Schools	Caledonia, MI
42	55.1	Lansing Central SD	Lansing, NY	102	53.9	Wickliffe City SD	Wickliffe, OH
43	55.0	Hamtramck Public Schools	Hamtramck, MI	103	53.9	Glenwood Community SD	Glenwood, IA
44	54.9	Ridgefield Boro	Ridgefield, NJ	104	53.9	Mayfield Independent	Mayfiel, KY
45	54.9	Bergen County Vocational	Paramus, NJ	105	53.9	Sanger ISD	Sanger, TX
46	54.9	Alliance Public Schools	Alliance, NE	106	53.9	West Oso ISD	Corpus Christi, TX
47	54.9	Colbert County	Tuscumbia, AL	107	53.9	Royse City ISD	Royse City, TX
48	54.8	West ISD	West, TX	108	53.9	West De Pere	De Pere, WI
49	54.8	Madison County SD	Madison, FL	109	53.8	Fenton Community HSD 100	Bensenville, IL
50	54.7	Lorena ISD	Lorena, TX	110	53.8	Buchanan Community Schools	Buchanan, MI
51	54.7	Attica Central SD	Attica, NY	111	53.8	Tuscarawas Valley Local SD	Zoarville, OH
52	54.7	Westonka	Minnetrista, MN	112	53.8	Independence	Independence, KS
53	54.6	Greater New Bedford	New Bedford, MA	113	53.8	Sinton ISD	Sinton, TX
54	54.6	Osceola SD	Osceola, AR	114	53.8	Perry Community SD	Perry, IA
55	54.6	Mason County Central Schools	Scottville, MI	115	53.8	Mayfield City SD	Highland Hgts, OH
56	54.6	Harrison Hills City SD	Hopedale, OH	116	53.8	Dade County	Trenton, GA
57	54.6	Breathitt County	Jackson, KY	117	53.8	Berlin-Milan Local SD	Milan, OH
58	54.6	Orange City SD	Cleveland, OH	118	53.8	Fremont County SD # 1	Lander, WY
59	54.5	Brewer School Department	Brewer, ME	119	53.8	Rocori	Cold Spring, MN
60	54.5	Crenshaw County	Luverne, AL	119	53.8	Three Rivers Community Schools	Three Rivers, MI

This section ranks 120 school districts at both the "top" and "bottom" of each category for a total of 240 districts per category. The "top" list (descending order) appears first, followed by the "bottom" list (ascending order). Ranking tables cover public school districts serving 1,500 or more students.

Male Students
School districts ranked in *ascending* order

Rank	Percent	District Name	City, State	Rank	Percent	District Name	City, State
1	36.3	Florida Virtual School	Orlando, FL	61	48.9	Cromwell SD	Cromwell, CT
2	43.1	Essex County Voc-Tech	West Orange, NJ	62	48.9	Madison County Public Schools	Madison, VA
3	45.7	Electronic Classrm of Tomorrow	Columbus, OH	63	48.9	Highland Park City Schools	Highland Park, MI
4	46.4	Detroit Acad of Arts & Sciences	Detroit, MI	64	48.9	Monroe	Monroe, WI
5	46.6	South Texas ISD	Mercedes, TX	65	48.9	East Cleveland City SD	East Cleveland, OH
6	46.8	Norwich Free Academy	Norwich, CT	66	48.9	MSAD 51 Cumberland	Cumberland Ctr, ME
7	46.9	North Adams	North Adams, MA	67	49.0	Belding Area SD	Belding, MI
8	46.9	Julian Union Elementary	Julian, CA	68	49.0	Fremont County SD #25	Riverton, WY
9	47.0	Nyc Alternative HS District	New York, NY	69	49.0	Norwich City SD	Norwich, NY
10	47.3	Gorman Elementary	Gorman, CA	70	49.0	Pearl River Union Free SD	Pearl River, NY
11	47.4	Basehor-Linwood	Basehor, KS	71	49.0	Western Placer Unified	Lincoln, CA
12	47.5	Ramapo-Indian Hill Reg	Franklin Lakes, NJ	72	49.0	San Diego ISD	San Diego, TX
13	47.6	Danvers	Danvers, MA	73	49.0	Bayless	St Louis, MO
14	47.6	Johnstown City SD	Johnstown, NY	74	49.0	Weiser District	Weiser, ID
15	47.7	Salem City	Salem, NJ	75	49.0	Newaygo Public SD	Newaygo, MI
16	47.8	Doniphan R-I	Doniphan, MO	76	49.0	Essex County Public Schools	Tappahannock, VA
17	47.8	Lebanon SD	Lebanon, CT	77	49.1	Mathis ISD	Mathis, TX
18	47.9	Paris-Union SD 95	Paris, IL	78	49.1	Westbury Union Free SD	Old Westbury, NY
19	48.0	Concord	Concord, MA	79	49.1	Hazlet Twp	Hazlet, NJ
20	48.0	Sheffield-Sheffield Lake City SD	Sheffield Vlg, OH	80	49.1	Warrensville Heights City SD	Warrensville Hgts, OH
21	48.0	Mainland Regional	Linwood, NJ	81	49.1	Buckeye Local SD	Ashtabula, OH
22	48.0	King Philip	Wrentham, MA	82	49.1	Clearview Local SD	Lorain, OH
23	48.0	Southeast Dubois County Sch Corp	Ferdinand, IN	83	49.1	Mount Vernon SD 80	Mount Vernon, IL
24	48.1	Carroll Community SD	Carroll, IA	84	49.1	Regional SD 14	Woodbury, CT
25	48.1	Galion City SD	Galion, OH	85	49.1	Clinton City Schools	Clinton, NC
26	48.1	Pitman Boro	Pitman, NJ	86	49.1	Locust Valley Central SD	Locust Valley, NY
27	48.1	Byng	Ada, OK	87	49.1	Kewaskum	Kewaskum, WI
28	48.2	Pojoaque Valley Public Schools	Santa Fe, NM	88	49.1	Garrett-Keyser-Butler Com	Garrett, IN
29	48.2	Altmar-Parish-Williamstown Cent SD	Parish, NY	89	49.1	Webster County	Dixon, KY
30	48.2	Orange Grove ISD	Orange Grove, TX	90	49.1	Cheektowaga-Maryvale Union Free SD	Cheektowaga, NY
31	48.3	MSAD 05 Rockland	Rockland, ME	91	49.1	Greene County SD	Leakesville, MS
32	48.3	Las Vegas City Public Schools	Las Vegas, NM	92	49.1	Cincinnati City SD	Cincinnati, OH
33	48.5	Saddle Brook Twp	Saddle Brook, NJ	93	49.1	Monson	Monson, MA
34	48.5	Prairie Heights Com Sch Corp	Lagrange, IN	94	49.1	Batavia City SD	Batavia, NY
35	48.5	Grady County	Cairo, GA	94	49.1	Wylie ISD	Abilene, TX
36	48.5	Mount Pleasant Community SD	Mount Pleasant, IA	96	49.1	Fullerton Joint Union High	Fullerton, CA
37	48.6	Wisconsin Dells	Wisconsin Dells, WI	97	49.1	Stewartville	Stewartville, MN
38	48.6	Mother Lode Union Elementary	Placerville, CA	98	49.1	Ipswich	Ipswich, MA
39	48.6	Canastota Central SD	Canastota, NY	99	49.1	Proctor	Proctor, MN
40	48.6	China Spring ISD	Waco, TX	100	49.2	Floyd County Public Schools	Floyd, VA
41	48.6	Zane Trace Local SD	Chillicothe, OH	101	49.2	Pennfield SD	Battle Creek, MI
42	48.6	Canton Public SD	Canton, MS	102	49.2	Center ISD	Center, TX
43	48.6	West Delaware County Community SD	Manchester, IA	103	49.2	Mcfarland Unified	Mcfarland, CA
44	48.6	East Carroll Parish School Board	Lake Providence, LA	104	49.2	Jamesville-Dewitt Central SD	Dewitt, NY
45	48.7	Weston SD	Weston, CT	105	49.2	Geneva City SD	Geneva, NY
46	48.7	Marlboro Central SD	Marlboro, NY	106	49.2	Alleghany County Schools	Sparta, NC
47	48.7	Lunenburg County Public Schools	Victoria, VA	107	49.2	Sherburne-Earlville Central SD	Sherburne, NY
48	48.7	Farmersville Unified	Farmersville, CA	108	49.2	Clay County SD	Clay, WV
49	48.7	Littleton	Littleton, MA	109	49.2	Screven County	Sylvania, GA
50	48.7	Stafford SD	Stafford Spgs, CT	110	49.2	Central Montcalm Public Schools	Stanton, MI
51	48.7	Akron Central SD	Akron, NY	111	49.2	New York City Geographic Dist 15	Brooklyn, NY
52	48.8	Clare Public Schools	Clare, MI	112	49.2	Oakwood City SD	Dayton, OH
53	48.8	Masconomet	Topsfield, MA	113	49.2	Penn Yan Central SD	Penn Yan, NY
54	48.8	Nooksack Valley SD 506	Everson, WA	114	49.2	Gasconade County R-II	Owensville, MO
55	48.8	Marble Falls ISD	Marble Falls, TX	115	49.2	Pelham SD	Windham, NH
56	48.8	Mount Sinai Union Free SD	Mount Sinai, NY	116	49.3	Zanesville City SD	Zanesville, OH
57	48.8	Claiborne County SD	Port Gibson, MS	117	49.3	Marshall	Marshall, MN
58	48.8	Centerville Community SD	Centerville, IA	118	49.3	Suffield SD	Suffield, CT
59	48.8	Sussex-Wantage Regional	Wantage, NJ	119	49.3	East St Louis SD 189	E Saint Louis, IL
60	48.9	Crookston	Crookston, MN	120	49.3	El Segundo Unified	El Segundo, CA

This section ranks 120 school districts at both the "top" and "bottom" of each category for a total of 240 districts per category. The "top" list (descending order) appears first, followed by the "bottom" list (ascending order). Ranking tables cover public school districts serving 1,500 or more students.

Female Students

School districts ranked in *descending* order

Rank	Percent	District Name	City, State	Rank	Percent	District Name	City, State
1	63.6	Florida Virtual School	Orlando, FL	61	51.0	Cromwell SD	Cromwell, CT
2	56.8	Essex County Voc-Tech	West Orange, NJ	62	51.0	Madison County Public Schools	Madison, VA
3	54.2	Electronic Classrm of Tomorrow	Columbus, OH	63	51.0	Highland Park City Schools	Highland Park, MI
4	53.5	Detroit Acad of Arts & Sciences	Detroit, MI	64	51.0	Monroe	Monroe, WI
5	53.3	South Texas ISD	Mercedes, TX	65	51.0	East Cleveland City SD	East Cleveland, OH
6	53.1	Norwich Free Academy	Norwich, CT	66	51.0	MSAD 51 Cumberland	Cumberland Ctr, ME
7	53.0	North Adams	North Adams, MA	67	50.9	Belding Area SD	Belding, MI
8	53.0	Julian Union Elementary	Julian, CA	68	50.9	Fremont County SD #25	Riverton, WY
9	52.9	Nyc Alternative HS District	New York, NY	69	50.9	Norwich City SD	Norwich, NY
10	52.6	Gorman Elementary	Gorman, CA	70	50.9	Pearl River Union Free SD	Pearl River, NY
11	52.5	Basehor-Linwood	Basehor, KS	71	50.9	Western Placer Unified	Lincoln, CA
12	52.4	Ramapo-Indian Hill Reg	Franklin Lakes, NJ	72	50.9	San Diego ISD	San Diego, TX
13	52.3	Danvers	Danvers, MA	73	50.9	Bayless	St Louis, MO
14	52.3	Johnstown City SD	Johnstown, NY	74	50.9	Weiser District	Weiser, ID
15	52.2	Salem City	Salem, NJ	75	50.9	Newaygo Public SD	Newaygo, MI
16	52.1	Doniphan R-I	Doniphan, MO	76	50.9	Essex County Public Schools	Tappahannock, VA
17	52.1	Lebanon SD	Lebanon, CT	77	50.8	Mathis ISD	Mathis, TX
18	52.0	Paris-Union SD 95	Paris, IL	78	50.8	Westbury Union Free SD	Old Westbury, NY
19	51.9	Concord	Concord, MA	79	50.8	Hazlet Twp	Hazlet, NJ
20	51.9	Sheffield-Sheffield Lake City SD	Sheffield Vlg, OH	80	50.8	Warrensville Heights City SD	Warrensville Hgts, OH
21	51.9	Mainland Regional	Linwood, NJ	81	50.8	Buckeye Local SD	Ashtabula, OH
22	51.9	King Philip	Wrentham, MA	82	50.8	Clearview Local SD	Lorain, OH
23	51.9	Southeast Dubois County Sch Corp	Ferdinand, IN	83	50.8	Mount Vernon SD 80	Mount Vernon, IL
24	51.8	Carroll Community SD	Carroll, IA	84	50.8	Regional SD 14	Woodbury, CT
25	51.8	Galion City SD	Galion, OH	85	50.8	Clinton City Schools	Clinton, NC
26	51.8	Pitman Boro	Pitman, NJ	86	50.8	Locust Valley Central SD	Locust Valley, NY
27	51.8	Byng	Ada, OK	87	50.8	Kewaskum	Kewaskum, WI
28	51.7	Pojoaque Valley Public Schools	Santa Fe, NM	88	50.8	Garrett-Keyser-Butler Com	Garrett, IN
29	51.7	Altmar-Parish-Williamstown Cent SD	Parish, NY	89	50.8	Webster County	Dixon, KY
30	51.7	Orange Grove ISD	Orange Grove, TX	90	50.8	Cheektowaga-Maryvale Union Free SD	Cheektowaga, NY
31	51.6	MSAD 05 Rockland	Rockland, ME	91	50.8	Greene County SD	Leakesville, MS
32	51.6	Las Vegas City Public Schools	Las Vegas, NM	92	50.8	Cincinnati City SD	Cincinnati, OH
33	51.4	Saddle Brook Twp	Saddle Brook, NJ	93	50.8	Monson	Monson, MA
34	51.4	Prairie Heights Com Sch Corp	Lagrange, IN	94	50.8	Batavia City SD	Batavia, NY
35	51.4	Grady County	Cairo, GA	94	50.8	Wylie ISD	Abilene, TX
36	51.4	Mount Pleasant Community SD	Mount Pleasant, IA	96	50.8	Fullerton Joint Union High	Fullerton, CA
37	51.3	Wisconsin Dells	Wisconsin Dells, WI	97	50.8	Stewartville	Stewartville, MN
38	51.3	Mother Lode Union Elementary	Placerville, CA	98	50.8	Ipswich	Ipswich, MA
39	51.3	Canastota Central SD	Canastota, NY	99	50.8	Proctor	Proctor, MN
40	51.3	China Spring ISD	Waco, TX	100	50.7	Floyd County Public Schools	Floyd, VA
41	51.3	Zane Trace Local SD	Chillicothe, OH	101	50.7	Pennfield SD	Battle Creek, MI
42	51.3	Canton Public SD	Canton, MS	102	50.7	Center ISD	Center, TX
43	51.3	West Delaware County Community SD	Manchester, IA	103	50.7	Mcfarland Unified	Mcfarland, CA
44	51.3	East Carroll Parish School Board	Lake Providence, LA	104	50.7	Jamesville-Dewitt Central SD	Dewitt, NY
45	51.2	Weston SD	Weston, CT	105	50.7	Geneva City SD	Geneva, NY
46	51.2	Marlboro Central SD	Marlboro, NY	106	50.7	Alleghany County Schools	Sparta, NC
47	51.2	Lunenburg County Public Schools	Victoria, VA	107	50.7	Sherburne-Earlville Central SD	Sherburne, NY
48	51.2	Farmersville Unified	Farmersville, CA	108	50.7	Clay County SD	Clay, WV
49	51.2	Littleton	Littleton, MA	109	50.7	Screven County	Sylvania, GA
50	51.2	Stafford SD	Stafford Spgs, CT	110	50.7	Central Montcalm Public Schools	Stanton, MI
51	51.2	Akron Central SD	Akron, NY	111	50.7	New York City Geographic Dist 15	Brooklyn, NY
52	51.1	Clare Public Schools	Clare, MI	112	50.7	Oakwood City SD	Dayton, OH
53	51.1	Masconomet	Topsfield, MA	113	50.7	Penn Yan Central SD	Penn Yan, NY
54	51.1	Nooksack Valley SD 506	Everson, WA	114	50.7	Gasconade County R-II	Owensville, MO
55	51.1	Marble Falls ISD	Marble Falls, TX	115	50.7	Pelham SD	Windham, NH
56	51.1	Mount Sinai Union Free SD	Mount Sinai, NY	116	50.6	Zanesville City SD	Zanesville, OH
57	51.1	Claiborne County SD	Port Gibson, MS	117	50.6	Marshall	Marshall, MN
58	51.1	Centerville Community SD	Centerville, IA	118	50.6	Suffield SD	Suffield, CT
59	51.1	Sussex-Wantage Regional	Wantage, NJ	119	50.6	East St Louis SD 189	E Saint Louis, IL
60	51.0	Crookston	Crookston, MN	120	50.6	El Segundo Unified	El Segundo, CA

This section ranks 120 school districts at both the "top" and "bottom" of each category for a total of 240 districts per category. The "top" list (descending order) appears first, followed by the "bottom" list (ascending order). Ranking tables cover public school districts serving 1,500 or more students.

Female Students
School districts ranked in *ascending* order

Rank	Percent	District Name	City, State	Rank	Percent	District Name	City, State
1	8.5	Corrections SD 428 Dept of	Springfield, IL	61	45.4	Brown Deer	Brown Deer, WI
2	24.1	Boces Nassau	Garden City, NY	62	45.5	Litchfield SD	Litchfield, NH
3	25.9	Boces Eastern Suffolk (Suffolk I)	Patchogue, NY	63	45.5	Southeast Local SD	Apple Creek, OH
4	26.4	San Bernardino Co Off of Education	San Bernardino, CA	64	45.5	Little Chute Area	Little Chute, WI
5	28.3	Burlington County Spec Serv	Mount Holly, NJ	65	45.5	Franklin County SD	Meadville, MS
6	28.5	Macomb ISD	Clinton Twp, MI	66	45.5	Highland Central SD	Highland, NY
7	28.9	Mercer County Special Service	Trenton, NJ	67	45.5	Mercer County	Harrodsburg, KY
8	30.6	Los Angeles Co Office of Education	Downey, CA	68	45.6	St Marys City SD	Saint Marys, OH
9	30.9	Specl. Sch. Dst. St. Louis Co.	Town & Ctry, MO	69	45.6	Monroe County	Tompkinsville, KY
10	31.3	Coxsackie-Athens Central SD	Coxsackie, NY	70	45.6	Orrville City SD	Orrville, OH
11	32.2	Kern County Office of Education	Bakersfield, CA	71	45.6	Cameron R-I	Cameron, MO
12	32.2	Santa Clara Co Off of Education	San Jose, CA	72	45.6	Tallmadge City Schools	Tallmadge, OH
13	32.7	Fresno County Office of Education	Fresno, CA	73	45.6	Cascade Union Elementary	Anderson, CA
14	33.0	Taos Municipal Schools	Taos, NM	74	45.7	Clio Area SD	Clio, MI
15	33.9	Tulare County Office of Education	Visalia, CA	75	45.7	Genoa Area Local SD	Genoa, OH
16	35.5	Bergen County Special Service	Paramus, NJ	76	45.7	Diboll ISD	Diboll, TX
17	35.8	State Vocational-Technical Schools	Middletown, CT	77	45.7	Sullivan	Sullivan, MO
18	38.7	San Joaquin Co Off of Education	Stockton, CA	78	45.7	Franklin Twp	Franklinville, NJ
19	39.1	Orange County Office of Education	Costa Mesa, CA	79	45.8	Union Local SD	Morristown, OH
20	39.5	Riverside Co Office of Education	Riverside, CA	80	45.8	Evans County	Claxton, GA
21	39.6	Maricopa County Regional District	Phoenix, AZ	81	45.8	Logan-Rogersville R-VIII	Rogersville, MO
22	40.6	Area Coop Educational Services	North Haven, CT	82	45.8	El Dorado	El Dorado, KS
23	40.9	San Diego Co Office of Education	San Diego, CA	83	45.8	Shepherd ISD	Shepherd, TX
24	41.5	Middlesex County Vocational	E Brunswick, NJ	84	45.8	Coldspring-Oakhurst Cons	Coldspring, TX
25	41.9	Vassar Public Schools	Vassar, MI	85	45.9	Bloomfield SD	Bloomfield, CT
26	41.9	Fremont County Joint District	St. Anthony, ID	86	45.9	Mannheim SD 83	Franklin Park, IL
27	42.2	Intermediate SD 287	Plymouth, MN	87	45.9	Jacksonville City	Jacksonville, AL
28	43.4	Rochester SD 401	Rochester, WA	88	45.9	Aspen 1	Aspen, CO
29	43.6	Broadalbin-Perth Central SD	Broadalbin, NY	89	45.9	Sweeny ISD	Sweeny, TX
30	43.8	Hudson City SD	Hudson, NY	90	45.9	Western Maricopa Ed Ctr (West-Mec)	Phoenix, AZ
31	43.8	Martin County	Inez, KY	91	45.9	Two Rivers	Two Rivers, WI
32	44.1	East Valley Institute of Tech	Mesa, AZ	92	46.0	Atlantic Community SD	Atlantic, IA
33	44.4	Monmouth County Vocational	Colts Neck, NJ	93	46.0	Moraga Elementary	Moraga, CA
34	44.4	Washtenaw ISD	Ann Arbor, MI	94	46.0	North Arlington Boro	North Arlington, NJ
35	44.7	Berlin SD	Berlin, NH	95	46.0	Beachwood City SD	Beachwood, OH
36	44.7	Fonda-Fultonville Central SD	Fonda, NY	96	46.0	Tecumseh	Tecumseh, OK
37	44.7	Mantua Twp	Sewell, NJ	97	46.0	Wilton SD	Wilton, CT
38	44.7	Watkins Glen Central SD	Watkins Glen, NY	98	46.0	Plattsmouth Community Schools	Plattsmouth, NE
39	44.7	Pike County	Troy, AL	99	46.0	Winters Joint Unified	Winters, CA
40	44.7	Spooner	Spooner, WI	100	46.0	Canton Local SD	Canton, OH
41	44.7	Lower Twp	Cape May, NJ	101	46.0	Caledonia Community Schools	Caledonia, MI
42	44.8	Lansing Central SD	Lansing, NY	102	46.0	Wickliffe City SD	Wickliffe, OH
43	44.9	Hamtramck Public Schools	Hamtramck, MI	103	46.0	Glenwood Community SD	Glenwood, IA
44	45.0	Ridgefield Boro	Ridgefield, NJ	104	46.0	Mayfield Independent	Mayfiel, KY
45	45.0	Bergen County Vocational	Paramus, NJ	105	46.0	Sanger ISD	Sanger, TX
46	45.0	Alliance Public Schools	Alliance, NE	106	46.0	West Oso ISD	Corpus Christi, TX
47	45.0	Colbert County	Tuscumbia, AL	107	46.0	Royse City ISD	Royse City, TX
48	45.1	West ISD	West, TX	108	46.0	West De Pere	De Pere, WI
49	45.1	Madison County SD	Madison, FL	109	46.1	Fenton Community HSD 100	Bensenville, IL
50	45.2	Lorena ISD	Lorena, TX	110	46.1	Buchanan Community Schools	Buchanan, MI
51	45.2	Attica Central SD	Attica, NY	111	46.1	Tuscarawas Valley Local SD	Zoarville, OH
52	45.2	Westonka	Minnetrista, MN	112	46.1	Independence	Independence, KS
53	45.3	Greater New Bedford	New Bedford, MA	113	46.1	Sinton ISD	Sinton, TX
54	45.3	Osceola SD	Osceola, AR	114	46.1	Perry Community SD	Perry, IA
55	45.3	Mason County Central Schools	Scottville, MI	115	46.1	Mayfield City SD	Highland Hgts, OH
56	45.3	Harrison Hills City SD	Hopedale, OH	116	46.1	Dade County	Trenton, GA
57	45.3	Breathitt County	Jackson, KY	117	46.1	Berlin-Milan Local SD	Milan, OH
58	45.3	Orange City SD	Cleveland, OH	118	46.1	Fremont County SD # 1	Lander, WY
59	45.4	Brewer School Department	Brewer, ME	119	46.1	Rocori	Cold Spring, MN
60	45.4	Crenshaw County	Luverne, AL	119	46.1	Three Rivers Community Schools	Three Rivers, MI

This section ranks 120 school districts at both the "top" and "bottom" of each category for a total of 240 districts per category. The "top" list (descending order) appears first, followed by the "bottom" list (ascending order). Ranking tables cover public school districts serving 1,500 or more students.

Individual Education Program (IEP) Students
School districts ranked in *descending* order

Rank	Percent	District Name	City, State	Rank	Percent	District Name	City, State
1	76.7	Riverside Co Office of Education	Riverside, CA	61	23.9	Florence County SD 05	Johnsonville, SC
2	67.8	Fresno County Office of Education	Fresno, CA	62	23.9	Lauderdale County SD	Ripley, TN
3	55.4	Los Angeles Co Office of Education	Downey, CA	63	23.8	Woonsocket SD	Woonsocket, RI
4	54.9	Kern County Office of Education	Bakersfield, CA	64	23.8	Overton County SD	Livingston, TN
5	34.9	Intermediate SD 287	Plymouth, MN	65	23.8	Camden County Vocational	Sicklerville, NJ
6	34.5	Area Coop Educational Services	North Haven, CT	66	23.7	Winston County	Double Springs, AL
7	31.8	Burlington County Vocational	Westampton Twp, NJ	67	23.7	Jackson-Madison Consolidated	Jackson, TN
8	31.5	Los Alamos Public Schools	Los Alamos, NM	68	23.7	Hawkins County SD	Rogersville, TN
9	29.8	Bledsoe County SD	Pikeville, TN	69	23.6	Cumberland SD	Cumberland, RI
10	29.7	San Joaquin Co Off of Education	Stockton, CA	70	23.5	Pawtucket SD	Pawtucket, RI
11	29.5	Harrison Hills City SD	Hopedale, OH	71	23.5	Dayton City SD	Dayton, OH
12	29.2	Unicoi SD	Erwin, TN	72	23.5	San Diego Co Office of Education	San Diego, CA
13	28.8	Grundy County SD	Altamont, TN	73	23.4	Dixie County SD	Cross City, FL
14	28.6	Oak Ridge City SD	Oak Ridge, TN	74	23.4	Sto-Rox SD	Mckees Rocks, PA
15	28.2	Newport SD	Newport, RI	75	23.3	Upper Twp	Petersburg, NJ
16	27.4	Mount Vernon SD 80	Mount Vernon, IL	76	23.3	Washington	Washington, MO
17	27.3	Baldwin County	Bay Minette, AL	77	23.2	Greene County SD	Greeneville, TN
18	26.6	Benton Community School Corp	Fowler, IN	78	23.2	South Bend Community Sch Corp	South Bend, IN
19	26.5	Johnston SD	Johnston, RI	79	23.2	Muncie Community Schools	Muncie, IN
20	26.4	Greeneville City SD	Greeneville, TN	80	23.2	Belleville SD 118	Belleville, IL
21	26.4	Carlsbad Municipal Schools	Carlsbad, NM	81	23.1	Bloomfield Municipal Schools	Bloomfield, NM
22	26.2	Anderson County School Distrct	Clinton, TN	82	23.1	Florence County SD 03	Lake City, SC
23	26.2	North Putnam Community Schools	Bainbridge, IN	83	23.0	Union County	Morganfiel, KY
24	26.0	Barnegat Twp	Barnegat, NJ	84	23.0	Los Lunas Public Schools	Los Lunas, NM
25	25.7	Lower Cape May Regional	Cape May, NJ	85	23.0	Claiborne County SD	Tazewell, TN
26	25.6	New Castle Community Sch Corp	New Castle, IN	86	23.0	West Warwick SD	West Warwick, RI
27	25.4	Gilchrist County SD	Trenton, FL	87	23.0	Lake Villa CCSD 41	Lake Villa, IL
28	25.4	Wilkinsburg Borough SD	Wilkinsburg, PA	88	23.0	West ISD	West, TX
29	25.3	Prentiss County SD	Booneville, MS	89	23.0	Frankfort Community Unit SD 168	West Frankfort, IL
30	25.2	Richmond Community School Corp	Richmond, IN	90	22.9	Dickson County SD	Dickson, TN
31	25.2	Roswell Independent Schools	Roswell, NM	91	22.9	Streator Elem SD 44	Streator, IL
32	25.1	Greater Lowell Voc Tec	Tyngsborough, MA	92	22.8	East Providence SD	E Providence, RI
33	25.0	Central Falls SD	Central Falls, RI	93	22.8	Belen Consolidated Schools	Belen, NM
34	25.0	Meriwether County	Greenville, GA	94	22.7	Zanesville City SD	Zanesville, OH
35	24.9	Madison County SD	Madison, FL	95	22.7	Breathitt County	Jackson, KY
36	24.9	Las Cruces Public Schools	Las Cruces, NM	96	22.7	Lafayette School Corporation	Lafayette, IN
37	24.9	Warren County SD	Mcminnville, TN	97	22.7	Herrin CUSD 4	Herrin, IL
38	24.8	Redford Union SD	Redford, MI	98	22.7	M S D Mount Vernon	Mount Vernon, IN
39	24.8	Marshall	Marshall, MO	99	22.6	Clay County	Manchester, KY
40	24.8	Lancaster SD	Lancaster, PA	100	22.6	Huntsville City	Huntsville, AL
41	24.8	Dekalb County SD	Smithville, TN	101	22.6	Chester-Upland SD	Chester, PA
42	24.7	Keansburg Boro	Keansburg, NJ	102	22.6	Aztec Municipal Schools	Aztec, NM
43	24.6	Shelby County	Columbiana, AL	103	22.6	Truth Or Consequences Schools	Truth or Conseq, NM
44	24.5	Lovington Public Schools	Lovington, NM	104	22.5	South Kingstown SD	Wakefield, RI
45	24.5	Charleston CUSD 1	Charleston, IL	105	22.5	Calhoun County SD	Blountstown, FL
46	24.5	Narragansett SD	Narragansett, RI	106	22.5	Jennings County Schools	North Vernon, IN
47	24.4	Grand Rapids Public Schools	Grand Rapids, MI	107	22.4	Homewood City	Homewood, AL
48	24.4	Dyer County SD	Dyersburg, TN	108	22.4	Tiverton SD	Tiverton, RI
49	24.3	Floyd County	Rome, GA	109	22.4	Cobre Consolidated Schools	Bayard, NM
50	24.2	Bradford County SD	Starke, FL	110	22.4	Bristol Warren RD	Bristol, RI
51	24.1	Pinelands Regional	Tuckerton, NJ	111	22.4	Shelby County SD	Memphis, TN
52	24.0	Union County SD	Maynardville, TN	112	22.4	Bamberg County SD 01	Bamberg, SC
53	24.0	Madison Consolidated Schools	Madison, IN	113	22.4	Summers County SD	Hinton, WV
54	24.0	Peoria SD 150	Peoria, IL	114	22.4	Northeast School Corp	Hymera, IN
55	24.0	Saco School Department	Saco, ME	115	22.3	Richland	Richland Ctr, WI
56	24.0	Kokomo-Center Twp Con Sch Corp	Kokomo, IN	116	22.3	Sussex-Wantage Regional	Wantage, NJ
57	24.0	Levy County SD	Bronson, FL	117	22.3	East Longmeadow	East Longmeadow, MA
58	23.9	Southwest School Corp	Sullivan, IN	118	22.3	Pike County	Troy, AL
59	23.9	Sequatchie County SD	Dunlap, TN	119	22.3	Antioch CCSD 34	Antioch, IL
60	23.9	Randolph Central School Corp	Winchester, IN	120	22.2	Venus ISD	Venus, TX

This section ranks 120 school districts at both the "top" and "bottom" of each category for a total of 240 districts per category. The "top" list (descending order) appears first, followed by the "bottom" list (ascending order). Ranking tables cover public school districts serving 1,500 or more students.

Individual Education Program (IEP) Students

School districts ranked in *ascending* order

Rank	Percent	District Name	City, State	Rank	Percent	District Name	City, State
1	0.0	Beardsley Elementary	Bakersfield, CA	59	5.9	Riverdale Joint Unified	Riverdale, CA
1	0.0	Bergen County Special Service	Paramus, NJ	62	6.0	Mother Lode Union Elementary	Placerville, CA
1	0.0	Burlington County Spec Serv	Mount Holly, NJ	62	6.0	Seymour SD	Seymour, CT
1	0.0	Central Ariz Valley Inst of Tech	Coolidge, AZ	64	6.1	Branford SD	Branford, CT
1	0.0	East Valley Institute of Tech	Mesa, AZ	65	6.2	Bow SD	Bow, NH
1	0.0	Florida Virtual School	Orlando, FL	65	6.2	Cupertino Union School	Cupertino, CA
1	0.0	Mercer County Special Service	Trenton, NJ	65	6.2	Gainesville City	Gainesville, GA
1	0.0	Monmouth County Vocational	Colts Neck, NJ	65	6.2	Western Pennsylvania Cyber CS	Midland, PA
1	0.0	Mount Anthony UHSD 14	Bennington, VT	69	6.3	Hidalgo ISD	Hidalgo, TX
1	0.0	N. Little Rock SD	N Little Rock, AR	69	6.3	Mission Cons ISD	Mission, TX
1	0.0	Navit	Snowflake, AZ	69	6.3	Parlier Unified	Parlier, CA
1	0.0	NE Arizona Tech Inst of Voc Ed	Kayenta, AZ	69	6.3	Progreso ISD	Progreso, TX
1	0.0	Pinkerton Academy SD	Derry, NH	73	6.4	Archuleta County 50 Jt	Pagosa Springs, CO
1	0.0	Santa Rita Union Elementary	Salinas, CA	73	6.4	Calexico Unified	Calexico, CA
1	0.0	Western Maricopa Ed Ctr (West-Mec)	Phoenix, AZ	73	6.4	Wheatland Elementary	Wheatland, CA
1	0.0	Westwood Unified	Westwood, CA	76	6.5	Alisal Union Elementary	Salinas, CA
1	0.0	Willows Unified	Willows, CA	76	6.5	MSAD 51 Cumberland	Cumberland Ctr, ME
18	0.4	Oro Grande Elementary	Oro Grande, CA	78	6.6	Jefferson Elementary	Daly City, CA
19	1.5	Coldwater Community Schools	Coldwater, MI	78	6.6	Winton Elementary	Winton, CA
20	1.7	Peach Springs Unified District	Peach Springs, AZ	80	6.7	Dinuba Unified	Dinuba, CA
21	2.7	Quincy Community SD	Quincy, MI	80	6.7	Shasta Union High	Redding, CA
22	3.0	Lindsay Unified	Lindsay, CA	80	6.7	South Texas ISD	Mercedes, TX
23	3.2	Escalon Unified	Escalon, CA	80	6.7	Tolleson Elementary District	Tolleson, AZ
23	3.2	Galena City SD	Galena, AK	84	6.8	Bangor Public Schools (Van Buren)	Bangor, MI
23	3.2	Marlboro County SD	Bennettsville, SC	84	6.8	Corcoran Joint Unified	Corcoran, CA
26	3.3	Butte County Joint District	Arco, ID	84	6.8	Madera Unified	Madera, CA
27	3.4	Chowchilla Elementary	Chowchilla, CA	84	6.8	Manasquan Boro	Manasquan, NJ
27	3.4	Cutler-Orosi Joint Unified	Orosi, CA	84	6.8	Roaring Fork Re-1	Glenwood Spgs, CO
27	3.4	Mattawan Consolidated School	Mattawan, MI	84	6.8	Templeton Unified	Templeton, CA
30	3.9	Julian Union High	Julian, CA	84	6.8	Wasco Union Elementary	Wasco, CA
31	4.0	Belcourt 7	Belcourt, ND	91	6.9	Anthony Wayne Local SD	Whitehouse, OH
32	4.3	Earlimart Elementary	Earlimart, CA	91	6.9	Jefferson Elementary	Tracy, CA
32	4.3	Golden Plains Unified	San Joaquin, CA	91	6.9	Red Bluff Union Elementary	Red Bluff, CA
32	4.3	Lynwood Unified	Lynwood, CA	91	6.9	San Carlos Elementary	San Carlos, CA
35	4.4	Champion Local SD	Warren, OH	91	6.9	Walnut Valley Unified	Walnut, CA
36	4.5	Burton Elementary	Porterville, CA	96	7.0	Arrowhead UHS	Hartland, WI
36	4.5	Mendota Unified	Mendota, CA	96	7.0	Imperial Unified	Imperial, CA
38	4.7	Aspen 1	Aspen, CO	96	7.0	Nuview Union Elementary	Nuevo, CA
38	4.7	Brookfield SD	Brookfield, CT	96	7.0	Santa Maria-Bonita Elementary	Santa Maria, CA
38	4.7	Detroit Acad of Arts & Sciences	Detroit, MI	96	7.0	Soledad Unified	Soledad, CA
38	4.7	Los Banos Unified	Los Banos, CA	101	7.1	Brawley Elementary	Brawley, CA
38	4.7	Woodlake Union Elementary	Woodlake, CA	101	7.1	Del Paso Heights Elementary	Sacramento, CA
43	4.8	Live Oak Unified	Live Oak, CA	101	7.1	El Segundo Unified	El Segundo, CA
44	4.9	Mars Area SD	Mars, PA	101	7.1	Flathead HS	Kalispell, MT
45	5.1	Cheyenne Mountain 12	Colorado Spgs, CO	101	7.1	Fullerton Joint Union High	Fullerton, CA
45	5.1	Rescue Union Elementary	Rescue, CA	101	7.1	Hoover City	Hoover, AL
47	5.2	Buckeye Union Elementary	Shingle Springs, CA	101	7.1	Pinon Unified District	Pinon, AZ
47	5.2	Compton Unified	Compton, CA	101	7.1	Pleasant Valley Community SD	Pleasant Valley, IA
47	5.2	Hanford Elementary	Hanford, CA	101	7.1	Wilmer-Hutchins ISD	Dallas, TX
50	5.3	Salinas City Elementary	Salinas, CA	101	7.1	Yuba City Unified	Yuba City, CA
50	5.3	West Covina Unified	West Covina, CA	111	7.2	Berlin SD	Berlin, NH
52	5.4	Ohio Virtual Academy	Maumee, OH	111	7.2	Corrections SD 428 Dept of	Springfield, IL
53	5.5	Exeter Union Elementary	Exeter, CA	111	7.2	Gorman Elementary	Gorman, CA
53	5.5	Mount Mansfield Usd 17	Jericho, VT	111	7.2	Jefferson Union High	Daly City, CA
55	5.6	Cloverdale Unified	Cloverdale, CA	111	7.2	Ridgefield Boro	Ridgefield, NJ
55	5.6	Farmersville Unified	Farmersville, CA	116	7.3	Academy 20	Colorado Spgs, CO
55	5.6	Norris Elementary	Bakersfield, CA	116	7.3	Colorado Springs 11	Colorado Spgs, CO
55	5.6	Porterville Unified	Porterville, CA	116	7.3	Copiah County SD	Hazlehurst, MS
59	5.9	Corning Union Elementary	Corning, CA	116	7.3	Inglewood Unified	Inglewood, CA
59	5.9	Pennsylvania Virtual CS	Norristown, PA	116	7.3	Palo Verde Unified	Blythe, CA

This section ranks 120 school districts at both the "top" and "bottom" of each category for a total of 240 districts per category. The "top" list (descending order) appears first, followed by the "bottom" list (ascending order). Ranking tables cover public school districts serving 1,500 or more students.

English Language Learner (ELL) Students

School districts ranked in *descending* order

Rank	Percent	District Name	City, State	Rank	Percent	District Name	City, State
1	96.2	Lower Yukon SD	Mountain Vlg, AK	61	53.1	Presidio ISD	Presidio, TX
2	94.8	Gadsden Elementary District	San Luis, AZ	62	52.9	Magnolia Elementary	Anaheim, CA
3	89.6	Todd County SD 66-1	Mission, SD	63	52.3	Donna ISD	Donna, TX
4	85.7	Snohomish SD 201	Snohomish, WA	64	52.2	King City Union Elementary	King City, CA
5	83.0	Earlimart Elementary	Earlimart, CA	65	51.7	Lynwood Unified	Lynwood, CA
6	81.8	Zuni Public Schools	Zuni, NM	66	51.6	Whiteriver Unified District	Whiteriver, AZ
7	74.5	Mendota Unified	Mendota, CA	67	51.2	Delhi Unified	Delhi, CA
8	73.8	Lamont Elementary	Lamont, CA	68	50.9	Ocean View Elementary	Oxnard, CA
9	73.1	Calexico Unified	Calexico, CA	69	50.2	Rio Grande City CISD	Rio Grande City, TX
10	72.5	Bering Strait SD	Unalakleet, AK	70	50.0	Brownsville ISD	Brownsville, TX
11	72.3	Somerton Elementary District	Somerton, AZ	71	49.7	Storm Lake Community SD	Storm Lake, IA
12	71.4	Orting SD 344	Orting, WA	72	49.6	Alhambra Elementary District	Phoenix, AZ
13	70.6	Ganado Unified District	Ganado, AZ	73	49.6	Phoenix Elementary District	Phoenix, AZ
14	69.2	Ravenswood City Elementary	East Palo Alto, CA	74	49.6	Santa Paula Elementary	Santa Paula, CA
15	69.1	Alisal Union Elementary	Salinas, CA	75	49.5	Dodge City	Dodge City, KS
16	69.0	Lennox Elementary	Lennox, CA	76	49.3	Santa Maria-Bonita Elementary	Santa Maria, CA
17	68.6	San Ysidro Elementary	San Ysidro, CA	77	49.3	Ontario-Montclair Elementary	Ontario, CA
18	68.4	Hatch Valley Public Schools	Hatch, NM	78	49.1	San Juan SD	Blanding, UT
19	67.7	Chinle Unified District	Chinle, AZ	79	49.1	Garden Grove Unified	Garden Grove, CA
20	67.5	Reef-Sunset Unified	Avenal, CA	80	49.1	Redwood City Elementary	Redwood City, CA
21	67.2	Hamtramck Public Schools	Hamtramck, MI	81	48.0	Delano Joint Union High	Delano, CA
22	67.1	Coachella Valley Unified	Thermal, CA	82	48.0	Pojoaque Valley Public Schools	Santa Fe, NM
23	66.8	Arvin Union Elementary	Arvin, CA	83	47.7	Central Consolidated Schools	Shiprock, NM
24	66.6	West Las Vegas Public Schools	Las Vegas, NM	84	47.6	La Joya ISD	La Joya, TX
25	66.0	Bellevue Union Elementary	Santa Rosa, CA	85	47.3	Progreso ISD	Progreso, TX
26	65.7	Livingston Union Elementary	Livingston, CA	86	46.9	Northwest Arctic SD	Kotzebue, AK
27	65.1	Murphy Elementary District	Phoenix, AZ	87	46.9	Roma ISD	Roma, TX
28	64.9	Cashmere SD 222	Cashmere, WA	88	46.8	Gadsden Independent Schools	Anthony, NM
29	63.8	Parlier Unified	Parlier, CA	89	46.8	Perris Elementary	Perris, CA
30	63.5	Kayenta Unified District	Kayenta, AZ	90	46.7	Weaver Union Elementary	Merced, CA
31	62.8	Lower Kuskokwim SD	Bethel, AK	91	46.4	Clint ISD	El Paso, TX
32	62.5	Pinon Unified District	Pinon, AZ	92	46.3	Farmersville Unified	Farmersville, CA
33	62.4	Anaheim Elementary	Anaheim, CA	93	45.8	Balsz Elementary District	Phoenix, AZ
34	62.1	North Slope Borough SD	Barrow, AK	94	45.6	Pajaro Valley Unified School	Watsonville, CA
35	62.0	Laredo ISD	Laredo, TX	95	45.4	Paramount Unified	Paramount, CA
36	61.7	Soledad Unified	Soledad, CA	96	45.2	Oxnard Elementary	Oxnard, CA
37	60.9	Isaac Elementary District	Phoenix, AZ	97	45.2	Tuba City Unified District	Tuba City, AZ
38	60.7	Santa Ana Unified	Santa Ana, CA	98	45.2	United ISD	Laredo, TX
39	60.6	Alum Rock Union Elementary	San Jose, CA	99	45.2	El Monte City Elementary	El Monte, CA
40	60.5	Nogales Unified District	Nogales, AZ	100	45.1	Pomona Unified	Pomona, CA
41	60.4	Creighton Elementary District	Phoenix, AZ	101	45.1	Buena Park Elementary	Buena Park, CA
42	59.0	Gonzales Unified	Gonzales, CA	102	44.7	Bethel SD 403	Spanaway, WA
43	59.0	East Holmes Local Schools	Berlin, OH	103	44.7	Cartwright Elementary District	Phoenix, AZ
44	58.3	Lindsay Unified	Lindsay, CA	104	44.5	El Centro Elementary	El Centro, CA
45	58.2	National Elementary	National City, CA	105	44.3	Hueneme Elementary	Port Hueneme, CA
46	57.7	Santa Cruz Valley Unified District	Rio Rico, AZ	106	44.3	La Habra City Elementary	La Habra, CA
47	57.5	Mountain View Elementary	El Monte, CA	107	44.3	Hawthorne Elementary	Hawthorne, CA
48	57.4	Cutler-Orosi Joint Unified	Orosi, CA	108	44.3	Fabens ISD	Fabens, TX
49	57.0	Greenfield Union Elementary	Greenfield, CA	109	44.2	Richland Union Elementary SD	Shafter, CA
50	56.8	Golden Plains Unified	San Joaquin, CA	110	44.1	Salinas City Elementary	Salinas, CA
51	55.9	Winton Elementary	Winton, CA	111	43.8	Union City	Union City, NJ
52	55.7	Douglas Unified District	Douglas, AZ	112	43.7	Bernalillo Public Schools	Bernalillo, NM
53	55.7	Delano Union Elementary	Delano, CA	113	43.7	Los Angeles Unified	Los Angeles, CA
54	55.5	Macomb ISD	Clinton Twp, MI	114	43.5	Garvey Elementary	Rosemead, CA
55	54.9	Mt. Pleasant Elementary	San Jose, CA	115	43.4	Weld County SD Re-8	Fort Lupton, CO
56	54.3	Valley View ISD	Pharr, TX	116	43.3	Montebello Unified	Montebello, CA
57	54.0	Hidalgo ISD	Hidalgo, TX	117	43.1	Holtville Unified	Holtville, CA
58	54.0	San Elizario ISD	San Elizario, TX	118	43.0	Edcouch-Elsa ISD	Edcouch, TX
59	54.0	Franklin-Mckinley Elementary	San Jose, CA	119	43.0	Sunnyside Unified District	Tucson, AZ
60	53.7	Compton Unified	Compton, CA	120	42.9	Westminster Elementary	Westminster, CA

This section ranks 120 school districts at both the "top" and "bottom" of each category for a total of 240 districts per category. The "top" list (descending order) appears first, followed by the "bottom" list (ascending order). Ranking tables cover public school districts serving 1,500 or more students.

English Language Learner (ELL) Students

School districts ranked in *ascending* order

Rank	Percent	District Name	City, State
1	0.0	Aberdeen SD	Aberdeen, MS
1	0.0	Adams-Friendship Area	Friendship, WI
1	0.0	Airport Community SD	Carleton, MI
1	0.0	Albion Public Schools	Albion, MI
1	0.0	Algonac Community SD	Algonac, MI
1	0.0	Allen County	Scottsville, KY
1	0.0	Allen Park Public Schools	Allen Park, MI
1	0.0	Alma Public Schools	Alma, MI
1	0.0	Almont Community Schools	Almont, MI
1	0.0	Alpena Public Schools	Alpena, MI
1	0.0	Amanda-Clearcreek Local SD	Amanda, OH
1	0.0	Amery	Amery, WI
1	0.0	Amherst Ex Vill SD	Amherst, OH
1	0.0	Anacortes SD 103	Anacortes, WA
1	0.0	Anchor Bay SD	New Baltimore, MI
1	0.0	Anthony Wayne Local SD	Whitehouse, OH
1	0.0	Antigo	Antigo, WI
1	0.0	Arlington SD 16	Arlington, WA
1	0.0	Armada Area Schools	Armada, MI
1	0.0	Arrowhead UHS	Hartland, WI
1	0.0	Ashburnham-Westminster	Westminster, MA
1	0.0	Ashland	Ashland, WI
1	0.0	Ashwaubenon	Green Bay, WI
1	0.0	Atchison Public Schools	Atchison, KS
1	0.0	Atlantic Community SD	Atlantic, IA
1	0.0	Augusta	Augusta, KS
1	0.0	Ava R-I	Ava, MO
1	0.0	Avondale SD	Auburn Hills, MI
1	0.0	Bamberg County SD 01	Bamberg, SC
1	0.0	Bangor Public Schools (Van Buren)	Bangor, MI
1	0.0	Bangor Township Schools	Bay City, MI
1	0.0	Baraboo	Baraboo, WI
1	0.0	Basehor-Linwood	Basehor, KS
1	0.0	Bath County	Owingsv, KY
1	0.0	Beaver Local SD	Lisbon, OH
1	0.0	Beaverton Rural Schools	Beaverton, MI
1	0.0	Beecher Community SD	Flint, MI
1	0.0	Belcourt 7	Belcourt, ND
1	0.0	Bell County	Pineville, KY
1	0.0	Bellaire Local SD	Bellaire, OH
1	0.0	Bendle Public Schools	Burton, MI
1	0.0	Benjamin Logan Local SD	Bellefontaine, OH
1	0.0	Benton Carroll Salem Local SD	Oak Harbor, OH
1	0.0	Benton Community SD	Van Horne, IA
1	0.0	Benton Harbor Area Schools	Benton Harbor, MI
1	0.0	Benzie County Central Schools	Benzonia, MI
1	0.0	Bergen County Special Service	Paramus, NJ
1	0.0	Berlin Area	Berlin, WI
1	0.0	Berlin SD	Berlin, NH
1	0.0	Berrien County	Nashville, GA
1	0.0	Bethel-Tate Local SD	Bethel, OH
1	0.0	Big Rapids Public Schools	Big Rapids, MI
1	0.0	Black River Falls	Black River Fls, WI
1	0.0	Black River Local SD	Sullivan, OH
1	0.0	Blackstone-Millville	Blackstone, MA
1	0.0	Blanchester Local SD	Blanchester, OH
1	0.0	Board of Educ Garrett County	Oakland, MD
1	0.0	Bonner Springs	Bonner Springs, KS
1	0.0	Brainerd	Brainerd, MN
1	0.0	Brandywine Public SD	Niles, MI

Rank	Percent	District Name	City, State
1	0.0	Breathitt County	Jackson, KY
1	0.0	Breitung Township Schools	Kingsford, MI
1	0.0	Bremen City	Bremen, GA
1	0.0	Bridgeport-Spaulding Community SD	Bridgeport, MI
1	0.0	Brighton Area Schools	Brighton, MI
1	0.0	Brooke County SD	Wellsburg, WV
1	0.0	Brown Deer	Brown Deer, WI
1	0.0	Buchanan Community Schools	Buchanan, MI
1	0.0	Buckeye Local SD	Medina, OH
1	0.0	Buckeye Local SD	Rayland, OH
1	0.0	Buckeye Valley Local SD	Delaware, OH
1	0.0	Burke County	Waynesboro, GA
1	0.0	Burlington County Spec Serv	Mount Holly, NJ
1	0.0	Butte County Joint District	Arco, ID
1	0.0	Butte Elem	Butte, MT
1	0.0	Butte HS	Butte, MT
1	0.0	Butts County	Jackson, GA
1	0.0	Byron	Byron, MN
1	0.0	Byron Center Public Schools	Byron Center, MI
1	0.0	Cadillac Area Public Schools	Cadillac, MI
1	0.0	Caldwell County	Princeton, KY
1	0.0	Caldwell Parish School Board	Columbia, LA
1	0.0	Caledonia Community Schools	Caledonia, MI
1	0.0	Cambridge City SD	Cambridge, OH
1	0.0	Camden County Vocational	Sicklerville, NJ
1	0.0	Campbellsport	Campbellsport, WI
1	0.0	Capac Community SD	Capac, MI
1	0.0	Caro Community Schools	Caro, MI
1	0.0	Carrollton Ex Vill SD	Carrollton, OH
1	0.0	Carrollton SD	Saginaw, MI
1	0.0	Carter County	Grayson, KY
1	0.0	Carver	Carver, MA
1	0.0	Casey County	Liberty, KY
1	0.0	Catahoula Parish School Board	Harrisonburg, LA
1	0.0	Cedarburg	Cedarburg, WI
1	0.0	Celina City SD	Celina, OH
1	0.0	Center Line Public Schools	Center Line, MI
1	0.0	Central Ariz Valley Inst of Tech	Coolidge, AZ
1	0.0	Central Berkshire	Dalton, MA
1	0.0	Central Clinton Community SD	De Witt, IA
1	0.0	Central Montcalm Public Schools	Stanton, MI
1	0.0	Central R-III	Park Hills, MO
1	0.0	Champion Local SD	Warren, OH
1	0.0	Chanute Public Schools	Chanute, KS
1	0.0	Charlotte Public Schools	Charlotte, MI
1	0.0	Charlton County	Folkston, GA
1	0.0	Cheboygan Area Schools	Cheboygan, MI
1	0.0	Chelsea SD	Chelsea, MI
1	0.0	Cheney SD 360	Cheney, WA
1	0.0	Chesaning Union Schools	Chesaning, MI
1	0.0	Chillicothe City SD	Chillicothe, OH
1	0.0	Chillicothe R-II	Chillicothe, MO
1	0.0	Chippewa Falls Area	Chippewa Falls, WI
1	0.0	Chippewa Hills SD	Remus, MI
1	0.0	Choctaw County	Butler, AL
1	0.0	Choctaw County SD	Ackerman, MS
1	0.0	Circle	Towanda, KS
1	0.0	Claiborne County SD	Port Gibson, MS
1	0.0	Claiborne Parish School Board	Homer, LA
1	0.0	Clarenceville SD	Livonia, MI

This section ranks 120 school districts at both the "top" and "bottom" of each category for a total of 240 districts per category. The "top" list (descending order) appears first, followed by the "bottom" list (ascending order). Ranking tables cover public school districts serving 1,500 or more students.

Migrant Students

School districts ranked in *descending* order

Rank	Percent	District Name	City, State	Rank	Percent	District Name	City, State
1	90.6	Robstown ISD	Robstown, TX	61	28.8	Fillmore Unified	Fillmore, CA
2	58.1	King City Joint Union High	King City, CA	62	28.5	Dequeen SD	De Queen, AR
3	55.4	Wasco Union Elementary	Wasco, CA	63	28.0	Morrow SD 1	Lexington, OR
4	53.4	Golden Plains Unified	San Joaquin, CA	64	27.8	North Monterey County Unified	Moss Landing, CA
5	53.1	Lexington Public Schools	Lexington, NE	65	27.7	La Joya ISD	La Joya, TX
6	51.4	Reef-Sunset Unified	Avenal, CA	66	27.6	Windham SD	Willimantic, CT
7	50.3	Firebaugh-Las Deltas Joint Unified	Firebaugh, CA	67	27.0	Kerman Unified	Kerman, CA
8	49.4	Alisal Union Elementary	Salinas, CA	68	26.7	Ocean View Elementary	Oxnard, CA
9	49.2	Gonzales Unified	Gonzales, CA	69	26.3	Liberal	Liberal, KS
10	47.1	Clinton	Clinton, OK	70	26.2	Escalon Unified	Escalon, CA
11	46.2	Arvin Union Elementary	Arvin, CA	71	26.1	Crystal City ISD	Crystal City, TX
12	46.2	Hereford ISD	Hereford, TX	72	25.8	Brawley Union High	Brawley, CA
13	45.7	Pajaro Valley Unified School	Watsonville, CA	73	25.5	Riverbank Unified	Riverbank, CA
14	45.2	Richland Union Elementary SD	Shafter, CA	74	25.5	Lyford CISD	Lyford, TX
15	45.0	Mendota Unified	Mendota, CA	75	25.3	River Delta Joint Unified	Rio Vista, CA
16	44.9	Lamont Elementary	Lamont, CA	76	25.0	So Sioux City Community Schs	So Sioux City, NE
17	44.7	Dumas ISD	Dumas, TX	77	24.9	Presidio ISD	Presidio, TX
18	44.6	Mcfarland Unified	Mcfarland, CA	78	24.9	Weld County SD Re-8	Fort Lupton, CO
19	42.6	Guymon	Guymon, OK	79	24.6	Brawley Elementary	Brawley, CA
20	41.9	Progreso ISD	Progreso, TX	80	24.4	Santa Paula Elementary	Santa Paula, CA
21	40.7	Parlier Unified	Parlier, CA	81	24.2	Mount Pleasant ISD	Mt Pleasant, TX
22	40.6	Raymondville ISD	Raymondville, TX	82	24.1	Hueneme Elementary	Port Hueneme, CA
23	39.9	Delano Union Elementary	Delano, CA	83	23.8	Coachella Valley Unified	Thermal, CA
24	39.9	Mathis ISD	Mathis, TX	84	23.2	Lower Kuskokwim SD	Bethel, AK
25	39.6	Salinas City Elementary	Salinas, CA	85	23.2	Santa Maria Joint Union High	Santa Maria, CA
26	39.0	Greenfield Union Elementary	Greenfield, CA	86	23.0	Calexico Unified	Calexico, CA
27	38.9	King City Union Elementary	King City, CA	87	22.8	Mercedes ISD	Mercedes, TX
28	38.2	Riverdale Joint Unified	Riverdale, CA	88	22.7	Patterson Joint Unified	Patterson, CA
29	37.7	Storm Lake Community SD	Storm Lake, IA	89	22.7	Carpinteria Unified	Carpinteria, CA
30	37.2	Corcoran Joint Unified	Corcoran, CA	90	22.4	Santa Maria-Bonita Elementary	Santa Maria, CA
31	36.8	Dodge City	Dodge City, KS	91	22.3	Hughson Unified	Hughson, CA
32	36.7	Fairfax Elementary	Bakersfield, CA	92	22.0	Greenfield Union Elementary	Bakersfield, CA
33	36.5	Lindsay Unified	Lindsay, CA	93	21.1	Newman-Crows Landing Unified	Newman, CA
34	36.4	Ontario SD 8c	Ontario, OR	94	21.1	Fort Morgan Re-3	Fort Morgan, CO
35	36.4	Delano Joint Union High	Delano, CA	95	21.0	Crete Public Schools	Crete, NE
36	36.2	San Felipe-Del Rio Cons I	Del Rio, TX	96	20.8	Ukiah Unified	Ukiah, CA
37	35.9	Coalinga-Huron Joint Unified	Coalinga, CA	97	20.6	Healdsburg Unified	Healdsburg, CA
38	33.9	Bering Strait SD	Unalakleet, AK	98	20.5	Taft City Elementary	Taft, CA
39	33.2	Woodlake Union Elementary	Woodlake, CA	99	20.3	Hermiston SD 8	Hermiston, OR
40	33.2	Earlimart Elementary	Earlimart, CA	100	20.2	Jefferson County SD 509J	Madras, OR
41	33.0	Weslaco ISD	Weslaco, TX	101	20.1	North Slope Borough SD	Barrow, AK
42	32.1	Lower Yukon SD	Mountain Vlg, AK	102	19.4	Hood River County SD	Hood River, OR
43	32.1	Farmersville Unified	Farmersville, CA	103	19.3	Live Oak Unified	Live Oak, CA
44	31.8	Soledad Unified	Soledad, CA	104	19.3	Gustine Unified	Gustine, CA
45	31.7	Rio Elementary	Oxnard, CA	105	19.3	Central Union High	El Centro, CA
46	31.3	Denison Community SD	Denison, IA	106	19.1	Perryton ISD	Perryton, TX
47	31.3	Edcouch-Elsa ISD	Edcouch, TX	107	18.9	Bakersfield City Elementary	Bakersfield, CA
48	31.3	Northwest Arctic SD	Kotzebue, AK	108	18.7	Lemoore Union Elementary	Lemoore, CA
49	31.2	Salinas Union High	Salinas, CA	109	18.7	Perry Community SD	Perry, IA
50	31.0	Hardee County SD	Wauchula, FL	110	18.5	Great Bend	Great Bend, KS
51	30.5	Rio Grande City CISD	Rio Grande City, TX	111	18.4	Atkinson County	Pearson, GA
52	30.4	San Benito High	Hollister, CA	112	18.4	Oxnard Union High	Oxnard, CA
53	30.2	Holtville Unified	Holtville, CA	113	18.4	Winters Joint Unified	Winters, CA
54	30.0	Hendry County SD	La Belle, FL	114	18.4	Hanford Elementary	Hanford, CA
55	29.8	Woodburn SD 103	Woodburn, OR	115	18.3	Cloverdale Unified	Cloverdale, CA
56	29.2	Donna ISD	Donna, TX	116	18.1	San Elizario ISD	San Elizario, TX
57	29.2	Hollister SD	Hollister, CA	117	18.0	Santa Paula Union High	Santa Paula, CA
58	29.2	Roma ISD	Roma, TX	118	18.0	Gridley Unified	Gridley, CA
59	29.0	Linden Unified	Linden, CA	119	17.7	Dinuba Unified	Dinuba, CA
60	28.8	Alamosa RE-11J	Alamosa, CO	120	17.5	Dos Palos Oro Loma Jt. Unified	Dos Palos, CA

This section ranks 120 school districts at both the "top" and "bottom" of each category for a total of 240 districts per category. The "top" list (descending order) appears first, followed by the "bottom" list (ascending order). Ranking tables cover public school districts serving 1,500 or more students.

Migrant Students

School districts ranked in *ascending* order

Rank	Percent	District Name	City, State	Rank	Percent	District Name	City, State
1	0.0	Aberdeen SD 06-1	Aberdeen, SD	1	0.0	Appomattox County Public Schools	Appomattox, VA
1	0.0	Abilene ISD	Abilene, TX	1	0.0	Aptakisic-Tripp CCSD 102	Buffalo Grove, IL
1	0.0	Abington	Abington, MA	1	0.0	Arab City	Arab, AL
1	0.0	Abington SD	Abington, PA	1	0.0	Archuleta County 50 Jt	Pagosa Springs, CO
1	0.0	Academy 20	Colorado Spgs, CO	1	0.0	Ardmore	Ardmore, OK
1	0.0	Acalanes Union High	Lafayette, CA	1	0.0	Argo Community HSD 217	Summit, IL
1	0.0	Acton-Boxborough	Acton, MA	1	0.0	Arkadelphia SD	Arkadelphia, AR
1	0.0	Ada	Ada, OK	1	0.0	Arlington	Arlington, MA
1	0.0	Adams-Cheshire	Cheshire, MA	1	0.0	Arlington County Public Schools	Arlington, VA
1	0.0	Adams-Friendship Area	Friendship, WI	1	0.0	Arlington Heights SD 25	Arlington Hgts, IL
1	0.0	Addison SD 4	Addison, IL	1	0.0	Armstrong SD	Ford City, PA
1	0.0	Adelanto Elementary	Adelanto, CA	1	0.0	Arrowhead UHS	Hartland, WI
1	0.0	Adlai E Stevenson Dist 125	Lincolnshire, IL	1	0.0	Asbury Park City	Asbury Park, NJ
1	0.0	Affton 101	St Louis, MO	1	0.0	Ashburnham-Westminster	Westminster, MA
1	0.0	Agawam	Feeding Hills, MA	1	0.0	Ashdown SD	Ashdown, AR
1	0.0	Alamo Heights ISD	San Antonio, TX	1	0.0	Asheville City Schools	Asheville, NC
1	0.0	Alamogordo Public Schools	Alamogordo, NM	1	0.0	Ashland	Ashland, MA
1	0.0	Albany	Albany, MN	1	0.0	Ashland	Ashland, WI
1	0.0	Albany City Unified	Albany, CA	1	0.0	Ashwaubenon	Green Bay, WI
1	0.0	Albany County SD #1	Laramie, WY	1	0.0	Aspen 1	Aspen, CO
1	0.0	Albert Gallatin Area SD	Uniontown, PA	1	0.0	Astoria SD 1	Astoria, OR
1	0.0	Albert Lea	Albert Lea, MN	1	0.0	Atchison Public Schools	Atchison, KS
1	0.0	Albertville City	Albertville, AL	1	0.0	Athens City	Athens, AL
1	0.0	Albuquerque Public Schools	Albuquerque, NM	1	0.0	Athol-Royalston	Athol, MA
1	0.0	Alexander City	Alexander City, AL	1	0.0	Atlanta City	Atlanta, GA
1	0.0	Alexander County Schools	Taylorsville, NC	1	0.0	Atlantic Community SD	Atlantic, IA
1	0.0	Alexandria	Alexandria, MN	1	0.0	Attalla City	Attalla, AL
1	0.0	Alexandria City Public Schools	Alexandria, VA	1	0.0	Auburn City	Auburn, AL
1	0.0	Alhambra Elementary District	Phoenix, AZ	1	0.0	Auburn Washburn	Topeka, KS
1	0.0	Alief ISD	Houston, TX	1	0.0	Audubon Boro	Audubon, NJ
1	0.0	Alleghany County Public Schools	Covington, VA	1	0.0	Augusta	Augusta, KS
1	0.0	Alpine Union Elementary	Alpine, CA	1	0.0	Aurora West Unit SD 129	Aurora, IL
1	0.0	Alsip-Hazlgrn-Oaklwn SD 126	Alsip, IL	1	0.0	Austin	Austin, MN
1	0.0	Alta Loma Elementary	Alta Loma, CA	1	0.0	Autauga County	Prattville, AL
1	0.0	Alton Community Unit SD 11	Alton, IL	1	0.0	Avery County Schools	Newland, NC
1	0.0	Altoona Area SD	Altoona, PA	1	0.0	Avon SD	Avon, CT
1	0.0	Amador County Unified	Jackson, CA	1	0.0	Aztec Municipal Schools	Aztec, NM
1	0.0	Ambridge Area SD	Ambridge, PA	1	0.0	Baker SD 5J	Baker City, OR
1	0.0	Amery	Amery, WI	1	0.0	Bald Eagle Area SD	Wingate, PA
1	0.0	Ames Community SD	Ames, IA	1	0.0	Baldwin County	Bay Minette, AL
1	0.0	Amesbury	Amesbury, MA	1	0.0	Baldwin County	Milledgeville, GA
1	0.0	Amherst SD	Amherst, NH	1	0.0	Baldwin-Whitehall SD	Pittsburgh, PA
1	0.0	Amory SD	Amory, MS	1	0.0	Ball Chatham CUSD 5	Chatham, IL
1	0.0	Amphitheater Unified District	Tucson, AZ	1	0.0	Balsz Elementary District	Phoenix, AZ
1	0.0	Anadarko	Anadarko, OK	1	0.0	Bandera ISD	Bandera, TX
1	0.0	Andalusia City	Andalusia, AL	1	0.0	Bangor Area SD	Bangor, PA
1	0.0	Andover	Andover, KS	1	0.0	Banning Unified	Banning, CA
1	0.0	Ankeny Community SD	Ankeny, IA	1	0.0	Baraboo	Baraboo, WI
1	0.0	Annandale	Annandale, MN	1	0.0	Barbour County SD	Philippi, WV
1	0.0	Anniston City	Anniston, AL	1	0.0	Bardstown Ind	Bardstown, KY
1	0.0	Annville-Cleona SD	Annville, PA	1	0.0	Barnegat Twp	Barnegat, NJ
1	0.0	Anoka-Hennepin	Coon Rapids, MN	1	0.0	Barrington CUSD 220	Barrington, IL
1	0.0	Anson County Schools	Wadesboro, NC	1	0.0	Barstow Unified	Barstow, CA
1	0.0	Ansonia SD	Ansonia, CT	1	0.0	Bartlesville	Bartlesville, OK
1	0.0	Antigo	Antigo, WI	1	0.0	Bartow County	Cartersville, GA
1	0.0	Antioch CCSD 34	Antioch, IL	1	0.0	Basehor-Linwood	Basehor, KS
1	0.0	Apache Junction Unified District	Apache Junction, AZ	1	0.0	Batavia Unit SD 101	Batavia, IL
1	0.0	Apollo-Ridge SD	Spring Church, PA	1	0.0	Bayless	St Louis, MO
1	0.0	Apple Valley Unified	Apple Valley, CA	1	0.0	Bayonne City	Bayonne, NJ
1	0.0	Appleton Area	Appleton, WI	1	0.0	Beach Park CCSD 3	Beach Park, IL

This section ranks 120 school districts at both the "top" and "bottom" of each category for a total of 240 districts per category. The "top" list (descending order) appears first, followed by the "bottom" list (ascending order). Ranking tables cover public school districts serving 1,500 or more students.

Students Eligible for Free Lunch Program

School districts ranked in *descending* order

Rank	Percent	District Name	City, State
1	99.6	Delano Union Elementary	Delano, CA
2	99.5	Isaac Elementary District	Phoenix, AZ
3	99.5	Holly Springs SD	Holly Springs, MS
4	99.4	Los Nietos Elementary	Whittier, CA
5	99.4	National Elementary	National City, CA
6	99.4	Somerton Elementary District	Somerton, AZ
7	99.4	Greenwood Public SD	Greenwood, MS
8	99.4	Jefferson Davis County SD	Prentiss, MS
9	99.4	Claiborne County SD	Port Gibson, MS
10	99.4	Jefferson County SD	Fayette, MS
11	99.3	Forrest City SD	Forrest City, AR
12	99.3	Blytheville SD	Blytheville, AR
13	99.3	Noxubee County SD	Macon, MS
14	99.2	Leflore County SD	Greenwood, MS
15	99.2	South Pike SD	Magnolia, MS
16	99.2	Wilkinson County SD	Woodville, MS
17	99.0	Quitman County SD	Marks, MS
18	99.0	Lamont Elementary	Lamont, CA
19	98.6	Coahoma County SD	Clarksdale, MS
20	98.4	Reef-Sunset Unified	Avenal, CA
21	97.3	Todd County SD 66-1	Mission, SD
22	97.0	Osceola SD	Osceola, AR
23	95.9	Wilcox County	Camden, AL
24	95.4	Holmes County SD	Lexington, MS
25	94.4	Humphreys County SD	Belzoni, MS
26	93.8	Canton Public SD	Canton, MS
27	93.2	Perry County	Marion, AL
28	91.2	W Harvey-Dixmoor PS Dist 147	Harvey, IL
29	90.9	Murphy Elementary District	Phoenix, AZ
30	90.7	Del Paso Heights Elementary	Sacramento, CA
31	90.3	Mccomb SD	Mccomb, MS
32	90.0	Yazoo City Municipal SD	Yazoo City, MS
33	89.6	Hazlehurst City SD	Hazlehurst, MS
34	88.9	Lowndes County	Hayneville, AL
35	88.5	Mendota Unified	Mendota, CA
36	88.4	San Elizario ISD	San Elizario, TX
37	87.8	Earlimart Elementary	Earlimart, CA
38	87.6	Union City	Union City, NJ
39	87.5	Tunica County SD	Tunica, MS
40	87.4	Western Line SD	Avon, MS
41	87.4	Compton Unified	Compton, CA
42	87.3	Lee County SD	Marianna, AR
43	86.9	East Carroll Parish School Board	Lake Providence, LA
44	86.7	Gadsden Independent Schools	Anthony, NM
45	86.6	Golden Plains Unified	San Joaquin, CA
46	85.6	Balsz Elementary District	Phoenix, AZ
47	85.1	Greene County	Eutaw, AL
48	85.1	Aberdeen SD	Aberdeen, MS
49	85.0	Indianola SD	Indianola, MS
50	84.8	Bullock County	Union Springs, AL
51	84.8	Creighton Elementary District	Phoenix, AZ
52	84.6	Robstown ISD	Robstown, TX
53	84.5	Alhambra Elementary District	Phoenix, AZ
54	84.4	North Panola Schools	Sardis, MS
55	84.4	Brooks County ISD	Falfurrias, TX
56	84.2	Greenville Public Schools	Greenville, MS
57	84.1	Williamsburg County SD	Kingstree, SC
58	83.7	Sunflower County SD	Indianola, MS
59	83.2	Natchez-Adams SD	Natchez, MS
60	82.7	San Diego Co Office of Education	San Diego, CA
61	82.7	Ganado Unified District	Ganado, AZ
62	82.4	Soledad Unified	Soledad, CA
63	82.1	Taos Municipal Schools	Taos, NM
64	81.4	Cutler-Orosi Joint Unified	Orosi, CA
65	81.2	Sunnyside Unified District	Tucson, AZ
66	81.1	Sumter County	Livingston, AL
67	81.0	Harvey SD 152	Harvey, IL
68	80.9	Madison Parish School Board	Tallulah, LA
69	80.6	Randolph County	Cuthbert, GA
70	80.6	Benton Harbor Area Schools	Benton Harbor, MI
71	80.6	Muskegon Heights SD	Muskegon Hgts, MI
72	80.6	Wasco Union Elementary	Wasco, CA
73	80.4	Chelsea	Chelsea, MA
74	80.2	Clint ISD	El Paso, TX
75	79.9	Laurel SD	Laurel, MS
76	79.8	Marengo County	Linden, AL
77	79.1	Orangeburg County SD 03	Holly Hill, SC
78	78.9	Rio Grande City CISD	Rio Grande City, TX
79	78.9	Allendale County SD	Allendale, SC
80	78.7	Woodlake Union Elementary	Woodlake, CA
81	78.7	Hatch Valley Public Schools	Hatch, NM
82	78.6	Jefferson County	Louisville, GA
83	78.5	Dollarway SD	Pine Bluff, AR
84	78.5	Mountain View Elementary	El Monte, CA
85	78.1	Selma City	Selma, AL
86	78.1	El Monte City Elementary	El Monte, CA
87	78.0	Chicago Heights SD 170	Chicago Heights, IL
88	77.9	Coachella Valley Unified	Thermal, CA
89	77.6	Mcfarland Unified	Mcfarland, CA
90	77.5	Fairfax Elementary	Bakersfield, CA
91	77.5	St. Louis City	St Louis, MO
92	77.4	Red River Parish School Board	Coushatta, LA
93	77.4	East Tallahatchie Consol SD	Charleston, MS
94	77.3	Clarksdale Municipal SD	Clarksdale, MS
95	77.0	Richland Union Elementary SD	Shafter, CA
96	76.8	Tuba City Unified District	Tuba City, AZ
97	76.7	Perris Elementary	Perris, CA
98	76.6	City of Bogalusa School Board	Bogalusa, LA
99	76.5	Lee County SD	Bishopville, SC
100	76.4	School City of East Chicago	East Chicago, IN
101	76.3	Bakersfield City Elementary	Bakersfield, CA
102	76.2	Woodburn SD 103	Woodburn, OR
103	76.2	Laveen Elementary District	Laveen, AZ
104	76.2	Iberville Parish School Board	Plaquemine, LA
105	76.1	Oklahoma City	Oklahoma City, OK
106	76.1	Dooly County	Vienna, GA
107	76.1	Winton Elementary	Winton, CA
108	75.9	Red Lake	Red Lake, MN
109	75.7	Anniston City	Anniston, AL
110	75.6	Osborn Elementary District	Phoenix, AZ
111	75.6	Florence County SD 03	Lake City, SC
112	75.5	Asbury Park City	Asbury Park, NJ
113	75.4	East Feliciana Parish School Board	Clinton, LA
114	75.4	Fowler Elementary District	Phoenix, AZ
115	75.4	San Ysidro Elementary	San Ysidro, CA
116	75.3	Saint John the Baptist Parish SB	Reserve, LA
117	75.2	Prairie-Hills Elem SD 144	Markham, IL
118	75.2	Conecuh County	Evergreen, AL
119	74.8	Halifax County Schools	Halifax, NC
120	74.7	Camden City	Camden, NJ

This section ranks 120 school districts at both the "top" and "bottom" of each category for a total of 240 districts per category. The "top" list (descending order) appears first, followed by the "bottom" list (ascending order). Ranking tables cover public school districts serving 1,500 or more students.

Students Eligible for Free Lunch Program

School districts ranked in *ascending* order

Rank	Percent	District Name	City, State	Rank	Percent	District Name	City, State
1	0.0	Acton-Agua Dulce Unified	Acton, CA	59	0.2	Verona Boro	Verona, NJ
1	0.0	Aspen 1	Aspen, CO	62	0.3	Holmdel Twp	Holmdel, NJ
1	0.0	Bremen Community HS District 228	Midlothian, IL	62	0.3	SD of the Chathams	Chatham, NJ
1	0.0	Burbank SD 111	Burbank, IL	62	0.3	Tenafly Boro	Tenafly, NJ
1	0.0	Carlynton SD	Carnegie, PA	62	0.3	Wyckoff Twp	Wyckoff, NJ
1	0.0	Community Consolidated S D 93	Carol Stream, IL	66	0.4	Acalanes Union High	Lafayette, CA
1	0.0	Community High SD 117	Lake Villa, IL	66	0.4	Kinnelon Boro	Kinnelon, NJ
1	0.0	Community High SD 94	West Chicago, IL	66	0.4	Mt Lebanon SD	Pittsburgh, PA
1	0.0	Cons High SD 230	Orland Park, IL	66	0.4	N Hunt/Voorhees Regional	Annandale, NJ
1	0.0	Deerfield SD 109	Deerfield, IL	66	0.4	Watchung Hills Regional	Warren, NJ
1	0.0	Duxbury	Duxbury, MA	71	0.5	Caldwell-West Caldwell	West Caldwell, NJ
1	0.0	Fenton Community HSD 100	Bensenville, IL	71	0.5	Chagrin Falls Ex Vill SD	Chagrin Falls, OH
1	0.0	Florida Virtual School	Orlando, FL	71	0.5	Glen Rock Boro	Glen Rock, NJ
1	0.0	Flossmoor SD 161	Chicago Heights, IL	71	0.5	Hanover Twp	Whippany, NJ
1	0.0	Frankfort CCSD 157c	Frankfort, IL	71	0.5	La Canada Unified	La Canada, CA
1	0.0	Fremont SD 79	Mundelein, IL	71	0.5	Livingston Twp	Livingston, NJ
1	0.0	Geneva Community Unit SD 304	Geneva, IL	71	0.5	Millburn Twp	Millburn, NJ
1	0.0	Glen Ellyn CCSD 89	Glen Ellyn, IL	71	0.5	Montgomery Twp	Skillman, NJ
1	0.0	Glen Ellyn SD 41	Glen Ellyn, IL	71	0.5	Montville Twp	Montville, NJ
1	0.0	Glen Ridge Boro	Glen Ridge, NJ	71	0.5	Warren Twp	Warren, NJ
1	0.0	Grayslake Community High SD 127	Grayslake, IL	71	0.5	Washington Twp	Long Valley, NJ
1	0.0	Gurnee SD 56	Gurnee, IL	71	0.5	West Morris Regional	Chester, NJ
1	0.0	Highland Park ISD	Dallas, TX	83	0.6	Granville Ex Vill SD	Granville, OH
1	0.0	Hinsdale Twp HSD 86	Hinsdale, IL	83	0.6	Oakwood City SD	Dayton, OH
1	0.0	Homer Community CSD 33c	Homer Glen, IL	83	0.6	Orinda Union Elementary	Orinda, CA
1	0.0	Indian Prairie CUSD 204	Aurora, IL	83	0.6	Saratoga Union Elementary	Saratoga, CA
1	0.0	Keeneyville SD 20	Hanover Park, IL	87	0.7	Berkeley Heights Twp	Berkeley Hgts, NJ
1	0.0	Kirby SD 140	Tinley Park, IL	87	0.7	Bernards Twp	Basking Ridge, NJ
1	0.0	Lake Forest Community HS Dist 115	Lake Forest, IL	87	0.7	Colts Neck Twp	Colts Neck, NJ
1	0.0	Lake Forest SD 67	Lake Forest, IL	87	0.7	New Providence Boro	New Providence, NJ
1	0.0	Lake Park Community HSD 108	Roselle, IL	87	0.7	Oakland Boro	Oakland, NJ
1	0.0	Lansing SD 158	Lansing, IL	87	0.7	Southborough	Northborough, MA
1	0.0	Libertyville SD 70	Libertyville, IL	87	0.7	Waldwick Boro	Waldwick, NJ
1	0.0	Lincolnshire-Prairieview S D 103	Lincolnshire, IL	94	0.8	Council Rock SD	Newtown, PA
1	0.0	Los Alamos Public Schools	Los Alamos, NM	94	0.8	Downers Grove Grade SD 58	Downers Grove, IL
1	0.0	Lyons Twp HSD 204	La Grange, IL	94	0.8	Hopewell Valley Regional	Pennington, NJ
1	0.0	Minooka Community HS District 111	Minooka, IL	94	0.8	Indian Hill Ex Vill SD	Cincinnati, OH
1	0.0	Mountain Brook City	Mountain Brook, AL	94	0.8	Ridgewood Village	Ridgewood, NJ
1	0.0	Niles Twp Community High SD 219	Skokie, IL	94	0.8	San Marino Unified	San Marino, CA
1	0.0	Northbrook SD 28	Northbrook, IL	94	0.8	Upper Arlington City SD	Upper Arlington, OH
1	0.0	Oak Lawn-Hometown SD 123	Oak Lawn, IL	101	0.9	Branchburg Twp	Branchburg, NJ
1	0.0	Orland SD 135	Orland Park, IL	101	0.9	Cedar Grove Twp	Cedar Grove, NJ
1	0.0	Ottawa Twp HSD 140	Ottawa, IL	101	0.9	Clark Twp	Clark, NJ
1	0.0	Park Ridge CCSD 64	Park Ridge, IL	101	0.9	Clinton Twp	Annandale, NJ
1	0.0	Pennsylvania Virtual CS	Norristown, PA	101	0.9	Garnet Valley SD	Glen Mills, PA
1	0.0	Piedmont City Unified	Piedmont, CA	101	0.9	Haddonfield Boro	Haddonfield, NJ
1	0.0	Prospect Heights SD 23	Prospect Hgts, IL	101	0.9	Hopkinton	Hopkinton, MA
1	0.0	Queen Bee SD 16	Glendale Hgts, IL	101	0.9	Los Gatos-Saratoga Jt Union High	Los Gatos, CA
1	0.0	Ramapo-Indian Hill Reg	Franklin Lakes, NJ	101	0.9	Marlboro Twp	Marlboro, NJ
1	0.0	Schaumburg CCSD 54	Schaumburg, IL	101	0.9	Mercer Island SD 400	Mercer Island, WA
1	0.0	Warren Twp High SD 121	Gages Lake, IL	101	0.9	Naperville C U Dist 203	Naperville, IL
1	0.0	Western Pennsylvania Cyber CS	Midland, PA	101	0.9	Oak Park Unified	Oak Park, CA
1	0.0	Westwood	Westwood, MA	101	0.9	Readington Twp	Whitehouse Stn, NJ
1	0.0	Wilmette SD 39	Wilmette, IL	101	0.9	Upper Saint Clair SD	Pittsburgh, PA
1	0.0	Winnetka SD 36	Winnetka, IL	115	1.0	Bedford SD	Bedford, NH
1	0.0	Yorkville Community Unit SD 115	Yorkville, IL	115	1.0	Eanes ISD	Austin, TX
57	0.1	Everman ISD	Everman, TX	115	1.0	Elmhurst SD 205	Elmhurst, IL
57	0.1	Northern Valley Regional	Demarest, NJ	115	1.0	Galena City SD	Galena, AK
59	0.2	Franklin Lakes Boro	Franklin Lakes, NJ	115	1.0	Lower Moreland Township SD	Huntingdon Vly, PA
59	0.2	Lafayette Elementary	Lafayette, CA	115	1.0	Lynnfield	Lynnfield, MA

This section ranks 120 school districts at both the "top" and "bottom" of each category for a total of 240 districts per category. The "top" list (descending order) appears first, followed by the "bottom" list (ascending order). Ranking tables cover public school districts serving 1,500 or more students.

Students Eligible for Reduced-Price Lunch Program

School districts ranked in *descending* order

Rank	Percent	District Name	City, State	Rank	Percent	District Name	City, State
1	26.0	South Whittier Elementary	Whittier, CA	61	16.3	Chula Vista Elementary	Chula Vista, CA
2	22.8	Little Lake City Elementary	Santa Fe Spgs, CA	62	16.3	Robla Elementary	Sacramento, CA
3	22.6	Twin Ridges Elementary	North San Juan, CA	63	16.2	Othello SD 147	Othello, WA
4	22.2	Chandler Unified District	Chandler, AZ	64	16.2	Emery SD	Huntington, UT
5	21.7	Anaheim Elementary	Anaheim, CA	65	16.2	Romoland Elementary	Homeland, CA
6	21.6	Santa Paula Elementary	Santa Paula, CA	66	16.1	Livingston Union Elementary	Livingston, CA
7	20.9	Rosemead Elementary	Rosemead, CA	67	16.1	Hampshire County SD	Romney, WV
8	20.6	Central Union Elementary	Lemoore, CA	68	16.1	Vernon Parish School Board	Leesville, LA
9	20.3	Downey Unified	Downey, CA	69	16.1	Douglas SD 51-1	Box Elder, SD
10	20.1	Standard Elementary	Bakersfield, CA	70	16.1	Moreno Valley Unified	Moreno Valley, CA
11	19.6	Hemet Unified	Hemet, CA	71	16.1	South Bay Union Elementary	Imperial Beach, CA
12	19.4	Hillside Twp	Hillside, NJ	72	16.0	Burton Elementary	Porterville, CA
13	19.4	Cucamonga Elementary	Rcho Cucamong, CA	73	16.0	Cherokee County Schools	Murphy, NC
14	19.4	Garfield City	Garfield, NJ	74	16.0	Enterprise Elementary	Redding, CA
15	19.3	Cobre Consolidated Schools	Bayard, NM	75	16.0	Buchanan County Public Schools	Grundy, VA
16	19.2	Jefferson Elementary	Daly City, CA	76	16.0	Sweetwater Union High	Chula Vista, CA
17	19.1	Salinas City Elementary	Salinas, CA	77	16.0	Jay	Jay, OK
18	19.1	Silver Valley Unified	Yermo, CA	78	15.9	Rio Elementary	Oxnard, CA
19	19.1	Locust Grove	Locust Grove, OK	79	15.9	Whittier City Elementary	Whittier, CA
20	18.9	Ocean View Elementary	Oxnard, CA	80	15.9	Tahlequah	Tahlequah, OK
21	18.7	Alisal Union Elementary	Salinas, CA	81	15.9	Iola	Iola, KS
22	18.7	Geary County Schools	Junction City, KS	82	15.9	West Bonner County District	Sandpoint, ID
23	18.6	N Sanpete SD	Mt Pleasant, UT	83	15.8	Checotah	Checotah, OK
24	18.5	Brookings-Harbor SD 17c	Brookings, OR	84	15.8	El Rancho Unified	Pico Rivera, CA
25	18.4	Cascade Union Elementary	Anderson, CA	85	15.8	Bristow	Bristow, OK
26	18.3	Val Verde Unified	Perris, CA	86	15.8	Kalkaska Public Schools	Kalkaska, MI
27	18.2	Azusa Unified	Azusa, CA	87	15.7	Littleton Elementary District	Cashion, AZ
28	18.1	Lemon Grove Elementary	Lemon Grove, CA	88	15.7	Santa Cruz Valley Unified District	Rio Rico, AZ
29	17.9	Beaumont Unified	Beaumont, CA	89	15.7	Screven County	Sylvania, GA
30	17.8	Pittsburg Unified	Pittsburg, CA	90	15.7	Millard SD	Delta, UT
31	17.6	Hardy County SD	Moorefield, WV	91	15.7	Clover Park SD 400	Lakewood, WA
32	17.5	Passaic County Vocational	Wayne, NJ	92	15.6	Lower Twp	Cape May, NJ
33	17.4	Somerville	Somerville, MA	93	15.6	Hawthorne Elementary	Hawthorne, CA
34	17.4	Monroe County SD	Union, WV	94	15.6	Juab SD	Nephi, UT
35	17.4	Lexington Public Schools	Lexington, NE	95	15.6	Carpinteria Unified	Carpinteria, CA
36	17.2	Dover Town	Dover, NJ	96	15.6	Pleasantville City	Pleasantville, NJ
37	17.2	Palmdale Elementary	Palmdale, CA	97	15.5	Bayless	St Louis, MO
38	17.1	West Covina Unified	West Covina, CA	98	15.5	Brooklyn Center	Brooklyn Center, MN
39	17.1	Lawndale Elementary	Lawndale, CA	99	15.5	Deer Park SD 414	Deer Park, WA
40	17.1	Essex County Voc-Tech	West Orange, NJ	100	15.5	Farwell Area Schools	Farwell, MI
41	17.0	Greenfield Union Elementary	Greenfield, CA	101	15.5	Chino Valley Unified District	Chino Valley, AZ
42	17.0	Knob Noster R-VIII	Knob Noster, MO	102	15.4	Pocahontas SD	Pocahontas, AR
43	16.9	Calexico Unified	Calexico, CA	103	15.4	Killeen ISD	Killeen, TX
44	16.8	Rabun County	Clayton, GA	104	15.4	Vinita	Vinita, OK
45	16.8	Bellevue Union Elementary	Santa Rosa, CA	105	15.4	Empire Union Elementary	Modesto, CA
46	16.8	Santa Ana Unified	Santa Ana, CA	106	15.4	Berwyn South SD 100	Berwyn, IL
47	16.7	Hueneme Elementary	Port Hueneme, CA	107	15.4	Noble	Noble, OK
48	16.6	Ashe County Schools	Jefferson, NC	108	15.4	Lindenwold Boro	Lindenwold, NJ
49	16.6	S Sanpete SD	Manti, UT	109	15.3	Barbour County SD	Philippi, WV
50	16.6	Santa Barbara Elementary	Santa Barbara, CA	110	15.3	Hacienda La Puente Unified	City of Industry, CA
51	16.6	Bertie County Schools	Windsor, NC	111	15.3	Klamath Falls City Schools	Klamath Falls, OR
52	16.5	Avery County Schools	Newland, NC	112	15.3	Long Branch City	Long Branch, NJ
53	16.5	Keansburg Boro	Keansburg, NJ	113	15.3	Lowell	Lowell, MA
53	16.5	Medical Lake SD 326	Medical Lake, WA	114	15.3	Atwater Elementary	Atwater, CA
55	16.5	Westwood Community Schools	Dearborn Hgts, MI	115	15.3	Grove	Grove, OK
56	16.4	King City Union Elementary	King City, CA	116	15.3	Gonzales Unified	Gonzales, CA
57	16.4	Ravenswood City Elementary	East Palo Alto, CA	117	15.3	Parker Unified SD	Parker, AZ
58	16.4	Winston County	Double Springs, AL	118	15.3	Salinas Union High	Salinas, CA
59	16.3	Fowler Elementary District	Phoenix, AZ	119	15.2	Van Dyke Public Schools	Warren, MI
60	16.3	Oxnard Elementary	Oxnard, CA	120	15.2	Banning Unified	Banning, CA

This section ranks 120 school districts at both the "top" and "bottom" of each category for a total of 240 districts per category. The "top" list (descending order) appears first, followed by the "bottom" list (ascending order). Ranking tables cover public school districts serving 1,500 or more students.

Students Eligible for Reduced-Price Lunch Program

School districts ranked in *ascending* order

Rank	Percent	District Name	City, State	Rank	Percent	District Name	City, State
1	0.0	Acton-Agua Dulce Unified	Acton, CA	1	0.0	Lansing SD 158	Lansing, IL
1	0.0	Amherst-Pelham	Amherst, MA	1	0.0	Leflore County SD	Greenwood, MS
1	0.0	Andover	Andover, MA	1	0.0	Libertyville SD 70	Libertyville, IL
1	0.0	Belmont-Redwood Shores Elementary	Belmont, CA	1	0.0	Lincolnshire-Prairieview S D 103	Lincolnshire, IL
1	0.0	Blytheville SD	Blytheville, AR	1	0.0	Los Alamos Public Schools	Los Alamos, NM
1	0.0	Bremen Community HS District 228	Midlothian, IL	1	0.0	Los Gatos-Saratoga Jt Union High	Los Gatos, CA
1	0.0	Burbank SD 111	Burbank, IL	1	0.0	Los Nietos Elementary	Whittier, CA
1	0.0	Burlington	Burlington, MA	1	0.0	Lyons Twp HSD 204	La Grange, IL
1	0.0	Carlynton SD	Carnegie, PA	1	0.0	Masconomet	Topsfield, MA
1	0.0	Catalina Foothills Unified Dist	Tucson, AZ	1	0.0	Melrose	Melrose, MA
1	0.0	Chelsea	Chelsea, MA	1	0.0	Minooka Community HS District 111	Minooka, IL
1	0.0	Claiborne County SD	Port Gibson, MS	1	0.0	Moraga Elementary	Moraga, CA
1	0.0	Clinton Twp	Annandale, NJ	1	0.0	Mountain Brook City	Mountain Brook, AL
1	0.0	Coahoma County SD	Clarksdale, MS	1	0.0	National Elementary	National City, CA
1	0.0	Community Consolidated S D 93	Carol Stream, IL	1	0.0	Niles Twp Community High SD 219	Skokie, IL
1	0.0	Community High SD 117	Lake Villa, IL	1	0.0	North Shore SD 112	Highland Park, IL
1	0.0	Community High SD 94	West Chicago, IL	1	0.0	Northbrook SD 28	Northbrook, IL
1	0.0	Cons High SD 230	Orland Park, IL	1	0.0	Noxubee County SD	Macon, MS
1	0.0	Corrections SD 428 Dept of	Springfield, IL	1	0.0	Oak Lawn-Hometown SD 123	Oak Lawn, IL
1	0.0	Deerfield SD 109	Deerfield, IL	1	0.0	Orinda Union Elementary	Orinda, CA
1	0.0	Delano Union Elementary	Delano, CA	1	0.0	Orland SD 135	Orland Park, IL
1	0.0	Denville Twp	Denville, NJ	1	0.0	Oro Grande Elementary	Oro Grande, CA
1	0.0	Duxbury	Duxbury, MA	1	0.0	Osceola SD	Osceola, AR
1	0.0	East Longmeadow	East Longmeadow, MA	1	0.0	Ottawa Twp HSD 140	Ottawa, IL
1	0.0	Everman ISD	Everman, TX	1	0.0	Park Ridge CCSD 64	Park Ridge, IL
1	0.0	Fenton Community HSD 100	Bensenville, IL	1	0.0	Pascack Valley Regional	Montvale, NJ
1	0.0	Florida Virtual School	Orlando, FL	1	0.0	Pennsylvania Virtual CS	Norristown, PA
1	0.0	Flossmoor SD 161	Chicago Heights, IL	1	0.0	Piedmont City Unified	Piedmont, CA
1	0.0	Forrest City SD	Forrest City, AR	1	0.0	Prospect Heights SD 23	Prospect Hgts, IL
1	0.0	Framingham	Framingham, MA	1	0.0	Queen Bee SD 16	Glendale Hgts, IL
1	0.0	Frankfort CCSD 157c	Frankfort, IL	1	0.0	Quitman County SD	Marks, MS
1	0.0	Franklin	Franklin, MA	1	0.0	Reef-Sunset Unified	Avenal, CA
1	0.0	Franklin Lakes Boro	Franklin Lakes, NJ	1	0.0	Sandwich	Sandwich, MA
1	0.0	Fremont SD 79	Mundelein, IL	1	0.0	Schaumburg CCSD 54	Schaumburg, IL
1	0.0	Geneva Community Unit SD 304	Geneva, IL	1	0.0	Somerton Elementary District	Somerton, AZ
1	0.0	Glen Ellyn CCSD 89	Glen Ellyn, IL	1	0.0	South Hadley	South Hadley, MA
1	0.0	Glen Ellyn SD 41	Glen Ellyn, IL	1	0.0	South Pike SD	Magnolia, MS
1	0.0	Glen Ridge Boro	Glen Ridge, NJ	1	0.0	Tempe Union High SD	Tempe, AZ
1	0.0	Grayslake Community High SD 127	Grayslake, IL	1	0.0	Todd County SD 66-1	Mission, SD
1	0.0	Greater New Bedford	New Bedford, MA	1	0.0	Warren Twp	Warren, NJ
1	0.0	Greenwood Public SD	Greenwood, MS	1	0.0	Warren Twp High SD 121	Gages Lake, IL
1	0.0	Gurnee SD 56	Gurnee, IL	1	0.0	Western Pennsylvania Cyber CS	Midland, PA
1	0.0	Hanover Twp	Whippany, NJ	1	0.0	Westwood	Westwood, MA
1	0.0	Highland Park ISD	Dallas, TX	1	0.0	Wilkinson County SD	Woodville, MS
1	0.0	Hinsdale Twp HSD 86	Hinsdale, IL	1	0.0	Wilmette SD 39	Wilmette, IL
1	0.0	Holly Springs SD	Holly Springs, MS	1	0.0	Winchester	Winchester, MA
1	0.0	Homer Community CSD 33c	Homer Glen, IL	1	0.0	Winnetka SD 36	Winnetka, IL
1	0.0	Hopkinton	Hopkinton, MA	1	0.0	Yorkville Community Unit SD 115	Yorkville, IL
1	0.0	Indian Prairie CUSD 204	Aurora, IL	109	<0.1	Newark Unified	Newark, CA
1	0.0	Isaac Elementary District	Phoenix, AZ	109	<0.1	West Morris Regional	Chester, NJ
1	0.0	Jefferson County SD	Fayette, MS	109	<0.1	Wyckoff Twp	Wyckoff, NJ
1	0.0	Jefferson Davis County SD	Prentiss, MS	112	0.1	Acalanes Union High	Lafayette, CA
1	0.0	Keeneyville SD 20	Hanover Park, IL	112	0.1	Cedar Grove Twp	Cedar Grove, NJ
1	0.0	Kinnelon Boro	Kinnelon, NJ	112	0.1	Central Community Unit SD 301	Burlington, IL
1	0.0	Kirby SD 140	Tinley Park, IL	112	0.1	Chagrin Falls Ex Vill SD	Chagrin Falls, OH
1	0.0	Lafayette Elementary	Lafayette, CA	112	0.1	Downers Grove Grade SD 58	Downers Grove, IL
1	0.0	Lake Forest Community HS Dist 115	Lake Forest, IL	112	0.1	Holmdel Twp	Holmdel, NJ
1	0.0	Lake Forest SD 67	Lake Forest, IL	112	0.1	King Philip	Wrentham, MA
1	0.0	Lake Park Community HSD 108	Roselle, IL	112	0.1	Littleton	Littleton, MA
1	0.0	Lamont Elementary	Lamont, CA	112	0.1	Lyford CISD	Lyford, TX

This section ranks 120 school districts at both the "top" and "bottom" of each category for a total of 240 districts per category. The "top" list (descending order) appears first, followed by the "bottom" list (ascending order). Ranking tables cover public school districts serving 1,500 or more students.

Student/Teacher Ratio

School districts ranked in *descending* order

Rank	Ratio	District Name	City, State	Rank	Ratio	District Name	City, State
1	98.1	Northview Public SD	Grand Rapids, MI	60	24.3	King City Joint Union High	King City, CA
2	95.1	Mason Consol Schools (Monroe)	Erie, MI	62	24.2	Alpine SD	American Fork, UT
3	83.0	Peach Springs Unified District	Peach Springs, AZ	62	24.2	Saddleback Valley Unified	Mission Viejo, CA
4	63.6	Galena City SD	Galena, AK	64	24.1	Anderson Union High	Anderson, CA
5	54.2	Lansing Public SD	Lansing, MI	64	24.1	Chino Valley Unified	Chino, CA
6	53.2	Western Pennsylvania Cyber CS	Midland, PA	64	24.1	Corvallis SD 509J	Corvallis, OR
7	46.3	Pennsylvania Virtual CS	Norristown, PA	64	24.1	Hanford Joint Union High	Hanford, CA
8	43.9	North Branch Area Schools	North Branch, MI	64	24.1	Pembroke	Pembroke, MA
9	42.6	Washtenaw ISD	Ann Arbor, MI	64	24.1	Santa Paula Elementary	Santa Paula, CA
10	42.5	Edison-Friendship Public Charter	Washington, DC	64	24.1	Victor Elementary	Victorville, CA
11	39.6	Ohio Virtual Academy	Maumee, OH	71	24.0	Alta Loma Elementary	Alta Loma, CA
12	36.6	Corrections SD 428 Dept of	Springfield, IL	71	24.0	Brawley Union High	Brawley, CA
12	36.6	Electronic Classrm of Tomorrow	Columbus, OH	71	24.0	Central Union High	El Centro, CA
12	36.6	Jackson Public Schools	Jackson, MI	71	24.0	Hesperia Unified	Hesperia, CA
15	34.6	Western Placer Unified	Lincoln, CA	71	24.0	Nebo SD	Spanish Fork, UT
16	34.4	Saginaw ISD	Saginaw, MI	76	23.9	Alisal Union Elementary	Salinas, CA
17	34.2	Highland Park City Schools	Highland Park, MI	76	23.9	Fountain 8	Fountain, CO
18	31.9	Okemos Public Schools	Okemos, MI	76	23.9	Higley Unified District	Higley, AZ
19	31.8	Honors Academy	Dallas, TX	76	23.9	Lincoln County SD	Newport, OR
20	31.4	Butte County Joint District	Arco, ID	76	23.9	Montebello Unified	Montebello, CA
21	30.5	Greenfield Union Elementary	Greenfield, CA	76	23.9	Oregon Trail SD 46	Sandy, OR
22	29.8	Gorman Elementary	Gorman, CA	76	23.9	Shasta Union High	Redding, CA
23	29.0	Fullerton Joint Union High	Fullerton, CA	76	23.9	South Pasadena Unified	South Pasadena, CA
24	27.2	Fern Ridge SD 28J	Elmira, OR	84	23.8	Colorado River Union High SD	Fort Mojave, AZ
24	27.2	Oroville Union High	Oroville, CA	84	23.8	Fountain Valley Elementary	Fountain Valley, CA
26	26.8	Lynwood Unified	Lynwood, CA	84	23.8	Hillsboro SD 1J	Hillsboro, OR
27	26.6	Santa Paula Union High	Santa Paula, CA	84	23.8	Oxford Area Community Schools	Oxford, MI
28	26.4	Antelope Valley Union High	Lancaster, CA	84	23.8	Rim of the World Unified	Lake Arrowhead, CA
29	26.3	Huntington Beach Union High	Huntington Bch, CA	89	23.7	Delano Joint Union High	Delano, CA
30	26.1	Oxnard Union High	Oxnard, CA	89	23.7	Junction City SD 69	Junction City, OR
31	25.9	Banning Unified	Banning, CA	89	23.7	Yucaipa-Calimesa Jt. Unified	Yucaipa, CA
32	25.8	San Benito High	Hollister, CA	92	23.6	Central Elementary	Rcho Cucamong, CA
33	25.7	Gadsden Elementary District	San Luis, AZ	92	23.6	Compton Unified	Compton, CA
33	25.7	Lebanon Community SD 9	Lebanon, OR	92	23.6	Juab SD	Nephi, UT
35	25.6	El Monte Union High	El Monte, CA	92	23.6	Jurupa Unified	Riverside, CA
35	25.6	Victor Valley Union High	Victorville, CA	92	23.6	Las Virgenes Unified	Calabasas, CA
35	25.6	Whittier Union High	Whittier, CA	92	23.6	Livermore Valley Joint Unified	Livermore, CA
38	25.4	Anaheim Union High	Anaheim, CA	92	23.6	San Marcos Unified	San Marcos, CA
39	25.2	Perris Union High	Perris, CA	92	23.6	Southern Kern Unified	Rosamond, CA
39	25.2	William S. Hart Union High	Santa Clarita, CA	100	23.5	Centinela Valley Union High	Lawndale, CA
41	25.0	Alhambra City High	Alhambra, CA	100	23.5	Fremont Union High	Sunnyvale, CA
41	25.0	Campbell Union High	San Jose, CA	100	23.5	Garden Grove Unified	Garden Grove, CA
41	25.0	Eagle Point SD 9	Eagle Point, OR	100	23.5	Merced Union High	Atwater, CA
41	25.0	Santa Cruz City High	Soquel, CA	100	23.5	Placer Union High	Auburn, CA
45	24.9	Tehachapi Unified	Tehachapi, CA	100	23.5	Ramona City Unified	Ramona, CA
46	24.8	Chaffey Joint Union High	Ontario, CA	100	23.5	Romoland Elementary	Homeland, CA
46	24.8	Escondido Union High	Escondido, CA	100	23.5	Sonora Union High	Sonora, CA
48	24.7	Baldwin Park Unified	Baldwin Park, CA	100	23.5	Tustin Unified	Tustin, CA
48	24.7	Charter Oak Unified	Covina, CA	109	23.4	Crown Point Community Sch Corp	Crown Point, IN
48	24.7	Modesto City High	Modesto, CA	109	23.4	Oregon City SD 62	Oregon City, OR
48	24.7	Santa Maria Joint Union High	Santa Maria, CA	111	23.3	Apple Valley Unified	Apple Valley, CA
52	24.6	Central Point SD 6	Central Point, OR	111	23.3	Fontana Unified	Fontana, CA
52	24.6	San Dieguito Union High	Encinitas, CA	111	23.3	Fullerton Elementary	Fullerton, CA
52	24.6	Tulare Joint Union High	Tulare, CA	111	23.3	Glendora Unified	Glendora, CA
55	24.5	Huntington Beach City Elementary	Huntington Bch, CA	111	23.3	Los Alamitos Unified	Los Alamitos, CA
55	24.5	Jordan SD	Sandy, UT	111	23.3	Oro Grande Elementary	Oro Grande, CA
55	24.5	Liberty Union High	Brentwood, CA	117	23.2	Downey Unified	Downey, CA
55	24.5	Palmdale Elementary	Palmdale, CA	117	23.2	El Centro Elementary	El Centro, CA
55	24.5	Val Verde Unified	Perris, CA	117	23.2	Irvine Unified	Irvine, CA
60	24.3	Adelanto Elementary	Adelanto, CA	117	23.2	La Canada Unified	La Canada, CA

This section ranks 120 school districts at both the "top" and "bottom" of each category for a total of 240 districts per category. The "top" list (descending order) appears first, followed by the "bottom" list (ascending order). Ranking tables cover public school districts serving 1,500 or more students.

Student/Teacher Ratio

School districts ranked in *ascending* order

Rank	Ratio	District Name	City, State	Rank	Ratio	District Name	City, State
1	0.6	Specl. Sch. Dst. St. Louis Co.	Town & Ctry, MO	60	10.7	Augusta Public Schools	Augusta, ME
2	3.2	Boces Eastern Suffolk (Suffolk I)	Patchogue, NY	60	10.7	Dryden Central SD	Dryden, NY
3	3.8	Boces Nassau	Garden City, NY	60	10.7	Great Neck Union Free SD	Great Neck, NY
4	5.3	Bergen County Special Service	Paramus, NJ	60	10.7	Harrisonburg City Public Schools	Harrisonburg, VA
5	6.4	Mercer County Special Service	Trenton, NJ	60	10.7	North Slope Borough SD	Barrow, AK
6	7.2	Monmouth County Vocational	Colts Neck, NJ	60	10.7	Phillipsburg Town	Phillipsburg, NJ
7	7.4	Macomb ISD	Clinton Twp, MI	60	10.7	Staunton City Public Schools	Staunton, VA
8	8.1	Burlington County Spec Serv	Mount Holly, NJ	68	10.8	Arlington County Public Schools	Arlington, VA
9	8.4	Watertown	Watertown, MA	68	10.8	Falls Church City Public Schools	Falls Church, VA
10	8.5	Intermediate SD 287	Plymouth, MN	68	10.8	Huber Heights City SD	Huber Heights, OH
11	8.7	Middlesex County Vocational	E Brunswick, NJ	68	10.8	MSAD 03 Unity	Unity, ME
12	8.8	Santa Clara Co Off of Education	San Jose, CA	68	10.8	MSAD 43 Mexico	Mexico, ME
13	9.2	Akron Public Schools	Akron, OH	68	10.8	Mineola Union Free SD	Mineola, NY
13	9.2	Area Coop Educational Services	North Haven, CT	68	10.8	Oyster Bay-East Norwich Central SD	Oyster Bay, NY
15	9.3	El Dorado	El Dorado, KS	68	10.8	Prentiss County SD	Booneville, MS
15	9.3	Pleasantville City	Pleasantville, NJ	68	10.8	Rockville Centre Union Free SD	Rockville Ctre, NY
15	9.3	Red Lake	Red Lake, MN	77	10.9	Bridgeton City	Bridgeton, NJ
18	9.4	Bergen County Vocational	Paramus, NJ	77	10.9	Essex Community Education Ctr	Essex Junction, VT
18	9.4	Leavenworth	Leavenworth, KS	77	10.9	Hartford SD	White River Jct, VT
20	9.7	Asbury Park City	Asbury Park, NJ	77	10.9	Mount Pleasant Central SD	Thornwood, NY
20	9.7	Gloucester City	Gloucester City, NJ	77	10.9	New Brunswick City	New Brunswick, NJ
20	9.7	Keansburg Boro	Keansburg, NJ	77	10.9	Paterson City	Paterson, NJ
23	9.8	Belcourt 7	Belcourt, ND	77	10.9	Wells-Ogunquit CSD	Wells, ME
23	9.8	MSAD 61 Bridgton	Bridgton, ME	77	10.9	Wilkinsburg Borough SD	Wilkinsburg, PA
23	9.8	Mountain Lakes Boro	Mountain Lakes, NJ	85	11.0	Camden City	Camden, NJ
26	9.9	Cambridge	Cambridge, MA	85	11.0	Charlottesville City Pub Schools	Charlottesville, VA
26	9.9	Greater New Bedford	New Bedford, MA	85	11.0	Greene County Public Schools	Stanardsville, VA
28	10.0	Hoboken City	Hoboken, NJ	85	11.0	Hastings-On-Hudson Union Free SD	Hastings-on-Hud, NY
28	10.0	Leonia Boro	Leonia, NJ	85	11.0	Smyth County Public Schools	Marion, VA
28	10.0	Long Branch City	Long Branch, NJ	85	11.0	South Portland School Department	South Portland, ME
28	10.0	MSAD 34 Belfast	Belfast, ME	85	11.0	Syosset Central SD	Syosset, NY
32	10.1	Dunkirk City SD	Dunkirk, NY	92	11.1	Bristol Warren RD	Bristol, RI
32	10.1	Jericho Union Free SD	Jericho, NY	92	11.1	Buchanan County Public Schools	Grundy, VA
32	10.1	Lawrence Union Free SD	Lawrence, NY	92	11.1	East Greenwich SD	East Greenwich, RI
32	10.1	MSAD 09 Farmington	New Sharon, ME	92	11.1	Fredonia Central SD	Fredonia, NY
36	10.2	Ocean City	Ocean City, NJ	92	11.1	Medford	Medford, MA
36	10.2	Southampton Union Free SD	Southampton, NY	92	11.1	North Rose-Wolcott Central SD	Wolcott, NY
38	10.3	Auburn School Department	Auburn, ME	92	11.1	North Shore Central SD	Sea Cliff, NY
38	10.3	Burlington City	Burlington, NJ	92	11.1	Pinelands Regional	Tuckerton, NJ
38	10.3	Capitol Region Education Council	Hartford, CT	92	11.1	San Bernardino Co Off of Education	San Bernardino, CA
38	10.3	Lee County Public Schools	Jonesville, VA	92	11.1	Winfield	Winfield, KS
38	10.3	Plattsburgh City SD	Plattsburgh, NY	102	11.2	Bristol City Public Schools	Bristol, VA
43	10.4	Bath School Department	Bath, ME	102	11.2	Fresno County Office of Education	Fresno, CA
43	10.4	Carle Place Union Free SD	Carle Place, NY	102	11.2	Grayson County Public Schools	Independence, VA
43	10.4	Passaic County Vocational	Wayne, NJ	102	11.2	Greenburgh Central SD	Hartsdale, NY
43	10.4	State Vocational-Technical Schools	Middletown, CT	102	11.2	Harrison Central SD	Harrison, NY
47	10.5	Alexandria City Public Schools	Alexandria, VA	102	11.2	Herricks Union Free SD	New Hyde Park, NY
47	10.5	Beachwood City SD	Beachwood, OH	102	11.2	Holyoke	Holyoke, MA
47	10.5	Elizabeth City	Elizabeth, NJ	102	11.2	King William County Public Schools	King William, VA
47	10.5	Greater Lowell Voc Tec	Tyngsborough, MA	102	11.2	Lindenwold Boro	Lindenwold, NJ
47	10.5	Narragansett SD	Narragansett, RI	102	11.2	MSAD 52 Turner	Turner, ME
47	10.5	Todd County SD 66-1	Mission, SD	102	11.2	MSAD 54 Skowhegan	Skowhegan, ME
47	10.5	Waltham	Waltham, MA	102	11.2	Montgomery County Public Schools	Christiansburg, VA
47	10.5	Warren Twp	Warren, NJ	102	11.2	Pemberton Twp	Pemberton, NJ
47	10.5	Westbrook School Department	Westbrook, ME	102	11.2	Rockbridge County Public Schools	Lexington, VA
47	10.5	Westhampton Beach Union Free SD	Westhampton Bch, NY	102	11.2	Towns County	Hiawassee, GA
57	10.6	MSAD 40 Waldoboro	Warren, ME	102	11.2	Waterville Public Schools	Waterville, ME
57	10.6	Sherburne-Earlville Central SD	Sherburne, NY	118	11.3	Adirondack Central SD	Boonville, NY
57	10.6	Woodbury City	Woodbury, NJ	118	11.3	Colonial Hgts City Public Schools	Colonial Hgts, VA
60	10.7	Aberdeen SD	Aberdeen, MS	118	11.3	Lebanon SD	Lebanon, NH

This section ranks 120 school districts at both the "top" and "bottom" of each category for a total of 240 districts per category. The "top" list (descending order) appears first, followed by the "bottom" list (ascending order). Ranking tables cover public school districts serving 1,500 or more students.

Student/Librarian Ratio

School districts ranked in *descending* order

Rank	Ratio	District Name	City, State		Rank	Ratio	District Name	City, State
1	88,150.0	Campbell County Public Schools	Rustburg, VA		61	7,405.6	Fremont Unified	Fremont, CA
2	69,746.7	Jurupa Unified	Riverside, CA		62	7,343.8	Peoria Unified SD	Glendale, AZ
3	67,213.3	Escondido Union Elementary	Escondido, CA		63	7,301.4	Tracy Joint Unified	Tracy, CA
4	54,235.0	Lucia Mar Unified	Arroyo Grande, CA		64	7,294.5	San Marcos Unified	San Marcos, CA
5	49,746.0	Capistrano Unified	San Juan Capis, CA		65	7,273.0	New Bedford	New Bedford, MA
6	41,850.0	Milford	Milford, MA		66	7,247.0	Jackson Public Schools	Jackson, MI
7	41,343.0	Fontana Unified	Fontana, CA		67	7,234.7	Victor Valley Union High	Victorville, CA
8	36,046.7	Antioch Unified	Antioch, CA		68	7,196.5	Natomas Unified	Sacramento, CA
9	23,272.0	Oak Grove Elementary	San Jose, CA		69	7,127.5	Temple City Unified	Temple City, CA
10	22,588.0	Etiwanda Elementary	Etiwanda, CA		70	7,110.0	Charter Oak Unified	Covina, CA
11	20,083.3	North Monterey County Unified	Moss Landing, CA		71	7,046.7	Live Oak Elementary	Santa Cruz, CA
12	19,287.0	Baldwin Park Unified	Baldwin Park, CA		72	7,019.5	Pleasanton Unified	Pleasanton, CA
13	19,272.7	San Bernardino City Unified	San Bernardino, CA		73	7,010.0	Barstow Unified	Barstow, CA
14	18,384.0	Rowland Unified	Rowland Heights, CA		74	7,002.5	Sierra Sands Unified	Ridgecrest, CA
15	16,687.5	Santa Maria Joint Union High	Santa Maria, CA		75	6,987.0	Wachusett	Jefferson, MA
16	16,463.0	Lansing Public SD	Lansing, MI		76	6,850.0	Culver City Unified	Culver City, CA
17	16,243.0	Compton Unified	Compton, CA		77	6,846.0	Claremont Unified	Claremont, CA
18	14,765.3	Antelope Valley Union High	Lancaster, CA		78	6,842.0	Washington Unified	West Sacramento, CA
19	14,621.0	Coachella Valley Unified	Thermal, CA		79	6,828.0	Ukiah Unified	Ukiah, CA
20	14,544.6	San Juan Unified	Carmichael, CA		80	6,631.4	Lodi Unified	Lodi, CA
21	13,963.3	Amherst Ex Vill SD	Amherst, OH		81	6,578.0	Monrovia Unified	Monrovia, CA
22	13,963.0	Panama Buena Vista Union Elem	Bakersfield, CA		82	6,551.7	Big Spring ISD	Big Spring, TX
23	13,887.0	Vacaville Unified	Vacaville, CA		83	6,530.5	Desert Sands Unified	La Quinta, CA
24	13,585.0	Upland Unified	Upland, CA		84	6,486.0	Klamath County SD	Klamath Falls, OR
25	12,749.5	Hacienda La Puente Unified	City of Industry, CA		85	6,441.0	Manhattan Beach Unified	Manhattan Beach, CA
26	12,629.0	Visalia Unified	Visalia, CA		86	6,379.0	Danville CCSD 118	Danville, IL
27	12,574.8	Santa Ana Unified	Santa Ana, CA		87	6,333.0	Round Lake Area Schs - Dist 116	Round Lake, IL
28	12,557.0	Whittier Union High	Whittier, CA		88	6,159.0	Redmond SD 2J	Redmond, OR
29	12,556.4	Fullerton Elementary	Fullerton, CA		89	6,082.0	Selma Unified	Selma, CA
30	11,829.0	Los Angeles Co Office of Education	Downey, CA		90	5,917.0	Maywood-Melrose Park-Broadview-89	Melrose Park, IL
31	11,113.3	Chino Valley Unified	Chino, CA		91	5,903.0	Northmont City SD	Englewood, OH
32	10,999.5	Corona-Norco Unified	Norco, CA		92	5,838.0	Shasta Union High	Redding, CA
33	10,863.5	Simi Valley Unified	Simi Valley, CA		93	5,826.7	Murrieta Valley Unified	Murrieta, CA
34	10,656.3	Los Angeles Unified	Los Angeles, CA		94	5,796.7	Sanger Unified	Sanger, CA
35	10,621.0	Alameda City Unified	Alameda, CA		95	5,779.5	Lompoc Unified	Lompoc, CA
36	10,192.0	Mountain View Elementary	El Monte, CA		96	5,749.0	Madera Unified	Madera, CA
37	10,056.0	Penn-Harris-Madison Sch Corp	Mishawaka, IN		97	5,735.0	Blackstone-Millville	Blackstone, MA
38	9,992.0	Arcadia Unified	Arcadia, CA		98	5,718.2	Porterville Unified	Porterville, CA
39	9,970.0	Rio Linda Union Elementary	Rio Linda, CA		99	5,679.0	Bethel SD 52	Eugene, OR
40	9,918.0	Beaumont Unified	Beaumont, CA		100	5,676.0	Forest Grove SD 15	Forest Grove, OR
41	9,829.0	Lynwood Unified	Lynwood, CA		101	5,674.3	Napa Valley Unified	Napa, CA
42	9,591.0	Pittsburg Unified	Pittsburg, CA		102	5,656.8	Manteca Unified	Manteca, CA
43	9,580.0	Indian Valley Local SD	Gnadenhutten, OH		103	5,621.0	Oceanside Unified	Oceanside, CA
44	9,475.0	Tustin Unified	Tustin, CA		104	5,618.0	Rim of the World Unified	Lake Arrowhead, CA
45	8,924.7	Placentia-Yorba Linda Unified	Placentia, CA		105	5,575.0	Dysart Unified District	El Mirage, AZ
46	8,880.0	Morgan Hill Unified	Morgan Hill, CA		106	5,545.0	Sweetwater ISD	Sweetwater, TX
47	8,853.0	Pomona Unified	Pomona, CA		107	5,542.0	Dinuba Unified	Dinuba, CA
48	8,837.3	Saddleback Valley Unified	Mission Viejo, CA		108	5,541.3	Colton Joint Unified	Colton, CA
49	8,570.0	Bear Valley Unified	Big Bear Lake, CA		109	5,531.0	Kalamazoo Public SD	Kalamazoo, MI
50	8,409.7	Torrance Unified	Torrance, CA		110	5,517.0	Atascadero Unified	Atascadero, CA
51	8,406.2	Oakland Unified	Oakland, CA		111	5,507.3	Brighton 27J	Brighton, CO
52	8,160.0	Orange Grove ISD	Orange Grove, TX		112	5,504.8	Chico Unified	Chico, CA
53	8,152.0	Grossmont Union High	La Mesa, CA		113	5,473.0	Dekalb Community Unit SD 428	De Kalb, IL
54	8,057.0	Redondo Beach Unified	Redondo Beach, CA		114	5,444.0	Rockland	Rockland, MA
55	7,951.0	Alisal Union Elementary	Salinas, CA		115	5,296.7	Buna ISD	Buna, TX
56	7,924.0	Glendora Unified	Glendora, CA		116	5,259.5	South-Western City SD	Grove City, OH
57	7,910.0	Placer Union High	Auburn, CA		117	5,257.5	Woodland Joint Unified	Woodland, CA
58	7,832.0	Temecula Valley Unified	Temecula, CA		118	5,241.0	Prescott Unified District	Prescott, AZ
59	7,421.0	Newark Unified	Newark, CA		119	5,236.0	Humboldt Unified District	Prescott Valley, AZ
60	7,414.3	Conejo Valley Unified	Thousand Oaks, CA		120	5,213.3	Bullard ISD	Bullard, TX

This section ranks 120 school districts at both the "top" and "bottom" of each category for a total of 240 districts per category. The "top" list (descending order) appears first, followed by the "bottom" list (ascending order). Ranking tables cover public school districts serving 1,500 or more students.

Student/Librarian Ratio

School districts ranked in *ascending* order

Rank	Ratio	District Name	City, State	Rank	Ratio	District Name	City, State
1	120.3	Specl. Sch. Dst. St. Louis Co.	Town & Ctry, MO	61	363.8	Malvern SD	Malvern, AR
2	231.6	Conecuh County	Evergreen, AL	62	363.9	Moss Point Separate SD	Moss Point, MS
3	240.6	Avery County Schools	Newland, NC	63	364.3	Oneida City SD	Oneida, NY
4	277.8	Aberdeen SD	Aberdeen, MS	64	365.1	Magoffin County	Salyersville, KY
5	281.8	Grayson County Public Schools	Independence, VA	65	366.0	Batesville SD	Batesville, AR
6	289.4	Lebanon SD	Lebanon, NH	66	366.3	Currituck County Schools	Currituck, NC
7	294.0	Mohawk Trail	Shelburne Falls, MA	67	366.4	Lincoln Parish School Board	Ruston, LA
8	297.1	Western Line SD	Avon, MS	68	367.0	Chapel Hill-Carrboro Schools	Chapel Hill, NC
9	298.8	Circle	Towanda, KS	69	367.6	W Harvey-Dixmoor PS Dist 147	Harvey, IL
10	303.2	Cameron Parish School Board	Cameron, LA	70	368.2	Elizabethton City SD	Elizabethton, TN
11	306.2	Monmouth Unit SD 38	Monmouth, IL	71	368.5	Cedar Grove Twp	Cedar Grove, NJ
12	310.2	Coahoma County SD	Clarksdale, MS	72	369.4	Missoula Elem	Missoula, MT
13	312.6	Wilkinson County SD	Woodville, MS	73	370.8	Buhler	Buhler, KS
14	313.4	Regional SD 18	Old Lyme, CT	74	370.9	Adair County	Columbia, KY
15	313.5	Choctaw County SD	Ackerman, MS	75	372.5	Mayfield Independent	Mayfiel, KY
16	316.5	Prentiss County SD	Booneville, MS	76	373.8	Tunica County SD	Tunica, MS
17	318.5	Yancey County Schools	Burnsville, NC	77	374.3	Monroe County	Tompkinsville, KY
18	319.9	Clayton	Clayton, MO	78	374.6	Central R-III	Park Hills, MO
19	321.3	Fayette County SD	Somerville, TN	78	374.6	Columbia SD	Columbia, MS
20	325.1	Dickenson County Public Schools	Clintwood, VA	80	375.3	Santa Cruz City Elementary	Soquel, CA
20	325.1	Jackson County	Mckee, KY	81	375.4	Billings Elem	Billings, MT
22	325.6	Rockbridge County Public Schools	Lexington, VA	81	375.4	Smithville R-II	Smithville, MO
23	327.3	Cleveland SD	Cleveland, MS	83	375.5	Bay St Louis Waveland SD	Bay St Louis, MS
24	328.8	Clay County	Manchester, KY	83	375.5	Sunflower County SD	Indianola, MS
25	331.0	San Juan SD	Blanding, UT	85	375.8	Henderson County SD	Lexington, TN
26	331.2	Ashdown SD	Ashdown, AR	85	375.8	Red Lake	Red Lake, MN
27	331.7	Buchanan County Public Schools	Grundy, VA	87	376.0	Iola	Iola, KS
28	333.6	Mitchell County Schools	Bakersville, NC	87	376.0	Webster County SD	Eupora, MS
29	335.0	Osceola SD	Osceola, AR	89	376.6	Stuttgart SD	Stuttgart, AR
29	335.0	School of the Osage R-II	Lake Ozark, MO	90	377.3	Libby K-12 Schools	Libby, MT
31	335.3	Winnetka SD 36	Winnetka, IL	91	377.5	Buckingham County Public Schools	Buckingham, VA
32	336.0	Athens City Elementary SD	Athens, TN	92	378.2	Perry County	Hazard, KY
33	336.3	Kalispell Elem	Kalispell, MT	93	378.3	Northampton County Schools	Jackson, NC
34	339.3	Lee County Public Schools	Jonesville, VA	94	378.9	Anniston City	Anniston, AL
35	339.5	Scott County Public Schools	Gate City, VA	95	379.2	Locust Valley Central SD	Locust Valley, NY
36	340.8	Louisville Municipal SD	Louisville, MS	96	379.8	Concordia Parish School Board	Vidalia, LA
37	341.1	Morgan County R-II	Versailles, MO	97	382.0	Cherokee County Schools	Murphy, NC
38	344.4	Winston County	Double Springs, AL	97	382.0	Daingerfield-Lone Star Is	Daingerfield, TX
39	346.8	South Pike SD	Magnolia, MS	99	383.0	Waynesville R-VI	Waynesville, MO
40	347.5	Kosciusko SD	Kosciusko, MS	100	383.6	Walthall County SD	Tylertown, MS
41	347.9	Robeson County Schools	Lumberton, NC	101	385.3	Alleghany County Schools	Sparta, NC
42	349.2	MSAD 40 Waldoboro	Warren, ME	102	385.6	Hartford SD	White River Jct, VT
43	350.6	Danville Independent	Danville, KY	102	385.6	Lasalle Parish School Board	Jena, LA
44	351.8	Martin County Schools	Williamston, NC	104	385.8	Dollarway SD	Pine Bluff, AR
45	352.9	Madison Boro	Madison, NJ	105	385.9	Asheville City Schools	Asheville, NC
46	353.6	Summit Re-1	Frisco, CO	106	386.0	Athens City	Athens, AL
47	353.9	W Baton Rouge Parish SB	Port Allen, LA	106	386.0	Bertie County Schools	Windsor, NC
48	355.6	Union County SD	New Albany, MS	108	387.0	Elk Rapids Schools	Elk Rapids, MI
49	356.2	Scott County SD	Forest, MS	109	387.1	Greenup County	Greenup, KY
49	356.2	Wythe County Public Schools	Wytheville, VA	110	387.2	Northborough	Northborough, MA
51	357.0	Oneonta City SD	Oneonta, NY	111	387.3	Bristol City Public Schools	Bristol, VA
52	357.3	North Panola Schools	Sardis, MS	112	387.8	Forrest County SD	Hattiesburg, MS
53	357.6	Cushing	Cushing, OK	112	387.8	Seminole	Seminole, OK
54	358.4	Lincoln County SD	Brookhaven, MS	114	388.1	Sabine Parish School Board	Many, LA
55	359.2	Breathitt County	Jackson, KY	115	389.4	Harlan County	Harlan, KY
56	359.6	Decatur City	Decatur, GA	116	389.7	Selma City	Selma, AL
57	360.7	Augusta	Augusta, KS	117	390.4	Choctaw County	Butler, AL
58	361.8	Ashland Ind	Ashland, KY	118	390.5	Tonawanda City SD	Tonawanda, NY
59	362.8	Uinta County SD #1	Evanston, WY	119	390.6	Watauga County Schools	Boone, NC
60	363.2	Clinton	Clinton, OK	120	390.7	Ladue	St Louis, MO

This section ranks 120 school districts at both the "top" and "bottom" of each category for a total of 240 districts per category. The "top" list (descending order) appears first, followed by the "bottom" list (ascending order). Ranking tables cover public school districts serving 1,500 or more students.

Student/Counselor Ratio

School districts ranked in *descending* order

Rank	Ratio	District Name	City, State	Rank	Ratio	District Name	City, State
1	44,075.0	Campbell County Public Schools	Rustburg, VA	61	3,126.0	Fowler Elementary District	Phoenix, AZ
2	21,963.0	Anaheim Elementary	Anaheim, CA	62	3,122.0	Harvey SD 152	Harvey, IL
3	20,408.0	Saugus Union Elementary	Santa Clarita, CA	63	3,075.0	Belmont-Redwood Shores Elementary	Belmont, CA
4	14,975.0	Huntington Beach Union High	Huntington Bch, CA	64	3,071.0	Santa Rita Union Elementary	Salinas, CA
5	12,403.3	Alhambra City Elementary	Alhambra, CA	65	2,989.6	Schaumburg CCSD 54	Schaumburg, IL
6	10,973.3	Garvey Elementary	Rosemead, CA	66	2,976.0	Keppel Union Elementary	Pearblossom, CA
7	9,715.0	Encinitas Union Elementary	Encinitas, CA	67	2,948.3	Maricopa County Regional District	Phoenix, AZ
8	8,834.0	Redwood City Elementary	Redwood City, CA	68	2,940.0	Arvin Union Elementary	Arvin, CA
9	8,575.0	Bellevue Union Elementary	Santa Rosa, CA	69	2,906.0	Mt. Pleasant Elementary	San Jose, CA
10	8,382.0	Creighton Elementary District	Phoenix, AZ	70	2,872.3	Orange County Office of Education	Costa Mesa, CA
11	8,231.5	Lansing Public SD	Lansing, MI	71	2,854.0	Casa Grande Elementary District	Casa Grande, AZ
12	7,928.0	Goleta Union Elementary	Goleta, CA	72	2,810.2	Chula Vista Elementary	Chula Vista, CA
13	7,826.7	Santa Rosa Elementary	Santa Rosa, CA	73	2,801.0	Cambrian Elementary	San Jose, CA
14	7,024.0	Wheeling CCSD 21	Wheeling, IL	74	2,796.0	Bethalto CUSD 8	Bethalto, IL
15	6,629.0	Glendale Elementary District	Glendale, AZ	75	2,780.0	Phoenix Elementary District	Phoenix, AZ
16	6,242.0	Hollister SD	Hollister, CA	76	2,756.4	Alum Rock Union Elementary	San Jose, CA
17	6,162.5	Linden Unified	Linden, CA	77	2,659.2	Marysville Joint Unified	Marysville, CA
18	6,007.8	Antioch Unified	Antioch, CA	78	2,630.1	Mt. Diablo Unified	Concord, CA
19	5,956.0	Richland Union Elementary SD	Shafter, CA	79	2,626.5	Madison Elementary District	Phoenix, AZ
20	5,684.0	Palmdale Elementary	Palmdale, CA	80	2,610.0	Little Lake City Elementary	Santa Fe Spgs, CA
21	5,236.4	Capistrano Unified	San Juan Capis, CA	81	2,595.0	King City Union Elementary	King City, CA
22	5,213.0	Electronic Classrm of Tomorrow	Columbus, OH	82	2,587.0	Murphy Elementary District	Phoenix, AZ
23	5,096.0	Mountain View Elementary	El Monte, CA	83	2,563.5	San Ysidro Elementary	San Ysidro, CA
24	5,064.0	Benton Harbor Area Schools	Benton Harbor, MI	84	2,525.9	Palatine CCSD 15	Palatine, IL
25	5,019.0	Ravenswood City Elementary	East Palo Alto, CA	85	2,483.0	Cartwright Elementary District	Phoenix, AZ
26	4,902.5	Victor Elementary	Victorville, CA	86	2,477.7	Westside Union Elementary	Lancaster, CA
27	4,640.0	Moraga Elementary	Moraga, CA	87	2,416.0	Tehachapi Unified	Tehachapi, CA
28	4,501.7	Ontario-Montclair Elementary	Ontario, CA	88	2,385.0	Los Nietos Elementary	Whittier, CA
29	4,487.0	Oakley Union Elementary	Oakley, CA	89	2,382.0	Atwater Elementary	Atwater, CA
30	4,344.3	Selma Unified	Selma, CA	90	2,363.0	Coopersville Public SD	Coopersville, MI
31	4,264.0	Eureka Union Elementary	Granite Bay, CA	91	2,341.0	Saddleback Valley Unified	Mission Viejo, CA
32	4,254.0	Hueneme Elementary	Port Hueneme, CA	92	2,333.9	National Elementary	National City, CA
33	4,248.0	Elmont Union Free SD	Elmont, NY	93	2,331.3	Bonsall Union Elementary	Bonsall, CA
34	4,081.7	Savanna Elementary	Anaheim, CA	94	2,330.0	Hilmar Unified	Hilmar, CA
35	4,028.0	CCSD 181	Hinsdale, IL	95	2,329.0	Alpine Union Elementary	Alpine, CA
36	3,953.3	East Maine SD 63	Des Plaines, IL	96	2,327.4	Washington Elementary District	Phoenix, AZ
37	3,918.0	Addison SD 4	Addison, IL	97	2,293.0	Newman-Crows Landing Unified	Newman, CA
38	3,834.6	Rio Linda Union Elementary	Rio Linda, CA	98	2,283.0	Ridgeland SD 122	Oak Lawn, IL
39	3,820.0	SD 45 Dupage County	Villa Park, IL	99	2,275.2	Sacramento City Unified	Sacramento, CA
40	3,761.0	Enterprise Elementary	Redding, CA	100	2,274.0	Lyons SD 103	Lyons, IL
41	3,731.0	Campbell Union Elementary	Campbell, CA	101	2,273.5	Union Elementary	San Jose, CA
42	3,687.3	Kalamazoo Public SD	Kalamazoo, MI	102	2,270.0	Dassel-Cokato	Cokato, MN
43	3,647.3	Cupertino Union School	Cupertino, CA	103	2,241.0	Oxford	Oxford, MA
44	3,634.7	Fullerton Elementary	Fullerton, CA	104	2,240.4	Escondido Union Elementary	Escondido, CA
45	3,514.0	San Diego Co Office of Education	San Diego, CA	105	2,219.0	Mundelein Elem SD 75	Mundelein, IL
46	3,510.0	Mohave Valley Elementary District	Mohave Valley, AZ	106	2,214.1	Lakeside Union Elementary	Lakeside, CA
47	3,490.8	Panama Buena Vista Union Elem	Bakersfield, CA	107	2,210.5	North Shore SD 112	Highland Park, IL
48	3,487.0	Kildeer Countryside CCSD 96	Buffalo Grove, IL	108	2,202.0	Park Ridge CCSD 64	Park Ridge, IL
49	3,485.5	Magnolia Elementary	Anaheim, CA	109	2,182.0	Taft City Elementary	Taft, CA
50	3,482.0	Mountain View Elementary	Ontario, CA	110	2,171.0	Muskegon Heights SD	Muskegon Hgts, MI
51	3,471.0	Chicago Heights SD 170	Chicago Heights, IL	111	2,168.0	Kingsburg Elementary Charter	Kingsburg, CA
52	3,346.7	Wiseburn Elementary	Hawthorne, CA	112	2,161.3	Lawndale Elementary	Lawndale, CA
53	3,346.3	Cajon Valley Union Elementary	El Cajon, CA	113	2,143.0	Baldwin Park Unified	Baldwin Park, CA
54	3,345.0	Walnut Creek Elementary	Walnut Creek, CA	114	2,123.4	Tulare City Elementary	Tulare, CA
55	3,336.0	Newhall Elementary	Valencia, CA	115	2,118.1	Lafayette Elementary	Lafayette, CA
56	3,184.2	Livermore Valley Joint Unified	Livermore, CA	116	2,116.0	Rosedale Union Elementary	Bakersfield, CA
57	3,169.0	Pacifica SD	Pacifica, CA	117	2,112.0	Queen Bee SD 16	Glendale Hgts, IL
58	3,157.0	Deerfield SD 109	Deerfield, IL	118	2,111.0	Round Lake Area Schs - Dist 116	Round Lake, IL
59	3,135.0	Waterford Unified	Waterford, CA	119	2,096.0	Millbrae Elementary	Millbrae, CA
60	3,133.0	Fruitvale Elementary	Bakersfield, CA	120	2,092.0	Gladwin Community Schools	Gladwin, MI

This section ranks 120 school districts at both the "top" and "bottom" of each category for a total of 240 districts per category. The "top" list (descending order) appears first, followed by the "bottom" list (ascending order). Ranking tables cover public school districts serving 1,500 or more students.

Student/Counselor Ratio

School districts ranked in *ascending* order

Rank	Ratio	District Name	City, State	Rank	Ratio	District Name	City, State
1	89.2	Monmouth County Vocational	Colts Neck, NJ	61	210.4	Claremont SD	Claremont, NH
2	112.7	Specl. Sch. Dst. St. Louis Co.	Town & Ctry, MO	62	212.2	Lafayette Parish School Board	Lafayette, LA
3	141.6	Todd County SD 66-1	Mission, SD	63	212.8	Northern Burlington Reg	Columbus, NJ
4	145.1	Passaic County Vocational	Wayne, NJ	63	212.8	Norwich Free Academy	Norwich, CT
5	149.5	E Baton Rouge Parish SB	Baton Rouge, LA	65	213.4	Watchung Hills Regional	Warren, NJ
6	151.4	Mount Anthony UHSD 14	Bennington, VT	66	213.9	Essex County Voc-Tech	West Orange, NJ
7	152.1	Salem SD	Salem, NH	66	213.9	Natrona County SD #1	Casper, WY
8	152.7	Camden County Vocational	Sicklerville, NJ	68	214.0	Cameron Parish School Board	Cameron, LA
9	155.6	Bergen County Vocational	Paramus, NJ	69	214.1	Allen Parish School Board	Oberlin, LA
10	156.4	N Hunt/Voorhees Regional	Annandale, NJ	70	214.7	Black Horse Pike Regional	Blackwood, NJ
11	158.2	Sweetwater County SD #1	Rock Springs, WY	70	214.7	Jefferson Parish School Board	Harvey, LA
12	158.5	City of Bogalusa School Board	Bogalusa, LA	72	215.5	Rutland City SD	Rutland, VT
13	159.0	Boces Eastern Suffolk (Suffolk I)	Patchogue, NY	73	215.9	Westhampton Beach Union Free SD	Westhampton Bch, NY
14	161.3	Ascension Parish School Board	Donaldsonville, LA	74	216.0	Plaquemines Parish School Board	Port Sulphur, LA
15	163.1	Lafourche Parish School Board	Thibodaux, LA	75	216.9	Lake Forest Community HS Dist 115	Lake Forest, IL
16	164.7	Albany County SD #1	Laramie, WY	76	217.0	Kingsway Regional	Woolwich Twp, NJ
17	165.1	Laconia SD	Laconia, NH	77	217.3	Waterville Public Schools	Waterville, ME
18	165.6	Saint Tammany Parish School Board	Covington, LA	78	218.6	Park County SD # 6	Cody, WY
19	167.1	Community High SD 128	Libertyville, IL	79	218.7	Avery County Schools	Newland, NC
20	167.8	Caddo Parish School Board	Shreveport, LA	80	218.8	Auburn School Department	Auburn, ME
20	167.8	Morris Hills Regional	Rockaway, NJ	80	218.8	Dansville Central SD	Dansville, NY
22	169.8	Essex Community Education Ctr	Essex Junction, VT	82	218.9	Newfound Area SD	Bristol, NH
23	170.5	Milton Id SD	Milton, VT	82	218.9	Pinelands Regional	Tuckerton, NJ
23	170.5	State Vocational-Technical Schools	Middletown, CT	84	219.4	Mountain Grove R-III	Mountain Grove, MO
25	173.2	Washington Parish School Board	Franklinton, LA	85	220.5	MSAD 34 Belfast	Belfast, ME
26	175.8	Regional SD 05	Woodbridge, CT	86	221.1	Jefferson Davis Parish SB	Jennings, LA
27	176.5	Saint John the Baptist Parish SB	Reserve, LA	86	221.1	Southampton Union Free SD	Southampton, NY
28	176.9	Ramapo-Indian Hill Reg	Franklin Lakes, NJ	88	221.3	Converse County SD #1	Douglas, WY
29	179.7	Portsmouth SD	Portsmouth, NH	89	221.9	Vineland City	Vineland, NJ
30	183.9	West Morris Regional	Chester, NJ	89	221.9	Wayne Central SD	Ontario Center, NY
31	185.3	Vermilion Parish School Board	Abbeville, LA	91	222.0	Sewanhaka Central High SD	Floral Park, NY
32	187.1	Hunterdon Central Reg	Flemington, NJ	92	222.1	Clinton County	Albany, KY
33	187.2	Hartford SD	White River Jct, VT	93	223.3	Park County SD # 1	Powell, WY
34	187.3	Webster Parish School Board	Minden, LA	94	223.5	MSAD 52 Turner	Turner, ME
35	189.1	Salamanca City SD	Salamanca, NY	95	224.9	Burlington SD	Burlington, VT
36	191.6	Sheridan County SD #2	Sheridan, WY	95	224.9	Livingston ISD	Livingston, TX
37	192.7	Northern Valley Regional	Demarest, NJ	97	225.1	Acton-Boxborough	Acton, MA
38	193.0	Acadia Parish School Board	Crowley, LA	98	225.2	Pinkerton Academy SD	Derry, NH
39	193.3	MSAD 03 Unity	Unity, ME	99	225.3	Sanborn Regional SD	Kingston, NH
40	194.0	Fremont County SD #25	Riverton, WY	99	225.3	Springfield Twp	Springfield, NJ
40	194.0	Keene SD	Keene, NH	101	226.1	Campbell County SD #1	Gillette, WY
42	194.9	Evanston Twp HSD 202	Evanston, IL	102	226.3	Brewer School Department	Brewer, ME
43	195.1	Township High SD 113	Highland Park, IL	103	226.5	Saint Mary Parish School Board	Centerville, LA
44	196.0	Mundelein Cons High SD 120	Mundelein, IL	104	227.3	City of Monroe School Board	Monroe, LA
45	197.4	East Feliciana Parish School Board	Clinton, LA	104	227.3	Pointe Coupee Parish School Board	New Roads, LA
46	198.1	Eastern Camden County Reg	Voorhees, NJ	106	227.4	Northfield Twp High SD 225	Glenview, IL
47	200.1	Rapides Parish School Board	Alexandria, LA	107	228.1	Nauset	Orleans, MA
48	200.2	Lenape Regional	Shamong, NJ	108	228.7	Pearsall ISD	Pearsall, TX
49	200.3	Burlington County Vocational	Westampton Twp, NJ	109	229.0	Adlai E Stevenson Dist 125	Lincolnshire, IL
50	200.5	Pascack Valley Regional	Montvale, NJ	109	229.0	Carroll County	Carrollton, KY
51	203.8	Sweetwater County SD #2	Green River, WY	109	229.0	Iberia Parish School Board	New Iberia, LA
52	204.1	Amherst-Pelham	Amherst, MA	112	230.3	Oneonta City SD	Oneonta, NY
53	204.8	Township High SD 214	Arlington Hgts, IL	113	230.6	Indian Hill Ex Vill SD	Cincinnati, OH
54	206.1	Fremont County SD # 1	Lander, WY	114	231.1	South Portland School Department	South Portland, ME
55	206.4	Goshen County SD #1	Torrington, WY	115	232.0	Greater New Bedford	New Bedford, MA
56	207.0	Oyster River Coop SD	Durham, NH	116	232.3	Ironton City SD	Ironton, OH
57	207.6	Masconomet	Topsfield, MA	117	232.4	Elgin Local SD	Marion, OH
58	208.9	Terrebonne Parish School Board	Houma, LA	117	232.4	Mcallen ISD	Mcallen, TX
59	209.8	Exeter Region Cooperative SD	Exeter, NH	119	233.0	Red River Parish School Board	Coushatta, LA
60	210.2	Lebanon SD	Lebanon, NH	120	233.2	Board of Ed of Kent County	Chestertown, MD

This section ranks 120 school districts at both the "top" and "bottom" of each category for a total of 240 districts per category. The "top" list (descending order) appears first, followed by the "bottom" list (ascending order). Ranking tables cover public school districts serving 1,500 or more students.

Current Spending per Student in FY2003
School districts ranked in *descending* order

Rank	Dollars	District Name	City, State
1	71,341	Gorman Elementary	Gorman, CA
2	63,340	Santa Clara Co Off of Education	San Jose, CA
3	54,368	Tulare County Office of Education	Visalia, CA
4	45,766	San Bernardino Co Off of Education	San Bernardino, CA
5	45,427	San Diego Co Office of Education	San Diego, CA
6	41,852	Riverside Co Office of Education	Riverside, CA
7	40,267	Los Angeles Co Office of Education	Downey, CA
8	39,428	Bergen County Special Service	Paramus, NJ
9	38,535	Kern County Office of Education	Bakersfield, CA
10	35,115	Fresno County Office of Education	Fresno, CA
11	32,907	Mercer County Special Service	Trenton, NJ
12	31,812	Burlington County Spec Serv	Mount Holly, NJ
13	31,262	San Joaquin Co Off of Education	Stockton, CA
14	24,805	Bergen County Vocational	Paramus, NJ
15	22,784	Asbury Park City	Asbury Park, NJ
16	22,637	North Slope Borough SD	Barrow, AK
17	22,131	Westwood Unified	Westwood, CA
18	21,614	Monmouth County Vocational	Colts Neck, NJ
19	21,067	Oyster Bay-East Norwich Central SD	Oyster Bay, NY
20	20,835	Cambridge	Cambridge, MA
21	20,689	Southampton Union Free SD	Southampton, NY
22	20,642	Hoboken City	Hoboken, NJ
23	20,639	Manhasset Union Free SD	Manhasset, NY
24	20,350	Middlesex County Vocational	E Brunswick, NJ
25	20,319	Bering Strait SD	Unalakleet, AK
26	20,305	Mineola Union Free SD	Mineola, NY
27	20,216	Lawrence Union Free SD	Lawrence, NY
28	19,950	Greenburgh Central SD	Hartsdale, NY
29	19,936	Roslyn Union Free SD	Roslyn, NY
30	19,799	Great Neck Union Free SD	Great Neck, NY
31	19,771	Jericho Union Free SD	Jericho, NY
32	19,455	Locust Valley Central SD	Locust Valley, NY
33	19,392	North Shore Central SD	Sea Cliff, NY
34	19,113	Passaic County Vocational	Wayne, NJ
35	19,083	Pascack Valley Regional	Montvale, NJ
36	18,841	East Williston Union Free SD	Old Westbury, NY
37	18,756	Northern Valley Regional	Demarest, NJ
38	18,577	Carle Place Union Free SD	Carle Place, NY
39	18,517	Newark City	Newark, NJ
40	18,508	Harrison Central SD	Harrison, NY
41	18,489	Orange County Office of Education	Costa Mesa, CA
42	18,418	White Plains City SD	White Plains, NY
43	18,192	Northwest Arctic SD	Kotzebue, AK
44	18,180	New Brunswick City	New Brunswick, NJ
45	18,010	Bedford Central SD	Mount Kisco, NY
46	17,826	Township High SD 113	Highland Park, IL
47	17,822	Briarcliff Manor Union Free SD	Briarcliff Manor, NY
48	17,805	Englewood City	Englewood, NJ
49	17,705	Huntington Union Free SD	Huntington Stn, NY
50	17,632	Evanston Twp HSD 202	Evanston, IL
51	17,527	Hewlett-Woodmere Union Free SD	Woodmere, NY
52	17,511	Port Washington Union Free SD	Pt Washington, NY
53	17,415	Schalmont Central SD	Schenectady, NY
54	17,371	Syosset Central SD	Syosset, NY
55	17,270	Trenton City	Trenton, NJ
56	17,088	Long Beach City SD	Long Beach, NY
57	17,048	Lower Kuskokwim SD	Bethel, AK
58	17,024	Camden County Vocational	Sicklerville, NJ
59	16,955	Wyandanch Union Free SD	Wyandanch, NY
60	16,952	Beachwood City SD	Beachwood, OH
61	16,867	Scarsdale Union Free SD	Scarsdale, NY
62	16,829	E Ramapo Central SD (Sprg Valley)	Spring Valley, NY
63	16,786	Mount Pleasant Central SD	Thornwood, NY
64	16,766	Onteora Central SD	Boiceville, NY
65	16,643	Malverne Union Free SD	Malverne, NY
66	16,634	Julian Union High	Julian, CA
67	16,562	East Hampton Union Free SD	East Hampton, NY
68	16,514	Nanuet Union Free SD	Nanuet, NY
69	16,491	Keansburg Boro	Keansburg, NJ
70	16,487	Plainview-Old Bethpage Central SD	Plainview, NY
71	16,452	Pleasantville City	Pleasantville, NJ
72	16,421	Roosevelt Union Free SD	Roosevelt, NY
73	16,420	Peekskill City SD	Peekskill, NY
74	16,413	Central Islip Union Free SD	Central Islip, NY
75	16,376	Lower Merion SD	Ardmore, PA
76	16,303	Nyack Union Free SD	Nyack, NY
77	16,299	Katonah-Lewisboro Union Free SD	South Salem, NY
78	16,275	Burlington County Vocational	Westampton Twp, NJ
79	16,213	Essex County Voc-Tech	West Orange, NJ
80	16,116	Union Free SD of the Tarrytowns	Sleepy Hollow, NY
81	16,093	Rockville Centre Union Free SD	Rockville Ctre, NY
82	16,089	Morris SD	Morristown, NJ
83	16,074	Ramapo-Indian Hill Reg	Franklin Lakes, NJ
84	16,026	Uniondale Union Free SD	Uniondale, NY
85	15,929	Chappaqua Central SD	Chappaqua, NY
86	15,888	Jersey City	Jersey City, NJ
87	15,866	Westhampton Beach Union Free SD	Westhampton Bch, NY
88	15,830	Haverstraw-Stony Point Central SD	Garnerville, NY
89	15,829	Hempstead Union Free SD	Hempstead, NY
90	15,760	Rye City SD	Rye, NY
91	15,746	New Trier Twp HSD 203	Northfield, IL
92	15,744	Amityville Union Free SD	Amityville, NY
93	15,738	Northfield Twp High SD 225	Glenview, IL
94	15,704	Hendrick Hudson Central SD	Montrose, NY
95	15,621	Morris Hills Regional	Rockaway, NJ
96	15,586	Long Branch City	Long Branch, NJ
97	15,564	Passaic City	Passaic, NJ
98	15,505	Herricks Union Free SD	New Hyde Park, NY
99	15,491	Mamaroneck Union Free SD	Mamaroneck, NY
100	15,344	South Orangetown Central SD	Blauvelt, NY
101	15,316	Westbury Union Free SD	Old Westbury, NY
102	15,257	Irvington Township	Irvington, NJ
103	15,225	East Orange	East Orange, NJ
103	15,225	Somers Central SD	Lincolndale, NY
105	15,208	Mountain Lakes Boro	Mountain Lakes, NJ
105	15,208	Teaneck Twp	Teaneck, NJ
107	15,185	City of Orange Twp	Orange, NJ
108	15,138	Ellenville Central SD	Ellenville, NY
109	15,137	High Point Regional	Sussex, NJ
110	15,125	Glen Cove City SD	Glen Cove, NY
111	15,122	Camden City	Camden, NJ
112	15,100	Lakewood Twp	Lakewood, NJ
113	15,081	Oak Park & River Forest Dist 200	Oak Park, IL
113	15,081	South Country Central SD	E Patchogue, NY
115	15,032	Ossining Union Free SD	Ossining, NY
116	14,973	West Hempstead Union Free SD	W Hempstead, NY
117	14,966	Paterson City	Paterson, NJ
118	14,959	Waltham	Waltham, MA
119	14,947	Ocean City	Ocean City, NJ
120	14,946	Eastchester Union Free SD	Eastchester, NY

This section ranks 120 school districts at both the "top" and "bottom" of each category for a total of 240 districts per category. The "top" list (descending order) appears first, followed by the "bottom" list (ascending order). Ranking tables cover public school districts serving 1,500 or more students.

Current Spending per Student in FY2003

School districts ranked in *ascending* order

Rank	Dollars	District Name	City, State	Rank	Dollars	District Name	City, State
1	4,097	Honors Academy	Dallas, TX	61	4,987	Kuna Joint District	Kuna, ID
2	4,260	Bullhead City Elementary District	Bullhead City, AZ	62	4,992	Post Falls District	Post Falls, ID
3	4,285	Mohave Valley Elementary District	Mohave Valley, AZ	63	4,996	Claremore	Claremore, OK
3	4,285	Ohio Virtual Academy	Maumee, OH	64	4,997	Bixby	Bixby, OK
5	4,339	Nebo SD	Spanish Fork, UT	65	4,999	Fountain Hills Unified District	Fountain Hills, AZ
6	4,374	Tooele SD	Tooele, UT	66	5,002	Murray SD	Murray, UT
7	4,413	Alpine SD	American Fork, UT	67	5,013	Prescott Unified District	Prescott, AZ
8	4,444	Desoto County SD	Hernando, MS	68	5,025	Noble	Noble, OK
9	4,475	Lake Havasu Unified District	Lk Havasu City, AZ	69	5,029	Lewis County SD	Hohenwald, TN
10	4,520	Jordan SD	Sandy, UT	70	5,032	Lakeland District	Rathdrum, ID
11	4,521	Weber SD	Ogden, UT	71	5,034	Marana Unified District	Marana, AZ
12	4,524	Washington SD	St George, UT	71	5,034	Show Low Unified District	Show Low, AZ
13	4,595	Granite SD	Salt Lake City, UT	71	5,034	Yazoo City Municipal SD	Yazoo City, MS
14	4,606	North Pike SD	Summit, MS	74	5,037	Yuma Elementary District	Yuma, AZ
15	4,660	Marshall County SD	Holly Springs, MS	75	5,043	Jackson County SD	Vancleave, MS
16	4,686	Juab SD	Nephi, UT	76	5,050	Kingman Unified SD	Kingman, AZ
17	4,692	Davis SD	Farmington, UT	77	5,056	Deer Valley Unified District	Phoenix, AZ
18	4,698	Gilbert Unified District	Gilbert, AZ	78	5,061	Scott County SD	Forest, MS
19	4,728	Box Elder SD	Brigham City, UT	79	5,062	Carterville CUSD 5	Carterville, IL
20	4,733	Pearl River County SD	Carriere, MS	80	5,063	Bonneville Joint District	Idaho Falls, ID
21	4,746	Preston Joint District	Preston, ID	81	5,066	Meridian Joint District	Meridian, ID
22	4,775	Rhea County SD	Dayton, TN	82	5,074	Shelley Joint District	Shelley, ID
23	4,776	Chino Valley Unified District	Chino Valley, AZ	83	5,081	Iron SD	Cedar City, UT
24	4,781	Western Pennsylvania Cyber CS	Midland, PA	84	5,083	Littleton Elementary District	Cashion, AZ
25	4,786	Mannford	Mannford, OK	85	5,090	Coweta	Coweta, OK
26	4,788	Pendergast Elementary District	Phoenix, AZ	86	5,091	Leake County SD	Carthage, MS
27	4,793	Avondale Elementary District	Avondale, AZ	87	5,093	Peoria Unified SD	Glendale, AZ
28	4,805	Piedmont	Piedmont, OK	88	5,097	Skiatook	Skiatook, OK
29	4,819	Electronic Classrm of Tomorrow	Columbus, OH	89	5,101	Copiah County SD	Hazlehurst, MS
30	4,822	Collinsville	Collinsville, OK	89	5,101	Ozark R-VI	Ozark, MO
31	4,829	Morgan SD	Morgan, UT	91	5,106	Glenpool	Glenpool, OK
32	4,831	Chester County SD	Henderson, TN	92	5,107	Grenada SD	Grenada, MS
33	4,832	Gadsden Elementary District	San Luis, AZ	93	5,112	Owasso	Owasso, OK
34	4,833	Sierra Vista Unified District	Sierra Vista, AZ	94	5,115	Macon County SD	Lafayette, TN
35	4,845	Canton Public SD	Canton, MS	95	5,117	Detroit Acad of Arts & Sciences	Detroit, MI
36	4,853	Santa Cruz Valley Unified District	Rio Rico, AZ	96	5,120	Genoa Kingston CUSD 424	Genoa, IL
37	4,858	Summit Hill SD 161	Frankfort, IL	97	5,122	Choctaw/Nicoma Park	Choctaw, OK
38	4,871	Litchfield Elementary District	Litchfield Park, AZ	98	5,129	Payson Unified District	Payson, AZ
38	4,871	Logan SD	Logan, UT	99	5,132	Amphitheater Unified District	Tucson, AZ
40	4,886	Glendale Elementary District	Glendale, AZ	100	5,141	Itawamba County SD	Fulton, MS
41	4,891	Wasatch SD	Heber City, UT	101	5,143	Bedford County SD	Shelbyville, TN
42	4,910	Gibson Special District	Dyer, TN	102	5,150	Union	Tulsa, OK
43	4,913	Wylie ISD	Abilene, TX	103	5,167	Lauderdale County SD	Meridian, MS
44	4,916	Lincoln County SD	Brookhaven, MS	103	5,167	Mokena SD 159	Mokena, IL
45	4,918	White County SD	Sparta, TN	105	5,168	Pryor	Pryor, OK
46	4,947	Cartwright Elementary District	Phoenix, AZ	106	5,170	Montgomery County Schools	Clarksville, TN
47	4,948	Western Placer Unified	Lincoln, CA	107	5,175	Dysart Unified District	El Mirage, AZ
48	4,950	Hilldale	Muskogee, OK	108	5,176	Maricopa County Regional District	Phoenix, AZ
48	4,950	Kyrene Elementary District	Tempe, AZ	109	5,180	Humboldt Unified District	Prescott Valley, AZ
50	4,955	Cleveland	Cleveland, OK	110	5,187	Blue Ridge Unified District	Lakeside, AZ
51	4,958	Smith County SD	Carthage, TN	110	5,187	Yuma Union High SD	Yuma, AZ
52	4,970	Alhambra Elementary District	Phoenix, AZ	112	5,188	Smith County SD	Raleigh, MS
53	4,973	Cache SD	Logan, UT	113	5,190	Senatobia Municipal SD	Senatobia, MS
53	4,973	Crane Elementary District	Yuma, AZ	114	5,201	Vail Unified District	Vail, AZ
55	4,974	Mustang	Mustang, OK	115	5,205	Houston SD	Houston, MS
55	4,974	Republic R-III	Republic, MO	116	5,206	Hardeman County School Distrct	Bolivar, TN
57	4,975	Safford Unified District	Safford, AZ	116	5,206	Meigs County SD	Decatur, TN
58	4,979	Union County SD	New Albany, MS	118	5,208	South Tippah SD	Ripley, MS
59	4,985	George County SD	Lucedale, MS	119	5,211	Ocean Springs SD	Ocean Springs, MS
60	4,986	Lorena ISD	Lorena, TX	120	5,213	Hickman County SD	Centerville, TN

This section ranks 120 school districts at both the "top" and "bottom" of each category for a total of 240 districts per category. The "top" list (descending order) appears first, followed by the "bottom" list (ascending order). Ranking tables cover public school districts serving 1,500 or more students.

Number of Diploma Recipients

School districts ranked in *descending* order

Rank	Number	District Name	City, State	Rank	Number	District Name	City, State
1	37,915	New York City Public Schools	Brooklyn, NY	61	3,309	Tucson Unified District	Tucson, AZ
2	27,720	Los Angeles Unified	Los Angeles, CA	62	3,304	Guilford County Schools	Greensboro, NC
3	16,638	Dade County SD	Miami, FL	63	3,292	Chesterfield County Public Schools	Chesterfield, VA
4	15,653	City of Chicago SD 299	Chicago, IL	64	3,222	Fort Worth ISD	Fort Worth, TX
5	11,654	Broward County SD	Fort Lauderdale, FL	65	3,208	North East ISD	San Antonio, TX
6	10,452	Hawaii Department of Education	Honolulu, HI	66	3,196	Prince William Co Public Schools	Manassas, VA
7	10,450	Fairfax County Public Schools	Fairfax, VA	67	2,992	Antelope Valley Union High	Lancaster, CA
8	10,215	Clark County SD	Las Vegas, NV	68	2,990	Howard County Pub Schls System	Ellicott City, MD
9	8,559	Philadelphia City SD	Philadelphia, PA	69	2,934	Greenville County SD	Greenville, SC
10	8,282	Montgomery County Public Schls	Rockville, MD	70	2,922	Cherry Creek 5	Greenwood Vlg, CO
11	7,968	Hillsborough County SD	Tampa, FL	71	2,905	Huntington Beach Union High	Huntington Bch, CA
12	7,945	Houston ISD	Houston, TX	72	2,894	District of Columbia Pub Schls	Washington, DC
13	7,687	Palm Beach County SD	West Palm Beach, FL	73	2,875	Arlington ISD	Arlington, TX
14	7,552	Prince Georges Co Public Schools	Upper Marlboro, MD	74	2,854	Mobile County	Mobile, AL
15	7,361	Orange County SD	Orlando, FL	75	2,851	Washoe County SD	Reno, NV
16	6,859	Baltimore County Public Schls	Towson, MD	76	2,846	Lee County SD	Fort Myers, FL
17	6,532	Dallas ISD	Dallas, TX	77	2,842	Ysleta ISD	El Paso, TX
18	6,504	San Diego Unified	San Diego, CA	78	2,816	Boston	Boston, MA
19	6,116	Gwinnett County	Lawrenceville, GA	79	2,815	E Baton Rouge Parish SB	Baton Rouge, LA
20	5,741	Kern Union High	Bakersfield, CA	79	2,815	Modesto City High	Modesto, CA
21	5,540	Detroit City SD	Detroit, MI	79	2,815	Township High SD 214	Arlington Hgts, IL
22	5,413	Pinellas County SD	Largo, FL	82	2,809	Cumberland County Schools	Fayetteville, NC
23	5,411	Wake County Schools	Raleigh, NC	83	2,795	Plano ISD	Plano, TX
24	5,334	Jefferson County R-1	Golden, CO	84	2,738	Garden Grove Unified	Garden Grove, CA
25	5,260	Duval County SD	Jacksonville, FL	85	2,728	Elk Grove Unified	Elk Grove, CA
26	5,231	Cobb County	Marietta, GA	86	2,727	San Antonio ISD	San Antonio, TX
27	5,087	Charlotte-Mecklenburg Schools	Charlotte, NC	87	2,726	Alpine SD	American Fork, UT
28	4,932	Jefferson County	Louisville, KY	88	2,725	Township HSD 211	Palatine, IL
29	4,916	Jordan SD	Sandy, UT	89	2,689	Garland ISD	Garland, TX
30	4,768	Sweetwater Union High	Chula Vista, CA	90	2,678	Tempe Union High SD	Tempe, AZ
31	4,708	Albuquerque Public Schools	Albuquerque, NM	91	2,670	Fullerton Joint Union High	Fullerton, CA
32	4,664	Long Beach Unified	Long Beach, CA	92	2,644	Capistrano Unified	San Juan Capis, CA
33	4,524	Baltimore City Public Schools Sys	Baltimore, MD	93	2,629	Seattle SD 1	Seattle, WA
34	4,467	East Side Union High	San Jose, CA	94	2,612	Denver County 1	Denver, CO
35	4,466	Anne Arundel County Pub Schls	Annapolis, MD	95	2,609	Glendale Union High SD	Glendale, AZ
36	4,455	Virginia Beach City Public Schls	Virginia Beach, VA	95	2,609	Nashville-Davidson County SD	Nashville, TN
37	4,387	Grossmont Union High	La Mesa, CA	97	2,600	Columbus Public Schools	Columbus, OH
38	4,191	Dekalb County	Decatur, GA	98	2,592	Portland SD 1J	Portland, OR
39	4,170	Granite SD	Salt Lake City, UT	99	2,553	Knox County SD	Knoxville, TN
40	4,014	Mesa Unified District	Mesa, AZ	100	2,550	Shelby County SD	Memphis, TN
41	3,938	Cypress-Fairbanks ISD	Houston, TX	101	2,529	Oxnard Union High	Oxnard, CA
42	3,933	Memphis City SD	Memphis, TN	102	2,505	Anchorage SD	Anchorage, AK
43	3,928	Northside ISD	San Antonio, TX	103	2,484	Santa Ana Unified	Santa Ana, CA
44	3,912	Milwaukee	Milwaukee, WI	104	2,465	Frederick County Board of Ed	Frederick, MD
45	3,873	Chaffey Joint Union High	Ontario, CA	105	2,453	Pasco County SD	Land O' Lakes, FL
46	3,815	Polk County SD	Bartow, FL	106	2,443	Cleveland Municipal City SD	Cleveland, OH
47	3,765	Davis SD	Farmington, UT	107	2,425	Harford County Public Schools	Bel Air, MD
48	3,721	Fresno Unified	Fresno, CA	108	2,400	Henrico County Public Schools	Richmond, VA
49	3,705	Austin ISD	Austin, TX	109	2,393	William S. Hart Union High	Santa Clarita, CA
50	3,688	Anaheim Union High	Anaheim, CA	110	2,372	Anoka-Hennepin	Coon Rapids, MN
51	3,630	Fort Bend ISD	Sugar Land, TX	111	2,320	Escambia County SD	Pensacola, FL
52	3,578	Brevard County SD	Viera, FL	112	2,298	Chesapeake City Public Schools	Chesapeake, VA
53	3,556	San Juan Unified	Carmichael, CA	113	2,278	Jefferson County	Birmingham, AL
54	3,534	Phoenix Union High SD	Phoenix, AZ	114	2,271	Forsyth County Schools	Winston Salem, NC
55	3,471	Orleans Parish School Board	New Orleans, LA	115	2,270	Atlanta City	Atlanta, GA
56	3,420	Seminole County SD	Sanford, FL	116	2,267	Lewisville ISD	Flower Mound, TX
57	3,399	San Francisco Unified	San Francisco, CA	117	2,261	Jefferson Parish School Board	Harvey, LA
58	3,386	Volusia County SD	Deland, FL	118	2,251	Riverside Unified	Riverside, CA
59	3,360	Fulton County	Atlanta, GA	119	2,237	Sacramento City Unified	Sacramento, CA
60	3,353	El Paso ISD	El Paso, TX	120	2,230	Poway Unified	Poway, CA

This section ranks 120 school districts at both the "top" and "bottom" of each category for a total of 240 districts per category. The "top" list (descending order) appears first, followed by the "bottom" list (ascending order). Ranking tables cover public school districts serving 1,500 or more students.

Number of Diploma Recipients
School districts ranked in *ascending* order

Rank	Number	District Name	City, State	Rank	Number	District Name	City, State
1	0	Amsterdam City SD	Amsterdam, NY	58	53	North Panola Schools	Sardis, MS
1	0	Bergen County Special Service	Paramus, NJ	62	54	Terrell County	Dawson, GA
1	0	Bonsall Union Elementary	Bonsall, CA	62	54	Todd County SD 66-1	Mission, SD
1	0	Burlington County Spec Serv	Mount Holly, NJ	64	55	Bledsoe County SD	Pikeville, TN
1	0	Central Ariz Valley Inst of Tech	Coolidge, AZ	64	55	Henderson County SD	Lexington, TN
1	0	Corrections SD 428 Dept of	Springfield, IL	64	55	Zuni Public Schools	Zuni, NM
1	0	Creighton Elementary District	Phoenix, AZ	67	56	Sunflower County SD	Indianola, MS
1	0	East Valley Institute of Tech	Mesa, AZ	67	56	West Oso ISD	Corpus Christi, TX
1	0	Escondido Union Elementary	Escondido, CA	69	57	Dooly County	Vienna, GA
1	0	Glendale Elementary District	Glendale, AZ	69	57	Forrest County SD	Hattiesburg, MS
1	0	Hampton Bays Union Free SD	Hampton Bays, NY	69	57	Western Pennsylvania Cyber CS	Midland, PA
1	0	Lawndale Elementary	Lawndale, CA	72	58	Conecuh County	Evergreen, AL
1	0	Lennox Elementary	Lennox, CA	72	58	Forest Municipal SD	Forest, MS
1	0	Lindenwold Boro	Lindenwold, NJ	72	58	Vail Unified District	Vail, AZ
1	0	Litchfield SD	Litchfield, NH	75	62	Florence County SD 05	Johnsonville, SC
1	0	Madison Elementary District	Phoenix, AZ	75	62	Hatch Valley Public Schools	Hatch, NM
1	0	Mercer County Special Service	Trenton, NJ	77	63	Beecher Community SD	Flint, MI
1	0	Minooka Community HS District 111	Minooka, IL	77	63	Coahoma County SD	Clarksdale, MS
1	0	Navit	Snowflake, AZ	77	63	East Holmes Local Schools	Berlin, OH
1	0	Nuview Union Elementary	Nuevo, CA	80	65	Bendle Public Schools	Burton, MI
1	0	Oak Park & River Forest Dist 200	Oak Park, IL	80	65	Jefferson City	Jefferson, GA
1	0	Passaic City	Passaic, NJ	80	65	Quitman County SD	Marks, MS
1	0	Pde Division of Data Services	Harrisburg, PA	80	65	Trinidad 1	Trinidad, CO
1	0	Pekin Public SD 108	Pekin, IL	80	65	Tunica County SD	Tunica, MS
1	0	Plumsted Twp	New Egypt, NJ	80	65	Woodbridge SD	Greenwood, DE
1	0	Public Schools of Petoskey	Petoskey, MI	86	66	Caldwell Parish School Board	Columbia, LA
1	0	Ravenswood City Elementary	East Palo Alto, CA	86	66	Wyandanch Union Free SD	Wyandanch, NY
1	0	Red Bluff Union Elementary	Red Bluff, CA	88	67	Dalhart ISD	Dalhart, TX
1	0	San Bernardino Co Off of Education	San Bernardino, CA	88	67	Douglas	Douglas, MA
1	0	Scotts Valley Unified	Scotts Valley, CA	88	67	Westwood Community Schools	Dearborn Hgts, MI
1	0	Tempe Elementary District	Tempe, AZ	91	68	Greene County	Eutaw, AL
1	0	Wheatland Elementary	Wheatland, CA	91	68	Northwest Arctic SD	Kotzebue, AK
33	1	Keyes Union Elementary	Keyes, CA	91	68	Sutherlin SD 130	Sutherlin, OR
33	1	Mannheim SD 83	Franklin Park, IL	94	69	Cleveland	Cleveland, OK
33	1	Watertown SD 14-4	Watertown, SD	94	69	Heard County	Franklin, GA
36	3	Redding Elementary	Redding, CA	94	69	Mcintosh County	Darien, GA
36	3	Redwood City Elementary	Redwood City, CA	94	69	Tri County Area Schools	Sand Lake, MI
38	4	Cheney SD 360	Cheney, WA	98	70	Hutto ISD	Hutto, TX
38	4	Windham School Department	Windham, ME	98	70	Michigan Center SD	Michigan Center, MI
40	10	Riverside SD 416	Chattaroy, WA	98	70	North Pike SD	Summit, MS
41	11	Norwich SD	Norwich, CT	98	70	Royal ISD	Brookshire, TX
42	13	Lakeside Union Elementary	Lakeside, CA	102	71	Gallatin County	Warsaw, KY
43	18	Capitol Region Education Council	Hartford, CT	102	71	Salamanca City SD	Salamanca, NY
44	24	Area Coop Educational Services	North Haven, CT	104	72	Candler County	Metter, GA
44	24	Tulare County Office of Education	Visalia, CA	104	72	Shaker Regional SD	Belmont, NH
46	28	Gorman Elementary	Gorman, CA	104	72	Wahluke SD 73	Mattawa, WA
47	31	Electronic Classrm of Tomorrow	Columbus, OH	104	72	Wilkinson County SD	Woodville, MS
48	32	Waterford Unified	Waterford, CA	108	73	Coosa County	Rockford, AL
49	33	Julian Union Elementary	Julian, CA	108	73	Croton-Harmon Union Free SD	Croton-On-Hud, NY
49	33	Twin Ridges Elementary	North San Juan, CA	108	73	Muskegon Heights SD	Muskegon Hgts, MI
51	36	Butte County Joint District	Arco, ID	108	73	Pelham City	Pelham, GA
52	39	Red Lake	Red Lake, MN	108	73	White Cloud Public Schools	White Cloud, MI
53	45	Westwood Unified	Westwood, CA	113	74	Cairo-Durham Central SD	Cairo, NY
54	46	Godfrey-Lee Public Schools	Wyoming, MI	113	74	Hastings-On-Hudson Union Free SD	Hastings-on-Hud, NY
55	47	Bering Strait SD	Unalakleet, AK	113	74	Humphreys County SD	Belzoni, MS
55	47	Peach Springs Unified District	Peach Springs, AZ	113	74	Jasper County	Monticello, GA
57	50	Lower Yukon SD	Mountain Vlg, AK	113	74	Newton County SD	Decatur, MS
58	53	Atkinson County	Pearson, GA	113	74	Sto-Rox SD	Mckees Rocks, PA
58	53	East Tallahatchie Consol SD	Charleston, MS	113	74	Truth Or Consequences Schools	Truth or Conseq, NM
58	53	Maywood-Melrose Park-Broadview-89	Melrose Park, IL	113	74	Wilkinsburg Borough SD	Wilkinsburg, PA

This section ranks 120 school districts at both the "top" and "bottom" of each category for a total of 240 districts per category. The "top" list (descending order) appears first, followed by the "bottom" list (ascending order). Ranking tables cover public school districts serving 1,500 or more students.

High School Drop-out Rate
School districts ranked in *descending* order

Rank	Percent	District Name	City, State	Rank	Percent	District Name	City, State
1	31.3	Amityville Union Free SD	Amityville, NY	60	12.2	Wenatchee SD 246	Wenatchee, WA
2	30.6	Norwich SD	Norwich, CT	62	12.1	Dooly County	Vienna, GA
3	29.1	Seminole County	Donalsonville, GA	62	12.1	Jenkins County	Millen, GA
4	26.8	Whiteriver Unified District	Whiteriver, AZ	62	12.1	Little Rock SD	Little Rock, AR
5	25.8	Western Pennsylvania Cyber CS	Midland, PA	62	12.1	Oklahoma City	Oklahoma City, OK
6	24.4	Seattle SD 1	Seattle, WA	62	12.1	Peoria SD 150	Peoria, IL
7	22.6	West Valley SD 363	Spokane, WA	62	12.1	Red Lake	Red Lake, MN
8	22.1	Wapato SD 207	Wapato, WA	68	12.0	Elma SD 68	Elma, WA
9	21.0	Coolidge Unified District	Coolidge, AZ	68	12.0	Hancock County	Sparta, GA
10	20.5	Red River Parish School Board	Coushatta, LA	70	11.9	Aberdeen SD 5	Aberdeen, WA
11	18.9	Diboll ISD	Diboll, TX	70	11.9	Longview SD 122	Longview, WA
12	18.8	Lower Yukon SD	Mountain Vlg, AK	72	11.8	Lackawanna City SD	Lackawanna, NY
13	18.7	Pinon Unified District	Pinon, AZ	73	11.7	Anniston City	Anniston, AL
14	18.4	Schenectady City SD	Schenectady, NY	73	11.7	Murray County	Chatsworth, GA
14	18.4	Yakima SD 7	Yakima, WA	73	11.7	Page Unified District	Page, AZ
16	18.3	Todd County SD 66-1	Mission, SD	76	11.6	Everett SD 2	Everett, WA
17	17.6	City of Chicago SD 299	Chicago, IL	76	11.6	Pointe Coupee Parish SB	New Roads, LA
18	17.5	Roosevelt Union Free SD	Roosevelt, NY	78	11.5	Baltimore City Public Schools	Baltimore, MD
19	17.3	Chinle Unified District	Chinle, AZ	78	11.5	Pleasantville City	Pleasantville, NJ
19	17.3	Excelsior Springs 40	Excelsior Spgs, MO	80	11.3	Danville CCSD 118	Danville, IL
21	17.1	Sunnyside SD 201	Sunnyside, WA	81	11.2	Copiah County SD	Hazlehurst, MS
22	16.9	Ledyard SD	Ledyard, CT	81	11.2	Phoenix Union High SD	Phoenix, AZ
22	16.9	Lower Kuskokwim SD	Bethel, AK	81	11.2	Salt Lake City SD	Salt Lake City, UT
24	16.8	Chatham County	Savannah, GA	81	11.2	Waukegan CUSD 60	Waukegan, IL
25	16.6	Tuba City Unified District	Tuba City, AZ	81	11.2	Wilkinsburg Borough SD	Wilkinsburg, PA
26	16.0	Canton City SD	Canton, OH	86	11.1	Juneau Borough Schools	Juneau, AK
27	15.9	Safford Unified District	Safford, AZ	87	11.0	Dysart Unified District	El Mirage, AZ
28	15.5	Gainesville City	Gainesville, GA	87	11.0	Fairbanks North Star Boro SD	Fairbanks, AK
29	15.4	Belcourt 7	Belcourt, ND	87	11.0	Greene County	Eutaw, AL
29	15.4	Peach County	Fort Valley, GA	87	11.0	Higley Unified District	Higley, AZ
29	15.4	White River SD 416	Buckley, WA	87	11.0	Mitchell County	Camilla, GA
32	15.1	Cleveland Municipal City SD	Cleveland, OH	87	11.0	Whitfield County	Dalton, GA
33	14.8	Renton SD 403	Renton, WA	93	10.9	Casa Grande Union High SD	Casa Grande, AZ
34	14.2	New York City Public Schools	Brooklyn, NY	93	10.9	Madison Parish School Board	Tallulah, LA
35	14.1	Bering Strait SD	Unalakleet, AK	93	10.9	Omaha Public Schools	Omaha, NE
35	14.1	Camden City	Camden, NJ	93	10.9	South Pike SD	Magnolia, MS
35	14.1	Omak SD 19	Omak, WA	93	10.9	Walker County	Lafayette, GA
38	14.0	Sumter County	Americus, GA	93	10.9	Wayne County	Jesup, GA
38	14.0	Trenton City	Trenton, NJ	99	10.8	Atkinson County	Pearson, GA
40	13.9	Clover Park SD 400	Lakewood, WA	99	10.8	East Valley SD 90	Yakima, WA
40	13.9	Intermediate SD 287	Plymouth, MN	99	10.8	Long County	Ludowici, GA
40	13.9	Parker Unified SD	Parker, AZ	99	10.8	Portland SD 1J	Portland, OR
43	13.8	Espanola Municipal Schools	Espanola, NM	103	10.7	Clarke County	Athens, GA
44	13.7	Colonial SD	New Castle, DE	103	10.7	Decatur SD 61	Decatur, IL
44	13.7	Woodbridge SD	Greenwood, DE	103	10.7	East Cleveland City SD	East Cleveland, OH
46	13.6	Colorado River Union High SD	Fort Mojave, AZ	103	10.7	Helena/West Helena SD	Helena, AR
46	13.6	Toppenish SD 202	Toppenish, WA	103	10.7	Lancaster SD	Lancaster, PA
48	13.5	Sedro-Woolley SD 101	Sedro Woolley, WA	103	10.7	Poughkeepsie City SD	Poughkeepsie, NY
49	13.4	Mcintosh County	Darien, GA	109	10.6	Leflore County SD	Greenwood, MS
49	13.4	New London SD	New London, CT	110	10.5	Christina SD	Newark, DE
51	13.2	Spalding County	Griffin, GA	110	10.5	Holbrook Unified District	Holbrook, AZ
52	13.1	Bremerton SD 100	Bremerton, WA	110	10.5	Oak Harbor SD 201	Oak Harbor, WA
53	13.0	Rochester City SD	Rochester, NY	110	10.5	Putnam County	Eatonton, GA
54	12.9	Marion County	Buena Vista, GA	110	10.5	Vancouver SD 37	Vancouver, WA
55	12.5	City of Monroe School Board	Monroe, LA	110	10.5	Window Rock Unified District	Ft Defiance, AZ
55	12.5	Minneapolis	Minneapolis, MN	116	10.4	Brantley County	Nahunta, GA
55	12.5	Taylor County	Butler, GA	116	10.4	Valdosta City	Valdosta, GA
58	12.4	Kingman Unified SD	Kingman, AZ	118	10.3	Bibb County	Macon, GA
59	12.3	Sunnyside Unified District	Tucson, AZ	118	10.3	Haralson County	Buchanan, GA
60	12.2	Lima City SD	Lima, OH	118	10.3	Jasper County	Monticello, GA

This section ranks 120 school districts at both the "top" and "bottom" of each category for a total of 240 districts per category. The "top" list (descending order) appears first, followed by the "bottom" list (ascending order). Ranking tables cover public school districts serving 1,500 or more students.

High School Drop-out Rate

School districts ranked in *ascending* order

Rank	Percent	District Name	City, State	Rank	Percent	District Name	City, State
1	0.0	Amery	Amery, WI	1	0.0	Northern Valley Regional	Demarest, NJ
1	0.0	Anderson Community School Corp	Anderson, IN	1	0.0	Old Saybrook SD	Old Saybrook, CT
1	0.0	Athens City Elementary SD	Athens, TN	1	0.0	Pekin Public SD 108	Pekin, IL
1	0.0	Avon Community School Corp	Avon, IN	1	0.0	Pequannock Twp	Pompton Plains, NJ
1	0.0	Avon SD	Avon, CT	1	0.0	Putnam Valley Central SD	Putnam Valley, NY
1	0.0	Baugo Community Schools	Elkhart, IN	1	0.0	Ramsey Boro	Ramsey, NJ
1	0.0	Benton Community School Corp	Fowler, IN	1	0.0	Regional SD 16	Prospect, CT
1	0.0	Bergen County Vocational	Paramus, NJ	1	0.0	Ridgefield Boro	Ridgefield, NJ
1	0.0	Bound Brook Boro	Bound Brook, NJ	1	0.0	Rocky Hill SD	Rocky Hill, CT
1	0.0	Brandon Valley SD 49-2	Brandon, SD	1	0.0	Scarborough School Department	Scarborough, ME
1	0.0	Briarcliff Manor Union Free SD	Briarcliff Manor, NY	1	0.0	School Town of Highland	Highland, IN
1	0.0	Byram Hills Central SD	Armonk, NY	1	0.0	School Town of Speedway	Speedway, IN
1	0.0	Canton SD	Canton, CT	1	0.0	Seymour Community	Seymour, WI
1	0.0	Chappaqua Central SD	Chappaqua, NY	1	0.0	Shaker Heights City SD	Shaker Heights, OH
1	0.0	Chatham Central SD	Chatham, NY	1	0.0	Shelbyville Central Schools	Shelbyville, IN
1	0.0	Cold Spring Harbor Central SD	Cold Sprg Harbor, NY	1	0.0	Shenendehowa Central SD	Clifton Park, NY
1	0.0	Danville Community School Corp	Danville, IN	1	0.0	Shorewood	Shorewood, WI
1	0.0	East Holmes Local Schools	Berlin, OH	1	0.0	South Madison Com Sch Corp	Pendleton, IN
1	0.0	East Noble School Corp	Kendallville, IN	1	0.0	Southeast Dubois County Sch Corp	Ferdinand, IN
1	0.0	East Williston Union Free SD	Old Westbury, NY	1	0.0	Sparta CUSD 140	Sparta, IL
1	0.0	Eastbrook Community Sch Corp	Marion, IN	1	0.0	Springfield Twp	Springfield, NJ
1	0.0	Edgemont Union Free SD	Scarsdale, NY	1	0.0	Switzerland County School Corp	Vevay, IN
1	0.0	Edgerton	Edgerton, WI	1	0.0	Upper Saint Clair SD	Pittsburgh, PA
1	0.0	Edina	Edina, MN	1	0.0	Verona Area	Verona, WI
1	0.0	Electronic Classrm of Tomorrow	Columbus, OH	1	0.0	Vincennes Community Sch Corp	Vincennes, IN
1	0.0	Ft Leavenworth	Ft Leavenworth, KS	1	0.0	Waconia	Waconia, MN
1	0.0	Glen Rock Boro	Glen Rock, NJ	1	0.0	Wautoma Area	Wautoma, WI
1	0.0	Greensburg Community Schools	Greensburg, IN	1	0.0	Waverly-Shell Rock Community SD	Waverly, IA
1	0.0	Gretna Public Schools	Gretna, NE	1	0.0	West Lafayette Com School Corp	West Lafayette, IN
1	0.0	Haddonfield Boro	Haddonfield, NJ	1	0.0	West Noble School Corporation	Ligonier, IN
1	0.0	Hampton Bays Union Free SD	Hampton Bays, NY	1	0.0	Westfield-Washington Schools	Westfield, IN
1	0.0	Hancock County	Hawesville, KY	1	0.0	Westmont Hilltop SD	Johnstown, PA
1	0.0	High Point Regional	Sussex, NJ	1	0.0	Weston SD	Weston, CT
1	0.0	Highland Park Boro	Highland Park, NJ	1	0.0	Whitnall	Greenfield, WI
1	0.0	Hopewell Valley Regional	Pennington, NJ	1	0.0	Wyoming City SD	Wyoming, OH
1	0.0	Hudson	Hudson, WI	1	0.0	Zionsville Community Schools	Zionsville, IN
1	0.0	Huntington County Com Sch Corp	Huntington, IN	97	0.1	Aledo ISD	Aledo, TX
1	0.0	Kinnelon Boro	Kinnelon, NJ	97	0.1	Bernards Twp	Basking Ridge, NJ
1	0.0	Kokomo-Center Twp Con Sch Corp	Kokomo, IN	97	0.1	Crown Point Community Sch Corp	Crown Point, IN
1	0.0	Kosciusko SD	Kosciusko, MS	97	0.1	De Forest Area	De Forest, WI
1	0.0	Lakeland School Corporation	Lagrange, IN	97	0.1	Essex County Voc-Tech	West Orange, NJ
1	0.0	Liberty Central SD	Liberty, NY	97	0.1	Euclid City SD	Euclid, OH
1	0.0	Livingston Twp	Livingston, NJ	97	0.1	Franklin Public	Franklin, WI
1	0.0	Lodi	Lodi, WI	97	0.1	Griffith Public Schools	Griffith, IN
1	0.0	M S D Decatur Township	Indianapolis, IN	97	0.1	Hawthorne Boro	Hawthorne, NJ
1	0.0	M S D Pike Township	Indianapolis, IN	97	0.1	Holmdel Twp	Holmdel, NJ
1	0.0	MSAD 05 Rockland	Rockland, ME	97	0.1	Jericho Union Free SD	Jericho, NY
1	0.0	MSAD 34 Belfast	Belfast, ME	97	0.1	Kimberly Area	Kimberly, WI
1	0.0	Madison Boro	Madison, NJ	97	0.1	Lauderdale County	Florence, AL
1	0.0	Madison Consolidated Schools	Madison, IN	97	0.1	Levittown Union Free SD	Levittown, NY
1	0.0	Manchester Community Schools	N Manchester, IN	97	0.1	Lindenhurst Union Free SD	Lindenhurst, NY
1	0.0	Mannheim SD 83	Franklin Park, IL	97	0.1	Monroe SD	Monroe, CT
1	0.0	Mequon-Thiensville	Mequon, WI	97	0.1	Mountain Brook City	Mountain Brook, AL
1	0.0	Michigan City Area Schools	Michigan City, IN	97	0.1	Northwest Allen County Schools	Fort Wayne, IN
1	0.0	Millburn Twp	Millburn, NJ	97	0.1	Owego-Apalachin Central SD	Owego, NY
1	0.0	Monmouth County Vocational	Colts Neck, NJ	97	0.1	Paramus Boro	Paramus, NJ
1	0.0	New Providence Boro	New Providence, NJ	97	0.1	Pascack Valley Regional	Montvale, NJ
1	0.0	North Arlington Boro	North Arlington, NJ	97	0.1	Rockville Centre Union Free SD	Rockville Ctre, NY
1	0.0	North Babylon Union Free SD	North Babylon, NY	97	0.1	Roslyn Union Free SD	Roslyn, NY
1	0.0	North Montgomery Com Sch Corp	Crawfordsville, IN	97	0.1	Rutherford Boro	Rutherford, NJ

This section ranks 120 school districts at both the "top" and "bottom" of each category for a total of 240 districts per category. The "top" list (descending order) appears first, followed by the "bottom" list (ascending order). Ranking tables cover public school districts serving 1,500 or more students.

A

Abbeville County SD Abbeville, SC, 1174
ABC Unified Cerritos, CA, 99
Aberdeen SD 06-1 Aberdeen, SD, 1193
Aberdeen SD 5 Aberdeen, WA, 1359
Aberdeen SD Aberdeen, MS, 694
Abilene ISD Abilene, TX, 1277
Abington SD Abington, PA, 1123
Abington Heights SD Clarks Summit, PA, 1113
Abington Abington, MA, 566
Academy 20 Colorado Springs, CO, 198
Acadia Parish School Board Crowley, LA, 502
Acalanes Union High Lafayette, CA, 87
Accomack County Public Schools Accomac, VA, 1328
Acton-Agua Dulce Unified Acton, CA, 99
Acton-Boxborough Acton, MA, 556
Acton Acton, MA, 556
Ada Ada, OK, 1053
Adair County Columbia, KY, 472
Adams 12 Five Star Schools Thornton, CO, 196
Adams County 14 Commerce City, CO, 196
Adams County/Ohio Valley Local SD West Union, OH, 966
Adams-Arapahoe 28J Aurora, CO, 196
Adams-Cheshire Cheshire, MA, 547
Adams-Friendship Area Friendship, WI, 1400
Addison SD 4 Addison, IL, 340
Adelanto Elementary Adelanto, CA, 128
Adirondack Central SD Boonville, NY, 878
Adlai E Stevenson Dist 125 Lincolnshire, IL, 350
Adrian City SD Adrian, MI, 608
Affton 101 St Louis, MO, 727
Agawam Feeding Hills, MA, 553
Agua Fria Union High SD Avondale, AZ, 41
Aiken County SD Aiken, SC, 1174
Airport Community SD Carleton, MI, 614
Akron Central SD Akron, NY, 859
Akron Public Schools Akron, OH, 1012
Alachua County SD Gainesville, FL, 252
Alamance-Burlington Schools Burlington, NC, 932
Alameda City Unified Alameda, CA, 84
Alamo Heights ISD San Antonio, TX, 1230
Alamogordo Public Schools Alamogordo, NM, 842
Alamosa RE-11J Alamosa, CO, 196
Albany City SD Albany, NY, 852
Albany City Unified Albany, CA, 84
Albany County SD #1 Laramie, WY, 1434
Albany Albany, MN, 670
Albemarle County Public Schools Charlottesville, VA, 1328
Albert Gallatin Area SD Uniontown, PA, 1111
Albert Lea Albert Lea, MN, 660
Albertville City Albertville, AL, 16
Albion Central SD Albion, NY, 883
Albion Public Schools Albion, MI, 593
Albuquerque Public Schools Albuquerque, NM, 840
Alcorn SD Corinth, MS, 684
Alden Central SD Alden, NY, 859
Aldine ISD Houston, TX, 1250
Aledo ISD Aledo, TX, 1270
Alexander City Alexander City, AL, 19
Alexander County Schools Taylorsville, NC, 932
Alexander Local SD Albany, OH, 967
Alexandria City Public Schools Alexandria, VA, 1328
Alexandria Com School Corp Alexandria, IN, 406
Alexandria Alexandria, MN, 660
Algonac Community SD Algonac, MI, 626
Alhambra City Elementary Alhambra, CA, 99
Alhambra City High Alhambra, CA, 100
Alhambra Elementary District Phoenix, AZ, 41
Alice ISD Alice, TX, 1259
Alief ISD Houston, TX, 1250
Alisal Union Elementary Salinas, CA, 114
Allegan Public Schools Allegan, MI, 590
Alleghany County Public Schools Covington, VA, 1328
Alleghany County Schools Sparta, NC, 932
Allen County Scottsville, KY, 472

Allen ISD Allen, TX, 1236
Allen Parish School Board Oberlin, LA, 502
Allen Park Public Schools Allen Park, MI, 630
Allendale County SD Allendale, SC, 1174
Allendale Public SD Allendale, MI, 622
Allentown City SD Allentown, PA, 1118
Alliance City SD Alliance, OH, 1010
Alliance Public Schools Alliance, NE, 752
Alma Public Schools Alma, MI, 600
Alma SD Alma, AR, 65
Almont Community Schools Almont, MI, 608
Alpena Public Schools Alpena, MI, 590
Alpine SD American Fork, UT, 1315
Alpine Union Elementary Alpine, CA, 132
Alsip-Hazlgrn-Oaklwn SD 126 Alsip, IL, 327
Alta Loma Elementary Alta Loma, CA, 128
Altmar-Parish-Williamstown Central SD Parish, NY, 883
Alton Community Unit SD 11 Alton, IL, 355
Altoona Area SD Altoona, PA, 1096
Altus Altus, OK, 1049
Alum Rock Union Elementary San Jose, CA, 143
Alvarado ISD Alvarado, TX, 1259
Alvin ISD Alvin, TX, 1232
Alvord Unified Riverside, CA, 122
Amador County Unified Jackson, CA, 86
Amanda-Clearcreek Local SD Amanda, OH, 980
Amarillo ISD Amarillo, TX, 1271
Ambridge Area SD Ambridge, PA, 1092
Amelia County Public Schools Amelia, VA, 1328
American Falls Joint District American Falls, ID, 319
Amery Amery, WI, 1412
Ames Community SD Ames, IA, 443
Amesbury Amesbury, MA, 550
Amherst Central SD Amherst, NY, 859
Amherst County Public Schools Amherst, VA, 1328
Amherst Ex Vill SD Amherst, OH, 994
Amherst SD Amherst, NH, 769
Amherst-Pelham Amherst, MA, 555
Amityville Union Free SD Amityville, NY, 890
Amory SD Amory, MS, 694
Amphitheater Unified District Tucson, AZ, 50
Amsterdam City SD Amsterdam, NY, 868
Anacortes SD 103 Anacortes, WA, 1366
Anadarko Anadarko, OK, 1046
Anaheim Elementary Anaheim, CA, 117
Anaheim Union High Anaheim, CA, 117
Anchor Bay SD New Baltimore, MI, 609
Anchorage SD Anchorage, AK, 32
Andalusia City Andalusia, AL, 7
Anderson Community School Corp Anderson, IN, 406
Anderson County School Distrct Clinton, TN, 1201
Anderson County SD 01 Williamston, SC, 1174
Anderson County SD 02 Honea Path, SC, 1174
Anderson County SD 03 Iva, SC, 1174
Anderson County SD 04 Pendleton, SC, 1174
Anderson County SD 05 Anderson, SC, 1175
Anderson County Lawrenceburg, KY, 472
Anderson Union High Anderson, CA, 148
Andover Andover, KS, 454
Andover Andover, MA, 550
Andrews ISD Andrews, TX, 1227
Angleton ISD Angleton, TX, 1232
Ankeny Community SD Ankeny, IA, 440
Ann Arbor Public Schools Ann Arbor, MI, 628
Annandale Annandale, MN, 672
Anne Arundel County Pub Schls Annapolis, MD, 536
Anniston City Anniston, AL, 5
Annville-Cleona SD Annville, PA, 1117
Anoka-Hennepin Coon Rapids, MN, 656
Anson County Schools Wadesboro, NC, 932
Ansonia SD Ansonia, CT, 220
Antelope Valley Union High Lancaster, CA, 100
Anthony Wayne Local SD Whitehouse, OH, 995
Antigo Antigo, WI, 1406
Antioch CCSD 34 Antioch, IL, 350
Antioch Unified Antioch, CA, 87

Apache Junction Unified District Apache Junction, AZ, 51
Apollo-Ridge SD Spring Church, PA, 1091
Apple Valley Unified Apple Valley, CA, 128
Appleton Area Appleton, WI, 1410
Appling County Baxley, GA, 270
Appomattox County Public Schools Appomattox, VA, 1329
Appoquinimink SD Odessa, DE, 238
Aptakisic-Tripp CCSD 102 Buffalo Grove, IL, 350
Arab City Arab, AL, 16
Aransas County ISD Rockport, TX, 1228
Aransas Pass ISD Aransas Pass, TX, 1273
Arcadia Unified Arcadia, CA, 100
Archuleta County 50 Jt Pagosa Springs, CO, 197
Ardmore Ardmore, OK, 1047
Ardsley Union Free SD Ardsley, NY, 900
Area Cooperative Educational Services North Haven, CT, 220
Argo Community HSD 217 Summit, IL, 327
Arkadelphia SD Arkadelphia, AR, 64
Arkansas City Arkansas City, KS, 455
Arlington Central SD Poughkeepsie, NY, 858
Arlington County Public Schools Arlington, VA, 1329
Arlington Heights SD 25 Arlington Heights, IL, 328
Arlington ISD Arlington, TX, 1275
Arlington SD 16 Arlington, WA, 1367
Arlington Arlington, MA, 556
Armada Area Schools Armada, MI, 609
Armstrong SD Ford City, PA, 1092
Arrowhead Uhs Hartland, WI, 1418
Artesia Public Schools Artesia, NM, 841
Arvin Union Elementary Arvin, CA, 94
Asbury Park City Asbury Park, NJ, 805
Ascension Parish School Board Donaldsonville, LA, 502
Ashburnham-Westminster Westminster, MA, 569
Ashdown SD Ashdown, AR, 70
Ashe County Schools Jefferson, NC, 932
Asheboro City Schools Asheboro, NC, 945
Asheville City Schools Asheville, NC, 933
Ashland City SD Ashland, OH, 966
Ashland Ind Ashland, KY, 473
Ashland SD 5 Ashland, OR, 1070
Ashland Ashland, MA, 557
Ashland Ashland, WI, 1400
Ashtabula Area City SD Ashtabula, OH, 966
Ashwaubenon Green Bay, WI, 1400
Aspen 1 Aspen, CO, 202
Assumption Parish School Board Napoleonville, LA, 502
Astoria SD 1 Astoria, OR, 1067
Atascadero Unified Atascadero, CA, 139
Atchison Public Schools Atchison, KS, 454
Athens Area SD Athens, PA, 1097
Athens City Elementary SD Athens, TN, 1210
Athens City SD The Plains, OH, 967
Athens City Athens, AL, 14
Athens ISD Athens, TX, 1253
Athol-Royalston Athol, MA, 569
Atkinson County Pearson, GA, 270
Atlanta City Atlanta, GA, 278
Atlanta ISD Atlanta, TX, 1236
Atlantic City Atlantic City, NJ, 782
Atlantic Community SD Atlantic, IA, 435
Attalla City Attalla, AL, 10
Attica Central SD Attica, NY, 905
Attleboro Attleboro, MA, 547
Atwater Elementary Atwater, CA, 112
Auburn City SD Auburn, NY, 855
Auburn City Auburn, AL, 14
Auburn School Department Auburn, ME, 522
Auburn SD 408 Auburn, WA, 1360
Auburn Union Elementary Auburn, CA, 121
Auburn Washburn Topeka, KS, 461
Auburn Auburn, MA, 569
Audubon Boro Audubon, NJ, 791
Augusta County Public Schools Fishersville, VA, 1329
Augusta Public Schools Augusta, ME, 524
Augusta Augusta, KS, 454

C

Cabarrus County Schools Concord, NC, 934
Cabell County SD Huntington, WV, 1386
Cabot SD Cabot, AR, 70
Cabrillo Unified Half Moon Bay, CA, 140
Cache SD Logan, UT, 1312
Caddo Parish School Board Shreveport, LA, 503
Cadillac Area Public Schools Cadillac, MI, 634
Caesar Rodney SD Wyoming, DE, 238
Cahokia Community Unit SD 187 Cahokia, IL, 362
Cairo-Durham Central SD Cairo, NY, 864
Cajon Valley Union Elementary El Cajon, CA, 132
Calallen ISD Corpus Christi, TX, 1268
Calaveras Unified San Andreas, CA, 87
Calcasieu Parish School Board Lake Charles, LA, 503
Caldwell County Schools Lenoir, NC, 934
Caldwell County Princeton, KY, 474
Caldwell District Caldwell, ID, 316
Caldwell ISD Caldwell, TX, 1234
Caldwell Parish School Board Columbia, LA, 503
Caldwell-West Caldwell West Caldwell, NJ, 795
Caledonia Community Schools Caledonia, MI, 605
Calexico Unified Calexico, CA, 93
Calhoun City Calhoun, GA, 279
Calhoun County ISD Port Lavaca, TX, 1234
Calhoun County SD Blountstown, FL, 252
Calhoun County SD Pittsboro, MS, 684
Calhoun County SD St Matthews, SC, 1175
Calhoun County Anniston, AL, 5
Calloway County Murray, KY, 475
Calvert County Public Schools Prince Frederick, MD, 536
Camas SD 117 Camas, WA, 1357
Cambria Heights SD Patton, PA, 1100
Cambrian Elementary San Jose, CA, 143
Cambridge City SD Cambridge, OH, 985
Cambridge-Isanti Cambridge, MN, 663
Cambridge Cambridge, MA, 557
Camden Central SD Camden, NY, 878
Camden City Camden, NJ, 791
Camden County Schools Camden, NC, 934
Camden County Vocational Sicklerville, NJ, 792
Camden County Kingsland, GA, 272
Camden Fairview SD Camden, AR, 71
Camdenton R-III Camdenton, MO, 713
Cameron ISD Cameron, TX, 1266
Cameron Parish School Board Cameron, LA, 503
Cameron R-I Cameron, MO, 715
Campbell City SD Campbell, OH, 997
Campbell County Public Schools Rustburg, VA, 1330
Campbell County School Distrct Jacksboro, TN, 1202
Campbell County SD #1 Gillette, WY, 1434
Campbell County Alexandria, KY, 475
Campbell Union Elementary Campbell, CA, 143
Campbell Union High San Jose, CA, 143
Campbellsport Campbellsport, WI, 1404
Canal Winchester Local SD Canal Winchester, OH, 981
Canandaigua City SD Canandaigua, NY, 881
Canastota Central SD Canastota, NY, 866
Canby SD 86 Canby, OR, 1066
Candler County Metter, GA, 272
Canfield Local SD Canfield, OH, 997
Cannon County SD Woodbury, TN, 1202
Canon City Re-1 Canon City, CO, 200
Canon-Mcmillan SD Canonsburg, PA, 1132
Canton Central SD Canton, NY, 889
Canton City SD Canton, OH, 1010
Canton ISD Canton, TX, 1279
Canton Local SD Canton, OH, 1010
Canton Public SD Canton, MS, 693
Canton SD Canton, CT, 215
Canton Union SD 66 Canton, IL, 345
Canton Canton, MA, 563
Canutillo ISD El Paso, TX, 1243
Canyon ISD Canyon, TX, 1272
Capac Community SD Capac, MI, 626

Cape Elizabeth School Department Cape Elizabeth, ME, 522
Cape Girardeau 63 Cape Girardeau, MO, 713
Cape Henlopen SD Lewes, DE, 239
Capistrano Unified San Juan Capistrano, CA, 117
Capital SD Dover, DE, 238
Capitol Region Education Council Hartford, CT, 215
Carbon County SD #1 Rawlins, WY, 1434
Carbon SD Price, UT, 1312
Caribou School Department Caribou, ME, 522
Carl Junction R-I Carl Junction, MO, 720
Carle Place Union Free SD Carle Place, NY, 869
Carlinville CUSD 1 Carlinville, IL, 355
Carlisle Area SD Carlisle, PA, 1105
Carlisle Local SD Carlisle, OH, 1017
Carlsbad Municipal Schools Carlsbad, NM, 841
Carlsbad Unified Carlsbad, CA, 132
Carlynton SD Carnegie, PA, 1087
Carman-Ainsworth Community Schools Flint, MI, 597
Carmel Central SD Patterson, NY, 885
Carmel Clay Schools Carmel, IN, 397
Carmel Unified Carmel, CA, 114
Caro Community Schools Caro, MI, 627
Caroline County Board of Ed Denton, MD, 536
Caroline County Public Schools Bowling Green, VA, 1330
Carpinteria Unified Carpinteria, CA, 142
Carrizo Springs Cons ISD Carrizo Springs, TX, 1242
Carroll Community SD Carroll, IA, 435
Carroll County Public Schools Hillsville, VA, 1330
Carroll County Public Schools Westminster, MD, 536
Carroll County Carrollton, GA, 273
Carroll County Carrollton, KY, 475
Carroll ISD Grapevine, TX, 1275
Carrollton City Carrollton, GA, 273
Carrollton Ex Vill SD Carrollton, OH, 970
Carrollton SD Saginaw, MI, 624
Carrollton-Farmers Branch Carrollton, TX, 1238
Carson City SD Carson City, NV, 762
Carter County SD Elizabethton, TN, 1202
Carter County Grayson, KY, 475
Carteret Boro Carteret, NJ, 802
Carteret County Public Schools Beaufort, NC, 934
Cartersville City Cartersville, GA, 271
Carterville CUSD 5 Carterville, IL, 367
Carthage Central SD Carthage, NY, 864
Carthage ISD Carthage, TX, 1270
Carthage R-IX Carthage, MO, 720
Cartwright Elementary District Phoenix, AZ, 42
Caruthersville 18 Caruthersville, MO, 724
Carver Carver, MA, 566
Cary CCSD 26 Cary, IL, 356
Casa Grande Elementary District Casa Grande, AZ, 51
Casa Grande Union High SD Casa Grande, AZ, 51
Cascade SD 5 Turner, OR, 1073
Cascade Union Elementary Anderson, CA, 148
Casey County Liberty, KY, 476
Cashmere SD 222 Cashmere, WA, 1356
Cassia County Joint District Burley, ID, 316
Cassville R-IV Cassville, MO, 712
Castaic Union Elementary Valencia, CA, 101
Castleberry ISD Fort Worth, TX, 1276
Castro Valley Unified Castro Valley, CA, 84
Caswell County Schools Yanceyville, NC, 934
Catahoula Parish School Board Harrisonburg, LA, 504
Catalina Foothills Unified District Tucson, AZ, 50
Catasauqua Area SD Catasauqua, PA, 1118
Catawba County Schools Newton, NC, 935
Catoosa County Ringgold, GA, 273
Catoosa Catoosa, OK, 1054
Catskill Central SD Catskill, NY, 864
Cave Creek Unified District Cave Creek, AZ, 42
Cazenovia Central SD Cazenovia, NY, 866
CCSD 181 Hinsdale, IL, 341
Cedar Falls Community SD Cedar Falls, IA, 434
Cedar Grove Twp Cedar Grove, NJ, 795
Cedar Hill ISD Cedar Hill, TX, 1238

Cedar Rapids Community SD Cedar Rapids, IA, 439
Cedar Springs Public Schools Cedar Springs, MI, 605
Cedarburg Cedarburg, WI, 1411
Celina City SD Celina, OH, 1000
Centennial SD 28J Portland, OR, 1074
Centennial SD Warminster, PA, 1098
Centennial Circle Pines, MN, 656
Center 58 Kansas City, MO, 718
Center Area SD Monaca, PA, 1092
Center Grove Com Sch Corp Greenwood, IN, 402
Center ISD Center, TX, 1274
Center Joint Unified Antelope, CA, 126
Center Line Public Schools Center Line, MI, 609
Centerville City SD Centerville, OH, 1001
Centerville Community SD Centerville, IA, 434
Centerville-Abington Com Schs Centerville, IN, 417
Centinela Valley Union High Lawndale, CA, 101
Central Arizona Valley Institute of Technology Coolidge, AZ, 51
Central Berkshire Dalton, MA, 547
Central Bucks SD Doylestown, PA, 1098
Central Cambria SD Ebensburg, PA, 1100
Central Clinton Community SD De Witt, IA, 436
Central Columbia SD Bloomsburg, PA, 1104
Central Community Unit SD 301 Burlington, IL, 347
Central Consolidated Schools Shiprock, NM, 843
Central Dauphin SD Harrisburg, PA, 1106
Central Elementary Rancho Cucamonga, CA, 129
Central Falls SD Central Falls, RI, 1165
Central Greene SD Waynesburg, PA, 1112
Central ISD Pollok, TX, 1227
Central Islip Union Free SD Central Islip, NY, 891
Central Kitsap SD 401 Silverdale, WA, 1363
Central Montcalm Public Schools Stanton, MI, 615
Central Point SD 6 Central Point, OR, 1070
Central R-III Park Hills, MO, 726
Central Regional Bayville, NJ, 811
Central SD 13J Independence, OR, 1075
Central Square Central SD Central Square, NY, 883
Central Unified Fresno, CA, 90
Central Union Elementary Lemoore, CA, 97
Central Union High El Centro, CA, 93
Central Valley SD 356 Greenacres, WA, 1369
Central York SD York, PA, 1135
Centralia Elementary Buena Park, CA, 117
Centralia SD 401 Centralia, WA, 1364
Ceres Unified Ceres, CA, 152
Chaffey Joint Union High Ontario, CA, 129
Chagrin Falls Ex Vill SD Chagrin Falls, OH, 975
Chambers County Lafayette, AL, 5
Chambersburg Area SD Chambersburg, PA, 1112
Champaign Community Unit SD 4 Champaign, IL, 326
Champion Local SD Warren, OH, 1015
Chandler Unified District Chandler, AZ, 42
Channelview ISD Channelview, TX, 1250
Chanute Public Schools Chanute, KS, 459
Chapel Hill ISD Tyler, TX, 1274
Chapel Hill-Carrboro Schools Chapel Hill, NC, 943
Chappaqua Central SD Chappaqua, NY, 901
Chardon Local SD Chardon, OH, 984
Chariho RD Wood River Junct., RI, 1167
Charleroi SD Charleroi, PA, 1132
Charles City Community SD Charles City, IA, 437
Charleston County SD Charleston, SC, 1175
Charleston CUSD 1 Charleston, IL, 327
Charlotte County Public Schools Charlotte Court House, VA, 1331
Charlotte County SD Port Charlotte, FL, 253
Charlotte Public Schools Charlotte, MI, 596
Charlotte-Mecklenburg Schools Charlotte, NC, 942
Charlottesville City Public Schools Charlottesville, VA, 1331
Charlton County Folkston, GA, 273
Charter Oak Unified Covina, CA, 101
Chartiers Valley SD Pittsburgh, PA, 1087
Chaska Chaska, MN, 658

Chatham Central SD Chatham, NY, 857
Chatham County Schools Pittsboro, NC, 935
Chatham County Savannah, GA, 273
Chattooga County Summerville, GA, 273
Cheatham County School Distrct Ashland City, TN, 1202
Cheboygan Area Schools Cheboygan, MI, 595
Checotah Checotah, OK, 1051
Cheektowaga Central SD Cheektowaga, NY, 859
Cheektowaga-Maryvale Union Free SD Cheektowaga, NY, 860
Cheektowaga-Sloan Union Free SD Sloan, NY, 860
Chehalis SD 302 Chehalis, WA, 1364
Chelmsford North Chelmsford, MA, 557
Chelsea SD Chelsea, MI, 628
Chelsea Chelsea, MA, 568
Cheltenham Township SD Elkins Park, PA, 1123
Chenango Forks Central SD Binghamton, NY, 853
Chenango Valley Central SD Binghamton, NY, 853
Cheney SD 360 Cheney, WA, 1369
Cherokee County Schools Murphy, NC, 935
Cherokee County SD Gaffney, SC, 1176
Cherokee County Canton, GA, 274
Cherokee County Centre, AL, 5
Cherry Creek 5 Greenwood Village, CO, 197
Cherry Hill Twp Cherry Hill, NJ, 792
Chesaning Union Schools Chesaning, MI, 624
Chesapeake City Public Schools Chesapeake, VA, 1331
Cheshire SD Cheshire, CT, 221
Chester County SD Chester, SC, 1176
Chester County SD Henderson, TN, 1203
Chester-Upland SD Chester, PA, 1107
Chesterfield County Public Schools Chesterfield, VA, 1331
Chesterfield County SD Chesterfield, SC, 1176
Chestnut Ridge SD Fishertown, PA, 1093
Cheyenne Mountain 12 Colorado Springs, CO, 198
Chicago Heights SD 170 Chicago Heights, IL, 329
Chichester SD Boothwyn, PA, 1107
Chickasha Chickasha, OK, 1049
Chico Unified Chico, CA, 86
Chicopee Chicopee, MA, 554
Chillicothe City SD Chillicothe, OH, 1008
Chillicothe R-II Chillicothe, MO, 722
Chilton County Clanton, AL, 6
China Spring ISD Waco, TX, 1264
Chinle Unified District Chinle, AZ, 40
Chino Valley Unified District Chino Valley, AZ, 52
Chino Valley Unified Chino, CA, 129
Chippewa Falls Area Chippewa Falls, WI, 1401
Chippewa Hills SD Remus, MI, 613
Chippewa Valley Schools Clinton Township, MI, 610
Chisago Lakes Lindstrom, MN, 658
Chittenango Central SD Chittenango, NY, 866
Choctaw County SD Ackerman, MS, 685
Choctaw County Butler, AL, 6
Choctaw/Nicoma Park Choctaw, OK, 1051
Chowchilla Elementary Chowchilla, CA, 111
Christian County Hopkinsville, KY, 476
Christina SD Newark, DE, 239
Chula Vista Elementary Chula Vista, CA, 133
Churchill County SD Fallon, NV, 762
Churchville-Chili Central SD Churchville, NY, 866
Cicero SD 99 Cicero, IL, 329
Cincinnati City SD Cincinnati, OH, 985
Cinnaminson Twp Cinnaminson, NJ, 789
Circle Towanda, KS, 454
Circleville City SD Circleville, OH, 1005
Citrus County SD Inverness, FL, 253
City of Baker SD Baker, LA, 504
City of Bogalusa School Board Bogalusa, LA, 511
City of Chicago SD 299 Chicago, IL, 329
City of Monroe School Board Monroe, LA, 508
City of Orange Twp Orange, NJ, 795
Claiborne County SD Port Gibson, MS, 685
Claiborne County SD Tazewell, TN, 1203
Claiborne Parish School Board Homer, LA, 504
Clare Public Schools Clare, MI, 595

Claremont SD Claremont, NH, 773
Claremont Unified Claremont, CA, 101
Claremore Claremore, OK, 1054
Clarence Central SD Clarence, NY, 860
Clarenceville SD Livonia, MI, 618
Clarendon County SD 02 Manning, SC, 1176
Clark County SD Las Vegas, NV, 762
Clark County Winchester, KY, 476
Clark Twp Clark, NJ, 818
Clark-Pleasant Com School Corp Whiteland, IN, 402
Clark-Shawnee Local SD Springfield, OH, 970
Clarke County Public Schools Berryville, VA, 1331
Clarke County Athens, GA, 274
Clarke County Grove Hill, AL, 6
Clarksdale Municipal SD Clarksdale, MS, 685
Clarkston Community SD Clarkston, MI, 618
Clarkston SD 250 Clarkston, WA, 1356
Clarkstown Central SD New City, NY, 886
Clarksville SD Clarksville, AR, 69
Clay Community Schools Knightsville, IN, 392
Clay County SD Clay, WV, 1386
Clay County SD Green Cove Springs, FL, 253
Clay County Ashland, AL, 6
Clay County Manchester, KY, 476
Claymont City SD Dennison, OH, 1016
Clayton County Jonesboro, GA, 274
Clayton Clayton, MO, 727
Clear Creek ISD League City, TX, 1246
Clear Fork Valley Local SD Bellville, OH, 1007
Clearfield Area SD Clearfield, PA, 1103
Clearview Local SD Lorain, OH, 994
Clearview Regional Mullica Hill, NJ, 797
Cleburne County Heflin, AL, 6
Cleburne ISD Cleburne, TX, 1259
Clermont Northeastern Local SD Batavia, OH, 972
Cleveland City SD Cleveland, TN, 1202
Cleveland County Schools Shelby, NC, 936
Cleveland Hill Union Free SD Cheektowaga, NY, 860
Cleveland Hts-Univ Hts City SD University Heights, OH, 975
Cleveland ISD Cleveland, TX, 1262
Cleveland Municipal City SD Cleveland, OH, 975
Cleveland SD Cleveland, MS, 684
Cleveland Cleveland, OK, 1053
Cliffside Park Boro Cliffside Park, NJ, 783
Clifton City Clifton, NJ, 813
Clint ISD El Paso, TX, 1243
Clinton Central SD Clinton, NY, 878
Clinton City Schools Clinton, NC, 946
Clinton Community SD Clinton, IA, 436
Clinton County Albany, KY, 476
Clinton CUSD 15 Clinton, IL, 340
Clinton Public SD Clinton, MS, 688
Clinton SD Clinton, CT, 219
Clinton Twp Annandale, NJ, 800
Clinton-Massie Local SD Clarksville, OH, 972
Clinton Clinton, MA, 569
Clinton Clinton, MO, 718
Clinton Clinton, OK, 1048
Clintondale Community Schools Clinton Township, MI, 610
Clintonville Clintonville, WI, 1419
Clio Area SD Clio, MI, 597
Cloquet Cloquet, MN, 657
Clover Park SD 400 Lakewood, WA, 1365
Cloverdale Unified Cloverdale, CA, 150
Cloverleaf Local SD Lodi, OH, 999
Clovis Municipal Schools Clovis, NM, 840
Clovis Unified Clovis, CA, 90
Clyde-Green Springs Ex Vill SD Clyde, OH, 1009
Coachella Valley Unified Thermal, CA, 123
Coahoma County SD Clarksdale, MS, 686
Coal City CUSD 1 Coal City, IL, 345
Coalinga-Huron Joint Unified Coalinga, CA, 90
Coatesville Area SD Coatesville, PA, 1102
Cobb County Marietta, GA, 274
Cobleskill-Richmondville Central SD Cobleskill, NY, 888

Cobre Consolidated Schools Bayard, NM, 841
Cocalico SD Denver, PA, 1114
Cocke County SD Newport, TN, 1203
Coeur D Alene District Coeur D Alene, ID, 317
Coffee County SD Manchester, TN, 1203
Coffee County Douglas, GA, 274
Coffee County Elba, AL, 6
Coffeyville Coffeyville, KS, 459
Cohoes City SD Cohoes, NY, 852
Colbert County Tuscumbia, AL, 7
Colchester SD Colchester, CT, 224
Colchester SD Colchester, VT, 1322
Cold Spring Harbor Central SD Cold Spring Harbor, NY, 891
Coldspring-Oakhurst Cons Coldspring, TX, 1272
Coldwater Community Schools Coldwater, MI, 593
Coldwater Ex Vill SD Coldwater, OH, 1000
College Community SD Cedar Rapids, IA, 439
College Station ISD College Station, TX, 1233
Colleton County SD Walterboro, SC, 1176
Collier County SD Naples, FL, 253
Collingswood Boro Collingswood, NJ, 792
Collinsville CUSD 10 Collinsville, IL, 355
Collinsville Collinsville, OK, 1055
Coloma Community Schools Coloma, MI, 592
Colonial Heights City Public Schools Colonial Heights, VA, 1331
Colonial SD New Castle, DE, 239
Colonial SD Plymouth Meeting, PA, 1123
Colorado River Union High SD Fort Mojave, AZ, 48
Colorado Springs 11 Colorado Springs, CO, 199
Colquitt County Moultrie, GA, 274
Colton Joint Unified Colton, CA, 129
Colts Neck Twp Colts Neck, NJ, 805
Columbia 93 Columbia, MO, 712
Columbia Community Unit SD 4 Columbia, IL, 358
Columbia County SD Lake City, FL, 253
Columbia County Appling, GA, 275
Columbia Falls Elem Columbia Falls, MT, 744
Columbia Heights Columbia Heights, MN, 656
Columbia SD Brooklyn, MI, 603
Columbia SD Columbia, MS, 693
Columbia-Brazoria ISD West Columbia, TX, 1232
Columbus County Schools Whiteville, NC, 936
Columbus ISD Columbus, TX, 1237
Columbus Municipal SD Columbus, MS, 693
Columbus Public Schools Columbus, NE, 754
Columbus Public Schools Columbus, OH, 981
Colville SD 115 Colville, WA, 1370
Comal ISD New Braunfels, TX, 1237
Commack Union Free SD East Northport, NY, 891
Commerce ISD Commerce, TX, 1257
Community Consolidated S D 93 Carol Stream, IL, 341
Community Consolidated SD 46 Grayslake, IL, 350
Community Consolidated SD 62 Des Plaines, IL, 329
Community CSD 168 Sauk Village, IL, 329
Community CSD 59 Arlington Heights, IL, 329
Community High SD 117 Lake Villa, IL, 350
Community High SD 128 Libertyville, IL, 351
Community High SD 155 Crystal Lake, IL, 357
Community High SD 218 Oak Lawn, IL, 330
Community High SD 94 West Chicago, IL, 341
Community High SD 99 Downers Grove, IL, 341
Community Schools of Frankfort Frankfort, IN, 392
Community Unit SD 200 Wheaton, IL, 341
Community Unit SD 300 Carpentersville, IL, 347
Compton Unified Compton, CA, 102
Comstock Park Public Schools Comstock Park, MI, 605
Comstock Public Schools Kalamazoo, MI, 604
Concord Community Schools Elkhart, IN, 395
Concord SD Concord, NH, 771
Concord Concord, MA, 558
Concordia Parish School Board Vidalia, LA, 504
Conecuh County Evergreen, AL, 7
Conejo Valley Unified Thousand Oaks, CA, 157
Conestoga Valley SD Lancaster, PA, 1115

M

Parkway C-2 Chesterfield, MO, 729

Parlier Unified Parlier, CA, 92

Parma City SD Parma, OH, 977

Parsippany-Troy Hills Twp Parsippany, NJ, 810

Parsons Parsons, KS, 458

Pasadena ISD Pasadena, TX, 1252

Pasadena Unified Pasadena, CA, 107

Pascack Valley Regional Montvale, NJ, 786

Pascagoula SD Pascagoula, MS, 690

Pasco County SD Land O' Lakes, FL, 259

Pasco SD 001 Pasco, WA, 1359

Paso Robles Joint Unified Paso Robles, CA, 139

Pasquotank County Schools Elizabeth City, NC, 944

Pass Christian Public SD Pass Christian, MS, 688

Passaic City Passaic, NJ, 813

Passaic County Vocational Wayne, NJ, 813

Patchogue-Medford Union Free SD Patchogue, NY, 894

Paterson City Paterson, NJ, 814

Patrick County Public Schools Stuart, VA, 1339

Patterson Joint Unified Patterson, CA, 153

Pattonville R-III St Ann, MO, 729

Paulding County Dallas, GA, 287

Paulding Ex Vill SD Paulding, OH, 1005

Paulsboro Boro Paulsboro, NJ, 798

Paw Paw Public SD Paw Paw, MI, 628

Pawtucket SD Pawtucket, RI, 1167

Payette Joint District Payette, ID, 319

Payson Unified District Payson, AZ, 41

Pde Division of Data Services Harrisburg, PA, 1107

Peabody Peabody, MA, 552

Peach County Fort Valley, GA, 287

Peach Springs Unified District Peach Springs, AZ, 48

Pearl Public SD Pearl, MS, 697

Pearl River County SD Carriere, MS, 695

Pearl River Union Free SD Pearl River, NY, 886

Pearland ISD Pearland, TX, 1233

Pearsall ISD Pearsall, TX, 1246

Pecos-Barstow-Toyah ISD Pecos, TX, 1272

Peekskill City SD Peekskill, NY, 903

Pekin Community HSD 303 Pekin, IL, 363

Pekin Public SD 108 Pekin, IL, 364

Pelham City Pelham, GA, 285

Pelham SD Windham, NH, 771

Pelham Union Free SD Pelham, NY, 903

Pell City Pell City, AL, 18

Pella Community SD Pella, IA, 440

Pemberton Twp Pemberton, NJ, 791

Pembroke SD Pembroke, NH, 771

Pembroke Pembroke, MA, 567

Pen Argyl Area SD Pen Argyl, PA, 1127

Pender County Schools Burgaw, NC, 944

Pendergast Elementary District Phoenix, AZ, 45

Pendleton County Falmouth, KY, 486

Pendleton SD 16 Pendleton, OR, 1075

Penfield Central SD Penfield, NY, 867

Peninsula SD 401 Gig Harbor, WA, 1365

Penn Cambria SD Cresson, PA, 1100

Penn Hills SD Pittsburgh, PA, 1089

Penn Manor SD Millersville, PA, 1116

Penn Yan Central SD Penn Yan, NY, 905

Penn-Delco SD Aston, PA, 1108

Penn-Harris-Madison Sch Corp Mishawaka, IN, 414

Penn-Trafford SD Harrison City, PA, 1135

Penncrest SD Saegertown, PA, 1105

Pennfield SD Battle Creek, MI, 594

Pennridge SD Perkasie, PA, 1098

Penns Grv-Carney's Pt Reg Penns Grove, NJ, 814

Penns Valley Area SD Spring Mills, PA, 1101

Pennsauken Twp Pennsauken, NJ, 793

Pennsbury SD Fallsington, PA, 1098

Pennsville Pennsville, NJ, 814

Pennsylvania Virtual CS Norristown, PA, 1124

Pentucket West Newbury, MA, 552

Peoria SD 150 Peoria, IL, 360

Peoria Unified SD Glendale, AZ, 46

Peotone CUSD 207u Peotone, IL, 366

Pequannock Twp Pompton Plains, NJ, 810

Pequea Valley SD Kinzers, PA, 1116

Perham Perham, MN, 666

Perkins Local SD Sandusky, OH, 979

Perkiomen Valley SD Collegeville, PA, 1125

Perquimans County Schools Hertford, NC, 944

Perris Elementary Perris, CA, 124

Perris Union High Perris, CA, 125

Perry Community SD Perry, IA, 436

Perry County 32 Perryville, MO, 724

Perry County Hazard, KY, 487

Perry County Marion, AL, 17

Perry Local SD Massillon, OH, 1012

Perry Local SD Perry, OH, 991

Perry Public SD Perry, MI, 626

Perrysburg Exempted Village Perrysburg, OH, 1020

Perryton ISD Perryton, TX, 1269

Person County Schools Roxboro, NC, 944

Perth Amboy City Perth Amboy, NJ, 804

Peru Central SD Peru, NY, 856

Peru Community Schools Peru, IN, 409

Petal SD Petal, MS, 687

Petaluma City Elementary Petaluma, CA, 150

Petaluma Joint Union High Petaluma, CA, 151

Peters Township SD Mcmurray, PA, 1132

Petersburg City Public Schools Petersburg, VA, 1339

Pewaukee Pewaukee, WI, 1419

Pflugerville ISD Pflugerville, TX, 1279

Pharr-San Juan-Alamo ISD Pharr, TX, 1255

Phelps-Clifton Springs Central SD Clifton Springs, NY, 881

Phenix City Phenix City, AL, 18

Philadelphia City District Philadelphia, PA, 1128

Philipsburg-Osceola Area SD Philipsburg, PA, 1104

Phillipsburg Town Phillipsburg, NJ, 820

Philomath SD 17J Philomath, OR, 1066

Phoenix Central SD Phoenix, NY, 884

Phoenix Elementary District Phoenix, AZ, 46

Phoenix Union High SD Phoenix, AZ, 46

Phoenix-Talent SD 4 Phoenix, OR, 1070

Phoenixville Area SD Phoenixville, PA, 1103

Picayune SD Picayune, MS, 696

Pickens County SD Easley, SC, 1182

Pickens County Carrollton, AL, 17

Pickens County Jasper, GA, 287

Pickerington Local SD Pickerington, OH, 980

Piedmont City Unified Piedmont, CA, 85

Piedmont Piedmont, OK, 1046

Pierce County Blackshear, GA, 287

Pierre SD 32-2 Pierre, SD, 1193

Pike County School Corp Petersburg, IN, 411

Pike County Pikeville, KY, 487

Pike County Troy, AL, 17

Pike County Zebulon, GA, 287

Pike-Delta-York Local SD Delta, OH, 983

Pinconning Area Schools Pinconning, MI, 592

Pine Bluff SD Pine Bluff, AR, 69

Pine Bush Central SD Pine Bush, NY, 882

Pine City Pine City, MN, 667

Pine Grove Area SD Pine Grove, PA, 1129

Pine Hill Boro Pine Hill, NJ, 793

Pine Tree ISD Longview, TX, 1248

Pine-Richland SD Gibsonia, PA, 1089

Pinelands Regional Tuckerton, NJ, 812

Pinellas County SD Largo, FL, 259

Piner-Olivet Union Elementary Santa Rosa, CA, 151

Pinkerton Academy SD Derry, NH, 772

Pinon Unified District Pinon, AZ, 49

Piqua City SD Piqua, OH, 1000

Piscataway Twp Piscataway, NJ, 804

Pitman Boro Pitman, NJ, 798

Pitt County Schools Greenville, NC, 944

Pittsburg ISD Pittsburg, TX, 1236

Pittsburg Unified Pittsburg, CA, 88

Pittsburg Pittsburg, KS, 455

Pittsburgh SD Pittsburgh, PA, 1089

Pittsfield Pittsfield, MA, 547

Pittsford Central SD Pittsford, NY, 868

Pittsgrove Twp Pittsgrove, NJ, 814

Pittston Area SD Pittston, PA, 1120

Pittsylvania County Public Schools Chatham, VA, 1340

Placentia-Yorba Linda Unified Placentia, CA, 120

Placer Union High Auburn, CA, 121

Plain Local SD Canton, OH, 1012

Plain Local SD New Albany, OH, 982

Plainedge Union Free SD North Massapequa, NY, 874

Plainfield City Plainfield, NJ, 818

Plainfield Community Sch Corp Plainfield, IN, 399

Plainfield SD 202 Plainfield, IL, 366

Plainfield SD Plainfield, CT, 227

Plainview ISD Plainview, TX, 1249

Plainview-Old Bethpage Central SD Plainview, NY, 874

Plainville SD Plainville, CT, 217

Plainwell Community Schools Plainwell, MI, 590

Plano ISD Plano, TX, 1237

Plaquemines Parish School Board Port Sulphur, LA, 508

Platte County R-III Platte City, MO, 725

Platteville Platteville, WI, 1404

Plattsburgh City SD Plattsburgh, NY, 856

Plattsmouth Community Schools Plattsmouth, NE, 752

Pleasant Grove ISD Texarkana, TX, 1232

Pleasant Hill R-III Pleasant Hill, MO, 714

Pleasant Ridge Union Elementary Grass Valley, CA, 116

Pleasant Valley Community SD Pleasant Valley, IA, 442

Pleasant Valley School Camarillo, CA, 158

Pleasant Valley SD Brodheadsville, PA, 1123

Pleasanton ISD Pleasanton, TX, 1228

Pleasanton Unified Pleasanton, CA, 85

Pleasantville City Pleasantville, NJ, 783

Pleasantville Union Free SD Pleasantville, NY, 903

Plum Borough SD Plum, PA, 1089

Plumas Unified Quincy, CA, 122

Plumsted Twp New Egypt, NJ, 812

Plymouth Community School Corp Plymouth, IN, 409

Plymouth SD Terryville, CT, 218

Plymouth-Canton Community Schools Plymouth, MI, 632

Plymouth Plymouth, MA, 567

Plymouth Plymouth, WI, 1415

Pocahontas SD Pocahontas, AR, 72

Pocatello District Pocatello, ID, 314

Pocono Mountain SD Swiftwater, PA, 1123

Point Isabel ISD Port Isabel, TX, 1235

Point Pleasant Boro Point Pleasant, NJ, 812

Pointe Coupee Parish School Board New Roads, LA, 508

Pojoaque Valley Public Schools Santa Fe, NM, 844

Poland Local SD Poland, OH, 998

Polk County Schools Columbus, NC, 945

Polk County SD Bartow, FL, 260

Polk County SD Benton, TN, 1211

Polk County Cedartown, GA, 287

Pomona Unified Pomona, CA, 107

Pompton Lakes Boro Pompton Lakes, NJ, 814

Ponca City Ponca City, OK, 1049

Pontiac City SD Pontiac, MI, 620

Pontotoc City Schools Pontotoc, MS, 696

Pontotoc County SD Pontotoc, MS, 697

Poplar Bluff R-I Poplar Bluff, MO, 713

Poplarville Separate SD Poplarville, MS, 696

Poquoson City Public Schools Poquoson, VA, 1340

Port Angeles SD 121 Port Angeles, WA, 1357

Port Arthur ISD Port Arthur, TX, 1258

Port Chester-Rye Union Free SD Port Chester, NY, 904

Port Clinton City SD Port Clinton, OH, 1004

Port Huron Area SD Port Huron, MI, 626

Port Jervis City SD Port Jervis, NY, 882

Port Neches-Groves ISD Port Neches, TX, 1259

Port Townsend SD 50 Port Townsend, WA, 1360

Port Washington Union Free SD Port Washington, NY, 874

Port Washington-Saukville Port Washington, WI, 1412

Portage Community Portage, WI, 1401

Portage Public Schools Portage, MI, 604

Portage Township Schools Portage, IN, 412

Portales Municipal Schools Portales, NM, 843

South Windsor SD South Windsor, CT, 217
South-Western City SD Grove City, OH, 982
Southampton County Public Schools Courtland, VA, 1343
Southampton Union Free SD Southampton, NY, 896
Southborough Northborough, MA, 572
Southbridge Southbridge, MA, 572
Southeast Delco SD Folcroft, PA, 1108
Southeast Dubois County Sch Corp Ferdinand, IN, 394
Southeast Local SD Apple Creek, OH, 1019
Southeast Local SD Ravenna, OH, 1007
Southeast Polk Community SD Runnells, IA, 441
Southeastern School Corp Walton, IN, 392
Southern Hancock County Com Sch Corp New Palestine, IN, 398
Southern Kern Unified Rosamond, CA, 97
Southern Lehigh SD Center Valley, PA, 1119
Southern Regional Manahawkin, NJ, 813
Southern Tioga SD Blossburg, PA, 1130
Southern York County SD Glen Rock, PA, 1137
Southfield Public SD Southfield, MI, 621
Southgate Community SD Southgate, MI, 633
Southington SD Southington, CT, 217
Southmoreland SD Scottdale, PA, 1135
Southside ISD San Antonio, TX, 1231
Southwest Dubois County Sch Corp Huntingburg, IN, 394
Southwest ISD San Antonio, TX, 1231
Southwest Licking Local SD Etna, OH, 993
Southwest Local SD Harrison, OH, 987
Southwest School Corp Sullivan, IN, 415
Southwestern Central SD At Jamestown Jamestown, NY, 855
Southwestern CUSD 9 Piasa, IL, 355
Southwick-Tolland Southwick, MA, 555
Spackenkill Union Free SD Poughkeepsie, NY, 859
Spalding County Griffin, GA, 289
Sparta Area Schools Sparta, MI, 607
Sparta Area Sparta, WI, 1410
Sparta CUSD 140 Sparta, IL, 360
Sparta Twp Sparta, NJ, 817
Spartanburg County SD 01 Campobello, SC, 1182
Spartanburg County SD 02 Spartanburg, SC, 1182
Spartanburg County SD 03 Glendale, SC, 1183
Spartanburg County SD 04 Woodruff, SC, 1183
Spartanburg County SD 05 Duncan, SC, 1183
Spartanburg County SD 06 Spartanburg, SC, 1183
Spartanburg County SD 07 Spartanburg, SC, 1183
Spearfish SD 40-2 Spearfish, SD, 1194
Special School District - St. Louis County Town & Country, MO, 729
Spencer Community SD Spencer, IA, 435
Spencer County Taylorsvil, KY, 488
Spencer-E Brookfield Spencer, MA, 572
Spencer-Owen Community Schools Spencer, IN, 411
Spencerport Central SD Spencerport, NY, 868
Splendora ISD Splendora, TX, 1267
Spokane SD 81 Spokane, WA, 1370
Spooner Spooner, WI, 1417
Spotswood Boro Spotswood, NJ, 805
Spotsylvania County Public Schools Spotsylvania, VA, 1343
Spring Branch ISD Houston, TX, 1252
Spring Cove SD Roaring Spring, PA, 1096
Spring Grove Area SD Spring Grove, PA, 1137
Spring Hill ISD Longview, TX, 1248
Spring Hill Spring Hill, KS, 457
Spring ISD Houston, TX, 1252
Spring Lake Park Spring Lake Park, MN, 656
Spring Lake Public Schools Spring Lake, MI, 623
Spring-Ford Area SD Collegeville, PA, 1125
Springboro Community City SD Springboro, OH, 1018
Springdale SD Springdale, AR, 74
Springfield City SD Springfield, OH, 971
Springfield Local Schools Holland, OH, 996
Springfield Local SD Akron, OH, 1014
Springfield R-XII Springfield, MO, 717
Springfield SD 186 Springfield, IL, 362

Springfield SD 19 Springfield, OR, 1072
Springfield SD Springfield, PA, 1109
Springfield Township SD Oreland, PA, 1125
Springfield Twp Springfield, NJ, 819
Springfield Springfield, MA, 555
Springtown ISD Springtown, TX, 1270
Springville-Griffith Institute Central SD Springville, NY, 862
St Charles CUSD 303 Saint Charles, IL, 348
St Clair County Ashville, AL, 19
St Clairsville-Richland City SD Saint Clairsville, OH, 968
St Helens SD 502 St Helens, OR, 1068
St Marys City SD Saint Marys, OH, 967
St Vrain Valley RE-1J Longmont, CO, 197
St. Anthony-New Brighton St. Anthony, MN, 662
St. Charles R-VI St Charles, MO, 726
St. Clair R-XIII St Clair, MO, 716
St. Cloud St. Cloud, MN, 670
St. Francis St. Francis, MN, 656
St. James R-I St James, MO, 724
St. Johns County SD St. Augustine, FL, 260
St. Johns Public Schools St. Johns, MI, 596
St. Joseph Public Schools St. Joseph, MI, 593
St. Joseph St Joseph, MO, 713
St. Louis City St Louis, MO, 730
St. Louis County Virginia, MN, 670
St. Louis Park St. Louis Park, MN, 662
St. Lucie County SD Fort Pierce, FL, 261
St. Michael-Albertville St. Michael, MN, 672
St. Paul St. Paul, MN, 668
St. Peter St. Peter, MN, 665
Stafford County Public Schools Stafford, VA, 1343
Stafford Municipal School Stafford, TX, 1245
Stafford SD Stafford Springs, CT, 226
Stafford Twp Manahawkin, NJ, 813
Stamford SD Stamford, CT, 214
Standard Elementary Bakersfield, CA, 97
Standish-Sterling Community Schools Standish, MI, 591
Stanislaus Union Elementary Modesto, CA, 153
Stanly County Schools Albemarle, NC, 946
Stanwood-Camano SD 401 Stanwood, WA, 1368
Star City SD Star City, AR, 70
Starkville SD Starkville, MS, 695
Starpoint Central SD Lockport, NY, 877
State College Area SD State College, PA, 1102
State Vocational-Technical Schools Middletown, CT, 220
Staunton City Public Schools Staunton, VA, 1343
Ste. Genevieve County R-II Ste Genevieve, MO, 730
Steamboat Springs Re-2 Steamboat Springs, CO, 203
Steel Valley SD Munhall, PA, 1090
Steger SD 194 Steger, IL, 338
Steilacoom Historical SD Steilacoom, WA, 1366
Stephens County Toccoa, GA, 289
Stephenville Stephenville, TX, 1244
Sterling C U Dist 5 Sterling, IL, 364
Steubenville City SD Steubenville, OH, 990
Stevens Point Area Stevens Point, WI, 1412
Stewart County SD Dover, TN, 1213
Stewartville Stewartville, MN, 666
Stillwater Stillwater, MN, 671
Stillwater Stillwater, OK, 1053
Sto-Rox SD Mckees Rocks, PA, 1090
Stockbridge Community Schools Stockbridge, MI, 601
Stockton City Unified Stockton, CA, 138
Stokes County Schools Danbury, NC, 946
Stone County SD Wiggins, MS, 698
Stoneham Stoneham, MA, 561
Stonington SD Old Mystic, CT, 225
Stoughton Area Stoughton, WI, 1402
Stoughton Stoughton, MA, 565
Stow-Munroe Falls City SD Stow, OH, 1014
Stratford SD Stratford, CT, 214
Streator Elem SD 44 Streator, IL, 349
Streetsboro City Schools Streetsboro, OH, 1007
Strongsville City SD Strongsville, OH, 978
Stroudsburg Area SD Stroudsburg, PA, 1123

Struthers City SD Struthers, OH, 998
Sturgis Public Schools Sturgis, MI, 627
Stuttgart SD Stuttgart, AR, 63
Sudbury Sudbury, MA, 561
Suffield SD Suffield, CT, 218
Suffolk City Public Schools Suffolk, VA, 1343
Sugarcreek Local SD Bellbrook, OH, 984
Sullivan County School Distrct Blountville, TN, 1214
Sullivan West Central SD Callicoon, NY, 897
Sullivan Sullivan, MO, 716
Sulphur Springs ISD Sulphur Springs, TX, 1256
Sulphur Springs Union Elementary Canyon Country, CA, 109
Sultan Home School Sultan, WA, 1369
Summers County SD Hinton, WV, 1392
Summit City Summit, NJ, 819
Summit Hill SD 161 Frankfort, IL, 366
Summit Re-1 Frisco, CO, 203
Summit SD 104 Summit, IL, 338
Sumner County SD Gallatin, TN, 1214
Sumner SD #320 Sumner, WA, 1366
Sumter County SD 02 Sumter, SC, 1183
Sumter County SD 17 Sumter, SC, 1183
Sumter County SD Bushnell, FL, 261
Sumter County Americus, GA, 289
Sumter County Livingston, AL, 19
Sun Prairie Area Sun Prairie, WI, 1403
Sunflower County SD Indianola, MS, 698
Sunman-Dearborn Com Sch Corp Sunman, IN, 393
Sunnyside SD 201 Sunnyside, WA, 1373
Sunnyside Unified District Tucson, AZ, 50
Sunnyvale Elementary Sunnyvale, CA, 147
Superior Superior, WI, 1403
Surry County Schools Dobson, NC, 947
Susquehanna Township SD Harrisburg, PA, 1107
Susquehanna Valley Central SD Conklin, NY, 853
Susquenita SD Duncannon, PA, 1128
Sussex-Wantage Regional Wantage, NJ, 817
Sutherlin SD 130 Sutherlin, OR, 1069
Sutton Sutton, MA, 572
Suwannee County SD Live Oak, FL, 261
Swain County Schools Bryson City, NC, 947
Swampscott Swampscott, MA, 553
Swan Valley SD Saginaw, MI, 625
Swansea Swansea, MA, 549
Swanton Local SD Swanton, OH, 983
Swartz Creek Community Schools Swartz Creek, MI, 599
Sweeny ISD Sweeny, TX, 1233
Sweet Home Central SD Amherst, NY, 862
Sweet Home SD 55 Sweet Home, OR, 1072
Sweetwater County SD #1 Rock Springs, WY, 1436
Sweetwater County SD #2 Green River, WY, 1436
Sweetwater ISD Sweetwater, TX, 1268
Sweetwater Union High Chula Vista, CA, 137
Switzerland County School Corp Vevay, IN, 415
Switzerland of Ohio Local SD Woodsfield, OH, 1001
Sycamore Community City SD Cincinnati, OH, 987
Sycamore CUSD 427 Sycamore, IL, 340
Sylacauga City Sylacauga, AL, 19
Sylvan Union Elementary Modesto, CA, 153
Sylvania City SD Sylvania, OH, 996
Syosset Central SD Syosset, NY, 875
Syracuse City SD Syracuse, NY, 880

T

Tacoma SD 10 Tacoma, WA, 1366
Taconic Hills Central SD Craryville, NY, 857
Taft City Elementary Taft, CA, 97
Tahlequah Tahlequah, OK, 1047
Tahoe-Truckee Joint Unified Truckee, CA, 122
Tahoma SD 409 Maple Valley, WA, 1363
Talawanda City SD Oxford, OH, 970
Talbot County Public Schools Easton, MD, 539
Talladega City Talladega, AL, 19
Talladega County Talladega, AL, 19

U

V

Catskill, NY, 864
Cave Creek, AZ, 42
Cazenovia, NY, 866
Cedar City, UT, 1313
Cedar Falls, IA, 434
Cedar Grove, NJ, 795
Cedar Hill, TX, 1238
Cedar Lake, IN, 405
Cedar Rapids, IA, 439
Cedar Springs, MI, 605
Cedarburg, WI, 1411
Cedartown, GA, 287
Celina, OH, 1000
Center Line, MI, 609
Center Valley, PA, 1119
Center, TX, 1274
Centereach, NY, 894
Centerville, IA, 434
Centerville, IN, 417
Centerville, LA, 510
Centerville, OH, 1001
Centerville, TN, 1207
Central Falls, RI, 1165
Central Islip, NY, 891
Central Point, OR, 1070
Central Square, NY, 883
Central Valley, NY, 882
Centralia, WA, 1364
Centre, AL, 5
Centreville, AL, 4
Centreville, MD, 538
Ceres, CA, 152
Cerritos, CA, 99
Chagrin Falls, OH, 975, 984
Chalmette, LA, 509
Chambersburg, PA, 1112
Champaign, IL, 326
Champlain, NY, 856
Chandler, AZ, 42
Channelview, TX, 1250
Chanute, KS, 459
Chapel Hill, NC, 943
Chappaqua, NY, 901
Chardon, OH, 984
Charleroi, PA, 1132
Charles City, IA, 437
Charles Town, WV, 1388
Charleston, IL, 327
Charleston, MS, 698
Charleston, SC, 1175
Charleston, WV, 1388
Charlestown, NH, 774
Charlotte Court House, VA, 1331
Charlotte, MI, 596
Charlotte, NC, 942
Charlottesville, VA, 1328, 1331
Chaska, MN, 658
Chatham, IL, 361
Chatham, NJ, 810
Chatham, NY, 857
Chatham, VA, 1340
Chatom, AL, 20
Chatsworth, GA, 286
Chattanooga, TN, 1206
Chattaroy, WA, 1370
Cheboygan, MI, 595
Checotah, OK, 1051
Cheektowaga, NY, 859, 860
Chehalis, WA, 1364
Chelsea, MA, 568
Chelsea, MI, 628
Cheney, WA, 1369
Chepachet, RI, 1166
Cherry Hill, NJ, 792
Chesaning, MI, 624
Chesapeake, VA, 1331

Cheshire, CT, 221
Cheshire, MA, 547
Chester, NJ, 811
Chester, PA, 1107
Chester, SC, 1176
Chesterfield, MO, 729
Chesterfield, SC, 1176
Chesterfield, VA, 1331
Chesterland, OH, 984
Chesterton, IN, 411
Chestertown, MD, 538
Cheyenne, WY, 1435
Chicago Heights, IL, 328, 329, 331
Chicago, IL, 329
Chickasha, OK, 1049
Chico, CA, 86
Chicopee, MA, 554
Chillicothe, IL, 360
Chillicothe, MO, 722
Chillicothe, OH, 1008, 1009
Chinle, AZ, 40
Chino Valley, AZ, 52
Chino, CA, 129
Chipley, FL, 262
Chippewa Falls, WI, 1401
Chittenango, NY, 866
Choctaw, OK, 1051
Chowchilla, CA, 111
Christiansburg, VA, 1338
Chula Vista, CA, 133, 137
Churchville, NY, 866
Cicero, IL, 329, 332
Cincinnati, OH, 972, 985, 986, 987
Cinnaminson, NJ, 789
Circle Pines, MN, 656
Circleville, OH, 1005
City Of Industry, CA, 104
Clanton, AL, 6
Clare, MI, 595
Claremont, CA, 101
Claremont, NH, 773
Claremore, OK, 1054
Clarence, NY, 860
Clark, NJ, 818
Clarkesville, GA, 280
Clarks Summit, PA, 1113
Clarksburg, NJ, 807
Clarksburg, WV, 1388
Clarksdale, MS, 685, 686
Clarkston, MI, 618
Clarkston, WA, 1356
Clarksville, AR, 69
Clarksville, OH, 972
Clarksville, TN, 1211
Claxton, GA, 277
Clay, WV, 1386
Claymont, DE, 238
Claysville, PA, 1132
Clayton, GA, 288
Clayton, IN, 399
Clayton, MO, 727
Clearfield, PA, 1103
Cleburne, TX, 1259
Cleveland, GA, 292
Cleveland, MS, 684
Cleveland, OH, 975, 977
Cleveland, OK, 1053
Cleveland, TN, 1202
Cleveland, TX, 1262
Cleves, OH, 987
Cliffside Park, NJ, 783
Clifton Park, NY, 887
Clifton Springs, NY, 881
Clifton, NJ, 813
Clinton Township, MI, 610, 611
Clinton, CT, 219

Clinton, IA, 436
Clinton, IL, 340
Clinton, IN, 416
Clinton, LA, 505
Clinton, MA, 569
Clinton, MO, 718
Clinton, MS, 688
Clinton, NC, 946
Clinton, NY, 878
Clinton, OK, 1048
Clinton, SC, 1179
Clinton, TN, 1201
Clintonville, WI, 1419
Clintwood, VA, 1332
Clio, MI, 597
Cloquet, MN, 657
Clover, SC, 1184
Cloverdale, CA, 150
Clovis, CA, 90
Clovis, NM, 840
Clyde, OH, 1009
Coal City, IL, 345
Coal Township, PA, 1128
Coalinga, CA, 90
Coatesville, PA, 1102
Cobleskill, NY, 888
Cochran, GA, 271
Cody, WY, 1435
Coeur D Alene, ID, 317
Coffeyville, KS, 459
Cohoes, NY, 852
Cokato, MN, 665
Colchester, CT, 224
Colchester, VT, 1322
Cold Spring Harbor, NY, 891
Cold Spring, MN, 670
Coldspring, TX, 1272
Coldwater, MI, 593
Coldwater, OH, 1000
Colfax, LA, 505
College Station, TX, 1233
Collegeville, PA, 1125
Collingswood, NJ, 792
Collins, MS, 686
Collinsville, IL, 355
Collinsville, OK, 1055
Collinsville, VA, 1335
Coloma, MI, 592
Colonial Heights, VA, 1331
Colorado Springs, CO, 198, 199
Colton, CA, 129
Colts Neck, NJ, 805, 807
Columbia City, IN, 418
Columbia Falls, MT, 744
Columbia Heights, MN, 656
Columbia, IL, 358
Columbia, KY, 472
Columbia, LA, 503
Columbia, MO, 712
Columbia, MS, 693, 694
Columbia, SC, 1182
Columbia, TN, 1210
Columbiana, AL, 18
Columbus, GA, 286
Columbus, IN, 390
Columbus, MS, 693
Columbus, NC, 945
Columbus, NE, 754
Columbus, NJ, 790
Columbus, OH, 981
Columbus, TX, 1237
Colville, WA, 1370
Commerce City, CO, 196
Commerce, TX, 1257
Compton, CA, 102
Comstock Park, MI, 605

Concord, CA, 88
Concord, MA, 558
Concord, NC, 934
Concord, NH, 771
Conklin, NY, 853
Conneaut, OH, 967
Connell, WA, 1359
Connellsville, PA, 1111
Connersville, IN, 396
Conroe, TX, 1267
Constantine, MI, 627
Converse, IN, 409
Conway, AR, 67
Conway, SC, 1179
Conyers, GA, 288
Cookeville, TN, 1211
Coolidge, AZ, 51
Coon Rapids, MN, 656
Coopersville, MI, 622
Coos Bay, OR, 1068
Copiague, NY, 892
Copley, OH, 1013
Coppell, TX, 1239
Copperas Cove, TX, 1238
Corbin, KY, 490
Corcoran, CA, 98
Cordele, GA, 275
Cordova, SC, 1181
Corinth, MS, 684
Corning, CA, 154
Cornwall On Hudson, NY, 881
Corona, CA, 133
Coronado, CA, 133
Corpus Christi, TX, 1268, 1269
Corry, PA, 1109
Corsicana, TX, 1268
Cortez, CO, 202
Cortland, NY, 857
Cortland, OH, 1015
Corunna, MI, 625
Corvallis, OR, 1066
Corydon, IN, 399
Coshocton, OH, 973
Costa Mesa, CA, 119, 120
Cottage Grove, MN, 671
Cottage Grove, OR, 1072
Cottonwood, AZ, 52
Council Bluffs, IA, 441
Country Club Hill, IL, 330
Courtland, VA, 1343
Coushatta, LA, 509
Coventry, CT, 225
Coventry, RI, 1164
Covina, CA, 101, 102
Covington, GA, 286
Covington, KY, 481
Covington, LA, 510
Covington, TN, 1214
Covington, VA, 1328
Coweta, OK, 1057
Coxsackie, NY, 864
Craig, CO, 201
Crandall, TX, 1260
Cranford, NJ, 818
Cranston, RI, 1165
Craryville, NY, 857
Crawfordsville, IN, 409, 410
Crawfordville, FL, 262
Crescent City, CA, 89
Cresco, IA, 437
Cresskill, NJ, 783
Cresson, PA, 1100
Crete, IL, 364
Crete, NE, 755
Crockett, CA, 87
Crockett, TX, 1256
Cromwell, CT, 219

Crookston, MN, 667
Crosby, TX, 1250
Cross City, FL, 254
Crossett, AR, 63
Crossville, TN, 1204
Croswell, MI, 625
Croton-On-Hudson, NY, 901
Crowley, LA, 502
Crowley, TX, 1276
Crown Point, IN, 404
Crystal City, TX, 1284
Crystal Lake, IL, 357
Cudahy, WI, 1408
Cuero, TX, 1241
Cullman, AL, 8
Culpeper, VA, 1332
Culver City, CA, 102
Cumberland Ctr., ME, 523
Cumberland, MD, 536
Cumberland, RI, 1166
Cumming, GA, 278
Cupertino, CA, 144
Currituck, NC, 937
Cushing, OK, 1053
Cutchogue, NY, 894
Cuthbert, GA, 288
Cuyahoga Falls, OH, 1013
Cynthiana, KY, 480
Cypress, CA, 118

D

Dadeville, AL, 19
Dahlonega, GA, 284
Daingerfield, TX, 1268
Daleville, AL, 8
Dalhart, TX, 1238
Dallas Center, IA, 436
Dallas, GA, 287
Dallas, OR, 1075
Dallas, PA, 1119
Dallas, TX, 1239, 1240
Dallastown, PA, 1136
Dalton, GA, 292, 293
Dalton, MA, 547
Daly City, CA, 140
Danbury, CT, 212
Danbury, NC, 946
Dandridge, TN, 1208
Danielson, CT, 226
Danielsville, GA, 284
Dannemora, NY, 857
Dansville, NY, 865
Danvers, MA, 550
Danville, CA, 88
Danville, IL, 364
Danville, IN, 399
Danville, KY, 474
Danville, PA, 1126
Danville, VA, 1332
Dardanelle, AR, 74
Darien, CT, 212
Darien, GA, 285
Darien, IL, 341
Darlington, SC, 1176
Davenport, IA, 442
Davis, CA, 159
Davison, MI, 598
Dawson, GA, 290
Dawsonville, GA, 276
Dayton, OH, 1001, 1002
Dayton, TN, 1212
Dayton, TX, 1262
De Forest, WI, 1401
De Kalb, IL, 340
De Pere, WI, 1400, 1401
De Queen, AR, 73

Temecula, CA, 125
Tempe, AZ, 44, 46, 47
Temperance, MI, 614
Temple City, CA, 109
Temple, TX, 1230
Templeton, CA, 139
Tenafly, NJ, 788
Terre Haute, IN, 416
Terrell, TX, 1261
Terryville, CT, 218
Tewksbury, MA, 561
Texarkana, AR, 70
Texarkana, TX, 1232
Texas City, TX, 1247
The Dalles, OR, 1076
The Plains, OH, 967
Thermal, CA, 123
Thibodaux, LA, 507
Thief River Falls, MN, 667
Thomaston, GA, 291
Thomasville, AL, 6
Thomasville, GA, 290
Thomasville, NC, 937
Thomson, GA, 285
Thornton, CO, 196
Thorntown, IN, 391
Thornville, OH, 1005
Thornwood, NY, 903
Thousand Oaks, CA, 157
Three Rivers, MI, 627
Throop, PA, 1114
Tiffin, OH, 1010
Tifton, GA, 290
Tigard, OR, 1076
Tillamook, OR, 1075
Tilton, NH, 768
Tinley Park, IL, 332, 338
Tinton Falls, NJ, 808
Tipp City, OH, 1000
Tipton, IN, 416
Titusville, PA, 1131
Tiverton, RI, 1165
Toccoa, GA, 289
Toledo, OH, 996
Tolland, CT, 226
Tolleson, AZ, 47
Tomah, WI, 1410
Tomahawk, WI, 1407
Tomball, TX, 1252
Tompkinsville, KY, 485
Toms River, NJ, 813
Ton0pah, NV, 763
Tonawanda, NY, 862
Tonganoxie, KS, 458
Tontogany, OH, 1020
Tooele, UT, 1315
Topeka, IN, 404
Topeka, KS, 461, 462
Toppenish, WA, 1373
Topsfield, MA, 552
Topsham, ME, 526
Topton, PA, 1094
Torrance, CA, 109
Torrington, CT, 219
Torrington, WY, 1434
Towanda, KS, 454
Towanda, PA, 1097
Town & Country, MO, 729
Townsend, MA, 560
Towson, MD, 536
Tracy, CA, 137, 138
Trafalgar, IN, 402
Traverse City, MI, 600
Travis Afb, CA, 149
Trenton, FL, 254
Trenton, GA, 275

Trenton, MI, 633
Trenton, NJ, 802
Trenton, OH, 969
Trinidad, CO, 201
Trotwood, OH, 1002
Troy, AL, 17, 18
Troy, IL, 356
Troy, MI, 621
Troy, MO, 722
Troy, NC, 942
Troy, NY, 885, 886
Troy, OH, 1001
Troy, PA, 1097
Truckee, CA, 122
Trumann, AR, 71
Trumbull, CT, 214
Truth Or Conseq, NM, 844
Tuba City, AZ, 41
Tuckerton, NJ, 812
Tucson, AZ, 50, 51
Tukwila, WA, 1363
Tulare, CA, 156
Tullahoma, TN, 1203
Tulsa, OK, 1056
Tumwater, WA, 1371
Tunica, MS, 699
Tunkhannock, PA, 1135
Tupelo, MS, 692
Turbotville, PA, 1128
Turlock, CA, 154
Turner, ME, 522
Turner, OR, 1073
Tuscaloosa, AL, 20
Tuscumbia, AL, 7
Tuskegee, AL, 15
Tustin, CA, 120
Twentynine Palms, CA, 130
Twin Falls, ID, 319
Twinsburg, OH, 1014
Two Harbors, MN, 664
Two Rivers, WI, 1407
Tyler, TX, 1274
Tylertown, MS, 700
Tyngsborough, MA, 558, 561
Tyrone, PA, 1097

U

Ukiah, CA, 112
Ulysses, KS, 456
Unalakleet, AK, 33
Union City, CA, 85
Union City, NJ, 800
Union City, TN, 1211
Union Springs, AL, 4
Union, MO, 717
Union, NJ, 819
Union, SC, 1184
Union, WV, 1390
Uniondale, NY, 875
Uniontown, PA, 1111
Unity, ME, 527
University City, MO, 729
University Heights, OH, 975
University Pla, WA, 1366
Upland, CA, 131
Upper Arlington, OH, 982
Upper Marlboro, MD, 538
Upper Sandusky, OH, 1020
Urbana, IL, 326
Urbana, OH, 970
Urbandale, IA, 441
Utica, NY, 879
Utica, OH, 993
Uvalde, TX, 1279
Uxbridge, MA, 573

V

Vacaville, CA, 149
Vail, AZ, 51
Valatie, NY, 857
Valdosta, GA, 284
Valencia, CA, 101, 107
Vallejo, CA, 149
Valley Center, CA, 137
Valley Center, KS, 461
Valley Stream, NY, 875, 876
Valparaiso, IN, 412
Van Buren, AR, 66
Van Horne, IA, 434
Van Wert, OH, 1017
Van, TX, 1280
Vanceburg, KY, 483
Vancleave, MS, 689
Vancouver, WA, 1357, 1358
Vandalia, IL, 345
Vandalia, OH, 1003
Vandergrift, PA, 1134
Vashon, WA, 1363
Vassar, MI, 627
Ventura, CA, 159
Venus, TX, 1260
Vermilion, OH, 979
Vermontville, MI, 597
Vernal, UT, 1315
Vernon Hills, IL, 351
Vernon, AL, 13
Vernon, CT, 226
Vernon, NJ, 817
Vernon, TX, 1282
Vero Beach, FL, 256
Verona, NJ, 797
Verona, NY, 878
Verona, WI, 1403
Versailles, IN, 413
Versailles, KY, 490
Versailles, MO, 723
Vestal, NY, 854
Vevay, IN, 415
Vicksburg, MI, 605
Vicksburg, MS, 700
Victor, NY, 881
Victoria, TX, 1280
Victoria, VA, 1337
Victorville, CA, 132
Vidalia, GA, 291
Vidalia, LA, 504
Vidor, TX, 1270
Vienna, GA, 276
Viera, FL, 252
Villa Park, IL, 342, 344
Ville Platte, LA, 505
Vilonia, AR, 67
Vincennes, IN, 402
Vincent, OH, 1018
Vineland, NJ, 795
Vinita, OK, 1047
Vinton, IA, 434
Virginia Beach, VA, 1344
Virginia, MN, 670
Visalia, CA, 156
Vista, CA, 137
Voorhees, NJ, 792, 793

W

W Columbia, SC, 1180
Wabash, IN, 417
Waco, TX, 1264, 1265
Waconia, MN, 658
Wadesboro, NC, 932
Wadsworth, OH, 999
Wagoner, OK, 1057

Wahpeton, ND, 960
Wakefield, MA, 561
Wakefield, RI, 1168
Waldron, AR, 73
Waldwick, NJ, 788
Wales, WI, 1418
Walhalla, SC, 1181
Walkerton, IN, 414
Wall, NJ, 808
Walla Walla, WA, 1371
Walled Lake, MI, 621
Waller, TX, 1280
Wallingford, CT, 223
Wallingford, PA, 1109
Wallkill, NY, 899
Walnut Creek, CA, 89
Walnut, CA, 109
Walpole, MA, 565
Walterboro, SC, 1176
Waltham, MA, 561
Walton, IN, 392
Wantage, NJ, 817
Wantagh, NY, 876
Wapakoneta, OH, 968
Wapato, WA, 1373
Wappingers Falls, NY, 859
Wareham, MA, 568
Warminster, PA, 1098
Warr Acres, OK, 1052
Warren, AR, 64
Warren, ME, 525
Warren, MI, 610, 612
Warren, NJ, 816
Warren, OH, 1015, 1016
Warrensburg, MO, 721
Warrensville Heights, OH, 978
Warrenton, MO, 731
Warrenton, NC, 948
Warrenton, VA, 1333
Warsaw, IN, 403
Warsaw, KY, 478
Warsaw, MO, 712
Warsaw, OH, 974
Wartburg, TN, 1211
Warwick, NY, 883
Warwick, RI, 1164
Wasco, CA, 97
Waseca, MN, 671
Washington Court Hou, OH, 980
Washington, DC, 246
Washington, GA, 293
Washington, IA, 443
Washington, IN, 393
Washington, MO, 717
Washington, NC, 933
Washington, NJ, 820
Washington, PA, 1132, 1133
Washingtonville, NY, 883
Washougal, WA, 1358
Waterboro, ME, 527
Waterbury, CT, 223
Waterford, CA, 154
Waterford, CT, 225
Waterford, MI, 621
Waterford, PA, 1110
Waterford, WI, 1413
Waterloo, IA, 434
Waterloo, IL, 358
Waterloo, IN, 393
Waterloo, NY, 889
Watertown, CT, 219
Watertown, MA, 562
Watertown, NY, 865
Watertown, SD, 1193
Watertown, WI, 1405
Waterville, ME, 525

Watkins Glen, NY, 889
Watkinsville, GA, 286
Watsonville, CA, 147
Wauchula, FL, 255
Wauconda, IL, 353
Waukee, IA, 436
Waukegan, IL, 354
Waukesha, WI, 1419
Waunakee, WI, 1403
Waupaca, WI, 1420
Waupun, WI, 1404
Wausau, WI, 1407
Wauseon, OH, 983
Wautoma, WI, 1420
Wauwatosa, WI, 1409
Waverly, IA, 434
Waverly, NE, 754
Waverly, NY, 897
Waverly, OH, 1006
Waverly, TN, 1207
Waxahachie, TX, 1244
Waycross, GA, 292
Wayland, MA, 562
Wayland, MI, 590
Wayland, NY, 890
Wayne, NJ, 813, 814
Wayne, PA, 1108
Wayne, WV, 1392
Waynesboro, GA, 272
Waynesboro, MS, 700
Waynesboro, PA, 1112
Waynesboro, TN, 1215
Waynesboro, VA, 1344
Waynesburg, PA, 1112
Waynesville, MO, 725
Waynesville, NC, 940
Wayzata, MN, 662
Weatherford, OK, 1048
Weatherford, TX, 1271
Webb City, MO, 720
Webster City, IA, 437
Webster Groves, MO, 730
Webster Springs, WV, 1392
Webster, MA, 573
Webster, NY, 868
Wedowee, AL, 18
Weiser, ID, 319
Welch, WV, 1389
Wellesley, MA, 565
Wellington, KS, 462
Wellington, OH, 995
Wells, ME, 528
Wellsboro, PA, 1130
Wellsburg, WV, 1386
Wellston, OH, 990
Wenatchee, WA, 1357
Wenham, MA, 551
Wentzville, MO, 726
Weslaco, TX, 1256
West Allis, WI, 1409
West Atlantic City, NJ, 782
West Babylon, NY, 896
West Bend, WI, 1417
West Bloomfield, MI, 621
West Branch, MI, 622
West Caldwell, NJ, 795
West Carrollton, OH, 1003
West Chazy, NY, 856
West Chester, PA, 1103
West Chicago, IL, 341, 344
West Columbia, TX, 1232
West Covina, CA, 109
West Deptford, NJ, 799
West Des Moines, IA, 441
West Fargo, ND, 960
West Frankfort, IL, 345

Sedgwick Press
Education Directories

Educators Resource Directory, 2005/06

Educators Resource Directory is a comprehensive resource that provides the educational professional with thousands of resources and statistical data for professional development. This directory saves hours of research time by providing immediate access to Associations & Organizations, Conferences & Trade Shows, Educational Research Centers, Employment Opportunities & Teaching Abroad, School Library Services, Scholarships, Financial Resources, Professional Consultants, Computer Software & Testing Resources and much more. Plus, this comprehensive directory also includes a section on Statistics and Rankings with over 100 tables, including statistics on Average Teacher Salaries, SAT/ACT scores, Revenues & Expenditures and more. These important statistics will allow the user to see how their school rates among others, make relocation decisions and so much more. For quick access to information, this directory contains four indexes: Entry & Publisher Index, Geographic Index, a Subject & Grade Index and Web Sites Index. *Educators Resource Directory* will be a well-used addition to the reference collection of any school district, education department or public library.

"Recommended for all collections that serve elementary and secondary school professionals." –Choice

1,000 pages; Softcover ISBN 1-59237-080-2, $145.00 ♦ Online Database $195.00 ♦ Online Database & Directory Combo $280.00

The Complete Learning Disabilities Directory, 2005

The Complete Learning Disabilities Directory is the most comprehensive database of Programs, Services, Curriculum Materials, Professional Meetings & Resources, Camps, Newsletters and Support Groups for teachers, students and families concerned with learning disabilities. This information-packed directory includes information about Associations & Organizations, Schools, Colleges & Testing Materials, Government Agencies, Legal Resources and much more. For quick, easy access to information, this directory contains four indexes: Entry Name Index, Subject Index and Geographic Index. With every passing year, the field of learning disabilities attracts more attention and the network of caring, committed and knowledgeable professionals grows every day. This directory is an invaluable research tool for these parents, students and professionals.

"Due to its wealth and depth of coverage, parents, teachers and others… should find this an invaluable resource." –Booklist

900 pages; Softcover ISBN 1-59237-092-6, $145.00 ♦ Online Database $195.00 ♦ Online Database & Directory Combo $280.00

Universal Reference Publications
Statistical & Demographic Reference Books

The Value of a Dollar 1600-1859, The Colonial Era to The Civil War

Following the format of the widely acclaimed, T*he Value of a Dollar, 1860-2004, The Value of a Dollar 1600-1859, The Colonial Era to The Civil War* records the actual prices of thousands of items that consumers purchased from the Colonial Era to the Civil War. Our editorial department had been flooded with requests from users of our Value of a Dollar for the same type of information, just from an earlier time period. This new volume is just the answer – with pricing data from 1600 to 1859. Arranged into five-year chapters, each 5-year chapter includes a Historical Snapshot, Consumer Expenditures, Investments, Selected Income, Income/Standard Jobs, Food Basket, Standard Prices and Miscellany. There is also a section on Trends. This informative section charts the change in price over time and provides added detail on the reasons prices changed within the time period, including industry developments, changes in consumer attitudes and important historical facts. This fascinating survey will serve a wide range of research needs and will be useful in all high school, public and academic library reference collections.

600 pages; Hardcover ISBN 1-59237-094-2, $135.00

The Value of a Dollar 1860-2004, Third Edition

A guide to practical economy, *The Value of a Dollar* records the actual prices of thousands of items that consumers purchased from the Civil War to the present, along with facts about investment options and income opportunities. This brand new Third Edition boasts a brand new addition to each five-year chapter, a section on Trends. This informative section charts the change in price over time and provides added detail on the reasons prices changed within the time period, including industry developments, changes in consumer attitudes and important historical facts. Plus, a brand new chapter for 2000-2004 has been added. Each 5-year chapter includes a Historical Snapshot, Consumer Expenditures, Investments, Selected Income, Income/Standard Jobs, Food Basket, Standard Prices and Miscellany. This interesting and useful publication will be widely used in any reference collection.

"Recommended for high school, college and public libraries." –ARBA

600 pages; Hardcover ISBN 1-59237-074-8, $135.00

To preview any of our Directories Risk-Free for 30 days, call (800) 562-2139 or fax to (518) 789-0556

Working Americans 1880-1999
Volume I: The Working Class, Volume II: The Middle Class, Volume III: The Upper Class

Each of the volumes in the *Working Americans 1880-1999* series focuses on a particular class of Americans, The Working Class, The Middle Class and The Upper Class over the last 120 years. Chapters in each volume focus on one decade and profile three to five families. Family Profiles include real data on Income & Job Descriptions, Selected Prices of the Times, Annual Income, Annual Budgets, Family Finances, Life at Work, Life at Home, Life in the Community, Working Conditions, Cost of Living, Amusements and much more. Each chapter also contains an Economic Profile with Average Wages of other Professions, a selection of Typical Pricing, Key Events & Inventions, News Profiles, Articles from Local Media and Illustrations. The *Working Americans* series captures the lifestyles of each of the classes from the last twelve decades, covers a vast array of occupations and ethnic backgrounds and travels the entire nation. These interesting and useful compilations of portraits of the American Working, Middle and Upper Classes during the last 120 years will be an important addition to any high school, public or academic library reference collection.

"These interesting, unique compilations of economic and social facts, figures and graphs will support multiple research needs. They will engage and enlighten patrons in high school, public and academic library collections." –Booklist

Volume I: The Working Class ◆ 558 pages; Hardcover ISBN 1-891482-81-5, $145.00
Volume II: The Middle Class ◆ 591 pages; Hardcover ISBN 1-891482-72-6; $145.00
Volume III: The Upper Class ◆ 567 pages; Hardcover ISBN 1-930956-38-X, $145.00

Working Americans 1880-1999 Volume IV: Their Children

This Fourth Volume in the highly successful *Working Americans 1880-1999* series focuses on American children, decade by decade from 1880 to 1999. This interesting and useful volume introduces the reader to three children in each decade, one from each of the Working, Middle and Upper classes. Like the first three volumes in the series, the individual profiles are created from interviews, diaries, statistical studies, biographies and news reports. Profiles cover a broad range of ethnic backgrounds, geographic area and lifestyles – everything from an orphan in Memphis in 1882, following the Yellow Fever epidemic of 1878 to an eleven-year-old nephew of a beer baron and owner of the New York Yankees in New York City in 1921. Chapters also contain important supplementary materials including News Features as well as information on everything from Schools to Parks, Infectious Diseases to Childhood Fears along with Entertainment, Family Life and much more to provide an informative overview of the lifestyles of children from each decade. This interesting account of what life was like for Children in the Working, Middle and Upper Classes will be a welcome addition to the reference collection of any high school, public or academic library.

600 pages; Hardcover ISBN 1-930956-35-5, $145.00

Working Americans 1880-2003 Volume V: Americans At War

Working Americans 1880-2003 Volume V: Americans At War is divided into 11 chapters, each covering a decade from 1880-2003 and examines the lives of Americans during the time of war, including declared conflicts, one-time military actions, protests, and preparations for war. Each decade includes several personal profiles, whether on the battlefield or on the homefront, that tell the stories of civilians, soldiers, and officers during the decade. The profiles examine: Life at Home; Life at Work; and Life in the Community. Each decade also includes an Economic Profile with statistical comparisons, a Historical Snapshot, News Profiles, local News Articles, and Illustrations that provide a solid historical background to the decade being examined. Profiles range widely not only geographically, but also emotionally, from that of a girl whose leg was torn off in a blast during WWI, to the boredom of being stationed in the Dakotas as the Indian Wars were drawing to a close. As in previous volumes of the *Working Americans* series, information is presented in narrative form, but hard facts and real-life situations back up each story. The basis of the profiles come from diaries, private print books, personal interviews, family histories, estate documents and magazine articles. For easy reference, *Working Americans 1880-2003 Volume V: Americans At War* includes an in-depth Subject Index. The *Working Americans* series has become an important reference for public libraries, academic libraries and high school libraries. This fifth volume will be a welcome addition to all of these types of reference collections.

600 pages; Hardcover ISBN 1-59237-024-1; $145.00
Five Volume Set (Volumes I-V), Hardcover ISBN 1-59237-034-9, $675.00

Working Americans 1880-2005 Volume VI: Women at Work

Unlike any other volume in the *Working Americans* series, this Sixth Volume, is the first to focus on a particular gender of Americans. *Volume VI: Women at Work*, traces what life was like for working women from the 1860's to the present time. Beginning with the life of a maid in 1890 and a store clerk in 1900 and ending with the life and times of the modern working women, this text captures the struggle, strengths and changing perception of the American woman at work. Each chapter focuses on one decade and profiles three to five women with real data on Income & Job Descriptions, Selected Prices of the Times, Annual Income, Annual Budgets, Family Finances, Life at Work, Life at Home, Life in the Community, Working Conditions, Cost of Living, Amusements and much more. For even broader access to the events, economics and attitude towards women throughout the past 130 years, each chapter is supplemented with News Profiles, Articles from Local Media, Illustrations, Economic Profiles, Typical Pricing, Key Events, Inventions and more. This important volume illustrates what life was like for working women over time and allows the reader to develop an understanding of the changing role of women at work. These interesting and useful compilations of portraits of women at work will be an important addition to any high school, public or academic library reference collection.

600 pages; Hardcover ISBN 1-59237-063-2; $145.00
Six Volume Set (Volumes I-VI), Hardcover ISBN 1-59237-063-2, $810.00

America's Top-Rated Cities, 2006

America's Top-Rated Cities provides current, comprehensive statistical information and other essential data in one easy-to-use source on the 100 "top" cities that have been cited as the best for business and living in the U.S. This handbook allows readers to see, at a glance, a concise social, business, economic, demographic and environmental profile of each city, including brief evaluative comments. In addition to detailed data on Cost of Living, Finances, Real Estate, Education, Major Employers, Media, Crime and Climate, city reports now include Housing Vacancies, Tax Audits, Bankruptcy, Presidential Election Results and more. This outstanding source of information will be widely used in any reference collection.

"The only source of its kind that brings together all of this information into one easy-to-use source. It will be beneficial to many business and public libraries." —ARBA

2,500 pages, 4 Volume Set; Softcover ISBN 1-59237-076-4, $195.00

America's Top-Rated Smaller Cities, 2004/05

A perfect companion to *America's Top-Rated Cities*, *America's Top-Rated Smaller Cities* provides current, comprehensive business and living profiles of smaller cities (population 25,000-99,999) that have been cited as the best for business and living in the United States. Sixty cities make up this 2004 edition of *America's Top-Rated Smaller Cities*, all are top-ranked by Population Growth, Median Income, Unemployment Rate and Crime Rate. City reports reflect the most current data available on a wide-range of statistics, including Employment & Earnings, Household Income, Unemployment Rate, Population Characteristics, Taxes, Cost of Living, Education, Health Care, Public Safety, Recreation, Media, Air & Water Quality and much more. Plus, each city report contains a Background of the City, and an Overview of the State Finances. *America's Top-Rated Smaller Cities* offers a reliable, one-stop source for statistical data that, before now, could only be found scattered in hundreds of sources. This volume is designed for a wide range of readers: individuals considering relocating a residence or business; professionals considering expanding their business or changing careers; general and market researchers; real estate consultants; human resource personnel; urban planners and investors.

"Provides current, comprehensive statistical information in one easy-to-use source... Recommended for public and academic libraries and specialized collections." —Library Journal

1,100 pages; Softcover ISBN 1-59237-043-8, $160.00

Profiles of America: Facts, Figures & Statistics for Every Populated Place in the United States

Profiles of America is the only source that pulls together, in one place, statistical, historical and descriptive information about every place in the United States in an easy-to-use format. This award winning reference set, now in its second edition, compiles statistics and data from over 20 different sources – the latest census information has been included along with more than nine brand new statistical topics. This Four-Volume Set details over 40,000 places, from the biggest metropolis to the smallest unincorporated hamlet, and provides statistical details and information on over 50 different topics including Geography, Climate, Population, Vital Statistics, Economy, Income, Taxes, Education, Housing, Health & Environment, Public Safety, Newspapers, Transportation, Presidential Election Results and Information Contacts or Chambers of Commerce. Profiles are arranged, for ease-of-use, by state and then by county. Each county begins with a County-Wide Overview and is followed by information for each Community in that particular county. The Community Profiles within the county are arranged alphabetically. *Profiles of America* is a virtual snapshot of America at your fingertips and a unique compilation of information that will be widely used in any reference collection.

A Library Journal Best Reference Book *"An outstanding compilation." —Library Journal*

10,000 pages; Four Volume Set; Softcover ISBN 1-891482-80-7, $595.00

To preview any of our Directories Risk-Free for 30 days, call (800) 562-2139 or fax to (518) 789-0556

The Comparative Guide to American Suburbs, 2005

The Comparative Guide to American Suburbs is a one-stop source for Statistics on the 2,000+ suburban communities surrounding the 50 largest metropolitan areas – their population characteristics, income levels, economy, school system and important data on how they compare to one another. Organized into 50 Metropolitan Area chapters, each chapter contains an overview of the Metropolitan Area, a detailed Map followed by a comprehensive Statistical Profile of each Suburban Community, including Contact Information, Physical Characteristics, Population Characteristics, Income, Economy, Unemployment Rate, Cost of Living, Education, Chambers of Commerce and more. Next, statistical data is sorted into Ranking Tables that rank the suburbs by twenty different criteria, including Population, Per Capita Income, Unemployment Rate, Crime Rate, Cost of Living and more. *The Comparative Guide to American Suburbs* is the best source for locating data on suburbs. Those looking to relocate, as well as those doing preliminary market research, will find this an invaluable timesaving resource.

"Public and academic libraries will find this compilation useful...The work draws together figures from many sources and will be especially helpful for job relocation decisions." – Booklist

1,700 pages; Softcover ISBN 1-59237-004-7, $130.00

Crime in America's Top-Rated Cities, 2000

This volume includes over 20 years of crime statistics in all major crime categories: violent crimes, property crimes and total crime. *Crime in America's Top-Rated Cities* is conveniently arranged by city and covers 76 top-rated cities. *Crime in America's Top-Rated Cities* offers details that compare the number of crimes and crime rates for the city, suburbs and metro area along with national crime trends for violent, property and total crimes. Also, this handbook contains important information and statistics on Anti-Crime Programs, Crime Risk, Hate Crimes, Illegal Drugs, Law Enforcement, Correctional Facilities, Death Penalty Laws and much more. A much-needed resource for people who are relocating, business professionals, general researchers, the press, law enforcement officials and students of criminal justice.

"Data is easy to access and will save hours of searching." –Global Enforcement Review

832 pages; Softcover ISBN 1-891482-84-X, $155.00

The Asian Databook: Statistics for all US Counties & Cities with Over 10,000 Population

This is the first-ever resource that compiles statistics and rankings on the US Asian population. *The Asian Databook* presents over 20 statistical data points for each city and county, arranged alphabetically by state, then alphabetically by place name. Data reported for each place includes Population, Languages Spoken at Home, Foreign-Born, Educational Attainment, Income Figures, Poverty Status, Homeownership, Home Values & Rent, and more. Next, in the Rankings Section, the top 75 places are listed for each data element. These easy-to-access ranking tables allow the user to quickly determine trends and population characteristics. This kind of comparative data can not be found elsewhere, in print or on the web, in a format that's as easy-to-use or more concise. A useful resource for those searching for demographics data, career search and relocation information and also for market research. With data ranging from Ancestry to Education, *The Asian Databook* presents a useful compilation of information that will be a much-needed resource in the reference collection of any public or academic library along with the marketing collection of any company whose primary focus in on the Asian population.

1,000 pages; Softcover ISBN 1-59237-044-6 $150.00

The Hispanic Databook: Statistics for all US Counties & Cities with Over 10,000 Population

Previously published by Toucan Valley Publications, this second edition has been completely updated with figures from the latest census and has been broadly expanded to include dozens of new data elements and a brand new Rankings section. The Hispanic population in the United States has increased over 42% in the last 10 years and accounts for 12.5% of the total US population. For ease-of-use, *The Hispanic Databook* presents over 20 statistical data points for each city and county, arranged alphabetically by state, then alphabetically by place name. Data reported for each place includes Population, Languages Spoken at Home, Foreign-Born, Educational Attainment, Income Figures, Poverty Status, Homeownership, Home Values & Rent, and more. Next, in the Rankings Section, the top 75 places are listed for each data element. These easy-to-access ranking tables allow the user to quickly determine trends and population characteristics. This kind of comparative data can not be found elsewhere, in print or on the web, in a format that's as easy-to-use or more concise. A useful resource for those searching for demographics data, career search and relocation information and also for market research. With data ranging from Ancestry to Education, *The Hispanic Databook* presents a useful compilation of information that will be a much-needed resource in the reference collection of any public or academic library along with the marketing collection of any company whose primary focus in on the Hispanic population.

"This accurate, clearly presented volume of selected Hispanic demographics is recommended for large public libraries and research collections."-Library Journal

1,000 pages; Softcover ISBN 1-59237-008-X, $150.00

To preview any of our Directories Risk-Free for 30 days, call (800) 562-2139 or fax to (518) 789-0556

Ancestry in America: A Comparative Guide to Over 200 Ethnic Backgrounds

This brand new reference work pulls together thousands of comparative statistics on the Ethnic Backgrounds of all populated places in the United States with populations over 10,000. Never before has this kind of information been reported in a single volume. Section One, Statistics by Place, is made up of a list of over 200 ancestry and race categories arranged alphabetically by each of the 5,000 different places with populations over 10,000. The population number of the ancestry group in that city or town is provided along with the percent that group represents of the total population. This informative city-by-city section allows the user to quickly and easily explore the ethnic makeup of all major population bases in the United States. Section Two, Comparative Rankings, contains three tables for each ethnicity and race. In the first table, the top 150 populated places are ranked by population number for that particular ancestry group, regardless of population. In the second table, the top 150 populated places are ranked by the percent of the total population for that ancestry group. In the third table, those top 150 populated places with 10,000 population are ranked by population number for each ancestry group. These easy-to-navigate tables allow users to see ancestry population patterns and make city-by-city comparisons as well. Plus, as an added bonus with the purchase of *Ancestry in America*, a free companion CD-ROM is available that lists statistics and rankings for all of the 35,000 populated places in the United States. This brand new, information-packed resource will serve a wide-range or research requests for demographics, population characteristics, relocation information and much more. *Ancestry in America: A Comparative Guide to Over 200 Ethnic Backgrounds* will be an important acquisition to all reference collections.

"This compilation will serve a wide range of research requests for population characteristics
… it offers much more detail than other sources." –Booklist

1,500 pages; Softcover ISBN 1-59237-029-2, $225.00

The American Tally: Statistics & Comparative Rankings for U.S. Cities with Populations over 10,000

This important statistical handbook compiles, all in one place, comparative statistics on all U.S. cities and towns with a 10,000+ population. *The American Tally* provides statistical details on over 4,000 cities and towns and profiles how they compare with one another in Population Characteristics, Education, Language & Immigration, Income & Employment and Housing. Each section begins with an alphabetical listing of cities by state, allowing for quick access to both the statistics and relative rankings of any city. Next, the highest and lowest cities are listed in each statistic. These important, informative lists provide quick reference to which cities are at both extremes of the spectrum for each statistic. Unlike any other reference, *The American Tally* provides quick, easy access to comparative statistics – a must-have for any reference collection.

"A solid library reference." –Bookwatch

500 pages; Softcover ISBN 1-930956-29-0, $125.00

The Grey House Handbook on Alternative Energy, 2006

This is the first ever resource to pull together information, resources and statistics for all types of Alternative Energy, including Hydro, Wind, Solar, Coal, Natural Gas and Atomic Energy sources. The Handbook begins with an informative Introduction to Alternative Energy Resources, including editorial on the history of energy, the necessity of using alternative energy, conservation and the economics of using alternative energy sources. Plus, handy charts are also included that cover uses of energy sources today; forecasts of energy sources and the availability of energy sources in the future. Next, readers will find chapters on each Type of Energy Source. Chapters begin with an Introduction to the specific energy source, History, Strengths & Drawbacks, Industrial & Residential Use and Trends. Several articles are also included for each energy source, followed by Resources, including Associations, Magazines, Trade Shows and Vendors. The Grey House Handbook on Alternative Energy also contains a informative, useful section on Statistics. These charts allow for easy location of very specific data. A handy Glossary and section on Public Energy Companies is also included for easy reference. Three indexes, Product Index, Subject Index and Entry Name Index allow the user to locate specific resources quickly and easily. As the need for alternative energy sources continues to grow, having access to these resources will become more and more important. This first edition will prove useful to the reference collections public and academic libraries.

800 pages; Softcover ISBN 1-59237-134-5; $165.00

The Environmental Resource Handbook, 2005/06

The Environmental Resource Handbook is the most up-to-date and comprehensive source for Environmental Resources and Statistics. Section I: Resources provides detailed contact information for thousands of information sources, including Associations & Organizations, Awards & Honors, Conferences, Foundations & Grants, Environmental Health, Government Agencies, National Parks & Wildlife Refuges, Publications, Research Centers, Educational Programs, Green Product Catalogs, Consultants and much more. Section II: Statistics, provides statistics and rankings on hundreds of important topics, including Children's Environmental Index, Municipal Finances, Toxic Chemicals, Recycling, Climate, Air & Water Quality and more. This kind of up-to-date environmental data, all in one place, is not available anywhere else on the market place today. This vast compilation of resources and statistics is a must-have for all public and academic libraries as well as any organization with a primary focus on the environment.

"…the intrinsic value of the information make it worth consideration by libraries with
environmental collections and environmentally concerned users." –Booklist

1,000 pages; Softcover ISBN 1-59237-090-X, $155.00 ◆ Online Database $300.00

To preview any of our Directories Risk-Free for 30 days, call (800) 562-2139 or fax to (518) 789-0556

Weather America, A Thirty-Year Summary of Statistical Weather Data and Rankings

This valuable resource provides extensive climatological data for over 4,000 National and Cooperative Weather Stations throughout the United States. *Weather America* begins with a new Major Storms section that details major storm events of the nation and a National Rankings section that details rankings for several data elements, such as Maximum Temperature and Precipitation. The main body of *Weather America* is organized into 50 state sections. Each section provides a Data Table on each Weather Station, organized alphabetically, that provides statistics on Maximum and Minimum Temperatures, Precipitation, Snowfall, Extreme Temperatures, Foggy Days, Humidity and more. State sections contain two brand new features in this edition – a City Index and a narrative Description of the climatic conditions of the state. Each section also includes a revised Map of the State that includes not only weather stations, but cities and towns.

"Best Reference Book of the Year." –Library Journal

2,013 pages; Softcover ISBN 1-891482-29-7, $175.00

Sedgwick Press
Health Directories

The Complete Directory for People with Disabilities, 2006

A wealth of information, now in one comprehensive sourcebook. Completely updated, this edition contains more information than ever before, including thousands of new entries and enhancements to existing entries and thousands of additional web sites and e-mail addresses. This up-to-date directory is the most comprehensive resource available for people with disabilities, detailing Independent Living Centers, Rehabilitation Facilities, State & Federal Agencies, Associations, Support Groups, Periodicals & Books, Assistive Devices, Employment & Education Programs, Camps and Travel Groups. Each year, more libraries, schools, colleges, hospitals, rehabilitation centers and individuals add *The Complete Directory for People with Disabilities* to their collections, making sure that this information is readily available to the families, individuals and professionals who can benefit most from the amazing wealth of resources cataloged here.

"No other reference tool exists to meet the special needs of the disabled in one convenient resource for information." –Library Journal

1,200 pages; Softcover ISBN 1-59237-083-7, $165.00 ◆ Online Database $215.00 ◆ Online Database & Directory Combo $300.00

The Complete Directory for People with Chronic Illness, 2005/06

Thousands of hours of research have gone into this completely updated 2005/06 edition – several new chapters have been added along with thousands of new entries and enhancements to existing entries. Plus, each chronic illness chapter has been reviewed by an medical expert in the field. This widely-hailed directory is structured around the 90 most prevalent chronic illnesses – from Asthma to Cancer to Wilson's Disease – and provides a comprehensive overview of the support services and information resources available for people diagnosed with a chronic illness. Each chronic illness has its own chapter and contains a brief description in layman's language, followed by important resources for National & Local Organizations, State Agencies, Newsletters, Books & Periodicals, Libraries & Research Centers, Support Groups & Hotlines, Web Sites and much more. This directory is an important resource for health care professionals, the collections of hospital and health care libraries, as well as an invaluable tool for people with a chronic illness and their support network.

"A must purchase for all hospital and health care libraries and is strongly recommended for all public library reference departments." –ARBA

1,200 pages; Softcover ISBN 1-59237-081-0, $165.00 ◆ Online Database $215.00 ◆ Online Database & Directory Combo $300.00

The Complete Mental Health Directory, 2006

This is the most comprehensive resource covering the field of behavioral health, with critical information for both the layman and the mental health professional. For the layman, this directory offers understandable descriptions of 25 Mental Health Disorders as well as detailed information on Associations, Media, Support Groups and Mental Health Facilities. For the professional, *The Complete Mental Health Directory* offers critical and comprehensive information on Managed Care Organizations, Information Systems, Government Agencies and Provider Organizations. This comprehensive volume of needed information will be widely used in any reference collection.

"... the strength of this directory is that it consolidates widely dispersed information into a single volume." –Booklist

800 pages; Softcover ISBN 1-59237-124-8, $165.00 ◆ Online Database $215.00 ◆ Online & Directory Combo $300.00

Older Americans Information Directory, 2004/05

Completely updated for 2004/05, this Fifth Edition has been completely revised and now contains 1,000 new listings, over 8,000 updates to existing listings and over 3,000 brand new e-mail addresses and web sites. You'll find important resources for Older Americans including National, Regional, State & Local Organizations, Government Agencies, Research Centers, Libraries & Information Centers, Legal Resources, Discount Travel Information, Continuing Education Programs, Disability Aids & Assistive Devices, Health, Print Media and Electronic Media. Three indexes: Entry Index, Subject Index and Geographic Index make it easy to find just the right source of information. This comprehensive guide to resources for Older Americans will be a welcome addition to any reference collection.

"Highly recommended for academic, public, health science and consumer libraries..." –Choice

1,200 pages; Softcover ISBN 1-59237-037-3, $165.00 ◆ Online Database $215.00 ◆ Online Database & Directory Combo $300.00

To preview any of our Directories Risk-Free for 30 days, call (800) 562-2139 or fax to (518) 789-0556

The Complete Directory for Pediatric Disorders, 2004/05

This important directory provides parents and caregivers with information about Pediatric Conditions, Disorders, Diseases and Disabilities, including Blood Disorders, Bone & Spinal Disorders, Brain Defects & Abnormalities, Chromosomal Disorders, Congenital Heart Defects, Movement Disorders, Neuromuscular Disorders and Pediatric Tumors & Cancers. This carefully written directory offers: understandable Descriptions of 15 major bodily systems; Descriptions of more than 200 Disorders and a Resources Section, detailing National Agencies & Associations, State Associations, Online Services, Libraries & Resource Centers, Research Centers, Support Groups & Hotlines, Camps, Books and Periodicals. This resource will provide immediate access to information crucial to families and caregivers when coping with children's illnesses.

"Recommended for public and consumer health libraries." –Library Journal

1,200 pages; Softcover ISBN 1-59237-045-4, $165.00 ◆ Online Database $215.00 ◆ Online Database & Directory Combo $300.00

The Complete Directory for People with Rare Disorders

This outstanding reference is produced in conjunction with the National Organization for Rare Disorders to provide comprehensive and needed access to important information on over 1,000 rare disorders, including Cancers and Muscular, Genetic and Blood Disorders. An informative Disorder Description is provided for each of the 1,100 disorders (rare Cancers and Muscular, Genetic and Blood Disorders) followed by information on National and State Organizations dealing with a particular disorder, Umbrella Organizations that cover a wide range of disorders, the Publications that can be useful when researching a disorder and the Government Agencies to contact. Detailed and up-to-date listings contain mailing address, phone and fax numbers, web sites and e-mail addresses along with a description. For quick, easy access to information, this directory contains two indexes: Entry Name Index and Acronym/Keyword Index along with an informative Guide for Rare Disorder Advocates. The Complete Directory for People with Rare Disorders will be an invaluable tool for the thousands of families that have been struck with a rare or "orphan" disease, who feel that they have no place to turn and will be a much-used addition to the reference collection of any public or academic library.

"Quick access to information... public libraries and hospital patient libraries will find this a useful resource in directing users to support groups or agencies dealing with a rare disorder." –Booklist

726 pages; Softcover ISBN 1-891482-18-1, $165.00

The Directory of Drug & Alcohol Residential Rehabilitation Facilities

This brand new directory is the first-ever resource to bring together, all in one place, data on the thousands of drug and alcohol residential rehabilitation facilities in the United States. *The Directory of Drug & Alcohol Residential Rehabilitation Facilities* covers over 1,000 facilities, with detailed contact information for each one, including mailing address, phone and fax numbers, email addresses and web sites, mission statement, type of treatment programs, cost, average length of stay, numbers of residents and counselors, accreditation, insurance plans accepted, type of environment, religious affiliation, education components and much more. It also contains a helpful chapter on General Resources that provides contact information for Associations, Print & Electronic Media, Support Groups and Conferences. Multiple indexes allow the user to pinpoint the facilities that meet very specific criteria. This time-saving tool is what so many counselors, parents and medical professionals have been asking for. *The Directory of Drug & Alcohol Residential Rehabilitation Facilities* will be a helpful tool in locating the right source for treatment for a wide range of individuals. This comprehensive directory will be an important acquisition for all reference collections: public and academic libraries, case managers, social workers, state agencies and many more.

"This is an excellent, much needed directory that fills an important gap..." –Booklist

300 pages; Softcover ISBN 1-59237-031-4, $135.00

To preview any of our Directories Risk-Free for 30 days, call (800) 562-2139 or fax to (518) 789-0556

Sedgwick Press
Hospital & Health Plan Directories

The Comparative Guide to American Hospitals

This brand new title is the first ever resource to compare all of the nation's hospitals by 17 measures of quality in the treatment of heart attack, heart failure and pneumonia. This data is based on the recently announced Hospital Compare, produced by Medicare, and is available in print and in a unique and user-friendly format from Grey House Publishing, along with extra contact information from Grey House's *Directory of Hospital Personnel*. *The Comparative Guide to American Hospitals* provides a snapshot profile of each of the nations 6,000 hospitals. These informative profiles illustrate how the hospital rates in 17 important areas: Heart Attack Care (% who receive Aspirin at Arrival, Aspirin at Discharge, ACE Inhibitor for LVSD, Beta Blocker at Arrival, Beta Blocker at Discharge, Thrombolytic Agent Received, PTCA Received and Adult Smoking Cessation Advice); Heart Failure (% who receive LVF Assessment, ACE Inhibitor for LVSD, Discharge Instructions, Adult Smoking Cessation Advice); and Pneumonia (% who receive Initial Antibiotic Timing, Pneumococcal Vaccination, Oxygenation Assessment, Blood Culture Performed and Adult Smoking Cessation Advice). Each profile includes the raw percentage for that hospital, the state average, the US average and data on the top hospital. For easy access to contact information, each profile includes the hospitals address, phone and fax numbers, email and web addresses, type and accreditation along with 5 top key administrations. These profiles will allow the user to quickly identify the quality of the hospital and have the necessary information at their fingertips to make contact with that hospital. Most importantly, *The Comparative Guide to American Hospitals* provides an easy-to-use Ranking Table for each of the data elements to allow the user to quickly locate the hospitals with the best level of service. This brand new title will be a must for the reference collection at all public, medical and academic libraries.

2,500 pages; Softcover ISBN 1-59237-109-4 $175.00

The Directory of Hospital Personnel, 2006

The Directory of Hospital Personnel is the best resource you can have at your fingertips when researching or marketing a product or service to the hospital market. A "Who's Who" of the hospital universe, this directory puts you in touch with over 150,000 key decision-makers. With 100% verification of data you can rest assured that you will reach the right person with just one call. Every hospital in the U.S. is profiled, listed alphabetically by city within state. Plus, three easy-to-use, cross-referenced indexes put the facts at your fingertips faster and more easily than any other directory: Hospital Name Index, Bed Size Index and Personnel Index. *The Directory of Hospital Personnel* is the only complete source for key hospital decision-makers by name. Whether you want to define or restructure sales territories… locate hospitals with the purchasing power to accept your proposals… keep track of important contacts or colleagues… or find information on which insurance plans are accepted, *The Directory of Hospital Personnel* gives you the information you need – easily, efficiently, effectively and accurately.

"Recommended for college, university and medical libraries." –ARBA

2,500 pages; Softcover ISBN 1-59237-107-8 $275.00 ◆ Online Database $545.00 ◆ Online Database & Directory Combo, $650.00

The Directory of Health Care Group Purchasing Organizations, 2006

This comprehensive directory provides the important data you need to get in touch with over 800 Group Purchasing Organizations. By providing in-depth information on this growing market and its members, *The Directory of Health Care Group Purchasing Organizations* fills a major need for the most accurate and comprehensive information on over 800 GPOs – Mailing Address, Phone & Fax Numbers, E-mail Addresses, Key Contacts, Purchasing Agents, Group Descriptions, Membership Categorization, Standard Vendor Proposal Requirements, Membership Fees & Terms, Expanded Services, Total Member Beds & Outpatient Visits represented and more. Five Indexes provide a number of ways to locate the right GPO: Alphabetical Index, Expanded Services Index, Organization Type Index, Geographic Index and Member Institution Index. With its comprehensive and detailed information on each purchasing organization, *The Directory of Health Care Group Purchasing Organizations* is the go-to source for anyone looking to target this market.

"The information is clearly arranged and easy to access…recommended for those needing this very specialized information." –ARBA

1,000 pages; Softcover ISBN 1-59237-0091-8, $325.00 ◆ Online Database, $650.00 ◆ Online Database & Directory Combo, $750.00

To preview any of our Directories Risk-Free for 30 days, call (800) 562-2139 or fax to (518) 789-0556

The HMO/PPO Directory, 2006

The HMO/PPO Directory is a comprehensive source that provides detailed information about Health Maintenance Organizations and Preferred Provider Organizations nationwide. This comprehensive directory details more information about more managed health care organizations than ever before. Over 1,100 HMOs, PPOs and affiliated companies are listed, arranged alphabetically by state. Detailed listings include Key Contact Information, Prescription Drug Benefits, Enrollment, Geographical Areas served, Affiliated Physicians & Hospitals, Federal Qualifications, Status, Year Founded, Managed Care Partners, Employer References, Fees & Payment Information and more. Plus, five years of historical information is included related to Revenues, Net Income, Medical Loss Ratios, Membership Enrollment and Number of Patient Complaints. Five easy-to-use, cross-referenced indexes will put this vast array of information at your fingertips immediately: HMO Index, PPO Index, Other Providers Index, Personnel Index and Enrollment Index. *The HMO/PPO Directory* provides the most comprehensive information on the most companies available on the market place today.

> *"Helpful to individuals requesting certain HMO/PPO issues such as co-payment costs, subscription costs and patient complaints. Individuals concerned (or those with questions) about their insurance may find this text to be of use to them." -ARBA*

600 pages; Softcover ISBN 1-59237-100-0, $275.00 ◆ Online Database, $495.00 ◆ Online Database & Directory Combo, $600.00

The Directory of Independent Ambulatory Care Centers

This first edition of *The Directory of Independent Ambulatory Care Centers* provides access to detailed information that, before now, could only be found scattered in hundreds of different sources. This comprehensive and up-to-date directory pulls together a vast array of contact information for over 7,200 Ambulatory Surgery Centers, Ambulatory General and Urgent Care Clinics, and Diagnostic Imaging Centers that are not affiliated with a hospital or major medical center. Detailed listings include Mailing Address, Phone & Fax Numbers, E-mail and Web Site addresses, Contact Name and Phone Numbers of the Medical Director and other Key Executives and Purchasing Agents, Specialties & Services Offered, Year Founded, Numbers of Employees and Surgeons, Number of Operating Rooms, Number of Cases seen per year, Overnight Options, Contracted Services and much more. Listings are arranged by State, by Center Category and then alphabetically by Organization Name. Two indexes provide quick and easy access to this wealth of information: Entry Name Index and Specialty/Service Index. *The Directory of Independent Ambulatory Care Centers* is a must-have resource for anyone marketing a product or service to this important industry and will be an invaluable tool for those searching for a local care center that will meet their specific needs.

> *"Among the numerous hospital directories, no other provides information on independent ambulatory centers. A handy, well-organized resource that would be useful in medical center libraries and public libraries." –Choice*

986 pages; Softcover ISBN 1-930956-90-8, $185.00 ◆ Online Database, $365.00 ◆ Online Database & Directory Combo, $450.00

To preview any of our Directories Risk-Free for 30 days, call (800) 562-2139 or fax to (518) 789-0556

The Directory of Venture Capital & Private Equity Firms, 2006

This edition has been extensively updated and broadly expanded to offer direct access to over 2,800 Domestic and International Venture Capital Firms, including address, phone & fax numbers, e-mail addresses and web sites for both primary and branch locations. Entries include details on the firm's Mission Statement, Industry Group Preferences, Geographic Preferences, Average and Minimum Investments and Investment Criteria. You'll also find details that are available nowhere else, including the Firm's Portfolio Companies and extensive information on each of the firm's Managing Partners, such as Education, Professional Background and Directorships held, along with the Partner's E-mail Address. *The Directory of Venture Capital & Private Equity Firms* offers five important indexes: Geographic Index, Executive Name Index, Portfolio Company Index, Industry Preference Index and College & University Index. With its comprehensive coverage and detailed, extensive information on each company, *The Directory of Venture Capital & Private Equity Firms* is an important addition to any finance collection.

"The sheer number of listings, the descriptive information provided and the outstanding indexing make this directory a better value than its principal competitor, Pratt's Guide to Venture Capital Sources. Recommended for business collections in large public, academic and business libraries." –Choice

1,300 pages; Softcover ISBN 1-59237-102-7, $450.00 ◆ Online Database (includes a free copy of the directory) $889.00

The Directory of Mail Order Catalogs, 2006

Published since 1981, this updated edition features 100% verification of data and is the premier source of information on the mail order catalog industry. Details over 12,000 consumer catalog companies with 44 different product chapters from Animals to Toys & Games. Contains detailed contact information including e-mail addresses and web sites along with important business details such as employee size, years in business, sales volume, catalog size, number of catalogs mailed and more. Four indexes provide quick access to information: Catalog & Company Name Index, Geographic Index, Product Index and Web Sites Index.

"This is a godsend for those looking for information." –Reference Book Review

1,700 pages; Softcover ISBN 1-59237-103-5 $250.00 ◆ Online Database (includes a free copy of the directory) $495.00

The Directory of Business to Business Catalogs, 2006

The completely updated *Directory of Business to Business Catalogs*, provides details on over 6,000 suppliers of everything from computers to laboratory supplies… office products to office design… marketing resources to safety equipment… landscaping to maintenance suppliers… building construction and much more. Detailed entries offer mailing address, phone & fax numbers, e-mail addresses, web sites, key contacts, sales volume, employee size, catalog printing information and more. Jut about every kind of product a business needs in its day-to-day operations is covered in this carefully-researched volume. Three indexes are provided for at-a-glance access to information: Catalog & Company Name Index, Geographic Index and Web Sites Index.

"An excellent choice for libraries… wishing to supplement their business supplier resources." –Booklist

800 pages; Softcover ISBN 1-59237-105-1, $165.00 ◆ Online Database (includes a free copy of the directory) $325.00

Sports Market Place Directory, 2005

For over 20 years, this comprehensive, up-to-date directory has offered direct access to the Who, What, When & Where of the Sports Industry. With over 20,000 updates and enhancements, the *Sports Market Place Directory* is the most detailed, comprehensive and current sports business reference source available. In 1,800 information-packed pages, *Sports Market Place Directory* profiles contact information and key executives for: Single Sport Organizations, Professional Leagues, Multi-Sport Organizations, Disabled Sports, High School & Youth Sports, Military Sports, Olympic Organizations, Media, Sponsors, Sponsorship & Marketing Event Agencies, Event & Meeting Calendars, Professional Services, College Sports, Manufacturers & Retailers, Facilities and much more. *The Sports Market Place Directory* provides organization's contact information with detailed descriptions including: Key Contacts, physical, mailing, email and web addresses plus phone and fax numbers. Plus, nine important indexes make sure that you can find the information you're looking for quickly and easily: Entry Index, Single Sport Index, Media Index, Sponsor Index, Agency Index, Manufacturers Index, Brand Name Index, Facilities Index and Executive/Geographic Index. For over twenty years, *The Sports Market Place Directory* has assisted thousands of individuals in their pursuit of a career in the sports industry. Why not use "THE SOURCE" that top recruiters, headhunters and career placement centers use to find information on or about sports organizations and key hiring contacts.

1,800 pages; Softcover ISBN 1-59237-077-2, $225.00 ◆ CD-ROM $479.00

Thomas Food and Beverage Market Place, 2006

Thomas Food and Beverage Market Place is bigger and better than ever with thousands of new companies, thousands of updates to existing companies and two revised and enhanced product category indexes. This comprehensive directory profiles over 18,000 Food & Beverage Manufacturers, 12,000 Equipment & Supply Companies, 2,200 Transportation & Warehouse Companies, 2,000 Brokers & Wholesalers, 8,000 Importers & Exporters, 900 Industry Resources and hundreds of Mail Order Catalogs. Listings include detailed Contact Information, Sales Volumes, Key Contacts, Brand & Product Information, Packaging Details and much more. *Thomas Food and*

To preview any of our Directories Risk-Free for 30 days, call (800) 562-2139 or fax to (518) 789-0556

Beverage Market Place is available as a three-volume printed set, a subscription-based Online Database via the Internet, on CD-ROM, as well as mailing lists and a licensable database.

"An essential purchase for those in the food industry but will also be useful in public libraries where needed. Much of the information will be difficult and time consuming to locate without this handy three-volume ready-reference source." –ARBA

8,500 pages, 3 Volume Set; Softcover ISBN 1-59237-096-9, $495.00 ◆ CD-ROM $695.00 ◆ CD-ROM & 3 Volume Set Combo $895.00 ◆ Online Database $695.00 ◆ Online Database & 3 Volume Set Combo, $895.00

The Grey House Biometric Information Directory, 2006

The Biometric Information Directory is the only comprehensive source for current biometric industry information. This 2006 edition is the first published by Grey House. With 100% updated information, this latest edition offers a complete, current look, in both print and online form, of biometric companies and products – one of the fastest growing industries in today's economy. Detailed profiles of manufacturers of the latest biometric technology, including Finger, Voice, Face, Hand, Signature, Iris, Vein and Palm Identification systems. Data on the companies include key executives, company size and a detailed, indexed description of their product line. Plus, the Directory also includes valuable business resources, and current editorial make this edition the easiest way for the business community and consumers alike to access the largest, most current compilation of biometric industry information available on the market today. The new edition boasts increased numbers of companies, contact names and company data, with over 700 manufacturers and service providers. Information in the directory includes: Editorial on Advancements in Biometrics; Profiles of 700+ companies listed with contact information; Organizations, Trade & Educational Associations, Publications, Conferences, Trade Shows and Expositions Worldwide; Web Site Index; Biometric & Vendors Services Index by Types of Biometrics; and a Glossary of Biometric Terms. This resource will be an important source for anyone who is considering the use of a biometric product, investing in the development of biometric technology, support existing marketing and sales efforts and will be an important acquisition for the business reference collection for large public and business libraries.

800 pages; Softcover ISBN 1-59237-121-3, $225

The Grey House Homeland Security Directory, 2006

This updated edition features the latest contact information for government and private organizations involved with Homeland Security along with the latest product information and provides detailed profiles of nearly 1,000 Federal & State Organizations & Agencies and over 3,000 Officials and Key Executives involved with Homeland Security. These listings are incredibly detailed and include Mailing Address, Phone & Fax Numbers, Email Addresses & Web Sites, a complete Description of the Agency and a complete list of the Officials and Key Executives associated with the Agency. Next, *The Grey House Homeland Security Directory* provides the go-to source for Homeland Security Products & Services. This section features over 2,000 Companies that provide Consulting, Products or Services. With this Buyer's Guide at their fingertips, users can locate suppliers of everything from Training Materials to Access Controls, from Perimeter Security to BioTerrorism Countermeasures and everything in between – complete with contact information and product descriptions. A handy Product Locator Index is provided to quickly and easily locate suppliers of a particular product. Lastly, an Information Resources Section provides immediate access to contact information for hundreds of Associations, Newsletters, Magazines, Trade Shows, Databases and Directories that focus on Homeland Security. This comprehensive, information-packed resource will be a welcome tool for any company or agency that is in need of Homeland Security information and will be a necessary acquisition for the reference collection of all public libraries and large school districts.

"Compiles this information in one place and is discerning in content. A useful purchase for public and academic libraries." –Booklist

800 pages; Softcover ISBN 1-59237-084-5, $195.00 ◆ Online Database (includes a free copy of the directory) $385.00

The Grey House Transportation Security Directory & Handbook, 2005

This brand new title is the only reference of its kind that brings together current data on Transportation Security. With information on everything from Regulatory Authorities to Security Equipment, this top-flight database brings together the relevant information necessary for creating and maintaining a security plan for a wide range of transportation facilities. With this current, comprehensive directory at the ready you'll have immediate access to: Regulatory Authorities & Legislation; Information Resources; Sample Security Plans & Checklists; Contact Data for Major Airports, Seaports, Railroads, Trucking Companies and Oil Pipelines; Security Service Providers; Recommended Equipment & Product Information and more. Using the *Grey House Transportation Security Directory & Handbook*, managers will be able to quickly and easily assess their current security plans; develop contacts to create and maintain new security procedures; and source the products and services necessary to adequately maintain a secure environment. This valuable resource is a must for all Security Managers at Airports, Seaports, Railroads, Trucking Companies and Oil Pipelines.

800 pages; Softcover ISBN 1-59237-075-6, $195

To preview any of our Directories Risk-Free for 30 days, call (800) 562-2139 or fax to (518) 789-0556

The Grey House Safety & Security Directory, 2006

The Grey House Safety & Security Directory is the most comprehensive reference tool and buyer's guide for the safety and security industry. Arranged by safety topic, each chapter begins with OSHA regulations for the topic, followed by Training Articles written by top professionals in the field and Self-Inspection Checklists. Next, each topic contains Buyer's Guide sections that feature related products and services. Topics include Administration, Insurance, Loss Control & Consulting, Protective Equipment & Apparel, Noise & Vibration, Facilities Monitoring & Maintenance, Employee Health Maintenance & Ergonomics, Retail Food Services, Machine Guards, Process Guidelines & Tool Handling, Ordinary Materials Handling, Hazardous Materials Handling, Workplace Preparation & Maintenance, Electrical Lighting & Safety, Fire & Rescue and Security. The Buyer's Guide sections are carefully indexed within each topic area to ensure that you can find the supplies needed to meet OSHA's regulations. Six important indexes make finding information and product manufacturers quick and easy: Geographical Index of Manufacturers and Distributors, Company Profile Index, Brand Name Index, Product Index, Index of Web Sites and Index of Advertisers. This comprehensive, up-to-date reference will provide every tool necessary to make sure a business is in compliance with OSHA regulations and locate the products and services needed to meet those regulations.

"Presents industrial safety information for engineers, plant managers, risk managers, and construction site supervisors..." –Choice

1,500 pages, 2 Volume Set; Softcover ISBN 1-59237-104-3, $225.00

The Grey House Performing Arts Directory, 2005

The Grey House Performing Arts Directory is the most comprehensive resource covering the Performing Arts. This important directory provides current information on over 8,500 Dance Companies, Instrumental Music Programs, Opera Companies, Choral Groups, Theater Companies, Performing Arts Series and Performing Arts Facilities. Plus, this edition now contains a brand new section on Artist Management Groups. In addition to mailing address, phone & fax numbers, e-mail addresses and web sites, dozens of other fields of available information include mission statement, key contacts, facilities, seating capacity, season, attendance and more. This directory also provides an important Information Resources section that covers hundreds of Performing Arts Associations, Magazines, Newsletters, Trade Shows, Directories, Databases and Industry Web Sites. Five indexes provide immediate access to this wealth of information: Entry Name, Executive Name, Performance Facilities, Geographic and Information Resources. *The Grey House Performing Arts Directory* pulls together thousands of Performing Arts Organizations, Facilities and Information Resources into an easy-to-use source – this kind of comprehensiveness and extensive detail is not available in any resource on the market place today.

"Immensely useful and user-friendly ... recommended for public, academic and certain special library reference collections." –Booklist

1,500 pages; Softcover ISBN 1-59237-023-3, $185.00 ◆ Online Database $335.00

New York State Directory, 2005/06

The New York State Directory, published annually since 1983, is a comprehensive and easy-to-use guide to accessing public officials and private sector organizations and individuals who influence public policy in the state of New York. *The New York State Directory* includes important information on all New York state legislators and congressional representatives, including biographies and key committee assignments. It also includes staff rosters for all branches of New York state government and for federal agencies and departments that impact the state policy process. Following the state government section are 25 chapters covering policy areas from agriculture through veterans' affairs. Each chapter identifies the state, local and federal agencies and officials that formulate or implement policy. In addition, each chapter contains a roster of private sector experts and advocates who influence the policy process. The directory also offers appendices that include statewide party officials; chambers of commerce; lobbying organizations; public and private universities and colleges; television, radio and print media; and local government agencies and officials.

New York State Directory - 800 pages; Softcover ISBN 1-59237-093-4; $129.00
New York State Directory with Profiles of New York – 2 volumes; 1,600 pages; Softcover ISBN 1-59237-095-0; $195

To preview any of our Directories Risk-Free for 30 days, call (800) 562-2139 or fax to (518) 789-0556

Profiles of New York, 2005/06 ◆ Profiles of Florida, 2005/06 ◆ Profiles of Texas, 2005/06

Packed with over 50 pieces of data that make up a complete, user-friendly profile of each state, these directories go even further by then pulling selected data and providing it in ranking list form for even easier comparisons between the 100 largest towns and cities! The careful layout gives the user an easy-to-read snapshot of every single place and county in the state, from the biggest metropolis to the smallest unincorporated hamlet. The richness of each place or county profile is astounding in its depth, from history to weather, all packed in an easy-to-navigate, compact format. No need for piles of multiple sources with this volume on your desk. Here is a look at just a few of the data sets you'll find in each profile: History, Geography, Climate, Population, Vital Statistics, Economy, Income, Taxes, Education, Housing, Health & Environment, Public Safety, Newspapers, Transportation, Presidential Election Results, Information Contacts and Chambers of Commerce. As an added bonus, there is a section on Selected Statistics, where data from the 100 largest towns and cities is arranged into easy-to-use charts. Each of 22 different data points has its own two-page spread with the cities listed in alpha order so researchers can easily compare and rank cities. A remarkable compilation that offers overviews and insights into each corner of the state, *Profiles of New York*, *Profiles of Florida* and *Profiles of Texas* go beyond Census statistics, beyond metro area coverage, beyond the 100 best places to live. Drawn from official census information, other government statistics and original research, you will have at your fingertips data that's available nowhere else in one single source. Data will be published on additional states in 2006 and 2007.

Profiles of New York, 2005/06: 800 pages; Softcover ISBN 1-59237-108-6; $129.00
Profiles of Florida, 2005/06: 800 pages; Softcover ISBN 1-59237-110-8; $129.00
Profies of Texas, 2005/06: 800 pages; Softcover ISBN 1-59237-111-6; $129.00

Research Services Directory: Commercial & Corporate Research Centers

This Ninth Edition provides access to well over 8,000 independent Commercial Research Firms, Corporate Research Centers and Laboratories offering contract services for hands-on, basic or applied research. *Research Services Directory* covers the thousands of types of research companies, including Biotechnology & Pharmaceutical Developers, Consumer Product Research, Defense Contractors, Electronics & Software Engineers, Think Tanks, Forensic Investigators, Independent Commercial Laboratories, Information Brokers, Market & Survey Research Companies, Medical Diagnostic Facilities, Product Research & Development Firms and more. Each entry provides the company's name, mailing address, phone & fax numbers, key contacts, web site, e-mail address, as well as a company description and research and technical fields served. Four indexes provide immediate access to this wealth of information: Research Firms Index, Geographic Index, Personnel Name Index and Subject Index.

"An important source for organizations in need of information about laboratories, individuals and other facilities." –ARBA

1,400 pages; Softcover ISBN 1-59237-003-9, $395.00 ◆ Online Database (includes a free copy of the directory) $850.00

International Business and Trade Directories

Completely updated, the Third Edition of *International Business and Trade Directories* now contains more than 10,000 entries, over 2,000 more than the last edition, making this directory the most comprehensive resource of the worlds business and trade directories. Entries include content descriptions, price, publisher's name and address, web site and e-mail addresses, phone and fax numbers and editorial staff. Organized by industry group, and then by region, this resource puts over 10,000 industry-specific business and trade directories at the reader's fingertips. Three indexes are included for quick access to information: Geographic Index, Publisher Index and Title Index. Public, college and corporate libraries, as well as individuals and corporations seeking critical market information will want to add this directory to their marketing collection.

"Reasonably priced for a work of this type, this directory should appeal to larger academic, public and corporate libraries with an international focus." –Library Journal

1,800 pages; Softcover ISBN 1-930956-63-0, $225.00 ◆ Online Database (includes a free copy of the directory) $450.00

To preview any of our Directories Risk-Free for 30 days, call (800) 562-2139 or fax to (518) 789-0556